Eight Simple Guides for the Use of this Dictionary

This DICTIONARY has been designed to give you the word or the meaning you desire; and it has been designed to lead you directly to it. By following these eight simple guides you will arrive at the word or the meaning you desire with certainty, with speed, and with the utmost ease.

1. Look up idioms under the noun, whether the idiom consists of a preposition and a noun or a verb and a noun (See Explanatory Note 29, p. xiv).
2. Look up prepositions under the word (verb or noun) associated syntactically with them; also under the prepositions themselves (See Explanatory Note 37, p. xvi).
3. Look up the adjective meanings of a word at the beginning of the entry, the verb meanings at the end, and other meanings in between, according to the functional sequence established for the treatment of words on the basis of the parts of speech (See Explanatory Note 23, p. xiii). You will be greatly aided in finding changes in part of speech by the boldface perpendicular lines used in many entries (See Explanatory Note 38, p. xvi).
4. Look up abbreviations and proper nouns in the same alphabetical listing as common words (See Explanatory Note 19, p. xiii).
5. Look up all words spelled alike under one and the same entry, whether spelled with an initial capital or not (See Explanatory Notes 21 and 22, p. xiii).
6. Look up feminine nouns that have identical spelling with the feminine form of an adjective under the masculine form of the adjective (See Explanatory Note 24, p. xiii).
7. Look up verb phrases under the transitive or intransitive treatment of the verb according as the verb (not the verb phrase as a whole) is transitive or intransitive (See Explanatory Note 36, p. xvi).
8. Look up English solid, hyphenated, and spaced compounds as lexical units. For example, *soft-boiled egg* is found as a separate entry and not under *soft* or *boiled* or *egg* (See Explanatory Note 27, p. xiv).

Ocho Sencillas Indicaciones para el Uso de este Diccionario

Este DICCIONARIO ha sido planeado para proporcionar al usuario la palabra o la acepción deseada; y para conducirle de un modo directo a dicha palabra o acepción. Siguiendo estas ocho sencillas indicaciones, encontrará el usuario la palabra o la acepción que desea con seguridad, con rapidez y con la mayor facilidad.

1. Búsquense los modismos bajo el nombre, sea un modismo que conste de una preposición y un nombre o uno que conste de un verbo y un nombre (Véase Nota Explicativa 29, pág. xiv).
2. Búsquense las preposiciones bajo la palabra (verbo o nombre) que va asociada con ellas sintácticamente; y también bajo las preposiciones mismas (Véase Nota Explicativa 37, pág. xvi).
3. Búsquense las acepciones adjetivales de las palabras al principio del artículo, las acepciones verbales al fin y las demás acepciones entre ambas, según el orden funcional establecido para el tratamiento de las palabras a base de las partes de la oración (Véase Nota Explicativa 23, pág. xiii). Las líneas perpendiculares impresas en negrillas, que se encuentran en muchos artículos, ayudarán muchísimo a hallar cambios de una parte de la oración a otra (Véase Nota Explicativa 38, pág. xvi).
4. Búsquense las abreviaturas y los nombres propios en la misma lista alfabética de las palabras comunes (Véase Nota Explicativa 19, pág. xiii).
5. Búsquense todas las palabras escritas de la misma manera bajo un mismo artículo, ya sea que vayan escritas con mayúscula inicial o no (Véanse Notas Explicativas 21 y 22, pág. xiii).
6. Búsquense los nombres femeninos que se escriben de la misma manera que la forma femenina de un adjetivo bajo la forma masculina del adjetivo (Véase Nota Explicativa 24, pág. xiii).
7. Búsquense las frases verbales bajo el tratamiento transitivo o intransitivo del verbo según que el verbo (y no la frase verbal en su conjunto) sea transitivo o intransitivo (Véase Nota Explicativa 36, pág. xvi).
8. Búsquense como unidades léxicas independientes los compuestos ingleses sólidos, los unidos con guión y los escritos como dos o más vocablos separados. Por ejemplo, *soft-boiled egg* se encuentra como artículo separado y no bajo *soft* ni bajo *boiled* ni bajo *egg* (Véase Nota Explicativa 27, pág. xiv).

The Williams
SPANISH & ENGLISH DICTIONARY

EXPANDED EDITION

The Williams
SPANISH & ENGLISH DICTIONARY

EXPANDED EDITION

Edwin B. Williams
University of Pennsylvania

SPANISH-ENGLISH ENGLISH-SPANISH

complete in one volume

NELSON

Thomas Nelson and Sons Ltd
36 Park Street London W1Y 4DE

PO Box 18123 Nairobi Kenya

Thomas Nelson (Australia) Ltd
171-5 Bank Street South Melbourne
Victoria 3205

Thomas Nelson and Sons (Canada) Ltd
81 Curlew Drive Don Mills Ontario

Thomas Nelson (Nigeria) Ltd
PO Box 336 Apapa Lagos

0 17 146065 0

Printed in the United States of America

Preface

A bilingual dictionary is a bridge between two cultures. If these two cultures are among the great cultures of the world, it is important that this bridge be a sturdy and trustworthy medium through which they may become better known to each other and through which they may collaborate to their mutual enhancement and the benefit of the world at large.

It was with the purpose of building this bridge between Anglo-Saxon and Hispanic culture on a sounder footing than had ever been done before that I embarked on the task of designing and compiling this dictionary over fifteen years ago.

At the outset it was necessary to establish principles for the treatment of words, criteria for their acceptance, and standards for the relative space to be accorded them. It was also necessary to survey the history and current status of English lexicography, Spanish lexicography, and English and Spanish bilingual lexicography, as I had been doing for many years prior to the initiation of this work and as I continued to do throughout its compilation, its revision, and its subsequent expansion.

This has involved considerations of frequency and range. Probably at no time in the history of the world has language change been more rapid than in the past fifteen or twenty years. The acceleration of events, the rise of new concepts of life and government, the spread of new interests, the invention of new devices, and the discovery of new relationships in matter, individuals, and societies have brought into English and Spanish thousands of new words and meanings. Obsolete Spanish and English words, many of them not indicated as such in other dictionaries, many of them of little relative value, and many of them carried over from dictionary to dictionary during the past century, had to be eliminated to make way for

Prólogo

Un diccionario bilingüe es un puente entre dos culturas. Si estas dos culturas se hallan entre las culturas mayores del mundo, es importante que este puente sea de solidez y confianza tales que permita que a través de él se compenetren mejor la una con la otra y puedan colaborar hacia su mutua superación y para beneficio del mundo entero.

Fué con el propósito de construir este puente entre la cultura anglosajona y la hispánica sobre bases más firmes que jamás antes haya tenido, por lo que yo me empeñé en la tarea de planear y compilar este diccionario hace más de quince años.

Como punto de partida era necesario establecer principios para el modo de considerar las palabras, criterios para su aceptación y normas para el espacio relativo que se les debía fijar. También era necesario estudiar la historia y el estado actual de la lexicografía inglesa, la lexicografía española y la lexicografía bilingüe inglesa y española, cosa que había estado haciendo durante muchos años antes de iniciar esta obra y que continué haciendo durante su compilación, su revisión y su ampliación ulterior.

En esto han intervenido consideraciones de frecuencia y extensión. Probablemente jamás en la historia del mundo haya habido cambios en el idioma más rápidos que en los últimos quince o veinte años. La aceleración de los sucesos, el surgimiento de nuevos conceptos de vida y de gobierno, el acrecentamiento de nuevos intereses, la invención de nuevos dispositivos y el descubrimiento de nuevas relaciones en la materia, los individuos y las sociedades han injertado en el inglés y el español millares de nuevas palabras y de significados nuevos. Las palabras españolas e inglesas desusadas, muchas de ellas ni indicadas como tales en otros diccionarios, muchas de ellas relativamente de poco valor y muchas de ellas pasadas de diccionario en diccionario durante el último siglo tuvieron que eliminarse para hacer lugar a las palabras de importancia incuestionable de hoy día en

words of unquestioned importance today in all branches of human knowledge and human activity and interest, such as literature, music, art, archeology, philosophy, psychology, anthropology, religion, agriculture, engineering, chemistry, mathematics, physics, astronomy, business, commerce, industry, medicine, surgery, dentistry, veterinary medicine, international law, diplomacy, sports, and games. And special attention has been given to the neologisms of both English and Spanish connected with jet propulsion, nuclear physics, the wonder drugs, radio, television, aeronautics, aerospace technology, rocketry, astronautics, etc.

A bilingual and bidirectional dictionary should fulfill four purposes. For example, a Spanish and English bilingual dictionary should provide (1) Spanish words which an English-speaking person wishes to use in speech or writing (by means of the English-Spanish part), (2) English meanings of Spanish words which an English-speaking person encounters in speech or writing (by means of the Spanish-English part), (3) English words which a Spanish-speaking person wishes to use in speech or writing (by means of the Spanish-English part), and (4) Spanish meanings of English words which a Spanish-speaking person encounters in speech or writing (by means of the English-Spanish part). Thus two purposes serve the English-speaking person, two the Spanish-speaking person. And thus each of the two parts had to be designed to fulfill two purposes.

Much research in many fields of knowledge has been necessary to solve the problems of translation. Chemical, mineralogical, biochemical, and pharmaceutical glosses have been compiled on the basis of chemical formulae. Botanical, entomological, ichthyological, ornithological, zoölogical, and some bacteriological and virological glosses have been compiled on the basis of the Latin names of the

todos los ramos del conocimiento humano, y en las actividades e intereses humanos, como son la literatura, la música, el arte, la arqueología, la filosofía, la psicología, la antropología, la religión, la agricultura, la ingeniería, la química, las matemáticas, la física, la astronomía, el comercio, la industria, la medicina, la cirujía, la odontología, la medicina veterinaria, el derecho internacional, la diplomacia, los deportes y los juegos. Y se ha prestado atención especial a los neologismos tanto de inglés como de español, relacionados con la propulsión a chorro, la física nuclear, las drogas milagrosas, la radio, la televisión, la aeronáutica, la tecnología aero-espacial, la cohetería, la astronáutica, etc.

Un diccionario bilingüe y bidireccional debiera cumplir cuatro propósitos. Por ejemplo, un diccionario bilingüe español e inglés debiera proveer (1) palabras en español que una persona de habla inglesa desee emplear en la conversación o en la escritura—usando la parte de inglés-español, (2) los significados ingleses de palabras españolas que una persona de habla inglesa encuentre en el discurso o en la lectura—usando la parte de español-inglés, (3) palabras en inglés que una persona de habla hispana desee emplear en la conversación o en la escritura—usando la parte de español-inglés y (4) los significados españoles de palabras inglesas que una persona de habla hispana encuentre en el discurso o en la lectura —usando la parte de inglés-español. De esta manera dos propósitos sirven a la persona de habla inglesa, dos a la persona de habla hispana. Y fué por esto que se idearon las dos partes del diccionario para que cada una cumpliera plenamente sus dos propósitos.

Han sido necesarias muchas pesquisas en todos los terrenos del conocimiento para solventar los problemas de la traducción. Se han compilado las glosas químicas, mineralógicas, bioquímicas y farmacéuticas a base de fórmulas químicas. Se han compilado las glosas botánicas, entomológicas, ictiológicas, ornitológicas, zoológicas y algunas bacteriológicas y virológicas

genus and species. And although etymologies are not included, the study of the etymology and phonology of words has often contributed to the precise solution of many difficult translations.

The two parts have been compiled concurrently and thus have an intimate structural relationship seldom found in bilingual dictionaries. The Spanish is both peninsular and Spanish American, while the English is both American and British. The work contains over 130,000 separate entries about equally divided between the two parts. These entries are enriched by the inclusion of thousands of idioms, and the language of everyday life is presented in words and phrases in both parts.

Two grammars, an English grammar written in Spanish and a Spanish grammar written in English, present in full detail the pronunciation of both languages and the inflection of nouns, adjectives, and verbs. English pronunciation, with variants, is shown by a simplified adaptation of the International Phonetic Alphabet.

The work of revision and expansion was begun immediately after the appearance of the first edition early in 1955 and has been carried on without interruption since that time. In this period many mighty changes have taken place in the world and these changes have brought into existence many new words and meanings, and many new ideas about lexicography also. In 1956 the Spanish Academy published the eighteenth edition of its dictionary and while it sanctioned some new words in this edition and displayed a slight tendency toward permissiveness in matters of pronunciation and spelling in its *Nuevas normas* of 1959 it remains basically prescriptive in theory and practice. In 1961 the G. and C. Merriam Company published Webster's *Third New International Dictionary Unabridged.* This work is extremely permissive, partic-

a base de los nombres latinos de los géneros y las especies. Y aunque no se han incluído las etimologías, el estudio de la etimología y la fonología ha contribuído a menudo a dar con la solución precisa de muchas traducciones difíciles.

Las dos partes se han compilado concurrentemente, con lo que tienen una relación estructural íntima que rara vez se encuentra en los diccionarios bilingües. El español es tanto el peninsular como el de la América Hispana, al igual que el inglés es tanto el que se usa en los Estados Unidos de Norteamérica como el de las islas Británicas. La obra contiene más de 130.000 artículos distintos que están más o menos igualmente divididos en ambas partes. Estos artículos están enriquecidos con la inclusión de miles de modismos y el idioma de la vida cotidiana se presenta en palabras y frases en ambas partes.

Dos gramáticas, una de inglés escrita en español y otra de español escrita en inglés, presentan con todo detalle la pronunciación de ambos idiomas y la inflexión de los nombres, adjetivos y verbos. La pronunciación del inglés, con sus variantes, se enseña mediante una adaptación simplificada del alfabeto fonético internacional.

La tarea de revisión y ampliación se inició a raíz de la aparición de la primera edición a principios de 1955 y se ha llevado a cabo sin interrupción desde aquel entonces. Durante este lapso muchos y grandes cambios han ocurrido en el mundo, cambios que han dado origen a muchas palabras y acepciones nuevas, como también nuevas ideas en el campo de la lexicografía. En 1956 la Real Academia Española publicó la décimoctava edición de su diccionario y aunque sancionó algunas palabras nuevas y demostró una ligera tendencia hacia lo permisivo en cuanto a pronunciación y ortografía en sus *Nuevas normas* de 1959, permanece fundamentalmente prescriptiva tanto en la teoría como en la práctica. En 1961 la Compañía G. and C. Merriam publicó *Webster's Third New International Dictionary Unabridged.* Esta obra es sumamente

ularly in the matter of usage, and has awakened increased interest in problems of lexicography and language in academic circles and the press.

In this Expanded Edition I have chosen an eclectic course between the prescriptiveness of the Academy and the permissiveness of Webster's Third. I have emphasized the language of contemporary literature, the language of everyday speech, and the language of science and technology and thus have introduced thousands of new words and meanings of varied status, many of which have not appeared in any other monolingual or bilingual dictionary. At the same time, feeling that the status of a word is just as important as any other aspect of the word, especially for users of a foreign tongue, I have labeled all words that deviate from standard usage with the labels that have been customarily used for the purpose.

In addition to the large increase in the main body of the dictionary I have inserted in the Center Section the following new features: a Breve historia de la lengua inglesa, a Brief History of the Spanish Language, a table of Model Regular Verbs (so arranged as to show the parallelisms of the simple and compound tenses), tables of Spanish and English Cognates, an abstract of the *Nuevas normas de prosodia y ortografía* of the Spanish Academy, and Conversion Tables (for converting elements of the British and American system of weights and measures into the metric system and vice versa).

This dictionary was originally conceived with the hope that it would contribute to greater understanding between Spanish-speaking and English-speaking peoples and thus to universal peace among the nations of the world. It should be mentioned now that this same hope was ever-present in the work of revision and expansion.

permisiva, especialmente en cuestiones de uso, y ha despertado mucho mayor interés en los problemas de la lexicografía y el lenguaje en los círculos académicos y en la prensa.

En esta Edición Aumentada he seguido un camino ecléctico entre el prescriptivo de la Academia y el permisivo del nuevo Webster. He hecho hincapié en el lenguaje de la literatura contemporánea, el lenguaje de uso diario y el lenguaje científico y tecnológico, con lo que he introducido miles de palabras y acepciones nuevas de diferentes categorías, muchas de las cuales no figuran en ningún otro diccionario monolingüe ni bilingüe. Al mismo tiempo, convencido de que la categoría de una palabra es tan importante como cualquier otro aspecto de ella, especialmente para los usuarios de una lengua extranjera, he calificado todas las palabras que se apartan del uso ordinario con las designaciones que se emplean habitualmente para tal efecto.

Además del gran aumento en el texto del diccionario, he incluído en la Sección Central los siguientes elementos nuevos: una Breve historia de la lengua inglesa, una Brief History of the Spanish Language, un cuadro de Modelos de conjugación de los verbos regulares (dispuesto de modo que demuestra el paralelismo de los tiempos simples y compuestos), tablas de palabras cognadas españolas e inglesas, un resumen de las *Nuevas normas de prosodia y ortografía* de la Real Academia Española y Tablas de conversión (para convertir elementos del sistema británico y norteamericano de pesas y medidas en el sistema métrico y viceversa).

Este diccionario se concibió desde el principio con la esperanza de que contribuiría a un mayor entendimiento entre los pueblos hispanohablantes y anglohablantes y por tanto a la paz universal entre las naciones del mundo. Cabe ahora mencionar que esta misma esperanza ha estado siempre presente en la obra de revisión y ampliación.

Philadelphia—EDWIN B. WILLIAMS

Table of Contents — Índice de Materias

Explanatory Notes

1. Subject and usage labels are printed in roman and in parentheses and refer to the preceding entry or phrase (printed in boldface).

arco *m* (geom. & elec.) arc; (anat. & arch.) arch
shy [ʃaɪ] *adj* . . . ; **to be shy on** (slang) estar escaso de

However, when they come immediately, i.e., without any intervening punctuation mark, after a target word, they refer to that target word and the preceding words grouped with it if there are any.

sidewalk [ˈsaɪd,wɔk] *s* acera; banqueta, vereda (Am.)

2. Subject and usage labels are generally in the form of abbreviations but they are sometimes full English words.

entropy [ˈɛntrəpɪ] *s* (*pl:* **-pies**) (thermodynamics) entropía

3. Subject and usage labels are designed to be readily understood by both English-speaking and Spanish-speaking persons. In case of uncertainty ready reference can be had to the single alphabetical list of them on the end papers at the end of this book.

4. The subject label (bot.) is used with names of plants but not with names of fruits.

toronjo *m* (bot.) grapefruit
toronja *f* grapefruit (*fruit*)

5. In view of the fact that bilingual dictionaries are consulted more frequently and by a larger number of users in pursuit of the meaning of foreign words than of foreign words themselves, definitions, particularizing words and phrases, and synonyms used to particularize are provided in the target language. They are printed in italics and in parentheses, and refer to the preceding word or phrase (printed in ordinary roman).

Notas Explicativas

1. Las designaciones de tema y uso se han impreso en letra redonda y entre paréntesis y se refieren al vocablo o frase que anteceden (impresos en negrillas);

Sin embargo, cuando siguen inmediatamente, es decir, sin signo de puntuación intermedia, a un vocablo de la lengua-traductora, se refieren a este vocablo y los vocablos precedentes agrupados con él si los hay.

2. Las designaciones de tema y uso se dan generalmente en forma de abreviaturas pero algunas veces se dan las palabras completas en inglés.

3. Las designaciones de tema y uso se escriben de manera que sean de facilísima comprensión tanto para las personas de habla inglesa como para las de habla hispana. En caso de duda se puede hacer pronta consulta en la única lista alfabética de las mismas en las guardas al final de este libro.

4. La designación de tema (bot.) se usa con los nombres de las plantas pero no con los nombres de los frutos.

5. En vista de que los diccionarios bilingües se consultan más frecuentemente y por un número mayor de usuarios en busca de las acepciones de palabras extranjeras que de las palabras extranjeras mismas, las definiciones, los vocablos y frases particularizantes y los sinónimos que se usan con fines particularizadores van suministrados en la lengua-traductora. Van impresos en itálicas y entre paréntesis y se refieren al vocablo o frase que anteceden (impresos en redondas corrientes).

DEFINITION:	**oriente** *m* east; . . . ; orient (*luster of the pearl*)
PARTICULARIZING WORD:	**suicide** [ˈsuɪsaɪd] o [ˈsjuɪsaɪd] *s* suicidio (*acción*); suicida (*persona*)
PARTICULARIZING PHRASE:	**shutter** [ˈʃʌtər] *s* cerrador; . . . contraventana (*para el exterior de las vidrieras*)
SYNONYM:	**férvido -da** *adj* fervid (*hot, boiling; vehement*)

6. The particularizing word or phrase may be (a) a noun (to particularize the meaning of an adjective), (b) a noun in apposition (to particularize the meaning of another noun), (c) a direct object (to particularize the meaning of a verb), (d) a subject (to particularize the meaning of a verb), (e) an adjectival expression (to particularize the meaning of a noun), or (f) an adverbial expression (to particularize the meaning of a verb).

6. El vocablo o frase particularizante puede ser (a) un substantivo (para particularizar el significado de un adjetivo), (b) un substantivo en aposición (para particularizar el significado de otro sustantivo), (c) un complemento directo (para particularizar el significado de un verbo), (d) un sujeto (para particularizar el significado de un verbo), (e) una expresión adjetival (para particularizar el significado de un sustantivo) o (f) una expresión adverbial (para particularizar el significado de un verbo).

(a) **desperate** ['dɛspərɪt] *adj* . . . ; heroico (*p.ej., remedio*)
(b) **homicidio** *m* homicide (*act*)
(c) **pack** [pæk] *s* . . . ; *va* . . . ; hacer (*el baúl, la maleta*)
(d) **sag** [sæg] *s* . . . ; *vn* bajar (*los precios*)
(e) **abismo** *m* abyss; trough (*of a wave*)
(f) **felpar** *va* . . . ; (poet.) to carpet (*with grass or flowers*)

7. The Latin names of genus and species are given when needed for purposes of particularization.

7. Los nombres en latín de los géneros y las especies se dan cuando se necesitan para particularizar.

oso marino (zool.) fur seal (*Callorhinus alascanus*)

8. Abbreviations of grammatical terms are printed in italics and not in parentheses and refer to the preceding entry (printed in boldface).

8. Las abreviaturas de términos gramaticales se han impreso en itálicas y no entre paréntesis y se refieren al artículo antecedente (en negrillas).

danés -nesa *adj* Danish; *mf* Dane; *m* Danish (*language*)

9. The abbreviations *(cap.)* and *(l.c.)* are printed in italics and in parentheses, refer to the preceding entry, and are placed before the abbreviation indicating the part of speech.

9. Las abreviaturas *(cap. = mayúscula)* y *(l.c. = minúscula)* se han impreso en itálicas y entre paréntesis, se refieren al artículo antecedente y se han colocado antes de la abreviatura que indica la parte de la oración.

python ['paɪθɑn] o ['paɪθən] *s* (zool.) pitón; (*cap.*) *s* (myth.) Pitón
Henry ['hɛnrɪ] *s* Enrique; (*l.c.*) *s* (*pl:* **-ries** o **-rys**) (elec.) henrio

10. Irregular plurals are printed in boldface and in parentheses and are placed after the abbreviation indicating the part of speech, except that irregular Spanish plurals that apply to both the noun and adjective use of a word are placed immediately after the entry, that is, before the abbreviation *adj*.

10. Los plurales irregulares se han impreso en negrillas y entre paréntesis y se han colocado después de la abreviatura que indica la parte de la oración, excepto los plurales irregulares en español que se aplican tanto al substantivo como al adjetivo que se han colocado inmediatamente después del artículo, es decir, antes de la abreviatura *adj*.

tooth [tuθ] *s* (*pl:* **teeth**) diente
infeliz (*pl:* **-lices**) *adj* unhappy; (coll.) simple and good-natured; *m* wretch, poor soul

11. Irregular English comparatives and superlatives are printed in boldface and in parentheses and are placed after the abbreviation indicating the part of speech.

11. Los comparativos y superlativos irregulares en inglés se han impreso en negrillas y entre paréntesis y se han colocado después de la abreviatura que indica la parte de la oración.

hot [hɑt] *adj* (*comp:* **hotter;** *super:* **hottest**) caliente

12. The irregular forms of English verbs are printed in boldface and in parentheses and are placed before the abbreviation indicating the part of speech.

12. Las formas irregulares de los verbos ingleses se han impreso en negrillas y entre paréntesis y se han colocado antes de la abreviatura que indica la parte de la oración.

run [rʌn] *s* carrera; . . . (*pret:* **ran**; *pp:* **run**; *ger:* **running**) *va* correr

13. Irregular plural endings are shown by giving that part of the word that is necessary to complete the form after dropping the last orthographic syllable of the singular.

13. Las terminaciones irregulares del plural se han indicado dando la parte de la palabra necesaria para completar la forma después de suprimir la última sílaba ortográfica del singular.

cemetery [ˈsɛmɪˌtɛrɪ] *s* (*pl:* **-ies**) cementerio

14. The same method is used to show the irregular endings of English comparatives, superlatives, preterits, past participles, and gerunds.

14. El mismo método se usa para enseñar las terminaciones irregulares de los comparativos, superlativos, pretéritos, participios y gerundios ingleses.

happy [ˈhæpɪ] *adj* (*comp:* **-pier**; *super:* **-piest**) feliz
forget [fɔrˈgɛt] (*pret:* **-got**; *pp:* **-gotten** o **-got**; *ger:* **-getting**) *va* olvidar

15. Key forms of English and Spanish verbs are listed as separate entries with cross reference to the infinitive.

15. Las formas principales de los verbos en inglés y español se han incluído como artículos separados, con referencia al infinitivo.

forgiven [fɔrˈgɪvən] *pp de* **forgive**
tuve *1st sg pret ind of* **tener**

16. Numbers referring to the model conjugations of irregular Spanish verbs are placed before the abbreviation indicating the part of speech. If the verb may also be conjugated regularly, this is indicated by the addition of '**& regular**'.

16. Los números que se refieren a las conjugaciones modelo de los verbos irregulares españoles se han colocado antes de la abreviatura que indica la parte de la oración. Si el verbo se conjuga también regularmente, se indica, añadiendo '**& regular**'.

poner §69 *va* to put, place, lay, set
vidriar §90 & regular *va* to glaze

Some model conjugations show a combination of two irregularities.

Algunas conjugaciones modelo muestran una combinación de dos irregularidades.

torcer §87 *va* to twist; to bend; to turn

17. The regimen of English and Spanish verbs is shown with respect to a following noun, infinitive, or gerund.

17. El régimen de los verbos ingleses y españoles se ha dado respecto al nombre, infinitivo o gerundio que sigue.

set [sɛt] . . . *va* . . . ; **to set afire** poner fuego a, pegar fuego a
keep [kip] . . . *va* . . . ; **to keep** + *ger* hacer + *inf*, p.ej., **I am sorry to keep you waiting** siento hacerle esperar

18. Some verbs, traditionally considered to be intransitive but actually transitive, are designated as transitive for the first time herein.

18. Algunos verbos, tradicionalmente considerados intransitivos pero que realmente son transitivos, se designan como transitivos por primera vez.

agradar *va* to please

19. Abbreviations and proper nouns are all included in the alphabetical body of the dictionary.

19. Las abreviaturas y los nombres propios están todos incluídos en el cuerpo alfabético del diccionario.

jeopardy ['dʒɛpərdɪ] *s* riesgo, peligro
Jephthah ['dʒɛfθə] *s* (Bib.) Jefté
Jer. abr. de **Jeremiah**

20. Proper nouns include given names, place names, Biblical names, mythological names, classical names, gentile nouns, and the names of some of the great figures of history.

20. Los nombres propios incluyen los nombres de pila y de lugares, nombres bíblicos, mitológicos, clásicos, gentilicios y los de algunas de las grandes figuras de la historia.

21. Words with the same spelling are combined in a single entry regardless of variation in part of speech, meaning, etymology, or pronunciation.

21. Las palabras escritas con las mismas letras se combinan en un solo artículo a pesar de su diferencia como partes de la oración, y de su significado, etimología o pronunciación.

wind [wɪnd] *s* viento . . . ; [waɪnd] *s* vuelta, recodo; . . . *va* enrollar, envolver; [waɪnd] o [wɪnd] . . . *va* sonar (*un instrumento de viento*)

22. Accordingly, common nouns and proper nouns that are spelled alike except for the initial capital are combined in a single entry.

22. De acuerdo con lo anterior, los nombres comunes y los nombres propios escritos con las mismas letras, excepto la mayúscula inicial, se han combinado en un solo artículo.

scotia ['skoʃɪə] o ['skoʃə] *s* (arch.) escocia, nacela; (*cap.*) ['skoʃə] *s* (poet.) Escocia

23. All words are treated in a fixed functional sequence, as follows: adjective, adverb, preposition, conjunction, interjection, noun, transitive verb, intransitive verb, and reflexive verb.

23. Todas las palabras se han tratado en su función fija y consecutiva, como sigue: adjetivo, adverbio, preposición, conjunción, interjección, sustantivo, verbo transitivo, verbo intransitivo y verbo reflexivo.

after ['æftər] o ['ɑftər] *adj* siguiente; *adv* después; *prep* después de; según; *conj* después que o después de que
acostar §77 *va* to lay, to lay down; to put to bed; (naut.) to bring alongside, to bring inshore; *vn* to lean, list; *vr* to lie down, to go to bed; (Am.) to be confined (with child)

Occasional exceptions occur, particularly in English nouns whose adjective function is sometimes treated in second place.

Sin embargo, se dan excepciones, particularmente con sustantivos ingleses cuya función adjetival se ha tratado a veces en segundo lugar.

university [ˌjunɪ'vʌrsɪtɪ] *s* (*pl:* **-ties**) universidad; *adj* universitario

24. If a Spanish feminine noun is the same in form as the feminine form of an adjective, it is entered under the adjective.

24. Si un nombre femenino español está en la forma misma que la forma femenina de un adjetivo, se lo inserta bajo el adjetivo.

alazán -zana *adj* sorrel, reddish-brown; *mf* sorrel horse; *f* wine press; olive-oil press

If this removes it from its alphabetical position, it is entered also in its alphabetical position with a cross reference to the adjective.

Si esto saca el nombre de su lugar alfabético, se lo inserta también en el lugar que le corresponda alfabéticamente y con una referencia al adjetivo.

fecha *f* see **fecho**
fechación *f* dating
fechador *m* (Am.) canceling stamp
fechar *va* to date
fecho -cha *adj* issued, executed; *f* date

25. The gender of the first noun of a pair of Spanish nouns separated by 'or' is indicated only after the second noun if both nouns are masculine and the first one ends in o or if both nouns are feminine and the first one ends in a.

25. El género del primer nombre de un par de nombres españoles separados por 'or' se indica sólo después del segundo nombre si ambos nombres son masculinos y el primero termina con **o**, o si ambos nombres son femeninos y el primero termina con **a**.

hartazgo or **hartazón** *m* fill, bellyful
Antígona or **Antígone** *f* (myth.) Antigone

26. A masculine and a feminine noun differing only in ending are combined in one entry if they have at least one meaning in common.

26. Un nombre masculino y uno femenino que difieren sólo en su terminación se combinan en un solo artículo si tienen por lo menos un significado que les sea común.

nieto -ta *mf* grandchild; *m* grandson; *f* granddaughter

27. All compound English words, whether written with hyphens or as two or more separate words, are listed as separate entries. The pronunciation of the elements not joined by a hyphen is given only if the word does not exist elsewhere in the dictionary as a separate entry.

27. Todas las palabras inglesas compuestas, bien se escriban con guiones o bien como dos o más palabras separadas, están incluídas como artículos separados. La pronunciación de los elementos que no van unidos por un guión se ha dado solamente si la palabra no existe en otra parte del diccionario como artículo separado.

acetic acid *s* (chem.) ácido acético
Saint Vitus's dance ['vaɪtəsɪz] *s* (path.) baile de San Vito

28. Spanish expressions consisting of a noun and an adjective or a noun and an adjective phrase are listed under the noun.

28. Las expresiones españolas que constan de un nombre y un adjetivo o de un nombre y una frase adjetival se han insertado bajo el nombre.

ácido -da *adj* acid; . . . ; *m* (chem.) acid; **ácido acético** acetic acid
avión *m* airplane; (orn.) martin; . . . ; **avión de caza** (aer.) pursuit plane

29. Prepositional phrases and expressions containing a verb and a noun are listed under the noun.

29. Las frases preposicionales y las expresiones que contienen un verbo y un nombre se incluyen bajo el nombre.

quiet ['kwaɪət] *adj* quieto; . . . ; *s* quietud; **on the quiet** a las calladas, de callada
pie *m* foot; . . . **perder pie** to lose one's footing

30. All subentries are listed alphabetically, those in which the entry word is not the first word coming before those in which it is.

30. Todos los artículos secundarios están en lista alfabética, poniéndose en primer lugar aquéllos cuya primera palabra no es la del artículo principal y en segundo lugar aquéllos cuya primera palabra lo es.

vino *m* wine; **bautizar** or **cristianizar el vino** to water wine; **dormir el vino** to sleep off a drunk; **tener mal vino** to be a quarrelsome drunk; **vino cubierto** dark-red wine; **vino de cuerpo** strong-bodied wine; **vino de Jerez** sherry wine; . . . ; **vino generoso** generous rich wine

31. The pronunciation of all English words is shown by a simplified adaptation of the International Phonetic Alphabet. (See note 27 above.) And common variant pronunciations are also given.

31. La pronunciación de todas las palabras inglesas se indica por medio de una adaptación simplificada del alfabeto fonético internacional. (Véase la nota 27.) Y también se dan las variaciones de pronunciación comunes.

laugh [læf] o [lɑf] *s* risa
long [lɔŋ] o [lɑŋ] *adj* (*comp:* **longer** [ˈlɔŋgər] o [ˈlɑŋgər]; *super:* **longest** [ˈlɔŋgɪst] o [ˈlɑŋgɪst]) largo

32. The Spanish conjunction **o** is always changed to **u** before English orthographic **o** but is only changed to **u** before the phonetic symbols [ɔ] and [o].

32. La conjunción española **o** se cambia siempre en **u** antes de la **o** ortográfica inglesa, pero se cambia en **u** antes de los únicos símbolos fonéticos [ɔ] y [o].

octet u **octette** [ɑkˈtɛt] *s* (mus.) octeto; (pros.) octava; grupo de ocho
orange [ˈɑrɪndʒ] u [ˈɔrɪndʒ] *s* naranja (*fruto*)
overt [ˈovʌrt] u [oˈvʌrt] *adj* abierto, manifiesto; premeditado
octavo [ɑkˈtevo] o [ɑkˈtɑvo] *adj* en octavo; *s* (*pl:* **-vos**) libro en octavo

33. The two parts of the dictionary are the converse of each other. However, they are not symmetrical because of differences in lexicographical procedure particularly in the matter of the treatment of compounds. (See notes 27 and 28 above.)

33. Las dos partes del diccionario son recíprocas la una de la otra. Con todo, no son simétricas a causa de las diferencias de procedimiento lexicográfico en cuanto al tratamiento de los compuestos. (Véanse notas 27 y 28 arriba.)

34. Grammatical information (pronunciation of English words, part of speech, gender of Spanish nouns, feminine of Spanish adjectives, and irregular forms of inflected words) is given for the source language in each part of the dictionary.

34. Los informes gramaticales (pronunciación de las palabras inglesas, parte de la oración, género de los nombres españoles, forma femenina de los adjetivos españoles y formas irregulares de palabras sujetas a la flexión) se dan para la lengua-fuente en las dos partes del diccionario.

hindú -dúa *adj & mf* (*pl:* **-dúes -dúas**) Hindu or Hindoo
get [gɛt] (*pret:* **got;** *pp:* **got** o **gotten;** *ger:* **getting**) *va* obtener, recibir

However, in order to match the meanings of the two languages, syntactical and lexical construction is shown in both the source and the target languages. Thus a transitive verb or expression is glossed by a transitive verb or expression, an intransitive verb or expression by an intransitive verb or expression, a mass noun by a mass noun, and a countable by a countable or by a mass noun accompanied by an appropriate counter.

Sin embargo, para igualar las acepciones de los dos idiomas, la construcción sintáctica y léxica se muestra tanto en la lengua-fuente como en la lengua-traductora. Así, un verbo o giro transitivo va glosado por un verbo o giro transitivo, uno intransitivo por uno intransitivo, un nombre no contable por un nombre no contable y uno contable por uno contable o por uno no contable acompañado de una palabra que hace posible la enumeración.

rival [ˈraɪvəl] *s* . . . ; *va* rivalizar con
mueble *adj* . . . ; *m* piece of furniture; cabinet (*e.g., of a radio*); **muebles** *mpl* furniture

When the gender of a Spanish noun varies with its meaning, it is also shown in the English-Spanish part of the dictionary.

Cuando el género de un nombre español varía con su acepción, aquél se indica también en la parte de inglés-español del diccionario.

order [ˈɔrdər] *s* orden *m* (*sucesión metódica de la cosas; . . .*); orden *f* (*mandato; . . .*)

35. When the subject and/or object of a verb are necessary to the understanding of the translation of the verb, although not part of the translation, they are included in parentheses and printed in italics.

35. Cuando el sujeto o el objeto o ambos son necesarios para la comprensión de la traducción del verbo, aunque no forman parte de dicha traducción, se encierran entre paréntesis y se imprimen en itálicas.

grabar *va* . . . ; to record (*a sound, a song, a phonograph record, etc.*)
frost [frɔst] o [frɑst] *s* . . . ; *va* . . . ; escarchar (*p.ej., confituras*); quemar (*el hielo las plantas*); deslustrar (*el vidrio*)

As personal a is considered to be part of the object, it is included in parentheses with the object.

Ya que se considera a la preposición a antes del acusativo como parte inseparable de dicho acusativo, se encierra dentro del mismo paréntesis.

trap . . . *va* entrampar; atrapar (*a un ladrón*)
pass . . . *va* . . . aprobar (*un proyecto de ley; un examen; a un alumno*)

36. Verb phrases in which the verb is transitive are entered under the treatment of the transitive verb, those in which the verb is intransitive under the treatment of the intransive verb. Thus the same verb phrase often occurs twice in the same vocabulary entry.

36. Las frases verbales en las cuales el verbo es transitivo se presentan bajo el tratamiento del verbo transitivo y aquellas en las cuales el verbo es intransitivo bajo el tratamiento del verbo intransitivo. De suerte que la misma frase verbal se encuentra a menudo dos veces en el mismo artículo.

take [tek] *s* . . . ; . . . ; *va* . . . ; **to take off** quitarse (*p.ej., el sombrero*); descontar; (coll.) imitar, parodiar; . . . ; *vn* . . . ; **to take off** levantarse; salir; (aer.) despegar

Accordingly, although the verb phrase as a whole may be transitive, it is entered under the treatment of the intransitive verb when the verb itself of the verb phrase is intransitive.

Por consiguiente, aunque la frase verbal en su conjunto pueda ser transitiva, se encontrará bajo el tratamiento del verbo intransitivo cuando el verbo mismo de la frase verbal es intransitivo.

taste [test] *s* . . . ; *va* gustar; probar; *vn* saber; **to taste like** u **of** saber a

37. While prepositions are treated comprehensively in their alphabetical position in the dictionary, they are treated also and with more direct applicability and usefulness under the words (verbs and nouns) with which they are closely associated syntactically and idiomatically.

37. Al paso que las preposiciones van tratadas detalladamente en su puesto alfabético en el diccionario, van tratadas también y con aplicación y utilidad más directas bajo los vocablos (verbos y nombres) con los cuales están asociadas sintáctica e idiomáticamente.

jump [dʒʌmp] *s* . . . ; *vn* . . . ; **to jump at** saltar sobre; apresurarse a aceptar (*una invitación*); apresurarse a aprovechar (*la oportunidad*)

38. In long or complicated vocabulary entries, change in part of speech, inflection, function of verbs (transitive, intransitive, etc.), gender of Spanish nouns, and pronunciation of English words is marked with a boldface perpendicular line in place of the usual semicolon.

38. En los artículos largos o complicados, los cambios en la parte de la oración, la flexión, la función de los verbos (transitiva, intransitiva, etc.), el género de los nombres españoles y la pronunciación de las palabras inglesas van señalados con una línea perpendicular impresa en negrilla en vez del punto y coma de costumbre.

pick [pɪk] *s* pico; . . . ; flor (*lo más excelente*) **|** *va* escoger; recoger (*p.ej., flores*)
corte *m* cut; . . . ; **corte de traje** suiting **|** *f* court; yard

A, a *f* first letter of the Spanish alphabet
A. abr. of **Alteza & aprobado**
a *prep* (to indicate place whither) to, e.g., **va a Buenos Aires** he is going to Buenos Aires; **bajan a la estación** they are going down to the station; **viaje a la luna** trip to the moon; (as indirect object) to, e.g., **escribo a Carlos** I am writing to Charles; **dieron algo al pobre** they gave something to the beggar; (to express addition) to, e.g., **añade agua al vino** he adds water to the wine; (with a following infinitive after certain verbs) to, e.g., **voy a hacerlo** I am going to do it; **aprendemos a bailar** we are learning to dance; **comienza a llover** it is beginning to rain; (with a following infinitive in certain expressions) to, e.g., **a decir verdad** to tell the truth; (with a following infinitive to express condition) if, unless, e.g., **a no ser por** if it were not for, but for; **a saberlo yo** if I had known it; **a no venir él** unless he comes; (to express limit of change or motion in time or place) to, e.g., **de la juventud a la vejez** from youth to old age; **de las tres a las cuatro de la tarde** from three to four in the afternoon; **de calle a calle** from street to street; (in idiomatic expressions) to, e.g., **cara a cara** face to face; **a mi gusto** to my taste; (to indicate location) at, e.g., **sentado a la mesa** seated at the table; **me esperaba a la puerta** he was waiting for me at the door; **a tres kilómetros de Madrid** at three kilometers from Madrid; **a lo lejos** at a distance; **a veinticinco grados sobre cero** at twenty-five degrees above zero; (in telling time) at, e.g., **a los ocho** at eight o'clock; **a medianoche** at midnight; (to express price, rate, etc.) at, e.g., **a cien pesetas la libra** at a hundred pesetas a pound; **a veinte nudos** at twenty knots; (in idiomatic expressions) at, e.g., **a la vista** at sight; **al fin** at last; **al principio** at the beginning; **al menos** at least; **a solicitud de** at the request of; **a veces** at times; **a la ventura** at random; after, e.g., **a los dos meses** after two months; by, e.g., **hecho a mano** made by hand; **a fuerza de** by dint of; **a la luz de la luna** by moonlight; **al año** by the year; **dos a dos** two by two; **poco a poco** little by little; from, e.g., **compré el cuadro a Carlos** I bought the picture from Charles; **gané la apuesta a Juan** I won the bet from John; **quité la navaja al gamberro** I took the knife from the hoodlum; **a lo que veo** from what I see; in, e.g.; **a guisa de** in the manner of; **al aire libre** in the open air; **a mi servicio** in my service; **a poco** in a little while; **a pesar de** in spite of; **a la francesa** in the French manner; **a lo rústico** in rustic style; on, e.g., **a causa de** on account of; **a bordo** on board; **al día siguiente** on the following day; **a caballo** on horseback; **a pie** on foot; **a la derecha** on the right; **a condición de que** on condition that; **al contrario** on the contrary; within, e.g., **al alcance de** within reach of; (to indicate the addition of another substance or ingredient), e.g., **acero al carbono** carbon steel; **bronce al aluminio** aluminum bronze; (to indicate a substance with which an object is treated or prepared), e.g., **cuadro al óleo** oil painting; (to indicate the direct object with substantives standing for definite persons and personified abstractions, in grammatical language after such verbs as **modificar** and **regir,** and sometimes with place names that are used without the definite article), e.g., **quieren al niño** they love the child; **encontré a Pedro** I met Peter; **no vi a nadie** I saw nobody; **llama a la Muerte** he summons Death; **el adjetivo modifica al nombre** the adjective modifies the noun; **visitó (a) Madrid el año pasado** he visited Madrid last year; (in certain miscellaneous phrases), e.g., **¡al ladrón!** stop thief!; **a lo que dice** according to what he says; **a lo que parece** as it seems; **a que no . . .** I'll bet . . . not, e.g., **a que no sabe Vd. mi nombre** I'll bet you don't know my name; **¡a ver!** let's see!; **al** + *inf* on + *ger*, e.g., **al llegar a la oficina** on arriving at the office
Aarón *m* (Bib.) Aaron
ab. abr. of **abad**
aba *f* aba (*woolen cloth and garment*)
ababa *f* or **ababol** *m* (bot.) poppy
abacá *m* (bot.) abacá (*plant and fiber*)
abacería *f* grocery, grocery store
abacero -ra *mf* grocer
abacial *adj* abbatial
ábaco *m* abacus; (arch.) abacus; (min.) wash-trough
abacorar *va* (Am.) to press closely, to attack boldly, to undertake with daring; (Am.) to monopolize; (Am.) to catch, to surprise; *vn* (Am.) to hold improperly (*in dancing*)
abactor *m* cattle thief
abad *m* abbot; (dial.) parish priest
abadejo *m* (ichth.) codfish; (ent.) Spanish fly, blister beetle; (orn.) wren, firecrest; **abadejo largo** (ichth.) ling
abadengo -ga *adj* abbatial; *m* abbacy (*estate and jurisdiction*)
abadernar *va* (naut.) to fasten with short ropes
abadesa *f* abbess; (Am.) proprietress of a bawdy house
abadía *f* abbey; abbacy
abadiato *m* abbacy
abafo -fa *adj* undyed
abajadero *m* slope, incline
abajador *m* stable boy; (min.) pit boy; (surg.) depressor
abajeño -ña *adj* (Am.) (pertaining to the) lowland; *mf* (Am.) lowlander
abajero -ra *adj* (Am.) lower, under; *f* (Am.) bellyband, belly strap; (Am.) saddlecloth
abajino -na *adj* (Chile) Northern; *mf* (Chile) Northerner
abajo *adv* down, below, underneath; downwards; downstairs; **más abajo de** lower than (*below*); **río abajo** downstream; **abajo de** down; *interj* down with . . . !
abalanzar §76 *va* to balance, to weigh; to hurl; *vr* to hurl oneself, to rush; to venture; (Am.) to rear (*said of a horse*); **abalanzarse a** to spring at; to rush into; **abalanzarse sobre** to pounce upon
abalaustrado -da *adj* var. of **balaustrado**
abaldonamiento *m* debasement, affront
abaldonar *va* to debase, affront
abaleador -dora *mf* farmer who sweeps up after winnowing
abalear *va* (agr.) to sweep up (*grain*) after winnowing; (Am.) to shoot
abaleo *m* (agr.) sweeping up after winnowing; (Am.) shooting
abalizar §76 *va* (naut.) to mark with buoys; *vr* (naut.) to take bearings
abalone *m* (zool.) abalone
abalorio *m* glass bead; beadwork; **no valer un abalorio** to be not worth a continental
abaluartar *va* to bulwark, to fortify with bastions
aballestar *va* (naut.) to haul, to pull
abama *f* (bot.) bog asphodel
abanar *va* to fan
abandalizar §76 *va & vr* var. of **abanderizar**

abanderado -da *adj* standardbearing; (mil.) color; *m* standardbearer, flagman
abanderar *va* (naut.) to register (*a ship*)
abanderizador -dora *mf* agitator; revolutionist
abanderizar §76 *va* to organize into bands; *vr* to band together
abandonado -da *adj* abandoned; slovenly
abandonamiento *m* abandon, abandoning
abandonar *va* to abandon; *vr* to abandon oneself, to yield, to give up
abandonismo *m* defeatism
abandonista *adj & mf* defeatist
abandono *m* abandon, abandonment; **darse al abandono** to go to the dogs
abanicada *f* fanning, fanning motion
abanicar §86 *va* to fan
abanicazo *m* tap with a fan, blow with a fan; big fan; blast (*e.g., of hot air*)
abanico *m* fan; fan-shaped object; (coll.) sword; (arch.) fanlight, fan window; (naut.) derrick, crane; (Am.) semaphore; **en abanico** fan-shaped; **abanico de chimenea** fire screen
abanillo *m* frilled collar; fan
abanino *m* frill, ruff
abaniquear *va* to fan
abaniqueo *m* fanning; gesticulation; (aut.) shimmy (*of front wheels*)
abaniquería *f* fanmaker's shop; fan store
abaniquero -ra *mf* fanmaker; fan dealer
abano *m* fan; ceiling fan, flychaser
abanto -ta *adj* skittish, shy, timid; *m* (orn.) Egyptian vulture
abañar *va* to sift, to grade by sifting
abaratamiento *m* cheapening
abaratar *va* to cheapen, to make cheap; to lower (*prices*); *vn & vr* to get cheap
abarca *f* sandal; wooden shoe
abarcado -da *adj* sandaled
abarcador -dora *adj* inclusive
abarcadura *f* or **abarcamiento** *m* embrace; inclusion, inclusiveness, encompassment
abarcar §86 *va* to embrace; to include, take in, encompass; to surround, enclose; (Am.) to corner, to monopolize; **quien mucho abarca poco aprieta** grasp all, lose all
abarcón *m* pole ring of carriage
abarloar *va* (naut.) to bring alongside
abarquero -ra *mf* sandal maker; sandal dealer
abarquillamiento *m* curling up
abarquillar *va & vr* to curl up
abarracar §86 *vn* to set up barracks; *vr* to go into barracks
abarrado -da *adj* blemished with stripes
abarraganamiento *m* illicit cohabitation
abarraganar *vr* to cohabit illicitly
abarrajar *va* to overwhelm (*an enemy*); to throw hard; *vr* to stumble, slip, fall
abarrancadero *m* place full of pitfalls, hard road, difficult situation
abarrancamiento *m* fall into a ditch; obstruction; (naut.) running aground; predicament
abarrancar §86 *va* to open cracks or fissures in; to throw into an opening; to stop up; *vn* (naut.) to run aground; *vr* to fall into an opening or ditch; to become stopped up; (naut.) to run aground; to get into a jam
abarrar *va* to throw hard
abarredera *f* broom; sweeper
abarrotar *va* to bar, fasten with bars; to bind, fasten; (naut.) to stow or pack (*cargo*); to overstock; to jam, to pack (*e.g., a theater*); *vn* (cards) to finesse; *vr* (Am.) to become a glut in the market
abarrote *m* (naut.) packing; **abarrotes** *mpl* (Am.) groceries
abarrotería *f* (Am.) grocery, grocery store
abarrotero -ra *mf* (Am.) grocer
abasidas *mpl* Abbassides
abastardar *va* to degrade; *vn* to degenerate
abastecedor -dora supplying; *mf* supplier, provider
abastecer §34 *va* to supply, provide, provision
abastecimiento *m* supplying, provisioning
abastero *m* (Am.) wholesale cattle dealer
abastionar *va* to fortify with bastions
abasto *m* supply; provisioning; tavern; **dar abasto** to be sufficient; **dar abasto a** to satisfy; to supply
abatanado -da *adj* skilled
abatanar *va* to beat or full (*cloth*); to beat, to whip; to overcome, to conquer
abatatar *va* (Am.) to intimidate; *vr* (Am.) to get timid; (Am.) to become agitated
abate *m* abbé
abatí *m* (Am.) corn; (Am.) corn whiskey
abatible *adj* collapsible, folding
abatido -da *adj* downcast; abject, contemptible; depreciated; *f* (fort.) abatis
abatimiento *m* knocking down; lowering; shooting down; dismantling; depression, discouragement; (aer.) leeway, drift angle; (naut.) leeway
abatir *va* to knock down; to take down, to lower; to shoot down; to take apart; to humble; to depress, to discourage; to draw (*a line*); *vn* (aer.) to drift; (naut.) to have leeway; *vr* to be humbled; to become discouraged; to swoop down; to drop, to fall
abayado -da *adj* berry-like
abazón *m* cheek pouch (*of monkeys*)
abdicación *f* abdication; renouncing
abdicar §86 *va* to abdicate; to renounce; *vn* to abdicate; **abdicar de** to renounce; **abdicar en** to abdicate in favor of
abdomen *m* (anat. & zool.) abdomen
abdominal *adj* abdominal
abducción *f* (physiol. & log.) abduction
abducir §38 *va* (physiol.) to abduct
abductor -tora *adj* (physiol.) abducent; *m* (physiol.) abductor
abecé *m* A B C (*alphabet; elements of a subject*)
abecedario *m* A B C's; primer; **abecedario manual** manual alphabet
abedul *m* (bot.) birch
abeja *f* (ent.) bee; **abeja albañila** (ent.) mason bee; **abeja carpintera** (ent.) carpenter bee; **abeja de miel** or **doméstica** (ent.) honeybee; **abeja machiega, maesa** or **maestra** queen bee; **abeja neutra** or **obrera** worker (*bee*); **abeja reina** queen bee
abejar *m* apiary
abejarrón *m* (ent.) bumblebee
abejaruco *m* (orn.) bee eater
abejear *vn* to swarm; to buzz
abejeo *m* swarming; buzzing
abejero -ra *adj* (pertaining to the) bee; *mf* beekeeper; *m* (orn.) bee eater; *f* apiary; (bot.) balm (*Melissa officinalis*)
abejón *m* (ent.) bumblebee; (ent.) drone
abejorreo *m* buzz, buzzing
abejorro *m* (ent.) bumblebee; (ent.) cockchafer
abejuno -na *adj* (pertaining to the) bee
Abelardo *m* Abelard
abelmosco *m* (bot.) abelmosk
abellacado -da *adj* mean, villainous
abellacar §86 *va* to make mean; *vr* to become mean
abellotado -da *adj* acorn-shaped
abemoladamente *adv* sweetly, softly
abemolar *va* to soften, ease (*the voice*); (mus.) to mark with a flat
abencerraje *adj* (coll.) coarse, ill-mannered; **abencerrajes** *mpl* Abencerrages (*Moorish family in Granada in fifteenth century*)
abéndula *f* vane (*of water wheel*)
aberenjenado -da *adj* eggplant-shaped, eggplant-colored
aberración f aberration; (astr. & opt.) aberration; **aberración cromática** (opt.) chromatic aberration
aberrante *adj* aberrant
aberrar *vn* to err, be mistaken
aberrugado -da *adj* warty
abertal *adj* easily split or cracked; badly fenced; *m* crack, opening
abertura *f* aperture; opening; crack, slit, crevice; wide valley; cove, inlet; openness, frankness; (phonet.) opening
abesana *f* var. of **besana**
abesón *m* (bot.) dill
abestiado -da *adj* beast-like, bestialized
abéstola *f* plowstaff
abetal *m* fir forest
abete *m* pair of hooks used to hold cloth on the cutting table; (bot.) fir
abetinote *m* fir rosin

abeto *m* (bot.) fir; **abeto blanco, abeto de hojas de tejo** or **abeto plateado** (bot.) silver fir; **abeto del Norte, abeto falso** or **abeto rojo** (bot.) spruce
abetuna *f* fir sprout
abetunar *va* var. of **embetunar**
abey *m* (bot.) jacaranda
abiar *m* (bot.) oxeye
Abidos *f* Abydos
abierto -ta *adj* open; frank; (Am.) generous; (Am.) conceited; **a cielo abierto** in the open air; **a pecho abierto** frankly; *pp of* **abrir;** *f* vent (*in coat*)
abigarrado -da *adj* variegated, motley; incoherent, confused
abigarrar *va* to paint in several colors; to daub in several colors, to streak
abigeato *m* cattle stealing
abigeo *m* cattle thief, rustler
abigotado -da *adj* mustachioed
abijar *va* (Am.) to incite, sic (*a dog*); (Am.) to scare away (*cattle*)
abintestato *m* (law) settlement of an intestate estate
ab intestato *adv* (Lat.) intestate; (coll.) neglected, unprotected
abiogénesis *f* abiogenesis
abiosis *f* abiosis
abiótico -ca *adj* abiotic
abirritación *f* abirritation
abirritante *adj* abirritant
abirritar *va* (med.) to abirritate
abisagrar *va* to put hinges on
abisal *adj* abyssal
abiselar *va* to bevel
abisinio -nia *adj & mf* Abyssinian; *m* Abyssinian (*language*); (*cap.*) *f.* Abyssinia
abismal *adj* abysmal; *m* shingle nail, slate nail; pin, peg
abismar *va* to cast into an abyss; to cast down; to humble; to spoil, ruin; *vr* to cave in; to sink; to be humbled; to give oneself up (*e.g., to sorrow, meditation*); to lose oneself (*e.g., in reading*); (Am.) to be surprised
abismático -ca *adj* abysmal
abismo *m* abyss; trough (*of a wave*)
abita *f* var. of **bita**
abitaque *m* joist, beam, rafter
abitar *va* (naut.) to bitt
abitón *m* (naut.) bitt, topsail bitt
abizcochado -da *adj* biscuit-like; bisque-like
abjuración *f* abjuration, abjurement
abjurar *va* to abjure; *vn* to perjure oneself; **abjurar de** to abjure
ab.[l] abr. de **abril**
ablación *f* (surg.) ablation
ablactación *f* ablactation, weaning
ablactar *va* to ablactate, to wean
ablana *f* (prov.) hazelnut
ablandabrevas *mf* (*pl:* **-vas**) (coll.) good-for-nothing
ablandador -dora *adj* soothing, mollifying
ablandahigos *mf* (*pl:* **-gos**) (coll.) good-for-nothing
ablandamiento *m* softening; soothing, mollification; softening up (*by bombardment*)
ablandar *va* to soften; to soothe, mollify; to loosen (*bowels*); to soften up (*by bombardment*); *vn* to moderate (*said of weather*); *vr* to soften; to relent; to moderate (*said of weather*)
ablandativo -va *adj* soothing, mollifying
ablandecer §34 *va* to soften
ablano *m* (prov.) hazel
ablaqueación *f* hollow for water or air around plants and trees
ablativo *m* (gram.) ablative, ablative case; **ablativo absoluto** (gram.) ablative absolute
ablefaria *f* ablepharia
ablegado *m* (eccl.) ablegate
ablegar §59 *va* to send away, to get rid of
ablepsia *f* ablepsia
ablución *f* ablution
abluente *adj & m* (med.) detergent
abnegación *f* abnegation
abnegar §29 *va & vr* to abnegate
abobado -da *adj* stupid, stupid-looking
abobamiento *m* stupidity
abobar *va* to make stupid; *vr* to grow stupid
abocadear *va* to tear away or out by mouthfuls
abocado -da *adj* vulnerable; mild, smooth (*wine*); **abocado a** verging on
abocamiento *m* biting; approach; meeting, interview
abocar §86 *va* to bite, seize with the mouth; to transfer by pouring; to bring up, bring nearer; *vn* (naut.) to enter a river, channel, etc.; **abocar en** (naut.) to enter into the mouth of (*a river, channel, etc.*); *vr* to approach; to have an interview
abocardado -da *adj* bell-mouthed
abocardar *va* to widen or spread the mouth of (*a tube or pipe*)
abocardo *m* var. of **alegra**
abocetar *va* to sketch; to paint hastily
abocinamiento *m* flare, flaring
abocinar *va* to shape like a trumpet; to flare; *vn* to fall on the face; *vr* to take the shape of a trumpet; to flare; to walk with head lowered (*said of a horse*)
abochornado -da *adj* overheated; flushed, ashamed
abochornar *va* to burn up, overheat; to make blush; *vr* to blush; to wilt, wither
abofellar *va & vn* to puff out, to swell
abofeteador -dora *adj* slapping; insulting; *mf* slapper; insulter
abofetear *va* to slap in the face
abogacía *f* law, legal profession
abogada *f* lawyeress (*woman lawyer; lawyer's wife*)
abogadear *vn* (coll.) to be a poor lawyer; (coll.) to be a shyster; (coll.) to talk in legal jargon
abogaderas *fpl* (Am.) specious arguments, quibbling
abogadesco -ca *adj* lawyerish, lawyerlike
abogadil *adj* lawyerish
abogadismo *m* legal interference
abogado *m* mediator; lawyer; **abogado del diablo** (eccl. & fig.) devil's advocate; **abogado de secano** quack lawyer, quack, charlatan; **abogado firmón** shyster who will sign anything; **abogado trampista** shyster
abogalia or **abogalla** *f* (bot.) nutgall
abogar §59 *vn* to plead, intercede; **abogar por** to advocate, to back
abohardillado -da *adj* var. of **abuhardillado**
abolengo *m* ancestry, descent; inheritance
abolición *f* revocation, repeal; (hist.) abolition
abolicionismo *m* abolitionism
abolicionista *mf* abolitionist
abolir §53 *va* to revoke, to repeal
abolorio *m* ancestry
abolsado -da *adj* full of pockets, puckered, baggy
abolsar *vr* to form pockets, to get baggy
abollado -da *adj* rough, uneven; fluted, frilled; *m* puffs, tufts (*in a dress*)
abolladura *f* dent; embossing; bump, bruise
abollar *va* to dent; to emboss; to bump, to bruise; to stun; *vr* to dent, be dented; to get bumped, to get bruised
abollonadura *f* embossing
abollonar *va* to emboss
abomaso *m* (anat.) abomasum
abombar *va* to make convex, to make bulge; to crown (*a road*); (coll.) to stun, confound; *vr* (Am.) to rot, decompose; (Am.) to get drunk
abominable *adj* abominable
abominación *f* abomination
abominar *va* to abominate; *vn* **abominar de** to abominate
abonable *adj* payable
abonado -da *adj* trustworthy; likely; *mf* subscriber; commuter
abonador -dora *mf* guarantor, surety; (agr.) manurer; *m* cooper's auger; *f* (agr.) fertilizer spreader (*implement*)
abonamiento *m* vouching, backing; bail, security
abonanzar §76 *vn* to clear up (*said of weather or a complicated situation*); (naut.) to abate, become less rough (*said of wind or sea*)
abonar *va* to vouch for, to answer for; to certify; to improve; to fertilize; to take the subscription of; to pay; to credit; **abonar en cuenta a** to credit to the account of; *vn* to clear up (*said of the weather*); *vr* to subscribe
abonaré *m* promissory note

abono *m* manure, fertilizer; subscription; credit; instalment; voucher, guarantee; **ser de abono** to be to the good; **abono compuesto** (agr.) compost; **abono verde** (agr.) leaf mold
aboquillado -da *adj* tipped (*cigaret*)
aboquillar *va* to put a mouth or nozzle on; to widen, to widen the mouth of; to bevel
abordable *adj* approachable
abordador *m* (naut.) boarder
abordaje *m* (naut.) boarding; (naut.) collision, running afoul
abordar *va* to approach; to accost; to undertake, to plan; (naut.) to board (*said of one ship with respect to another*); (naut.) to run afoul of; (naut.) to dock; *vn* (naut.) to run afoul; (naut.) to put in, put into port
abordo *m* (naut.) var. of **abordaje**
abordonado -da *adj* (Am.) striped, ribbed
aborigen *adj & m* aboriginal; **aborígenes** *mpl* aborigines
aborlonado -da *adj* (Am.) ribbed
aborrachado -da *adj* bright red
aborrascar §86 *vr* to get stormy
aborrecedor -dora *adj* abhorring, hating; *mf* abhorrer, hater
aborrecer §34 *va* to abhor, hate, detest; to bore; to alienate, antagonize; to abandon or desert (*eggs or young*); (coll.) to waste, throw away; *vr* to be bored
aborrecible *adj* abhorrent, detestable
aborrecimiento *m* abhorrence, hate, detestation
aborregado -da *adj* fleecy (*clouds*); mackerel (*sky*)
aborregar §59 *vr* to get covered with light fleecy clouds; to fall madly in love; (Am.) to get dull or stupid
aborricar §86 *vr* var. of **emborricar**
abortamiento *m* abortion
abortar *va & vn* to abort
abortista *mf* abortionist
abortivo -va *adj* abortive; *m* abortive medicine
aborto *m* abortion; **aborto de la naturaleza** monster
abortón *m* abortion (*of an animal*); skin of aborted lamb
aborujar *va* to pack, make lumpy; *vr* to get lumpy; to be wrapped up
abosar *va* (Am.) to revive (*cock in cockfighting*)
abotagado -da *adj* bloated, swollen
abotagamiento *m* bloating, swelling
abotagar §59 *vr* to get bloated, to swell up
abotellar *vr* to get full of bubbles (*said of glass*)
abotijar *vr* to become pot-bellied
abotinado -da *adj* boot-shaped; closed over instep (*said of trousers*); having feet of different color from rest of leg
abotonador *m* buttonhook
abotonar *va* to button; *vn* to bud; to form buttons (*said of an egg cracked while boiling*)
abovedado -da *adj* arched, vaulted; *m* vaulting
abovedar *va* to arch, to vault; to crown (*a road*)
aboyado -da *adj* with oxen (*said of a place that is so rented*)
aboyar *va* (naut.) to lay buoys in, to mark with buoys
abozalar *va* to muzzle
abra *f* bay, cove; vale, valley; crack, fissure; (Am.) clearing
abracadabra *m* abracadabra
abracadabrante *adj* (hum.) killing, amazing, breath-taking
abracapalo *m* (bot.) tropical American orchid (*Epidendrum nodosum*)
abracijo *m* (coll.) hug, embrace
Abrahán *m* Abraham
abrahonar *va* to seize by the clothing
abrasador -dora *adj* very hot, burning
abrasamiento *m* catching fire, burning; ardor, passion
abrasar *va* to set afire, to burn; to destroy by gunfire; to parch; to nip (*said of cold*); to squander (*money*); to shame; *vn* to burn; *vr* to burn; to be parched; to be nipped (*by cold*); (fig.) to be on fire (*i.e., to be very hot; to be agitated by violent passion*)
abrasilado -da *adj* Brazil-red
abrasión *f* abrasion; erosion; (med.) abrasion; intestinal irritation
abrasivo -va *adj & m* abrasive
abrazadera *f* band, clasp, clamp; tieback; (print.) bracket; (aut.) snap-on; **abrazadera para papeles** paper clip
abrazador -dora *adj* embracing
abrazamiento *m* embracing
abrazar §76 *va* to embrace; to clasp, throw one's arms around; to include, take in, take up; to embrace (*e.g., Catholicism*); *vr* to embrace; **abrazarse a, con** or **de** to embrace; to clasp, throw one's arms around
abrazo *m* hug, embrace
abrebocas *m* (*pl:* **-cas**) (surg.) mouth prop, mouth gag
abrebotellas *m* (*pl:* **-llas**) bottle opener
abrecarta *m* (*pl:* **-tas**) knife (*for slitting envelopes*)
abrecoches *m* (*pl:* **-ches**) doorman
ábrego *m* southwest wind
abrelatas *m* (*pl:* **-tas**) can opener; tin opener (Brit.)
abrenuncio *interj* fie!; by no means!
abreostras *m* (*pl:* **-tras**) oyster knife
abrevadero *m* drinking trough, watering place
abrevador -dora *adj* watering; *mf* one who waters livestock; *m* drinking trough
abrevar *va* to water (*cattle*); to give a drink to; to irrigate; to wet, soak; to size (*before painting*); to wet down (*a wall—for stuccoing*); *vn* to water cattle; to drink, to quench the thirst; *vr* to drink, to quench the thirst; **abrevarse en** to be bathed in (*e.g., blood, tears*)
abreviación *f* abbreviation (*making shorter*); abridgment; lessening, shortening; hastening
abreviadamente *adv* in an abridged form, summarily
abreviado -da *adj* abridged, condensed, summary
abreviador -dora *adj* abbreviating; abridging; shortening; *mf* abbreviator; *m* (eccl.) abbreviator
abreviaduría *f* (eccl.) office of papal abbreviator
abreviamiento *m* var. of **abreviación**
abreviar *va* to abbreviate; to abridge; to lessen, shorten, lighten; to cut short; to hasten; *vn* to be quick; **¡abrevia!** hurry!; **abreviar con** to make short work of; **abreviar en** + *inf* to be brief in + *ger*, to not take long to + *inf*
abreviatura *f* abbreviation (*shortened form*); **en abreviatura** in abbreviation; (coll.) in a hurry
abreviaturía *f* var. of **abreviaduría**
abribonar *vr* to become a loafer; to become a rascal
abridero -ra *adj & m* freestone
abridor -dora *adj* opening; *m* opener (*person or thing*); freestone; grafting knife; child's gold eardrop; **abridor de botellas** bottle opener; **abridor de guantes** glove stretcher; **abridor de láminas** engraver; **abridor de latas** can opener; **abridor en hueco** diesinker
abrigadero *m* shelter, windbreak
abrigado -da *adj* (Am.) heavy, warm (*clothes*); *m & f* shelter, windbreak
abrigador -dora *adj* warm (*clothing*); (Am.) concealing; *mf* (Am.) concealer; *m* (Am.) jacket
abrigaño *m* shelter, windbreak
abrigar §59 *va* to shelter; to help, protect; to nourish, cherish, foster (*hopes, plans, etc.*); *vr* to take shelter; to wrap oneself up
abrigo *m* shelter; aid, support; fostering; cover, wrap; overcoat; (naut.) harbor, shelter; **al abrigo de** protected from, sheltered from, under the protection of; **de mucho abrigo** heavy (*said of clothing*); **abrigo antiaéreo** air-raid shelter; **abrigo de entretiempo** topcoat, spring-and-fall coat
ábrigo *m* var. of **ábrego**
abril *m* April; springtime (*of life*); summer (*i.e., year*), e.g., **tener quince abriles** to have seen fifteen summers; **estar hecho un abril** to be all dressed up, to be dressed to kill; **los dieciséis abriles** sweet sixteen
abrileño -ña *adj* (pertaining to) April
abrillantador *m* cutter and polisher of precious stones

abrillantamiento *m* cutting into facets; shining, polishing, brightening
abrillantar *va* to cut into facets, to cut facets in; to shine, polish, brighten; to enhance
abrimiento *m* opening
abrir *m* opening; **en un abrir y cerrar de ojos** (coll.) in the twinkling of an eye; **§17,** 9 *va* to open; to unlock, unfasten; to engrave, carve; (Am.) to clear (*woodland*); to whet (*the appetite*); to dig (*the foundations*); *vn* to open; *vr* to open; **abrirse a** or **con** to open up to, to unbosom oneself to
abrochador *m* buttonhook
abrochadura *f* or **abrochamiento** *m* buttoning, hooking, fastening
abrochar *va* to button, to hook, to fasten
abrogación *f* abrogation
abrogar §59 *va* abrogate
abrojal *m* thistly spot of ground
abrojín *m* (zool.) purple shell
abrojo *m* (bot. & mil.) caltrop; thistle, thorn; thorny tip of scourge; **abrojos** *mpl* (naut.) hidden rocks
abroma *m* (bot.) devil's-cotton
abromado -da *adj* darkened with heavy mist or clouds
abromar *vr* (naut.) to get covered with shipworms
abroncar §86 *va* to embarrass, ridicule; (coll.) to bore, annoy
abroquelado -da *adj* shaped like a shield
abroquelar *va* (naut.) to boxhaul; *vr* to shield oneself
abrótano *m* (bot.) southernwood; **abrótano hembra** (bot.) lavender cotton
abrotoñar *vn* to bud, to sprout
abrumador -dora *adj* crushing, oppressing, wearisome; overwhelming
abrumar *va* to crush, oppress, weary; to overwhelm; to annoy; *vr* to get foggy
abrupto -ta *adj* abrupt, steep; rough, rugged
abrutado -da *adj* brutalized, brutish, bestial
Absalón *m* (Bib.) Absalom
absceso *m* (path.) abscess; **absceso de fijación** (med.) fixation abscess
abscisa *f* (geom.) abscissa
abscisión *f* abscission
absenta *f* absinthe (*drink*)
absentismo *m* absenteeism
absentista *mf* absentee; absentee landlord
ábsida *f* or **ábside** *m* (arch.) apse
absidiolas *fpl* (arch.) apse chapels
absidiolo *m* (arch.) apsidiole
absintina *f* (chem.) absinthin
absintio *m* (bot.) absinthe
absintismo *m* (path.) absinthism
absolución *f* absolution; **absolución de la demanda** (law) dismissal of complaint, finding for the defendant; **absolución de la instancia** (law) dismissal of the case; **absolución libre** (law) acquittal, verdict of not guilty
absoluta *f* see **absoluto**
absolutismo *m* absolutism
absolutista *mf* absolutist
absoluto -ta *adj* absolute; (coll.) arbitrary, despotic; *m* absolute; **en absoluto** absolutely; absolutely not; *f* dogmatic statement; (log.) universal proposition; (mil.) discharge
absolvederas *fpl;* **tener buenas absolvederas** (coll.) to be an indulgent confessor
absolver §63 & §17, 9 *va* to absolve; (law) to acquit
absorbencia *f* absorbency
absorbente *adj* absorbent; absorbing; *m* absorbent; **absorbente higiénico** sanitary napkin
absorber *va* to absorb; to use up, wipe out; to attract, captivate
absorbible *adj* absorbable
absorción *f* absorption
absortar *va* to entrance; *vr* to be entranced
absorto -ta *adj* absorbed; entranced
abstemio -mia *adj* abstemious; *mf* abstemious person
abstención *f* abstention
abstencionismo *m* nonparticipation (*especially in political matters*)
abstencionista *adj* nonparticipating; *mf* nonparticipant
abstendré *1st sg fut ind of* **abstener**
abstener §85 *vr* to abstain, to refrain; **abstenerse de** + *inf* to abstain or refrain from + *ger*
abstengo *1st sg pres ind of* **abstener**
abstergente *adj & m* abstergent
absterger §49 *va* to cleanse (*a wound*)
abstersión *f* abstersion
abstersivo -va *adj* abstersive
abstinencia *f* abstinence
abstinente *adj* abstinent, abstemious; *mf* abstainer
abstracción *f* abstraction; withdrawal, retirement; **hacer abstracción de** to take away, leave out of account, disregard
abstraccionismo *m* (f.a.) abstractionism
abstraccionista *adj & mf* (f.a.) abstractionist
abstractivamente *adv* abstractly
abstracto -ta *adj* abstract; **en abstracto** in the abstract
abstraer §88 *va* to abstract (*a quality*); *vn* **abstraer de** to do without, leave aside; *vr* to be abstracted or absorbed; **abstraerse de** to do without, leave aside
abstraído -da *adj* withdrawn, in seclusion; abstracted, absorbed
abstraigo *1st sg pres ind of* **abstraer**
abstraje *1st sg pret ind of* **abstraer**
abstruso -sa *adj* abstruse
abstuve *1st sg pret ind of* **abstener**
absuelto -ta *pp of* **absolver**
absurdidad *f* absurdity
absurdo -da *adj* absurd; *m* absurdity
abubilla *f* (orn.) hoopoe
abuchear *va & vn* to boo, to hoot
abucheo *m* booing, hooting
abuela *f* see **abuelo**
abuelastra *f* stepgrandmother
abuelastro *m* stepgrandfather
abuelo -la *mf* grandparent; *m* grandfather; **abuelos** *mpl* grandparents; grandfather and grandmother; ancestors; *f* grandmother; old woman; **cuénteselo a su abuela** (coll.) tell that to the marines
abuenar *va* to calm, pacify
abufar *vr* (Am.) to swell
abuhardillado -da *adj* (arch.) dormered
abulense *adj* (pertaining to) Ávila; *mf* native or inhabitant of Ávila
abulia *f* apathy; (psychopath.) abulia
abúlico -ca *adj* apathetic; *mf* apathetic person
abultado -da *adj* bulky, massive
abultamiento *m* enlarging; bulk
abultar *va* to enlarge; (fig.) to enlarge, exaggerate; *vn* to be bulky
abundamiento *m* abundance, plenty; **a mayor abundamiento** furthermore; with all the more reason
abundancia *f* abundance
abundante *adj* abundant
abundar *vn* to abound; **abundar de** to abound in or with; **abundar en** to abound in or with; to espouse (*an opinion*)
abundo or **abundosamente** *adv* abundantly
abundoso -sa *adj* abundant
abuñolar §77 *va* to fry (*eggs*) fluffy and brown; to rumple, crumple
abuñuelar *va* var. of **abuñolar**
abur *interj* (coll.) bye-bye!, so long!
aburar *va* to burn up
aburelado -da *adj* reddish brown
aburguesado -da *adj* middle-class
aburguesar *vr* to become bourgeois, to become middle-class
aburilar *va* to engrave (with a burin)
aburrición *f* (coll.) boredom
aburrido -da *adj* bored; tiresome, boring
aburrimiento *m* boredom
aburrir *va* to bore, weary, tire; to abandon, desert; (coll.) to spend, put in, while away; (coll.) to venture; *vr* to get bored; **aburrirse con, de,** or **por** to get bored with
aburujar *va & vr* var. of **aborujar**
abusar *vn* to go too far, to take advantage; **abusar de** to abuse (*to make bad use of*); to take advantage of, to impose on or upon
abusión *f* abuse; superstition; omen, augury; (rhet.) catachresis
abusionero -ra *adj* superstitious

abusivo -va *adj* abusive (*wrongly used*)
abuso *m* abuse (*misuse; bad practice, injustice*); imposition
abusón -sona *adj* (coll.) presumptuous; *mf* (coll.) imposer
abutilón *m* (bot.) flowering maple
abyección *f* abjectness, abjection
abyecto -ta *adj* abject
A.C. abr. of **año de Cristo**
acá *adv* here, around here; **de ayer acá** since yesterday; **¿de cuándo acá?** since when?; **desde entonces acá** since then, since that time; **más acá** here closer; **muy acá** right here
acabable *adj* achievable, attainable; endable
acabado -da *adj* finished, complete, perfect; worn-out, exhausted; *m* finish
acabador -dora *adj* finishing; *mf* finisher
acabalar *va* to complete
acaballadero *m* stud farm; mating season
acaballado -da *adj* horselike, like a horse's
acaballar *va* to cover (*a mare*)
acaballerado -da *adj* gentlemanly
acaballerar *va* to treat as a gentleman; *vr* to behave like a gentleman
acaballonar *va* (agr.) to ridge, to work ridges in
acabamiento *m* completion, finishing; end; exhaustion; death
acabar *va* to end, terminate, finish, complete; (Am.) to flay, excoriate; *vn* to end, come to an end; to die; **no acabar de decidirse** to be unable to make up one's mind; **acabar con** to finish, put an end to, wipe out; to end in; **acabar de** + *inf* to finish + *ger;* to have just + *pp*, e.g., **acabo de llegar** I have just arrived; **acababa de llegar** I had just arrived; **acabar por** to end in; **acabar por** + *inf* to end or finish by + *ger; vr* to end, come to an end; to be exhausted; to be all over; to run out of, e.g., **se me acabó el pan** I have run out of bread
acabestrar *va* to accustom to the halter
acabestrillar *vn* to go hunting with an ox as a shield
acabildar *va* to organize into a group
acabo *m* completion
acabóse *m* (coll.) windup, pay-off, limit
acacia *f* (bot.) acacia; **acacia bastarda** (bot.) blackthorn; **acacia de tres espinas** (bot.) honey locust; **acacia falsa** (bot.) acacia, locust tree; **acacia rosa** (bot.) rose acacia
acachetar *va* (taur.) to finish off with the dagger
acachetear *va* to pat, to slap
academia *f* academy; (f.a.) academy figure; **Academia General del Aire** Air Force Academy (U.S.A.); Royal Air Force College (Brit.); **Academia General Militar** Military Academy (U.S.A.); Royal Military College (Brit.)
académico -ca *adj* academic (*pertaining to an academy or school; classical, literary; theoretical; mannered*); *mf* academician; member (*of an academy*)
academizar §76 *va* to academize
Academo *m* (myth.) Academus
Acadia *f* Acadia
acadiense *adj & mf* Acadian
acaecedero -ra *adj* possible
acaecer §34 *vn* to happen, occur
acaecimiento *m* happening, occurrence
acafresna *f* (bot.) service tree
acajú *m* (*pl:* **-júes**) (bot.) cashew tree
acalabrotado -da *adj* (naut.) cable-laid
acalabrotar *va* (naut.) to weave into a cable of three ropes of three strands each
acalambrar *vr* to contract with cramps (*said of muscles*)
acalefo -fa *adj & m* (zool.) acalephan
acalenturar *vr* to become feverish
acalia *f* (bot.) marsh mallow
acalicino -na *adj* (bot.) acalycine
acalorado -da *adj* fiery, excited; warm; heated
acalorar *va* to warm, to heat; to encourage, incite, inspire; to stir up, inflame; *vr* to warm up; to become heated
acalote *m* (Am.) stretch of river cleared of floating vegetation; (orn.) Mexican wood ibis
acallantar or **acallar** *va* to silence, to quiet, to pacify; to silence by bribery
acaller *m* (archaic) potter
acamaleonado -da *adj* chameleon-like
acamar *va* to blow over, to beat down (*said of wind or rain acting on plants*)
acampador -dora *mf* camper
acampamento *m* camping; camp, encampment
acampanado -da *adj* bell-shaped
acampanar *va* to shape like a bell; *vr* to become bell-shaped
acampar *va, vn & vr* to encamp
acampo *m* pasture, grassland
ácana *m & f* (bot.) mastic bully, mastic tree, wild olive (*Sideroxylon mastichodendron*); (bot.) acana (*Labourdonnaisia albescens*)
acanalado -da *adj* channeled; fluted, grooved
acanalador *m* grooving plane
acanaladura *f* fluting, groove, striation; corrugation
acanalar *va* to flute, to groove; to corrugate; to channel
acanallado -da *adj* vile, degraded
acandilado -da *adj* peaked, pointed; (coll.) erect
acanelado -da *adj* cinnamon-colored, cinnamon-flavored
acanelonar *va* to flog with cat-o'-nine-tails
acanillado -da *adj* striped, ribbed
acanilladura *f* flaw, uneven weaving
acansinar *vr* (coll.) to get tired, to become lazy
acantáceo -a *adj* (bot.) acanthaceous
acantalear *vn* (prov.) to hail hen's eggs; (prov.) to rain pitchforks
acantarar *va* to measure by pitcherfuls
acantilado -da *adj* full of rocks (*said of surface of sea*); steep, precipitous; *m* cliff, escarpment, palisade
acantilar *va* (naut.) to run (*a ship*) on the rocks; to dredge; *vr* (naut.) to run on the rocks
acantio *m* (bot.) cotton thistle, Scotch thistle
acanto *m* (bot. & arch.) acanthus
acantocéfalo -la *adj & m* (zool.) acanthocephalan
acantonamiento *m* (mil.) cantonment, quarters; (mil.) quartering
acantonar *va* (mil.) to canton, to quarter; *vr* (mil.) to be cantoned, to be quartered; **acantonarse en** to limit one's activities (*studies, interests, etc.*) to
acantopterigio -gia *adj & m* (ichth.) acanthopterygian
acañaverear *va* to wound with sharp-pointed reeds
acañonear *va* to cannonade
acaparador -dora *adj* monopolizing; absorbing, engrossing; *mf* monopolizer
acaparamiento *m* monopolizing, monopoly; hoarding
acaparar *va* to monopolize; to corner; to hoard; (fig.) to monopolize (*e.g., the conversation*); to seize, grasp
acaparrar *vr* to come to terms, to make a deal
acaparrosado -da *adj* blotchy (*said of, e.g., the complexion*)
acapizar §76 *vr* (coll.) to grapple, to come to grips
acaponado -da *adj* effeminate, unmanly
acaracolado -da *adj* spiral, winding
acarambanado -da *adj* var. of **carambanado**
acaramelado -da *adj* carameled; caramel-colored; (coll.) overpolite, oversweet
acaramelar *va* to caramel, to caramelize; *vr* to caramel, to caramelize; (coll.) to be oversweet (*especially toward a woman*)
acarar *va* to bring face to face
acardenalar *va* to make black-and-blue; *vr* to get black-and-blue
acareamiento *m* facing, confronting
acarear *va* to bring face to face; to face, confront, brave
acariciador -dora *adj* caressing; *mf* caresser
acariciar *va* to caress; to cherish (*to treat with affection; to cling to, e.g., a hope*)
acárido *m* (zool.) acarid, mite
acarnerado -da *adj* sheeplike
ácaro *m* (zool.) acarus, mite; **ácaro de la sarna** (ent.) itch mite; **ácaro del queso** or **ácaro doméstico** (ent.) cheese mite
acaroide *f* acaroid gum or resin
acarpo -pa *adj* (bot.) acarpous

acarraladura *f* (Am.) run (*in stockings*)
acarralar *va* to drop (*a thread*); *vr* to be nipped by the frost (*said of grapes*)
acarrar *vr* to seek the shade (*said of sheep*)
acarreadizo -za *adj* transportable
acarreador -dora *adj* carrying, transporting; *mf* carrier; *m* carrier of grain to thrashing floor
acarreamiento *m* cartage, carrying, transportation
acarrear *va* to cart, to transport, to carry along; to cause, to entail, to occasion; *vr* to bring upon oneself, incur
acarreo *m* cartage, drayage
acartonado -da *adj* like cardboard; wizened
acartonar *vr* (coll.) to dry up like cardboard, to shrivel up, to become wizened
acasamatado -da *adj* casemated
acaserado -da *adj* (Am.) regular; (Am.) home-loving; *mf* (Am.) regular customer; (Am.) homebody, stay-at-home
acaserar *vr* (Am.) to be a regular customer; (Am.) to become attached; (Am.) to be a stay-at-home
acaso *m* chance, accident; **al acaso** at random; *adv* maybe, perhaps; **por si acaso** in case; for any eventuality
acastañado -da *adj* chestnut-colored
acastorado -da *adj* (like) beaver
acatable *adj* worthy of respect
acatadamente *adv* respectfully
acataléctico -ca or **acatalecto -ta** *adj & m* acatalectic
acatalepsia *f* (philos.) acatalepsy; (med.) acatalepsia
acatamiento *m* reverence, awe
acatar *va* to revere, to hold in awe; to observe
acatarrar *va* (Am.) to bother, molest; *vr* to catch cold; (Am.) to get tipsy
Acates *m* (myth.) Achates
acatólico -ca *adj* non-Catholic
acaudalado -da *adj* rich, well-to-do
acaudalar *va* to accumulate, acquire (*knowledge, money, etc.*)
acaudillador -dora *adj* leading, commanding; *mf* leader, commander
acaudillamiento *m* leading, command
acaudillar *va* to lead, command; to be the leader of; to direct; *vr* to choose a leader
acaule *adj* (bot.) acaulescent
Acaya *f* Achaea
acceder *vn* to accede; to agree; **acceder a** + *inf* to agree to + *inf*
accesibilidad *f* accessibility
accesible *adj* accessible; attainable; approachable
accesión *f* accession, acquiescence; accessory; access, entry; (med.) attack of intermittent fever
accesional *adj* intermittent
accésit *m* second prize, honorable mention
acceso *m* access, approach; attack, fit, spell, e.g., **acceso de tos** coughing spell, fit of coughing; access, outburst (*e.g., of anger*); **acceso del Sol** (astr.) apparent motion of the sun toward the equator; **acceso dirigido desde tierra** (aer.) ground-controlled approach; **acceso forzoso** (law) easement, right of way; **acceso prohibido** no admittance
accesorio -ria *adj* accessory; *m* accessory, fixture, attachment; **accesorios** *mpl* (theat.) properties; **accesorias** *fpl* annex (*building*)
accidentado -da *adj* agitated, troubled; stormy, restless; rough, uneven; *mf* victim, casualty
accidental *adj* accidental; acting, temporary, pro tem; *m* (mus.) accidental
accidentalizar §76 *va* (mus.) to mark with accidentals
accidentar *va* to injure, hurt; *vr* to faint
accidente *m* accident; roughness, unevenness (*in a surface*); fainting spell; (gram. & mus.) accident; **por accidente** by accident
Accio *m* Actium
acción *f* action; (com.) share (*of stock*); (com.) stock certificate; **en acción** in action; **acción de gracias** thanksgiving; **acción de guerra** battle; **acción directa** direct action; **acción eslabonada** (phys.) chain reaction; **acción liberada** (com.) stock dividend; (com.) paid-up stock
accionado *m* action (*mechanism*)
accionar *va* (mach.) to drive; *vn* to gesticulate
accionista *mf* shareholder, stockholder; **accionista que como tal figura en el libro-registro de la compañía** stockholder of record
accipitre *m* (orn.) goshawk; (surg.) accipiter
acebadamiento *m* var. of **encebadamiento**
acebadar *va & vr* var. of **encebadar**
acebal *m*, **acebeda** *f*, or **acebedo** *m* plantation of holly trees
acebo *m* (bot.) holly, ilex
acebollado -da *adj* having cup shake or ring shake (*said of timber*); like an onion
acebolladura *f* cup shake, ring shake
acebrado -da *adj* var. of **cebrado**
acebuchal *adj* (pertaining to the) wild olive; *m* grove of wild olives
acebuche *m* (bot.) wild olive (*tree*)
acebucheno -na *adj* (pertaining to the) wild olive
acebuchina *f* wild olive (*fruit*)
acecido *m* var. of **acezo**
acecinar *va* to dry-cure, to dry-salt; *vr* to get thin and wrinkled
acechadera *f* ambush
acechador -dora *adj* spying; *mf* spyer, person who spies
acechamiento *m* or **acechanza** *f* spying, watching
acechar *va* to spy on, to watch
aceche *m* copperas
acecho *m* spying; **al acecho** or **en acecho** spying, on the watch
acechón -chona *adj* (coll.) spying; **hacer la acechona** (coll.) to spy, to lie in ambush, to watch
acedar *va* to make sour; (fig.) to sour, to embitter; *vr* to turn sour; to wither
acedera *f* (bot.) sorrel (*Rumex acetosa*); **acedera menor** (bot.) oxalis, wood sorrel
acederaque *m* (bot.) China tree, bead tree, azederach
acederilla *f* (bot.) sheep sorrel; (bot.) oxalis, wood sorrel
acedía *f* sourness, acidity; crabbedness, unpleasantness; heartburn; (ichth.) plaice
acedo -da *adj* sour, tart, acid; crabbed, disagreeable
acéfalo -la *adj* acephalous
aceguero *m* woodsman who gathers dead timber
aceitada *f* spilt oil; cake made with oil
aceitado *m* oiling, lubricating
aceitar *va* to oil, apply oil to
aceitazo *m* thick dirty oil
aceite *m* oil; olive oil; (paint.) medium; **dejarle a uno freír en su aceite** (coll.) to let someone stew in his own juice; **aceite alcanforado** camphorated oil; **aceite combustible** fuel oil; **aceite de algodón** cottonseed oil; **aceite de ballena** whale oil; **aceite de ben** oil of ben, behen oil; **aceite de cacahuete** peanut oil; **aceite de coco** coconut oil; **aceite de colza** colza oil, rape oil; **aceite de comer** table oil; **aceite de creosota** creosote oil; **aceite de crotón** croton oil; **aceite de esperma** sperm oil; **aceite de fusel** fusel oil; **aceite de gaulteria** oil of wintergreen; **aceite de hígado de bacalao** cod-liver oil; **aceite de linaza** linseed oil; **aceite de Macasar** Macassar oil; **aceite de nerolí** (chem.) neroli oil; **aceite de oliva** olive oil; **aceite de palma** palm oil; **aceite de palo** copaiba balsam; **aceite de pescado** fish oil; **aceite de pie de buey** neat's-foot oil; **aceite de ricino** castor oil; **aceite de vitriolo** oil of vitriol; **aceite esencial** essential oil; **aceite esencial de rosas** attar of roses; **aceite mineral** mineral oil; **aceite secante** (paint.) drying oil; **aceite vegetal** vegetable oil; **aceite volátil** volatile oil
aceitera *f* see **aceitero**
aceitería *f* oil shop; oil business
aceitero -ra *adj* (pertaining to) oil; *mf* oil dealer; oiler; *f* oilcan; (mach.) oil cup; (ent.) oil beetle; **aceiteras** *fpl* cruet stand
aceitillo *m* thin oil; (Am.) oil perfume; (bot.) mountain damson (*Simarouba amara*); (bot.) snowberry (*Chiococca*)

aceitón *m* thick dirty oil; olive oil dregs
aceitoso -sa *adj* oily, greasy
aceituna *f* olive (*fruit*); **llegar a las aceitunas** (coll.) to arrive late; **aceituna corval** jumbo olive; **aceituna de la reina** or **aceituna gordal** queen olive; **aceituna manzanilla** little round olive, manzanilla; **aceituna negra** ripe olive; **aceituna rellena** stuffed olive; **aceituna zapatera** spoilt olive; **aceituna zorzaleña** crescent olive
aceitunado -da *adj* olive, olive-colored; *f* olive harvest; batch of olives
aceitunero -ra *mf* olive dealer; olive picker; *m* olive storehouse
aceituní *m* (*pl:* **-níes**) rich medieval oriental fabric; arabesque; olive-colored velvet
aceitunil *adj* olive, olive-colored
aceitunillo *m* (bot.) West Indian storax (*Agotoxylum punctatum*)
aceituno *m* (bot.) olive (*tree*)
acelajado -da *adj* cloud-colored
acelajar *vr* to get cloudy
aceleración *f* hastening; acceleration
acelerada *f* (aut.) speed-up (*of motor*)
aceleradamente *adv* hastily, hurriedly
acelerador -dora or **-triz** (*pl:* **-trices**) *adj* hastening; accelerating; *m* (aut.) accelerator
aceleramiento *m* var. of **aceleración**
acelerar *va* to hasten, hurry; to accelerate; to advance (*e.g., a date*); *vr* to hasten, hurry; to accelerate
acelerómetro *m* (aer.) accelerometer
acelerón *m* acceleration, speed-up
acelga *f* (bot.) Swiss chard; **acelga silvestre** (bot.) sea lavender
acémila *f* beast of burden, sumpter, mule; (coll.) drudge; (coll.) beast, brute
acemilar *adj* (pertaining to the) mule; (pertaining to the) stable
acemilería *f* mule stable
acemilero -ra *adj* (pertaining to the) stable; *m* muleteer
acemita *f* bran bread
acemite *m* bran and flour mixed; porridge
acendrado -da *adj* pure, refined; stainless, spotless
acendrar *va* to purify, refine; to make stainless
acensuar §33 *va* to tax (*a possession*)
acento *m* accent; **acento agudo** acute accent; **acento circunflejo** circumflex accent; **acento de altura** pitch accent; **acento grave** grave accent; **acento ortográfico** written accent; **acento primario** primary accent; **acento prosódico** stress accent; **acento secundario** secondary accent; **acento tónico** tonic accent
acentuación *f* accentuation; emphasis
acentuadamente *adv* with an accent; markedly
acentual *adj* accentual
acentuar §33 *va* to accent; to accentuate, emphasize; *vr* to be accentuated, to become marked, to be aggravated; to become heavy, become bulky
aceña *f* water-driven flour mill
aceñero *m* miller in a water-driven flour mill
acepar *vn* to take root
acepción *f* acception, acceptation, meaning; **acepción de personas** partiality, discrimination
acepillado *m* planing
acepilladora *f* planer, planing machine
acepilladura *f* planing; **acepilladuras** *fpl* shavings, turnings
acepillar *va* to plane; to brush; (coll.) to polish, to smooth
aceptabilidad *f* acceptability
aceptable *adj* acceptable
aceptación *f* acceptance; (com.) acceptance; **aceptación de personas** partiality, discrimination
aceptador -dora *adj* accepting; *mf* acceptor
aceptante *adj* accepting; *mf* acceptor; (com.) acceptor
aceptar *va* to accept; (com.) to accept; **aceptar a** + *inf* to agree to + *inf*
acepto -ta *adj* acceptable, welcome
acequia *f* drain, irrigation ditch
acequiar *va* to build drains or irrigation ditches in, to equip with drains or irrigation ditches; *vn* to build drains or irrigation ditches
acequiero *m* irrigation ditch tender
acera *f* sidewalk; row of houses; (arch.) facing (*of wall*)
aceráceo -a *adj* (bot.) aceraceous
acerado -da *adj* (pertaining to) steel; sharp, cutting, biting
acerar *va* to acierate; to lay sidewalks in or along; to make sharp or biting; to harden, to steel; to face (*a wall*); to stucco; *vr* to harden, to get hard, cruel, or pitiless; to steel oneself
acerato -ta *adj* (zool.) acerous (*without horns*)
acerbidad *f* acerbity
acerbo -ba *adj* sour, bitter; harsh, sharp, cruel
acerca *adv* **acerca de** about, concerning, with regard to
acercamiento *m* approach, bringing near, drawing near, rapprochement
acercar §86 *va* to bring near or nearer; *vr* to approach, come near or nearer; to be warm (*i.e., near what one is looking for*); **acercarse a** to approach; **acercarse a** + *inf* to come near (in order) to + *inf*
ácere *m* var. of **arce**
acería *f* steel mill
acerico *m* small cushion; pincushion
acerilla *f* stronghold or tower on a cliff
acerillo *m* var. of **acerico**
acerina *f* see **acerino**
acerineo -a *adj* (bot.) aceraceous
acerino -na *adj* (poet.) steel; *f* (ichth.) ruff
acernadar *va* var. of **encernadar**
acero *m* steel; sword, weapon; courage, spirit; **aceros** *mpl* temper; (coll.) appetite; **tener buenos aceros** (coll.) to have a lot of courage; (coll.) to be good and hungry; **acero adamascado** Damascus steel, damask steel; **acero al hogar abierto** open-hearth steel; **acero al manganeso** manganese steel; **acero al molibdeno** molybdenum steel; **acero al níquel** nickel steel; **acero al vanadio** vanadium steel; **acero Bessemer** Bessemer steel; **acero colado** cast steel; **acero damasquino** Damascus steel, damask steel; **acero de aleación** alloy steel; **acero de alta velocidad** or **de corte rápido** high-speed steel; **acero de crisol** crucible steel; **acero de herramientas** tool steel; **acero dulce** soft steel; **acero duro** hard steel; **acero fundido** cast steel; **acero inmanchable** or **inoxidable** stainless steel; **acero intermedio** or **mediano** medium steel; **acero rápido** high-speed steel; **acero suave** soft steel
acerocromo *m* chromium steel, chrome steel
acerola *f* azarole, Neapolitan medlar (*fruit*)
acerolo *m* (bot.) azarole, Neapolitan medlar (*shrub*)
aceroníquel *m* nickel steel
aceroso -sa *adj* (bot.) acerose or acerous
acérrimo -ma *adj super* very acrid; very strong, vigorous or tenacious; very bitter (*e.g., enemy*)
acerrojar *va* to bolt, to fasten or lock with a bolt
acertado -da *adj* right, fit; sure, skillful; sure, well-aimed
acertador -dora *adj* skillful; *mf* good guesser
acertajo *m* (coll.) var. of **acertijo**
acertamiento *m* var. of **acierto**
acertante *mf* winner
acertar §18 *va* to hit, to hit upon; to guess right, to figure out correctly; to find, to find easily; to do (*something*) right or skillfully; *vn* to be right, to succeed; to guess right; to grow, to thrive (*said of plants*); **acertar a** + *inf* to happen to + *inf;* to succeed in + *ger;* **acertar con** to find, to find easily; to come upon, to happen upon
acertijo *m* riddle, conundrum
aceruelo *m* small packsaddle; pincushion
acervo *m* heap; store, fund, hoard; joint property; **acervo común** undivided estate
acérvula *f* (anat.) acervulus cerebri, brain sand
acetábulo *m* (anat., bot. & zool.) acetabulum
acetanilida *f* (chem.) acetanilid
acetato *m* (chem.) acetate; **acetato de vinilo** (chem.) vinyl acetate
acético -ca *adj* (chem.) acetic

acetificación *f* acetification
acetificar §86 *va & vr* to acetify
acetilénico -ca *adj* acetylene; acetylenic
acetileno *m* (chem.) acetylene
acetilo *m* (chem.) acetyl
acetímetro *m* acetometer
acetín *m* (bot.) barberry
acetona *f* (chem.) acetone
acetonemia *f* (path.) acetonemia
acetonuria *f* (path.) acetonuria
acetosa *f* see **acetoso**
acetosilla *f* var. of **acederilla**
acetoso -sa *adj* acetous; *f* (bot.) sorrel
acetre *m* small bucket; holy-water vessel
acezar §76 *vn* to pant, to gasp
acezo *m* panting, gasping
acezoso -sa *adj* panting, gasping
aciago -ga *adj* unlucky, ill-fated, evil
acial *m* barnacles or twitch (*device to keep an animal still*); (her.) barnacles
aciano *m* (bot.) bluebottle, cornflower
aciar *m* var. of **acial**
acíbar *m* aloes; bitterness, sorrow
acibarar *va* to make bitter with aloes; to embitter
aciberar *va* to grind fine
acicalado -da *adj* dressy; dressed up, spruced up; shiny; *m* polish, burnish
acicalador -dora *adj* polishing, burnishing; *m* polishing tool, burnishing tool
acicaladura *f* or **acicalamiento** *m* polishing, burnishing; polish; dressiness
acicalar *va* to polish, burnish (*e.g., a sword*); to dress, to dress up; (mas.) to finish, to point (*a wall*); *vr* to get dressed up
acicate *m* long-pointed spur; incentive, inducement
acíclico -ca *adj* acyclic
aciculado -da *adj* (bot. & zool.) aciculate
acicular *adj* acicular
aciche *m* paver's hammer
acidalio -lia *adj* (myth.) Acidalian (*pertaining to Venus*)
acidaque *m* Mohammedan's dowry to his wife
acidez *f* acidity
acidífero -ra *adj* acidiferous
acidificación *f* acidification
acidificar §86 *va & vr* to acidify
acidímetro *m* acidimeter
acidioso -sa *adj* lazy, lax
ácido -da *adj* acid; (chem.) acid; (petrog.) acid, acidic; *m* (chem.) acid; **ácido acético** acetic acid; **ácido acrílico** acrylic acid; **ácido arábico** arabic acid; **ácido arsénico** arsenic acid; **ácido ascórbico** ascorbic acid; **ácido barbitúrico** barbituric acid; **ácido benzoico** benzoic acid; **ácido bórico** boric acid, boracic acid; **ácido bromhídrico** hydrobromic acid; **ácido butírico** butyric acid; **ácido carbólico** carbolic acid; **ácido carbónico** carbonic acid; **ácido cerótico** cerotic acid; **ácido cianhídrico** hydrocyanic acid; **ácido ciánico** cyanic acid; **ácido cítrico** citric acid; **ácido clorhídrico** hydrochloric acid; **ácido clórico** chloric acid; **ácido esteárico** stearic acid; **ácido férrico** ferric acid; **ácido fluorhídrico** hydrofluoric acid; **ácido fólico** folic acid; **ácido fórmico** formic acid; **ácido fosfórico** phosphoric acid; **ácido fosforoso** phosphorous acid; **ácido fulmínico** fulminic acid; **ácido gálico** gallic acid; **ácido glicérico** glyceric acid; **ácido graso** fatty acid; **ácido hipocloroso** hypochlorous acid; **ácido hipofosfórico** hypophosphoric acid; **ácido hipofosforoso** hypophosphorous acid; **ácido hiposulfuroso** hyposulfurous acid; **ácido láctico** lactic acid; **ácido levulínico** levulinic acid; **ácido málico** malic acid; **ácido mangánico** manganic acid; **ácido metacrílico** methacrylic acid; **ácido muriático** muriatic acid; **ácido nicotínico** nicotinic acid; **ácido nítrico** nitric acid; **ácido nucleico** or **nucleínico** nucleic acid; **ácido oleico** oleic acid; **ácido oxálico** oxalic acid; **ácido pantoténico** pantothenic acid; **ácido perclórico** perchloric acid; **ácido permangánico** permanganic acid; **ácido pícrico** picric acid; **ácido prúsico** prussic acid; **ácido salicílico** salicylic acid; **ácido sulfhídrico** sulfhydric or sulphydric acid (*hydrogen sulfide*); **ácido sulfúrico** sulfuric acid; **ácido sulfuroso** sulfurous acid; **ácido tánico** tannic acid; **ácido tantálico** tantalic acid; **ácido tártrico** tartaric acid; **ácido tiociánico** thiocyanic acid; **ácido tiónico** thionic acid; **ácido tiosulfúrico** thiosulfuric acid; **ácido úrico** uric acid; **ácido yodhídrico** hydriodic acid
acidófilo -la *adj & m* acidophil
acidógeno -na *adj* acid-forming (*said of food*)
acidómetro *m* hydrometer
acidosis *f* (path.) acidosis
acidular *va* to acidulate, to make sour; to saturate (*water*) with carbonic acid; *vr* to get sour
acídulo -la *adj* acidulous
acierto *m* lucky hit, good shot; good guess; tact, prudence; skill, ability; success; accuracy, precision; rightness
ácigos *m* (anat.) azygos
aciguatado -da *adj* suffering from fish poisoning; yellowish, jaundiced
aciguatar *vr* to be sick with fish poisoning
acijado -da *adj* greenish
acije *m* copperas
acijoso -sa *adj* containing copperas, like copperas
acimboga *f* citron (*fruit*)
ácimo -ma *adj* var. of **ázimo**
acimut *m* (*pl:* **-muts**) azimuth
acimutal *adj* azimuthal
acintle *m* (orn.) helldiver, pied-billed grebe
ación *f* stirrup strap
acipado -da *adj* close-woven
acirate *m* boundary ridge; ridge between two furrows; rectangular flower plot; walk between rows of trees
acitara *f* zither; wall, railing, parapet; chair cover, saddle cover
acitrón *m* candied citron
acivilar *vr* (Am.) to be married by civil ceremony
aclamación *f* acclaim, acclamation, applause; **por aclamación** by acclamation
aclamador -dora *adj* acclaiming, applauding; *mf* acclaimer, applauder
aclamar *va & vn* to acclaim, to applaud
aclaración *f* brightening; rinsing; clearing; explanation
aclarador -dora *adj* explanatory
aclarar *va* to brighten, to brighten up; to make clear, to thin; to rinse; to clear out (*e.g., a thicket*); to explain; *vn* to brighten, to get bright; to clear up; to dawn; *vr* to brighten, to get bright; to clear up
aclaratorio -ria *adj* explanatory
aclástico -ca *adj* (opt.) aclastic
acleido -da *adj & m* (anat.) acleidian
aclimatación *f* acclimation, acclimatization
aclimatar *va & vr* to acclimate, to acclimatize
aclínico -ca *adj* (phys.) aclinic; *m* opera glasses
aclocar §95 *vn* to brood; *vr* to brood; to sprawl; to squat
aclorhidria *f* (path.) achlorhydria
acmé *m* (med.) acme
acne *f* (path.) acne
acobardamiento *m* intimidation; cowardliness
acobardar *va* to cow, to intimidate; *vr* to become frightened
acobijar *va* (agr.) to hill
acobijo *m* (agr.) hill
acobrado -da *adj* coppery
acoceador -dora *adj* kicking
acoceamiento *m* kicking; (coll.) ill-treatment
acocear *va* to kick; (coll.) to ill-treat, to trample upon
acocil *m* (zool.) Mexican crayfish (*Cambarus montezumae*); **estar como un acocil** (Am.) to blush, to flush
acocotar *va* var. of **acogotar**
acocote *m* (Am.) long gourd used to suck out the juice of the maguey
acochar *vr* to crouch, to squat, to stoop over
acochinar *va* (coll.) to corner and slay; to humble, to scare; to corner (*in checkers*); *vr* to wallow; to get smeared up
acodado -da *adj* bent in an elbow
acodadura *f* bending; leaning; (hort.) layerage

acodalamiento *m* propping, shoring
acodalar *va* to prop up, to shore up
acodar *va* to lean (*e.g., the arm*); (hort.) to layer; to prop; to square (*timber*); *vr* to lean (on the elbows)
acoderar *va* (naut.) to tie up alongside the dock, to moor with a spring, to moor broadside
acodiciar *va* to covet; *vr* **acodiciarse a** or **de** to covet
acodillar *va* to bend into an elbow; *vr* to double up; to bow, to bend, to crumple
acodo *m* (hort.) layer
acogedizo -za *adj* easy to gather, gathered at random
acogedor -dora *adj* welcoming, kindly; *mf* welcomer
acoger §49 *va* to welcome, receive; to accept; *vr* to take refuge; **acogerse a** to take refuge in; to have recourse to
acogeta *f* shelter, cover, refuge
acogible *adj* welcome, acceptable
acogido -da *mf* inmate of poorhouse; *m* flock admitted to pasture for a price; *f* welcome, reception; meeting place, confluence; refuge; shelter; protection; (com.) acceptance; **dar acogida a** (com.) to honor (*e.g., a draft*); **tener buena acogida** to be well received
acogimiento *m* welcome, welcoming
acogollar *va* to cover up (*plants*); *vn & vr* to sprout, to bud
acogombradura *f* (agr.) hilling
acogombrar *va* (agr.) to hill (*plants*)
acogotar *va* to kill with a blow on the back of the neck; to knock down by grabbing by the back of the neck; to conquer, to subdue
acohombrar *va* var. of **acogombrar**
acojinamiento *m* (mach.) cushioning
acojinar *va* to quilt, to pad; to stuff; (mach.) to cushion (*a piston*)
acolada *f* accolade; (arch., mus. & paleog.) accolade
acolar *va* (her.) to unite (*two coats of arms*) under one crest; (her.) to add (*certain distinctive symbols*) to the escutcheon
acolchado *m* cushions (*of a carriage or auto*); riprap; revetment of straw and reeds
acolchar *va* to quilt, to pad; (naut.) to intertwine (*strands*)
acolchonar *va* (Am.) var. of **acolchar**
acolitado *m* (eccl.) order of acolyte
acolitazgo *m* (eccl.) acolythate; (eccl.) order of acolyte; acolytes (*of a church*)
acólito *m* acolyte; altar boy; (coll.) satellite, shadow
acología *f* acology
acollador *m* (naut.) lanyard
acollar §77 *va* to surround (*base of tree trunk*) with earth; to shear the neck of (*sheep*); (naut.) to haul on (*the lanyards*); (naut.) to calk
acollarado -da *adj* ring-necked (*said of animals*)
acollarar *va* to put a collar on; to hitch up; to leash; *vr* (coll.) to get married
acollonar *va* (coll.) to scare, to intimidate
acombar *va* var. of **combar**
acomedido -da *adj* (Am.) obliging
acomedir §94 *vr* (Am.) to be obliging
acomejenar *vr* (Am.) to become infested with termites
acometedor -dora *adj* aggresive; enterprising; *mf* aggressor; enterprising person
acometer *va* to attack; to overcome suddenly; to undertake; to widen into; *vn* to attack
acometida *f* attack, assault; house or service connection (*of wires or pipes*)
acometimiento *m* attack, assault; temptation; sewer connection
acometividad *f* aggressiveness
acomodable *adj* adaptable
acomodación *f* accommodation, arrangement; (physiol.) accommodation
acomodadizo -za *adj* accommodating, obliging
acomodado -da *adj* convenient, suitable; moderately priced; comfort-loving; well-to-do
acomodador -dora *adj* accommodating, obliging; *mf* usher (*in theaters*); *f* usherette
acomodamiento *m* convenience, suitability; transaction
acomodar *va* to accommodate, to arrange; to usher (*in theaters*); to reconcile; to suit; to supply, furnish; *vn* to be suitable, be fitting; *vr* to comply, adapt oneself; to come to terms; **acomodarse a** or **con** to comply with; **acomodarse a** + *inf* to settle down to + *inf;* **acomodarse de** to supply oneself with, to be supplied with; to hire out as
acomodaticio -cia *adj* accommodating, obliging; sycophantic; (iron.) elastic
acomodo *m* arrangement, adjustment; lodgings; job, position; (Am.) neatness, tidiness, spruceness
acompañado -da *adj* accompanied, attended; busy, frequented; (Am.) tipsy; *mf* consultant; *m* (Am.) sewer covering
acompañador -dora *adj* accompanying, attending; *mf* companion, attendant; accompanist
acompañamiento *m* accompaniment; retinue, escort; (mus.) accompaniment; (theat.) supernumeraries, extras; (Am.) food eaten with coffee, tea, or chocolate
acompañanta *f* female companion, attendant, or escort; (mus.) woman accompanist; (prov.) governess
acompañante *adj* accompanying; *m* companion, attendant, escort; (mus.) accompanist
acompañar *va* to accompany, go with; to enclose (*in a letter, etc.*); to share with, to sympathize with; (mus.) to accompany; (Am.) to point (*e. g., brickwork*); *vr* to consult
acompasado -da *adj* rhythmic, regular; slow; easy-going, steady; cautious
acompasar *va* to measure with a compass; to make rhythmical; to mark the rhythm or cadence of; to distribute evenly
acomplexionado -da *adj* var. of **complexionado**
acomunar *vr* to join forces, make common cause
acón *m* (Am.) flatboat
aconcagüés -güesa or **aconcagüino -na** *adj* (pertaining to) Aconcagua; *mf* native or inhabitant of Aconcagua
aconchabar *vr* (coll.) to confabulate, to conspire, to gang up
aconchar *va* to make shell-like; to push to safety; (naut.) to beach, to run aground; (Am.) to shame; *vr* to become shell-like; to take shelter; (naut.) to become beached, to run aground; (Am.) to be a sponger; to form a deposit
acondicionado -da *adj* conditioned; **bien acondicionado** well-disposed; in good condition; of good quality; **mal acondicionado** ill-disposed; in bad condition; of poor quality
acondicionador -dora *adj* conditioning; *mf* conditioner; **acondicionador de aire** air conditioner
acondicionamiento *m* conditioning; municipal testing bureau of silk and cotton fabrics; **acondicionamiento del aire** air conditioning
acondicionar *va* to condition, to arrange, make fit; to put in condition; to repair; to season; *vr* to qualify; to get placed, find a job
acongojadamente *adv* sorrowfully, with anguish
acongojar *va* to grieve, afflict, to distress; *vr* to grieve, be distressed; to faint
aconitina *f* (chem.) aconitine
acónito *m* (bot.) aconite, monkshood
aconsejable *adj* advisable
aconsejador -dora *adj* counseling, advising; *mf* counselor, adviser
aconsejar *va* to advise, to counsel, to warn; **aconsejar** + *inf* to advise to + *inf;* *vr* to seek advice, to get advice; **aconsejarse de** or **con** to advise with, to consult with, to seek or get advice from; **aconsejarse mejor** to think better of it
aconsonantar *va & vn* to rhyme
acontecedero -ra *adj* possible
acontecer §34 *vn* to happen
acontecimiento *m* happening, event
acopar *va* to make cuplike, to hollow out; *vn* to spread out
acopetado -da *adj* crested, tufted

acopiador -dora *adj* gathering; *mf* gatherer, collector, buyer; monopolist; (Am.) agricultural export buyer
acopiamiento *m* gathering, collecting; supply, store
acopiar *va* to gather together
acopio *m* gathering, collecting; assortment, stock; abundance
acoplado *m* (Am.) trailer; (Am.) tow (*of barges*)
acoplador *m* (mach. & rad.) coupler
acopladura *f* joining, fitting
acoplamiento *m* coupling, joining; connection, joint, splice; (elec.) connection, hookup; (Am.) clutch; (Am. rail.) coupling; **acoplamiento de cono** cone coupling; **acoplamiento de fricción** friction coupling; (Am.) friction clutch; **acoplamiento de manguito** sleeve coupling; **acoplamiento de rebajo** (carp.) rabbeted joint; **acoplamiento en serie** (elec.) series connection; **acoplamiento inductivo** (elec.) linkage, flux linkage; **acoplamiento universal** universal joint
acoplar *va* to join, couple, fit together; to hitch; to bring together for breeding; to unite, reconcile; (elec.) to connect, to hook up; (Am. rail.) to couple (*cars*); *vr* to be reconciled; to be intimate; to mate
acoquinamiento *m* intimidation
acoquinar *va* to intimidate
acorar *va* to oppress, afflict; (Am.) to intimidate, to quiet; *vr* to be grieved; to be stifled; to wilt, to die (*said of plants*)
acorazado -da *adj* armored, armor-plated; ironclad; (coll.) forbidding, contrary; *m* battleship; ironclad; **acorazado de bolsillo** pocket battleship
acorazamiento *m* armor, armor-plating
acorazar §76 *va* to cover with armor, to armor-plate; *vr* (coll.) to steel oneself
acorazonado -da *adj* heart-shaped
acorchamiento *m* withering, shriveling
acorchar *va* to turn into cork, to give an appearance of cork to; to line with cork; *vr* to become cork-like or spongy; to dry up, wither, shrivel; to become corky or pithy; to get sluggish, to get numb; to become morally benumbed
acorchetar *va* to bracket
acordada *f* decree, order; authorization; curved ruler
acordadamente *adv* by common consent; after due reflection
acordancia *f* harmony, agreement
acordar §77 *va* to decide, to agree upon; to grant, to authorize; to reconcile, to harmonize; to arrange; to make smooth; to make level or flush; to remind, to remind of; to tune; *vn* to agree, be in agreement; to blend, to harmonize; **acordar** + *inf* to agree to + *inf; vr* to be agreed, reconciled, harmonized; to remember; **si mal no me acuerdo** (coll.) if I remember correctly; **acordarse de** to remember; **acordarse de** + *inf* to remember to + *inf*, e.g., **se acordó de hacerlo** he remembered to do it; **acordarse de** + *perf inf* to remember + *ger*, e.g., **se acordaba de haberlo hecho** he remembered doing it
acorde *adj* agreed, in accord; harmonious, in tune; *m* accord, harmony; (mus.) chord
acordelar *va* to align with a cord, to measure with a cord, to lay out with a chalk line
acordemente *adv* var. of **acordadamente**
acordeón *m* accordion; **en acordeón** accordion (*pleats*)
acordeonado -da *adj* accordion (*pleats*)
acordeonista *mf* accordionist
acordonamiento *m* cording, lacing; milling, knurling; drawing a cordon around a place; roping off
acordonar *va* to cord, to lace, to fasten with cords; to mill, bead, knurl (*coins, etc.*); to draw a cordon around, to surround; to rope off (*a street*); (Am.) to align, to lay out by line
acores *mpl* (path.) milk crust
acornar §77 *va* to attack with the horns, to butt, to gore; to shape like a horn; to make horny; *vn* to become horn-shaped; to become horny; to grow horns
acorneador -dora *adj* butting; *mf* animal given to butting
acornear *va* to butt; (Am.) to drive away, put to flight
ácoro *m* (bot.) sweet flag; **ácoro bastardo, falso** or **palustre** (bot.) flagon
acorralamiento *m* corralling, cornering; intimidation
acorralar *va* to corral, to corner; to intimidate
acorrucar §86 *vr* to crouch, to huddle; to curl up to keep warm
acortamiento *m* cutting down, shortening, slackening; shrinking, contraction; (astr.) curtation
acortar *va* to cut down, to shorten, to reduce; to check, stop; to pull up (*a horse*); to slacken (*speed*); (Am.) to tone down (*a statement*); **acortar la vela** (naut.) to shorten sail; *vr* to become shorter; to be timid; to hold back; to slow down; to shrink, to contract
acorullar *va* (naut.) to ship (*oars*)
acorvar *va* to curve, to bend
acosamiento *m* var. of **acoso**
acosar *va* to harass, to pursue relentlessly; (taur.) to corral and test the mettle of
acosijar *va* (Am.) var. of **acosar**
acoso *m* harassment, relentless pursuit; (taur.) corralling and testing the mettle of a bull
acostado -da *adj* lying down; leaning, bent over; in bed; closely related; friendly; favored; (naut.) on beam ends; *f* (Am.) childbirth; (Am.) (sexual) intercourse
acostamiento *m* laying down; lying down, reclining; support, favor, protection; (archaic) stipend, emolument
acostar §77 *va* to lay, to lay down; to put to bed; (naut.) to bring alongside, to bring inshore; *vn* to lean, to list; *vr* to lie down, to go to bed; (Am.) to be confined (with child)
acostillado -da *adj* ribbed
acostumbrado -da *adj* accustomed; usual, customary
acostumbrar *va* to accustom; **acostumbrar a** + *inf* to accustom (*someone*) to + *inf; vn* to be accustomed; **acostumbrar** + *inf* or **acostumbrar a** + *inf* to be accustomed to + *inf; vr* to accustom oneself; to become accustomed; **acostumbrarse a** + *inf* to be or become accustomed to + *inf*
acotación *f* boundary mark, landmark; annotation, marginal note; elevation mark
acotada *f* tree nursery
acotamiento *m* boundary mark, landmark; annotation, marginal note; elevation mark; stage direction; (Am.) shoulder (*of road*)
acotar *va* to survey, to map, to mark off; to annotate; to fix, to set up; to admit, to accept; to check, to verify; to vouch for; to choose, to select; to pollard, to cut off top branches of; to mark elevations on (*maps, etc.*)
acotiledón -dona *adj* (bot.) acotyledonous; *m* (bot.) acotyledon
acotiledóneo -a *adj* (bot.) acotyledonous
acotillo *m* sledge hammer
acoyotado -da *adj* (Am.) coyote-colored
acoyundar *va* to yoke (*oxen*)
acoyuntar *va* to yoke (*two horses of different owners*)
acoyuntero *m* farmer who yokes his horse with that of another farmer
acre *adj* acrid; austere, severe; biting, mordant; quarrelsome; *m* acre
acreaje *m* (Am.) acreage
acrecencia *f* increase, growth; accrual
acrecentamiento *m* accretion; increase, growth; promotion
acrecentar §18 *va* to increase; to promote, to foster, to make flourish; *vr* to increase, to grow; to bud, to blossom
acrecer §34 *va* to increase, enlarge; *vn* (law) to devolve or to be added (*said of share of an estate given up by an heir voluntarily or by death*); *vr* to increase, to grow larger
acreción *f* (mineral. & path.) accretion
acreditación *f* accreditation; (educ.) accreditation
acreditar *va* to accredit; to credit, to give a reputation to; to credit to; to get the reputation for; to do credit to; (com.) to credit; (educ.) to

accredit; *vr* to get a reputation; **acreditarse de loco** to act crazy
acreedor -dora *adj* accrediting, crediting; deserving; **acreedor a** deserving of; *mf* creditor; **acreedor hipotecario** mortgagee
acreencia *f* (Am.) balance in favor of creditor
acribador -dora *adj* sifting; *mf* sifter
acribadura *f* sifting; (fig.) riddling
acribar *va* to sift; (fig.) to riddle
acribillar *va* to riddle; to riddle with wounds, bites, stings, etc.; (coll.) to harass, to plague, to pester; **acribillar a balazos** to riddle with bullets; **acribillar a preguntas** to riddle with questions
acriflavina *f* (pharm.) acriflavine
acrílico -ca *adj* (chem.) acrylic
acriminación *f* incrimination; exaggeration of guilt
acriminador -dora *adj* incriminating; *mf* accuser
acriminar *va* to incriminate, to accuse; to exaggerate the gravity of (*a defect, weakness, misdeed, etc.*)
acrimonia *f* acridness; acrimony
acrimonioso -sa *adj* acrid; acrimonious
acriollar *vr* (Am.) to take on Spanish American ways
acrisolado -da *adj* pure; tried, tested; honest, reliable
acrisolar *va* to purify; to bring out, to reveal (*the truth*)
acristalado -da *adj* glass-enclosed, glassed-in
acristianar *va* (coll.) to Christianize; (coll.) to christen, to baptize; to beautify; *vr* (coll.) to become Christian, to get religious
acritud *f* var. of **acrimonia**
acrobacia *f* acrobatics (*feats or performances*)
acróbata *mf* acrobat
acrobático -ca *adj* acrobatic
acrobatismo *m* acrobatics (*art or profession*)
acrofobia *f* (path.) acrophobia
acrógena *f* (bot.) acrogen
acromático -ca *adj* achromatous; (opt., biol. & mus.) achromatic
acromatina *f* (biol.) achromatin
acromatismo *m* achromatism
acromatizar §76 *va* to achromatize
acromatopsia *f* (path.) achromatopsia, color blindness
acromatosis *f* (path.) achromatosis
acromegalia *f* (path.) acromegaly
acrónimo *m* acronym
acrópolis *f* (*pl:* **-lis**) acropolis; **la Acrópolis** the Acropolis
acrósporo *m* (bot.) acrospore
acróstico -ca *adj* acrostical; *m* acrostic
acrostolio *m* (naut.) rostrum, acroterium; (naut.) spur, beak, ram (*of classical war vessel*)
acrotera *f* (arch.) acroterium
acta *f* minutes; certificate of election; **actas** *fpl* lives (*of saints, martyrs, etc.*); transactions (*of a learned society*); **levantar acta** to draw up the minutes; **tomar acta de** (coll.) to take note of; **acta de matrimonio** marriage certificate; **acta de nacimiento** birth certificate; **acta de nacionalidad** (naut.) registry certificate; **acta notarial** affidavit; **Actas de los Apóstoles** (Bib.) Acts of the Apostles
actea *f* (bot.) danewort, dwarf elder
actinia *f* (zool.) actinia, sea anemone
actínico -ca *adj* actinic
actinio *m* (chem.) actinium
actinismo *m* actinism
actinómetro *m* actinometer
actinomicina *f* (pharm.) actinomycin
actinomicosis *f* (path.) actinomycosis
actitud *f* attitude; (fig.) attitude (*feeling, outlook*); **en actitud de** + *inf* showing an intention to + *inf*, getting ready to + *inf*
activación *f* activation, promotion
activador -dora *adj* activating, moving; *mf* activator, mover; *m* (chem.) activator
activar *va* to activate; to expedite, to hasten
actividad *f* activity; **en actividad** active, operating; **en plena actividad** in full swing
activista *mf* activist
activo -va *adj* active; *m* (com.) assets; (com.) credit side (*of an account*); **en activo** in active service
acto *m* act; event; public function; commencement (*of school*); (theat.) act; (educ.) thesis; sexual intercourse; **en el acto** at once; on the spot; **hacer acto de presencia** to honor with one's presence, to pay one's respects in person; **acto continuo** right afterwards; **acto de presencia** formal attendance; **acto inaugural** opening, opening ceremonies, dedication; **Actos de los Apóstoles** (Bib.) Acts of the Apostles; **acto seguido** right afterwards; **acto seguido de** right after
actor *m* actor, agent; (theat.) actor; (law) actor, plaintiff; **primer actor** (theat.) leading man; **actor de carácter** (theat.) character actor
actora *f* (law) actor, plaintiff (*woman*)
actriz *f* (*pl:* **-trices**) (theat.) actress; **primera actriz** (theat.) leading lady
actuación *f* action; activity; operation; performance; acting; behavior
actuado -da *adj* skilled, experienced
actual *adj* present, present-day; up-to-date
actualidad *f* present time; present condition; timeliness; question of the moment; **actualidades** *fpl* current events; newsreel; **en la actualidad** at the present time; **ser de gran actualidad** to be of great importance at the moment; **actualidad gráfica** news in pictures; **actualidad escénica** theater news
actualizar §76 *va* to make up-to-date, to bring up to date
actualmente *adv* at present, at the present time
actuar §33 *va* to actuate, to put into action; *vn* to act; to perform; to take action; **actuar de** to act as; **actuar sobre** to act on or upon
actuarial *adj* actuarial
actuario -ria *adj* actuarial; *mf* actuary; **actuario de seguros** actuary
acuadrillar *va* to band together; to command (*a band*); *vr* to band together
acuafortista *mf* etcher, aquafortist
acuantiar §90 *va* to fix or set the amount of
acuaplano *m* aquaplane
acuarela *f* water color
acuarelista *mf* water-colorist, aquarellist
acuario *m* aquarium; (*cap.*) *s* (astr.) Aquarius
acuartelado -da *adj* (her.) quartered
acuartelamiento *m* quartering, billeting; quarters; (her.) quartering
acuartelar *va* to quarter, to billet; to divide (*land*) into lots; (naut.) to bear (*sail*) to windward; (her.) to quarter (*a shield*); *vr* to quarter, take up quarters; to withdraw, retire
acuarteronado -da *adj* & *mf* mulatto, quadroon
acuartillar *vn* to bend in the quarters under a heavy load or through weakness
acuático -ca or **acuátil** *adj* aquatic
acuatinta *f* aquatint
acuatintista *mf* aquatinter
acuatizaje *m* (aer.) alighting on water
acuatizar §76 *vn* (aer.) to alight on water
acubilar *va* to round up (*cattle*) for the night
acucia *f* zeal, diligence, haste; keen desire; sharpness (*of pain*)
acuciadamente *adv* zealously, hastily; keenly, eagerly
acuciador -dora *adj* keen, excruciating
acuciamiento *m* goading, prodding, hastening
acuciante *adj* keen, burning (*desire*); acute (*problem*)
acuciar *va* to goad, to prod, to hasten; to harass; to desire keenly; *vr* to hasten
acucioso -sa *adj* zealous, hasty; keen, eager
acuclillar *vr* to squat, to crouch down
acucharado -da *adj* spoon-shaped
acuchilladizo *m* gladiator; fencer
acuchillado -da *adj* knife-shaped, knife-like; full of stabs; cautious through bitter experience; slashed (*said of a garment*)
acuchillador -dora *mf* stabber, fighter, bully
acuchillar *va* to stab; to stab to death; to slash (*a garment*); to smooth down (*a piece of wood*); to cleave (*the air*); *vr* to fight with knives or swords
acudimiento *m* aid, succor; approach

acudir *vn* to come up, to respond; to come to the rescue; to hang around; to apply, to resort; to produce, to yield; **acudir a** + *inf* to come to + *inf*
acueducto *m* aqueduct; (anat.) aqueduct
ácueo -a *adj* aqueous
acuerdado -da *adj* aligned with a cord or rope
acuerdo *m* accord; agreement; memory, remembrance; **de acuerdo** in accord; **de acuerdo con** in accord with; **de común acuerdo** with one accord; **estar en su acuerdo** to be in one's right mind; **estar, quedar,** or **ponerse de acuerdo** to be in agreement; **llegar a un acuerdo con** to come to an understanding with; **volver en su acuerdo** to come to; to change one's mind
acuernar *va* (taur.) to look at or butt toward one side, to have the habit or defect of attacking on only one side
acuerpar *va* (Am.) to back up, defend
acuidad *f* acuity; visual acuity
acuitadamente *adv* with grief, sorrowfully, grievously
acuitar *va* to afflict, to grieve; *vr* to grieve, to be grieved
acular *va* to back up; (coll.) to force into a corner; *vr* (naut.) to back up on a shoal
acullá *adv* yonder, over there
acumen *m* acumen, keenness
acuminado -da *adj* acuminate; (bot. & zool.) acuminate
acumulación *f* accumulation
acumulador -dora *adj* accumulating; *mf* accumulator; *m* (elec.) storage battery; **acumulador de ferro-níquel** (elec.) iron-nickel alkaline cell; **acumulador de plomo-ácido** (elec.) lead acid cell; **acumulador flotante** (elec.) floating battery; **acumulador hierro-níquel** (elec.) iron-nickel alkaline cell; **acumulador níquel-cadmio** (elec.) nickel-cadmium battery
acumular *va* to accumulate, to gather; to store up; to charge with; *vn* to accumulate; *vr* to accumulate, to gather
acumulativo -va *adj* cumulative
acúmulo *m* accumulation; (bact.) clump
acunar *va* to rock in a cradle, to cradle; (fig.) to cradle (*to nurture during infancy*)
acuñación *f* coining, minting; wedging
acuñador *m* coiner, minter; wedge; tamper; (print.) shooting stick
acuñar *va* to coin, to mint; to wedge; to key, to lock; to tamp (*ties*); (print.) to quoin
acuosidad *f* wateriness, aqueousness
acuoso -sa *adj* watery, aqueous; juicy
acupuntura *f* (surg.) acupuncture
acurrucar §86 *va* to wrap up; *vr* to huddle; to squat
acusable *adj* accusable
acusación *f* accusation
acusado -da *adj* accused; marked; *mf* accused
acusador -dora *adj* accusing; *mf* accuser
acusar *va* to accuse; to show; to acknowledge (*receipt*); to announce (*winning cards*); **acusar de** + *inf* to accuse of + *ger; vr* to confess; **acusarse de** to confess (*a crime*); to confess being; **acusarse de haber** + *pp* to confess having + *pp*
acusativo -va *adj* accusative, accusing; (gram.) accusative; *m* (gram.) accusative
acusatorio -ria *adj* accusatory
acuse *m* acknowledgment (*of receipt*); announcement (*of winning cards*); winning card; **acuse de recibo** acknowledgment of receipt
acusete *m* talebearer, informer
acusón -sona *adj* (coll.) talebearing; *mf* (coll.) tattler, talebearer
acústico -ca *adj* acoustic; *m* hearing aid; *f* (phys.) acoustics; **acústica arquitectural** acoustics (*acoustic properties of a room or building*)
acusticón *m* acousticon
acusuco *m* (Am.) wild desire, great anxiety
acutángulo -la *adj* acute-angled
acutí *m* (*pl:* **-tíes**) (zool.) agouti
achacar §86 *va* to impute, to attribute
achacoso -sa *adj* sickly, ailing; indisposed
achaflanar *va* to chamfer, to bevel
achagrinado -da *adj* shagreen, shagreened
achampañado -da *adj* sparkling, effervescent, like champagne
achantar *vr* (coll.) to hide away from danger; (coll.) to comply, to submit
achaparrado -da *adj* stubby; chubby; runty
achaparrar *vr* to grow stunted
achaque *m* sickliness, unhealthiness; indisposition; weakness, fault; (coll.) monthlies; (coll.) pregnancy; excuse, pretext; matter, subject; (law) fine
achaquiento -ta *adj* var. of **achacoso**
acharolar *va* var. of **charolar**
achatamiento *m* flattening
achatar *va* to flatten; *vr* to get flat
achicado -da *adj* childish, childlike; abashed; disconcerted, confused
achicador *m* scoop (*for bailing water*); bailer
achicadura *f* or **achicamiento** *m* reduction in size; bailing
achicar §86 *va* to make smaller; to humble, to intimidate; to drain, to bail out; to make childish; (Am.) to kill
achicoria *f* (bot.) chicory
achicharradero *m* inferno (*any hot place*)
achicharrar *va* to scorch; to bother, to bedevil; *vr* to get scorched
achichinque *m* (min.) scooper, bailer (*workman*)
achilenado -da *adj* (Am.) like a Chilean; (Am.) pro-Chilean
achinado -da *adj* Chinese-looking; (Am.) half-breed; (Am.) degraded; (Am.) copper-colored; (Am.) Indian-looking (*in color or features*)
achinar *va* (coll.) to intimidate, scare
achinelado -da *adj* slipper-shaped
achiotal *m* plantation of annatto trees
achiote *m* (bot.) annatto tree
achique *m* bailing, scooping, draining
achispado -da *adj* tipsy
achispar *va* to make tipsy; *vr* to get tipsy
-acho -cha *suffix aug & pej* e.g., **hombracho** husky big fellow; **populacho** mob, rabble; **terminacho** vulgar term
achocadura *f* hurling or dashing against a wall; hitting, striking, stoning
achocar §86 *va* to hurl or dash against a wall; to hit, to strike, to stone; (coll.) to hoard
achocolatado -da *adj* chocolate, chocolate-colored
achochar *vr* (coll.) to begin to dote, to go into one's dotage
acholado -da *adj* (Am.) part white, part Indian; (Am.) abashed, cowed
acholar *vr* (Am.) to be abashed, to be ashamed
achote *m* var. of **achiote**
achubascar §86 *vr* to get cloudy and threatening (*said of the sky*)
achucutar or **achucuyar** *vr* (Am.) to become discouraged; (Am.) to wither, to spoil
achuchar *va* to incite, urge on; (coll.) to crumple, crush; to push around, jostle
achuchón *m* (coll.) crumpling, crushing; jostling
achulado -da *adj* (coll.) rough, tough
achulapar or **achular** *vr* to get rough and ill-mannered
achunchar *va* (Am.) to embarrass, to foil; (Am.) to cast the evil eye on
achuñuscar §86 *va* to crumple, to crush
achura *f* (Am.) guts (*of an animal*)
Ada *f* Ada
adafina *f* Jewish stew
adagio *m* adage; (mus.) adagio
adala *f* (naut.) pump dale
adalid *m* chief, commander; guide, leader; champion (*of a cause, a movement, etc.*)
adamado -da *adj* womanish, soft; chic, stylish; gaudy (*said of a woman*)
adamantino -na *adj* adamantine
adamar *vr* to become thin, to become effeminate, to look like a woman
adamas *m* adamant, diamond
adamascado -da *adj* damask; damascene
adamascar §86 *va* to damask (*to weave like damask*); to damascene
adámico -ca *adj* Adamic; left by the tide (*said of sand and other sediment*)
Adán *m* Adam; (*l.c.*) *m* (coll.) dirty, ragged fellow; (coll.) lazy, careless fellow

adaptabilidad *f* adaptability
adaptable *adj* adaptable
adaptación *f* adaptation
adaptador *m* adapter
adaptante *adj* adapting, adaptive
adaptar *va* to adapt, to fit
adaraja *f* (mas.) toothing
adarce *m* dried salt froth, incrustation of salt spray
adarga *f* oval or heart-shaped leather shield
adargar **§59** *va* to shield, protect
adarme *m* sixteenth part of ounce (*179 centigrams*); bit, driblet
adarvar *va* to stun, to bewilder; *vr* to be stunned, to be overwhelmed
adarve *m* (fort.) walk behind parapet on top of wall
adatar *va* to enter in a ledger; to credit
adaza *f* (bot.) sorghum
A. de C. abr. of **año de Cristo**
adecenamiento *m* grouping or dividing in tens
adecenar *va* to group or divide in tens
adecentar *va* to make decent or proper; to tidy up, to clean up; *vr* (coll.) to put on a clean shirt, to dress up
adecuación *f* fitting, adaptation
adecuado -da *adj* fitting, suitable
adecuar *va* to fit, adapt
adefagia *f* voracity
adéfago -ga *adj* voracious
adefesio *m* (coll.) nonsense, absurdity; (coll.) outlandish outfit; (coll.) ridiculous fellow, queer-looking guy; **decir** or **hablar adefesios** to talk nonsense
adefina *f* var. of **adafina**
adehala *f* gratuity, extra, perquisite
adehesamiento *m* converting into pasture
adehesar *va* to convert into pasture
Adelaida *f* Adelaide
adelantadamente *adv* beforehand, in advance
adelantado -da *adj* precocious; bold, rash; fast (*said of a watch or clock*); **por adelantado** in advance; *m* (archaic) governor of a province
adelantamiento *m* anticipation; advancement, progress, improvement, promotion
adelantar *va* to move forward, to move ahead; to get ahead of, to outstrip; to hasten (*e.g., one's step*); to advance, promote; to make (*e.g., payment*) in advance; to improve; *vn* to advance, get along, improve; to be fast (*said of a watch or clock*); *vr* to move forward, to move ahead; to gain, be fast (*said of a watch or clock*); **adelantarse a** or **de** to get ahead of, to outstrip
adelante *adv* ahead; forward; in the opposite direction, e.g., **un hombre que viene por el camino adelante** a man coming in the opposite direction; **de aquí en adelante** from now on, henceforth; **en adelante** in the future; **hacia adelante** forward; **más adelante** farther on; later; *interj* ahead!, go ahead!; come in!
adelanto *m* advance, progress; advancement; payment in advance
adelfa *f* (bot.) oleander, rosebay
adelfal *m* field of oleanders
adelfilla *f* (bot.) spurge laurel; **adelfilla pelosa** (bot.) willow herb (*Epilobium hirsutum*)
adelgazamiento *m* thinness, slenderness; hairsplitting
adelgazar **§76** *va* to make thin or slender; to taper; to purify, refine; to split hairs regarding; **adelgazar el entendimiento** to sharpen one's wits; **adelgazar la voz** to raise the pitch of one's voice; *vn* to get thin or slender; *vr* to get thin or slender; to taper; to split hairs
Adelina *f* Adeline
adema *f* var. of **ademe**
ademador *m* (min.) shorer
ademán *m* attitude; gesture; (paint. & sculp.) attitude; **ademanes** *mpl* manners; **en ademán de** + *inf* showing an intention to + *inf*, getting ready to + *inf*; **hacer ademán de** + *inf* to make a move to + *inf*
ademar *va* (min.) to shore, to shore up
además *adv* moreover, besides; **además de** in addition to, besides
ademe *m* (min.) shore, strut, prop; shoring
Adén *m* Aden
adenia *f* (path.) adenia
adenitis *f* (path.) adenitis
adenoidectomía *f* adenoidectomy
adenoideo -a *adj* adenoid, adenoidal
adenoma *m* (path.) adenoma
adensar *vr* to become thick or thicker
adentellar *va* to sink one's teeth into; to criticize bitingly; (mas.) to leave toothing in (*e.g., a wall*)
adentrar *vn & vr* to go in, to go into; **adentrarse en el mar** to go further out to sea
adentro *adv* inside, within; **mar adentro** out at sea; **ser muy de adentro** to be like a member of the family; **tierra adentro** inland; **adentros** *mpl* very inmost being, very inmost thoughts; **en** or **para sus adentros** to oneself, to himself, etc.
adepto -ta *adj* adept; *mf* follower; adept (*in alchemy, magic, etc.*)
aderezamiento *m* dressing; adornment, embellishment
aderezar **§76** *va* to dress, to prepare, to embellish; to cook, to season; to repair; to mix (*drinks*); to lead, show the way to; *vr* to dress, to get ready
aderezo *m* dressing; seasoning, condiment; adornment, finery; equipment; set of jewels
aderra *f* rope made of esparto; trappings; trimmings; stiffening
adestrado -da *adj* (her.) dexterwise
adestrador -dora *adj & mf* var. of **adiestrador**
adestrar **§18** *va & vr* var. of **adiestrar**
adeudado -da *adj* indebted, in debt
adeudar *va* to owe; to be liable or subject to (*duties, taxes, etc.*); to charge, to debit; *vn* to become related by marriage; *vr* to run into debt, to become indebted
adeudo *m* debt, indebtedness; custom duty; charge, debit
adherencia *f* adhesion (*sticking fast*); bond, relationship; (path. & phys.) adhesion; **tener adherencias** to have connections
adherente *adj* adherent; *m* adherent; requisite; accessory; dressing
adherir **§62** *vn & vr* to adhere, to stick; **adherir a** or **adherirse a** to be attached to; to espouse, to embrace
adhesión *f* adherence or adhesion (*steady attachment*); (phys.) adhesion
adhesividad *f* adhesiveness; addiction; sociability
adhesivo -va *adj & m* adhesive
adiabático -ca *adj* adiabatic
adiafa *f* (archaic) treat or gift to sailors at the end of a voyage
adiaforesis *f* (path.) adiaphoresis
adiamantado -da *adj* diamondlike
adición *f* addition; marginal note (*on bill or account*); (Am.) check (*in hotel or restaurant*); **adición de la herencia** (law) acceptance of an inheritance
adicional *adj* additional
adicionar *va* to add; to add to
adicto -ta *adj* devoted; belonging, supporting; adjunct; *mf* devotee; supporter, partisan
adiestrable *adj* trainable; docile
adiestrador -dora *adj* training; teaching; *mf* trainer; teacher; guide
adiestramiento *m* training; teaching; leading
adiestrar *va* to train; to teach; to lead, direct, guide; *vr* to train, to practice; **adiestrarse a** + *inf* to train oneself to + *inf*, to practice + *ger*
adietar *va* to put on a diet
adifés *adv* (Am.) on purpose
adinamia *f* (path.) adynamia
adinámico -ca *adj* adynamic
adinerado -da *adj* moneyed, wealthy
adinerar *va* (prov.) to turn into cash; *vr* (coll.) to get rich
adintelado -da *adj* straight, flat (*said of an arch or vault*)
adiós *m* (*pl:* **adioses**) adieu, good-by; *interj* adieu!, good-by!; hello!
adiosito *interj* bye-bye!
adipocira *f* adipocere
adiposidad *f* adiposity
adiposis *f* (path.) adiposis
adiposo -sa *adj* adipose

adipsia *f* (path.) adipsia
adir *va* (law) to accept (*an inheritance*)
aditamento *m* addition; attachment, accessory
aditivo -va *adj & m* additive
adiva *f* (zool.) jackal; **adivas** *fpl* (vet.) vives
adive *m* (zool.) jackal
adivina *f* see **adivino**
adivinable *adj* guessable
adivinación *f* prophecy; guessing, divination; solving; **adivinación del pensamiento** mind reading
adivinador -dora *adj* divinatory; *mf* prophesier; guesser, diviner; good guesser; **adivinador del pensamiento** mind reader
adivinaja *f* (coll.) riddle, puzzle
adivinamiento *m* var. of **adivinación**
adivinanza *f* riddle; divination, guess
adivinar *va* to prophesy; to guess, to divine; to solve (*a riddle or puzzle*); to read (*someone's mind or thoughts*); *vn* to divine
adivinatorio -ria *adj* divining, divinatory
adivino -na *mf* fortuneteller, soothsayer, prophet; guesser; *m* (ent.) praying mantis; *f* (prov.) riddle, puzzle
adjetivación *f* modification; adjective use
adjetivadamente *adv* adjectively
adjetival *adj* adjectival
adjetivar *va* to modify (*a noun*); to apply an epithet to; to use as an adjective; *vr* to become an adjective
adjetivo -va *adj* adjective, adjectival; *m* adjective; **adjetivo gentilicio** adjective of nationality
adjudicación *f* adjudging, awarding
adjudicador -dora *adj* adjudging; *mf* adjudger
adjudicar §86 *va* to adjudge (*to award*); *vr* to appropriate
adjudicatario -ria *mf* awardee, grantee
adjuntar *va* to join, connect; to add; to enclose (*in a letter*)
adjunto -ta *adj* adjunct; added, attached; enclosed (*in a letter*); *mf* adjunct, associate; *m* (gram.) adjunct
adjuración *f* (archaic) conjuration (*invoking by a sacred name*)
adlátere *m* var. of **a látere**
Admeto *m* (myth.) Admetus
adminicular *va* (law) to strengthen, reinforce
adminículo *m* adminicle, aid, auxiliary; accessory, gadget; meddler; (law) adminicle (*corroborative proof*); **adminículos** *mpl* emergency equipment
administración *f* administration
administrador -dora *adj* administrating; *mf* administrator; **administrador de aduanas** collector of customs; **administrador de correos** postmaster; **administrador judicial** administrator (*of an estate*); **administradora judicial** administratrix (*of an estate*)
administrar *va* to administer
administrativo -va *adj* administrative
admirabilísimo -ma *adj super* very or most admirable
admirable *adj* admirable
admiración *f* admiration; wonder; exclamation point
admirador -dora *adj* admiring; (coll.) beauty-loving; *mf* admirer; (coll.) beauty-lover, devotee of the fair sex
admirando -da *adj* admirable
admirar *va* to admire; to surprise; *vr* to admire, to wonder; **admirarse de** to wonder at
admirativo -va *adj* admiring; admirable
admisibilidad *f* admissibility
admisible *adj* admissible; allowable
admisión *f* admission; (mach.) intake
admitancia *f* (elec.) admittance
admitir *va* to admit; to allow, to allow for; to accept, recognize; **admitir** + *inf* to agree to + *inf*
admonición *f* admonition
adm.or abr. of **administrador**
adnato -ta *adj* (bot. & zool.) adnate; *f* (anat.) conjunctiva
-ado -da *suffix adj* -ate, e.g., **separado** separate; **apasionado** passionate; -ed, e.g., **bienaventurado** blessed; -y, e.g., **ondulado** wavy; -shaped, e.g., **acorazonado** heart-shaped; -colored, e.g., **naranjado** orange-colored; (bot. & zool.) -ate, e.g., **cordado** chordate; **espatulado** spatulate; *suffix m* -acy, e.g., **papado** papacy; -ate, e.g., **prelado** prelate; **senado** senate; -ful, e.g., **brazado** armful; **puñado** handful; -ing, e.g., **pisonado** tamping; **planchado** ironing; *suffix f* -ad, e.g., **tríada** triad; **Ilíada** Iliad; -ade, e.g., **brigada** brigade; **limonada** lemonade; **mascarada** masquerade; -ful, e.g., **cucharada** spoonful; **palada** shovelful; blow, stroke, stab, e.g., **martillada** blow or stroke with a hammer; **plumada** stroke of pen; **puñalada** stab with a dagger; pack, drove, e.g., **perrada** pack of dogs; **vacada** drove of cattle
adobado *m* pickled meat
adobador -dora *mf* repairer, dresser; pickler; tanner
adobajes *mpl* pickled meat in barrels
adobar *va* to repair, restore; to prepare, to dress; to trim (*a lamp*); to cook, stew; to pickle (*meat, fish*); to tan (*hides*); to fertilize; to hammer and fit (*a horseshoe*)
adobasillas *m* (*pl:* **-llas**) chair mender
adobe *m* adobe
adobeño -ña *adj* adobe-like; (pertaining to the) adobe
adobera *f* adobe mould; adobe factory; (Am.) adobe-shaped cheese; (Am.) mould for adobe-shaped cheese
adobería *f* adobe factory; tannery
adobino -na *adj* (pertaining to the) adobe
adobo *m* repairing; dressing; trimming; cooking; pickling, pickle, pickled meat or fish; tanning, tanning mixture
adocenado -da *adj* commonplace, ordinary
adocenar *va* to arrange or divide in dozens; to confuse with the rabble, to put in a lower class
adoctrinamiento *m* indoctrination, teaching, instruction
adoctrinar *va* to indoctrinate, to teach, to instruct
adolecer §34 *vn* to fall sick, become ill; **adolecer de** to suffer from; (fig.) to suffer from; *vr* to sympathize, be sorry
adolescencia *f* adolescence
adolescente *adj & mf* adolescent
Adolfo *m* Adolph
adolorado -da or **adolorido -da** *adj* sore, aching; grieving, sorrowful
adomiciliar *va & vr.* var. of **domiciliar**
adonde *conj* where, whither
adónde *adv* where?, whither?; where, whither, e.g., **dígame Vd. adónde va** tell me where you are going
adondequiera *adv* anywhere; **adondequiera que** wherever, whithersoever
adónico -ca *adj & m* Adonic
adonis *m* (*pl:* **-nis**) Adonis (*handsome young man*); (*cap.*) *s* (myth.) Adonis
adonizar §76 *vn & vr* to be a dandy, to be dandified; to be puffed up, be conceited
adopción *f* adoption
adopcionismo *m* adoptionism
adopcionista *adj & m* adoptionist
adoptable *adj* adoptable
adoptador -dora or **adoptante** *adj* adopting; *mf* adopter
adoptar *va* to adopt
adoptivo -va *adj* adoptive; strange, artificial, sham
adoquín *m* paving stone, paving block; dolt
adoquinado *m* cobblestone paving
adoquinar *va* to pave, to pave with cobblestones
-ador -dora *suffix adj* -ing, e.g., **acusador** accusing; **trabajador** working, hard-working; *suffix mf* -er, e.g., **acusador** accuser; **trabajador** worker; *suffix m* -er, e.g., **mostrador** counter; *suffix f* -er, e.g., **apisonadora** road roller
ador *m* turn to irrigate
adorable *adj* adorable
adoración *f* adoration, worship; **Adoración de los Reyes** (eccl.) Epiphany
adorador -dora *adj* adoring, worshiping; *mf* adorer, worshiper; **adorador del fuego** fire worshiper; *m* suitor
adorar *va & vn* to adore, to worship

adormecedor -dora *adj* soporific, sleep-producing
adormecer §34 *va* to put to sleep; to calm, lull, ease; to quiet; *vr* to go to sleep, to fall asleep; to get numb; **adormecerse en** to persist in (*vices, pleasures, etc.*)
adormecido -da *adj* sleepy, drowsy; numb; calm, inactive
adormecimiento *m* falling asleep; sleepiness; numbness
adormidera *f* (bot.) opium poppy; **adormidera espinosa** (bot.) prickly poppy
adormilar *vr* to doze
adormir §45 *va* to put to sleep; *vr* to go to sleep
adormitar *vr* to doze
adornado -da *adj* adorned, ornate; gifted, endowed; *m* adornment
adornar *va* to adorn; to embroider (*a story*)
adornista *mf* decorator
adorno *m* adornment, decoration; **adornos** *mpl* finery; **de adorno** ornamental (*e.g., plants*); **adorno de escaparate** window dressing; (fig.) window dressing
adosado -da *adj* (her.) addorsed
adosar *va* to lean; to push close; **adosar a** to lean (*something*) against; to push close to; to place with the back against
adquirente *mf* acquirer, purchaser
adquiridor -dora *mf* acquirer
adquirir §56 *va* to acquire
adquisición *f* acquisition, acquirement
adquisidor -dora *mf* acquirer
adquisitivo -va *adj* (law) acquisitive
adquisividad *f* acquisitiveness
adra *f* turn; section of people of a town
adraganto *m* (bot.) tragacanth
adral *m* sideboard (*of a wagon*)
adrede or **adredemente** *adv* on purpose, purposely
adrenalina *f* (physiol. & pharm.) adrenalin
adresógrafo *m* addressograph
adrián *m* bunion; nest of magpies
Adriano *m* Adrian; Hadrian
Adriático -ca *adj* & *m* Adriatic
adrizar §76 *va* (naut.) to right, to straighten
adscribir §17, 9 *va* to attribute; to assign, appoint
adscripción *f* attribution; assignment, appointment
adscripto -ta or **adscrito -ta** *pp of* **adscribir**
adsorbente *adj* adsorptive
adsorber *va* to adsorb
adsorción *f* adsorption
aduana *f* customhouse; **aduana seca** inland customhouse
aduanar *va* to enter (*goods*) at the customhouse; to pay duty on
aduanero -ra *adj* (pertaining to the) customhouse; *m* customhouse officer
aduanilla *f* (prov.) general store
aduar *m* Arab settlement; gipsy camp; (Am.) Indian camp or ranch
adúcar *m* floss, coarse silk; coarse silk cloth
aducción *f* adduction; (physiol.) adduction
aducir §38 *va* to adduce; (physiol.) to adduct
aductor *adj* (physiol.) adducent; *m* (physiol.) adductor
aduendado -da *adj* fairylike
adueñar *vr* to take possession
adufa *f* lock, sluice
adufe *m* tambourine; (coll.) rattle-brained person
aduja *f* (naut.) turn, coil, fake
adujada *f* (naut.) coil (*of rope or cable*)
adujar *va* (naut.) to coil (*a rope or cable*); *vr* (naut.) to curl up (*e.g., to sleep*)
aduje *1st sg pret ind of* **aducir**
adula *f* common pasture
adulación *f* adulation
adulador -dora *adj* adulating, fawning; *m* adulator; *f* adulatress
adular *va* to adulate, to flatter, to fawn on
adularia *f* (mineral.) adularia
adulatorio -ria *adj* adulatory
adulón -lona *adj* (coll.) fawning, groveling; *mf* (coll.) bootlicker
adúltera *f* see **adúltero**
adulteración *f* adulteration
adulterante *adj* & *m* adulterant
adulterar *va* to adulterate; to wangle (*an account*); *vn* to adulterize, to commit adultery; *vr* to become adulterated
adulterino -na *adj* adulterine, adulterous; bastard; false, fake
adulterio *m* adultery
adúltero -ra *adj* adulterous; *m* adulterer; *f* adulteress
adultez *f* (Am.) adulthood
adulto -ta *adj* & *mf* adult
adulzar §76 *va* to sweeten; to make more ductile, to soften (*metals*)
adumbración *f* (paint.) shadow
adumbrar *va* to shade; to conceal
adunación *f* or **adunamiento** *m* uniting, gathering
adunar *va* & *vr* to unite, join, gather
adunco -ca *adj* arched, curved
adunia *adv* in abundance
adustez *f* grimness, sternness, sullenness, gloominess
adustión *f* (surg.) cauterization
adusto -ta *adj* scorching hot; grim, stern, sullen, gloomy
aduzco *1st sg pres ind of* **aducir**
advendré *1st sg fut ind of* **advenir**
advenedizo -za *adj* foreign; strange; immigrant; parvenu, upstart; (Am.) inexperienced; *mf* foreigner; stranger, newcomer, outsider; immigrant; parvenu, upstart; nouveau riche; (Am.) novice, beginner
advengo *1st sg pres ind of* **advenir**
advenidero -ra *adj* coming, future
advenimiento *m* advent, coming; accession (*of a pontiff or sovereign*); **esperar el santo advenimiento** (coll.) to wait in vain; **segundo advenimiento** Second Advent
advenir §92 *vn* to come, to arrive; to happen
adventicio -cia *adj* adventitious; (anat., biol. & med.) adventitious; *f* (anat.) adventitia
adventismo *m* Adventism
adventista *mf* Adventist
adverado -da *adj* certified
adverbial *adj* adverbial
adverbializar §76 *va* to adverbialize
adverbio *m* adverb
adversario -ria *mf* adversary; **adversarios** *mpl* adversaria (*notes*)
adversativo -va *adj* & *f* (gram.) adversative
adversidad *f* adversity (*misfortune*)
adverso -sa *adj* adverse
advertencia *f* observation; notice, remark; warning; foreword
advertidamente *adv* deliberately, on purpose; with open eyes
advertido -da *adj* capable, clever, wide-awake
advertir §62 *va* to notice, observe; to point out; to notify, warn, advise; *vn* **advertir en** to notice, observe; to take into account; *vr* to notice, become aware
Adviento *m* (eccl.) Advent
advine *1st sg pret ind of* **advenir**
advocación *f* name given to a church, chapel, or altar in dedication to the Virgin or a saint
adyacencia *f* adjacency
adyacente *adj* adjacent
adyuvante *adj* & *m* adjuvant
aechadero *m* sifting floor
aechador -dora *adj* sifting; *mf* sifter
aechaduras *fpl* siftings, chaff
aechar *va* to sift (*grain*)
aecho *m* sifting (*of grain*)
Aelfrico *m* Aelfric
aeración *f* aeration; ventilation; air conditioning
aerear *va* to aerate
aéreo -a *adj* aerial, (pertaining to) air; overhead, elevated; light, airy, fanciful; (poet.) tall, lofty
aerífero -ra *adj* aeriferous
aerificación *f* aerification
aerificar §86 *va* to aerify
aeriforme *adj* aeriform
aéro-atómico -ca *adj* air-atomic
aeróbico -ca *adj* (bact.) aerobic
aerobio *m* (bact.) aerobe
aerobús *m* passenger plane

aerodinámico -ca *adj* aerodynamic; streamlined; *f* aerodynamics
aeródromo *m* aerodrome, airdrome; **aeródromo de urgencia** (aer.) emergency landing field
aeroembolismo *m* (path.) aeroembolism
aeroescala *f* var. of **aeroscala**
aerofagia or **aerofagía** *f* (path.) aerophagia, air swallowing
aerofaro *m* aerial beacon
aerofluyente *adj* streamlined
aerofobia *f* (path.) aerophobia
aeroforme *adj* streamlined
aeróforo -ra *adj* aeriferous; *m* (med. & min.) aerophore
aerofoto *f* aerophotograph
aerofotografía *f* aerophotography (*art or process*); aerophotograph (*picture*)
aerofotografiar §90 *va* to photograph from the air
aerofumigación *f* crop dusting
aerógrafo *m* atomizer, air brush
aerograma *m* aerogram (*message carried by aircraft; radiogram*)
aerolínea *f* air line
aerolito *m* aerolite
aerología *f* aerology
aerólogo -ga *mf* aerologist
aeromancía *f* aeromancy
aeromántico -ca *adj* aeromantic; *mf* aeromancer
aeromapa *m* air map
aeromecánico -ca *adj* aeromechanical; *f* aeromechanics
aeromedicina *f* aviation medicine
aerómetro *m* aerometer
aeromodelismo *m* model-airplane building
aeromodelista *mf* model-airplane builder
aeromodelo *m* model airplane
aeromotor *m* windmill; aeromotor, aircraft motor
aeromoza *f* (aer.) air hostess, stewardess
aeronato -ta *adj* born in an aircraft in flight
aeronauta *mf* aeronaut
aeronáutico -ca *adj* aeronautic, aeronautical; *m* aeronautical engineer; *f* aeronautics
aeronave *f* airship; **aeronave cohete** rocket ship
aeropista *f* (aer.) landing strip
aeroplano *m* aeroplane
aeroplano-nodriza *m* (aer.) tanker plane
aeropostal *adj* air-mail
aeropropulsor *m* (aer.) airplane engine; **aeropropulsor por reacción** (aer.) jet engine
aeropuerto *m* airport
aeroscala *f* (aer.) fuel stop, transit point
aeroscopio *m* aeroscope
aerosol *m* (physical chem.) aerosol
aerostación *f* aerostation
aeróstata *mf* aerostat (*person*)
aerostático -ca *adj* aerostatic, aerostatical; *f* aerostatics
aeróstato *m* aerostat (*craft*)
aerostero -ra *adj* (pertaining to) aviation; *m* flyer; airman (*enlisted man*)
aeroterapia *f* aerotherapeutics, aerotherapy
aeroterrestre *adj* air-ground
aerotransportado -da *adj* airborne
aerovía *f* airway
afabilidad *f* affability
afabilísimo -ma *adj super* very or most affable
afable *adj* affable
afabulación *f* putting into the form of a fable; moral of a fable
afabular *va* to put into the form of a fable
áfaca *f* (bot.) lathyrus
afamado -da *adj* famed, noted, famous
afamar *va* to make famous; *vr* to become famous
afán *m* hard work; physical labor; anxiety, worry; zeal, eagerness; task, duty
afanadamente *adv* laboriously, zealously
afanador -dora *adj* hard-working, laborious; *mf* hard-worker, toiler
afanar *va* to press, harass, hurry; *vn* to strive, toil, labor; *vr* to busy oneself; to strive, toil, labor; **afanarse** + *ger* to busy oneself + *ger;* **afanarse en** or **por** + *inf* to strive to + *inf*
afaníptero -ra *adj* (zool.) aphanipterous
afanita *f* var. of **anfíbolita**
afanoso -sa *adj* hard, heavy, laborious; hard-working
afarallonado -da *adj* craggy, cliffy
afarolar *vr* (Am.) to get all excited, to make a fuss
afasia *f* (path.) aphasia
afeamiento *m* making ugly, defacement; blame, condemnation
afear *va* to make ugly, to deform, deface; to blame, condemn
afeblecer §34 *vr* to grow thin, to grow feeble
afección *f* affection; change, effect; (med.) affection
afectabilidad *f* susceptibility
afectable *adj* susceptible
afectación *f* affectation
afectado -da *adj* affected
afectar *va* to affect (*to pretend to have or feel; to assume*); to desire eagerly; to earmark; to sadden, afflict; to mortgage, to encumber; *vr* to be moved or stirred
afectivo -va *adj* affective, emotional
afecto -ta *adj* fond; annexed, attached; inclined, subject; harmed; **afecto de** affected with (*a disease*); *m* emotion; affection; moral instinct; **afecto moral** or **afecto superior** sense of human dignity
afectuosidad *f* affection, fondness
afectuoso -sa *adj* affectionate
afeitada *f* (Am.) shave, shaving
afeitadera *f* safety razor
afeitado *m* shave, shaving
afeitanar *va* (mach.) to cut off, to shear off
afeitar *va* to shave; to adorn, embellish; to paint (*e.g., the face*); to trim (*horse's mane or tail; branches, leaves of plant*); (taur.) to shave (*the bull's horns*); *vr* to shave; to paint; to become bored
afeite *m* fixing, arranging, adornment; cosmetic, make-up; grease paint, rouge
afelio *m* (astr.) aphelion
afelpar *va* to make like velvet or plush
afeminación *f* effeminacy; effemination
afeminado -da *adj* effeminate
afeminamiento *m* effeminacy; effemination
afeminar *va & vr* to effeminate
aferente *adj* (physiol.) afferent
aféresis *f* (*pl:* **-sis**) (gram.) aphaeresis
aferrado -da *adj* stubborn, obstinate
aferramiento *m* seizing, grasping; (naut.) mooring, anchoring; (naut.) furling; insistence, persistence
aferrar *va* to seize, grasp; to catch; to hook; (naut.) to moor, anchor; (naut.) to furl; *vn* (naut.) to moor, anchor; to insist; **aferrar a, con** or **en** to stick to (*e.g., an opinion*); **aferrar de** or **en** to seize, grasp; *vr* to interlock, to hook together; to insist; to cling; **aferrarse a, con,** or **en** to stick to (*e.g., an opinion*)
aferruzado -da *adj* angry, irate
afestonado -da *adj* festooned
Afganistán, el Afghanistan
afgano -no *adj & mf* Afghan; *m* Afghan (*language*)
afianzable *adj* bailable
afianzamiento *m* guarantee, security, bail; support, prop; fastening; (fig.) backing, support
afianzar §76 *va* to guarantee, to vouch for; to fasten; to support, to prop up; to grasp; (fig.) to support, to back, to strengthen; *vr* to hold fast, to steady oneself
afición *f* fondness, liking, taste; zeal, ardor; fans, public; **de afición** as an amateur; (sport) amateur; **tomar afición a** to take a liking to; **afición ciega razón** love is blind
aficionado -da *adj* fond; amateur; *mf* amateur; lover, follower, fan
aficionar *va* to cause to like; *vr* **aficionarse a** to become fond of; to become a lover or follower of; **aficionarse a** + *inf* to become fond of + *ger*
afiche *m* (Am.) poster
afidávit *m* affidavit
afídidos or **áfidos** *mpl* (ent.) aphides
afiebrado -da *adj* feverish
afijación *f* (gram.) affixation

afijo *adj masc* (gram.) conjunctive (*pronoun*); *m* (gram.) affix
afiladera *f* grindstone
afilado -da *adj* sharp; pointed; peaked
afilador -dora *adj* sharpening; *m* sharpener, grinder (*person*); steel, knife sharpener; razor strop
afiladura *f* grinding, sharpening
afilalápices *m* (*pl:* **-ces**) pencil sharpener
afilamiento *m* peakedness (*of nose, fingers, face, etc.*)
afilar *va* to whet, grind, sharpen; to put a point or edge on; to strop (*a razor*); *vr* to sharpen, get sharp; to get thin or pointed (*said of nose, fingers, face, etc.*)
afiliación *f* affiliation
afiliar §90 & regular *va & vr* to affiliate; **afiliarse a** to affiliate oneself with, to affiliate with
afiligranado -da *adj* filigreed; fine, delicate; thin, slender
afiligranar *va* to filigree; to adorn, embellish
áfilo -la *adj* (bot.) aphyllose
afilón *m* steel, knife sharpener; razor strop
afilorar *va* (Am.) to adorn, bedeck
afilosofado -da *adj* like a philosopher, having the pretentions of a philosopher
afín *adj* near, bordering; like, similar; related; *mf* relative by marriage
afinación *f* refining, completion; (mus.) tuning
afinadamente *adv* completely, perfectly; smoothly, delicately
afinador *m* (mus.) tuner (*person*); (mus.) tuning hammer, tuning key
afinadura *f* var. of **afinación**
afinamiento *m* refining, completion; (mus.) tuning; refinement
afinar *va* to purify, refine, polish, perfect; to trim (*edges of a book*); (mus.) to tune; (mus.) to sing or play in tune
afincado -da *adj* owning real estate
afincamiento *m* settlement, location
afincar §86 *vn & vr* var. of **fincar**
afinidad *f* affinity; (biol. & chem.) affinity; **por afinidad** by marriage
afino *m* refinement (*of metals*)
afirmación *f* affirmation
afirmadamente *adv* firmly
afirmador -dora *adj* affirming; *mf* affirmer
afirmar *va* to strengthen, secure, fasten; to assert, to affirm; *vn* to affirm; *vr* to be fastened, to hold fast; to make oneself firm, to steady oneself
afirmativo -va *adj & f* affirmative
afistular *va* to make fistulous
aflato *m* wind, draft; (fig.) afflatus
aflautado -da *adj* high-pitched; fluty, flutelike
aflechado -da *adj* arrow-shaped; (bot.) sagittate
aflicción *f* affliction, sorrow, grief
aflictivo -va *adj* afflictive
aflicto -ta *adj* afflicted
afligidamente *adv* sorrowfully, with affliction
afligimiento *m* var. of **aflicción**
afligir §42 *va* to afflict, to grieve; *vr* to grieve; **afligirse de** + *inf* to be grieved at + *ger;* **afligirse con, de,** or **por** to be grieved at
afilijón -jona *adj* (Am.) gloomy, weepy
aflogístico -ca *adj* aphlogistic
aflojamiento *m* slackening, relaxing; loosening; diminution, abatement
aflojar *va* to slacken, to relax, to let go; to loosen (*e.g., a screw, the bowels*); *vn* to slacken, to relax, to slow up; to lessen, to abate; *vr* to come loose; to slacken; (Am.) to break wind
aflorado -da *adj* fine, elegant, excellent; (pertaining to) flour
afloramiento *m* (min.) outcrop, outcropping
aflorar *va* to sift; *vn* to crop out, crop up; (min.) to crop out, to outcrop
afluencia *f* flowing; inflow, influx; flow; rush (*of people*); affluence, abundance; crowd, jam; fluency, eloquence
afluente *adj* flowing; affluent, abundant; fluent, eloquent; *m* affluent, tributary
afluir §41 *vn* to flow, to inflow; to pour (*said of a crowd of people, of a river, etc.*)
aflujo *m* (med.) afflux
afmo. or **af.**^mo^ abr. of **afectísimo**
afofar *va* to make fluffy, make spongy; *vr* to become fluffy, become spongy
afogarar *va & vr* to burn
afollar §77 *va* to blow (with bellows); to fold in the shape of bellows
afondar *va, vn & vr* to sink
afonía *f* (path.) aphonia
afónico -ca *adj* (path. & phonet.) aphonic
afonización *f* (phonet.) unvoicing
afonizar §76 *va & vr* to unvoice
áfono -na *adj* aphonous
aforado -da *adj* privileged; assessed
aforador *m* gauger; appraiser; stream gauge; (coll.) winebibber
aforamiento *m* gauging, measuring; appraisement
aforar *va* to gauge, to measure; to appraise; (hyd.) to gauge; (law) to grant by emphyteusis; **§77** *va* to privilege, to grant privileges to (*a town*)
aforestalación *f* afforestation
aforismo *m* aphorism
aforístico -ca *adj* aphoristic
aforo *m* gauging, measuring; appraisement; seating capacity
aforrar *va* to line; (naut.) to serve (*a cable*); *vr* to put on heavy underwear; (coll.) to gorge
aforro *m* lining; (naut.) serving
afortunado -da *adj* fortunate; happy; stormy, tempestuous; *mf* lucky person
afortunar *va* to make happy
afosar *vr* (mil.) to entrench, dig in
afoscar §86 *vr* to become misty or hazy
afrailar *va* to cut back, to trim (*trees, branches of trees*)
afrancesado -da *adj* Frenchified; *adj & mf* Francophile (*especially as applied to Spaniards in the eighteenth and nineteenth centuries*)
afrancesamiento *m* Francophilism; Gallicization
afrancesar *va* to Frenchify; to Gallicize; *vr* to Frenchify; to Gallicize; to become a Francophile
afrecho *m* bran
afrenillar *va* (naut.) to bridle (*the oars*)
afrenta *f* affront
afrentar *va* to affront; *vr* to be ashamed
afrentoso -sa *adj* insulting, ignominious
afretar *va* (naut.) to scrub and clean (*the hull*)
África *f* Africa; **el África del Norte** North Africa; **el África del Sudoeste** South-West Africa; **el África Ecuatorial Francesa** French Equatorial Africa; **el África Occidental Francesa** French West Africa; **el África Occidental Portuguesa** Portuguese West Africa; **el África Oriental Portuguesa** Portuguese East Africa
africado -da *adj* (phonet.) affricative; *f* (phonet.) affricate
africanista *mf* Africanist
africano -na *adj & mf* African
áfrico *m* var. of **ábrego**
afriza *f* (orn.) surfbird
afroamericano -na *adj & mf* Afro-American
afro-asiático -ca *adj* Afro-Asian
afrodisia *f* (path.) aphrodisia
afrodisíaco -ca *adj & m* aphrodisiac
Afrodita *f* (myth.) Aphrodite; (zool.) Aphrodite (*marine annelid*)
afronitro *m* wall saltpeter
afrontamiento *m* confrontation; meeting face to face
afrontar *va* to confront, to bring face to face; to face, to defy, to meet face to face; *vr* **afrontarse con** to confront, to meet face to face
afta *f* (path.) aphtha
af.^to^ abr. of **afecto**
aftoso -sa *adj* aphthous; *f* (Am.) foot-and-mouth disease
afuera *adv* outside; *interj* look out!, gangway!; **afueras** *fpl* outskirts
afuetear *va* (Am.) to whip, to flog
afufa *f* (coll.) flight
afufar *vn & vr* (coll.) to flee, run away
afufón *m* (coll.) flight
afusión *f* (med.) affusion
afuste *m* (mil.) gun carriage

afutrar *vr* (Am.) to doll up
agachada *f* trick, wile; trickiness
agachadiza *f* (orn.) snipe; **hacer la agachadiza** (coll.) to duck (*to avoid being seen or as if to avoid being seen*)
agachar *va* (coll.) to bow, to lower (*e.g., the head*); *vr* (coll.) to crouch, squat; (coll.) to cower; (coll.) to fade out of sight
agalbanado -da *adj* var. of **galbanoso**
agalerar *va* (naut.) to tip (*an awning*)
agáloco *m* (bot.) agalloch, eaglewood
agalla *f* (bot.) nutgall; gill (*of fish*); ear lobe (*of bird*); windgall (*of horse*); **agallas** *fpl* beaks (*of shuttle*); tonsils; tonsilitis; (coll.) courage, energy, guts
agallado -da *adj* galled; *m* decoction of gallnuts
agallón *m* (bot.) large gallnut; hollow silver bead; large wooden bead
agalludo -da *adj* (Am.) stingy; (Am.) cunning; (Am.) daring, bold
Agamenón *m* (myth.) Agamemnon
agamí *m* (*pl:* **-míes**) (orn.) trumpeter
agamitar *vn* to bleat like a small deer
ágamo -ma *adj* (biol.) agamic
agamogénesis *f* (biol.) agamogenesis
agamuzado -da *adj* var. of **gamuzado**
agangrenar *vr* to gangrene
Aganipe *f* (myth.) Aganippe
ágape *m* banquet; love feast
agar-agar *m* agar, agar-agar
agarbado -da *adj* var. of **garboso**
agarbanzado -da *adj* like a chickpea; of the color of chickpeas
agarbanzar **§76** *vn* to bud, sprout
agarbar *vr* to crouch, stoop, cower
agarbillar *va* to tie or bind in sheaves
agareno -na *adj* & *mf* Mohammedan
agárico *m* (bot.) agaric; **agárico blanco** (pharm.) agaric
agarrada *f* see **agarrado**
agarradero *m* handle; hold, grip; (coll.) shelter, protection; (naut.) anchorage
agarrado -da *adj* stingy, close-fisted; *f* (coll.) scrap, fight, brawl
agarrador -dora *adj* grasping, seizing; *m* flatiron holder; bailiff
agarrafar *va* (coll.) to grab, to clutch, to clinch
agarrar *va* to grasp, grab; to catch, take hold of; to filch; (coll.) to get, obtain; *vn* to take hold; to take root; to stick (*said of paint*); **agarrar de** to take hold of; **agarrar para** (Am.) to strike out for; *vr* to grasp each other, to grapple; to have a good hold, be on a sound footing; to worry; (coll.) to take hold of (*said of a disease*), e.g., **se le agarró la calentura** (coll.) the fever took hold of him; **agarrarse a** or **de** to seize, take a firm hold of
agarre *m* var. of **agarradero**
agarro *m* grasp, hold
agarrochador *m* goader
agarrochar *va* to goad, to prick with a spear
agarrón *m* (Am.) grab; (Am.) jerk; (Am.) hard throw; (Am.) row, fight, brawl
agarrotamiento *m* binding, jamming; stiffness
agarrotar *va* to bind with ropes; to squeeze hard, to pinch; to garrote; *vr* to get stiff, to get numb; to stick, get stuck; to bind, to jam
agasajador -dora *adj* kind, considerate, attentive
agasajar *va* to treat affectionately, to entertain royally, to shower with attentions, to lionize
agasajo *m* kindness, attention, show of affection; lionization; gift, favor; treat, refreshment; party (*in honor of someone*)
ágata *f* (mineral.) agate; (*cap.*) *s* Agatha; **ágata musgosa** (mineral.) moss agate
agavanza *f* dog rose (*fruit*)
agavanzo *m* (bot.) dog rose (*plant and fruit*)
agave *f* (bot.) agave
agavillador -dora *mf* binder (*of sheaves*); *f* binder (*machine*)
agavillar *va* to tie or bind in sheaves; *vr* to band together, to gang up
agazapar *va* (coll.) to seize, to grab; *vr* (coll.) to hide; (coll.) to crouch, to squat
agencia *f* agency; (Am.) pawnshop; **agencia de noticias** news agency
agenciar *va* to promote, to manage to bring about; *vr* to get along; to manage; to be put into effect
agencioso -sa *adj* active, diligent
agenda *f* notebook; agenda
agenesia *f* (physiol.) agennesis
agente *m* agent; policeman; (gram.) agent; **agente consular** consular agent; **agente de policía** policeman; detective; **agente provocador** agent provocateur; **agente reductor** (chem.) reducing agent; **agente secreto** secret agent; **agente viajero** agent, traveling salesman
Ageo *m* (Bib.) Haggai
agérato *m* (bot.) ageratum; (bot.) sweet maudlin
agermanar *vr* to join a gang of thieves; (Am.) to become Germanized, to imitate the Germans
agestado -da *adj* featured; **bien agestado** well-featured; **mal agestado** ill-featured
agestión *f* accumulation
ageusia *f* (path.) ageusia
agibílibus *m* (*pl:* **-bus**) (coll.) smartness, ability to look out for oneself; (coll.) smart fellow, fellow who knows how to look out for himself
agible *adj* feasible, workable
agigantado -da *adj* gigantic; notable, extraordinary
agigantar *va* to make huge, enormous, or immense; *vr* to become huge, enormous, or immense
ágil *adj* agile; light, flexible
agilidad *f* agility; lightness
agilitar or **agilizar** **§76** *va* to make agile, to limber; to enable; *vr* to limber up
agio *m* agio; speculation; usury
agiotador *m* speculator; usurer
agiotaje *m* var. of **agio**
agiotar *vn* to speculate; to practice usury
agiotista *m* var. of **agiotador**
agitable *adj* agitable
agitación *f* agitation
agitado -da *adj* agitated, excited; blustering; rough (*sea*); exalted
agitador -dora *adj* agitating; *mf* agitator; *m* agitator, stirrer, shaker
agitanado -da *adj* gypsylike, gypsy
agitar *va* to agitate, to shake, to wave; to stir; to excite; *vn* to agitate (*to stir up discussion*); *vr* to be agitated; to shake, to wave; to get excited; to get rough (*said of the sea*)
Aglaya *f* (myth.) Aglaia
aglobar *va* to make into a ball, to heap together; to include
aglomeración *f* agglomeration; built-up area; density (*of building*); crowd
aglomerado -da *adj* agglomerate; (bot.) agglomerate; *m* briquet, coal briquet; (geol.) agglomerate
aglomerante *m* agglomerant, binder
aglomerar *va* & *vr* to agglomerate
aglutinación *f* agglutination
aglutinado -da *adj* agglutinate
aglutinante *adj* agglutinative; *m* sticking plaster; cementing material; (elec.) binder
aglutinar *va* to agglutinate; to stick together; to bind; *vr* to agglutinate; to cake
aglutinina *f* (biochem.) agglutinin
agnación *f* agnation
agnado -da *adj* & *mf* agnate
agnición *f* (rhet.) recognition
agnocasto *m* (bot.) agnus castus, chaste tree
agnosticismo *m* agnosticism
agnóstico -ca *adj* & *mf* agnostic
agnusdéi *m* Agnus Dei
agobiado -da *adj* weighed down; bent over
agobiador -dora or **agobiante** *adj* exhausting, oppressive
agobiar *va* to bow, to weigh down, to overburden; to exhaust, oppress; *vr* to bow, to be bowed; **agobiarse con, de,** or **por** to be weighed down or overburdened with
agobio *m* bowing; burden, exhaustion, oppression
agogía *f* water outlet, drainage canal
agolpamiento *m* thronging, crowding, rush
agolpar *vr* to throng, crowd together, flock
agonal *adj* agonistic; **agonales** *fpl* agones

agonía *f* agony (*anguish; death struggle*); yearning; end; **agonías** *m* (coll.) whiner, gloomy person
agónico -ca *adj* (pertaining to) death or dying; agonic
agonioso -sa *adj* (coll.) petulant, insistent
agonístico -ca *adj* agonistic; *f* agonistics
agonizante *adj* dying; *mf* dying person; *m* monk of the order of St. Camillus who assists the dying; prompter at university examinations
agonizar §76 *va* to assist or attend (*the dying*); (coll.) to harass, importune; *vn* to be in the throes of death; to be dying out (*said, e.g., of a fire*)
ágono -na *adj* (geom.) agonic
ágora *f* agora
agorador -dora *adj & mf* var. of **agorero**
agorafobia *f* (psychopath.) agoraphobia
agorar §19 *va* to predict, foretell, have a presentiment of; to prophesy
agorero -ra *adj* fortunetelling; ill-omened; superstitious; *mf* fortuneteller; foreteller of doom
agorgojar *vr* to be infested with grubs, mites, etc. (*said of grain*)
agostadero *m* summer pasture; summer-pasture time
agostamiento *m* burning, parching, withering
agostar *va* to burn up, parch, wither; to plow to get rid of August weeds; to kill untimely; *vn* to burn up, parch, wither; to graze on stubbles in the dry season; to spend August; *vr* to fade away (*said of hope, happiness, etc.*)
agosteño -ña *adj* (pertaining to) August
agostero -ra *adj* (pertaining to) August; *m* harvest helper; religious mendicant begging grain at harvest time
agostino -na *adj* (pertaining to) August
agostizo -za *adj* sickly, scrawny; (pertaining to) August; born in August
agosto *m* August; harvest, crop; harvest time; **hacer su agosto** (coll.) to make hay while the sun shines
agotable *adj* exhaustible
agotado -da *adj* exhausted; sold out; out-of-print
agotador -dora *adj* exhausting
agotamiento *m* exhaustion; draining; consumption
agotar *va* to wear out, exhaust, use up; to drain, drain off; to run through (*money*); *vr* to become exhausted, to be used up; to give out; to go out of print, to go out of stock, to be selling out
agovía *f* var. of **alborga**
agracejina *f* barberry (*fruit*)
agracejo *m* stunted little grape; (bot.) barberry; (prov.) fallen olive (*before ripening*)
agraceño -ña *adj* tart, sour
agracero -ra *adj* yielding unripe grapes; *f* cruet for green-grape juice
agraciado -da *adj* graceful, charming; pretty, nice; *mf* winner
agraciar *va* to grace, make graceful; to favor, honor, reward; to award; to pardon
agracillo *m* (bot.) barberry
agradabilidad *f* agreeableness
agradabilísimo -ma *adj super* very or most agreeable
agradable *adj* agreeable
agradar *va* to please, to be pleasing to; **agradar** + *inf* to please (*someone*) to + *inf*, to like to + *inf*; *vn* to be pleasing; *vr* to be pleased; **agradarse de** to be pleased at
agradecer §34 *va* to thank; to reward; to be thankful or grateful for; **agradecerle a uno (que)** + *subj* to thank someone to + *inf*, e.g., **le agradeceremos llene la adjunta tarjeta** we will thank you to fill out the enclosed card; **agradecerle a uno una cosa** to thank a person for something
agradecido -da *adj* thankful, grateful; rewarding
agradecimiento *m* thanks, thankfulness, gratefulness
agrado *m* affability; pleasure, liking; **ser del agrado de** to be to the liking of
agramadera *f* scutch, brake
agramador -dora *adj* hemp-braking, flax-braking; *m* scutcher (*person*); scutch (*instrument*)
agramaduras *fpl* hemp refuse
agramar *va* to scutch, to brake (*flax or hemp*)
agramilar *va* to trim (*bricks*); to paint to resemble bricks; to mark out, to mark with a marking gauge
agramiza *f* stalk of hemp; hemp refuse
agrandamiento *m* enlargement, aggrandizement
agrandar *va* to enlarge, aggrandize; *vr* to grow larger; to aggrandize oneself
agranelar *va* to grain, to pebble (*leather*)
agranitado -da *adj* granitelike, granite
agranujado -da *adj* grain-shaped, grainlike, grained; pimply; rascally
agranujar *va* to grain, give a granular finish to; *vr* to become grained; (coll.) to turn into a rascal, to get to be worthless
agrarianismo *m* agrarianism
agrariense *adj & mf* agrarian
agrario -ria *adj* agrarian
agravación *f* aggravation, exaggeration, worsening
agravador -dora *adj* aggravating, oppressing
agravamiento *m* var. of **agravación**
agravante *adj* aggravating
agravar *va* to weigh down, make heavier; to increase (*taxes*); to aggravate; to make worse; to exaggerate; to oppress; *vr* to become aggravated; to get worse
agravatorio -ria *adj* aggravating; (law) mandatory
agraviamiento *m* wrong, offensiveness
agraviante *adj* offending, offensive
agraviar *va* to wrong, to offend; *vr* to take offense; **agraviarse de** or **por** to be offended at
agravio *m* wrong, offense; burden, weight; **agravios de hecho** assault and battery
agravioso -sa *adj* offensive, insulting
agraz *m* (*pl:* **-graces**) sour grape, sour grapes; sour-grape juice; (bot.) red-berried mistletoe; (bot.) mountain currant; (coll.) bitterness, displeasure; **echar el agraz en el ojo a** to hurt, to injure the feelings of; **en agraz** prematurely
agrazada *f* verjuice, green-grape juice
agrazar §76 *va* to annoy, embitter; *vn* to taste sour, have a sour taste
agrazón *m* wild grape; wild-gooseberry bush; (coll.) displeasure, annoyance
agrecillo *m* (bot.) barberry
agredir §53 *va* to attack, assault; to insult
agregación *f* aggregation
agregado -da *mf* (Am.) tenant farmer; (Am.) household guest; *m* aggregate; concrete block; acting employee; attaché
agregar §59 *va* to add; to annex; to attach, to detail; to admit; to appoint; *vr* to join; to intrude
agremán *m* braid, ribbon
agremiación *f* unionization
agremiado *m* union man, unionist
agremiar *va* to unionize; *vr* to become unionized
agresión *f* aggression
agresividad *f* aggressiveness, self-assertion
agresivo -va *adj* aggressive; offensive
agresor -sora *adj* aggressive; *mf* aggressor
agreste *adj* rustic, country; wild, rough; uncouth
agrete *adj* sourish
agriar §90 & regular *va* to make sour; to exasperate, to aggravate; *vr* to sour, turn sour; to become exasperated
agriaz *m* (*pl:* **-griaces**) (bot.) China tree
agrícola *adj* agricultural; (pertaining to the) farm; *mf* agriculturalist
agricultor -tora *mf* agriculturalist, agriculturist; farmer
agricultura *f* agriculture
agridulce *adj* bittersweet
agriera *f* (Am.) heartburn
agrietamiento *m* cracking; crack
agrietar *va & vr* to crack
agrifolio *m* (bot.) holly
agrilla *f* var. of **acedera**
agrillar *vr* var. of **grillar**
agrimensor *m* surveyor

agrimensura *f* surveying
agrimonia *f* (bot.) agrimony
agringar §59 *vr* (Am.) to act like a gringo
agrio -gria *adj* sour, acrid; citrus (*fruit*); uneven, rough; brittle, unmalleable; (fig.) sour, mordant; *m* sour juice; sour gravy; **agrios** *mpl* citrus fruit; citrus fruit trees; citrus juices
agrión *m* (bot.) China tree; (vet.) callus on horse's knee
Agripa *m* Agrippa
agripalma *f* (bot.) motherwort
agrisado -da *adj* grayish
agrisetado -da *adj* flowered-silk
agro *m* land, countryside
agronometría *f* soil science
agronomía *f* agronomy
agronómico -ca *adj* agronomic
agrónomo *m* agronomist
agropecuario -ria *adj* farm, farming (*pertaining to cattle and crop raising*)
agróstide *f* (bot.) redtop
agrumar *va & vr* to clot, to curd
agrupación *f* grouping, group, cluster, crowd
agrupar *va & vr* to group, to cluster
agrura *f* sourness, acerbity; citrus fruit trees; **agruras** *fpl* citrus fruit
ag.to abr. of **agosto**
agua *f* water; tide; slope (*of a roof*); (naut.) leak; (naut.) sea route; **aguas** *fpl* waters, mineral springs; water, urine; water, sparkle (*of precious stones*); watered effect (*e.g., of silk*); **bailarle a uno el agua** to dance attendance on a person; **cubrir aguas** to have under roof; to have the roof put on; **cubrir aguas en** to put the roof on (*a new building*); **entre aguas** floating under water; **entre dos aguas** (coll.) undecided, without taking sides; **hacer agua** (naut.) to make water (*to leak*); **hacer aguas** to make water (*to urinate*); **hacerle a uno la boca agua** to make one's mouth water; **hacerse** or **volverse agua de cerrajas** (coll.) to fizzle out, to flop; **hacerse agua en la boca** to melt in one's mouth; **¡hombre al agua!** man overboard!; **pescar en agua turbia** (coll.) to fish in troubled waters; **tan claro como el agua** as clear as crystal; **agua abajo** downstream; **agua amoniacal** (chem.) ammonia water; **agua arriba** upstream; **agua bendita** holy water; **agua blanda** soft water; **agua corriente** running water; **agua de alhucema** lavender water; **agua de azahar** orange-flower water; **agua de cepas** (coll.) wine; **agua de cerrajas** (coll.) trash, trifle; **agua de Colonia** eau de Cologne; **agua de cristalización** (chem.) water of crystallization; **agua delgada** soft water; **agua de bebida** drinking water; **agua de espliego** lavender water; **agua de Javel** Javel water; **agua de nafa** orange-flower water; **agua de pantoque** (naut.) bilge water; **agua de pie** running water; **agua de rosas** rose water; **agua de seltz** seltzer water; **agua de socorro** emergency baptism; **agua de Vichy** Vichy water; **agua dulce** fresh water; **agua fuerte** aqua fortis; etching; **agua gaseosa** carbonated water; **agua helada** ice water; **agua herrada** water in which a red-hot iron has been cooled; **agua lluvia** rain water; **agua manantial** spring water; **agua mineral** mineral water; **agua mineromedicinal** mineral water (*for medicinal use*); **agua nieve** sleet; **agua oxigenada** hydrogen peroxide; **agua pesada** (chem.) heavy water; **agua regia** aqua regia; **aguas de albañal** sewage; **aguas de creciente** rising tide; **aguas de menguante** ebb tide; **aguas madres** mother liquid; **aguas mayores** equinoctial tide; feces; **aguas menores** ordinary tide; urine, urination; **aguas muertas** neap tide; **aguas negras** sewage; **aguas vivas** spring tide; **agua viento** driving rain, driving rain and snow; **agua viva** running water, spring
aguacatal *m* avocado orchard
aguacate *m* (bot.) avocado (*tree and fruit*); pear-shaped emerald
aguacero *m* shower, heavy shower
aguacibera *f* water to start growth in new-sown ground
aguacha *f* foul, stagnant water
aguachar *m* pool, puddle; *va* to flood; (Am.) to tame, domesticate; *vr* (Am.) to get fat (*said of horses*)
aguacharnar *va* to flood
aguachento -ta *adj* (Am.) watery (*e.g., fruit*)
aguachinar *va* (dial.) var. of **aguacharnar**
aguachirle *m* cheap wine; slosh, slipslop; trifle
aguada *f* see **aguado**
aguadero -ra *adj* rain, e.g., **capa aguadera** rain cloak; *m* watering place; **aguaderas** *fpl* framework for water vessels on horseback or muleback; (orn.) upper wing coverts
aguadija *f* water in a pimple or sore
aguado -da *adj* watery, watered; soaked; abstemious; spoiled, interrupted; (Am.) weak, washed out; *f* source of water; mine flood; water coloring; water color; gouache (*method and picture*); (naut.) water supply; (rail.) watering station; **hacer aguada** (naut.) to take water
aguador -dora *mf* water carrier, water vendor; *m* paddle, bucket (*of waterwheel*); (orn.) black phoebe
aguaducho *m* stall for selling water, refreshment stand; flood, freshet
aguadura *f* (vet.) hoof abscess; (vet.) surfeit
aguafiestas *mf* (*pl:* **-tas**) kill-joy, wet blanket, crapehanger
aguafortista *mf* etcher, aquafortist
aguafuerte *f* aqua fortis; etching; **grabar al aguafuerte** to etch
aguafuertista *mf* etcher, aquafortist
aguagoma *f* gum water
aguaitacamino *m* (orn.) goatsucker
aguaitada *f* (Am.) var. of **aguaitamiento**
aguaitamiento *m* spying, watching
aguaitar *va* to spy upon, lie in wait for
aguajaque *m* fennel gum
aguajas *fpl* var. of **ajuagas**
aguaje *m* watering place; water supply; strong sea current; tidal wave; wake (*of ship*)
agualluvia *f* rain water
aguamala *f* (zool.) jellyfish
aguamanil *m* ewer, wash jug, wash pitcher; washstand
aguamanos *m* (*pl:* **-nos**) water for washing hands; washstand
aguamar *m* (zool.) jellyfish
aguamarina *f* aquamarine (*mineral and color*)
aguamarincrisolita *f* (mineral.) aquamarine chrysolite
aguamasa *f* (Am.) crushed corn washings
aguamelado -da *adj* soaked or bathed in honey and water
aguamiel *f* hydromel, honey and water; maguey juice
aguanieve *f* sleet
aguanieves *f* (*pl:* **-ves**) (orn.) wagtail
aguanosidad *f* wetness, wateriness; aqueous substance (*in the body*)
aguanoso -sa *adj* wet, watery, soaked
aguantable *adj* tolerable, bearable, endurable
aguantaderas *fpl* (coll.) long-suffering, forbearance
aguantar *va* to hold (*e.g., one's breath*); to hold back (*laughter*); to hold up, sustain; to bear, endure, tolerate, stand; *vn* to last, hold out; *vr* to restrain oneself; to hold on
aguante *m* patience, endurance; strength, vigor
aguañón *adj* see **maestro**
aguapié *m* small wine; slosh, slipslop; running water
aguar §23 *va* to water; to spoil, mar, throw cold water on; to lighten (*a burden*); *vr* to collapse from overwork or drinking when overheated (*said of beasts of burden*); to flood; to become thin or watery
aguardada *f* wait, waiting
aguardadero *m* var. of **aguardo**
aguardador -dora *adj* waiting; *mf* person who waits
aguardar *va* to await, to wait for; to give an extension of time to; *vn* to wait; **aguardar a** + *inf* to wait to + *inf;* **aguardar a que** + *subj* to wait until + *ind*
aguardentado -da *adj* brandied; tipsy, drunk
aguardentería *f* liquor store

aguardentero -ra *mf* brandy maker; brandy vendor; *f* liquor flask, brandy flask
aguardentoso -sa *adj* brandy; brandyish; whisky (*voice*)
aguardiente *m* brandy; rum, spirituous liquor (*any intoxicating liquor*); **aguardiente de cabeza** first running (*from still*); **aguardiente de caña** rum; **aguardiente de cerezas** cherry brandy; **aguardiente de manzana** applejack
aguardillado -da *adj* having a garret; like a garret
aguardo *m* hiding place, hunter's blind
aguarrás *m* (*pl:* **-rrases**) oil of turpentine
aguasal *f* brine; pickle
aguasar *vr* to become countrified
aguasol *m* chickpea mildew; (Am.) corn stubble
aguate *m* (Am.) prickle (*of cactus, etc.*)
aguatero -ra *mf* (Am.) water carrier, water vendor
aguatinta *f* var. of **acuatinta**
aguatocha *f* water pump
aguatoso -sa *adj* (Am.) spiny, prickly
aguaturma *f* (bot.) Jerusalem artichoke (*plant and tuber*)
aguaverde *f* (zool.) green jellyfish
aguaviento *m* driving rain, driving rain and snow
aguavientos *m* (*pl:* **-tos**) (bot.) Jerusalem sage
aguavilla *f* (bot.) bearberry
aguaza *f* aqueous humor; sap
aguazal *m* pool, puddle
aguazar §76 *va* to make marshy; to flood; *vr* to become marshy
aguazo *m* (paint.) gouache (*picture*)
aguazoso -sa *adj* var. of **aguanoso**
aguazul *m* or **aguazur** *m* var. of **algazul**
agudeza *f* acuteness; acuity; sharpness; briskness; witticism
agudización *f* sharpening; aggravation
agudizar §76 *va* to sharpen, make more acute; *vr* to become aggravated, to get worse
agudo -da *adj* acute; sharp; keen; brisk; witty; (gram.) oxytone
Águeda *f* Agatha
agüera *f* irrigation ditch
agüero *m* augury; forecast; omen, sign; **ser de buen agüero** to augur well; **ser de mal agüero** to augur ill
aguerrido -da *adj* inured to war, inured, hardened
aguerrir §53 *va* to inure to war, to inure, to harden; *vr* to become inured to war, to become inured, to become hardened
aguijada *f* goad, spur; plowstaff
aguijador -dora *adj* goading, inciting; *mf* goader, inciter
aguijadura *f* goading, inciting
aguijar *va* to goad, incite, urge on, hasten; to hasten (*one's steps*); *vn* to hurry along, to move fast
aguijón *m* spur, goad; sting (*of insects*); prickle, thorn (*of plants*); stimulus, incitement; **cocear** or **dar coces contra el aguijón** (coll.) to kick against the pricks
aguijonada *f* prick, sting; prick with goad or spur
aguijonar *va* var. of **aguijonear**
aguijonazo *m* var. of **aguijonada**
aguijonear *va* to goad, spur, incite, urge on; to sting
águila *f* (orn.) eagle; (fig.) eagle (*emblem; U.S. coin*); (Am.) swindler, cheat; (*cap.*) *f* (astr.) Eagle; **águila barbuda** (orn.) bearded eagle, bearded vulture, lammergeier; **águila caudal** (orn.) golden eagle; **águila de cabeza blanca** (orn.) bald eagle, white-headed eagle; **águila gallinera** (orn.) Egyptian vulture; **águila imperial** (orn.) imperial eagle; **águila marina** (orn.) sea eagle, white-tailed eagle; **águila moneva** (orn.) harpy eagle (*Pithecophaga jefferyi*); **águila pescadora** (orn.) fish hawk; **águila ratonera** (orn.) buzzard; **águila real** (orn.) golden eagle; *m* lively person, keen person; (ichth.) eagle ray
aguileño -ña *adj* aquiline; sharp-featured; *f* (bot.) columbine
aguilera *f* eagle's nest, eyrie
aguilón *m* large eagle; boom, jib (*of crane or derrick*); gable (*of roof*); slate or tile cut obliquely; square terra-cotta pipe
aguilucho *m* (orn.) eaglet
agüilla *f* moisture, seepage
aguinaldo *m* Christmas gift, Epiphany gift; (bot.) bindweed; (Am.) Christmas carol
agüista *mf* resorter, frequenter of a spa
aguja *f* needle (*for sewing; of phonograph; obelisk*); bodkin; hatpin; steeple, spire; hand (*of watch, clock, etc.*); pointer (*of dial, etc.*); style (*of sundial*); (rail.) switch rail; (ichth.) sailfish; (ichth.) needlefish; (bot.) lady's-comb; needlework; **agujas** *fpl* ribs (*of animal*); (rail.) switch; **alabar sus agujas** to blow one's own horn; **buscar una aguja en un pajar** to look for a needle in a haystack; **cuartear la aguja** (naut.) to box the compass; **aguja capotera** darning needle; sail needle; **aguja colchonera** tufting needle; **aguja de coser** sewing needle; **aguja de gancho** crochet needle; **aguja de hacer media** knitting needle; **aguja de mar** (ichth.) garfish; (ichth.) sailfish; **aguja de marear** mariner's needle, ship's needle; **aguja descarriladora** derail switch; **aguja de zurcir** darning needle; **aguja hipodérmica** hypodermic needle; **aguja imanada** or **magnética** magnetic needle; **aguja para marcar** center punch; **aguja salmera** upholsterer's needle; **aguja saquera** pack needle, packing needle
agujazo *m* prick or jab with a needle
agujerar or **agujerear** *va* to pierce, perforate, make a hole or holes in
agujería *f* needle factory
agujero *m* hole; maker or vendor of needles; pincushion; **quien acecha por agujero, ve su duelo** curiosity killed a cat; **agujero de hombre** manhole
agujeruelo *m* little hole
agujeta *f* needle (*of a syringe*); shoestring; (archaic) lace, string, or shoestring with tips; (orn.) godwit; **agujetas** *fpl* stitches, twinges
agujetería *f* (archaic) shoestring shop
agujetero -ra *mf* (archaic) maker or vendor of shoestrings; switch tender; *m* (Am.) needle case, pincushion
agujón *m* hatpin; (ichth.) needlefish
agujuela *f* brad
aguosidad *f* wateriness; aqueous humor, lymph
aguoso -sa *adj* watery
agur *interj* (coll.) bye-bye!, so long!
agusanamiento *m* worminess
agusanar *vr* to get wormy
Agustín *m* Austin, Augustine; **San Agustín** Saint Augustine; St. Augustine (*Florida city*)
agustinianismo *m* Augustinianism
agustiniano -na or **agustino -na** *adj & mf* Augustinian
agutí *m* (*pl:* **-tíes**) var. of **acutí**
aguzadero -ra *adj* sharpening; *m* place where wild boars whet their tusks; *f* sharpener, whetstone
aguzador -dora *adj* sharpening; *mf* sharpener; *f* drill sharpener
aguzadura *f* sharpening; steel or iron for ploughshare
aguzamiento *m* sharpening
aguzanieves *f* (*pl:* **-ves**) (orn.) wagtail
aguzar §76 *va* to sharpen, to point, to whet; to incite, stir up; to stare at; **aguzar las orejas** to prick up one's ears; **aguzar la vista** to look sharp; **aguzar los dientes** (coll.) to whet one's appetite
aguzonazo *m* lunge, thrust, stab
ah *interj* ah!; **¡ah del barco!** ship ahoy!
ah-chís *interj* kerchoo!
ahebrado -da *adj* fibrous, thready
ahechadero *m* var. of **aechadero**
ahechador -dora *adj & mf* var. of **aechador**
ahechaduras *fpl* var. of **aechaduras**
ahechar *va* var. of **aechar**
ahecho *m* var. of **aecho**
ahelear *va* to make bitter; *vn* to taste bitter
ahelgado -da *adj* jag-toothed, snaggle-toothed
aherrojamiento *m* fettering, shackling
aherrojar *va* to fetter, to shackle; to subjugate, oppress

aherrumbrar *va* to rust; to give the taste or color of iron to; *vr* to rust; to take on the taste or color of iron
ahervorar *vr* to generate heat (*said of stored grain*)
ahí *adv* there; **de ahí que** with the result that; **por ahí** that way; about, more or less
ahidalgado -da *adj* noble, high-born, chivalrous
ahigadado -da *adj* liver-colored; (archaic) fearless, intrepid
ahijadero *m* (prov.) sheep nursery
ahijado -da *mf* godchild; protégé
ahijar §99 *va* to adopt; to impute; *vn* to beget offspring; to sprout
ahilar §99 *va* to line up; *vn* to go in single file; *vr* to faint from hunger; to grow thin through illness; to grow poorly; to turn, to grow sour (*said, e.g., of wine*)
ahílo *m* faintness, weakness
ahincadamente *adv* hard, insistently, earnestly
ahincar §86 & §99 *va* to press, urge; to importune; *vr* to hasten
ahínco *m* earnestness, zeal, ardor
ahitar §99 *va* to surfeit, cloy, satiate, stuff; *vr* to get surfeited
ahitera *f* (coll.) acute indigestion, bellyache
ahíto -ta *adj* surfeited, gorged, stuffed; disgusted, fed up; having indigestion; *m* surfeit; indigestion
ahobachonado -da *adj* (coll.) lazy, shiftless
ahobachonar *vr* (coll.) to become lazy or shiftless
ahocicar §86 *va* to stick the nose of (*a dog or cat*) in the dirt it has made; (coll.) to get the best of (*a person*) in an argument; *vn* (naut.) to dip the bows under; (Am.) to give in (*in an argument*)
ahocinado *m* gorge, narrow passage (*in stream or river*)
ahocinar *vr* to pass through a narrow gorge (*said of streams, rivers, etc.*)
ahogadero *m* hangman's rope; crowded place; throatband, throatlatch
ahogadizo -za *adj* easily drowned or stifled; dry, pulpy, hard to swallow (*said of fruit*); sinkable, nonfloating (*said of wood*)
ahogado -da *adj* drowned, suffocated; close, unventilated; sunk, swamped, overwhelmed; **morir** or **perecer ahogado** to drown; *mf* drowned person, suffocated person
ahogador -dora *mf* choker; *m* choker, collar
ahogamiento *m* drowning; suffocation, choking
ahogar §59 *va* to drown; to suffocate, smother, quench, choke; to slake (*lime*); to soak (*plants*); to oppress; to kill (*e.g., a legislative bill*); to quench, extinguish; to stalemate; to drown (*e.g., one's sorrows*); *vr* to drown, suffocate, smother; to drown oneself
ahogo *m* oppression, constriction; shortness of breath; great sorrow or affliction; pinch, stringency
ahoguijo *m* (vet.) quinsy
ahoguío *m* oppression or constriction (of the chest)
ahombrado -da *adj* (coll.) mannish
ahombrar *vr* to become mannish
ahondar *va* to deepen; to make deeper, to dig deeper; to probe, to go deep into, to study thoroughly; *vn* to go deep; to go deeper; to sink, to dip; to become thoroughly versed; *vr* to go deep; to sink, to dip
ahonde *m* deepening; digging; probing
ahora *adv* now; in a little while; a little while ago; **de ahora en adelante** from now on; **por ahora** for the present; **ahora bien** now then, so then; **ahora mismo** right now; **ahora que** but
ahorcado -da *adj* hanging, hanging by the neck; ruined; grieved; anxious, worried; *mf* hangee, person who has been hanged or who has hanged himself; person condemned to be hanged
ahorcadura *f* hanging
ahorcajar *vr* to sit astride, to get astride; **ahorcajarse en** to sit astraddle on, to straddle
ahorcaperro *m* (naut.) slip knot; (naut.) running bowline
ahorcar §86 *va* to hang (*to execute*); *vr* to hang, be hanged; to hang oneself; (mach.) to jam, get caught
ahorita *adv* (coll.) right now, right away; (coll.) just now, a minute ago
ahormar *va* to put on a form or last; to shape, fit, adjust; to break in (*e.g., shoes*); to mold (*someone's character*)
ahornagamiento *m* parching
ahornagar §59 *vr* to become parched (*said of the earth and its crops*)
ahornar *va* to put into the oven or furnace; *vr* to burn on the outside before being baked inside (*said of bread*)
ahorquillado -da *adj* forked; (shaped like a) hairpin
ahorquillar *va* to prop up (*limbs of trees*) with forks; to shape like a fork or a hairpin
ahorrable *adj* easy to save or spare
ahorradamente *adv* freely, easily
ahorrado -da *adj* saving, thrifty; free, emancipated
ahorrador -dora *adj* saving; freeing; *mf* saver; emancipator
ahorramiento *m* saving, economy; emancipation
ahorrar *va* to save, to spare; to free (*e.g., a slave*); *vr* to save or spare oneself; **no ahorrarse con nadie** or **no ahorrárselas con nadie** to be afraid of nobody
ahorrativa *f* see **ahorrativo**
ahorratividad *f* frugality; (coll.) stinginess
ahorrativo -va *adj* saving, thrifty, stingy; *f* economy
ahorrillos *mpl* small savings
ahorro *m* economy; saving (*e.g., of time*); **ahorros** *mpl* savings
ahoyadura *f* digging holes; hole
ahoyar *va* to dig holes in
ahuate *m* (Am.) prickly down (*of certain plants*)
ahuatoso -sa *adj* (Am.) spiny, prickly
ahuchador -dora *adj* hoarding, miserly; *mf* hoarder, miser
ahuchar §99 *va* to hoard
ahuchear *va* to whistle at, to hiss
ahucheo *m* whistling, hissing
ahuecado -da *adj* hollow; (fig.) hollow (*sound, voice*)
ahuecador *m* crinoline; hoops (*of hoop skirt*); curved chisel
ahuecamiento *m* hollowing; hollow, hollowness; loosening, softening; swaggering
ahuecar §86 *va* to hollow, hollow out; to loosen, soften, fluff up (*earth, wool, etc.*); to make (*the voice*) deep and solemn; *vn* (coll.) to beat it; *vr* to swagger, to put on airs
ahuehué *m* or **ahuehuete** *m* (Am.) Montezuma cypress
ahuesado -da *adj* bonelike, bony
ahuevar *va* to make egg-shaped; to clarify (*wine*) with white of eggs
ahumada *f* see **ahumado**
ahumadero *m* smokehouse
ahumado -da *adj* smoked, smoky; (Am.) drunk; *m* smoking, curing; *f* smoke signal
ahumamiento *m* smoking, curing with smoke
ahumar §99 *va* to treat with smoke, to fill with smoke, to cure with smoke; *vn* to be smoky, to emit smoke; *vr* to get smoked up; to look smoky, to taste smoky; (coll.) to get tipsy, get drunk
ahurragado -da *adj* badly cultivated
ahusado -da *adj* tapering; spindle-shaped
ahusamiento *m* taper, tapering
ahusar *va & vr* §99 *va & vr* to taper
ahuyentar *va* to put to flight; to scare away; to drive away, to drive out, banish; *vr* to flee, run away
aijada *f* goad, spur
ailanto *m* (bot.) ailanthus
aína or **aínas** *adv* (archaic) soon; (archaic) easily; (archaic) almost
aindiado -da *adj* (Am.) Indian-looking
airado -da *adj* angry, irate; wild, violent; depraved
airamiento *m* anger, wrath

airar §75 *va* to anger; *vr* to get angry; **airarse con** or **contra** to get angry with (*a person*); **airarse de** or **por** to get angry at (*a thing*)
aire *m* air; pace (*way of stepping: walk, trot, gallop, etc.*); **al aire libre** in the open air; **darse aire** to fan oneself; **darse aires** to put on airs; **darse aires de** to claim to be, to boast of being; **estar en el aire** (coll.) to be in the wind (*to be impending*); **¿qué aires traen a Vd. acá?** (coll.) what brings you here?, what are you doing here?; **tomar el aire** to go out to get some fresh air, to go out for a walk; **volar por los aires** to fly through the air; **aire acondicionado** air conditioning; **aire colado** cold draft; **aire comprimido** compressed air; **aire detonante** firedamp; **aire líquido** liquid air
aireación *f* aeration
airear *va* to air, ventilate; to aerate; *vr* to get aired, to take the air; to catch a cold
airón *m* aigrette; panache; (elec.) aigrette; (orn.) heron, gray heron
airosidad *f* gracefulness, elegance, majesty
airoso -sa *adj* airy; drafty; breezy; graceful, light; grand, resplendent; successful; **quedar** or **salir airoso** to come off with flying colors
aislación *f* insulation; **aislación de sonido** soundproofing
aislacionismo *m* isolationism
aislacionista *adj & mf* isolationist
aisladamente *adv* singly, alone
aislador -dora *adj* isolating; insulating; *m* (elec.) insulator
aislamiento *m* isolation, detachment; insulation; insulating material
aislar §75 *va* to isolate; to detach, separate; to insulate; *vr* to be isolated, to live in seclusion
ajá *interj* (coll.) fine!, good!, aha!
ajada *f* garlic sauce
ajadizo -za *adj* easily mussed or crumpled
ajadura *f* withering; mussing; tampering; wear and tear
ajaja *f* (orn.) spoonbill
ajamiento *m* withering; mussing, rumpling; tampering; abuse, insult
ajamonar *vr* (coll.) to get fat and middle-aged (*said of a woman*); (Am.) to wither, to dry up
ajaquecar §86 *vr* to get a headache
ajar *m* garlic field; *va* to wither; to muss, rumple; to tamper with; to abuse; *vr* to wither, to wither away, to waste away; to get mussed
ajaraca *f* (arch.) arabesque
ajarafe *m* tableland; flat roof, terrace
ajardinar *va* to landscape
aje *m* complaint, indisposition, weakness
ajedrea *f* (bot.) savory; **ajedrea de jardín** (bot.) savory, summer savory
ajedrecista *mf* chess player
ajedrez *m* chess; chess set
ajedrezado -da *adj* checkered; *m* checkerwork
ajedrista *mf* chess player
ajenabe *m* or **ajenabo** *m* (bot.) mustard
ajengibre *m* var. of **jengibre**
ajenjo *m* (bot.) absinthe, wormwood; absinthe (*drink*)
ajeno -na *adj* another's; contrary, inappropriate; free; foreign; different; insane; **estar ajeno de** (coll.) to be uninformed about, be unaware of; **estar ajeno de sí** to be detached, distinterested; **ajeno a** unbecoming to; not connected with; unmindful of
ajenuz *m* (bot.) love-in-a-mist
ajeo *m* cry of hunted partridge
ajerezado -da *adj* sherry-type (*wine*)
ajesuitado -da *adj* (Am.) jesuitical (*crafty*)
ajete *m* young garlic; garlic sauce
ajetrear *va* to harass, to exhaust; *vr* to bustle about, to wear oneself out
ajetreo *m* bustle
ají *m* (*pl:* **ajíes**) (bot.) chili (*plant and fruit*); chili sauce; **ponerse como un ají** (Am.) to turn red as a tomato
ajiaceite *m* garlic and olive-oil sauce
ajiaco *m* (Am.) chili sauce; (Am.) Spanish stew seasoned with garlic; **estar como ajiaco** (Am.) to be in a bad humor
ajicola *f* (paint.) glue made of boiled animal skins and garlic
ajilimoje *m* or **ajilimójili** *m* (coll.) pepper-and-garlic sauce; **ajilimojes** *mpl* or **ajilimójilis** *mpl* (coll.) accessories
ajillo *m* (bot.) woody vine of trumpet-creeper family (*Cydista aequinoctialis*)
ajimez *m* (*pl:* **-meces**) (arch.) mullioned window
ajipa *f* (bot.) artichoke, Jerusalem artichoke
ajipuerro *m* (bot.) wild leek
ajironar *va* to trim with braid; to tear into shreds
-ajo -ja *suffix dim & pej* e.g., **colgajo** rag, tatter; **lagunajo** puddle; **migaja** crumb
ajo *m* (bot.) garlic; clove of garlic; garlic sauce; face paint; (coll.) shady business; (coll.) obscenity; **ajos** *mpl* garlic; **harto de ajos** ill-bred; **revolver el ajo** (coll.) to stir up a row; **tieso como un ajo** proud and haughty; **ajo blanco** (bot.) garlic; Andalusian garlic sauce; **ajo de chalote** (bot.) shallot; **ajo moruno** (bot.) chive; **ajo silvestre** (bot.) moly (*Allium moly*); *interj* goo!, dada! (*to make a baby talk*)
ajobar *va* (coll.) to carry on one's back, to struggle along with
ajobilla *f* (zool.) clam
ajobo *m* burdening, burden, heavy load, heavy task
ajolote *m* (zool.) axolotl, mud puppy
ajomate *m* (bot.) conferva
ajonje *m* birdlime
ajonjear *va* (*Am.*) to fondle, caress
ajonjera *f* or **ajonjero** *m* (bot.) carline thistle
ajonjolí *m* (*pl:* **-líes**) (bot.) sesame
ajoqueso *m* dish of garlic and cheese
ajorca *f* bracelet, anklet, bangle
ajornalar *va* to hire by the day; *vr* to hire out by the day
ajote *m* (bot.) water germander
ajuagas *fpl* (vet.) malanders
ajuanetado -da *adj* bunionlike; having bunions
ajuar *m* housefurnishings; bridal equipment, trousseau; **ajuar de cocina** kitchen utensils
ajudiado -da *adj* Jewish, Jewlike
ajuiciado -da *adj* wise, sensible, prudent
ajuiciar *va* to bring to one's senses; *vn & vr* to come to one's senses, to mend one's ways
ajumar *vr* (Am.) to get drunk
ajustado -da *adj* just, right; close-fitting, tight
ajustador *m* jacket, close-fitting jacket; corselet; finisher, fitter; (print.) pager
ajustamiento *m* var. of **ajuste**
ajustar *va* to fit, adapt, adjust; to engage, hire; to arrange, arrange for; to reconcile; to settle; to fasten (*e.g., one's safety belt*); (print.) to page; **ajustar cuentas con** to settle accounts with; *vn* to fit; *vr* to fit; to get adjusted; to engage oneself; to be engaged, be hired; to hire out; to come to an agreement; **ajustarse a** + *inf* to agree to + *inf*
ajuste *m* fit (*of clothes*); fitting, adjustment; hiring; arrangement; reconciliation; settlement; agreement; (print.) paging
ajusticiado -da *mf* executed criminal
ajusticiar *va* to punish with death, to execute
al contraction of **a** and **el; al** + *inf* on + *ger*, e.g., **al llegar** on arriving
ala *f* wing; brim (*of hat*); auricle (*of heart*); fin (*of fish, torpedo, etc.*); leaf (*of door, table, etc.*); flange; mudguard; (naut.) studdingsail; (theat.) wing; **alas** *fpl* boldness; courage; importance; **ahuecar el ala** (coll.) to beat it; **caérsele a uno las alas** to lose heart; **cortarle a uno las alas** to clip one's wings; **volar con sus propias alas** to stand on one's own feet; **ala en delta** (aer.) delta wing; **ala en flecha** (aer.) backswept wing; *m* (sport) wing; (football) end
Alá *m* Allah
alabado *m* hymn in praise of the sacrament
alabador -dora *adj* eulogistic; *mf* praiser
alabamiento *m* praise
alabamio *m* (chem.) alabamine
alabancero -ra *adj* (coll.) fawning, flattering
alabancioso -sa *adj* (coll.) boastful
alabanza *f* praise; **amontonar alabanzas sobre** to heap praises on
alabar *va* to praise; *vr* to be pleased or satisfied; to boast; **alabarse de** to boast of being
alabarda *f* halberd

alabardado -da *adj* halberd-shaped; (bot.) hastate
alabardazo *m* blow or wound with a halberd
alabardero *m* halberdier; (theat.) paid applauder, claqueur
alabastrado -da *adj* alabaster, like alabaster
alabastrino -na *adj* alabastrine; *f* translucent sheet of alabaster
alabastro *m* alabaster
álabe *m* drooping branch of tree; bucket, paddle (*of water wheel*); wooden cog (*in flour mill*); side mat (*in wagons*)
alabear *va & vr* to warp
alábega *f* (bot.) basil
alabeo *m* warping
alacena *f* closet set in wall, cupboard; (naut.) locker
alacrán *m* (ent.) scorpion; link (*on metal button*); bridle-curb (*of harness*); **alacrán cebollero** (ent.) mole cricket; **alacrán marino** (ichth.) angler
alacranado -da *adj* stung by a scorpion; vice-ridden, disease-ridden
alacranera *f* (bot.) scorpion grass
alacridad *f* alacrity
alacha *f* or **alache** *m* (ichth.) anchovy
alada *f* see **alado**
aladares *mpl* hair falling over the temples
aladica *f* winged ant
aladierna *f* (bot.) evergreen buckthorn, alatern
Aladino *m* Aladdin
alado -da *adj* alate; winged (*having wings; swift*); *f* fluttering of wings
aladrero *m* (min.) timberman; (prov.) plowmaker
aladroque *m* (ichth.) anchovy
alafia *f* (coll.) pardon
álaga *f* (bot.) spelt
alagadizo -za *adj* subject to flooding
alagar §59 *va* to flood, to make ponds or lakes in
alagartado -da *adj* motley, variegated
alajú *m* (*pl:* **-júes**) paste made of nuts, honey, and spices
ALALC *f* abr. of **Asociación Latinoamericana de Libre Comercio**
alamar *m* frog (*button and loop on garments*)
alambicado -da *adj* distilled; overrefined, precious, oversubtle; doled out sparingly
alambicamiento *m* distillation; overrefinement, affectation, pedantry
alambicar §86 *va* to distill; to scrutinize; to refine to excess, make oversubtle; to sell cheap with a large turnover
alambique *m* still, alembic; **por alambique** sparingly
alambor *m* beveling; (fort.) scarp
alamborado -da *adj* beveled, sloped
alambrado -da *adj* (pertaining to) wire; *m* wire mesh, chicken wire; (mil.) wire entanglement; *f* wire mesh, chicken wire; wire fence; (mil.) barbed wire, wire entanglement; (elec.) wiring
alambraje *m* (elec.) wiring
alambrar *va* to enclose with wire, to fence with wire, to string with wire; to wire (*for electricity*)
alambre *m* wire; **alambre cargado** live wire; **alambre de entrada** (rad.) lead-in wire; **alambre de espino** or **de púas** barbed wire; **alambre de tierra** (rad.) ground wire; **alambre gemelo** (telv.) twin lead; **alambre para artefactos** (elec.) fixture wire; **alambre para timbres eléctricos** annunciator wire; **alambre sin aislar** bare wire
alambrecarril *m* aerial railway, cable or funicular railway, cableway, rope railway
alambrera *f* see **alambrero**
alambrería *f* wire shop
alambrero -ra *mf* wireworker; *m* (coll.) telegraph maintenance man; *f* screen; bell-shaped screen to place over a fire or embers; screen cover for food
alámbrico -ca *adj* wire
alambrista *mf* tightrope walker
alameda *f* poplar grove; tree-lined walk or avenue, mall
alamín *m* inspector of weights and measures; irrigation superintendent
álamo *m* (bot.) poplar; **álamo blanco** (bot.) white poplar; **álamo de Italia** (bot.) Lombardy poplar; **álamo negro** (bot.) black poplar; **álamo temblón** (bot.) aspen
alampar *vr* to have a craving; **alamparse por** to crave
alamud *m* bolt for door or window
alanceado -da *adj* (bot.) lanceolate
alanceador *m* spearman
alancear *va* to spear, to lance
alandrear *vr* to become dry, stiff, and white (*said of silkworms*)
alanés *m* large Mexican deer
alano *m* mastiff, great Dane; (*cap.*) *m* Alan, Allen
alantoideo -a *adj* allantoid
alantoides *f* (anat.) allantois
alanzar §76 *va* to strike or wound with a lance, to spear
alaqueca *f* (mineral.) carnelian
alar *adj* wing; (bot.) alar; *m* overhanging roof; horsehair snare; *va* (naut.) to haul
alárabe or **alarbe** *adj* Arabic, Arabian; *mf* Arab, Arabian; rough, unmannerly person
alarde *m* (mil.) review; show, display, ostentation; **hacer alarde de** to make a show of, to boast of
alardear *vn* to boast, brag, show off; **alardear de** to boast of
alardoso -sa *adj* showy, ostentatious
alargada *f* extension, lengthening; **dar la alargada** (Am.) to let out more string (*for a kite*)
alargadera *f* (chem.) adapter; (mach.) extension
alárgama *f* (bot.) African rue
alargamiento *m* lengthening, extension, prolongation; increase
alargar §59 *va* to lengthen, extend, stretch, prolong; to increase; to hand, to reach; to let out, to pay out (*e.g., a rope*); *vr* to go away, withdraw, separate; to lengthen, be prolonged; to expatiate, be long-winded
alarguez *m* (bot.) rosewood
alaria *f* smoothing tool (*of potters*)
Alarico *m* Alaric
alarida *f* shouting, yelling, uproar
alarido *m* shout, yell, howl, whoop, squeal
alarifazgo *m* profession of architect
alarife *m* architect; builder; (Am.) clever fellow, sharper
alario -ria *adj* alary
alarma *f* alarm; (aer.) alert; **falsa alarma** false alarm; **alarma aérea** air-raid warning; **alarma de incendios** fire alarm; **alarma de ladrones** burglar alarm
alarmante *adj* alarming
alarmar *va* to alarm; to call to arms; *vr* to become alarmed
alármega *f* var. of **alárgama**
alarmista *mf* alarmist
alaroz *m* (*pl:* **-roces**) framework closing a doorway with opening for small door; mullion
alastrar *va* to throw back (*the ears*); (naut.) to ballast; *vr* to lie flat, to cower (*said of hunted animals*)
a látere *m* (coll.) side-kick
alaterno *m* var. of **aladierna**
alatinadamente *adv* according to Latin, like Latin
alatinado -da *adj* affected, puristic
alatrón *m* wall saltpeter
alavanco *m* wild duck
alavense or **alavés -vesa** *adj* (pertaining to) Álava; *mf* native or inhabitant of Álava
alazán -zana *adj* sorrel, reddish-brown; *mf* sorrel horse; *f* wine press; olive-oil press
alazo *m* blow or stroke with a wing
alazor *m* (bot.) safflower, bastard saffron
alba *f* see **albo**
albacara *f* (fort.) projecting tower
albacea *m* executor; **albacea dativo** executor appointed by the court; *f* executrix
albaceazgo *m* executorship
albacora *f* (ichth.) albacore; (ichth.) swordfish; early fig
albada *f* dawn; aubade, morning music; (bot.) soapwort
albahaca *f* (bot.) basil

albahaquero *m* flowerpot
albaicín *m* hilly quarter (*of a town*); (*cap.*) *m* gypsy cave-dwelling quarter of Granada, Spain
albaida *f* (bot.) anthyllis
albalá *m & f* (*pl:* **-laes**) (archaic) royal letter patent; (archaic) statement, proof; (archaic) customhouse receipt
albanega *f* hair net; net for catching small game
albanés -nesa or **albano -na** *adj & mf* Albanian; *m* Albanian (*language*)
Albania *f* Albania
albañal *m* sewer, drain; slop basin, slop can, slop jar
albañalero *m* slop man; sewer cleaner
albañil *m* mason, bricklayer
albañila *f* (ent.) mason bee
albañilería *f* masonry, brickwork, bricklaying
albaquía *f* balance due
albar *adj* white; *va* to whiten, to shine; to make (*iron*) red-hot
albarán *m* rent sign; duplicate list of purchases
albarazado -da *adj* whitish; leprous; streaked with black, yellow, and red; (Am.) of mixed white, Chinese, and Indian blood
albarazo *m* (path.) tetter, ringworm; (path.) alphos
albarca *f* sandal
albarcoque *m* apricot (*fruit*)
albarcoquero *m* (bot.) apricot tree
albarda *f* packsaddle
albardado -da *adj* saddleback (*with back of a different color*)
albardar *va* to put a packsaddle on; to lard (*fowls*)
albardear *va* (Am.) to vex, annoy
albardela *f* small saddle, training saddle
albardería *f* packsaddle shop
albardero *m* packsaddle maker or vendor
albardilla *f* small packsaddle; thick coat of wool; shoulder pad (*for carrying water*); iron holder, pot holder; cope, coping; raised earthen border (*of walk or garden*); larding (*for fowl*)
albardín *m* (bot.) matweed
albardón *m* large packsaddle; saddle pad
albarejo *m* white wheat, summer wheat
albareque *m* fishing net
albarico *m* white wheat, summer wheat
albaricoque *m* apricot (*fruit*)
albaricoquero *m* (bot.) apricot tree
albarillo *m* lively dance tune; white apricot
albarizo -za *adj* whitish; *f* saltwater pond or lake
albarrada *f* dry wall; earthen wall; entrenchment, defensive earthwork
albarranilla *f* (bot.) squill
albarrano -na *adj & mf* (dial.) gypsy; see **cebolla & torre**
albarraz *m* (bot.) stavesacre
albatros *m* (*pl:* **-tros**) (orn.) albatross
albayaldar *va* to coat or cover with white lead
albayalde *m* white lead
albazano -na *adj* dark-chestnut
albear *vn* to turn white; (Am.) to get up early
albedrío *m* free will; caprice, fancy, wilfulness; (law) precedent, unwritten law; **al albedrío de** according to the pleasure of; **libre albedrío** free will
albéitar *m* veterinarian
albeitería *f* veterinary medicine, veterinary surgery
albellanino *m* (bot.) cornel tree
albellón *m* sewer, drain
albenda *f* embroidered white linen hangings
albendera *f* (archaic) gadabout
albengala *f* turban gauze
albéntola *f* fine-meshed fishing net
alberca *f* pond, pool, tank, reservoir, cistern; (Am.) swimming pool; **en alberca** roofless
albérchiga *f* clingstone peach
albérchigo *m* (bot.) clingstone-peach tree; clingstone peach; (prov.) apricot
alberchiguero *m* (bot.) clingstone-peach tree
albergada *f* cover, shelter, protection
albergar §59 *va* to shelter, harbor; to lodge, give lodging to; to house; *vn & vr* to take shelter; to lodge, to take lodgings
albergue *m* shelter, refuge, lodging; lair, burrow, den; **albergue de carretera** wayside inn
albericoque *m* apricot (*fruit*)
albero -ra *adj* white; *m* white earth, pipe clay; dishcloth
alberquero *m* tender of tanks or pools
Alberto *m* Albert; **Alberto Magno** Albertus Magnus
albica *f* white clay
albicante *adj* whitening, bleaching
albido -da *adj* whitish
albigense *adj* Albigensian; **albigenses** *mpl* Albigenses
albihar *m* (bot.) oxeye
albillo -lla *adj* white (*grape or wine*)
albín *m* hematite; dark carmine
albina *f* see **albino**
albinismo *m* albinism
albino -na *adj* albinic; *mf* albino; *f* salt-water marsh, salt deposit
Albión *f* (poet.) Albion (*England*)
albita *f* (mineral.) albite
albitana *f* fence to protect plants; (naut.) apron
albo -ba *adj* (poet.) white, snow-white; *f* dawn; alb (*priest's white linen robe*)
alboaire *m* glazed tiling (*in archways and vaulted roofs*)
albohol *m* (bot.) lesser bindweed
albollón *m* sewer, drain
albóndiga *f* meat ball, fish ball
albondigón *m* hamburger, Hamburg steak
alboque *m* flageolet, pastoral pipe; small cymbal
albor *m* whiteness; dawn; **albor de la vida** childhood, youth; **albores** *mpl* dawn
alborada *f* dawn; aubade, morning music; dawn attack; reveille; morning watch
albórbola *f* shouting, cheering, joyful yelling
alborear *vn* to dawn
alborga *f* matweed sandal
albornía *f* large glazed earthenware vessel
alborno *m* alburnum, sapwood
albornoz *m* (*pl:* **-noces**) coarse woolen stuff, terry cloth; burnoose; beach robe, bathrobe (*of terry cloth*); cardigan
alboronía *f* stew of eggplant, tomatoes, squash, and peppers
alboroque *m* treat given at the close of a deal
alborotadizo -za *adj* excitable, jumpy
alborotado -da *adj* hasty, rash
alborotador -dora *adj* inciting to riot; *mf* agitator, rioter
alborotapueblos *mf* (*pl:* **-blos**) (coll.) rabble rouser; (coll.) gay noisy person
alborotar *va* to agitate, stir up, arouse, excite; *vn* to make a racket, to clatter; to rampage; *vr* to become agitated, get excited; to riot; to get rough (*said of the sea*)
alboroto *m* agitation, disturbance, excitement; riot, noise, uproar; **alborotos** *mpl* (Am.) honey-coated popcorn
alborozador -dora *adj* cheering, joy-bringing; *mf* bringer of joy and gladness
alborozar §76 *va* to cheer, gladden, overjoy
alborozo *m* joy, merriment
albotín *m* (bot.) terebinth
albriciar *va* (archaic) to bring good news to, to reward for good news, to congratulate
albricias *fpl* reward for good news; present asked for or given on the occasion of some happy event; **en albricias de** as a token of; *interj* good news!, congratulations!
albudeca *f* tasteless melon; watermelon
albufera *f* saltwater lagoon
albugíneo -a *adj* albugineous
albugo *m* (path.) albugo; white spot (*on nails*)
albuhera *f* lake, lagoon, reservoir
álbum *m* (*pl:* **álbumes**) album; **álbum de recortes** scrapbook
albumen *m* (bot.) albumen
albúmina *f* (biochem.) albumin
albuminado -da *adj* albuminous; covered with a coat of albumin
albuminaje *m* (phot.) emulsification
albuminar *va* (phot.) to emulsify
albuminímetro *m* albuminimeter
albuminoide *m* albuminoid

albuminoideo -a *adj* albuminoid
albuminoso -sa *adj* albuminous
albuminuria *f* (path.) albuminuria
albur *m* (ichth.) dace; first two cards drawn by banker at monte (*card game*); risk, chance, hazard
albura *f* pure whiteness; white of egg; alburnum
alburno *m* var. of **alborno**
alca *f* (orn.) auk
alcabala *f* (archaic) sales tax; **alcabala del viento** (archaic) sales tax paid by outside merchant
alcabalero *m* (archaic) sales-tax collector
alcacel *m* or **alcacer** *m* (bot.) green barley
alcací *m* (*pl:* **-cíes**) (bot.) wild artichoke
alcachofa *f* (bot.) artichoke (*plant and head*)
alcachofado -da *adj* artichoke-shaped; *m* artichoke stew
alcachofal *m* artichoke bed; field of wild artichokes
alcachofero -ra *adj* (yielding the) artichoke; *mf* artichoke seller; *f* (bot.) artichoke
alcahaz *m* (*pl:* **-haces**) large bird cage
alcahazada *f* cageful of birds
alcahazar **§76** *va* to put or keep (*birds*) in a cage
alcahuete -ta *mf* bawd, procurer, go-between; harborer, screen, fence (*for criminals or stolen goods*); (coll.) schemer; (coll.) gossip, talebearer; *m* (theat.) curtain dropped for short intermission
alcahuetear *va* to procure (*for prostitution*); to harbor (*criminals or stolen goods*); (coll.) to scheme for; *vn* to pander
alcahuetería *f* pandering, procuring; harboring (*of criminals or stolen goods*); (coll.) trick, deceit, scheming
alcaicería *f* raw-silk market or exchange, bazaar
alcaide *m* governor or warden of a castle, fortress, or prison
alcaidesa *f* governor's lady, warden's wife, jailer's wife
alcaidía *f* position of governor or warden of a castle, fortress, or prison; governor's house, warden's house
alcalaíno -na *adj* (pertaining to) Alcalá de Henares, Alcalá de los Gazules, or Alcalá la Real (*Spanish cities*); *mf* native or inhabitant of Alcalá de Henares, Alcalá de los Gazules, or Alcalá la Real
alcalareño -ña *adj* (pertaining to) Alcalá de Guadaira, Alcalá del Río, or Alcalá del Valle (*Spanish cities*); *mf* native or inhabitant of Alcalá de Guadaira, Alcalá del Río, or Alcalá del Valle
alcaldada *f* abuse of authority, petty tyranny
alcalde *m* mayor, chief burgess; **tener el padre alcalde** to have a friend at court; **alcalde de monterilla** small-town mayor; **alcalde ordinario** mayor and justice of the peace combined, in colonial times
alcaldear *vn* to lord it, to be bossy
alcaldesa *f* mayoress
alcaldesco -ca *adj* (coll.) mayoral, mayor's
alcaldía *f* mayoralty; town hall, city hall
alcalescencia *f* (chem.) alkalescence
alcalescente *adj* (chem.) alkalescent
álcali *m* (chem.) alkali; **álcalis térreos** (chem.) alkaline earths
alcalímetro *m* alkalimeter
alcalinidad *f* alkalinity
alcalino -na *adj* alkaline
alcalinotérreo -rrea *adj* (chem.) alkaline-earth
alcalizar **§76** *va* to alkalize
alcaloide *m* alkaloid
alcalóidico -ca *adj* alkaloidal
alcalosis *f* (physiol.) alkalosis
alcaller *m* potter; pottery
alcallería *f* pottery, collection of pottery
alcamonías *fpl* aromatic seeds for flavoring; *m* (coll.) pander, go-between
alcana *f* (bot.) henna; (bot.) alkanet
alcance *m* pursuit; special delivery (*of mail*); late news (*in newspapers*); reach, arm's length; range (*e.g., of a gun*); scope, purview; extent; capacity, comprehension, intelligence; import, significance; coverage; balance due; deficit; **al alcance de** within reach of, within range of; **al alcance de la mano** within reach; **andarle** or **irle a uno en los alcances** to spy on a person; **dar alcance a** to catch up with; **de cortos alcances** of limited intelligence; **de gran alcance** long-range; **seguir los alcances a** to pursue; **alcance agresivo** striking range; **alcance de la vista** eyesight, eyeshot; **alcance del oído** earshot
alcancía *f* child's bank; bin, hopper, chute; (mil.) grenade; (Am.) poor box
alcándara *f* (archaic) perch for falcons; (archaic) clothes rack
alcandía *f* (bot.) sorghum, Indian millet
alcandial *m* field of sorghum
alcandora *f* signal fire, beacon
alcanfor *m* camphor
alcanforada *f* (bot.) stinking ground pine (*Camphorosma monspeliacum*)
alcanforar *va* to camphorate; *vr* (Am.) to hide, to disappear
alcanforero *m* (bot.) camphor tree
alcántara *f* cover for velvet in the loom
alcantarilla *f* drain, conduit, sewer, culvert; small bridge
alcantarillado *m* sewering, sewage system
alcantarillar *va* to sewer, to lay sewers in
alcanzable *adj* attainable
alcanzadizo -za *adj* reachable, attainable
alcanzado -da *adj* needy, hard up
alcanzadura *f* (vet.) attaint
alcanzar **§76** *va* to catch up to, to overtake; to reach; to grasp; to perceive (*to see, hear, smell*); to live through; to obtain, to attain; to understand; **alcanzar de cuenta a** to find lacking; **alcanzar en** to find (*someone*) indebted for the amount of; *vn* to succeed; to carry (*said of firearm*); **alcanzar a** + *inf* to manage to + *inf;* **alcanzar a** or **hasta** to attain to, to reach, to reach up to; **alcanzar a oír** to manage to hear, to overhear; **alcanzar a ver** to catch sight of, to set sight on; **alcanzar para** to be sufficient for; *vr* to overreach (*said of a horse*)
alcaparra *f* (bot.) caper (*plant and berry*)
alcaparrado -da *adj* prepared with capers
alcaparral *m* caper field
alcaparrera *f* or **alcaparro** *m* (bot.) caper (*plant*)
alcaparrón *m* caper (*bud or berry*)
alcaparrosa *f* var. of **caparrosa**
alcaraván *m* (orn.) stone curlew, thick-knee
alcaravea *f* (bot.) caraway (*plant and seed*)
alcarceña *f* (bot.) tare
alcarcil *m* artichoke, wild artichoke
alcarracero -ra *mf* maker of unglazed porous jugs; *m* shelf or cupboard for unglazed porous jugs
alcarraza *f* unglazed porous jug (*for cooling water by evaporation*)
alcarria *f* barren plateau
alcartaz *m* (*pl:* **-taces**) paper cone
alcatara *f* (archaic) still
alcatifa *f* fine rug or carpet; filling of earth or cinders under tile or brick
alcatraz *m* (*pl:* **-traces**) (orn.) gannet, solan; (orn.) pelican; (bot.) arum; paper cone
alcaucí *m* (*pl:* **-cíes**) (bot.) wild artichoke
alcauciar *va* (Am.) to shoot to death
alcaudón *m* (orn.) shrike
alcayata *f* tenterhook; meat hook; spike
alcazaba *f* fortress (*within a walled town*)
alcázar *m* alcazar, fortress; castle, royal palace; (naut.) quarterdeck
alcazuz *m* (bot.) licorice
alc.^de^ abr. of **alcalde**
alce *m* (zool.) elk, moose; cut (*in card playing*)
alcedo *m* maple grove
alcélafo *m* (zool.) bubal, hartebeest
Alcestes *f* (myth.) Alcestis
Alcibíades *m* Alcibiades
alcino *m* (bot.) wild basil
alción *m* (orn.) kingfisher, halcyon; (myth.) halcyon; (*cap.*) *m* (astr.) Alcyone
alciónеos *mpl* (meteor. & myth.) halcyon days
alcista *adj* bullish (*tending to rise in price*); rising, upward (*e.g., trend in cost of living*); *mf* bull (*in stock market*)

Alcmena *f* (myth.) Alcmene
alcoba *f* bedroom; **alcoba de respeto** guest room
alcocarra *f* grimace, face
alcofa *f* rush or wicker basket or hamper
alcohol *m* alcohol; kohl; (mineral.) galena; **alcohol absoluto** absolute alcohol; **alcohol de grano** grain alcohol; **alcohol de madera** wood alcohol; **alcohol desnaturalizado** denatured alcohol; **alcohol etílico** ethyl alcohol; **alcohol metílico** methyl alcohol, wood alcohol; **alcohol para fricciones** rubbing alcohol; **alcohol vinílico** vinyl alcohol
alcoholado -da *adj* having dark hair around the eyes (*said of an animal*); *m* (pharm.) alcoholate, spirit
alcoholar *va* to distill alcohol from; to blacken with kohl
alcoholato *m* (pharm.) alcoholate
alcoholaturo *m* (pharm.) alcoholature
alcoholero -ra *adj* (pertaining to) alcohol; *f* vessel for holding kohl (*cosmetic*); alcohol plant or factory
alcohólico -ca *adj* alcoholic; (med.) alcoholic; *mf* (med.) alcoholic
alcoholímetro *m* alcoholometer
alcoholismo *m* (path.) alcoholism
alcoholización *f* alcoholization
alcoholizado -da *adj & mf* (med.) alcoholic
alcoholizar §76 *va* to alcoholize; to fortify (*wines*); *vr* to become alcoholic
alcolla *f* large glass pitcher, vial, or cruet
alconcilla *f* rouge
alcor *m* hill, eminence
Alcorán *m* Alcoran, Koran
alcoránico -ca *adj* Koranic
alcoranista *m* Koranist
alcornocal *m* woods or forest of cork oaks
alcornoque *m* (bot.) cork oak; (coll.) blockhead
alcornoqueño -ña *adj* cork-oak
alcorque *m* cork-soled shoe; trench around base of plant or tree to hold irrigation water
alcorza *f* frosting of sugar and starch; **ser una alcorza** (Am.) to be a crybaby
alcorzar §76 *va* to frost with sugar and starch; to adorn
alcotán *m* (orn.) lanner
alcotana *f* mason's or bricklayer's pickaxe
alcrebite *m* sulfur
alcribís *m* tuyère
alcubilla *f* basin, reservoir
alcucero -ra *adj* (coll.) sweet-toothed; (coll.) greedy; *mf* maker or vendor of olive-oil cans
Alcuino *m* Alcuin
alcurnia *f* ancestry, lineage, family
alcuza *f* olive-oil can; (Am.) water jug; (Am.) earthen bottle; (Am.) caster
alcuzada *f* canful of olive oil
alcuzcuz *m* couscous
aldaba *f* knocker, door knocker; bolt, crossbar; latch; hitching ring; **tener buenas aldabas** to have pull, to have influence; **aldaba dormida** deadlatch
aldabada *f* knock with a door knocker; sudden fright or shock
aldabazo *m* sharp knock with a door knocker
aldabear *vn* to knock with a door knocker
aldabeo *m* knocking with a door knocker
aldabía *f* crossbeam (*of door or partition*)
aldabilla *f* hook or catch (*for door or window*)
aldabón *m* knocker, door knocker; trunk or chest handle
aldabonazo *m* knock with a door knocker; sharp knock with a door knocker
aldea *f* village
aldeaniego -ga *adj* village, rustic, peasant
aldeano -na *adj* village; country, rustic; *mf* villager
Aldebarán *m* (astr.) Aldebaran
aldehido *m* (chem.) aldehyde
aldehuela *f* little village, hamlet
aldeorrio or **aldeorro** *m* small backward village
alderredor *adv* around, about
aldino -na *adj* Aldine
aldiza *f* (bot.) bluebottle, cornflower
aldora *f* (bot.) sorghum
aldrán *m* country wine peddler
aleación *f* alloy
alear *va* to alloy; to ally; *vn* to beat the wings; to move the arms up and down (*like wings*); to convalesce
aleatorio -ria *adj* aleatory
alebrar §18 *vr* to lie flat (*like a rabbit*); to cower
alebrastar or **alebrestar** *vr* to lie flat (*like a rabbit*); to cower; (Am.) to rear; (Am.) to dash along; (Am.) to fall in love; (Am.) to become frightened; (Am.) to brighten up, to cheer up; (Am.) to get tipsy
alebronar *va* to cow, to intimidate; to frighten; *vr* to lie flat (*like a rabbit*); to cower; to become frightened
aleccionador -dora *adj* instructive, enlightening
aleccionamiento *m* instruction; training, coaching
aleccionar *va* to teach, instruct; to train, coach
alece *m* (ichth.) anchovy; ragout of fish liver
alecrín *m* (ichth.) tiger shark (*Galeocerdo arcticus*); (bot.) South American hardwood (*Holocalyx balansae*)
aleche *m* (ichth.) anchovy
alechugar §59 *va* to curl in the shape of a lettuce leaf; to curl, fold, pleat, frill
alechuguinar *va* to make foppish; *vr* to become foppish, become a dude
aleda *f* propolis
aledaño -ña *adj* bordering; attached; *m* border, boundary
alefangina *f* (archaic) purgative pill containing aloes, nutmeg, etc.
alefriz *m* (naut.) rabbet, mortise
alegación *f* allegation
alegamar *va* to fertilize with silt; *vr* to get full of silt
alegar §59 *va* to allege; *vn* (law) to plead
alegato *m* allegation; (law) allegation; (law) summing up, brief
alegoría *f* allegory
alegórico -ca *adj* allegoric
alegorizar §76 *va* to allegorize
alegra *f* (naut.) pump auger
alegrador -dora *adj* cheering; *m* spill (*twisted paper for lighting*); reamer; **alegradores** *mpl* (taur.) banderillas
alegrar *va* to cheer, make glad; to brighten, enliven; to stir up (*a fire*); (naut.) to widen (*a hole*); *vr* to be glad, to rejoice; (coll.) to get tipsy; **alegrarse de, con,** or **por** to be glad of or because of; **alegrarse de** + *inf* to be glad to + *inf*
alegre *adj* glad, joyful; bright, gay; cheerful, merry, light-hearted; careless, reckless; (coll.) off-color; (coll.) tipsy; **alegre de cascos** scatterbrained
alegreto *m* (mus.) allegretto
alegría *f* joy, cheer, gladness; brightness, gaiety; (bot.) sesame; nougat of honey and sesame seeds; **alegría secreta, candela muerta** all who joy would win must share it
alegro *m* (mus.) allegro
alegrón *m* sudden upsurge of joy; flare-up, sudden blaze; (Am.) flirt
alejado -da *adj* distant, remote
alejamiento *m* farness, distance; removal, withdrawal; estrangement
Alejandría *f* Alexandria
alejandrino -na *adj* Alexandrian; Alexandrine; *mf* Alexandrine (*native or inhabitant of Alexandria*); *m* Alexandrine (*verse of twelve syllables in English, fourteen in Spanish*)
Alejandro *m* Alexander; **Alejandro Magno** Alexander the Great
alejar *va & vr* to move aside, to move away, to keep at a distance
alejijas *fpl* barley porridge
Alejo *m* Alexis
alejur *m* var. of **alajú**
alelado -da *adj* stunned, dumbfounded
alelamiento *m* stupidity, imbecility
alelar *va* to make stupid, to stupefy; *vr* to grow stupid or dull
alelí *m* (*pl:* **-líes**) (bot.) gillyflower
aleluya *m & f* hallelujah; *m* Easter time; *f* prints distributed at church on Holy Saturday; (bot.) hallelujah, wood sorrel; doggerel; daub; bag of bones, skinny fellow; **aleluya navideña** Christmas card; *interj* hallelujah!

alema *f* allotment of irrigation water; **alemas** *fpl* (Am.) public baths
alemán -mana *adj & mf* German; *m* German (*language*); *f* allemande (*dance*)
alemanda *f* allemande (*dance*)
alemanesco -ca *adj* var. of **alemanisco**
Alemania *f* Germany; **la Alemania Occidental** West Germany; **la Alemania Oriental** East Germany
alemánico -ca *adj* Germanic
alemanisco -ca *adj* damask; Germanic; *m* damask table linen
alentado -da *adj* brave, spirited; haughty, gallant; (Am.) well, in good health; *f* long breath, deep breath; **de una alentada** without catching one's breath
alentador -dora *adj* encouraging
alentar **§18** *va* to encourage, inspire, cheer; **alentar a** + *inf* to encourage to + *inf; vn* to breathe; *vr* to get well, to recover
aleonado -da *adj* tawny, fulvous
aleonar *va* (Am.) to stir up, agitate
alepantado -da *adj* (Am.) distracted, fascinated
alepídoto -ta *adj* (ichth.) alepidote
alepín *m* bombazine
Alepo *m* Aleppo
alerce *m* (bot.) larch; **alerce africano** (bot.) sandarac
alergeno *m* (immun.) allergen
alergia *f* (path.) allergy
alérgico -ca *adj* allergic
alero *m* eaves; mudguard, splashboard
alerón *m* (aer.) aileron
alerta *m, adv & interj* see **alerto**
alertar *va* to alert
alerto -ta *adj* alert, watchful, vigilant; **alerta** *m* (mil.) alert; (mil.) watchword; **alerta** *adv* on the alert, alertly, watchfully; **estar alerta** to be on the alert; **alerta** *interj* watch out!, look out!
alesaje *m* bore (*of cylinder of motor*)
alesna *f* awl
alesnado -da *adj* awl-shaped; pointed; (bot.) subulate
aleta *f* small wing; fin (*of fish, etc.*); leaf (*of hinge*); blade (*of propeller*); (naut.) fashion piece; (aut.) fender, mudguard; (coll.) fin (*hand, arm*)
aletada *f* beating of wings, fluttering
aletargamiento *m* numbness, lethargy
aletargar **§59** *va* to benumb, to make lethargic; *vr* to get benumbed, to fall into a lethargy
aletazo *m* stroke or flap of wing or fin
aletear *vn* to flutter, to beat or flap the wings or fins
aleteo *m* fluttering, flapping, beating; palpitation (*of heart*)
aleto *m* (orn.) osprey
aletría *f* (prov.) noodles, spaghetti
aleudar *va* to leaven, to ferment with yeast; *vr* to rise, become fermented
aleurona *f* (biochem.) aleurone
aleutiano -na *adj* Aleutian; *mf* Aleut, Aleutian (*native or inhabitant*); *m* Aleut (*language*)
aleve *adj* treacherous, perfidious; *mf* traitor, rebel; *m* treachery, perfidy
alevilla *f* (ent.) moth
alevosa *f* see **alevoso**
alevosía *f* treachery, perfidy
alevoso -sa *adj* treacherous, perfidious; *f* (vet.) frogtongue
alexia *f* (psychopath.) alexia
alexifármaco -ca *adj & m* alexipharmic
alexina *f* (biochem.) alexin
aleya *f* verse of the Koran
alezo *m* drawsheet (*in hospitals*)
alfa *f* alpha; **alfa y omega** alpha and omega
alfábega *f* (bot.) basil
alfabético -ca *adj* alphabetic
alfabetización *f* alphabetization; (Am.) teaching illiterates to read and write
alfabetizar **§76** *va* to alphabetize; (Am.) to teach (*a person*) to read and write
alfabeto *m* alphabet; **alfabeto Morse** (telg.) Morse code; **alfabeto para sordomudos** deaf-and-dumb alphabet
alfaguara *f* gushing spring
alfaida *f* tidewater (*in a river*)
alfajía *f* quartering for doorframe or window frame; (prov.) roof timber
alfajor *m* var. of **alajú**
alfalfa *f* (bot.) alfalfa
alfalfal *m* alfalfa field
alfalfe *m* var. of **alfalfa**
alfana *f* big, fiery horse
alfaneque *m* (orn.) buzzard; (archaic) campaign tent
alfanjado -da *adj* cutlass-shaped
alfanjazo *m* stroke or wound with a cutlass
alfanje *m* cutlass; (ichth.) swordfish
alfaque *m* bar, shoal
alfaquí *m* (*pl:* **-quíes**) alfaqui (*expounder of the Koran*)
alfar *adj* galloping with front feet and trotting with rear feet; *m* pottery; clay; *vn* to gallop with front feet and trot with rear feet; (naut.) to pitch
alfaraz *m* (*pl:* **-races**) Moorish light-cavalry horse
alfarda *f* tax levied on Jews and Moors; special tax; (arch.) light beam
alfardilla *f* binding, trimming, gold or silver braid
alfardón *m* ring, washer; tax
alfarería *f* pottery; pottery store or stand; potter's workshop
alfarero *m* potter
alfargo *m* press of olive-oil mill
alfarje *m* olive crusher; carved and paneled ceiling
alfarjía *f* quartering for doorframe or window frame
alféizar *m* splay of door or window; embrasure
alfeñicar **§86** *vr* (coll.) to become extremely thin; (coll.) to be finical, to be too nice
alfeñique *m* almond-flavored sugar paste; (coll.) thin, delicate person; prudery, squeamishness
Alfeo *m* (myth.) Alpheus
alferazgo ensigncy; second lieutenancy
alferecía *f* epilepsy; ensigncy; second lieutenancy
alférez *m* (*pl:* **-reces**) (mil.) second lieutenant; (mil.) subaltern (Brit.); **alférez de fragata** (nav.) ensign; **alférez de navío** (nav.) lieutenant (j.g.)
alficoz *m* (*pl:* **-coces**) (bot.) cucumber (*plant and fruit*)
alfil *m* bishop (*in chess*)
alfiler *m* pin; (elec.) prong (*of a tube*); **alfileres** *mpl* pin money; **de veinticinco alfileres** or **con todos sus alfileres** (coll.) dressed to kill; **no estar con sus alfileres** (coll.) to be in a bad humor; **pedir para alfileres** (coll.) to ask for a tip; (coll.) to ask for pin money; **pegar** or **prender con alfileres** (coll.) to put together in a shaky way; (coll.) to learn superficially; **alfiler de corbata** stickpin, scarfpin; **alfiler de madera** clothespin; **alfiler de París** wire nail; **alfiler de seguridad** safety pin
alfilerar *va* to pin, pin up
alfilerazo *m* pinprick; (fig.) dig, jab, innuendo
alfilerillo *m* finishing nail
alfiletero *m* pincase, needlecase
alfitete *m* semolina
alfolí *m* (*pl:* **-líes**) granary; salt warehouse
alfoliar **§90** *va* (archaic) to store (*grain or salt*)
alfolla *f* hook, clasp; purple brocade
alfombra *f* carpet, rug; (path.) German measles; **alfombra de baño** bath mat; **alfombra de rezo** prayer rug; **alfombra mágica** magic carpet
alfombrado *m* carpeting
alfombrar *va* to carpet
alfombrero -ra *mf* carpet maker
alfombrilla *f* rug, runner; door mat; (path.) German measles
alfombrista *mf* carpet dealer; carpet repairer
alfóncigo *m* (bot.) pistachio (*tree and seed*)
alfonsí *adj masc* (*pl:* **-síes** or **-sinos**) Alphonsine
alfónsigo *m* var. of **alfóncigo**
alfonsino -na *adj* Alphonsine
Alfonso *m* Alphonso; **Alfonso el Sabio** Alphonso the Wise
alforfón *m* (bot.) buckwheat

alforjas *fpl* saddlebags, knapsack; provisions for traveling
alforjón *m* (bot.) buckwheat
alforza *f* pleat, tuck; innermost heart; (coll.) scar
alforzar §76 *va* to pleat, to tuck
alfoz *m* (*pl:* **-foces**) narrow mountain pass; district, dependence; outskirts
Alfredo *m* Alfred; **Alfredo el Grande** Alfred the Great
alga *f* (bot.) alga; (bot.) seaweed
algaba *f* woods, thicket
algaida *f* jungle, brush, thicket; sandbank, dune
algalia *f* civet; (surg.) catheter; *m* (zool.) civet cat
algaliar *va* to perfume with civet
algara *f* thin skin (*of egg, onion, etc.*); raiding cavalry; cavalry raid
algarabía *f* Arabic; (coll.) gibberish, jabber; (*coll.*) din, clamor, uproar, confusion; (bot.) broomweed; (zool.) fulvous tree duck
algaracear *vn* (Am.) to spit snow, to snow lightly
algarada *f* outcry; catapult (*of ancient Romans*)
algarero -ra *adj* chattering, talkative; *m* raiding cavalryman
algarrada *f* catapult (*of ancient Romans*); bull baiting; fight with young bulls; driving bulls into pen
algarroba *f* (bot.) vetch; carob bean, locust bean
algarrobilla *f* (bot.) vetch
algarrobo *m* (bot.) carob; **algarrobo loco** (bot.) Judas tree; **algarrobo negro** (bot.) mesquite, honey mesquite
algazara *f* Moorish battle cry; uproar, tumult, din
algazul *m.* (bot.) ice plant
álgebra *f* algebra
algebraico -ca or **algébrico -ca** *adj* algebraic
algebrista *mf* algebraist
algecireño -ña *adj* (pertaining to) Algeciras; *mf* native or inhabitant of Algeciras
algidez *f* abnormal coldness
álgido -da *adj* cold, chilly; (bot. & zoöl.) of the frigid zone; (coll.) most active, most intense, decisive
algo *pron indef* something; **¿algo más?** anything else?; **algo por el estilo** something of the sort; *adv* somewhat, rather, a little
algodón *m* cotton; cotton wadding (*for ears*); (bot.) cotton plant; **estar criado entre algodones** to be brought up in comfort; **algodón de altura** upland cotton; **algodón en hojas** cotton batting; **algodón en rama** raw cotton, cotton wool; **algodón hidrófilo** absorbent cotton; **algodón pólvora** guncotton
algodonal *m* cotton plantation, cotton field
algodonar *va* to fill or stuff with cotton
algodoncillo *m* piece of cotton (*for the ear*); (bot.) milkweed, swamp milkweed
algodonería *f* cotton factory; cotton manufacture; cotton plantation
algodonero -ra *adj* (pertaining to) cotton; *mf* cotton dealer, cotton broker; cotton grower; *m* Levant cotton
algodonoso -sa *adj* cottony
algología *f* algology
algonquino -na *adj* (philol.) Algonquian; (geol.) Algonkian; *m* Algonquin (*North American Indian and his language*); (philol.) Algonquian; *f* (geol.) Algonkian
algor *m* (path.) algor
algorfa *f* grain loft
algorín *m* olive bin
algoritmia *f* (math.) algorism
algorítmico -ca *adj* algorithmic
algoritmo *m* (math.) algorism
algoso -sa *adj* algous
alguacil *m* bailiff, alguazil; (taur.) mounted police officer who heads the processional entrance of the bullfighters; (ent.) jumping spider
alguacilazgo *m* bailiwick
alguacilillo *m* (taur.) mounted police officer who heads the processional entrance of the bullfighters; (ent.) jumping spider
alguarín *m* (prov.) storeroom; (prov.) flour trough (*in flour mill*); (prov.) olive trough
alguaza *f* (prov.) hinge
Alguer Alghero (*Catalan-speaking Sardinian city*)
alguien *pron indef* somebody, someone
algún *adj indef* apocopated form of **alguno**, used only before masculine singular nouns and adjectives; *adv* **algún tanto** somewhat, a little
alguno -na *adj indef* some, any; (after noun) not any; **alguno de ellos** one or another of them; **alguno que otro** some or another, an occasional; **alguna vez** sometimes; ever, e.g., **¿Ha estado Vd. alguna vez en España?** Have you ever been in Spain?; *pron indef* someone, some one; **algunos** some; **algunos de entre** some of
alhaja *f* jewel, gem, ornament, fine piece of furniture; (fig.) gem (*thing*); (coll.) gem (*person*); **buena alhaja** a sly fellow, a bad egg
alhajar *va* to bejewel; to furnish, to appoint
alhámega *f* var. of **alárgama**
alhamel *m* (prov.) beast of burden; (prov.) messenger; (prov.) muleteer
alhandal *m* colocynth, bitter apple (*fruit*)
alharaca *f* fuss, outcry, ado, ballyhoo; **hacer alharacas** to make a fuss
alharaquiento -ta *adj* fussy, emotional, strident, clamorous
alhárgama or **alharma** *f* var. of **alárgama**
alhelí *m* (*pl:* **-líes**) (bot.) gillyflower
alhelicillo *m* (bot.) alyssum, sweet alyssum
alheña *f* (bot.) henna; powdered henna; blight, mildew; **hecho alheña** or **molido como una alheña** (coll.) all fagged out
alheñar *va* to henna; to mildew, to blight; *vr* to henna (*e.g., one's hair*); to become mildewed, to become blighted
alhócigo *m* var. of **alfóncigo**
alhoja *f* (orn.) lark
alholva *f* (bot.) fenugreek (*plant and seed*)
alhóndiga *f* grain exchange
alhorma *f* Moorish camp; Moorish sanctuary or place of refuge (*around the tomb of a holy man*)
alhorre *m* meconium; skin eruption of newborn child
alhoz *m* (*pl:* **-hoces**) (archaic) var. of **alfoz**
alhucema *f* (bot.) lavender (*plant and dried flowers and leaves*)
alhumajo *m* pine needles
alhurreca *f* var. of **adarce**
aliabierto -ta *adj* with wings spread
aliacán *m* (path.) jaundice
aliacanado -da *adj* jaundiced
aliáceo -a *adj* garlicky
aliado -da *adj* allied; *mf* ally
aliadófilo -la *adj & mf* pro-Ally
aliaga *f* (bot.) furze, gorse
aliagar *m* furze field
alianza *f* alliance; wedding ring; (Bib.) covenant; **Santa Alianza** Holy Alliance; **Triple Alianza** Triple Alliance; **Alianza para el progreso** Alliance for Progress
aliar §90 *va* to ally; *vr* to become allied; to form an alliance
aliara *f* drinking horn
aliaria *f* (bot.) garlic mustard
alias *m & adv* alias
aliblanca *f* (orn.) white-winged dove
alible *adj* nourishing, nutritive
álica *f* porridge of corn, wheat, and pulse
alicaído -da *adj* with drooping wings; (coll.) drooping, crestfallen; (coll.) discouraged, downhearted; (coll.) discountenanced
alicántara *f* (zool.) viper
alicante *m* (zool.) viper; Alicante wine
alicantino -na *adj* (pertaining to) Alicante; *mf* native or inhabitant of Alicante; *f* (coll.) trick, ruse
alicatado *m* tiling with arabesque designs
alicatar *va* to tile
alicates *mpl* pliers
Alicia *f* Alice; **Alicia en el país de las maravillas** Alice in Wonderland
aliciente *m* attraction, inducement, incentive
alicortar *va* to cut the wings of, to wing (*to wound*)
alicuanta *adj fem* (math.) aliquant
alícuota *adj fem* (math.) aliquot
alidada *f* alidade
alienable *adj* alienable

alienación *f* alienation; rapture
alienado -da *adj* insane; enraptured; distracted; *mf* insane person
alienar *va* to alienate; to enrapture
alienismo *m* alienism (*profession of alienist*)
alienista *mf* alienist
aliento *m* breath, breathing; enterprise, courage, spirit; **cobrar aliento** to revive, to take heart; **contener el aliento** to hold one's breath; **dejar sin aliento** to leave breathless; **de mucho aliento** long, endless, arduous (*work*); **de un aliento** without catching one's breath; without stopping; **mal aliento** bad breath; **nuevo aliento** second wind; **sin aliento** out of breath; **tomar aliento** to catch one's breath
alifafe *m* (vet.) tumor on horse's hock; (coll.) complaint, indisposition
alifar *va* (prov.) to polish, to burnish
alifara *f* (prov.) light lunch
alifático -ca *adj* (chem.) aliphatic
alífero -ra *adj* winged
aliforme *adj* wing-shaped
aligación *f* or **aligamiento** *m* bond, tie, connection; alloy
aligar §59 *vr* to band together
aligeramiento *m* lightening; easing, alleviation; shortening; hastening
aligerar *va* to lighten; to ease, alleviate; to shorten; to hasten
alígero -ra *adj* (poet.) winged
aligonero *m* var. of **almez**
aligustre *m* (bot.) privet; **aligustre del Japón** (bot.) wax privet
aligustrón *m* (bot.) wax privet
alijado -da *adj* (naut.) light, unloaded
alijador *m* lighter (*ship*); lighterman; cotton ginner (*person*); smuggler; sander, sandpaperer
alijar *m* wasteland; Moorish tile; **alijares** *mpl* outlying commons; *va* to unload, to lighten (*a ship*); to unload (*contraband*); to gin (*cotton*); to sandpaper
alijarar *va* to apportion (*wasteland*) for cultivation
alijarero *m* farmer of wasteland
alijo *m* lighterage; ginning; smuggling; smuggled goods; contraband; (Am.) locomotive tender
alilaya *f* (Am.) flimsy excuse
alileno *m* (chem.) allylene
alilo *m* (chem.) allyl
alimaña *f* animal, small predatory animal, varmint
alimañero *m* gamekeeper who watches for and destroys predatory animals
alimentación *f* alimentation, nourishment, feed, feeding; **alimentación forzada** (mach.) force feed; (med.) force-feeding
alimentador -dora *adj* nourishing; *mf* nourisher; *m* stoker (*machine*); (elec.) feeder
alimentar *va* to nourish, to feed; to sustain, to maintain; to foster, to cherish; *vn* to be nourishing; *vr* to feed; **alimentarse con** or **de** to feed on or upon
alimentario -ria *adj* alimentary (*providing support*); *mf* pensioner
alimenticio -cia *adj* alimentary, nourishing, nutritional, food
alimentista *mf* pensioner
alimento *m* food, nourishment, aliment; encouragement, support; **alimentos** *mpl* foodstuffs; alimony; allowance; **alimento combustible** or **energético** carbohydrate; **alimento plástico** or **reparador** protein; **alimento respiratorio** or **termógeno** carbohydrate
alimentoso -sa *adj* nutritious
álimo *m* (bot.) saltbush
alimoche *m* (orn.) Egyptian vulture, Pharaoh's chicken
alimón; al alimón (taur.) with the cape held by two toreros
alimonado -da *adj* lemon (*in form, appearance, or color*)
alimonar *vr* to turn yellow (*said of leaves*)
alindado -da *adj* vain, foppish, dandified, mincing
alindamiento *m* marking off, setting boundaries
alindar *va* to mark off; to prettify; *vn* to border, be contiguous
alindongar §59 *vr* (dial.) to overdress
alineación *f* alignment; (eng.) alignment; **fuera de alineación** out of alignment
alineador -dora *adj* aligning; *mf* aligner
alineamiento *m* building line; (archeol.) alignment
alinear *va & vr* to align, to line up
aliñar *va* to season, to dress (*food*); (Am.) to set (*a broken bone*)
aliño *m* seasoning, dressing; preparation; **aliño francés** French dressing
aliñoso -sa *adj* seasoned; careful, attentive
alioli *m* garlic and olive-oil sauce
alionar *va* (Am.) to stir up, agitate
alionín *m* (orn.) bottle tit
alipata *m* (bot.) blind-your-eyes, poison tree
alípede *adj* (poet.) winged, nimble, swift
alípedo -da *adj & mf* aliped
aliquebrado -da *adj* (coll.) drooping, crestfallen
aliquebrar §18 *va* to break the wings of
alirado -da *adj* lyrate, lyre-shaped
alirrojo -ja *adj* red-winged
alisado *m* (action of) smoothing
alisador -dora *adj* polishing; *mf* smoother, polisher, finisher; *m* smoothing iron, smoothing blade; *f* surfacing machine, road scraper
alisadura *f* smoothing, polishing; surfacing; **alisaduras** *fpl* turnings, cuttings, shavings
alisar *m* alder grove or plantation; *va* to smooth; to sleek; to iron lightly
aliseda *f* alder grove or plantation
alisios *mpl* trade winds
alisma *f* (bot.) water plantain
aliso *m* (bot.) alder
alistador -dora *mf* enlister, enroller, recruiter
alistamiento *m* enlistment, enrolment, recruitment
alistar *va* to list; to enlist, enroll; to prepare, arrange; to stripe; *vr* to enlist, enroll; to get ready
aliteración *f* alliteration; paronomasia
aliterado -da *adj* alliterative
alitierno *m* (bot.) mock privet
aliviador -dora *adj* alleviative
alivianar *va* (Am.) to make lighter (*in weight*)
aliviar *va* to lighten; to alleviate, mitigate, soothe; to hasten, speed up
alivio *m* alleviation, relief
alizar *m* tile dado; tile (*of a dado*)
alizarina *f* (chem.) alizarin
aljaba *f* quiver
aljama *f* Moorish gathering, Jewish gathering; mosque, synagogue; Moorish quarter, ghetto
aljamía *f* Spanish of Moors or Jews; Spanish written in Arabic characters
aljamiado -da *adj* aljamía-speaking; written in Arabic characters (*said of Spanish*)
aljarafe *m* tableland; flat roof, terrace
aljarfa *f* or **aljarfe** *m* thick central part of fishing net
aljerife *m* large fishing net
aljévena *f* (prov.) washbowl, basin
aljez *m* gypsum
aljezar *m* gypsum pit
aljezón *m* gypsum rubbish
aljibe *m* tank barge, water tender; oil tanker; cistern, reservoir
aljibero *m* tender of a cistern or reservoir
aljofaina *f* washbowl, basin
aljófar *m* imperfect pearl; pearl trimming; (fig.) dewdrop
aljofarar *va* to adorn with pearls; to bepearl
aljofifa *f* floor mop
aljofifar *va* to mop (*a tiled floor*)
aljonje *m* birdlime
aljonjera *f* or **aljonjero** *m* (bot.) carline thistle
aljonjolí *m* (*pl:* **-líes**) (bot.) sesame
aljor *m* gypsum
aljorozar §76 *va* (Am.) to smooth, to make smooth with plaster
aljuba *f* jubbah
alma *f* see **almo**
almacén *m* warehouse; store, department store; (phot.) magazine; (fig.) storehouse; (Am.) grocery store; **gastar (mucho) almacén** (coll.) to dress gaudily, be gaudily

dressed; (coll.) to be long-winded; **grandes almacenes** department store; **almacén de placas** (phot.) plateholder
almacenaje *m* storage (*cost, charges*)
almacenamiento *m* storage, storing
almacenar *va* to store; to store up, hoard
almacenero *m* storekeeper; warehouseman
almacenista *mf* shop owner; store clerk; warehouseman; (Am.) wholesale grocer
almacería *f* covered seedbed
almáciga *f* seedbed (*for later transplantation*); mastic
almacigar **§59** *va* to scent or treat with mastic
almácigo *m* (bot.) mastic tree; seedbed
almaciguero -ra *adj* (pertaining to a) seedbed
almádana or **almádena** *f* stone hammer, spalling hammer
almadía *f* Hindoo canoe; raft
almadiar *vr* to get sick, become nauseated
almadiero *m* paddler, canoeist; raftsman
almádina *f* var. of **almádana**
almadraba *f* tuna fishing; tuna fishery; tuna-fish net
almadrabero -ra *adj* tuna-fishing; *mf* tuna fisher
almadraque *m* cushion, pillow; mattress
almadreña *f* wooden shoe
almaganeta *f* var. of **almádana**
almagesto *m* almagest
almagra *f* red ocher, ruddle
almagrado -da *adj* red-ocher (*color*)
almagradura *f* coloring with red ocher
almagral *m* ocher deposit
almagrar *va* to color with red ocher; to make bloody; (slang) to make bleed, to draw blood on; to stigmatize, to defame
almagre *m* red ocher
almagrero -ra *adj* red-ocher-bearing; *f* ocher deposit; ocher can
almaizal *m* or **almaizar** *m* Moorish gauze veil; (eccl.) humeral veil
almajal *m* var. of **almarjal**
almajaneque *m* (mil.) battering ram
almajar *m* var. of **almarjal**
almajara *f* (hort.) hotbed, forcing bed
almajo *m* var. of **almarjo**
almalafa *f* Moorish robe
almanaque *m* almanac; calendar; **hacer almanaques** (coll.) to meditate, to muse; **ser un almanaque del año pasado** to be out of date
almanaquero -ra *mf* maker or vendor of almanacs
almancebe *m* Guadalquivir fishing net
almandina *f* deep-red garnet
almánguena *f* red ocher
almanta *f* space between rows of trees; ground between two large furrows
almarada *f* poniard with triangular blade; wooden-handled poker; rope-sandalmaker's needle
almarbatar *va* to join (*two pieces of wood*)
almarcha *f* town on marshy ground
almarga *f* marlpit
almarjal *m* glasswort field; marsh, fen
almarjo *m* (bot.) glasswort; (chem.) barilla
almaro *m* (bot.) germander
almarrá *m* (*pl:* **-rraes**) cotton gin
almarraja or **almarraza** *f* glass sprinkling vessel
almártaga *f* (archaic) headstall; litharge
almártega *f* litharge
almártiga *f* (archaic) headstall
almartigón *m* halter (*for tying horse to manger*)
almaste *m*, **almástec** *m*, or **almástiga** *f* mastic
almatrero *m* shad fisherman
almatriche *m* irrigation trench
almatroque *m* shad net
almatroste *m* (Am.) var. of **armatoste**
almazara *f* oil mill, oil press
almazarero *m* oil-mill operator
almazarrón *m* red ocher
almea *f* almeh (*Oriental singing and dancing girl*); liquid storax; storax bark
almear *m* shock, stack; loft
almecina *f* var. of **almeza**
almeja *f* (zool.) clam; **almeja de los estanques** (zool.) swan mussel; **almeja redonda** (zool.) quahog, hard-shelled clam
almejar *m* clam bed
almejía *f* Moorish cloak of rough cloth
almena *f* (fort.) merlon
almenado -da *adj* battlemented, crenelated; *m* battlement
almenaje *m* battlement, battlements
almenar *s* cresset; *va* (fort.) to crenelate, to line or top with merlons
almenara *f* beacon fire; chandelier; overflow ditch, return ditch
almendra *f* almond (*fruit and stone; almond-shaped glass, diamond, etc.*); kernel (*of drupaceous fruit*); **almendra amarga** bitter almond; **almendra de Málaga** Jordan almond; **almendra garapiñada** praline
almendrado -da *adj* almond-shaped; *m* macaroon; *f* drink of milk and almonds; compliment
almendral *m* almond grove
almendrate *m* almond stew
almendrera *f* (bot.) almond tree; **florecer la almendrera** (coll.) to turn gray prematurely
almendrero *m* (bot.) almond tree; dish for almonds
almendrilla *f* almond-shaped file; fine gravel; buckwheat coal
almendro *m* (bot.) almond tree; **almendro amargo** (bot.) bitter almond
almendrón *m* (bot.) Malabar almond (*tree and nut*); (bot.) Brazil-nut tree; (bot.) Jamaica bayberry
almendruco *m* green almond
almenilla *f* merlon-shaped trimming
almeriense *adj* (pertaining to) Almería; *mf* native or inhabitant of Almería
almete *m* armet; soldier wearing armet
almez *m* (*pl:* **-meces**) (bot.) hackberry, nettle tree
almeza *f* hackberry (*fruit*)
almezo *m* (bot.) hackberry, nettle tree
almiar *m* haystack, hayrick
almíbar *m* simple syrup; fruit juice; **estar hecho un almíbar** (coll.) to be as sweet as pie
almibarado -da *adj* syrupy; (coll.) sugary, honeyed, flattering
almibarar *va* to preserve in syrup; to honey (*one's words*)
almicantarada or **almicantarat** *f* (astr.) almucantar
almidón *m* starch; **almidón de maíz** cornstarch
almidonado -da *adj* starched; (coll.) spruce, dapper; *m* starching
almidonar *va* to starch
almidonería *f* starch factory
almijar *m* place for drying olives or grapes before pressing
almilla *f* bodice, close-fitting jacket; undervest; (carp.) tenon; breast of pork
almimbar *m* mimbar (*pulpit in a mosque*)
alminar *m* minaret
almiranta *f* admiral's wife; flagship
almirantazgo *m* admiralty
almirante *m* admiral; female headgear; cone shell; (prov.) swimming coach
almirez *m* (*pl:* **-reces**) metal mortar
almizclar *va* to perfume with musk
almizcle *m* musk
almizcleño -ña *adj* musky; *f* (bot.) grape hyacinth
almizclero -ra *adj* musky; *m* (zool.) musk deer; *f* (zool.) muskrat
almo -ma *adj* (poet.) nourishing; (poet.) sacred, venerable; *f* soul, heart, spirit; living soul (*person*); strength, vigor; crux, heart (*of the matter*); pith (*of plants*); darling, sweetheart; bore (*of gun*); web (*of rail, etc.*); (elec.) core (*of cable*); newel (*of staircase*); (mus.) sounding-post (*of violin, etc.*); **dar el alma, entregar el alma, rendir el alma** to give up the ghost; **estar con el alma en la boca** or **entre los dientes** (coll.) to have one's heart in one's boots or mouth
almocadén *m* (archaic) infantry officer; (archaic) cavalry officer in command of a platoon; petty officer (*in Morocco*)
almocafre *m* dibble, weeding hoe

almocárabes *mpl* or **almocarbes** *mpl* (arch.) intertwining spiral or scroll-like figures
almocatracía *f* (archaic) duty on woolen goods
almocela *f* farmer's straw mattress; (archaic) hood
almocrate *m* (chem.) sal ammoniac
almocrí *m* (*pl:* **-críes**) reader of Koran in a mosque
almodí *m* (*pl:* **-díes**) public grain exchange
almodón *m* flour made from dampened wheat
almodrote *m* sauce of oil, cheese, and garlic; (coll.) mixture, hodgepodge
almófar *m* (arm.) mail coif (*worn under helmet*)
almofía *f* brass washbasin
almofrej *m* or **almofrez** *m* traveling bag for bedding
almogama *f* (naut.) var. of **redel**
almogárabe *m* (mil.) raider, forager
almogataz *m* Christianized Moor in Spanish army in Africa
almogávar *m* (mil.) raider, forager
almogavarear *vn* to go raiding, to go foraging
almogavaría or **almogavería** *f* (mil.) raiding troops, raiding party
almohada *f* pillow; cushion; pillowcase; (naut.) pillow; **consultar con la almohada** to sleep a thing over; **dar almohada a** (hist.) to raise to the nobility (*by the queen's inviting a woman to sit at her side on a cushion*); **almohada de aire** air cushion
almohade *adj* Almohade; **almohades** *mpl* Almohades (*Islamitic sect which controlled the Mussulman territory of North Africa and Spain in the 12th and 13th centuries*)
almohadilla *f* small pillow or cushion; sewing cushion; pad; harness pad; callus (*from saddle or harness*); cushion (*pad for gold leaf*); (arch.) bossage (*of an ashlar*); (arch.) bolster; (baseball) bag; **almohadilla higiénica** sanitary napkin; **almohadilla caliente eléctrica** electric hot pad, electric heating pad
almohadillado -da *adj* padded, cushioned; ashlared; *m* bossage; ashlar; **almohadillado rústico** rusticated or quarry-faced ashlar
almohadillar *va* to pad, to cushion; to dress (*an ashlar*)
almohadón *m* large pillow or cushion, round cushion, hassock; (arch.) springer
almohatre *m* (chem.) sal ammoniac
almohaza *f* currycomb
almohazador *m* currier, groom
almohazar **§76** *va* to curry, to currycomb
almojábana *f* cheese cake; cruller
almojarifazgo *m* import duty, export duty; custom house
almojarife *m* royal tax collector, revenue officer, customhouse officer
almojaya *f* (carp.) putlog
almona *f* shad fishery; (archaic) public stores; (prov.) soap factory
almóndiga *f* meat ball, fish ball
almoneda *f* auction; clearance sale
almonedar or **almonedear** *va* to auction; to sell out
almonedero *m* auctioneer
almoraduj *m* or **almoradux** *m* (bot.) sweet marjoram
almorávid *adj* Almoravide; **almorávides** *mpl* Almoravides (*North African tribe which dominated Arabic Spain from 1093 to 1148*)
almorejo *m* (bot.) bottle grass (*Setaria glauca*)
almorí *m* (*pl:* **-ríes**) honey cake
almoronía *f* var. of **alboronía**
almorranas *fpl* (path.) piles, hemorrhoids
almorraniento -ta *adj* suffering from piles
almorrefa *f* triangular tile
almorta *f* (bot.) grass pea
almorzada *f* double handful
almorzar **§52** *va* to eat for lunch, to lunch on; *vn* to have lunch, to lunch
almotacén *m* inspector of weights and measures; inspector's office
almotacenazgo *m* office of inspector of weights and measures
almotacenía *f* inspector's fee; office of inspector of weights and measures
almozala *f* quilt, blanket
almozárabe *adj* Mozarabic; *mf* Mozarab
almud *m* almud (*dry measure: 2 to 21 qts.; liquid measure: 5 to 32 qts.*)
almudada *f* ground sown with one almud of seed
almudero *m* keeper of dry measures
almudí *m* (*pl:* **-díes**) public grain exchange
almudín *m* var. of **almudí**
almuecín *m* or **almuédano** *m* muezzin
almuérdago *m* var. of **muérdago**
almuerza *f* double handful
almuerzo *m* lunch; luncheon set (*of dishes*)
almunia *f* orchard, farm
alnado -da *mf* stepchild
alnico *m* alnico (*alloy*)
aló *interj* (Am.) hello!, hey!
alobadado -da *adj* bitten by a wolf; (vet.) having carbuncular tumors
alobunado -da *adj* wolflike, wolf-colored
alocado -da *adj* mad, wild, reckless, foolish; *mf* madcap
alocar **§86** *va* to drive mad or crazy
alocución *f* allocution, address, speech
alodial *adj* (law) alodial
alodio *m* (law) alodium
áloe or **aloe** *m* (bot.) aloe; (pharm.) aloes
aloético -ca *adj* aloetic
alófana *f* (chem.) allophane
alogamia *f* (bot.) allogamy
aloína *f* (chem. & pharm.) aloin
aloja *f* metheglin, mead
alojado -da *mf* (Am.) guest, lodger; *m* soldier billeted in a private house
alojamiento *m* lodging; housing; quartering, billeting; lodgings, quarters; (naut.) crew's quarters
alojar *va* to lodge; to quarter, billet (*troops*); *vn & vr* to lodge; to be quartered or billeted
alojería *f* metheglin shop, mead shop
alojero -ra *mf* metheglin mixer or vendor; (theat.) box near the pit
alomado -da *adj* high-backed
alomar *va* to plow in wide furrows; *vr* to become strong in back and loins (*said of a horse*)
alón *m* wing without feathers
alondra *f* (orn.) lark; **alondra azul** (orn.) blue grosbeak
alongamiento *m* lengthening, prolongation; extension; distance, separation
alongar **§79** *va* to lengthen, prolong; to stretch, extend; to remove, to put at a distance; *vr* to move away
alópata *mf* allopath
alopatía *f* allopathy
alopático -ca *adj* allopathic
alopecia *f* (path.) alopecia
alopecuro *m* (bot.) foxtail grass
alopiado -da *adj* opiate
aloque *adj* light-red (*said of wine*); *m* light-red wine; mixture of light-red and white wine
aloquecer **§34** *vr* to go crazy, to lose one's mind
aloquín *m* stone inclosure of a wax bleachery
alosa *f* (ichth.) shad
alotar *va* (naut.) to reef, to stow
alotropía *f* allotropy
alotrópico -ca *adj* allotropic
alotropismo *m* allotropism
alotropo *m* allotrope
alpaca *f* (zool.) alpaca; alpaca (*wool and cloth; glossy black cloth made of wool and cotton*); German silver
alpañata *f* chamois skin, soft leather (*for polishing pottery before baking*)
alpargata *f* hemp sandal; espadrille
alpargatado -da *adj* shaped like a hemp sandal
alpargatar *vn* to make hemp sandals
alpargate *m* var. of **alpargata**
alpargatería *f* hemp-sandal shop or factory
alpargatero -ra *mf* maker or seller of hemp sandals
alpargatilla *mf* crafty, sneaking person
alpechín *m* foul-smelling juice that oozes from a heap of olives
alpechinera *f* vat for catching juice oozing from a heap of olives
alpende *m* tool house, tool shed; lean-to, penthouse
alpérsico *m* (bot.) peach (*tree and fruit*)

Alpes *mpl* Alps; **Alpes dináricos** Dinaric Alps; **Alpes julianos** Julian Alps; **Alpes réticos** Rhaetian Alps
alpestre *adj* alpine; Alpine
alpicoz *m* (*pl:* **-coces**) (prov.) var. of **alficoz**
alpinismo *m* Alpinism, mountain climbing
alpinista *mf* Alpinist, mountain climber
alpino -na *adj* Alpine
alpiste *m* (bot.) canary grass; alpist, canary seed, birdseed; **dejar alpiste a uno** (coll.) to disappoint someone; **quedarse alpiste** (coll.) to be disappointed
alpistela *f* sesame-seed cake
alpistero -ra *adj* canary-grass; canary-seed; *f* sesame-seed cake
alpujarreño -ña *adj* pertaining to the Alpujarras; *mf* native or inhabitant of the Alpujarras
alquequenje *m* (bot.) winter cherry, alkekengi
alquería *f* farmhouse
alquermes *m* kermes-colored alcoholic drink
alquerque *m* place in olive-oil mill for shredding crushed residue from first pressing
alquez *m* (*pl:* **-queces**) wine measure of 193 liters
alquibla *f* kiblah (*direction to which Moslems turn in prayer*)
alquicel *m* or **alquicer** *m* Moorish cloak; fabric for covering furniture
alquifol *m* alquifou (*lead sulfide for glazing pottery*)
alquila *f* "for hire" sign on a cab
alquilable *adj* rentable, for rent
alquiladizo -za *adj* for rent, for hire; hireling; *mf* hireling
alquilador -dora *mf* renter, hirer; proprietor, tenant
alquilamiento *m* rent, renting, hire, hiring
alquilar *va* to rent, to let, to hire; *vr* to hire, hire out; to be for rent; **se alquila** for rent
alquilate *m* (dial.) sales tax
alquiler *m* rent, rental, hire; **de alquiler** for hire; **alquiler de coches** car-rental service; **alquiler sin chófer** drive-yourself service
alquilón -lona *adj* cheap to rent, easy to hire; hireling; *mf* hireling; *m* hired cab or coach; *f* charwoman, cleaning woman
alquimia *f* alchemy
alquímico -ca *adj* alchemical
alquimila *f* (bot.) lady's-mantle, lion's-foot
alquimista *m* alchemist
alquinal *m* woman's headdress or veil
alquitara *f* still, alembic
alquitarar *va* to distil
alquitira *f* (bot.) tragacanth
alquitrán *m* tar; pitch; **alquitrán de hulla** coal tar; **alquitrán vegetal** wood tar
alquitranado -da *adj* (pertaining to) tar, tarred; *m* tarred cloth, tarpaulin
alquitranadora *f* tar-spraying machine
alquitranar *va* to tar
alrededor *adv* around; **alrededor de** around, about; (coll.) about (*practically*); **alrededores** *mpl* environs, outskirts
alrota *f* coarse tow, waste tow
Alsacia *f* Alsace
Alsacia-Lorena *f* Alsace-Lorraine
alsaciano -na *adj & mf* Alsatian
álsine *m* (bot.) chickweed
alta *f* see **alto**
altabaque *m* wicker basket, sewing basket
altabaquillo *m* (bot.) lesser bindweed
altaico -ca *adj* Altaic
altamente *adv* exceedingly, extremely
altamisa *f* var. of **artemisa**
altanería *f* upper air; soaring; falconry; haughtiness, arrogance
altanero -ra *adj* soaring, towering; haughty, arrogant
altanos *mpl* (naut.) winds blowing alternately offshore and off the sea
altar *m* altar; (found.) altar, flue bridge; **conducir al altar** to lead to the altar; **altar mayor** high altar
altaricón -cona *adj* (coll.) strapping, big and husky
altarreina *f* (bot.) yarrow
altavoz *m* (*pl:* **-voces**) (rad.) loudspeaker
altea *f* (bot.) althea
altear *vr* to rise, stand out
alterabilidad *f* alterability
alterable *adj* alterable
alteración *f* alteration; disturbance; agitation, irritation; uneven pulse, fast pulse; disorder, uprising; quarrel, altercation
alteradizo -za *adj* changeable, fickle
alterado -da *adj* altered; disturbed, agitated, upset; angered
alterante *adj & m* (med.) alterative
alterar *va* to alter; to disturb, to upset; to corrupt, to falsify; to agitate, irritate; to lessen, to cool; *vr* to alter; to be disturbed; to become agitated, to get irritated; to flutter (*said of the pulse*); to lessen, to cool
alterativo -va *adj* alterative (*causing change*)
altercación *f* or **altercado** *m* altercation, bickering
altercador -dora *adj* wrangling, bickering; *mf* wrangler, bickerer
altercar §86 *vn* to altercate, to wrangle, argue, bicker
álter ego (Lat.) alter ego
alternación *f* alternation
alternadamente *adv* alternately
alternador *m* (elec.) alternator
alternancia *f* (elec.) alternation; **alternancia de generaciones** (biol.) alternation of generations
alternante *adj* alternate, alternating
alternar *va* to alternate; to vary; *vn* to alternate; to take turns; **alternar con** to go around with, be friendly with
alternativo -va *adj* alternating; *f* alternative, option; alternation; (taur.) ceremony by which a senior matador authorizes a novice matador to kill the bull, thus making the novice a full-fledged matador; **alternativas** *fpl* ups and downs; **tomar la alternativa** (taur.) to be dubbed a matador; **alternativa de cosechas** rotation of crops
alterno -na *adj* alternating; (bot. & geom.) alternate
alteroso -sa *adj* (naut.) top-heavy
alteza *f* height, elevation, sublimity; (*cap.*) s Highness (*title*)
altibajo *m* velvet brocade; downward cut or thrust (*with a sword*); **altibajos** *mpl* bumps, uneven ground; ups and downs, vicissitudes
altilocuencia *f* grandiloquence
altilocuente or **altílocuo -cua** *adj* grandiloquent
altillo *m* hillock; balcony (*in a store or shop, used as an office*); (Am.) attic
altimetría *f* altimetry
altímetro -tra *adj* altimetrical; *m* altimeter
altiplanicie *f* high plateau; (Am.) highland plain
altiplano *m* (Am.) highland plain
altísimo -ma *adj super* most high, very high; **el Altísimo** the Most High (*God*)
altisonancia *f* high-flown language
altisonante or **altísono -na** *adj* high-flown; high-sounding
altitonante *adj* (poet.) thundering
altitud *f* altitude
altivar *vr* to put on airs, to act haughtily
altivecer §34 *va* to make haughty; *vr* to act haughtily, to become haughty
altivez *f* or **altiveza** *f* pride, haughtiness, arrogance
altivo -va *adj* proud, haughty, arrogant
alto -ta *adj* high; upper; deep; tall; loud; top; late (*hours*); early, remote (*e.g., Middle Ages*); arduous; noble, eminent; enormous; **de alto bordo** (naut.) of several decks, sea-going; (fig.) of importance; (fig.) high-up; **alta mar** high seas; **altas clases** upper classes; **altas horas** late hours; **alta traición** high treason; **alto horno** blast furnace; **alto relieve** altorelievo, high relief; **alto** *adv* high up; loud, aloud, loudly; **alto** *interj* halt!; **¡alto ahí!** halt!, stop there!; **¡alto al fuego!** (mil.) cease fire!; **¡alto de aquí!** (coll.) out of here!; *m* height, altitude; depth; story, floor; roadbed; stop, halt; (mus.) alto; (Am.) pile, heap; **de alto a bajo** from top to bottom; **de lo alto** from above; **en alto** up high, up above; upward; **en lo alto de** on top of; **hacer alto** to

stop, to halt; **pasar por alto** to overlook, disregard, forget; **pasársele a uno por alto** to overlook, e.g., **eso se nos pasó por alto** we overlooked that; **ponerse tan alto** to take offense, to become hoity-toity; **alto el fuego** (mil.) cease fire; *f* courtly dance of German origin; dancing exercise; fencing bout; certificate of discharge from hospital; (mil.) certificate of induction into active service; acceptance as member of society or profession; **dar de alta** to discharge (*a patient*) from the hospital; (mil.) to admit, to enroll; **darse de alta** to join, become a member, be admitted; (mil.) to report for duty

altoalemán -mana *adj* High-German; *m* High German; **antiguo altoalemán** Old High German; **medio altoalemán** Middle High German

altocúmulo *m* (meteor.) alto-cumulus

altoestrato *m* var. of **altostrato**

altoparlante *m* (rad.) loudspeaker; **altoparlante dinámico** (rad.) dynamic speaker; **altoparlante electromagnético** (rad.) electromagnetic speaker

altostrato *m* (meteor.) alto-stratus

altozanero *m* (Am.) errand boy

altozano *m* hillock, knoll; hilly part of town; (Am.) paved terrace

altramuz *m* (*pl:* **-muces**) (bot.) lupine (*plant and seed*); (eccl.) voting bean

altruísmo *m* altruism

altruísta *adj* altruistic; *mf* altruist

altura *f* height, altitude; high seas; loftiness; (mus.) pitch; (naut.) latitude; point, stage, juncture; **alturas** *fpl* Heaven; **a estas alturas** at this point, at this juncture; **a la altura de** (naut.) off; **estar a la altura de** to be up to, to be equal to (*a task, undertaking, etc.*); **estar a la altura de las circunstancias** (coll.) to rise to the occasion; **por estas alturas** (coll.) around here; **altura de la vegetación** timber line

alúa *f* (ent.) fire beetle

alubia *f* string bean

aluciar *va* to shine, polish; *vr* to get dressed up

alucinación *f* hallucination

alucinadamente *adv* deludedly, with delusion

alucinador -dora *adj* hallucinatory, delusive

alucinamiento *m* (act of) hallucinating

alucinante *adj* dazzling

alucinar *va* to hallucinate, to delude; *vr* to be deluded, be dazzled

alucita *f* (ent.) moth

alucón *m* (orn.) tawny owl

alud *m* avalanche; (fig.) avalanche

aluda *f* see **aludo**

aludel *m* (chem.) aludel

aludido -da *adj* above-mentioned; alluded to

aludir *va* to allude to; *vn* to allude

aludo -da *adj* large-winged; *f* (ent.) winged ant

alula *f* (orn. & ent.) alula

alumbrado -da *adj* lighted; enlightened; (coll.) tipsy; (chem.) aluminous; *m* lighting, lighting system; **alumbrado de arco** arc light, arc lighting; **alumbrado fluorescente** fluorescent lighting; **alumbrado reflejado** indirect lighting; **alumbrados** *mpl* Illuminati (*mystical Spanish sect of 16th century*)

alumbrador -dora *adj* lighting, illuminating; enlightening; *mf* lighter; enlightener

alumbramiento *m* lighting; childbirth, accouchement; discovery and elevation of subterranean water

alumbrar *va* to light, illuminate; to show the way with a light to; to give sight to (*the blind*); to enlighten; to find (*subterranean water*); to remove the earth from around (*a vine*); to treat with alum; *vn* to have a child, to give birth; *vr* (coll.) to get tipsy

alumbre *m* (chem.) alum; **alumbre de cromo** (chem.) chrome alum; **alumbre de rasuras** (chem.) potassium carbonate; **alumbre de roca** (mineral.) alum rock; **alumbre sacarino** or **zacarino** saccharine alum

alumbrera *f* alum mine

alumbroso -sa *adj* aluminous

alúmina *f* (mineral.) alumina

aluminato *m* (chem.) aluminate

alumínico -ca *adj* aluminic

aluminio *m* (chem.) aluminum

aluminita *f* (mineral.) aluminite

aluminoso -sa *adj* aluminous

aluminotermia *f* aluminothermy

alumnado *m* student body; boarding school

alumno -na *mf* foster child; ward; pupil, student; **alumno de las Musas** poet

alunado -da *adj* lunatic; long-tusked (*said of a wild boar*); spoiled (*said of bacon*); (vet.) suffering from spasms

alunar *vr* to spoil (*said of bacon*); to have a crazy streak, to be not all there

alunita *f* (mineral.) alunite

alunizar §76 *vn* to land on the moon

alusión *f* allusion

alusivo -va *adj* allusive

alustrar *va* to polish, to put a shine on, to give luster to

alútero *m* (ichth.) filefish

alutrado -da *adj* otter-colored

aluvial *adj* alluvial

aluvión *m* alluvion; alluvium; (law) alluvion; (fig.) flood

aluzar §76 *va* (dial. & Am.) to light, illuminate

alveario *m* (anat.) alveary

álveo *m* bed of a stream

alveolar *adj* (anat. & phonet.) alveolar

alvéolo *m* (anat., phonet. & zool.) alveolus; bucket (*of a water wheel*)

alverja or **alverjana** *f* var. of **arveja**

alverjilla *f* (Am.) sweet pea

alverjón *m* (bot.) grass pea

alvino -na *adj* (med.) alvine

alza *f* rise, advance (*e.g., in prices*); leather between last and shoe; (print.) overlay; rear sight (*of firearms*); **jugar al alza** to bull the market

alzacuello *m* stock (*kind of cravat*)

alzada *f* see **alzado**

alzadamente *adv* for a cash settlement, for a lump sum

alzadizo -za *adj* easy to lift, easy to raise

alzado -da *adj* raised, lifted; fixed, settled; *m* cash settlement, lump sum; (arch.) front elevation; (b.b.) quire, gathering; (naut.) height (*of a ship*); *f* height (*of horse at withers*); (law) appeal

alzadura *f* raising, lifting

alzafuelles *mf* (*pl:* **-lles**) (coll.) flatterer, fawner; (Am.) squealer

alzamiento *m* raising, lifting; rise (*in prices*); overbid; uprising, insurrection; fraudulent bankruptcy

alzapaño *m* curtain hook, curtain holder; tieback

alzapié *m* snare, trap

alzaprima *f* lever, crowbar; wedge; (mus.) bridge (*in string instruments*)

alzaprimar *va* to raise with a lever or wedge; to arouse, incite, stir up

alzapuertas *m* (*pl:* **-tas**) dumb player, actor of small parts, supernumerary

alzar §76 *va* to raise, lift, elevate, heave, hoist; to pick up; to carry off; to hide, lock up; to cut (*cards*); to elevate (*the host*); (b.b.) to gather; *vr* to rise, get up; to revolt; to become fraudulently bankrupt; to leave with one's winnings; (Am.) to run away; **alzarse a mayores** to get stuck up; **alzarse con** to flee with (*e.g., money*)

alzaválvulas *m* (*pl:* **-las**) (mach.) tappet

allá *adv* there, yonder; back there, long ago; **el más allá** the beyond (*life after death*); **más allá** farther away, farther over there, farther on; **más allá de** beyond; **no estar muy allá** (coll.) to not be very well; **por allá** thereabouts; that way; **tan allá** so far away; **allá en** over in; back in

allanador -dora *adj* leveling, flattening; *mf* leveler; *m* book for keeping gold leaf

allanamiento *m* leveling, flattening; submission, acquiescence; **allanamiento a la demanda** (law) acceptance of defendant's claim; **allanamiento de morada** housebreaking

allanar *va* to level, smooth, flatten; to overcome, iron out, get around (*e.g., a difficulty*); to subdue; to admit into; to break into (*a house*); *vn* to level off; *vr* to tumble down; to yield, submit; to humble oneself

allegadizo -za *adj* gathered or piled up at random
allegado -da *adj* near, close; related; partisan; (Am.) foster; *mf* relative; partisan, follower
allegador -dora *mf* gatherer, reaper; *m* board on which thrashed wheat is gathered
allegamiento *m* collecting, gathering, reaping; relationship, union, close friendship
allegar §59 *va* to collect, gather, reap; to add; *vn* to approach, to arrive; *vr* to approach, to arrive; **allegarse a** to become attached to, to become a follower of, to agree with
allende *adv* beyond, elsewhere; **de allende y de aquende** from both sides; **allende de** besides, in addition to; *prep* beyond; **de allende los mares** from overseas
allí *adv* there; then; **de allí que** with the result that; **por allí** that way; **allí dentro** in there
alloza *f* green almond
allozar *m* almond plantation or grove
allozo *m* (bot.) almond tree; (bot.) wild almond tree
alludel *m* var. of **aludel**
allulla *f* (Am.) corn-meal bread
ama *f* mistress (*of a household*); housekeeper; housewife, lady of the house; owner, landlady, proprietress; landlord's wife; **ama de brazos** child's nurse; **ama de casa** housewife; **ama de cría** wet nurse; **ama de gobierno** housekeeper; **ama de leche** wet nurse; **ama de llaves** housekeeper; **ama seca** dry nurse
amabilidad *f* amiability
amabilísimo -ma *adj super* very or most amiable or kind
amable *adj* amiable, affable, kind, lovable
amacayo *m* (bot.) jacobean lily
amaceno -na *adj* Damascene; *m* (bot.) damson (*tree*); *f* damson (*fruit*)
amacollar *vn & vr* to put forth clusters or bunches (*of sprouts*)
amachetear *va* to strike with a machete, to hack at
amachinar *vr* (Am.) to cohabit, to get intimate
amacho -cha *adj* (Am.) strong, vigorous, outstanding
amadís *m* chivalrous man
amado -da *adj & mf* beloved
amador -dora *adj* loving, fond; *mf* lover
amadrigar §59 *va* to welcome, take, shelter, receive with open arms; *vr* to burrow, to hole up; to seclude oneself, to live in retirement
amadrinar *va* to couple, yoke together; to act as godmother to, to act as bridesmaid to; (naut.) to fasten together, to splice; to sponsor, to second, to sanction; to reinforce, to strengthen
amaestramiento *m* teaching, coaching; training
amaestrar *va* to teach, to coach; to train (*an animal*)
amagamiento *m* (Am.) fissure, cleft
amagar §59 *va* to threaten, to hint, to show signs of; to feint; (dial.) to hide; *vn* to threaten, to look threatening, to be impending; **amagar a** + *inf* to move to + *inf;* to threaten to + *inf; vr* (dial.) to hide
amago *m* threat, menace; sign, indication, symptom; feint
ámago *m* beebread; nausea, loathing, disgust
amainar *va* (naut.) to lower, to shorten (*a sail*); to lessen, relax; *vn* to subside, die down (*said, e.g., of the wind*); to lessen; to yield; *vr* to lessen; to yield
amaine *m* (naut.) lowering, shortening; lessening, slacking; subsiding; yielding
amaitinar *va* to watch, to spy upon
amajadar *va* to fertilize (*a field*) with sheep; *vn* to seek shelter in the fold
amalayar *va* (Am.) to yearn for
amalecita *m* (Bib.) Amalekite
amalgama *f* (chem., mineral. & fig.) amalgam
amalgamación *f* amalgamation; (min.) amalgamation process
amalgamar *va & vr* (chem. & fig.) to amalgamate
Amalia *f* Amelia
amamantamiento *m* nursing, suckling
amamantar *va* to nurse, to suckle
amán *m* amnesty; (*cap.*) *m* (Bib.) Haman
amancebamiento *m* concubinage, cohabitation
amancebar *vr* to live in concubinage, to cohabit
amancillar *va* to stain, spot; to sully, tarnish, defame
amanecer *m* dawn, daybreak; **al amanecer** at daybreak; §34 *va* (poet.) to light up, illuminate; *vn* to dawn, to begin to get light; to begin to appear; to start the day, to get awake; **amanecer en** to be at (*a certain place*) at daybreak or in the morning; to awaken in
amanecida *f* dawn, daybreak
amanerado -da *adj* mannered, affected
amaneramiento *m* mannerism, affectation
amanerar *vr* to indulge in mannerisms, to become affected, to act affectedly
amanita *f* (bot.) amanita
amanojado -da *adj* bunchy
amanojar *va* to gather by the handful, to gather in bunches
amansador -dora *adj* taming; soothing, appeasing; *mf* tamer; horse breaker; soother, appeaser
amansamiento *m* taming, subduing; soothing, appeasement; tameness
amansar *va* to tame (*an animal*); to break (*a horse*); to soothe, to appease
amanse *m* (Am.) var. of **amansamiento**
amantar *va* to cloak, to blanket
amante *adj* fond, loving; *mf* (Am.) lover, paramour; *m* lover; (naut.) lift; *f* lover, sweetheart
amantillar *va* (naut.) to hoist by hauling on the lifts
amantillo *m* (naut.) lift, topping lift
amanuense *mf* amanuensis
amañado -da *adj* skilful, clever; faked; stacked (*said of cards*)
amañar *va* to do skilfully or cleverly; to fake; *vr* to be handy, to acquire skill, to become expert; **amañarse a** + *inf* to settle down to + *inf*
amaño *m* skill, cleverness, aptitude; **amaños** *mpl* tools, implements; machinations, trickery
amapola *f* (bot.) poppy, corn poppy
amar *va* to love
amaracino -na *adj* (pertaining to) sweet marjoram
amáraco *m* (bot.) sweet marjoram
amaraje *m* (aer.) alighting on water
amarantáceo -a *adj* (bot.) amaranthaceous
amarantino -na *adj* amaranthine; *f* (bot.) globe amaranth
amaranto *m* (bot.) amaranth
amarar *vn* (aer.) to alight on water
amarchantar *vr* (Am.) to become a customer, to deal regularly
amarescente *adj* bitterish
amargaleja *f* sloe (*fruit*)
amargar §59 *va* to make bitter; to embitter; to spoil (*a party, an evening*); *vn & vr* to become bitter; to become embittered
amargo -ga *adj* bitter; grievous; grieved; *m* bitterness; bitter-almond candy; **amargos** *mpl* bitters
amargón *m* (bot.) dandelion
amargor *m* bitterness; sorrow, grief
amargoso -sa *adj* bitter
amarguera *f* (bot.) shrubby hare's-ear
amarguillo -lla *adj* bitterish
amargura *f* bitterness; sorrow, grief
amaricado -da *adj* (coll.) effeminate
amarilis *f* (bot.) amaryllis; (*cap.*) *s* Amaryllis (*shepherdess*)
amarilla *f* see **amarillo**
amarillear *vn* to show yellow, to be yellowish
amarillecer §34 *vn* to become yellow
amarillejo -ja or **amarillento -ta** *adj* yellowish
amarilleo *m* showing yellow, yellowishness
amarillez *f* yellowness
amarillo -lla *adj* yellow; *m* yellow; jaundice; drowsiness of silk worms in damp weather; **amarillo indio** Indian yellow; *f* (vet.) sheep jaundice
amarilloso -sa *adj* yellowish
amarinar *va* to salt (*fish*); to man (*a ship*)
amariposado -da *adj* butterfly-shaped
amaro *m* (bot.) clary

amarra *f* martingale; (naut.) mooring line or cable; **amarras** *fpl* protection, support; **falsa amarra** (naut.) guest rope
amarradero *m* hitching post, hitching ring; tying place, ring for tying something; (naut.) bollard, mooring post; (naut.) mooring berth
amarradijo *m* (Am.) granny knot, bad knot
amarradura *f* mooring, moorage
amarraje *m* moorage (*charge for mooring*)
amarrar *va* to moor, lash, tie up; to stack (*cards*)
amarrazones *mpl* (naut.) ground tackle
amarre *m* mooring, tying, fastening; tie, splice; mooring rope, line, or cable; stacking (*cards*)
amarro *m* mooring line or cable; (Am.) pack of cigarets
amartelado -da *adj* amorous, in love; **estar amartelado** (coll.) to be cuddly
amartelamiento *m* (coll.) lovemaking, infatuation
amartelar *va* to make love to, to court, to woo; to love with devotion; to make jealous, to infatuate; *vr* to fall in love; to get jealous, to become infatuated
amartillar *va* to hammer; to cock (*a gun*)
amasada *f* (Am.) batch of dough; (Am.) batch of mortar
amasadera *f* kneading trough, kneading board, kneading machine
amasadero *m* kneading room
amasador -dora *adj* kneading; *mf* kneader; baker; *m* kneading room
amasadura *f* kneading; batch of dough
amasamiento *m* kneading; massaging
amasandería *f* (Am.) small bakery, small baker's shop
amasandero *m* (Am.) small baker
amasar *va* to knead; to prepare, to arrange; to massage; to cook up (*e.g., an intrigue*); to amass (*money, a fortune*)
amasijo *m* kneading; batch of dough; batch of mortar; job, task; plot, intrigue; medley, hodgepodge
Amata *f* Amy
amate *m* (bot.) rubber plant (*Ficus elastica*); (bot.) benjamin tree (*Ficus benjamina*)
amatista *f* amethyst
amativo -va *adj* amative
amatorio -ria *adj* amatory
amaurosis *f* (path.) amaurosis
amayorazgar §59 *va* (law) to entail, to leave in entail
amazacotado -da *adj* heavy, thick; ponderous, stodgy, awkward, clumsy
amazona *f* amazon (*masculine woman*); equestrienne, horsewoman; riding habit (*of woman*); ostrich plume; (orn.) Amazon (*parrot*); (myth.) Amazon
Amazonas *m* Amazon (*river*)
Amazonia *f* see **amazonio**
amazónico -ca *adj* Amazonian
amazonio -nia *adj* Amazonian; (*cap.*) *f* basin of the Amazon and its tributaries
amazonita *f* (mineral.) amazonite
ambages *mpl* ambages, quibbling, ambiguity; **sin ambages** without beating about the bush
ambagioso -sa *adj* ambagious, roundabout, ambiguous
ámbar *m* amber; **ámbar gris** ambergris; **ámbar negro** black amber
ambarino -na *adj* (pertaining to) amber; *f* musk, civet
Amberes *f* Antwerp
amberino -na *adj* (pertaining to) Antwerp; *mf* native or inhabitant of Antwerp
ambición *f* ambition
ambicionar *va* to be ambitious for, to desire earnestly, to strive for; **ambicionar** + *inf* to be ambitious to + *inf*
ambicioso -sa *adj* ambitious; eager, greedy; climbing, clinging (*plant, vine*); **ambicioso de figurar** social climber
ambidexteridad *f* or **ambidextrismo** *m* ambidexterity
ambidextro -tra *adj* ambidextrous
ambientación *f* atmosphere
ambiental *adj* environmental
ambientar *va* to give atmosphere to; to acclimate
ambiente *adj* ambient; *m* atmosphere; (fig.) atmosphere
ambigú *m* (*pl:* **-gúes**) buffet supper; buffet, refreshment bar, refreshment counter
ambigüedad *f* ambiguity
ambiguo -gua *adj* ambiguous; (gram.) common (*gender*)
ambir *m* (Am.) tobacco juice (*in pipestem*); (Am.) tobacco stain (*on fingers*)
ámbito *m* ambit, contour; limit, boundary line; compass, scope
ambivalencia *f* (psychol.) ambivalence
ambivalente *adj* ambivalent
amblador -dora *adj* ambling; *mf* ambler
ambladura *f* amble
amblar *vn* to amble, to pace
ambleo *m* short, thick wax candle; candlestick
ambligonio -nia *adj* (geom.) obtuse-angled
ambliopía *f* (path.) amblyopia
ambo *m* two-number combination in a lottery; (Am.) two-piece suit
ambón *m* ambo
ambos -bas *adj & pron indef* both; **ambos a dos** both
ambrosía *f* (bot., myth. & fig.) ambrosia
ambrosíaco -ca *adj* ambrosial
ambrosiano -na *adj* Ambrosian
Ambrosio *m* Ambrose
ambucia *f* (Am.) gluttony, greediness
ambuesta *f* double handful
ambulacral *adj* (zool.) ambulacral
ambulacro *m* hall, passage; (zool.) ambulacrum
ambulancia *f* ambulance; (mil.) field hospital; **ambulancia de correos** railway post office, post office car; **ambulancia de vía férrea** (mil.) hospital train
ambulanciero -ra *mf* ambulance driver
ambulante *adj* ambulant, walking; *m* railway mail clerk
ambular *vn* to ambulate
ambulativo -va *adj* roving, wandering
ambulatorio -ria *adj* ambulatory
ambustión *f* burning, scalding; (surg.) cauterization
ameba *f* var. of **amiba**
amebeo *m* amoebaeum (*dialogue in verse*)
amechar *va* to put a wick in; to lard (*meat, etc.*)
amedrentador -dora *adj* frightening; *mf* frightener
amedrentar *va* to frighten, scare; *vr* to get scared
amelanquier *m* (bot.) chokeberry
amelga *f* ridge between plowed furrows; plot of ground marked for planting
amelgado -da *adj* unevenly sown, unevenly growing; *m* (prov.) boundary mound
amelgar §59 *va* to plow regularly; to mark off with mounds to show boundaries
amelonado -da *adj* melon-shaped; (coll.) lovesick
amelonar *vr* (coll.) to fall madly in love
amén *m & interj* amen; **decir a todo amén** (coll.) to agree with everything; **en un decir amén** (coll.) in a jiffy; **amén de** (coll.) aside from, except for; (coll.) in addition to, besides
amenaza *f* threat, menace
amenazador -dora *adj* threatening, menacing; *mf* threatener
amenazante *adj* threatening, menacing, impending
amenazar §76 *va & vn* to threaten; **amenazar** + *inf* or **amenazar con** + *inf* to threaten to + *inf*
amenguamiento *m* lessening, diminution; belittlement; defamation
amenguar §23 *va* to lessen, diminish; to belittle, depreciate; to defame
amenidad *f* amenity
amenizar §76 *va* to make pleasant, to make agreeable, to add charm to
ameno -na *adj* pleasant, agreeable, charming
amenorrea *f* (path.) amenorrhea
amentáceo -a *adj* (bot.) amentaceous
amentar §18 *va* to fasten with a strap; to lace (*footwear*)
amento *m* (bot.) ament, catkin, cattail; (archaic) leather strap; (obs.) shoelace
ameos *m* (*pl:* **-os**) (bot.) bishop's-weed

amerar *va* to mix, to mix with water; *vr* to soak in, to percolate
amerengado -da *adj* like meringue; sweet, sugary; (coll.) prudish, overnice, prissy
América *f* America; **la América Central** Central America; **la América del Norte** North America; **la América del Sur** South America; **la América Latina** Latin America; **la Pequeña América** Little America (*Antarctic base*)
americana *f* see **americano**
americanismo *m* Americanism; (Am.) U.S. interference in the affairs of other nations of the Western Hemisphere
americanista *mf* Americanist
americanización *f* Americanization
americanizar §76 *va* to Americanize; *vr* to Americanize, to become Americanized
americano -na *adj & mf* American; Spanish American; *f* sack coat; **americana sport** sport coat
americio *m* (chem.) americium
americomanía *f* Americomania
amerindio -dia *adj* Amerindian; *mf* Amerind, Amerindian
amerizar §76 *vn* var. of **amarar**
amestizado -da *adj* like a half-breed
ametalado -da *adj* metallic; (fig.) metallic (*said, e.g., of voice*)
ametista *f* var. of **amatista**
ametrallador *m* machine gunner
ametralladora *f* machine gun; **ametralladora antiaérea** anti-aircraft gun
ametrallar *va* to machine-gun
ametropía *f* (path.) ametropia
amezquinar *vr* to complain
amezquindar *vr* to become sad
amia *f* (ichth.) cub shark; (ichth.) bowfin
amianto *m* asbestos
amiba *f* (zool.) amoeba
amibiano -na *adj* amoebic
amibo *m* var. of **amiba**
amiboideo -a *adj* amoeboid
amicísimo -ma *adj super* very or most friendly
amida *f* (chem.) amide
amidina *f* (chem.) amidine
amidógeno *m* (chem.) amidogen
amidol *m* (chem.) amidol
amiento *m* (archaic) leather strap; (obs.) shoelace
amiga *f* see **amigo**
amigabilidad *f* amicability, friendliness
amigable *adj* amicable, friendly; harmonious, concordant
amigacho *m* (coll.) chum, crony, husband's side-kick; (coll.) sugar daddy
amigar §59 *va* to bring together, to make friendly; *vr* to become friendly; to cohabit
amígdala *f* (anat.) amygdala; (anat.) tonsil; **amígdala palatina** (anat.) tonsil
amigdalina *f* (chem.) amygdalin
amigdalitis *f* (path.) tonsillitis
amigdaloide *adj* (mineral.) amygdaloid, amygdaloidal
amigdalotomía *f* (surg.) tonsillectomy
amigo -ga *adj* friendly; fond; **hacerse amigo de** to make friends with; **ser amigo de** to be fond of, to have a liking for; *mf* friend; sweetheart; **amigo del alma** or **amigo del corazón** bosom friend; *m* male paramour; *f* mistress, concubine; schoolmistress; kindergarten, girls' school; **amiga de noche** (bot.) tuberose
amigote *m* (coll.) old friend, pal
amiláceo -a *adj* amylaceous, starchy
amilanado -da *adj* cowardly; lazy
amilanamiento *m* terror, intimidation
amilanar *va* to terrify, intimidate, cow; *vr* to be terrified, be intimidated, be cowed
amilasa *f* (biochem.) amylase
Amílcar *m* Hamilcar
amileno *m* (chem.) amylene
amílico -ca *adj* (chem.) amylic; *m* (slang) rotgut, poor wine
amilo *m* (chem.) amyl
amiloideo -a *adj* amyloid
amiloidosis *f* (path.) amyloidosis
amilopsina *f* (chem.) amylopsin
amillaramiento *m* tax assessment
amillarar *va* to assess (*property*) for taxes
amillonado -da *adj* extremely rich
amimar *va* to pet, fondle, indulge
amina *f* (chem.) amine
amínico -ca *adj* (chem.) aminic
aminoácidos *mpl* (chem.) amino acids
aminoración *f* lessening, diminution; weakening
aminorar *va* to lessen, diminish; to weaken
amir *m* amir
amistad *f* friendship; friendly connection, friend; kindness; cohabitation, concubinage; affinity; **hacer las amistades** (coll.) to make up; **romper las amistades** (coll.) to fall out, to become enemies; **trabar amistad** to strike up a friendship
amistar *va* to bring together, to make friendly; *vr* to become friends, to become reconciled
amistoso -sa *adj* friendly
amitigar §59 *va* var. of **mitigar**
amito *m* (eccl.) amice
amitosis *f* (biol.) amitosis
amnesia *f* (path.) amnesia
amnésico -ca *adj* amnesic
amnícola *adj* growing along rivers
amnios *m* (*pl:* **-nios**) (anat.) amnion
amniota *adj & m* (zool.) amniote
amniótico -ca *adj* (anat.) amniotic
amnistía *f* amnesty
amnistiar §90 *va* to amnesty, to grant amnesty to
am.º abr. of **amigo**
amo *m* master (*of a household*); head of family; owner, landlord, proprietor; foster father; boss, foreman, overseer; **amos** *mpl* master and mistress; landlord and his wife; **el amo grande** (coll.) God; **ser el amo del cotarro** (dial.) to rule the roost
amoblar §77 *va* to furnish
amodita *f* (zool.) horned serpent
amodorrado -da *adj* drowsy, numb, sleepy
amodorramiento *m* drowsiness, numbness, sleepiness
amodorrante *adj* soporific; numbing
amodorrar *vr* to get drowsy; to grow numb; to fall asleep
amodorrecer §34 *va* to make drowsy, to make numb
amodorrido -da *adj* drowsy, numb, sleepy
amófilo *m* (ent.) sand wasp
amogotado -da *adj* knoll-shaped, humped
amohecer §34 *va & vr* to mold, mildew, rust
amohinar §99 *va* to vex, annoy; *vr* to get vexed, be annoyed
amojamar *va* to dry and salt (*tuna fish*); *vr* to wither, dry up
amojelar *va* (naut.) to seize (*a cable*)
amojonamiento *m* marking with landmarks; landmarks
amojonar *va* to mark off with landmarks, to put landmarks on
amoladera *f* grindstone, whetstone
amolador -dora *adj* grinding, sharpening; (coll.) boring, annoying, tedious; *mf* grinder, sharpener; *f* grinder, grinding machine
amoladura *f* grinding, sharpening; **amoladuras** *fpl* grindings
amolar §77 *va* to grind, sharpen; (coll.) to bore, annoy
amoldamiento *m* molding, fitting, modeling
amoldar *va* to mold, pattern, adjust, adapt, fit, model; *vr* to mold oneself, pattern oneself
amole *m* soap root, soap bark
amollar *va* (naut.) to ease off, to pay out (*rope, cable, etc.*); *vn* to play low (*in card games*); to yield, give, give in
amollentar *va* to soften
amolletado -da *adj* roll-shaped, loaf-shaped
amomo *m* (bot.) amomum
amonar *vr* (coll.) to get drunk
amondongado -da *adj* (coll.) flabby
amonedación *f* coining, coinage
amonedar *va* to coin, to mint
amonestación *f* admonition; marriage banns; **correr las amonestaciones** to publish the banns
amonestador -dora *adj* admonishing; *mf* admonisher
amonestamiento *m* admonishment

amonestar *va* to admonish; to publish the banns of
amoniacal *adj* ammoniacal
amoníaco -ca *adj* ammoniac, ammoniacal; *m* (chem.) ammonia; ammoniac (*gum resin*); **amoníaco líquido** (chem.) liquid ammonia
amónico -ca *adj* ammonic, (pertaining to) ammonium
amonio *m* (chem.) ammonium
amonita *f* (pal.) ammonite; *mf* (Bib.) Ammonite
amontar *va* to put to flight; *vr* to take cover, to flee to the woods
amontazgar §59 *va* var. of **montazgar**
amontillado *m* pale dry sherry
amontonador -dora *adj* heaping, accumulating, hoarding; *mf* gatherer, accumulator, hoarder
amontonamiento *m* heaping, piling, accumulation; hoarding, hoard
amontonar *va* to heap, pile, accumulate, hoard; *vr* to pile up, to collect, to gather; to be crowded, to crowd; (coll.) to get angry; to cohabit
amor *m* love; beloved; (*cap.*) *m* Cupid, Amor; **amores** *mpl* amour, love affair; (bot.) hedgehog parsley; **al amor del agua** with the current; obligingly; **al amor de la lumbre** at the fireside, in the warmth of the fire; **a su amor** at ease, leisurely; **de mil amores** with the greatest pleasure; **amor al uso** (bot.) cotton rose; **amor cortés** courtly love; **amor de hortelano** (bot.) bedstraw; **amor platónico** Platonic love; **amor propio** amour-propre
amoral *adj* amoral, unmoral
amoralidad *f* amorality
amoratado -da *adj* black-and-blue
amoratar *va* to turn purple; to make black and blue; *vn* to turn purple; to get black and blue
amorcillo *m* flirtation, passing fancy; (f.a.) little Cupid
amordazamiento *m* muzzling; (fig.) muzzling, gag
amordazar §76 *va* to muzzle; to gag; (fig.) to muzzle, to gag
amorecer §34 *va* to cover or serve (*a female sheep*); *vr* to be in rut (*said of sheep*)
amorfia *f* amorphia; organic deformity
amorfismo *m* amorphism
amorfo -fa *adj* amorphous
amorgar §59 *va* to drug (*fish*) with olive pulp
amoricones *mpl* (coll.) love glances, flirtations
amorío *m* (coll.) love-making; (coll.) love affair, flirtation
amoriscado -da *adj* Moorish, Moorish-looking
amormado -da *adj* suffering from glanders
amormío *m* (bot.) sea daffodil
amoroso -sa *adj* amorous; loving, affectionate; soft, malleable; mild, pleasant
amorrar *va* (naut.) to make pitch at the bow; (naut.) to beach head-on; *vn & vr* to hang one's head; (coll.) to sulk, to brood; (naut.) to dip the bows under
amorronar *va* (naut.) to roll and knot (*a flag*) to make a waft for hoisting as a signal of distress
amortajar *va* to shroud, to cover with a shroud, to lay out; to mortise
amortecer §34 *va* to lessen, deaden, muffle, tone down; *vr* to die away, to become faint, to be muffled; to faint
amortecimiento *m* lessening, deadening, muffling; faint, fainting; faintness
amortiguación *f* deadening, muffling; lessening, softening; dimming, damping; cushioning, absorbing; **amortiguación de las crecidas** flood control
amortiguador -dora *adj* deadening, muffling; lessening, softening; dimming, damping; *mf* deadener; lessener; dimmer, damper; *m* shock absorber; door check; bumper (*of automobile*); **amortiguador de luz** (aut.) dimmer; **amortiguador de ruido** (mach.) muffler
amortiguamiento *m* var. of **amortiguación**
amortiguar §23 *va* to deaden, muffle; to lessen, soften, tone down; to dim, to damp; to cushion (*a blow or shock*); to absorb (*a shock*); (elec.) to damp (*electromagnetic waves*)
amortizable *adj* amortizable
amortización *f* amortization, amortizement
amortizar §76 *va* to amortize; to pay off; to refund; to eliminate (*a position, office, etc.*)
Amós *m* Amos
amoscar §86 *vr* to become annoyed, peeved, or miffed
amostachado -da *adj* mustachioed
amostazar §76 *va* (coll.) to anger, provoke; *vr* (coll.) to become angry, get provoked
amotinado -da *adj* mutinous, rebellious, riotous; *mf* mutineer, insurgent, rebel
amotinador -dora *adj* rabble-rousing; mutinous, riotous; *mf* rabble rouser, mutineer, insurgent
amotinamiento *m* mutiny, uprising, insurrection
amotinar *va* to stir up, to upset; to incite to riot or mutiny; *vr* to be stirred up, to be upset; to rise up, to rebel, to riot, to mutiny
amover §63 *va* to remove, discharge, dismiss
amovibilidad *f* removability
amovible *adj* removable; detachable
ampalagua *f* (zool.) large boa
amparador -dora *adj* protecting, sheltering; *mf* protector, helper
amparar *va* to protect, shelter; *vr* to seek shelter; to defend oneself, to protect oneself; **ampararse a** to have recourse to, to seek the protection of; **ampararse de** to seek the protection of; to avail oneself of
amparito *m* stall (*e.g., in a market*)
amparo *m* protection, shelter, refuge; stall (*e.g., in a market*); aid, favor; (*cap.*) *f* Amparo (*female name*)
ampélido *m* (orn.) waxwing
ampelita *f* (mineral.) ampelite
ampelografía *f* ampelography
amper *m* (elec.) ampere
amperaje *m* (elec.) amperage
amperímetro *m* (elec.) ammeter; **amperímetro de hilo caliente** (elec.) hot-wire ammeter
amperio *m* (elec.) ampere; **amperio hora** *m* (*pl:* **amperios hora**) (elec.) ampere-hour
amperio-vuelta *f* (*pl:* **amperios-vueltas**) (elec.) ampere turn
amperómetro *m* var. of **amperímetro**
ampervuelta *f* (*pl:* **-tas**) (elec.) ampere turn
amplexicaulo -la *adj* (bot.) amplexicaul, amplexicauline
ampliación *f* amplification, enlargement, extension; (phot.) enlarging, enlargement
ampliador -dora *adj* amplifying, enlarging; *mf* amplifier, enlarger; *f* (phot.) enlarger
ampliar §90 *va* to amplify, enlarge, extend, broaden; (phot.) to enlarge
ampliativo -va *adj* amplifying, enlarging, amplificatory
amplificación *f* amplification; (elec.) amplification; **amplificación en cascada** (elec.) cascade amplification
amplificador -dora *adj* amplifying; *mf* amplifier; *m* (elec.) amplifier; **amplificador de poder** or **de potencia** (rad.) power amplifier
amplificar §86 *va* to amplify; (elec.) to amplify
amplificativo -va *adj* amplificative
amplio -plia *adj* ample; full, roomy; prolix; bold
amplitud *f* amplitude; roominess; (astr., elec. & mech.) amplitude
ampo *m* dazzling white; snowflake; **como el ampo de la nieve** white as the driven snow
ampolla *f* blister; bubble; cruet; round-bellied bottle; (med.) ampoule; (anat., bot., eccl., hist. & zool.) ampulla; bulb (*of electric-light or vacuum tube*)
ampollar *adj* blisterlike; bubble-shaped; bottle-shaped; bulbous; *va* to blister; to make bulbous; to hollow, to distend; *vr* to blister; to get bulbous; to be hollowed out, to distend
ampolleta *f* small vial, small bottle, small cruet; sandglass, hourglass; time taken by sand to run from top of sandglass; bulb, light bulb
ampulosidad *f* pomposity, bombast
ampuloso -sa *adj* pompous, bombastic
amputación *f* amputation
amputar *va* amputate
amuchachado -da *adj* boyish, boylike
amueblar *va* to furnish
amugamiento *m* setting up landmarks
amugronamiento *m* (hort.) layering

amugronar *va* (hort.) to layer
amujerado -da *adj* womanish, womanlike, effeminate
amujeramiento *m* womanishness, effeminacy
amulatado -da *adj* mulattolike
amuleto *m* amulet
amunicionar *va* to ammunition, supply with ammunition
amunucar §86 *vr* to grow sulky, to pout, scowl
amuñecado -da *adj* doll-like, puppetlike
amura *f* (naut.) tack of a sail; (naut.) beam of ship at one-eighth its length, measured from bow; **cambiar de amura** (naut.) to go about, to come about
amurada *f* (naut.) ship's side (*from within*)
amurallar *va* to wall, to wall in
amurar *va* (naut.) to fasten (*corner of sail*) for tacking; (naut.) to haul on (*a sail*) by the tack; *vn* (naut.) to tack
amurcar §86 *va* to gore
amurco *m* goring
amurillar *va* (hort.) to pile up earth around (*a tree*)
amurrar *vr* (Am.) to become glum, to become downcast
amurriar *vr* (prov.) var. of **amurrar**
amusco -ca *adj* brown
amusgar §59 *va* to throw back (*the ears*); to squint (*the eyes*) to see better
amustiar *va & vr* to wither
Ana *f* Ann, Anna, Anne; **Ana Bolena** Anne Boleyn: **Ana de Austria** Anne of Austria; **Ana Estuardo** Queen Anne; (*l.c.*) *f* ell (*measure*)
anabaptismo *m* Anabaptism
anabaptista *adj & mf* Anabaptist
anabas *s* (*pl:* **-bas**) (ichth.) anabas, climbing fish
anabiosis *f* anabiosis
anabólico -ca *adj* anabolic
anabolismo *m* (biol.) anabolism
anacarado -da *adj* mother-of-pearl (*in appearance*)
anacardiáceo -a *adj* (bot.) anacardiaceous
anacárdico -ca *adj* (chem.) anacardic
anacardo *m* (bot.) cashew (*tree and nut*)
anaco *m* (Peru & Bolivia) slit skirt of Indian women; (Ecuador) hair worn in single braid
anacoluto *m* (gram.) anacoluthon
anaconda *f* (zool.) anaconda
anacoreta *m* anchorite; *f* anchoress
anacorético -ca *adj* anchoritic
anacoretismo *m* anchoritism
Anacreonte *m* Anacreon
anacreóntico -ca *adj* Anacreontic
anacrónico -ca *adj* anachronistic, anachronous
anacronismo *m* anachronism
ánade *mf* duck; goose; **ánade cucharetero** (orn.) shoveler; **ánade negro** (orn.) black scoter; **ánade salvaje** (orn.) mallard; **ánade silbador** (orn.) European widgeon
anadear *vn* to waddle
anadeja *f* duckling
anadeo *m* waddle, waddling
anadino -na *mf* duckling
anadón *m* duckling; nonfloating log
anadromo -ma *adj* anadromous
anaeróbico -ca *adj* anaerobic
anaerobio -bia *adj* anaerobic; *m* anaerobe
anafase *f* (biol.) anaphase
anafe *m* portable brazier
anafilaxis *f* (path.) anaphylaxis
anáfora *f* (rhet. & astrol.) anaphora
anafre *m* portable brazier
anafrodisia *f* (med.) anaphrodisia
anafrodisíaco -ca *adj & m* (med.) anaphrodisiac
anafrodita *adj* anaphroditous; sexually abstinent
anáglifo *m* anaglyph
anagnórisis *f* (rhet.) anagnorisis
anagoge *m* or **anagogía** *f* anagogics; mystical rapture, divine rapture
anagrama *m* anagram; **anagramas** *mpl* anagrams (*game*)
anagramático -ca *adj* anagrammatic, anagrammatical
anagramatismo *m* anagrammatism
anal *adj* (anat.) anal
analectas *fpl* analecta, analects
analéptico -ca *adj* analeptic
anales *mpl* annals
analfabético -ca *adj* illiterate
analfabetismo *m* illiteracy
analfabeto -ta *adj & mf* illiterate
analgeno *m* (pharm.) analgen
analgesia *f* (physiol.) analgesia; (med.) general anesthesia
analgésico -ca *adj & m* analgesic
analgesina *f* (pharm.) antipyrene
análisis *m & f* (*pl:* **-sis**) analysis; **análisis cualitativo** (chem.) qualitative analysis; **análisis cuantitativo** (chem.) quantitative analysis; **análisis espectral** spectrum analysis; **análisis gramatical** parsing
analista *mf* annalist; analyst (*analyzer; psychoanalyst*)
analítico -ca *adj* analytic, analytical; *f* (philos.) analytics
analizable *adj* analyzable
analizador -dora *mf* analyzer; analyst; *m* (opt.) analyzer
analizar §76 *va* to analyze; **analizar gramaticalmente** to parse
analogía *f* analogy; (gram.) inflection
analógico -ca *adj* analogical
análogo -ga *adj* analogous; similar; *m* analogue; (biol.) analogue
anamita *adj & mf* Annamese
anamniótico -ca *adj* anamniotic
anamorfosis *f* (*pl:* **-sis**) anamorphosis; (biol. & bot.) anamorphosis
ananá *m* (*pl:* **-naes**) (bot.) pineapple (*plant and fruit*)
ananás *m* var. of **ananá**
Ananías *m* (Bib.) Ananias
anapelo *m* (bot.) wolfsbane
anapéstico -ca *adj* anapestic
anapesto *m* anapest
anaplastia *f* (surg.) anaplasty
anaplástico -ca *adj* anaplastic
anaptixis *f* (phonet.) anaptyxis
anaquel *m* shelf (*in wall, closet, store, etc.*)
anaquelería *f* shelving
anaranjado -da *adj & m* orange (*color*); **anaranjado de metilo** methyl orange
anarquía *f* anarchy
anárquico -ca *adj* anarchic, anarchical
anarquismo *m* anarchism
anarquista *adj* anarchistic; *mf* anarch, anarchist
anarquizar §76 *va* to spread anarchism in (*a country or people*)
anasarca *f* (path.) anasarca
anascote *m* serge-like woolen material
anastasia *f* (bot.) mugwort
anastático -ca *adj* anastatic
anastigmático -ca *adj* (opt.) anastigmatic
anastomizar §76 *vr* var. of **anastomosar**
anastomosar *vr* to anastomose
anastomosis *f* (*pl:* **-sis**) (anat. & biol.) anastomosis
anastomótico -ca *adj* anastomotic
anástrofe *f* (gram.) anastrophe
anata *f* yearly income
anatema *m & f* anathema
anatematismo *m* anathematism, anathematization
anatematización *f* anathematization
anatematizar §76 *va* anathematize
anatifa *f* (zool.) goose barnacle
anatolio -lia *adj & mf* Anatolian
anatomía *f* anatomy; **anatomía macroscópica** gross anatomy
anatómico -ca *adj* anatomic, anatomical; *mf* anatomist
anatomista *mf* anatomist
anatomizar §76 *va* to anatomize; (paint. & sculp.) to bring out or emphasize (*the bones and muscles*)
anavajado -da *adj* knife-scarred
anavia *f* (prov.) bilberry
Anaxágoras *m* Anaxagoras
Anaximandro *m* Anaximander
anca *f* croup, haunch; rump, buttock; **a ancas** or **a las ancas** mounted behind another person (*on horseback*); **no sufrir ancas** (coll.) to take no joking

ancado -da *adj* (vet.) stringhalted, stringtied; seated behind another person (*on same mount*); *m* (vet.) stringhalt
ancestral *adj* ancestral
ancianidad *f* old age
anciano -na *adj* old, aged; *m* old man; (eccl.) elder; **el anciano de los días** Ancient of Days (*God*); *f* old woman
ancilar *adj* ancillary
ancla *f* (naut.) anchor; **echar anclas** to cast anchor; **levar anclas** to weigh anchor; **ancla de la esperanza** (naut.) sheet anchor
ancladero *m* anchorage, anchoring place
anclaje *m* anchorage; (dent.) anchor
anclar *vn* to anchor, to drop anchor
anclote *m* small anchor, kedge anchor
anclotillo *m* kedge anchor
ancolia *f* (bot.) columbine
ancón *m* (anat. & arch.) ancon; cove, bay
anconada *f* cove, bay
áncora *f* (naut., horol. & fig.) anchor
ancoraje *m* anchorage; anchoring; anchors
ancorar *vn* to anchor, to drop anchor
ancorca *f* yellow ocher
ancorel *m* stone sinker for fishing nets
ancorería *f* anchor foundry
ancorero *m* anchor smith
ancudo -da *adj* big-rumped
ancusa *f* (bot.) alkanet; **ancusa de tintes** (bot.) alkanet (*Alkanna tinctoria*)
ancusina *f* (chem.) alkanet
anchar *va, vn & vr* to widen, extend, enlarge
ancheta *f* small lot (*of goods*); gain, profit
anchicorto -ta *adj* wider than long; wide and short
ancho -cha *adj* broad, wide; full, ample, lax, loose, loose-fitting; **a sus anchas** in comfort, at ease, as one pleases; **ancho de conciencia** indulgent; free, lax; self-indulgent; *m* width, breadth; **ancho de vía** (rail.) track gauge
anchoa *f* (ichth.) anchovy; **anchoa de banco** (ichth.) bluefish
anchor *m* var. of **anchura**
anchova *f* (ichth.) anchovy
anchuelo -la *adj* widish, rather wide
anchura *f* width, breadth; extension; fullness, ampleness; ease, comfort, freedom, looseness
anchuroso -sa *adj* broad, wide, spacious
andada *f* see **andado**
andadero -ra *adj* passable, fit to walk or pass through; wandering, gadding; **andaderas** *fpl* gocart, walker (*to support child learning to walk*)
andado -da *adj* trodden, frequented; ordinary, common; worn, used; *f* thin, hard-baked cake or cracker; **andadas** *fpl* tracks (*of wild animals*); **volver a las andadas** (coll.) to backslide, to return to one's old tricks
andador -dora *adj* walking, fast-walking, swift; wandering, gadding; *mf* walker, runner; fast mover; great traveler; gadabout; *m* court messenger; footpath; **andadores** *mpl* leading strings (*to support child learning to walk*)
andadura *f* gait; walking, running; pace, amble
andahuertas *f* (*pl:* **-tas**) (orn.) garden warbler, whitethroat
Andalucía *f* Andalusia
andalucismo *m* Andalusianism
andalucita *f* (mineral.) andalusite
andaluz -luza *adj & mf* Andalusian; *m* Andalusian (*dialect*)
andaluzada *f* (coll.) tall story, Andalusian boastfulness
andamiada *f* or **andamiaje** *m* scaffolding, staging
andamio *m* scaffold; platform; skeleton; **andamio suspendido** hanging scaffold
andana *f* row, line, tier; **llamarse andana** (coll.) to take back a promise
andanada *f* (naut.) broadside; (taur.) covered section at top of grandstand; (coll.) scolding; (fig.) fusillade (*e.g., of questions*); **soltar la** or **una andanada a** to rake over the coals
andancia *f* (Am. & prov.) slight epidemic
andaniño *m* gocart (*to support child learning to walk*)
andante *adj* walking; errant; *m* (mus.) andante
andantesco -ca *adj* chivalrous, quixotic, (pertaining to a) knight-errant
andantino *m* (mus.) andantino
andanza *f* fate, fortune; (archaic) act, happening
andar *m* walk, gait, pace; go; passing (*e.g., of time*); **a largo andar** in time; **a más andar** at full speed ‖ §20 *va* to go (*e.g., two miles*); to go down or up (*a road*) ‖ *vn* to go, to move, to walk, to run; to go about, to travel; to act, to behave; to go, to run, to work (*said, e.g., of a clock*); to be, to feel; to continue, to keep on; to amble, to pace; to sail; to go by, to pass, to elapse (*said of time*); **¡anda!** (coll.) come now!; (coll.) fine!; (coll.) cut it out!; **andar a caballo** to ride horseback; **andar a gatas** to go on all fours; **andar andando** (Am.) to chase around; **andar bien** to keep good time (*said of a clock*); **andar bien de** to be well supplied with; **andar con** to handle; **andar en** to be engaged in; to be going on (*so many years old*); (coll.) to poke into; **andar en cuestiones** to wrangle; **andar reñidos** to be on bad terms ‖ *vr* to go by, to pass, to elapse (*said of time*); to go off, to go away; **andarse en** to give way to, to indulge in; (coll.) to poke into; **andarse por las ramas** to beat about the bush; **andarse sin** + *inf* to go or to do without + *ger*
andaraje *m* bucket wheel of noria; frame of garden roller
andariego -ga *adj* wandering, roving, gadding; swift, fleet-footed
andarín -rina *adj* fast-moving; *mf* fast walker, fast runner; professional runner; *f* (orn.) swallow
andarivel *m* ferry cable; cable ferry; aerial tramway, cableway; (naut.) hand rope; gantline
andarríos *m* (*pl:* **-rríos**) (orn.) wagtail
andas *fpl* litter; stretcher; bier with shafts; portable platform; **en andas** in triumph
andén *m* railway platform; boat landing; footpath; side path; sidewalk (*especially on bridge*)
andero *m* litter bearer; stretcher-bearer; bier bearer
Andes *mpl* Andes
andinismo *m* mountain climbing in the Andes
andinista *mf* mountain climber in the Andes
andino -na *adj & mf* Andean
ándito *m* exterior balcony (*going around or almost around a building*)
andolina *f* (orn.) swallow
andorga *f* (coll.) belly; **llenar la andorga** (coll.) to stuff oneself, to gorge
andorina *f* (orn.) swallow
andorra *f* (coll.) gadder (*woman*)
andorrano -na *adj & mf* Andorran
andorrear *vn* to gad about, to walk the streets, to tramp
andorrero -ra *adj* gadding, gadding about; *mf* gadder, wanderer
andosco -ca *adj* two-year-old (*cattle*)
andrajero -ra *mf* ragpicker
andrajo *m* rag, tatter; ragamuffin, scalawag; **estar en andrajos** to be in rags
andrajoso -sa *adj* ragged, raggedy
Andrés *m* Andrew
andrina *f* var. of **endrina**
andrino *m* var. of **endrino**
androceo *m* (bot.) androecium
Androcles *m* Androcles
androfobia *f* androphobia
andrógeno *m* (biochem.) androgen
andrógino -na *adj* androgynous; (bot.) androgynous; *mf* androgyne; *m* (bot.) androgyne
androide *m* android (*manlike automaton*)
Andrómaca *f* (myth.) Andromache
Andrómeda *f* (myth. & astr.) Andromeda
andrómina *f* (coll.) fraud, deceit, trick, lie, fib
androsemo *m* (bot.) androseme
androsfinge *m & f* (archeol.) androsphinx
androsterona *f* (biochem.) androsterone
andulario *m* long, trailing gown
andullo *m* fender, shield; plug tobacco; rolled tobacco leaf, pigtail
andurriales *mpl* byways, lonely spot, out-of-the-way place
anduve *1st sg pret ind of* **andar**

anea *f* (bot.) cattail, bulrush, reed mace (*Typha angustifolia*); (bot.) cattail, bulrush (*Typha latifolia*)
aneblar §18 *va* to cloud, darken; to cast a cloud over; *vr* to become clouded, get dark
anécdota *f* anecdote
anecdotario *m* stock or fund of anecdotes, collection of anecdotes
anecdótico -ca *adj* anecdotal
anecdotista *mf* anecdotist
anega *f* (bot.) dill
anegable *adj* subject to flooding
anegación *f* flooding; drowning; annihilation
anegadizo -za *adj* subject to frequent flooding; heavier-than-water
anegamiento *m* var. of **anegación**
anegar §59 *va* to flood; to drown; to sink; to annihilate; (aut.) to flood (*carburetor*); *vr* to become flooded; to drown; to sink; to be annihilated; (aut.) to become flooded; **anegarse en llanto** to be bathed in tears
anegociado -da *adj* busy, full of business
anejar *va* var. of **anexar**
anejín *m* or **anejir** *m* rhymed proverb set to music
anejo -ja *adj* annexed, attached; accessory; dependent; *m* annex; dependency; dependent church or benefice; supplement (*to a periodical*)
aneldo *m* (bot.) dill
aneléctrico -ca *adj & m* (phys.) anelectric
anélido -da *adj & m* (zool.) annelid
anemia *f* (path.) anemia; **anemia de los mineros** or **de los túneles** (path.) hookworm disease, tunnel disease; **anemia perniciosa** (path.) pernicious anemia
anémico -ca *adj* anemic
anemometría *f* anemometry
anemómetro *m* anemometer
anemona, anemone *f* or **anémone** *f* (bot.) anemone; **anemona de mar** (zool.) sea anemone
anemoscopio *m* anemoscope
anepigráfico -ca *adj* anepigraphic
anequín; a anequín or **de anequín** on a piecework basis (*for shearing sheep*)
aneroide *adj* aneroid
anestesia *f* anesthesia; **anestesia cruzada** crossed anesthesia; **anestesia de bloque** block anesthesia; **anestesia de conducción** conduction anesthesia; **anestesia espinal** spinal anesthesia; **anestesia general** general anesthesia; **anestesia local** local anesthesia; **anestesia medular** spinal anesthesia; **anestesia regional** conduction anesthesia
anestesiador *m* anesthetist
anestesiar *va* anesthetize
anestésico *adj & m* anesthetic
anestesiología *f* anesthesiology
anestesiólogo -ga *mf* anesthesiologist
anestesista *mf* anesthetist
anestético -ca *adj* anesthetic
aneurisma *m & f* (path.) aneurysm
aneurismático -ca *adj* aneurysmatic
anexar *va* to annex; to attach, append; to enclose
anexidades *fpl* annexes, supplements, appurtenances
anexión *f* annexation
anexionar *va* var. of **anexar**
anexionismo *m* annexationism
anexionista *adj & mf* annexationist
anexo -xa *adj* annexed, attached; accessory; dependent; *m* annex; dependency; **anexos** *mpl* (anat.) adnexa
anfesibena *f* var. of **anfisbena**
anfetamina *f* (pharm.) amphetamine
anfibio -bia *adj* amphibian; amphibious; *m* (aer. & biol.) amphibian
anfíbol *m* (mineral.) amphibole
anfibolita *f* (geol.) amphibolite
anfibología *f* amphibology
anfibológico -ca *adj* amphibological
anfíbraco *m* amphibrach
anfión *m* opium; (*cap.*) *m* (myth.) Amphion
anfípodo -da *adj & m* (zool.) amphipod
anfisbena *f* (zool.) amphisbaena
anfiscios *mpl* amphiscians (*inhabitants of tropics*)
anfiteatro *m* amphitheater; dissecting room
Anfitrión *m* (myth.) Amphitryon; (*l.c.*) *m* (coll.) host, lavish host; (coll.) escort (*of a lady*)
Anfitrite *f* (myth. & zool.) Amphitrite
anfiumo *m* (zool.) congo snake
ánfora *f* amphora; (eccl.) cruet for consecrated oils; (Am.) voting urn
anfractuosidad *f* anfractuosity
anfractuoso -sa *adj* anfractuous, winding, sinuous, tortuous
angalete *m* (Am.) miter box
angaria *f* (law) angaria
angarillas *fpl* handbarrow; panniers; cruet stand
angaripola *f* coarse colored linen; **angaripolas** *fpl* (coll.) gaudy trimmings, garish adornments
ángaro *m* beacon fire
angarrio *m* (Am.) living skeleton
angas *fpl;* **por angas o por mangas** (Am.) one way or another, by hook or by crook
angazo *m* rake for gathering shellfish
ángel *m* angel; grace, charm; **ángel caído** fallen angel; **ángel custodio** or **de la guarda** guardian angel; **ángel de mar** (ichth.) angelfish; **ángel patudo** (coll.) wolf in sheep's clothing; **tener ángel** to have charm
Angela *f* Angela; **¡Angela María!** I get you!
angélica *f* see **angélico**
angelical *adj* angelic or angelical
angelico *m* little imp of an angel
angélico -ca *adj* angelic or angelical; *f* (bot.) angelica; **angélica carlina** (bot.) carline thistle
angelín *m* (bot.) angelin
angelito *m* little angel; (fig.) little angel (*winsome or well-behaved child*)
angelón *m* large angel; **angelón de retablo** (coll.) awkward fat and chubby person
angelote *m* large figure of an angel; chubby child; (ichth.) angelfish
ángelus *m* (*pl:* **-lus**) Angelus
angevino -na *adj & mf* Angevin
angina *f* (path.) angina; **angina de pecho** (path.) angina pectoris
angiocolitis *f* (path.) angiocholitis
angiografía *f* (anat.) angiography
angiología *f* angiology
angiospermo -ma *adj* (bot.) angiospermous; *f* (bot.) angiosperm
angla *f* see **anglo**
anglesita *f* (mineral.) anglesite
Anglia *f* Anglia
anglicanismo *m* Anglicanism
anglicano -na *adj & mf* Anglican
anglicismo *m* Anglicism
anglicización *f* Anglicization
anglo -gla *adj* Anglian; *mf* Anglian; **anglos** *mpl* Angles; *f* cape, promontory
angloamericano -na *adj & mf* Anglo-American
anglocatolicismo *m* Anglo-Catholicism
anglocatólico -ca *adj & mf* Anglo-Catholic
angloespañol -ñola *adj* English-Spanish
anglófilo -la *adj & mf* Anglophile
anglofobia *f* Anglophobia
anglófobo -ba *adj & mf* Anglophobe
angloíndio -da *adj & mf* Anglo-Indian
angloiranio -nia *adj & mf* Anglo-Iranian
anglomanía *f* Anglomania
anglómano -na *mf* Anglomaniac
anglonormando -da *adj & mf* Anglo-Norman; *m* Anglo-Norman (*dialect*)
anglonorteamericano -na *adj & mf* Anglo-American
angloparlante *adj* English-speaking; *mf* speaker of English
anglosajón -jona *adj & mf* Anglo-Saxon; *m* Anglo-Saxon (*language*)
angora *mf* Angora (*cat or goat*)
angostar *va* to narrow, tighten, contract
angosto -ta *adj* narrow
angostura *f* narrowness; narrow place or passage; narrows; angostura (*medicinal bark*)
angosturina *f* (pharm.) angostura bitters
angra *f* cove, inlet
angrelado -da *adj* (her.) engrailed
angstrom *m* (*pl:* **-troms**) (phys.) angstrom
anguarina *f* sleeveless smock frock

anguila *f* (ichth.) eel; lash, whip; wiry fellow; **anguilas** *fpl* ways (*for launching a ship*); **escurrirse como una anguila** to be as slippery as an eel; **anguila agachadiza** (ichth.) snipe eel; **anguila de barro** (ichth.) mud eel; **anguila de cabo** (archaic) whip (*for flogging galley slaves*); **anguila eléctrica** (ichth.) electric eel
anguilazo *m* (naut.) lash (*stroke with rope's end*)
anguilero -ra *adj* for eels; *f* eel garth; eel basket
anguílula *f* (zool.) eelworm; **anguílula del vinagre** (zool.) vinegar eel
anguina *f* (vet.) inguinal vein
angula *f* grig (*young eel*)
angular *adj* angular
angularidad *f* angularity
angulemia *f* coarse cloth of hemp or tow; (*cap.*) *f* Angoulême; **angulemas** *fpl* flattery, coaxing
ángulo *m* angle; corner; **de ángulo ancho** (phot.) wide-angle; **en ángulo** at an angle; **ángulo agudo** acute angle; **ángulo complementario** complementary angle; **ángulo de ataque** (aer.) angle of attack; **ángulo de deriva** (aer. & naut.) drift angle; **ángulo de incidencia** (phys.) angle of incidence; **ángulo facial** facial angle; **ángulo obtuso** obtuse angle; **ángulo recto** right angle; **ángulos adyacentes** adjacent angles; **ángulos alternos** alternate angles
angulosidad *f* angularity
anguloso -sa *adj* angular (*said, e.g., of features*)
angurria *f* (coll.) strangury; (Am.) raging hunger
angustia *f* anguish, distress, affliction
angustiado -da *adj* distressed, grieved; greedy, grasping, mean
angustiar *va* to distress, afflict
angustioso -sa *adj* distressed, afflicted; grievous, worrisome
angustura *f* angostura (*medicinal bark*)
anhelación *f* panting, gasping; yearning
anhelante *adj* panting, gasping; eager, yearning
anhelar *va* to desire eagerly, to crave, to covet; *vn* to gasp, to pant; **anhelar** + *inf* to long to, to yearn to + *inf;* **anhelar por** to long for, to yearn for
anhélito *m* shortness of breath, hard breathing
anhelo *m* yearning, longing; gasp
anheloso -sa *adj* panting, breathless; eager, yearning
anhídrido *m* (chem.) anhydrid; **anhídrido carbónico** (chem.) carbon dioxide
anhidrita *f* (mineral.) anhydrite
anhidro -dra *adj* (chem.) anhydrous
anhima *f* (orn.) screamer
anhinga *f* (orn.) snakebird
aní *m* (*pl:* **-níes**) (orn.) ani
Aníbal *m* Hannibal
anidación *f* nesting
anidar *va* to shelter, take in; *vn & vr* to nestle, make one's nest; to live, dwell
anieblar *va & vr* var. of **aneblar**
aniego *m* var. of **anegación**
anilina *f* (chem.) anilin
anilla *f* curtain ring; ring, hoop; ring (*for gymnastics*); bow or loop (*of key*)
anillado -da *adj* ringed, ring-shaped, annulated; *m* (zool.) annelid
anillar *va* to form into rings or hoops; to make rings in; to fasten with rings or hoops; to put a ring on
anillejo or **anillete** *m* little ring, ringlet
anillo *m* ring; cigar band; (anat., arch. & bot.) annulus; (her. & zool.) annulet; (naut.) grommet; **de anillo** honorary; **venir como anillo al dedo** (coll.) to fit the case perfectly, to come in the nick of time; **anillo de boda** wedding ring; **anillo de collera** terret; **anillo de compromiso** engagement ring; **anillo de émbolo** piston ring; **Anillo del Nibelungo** (myth.) Ring of the Nibelung; **anillo de pedida** engagement ring; **anillos de Saturno** (astr.) rings of Saturn; **anillo sigilar** seal ring, signet ring
ánima *f* soul; soul in purgatory; bore (*of firearm*); (elec.) core (*of cable*); (found.) core (*of a mold*); web (*of rail*); **ánimas** *fpl* (eccl.) ringing of bells at sunset for prayers for souls in purgatory
animación *f* animation; liveliness; bustle, movement
animado -da *adj* animate; lively, animated
animador -dora *adj* animating; enlivening; encouraging, inspiring; *mf* animator; enlivener; inspirer; (mov.) animator; *m* master of ceremonies (*in night club, radio, etc.*)
animadversión *f* animadversion; enmity, ill will
animal *adj & m* animal
animalada *f* (coll.) stupidity
animálculo *m* animalcule
animalejo *m* little animal
animalia *f* animals, animal kingdom
animalidad *f* animality
animalismo *m* animalism
animalista *adj* animalistic; *mf* animalist
animalización *f* animalization
animalizar **§76** *va* to animalize; *vr* to become animalized
animalote *m* big animal
animalucho *m* ugly animal; (coll.) big ignoramus
animar *va* to animate; to enliven; to encourage; to strengthen; to drive, impel; **animar a** + *inf* to encourage to + *inf; vr* to become enlivened; to take heart, cheer up, feel encouraged
anime *m* (bot.) courbaril (*tree and resin*)
animero *m* beggar for souls in purgatory
anímico -ca *adj* psychic
animismo *m* animism
animista *adj* animistic; *mf* animist
animita *f* (Am.) firefly
ánimo *m* soul; spirit; will, intention; attention, mind, thought; courage, valor; encouragement; **dar ánimo** or **ánimos a** to give encouragement to; **esparcir el ánimo** to relax, take it easy; **tener ánimo de** + *inf* to intend to + *inf*
animosidad *f* animosity; bravery, courage
animoso -sa *adj* brave, courageous, spirited
aniñado -da *adj* childish, babyish; (pertaining to a) baby
aniñar *vr* to become childish, to act childishly
anión *m* (elec.) anion
aniquilación *f* annihilation
aniquilador -dora *adj* annihilating, destructive, exhausting; *mf* annihilator, destroyer
aniquilamiento *m* annihilation
aniquilar *va* to annihilate; to destroy, exhaust; *vr* to be annihilated, to be wiped out; to decline, decay, waste away; to be humbled
anís *m* (bot.) anise (*plant and seed*); anise-flavored brandy
anisado -da *adj* anisated, flavored with anise; *m* anise-flavored brandy
anisar *m* patch of anise; *va* to anisate, to flavor with anise
anisete *m* anisette
anisillo *m* appetizer, relish
anisofilo -la *adj* (bot.) anisophyllous
anisómero -ra *adj* (bot.) anisomerous
anisométrico -ca *adj* (mineral.) anisometric
anivelar *va* to level; to even
aniversario -ria *adj & m* anniversary
anjeo *m* coarse linen; burlap
anmetro *m* (elec.) ammeter
ano *m* (anat.) anus
anoche *adv* last night
anochecedor -dora *adj* nocturnal, staying up late; *mf* night owl, nighthawk
anochecer *m* dusk, twilight, nightfall; **§34** *vn* to grow dark; to be, arrive, or happen at nightfall; to end the day, go to sleep; *vr* to get dark; to get cloudy; (coll.) to slip away, to hide
anochecida *f* nightfall
anódico -ca *adj* anode, anodic
anodinia *f* anodynia
anodino -na *adj* anodyne; insignificant; innocuous; *m* anodyne
anodizar **§76** *va* (metal.) to anodize
ánodo *m* (elec.) anode

anofeles *m* (*pl:* **-les**) (ent.) anopheles
anomalía *f* anomaly
anomalístico -ca *adj* (astr.) anomalistic
anómalo -la *adj* anomalous
anomuro -ra *adj & m* (zool.) anomuran
anón *m* or **anona** *f* (bot.) soursop
anonáceo -a *adj* (bot.) annonaceous
anonadación *f* or **anonadamiento** *m* annihilation, destruction; humiliation; discouragement
anonadar *va* to annihilate, destroy; to crush, overwhelm; to humiliate; *vr* to be humiliated; to be discouraged, be crushed
anonimato *m* or **anonimia** *f* anonymity
anónimo -ma *adj* anonymous; *m* anonym; anonymous letter, unsigned letter; anonymity; **conservar** or **guardar el anónimo** to preserve one's anonymity
anorexia *f* (path.) anorexia
anormal *adj* abnormal
anormalidad *f* abnormality
anorza *f* (bot.) bryony (*Bryonia alba*)
anosmia *f* (path.) anosmia
anotación *f* annotation; note, record; comment; (Am.) score (*in games*)
anotador -dora *mf* annotation; *m* (Am.) score card
anotar *va* to annotate; to note, to jot down; to comment on; to point out; to score (*a point*)
anovelado -da *adj* novelistic
anoxemia *f* (path.) anoxemia
anqueta *f* small rump; **estar de media anqueta** (coll.) to be uncomfortably seated
anquialmendrado -da *adj* narrow-rumped (*said of a horse*)
anquiboyuno -na *adj* bony-rumped (*said of a horse*)
anquiderribado -da *adj* low-buttocked (*said of a horse*)
anquilosar *va & vr* to ankylose
anquilosis *f* (path.) ankylosis
anquirredondo -da *adj* round-rumped (*said of a horse*)
anquiseco -ca *adj* thin-rumped (*said of a horse*)
Anquises *m* (myth.) Anchises
ansa *f* hanse (*medieval guild*)
ánsar *m* (orn.) goose; wild goose; (orn.) tule goose; **ánsar blanco** (orn.) lesser snow goose
ansarería *f* goose farm
ansarero -ra *mf* gooseherd; *f* goosegirl
ansarino -na *adj* anserine; *m* gosling
ansarón *m* goose, large goose
anseático -ca *adj* Hanseatic
Anselmo, San Saint Anselm
ansia *f* anxiety; anguish; longing, yearning; **ansias** *fpl* nausea
ansiadamente *adv* anxiously, yearningly
ansiar §90 & regular *va* to long for, yearn for, covet; **ansiar** + *inf* to yearn to, to be eager to + *inf; vn* (coll.) to be madly in love; **ansiar por** (coll.) to be madly in love with
ansiedad *f* anxiety, worry; pain
ansioso -sa *adj* anxious; anguished; longing, yearning; covetous
ant. abr. of **anticuado**
anta *f* (zool.) elk; (archeol.) menhir; (arch.) anta
antagalla *f* (naut.) spritsail reef band
antagónico -ca *adj* antagonistic
antagonismo *m* antagonism
antagonista *mf* antagonist
antañazo *adv* (coll.) a long time ago
antaño *adv* last year; of yore, long ago
antañón -ñona *adj* ancient, very old
Antarés *m* (astr.) Antares
antártico -ca *adj* antarctic; (*cap.*) *m* Antarctic (*ocean*); **la Antártica** Antarctica (*continent*)
Antártida, la Antarctica (*continent*)
-ante *suffix adj* -ing, e.g., **amante** loving; **hispanohablante** Spanish-speaking
ante *m* (zool.) elk; elk skin, buff; first course (*of a meal*); *prep* before, in the presence of; in front of; at, with; **ante todo** first of all
anteado -da *adj* buff (*orange yellow*)
antealtar *m* (eccl.) chancel
anteanoche *adv* night before last
anteanteanoche *adv* three nights ago
anteanteayer *adv* three days ago
anteantier *adv* (coll.) three days ago
anteayer *adv* day before yesterday
antebrazo *m* forearm
antecama *f* bedside rug
antecámara *f* antechamber, anteroom; lobby, hall
antecapilla *f* (eccl.) antechapel
antecedente *adj* antecedent; *m* antecedent; (gram., log. & math.) antecedent; **antecedentes** *mpl* antecedents
anteceder *va* to precede, go before
antecesor -sora *adj* preceding; *mf* predecessor; ancestor
anteclásico -ca *adj* preclassical
antecoger §49 *va* to drag or pull forward
antecolumna *f* (arch.) free column
antecoro *m* (arch.) antechoir
antecos *mpl* antiscians
antedata *f* antedate
antedatar *va* to antedate
antedecir §37 *va* (archaic) to foretell, predict
antedespacho *m* front office
antedía *adv* the day before, a day or two before
antedicho -cha *adj* aforesaid, aforementioned; *pp of* **antedecir**
antedigo *1st sg pres ind of* **antedecir**
antedije *1st sg pret ind of* **antedecir**
antediluviano -na *adj* antediluvian
antediré *1st sg fut ind of* **antedecir**
antefija *f* (arch.) antefix; gable end
antefirma *f* formal close (*of a letter*); title above signature
antefoso *m* (fort.) outer moat
antehistórico -ca *adj* prehistoric
anteiglesia *f* church porch; parochial church; parish
antelación *f* previousness, anticipation, planning; **con antelación** in advance
antelio *m* (meteor.) anthelion
antemano; de antemano beforehand, in advance
antemeridiano -na *adj* antemeridian
antemio or **antemión** *m* (f.a.) anthemion
antemural *m* (fort.) rampart, outwork; (fig.) rampart, defense, protection
antena *f* (ent.) antenna; (rad.) aerial, antenna; (naut.) lateen yard; **en antena** (rad.) on the air; **llevar a las antenas** (rad.) to put on the air; **antena de cuadro** (rad.) loop aerial or antenna; **antena de interior** (rad.) indoor aerial or antenna; **antena de amarre** (aer.) mooring mast (*of a dirigible*); **antena de radar** radar screen; **antena de rastreo** tracking antenna; **antena dipolo** (rad.) dipole antenna; **antena direccional** (rad.) directional antenna; **antena interior incorporada** (rad.) built-in antenna
antenacido -da *adj* born prematurely
antenado -da *adj* (ent.) provided with antennae; *mf* stepchild
antenatal *adj* antenatal
antenoche *adv* night before last; before sunset
antenombre *m* title, honorific
anténulas *fpl* feelers; antenules
antenupcial *adj* antenuptial
Anteo *m* (myth.) Antaeus
anteojera *f* spectacle case; patch (*worn over eye*); blinder, blinker
anteojero *m* maker or vendor of spectacles or eyeglasses
anteojo *m* eyeglass; spyglass, telescope; **anteojos** *mpl* spectacles, eyeglasses; opera glasses; binoculars; blinkers (*for horses*); **anteojo de larga vista** long-range telescope; **anteojo prismático** prism binocular; **anteojos bifocales** bifocals; **anteojos de campaña** field glass; **anteojos de predicador** pulpit glasses
antepagar §59 *va* to pay in advance
antepalco *m* (theat.) small antechamber to a box
antepasado -da *adj* before last, e.g., **la semana antepasada** the week before last; **antepasados** *mpl* ancestors
antepecho *m* railing, guardrail; sill; parapet, breastwork; breast collar (*of harness*); footboard (*of carriage*)
antepenúltimo -ma *adj* antepenultimate; *f* antepenult

antepondré *1st sg fut ind of* **anteponer**
anteponer **§69** *va* to place before, place in front; to prefer; *vr* to get ahead; **anteponerse a** to get ahead of, overcome
antepongo *1st sg pres ind of* **anteponer**
anteportada *f* (print.) bastard title, half title
anteportal *m* porch, vestibule, entry
anteproyecto *m* preliminary sketch or plan; first draft
antepuerta *f* portière; (fort.) counterport
antepuerto *m* entrance to a mountain pass; (naut.) outer port; (naut.) outer anchorage
antepuesto -ta *pp of* **anteponer**
antepuse *1st sg pret ind of* **anteponer**
antera *f* (bot.) anther
anterea *f* (ent.) tussah (*silkworm*)
anteridio *m* (bot.) antheridium
anterior *adj* anterior, front, previous, preceding; earlier; front (*tooth*); (phonet.) front; **anterior a** previous to, earlier than
anterioridad *f* anteriority, priority, precedence; **con anterioridad** previously; **con anterioridad a** previous to, prior to
antero *m* tanner, leather dresser
anterozoide *m* (bot.) antherozoid
antes *adv* before, formerly; previously; sooner, soonest; rather; **cuanto antes** or **lo más antes** as soon as possible; **antes bien** rather, on the contrary; **antes de** before (*in time*); **antes de** + *inf* before + *ger;* **antes que** rather than; **antes (de) que** before (*in time*)
antesacristía *f* anteroom to the sacristy
antesala *f* antechamber; waiting room (*e.g., of a doctor's office*); **hacer antesala** to dance attendance, to kick one's heels
antesis *f* (bot.) anthesis
antestatura *f* (fort.) makeshift barricade or entrenchment
antetemplo *m* (arch.) porch, portico
antever **§93** *va* to foresee
anteversión *f* (bot.) anteversion
antevíspera *f* two days before
antevisto -ta *pp of* **antever**
anti- *prefix* anti-, e.g., **antisemítico** anti-Semitic; **antitoxina** antitoxin; **antipapa** antipope; ant-, e.g., **antiácido** antacid; contra-, e.g., **anticonceptivo** contraceptive; in-, e.g., **antiartístico** inartistic; non-, eg., **antirresbaladizo** nonskid; -proof, e.g., **antisonoro** soundproof; **antitérmico** heatproof; un-, e.g., **anticientífico** unscientific; **antideportivo** unsportsmanlike; **antieconómico** uneconomic
antiácido -da *adj & m* antacid
antiaéreo -a *adj* anti-aircraft; *m* anti-aircraft gun
antiafrodisíaco -ca *adj & m* (med.) anaphrodisiac
antialcohólico -ca *adj* antialcoholic; antisaloon (*league, propaganda, etc.*)
antialcoholismo *m* antialcoholism
antiar *m* antiar (*poisonous gum*)
antiarina *f* (chem.) antiarin
antiartístico -ca *adj* inartistic
antibactérico -ca *adj* antibacterial
antibiosis *f* (biol.) antibiosis
antibiótico -ca *adj & m* antibiotic
anticartel *adj invar* antitrust
anticatarral *adj & m* anticatarrhal
anticátodo *m* anticathode
anticatólico -ca *adj & mf* anti-Catholic
anticiclón *m* (meteor.) anticyclone
anticiclonal *adj* anticyclonic
anticientífico -ca *adj* unscientific
anticipación *f* anticipation; advance; **con anticipación** in advance
anticipada *f* see **anticipado**
anticipadamente *adv* in advance, beforehand
anticipado -da *adj* advance (*e.g., payment*); *f* unexpected thrust, treacherous attack
anticipar *va* to anticipate, advance, accelerate, hasten; to move up, to move ahead (*a scheduled event*); to advance (*money*); to lend; *vr* to happen early, take place earlier; **anticiparse a** to anticipate, get ahead of; **anticiparse a** + *inf* to + *inf* ahead of time, e.g., **se anticipó a salir sin esperar a sus amigos** he left ahead of time without waiting for his friends
anticipo *m* anticipation; forehandedness; deposit, advance payment; retaining fee
anticlerical *adj* anticlerical
anticlericalismo *m* anticlericalism
anticlímax *m* (rhet.) anticlimax
anticlinal *adj* anticlinal; *m* (geol.) anticline
anticlinorio *m* (geol.) anticlinorium
anticloro *m* (chem.) antichlor
anticomunista *adj & mf* anticommunist
anticoncepción *f* contraconception
anticonceptivo -va *adj & m* contraconceptive
anticongelante *m* antifreeze
anticonstitucional *adj* unconstitutional
anticresis *f* (*pl:* **-sis**) (law) antichresis
anticrético -ca *adj* antichretic
anticristiano -na *adj & mf* anti-Christian
Anticristo *m* Antichrist
anticuado -da *adj* antiquated; obsolete; old-fashioned
anticuar *va* to antiquate, make out of date; *vr* to become antiquated
anticuario -ria *adj* antiquarian; *m* antiquarian or antiquary; antique dealer
anticuerpo *m* (bact.) antibody
antidáctilo *m* anapest
antidemocrático -ca *adj* antidemocratic
antideportivo -va *adj* unsportsmanlike
antiderrapante *adj* nonskid
antideslizante *adj* nonslipping; nonskid
antideslumbrante *adj* antiglare
antidetonante *adj & m* antiknock
antídoto *m* antidote; (fig.) antidote
antieconómico -ca *adj* uneconomic or uneconomical
antiemético -ca *adj & m* antiemetic
antier *adv* (coll.) day before yesterday
antiesclavista *adj* antislavery; *m* abolitionist
antiescorbútico -ca *adj & m* antiscorbutic
antiespañol -la *adj* anti-Spanish
antiespasmódico -ca *adj* antispasmodic
antiestético -ca *adj* unesthetic
antifaz *m* (*pl:* **-faces**) veil, mask
antifederalista *adj* antifederal; *m* antifederalist
antiflogístico -ca *adj* antiphlogistic
antífona *f* (eccl.) antiphon; anthem
antifonal or **antifonario -ria** *adj & m* antiphonal
antifonero *m* precentor
antífrasis *f* (rhet.) antiphrasis
antifricción *m* antifriction; antifriction metal
antigás *adj invar* protecting from poisonous gases, gas (*e.g., mask*)
antigénico -ca *adj* antigenic
antígeno *m* (bact.) antigen
Antígona or **Antígone** *f* (myth.) Antigone
antigramatical *adj* ungrammatical
antigripal *adj* antigrippe
antigualla *f* antique; old story; ancient custom; (coll.) relic, antique; (coll.) faded rose, has-been
antiguar **§23** *vn* to attain seniority; *vr* to attain seniority; to become antiquated
antigüedad *f* antiquity; seniority; **antigüedades** *fpl* antiquities
antiguo -gua *adj* old; ancient; antique; **a la antigua** or **a lo antiguo** in the ancient manner; in an old-fashioned way; **de antiguo** from days gone by, from time immemorial; **en lo antiguo** in ancient times; *mf* old member; veteran; senior; **los antiguos** the ancients
antiherrumbroso -sa *adj* rustless, rust-resisting
antihistamina *f* (pharm.) antihistamine
antihistamínico -ca *adj & m* (pharm.) antihistamine
antiinflacionista *adj* anti-inflationary
antijudío -a *adj* anti-Jewish
antilogaritmo *m* (math.) antilogarithm
antílope *m* (zool.) antelope
antillano -na *adj & mf* Antillean, West Indian
Antillas *fpl* Antilles; **Antillas Francesas** French West Indies; **Antillas Mayores** Greater Antilles; **Antillas Menores** Lesser Antilles
antimacasar *m* antimacassar
antimateria *f* (phys.) antimatter
antimilitarismo *m* antimilitarism
antimilitarista *adj & mf* antimilitarist
antimonárquico -ca *adj* antimonarchical
antimonial *adj* (chem.) antimonial

antimonio *m* (chem.) antimony

antimonita *f* (chem. & mineral.) antimonite

antinatural *adj* unnatural

antinodo *m* (phys.) antinode

antinomia *f* antinomy

antinómico -ca *adj* antinomic

antiobrero -ra *adj* antilabor

Antíoco *m* Antiochus

antioqueno -na *adj & mf* Antiochian

antioqueño -ña *adj* (pertaining to) Antioquia, S.A.; *mf* native or inhabitant of Antioquia

Antioquía *f* Antioch

antipapa *m* antipope

antipara *f* folding screen; gaiter

antiparásito *m* (rad.) static eliminator

antiparras *fpl* (coll.) spectacles, eyeglasses

antipartido *adj invar & m* antiparty

antipatía *f* dislike, antipathy

antipático -ca *adj* disagreeable; antipathetic

antipatinador -dora *adj* nonskid

antipatizar §76 *vn* (Am.) to feel antipathy, arouse antipathy, be repugnant

antipatriótico -ca *adj* unpatriotic

antipendio *m* (eccl.) antependium

antipirético -ca *adj & m* antipyretic

antipirina *f* (pharm.) antipyrine

antípoda *adj* antipodal; *m* antipode (*anything directly opposite*); **antípodas** *mpl* antipodes (*places and people*); **Antípodas** *fpl* Antipodes (*islands*)

antipoliomielítico -ca *adj* antipolio

antiprotón *m* (phys. & chem.) antiproton

antiproyectil *adj* antimissile

antiquísimo -ma *adj super* very old; very or most ancient

antirrábico -ca *adj* antirabic

antirraquítico -ca *adj & m* antirachitic

antirreligioso -sa *adj* antireligious

antirresbaladizo -za *adj* nonskid

antirrino *m* (bot.) snapdragon

antiscios *mpl* antiscians of the temperate zones

antisemita *mf* anti-Semite

antisemítico -ca *adj* anti-Semitic

antisemitismo *m* anti-Semitism

antisepsia or **antisepsis** *f* antisepsis

antiséptico -ca *adj & m* antiseptic

antisísmico -ca *adj* earthquake-proof

antisocial *adj* antisocial

antisonoro -ra *adj* soundproof

antisoviético -ca *adj* anti-Soviet

Antístenes *m* Antisthenes

antistrofa *f* antistrophe

antisubmarino -na *adj* antisubmarine

antitanque *adj* (*pl:* **-ques**) antitank

antitérmico -ca *adj* heatproof; antipyretic

antítesis *f* (*pl:* **-sis**) antithesis

antitético -ca *adj* antithetical

antitóxico -ca *adj* antitoxic

antitoxina *f* (bact.) antitoxin

antitrago *m* (anat.) antitragus

antiveneno *m* antivenin

antiviral or **antivirulento -ta** *adj* antiviral

antiviviseccionista *adj & mf* antivivisectionist

antociana or **antocianina** *f* (biochem.) anthocyanin

antodio *m* (bot.) anthodium

antófilo -la *adj* flower-loving; *mf* flower lover

antofita *f* (bot.) anthophyte

antojadizo -za *adj* fickle, capricious, whimsical

antojado -da *adj* desirous, eager

antojar *vr* to seem; *vr & impers* to fancy, take a sudden fancy to or for; to seem, seem likely, imagine, e.g., **se me antoja que va a llover** it seems to me that it is going to rain; **antojársele a uno** + *inf* to have or take a notion to + *inf*, e.g., **se me antoja ir a paseo** I have a notion to go for a walk

antojera *f* blinker, blinder (*for horses*)

antojito *m* (Am.) tidbit, delicacy

antojo *m* passing fancy, whim, caprice; hasty judgment; **antojos** *mpl* moles, spots, warts; **a su antojo** as one pleases

antojuelo *m* whim, vagary

antología *f* anthology

antólogo -ga *mf* anthologist

Antón *m* Antony, Anthony

Antonieta *f* Antoinette

antónimo -ma *adj* antonymous; *m* antonym

Antonino *m* Antoninus

Antonio *m* Anthony, Antonius

antonomasia *f* (rhet.) antonomasia

Antoñito *m* Tony

antorcha *f* torch; **antorcha a soplete** blowtorch

antorchar *va* var. of **entorchar**

antorchero *m* torch holder or socket; cresset

antozoos *mpl* (zool.) anthozoans

antraceno *m* (chem.) anthracene

antracita *f* anthracite

antracitoso -sa *adj* anthracite

antracnosis *f* (bot.) anthracnose

ántrax *m* (path.) anthrax

antreno *m* (ent.) museum beetle

antro *m* antrum, cavern; den (*e.g., of crooks*); (anat.) antrum; **antro de Highmoro** (anat.) antrum of Highmore; **antro timpánico** (anat.) tympanic antrum

antropofagía *f* anthropophagy

antropófago -ga *adj* anthropophagic; **antropófagos** *mpl* anthropophagi

antropoide *adj* anthropoid; *m* (orn.) demoiselle

antropoideo -a *adj* anthropoidal; *m* (zool.) anthropoid, anthropoid ape

antropología *f* anthropology

antropológico -ca *adj* anthropological

antropólogo -ga *mf* anthropologist

antropometría *f* anthropometry

antropométrico -ca *adj* anthropometric

antropomórfico -ca *adj* anthropomorphic

antropomorfismo *m* anthropomorphism

antropomorfo -fa *adj* anthropomorphous; **antropomorfos** *mpl* (zool.) anthropoids

antropopiteco *m* (pal.) Anthropopithecus

antruejo *m* carnival (*the three days before Lent*)

antuviada *f* (coll.) sudden blow or bump

antuviar *va* (coll.) to strike or bump suddenly or without warning, to be first to strike

antuvión *m* (coll.) sudden blow or attack; **de antuvión** (coll.) suddenly, unexpectedly

anual *adj* annual

anualidad *f* annuity; year's pay; annual occurrence; annual payment

anuario *m* yearbook; directory; bulletin, catalogue (*e.g., of a university*); **anuario telefónico** telephone directory

anúbada *f* call to arms; feudal service; tribute paid in lieu of service

anubarrado -da *adj* cloudy, overcast; with clouds painted in

anublado -da *adj* (slang) blind

anublar *va* to cloud; to dim, darken, to obscure; to wither, to dry up (*plants*); *vr* to become cloudy; to be withered; to fade away (*said, e.g., of one's hopes*)

anublo *m* var. of **añublo**

anudar *va* to knot, to tie, to fasten; to join, to unite; to take up again (*a story*); *vr* to get knotted; to unite, be united; to fade away, wither, wilt, fail; **se le anudó la garganta** he got a lump in his throat; **se le anudó la lengua** his tongue stuck in his throat

anuencia *f* consent

anuente *adj* consenting

anulable *adj* voidable

anulación *f* annulment; nullification, revocation; cancellation; removal, discharge

anular *adj* annular; *m* ring finger; *va* to annul; to nullify, revoke; to cancel; to remove, unseat, discharge; *vr* to be deprived of authority; to be passed over; to be humiliated

anuloso -sa *adj* annular; full of rings

anunciación *f* announcement, annunciation; (*cap.*) *f* Annunciation

anunciador -dora *adj* advertising; *mf* announcer; annunciator; advertiser

anunciante *adj* advertising; *mf* advertiser

anunciar *va* to announce, to annunciate; to forebode; to advertise

anuncio *m* announcement; harbinger; omen; advertisement; **anuncios clasificados (en secciones)** classified advertisements; **anuncios por palabras** classified advertisements at so much per word

anuo -nua *adj* annual

anúteba *f* var. of **anúbada**

anverso *m* obverse

anzuelo *m* fishhook; lure, attraction; **picar en el anzuelo** or **tragar el anzuelo** (fig.) to swallow the bait, swallow the hook
añacal *m* carrier of grain to the mill; board for carrying bread
añacalero *m* (prov.) hod carrier
añada *f* year, season (*speaking of weather or crops*); vintage wine; tract of cultivated land
añadible *adj* addible
añadido -da *adj* added, additional; *m* false hair, switch
añadidura *f* addition, increase; extra weight, extra measure; **de añadidura** extra, into the bargain; **por añadidura** besides, after all
añadir *va* to add; to add to
añafea *f* rag paper, brown paper
añafil *m* straight Moorish trumpet
añagaza *f* bird call; decoy, lure; trap, trick
añal *adj* annual; year-old; *mf* year-old calf, kid, or lamb; *m* memorial a year after death
añalejo *m* (eccl.) liturgical calendar, ordinal
añascar §86 *va* (coll.) to gather together bit by bit
añejamiento *m* aging; turning stale
añejar *va* to age; to make stale; *vr* to age, become aged; to improve with age; to grow stale
añejo -ja *adj* aged (*said, e.g., of wine*); old, stale; musty, rancid
añicos *mpl* pieces, bits, shreds; **hacer añicos** to tear to smithereens; **hacerse añicos** (coll.) to take great pains, to wear oneself out
añil *m* (bot.) anil (*plant, color, and dye*); bluing (*for laundering*); indigo (*of the solar spectrum*)
añilar *va* to dye with indigo; to blue (*clothes*)
añilería *f* anil or indigo plantation; anil mill, indigo works
añinero *m* dresser of lambskin; dealer in lambskin
añinos *mpl* unshorn lambskin; lamb's wool
año *m* year; **años** *mpl* birthday; **cumplir años** to have a birthday; **cumplir . . . años** to be . . . years old, to reach the age of; **¡Feliz Año Nuevo!** Happy New Year!; **por los años de . . .** about the year . . . ; **tener . . . años (de edad)** to be . . . years old; **año anomalístico** (astr.) anomalistic year; **año astronómico** astronomical year; **año bisiesto** leap year; **año civil** calendar year, civil year; **año de Cristo** anno Domini; **año de gracia** year of grace; **año de nuestra salud** year of our Lord; **año económico** fiscal year; **año escolar** or **año lectivo** school year; **año lunar** lunar year; **año luz** (*pl:* **años luz**) (astr.) light-year; **año nuevo** new year; **año solar** solar year; **año trópico** (astr.) tropical year
añojal *m* fallow land
añojo -ja *mf* year-old calf or lamb
añoranza *f* loneliness, longing, sorrow, grief
añorar *va* to long for, to miss, to sorrow for, to grieve over; *vn* to pine, to sorrow, to grieve
añoso -sa *adj* old, aged, heavy with years
añublado -da *adj* var. of **anublado**
añublar *va & vr* var. of **anublar**
añublo *m* blight, mildew
añudar *va & vr* var. of **anudar**
añusgar §59 *vn* to strangle, choke; to get angry
aojada *f* (Am.) skylight; (Am.) transom
aojador -dora *mf* hoodoo
aojadura *f* or **aojamiento** *m* spell, curse; evil eye, bad luck
aojar *va* to cast the evil eye upon, to hoodoo, to jinx
aojo *m* evil eye, bad luck
aonio -nia *adj* Aonian
aoristo *m* (gram.) aorist
aorta *f* (anat.) aorta
aórtico -ca *adj* aortic
aovado -da *adj* oval, egg-shaped
aovar *vn* to lay eggs
aovillar *vr* to form a ball, curl up, shrink
ap. abr. of **aparte** & **apóstol**
apabilar *va* to trim (*a wick*)
apabullar *va* (coll.) to mash, crush, flatten; (coll.) to squelch
apabullo *m* (coll.) mashing, crushing, flattening; (coll.) squelching
apacentadero *m* pasture, grazing ground
apacentador -dora *adj* pasturing, grazing; nourishing; encouraging, fostering; *mf* nourisher, fosterer; *m* shepherd, herdsman
apacentamiento *m* pasturage, grazing; feed, fodder; fuel
apacentar §18 *va* to pasture, to graze; (fig.) to feed; *vr* to pasture, to graze; to feed; **apacentarse con** or **de** to feed on
apacibilidad *f* peacefulness; mildness, gentleness
apacible *adj* peaceful; mild, gentle
apaciguador -dora *adj* pacifying, calming, appeasing; *mf* pacifier, calmer, appeaser
apaciguamiento *m* pacification, calming, appeasement
apaciguar §23 *va* to pacify, calm, appease; *vr* to become peaceful, to grow calm, to calm down
apache *m* apache (*bandit*); Apache (*Indian*)
apacheta *f* (Am.) devotional heap of stones at the top of a mountain road
apachico *m* (Am.) package, bundle
apachurrar *va* (Am.) to mash, to crush, to mangle
apadrinador -dora *adj* sponsoring; backing, protecting; *mf* sponsor, backer, supporter; protector; *m* patron; second (*in a duel*); *f* patroness
apadrinamiento *m* sponsorship, sponsoring, support
apadrinar *va* to sponsor; to act as godfather for; to be best man for; to second (*in a duel*); to back, to support; to take under one's wing; to ride alongside (*a rider on a partly broken horse*)
apagable *adj* extinguishable
apagabroncas *m* (*pl:* **-cas**) (coll.) bouncer
apagachispas *m* (*pl:* **-pas**) (elec.) spark arrester
apagadizo -za *adj* fire-resisting
apagado -da *adj* out (*said of fire or light*); dull, weak, dim; calm, listless, spiritless; timid; slaked (*lime*)
apagador -dora *adj* extinguishing; dimming; muffling; *mf* extinguisher (*person*); *m* extinguisher (*of a candle*); damper (*of piano*)
apagafuego *m* fire extinguisher
apagaincendios *m* (*pl:* **-dios**) fire extinguisher
apagamiento *m* extinguishing; dimming, dulling; muffling; subsiding
apagapenoles *mpl* (naut.) leech lines
apagar §59 *va* to put out, to extinguish; to turn off (*lights, electric current, radio, etc.*); to tone down (*light or color*); to damp, to muffle (*sound*); to slake (*lime*); to silence (*enemy fire*); to quench (*thirst*); to soothe, to calm, to deaden (*pain*); *vn* **¡apaga y vámonos!** (coll.) dry up!; *vr* to go out, to be extinguished; to subside, to calm down, to die away, to fade away
apagavelas *m* (*pl:* **-las**) candle extinguisher, snuffers
apagón -gona *adj* (Am.) fire-resisting; *m* blackout (*as military precaution*); darkness (*e.g., from failure of electricity*)
apagoso -sa *adj* (Am.) poorly burning
apainelado -da *adj* (arch.) basket-handle (*said of an arch*)
apaisado -da *adj* elongated, oblong
apajarado -da *adj* (Am.) scatterbrained, flighty
apalabrar *va* to bespeak, to engage; to discuss, to consider; *vr* to agree, to come to an agreement
apalache *adj* Appalachian; **Apalaches** *mpl* Appalachians (*mountains*)
apalachina *f* (bot.) yaupon
apalancar §86 *va* to move or raise with a lever, to move or raise with a crowbar
apaleamiento *m* shoveling; beating, thrashing; piling, heaping
apalear *va* to shovel; to beat, thrash, drub; to pile up, to heap up
apaleo *m* thrashing; piling, heaping
apanalado -da *adj* honeycombed
apancle *m* (Am.) irrigation ditch
apancora *f* (zool.) spiny crab; (zool.) sea hedgehog
apandar *va* (coll.) to steal, to swipe
apandillar *va* to form into bands, form into gangs; *vr* to band together

apandorgar §59 *vr* (coll.) to get fat, put on weight; (Am.) to get lazy
apanojado -da *adj* (bot.) panicled
apantallar *va* (elec.) to shield, to screen; (Am.) to dazzle, to amaze
apantanar *va* to make swampy or marshy; to stick in a swamp; *vr* to get swampy or marshy; to get stuck in a swamp, get stuck in the mud
apantuflado -da *adj* slipper-shaped
apañado -da *adj* clothlike, thick-textured; clever, handy; fit, suitable
apañadura *f* grasping; stealing; repairing, repair, patch; trimming, edging
apañar *va* to pick up, to grasp; to seize, to steal; to dress; to repair, to mend; (coll.) to wrap up; *vr* (coll.) to be handy
apaño *m* grasping; stealing; repairing, repair; skill, handiness
apañuscar §86 *va* (coll.) to rumple, crumple; (coll.) to steal, to swipe; (Am.) to jam, to crowd
apapagayado -da *adj* parrot-like; shaped like the beak of a parrot
apar *m* or **apara** *m* (zool.) three-banded armadillo
aparador *m* sideboard, dresser, buffet; serving table; showcase; workshop
aparadura *f* (naut.) garboard, garboard strake
aparar *va* to prepare, to arrange; to adorn, to dress; to block, to head off; to stretch out the hands, cloak, or skirt to catch; to dress, to cultivate (*plants*); to close (*uppers of shoes*); (carp.) to dub (*with adz*)
aparasolado -da *adj* parasol-shaped; (bot.) umbellate
aparatar *vr* to get ready; to get dressed up; (prov. & Am.) to get cloudy, to look threatening
aparato *m* preparation; apparatus, device; display, ostentation, show; exaggeration, embroidery; literary baggage; sign; radio set; television set; telephone; (coll.) airplane; (anat.) apparatus; (surg.) application, bandage; (theat.) scenery, properties; (med.) syndrome; **ponerse al aparato** to come or to go to the phone; **aparato auditivo** hearing aid; **aparato crítico** apparatus criticus; **aparato de relojería** clockwork; **aparato fotográfico** camera; **aparato pulverizador** sprayer, spray outfit; **aparatos sanitarios** bathroom fixtures; **aparato tomavistas** motion-picture camera
aparatosidad *f* ostentation, showiness, pomposity
aparatoso -sa *adj* ostentatious, showy, pompous
aparcamiento *m* parking
aparcar §86 *va & vn* (aut. & mil.) to park
aparcería *f* (com.) partnership
aparcero -ra *mf* (com.) partner; sharer, coheir; sharecropper; (Am.) customer
apareamiento *m* making even; pairing, mating, matching
aparear *va* to make even; to pair, to mate, to match; *vr* to match; to pair, to mate
aparecer §34 *vn & vr* to appear; to turn up, to show up
aparecido *m* ghost, specter
aparecimiento *m* appearance
aparedar *va* to wall up
aparejado -da *adj* ready, fit, suitable
aparejador *m* foreman, overseer, supervisor, builder; (naut.) rigger
aparejar *va* to prepare; to threaten; to harness; to dress, to process; to prime, to size; (naut.) to rig, to rig out; (Am.) to pair, to mate (*animals*); *vr* to prepare, to get ready; to get dressed up
aparejería *f* (Am.) harness shop
aparejo *m* preparation, arrangement; harness, riding gear; (mas.) bond, bonding; set, kit, equipment; (naut.) rigging, sails and rigging; (naut.) gear, tackle, block and tackle; priming, sizing, filler; **aparejos** *mpl* tools, instruments, implements, equipment, accessories; **aparejo de gata** (naut.) cat tackle; **aparejo flamenco** or **holandés** (mas.) Flemish bond; **aparejo inglés** (mas.) English bond
aparentar *va* to feign, pretend, affect; to look to be (*so many years old*); **aparentar** + *inf* to seem to + *inf*; to pretend to + *inf*
aparente *adj* apparent, seeming; visible, evident; right, proper, suitable
aparición *f* appearance; apparition
apariencia *f* appearance, aspect; probability, sign, indication; **juzgar por las apariencias** to judge by appearances; **las apariencias engañan** things are not what they seem; **salvar las apariencias** to keep up appearances, to save face
aparqueamiento *m* parking
aparquear *va* (mil. & aut.) to park
aparqueo *m* var. of **aparqueamiento**
aparrado -da *adj* viny, vinelike, shrubby; chunky, stubby; spreading
aparragar §59 *vr* (Am.) to squat, crouch, bend
aparrar *va* to espalier; *vr* to spread; (Am.) to squat, crouch; to be chunky
aparroquiado -da *adj* established in a parish; having many customers, patients, or clients
aparroquiar *va* to get customers, patients, or clients for; *vr* to get customers, patients, or clients
apartadero *m* siding, sidetrack; turnout; road fork; sorting room (*for driving bulls into individual pens before fight*)
apartadijo *m* small part; alcove, offset, recess; **hacer apartadijos de** to break up, break apart
apartadizo -za *adj* shy, diffident, retiring; *m* alcove, offset, recess
apartado -da *adj* separated; distant, remote; aloof; different; side or back (*e.g., road*); *m* side room; distribution; post-office box; section; vocabulary entry; penning of bulls; governing board of cattle dealers; **hacer el apartado de** to distribute, to separate
apartador -dora *mf* separator, divider, sorter; *m* (Am.) stick (*for driving cattle*)
apartamento *m* apartment, apartment house
apartamiento *m* separation; withdrawal, retirement; remoteness, remote spot; aloofness; coldness, indifference; apartment
apartar *va* to separate; to take aside; to turn aside; to move away, push away; (law) to set aside, to waive; (rail.) to shunt; to sort (*cattle*); to pen (*bulls*); *vr* to separate; to move away, keep away, turn aside, stand aside; to withdraw, retire; to get divorced; (law) to withdraw from a suit, to desist
aparte *adv* apart, aside; **esto aparte** aside from this; **aparte de** apart from; *adj* separate; *prep* apart from; *m* aside (*remark*); indented line, new paragraph
apartidar *va* to back, support; *vr* to take sides
aparvar *va* to arrange (*grain*) for thrashing; to heap, gather together
apasionado -da *adj* passionate; passionately fond, devoted; tender, sore (*said of a part of body*); tender, loving; **apasionado a** or **por** passionately fond of, devoted to; *m* lover
apasionamiento *m* passion, enthusiasm, intense emotion; violence, vehemence
apasionante *adj* stirring, thrilling
apasionar *va* to appeal deeply to, make enthusiastic, arouse passionately; to afflict; *vr* to become impassioned; to fall madly in love; to be stirred up; **apasionarse de** or **por** to fall madly in love with, be crazy about
apasote *m* (bot.) wormseed
apaste *m* (Am.) earthen bowl, earthen vat
apatanado -da *adj* coarse, farmerish
apatía *f* apathy
apático -ca *adj* apathetic
apatita *f* (mineral.) apatite
apátrida *adj* stateless, without a country; *mf* stateless person, expatriate; *m* man without a country
apatuscar §86 *va* (slang) to do in a hurry, to botch
apatusco *m* (coll.) ornament, finery, trimming
apayasar *va* to make clownish; *vr* to be clownish, act the clown
apazote *m* var. of **apasote**
apdo. abr. of **apartado**
apea *f* hobble (*for horses*)

apeadero *m* horse block, carriage block; (rail.) flag stop, wayside station; platform, landing; resting place; temporary lodging, place to stay
apeador *m* surveyor
apealar *va* (Am.) to hobble (*a horse*)
apeamiento *m* dismounting, alighting; propping; surveying
apear *va* to dismount, help dismount; to help down, help out; to bring down, to fell; to remove, discharge; to overcome (*a difficulty*); to prop, prop up; to wedge, to block (*a wheel*); (coll.) to dissuade; to hobble, to fetter (*animals*); to survey; *vr* to dismount, alight, get off, get out; (coll.) to be dissuaded, back down; to stay, to stop, to put up
apechugar §59 *va* (Am.) to grab, seize forcibly; *vn* to push with the chest; **apechugar con** (coll.) to make the best of, to put up with
apedazar §76 *va* to piece out, to mend, to patch; to cut in pieces; to tear to pieces
apedernalado -da *adj* flinty, hard as flint; stonyhearted
apedreado -da *adj* variegated; speckled; pockmarked
apedreador -dora *adj* stoning, stone-throwing; *mf* stone thrower
apedreamiento *m* stoning; lapidation; pitting; hail, hailstorm; damage from hail
apedrear *va* to stone, throw stones at; to cut with stones, hail, etc.; to lapidate; to stone to death; to pit; *vn* to hail; *vr* to be damaged by hail; to become pitted
apedreo *m* var. of **apedreamiento**
apegadamente *adv* affectionately, devotedly
apegar §59 *vr* to become attached, to grow fond; **apegarse a** to become attached to, to grow fond of
apego *m* attachment, fondness
apelable *adj* appealable
apelación *f* appeal; (law) appeal; (coll.) medical consultation; (coll.) help, remedy
apelado -da *mf* (law) appellee
apelambrar *va* to flesh, to remove hair from (*hides*)
apelante *adj & mf* (law) appellant
apelar *vn* to appeal, make an appeal; to have recourse; to refer; (law) to appeal; **apelar de** (law) to appeal from
apelativo -va *adj & m* (gram.) appellative
apeldar *vn* (coll.) to flee, run away; **apeldarlas** (coll.) to run away
apelde *m* (coll.) flight; dawn bell (*in Franciscan monasteries*)
Apeles *m* Apelles
apelmazado -da *adj* compressed, compact; heavy, clumsy (*writing*)
apelmazamiento *m* compactness
apelmazar §76 *va* to compress, squeeze together; *vr* to cake
apelotonar *va* to form into a ball, make a ball of; *vr* to form a ball or balls, to curl up
apellar *va* to dress, soften (*leather*)
apellidamiento *m* calling, naming, appellation
apellidar *va* to call, to name; to call by one's surname
apellido *m* name; surname, last name, family name; cognomen, epithet, nickname; **apellido de soltera** maiden name
apenachado -da *adj* plumed, crested
apenar *va* to cause sorrow to; *vr* to grieve
apenas *adv* scarcely, hardly; with difficulty; **apenas si** scarcely, hardly; *conj.* no sooner, as soon as
apencar §86 *vn* (coll.) to buck up, to face the music
apendectomía *f* (surg.) appendectomy
apéndice *m* appendix, appendage; (aer.) appendix; (biol.) appendage; **apéndice cecal, vermicular,** or **vermiforme** (anat.) vermiform appendix
apendicectomía *f* (surg.) appendectomy
apendicitis *f* (path.) appendicitis
apendicitomía *f* var. of **apendicectomía**
apendicular *adj* appendicular
Apeninos *mpl* Apennines
apeñuscar §86 *va* var. of **apañuscar**
apeo *m* dismounting, alighting; felling; propping; survey, surveying; surveyor's plan
apeonar *vn* to run (*said of birds*)
apepsia *f* (path.) apepsia
aperador *m* farmer; wheelwright; (min.) foreman
aperar *va* to make (*wagons, farm equipment, etc.*); to repair
apercancar §86 *vr* (Am.) to rust, to mold, get moldy
apercepción *f* (philos.) apperception
aperceptivo -va *adj* (philos.) apperceptive
apercibimiento *m* preparation, provision; warning, notice; (law) summons
apercibir *va* to prepare; to provide; to warn; to perceive; (law) to summon; (Am.) to collect; *vr* to get ready; to be provided; **apercibirse de** to provide oneself with; to notice, to observe
apercollar §77 *va* (coll.) to grab by the neck; (coll.) to grab, to snatch; (coll.) to club, to stun or to kill by a blow on the back of the neck
aperchar *va* (Am.) to pile, to heap, to stack up
aperdigar §59 *va* to brown, to broil slightly
apergaminar *vr* to get like parchment; (coll.) to dry up, to become yellow and wrinkled
aperiódico -ca *adj* aperiodic
aperitivo -va *adj* (med.) aperitive; *m* (med.) aperitive; apéritif, appetizer
aperlado -da *adj* pearly, pearl-colored
apernar *va* to bolt, to pin; **§18** *va* to seize (*game*) by the leg (*said of hunting dogs*)
apero *m* tools, equipment, outfit, gear; sheepfold; (Am.) saddle, riding gear
aperreador -dora *adj* (coll.) worrisome, harassing, tiresome; *mf* (coll.) plague, bore
aperrear *va* to set the dogs on; (coll.) to worry, harass, plague, pester; *vr* (coll.) to be worried, harassed, plagued
aperreo *m* (coll.) worry, harassment, toil
apersogar §59 *va* to tether (*an animal*), to tie by the neck
apersonado -da *adj;* **bien apersonado** presentable; **mal apersonado** unpresentable
apersonamiento *m* personal appearance; (law) appearance
apersonar *vr* to appear in person; to have an interview; (law) to appear
apertura *f* opening, beginning; opening a will; (chess) opening
apesadumbrar *va* to grieve, distress; *vr* to grieve, be distressed; **apesadumbrarse con** or **de** to be grieved at, be distressed at
apesaradamente *adv* sadly, sorrowfully
apesarar *va & vr* var. of **apesadumbrar**
apesgar §59 *va* to overwhelm, overburden
apestado -da *adj* nauseated; pestilential
apestar *va* to infect with a plague; to corrupt, vitiate; (coll.) to sicken, nauseate, plague; to infest, fill; *vn* to stink; *vr* to be infected with a plague; to become vitiated
apestoso -sa *adj* pestilent, infected; sickening; annoying; stinking
apétalo -la *adj* (bot.) apetalous
apetecedor -dora *adj* hungering, thirsting, craving, longing
apetecer §34 *va* to hunger for, to thirst for, to crave, to long for
apetecible *adj* desirable; appetizing, tempting
apetencia *f* hunger, appetite, craving
apetite *m* sauce, appetizer; incentive, inducement
apetitivo -va *adj* appetitive; appetizing
apetito *m* appetite; **abrir el apetito** to whet the appetite
apetitoso -sa *adj* appetizing, tasty; gourmand
ápex *m* apex; (gram. & hist.) apex
apezonado -da *adj* nipple-shaped
apezuñar *vn* to dig the hoofs into the ground
apiadar *va* to move to pity; to take pity on; *vr* to have pity; **apiadarse de** to have pity on
apiaradero *m* shepherd's account of the heads of his flock
apiario -ria *adj* beelike; *m* apiary
apical *adj* apical; (phonet.) apical
apicarar *vr* to go to the bad, become depraved
ápice *m* apex; crux; bit, whit, iota; **estar en los ápices de** (coll.) to be up in, to know all about
apícola *adj* apicultural; *mf* apiculturist
apículo *m* apiculus

apicultor -tora *mf* apiculturist
apicultura *f* apiculture
apilada *f* dried chestnut
apilamiento *m* piling, heaping, pile
apilar *va & vr* to pile, pile up
apilonar *va* (Am.) to pile, to pile up
apimpollar *vr* to sprout, to put forth shoots
apiñado -da *adj* cone-shaped; packed, congested
apiñadura *f* or **apiñamiento** *m* squeezing; crowding, jamming; crowd, jam
apiñar *va* to bunch, to squeeze together, to crowd, to jam; *vr* to bunch, be squeezed together; to crowd, become crowded or jammed; to grow densely
apio *m* (bot.) celery; celery plant, celery stalk; **apio de ranas** (bot.) field buttercup, blister plant
apiolar *va* to gyve (*falcons*); to tie up (*the legs of a dead animal*); (coll.) to seize, arrest; (coll.) to kill
apio-nabo *m* (bot.) celeriac
apipar *vr* (coll.) to gorge with food and drink
apirético -ca *adj* apyretic
apirexia *f* (path.) apyrexia
apiri *m* (Am.) mine worker
apisonado *m* tamping, packing
apisonador -dora *adj* tamping; rolling; *mf* tamper (*person*); *m & f* road roller; roller; **apisonador de vapor** or **apisonadora movida a vapor** steam roller; *m* tamper (*tool*)
apisonamiento *m* tamping; rolling
apisonar *va* to tamp, to pack down; to roll
apitonar *va* to pierce, to break through; to peck at; *vn* to begin to show; to bud, to sprout; *vr* (coll.) to abuse each other, to exchange insults
apizarrado -da *adj* slate, slate-colored
aplacable *adj* placable, appeasable
aplacador -dora *adj* placating, appeasing; *mf* placator, appeaser
aplacamiento *m* placation, appeasement, calming
aplacar §86 *va* to placate, appease, pacify, calm, satisfy; to quench (*thirst*)
aplacer §34 *va* to please, satisfy; *vr* to be pleased, to take pleasure
aplacerado -da *adj* smooth and shallow (*said of bottom of sea*)
aplacible *adj* pleasant
aplacimiento *m* pleasure, enjoyment
aplanadera *f* road drag, leveler, roller, road roller; tamper
aplanador -dora *adj* smoothing, leveling; *m* roller
aplanamiento *m* smoothing, leveling; planishing
aplanar *va* to smooth, make even; to planish; (coll.) to astound; *vr* to collapse, fall over; to become discouraged
aplanchado *m* ironing
aplanchador -dora *mf* ironer
aplanchar *va* to iron (*clothing*)
aplanético -ca *adj* (opt.) aplanatic
aplantillar *va* to carve to measure
aplastador -dora *adj* var. of **aplastante**
aplastamiento *m* flattening, smashing; (coll.) dumbfounding
aplastante *adj* astounding, dumbfounding
aplastapapeles *m* (*pl:* **-les**) (Am.) paperweight
aplastar *va* to flatten, smash, crush; (coll.) to leave speechless; (Am.) to weary, to bore; *vr* to become flat; (coll.) to be left speechless
aplaudidor -dora *adj* applauding; *mf* applauder
aplaudir *va & vn* to applaud
aplauso *m* applause; **aplausos** *mpl* applause
aplayar *vn* to overflow, to flood (*said of a river*)
aplazamiento *m* convening; summons; postponement
aplazar §76 *va* to convene; to summon; to postpone; to set a time or date for
aplebeyar *va* to degrade; *vr* to be degraded, to lower oneself
aplicabilidad *f* applicability
aplicable *adj* applicable
aplicación *f* application; diligence; appliqué
aplicado -da *adj* studious, industrious; applied; appliqué
aplicar §86 *va* to apply; to assign; to attribute; (law) to adjudge; *vr* to apply (*be pertinent*); to apply oneself; to devote oneself
aplomado -da *adj* lead-colored; solemn, serious
aplomar *va* to plumb (*with plumb line*); to make straight or vertical; *vn* to plumb, be vertical; *vr* to collapse, fall to the ground
aplomo *m* seriousness, gravity; aplomb, self-possession
apnea *f* (path.) apnea
apocado -da *adj* irresolute, diffident, vacillating, of little courage; humble, lowly
Apocalipsis *m* (Bib.) Apocalypse
apocalíptico -ca *adj* apocalyptic; (fig.) apocalyptic
apocamiento *m* irresolution, diffidence, vacillation, lack of courage; depression, low spirits
apocar §86 *va* to cramp, contract, restrict; to make smaller, to narrow; to humble, belittle; *vr* to humble oneself
apocárpico -ca *adj* (bot.) apocarpous
apócema *f* or **apócima** *f* (pharm.) apozem, decoction
apocináceo -a *adj* (bot.) apocynaceous
apocopar *va* (gram.) to apocopate
apócope *f* (gram.) apocope
apócrifo -fa *adj* apocryphal; Apocryphal
apodar *va* to nickname; to make fun of; to curse, slander
apoderado -da *adj* empowered, authorized; *m* proxy; attorney; agent (*e.g., of a bullfighter*)
apoderar *va* to empower, to grant the power of attorney to; *vr* **apoderarse de** to take hold of, to seize, to grasp; to take possession of
apodíctico -ca *adj* (log.) apodictic
apodo *m* nickname, sobriquet
ápodo -da *adj* apodal
apódosis *f* (*pl:* **-sis**) (gram.) apodosis
apófige *f* (arch.) apophyge
apófisis *f* (*pl:* **-sis**) (anat. & zool.) process; (anat., bot., geol. & zool.) apophysis; (bot.) struma; **apófisis alveolar** (anat.) alveolar process; **apófisis coracoides** (anat.) coracoid process; **apófisis estiloides** (anat.) styloid process
apofonía *f* (phonet.) ablaut
apogeo *m* (astr. & fig.) apogee
apógrafo *m* apograph, copy
apolillado -da *adj* mothy, moth-eaten
apolilladura *f* moth hole
apolillar *va* to eat (*said of moths*); *vr* to become moth-eaten
Apolo *m* (myth.) Apollo
apologético -ca *adj* apologetic; *f* apologetics
apología *f* apology, apologia
apologista *mf* apologist
apologizar §76 *va* to praise, to defend; *vn* to apologize (*to offer a defense*)
apólogo *m* apologue
apoltronado -da *adj* loafing, idle, lazy
apoltronar *vr* to loaf around, to become lazier and lazier; to sprawl
Apollión *m* (Bib.) Apollyon
apomazar §76 *va* to smooth or polish with pumice stone
apomorfina *f* (pharm.) apomorphine
aponeurosis *f* (*pl:* **-sis**) (anat.) aponeurosis
aponeurótico -ca *adj* aponeurotic
aponeurótomo *m* (surg.) aponeurotome
apontaje *m* var. of **apontizaje**
apontar *vn* var. of **apontizar**
apontizaje *m* (aer.) deck-landing
apontizar §76 *vn* to deck-land
apontocar §86 *va* to prop up
apoplejía *f* (path.) apoplexy
apoplético -ca *adj & mf* apoplectic
apoquinar *vn* (slang) to come across, to cough up
aporcado *m* or **aporcadura** *f* (agr.) hilling
aporcar §86 *va* (agr.) to hill (*plants*)
aporcelanado -da *adj* procelainlike; porcelanic
aporisma *m* (path.) ecchymoma
aporismar *vr* to become an ecchymoma
aporrar *vn* (coll.) to be unable to say a word; *vr* (coll.) to be a bore, be a nuisance
aporreado -da *adj* poor, wretched; rascally; *m* (Am.) chopped beef stew
aporreadura *f* or **aporreamiento** *m* cudgeling, beating, clubbing

aporrear *va* to cudgel, beat, club; to annoy, bother; *vr* to get a beating; to drudge, slave
aporreo *m* var. of **aporreadura**
aportación *f* addition, contribution; (law) dowry, portion
aportadera *f* pannier or box (*to be carried on each side of a beast's back*); grape tub
aportadero *m* (naut.) port, harbor; stopping place, outlet
aportar *va* to bring, contribute; to lead; to provide; to bring as dowry; to bring (*one's proper share*); *vn* (naut.) to reach port; to come out at an unexpected place, to show up
aporte *m* (Am.) contribution
aportillar *va* to breach, break open, break down; *vr* to collapse, tumble down
aposentador *m* host; (mil.) billeter
aposentamiento *m* lodging; settling down, taking one's place
aposentar *va* to put up, to lodge; *vr* to take lodging; to take one's place
aposento *m* room; inn; lodging; box (*in ancient theaters*)
aposesionar *va* to give possession to; *vr* to take possession
aposición *f* (gram.) apposition
apositivo -va *adj & m* (gram.) appositive
apósito *m* (med.) external application
aposta or **apostadamente** *adv* (coll.) on purpose
apostadero *m* stand, station, post; (mil.) post; (naut.) naval station; (naut.) naval district
apostador -dora *mf* or **apostante** *mf* bettor
apostal *m* good spot for fishing
apostar *va* to post, to station; §77 *va* to bet, to wager; *vn* to bet; to compete; **apostar a que** to bet that; **apostar a** or **por** to bet on (*e.g., a horse*); *vr* to compete; **apostárselas a** or **con** (coll.) to compete with
apostasía *f* apostasy
apóstata *mf* apostate
apostatar *vn* apostatize
apostema *f* (path.) abscess, aposteme
apostemar *va* to form an abscess in; *vr* to abscess, become abscessed
apostematoso -sa *adj* apostematous
apostemero *m* (surg.) lancet
apostilla *f* note, comment
apostillar *va* to annotate (*a text*); *vr* to break out in pimples
apóstol *m* apostle; **apóstol de las gentes** or **los gentiles** (Bib.) Apostle of the Gentiles
apostolado *m* apostolate
apostólicamente *adv* apostolically; (coll.) poorly, unostentatiously
apostólico -ca *adj* apostolic or apostolical
apostrofar *va* to apostrophize; to scold, insult; to write with an apostrophe
apóstrofe *m & f* apostrophe (*addressed to absent person*); scolding, insult
apóstrofo *m* (gram.) apostrophe
apostura *f* gracefulness, neatness, spruceness; bearing
apotegma *m* apothegm (*short, instructive saying*)
apotema *f* (geom.) apothem
apoteósico -ca *adj* deific, deifying; glorifying
apoteosis *f* (*pl:* **-sis**) apotheosis
apotrerar *va* (Am.) to take (*horses*) to pasture
apoyabrazos *m* (*pl:* **-zos**) armrest
apoyador *m* bracket, support
apoyadura *f* flow of milk to the udders
apoyalibros *m* (*pl:* **-bros**) book end
apoyapié *m* or **apoyapiés** *m* (*pl:* **-piés**) (aut.) footrest
apoyar *va* to lean, rest, support; to hold up, prop; to back, abet; to droop (*the head; said of horses*); *vn* to lean, rest, be supported; *vr* to lean, rest, be supported; to depend, be based; **apoyarse en** to lean on; to rely on; to stress
apoyatura *f* (mus.) appoggiatura, grace note
apoyo *m* prop, support; backing, approval, aid, protection
apraxia *f* (path.) apraxia
apreciable *adj* appreciable; estimable; (coll.) nice, fine (*person*)
apreciación *f* appreciation, appraisal; smallest reading (*of an instrument or gauge*)
apreciadamente *adv* appreciatively
apreciador -dora *mf* appraiser
apreciar *va* to appreciate; to appraise, to estimate; to esteem
apreciativo -va *adj* appreciable (*e.g., error*)
aprecio *m* appreciation, esteem
aprehender *va* to apprehend, catch; to conceive, think; to seize, attach (*property*)
aprehensión *f* apprehension (*capture; fear*); (law) seizure, attachment
aprehensivo -va *adj* apprehensive (*perceptive; afraid, worried*)
aprehensor -sora *mf* captor
apremiadamente *adv* with insistence, urgently
apremiador -dora *adj* pressing, compelling; *mf* compeller
apremiante *adj* insistent, urgent
apremiar *va* to press, urge; to compel, force; to hurry; to harass, oppress; **apremiar** + *inf* to be urgent to + *inf*
apremio *m* pressure, constraint; compulsion; oppression; (law) judicial writ (*to compel payment or fulfilment*)
aprendedor -dora *adj* learning; *mf* learner
aprender *va & vn* to learn; **aprender a** + *inf* to learn to + *inf*
aprendiz -diza *mf* apprentice, beginner; **aprendiz de imprenta** printer's devil
aprendizaje *m* learning; apprenticeship; **hacer su aprendizaje** to serve one's apprenticeship; **pagar el aprendizaje** (coll.) to pay for one's inexperience
aprensador -dora *adj* pressing; *mf* presser
aprensar *va* to press; to crush, oppress
aprensión *f* apprehension (*fear, worry*); notion, strange idea; (coll.) shame
aprensivo -va *adj* apprehensive (*afraid, worried*)
apresador -dora *adj* seizing; *mf* captor
apresamiento *m* seizing; clutch, hold; capture
apresar *va* to seize, grasp; to capture, take prisoner
apreso -sa *adj* rooted, well rooted
aprestador *m* primer (*for paint*)
aprestar *va* to prepare, make ready; to prime (*for painting*); to size; *vr* to prepare, get ready; **aprestarse a** + *inf* to prepare to + *inf*, to get ready + *inf*
apresto *m* preparation, readiness; outfit, equipment; priming; size, sizing
apresuración *f* haste, hastening
apresuradamente *adv* hastily
apresuramiento *m* haste, hastiness, hastening
apresurar *va & vr* to hasten, hurry; **apresurarse a** + *inf* to hasten to + *inf*, to hurry to + *inf*
apretadamente *adv* hard, tight; tightly, closely
apretadera *f* strap, rope (*for tying, e.g., a trunk*); **apretaderas** *fpl* (coll.) insistence, pressure
apretadero *m* truss
apretadizo -za *adj* easily compressed
apretado -da *adj* tight, compact; difficult, dangerous; (coll.) stingy; close, intimate; strict; dense, thick; (coll.) dangerously ill
apretador *m* tightener; corset; hair net
apretadura *f* tightening; squeezing; compression
apretar §18 *va* to tighten; to squeeze; to contract; to fit tight, to pinch; to press (*e.g., a button*); to hold tight, to hug; to importune, to hurry; to pursue closely, to harass; to treat harshly; to beset, to distress, to afflict; to dun; to make more severe; to clench (*the fists, the teeth*); to shake (*hands*); *vn* to get worse; to pinch; to insist; **¡aprieta!** (coll.) get out!, nonsense!; **apretar a correr** (coll.) to strike out on a run; **apretar con** (coll.) to close in on, to attack; *vr* to narrow, be compressed; to grieve, be distressed; to skimp; (Am.) to gorge
apretazón *f* (Am.) var. of **apretadura**
apretón *m* sudden pressure; quick hug; struggle, conflict; dash, short run; **apretón de manos** handshake
apretujar *va* (coll.) to jam, to press hard, to keep on pressing or squeezing; *vr* (coll.) to jam, to be packed in
apretujón *m* (coll.) hard squeeze
apretura *f* jam, crush; fix; distress, tightness, constriction; difficulty, trouble; need, want

aprietapapeles *m* (*pl:* **-les**) paper finger (*of typewriter*)
aprietarropa *m* clothespin
aprietatuercas *m* (*pl:* **-cas**) wrench; spintight, nut-driver
apriete *m* tightening
aprieto *m* jam, crush; fix; **poner en aprieto** to put pressure on, to put on the spot; **sacar de un aprieto** to get (*someone*) out of a jam
aprioridad *f* (philos.) apriority
apriorismo *m* (philos.) apriorism
apriorístico -ca *adj* aprioristic
aprisa *adv* fast, quickly, hurriedly
apriscar §86 *va* to gather (*sheep*) into the fold
aprisco *m* sheepfold; place of refuge
aprisionar *va* to imprison; to shackle; to tie, bind
aproar *vn* (naut.) to turn the prow
aprobación *f* approbation, approval; pass, passing grade
aprobado -da *adj* excellent, estimable; *m* pass (*mark of passing an examination*)
aprobante *adj* approving
aprobar §77 *va* to approve; to pass (*a student; an examination; a course*); *vn* to approve; to pass
aproches *mpl* access, approach; neighborhood; (mil.) approaches
aprontamiento *m* quick preparation, ready delivery
aprontar *va* to prepare quickly, to hand over without delay, to have ready
apropiable *adj* appropriable
apropiación *f* giving, gift; fitting, adaptation; appropriation
apropiado -da *adj* appropriate, proper, fitting
apropiar *va* to give, to give possession of; to fit, adapt, apply; *vr* to appropriate; **apropiarse de una cosa** or **apropiarse una cosa** to appropriate something
apropincuar *vr* (hum.) to approach, come near
apropósito *m* (theat.) occasional play
aprovechable *adj* available, usable
aprovechado -da *adj* saving, thrifty; miserly, stingy; diligent, studious, industrious; well-spent (*said of time*); *m* opportunist
aprovechamiento *m* use; profit, advantage; progress; improvement; progress in school; harnessing (*e.g., of waterfalls*)
aprovechar *va* to make use of, benefit from, profit by, take advantage of; to harness (*e.g., a waterfall*); *vn* to be useful, to avail; to progress, to improve; *vr* **aprovecharse de** to avail oneself of, to take advantage of
aprovisionador *m* supplier
aprovisionamiento *m* supplying; supplies, supply
aprovisionar *va* to supply, furnish, provision
aproximación *f* nearness, closeness; approximation; approach; rapprochement; consolation prize (*in a lottery*); **aproximación controlada desde tierra** (aer.) ground-controlled approach
aproximado -da *adj* approximate
aproximar *va* to bring near or nearer; to approximate; *vr* to come near or nearer; to approximate
aproximativo -va *adj* approximate
ápside *m* (astr.) apsis
apsiquia *f* (path.) apsychia
áptero -ra *adj* apterous
aptitud *f* aptitude; suitability
apto -ta *adj* apt; suitable; **apto para** + *inf* quick to + *inf;* suitable for + *ger*
apuesto -ta *adj* elegant, bedecked, spruce; *f* bet, wager
Apuleyo *m* Apuleius
apulgarar *vn* to press the or one's thumb; *vr* (coll.) to spot with mildew (*said of clean wash*)
apulso *m* (astr.) appulse; (opt.) contact of heavenly body with vertical wire of reticle
apunar *vr* (Am.) to suffer from mountain sickness
apuntación *f* pointing, aiming; note, annotation; scoring; (mus.) notation; composition of music; **apuntaciones** *fpl* (mus.) transcription for voice
apuntado -da *adj* pointed, sharp; (her.) counterpointed; (Am.) tipsy
apuntador *m* (theat.) prompter
apuntalamiento *m* prop, propping, underpinning
apuntalar *va* to prop, prop up, underpin
apuntamiento *m* pointing, aiming; note; sketch, outline; judicial report
apuntar *va* to point at; to point out, to mark; to note, to take note of; to aim; to aim at; to sharpen; to stitch; to darn; to patch; to fasten up, to fasten temporarily; to prompt (*a student in an examination*); to correct, to set aright; to put up, to stake; to sketch, to outline; (theat.) to prompt; *vn* to begin to appear; to dawn; to hint; **apuntar y no dar** (coll.) to fail to come through; *vr* to begin to sour (*said of wine*); (coll.) to get tipsy; to register, to sign up
apunte *m* note; sketch; prompter; promptbook; stake; rascal
apuntillar *va* (taur.) to finish off with the dagger
apuñadar *va* (prov.) to punch with the fist
apuñalado -da *adj* dagger-shaped
apuñalar *va* to stab
apuñar *va* to seize with the fist; to punch with the fist; *vn* to tighten one's hand
apuñear or **apuñetear** *va* (coll.) to punch with the fist
apuracabos *m* (*pl:* **-bos**) save-all (*candlestick in which candle burns to very end*)
apuración *f* purification; verification; consumption; annoyance, worry; hurry
apuradamente *adv* (coll.) precisely, punctually; (coll.) carefully; (coll.) with difficulty
apurado -da *adj* needy, hard up; hard, dangerous; (coll.) hurried, rushed
apurador -dora *adj* purifying, refining; exhausting; *m* save-all (*candlestick in which candle burns to very end*)
apuramiento *m* draining; verification, check
apuranieves *m* (*pl:* **-ves**) (orn.) wagtail
apurar *va* to purify, refine; to verify, clarify, clear up; to carry out, finish; to exhaust, drain, use up; to annoy; to hurry, press; *vr* to grieve, worry, fret; (Am.) to hurry, hasten; **apurarse por** + *inf* to strive to + *inf*
apure *m* (min.) refining, refinement
apurismado -da *adj* (Am.) weak, sickly
apuro *m* need, want, fix; grief, sorrow, affliction; (Am.) haste, urgency; **estar en el mayor apuro** to be in a bad fix, to be up against it, to be in dire straits
aquejar *va* to grieve, afflict, weary; to harass; *vr* to hurry; to complain
aquejoso -sa *adj* sad, afflicted, grieved
aquel, aquella *adj dem* (*pl:* **aquellos, aquellas**) that, that . . . yonder
aquél, aquélla *pron dem* (*pl:* **aquéllos, aquéllas**) that one, that one yonder; the one; the former; the first (*of three*); *m* (coll.) charm, appeal
aquelarre *m* witches' Sabbath
aquello *pron dem neut* that; that thing, that matter
aquende *adv* on this side; *prep* on this side of; **de aquende** on this side of
aquénico -ca *adj* achenial
aquenio *m* (bot.) achene
aqueo -a *adj & mf* Achaean
aquerenciar *vr* to become fond; **aquerenciarse a** to become fond of, to become attached to
Aqueronte *m* (myth.) Acheron
aquí *adv* here; **de aquí** from here; hence; **de aquí a** in, within; **de aquí en adelante** from now on; **de aquí que** hence; **por aquí** hereabouts; this way; **aquí dentro** in here
aquiescencia *f* acquiescence
aquiescente *adj* acquiescent
aquietar *va* to quiet, calm, pacify; *vr* to quiet down, become calm
aquilatamiento *m* assay; weighing, estimation, checking
aquilatar *va* to assay; to weigh the merit of, to check, to appreciate
aquilea *f* (bot.) yarrow
Aquiles *m* (myth.) Achilles
aquilino -na *adj* (poet.) aquiline
aquilón *m* north wind; north
aquilonal *adj* north-wind; northern; (pertaining to) winter

aquillado -da *adj* keel-shaped, keellike; wide-keeled
Aquisgrán *m* Aachen, Aix-la-Chapelle
aquistar *va* to get, acquire, win
Aquitania *f* Aquitaine
aquitánico -ca *adj* Aquitanian
aquitano -na *adj & mf* Aquitanian
aquivo -va *adj & mf* var. of **aqueo**
ara *f* altar; altar slab; communion table; **en aras de** in honor of; *m* (orn.) macaw
árabe *adj* Arab, Arabic; (arch.) Moresque; *mf* Arab; *m* Arabic (*language*)
arabesco -ca *adj* Arabic; (f.a.) arabesque; *m* (f.a.) arabesque
Arabia, la Arabia; **la Arabia Saudita** Saudi Arabia
arábico -ca *adj* Arabic
arábigo -ga *adj* Arabian, Arabic; *m* Arabic (*language*); **estar en arábigo** (coll.) to be Greek (*i.e., hard to understand*); **hablar en arábigo** (coll.) to talk gibberish
arabismo *m* Arabism
arabista *mf* Arabist
arabizar §76 *va* to Arabize, to make Arabic
arable *adj* arable
aracanga *m* (orn.) macaw
aráceo -a *adj* (bot.) araceous
Aracne *f* (myth.) Arachne
arácnido -da *adj* (zool.) arachnid, arachnidan; *m* (zool.) arachnid
aracnoides *m* (*pl:* **-des**) (anat.) arachnoid
arada *f* plowed land; plowing; day's plowing by a yoke of oxen
arado *m* plow; plowshare
arador *m* plowman; (ent.) itch mite
aradura *f* plowing
Aragón *m* Aragon (*river, region, and former kingdom of Spain*)
aragonés -nesa *adj & mf* Aragonese; *m* Aragonese (*dialect*)
aragonesismo *m* Aragonese expression or idiom
aragonita *f* or **aragonito** *m* (mineral.) aragonite
araguato *m* (zool.) ursine howler
aralia *f* (bot. & pharm.) aralia; (bot.) spikenard
araliáceo -a *adj* (bot.) araliaceous
aramaico -ca *adj & m* Aramaic (*language*)
arambel *m* hangings; rag, shred
arameo -a *adj* Aramaean; Aramaic; *mf* Aramaean; *m* Aramaic (*language*)
aramio *m* fallow land, fallow field
arana *f* trick, cheat
arancel *m* tariff
arancelario -ria *adj* (pertaining to) tariff, customs
arandanedo *m* bilberry patch; cranberry bog
arándano *m* (bot.) bilberry, whortleberry; **arándano agrio** (bot.) cranberry; **arándano encarnado** (bot.) mountain cranberry, cowberry
arandela *f* (mach.) washer; bobèche, disk to catch drippings of candle; guard on handle of lance; candle stand; (naut.) half-port
arandillo *m* (orn.) marsh warbler
aranero -ra *adj* cheating, tricky, swindling; *mf* cheat, trickster, swindler
araña *f* (ent. & mach.) spider; crowfoot (*to suspend awnings, etc.*); (ichth.) stingbull, greater weever; (bot.) love-in-a-mist; chandelier; (coll.) thrifty, calculating person; whore; **araña de mar** (zool.) spider crab; **araña de sobremesa** candelabrum; **araña epeira** (ent.) cross spider
arañada *f* scratch
arañador -dora *adj* scratching; *mf* scratcher; burler; scraper (*penurious saver; poor fiddler*); *m* burling iron
arañamiento *m* scratching, scratch; scraping
arañar *m* scratch; **arañar de la aguja** needle scratch; *va* to scratch; to scrape; (coll.) to scrape together; *vr* to scratch
arañazo *m* scratch (*with fingernail, pin, etc.*)
arañero -ra *adj* wild, haggard (*said of birds*)
araño *m* scratching, scratch
arañuela *f* (bot.) love-in-a-mist
arañuelo *m* (ent.) red spider; (ent.) spider grub; bird net
aráquida *f* peanut
arar *m* (bot.) sandarac tree; *va* to plow
arasá *m* (Am.) guava (*tree and fruit*)
araucanista *mf* Araucanist (*authority on Araucanian language and customs*)
araucano -na *adj* Araucanian; *mf* Araucanian, Araucan; *m* Araucanian or Araucan (*language*)
araucaria *f* (bot.) araucaria, Norfolk Island pine
arbalestrilla *f* (math.) arbalest, cross-staff
arbellón *m* sewer, drain, gutter
arbitrable *adj* arbitrable
arbitrador -dora *adj* arbitrating; *m* arbitrator; *f* arbitress
arbitraje *m* arbitration, arbitrage; **arbitraje de cambio** arbitrage of exchange
arbitral *adj* arbitral
arbitramento or **arbitramiento** *m* arbitrament
arbitrar *va* to arbitrate; to referee; (sport) to umpire; to contrive, bring together, assemble; *vn* to arbitrate; to referee; (sport) to umpire; *vr* to manage well; (coll.) to manage to get along well
arbitrariedad *f* abuse, outrage, arbitrary act
arbitrario -ria *adj* arbitrary
arbitrio *m* free will; means, ways, expedient; adjudication; **arbitrios** *mpl* excise taxes
arbitrista *mf* cure-all politician, wild-eyed dreamer
árbitro -tra *adj* independent, autonomous; *m* arbiter; (sport) umpire; *f* arbitress
árbol *m* tree; newel (*of winding stairs*); body (*of shirt*); (mach.) shaft, arbor, axle, spindle; (naut.) mast; (print.) shank; **árbol de Judas** or **de Judea** (bot.) Judas tree; **árbol de la cera** (bot.) wax myrtle (*Myrica cerifera*); (bot.) wax tree (*Rhus verniciflus; Myrica cerifera*); (bot.) wax palm (*Ceroxylon andicolum*); **árbol de la ciencia del bien y del mal** (Bib.) tree of knowledge of good and evil; **árbol del alcanfor** (bot.) camphor tree; **árbol de la leche** (bot.) cow tree; **árbol del amor** (bot.) Judas tree; **árbol de las calabazas** (bot.) calabash tree; **árbol de la vida** (Bib. & bot.) tree of life; (anat.) arbor vitae; **árbol del caucho** (bot.) rubber plant; **árbol del cielo** (bot.) tree of heaven; **árbol del diablo** (bot.) sandbox tree; **árbol de levas** (mach.) camshaft; **árbol del pan** (bot.) breadfruit, breadfruit tree; **árbol del paraíso** (bot.) China tree; **árbol del tomate** (bot.) tomato tree; **árbol del viajero** (bot.) traveler's tree; **árbol de mando** (mach.) drive shaft; **árbol de María** (bot.) calaba; **árbol de Navidad** Christmas tree; **árbol de pie** seedling; **árbol de sombra** shade tree; **árbol de vaca** (bot.) cow tree; **árbol frutal** fruit tree; **árbol genealógico** genealogical tree, family tree; **árbol motor** (mach.) drive shaft
arbolado -da *adj* wooded; high (*seas*); *m* woodland
arboladura *f* (naut.) masts and spars
arbolar *va* to hoist; to raise, set up; (naut.) to mast (*a ship*); *vr* to rear on the hind feet
arbolario -ria *adj & mf* (coll.) scatterbrain
arboleda *f* grove
arboledo *m* woodland
arbolejo *m* little tree
arbolete *m* little tree; branch on which to fasten lime twigs (*to catch birds*)
arbolillo *m* little tree; side of a blast furnace
arbolista *mf* arborist
arbollón *m* sewer, drain
arborecer §34 *vn* to grow, develop (*said of trees*)
arbóreo -a *adj* arboreal
arborescencia *f* arborescence
arborescente *adj* arborescent
arboricultor *m* arboriculturist
arboricultura *f* arboriculture
arboriforme *adj* arboriform
arborización *f* (anat. & mineral.) arborization
arborizado -da *adj* treelike
arbotante *m* (arch.) flying buttress
arbustivo -va *adj* shrubby
arbusto *m* (bot.) shrub
arca *f* chest, coffer; tank, reservoir; ark; tempering oven; **arcas** *fpl* coffers (*e.g., of the State*); hollow below the ribs; **arca cerrada**

pure heart of a maiden; quiet person; unknown quantity (*person*); **arca de agua** water tower; **arca de la alianza** (Bib.) ark of the covenant; **arca de Noé** Noah's ark; (coll.) lumber room; (coll.) house in which all sorts and conditions of people live
arcabucear *va* to shoot with a harquebus, to kill with a harquebusade
arcabucería *f* troop of harquebusiers; harquebuses; harquebusade; harquebus factory
arcabucero *m* harquebusier; harquebus maker
arcabuco *m* craggy thicket
arcabuz *m* (*pl:* **-buces**) harquebus
arcabuzazo *m* harquebus shot or wound
arcacil *m* (bot.) artichoke
arcada *f* (arch.) arcade; archway; (mus.) stroke of bow; **arcadas** *fpl* retching
árcade *adj & mf* Arcadian
Arcadia, la Arcadia
arcádico -ca *adj* (fig.) Arcadian (*simple, rural*)
arcadio -dia *adj & mf* Arcadian
arcaduz *m* (*pl:* **-duces**) *m* pipe, conduit; bucket; means, way
arcaico -ca *adj* archaic; (geol.) Archeozoic
arcaísmo *m* archaism
arcaísta *mf* archaist
arcaizante *adj* obsolescent; using obsolescent forms
arcaizar §97 *va & vn* to archaize
arcángel *m* archangel
arcangélico -ca *adj* archangelic
arcano -na *adj* arcane, hidden, secret; *m* arcanum
arcar §86 *va* to arch; to beat (*wool*)
arce *m* (bot.) maple; **arce blanco** (bot.) sycamore; **arce del azúcar** (bot.) sugar maple
arcedianato *m* archdeaconry
arcediano *m* archdeacon
arcedo *m* maple grove
arcén *m* border, edge, brim; curbstone (*of well*)
arcilla *f* clay; **arcilla figulina** potter's clay, argil
arcillar *va* to clay; (agr.) to clay
arcilloso -sa *adj* clayey
arciprestazgo *m* archpriesthood
arcipreste *m* archpriest
arco *m* (geom. & elec.) arc; (anat. & arch.) arch; bow; hoop; (sport) goal post; **arco abocinado** splayed arch; **arco adintelado** horizontal or straight arch; **arco apainelado** basket-handle arch; **arco arábigo** Moorish arch; **arco botarete** (arch.) flying buttress; **arco carpanel** basket-handle arch; **arco cigomático** (anat.) zygomatic arch; **arco conopial** ogee arch; **arco de herradura** horseshoe arch; **arco de medio punto** semicircular arch; **arco de todo punto** Gothic arch; **arco de triunfo** triumphal arch; memorial arch; **arco elíptico** elliptical arch; **arco en rampa** rampant arch; **arco escarzano** segmental arch; **arco iris** rainbow; **arco ojival** pointed arch; **arco peraltado** stilted arch; **arco por tranquil** rampant arch; **arco trebolado** trefoil arch; **arco triunfal** triumphal arch; memorial arch
arcón *m* bin, bunker; large chest
arcosa *f* (geol.) arkose
archi- *prefix* (coll.) very, extremely, e.g., **archiconocido** extremely well-known; **archiridículo** very silly
archi *adj* (coll.) super (*excellent, superfine*)
archicofradía *f* privileged brotherhood
archidiácono *m* archdeacon
archidiócesis *f* (*pl:* **-sis**) var. of **arquidiócesis**
archiducado *m* archduchy
archiducal *adj* archducal
archiduque *m* archduke
archiduquesa *f* archduchess
archienemigo *m* archenemy (*chief enemy*)
archilaúd *m* (mus.) large lute
archimillonario -ria *adj & mf* multimillionaire
archipámpano *m* (hum.) self-styled or imaginary tycoon
archipiélago *m* archipelago; (coll.) labyrinth, entanglement; (*cap.*) *m* Aegean Sea, Archipelago; **archipiélago de Francisco José** Franz Josef Land; **archipiélago de Joló** or **de Sulú** Sulu Archipelago; **archipiélago Malayo** Malay Archipelago
archivador -dora *adj* filing; *mf* file clerk; *m* filing cabinet; letter file
archivar *va* to file; to file away; to deposit in the archives; (coll.) to hide away
archivero *m* archivist; city clerk
archivista *m* archivist
archivo *m* archives; file, files; filing; public records; (fig.) model (*e.g., of perfection*); (Am.) office
archivolta *f* (arch.) archivolt
arda *f* (zool.) squirrel
ardalear *vn* to fail to fill out (*said of bunches of grapes*)
árdea *f* var. of **alcaraván**
ardeida *f* (orn.) heron
ardentía *f* heartburn; (naut.) phosphorescence (*of water*)
ardentísimo -ma *adj super* very or most ardent; very or most passionate; bright red
arder *va* to burn; (Am.) to itch; *vn* to burn, to blaze; (poet.) to shine, flash; **estar que arde** to be coming to a head, to be near the breaking point; **arder de** or **en** to burn with (*e.g., love, hate*); **arder en** to be ablaze with (*e.g., war*); **arder por** + *inf* to be burning to + *inf;* **arder sin llamas** to smolder; *vr* to burn; to burn up (*said of grain in hot, dry weather*)
ardero *m* squirrel dog
ardid *m* trick, artifice, ruse
ardido -da *adj* spoiled, burnt-up (*said of grain, olives, etc.*); bold, intrepid; (Am.) angry
ardiendo *adj invar* burning, hot
ardiente *adj* ardent, burning; passionate, fiery; feverish; red
ardilla *f* (zool.) squirrel; **andar como una ardilla** to be always on the go, to flit about; **ardilla de tierra** (zool.) gopher; **ardilla gris** (zool.) gray squirrel; **ardilla ladradora** (zool.) prairie dog; **ardilla listada** (zool.) chipmunk; **ardilla voladora** (zool.) flying squirrel
ardillón *m* (zool.) gopher (*Spermophilus*)
ardimiento *m* burning; intrepidity, courage
ardiondo -da *adj* intrepid, courageous
ardite *m* old Spanish coin of little value; **no me importa un ardite** (coll.) I don't care a hang; **no valer un ardite** (coll.) to be not worth a continental
ardor *m* ardor, heat, excitement, vehemence; zeal, eagerness; intrepidity, courage, dash
ardoroso -sa *adj* burning, fiery, enthusiastic; restive, balky
arduidad *f* arduousness
arduo -dua *adj* arduous, hard
área *f* area; are (*surface measure*); **área de la libra esterlina** sterling block
areca *f* (bot.) areca (*palm and nut*)
arefacción *f* drying
arel *m* large sieve (*for grain*)
arelar *va* to sieve or sift (*grain*)
arena *f* sand; grit, grindings; arena; **arenas** *fpl* arena; (path.) stones (*in bladder*); **arena de estufa** or **arena seca** (found.) dry sand; **arena movediza** quicksand; **arena verde** (found.) green sand
arenáceo -a *adj* arenaceous
arenación *f* sanding; mixing sand and lime; (med.) arenation
arenal *m* sandy ground, sand pit; desert; quicksand
arenalejo *m* small sandy spot
arenar *va* to spread sand over; to sand, to rub or polish with sand; *vn* to become covered with sand; (naut.) to run aground on sand
arenario -ria *adj* (living in) sand; *f* (bot.) sandwort
arencar §86 *va* to cure (*sardines*) like herring
arenero -ra *adj* (for) sand; *mf* sand dealer; *m* (rail.) sandbox; (taur.) boy who spreads and smooths sand after each bullfight
arenga *f* harangue; (coll.) scolding
arengador -dora *mf* haranguer; (coll.) scold
arengar §59 *va & vn* to harangue; (coll.) to scold
arenilla *f* fine sand used to dry wet ink, pounce; **arenillas** *fpl* granulated saltpeter; (path.) stones (*in bladder*)

arenillero *m* var. of **salvadera**
arenisco -ca *adj* sandy, gritty; (pertaining to) sand; *f* (mineral.) sandstone; **arenisca verde** greensand
arenoso -sa *adj* sandy
arenque *m* (ichth.) herring; **arenque de ojos grandes** (ichth.) walleyed herring
arenquero -ra *mf* herring vendor; *f* herring net; (slang) coarse, shameless woman
aréola *f* (anat., bot., path. & zool.) areola
areolar *adj* areolar
areometría *f* hydrometry
areométrico -ca *adj* hydrometric
areómetro *m* areometer, hydrometer
Areópago *m* Areopagus
areóstilo *m* (arch.) areostyle
arepa *f* (Am.) corn griddle cake
Ares *m* (myth.) Ares
arestín *m* (vet.) thrush
arete *m* eardrop, earring
Aretusa *f* (myth.) Arethusa
arfada *f* (naut.) pitching
arfar *vn* (naut.) to pitch
argadijo or **argadillo** *m* reel, bobbin; (coll.) blustering fellow
argado *m* prank, trick
argal *m* wine stone
argala *f* (orn.) adjutant, adjutant bird
argalí *m* (*pl:* **-líes**) (zool.) argali
argalia *f* (surg.) catheter
argallera *f* croze, crozing saw
argamandel *m* rag, tatter
argamandijo *m* (coll.) set of small tools or utensils
argamasa *f* mortar; **argamasa hidráulica** hydraulic mortar
argamasar *va* to mix (*mortar*); to mortar, to plaster; *vn* to make mortar
argamasilla *f* fine mortar
argamasón *m* large dry piece of mortar
argán *m* (bot.) argan tree; argan (*fruit of argan tree*); (mus.) Arab organ
árgana *f* (mach.) crane; wicker basket for packsaddles
arganeo *m* (naut.) anchor ring
argavieso *m* thunderstorm
argayar *v impers* to be a landslide
argayo *m* landslide; **argayo de nieve** (prov.) avalanche
argel *adj* with right hind foot white (*said of a horse*); (coll.) wretched, unfortunate; (*cap.*) *f* Algiers
Argelia *f* Algeria
argelino -na *adj & mf* Algerian
argemone *f* (bot.) argemone, prickly poppy; **argemone mejicana** (bot.) Mexican poppy
argén *m* (her.) argent
argentado -da *adj* silver-plated; silvery; slashed (*said of shoes*)
argentán *m* German silver
argentar *va* to silver; to trim with silver; to give a silver finish to; (fig.) to silver; *vr* (fig.) to silver
argentario *m* silversmith; master of the mint
argénteo -a *adj* silvery; silver-plated
argentería *f* embroidery of silver or gold
argentero *m* silversmith
argentífero -ra *adj* argentiferous
argentina *f* & **Argentina, la** see **argentino**
argentinismo *m* Argentinism
argentinizar §76 *va* to Argentinize; *vr* to become Argentinized
argentino -na *adj* argentine, silvery; Argentine; *mf* Argentine, Argentinean; *m* argentino (*coin*); *f* (mineral.) argentine; (bot.) silverweed; **la Argentina** Argentina, the Argentine
argentista *m* freesilverite
argento *m* (poet.) argent, silver; **argento vivo** quicksilver; **argento vivo sublimado** (chem.) corrosive sublimate
argentoso -sa *adj* mixed with silver
argila or **argilla** *f* var. of **arcilla**
argiloso -sa *adj* var. of **arcilloso**
argirol *m* argyrol
argivo -va *adj & mf* Argive
argo *m* (chem.) argon
argólico -ca *adj* Argolic
Argólida or **Argólide, la** Argolis
argolla *f* large iron ring; staple; croquet (*game*); ring (*put in the snout of an animal*)
argolleta *f* little iron ring
argoma *f* (bot.) furze, gorse
argón *m* (chem.) argon
argonauta *m* (myth.) Argonaut; (zool.) argonaut, paper nautilus
argonáutico -ca *adj* (myth.) Argonautic
Argos *f* Argos (*ancient Greek town*); (myth.) Argo (*ship*); (astr.) Argo; *m* (myth.) Argus (*monster*); (*l.c.*) *m* Argus (*watchful person*); **ser un argos, estar hecho un argos** to be Argus-eyed
argucia *f* subtlety, sophistry; trick, deceit
argüe *m* capstan
arguellar *vr* (dial.) to become emaciated, to lose weight
arguello *m* (dial.) emaciation, loss of weight
árguenas or **árgueñas** *fpl* handbarrow; saddlebags
argüir §21 *va* to argue (*to indicate, to prove; to accuse*); *vn* to argue; **argüir contra** to argue against
argumentación *f* argumentation
argumentador -dora *adj* argumentative; *mf* arguer
argumental *adj* of the argument
argumentar *va & vn* to argue
argumentativo -va *adj* argumentative (*containing argument*)
argumentista *mf* arguer
argumento *m* argument; **argumento ontológico** (philos.) ontological argument
aria *f* see **ario**
Ariadna *f* (myth.) Ariadne
aricado *m* light plowing, cross harrowing
aricar §86 *va* to plow lightly, to harrow crosswise
aridecer §34 *va* to make dry or arid; *vn & vr* to become dry or arid
aridez *f* aridity, dryness
árido -da *adj* arid; (fig.) dry (*dull, boring*); **áridos** *mpl* dry commodities
Aries *m* (astr.) Aries
arieta *f* (mus.) arietta, short air
ariete *m* battering ram; **ariete hidráulico** hydraulic ram
arietino -na *adj* like a ram's head
arijo -ja *adj* easily tilled or cultivated
arilado -da *adj* (bot.) arillate, ariled
arilo *m* (bot.) aril
arillo *m* earring; frame for neck stock (*of clerics*)
arimez *m* projection (*in a building*)
arincar §86 *vr* (Am.) to be or become constipated
ario -ria *adj & mf* Aryan; *f* (mus.) aria
arísaro *m* (bot.) wake-robin
arisblanco -ca *adj* white-bearded (*said of wheat*)
arisco -ca *adj* churlish, surly, shy; wicked, vicious
arisema *f* (bot.) Indian turnip, jack-in-the-pulpit
arisnegro -gra or **arisprieto -ta** *adj* black-bearded (*said of wheat*)
arista *f* (arch.) arris; (bot.) awn; (geom.) edge; **arista de encuentro** (arch.) groin
aristado -da *adj* (bot.) bearded, awned
aristarco *m* Aristarch, severe critic
Arístides *m* Aristides
aristocracia *f* aristocracy
aristócrata *mf* aristocrat
aristocrático -ca *adj* aristocratic
aristocratizar §76 *va* to give aristocratic form to (*the government*); to infuse with aristocratic ideas; *vn* to act aristocratically; *vr* to become aristocratic; to become an aristocrat
Aristófanes *m* Aristophanes
aristofánico -ca *adj* Aristophanic; *m* (rhet.) Aristophanic
aristoloquia *f* (bot.) birthwort
aristón *m* (arch.) edge, corner; (arch.) groin rib; (mus.) hand organ
aristoso -sa *adj* bearded, many-bearded (*said of wheat*)
Aristóteles *m* Aristotle
aristotélico -ca *adj & mf* Aristotelian
aristotelismo *m* Aristotelianism

aritmético -ca *adj* arithmetical; *mf* arithmetician; *f* arithmetic
aritmo -ma *adj* arrhythmic
aritmomanía *f* arithmomania
aritmómetro *m* arithmometer
arjorán *m* (bot.) Judas tree
arlequín *m* harlequin; harlequin ice cream, Neapolitan ice cream; **arlequín de Cayena** (ent.) harlequin beetle; (*cap.*) *m* Harlequin
arlequina *f* harlequina; burlesque dance; music for such a dance
arlequinada *f* harlequinade
arlequinesco -ca *adj* harlequin, harlequinesque
arlo *m* (bot.) barberry; fruit hung up for keeping
arlota *f* var. of **alrota**
arma *f* arm, weapon; branch of the service (*army, navy, air force*); **¡a las armas!** to arms!; **alzarse en armas** to rise up, rebel; **jugar a las armas** to fence; **llevar las armas** to bear arms; **pasar por las armas** to execute by shooting; **presentar armas** to present arms; **rendir las armas** to lay down one's arms; **sobre las armas** under arms; **tocar al arma** or **tocar arma** to sound the call to arms; **tomar (las) armas** to take up arms; **arma al hombro** (mil.) right shoulder arms; **arma atómica** atomic weapon; **arma blanca** steel blade (*sword*); **arma corta** pistol; **arma de fuego** firearm; **arma negra** foil; **armas parlantes** (her.) canting arms, rebus
armada *f* see **armado**
armadera *f* (naut.) main timber
armadía *f* raft, float
armadija *f* or **armadijo** *m* trap, snare
armadillo *m* (zool.) armadillo; **armadillo de tres fajas** (zool.) three-banded armadillo
armado -da *adj* armed; reinforced (*concrete*); (her.) armed; *m* man in armor in processions of Holy Week; *f* fleet, armada; navy; **Armada Invencible** Invincible Armada
armador -dora *adj* shipbuilding; *m* shipowner, outfitter; privateer; jacket
armadura *f* armature, armor; frame, framework, support; skeleton; guard (*around a tree*); (elec.) armature (*of condenser, magnet, motor, etc.*); (mach.) assembly; (mus.) key signature; reinforcement (*of concrete*); **armadura de pendolón** king truss
armaga *f* (bot.) rue
Armagedón *m* (Bib.) Armageddon
armajal *m* marsh, moor, fen
armajo *m* (bot.) glasswort
armamentario *m* medical arsensal
armamentismo *m* military preparedness
armamentista *adj* (pertaining to) armament; militarist; *mf* advocate of military preparedness; arms dealer
armamento *m* armament
armar *va* to arm; to load (*a weapon*); to fix (*a bayonet*); to mount, assemble, put together, set, adjust; to build, establish; to equip; to suit, fit, become; to reinforce (*e.g., concrete*); (coll.) to cause, start, stir up, cook up; (coll.) to arrange, prepare; (naut.) to fit out, to commission; **armar caballero** to knight; **armarla** (coll.) to start a row; (coll.) to cheat; *vn* to suit, be becoming; *vr* to arm, to arm oneself; to get ready; to become erect; (coll.) to start, break out; (Am.) to balk, be balky; (Am.) to make a killing; **armarse con** (coll.) to hold on to unfairly, to refuse to give up
armario *m* closet, wardrobe; **armario de luna** wardrobe with mirror in door; **armario frigorífico** refrigerator
armatoste *m* hulk (*crude, heavy machine or piece of furniture; fat, clumsy person*)
armazón *f* frame, framework; assemblage; skeleton; (aer.) chassis; (Am.) shelving
armella *f* screw eye, eyebolt
armelluela *f* little screw eye
armenio -nia *adj & mf* Armenian; *m* Armenian (*language*); (*cap.*) *f* Armenia
armería *f* arms museum; armory (*manufactory; art of armorer*); arms shop; (her.) armory
armero *m* armorer, gunsmith; rack or stand for arms, armrack
armífero -ra *adj* warlike
armígero -ra *adj* (poet.) bearing arms; warlike; *m* armor-bearer
armilar *adj* armillary
armilla *f* (arch.) astragal (*molding*); (arch.) surbase
arminianismo *m* Arminianism
arminiano -na *adj & mf* Arminian
Arminio *m* Arminius
armiñado -da *adj* ermine; ermined
armiño *m* (zool. & her.) ermine; **armiño de cola larga** (zool.) long-tailed weasel
armipotente *adj* (poet.) mighty in war
armisonante *adj* (poet.) resounding with arms
armisticio *m* armistice
armón *m* (arti.) limber
armonía *f* harmony
armónico -ca *adj & m* (mus. & phys.) harmonic; *f* (mus.) harmonica; **armónica de boca** (mus.) mouth organ
armonio *m* (mus.) harmonium
armonioso -sa *adj* harmonious
armonización *f* harmonization
armonizar §76 *va & vn* to harmonize
armuelle *m* (bot.) orach
arna *f* beehive
arnacho *m* (bot.) restharrow
Arnaldo *m* Arnold
arnaúte *adj & mf* (archaic) Albanian
arnés *m* armor, coat of mail; harness; **arneses** *mpl* harness, trappings; outfit, equipment; accessories
árnica *f* (bot. & pharm.) arnica
aro *m* hoop; rim; (croquet) hoop, wicket; (bot.) cuckoopint; **entrar por el aro** (coll.) to have to go ahead against one's will; **aro de émbolo** piston ring; **aro de Etiopía** (bot.) arum, arum lily, calla lily
aroma *f* aroma (*flower*); *m* aroma, fragrance; aromatic gum, herb, balm, or wood
aromaticidad *f* aromacity
aromático -ca *adj* aromatic; *m* (chem. & med.) aromatic; *f* (bot.) aromatic
aromatización *f* aromatization
aromatizar §76 *va* to aromatize; to flavor
aromo *m* (bot.) aroma, huisache (*tree*)
aromoso -sa *adj* aromatic
arón *m* (bot.) cuckoopint; (*cap.*) *m* (Bib.) Aaron
arpa *f* (mus.) harp; **arpa eolia** aeolian harp
arpado -da *adj* toothed, jagged; (poet.) singing (*said of birds*)
arpadura *f* scratch
arpar *va* to tear, rend, claw, scratch
arpegio *m* (mus.) arpeggio
arpella *f* (orn.) marsh harrier
arpeo *m* (naut.) grappling iron
arpía *f* (coll.) ugly shrew, jade; (coll.) harpy (*rapacious person*); (myth.) Harpy
arpillera *f* burlap, bagging, sackcloth
arpista *mf* harpist
arpón *m* harpoon
arponado -da *adj* like a harpoon
arponar or **arponear** *va* to harpoon; *vn* to wield the harpoon with skill
arponero *m* harpoon maker; harpooner
arqueada *f* (mus.) bow (*stroke with bow*)
arqueador *m* ship gauger; wool beater
arqueaje *m* or **arqueamiento** *m* (naut.) gauging; (naut.) tonnage
arquear *va* to arch; to beat (*wool*); to gauge (*a ship*); to check; to audit (*cash and other assets in hand*); *vn* to retch, be nauseated; *vr* to arch
arquegonio *m* (bot.) archegonium
arqueo *m* arching; (naut.) gauging; (naut.) tonnage; check, checking; audit of cash in hand
arqueología *f* archeology
arqueológico -ca *adj* archeological
arqueólogo -ga *mf* archeologist
arqueozoico -ca *adj* (geol.) Archeozoic
arquería *f* arcade, series of arches
arquero *m* archer, bowman; bow maker; treasurer, cashier; (sport) goalkeeper
arquetipo *m* archetype
arquibanco *m* bench with drawers under seat
arquidiócesis *f* (*pl:* **-sis**) archdiocese
arquiepiscopal *adj* archiepiscopal
Arquímedes *m* Archimedes
arquimédico -ca *adj* Archimedean
arquimesa *f* writing desk

arquisinagogo *m* chief rabbi
arquitecto *m* architect; **arquitecto de jardines** landscape gardener; **arquitecto paisajista** landscape architect
arquitectónico -ca *adj* architectonic
arquitectura *f* architecture
arquitectural *adj* architectural
arquitrabe *m* (arch.) architrave
arquivolta *f* var. of **archivolta**
arrabá *m* (*pl:* **-baes**) (arch.) semirectangular frame around Moorish arch
arrabal *m* suburb; **arrabales** *mpl* outskirts, environs
arrabalero -ra *adj* suburban; (coll.) ill-bred; *mf* suburbanite
arrabio *m* pig iron
arracacha *f* (bot.) arracacha; (Am.) stupidity
arracada *f* earring, earring with pendant
arracimado -da *adj* clustered
arracimar *vr* to cluster, to bunch
arraclán *m* (bot.) alder buckthorn
arráez *m* Moorish chieftain; master of a Moorish ship
arraigadamente *adv* firmly, securely
arraigado -da *adj* rooted; deep-rooted; owning property; **arraigadas** *fpl* (naut.) futtock shrouds
arraigamiento *m* taking root; deep-seated habit
arraigar **§59** *va* to establish, strengthen; *vn* to take root, become deep-rooted; *vr* to take root; to get settled, become a property owner
arraigo *m* rootage, taking root; solidity, stability, settling; property, real estate
arralar *vn* to become thin or sparse; to yield thin bunches of grapes
arramblar *va* to cover with sand and gravel (*said of a stream or torrent*); to sweep away; *vn* to make off; *vr* to be covered with sand and gravel
arrancacepas *m* (*pl:* **-pas**) stump puller
arrancaclavos *m* (*pl:* **-vos**) nail claw, nail extractor
arrancada *f* see **arrancado**
arrancadera *f* leading bell (*for cattle*)
arrancadero *m* starting point (*in a race*)
arrancado -da *adj* (coll.) poor, penniless; *f* start; sudden start; (rail.) jerky start; (naut.) quick start, sudden pick-up; (taur.) sudden charge (*of bull*)
arrancador -dora *adj* extracting; *m* (aut.) starter; **arrancador automático** (aut.) self-starter; *f* extracting machine
arrancadura *f* or **arrancamiento** *m* pulling out, extraction; snatching
arrancapinos *m* (*pl:* **-nos**) (coll.) dwarf (*little fellow*); (coll.) giant (*big fellow*)
arrancar **§86** *va* to root up, to pull out, to pull up; to snatch, to snatch away, to tear away; to wrest, to wring; to draw forth (*e.g., tears*); to make (*a ship*) go faster; **arrancar a** to snatch from, snatch away from; *vn* to start; to start on a run; to set sail; (coll.) to leave, go away; (arch.) to spring (*said of an arch or vault*); (taur.) to rush forward; **arrancar de** to come from, originate in
arrancarraíces *m* (*pl:* **-rraíces**) root puller
arrancasiega *f* pulling up the short grain while mowing
arrancasondas *m* (*pl:* **-das**) drill extractor, grab
arranciar *vr* to get rancid
arranchar *va* to arrange, put in order; (naut.) to brace sharp up, to haul close aft; (naut.) to skirt, to sail close to; *vr* to gather together, to live in the same barracks, to mess together
arranque *m* pulling up; impulse, fit; sudden start, jerk; outburst, sally (*of wit, etc.*); (arch.) spring (*of an arch*); start, starting; (aut.) starter, starting gear, starting; **arranque a mano** (aut.) hand cranking; **arranque automático** (aut.) self-starter, self-starting
arrapar *va* (slang) to snatch away
arrapiezo *m* rag, tatter; (coll.) whippersnapper
arrapo *m* rag, tatter
arras *fpl* deposit, pledge, earnest money; dowry; thirteen coins given by bridegroom to bride at wedding
arrasado -da *adj* satin; satiny
arrasadura *f* leveling with a strickle
arrasamiento *m* razing, demolition
arrasar *va* to smooth, to level; to rase, wreck, flatten, demolish; to fill to the brim; to strike, to level with a strickle; *vn* to clear up, to get clear (*said of sky*); *vr* to clear up, to get clear (*said of sky*); **arrasarse de** or **en agua** or **lágrimas** to fill with tears (*said of the eyes*)
arrastraculo *m* (naut.) driver, water sail
arrastradamente *adv* (coll.) imperfectly; (coll.) laboriously, arduously; (coll.) penuriously; (coll.) unhappily
arrastradera *f* (naut.) lower studding sail; trail rope, guide rope (*of balloon*)
arrastradero *m* log path, dragging road; place where dead animals are dragged from bull ring
arrastradizo -za *adj* dangling; trailing; beaten, frequented; cringing
arrastrado -da *adj* poor, wretched, miserable; (coll.) knavish, rascally; *mf* (coll.) knave, rascal
arrastramiento *m* dragging; crawling
arrastrar *va* to drag; to drag along, drag on; to drag down; to impel; to compel, to necessitate; **traer arrastrado** or **arrastrando** to weary, to harass; **arrastrar a uno a** + *inf* to drag or draw someone into + *ger*; *vn* to crawl, creep; to drag, trail, touch the floor or the ground; *vr* to crawl, creep; to drag, trail, touch the floor or the ground; to trail (*said of a plant or vine*); to drag on; to cringe
arrastre *m* drag, dragging; haulage, hauling; washout; crawl, crawl stroke; influence, force; (Am.) drag (*political or social influence*); (min.) slope of an adit; (taur.) dragging dead bull from the arena; **arrastre de espalda** backstroke (*in swimming*)
arratonado -da *adj* eaten by mice, eaten by rats
arrayán *m* (bot.) myrtle; **arrayán brabántico** (bot.) wax myrtle, bayberry
arrayanal *m* myrtle field
arrayanilla *f* (bot.) Saint-Andrew's-cross
arráyaz *m* or **arraz** *m* var. of **arráez**
arre *m* (coll.) nag, old nag; *interj* gee!, get up!
arreador *m* foreman, overseer; muleteer; (Am.) whip
arrear *va* to drive (*horses, mules, etc.*); to prod; to harness; *vn* (coll.) to hurry along; **¡arrea!** (coll.) get moving!; (coll.) do tell!; *vr* to be ruined, lose all one's money
arrebañaderas *fpl* grapnel (*for pulling something out of a well*)
arrebañador -dora *mf* gatherer, collector, scraper
arrebañadura *f* (coll.) gathering-up; **arrebañaduras** *spl* leavings gathered together
arrebañar *va* to gather up; to eat up
arrebatadamente *adv* headlong, recklessly
arrebatadizo -za *adj* excitable, inflammable
arrebatado -da *adj* reckless, rash, impetuous; ruddy, flushed (*said of countenance*)
arrebatador -dora *adj* captivating; raging, furious; stirring, exciting
arrebatamiento *m* snatching away, carrying off; captivation; rage, fury; rapture, ecstasy
arrebatar *va* to snatch; to carry away, carry off; to attract, captivate; to move, stir; to parch (*grain*); **arrebatar a** to snatch from, snatch away from; *vn* to snatch, grab; *vr* to be parched (*said of grain*); to be burned (*by excessive cooking*); to be carried away (*by some passion or emotion*)
arrebatiña *f* grabbing, scramble, scuffle
arrebato *m* rage, fury; rapture, ecstasy
arrebol *m* red (*of sunrise or sunset*); rouge; rosiness (*of cheeks*); **arreboles** *mpl* red clouds; **arrebol alpestre** alpenglow
arrebolada *f* red clouds (*of sunrise or sunset*)
arrebolar *va* to redden, make red; to rouge; *vr* to redden, turn red; to rouge
arrebolera *f* rouge case; (bot.) four-o'clock, marvel-of-Peru
arrebollar *vr* (prov.) to fall or rush headlong
arrebozar **§76** *va* to muffle; *vr* to muffle or wrap up one's face; to cluster, to swarm
arrebujadamente *adv* in confusion; equivocally; vaguely

arrebujar *va* to jumble together; to wrap, to cover; *vr* to wrap oneself all up
arreciar *vn* to grow worse, become more severe or violent; to rage; *vr* to grow worse, become more severe or violent; to grow stronger, to take on weight
arrecife *m* stone-paved road; stone ditch, dike; (naut.) reef; **arrecife de coral** coral reef
arrecir §53 *vr* to grow stiff with cold
arrechucho *m* (coll.) fit, impulse, impulsive act; (coll.) slight indisposition
arredilar *va* to fold, to corral
arredomado -da *adj* sly, canny
arredondear *va* to round off; *vr* to get round, become rounded
arredramiento *m* driving back; backing out; fear
arredrar *va* to drive back; to frighten; *vr* to move away; to draw back, to shrink; to be frightened
arregazado -da *adj* tucked up; turned up
arregazar §76 *va* to tuck up
arreglado -da *adj* regular; moderate; reasonable; moderately fixed; neat, orderly
arreglar *va* to adjust, regulate, settle; to put in order, arrange; to fix, to repair; (coll.) to alter (*to castrate or to spay*); *vr* to adjust, settle; to arrange; to conform; **arreglarse con** to come to terms with, to reach an agreement with; **arreglárselas** (coll.) to manage all right, to shift
arreglo *m* adjustment; arrangement; settlement; rule, order; agreement; **con arreglo a** according to
arregostar *va* to lure, entice; *vr* (coll.) to take a liking
arregosto *m* (coll.) liking, taste
arrejacar §86 *va* to harrow, rake, or hoe crosswise (*i.e., across the furrows*)
arrejaco *m* (orn.) blackmartin, European swift
arrejada *f* plowstaff
arrejaque *m* three-pronged fishing fork; (orn.) blackmartin, European swift
arrejerar *va* (naut.) to anchor with two anchors fore and one aft
arrellanar *vr* to loll, to sprawl, to sprawl in one's seat; to enjoy one's work
arremangado -da *adj* turned up, tucked up, upturned
arremangar §59 *va* to turn up (*sleeves*); to tuck up (*dress*); *vr* to turn up one's sleeves; to tuck up one's dress; (coll.) to take a firm stand; to be turned up
arremango *m* turning up, tucking up; sleeve turned up, dress tucked up; boldness, dash; **arremangos** *mpl* threats
arrematar *va* to finish, terminate
arremetedero *m* (mil.) place to attack a fortress
arremetedor -dora *adj* attacking; *mf* attacker, aggressor
arremeter *va* to spur (*a horse*); to attack, to assail; *vn* to rush forth, to attack; to offend, be offensive (*to look at*); **arremeter con, contra,** or **para** to rush upon, to attack
arremetida *f* or **arremetimiento** *m* attack; sudden start (*of a horse*); short, wild run; push
arremolinar *vr* to crowd, to crush; to mill about; to whirl
arrendable *adj* rentable
arrendación *f* var. of **arrendamiento**
arrendadero *m* ring in manger to which horses are tied
arrendado -da *adj* obedient to the reins
arrendador -dora *mf* renter; tenant; *m* landlord; ring in manger to which horses are tied; *f* landlady
arrendajo *m* (orn.) jay; (coll.) mimic
arrendamiento *m* rent, rental, renting; lease
arrendar §18 *va* to rent (*to grant or take temporary possession of*); to tie (*a horse*); to bridle; to rein; to mimic; *vr* to rent, be rented
arrendatario -ria *mf* renter, tenant
arreo *m* adornment, dress; piece of harness; **arreos** *mpl* female headdress; appurtenances, accessories; harness, trappings; *adv* successively, without interruption
arrepápalo *m* fritter
arrepentido -da *adj* repentant; *mf* penitent; *f* penitent woman who has retired to a convent
arrepentimiento *m* repentance; curl on neck; repair to a painting
arrepentir §62 *vr* to repent, be repentant; to back down, back out; **arrepentirse de** to repent (*some deed, a sin, etc.*); **arrepentirse de haber** + *pp* to repent having + *pp*
arrepistar *va* to grind (*rags*) into pulp
arrepisto *m* grinding of rags
arrepollado -da *adj* cabbage-headed
arrepticio -cia *adj* possessed by the devil
arrequesonar *vr* to curdle
arrequives *mpl* finery; (coll.) attendant circumstances
arrestado -da *adj* bold, audacious
arrestar *va* to arrest, to take prisoner; *vr* to rush ahead boldly; **arrestarse a** to rush boldly into
arresto *m* arrest, imprisonment; boldness, daring; **bajo arresto** under arrest
arretín *m* moreen
arrevesado -da *adj* complex, intricate; wild, unmanageable
arrezafe *m* field full of brambles
arrezagar §59 *va* to tuck up; to raise (*e.g., the hand*)
arria *f* drove (*of horses*)
arriada *f* flood
arrial *m* var. of **arriaz**
arrianismo *m* Arianism
arriano -na *adj* & *mf* Arian
arriar §90 *va* to flood; (naut.) to lower, to strike; (naut.) to loosen, slacken, let loose; *vr* to become flooded
arriata *f* or **arriate** *m* border, edge (*in garden*); trellis; highway, road
arriaz *m* (*pl:* **arriaces**) quillon (*of sword*); hilt
arriba *adv* up, upward; above, on high; upwards; upstairs; uptown; on top; (naut.) aloft; upwards of, e.g., **tiene doce años arriba** he is upwards of twelve years old; **calle arriba** up the street; **de arriba** from above; **de arriba abajo** from top to bottom, from the top down, from head to foot, from beginning to end; superciliously; **más arriba de** higher than, above; **río arriba** upstream; **arriba de** up; *interj* up with . . . !
arribada *f* arrival (*by sea*); **de arribada** (naut.) emergency
arribaje *m* (naut.) arrival; (naut.) landing beach
arribar *vn* to put into port; to arrive; (naut.) to fall off to leeward; (coll.) to come back (*in health or fortune*); **arribar a** + *inf* to manage to + *inf*
arribazón *m* abundance of fish in port and along the coast; abundance
arribeño -ña *adj* (Am.) upland, highland; *mf* (Am.) uplander, highlander
arribismo *m* ruthless ambition
arribista *adj* & *mf* upstart, parvenu
arribo *m* arrival
arricés *m* buckle of stirrup strap
arricete *m* shoal, bar
arridar *va* (naut.) to haul taut
arriendo *m* var. of **arrendamiento**
arrieraje *m* (Am.) muleteers; (Am.) driving of pack animals
arriería *f* driving of pack animals
arriero *m* driver of pack animal, muleteer
arriesgado -da *adj* risky, dangerous; bold, daring
arriesgar §59 *va* to risk, to jeopardize; *vr* to take a risk, to expose oneself to danger; **arriesgarse a** + *inf* to risk + *ger;* **arriesgarse en** to venture on; **arriesgarse fuera** to venture abroad, to venture out; **quien no se arriesga no pasa la mar** nothing venture, nothing win
arriesgón *m* (coll.) risk, venture
arrimadero *m* support; wainscot, wainscoting
arrimadillo *m* mat, matting (*fastened to wall*); wainscot, wainscoting; pitching pennies (*boy's game*)
arrimadizo -za *adj* movable; parasitic; *mf* sycophant
arrimador *m* backlog in fireplace

arrimadura *f* moving near
arrimar *va* to move up, bring close; to give (*a blow, punch, kick, etc.*); to get rid of, remove; to abandon, neglect; to give up (*a position, profession, etc.*); (naut.) to stow; **arrimar el hombro** to put one's shoulder to the wheel; *vr* to move up, come close; to gather together; (taur.) to work close to the bull; **arrimarse a** to come close to; to draw up to (*e.g., the curb*); to lean against; to get to (*the point*); to depend on, to trust; to snuggle up to
arrime *m* spot near goal (*in bowling*)
arrimo *m* moving near; support; help, aid; favor, protection; fondness, attachment; party wall; idle wall
arrimón *m* loafer, idler; **estar de arrimón** to hang around watching; **hacer de arrimón** (coll.) to hold on to the wall (*for fear of falling from drunkenness*)
arrinconado -da *adj* distant, remote, out of the way; forgotten, neglected, shelved
arrinconamiento *m* retirement, seclusion
arrinconar *va* to corner; to put away in a corner, to lay aside; to get rid of, remove; to abandon, neglect, shelve; *vr* (coll.) to live in seclusion, to withdraw from the world
arriñonado -da *adj* kidney-shaped
Arrio *m* Arius
arriostramiento *m* brace, bracing
arriostrar *va* to brace, to stay
arriscado -da *adj* bold, enterprising; free, brisk, easy; craggy
arriscamiento *m* risk, risk taking
arriscar §86 *va* to risk; *vr* to take a risk; to be vain; to plunge over a cliff (*said of cattle*)
arrisco *m* risk
arritmia *f* (path.) arrhythmia
arrítmico -ca *adj* arrhythmic
arrivismo *m* var. of **arribismo**
arrivista *adj & mf* var. of **arribista**
arrizafa *f* garden, park
arrizar §76 *va* (naut.) to reef, stow, lash
arrizo -za *adj* (bot.) arrhizal or arrhizous
arroaz *m* (*pl:* **-aces**) (zool.) dolphin
arroba *f* arroba (*Spanish weight of about 25 lbs. and Spanish liquid measure of varying value*)
arrobadizo -za *adj* easily entranced, always entranced; feigning entrancement
arrobador -dora *adj* entrancing
arrobamiento *m* entrancement, ecstasy
arrobar *va* to entrance; *vr* to be entranced
arrobero -ra *adj* weighing an arroba; *mf* local baker
arrobo *m* ecstasy
arrocabe *m* top crossbeam; wooden frieze
arrocero -ra *adj* (pertaining to) rice; *mf* rice grower, rice dealer; *m* (orn.) redwing, red-winged blackbird
arrocinado -da *adj* nag-like, worn-out; bestial; (slang) ignorant, stupid
arrocinar *va* to bestialize; *vr* to become bestialized; to fall madly in love
arrodajar *vr* (Am.) to sit down with one's legs crossed
arrodelar *va* to protect with a buckler; *vr* to be protected or armed with a buckler
arrodillado -da *adj* kneeling, on bended knee
arrodilladura *f* or **arrodillamiento** *m* kneeling
arrodillar *va* to make (*someone*) kneel; *vn & vr* to kneel, to kneel down
arrodrigar §59 *va* to prop (*vines*)
arrodrigonar *va* to prop (*vines*)
arrogación *f* adoption; arrogation
arrogancia *f* arrogance; gracefulness, elegance, majesty
arrogante *adj* arrogant; graceful, elegant, majestic
arrogar §59 *va* to adopt; *vr* to arrogate, to arrogate to oneself
arrojadizo -za *adj* easily thrown; to be thrown, for throwing
arrojado -da *adj* bold, dashing, fearless, foolhardy
arrojallamas *m* (*pl:* **-mas**) (mil.) flame thrower
arrojar *va* to throw, hurl; to emit, shed; to bring forth (*shoots, sprouts*); to yield; *vr* to throw oneself; to rush; to rush recklessly
arroje *m* (theat.) man who drops as counterweight to raise the curtain; **arrojes** *mpl* (theat.) stand from which he drops; (theat.) stage to right of spectators
arrojo *m* boldness, dash, fearlessness
arrollado *m* (elec.) coil
arrollador -dora *adj* violent, sweeping, devastating; *m* windlass; *f* (ent.) sewer, leaf sewer
arrollamiento *m* rolling, winding; (elec.) winding; **arrollamiento del inducido** (elec.) armature winding; **arrollamiento inductor** (elec.) field winding
arrollar *va* to roll; to roll up; to wind, to coil; to sweep away; to rout (*enemy*); to dumbfound, leave speechless; to ride roughshod over; (coll.) to knock down, to run over
arromadizar §76 *va* to give a cold to; *vr* to catch cold
arromanzar §76 *va* (archaic) to put into the vernacular (*i.e., any Romance language*), to translate into Spanish
arromar *va* to blunt, to dull; *vr* to get dull
arromper *va* (coll.) to plow (*untilled ground*)
arrompido *m* newly broken ground
arronzar §76 *va* (naut.) to move with levers; (naut.) to haul and shore (*the anchor*); *vn* (naut.) to drift to leeward
arropamiento *m* wrapping
arropar *va* to wrap, wrap up; to mix syrup with (*wine*); *vr* to wrap oneself up, to bundle up
arrope *m* grape syrup; honey syrup
arropea *f* irons, fetters, shackles
arropera *f* vessel for grape syrup
arropía *f* taffy
arropiero -ra *mf* maker or vendor of grape juice syrup
arrostrado -da *adj* featured; **bien arrostrado** well-featured; **mal arrostrado** ill-featured
arrostrar *va* to face; to overcome; to show a liking for, to show an inclination for; *vn* to face; **arrostrar con** or **por** to face, to resist; *vr* to rush into the fight; **arrostrarse con** to defy
arroyada *f* gully; channel; freshet, flood
arroyadero *m* gully; channel
arroyar *va* to make gullies in (*said of the rain*); *vn* to pour, to come down in torrents; *vr* to get full of gullies (*from the rain*); to blight, be blighted
arroyo *m* stream, rivulet, brook; gutter (*in street*); street; (fig.) stream (*of tears, blood, etc.*); **estar en el arroyo** (coll.) to be homeless; **plantar** or **poner en el arroyo** (coll.) to put out of the house
arroyuela *f* (bot.) loosestrife
arroyuelo *m* little stream, rill
arroz *m* (bot.) rice (*plant and grain or seeds*); **arroz de los pieles rojas** (bot.) Indian rice, wild rice
arrozal *m* rice field
arruar §33 *vn* to grunt (*said of wild boar*)
arrufadura *f* (naut.) sheer
arrufar *va* to wrinkle (*one's brow*); to scold; (naut.) to form the sheer of; *vn* (naut.) to be curved upward
arrufianar *vr* to be foul, to be depraved; to pander, be a panderer
arrufo *m* var. of **arrufadura**
arruga *f* wrinkle; crease, rumple
arrugación *f* or **arrugamiento** *m* wrinkling; creasing, rumpling, crumpling
arrugar §59 *va* to wrinkle; to crease, rumple, crumple; to knit (*the brow*); *vr* to wrinkle, become wrinkled; to crease, rumple, crumple; to shrink, to shrivel
arrugia *f* gold mine
arruinador -dora *adj* ruining, destructive; *mf* ruiner, destroyer
arruinamiento *m* ruin, ruination, destruction, demolition
arruinar *va* to ruin, destroy, demolish; *vr* to go to ruin, to be destroyed
arrullar *va* to coo to; to lull to sleep, to sing to sleep; (coll.) to court, to woo; *vn* to coo; *vr* to bill (*said of doves*); to coo
arrullo *m* cooing and billing; lullaby
arruma *f* (naut.) division or partition in hold (*for stowing cargo*)

arrumaco *m* caress; odd dress or adornment; flattery, pretense; **arrumacos** *mpl* show of affection
arrumaje *m* (naut.) good stowage; (naut.) ballast
arrumar *va* (naut.) to stow; *vr* (naut.) to become overcast
arrumazón *f* (naut.) stowing; (naut.) good stowage; (naut.) ballast; (naut.) overcast horizon
arrumazonar *vr* to become overcast (*said of sky or horizon*)
arrumbadas *fpl* (naut.) wales of a row galley
arrumbamiento *m* (naut.) bearing, direction
arrumbar *va* to cast aside; to neglect, pay no attention to; to sweep aside, to silence; to line up (*wine casks*) along the wall of a wine cellar; (naut.) to determine the lay of (*a coast*); *vn* (naut.) to take bearings; *vr* (naut.) to take bearings; to get seasick
arrumbe *m* (Am.) rust
arrurruz *m* arrowroot (*starch*)
arsáfraga *f* (bot.) water parsnip
arsenal *m* arsenal, armory; shipyard, navy yard, dockyard; (fig.) arsenal
arseniato *m* (chem.) arsenate
arsenical *adj* arsenical
arsénico -ca *adj* arsenical; (chem.) arsenic; *m* (chem. & mineral.) arsenic
arsenioso -sa *adj* (chem.) arsenious
arsenito *m* (chem.) arsenite
arseniuro *m* (chem.) arsenide
arsfenamina *f* (pharm.) arsphenamine
arsolla *f* var. of **arzolla**
art. abr. of **artículo**
arta *f* (bot.) plantain; **arta de agua** (bot.) fleawort
Artajerjes *m* Artaxerxes
artanica or **artanita** *f* (bot.) cyclamen, sowbread
arte *m & f* art; trick, cunning; knack; fishing gear; **bellas artes** fine arts; **el séptimo arte** moving pictures; **no tener arte ni parte en** to have nothing to do with; **arte cisoria** (cook.) art of carving; **arte manual** craft; **arte mayor** Spanish verse of ten to twelve syllables with the following rhyme scheme: abbaacca; **arte menor** Spanish verse of six to eight syllables, sometimes in the form of a quatrain; **arte plumaria** art of embroidering featherwork; **artes gráficas** graphic arts; **artes liberales** *fpl* liberal arts; **arte típico** native craft; **artes y oficios** arts and crafts
artefacto *m* device, contrivance, appliance, fixture, artifact; (biol.) artifact; **artefactos de alumbrado** lighting fixtures; **artefactos sanitarios** bathroom fixtures
artejo *m* knuckle (*of fingers*); (zool.) arthromere
Artemis *f* (myth.) Artemis
artemisa *f* (bot.) mugwort, sagebrush; (*cap.*) *f* (myth.) Artemis
artemisia *f* (bot.) mugwort, sagebrush
artera *f* see **artero**
arteria *f* (anat.) artery; (elec.) feeder; (fig.) artery (*main highway*)
artería *f* craftiness, cunning; (slang) rascality
arterial *adj* arterial
arterialización *f* arterialization
arterializar §76 *va* to arterialize
arterioesclerosis *f* var. of **arteriosclerosis**
arteriola *f* arteriole
arteriosclerosis *f* (path.) arteriosclerosis
arterioso -sa *adj* arterious
arteritis *f* (path.) arteritis
artero -ra *adj* sly, cunning, artful; *f* bread stamp (*iron for marking bread to be sent to common bakery*)
arteroesclerosis *f* var. of **arteriosclerosis**
artesa *f* trough, kneading trough; Indian canoe
artesanado *m* craftsmen, mechanics
artesanía *f* craftsmanship; craftsmen, mechanics
artesano -na *mf* artisan, craftsman; *f* craftswoman
artesiano -na *adj* Artesian; artesian (*well*)
artesilla *f* small trough; trough in bucket wheel
artesón *m* kitchen tub; (arch.) coffer, caisson
artesonado -da *adj* (arch.) caissoned; *m* (arch.) caissoned ceiling
artesonar *va* (arch.) to adorn (*a ceiling or vault*) with caissons
artesuela *f* small trough, small bowl
artético -ca *adj & mf* arthritic
ártico -ca *adj* arctic; (*cap.*) *m* Arctic (*ocean*)
articulación *f* articulation; (anat., bot. & zool.) articulation, joint; (phonet.) articulation; **articulación universal** (aut.) universal joint
articulado -da *adj* articulate; articulated; *m* series of articles; (law) series of proofs; (zool.) articulate
articular *adj* articular; *va & vr* to articulate; to article; to question
articulista *mf* writer of articles
artículo *m* article; item; joint (*part between two articulations*); entry (*each alphabetized word in a dictionary, etc.*); (anat. & bot.) articulation; **artículo de costumbres** (lit.) article on manners and customs; **artículo definido** or **determinado** (gram.) definite article; **artículo de fondo** leader, editorial; **artículo indefinido** or **indeterminado** (gram.) indefinite article; **artículos de consumo** consumers' goods; **artículos de cuero** leather goods; **artículos de deporte** sporting goods; **artículos del culto** church supplies; **artículos de primera necesidad** basic commodities; **artículos para caballeros** men's furnishings
artífice *mf* artificer; craftsman (*artist*)
artificial *adj* artificial
artificiero *m* fireworks manufacturer; (mil.) artificer
artificio *m* artifice; craft, workmanship; device, appliance; trick, ruse; cunning
artificioso -sa *adj* skillful, ingenious; wary, cunning, artful, scheming, tricky, fake, deceptive
artiga *f* (agr.) burning and breaking a field; field burned and broken
artigar §59 *va* (agr.) to burn clear and break (*a field, etc.*)
artilugio *m* (coll.) jigger, thingamajig; (coll.) scheme, trick
artillado *m* artillery
artillar *va* to arm or equip with artillery
artillería *f* artillery; **artillería de sitio** siege artillery
artillero *m* artilleryman; artillerist
artimaña *f* trap; (coll.) trick, cunning
artimón *m* (naut.) mizzenmast
artina *f* boxthorn berry
artiodáctilo -la *adj & m* (zool.) artiodactyl
artista *mf* artist
artístico -ca *adj* artistic
art.º abr. of **artículo**
arto *m* (bot.) boxthorn
artolas *fpl* mule chair, cacolet
artralgia *f* (path.) arthralgia, pain in the joints
artrítico -ca *adj & mf* arthritic
artritis *f* (path.) arthritis; **artritis reumatoidea** (path.) rheumatoid arthritis
artrómera *f* (zool.) arthromere
artrópodo -da *adj & m* (zool.) arthropod
arturiano -na or **artúrico -ca** *adj* Arthurian
Arturo *m* Arthur; (astr.) Arcturus; **el rey Arturo** King Arthur
Artús *m* Arthur (*king*)
arugas *fpl* (bot.) camomile
árula *f* small altar
arundíneo -a *adj* arundineous, reedy
aruñar *va* (coll.) to scratch
aruñazo *m* (coll.) scratch
arúspice *m* haruspex, diviner, soothsayer
aruspicina *f* haruspicy, divination
arveja *f* (bot.) vetch, spring vetch, tare; (bot.) vetchling; (bot.) pea
arvejal *m* vetch field
arvejana *f* var. of **arveja**
arvejo *m* (bot.) pea
arvense *adj* (growing in a) field
arvícola *f* (zool.) vole, water rat
arz. abr. of **arzobispo**
arzbpo. abr. of **arzobispo**
arzobispado *m* archbishopric

arzobispal *adj* archiepiscopal
arzobispo *m* archbishop
arzolla *f* (bot.) centaury; (bot.) milk thistle
arzón *m* saddletree; **arzón delantero** saddlebow; **arzón trasero** cantle
as *m* ace (*in cards, dice, tennis, aviation*); **as de fútbol** football star; **as de guía** (naut.) bowline, bowline knot; **as del volante** (aut.) speed king
asa *f* handle (*of jug, basket, etc.*); juice; opportunity, pretext; (bact.) loop; **asa dulce** (pharm.) gum benzoin; **asa fétida** asafetida
asacar §86 *va* to produce, invent; to feign; to impute, attribute
asación *f* roasting; (pharm.) decoction
asadero -ra *adj* for roasting; *m* oven (*hot place*); (Am.) fresh cheese
asado -da *adj* roasted; **bien asado** well-done, done brown; **poco asado** rare, underdone; *m* roasting; roast
asador *m* spit; roasting jack
asadura *f* entrails; liver; (fig.) sluggishness; **asadura de puerco** haslet
asaetear *va* to shoot with an arrow; to wound or kill with an arrow; to bother, harass
asaetinado -da *adj* sateen
asafétida *f* asafetida
asainetado -da *adj* farcical
asalariado -da *adj* wage-earning; *mf* wage earner
asalariar *va* to fix wages for; *vr* to work for wages
asalmonado -da *adj* salmon-like; salmon, salmon-colored
asaltante *mf* assailant
asaltar *va* to assault, assail, storm; to overtake, come suddenly upon (*a person*)
asalto *m* assault, attack; surprise party; (box.) round; **tomar por asalto** to take by storm
asamblea *f* assembly, assemblage; (mil.) assembly; **Asamblea General** General Assembly
asambleísta *mf* member of an assembly; *m* assemblyman
asar *va* to roast; to bother, annoy, pursue; *vr* to be burning up, be exceedingly hot
asarabácara *f* (bot.) asarabacca
asarero *m* (bot.) blackthorn
asargado -da *adj* twilled, serge
ásaro *m* (bot.) asarabacca
asativo -va *adj* (pharm.) boiled in its own juice
asaz *adj & adv* (poet.) enough, aplenty
asbestino -na *adj* (pertaining to) asbestos
asbesto *m* asbestos
asca *f* (bot.) ascus
ascalonia *f* (bot.) shallot
áscar *m* army (*in Morocco*)
áscari *m* soldier (*in Morocco*)
ascáride *f* (zool.) ascarid
ascendencia *f* ancestry, line
ascendente *adj* up, ascending, ascendant; *m* (astrol.) ascendant
ascender §66 *va* to promote; *vn* to ascend, go up; to be advanced, be promoted; **ascender a** to amount to
ascendiente *adj* up, ascending, ascendant; *mf* ancestor; *m* ascendancy
ascensión *f* ascension; exaltation; (*cap.*) *f* Ascension (*ascending of Jesus; church festival; island of Atlantic*); **ascensión recta** (astr.) right ascension
ascensional *adj* ascensional
ascensionista *mf* balloonist; mountain climber
ascenso *m* ascent, promotion
ascensómetro *m* (aer.) climb indicator
ascensor *m* elevator; freight elevator; **ascensor hidráulico** hydraulic elevator
ascensorista *mf* elevator operator
asceta *mf* ascetic
ascético -ca *adj* ascetic
ascetismo *m* asceticism
ascidia *f* (zool.) ascidian
ascios *mpl* ascians
asciro *m* (bot.) St.-Andrew's-cross
ascitis *f* (path.) ascites
Asclepio *m* (myth.) Asclepius
asco *m* loathing, nausea, disgust; disgusting thing; **dar asco** (coll.) to turn the stomach, to disgust; **estar hecho un asco** (coll.) to be filthy; **hacer ascos de** (coll.) to turn one's nose up at, to pretend to be contemptuous of; **tener asco a** to be disgusted with, to have enough of
ascomiceto -ta *adj* (bot.) ascomycetous; *m* (bot.) ascomycete
ascón *m* (zool.) ascon
ascórbico -ca *adj* ascorbic
ascospora *f* (bot.) ascospore
ascua *f* ember; **arrimar el ascua a su sardina** to know how to take care of oneself; **estar en** or **sobre ascuas** (coll.) to be worried to death; **sacar el ascua con la mano del gato** or **con mano ajena** (coll.) to get someone else to pull one's chestnuts out of the fire; **¡ascuas!** ouch!
Asdrúbal *m* Hasdrubal
aseado -da *adj* clean, neat, tidy
asear *va* to adorn, clean up, polish, embellish; *vr* to clean up, tidy up
asechamiento *m* or **asechanza** *f* trap, snare, waylaying
asechar *va* to waylay, ambush
asecho *m* var. of **asechamiento**
asedado -da *adj* silken
asedar *va* to make (*e.g., flax*) soft as silk
asediador -dora *adj* besieging; *mf* besieger
asediar *va* to besiege, to blockade; (fig.) to besiege, to harass; to make love to, to throw oneself at
asedio *m* siege, blockade
aseglarar *vr* to act like a layman, to look like a layman
asegundar *va* to repeat at once
asegurable *adj* insurable
aseguración *f* insurance; insurance policy
asegurado -da *adj* assured; insured; *mf* insured
asegurador -dora *adj* insuring, underwriting; *mf* insurer, underwriter; fastener, fastening
aseguramiento *m* assurance; insurance; pass, permit; fastening
aseguranza *f* (prov.) firmness, security; (Am.) insurance
asegurar *va* to secure, make secure, fasten; to assure, guarantee; to assert; to seize, imprison; to insure; *vr* to make oneself secure; to make onself sure; to take out insurance
aseidad *f* (theol.) aseity
asemejar *va* to make like; to compare; to resemble; *vn & vr* to be similar; **asemejar a** or **asemejarse a** to be like, to resemble
asendereado -da *adj* beaten, frequented; overwhelmed with work or trouble
asenderear *va* to cut or open a path through; to pursue through paths and by-paths
asenso *m* assent; credence
asentada *f* see **asentado**
asentaderas *fpl* (coll.) buttocks
asentadillas; a asentadillas sidesaddle, woman-fashion
asentado -da *adj* sedate, judicious; stable, permanent; *f* sitting; **de una asentada** at one sitting
asentador *m* stonemason; strap, razor strop; wholesale merchant; turning chisel; **asentador de vía** (rail.) road foreman, roadmaster
asentamiento *m* establishment; settlement, settling; plot, land; judgment, wisdom
asentar §18 *va* to seat; to place; to fix, establish, found; to tamp down, to smooth, to level; to hone, sharpen; to note, to enter (*e.g., in a ledger*); to impart (*a blow*); to impress (*on the mind*); to affirm; to guess, suppose; (law) to award; to settle (*food with a drink*); *vn* to be suitable, be becoming; *vr* to sit down; to establish oneself, to be established; to not be digested (*said of food*); to settle (*said of a liquid or a building*)
asentimiento *m* assent
asentir §62 *vn* to assent
asentista *m* army contractor; builder, contractor
aseñorado -da *adj* pompous, lordly
aseo *m* cleanliness, neatness, tidiness; toilet, powder room
asepsia *f* (med.) asepsis
aséptico -ca *adj* aseptic
asequible *adj* accessible, obtainable

aserción *f* assertion
aserradero *m* sawmill
aserradizo -za *adj* for sawing; sawed
aserrado -da *adj* serrate, dented
aserrador -dora *adj* saw, sawing; *m* sawer, sawyer; (coll.) scraper, fiddler; *f* power saw
aserradura *f* saw cut; **aserraduras** *fpl* sawings, sawdust
aserraduría *f* sawmill
aserrar §18 *va* to saw
aserrería *f* sawmill
aserrín *m* sawdust
aserruchar *va* to saw (*with a handsaw*)
asertivo -va *adj* assertive
aserto *m* assertion
asesar *vn* to become wise, to get sense
asesinar *va* to assassinate, murder; to plague, harass
asesinato *m* assassination, murder; **asesinato ritual** ritual murder
asesino -na *adj* murderous; *mf* assassin, murderer; *m* traitor, betrayer; *f* murderess
asesor -sora *adj* advising, advisory; *mf* adviser
asesoramiento *m* advising, counseling
asesorar *va* to advise; *vr* to seek advice; to get advice
asesoría *f* advising; adviser's fee; adviser's office
asestadura *f* aiming; shooting, firing
asestar *va* to aim; to shoot, fire; to deal (*a blow*); to try to hurt
aseveración *f* asseveration
aseveradamente *adv* positively, affirmatively
aseverar *va* to asseverate
aseverativo -va *adj* asseverative; (gram.) declarative (*sentence*)
asexual *adj* asexual
asfaltado -da *adj* (pertaining to) asphalt; *m* asphalting; asphalt paving
asfaltar *va* to asphalt
asfáltico -ca *adj* asphaltic, asphalt
asfalto *m* asphalt; (mineral.) asphalt
asfíctico -ca *adj* asphyctic, asphyxial
asfixia *f* asphyxiation; (path.) asphyxia
asfixiante *adj* asphyxiating
asfixiar *va* to asphyxiate; *vr* to be asphyxiated
asfíxico -ca *adj* var. of **asfíctico**
asfódelo *m* (bot.) asphodel
asgo *1st sg pres ind of* **asir**
así *adv* so, thus; **y así sucesivamente** and so on; **así así** so so; **así . . . como** both . . . and; **así como** as soon as; as well as; **así no más** (Am.) so so; **así que** as soon as; so that, with the result that; **así y todo** even so, anyhow; **por decirlo así** so to speak; *adj* such, e.g., **un hombre así** such a man; *conj* although; would that . . . !
Asia *f* Asia; **el Asia Menor** Asia Minor; **el Asia sudoriental** Southeast Asia
asiaticismo *m* Asiaticism
asiático -ca *adj & mf* Asian, Asiatic
asibilación *f* (phonet.) assibilation
asibilar *va & vr* (phonet.) to assibilate
asidera *f* (Am.) saddle strap with ring at each end
asidero *m* handle; handhold; (fig.) handle (*occasion, pretext*)
asiduidad *f* assiduity; frequency, persistence
asiduo -dua *adj* assiduous; frequent, persistent
asiento *m* seat; site; settling (*of a building*); bottom (*e.g., of a bottle or chair*); sediment; list, roll; collar band; entry (*e.g., in ledger*); indigestion; trading contract; wisdom, judgment, maturity; **asientos** *mpl* buttocks; **hacer asiento** to settle (*said of a building*); **tome Vd. asiento** have a seat; **asiento de pastor** (bot.) blue genista; **asiento de rejilla** cane seat; **asiento de válvula** valve seat; **asiento lanzable** (aer.) ejection seat
asignable *adj* assignable
asignación *f* assignation; salary; allowance
asignado *m* assignat (*paper money in French Revolution*)
asignar *va* to assign
asignatura *f* course, subject (*in school*)
asilado -da *mf* inmate (*in an asylum or home*)
asilar *va* to shelter, give refuge to; to place in an asylum; (agr.) to silo, to ensile; *vr* to take refuge, to take refuge in an asylum; to be placed in an asylum; (archaic) to seek sanctuary
asilo *m* asylum; home (*for sick, poor, etc.*); refuge, shelter, protection; (ent.) robber fly, hawk fly; **asilo de huérfanos** orphan asylum; **asilo de locos** insane asylum; **asilo de pobres** poorhouse; **asilo nocturno** night shelter, flophouse
asilla *f* fastener; slight pretext; collarbone; **asillas** *fpl* shoulder pole (*for carrying equal weights on each side*)
asimetría *f* asymmetry
asimétrico -ca *adj* asymmetric or asymmetrical
asimiento *m* seizing, grasp; attachment, affection
asimilable *adj* assimilable
asimilación *f* assimilation; understanding (*of another person, of a role, of a character*)
asimilar *va* to assimilate; to compare; to take in; *vn* to assimilate; to be alike; *vr* to assimilate (*e.g., food, knowledge*); **asimilarse a** to resemble
asimilativo -va *adj* assimilative
asimina *f* (bot.) papaw
asimismo *adv* in like manner, likewise, also
asimplado -da *adj* simple, simple-looking
asincrónico -ca *adj* asynchronous
asincronismo *m* asynchronism
asíndeton *m* (rhet.) asyndeton
asinino -na *adj* var. of **asnino**
asíntota *f* (math.) asymptote
asir §22 *va* to seize, grasp; **tener asido** to hold on to; **asidos del brazo** arm in arm; *vn* to take root; *vr* to take hold; to fight, grapple; **asirse a** or **de** to seize, grasp, take hold of; **asirse con** to grapple with
Asiria *f* see **asirio**
asiriano -na *adj & mf* (archaic) Assyrian
asirio -ria *adj & mf* Assyrian; *m* Assyrian (*language*); (*cap.*) *f* Assyria
asiriología *f* Assyriology
asiriólogo -ga *mf* Assyriologist
Asís *f* Assisi
asistencia *f* attendance; assistence; reward; social work; persons present, audience; (Am.) upstairs parlor; (Am.) boarding house; (Am.) board; **asistencias** *fpl* allowance, support
asistencial *adj* of assistance
asistenta *f* (female) attendant, handmaid; day maid, charwoman
asistente *adj* attendant; attending, present; *m* assistant; attendant; bystander, spectator, person present; (mil.) orderly
asistido -da *mf* (Am.) roomer, boarder; *m* (Am.) miner
asistir *va* to assist, aid, help; to attend, to accompany; to serve, wait on; to take care of; *vn* to be present; to follow suit; **asistir a** to be present at, to attend
asistolia *f* (path.) asystole
asistólico -ca *adj* asystolic
asma *f* (path.) asthma
asmático -ca *adj & mf* asthmatic
Asmodeo *m* Asmodeus
asna *f* she-ass, jenny ass; **asnas** *fpl* rafters
asnacho *m* (bot.) restharrow
asnada *f* (coll.) asininity
asnado *m* (min.) side-wall timber
asnal *adj* (pertaining to a) donkey; (coll.) bestial, brutish
asnalmente *adv* (coll.) riding on a donkey; (coll.) bestially, brutishly
asnallo *m* (bot.) restharrow
asnaucho *m* (bot.) Spanish paprika
asnería *f* asses; asininity
asnilla *f* prop; shoring; trestle, sawbuck
asnino -na *adj* (pertaining to a) donkey
asno *m* ass, donkey, jackass; (fig.) ass
asobarcar §86 *va* to take under the arm; to lift high (*one's skirts*)
asobinar *vr* to be sprawled out helpless; to fall in a lump
asocarronado -da *adj* crafty, cunning
asociación *f* association; (sport) association football, soccer
asociacionismo *m* (psychol.) associationism
asociado -da *adj* associated; associate; *mf* associate, partner

asociamiento *m* association
asociar *va* to associate; to take as partner; *vr* to associate; to become a partner; to become partners
asociativo -va *adj* associative
asolación *f* destruction, razing
asolador -dora *adj* destructive; *mf* destroyer
asolamiento *m* destruction, razing
asolanar *va* to parch, dry up (*said of the east wind*); *vr* to be too early, to ripen too early
asolapar *va* to make (*e.g., a tile*) overlap
asolar *va* to parch, burn; *vr* to become parched; **§77** *va* to knock down, to destroy, to raze; *vr* to settle (*said of a liquid*)
asoldadar *va* var. of **asoldar**
asoldar §77 *va* to hire
asolear *va* to sun; *vr* to bask; to get sunburned
asoleo *m* sunning, basking
asomado -da *adj* leaning, leaning out; tipsy; *f* brief appearance; spot from which something is first seen
asomar *va* to show, to stick out (*e.g., one's head*); to let show; *vn* to begin to show or appear; to show; *vr* to show, to stick out; to lean out; (coll.) to begin to get tipsy, to get tipsy; **asomarse a mirar** to lean out to look; to come out to look around; **asomarse a ver** to take a look at, to look in at, to look out at
asombradizo -za *adj* timid, shy
asombrador -dora *adj* astonishing, amazing
asombrar *va* to shade; to darken (*a color*); to frighten; to astonish, amaze; *vr* to be frightened; to be astonished or amazed; **asombrarse con** or **de** to be amazed at; **asombrarse de** + *inf* to be amazed to + *inf*
asombro *m* fear, fright, scare; astonishment, amazement; wonder; **no volver de su asombro** to not be able to get over it
asombroso -sa *adj* astonishing, amazing
asomo *m* appearance; sign, indication; **ni por asomo** by no means, not by a long shot
asonada *f* mob; row
asonancia *f* assonance; correspondence
asonantado -da *adj* assonanced
asonantar *va* to make assonant; *vn* to assonate
asonante *adj* assonant; *m & f* assonance (*sound, syllable, or letter*)
asonar §77 *vn* to assonate
asordar *va* to deafen
asosegar §29 *va* to calm, quiet; *vn & vr* to become calm, quiet down
asotanar *va* to dig or excavate for a cellar
aspa *f* X-shaped figure, crosspiece, cross stud; reel; wheel (*of windmill*); vane (*of windmill*); propeller blade; **en aspa** crosswise
aspadera *f* reel
aspado -da *adj* cross-shaped; with the arms outstretched; (coll.) tight-laced
aspador -dora *mf* reeler; *m* reel
aspálato *m* (bot.) rosewood
aspalto *m* (paint.) dark glaze
aspar *va* to reel; to crucify; (coll.) to vex, annoy; *vr* to writhe; to strive, take great pains
aspaventero -ra *adj* fussy, excitable; *mf* fussy, excitable person
aspaviento *m* fuss, excitement
aspear *vr* to bruise one's feet, to become footsore
aspecto *m* aspect; (astr., astrol. & gram.) aspect; **al** or **a primer aspecto** at first sight
asperarteria *f* (anat.) windpipe, trachea
asperear *vn* to taste bitter
asperete *m* bitterness, sourness
aspereza *f* roughness; harshness; bitterness, sourness; rudeness, coarseness, gruffness; asperity; **limar asperezas** (fig.) to smooth away the rough edges
asperiego -ga *adj* cider (*apple or apple tree*)
asperilla *f* (bot.) woodruff
asperillo *m* bitterness, sourness
asperjar *va* to sprinkle; to sprinkle with holy water
áspero -ra *adj* rough; harsh; bitter, tart; sour; rude, coarse, gruff; (phonet.) rough (*breathing*)
asperón *m* sandstone, grit, gritstone; grindstone
asperonar *va* to grind with sandstone and water, to rub with sandstone
aspérrimo -ma *adj super* very or most rough
aspersión *f* aspersion (*sprinkling*); sprinkling; spraying
aspersor *m* sprinkler
aspersorio *m* sprinkler, water sprinkler
áspid *m* or **áspide** *m* (zool.) asp, aspic
aspidistra *f* (bot.) aspidistra
aspillera *f* (fort.) embrasure, loophole; (fort.) machicolation
aspillerar *va* to embrasure; to machicolate
aspiración *f* aspiration; inhalation; suction; draft; intake; (mus.) short pause
aspirado -da *adj & f* (phonet.) aspirate
aspirador -dora *adj* (pertaining to) suction; *mf* inhaler; *m* aspirator; **aspirador de gasolina** (aut.) vacuum tank; **aspirador** or **aspiradora de polvo** vacuum cleaner
aspirante *adj* (pertaining to) suction; *m* applicant, candidate; **aspirante a cabo** (mil.) private first class; **aspirante de marina** (naut.) midshipman
aspirar *va* to suck, draw in; to inhale; (phonet.) to aspirate; *vn* to aspire; to inhale; **aspirar a** to aspire after or to; **aspirar a** + *inf* to aspire to + *inf*
aspirina *f* (pharm.) aspirin
asplenio *m* (bot.) spleenwort
asquear *va* to loathe, be nauseated at; *vn* to be nauseated
asquerosidad *f* loathsomeness; nausea; squeamishness
asqueroso -sa *adj* loathsome, disgusting; nauseated; squeamish
asta *f* spear; shaft; mast, flagpole, staff; handle (*of brush*); horn; antler; **a media asta** at half-mast; **dejar en las astas del toro** (coll.) to leave high and dry
ástaco *m* (zool.) crawfish, crayfish
astado -da *adj* horny; horned; *m* bull
astático -ca *adj* astatic
astatino or **ástato** *m* (chem.) astatine
astenia *f* (path.) asthenia
asténico -ca *adj & mf* asthenic
aster or **áster** *m & f* (bot. & biol.) aster
asteria *f* (mineral.) asteriated opal; (zool.) starfish
asterisco *m* asterisk
asterismo *m* (astr. & phys.) asterism
asteroide *adj* asteroid (*starlike*); *m* (astr.) asteroid
asteroideo -a *adj & m* (zool.) asteroidean
Astianacte *m* (myth.) Astyanax
astigmático -ca *adj* astigmatic
astigmatismo *m* (med.) astigmatism
astigmómetro *m* astigmometer
astil *m* handle (*of an ax*); shaft (*of arrow, of feather*); beam (*of balance*)
astilla *f* chip, splinter
astillar *va* to chip, to splinter; *vr* to chip, to splinter; (coll.) to be bursting (*with too much food or drink*)
astillazo *m* blow from flying chip
Astillejos *mpl* (astr.) Castor and Pollux
astillero *m* rack for spears, lances, etc.; shipyard, dockyard
astilloso -sa *adj* splintery
astorgano -na *adj* (pertaining to) Astorga; *mf* native or inhabitant of Astorga
astracán *m* astrachan; (theat.) drama of puns
astracanada *f* (coll.) cheap farce
astrágalo *m* (anat., arch. & arti.) astragal; (bot.) milk vetch
astral *adj* astral
astrancia *f* (bot.) astrantia; **astrancia mayor** (bot.) black sanicle, masterwort
astreñir §74 *va* var. of **astringir**
astricción *f* astriction
astrictivo -va *adj* astrictive
astrífero -ra *adj* (poet.) starry
astringencia *f* astringency
astringente *adj & m* astringent
astringir §42 *va* to constrict, compress; to bind, compel
astriñir §25 *va* var. of **astringir**
astro *m* star, heavenly body; (fig.) star, luminary, leading light; **el astro de la noche** the moon; **el astro del día** the sun
astródomo *m* (aer.) astrodome
astrofísico -ca *adj* astrophysical; *f* astrophysics

astrofotografía *f* astrophotography
astrofotometría *f* astrophotometry
astrolabio *m* (astr.) astrolabe
astrologar §59 *va & vn* to astrologize
astrología *f* astrology
astrológico -ca *adj* astrological
astrólogo -ga *adj* astrological; *mf* astrologer
astronauta *m* astronaut
astronáutico -ca *adj* astronautic or astronautical; *f* astronautics
astronave *f* spaceship; **astronave tripulada** manned spaceship
astronavegación *f* space travel; astronavigation
astronomía *f* astronomy
astronómico -ca *adj* astronomic or astronomical; (coll.) astronomic or astronomical (*exceedingly large*)
astrónomo -ma *mf* astronomer
astroso -sa *adj* unfortunate, ill-fated; vile, contemptible; (coll.) shabby, ragged
astucia *f* astuteness; cunning; trick, artifice
astucioso -sa *adj* astute, cunning
astur *adj & mf* var. of **asturiano**
asturianismo *m* Asturian word or expression
asturiano -na *adj & mf* Asturian; *m* Asturian (*dialect*)
Asturias *f* Asturias
asturión *m* (ichth.) sturgeon; pony
astuto -ta *adj* **astute, cunning, sly; tricky**
asuardado -da *adj* spotted, stained
asuertado -da *adj* (Am.) lucky, fortunate
asueto *m* day off, short time off, brief vacation; (coll.) leisure, diversion, amusement
asumir *va* to assume (*command, responsibilities, great proportions, etc.*); to raise, elevate (*to a dignity*); *vr* to assume
asunción *f* assumption; elevation (*to a dignity*); (*cap.*) *f* (eccl.) Assumption; Asunción (*city*)
asuncionista *mf* Assumptionist
asunto *m* subject, matter; business, affair; theme; **asuntos exteriores** foreign affairs
asuramiento *m* burning; parching; worriment
asurar *va* to burn (*food*); to parch (*said of hot sun*); to worry, harass; *vr* to be burned; to be parched; to be worried or annoyed; to be burning up, be roasting
asurcano -na *adj* neighboring (*said of fields and their farmers*)
asurcar §86 *va* to furrow, to plow
asustadizo -za *adj* shy, scary, skittish
asustador -dora *adj* frightening
asustar *va* to scare, frighten; *vr* to be scared, frightened; **asustarse de, con,** or **por** to be frightened at; **asustarse de** + *inf* to be frightened to, to be afraid to + *inf*
atabacado -da *adj* tobacco-colored
atabal *m* kettledrum; kettledrummer; timbrel
atabalear *vn* to stamp (*said of a horse*); to drum (*with the fingers*)
atabalero *m* kettledrummer
atabanado -da *adj* with white spots (*said of a horse*)
atabardillado -da *adj* like spotted fever
atabe *m* vent (*in a pipe*)
atabernado -da *adj* sold by the glass (*said of wine*)
atabladera *f* drag (*for smoothing or leveling*)
atablar *va* to drag (*e.g., a field for leveling*)
atacable *adj* attackable, assailable
atacadera *f* blaster's rammer, tamping stick
atacado -da *adj* undecided, irresolute; stingy, mean
atacador -dora *mf* aggressor; *m* ramrod, rammer
atacadura *f* attaching, fastening, buttoning; (min.) plugging (*of blasting-powder holes*)
atacamita *f* (mineral.) atacamite
atacante *adj* attacking; *mf* attacker
atacar §86 *va* to attach, fasten, button, buckle; to pack, to jam; to ram, tamp; to attack; to corner, to contradict
atacir *m* (astrol.) division of celestial sphere into twelve houses
ataderas *fpl* (coll.) garters
atadero *m* cord, rope; place for tying; **no tener atadero** (coll.) to be in disorder; (coll.) to be full of nonsense
atadijo *m* (coll.) loose package
atado -da *adj* timid, shy; weak, irresolute; insignificant; hampered, cramped; *m* pack, bundle, roll
atador -dora *adj* binding; *mf* binder; *f* binding machine; **atadores** *mpl* bonnet strings
atadura *f* tying, binding, fastening; string, rope; knot, connection; bond, union; obstacle, shackle
atafagar §59 *va* to suffocate (*especially with strong odors*); to bother, harass
atafea *f* surfeit
atafetanado -da *adj* like taffeta
ataguía *f* cofferdam
ataharre *m* breeching
atahona *f* var. of **tahona**
atahorma *f* (orn.) harrier eagle
ataifor *m* round Moorish table
atairar *va* to put molding in (*doors and windows*)
ataire *m* molding
atajadero *m* dike, levee (*for directing and controlling irrigation*)
atajadizo *m* partition, wall
atajador *m* interceptor; (mach.) arrester; (Am.) stable boy
atajar *va* to stop, arrest, intercept, interrupt; to partition off; to take a short cut to meet or to head off; to cross off; *vn* to take a short cut; *vr* to be abashed, be confused with fear or shame
atajo *m* short cut; cut (*e.g., in a play*); flock; (fig.) short cut; **echar por el atajo** to duck (*to get expeditiously out of an unpleasant situation*)
atalajar *va* to harness and hitch
atalaje *m* harness; (coll.) outfit, equipment
atalantar *va* to please, to suit; to stun, daze; *vr* to be stunned
atalaya *f* watchtower; height, elevation; *m* guard, lookout
atalayador -dora *mf* lookout; spy, prier
atalayar *va* to watch from a watchtower; to spy on
atalayero *m* (mil.) scout
ataludar *va* to slope, batter
atalvina *f* var. of **talvina**
atamán *m* var. of **hetmán**
atamiento *m* (coll.) pusillanimity, timidity
atanasia *f* athanasia (*immortality*); (bot.) costmary; (print.) English (*14 points*)
atanasiano -na *adj* Athanasian
Atanasio, San Saint Athanasius
atanor *m* water pipe; athanor
atanquía *f* (coll.) depilatory ointment; coarse silk, floss
atañadero -ra *adj* applicable; concerning, pertaining
atañer §84 *va* to concern
atapar *va* to cover, cover up, hide; to stop up, plug
ataque *m* attack; (mil.) offensive trenches; **ataque aéreo** air attack, air raid; **ataque cardíaco** or **ataque de corazón** heart attack; **ataque en picado** (aer.) diving attack; **ataque por sorpresa** surprise attack
ataquiza *f* (hort.) layering
ataquizar §76 *va* (hort.) to layer (*a vine*)
atar *va* to tie, fasten, lace; to paralyze; **no atar ni desatar** (coll.) to talk nonsense; (coll.) to get nowhere, to lead nowhere; *vr* to stick (*to, e.g., an opinion*); to get tied up (*e.g., in difficulties*)
ataracea *f* marquetry, inlaid work; inlaid floor
ataracear *va* to inlay, to adorn with marquetry
atarantado -da *adj* bitten by a tarantula; scared, bewildered; (coll.) restless, boisterous
atarantamiento *m* stunning, daze, bewilderment
atarantar *va* to stun, daze; *vr* to be stunned
ataraxia *f* ataraxia
ataráxico -ca *adj* ataractic
atarazana *f* shipyard; spinner's shed; (prov.) wine vault
atarazar §76 *va* to bite, to tear or lacerate with the teeth
atardecer *m* late afternoon; §34 *vn* to draw towards evening; to be, arrive, or happen in the late afternoon
atareado -da *adj* busy

atarear *va* to assign a task to, to give a job to; *vr* to toil, to overwork; **atarearse a** + *inf* to be busy + *ger;* **atarearse con** or **en** to busy oneself with
atarjea *f* culvert, drainpipe, sewer; sewer connection (*from house*); **atarjea de alimentación** (rail.) feed trough, track tank
atarquinar *va* to cover with mud; *vr* to get covered with mud, to silt up
atarraga *f* (bot.) elecampane
atarragar §59 *va* to hammer and fit (*a horseshoe*)
atarrajar *va* to thread, to tap
atarraya *f* casting net
atarugamiento *m* (coll.) confusion, timidity, bashfulness
atarugar §59 *va* to fasten with pegs, pins, or wedges; to plug, to plug up; to stuff, fill; (coll.) to silence, shut up; *vr* (coll.) to get confused (*in speech*)
atasajar *va* to jerk (*meat*); to slash, hack; (coll.) to stretch across a horse
atascadero *m* mudhole, bog; obstruction, interference
atascamiento *m* obstruction; (path.) compression, constriction
atascar §86 *va* to stop, stop up, clog; *vr* to become stopped up, to clog; to get stuck (*in the mud*); to stuff, to stuff oneself; (coll.) to get stuck (*in speech*)
atasco *m* clogging, jamming, sticking; obstruction
ataúd *m* casket, coffin
ataudado -da *adj* coffin-shaped
ataujía *f* damascene, damascene work (*incrustation of gold or silver wire and enamel in steel or copper*); (Am.) conduit, drain
ataujiado -da *adj* damascene, damascened (*having gold or silver wire incrusted in steel or copper*)
ataujiar §90 *va* to damascene (*to adorn with gold or silver wire or enamel incrusted in steel or copper*)
ataurique *m* (arch.) Moorish ornamental plasterwork; carved foliage
ataviar §90 *va* to dress, dress up, adorn
atávico -ca *adj* atavistic
atavío *m* dress, adornment; **atavíos** *mpl* finery
atavismo *m* (biol.) atavism
ataxia *f* ataxia; (path.) ataxia; **ataxia locomotriz progresiva** (path.) locomotor ataxia
atáxico -ca *adj & mf* ataxic
Até *f* (myth.) Ate
atediante *adj* boring, tiresome
atediar *va* to bore, tire; *vr* to become bored, be bored
ateísmo *m* atheism
ateísta *adj & mf* atheist
ateístico -ca *adj* atheistic
atejado -da *adj* overlapping
ateje *m* (bot.) tropical tree of genus *Cordia*
atejonar *vr* (Am.) to squat, cower, duck, hide; (Am.) to become sly, cunning
atelaje *m* harness; team
atemorizar §76 *va* to scare, frighten; *vr* to become scared, become frightened; **atemorizarse de** or **por** to become scared or frightened at
atemperación *f* tempering, moderation; adjusting; cooling
atemperante *adj* tempering, softening; cooling
atemperar *va* to temper, soften, moderate; to adjust, accommodate; to cool; to condition (*air*)
atemporalado -da *adj* stormy, tempestuous
Atena *f* (myth.) Athena
atenacear *va* to tear the flesh of (*a person*) with nippers; to tie down; to torture
Atenas *f* Athens
atenazar §76 *va* var. of **atenacear**
atención *f* attention; **atenciones** *fpl* attentions (*acts of courtesy, etc.*); business, duties, responsibilities; **en atención a** in view of; *interj* attention!; (mil.) attention!
atendedor -dora *mf* (print.) copyholder (*reader who follows copy as proofreader reads aloud*)
atendencia *f* attention, attending
atender §66 *va* to attend to, pay attention to; to take care of; *vn* to attend, pay attention; (print.) to follow copy as proofreader reads aloud; **atender por** to answer to the name of (*said of an animal*)
atendible *adj* worthy of attention
atendré *1st sg fut ind of* **atener**
Atenea *f* see **ateneo**
atenebrar *vr* to become dark
ateneo -a *adj & mf* (poet.) Athenian; *m* athenaeum; (*cap.*) *f* (myth.) Athena
atener §85 *vr* to abide; to depend, to rely; **atenerse a** to abide by; to depend on, to rely on
atengo *1st sg pres ind of* **atener**
ateniense *adj & mf* Athenian
atentación *f* illegality
atentadamente *adv* illegally; cautiously
atentado -da *adj* prudent, moderate; cautious; *m* attempt, assault; crime
atentar *va* to do illegally; to attempt, to try to commit; *vn* to attempt a crime; **atentar a** or **contra** to attempt (*e.g., the life of a person*); **§18** *vr* to grope; to restrain oneself
atentatorio -ria *adj* offensive; **atentatorio a** violating
atento -ta *adj* attentive; kind; polite, courteous; *f* favor (*letter of which one acknowledges receipt*)
atenuación *f* attenuation; extenuation (*of guilt, offense, etc.*); (rhet.) litotes
atenuar §33 *va* to attenuate; to extenuate (*to make seem less serious*); *vn* to attenuate
ateo -a *adj* atheist, atheistic; *mf* atheist
atercianado -da *adj* suffering from tertian fever; *mf* person suffering from tertian fever
aterciopelado -da *adj* velvety
aterecer §34 *vr* to become stiff with cold
aterimiento *m* stiffness from cold
aterir §53 *vr* to become stiff with cold
atermancia *f* (phys.) athermancy
atérmano -na *adj* athermanous
aterosclerosis *f* (path.) atherosclerosis
aterrada *f* (naut.) landfall (*making or sighting land*)
aterrador -dora *adj* frightful, dreadful
aterrajar *va* to thread, to tap
aterraje *m* landing (*of boat or aircraft*)
aterramiento *m* ruin, destruction; terror; discouragement; landing
aterrar *va* to terrify; *vr* to become terrified; **§18** *va* to demolish, destroy; to cover with earth, to earth up; (min.) to dump; *vn* to land; *vr* to keep or stand inshore; **navegar aterrado** (naut.) to sail inshore
aterrizaje *m* (aer.) landing; **aterrizaje a ciegas** (aer.) blind landing; **aterrizaje aplastado** or **en desplome** (aer.) pancake landing; **aterrizaje forzado** or **forzoso** (aer.) forced landing; **aterrizaje sobre tres puntos** (aer.) three-point landing
aterrizar §76 *vn* (aer.) to land
aterronado -da *adj* lumpish, cloddy
aterronar *va* to make lumpy, to clod; *vr* to become lumpy, to cake
aterrorizar §76 *va* to terrify
atesar §18 *va* (naut.) to haul taut
atesoramiento *m* hoarding
atesorar *va* to treasure, hoard up; to possess (*virtues, charm, etc.*)
atestación *f* attestation
atestado -da *adj* stubborn; *m* (law) attestation; **atestados** *mpl* (law) testimonials
atestadura *f* packing, cramming, stuffing; must for filling up casks
atestamiento *m* packing, cramming, stuffing
atestar *va* (law) to attest; **§18 & regular** *va* to pack, to stuff, to cram; to fill up (*wine casks*); (coll.) to stuff (*with food*)
atestiguación *f* or **atestiguamiento** *m* attestation, testifying, deposition, corroboration
atestiguar §23 *va* to attest, to testify, to depose
atetado -da *adj* mammiform
atetar *va* to suckle
atetillar *va* (agr.) to make a pit around (*trunk of tree*), leaving some earth close to trunk
atezado -da *adj* tan; black
atezamiento *m* tanning; blackening

atezar §76 *va* to tan; to blacken; *vr* to tan; to become tanned; to get black
atibar *va* (min.) to fill up with muck and rubbish
atiborrar *va* to stuff; (coll.) to stuff (*with food*); *vr* (coll.) to stuff, to stuff oneself (*with food*)
Ática *f* see **ático**
aticismo *m* Atticism
aticista *mf* Atticist
ático -ca *adj & mf* Attic; *m* (anat. & arch.) attic; **el Ática** Attica
atierre *m* (min.) cave-in, deads; (Am.) filling with earth
atiesador *m* stiffener, stiffening
atiesamiento *m* stiffening
atiesar *va* to stiffen; to tighten; *vr* to stiffen, become stiff; to tighten, become tight
atifle *m* potter's trivet
atigrado -da *adj* tigerish; tiger-marked
atigrar *va* to mark like a tiger; *vr* to become tigerish
atijara *f* goods, business; transportation (*cost*); reward
Atila *m* Attila
atildado -da *adj* neat, stylish
atildadura *f* or **atildamiento** *m* marking with tilde; faultfinding; neatness, adornment, elegance
atildar *va* to put a tilde, dash, or accent mark over; to note, point out, find fault with; to clean, fix up, trim, adorn
atinado -da *adj* wise, keen, careful
atinar *va* to find, to come upon; *vn* to guess, guess right; to apply, be right; **atinar a** to guess; to find, to come upon; to hit (*e.g., the target*); **atinar a** + *inf* to manage to + *inf*, to succeed in + *ger*; **atinar con** to guess; to find, to come upon, to hit upon; **atinar en** to guess, guess right, hit upon
atíncar *m* borax
atinconar *va* (min.) to prop up, to shore up
atípico -ca *adj* atypical
atiplar *va* (mus.) to raise the pitch of to treble; *vr* (mus.) to rise to treble
atirantar *va* to make taut; to brace with stays or ties
atiriciar *vr* to become jaundiced
atisbadero *m* peephole
atisbador -dora *adj* watching, spying; *mf* watcher, spy
atisbadura *f* watching, spying
atisbar *va* to watch, spy on, observe
atisbo *m* watching, spying, observation; sign, token, show
atisuado -da *adj* like tissue
atizadero *m* poker; coal mouth (*of furnace*)
atizador -dora *adj* inciting, stirring; *m* poker; feeder
atizar §76 *va* to stir, to poke; to snuff; to rouse, to stir up; (coll.) to give, to let go (*e.g., a kick*)
atizonar *va* to bond with headers; to embed in a wall; (agr.) to smut, to taint with smut; *vn* (agr.) to smut, to blight
atlante *m* strong man; **atlantes** *mpl* (arch.) atlantes; (*cap.*) *m* (myth.) Atlas
atlántico -ca *adj* Atlantic; Atlantean; (*cap.*) *m* Atlantic (*ocean*)
Atlántida *f* Atlantis; **Atlántidas** *fpl* (astr. & myth.) Atlantides
atlas *m* (*pl:* **-las**) atlas (*book of maps; size of paper*); (anat.) atlas; (*cap.*) *m* (myth.) Atlas; **el Atlas** the Atlas Mountains
atleta *mf* athlete; athletic person; intellectual giant; great figure (*e.g., of literature*); champion (*of a cause*)
atlético -ca *adj* athletic; *f* athletics (*art or skill*)
atletismo *m* athletics (*principles of athletic training; games, sports, etc.*)
atmósfera *f* atmosphere; (fig.) atmosphere
atmosférico -ca *adj* atmospheric
atoar *va* (naut.) to tow; (naut.) to warp
atocinado -da *adj* (coll.) fat, fleshy
atocinar *va* to cut up (*a pig*); to make into bacon; (coll.) to assassinate; *vr* (coll.) to become angry; (coll.) to fall madly in love
atocha *f* (bot.) esparto
atochada *f* dike of esparto grass and mud
atochal *m* esparto field
atochar *m* esparto field; *va* to stuff or fill with esparto; to stuff or fill; *vr* (naut.) to jam
atochón *m* (bot.) esparto; (bot.) esparto panicle
atol *m* or **atole** *m* (Am.) atole (*drink made of maize meal*)
atolón *m* atoll
atolondrado -da *adj* amazed, bewildered; scatterbrained, reckless
atolondramiento *m* amazement, bewilderment; thoughtlessness, recklessness
atolondrar *va* to amaze, bewilder; *vr* to become amazed, become bewildered
atolladero *m* mudhole; difficulty, obstruction, blind alley, dead end
atollar *vn* to get stuck in the mud or in a mudhole; *vr* to get stuck in the mud or in a mudhole; (coll.) to get stuck
atomicidad *f* (chem.) atomicity
atómico -ca *adj* atomic
atomismo *m* atomism
atomista *mf* atomist
atomístico -ca *adj* atomistic; *f* atomistics
atomizador *m* atomizer
atomizar §76 *va* to atomize
átomo *m* atom; (chem.) atom; **átomo cálido** (phys.) hot atom
átomo-gramo *m* (*pl:* **átomos-gramos**) (chem.) gram atom
atonal *adj* (mus.) atonal
atonalidad *f* (mus.) atonality
atonalismo *m* (mus.) atonalism
atondar *va* to spur (*a horse*)
atonía *f* (path. & phonet.) atony; (phonet.) lack of stress
atonicidad *f* (med.) atonicity
atónico -ca *adj* (gram. & med.) atonic
atónito -ta *adj* overwhelmed, aghast
átono -na *adj* (gram. & med.) atonic
atontadamente *adv* stupidly
atontamiento *m* stunning, stupefaction; confusion, bewilderment; stupidity, imbecility
atontar *va* to stun, stupefy; to confuse, bewilder; *vr* to become stunned, become stupefied; to become confused, become bewildered
atoramiento *m* sticking; choking; obstruction
atorar *va* to obstruct; *vn* to stick; *vr* to stick; to choke; §77 *va* to chop (*wood*)
atormentador -dora *adj* tormenting; *mf* tormentor; torturer
atormentar *va* to torment; to torture
atornillar *va & vr* to screw, to screw on
atorozonar *vr* (vet.) to suffer from colic
atorrante *adj & mf* (Am.) good-for-nothing
atortolar *va* to rattle, intimidate; *vr* to become rattled or intimidated
atortorar *va* (naut.) to frap (*a cable*)
atortujar *va* to squeeze, to flatten
atosigador -dora *mf* poisoner; urger
atosigamiento *m* poisoning; pressing, urging
atosigar §59 *va* to poison; to press, harass; *vr* to be hurried
atrabajado -da *adj* overworked; belabored
atrabancar §86 *va & vn* to get through in a hurry
atrabanco *m* hurry, precipitation
atrabiliario -ria *adj* atrabilious
atrabilis *f* (med.) black bile; (fig.) ill-humor
atracadero *m* (naut.) landing, wharf, berth
atracado -da *adj* (coll.) stuffed; *f* (naut.) bringing alongside, mooring
atracador *m* (slang) holdup man
atracar §86 *va* to bring up; (naut.) to bring alongside; to waylay, to hold up; (coll.) to stuff (*with food and drink*); *vn* (naut.) to come alongside; *vr* (coll.) to stuff (*to eat and drink too much*); (Am.) to fight, quarrel
atracazón *m* (Am.) jam, mob
atracción *f* attraction; amusement (*in vaudeville, a circus, etc.*); **atracción capilar** (phys.) capillary attraction
atraco *m* holdup
atracón *m* (coll.) stuffing, gluttony
atractivo -va *adj* attractive; *m* attraction; attractiveness
atractriz (*pl:* **-trices**) *adj fem* attracting; *f* (phys.) force of attraction
atraer §88 *va* to attract; to draw (*e.g., a crowd*); *vr* to be attracted; to draw (*applause*)
atrafagar §59 *vn* to toil, make a great effort

atragantado -da *adj* choking (*with strong emotion*)
atragantamiento *m* choking
atragantar *va* to choke down; *vr* to choke; (coll.) to get mixed up (*in one's speech*); **atragantarse con** to choke on
atraíble *adj* attractable
atraicionar *va* to betray
atraidorado -da *adj* treacherous, traitorous
atraigo *1st sg pres ind of* **atraer**
atraillar §75 *va* to leash; to pursue (*game*) with a dog in leash
atraimiento *m* attracting, attraction
atraje *1st sg pret ind of* **atraer**
atrampar *vr* to be trapped, to fall in the trap; to stop up (*said, e.g., of a pipe*); to catch, to stick (*said of bolt of lock that cannot be opened*); (coll.) to get entangled, to get stuck
atramuz *m* (*pl:* **-muces**) var. of **altramuz**
atrancar §86 *va* to bar; to obstruct; *vn* (coll.) to stride, take large strides; (coll.) to read hastily and skipping words; *vr* (Am.) to be insistent
atranco or **atranque** *m* mudhole; difficulty, obstruction
atrapador *m* (mach.) trap, collector
atrapamoscas (*pl:* **-cas**) *f* (bot.) Venus's-flytrap
atrapar *va* (coll.) to catch, to trap (*especially, person or animal that is fleeing*); (coll.) to get (*something good or advantageous*); (coll.) to trap, take in, deceive
atraque *m* (naut.) bringing alongside, mooring
atrás *adv* back, backward; behind; previously; **desde muy atrás** a long time ago; for a long time; **días atrás** days ago; **hacerse atrás** to back up, move back, fall back; **hacia atrás** backwards; (coll.) the wrong way; **ir para atrás** to look younger every day; **atrás de** back of, behind; *interj* back up!, back out!
atrasado -da *adj* slowed, late; slow (*said of a watch or clock*); hard up, needy; back; past; due; in arrears; retarded; (coll.) backward, slow to learn; **mentalmente atrasado** mentally retarded; **atrasado de medios** poor, impoverished; **atrasado de noticias** behind the times; **atrasado en pagos** in arrears
atrasar *va* to slow, slow down; to slow down, retard (*watch or clock*); to set back, to turn back (*hands of watch or clock*); to leave behind; to hold back, to delay; to postdate (*an event, document, etc.*); *vn* to go slow, to be slow (*said of a watch or clock*); *vr* to go slow, to be slow; to lose time; to stay back, stay behind; to lag; to be late; to be in debt
atraso *m* slowness, delay; backwardness; lag
atravesado -da *adj* squint-eyed; crossbred, mongrel; wicked, treacherous, vile
atravesador -dora *adj* crossing; monopolizing; *m* (elec.) bushing (*of a transformer*)
atravesaño *m* var. of **travesaño**
atravesar §18 *va* to put or lay (*e.g., a piece of timber*) across; to cross, to go through, to go over, to go across; to pierce; to cast the evil eye upon; to put up, to stake, to wager; to buy (*goods*) wholesale in order to sell retail; **atravesar . . . en** to put or lay (*e.g., a piece of timber*) across (*e.g., a street*); *vr* to butt in; to wrangle, fight; to get stuck (*said e.g., of a bone in the throat*)
atrayente *adj* attractive
atreguado -da *adj* mad, deranged; under truce
atreguar §23 *va* to give a truce to; to grant an extension; *vr* to agree to a truce
atrenzo *m* (Am.) conflict, difficulty
Atreo *m* (myth.) Atreus
atresia *f* (med.) atresia
atresnalar *va* (agr.) to arrange (*sheaves*) in shocks
atrever *vr* to dare, to make bold; **atreverse a** to venture, to dare to undertake; **atreverse a** + *inf* to dare to + *inf;* **atreverse con** or **contra** to be impudent toward
atrevido -da *adj* bold, daring; impudent, forward
atrevimiento *m* boldness, daring; impudence, effrontery
atrezo *m* stage equipment, properties
atribución *f* attribution; assignment, power, function
atribuíble *adj* attributable
atribuir §41 *va* to attribute; to assign
atribulación *f* tribulation, grieving
atribular *va* to grieve, afflict; *vr* to grieve, be grieved, lose heart
atributivo -va *adj* attributive; (gram.) attributive
atributo *m* attribute; (gram.) attribute
atrición *f* (phys. & theol.) attrition; (path.) bruise
atril *m* lectern; music stand
atrilera *f* ornamental cover of lectern or choir desk
atrincheramiento *m* intrenchment
atrincherar *va* to intrench, to fortify with trenches; *vr* to intrench, to dig in
atrio *m* atrium; hall, vestibule; parvis; (anat.) atrium
atrípedo -da *adj* (zool.) black-footed
atrirrostro -tra *adj* black-beaked
atrito -ta *adj* contrite
atrocidad *f* atrocity; (coll.) enormity; (coll.) stupidity; **¡qué atrocidad!** (coll.) how terrific!
atrochar *vn* to go by cross paths, to take a short cut
atrofia *f* atrophy
atrofiar *va & vr* to atrophy
atrojar *va* to garner (*grain*); *vr* (Am.) to be befuddled, to not know which way to turn
atrompetado -da *adj* bell-mouthed, trumpet-shaped
atronado -da *adj* reckless, thoughtless
atronador -dora *adj* deafening
atronadura *f* fissure in trunk of tree; (vet.) crepance
atronamiento *m* deafening; stun, stunning; (vet.) crepance
atronar §77 *va* to deafen; to stun; to stop the ears of (*a horse*); to kill (*a bull*) by blow on nape of neck; *vn* to thunder; *vr* to be frightened at thunder (*said of chickens and silkworms*)
atronerar *va* (fort.) to make embrasures in
atropar *va* to round up in a gang; to gather (*grain, hay, etc.*); *vr* to gang together
atropellado -da *adj* hasty; violent, brusk; tumultous; sickly, decrepit
atropellador -dora *mf* trampler; brash person
atropellamiento *m* trampling; upsetting; abuse, insult
atropellaplatos *f* (*pl:* **-tos**) (coll.) slap-bang maid
atropellar *va* to trample under foot; to run over; to knock down; to push one's way through; to ride roughshod over or through; to do hurriedly; to disregard, to violate; *vn* to act hastily or recklessly; **atropellar por** to push one's way through; to disregard, to violate; *vr* to act hastily or recklessly
atropello *m* trampling; upsetting; (act of) running down, running over; abuse, insult; outrage, excess
atropina *f* (chem. & pharm.) atropine
Átropos *f* (myth.) Atropos
atroz *adj* (*pl:* **-troces**) atrocious; (coll.) huge, enormous
atruhanado -da *adj* scurrilous
atto. or **att.º** abr. of **atento**
atuendo *m* pomp, show; dress, adornment
atufamiento *m* anger, vexation, annoyance
atufar *va* to anger, vex, irritate; *vr* to get angry; to turn sour (*said of wine*); to get smelly (*said of food*); **atufarse con, de** or **por** to get angry at
atufo *m* anger, vexation, irritation
atumultuar §33 *va & vr* var. of **tumultuar**
atún *m* (ichth.) tuna, tunny
atunara *f* tuna fishery
atunero -ra *mf* tuna dealer; *m* tuna fisherman; *f* tuna fishhook
aturar *va* (coll.) to close up tight
aturbonar *vr* to become overcast with thunderclouds
aturdido -da *adj* thoughtless, scatterbrained, reckless
aturdidor -dora *adj* amazing, bewildering, perplexing, deafening

aturdimiento *m* stun, stunning; amazement, bewilderment, confusion
aturdir *va* to stun; to amaze, bewilder, perplex; *vr* to be stunned; to be amazed, to become bewildered, to become perplexed
aturrullamiento *m* (coll.) bewilderment, perplexity
aturrullar *va* (coll.) to bewilder, to perplex, to dumbfound; *vr* (coll.) to become bewildered, become perplexed, become dumbfounded
atusar *va* to trim (*the hair*); to smooth (*the hair with hand and comb*); to trim (*plants*); *vr* to dress too fancily
atutía *f* tutty
atuve *1st sg pret ind of* **atener**
auca *f* (orn.) goose; (Am.) derby hat
audacia *f* audacity
audaz *adj* (*pl:* **-daces**) audacious
audibilidad *f* audibility
audible *adj* audible
audición *f* hearing; audition; concert; (law) hearing; (rad.) listening
audiencia *f* audience; audience chamber; hearing, listening; (law) hearing; royal tribunal; high court of justice (*in Spanish colony*); provincial high court
audífono *m* audiphone; hearing aid; earphone; handset
audímetro *m* audiometer
audiofrecuencia *f* (rad.) audio frequency
audiología *f* audiology
audiómetro *m* audiometer
audión *m* (rad.) audion
audio-visual *adj* audio-visual
auditivo -va *adj* auditory; *m* earpiece (*of telephone*)
auditor *m* judge advocate; auditor (*in school*); listener (*to radio*); (com.) auditor; **auditor de guerra** judge advocate (*in army*); **auditor de marina** judge advocate (*in navy*)
auditoría *f* judge advocate's office; (com.) auditorship
auditorio *m* audience; auditorium; studio, radio studio
auge *m* height, acme, zenith; boom; vogue; (astr.) apogee; **cobrar nuevo auge** to take on new life; **estar en auge** to be booming; to be in vogue; **tomar auge** to have great vogue, to be all the rage
augita *f* (mineral.) augite
augur *m* augur
auguración *f* auguring
augurado *m* augurate
augural *adj* augural, ominous, portentous
augurar *va* to augur; (Am.) to wish; *vn* to augur
augurio *m* augury; (Am.) wish, good wish
augustal *adj* Augustan
augusto -ta *adj* august; (*cap.*) *m* Augustus
aula *f* classroom, lecture room; (anat.) aula; (poet.) palace; **aula magna** assembly hall
aulaga *f* (bot.) furze, gorse
aulagar *m* furze field, gorse field
áulico -ca *adj* aulic; *m* aulic; courtier
aulladero *m* place where animals gather and howl
aullador -dora *adj* howling; *mf* howler; *m* (zool.) howler, howling monkey
aullar §75 *vn* to howl
aullido *m* howl; (rad.) howling, squealing
aúllo *m* howl
aumentación *f* (rhet.) climax; (her.) augmentation
aumentado -da *adj* (mus.) augmented
aumentador -dora *adj* increasing, amplifying; *m* booster
aumentar *va* to augment, increase, enlarge; to promote; (coll.) to exaggerate; *vn* to augment, increase; *vr* to augment, increase; to multiply
aumentativo -va *adj* & *m* (gram.) augmentative
aumento *m* augmentation, increase, enlargement; promotion; **ir en aumento** to be on the increase
aun *adv* still; even; also; **ni aun** not even; neither; **aun cuando** although
aún *adv* still, yet
aunar §75 *va* to join, unite; to mix, combine; *vr* to join, unite; to combine
aunque *conj* although, even though
aúpa *interj* up, up!; **de aúpa** (coll.) swanky
aupar §75 *va* (coll.) to help up; to extol, praise; *vr* (coll.) to arise, to rise up, to be extolled, be praised
aura *f* gentle breeze; breath; popularity; dawn; orange (*color*); (orn.) turkey buzzard; (med.) aura
aural *adj* aural
Aureliano *m* Aurelian
Aurelio, Marco Marcus Aurelius
áureo -a *adj* aureate
aureola or **auréola** *f* (meteor. & theol.) aureole; (f.a. & fig.) aureole, halo
aureolar *va* to aureole, to halo; (Am.) to glorify
aureomicina *f* (pharm.) aureomycin
aurícula *f* (anat.) auricle; (bot.) auricula
auriculado -da *adj* (bot. & zool.) auriculate
auricular *adj* auricular; (anat.) auricular; *m* earpiece, receiver (*of telephone*); little finger; **auricular de casco** headphone
aurífero -ra *adj* auriferous, gold-bearing
auriga *m* (poet.) coachman, charioteer; (*cap.*) *m* (astr.) Auriga
aurista *mf* aurist
aurora *f* aurora, dawn; roseate hue; pink cheeks; (bot.) flower of an hour; (fig.) dawn, harbinger; (*cap.*) *f* (myth.) Aurora; **aurora austral** (meteor.) aurora australis; **aurora boreal** (meteor.) aurora borealis; **aurora polar** (meteor.) aurora
auroral *adj* auroral
aurorino -na *adj* (poet.) auroral
aurragado -da *adj* badly cultivated
aurúspice *m* var. of **arúspice**
auscultación *f* auscultation
auscultar *va* to auscultate; to sound out; *vn* to auscultate
ausencia *f* absence
ausentado -da *adj* absent
ausentar *va* to send away; *vr* to absent oneself
ausente *adj* absent; absent-minded; *mf* absentee;; *m* (law) missing person
ausentismo *m* absenteeism
auspiciar *va* (Am.) to support, foster, back
auspicio *m* auspice; **bajo los auspicios de** under the auspices of
auspicioso -sa *adj* (Am.) auspicious
austeridad *f* austerity
austero -ra *adj* austere; harsh, astringent; penitent; honest, incorruptible
austral *adj* austral
Australasia, la Australasia
australasiático -ca *adj* & *mf* Australasian
australasino -na *adj* Australasian
Australia *f* Australia
australiano -na *adj* & *mf* Australian
Austria *f* Austria
austríaco -ca *adj* & *mf* Austrian
Austria-Hungría *f* Austria-Hungary
austro *m* south wind
austrohúngaro -ra *adj* & *mf* Austro-Hungarian
autarcía *f* autarky (*economic self-sufficiency*)
autárcico -ca *adj* autarkic or autarkical
autarquía *f* autarchy; autarky (*economic self-sufficiency*)
autárquico -ca *adj* autarchic or autarchical; autarkic or autarkical
auténtica *f* see **auténtico**
autenticación *f* authentication
autenticar §86 *va* to authenticate
autenticidad *f* authenticity
auténtico -ca *adj* authentic; real; *f* certification; certificate; **auténticas** *fpl* Authentics (*Novels of Justinian*)
autillo *m* (orn.) tawny owl; particular decree of Inquisition
auto *m* edict, judicial decree; short Biblical play; miracle play; auto; **auto de fe** auto-da-fe; **auto de prisión** commitment, warrant for arrest; **auto sacramental** Biblical play following a procession in honor of the Sacrament
autoanálisis *m* self-analysis
autobiografía *f* autobiography
autobiográfico -ca *adj* autobiographical
autobiógrafo -fa *mf* autobiographer

autoblasto *m* (biol.) autoblast
autobomba *f* motor pumper; motor fire engine
autobombo *m* self-glorification
autobote *m* powerboat, motorboat
autobús *m* (*pl:* **-buses**) bus, autobus
autocamión *m* autotruck, motor truck
autocar *m* bus, interurban bus; **sightseeing bus**
autocarril *m* (rail.) motorcar
autocasa *f* trailer (*mobile house*)
autocebante *adj* self-priming
autoclave *f* autoclave
autoconciencia *f* self-consciousness
autocracia *f* autocracy
autócrata *mf* autocrat
autocrático -ca *adj* autocratic
autocrítica *f* self-examination; self-criticism; criticism of a work by its author
autoctonía *f* autochthony
autóctono -na *adj* autochthonous; native; *mf* autochthon; native
autodefensa *f* self-defense
autodestrucción *f* self-destruction
autodeterminación *f* or **autodeterminismo** *m* (pol.) self-determination
autodidacto -ta *adj* self-taught, self-educated
autodidaxia *f* self-instruction
autodirigido -da *adj* self-directed
autodisciplina *f* self-discipline
autodominio *m* self-control
autódromo *m* automobile race course
autoencendido *m* self-ignition, pre-ignition
autoenfriamiento *m* self-cooling
autoengaño *m* self-deception
autoenseñanza *f* self-instruction
auto-escuela *f* driving school
autofecundación *f* (bot.) close fertilization
autofretage *m* autofrettage
autogénesis *f* (biol.) autogenesis
autógeno -na *adj* autogenous; *f* welding
autogiro *m* autogiro
autogobierno *m* self-government
autografía *f* autography
autografiar §90 *va* to autograph
autográfico -ca *adj* autographic
autógrafo -fa *adj & m* autograph
autohipnosis *f* autohypnosis, self-hypnotism
autoinducción *f* (elec.) self-induction
autoinducido -da *adj* (elec.) self-induced
autoinductancia *f* (elec.) self-inductance
autoinfección *f* (path.) autoinfection
autointoxicación *f* (path.) autointoxication
autolicuador *m* juice extractor
autolimpiador -dora *adj* self-cleaning
automacia *f* automatism
autómata *m* automaton; (coll.) automaton (*person*)
automático -ca *adj* automatic
automatismo *m* automatism
automatización *f* automation
automatizar §76 *va* to automate; (coll.) to make an automaton of, to deprive of independence
automotor -tora *adj* automotive; self-propelling; self-moving; *m* railway motor coach
automotriz *f* (*pl:* **-trices**) rail car, self-propelled railroad car
automóvil *adj & m* automobile
automovilismo *m* motoring; automobile industry
automovilista *adj* (pertaining to the) automobile; *mf* automobilist, motorist
automovilístico -ca *adj* (pertaining to the) automobile
autonomía *f* autonomy; cruising radius (*of a boat, airplane, etc.*)
autonómico -ca *adj* autonomic
autonomista *mf* autonomist
autónomo -ma *adj* autonomous, independent
autopiano *m* (Am.) player piano
autopista *f* automobile road, turnpike
autoplastia *f* (surg.) autoplasty
autoplástico -ca *adj* autoplastic
autopolinización *f* (bot.) self-pollination
autopolinizar §76 *va* (bot.) to self-pollinate
autopropulsado -da *adj* self-propelled
autopropulsión *f* self-propulsion
autopropulsor -sora *adj* self-propelling
autoprotección *f* self-protection
autopsia *f* autopsy
autopsiar *va* to autopsy
autópsido -da *adj* (mineral.) having metallic luster
autor -tora *mf* author; perpetrator (*of crime*); (archaic) theatrical manager; *f* authoress
autoría *f* (archaic) management of a theater
autoridad *f* authority; pomp, show, display
autoritario -ria *adj* authoritarian; authoritative; *mf* authoritarian
autoritarismo *m* authoritarianism
autorización *f* authorization
autorizado -da *adj* authoritative
autorizamiento *m* var. of **autorización**
autorizar §76 *va* to authorize; to legalize; to exalt, to enhance; **autorizar a** or **para** + *inf* to authorize to + *inf*
autorradio *m* auto radio
autorreactor *m* (aer.) ram-jet engine
autorregistrador -dora *adj* self-recording
autorregulador -dora *adj* self-regulating
autorretrato *m* self-portrait
autorriel *m* railway motor coach
autoservicio *m* self-service
auto-stop *m* hitchhiking; **hacer auto-stop** to hitchhike
autosuficiencia *f* self-sufficiency
autosuficiente *adj* self-sufficient
autosugestión *f* autosuggestion
autosuperar *vr* to outdo oneself
autotaponador -dora *adj* self-sealing
auto-teatro *m* drive-in motion-picture theater
autotécnica *f* automotive engineering
autotécnico *m* automotive engineer
autótrofo -fa *adj* (bot.) autotrophic
autotropismo *m* (bot.) autotropism
autovía *f* automobile road, turnpike; *m* railway motor coach
autunita *f* (mineral.) autunite
Auvernia *f* Auvergne
auxiliador -dora *adj* helping, aiding; *mf* helper, aider
auxiliante *adj* helping, aiding
auxiliar *adj* auxiliary; (gram.) auxiliary; *mf* auxiliary; aid, assistant; substitute teacher, professor's assistant; *m* (gram.) auxiliary (*verb*); **§90 & regular** *va* to help, aid, assist; to attend (*a dying person*)
auxiliaría *f* substitute teaching position; assistantship
auxilio *m* help, aid, assistance, relief; **acudir en auxilio a** or **de** to come to the help of; **primeros auxilios** first aid; **auxilio en carretera** (aut.) road service; **auxilio social** social work
auxocromo *m* (chem.) auxochrome
avacado -da *adj* cowlike, slow, heavy
avadar *vn & vr* to become fordable
avahar *va* to steam; to warm with vapor or breath; *vn* to steam, give out vapor; *vr* to steam, give out vapor; to warm one's hands with one's breath
aval *m* indorsement, backing; countersignature
avalancha *f* avalanche; (fig.) avalanche
avalar *va* (com.) to guarantee with an indorsement; to answer for (*a person*) with an indorsement; to enhance; to sanction; *vn* to shake with an earthquake
avalentado -da *adj* of a boaster or braggart; swaggering, bullying (*manner*)
avalentonado -da *adj* arrogant, boastful
avalo *m* slight movement; earthquake
avalorar *va* to estimate; to encourage
avaluación *f* valuation, appraisal
avaluar §33 *va* to appraise, estimate
avalúo *m* var. of **avaluación**
avallar *va* to wall in, to fence in
avambrazo *m* armlet (*of armor*)
avance *m* advance; payment in advance; removable front (*of carriage body*); (com.) balance; (com.) estimate; (mil.) advance, attack; (elec. & mach.) lead; (mach.) feed; (mov.) preview; **avance del encendido** (mach.) spark lead
avante *adv* (naut.) fore; **tomar por avante** (naut.) to broach to
avantrén *m* (mil.) limber
avanzado -da *adj* advanced; **avanzado de años** or **de edad** advanced in years; *f* (mil.) outpost, advance guard; (fig.) vanguard

avanzar §76 *va* to propose; to advance, increase; *vn* to advance; (com.) to have a favorable balance; (Am.) to vomit; *vr* to advance
avanzo *m* (com.) balance; (com.) estimate
avaricia *f* avarice
avaricioso -sa *adj* avaricious
avariento -ta *adj* avaricious, miserly; *mf* miser
avaro -ra *adj* miserly; *mf* miser
avasallamiento *m* subjection, enslavement
avasallar *va* to subject, enslave; *vr* to become a subject or vassal; to submit
avatar *m* avatar
ave *f* bird; fowl; **ave canora** songbird; **ave de corral** barnyard fowl; **ave del paraíso** bird of paradise; **ave de mar** seafowl; **ave de paso** bird of passage; (fig.) bird of passage; **ave de rapiña** bird of prey; **ave fría** (orn.) lapwing; **ave lira** (orn.) lyrebird; **ave nocturna** night bird; (fig.) night owl; **aves de cetrería** hawking birds; **ave tonta** (orn.) yellowhammer; **ave toro** (orn.) bittern, European bittern; **ave viajera** migratory bird; **ave zancuda** (orn.) wading bird
avecilla *f* birdie; **avecilla de las nieves** (orn.) wagtail
avecinar *va* to bring near; to domicile; *vr* to approach; to take up residence
avecindamiento *m* domicile; domiciliation
avecindar *va* to domicile; *vr* to take up residence, become a resident
avechucho *m* ugly bird; (coll.) scalawag, bum
avefría *f* (orn.) lapwing
avejentado -da *adj* aged, old-looking
avejentar *va & vr* to age before one's time
avejigar §59 *va, vn & vr* to vesicate, to blister
avellana *f* hazelnut; **avellana de la India** or **avellana índica** myrobalan
avellanado -da *adj* hazel, nut-brown; shriveled
avellanador *m* countersink, countersinking bit
avellanal *m* hazel plantation
avellanar *m* hazel plantation; *va* to countersink; *vr* to shrivel, shrivel up
avellaneda *f* or **avellanedo** *m* hazel plantation
avellanero -ra *mf* vendor of hazelnuts; *f* (bot.) hazel, hazel tree
avellano *m* (bot.) hazel
avemaría *f* Ave Maria; **al avemaría** at sunset; **en un avemaría** (coll.) in a twinkle; **saber como el avemaría** (coll.) to have a ready knowledge of
Ave María *interj* gracious goodness!
avena *f* (bot.) oats (*plant or seed*); (poet.) oat (*reed instrument*)
avenado -da *adj* fickle; crazy
avenal *m* oat field
avenamiento *m* draining, drainage
avenar *va* to drain
avenate *m* oatmeal gruel; (prov.) fit of madness
avendré *1st sg fut ind of* **avenir**
avenencia *f* deal, bargain; agreement
avengo *1st sg pres ind of* **avenir**
avenido -da *adj;* **bien avenidos** in agreement; **mal avenidos** in disagreement; *f* avenue; allée; flood, freshet; assemblage, gathering
avenidor -dora *mf* reconciler, mediator
avenimiento *m* reconciliation; agreement
avenir §92 *va* to reconcile; *vr* to agree, be reconciled; **avenirse a** to correspond to; to harken to; **avenirse a** + *inf* to agree to + *inf;* **avenirse con** to get along with
aventador -dora *adj* winnowing; *mf* winnower; *m* winnowing rake; blower, fan; esparto fan (*for fanning fire*); *f* winnowing machine
aventadura *f* (vet.) windgall
aventajado -da *adj* superior, outstanding, excellent; advantageous
aventajar *va* to advance, to raise, to give an advantage to; to put ahead, to prefer; to excel; *vr* to advance, to win an advantage; to excel
aventamiento *m* fanning; blowing; winnowing
aventar §18 *va* to fan; to blow; to winnow; to scatter to the winds; (coll.) to expel, drive away; *vr* to swell, swell up; (coll.) to flee, run away
aventón *m* (Am.) push; (Am.) lift (*free ride*); **pedir aventón** (Am.) to hitchhike
aventura *f* adventure; risk, danger, peril
aventurado -da *adj* venturesome, hazardous
aventurar *va* to adventure; to adventure, to hazard (*an opinion*); *vr* to adventure, take a risk; **aventurarse a** + *inf* to venture to + *inf;* to risk + *ger;* **quien no se aventura no pasa el mar** nothing venture nothing win
aventurero -ra *adj* adventurous, adventuresome, venturesome; *m* adventurer, soldier of fortune; *f* adventuress
avergonzar §98 *va* to shame, to put to shame; to embarrass; *vr* to be ashamed; to be embarrassed; **avergonzarse de** + *inf* to be ashamed to + *inf*
avería *f* aviary; flock of birds; breakdown, failure, damage, defect; (com.) damage; (naut.) average; **localizar averías** to shoot trouble; **avería gruesa** (naut.) general or gross average
averiable *adj* damageable, perishable
averiar §90 *va* to damage; *vr* to suffer damage, be damaged; to break down
averiguable *adj* ascertainable
averiguación *f* ascertainment; inquiry
averiguador -dora *adj* investigating, inquiring; *mf* investigator, inquirer
averiguamiento *m* var. of **averiguación**
averiguar §23 *va* to ascertain, find out
averío *m* flock of birds
Averno *m* (myth.) Avernus; hell
averroísmo *m* Averroism
averroísta *mf* Averroist
averrugado -da *adj* full of warts, warty
averrugar §59 *vr* to become warty
aversión *f* aversion; **cobrar aversión a** to take a dislike for
avestruz *m* (*pl:* **-truces**) (orn.) ostrich; (coll.) blockhead; **avestruz de América** or **de la pampa** (orn.) American ostrich, rhea
avetado -da *adj* veined, streaked
avetarda *f* var. of **avutarda**
avetoro *m* (orn.) bittern, European bittern
avezar §76 *va* to accustom; *vr* to become accustomed; **avezarse a** + *inf* to accustom oneself to + *inf*, to become accustomed to + *inf*
aviación *f* aviation; aviation corps
aviador -dora *adj* preparing, equipping; flying; *mf* preparer, equipper; aviator, flyer; *m* aviator, airman; (mil.) airman; (naut.) caulker's auger; (Am.) mining moneylender; **aviador postal** air-mail pilot; *f* airwoman, aviatrix
aviar *adj* (pertaining to a) bird; §90 *va* to get ready, prepare; (coll.) to equip, provide; (Am.) to lend (*money or equipment*); **estar, encontrarse** or **quedar aviado** (coll.) to be in a mess, to be in a jam; **dejar aviado** (coll.) to leave in the lurch; *vn* (coll.) to hurry, make haste; (aer.) to take off
aviatorio -ria *adj* (pertaining to) aviation
aviatriz *f* (*pl:* **-trices**) aviatrix
avícola *adj* bird-raising
avicultor *m* bird fancier, bird keeper
avicultura *f* aviculture
avidez *f* avidity, greediness
ávido -da *adj* avid, greedy, thirsty
aviejar *va & vr* to age before one's time
avienta *f* winnowing
aviento *m* long-pronged rakelike winnowing fork; pitchfork
avieso -sa *adj* distorted, irregular; evil-minded, perverse
avigorar *va* to invigorate, revive
avilantar *vr* to be insolent
avilantez *f* or **avilanteza** *f* boldness, insolence; meanness
avilés -lesa *adj* (pertaining to) Ávila; *mf* native or inhabitant of Ávila
avillanado -da *adj* rustic, peasant
avillanamiento *m* boorishness, debasement
avillanar *va* to make boorish, to debase; *vr* to become boorish, to become debased
avinagrado -da *adj* (coll.) vinegarish, crabbed
avinagrar *va* to sour, to make sour; *vr* to sour, to turn sour; to turn into vinegar
avine *1st sg pret ind of* **avenir**
aviniendo *ger of* **avenir**
Aviñón *f* Avignon
aviñonense or **aviñonés -nesa** *adj* (pertaining to) Avignon; *mf* native or inhabitant of Avignon

avío *m* preparation, provision; (Am.) loan; **avíos** *mpl* tools, equipment, outfit; **¡al avío!** hurry up!
avión *m* airplane; (orn.) martin; **avión a turbohélice** (aer.) turbo-prop plane; **avión birreactor** (aer.) twin-jet plane; **avión cohete** (aer.) rocket plane; **avión convertible** (aer.) convertiplane; **avión de caza** (aer.) pursuit plane; **avión de combate** (aer.) fighter; **avión a chorro, de chorro, de propulsión a chorro** or **a reacción** (aer.) jet plane; **avión de transporte** (aer.) transport; **avión de travesía** (aer.) air liner; **avión interceptor** (aer.) interceptor; **avión militar** (aer.) warplane; **avión transporte** (aer.) transport
avión-correo *m* mailplane
avioneta *f* (aer.) small plane
avión-nodriza *m* var. of **aeroplano-nodriza**
avisacoches *m* (*pl:* **-ches**) car caller
avisado -da *adj* prudent, wise; **mal avisado** rash, thoughtless
avisador -dora *adj* warning; *mf* informer, announcer; adviser, admonisher; *m* electric bell; **avisador de incendio** fire alarm
avisar *va* to advise, inform; to warn, admonish; to report on; **avisar a una persona una cosa** to notify a person of or about something
aviso *m* advice, information, notice; warning, admonishment; prudence, attention, care; dispatch boat; **poner sobre aviso de** to keep (*someone*) on the lookout for; **sobre aviso** on the lookout, on the watch
avispa *f* (ent.) wasp; crafty person; **avispa cavadora** (ent.) digger wasp; **avispa de barro** (ent.) mason wasp
avispado -da *adj* (coll.) brisk, lively, clever, wide-awake
avispar *va* to spur (*a horse*); (coll.) to stir up, prod, enliven; *vr* (coll.) to become stirred up; to fret, to worry
avispero *m* wasp's nest; swarm of wasps; mass of boils; (coll.) mess, complicated affair
avispón *m* (ent.) hornet
avistar *va* to descry; *vr* to have an interview
avitaminosis *f* (path.) avitaminosis
avitelado -da *adj* (pertaining to or like) vellum
avituallamiento *m* victualing, provisioning
avituallar *va* to victual; to supply, to provision; *vr* to victual
avivadamente *adv* briskly, lively
avivador -dora *adj* reviving, enlivening; *m* (arch.) quirk; plane for making quirks
avivamiento *m* reviving, enlivening
avivar *va* to revive, enliven, brighten; *vn & vr* to revive, brighten
avizor *m* watcher; **avizores** *mpl* (slang) eyes
avizorador -dora *mf* watcher, spyer
avizorar *va* to watch; *vr* to hide and watch, to spy
avocación *f* or **avocamiento** *m* (law) removal to a superior court
avocar §86 *va* (law) to remove to a superior court
avoceta *f* (orn.) avocet
avolcanado -da *adj* volcanic
avora *f* (bot.) oil palm
avucasta *f* var. of **avutarda**
avugo *m* small early pear
avuguero *m* (bot.) pear tree
avulsión *f* (law) avulsion; (surg.) extirpation, excision
avuncular *adj* avuncular
avutarda *f* (orn.) great bustard
avutardado -da *adj* like a great bustard
ax *interj* ow!, ouch!
axial or **axil** *adj* axial
axila *f* (anat. & zool.) axilla; (bot.) axil or axilla
axilar *adj* axile; axillar; axillary; *f* (ent.) axillar
axinita *f* (mineral) axinite
axiología *f* axiology
axioma *m* axiom
axiomático -ca *adj* axiomatic
axión *m* (anat.) axion
axis *m* (*pl:* **-xis**) (anat.) axis; (zool.) axis deer
axo *m* square woolen cloth, worn by Peruvian women
axoideo -a *adj* (anat.) axoid, axoidean
axón *m* (anat.) axon; (anat. & physiol.) axon or axone
ay *m* sigh; *interj* alas!; ouch!; **¡ay de . . . !** woe to . . . !; **¡ay de mí!** ay me!, woe is me!
aya *f* governess, instructress
ayate *m* (Am.) cloth of maguey fiber
ayatito *m* (bot.) sego, sego lily
Áyax *m* (myth.) Ajax; **Áyax el Pequeño** (myth.) Ajax the Less
ayear *vn* to sigh, to utter sighs
ayeaye *m* (zool.) aye-aye
ayer *adv & m* yesterday
ayo *m* tutor
ayocote *m* (bot.) scarlet runner, scarlet runner bean
ayuda *f* aid, help, assistance; enema; **ayuda de parroquia** chapel of ease; *m* page; **ayuda de cámara** valet de chambre
ayudador -dora *adj* helping; *mf* helper
ayudanta *f* aid, assistant; (Am.) substitute (*teacher*); **ayudanta de cocina** kitchenmaid
ayudante *m* aid, assistant; (mil.) adjutant; **ayudante de campo** (mil.) aide-de-camp; **ayudante de profesor** assistant professor; **ayudante general** (mil.) adjutant general; *adj* assistant, adjutant
ayudantía *f* assistantship; (mil.) adjutancy
ayudar *va* to aid, help, assist; **ayudar a** + *inf* to help to + *inf*, to help + *inf*
ayuga *f* (bot.) mock cypress
ayunador -dora *adj* fasting; *mf* faster
ayunar *vn* to fast; to deprive oneself; (coll.) to go hungry
ayuno -na *adj* fasting; deprived; uninformed; **en ayunas** or **en ayuno** fasting, before breakfast; **estar** or **quedarse en ayunas** or **en ayuno** to be uninformed; to not catch on, to miss the point; *m* fast, fasting; **ayuno natural** fasting from midnight on
ayunque *m* anvil
ayuntamiento *m* town or city council, municipal government; town or city hall; sexual intercourse
ayustar *va* (naut.) to splice; (naut.) to scarf
ayuste *m* (naut.) splicing, splice; (naut.) scarfing, scarf
azabachado -da *adj* jet, jet-black
azabache *m* (mineral.) jet; (orn.) coal titmouse; **azabaches** *mpl* jet trinkets
azabachero *m* jet worker; jet vendor
azabara *f* (bot.) aloe
azacán -cana *adj* menial, drudging; *mf* drudge; *m* water carrier
azacanar *vr* to toil, drudge
azacaya *f* (prov.) water pipe
azache *adj* inferior (*said of silk from outside of cocoon*)
azada *f* hoe; blow with hoe
azadazo *m* blow with hoe
azadilla *f* little hoe; dibble, weeding hoe
azadón *m* hoe; grub hoe; **azadón de peto** or **de pico** mattock
azadonada *f* blow with a hoe
azadonar *va* to hoe, hoe up, dig with a hoe
azadonazo *m* var. of **azadonada**
azadonero *m* hoer
azafata *f* lady of the queen's wardrobe; (aer.) air hostess, stewardess
azafate *m* low, flat basket, tray, waiter
azafrán *m* (bot.) saffron; saffron (*stigmas and color*); (naut.) rudder frame; **azafrán bastardo, romí,** or **romín** (bot.) bastard saffron
azafranado -da *adj* saffron, saffroned
azafranal *m* saffron plantation
azafranar *va* to saffron (*to color or flavor*)
azafranero -ra *mf* saffron grower; saffron dealer
azagadero or **azagador** *m* cattle path
azagaya *f* assagai, javelin
azahar *m* orange blossom, lemon blossom, citron blossom
azainadamente *adv* perfidiously
azalá *m* (*pl:* **-laes**) Mohammedan prayer
azalea *f* (bot.) azalea
azamboa *f* citron (*fruit*)
azamboero *m* or **azamboo** *m* (bot.) citron (*tree*)
azanahoriate *m* preserved carrot; (coll.) insincere flattery

azanca *f* underground spring
azar *m* chance, hazard; accident, misfortune; fate, lot, destiny; losing card; losing throw (*at dice*); Jonah (*that which brings bad luck*); cushion side (*of billiard pocket*); hazard (*in a game*); **al azar** at random
azarandar *va* var. of **zarandar**
azarar *vr* to go awry; to get rattled
azarbe *m* irrigation trench
azarbeta *f* little irrigation trench
azarcón *m* minium; earthen pot; bright orange (*color*)
azarja *f* reel for winding raw silk
azarolla *f* var. of **acerola**
azarollo *m* var. of **acerolo**
azaroso -sa *adj* risky, hazardous; unfortunate
Azerbeiyán, el Azerbaijan
ázimo -ma *adj* azymous, unleavened
azimut *m* (*pl:* **-muts**) var. of **acimut**
azimutal *adj* var. of **acimutal**
aznacho *m* (bot.) Scotch pine
aznallo *m* (bot.) Scotch pine; (bot.) restharrow
-azo -za *suffix aug* e.g., **bribonazo** big rascal; **bocaza** big mouth; *suffix m* blow, e.g., **escobazo** blow with a broom; **puñetazo** blow with the fist, punch; shot, e.g., **cañonazo** cannon shot; **fusilazo** gunshot; wound, e.g., **flechazo** arrow wound; **sablazo** saber wound
azoado -da *adj* nitrogenous
azoar *va* to fix nitrogen in
azoato *m* nitrate
ázoe *m* (chem.) azote, nitrogen
azofaifa *f* var. of **azufaifa**
azofaifo *m* var. of **azufaifo**
azófar *m* brass, latten
azogado -da *adj* (coll.) restless, fidgety, turbulent; *m* quicksilver foil (*of a mirror*); **temblar como un azogado** (coll.) to shake like a leaf
azogamiento *m* quicksilver coating, silvering; (coll.) shaking, agitation, confusion
azogar §59 *va* to coat with quicksilver, to silver (*a mirror*); *vr* to have mercurialism or mercury poisoning; (coll.) to shake, to become agitated, to become confused
azogue *m* quicksilver, mercury; market place; (coll.) mirror; **ser un azogue** (coll.) to be restless
azoguejo *m* small market place
azoguería *f* amalgamation works
azoguero *m* amalgamator; dealer in quicksilver
azoico -ca *adj* (chem. & geol.) azoic
azolar §77 *va* to adz, to dub
azolvar *vr* to silt up, become obstructed
azor *m* (orn.) goshawk
azoramiento *m* excitement, confusion
azorar *va* to abash, disturb; to excite, stir up; *vr* to be abashed, be disturbed; to get excited, become upset
Azores *fpl* Azores
azorramiento *m* drowsiness; heavy-headedness; headache
azorrar *va* (naut.) to overload (*a boat*); *vr* to get drowsy; (naut.) to become threatening (*said of the atmosphere*); (naut.) to pitch (*from being overloaded*); (slang) to get drunk
azotable *adj* deserving a beating
azotacalles *mf* (*pl:* **-lles**) (coll.) gadabout, loafer; *f* (coll.) piano teacher
azotado -da *adj* variegated; *m* criminal whipped in public; penitent
azotador -dora *adj* whipping; *mf* whipper, flogger
azotaina *f* (coll.) whipping, flogging, spanking
azotalenguas *f* (bot.) bedstraw
azotar *va* to whip, to horsewhip, to scourge; to beat with the tail or the wings; to flail; to beat upon, beat down upon
azotazo *m* lash, lashing; slap, spanking
azote *m* whip; lash, spanking; (fig.) scourge; **el azote de Dios** the Scourge of God (*Attila*); **azotes y galeras** (coll.) tiresome fare
azotea *f* flat roof
azotina *f* (coll.) var. of **azotaina**
azteca *adj & mf* Aztec; *m* Aztec (*language*)
aztor *m* var. of **azor**
azúcar *m & f* sugar; **azúcar blanco** refined sugar; **azúcar cande** or **candi** rock candy; **azúcar de arce** maple sugar; **azúcar de flor** refined sugar; **azúcar de fruta** (chem.) fruit sugar; **azúcar de leche** sugar of milk; **azúcar de malta** malt sugar; **azúcar de plomo** (chem.) sugar of lead; **azúcar de remolacha** beet sugar; **azúcar de uva** grape sugar; **azúcar en polvo** powdered sugar; **azúcar en terrón** lump sugar; **azúcar moreno** or **negro** brown sugar
azucarado -da *adj* sugared, sugary; (coll.) sugary
azucarar *va* to sugar, to coat or ice with sugar; (coll.) to sugar, sugar over
azucarera *f* see **azucarero**
azucarería *f* (Am.) sugar store
azucarero -ra *adj* (pertaining to) sugar; *m* sugar master, sugar expert; confectioner; sugar bowl; (orn.) honey creeper; *f* sugar bowl; sugar refinery
azucarillo *m* brittle sugar bar (*made of sugar, white of egg, and lemon juice and used to sweeten water*)
azucena *f* (bot.) Madonna lily; **azucena amarilla** (bot.) day lily; **azucena atigrada** (bot.) tiger lily
azucenilla *f* (bot.) night-blooming gladiolus (*Gladiolus tristis*)
azuche *m* pile shoe
azud *m* or **azuda** *f* irrigation water wheel; dam, diversion dam
azuela *f* adz, chip ax
azufaifa *f* jujube (*fruit*)
azufaifo *m* (bot.) jujube (*tree*)
azufrado -da *adj* (pertaining to or like) sulfur; *m* sulfuring
azufrador -dora *adj* sulfuring; *m* drying machine; sulfuring machine (*for grapevines*)
azufral *m* sulfur mine
azuframiento *m* sulfuring, sulfuration
azufrar *va* to sulfur, sulfurate, sulphurize
azufre *m* (chem.) sulfur; brimstone; **azufre cañón** or **en canuto** roll sulfur; **azufre vegetal** (bot.) club moss
azufrera *f* sulfur mine
azufrón *m* powdered pyrites
azufroso -sa *adj* sulphury, sulphureous
azul *adj & m* blue; **dar el azul a** (coll.) to put on probation; **azul celeste** sky blue; **azul de mar** navy blue; **azul de metileno** methylene blue; **azul de Prusia** Prussian blue; **azul de ultramar** ultramarine (*pigment and color*); **azul marino** navy blue; **azul turquesa** turquoise blue; **azul turquí** indigo (*color*)
azulado -da *adj* blue, bluish
azulaque *m* var. of **zulaque**
azular *va* to color blue, to dye blue; *vr* to turn blue
azulear *va* to turn blue; *vn* to have a bluish cast, to look bluish, to turn blue
azulejar *va* to tile, cover with tiles
azulejería *f* tilework; tilemaking
azulejero *m* tilemaker
azulejo *m* glazed colored tile; (bot.) bluebottle, bachelor's-button; (orn.) bee eater; (orn.) indigo bunting; **azulejo antisonoro** acoustical tile
azulenco -ca *adj* blue, bluish
azulete *m* bluish cast, bluish hue; bluing
azulino -na *adj* bluish
azuloso -sa *adj* (Am.) bluish
azumar *va* to dye and oil (*the hair*)
azumbrado -da *adj* measured in azumbres; (coll.) drunk
azumbre *m* azumbre (*liquid measure: about 2 liters*)
azur *m* (her.) azure
azurita *f* (mineral.) azurite
azuzamiento *m* sicking; (coll.) teasing
azuzar §76 *va* to sic (*a dog*); (coll.) to tease, stir up, incite
azuzón -zona *mf* (slang) troublemaker

B

B, b *f* second letter of the Spanish alphabet
B. abr. of **Beato** and **Bueno** (*en examen*)
baba *f* drivel, spittle, slobber; mucus (*viscid animal secretion*); **caérsele a uno la baba** (coll.) to be overwhelmed with joy
babada *f* (vet.) stifle
babador *m* bib; apron top
babaza *f* froth, slobber; slime; (zool.) slug
babazorro *m* (coll.) boor, ill-bred fellow
babear *vn* to slobber, to drivel; to foam, to froth; (coll.) to be fascinated (*by a person of the opposite sex*); (coll.) to be overattentive (*to a woman*)
babel *m & f* babel, bedlam, confusion; (*cap.*) *m & f* Babel
babeo *m* slobbering, driveling
babera *f* beaver (*of helmet*); bib
babero *m* bib
baberol *m* beaver (*of helmet*)
Babia *f* mountainous region of León; **estar en Babia** to be absent-minded, to be stargazing
babicha *mf* (Am.) Italian; *m* (Am.) Italian (*language*); (Am.) cigar stump; **babichas** *fpl* (Am.) leavings; (Am.) dregs of pulque
babieca *adj* (coll.) simple, ignorant; *mf* (coll.) simpleton, ignoramus
Babilonia *f* see **babilonio**
babilónico -ca *adj* Babylonian; (fig.) Babylonian (*magnificent*)
babilonio -nia *adj & mf* Babylonian; *f* babel; confusion; (*cap.*) *f* Babylonia (*ancient empire*); Babylon (*ancient city; any great, rich, and wicked city*)
babilla *f* (vet.) stifle
babirusa *m* (zool.) babirusa
bable *m* Asturian (*dialect*); patois
babor *m* (naut.) port, larboard; **a babor** (naut.) aport; **de babor a estribor** (naut.) athwartships
babosa *f* see **baboso**
babosear *va* to slobber over
baboso -sa *adj* slobbery; immature, unfit; filthy, unkempt; (coll.) mushy (*with women*); (Am.) idiotic; *mf* (Am.) fool; *m* (ichth.) butterfly fish; *f* (zool.) slug
babucha *f* slipper; mule, heelless slipper
babuíno *m* (zool.) baboon
baca *f* top of stagecoach (*for passengers or baggage*); rainproof cover for stagecoach
bacalada *f* cured codfish
bacaladero -ra *adj* (pertaining to) codfish
bacalao or **bacallao** *m* codfish; (coll.) shriveled person; (Am.) cold-blooded person
bacallar *m* peasant, country fellow
bacán *m* (Am.) sport, bawd, pimp
bacanal *adj* bacchanal; bacchanalian; *f* bacchanal, bacchanalia (*orgy*); **bacanales** *fpl* bacchanals, Bacchanalia
bacante *f* bacchante; drunken, riotous woman; **bacantes** *fpl* Bacchae
bácara *f* (bot.) clary
bacará *m* baccara
bácaris *f* var. of **bácara**
bacelar *m* grape arbor; new vineyard
bacera *f* (vet.) anthrax, splenic fever
baceta *f* widow (*in card playing*)
bacía *f* basin, vessel; shaving dish
bacífero -ra *adj* (bot.) bacciferous
báciga *f* three-card game
bacilar *adj* bacillary
bacilo *m* bacillus; (anat.) rod (*in retina*)
bacillar *m* grape arbor; new vineyard
bacín *m* big chamber pot; poor box; (coll.) cur
bacinada *f* contents thrown from chamber pot; (coll.) contemptible action
bacinero -ra *mf* person who passes the plate for the poor box
bacineta *f* little chamber pot; small poor box; pan (*of gunlock*)
bacinete *m* basinet; cuirassier; (anat.) pelvis
bacinica or **bacinilla** *f* little chamber pot; small poor box
Baco *m* (myth.) Bacchus; (fig.) wine
baconiano -na *adj* Baconian
baconista *mf* Baconian
bacteria *f* bacterium
bacteriano -na *adj* bacterial
bactericida *adj* bactericidal; *m* bactericide
bacteriófago *m* (bact.) bacteriophage
bacteriólisis *f* bacteriolysis
bacteriología *f* bacteriology
bacteriológico -ca *adj* bacteriological
bacteriólogo -ga *mf* bacteriologist
bacteriostasis *f* (bact.) bacteriostasis
bacteriostático -ca *adj* bacteriostatic
bactriano -na *adj & mf* Bactrian
báculo *m* stick, staff; aid, consolation; **báculo del obispo, báculo pastoral** crozier, bishop's crozier
bache *m* hole, rut, pothole; sweating room for sheep (*to prepare them for shearing*); (radar) blip; **bache aéreo** (aer.) air pocket
bachear *va* to fill the ruts and holes in (*a road*)
bachiller -llera *adj* garrulous, loquacious; *mf* garrulous person, babbler; **bachiller** *mf* bachelor (*holder of degree*)
bachilleramiento *m* conferring the bachelor's degree; receiving the bachelor's degree
bachillerar *va* to confer the bachelor's degree on; *vr* to receive the bachelor's degree
bachillerato *m* baccalaureate, bachelor's degree
bachillerear *vn* to babble, prattle
bachillería *f* (coll.) babble, prattle; (coll.) gossip, groundless rumor
bachorno *m* (Am.) drudgery
bachornoso -sa *adj* (Am.) toilsome, laborious
bada *f* (zool.) rhinoceros
badajada *f* stroke (*of a bell*); (coll.) idle talk, nonsense
badajazo *m* stroke (*of a bell*)
badajear *vn* (coll.) to talk nonsense
badajo *m* clapper (*of bell*); (coll.) prattler, blatherskite
badajocense or **badajoceño -ña** *adj* (pertaining to) Badajoz; *mf* native or inhabitant of Badajoz
badal *m* muzzle; twitch (*to twist a horse's lip*)
badán *m* trunk (*of animal body*)
badana *f* (dressed) sheepskin; **zurrarle a uno la badana** (coll.) to tan someone's hide; (coll.) to give one a raking over the coals
badazas *fpl* (naut.) bonnet lacing
badea *f* tasteless melon; (coll.) dullard; (coll.) triviality
badén *m* gully, gutter (*channel made by rain water*); thank-you-ma'am; paved trench for a stream across a road; dry bed of stream
baderna *f* (naut.) thrummed cable
badián *m* (bot.) Chinese anise
badiana *f* (bot.) Chinese anise; badian (*fruit*)
badil *m* fire shovel
badila *f* fire shovel; **dar con la badila en los nudillos a** to rap the knuckles of; **badila de mesa** crumb tray
badilazo *m* blow with a fire shovel
badilejo *m* mason's trowel
badomía *f* nonsense, absurdity
badulaque *m* (coll.) nincompoop; (obs.) paint, make-up; (obs.) chopped-lung stew; (Am.) hell-raiser
Baedeker *m* Baedeker (*guidebook*)
baga *f* head of flax; (prov.) rope used to tie packs on beasts of burden

bagacera *f* bagasse drier
bagaje *m* beast of burden; military baggage
bagajero *m* driver of army beasts
bagar §59 *vn* to go to seed (*said of flax*)
bagarino *m* volunteer oarsman, paid oarsman (*not a slave*)
bagasa *f* prostitute, harlot, loose woman
bagatela *f* trinket; bagatelle, triviality; pinball
bagazo *m* bagasse; pressed pulp; flax straw, flax husk
bagre *adj* (Am.) showy, gaudy; (Am.) coarse, ill-bred; *m* (ichth.) catfish
bagual *adj* (Am.) wild, untamed; (Am.) dull, doltish
baguarí *m* (*pl:* **-ríes**) (orn.) South American crane
baguío *m* baguio (*cyclone in the Philippine Islands*)
bah *interj* bah!
baharí *m* (*pl:* **-ríes**) (orn.) sparrow hawk
bahía *f* bay
bahorrina *f* (coll.) slop; (coll.) riffraff
bahuno -na *adj* var. of **bajuno**
baila *f* (ichth.) hogfish
bailable *adj* danceable; with dancing; *m* ballet
bailadero *m* public dance hall, dance floor
bailador -dora *mf* dancer
bailar *va* to dance (*e.g., a polka*); to spin (*a top*); *vn* to dance; (fig.) to dance; to spin (*said of a top*); to wobble
bailarín -rina *mf* dancer; *m* dancer (*professional*); **bailarín de cuerda** ropedancer; *f* ballerina; **bailarina ombliguista** (coll.) belly dancer
baile *m* dance, ball; ballet; bailiff; **baile de etiqueta** dress ball, formal dance; **baile de los globos** bubble dance; **baile de máscaras** masquerade ball; **baile de San Vito** (path.) Saint Vitus's dance; **baile de trajes** costume ball, fancy ball; **baile serio** dress ball, formal dance
bailete *m* short ballet
bailía *f* bailiwick
bailiaje *m* commandery in the order of Malta
bailiazgo *m* bailiwick
bailío *m* knight commander of Malta
bailotear *vn* (coll.) to dance a lot and without grace, to hop about
bailoteo *m* (coll.) awkward dancing, hopping around
baivel *m* bevel square
baja *f* see **bajo**
bajá *m* (*pl:* **-jaes**) pasha
bajaca *f* (Am.) hair ribbon
bajada *f* slope; descent; swoop; (rad.) lead-in wire; **bajada de aguas** spout, downspout; **bajada de antena** (rad.) lead-in wire
bajadizo -za *adj* sloping gently, easy to go down
bajagua *f* (Am.) poor tobacco
bajamanero *m* (slang) sneak thief
bajamar *f* (naut.) low tide
bajar *va* to lower, to let down; to bring down; to descend, to go down (*stairs*); to bend down; to humble; *vn* to go down, to come down; to get off; **bajar de** to get off (*e.g., a trolley car*); *vr* to bend down; to humble oneself
bajel *m* ship, vessel
bajelero *m* boatman, skipper, master
bajero -ra *adj* lower, under
bajete *m* (coll.) shorty; (mus.) baritone; (mus.) counterpoint exercise
bajeza *f* lowness; lowliness, meanness, vileness
bajial *m* (Am.) winter marshland
bajío *m* shoal, sand bank; (Am.) lowland
bajista *mf* bear (*in stock market*); (mus.) bass viol player
bajo -ja *adj* low, lower, under; short (*in stature*); common, mean, vile; shallow; downcast; poor (*wine*); (mus.) bass; **por lo bajo** on the sly, secretly; (coll.) under one's breath; **bajo de cuerpo** short; *m* shoal, sandbank; (mus.) bass (*voice, score, singer, instrument, etc.*); **bajo profundo** (mus.) basso profundo; *f* fall, drop (*in prices*); casualty (*in war*); canceled subscription; **dar baja, ir de baja** or **ir en baja** to go down, to decline (*said, e.g., of prices*); **dar de baja** to drop (*from a list, society, etc.*); (mil.) to mark absent; **darse de baja** to drop out; **jugar a la baja** to bear the market; **bajo** *adv* down; low, in a low voice; **bajo** *prep* under
bajoalemán -mana *adj* Low-German; *m* Low German
bajoca *f* (prov.) string bean; (prov.) dead silkworm
bajón *m* decline, drop (*in health, wealth, etc.*); (mus.) bassoon; bassoon player
bajonista *mf* bassoon player, bassoonist
bajorrelieve *m* bas-relief
bajuno -na *adj* low, mean, vile
bajura *f* lowness, low or deep place, depth; shortness (*of stature*)
bakelita *f* var. of **baquelita**
Bakú *f* Baku
bala *f* bullet; bale (*of paper, cotton, etc.*); **bala dumdum** dumdum bullet; **bala fría** spent bullet; **bala perdida** stray bullet; **balas enramadas** (mil.) chain shot
Balaán *m* (Bib.) Balaam
balaca *f* (Am.) boast, boasting, bravado
balacera *f* (Am.) firing, shooting, stray shooting
balada *f* ballad; (mus.) ballade
baladí *adj* (*pl:* **-díes**) frivolous, trivial, paltry
balador -dora *adj* bleating, baaing
baladrar *vn* to scream, screech, whoop
baladre *m* (bot.) oleander, rosebay
baladrero -ra *adj* screaming, screeching; loud-mouthed
baladro *m* scream, screech, whoop
baladrón -drona *adj* boastful; *mf* boaster, braggart
baladronada *f* boasting, bragging; boastful word or deed
baladronear *vn* to boast, brag; to speak or act boastfully
bálago *m* chaff (*of hay or rye*); heap of chaff; soapsuds
balaguero *m* heap of chaff
balaj *m* or **balaje** *m* balas (*ruby spinel*)
balalaika *f* (mus.) balalaika
balance *m* rocking, swinging; hesitation, uncertainty; (com.) balancing, balance, balance sheet; (aer. & naut.) rolling; (Am.) rocking chair
balancear *va* to balance; *vn* to rock, swing; *vr* to rock, swing; to hesitate, waver
balanceo *m* balancing; rocking, swinging; hesitation
balancero *m* var. of **balanzario**
balancín *m* balance beam; rocker arm; singletree; (naut.) outrigger (*e.g., of canoe*); ropewalker's balancing pole; seesaw; balancer, halter (*of insect*)
balandra *f* (naut.) sloop
balandrán *m* cassock
balandro *m* (naut.) small sloop, fishing smack
bálano or **balano** *m* (anat.) glans of penis; (zool.) acorn barnacle
balante *adj* bleating
balanza *f* balance, scales; comparison, judgment; **en balanza** in the balance; **balanza de comercio** balance of trade; **balanza de compensación** (horol.) compensation balance; **balanza de pagos** balance of payments; **balanza de precisión** precision balance; **balanza de torsión** (phys.) torsion balance: (*cap.*) *f* (astr.) Scales
balanzario *m* weighmaster (*in mint*)
balanzón *m* cleaning pan (*of silversmith*)
balar *vn* to bleat; **balar por** (coll.) to pine for, to cry for
balarrasa *f* (coll.) strong brandy
balastar *va* (rail.) to ballast
balasto *m* (rail.) ballast
balata *f* (bot.) balata, bully tree
balate *m* terrace; narrow slope; edge, border (*of a ditch*); (zool.) slug
balausta *f* balausta (*any fruit like pomegranate*)
balaustra *f* (bot.) pomegranate tree
balaustrado -da *adj* balustered; *m* balustrade, circle of balusters; *f* balustrade, banisters
balaustrar *va* to adorn or enclose with a balustrade
balaustre *m* or **balaústre** *m* baluster, banister
balay *m* (Am.) wicker basket

balazo *m* shot; bullet wound; **acribillar a balazos** to riddle with bullets
balboa *m* balboa (*monetary unit of Panama*)
balbucear *va* to stammer (*e.g., excuses*); *vn* to stammer, stutter; to babble, prattle
balbucencia *f* or **balbuceo** *m* stammering, stuttering; babbling, prattling
balbucir §53 *vn* var. of **balbucear**
Balcanes, los the Balkans
balcánico -ca *adj* Balkan
balcanizar §76 *va* to Balkanize
balcarrotas *fpl* (Am.) sideburns, side whiskers; (Am.) locks of hair falling over sides of face
balcón *m* balcony; railing; large window with balcony
balconaje *m* balconies, row of balconies
balconcillo *m* little balcony
balda *f* see **baldo**
baldadura *f* or **baldamiento** *m* incapacity, disability
baldaquín *m* or **baldaquino** *m* baldachin, canopy, dais; (arch.) baldachin, ciborium
baldar *va* to cripple; to incapacitate; to inconvenience; to ruff, to trump
balde *m* bucket, pail; **de balde** free, for nothing; over, in excess; idle; **en balde** in vain
baldear *va* to wash (*decks, floors, etc.*) with pails of water; to bail out (*a ditch*)
baldeo *m* deckswabbing
baldés *m* sheepskin for gloves
baldío -a *adj* untilled, uncultivated; idle, lazy; careless; vagabond; vain, useless; baseless, unfounded; *m* wasteland
baldo -da *adj* lacking, out of (*a suit of cards*); *m* lack (*of a suit*); *f* closet shelf
baldón *m* insult, affront; blot, stain, disgrace
baldonar *va* to insult, to affront; to stain, disgrace
baldosa *f* floor tile, paving tile; (Am.) gravestone
baldosado *m* tile flooring, tile paving
baldosar *va* to floor or pave with tile
baldosilla *f* or **baldosín** *m* small square paving tile
baldosón *m* large paving tile, flagstone
baldragas *m* (*pl:* **-gas**) (coll.) easy-going fellow
Balduíno *m* Baldwin
balduque *m* narrow red tape
balear *adj* Balearic; *mf* native or inhabitant of the Balearic Islands; **las Baleares** the Balearic Islands; *va* (Am.) to shoot at, to shoot, to shoot to death
baleárico -ca *adj* Balearic
baleo *m* round mat; esparto fan (*for fanning fire*)
balería *f* or **balerío** *m* stock of balls or bullets (*of an army or fort*)
balero *m* bullet mold
baleta *f* small bale, small bundle
baliaga *adj* & *mf* Balinese
balido *m* bleat, bleating
balín *m* small bullet; **balines** *mpl* shot, buckshot
balinés -nesa *adj* & *mf* Balinese
balista *f* ballista
balístico -ca *adj* ballistic; *f* ballistics
balistocardiografía *f* ballistocardiography
balistocardiógrafo *m* ballistocardiograph
balistocardiograma *m* ballistocardiogram
balita *f* small bullet; small bale; (Am.) marble
balitadera *f* deer call
balitar or **baliteear** *vn* to bleat all the time
baliza *f* buoy, beacon; danger signal (*on highway undergoing repairs*)
balizaje *m* (naut.) system of buoys; (aer.) airway lighting
balizamiento *m* marking with buoys or beacons
balizar §76 *va* to mark with buoys or beacons; to show, to mark off
balneario -ria *adj* bathing, mineral, medicinal; *m* spa, watering place
balneoterapia *f* treatment with baths, balneotherapy
balomano *m* handball
balompédico -ca *adj* (pertaining to) football, soccer
balompié *m* football, soccer
balón *m* football; bale; balloon; **balón a mano** handball
baloncestista *mf* basketball player
baloncestístico -ca *adj* (pertaining to) basketball
baloncesto *m* basketball
balota *f* small ball (*used in voting*); ballot
balotada *f* ballotade (*leap of horse*)
balotaje *m* (Am.) balloting
balotar *vn* to ballot
balsa *f* raft, balsa; float; pool, puddle; (bot.) balsa, corkwood
balsadera *f* or **balsadero** *m* ferry
balsamea *f* (bot.) balm of Gilead
balsamera or **balsamerita** *f* flask for balsam
balsámico -ca *adj* balsamic, balmy; soothing, healing
balsamina *f* (bot.) balsam apple; (bot.) balsam (*Impatiens balsamina*); **balsamina de jardín** (bot.) garden balsam
balsamita *f* (bot.) hedge mustard; (bot.) feverfew; (bot.) wall rocket; **balsamita mayor** (bot.) costmary; **balsamita menor** (bot.) tansy
bálsamo *m* balsam, balm; (fig.) balm (*something soothing*); **bálsamo de Judea** or **de la Meca** balm of Gilead (*resin and ointment*); **bálsamo de Tolú** tolu or tolu balsam
balsar *m* (Am.) swamp covered with underbrush
balsear *va* to cross (*a stream*) by ferry or raft, to ferry across (*a stream*)
balsero *m* ferryman
balso *m* rope netting; (bot.) corkwood
balsopeto *m* (coll.) bosom; (coll.) pouch worn on bosom
Baltasar *m* Balthasar; (Bib.) Belshazzar
bálteo *m* (arch.) balteus, baluster (*of Ionic capital*); (archaic) balteus (*kind of baldric*)
báltico -ca *adj* Baltic; (*cap.*) *m* Baltic
balto -ta *mf* Balt
baluarte *m* (fort. & fig.) bulwark
balumba *f* great bulk
balumbo *m* bulk, bulky thing
ballena *f* whale; whalebone; corset steel, stay; **la Ballena** (astr.) Cetus, the Whale
ballenato *m* whale calf
ballener *m* whale-shaped vessel (*of Middle Ages*)
ballenero -ra *adj* (pertaining to) whaling; *m* whaler (*person and ship*); (naut.) whaleboat (*long rowboat with a bold sheer at both ends*)
ballesta *f* crossbow, arbalest; carriage spring; auto spring
ballestada *f* crossbow shot
ballestazo *m* hit or wound from crossbow shot
ballestear *va* to shoot or to shoot at with a crossbow
ballestera *f* loophole for crossbows
ballestería *f* archery; bowmen; bowmen's quarters; store of crossbows
ballestero *m* crossbowman; maker of crossbows; royal armorer
ballestilla *f* singletree; (vet.) fleam; (naut.) forestaff, cross-staff
ballestrinque *m* (naut.) clove hitch
ballet *m* (*pl:* **-llets**) ballet
ballico *m* (bot.) Italian rye grass; **ballico perenne** (bot.) cockle, rye grass
ballueca *f* (bot.) wild oats
bamba *f* fluke (*in billiards*)
bambalear *vn* & *vr* var. of **bambolear**
bambalina *f* (theat.) flies, borders
bambalúa *m* (Am.) clumsy fellow
bambanear *vn* & *vr* var. of **bambolear**
bambarotear *vn* to be loud and noisy, to make a racket
bambarria *f* fluke, scratch (*in billiards*); *mf* dolt, idiot
bambarrión *m* (coll.) big fluke; (coll.) big idiot
bambochada *f* (paint.) drinking scene, scene of revelry
bamboche *m* (coll.) plump, ruddy fellow
bamboleante *adj* swinging, swaying
bambolear *vn* & *vr* to swing, sway, reel, totter, wobble
bamboleo *m* swinging, swaying, reeling, tottering, wobbling

bambolla *f* (coll.) show, sham; pageantry
bambollero -ra *adj* (coll.) showy, flashy
bambonear *vn & vr* var. of **bambolear**
bamboneo *m* var. of **bamboleo**
bambú *m* (*pl:* **-búes**) (bot.) bamboo (*plant and hollow stems*)
bambuche *m* (Am.) ridiculous clay figure
bamburé *m* (Am.) large toad
banana *f* (bot.) banana (*tree and fruit*); (rad.) plug
bananal *m* banana plantation
bananero -ra *adj* (pertaining to the) banana; *m* (bot.) banana tree
banano *m* (bot.) banana tree
banas *fpl* (Am.) banns
banasta *f* large basket, hamper
banastero -ra *mf* basket maker
banasto *m* large round basket
Banato, el the Banat
banca *f* bench; stand, fruit stand; banking; bank (*especially in gambling*); **hacer saltar la banca** to break the bank (*in gambling*); **tener banca** (coll.) to be influential; **banca de hielo** iceberg, ice field
bancada *f* large stone bench; bedframe, solepiece; thwart; (min.) stope
bancal *m* oblong plot, oblong orchard; terrace; bench cover
bancario -ria *adj* banking, bank
bancarrota *f* bankruptcy; (fig.) bankruptcy (*utter ruin*); **hacer bancarrota** to go bankrupt
bancarrotero -ra *adj & mf* bankrupt
bance *m* rail (*used to close a road*)
banco *m* bench; bank; school (*of fish*); **banco de ahorros** savings bank; **banco de emisión** bank of issue; **banco de hielo** iceberg; **banco de liquidación** clearing house; **banco de nieblas** fog bank; **banco de pruebas** testing bench; **banco de sangre** blood bank
banda *f* band; ribbon, sash; faction, party; gang; flock; bank, shore; border, edge; side; cushion (*of billiard table*); (mus. & rad.) band; **allá de la otra banda** on the other side; **de la banda de allá de** on the other side of; **irse a la banda** (naut.) to list; **banda de rodamiento** (aut.) tread; **banda de tambores** drum corps; **Banda Oriental** East Bank or Side (*Uruguay*); **bandas laterales** (rad.) sidebands; **banda sonora** (mov.) sound track; **banda transportadora** belt conveyor
bandada *f* flock of birds; (coll.) flock (*of people*)
bandaje *m* tire
bandarria *f* (naut.) iron maul, sledge hammer
bandazo *m* swerving, zigzagging; (naut.) blow of wave on side of ship; (naut.) lurch, violent jolt to one side
bandeado -da *adj* banded, striped
bandear *va* (Am.) to cross, go through; (Am.) to swim across; (Am.) to pursue, make love to; *vr* (Am.) to manage, to get along
bandeja *f* tray; (Am.) dish
bandera *f* flag, banner; **a banderas desplegadas** in the open; **con banderas desplegadas** (mil.) with flying colors (*with flags unfurled and waving*); **bandera blanca** white flag; **bandera de parlamento** or **de paz** flag of truce; **bandera de proa** (naut.) jack; **bandera morrón** waft, weft; **bandera negra** black flag (*of pirates*)
bandereta *f* banneret
bandería *f* band, faction
banderilla *f* banderilla (*barbed dart with banderole*); (print.) paper with corrections pasted on proof; **clavar, plantar** or **poner una banderilla a** (coll.) to taunt, to be sarcastic to; (coll.) to hit for a loan; **banderillas de fuego** (taur.) banderillas with firecrackers attached
banderillear *va* to thrust banderillas into (*neck or shoulder of bull*)
banderillero *m* banderillero (*bullfighter who thrusts banderillas into neck or shoulders of bull*)
banderín *m* little flag, banneret; camp colors; recruiting post; (rail.) flag
banderita *f* banderole
banderizar **§76** *va & vr* var. of **abanderizar**
banderizo -za *adj* factional; fiery, excitable; seditious; *mf* factionist, partisan
banderola *f* banderole; (surv.) fanion; (Am.) transom
bandicut *m* (zool.) bandicoot
bandidaje *m* banditry; gang of bandits
bandido *m* bandit, outlaw
bandín *m* (naut.) stern seat
bandítismo *m* banditry
bando *m* edict, proclamation; faction, party; side (*e.g., in bridge*); **bando de destierro** ban
bandola *f* mandolin; (naut.) jury mast; (Am.) red flag (*of bullfighters*)
bandolera *f* bandoleer; female bandit, moll; **en bandolera** across the shoulders
bandolerismo *m* brigandage
bandolero *m* brigand, robber, highwayman
bandolín *m* var. of **bandola**
bandolina *f* (mus.) mandolin; pomade, hair grease
bandolón *m* (mus.) mandola
bandujo *m* sausage
bandullo *m* (coll.) belly, guts, bowels
bandurria *f* (mus.) bandurria (*instrument of lute family*)
baniano *m* banian; (bot.) banian
banjo *m* banjo
banjoísta *mf* banjoist
bánova *f* light bedcover; (prov.) bedquilt
banquero *m* banker
banqueta *f* stool, footstool; (eng. & fort.) banquette; (Am.) sidewalk
banquete *m* banquet
banquetear *va, vn & vr* to banquet
banquillo *m* bench; footstool; defendant's seat; (Am.) scaffold
banquisa *f* iceberg, floe, ice field
bantu (*pl:* **-tus**) *adj & mf* Bantu
bantú (*pl:* **-tús** *or* **-túes**) *adj & mf* var. of **bantu**
banzo *m* cheek (*of a frame*)
baña *f* water hole, bathing hole (*for animals*)
bañadera *f* (Am.) bathtub
bañadero *m* var. of **bañil**
bañado *m* chamber pot; (Am.) marshy land
bañador -dora *adj* bathing; *mf* bather; *m* bathing tub or trough; bathing suit
bañar *va* to bathe; to dip; to coat by dipping; (fig.) to cover (*e.g., with glory*); (fig.) to overspread (*e.g., with smiles*); **estar bañado en agua de rosas** to walk on air; *vr* to bathe
bañero -ra *mf* bathhouse proprietor; bath attendant; *m* dipping tub (*for candle makers*); *f* bathtub
bañil *m* water hole, wallow (*where wild animals bathe*)
bañista *mf* bather; resorter, frequenter of a spa or seaside resort
baño *m* bath; bathing; bathroom; bathtub; bagnio (*Moorish or Turkish prison*); cover, coating; **baño de asiento** sitz bath; **baño de ducha** or **de lluvia** shower bath; **baño de maría** or **baño maría** double boiler, water bath, bain-marie; **baño del sol** sun bath; **baño de vapor** steam bath; **baño para pájaros** bird bath; **baño turco** Turkish bath
bañomaría *m* double boiler, water bath, bain-marie
bao *m* (naut.) beam, cross timber; **bao mayor** (naut.) beam (*main horizontal support*)
baobab *m* (bot.) baobab
baptista *adj & mf* Baptist
baptisterio *m* baptistry
baque *m* thud, thump; bump, bruise
baquelita *f* bakelite
baqueta *f* ramrod; drumstick; **a baqueta** or **a la baqueta** harshly, scornfully; **correr baquetas** or **pasar por baquetas** (mil. & fig.) to run the gauntlet
baquetazo *m* blow with a ramrod
baquetear *va* to make run the gauntlet; to inure; to bother, to disturb
baquetudo -da *adj* (Am.) sluggish, slow, phlegmatic
baquía *f* familiarity with region (*roads, paths, rivers etc.*); (Am.) skill, manual dexterity
baquiano -na *adj* skilful, expert; *mf* guide, pathfinder
baquiar *va* (Am.) to train (*animals*)

báquico -ca *adj* Bacchic; bacchic (*drunken, riotous*)
baquira or **báquira** *mf* (zool.) peccary
bar *m* bar, barroom; cocktail bar
barahúnda *f* uproar, tumult
baraja *f* deck or pack (*of playing cards*); confusion, mix-up; gang, mob; **jugar con dos barajas** (coll.) to act with duplicity, to be a double-crosser; **peinar la baraja** to riffle the cards
barajado *m* shuffling
barajadura *f* shuffling; quarrel, dispute
barajar *va* to shuffle (*playing cards*); to mix; to bandy about; (Am.) to parry, ward off; (Am.) to catch; *vn* to fight, quarrel; *vr* to become jumbled; to get mixed up
Barajas international airport of Madrid
barajones *mpl* (prov.) skis
baranda *f* railing; cushion (*of billiard table*)
barandaje *m* or **barandajo** *m* railing, balustrade
barandal *m* upper or lower rail of balustrade; railing, balustrade
barandilla *f* railing, balustrade; (naut.) guardrail
baranguay *m* baranguay (*Philippine canoe or boat; Philippine village of 50 to 100 families*)
barata *f* see **barato**
baratador -dora *mf* barterer
baratar *vn* (archaic) to barter
baratear *va* to sell cheaply, to sell at a bargain
baratería *f* (law) barratry; **baratería de capitán** or **patrón** (naut. law) barratry
baratero -ra *adj* (Am.) cheap (*charging low prices*); *m* fellow who exacts money from winning gamblers; (Am.) haggler
baratía *f* (Am.) cheapness
baratija *f* trinket, trifle
baratillero -ra *mf* second-hand dealer
baratillo *m* second-hand goods; second-hand shop; bargain counter; bargain sale; **de baratillo** cheap, second-rate
barato -ta *adj* cheap; *m* bargain sale; **dar de barato** (coll.) to admit for the sake of argument; **de barato** gratis, free; **echar** or **meter a barato** (coll.) to heckle; (coll.) to sneer at; *f* barter; cheapness; (Am.) bargain sale; **barato** *adv* cheap
báratro *m* (poet.) hell, inferno
baratura *f* cheapness
baraúnda *f* uproar, tumult
baraustar §75 *va* to aim; to ward off
barba *f* chin; beard, whiskers; deckle edge, rough edge; gill or wattle (*of fowl*); (bot.) beard; (mach.) burr; **echarle a las barbas a uno** to throw in one's teeth; **hacer la barba** to shave (oneself); **hacer la barba a** to shave; to bore, annoy; to fawn on; **mentir por la barba** (coll.) to tell fish stories; **por barba** apiece; **barba cabruna** (bot.) goatsbeard; **barba de capuchino** (bot.) clover dodder; **barba de Júpiter** (bot.) houseleek; **barba española** (bot.) Spanish moss, Florida moss; **barbas de viejo** (bot.) Spanish moss, Florida moss; *m* (theat.) old man; **Barba Azul** Bluebeard
barbacana *f* (fort.) barbican; churchyard wall
barbacoa *f* (Am.) barbecue
barbada *f* see **barbado; la Barbada** see **barbado**
barbadejo *m* (bot.) wayfaring tree
barbadija *f* (bot.) laurustine
barbado -da *adj* bearded; barbed; deckle-edged; *m* shoot, sucker, seedling for transplanting; **plantar de barbado** to transplant (*a seedling*); *f* lower jaw of horse; bridle curb; (ichth.) dab; **la Barbada** Barbados
barbaja *f* (bot.) cut-leaved viper's-grass; **barbajas** *fpl* (agr.) first roots
barbaján *m* (Am.) rustic, hayseed
barbar *vn* to grow a beard; to breed bees; to strike root
barbárico -ca *adj* barbaric
barbaridad *f* barbarism; outrage; nonsense; (coll.) huge amount; **¡qué barbaridad!** how awful!
barbarie *f* barbarism, barbarity
barbarismo *m* (gram.) barbarism; illiteracy; barbarity; outrage; barbarians
barbarizar §76 *va* to make barbarous; to fill with barbarisms; *vn* to make atrocious remarks
bárbaro -ra *adj* barbaric; barbarous; *mf* barbarian
barbarote -ta *adj* (coll.) cruel; (coll.) coarse
barbaza *f* shaggy beard
barbear *va* to reach with the chin; to be as high as; (Am.) to shave; (Am.) to flatter; *vn* to reach the same height; **barbear con** to be as high as
barbechada *f* fallowing
barbechar *va* to plow for seeding; to fallow
barbechera *f* series of fallows; fallowing; fallowing season
barbecho *m* fallow
barbera *f* see **barbero**
barbería *f* barbershop; barbering
barberil *adj* (pertaining to a) barber
barbero -ra *adj* (Am.) fawning, flattering; *m* barber; *f* barber's wife
barbeta *f* (fort.) barbette; (naut.) racking; **a barbeta** in barbette
barbián -biana *adj* (coll.) dashing, bold, handsome
barbibermejo -ja *adj* red-bearded
barbiblanco -ca *adj* var. of **barbicano**
barbicacho *m* chin ribbon or strap, cap or hat string
barbicano -na *adj* gray-bearded, white-bearded
barbiespeso -sa *adj* heavy-bearded, thick-bearded
barbihecho -cha *adj* fresh-shaved
barbilampiño -ña *adj* smooth-faced, beardless
barbilindo -da *adj* dapper, dandified
barbiluengo -ga *adj* long-bearded
barbilla *f* tip of chin; (carp.) rabbet; barbel (*growth in mouth of fish*)
barbillera *f* tuft of tow; chin strap (*to hold mouth of corpse shut*)
barbinegro -gra *adj* black-bearded
barbiponiente *adj* (coll.) beginning to grow a beard; (coll.) beginning, apprenticed
barbiquejo *m* chin strap, hat guard; (naut.) bobstay
barbirrubio -bia *adj* blond-bearded
barbirrucio -cia *adj* gray-bearded, with a grizzled beard
barbitaheño -ña *adj* red-bearded
barbitonto -ta *adj* simple, simple-looking
barbiturato *m* (chem.) barbiturate
barbitúrico -ca *adj* (chem.) barbituric
barbo *m* (ichth.) barbel; **barbo de mar** (ichth.) red mullet
barbón *m* bearded man; billy goat; Carthusian lay brother; (coll.) graybeard, solemn old person
barboquejo *m* var. of **barbiquejo**
barbotar *va & vn* to mutter, to mumble
barbote *m* beaver (*of helmet*)
barbotear *vn* to mumble
barboteo *m* mumbling
barbudo -da *adj* bearded, long-bearded, heavy-bearded; *m* shoot, sucker, seedling for transplanting
barbulla *f* (coll.) uproar, clamor, hubbub, hullabaloo
barbullar *va* to daub; *vn* (coll.) to blabber, to make a hullabaloo
barbullón -llona *adj* loudmouthed; *mf* noisy talker
barbuquejo *m* var. of **barbiquejo**
barca *f* small boat; (naut.) bark, barque
barcada *f* boatload; boat trip
barca-goleta *f* (naut.) barkentine
barcaje *m* ferrying; boat fare
barcal *m* wooden bowl or trough; dog dish
barcarola *f* (mus.) barcarole; rowing song
barcarrón *m* (naut.) hooker, tub
barcaza *f* lighter, barge; lighterage
barcelonés -nesa *adj* (pertaining to) Barcelona; *mf* native or inhabitant of Barcelona
barceno -na *adj* ruddy, auburn
barceo *m* (bot.) matweed
barcia *f* chaff
barcinar *va* (prov.) to gather in (*grain*)
barcino -na *adj* reddish-brown and white; *mf* (Am.) turncoat (*in politics*); *f* load of hay or straw; straw-net bag

barco *m* boat, vessel; shallow ravine; **el Barco fantasma** the Flying Dutchman; **barco marinero** good sailer; **barco náufrago** shipwreck; **barco velero** fast sailer
barcolongo or **barcoluengo** *m* (hist.) round-bow sailing vessel; (hist.) long, narrow two-master
barcón *m* large boat
barchilón -lona *mf* (Am.) orderly, nurse
barda *f* bard, horse armor; thatch; hedge; (naut.) low black cloud
bardaguera *f* (bot.) osier
bardal *m* thatched fence or wall
bardana *f* (bot.) burdock; **bardana menor** (bot.) cocklebur (*Xanthium strumarium*); (bot.) hedgehog parsley
bardar *va* to thatch; to bard (*a horse*)
bardiota *m* (archaic) Byzantine imperial guard
bardo *m* bard
bardoma *f* (prov.) filth, dirt, dung
baremo *m* ready reckoner; arithmetic (*book*); scale (*of marks, salaries, etc.*); table of rates
barés *m* barège
barga *f* river barge
bargueño *m* fancy inlaid gilt secretary
baribal *m* (zool.) black bear
bario *m* (chem.) barium
barisfera *f* (geol.) barysphere
barita *f* (mineral.) baryta
baritel *m* hoist, windlass
baritina *f* (chem.) barite
barítono *m* (mus.) baritone
barjuleta *f* knapsack, haversack; tool bag
barloar *va* (naut.) to bring alongside; *vn & vr* (naut.) to come alongside
barloas *fpl* (naut.) relieving tackles
barloventear *vn* (naut.) to ply or turn to windward; to wander from place to place
barlovento *m* (naut.) windward
barman *m* (*pl:* **-mans**) bartender
barnacla *f* (zool.) barnacle; (orn.) sea goose
barniz *m* (*pl:* **-nices**) varnish; glaze (*on pottery*); face paint; gloss, polish; smattering; **dar de barniz** to varnish (*e.g., a piece of furniture*); **barniz del Japón** (bot.) tree of heaven; **barniz aislador** electric varnish
barnizado *m* varnish, varnishing, coat of varnish; (f.a.) varnishing day
barnizador -dora *adj* varnishing; glazing; *mf* varnisher; glazer
barnizar **§76** *va* to varnish; to glaze (*pottery*); to polish, to shine
barógrafo *m* barograph
barograma *m* barogram
barométrico -ca *adj* barometric
barómetro *m* barometer; (fig.) barometer; **barómetro aneroide** aneroid barometer
barón *m* baron
baronaje *m* or **baronato** *m* baronage
baronesa *f* baroness
baronía *f* barony, baronage
baronial *adj* baronial
baroscopio *m* baroscope
barquear *va* to cross (*e.g., a river*) in a boat; *vn* to cross or go across in a boat
barqueo *m* boating, crossing in a boat
barquero *m* boatman
barquía *f* fishing boat, fishing smack
barquilla *f* cone mold; (aer.) nacelle; (naut.) log; log chip; **barquilla transbordadora** transporter car
barquillero -ra *mf* maker or seller of cones; *m* cone mold; waffle iron; harbor boatman; **barquillero de los estanques** (ent.) back swimmer
barquillo *m* cone (*e.g., for ice cream*); waffle; wafer stick
barquín *m* bellows
barquinazo *m* (coll.) hard jolt, fall, or upset of a carriage
barquinera *f* bellows
barquino *m* wineskin
barra *f* bar (*of metal, etc.; of sand in river or ocean; military badge; counter of barroom*); stick (*of dynamite*); railing in courtroom; (her. & mus.) bar; (mach.) rod; gross-spun or colored thread (*in a fabric*); **barra colectora** (elec.) bus bar; **barra de balas** bar bell; **barra de labios** or **para los labios** lipstick; **barra imantada** bar magnet; **barras paralelas** (sport) parallel bars
barrabás *m* (fig.) devil; (*cap.*) *m* (Bib.) Barabbas
barrabasada *f* devilishness, fiendish act
barraca *f* cabin, hut; small country house; (Am.) storage shed
barracón *m* barracks; fair booth; (mil.) permanent quarters
barracuda *f* (ichth.) barracuda
barragán *m* barragan; barragan raincoat
barragana *f* concubine
barraganería *f* concubinage
barraganete *m* (naut.) top-timber
barramunda *f* (ichth.) Burnett salmon; (ichth.) arapaima
barranca *f* ravine, gorge, gully; (Am.) channel made by running water
barrancal *m* locality full of ravines, place full of gullies
barranco *m* ravine, gorge, gully; (Am.) cliff, precipice; great difficulty, obstruction
barrancoso -sa *adj* full of ravines, gorges, or gullies; broken, uneven; steep, precipitous
barranquear *va* to drag (*logs*) down a ravine
barranquera *f* ravine, gorge, gully
barrar *va* to daub, smear; to bar, barricade
barreal *m* (Am.) mudhole, quagmire
barrear *va* to barricade; to bar, fasten with a bar; (prov.) to strike out, cross off; *vn* to graze one's opponent's armor; *vr* (prov.) to wallow in the mud (*said of wild boar*)
barreda *f* barrier
barredero -ra *adj* sweeping; drag; *m* baker's mop; *f* street sweeper; **barredera de alfombras** carpet sweeper
barredor -dora *adj* sweeping; *mf* sweeper; **barredora de nieve** snowplow
barredura *f* sweeping; **barreduras** *fpl* sweepings, refuse
barrejobo *m* (Am.) clearing, clean sweep
barreminas *m* (*pl:* **-nas**) (nav.) mine sweeper
barrena *f* drill, auger, gimlet; bit (*of drill*); crowbar; (aer.) spin; **entrar en barrena** (aer.) to go into a spin
barrenado -da *adj* drilled; (coll.) mad, crazy
barrenar *va* to drill; to scuttle (*a ship*); to undo, upset; to violate
barrendero -ra *mf* sweeper (*person*)
barrendo *m* (Am.) wildcat
barrenero *m* drill maker, drill dealer; (min.) driller, blaster
barrenillo *m* (ent.) boring insect, borer
barreno *m* large drill; bored hole; blast hole; pride, haughtiness; (Am.) mania, pet idea; **dar barreno a** to scuttle (*a ship*)
barreña *f* or **barreño** *m* dishpan
barrer *va* to sweep, to sweep away, to sweep clean; to graze; *vn* to sweep; **barrer hacia dentro** to look out for oneself; *vr* (Am.) to shy (*said of a horse*)
barrera *f* barrier; (mil.) barricade; (mil.) barrage; clay pit; crockery cupboard; gate; tollgate; (rail.) crossing gate; (taur.) wooden barrier or fence around inside of bull ring; (taur.) first row of seats; **barrera aduanera** customs barrier; **barrera de arrecifes** barrier reef; **barrera de globos** balloon barrage; **barrera del idioma** language barrier; **barrera del sonido** or **barrera sónica** sonic barrier; **barrera de paso a nivel** (rail.) crossing gate; **barrera térmica** thermal barrier
barrero *m* potter; mudhole; (Am.) salt marsh
barreta *f* small bar; shoe lining
barretear *va* to bar, fasten with a bar; to line (*a shoe*)
barretina *f* Catalan beret
barriada *f* ward, quarter, district, precinct; houses on edge of town
barrica *f* cask, large cask
barricada *f* barricade
barrido *m* sweeping, sweepings
barriga *f* belly; (fig.) belly (*of a container*); bulge (*in a wall*)
barrigón -gona or **barrigudo -da** *adj* big-bellied
barriguera *f* bellyband, cinch, girth
barril *m* barrel; earthen water jug
barrilamen *m* stock of barrels or casks
barrilejo *m* rundlet, small barrel

barrilería *f* stock of barrels or casks; barrel factory, barrel shop
barrilero *m* cooper, barrel maker, barrel dealer
barrilete *m* dog, clamp; (naut.) mouse; (zool.) fiddler crab; keg
barrilla *f* (bot. & chem.) barilla
barrillar *m* barilla plantation; barilla pit
barrillero -ra *adj* barilla-yielding
barrillo *m* pimple
barrio *m* ward, quarter, precinct; suburb; **andar** or **estar vestido de barrio** (coll.) to be dressed plainly; **el otro barrio** (coll.) the other world; **barrio bajo** slums; **barrio comercial** shopping district, business district; **Barrio Latino** Latin Quarter; **barrios externos** suburbs
barrisco; a barrisco jumbled together, indiscriminately
barrita *f* little bar; **barrita de pan** roll
barritar *vn* to trumpet (*said of elephants*)
barrizal *m* mudhole, mire
barro *m* mud; clay; earthenware; pimple, whelk
barroco -ca *adj & m* baroque
barrocho *m* barouche
barrón *m* large bar; (bot.) beach grass
barroquismo *m* baroque style, baroque taste; extravagance, bad taste
barroso -sa *adj* muddy; pimply
barrote *m* bar, heavy bar; bolt; cross brace
barrueco *m* baroque pearl
barrumbada *f* boast; boastful extravagance
barruntador -dora *adj* conjecturing, guessing; *mf* guesser
barruntamiento *m* conjecturing, guessing
barruntar *va* to conjecture, guess; to sense
barrunte *m* or **barrunto** *m* conjecture, guess; sign, token, show
bartola; a la bartola carelessly, in a carefree manner
bartolillo *m* little meat pie; cream tart
bartolina *f* (Am.) cell, dungeon; (Am.) solitary confinement
Bartolomé *m* Bartholomew
bártulos *mpl* household tools; dealings, business; steps, means, way; **liar los bártulos** (coll.) to pack up, to gather one's belongings; **preparar los bártulos** (coll.) to get set, to lay one's plans
Baruc *m* (Bib.) Baruch
baruca *f* (coll.) snare, trap
barullo *m* tumult, uproar, confusion
barzal *m* bramblebush, thicket
barzoi *m* borzoi (*Russian wolfhound*)
barzón *m* loitering, wandering, saunter, stroll; ring or loop of a yoke
barzonear *vn* to loiter, to wander around, to saunter, to stroll
basa *f* (arch.) base; basis, foundation
basada *f* stocks (*for shipbuilding*)
basal *adj* basal, basic
basáltico -ca *adj* basaltic, basalt
basalto *m* basalt
basamento *m* (arch.) base and pedestal (*of a column*)
basanita *f* basalt; (petrog.) basanite
basar *va* to base; to support; *vr* **basarse en** to base one's judgment on, to rely on
basáride *f* (zool.) cacomistle
basca *f* nausea, squeamishness; (coll.) fit of temper, angry mood
bascosidad *f* filth, dirt
bascoso -sa *adj* nauseated, squeamish
báscula *f* platform scale
bascular *vn* to tip, tilt, rock
base *f* base; basis; **a base de** on the basis of; **primera base** *f* (baseball) first base (*station*); **primera base** *m* (baseball) first base, first baseman (*player*); **segunda base** *f* (baseball) second base (*station*); **segunda base** *m* (baseball) second base, second baseman (*player*); **tercera base** *f* (baseball) third base (*station*); **tercera base** *m* third base, third baseman (*player*); **base aérea** air base; **base aeronaval** naval air base; **base robada** (baseball) stolen base
basebolista *mf* baseball player
basicidad *f* (chem.) basicity
básico -ca *adj* basic; (chem.) basic
basidio *m* (bot.) basidium
basidiomiceto *m* (bot.) basidiomycete
basilar *adj* basilar
Basilea *f* Basle, Basel
basílica *f* basilica; (anat.) basilic vein
basiliense *adj* (pertaining to) Basle; *mf* native or inhabitant of Basle
basilio -lia *adj & m* Basilian
basilisco *m* (zool. & myth.) basilisk; **estar hecho un basilisco** to be in a rage
basquear *vn* to be nauseated
basquetbol *m* basketball
basquetbolista *mf* basketball player
basquiña *f* basquine; skirt
basta *f* see **basto**
bastaje *m* porter, errand boy
bastante *adj* enough, sufficient; *adv* enough; fairly, rather
bastantear *va* (law) to recognize as valid, to admit the legality of
bastantemente *adv* sufficiently
bastanteo *m* (law) recognition, admission, validation
bastar *vn* to suffice, be enough, be more than enough, to abound; **¡basta!** that'll do!, cut it out!; **bastar** + *inf* or **bastar con** + *inf* to be enough to + *inf*; **bastar a** or **para** + *inf* to suffice to + *inf*; *vr* to be self-sufficient; **bastarse a sí mismo** to be sufficient unto oneself
bastarda *f* see **bastardo**
bastardear *va* to debase; to adulterate, contaminate; *vn* to degenerate, deteriorate, decline
bastardelo *m* notary's notebook
bastardía *f* bastardy; meanness, wickedness, indignity
bastardillo -lla *adj* (print.) italic; *f* (print.) italics
bastardo -da *adj & mf* bastard; *m* (print.) bastard type; (naut.) parrel rope; *f* bastard file
baste *m* stitch; saddle pad
bastear *va* to baste, to tack; to tuft
bastedad *f* coarseness, rudeness, roughness
bastero *m* maker or seller of packsaddles; harness maker
basteza *f* var. of **bastedad**
bastidor *m* frame; stretcher (*for canvas*); wing (*of stage scenery*); (phot.) plate holder; **entre bastidores** (theat. & fig.) behind the scenes
bastilla *f* (sew.) hem; bastille (*small fortress*)
bastillar *va* (sew.) to hem
bastimentar *va* to supply, provision
bastimento *m* vessel; supplies, provisions
bastión *m* bastion
bastionado -da *adj* (fort.) bastioned
basto -ta *adj* coarse, rude, rough; *m* packsaddle; club (*playing card*); **bastos** *mpl* clubs (*suit of playing cards*); **el basto** the ace of clubs; *f* coarse stitch; basting; basting stitch
bastón *m* cane, staff, baton; **empuñar el bastón** to seize the reins; **meter el bastón** to intercede; **bastón de esquiar** ski pole or stick; **bastón de estoque** sword cane
bastonada *f* or **bastonazo** *m* bastinado
bastoncillo *m* small cane or stick; narrow trimming lace; (anat.) rod (*in retina*)
bastoncito *m* (bact.) rod
bastonear *va* to cane, to beat, to cudgel
bastoneo *m* caning, beating, cudgeling
bastonera *f* cane stand, umbrella stand
bastonería *f* cane making; cane shop
bastonero *m* cane maker, cane dealer; master of ceremonies at a ball; jailer's assistant
basura *f* sweepings; rubbish, refuse, trash; horse manure
basural *m* (Am.) dump, trash pile; (Am.) manure pile
basurero *m* rubbish collector, trash collector; trash can; rubbish dump
basuriento -ta *adj* (Am.) full of rubbish or trash, dirty
bata *f* smock; dressing gown, wrapper; **bata de baño** bathrobe
Bataán, el Bataan
batacazo *m* thud, bump
bataclán *m* (Am.) burlesque show
bataclana *f* (Am.) show girl, stripteaser; (Am.) pinup girl
batahola *f* (coll.) hubbub, uproar

batalla *f* battle, fight; joust, tournament; wheel base; seat (*of saddle*); worry, uneasiness; (paint.) battle piece; **en batalla** in battle array; **librar batalla** to do battle, to join battle; **batalla campal** pitched battle
batallador -dora *adj* battling; *mf* battler; fighter; fencer
batallar *vn* to battle, fight, struggle; to fence; to hesitate, waver
batallola *f* (naut.) rail
batallón *m* (mil. & fig.) battalion
batán *m* fulling mill
batanar *va* to beat or full (*cloth*); to beat, to whip; to overcome, conquer
batanear *va* to beat, to thrash
batanero *m* fuller
batanga *f* bamboo outrigger (*in Philippine Islands*)
bataola *f* var. of **batahola**
batata *f* (bot.) sweet potato (*plant and tuber*); (Am.) timidity, bashfulness
batatal *m* sweet-potato field or patch
batatazo *m* (Am.) fluke, stroke of luck; **dar batatazo** (Am.) to win against all odds (*in a horse race*)
bátavo -va *adj & mf* Batavian
batayola *f* (naut.) rail
batazo *m* (baseball) hit; **buen batazo** (baseball) fair ball; **mal batazo** (baseball) foul ball
bate *m* beating, shaking; tamping pick; baseball bat
batea *f* tray; painted wooden tray; flat-bottomed boat; tray (*e.g., of a trunk*); (rail.) flatcar; (min.) washing trough
bateado *m* (baseball) batting
bateador -dora *adj* (baseball) batting, at bat; *mf* (baseball) batter
batear *va & vn* (baseball) to bat
batel *m* small boat, skiff
batelero *m* boatman
bateo *m* (coll.) baptism; (baseball) batting
batería *f* battery; battering; (elec.) battery (*two or more cells connected together*); (baseball) battery; footlights; **batería de cocina** set of kitchen utensils
batey *m* (Am.) sugar refinery; (Am.) sugar-refining machinery
batibio *m* (zool.) bathybius
batiborrillo or **batiburrillo** *m* hodgepodge
baticola *f* crupper
batida *f* see **batido**
batidera *f* mortar hoe, concrete hoe; stirrer; device for cutting honeycombs
batidero *m* constant beating or striking; rough ground; (fig.) going and coming; **batideros** *mpl* (naut.) washboard; (naut.) patch (*to protect sails from rubbing*)
batido -da *adj* beaten (*path*); chatoyant (*silk*); *m* batter; milk shake; beating; beat; (rad.) beat; *f* battue; search, reconnoitering
batidor *m* beater (*person or device*); scout, ranger; haircomb; (mus.) finger board; **batidor de oro** goldbeater
batidora *f* beater, mixer (*device*)
batiente *m* jamb; door (*each of a pair of double doors*)· damper (*of a piano*)
batihoja *m* goldbeater; sheet-metal worker
batimento *m* (paint.) shade, shading, shadow
batimiento *m* beating; (phys.) beat
batín *m* smoking jacket
batintín *m* (mus.) Chinese gong
bationdeo *m* flapping (*of a curtain, flag, etc.*)
batiportar *va* (naut.) to house (*a gun*)
batiporte *m* (naut.) sill (*of gun ports*)
batir *va* to beat; to beat down; to clap (*the hands*); to coin; **batir las olas** to ply the seas; **batir los talones** to take to one's heels; **batir tiendas** (mil.) to strike camp; *vr* to fight
batiscafo *m* bathyscaphe
batisfera *f* bathysphere
batista *f* cambric; **batista de Escocia** batiste
batitú *m* (*pl:* **-túes**) (orn.) upland plover
bato *m* rustic, simpleton ; (orn.) wood ibis
batojar *va* to beat down (*fruit from a tree*)
batolito *m* (geol.) batholith
batología *f* battology
batómetro *m* bathometer
batracio *adj & m* (zool.) batrachian
batucar §86 *va* to shake, to shake up, to stir together
batuda *f* jumping (*on a springboard*)
batueco -ca *adj* stupid, foolish, simple
batuque *m* (Am.) uproar, rumpus; (Am.) jamboree; **armar un batuque** (Am.) to raise a row
batuquear *va* var. of **batucar**
baturrillo *m* hodgepodge
baturro -rra *adj* (dial.) countrified; *mf* (dial.) peasant
batuta *f* (mus.) baton; **llevar la batuta** (coll.) to be in charge, to boss the show
Baucis *f* (myth.) Baucis
baúl *m* trunk; (coll.) belly; **baúl mundo** Saratoga trunk; **baúl perchero** or **ropero** wardrobe trunk
baulería *f* trunk shop
baulero *m* trunk maker or dealer
bauprés *m* (naut.) bowsprit
bausán -sana *adj* (Am.) idle, loafing; *mf* fool, idiot; (Am.) loafer; *m & f* straw soldier (*figure stuffed with straw*)
bautismal *adj* baptismal
bautismo *m* baptism; (eccl.) baptism; **bautismo de aire** first flight in an airplane; **bautismo de fuego** baptism of fire
bautista *adj* Baptist; *mf* baptizer; Baptist; **el Bautista** (Bib.) John the Baptist
bautisterio *m* baptistery
bautizar §76 *va* to baptise (*a person, a ship; to give a name to*); to throw water on (*a person*); (coll.) to dilute, to water (*wine*)
bautizo *m* baptism; christening party
bauxita *f* (mineral.) bauxite
bávaro -ra *adj & mf* Bavarian; *m* Bavarian (*dialect*)
Baviera *f* Bavaria; (*l.c.*) *f* (Am.) Bavarian beer, Munich beer
baya *f* see **bayo**
bayadera *f* bayadere (*female dancer and singer of India*)
bayal *adj* berry-like; bay; *m* lever used for turning stones
Bayardo, señor de seigneur de Bayard
bayeta *f* baize; floor mop
bayetón *m* bearskin (*shaggy woolen cloth for overcoats*)
bayo -ya *adj* bay; *m* bay; silkworm used as bait; *f* berry; (coll.) fun, joke, trick
Bayona *f* Bayonne
bayonense or **bayonés -nesa** *adj* (pertaining to) Bayonne; *mf* native or inhabitant of Bayonne
bayoneta *f* bayonet; (bot.) Spanish bayonet, Spanish dagger; **bayonetas** *fpl* troops, army; **bayoneta espada** sword bayonet
bayonetazo *m* bayonet thrust, bayonet wound
bayonetear *va* (Am.) to bayonet
bayuca *f* (coll.) inn, tavern, drinking place
baza *f* see **bazo**
bazar *m* bazar
bazo -za *adj* yellowish-brown; *m* yellowish brown; (anat.) spleen; *f* trick (*cards in one round*); **hacer baza** (coll.) to get along, to succeed; **meter baza (en)** (coll.) to butt in; **no dejar meter baza** (coll.) to not let (*a person*) get a word in edgewise; **baza rápida** (cards) quick trick
bazofia *f* offal, refuse, garbage, hogwash
bazuca *f* (mil.) bazooka (*portable rocket launcher*)
bazucar §86 *va* to stir by shaking; to tamper with
bazuquear *va* var. of **bazucar**
bazuqueo *m* stirring, shaking; **bazuqueo gástrico** intestinal rumblings
be *m* baa
beatería *f* cant, hypocrisy, sanctimony
beaterio *m* house of lay sisters
beatificación *f* beatification
beatificar §86 *va* to beatify
beatífico -ca *adj* beatific
beatilla *f* betille, fine linen
beatísimo -ma *adj super* most holy; **Beatísima madre** Holy Mother; **Beatísimo padre** Holy Father
beatitud *f* beatitude; Beatitude (*Pope*)
beato -ta *adj* happy, blessed; beatified; devout; prudish, bigoted; *mf* beatified person; devout

person; prude, bigot; *m* man who wears clerical dress but is not in a religious community; (coll.) churchgoer; *f* charity worker (*woman*); lay sister
beatón -tona *adj* hypocritical, bigoted; *mf* hypocrite, bigot
Beatriz *f* Beatrice
beatucho -cha *mf* (coll.) scheming hypocrite
bebé *m* baby; doll
bebeco -ca *adj* (Am.) albino
bebedero -ra *adj* drinkable; *m* water trough; drinking dish or pan (*for animals*); spout (*of drinking vessel*); (found.) sprue
bebedizo -za *adj* drinkable; *m* potion (*medicinal or poisonous*); philter
bebedor -dora *adj* drinking; *mf* drinker; hard drinker, toper
beber *m* drink, drinking; *va* to drink; to drink in; **beber los vientos por** to sigh for, to long for; *vn* to drink; **beber a la salud de** to drink to the health of; **beber de** or **en** to drink out of; **beber por la salud de** to drink to the health of; *vr* to drink, to drink up; (fig.) to drink in (*e.g., a book*)
beberrón -rrona *adj* (coll.) hard-drinking, drunk; *mf* (coll.) hard drinker, drunk, drunkard
bebestible *adj* drinkable; *m* drink
bebezón *m* (Am.) drunk, spree, drinking party
bebible *adj* (coll.) pleasant, drinkable
bebido -da *adj* tipsy; *f* drink; (Am.) potion, medicine; (prov.) break for a bite and a drink
bebirina *f* (pharm.) bebeerine
bebistrajo *m* (coll.) unpalatable drink, dose
beborrotear *vn* (coll.) to sip, to tipple
beca *f* scholarship, fellowship; sash worn over academic gown
becabunga *f* (bot.) brooklime
becacín *m* (orn.) whole snipe
becacina *f* (orn.) great or double snipe
becado -da *mf* (Am.) var. of **becario;** *f* (orn.) woodcock; **becada de los pantanos** (orn.) jacksnipe
becafigo *m* (orn.) beccafico, figpecker
becar §86 *va* (Am.) to grant a scholarship or fellowship to
becardón *m* (orn.) snipe
becario -ria *mf* scholar, fellow, holder of a scholarship or fellowship
becerra *f* see **becerro**
becerrada *f* (taur.) fight of yearling calves
becerrero *m* keeper of herds of yearling calves
becerril *adj* (pertaining to a) calf
becerrillo *m* calfskin
becerro -rra *mf* yearling calf; *m* calfskin; **becerro de oro** (Bib. & fig.) golden calf; **becerro marino** (zool.) sea calf; *f* (bot.) snapdragon
becoquín *m* cap with strap under the chin
becoquino *m* (bot.) honeywort
becuadro *m* (mus.) natural sign
bechamela *f* béchamel sauce
Bechuanalandia, la Bechuanaland
bedano *m* heavy chisel
bedel *m* beadle
bedelía *f* beadleship
bedelio *m* bdellium
beduíno -na *adj & mf* Bedouin; *m* barbarian
befa *f* see **befo**
befar *va* to jeer at, to scoff at; *vn* to move the lips (*said of a horse*)
befo -fa *adj* blobber (*lip*); blobber-lipped; knock-kneed; *m* lip (*of an animal*); monkey; *f* jeer, scoff
begonia *f* (bot.) begonia
begoniáceo -a *adj* (bot.) begoniaceous
behaviorismo *m* behaviorism
behén *m* var. of **ben**
behetría *f* confusion, disorder, pandemonium
béisbol *m* baseball
beisbolero -ra or **beisbolista** *mf* (Am.) baseball player
bejín *m* (bot.) puffball; (coll.) touchy person, cross child
bejuco *m* (bot.) liana; **bejuco de corona** (bot.) bull briar
bejuquillo *m* Chinese gold necklace; ipecac
Belcebú *m* (Bib.) Beelzebub
belcho *m* (bot.) joint fir
beldad *f* beauty (*quality of beautiful; beautiful woman*)
beldar §18 *va* to winnow with a rakelike fork
belemnita *f* (pal.) belemnite
belén *m* crèche; (coll.) confusion, bedlam; (coll.) madhouse; risk, hazard; (slang) gossip, lie; (*cap.*) *m* Bethlehem
beleño *m* (bot.) henbane
belérico *m* (bot.) myrobalan
Belerofonte *m* (myth.) Bellerophon
belesa *f* (bot.) leadwort
belez *m* or **belezo** *m* jar, vessel; piece of furniture
belfo -fa *adj* blobber (*lip*); blobber-lipped; *m* lip (*of an animal*); blobber lip
belga *adj & mf* Belgian
bélgico -ca *adj* Belgian; (*cap.*) *f* Belgium
Belgrado *f* Belgrade
Bélice Belize
belicismo *m* war spirit, militarism
belicista *adj* war, militaristic
bélico -ca *adj* warlike
belicosidad *f* bellicosity
belicoso -sa *adj* bellicose
beligerancia *f* belligerence, belligerency
beligerante *adj & m* belligerent
belígero -ra *adj* (poet.) warlike
belio *m* (phys.) bel
Belisario *m* Belisarius
belísono -na *adj* with warlike sound
belitre *adj* (coll.) low, mean, vile; *m* rogue, scoundrel
belorta *f* clasp ring of plow
Beltrán *m* Bertram
beltranear *vn* (coll.) to be crude, to be uncouth
Beluchistán, el Baluchistan
beluga *f* (zool.) beluga
belvedere *m* belvedere
bellacada *f* var. of **bellaquería**
bellaco -ca *adj* sly, cunning; wicked, knavish; balky; *mf* scoundrel, knave
belladona *f* (bot.) belladonna, banewort; (pharm.) belladonna
bellaquear *vn* to deceive, to cheat, to be crooked; to rear; (Am.) to be stubborn
bellaquería *f* slyness, cunning; wickedness, knavery
belleza *f* beauty (*quality of beautiful; beautiful woman*)
bello -lla *adj* beautiful, fair; **bello ideal** beau ideal; **la Bella durmiente** Sleeping Beauty
bellorio -ria *adj* mouse-colored
bellorita *f* (bot.) English daisy
bellota *f* acorn; acorn-shaped perfume box; (zool.) acorn barnacle; carnation bud; (coll.) Adam's apple; **bellota de mar** or **marina** (zool.) sea urchin
bellote *m* round-headed spike
bellotear *vn* to feed on acorns (*said of pigs*)
bellotero -ra *mf* acorn gatherer or vendor; *f* acorn season; acorn crop
bembo -ba *adj* (Am.) thick-lipped; (Am.) snouty; *mf* (Am.) thicklips (*person*); (Am.) simpleton; *m* (Am.) thick lip
bembón -bona *adj* (Am.) thick-lipped; (Am.) snouty
bemol *adj* (mus.) flat; *m* (mus.) flat; **doble bemol** (mus.) double flat; **tener bemoles** or **tener tres bemoles** (coll.) to be full of difficulties, to be a tough job
bemolado -da *adj* (mus.) flat, lowered a semitone
ben *m* (bot.) horse-radish tree
bencedrina *f* (pharm.) benzedrine
benceno *m* (chem.) benzene
bencidina *f* (chem.) benzidine
bencina *f* benzine
bendecidor -dora *adj* blessing, giving blessings
bendecir §24 *va* to bless; to consecrate; to extol
bendición *f* benediction, blessing; grace (*at table*); **bendiciones** *fpl* wedding ceremony; **de bendición** legitimate; **que es una bendición** abundantly, with the greatest ease; **echar la bendición a** (coll.) to have nothing to do with, to say good-bye to; **bendición de la mesa** grace; **bendiciones nupciales** wedding ceremony
bendigo *1st sg pres ind of* **bendecir**

bendije *1st sg pret ind of* **bendecir**
bendito -ta *adj* saintly, blessed; happy; simple, silly; holy (*water*); **como el pan bendito** (coll.) as easy as pie; **ser un bendito** (coll.) to be a simpleton, be a simple-minded soul
benedícite *m* (eccl.) Benedicite; (coll.) benedicite (*as at table*)
benedictino -na *adj & mf* Benedictine; *m* benedictine (*liqueur*)
Benedicto *m* Benedict (*pope*)
benedictus *m* (eccl.) Benedictus
beneficencia *f* beneficence, charity, welfare; public welfare
beneficentísimo -ma *adj super* very or most beneficent or charitable
beneficiación *f* benefit; cultivation; exploitation; reduction, processing (*of ores*)
beneficiado -da *mf* person receiving the proceeds of a benefit performance; *m* (eccl.) beneficiary
beneficial *adj* pertaining to ecclesiastical benefices
beneficiar *va* to benefit; to cultivate (*land*); to exploit, to work (*a mine*); to reduce, to process (*ores*); to season; to serve (*a certain region or part of country*); (com.) to discount; (Am.) to slaughter (*cattle*); *vn* to benefit; *vr* **beneficiarse de** to take advantage of
beneficiario -ria *mf* beneficiary
beneficio *m* beneficence, benefaction; yield, profit; benefit; (theat.) benefit, benefit performance; (eccl.) benefice; exploitation (*of a mine*); smelting, ore reduction; **a beneficio de** for the benefit of
beneficioso -sa *adj* beneficial, profitable
benéfico -ca *adj* beneficent, charitable, benevolent; beneficial
benemérito -ta *adj* worthy, meritorious; *mf* worthy, notable; **benemérito de la patria** national hero
beneplácito *m* approval, consent
benevolencia *f* benevolence
benevolentísimo -ma *adj super* very or most benevolent or kind
benévolo -la *adj* benevolent, kind
Bengala *f* Bengal; (*l.c.*) *f* Bengal hemp; Bengal light; (aer.) flare
bengalí (*pl:* **-líes**) *adj & mf* Bengalese, Bengali; *m* Bengali (*language*); (orn.) Bengali
bengalina *f* bengaline
benignidad *f* benignity, benignancy
benigno -na *adj* benign, benignant, mild, kind; (path.) benign, benignant
benito -ta *adj & mf* Benedictine; (*cap.*) *m* Benedict
benjamín *m* baby (*youngest child*); (*cap.*) *m* Benjamin
benjuí *m* benzoin (*fragrant resin*)
bentos *m* (biol.) benthos
benzoato *m* (chem.) benzoate
benzoico -ca *adj* (chem.) benzoic
benzoin *m* (bot.) benzoin
benzoína *f* (chem.) benzoin
benzol *m* (chem.) benzol; (chem.) benzene
beocio -cia *adj* Boeotian; (fig.) Boeotian (*dull, stupid*); *mf* Boeotian; **la Beocia** Boeotia
beodez *f* drunkenness
beodo -da *adj & mf* drunk
beorí *m* (*pl:* **-ríes**) (zool.) American tapir
beque *m* (naut.) head (*of ship*); (naut.) beakhead
berberecho *m* (zool.) cockle (*Cardium edule*)
berberí (*pl:* **-ríes**) *adj & mf* Berber; *m* Berber (*language*); mother-of-pearl
Berbería *f* Barbary
berberís *m* (*pl:* **-rises**) (bot.) barberry (*shrub and fruit*)
berberisco -ca *adj & mf* var. of **bereber**
bérbero *m* (bot.) barberry (*shrub and fruit*)
berbiquí *m* (*pl:* **-quíes**) brace, carpenter's brace; **berbiquí y barrena** brace and bit
berceo *m* (bot.) matweed
bercial *m* field of matweed
bereber *adj & mf* Berber; *m* Berber (*language*)
berenjena *f* (bot.) eggplant
berenjenal *m* bed of eggplants; (coll.) predicament, kettle of fish, e.g., **en buen berenjenal nos hemos metido** (coll.) this is a fine kettle of fish we've got into
bergamota *f* bergamot (*lime; pear; perfume; snuff*)
bergamote *m* or **bergamoto** *m* (bot.) bergamot (*lime tree; pear tree*)
bergante *m* scoundrel, rascal
bergantín *m* (naut.) brig; **bergantín goleta** (naut.) brigantine, hermaphrodite brig
beriberi *m* (path.) beriberi
berilio *m* (chem.) beryllium
berilo *m* (mineral.) beryl
berkelio *m* (chem.) berkelium
Berlín *m* Berlin
berlina *f* berlin (*carriage*); closed front compartment (*of stagecoach or railroad car*); **en berlina** in a ridiculous position
berlinés -nesa *adj* (pertaining to) Berlin; *mf* Berliner
Berlín-Este, el East Berlin
berlinga *f* clothes pole; poker
berlingar §59 *va* to stir (*molten mass*) with poker
Berlín-Oeste, el West Berlin
berma *f* (fort.) berm
bermejear *vn* to turn bright red; to look bright red
bermejizo -za *adj* reddish; *m* (zool.) fruit bat, flying fox
bermejo -ja *adj* vermilion, bright red
bermejón -jona *adj* red, reddish
bermejuela *f* (ichth.) bitterling
bermejura *f* bright redness
bermellón *m* vermilion
Bermudas, las Bermuda
bermudeño -ña *adj & mf* Bermudian
Berna *f* Bern
Bernabé *m* Barnaby
bernardina *f* (coll.) tall story, extravagant boastful lie
bernardo -da *adj* Bernardine; *m* Bernardine monk; *f* Bernardine nun; (*cap.*) *m* Bernard
bernegal *m* drinking cup with scalloped edge
bernés -nesa *adj & mf* Bernese
bernia *f* rug; rug cloak
bernicla *f* (orn.) barnacle goose
berra *f* tall water cress
berraza *f* (bot.) water parsnip; tall water cress
berrear *vn* to low, to bellow
berrenchín *m* strong breath of angry boar; (coll.) rage, tantrum
berrendo -da *adj* two-colored; spotted; *m* (zool.) pronghorn
berrera *f* (bot.) water parsnip
berrido *m* lowing, bellowing; screech
berrín *m* (coll.) touchy person, cross child; small water cress
berrinche *m* (coll.) rage, tantrum
berrinchudo -da *adj* (Am.) cross, irascible
berrizal *m* water-cressy place
berro *m* (bot.) water cress (*plant and leaves that are used for salad*); **berro de caballo** (bot.) brooklime
berrocal *m* rocky spot
berroqueño -ña *adj* hard, resistant; hardened, hard-hearted; see **piedra**
berrueco *m* granite rock; baroque pearl; (path.) iritis
berta *f* bertha (*collar*); (*cap.*) *f* Bertha; (coll.) Bertha (*German cannon*)
bertillonaje *m* Bertillon system, bertillonnage
berza *f* (bot.) cabbage; **berzas** *fpl* cabbage (*for eating*); **mezclar berzas con capachos** (coll.) to bring up something irrelevant
berzal *m* cabbage patch
besador -dora *adj* kissing, fond of kissing
besalamano *m* unsigned note, written in the third person and marked B.L.M. (*kisses your hand*)
besamanos *m* levee, visit at court; throwing kisses
besamela *f* var. of **bechamela**
besana *f* furrowing; first furrow
besar *va* to kiss; (coll.) to graze, to touch; **a besar** (naut.) chock-a-block; **besar la mano** or **los pies** to give regards, to pay respects; *vr* (coll.) to bump heads together
Besarabia, la Bessarabia
besico *m* little kiss; **besico de monja** (bot.) Canterbury bell; (bot.) balloon vine, Indian heart

beso *m* kiss; kissing crust (*of bread*); bump; **beso de Judas** Judas kiss; **beso sonado** buss
bestezuela *f* little beast
bestia *f* beast; **gran bestia** (zool.) tapir; **bestia de carga** beast of burden; *mf* dunce, boor; *adj* stupid, boorish
bestiaje *m* beasts of burden
bestial *adj* beastly, bestial; (coll.) terrific (*extraordinarily great, intense, fine, beautiful, etc.*)
bestialidad *f* beastliness, bestiality; (coll.) stupidity
bestializar §76 *vr* to live like a beast, to become bestialized
bestiario *m* gladiator; bestiary
bestiaza *f* big beast; big fool
bestión *m* big beast; big brute (*person*); (arch.) grotesque animal figure, chimera
béstola *f* plowstaff
besucador -dora *adj* (coll.) kissing; *mf* (coll.) kisser
besucar §86 *va* (coll.) var. of **besuquear**
besucón -cona *adj* (coll.) kissing; *mf* (coll.) kisser
besugo *m* (ichth.) sea bream; (ichth.) red porgy
besuguero -ra *mf* fishmonger who sells sea breams; *f* fishing boat, fishing boat for fishing sea breams; fish pan for cooking sea breams
besuguete *m* (ichth.) little sea bream
besuquear *va* (coll.) to kiss repeatedly, to keep on kissing
besuqueo *m* (coll.) kissing, repeated kissing
beta *f* string, line, tape; beta
betabel *m* (Am.) beet
Betania *f* (Bib.) Bethany
betarraga or **betarrata** *f* (bot.) beet
betatrón *m* (phys.) betatron
betel *m* (bot.) betel
Betelgeuze *f* (astr.) Betelgeuse
bético -ca *adj* & *mf* Andalusian
betijo *m* stick fastened in the mouth of young goats to keep them from suckling but not from grazing
Betis *m* ancient name of the Guadalquivir
betlemita *mf* Bethlehemite
betónica *f* (bot.) hedge nettle, betony
Betsabé *f* (Bib.) Bathsheba
Betsaida *f* (Bib.) Bethsaida
betuláceo -a *adj* (bot.) betulaceous
betuminoso -sa *adj* var. of **bituminoso**
betún *m* bitumen; shoe polish, shoe blacking; (mach.) packing; **betún de Judea** bitumen of Judea, Jew's pitch; **betún de saliva** (coll.) elbow grease
betunería *f* pitch shop
betunero *m* pitch dealer
bezante *m* bezant (*coin*); (f.a. & her.) bezant
bezo *m* blubber lip; proud flesh
bezoar *m* bezoar
bezudo -da *adj* thick-lipped
biangular *adj* biangular
biatómico -ca *adj* (chem.) biatomic
biaxil *adj* biaxial
biaza *f* saddlebag
bibásico -ca *adj* (chem.) dibasic
biberón *m* nursing bottle
bibijagua *f* (ent.) leaf-cutting ant; (Am.) hustler
Biblia *f* Bible
biblicista *mf* Biblicist
bíblico -ca *adj* Biblical
bibliófilo -la *mf* bibliophile
bibliografía *f* bibliography
bibliográfico -ca *adj* bibliographic or bibliographical
bibliógrafo -fa *mf* bibliographer
bibliomanía *f* bibliomania
bibliómano -na *adj* & *mf* bibliomaniac
biblioteca *f* library; **biblioteca de consulta** reference library; **biblioteca de préstamo** lending library; **biblioteca rodante** bookmobile
bibliotecario -ria *mf* librarian
B.I.C. abr. of **Brigada de Investigación Criminal**
bical *m* (ichth.) male salmon
bicameral *adj* bicameral
bicarbonato *m* (chem.) bicarbonate; **bicarbonato sódico** or **de sosa** (chem.) bicarbonate of soda
bicéfalo -la *adj* bicephalous
bicentenario -ria *adj* & *m* bicentenary or bicentennial
bíceps *m* (*pl:* **-ceps**) (anat.) biceps
bicerra *f* (zool.) wild goat, mountain goat
bici *f* (coll.) bike (*bicycle*)
bicicleta *f* bicycle
biciclista *mf* bicyclist
biciclo *m* velocipede
bicilíndrico -ca *adj* two-cylinder
bicípite *adj* bicipital
bicoca *f* trifle, bagatelle
bicolor *adj* bicolor, bicolored
bicóncavo -va *adj* biconcave
biconvexo -xa *adj* biconvex
bicoquete *m* or **bicoquín** *m* two-pointed skullcap
bicorne *adj* (poet.) two-horned, two-pointed
bicornio *m* two-cornered hat
bicos *mpl* gold studs (*for velvet caps*)
bicromato *m* (chem.) bichromate
bicromía *f* two-color print
bicuento *m* (archaic) trillion (U.S.A.) (*one million million*)
bicuspidado -da *adj* bicuspidate
bicúspide *adj* bicuspid; (anat.) bicuspid; *m* (anat.) bicuspid
bicha *f* (superstitious use) snake; (archeol.) grotesque animal figure, chimera
bichero *m* boat hook
bicho *m* bug, vermin; beast; fighting bull; fool, simpleton; (coll.) brat, imp; **de puro bicho** (Am.) out of spite, out of pure envy; **mal bicho** wicked fellow, evil schemer; ferocious bull; **tener bicho** (Am.) to have a wild thirst; **bicho viviente** (coll.) living soul
bidé *m* bidet (*tub for sitz bath*)
bidente *adj* bidentate; *m* weeding hoe
bidón *m* can, tin can; drum (*container*)
biela *f* (mach.) connecting rod; (aut.) tie rod (*of steering system*)
bielda *f* wooden rake; winnowing
bieldar *va* to winnow with a rakelike fork
bieldo or **bielgo** *m* rakelike winnowing fork
bielorruso -sa *adj* & *mf* Byelorussian
bien *adv* well; properly, all right, readily; about; very, fully; indeed; **ahora bien** now then; **de bien en mejor** better and better; **más bien** rather; somewhat; **o bien** or else; **por bien** willingly; **si bien** while, though; **tener a bien** to deem wise or proper; **tener a bien** + *inf* to see fit to + *inf*; **y bien** now then, well; **bien a bien** willingly; **bien así como** or **bien como** just as; **bien que** although ‖ *conj* **no bien** as soon as, just as; scarcely; **bien . . . bien** either . . . or ‖ *m* good, welfare; property, piece of property; dearest, darling; **en bien de** for the sake of, for the benefit of; **bienes** *mpl* wealth, riches, property, possessions; **bienes de consumo** consumers' goods; **bienes de fortuna** worldly possessions; **bienes de producción** producers' goods; **bienes dotales** dower; **bienes gananciales** property acquired during married life; **bienes inmuebles** real estate; **bienes mostrencos** unclaimed property; **bienes muebles** personal property; **bienes parafernales** (law) paraphernalia; **bienes raíces** real estate; **bienes relictos** estate (*left by a decedent*); **bienes semovientes** livestock
bienal *adj* & *f* biennial
bienamado -da *adj* dearly beloved
bienandante *adj* happy, prosperous
bienandanza *f* happiness, prosperity, welfare
bienaventurado -da blissful, happy; blessed; simple
bienaventuranza *f* bliss, blessedness; well-being; **las bienaventuranzas** (theol.) the Beatitudes
bienestar *m* well-being, welfare, abundance
bienfortunado -da *adj* fortunate, lucky
biengranada *f* (bot.) botryoid goosefoot
bienhablado -da *adj* well-spoken
bienhadado -da *adj* fortunate, lucky
bienhechor -chora *adj* beneficent; *m* benefactor; *f* benefactress
bienhechuría *f* (Am.) improvements (*to real estate*)
bienintencionado -da *adj* well-meaning

bienio *m* biennium
bienllegada *f* welcome
bienmandado -da *adj* obedient, submissive
bienmesabe *m* meringue batter
bienoliente *adj* fragrant
bienparecer *m* compromise to save face
bienpareciente *adj* good-looking
bienquerencia *f* affection, fondness, good will
bienquerer *m* affection, fondness, good will; **§70** *va* to like, to be fond of, to be well-disposed toward
bienqueriente *adj* affectionate, fond, well-disposed
bienquerré *1st sg fut ind of* **bienquerer**
bienquise *1st sg pret ind of* **bienquerer**
bienquistar *va* to bring together, to reconcile; *vr* to become reconciled
bienquisto -ta *adj* well-thought-of
bienteveo *m* elevated wigwam from which to watch the vineyard; (orn.) Derby flycatcher
bienvenido -da *adj* welcome; *f* safe arrival; welcome; **dar la bienvenida a** to welcome
bienvivir *vn* to live in comfort; to live right
bies *m* bias
bifásico -ca *adj* (elec.) two-phase, diphase
bífero -ra *adj* (bot.) biferous
bífido -da *adj* bifid
bifilar *adj* bifilar; (elec.) two-wire
bifloro -ra *adj* biflorous
bifocal *adj* bifocal
biforme *adj* biform
bifronte *adj* (poet.) double-faced
biftec *m* (*pl:* **-tecs**) beefsteak
bifurcación *f* bifurcation; branch; junction
bifurcado -da *adj* bifurcate, forked
bifurcar §86 *vr* to bifurcate, to fork, to branch
biga *f* two-horse carriage; (poet.) team of two horses
bigamia *f* bigamy
bígamo -ma *adj* bigamous; *mf* bigamist
bigardear *vn* (coll.) to bum around
bigardía *f* licentiousness; perversity; fake, dissimulation
bigardo -da *adj* licentious; wanton, perverse
bigardón -dona *adj* licentious; wanton, perverse; (dial.) lank and overgrown
bígaro *m* (zool.) sea snail, periwinkle
bigarrado -da *adj* var. of **abigarrado**
bigarro *m* var. of **bígaro**
bignonia *f* (bot.) bignonia
bigorneta *f* small anvil, stake
bigornia *f* two-horned anvil
bigote *m* mustache; (print.) dash rule; (found.) slag tap; **no tener malos bigotes** (coll.) to be not bad-looking (*said of a girl or woman*); **tener bigotes** (coll.) to have a mind of one's own; **bigote de gato** (rad.) cat whisker
bigotera *f* chamois mustache protector (*to keep points of mustache straight*); smear on upper lip; folding carriage seat; bow compass
bigotudo -da *adj* mustachioed
bija *f* (bot.) annatto tree; annatto (*dyestuff*)
bilabiado -da *adj* (bot.) bilabiate
bilabial *adj* & *f* (phonet.) bilabial
bilateral *adj* bilateral
bilbaíno -na *adj* (pertaining to) Bilbao; *mf* native or inhabitant of Bilbao
biliar or **biliario -ria** *adj* biliary
bilingüe *adj* bilingual
bilingüismo *m* bilingualism
bilioso -sa *adj* bilious; (fig.) bilious
bilirrubina *f* (biochem.) bilirubin
bilis *f* (physiol. & fig.) bile; **descargar la bilis** to vent one's spleen
bilítero -ra *adj* biliteral
biliverdina *f* (biochem.) biliverdin
bilobular *adj* bilobular
bilocación *f* bilocation
bilocar §86 *vr* to be in two places at the same time
bilocular *adj* bilocular
biltrotear *vn* (coll.) to gad, run around
biltrotera *f* (coll.) gadabout
billa *f* pocketing a ball after it has struck another
billalda *f* tipcat (*boys' game*)
billar *m* billiards; billiard table; billiard room, billiard hall; **billar romano** pinball
billarda *f* var. of **billalda**
billarista *mf* (coll.) billiardist, billiard player
billetaje *m* tickets
billete *m* ticket; note; bill; **medio billete** half fare; **billete de abono** season ticket; commutation ticket; **billete de banco** bank note; **billete de ida y vuelta** round-trip ticket; **billete de regalo** complimentary ticket; **billete kilométrico** mileage book
billetero -ra *mf* vendor of lottery tickets; *m* & *f* billfold
billón *m* British billion; trillion (*in U.S.A.*)
billonario -ria *adj* & *mf* billionaire
billonésimo -ma *adj* & *m* billionth
bímano -na *adj* bimanous, two-handed; **bímanos** *mpl* (zool.) Bimana
bimanual *adj* bimanual, two-handed
bimba *f* (coll.) high hat
bimembre *adj* having two members, two-part
bimensual *adj* semimonthly
bimestral *adj* bimonthly
bimestre *adj* bimonthly; *m* period of two months; bimonthly payment (*of salary, debt, etc.*)
bimetal *m* two-metal element (*e.g., of thermostat*)
bimetálico -ca *adj* bimetallic
bimetalismo *m* bimetallism
bimetalista *adj* bimetallist, bimetallistic; bimetallic; *mf* bimetallist
bimotor *adj* twin-motor; *m* twin-motor plane
bina *f* second plowing or digging
binación *f* (eccl.) bination
binadera *f* weeding fork
binado -da *adj* (bot.) binate
binador -dora *adj* weeding; *mf* weeder; *f* weeding fork
binar *va* to plow or dig the second time; *vn* (eccl.) to celebrate two masses on the same day
binario -ria *adj* binary
binaural or **binauricular** *adj* binaural
binazón *f* second plowing or digging
binocular *adj* binocular
binóculo *m* binocle, binocular; spectacles, lorgnette
binomial *adj* binomial
binomio -mia *adj* binomial; *m* pair of names; hyphenated name; (alg. & biol.) binomial; **binomio de Newton** (alg.) binomial theorem
bínubo -ba *adj* twice married
binza *f* pellicle (*of eggshell; of onion*)
biodinámico -ca *adj* biodynamic; *f* biodynamics
biofísico -ca *adj* biophysical; *f* biophysics
biogénesis *f* (biol.) biogenesis
biografía *f* biography
biografiado -da *mf* biographee
biográfico -ca *adj* biographic or biographical
biógrafo -fa *mf* biographer
biología *f* biology
biológico -ca *adj* biologic or biological
biólogo -ga *mf* biologist
biombo *m* screen, folding screen
biomédico -ca *adj* biomedical
biometría *f* biometry
biométrico -ca *adj* biometric or biometrical
biopsia *f* (med.) biopsy
bioquímico -ca *adj* biochemical; *mf* biochemist; *f* biochemistry
biostático -ca *adj* biostatic or biostatical; *f* biostatics
biota *f* biota
biótico -ca *adj* biotic or biotical
biotipo *m* (biol.) biotype
biotita *f* (mineral.) biotite
bióxido *m* (chem.) dioxide
bíparo -ra *adj* (bot. & zool.) biparous
bipartición *f* bipartition, fission, splitting
bipartido -da or **bipartito -ta** *adj* bipartite
bípede *adj* biped
bípedo -da *adj* & *m* biped
bipersonal *adj* for two people
bipétalo -la *adj* (bot.) bipetalous
bipinado -da *adj* (bot.) bipinnate
biplano *m* (aer.) biplane
biplaza *m* (aer.) two-seater
bipolar *adj* bipolar; (elec.) double-pole
biribís *m* roulette
biricú *m* (*pl:* **-cúes**) sword belt
birimbao *m* (mus.) jews'-harp

birlar *va* to throw (*ball*) second time from place where it stopped; (coll.) to knock down with one blow, to kill with one shot; (coll.) to filch, to swipe; (coll.) to outwit
birlí *m* (*pl:* **-líes**) (print.) blank lower part (*of printed page*)
birlibirloque; por arte de birlibirloque magically, by magic
birlocha *f* kite
birlocho *m* surrey
birlón *m* (prov.) head pin (*in bowling*)
birlonga *f* omber (*card game*); **a la birlonga** (coll.) carelessly, sloppily
Birmania *f* Burma
birmano -na *adj* & *mf* Burmese; *m* Burmese (*language*)
birreactor *adj masc* (aer.) twin-jet
birrectángulo -la *adj* (geom.) birectangular
birrefringencia *f* birefringence
birreme *adj* & *f* bireme
birreta *f* biretta; (coll.) cardinalate
birrete *m* biretta; academic cap, mortarboard
birretina *f* small biretta, small cap; hussar's cap, grenadier's cap
birria *f* wobble (*of a spinning top*); clown; mess, sight; (Am.) grudge; **de birria** (Am.) half-heartedly
bis *adv* (mus.) bis; *interj* (theat.) encore!; *m* (theat.) encore
bisabuelo -la *mf* great-grandparent; *m* great-grandfather; *f* great-grandmother
bisagra *f* hinge; shoemaker's polisher of boxwood
bisanuo -nua *adj* (bot.) biennial
bisar *va* to repeat (*a song, performance, recitation, etc.*)
bisayo -ya *adj* & *mf* Bisayan or Visayan
bisbís *m* roulette
bisbisar *va* (coll.) to mutter, to mumble
bisbiseo *m* (coll.) muttering, mumbling
bisbita *f* (orn.) pipit, titlark
bisecar §86 *va* (geom.) to bisect
bisección *f* (geom.) bisection
bisector -triz *adj* (*pl:* **-tores -trices**) (geom.) bisecting; *f* (*pl:* **-trices**) (geom.) bisector or bisectrix
bisel *m* bevel, bevel edge
biselar *va* to bevel
bisemanal *adj* semiweekly, biweekly
bisexual *adj* & *m* bisexual
bisiesto -ta *adj* bissextile, leap (*year*); *m* bissextile, leap year; **mudar bisiesto** or **de bisiesto** (coll.) to change one's tune, to change one's ways
bisílabo -ba *adj* bisyllabic
bismutismo *m* (path.) bismuth poisoning
bismutita *f* (mineral.) bismutite
bismuto *m* (chem.) bismuth
bisnieto -ta *mf* great-grandchild; *m* great-grandson; *f* great-granddaughter
biso *m* (hist. & zool.) byssus
bisojo -ja *adj* squint-eyed, cross-eyed; *mf* cross-eyed person
bisonte *m* (zool.) bison; (zool.) buffalo
bisoñada *f* (coll.) greenhorn stunt or remark
bisoñé *m* wig for front of head
bisoñería *f* (coll.) var. of **bisoñada**
bisoño -ña *adj* green, inexperienced; (mil.) raw; *mf* greenhorn, rookie
bispón *m* roll of oilcloth
bisté *m* or **bistec** *m* beefsteak
bistorta *f* (bot.) bistort
bistre *m* (paint.) bister
bistrecha *f* advance, advance payment
bisturí *m* (*pl:* **-ríes**) (surg.) bistoury, lancet
bisulco -ca *adj* cloven-footed
bisulfato *m* (chem.) bisulfate
bisulfito *m* (chem.) bisulfite
bisulfuro *m* (chem.) bisulfide
bisunto -ta *adj* dirty, greasy
bisutería *f* costume jewelry, imitation jewelry
bita *f* (naut.) bitt; **bita de linguete** (naut.) pawl bitt; **bita de remolque** (naut.) towing bitt
bitácora *f* (naut.) binnacle
bitadura *f* (naut.) cable bitt
bitongo -ga *adj* (coll.) overgrown (*child*)
bitoque *m* bung; plug (*for muzzle of gun*)
bitor *m* (orn.) corn crake
bitter *m* bitters
bituminizar §76 *vr* to become bituminized
bituminoso -sa *adj* bituminous
bivalencia *f* (chem.) bivalence
bivalente *adj* (chem.) bivalent
bivalvo -va *adj* bivalve
bixáceo -a *adj* (bot.) bixaceous
biyugado -da *adj* (bot.) bijugate
biza *f* (ichth.) striped tunny
Bizancio *m* Byzantium
bizantino -na *adj* & *mf* Byzantine
bizarrear *vn* to act gallantly, to be magnanimous
bizarría *f* gallantry; loftiness, magnanimity; (arch.) bizarrerie
bizarro -rra *adj* gallant; lofty, magnanimous
bizaza *f* leather saddlebag
bizcar §86 *va* to wink (*the eye*); *vn* to squint
bizco -ca *adj* squint-eyed, cross-eyed; **quedarse bizco** (coll.) to be dazzled, be dumfounded; *mf* cross-eyed person
bizcochada *f* biscuit soup; slit roll
bizcochar *va* to bake a second time
bizcochero -ra *adj* (pertaining to a) biscuit or cake; *mf* biscuit or cake maker or dealer
bizcocho *m* biscuit (*bread and pottery*); cake, sponge cake; hardtack; bisque (*unglazed ceramic ware*); **bizcocho borracho** tipsy cake
bizcorneto -ta *adj* (Am.) squint-eyed, cross-eyed
bizcotela *f* sponge cake with icing
bizma *f* poultice
bizmar *va* to poultice
bizna *f* membrane (*between kernels of a nut*)
biznaga *f* (bot.) bishop's-weed; toothpick (*made from this plant*); (Am.) fishhook cactus
biznieto -ta *mf* var. of **bisnieto**
bizquear *vn* to squint
blanca *f* see **blanco**
blancazo -za *adj* (coll.) whitish
blanco -ca *adj* white (*like snow; applies also to grapes, wine, etc.*); fair (*complexion*); blank; water (*power*); (coll.) yellow (*cowardly*); *mf* white (*person*); (coll.) coward; *m* white (*color*); white star, white spot (*on horse*); blank; blank space; white page; interval; target; aim, goal; sizing; (print.) blank form; (her.) argent; **calentar al blanco** to heat to a white heat; **dar en el blanco** or **hacer blanco** to hit the mark; **en blanco** blank; **hacer blanco en** to hit; **quedarse en blanco** to fail to grasp the point; to be disappointed; **blanco abatible** collapsible target; **blanco de ballena** spermaceti; **blanco de España** whiting; **blanco de huevo** eggshell cosmetic; white of egg; **blanco de la uña** half moon of fingernail; **blanco del ojo** white of the eye; **blanco de plomo** white lead; *f* old coin of varying values; (mus.) minim; (*cap.*) *f* Blanch; **estar sin blanca** or **no tener blanca** to be broke; **blanca morfea** (vet.) tetter, ringworm; **Blanca Nieves** Snow White
blancor *m* whiteness
blancote -ta *adj* very white; dirty-white; (coll.) cowardly; *mf* (coll.) coward
blancura *f* whiteness; **blancura del ojo** (vet.) white spot on cornea
blancuzco -ca *adj* whitish; dirty-white
blandeador -dora *adj* softening, convincing
blandear *va* to soften, to convince, to persuade; to brandish; *vn* & *vr* to soften, to yield, to give in; to brandish
blandengue *adj* soft, easy-going; colorless, without character; *m* Argentine lancer
blandiente *adj* swaying, brandishing
blandir §53 *va, vn* & *vr* to brandish
blando -da *adj* bland, soft; tender (*eyes*); soft (*soap*); flabby; sensual; exquisite; indulgent; (coll.) cowardly; (phys.) soft (*ray; vacuum tube*); (mus.) flat; **más blando que una breva** (coll.) sweet as pie; **blando** *adv* softly, gently
blandón *m* wax candle; candlestick
blandujo -ja *adj* (coll.) softish
blandura *f* blandness, softness, gentleness; flattery, flirtation; white cosmetic; application, emolient; flabbiness; sensuality; mild weather
blandurilla *f* lavender pomade
blanduzco -ca *adj* (coll.) softish

blanqueación *f* whitening, bleaching; whitewashing; blanching
blanqueador -dora *adj* whitening, bleaching; whitewashing; *mf* whitener, bleacher; whitewasher
blanqueadura *f* or **blanqueamiento** *m* whitening, bleaching; whitewashing; blanching
blanquear *va* to whiten, to bleach; to whitewash; to tin; to blanch (*metals*); (cook. & hort.) to blanch; to wax (*honeycomb*); *vn* to blanch, to turn white
blanquecer §34 *va* to whiten, to bleach; to blanch (*metals*)
blanquecimiento *m* bleaching; blanching of metals
blanquecino -na *adj* whitish
blanqueo *m* whitening, bleaching; whitewashing; blanching
blanquería *f* bleachery
blanquete *m* white cosmetic
blanquición *f* blanching of metals
blanquillo -lla *adj* whitish; white (*wheat, bread*); *m* (Am.) egg; (Am.) white peach
blanquimento or **blanquimiento** *m* bleacher, bleaching solution
blanquinoso -sa *adj* whitish
blanquizal *m* or **blanquizar** *m* chalk pit
blanquizco -ca *adj* white, whitish
blao *m* (her.) azure
blasfemador -dora or **blasfemante** *adj* blaspheming, blasphemous; *mf* blasphemer
blasfemar *vn* to blaspheme; **blasfemar contra** to blaspheme, to blaspheme against; **blasfemar de** to blaspheme, to curse (*e.g., virtue*)
blasfematorio -ria *adj* blasphemous
blasfemia *f* blasphemy; vile insult
blasfemo -ma *adj* blasphemous; *mf* blasphemer
blasón *m* heraldry, blazon; armorial bearings; (her.) charge; honor, glory
blasonador -dora *adj* boasting, bragging
blasonar *va* to emblazon (*heraldic shield*); (fig.) to emblazon, to extol; *vn* to boast, to brag; **blasonar de** to boast of being
blasonería *f* boasting, bragging
blastema *m* (embryol.) blastema
blastocele *m* (embryol.) blastocoele
blastocisto *m* (embryol.) blastocyst
blastodermo *m* (embryol.) blastoderm
blástula *f* (embryol.) blastula
bledo *m* (bot.) blite, goosefoot; (bot.) prostrate pigweed; **no dársele a uno un bledo de** (coll.) to not matter to a person, e.g., **no se me da un bledo de ello** that does not matter to me, that is of no importance to me
blefaritis *f* (path.) blepharitis
blenda *f* (mineral.) blende, zinc sulfide
blenia *f* (ichth.) blenny
blenorrea *f* (path.) blennorrhea
blinda *f* (fort.) blind
blindado -da *adj* shielded, armored
blindaje *m* (fort.) blindage; (naut.) armor; (elec.) shield
blindar *va* to armor; to armor-plate; (elec.) to shield
b.l.m. or **B.L.M.** abr. of **besa la mano**
bloc *m* (*pl:* **bloques**) pad (*of note paper*); tear-off calendar
blocao *m* (fort.) blockhouse
blof *m* bluff
blofeador -dora *adj* bluffing; *mf* bluffer
blofear *vn* to bluff
blonda *f* see **blondo**
blondina *f* narrow blond lace
blondo -da *adj* blond, flaxen, light; (Am.) curly; *f* blond lace
bloque *m* block; (mach.) cylinder block; pad; (print.) block; (pol.) block, bloc; block, lot (*of merchandise*); **bloque de hormigón** concrete block
bloqueador -dora *adj* blockading; *mf* blockader
bloquear *va* (mil. & naut.) to blockade; to brake (*car, train, etc.*); to block; (com.) to freeze
bloqueo *m* (mil. & naut.) blockade; (com.) freezing; **burlar, forzar** or **violar el bloqueo** to run the blockade; **bloqueo en el papel** paper blockade; **bloqueo horizontal** (telv.) horizontal hold; **bloqueo vertical** (telv.) vertical hold
b.l.p. or **B.L.P.** abr. of **besa los pies**
blufar *vn* var. of **blofear**
blusa *f* blouse; shirtwaist
B.mo P.e abr. of **Beatísimo Padre**
boa *f* (zool.) boa, boa constrictor; *m* boa (*scarf*)
Boadicea *f* Boadicea
boardilla *f* var. of **buhardilla**
boato *m* show, pomp; pageantry
bobada *f* folly, foolishness
bobalías *mf* (coll.) dolt, dunce, ass
bobalicón -cona *adj* (coll.) stupid, silly; *mf* (coll.) nitwit
bobatel *m* (coll.) simpleton
bobático -ca *adj* (coll.) foolish, silly, stupid (*deed or remark*)
bobear *vn* to talk nonsense, to act like a fool; to dawdle, to fool around
bobera *f* (Am.) folly, foolishness
bobería *f* folly, foolishness; trifle
bóbilis; de bóbilis bóbilis (coll.) for nothing; (coll.) without effort
bobillo *m* round glazed pitcher; lace worn around open neck
bobina *f* bobbin; (elec.) coil; **bobina de cesto** (rad.) basket coil; **bobina de chispas** spark coil; **bobina de choque** (elec.) choke coil; **bobina de encendido** spark coil, ignition coil; **bobina de impedancia** (elec.) impedance coil; **bobina de panal** (rad.) honeycomb coil; **bobina de regeneración** (rad.) tickler coil; **bobina de sintonía** (rad.) tuning coil; **bobina móvil** (rad.) voice coil; (elec.) moving coil; **bobina térmica** (elec.) heating coil; **bobina tipo canasto** (rad.) basket-weave coil
bobinado *m* (elec.) winding
bobinadora *f* winding machine
bobinar *va* to wind
bobiné *m* (Am.) bobbinet
bobo -ba *adj* simple, stupid; **bobo con** crazy about, mad about; *mf* simpleton, dunce; clown, jester
boca *f* mouth; taste, flavor; speech; entrance, portal (*to tunnel, subway, etc.*); pit (*of stomach*); **a boca** by word of mouth; **a boca de cañón** at close range; **a boca de jarro** without moderation (*with reference to drinking*); at close range; **a pedir de boca** to one's heart's content; exactly right; **buscar a uno la boca** to draw someone out; **decir con la boca chica** or **chiquita** (coll.) to offer as a mere formality; **decir** (*uno*) **lo que se le viene a la boca** (coll.) to say whatever comes into one's mind; **hablar por boca de ganso** (coll.) to say what one is told to say; **hacer boca** (coll.) to have some hors d'oeuvres; **meterse en la boca del león** (coll.) to put one's head in the lion's mouth; **no decir esta boca es mía** (coll.) to not say a word, to not say boo; **venirse a la boca a** to taste bad to, to regurgitate for; **boca abajo** face downward; **boca a boca** by word of mouth; **boca arriba** face upward; **boca de agua** hydrant; **boca de dragón** (bot.) snapdragon, dragon's-mouth; **boca de escorpión** evil tongue (*person*); **boca de gachas** (coll.) driveler; (coll.) babbler, jabberer; **boca del estómago** pit of stomach; **boca de riego** faucet, hydrant
bocabarra *f* (naut.) bar hole, socket (*of capstan*)
bocacalle *f* street entrance, street intersection
bocacaz *m* (*pl:* **-caces**) spillway, overflow
bocací *m* bocasine, colored buckram
bocacha *f* big mouth; wide-mouthed blunderbuss
bocadear *va* to break up, to divide into small parts or bits
bocadillo *m* thin middling linen; narrow tape or ribbon; snack; sandwich; stuffed roll; farmhand's bite or snack at ten A.M.; guava paste
bocadito *m* little bit; (Am.) cigarette (*wrapped in tobacco leaf*); **a bocaditos** piecemeal
bocado *m* mouthful, bite, morsel; bit; bridle; **bocados** *mpl* dried preserves; **con el bocado en la boca** (coll.) right after eating; **no te-**

ner para un bocado (coll.) to not have a cent, to be penniless; **bocado de Adán** Adam's apple; **bocado de gallina** (bot.) chickweed
bocadulce *m* (ichth.) smooth dogfish
bocal *m* narrow-mouthed pitcher; flume; narrows (*into a harbor*)
bocallave *f* keyhole
bocamanga *f* cuff, wristband; opening of sleeve
bocamina *f* mine entrance
bocanada *f* swallow; puff (*of smoke*); (coll.) boasting, bragging; **bocanada de gente** (coll.) rush, crush (*of people*); **bocanada de viento** gust of wind
bocarte *m* (min.) stamp mill
bocartear *va* to stamp, to crush (*ore*)
bocateja *f* front tile
bocatijera *f* carriage-pole socket
bocaza *f* big mouth; *mf* (coll.) blatherskite
bocazo *m* fizzle (*in blasting*)
bocear *vn* var. of **bocezar**
bocel *m* (arch.) solid cylindrical molding; edge (*of tumbler, etc.*); (carp.) molding plane; **cuarto bocel** (arch.) quarter round; **medio bocel** (arch.) half round
bocelar *va* to cut a molding on
bocelete *m* small molding plane
bocera *f* smear, stickiness (*on lips after eating or drinking*)
boceto *m* sketch, outline, model
bocezar §76 *vn* to move the lips from side to side (*said of animals*)
bocín *m* hubcap (*of carriage*); hubcap of bass mat (*of cart*); feed pipe of overshot wheel
bocina *f* horn, trumpet; sea shell used as horn; phonograph horn; auto horn; speaking trumpet, ear trumpet; (Am.) blowgun
bocinar *vn* to blow the horn; to speak through a speaking trumpet
bocinero *m* hornblower, trumpeter
bocio *m* (path.) goiter
bock *m* (*pl:* **bocks**) beer glass (*of a quarter liter*)
bocón -cona *adj* (coll.) bigmouthed; (coll.) boastful; *mf* (coll.) spread eagle, braggart
bocoy *m* large barrel
bocudo -da *adj* bigmouthed
bocha *f* bowling ball; **bochas** *fpl* bowling
bochar *va* (bowling) to hit and move (*another ball*)
bochazo *m* stroke of one ball against another
boche *m* small hole in ground (*for boys' games*); Boche (*German*); (Am.) slight; **dar boche a** (Am.) to slight, to rebuff
bochinche *m* uproar, tumult; (Am.) mess, row, riot
bochinchero -ra *mf* noisemaker; (Am.) disturber of the peace, rioter; (Am.) sporty-looking roughneck
bochista *mf* expert bowler
bochornazo *m* sultry weather, stuffy weather
bochorno *m* sultry weather; hot summer breeze; flush; embarrassment; slight
bochornoso -sa *adj* sultry; stuffy; embarrassing; shameful, infamous
boda *f* marriage, wedding; **boda de negros** (coll.) noisy party, orgy; **bodas de Camacho** banquet, lavish feast; **bodas de diamante** diamond wedding, diamond jubilee; **bodas de oro** golden wedding; **bodas de plata** silver wedding
bode *m* billy goat
bodega *f* wine cellar, wine vault; vintage; pantry; storage vault, warehouse; (coll.) cellar; (naut.) hold (*of ship*); (coll.) tank (*hard drinker*); (Am.) grocery store; (Am.) freight station
bodegón *m* cheap restaurant; taproom; (paint.) still life
bodegoncillo *m* cheap little eating house; **bodegoncillo de puntapié** hash house on wheels
bodegonear *vn* to hang around taprooms
bodegonero -ra *mf* chophouse keeper; *m* bartender; *f* barmaid
bodeguero -ra *mf* cellarer, owner or keeper of a wine cellar; (Am.) grocer
bodigo *m* offering in church of a roll of fine wheat; dullard
bodijo *m* (coll.) unequal match, misalliance; (coll.) quiet wedding, simple wedding
bodocazo *m* hit made with ball of clay shot from crossbow
bodón *m* pool or pond that dries up in summer
bodoque *m* ball of clay shot from crossbow; lump; (coll.) dolt, dullard
bodoquera *f* mold for clay balls; cradle of crossbow; blowgun, peashooter
bodorrio *m* (coll.) unequal match, misalliance; (Am.) wedding party
bodrio *m* soup made of leavings; poorly seasoned stew; mixture of hog's blood and onions
bóer (*pl:* **bóeres**) *adj & mf* Boer
boezuelo *m* small ox; stalking ox (*used in hunting partridges*)
bofe *m* (coll.) lung; **bofes** *mpl* lights (*of sheep, pigs, etc.*); **echar el bofe** or **los bofes** (coll.) to toil, to drudge, to strive; **echar el bofe** or **los bofes por** (coll.) to burn to get, to be crazy about
bofena *f* var. of **bofe**
bófeta *f* thin stiff cotton fabric
bofetada *f* slap in the face; **dar de bofetada a** to slap in the face
bofetán *m* var. of **bófeta**
bofetón *m* hard slap in the face; (theat.) revolving-door trick
boga *f* vogue; rowing; stroke; (ichth.) ox-eyed cackerel, boce; **en boga** in vogue; *mf* rower
bogada *f* stroke (of oars)
bogador -dora *mf* rower
bogar §59 *vn* to row; to sail
bogavante *m* strokesman; (zool.) lobster (*Homarus*)
bogie *m* (rail.) truck, bogie
bogotano -na *adj* (pertaining to) Bogotá; *mf* native or inhabitant of Bogotá
bohardilla *f* var. of **buhardilla**
bohemia & **Bohemia** *f* see **bohemio**
bohemiano -na *adj & mf* Bohemian
bohémico -ca *adj* Bohemian
bohemio -mia *adj & mf* Bohemian; gypsy; (fig.) Bohemian; *m* Bohemian (*language*); *f* (fig.) Bohemia; (fig.) Bohemianism; (Am.) wild oats; (*cap.*) *f* Bohemia
bohemo -ma *adj & mf* Bohemian
bohena *f* lung; pork-lung sausage
bohío *m* (Am.) hut; (Am.) brothel
bohordo *m* dart, short spear; (bot.) reed; (bot.) scape; (bot.) cattail spike
boicot *m* (*pl:* **-cots**) boycott
boicotear *va* to boycott
boicoteo *m* boycott, boycotting
boíl *m* ox stall
boina *f* beret
boira *f* mist, fog
boj *m* (bot.) boxwood; **boj de China** (bot.) orange jessamine
boja *f* (bot.) southernwood; bushes (*for rearing silkworms*)
bojar *va* to scrape (*leather*) clean; (naut.) to measure the perimeter of (*island or cape*); *vn* to measure (*said of the perimeter of island or cape*)
boje *m* var. of **boj**
bojear *va* (naut.) to measure the perimeter of (*island or cape*); *vn* (naut.) to measure (*said of the perimeter of island or cape*)
bojedal *m* growth of boxwood
bojeo *m* (naut.) measure of perimeter of island or cape; (naut.) perimeter of island or cape
bojiganga *f* traveling comedians; outlandish dress or disguise
bojo *m* (naut.) measure of perimeter of island or cape
bol *m* bowl; punch bowl; ninepin; dragnet; **bol arménico** or **de Armenia** Armenian bole
bola *f* ball; globe; bowling; shine, shoeshine; (cards) slam, grand slam; resentment; trick, deceit, lie; (naut.) signal made of two black disks crossed at right angles; (Am.) uprising, revolution; **bolas** *fpl* (Am.) bolas (*South American cowboy weapon*); **a bola vista** evidently, openly; **¡dale bola!** (coll.) that'll do!; **dejar rodar la bola** to let things take their course; **bola de alcanfor** camphor ball, moth ball; **bola de billar** billiard ball; **bola de**

cristal crystal ball (*used to divine the future*); **bola de nieve** snowball; (bot.) snowball; **bola de tenis** tennis ball; **bola negra** black ball; **bola rompedora** wrecking ball
bolada *f* throw (*of a ball*); love affair; lucky deal; (coll.) cinch; (Am.) prize (*in a raffle*)
bolado *m* meringue
bolanchera *f* (Am.) Paul Jones (*dance*)
bolandista *m* Bollandist
bolardo *m* (naut.) bollard
bolazo *m* hit with a ball; (Am.) nonsense; **de bolazo** (coll.) carelessly, hurriedly
bolchevique *adj & mf* Bolshevik
bolcheviquismo *m* Bolshevism
bolcheviquista *adj* Bolshevist, Bolshevistic; *mf* Bolshevist
bolchevismo *m* var. of **bolcheviquismo**
bolchevista *adj & mf* var. of **bolcheviquista**
bolchevización *f* Bolshevization
bolchevizar §76 *va* to Bolshevize
boldina *f* (pharm.) boldine
boldo *m* (bot.) boldo
bolea *f* (sport) volley
boleada *f* (Am.) shoeshine
boleador *m* (Am.) bootblack
boleadoras *fpl* (Am.) bola or bolas (*South American cowboy weapon*)
bolear *va* (coll.) to throw; (coll.) to play a mean trick on; to blackball; (Am.) to flunk; (Am.) to lasso with bolas; (Am.) to shine, to polish (*shoes*); *vn* to play for fun (*said of billiards and other games*); to bowl; to boast; to lie; *vr* to stumble; (Am.) to stumble and fall in a ball; (Am.) to falter, to waver; (Am.) to rear and tumble
boleo *m* bowling; bowling green; jolt, blow
bolero -ra *adj* truant; (coll.) lying; *mf* bolero dancer; (Am.) bootblack; *m* bolero (*dance and music; short jacket*); *f* bowling alley; **bolera encespada** bowling green
boleta *f* pass, entrance ticket; authorization; (mil.) billet; small package of tobacco; (Am.) certificate; (Am.) ballot
boletería *f* (Am.) ticket office
boletero *m* (Am.) ticket agent, ticket seller; (Am.) ticket collector
boletín *m* bulletin; ticket; pay warrant; (mil.) billet; **boletín de inscripción** registration form; **boletín de renovación** renewal form (*e.g., for subscription to a newspaper*)
boleto *m* ticket of admission; lottery ticket; (bot.) boletus, cepe; (Am.) ticket; **boleto de empeño** (Am.) pawn ticket; **boleto de señal** animal license, dog license
bolichada *f* fish caught with dragnet; (coll.) lucky break; **de una bolichada** (coll.) at one stroke
boliche *m* bowling; jack (*small ball for bowling*); bowling alley; small dragnet; small fish caught with dragnet; cup and ball (*game*); lead-smelting furnace; (naut.) bowline of a small sail; (Am.) store, shop; (Am.) hash house; (Am.) gambling den
bolichear *vn* (Am.) to fiddle around
bólido *m* (astr.) bolide, fireball; racer, racing car; (Am.) hot rod (*supercharged flivver*)
bolígrafo *m* ball point pen
bolillo *m* bobbin for making lace; form for stiffening lace cuffs; (zool.) coffin bone; (Am.) drumstick; (Am.) white bread; (Am. offensive) light-skinned person; (Am.) roll (*bread*); **bolillos** *mpl* candy bars
bolín *m* jack (*small ball for bowling*); **de bolín** (coll.) carelessly, thoughtlessly
bolina *f* (naut.) bowline; (naut.) flogging; (naut.) sounding line; (coll.) racket, row, dispute; **de bolina** (naut.) on a bowline, close-hauled; **echar de bolina** (coll.) to boast, brag; (coll.) to exaggerate
bolineador -dora *adj* (naut.) sailing well when close-hauled
bolinear *va* (naut.) to haul (*the bowline*); *vn* (naut.) to haul the bowline, to sail close-hauled; (naut.) to sail to windward
bolinero -ra *adj* (naut.) sailing well when close-hauled; (Am.) riotous, quarrelsome
bolisa *f* embers, hot coals
bolístico -ca *adj* bowling
bolívar *m* bolivar (*monetary unit of Venezuela*)
Bolivia *f* Bolivia
bolivianismo *m* Bolivianism
boliviano -na *adj & mf* Bolivian; *m* boliviano (*Bolivian monetary unit*)
bolo *m* ninepin, tenpin; dunce, ignoramus; bolus, big pill; bolt (*of food*); traveling comedians; newel (*of winding stairs*); (cards) slam; bolo (*Philippine knife*); **bolos** *mpl* bowling, ninepins, tenpins; **jugar a los bolos** to bowl
Bolonia *f* Bologna
bolonio *adj masc* (coll.) stupid, ignorant; *m* (coll.) ignoramus
boloñés -ñesa *adj & mf* Bolognese
bolsa *f* purse, pocketbook; bag, pouch; bag (*e.g., in trousers*); pouch (*e.g., of kangaroo*); (anat. & path.) pocket; (anat.) bursa; stock exchange, stock market; (min.) richest vein of gold; wealth, money; grant, award (*to a student, artist, etc.*); (box.) prize money; (Am.) pocket; **bolsas** *fpl* (anat.) scrotum; **jugar a la bolsa** to play the market, to speculate in stocks; **la bolsa o la vida** your money or your life; **no abrir fácilmente la bolsa** to be tight-fisted; **bolsa de agua caliente** hot-water bottle; **bolsa de hielo** ice bag; **bolsa de la tinta** ink sac; **bolsa de pastor** (bot.) shepherd's-purse; **bolsa de trabajo** employment bureau; **bolsa de viaje** traveling fellowship
bolsear *va* (Am.) to jilt; (Am.) to pick the pocket of; (Am.) to sponge on; *vn* (Am.) to pucker
bolsería *f* manufacture of purses, pocketbooks, or bags; purse, pocketbook, or bag business or store
bolsero -ra *mf* maker or seller of purses or pocketbooks; (Am.) sponger
bolsillero *m* pickpocket
bolsillo *m* pocket; pocketbook; money; **rascarse el bolsillo** (coll.) to fork out, to come across; **tener en el bolsillo** to have in one's pocket (*i.e., in one's control*); **bolsillo de parche** patch pocket
bolsín *m* curb market
bolsiquear *va* (Am.) to frisk the pockets of
bolsista *m* broker, stockbroker
bolso *m* bag, purse, pocketbook; (naut.) pocket (*in a sail*); **bolso de mano** handbag
bolsón *m* large purse; plank floor of olive crusher; (geol.) bolson; (mil.) pocket
bolsudo -da *adj* (Am.) baggy; (Am.) slow, heavy, lazy
bolla *f* (archaic) tax on manufacture of playing cards
bolladura *f* dent; embossing; bump, bruise
bollar *va* to mark (*fabrics*) with lead seal; to emboss
bollería *f* bakery, pastry shop
bollero -ra *mf* baker
bollo *m* bun, muffin; puff (*in a dress*); tuft (*in upholstery*); bump, lump, bruise; dent; (Am.) loaf of bread; **bollos** *mpl* (Am.) troubles, difficulties; **bollos de relieve** embossing, raised work
bollón *m* brass-headed nail or tack; (bot.) bud; button earring
bollonado -da *adj* trimmed with brass-headed nails or tacks
bomba *f* see **bombo**
bombacha *f* or **bombachas** *fpl* (Am.) loose-fitting breeches fastened at the bottom
bombacho *adj masc* loose-fitting (*breeches or trousers*)
bombar *va* to pump
bombarda *f* (archaic) bombard (*piece of ordnance; bomb vessel*); (mus.) borbardon (*organ stop and ancient wind instrument*)
bombardear *va* to bombard; to bomb; (phys.) to bombard
bombardeo *m* bombardment; bombing; **bombardeo de precisión** (aer.) precision bombing; **bombardeo de saturación** (aer.) saturation bombing; **bombardeo en picado** (aer.) dive bombing
bombardero -ra *adj* bombing; *m* bomber (*crewman and airplane*)
bombardino *m* (mus.) saxhorn

bombardón *m* (mus.) bass saxhorn
bomba-reloj *f* time bomb
bombasí *m* fustian
bombástico -ca *adj* bombastic
bombazo *m* bomb explosion; bomb hit; bomb damage
bombé *m* light two-wheeled carriage for two people
bombear *va* to bomb; (Am.) to pump; (Am.) to reconnoiter; to laud, to ballyhoo; to cheat; (Am.) to fire, to dismiss; *vr* to arch, to camber, to bulge
bombeo *m* bombing; (Am.) pumping; curving, bulging; crown (*of a road*)
bombero *m* pumper, pumpman; fireman (*who puts out fires*)
bombilla *f* lamp chimney; light bulb; thief tube; **bombilla de destello** or **bombilla relámpago** (phot.) flash bulb
bombillo *m* lamp chimney; light bulb; thief tube; (naut.) portable pump; trap (*in a toilet*)
bombín *m* derby, bowler
bombista *m* lamp maker; bomb maker; (coll.) booster
bombo -ba *adj* (coll.) dumfounded, aghast ‖ *m* bass drum; bass-drum player; (naut.) barge, lighter; ballyhoo; (Am.) lie, falsehood; **anunciar a bombo y platillo** (coll.) to ballyhoo; **dar bombo a** (coll.) to ballyhoo ‖ *f* pump; fire engine; bomb; lamp globe; high hat; (Am.) firecracker, skyrocket; **a prueba de bombas** bombproof; **caer como una bomba** (coll.) to fall like a bombshell; (coll.) to burst in unexpectedly; **dar a la bomba** (naut.) to use the pump (*in order to bail out water*); **estar en bomba** (Am.) to be drunk; **bomba alimenticia** feed pump; **bomba al vacío** vacuum pump; **bomba aspirante** suction pump; **bomba atómica** atomic bomb; **bomba centrífuga** centrifugal pump; **bomba cohete** rocket bomb; **bomba de cadena** chain pump; **bomba de carena** (naut.) bilge pump; **bomba de demolición** demolition bomb; **bomba de émbolo buzo** plunger pump; **bomba de engrase** grease gun; **bomba de fragmentación** fragmentation bomb; **bomba de hidrógeno** hydrogen bomb; **bomba de incendios** fire engine; **bomba de mano** hand pump, stirrup pump; (mil.) hand bomb; **bomba demoledora** demolition bomb; **bomba de neutrones** neutron bomb; **bomba de plástico** plastic bomb; **bomba de profundidad** depth bomb; **bomba de sentina** (naut.) bilge pump; **bomba estomacal** stomach pump; **bomba fétida** stink bomb; **bomba impelente** force or pressure pump; **bomba incendiaria** (mil.) incendiary bomb; **bomba volante** buzz bomb; **¡bomba!** attention, please!
bombón *m* bonbon
bombona *f* carboy
bombonaje *m* (bot.) jipijapa (*plant and leaves*)
bombonera *f* candy box, bonbonnière
bombonería *f* candy store
Bona *f* Bône
bonachón -chona *adj* (coll.) good-natured, unsuspecting
bonaerense *adj* (pertaining to) Buenos Aires; *mf* native or inhabitant of Buenos Aires
bonancible *adj* calm, gentle, serene
bonanza *f* (naut.) fair weather, clear skies; (min.) bonanza; (fig.) bonanza (*source of wealth*); **estar en bonanza** to be booming; **ir en bonanza** (naut. & fig.) to have clear sailing; (fig.) to get along famously
bonapartista *mf* Bonapartist
bonarense *adj & mf* var. of **bonaerense**
bonazo -za *adj* (coll.) kind, good-natured
bondad *f* kindness, goodness, gentleness, favor; **tener la bondad de** + *inf* to be good enough to + *inf*, please + *inf*
bondadoso -sa *adj* kind, good
bonderizar §76 *va* to bonderize
boneta *f* (naut.) bonnet
bonetada *f* raising one's hat (*in salutation*)
bonete *m* hat, cap; cap (*of academic dress*); secular cleric; glass candy bowl; (anat. & fort.) bonnet; **a tente bonete** (coll.) with persistence
bonetería *f* hat shop; hat business
bonetero *m* hat maker or dealer; (bot.) spindle tree
bonga *f* (bot.) areca
bongó *m* bongo (*Afro-Cuban drum*)
bonhomía *f* (Am.) bonhomie
boniato *m* var. of **buniato**
bonico -ca *adj* nice, pretty, neat
Bonifacio *m* Boniface
bonificación *f* rise, increase; increased output; allowance, discount; (bridge) bonus
bonificar §86 *va* to allow, to discount
bonina *f* (bot.) ringflower
bonísimo -ma *adj super* very good
bonítalo *m* (ichth.) bonito
bonitamente *adv* gropingly, stealthily, craftily; slowly, gradually
bonito -ta *adj* pretty; neat, spruce; *m* (ichth.) bonito
bonizal *m* growth of wild corn
bonizo *m* wild corn
bono *m* (com.) bond; scrip, voucher
bonote *m* cocoanut fiber, coir
bonzo *m* bonze, Buddhist monk
boñiga *f* cow dung
boñigo *m* pancake (*of cow dung*)
Bootes *m* (astr.) Boötes
boqueada *f* gasp of death
boquear *va* to pronounce, to utter; *vn* to gape, to gasp; to be in the throes of death; (coll.) to be about to end
boquera *f* sluice (*of irrigation canal*); window in hayloft; (path.) sore at angle of lips; (vet.) sore mouth
boquerel *m* nozzle
boquerón *m* wide opening, large hole; (ichth.) anchovy
boquete *m* gap, narrow passage; breach, opening
boquiabierto -ta *adj* open-mouthed
boquiancho -cha *adj* wide-mouthed
boquiangosto -ta *adj* narrow-mouthed
boquiblando -da *adj* tender-mouthed (*said of a horse*)
boquiconejuno -na *adj* rabbit-mouthed (*said of a horse*)
boquiduro -ra *adj* hard-mouthed (*said of a horse*)
boquifresco -ca *adj* fresh-mouthed (*said of a horse*); (coll.) outspoken
boquilla *f* opening in leg of trousers (*through which foot passes*); opening in irrigation canal; mouthpiece (*of wind instrument*); stem (*of pipe*); nozzle; burner; cigar holder, cigarette holder; clasp (*of purse*); **boquilla filtrónica** filter tip
boquimuelle *adj* tender-mouthed (*said of a horse*); easily duped or imposed upon; garrulous
boquín *m* coarse baize
boquinegro -gra *adj* black-mouthed (*said of an animal*); *m* (zool.) land snail (*Helix vermiculata*)
boquirrasgado -da *adj* wide-mouthed
boquirroto -ta *adj* wide-mouthed; (coll.) garrulous
boquirrubio -bia *adj* rosy-mouthed (*said of a child*); outspoken; garrulous; simple, naive; *m* (coll.) pretty boy
boquiseco -ca *adj* dry-mouthed
boquituerto -ta *adj* wry-mouthed, crooked-mouthed
boquiverde *adj* smutty, obscene, ribald
boracita *f* (mineral.) boracite
boratado -da *adj* borated
borato *m* (chem.) borato
bórax *m* (chem.) borax
borbollar or **borbollear** *vn* to bubble, to boil up
borbollón *m* bubbling, boiling; **a borbollones** impetuously, tumultuously
borbollonear *vn* to bubble, to boil up
Borbón *m* Bourbon
borbónico -ca *adj* Bourbonian or Bourbonic
borbonismo *m* Bourbonism
borbor *m* bubbling (*of spring water or boiling water*)
borborigmo *m* rumbling of the bowels
borboritar *vn* (coll.) to bubble, to boil up

borbotar or **borbotear** *vn* to bubble out, to bubble up
borboton *m* bubbling, boiling; **a borbotones** impetuously, tumultuously; **hablar a borbotones** (coll.) to speak in torrents
borceguí *m* (*pl:* **-guíes**) high shoe
borceguinería *f* shoeshop, shoe store
borceguinero -ra *mf* shoemaker; shoe dealer
borcellar *m* brim, edge (*of a container*)
borda *f* (naut.) gunwale; (naut.) mainsail (*of galley*); hut; **fuera de borda** outboard; **arrojar, echar** or **tirar por la borda** to throw overboard; (fig.) to throw overboard
bordada *f* (naut.) board (*stretch on one tack*); (coll.) walking back and forth; **dar bordadas** (naut.) to tack back and forth; (coll.) to keep walking back and forth
bordado *m* embroidering; embroidery; **bordado de realce** raised embroidery
bordador -dora *mf* embroiderer
bordadura *f* embroidery; (her.) bordure
bordaje *m* (naut.) side planks
bordar *va* to embroider; (fig.) to embroider, to embroider on
borde *m* edge, border, fringe; ledge; (naut.) board; **borde de ataque** (aer.) leading edge; **borde del mar** seaside, seashore; **borde de salida** (aer.) trailing edge; *adj* wild, uncultivated; bastard
bordeado -da *adj* hairbreadth, close, narrow
bordear *va* to border, to trim with a border; to skirt; (fig.) to border on; *vn* to stay on the edge; (naut.) to sail to windward
bordelés -lesa *adj* Bordelais, (pertaining to) Bordeaux; *mf* native or inhabitant of Bordeaux
bordillo *m* curb, curbing
bordo *m* (naut.) board; (naut.) tack; (Am.) ridge, furrow; (Am.) dike, dam; **a bordo** (naut.) on board; **al bordo** (naut.) alongside; **de alto bordo** (naut.) of several decks, seagoing; (fig.) of importance; (fig.) high-up; **rendir el bordo en** (naut.) to arrive at
bordón *m* pilgrim's staff; staff, guide (*person*); (mus.) bass string; (mus.) bass stop (*of organ*); (mus.) drone (*of bagpipe*); burden (*of poem or song*); pet word, pet phrase; snare (*of drum*)
bordoncillo *m* pet word, pet phrase
bordonear *vn* to grope along with a stick or cane; to go around begging
bordonería *f* groping; life of a tramp; tramping as a pilgrim
bordonero -ra *mf* tramp, vagabond
bordura *f* (her.) bordure
boreal *adj* boreal, northern
Bóreas *m* (myth.) Boreas; (*l.c.*) *m* Boreas (*north wind*)
borgoña *m* Burgundy (*wine*); **la Borgoña** Burgundy
borgoñés -ñesa or **borgoñón -ñona** *adj & mf* Burgundian; *m* Burgundian (*dialect*)
borgoñota *f* burgonet
bórico -ca *adj* (chem.) boric
boricua *adj & mf* (Am.) Puerto Rican
borinqueño -ña *adj & mf* Puerto Rican
borla *f* tassel; tuft; powder puff; tassel of academic cap; doctor's degree; **borlas** *fpl* (bot.) amaranth; **tomar la borla** to take a higher degree, to take the doctor's degree
borlar *vr* (Am.) to take a higher degree, to take the doctor's degree
borlilla *f* (bot.) anther
borlón *m* large tassel; dimity; **borlones** *mpl* (bot.) amaranth
borne *m* tip (*of lance*); (elec.) binding post, terminal; (bot.) flatpod; *adj* hard and brittle (*said of wood*)
borneadero *m* (naut.) berth of a ship at anchor; (naut.) turning basin
borneadizo -za *adj* easy to bend, easily warped
bornear *va* to twist, to bend; to model and carve (*a column or pillar*); to hoist and put (*building stones*) in place; to size up (*e.g., a board*) with one eye closed, to see if it is in line; *vn* (naut.) to swing at anchor; *vr* to warp, to bulge
borneo *m* twisting, bending; sway (*in dancing*); (naut.) swinging at anchor
borní *m* (*pl:* **-níes**) (orn.) marsh harrier
boro *m* (chem.) boron
borona *f* (bot.) millet; corn bread
boronía *f* var. of **alboronía**
borra *f* yearling ewe; thick wool; goat's hair; fuzz, nap; floss, burl; sediment, lees; trash, waste; (chem.) borax; **borra de algodón** cotton waste
borracha *f* see **borracho**
borrachear *vn* to booze; to rant, talk nonsense
borrachera *f* drunkenness; spree, carousing; high exaltation; (coll.) great nonsense; **tomar una borrachera** to go on a spree, go on a binge
borrachero *m* (bot.) stramonium
borrachez *f* drunkenness; mental aberration
borrachín *m* (coll.) drunk, drunkard
borracho -cha *adj* drunk; drinking; violet-colored; (coll.) blind, wild (*e.g., with jealousy*); **borracho perdido** blotto; *mf* drunk, drunkard; *f* (coll.) leather wine bottle
borrachuela *f* (bot.) darnel, bearded darnel
borrachuelo *m* brandied fritter
borrado *m* erasure
borrador *m* rough draft; rough copy; sketch; blotter, waste book, day book; (Am.) rubber eraser; (Am.) blackboard eraser
borradura *f* erasure
borraj *m* (chem.) borax
borraja *f* (bot.) borage
borrajear *va & vn* to scribble; to doodle
borrajo *m* embers, hot ashes
borrar *va* to efface, to strike out, to cross out; to erase, to rub out, to blot out; to blot, to smear with ink; to cloud, to darken, to obscure
borrasca *f* storm, tempest; danger, hazard; setback; revolution; (coll.) spree, orgy; (naut.) storm; **borrasca magnética** (phys.) magnetic storm
borrascoso -sa *adj* stormy; (fig.) stormy
borrasquero -ra *adj* (coll.) riotous, fond of revelry
borratintas *m* (*pl:* **-tas**) ink eradicator
borregada *f* flock of lambs
borrego -ga *mf* lamb; (coll.) simpleton; **borregos** *mpl* (coll.) fleecy clouds
borreguero -ra *adj* good for pasturing lambs; *mf* shepherd who tends lambs
borreguil *adj* (pertaining to a) lamb
borrén *m* saddle pad
borrica *f* she-ass; (coll.) stupid woman
borricada *f* drove of asses; ride on an ass; asininity
borrico *m* ass, donkey; sawhorse; (fig.) ass
borricón *m* or **borricote** *m* (coll.) drudge, plodder
borrilla *f* down, fuzz (*on fruit*)
borriquero *m* ass driver or tender
borriquete *m* sawhorse
borro *m* lamb (*between one and two years old*)
borrón *m* blot, ink blot; blemish; rough draft; first sketch; (fig.) blot, stain
borronear *va* to scribble; to outline
borroso -sa *adj* blurred, blurry, fuzzy; muddy, thick; dull, inconspicuous
borrumbada *f* var. of **barrumbada**
boruca *f* noise, uproar, hubbub
borujo *m* pack, lump; bagasse of olive pits
borujón *m* bump, lump; roll, bundle (*of clothing*)
borusca *f* dry leaves, falling leaves
boscaje *m* boscage; (paint.) woodland scene
boscoso -sa *adj* woodsy, bosky
Bósforo *m* Bosporus; (*l.c.*) *m* strait
bosníaco -ca or **bosnio -nia** *adj & mf* Bosnian
bosque *m* forest, woods, woodland; **bosque maderable** timberland
bosquecillo *m* copse, bosk
bosquejar *va* to sketch, to outline
bosquejo *m* sketch, outline
bosquete *m* woods, forest; grove
bosquimán *m* or **bosquimano** *m* Bushman (*roving hunter of South Africa*)
bosta *f* dung, manure
bostezador -dora *adj* always yawning

bostezar §76 *vn* to yawn, to gape
bostezo *m* yawn, gape; **bostezos** yawning
bostón *m* boston (*card game and dance*)
bostonar or **bostonear** *vn* to dance the boston
bostoniano -na *adj & mf* Bostonian
bóstrice *m* (bot.) bostryx
bota *f* see **boto**
botacuchar *vn* to meddle, to butt in
botado -da *adj* (Am.) (pertaining to a) foundling; (Am.) brazen; (Am.) simple, silly; (Am.) fired, discharged; (Am.) wasteful, prodigal, spendthrift; (Am.) cheap; (Am.) overcome with sleep from too much drinking; *mf* (Am.) foundling; *f* launching; staves for barrels; (Am.) firing (*of an employee*)
botador *m* pole (*to push a boat*); punch, nailset; nail puller; (dent.) pelican
botadura *f* launching
botafuego *m* linstock, match staff; (coll.) firebrand, quick temper (*person*)
botafumeiro *m* incensory; (coll.) flattery
botagueña *f* pork-haslet sausage
botalón *m* (naut.) boom; **botalón de foque** (naut.) jib boom; **botalón de petifoque** (naut.) flying jib boom
botamen *m* pots and jars of a drug store; (naut.) water casks on board
botana *f* plug, stopper; scar; patch, plaster; (Am.) hors d'oeuvre
botanga *f* (naut.) outrigger
botánico -ca *adj* botanic or botanical; *mf* botanist; *f* botany
botanista *mf* botanist
botanizar §76 *vn* to botanize
botar *va* to hurl, to fling; to throw away; to launch (*a boat*); to turn, to shift (*the helm or rudder*); (Am.) to waste, to squander; (Am.) to fire, to dismiss; *vn* to bounce; to jump, to caper; *vr* to buck (*to throw rider*); (Am.) to lie down
botaratada *f* (coll.) blustering, wildness; (coll.) smartness; (coll.) bragging; (Am.) profligacy
botarate *m* (coll.) blusterer, madcap; (coll.) smart aleck; (coll.) braggart; (Am.) spendthrift
botarel *m* (arch.) abutment, buttress
botarga *f* galligaskins; clownish outfit; clown
botasilla *f* (mil.) boots and saddles
botavante *m* (naut.) boarding pike
botavara *f* (naut.) sprit, gaff, boom, pole
bote *m* thrust, blow; jump, prance (*of horse*); small boat, rowboat; bounce; can; pot, jar; (Am.) jug, jail; (Am.) liquor bottle, gin bottle; **de bote en bote** (coll.) jammed, packed; **de bote y boleo** (coll.) hastily, thoughtlessly; **bote automóvil** powerboat; **bote de carnero** bucking of a horse; **bote de paso** ferryboat; **bote de porcelana** apothecary's jar; **bote de remos** rowboat; **bote de salvamento** or **bote salvavidas** lifeboat; **bote vivandero** bumboat; **bote volador** flying boat
botella *f* bottle; **botella de Leiden** (elec.) Leyden jar
botellazo *m* blow or hit with a bottle
botellería *f* bottle factory; bottles
botellero *m* bottle maker or dealer; bottle rack
botellón *m* (Am.) large water bottle; (Am.) carafe; (Am.) demijohn
botería *f* manufacture or business of wine bags, bottles, or casks; (naut.) wine casks
botero *m* maker or seller of wine bags, bottles, or casks; boatman, ferryman; skipper
botica *f* drug store, apothecary's shop; medicine; **de todo como en botica** (coll.) everything under the sun
boticario -ria *mf* druggist; *f* druggist's wife
botija *f* earthen jug; (Am.) buried treasure; (Am.) belly; **estar hecho una botija** (coll.) to be puffy, be puffed up; **decir más que botija verde a** or **poner como botija verde** (Am.) to heap insults on
botijero -ra *mf* maker or seller of earthen jars and jugs
botijo *m* earthen jar or jug with spout and handle; (coll.) chunky fellow
botilla *f* shoe; (Am.) bottle
botillería *f* ice-cream parlor, soft-drink store; liquor store; bar, saloon
botillero -ra *mf* ice-cream and soft-drink dealer; liquor dealer
botillo *m* leather wine bag
botín *m* boot; spat (*short gaiter*); buskin; booty, spoils; (Am.) sock
botina *f* high shoe
botinero -ra *adj* black-foot (*cattle*); *m* boot maker; boot dealer; (mil.) handler of booty
botiquín *m* medicine kit, medicine chest, first-aid kit; first-aid station; (Am.) retail wine store; **botiquín de emergencia** first-aid kit
botito *m* high shoe
botivoleo *m* (sport) hitting the ball on the bounce
boto -ta *adj* dull, blunt; (fig.) dull, slow; *m* leather wine or oil bag; *f* boot, shoe; leather wine bag; butt, pipe; water cask; liquid measure (*516 liters or 125 gallons*); **morir con las botas puestas** to die with one's boots on; **ponerse las botas** (coll.) to hit the jack pot, strike it rich; **bota de agua** gum boot; **bota de montar** riding boot
botón *m* button; knob; stem (*of watch*); tip (*of foil*); (bot.) bud; (elec.) push button; (mach.) crankpin; **botones** *msg* bellboy, bellhop, buttons; **botón de contacto** (elec.) push button; **botón de oro** (bot.) creeping crowfoot; (bot.) buttercup (*Ranunculus acris*); **botón de puerta** doorknob; **botón de sintonización** (rad.) tuning knob
botonadura *f* set of buttons
botonar *vn* (Am.) to bud
botonazo *m* thrust with foil
botoncillo *m* (bot.) buttonwood (*Conocarpus*)
botonería *f* button maker's shop
botonero -ra *mf* button maker or dealer; *f* (bot.) santolina; (elec.) panel of push buttons
bototo *m* (Am.) gourd for carrying water
botulismo *m* (path.) botulism
botuto *m* long stem of papaya; sacred war trumpet of Orinoco Indians
bou *m* (*pl:* **bous**) fishing by casting a net between two boats
bóveda *f* (arch.) vault, dome; cave, cavern; crypt; (anat.) vault; (aut.) cowl; **bóveda celeste** firmament, canopy of heaven; **bóveda claustral** (arch.) cloister vault; **bóveda de casquete esférico** (arch.) spherical vault; **bóveda en cañón** (arch.) barrel vault; **bóveda esquifada** (arch.) cavetto vault; **bóveda ojival** (arch.) quadripartite vault; **bóveda palatina** (anat.) palatine vault; **bóveda por arista** (arch.) cross vault; **bóveda vaída** (arch.) Byzantine dome or vault
bovedilla (arch.) small vault or arch; (naut.) counter
bóvido -da *adj* bovine, bovid
bovino -na *adj & m* bovine
boxeador *m* (sport) boxer; (Am.) brass knuckles
boxear *vn* to box
boxeo *m* boxing
bóxer *m* (*pl:* **bóxers**) boxer (*dog*); brass knuckles; Boxer (*of China*)
boxibalón *m* (sport) punching bag
boxístico -ca *adj* boxing
boya *f* (naut.) buoy; float (*for fishing net*); **boya de campana** (naut.) bell buoy; **boya pantalón** (naut.) breeches buoy; **boya salvavidas** (naut.) life buoy
boyada *f* drove of oxen
boyal *adj* (pertaining to) cattle
boyante *adj* buoyant; prosperous, lucky; (naut.) light (*carrying a small cargo or none at all*); (taur.) easy, mild
boyar *vn* to float, be afloat again
boyardo *m* boyar or boyard
boyazo *m* large ox
boyera or **boyeriza** *f* ox stable
boyerizo or **boyero** *m* oxherd, ox driver
boyezuelo *m* small ox, young ox
boyuno -na *adj* bovine
boza *f* (naut.) stopper
bozal *adj* just brought in (*said of Negro from Africa*); pure, unmixed (*said of Negro*); simple, stupid; wild, untamed; stammering (*child*); (coll.) novice, inexperienced; (Am.) speaking broken Spanish; *m* muzzle; bells on harness (*over nose of horse*); (Am.) headstall

bozo *m* down on upper lip; mouth, lips; lower part of face; headstall
B.p. abr. of **Bendición papal**
br. or **Br.** abr. of **bachiller**
Brabante *m* Brabant; (*l.c.*) *m* brabant (*linen*)
braceada *f* swinging the arms
braceador *m* brewer
braceaje *m* coining, minting; brewing; (found.) tapping; (naut.) fathoming, fathomage; (naut.) bracing the yards
bracear *va* to brew; (found.) to tap (*a furnace*); (naut.) to measure in fathoms; *vn* to swing the arms; to swim raising the arms out of the water; to struggle, to wrestle; (naut.) to brace the yards
braceo *m* swinging the arms; struggling
braceral *m* (arm.) brassart
bracero -ra *adj* (pertaining to the) arm; manual; thrown with the hand (*said of a weapon*); *m* man offering his arm to a lady; laborer; day laborer; brewer; sure-armed fellow (*in throwing or shooting*); **de bracero** arm in arm
bracete *m* small arm; **de bracete** (coll.) arm in arm
bracil *m* (arm.) brassart; upper arm
bracmán *m* var. of **brahmán**
braco -ca *adj* pug-nosed; *mf* setter (*dog*)
bráctea *f* (bot.) bract; (bot.) bractlet
bractéola *f* (bot.) bractlet, bracteole
bradicardia *f* (path.) bradycardia
bradipepsia *f* (path.) bradypepsia
brafonera *f* (arm.) rerebrace
braga *f* hoisting rope, lashing rope; diaper, clout; panties, step-ins; **bragas** *fpl* breeches, knickers, pants; panties, step-ins
bragado -da *adj* with the flanks of a different color from rest of body; wicked, ill-disposed; firm, energetic; *f* flat of the thigh (*of animals*)
bragadura *f* crotch
bragazas (*pl:* **-zas**) *adj* (coll.) easy, henpecked; *m* (coll.) easy mark, henpecked fellow
braguero *m* truss (*for rupture*); breeching (*of a gun*)
bragueta *f* fly (*flap on clothing*)
braguillas *m* (*pl:* **-llas**) (coll.) brat; boy wearing first pair of pants
Brahma *m* (rel.) Brahma
brahmán *m* Brahman
brahmanismo *m* Brahmanism
brahmín *m* var. of **brahmán**
brama *f* rut (*state and season*)
bramadera *f* whistle (*toy made to spin on end of a string*); horn call
bramadero *m* rutting or mating place (*of deer and other wild animals*)
bramador -dora *adj* roaring, howling
bramante *adj* roaring, howling; *m* twine, packthread; brabant (*linen*)
bramantesco -ca *adj* (arch.) Bramantesque
bramar *vn* to roar, to bellow; to storm, to bluster; (coll.) to cry out, to shriek
bramido *m* roar, bellow, howl; (coll.) outcry, shriek
branca *f* (archaic) point of horn; (archaic) row of prisoners; (obs.) branch of tree; **brancas** *fpl* (obs.) lion's claws; **branca ursina** (bot.) acanthus; **branca ursina alemana** or **espuria** (bot.) cow parsnip (*Heracleum sphodylium*)
brancada *f* dragnet, sweep net
brancal *m* frame (*of wagon or gun carriage*)
brandal *m* (naut.) backstay
Brandeburgo *m* Brandenburg (*city, province, and military decoration*)
brandís *m* greatcoat
branquia *f* (ichth.) gill, branchia
branquial *adj* branchial
branquífero -ra *adj* branchiferous
braña *f* summer pasture
braquial *adj* brachial
braquicéfalo -la *adj* (anthrop.) brachycephalic
braquigrafía *f* study of abbreviations
braquiópodo *m* (zool.) brachiopod
braquiuro -ra *adj* & *m* (zool.) brachyuran
brasa *f* live coal, red-hot charcoal; **estar en brasas** (coll.) to be on pins and needles; **estar hecho unas brasas** to be flushed, be red in the face
brasca *f* (found.) brasque, steep
brascar §86 *va* (found.) to brasque, to fettle
braserillo *m* small brazier
brasero *m* brazier; brasero (*place where heretics were burned*)
brasil *m* (bot.) brasiletto; brazilwood; Brazil red; rouge; **el Brasil** Brazil
brasilado -da *adj* Brazil-red
brasileño -ña *adj* & *mf* Brazilian
brasilete *m* (bot.) brasiletto; brazilwood
brasilina *f* (chem.) brazilin
brasmología *f* treatise on the tides; treatise on fermentation
bravamente *adv* bravely; well, skilfully; cruelly; hard, abundantly
bravata *f* bravado; **echar bravatas** to talk big
braveador -dora *adj* blustering, bullying; *mf* blusterer, bully
bravear *vn* to bluster, to boast, to four-flush
bravera *f* vent, chimney
braveza *f* fierceness, ferocity; bravery, courage; fury (*of the elements*)
bravío -vía *adj* fierce, ferocious, savage; wild, uncultivated; coarse, unpolished; (coll.) stubborn; *m* fierceness, ferocity
bravo -va *adj* brave; fine, excellent, great; elegant, spruce; (coll.) sumptuous, magnificent; wild, fierce, savage; game; rough (*sea; coast line*); angry, annoyed; (coll.) boasting, blustering; (coll.) ill-humored; strong (*chili*); (Am.) querulous; *m* bravo (*murderer*); **¡bravo!** bravo!
bravonel *m* braggart
bravucón -cona *adj* (coll.) four-flushing; *mf* (coll.) four-flusher
bravuconada *f* (coll.) four-flushing
bravura *f* fierceness, ferocity; gameness; bravery (*courage; fine appearance*); bravado, boasting; bruskness, ill-humor; (mus.) bravura
braza *f* (naut.) fathom; (naut.) brace (*rope*)
brazada *f* stroke with arms; armful; **brazada de pecho** breast stroke
brazado *m* armful, armload
brazaje *m* coining, minting; (naut.) fathomage
brazal *m* brassart (*of armor*); arm band; irrigation ditch; (naut.) headrail; **brazal de arquero** bracer
brazalete *m* bracelet; (arm.) brassart
brazo *m* arm (*of body, chair, sea, law, etc.*); foreleg (*of quadruped*); energy, enterprise; **brazos** *mpl* laborers, hands; backers, protectors; **a brazo partido** hand to hand; **asidos del brazo** arm in arm; **con los brazos abiertos** with open arms; **de brazos caídos** with arms folded; **hecho un brazo de mar** (coll.) gorgeously outfitted; **no dar su brazo a torcer** (coll.) to be stubborn, be persistent; **tener brazo** (coll.) to be husky; **brazo a brazo** hand to hand; **brazo derecho** right-hand man
brazofuerte *m* (zool.) ant bear
brazola *f* (naut.) coaming
brazolargo *m* (zool.) spider monkey
brazuelo *m* small arm; shoulder (*of animal*)
brea *f* tar, pitch, petroleum asphalt; (naut.) calking material; **brea seca** rosin
brear *va* (coll.) to abuse, to mistreat; (coll.) to play a joke on, to make fun of
brebaje *m* potion, dose; poison; unpleasantness; (naut.) grog
breca *f* (ichth.) dace; (ichth.) bleak
brecina *f* (bot.) broom heath
brécol *m* or **brécoles** *mpl* (bot.) broccoli
brecolera *f* woman who sells broccoli; (bot.) broccoli
brecha *f* breach, breakthrough; opening; impression; (geol.) breccia; **batir en brecha** (mil.) to breach; to get the better of; to floor
brega *f* struggle; fight, scrap, row; trick, joke; **andar a la brega** to toil, to work hard; **dar brega a** to play a trick on
bregar §59 *va* to work (*dough*) with a rolling pin; *vn* to struggle; to fight, to start a row; to toil, to work hard; to try hard to win out
brema *f* (ichth.) bream; (*cap.*) *f* Bremen
bremense *adj* (pertaining to) Bremen; *mf* native or inhabitant of Bremen

bren *m* bran
brenca *f* sluice post
Brenero *m* Brenner
breña *f* rough and brambly ground
breñal *m* or **breñar** *m* rough and brambly region
breñoso -sa *adj* rough and brambly; rocky, craggy
breque *m* (ichth.) bleak
bresca *f* honeycomb
brescar §86 *va* to extract honeycombs from (*a hive*)
Bretaña *f* Brittany; **la Gran Bretaña** Britain, Great Britain; (*l.c.*) *f* Brittany, Brittany cloth; (bot.) hyacinth
brete *m* fetters, shackles; tight spot, tight squeeze
bretón -tona *adj & mf* Breton; **bretones** *mpl* (bot.) Brussels sprouts
breva *f* purple fig, early fig; snap, cinch; flat cigar
breval *m* fig tree yielding early figs
breve *adj* short, brief; (gram.) short; **en breve** soon, shortly; in short; *m* apostolic brief; *f* (mus.) breve
brevedad *f* brevity, briefness, conciseness; **a** or **con la mayor brevedad** as soon as possible
brevete *m* note, memorandum
breviario *m* breviary, brief treatise; (eccl.) breviary; (print.) brevier
brevipenne *adj* (zool.) brevipennate
brezal *m* heath, moor
brezo *m* (bot.) heath, heather; **brezo albarino, blanco** or **castellano** (bot.) tree heath, brier
brezoso -sa *adj* heathery
briaga *f* hoisting rope, lashing rope; bass-weed rope
Briareo *m* (myth.) Briareus
briba *f* bumming, loafing; **andar a la briba** to bum around, to loaf around
bribón -bona *adj* bumming, loafing; rascally; *mf* bum, loafer; rascal, scoundrel
bribonada *f* rascality, knavery
bribonazo *m* big rascal
bribonear *vn* to bum around, to loaf; to be a rascal
bribonería *f* life of loafing; rascality
bricbarca *f* (naut.) bark
bricho *m* gold or silver spangle (*used in embroidery*)
brida *f* bridle; horsemanship; curb, check, restraint; splice plate; fishplate; flange; clamp; **bridas** *fpl* (rail.) couplers; (surg.) filaments around the lips of a wound; **a toda brida** at top speed
bridar *va* to flange
bridecú *m* (*pl:* **-cúes**) sword belt
bridón *m* small bridle; bridoon; horseman riding a bur saddle; horse fitted with a bur saddle; (poet.) spirited steed
brigada *f* brigade; squad, gang, party; fleet (*e.g., of tractors*); (mil.) brigade; (mil.) train; *m* (mil.) staff sergeant
brigadero *m* man in charge of military pack animals
brigadier *m* (mil.) brigadier, brigadier general
brigadiera *f* (coll.) brigadier general's wife
brigantino -na *adj* (pertaining to) Corunna; *mf* native or inhabitant of Corunna; *f* (arm.) brigandine
Brígida *f* Bridget
Briján *m;* **saber más que Briján** to be wide-awake, to be keen-witted
brillante *adj* brilliant, bright, shining; (fig.) brilliant; *m* brilliant (*sparkling stone*); metallic lustre
brillantez *f* brilliance; (fig.) brilliance
brillantina *f* brilliantine (*hair dressing; glossy fabric*); metal polish
brillar *vn* to shine, to sparkle
brillo *m* brilliance, brightness, lustre; splendor
brilloso -sa *adj* shiny
brin *m* fine canvas; (Am.) canvas (*for painting*)
brincar §86 *va* to bounce (*a child*) in one's arms; (coll.) to skip (*a word or passage*); to pass over (*another person because of a promotion*); *vn* to leap, to jump; (coll.) to be very touchy, to flare up
brinco *m* leap, jump; hop, bounce; fancy hair ornament; **en dos brincos** or **en un brinco** in an instant
brindador -dora *mf* toaster, person who proposes a toast
brindar *va* to offer; to invite; **brindar a** + *inf* to invite to + *inf;* **brindar a uno con una cosa** to offer someone something; *vn* to invite; to drink a toast; **brindar a** or **por** to drink to; to toast; **brindar con** to offer; *vr* to offer; **brindarse a** + *inf* to offer to + *inf*
brindis *m* (*pl:* **-dis**) toast (*to someone's health*); offer; invitation, treat; (taur.) dedication (*by the matador of the first bull killed to the presiding officer*)
brinquillo or **brinquiño** *m* gewgaw, trinket; Portuguese candy or sweet; **hecho un brinquiño** (coll.) all spruced up
brinza *f* (bot.) sprig, shoot, blade
briñón *m* nectarine (*fruit*)
brío *m* spirit; determination, enterprise; elegance; **cortar los bríos a uno** to cut someone's wings
briofita *f* (bot.) bryophyte
briol *m* (naut.) buntline
briología *f* bryology
brionia *f* (bot.) bryony
brios euphemistic form of **dios,** used in mild oaths
brioso -sa *adj* spirited; determined, enterprising; elegant
briqueta *f* briquet or briquette (*of coal*)
brisa *f* breeze; bagasse of pressed grapes; (poet.) zephyr
brisca *f* bezique (*card game*); brisque (*ace*)
briscado -da *adj* interwoven with silk and gold thread or silk and silver thread
briscar §86 *va* to weave with silk and gold or silver thread; to embroider with silk and gold or silver thread
Briseida *f* (myth.) Briseis
brisera *f* or **brisero** *m* (Am.) glass lamp shade
brisote *m* stormy breeze; steady, fresh breeze
brístol *m* Bristol board
británico -ca *adj* Britannic
britano -na *adj* British; *mf* Briton; Britisher; **los britanos** the British
briza *f* (bot.) quaking grass
brizar §76 *va* to rock in a cradle
brizna *f* chip, splinter, fragment; filament, string; blade (*e.g., of straw*); (fig.) grain (*of hope, conscience, etc.*)
briznoso -sa *adj* splintery; stringy
brizo *m* cradle
brl. abr. of **barril**
broa *f* biscuit, cracker; corn bread; shallow cove
broca *f* reel, bobbin (*in a shuttle*); drill, drill bit; shoemaker's tack; **broca de avellanar** countersinking bit; **broca de centrar** center drill
brocadillo *m* light brocade
brocado -da *adj* brocaded; *m* brocade
brocal *m* curbstone (*of well*); steel rim (*of shield*); cigarette holder; mouthpiece of leather wine bag
brocamantón *m* diamond brooch
brocatel *m* brocatel (*brocade and marble*)
brocino *m* bump, lump (*on head*)
bróculi *m* (bot.) broccoli
brocha *f* brush, stubby brush (*for painting, shaving, etc.*); loaded dice; **de brocha gorda** house (*painter*); (coll.) crude, heavy-handed
brochada *f* brush, stroke with a brush
brochal *m* header beam
brochar *va* (mach.) to broach
brochazo *m* dab, stroke (*with brush*)
broche *m* clasp, fastener, clip; hook and eye; brooch; hasp (*for book covers*); (Am.) cuff button; **broche de oro** punch line
brocheta *f* (cook.) skewer
brochón *m* large brush; whitewash brush, plasterer's brush
brodio *m* var. of **bodrio**
broma *f* joke, jest; fun, merriment; (cook.) oatmeal; (mas.) riprap; (zool.) shipworm; (Am.) disappointment; **de broma** in fun, as a joke; **decir en broma** to say jokingly; **gastar una broma (a)** to play a joke (on)

bromar *va* to gnaw, to bore (*said of a shipworm*)
bromato *m* (chem.) bromate
bromazo *m* poor joke
bromear *vn* to joke, to jest; to enjoy oneself, have a good time; to carouse, go on a spree; *vr* to joke, to jest; to chat and joke
bromeliáceo -a *adj* (bot.) bromeliaceous
bromhídrico -ca *adj* (chem.) hydrobromic
brómico -ca *adj* (chem.) bromic
bromista *adj* joking; *mf* joker
bromo *m* (chem.) bromin or bromine; (bot.) brome grass
bromurado -da *adj* (containing) bromine
bromuro *m* (chem.) bromide; **bromuro de potasio** (chem.) potassium bromide
bronca *f* see **bronco**
bronce *m* bronze (*alloy; object; powder*); (poet.) cannon, bell, trumpet, clarion; **bronce de aluminio** aluminum bronze; **bronce de campanas** bell metal; **bronce de magnesio** magnesium bronze; **bronce fosforoso** phosphor bronze
bronceado -da *adj* bronze, bronze-colored; tanned, sunburnt: *m* bronzing; bronze finish; bronze (*color*); tan, sunburn
broncear *va, vn & vr* to bronze; to tan
broncería *f* collection of bronzes; bronze work, brasswork; bronze or brass shop
broncíneo -a *adj* bronzelike
broncista *m* bronzesmith
bronco -ca *adj* coarse, rough; gruff, uncouth; raspy, harsh; hoarse; brittle (*metal*); *f* (coll.) row, wrangle, dispute; (coll.) poor joke; **armar una bronca** (coll.) to start a row
bronconeumonía *f* (path.) bronchopneumonia
broncorrea *f* (path.) bronchorrhea
broncoscopia *f* bronchoscopy
broncoscopio *m* bronchoscope
bronquedad *f* coarseness, roughness; gruffness, uncouthness; harshness; hoarseness; brittleness
bronquial *adj* bronchial
bronquina *f* (coll.) scrap, quarrel
bronquio *m* (anat.) bronchus, bronchial tube
bronquíolo *m* (anat.) bronchiole, smaller bronchus
bronquítico -ca *adj* bronchitic
bronquitis *f* (path.) bronchitis
brontosauro *m* (pal.) brontosaurus
broquel *m* shield, buckler; (fig.) shield
broquelar *vr* to shield oneself
broquelazo *m* stroke with a shield or buckler
broquelillo *m* earring
broqueta *f* (cook.) skewer, brochette
brota *f* shoot, bud
brotadura *f* sprouting, budding; springing, gushing; eruption (*of the skin*)
brótano *m* var. of **abrótano**
brotar *va* to sprout, to shoot forth; to cause, to produce; *vn* to sprout, to shoot forth, to bud; to spring, to gush; to break out (*on the skin*)
brote *m* shoot, bud; rash, pimples; breaking out in a rash; outburst; outbreak (*of a disease*); (dial.) bit, crumb, fragment
brótola *f* (ichth.) codling
broza *f* brushwood; rubbish, trash; brush, underbrush; printer's brush; (fig.) rubbish
brozar §76 *va* (print.) to brush, to clean with a brush
brozoso -sa *adj* rubbishy, full of rubbish
brucelosis *f* (path. & vet.) brucellosis
brucero *m* brush or broom maker or dealer
bruces *mpl* lips; **a** or **de bruces** face downward, on one's face, prone
brucina *f* (pharm.) brucine
brucita *f* (mineral.) brucite
brugo *m* (ent.) plant louse; (ent.) oak larva
bruja *f* (orn.) barn owl; witch, sorceress; (coll.) hag; (coll.) shrew; (Am.) spook (*person wrapped in sheet*)
Brujas *f* Bruges
brujear *vn* to practice witchcraft
brujería *f* witchcraft, sorcery, magic
brujesco -ca *adj* witch
brujidor *m* var. of **grujidor**
brujir *va* var. of **grujir**
brujo *m* sorcerer, magician, wizard; (fig.) wizard
brújula *f* magnetic needle; compass; sight (*hole for aiming*); (fig.) guide; (*cap.*) *f* (astr.) Compasses; **brújula de inducción terrestre** (aer.) earth induction compass; **perder la brújula** to lose one's touch
brujulear *va* to uncover (*one's cards*) gradually; (coll.) to guess, to suspect; *vn* to know one's way around
brulote *m* fire ship
bruma *f* fog, mist
brumador -dora *adj* var. of **abrumador**
brumal *adj* foggy, misty
brumar *va* to crush, to overwhelm; to annoy
brumazón *m* heavy fog, thick mist
brumo *m* pure coating wax
brumoso -sa *adj* foggy, misty
Brunilda *f* Brunhild
bruno -na *adj* dark brown, blackish; brown; *m* (bot.) black plum
bruñido *m* burnishing, polishing
bruñidor -dora *adj* burnishing, polishing; *mf* burnisher, polisher; *m* burnisher (*tool*)
bruñidura *f* or **bruñimiento** *m* burnishing, polishing
bruñir §25 *va* to burnish, to polish; (coll.) to put rouge on, to put make-up on
bruño *m* (bot.) black plum
bruñón *m* nectarine
brus *m* (naut.) deck mop
brusco -ca *adj* brusque; sudden; rough, gruff; sharp (*curve*); *m* (bot.) butcher's-broom; *f* camber, roundup; (Am.) brushwood
brusela *f* (bot.) myrtle, lesser periwinkle; **bruselas** *fpl* tweezers
Bruselas *f* Brussels
bruselense *adj* (pertaining to) Brussels; *mf* native or inhabitant of Brussels
brusquedad *f* brusqueness; suddenness; roughness, gruffness; sharpness (*of a curve*)
brutal *adj* brutal; sudden, unexpected; (coll.) terrific (*e.g., speed*); (coll.) stunning; (coll.) huge, colossal; *m* brute, beast
brutalidad *f* brutality; stupidity; (coll.) flock, slew
brutalizar §76 *va* to brutalize
brutear *vn* (Am.) to talk nonsense, to bungle
brutesco -ca *adj* grotesque
bruteza *f* brutality; roughness, lack of polish
bruto -ta *adj* brute, brutish; stupid, ignorant; rough; gross; crude; (coll.) big, huge; **en bruto** in the rough; *mf* brute (*person*); ignoramus; *m* brute (*animal*); (coll.) dolt; (*cap.*) *m* Brutus
bruza *f* horse brush; printer's brush
bruzar §76 *va* to brush, to clean with a brush
bu *m* (*pl:* **búes**) (coll.) bogeyman, bugaboo; **hacer el bu a** (coll.) to scare, to frighten, to say boo to; *interj* boo!
búa *f* pimple; (path.) bubo
buarro *m* var. of **buharro**
buba *f* (path.) syphilis; **bubas** *fpl* (path.) bubo
búbalo -la *mf* (zool.) bubal
bubón *m* (path.) bubo
bubónico -ca *adj* bubonic
buboso -sa *adj* buboed
bucal *adj* buccal
bucanero *m* buccaneer
bucare *m* or **búcare** *m* (bot.) bucare, coral tree
Bucarest *f* Bucharest
búcaro *m* fragrant clay; flower vase
buccino *m* (zool.) whelk
buceador -dora *mf* diver
buceamiento *m* diving
bucear *vn* to dive; to be a diver; to delve
Bucéfalo *m* Bucephalus; (*l.c.*) *m* (coll.) blockhead, jackass
buceo *m* diving
bucero -ra *adj* black-nosed (*said of a hound*)
bucinador *m* (anat.) buccinator
bucle *m* curl, ringlet, lock; bend, loop
buco *m* opening, gap; (zool.) buck
bucólico -ca *adj* bucolic; *m* bucolic poet; *f* bucolic (*poem*); (coll.) food; (coll.) meal
bucráneo *m* (arch.) bucranium
buchada *f* mouthful
buche *m* craw, crop, maw; belly; mouthful; bag, pucker (*in clothes*); bosom (*for secrets*); suck-

ling ass; **hacer buche** to be baggy, to pucker; **sacar el buche a uno** (coll.) to make someone tell all he knows
buchete *m* puffed-up cheek
buchón -chona *adj* (coll.) baggy, bulging; pouting (*pigeon*); *f* (orn.) pouter
buchú *m & f* (pharm.) buchu
Buda *m* Buddha
búdico -ca *adj* Buddhic
budín *m* pudding
budinera *f* pudding mold
budión *m* (ichth.) butterfly fish
budismo *m* Buddhism
budista *adj & mf* Buddhist
buega *f* (prov.) boundary mark
buen *adj* apocopated form of **bueno**, used only before masculine singular nouns
buenaboya *m* volunteer oarsman
buenamente *adv* easily, with ease; freely, voluntarily
buenandanza *f* var. of **bienandanza**
buenaventura *f* good luck; fortune (*told by fortuneteller*); **decirle a uno la buenaventura** to tell one's fortune, to tell someone his fortune
buenazo -za *adj* (coll.) kind, good-natured
buenísimo -ma *adj super* (coll.) very good
bueno -na *adj* good; kind; well; fine, e.g., **buen tiempo** fine weather; (iron.) fine; **a buenas** willingly; **a la buena de Dios** at random; **de buenas a primeras** suddenly; afresh, anew, from the beginning; **¿de dónde bueno?** (coll.) where do you come from?, what's the good news?; **el bueno de Juan** good old John; **estar de buenas** to be in a good mood; **por las buenas** willingly; **¡buena es ésa** or **ésta!** (coll.) that's a fine how-do-you-do!, that's a fine state of affairs!; **¡buenas!** greetings!; **¡bueno!** well!, all right!; that'll do!
Buenos Aires *m & f* Buenos Aires; **el Gran Buenos Aires** Greater Buenos Aires
buenpasar *m* well-being
buey *m* ox, bullock, steer; **trabajar como un buey** to work like an ox; **buey almizclado** or **almizclero** (zool.) musk ox; **buey de cabestrillo** ox used as a shield by hunter; **buey del Tibet** (zool.) yak; **buey giboso** (zool.) zebu; **buey suelto** (coll.) free agent; (coll.) bachelor; **buey marino** (zool.) sea cow (*Halicore*)
bueyuno -na *adj* bovine
buf *interj* (coll.) ugh!
bufa *f* see **bufo**
bufalino -na *adj* (pertaining to the) buffalo
búfalo -la *mf* (zool.) buffalo; **búfalo cafre** (zool.) Cape buffalo
bufanda *f* scarf, muffler
bufar *vn* to snort; (coll.) to snort, to puff (*e.g., with anger*); *vr* to swell, to heave
bufete *m* writing desk; law office; clients (*of lawyer*); (Am.) snack, refreshment; **abrir bufete** to open a law office
bufetillo *m* small desk
bufido *m* snort; (coll.) snort, puff (*e.g., of anger*)
bufo -fa *adj* farcical; clownish; *mf* buffoon; *f* jest, buffoonery
bufón -fona *adj* funny, comical, clownish; *mf* buffoon, clown; *m* fool, jester; peddler, street vendor
bufonada *f* jest, buffoonery; raillery, sarcasm
bufonear *vn* to play the clown; *vr* to jest, to make fun
bufonesco -ca *adj* farcical, clownish; coarse, rude, burlesque
bufonizar §76 *vn & vr* to jest, to make fun
bugalla *f* oak gall
buganvilla *f* (bot.) bougainvillea
bugle *m* (mus.) bugle
buglosa *f* (bot.) bugloss
buharda *f* dormer; dormer window; garret; (fort.) balcony, battlement (*designed for dropping weapons on attackers at foot of wall*)
buhardilla *f* dormer; dormer window; garret; (Am.) skylight
buharro *m* (orn.) scops owl
buhedera *f* loophole, embrasure
buhedo *m* pool or pond that dries up in summer; marl
búho *m* (orn.) eagle owl; (coll.) unsociable person; (slang) squealer
buhonería *f* peddler's kit; peddler's stock or wares
buhonero *m* peddler, hawker
buído -da *adj* sharp, pointed; fluted, grooved; weak, skinny
buitre *m* (orn.) vulture
buitrero -ra *adj* vulturine; *m* vulture hunter; *f* vulture trap
buitrón *m* fish trap (*made of osier*); partridge net; silver-smelting furnace; ashpit (*of furnace*)
Bujara *f* Bokhara or Bukhara (*city*); **la Bujara** Bokhara or Bukhara (*state*)
bujarasol *m* reddish fig (*of Murcia*)
buje *m* axle box, bushing
bujeda *f*, **bujedal** *m* or **bujedo** *m* var. of **bojedal**
bujería *f* bauble, gewgaw, trinket
bujeta *f* box made of boxwood; box, case; perfume bottle; perfume box
bujía *f* candle; candlestick; candle power; spark plug; (surg.) bougie; **bujía internacional** (phys.) international candle; **bujía normal** or **patrón** (phys.) standard candle
bujía-pie *m* (*pl:* **bujías-pies**) foot-candle
bujiería *f* chandlery
bula *f* bull, bulla
bulario *m* collection of papal bulls, bullary
bulbillo *m* (bot.) bulbil
bulbo *m* (anat. & bot.) bulb
bulboso -sa *adj* bulbous
bulerías *fpl* Andalusian song and dance
buleto *m* apostolic brief
bulevar *m* boulevard
Bulgaria *f* Bulgaria
búlgaro -ra *adj & mf* Bulgar, Bulgarian; *m* Bulgar, Bulgarian (*language*)
bulí *m* var. of **burí**
bulimia *f* (path.) bulimia (*insatiable hunger*)
bulímico -ca *adj & mf* bulimic, bulimiac
bulo *m* (coll.) false rumor
bulón *m* bolt; **bulón de grillete** shackle bolt
bulonar *va* to bolt
bulto *m* bulk, volume; bust, statue; bundle, package; piece of baggage; bump, swelling; form, body, shadow; (slang) carcass (*of a person*); (Am.) briefcase; **a bulto** broadly, by guess; **buscar el bulto a** (coll.) to lay for; **coger el bulto a** (coll.) to have in one's clutches; **de bulto** evident; (Am.) important; **escurrir** or **esquivar el bulto** (coll.) to duck, to dodge
bululú *m* (*pl:* **-lúes**) (archaic) strolling impersonator; (Am.) excitement, disturbance
bulla *f* noise, uproar; bustle, crowd
bullabesa *f* bouillabaisse
bullaje *m* crush, mix-up
bullanga *f* disturbance, riot
bullanguero -ra *adj* turbulent, rioting; *mf* disturber of the peace, rioter
bullebulle *mf* (coll.) bustler, busybody
bullente *adj* boiling, bubbling; frothy (*beer*); teeming, swarming
bullicio *m* bustle, rumble; brawl, wrangle; disturbance, excitement
bullicioso -sa *adj* bustling, rumbling; turbulent, restless; riotous; *mf* rioter
bullidor -dora *adj* bustling, turbulent
bullir §26 *va* to move, to budge; *vn* to boil, to bubble up; to swarm, to teem; to abound; to occur frequently; to bustle, to hustle; to stir, to budge; (coll.) to itch, be restless; *vr* to stir, to budge
bullón *m* bubbling dye (*in boiler*); stud (*for adorning bookbindings*); puff (*in a dress*)
bumerang *m* boomerang
buna *m* (chem.) buna
buniatal *m* sweet-potato patch
buniato *m* (bot.) sweet potato (*plant and tuber*)
bunio *m* (bot.) hardened bulb; (path.) bunion
buñolería *f* doughnut bakery
buñolero -ra *mf* doughnut maker or dealer
buñuelo *m* doughnut, cruller; (coll.) botch
bupresto *m* (ent.) buprestid, buprestid beetle

buque *m* capacity; hull (*of ship*); ship, vessel; (mus.) resonance box (*e.g., of guitar*); **buque almirante** admiral (*flagship of admiral*); **buque a rotores** rotor ship; **buque cablero** cable ship; **buque carguero** freighter; **buque cisterna** tanker; **buque correo** mailboat; **buque de cruz** square-rigger; **buque de desembarco** (nav.) landing craft, landing ship (*LST*); **buque de doble hélice** twin-screw ship; **buque de guerra** warship; **buque de ruedas** paddle-wheel steamer; **buque de transporte** transport; **buque de vapor** steamer, steamship; **buque de vela** sailboat; **buque escucha** vedette; **buque escuela** school ship; (nav.) training ship; **buque fanal** or **faro** lightship; **buque gemelo** sister ship; **buque hospital** hospital ship; **buque madre** (nav.) mother ship; **buque mercante** merchantman, merchant vessel; **buque portaminas** mine layer; **buque tanque** tanker; **buque teatro** showboat; **buque trampa** tramp steamer; **buque transbordador** train ferry; **buque velero** sailing vessel
buqué *m* bouquet (*of wine*)
buquetero *m* (Am.) flower vase
bura *m* (zool.) blacktail
burato *m* Canton crepe; transparent cloak or veil
burbuja *f* bubble
burbujear *vn* to bubble, to burble
burbujeo *m* bubbling, burbling
burchaca *f* var. of **burjaca**
burche *f* tower (*for defense*)
burda *f* see **burdo**
burdégano *m* hinny
burdel *m* brothel; disorderly house; *adj* libidinous, vicious
Burdeos *f* Bordeaux; (*l.c.*) *m* (*pl:* **burdeos**) Bordeaux (*wine*)
burdo -da *adj* coarse; *f* (naut.) backstay
burel *m* fid (*for opening strands of rope*)
bureo *m* court for trial of persons of royal household; amusement, diversion
bureta *f* (chem.) burette
burga *f* hot springs
burgado *m* (zool.) small brown snail
burgalés -lesa *adj* (pertaining to) Burgos; *mf* native or inhabitant of Burgos
burgo *m* (archaic) town, village
burgomaestre *m* burgomaster
burgrave *m* burgrave
burgraviato *m* burgraviate
burgués -guesa *adj* bourgeois, middle-class; (pertaining to a) town; *mf* bourgeois, person of the middle class; townsman
burguesía *f* bourgeoisie, middle class, **alta burguesía** upper middle class
burí *m* (bot.) buri palm, talipo palm
buriel *adj* dark red; *m* coarse woolen cloth
buril *m* burin, graver; (fig.) burin (*style or manner of engraver*); (dent.) explorer
burilada *f* stroke or mark made with a burin or chisel; shaving or chip cut with a burin or chisel; slither of silver to be assayed
buriladura *f* engraving; chiseling
burilar *va* to engrave with a burin; to chisel (*marble*)
burjaca *f* leather bag of pilgrim or beggar
burla *f* ridicule; sneering, scoffing; joke, jest; trick, deception; **de burlas** in fun, for fun; **burla burlando** by joking; unawares; on the quiet; **burla pesada** rough joke; **burlas aparte** joking aside
burladero *m* safety island, safety zone; covert in a bull ring; safety niche or recess in a tunnel
burlador -dora *adj* ridiculing; joking, jesting; disappointing; seducing; *mf* wag, jester, practical joker; *m* seducer of women; drinking cup full of holes (*used as a trick for the unwary*); hidden jet of water (*to squirt the unwary*)
burlar *va* to ridicule; to trick, to deceive, to disappoint; to outwit, to frustrate, to elude; to seduce (*a woman*); *vn* to scoff; **burlar de** to make fun of, to scoff at; *vr* to joke, to jest; **burlarse de** to make fun of, to scoff at
burlería *f* trick, deception; illusion; fish story, fairy tale; scorn, derision
burlesco -ca *adj* (coll.) funny, comic, jocular
burlete *m* weather strip or stripping
burlisto -ta *mf* (Am.) joker, jester; **burlisto grande** (orn.) Couch's kingbird
burlón -lona *adj* joking, jesting; *mf* joker, jester; *m* (orn.) mocking bird
burlonería *f* slyness, cunning
buró *m* (*pl:* **-rós**) writing desk, bureau; (Am.) night table
burocracia *f* bureaucracy
burócrata *mf* bureaucrat; jobholder
burocrático -ca *adj* bureaucratic
burra *f* see **burro**
burrada *f* drove of asses; asininity
burrajear *va* to scribble; to doodle
burrajo -ja *adj* (Am.) coarse, stupid; *m* dry stable dung (*used for fuel*)
burreño *m* var. of **burdégano**
burrero *m* herdsman who sells ass's milk; (Am.) owner or driver of asses
burrillo *m* liturgical calendar
burro -rra *adj* stupid, asinine; *m* jackass, donkey, burro; sawbuck, sawhorse; windlass; (naut.) feed pump; (Am.) stepladder; (fig.) jackass; **burro cargado de letras** (coll.) learned jackass; **burro de carga** drudge, slave (*man*); *f* she-ass; (fig.) ass, stupid woman; drudge, slave (*woman*)
burrumbada *f* (coll.) var. of **barrumbada**
bursátil *adj* stock, stock-market
bursitis *f* (path.) bursitis
burujo *m* var. of **borujo**
burujón *m* var. of **borujón**
busaca *f* (Am.) pocket (*of pool table*); (Am.) bag
busardo *m* (orn.) buzzard; (orn.) marsh harrier
busca *f* search, hunt, pursuit; (hunt.) party of beaters; **buscas** *fpl* (Am.) perquisites
buscada *f* search, hunt, pursuit
buscador -dora *adj* searching; **buscador del blanco** (mil.) homing (*e.g., torpedo*); *mf* searcher, seeker; *m* (astr.) finder
buscahuella *m* (aut.) spotlight
buscaniguas *m* (*pl:* **-guas**) (Am.) snake (*kind of firecracker*)
buscapié *m* hint; key (*to interpret obscure passages*); **buscapiés** *msg* (*pl:* **-piés**) snake, serpent (*kind of firecracker*)
buscapleitos *mf* (*pl:* **-tos**) (Am.) troublemaker
buscapolos *m* (*pl:* **-los**) (elec.) pole finder
buscar §86 *va* to look for, to hunt for, to seek, to seek out; (Am.) to provoke; **buscar tres pies al gato** to pick a quarrel; *vr* to be selfish, to look out for oneself; **buscársela** (coll.) to manage to get along; (coll.) to ask for it, to be looking for trouble
buscareta *f* (orn.) wren
buscarruidos *m* (*pl:* **-dos**) (coll.) troublemaker
buscavidas *mf* (*pl:* **-das**) (coll.) snoop, busybody; (coll.) hustler
busco *m* miter sill (*of canal-lock gate*)
buscón -cona *mf* seeker, investigator, checker; petty thief; *m* (min.) prospector; *f* (coll.) loose woman
busilis *m* (*pl:* **-lis**) (coll.) difficulty, trouble; (coll.) dough (*money*); secret, mystery; **ahí está el busilis** (coll.) that's the trouble; **dar en el busilis** (coll.) to put one's finger on the trouble
búsqueda *f* search, hunt, pursuit
busto *m* bust
bustrófedon *m* boustrophedon
butaca *f* armchair, easy chair; orchestra seat
butacama *f* (aer. & rail.) sleeper seat
butacón *m* large easy chair
butadieno *m* (chem.) butadiene
butano *m* (chem.) butane
buteno *m* (chem.) butene
butifarra *f* Catalonian sausage; loose sock or stocking; (Am.) ham sandwich
butifarrero -ra *mf* maker or seller of Catalonian sausages
butileno *m* (chem.) butylene
butilo *m* (chem.) butyl
butiondo -da *adj* lewd, lustful
butírico -ca *adj* (chem.) butyric
butirina *f* (chem.) butyrin
butiro *m* butter

butirómetro *m* butyrometer
butiroso -sa *adj* butyrous
butomáceo -a *adj* (bot.) butomaceous
butrino *m* fish trap (*made of osier*)
butrón *m* var. of **buitrón**
butuco -ca *adj* (Am.) thick, stumpy
buxáceo -a *adj* (bot.) buxaceous
buyo *m* buyo (*chewing paste*)
buz *m* (*pl:* **buces**) kiss of gratitude, kiss of reverence; lip; **hacer el buz** (coll.) to bow and scrape
buzamiento *m* (geol.) dip
buzar §76 *vn* (geol.) to dip
buzarda *f* (naut.) breasthook
buzo *m* diver (*especially in diving suit*); (orn.) buzzard; **buzo de los pantanos** (orn.) marsh harrier
buzón *m* canal, conduit; lid, cover; sluice (*of water course of mill*); (found.) plug; mailbox, letter box; letter drop; **buzón de alcance** special-delivery box; mailbox for last-minute mail

C

C, c *f* third letter of the Spanish alphabet
c. abr. of **capítulo, compañía, corriente** & **cuenta**
c/ abr. of **caja, cargo, contra** & **corriente**
c.ª abr. of **compañía**
c/a abr. of **cuenta abierta**
C.A. abr. of **corriente alterna**
ca *interj* (coll.) oh no!
Caaba *f* Kaaba (*at Mecca*)
caama *m* (zool.) hartebeest
cabal *adj* exact; complete, perfect, finished; **no estar en sus cabales** to be not all there, to not be in one's right mind; *adv* exactly; completely; *interj* right!
cábala *f* cabal; cabala; divination; lucky number (*to try for the lottery*); **cábalas** *fpl* guess, supposition
cabalgada *f* raid by horseback; booty brought back from a raid by horseback
cabalgador -dora *adj* upper (*said of one of crossed knees*); *m* rider, horseman; *f* rider, horsewoman
cabalgadura *f* mount, riding horse, riding animal; beast of burden; (coll.) nag
cabalgar §59 *va* to ride (*a horse*); to mount (*a gun*); to cover (*a mare*); *vn* to ride horseback, to go horseback riding; to gallop; **cabalgar sobre** to run over into (*the next line; said of the sense of a line of poetry*)
cabalgata *f* cavalcade
cabalista *mf* cabalist; schemer
cabalístico -ca *adj* cabalistic
cabalizar §76 *vn* to practice cabala
caballa *f* (ichth.) mackerel
caballada *f* drove of horses
caballaje *m* stud service; stud price; (Am.) horsepower
caballar *adj* (pertaining to the) horse, equine
caballazo *m* large heavy horse; (Am.) jolt with a horse, trampling with a horse
caballear *vn* (coll.) to go horseback riding, to like to go horseback riding
caballejo *m* little horse; nag; horse (*instrument of torture*)
caballerango *m* (Am.) stableman, horse trainer
caballerato *m* pontifical benefice granted to married layman
caballerear *vn* to claim to be a knight, to act the knight; to pretend to be somebody
caballeresco -ca *adj* knightly, chivalric; gentlemanly; quixotic
caballerete *m* (coll.) dude
caballería *f* horse, mule; mount; (mil.) cavalry; knights; knighthood, chivalry; order of knights; knight's share of booty; land measure of varying size in Spain and Spanish America; **andarse en caballerías** (coll.) to be over-obsequious, to outdo oneself in compliments; **caballería andante** errantry, knight-errantry; **caballería ligera** (mil.) light horse, light cavalry; **caballería mayor** saddle horse; **caballería menor** ass, jackass
caballeriza *f* stable; stable hands
caballerizo *m* groom, stableman; **caballerizo mayor del rey** royal master of the horse
caballero -ra *adj* mounted, riding; gentlemanly; obstinate, persistent; *m* knight, nobleman; mister; gentleman; cavalier, rider, horseman; (fort.) cavalier; (orn.) sandpiper; **armar caballero** to knight; **ir caballero en** to ride (*e.g., a horse, mule*); **caballero andante** knight errant; **caballero cubierto** grandee who did not have to uncover in presence of king; boorish fellow who stands with his hat on; **caballero de industria** knave, adventurer, sharper; **Caballero de la triste figura** Knight of the Rueful Countenance (*Don Quijote*); **caballero del cisne** (myth.) swan knight; **caballero del Temple** Templar, Knight Templar
caballerosidad *f* chivalry, gentlemanliness
caballeroso -sa *adj* chivalrous, gentlemanly
caballeta *f* (ent.) grasshopper
caballete *m* small horse; hip, ridge (*of roof*); ridge (*between furrows*); easel; trestle, horse, sawbuck; gantry, barrelstand; horse (*instrument of torture*); hemp brake; chimney cap; bridge (*of nose*); breastbone; (Am.) rest (*for knife and fork*); **Caballete del pintor** (astr.) Painter's Easel
caballista *m* horseman; horsebreaker; cowboy; (dial.) mounted highwayman; *f* horsewoman
caballito *m* little horse; hobbyhorse (*stick with horse's head*); **caballitos** *mpl* merry-go-round; mechanical horse race (*for gambling*); **caballito del diablo** (ent.) dragonfly, darning needle; **caballito de mar** (ichth.) sea horse
caballo *m* horse; knight (*in chess*); playing card (*figure on horseback*) equivalent to queen; **caballos** *mpl* (mil.) horse, cavalry; **a caballo** on horseback; **a caballo de** astride; **a mata caballo** at breakneck speed; **de a caballo** mounted; **ir a caballo** to go or to ride horseback; **montar a caballo** to ride horseback; **un sesenta caballos** a sixty-horsepower automobile; **caballo aguililla** (Am.) swift-pacing horse; **caballo blanco** angel (*financial backer*); **caballo de agua** (zool.) river horse; (ichth.) sea horse; **caballo de aldaba** horse kept for gala occasions; **caballo de batalla** battle horse, charger; forte, specialty; main point (*of an argument*); **caballo de carga** pack horse; **caballo de carrera** race horse; **caballo de frisa** (mil.) cheval-de-frise; **caballo de fuerza** (mech.) French or metric horsepower (*736 watts*); **caballo de guerra** charger; **caballo del diablo** (ent.) dragonfly, darning needle; **caballo de mar** (zool.) river horse; (ichth.) sea horse; **caballo de montar** or **de silla** saddle horse; **caballo de palo** (coll.) ship, vessel; (coll.) wooden horse (*used for punishment*); **caballo de posta** post horse; **caballo de regalo** horse kept for gala occasions; **caballo de tiro** draft horse; **caballo de Troya** Trojan horse; **caballo de vapor** (mech.) French horsepower or metric horsepower (*736 watts*); **caballo de vapor inglés** horsepower (*746 watts*); **caballo entero** stallion; **caballo hora** (*pl:* **caballos hora**) (mech.) horsepower-hour; **caballo marino** (zool.) river horse; (ichth. & zool.) sea horse; **caballo mecedor** rocking horse, hobbyhorse; **caballo padre** stallion; **caballo regalado** gift horse, e.g., **a caballo regalado no se le mira el diente** never look a gift horse in the mouth; **caballo semental** studhorse
caballón *m* big clumsy horse; ridge (*between furrows*); dike, levee
caballuno -na *adj* (pertaining to the) horse, horselike
cabaña *f* cabin, hut; hovel; rustic bower (*in a garden*); drove, flock; flock of sheep and ewes; livestock; drove of grain-carrying horses or mules; (hunt.) shelter; (paint.) pastoral scene; balk line (*in billiards*); cattle-breeding ranch
cabañal *adj* sheep-and-cattle (*path*); *m* village of cabins or huts
cabañería *f* shepherd's weekly ration
cabañero -ra *adj* sheep-and-cattle; grain-carrying; *m* shepherd; drover
cabañil *adj* shepherd's-cabin; *m* mule-driver

cabañuelas *fpl* weather forecasting in January and August; first summer rains (*in Argentina and Bolivia*); winter rain (*in Mexico*); (archaic) Feast of Tabernacles (*in Toledo*); **estar cogiendo cabañuelas** (Am.) to be out of work
cabaret *m* (*pl:* **-rets**) cabaret, night club
cabe *m* stroke of ball; **dar un cabe a** (coll.) to hurt, to harm; **cabe de pala** (coll.) lucky break; *prep* (archaic & poet.) near, at the side of
cabeceada *f* (Am. & dial.) nod
cabeceado *m* thick stroke (*of certain letters*)
cabeceamiento *m* var. of **cabeceo**
cabecear *va* to write (*letters*) with thick strokes; to bind (*e.g., a rug*); to put a headband on (*a book*); to head (*wine*); to put a new foot on (*a stocking*); *vn* to nod (*in sleep*); to bob the head; to shake one's head (*in negation*); to slip to one side, to hang over; to lurch; (naut.) to pitch
cabeceo *m* nod, bob, shake (*of the head*); lurching; (naut.) pitch, pitching
cabecera *f* head (*of bed, table, etc.*); bedside; headboard; headwall; headwaters; end (*of house, lot, or field*); heading (*e.g., of a chapter of a book*); (print.) headpiece; headline (*of newspaper*); (law) heading (*of a document*); capital, county seat; fortified point on a bridge; pillow, bolster; **asistir** or **estar a la cabecera de un enfermo** to be in constant attendance on a sick person; **cabecera de cartel** (theat.) top billing; **cabecera de puente** (mil.) bridgehead
cabeciancho -cha *adj* broad-headed
cabeciduro -ra *adj* (Am.) stubborn
cabecilla *mf* (coll.) scalawag; *m* rebel leader; gang leader; ringleader
cabellar *vn* to grow hair; to put on false hair; *vr* to put on false hair
cabellera *f* head of hair; switch of hair; (astr.) coma (*of comet*); (bot.) mistletoe (*Phoradendron*)
cabello *m* hair (*of head*); **cabellos** *mpl* hair (*of head*); corn silk; **asirse de un cabello** (coll.) to be out for the main chance; **cortar un cabello en el aire** to have keen insight; **en cabello** with one's hair down; **en cabellos** bareheaded; **estar pendiente de un cabello** to be hanging by a hair; **traer por los cabellos** to drag in irrelevantly; **cabello del rey** (bot.) Florida moss, Spanish moss; **cabello de Venus** (bot.) maidenhair; **cabello merino** thick curly hair; **cabellos de ángel** fine vermicelli
cabelludo -da *adj* hairy, shaggy; fibrous
caber §27 *vn* to fit, to go; to have enough room; to be admitted; to be possible; to befall, to happen; **no cabe duda** there is no doubt; **no cabe más** that's the limit; **no caber de** to be bursting with (*e.g., joy*); **no caber en sí** to be beside oneself; to be puffed up with conceit; **todo cabe en** anything (*bad*) can be expected of; **caber** + *inf* to be possible to + *inf;* **caber a** to happen to, to befall; **caber por** to be able to get through (*e.g., a door*)
cabero -ra *adj* (Am.) end, last; *m* (prov. & Am.) handle maker (*for farm implements*)
cabestraje *m* halters; fee paid to cattle drover
cabestrante *m* var. of **cabrestante**
cabestrar *va* to halter, put a halter on; *vn* to hunt using an ox as shield
cabestrear *va* (Am.) to lead by the halter; *vn* to be lead easily by the halter
cabestrería *f* halter shop
cabestrero -ra *adj* (dial.) wild but yielding to the halter; *m* maker and seller of halters and hemp ware
cabestrillo *m* sling (*to support hurt arm*); little chain worn as necklace; (carp.) strap, diagonal tie
cabestro *m* halter; trained ox, leading ox; (coll.) pander, pimp; (surg.) sling for broken jaw; **llevar** or **traer del cabestro** (coll.) to lead by the halter; (fig.) to lead by the nose
cabete *m* metal tip (*of rope*)
cabeza *f* head (*top part of body of man or animal; brains, intelligence; judgment; top part of page, of nail or pin, of a hammer; top of mountain; origin, source, e.g., of a river; front of a procession, army, etc.; chief, leader; chief command, leadership; person; individual; point of an arrow; rounded top of cabbage or lettuce; recording or reproducing part of tape recorder*); capital (*e.g., of a country*); **alzar la cabeza** (coll.) to be on one's feet (*after poverty or misfortune*); (coll.) to be up and around (*after an illness*); **andársele a uno la cabeza** (coll.) to be in a whirl; (coll.) to be on the skids; **calentarse la cabeza** (coll.) to be mentally exhausted; **dar de cabeza** (coll.) to lose one's wealth or standing; **dar en la cabeza a** to frustrate, to thwart; **de cabeza** on end; head first; by heart; on one's own, of one's own invention; **flaco de cabeza** befuddled, confused; **hacer cabeza** to be the head (*e.g., of a business*); **henchir la cabeza de viento a** (coll.) to flatter, to puff up; **ir cabeza abajo** (coll.) to be going downhill, to be on the decline; **irse de la cabeza** to go out of one's mind; **levantar la cabeza** (coll.) to be on one's feet (*after poverty or misfortune*); (coll.) to be up and around (*after an illness*); **mala cabeza** headstrong person; **meterse de cabeza** (coll.) to plunge headlong (*into a deal or business*); **metérsele a uno en la cabeza una cosa** (coll.) to get something in one's head; (coll.) to be bullheaded about something; **no levantar cabeza** to be deep in work, to be busy reading and writing; **no tener dónde volver la cabeza** to not know where to look for help; **otorgar de cabeza** to nod assent; **pasarle a uno por la cabeza** (coll.) to come into one's head; **perder la cabeza** to become befuddled, to go out of one's mind; **por su cabeza** on one's own (*without seeking advice*); **quebrantar la cabeza a** to humble the pride of; to bore to death; **quebrarse la cabeza** (coll.) to seek with diligence; **quebrarse la cabeza con** (coll.) to bother one's head about; **quitar a uno de la cabeza alguna cosa** (coll.) to put something out of someone's head; **romperse la cabeza** (coll.) to rack one's brains; **sentar la cabeza** (coll.) to settle down; **subírsele a uno a la cabeza** to go to one's head (*said of wine, success, etc.*); **tocado de la cabeza** (coll.) touched in the head; **cabeza de ajo** or **ajos** bulb of garlic; **cabeza de borrado** erase head (*of tape recorder*); **cabeza de combate** war head; **cabeza de chorlito** (coll.) scatterbrains; (Am.) forgetful person; **cabeza de la biela** (mach.) big end; **cabeza de lectura** playback head; **cabeza de mina** mine entrance; **cabeza de motín** ringleader; **cabeza de olla** (zool.) blackfish; **cabeza de partido** county seat; **cabeza de perro** (bot.) pilewort; **cabeza de playa** (mil.) beachhead; **cabeza de puente** (mil.) bridgehead; **cabeza de registro** or **cabeza grabadora** recording head; **cabeza de turco** (naut.) Turk's-head; (coll.) scapegoat, butt; **cabeza dura** (coll.) thick head (*person*); **cabeza mayor** head of cattle; **cabeza menor** head of sheep, goats, etc.; **cabeza perdida** countersunk head; **cabeza redonda** (coll.) blockhead
cabezada *f* butt (*with the head*); blow on the head; nod; headstall (*of a bridle*); pitch, pitching (*of a ship*); instep (*of boot*); (b.b.) headband; **dar cabezadas** to nod
cabezal *m* small pillow; bolster; header, header brick; (print.) heading; straw mattress of peasants; (surg.) compress; (mach.) headstock (*of a lathe*)
cabezalero -ra *mf* (law) executor
cabezazo *m* butt (*with the head*)
cabezo *m* hillock; summit, top; reef
cabezón -zona *adj* big-headed; headstrong; *m* hole for the head (*in a garment*); collarband; **llevar** or **traer de los cabezones** (coll.) to lead by the nose; **cabezón de serreta** cavesson
cabezonada *f* (coll.) stubbornness
cabezorro *m* (coll.) big misshapen head
cabezota *adj* (coll.) stubborn; *mf* (coll.) stubborn person; (coll.) big-headed person
cabezudo -da *adj* big-headed; (coll.) headstrong; heady (*wine*); *m* big-headed dwarf (*in carnival processions*); (ichth.) striped mullet

cabezuela *f* little head; coarse flour, middling; (bot.) capitulum or head (*inflorescence*); rose bud for making rose water; (bot.) broom centaury, cornflower
cabida *f* space, room, capacity; expanse; **dar cabida a** to make room for; **tener cabida** or **gran cabida** to have pull, to be in favor; **tener cabida en** to have a place in, to be included in
cabila *f* tribe (*in Morocco*)
cabildada *f* (coll.) hasty and unwise action of a chapter or council
cabildear *vn* to lobby
cabildeo *m* lobbying
cabildero *m* lobbyist
cabildo *m* cathedral chapter; chapter meeting; municipal council; council room; town hall
cabilla *f* steel bar, dowel, driftbolt; (naut.) belaying pin
cabillo *m* stalk, stem; end (*of a rope*)
cabillón *m* rung of rope ladder
cabimiento *m* space, room, capacity
cabina *f* cabin; cab (*e.g., of a truck*); booth (*for telephoning; for listening to phonograph records*); (aer.) cabin; (sport) dressing room; **cabinas de audición independientes** private listening booths
cabio *m* joist, rafter; trimmer; lintel, crosspiece
cabizbajo -ja *adj* crestfallen
cable *m* cable, rope, hawser; cable's length; (telg.) cable; **cable coaxial** coaxial cable; **cable de alambre** stranded cable; **cable de remolque** towline, towrope; **cable de retén** guy, guy wire
cableado *m* (elec.) cable (*in auto, radio, etc.*)
cablear *va* to fashion into a cable
cablecarril *m* cableway
cablegrafiar §90 *va & vn* to cable
cablegráfico -ca *adj* cable
cablegrama *m* cablegram, cable
cablero -ra *adj* cable (*e.g., ship*); *m* cable ship
cabo *m* end; handle; cape; small bundle; filament, thread, string; end, bit, small piece; chief, boss, foreman; finish, perfection; (naut.) cord, rope, cable; (mil.) corporal; **cabos** *mpl* eyes, eyebrows and hair; paws, nose, and mane (*of horse*); duds, pieces of clothing; miscellanies; **al cabo** finally, after all, **al cabo de** after, at the end of; **atar cabos** (coll.) to put two and two together; **dar cabo a** to finish, to perfect; **dar cabo de** to put an end to, to destroy; **El Cabo** Cape Town; **estar al cabo de** (coll.) to be informed about; **llevar a cabo** to carry out, accomplish; **ponerse al cabo de** to catch on to, to get the point of; **por ningún cabo** by no means; **cabo de año** anniversary memorial service; **Cabo de Buena Esperanza** Cape of Good Hope; **cabo de desgarre** (aer.) rip cord; **cabo de escuadra** (mil.) corporal; **Cabo de Hornos** Cape Horn; **cabo de maestranza** (naut.) foreman (*of a brigade of workmen*); **cabo de mar** (naut.) petty officer; **cabo de plumas** (Am.) penholder; **Cabo Finisterre** Cape Finisterre (*headland in northwest Spain*); Land's End (*southwest tip of England*); **cabo negro** (bot.) fishtail palm; **cabo suelto** (coll.) loose end (*unfinished business*); **Cabo Verde** Cape Verde
cabotaje *m* coasting trade, coastal traffic
cabra *f* (zool.) goat; (hist.) catapult; (Am.) loaded die; **cabra bezoar** (zool.) ibex (*Capra aegagrus*); **cabra de almizcle** (zool.) musk deer; **cabra montés** (zool.) ibex, wild goat
cabrahigadura *f* caprification
cabrahigal *m* field of caprifigs or wild figs
cabrahigar *m* field of caprifigs or wild figs; §59 *va* to caprificate
cabrahigo *m* (bot.) caprifig, wild fig (*tree and fruit*)
cabrajo *m* (zool.) lobster (*Homarus vulgaris*)
cabré *1st sg fut ind of* **caber**
cabrear *va* (vulg.) to burn up, exasperate; *vr* (Am.) to jump around
cabrera *f* goatherd (*woman*)
cabrería *f* goat-milk dairy; goat stable
cabrerizo -za *adj* goatish; *m* goatherd; *f* goat stable; goatherds' hut
cabrero *m* goatherd
cabrestante *m* capstan; **guarnir el cabrestante** to rig the capstan; **cabrestante para remolcar** towing winch
cabria *f* three-legged derrick, crab
cabrieta *f* jack, lifting jack
cabrilla *f* sawbuck, sawhorse; leg of a three-legged derrick; (ichth.) grouper; (ichth.) serran; **cabrillas** *fpl* (naut.) whitecaps; leg burns or blisters; game of skipping stones on water; (*cap.*) *fpl* (astr.) Pleiades
cabrillear *vn* to caper, to prance, to frisk; to sparkle, to flash; (naut.) to form whitecaps; (med.) to beat irregularly (*said of heart*)
cabrilleo *m* (naut.) forming of whitecaps
cabrio *m* rafter; joist
cabrío -a *adj* goatish; of goats; *m* herd of goats
cabriola *f* caper; skip, gambol; somersault; **dar** or **hacer cabriolas** to cut capers
cabriolar *vn* to caper, to prance, to frisk
cabriolé *m* cabriolet (*carriage and automobile*)
cabriolear *vn* to caper, to prance, to frisk
cabritero -ra *mf* dealer in kids (*young goats*)
cabritilla *f* kid, kidskin
cabrito *m* kid; **cabritos** *mpl* (Am.) popcorn
cabrón *m* buck, billy goat; complaisant husband, cuckold
cabronada *f* (coll.) indignity, shamelessness; (coll.) necessary evil
cabrón-emisario *m* (Bib.) scapegoat
cabruno -na *adj* (pertaining to the) goat
cabujón *m* uncut ruby; nail with diamond-shaped head; convex polished but uncut precious stone; **cabujones** *mpl* (print.) headpiece
cabuya *f* (bot.) century plant; pita fiber, pita hemp; rope, pita rope; (naut.) small ropes; **ponerse en la cabuya** (Am.) to catch on, to become fully informed
cabuyera *f* hammock cords
cabuyería *f* (naut.) small ropes
cacahuacintli *m* (Am.) hominy
cacahual *m* cacao plantation
cacahuate *m*, **cacahuete** *m* or **cacahuey** *m* (bot.) peanut (*plant, pod, and seed*)
cacahuetero -ra *mf* peanut vendor
cacalote *m* (Am.) raven; (Am.) popcorn; (Am.) break, blunder
cacao *m* (bot.) cacao (*tree and seed*); (Am.) chocolate; **pedir cacao** (Am.) to beg for mercy
cacaotal *m* var. of **cacahual**
cacaotero *m* (bot.) cacao (*tree*)
cacaraña *f* pit, pock (*in face*)
cacarañado -da *adj* pitted, pocked, pock-marked
cacarañar *va* (Am.) to pit
cacareador -dora *adj* cackling; (coll.) boasting
cacarear *va* (coll.) to exaggerate, exaggerate the importance of (*one's doings*); *vn* to cackle; to crow
cacareo *m* cackling; crowing; crying, yelling; (coll.) crowing, boasting
cacarizo -za *adj* (Am.) pock-marked
cacatúa *f* (orn.) cockatoo
cacaxtle *m* (Am.) crate
cacea *f* trolling; **pescar a la cacea** to troll
cacear *va* to stir with a dipper or ladle; *vn* to troll
caceo *m* stirring with a ladle; trolling
cacera *f* irrigating ditch or canal
cacería *f* hunt; hunting party; bag (*game caught*); (paint.) hunting scene
cacerina *f* cartridge pouch
cacerola *f* casserole, saucepan; (chem.) casserole
caceta *f* apothecaries' brass straining dipper
cacica *f* female Indian chief; chief's wife
cacicato or **cacicazgo** *m* position or territory of Indian chief; (coll.) bossism (*in politics*)
cacillo *m* small ladle or dipper; pannikin
cacimba *f* hole dug in beach for drinking water; bucket; (Am.) tub for collecting rain water
cacique *m* Indian chief; bossy person; (coll.) boss (*in politics*); (orn.) cacique; **cacique veranero** (orn.) hangbird, Baltimore oriole
caciquesco -ca *adj* (coll.) (pertaining to a) boss
caciquismo *m* (coll.) bossism
cacle *m* (Am.) leather sandal; (Am.) footwear
caco *m* pickpocket; (coll.) coward

cacodilato *m* (chem.) cacodylate
cacodílico -ca *adj* (chem.) cacodylic
cacofonía *f* cacophony
cacofónico -ca *adj* cacophonous
cacomite *m* (bot.) tigerflower
cacoquimia *f* (path.) cacochymia
cactáceo -a *adj* (bot.) cactaceous
cacto *m* (bot.) cactus
cacumen *m* (coll.) acumen
cacha *f* see **cacho**
cachaco -ca *adj* (Am.) sporty; *m* (Am.) sport
cachada *f* (Am.) thrust or wound made with the horns
cachalote *m* (zool.) sperm whale, cachalot
cachamarín *m* (naut.) coasting lugger
cachanilla *f* (bot.) arrowweed, arrowwood
cachano *m* (coll.) the devil; **llamar a cachano** (coll.) to ask in vain
cachapa *f* (Am.) corn bread
cachar *va* to break to pieces; to split (*wood*); to plough up
cacharpari *m* (Am.) farewell party, send-off party
cacharrería *f* crockery shop
cacharrero -ra *mf* crockery dealer
cacharro *m* crock, coarse earthen pot; piece of crockery (*still useful*); piece of junk (*any old machine that does not work well*); (Am.) notion, trinket
cachava *f* shinny (*game and stick*); crook, staff
cachavazo *m* stroke with shinny stick
cachaza *f* (coll.) slowness, sloth, phlegm; rum; first froth on boiling cane juice
cachazudo -da *adj* slow, slothful, phlegmatic; *mf* sluggard; *m* (zool.) tobacco worm
cache *adj* (Am.) slovenly
cachear *va* to frisk (*for weapons*)
cachemarín *m* (naut.) coasting lugger
cachemir *m* var. of **casimir**
cachemira *f* var. of **casimir;** (*cap.*) Cashmere
cacheo *m* frisking
cachera *f* homespun
cachería *f* (Am.) slovenliness; (Am.) small shop
cacheta *f* ward (*of lock*)
cachetada *f* (Am. & Canary Islands) slap in the face
cachete *m* punch in the face; cheek, swollen cheek; dagger
cachetero *m* dagger, short poniard; dagger man, puntillero (*bullfighter who gives coup de grâce with dagger*)
cachetina *f* (coll.) fist fight, brawl
cachetudo -da *adj* round-cheeked
cachicamo *m* (zool.) armadillo
cachicán *m* foreman, overseer; (coll.) sly fellow
cachicuerno -na *adj* horn-handled (*said of a weapon*)
cachidiablo *m* (coll.) hobgoblin; (coll.) person disguised as the devil; *adj* (coll.) mischievous, impish; (coll.) wild, unruly
cachifollar *va* (coll.) to make fun of, to humiliate
cachigordete -ta *adj* (coll.) stubby
cachigordo -da *adj* (coll.) squat
cachillada *f* breed, litter
cachimba *f* (Am.) spring, well; (Am.) pipe (*for smoking tobacco*); (Am.) pistol, revolver; (Am.) empty cartridge
cachimbo *m* (Am.) pipe; (Am.) sugar mill; **chupar cachimbo** (Am.) to smoke a pipe; (Am.) to suck its finger (*said of a baby*)
cachipolla *f* (ent.) shad fly, dayfly
cachiporra *f* billy, bludgeon
cachiporrazo *m* blow with a billy or bludgeon
cachirulo *m* liquor container; (naut.) small three-master; (slang) beau, lover; (prov.) kite; (prov.) hat, cap; (Am.) cloth or chamois patch (*for trousers*)
cachivache *m* (coll.) faker; **cachivaches** *mpl* broken crockery; pots and pans, kitchenware; trash, junk
cacho -cha *adj* bent, crooked; *m* crumb, bit, slice; (ichth.) chub; (Am.) horn; *f* side of the handle of a folding knife or razor; buttock (*of rabbit*); **hasta las cachas** (coll.) over head and ears
cacholas *fpl* (naut.) cheeks of the masts
cachón *m* breaker (*wave*); splashing jet of water; rapids (*in a river*); **cachones** *mpl* surf
cachondo -da *adj* in rut; (coll.) passionate; (slang) sexy (*woman*)
cachopín -pina *mf* var. of **cachupín**
cachorreñas *fpl* garlic soup
cachorrillo *m* pocket pistol; pup, cub
cachorro -rra *mf* pup, whelp, cub; *m* pocket pistol
cachú *m* (*pl:* **-chúes**) catechu
cachucha *f* rowboat; cap; cachucha (*Andalusian dance*)
cachuchero *m* maker or seller of caps; maker or seller of pincases
cachucho *m* oil measure equal to a sixth of a pound; pincase; rowboat; (ichth.) red West Indian snapper
cachuela *f* pork fricassee; fricassee of rabbit livers, hearts, and kidneys; gizzard
cachuelo *m* (ichth.) dace; (Am.) tip
cachumbo *m* (Am.) fruit shell (*used to make cups and other vessels*); (Am.) curl, corkscrew curl
cachunde *m* (pharm.) aromatic troche or pastil; catechu
cachupín -pina *mf* Spanish settler in America; *f* (Am.) strait jacket (*used for torture of prisoners*)
cachupinada *f* (coll.) gaudy party, gaudy gathering
cachurear *vn* (Am.) to rummage through the rubbish or trash
cachurrera menor *f* (bot.) cocklebur (*Xanthium spinosum*)
cada *adj indef* each; every (*followed by a numeral*), e.g., **cada tres meses** every three months; **cada tercer día** every third day; **cada cual** each one; **cada cuánto** how often; **cada día** + *comp* more and more; **cada quisque** (coll.) each one; **cada uno** each one; **cada vez** + *comp* more and more; **cada y siempre que** as soon as; *m* (bot.) juniper
cadahalso *m* wooden shed or shack
cadalecho *m* bed of branches
cadalso *m* stand, platform; scaffold
cadañego -ga *adj* annual, yearly
cadañero -ra *adj* annual, yearly; of a year's duration; having offspring every year
cadarzo *m* floss, floss silk (*threads of outer part of cocoon*)
cádava *f* (prov.) burnt stump of furze
cadáver *m* corpse, cadaver
cadavérico -ca *adj* cadaverous
cadejo *m* entangled hair; small hank or skein; batch of thread for making tassels
cadena *f* chain; chain gang; tie, brace; (chem. & rad.) chain; **cadena antideslizante** or **antirresbaladiza** tire chain; **cadena de agrimensor** surveyor's chain; **cadena de distribución** (aut.) timing chain; **cadena lateral** (chem.) side chain; **cadena para neumático** tire chain; **cadena perpetua** life imprisonment; **cadena sin fin** endless chain
cadencia *f* cadence; (mus.) cadence; (mus.) cadenza; **cadencia del paso** (mil.) cadence; **cadencia perfecta** (mus.) perfect cadence
cadencioso -sa *adj* rhythmical, cadenced
cadenear *va* to measure with the chain
cadenero *m* chainman, lineman
cadeneta *f* chain stitch; (b.b.) headband
cadenilla *f* small chain; **cadenilla de tiro** (elec.) pull chain
cadente *adj* declining, on the decline; rhythmic
cadera *f* (anat.) hip; flank (*of animal*); (zool.) coxa (*of arthropod*); **caderas** *fpl* bustle
caderillas *fpl* bustle
caderudo -da *adj* big-hipped
cadetada *f* (coll.) thoughtlessness, inconsiderate act
cadete *m* cadet; (Am.) apprentice
cadí *m* (*pl:* **-díes**) cadi
cadillar *m* field of hedgehog parsley
cadillo *m* (bot.) hedgehog parsley; (bot.) burdock; bristle, burr; **cadillos** *mpl* fag end, thrums
cadmeo -a *adj* Cadmean
cadmía *f* oxide of zinc which collects in the chimney of zinc-subliming furnaces

cadmio *m* (chem.) cadmium
Cadmo *m* (myth.) Cadmus
cadozo *m* whirlpool (*in river*)
caducar §86 *vn* to dote, to be in one's dotage; to be worn out, to be out-of-date; (com. & law) to lapse, to expire
caduceo *m* caduceus
caducidad *f* caducity (*feebleness, decrepitude; transitoriness*); (law) caducity (*lapse, expiration*); **incurrir en caducidad** to lapse, expire
caduco -ca *adj* caducous (*feeble, decrepit; transitory*); (bot. & law) caducous
caduquez *f* caducity
caedizo -za *adj* ready to fall, falling; fragile; weak, timid; (bot.) deciduous; **hacer caedizo** to drop, to lose (*on purpose*); *m* (Am.) lean-to
caedura *f* loose threads that fall from loom
caer §28 *vn* to fall, to tumble, to fall off; to droop; to be located, to be found; to fall due; to become faint (*said of colors*); to decline (*said of sun, day, wind, etc.*); to fall (*to be killed, e.g., in battle*); **estar al caer** to be about to happen; **no caigo** (coll.) I don't get it; **caer a** to face, to overlook; **caer bien** to fit, to hang well; to become, be becoming; to ride well; (coll.) to make a hit; **caer del burro** (fig.) to come down off one's horse; **caer de pies** to land on one's feet; **caer de plano** to fall flat; **caer en** to be found on or in (*a certain page or chapter*); **caer en cama** to fall ill; **caer en gracia** to be in favor; **caer en la cuenta** to catch on, to get the point; **caer enfermo** to fall ill; **caer en que** to realize that; **caer mal** to fit badly; to be unbecoming; to ride badly; (coll.) to fall flat ‖ *vr* to fall, to fall down; to be located, to be found; **caerse de sí mismo, caerse de su peso** or **caerse de suyo** to be self-evident; **caerse muerto de** to be struck dumb with (*e.g., fear*); **caerse redondo** to fall unconscious
Cafarnaúm Capernaum
café *m* coffee; coffee house; café; (bot.) coffee tree; (Am.) displeasure, unpleasant time; **café cantante** night club; **café de maquinilla** drip coffee; **café solo** black coffee; *adj* (Am.) tan, brown
café-concierto *m* (*pl:* **café-conciertos**) cabaret
cafeína *f* (pharm.) caffein
cafetal *m* coffee plantation
cafetán *m* caftan
cafetera *f* see **cafetero**
cafetería *f* cafeteria; (Am.) retail coffee shop
cafetero -ra *adj* (pertaining to) coffee; *mf* coffeegrower, coffee planter; coffee-bean picker, coffee gatherer; coffee seller; *f* coffee pot; **cafetera eléctrica** electric percolator
cafetín *m* small coffee shop
cafeto *m* (bot.) coffee plant, coffee tree
cáfila *f* (coll.) flock (*of people, animals, or things*); caravan
cafre *adj* & *mf* Kaffir or Kafir; savage; rustic, peasant
caftán *m* caftan
cagaaceite *m* (orn.) missel thrush
cagaestacas *m* (*pl:* **-cas**) (orn.) chat
cagafierro *m* slag, scoria
cagajón *m* horse or mule dung
cagalaolla *m* (coll.) clown, masquerader
cágalo *m* (orn.) jaeger
cagar §59 *va* (coll.) to spot, to spoil; *vn* to defecate; *vr* to defecate; to become frightened
cagarrache *m* washer of olive pits (*in olive-oil mill*); (orn.) missel thrush
cagarria *f* (bot.) morel
cagarruta *f* cow or sheep dung
cagatintas *m* (*pl:* **-tas**) (scornful) clerk, office worker
cagón -gona *adj* (coll.) cowardly; *mf* (coll.) coward
caguanete *m* cotton wool
cahiz *m* (*pl:* **-hices**) cahiz (*18.9 bushels*)
cahuama *f* (Am.) sea turtle
caico *m* (naut.) reef, shoal
caído -da *adj* fallen; turndown (*collar*); weak, languid; crestfallen; drooping (*eyelid, shoulder, etc.*); **caído en desuso** obsolete; **caídos** *mpl* income due; (min.) fallen material; **los caídos** the fallen (*in battle*); *f* fall, tumble; drop; collapse, failure; slip, blunder, lapse; fold (*e.g., of a curtain*); hang (*e.g., of clothing, of a curtain*); flop (*of a play*); (geol.) dip; (hyd.) head; (min.) slip; (naut.) calm; (naut.) depth or drop (*of a sail*); **caídas** *fpl* falling ends; coarse wool; (coll.) witticism; **a la caída de la hoja** in autumn; **a la caída de la tarde** in the late afternoon; **a la caída del sol** at sunset; **La Caída** the Fall (*sin of Adam*); **caída de agua** waterfall; **caída pluvial** rainfall; **caída radiactiva** (phys.) fallout
Caifás *m* (Bib.) Caiaphas
caigo *1st sg pres ind of* **caer**
caimán *m* (zool.) alligator, caiman; (coll.) schemer, sharper
caimiento *m* fall; weakness, decline
caimito *m* (bot.) star apple (*tree and fruit*)
Caín *m* (Bib.) Cain; **pasar las de Caín** to have a terrible time
caique *m* (naut.) caïque
cairel *m* wig; fringe; (arch. & naut.) breastrail
cairelar *va* to fringe, to trim with fringe
cairino -na *adj* & *mf* var. of **cairota**
Cairo, El Cairo
cairota *adj* (pertaining to) Cairo; *mf* native or inhabitant of Cairo
caja *f* box, case, chest; safe, strongbox; cashbox; cash; cashier's office; desk (*where bills are paid in a hotel*); coffin; case (*of watch*); drum; set (*of false teeth*); (elec.) box (*for switches, outlets, etc.*); cabinet (*e.g., of a radio*); body (*of carriage or car*); stock (*of firearm*); hole, hollow; socket; (carp.) mortise, recess; (elec.) jack; (mach.) housing, casing; shaft, well (*of staircase, elevator, etc.*); drum case or frame, drum; (print.) case; (bot.) capsule; **a caja y espiga** (carp.) mortise-and-tenon; **de caja alta** (print.) upper-case; **de caja baja** (print.) lower-case; **despedir** or **echar con cajas destempladas** (coll.) to send packing, to give the gate; **en caja** (coll.) in good shape, in good health; **caja clara** snare drum; **caja de aceite** (mach.) oil cup; **caja de ahorros** savings bank; **caja de cambio de marchas** (aut.) transmission-gear box; **caja de caudales** safe; **caja de cigüeñal** (aut.) crankcase; **caja de colores** paintbox; **caja de conexiones** (elec.) joint box, junction box; **caja de contacto** (elec.) receptacle; **caja de cortar al sesgo** (carp.) miter box; **caja de distribución** (mach.) valve chest; (elec.) junction box; **caja de embalaje** packing box or case; **caja de enchufe** (elec.) outlet; **caja de engranajes** gear case; **caja de fuego** firebox; **caja de fusibles** (elec.) fuse box; **caja de herramientas** tool box, tool chest; **caja de grasa** journal box; **caja de humos** smokebox; **caja de ingletes** (carp.) miter box; **caja de jubilaciones** pension fund; **caja del diferencial** (aut.) differential housing; **caja del eje** (mach.) journal box; **caja de menores** petty cash; **caja de música** music box; **caja de Pandora** (myth.) Pandora's box; **caja de Petri** Petri dish; **caja de puente trasero** (aut.) rear-axle housing; **caja de reclutamiento** (mil.) recruiting service; **caja de registro** manhole (*in street*); **caja de reloj** watchcase; **caja de resonancia** (mus. & fig.) sounding board; **caja de salida** (elec.) outlet box; **caja de sebo** (mach.) grease cup; **caja de seguridad** bank vault, safe; safe-deposit box; **caja de sorpresa** jack-in-the-box; **caja de vapor** steam box or chest; **caja de velocidades** (aut.) transmission-gear box; **caja de volquete** dump body (*of truck*); **caja fuerte** safe, bank vault; **caja postal de ahorros** postal or post-office savings; **caja registradora** cash register; **caja sorpresa** jack-in-the-box; **caja y espiga** (carp.) mortise and tenon
caja-dique *m* cofferdam
cajel *adj* see **naranja**
cajera *f* see **cajero**
cajería *f* box business, box store
cajero -ra *mf* boxmaker; teller, cashier; *f* groove, channel, recess
cajeta *f* little box; cigar case; (naut.) sennit; (Am.) butterscotch; *m* dude, sport, city guy
cajetilla *f* pack (*of cigarettes*)

cajetín *m* stamp, rubber stamp; (print.) box (*of type-holding tray*); (elec.) molding
cajiga *f* (bot.) gall oak
cajigal *m* grove of gall oaks
cajista *mf* (print.) compositor, typesetter
cajo *m* flange (*on back of book for boards to fit in*)
cajón *m* big box or case; bin; drawer; locker; space between shelves; stall, booth; shed; bier, coffin; (mil.) caisson; (taur.) box for transporting bulls; (Am.) dry-goods store; **ser de cajón** (coll.) to be customary; **cajón de aire comprimido** (eng.) caisson; **cajón de sastre** (coll.) odds and ends; (coll.) muddlehead; **cajón de suspensión** (naut.) caisson; **cajón hidráulico** (eng.) caisson
cajonada *f* (naut.) lockers
cajonera *f* chest of drawers in vestry; (hort.) cold frame
cajonería *f* set of drawers
cajuela *f* small box or case; groove, recess; (Am.) auto trunk
cal *f* lime; **de cal y canto** (coll.) strong, robust; **cal apagada** or **muerta** slaked lime; **cal hidráulica** hydraulic lime; **cal sodada** soda lime; **cal viva** quicklime
cala *f* cove, inlet; fishing ground; plug (*cut to sample a melon*); test core, test boring; (med.) suppository; (naut.) hold; (bot.) calla (*Zantedeschia aethiopica and Calla palustris*); **cala de construcción** (naut.) slip
calabacear *va* (coll.) to flunk; (coll.) to jilt
calabacero -ra *mf* calabash or pumpkin seller; *m* (bot.) calabash tree; *f* (bot.) calabash, pumpkin, squash
calabacilla *f* gourd-shaped eardrop; (bot.) squirting cucumber
calabacín *m* (bot.) small cylindrical calabash; (coll.) dolt
calabacinate *m* fried calabash or pumpkin
calabacino *m* gourd (*used as bottle, bowl, etc.*)
calabaza *f* calabash, pumpkin, squash, gourd (*fruit*); calabash, gourd (*bottle or bowl*); (coll.) dolt; **dar calabazas a** (coll.) to give the cold shoulder to; (coll.) to flunk; (coll.) to jilt; **salir calabaza** (coll.) to be a flop, to be a fizzle
calabazada *f* butt (*with the head*); blow on the head; **darse de calabazadas por** + *inf* (coll.) to break one's back to, to rack one's brains to + *inf*
calabazar *m* calabash or pumpkin plot
calabazate *m* candied calabash or pumpkin
calabazazo *m* blow with a pumpkin; (coll.) bump on the head
calabazo *m* gourd; wine gourd; (Am.) calabash (*drum*)
calabobos *m* (*pl:* **-bos**) (coll.) drizzle
calabocero *m* jailer
calabozaje *m* prisoner's fee to jailer
calabozo *m* calaboose, dungeon; cell; prison cell; (agr.) pruning hook, mattock
calabrés -bresa *adj & mf* Calabrian
calabriada *f* mixture, hodgepodge
calabriar *va* to mix up
calabrotar *va* var. of **acalabrotar**
calabrote *m* (naut.) cable-laid rope
calada *f* soaking; lowering of fishing net; diving, plunging; swoop (*of bird of prey*); openwork watchcase; **dar una calada a** (coll.) to rake over the coals
caladero *m* place for lowering fishing nets
caladio *m* (bot.) caladium
caladizo -za *adj* runny
calado *m* openwork, fretwork; plug (*in melon*); depth (*of water*); (naut.) draught; (sew.) drawn work; **en iguales calados** (naut.) on even keel
calador *m* borer, maker of openwork; calking iron; (surg.) probe
caladre *f* (orn.) calander
caladura *f* plugging (*a melon*)
calafate *m* calker; shipwright
calafateador *m* calker
calafatear *va* to calk; (mas.) to point; to plug, plug up
calafateo *m* calking
calafatería *f* calking; union or guild of calkers
calafatín *m* calker's boy or mate
calafraga *f* (bot.) saxifrage
calagozo *m* (agr.) pruning hook, mattock
calahorra *f* public granary; agency providing bread for poor
calaíta *f* (mineral.) turquoise
calaje *m* (elec.) angular displacement
calamaco *m* calamanco
calamar *m* (zool.) squid (*Loligo*); **calamar volante** (zool.) squid (*Ommastrephes*)
calamarera *f* squid-jigger
calambac *m* calambac (*wood*)
calambre *m* cramp; **calambre de los escribientes** writer's cramp; **calambre de los telegrafistas** telegrapher's cramp
calambuco -ca *adj* (Am.) pious, devout; *m* (bot.) calaba; (Am.) can, pail
calamento *m* submerging the fishing net: (bot.) calamint
calamidad *f* calamity
calamina *f* (mineral.) calamine
calaminta *f* (bot.) calamint
calamistro *m* (zool.) calamistrum
calamita *f* loadstone; magnetic needle
calamitoso -sa *adj* calamitous
cálamo *m* reed, stalk; (bot.) calamus, sweet flag; (poet.) reed, flute; (poet.) pen; **cálamo aromático** (bot.) sweet flag; (pharm.) calamus
calamocano -na *adj* (coll.) tipsy; (coll.) doddering
calamoco *m* icicle
calamocha *f* dark yellow ocher; (coll.) head
calamón *m* (orn.) sultana; brass tack; stay of the beam of an olive-oil mill
calamorra *f* (coll.) head; *adj* woolly-faced (*sheep*)
calamorrada *f* (coll.) butt (*with the head*)
calamorrazo *m* (coll.) bump on the head
calandraca *f* (naut.) hardtack and soup
calandrajo *m* rag; rag hanging from clothing; (coll.) sap, fool
calandrar *va* to calender (*paper*)
calandria *f* calender (*for giving paper glossy finish*); (orn.) calander; (chem.) calandria; treadmill cage (*of a hoisting whim*); person feigning illness in order to get into a hospital; (Am.) victoria (*coach*)
cálanis *m* (pharm.) calamus
calaña *f* model, sample, pattern; kind, nature, character, caliber; fan; guardrail, parapet
calañés *m* Andalusian hat with turned-up brim and low cone-shaped crown
cálao *m* (orn.) hornbill; **cálao rinoceronte** (orn.) rhinoceros hornbill
calapatillo *m* (ent.) weevil
calapé *m* (Am.) turtle roasted in its shell
calapuerta *f* holdback (*device to hold door open*)
calar *adj* lime, limy; *m* limestone quarry; *va* to pierce, perforate, permeate; to wedge; to soak; to cut openwork in (*paper, metal, etc.*); to cut a plug in (*a melon*); to make a core boring in; to bend (*a weapon*) forward; to fix (*a bayonet*); to lower (*a fishing net*) in the water; to sink (*a caisson*); to lower (*a drawbridge*); to treat with lime; (naut. & weaving) to draw; (coll.) to size up (*a person*); (coll.) to see through (*a person*); to slip in; (slang) to pick (*a pocket*); (Am.) to stare at; *vn* to cut, to hurt; to penetrate; (naut.) to draw; *vr* to become soaked or drenched; to slip in; to squeeze in; to swoop down (*said of birds of prey*); (coll.) to pull (*one's hat*) down on one's head; to stick (*one's glasses*) on; to miss fire; **calarse en** to slip in or into; **calarse hasta los huesos** to get soaked to the skin
calato -ta *adj* (Am.) naked
calatraveño -ña *adj* (pertaining to) Calatrava; *mf* native or inhabitant of Calatrava
calavera *f* skull; death's-head; (Am.) tail light; *m* daredevil, reckless fellow; roué, libertine
calaverada *f* recklessness, reckless act, escapade
calaverar *vn* (coll.) to become bald
calaverear *va* to make ugly, make hideous; *vn* (coll.) to act recklessly; (Am.) to carouse, to lead a wild life
calbote *m* chestnut or acorn bread; (dial.) roasted chestnut; **calbotes** *mpl* (dial.) string beans
calca *f* tracing; copy; (dial.) granary
calcado *m* tracing

calcador -dora *mf* tracer (*person*); *m* tracer (*instrument*)
calcadura *f* tracing
calcáneo *m* (anat.) calcaneus
calcañal *m* or **calcañar** *m* heel
calcar §86 *va* to trace; to copy, to imitate; to trample or tread on; **calcar en** to model (*e.g., one's style*) on
calcáreo -a *adj* calcareous
Calcas *m* (myth.) Calchas
calce *m* wedge; iron tire; iron tip, iron trimming; (Am.) foot, bottom (*of a document*)
calcedonia *f* (mineral.) chalcedony; (*cap.*) *f* Chalcedon
calceolaria *f* (bot.) calceolaria
calcés *m* (naut.) masthead
calceta *f* stocking; shackle, fetter; **hacer calceta** to knit
calcetería *f* hosiery; hosiery shop
calcetero -ra *mf* stocking maker or mender; hosier
calcetín *m* sock
calcetón *m* knitted stocking
calcicloro *m* (chem.) calcium chloride
cálcico -ca *adj* (chem.) calcic
calcífero -ra *adj* calciferous
calcificación *f* calcification
calcificar §86 *va & vr* to calcify
calcímetro *m* calcimeter
calcina *f* concrete
calcinación *f* calcination
calcinar *va & vr* to calcine; to burn
calcio *m* (chem.) calcium
calcita *f* (mineral.) calcite
calcitrapa *f* (bot.) star thistle
calco *m* tracing; copy, imitation
calcografía *f* chalcography; chalcograph; chalcograph shop; collection of chalcographs
calcográfico -ca *adj* chalcographic or chalcographical
calcógrafo *m* chalcographer
calcomanía *f* decalcomania
calcopirita *f* (mineral.) chalcopyrite
calculable *adj* calculable
calculadamente *adv* in a calculating way; deliberately
calculador -dora *adj* calculating; *mf* computer, calculator; *f* computer, calculating machine
calcular *va & vn* to calculate; to reckon
calculatorio -ria *adj* calculative
calculista *adj* planning, scheming; *mf* planner, schemer; rapid calculator
cálculo *m* calculation; conjecture; reflection; (math. & path.) calculus; **cálculo biliario** gallstone; **cálculo diferencial** (math.) differential calculus; **cálculo infinitesimal** (math.) infinitesimal calculus; **cálculo integral** (math.) integral calculus; **cálculo renal** (path.) kidney stone
calculosis *f* (path.) gallstones
calculoso -sa *adj* (path.) calculous; *mf* sufferer from gallstones
Calcuta *f* Calcutta
calchona *f* (Am.) bogey, goblin; (Am.) witch, hag
calda *f* warming, heating; **caldas** *fpl* hot baths, hot springs
caldaico -ca *adj* Chaldaic
Caldea *f* see **caldeo**
caldeamiento *m* heating
caldear *va* to heat, heat up; to weld; *vr* to become heated; to get overheated; (Am.) to get drunk; (Am.) to become overwrought
caldeo -a *adj & mf* Chaldean; *m* Chaldean (*language*); warming, heating; welding; (*cap.*) *f* Chaldea
caldera *f* boiler; pot, kettle; case of kettledrum; (min.) sump; (Am.) coffee pot, teapot; **las calderas de Pero Botero** (coll.) hell; **caldera de jabón** soap factory; **caldera de vapor** steam boiler; **caldera tubular de agua** water-tube boiler; **caldera tubular de humo** fire-tube boiler
calderada *f* boiler, kettle (*amount kettle or boiler can hold*)
calderería *f* boilermaking; boiler shop
calderero *m* boilermaker
caldereta *f* holy-water pot; fish stew; lamb stew
calderilla *f* holy-water vessel; bottom of a well; gutter; (bot.) currant; (min.) blind shaft, winze; copper coin; small change
caldero *m* kettle, pot, copper; (Am.) coffee pot, teapot; **caldero de colada** (found.) ladle
calderón *m* caldron; (mus.) pause (*hold and its symbol*); (print.) paragraph (*mark*); (zool.) blackfish, black whale; **calderones** *mpl* (bot.) globeflower
calderoniano -na *adj* Calderonian
calderuela *f* small kettle; vessel containing the light that hunters use to dazzle and catch partridges
caldillo *m* light broth; sauce for fricassee
caldo *m* broth, bouillon; sauce, dressing, gravy; salad dressing; liquid; (Am.) simple syrup; (Am.) sugar-cane juice; **caldos** *mpl* wet goods (*wine, olive oil, cider, vinegar, brandy, etc.*); spirituous liquors; **hacer el caldo gordo a** (coll.) to play into the hands of; **caldo de Burdeos** (hort.) Bordeaux mixture; **caldo de carne** beef tea; **caldo de cultivo** (bact.) broth; **caldo de la reina** eggnog
caldoso -sa *adj* full of broth
calducho *m* hogwash, slop
caldudo -da *adj* fond of broth; *f* (Am.) pie made of eggs, olives, and raisins
cale *m* slap, smack
calé *m* (slang) gypsy
calecer §34 *vn* to become hot
caledonio -nia *adj & mf* Caledonian
calefacción *f* heat, heating; **calefacción a panel radiante** radiant-panel heat; **calefacción a** or **por vapor** steam heat; **calefacción a vapor de baja presión** vapor heat; **calefacción central** central heating (*of a single building or house*); **calefacción por agua caliente** hot-water heat; **calefacción por aire caliente** hot-air heat
calefaccionar *va* to heat
calefaccionista *m* heating contractor
calefaciente *adj* (med.) heating, calefacient
calefactor *m* heater; heater man (*man who makes, installs, or repairs heating equipment*); (rad.) heater, heater element
calefactorio *m* calefactory (*in convents*)
calefón *m* (Am.) hot-water heater
caleidoscopio *m* var. of **calidoscopio**
calendar *va* to date (*a document*)
calendario *m* calendar; **hacer calendarios** (coll.) to meditate, to muse; (coll.) to make hasty and unfounded prophecies; **calendario escolar** school calendar; **calendario exfoliador** tear-off calendar; **calendario juliano** Julian calendar; **calendario gregoriano** Gregorian calendar; **calendario hebreo** Hebrew calendar
calendarista *mf* calendar maker
calendas *fpl* calends or kalends; **calendas griegas** Greek calends (*time that will never come*)
caléndula *f* (bot.) calendula
calentador -dora *adj* heating; *m* heater; warming pan; (coll.) turnip (*watch*); **calentador a gas** gas heater; **calentador de agua** water heater; **calentador de cama** warming pan
calentamiento *m* heating; inflammation (*e.g., of a sore*)
calentar §18 *va* to heat, heat up; to warm up; to warm (*a chair*); to hold (*a ball*) a moment before throwing it; (coll.) to beat; (Am.) to annoy, bother; **calentar al blanco** to make white-hot; **calentar al rojo** to make red-hot; *vr* to warm oneself; to heat up, to run hot; to warm up; to become heated (*in an argument*); to be in heat (*said of animals*); (Am.) to become annoyed; **calentarse la cabeza** to rack one's brains
calentón *m* (coll.) warm-up; (Am.) heater; **darse un calentón** (coll.) to come in and warm up
calentura *f* (path.) calenture, fever
calenturiento -ta *adj* feverish; exalted; (Am.) tubercular
calenturón *m* high fever
calenturoso -sa *adj* feverish
caleño -ña *adj* (pertaining to) lime
calepino *m* Latin dictionary
calera *f* see **calero**

calería *f* lime pit (*where lime is made and sold*)
calero -ra *adj* (pertaining to) lime; *m* lime burner; lime dealer; *f* limekiln; limestone quarry
calesa *f* chaise (*two-wheeled carriage*)
calesera *f* Andalusian jacket, bolero jacket
calesero *m* driver of a chaise
calesín *m* light chaise, fly
calesinero *m* driver of a light chaise
caleta *f* small inlet, cove
caletre *m* (coll.) judgment, acumen, brains
cali *m* (chem.) alkali
calibeado -da *adj* chalybeate
calíbeo -a *adj* steel-blue, chalybeous
calibración *f* calibration
calibrado *m* calibrating, calibration
calibrador *m* calipers; gauge; **calibrador de alambre** wire gauge; **calibrador fijo** caliper gauge
calibrar *va* to calibrate; to gauge
calibre *m* caliber; gauge; bore; calipers; (rail.) track gauge; (coll.) caliber (*quality of a thing*)
calicanto *m* stone masonry
calicata *f* (min.) test pit
calicó *m* calico
calicular *adj* (bot.) calycular
calículo *m* (anat. & zool.) calicle or calyculus; (bot.) calycle or epicalyx
caliche *m* pebble in a brick; flake or crust of lime
calidad *f* quality; qualification; capacity; condition, term; importance; nobility; **calidades** *fpl* moral qualities; **a calidad de que** provided, provided that; **en calidad de** in the capacity of, in quality of
calidez *f* warmth; heat, fire
cálido -da *adj* warm, hot (*climate, country*); hot, burning; warm (*color; welcome*)
calidoscópico -ca *adj* kaleidoscopic; (fig.) kaleidoscopic
calidoscopio *m* kaleidoscope; (fig.) kaleidoscope
calientacamas *m* (*pl:* **-mas**) bed warmer
calientapiés *m* (*pl:* **-piés**) foot warmer
calientaplatos *m* (*pl:* **-tos**) plate warmer, hot plate
caliente *adj* hot; heated; fiery; hot or warm (*near what one is looking for*); hot (*in rut*); **en caliente** while hot; at once; **caliente de cascos** hot-headed
califa *m* caliph
califato *m* caliphate
calificable *adj* qualifiable
calificación *f* qualification; proof; judgment; grade, mark (*in an examination*); standing (*in school*)
calificado -da *adj* attested, proved, qualified, competent
calificador -dora *mf* qualifier; censor; (eccl.) qualificator
calificar §86 *va* to qualify, to characterize; to ennoble; to attest, to certify; to mark (*an examination paper*); (Am.) to register (*as a voter*); *vr* to give legal proof of one's noble birth; (Am.) to register (*as a voter*)
calificativo -va *adj* qualifying; (gram.) qualifying; *m* grade, mark (*in school*); (gram.) qualifier
California *f* see **californio**
californiano -na *adj & mf* Californian
califórnico -ca *adj* Californian
californio -nia *adj & mf* Californian; *m* (chem.) californium; (*cap.*) *f* California; **Baja California** Lower California
cáliga *f* caliga (*of Roman soldier; of bishop*)
caligine *f* (poet.) mist, darkness
caliginoso -sa *adj* (poet.) misty, dark
caligrafía *f* calligraphy, penmanship
calígrafo -fa *mf* calligrapher, good penman
caligráfico -ca *adj* calligraphic
calima *f* haze; (naut.) buoy made of a string of corks
calimaco *m* calamanco
calimbo *m* quality, character, brand
calimoso -sa *adj* hazy
calina *f* haze
calinoso -sa *adj* hazy
Calíope *f* (myth.) Calliope
calípedes *m* (*pl:* **-des**) (zool.) sloth
calipso *m* calypso (*improvised song*); *f* (bot.) calypso; (*cap.*) *f* (myth.) Calypso
calisaya *f* (pharm.) calisaya bark
calistenia *f* calisthenics
calisténico -ca *adj* calisthenic
Calisto *f* (myth.) Callisto
cáliz *m* (*pl:* **-lices**) (anat. & bot.) calyx; (bot., eccl. & poet.) chalice; cup of bitterness or sorrow; block (*to shape a hat*)
calizo -za *adj* (pertaining to) limestone or lime; *f* limestone
calma *f* see **calmo**
calmante *adj* soothing; (med.) sedative; *m* (med.) sedative; **calmante del dolor** pain reliever
calmar *va* to calm, to quiet; *vn* to abate, be becalmed; *vr* to calm, calm down
calmazo *m* (naut.) dead calm
calmear *vn* to ease up, to lessen (*said, e.g., of anger*)
calmo -ma *adj* barren, treeless; calm, quiet; *f* calm, calm weather; quiet, tranquillity; slowness, laziness; suspension, letup; (naut.) calm; **en calma** in abeyance, in suspension; (com.) steady (*market*); (naut.) calm, smooth (*sea*); **calma chicha** or **muerta** dead calm
calmoso -sa *adj* calm; (coll.) slow, lazy, sluggish
calmudo -da *adj* calm; (naut.) calm, light (*wind*); (Am.) easy-going
caló *m* gipsy slang, underworld slang
calobiótica *f* right living; innate sense of order
calofriar §90 *vr* to chill, become chilled
calofrío *m* chill
calomel *m* or **calomelanos** *mpl* (pharm.) calomel
calón *m* rod for spreading nets; rod for measuring depth of water
calor *m* heat; warmth; heat wave; (fig.) heat, heatedness; (fig.) warmth, enthusiasm; **hacer calor** to be warm, to be hot (*said of weather*); **tener calor** to be warm, to be hot (*said of a person*); **calor específico** specific heat
caloría *f* (phys. & physiol.) calorie; **caloría gramo** or **caloría pequeña** gram calorie or small calorie; **caloría kilogramo** or **caloría grande** kilogram calorie or large calorie
caloricidad *f* (physiol.) caloricity
calórico -ca *adj* caloric; *m* (old chem.) caloric
calorífero -ra *adj* heat-producing; *m* heating system; heater, furnace; foot warmer
calorificación *f* calorification
calorífico -ca *adj* calorific
calorífugo -ga *adj* heat-resisting; noncombustible
calorimetría *f* calorimetry
calorimétrico -ca *adj* calorimetric or calorimetrical
calorímetro *m* calorimeter
caloroso -sa *adj* warm, hot; (fig.) warm, enthusiastic
calosfrío *m* chill
calostro *m* colostrum
calotear *va* (Am.) to cheat, to gyp
caloyo *m* new-born lamb or kid; raw recruit
calpense *adj* (pertaining to) Gibraltar; *mf* native of Gibraltar
calpul *m* (Am.) gathering, assembly; (Am.) Indian mound
calseco -ca *adj* cured with lime
calta *f* (bot.) caltha, marsh marigold
calumnia *f* calumny, slander
calumniador -dora *adj* slanderous; *m* calumniator, slanderer
calumniar *va* to calumniate, to slander
calumnioso -sa *adj* calumnious, slanderous
caluroso -sa *adj* warm, hot; (fig.) warm, enthusiastic
calva *f* see **calvo**
Calvario *m* (Bib.) Calvary; (*l.c.*) *m* calvary (*representation of crucifixion*); (fig.) cross (*suffering*); (coll.) series of misfortunes or sorrows; (coll.) debts; (coll.) baldy, bald fellow; (anat.) calvaria
calvatrueno *m* (coll.) complete baldness; (coll.) madcap, crazy fellow
calvero *m* clearing; clay pit

calvete *adj* baldish, somewhat bald
calvez *f* or **calvicie** *f* baldness
calvijar *m* var. of **calvero**
calvinismo *m* Calvinism
calvinista *adj* Calvinist; Calvinistic; *mf* Calvinist
Calvino *m* Calvin
calvo -va *adj* bald; bare, barren; *f* bald spot; barren spot, clearing; **calva de almete** crest of helmet
calza *f* (coll.) stocking; wedge; ribbon (*tied to an animal to distinguish it from others*); (Am.) gold filling (*of tooth*); **calzas** *fpl* hose, tights; breeches; shackles; **echarle a uno una calza** (coll.) to have someone's number; **en calzas prietas** in a tight fix; **tomar calzas de Villadiego** (coll.) to beat it; **calzas atacadas** patched breeches
calzacalzón *m* galligaskins
calzada *f* see **calzado**
calzadera *f* hemp cord (*for tying sandals*); brake block
calzado -da *adj* calced (*said, e.g., of a friar*); having feet of a different color (*said of an animal*); having feathers on the legs and feet (*said of birds*); *m* footwear; *f* causeway, highway; sidewalk; **Calzada de los Gigantes** Giant's Causeway (*in Ireland*)
calzador *m* shoehorn
calzadura *f* putting on shoes; wooden tire
calzar **§76** *va* to shoe, put shoes on, provide shoes for; to wear (*a certain size of shoe or glove*); to take (*a certain caliber of bullet*); to fit (*a person; said of a shoe*); to wedge, to shim, to chock; to scotch (*a wheel*); to block up, to put a wedge under (*e.g., the leg of a table*); (naut.) to chock; to tip, to trim with iron; (print.) to raise, to underlay; (Am.) to fill (*a tooth*); (hort.) to hill (*plants*); *vn* (Am.) to get the place sought for; **calzar bien** to wear good footwear; **calzar mal** to wear poor footwear; **calzar poco** (coll.) to not be very bright; *vr* to get a good position, to make a fortune; to put on (*shoes or gloves*); to wear
calzo *m* wedge, shim; (mach.) shoe; (mech.) fulcrum; (naut.) skid, chock; (print.) underlay
calzón *m* ombre (*game of cards*); roofer's strap (*to keep from slipping*); **calzones** *mpl* breeches; shorts; (Am.) trousers; (Am.) drawers; **calzarse** or **ponerse los calzones** (coll.) to wear the trousers
calzonarias *fpl* (Am.) suspenders
calzonazos *m* (*pl:* **-zos**) (coll.) softy, easygoing fellow, jellyfish
calzoncillos *mpl* drawers, underdrawers; shorts
calzoneras *fpl* (Am.) trousers buttoned down the sides
calzonudo -da *adj* (Am.) stupid, inept
calzorras *m* (*pl:* **-rras**) (coll.) var. of **calzonazos**
callado -da *adj* silent, quiet; secret; vague, mysterious; unmentioned; **estarse callado** to keep quiet; *f* (naut.) drop, abatement; dish of tripe; **a las calladas** (coll.) on the quiet; **dar la callada por respuesta** (coll.) to answer with silence; **de callada** (coll.) on the quiet
callamiento *m* silencing, quieting
callana *f* (Am.) crude Indian baking bowl; (Am.) flowerpot; (Am.) big watch; (Am.) useful slag; (Am.) metal-testing crucible
callandico or **callandito** *adv* (coll.) secretly, stealthily, softly
callao *m* pebble
callar *va* to silence, to hush up; to not mention; to keep (*a secret*); to quiet, to calm; *vn* to be silent, to keep silent, to become silent; to keep quiet, to stop playing or singing; **quien calla otorga** silence gives consent; **¡calla!** or **¡calle!** how strange!, you don't mean it!; *vr* to be silent, to keep silent, to become silent; to keep quiet, to stop playing or singing; to keep (*something*) to oneself; **callarse la boca** to shut up
calle *f* street; excuse, pretext; **abrir calle** (coll.) to open a path, to clear the way; **alborotar la calle** (coll.) to stir up the neighborhood; **dejar en la calle** (coll.) to deprive of one's livelihood; **echar a la calle** (coll.) to put out of the house; **hacer calle** (coll.) to open a path, to clear the way; **llevar** (or **llevarse**) **la calle a** to overwhelm; to confound, to silence; **para la calle** to take out (*said of food bought in a restaurant*); **quedarse en la calle** (coll.) to be at the end of one's means; **calle de árboles** alley, avenue of trees; **calle de travesía** cross street; **calle mayor** main street
callear *va* to clear (*passages between rows of vines*) of straggling stems and branches
calleja *f* side street, alley, by-street; (coll.) evasion, subterfuge, pretext; **sépase, ahora se sabrá, ya se verá** or **ya verán quién es Calleja** (coll.) you'll find out who I am; (coll.) you'll find out who he is
callejear *vn* to walk the streets, to loaf around the streets
callejeo *m* walking the streets, loafing around
callejero -ra *adj* (pertaining to the) street; fond of walking the streets; gadabout; *m* list of streets, street guide; addresses of newspaper subscribers
callejo *m* pitfall, trap
callejón *m* lane, alley; (taur.) passageway between barrier and stands; **callejón sin salida** blind alley; (coll.) impasse, deadlock
callejuela *f* side street, by-street, alley; (coll.) evasion, subterfuge, pretext
callialto -ta *adj* high-calked (*horseshoe*)
callicida *m & f* corn cure, corn remover
callista *mf* corncutter, chiropodist
callo *m* callus; corn (*on foot*); calk (*of horseshoe*); **callos** *mpl* tripe; **criar, hacer** or **tener callos** (coll.) to become callous (*unfeeling*)
callón *m* sharpening stone (*especially for awls*)
callonca *adj* half-roasted (*said of a chestnut or acorn*)
callosa *f* see **calloso**
callosidad *f* callosity
calloso -sa *adj* callous; *f* (bot. & biochem.) callose
cama *f* bed; couch; straw bedding or litter (*for animals*); lair; floor (*of wagon or cart*); side of melon resting on the ground; sheath (*of plow*); **caer en cama** or **en la cama** to fall sick; **estar en cama** to be confined to bed; **guardar cama** or **la cama** or **hacer cama** to be sick in bed; **hacer cama redonda** (coll.) to all sleep in the same bed; **hacer la cama** to make the bed; **hacerle la cama a uno** to work to harm someone behind his back; **media cama** single bed; **tenderle la cama a uno** (coll.) to set a trap for someone; (Am.) to help someone in his love affairs; **cama camera** single bed; **cama de matrimonio** double bed; **cama imperial** four-poster; **cama sencilla** single bed; **camas gemelas** twin beds; **cama turca** day bed (*couch without head and foot pieces*)
camachuelo *m* (orn.) linnet
camada *f* brood, litter; gang, den (*of thieves*); layer, stratum
camafeo *m* cameo
camal *m* halter of hemp; pole from which dead pig is hung; (arm.) camail
camaleón *m* (zool.) chameleon; (coll.) chameleon (*changeable person*)
cama-litera *f* (*pl:* **camas-literas**) double-decker (*bed*)
camamila *f* (bot.) camomile
camándula *f* rosary of one or three decades; (coll.) trickery, hypocrisy; **tener muchas camándulas** (coll.) to be full of tricks, to be full of hypocrisy
camandulear *vn* to be a hypocrite, to be untrustworthy
camandulería *f* prudery, priggishness; flattery
camandulero -ra *adj* (coll.) hypocritical, fawning; *mf* (coll.) hypocrite, flatterer
cámara *f* hall, parlor; chamber; bedroom; board, council; royal chamber; chamber, breech (*of firearm*); mow, granary; icebox; (aut.) inner tube; (min.) stall, chamber; (naut.) cabin; (nav.) wardroom; (aer.) cockpit; (anat.) chamber, cavity; (opt. & phot.) camera; bowels; **cámaras** *fpl* loose bowels; **de cámara** royal, e.g., **médico de cámara** royal physician; **irse de cámaras** to have an accident, to dirty oneself;

cámara agrícola grange (*organization of farmers*); **Cámara alta** Upper House; **cámara a popa** (naut.) stern sheets; **cámara apostólica** camera, papal treasury; **cámara ardiente** funeral chamber; **Cámara baja** Lower House; **cámara cinematográfica** motion-picture camera; **cámara clara** (opt.) camera lucida; **cámara compensadora** (com.) clearing house; **cámara de aire** (aut.) inner tube; (aer.) gasbag; **cámara de aire comprimido** pneumatic caisson; **cámara de combustión** (mach.) combustion chamber; **cámara de comercio** chamber of commerce; **cámara de compensación** (com.) clearing house; (hyd.) surge tank, surge chamber; **cámara de descompresión** decompression chamber; **cámara de fuelle** folding camera; **cámara de gas** or **de gases** gas chamber; **cámara de ionización** (phys.) ionization chamber; **cámara de las máquinas** (naut.) engine room; **Cámara de los Comunes** (Brit.) House of Commons; **Cámara de los Lores** (Brit.) House of Lords; **cámara de niebla** (phys.) cloud chamber; **cámara de oxígeno** (med.) oxygen tent; **cámara de pleno** plenum chamber; **Cámara de Representantes** (U.S.A.) House of Representatives; **cámara estrellada** Star Chamber (*in England*); **cámara fotográfica** camera; **cámara frigorífica** cold-storage room; **cámara indiscreta** candid camera; **cámara mortuoria** funeral chamber; **cámara múltiple** multiple-lens camera; **cámara oscura** (opt.) camera obscura; **cámara plegadiza** folding camera; **cámara televisora** television camera; *m* (mov.) cameraman
camarada *m* comrade, companion
camaradería *f* comradeship, camaraderie
camaraje *m* granary rent
camaranchón *m* garret, storeroom; (fig.) recess
camarera *f* waitress; maid, chambermaid; head maid; stewardess (*on ship or plane*); lady in waiting
camarero *m* waiter; valet; chamberlain; steward (*on ship or plane*)
camareta *f* (naut.) small cabin, deck cabin, midshipman's cabin
camariento -ta *adj* suffering from diarrhea
camarilla *f* camarilla, palace coterie, clique, cabal
camarín *m* boudoir; side room; (theat.) dressing room; niche behind altar containing an image; elevator car, shaft cage
camarista *m* minister of the royal council; *f* lady in waiting
camarlengo *m* papal chamberlain; lord in waiting of the kings of Aragon
cámaro *m* var. of **camarón**
camarógrafo *m* cameraman
camarón *m* (zool.) shrimp; (zool.) prawn (*Palaemon*); (Am.) tip, fee
camaronero -ra *mf* shrimp or prawn seller; *f* shrimp net
camarote *m* (naut.) stateroom, cabin
camasquince *mf* (*pl:* **camasquince**) (coll.) meddlesome person, kibitzer
camastro *m* rickety old bed; inclined bunk in barracks or guardhouse
camastrón -trona *adj* (coll.) tricky; *mf* (coll.) tricky person; (coll.) loafer
camastronería *f* (coll.) trickiness
cambalachar *va & vn* to swap, to exchange, to barter, to dicker
cambalache *m* swap, exchange, barter
cambalachear *va & vn* var. of **cambalachar**
cámbaro *m* (zool.) green crab
cambiable *adj* changeable; exchangeable
cambiacorrea *m* belt shifter
cambiadiscos *m* (*pl:* **-cos**) record changer
cambiadizo -za *adj* fickle, inconsistent
cambiador -dora *adj* exchanging, bartering; *m* (Am.) switch; (Am.) switchman; **cambiador de discos** record changer; **cambiador de frecuencia** (elec.) frequency changer
cambial *adj* (com.) (pertaining to) exchange
cambiamiento *m* change
cambiante *adj* changing; fickle; *mf* money changer; **cambiantes** *mpl* iridescence
cambiar *va* to change; to exchange; **cambiar el saludo** to exchange salutes; to exchange greetings; *vn* to change; **cambiar de** to change (*e.g., hats, clothes, trains*); **cambiar de sombrero con alguien** to exchange hats with someone; **cambiar de marcha** to shift gears; *vr* to change
cambiavía *m* (Am.) switch, turnout; (Am.) switchman
cambiazo *m* (coll.) gyp, fake, fraudulent exchange
cambija *f* raised water tank
cambín *m* fishing basket made of reeds
cambio *m* change; exchange; rate of exchange; (bot.) cambium; (aut.) shift; (rail.) switch; **en cambio** on the other hand; **en cambio de** in exchange for; instead of; **libre cambio** free trade; **cambio de hoja** change of subject; **cambio de hora** change of time; **cambio de marchas** or **de velocidades** (aut.) gearshift; **cambio de vía** (Am.) switch; **cambio exterior** or **extranjero** foreign exchange; **cambio minuto** change, small change
Cambises *m* Cambyses
cambista *mf* moneychanger, money broker; banker; *m* (Am.) switchman
cámbium *m* (*pl:* **-ums**) (bot.) cambium
cambocho -cha *adj* (Am.) bowlegged
Camboya *f* Cambodia
camboyano -na *adj & mf* Cambodian; *m* Cambodian (*language*)
cambray *m* chambray
cambrayón *m* cambric
cambriano -na or **cámbrico -ca** *adj & mf* Cambrian; *adj & m* (geol.) Cambrian
cambrina *f* (bot.) phlox
cambrón *m* (bot.) buckthorn; (bot.) boxthorn; (bot.) bramble; **cambrones** *mpl* (bot.) Christ's-thorn
cambronal *m* thicket of buckthorn, boxthorn, or brambles
cambronera *f* (bot.) boxthorn
cambuj *m* mask; cap used to keep baby's head straight
cambujo -ja *adj* reddish black (*donkey*); (Am.) half-breed; *mf* (Am.) half-breed
cambullón *m* (Am.) collusion, scheming, trickery; (Am.) trade, barter
cambur *m* (bot.) banana tree
camedrio *m* (bot.) germander, wall germander; **camedrio acuático** (bot.) water germander; **camedrio de los bosques** (bot.) wood germander
camelar *va* (coll.) to flirt with; (coll.) to cajole, to deceive
camelia *f* (bot.) camellia
camelina *f* (bot.) gold-of-pleasure, madwort
camelo *m* (coll.) flirtation; (coll.) joke; **dar camelo a** (coll.) to make fun of
camelote *m* camlet
camella *f* she-camel; ridge (*between furrows*); bow (*of yoke*); feed trough
camellería *f* camel stable; job of camel driver; camels
camellero *m* camel driver
camello *m* (zool.) camel; (naut.) camel (*to lift vessels*); **camello bactriano** (zool.) Bactrian camel; **camello pardal** (zool.) camelopard (*giraffe*)
camellón *m* drinking trough; sawhorse; ridge (*between furrows*); flower bed; camlet (*cloth*); (Am.) parkway
camena *f* (poet.) muse
camerino *m* (theat.) dressing room (*especially of star*)
camero -ra *adj* (pertaining to a) bed; single (*bed*); *mf* bedmaker; maker of bedding, maker of bed accessories; renter of beds; *m* (Am.) highway; *f* single bed
Camerón *m* Cameroons; **el Camerón francés** Cameroun
cámica *f* (Am.) slope of roof
camilla *f* stretcher; couch; table with heater underneath
camillero *m* stretcher-bearer
caminador -dora *adj* walking
caminante *adj* traveling; *mf* walker; traveler; passer-by; *m* groom who walks in front of master's horse

caminar *va* to walk (*a certain distance*); *vn* to travel, to journey; to go, to walk, to move; (coll.) to act, to behave
caminata *f* (coll.) hike, long walk; (coll.) jaunt, outing
caminero -ra *adj* (pertaining to a) road, highway; traveling, walking; *m* road laborer, road worker
camino *m* road, way, course, path; journey; runner (*on table or floor*); **abrir camino** to open a path or way; to find a way; **allanar el camino** (coll.) to smooth the way; **a medio camino (entre)** halfway (*between*); **de camino** in passing, on the way; traveling (*clothes, bags, etc.*); **echar camino adelante** to strike out; **en camino** on one's way; **ir de camino** to journey, to travel; **ir fuera de camino** to be mistaken; to be slipshod; to be out of all reason; **llevar camino de** + *inf* to show signs of + *ger;* **partir el camino con** to meet halfway; **traer a buen camino** to set right, to put back on the right path; **camino carretero** or **carretil** wagon or carriage road; **camino cubierto** (fort.) covered way; **camino de** on the way to; **camino de cintura** or **circunvalación** belt line; **camino de herradura** bridle path; **camino de hierro** railway; **camino de rueda** wagon or carriage road; **Camino de Santiago** Way of or to St. James (*Milky Way*); **camino de sirga** towpath; **camino real** highroad, highway; (fig.) highroad; **camino trillado** beaten path; **camino vecinal** town or county road
camión *m* camion; truck, motor truck; (Am.) bus, jitney; **camión cisterna** tank truck; **camión volquete** dump truck
camionaje *m* trucking, truckage
camionero -ra *adj* truck, trucking; *m* trucker, teamster
camioneta *f* light truck; (Am.) station wagon
camión-grúa *m* tow truck
camionista *m* trucker, teamster
camisa *f* shirt; chemise; (mach.) jacket, casing; (mach.) lining; thin skin (*of fruit*); slough (*of serpent*); mantle (*of gaslight*); folder (*for papers*); jacket (*of a book*); **cambiarse la camisa** to become a turncoat; **en camisa** in shirt sleeves; without dowry; **meterse en camisa de once varas** (coll.) to attend to other people's business; **perder hasta la camisa** to lose one's shirt; **camisa de agua** water jacket; **camisa de dormir** nightshirt; **camisa de fuerza** strait jacket; **camisa negra** *m* black shirt (*Fascist*); **camisa refrigerante** cooling jacket; **camisa parda** *m* brown shirt (*Nazi*)
camisería *f* shirt factory; shirt store, haberdashery
camisero -ra *mf* shirt maker; shirt dealer, haberdasher
camiseta *f* undershirt; sport shirt; mantle (*of gaslight*)
camisola *f* stiff shirt; ruffled shirt
camisolín *m* dickey, shirt front
camisón *m* nightshirt; shirt; (Am.) chemise
camisote *m* hauberk, haubergeon
camita *mf* Hamite; *f* little bed
camítico -ca *adj* Hamitic
camomila *f* (bot. & pharm.) camomile
camón *m* large bed; portable throne; (arch.) oriel; (arch.) arched rafter; felloe, section of a felloe; **camón de vidrios** glass partition
camorra *f* (coll.) quarrel, row; (dial.) hot dog; (*cap.*) *f* Camorra; **armar camorra** (coll.) to raise a row; **buscar camorra** (coll.) to look for trouble
camorrear *vn* (Am.) to quarrel
camorrero -ra *adj & mf* (Am.) var. of **camorrista**
camorrista *adj* (coll.) quarrelsome; *mf* (coll.) quarrelsome person; *m* Camorrist
camote *m* (Am.) sweet potato (*plant and tuber*); (Am.) onion; (Am.) rascal; (Am.) simpleton; **tomar un camote** (Am.) to become infatuated; **tragar camote** (Am.) to stammer, to falter
camotear *va* (Am.) to snitch; *vn* (Am.) to wander around aimlessly
campa *adj* treeless (*land*)
campal *adj* in the open country; pitched (*battle*)
campamento *m* encampment; camp
campamiento *m* excelling; show, display
campana *f* bell; canopy (*of electrical fixture*); bell glass, bell jar; (arch.) bell; parish, parish church; (Am.) spy, lookout; **a campana herida** or **tañida** with bell ringing; **por campana de vacante** (Am.) very seldom; **campana de buzo** diving bell; **campana de chimenea** funnel of a chimney; **campana de freno** (aut.) brake drum; **campana de vidrio** bell glass, bell jar; **campana eléctrica** electric bell
campanada *f* stroke of a bell; ringing of a bell; scandal (*sensational happening*)
campanario *m* belfry, bell tower, campanile; carillon
campanear *va* to ring (*bells*); to bruit about; *vn* to ring the bells, to ring the bells frequently; *vr* (coll.) to sway, to strut
campanela *f* rotation on one foot (*in Spanish dance*)
campaneo *m* bell ringing, frequent bell ringing; (coll.) sway, strut
campanero *m* bell founder; bell ringer; (ent.) praying insect; (orn.) bellbird
campaneta *f* small bell
campanil *adj* bell (*metal*); *m* belfry, bell tower
campanilla *f* bell, hand bell, doorbell; bubble; tassel; (anat.) uvula; (bot.) bellbind; **de campanillas** or **de muchas campanillas** (coll.) of great importance, of distinction; **campanilla de invierno** (bot.) snowdrop; **campanilla de otoño** (bot.) autumn snowflake; **campanilla de primavera** (bot.) spring snowflake; **campanilla eléctrica** electric bell
campanillazo *m* loud ring
campanillear *vn* to ring, to keep on ringing
campanilleo *m* ringing the bell
campanillero *m* bellman
campano *m* cowbell
campanología *f* campanology
campanólogo -ga *mf* campanologist
campante *adj* (coll.) proud, satisfied; (coll.) cheerful, buoyant
campanudo -da *adj* bell-shaped; wide, spreading; pompous, high-sounding
campánula *f* (bot.) bellflower, bluebell, campanula
campanuláceo -a *adj* (bot.) campanulaceous
campaña *f* (mil. & fig.) campaign; (naut.) cruise; level countryside; shift, work shift
campañol *m* (zool.) vole, meadow mouse
campar *vn* to excel, stand out; to camp; **campar por su cuenta** or **por sus respetos** (coll.) to do as one pleases
campeador *adj & m* champion in battle (*applied to the Cid*)
campear *vn* to go to pasture; to come out of the ground, come out of their lairs (*said of rabbits, etc.*); to grow green (*said of fields*); to work in the fields; to show up, to appear; to stand out; (mil.) to campaign; (mil.) to reconnoiter; (Am.) to round up the cattle
campecico, campecillo or **campecito** *m* little field
campechana *f* see **campechano**
campechanería or **campechanía** *f* (coll.) frankness, heartiness, good humor
campechano -na *adj* (coll.) frank, hearty, good-humored; *f* (Am.) mixed drink; (Am.) hammock
campeche *m* (bot.) logwood (*tree and wood*)
campeón *m* champion; (fig.) champion
campeona *f* championess
campeonato *m* championship
campeonil *adj* (pertaining to a) championship
campero -ra *adj* in the open, unsheltered; sleeping in the open (*said of domestic animals*); (Am.) good at farming; *m* farming friar or monk
campesino -na *adj* country; peasant; *mf* peasant; farmer; *m* countryman; *f* countrywoman
campestre *adj* country
campilán *m* campilan (*straight-edged sword of the Moros*)
campillo *m* small field; commons
campiña *f* stretch of farm land, countryside

campirano -na *adj & mf* (Am.) peasant; *m* (Am.) cowboy, broncobuster
campo *m* field; country; countryside; camp; crop; (her., phys. & sport) field; (fig.) field (*of various activities*); campus; ground, background; side (*in a contest*); **a campo raso** in the open; **a campo traviesa** or **travieso** across the fields, across country; **dar campo a** to give free range to; **en campo ajeno** (sport) away from home; **en campo propio** (sport) at home; **levantar el campo** (mil.) to break camp; (fig.) to consider finished, to give up; **quedar en el campo** to fall in battle or in a duel; **campo de Agramonte** bedlam; **campo de batalla** battlefield, battleground; **campo de concentración** concentration camp; **campo de deportes** athletic field; **campo de ejercicios** drill ground; **campo de emergencia** (aer.) emergency landing field; **campo de internamiento** internment camp; **campo de juego** playground; **campo del honor** field of honor (*of battle or duel*); **campo de minas** (mil. & nav.) mine field; **campo de pastoreo** grassland; **campo de pruebas** testing grounds; **campo de tiro** range, shooting range; **campo de trabajo** labor camp; **campo magnético** magnetic field; **campo raso** open country; **campo santo** cemetery; **campos elíseos** or **elisios** (myth.) Elysian Fields; **Campos Elíseos** Champs Elysées (*avenue in Paris*)
camposanto *m* cemetery
camuesa *f* pippin, sweeting (*apple*)
camueso *m* (bot.) pippin (*tree*); (coll.) simpleton, ignoramus
camuflaje *m* camouflage
camuflar *va* to camouflage
camuñas *fpl* mixture of seeds (*except wheat, barley, and rye*); *m* (*pl:* **-ñas**) goblin, bugaboo
can *m* dog; trigger (*of gun*); shoulder; bracket, corbel; khan; **Can mayor** (astr.) Canis Major, Great Dog; **Can menor** (astr.) Canis Minor, Little Dog
cana *f* see **cano**
Canaán, Tierra de (Bib.) Canaan, Land of Canaan
canabíneo -a *adj* (bot.) cannabinaceous
canáceo -a *adj* (bot.) cannaceous
Canadá, el Canada
canadiense *adj & mf* Canadian
canadillo *m* (bot.) joint fir
canal *m* canal; channel; (anat.) canal, duct; (rad. & telv.) channel; **el canal Ambrosio** Ambrose Channel; **Gran Canal** Grand Canal (*of China*); **canal de la Florida** Florida Straits; **canal de la Mancha** English Channel; **canal de Panamá** Panama Canal; **canal de Suez** Suez Canal; **canal digestivo** (anat.) alimentary canal; **Canal Grande** Grand Canal (*of Venice*); **canal semicircular** (anat.) semicircular canal ‖ *f* channel; gutter (*of roof*); gutter tile; pipe; conduit; long, narrow valley; fore edge (*of book*); groove, flute; dressed animal; **abierto en canal** split wide open; **abrir en canal** to cut in the middle from top to bottom; **canal para alambres** (elec.) conduit
canalado -da *adj* fluted, grooved, corrugated
canaladura *f* fluting, flute
canaleja *f* mill spout; (bot.) death cup
canaleta *f* wooden trough
canalete *m* paddle (*for canoeing*)
canalí *m* (*pl:* **-líes**) (Am.) paddle (*for canoeing*)
canalización *f* canalization; channeling; main, mains; piping; duct; installation of ducts; (elec.) wiring; (rad.) channeling; **canalización de consumo** (elec.) house current
canalizar §76 *va* to canalize; to pipe; to channel; (elec.) to wire
canalizo *m* (naut.) narrow channel, fairway
canalón *m* spout (*on side of house*); shovel hat; icicle; **canalones** *mpl* ravioli; **canalón de acera** cast-iron drain under sidewalk
canalla *f* (coll.) canaille, riffraff; *m* (coll.) cur, roughneck
canallada *f* meanness, currishness
canallesco -ca *adj* mean, low, base
canana *f* cartridge belt
cananeo -a *adj & mf* (Bib.) Canaanite
canapé *m* sofa; canapé (*appetizer*); **canapé cama** day bed
Canarias *fpl* see **canario**
canariense *adj & mf* Canarian
canariera *f* large cage for raising canaries
canario -ria *adj & mf* Canarian; *m* (orn.) canary, canary bird; (Am.) canary (*color*); (Am.) generous tipper; **Canarias** *fpl* Canaries; **¡canario!** great Scott!
canasta *f* basket, washbasket; canasta (*card game*)
canastada *f* basketful
canastería *f* basket business; baskets
canastero -ra *mf* basketmaker, basket dealer
canastilla *f* basket; layette; trousseau; **canastilla de la costura** sewing basket
canastillo *m* wicker tray
canasto *m* hamper; **¡canastos!** confound it!
canastro *m* hamper
cancagua *f* (Am.) fine building sand
cáncamo *m* (naut.) eyebolt; **cáncamo de argolla** ringbolt
cancamurria *f* (coll.) gloominess, blues
cancamusa *f* (coll.) ruse, artifice, fraud
cancán *m* cancan
cancanear *vn* (coll.) to stroll, to loaf about; (Am.) to stutter
cancaneo *m* (Am.) stuttering
cáncano *m* (coll.) louse
cancel *m* storm door; (Am.) folding screen
cancela *f* iron grating, iron door or gate
cancelación or **canceladura** *f* annulment, cancellation
cancelar *va* to annul, to cancel; to dispel, wipe out; to liquidate, pay off (*a debt*)
cancelaría *f* papal chancery
cancelariato *m* (eccl.) chancellorship
cancelario *m* (eccl.) chancellor (*who grants degrees*)
cáncer *m* (path.) cancer; (*cap.*) *m* (astr.) Cancer, Crab
cancerado -da *adj* cancerous; suffering from cancer; evil, corrupt
cancerar *va* to consume, destroy; to scold, punish; *vr* to have cancer; to become cancerous; to become depraved
Cancerbero *m* (myth. & fig.) Cerberus
cancerígeno -na *adj* cancerigenic
cancerología *f* study of cancer
cancerólogo -ga *mf* cancer expert, cancer specialist
canceroso -sa *adj* cancerous
cancilla *f* lattice gate (*of garden, barnyard, etc.*)
canciller *m* chancellor; **Canciller de hierro** Iron Chancellor (*Bismarck*); **Canciller del echiquier** (Brit.) Chancellor of the Exchequer; **Canciller mayor de Castilla** (archaic) Archbishop of Toledo
cancilleresco -ca *adj* (pertaining to a) chancellor or chancellery; formal, ceremonious
cancillería *f* chancellery, chancery; chancellorship
canción *f* song; lyric poem; **volver a la misma canción** (coll.) to sing the same old song; **canción de cuna** cradlesong; **canción popular** popular song; folk song
cancionero *m* anthology, collection of verse
cancioneta *f* canzonet
cancionista *mf* singer; song composer; *m* songster; *f* songstress
cancón *m* (coll.) bugaboo; **hacer un cancón a** (Am.) to threaten, to bluff
cancro *m* (path.) cancer; (bot.) canker
cancroide *m* (path.) cancroid tumor
cancroideo -a *adj* cancroid
cancha *f* (sport) field, ground; race track; golf links; cockpit; path, way; (Am.) roasted beans or corn; **estar en su cancha** (Am.) to be in one's element; **cancha de tenis** tennis court; *interj* (Am.) gangway!
canchal *m* rocky ground or region
canchalagua *f* (bot.) gentian
cancho *m* boulder, rock; rocky ground
candado *m* padlock; **candados** *mpl* lateral lacunae (*of horse's hoof*)
candaliza *f* (naut.) brail
candar *va* to lock; to shut, to close up
candeda *f* chestnut blossom

candela *f* candle, taper; flare, torch; fire, light; candlestick; candle power; chestnut bloom; **en candela** (naut.) vertical; **candela romana** Roman candle
candelabro *m* candelabrum
candelada *f* bonfire; candles
candelaria *f* Candlemas; (bot.) great mullein
candelecho *m* elevated wigwam from which to watch the vineyard
candelerazo *m* blow with a candlestick
candelero *m* candlestick; metal olive-oil lamp; fishing torch; stanchion; **en candelero** in a position of authority
candeleta *f* (naut.) brail
candelilla *f* (surg.) bougie, catheter; (bot.) catkin; (Am.) glowworm; (Am.) ignis fatuus; **hacerle a uno candelillas** (coll.) to sparkle, to flash (*said of the eyes of a tipsy person*)
candelita *f* (orn.) redstart, warbler
candeliza *f* (naut.) brail
candelizo *m* (coll.) icicle
candencia *f* candescence
candente *adj* candent, candescent; red-hot
candidación *f* candying of sugar
candidato -ta *mf* candidate
candidatura *f* slate, list of candidates; candidacy
candidez *f* candor; innocence, simple-mindedness, gullibility; silly remark
cándido -da *adj* candid; innocent, simple-minded, gullible; white, snowy
candiel *m* meringue
candil *m* olive-oil lamp; tine (*of antler*); (Am.) chandelier; **candiles** *mpl* (bot.) wake-robin; (Am.) icicles
candilada *f* oil spilt from a lamp
candileja *f* lampion; oil receptacle (*of lamp*); (bot.) corn cockle; **candilejas** *fpl* footlights
candilejo *m* small oil lamp; sunset glow; (bot.) corn cockle; **candilejos** *mpl* (bot.) wake-robin
candilera *f* (bot.) lampwick
candiletear *vn* (prov.) to snoop
candiletero -ra *mf* (prov.) snooper
candiota *f* wine barrel; large earthen wine jug
candiotera *f* wine cellar; storage for wine barrels or jugs
candongo -ga *adj* (coll.) fawning, scheming; (coll.) loafing; *mf* (coll.) fawner, schemer; (coll.) loafer, shirker; *f* (coll.) fawning, scheming; (coll.) teasing; (coll.) draft mule; **dar candonga a** (coll.) to kid, to tease
candonguear *va* (coll.) to kid, to tease, to jolly; *vn* (coll.) to scheme one's way out of work
candonguero -ra *adj* (coll.) kidding, teasing
candor *m* candor; pure whiteness
candoroso -sa *adj* candid, frank, simple
caneca *f* glazed earthen bottle
canecillo *m* (arch.) corbel, console; bracket, support
canela *f* see **canelo**
canelado -da *adj* cinnamon-colored, cinnamon-flavored
canelero *m* (bot.) cinnamon (*tree or shrub*)
canelina *f* canella alba
canelo -la *adj* cinnamon, cinnamon-colored; *m* cinnamon (*tree or shrub*); *f* cinnamon (*bark and spice*); (coll.) something peachy; **canela de la China** (pharm.) cassia; **canela de Magallanes** Winter's bark
canelón *m* spout; icicle (*hanging from spout*); (sew.) tubular trimming; cinnamon candy; heavy end of whip
canequí *m* cannequin (*cotton cloth*)
canesú *m* (*pl:* **-súes**) guimpe
caney *m* (Am.) cabin, hut; (Am.) abode of an Indian chief; (Am.) bend (*in a river*)
canfín *m* (Am.) petroleum
canfinflero or **canflinflero** *m* (Am.) bawd, pimp
canga *f* cangue
cangilón *m* large pitcher or jug (*of earthenware or metal*); bucket (*of a bucket wheel*); dipper, scoop (*of a dredge*); (Am.) rut, wagon rut
cangreja *f* (naut.) fore-and-aft sail; **cangreja de mesana** (naut.) jigger; **cangreja de popa** (naut.) spanker
cangrejal *m* (Am.) crab bed
cangrejero -ra *mf* crab seller or dealer; *f* crab nest, crab bed
cangrejo *m* (zool.) crab; (naut.) gaff, spanker gaff; **sacar cangrejos** (rowing) to catch a crab; **cangrejo bayoneta** (zool.) king crab, horseshoe crab; **cangrejo de mar** (zool.) green crab; **cangrejo de río** (zool.) crawfish; **cangrejo ermitaño** (zool.) hermit crab
cangrejuelo *m* little crab
cangrenar *vr* to gangrene, to become gangrenous
canguelo *m* (slang) fear
canguro *m* (zool.) kangaroo
caníbal *adj & mf* cannibal
canibalino -na *adj* cannibalistic
canibalismo *m* cannibalism
canica *f* marbles (*game*); marble
canicie *f* whiteness (*of hair*)
canícula *f* dog days; (*cap.*) *f* (astr.) Dog Star
canicular *adj* canicular; **caniculares** *mpl* canicular days, dog days
caniculario *m* beadle who keeps dogs out of church
cánido -da *adj* canine; *m* (zool.) canid
canijo -ja *adj* (coll.) sickly, infirm; *mf* (coll.) sickly person, weakling
canil *m* dog bread, dog cake
canilla *f* armbone, shinbone; tap (*in cask or barrel*); reel, bobbin; stripe, rib (*in cloth*)
canillado -da *adj* striped, ribbed
canillero -ra *mf* reel or bobbin maker; *m* taphole (*in cask or barrel*); (bot.) European elder; *f* shin guard; greave, jambe, jambeau
caninez *f* mad hunger
canino -na *adj* canine; *m* (anat.) canine, canine tooth; *f* dog excrement
caniquí *m* cannequin (*cotton cloth*)
canisté *m* or **canistel** *m* (bot.) lucuma; canistel (*fruit*)
canje *m* exchange
canjeable *adj* exchangeable
canjear *va* to exchange
cano -na *adj* gray, gray-haired; hoary, old; (poet.) white; *f* gray hair; measure equal to about two yards; (bot.) American fan palm; (Am.) jail; **echar una cana al aire** (coll.) to go on a lark, to cut loose
canoa *f* canoe; launch; (Am.) trough; **canoa automóvil** launch, motorboat
canoero -ra *mf* canoeist
canófilo -la *mf* dog fancier
canon *m* canon; (Bib., eccl. & mus.) canon; (eccl.) Canon (*part of the Mass which begins with Te igitur*); norm of human beauty; rate; royalty; tax; **cánones** *mpl* canon law; **gran canon** (print.) canon
canonesa *f* canoness
canonical *adj* canonical
canonicato *m* canonicate, canonry
canónico -ca *adj* (Bib. & eccl.) canonical; *f* (eccl.) canonical life
canóniga *f* (coll.) nap before eating
canónigo *m* canon (*churchman*)
canonista *m* canonist, canon lawyer
canonización *f* canonization
canonizar §76 *va* to canonize; to applaud, to approve
canonjía *f* canonry; (coll.) sinecure
canoro -ra *adj* singing, musical; sweet-singing (*bird*)
canoso -sa *adj* gray-haired, hoary
canotié *m* straw hat (*with low, flat crown*)
cansado -da *adj* tired, weary; worn-out, exhausted; tiresome, wearisome
cansancio *m* tiredness, weariness, fatigue
cansar *va* to tire; to weary, to bore; to harass; to exhaust (*a soil*); *vn* to tire, be tiresome; *vr* to tire, get tired; **cansarse de** + *inf* to get tired of + *ger;* **cansarse en** + *inf* to get tired + *ger*
cansera *f* (coll.) boredom, harassment
cansino -na *adj* tired, exhausted (*said of an animal*)
cantable *adj* singable; tuneful; sung slowly; *m* lyric (*words of musical passage of zarzuela*); musical passage (*of zarzuela*); (mus.) cantabile (*melodious, flowing passage*)
cantábrico -ca *adj* Cantabrian
cantada *f* (mus.) cantata
cantador -dora *mf* singer (*of popular songs*)
cantal *m* stone block; stony ground

cantalear *vn* to coo
cantaleta *f* tin-pan serenade, charivari, callithump; (Am.) constant scolding; **dar cantaleta a** (Am.) to make fun of, to laugh at; **la misma cantaleta** (Am.) the same old song
cantaletear *va* (Am.) to keep repeating, to say over and over again; (Am.) to make fun of, to laugh at
cantalinoso -sa *adj* rocky, stony (*ground*)
cantalupo *m* cantaloupe
cantamisano *m* var. of **misacantano**
cantante *adj* singing; *mf* singer; **cantante de ópera** opera singer
cantar *m* song; singing; chant; **ése es otro cantar** (coll.) that's another story; **cantar de gesta** (lit.) geste, romance; **Cantar de los Cantares** (Bib.) Song of Songs; *va* to sing; to sing of; to chant; **cantarlas claras** (coll.) to speak out; *vn* to sing; to chant; (coll.) to peach, to squeal; (coll.) to creak, to squeak; (naut.) to sing chanteys; (naut.) to whistle an order; **cantar de plano** (coll.) to make a full confession
cántara *f* jug; liquid measure equal to 13.16 liters
cantarada *f* jugful
cantarera *f* shelf for jugs
cantarería *f* jug shop, pottery
cantarero *m* potter
cantárida *f* (ent.) cantharis, Spanish fly; (pharm.) cantharides; blister plaster of cantharides; blister raised by cantharides
cantarilla *f* earthen jar
cantarillo *m* small jug
cantarín -rina *adj* fond of singing, always singing; *mf* singer, professional singer
cántaro *m* jug; jugful; ballot box; **llover a cántaros** to rain pitchforks
cantata *f* (mus.) cantata
cantatriz *f* (*pl:* **-trices**) singer, songstress
cantazo *m* blow with a big stone
cante *m* singing; popular song; **cante hondo, jondo** or **flamenco** Andalusian gypsy song or singing
canteado -da *adj* on edge, laid on edge
cantear *va* to pitch (*a stone*); to lay on edge
cantera *f* quarry, stone pit; talent, genius
cantería *f* stonecutting, stonework; stoneyard; masonry
canterios *mpl* roof girders
cantero *m* stonecutter; crust (*e.g., of bread*)
canticio *m* (coll.) tiresome singing
cántico *m* canticle; song
cantidad *f* quantity; **cantidad de movimiento** (mech.) momentum
cantiga *f* poem (*of troubadours*)
cantil *m* shelf (*on coast or under sea*); cliff
cantilena *f* song, ballad; cantilena; **la misma cantilena** (coll.) the same old song
cantillo *m* corner; pebble, little stone; jackstone; **cantillos** *mpl* jackstones
cantimplora *f* siphon; carafe, decanter; water bottle, canteen; wine flask; (eng.) weep hole; (Am.) powder flask; (Am.) mumps
cantina *f* canteen; wine cellar; lunchroom, luncheonette; lunch box; (rail.) station restaurant; (Am.) barroom
cantinela *f* var. of **cantilena**
cantinera *f* female sutler, vivandière; barmaid
cantinero *m* barkeeper, bartender
cantizal *m* stony ground
canto *m* song; singing; chant; canto; song (*lyric or ballad*); edge; corner; fore edge (*of book*); back (*of knife*); stone, pebble; crust (*of bread*); thickness (*e.g., of a board*); **de canto** on edge; on end; **canto ambrosiano** Ambrosian chant; **canto de corte** cutting edge; **canto del cisne** swan song; **canto flamenco** flamenco (*Andalusian gypsy singing*); **canto gregoriano** Gregorian chant; **canto llano** plain chant, plain song; **canto pelado** or **rodado** round stone, boulder
cantón *m* canton; region; cantonment; corner; (her.) canton
cantonado -da *adj* (her.) cantoned; *f* (archaic) corner; **dar cantonada a** (coll.) to shake off
cantonal *adj* cantonal
cantonalismo *m* cantonalism
cantonar *va & vr* var. of **acantonar**
cantonear *vn* to loaf at street corners; *vr* (coll.) to strut
cantonero -ra *mf* corner loafer; *m* gilding iron (*of bookbinder*); *f* angle iron, corner band, reinforcement (*of corner or edge*); corner shelf, corner table; streetwalker
cantonés -nesa *adj & mf* Cantonese
cantor -tora *adj* singing; sweet-singing; *m* singer, songster; minstrel; choirmaster; bard, poet; *f* songstress
cantoral *m* book of devotions
Cantórbery Canterbury
cantorral *m* stony ground
cantoso -sa *adj* stony, rocky
cantuariense *adj & mf* Canterburian
cantueso *m* (bot.) French lavender, stechados
canturía *f* vocal music; singing exercise; monotonous singing; singing quality (*of a composition*)
canturrear *va* (coll.) to hum, to sing; *vn* (coll.) to hum, to sing in a low voice
canturreo *m* (coll.) humming, singing in a low voice, crooning
canturriar *va & vn* (coll.) var. of **canturrear**
cánula *f* (surg.) cannula
canular *adj* cannular
canut *m* (orn.) knot
canutero *m* pincase
canutillo *m* var. of **cañutillo**
canuto *m* var. of **cañuto**
caña *f* cane, reed; stem, stalk; pipe; (bot.) giant reed; long bone (*of leg or arm*); leg (*of boot or stocking*); marrow; tipstock (*of firearm*); shank (*of anchor, drill, column, etc.*); wineglass (*stemless*); small glass (*of beer*); mine gallery; (naut.) tiller; (Am.) rum; (Am.) bluff; (Am.) boasting; **caña brava asiática** (bot.) bamboo; **caña de azúcar** sugar cane; **caña de Bengala** (bot.) rattan palm (*Calamus rotang*); **caña de Indias** (bot.) Indian reed, canna; **caña del pulmón** windpipe; **caña de pescar** fishing rod; **caña dulce** or **melar** sugar cane
cañacoro *m* (bot.) canna, Indian shot, Indian reed
cañada *f* gully, gulch; cattle path; (Am.) brook
cañadilla *f* (zool.) purple shell
cañafístola or **cañafístula** *f* (bot.) drumstick tree; cañafistula (*pods*)
cañaheja or **cañaherla** *f* (bot.) giant fennel
cañal *m* growth of reeds; fishgarth made of reeds, fishing channel
cañamar *m* hemp field
cañamazo *m* canvas; burlap; canvas for colored embroidery; embroidered hemp
cañamelar *m* sugar-cane plantation
cañameño -ña *adj* hempen, made of hemp
cañamiel *f* sugar cane
cañamiza *f* hemp refuse, hemp bagasse
cáñamo *m* (bot.) hemp (*plant and fiber*); hempen cloth; **cáñamo de Bengala** (bot.) sunn hemp; **cáñamo de Manila** Manila hemp; **cáñamo sisal** sisal hemp
cañamón *m* hempseed; **cañamones** *mpl* birdseed
cañamoncillo *m* fine mixing sand
cañamonero -ra *mf* hempseed vendor
cañar *m* growth of reeds; fishgarth made of reeds
cañareja *f* var. of **cañaheja**
cañariego -ga *adj* of a sheep that has died on the sheep path (*said of skin or hide*); accompanying the flock migrating between the north and south of Spain (*said of men, horses, and dogs*)
cañarroya *f* (bot.) wallwort
cañavera *f* (bot.) ditch reed
cañaveral *m* canebrake; reed field; sugar-cane plantation
cañaverear *va* var. of **acañaverear**
cañazo *m* blow with a reed or cane
cañedo *m* var. of **cañaveral**
cañería *f* pipe, pipe line; (mus.) organ pipes; **cañería de arcilla vitrificada** sewer pipe, soil pipe; **cañería maestra** main, gas or water main
cañero *m* pipe fitter, plumber; (dial.) angler; (Am.) sugar-cane dealer
cañeta *f* (bot.) ditch reed

cañete *m* small tube or pipe
cañilavado -da *adj* small-limbed (*said of a horse*)
cañista *m* pipe fitter, plumber
cañiza *f* coarse linen
cañizal *m* var. of **cañaveral**
cañizo *m* hurdle of reeds (*for drying fruit, rearing silkworms, shearing hats, etc.*); web of reeds and rope (*used as lath for ceilings*); (naut.) flake
caño *m* tube, pipe; ditch; gutter, sewer; channel (*into harbor or bay*); (mus.) organ pipe; mine gallery; spurt, jet; spout; cellar or cave for cooling water; wine cellar; **llover a caño libre** (coll.) to rain buckets
cañón *m* tube, pipe; cannon; barrel (*of gun*); shaft (*of column, elevator, etc.*); well (*of staircase*); (min.) gallery; shank (*of key*); stem (*of pipe, of feather*); quill; pinfeather; canyon; **cañón antiaéreo** anti-aircraft gun; **cañón antitanque** antitank gun; **cañón cohete** (mil.) rocket gun; **cañón de campaña** fieldpiece; **cañón de chimenea** flue, chimney flue; **cañón lanzaarpones** harpoon gun; **cañón lanzacabos** or **lanzacables** life-saving gun; **cañón obús** howitzer; **cañón rayado** rifled gun barrel
cañonazo *m* cannon shot
cañonear *va* to cannonade
cañoneo *m* cannonade, cannonry
cañonera *f* see **cañonero**
cañonería *f* cannon, cannonry; (mus.) set of organ pipes
cañonero -ra *adj* armed (*boat*); *m* gunner, cannoneer; gunboat; *f* (fort.) embrasure; (mil.) canteen (*store*); (Am.) holster
cañoto *m* (bot.) ditch reed
cañucela *f* slender cane or reed
cañuela *f* (bot.) fescue grass; **cañuela de oveja** (bot.) sheep's fescue
cañutazo *m* (coll.) gossip
cañutería *f* gold or silver embroidery; (mus.) set of organ pipes
cañutero *m* pincase
cañutillo *m* glass tube; bugle (*tubular glass bead*); gold or silver twist for embroidery
cañuto *m* internode (*of reed*); (coll.) gossip; tube, tubular container
caoba *f* (bot.) mahogany (*tree and wood*)
caobana *f* (archaic) mahogany (*tree*)
caobo *m* (bot.) mahogany (*tree*)
caolín *m* kaolin or kaoline
caos *m* chaos
caótico -ca *adj* chaotic
cap. abr. of **capitán** & **capítulo**
capa *f* cape, cloak, mantle; layer, bed; scum; coat (*e.g., of paint*); (mas.) bed, course; cigar wrapper; (anat. & geol.) stratum; (eccl.) cope; (naut.) primage; (fig.) cloak, mask; **a capa y espiga** mortise and tenon; **aguantarse a la capa** (naut.) to lie to; **andar de capa caída** (coll.) to be in a bad way (*in business, health, etc.*); **de capa y espada** cloak-and-sword; **de capa y gorra** plainly, informally; **estarse a la capa** (naut.) to lie to; **hacer de su capa un sayo** (coll.) to tend to one's own business, to keep one's own counsel; **so capa de** under the guise of, under the pretense of; **capa anual** (bot.) annual ring; **capa de balasto** (rail.) roadbed; **capa de Heaviside** (rad.) Heaviside layer; **capa del cielo** canopy of heaven; **capa de paseo** (taur.) dress cape; **capa freática** (eng.) water table; **capa magna** (eccl.) bishop's cope; **capa pluvial** (eccl.) cope, pluvial; **capa rota** (coll.) decoy, blind
capacete *m* casque, helmet
capacidad *f* capacity; capability; (elec. & phys.) capacity; **capacidad distribuída** (rad.) distributed capacity
capacitación *f* qualification, (act of) qualifying
capacitancia *f* (elec.) capacitance
capacitar *va* to enable, to qualify; to empower, to commission; *vr* to become enabled, become qualified
capacitor *m* (elec.) capacitor
capacha *f* frail, hamper; basket lid
capachero *m* porter or carrier using a basket
capacho *m* frail, hamper; basket lid; hempen pressing bag (*used in olive-oil presses*); bricklayer's hod; (orn.) barn owl
capada *f* (coll.) capeful (*contents of cape held as if it were an apron*)
capadocio -cia *adj* & *mf* Cappadocian
capador *m* gelder, castrator; gelder's whistle
capadura *f* gelding, castration; scar left by castration; second cutting of tobacco used for filling or wrappers
capar *va* to geld, to castrate; to curtail, to cut down
caparazón *m* caparison; horse blanket; feed bag; shell (*of insects or crustaceans*); carcass of fowl
caparidáceo -a *adj* (bot.) capparidaceous
caparra *f* cattle tick, sheep tick; earnest money
caparrón *m* (bot.) blossom
caparrosa *f* (chem.) vitriol; **caparrosa azul** (chem.) blue vitriol; **caparrosa blanca** (chem.) white vitriol; **caparrosa verde** (chem.) copperas, green vitriol
capataz *m* (*pl:* **-taces**) overseer, foreman; warden, steward
capaz *adj* (*pl:* **-paces**) capable, competent; capacious, spacious; **capaz de** capable of; with a capacity of; **capaz para** capable in; competent for; with room for
capazo *m* two-handled rush basket; blow with cloak
capciosidad *f* craftiness, deception
capcioso -sa *adj* crafty, deceptive
capea *f* (taur.) waving of cape at bull; (taur.) amateur free-for-all bullfight
capeador *m* (taur.) capeador (*bullfighter who waves cape before bull*)
capear *va* to take the cloak or cape away from; (coll.) to duck, dodge (*something unpleasant*); (taur.) to wave or flourish the cape at (*the bull*); (naut.) to weather (*a storm*); (coll.) to beguile, to take in; *vn* (naut.) to lay to; (Am.) to play hooky, to cut class
capeja *f* shabby cloak or cape
capelán *m* (ichth.) capelin
capelina *f* (surg.) capeline
capelo *m* cardinal's hat; cardinalate; **capelo rojo** red hat (*cardinal's hat; cardinalate*)
capellada *f* tip, toe piece (*of shoe*); patch on the vamp
capellán *adj masc* (Am.) fortune-hunting; *m* chaplain; (Am.) fortune hunter; **capellán castrense** or **de ejército** army chaplain; **capellán de la armada** or **de navío** navy chaplain
capellanía *f* fund left for religious purposes; chaplaincy
capellina *f* (arm. & surg.) capeline; (archaic) peasant's hood
capeo *m* (taur.) capework, waving of cape before bull
capeón *m* (taur.) young bull excited by waving of cape
capero *m* priest who wears a cope; cloak rack
caperucita *f* small pointed hood; **Caperucita Encarnada** or **Roja** Red Ridinghood, Little Red Ridinghood
caperuza *f* pointed hood; chimney cap; pipe cap; mantle (*of gaslight*); (mach.) hood
capeta *f* short cape
capetiano -na or **capetino -na** *adj* & *mf* Capetian
capialzado *m* curve or bend of arch; flashing over door or window
capialzar **§76** *va* to bend the face of (*an arch or lintel*) into an outward slope
capialzo *m* (arch.) slope of intrados
capibara *f* (zool.) capybara (*South American rodent*)
capicúa *m* palindrome
capiculado -da *adj* (philately) tête-bêche
capichola *f* ribbed silk
capigorra *m*, **capigorrón** *m* or **capigorrista** *m* (coll.) idler, loafer; dull cleric
capilar *adj* capillary; of the hair; *m* (anat.) capillary
capilaridad *f* capillarity
capilla *f* hood, cowl; chapel; death house; (mach.) bonnet, hood, cowl; (print.) proof sheet, advance sheet; (coll.) friar; **estar en**

capilla or **en la capilla** to be in the death house; (coll.) to be on pins and needles; (coll.) to be jittery about taking an examination; **estar expuesto en capilla ardiente** to be on view, to lie in state; **capilla ardiente** funeral chapel; oratory set up for funeral in the home; pallbearers; **capilla de la muerte** death house; **capilla mayor** chapel behind the high altar; **Capilla sixtina** Sistine Chapel

capillada *f* hoodful; blow with a hood

capillejo *m* skein of sewing silk

capiller *m* or **capillero** *m* chapelman, warden of a chapel, churchwarden

capilleta *f* small chapel; chapel-shaped niche

capillo *m* baby cap; hood; hood (*of falcon*); baptismal cap; cap of distaff; toe lining (*of shoe*); filler (*for cigars*); rabbit net; bud (*especially of rose*); cocoon; (metal.) cupel; (anat.) prepuce

capilludo -da *adj* like a hood or cowl; wearing a hood or cowl

capipardo *m* workingman

capirotada *f* dressing of eggs, herbs, garlic, etc.

capirotazo *m* fillip

capirote *m* hood (*covering face*); doctor's hood; cardboard or paper cone (*worn on head*); hood (*of falcon*); folding top (*of carriage*); fillip; *adj* with head of different color from that of body (*said of cattle*)

capirucho *m* (coll.) hood

capisayo *m* mantelet; bishop's vesture

capiscol *m* precentor

capitación *f* capitation; poll tax

capitado -da *adj* (bot.) capitate

capital *adj* capital; paramount; main, principal; essential; mortal (*enemy*); **lo capital** the main thing, the essential point; *m* capital; husband's estate at marriage; **capital circulante** (econ.) circulating capital; **capital de inversión** investment capital; **capital fijo** fixed capital; **capital lucrativo** productive capital; **capital social** capital stock; *f* capital (*city*); (fort.) capital

capitalidad *f* status as capital (*city*)

capitalino -na *adj* (Am.) of the capital; *mf* (Am.) dweller in the capital, native or inhabitant of the capital

capitalismo *m* capitalism

capitalista *adj* capitalist, capitalistic; *mf* capitalist; investor, share holder; *m* (taur.) apprentice bullfighter; (taur.) spectator who jumps into the ring at the end of the last fight

capitalización *f* capitalization; compounding (*of interest*)

capitalizar §76 *va* to capitalize; to compound (*interest*)

capitalmente *adv* mortally

capitán *m* leader; captain (*e.g., of a football team*); (mil., naut. & nav.) captain; **capitán de bandera** (nav.) flag captain; **capitán de corbeta** (nav.) lieutenant commander; **capitán de fragata** (nav.) commander; **capitán del puerto** harbor master; **capitán de navío** (nav.) captain; **capitán general** (mil.) general (*of highest rank*); captain general; **capitán general de ejército** (mil.) General of the Army; **capitán general de la armada** (nav.) Admiral of the Fleet; **capitán preboste** (mil.) provost marshal

capitana *f* (nav.) flagship; captain's wife; (coll.) female leader

capitanear *va* to captain; to lead, to command

capitanía *f* captaincy; captainship; (mil.) company; anchorage (*toll*); **capitanía general** captain-generalcy

capitel *m* (arch.) capital; (arch.) spire; (tech.) capital (*of a still*)

capitolino -na *adj* Capitoline

capitolio *m* capitol; (*cap.*) *m* Capitol

capitón *m* (ichth.) striped mullet

capitoste *m* (coll.) boss, head

capítula *f* chapter (*passage of Scripture*)

capitulación *f* agreement; capitulation; **capitulaciones** *fpl* marriage contract, articles of marriage

capitular *adj* capitular; *m* capitulary; **capitulares** *fpl* (hist.) capitularies; *va* to accuse, to impeach; to agree on (*terms*); *vn* to capitulate; **capitular con** to capitulate to (*an enemy*); to compound or compromise with (*e.g., one's conscience*)

capitulario *m* prayer book

capitulear *vn* (Am.) var. of **cabildear**

capituleo *m* (Am.) var. of **cabildeo**

capítulo *m* chapter; chapter house; commission, errand; reprimand, reproof; (coll.) subject, matter; **llamar** or **traer a capítulo** to take to task, to bring to book; **capítulos** *mpl* main points (*of a speech or writing*); characteristics; **capítulos matrimoniales** articles of marriage

capizana *f* (arm.) crinière

cap.^{n} abr. of **capitán**

capnomancia *f* capnomancy

cap.^{o} abr. of **capítulo**

capó *m* (*pl;* **-pós**) (aut.) hood

capoc *m* kapok

capolar *va* to chop, mince, hash; (dial.) to cut the throat of, to behead

capón -pona *adj* castrated; *m* eunuch; capon; fillip on the head; bundle of brushwood; (naut.) anchor stopper; *f* (mil. & nav.) shoulder strap

caponar *va* (agr.) to tie up (*a vine*)

caponera *f* cage or coop for fattening capons; (fort.) caponier; (coll.) hospitable house, place of welcome; (coll.) coop (*jail*)

capoquero *m* (bot.) kapok tree, silk-cotton tree

caporal *m* chief, leader; cattle boss

capota *f* head of the teasel; capote (*top of a vehicle; bonnet with strings*); (aer.) cowling; (aut.) top

capotaje *m* somersault, upset

capotar *vn* to turn somersault (*said of a car*); (aer.) to nose over

capote *m* capote (*cloak*); mass of heavy clouds; bullfighter's bright-colored cape; (coll.) frown; (Am.) thrashing, beating; **dar capote a** (coll.) to flabbergast; (coll.) to leave (*a late-comer*) without anything to eat; (coll.) to not let (*someone*) take a single trick; (Am.) to take in, to bamboozle; **decir para su capote** to say to oneself; **echar un capote** (coll.) to turn the conversation; **capote de monte** poncho

capotear *va* to duck (*a responsibility*); (coll.) to beguile, take in; (taur.) to wave or flourish the cape at (*the bull*); (theat.) to cut, to make cuts in (*a performance*)

capoteo *m* (taur.) waving of cape before bull

capotillo *m* cape, mantelet

capotudo -da *adj* frowning

capp.^{n} abr. of **capellán**

caprario -ria *adj* capric

Capricornio *m* (astr.) Capricorn; (*l.c.*) *m* (ent.) capricorn beetle

capricho *m* caprice; whim, fancy; keen desire; (mus.) capriccio, caprice

caprichoso -sa *adj* capricious; whimsical, willful

caprichudo -da *adj* whimsical, willful

caprifoliáceo -a *adj* (bot.) caprifoliaceous

caprino -na *adj* (pertaining to the) goat

capriotada *f* (Am.) goat's-milk pudding

caprípede or **caprípedo -da** *adj* (poet.) goat-footed

capsaicina *f* (chem.) capsaicin

cápsula *f* cap (*of a bottle*); laboratory dish; cartridge; capsule (*of space rocket*); (anat., bot., pharm. & zool.) capsule; **cápsula de cristal** (elec.) crystal cartridge; **cápsula fulminante** percussion cap; **cápsula manométrica** manometric capsule

capsular *adj* capsular; *va* to cap (*a bottle*)

captación *f* attraction, attractiveness; capture; winning; harnessing (*of water*); catchment; (rad.) tuning, tuning in, picking up; uptake (*of radioactive tracer*)

captalización *f* (wine mfg.) chaptalization

captalizar §76 *va* to chaptalize

captar *va* to catch; to attract, to win, to capture (*e.g., confidence or affection*); to impound (*water*); to harness (*a waterfall*); to tune in (*a radio station*); to get, to pick up (*a radio signal*); to grasp, to get (*what someone says*); *vr* to attract, to win

captor *m* captor

captura *f* capture; catch

capturar *va* to capture

capuana *f* (coll.) beating, whipping
capucha *f* cowl; circumflex accent
capuchina *f* Capuchin nun; (bot.) Indian cress, garden nasturtium; (orn.) capuchin (*pigeon*); confection of egg yolks; (Am.) latch (*of door or window*)
capuchino *m* Capuchin (*monk*); (zool.) capuchin (*monkey*)
capucho *m* cowl, hood, capuchin
capuchón *m* lady's cloak with hood; short domino; (aut.) valve cap
capulí *m* (*pl:* **-líes**) (bot.) capulin; (bot.) calabur tree
capulín *m* var. of **capulí**
capullo *m* cocoon; coarse spun silk; acorn cup; bud (*especially of rose*); (anat.) prepuce; **en capullo** (coll.) in embryo
capuz *m* (*pl:* **-puces**) cowl; hooded cloak; dive, duck
capuza *f* (Am.) branding iron
capuzar §76 *va* to duck; (naut.) to load (*a boat*) so that it draws more at the bow
caquéctico -ca *adj* cachectic or cachectical
caquexia *f* (path.) cachexia
caqui *m* (bot.) kaki, Japanese persimmon; khaki; *adj* khaki
caquinos *mpl* (Am.) cachinnation, uproarious laughter
cara *f* see **caro**
carabao *m* (zool.) carabao
cárabe *m* amber
carabela *f* (naut.) caravel
carabelón *m* small caravel
carabina *f* carbine; (coll.) chaperon; **ser la carabina de Ambrosio** (coll.) to be worthless
carabinazo *m* shot with a carbine; carbine wound
carabinero *m* carabineer; revenue guard
cárabo *m* (orn.) tawny owl; (ent.) carabus
caracal *m* (zool.) caracal
caracol *m* (zool.) snail; snail shell; sea shell; curl (*in hair*); spit curl; caracole (*of horse*); winding or spiral stairs; (anat.) cochlea; (arch.) spiral; (horol.) fusee; **¡caracoles!** confound it!; good gracious!; **hacer caracoles** to zigzag; **caracol real** (bot.) snailflower, corkscrew flower
caracola *f* (zool.) triton (*marine snail*); conch, triton (*shell*); trumpet
caracolada *f* fricassee of snails
caracolear *vn* (equit.) to caracole
caracolejo *m* small snail; small shell
caracolero -ra *mf* snail gatherer, snail vendor; *f* (bot.) pellitory
caracolillo *m* (bot.) Australian pea; pea-bean coffee; veined mahogany; **caracolillos** *mpl* shell-work trimmings or fringes; **caracolillo de olor** (bot.) sweet pea
caracolito *m* (bot.) gromwell
carácter *m* (*pl:* **caracteres**) character; (bot., zool., print. & theol.) character; brand (*on cattle*); **carácter adquirido** (biol.) acquired character; **carácter de imprenta** (print.) type; **carácter de letra** hand, handwriting; **carácter hereditario** (biol.) inherited character; **carácter recesivo** (biol.) recessive character
característico -ca *adj* characteristic; *m* (theat.) old man; *f* characteristic; (math. & rad.) characteristic; (theat.) old woman
caracterización *f* characterization
caracterizado -da *adj* distinguished, outstanding
caracterizar §76 *va* to characterize; to confer a distinction on; to play (*a rôle*) effectively; *vr* (theat.) to dress and paint for a rôle
caracul *m* caracul (*curly fur*)
caracha *m* or **carache** *m* (vet.) itch, mange (*on llamas*)
caracho -cha *adj* violet-colored
carado -da *adj:* **bien carado** good-faced, kind-faced; **mal carado** evil-faced
caradura *m* (coll.) scoundrel
caragilate *m* (bot.) black-eyed bean
caramanchel *m* (naut.) roof or cover of hatchway; (coll.) refreshment stand
caramanchón *m* var. of **camaranchón**
caramba *interj* confound it!; gracious me!
carambanado -da *adj* frozen, frozen into an icicle
carámbano *m* icicle
carambillo *m* (bot.) saltwort
carambola *f* carom; (bot.) carambola (*tree and fruit*); trick, cheat; chance; (fig.) double shot; **por carambola** deviously; by chance, by luck
carambolear *vn* to carom
carambolero *m* (bot.) carambola (*tree*); lucky fellow
carambolista *mf* good carom shot (*person*)
carambolo *m* (bot.) carambola (*tree*)
caramel *m* (ichth.) atherine, silversides
caramelizar §76 *va & vr* to caramelize
caramelo *m* caramel; lozenge, drop (*candy*)
caramilla *f* (mineral.) calamine
caramillar *m* growth of saltwort
caramillo *m* (bot.) saltwort; (mus.) shawm; crooked or shaky heap; gossiping, scheming
caramilloso -sa *adj* (coll.) var. of **quisquilloso**
carantamaula *f* (coll.) ugly false face; (coll.) ugly mug (*person*)
carantoña *f* (coll.) ugly false face, ugly face; (coll.) ugly old woman all dressed up and painted; **carantoñas** *fpl* (coll.) fawning, wheedling
carantoñero -ra *mf* (coll.) fawner, wheedler
caraña *f* caranna, caranna gum
carapacho *m* carapace; **meterse en su carapacho** to retire into one's shell; **salir del carapacho** to come out of one's shell
carapato *m* castor oil
carape *interj* var. of **caramba**
caraqueño -ña *adj* (pertaining to) Caracas; *mf* native or inhabitant of Caracas
carasol *m* solarium, sun porch, sunroom
carátula *f* mask; wire mask (*of beekeeper*); (Am.) title page; (Am.) face (*of watch*); (fig.) stage, theater
caratulero -ra *mf* mask maker or dealer
carava *f* peasant holiday gathering
caravana *f* caravan; (coll.) caravan (*band of travelers*)
caravanera *f* caravansary
caravanero *m* caravanner, caravanist
caravansera *f*, **caravanserrallo** *m* or **caravasar** *m* caravansary
caray *m* (zool.) tortoise; tortoise shell; *interj* confound it!; gracious me!
carbinol *m* (chem.) carbinol
carbodinamita *f* carbodynamite
carbohidrato *m* (chem.) carbohydrate
carbohielo *m* dry ice
carbol *m* (chem.) phenol
carbólico -ca *adj* carbolic
carbolíneo *m* carbolineum
carbolización *f* creosoting
carbolizar §76 *va* to creosote
carbón *m* coal; charcoal; black crayon, carbon pencil; (elec.) carbon (*of a battery or an arc lamp*); (agr.) smut; **carbón animal** boneblack; **carbón antracitoso** anthracite coal; **carbón bituminoso** bituminous coal; **carbón de bujía** cannel coal; **carbón de leña** charcoal; **carbón de llama corta** hard coal; **carbón de llama larga** soft coal; **carbón de piedra** coal; **carbón graso** soft coal; **carbón mate** cannel coal; **carbón mineral** coal; **carbón tal como sale** run-of-mine coal; **carbón vegetal** charcoal
carbonada *f* charge of coal (*for furnace*); broiled meat; pancake
carbonado *m* carbonado, carbon diamond
carbonalla *f* refractory mortar for hearth of reverberatory furnace
carbonatar *va* to carbonate
carbonato *m* (chem.) carbonate; **carbonato de calcio** (chem.) calcium carbonate; **carbonato de potasio** (chem.) potassium carbonate; **carbonato de sodio** (chem.) sodium carbonate
carboncillo *m* fine coal; charcoal (*pencil*); black sand; carbon (*in cylinder*)
carbonear *va* to make charcoal of, turn into charcoal
carboneo *m* charcoal burning
carbonera *f* see **carbonero**
carbonería *f* coalyard; charcoal store; coal shed

carbonero -ra *adj* (pertaining to) coal, charcoal; coaling; *mf* coaldealer; charcoal burner; *f* charcoal kiln; bunker, coal bunker; coalbin; (Am.) coal mine
carbónico -ca *adj* carbonic
carbonífero -ra *adj* carboniferous; (geol.) Carboniferous; *m* (geol.) Carboniferous
carbonilo *m* (chem.) carbonyl
carbonilla *f* fine coal, pulverized coal; cinders; (aut.) carbon (*in cylinders*)
carbonización *f* carbonization
carbonizar *va & vr* to carbonize, to char; to burn up
carbono *m* (chem.) carbon
carbonoso -sa *adj* carbonaceous
carborundo *m* carborundum
carboxilo *m* (chem.) carboxyl
carbunclo *m* carbuncle (*ruby or garnet*); (path. & vet.) carbuncle
carbunco *m* (path. & vet.) carbuncle
carbúnculo *m* carbuncle (*ruby or garnet*)
carburación *f* carburetion
carburador *m* carburetor
carburante *m* fuel (*gas or liquid*)
carburar *va* to carburet
carburo *m* (chem.) carbide (*especially calcium carbide*); **carburo de calcio** (chem.) calcium carbide
carcacha *f* (Am.) jalopy
carcaj *m* quiver; socket or bucket (*for holding standard surmounted by cross*); (Am.) rifle case
carcajada *f* outburst of laughter, burst of laughter
carcamal *adj* (coll.) infirm; *m* (coll.) infirm old person
carcamán *m* tub (*clumsy boat*)
carcasa *f* (mil.) carcass; (mach.) frame
Carcasona *f* Carcassonne
cárcava *f* gully; ditch, earthwork; grave
carcavón *m* gully, gorge
carcavuezo *m* deep pit
carcax *m* (*pl:* **-cajes**) var. of **carcaj**
carcayú *m* (*pl:* **-yúes**) (zool.) wolverine, glutton
carcaza *f* var. of **carcaj**
cárcel *f* jail, prison; groove in which sluice gate slides; (carp.) clamp (*for holding together boards to be glued*)
carcelaje *m* jailer's fee; imprisonment
carcelario -ria *adj* (pertaining to) jail
carcelería *f* imprisonment; bail
carcelero -ra *adj* (pertaining to) jail; *mf* jailer, warden
carcinógeno *m* (path.) carcinogen
carcinoma *m* (path.) carcinoma
cárcola *f* treadle of a loom
carcoma *f* (ent.) wood borer; dust made by wood borer; anxiety; spendthrift; bore, pest (*person*)
carcomer *va* to bore; to gnaw away, gnaw away at, to undermine; *vr* to become undermined; to become worm-eaten
carda *f* carding; teasel (*head of plant; device for raising nap*); card (*brush*); rebuke; **carda para limas** file brush or card
cardada *f* carding (*roll of wool from carding machine*)
cardador -dora *mf* carder (*of wool*); *m* (zool.) julid, millepede
cardal *m* var. of **cardizal**
cardamina *f* (bot.) pepper cress
cardamomo *m* (bot.) cardamom
cardán *m* (mach.) universal joint
cardar *va* to card; to rebuke
cardelina *f* (orn.) linnet
cardenal *m* (eccl.) cardinal; (orn.) cardinal, cardinal bird; black-and-blue mark; **cardenal de Virginia** (orn.) eastern cardinal
cardenalato *m* cardinalate
cardenalicio -cia *adj* (pertaining to a) cardinal
cardencha *f* (bot.) teasel; card (*brush*)
cardenchal *m* teasel field
cardenillo *m* verdigris
cárdeno -na *adj* purple, violet; gray (*bull*); opaline (*water*)
cardería *f* carding shop
cardíaca *f* see **cardíaco**
cardiáceo -a *adj* heart-shaped
cardíaco -ca *adj* cardiac; *mf* cardiac (*sufferer from heart disease*); *f* (bot.) motherwort
cardias *m* (*pl:* **-dias**) (anat.) cardia
cardillar *m* field of Spanish oyster plants
cardillo *m* (bot.) Spanish oyster plant, golden thistle
cardinal *adj* cardinal
cardinas *fpl* (arch.) thistle leaves
cardiografía *f* cardiography
cardiógrafo *m* cardiograph
cardiograma *m* cardiogram
cardiología *f* cardiology
cardiovascular *adj* cardiovascular
carditis *f* (path.) carditis
cardizal *m* field full of thistles or brambles
Card.[l] abr. of **Cardenal**
cardo *m* (bot., arch. & her.) thistle; file brush or card; **cardo ajonjero** (bot.) carline thistle; **cardo alcachofero** (bot.) artichoke; **cardo bendito** (bot.) blessed thistle; **cardo borriqueño** or **borriquero** (bot.) cotton thistle, Scotch thistle; **cardo corredor** (bot.) field eryngo; **cardo de cardadores** (bot.) fuller's teasel; **cardo de comer** (bot.) cardoon; **cardo estrellado** (bot.) star thistle; **cardo lechar, lechero** or **mariano** (bot.) milk thistle; **cardo negro** (bot.) Canada thistle; **cardo santo** (bot.) holy thistle; **cardo yesquero** (bot.) cotton thistle; (bot.) globe thistle
cardón *m* carding; (bot.) teasel, wild teasel
cardoncillo *m* (bot.) milk thistle
carducha *f* big iron carding brush
cardume *m* or **cardumen** *m* school (*of fish*)
carduzal *m* var. of **cardizal**
carduzar §76 *va* to card (*wool*); (hum.) to scratch with the nails
carear *va* to bring face to face; to compare; to lead (*cattle*); *vn* to face; **carear a** to face, to overlook (*e.g., a garden, the street*); *vr* to come face to face, to meet face to face; **carearse con** to face (*especially firmly or hostilely*)
carecer §34 *vn* to be in want; **carecer de** to lack, be in need of
carecimiento *m* lack, want, need
carelio -lia *adj & mf* Karelian; (*cap.*) *f* Karelia
carena *f* (naut.) careen, careening (*cleaning and caulking*); (naut.) bottom (*part underwater*); (coll.) chiding, jeering, mocking; (poet.) bottom, ship; **dar carena a** (naut.) to careen (*to clean and caulk*)
carenadura *f* (naut.) careenage
carenar *va* (naut.) to careen (*to clean and caulk*)
carencia *f* lack, want, need, deficiency
carencial *adj* deficiency
carenero *m* (naut.) careener
carente *adj* lacking, devoid; **carente de** lacking, devoid of, in need of
careo *m* meeting, confrontation; comparison
carero -ra *adj* (coll.) dear, expensive (*charging high prices*)
carestía *f* scarcity; want; high cost of living, high prices; **carestía de la vida** high cost of living
careto -ta *adj* marked with a blaze (*said of a horse or cow*); *f* mask; fencing mask; **quitar la careta a** to unmask; **careta antigás** gas mask
carey *m* (zool.) hawksbill turtle; tortoise shell
carga *f* loading; load; freight, cargo; burden; weight; anxiety, worry; charge (*of a cannon, furnace, etc.*); responsibility, charge, obligation; (mil. & elec.) charge; (hyd.) head; (elec.) load; **a cargas** (coll.) in abundance; **con plena carga** (elec. & mach.) at full load; **echar la carga a** to put the blame on; **volver a la carga** to not give up, to keep coming back; **carga de caballería** cavalry charge; **carga de camión** truckload; **carga de espacio** (elec.) space charge; **carga de familia** dependent; **carga de profundidad** depth charge; **carga prosódica** (gram.) stress, stress accent; **carga pública** public charge (*person who is a burden or responsibility to the state or local government*); **carga útil** pay load
cargadero *m* loading platform; freight station; hopper, mouth of furnace; (arch.) lintel

cargadilla *f* (coll.) debt and accrued interest
cargado -da *adj* loaded; overcast, cloudy; sultry; strong, thick; copious; big with young; charged, hot (*wire*); **cargado de años** up in years; **cargado de espaldas** stoop-shouldered
cargador *m* loader, stevedore; stoker; ramrod; rammer; carrier, porter; **cargador de acumulador** (elec.) battery charger
cargamento *m* load; cargo, shipment; dependents
cargante *adj* (coll.) boring, annoying, tiresome
cargar **§59** *va* to load; to load up, to overload; to weigh down on, to burden; to increase (*taxes*); to load (*a gun, a furnace, dice, etc.*); to charge; (mil. & elec.) to charge; to play (*a higher card*); (coll.) to weary, to bore; (coll.) to annoy; (coll.) to flunk; (Am.) to carry; (Am.) to wear; (Am.) to punish; **cargar a una persona** to place (*e.g., a task*) on someone; to entrust (*e.g., a responsibility*) to someone; to impose (*e.g., a tax*) on someone; to charge someone with (*an offense or crime*); **cargar a una persona de** to charge someone with being ‖ *vn* to load; to turn (*said of wind*); to incline, to tip; (phonet.) to fall (*said of accent*); to crowd; (coll.) to overeat, to drink too much; **cargar con** to pick up, to carry; to walk away with, steal; to take upon oneself; to shoulder (*a gun*); **cargar sobre** to rest on; to devolve on; to pester, to importune ‖ *vr* to turn (*said of wind*); to become overcast; (coll.) to become bored; (coll.) to become annoyed; (coll.) to break; **cargarse de** to have in abundance, to be overloaded with; to be bathed in (*tears*); (coll.) to get rid of
cargareme *m* voucher, deposit voucher
cargazón *f* cargo; heaviness (*in stomach, head, etc.; in literary style*); mass of heavy clouds; share, portion
cargo *m* burden, weight; blame, charge; job, post, position, duty; management; care, charge, responsibility; (law) count; (com.) charge; pile of olive-oil bags; load of pressed grapes; (naut.) freighter; **a cargo de** in charge of (*a person*); **girar a cargo de** (com.) to draw on; **hacer cargo a uno de una cosa** to charge someone with something; **hacerse cargo de** to take charge of; to look into; to grasp, to realize; to understand; **hacerse cargo de** + *inf* to take it upon oneself to + *inf;* **librar a cargo de** (com.) to draw on; **ser en cargo a** to be indebted to; **tomar a su cargo** to take upon oneself; **vestir el cargo** to look the part; **cargo de conciencia** sense of guilt, burden on one's conscience
cargoso -sa *adj* burdensome, onerous; annoying, bothersome
carguero -ra *adj* of burden (*said of animals*); freight, freight-carrying; *m* (Am.) beast of burden
carguío *m* load; cargo, freight
cari *m* curry (*sauce, powder, or stew*)
caria *f* (arch.) shaft (*of column*)
cariacedo -da *adj* sour-faced, unpleasant
cariacontecido -da *adj* (coll.) woebegone, down in the mouth
cariacuchillado -da *adj* scar-faced
cariado -da *adj* carious
cariadura *f* (path.) caries
cariaguileño -ña *adj* (coll.) sharp-featured
carialegre *adj* (coll.) smiling
cariampollado -da or **cariampollar** *adj* (coll.) fat-cheeked, round-faced
cariancho -cha *adj* (coll.) broad-faced
cariar **§90** *va* to decay, cause to decay; *vr* to decay, become decayed
cariátide *f* (arch.) caryatid
caríbal *adj & mf* (obs.) var. of **caníbal**
Caribdis *f* (geog. & myth.) Charybdis
caribe *adj* Caribbean; *mf* Carib; *m* brute, savage; (ichth.) caribe
caribú *m* (*pl:* **-búes**) (zool.) caribou
caricato *m* buffo, buffoon
caricatura *f* caricature; cartoon
caricaturar *va* to caricature
caricaturesco -ca *adj* in caricature
caricaturista *mf* caricaturist; cartoonist
caricaturizar **§76** *va* to caricature
caricia *f* caress, petting; endearment
caricioso -sa *adj* caressing, affectionate
caricuerdo -da *adj* (coll.) wise-looking
carichato -ta *adj* flat-faced
caridad *f* charity
caridelantero -ra *adj* (coll.) forward, brazen
caridoliente *adj* sad-looking
cariedón *m* (ent.) weevil
carientismo *m* (rhet.) disguised irony
caries *f* (path.) caries, decay (*e.g., of teeth*); (agr.) blight
carifruncido -da *adj* (coll.) wrinkle-faced
carigordo -da *adj* (coll.) fat-faced
cariharto -ta *adj* (coll.) round-faced
carilampiño -ña *adj* (Am.) smooth-faced, beardless
carilargo -ga *adj* (coll.) long-faced
carilucio -cia *adj* (coll.) glossy-faced
carilla *f* mask (*of beekeeper*); page (*of book*)
carilleno -na *adj* (coll.) full-faced
carillón *m* (mus.) carillon
carimbar *va* (Am.) to brand
carimbo *m* (Am.) branding iron
carinegro -gra *adj* swarthy; blackface
cariño *m* love, affection; fondness, fond attention; (Am.) gift, present; **cariños** *mpl* words of love, show of affection
cariñoso -sa *adj* loving, affectionate, endearing
cariocinesis *f* (biol.) karyokinesis
cariofiláceo -a *adj* (bot.) caryophyllaceous
cariofilata *f* (bot.) avens; **cariofilata acuática** (bot.) purple or water avens
cariomitoma *m* (biol.) karyomitome
carioplasma *m* (biol.) karyoplasm
cariópside *f* (bot.) caryopsis
carioquinesis *f* var. of **cariocinesis**
cariosoma *m* (biol.) karyosome
cariotina *f* (biol.) karyotin
cariparejo -ja *adj* (coll.) impassive, stone-faced
carirraído -da *adj* (coll.) brazen-faced
carirredondo -da *adj* (coll.) round-faced
carisea *f* kersey
cariseto *m* coarse wool
carisma *m* (theol.) charism
carita *f* little face; (bot.) mesquite; **dar** or **hacer carita** (Am.) to smile back (*said of a woman flirting*); **carita blanca** (zool.) capuchin (*monkey*)
caritativo -va *adj* charitable; **caritativo con, para** or **para con** charitable to or toward
cariz *m* appearance (*of sky or weather*); (coll.) look, aspect
carlanca *f* dog collar with sharp points around it (*to protect the dog*); **tener muchas carlancas** (coll.) to be underhanded
carlancón -cona *adj* underhanded; *mf* underhanded person
carlear *vn* to pant
carleta *f* file; French slate
carlina *f* (bot.) carline thistle
carlinga *f* (aer.) cockpit; (naut.) mast step
carlismo *m* Carlism
carlista *adj & mf* Carlist
carlita *f* eyeglass, lens
Carlitos *m* Charlie
Carlomagno *m* Charlemagne
Carlos *m* Charles
Carlota *f* Charlotte; (*l.c*) *f* charlotte (*pudding*); **carlota rusa** charlotte russe
carlovingio -gia *adj & m* Carlovingian
carmañola *f* carmagnole (*jacket, song, and dance*)
carme *m* villa, country house and garden
Carmela *f* Carmela (*familiar form of Carmen*)
carmelina *f* second crop of vicuña wool
carmelita *adj* (Am.) brown; *adj & mf* Carmelite; *f* nasturtium bud (*used in salads*)
carmelitano -na *adj* Carmelite
carmen *m* carmen, song, poem; villa, country house and garden; (*cap.*) *f* Carmen; Order of Our Lady of Mount Carmel
carmenador *m* teasler (*man or machine*); haircomb
carmenadura *f* teasling
carmenar *va* to unravel, disentangle; to teasel; (coll.) to pull the hair of; (coll.) to fleece, to swindle; *vr* to come unraveled

carmes *m* var. of **quermes**
carmesí (*pl:* **-síes**) *adj* crimson; *m* crimson; kermes powder; red silk (*fabric*)
carmín *m* carmine (*dyestuff and color*); (bot.) wild rose; (bot.) pokeweed; **carmín de índigo** indigo extract
carminar *va* to carmine; *vr* to become carmine (*in color*)
carminativo -va *adj & m* (med.) carminative
carmíneo -a *adj* carmine
carminita *f* (mineral.) carminite
carnada *f* bait; (coll.) bait, lure, trap
carnadura *f* muscularity, flesh, strength
carnaje *m* salt beef, jerked beef
carnal *adj* carnal; full (*brother, cousin, etc.*); *m* non-Lenten period
carnalidad *f* carnality
carnalita *f* (mineral.) carnallite
carnaval *m* carnival
carnavalada *f* carnival stunt
carnavalesco -ca *adj* (pertaining to) carnival
carnaza *f* inner face of hide or skin; bait; (coll.) fleshiness (*of a person*)
carne *f* flesh; meat; preserves; **cobrar carnes** (coll.) to put on flesh; **criar carnes** to put on fat, put on weight; **echar carnes** (coll.) to put on flesh; **en carnes** naked; without dowry; **en carne viva** raw (*skin or sore*); **en vivas carnes** naked; **no ser carne ni pescado** to be neither fish nor fowl, to be nondescript, to be colorless; **perder carnes** to lose flesh; **poner toda la carne en el asador** (coll.) to stake all, to put all one's eggs in one basket; **ser de carne y hueso** (coll.) to be only human; **temblarle a uno las carnes** (coll.) to be in deathly fear; **tener carne de perro** (coll.) to have an iron constitution; **carne asada al horno** baked meat; **carne asada en parrillas** broiled meat; **carne cediza** tainted meat; **carne de cañón** cannon fodder; **carne de cerdo** pork; **carne de cordero** lamb; **carne de gallina** goose flesh, goose pimples; **carne de horca** gallows bird; **carne de membrillo** preserved quinces; **carne de pelo** rabbit meat; **carne de pluma** fowl (*as food*); **carne de puerco** pork; **carne de res** (Am.) beef; **carne de ternera** veal; **carne de vaca** beef; **carne de venado** venison; **carne fiambre** cold meat; **carne mollar** lean meat; **carne sin hueso** (coll.) cinch, snap; **carne y sangre** flesh and blood
carneada *f* (Am.) butchering
carnear *va* (Am.) to slaughter, to butcher; (Am.) to take in, to deceive
carnecilla *f* bump, lump (*on body*)
carnerada *f* flock of sheep
carneraje *m* sheep tax
carnereamiento *m* penalty for damage caused by sheep
carnerear *va* to kill (*sheep and cattle*) for damage they caused
carnerero *m* shepherd
carneril *adj* (pertaining to) sheep
carnerismo *m* (Am.) sheepishness
carnero *m* (zool.) sheep; mutton; battering ram; (dial.) sheepskin; (Am.) sheep (*person*); charnel; charnel house; family vault; **cantar para el carnero** (Am.) to die; **no hay tales carneros** there's no truth to it; **carnero ciclán** (vet.) cryptorchid; **carnero de la sierra** or **de la tierra** (Am.) alpaca, vicuña, llama; **carnero del Cabo** (orn.) albatross; **carnero de simiente** ram for breeding; **carnero marino** seal; **carnero llano** wether
carneruno -na *adj* (pertaining to) sheep; sheeplike, rammish
carnestolendas *fpl* Shrovetide, carnival
carnet *m* (*pl:* **-nets**) notebook; bankbook; dance card; **carnet de chófer** driver's license, operator's license; **carnet de identidad** identification card
carnicería *f* meat market, butcher shop; (fig.) carnage
carnicero -ra *adj* carnivorous; bloodthirsty; fattening (*said of pasture*); (coll.) meat-devouring; *mf* butcher; (fig.) butcher (*person guilty of cruel slaughter*); *m* (zool.) carnivore
cárnico -ca *adj* (pertaining to) meat
carnicol *m* half of cloven hoof
carnificación *f* (path.) carnification
carnificar §86 *vr* to carnify
carniseco -ca *adj* skinny
carnívoro -ra *adj* carnivorous; *m* (zool. & bot.) carnivore
carniza *f* (coll.) offal (*of butchered animal*); (coll.) decayed meat
carnosidad *f* fleshiness, corpulence; proud flesh; carnosity
carnosina *f* (chem.) carnosine
carnoso -sa *adj* fleshy; marrowy; meaty (*of meat; like meat*)
carnotita *f* (mineral.) carnotite
carnudo -da *adj* fleshy
carnuza *f* coarse cheap meat
caro -ra *adj* dear, expensive; dear, beloved ‖ **caro** *adv* dear ‖ *f* face; look; mien, countenance; front, façade; facing; flat surface; heads (*of coin*); face (*of coin or medal*); side (*of phonograph record*); **a cara descubierta** openly; **a cara o cruz** heads or tails; **a dos caras** two-facedly; **dar la cara** to be willing to take the consequences; **dar la cara por otro** (coll.) to answer for someone else; **darle en cara a uno** to cast or throw in one's teeth; **de cara** opposite, facing; in the face; **echar a cara o cruz** to flip up, to flip a coin; **echarle en cara a uno** to cast or throw in one's teeth; **hacer cara a** to face, to resist, to meet boldly; **lavar la cara a** (coll.) to fawn on; **no volver la cara atrás** to not flinch; **tener buena cara** to look well; to look good; **tener cara de** + *inf* to look as if + *cond*, e.g., **esta tela tiene cara de romperse pronto** this cloth looks as if it would tear soon; **tener mala cara** to look ill; to look bad; **cara a** facing; **cara a cara** face to face; **cara adelante** facing forward; **cara al público** with an audience; **cara atrás** facing backward; **cara de acelga** (coll.) sallow face; **cara de ajo** (coll.) vinegar face; **cara de aleluya** (coll.) cheerful face; **cara de corcho** (coll.) shamelessness; **cara de cuaresma** dismal countenance; **cara de cuchillo** (coll.) hatchet face; **cara de hereje** (coll.) baboon, fright; **cara de pascua** (coll.) smiling face; **cara de rallo** (coll.) pocked face; **cara de viernes** (coll.) wan face, sorry countenance; **cara de vinagre** (coll.) sour face, vinegar aspect; **cara dura** (coll.) cheeky
caroca *f* paintings hung in streets in public celebrations; clownish farce; (coll.) false affection, hypocrisy
carocha *f* eggs (*of insect*)
carochar *vn* to lay eggs (*said of an insect*)
Carolina *f* see **carolino**
carolingio -gia *adj & m* Carolingian
carolino -na *adj* Caroline; (*cap.*) *f* Caroline; **la Carolina del Norte** North Carolina; **la Carolina del Sur** South Carolina
caromomia *f* dry flesh of a mummy (*once used in medicine*)
Carón *m* (myth.) Charon
carona *f* saddle padding; saddlecloth; part of back where saddle rests
Caronte *m* (myth.) Charon
caroñoso -sa *adj* full of galls, full of sores (*said of an old horse*)
caroquero -ra *adj* fawning, flattering; *mf* fawner, flatterer
carosis *f* (path.) deep stupor
caroteno *m* (chem.) carotene
carótida *f* (anat.) carotid
carotídeo -a *adj* carotid
carotina *f* var. of **caroteno**
carozo *m* corncob; (dial.) core (*e.g., of an apple*)
carpa *f* (ichth.) carp; part of a bunch of grapes; (Am.) awning, tent, circus tent; **carpa dorada** goldfish
carpanel *adj* see **arco**
carpanta *f* (coll.) raging hunger
Cárpatos *mpl* Carpathians, Carpathian Mountains
carpe *m* (bot.) hornbeam, yoke elm
carpedal *m* woods or growth of hornbeams
carpelar *adj* carpellary, carpellate
carpelo *m* (bot.) carpel

carpeta *f* table cover; folder; portfolio; invoice; curtain over tavern door; coating; paving; (Am.) office desk; (Am.) bookkeeping department; (Am.) slab
carpetazo *m* blow with a table cover; **dar carpetazo a** to table, to shelve, to set aside, to pigeonhole
carpetero *m* filing cabinet
carpiano -na *adj* (anat.) carpal
carpidor *m* (Am.) weeder (*tool*)
carpincho *m* (zool.) capybara (*South American rodent*)
carpintear *vn* to carpenter
carpintería *f* carpentry, carpentering; carpenter shop; **carpintería de modelos** patternmaking; **carpintería de taller** millwork
carpinteril *adj* (pertaining to a) carpenter
carpintero *m* carpenter; (orn.) woodpecker; **carpintero de armar** framer; **carpintero de banco** shop carpenter; **carpintero de blanco** joiner; **carpintero de buque** ship carpenter, shipwright; **carpintero de carreta** wheelwright; **carpintero de fino** joiner; **carpintero de navío** ship carpenter, shipwright; **carpintero de obra de afuera** framer; **carpintero de prieto** wheelwright; **carpintero de ribera** ship carpenter, shipwright; **carpintero modelista** patternmaker; **carpintero naval** ship carpenter, shipwright
carpir *va* to stun, to knock out; (Am.) to weed
carpo *m* (anat.) carpus
carpobálsamo *m* (bot.) balm of Gilead (*tree and fruit*)
carpología *f* carpology
carquerol *m* treadle cord (*of loom*)
carquesa *f* carquaise (*glass-annealing furnace*)
carraco -ca *adj* (coll.) old, decrepit; *f* (naut.) carrack (*galleon*); piece of junk; tub, hulk (*clumsy old boat*); rattle; ratchet, ratchet brace; **la Carraca** Cádiz navy yard
carrada *f* cartful, cartload
carragaen *m* (bot.) carrageen
carral *m* wine barrel
carraleja *f* (ent.) oil beetle
carralero *m* cooper
carranca *f* var. of **carlanca**
carranza *f* iron point (*on dog collar*)
carraón *m* spelt
carrasca *f* (bot.) kermes oak
carrascal *m* growth of kermes oaks; (Am.) stony place
carrasco *m* var. of **carrasca**
carrascoso -sa *adj* full of kermes oaks
carraspada *f* negus (*drink*)
carraspear *vn* to be hoarse, to hawk
carraspeño -ña *adj* rough, harsh; hoarse
carraspeo *m* hoarseness, hawking
carraspera *f* (coll.) hoarseness
carraspique *m* (bot.) candytuft
carrasposo -sa *adj* chronically hoarse; (Am.) rough
carrasqueño -ña *adj* kermes-oak; (coll.) rough
carrasquera *f* var. of **carrascal**
carrasquilla *f* (bot.) germander
carrejo *m* hall
carrera *f* run; race; race track; stretch, course; career; road; avenue, boulevard; row, line; part (*in hair*); rafter, girder, joist; (mach.) stroke (*of piston*); run (*in stocking*); (mus.) run; (naut.) route, run; **carreras** *fpl* horse racing, turf; **a carrera abierta** at full speed; **a la carrera** running; **dar carrera a** to provide an education for; **de carrera** hastily; without thinking; career (*used as adj*); **no poder hacer carrera con** (coll.) to make no headway with, to be unable to bring to reason; **tomar carrera** to take a running start (*before a jump*); **carrera al trote** trotting race; **carrera a pie** foot race; **carrera armamentista** or **carrera de los armamentos** armament race; **carrera a reclamar** selling race; **carrera ascendente** upstroke; **carrera de admisión** or **aspiración** intake stroke; **carrera de baquetas** (mil. & fig.) gauntlet; **carrera de caballos** horse race; **carrera de compresión** compression stroke; **carrera de consolación** (sport) consolation race; **carrera de encendido** ignition stroke; **carrera de escape** exhaust stroke; **carrera de expansión** expansion stroke; **carrera de galgos** greyhound race; **carrera de Indias** trade with South America (*from Spain*); **carrera de ladrillos** course of brick; **carrera de campanario** (sport) steeplechase; **carrera de maratón** (sport) marathon race; **carrera de obstáculos** obstacle race; steeplechase; **carrera de relevos** (sport) relay race; **carrera de resistencia** (sport) endurance race; **carrera descendente** downstroke; **carrera de vallas** (sport) hurdles, hurdle race; **carrera de ventas** selling race; **carrera espacial** space race; **carrera motriz** power stroke
carrerilla *f* (mus.) run of an octave
carrerista *mf* race-track fan; bicycle racer; race-track bettor; auto racer; *m* outrider; *f* (slang) streetwalker; *adj* horsy
carrero *m* cartwright; driver, teamster; track; (naut.) wake; handcar driver
carreta *f* cart
carretada *f* cartful, cartload; (coll.) great amount, great number; **a carretadas** (coll.) in abundance, in flocks
carretaje *m* cartage, drayage
carretal *m* rough ashlar stone
carrete *m* spool, bobbin, reel; fishing reel; (elec.) coil; **carrete de encendido** (aut.) ignition coil; **carrete de inducción** (elec.) induction coil; **carrete de película** film spool; **carrete de resistencia** (elec.) resistance coil; **carrete primario** (elec.) primary coil; **carrete secundario** (elec.) secondary coil
carretear *va* to cart, to haul; to drive (*a cart*); (aer.) to taxi; *vn* (aer.) to taxi; *vr* to pull hard (*said of oxen or mules*)
carretel *m* (naut.) reel, spool; (naut.) log reel; marking line (*of ship carpenter*); (prov.) fishing reel
carretela *f* calash
carretera *f* see **carretero**
carretería *f* carts, wagons; cart or wagon shop; cartwright work, wagon work; carting business
carreteril *adj* driver's, teamster's
carretero -ra *adj* (pertaining to a) wagon or carriage; *m* cartwright, wheelwright; driver, carter, teamster; charioteer; **jurar como un carretero** (coll.) to swear like a trooper; *f* highway; **carretera biviaria** two-lane highway; **carretera de cuatro vías** four-lane highway; **carretera de peaje** turnpike; **carretera de vía libre** express highway; **carretera matriz** through highway
carretil *adj* (pertaining to a) cart
carretilla *f* wheelbarrow; truck, baggage truck; gocart (*for learning to walk*); snake, serpent (*kind of firecracker*); pastry tube; **de carretilla** by rote, by heart, mechanically; **carretilla de mano** handcart
carretillada *f* wheelbarrow load; baggage-truck load
carretillero *m* wheelbarrow man; baggageman (*who pushes a truck*)
carretón *m* cart; gocart; portable grindstone (*with treadle*); (rail.) truck; **carretón de lámpara** pulley for raising and lowering lamps in church; **carretón de remolque** trailer
carretonada *f* cartload
carretonero *m* cart driver, cart pusher; drayman
carricera *f* (bot.) plume grass
carricoche *m* covered cart; old hack; (dial.) dung cart
carricuba *f* street sprinkler
carriego *m* fish trap (*made of osier*); basket for bleaching flax
carril *m* track, rut; furrow; lane, narrow road; rail; **carril de cremallera** rack rail; **carril de toma** (elec.) third rail
carrilada *f* track, rut
carrilera *f* track, rut; (Am.) sidetrack
carrilero *m* (Am.) railroader; (Am.) thief, bandit
carrillada *f* fat in hog's jowls; **carrilladas** *fpl* quaking of jaws
carrillar *m* (naut.) hoisting tackle
carrillera *f* jaw; chin strap, chin stay; cheekpiece (*of armor*)

carrillo *m* cheek; pulley; cart, truck; **comer a dos carrillos** (coll.) to have two sources of income; (coll.) to play both sides, to keep in with both sides
carrilludo -da *adj* round-cheeked
carriola *f* cariole; trundle bed, truckle bed
carrizada *f* (naut.) string of barrels being towed
carrizal *m* growth of ditch reed
carrizo *m* (bot.) ditch reed; **carrizo de las pampas** (bot.) pampas grass
carro *m* cart, wagon; truck; car, auto; railway car; streetcar; chariot; (mach.) carriage (*e.g., of a typewriter*); cartload, wagonload; carload; **el Carro** (astr.) the Dipper; **pare Vd. el carro** (coll.) hold your horses (*restrain yourself*); **tirar del carro** (coll.) to do all the work; **untar el carro** (coll.) to bribe; **carro alegórico** float (*in a parade*); **carro blindado** (mil.) armored car; **carro completo** (rail.) carload lot; **carro correo** (rail.) mail car; **carro cuba** (rail.) tank car; **carro de asalto** (mil.) heavy tank; **carro de carga** (rail.) freight car; **carro de combate** (mil.) combat car, tank; **carro de equipajes** (rail.) baggage car; **carro de guerra** chariot; **carro de hacienda** (Am.) stock car, cattle car; **carro de mudanza** moving van; **carro de plataforma** (rail.) flatcar; **carro de remolque** trailer; **carro de riego** street sprinkler; **carro entero** (rail.) carload lot; **carro frigorífico** (rail.) refrigerator car; **carro fuerte** platform carriage; **carro fúnebre** hearse; **carro ganadero** stock car, cattle car; **Carro Mayor** (astr.) Big Dipper; **Carro Menor** (astr.) Little Dipper; **carro nevera** (rail.) refrigerator car; **carro plano** (rail.) flatcar; **carro romano** chariot; **carro salón** (rail.) chair car; **carro transbordador** (rail.) transfer table, traverser
carró *m* (*pl:* **carrós**) (Am.) diamond (*playing card*); **carrós** *mpl* (Am.) diamonds (*suit of playing cards*)
carrocería *f* carriage shop; body (*e.g., of automobile*)
carrocero -ra *adj* (pertaining to a) carriage; (pertaining to a) body; *m* carriage maker, wheelwright
carrocín *m* shay (*light carriage*)
carrocha *f* eggs (*of insect*)
carrochar *vn* to lay eggs (*said of an insect*)
carromatero *m* cart driver
carromato *m* covered cart (*drawn by one horse or by two or more in single file*)
carrón *m* hod of bricks
carronada *f* carronade
carroña *f* see **carroño**
carroñar *va* to infect (*sheep*) with the scab
carroño -ña *adj* carrion (*rotten*); *f* carrion
carroñoso -sa *adj* carrion-smelling
carroza *f* coach, stately carriage; (naut.) awning; (Am.) hearse; **carroza alegórica** float
carruaje *m* carriage, vehicle
carruajero *m* driver, carriage driver
carruco *m* cart with solid wooden wheels
carrucha *f* pulley; reel, spool
carrujado -da *adj & m* var. of **encarrujado**
carrusel *m* cavalcade; carousel, merry-go-round
carsaya *f* kersey
carta *f* letter; chart; charter; playing card; map; bill of fare; **a carta cabal** thorough, in every respect; **a cartas vistas** with one's cards on the table; (coll.) with inside information; **a la carta** à la carte; **echar las cartas** to tell or read one's fortune with cards; **jugar a cartas vistas** to put one's cards on the table; (coll.) to act on inside information; **no saber a qué carta quedarse** to be unable to make up one's mind; **no ver carta** (coll.) to have a bad run of cards; **poner las cartas boca arriba** to put one's cards on the table; **tomar cartas en** (coll.) to get into, to take part in; **carta aérea** air-mail letter; **carta blanca** carte blanche; **carta certificada** registered letter; **carta credencial** (dipl.) credentials; **carta de crédito** letter of credit; **carta de fletamento** (naut.) charter party; **carta de marca** letter of marques; **carta de marear** ocean chart; **carta de Mercátor** (geog.) Mercator's chart; **carta de naturaleza** naturalization papers; **carta de pedido** letter ordering merchandise; **carta de presentación** letter of introduction; **carta de vecindad** registration certificate; **carta de venta** bill of sale; **carta general** form letter; **Carta Magna** Magna Charta; **carta meteorológica** weather map; **carta orden de crédito** (com.) letter of credit; **carta partida** (naut.) charter party; **carta por avión** air-mail letter; **carta postal** (Am.) postal card
cartabón *m* triangle (*used in drafting*); size stick (*for measuring foot*); gunner's quadrant; gusset plate; angle made by two slopes of a roof
cartagenero -ra *adj* (pertaining to) Cartagena; *mf* native or inhabitant of Cartegena
cartaginense or **cartaginés -nesa** *adj & mf* Carthaginian
Cartago *f* Carthage
cártama *f* or **cártamo** *m* (bot.) safflower, bastard saffron
cartapacio *m* notebook, memorandum book; dossier; satchel (*for schoolboy's books*); writing book (*with ruled lines for beginners*)
cartapel *m* silly document
cartazo *m* (coll.) letter or note of censure
cartear *vn* to play low cards (*to feel one's way*); *vr* to write to each other, to correspond
cartel *m* poster, placard, show bill; lampoon; cartel (*written challenge*); (econ.) cartel, trust; (dipl. & pol.) cartel; (taur.) fame, reputation; (theat.) bill; **dar cartel a** (coll.) to lend prestige to; (coll.) to headline; **se prohíbe fijar carteles** post no bills; **tener cartel** (slang) to make a hit, be the rage (*said of an actor, bullfighter, etc.*); **cartel de teatro** bill
cartela *f* (arch.) cartouche (*tablet for ornament or inscription*); bracket, support; tag, label; (arch.) bracket, console, corbel
cartelero -ra *adj* striking, catching, appealing; *m* billposter; *f* billboard; amusement page (*of newspaper*)
cartelista *mf* cartelist; lampooner; poster designer; billboard painter, sign painter
cartelón *m* show bill, poster; chart
carteo *m* correspondence, exchange of letters; play, playing (*of cards*)
cárter *m* (mach.) housing, case; **cárter de engranajes** (mach.) gear case; **cárter del cigüeñal** or **del motor** (mach.) crankcase
cartera *f* portfolio (*portable case for papers; office of minister; list of securities*); letter file, desk pad; pocket flap; (b.b.) tuck; **cartera de bolsillo** billfold, wallet
cartería *f* job of letter carrier; sorting room (*in post office*)
carterista *m* pickpocket
cartero *m* postman, mailman, letter carrier
cartesianismo *m* Cartesianism
cartesiano -na *adj & mf* Cartesian
carteta *f* lansquenet (*card game*)
cartilagíneo -a *adj* (ichth.) cartilaginous
cartilaginoso -sa *adj* cartilaginous, gristly; (ichth.) cartilaginous
cartílago *m* (anat.) cartilage
cartilla *f* primer, speller; short treatise; deposit book; identity card (*e.g., of servants*); liturgical calendar; **leer la cartilla a** (coll.) to lecture, to call down; **no estar en la cartilla** (coll.) to be unusual or extraordinary; **no saber la cartilla** (coll.) to be completely ignorant of the subject; **cartilla de abastecimiento** or **racionamiento** ration book
cartillero -ra *adj* (coll.) hackneyed; (coll.) ham
cartivana *f* (b.b.) hinge
cartografía *f* cartography
cartográfico -ca *adj* cartographic
cartógrafo -fa *mf* cartographer
cartolas *fpl* var. of **artolas**
cartomancía *f* fortunetelling with cards, cartomancy
cartómetro *m* chartometer
cartón *m* cardboard, pasteboard; carton, cardboard box; cartoon (*model for fresco, tapestry, etc.*); **cartón alquitranado** tar paper; **cartón de asbesto** asbestus board; **cartón de paja** strawboard; **cartón de yeso** plaster-

board, wallboard; **cartón embetunado** tar paper; **cartón piedra** papier-mâché; **cartón tabla** wallboard
cartonajes *mpl* cardboard products, cardboard boxes
cartoné; en cartoné (b.b.) in boards, bound in boards
cartonería *f* cardboard factory or shop; cardboard business
cartonero -ra *adj* (pertaining to) cardboard; *mf* cardboard maker or dealer
cartuchera *f* cartridge box; cartridge belt
cartucho *m* cartridge; roll of coins; paper cone or bag; (arch.) cartouche (*tablet for ornament or inscription*); **cartucho en blanco** blank cartridge
cartuja & **Cartuja** *f* see **cartujo**
cartujano -na *adj* & *m* Carthusian
cartujo -ja *adj* Carthusian; *m* Carthusian, Carthusian monk; (coll.) silent fellow, recluse; *f* Carthusian monastery, charterhouse; (*cap.*) *f* Carthusian order
cartulario *m* chartulary; archivist
cartulina *f* light or fine cardboard
cartusana *f* fancy braid
carúncula *f* (anat., bot. & zool.) caruncle; **carúncula lagrimal** (anat.) lachrymal caruncle
carunculado -da *adj* carunculate
caruncular *adj* caruncular
carvajal *m* woods of oak trees
carvajo or **carvallo** *m* (bot.) oak tree
carvi *m* caraway, caraway seeds
casa *f* house; home; household; apartment; firm; square (*e.g., of checkerboard*); **¡convida la casa!** the drinks are on the house!; **echar la casa por la ventana** (coll.) to go to a lot of expense (*to entertain or in other ways*); **empezar la casa por el tejado** to put the cart before the horse; **en casa** home, at home; **en casa de** at the home, office, shop, etc. of; **guardar la casa** to be confined to the house; **hacer casa** to get rich; **ir a buscar casa** to go house hunting; **no tener casa ni hogar** to have neither house nor home; **poner casa** to set up housekeeping; **por casa** at the house; **Casa Blanca** White House; **casa capitular** chapter house; **casa central** home office; **casa consistorial** town hall, city hall; **casa cuna** foundling home; **casa de asistencia** (Am.) boarding house; **casa de azotea** penthouse; **casa de banca** banking house; **casa de baños** bathhouse; **casa de beneficencia** settlement, settlement house; **casa de bombas** pump house; **casa de camas** bawdyhouse; **casa de campo** country house; **casa de caridad** poorhouse; **casa de citas** house of assignation; **casa de comercio** business house; **casa de comida** eating house; **casa de corrección** reform school, house of correction; **casa de correos** post office; **casa de departamentos** (Am.) apartment house; **casa de Dios** God's house, house of God (*church*); **casa de empeños** pawnshop; **casa de expósitos** foundling home or hospital; **casa de fieras** menagerie; **casa de huéspedes** boarding house; **casa de juego** gambling house; **casa de locos** madhouse; (fig.) madhouse; **casa de maternidad** maternity hospital; **casa de medianería** house between two others (*in a row*); **casa de modas** dress shop; **casa de moneda** mint; **casa de montería** hunting lodge; **casa de moradores** tenement house; **casa de niñas** disorderly house; **casa de oración** house of prayer; **casa de orates** insane asylum; **casa de placer** country house; **casa de posada** boarding house; **casa de postas** posthouse; **casa de préstamos** pawnshop; **casa de pupilos** boarding house; **casa de salud** private hospital; **casa de sanidad** health office; **casa de socorro** first-aid station, emergency hospital; **casa de tía** (coll.) jail; (hum.) tavern; **casa de vacas** dairy; **casa de vecindad** or **de vecinos** apartment house, tenement house; **casa editorial** publishing house; **casa grande** mansion; (hum.) big house (*jail*); **casa matriz** main office; **casa medianera** house between two others (*in a row*); **casa mortuoria** house of mourning (*where a death has occurred*); **casa pública** brothel; **casa real** royal palace; royal family; **Casa Rosada** Pink House (*official residence of chief executive of Argentina*); **casas baratas** low-cost housing; **casa solar** or **solariega** manor house, ancestral mansion
casabe *m* cassava flour; cassava bread; (ichth.) amberfish
casaca *f* dress coat, musketeer's coat; (coll.) wedding, marriage; **cambiar de casaca** or **volver casaca** or **la casaca** (coll.) to become a turncoat
casación *f* (law) cassation, annulment
casacón *m* greatcoat
casadero -ra *adj* marriageable
casado -da *adj* married; *mf* married person, spouse; *m* (print.) imposition
casal *m* country place; (Am.) pair (*male and female*)
casalicio *m* house, building, edifice
casamata *f* (fort. & naut.) casemate
casamentero -ra *adj* matchmaking; *mf* matchmaker
casamiento *m* marriage; wedding
Casandra *f* (myth. & fig.) Cassandra
casapuerta *f* vestibule, entrance
casaquilla *f* jacket
casar *m* hamlet; *va* to marry; to marry off (*a daughter*); to match, to harmonize; (law) to abrogate, annul, break; *vn* to marry, get married; to match, to harmonize; **casar con** to get married to; *vr* to marry, get married; **casarse con** to get married to; **casarse en segundas nupcias** to marry the second time; **no casarse con nadie** (coll.) to get tied up with nobody
casarón *m* large tumble-down house
casatienda *f* store and home in same building
casca *f* tanning bark; grape skins; marchpane
cascabel *m* tinkle bell, sleigh bell; rattlebrain; cascabel (*of a cannon*); **de cascabel gordo** (coll.) cheap, melodramatic; **ponerle cascabel al gato** (coll.) to bell the cat
cascabelada *f* noisy village celebration; (mus.) chimes (*of organ*); (coll.) piece of nonsense, indiscretion
cascabelear *va* (coll.) to cajole, to beguile; *vn* to jingle; (coll.) to behave in an inconsiderate manner
cascabeleo *m* jingle, jingling
cascabelero -ra *adj* (coll.) thoughtless, featherbrained; *mf* featherbrain; *m* baby's rattle
cascabelillo *m* little sweet plum
cascabelito *m* (bot.) locoweed
cascabillo *m* tinkle bell; glume, chaff, husk; cup of acorn
cascaciruelas *mf* (*pl:* **-las**) (coll.) contemptible good-for-nothing; **hacer lo que cascaciruelas** (coll.) to make a lot of fuss for nothing
cascado -da *adj* broken, infirm; weak, hollow (*voice*); *f* cascade, waterfall
cascadura *f* breaking, splitting
cascajal *m* or **cascajar** *m* place full of gravel, gravel pit; dump for grape skins
cascajera *f* place full of gravel, gravel pit
cascajero *m* (Am.) gravel pit; (Am.) gold mine not completely exhausted
cascajo *m* gravel, crushed stone; (coll.) broken crockery, rubbish, junk; **estar hecho un cascajo** (coll.) to be old and worn-out, to be a wreck
cascajoso -sa *adj* gravelly
cascamajar *va* to crush, to break up
cascamiento *m* breaking, splitting
cascanueces *m* (*pl:* **-ces**) nutcracker; (orn.) nutcracker
cascapiñones *m* (*pl:* **-nes**) pine-nut sheller; nutcracker for pine nuts; (orn.) hawfinch
cascar §86 *va* to crack, to split; (coll.) to break (*someone's health*); (coll.) to beat, to hit; *vn* to chatter; *vr* to crack, to split; (coll.) to break (*said of health, of the voice, etc.*)
cáscara *f* rind, peel, hull, shell; bark, crust; **¡cáscaras!** *interj* (coll.) upon my word!; **dar cáscaras de novillo a** (Am.) to whip, to beat; **ser de la cáscara amarga** (coll.) to be wild or flighty; (Am.) to be determined or resolute; **cáscara amarga** (pharm.) cascara

amarga; **cáscara rueda** (Am.) ring-around-a-rosy; **cáscara sagrada** (bot.) cascara or cascara buckthorn; (pharm.) cascara or cascara sagrada
cascarela *f* lansquenet (*card game*)
cascarilla *f* (pharm.) Peruvian bark, cinchona bark; (pharm.) cascarilla, sweetwood bark; foil (*metal*); powdered eggshell (*cosmetic*)
cascarillero -ra *mf* gatherer of cinchona, dealer in cinchona; *m* (bot.) cinchona
cascarillo *m* (bot.) cinchona
cascarón *m* eggshell; broken eggshell (*from which chick has emerged*); (arch.) calotte (*half cupola*); (Am.) cascaron (*filled with confetti*); **cascarón de nuez** (coll.) cockleshell (*light boat*)
cascarrabias *mf* (*pl:* **-bias**) (coll.) grouch, crab
cascarria *f* dried splashes of mud on lower part of clothing; (Am.) sheep dung stuck to wool
cascarrón -rrona *adj* (coll.) rough, harsh, gruff
cascarudo -da *adj* thick-shelled
cascaruleta *f* (coll.) chattering of teeth caused by hitting oneself on the chin
casco *m* skull; hoof; potsherd, broken piece; quarter (*of a fruit*); coat, shell (*of an onion*); crown (*of hat*); hulk (*of old ship*); hull (*of ship*); head (*of cask or barrel*); cask, vat, barrel; casque, headpiece; helmet (*of armor; of soldier, fireman, diver, etc.*); headset, headpiece; shell, container; bottle, liquid container; (dial. & Am.) slice (*e.g., of orange*); (mach.) shell, casing; tree (*of saddle*); **romperse los cascos** (coll.) to rack one's brains; **tener los cascos vacíos** (coll.) to be empty-headed; **casco de población** or **casco urbano** city limits
cascote *m* piece of rubble; rubbish, debris
cascudo -da *adj* large-hoofed
caseación *f* curdling
caseasa *f* (biochem.) casease
caseico -ca *adj* caseic
caseificación *f* (path.) caseation
caseificar §86 *va* to change into casein; to separate casein from (*milk*)
caseína *f* (biochem.) casein
caseinógeno *m* (biochem.) caseinogen
cáseo -a *adj* caseous; *m* curd
caseoso -sa *adj* caseous
casera *f* see **casero**
casería *f* country place, country house with outbuildings; housekeeping; (Am.) customers
caserío *m* country house; group of houses, hamlet
caserna *f* (fort.) armored barracks
casero -ra *adj* homemade; house (*e.g., dress*); home (*e.g., gathering*); home-loving; (sport) partial to home team; *mf* caretaker, janitor; renter; (Am.) huckster; *m* landlord; *f* landlady; housekeeper
caserón *m* var. of **casarón**
caseta *f* small house; bathhouse; stall (*at a fair*); booth
casetón *m* (arch.) coffer, caisson
casi *adv* almost, nearly; **casi casi** or **casi que** very nearly
casia *f* (bot.) cassia, stinking weed, ringworm bush
casicontrato *m* (law) quasi contract
casilla *f* hut, shack; cabin, booth; cab (*of locomotive or truck*); column or square (*on sheet of paper*); pigeonhole; square (*of checkerboard*); point (*of backgammon board*); ticket office; (aer.) nacelle, cockpit; (Am.) water closet; (Am.) bird trap; (Am.) post-office box; (dial.) lockup, jail; **sacar de sus casillas** (coll.) to jolt (*a person*) out of his old habits; (coll.) to drive crazy; **salir de sus casillas** (coll.) to forget oneself, to fly off the handle, to go wild; **casilla de correos** (Am.) post-office box
casillero -ra *mf* (rail.) crossing guard; *m* set of pigeonholes, filing cabinet; (sport) scoreboard
casimba *f* (Am.) well, spring
casimir *m* cashmere; cassimere
casino *m* casino; club; political club; clubhouse; recreation hall
Casio *m* Cassius
Casiopea *f* (myth. & astr.) Cassiopeia
casis *f* (bot.) cassis (*plant and liquor*); (zool.) queen conch
casiterita *f* (chem.) cassiterite
casitienda *f* var. of **casatienda**
casmodia *f* (path.) excessive yawning
caso *m* case; chance; event, happening; (gram. & med.) case; **dado caso que** supposing that; **de caso pensado** deliberately, on purpose; **en caso de** in case of, in the event of; **en el caso de que** in case; **en tal caso** in such a case; **en todo caso** in any case, at all events; **hacer al caso** (coll.) to be to the purpose; to be the point at issue; **hacer caso a** to mind, to notice; **hacer caso de** (coll.) to pay attention to, to take into account; **hacer caso omiso de** to pass over in silence, to not mention; **no venir al caso** to be beside the point; **poner por caso** to take as an example; **vamos al caso** (coll.) let's get to the point; **venir al caso** to be opportune, to be just the thing; **verse en el caso de** + *inf* to find oneself obliged to + *inf;* **caso de conformidad** in case you agree; **caso fortuito** mischance; act of God; **caso que** in case
casón *m* large house
casorio *m* (coll.) hasty marriage, unwise marriage
caspa *f* dandruff; scurf
caspera *f* fine comb for dandruff
caspiano -na *adj & mf* Caspian
caspicias *fpl* (coll.) offal, leavings
caspio -pia *adj & mf* Caspian
caspiroleta *f* (Am.) eggnog
cáspita *interj* well, well!, upon my word!
casposo -sa *adj* full of dandruff
casquería *f* tripe shop
casquero *m* tripe dealer
casquetazo *m* blow with the head
casquete *m* skullcap, calotte; cap; helmet; wig; canopy (*of parachute*); **casquete esférico** (geom.) zone of one base; **casquete polar** polar cap (*of Mars*); polar region (*of earth*)
casquiacopado -da *adj* cup-hoofed
casquiblando -da *adj* soft-hoofed
casquiderramado -da *adj* wide-hoofed
casquijo *m* gravel, ballast
casquilucio -cia *adj* (coll.) scatterbrained
casquilla *f* queen cell
casquillo *m* tip, cap, butt; ferrule; socket; sleeve, bushing; metal arrowhead; (Am.) horseshoe; cartridge case; metal part of pasteboard cartridge; **casquillos** *mpl* metal trimmings
casquimuleño -ña *adj* narrow-hoofed (*like mules*)
casquivano -na *adj* (coll.) scatterbrained
casta *f* see **casto**
Castálidas *fpl* (myth.) Castalides
castaña *f* see **castaño**
castañar *m*, **castañal** *m* or **castañeda** *f* woods of chestnut trees, chestnut grove
castañero -ra *mf* chestnut vendor; *m* (orn.) grebe
castañeta *f* castanet; snapping of the fingers; click with the tongue
castañetada *f* or **castañetazo** *m* click of castanets; cracking of roasting chestnut; cracking of joints
castañeteado *m* clicking of castanets
castañetear *va* to snap or to click (*the fingers*); to click off (*e.g., a seguidilla*) with the castanets; *vn* to click; to chatter (*said of teeth*); to crack (*said of knee joints*)
castañeteo *m* clicking (*of fingers or castanets*); chattering (*of teeth*)
castaño -ña *adj* chestnut, chestnut-colored ‖ *m* (bot.) chestnut, Spanish chestnut (*tree and wood*); chestnut (*color*); **pasar de castaño obscuro** (coll.) to be too much, to be too much trouble; **castaño de Indias** (bot.) horse chestnut ‖ *f* chestnut; demijohn; knot of hair, chignon; **sacarle a uno las castañas del fuego** to pull someone's chestnuts out of the fire; **castaña de Indias** horse chestnut; **castaña de Pará** Brazil nut
castañola *f* (ichth.) pomfret
castañuelo -la *adj* chestnut, chestnut-colored; *f* castanet; lewis (*used to hoist stones*); (bot.) plant of the sedge family (*Bulbocastanum in-*

crassatanum); **estar como unas castañuelas** (coll.) to be bubbling over with joy
castellán *m* castellan
castellana *f* see **castellano**
castellanismo *m* Castilianism
castellanización *f* Hispanicization
castellanizar §76 *va* to make (*a foreign word*) Spanish, to Hispanicize
castellano -na *adj & mf* Castilian; *m* Castilian, Spanish (*language*); castellan; lord of the castle; *f* chatelaine; assonanced octosyllabic verse of four lines
castellar *m* (bot.) St.-John's-wort
casticidad *f* purity, correctness (*in language*)
casticismo *m* purism
casticista *mf* purist
castidad *f* chastity, purity
castigable *adj* punishable
castigación *f* var. of **castigo**
castigadera *f* strap to tie clapper of wether's bell
castigador -dora *mf* punisher, castigator; *m* (coll.) seducer, Don Juan
castigar §59 *va* to punish, chastise; to castigate; to mortify (*the flesh*); to correct (*style, writing*); to cut down (*expenses*); (slang) to captivate, to break the heart of
castigo *m* punishment, chastisement; castigation; correction
Castilla *f* Castile; **¡ancha Castilla!** free and easy!; **Castilla la Nueva** New Castile; **Castilla la Vieja** Old Castile
castillaje *m* castle toll (*for passing through territory of castle*)
castillejo *m* small castle; gocart; scaffolding, trestlework
castillería *f* castle toll; castle-repair tax
castillete *m* small castle; **castillete de mina** gallows, headframe
castillo *m* castle; howdah; queen cell; **castillo en el aire** castle in Spain, castle in the air; **castillo de naipes** house of cards; **castillo de proa** (naut.) forecastle
castilluelo *m* castlet
castina *f* (metal.) limestone flux
castizo -za *adj* pure-blooded; pure, correct, chaste (*language*); real, genuine; prolific
casto -ta *adj* chaste, pure; *f* caste; race, breed; kind, quality; high breeding
castor *m* (zool.) beaver; beaver (*woolen cloth*)
Cástor *m* (myth., astr. & naut.) Castor; **Cástor y Pólux** (myth., astr. & naut.) Castor and Pollux
castorcillo *m* beaver cloth
castoreño *m* beaver (*hat*)
castóreo *m* castor, castoreum (*oily substance*)
castorina *f* beaver cloth; (chem.) castorin
castra *f* pruning; pruning season
castración *f* castration; pruning; extraction of honeycombs
castradera *f* honey extractor
castrador *m* castrator, sow-gelder
castradura *f* castration; scar left from castration
castrametación *f* (mil.) castrametation
castrapuercas *m* (*pl:* **-cas**) gelder's whistle
castrar *va* to castrate; to prune, cut back (*a plant*); to extract combs from (*hive*); to weaken
castrazón *f* extraction of honeycombs; season for extracting honeycombs
castrense *adj* (pertaining to the) army, military
castro *m* hopscotch; extraction of honeycombs; (dial.) headland
castrón *m* castrated goat
casual *adj* accidental, chance, casual; (gram.) case; **casuales** *mpl* priest's fee (*for baptism, marriage, funeral, etc.*)
casualidad *f* chance, accident; **por casualidad** by chance
casuarina *f* (bot.) beefwood, she-oak, swamp oak
casuario *m* (orn.) cassowary
casuca *f*, **casucha** *f* or **casucho** *m* shack, shanty
casuísta *adj* casuistic; *mf* casuist
casuístico -ca *adj* casuistic or casuistical; *f* casuistry; (med.) clinical report
casulla *f* chasuble
casullero *m* church-vestment tailor
cata *f* tasting, sampling; taste, sample; test pit; test boring
catabolismo *m* (biol.) catabolism
catacaldos *m* (*pl:* **-dos**) (coll.) rolling stone; (coll.) meddler, intruder
cataclísmico -ca *adj* cataclysmic
cataclismo *m* cataclysm
catacresis *f* (*pl:* **-sis**) (rhet.) catachresis
catacumba *f* catacomb
catadióptrico -ca *adj* (phys.) catadioptric
catador *m* taster, sampler
catadura *f* tasting, sampling; face, countenance
catafalco *m* catafalque
cataforesis *f* (med. & chem.) cataphoresis
catalán -lana *adj* Catalan; Catalonian; *mf* Catalan; *m* Catalan (*language*)
catalanidad *f* Catalan spirit or nature
catalanismo *m* Catalonian autonomy movement or doctrine; Catalanism (*word or expression*)
catalanista *mf* partisan of Catalonian autonomy; Catalanist (*one versed in Catalan*)
catalasa *f* (chem.) catalase
cataléctico -ca or **catalecto -ta** *adj* catalectic
catalejo *m* spyglass
catalepsia *f* (path.) catalepsis or catalepsy
cataléptico -ca *adj & mf* cataleptic
catalicón *m* var. of **diacatolicón**
Catalina *f* Catherine
catalineta *f* (ichth.) catalufa
catálisis *f* (chem.) catalysis
catalítico -ca *adj* catalytic
catalizador *m* (chem.) catalyst, catalyzer, catalytic agent
catalogación *f* cataloguing
catalogador -dora *adj* cataloguing
catalogar §59 *va* to catalogue
catálogo *m* catalogue
catalpa *f* (bot.) catalpa
catalufa *f* variegated carpet material; double taffeta; (ichth.) catalufa
Cataluña *f* Catalonia
catamarán *m* (naut.) catamaran
catán *m* catan, oriental cutlass
cataplasma *f* poultice; **cataplasma de mostaza** mustard plaster; *mf* (coll.) nuisance, pest, bore; (coll.) physical wreck (*person*)
cataplum *interj* bang!, boom!
catapulta *f* catapult; (aer.) catapult
catapultar *va* to catapult
catar *va* to taste, to sample; to look at, to examine, to check; to pass on; to look out for; to respect, to esteem; to extract combs from (*hive*)
cataraña *f* (orn.) sheldrake
catarata *f* cataract, waterfall; (path.) cataract; **abrirse las cataratas del cielo** to pour, to rain hard; **tener cataratas** (coll.) to be blind (*e.g., with ignorance*)
catarina *f* (Am.) pulque cup; (bot.) Mexican fire plant
catarral *adj* catarrhal
catarro *m* (path.) catarrh; head cold
catarroso -sa *adj* catarrhal; rheumy
catarsis *f* (aesthetics, med. & psychoanal.) catharsis
catártico -ca *adj* cathartic
catasalsas *mf* (*pl:* **-sas**) (coll.) var. of **catacaldos**
catastral *adj* cadastral
catastro *m* cadastre
catástrofe *f* catastrophe; (theat. & geol.) catastrophe
catastrófico -ca *adj* catastrophic
cataviento *m* (naut.) dogvane
catavino *m* cup for tasting wine; winetaster (*pipette*)
catavinos *m* (*pl:* **-nos**) winetaster (*person*); (coll.) rounder (*from one tavern to another*)
Catay *m* Cathay
cateador *m* prospecting hammer; (Am.) prospector
catear *va* to search for; to sample; (coll.) to flunk; (Am.) to explore, prospect for; (Am.) to break into, to search (*a house*)

catecismo *m* catechism
catecú *m* (*pl:* **-cúes**) catechu
catecumenado *m* catechumenate
catecúmeno -na *mf* (eccl. & fig.) catechumen
cátedra *f* chair, professorship; seat of the professor; class; subject; (eccl.) cathedra; **explicar una cátedra de** to hold a professorship of; **poner** or **sentar cátedra** to hold forth; **cátedra del Espíritu Santo** pulpit; **cátedra de San Pedro** Chair of Saint Peter (*papal see; actual chair*)
catedral *adj* & *f* cathedral
catedralicio -cia *adj* (pertaining to a) cathedral
catedralidad *f* status of a cathedral
catedrática *f* woman professor; professor's wife
catedrático *m* university professor; (eccl.) cathedraticum
categoría *f* category; class, kind; quality, condition; status, standing; **de categoría** of importance, prominent
categórico -ca *adj* categorical
catenario -ria *adj* catenary; *f* (math.) catenary
catenular *adj* catenulate
cateo *m* (Am.) sampling; (Am.) prospecting
catequesis *f* or **catequismo** *m* religious instruction, catechizing; teaching by questions and answers
catequista *mf* catechist
catequístico -ca *adj* catechistic (*pertaining to a catechism*); catechetical (*presented in the form of questions and answers*)
catequizador -dora *mf* forceful arguer
catequizante *adj* catechizing
catequizar **§76** *va* to catechize; to bring around, win over
caterva *f* throng, crowd, mob
catéter *m* (surg.) catheter
cateterismo *m* or **cateterización** *f* (surg.) catheterization
cateterizar **§76** *va* (surg.) catheterize
cateto -ta *mf* rustic, villager; *m* (geom.) leg (*of a right-angled triangle*)
catetómetro *m* (phys.) cathetometer
catilinaria *f* oration of Cicero against Catiline; vehement denunciation
catín *m* (metal.) copper crucible for forming rosettes
catión *m* (elec.) cation
catite *m* loaf of the finest sugar; light slap
cato *m* catechu
catódico -ca *adj* cathode, cathodic
cátodo *m* (elec.) cathode
catolicidad *f* catholicity; Catholicity, Catholicism
catolicísimo -ma *adj super* Most Catholic
catolicismo *m* Catholicism; **catolicismo romano** Roman Catholicism
católico -ca *adj* catholic; Catholic; **no estar muy católico** (coll.) to be under the weather; *mf* Catholic; **católico romano** Roman Catholic
catolizar **§76** *va* & *vr* to catholicize
Catón *m* Cato; (*l.c.*) *m* reader (*for children*); severe critic
catoniano -na *adj* Catonian
catóptrico -ca *adj* catoptric; *f* (opt.) catoptrics
catorce *adj* fourteen; **las catorce** two P.M.; *m* fourteen; fourteenth (*in dates*)
catorceavo -va *adj* & *m* var. of **catorzavo**
catorceno -na *adj* fourteenth
catorzavo -va *adj* & *m* fourteenth
catre *m* cot; **catre de tijera** folding cot
catrecillo *m* campstool, folding seat
catricofre *m* folding bed
catrín -trina *adj* (Am.) swell, sporty
Catulo *m* Catullus
caucáseo -a or **caucasiano -na** *adj* & *mf* Caucasian (*of the Caucasus*)
caucásico -ca *adj* & *mf* Caucasian (*white*)
Cáucaso *m* Caucasus
cauce *m* river bed; channel, trench; channel, passage; **cauce de salida** tailrace
caución *f* caution, precaution; (law) pledge, security, bond, bail
caucionar *va* to prevent (*harm or damage*); (law) to give security or bail for
cauchal *m* rubber plantation
cauchero -ra *adj* rubber; *m* rubber gatherer; rubber worker; *f* (bot.) rubber plant
caucho *m* rubber; (bot.) rubber plant; rubber raincoat; **caucho duro** or **endurecido** hard rubber; **caucho esponjoso** foam rubber; **caucho regenerado** reclaimed rubber; **caucho sintético** synthetic rubber; **caucho vulcanizado** vulcanized rubber
cauchotar *va* to rubberize, to cover with rubber
cauda *f* tail or train of bishop's cope
caudal *adj* of great volume (*e.g., river*); (zool.) caudal; *m* volume (*of water*); abundance; wealth; **caudal relicto** (law) estate
caudaloso -sa *adj* of great volume (*said of body or source of water*); abundant, wealthy
caudatario *m* priest who holds the train of bishop's cope
caudato -ta *adj* caudate
caudatrémula *f* (orn.) wagtail
caudillaje *m* leadership; (Am.) bossism
caudillo *m* chief, leader; military leader, chieftain, caudillo, head of the state
caudimano *adj* (zool.) having a prehensile tail (*like a beaver*)
caudón *m* (orn.) shrike
caulescente *adj* (bot.) caulescent
caulícolo *m* var. of **caulículo**
caulícula *f* (bot.) caulicle
caulículo *m* (arch.) cauliculus
cauri *m* cowrie (*shell used as money in parts of Africa*)
cauro *m* northwest wind
causa *f* cause; (law) cause, suit; (law) trial; (Am.) light lunch; (Am.) potato salad; **a** or **por causa de** on account of, because of; **hacer causa común con** to make common cause with
causador -dora *adj* causing; *mf* cause (*person*)
causahabiente *m* (law) assign
causal *adj* causal
causalidad *f* causality
causante *mf* cause (*person*); (law) principal, constituent
causar *va* to cause; (law) to sue
causativo -va *adj* causative
causear *va* (Am.) to defeat, overcome; *vn* (Am.) to have a bite, have a snack
causeo *m* (Am.) bite, snack
causídico -ca *adj* (law) causidical; *m* (law) advocate
causón *m* (path.) short intense fever
cáustica *f* see **cáustico**
causticar **§86** *va* to make caustic
causticidad *f* causticity; (fig.) causticity
cáustico -ca *adj* (chem., math., opt. & fig.) caustic; *m* (chem.) caustic; **cáustico lunar** lunar caustic; *f* (math. & opt.) caustic
cautela *f* caution; craft, cunning
cautelar *va* to prevent; *vr* to be on one's guard; **cautelarse de** to guard against
cauteloso -sa *adj* cautious, heedful, wary; crafty, cunning
cauterio *m* cautery; eradication (*of an evil*)
cauterización *f* cauterization
cauterizar **§76** *va* to cauterize; to eradicate (*an evil*); to brand
cautín *m* soldering iron
cautivar *va* to take prisoner; to attract, to win over; to charm, to captivate
cautiverio *m* or **cautividad** *f* captivity
cautivo -va *adj* & *mf* captive
cauto -ta *adj* cautious
cava *f* digging, cultivation (*of vines*); royal wine cellar; (fort.) moat; (anat.) vena cava
cavacote *m* mound made with a hoe and used as a marker
cavadizo -za *adj* soft, loose (*earth, sand*)
cavador *m* digger
cavadura *f* digging
cavalillo *m* irrigating ditch between two properties
cavar *va* to dig (*with hoe, etc.*); *vn* to go deep (*said, e.g., of a wound*); to paw; **cavar en** to go into thoroughly, to study deeply
cavatina *f* (mus.) cavatina; (dent.) cavity varnish
cavazón *f* digging
caverna *f* cavern

cavernícola *adj* cave-dwelling (*man or animal*); (coll.) reactionary; *mf* cave dweller; (coll.) political reactionary
cavernosidad *f* cave, cavern; hollowness; hollow sound
cavernoso -sa *adj* cavernous
caveto *m* (arch.) cavetto
cavia *f* trench around base of plant or tree to hold irrigation water; *m* (zool.) cavy
cavial *m* or **caviar** *m* caviar
cavicornio -nia *adj* (zool.) cavicorn
cavidad *f* cavity
cavilación *f* cavil, caviling; suspicion, mistrust; worry
cavilar *va* to cavil, to cavil at; *vn* to cavil; to worry, to fret
cavilosidad *f* suspicion, mistrust
caviloso -sa *adj* suspicious, mistrustful
cavitación *f* (mach. & path.) cavitation
cayada *f* or **cayado** *m* sheephook, shepherd's hook; crozier (*of bishop*); walking staff
Cayena *f* Cayenne
cayente *adj* falling
cayo *m* cay, key; **Cayo Hueso** Key West; **Cayos de la Florida** Florida Keys
cayote *m* var. of **chayote**
cayuco *m* (Am.) dugout canoe
caz *m* (*pl:* **caces**) millrace, flume; **caz de descarga** tailrace; **caz de traída** headrace
caza *f* chase, hunt, hunting; game; (aer.) pursuit; **a caza de** (coll.) in search of, on the hunt for; **andar a caza de** (coll.) to go hunting for; **dar caza** to give chase; **dar caza a** to go hunting for; to try to ferret out; to be on the lookout for; **ir de caza** to go hunting; **levantar la caza** (coll.) to try to attract attention; **llevar de caza** to take (*someone*) hunting; **caza al hombre** manhunt; **caza de grillos** fool's errand, wild-goose chase; **caza de pelo** fur, ground game; **caza de pluma** winged game; **caza mayor** big game; **caza menor** small game; *m* (aer.) pursuit plane; **caza de escolta** (aer.) escort fighter; **caza de reacción** or **caza reactor** (aer.) jet fighter
cazabe *m* cassava flour; cassava bread
cazabombardero *m* (aer.) fighter bomber
cazaclavos *m* (*pl:* **-vos**) nail puller
cazadero *m* hunting ground
cazador -dora *adj* hunting; chasing; *m* hunter; chaser; (mil.) chasseur; **cazador de alforja** trapper; **cazador de autógrafos** autograph seeker; **cazador de cabezas** head-hunter; **cazador furtivo** poacher; *f* huntress; jacket, hunting jacket
cazamoscas *m* (*pl:* **-cas**) (orn.) flycatcher
cazanoticias *m* (*pl:* **-cias**) newshawk
cazaperros *m* (*pl:* **-rros**) dogcatcher
cazar §76 *va* to chase; to hunt; to catch; (coll.) to wangle (*to get by scheming*); (coll.) to catch up (*in a mistake*); (coll.) to catch (*a mistake*); to take in (*to win over by trickery*); (naut.) to haul (*the sheets*) taut; **cazar vivo** to catch alive; *vn* to hunt; **cazar largo** (coll.) to be on one's toes, be alert
cazarratas *m* (*pl:* **-tas**) ratcatcher
cazarreactor *m* (aer.) jet fighter
cazasubmarinos *m* (*pl:* **-nos**) subchaser, submarine chaser
cazata *f* var. of **cacería**
cazatorpedero *m* (nav.) torpedo-boat destroyer
cazcalear *vn* (coll.) to buzz about
cazcarria *f* dried splashes of mud on lower part of clothing
cazcarriento -ta *adj* (coll.) splashed with mud
cazcorvo -va *adj* knock-kneed (*said of horses*)
cazo *m* dipper, ladle; glue pot; back of knife
cazolero *adj masc & m* var. of **cominero**
cazoleta *f* pan (*of musket lock*); bowl (*of tobacco pipe*); hand guard (*of sword*); boss (*of shield*); (mach.) pan, housing
cazoletero *adj masc & m* var. of **cominero**
cazolón *m* large earthen casserole
cazón *m* (ichth.) dogfish, shark; hunting dog; brown sugar
cazonal *m* tackle for shark fishing; (coll.) mess, entanglement
cazonete *m* (naut.) toggle
cazudo -da *adj* thick-backed (*said of a knife*)
cazuela *f* earthen casserole; minced meat and vegetables cooked in a casserole; (Am.) chicken stew; (theat.) upper gallery; (theat.) gallery for women
cazumbrar *va* to join (*staves of a barrel*) with oakum
cazumbre *m* cooper's oakum
cazumbrón *m* cooper
cazurrería *f* (coll.) sulkiness, sullenness
cazurro -rra *adj* (coll.) sulky, sullen
cazuz *m* (bot.) ivy
c.c. abr. of **centímetro cúbico** or **centímetros cúbicos** (*often used as a measure of cylinder displacement*)
C.C. abr. of **corriente continua**
C. de J. abr. of **Compañía de Jesús**
ce *interj* hey!, pst!
ceanoto *m* (bot.) New Jersey tea
cearina *f* (pharm.) cearin
ceba *f* fattening; feeding a furnace
cebada *f* barley; grain of barley; **cebada perlada** pearl barley
cebadal *m* barley field
cebadar *va* to feed barley to
cebadazo -za *adj* (pertaining to) barley
cebadera *f* nose bag; barley bin; hopper (*of furnace*); (naut.) spritsail
cebadero *m* barley dealer; mule carrying feed; lead mule; feeder of hawks; feeding place; mouth for charging a furnace or oven
cebadilla *f* (bot.) white hellebore; (bot.) sabadilla; hellebore snuff; sabadilla seeds (*used to kill head lice*)
cebador *m* priming horn; priming powder; (elec.) starter (*of fluorescent light*); (mach.) primer, priming cup
cebadura *f* fattening; priming
cebar *va* to fatten; to feed (*e.g., a furnace*); to bait (*a fishhook*); to prime (*gun, pump, gas engine, induction electric machine*); to light (*fireworks*); to start growth in (*new-sown ground*); to nourish (*e.g., anger, passion, hope; e.g., a person with hope*); to lure; to make (*a nut or screw*) catch; *vn* to take hold, to catch (*said of a nut or nail*); *vr* to rage (*said of a disease or epidemic*); **cebarse en** to become absorbed in; to vent one's fury on
cebo *m* feed, fattening; bait; incentive, lure; primer, charge; priming; **dar cebo a** to give grounds for; **cebo de fango** (ichth.) sand launce
cebolla *f* (bot.) onion (*plant and bulb*); bulb; strainer (*for foot valve*); oil receptacle (*of lamp*); **cebolla albarrana** (bot.) squill; **cebolla escalonia** (bot.) shallot
cebollada *f* onion stew; (bot.) globe daisy
cebollar *m* onion patch
cebollero -ra *adj* (pertaining to the) onion; *mf* onion dealer
cebolleta *f* tender onion; (bot.) Welsh onion
cebollino *m* young onion for transplanting; onion seeds; (bot.) chive; (bot.) onion set; **cebollino inglés** (bot.) Welsh onion
cebollón *m* large onion
cebolludo -da *adj* bulbous
cebón -bona *adj* fattened; *m* fattened animal
ceboncillo *m* fatling
ceborrincha *f* (bot.) wild onion
cebra *f* (zool.) zebra
cebrado -da *adj* having stripes like the zebra
cebratana *f* var. of **cerbatana**
cebruno -na *adj* var. of **cervuno**
cebú *m* (*pl:* **-búes**) (zool.) zebu
ceca *f* (archaic) mint; **andar de ceca en Meca** (coll.) to go from place to place, to go hither and thither
cecal *adj* caecal
cecear *vn* to lisp; to pronounce Spanish s like c and z (*i.e.,* [θ])
ceceo *m* lisping; pronunciation of Spanish s like c and z (*i.e.,* [θ])
ceceoso -sa *adj* lisping
cecial *m* fish dried and cured
cecidia *f* (bot.) gall, cecidium
Cecilia *f* Cecilia
Cecilio *m* Cecil
cecina *f* dried beef
cecinar *va* to dry-cure, to dry-salt
cecografía *f* writing of the blind

cecógrafo *m* device for helping the blind to write
cechero *m* (hunt.) watcher
ceda *f* bristle
cedacería *f* sieve shop
cedacero *m* sieve maker or dealer
cedacillo *m* (bot.) quaking grass
cedazo *m* sieve, bolt
cedazuelo *m* small sieve
ceder *va* to yield, give up, hand over, cede; *vn* to yield, give way, surrender; to decline, go down; to slacken, relax; **ceder de to give up** (*e.g., a claim*)
cedilla *f* cedilla
cedizo -za *adj* tainted, spoiled
cedoaria *f* (pharm.) zedoary
cedras *fpl* skin saddlebags
cedria *f* cedrium
cédride *f* cedar cone
cedrino -na *adj* cedar
cedro *m* (bot.) cedar; **cedro de España** (bot.) Spanish cedar; **cedro de las Antillas** (bot.) mahogany; **cedro del Líbano** (bot.) cedar of Lebanon; (fig.) potentate, tycoon; **cedro deodara** or **cedro de las Indias** (bot.) deodar; **cedro de Virginia** (bot.) juniper, red cedar; **cedro macho** (bot.) Spanish cedar
cédula *f* slip of paper or parchment; blank; form; certificate; government order; I.O.U.; **cédula de subscripción** subscription blank; **cédula de vecindad** identification papers; **cédula en blanco** blank check; **cédula personal** identification papers
cedular *va* to post, post up (*on the wall*)
cedulón *m* public notice, proclamation; lampoon
cefalalgia *f* (path.) cephalalgia, headache
cefalea *f* (path.) headache
cefálico -ca *adj* cephalic
cefalitis *f* (path.) encephalitis
céfalo *m* (ichth.) mullet, common mullet
cefalocordado -da *adj* (zool.) cephalochordate
cefalópodo -da *adj & m* (zool.) cephalopod
cefalotórax *m* (zool.) cephalothorax
cefeido -da *adj & f* (astr.) Cepheid; **cefeida variable** (astr.) Cepheid variable
Cefeo *m* (myth. & astr.) Cepheus
céfiro *m* zephyr (*wind; fabric*)
cegajo *m* two-year-old he-goat
cegajoso -sa *adj* blear, weepy
cegar §29 *va* to blind; to block, plug, stop up; to wall up (*door or window*); *vn* to go blind; to become blinded (*e.g., by passion*); *vr* to become blinded (*e.g., by passion*)
cegarra *adj* (coll.) near-sighted, dim-sighted
cegarrita *adj* (coll.) squinting (*to see better*)
cegato -ta *adj* (coll.) near-sighted, dim-sighted
cegatoso -sa *adj* blear, weepy
cegesimal *adj* (phys.) centimeter-gram-second
ceguedad *f* blindness
ceguera *f* blindness; disease causing blindness; **ceguera nocturna** night blindness
ceiba *f* (bot.) ceiba tree, God tree, silk-cotton tree; (bot.) sea moss
ceibal *m* growth of ceiba trees; growth of ceibos
ceibo *m* (bot.) ceibo
Ceilán *m* Ceylon
ceilanés -nesa *adj & mf* Ceylonese
ceja *f* brow; eyebrow; (fig.) brow (*of hill*); projection; edging; rim, edge; flange; path at edge of woods; (mus.) fret; (mus.) capotasto; (naut.) opening in clouds; (Am.) clearing for a road; **dar entre ceja y ceja a** (coll.) to say to one's face; **fruncir las cejas** to knit one's brow; **hasta las cejas** deep (*e.g., in work*); **quemarse las cejas** (coll.) to burn the midnight oil; **tener entre ceja y ceja** (coll.) to look on (*a person*) with disfavor; (coll.) to persist in (*an intention*)
cejadero *m* holdback (*on a carriage*)
cejador -dora *adj* (Am.) shy, balky (*horse*); *m* holdback (*on a carriage*)
cejar *vn* to back up; to turn back; to slacken, relax
cejijunto -ta *adj* (coll.) beetle-browed; (coll.) scowling, frowning
cejilla *f* (mus.) capotasto
cejo *m* morning mist over a river or stream; esparto cord
cejudo -da *adj* beetle-browed
cejuela *f* (mus.) capotasto
celada *f* ambush, trap; (arm.) sallet; **caer en la celada** to fall into the trap; **celada borgoñota** (arm.) burgonet
celador -dora *adj* watching, on guard; *mf* caretaker; *m* watchman; **maintenance man;** proctor
celaje *m* cloud effect; skylight, transom; harbinger; (naut.) clouds; (paint.) clouds, burst of light through clouds
celajería *f* (naut.) clouds, mass of clouds
celandés -desa *adj* (pertaining to) Zeeland; *mf* Zeelander
celar *va* to see to (*observance of laws*); to watch over, keep a check on (*e.g., employees*); to keep an eye on (*out of jealousy or other concern*); to hide, conceal; to carve; to engrave; *vn* **celar sobre** to see to (*observance of laws*); **celar por** to watch out for (*e.g., protection of someone or something*)
celastro *m* (bot.) staff tree
celda *f* cell (*of honeycomb; small room in convent, prison, etc.*); (aer.) cell; **celda de castigo** solitary confinement
celdilla *f* cell (*of honeycomb*); niche; cavity; (bot.) cell (*loculus*)
celebérrimo -ma *adj super* very or most celebrated
celebración *f* celebration; holding (*e.g., of a meeting*)
celebrante *adj* celebrating, officiating; *mf* celebrator; *m* celebrant (*priest*)
celebrar *va* to celebrate; to welcome (*to accept or look upon with pleasure or approval*); to hold (*e.g., an interview, meeting*); to perform (*e.g., a marriage*); to say (*Mass*); *vn* to celebrate (*to say Mass*); to be glad; **celebrar** + *inf* to be glad to + *inf; vr* to be celebrated; to take place
célebre *adj* celebrated, famous; (coll.) funny, witty; (Am.) pretty
celebridad *f* celebrity (*quality and person*); celebration, pageant
celedón *m* celadon green
celemín *m* celemin (*Spanish dry measure: about half peck*)
celenterado -da *adj & m* (zool.) coelenterate
célere *adj* rapid, swift, quick
celeridad *f* celerity
celerímetro *m* speed gauge
celesta *f* (mus.) celesta
celeste *adj* celestial; heavenly (*body*); sky-blue; (mus.) soft (*pedal*); *mf* Celestial (*Chinese*); *m* sky blue; (mus.) celesta (*organ stop*)
celestial *adj* celestial, heavenly; (fig.) celestial, heavenly; (coll.) stupid, silly
celestina *f* bawd, procuress, go-between; (mineral.) celestite, celestine
celíaco -ca *adj* (anat.) coeliac; *f* (path.) coeliac flux
celibato *m* celibacy; (coll.) bachelor
célibe *adj* celibate, single, unmarried; *mf* celibate, single person, unmarried person
célico -ca *adj* (poet.) celestial
celidonia *f* (bot.) celandine; **celidonia menor** (bot.) pilewort
celinda *f* (bot.) syringa, mock orange
celindrate *m* dish seasoned with coriander
celo *m* zeal; distrust, envy; heat, rut; **celos** *mpl* jealousy; **en celo** in rut, in heat; **tener celos** to be jealous
celofán *m* or **celofana** *f* cellophane
celoidina *f* (chem.) celloidin
celoma *m* (anat. & zool.) coelom
celomado -da *adj & m* (zool.) coelomate
celosía *f* jalousie, slatted shutter; lattice, latticework; jealousy; (her.) lattice
celoso -sa *adj* jealous; zealous; distrustful, suspicious; (naut.) unsteady
celotipia *f* jealousy
celsitud *f* elevation, grandeur
celta *adj* Celtic; *mf* Celt; *m* Celtic (*language*)
Celtiberia *f* Celtiberia
celtibérico -ca, celtiberio -ria, celtibero -ra or **celtíbero -ra** *adj & mf* Celtiberian
céltico -ca *adj* Celtic
celtismo *m* Celticism

celtista *mf* Celticist, Celtist
celtohispánico -ca or **celtohispano -na** *adj* Celto-Hispanic
célula *f* (biol., elec. & pol.) cell; (aer.) cell, plane cell, cellule; **célula cribosa** (bot.) sieve cell; **célula de selenio** selenium cell; **célula fotoeléctrica** photoelectric cell; **célula germen** (biol.) germ cell; **célula mitral** mitral cell; **célula nerviosa** nerve cell; **célula sanguínea** blood cell; **célula voltaica** voltaic cell
celulado -da *adj* celled
celular *adj* cellular; cell, e.g., **prisión celular** cell house
celulario -ria *adj* cellular
celulitis *f* (path.) cellulitis
celuloide *m* celluloid; (fig.) celluloid (*motion-picture film*); **llevar al celuloide** to put on the screen
celuloso -sa *adj* cellulous; *f* (chem.) cellulose
cellenco -ca *adj* (coll.) decrepit
cellisca *f* sleet, sleet storm
cellisquear *vn* to sleet
cello *m* hoop
cementación *f* (metal.) cementation, casehardening
cementar *va* (metal.) to cement, to caseharden
cementerio *m* cemetery
cementista *mf* cement worker
cemento *m* cement; concrete; (anat., dent. & geol.) cement; **cemento armado** reinforced concrete; **cemento de goma** rubber cement; **cemento de Pórtland** or **cemento pórtland** Portland cement
cementoso -sa *adj* cement-like, cementitious
cena *f* supper; (*cap.*) *f* Last Supper
cenaaoscuras *mf* (*pl:* **-ras**) (coll.) recluse; (coll.) skinflint
cenáculo *m* cénacle, literary group; (*cap.*) *m* Cenacle (*room of Last Supper*)
cenacho *m* market basket
cenadero *m* supper room; summerhouse
cenador -dora *mf* diner-out; *m* arbor, bower, summerhouse; gallery around patio (*in houses in Granada*)
cenaduría *f* (Am.) eating house
cenagal *m* quagmire; (fig.) quagmire
cenagoso -sa *adj* muddy, miry
cenar *va* to have (*e.g., chicken*) for supper; *vn* to sup, to have supper
cenceño -ña *adj* thin, slender, lean
cencerra *f* cowbell
cencerrada *f* (coll.) charivari (*to celebrate the nuptials of a widower*)
cencerrear *vn* to jingle cowbells continuously; to jangle, to rattle; (coll.) to play out of tune, to play on an instrument that is out of tune
cencerreo *m* jingling of cowbells; jangle, rattle
cencerro *m* cowbell; **a cencerros tapados** (coll.) cautiously, stealthily; **cencerro zumbón** bell worn by foremost or leading animal
cencerrón *m* bunch of grapes left on the vine
cencido -da *adj* untrodden
cendal *m* sendal; gauze; (eccl.) humeral veil; barbs of feather; illusion
cendolilla *f* flighty young girl
cendra *f* cupel paste
cendrada *f* cupel; cupel paste
cendradilla *f* cupellation furnace
cendrazo *m* cupellation residue
cenefa *f* border, trimming; orphrey (*of chasuble*); (arch.) border; (naut.) weather cloth; (naut.) top rim
cenestesia *f* (psychol.) coenesthesis
cení *m* fine brass or bronze
cenia *f* irrigation water wheel; bucket wheel; irrigated garden
cenicero *m* ashpan; ash tray; ashpit, ash dump
ceniciento -ta *adj* ashen, ash-gray; *f* person or thing unjustly despised or disregarded; **la Cenicienta** Cinderella
cenicilla *f* (bot.) oidium
cenit *m* (astr. & fig.) zenith
cenital *adj* zenith, zenithal
ceniza *f* see **cenizo**
cenizal *m* ashpit
cenizo -za *adj* ashen, ash-gray; *mf* (coll.) wet blanket; *m* (bot.) white goosefoot; (bot.) oidium; (coll.) Jonah, jinx, hoodoo; *f* ash; ashes; **cenizas** *fpl* ashes; (fig.) ashes (*mortal remains*); **huir de las cenizas y caer en las brasas** to jump from the frying pan into the fire; **cenizas de perla** pearlash; **cenizas de sosa** soda ash
cenizoso -sa *adj* ashy; ashen, ash-gray
cenobio *m* cenoby; (biol. & bot.) coenobium
cenobita *mf* cenobite
cenobitismo *m* cenobitism
cenojil *m* garter
cenotafio *m* cenotaph
cenote *m* (Am.) deep underground water reservoir
cenozoico -ca *adj* (geol.) Cenozoic
censal *adj* (pertaining to the) census
censatario -ria *mf* (law) lienee
censo *m* census; tax; perpetual lien or encumbrance; mortgage; **levantar el censo** to take the census; **ser un censo** (coll.) to be a constant drain (*on one's money*); **censo de por vida** life lien
censor *m* censor; censorious person; accountant; (educ.) proctor; **censor jurado de cuentas** certified public accountant
censorino -na or **censorio -ria** *adj* censorial; (educ.) proctorial
censual *adj* (pertaining to) census; (pertaining to a) lien
censualista *mf* (law) lienor
censuario *m* (law) lienee
censura *f* censure; censorship; censoring; **censura de cuentas** (com.) auditing
censurable *adj* censurable, reprehensible
censurador -dora *adj* censuring; censoring; *mf* censurer; censor
censurar *va* to censure; to censor
censurista *adj* censorious; *mf* censorious person, faultfinder
centaura or **centaurea** *f* (bot.) centaury; **centaura de jardín** (bot.) golden coreopsis
centauro *m* (myth.) centaur
centavo -va *adj* hundredth; *m* hundredth; cent
centella *f* flash (*of lightning; from flint*); (fig.) spark (*of genius; of love, etc.*); **echar centellas** (coll.) to blow up, hit the ceiling
centellador -dora *adj* flashing, sparkling, glimmering; *m* (phys.) scintillation counter
centellar or **centellear** *vn* to flash, to sparkle, to glimmer
centelleo *m* flashing, sparkling, glimmering
centellón *m* large flash or spark
centena *f* see **centeno**
centenada *f* hundred; **a centenadas** by the hundred
centenal *m* rye field; hundred
centenar *m* hundred; centenary (*celebration*); rye field; **a centenares** by the hundred
centenario -ria *adj* centenary or centennial; centenarian; *mf* centenarian; *m* centenary or centennial
centenaza *f* rye straw
centenero -ra *adj* good for growing rye (*said of soil*)
centeno -na *adj* hundredth; *m* (bot.) rye; *f* hundred; **las centenas** the hundreds (*the numbers 100, 200, 300, etc.*)
centesimal *adj* centesimal
centésimo -ma *adj* hundredth; *m* hundredth; (Am.) centime
centiárea *f* centiare
centígrado -da *adj* centigrade
centigramo *m* centigram
centilitro *m* centiliter
centiloquio *m* work of a hundred parts
centimano or **centímano** *adj* (myth.) hundred-handed
centímetro *m* centimeter
céntimo -ma *adj* hundredth; *m* hundredth; centime
centinela *mf* (may be used as feminine in speaking of a man) sentinel, sentry; watch, guard (*person*); **estar de centinela** to stand sentinel; **hacer centinela** to stand sentinel; to keep watch; **centinela de avanzada** vedette; **centinela de vista** prisoner's guard; **centinela perdida** (mil.) forlorn hope
centinodia *f* (bot.) knotgrass
centípedo *m* (zool.) centipede
centiplicado -da *adj* hundredfold

centipondio *m* hundredweight
centola or **centolla** *f* (zool.) thornback, maian (*Maia squinado*)
centón *m* crazy quilt; (lit.) cento
centraje *m* centering
central *adj* central; *f* main office, headquarters; (elec.) powerhouse; (telp.) central; (Am.) community sugar mill; **central de correos** main post office; **central de teléfonos** telephone exchange; **central generadora** (elec.) generating station; **central térmica** (elec.) steam power plant
centralilla *f* (telp.) local exchange, private exchange
centralismo *m* centralism
centralista *adj & mf* centralist
centralización *f* centralization
centralizar §76 *va & vr* to centralize
centrar *va* to center; (hunt.) to hit in the center; (mil.) to center (*fire, attack, etc.*); *vr* to center, be centered
céntrico -ca *adj* downtown; centric
centrifugadora *f* centrifugal machine
centrifugar §59 *va* to centrifuge
centrífugo -ga *adj* centrifugal; *f* centrifuge, centrifugal machine
centrípeto -ta *adj* centripetal
centrisco *m* (ichth.) shrimpfish
centrista *adj* (pertaining to the) center; *mf* (pol.) centrist
centro *m* center; middle; heart; business district, downtown; club; goal, purpose; **estar en su centro** to be in one's element; **centro de atracción** (astr.) center of attraction; **centro de control** control center; **centro de gravedad** (mech.) center of gravity; **centro de gravitación** (astr.) center of attraction; **centro de mesa** centerpiece; **centro de recepción** (mil.) reception center; **centro de substitución** (mil.) replacement center; **centro docente** educational institution; **centro ferroviario** rail center; **centro nervioso** (anat.) nerve center
Centro América *f* Central America
centroamericano -na *adj & mf* Central American
centrobárico -ca *adj* centrobaric
centroesfera *f* (biol.) centrosphere
centroeuropeo -a *adj* Central European
centrosoma *m* (biol.) centrosome
cénts. abr. of **céntimos**
centuplicar §86 *va* to centuple
céntuplo -pla *adj* centuple, hundredfold; *m* hundredfold
centuria *f* century; (hist.) century
centurión *m* centurion
cenzalino -na *adj* (pertaining to the) mosquito
cénzalo *m* (ent.) mosquito
cenzontle *m* (Am.) mocking-bird
ceñideras *fpl* overalls
ceñido -da *adj* tight, close-fitting; close; narrow-waisted, svelte, lithe; thrifty, economical
ceñidor *m* belt, girdle, sash
ceñidura *f* (act of) girding; fastening; abridgment
ceñiglo *m* (bot.) white goosefoot; **ceñiglo de jardín** (bot.) broom goosefoot
ceñir §74 *va* to gird; to encircle (*e.g., the brow*); to fasten around the waist, to fit around the waist; to fasten, to tie; to fit tightly; to abridge, shorten; (mil.) to besiege; *vn* (naut.) to sail close to the wind; *vr* to tighten one's belt, cut expenses; to limit oneself (*e.g., in words*); to adapt oneself; **ceñirse a** to hug, keep close to
ceño *m* frown; threatening aspect (*of clouds, sea, etc.*); band, ring, hoop; (vet.) dry and contracted hoof; **arrugar el ceño** to knit the brow, to frown
ceñoso -sa or **ceñudo -da** *adj* frowning; stern, grim, gruff
ceo *m* (ichth.) dory
cepa *f* stump (*of tree or plant*); stub (*of tail*); vinestalk; (arch.) footing; strain (*of a family*); **de buena cepa** of well-known quality
cepacaballo *m* (bot.) carline thistle
cepáceo -a *adj* garlicky
cepeda *f* land overgrown with heath
cepejón *m* thick end of broken branch; heavy root branching from trunk
cepellón *m* (hort.) ball (*left around root for transplanting*)
cepera *f* var. of **cepeda**
cepillado *m* var. of **acepillado**
cepilladura *f* var. of **acepilladura**
cepillar *va* var. of **acepillar**
cepillo *m* brush; (carp.) plane; charity box, poor box; (Am.) flatterer; **cepillo bocel** reed plane; **cepillo de alambre** wire brush; **cepillo de cabeza** hairbrush; **cepillo de dientes** toothbrush; **cepillo de ropa** or **para la ropa** clothesbrush; **cepillo para las uñas** nailbrush; **cepillo para los dientes** toothbrush
cepo *m* branch, bough; stock (*of anvil*); clamp, vise; snare, trap; reel (*for winding silk*); poor box; (naut.) stock (*of anchor*); stocks, pillory; **¡cepos quedos!** (coll.) quiet!, cut it out!
ceporro *m* old stump pulled up for firewood; (coll.) rude or uncouth fellow
cequia *f* var. of **acequia**
cera *f* wax; beeswax; wax candles (*burning at a function*); (orn.) cere; **ceras** *fpl* honeycomb; **hacer cera y pabilo de** (coll.) to lead by the nose; **ser como una cera** to be wax in one's hands; **cera aleda** bee glue; **cera de los oídos** earwax; **cera de lustrar** polishing wax; **cera de palma** palm wax; **cera de** or **para pisos** floor wax; **cera montana** montan wax
cerafolio *m* (bot.) chervil
cerámico -ca *adj* ceramic; *f* ceramics (*art; objects*); (archeol.) study of ceramics
ceramista *mf* ceramist
cerapez *m* shoemaker's wax
cerasta *f* or **ceraste** *m* (zool.) cerastes
ceratias *m* (astr.) twin-tailed comet
cerato *m* (pharm.) cerate
cerbatana *f* blowgun, peashooter; ear trumpet; (coll.) mouthpiece, spokesman, go-between
Cerbero *m* var. of **Cancerbero**
cerca *f* fence, wall; **cerca viva** hedge; *m* (coll.) close-up; **cercas** *mpl* (paint.) objects in foreground; **tener buen cerca** (coll.) to look good when close (*said of a person or thing*); *adv* near; **de cerca** near, nearly; at close range; **cerca de** near; about (*a certain number*); to, at the court of; **cerca de** + *inf* near + *ger*
cercado *m* fenced-in or walled-in garden or field; fence, wall
cercador -dora *adj* encircling, surrounding; *m* repoussé tool
cercanía *f* nearness, proximity; **cercanías** *fpl* neighborhood, vicinity
cercano -na *adj* near, close; adjoining, neighboring; **cercano a** + *inf* near + *ger*
cercar §86 *va* to fence in, to wall in, to hedge in; to encircle, to surround; to crowd around; (mil.) to besiege, lay siege to
cercén; a cercén all around, close
cercenador -dora *mf* clipper, trimmer
cercenadura *f* or **cercenamiento** *m* clipping, trimming; curtailment, reduction
cercenar *va* to clip, to trim, to trim the edges of; to curtail, to reduce
cerceta *f* (orn.) garganey; **cercetas** *fpl* spikes (*of young deer*); **cerceta de verano** (orn.) greenwing
cercillo *m* tendril (*of a vine*)
cerciorar *va* to inform, to assure (*a person*); *vr* to find out; **cerciorarse de** to find out about, to ascertain
cerco *m* fence, wall, enclosure; hoop; ring; rim, edge; casing or frame (*of door or window*); group, circle; (mil.) siege; (aut.) rim; iron tire; halo (*around sun or moon*); **alzar el cerco** (mil.) to raise the siege; **poner cerco a** (mil.) to lay siege to
cercopiteco *m* (zool.) cercopithecus, long-tailed African monkey
cercha *f* segment (*of rim of wheel*); (arch.) rib (*of center of arch*); flexible wooden rule for measuring concave or convex surfaces; (rail.) clearance gage
cerchar *va* (hort.) to layer
cerchón *m* (arch.) center, centering
cerda *f* bristle, horsehair; new-mown grain; snare (*to catch birds*); (zool.) sow
cerdada *f* herd of swine; swinishness

cerdamen *m* bunch of bristles (*for making brushes*)
cerdear *vn* to falter in the forelegs; to rasp, to grate (*said of a string instrument*); (coll.) to hold back, to look for excuses
Cerdeña *f* Sardinia; **la Cerdeña catalana** Alghero (*seaport in Sardinia where Catalan is still spoken*)
cerdo *m* (zool.) hog; dirty, sloppy fellow; ill-bred fellow; **cerdo de cría** pig not old enough to be slaughtered; **cerdo de mata** or **de muerte** pig old enough to be slaughtered; **cerdo de vida** pig not old enough to be slaughtered; **cerdo hormiguero** (zool.) aardvark; **cerdo marino** (zool.) porpoise, harbor porpoise
cerdoso -sa *adj* bristly
cerdudo -da *adj* bristly; hairy-chested
cereal *adj* & *m* cereal
cerealista *adj* (pertaining to) cereal, grain; *mf* grain producer, grain dealer
cerebelo *m* (anat.) cerebellum
cerebración *f* cerebration
cerebral *adj* cerebral
cerebro *m* (anat.) cerebrum (*brain; forebrain*); (fig.) brain, brains; **cerebro electrónico** electronic brain
cerebroespinal *adj* cerebrospinal
cereceda *f* cherry orchard
cerecilla *f* red pepper
ceremonia *f* ceremony; **de ceremonia** with all due ceremony; formal; **hacer ceremonias** to stand on ceremony; **por ceremonia** as a matter of form
ceremonial *adj* ceremonial; *m* ceremonial; (eccl.) ceremonial (*book*)
ceremoniático -ca *adj* extremely ceremonious
ceremoniero -ra *adj* (coll.) full of compliments
ceremonioso -sa *adj* ceremonious, overpolite; formal
céreo -a *adj* waxen
cerería *f* chandlery; royal chandlery
cerero *m* wax chandler; wax dealer; (bot.) wax myrtle; **cerero mayor** royal chandler
Ceres *f* (myth.) Ceres
ceresina *f* ceresin
cerevisina *f* brewers' yeast
cereza *f* cherry (*fruit*); cherry red (*of incandescent metals*)
cerezal *m* cherry orchard
cerezo *m* (bot.) cherry tree; cherry wood; **cerezo silvestre** (bot.) dogwood
céridos *mpl* (chem.) cerium metals
cerífero -ra *adj* ceriferous
ceriflor *f* (bot.) honeywort
cerilla *f* wax taper; wax match, paper match; earwax
cerillero -ra *mf* match vendor; *m* & *f* matchbox
cerillo *m* wax taper; (*dial.*) wax match
cerina *f* (chem.) cerin
cerio *m* (chem.) cerium
cerita *f* (mineral.) cerite
cermeña *f* pear (*fruit*)
cermeño *m* (bot.) pear tree; ill-bred fellow
cernada *f* cinder; leached ashes; sizing; (vet.) poultice made of ashes
cernadero *m* coarse linen cloth used for leaching ashes
cerne *m* heart (*of tree*)
cernedero *m* flour-sifter's apron; place for sifting flour
cernedor *m* screen, sieve, sifter
cerneja *f* or **cernejas** *fpl* fetlock (*tuft of hair*)
cernejudo -da *adj* heavily fetlocked
cerner §66 *va* to sift, to bolt; (Am.) to strain; to scan (*e.g., the horizon*); *vn* to bud, to blossom; to drizzle; *vr* to waddle; to soar, to hover; to impend, be imminent (*said of some evil or misfortune*); to threaten, to gather (*said, e.g., of a storm*); **cernerse sobre** to hang over (*to threaten*)
cernícalo *m* (orn.) sparrow hawk, kestrel; (coll.) rude ignoramus; **coger** or **pillar un cernícalo** (coll.) to get drunk
cernidillo *m* drizzle; waddling, wobbling
cernido *m* sifting; sifted flour
cernidura *f* sifting; **cerniduras** *fpl* screenings
cernir §43 *va* to sift
cero *m* zero; **ser un cero** or **ser un cero a la izquierda** (coll.) to not count, to be of no account; **cero absoluto** (phys.) absolute zero; **cero volado** (print.) superior zero, superior letter o
cerollo -lla *adj* mown while green and flexible
cerón *m* dross of honeycombs
ceroplástica *f* ceroplastics
ceroso -sa *adj* waxy
cerote *m* shoemaker's wax; (coll.) fright, fear
cerotear *va* to wax (*thread*); *vn* (Am.) to drip (*said of a candle*)
cerótico -ca *adj* (chem.) cerotic
cerquillo *m* fringe of hair around tonsure; welt (*of shoe*); (Am.) bangs
cerquita *adv* quite near, close by
cerrada *f* see **cerrado**
cerradero -ra *adj* lock; locking (*device*); *m* lock; keeper, strike (*of a lock*); purse strings; clasp; *f* lock; **echar la cerradera** (coll.) to turn a deaf ear
cerradizo -za *adj* easily locked
cerrado -da *adj* close, closed; secretive; obscure, incomprehensible; cloudy, overcast; sharp (*curve*); thick (*beard*); typical, out-and-out; (phonet.) close; (coll.) quiet, reserved; (coll.) dense, stupid; (coll.) with a heavy local accent; **cerrado de mollera** (coll.) crude, ignorant; *f* hide over backbone (*of an animal*)
cerrador -dora *adj* shutting, locking; *m* shutter; lock
cerradura *f* closing, shutting, locking; lock; **cerradura de cilindro** cylinder lock; **cerradura de dos vueltas** double-turn lock; **cerradura de embutir** mortise lock; **cerradura de golpe** or **de muelle** spring lock; **cerradura de seguridad** safety lock; **cerradura dormida** deadlock; **cerradura guarnecida al revés** rim lock; **cerradura recercada** mortise lock
cerraja *f* lock; (bot.) sow thistle; (bot.) corn sow thistle
cerrajear *vn* to be a locksmith
cerrajería *f* locksmith trade or business; locksmith's shop; light ironwork; hardware shop; builder's hardware
cerrajero *m* locksmith; hardware man, ironworker
cerrajón *m* big, steep hill
cerramiento *m* closing, shutting, locking; enclosure; partition wall; (arch.) roof
cerrar §18 *va* to close, to shut, to lock; to bolt; to turn off (*e.g., a radio*); to enclose; to clench (*the fist*); **cerrar con llave** to lock; **cerrar el ojo** (coll.) to close one's eyes (*to die*); *vn* to close; to close in, to make an attack; **cerrar con** to close in on (*an enemy*); **cerrar en falso** to not catch (*said of a door, lock, latch*); *vr* to close, to shut, to lock; to close, to heal (*said of a sore*); **cerrarse en** + *inf* to persist in + *ger;* **cerrarse en falso** to not heal right
cerrazón *f* gathering storm clouds; close-mindedness; (phonet.) closing (*of vowel*); (Am.) spur (*of mountain range*)
cerrejón *m* hillock
cerrero -ra *adj* running wild; unbroken (*colt*); (Am.) rough, unpolished; (Am.) bitter; (Am.) stubborn
cerreta *f* (naut.) headrail
cerril *adj* rough, uneven; wild, untamed; (coll.) rough, boorish
cerrilla *f* milling machine (*to mill coins*)
cerrillar *va* to mill, to knurl (*coins*)
cerrillo *m* (bot.) couch grass, twitch; (bot.) beard grass; **cerrillos** *mpl* milling cutter
cerrión *m* icicle
cerro *m* hill; neck of an animal; backbone; bunch of combed flax or hemp; **en cerro** bareback; **por los cerros de Úbeda** (coll.) off the track; (coll.) out of place, **echar por los cerros de Úbeda** (coll.) to talk nonsense
cerrojazo *m* slamming the bolt; **dar cerrojazo** to slam the bolt; (archaic) to adjourn (*the Cortes*) suddenly
cerrojillo *m* (orn.) coal titmouse
cerrojo *m* bolt
cerrón *m* burlap
cerruma *f* pastern

certamen *m* literary contest; match, contest; (obs.) challenge, duel, fight
certero -ra *adj* sure, certain, accurate; good (*shot*); well-aimed; well-informed
certeza *f* certainty
certidumbre *f* certainty; **certidumbre moral** moral certainty
certificable *adj* certifiable
certificación *f* certification; certificate
certificado -da *adj* registered; *m* registered letter or package; certificate; **certificado de estudios** (educ.) transcript; **certificado de origen** (com.) certificate of origin
certificar §86 *va* to certify; to certificate; to register (*a letter*); to assure
certificatorio -ria *adj* certificatory
certinidad *f* certainty
certísimo -ma *adj super* very or most certain
certitud *f* certainty
cerúleo -a *adj* cerulean
ceruma *f* var. of **cerruma**
cerumen *m* (physiol.) cerumen, earwax
cerusa *f* (chem.) ceruse
cerusita *f* (mineral.) cerussite
cerval *adj* deer; deerlike; intense (*fear*)
cervantesco -ca, cervántico -ca or **cervantino -na** *adj* (pertaining to) Cervantes
cervantismo *m* influence of Cervantes; expression or idiom of Cervantes
cervantista *mf* Cervantist
cervantófilo -la *mf* admirer of Cervantes; collector of editions of Cervantes
cervario -ria *adj* cervine, deer
cervatica *f* (ent.) green grasshopper
cervatillo *m* new-born fawn; (zool.) musk deer; (zool.) muntjac
cervato *m* fawn
cerveceo *m* fermentation of beer
cervecera *f* see **cervecero**
cervecería *f* brewery; beer saloon; **cervecería al aire libre** beer garden
cervecero -ra *adj* brewing; (pertaining to) beer; *mf* brewer; *f* (ichth.) alewife
cerveza *f* beer; **cerveza a presión** draught beer; **cerveza clara** light beer; **cerveza parda** dark beer; **cerveza de marzo** bock beer
cervicabra *f* (zool.) antelope
cervical *adj* cervical
cervicitis *f* (path.) cervicitis
cervicular *adj* cervical
cérvido -da *adj* (zool.) cervid
cervigón *m* var. of **cerviguillo**
cervigudo -da *adj* thick-necked
cerviguillo *m* thick nape of the neck, thick neck
cervillera *f* helmet
cervino -na *adj* cervine; **el Cervino** or **el monte Cervino** the Matterhorn
cerviola *f* (ichth.) amberfish
cerviz *f* (*pl:* **-vices**) (anat.) cervix; neck, nape of neck; base of brain; **bajar** or **doblar la cerviz** to humble oneself; **levantar la cerviz** to grow proud; **ser de dura cerviz** to be headstrong, be ungovernable
cervuno -na *adj* cervine, deer; deerlike; deerskin; deer-colored
cesación *f* or **cesamiento** *m* cessation, suspension
cesante *adj* jobless; out of office; on strike; on part pay; *mf* unemployed person; dismissed public employee
cesantía *f* dismissal; dismissal from public employment; pension of dismissed public employee; unemployment; unemployment compensation
cesar *va* to stop; (Am.) to dismiss; *vn* to cease, to stop, to desist; to quit, to leave; **sin cesar** ceaselessly; **cesar de** + *inf* to cease + *ger*
César *m* Caesar
Cesarea *f* Caesarea
cesáreo -a *adj* Caesarean (*imperial*); (surg.) Caesarean
cesariano -na *adj* Caesarean (*pertaining to Caesar*)
cesarismo *m* Caesarism
cese *m* cease; stoppage of salary; **cese de alarma** all-clear; **cese de fuego** cease fire
cesible *adj* (law) transferable
cesio *m* (chem.) cesium
cesión *f* cession; **cesión de bienes** (law) cessio bonorum
cesionario -ria *mf* grantee, assignee
cesionista *mf* grantor, assigner
cesonario -ria *mf* var. of **cesionario**
césped *m* or **céspede** *m* sod, turf, sward, lawn; (hort.) cortex growing over cut after pruning; **césped de Olimpo** (bot.) sea pink, thrift; **césped inglés** (bot.) Italian rye grass
cespedera *f* field or meadow where sod is cut
cespitar *vn* to waver, to totter
cespitoso -sa *adj* cespitose
cesta *f* basket; (sport) cesta, wickerwork racket; **cesta de costura** sewing basket
cestada *f* basketful
cestería *f* basketmaking; basket shop; basketwork
cestero -ra *mf* basketmaker, basket dealer
cesto *m* basket; washbasket; (hist.) cestus (*hand covering*); **estar hecho un cesto** (coll.) to be overcome with sleep or drink; **estar metido en el cesto** (coll.) to be peevish or fretful (*said of a child*); **ser un cesto** (coll.) to be crude and ignorant; **cesto de la colada** clothesbasket, washbasket
cestodo *m* (zool.) cestode
cestón *m* large basket; (fort.) gabion
cestonada *f* (fort.) gabionade
cesura *f* (pros.) caesura
cetáceo -a *adj* (zool.) cetacean, cetaceous; *m* (zool.) cetacean
cetano *m* (chem.) cetane
cetilo *m* (chem.) cetyl
cetina *f* whale oil, sperm oil; (chem.) cetin
cetoína *f* (ent.) flower beetle; **cetoína dorada** (ent.) rose chafer
cetona *f* (chem.) ketone
cetoria *f* fish tank, fishpond
cetrarina *f* (chem.) cetrarin
cetrería *f* falconry, hawking
cetrero *m* falconer; (eccl.) verger
cetrino -na *adj* sallow; jaundiced, melancholy
cetro *m* scepter; perch, roost (*for birds*); (eccl.) verge; **empuñar el cetro** to ascend the throne; **cetro de bufón** bauble; **cetro de locura** bauble, fool's scepter
ceugma *f* var. of **zeugma**
ceutí (*pl:* **-tíes**) *adj* (pertaining to) Ceuta; *mf* native or inhabitant of Ceuta
cf. abr. of **confesor**
cg. abr. of **centigramo** or **centigramos**
C.I. abr. of **cociente intelectual**
c.ía or **cía.** abr. of **compañía**
cía *f* (*anat.*) hipbone; (naut.) sternway
ciaboga *f* (naut.) turn, turning (*with oars or with rudder and engine*); **hacer ciaboga** to turn around in order to flee
cianamida *f* (chem.) cyanamide; **cianamida de calcio** (chem.) calcium cyanamide
cianato *m* (chem.) cyanate
cianea *f* (mineral.) lazulite
cianhídrico -ca *adj* (chem.) hydrocyanic
ciánico -ca *adj* (chem.) cyanic
cianita *f* (mineral.) cyanite
cianofíceo -a *adj & f* (bot.) cyanophycean
cianógeno *m* (chem.) cyanogen
cianosis *f* (path.) cyanosis
cianótico -ca *adj* (path.) cyanotic; cyanic (*blue*)
cianotipia *f* cyanotype, blueprinting
cianotipo *m* cyanotype, blueprint
cianuración *f* (min.) cyanide process
cianurar *va* to treat (*gold ore*) with the cyanide process
cianuro *m* (chem.) cyanide; **cianuro de potasio** or **cianuro potásico** (chem.) potassium cyanide; **cianuro de sodio** or **cianuro sódico** (chem.) sodium cyanide
ciar §90 *vn* (naut. & fig.) to back water
ciático -ca *adj* sciatic; *f* (path.) sciatica
cibal *adj* (pertaining to) food
cibeleo -a *adj* (poet.) of Cybele
Cibeles *f* (myth.) Cybele
cibera *f* wheat thrown into hopper to prime the mill; squashed fruit
cibernética *f* cybernetics
cibiaca *f* var. of **parihuela**
cíbolo -la *mf* (zool.) American bison
ciborio *m* (arch.) ciborium

cicatear *vn* (coll.) to be miserly, be stingy
cicatería *f* miserliness, stinginess
cicatero -ra *adj* miserly, stingy; *mf* miser, skinflint; *m* (slang) pickpocket
cicatrícula *f* (bot. & embryol.) cicatricle
cicatriz *f* (*pl:* **-trices**) cicatrix, scar; (bot.) cicatrix; (fig.) scar
cicatrización *f* cicatrization
cicatrizar §76 *va* to cicatrize, to heal; *vr* to cicatrize, to heal; to scar
cicércula or **cicercha** *f* (bot.) grass pea
cícero *m* (print.) pica
Cicerón *m* Cicero
cicerone *m* cicerone
ciceroniano -na *adj* Ciceronian
cicindela *f* (ent.) tiger beetle
cíclada *f* cyclas (*of Roman women*)
Cícladas *fpl* Cyclades
ciclamen *m* (bot.) cyclamen
ciclamina *f* (chem.) cyclamin
ciclamino *m* (bot.) cyclamen
ciclamor *m* (bot.) Judas tree
ciclar *va* to polish (*a precious stone*)
ciclatón *m* cyclas (*medieval tunic*); ciclatoun (*medieval fabric*)
cíclico -ca *adj* cyclic or cyclical
ciclismo *m* cycling, bicycling; bicycle racing
ciclista *mf* cyclist, bicyclist; bicycle racer
ciclización *f* (chem.) ring formation
ciclo *m* cycle; term (*in school*); **ciclo de Artús** (lit.) Arthurian Cycle; **ciclo de Carnot** (phys.) Carnot cycle; **ciclo de cuatro tiempos** (mach.) four-cycle; **ciclo de dos tiempos** (mach.) two-cycle; **ciclo del nitrógeno** nitrogen cycle; **ciclo de Metón** (astr.) Metonic cycle
cicloidal *adj* cycloid, cycloidal
cicloide *f* (geom.) cycloid
cicloideo -a *adj* var. of **cicloidal**
ciclómetro *m* cyclometer
ciclón *m* cyclone
ciclonal *adj* cyclonal
ciclónico -ca *adj* cyclonic
Cíclope *m* (myth.) Cyclops
ciclopentano *m* (chem.) cyclopentane
ciclópeo -a *adj* cyclopean; (myth.) Cyclopean
ciclópico -ca *adj* Cyclopic
cicloplejía *f* (path.) cycloplegia
ciclopropano *m* (chem.) cyclopropane
ciclorama *m* cyclorama
ciclostilo or **ciclóstilo** *m* mimeograph
ciclóstoma *m* (ichth.) cyclostome
ciclotrón *m* (phys.) cyclotron
-cico -ca *suffix dim* var. of **-ico** and attached to polysyllables ending in **d, e, n, r,** or an accented vowel, e.g., **duendecico** elfkin; **corazoncico** dear little heart; **mujercica** cute little woman
cicuta *f* (bot.) hemlock, poison hemlock; hemlock (*poison*); **cicuta acuática** (bot.) water hemlock; **cicuta mayor** (bot.) hemlock, poison hemlock; **cicuta menor** (bot.) fool's-parsley
cicutina *f* (chem.) coniine
cid *m* leader, hero; **el Cid Campeador** Spanish hero of the wars against the Moors in the eleventh century
cidiano -na *adj* of the Cid
Cidno *m* Cydnus
cidra *f* citron (*fruit of Citrus medica*); citrus (*fruit of any plant of the genus Citrus*)
cidrada *f* citron (*candied rind*)
cidral *m* citron grove; (bot.) citron (*tree*)
cidrato *m* citron (*fruit*)
cidrera *f* or **cidrero** *m* (bot.) citron tree
cidria *f* cedrium
cidro *m* (bot.) citron (*Citrus medica*); (bot.) citrus (*any plant of the genus Citrus*)
cidronela *f* (bot.) balm (*Melissa officinalis*)
ciegayernos *m* (*pl:* **-nos**) (coll.) fraud, sham, humbug
ciego -ga *adj* blind; stopped, blocked; dark, dense; blank; (arch.) blind (*window, door, etc.*); (fig.) blind, e.g., **ciego de ira** blind with anger; **ciego con celos** blind with jealousy; *mf* blind person; *m* blind man; blood pudding; *f* blind woman; **a ciegas** blindly; without watching, without looking; thoughtlessly
cieguecico -ca, cieguecillo -lla, cieguecito -ta or **cieguezuelo -la** *mf* little blind person
cielito *m* darling, dearie; (Am.) ring dance and song of the Gauchos
cielo *m* sky, heaven; skies, climate, weather; top, ceiling, roof; canopy (*of a bed*); Heaven; (paint.) sky; **a cielo abierto** in the open air, outdoors; **a cielo descubierto** openly; **a cielo raso** in the open air, outdoors; in the country; **bajado del cielo** (coll.) marvelous, perfect; **escupir al cielo** to have something boomerang; **llovido del cielo** (coll.) heaven-sent; **mover cielo y tierra** (coll.) to move heaven and earth; **poner en el cielo** or **en los cielos** (coll.) to praise to the skies; **séptimo cielo** seventh heaven; (fig.) seventh heaven (*perfect felicity*); **tomar el cielo con las manos** (coll.) to hit the ceiling; **¡vaya Vd. al cielo!** (coll.) tell that to the marines!; **venirse el cielo abajo** (coll.) to rain pitchforks; **ver el cielo abierto** or **los cielos abiertos** (coll.) to see the light, to see one's way out (*of a difficulty*); **cielo de la boca** roof of the mouth; **cielo del hogar** crown sheet (*of firebox*); **cielo máximo** (aer.) ceiling; **cielo raso** ceiling, flat ceiling
cielorraso *m* ceiling, flat ceiling
ciempiés *m* (*pl:* **-piés**) (zool.) centipede; (coll.) disconnected nonsense (*in writing*)
cien *adj* hundred, a hundred, one hundred; **los Cien Días** the Hundred Days; *m* (coll.) a hundred, one hundred; **cien por cien** or **por ciento** hundred-per-cent
ciénaga *f* marsh, moor; mudhole
ciencia *f* science; knowledge; learning; **a ciencia cierta** with certainty; **a ciencia y paciencia** on sufferance; **de ciencia cierta** with certainty; **gaya ciencia** gay science (*amatory poetry*); **ciencia cristiana** Christian Science; **ciencia exacta** exact science; **ciencia física** physical science; **ciencia infusa** afflatus, divine afflatus; **ciencia natural** natural science; **ciencia social** social science; **ciencias ocultas** occult sciences
cieno *m* mud, slime, silt
cienoso -sa *adj* muddy, slimy, silty
cientificismo *m* scientific method
científico -ca *adj* scientific; *mf* scientist
cientismo *m* scientism
cientista *mf* scientist
ciento *adj & m* hundred, a hundred, one hundred; **por ciento** per cent; **por cientos** by the hundred; **un ciento de** a hundred, one hundred
cientopiés *m* (*pl:* **-piés**) (zool.) centipede
cierna *f* (bot.) anther (*of flower of wheat, the vine, etc.*)
cierne *m* (bot.) budding, blossoming; **en cierne** in blossom; in its infancy
cierrarrenglón *m* marginal stop (*of typewriter*)
cierre *m* closing, shutting, locking; snap, clasp, fastener; latch, lock, window latch; choke (*of carburetor*); close (*e.g., of stock market*); shutdown; (com.) closing (*of an account*); **cierre de cañón** breechblock; **cierre de portada** metal shutter (*for store window or door*); **cierre de puertas** door check; **cierre hermético** weather stripping; **cierre hidráulico** water seal; **cierre metálico** sliding metal shutter (*for store window or door*); **cierre cremallera** or **relámpago** zipper
cierro *m* closing, shutting, locking; (Am.) wall, fence; (Am.) envelope; **cierro de cristales** glass-enclosed balcony or porch
cierto -ta *adj* certain; a certain; fixed; **estar en lo cierto** to be right; to be sure of oneself; **de cierto** or **por cierto** for certain; **no, por cierto** certainly not; **cierto** *adv* certainly, surely
cierva *f* (zool.) hind
ciervo *m* (zool.) deer, stag, hart; spit curl; **ciervo del Cabo** (zool.) hartebeest; **ciervo de Virginia** (zool.) white-tailed deer; **ciervo mulo** (zool.) mule deer; **ciervo volante** (ent.) stag beetle
cierzas *fpl* vine shoots
cierzo *m* cold north wind
cifosis *f* (path.) kyphosis

cifra *f* cipher, figure, number; character; abridgment, summary; device, monogram, cipher; sum, amount; **en cifra** in code; secretly, enigmatically; in brief; **cifra arábiga** Arabic figure
cifrado -da *adj* cipher
cifrador *m* cipher device
cifrar *va* to cipher, to code; to abridge, to summarize; to calculate; **cifrar la dicha en** to base one's happiness on; **cifrar la esperanza en** to place one's hope in
cifrario *m* (com.) code
cigala *f* (zool.) squilla; (zool.) Norway lobster
cigarra *f* (ent.) locust, harvest fly
cigarral *m* orchard and picnic grounds (*in or near Toledo*)
cigarrera *f* see **cigarrero**
cigarrería *f* cigar store
cigarrero -ra *mf* cigar maker; cigar seller, cigar dealer; *f* cigar cabinet, cigar case; pocket cigar case
cigarrillo *m* cigarette; **cigarrillo con filtro** filter cigarette
cigarrista *mf* chain smoker
cigarro *m* cigar; cigarette; **cigarro de hoja** (Am.) cigar; **cigarro de papel** cigarette; **cigarro puro** cigar
cigarrón *m* big cigar; (ent.) grasshopper
cigofiláceo -a *adj* (bot.) zygophyllaceous
cigoma *f* (anat.) zygoma
cigomático -ca *adj* (anat.) zygomatic
cigoñal *m* well sweep; (mach.) crankshaft
cigoñino *m* (orn.) young stork
cigoñuela *f* (orn.) stilt
cigoto *m* (biol.) zygote
ciguatera *f* fish poisoning
ciguato -ta *adj* sick with fish poisoning
cigüeña *f* (orn.) stork; (mach.) crank, winch; **recibir a la cigüeña** (fig.) to have a visit from the stork; **cigüeña negra** (orn.) black stork
cigüeñal *m* var. of **cigoñal**
cigüeñuela *f* small crank; (orn.) stilt
cija *f* sheepfold; hayloft
cilanco *m* pool left by receding stream
cilantro *m* (bot.) coriander
ciliado -da *adj* ciliate, ciliated; *m* (zool.) ciliate
ciliar *adj* (anat.) ciliary
cilicio *m* sackcloth, haircloth, hair shirt
cilindrada *f* piston displacement, cylinder capacity
cilindrado *m* rolling
cilindradora *f* road roller
cilindrar *va* to roll
cilíndrico -ca *adj* cylindric or cylindrical
cilindro *m* cylinder; roll, roller; (Am.) barrel organ; **un cuatro cilindros** a four-cylinder motor; **un dos cilindros** a two-cylinder motor; **un ocho cilindros en V** an eight-cylinder V motor; **cilindro de caminos** road roller
cilindroeje *m* (anat. & physiol.) axis cylinder
cilindroide *adj* cylindroid; *m* (geom. & med.) cylindroid
cilio *m* cilium, eyelash; (bot. & zool.) cilium
cilla *f* granary; tithe
cilleriza *f* nun in charge of housekeeping in a convent
cillerizo *m* tithe man
cillero *m* tithe man; tithe barn; wine cellar; storehouse
-cillo -lla *suffix dim* var. of **-illo** and attached to polysyllables ending in **d, e, n, r,** or an accented vowel, e.g., **nubecilla** little cloud; **jardincillo** small garden; **dolorcillo** little pain
cima *f* top (*of tree*); top, summit (*of mountain*); (bot.) cyme; (bot.) sprout; (fig.) top, height; **dar cima a** to carry out, to complete; **mirar por cima** to pay slight attention to; **por cima** (coll.) at the very top; **cima helicoidea** (bot.) helicoid cyme
cimacio *m* (arch.) cyma, ogee
cimarrón -rrona *adj* (Am.) shy, wild; (Am.) wild (*plant*); (Am.) black or bitter (*maté*); (Am.) fugitive (*slave*); (Am.) lazy (*sailor*); *mf* (Am.) fugitive slave; *m* (Am.) lazy sailor
cimarronear *vn* (Am.) to drink black maté; *vr* (Am.) to flee, run away (*said of a slave*)
cimbalaria *f* (bot.) Kenilworth ivy
cimbalero *m* (mus.) cymbalist
cimbalillo *m* small bell
cimbalista *m* (mus.) cymbalist
címbalo *m* (mus.) cymbal
cimbanillo *m* var. of **cimbalillo**
címbara *f* short, broad scythe or sickle
cimbel *m* stool pigeon, decoy pigeon; cord to which a decoy is attached
cimboga *f* citron (*fruit*)
cimborio or **cimborrio** *m* (arch.) dome; dome (*of steam boiler, tank car, etc.*)
cimbra *f* (arch.) centering; inside curvature of an arch or vault; (naut.) curvature of a board
cimbrado *m* bending body at the waist (*in a Spanish dance*)
cimbrar *va* to swing, to sway, to bend; (coll.) to beat with a stick, to thrash; (arch.) to build the centering for (*an arch or vault*); *vn* to swerve; *vr* to swing, to sway, to bend
cimbre *m* subterranean gallery
cimbreante *adj* flexible, pliant
cimbrear *va, vn & vr* var. of **cimbrar**
cimbreño -ña *adj* flexible, pliant; agile, willowy
cimbreo *m* swinging, swaying, bending
cimbronazo *m* blow with flat of sword; (Am.) earthquake
cimeno *m* (chem.) cymene
cimentación *f* foundation, laying a foundation
cimentar **§18** *va* to found; to lay the foundation for (*a wall, building, etc.; a science, religion, etc.*)
cimenterio *m* var. of **cementerio**
cimento *m* (geol.) cement
cimera *f* see **cimero**
cimerio -ria *adj & mf* Cimmerian
cimero -ra *adj* top, uppermost; *f* crest (*of helmet*); (her.) crest
cimicaria *f* (bot.) dwarf elder
cimiento *m* foundation, groundwork; basis, source; **abrir los cimientos** to dig the foundations, to break ground
cimillo *m* stool (*pole to which decoy is fastened*)
cimitarra *f* scimitar
cimo *m* (path.) zyme; **cimo excitador** (biol.) zymogen
cimofana *f* (mineral.) cymophane
cimogénesis *f* (biochem.) zymogenesis
cimógeno -na *adj* zymogenic; *m* (biochem. & biol.) zymogen
cimología *f* zymology
cimosis *f* (*pl:* **-sis**) zymosis
cimoso -sa *adj* (bot.) cymose
cimotecnia *f* var. of **cimurgia**
cimótico -ca *adj* zymotic
címrico -ca *adj & m* Cymric
cimurgia *f* zymurgy
cinabrio *m* cinnabar (*mineral and color*)
cinacina *f* (bot.) Jerusalem thorn
cinámico -ca *adj* (chem.) cinnamic
cinamomo *m* (bot.) bead tree; (bot.) oleaster, Russian olive
cinanquia *f* (path.) quinsy
cinc *m* (*pl:* **cinces**) (chem.) zinc
cinca *f* fault, error (*in bowling*)
cincar **§86** *va* to zinc
cincel *m* chisel, cutter, graver
cincelador *m* sculptor; engraver; stonecutter; chipping hammer
cinceladura *f* chiseling, carving, engraving
cincelar *va* to chisel, carve, engrave
cinceta *f* (orn.) pipit, titlark
cincino *m* (bot.) helicoid cyme
cincita *f* (mineral.) zincite
cinco *adj* five; **las cinco** five o'clock; *m* five; fifth (*in dates*); **decir a uno cuántas son cinco** (coll.) to tell someone what's what; **¡choque Vd. esos cinco!** or **¡vengan esos cinco!** (coll.) shake! (*i.e., shake hands!*)
cincocentista *adj* fifteenth-century; *m* (f.a.) cinquecentist
cincoenrama *f* (bot.) cinquefoil
cincograbado *m* zinc etching, zincograph
cincografía *f* zinc etching, zincography
cincomesino -na *adj* five-month-old
cincoso -sa *adj* zincous
cincuenta *adj & m* fifty
cincuentavo -va *adj & m* fiftieth

cincuentenario -ria *adj & m* semicentennial
cincuenteno -na *adj* fiftieth; *f* fifty
cincuentón -tona *adj & mf* quinquagenarian
cincha *f* cinch (*of saddle*); **a revienta cinchas** at breakneck speed; (Am.) unwillingly
cinchadura *f* cinching
cinchar *va* to cinch; to band, to hoop
cinchera *f* part of body where cinch is worn; (vet.) girth sore
cincho *m* sash, girdle; iron hoop; iron tire; (vet.) dry and contracted hoof
cinchuela *f* small cinch; narrow ribbon
cine *m* (coll.) movie, movies; **en cine** (coll.) in the movies; **cine en colores** (coll.) color movies; **cine en relieve** (coll.) three-dimensional movie; **cine hablado** (coll.) talkie; **cine mudo** (coll.) silent movie; **cine sonoro** (coll.) sound movie, talkie
cineasta *mf* motion-picture producer; movie fan; *m* movie actor; *f* movie actress
cinedrama *m* screenplay
cinegético -ca *adj* cynegetic; *f* cynegetics, hunting
cineísta *mf* var. of **cineasta**
cinelandia *f* (coll.) movieland
cinema *m* var. of **cine**
cinemadrama *m* photoplay
cinemateca *f* film library
cinemático -ca *adj* kinematic; *f* kinematics
cinematografía *f* cinematography
cinematografiar §90 *va & vn* to cinematograph, to film
cinematográfico -ca *adj* cinematographic, motion-picture
cinematografista *mf* motion-picture director
cinematógrafo *m* cinematograph, motion-picture projector, motion-picture theater; motion pictures
cineración *f* incineration
cinerario -ria *adj* cinerary; *f* (bot.) cineraria
cinéreo -a *adj* cinereous, ash-gray
cinericio -cia *adj* ashen; ash-gray
cinescopio *m* kinescope
cinestéreo *m* (mov.) three-D
cinestesia *f* kinaesthesia or kinesthesia
cinestésico -ca *adj* kinesthetic
cineteatro *m* movie house, motion-picture theater
cinético -ca *adj* kinetic; *f* kinetics
cingalés -lesa *adj* Singhalese; *mf* Singhalese; *m* Singhalese (*language*)
cíngaro -ra *adj* gypsy; *mf* zingaro
cinglado *m* shingling (*of iron*)
cinglador *m* shingler (*machine*)
cinglar *va* to shingle (*iron*); to scull (*to propel from the stern with one oar*)
cíngulo *m* cingulum (*of a priest's alb*); (anat., bot. & zool.) cingulum
cínico -ca *adj* cynic or cynical; Cynic; brazen, impudent; slovenly, untidy; *mf* cynic; *m* Cynic
cínife *m* (ent.) mosquito; (ent.) gallfly
cinismo *m* cynicism; Cynicism; brazenness, impudence
cinocéfalo -la *adj* cynocephalous; *m* (zool.) baboon
cinoglosa *f* (bot.) hound's-tongue
Cinosura *f* (astr.) Cynosure
cinquén *m* old Spanish coin (*five maravedis*)
cinquero *m* zinc worker, tinsmith
cinta *f* ribbon; tape, band, strip; film; measuring tape; curb (*along sidewalk*); (arch.) fillet, scroll; (Am.) can; **en cinta** tied down, repressed; **cinta adhesiva** adhesive tape; **cinta aisladora** or **aislante** friction tape; **cinta cinematográfica** moving-picture film; **cinta de embrague** (aut.) clutch band; **cinta de freno** (aut.) brake lining; **cinta de medir** tape measure; **cinta de teleimpresor** ticker tape; **cinta de transporte** belt conveyor; **cinta grabada de televisión** video tape; **cinta magnética** magnetic tape; **cinta magnetofónica** recording tape; **cinta métrica** tape measure; **cinta para cubrir** masking tape; **cinta perforada** paper tape, punched tape; **cinta pescadora** (elec.) fish wire
cintado -da *adj* beribboned
cintagorda *f* coarse hempen fishing net
cintarazo *m* blow with the flat of a sword
cintarear *va* (coll.) to strike with the broad of a sword
cinteado -da *adj* beribboned
cintería *f* ribbons; ribbon business; ribbon shop
cintero -ra *mf* ribbon weaver, ribbon dealer; *m* belt, girdle; hoisting line; (surv.) tapeman
Cintia *f* (myth.) Cynthia
cintilar *vn* var. of **centellear**
cintillo *m* hatband; ring set with precious stones, diamond ring; (Am.) hair ribbon
cinto *m* belt, girdle
cintra *f* (arch.) arch (*of an arch or vault*); **plena cintra** (arch.) semicircular arch
cintrado -da *adj* arched
cintradora *f* cambering machine
cintrar *va* to arch, bend, curve; to camber (*timber*)
cintrel *m* (arch.) guide rule for determining the angle of the various courses of an arch
cintura *f* waist; waistline; girdle; throat (*of chimney*); **meter en cintura** (coll.) to hold in check, to bring to reason
cinturón *m* sword belt; belt, sash; (fig.) belt, circle; **cinturón de castidad** chastity belt; **cinturón de asiento** seat belt; **cinturón de seguridad** safety belt (*of a lineman*); **cinturón de Venus** (myth.) cestus; (zool.) Venus's-girdle; **cinturón ortopédico** orthopedic belt; **cinturón salvavidas** (naut.) safety belt
cipariso *m* (poet.) cypress
cipayo *m* sepoy
ciperáceo -a *adj* (bot.) cyperaceous
cipo *m* memorial pillar; boundary stone; milestone, kilometer stone
cipote *adj* (Am.) stupid; (Am.) chubby, fat; *mf* (Am.) urchin, brat
ciprés *m* (bot.) cypress
cipresal *m* cypress grove
cipresino -na *adj* (pertaining to the) cypress
ciprino -na or **ciprio -pria** *adj & mf* Cyprian
cipripedio *m* (bot.) cypripedium
ciquiricata *f* (coll.) show of flattery, obsequiousness
circasiano -na *adj & mf* Circassian
Circe *f* (myth.) Circe; (*l.c.*) *f* cunning and deceitful woman
circense *adj* Circensian; (pertaining to a) circus
circinado -da *adj* (bot.) circinate
circo *m* circus; amphitheater; (geol.) cirque; **circo máximo** Circus Maximus
circón *m* (mineral.) zircon
circona *f* (chem.) zirconia
circonio *m* (chem.) zirconium
circuición *f* circling, surrounding
circuir §41 *va* to circle, to surround
circuito *m* circuit; race course; network (*of roads or railroads*); (elec.) circuit; **corto circuito** (elec.) short circuit; **circuito abierto** (elec.) open circuit; **circuito cerrado** (elec.) closed circuit; **circuito de filamento** (rad.) filament circuit; **circuito de placa** (rad.) plate circuit; **circuito de rejilla** (rad.) grid circuit; **circuito de retorno por tierra** (elec.) earth-return circuit; **circuito fantasma** (elec.) phantom circuit; **circuito impreso** (elec.) printed circuit
circulación *f* circulation; traffic; **circulación rodada** vehicular traffic
circulante *adj* circulating
circular *adj* circular; *f* circular, circular letter; *va* to circulate; *vn* to circulate; **circular por** to walk around (*e.g., a garden*)
circularidad *f* circularity
circulatorio -ria *adj* circulatory
círculo *m* circle; club; clubhouse; **cuadrar el círculo** to square the circle; **círculo horario** (astr.) hour circle; **círculo máximo** (astr. & geom.) great circle; **círculo menor** (astr. & geom.) small circle; **círculo parhélico** (meteor.) parheliacal ring, parhelic circle; **círculo polar antártico** antarctic circle; **círculo polar ártico** arctic circle; **círculo vicioso** vicious circle
circumambiente *adj* circumambient, surrounding
circumpolar *adj* circumpolar
circuncidar *va* to circumcise; to clip, diminish, curtail

circuncisión *f* circumcision
circunciso -sa *adj* circumcised
circundar *va* to surround, encompass, go around
circunferencia *f* circumference
circunferencial *adj* circumferential
circunferente *adj* surrounding
circunflejo -ja *adj* (anat. & gram.) circumflex; *m* (gram.) circumflex
circunfluente *adj* circumfluent
circunfuso -sa *adj* circumfused
circunlocución *f* or **circunloquio** *m* circumlocution
circunnavegación *f* circumnavigation
circunnavegador -dora *mf* circumnavigator
circunnavegar §59 *va* to circumnavigate
circunscribir §17, 9 *va* to circumscribe; (geom.) to circumscribe; *vr* to become circumscribed; to hold oneself down
circunscripción *f* circumscription; subdivision (*of an administrative, military, electoral, or ecclesiastical territory*)
circunscrito -ta *pp of* **circunscribir;** *adj* circumscript
circunspección *f* circumspection
circunspecto -ta *adj* circumspect
circunstancia *f* circumstance; **en las circunstancias presentes** under the circumstances; **circunstancias agravantes** aggravating circumstances; **circunstancias atenuantes** extenuating circumstances
circunstanciado -da *adj* circumstantial, detailed, minute
circunstancial *adj* circumstantial
circunstante *adj* present; surrounding; *mf* bystander, onlooker
circunterrestre *adj* around the earth
circunvalación *f* circumvallation; (fort.) circumvallation
circunvalar *va* to surround; (fort.) to circumvallate
circunvecino -na *adj* adjacent, neighboring, surrounding
circunvolar §77 *va* to fly around
circunvolución *f* circumvolution; convolution; (anat.) convolution; **circunvolución cerebral** (anat.) cerebral convolution; **circunvolución de Broca** (anat.) convolution of Broca
circunyacente *adj* circumjacent
cirenaico -ca *adj & mf* Cyrenaic; **la Cirenaica** Cyrenaica
Cirene *f* Cyrene (*city*)
cirial *m* (eccl.) processional candlestick
cirigallo -lla *mf* gadabout
cirigaña *f* (dial.) flattery; (dial.) triviality; (dial.) disappointment
cirílico -ca *adj* Cyrillic
Cirilo *m* Cyril
cirineo *m* (coll.) helper
cirio *m* (eccl.) wax candle; **cirio pascual** (eccl.) paschal candle
Ciro *m* Cyrus
cirolero *m* (bot.) plum tree
cirrípedo -da *adj & m* (zool.) cirriped
cirro *m* (bot., zool. & meteor.) cirrus; (path.) scirrhus
cirrocúmulo *m* (meteor.) cirro-cumulus
cirroestrato *m* var. of **cirrostrato**
cirrópodo -da *adj & m* (zool.) cirriped
cirrosis *f* (path.) cirrhosis
cirroso -sa *adj* cirrous; scirrhous
cirrostrato *m* (meteor.) cirro-stratus
cirrótico -ca *adj* cirrhotic
ciruela *f* plum (*fruit*); **ciruela claudia** greengage; **ciruela de América** coco plum; **ciruela de fraile** long green plum; **ciruela de yema** yellow plum; **ciruela pasa** prune; **ciruela verdal** greengage
ciruelo *m* (bot.) plum tree; (coll.) dolt
cirugía *f* surgery; **cirugía cosmética, decorativa** or **estética** face lifting; **cirugía mayor** major surgery; **cirugía menor** minor surgery; **cirugía nerviosa** neurosurgery; **cirugía ortopédica** orthopedic surgery; **cirugía plástica** plastic surgery
cirujano -na *mf* surgeon; *m* (ichth.) surgeonfish
cirujano-dentista *m* dental surgeon
cisalpino -na *adj* cisalpine
cisandino -na *adj* cisandine
cisatlántico -ca *adj* cisatlantic
cisca *f* (bot.) ditch reed; (bot.) cogon grass
ciscar §86 *va* (coll.) to dirty, to soil; *vr* to soil one's bed or one's clothes
cisco *m* slack, culm, coal dust; (coll.) uproar, row, wrangling; **meter cisco** (coll.) to stir up a row
ciscón *m* cinders
cisión *f* incision
cisípedo -da *adj* finger-footed
cisma *m* schism; discord
cismático -ca *adj* schismatic or schismatical; (Am.) fastidious; (Am.) gossipy; *mf* schismatic
cismontano -na *adj* cismontane, situated on this side of the mountains
cismoso -sa *adj* troublemaking; gossipy; *mf* troublemaker; gossip
cisne *m* (orn.) swan; (fig.) swan (*poet*); (*cap.*) *m* (astr.) Cygnus, Swan; **cisne de Mantua** Mantuan Swan (*Virgil*); **cisne dirceo** Dircaean Swan (*Pindar*)
cisoide *f* (geom.) cissoid
cispadano -na *adj* cispadane, situated on the Roman side of the river Po
cisquera *f* coal-dust shop
cisquero *m* coal-dust dealer; pounce bag
cistáceo -a *adj* (bot.) cistaceous
cistercience *adj & m* Cistercian
cisterna *f* cistern; (anat.) cistern; **cisterna de desagüe** catch basin
cisticerco *m* (zool.) cysticercus
cisticercosis *f* (path.) cysticercosis
cístico -ca *adj* (anat.) cystic; *m* (anat.) cystic duct
cistitis *f* (path.) cystitis
cistoscopio *m* cystoscope
cistotomía *f* (surg.) cystotomy
cisura *f* fissure; incision; (anat.) sulcus; **cisura de Rolando** (anat.) sulcus of Rolando
cita *f* date, engagement, appointment; citation; quotation; reference; **darse cita** to make a date, to have an appointment (*with each other*); **cita a ciegas** (coll.) blind date
citable *adj* quotable
citación *f* citation, quotation; (law) citation, summons
citado -da *adj* above-mentioned
citano -na *mf* (coll.) so-and-so
citar *va* to make an appointment with; to cite, to quote; (law) to cite, to summon; (taur.) to incite, to provoke; *vr* to have a date, to keep a date
citara *f* wall the thickness of a brick
cítara *f* (mus.) cithara; (mus.) cither; (mus.) zithern; (mus.) zither
citarilla *f* thin brick wall
citarón *m* masonry foundation
citasa *f* (biochem.) cytase
cite *m* (taur.) incitement, challenge
citereo -a *adj* (poet.) Cytherean; (*cap.*) *f* (myth.) Cytherea
citerior *adj* hither, nearer, situated on this side
citisina *f* (pharm.) cytisine
cítiso *m* (bot.) cytisus
-cito -ta *suffix dim* var. of **-ito** and attached to polysyllables ending in **d, e, n, r,** or an accented vowel, e.g., **ciudadcita** pretty little city; **madrecita** dear little mother; **Carmencita** little Carmen; **mujercita** nice little woman; **papacito** dear papa
cítola *f* millclapper
citología *f* cytology
citólogo -ga *mf* cytologist
citoplasma *m* (biol.) cytoplasm
citoplásmico -ca *adj* (biol.) cytoplasmic
citoquímica *f* cytochemistry
citote *m* (coll.) citation, summons
citramontano -na *adj* var. of **cismontano**
citrato *m* (chem.) citrate; **citrato de magnesia** (med.) citrate of magnesia
cítrico -ca *adj* (chem.) citric
citrícola *adj* citrus-growing
citrina *f* lemon oil; (biochem.) citrin
citrón *m* var. of **limón**
ciudad *f* city; city council; **ciudad Condal** Barcelona; **ciudad de David** City of David (*Jerusalem; Bethlehem*); **ciudad de Dios** City of God (*heaven*); **ciudad del amor fraternal**

City of Brotherly Love (*Philadelphia*); **ciudad del Apóstol** Santiago de Compostela; **ciudad de las siete colinas** City of the Seven Hills (*Rome*); **ciudad del Betis** Seville; **Ciudad del Cabo** Cape Town; **ciudad de los Califas** Cordova; **ciudad de los mástiles** City of Masts (*London*); **ciudad de los Reyes** Lima, Peru; **Ciudad del Vaticano** Vatican City; **ciudad de María Santísima** Seville; **Ciudad Eterna** Eternal City (*Rome*); **ciudad Imperial** or **Imperial ciudad** Toledo; **ciudad jardín** garden city; **ciudad libre** free city; **ciudad prohibida** Forbidden City (*Lhasa, capital of Tibet; walled section of Pekin*); **Ciudad Santa** Holy City (*Jerusalem, Rome, Mecca, etc.*); **Ciudad Vaticana** Vatican City; **Ciudad** City (*word written on an envelope to indicate that the letter is to go to the city in which it is mailed*)
ciudadanía *f* citizenship
ciudadano -na *adj* (pertaining to the) city; civic; citizen; *mf* citizen; urbanite; *f* citizeness
ciudadela *f* (fort.) citadel; (Am.) tenement house
civeta *f* (zool.) civet cat
civeto *m* civet
cívico -ca *adj* civic; public-spirited; domestic; *m* (coll.) policeman
civil *adj* civil; civilian; *mf* civilian; *m* policeman
civilidad *f* civility
civilista *mf* authority on civil law, professor of civil law; (Am.) antimilitarist
civilización *f* civilization
civilizador -dora *adj* civilizing
civilizar §76 *va & vr* to civilize
civismo *m* civism, good citizenship
cizalla *f* shears, sheet-metal shears; shearing machine; paper cutter; (surg.) bone forceps; chip, clipping (*of metal*); chips, shavings; **cizallas** *fpl* shears; **cizalla de guillotina** guillotine shears
cizallar *va* to shear
cizaña *f* (bot.) darnel; contagious vice, contaminating influence; discord; (Bib.) tare; **sembrar cizaña** to sow discord; **cizaña vivaz** (bot.) rye grass
cizañador -dora *mf* sower of discord, troublemaker
cizañamiento *m* sowing of discord, troublemaking
cizañar *va* to sow discord among, to alienate; *vn* to sow discord
cizañero -ra *mf* (coll.) sower of discord, troublemaker
cl. abr. of **centilitro** or **centilitros**
clac *m* (*pl:* **claques**) opera hat (*collapsible hat*); cocked hat
cladócero -ra *adj & m* (zool.) cladoceran
cladodio *m* (bot.) cladode, cladophyll
claitonia *f* (bot.) claytonia
clamar *va* to clamor for, cry out for; *vn* to clamor, cry out; **clamar al cielo** to cry to heaven; **clamar contra** to cry out against; **clamar por** to clamor for, cry out for
clámide *f* chlamys
clamor *m* clamor, outcry; plaint, whine; knell, toll
clamoreada *f* clamor, outcry; plaint, whine
clamorear *va* to clamor; *vn* to clamor; to toll
clamoreo *m* clamor, clamoring; toll, tolling
clamoroso -sa *adj* clamorous; crying, shrieking; buzzing (*noise*)
clan *m* clan
clandestinidad *f* clandestinity, secrecy, underhandedness
clandestinista *mf* (Am.) bootlegger
clandestino -na *adj* clandestine
clanga *f* (orn.) gannet, solan
clangor *m* (poet.) blare, sound of trumpet
claque *f* claque, hired clappers
clara & **Clara** *f* see **claro**
claraboya *f* skylight; transom; (arch.) bull's-eye; (arch.) clerestory
clarar *va* var. of **aclarar**
clarea *f* mulse, mulled wine
clarear *va* to brighten, light up; (Am.) to pierce through and through; *vn* to dawn; to clear up; *vr* to show through, be transparent (*said of a fabric*); (coll.) to show one's hand, give oneself away
clarecer §34 *vn* to dawn
clarens *m* (*pl:* **-rens**) clarence (*carriage*)
clareo *m* clearing (*of a thicket or woods*)
clarete *m* claret
clareza *f* clarity, clearness
claridad *f* clarity, clearness; brightness, brilliance, glory; blunt remark; **claridades** *fpl* plain language, simple truth
claridoso -sa *adj* (Am.) blunt, plain-talking
clarificación *f* clarification; brightening
clarificador *m* clarifier
clarificadora *f* (Am.) clarifier (*in sugar refining*)
clarificar §86 *va* to clarify; to brighten, light up; to clear (*e.g., a thicket*)
clarífico -ca *adj* bright, resplendent
clarimente *m* (archaic) face lotion
clarimento *m* (paint.) bright color
clarín *m* (mus.) clarion (*kind of trumpet; organ stop*); clarion player; fine cambric; (orn.) tropical thrush (*Myadestes unicolor*); (Am.) sweet pea
clarinada *f* clarion call; (coll.) uncalled-for remark
clarinazo *m* clarion call
clarinero *m* clarion player, bugler
clarinete *m* (mus.) clarinet; clarinetist
clarinetista *mf* clarinetist
clarión *m* chalk
clarioncillo *m* crayon
clarisa *f* Clare (*nun*)
clarividencia *f* clairvoyance (*clear-sightedness; supposed power to see things that are out of sight*)
clarividente *adj* clairvoyant; clear-sighted; *mf* clairvoyant (*person who claims to see things that are out of sight*)
claro -ra *adj* clear; bright; light (*in color*); thin (*liquid*); thin, sparse (*hair*); weak (*tea*); smart; famous, illustrious; light (*beer*); **a las claras** openly, publicly; clearly ‖ **claro** *adv* clearly; **¡claro!** sure!; of course!; **¡claro está!** or **¡claro que sí!** sure!, of course ‖ *m* gap, break; space, interval; glade, clearing; light (*window or opening*); skylight; (naut.) break (*in clouds*); **de claro en claro** obviously; from one end to the other; **pasar la noche de claro en claro** to not sleep a wink all night; **poner** or **sacar en claro** to explain, clear up; to copy (*a rough draft*); **claro de luna** brief moonlight (*on a dark night*) ‖ *f* white of egg; bald spot; thinly woven piece of cloth; temporary let-up or break (*in rain*) ‖ (*cap.*) *f* Clara, Clare
claror *m* brightness, splendor; **claror de luna** moonlight
claroscuro *m* (paint.) chiaroscuro; combination of fine and heavy strokes in penmanship
clarucho -cha *adj* (coll.) watery, thin
clase *f* class; classroom; **clases** *fpl* noncommissioned officers, warrant officers; **altas clases** upper classes; **fumarse la clase** (coll.) to cut class; **primera clase** (naut. & rail.) first class; **segunda clase** (naut. & rail.) second class; **tercera clase** (naut. & rail.) third class; **clase alta** upper class; **clase baja** lower class; **clase de cámara** or **clase intermedia** (naut.) cabin class; **clase de tropa** (mil.) noncommissioned officers; **clase media** middle class; **clase obrera** working class; **clases pasivas** pensioners; **clase turista** (aer. & naut.) tourist class
clasicismo *m* classicism
clasicista *adj* classicistic; *mf* classicist
clásico -ca *adj* classic, classical; outstanding; regular, everyday; *m* classic (*author*); classicist
clasificación *f* classification
clasificador -dora *adj* classifying; filing; *m* filing cabinet; (min.) classifier
clasificar §86 *va* to classify
clasismo *m* class discrimination
clasista *adj* (pertaining to) class; *mf* advocate of class discrimination
claudicación *f* limping, limp
claudicar §86 *vn* to limp; to bungle; (coll.) to back down
Claudio *m* Claude, Claudius

claustra *f* cloister
claustral *adj* cloistral
claustro *m* cloister; (anat.) claustrum; faculty (*of a school*)
claustrofobia *f* (path.) claustrophobia
cláusula *f* clause (*in a contract or other document*); (gram.) sentence; **cláusula de evicción de saneamiento** (law) warranty clause
clausulado -da *adj* choppy (*style*); *m* clauses, series of clauses
clausular *va* to close, finish; to terminate (*a contract*)
clausura *f* confinement, monastic life; adjournment, close; closing
clausurar *va & vr* to adjourn; to close
clava *f* club; (naut.) scupper; (anat.) clava
clavadista *mf* (Am.) diver
clavadizo -za *adj* nail-studded
clavado -da *adj* studded with nails; exact, precise; just right; stopped (*said of a watch*); sharp, e.g., **a las cinco clavadas** at five o'clock sharp; *m* (Am.) dive; **echar un clavado** (Am.) to take a dive
clavadura *f* pricking a horse's foot (*with horseshoe nail*)
clavar *va* to nail; to drive (*a nail*); to stick (*a dagger, a punch, etc.*); to prick (*a horse in shoeing*); to set (*a precious stone*); to fix (*eyes, attention, etc.*); (coll.) to cheat; *vr* (coll.) to get cheated; (Am.) to dive; **clavárselas** (Am.) to get drunk
clavaria *f* nail mould; (bot.) goatsbeard
clavazón *f* nails, stock of nails
clave *f* key (*to a code, puzzle, etc.*); (mus.) clef; (arch.) keystone; **echar la clave** to close, to wind up (*a deal, speech, etc.*); **clave de fa** (mus.) bass clef; **clave de sol** (mus.) treble clef; **clave telegráfica** (telg.) code word; *m* (mus.) harpsichord; *adj* key
clavel *m* (bot.) pink, carnation; **clavel coronado** (bot.) garden pink, grass pink; **clavel de China** (bot.) China pink; **clavel de las Indias** (bot.) French marigold; **clavel de ramillete** or **clavel de San Isidro** (bot.) sweet william; **clavel reventón** carnation, double-flowered carnation
clavelito *m* (bot.) dogbane
clavelón *m* (bot.) marigold
clavellina *f* (bot.) pink; **clavellina de pluma** (bot.) garden pink, grass pink
claveque *m* rock crystal (*cut to imitate a diamond*)
clavero -ra *mf* keeper of the keys; treasurer; *m* (bot.) clove tree; *f* nail hole; nail mould, heading stamp; line of boundary stones or landmarks
claveta *f* peg, wooden peg
clavete *m* tack; (mus.) plectrum
clavetear *va* to stud, to trim with studs, gold or silver tacks, etc.; to tip, to put a tip on (*a cord, string, ribbon, etc.*); to wind up, to settle
clavicordio *m* (mus.) clavichord
clavícula *f* (anat.) clavicle
claviculado -da *adj* (zool.) claviculate
clavicular *adj* clavicular
claviforme *adj* (bot. & zool.) clavate
clavija *f* pin, peg, dowel; treenail; (mach.) pintle; (mus.) peg (*of string instrument*); (elec.) plug; **apretar las clavijas a** (coll.) to put the screws on; **clavija de piso** (elec.) floor plug; **clavija hendida** cotter pin
clavijero *m* peg, hook, hanger; (mus.) pegbox (*e.g., of a guitar*); (mus.) wrest plank (*of piano*); (telp.) plug
clavillo or **clavito** *m* brad, tack; pin, rivet (*e.g., to hold scissors together*); (cook.) clove
clavo *m* nail; spike; corn (*on foot*); sharp pain; keen sorrow; headache; scab; (vet.) pastern tumor; (cook.) clove; (min.) rich vein; (Am.) drug on the market; **dar en el clavo** (coll.) to hit the nail on the head; **de clavo pasado** self-evident; easy; **remachar el clavo** (coll.) to make a bad situation worse; (coll.) to argue for a statement already proved; **clavo de alambre** wire nail; **clavo de especia** clove (*flower*); **clavo de herrar** horse nail, horseshoe nail; **clavo romano** brass-headed nail
claxon *m* klaxon
cleistógamo -ma *adj* (bot.) cleistogamous
clemátide *f* (bot.) clematis, virgin's-bower
clemencia *f* clemency
clemente *adj* clement; (*cap.*) *m* Clement
Cleón *m* Cleon
clepsidra *f* water clock, clepsydra
cleptomanía *f* kleptomania
cleptomaníaco -ca or **cleptómano -na** *adj & mf* kleptomaniac
clerecía *f* clergy; priesthood
clerical *adj* clerical; *m* clerical, clericalist
clericalismo *m* clericalism
clericato *m* or **clericatura** *f* clergy, priesthood
clerigalla *f* (scornful) priesthood, priests
clérigo *m* cleric, clergyman; (hist.) clerk (*scholar*); **clérigo de misa** priest
clerizón *m* chorister, acolyte
clerizonte *m* fake cleric; shabby priest
clero *m* clergy
clerofobia *f* priest hatred
clerófobo -ba *adj* priest-hating; *mf* priest hater
cleveíta *f* (mineral.) cleveite
cliché *m* cliché (*timeworn phrase or idea*)
cliente *mf* client; customer; patient (*of a physician*); guest (*of a hotel*)
clientela *f* clientele; customers; patronage, protection
clima *m* climate; (geog.) zone, country, clime; **clima artificial** air conditioning
climatérico -ca *adj* climacteric; (coll.) ill-humored; *m* climacteric
climaterio *m* climacteric
climático -ca *adj* climatic
climatización *f* air conditioning
climatizar **§76** to air-condition
climatología *f* climatology
clímax *m* (*pl:* **-max**) (rhet.) climax
clin *f* var. of **crin**
clincha *f* (box.) clinch
clínico -ca *adj* clinical; *mf* clinician; (archaic) person asking for deathbed baptism; *f* clinic; private hospital; **clínica de reposo** convalescent home, nursing home
clinómetro *m* clinometer
clinopodio *m* (bot.) calamint
Clío *f* (myth.) Clio
clípeo *m* (archeol., bot. & zool.) clypeus
clíper *m* (naut. & aer.) clipper
cliqueteo *m* click, clicking
clisado *m* (print.) plating
clisar *va* (print.) to plate
clisé *m* (print.) cliché, plate; (print.) electrotype; (phot.) plate (*positive or negative*)
clistel *m* or **clister** *m* (med.) clyster, enema
clisterizar **§76** *va* to clyster, to give an enema to; *vr* to give oneself an enema
clitelo *m* (zool.) clitellum
Clitemnestra *f* (myth.) Clytemnestra
clitómetro *m* clinometer
clítoris *m* (anat.) clitoris
clivoso -sa *adj* (poet.) sloping
clo *m* cluck
cloaca *f* sewer; (zool.) cloaca
clocar **§95** *vn* to cluck
Clodoveo *m* Clovis
Cloe *f* Chloe
clónico -ca *adj* clonic
clono *m* (path.) clonus
clopemanía *f* var. of **cleptomanía**
cloque *m* boat hook; harpoon to catch tuna fish
cloquear *va* to harpoon (*tuna fish*); *vn* to cluck
cloqueo *m* cluck, clucking
cloquera *f* broodiness (*of a hen*)
cloquero *m* tuna-fish harpooner
cloral *m* (chem.) chloral
clorato *m* (chem.) chlorate; **clorato de potasio** (chem.) potassium chlorate
clorhidrato *m* (chem.) hydrochlorate
clorhídrico -ca *adj* (chem.) hydrochloric
clórico -ca *adj* (chem.) chloric
Cloris *f* (myth.) Chloris
clorita *f* (mineral.) chlorite
clorítico -ca *adj* chloritic
clorito *m* (chem.) chlorite
cloro *m* (chem.) chlorine
clorofila *f* (bot. & biochem.) chlorophyll
clorofílico -ca *adj* chlorophyllous
clorofilina *f* (biochem.) chlorophyllin
clorofórmico -ca *adj* chloroformic

cloroformización *f* (med.) chloroformization, chloroforming
cloroformizar **§76** *va* (med.) to chloroform
cloroformo *m* (chem.) chloroform
cloromicetina *f* (pharm.) chloromycetin
cloropicrina *f* (chem.) chloropicrin
cloroplasto *m* (bot.) chloroplast
cloropreno *m* (chem.) chloroprene
clorosis *f* (bot. & path.) chlorosis; **clorosis de Egipto** (path.) hookworm disease
cloroso -sa *adj* (chem.) chlorous
clorótico -ca *adj* chlorotic
clortetraciclina *f* (pharm.) chlortetracycline
clorurar *va* to chloridize, to convert into a chloride
cloruro *m* (chem.) chloride; **cloruro amónico** (chem.) ammonium chloride; **cloruro de cal** (chem.) chloride of lime; **cloruro de calcio** (chem.) calcium chloride; **cloruro de etilo** (chem.) ethyl chloride; **cloruro mercúrico** (chem.) mercuric chloride
Cloto *f* (myth.) Clotho
club *m* (*pl:* **clubs**) club; **club náutico** yacht club
clubista *mf* club member
clueco -ca *adj* broody; (coll.) decrepit; *f* brooder (*hen*)
cluniacense *adj & m* Cluniac
cllo. abr. of **cuartillo**
cm. abr. of **centímetro** or **centímetros**
C.M.B. or **c.m.b.** abr. of **cuyas manos beso**
Cnosos *f* Knossos
coa *f* sharp stick used by Indians for tilling; (Am.) hoe; (Am.) jail slang
coacción *f* coercion, compulsion, coaction; enforcement
coaccionar *va* to force, to compel
coacervación *f* piling, heaping
coacervar *va* to pile, to heap up
coacreedor -ra *mf* cocreditor
coactar *va* to coerce, to force
coactivo -va *adj* coercive, compelling
coacusado -da *adj* jointly accused; *mf* codefendant
coadjutor -tora *mf* coadjutor; *f* coadjutrix
coadjutoría *f* coadjuvancy
coadministrador *m* coadministrator
coadunación *f* or **coadunamiento** *m* close union, coadunation
coadunar *va & vr* to join closely together
coadyutor *m* coadjutor
coadyuvante *m* state's attorney; (med.) adjuvant
coadyuvar *va* to help, aid; **coadyuvar a** + *inf* to help to + *inf; vn* to contribute
coagente *mf* coagent, associate
coagulación *f* coagulation; curdling
coagulador -dora *adj* coagulating, coagulative
coagulante *adj* coagulating, coagulative; *m* coagulant
coagular *va & vr* to coagulate; to curdle
coagulina *f* (biochem.) coagulin
coágulo *m* (physiol.) coagulum, clot
coala *m* (zool.) koala
coalescencia *f* coalescence
coalescente *adj* coalescent
coalición *f* coalition
coalicionista *mf* coalitionist
coaligar **§59** *vr* var. of **coligar**
coalla *f* (orn.) woodcock
coana *f* (anat.) choana
coapóstol *m* fellow apostle
coaptación *f* coaptation
coartación *f* limitation, restriction; (med.) coarctation; obligation to be ordained within a limited time in order to enjoy a benefice
coartada *f* alibi; **probar la coartada** to prove an alibi
coartar *va* to limit, restrict
coate -ta *adj & mf* (Am.) var. of **cuate**
coatí *m* (*pl:* **-tíes**) (zool.) coati
coautor -tora *mf* coauthor, fellow author
coaxial *adj* coaxial
coba *f* (coll.) trick; (coll.) cajolery; (coll.) chat
cobaltar *va* to plate with cobalt
cobáltico -ca *adj* (chem.) cobaltic
cobaltina *f* (mineral.) cobaltite or cobaltine
cobalto *m* (chem.) cobalt
cobarde *adj* cowardly; timid, faint-hearted; dim (*sight*); *mf* coward
cobardear *vn* to be cowardly; to be timid, faint-hearted
cobardía *f* cowardice; timidity, faint-heartedness
cobaya *m* or **cobayo** *m* (zool.) guinea pig
cobeligerante *m* cobelligerent
cobertera *f* lid, potlid; procuress
cobertizo *m* shed
cobertor *m* bedcover, bedspread
cobertura *f* cover; covering; ceremony of conferring title on grandee of Spain (*which consists of his putting his hat on in the presence of king*)
cobija *f* imbrex tile; short mantilla; blanket; (Am.) horse blanket; **cobijas** *fpl* (Am.) bedclothes; **cobija eléctrica** electric blanket
cobijamiento *m* covering, closing
cobijar *va* to cover, to close; to lodge; to shelter; **en todo lo que el sol cobija** under the sun
cobijo *m* covering, closing; lodging (*without meals*); shelter, protection
cobista *adj* (coll.) fawning, flattering; *mf* (coll.) fawner, flatterer
Coblenza *f* Coblenz
cobo *m* (zool.) purse crab; (Am.) blanket
cobra *f* (hunt.) retrieve, retrieval; rope for yoking oxen; mares hitched to tread grain; (zool.) cobra
cobrable or **cobradero -ra** *adj* collectable; recoverable
cobrador *m* collector; conductor, trolley conductor; retriever (*dog*)
cobranza *f* collection; cashing; retrieval (*of game*)
cobrar *va* to recover (*something lost*); to collect; to cash; to charge; to acquire, get, win; to pull in (*a rope*); (hunt.) to retrieve; (Am.) to dun; **cobrar afición, odio, etc. a** to take a liking, dislike, etc. for; **cobrar ánimo** to take courage; **cobrar carnes** to put on flesh; **cobrar fuerzas** to gain strength; *vn* to get hit, e.g., **vas a cobrar** you're going to get hit; *vr* to recover (*e.g., from fear*); to come to
cobre *m* copper; brasses (*kitchen utensils*); **cobres** (mus.) brasses; **batir el cobre** (coll.) to hustle, work with energy; **mostrar el cobre** (Am.) to show one's bad side; **cobre quemado** copper sulfate; **cobre verde** malachite
cobreado -da *adj* copperplated; *m* copperplating
cobreño -ña *adj* copper
cobrería *f* copper work; copperworks
cobrero *m* coppersmith
cobrizo -za *adj* copper-colored; cupreous
cobro *m* collection; cashing; **poner en cobro** to put in a safe place; **ponerse en cobro** to withdraw to a safe place
Coburgo Coburg
coca *f* (bot. & pharm.) coca; little, round berry; woman's hair on one side of part in the center; (coll.) head; (coll.) rap on the head with the knuckles; kink, knot (*in a rope*); (Am.) shell, rind; **de coca** (Am.) free; (Am.) in vain; **coca de Levante** (bot.) India berry tree
cocada *f* coconut candy, coconut bar
cocaína *f* cocaine
cocainismo *m* (path.) cocainism
cocainización *f* cocainization
cocainizar **§76** *va* to cocainize
cocar **§86** *va* (coll.) to make a face at, to make faces at; (coll.) to cajole; (coll.) to make eyes at, to flirt with
coccíneo -a *adj* purple
cocción *f* cooking, boiling; baking, burning (*of brick*)
cóccix *m* (*pl:* **-cix**) (anat.) coccyx
coceador -dora *adj* kicking (*animal*)
coceadura *f* or **coceamiento** *m* kicking
cocear *vn* to kick; (coll.) to balk, to resist
cocedero -ra *adj* easy to cook, boil, or bake; *m* cookery, boiling room
cocedizo -za *adj* easy to cook, boil, or bake
cocedor *m* workman in charge of boiling syrup (*for making wine*); cookery, boiling room
cocedura *f* var. of **cocción**
cocer **§30** *va* to cook; to boil; to bake (*bread, etc.*); to fire (*bricks*); to brew, to seethe; to di-

gest; to ret; *vn* to cook; to boil; to ferment; to seethe; *vr* to be in great sorrow; to be greatly inconvenienced; **no cocérsele a uno el pan** (coll.) to become intensely impatient
cocido -da *adj* (coll.) experienced, skilled; *m* olla, Spanish stew
cociente *m* (math.) quotient; **cociente intelectual** intelligence quotient
cocimiento *m* cooking, boiling; baking; decoction; bath for dyeing
cocina *f* kitchen; cuisine, cooking; stove; pottage of greens; **cocina de campaña** camp kitchen; **cocina de presión** pressure cooker; **cocina económica** kitchen range; **cocina sin fuego** fireless cooker
cocinar *va* to cook; (Am.) to bake; *vn* (coll.) to meddle
cocinero -ra *mf* cook
cocinilla *f* kitchenette; chafing dish; cooker; fireplace; **cocinilla sin fuego** fireless cooker; *m* (coll.) meddler
Cocito *m* (myth.) Cocytus
cóclea *f* endless screw; (anat.) cochlea
coclear *adj* cochlear
coclearia *f* (bot.) scurvy grass
coco *m* (bot.) coco, coconut palm or tree; coconut; coconut husk or shell; (bact.) coccus; percale; India berry; (ent.) scale insect; (orn.) white ibis; topknot, chignon; (coll.) bogeyman; (coll.) face, grimace; (Am.) derby hat; **hacer cocos** (coll.) to make a face, to make faces; (coll.) to cajole; (coll.) to make eyes, to flirt; **ser un coco** (coll.) to be ugly as the devil
cocobacilo *m* (bact.) coccobacillus
cocobolo *m* (bot.) sea grape; (bot.) cocobolo (*Dalbergia retusa*)
cocodriliano -na *adj & m* (zool.) crocodilian
cocodrilo *m* (zool.) crocodile
cocolmeca *f* (bot.) greenbrier
cócora *adj* (coll.) boresome, annoying; *mf* (coll.) bore
cocoso -sa *adj* gnawed by scale insects
cocotal *m* coconut grove
cocote *m* var. of **cogote**
cocotero *m* (bot.) coco, coconut palm or tree
coctel *m* or **cóctel** *m* cocktail; cocktail party
coctelera *f* cocktail shaker
cocuma *f* (Am.) roast corn on the cob
cocuyo *m* (bot.) ironwood; (ent.) fire beetle
cochambre *m* (coll.) filthy, stinking thing; (coll.) filthiness, dirtiness
cochambrería *f* (coll.) lot of filthy, stinking things
cochambrero -ra or **cochambroso -sa** *adj* (coll.) filthy and stinking
cocharro *m* wooden or stone cup, crock or bowl
cochastro *m* sucking wild boar
coche *m* carriage; coach; car; taxi; hog; **arrastrar coche** (coll.) to set up a coach, to live in style; **caminar en el coche de San Francisco** to go or to ride on shank's mare; **echar coche** to set up a coach; **coche automotor** rail car; **coche bar** (rail.) club car; **coche bomba** fire engine; **coche celular** Black Maria, prison van; **coche cuna** baby carriage; **coche de alquiler** cab, hack; **coche de carreras** (aut.) racing car; **coche de correos** (rail.) postal car, railroad mail car; **coche de deporte** (aut.) pleasure car; **coche de equipajes** (rail.) baggage car; **coche de mercancías** (rail.) freight car; **coche de muchos caballos** (aut.) high-powered car; **coche de paseo** (aut.) passenger car; **coche de plaza** or **de punto** hack; **coche de serie** (aut.) stock car; **coche de turismo** (aut.) touring car; **coche de viajeros** (rail.) passenger car; **coche fúnebre** or **mortuorio** hearse; **coche motor** motor coach; **coche usado** used car
cochear *vn* to drive a coach; to go driving
coche-bar *m* (*pl:* **coches-bares**) (rail.) club car
coche-cama *m* (*pl:* **coches-camas** or **coches-cama**) (rail.) sleeping car
cochecillo *m* little coach; wheel chair; **cochecillo para inválidos** wheel chair; **cochecillo para niño** baby carriage
coche-comedor *m* (*pl:* **coches-comedores**) (rail.) diner, dining car
coche-correo *m* (*pl:* **coches-correo**) (rail.) postal car, railroad mail car
coche-fumador *m* (*pl:* **coches-fumadores**) (rail.) smoker, smoking car
coche-habitación *m* (*pl:* **coches-habitación**) trailer
cochera *f* see **cochero**
coche-restaurante *m* (*pl:* **coches-restaurantes** or **coches-restaurante**) (rail.) diner, dining car
cocheril *adj* (coll.) (pertaining to a) coach; coachman's
cochero -ra *adj* easily boiled or cooked; *m* coachman; coach driver; **cochero de punto** hackman; *f* coachman's wife; coach house; livery stable; garage; carbarn
cocherón *m* large coach house; engine house, roundhouse
coche-salón *m* (*pl:* **coches-salones** or **coches-salón**) (rail.) parlor car, chair car
cochevira *f* lard
cochevís *m* (orn.) crested lark
cochifrito *m* fricassee of lamb or goat
cochinada *f* (coll.) piggishness, filthiness; (coll.) dirty trick
cochinata *f* (naut.) rider
cochinchina *f* Cochin (*fowl*); **la Cochinchina** Cochin China; **cochinchina enana** Cochin Bantam
cochinería *f* (coll.) piggishness, filthiness; (coll.) coarseness, baseness
cochinero -ra *adj* for hogs (*said of food*)
cochinilla *f* (ent.) cochineal insect; (zool.) wood louse; cochineal (*dyestuff*); **cochinilla de humedad** (zool.) sow bug; **cochinilla de la laca** (ent.) lac insect; **cochinilla de San José** (ent.) San Jose scale
cochinillo *m* sucking pig
cochino -na *adj* (coll.) piggish, dirty, filthy; (coll.) stingy; *mf* hog; (coll.) pig, dirty person; *m* (ichth.) oldwife; (metal.) pig; *f* sow; trollop (*slovenly woman*)
cochiquera *f* (coll.) var. of **cochitril**
cochite hervite *adv, adj & m* helter-skelter
cochitril *m* (coll.) pigsty; (coll.) den, filthy room, hovel
cochizo *m* (min.) rich vein
cocho -cha *mf* (dial.) hog
cochura *f* cooking, boiling, baking; batch of dough
coda *f* (carp.) corner block (*in form of triangular prism*); (mus.) coda
codadura *f* (hort.) layer
codal *adj* (pertaining to the) elbow; *m* elbowpiece (*of armor*); frame (*of saw*); strut, prop, shore, trench brace
codaste *m* (naut.) sternpost
codazo *m* nudge, poke with the elbow; **dar codazo a** (Am.) to tip, tip off
codear *vn* to elbow; (Am.) to sponge, sponge one's way; *vr* to hobnob; **codearse con** to hobnob with
codeína *f* (chem.) codein or codeine
codelincuencia *f* complicity
codelincuente *mf* accomplice
codeo *m* elbowing, nudging; (Am.) sponging
codera *f* elbow patch; itch on the elbow; (naut.) stern fast
codesera *f* growth of cytisus
codeso *m* (bot.) flatpod; (bot.) hairy cytisus
codeudor -dora *mf* codebtor
códice *m* codex
codicia *f* covetousness, cupidity, greed
codiciable *adj* covetable
codiciador -dora *adj* coveting; *mf* coveter
codiciar *va & vn* to covet
codicilar *adj* codicillary
codicilo *m* (law) codicil
codicioso -sa *adj* covetous, greedy, grasping; eager, anxious; **berserk** (*bull*); (coll.) hard-working, industrious
codificación *f* codification
codificar §86 *va* to codify
código *m* code; codex; Justinian code; **código civil** civil law; **código de honor** code of honor; **código de Justiniano** Justinian code; **código de señales** signal code; **código de señales marítimas** marine code; **código in-**

ternacional (telg.) international code; **código penal** penal code; **código telegráfico** telegraph code
codillo *m* knee (*of quadrupeds*); stirrup; (mach.) elbow; angle iron; bend; stump (*remaining on trunk after branch has been cut*); codille (*in game of omber*); **jugársela a uno de codillo** (coll.) to outwit someone; **tirar al codillo a** (coll.) to do everything possible to ruin (*someone*)
codo *m* elbow (*of arm or sleeve*); (mach.) elbow; cubit; **alzar** or **empinar el codo** (coll.) to drink, to crook the elbow; **dar de codo a** (coll.) to nudge; (coll.) to spurn; **hablar por los codos** (coll.) to talk too much; **hasta los codos** (coll.) up to the elbows; **mentir por los codos** (coll.) to lie like a trooper; **roerse los codos de hambre** (coll.) to be hard up, be in great want
codón *m* leather dock for horse's tail
codoñate *m* preserved quinces
codorniz *f* (*pl:* **-nices**) (orn.) quail
coeducación *f* coeducation
coeducacional *adj* coeducational
coeficiencia *f* common cause; cooperation, joint effort
coeficiente *m* (math. & phys.) coefficient; **coeficiente de dilatación** (phys.) coefficient of expansion; **coeficiente diferencial** (math.) differential coefficient; *adj* coefficient
coercer §91 *va* to coerce, to restrain
coerción *f* coercion, restraint; (phys.) coercive force
coercitivo -va *adj* coercive, restraining
coetáneo -a *adj & mf* contemporary
coeterno -na *adj* coeternal
coevo -va *adj* coeval
coexistencia *f* coexistence
coexistente *adj* coexistent
coexistir *vn* to coexist
coextender §66 *vr* to coextend
coextensión *f* coextension
coextensivo -va *adj* coextensive
cofa *f* (naut.) top
cofia *f* coif; hair net; (arm.) coif (*pad under helmet*)
cofiador *m* (law) joint bondsman or surety
cofiezuela *f* small coif; small hair net
cofín *m* basket, fruit basket
cofosis *f* (path.) cophosis, deafness
cofrada *f* sister, member
cofrade *mf* member, fellow member; *m* brother (*of a confraternity, etc.*); *f* sister (*of a confraternity, etc.*)
cofradía *f* confraternity, brotherhood, sisterhood; union, association
cofre *m* coffer, chest, trunk; (fort.) coffer; (ichth.) trunkfish; **cofre de equipajes** trunk (*of automobile*)
cofrero -ra *mf* trunk maker or dealer
cofto -ta *adj & mf* var. of **copto**
cogedero -ra *adj* ready to be picked; *m* handle; *f* rod for gathering esparto grass; box for catching bees; fruit picker (*pole with catch on end*)
cogedizo -za *adj* easy to pick
cogedor -dora *mf* picker, gatherer; *m* dustpan; coal shovel, ash shovel
cogedura *f* picking, gathering
cogegotas *m* (*pl:* **-tas**) drip pan
coger §49 *va* to pick, gather, collect; to seize, take hold of; to catch; to get; to overtake; to find; to take up, absorb; to hold; to cover, occupy; *vn* to be, to be located; (coll.) to fit; *vr* to get caught; (Am.) to steal; **cogerse los dedos** to burn one's fingers
cogetrapos *m* (*pl:* **-pos**) ragpicker, rag dealer
cogida *f* (coll.) picking, gathering, harvest; (taur.) hook (*with the horns*)
cogido *m* fold, gather (*in cloth*)
cogitabundo -da *adj* pensive, meditative
cogitativo -va *adj* cogitative (*possessing power of thought*)
cognación *f* blood relationship via the female line; relationship
cognado -da *adj & mf* cognate
cognaticio -cia *adj* cognatic
cognición *f* cognition (*process of knowing*)
cognomento *m* epithet, appellation
cognoscitivo -va *adj* cognitive
cogollo *m* heart (*of lettuce*); head (*of cabbage*); shoot (*of a plant*); top (*of tree*); (ent.) harvest fly; (fig.) cream, pick
cogombrillo *m* var. of **cohombrillo**
cogombro *m* (archaic) var. of **cohombro**
cogón *m* (bot.) cogon grass
cogorda *f* (bot.) bottle gourd
cogorza *f* (coll.) drunk, drunkenness
cogotazo *m* blow on the back of the neck
cogote *m* back of the neck; crest at back of helmet; **ser tieso de cogote** (coll.) to be stiff, be haughty
cogotera *f* havelock; sun curtain (*for horse's neck*)
cogotudo -da *adj* thick-necked; (coll.) proud, stiff-necked; (coll.) very rich; *m* (Am.) nouveau riche
cogucho *m* coarse sugar
cogujada *f* (orn.) crested lark
cogujón *m* point, tip, corner (*of a pillow, bag, etc.*)
cogujonero -ra *adj* with points or corners (*like those of a pillow*)
cogulla *f* cowl (*monk's hood and garment together*); **cogulla de fraile** (bot.) monkshood
cogullada *f* pendulous fold of skin under neck of hog
cohabitación *f* living together; cohabitation
cohabitar *vn* to dwell or live together; to cohabit
cohecha *f* (agr.) plowing just before sowing
cohechador -dora *adj* bribing; *mf* briber
cohechar *va* to bribe (*e.g., a judge*); (agr.) to plow just before sowing; *vn* to take a bribe
cohecho *m* bribing; (agr.) plowing season
cohen *mf* soothsayer; procurer
coheredera *f* coheiress
coheredero *m* coheir
coherencia *f* coherence
coherente *adj* coherent; (bot.) coherent
cohesión *f* cohesion; (phys.) cohesion
cohesivo -va *adj* cohesive
cohesor *m* (rad.) coherer
cohete *m* skyrocket; rocket; blasting fuse; (coll.) wind (*in intestines or being expelled*); **cohete de salvamento** (naut.) lifesaving rocket; **cohete de señales** (aer.) flare; *adj* (Am.) drunk
cohetear *va* (Am.) to blast
cohetería *f* rocketry
cohetero -ra *mf* maker or seller of skyrockets and fireworks; rocketeer
cohibición *f* restraint, restriction
cohibir §99 *va* to restrain, restrict, check
cohobación *f* cohobation, redistillation
cohobar *va* (chem.) to cohobate, redistil
cohobo *m* deerskin
cohollo *m* var. of **cogollo**
cohombral *m* cucumber patch
cohombrillo *m* (bot.) small cucumber; **cohombrillo amargo** (bot.) squirting cucumber
cohombro *m* (bot.) cucumber (*plant and fruit*); cucumber-shaped fritter; **cohombro de mar** (zool.) sea cucumber
cohonestar *va* to palliate, to gloss over, to rationalize
cohorte *f* cohort
coigual *adj & mf* coequal
coima *f* rake-off of operator of a gambling house; concubine; (Am.) bribe
coime *m* croupier; score keeper at billiards
coimero *m* croupier
coincidencia *f* coincidence; **en coincidencia con** in agreement with
coincidente *adj* coincident
coincidir *vn* to coincide; to come together; to agree
coinquilino -na *mf* joint tenant, cotenant
coinquinar *va* to stain, soil; *vr* to become sullied
cointeresado -da *adj* jointly interested; *mf* party having a joint interest
coipo or **coipu** *m* (zool.) coypu
coirón *m* (bot.) ichu
coito *m* coition, coitus
coja *f* see **cojo**
cojear *vn* to limp, to halt; to wobble (*said, e.g., of a table*); (coll.) to slip, to lapse (*into vice or error*); (fig.) to limp (*said of verse*); **saber**

de qué pie cojea alguien to know someone's weakness
cojera *f* limp, lameness
cojijo *m* bug; peeve
cojijoso -sa *adj* peevish, querulous
cojín *m* cushion
cojincillo *m* pad
cojinete *m* small cushion; sewing cushion; bearing; pillow block; (rail.) chair; **cojinete de balas** ball bearing; **cojinete de cono** cone bearing; **cojinete de rodillos** roller bearing
cojinillo *m* little cushion; holder (*to seize something hot*)
cojitranco -ca *adj* (scornful) mean and lame
cojo -ja *adj* lame, halt; crippled; wobbly (*table*); game (*leg*); shaky, unsound (*argument*); *mf* lame person; cripple; *f* (coll.) lewd woman
cojón *m* testicle
cojudo -da *adj* not castrated
cojuelo -la *adj* lame, crippled; *mf* cripple
cok *m* var. of **coque**
col. abr. of **colonia** & **columna**
col *f* (bot.) cabbage; **coles** *fpl* cabbage (*for eating*); **col de Bruselas** (bot.) Brussels sprouts; **col de Laponia** (bot.) Russian turnip; **col marina** (bot.) sea kale
col.ª abr. of **colonia** & **columna**
cola *f* tail; tail end; end seat; end, bottom (*e.g., of the class*); trail, train (*of a gown*); queue (*line of people*); glue; (fig.) tail (*e.g., of a comet, a coat*); **colas** *fpl* (min.) tailings; **a la cola** (coll.) behind; **hacer cola** (coll.) to stand in line, to queue; **tener** or **traer cola** (coll.) to have serious consequences; **cola de caballo** horsetail; (bot.) horsetail; **cola de gato** (meteor.) cat's-tail (*cirrus*); **cola del dragón** (astr.) dragon's tail; **cola del pan** bread line; **cola de milano** or **de pato** dovetail; **cola de perro** (bot.) crested dog's-tail; **cola de pescado** isinglass (*gelatin*); fish glue; **cola de rata** (bot.) bottle brush, field horsetail; **cola de retal** or **de retazo** (paint.) size, sizing; **cola de tijera** (orn.) frigate bird; **cola de zorra** (bot.) meadow foxtail; **cola de zorrillo** (bot.) hop tree; **cola negra** (zool.) blacktail, mule deer
colaboración *f* collaboration; contribution (*to a journal or symposium*)
colaboracionista *mf* collaborationist
colaborador -dora *adj* collaborating; *mf* collaborator; contributor
colaborar *vn* to collaborate; to contribute
colación *f* collation (*comparison; light lunch*); conferring (*e.g., of a degree*); parish land; **sacar a colación** (coll.) to bring up, make mention of; **traer a colación** (coll.) to bring in, to bring up; (coll.) to adduce as proof; (coll.) to lug in irrelevantly
colacionador -dora *mf* collator
colacionar *va* to collate
colactánea *f* foster sister
colactáneo *m* foster brother
colada *f* buck (*lye; bleached clothing*); bucking; cattle run; gulch; (metal.) tap; (coll.) good sword; **salir en la colada** (coll.) to come to light, be shown up, be exposed
coladera *f* strainer, colander
coladero *m* strainer, colander; narrow pass; (min.) winze, ore chute; (coll.) easy school, pipe course
coladizo -za *adj* runny
colador *m* strainer, colander
coladora *f* woman who bucks clothes
coladura *f* straining; (coll.) nonsense, lying
colágeno *m* (biochem.) collagen
colagogo -ga *adj & m* (med.) cholagogue
colaina *f* cup shake, ring shake
colambre *f* var. of **corambre**
colanilla *f* door or window bolt
colaña *f* low partition; solid or closed stair railing
colapez *f* or **colapiscis** *f* isinglass (*gelatin*)
colapsible *adj* collapsible
colapso *m* (path. & fig.) breakdown, collapse; **colapso nervioso** nervous breakdown
colapsoterapia *f* collapse therapy
colar *va* to confer (*a degree or an ecclesiastical benefit*); **§77** *va* to strain; to pour; to cast; to drive, bore; to sink (*a shaft*); to bleach (*washed clothes*) in hot lye, to buck; to pass off (*a bad coin*); **colar el hueso por** (coll.) to squeeze oneself through; *vn* to ooze, to run; to squeeze through; to come in (*said, e.g., of air through a narrow opening*); to slip in (*said of a remark*); (coll.) to drink wine; **no colar** (coll.) to not be believed; **colar a fondo** (naut.) to sink; *vr* to seep, percolate; to slip or sneak in; to slip through; to slip, make a slip; to talk nonsense, to lie; **colarse de gorra** (coll.) to crash the gate
colateral *adj* collateral; *mf* collateral (*relative*); *m* (com.) collateral
colativo -va *adj* collative; cleansing
colcótar *m* (chem.) colcothar
colcrén *m* cold cream
colcha *f* bedspread, counterpane, quilt
colchado -da *adj* quilted, padded; *m* quilting; lay (*in ropemaking*)
colchadura *f* quilting; (naut.) laying (*of ropes*)
colchar *va* to quilt; (naut.) to lay (*strands of rope*)
colchero -ra *mf* quilt maker
colchón *m* mattress; **colchón de aire** air mattress; **colchón de muelles** bedspring, spring mattress; **colchón de pluma** feather mattress; **colchón de tela metálica** wire bed, bedspring; **colchón de viento** air mattress
colchonería *f* wool shop; mattress, pillow, and cushion shop
colchonero -ra *mf* mattress maker
colchoneta *f* long cushion (*for a sofa or bench*)
coleada *f* wag of the tail; (Am.) throwing a bull by twisting its tail
coleador -dora *adj* tail-wagging
coleadura *f* wagging the tail; (taur.) twisting the bull's tail; (aer.) fishtail
colear *va* (taur.) to grab (*a bull*) by the tail; (Am.) to throw (*a bull*) by twisting its tail; (Am.) to nag, harass; (Am.) to trail after (*a person*); (Am.) to flunk (*a student*); (Am.) to be approaching (*a certain age*); *vn* to wag the tail; (aer.) to fishtail; (Am.) to sway (*said of a train*); **todavía colea** (coll.) it's still unsettled
colección *f* collection; (path.) abscess, gathering
coleccionador -dora *mf* collector (*e.g., of coins*)
coleccionar *va* to collect (*e.g., coins*)
coleccionista *mf* collector (*e.g., of coins*)
colecistectomía *f* (surg.) cholecystectomy
colecisto *m* (anat.) cholecyst
colecistostomía *f* (surg.) cholecystostomy
colecta *f* assessment; purse, money collected for charity; (eccl.) collect; (eccl.) collection
colectación *f* collection (*e.g., of taxes*)
colectar *va* to collect (*e.g., taxes*)
colecticio -cia *adj* new, green, untrained; omnibus (*volume*)
colectividad *f* collectivity; whole; group; community, whole community; collective ownership
colectivismo *m* collectivism
colectivista *adj* collectivistic; *mf* collectivist
colectivización *f* collectivization
colectivizar **§76** *va* to collectivize; *vr* to become collectivized
colectivo -va *adj* collective; group; (gram.) collective
colectomía *f* (surg.) colectomy
colector *m* collector (*e.g., of taxes*); trap, catch basin; sewer; (elec.) commutator; (elec.) collector; **colector de admisión** intake manifold; **colector de escape** exhaust manifold
colecturía *f* collectorship; collector's office; tax office
colédoco *m* (anat.) common bile duct
colega *mf* colleague
colegatario -ria *mf* (law) joint legatee, colegatary
colegiación *f* association, organization into an association
colegiado -da *adj* collegiate
colegial *adj* collegiate, college; *m* collegian
colegiala *f* collegian, co-ed
colegiar *vr* to form an association
colegiata *f* collegiate church
colegiatura *f* scholarship, fellowship

colegio *m* college; school, academy; student body; **Colegio de cardenales** College of Cardinals; **colegio electoral** electoral college; polls
colegir §72 *va* to gather, collect; to infer, to conclude
colegislador -dora *adj* colegislative
coleo *m* var. of **coleadura**
coleóptero -ra *adj* (ent.) coleopterous; *m* (ent.) coleopteran
coleorriza *f* (bot.) coleorhiza
colera *f* tail ornament (*for a horse*)
cólera *f* (physiol.) bile; anger, rage, choler; gummed white cotton fabric; **montar en cólera** to blow up, to hit the ceiling; *m* (path.) cholera; **cólera asiático** (path.) Asiatic cholera; **cólera de las gallinas** (vet.) chicken cholera; **cólera de los cerdos** (vet.) hog cholera; **cólera esporádico** (path.) cholera nostras; **cólera infantil** (path.) cholera infantum; **cólera morbo** (path.) cholera morbus; **cólera nostras** (path.) cholera nostras
colérico -ca *adj* choleric (*irascible*); choleraic (*pertaining to cholera*); sick with cholera; *mf* choleric or irritable person; person suffering from cholera
coleriforme *adj* choleriform
colerina *f* (path.) cholerine
colesterina *f* (biochem.) cholesterin
colesterol *m* (biochem.) cholesterol
coleta *f* pigtail; queue, cue; (coll.) postscript; (Am.) burlap; **cortarse la coleta** to quit the ring, give up bullfighting; to quit; **traer** o **tener coleta** (coll.) to lead to results of some moment
coletazo *m* lash, blow with the tail
coleteo *m* flop, flopping
coletero *m* (orn.) wren
coletillo *m* sleeveless jacket
coleto *m* buff jacket; (coll.) body, one's body, oneself; **decir para su coleto** (coll.) to say to oneself; **echarse al coleto** (coll.) to eat up, to drink up; (coll.) to read from cover to cover
coletudo -da *adj* (Am.) brazen, insolent
colgadero -ra *adj* fit to be hung up, fit to be kept; *m* hanger, hook; clothes rack
colgadizo -za *adj* hanging; lean-to, penthouse; *m* lean-to, penthouse
colgado -da *adj* pending, unsettled; drooping; **dejar colgado** (coll.) to frustrate, to disappoint; **quedarse colgado** (coll.) to be frustrated, to be disappointed
colgador *m* (print.) peel; clothes hanger
colgadura *f* hangings, drapery, tapestry
colgajo *m* rag, tatter; fruit hung up for keeping; (surg.) torn tissue (*used to heal over a wound*)
colgandero -ra *adj* hanging, suspended
colgante *adj* hanging; suspension; *m* hanger; drop, pendant; festoon; king post
colgar §79 *va* to hang; to drape, to adorn with hangings; to flunk; to give a birthday present to; to attribute, to blame; (coll.) to hang (*e.g., a criminal*); *vn* to hang; to dangle; to droop; to depend; (telp.) to hang up; **colgar de** to hang from; to hang on (*e.g., a nail*)
colibacilo *m* (bact.) coli
colibacilosis *f* (path.) colibacillosis
coliblanco -ca *adj* white-tailed
colibrí *m* (*pl:* **-bríes**) (orn.) humming bird
colicano -na *adj* white-tailed
cólico -ca *adj* (anat. & path.) colic; *m* (path.) colic; *f* (path.) upset stomach
colicuación *f* melting, fusion; (path.) colliquation
colicuar *va* to melt, dissolve
colicuecer §34 *va* var. of **colicuar**
coliche *m* (coll.) open house
coliflor *f* (bot.) cauliflower; (path.) cauliflower excrescence
coligación *f* connection, union; alliance
coligado -da *adj* bound together; allied; *mf* ally, confederate
coligadura *f* or **coligamiento** *m* var. of **coligación**
coligar §59 *vr* to join forces, make common cause
colilla *f* butt, stump (*of cigar*)
colillero -ra *mf* cigar-butt picker
colimación *f* (astr. & opt.) collimation
colimador *m* (opt.) collimator
colimbo *m* (orn.) grebe
colín -lina *adj* bobtailed (*horse or mare*); *m* (orn.) bobwhite; **colín de Virginia** (orn.) bobwhite
colina *f* hill, knoll; cabbage seed; cabbage nursery; (biochem.) choline
colinabo *m* (bot.) rutabaga
colindante *adj* adjacent, contiguous, neighboring
colindar *vn* to be adjacent, be contiguous
colineta *f* pretty dish of sweets; (Am.) macaroon
colino *m* cabbage seed; cabbage nursery
colinoso -sa *adj* hilly
coliquecer §34 *va* var. of **colicuar**
colirio *m* collyrium, eyewash
colirrábano *m* (bot.) kohlrabi
colirrojo *m* (orn.) redstart
colisa *f* (arti.) revolving platform; (arti.) swivel gun
coliseo *m* coliseum; (*cap.*) *m* Coliseum, Colosseum
colisión *f* collision; chafing, abrasion; bruise, bump
colista *mf* (hum.) queuer, person standing in line
colitigante *mf* colitigant
colitis *f* (path.) colitis
colmadamente *adv* in abundance
colmado -da *adj* abundant, full, overflowing; *m* sea-food restaurant; food store
colmar *va* to fill to overflowing; to fill, to stock; to fill in, to fill up; to crowd; to fulfill (*e.g., one's hopes*); to overwhelm; **colmar de** to shower with, to overwhelm with; **colmar el ojo** to fill the eye
colmena *f* beehive
colmenar *m* apiary
colmenero -ra *mf* beekeeper
colmenilla *f* (bot.) morel
colmillada *f* var. of **colmillazo**
colmillar *adj* (pertaining to an) eyetooth, tusk
colmillazo *m* bite with an eyetooth; gash made with a tusk
colmillejo *m* small eyetooth; small tusk
colmillo *m* eyetooth, canine tooth; tusk (*e.g., of elephant*); **enseñar los colmillos** (coll.) to show one's teeth; (coll.) to stiffen, show spirit; **escupir por el colmillo** (coll.) to boast, brag, bully; **tener el colmillo retorcido** (coll.) to be keen, be wide-awake
colmilludo -da *adj* having big eyeteeth; big-tusked; (coll.) keen, sharp-witted
colmo -ma *adj* filled to overflowing; *m* overflow, overflowing; (coll.) height, limit; thatch, thatched roof; topping (*e.g., of a dish of ice cream*); **a colmo** in abundance; **eso es el colmo** (coll.) that's the limit; **llegar a colmo** (coll.) to attain perfection; **llenar con colmo** to fill to overflowing; **para colmo de** to top off, as a finishing touch to
colobo *m* (zool.) guereza (*African monkey*)
colocación *f* placing; location; placement; investment; position, employment, job
colocar §86 *va* to place, to put; to locate; to invest; to find a place or position for; to set (*a trap*); to find an outlet for (*a product*); to lay (*a keel*); *vr* to get placed, find a job; to sell; (sport) to place (*said of a horse in a race*)
colocasia *f* (bot.) taro
colocolo *m* colocolo (*South American wildcat*); singing mouse of Chile; (Chile) imaginary fish-shaped or lizard-shaped monster hatched from a rotten egg
colocutor -tora *mf* collocutor, conferee; party (*to a conversation*)
colodión *m* (chem.) collodion
colodra *f* milk bucket; wine bucket; drinking horn; **ser una colodra** (coll.) to be a toper
colodrillo *m* back of neck
colofón *m* colophon; (fig.) finishing touch
colofonia *f* colophony, rosin
coloidal *adj* colloidal
coloide *adj* & *m* (chem.) colloid
coloideo -a *adj* colloid, colloidal
Colombia *f* Colombia; **la Colombia Británica** British Columbia

colombianismo *m* Colombianism
colombiano -na *adj & mf* Colombian
colombino -na *adj* Columbian (*pertaining to Columbus*); (*cap.*) *f* Columbine
colombio *m* (chem.) columbium
colombo *m* (pharm.) calumba
colombófilo -la *mf* pigeon fancier
colon *m* (anat.) colon; (gram.) main clause; (gram.) colon, semicolon; **colon imperfecto** (gram.) dependent clause; **colon perfecto** (gram.) independent clause, main clause
Colón *m* Columbus; (*l.c.*) *m* colon (*monetary unit of Costa Rica and El Salvador*)
colonato *m* colonialism
colonia *f* colony; cologne; silk ribbon (*about an inch and a half wide*); community, development; (Am.) sugar plantation; (*cap.*) *f* Cologne; **la Colonia del Cabo** Cape Colony; **colonia veraniega** summer colony
coloniaje *m* (Am.) colonial period; (Am.) colonial system; (Am.) slavery
colonial *adj* colonial; overseas; **coloniales** *mpl* imported foods
colonialismo *m* colonialism
colonialista *adj* colonial (*country*)
colónico -ca *adj* colonic
colonización *f* colonization; land settlement
colonizador -dora *adj* colonizing; *mf* colonizer, colonist
colonizar §76 *va & vn* to colonize, to settle
colono *m* colonist, settler; colonial; farmer; tenant farmer; (Am.) Indian peasant
coloquial *adj* colloquial
coloquíntida *f* (bot.) colocynth
coloquio *m* colloquy, talk, conference
color *m* color; coloring; paint; rouge; **colores** *mpl* colors (*flag*); **de color** colored (*not black or white; of some other race than the white*); tan (*e.g., shoes*); **en todo color** in full color; **mudar de color** to change color (*to turn pale; to blush*); **sacar los colores a** to make blush; **salirle a uno los colores** to blush; **so color de** under color of, under pretext of; **verlo todo de color de rosa** to see everything through rose-colored glasses; **color al óleo** (paint.) oil color; **colores complementarios** complementary colors; **colores de anilina** aniline dyes; **color local** (lit. & paint.) local color; **color muerto** o **quebrado** faded color, wan color
coloración *f* coloration, coloring
colorado -da *adj* colored; red, reddish; off-color (*joke*); colored, specious; **ponerse colorado** (coll.) to blush
coloradote -ta *adj* (coll.) ruddy, sanguine, blowzy
colorante *adj & m* coloring
colorar *va* to color; to dye; to stain
colorativo -va *adj* coloring
coloratura *f* (mus.) coloratura
colorear *va* to color; (fig.) to color, to palliate; *vn* to redden, turn red (*said, e.g., of ripening fruit*)
colorete *m* rouge; **ponerse colorete** to rouge, to make up
colorido -da *adj* colorful; *m* coloring; (fig.) coloring
colorimetría *f* colorimetry
colorímetro *m* colorimeter
colorín *m* (orn.) linnet; bright color
colorir §53 *va* to color; (fig.) to color; *vn* to take on color
colorista *mf* colorist
colosal *adj* colossal
colosense *adj & mf* Colossian
coloso *m* colossus; **coloso de Rodas** Colossus of Rhodes
colostomía *f* (surg.) colostomy
colquicina *f* (chem.) colchicine
cólquico *m* (bot.) colchicum, autumn crocus; (pharm.) colchicum
Cólquida, la Colchis
coludir *vn* to be in collusion
columbario *m* columbarium
columbino -na *adj* columbine, dovelike; simple, innocent
columbio *m* var. of **colombio**
columbrar *va* to glimpse, descry; to guess
columbrete *m* (naut.) reef
columela *f* (arch., anat., bot. & zool.) columella
columelar *adj* canine (*tooth*); *m* canine tooth
columna *f* column; **quinta columna** fifth column; **columna adosada** (arch.) engaged column; **columna cerrada** (mil.) close column; **columna de dirección** (aut.) steering column; **columna embebida** (arch.) engaged column; **columna entorchada** (arch.) wreathed column; **columna entregada** (arch.) engaged column; **columna mingitoria** public urinal; **columna rostral** rostral column; **columna salomónica** (arch.) twisted column; **columnas de Hércules** Pillars of Hercules; **columna vertebral** (anat.) vertebral column, spinal column; **columna volante** (mil.) flying column
columnación *f* (arch.) columniation
columnador *m* tabulator (*of typewriter*)
columnario -ria *adj* columnar
columnata *f* (arch.) colonnade; (arch.) columniation
columnista *mf* columnist
columpiar *va* to swing; *vr* to swing; to seesaw; (coll.) to swing, sway, swagger
columpio *m* swing; seesaw; (Am.) dip in the road
coluro *m* (astr.) colure
colusión *f* collusion
colusorio -ria *adj* collusive
colutorio *m* gargle
coluvie *f* (archaic) gang of thugs; sewer, mudhole
colza *f* (bot.) colza, rape
colla *f* collet (*of armor*); squally weather preceding monsoons; (naut.) last packing of oakum; row of fish traps
collada *f* pass (*through mountains*); (naut.) steady blow
collado *m* hill, height; pass (*through mountains*)
collar *m* necklace; cord or chain (*hung around neck to hold insignia*); dog collar, horse collar; collar, band (*placed on neck of a prisoner*); frill, ring (*of feathers of different colors around neck of bird*); (mach.) collar
collarejo *m* small necklace
collarín *m* stock (*worn by clergy*); collar (*of a coat*); frill (*around neck of bird or animal*); (arch.) gorgerin
collarino *m* (arch.) gorgerin
collazo *m* farmhand (*who has been given some land to work for himself*); bondsman, serf
colleja *f* (bot.) corn salad
collera *f* horse collar; collar (*breast harness*); chain gang; (Am.) pair of cuff links; **collera de yugo** oxbow
collerón *m* fancy horse collar
collón -llona *adj* (coll.) cowardly; *mf* (coll.) coward
collonada *f* (coll.) cowardice, cowardly act
collonería *f* (coll.) cowardice
coma *f* (gram.) comma (*used also for the decimal point in Spanish*); (arch.) miserere, misericord; **sin faltar una coma** (coll.) in minutest detail; *m* (path.) coma; **coma vigil** (path.) coma vigil
comabacilo *m* (bact.) comma bacillus
comadre *f* midwife; mother or godmother (*with respect to each other*); gossip; (coll.) woman friend (*of another woman*); (coll.) go-between
comadrear *vn* (coll.) to gossip, to go around gossiping; (Am.) to enjoy oneself
comadreja *f* (zool.) weasel
comadreo *m* (coll.) gossip, gossiping
comadrería *f* (coll.) gossiping, idle gossip
comadrero -ra *adj* (coll.) gossipy; *mf* (coll.) gossip (*person*)
comadrón *m* accoucheur, man midwife; gynecologist
comadrona *f* midwife
comal *m* (Am.) round earthenware griddle (*for corncakes*)
comalia or **comalía** *f* (vet.) dropsy
comalido -da *adj* sickly
comandancia *f* command (*position or function; territory; troops, ships, etc. under one who commands*); commander's office; (mil.) majority

comandanta *f* (coll.) wife of commander, commandant, or major; (nav.) flagship
comandante *m* (mil.) commander; (mil.) commandant; (mil.) major; **comandante en jefe** commander in chief
comandar *va* (mil. & nav.) to command
comandita *f* (com.) silent partnership
comanditar *va* (com.) to invest in (*an undertaking*) as a silent partner
comanditario -ria *adj* silent; silent-partnership; *mf* silent partner
comando *m* (mil.) command; (mil.) commando; control; **comando a distancia** remote control
comarca *f* region, territory, province
comarcal *adj* regional, provincial
comarcano -na *adj* regional; bordering, neighboring
comarcar §86 *va* to line up (*trees*) at equal distances in every direction; *vn* to border
comatoso -sa *adj* comatose
comátula *f* (zool.) feather star
comba *f* see **combo**
combadura *f* bending, curving, warping, bulging; bend, belly, sag; camber
combar *va* to bend, to curve; *vr* to bend, to curve, to warp, to bulge, to sag
combate *m* combat, fight; struggle; **fuera de combate** hors de combat; **triunfar por fuera de combate** (box.) to win by a knockout
combatido -da *adj* aggressive, militant
combatiente *adj* combatant; *m* combatant; (orn.) ruff
combatir *va* to combat, to fight; to beat, to beat upon; to harass; *vn* to combat; to struggle; *vr* to combat, to fight
combatividad *f* combativeness
combativo -va *adj* combative
combés *m* open space; (naut.) half deck
combinación *f* combination; combination (*underwear*); plan, scheme; **combinación de trenes** (rail.) connection
combinador *m* (elec.) controller
combinar *va* to combine, to bring together; to work out; (chem.) to combine; *vr* to combine; (chem.) to combine
combinatorio -ria *adj* combinatory; (math.) combinatorial
combleza *f* mistress (*of a married man*)
combo -ba *adj* bent, warped, crooked; *m* stand for casks; *f* bend, curve, warp, bulge; skipping rope; game of skipping rope; camber (*of road*); **hacer combas** (coll.) to sway, to swing; **saltar a la comba** to jump rope, to skip rope
comboso -sa *adj* bent, curved, arched, bulging
comburente *adj* supporting combustion; *m* supporter of combustion
combustibilidad *f* combustibility
combustible *adj* combustible; *m* combustible; fuel
combustión *f* combustion; **poner en combustión** to inflame, to stir up, to agitate; **combustión espontánea** spontaneous combustion
combusto -ta *adj* burnt
comedero -ra *adj* eatable; *m* manger, feed trough; dining room; (Am.) pasture; (Am.) hangout; **limpiarle a uno el comedero** (coll.) to deprive someone of his livelihood
comedia *f* comedy; play, drama; theater; comedia (*Spanish verse drama*); (fig.) farce; (fig.) drama; **hacer la comedia** (coll.) to pretend, make believe; **comedia cómica** comedy (*humorous play*); **comedia de capa y espada** cloak-and-sword play; **comedia de carácter** comedy of character; **comedia de costumbres** comedy of manners; **comedia de enredo** comedy of intrigue; **comedia de figurón** Spanish drama of the seventeenth century depicting a ridiculous or extravagant vice or character; **comedia devota** Spanish mystery play (*based on Eucharist*)
comediante -ta *mf* hypocrite; *m* actor; *f* actress, comedienne
comediar *va* to divide into equal parts, to divide in half
comedido -da *adj* courteous, polite; moderate, frugal; (Am.) meddlesome; (Am.) obliging
comedimiento *m* courtesy, politeness; moderation; (Am.) meddlesomeness
comedio *m* middle; interval
comediógrafo -fa *mf* playwright; comedian (*writer*)
comedión *m* dull, tiresome play
comedir §94 *vr* to be courteous; to be moderate, control oneself; (Am.) to meddle; (Am.) to be obliging; **comedirse a** + *inf* (Am.) to offer to, to volunteer to + *inf*
comedón *m* (path.) blackhead
comedor -dora *adj* heavy-eating, hungry; *m* dining room; eating place, restaurant; dining-room suite; **comedor de beneficencia** soup kitchen
comedorcito *m* dinette
comegente *m* (slang) man-eater
comején *m* (ent.) white ant, termite
comejenera *f* nest of white ants; (Am.) dive, den
comendador *m* knight commander; commander (*of a military order*); prelate of an order, Mercedarian prelate
comendadora *f* mother superior, Mercedarian mother superior
comendatario *m* (eccl.) commendatary, commendator
comendaticio -cia *adj* (eccl.) commendatory (*letter*)
comendatorio -ria *adj* commendatory (*letter or document*)
comendero *m* (hist.) commendator
comensal *mf* retainer, dependent, servant; table companion; fellow diner; (biol.) commensal
comensalía *f* house companionship, table companionship
comentador -dora *mf* commentator
comentar *va* to comment on, to expound; *vn* to comment; (coll.) to gossip
comentario *m* commentary; **comentarios** *mpl* (coll.) chit-chat, gossip
comentarista *mf* commentator
comento *m* comment; commentary; fiction, falsehood; deceit, cheat
comenzante *adj* beginning; *mf* beginner
comenzar §31 *va & vn* to begin, to start, to commence; **comenzar a** + *inf* to begin to + *inf;* **comenzar** + *ger* to begin + *ger;* **comenzar por** + *inf* to begin by + *ger*
comer *m* food; *va* to eat; to feed on; to gnaw, to gnaw away; to corrode; to consume; to fade; to enjoy (*an income*); (checkers & chess) to take; to itch; **sin comerlo ni beberlo** (coll.) without having anything to do with it; **tener qué comer** (coll.) to have enough to live on; **comer vivo** (coll.) to have it in for; *vn* to eat; to dine, have dinner; to itch; **comer de todo** to eat everything; *vr* to be eaten; to eat up; to bite (*one's nails*); (coll.) to consume (*money*); to skip, skip over; to nullify; **comerse unos a otros** (coll.) to be at loggerheads
comerciable *adj* marketable; sociable
comercial *adj* commercial
comercialidad *f* marketability
comercialización *f* commercialization
comercializar §76 *va* to commercialize
comerciante *adj* trading, of traders, of merchants; *mf* trader, merchant; **comerciante al por mayor** wholesaler; **comerciante al por menor** retailer; **comerciante comisionista** commission merchant; *m* tradesman
comerciar *vn* to deal, to trade; to have dealings
comercio *m* commerce, trade; business; business interests; business center; store, shop; firm; intercourse, illicit intercourse; **comercio de artículos de regalo** gift shop; **comercio exterior** foreign trade; **comercio interior** domestic commerce; **comercio sexual** sexual intercourse; **comercio social** social intercourse
comestible *adj* eatable, comestible; *m* food, foodstuff, comestible
cometa *m* (astr.) comet; *f* kite
cometario -ria *adj* (pertaining to a) comet
cometer *va* to entrust; to commit (*an undertaking to someone; a mistake, a sin, a crime*); to employ (*a figure of speech*)
cometido *m* assignment, commission, duty; commitment; purpose

comezón *f* itch; (fig.) itch
comible *adj* (coll.) fit to eat
comicastro *m* ham, ham actor
comicial *adj* comitial
comicidad *f* comedy, comicalness
comicios *mpl* comitia; election; voting; **acudir a los comicios** to go to the polls
cómico -ca *adj* comic or comical; dramatic; *mf* comedian; actor; **cómico de la legua** strolling actor, barnstormer; ham; *f* comedienne; actress
comida *f* see **comido**
comidilla *f* repast; (coll.) hobby; (coll.) talk, gossip; **comidilla de la ciudad, del pueblo** or **de la vecindad** (coll.) talk of the town
comido -da *adj* fed; finished eating; **estar comido** to have finished eating; **comido por servido** (coll.) unprofitable, not worth while; *f* eating; food; meal; dinner; **comida corrida** (Am.) table d'hôte; **comidas y camas** board and lodging
comienzo *m* beginning, start; **a comienzos de** around the beginning of (*e.g., the month*); **dar comienzo** to have its (or their) beginnings
comilitón *m* var. of **conmilitón**
comilitona *f* (coll.) spread, feast
comilón -lona *adj* (coll.) hearty, heavy-eating, voracious; *mf* (coll.) big eater; *f* (coll.) big meal, hearty meal, spread
comillas *fpl* quotation marks
cominear *vn* (coll.) to fuss around like a woman (*said of a man*)
cominería *f* (coll.) fussiness
cominero *adj masc* (coll.) fussy (*man*); *m* (coll.) fussy fellow, betty
Cominform *f* Cominform
cominillo *m* (bot.) cockle, darnel
comino *m* (bot.) cumin; cuminseed; **no valer un comino** (coll.) to be not worth a continental; **comino rústico** (bot.) laserwort
Comintern *f* Comintern
comiquear *vn* to put on amateur plays
comiquería *f* (coll.) group of ham actors; (coll.) educational farce
comiquillo *m* ham, ham actor
comisar *va* to attach, to seize; to confiscate
comisaría *f* commissariat; (Am.) police station
comisariato *m* commissariat
comisario *m* commissary; commissioner; commissar; (mil.) commissary; **alto comisario** high commissioner; **comisario de a bordo** (naut.) purser
comiscar §86 *va* (coll.) var. of **comisquear**
comisión *f* commission; committee; errand
comisionado -da *adj* commissioned; *mf* commissioner; committeeman
comisionar *va* to commission
comisionista *mf* commission agent; commission merchant; *adj* commission, working on a commission
comis.º abr. of **comisario**
comiso *m* attachment, seizure; confiscation; confiscated goods
comisquear *va* (coll.) to nibble at, keep nibbling at
comistión *m* commixture
comistrajo *m* (coll.) hodgepodge, mess
comisura *f* (anat., bot. & zool.) commissure; corner (*of lips, eyelids, etc.*)
comité *m* committee
comitente *adj & mf* constituent
comitiva *f* retinue, suite
cómitre *m* (naut.) galley boatswain
comiza *f* (ichth.) barbel
como *adv* as; like; how; so to speak, as it were; about; *conj* as; when; if; as soon as; so that; as long as; inasmuch as; that; **así como** as soon as; **la manera como** the way that; **tan luego como** as soon as; **como no** unless; **como no sea** unless it be; **como no sea para** + *inf* except to + *inf*, unless it be to + *inf*; **como que** because, inasmuch as; **como quien dice** so to speak; **como quiera que** however; since, inasmuch as; (archaic) although
cómo *adv* how?; why?; what?; how!; how, e.g., **no sé cómo explicar lo que hizo** I don't know how to explain what he did; **¿a cómo es . . . ?** how much is . . . ?; **¿cómo así?** how so?; **¿cómo no?** why not?; **¡cómo no!** (Am.) of course!
cómoda *f* see **cómodo**
comodable *adj* (law) susceptible of being lent
comodante *mf* (law) lender by commodation
comodatario -ria *mf* borrower by commodation
comodato *m* (law) commodation; (law) commodatum
comodidad *f* convenience; comfort; interest, advantage
comodidoso -sa *adj* (Am.) self-seeking
comodín *m* wild card, joker; gadget, jigger; excuse, alibi
comodista *adj* self-centered; selfish; comfort-loving
cómodo -da *adj* convenient, handy; comfortable (*person or thing*); comfort-loving; *f* commode, bureau, chest of drawers
comodón -dona *adj* (coll.) comfort-loving
comodoro *m* commodore
comoquiera *adv* anyway; **comoquiera que** however
comp.ª abr. of **compañía**
compacción *f* compactness
compacidad or **compactibilidad** *f* compressibility, contractility
compacto -ta *adj* compact; close (*e.g., weave*)
compadecer §34 *va* to pity, to feel sorry for; *vr* to harmonize; **compadecerse con** to harmonize with; **compadecerse de** to pity, to feel sorry for
compadecido -da *adj* sympathetic
compadraje *m* cabal, clique
compadrar *vn* to become a godfather; to become friendly; to be congenial
compadrazgo *m* compaternity; cabal, clique
compadre *m* father or godfather (*with respect to each other*); (coll.) friend, companion
compadrear *vn* (coll.) to be close friends; (Am.) to show off
compadrería *f* friendship, companionship
compadrito *m* (Am.) bully
compaginación *f* arrangement, ordering; (print.) paging
compaginador *m* (print.) pager
compaginar *va* to arrange, to put in order, to bring together; (print.) to page, page up, make up; *vr* to fit, agree, gee
companage *m* or **compango** *m* cold cuts, cold dish
compaña *f* (coll.) company; (archaic) family
compañerismo *m* good fellowship, comradeship, companionship
compañero -ra *mf* companion; mate; partner; **compañero de armas** companion-at-arms, comrade in arms; **compañero de cama** bedfellow; **compañero de cuarto** or **de habitación** roommate; **compañero de juego** playfellow, playmate; **compañero de trabajo** fellow worker; **compañero de viaje** fellow traveler (*communist sympathizer*); *f* helpmeet (*wife*)
compañía *f* company; society; (com., mil. & theat.) company; **hacerle compañía a una persona** to keep someone company; **compañía anónima** (com.) stock company; **compañía comanditaria** or **en comandita** (com.) commandite (*partnership with one or more silent partners*); **compañía de desembarco** (nav.) landing force; **Compañía de Jesús** Society of Jesus; **compañía del ahorcado** (coll.) unsteady or inconstant companion; **compañía de la legua** (theat.) strolling players; **compañía de seguros** insurance company; **compañía matriz** parent company
comparable *adj* comparable
comparación *f* comparison; (gram.) comparison
comparado -da *adj* comparative
comparador *m* (coll.) comparer; (phys.) comparator
comparar *va* to compare
comparativo -va *adj* comparative; (gram.) comparative; *m* (gram.) comparative; *f* (gram.) conjunction of comparison
comparecer §34 *vn* (law) to appear
compareciente *mf* (law) party appearing, party hereto
comparencia *f* (law) appearance
comparendo *m* (law) summons

comparición *f* (law) appearance; (law) summons
comparsa *f* (theat.) supernumeraries, extras; masquerade; *mf* (theat.) supernumerary, extra; (coll.) quiet person
comparte *mf* (law) joint party
compartidor -dora *mf* sharer, participant
compartimiento *m* division, distribution; compartment; (rail.) compartment; **compartimiento estanco** (naut.) watertight compartment
compartir *va* to divide; to share (*e.g., an opinion*)
compás *m* compass (*for showing directions*); compass or compasses (*for drawing curves, etc.*); (mus.) time, measure; (mus.) beat; (mus.) bar, measure; rule, measure; jurisdiction of a monastery; **a compás** (mus.) in time; **al compás de** in step with; **fuera de compás** (mus.) out of time, off beat; **llevar el compás** (mus.) to keep time; **perder el compás** (mus.) to get out of time; **compás de calibres** caliper compass, calipers; **compás de división** dividers; **compás mayor** (mus.) duple measure; **compás menor** (mus.) compound duple or quadruple time
compasado -da *adj* measured, moderate, prudent
compasar *va* to measure with a compass; to fit, to cut to size, to adapt or adjust with precision; (mus.) to mark off (*a composition*) in measures or bars
compasible *adj* pitiful; compassionate
compasillo *m* (mus.) compound duple or quadruple time
compasión *f* compassion; **mover a compasión** to move to compassion; **¡por compasión!** for pity's sake
compasionado -da *adj* passionate
compasivo -va *adj* compassionate
compaternidad *f* compaternity
compatibilidad *f* compatibility
compatible *adj* compatible
compatricio -cia or **compatriota** *mf* compatriot, fellow countryman
compatrón *m* var. of **compatrono**
compatrono -na *mf* joint patron
compeler *va* to compel; **compeler a** + *inf* to compel to + *inf*
compendiador -dora *adj* summarizing; *mf* summarizer
compendiar *va* to summarize, condense
compendiariamente *adv* in brief, in a word
compendio *m* compendium; **en compendio** in brief, in a word
compendioso -sa *adj* compendious
compendista *mf* writer of a compendium or digest; summarizer
compendizar §76 *va* var. of **compendiar**
compenetración *f* interpenetration, compenetration; mutual understanding
compenetrar *vr* to interpenetrate, to compenetrate; to have the same thoughts and feelings; to understand thoroughly; (Am.) to be convinced; **compenetrarse de** to absorb, take in
compensación *f* compensation; (com.) clearing; (sport) handicap (*in boat races*)
compensador -dora *adj* compensating; *m* compensator; compensating pendulum
compensar *va* to compensate; to compensate for, make up for; *vn* to compensate; *vr* to be compensated for
compensativo -va *adj* compensative
compensatorio -ria *adj* compensatory
competencia *f* competence or competency; adequacy, sufficiency; dispute; competition; area, domain, field; (law) competence or competency; **a competencia** in emulation, vying with each other; **de la competencia de** in the domain or bailiwick of; **en competencia de** in competition with; **sin competencia** unmatched (*e.g., prices*)
competente *adj* competent; adequate, sufficient; reliable; (law) competent
competer *vn* to be incumbent, to belong
competición *f* competition
competidor -dora *adj* competing; *mf* competitor
competir §94 *vn* to compete
compilación *f* compilation
compilador -dora *mf* compiler
compilar *va* to compile
compinche *mf* (coll.) chum, crony, pal
complacedero -ra or **complacedor -dora** *adj* pleasing
complacencia *f* complaisance; pleasure, satisfaction, complacency
complacer §34 *va* to please, to humor; *vr* to be pleased; **complacerse con, de** or **en** to be pleased with, take pleasure in, delight in; **complacerse** + *inf* or **en** + *inf* to be pleased to + *inf*, to take pleasure in + *ger*
complacido -da *adj* complacent, satisfied
complaciente *adj* complaisant; pleasing, agreeable; nice; indulgent
complacimiento *m* var. of **complacencia**
complejidad *f* complexity
complejo -ja *adj* complex; *m* complex; (psychol.) complex; **complejo B** (biochem.) B complex; **complejo de Electra** (psychoanal.) Electra complex; **complejo de Edipo** (psychoanal.) Oedipus complex; **complejo de inferioridad** inferiority complex
complementar *va* to complement
complementario -ria *adj* complementary
complemento *m* complement, addition; accessory; perfection, completion; (gram., math. & mus.) complement; **complemento directo** (gram.) direct object; **complemento indirecto** (gram.) indirect object
completamiento *m* completion
completar *va* to complete; to perfect
completas *fpl* see **completo**
completivo -va *adj* complemental; finished, perfect
completo -ta *adj* complete; full (*e.g., trolley car*); **completas** *fpl* (eccl.) compline, completory
complexidad *f* complexity
complexión *f* constitution; complexion
complexionado -da *adj* constituted; **bien complexionado** strong, robust; **mal complexionado** weak, frail
complexional *adj* constitutional
complexo -xa *adj* complex
complicación *f* complication
complicado -da *adj* complicated, complex
complicar §86 *va* to complicate; to involve; *vr* to become complicated; to become entangled or involved
cómplice *mf* accomplice, accessory
complicidad *f* complicity
complot *m* (*pl:* **-plots**) complot, plot, intrigue
complotar *vn* to complot, plot, intrigue
complutense *adj* (pertaining to) Alcalá de Henares; *mf* native or inhabitant of Alcalá de Henares; (*cap.*) *f* Complutensian Polyglot (*Bible polyglot printed in 1513-1517 in Alcalá de Henares*)
componado -da *adj* (her.) componé
compondré *1st sg fut ind of* **componer**
componedor -dora *mf* composer; compositor, typesetter; mender, repairer; arbitrator; **amigable componedor** (law) arbitrator; *m* (print.) stick, composing stick
componenda *f* compromise, deal; settlement; reconciliation
componente *adj* component; *m* component; member (*person*); *f* (mech.) component
componer §69 *va* to compose; to compound; (mus., lit. & print.) to compose; to make, to constitute; to arrange, to put in order; to mend, to repair; to adorn, to trim, to deck out; to pacify, to reconcile; to settle; (coll.) to strengthen, restore; (coll.) to settle (*the stomach*); to scheme up; (Am.) to set (*a bone*); *vn* to compose; *vr* to compose oneself; to get dressed; to make up (*with paint, powder, etc.; to become friends again*); **componerse de** to be composed of; **componerse con** to settle with, come to terms with; **componérselas** (coll.) to manage, to make out, to come to terms
componible *adj* adjustable; reparable, mendable; conciliable
comporta *f* grape basket or bucket
comportable *adj* bearable, tolerable
comportamentismo *m* (psychol.) behaviorism

comportamentista *adj* behavioristic; *mf* behaviorist
comportamiento *m* comportment, behavior, deportment
comportar *va* to bear, tolerate; (Am.) to entail; *vr* to comport oneself, to behave
comporte *m* behavior; bearing, carriage
comportería *f* grape-basket or grape-bucket business or shop
comportero -ra *mf* grape-basket or grape-bucket maker or dealer
composición *f* composition; settlement, compromise; agreement; composure; **hacer una composición de lugar** to size up the situation; to lay one's plans; **composición de fuerzas** (mech.) composition of forces
compositivo -va *adj* compositive, constituent; (gram.) combining (*particle*)
compositor -tora *mf* (mus.) composer; (Am.) trainer (*of race horses or fighting cocks*)
compostelano -na *adj* (pertaining to) Santiago de Compostela; *mf* native or inhabitant of Santiago de Compostela
compostura *f* composition, form, structure; agreement, settlement, adjustment; composure; circumspection; neatness, sleekness; repair, repairing; adulteration
compota *f* compote, preserves, sauce (*of fruit*)
compotera *f* compote, compotier
compound *adj indecl* (elec. & mach.) compound
compra *f* purchase, buy; shopping; day's marketing; **hacer compras** or **ir de compras** to go shopping
comprable, compradero -ra or **compradizo -za** *adj* purchasable
comprador -dora *adj* buying; *mf* buyer, purchaser; shopper
comprar *va* to buy, to purchase; (fig.) to buy, buy off (*by bribing*); **comprar a** or **de** to buy from; *vn* to shop
compraventa *f* transaction, buying and selling; second-hand business; (law) bargain
comprendedor -dora *adj* understanding
comprender *va* to understand; to comprehend; to comprize
comprensibilidad *f* comprehensibility
comprensible *adj* comprehensible, understandable
comprensión *f* comprehension, understanding; inclusion
comprensivo -va *adj* understanding; comprehensive; **comprensivo de** inclusive of
comprensor -sora *adj* inclusive, embracing; (theol.) blessed
compresa *f* (med.) compress; **compresa fría** (med.) cold pack; **compresa higiénica** sanitary napkin
compresibilidad *f* compressibility
compresible *adj* compressible
compresión *f* compression; (pros.) synaeresis
compresivo -va *adj* compressive
compresor -sora *adj* compressing; *m* compressor; (anat., mach. & surg.) compressor; *f* (mach.) compressor
comprimario -ria *mf* (theat.) singer playing second or supporting roles
comprimido -da *adj* compressed; flattened; *m* (pharm.) tablet
comprimir *va* to compress; to repress, to restrain; *vr* to become compressed, to flatten out; to control oneself
comprobable *adj* provable, verifiable
comprobación *f* checking, verification; proof; **comprobación de averías** trouble shooting
comprobante *adj* proving, verifying; *m* proof; certificate, voucher, warrant, claim check
comprobar §77 *va* to check, verify; to prove
comprofesor -sora *mf* colleague
comprometedor -dora *adj* (coll.) compromising
comprometer *va* to compromise, to involve, to bind; to endanger; to force, to oblige; to agree to entrust (*a matter to a third party*); *vr* to become compromised; to compromise oneself· to commit oneself; to become engaged; **comprometerse a** + *inf* to promise to + *inf*, to obligate oneself to + *inf*
comprometido -da *adj* awkward, embarrassing
comprometimiento *m* adjustment; danger, predicament; pledge, promise
compromisario -ria *mf* arbitrator, umpire; *m* electoral delegate
compromiso *m* compromise (*e.g., of a lawsuit*); engagement, appointment; commitment; pledge; compromising situation; embarrassment; betrothal; (canon law) compromise; **estar en compromiso** to be questioned, be in doubt; **poner en compromiso** to bring into question, cast doubt on
comprovincial *adj & m* (eccl.) comprovincial
comprovinciano -na *mf* comprovincial
comps. abr. of **compañeros**
compuerta *f* floodgate, sluice, lock; hatch, half door; draw (*of a drawbridge*); scapulary, shoulder strap (*to which cross was hung*)
compuestamente *adv* neatly, trimly; in an orderly fashion
compuesto -ta *adj* compound; composite; (gram.) compound; bedecked; composed, calm, circumspect; (arch.) Composite; *pp of* **componer;** *m* compound; composite; (chem.) compound; *f* (bot.) composite
compulsa *f* collating; (law) authentic copy
compulsación *f* collating
compulsar *va* to collate; (law) to make an authentic copy of
compulsión *f* compulsion
compulsivo -va *adj* compulsive, compulsory
compunción *f* compunction; sorrow, pity
compungido -da *adj* grieved, sorrowful, remorseful
compungir §42 *va* to make remorseful; *vr* to feel remorse, be remorseful
compungivo -va *adj* pricking, stinging
compurgación *f* (law) compurgation
compurgar §59 *va* (law) to try by compurgation; (Am.) to finish serving (*one's time in jail*)
compuse *1st sg pret ind of* **componer**
computación *f* computation
computar *va & vn* to compute
computista *mf* computer
cómputo *m* computation
comulgante *mf* (eccl.) communicant
comulgar §86 *va* to administer communion to; *vn* to take communion
comulgatorio *m* communion rail, altar rail; communion window (*in a nunnery*)
común *adj* common; (gram.) common; **común de dos** (gram.) common (*noun*); **común de tres** (gram.) common (*adjective or adjectival ending in Latin*); *m* community; commonalty; water closet; **el común de las gentes** the general run of people, the common run of people; **en común** in common; **por lo común** commonly
comuna *f* commune; (dial.) main irrigation channel; (*cap.*) *f* Commune
comunal *adj* common; communal, community; *m* commonalty, common people
comunero -ra *adj* popular (*well-liked*); *m* shareholder, joint owner; **comuneros** *mpl* commoners (*in pasture lands*)
comunicable *adj* communicable; sociable, communicative, companionable
comunicación *f* communication; report, paper; rhetorical question; **comunicaciones** *fpl* communications (*telephone, mail, etc.*)
comunicado *m* communiqué; letter to the editor; official notice
comunicador -dora *adj* communicating
comunicante *adj* communicant; communicating; *mf* communicant; writer (*person who writes to inform or request*)
comunicar §86 *va, vn & vr* to communicate
comunicativo -va *adj* communicative
comunidad *f* community; **comunidades** *fpl* popular uprisings (*especially in Castile under Charles I*); **de comunidad** jointly; **Comunidad Británica de Naciones** British Commonwealth of Nations; **comunidad de bienes** joint ownership
comunión *f* communion; political party; (eccl.) Communion; **comunión de los santos** (eccl.) communion of saints
comunismo *m* communism
comunista *adj* communist, communistic; *mf* communist
comunistizante *adj* communistically inclined; *mf* fellow traveler

comunistizar §76 *va* to communize; *vr* to become communistic
comunistoide *adj* fellow-traveling; *mf* fellow traveler
comunizar §76 *va* to communize
comuña *f* maslin (*mixture of wheat and rye*)
con *prep* with; in spite of; to, e.g., **amable con ella** kind to her; of: **soñar con** to dream of; **con** + *inf* by + *ger;* in spite of + *ger;* **con que** whereupon; and so; **con tal (de) que** provided that; **con todo** however, nevertheless
conación *f* (psychol.) conation
conato *m* endeavor, effort, try; attempt; (law) attempt, assault
concadenación *f* concatenation
concadenar *va* to concatenate, to link together
concambio *m* exchange
concanónigo *m* fellow canon
concatenación *f* concatenation
concatenar *va* to concatenate, to link together
concausa *f* concause, joint cause
concavidad *f* concavity
cóncavo -va *adj* concave; *m & f* concave, concavity, cavity
cóncavoconvexo -xa *adj* concavo-convex
concebible *adj* conceivable
concebir §94 *va & vn* to conceive
concedente *adj* conceding, concessive
conceder *va* to concede, admit; to grant
concedidamente *adv* admittedly, avowedly, concededly
concejal *m* alderman; councilman
concejala *f* alderman's wife; councilman's wife; councilwoman
concejil *adj* (pertaining to the) council; common, public
concejo *m* town council; town hall; council meeting; foundling
concento *m* harmonious singing
concentrabilidad *f* faculty of concentration
concentración *f* concentration
concentrado -da *adj* concentrated; uncommunicative
concentrar *va* to concentrate; to center; to restrain, conceal; *vr* to concentrate; to center
concéntrico -ca *adj* concentric or concentrical
concentuoso -sa *adj* harmonious
concepción *f* conception; Immaculate Conception; feast of the Immaculate Conception; **Inmaculada Concepción** Immaculate Conception
conceptear *vn* to be full of conceits, to be witty
conceptible *adj* conceivable
conceptismo *m* (lit.) conceptism
conceptista *adj & mf* (lit.) conceptist
conceptivo -va *adj* conceptive
concepto *m* concept; conceit, fancy, witticism; opinion, judgment; cause, reason; **¿bajo qué concepto?** from what point of view?, for what reason?; **en concepto de** under the head of; **tener buen concepto de** or **tener en buen concepto** to hold in high esteem, to have a high opinion of
conceptual *adj* conceptual
conceptualismo *m* (philos.) conceptualism
conceptualista *adj* (philos.) conceptualistic; *mf* (philos.) conceptualist
conceptuar §33 *va* to deem, to judge; **conceptuar a uno de** or **por** to deem someone to be
conceptuoso -sa *adj* witty, sententious, epigrammatic
concernencia *f* respect, connection, concern
concerniente *adj* relative, applicable; **concerniente a** concerning
concernir §43 *va* to concern
concertadamente *adv* in concert, in harmony
concertante *adj* contracting; (mus.) concertante; *m* (mus.) concertante; (mus.) finale (*of an act of an opera*)
concertar §18 *va* to concert; to arrange (*e.g., a marriage, peace*); to reconcile; to harmonize; to bargain for; to conclude (*an agreement*); to rouse (*game*); to mend, to repair; to set (*a broken bone*); to make agree; (gram.) to make agree; *vn* to concert; to harmonize; to agree; (gram.) to agree; *vr* to become reconciled, to come to terms; to harmonize; to agree; (Am.) to hire out
concertina *f* (mus.) concertina
concertino *m* (mus.) concertmaster
concertista *mf* (mus.) performer, soloist; (mus.) manager
concerto *m* (mus.) concerto
concesible *adj* grantable, concessible
concesión *f* concession, admission; grant
concesionario *m* concessionaire; dealer
concesivo -va *adj* concessive; (gram.) concessive
concia *f* forbidden section of woodland
conciencia *f* conscience; consciousness; awareness; **a conciencia** conscientiously; **en conciencia** in all conscience; **conciencia doble** (psycopath.) double consciousness
concienzudo -da *adj* conscientious, thorough
concierto *m* concert, agreement, harmony; (mus.) concert; (mus.) concerto; **de concierto** in concert
conciliable *adj* conciliable, reconcilable
conciliábulo *m* conciliabule
conciliación *f* conciliation; likeness, congruity; favor, esteem, protection
conciliador -dora *adj* conciliatory; *mf* conciliator
conciliar *adj* (pertaining to a) council; *m* council member; *va* to conciliate, to reconcile; to win; *vr* to win (*e.g., friendship*)
conciliativo -va *adj* conciliative
conciliatorio -ria *adj* conciliatory
concilio *m* (eccl.) council; council decrees; **concilio de Nicea** Nicene Council; **concilio de Trento** Council of Trent; **concilio ecuménico** (eccl.) ecumenical council
concisión *f* concision, conciseness
conciso -sa *adj* concise
concitación *f* agitation, incitement
concitador -dora *adj* inciting, stirring; *mf* agitator, inciter
concitar *va* to stir up, agitate, incite
concitativo -va *adj* inciting
conciudadano -na *mf* fellow citizen
conclave *m* or **cónclave** *m* conclave; (eccl.) conclave
conclavista *m* conclavist
concluir §41 *va* to conclude; to convince; to silence, to overwhelm; (fencing) to disarm (*an adversary*) by catching the hilt of his sword; *vn & vr* to conclude, to end; **concluir de** + *inf* to finish + *ger*
conclusión *f* conclusion; **en conclusión** in conclusion
conclusivo -va *adj* concluding, final
concluso -sa *adj* (law) closed, concluded (*said of a trial*)
concluyente *adj* conclusive, convincing
concoide *f* (geom.) conchoid
concoideo -a *adj* conchoidal; (mineral.) conchoidal
concoloro -ra *adj* concolorous
concomer *vr* (coll.) to shrug one's shoulders, to give a shrug, to fidget with an itch
concomimiento or **concomio** *m* (coll.) shrug, shrug of the shoulders, fidgets
concomitancia *f* concomitance
concomitante *adj & m* concomitant
concomitar *va* to accompany, work with, go with
concón *m* (orn.) tawny owl
concordación *f* harmonizing, combining, coördination
concordador -dora *adj* conciliating; *mf* conciliator
concordancia *f* concordance, agreement; (gram. & mus.) concord; **concordancias** *fpl* concordance (*list of words with references*)
concordante *adj* concordant
concordar §77 *va* to harmonize; to reconcile; (gram.) to make agree; *vn* to agree; (gram.) to agree; **concordar con** to agree with; (gram.) to agree with
concordata *f* or **concordato** *m* concordat; (eccl.) concordat
concorde *adj* in agreement
concordia *f* concord, harmony; agreement, settlement; double finger ring; **de concordia** by common consent
concreado -da *adj* (theol.) innate
concreción *f* concretion; (geol. & path.) concretion

concrecionar *va & vr* to concrete, to form into a mass, to form into concretions
concrescencia *f* concrescence; (biol.) concrescence; (path.) concretion
concretar *va* to concrete, make concrete; to specify; to explain; to thicken; to boil down (*a statement*); *vr* to limit oneself, to confine oneself; **concretarse a** + *inf* to limit oneself or confine oneself to + *inf*
concretera *f* (Am.) concrete mixer
concreto -ta *adj* concrete; *m* concretion; concrete; **en concreto** finally, to sum up
concubina *f* concubine
concubinario -ria *adj & m* concubinary
concubinato *m* concubinage
concúbito *m* coitus, concubitus
concuerda; por concuerda O.K. (*said of a true copy*)
conculcación *f* treading, trampling; violation
conculcar **§86** *va* to tread upon, trample under foot; to break, violate
concuñada *f* sister-in-law (*wife of one's husband's or wife's brother*)
concuñado *m* brother-in-law (*husband of one's wife's or husband's sister*)
concupiscencia *f* concupiscence
concupiscente *adj* concupiscent
concupiscible *adj* concupiscible
concurrencia *f* concurrence; attendance; crowd, gathering; competition, contest
concurrente *adj* concurrent; competing; *mf* contender
concurrido -da *adj* crowded, full of people
concurrir *vn* to concur; to gather, come together; to coincide (*in time*); to contend, to compete; **concurrir con** to come in with, to contribute (*e.g., money*)
concursado *m* (law) insolvent debtor
concursante *mf* competitor
concursar *va* (law) to declare insolvent
concurso *m* concourse, crowd; concurrence, backing, coöperation; contest, competition; show, exhibition (*with prizes*); (law) insolvency proceedings; **fuera de concurso** not competing; **concurso de acreedores** (law) meeting of creditors; **concurso hípico** horse show
concusión f concussion; extortion, shakedown; (path.) concussion
concusionario -ria *mf* extortioner
concha *f* shell; tortoise shell; shellfish; oyster; lower millstone; horseshoe bay; concha (*cigar*); sheltered inlet (*on seacoast*); (theat.) prompter's box; (anat.) concha; (arch.) conch, concha; **meterse en su concha** to retire into one's shell; **salir de la concha** to come out of one's shell; **tener muchas conchas** (coll.) to be sly, to be cunning; **concha de peregrino** scallop shell; (zool.) scallop; **concha de perla** mother-of-pearl
conchabanza *f* comfort; (coll.) ganging up
conchabar *va* to join, to unite; to mix (*wools of different qualities*); (Am.) to hire; (Am.) to get (*a job*); *vr* (coll.) to gang up; (Am.) to hire out
conchabero *m* (Am.) pieceworker
conchabo *m* (Am.) hiring; (Am.) hiring out; (Am.) work
conchado -da *adj* (zool.) shelled, shelly
conchesta *f* (dial.) snowdrift
conchil *m* (zool.) murex
conchudo -da *adj* (zool.) shelled, shelly; (coll.) sly, cunning, crafty
conchuela *f* (ent.) Mexican bean beetle
condado *m* earldom, countship; county
condal *adj* of an earl or count
conde *m* earl, count; gypsy chief; (dial.) foreman; **condes** *mpl* earl and countess, count and countess
condecoración *f* decoration (*especially with medal, badge, or ribbon; medal, badge, or ribbon itself*)
condecorar *va* to decorate (*with honors, medals, etc.*)
condena *f* sentence; penalty; transcript of sentence; **condena judicial** (law) conviction
condenación *f* condemnation; (theol.) damnation
condenado -da *adj* condemned; damned; (Am.) shrewd, clever; *mf* condemned; damned
condenador -dora *adj* condemning, incriminating; *mf* condemner
condenar *va* to condemn; to damn; to convict; to block up or shut off (*e.g., a window*); to close up, to padlock; **condenar a** + *inf* to condemn to + *inf; vr* to condemn oneself, confess one's guilt; to be damned (*to hell*)
condenatorio -ria *adj* condemnatory
condensación *f* condensation
condensador -dora *adj* condensing; *m* condenser; **condensador de derivación** or **de paso** (elec.) by-pass condenser; **condensador de placa** (rad.) plate condenser; **condensador de rejilla** (rad.) grid condenser; **condensador de sintonía** (rad.) tuning condenser; **condensador electrolítico** (rad.) electrolytic condenser; **condensador fijo** (elec.) fixed condenser; **condensador sintonizador** (rad.) tuning condenser; **condensador variable** (elec.) variable condenser
condensar *va* to condense; *vr* to condense, become condensed
condesa *f* countess; **condesa viuda** dowager countess
condescendencia *f* acquiescence, consent
condescender **§66** *vn* to acquiesce; **condescender a** to accede to; **condescender con** to yield to; **condescender en** + *inf* to acquiesce in + *ger*, to agree to + *inf*
condescendiente *adj* acquiescent, obliging
condestable *m* constable (*commander of armed forces in Middle Ages*); (nav.) deck petty officer, gunner
condestablesa *f* constable's wife
condestablía *f* constableship, constablewick
condición *f* condition, state; status, station, position; standing; circumstance; nature, temperament, character; **condiciones** *fpl* condition, state; aptitude, disposition; **a condición (de) que** on condition that, provided that; **tener condición** to have a bad temper
condicionado -da *adj* conditioned; conditional
condicional *adj* conditional; (gram.) conditional
condicionamiento *m* conditioning; adjustment; agreement
condicionar *va* to condition; to adjust; to prepare; (textiles) to condition; *vn* to agree, to fit
condigno -na *adj* condign (*punishment, censure*); appropriate, worthy; **condigno de** in accord with
cóndilo *m* (anat.) condyle
condimentación *f* seasoning
condimentar *va* to season, to treat with a condiment
condimento *m* condiment
condiscípulo *m* condisciple, fellow student
condolencia *f* condolence
condoler **§63** *vr* to condole, to sympathize; **condolerse de** to sympathize with, feel sorry for
condolido -da *adj* sad, sorrowful, touched
condominio *m* (law) joint ownership or possession; dual control, condominium
condómino *mf* (law) joint owner
condonación *f* condonation, forgiveness
condonante *adj* condoning, forgiving
condonar *va* to condone, to forgive
cóndor *m* (orn.) condor; **cóndor de California** (orn.) California condor
condotiero *m* condottiere
condrila *f* (bot.) gum succory
condrioma *m* (biol.) chondriome
condriosoma *m* (biol.) chondriosome
condrología *f* chondrology
conducción *f* leading, guiding; direction; conduction; transportation; piping; transfer, conveyance; (aut.) driving; agreement (*on prices or wages*); (phys. & physiol.) conduction; **conducción a derecha** or **a la derecha** (aut.) right-hand drive; **conducción a izquierda** or **a la izquierda** (aut.) left-hand drive; **conducción de noche** night driving; **conducción interior** (aut.) closed car
conducencia *f* conduction; transfer, conveyance
conducente *adj* conducive; leading
conducir **§38** *va* to lead, guide; to conduct, manage, direct; to convey, transport; to drive

(*a carriage, auto, etc.*); to hire, employ; *vn* to lead; to conduce, be suitable; *vr* to conduct oneself, behave
conducta *f* conduct, direction, management; guidance; conduct, behavior; convoy, conveyance; commission to enlist and bring in recruits; agreement made by a town with a doctor to attend its sick; **mejorar de conducta** to mend one's ways
conductancia *f* (elec.) conductance; **conductancia mutua** (elec.) mutual conductance
conductero *m* conductor of a convoy
conductibilidad *f* conductibility
conductible *adj* conductible
conductividad *f* conductivity
conductivo -va *adj* conductive
conducto *m* conduit, pipe; (elec.) conduit; (anat.) duct, canal; mediation, agency; channel; intermediary; **por conducto de** through; **conducto alimenticio** (anat.) alimentary canal; **conducto auditivo** (anat.) auditory canal; **conducto biliar** (anat.) bile duct; **conducto cístico** (anat.) cystic duct; **conducto de desagüe** sewer; (naut.) drain; **conducto de humo** flue; **conducto eyaculador** (anat.) ejaculatory duct; **conducto radicular** (anat. & dent.) root canal; **conducto regular** (mil.) channel; **conducto torácico** (anat.) thoracic duct
conductor -tora *adj* conducting, leading, guiding; (phys.) conductive; *m* conductor, leader, guide, mentor; driver, motorist; (phys. & rail.) conductor; (rail.) engineman, engine driver; (Am.) driver, teamster; **conductor huésped** (mus.) guest conductor
condueño *mf* part owner, joint owner
conduerma *f* (Am.) deep sleep, stupor
conduje *1st sg pret ind of* **conducir**
condumio *m* (coll.) grub, victuals; (coll.) food to eat with bread
conduplicado -da *adj* (bot.) conduplicate
conduplicación *f* (rhet.) reduplication
condutal *m* gutter, rain gutter
conduzco *1st sg pres ind of* **conducir**
conectador *m* connector; (elec.) connector; (elec.) outlet
conectar *va* to connect
conectivo -va *adj* connective
coneja *f* female rabbit
conejal *m* or **conejar** *m* rabbit warren
conejero -ra *adj* rabbit, rabbit-hunting; *mf* rabbit breeder; *f* burrow; rabbit warren; large cave; (coll.) joint, dive
conejillo *m* little rabbit; **conejillo de Indias** (zool.) guinea pig, cavy; (fig.) guinea pig
conejo *m* (zool.) rabbit; **conejo de Noruega** (zool.) lemming
conejuno -na *adj* (pertaining to a) rabbit; *f* cony, rabbit fur
conexidades *fpl* adjuncts, appurtenances
conexión *f* connection; **conexión en cascada** (elec.) cascade connection; **conexión en delta** (elec.) delta connection; **conexión en estrella** (elec.) star connection
conexionar *va* to connect; to put in touch; to compare, relate; *vr* to connect; to get in touch
conexivo -va *adj* connective
conexo -xa *adj* connected
conf. abr. of **confesor**
confabulación *f* confabulation; connivance, plotting, scheming, leaguing
confabulador -dora *mf* confabulator; conniver, plotter, schemer
confabular *vn* to confabulate; *vr* to connive, to plot, to scheme, to league together
confalón *m* gonfalon
confaloniero *m* gonfalonier
confección *f* making, confection; concoction; tailoring, suit making; ready-made suit; **confección a medida** made-to-order suit
confeccionado -da *adj* ready-made
confeccionar *va* to make (*e.g., a suit of clothes*); to make up (*a prescription*)
confeccionista *mf* ready-made clothier
confederación *f* confederation, confederacy, alliance, league
confederado -da *adj & mf* confederate
confederar *va & vr* to confederate
confederativo -va *adj* confederative
conferencia *f* conference; interview; lecture; **conferencia en la cumbre** summit conference
conferenciante *mf* lecturer; conferee
conferenciar *vn* to confer, hold an interview
conferencista *mf* (Am.) lecturer
conferir §62 *va* to confer, bestow, award; to compare; *vn* to confer; to lecture
confesa *f* see **confeso**
confesado -da *mf* (coll.) penitent
confesante *adj* confessing; *mf* confessor (*of guilt, fault, sin, etc.*)
confesar §18 *va* to confess; (eccl.) to confess (*sins; a sinner*); **confesar de plano** to confess openly; **confesar haber** + *pp* to confess having + *pp; vn & vr* to confess; (eccl.) to confess; **confesar** or **confesarse a** to confess to (*God*); **confesarse con** to confess to (*a priest*)
confesión *f* confession; faith, religion, denomination; **confesión de Augsburgo** Augsburg Confession
confesional *adj* confessional
confesionario *m* confessional; rule or code of confession
confesionista *mf* Confessionist, Lutheran
confeso -sa *adj* confessed; converted (*Jew*); *mf* converted Jew; *m* lay brother; *f* widow who has become a nun
confesonario *m* confessional
confesor *m* confessor (*believer; priest*)
confeti *m* confetti
confiabilidad *f* trustworthiness, reliability
confiable *adj* trustworthy, reliable
confiadamente *adv* trustingly, confidently
confiado -da *adj* confiding, unsuspecting; self-confident, haughty
confiador *m* var. of **cofiador**
confianza *f* confidence; self-confidence; familiarity, informality; **de confianza** reliable; **en confianza** trustingly; in confidence
confianzudo -da *adj* (coll.) overfriendly, overfamiliar, presumptuous; (Am.) meddlesome
confiar §90 *va* to entrust, confide; to give confidence to; **confiar algo a** or **en uno** to entrust something to someone; *vn & vr* to trust; **confiar** or **confiarse de** or **en** to trust in, rely on
confidencia *f* confidence; secret; **hacer confidencias a** to confide in
confidencial *adj* confidential
confidente -ta *adj* trustworthy, faithful; *mf* confident, confidant; informer, detective; spy, secret agent; *m* love seat; *f* confidante
configuración *f* configuration
configurar *va* to form, to shape
confín *adj* bordering; *m* confine, border, boundary; **los confines** the confines
confinación *f* var. of **confinamiento**
confinado -da *adj* confined (*kept in confines under surveillance*); *m* prisoner
confinamiento *m* confinement (*restraint under surveillance*)
confinante *adj* bordering
confinar *va* to confine (*to restrain within limits*); *vn* to border; **confinar con** to border on; *vr* to shut oneself up, to keep onself confined
confinidad *f* nearness, proximity
confirmación *f* confirmation
confirmadamente *adv* firmly, surely, approvingly
confirmador -dora or **confirmante** *adj* confirming, confirmatory; *mf* confirmer
confirmar *va* to confirm
confirmativo -va *adj* confirmative
confirmatorio -ria *adj* confirmatory
confiscación *f* confiscation
confiscar §86 *va* to confiscate
confitado -da *adj* hopeful, confident
confitar *va* to candy; to preserve; to sweeten
confite *m* candy, bonbon, confection; **confites** *mpl* candy; **morder en un confite** (coll.) to be very close, to be very intimate
confitería *f* confectionery; confectionery store
confitero -ra *mf* confectioner; *f* candy box; candy jar
confitura *f* confection, confiture, preserve
conflación *f* melting, smelting
conflagración *f* conflagration

conflagrar *va* to set fire to, to burn
conflátil *adj* fusible
conflicto *m* conflict; struggle, anguish; fix, jam
confluencia *f* confluence
confluente *adj* confluent; *m* confluence (*of rivers*)
confluir **§41** *vn* to flow together, to come together, to crowd, to meet
conformación *f* conformation
conformador *m* hat block; shoe tree; grader, road shaper
conformar *va* to conform; to adjust, harmonize; to shape; to block (*a hat*); *vn* to conform, to agree; *vr* to conform, to comply, to yield; **conformarse a** or **con** to resign oneself to, to submit to
conforme *adj* according, in agreement; conformable; **conforme con** in agreement with; resigned to; *adv* depending on circumstances; O.K.; **conforme a** according to, in accordance with; *conj* as; in proportion as, in the way that; as soon as; *m* approval
conformemente *adv* conformably; in agreement
conformidad *f* conformity, conformance; shape; compliance; forbearance; **de conformidad con** in accordance with, in agreement with; **en conformidad con** in compliance with
conformismo *m* conventionality; conformism
conformista *mf* conformist
confort *m* comfort
confortable *adj* comforting; comfortable (*e.g., chair, bed, room*)
confortación *f* comfort, consolation; strength, invigoration
confortador -dora *adj* comforting, consoling; *mf* comforter, consoler
confortamiento *m* var. of **confortación**
confortante *adj* comforting; tonic; *mf* comforter; *m* tonic; mitt
confortar *va* to comfort, console; to strengthen, enliven, invigorate
confortativo -va *adj* comforting, consoling; *m* comfort, consolation
conforte *m* var. of **confortación**
confr. abr. of **confesor**
confracción *f* breaking, fracture
confraternal *adj* confraternal
confraternar *vn* to be brotherly
confraternidad *f* confraternity
confraternizar **§76** *vn* to be brotherly; to fraternize
confricación *f* rubbing; (path.) chafing; masturbation; Lesbianism
confricar **§86** *va* to rub
confrontación *f* confrontation; propinquity; natural affinity, innate sympathy
confrontar *va* to confront (*to bring face to face; to compare*); *vn* to border; to get along, to agree; **confrontar con** to border on; to get along with, to agree with; *vr* to get along, to agree; **confrontarse con** to confront, to face; to get along with, to agree with
confucianismo *m* Confucianism
confucianista *adj & mf* Confucianist
confuciano -na *adj & mf* Confucian
Confucio *m* Confucius
confulgencia *f* combined brilliance
confundible *adj* confusable
confundimiento *m* confusion, bewilderment
confundir *va* to confuse; to mix, mix together, mix up; to confound; *vr* to become confused; to mix, to fuse; to become lost, become mingled (*e.g., in a crowd*)
confusión *f* confusion; **confusión de lenguas** (Bib.) confusion of tongues
confuso -sa *adj* confused; **en confuso** confusedly, in confusion
confutación *f* confutation
confutador -dora *adj* confutative; *mf* confuter
confutar *va* to confute
confutatorio -ria *adj* confutative
conga *f* see **congo**
congelación *f* congealing; freezing
congelador *m* freezer
congeladora *f* deep-freeze
congelamiento *m* var. of **congelación**
congelante *adj* freezing, refrigerant
congelar *va* to congeal; to freeze; (com.) to freeze (*assets, credits, etc.*); *vr* to congeal; to freeze
congelativo -va *adj* refrigerant
congénere *adj* congeneric; *m & f* congener; fellow
congenial *adj* congenial
congeniar *vn* to be congenial, to get along
congénito -ta *adj* congenital
congerie *f* congeries
congestión *f* congestion; (path.) congestion
congestionar *va* to congest; (path.) to congest; *vr* to congest, become congested
congestivo -va *adj* congestive
conglobación *f* conglobation; (fig.) concentration, integration
conglobar *va & vr* to conglobate, to form in a round mass
conglomeración *f* conglomeration
conglomerado -da *adj & m* conglomerate
conglomerar *va & vr* to conglomerate
conglutinación *f* conglutination
conglutinante *adj* conglutinant
conglutinar *va & vr* to conglutinate
conglutinativo -va *adj* conglutinative
congo -ga *adj & mf* Congo; *m* (zool.) congo monkey; (*cap.*) *m* Congo; **el Congo Belga** Belgian Congo; **el Congo Francés** French Congo; *f* (ent.) large poisonous ant; (zool.) hutia conga; (zool.) hutia carabali
congoja *f* anguish, grief
congojar *va & vr* var. of **acongojar**
congojoso -sa *adj* distressing; in anguish
congoleño -ña or **congolés -lesa** *adj & mf* Congoese or Congolese
congosto *m* canyon, narrow pass
congraciador -dora *adj* ingratiating
congraciamiento *m* ingratiation
congraciar *va* to win, win over; *vr* to win; **congraciarse con** to ingratiate oneself with
congratulación *f* congratulation
congratular *va* to congratulate; **congratular de** or **por** to congratulate on; *vr* to congratulate oneself, to rejoice
congratulatorio -ria *adj* congratulatory
congregación *f* congregation
congregacionalismo *m* congregationalism; Congregationalism
congregacionalista *adj* Congregational, Congregationalist; *mf* Congregationalist
congreganista *adj* congregational
congregar **§59** *va & vr* to congregate
congresal *mf* (Am.) var. of **congresista**
congresional *adj* congressional, Congressional
congresista *mf* delegate; member of congress; *m* congressman; *f* congresswoman
congreso *m* congress; meeting, convention; intercourse; **Congreso de los Diputados** Congress (*of Spanish or Spanish American Cortes*)
congrí *m* (Am.) rice and bean stew
congrio *m* (ichth.) conger, conger eel; (coll.) saphead, dope
congrua *f* see **congruo**
congruencia *f* congruence; congruity; (math.) congruence; (geom.) congruity
congruente *adj* congruent; appropriate; (geom.) congruent, congruous
congruo -grua *adj* congruous; *f* supplementary emolument; adequate income for one who is about to be ordained a priest
conicidad *f* conicity
conicina *f* (chem.) coniine
cónico -ca *adj* conic or conical; *f* (math.) conic section
conidio *m* (bot.) conidium
conidióforo *m* (bot.) conidiophore
conífero -ra *adj* (bot.) coniferous; *f* (bot.) conifer
coniforme *adj* coniform, cone-shaped
conirrostro -tra *adj* (orn.) conirostral
conivalvo -va *adj* (zool.) cone-shelled
coniza *f* (bot.) fleawort
conjetura *f* conjecture
conjeturador -dora *adj* guessing; *mf* guesser
conjetural *adj* conjectural
conjeturar *va & vn* to conjecture, to guess, to surmise
conjuez *m* (*pl:* **-jueces**) cojudge

conjugación *f* conjugation; (biol. & gram.) conjugation
conjugado -da *adj* (bot. & math.) conjugate; *f* (bot.) conjugate
conjugar §59 *va* to conjugate; (biol. & gram.) to conjugate; *vr* to conjugate, to be joined, be fused; (biol. & gram.) to conjugate
conjunción *f* conjunction; combination; (astr., astrol. & gram.) conjunction; **conjunción coordinante** (gram.) coördinating conjunction; **conjunción disyuntiva** (gram.) alternative conjunction; **conjunción dubitativa** (gram.) dubitative conjunction; **conjunción subordinante** (gram.) subordinating conjunction
conjuntado -da *adj* (theat.) well integrated
conjuntamente *adv* conjointly
conjuntar *va* to combine, to bring together
conjuntiva *f* see **conjuntivo**
conjuntival *adj* conjunctival
conjuntivitis *f* (path.) conjunctivitis
conjuntivo -va *adj* conjunctive; (gram.) conjunctive; *f* (anat.) conjunctiva
conjunto -ta *adj* conjoint, conjunct; joined, allied, related; joint; *m* whole, entirety, ensemble; group; unit; (mus.) ensemble (*whole effect of united performance*); (theat.) chorus; **de conjunto** general; united; **en conjunto** as a whole; **en su conjunto** in its entirety
conjura or **conjuración** *f* conspiracy, plot
conjurado -da *mf* conspirator
conjurador *m* conjurer (*one who entreats*)
conjuramentar *va* to swear in; *vr* to take an oath
conjurante *mf* conjurer (*one who entreats*)
conjurar *va* to swear in; to conjure (*to entreat*); to conjure away; *vn* to conspire, to plot; *vr* to conspire, to plot; to join in a conspiracy
conjuro *m* conjuration (*magic form of words*); conjuration of evil spirits; adjuration, entreaty
conllevador -dora *mf* co-worker; fellow sufferer
conllevancia *f* cooperation; mutual toleration
conllevar *va* to coöperate in bearing (*a task, burden, etc.*); to bear, tolerate (*a person*); to suffer (*adversity*)
conmemorable *adj* commemorable
conmemoración *f* commemoration; **en conmemoración de** in commemoration of
conmemorar *va* to commemorate
conmemorativo -va *adj* commemorative, memorial
conmemoratorio -ria *adj* commemoratory
conmensurabilidad *f* commensurability
conmensurable *adj* commensurable; commensurate
conmensuración *f* commensuration
conmensurar *va* to make commensurate, to commensurate
conmigo with me, with myself
conmilitón *m* companion-at-arms, fellow soldier
conminación *f* commination
conminar *va* to threaten; to threaten with punishment
conmiseración *f* commiseration
conmistión *f* commixture
conmisto -ta *adj* commingled
conmixtión *f* var. of **conmistión**
conmixto -ta *adj* var. of **conmisto**
conmoción *f* commotion, disturbance; shock; arousing, stirring; excitement
conmocionado -da *adj* jolted, shocked, stunned
conmoración *f* (rhet.) repetition, elaboration
conmovedor -dora *adj* stirring, moving, touching
conmover §63 *va* to stir, stir up; to move, to touch, to affect; to shake, to upset; *vr* to be moved, be touched, be affected
conmutable *adj* commutable
conmutación *f* commutation; (elec. & law) commutation
conmutador *m* (elec.) change-over switch, commutating switch; (elec.) commutator; **conmutador de cuatro terminales** (elec.) four-way switch; **conmutador de tres terminales** (elec.) three-way switch; **conmutador de doble caída** (elec.) double-throw switch
conmutar *va* to commute; (elec.) to commutate; (law) to commute
conmutativo -va *adj* commutative
conmutatriz *f* (*pl:* **-trices**) (elec.) converter
connacional *m* fellow countryman
connatural *adj* connatural, inborn, inherent
connaturalización *f* adaptation, acclimation
connaturalizar §76 *va* to make connatural; *vr* to become accustomed, become acclimated
connivencia *f* connivance
connivente *adj* conniving; (anat. & bot.) connivent
connotación *f* connotation; distant relationship
connotado -da *adj* (Am.) notable, outstanding; *m* distant relationship
connotar *va* to connote
connotativo -va *adj* connotative
connovicio -cia *mf* fellow novice, beginner, or apprentice
connubio *m* (poet.) marriage
connumerar *va* to mention; to connumerate
cono *m* (geom. & bot.) cone; **cono de poleas** cone pulley; **cono de proa** nose cone (*of a rocket*); **cono de sombra** (astr.) umbra; **cono de viento** (aer.) wind sock
conocedor -dora *adj* knowing, expert; *mf* connoisseur, judge
conocencia *f* (law) confession
conocer §32 *va* to know (*by reasoning or learning; by perception or the senses; to be acquainted with, to recognize*); to meet, to get to know; to tell, to distinguish; to know carnally; (law) to try (*a case*); *vn* to know; **conocer de** or **en** to know, to have a knowledge of; **conocer de** (law) to try (*a case*); *vr* to know oneself; to know each other; to meet, to meet each other, to get acquainted
conocible *adj* knowable
conocido -da *adj* familiar, well-known; illustrious, distinguished; *mf* acquaintance
conocimiento *m* knowledge; understanding; consciousness; acquaintance; (com.) bill of lading; **conocimientos** *mpl* knowledge; **hablar con pleno conocimiento de causa** to know what one is talking about; **obrar con conocimiento de causa** to know what one is doing, know what one is up to; **perder el conocimiento** to lose consciousness; **poner en conocimiento** to inform, to let know; **por su real conocimiento** (Am.) for real money; **recobrar el conocimiento** to regain consciousness; **venir en conocimiento de** to come to know, to find out, take cognizance of; **conocimiento de embarque** (com.) bill of lading
conoidal *adj* conoidal
conoide *adj* conoid; *m* (geom.) conoid
conoideo -a *adj* conoidal, cone-shaped
conopeo *m* canopy (*fixed over shrine or carried over exalted personage*)
conopial *adj* see **arco**
conozco *1st sg pres ind of* **conocer**
conque *adv* and so, so then, well; *m* (coll.) condition, terms, understanding
conquense *adj* (pertaining to) Cuenca; *mf* native or inhabitant of Cuenca, Spain
conquífero -ra *adj* conchiferous
conquiforme *adj* shell-shaped, conchiform
conquiliología *f* conchology
conquiliólogo -ga *mf* conchologist
conquista *f* conquest (*act; person or thing*); **conquista normanda** Norman Conquest
conquistable *adj* conquerable; easy to get, attainable
conquistador -dora *adj* conquering; *mf* conqueror; *m* lady-killer; conquistador (*Spanish conqueror in America in the sixteenth century*); **el Conquistador** the Conqueror (*William I of England, James I of Aragon, Alfonso I of Portugal*)
conquistar *va* to conquer (*by force of arms*); to win over; **conquistar algo a alguien** to win something from someone
Conrado *m* Conrad
conrear *va* to work over; to grease (*wool*); to plow a second time
conreinado *m* coreign
conreinar *vn* to reign jointly

consabido -da *adj* well-known, above-mentioned
consagración *f* consecration
consagrado -da *adj* consecrate, consecrated; hallowed (*ground*); sanctioned, established, time-honored; stock (*phrase*)
consagrante *adj* consecrating; *mf* consecrator
consagrar *va* to consecrate; to devote; to dedicate; to deify, to apotheosize; to authorize (*a new word or meaning*); *vr* to devote oneself (*e.g., to study*); to consecrate oneself; to make a name for oneself; **consagrarse a** + *inf* to devote oneself to + *inf*
consanguíneo -a *adj* consanguineous
consanguinidad *f* consanguinity
consciente *adj* conscious
conscripción *f* (mil.) conscription
conscripto *m* (mil.) draftee
consectario -ria *adj* next, adjoining; *m* corollary
consecución *f* obtaining, acquisition, attainment
consecuencia *f* consequence; consistency; **en consecuencia** accordingly; **guardar consecuencia** to remain consistent; **por consecuencia** consequently; **sacar en consecuencia** to prove, to show; **traer a consecuencia** to bring in, bring up
consecuente *adj* consecutive; consistent; *m* (log. & math.) consequent
consecutivo -va *adj* consecutive; (gram.) consecutive
conseguimiento *m* var. of **consecución**
conseguir §82 *va* to get, obtain; to bring about; **conseguir** + *inf* to succeed in + *ger*
conseja *f* story, fairy tale; cabal, conciliabule
consejero -ra *adj* advisory; *m* counselor, adviser; councilor; *f* counselor's wife; female adviser
consejo *m* advice, counsel; council; town or city council; board; **consejos** *mpl* advice; **tomar consejo** to take counsel, **un consejo** a piece of advice; **consejo de estado** council of state; **consejo de familia** board of guardians; **consejo de guerra** council of war; court-martial; **consejo de ministros** council of ministers, cabinet; **Consejo de Seguridad** Security Council
consenciente *adj* blinking at evil
consenso *m* consensus
consensual *adj* (law) consensual
consentido -da *adj* complaisant, indulgent (*husband*); pampered, spoiled; (Am.) proud, haughty
consentidor -dora *adj* acquiescent, yielding; (coll.) pampering; *mf* acquiescent person; (coll.) pamperer; *m* cuckold
consentimiento *m* consent
consentir §62 *va* to allow, permit, tolerate; to admit; to pamper, spoil; *vn* to consent; to believe; to weaken, become loose (*said, e.g., of a piece of furniture or its parts*); **consentir** + *inf* to believe, to think that + *ind*, e.g., **consentí morir helado** I thought that I was freezing to death; **consentir con** to be indulgent with; **consentir en** to consent to; **consentir en** + *inf* to consent to + *inf; vr* to begin to split or crack up; (Am.) to be proud
conserje *m* janitor, concierge, porter
conserjería *f* janitorship, janitor's quarters; porter's desk, conciergerie
conserva *f* conserve, preserves; preserved food; pickles; (naut.) convoy; **navegar en conserva** or **en la conserva** (naut.) to sail in a convoy; **conservas alimenticias** canned goods; **conserva trojezada** minced preserves
conservación *f* conservation; maintenance, upkeep; preservation; self-preservation; **conservación de la energía** (phys.) conservation of energy; **conservación de la masa** (phys.) conservation of mass; **conservación de la materia** (phys.) conservation of matter; **conservación de suelos** soil conservation
conservador -dora *adj* preservative; (pol.) conservative; *mf* (pol.) conservative; *m* conservator; curator
conservadorismo *m* var. of **conservadurismo**
conservaduría *f* curatorship
conservadurismo *m* conservatism; British Conservative Party
conservar *va* to conserve, keep, maintain; to preserve; **bien conservado** well-preserved; *vr* to keep; to take good care of oneself
conservatismo *m* (Am.) conservatism
conservativo -va *adj* preservative
conservatorio -ria *adj* conservatory; *m* conservatory, conservatoire; (Am.) conservatory (*greenhouse*)
conservera *f* see **conservero**
conservería *f* preserve making
conservero -ra *adj* preserve, canning (*business, industry, etc.*); *mf* preserver, preserve maker; canner; *f* cannery
considerabilísimo -ma *adj super* very great, quite considerable
considerable *adj* considerable; large, great
consideración *f* consideration; **cargar** or **fijar la consideración en** to consider carefully, to look into thoroughly; **en consideración** under consideration; **en consideración a** in consideration of; **ser de consideración** to be of importance, be of concern; **tomar en consideración** to take into consideration
consideradamente *adv* carefully, watchfully
considerado -da *adj* considered; considerate; respected, esteemed
considerando *m* whereas; **considerando que** whereas
considerar *va* to consider; to treat with respect
consigna *f* order; slogan; (mil.) watchword; (rail.) checkroom
consignación *f* consignment; (com.) consignment; **a consignación** (com.) on consignment
consignador *m* (com.) consignor
consignar *va* to consign; to assign; to tell, relate; to point out; to indicate, state; (com.) to consign
consignatario *m* consignatary; (com.) consignee
consigo with him, with her, with them, with you; with himself, with herself, with themselves, with yourself, with yourselves
consiguiente *adj* consequent; consequential; resultant; **ir** or **proceder consiguiente** to act consistently; *m* consequence, result; (log.) consequent; **por consiguiente** or **por el consiguiente** consequently, therefore
consiliario -ria *mf* counselor, adviser
consistencia *f* consistence or consistency
consistente *adj* consistent; consisting
consistir *vn* to consist; **consistir en** to consist in; to consist of; **consistir en** + *inf* to consist in + *ger*
consistorial *adj* consistorial; *m* member of a consistory; councilman
consistorio *m* consistory; town council; town hall; **Consistorio divino** Throne of God
cons.º abr. of **consejo**
consocio -cia *mf* copartner; companion, comrade, fellow member
consola *f* console, console table; bracket; (arch., mus. & rad.) console
consolación *f* consolation; (cards) consolation (*fine paid by loser*)
consolador -dora *adj* consoling; *mf* consoler
consolar §77 *va* to console
consolativo -va or **consolatorio -ria** *adj* consolatory
consólida *f* (bot.) comfrey; **consólida real** (bot.) delphinium, field larkspur
consolidación *f* consolidation
consolidado -da *adj* bonded (*debt*); **consolidados** *mpl* consolidated annuities
consolidar *va* to consolidate; to fund, to refund; to put together, to repair; *vr* to consolidate
consonancia *f* consonance or consonancy; harmony; rhyme; **en consonancia con** in accordance with
consonantado -da *adj* rhymed
consonante *adj* consonant; consonantal; rhyming; *m* rhyme word; *f* (gram.) consonant
consonántico -ca *adj* consonantal
consonar §77 *vn* to rhyme; (mus.) to be in harmony; to be harmonious

cónsone *adj* consonous, harmonious; *m* (mus.) chord
cónsono -na *adj* consonous, harmonious
consorcio *m* consortium; partnership; fellowship, harmony
consorte *mf* consort; companion, partner; **consortes** *mpl* (law) colitigants; (law) accomplices
conspicuo -cua *adj* distinguished, outstanding, conspicuous
conspiración *f* conspiracy
conspirado *m* conspirer, conspirator
conspirador -dora *mf* conspirer, conspirator
conspirar *vn* to conspire; **conspirar a** + *inf* to conspire to + *inf*
conspuir §41 *va* to decry, run down
Const. abr. of **Constitución**
constancia *f* constancy, steadiness; certainty; proof; (Am.) written evidence, documentary proof; **dejar constancia de** to prove, to establish
constante *adj* constant; clear, certain; *f* (math. & phys.) constant
constantemente *adv* constantly; surely, with certainty; regularly
Constantino *m* Constantine
Constantinopla *f* Constantinople
Constanza *f* Constance (*feminine proper name*)
constar *vn* to be clear, be certain; to be shown, be on record; to have the right rhythm (*said of verse*); **hacer constar** to state, to reveal; **constar de** to consist of, be composed of
constatación *f* proof, establishment (*of a fact*)
constatar *va* to state, show, establish, prove
constelación *f* (astr. & astrol.) constellation; climate, atmosphere; epidemic
constelar *va* to fill, cover, sprinkle
consternación *f* consternation
consternar *va* to dismay, terrify, consternate
constipación *f* cold, cold in the head; **constipación de vientre** constipation
constipado *m* cold, cold in the head
constipar *va* to cause (*someone*) to catch cold, to give a cold to; to constipate; to close or constrict (*pores or tissues*); to stop up (*nasal passages*); *vr* to catch cold; to become constipated
constitución *f* constitution
constitucional *adj* constitutional; *mf* constitutionalist
constitucionalidad *f* constitutionality
constituidor -dora *adj* constitutive
constituir §41 *va* to constitute; to set up, to establish; **constituir en** to force into; *vr* to constitute oneself; **constituirse en** or **por** to set oneself up as
constitutivo -va *adj & m* constituent
constituyente *adj* constituent; component; (pol.) constituent; *m* constituent; component; **constituyentes** *fpl* (pol.) constituent assembly
const.l abr. of **constitucional**
constreñidamente *adv* constrainedly
constreñimiento *m* constraint, compulsion
constreñir §74 *va* to constrain, to force; to compress, to oppress; to bind, make costive, constipate
constricción *f* constriction; (med.) constriction
constrictivo -va *adj* constrictive; styptic
constrictor -tora *adj* constricting; (med.) styptic; *m* (anat.) constrictor; (med.) styptic
constringente *adj* constringent
construcción *f* construction; structure, building; (gram.) construction; **construcción de buques, construcción naval** shipbuilding
constructivo -va *adj* constructive
constructor -tora *adj* constructing, building; construction (*e.g., company*); *mf* constructor, builder; **constructor de buques** shipbuilder
construir §41 *va* to construct; (geom. & gram.) to construct
constuprar *va* to defile, corrupt
consubstanciación *f* (theol.) consubstantiation
consubstancial *adj* consubstantial
consubstancialidad *f* consubstantiality
consuegra *f* mother-in-law of one's child
consuegro *m* father-in-law of one's child
consuelda *f* (bot.) comfrey; (bot.) prickly or rough comfrey; **consuelda mayor** (bot.) comfrey; **consuelda media** (bot.) bugle, bugleweed; **consuelda real** (bot.) field larkspur; **consuelda sarracena** (bot.) goldenrod (*Solidago virgaurea*)
consuelo *m* consolation; joy, comfort; **sin consuelo** inconsolably; (coll.) to excess, without limit; (*cap.*) *f* Consuelo (*woman's name*)
consueta *m* (theat.) prompter
consuetudinario -ria *adj* customary, consuetudinary; *mf* habitual sinner
cónsul *m* consul; **cónsul general** consul general
cónsula *f* consul's wife
consulado *m* consulate; consulship; **consulado general** consulate general
consular *adj* consular
consulesa *f* (coll.) consul's wife
consulta *f* consulting; consultation; opinion (*of lawyer, doctor, etc.*)
consultación *f* consultation
consultante *adj* consulting
consultar *va* to consult; to take up, to discuss; to advise; to hand down an opinion on; *vn* to consult
consultivo -va *adj* consultative
consultor -tora *adj* consulting; *mf* consultant
consultorio *m* information bureau; doctor's office, clinic
consumación *f* consummation; termination, extinction; **la consumación de los siglos** the end of the world
consumado -da *adj* consummate; fulfilled; *m* consommé
consumar *va* to consummate
consumero *m* (slang) tax collector (*at city gates*); (slang) guard stationed to prevent smuggling
consumible *adj* consumable
consumición *f* consumption; drink (*bought in a café or restaurant*)
consumido -da *adj* (coll.) weak, thin, emaciated, worn-out; (coll.) worrying, fretful
consumidor -dora *adj* consuming; *mf* consumer; customer (*of a café or restaurant*)
consumimiento *m* consumption, destruction
consumir *va* to consume; to take (*the Eucharist*); (coll.) to harass, vex, wear down; *vr* to consume, waste away, languish; to long, to yearn; (coll.) to become harassed or vexed
consumo *m* consumption (*e.g., of food*); consumers; **consumos** *spl* octroi, tax on provisions (*being brought into town*)
consunción *f* consumption, destruction; (path.) consumption
consuno; de consuno in accord, together
consuntivo -va *adj* consumptive, consuming
consustanciación *f* var. of **consubstanciación**
consustancial *adj* var. of **consubstancial**
consustancialidad *f* var. of **consubstancialidad**
contabilidad *f* calculability; accountancy, accounting, bookkeeping
contabilista *mf* accountant, bookkeeper
contabilizar §76 *va* to enter (*in ledger, on score card, etc.*)
contable *adj* countable; *m* accountant, bookkeeper
contactar *vn* to contact, be in contact
contacto *m* contact; (elec.) contact; **poner en contacto con** to put in contact or touch with; **ponerse en contacto con** to reach, to get in touch with
contactor *m* (elec.) contactor
contadero -ra *adj* countable; *m* narrow passage (*through which only one person or animal can pass at a time*)
contado -da *adj* scarce, rare; **contados -das** *adj pl* a few; **al contado** cash, for cash; **de contado** immediately, right away; **por de contado** naturally, of course
contador *m* counter; accountant; cash register; (law) auditor, receiver; meter (*for gas, water, electricity*); **contador automático** slot meter; **contador de abonado** house meter; **contador de centelleo** (phys.) scintillation counter; **contador de Geiger** (phys.) Geiger counter; **contador kilométrico** (aut.) speed-

ometer, odometer; **contador público titulado** certified public accountant
contaduría *f* accountancy; accountant's office; auditorship; (theat.) box office
contagiar *va* to affect by contagion; (fig.) to infect; (fig.) to communicate (*e.g., an emotion*); *vr* to become affected by contagion; (fig.) to become infected; **contagiarse de** to catch (*a disease*) by contagion
contagio *m* contagion
contagiosidad *f* contagiousness
contagioso -sa *adj* contagious
contal *m* string of beads for counting
contaminación *f* contamination; (philol.) contamination; (fig.) stain, blot
contaminador -dora *adj* contaminating
contaminar *va* to contaminate; to corrupt (*a text*); to profane, to break (*the law of God*); *vr* to become contaminated
contante *adj* ready (*money*)
contar **§77** *va* to count; to rate, consider; to charge, to debit; to tell, to relate; **dejarse contar diez** (box.) to take the count; **tiene sus días contados** or **sus horas contadas** his days are numbered; **contar . . . años** to be . . . years old; **contar una cosa por hecha** to consider a thing as good as done; *vn* to count; **a contar desde** beginning with; **contar con** to count on, rely on; to reckon with; **contar con** + *inf* to count on + *ger*, to expect to + *inf;* **contar con** or **por los dedos** to count on one's fingers
contario *m* var. of **contero**
contemperar *va* var. of **atemperar**
contemplación *f* contemplation; leniency, condescension; **gastar contemplaciones con** (coll.) to humor
contemplador -dora *adj* contemplating, contemplative; *mf* contemplator
contemplar *va* to contemplate; to be lenient to, to be condescending towards; *vn* to contemplate
contemplativo -va *adj* contemplative; lenient
contemporaneidad *f* contemporaneousness
contemporáneo -a *adj* contemporaneous; contemporary; *mf* contemporary (*person or thing*)
contemporización *f* temporizing, temporization
contemporizador -dora *adj* temporizing; *mf* temporizer
contemporizar **§76** *vn* to temporize
contén *m* curb; *2nd sg impv of* **contener**
contención *f* containment; containing, checking; contention, strife, emulation; (law) suit, litigation
contencioso -sa *adj* contentious; (law) contentious
contendedor *m* contestant
contender **§66** *vn* to contend, to contest
contendiente *adj* contending; *mf* contestant, contender
contendor *m* var. of **contendedor**
contendré *1st sg fut ind of* **contener**
contenencia *f* suspension in flight of birds of prey; (dancing) side step with pause
contener **§85** *va* to contain; *vr* to contain oneself
contengo *1st sg pres ind of* **contener**
contenido -da *adj* moderate, restrained; *m* contents; content
contenta *f* see **contento**
contentadizo -za *adj* easy to please; **bien contentadizo** easy to please; **mal contentadizo** hard to please
contentamiento *m* contentment
contentar *va* to content; (com.) to indorse; **ser de buen contentar** (coll.) to be easy to please; **ser de mal contentar** (coll.) to be hard to please; *vr* to be contented; **contentarse con** or **de** + *inf* to be satisfied with + *ger* or to + *inf*
contento -ta *adj* contented, glad; **no caber de contento** (coll.) to be bursting with joy; *m* contentment; **a contento** to one's satisfaction; *f* gift or treat to please someone; (com.) indorsement; (mil.) certificate of good conduct; (law) release
contera *f* tip (*e.g., of umbrella*); refrain; **por contera** (coll.) finally, at the end
contérmino -na *adj* conterminous
contero *m* (arch.) beading, beadwork
conterráneo -a *adj* of the same country; *m* fellow countryman; *f* fellow country woman
contertuliano -na or **contertulio -lia** *mf* party-goer, fellow member (*of a social group*)
contesta *f* (Am.) chat, conversation; (Am.) answer
contestable *adj* answerable
contestación *f* answer, reply; dispute, altercation; **contestación a la demanda** (law) answer, plea; **mala contestación** back talk, sauce
contestar *va* to answer; to confirm (*a witness, the deposition of a witness*); **contestar el timbre, la puerta, el teléfono, una carta, una pregunta, a una persona** to answer the bell, the door, the telephone, a letter, a question, a person; *vn* to answer; to agree; **contestar a** to answer (*e.g., a letter*)
conteste *adj* (law) confirming another witness; **estar contestes** to be in agreement
contexto *m* interweaving; interweaving of words; context
contextuar **§33** *va* to back with quotations
contextura *f* contexture; contexture of human body
conticinio *m* dead of night
contienda *f* contest, fight, dispute
contigo with thee, with you
contigüidad *f* contiguity
contiguo -gua *adj* contiguous
continencia *f* continence
continental *adj* continental; *m* office for local messages; local message
continente *adj* continent; *m* container; mien, countenance; bearing; continent; **Continente antártico** Antarctic Continent; **Continente Negro** Dark Continent
contingencia *f* contingency
contingente *adj* contingent; *m* contingent; share; quota; (mil.) contingent
contingible *adj* possible
continuación *f* continuation; continuance; **a continuación** later on, below; **a continuación de** right after; right behind
continuadamente *adv* continuously
continuador -dora *adj* continuing; *mf* continuer, continuator
continuar **§33** *va* to continue; *vn* to continue; **continuar** + *ger* to continue to + *inf*, to continue + *ger*; **continuará** to be continued (*said e.g., of a serial*); **continuar con** to continue with; to adjoin; *vr* to continue; **continuarse con** to connect with
continuativo -va *adj & f* (gram.) continuative
continuidad *f* continuity
continuo -nua *adj* continual; continuous; persevering; (mach.) endless; **a la continua** continuously; **de continuo** continuously; **continuo** *adv* continuously; *m* continuum; yeoman of the guard; **continuo espacio-temporal** or **continuo espacio tiempo** (phys.) space-time continuum
contómetro *m* comptometer
contonear *vr* to strut, to swagger
contoneo *m* strut, swagger
contorcer **§87** *vr* to twist oneself, to writhe
contorción *f* twisting, writhing, contortion
contornado -da *adj* (her.) contourné
contornar or **contornear** *va* to go around; to trace the contour of, to outline
contorneo *m* encircling; outline, outlining
contorno *m* contour, outline; **contornos** *mpl* environs; **en contorno** around, round about
contorsión *f* contortion
contorsionista *mf* contortionist
contra *prep* against; facing; *m* con (*opposite opinion*); (mus.) organ pedal; **contras** *mpl* lowest bass of organ; *f* (coll.) trouble, inconvenience; (fencing) counter; (Am.) play-off; (Am.) gift, extra (*to a customer*); **en contra de** against; **ir en contra de** to run counter to; **llevar la contra a** (coll.) to oppose, to disagree with
contraabertura *f* (surg.) counteropening
contraalmirante *m* rear admiral
contraamura *f* (naut.) preventer
contraantena *f* (rad.) counterpoise
contraaproches *mpl* (fort.) counterapproach

contraárbol *m* (mach.) countershaft
contraarmiños *mpl* (her.) ermines, counter-ermine
contraatacar §86 *va & vn* to counterattack
contraataguía *f* secondary cofferdam
contraataque *m* counterattack; **contraataques** *mpl* (fort.) fortified line of defense
contrabajo *m* (mus.) contrabass, double bass; (mus.) contrabassist
contrabajón *m* (mus.) double bassoon
contrabajonista *mf* double-bassoon player
contrabalancear *va* to counterbalance
contrabalanza *f* counterbalance; contrast
contrabandear *vn* to smuggle
contrabandista *adj* (pertaining to) contraband, smuggling; *mf* contrabandist, smuggler
contrabando *m* contraband; smuggling; **pasar de contrabando** to smuggle, to smuggle in; **contrabando de guerra** contraband of war
contrabarrera *f* (taur.) inner barrier; (taur.) second row of seats
contrabasa *f* pedestal
contrabatería *f* (mil.) counterbattery
contrabatir *va* (mil.) to fire back at (*enemy's battery*)
contrabolina *f* (naut.) auxiliary bowline
contrabóveda *f* (arch.) inverted vault or arch
contrabovedilla *f* (naut.) upper counter
contrabracear *va* to counterbrace
contrabranque *m* (naut.) stemson
contrabraza *f* (naut.) auxiliary brace
contrabrazo *m* drag link (*of steering gear*)
contrabrazola *f* (naut.) headledge
contracaja *f* (print.) upper right-hand corner of case for little-used type
contracalle *f* parallel side street
contracambio *m* exchange; (com.) re-exchange
contracanal *m* branch channel
contracarril *m* (rail.) guardrail
contracarta *f* var. of **contraescritura**
contracción *f* contraction; (econ.) recession
contracédula *f* counter decree
contracepción *f* contraception
contraceptivo -va *adj & m* contraceptive
contracifra *f* key to a cipher
contraclave *f* (arch.) voussoir next to keystone
contracodaste *m* (naut.) inner sternpost
contracorriente *f* countercurrent, crosscurrent; (fig.) backwash; **a contracorriente** upstream
contractable *adj* contractible
contráctil *adj* contractile; contractible, shrinkable
contractilidad *f* contractility
contractivo -va *adj* contractive
contracto -ta *adj* (gram.) contract
contractual *adj* contractual
contractura *f* contraction; (arch. & path.) contracture
contracuartelado -da *adj* (her.) counterquartered
contracurva *f* reverse curve
contrachapado *m* plywood
contradanza *f* contradance
contradecir §37 *va* to contradict; *vr* to contradict oneself
contradicción *f* contradiction
contradiciendo *ger of* **contradecir**
contradictor -tora *adj* contradictory (*person*); *mf* contradicter
contradictorio -ria *adj* contradictory; *f* (log.) contradictory
contradicho -cha *pp of* **contradecir**
contradigo *1st sg pres ind of* **contradecir**
contradije *1st sg pret ind of* **contradecir**
contradique *m* counterdike
contradiré *1st sg fut ind of* **contradecir**
contradriza *f* (naut.) auxiliary halyard
contradurmiente *m* (naut.) clamp
contraeje *m* (mach.) countershaft
contraelectromotriz *adj fem* counter electromotive
contraemboscada *f* counterambush
contraer §88 *va* to contract; to condense (*an idea*); (gram.) to contract; *vr* to contract; to be restricted; (Am.) to work hard, to apply oneself
contraescalón *m* riser (*of stairs*)
contraescarpa *f* (fort.) counterscarp
contraescota *f* (naut.) auxiliary sheet
contraescotín *m* (naut.) auxiliary topsail sheet
contraescritura *f* (law) countermand; (law) deed of invalidation
contraespía *mf* counterspy
contraespionaje *m* counterespionage
contraestimulante *m* (med.) counterstimulant
contrafagot *m* (mus.) contrafagotto, double bassoon
contrafajado -da *adj* (her.) counterfessed
contrafallar *va & vn* to overtrump
contrafallo *m* overtrump
contrafase *f* (rad.) push-pull amplification; **en contrafase** (rad.) push-pull
contrafigura *f* counterpart; (theat.) counterpart
contrafilo *m* back edge near the tip (*of a weapon*)
contraflorado -da *adj* (her.) counterflory
contrafoque *m* (naut.) foretopmast staysail
contrafoso *m* (theat.) subcellar; (fort.) outer ditch
contrafuerte *m* girth strap (*for saddletree*); stiffener for shoe (*inner strip of leather*); spur (*of mountain range*); (arch.) abutment, buttress, counterfort; (fort.) outwork, outer fort
contrafuga *f* (mus.) counterfugue
contragolpe *m* counterstroke; (path.) contrecoup; (mach.) return stroke; kickback; (box.) counter
contraguardia *f* (fort.) counterguard
contraguía *f* front left-hand animal in a team of four
contrahacedor -dora *adj* counterfeiting, imitative, fake; *mf* counterfeiter, imitator, fake; impersonator
contrahacer §55 *va* to counterfeit, imitate, copy; to forge; to feign; to mimic, impersonate; to pirate (*a book*); *vr* to feign
contrahago *1st sg pres ind of* **contrahacer**
contraharé *1st sg fut ind of* **contrahacer**
contrahaz *f* (*pl:* **-haces**) wrong side (*of cloth*)
contrahecho -cha *adj* counterfeit, faked; hunchbacked, deformed; *mf* hunchback; *pp of* **contrahacer**
contrahechura *f* counterfeit, fake
contrahice *1st sg pret ind of* **contrahacer**
contrahierba *f* (bot.) contrayerva; precaution
contrahilo; a contrahilo across the grain
contrahuella *f* riser (*of stairs*)
contraigo *1st sg pres ind of* **contraer**
contraindicación *f* (med.) contraindication
contraindicante *adj* (med.) contraindicating; *m* (med.) contraindicant
contraindicar §86 *va* (med.) to contraindicate
contrainteligencia *f* counterintelligence
contrairritación *f* (med.) counterirritation
contrairritante *adj & m* (med.) counterirritant
contraje *1st sg pret ind of* **contraer**
contralateral *adj* contralateral
contralecho; a contralecho (mas.) laid vertically
contralmirante *m* var. of **contraalmirante**
contralor *m* comptroller
contralto *m* (mus.) contralto (*voice*); *mf* (mus.) contralto (*person*)
contraluz *f* view against the light; **a contraluz** against the light
contramaestre *m* foreman; (naut.) boatswain; (nav.) warrant officer, petty officer; (orn.) tropic bird; **segundo contramaestre** (naut.) boatswain's mate; **contramaestre mayor de cargo** (nav.) chief petty officer
contramalla or **contramalladura** *f* double fishing net
contramandar *va* to countermand
contramandato *m* countermand
contramangas *fpl* oversleeves
contramanivela *f* drag link
contramano; a contramano the wrong way, in the wrong direction
contramarca *f* countermark
contramarcar §86 *va* to countermark
contramarco *m* (carp.) sash
contramarcha *f* countermarch; turning back; reverse, reversal; (naut.) evolution, maneuver; (mach.) fast and loose pulleys

contramarchar *vn* to countermarch; to turn back; to go into reverse, run in reverse
contramarea *f* (naut.) opposing tide
contramedida *f* countermeasure
contramesana *f* (naut.) aftermast
contramina *f* (mil.) countermine
contraminar *va* (mil. & fig.) to countermine
contramuralla *f* (fort.) countermure
contramuro *m* (arch.) low secondary wall; (fort.) countermure
contranatural *adj* unnatural
contraofensiva *f* (mil.) counteroffensive
contraorden *f* countermand, cancellation
contrapalado -da *adj* (her.) counterpaly
contrapalanquín *m* (naut.) auxiliary clew garnet
contrapar *m* rafter; eaves board
contraparte *f* counterpart (*complement*)
contrapartida *f* (com.) correction in double-entry bookkeeping
contrapás *m* half step (*in contredanse*); contredanse (*of Catalonia*)
contrapasamiento *m* going over to the other side, joining the other side
contrapasar *vn* to go over to the other side; (her.) to be counterpassant
contrapaso *m* back step; (mus.) counter passage
contrapeado *m* plywood
contrapear *va* (carp.) to place (*boards*) together with grains at right angles
contrapelo; a contrapelo against the hair; against the grain; backwards, the wrong way; **a contrapelo de** counter to, against
contrapesar *va* to offset, equalize, compensate, counterpoise, counterbalance
contrapeso *m* counterpoise, counterbalance, counterweight; makeweight (*to complete weight of meat, fish, etc.*); (rail.) counterbalance (*of locomotive wheel*)
contrapeste *m* pest preventive, remedy for the pest
contrapilastra *f* (carp.) astragal; (arch.) counterpilaster
contrapondré *1st sg fut ind of* **contraponer**
contraponer §69 *va* to set in front; to compare; to oppose; **contraponer a** to set up against; *vr* to be opposed, be opposite
contrapongo *1st sg pres ind of* **contraponer**
contraposición *f* contraposition; **en contraposición de** as contrasted with
contrapozo *m* counterblast
contrapresión *f* back pressure
contraproducente *adj* unproductive, self-defeating
contraproposición *f* counterproposition
contrapropuesta *f* counterproposal
contraprueba *f* (engraving) counterproof; (print.) second proof
contrapuerta *f* storm door; vestibule door; (fort.) counterport
contrapuesto -ta *pp of* **contraponer**
contrapunta *f* false edge (*of sword*); (mach.) tailstock
contrapuntante *mf* (mus.) counterpoint singer
contrapuntar *vr* var. of **contrapuntear**
contrapuntear *va* (mus.) to sing in counterpoint; *vn* to be sarcastic; *vr* to be sarcastic, to use abusive language; to be sarcastic to each other
contrapuntista *mf* (mus.) contrapuntist
contrapuntístico -ca *adj* (mus.) contrapuntal
contrapunto *m* (mus.) counterpoint
contrapunzar §76 *va* to rivet with a punch
contrapunzón *m* counterpunch; punch; nailset
contrapuse *1st sg pret ind of* **contraponer**
contraquilla *f* (naut.) keelson
contraria *f* see **contrario**
contrariar §90 *va* to oppose; to counteract, thwart; to annoy, provoke
contrariedad *f* contrariness, contrariety; opposition; interference, obstacle; annoyance, bother; disagreement, clash
contrario -ria *adj* contrary; opposite, opposed; hostile; harmful; *mf* enemy; opponent; rival; *m* opposite, contrary; contradiction; obstacle; **al contrario de** unlike; **en contrario** to the contrary; **por el** or **lo contrario** on the contrary; *f* contrary (*opposite*); **llevar la contraria a** (coll.) to oppose, to disagree with
contrarreclamación *f* counterclaim
contrarreconocimiento *m* (mil.) counterreconnaissance
contrarreferencia *f* cross reference
contrarreforma *f* counterreformation; (*cap.*) *f* Counter Reformation
contrarregistro *m* control (*of an account; of a scientific experiment*)
contrarreguera *f* lateral drain, cross ditch
contrarréplica *f* rejoinder; (law) rejoinder
contrarrestar *va* to resist, offset, counteract; (sport) to return (*a ball*)
contrarresto *m* resistance, counteraction; (sport) player who returns the ball
contrarretablo *m* (eccl.) altar slab
contrarrevolución *f* counterrevolution
contrarriel *m* (rail.) guardrail
contrarroda *f* (naut.) stemson
contrarronda *f* (mil.) counterround
contrarrotura *f* (vet.) plaster, poultice
contrasellar *va* to counterseal
contrasello *m* (hist.) counterseal
contrasentido *m* countersense, misinterpretation, mistranslation; contradiction; nonsense, piece of nonsense
contraseña *f* countersign, countermark; baggage check; (mil.) countersign, watchword; **contraseña de salida** (theat.) check
contrastar *va* to resist; to assay; to check (*weights and measures*); *vn* to resist; to contrast; **contrastar a, con** or **contra** to face up to
contraste *m* resistance; assay; assayer; assayer's office; assayer's seal; contrast; (naut.) sudden shift in the wind
contrata *f* contract
contratación *f* trade, commerce; deal, transaction; contract (*document*)
contratante *adj* contracting; *mf* contractor; covenanter, contracting party
contratar *va* to contract for; to engage, hire, take on
contratiempo *m* misfortune, disappointment, contretemps; (mus.) contretemps; **a contratiempo** (mus.) off beat
contratista *mf* contractor
contrato *m* contract; **contrato de compraventa** deal, bargain, contract
contratorpedero *m* (nav.) torpedo-boat destroyer
contratreta *f* counterplot
contratrinchera *f* var. of **contraaproches**
contratuerca *f* lock nut, jam nut
contravalación *f* (fort.) contravallation
contravalar *va* (fort.) to build a contravallation around or in front of
contravapor *m* back-pressure steam; **dar contravapor a** to reverse (*a steam engine*)
contravención *f* contravention, infringement, infraction
contravendré *1st sg fut ind of* **contravenir**
contraveneno *m* counterpoison; antidote; (fig.) antidote
contravengo *1st sg pres ind of* **contravenir**
contravenir §92 *vn* to act contrary; **contravenir a** to contravene, to infringe
contraventana *f* window shutter (*inside or outside*)
contraventar *va* to brace, to guy
contraventor -tora *adj* contravening; *mf* contravener
contravidriera *f* storm sash
contravine *1st sg pret ind of* **contravenir**
contraviniendo *ger of* **contravenir**
contrayente *adj* marriage-contracting; *mf* contracting party (*to a marriage*)
contrayerba *f* var. of **contrahierba**
contrecho -cha *adj* crippled, maimed
contribución *f* contribution; tax; **contribución de sangre** military service; **contribución directa** direct tax; **contribución indirecta** indirect tax; **contribución industrial** excise tax; **contribución territorial** land tax
contribuidor -dora *adj* contributory; taxpaying; *mf* contributor; taxpayer

contribuir §41 *va & vn* to contribute; **contribuir a** + *inf* to contribute to + *ger*
contribulado -da *adj* afflicted, grieved
contributario -ria *mf* fellow taxpayer
contributivo -va *adj* contributive, tax
contribuyente *adj* contributing; taxpaying; *mf* contributor; taxpayer
contrición *f* contrition
contrincante *m* opponent, rival, competitor
contristar *va* to sadden
contrito -ta *adj* contrite
control *m* check, control; control experiment; **control a cascada** (elec.) cascade control; **control de fuego** (nav.) fire control; **control de la frecuencia** (rad.) frequency control; **control de la natalidad** or **de los nacimientos** birth control; **control de volumen** (rad.) volume control; **control remoto** remote control
controlable *adj* controllable
controlar *va* to check, audit, control
controversia *f* controversy
controversista *mf* controversialist
controvertible *adj* controvertible
controvertir §62 *va* to controvert, dispute
contubernio *m* cohabitation; concubinage; vicious alliance
contumacia *f* contumacy; (law) contempt
contumaz *adj* (*pl:* **-maces**) contumacious; germ-bearing, disease-carrying; (law) guilty of contempt
contumelia *f* contumely
contumelioso -sa *adj* contumelious
contundencia *f* forcefulness, impressiveness
contundente *adj* bruising; forceful, impressive
contundir *va* to contuse, to bruise
conturbación *f* disquiet, anxiety, worry
conturbar *va* to disquiet, to upset, to trouble
contusión *f* contusion
contusionar *va* var. of **contundir**
contuso -sa *adj* bruised
contutor *m* coguardian
contuve *1st sg pret ind of* **contener**
convalecencia *f* convalescence
convalecer §34 *vn* to convalesce; to recover, get out of danger
convaleciente *adj & mf* convalescent
convalidación *f* confirming, confirmation
convalidar *va* to confirm
convección *f* (phys.) convection
convecino -na *adj* neighboring; *mf* fellow neighbor
conveler *vr* to twitch
convencedor -dora *adj* convincing; *mf* convincer
convencer §91 *va* to convince
convencible *adj* convincible
convencimiento *m* conviction; (act of) convincing
convención *f* convention
convencional *adj* conventional; *m* member of a convention
convencionalidad *f* conventionality
convencionalismo *m* conventionalism
convendré *1st sg fut ind of* **convenir**
convengo *1st sg pres ind of* **convenir**
convenible *adj* docile, compliant; reasonable, fair
conveniencia *f* propriety; fitness, suitability; advantage; agreement, conformity; convenience; **conveniencias** *fpl* property, income; perquisites; proprieties
convenienciero -ra *adj* selfish, thinking only of one's own convenience; comfort-loving
conveniente *adj* proper; fit, suitable; advantageous, profitable; convenient
convenio *m* covenant, pact; (com.) bankruptcy settlement
convenir §92 *vn* to be suitable, be becoming, be necessary, be important; to agree; to convene; **convenir** + *inf* to be important to + *inf;* **convenir en** + *inf* to agree to + *inf;* **conviene a saber** namely, to wit; *vr* to agree, come to an agreement; **convenirse en** + *inf* to agree to + *inf*
conventícula *f* or **conventículo** *m* conventicle
conventillo *m* (Am.) tenement house
convento *m* convent; monastery
conventual *adj & m* conventual
conventualidad *f* life in a convent or monastery; assignment to a convent or monastery
convergencia *f* convergence; concurrence, concordance
convergente *adj* convergent
converger §49 *vn* var. of **convergir**
convergir §42 *vn* to converge; to concur, concord
conversa *f* see **converso**
conversable *adj* conversable
conversación *f* conversation
conversacional *adj* conversational
conversador -dora *adj* conversing; *mf* conversationalist
conversar *vn* to converse; to live, dwell; to deal, traffic; (mil.) to wheel about
conversible *adj* var. of **convertible**
conversión *f* conversion; (alchem. & elec.) transformation; (rhet.) epistrophe; (mil.) conversion (*wheeling*); **conversión de la deuda** refunding of public debt
conversivo -va *adj* conversive
converso -sa *adj* converted; *mf* convert; *m* lay brother; *f* lay sister; (coll.) conversation, chat
conversor *m* (rad.) converter
convertibilidad *f* convertibility
convertible *adj* convertible
convertidor *m* (elec. & metal.) converter; (elec.) transformer; **convertidor Bessemer** Bessemer converter; **convertidor de frecuencia** (elec.) frequency converter; **convertidor de par** (aut.) torque converter; **convertidor sincrónico** (elec.) synchronous converter
convertiplano *m* (aer.) convertiplane
convertir §62 *va* to convert; to turn; *vr* to convert; to become converted; **convertirse en** to turn into, to become
convexidad *f* convexity
convexo -xa *adj* convex
convicción *f* conviction
convicto -ta *adj* convinced; convicted, found guilty; *mf* convict
convidado -da *mf* guest; *f* (coll.) treat (*to a drink*)
convidador -dora *adj* inviting; *mf* host
convidar *va* to invite; to treat; **convidar a** + *inf* to invite to + *inf;* to move to, to incite to + *inf;* **convidar a uno con una cosa** to offer something to someone; *vr* to volunteer one's services
convincente *adj* convincing
convine *1st sg pret ind of* **convenir**
conviniendo *ger of* **convenir**
convite *m* invitation; party, banquet; treat; **convite a escote** Dutch treat
convivencia *f* (act of) living together, life together
conviviente *adj* living together; *mf* companion
convivir *vn* to live together; **convivir con** to exist side by side with
convocación *f* convocation
convocador -dora *adj* summoning, convoking; *mf* convoker, convocator
convocar §86 *va* to convoke; to call (*a meeting, strike, etc.*)
convocatorio -ria *adj* summoning, convoking; *f* call, notice of a meeting
convolución *f* convolution
convolutado -da *adj* (bot.) convolute
convolvuláceo -a *adj* (bot.) convolvulaceous
convólvulo *m* (bot.) convolvulus; (ent.) measuring worm
convoy *m* convoy; (coll.) retinue; cruet stand; train, railway train
convoyar *va* to convoy
conv.te abr. of **conveniente**
convulsión *f* convulsion; (path.) convulsion
convulsionar *va* to convulse
convulsivo -va *adj* convulsive
convulso -sa *adj* convulsed, convulsive
convulsoterapia *f* (med.) convulsive treatment, shock treatment
conyugal *adj* conjugal
cónyuge *mf* spouse, consort, mate; **cónyuges** *mpl* couple, husband and wife
coñac *m* (*pl:* **-ñacs**) cognac
coolí *m* (*pl:* **-líes**) coolie
cooperación *f* coöperation

cooperador -dora *adj* coöperative; *mf* coöperator, co-worker
cooperar *vn* to coöperate; **cooperar a** + *inf* to coöperate in + *ger*
cooperario *m* coöperator, co-worker
cooperativo -va *adj* coöperative; *f* coöperative, coöperative society
coopositor -tora *mf* fellow competitor (*e.g., for a professorship*)
cooptación *f* coöptation
cooptar *va* coöpt
coordenado -da *adj* (math.) coördinate; *f* (math.) coördinate; **coordenadas cartesianas** (math.) Cartesian coördinates
coordinación *f* coördination
coordinado -da *adj & f* var. of **coordenado**
coordinador -dora *adj* coördinating; *mf* coördinator
coordinamiento *m* var. of **coordinación**
coordinante *adj* coördinating
coordinar *va & vn* to coördinate
coordinativo -va *adj* coördinative
copa *f* goblet, wineglass, cup, bowl; vase; crown (*of hat*); treetop; brazier; copa (*liquid measure equal to about a gill*); drink; sundae; (arch.) vase (*kind of finial*); roof or vault (*of a furnace*); playing card (*representing a bowl*) equivalent to heart; (sport) cup; (fig.) cup (*of sorrow, misfortune, etc.*); (*cap.*) *f* (astr.) Cup; **copas** *fpl* bosses of bridle; card suit corresponding to hearts; **tomarse una copa** to take a drink; **copa de oro** (bot.) California poppy
copado -da *adj* copped, crested; high-topped, bushy; *f* (orn.) crested lark
copaiba *f* (bot.) copaifera (*tree*); (pharm.) copaiba, copaiba balsam
copal *m* copal
copar *va* to cover (*the whole bet*); to sweep (*all posts in an election*); (mil.) to cut off and capture
coparticipación *f* joint partnership, copartnership, fellowship
copartícipe *mf* joint partner, copartner
copayero *m* (bot.) copaifera (*tree*)
cope *m* close-woven part of fishing net
copear *vn* to sell wine and liquor by the glass; to have a drink, to drink
copela *f* cupel
copelación *f* cupellation
copelar *va* to cupel
Copenhague *f* Copenhagen
copépodo -da *adj & m* (zool.) copepod
copera *f* cupboard, closet for glassware
copernicano -na *adj & mf* Copernican
Copérnico *m* Copernicus
copero *m* cupbearer; cabinet for wineglasses
copeta *f* small glass, small cup
copete *m* pompadour; tuft; forelock (*of horse*); crest (*of feathers; of a mountain*); top (*finial on piece of furniture*); topping (*e.g., of a dish of ice cream*); (carp.) triangular side of a hip roof; snobbishness; **de alto copete** important, aristocratic; **tener mucho copete** to be haughty, to be high-hat
copetudo -da *adj* copped, tufted; high, lofty; (coll.) haughty, snobbish; *f* (orn.) lark; (bot.) marigold
copey *m* (bot.) star-of-night; Ecuadoran bitumen
copia *f* abundance, plenty; copy; **copia al carbón** carbon copy; **copia del expediente académico** (educ.) transcript; **copia fiel** true copy
copiador -dora *adj* copying; *mf* copier, copyist; *m* letter book, letter file; duplicator, copying machine; *f* (mach.) copying lathe
copiante *mf* copier, copyist
copiar *va* to copy; to copy down
copihue *m* (bot.) Chilean bellflower (*Lapageria rosea*)
copiloto *m* (aer.) copilot
copilla *f* var. of **chofeta**
copiosidad *f* copiousness, abundance
copioso -sa *adj* copious, abundant; hearty (*meal*)
copista *mf* copyist, copier
copla *f* couplet; stanza; ballad, popular song; **coplas** *fpl* (coll.) verse, poetry; **coplas de ciego** (coll.) doggerel
coplear *vn* to compose or sing ballads
coplero -ra or **coplista** *mf* ballad vendor; poetaster
copo *m* flake; cot; bundle of cotton, flax, hemp, etc. (*to be spun*); bottom of purse net; fishing with purse net; **copo de nieve** snowflake
copón *m* large goblet, large cup; (eccl.) ciborium, pyx
coposesión *f* joint ownership
coposesor -sora *mf* joint owner
coposo -sa *adj* bushy, high-topped; flaky, woolly
copra *f* copra
copretérito *m* (gram.) imperfect (*indicative*)
coproducción *f* coproduction
coprolito *m* (pal.) coprolite
copropietario -ria *mf* joint owner
cóptico -ca *adj* Coptic
copto -ta *adj* Coptic; *mf* Copt (*person*); *m* Coptic (*language*)
copudo -da *adj* bushy, thick-topped (*tree or shrub*)
cópula *f* copula; (anat., gram., law, log. & med.) copula; (arch.) cupola
copulación *f* copulation
copular *vr* to copulate
copulativo -va *adj* copulative; *f* (gram.) copulative conjunction
coque *m* coke
coqueluche *f* (path.) whooping cough
coquera *f* head of a top; cavity or hollow in a stone; coke bin
coqueta *adj* coquettish, flirtatious; *f* coquette, flirt; roll, small loaf; blow on the palm of the hand with a ruler; dressing table
coquetear *vn* to flirt, to coquet; to try to please everybody
coqueteo *m* coquetting, flirting
coquetería *f* flirtation, coquetry; affectation, artificiality
coquetilla *f* little coquette
coquetismo *m* coquetry
coquetón -tona *adj* (coll.) coquettish, kittenish; *m* (coll.) ladykiller
coquificar §86 *va* to coke
coquina *f* (zool.) coquina, wedge shell
coquinero *m* (orn.) scaup, scaup duck
coquito *m* grimace made to make a baby laugh; cocoanut candy; (bot.) coquito, coquito palm; (orn.) Inca dove
coquizar §76 *va & vn* to coke
coráceo -a *adj* var. of **coriáceo**
coracero *m* cuirassier; (coll.) strong cigar
coracina *f* small breastplate
coracoideo -a *adj* coracoidal
coracoides *adj* coracoid; *m* (*pl:* **-des**) (anat.) coracoid
coracha *f* leather bag
corada *f* entrails
coraje *m* anger; mettle, spirit
corajina *f* (coll.) fit of anger
corajudo -da *adj* (coll.) ill-tempered
coral *adj* (mus.) choral; *m* (mus.) choral, chorale; (zool.) coral (*polyp, calcareous secretion, color, etc.*); (bot.) coral-bead tree; (bot.) coral vine; **corales** *mpl* coral beads; *f* (zool.) coral snake
coralero -ra *mf* worker or dealer in corals
coralífero -ra *adj* coralliferous
coralígeno -na *adj* coralligenous
coralilla *f* (bot.) pimpernel; (zool.) king snake
coralillo *m* (zool.) coral snake
coralino -na *adj* coralline; *f* (bot. & zool.) coralline
corambre *f* hides, skins; wine skin
corambrero *m* dealer in hides and skins
Corán *m* Koran
coránico -ca *adj* Koranic
coranvobis *m* (*pl:* **-bis**) (coll.) fat solemn-looking person
coraza *f* armor (*protective covering*); (arm. & zool.) cuirass; armor plate; (sport) guard, protector
coraznada *f* pith or marrow of pine tree; stew of animal hearts
corazón *m* heart; core; courage; (fig.) heart; **de corazón** heartily, sincerely; **decirle a uno el corazón una cosa** to have a presentiment of something; **hacer de tripas corazón** to pluck up courage; **llevar el co-**

razón en la mano to wear one's heart upon one's sleeve; **no tener corazón para** + *inf* to not have the heart to + *inf;* **partir** or **quebrantar el corazón de** to break the heart of; **corazón atlético** (path.) athlete's heart; **corazón grasoso** (path.) fatty heart
corazonada *f* impulsiveness; presentiment, hunch; (coll.) entrails
corazoncillo *m* (bot.) St.-John's-wort
corbachada *f* lash with a pizzle
corbacho *m* pizzle (*used as a whip*)
corbata *f* necktie, cravat; scarf; flap (*of a tire*); bow and streamer (*of a banner*); **corbata a la inglesa** ascot, ascot tie; **corbata a la mariposa** or **corbata de lazo** bow tie; **corbata de nudo corredizo** four-in-hand tie
corbatería *f* necktie shop
corbatero -ra *mf* necktie maker or dealer
corbatín *m* bow tie
corbato *m* cooler, cooling bath (*of a still*)
corbeta *f* (naut.) corvette, barque
corbona *f* basket
Córcega *f* Corsica
corcel *m* steed, charger
corcesca *f* barbed spear
corcino *m* small deer, young deer
corcova *f* hump, hunch
corcovado -da *adj* humpbacked, hunchbacked; *mf* humpback, hunchback
corcovar *va* to bend, to crook
corcovear *vn* to buck (*said of a horse*)
corcoveta *f* small hump; *mf* (coll.) humpback
corcovo *m* buck (*of a horse*); (coll.) crookedness
corcusido *m* (coll.) rough darning, rough patch
corcusir *va* (coll.) to darn or mend roughly
corcha *f* cork bark; cork bucket (*for cooling wine*); (naut.) laying of a rope
corchar *va* (naut.) to lay (*strands of rope*)
corche *m* cork-soled shoe
corchea *f* (mus.) quaver, eighth note
corchero -ra *adj* cork; *f* cork bucket (*for cooling wine*)
corcheta *f* eye (*of hook and eye*); rabbet (*in doorframe*)
corchete *m* hook and eye; hook (*of hook and eye*); (carp.) bench hook; bracket; horizontal brace; (print.) overrun; constable
corcho *m* cork; cork wine cooler; cork, cork stopper; cork-soled clog; cork box (*for carrying food*); cork mat; (angling) cork (*float*); beehive; **corcho bornizo** virgin cork; **corcho segundero** cork of second barking; **corcho virgen** virgin cork
corchoso -sa *adj* corky
corchotaponero -ra *adj* cork, cork-making, stopper-making (*industry*)
corda *f* (dial.) mountain range; **estar a la corda** (naut.) to be close-hauled, to be lying to
cordado -da *adj & m* (zool.) chordate
cordaje *m* cordage; strings of guitar; (naut.) rigging
cordal *m* (mus.) tailpiece (*of stringed instrument*); *f* wisdom tooth
cordato -ta *adj* cordate; (archaic) prudent, judicious
cordel *m* cord, string; five steps; cattle run; **a cordel** in a straight line; **cordel de la corredera** (naut.) log line
cordelado -da *adj* corded (*ribbon*)
cordelazo *m* lash with a rope
cordelejo *m* string; bantering; **dar cordelejo** to make fun, to banter
cordelería *f* cordmaking; cordage; cord shop; (naut.) rigging
cordelero -ra *mf* cordmaker, cord dealer
cordellate *m* grogram
cordera *f* ewe lamb; (fig.) lamb (*meek woman*)
cordería *f* cordage
corderilla *f* little ewe lamb
corderillo *m* lambskin (*dressed with wool on it*)
corderino -na *adj* (pertaining to a) lamb; *f* lambskin
cordero *m* lamb; lambskin (*dressed with wool on it*); (fig.) lamb (*meek fellow*); (*cap.*) *m* Lamb (*Christ*); **Divino Cordero** or **Cordero de Dios** Lamb of God; **cordero lechal** yeanling; **cordero pascual** paschal lamb; **cordero recental** sucking lamb
corderuela *f* little ewe lamb
corderuelo *m* little lamb
corderuna *f* lambskin
cordezuela *f* small cord or rope
cordíaco -ca *adj* var. of **cardíaco**
cordial *adj* cordial; middle (*finger*); *m* cordial, tonic
cordialidad *f* cordiality
cordiforme *adj* heart-shaped
cordila *f* (ichth.) young of the tunny
cordilla *f* guts of sheep (*fed to cats*)
cordillera *f* mountain range, chain of mountains
cordillerano -na *adj* Cordilleran
cordita *f* cordite
Córdoba *f* Cordova; (*l.c.*) *m* cordoba (*monetary unit of Nicaragua*)
cordobán *m* cordovan (*leather*)
cordobana; andar a la cordobana (coll.) to go naked
cordobanero *m* cordovan tanner
cordobés -besa *adj & mf* Cordovan
cordón *m* cordon (*cord or ribbon worn as ornament*); lace, lacing; milled edge of coin; strand (*of rope or wire*); (anat. & elec.) cord; (arch.) cordon, stringcourse, belt course; (fort., her., hort. & mil.) cordon; **cordones** *mpl* (mil.) aiguillettes; **cordón bleu** first-rate cook; **cordón espermático** (anat.) spermatic cord; **cordón sanitario** sanitary cordon; **cordón umbilical** (anat.) umbilical cord
cordonazo *m* blow with a cord or rope; **cordonazo de San Francisco** (naut.) autumn equinoctial storm
cordoncillo *m* rib, ridge; braid, piping; milling (*of coins*)
cordonería *f* cordmaking, ropemaking; lacemaking; lacework
cordonero -ra *mf* cordmaker, ropemaker; lacemaker
cordura *f* prudence, wisdom
corea *f* (path.) chorea; dance with singing; (*cap.*) *f* Corea or Korea; **la Corea del Norte** North Korea; **la Corea del Sur** South Korea
coreano -na *adj & mf* Corean or Korean; *m* Corean or Korean (*language*)
corear *va* to compose (*music*) for chorus; to accompany with a chorus, to choir; to answer in chorus; to join in singing (*a song*); to fawningly agree with (*someone's opinion*); *vn* to choir
corecico or **corecillo** *m* sucking pig
coreo *m* (pros.) choreus; (mus.) harmony
coreografía *f* choreography
coreográfico -ca *adj* choreographic
coreógrafo -fa *mf* choreographer
coreópsida *f* (bot.) coreopsis, calliopsis
corezuelo *m* sucking pig; skin of roast piglet
cori *m* (bot.) St.-John's-wort
coriáceo -a *adj* coriaceous
coriámbico -ca *adj & m* choriambic
coriambo *m* choriamb
coriandro *m* (obs.) var. of **cilantro**
coribante *m* Corybant (*priest of Cybele*)
corifeo *m* coryphaeus; (fig.) leader
coriláceo -a *adj* (bot.) corylaceous
corimbo *m* (bot.) corymb
corimboso -sa *adj* corymbose or corymbous
corindón *m* (mineral.) corundum
coríntico -ca *adj* Corinthian
corintio -tia *adj & mf* Corinthian
Corinto *f* Corinth
Coriolano *m* Coriolanus
corión *m* (embryol. & zool.) chorion; (anat. & zool.) corium
corista *mf* chorist; *m* choir priest; (theat.) chorus man; *f* (theat.) chorus girl, chorine
corito -ta *adj* naked; bashful, timid; *m* workman who carries the wine from press to vats; grape-treader
coriza *f* (path.) coryza; (prov.) sandal
corladura *f* gold varnish
corlar or **corlear** *va* to coat with gold varnish
corma *f* stocks (*for punishment*); annoyance, bother
cormo *m* (bot.) corm
cormofita *f* (bot.) cormophyte
cormorán *m* (orn.) cormorant
cornac *m* (*pl:* **-nacs**) or **cornaca** *m* mahout

cornáceo -a *adj* (bot.) cornaceous
cornada *f* thrust with horns; (fencing) upward thrust
cornadiza *f* stanchion (*for cattle*)
cornado *m* old copper coin; **no valer un cornado** (coll.) to be not worth a continental
cornadura *f* horns
cornal *m* strap for yoking oxen
cornalina *f* (mineral.) carnelian
cornalón *adj masc* big-horned (*said of a bull*)
cornamenta *f* horns, antlers
cornamusa *f* (mus.) bagpipe; (mus.) horn shaped like a French horn; (naut.) chock
cornatillo *m* horn-shaped olive
córnea *f* see **córneo**
corneador -dora *adj* butting, horning
corneal *adj* corneal
corneana *f* (geol.) hornfels
cornear *va* to butt, to horn
cornecico, cornecillo or **cornecito** *m* little horn
corneja *f* (orn.) crow, daw; (orn.) carrion crow; (orn.) scops owl
cornejo *m* (bot.) dogwood, cornel tree; **cornejo florido** (bot.) flowering dogwood; **cornejo hembra** (bot.) red dogwood; **cornejo macho** (bot.) cornelian cherry
Cornelia *f* Cornelia
cornelina *f* var. of **cornalina**
Cornelio *m* Cornelius
córneo -a *adj* horny, corneous; *f* (anat.) cornea; **córnea cónica** (path.) keratoconus; **córnea opaca** (anat.) sclera
cornerina *f* var. of **cornalina**
corneta *f* (mus.) bugle; (mus.) cornet; swineherd's horn; troop of horse; pennant; (mil.) cornet (*cavalry officer who carried flag*); **corneta acústica** ear trumpet; **corneta de llaves** cornet-à-pistons; **corneta de monte** hunting horn; *m* bugler; cornetist
cornete *m* (anat.) turbinated bone
cornetilla *f* hot pepper
cornetín *m* (mus.) cornet; cornetist
cornezuelo *m* (bot. & pharm.) ergot; crescent-shaped olive
corniabierto -ta *adj* with wide-spread horns
cornial *adj* horn-shaped
corniapretado -da *adj* with close-set horns
corniblanco -ca *adj* white-horned
cornicabra *f* (bot.) terebinth tree; crescent-shaped olive; (bot.) wild fig
córnico -ca *adj* Cornish; *m* Cornish (*language*)
cornicorto -ta *adj* short-horned
corniforme *adj* horn-shaped
cornigacho -cha *adj* with horns turned downward
cornígero -ra *adj* (poet.) horned
cornija *f* var. of **cornisa**
cornijal *m* corner (*of a cushion, building, etc.*); (eccl.) altar napkin
cornijón *m* (arch.) entablature; outer corner (*of a building*)
cornijuelo *m* (bot.) shadbush
cornil *m* var. of **cornal**
cornillo *m* (bot.) shadbush
corniola *f* var. of **cornalina**
cornisa *f* cornice (*of snow on a ridge*); (arch.) cornice
cornisamento or **cornisamiento** *m* (arch.) entablature
cornisón *m* var. of **cornijón**
corniveleto -ta *adj* with high, straight horns
corno *m* (bot.) dogwood; (mus.) horn; **corno inglés** (mus.) English horn
Cornualles *m* Cornwall
cornucopia *f* cornucopia; sconce with mirror
cornudilla *f* (ichth.) hammerhead
cornudo -da *adj* horned, antlered; cuckold; *m* cuckold
cornúpeta *adj* cornupete; *m* (coll.) bull
coro *m* chorus; choir; choir loft; (mus., arch. & theol.) choir; **a coros** alternately, responsively; **de coro** by heart; **hacer coro a** to echo; **coro mixto** mixed chorus
corocha *f* (ent.) vine fretter
corografía *f* chorography
corográfico -ca *adj* chorographic or chorographical
corógrafo -fa *mf* chorographer
coroideo -a *adj* choroid
coroides *adj & f* (anat.) choroid
corojo *m* or **corojo de Guinea** (bot.) African oil palm
corola *f* (bot.) corolla
corolario *m* corollary
corona *f* crown; wreath, garland; coronet; halo; tonsure; (astr., elec. & meteor.) corona; (dent.) crown; (vet.) coronet (*of horse's pastern*); crown (*coin*); **ceñir** or **ceñirse la corona** to assume the crown; **Corona austral** (astr.) Corona Australis; **Corona boreal** (astr.) Corona Borealis; **corona de flores** wreath, floral wreath; **corona de laurel** wreath, laurel wreath; **corona mural** (hist.) mural crown; **corona nupcial** bridal wreath
coronación *f* coronation, crowning; termination, completion
coronado *m* tonsured cleric; (bot.) aster, China aster
coronal *adj* coronal
coronamento or **coronamiento** *m* termination, completion; (arch.) crest, coping, top, crown; (naut.) taffrail
coronar *va* to crown; to cap, to top; (checkers) to crown
coronario -ria *adj* coronary; fine (*gold*); *f* second-hand wheel (*of clock or watch*)
corondel *m* (print.) column rule
coronel *m* colonel; (arch.) top molding; (her.) crown
coronela *f* colonel's wife
coronelato *m* (Am.) colonelcy
coronelía *f* colonelcy
coronilla *f* crown (*of head*); **andar** or **bailar de coronilla** (coll.) to grind away, to be hard at it; **dar de coronilla** (coll.) to bump one's head on the ground; **estar hasta la coronilla** (coll.) to be fed up
coronio *m* (chem.) coronium
coroza *f* conical paper hat worn as a mark of infamy; farmer's straw cape
corozo *m* (bot.) African oil palm; (bot.) cohune; cohune nut
corpa *f* (min.) lump of crude ore
corpachón *m* or **corpanchón** *m* (coll.) big body, big carcass; carcass of fowl
corpazo *m* (coll.) big body, big carcass
corpecico, corpecillo or **corpecito** *m* bodice, waist
corpiño *m* little body; bodice, waist; (Am.) brassière
corporación *f* corporation; association
corporal *adj* corporal, bodily; *m* (eccl.) corporal (*cloth*)
corporativo -va *adj* corporate, corporative
corpóreo -a *adj* corporeal
corpudo -da *adj* corpulent
corpulencia *f* corpulence
corpulento -ta *adj* corpulent; thick, heavy
Corpus *m* (eccl.) Corpus Christi
corpuscular *adj* corpuscular
corpúsculo *m* (bot. & physiol.) corpuscle; (chem. & phys.) corpuscle, particle; **corpúsculo de Malpighi** (anat.) Malpighian corpuscle
corral *m* corral, stockyard; barnyard; fishpond; open-air theater; blank left by a student in taking notes; **hacer corrales** (coll.) to play truant; **corral de madera** lumberyard; **corral de vacas** (coll.) pigpen (*place that is filthy or littered up*)
corralada *f* large corral
corralero -ra *adj* (pertaining to a) corral, barnyard; *mf* manure seller; *f* Andalusian dance and song; (dial.) hussy
corraliza *f* yard, court, corral
correa *f* leather strap, thong; leatheriness; (aer.) belt; (carp.) purlin; (mach.) belt, belting; (bot.) correa, native fuchsia; **correas** *fpl* duster made of strips of leather; **besar la correa** (coll.) to eat humble pie; **tener correa** (coll.) to take a kidding goodnaturedly; (coll.) to be tough; **correa conductora** belt conveyor; **correa de seguridad** (aer. & aut.) safety belt; **correa de ventilador** (aut.) fan belt; **correa de zapatos** leather shoestring; **correa transmisora** drive belt; **correa transportadora** belt conveyor

correaje *m* belts, belting
correal *m* deerskin (*used in garments*)
correar *va* to draw out (*wool*)
correazo *m* lash with a leather strap
correcalles *m* (*pl:* **-lles**) (coll.) loafer
correcamino *m* (orn.) road runner
corrección *f* correction; correctness
correccional *adj* & *m* correctional
correctivo -va *adj* corrective; (gram.) adversative; (gram.) restrictive; *m* corrective
correcto -ta *adj* correct
corrector -tora *adj* correcting, corrective; *m* corrector, correcting device; (print.) corrector, proofreader; superior, abbot (*in monastery of St. Francis of Paula*)
corredera *f* track, slide, rail, tongue, guide; shutter (*in a peephole*); upper millstone; race track; street; (mach.) slide valve; (ent.) roach; (naut.) log (*chip and line*); (naut.) log line; (surv.) target; **de corredera** sliding (*e.g., door*)
corredizo -za *adj* slide; sliding; slip
corredor -dora *adj* running; (orn.) ratite; *mf* runner; (sport) runner; (sport) racer; *m* corridor; porch, gallery; (com.) broker; (mil.) scout; (mil.) raider; (fort.) covert way; **corredor de apuestas** bookmaker, professional betting man; **corredor de bodas** (coll.) matchmaker; **corredor de noticias** (coll.) gossip; **corredor de posta** postrider; **Corredor Polaco** Polish Corridor; *f* (orn.) ratite
corredura *f* overflow
correduría *f* (com.) brokerage
correería *f* strap making; strap shop
correero -ra *mf* strap maker or seller
corregencia *f* coregency
corregente *mf* coregent
corregibilidad *f* corrigibility
corregible *adj* corrigible
corregidor -dora *adj* correcting; *m* corregidor (*Spanish magistrate; chief magistrate of Spanish town*); *f* wife of a corregidor
corregimiento *m* office of corregidor; district governed by a corregidor
corregir §72 *va* to correct; to temper, to lessen; *vr* to mend one's ways
corregüela or **correhuela** *f* (bot.) lesser bindweed; (bot.) knotgrass; **corregüela hembra** (bot.) mare's-tail
correinado *m* coreign
correjel *m* shoe leather, sole leather
correlación *f* correlation
correlacionar *va* & *vr* to correlate
correlativo -va *adj* & *m* correlative
correligionario -ria *mf* coreligionist, coreligionary; colleague, confederate
correncia *f* (coll.) looseness of the bowels; (coll.) bashfulness
correndilla *f* (coll.) short run, dash
correntío -a *adj* running; (coll.) free and easy, agile; *f* (coll.) looseness of the bowels
correntón -tona *adj* gadabout; jolly, full of fun
correntoso -sa *adj* (Am.) swift, rapid (*stream*)
correo *m* courier, postman; mail; post office; mail train; (law) accomplice; **correos** *mpl* postal service; **echar al correo** to mail, to post; **correo aéreo** air mail; **correo marítimo** packet boat; **correo urgente** special delivery
correón *m* large leather strap
correoso -sa *adj* leathery, tough
correr *va* to run, to race (*a horse*); to run (*a risk*); to traverse, travel over; to overrun; to chase, pursue; to slide; to turn (*a key*); to draw (*a curtain*); to embarrass; to confuse; to auction; to have (*e.g., the same fate or lot*); (slang) to cut (*class*); (naut.) to furl, unfurl (*a sail*); (naut.) to outride (*a storm*); to rob, get by robbery; (taur.) to fight (*a bull*); (Am.) to throw (*a person*) out; **correrla** (coll.) to carouse around at all hours of the night ‖ *vn* to run; to race; to flow; to blow; to pass, elapse; to pass, be accepted; to circulate, be common, be common talk; **a todo correr** at full speed; **a todo turbio correr** no matter how bad things are; **que corre** current (*e.g., month*); **correr a** to sell at or for; **correr a** + *inf* to run to + *inf;* **correr a cargo de** or **por cuenta de** to be under, be under the administration of; **correr con** to be in charge of, to be on good terms with; to defray (*an expense*); **correr por** to sell at or for; to be in the care or the hands of; *vr* to turn (*right or left*); to become embarrassed; to become confused; to be ashamed; to slide, to glide, to slip; to run (*said of a candle or a color*); to go too far
correría *f* excursion; raid, foray
correspondencia *f* correspondence; communication, contact (*between two places*); connection, interchange (*of road, subway, etc.*); agreement, harmony; **correspondencia urgente** special delivery
corresponder *vn* to correspond; to communicate (*said, e.g., of two rooms*); **corresponder a** to return, reciprocate (*affection, a favor, etc.*); to belong to, to concern; **corresponderle a uno** + *inf* to be up to someone to + *inf,* to be the turn of someone to + *inf; vr* to correspond (*to write to each other*); to be in agreement or harmony
correspondiente *adj* correspondent; corresponding; respective; *mf* correspondent
corresponsal *mf* correspondent
corresponsalía *f* post of newspaper correspondent
corretaje *m* brokerage
corretear *va* (coll.) to run up and down, to race around; *vn* (coll.) to hang around; (coll.) to romp, to race around
correteo *m* (coll.) hanging around; (coll.) romping
corretora *f* nun who directs the choir
correvedile *mf* or **correveidile** *mf* (*pl:* **-le**) (coll.) gossip, mischief-maker; (coll.) go-between, pimp
correverás *m* (*pl:* **-rás**) (coll.) mechanical toy
corrido -da *adj* in excess (*said of a weight or measure*); cursive; experienced; flowing, fluent: in sequence, continuous, unbroken; abashed, confused; (coll.) wise, sharp; (Am.) fixed-price (*meal*); **de corrido** fluently, unhaltingly; offhand; *m* shed along the wall of a corral; (Am.) ballad, street ballad; *f* race; bullfight; course, run, travel; **de corrida** fast, without stopping; **corrida de banco** (Am.) run on the bank; **corrida de toros** bullfight
corriente *adj* running (*water*); current; ordinary, common; regular, usual; well-known; permissible; fluent; good-natured; **corriente y moliente** (coll.) regular ‖ *adv* all right, O.K. ‖ *m* current month; **al corriente** on time, promptly; **estar al corriente (de)** to be posted (on), be informed (about), be aware (of); **poner al corriente (de)** to acquaint (with), to inform (about); **tener al corriente (de)** to keep (*someone*) posted (on), keep (*someone*) informed (about) ‖ *f* current, stream; (elec.) current; (fig.) current, stream; **dejarse llevar de la corriente, irse con** or **tras la corriente** (fig.) to follow the crowd; **llevarle a uno la corriente** (coll.) to kowtow to someone; **seguir la corriente** (fig.) to follow the crowd; to follow the line of least resistance; **ir** or **navegar contra la corriente** to go against the tide, to fight an uphill battle; **corriente alterna** or **alternativa** (elec.) alternating current; **corriente continua** (elec.) direct current; **corriente de aire** draft; **corriente de filamento** (rad.) filament current; **corriente de convección** (elec.) convection current; **corriente de Foucault** (elec.) eddy current, Foucault current; **Corriente del Golfo** Gulf Stream; **corriente del Japón** Japan current; **corriente de placa** (rad.) plate current; **corriente de rejilla** (rad.) grid current; **corriente de saturación** (phys.) saturation current; **corriente parásita** (elec.) eddy current; (rad.) static, interference; **corriente sanguínea** blood stream
corrientemente *adv* fluently; flatly, plainly
corrigendo -da *mf* inmate of a jail or reformatory
corrillero -ra *mf* loafer, lounger, idler
corrillo *m* huddle, clique
corrimiento *m* running, sliding, gliding; watery discharge, rheum; embarrassment, shyness; vine blight (*from frost, rain, etc.*); landslide; (elec.) creepage; **corrimiento de fase** (elec.) phase lag

corrincho *m* gathering of riffraff
corrivación *f* corrivation, construction that channels several streams together
corro *m* group or circle of people; ring (*space*); ring-around-a-rosy; **escupir en corro** to butt into the conversation; **hacer corro** to make room, to make an open space; **hacer corro aparte** to start a separate ring or faction; **corro de bruja** or **de brujas** fairy ring (*circle formed in grass by growth of certain fungi*)
corroboración *f* strengthening; corroboration
corroborante *adj* & *m* corroborant
corroborar *va* to strengthen; to corroborate
corroborativo -va *adj* corroborative
corrobra *f* var. of **alboroque**
corroer §78 *va* to corrode; (fig.) to corrode (*to prey upon, eat away at*); *vr* to corrode
corrompedor -dora *adj* corrupting; *mf* corrupter
corromper *va* to corrupt; to spoil; to rot; to bribe; to seduce; (coll.) to annoy, disturb, inconvenience; *vn* to smell bad; *vr* to become corrupted; to spoil, to become spoiled; to rot
corrosal *m* (bot.) soursop
corrosible *adj* corrodible, corrosible
corrosión *f* corrosion; (geol.) erosion
corrosivo -va *adj* & *m* corrosive
corr.te abr. of **corriente**
corrugación *f* contraction, shrinkage; wrinkling (*of skin*); corrugation
corrugado -da *adj* corrugated
corrugar §59 *va* to corrugate
corrumpente *adj* corrupting, corruptive; (coll.) annoying, bothersome
corrupción *f* corruption; corruptness; stink, stench
corruptela *f* corruption; abuse
corruptibilidad *f* corruptibility
corruptible *adj* corruptible
corruptivo -va *adj* corruptive
corruptor -tora *adj* & *mf* var. of **corrompedor**
corrusco *m* (coll.) piece of bread, crust of bread
corsa *f* see **corso**
corsario -ria *adj* (naut.) privateering; *mf* (croquet) rover (*player*); *m* (naut.) corsair (*pirate; pirate ship; privateer*); *f* (croquet) rover ball
corsé *m* corset
corsear *vn* (naut.) to privateer, to cruise as a privateer
corsetería *f* corset shop; corset business, corset manufacturing
corsetero -ra *mf* corset maker or dealer
corso -sa *adj* & *mf* Corsican; *m* Corsican (*dialect*); (naut.) privateering; (Am.) drive, promenade; **armar en corso** (naut.) to arm as a privateer; **ir a corso** (naut.) to cruise as a privateer; **llevar** or **traer a corso** to transport posthaste; *f* (naut.) day's voyage; (dial.) sled, drag
corta *f* see **corto**
cortaalambres *m* (*pl:* **-bres**) wire cutter; cold chisel
cortabolsas *m* (*pl:* **-sas**) (coll.) pickpocket
cortacallos *m* (*pl:* **-llos**) corncutter
cortacésped *m* lawn mower
cortacigarros *m* (*pl:* **-rros**) cigar cutter
cortacircuitos *m* (*pl:* **-tos**) (elec.) fuse
cortacorriente *m* (elec.) switch
cortada *f* see **cortado**
cortadero -ra *adj* easy to cut; *f* blacksmith's chisel; beekeeper's knife
cortadillo *m* drinking cup; **echar cortadillos** (coll.) to speak with affectation; (coll.) to drink wine
cortado -da *adj* proportioned; choppy (*style*); (Am.) hard up; *m* drinking cup; cup of coffee with a touch of milk; caper, cabriole (*in dancing*); *f* (Am.) cut; **cortada de pelo** (Am.) haircut
cortador -dora *adj* cutting; *m* cutter (*person who cuts out garments, etc.*); butcher; (anat.) cutter (*incisor*); *f* cutter, cutting machine; slicing machine; mower; cutting board
cortadura *f* cutting; cut; slit, slash; clipping, cutout; (fort.) parapet; (geog.) cut (*between mountains*); **cortaduras** *fpl* cuttings, trimmings, parings, shreds
cortafrío *m* cold chisel
cortafuego *m* (forestry) fireguard; fire wall
cortahielos *m* (*pl:* **-los**) icebreaker, iceboat
cortalápices *m* (*pl:* **-ces**) pencil sharpener
cortamente *adv* scantily, sparingly; curtly
cortante *adj* cutting, sharp; *m* butcher; butcher knife, cleaver
cortapapeles *m* (*pl:* **-les**) paper cutter, paper knife
cortapicos *m* (*pl:* **-cos**) (ent.) earwig; **cortapicos y callares** (coll.) little children should be seen and not heard
cortapiés *m* (*pl:* **-piés**) (coll.) cut or slash at the legs
cortapisa *f* trimming (*made of different material from dress*); charm, wit; terms, conditions (*of a gift*); difficulty, interference
cortaplumas *m* (*pl:* **-mas**) penknife, pocketknife
cortapuros *m* (*pl:* **-ros**) cigar cutter
cortar *va* to cut; to cut away, to trim; to clip; to cut down; to cut off; to cut out, omit; to cut short, to stop; to cut up; to carve; to engrave; to cleave, chop, hew, hack; to dock; to prune; (elec.) to cut off (*the current*); (aut.) to cut off (*the ignition*); (Am.) to pick, to harvest; **cortar bien** to pronounce (*a language*) well; to read (*verse*) well; **cortar mal** to pronounce (*a language*) poorly; to read (*verse*) poorly; **cortar por la mitad** to bisect ‖ *vn* to cut; to be cutting (*said of wind or cold*); **cortar de vestir** to cut cloth, cut a pattern; (coll.) to gossip, talk evil ‖ *vr* to become confused, become speechless; to chap, to crack (*said of skin*); to curdle, turn sour
cortarrenglón *m* marginal stop (*of typewriter*)
cortatubos *m* (*pl:* **-bos**) pipe cutter (*tool*)
cortaúñas *m* (*pl:* **-ñas**) nail clippers, nail cutters
cortavidrios *m* (*pl:* **-drios**) glass cutter
cortaviento *m* windshield
corte *m* cut; cutting; edge (*of knife, sword, book*); cross section; cut, fit (*of a garment*); piece of material (*for a suit, trousers, etc.*); cutting room (*of military tailor*); reconciliation; (elec.) break; **corte de pelo** haircut; **corte de pelo a cepillo** crew cut; **corte de traje** suiting ‖ *f* court; yard; stable, fold; (Am.) court (*of justice*); **Cortes** *fpl* Parliament; **darse corte** (Am.) to put on airs; **hacer la corte a** to pay court to (*a person in power, a woman*); **la Corte** the Capital (*Madrid*); **corte celestial** Heaven; **Corte Suprema** (Am.) Supreme Court
cortedad *f* shortness; smallness; scantiness; dullness; bashfulness, shyness; **cortedad de medios** or **recursos** lack of funds
cortejador -dora *adj* courting, wooing, courtly; *m* courter, wooer, courtier
cortejar *va* to escort, attend, court; to woo, to court (*a woman*)
cortejo *m* court, courting; courtship; homage; cortege; entourage; gift, treat; (coll.) beau, paramour
cortero *m* (Am.) day laborer
cortés *adj* courteous, gracious, polite
cortesana *f* see **cortesano**
cortesanazo -za *adj* overpolite, obsequious
cortesanía *f* courtliness, courtesy; fawning, flattery
cortesano -na *adj* of the court, courtlike; courtly, courteous; fawning, flattering; *m* courtier; fawner; flatterer; *f* courtesan
cortesía *f* courtesy, graciousness, politeness; expression of respect at end of a letter; title of honor; grace, favor; gift, present; (com.) days of grace; (print.) blank space at end or beginning of a chapter; bow; curtsy; **hacer una cortesía** to make a bow; to curtsy; **por cortesía** by courtesy
corteza *f* bark; peel, skin, rind; crust; coarseness, crudeness; (anat. & bot.) cortex; (orn.) sand grouse; **corteza del cascarillo** (pharm.) cinchona bark
cortezón *m* heavy bark or crust
cortezudo -da *adj* barky, corticated; crude, crusty, unpolished
cortezuela *f* thin bark; thin peel, skin, or rind
corticado -da *adj* corticate, corticated
cortical *adj* cortical

corticotropina *f* (physiol. & pharm.) corticotropin
cortijada *f* group of farmhouses
cortijero -ra *mf* farmer; *m* farm boss
cortijo *m* farmhouse, farm; **alborotar el cortijo** (coll.) to raise a row, cause a riot
cortil *m* barnyard
cortina *f* curtain; shade, screen; (fort.) curtain; **correr la cortina** to pull the curtain aside (*to reveal something hidden*); **cortina de bambú** (fig.) bamboo curtain; **cortina de hierro** (fig.) iron curtain; **cortina de humo** smoke screen; **cortina de muelle** sustaining wall (*of a dike*)
cortinaje *m* set of curtains, pair of curtains
cortinal *m* fenced-in and cultivated field near a farm or village
cortinilla *f* shade, window shade; carriage curtain
cortinón *m* big heavy curtain
cortiña *f* (prov.) garden patch
cortisona *f* or **cortisono** *m* (physiol. & pharm.) cortisone
corto -ta *adj* short; small; scant, wanting; slight; dull; bashful, shy; speechless; stingy; **a la corta o a la larga** sooner or later; **desde muy corta edad** from earliest childhood; **corto de alcances** limited, short-witted; **corto de manos** slow (*at work*); **corto de oído** hard of hearing; **corto de resuello** short of breath, short-winded; **corto de vista** shortsighted; *f* clearing, cutting, cutting or felling of trees; **corto** *adv* short
cortocircuitar *va* (elec.) to short-circuit
cortocircuito *m* (elec.) short circuit; **poner en cortocircuito** (elec.) to short-circuit; **ponerse en cortocircuito** (elec.) to short-circuit, be short-circuited
cortometraje *m* (mov.) short
cortón *m* (ent.) mole cricket
coruja *f* (orn.) barn owl
corulla *f* (naut.) cordage room (*in a galley*)
corundo *m* var. of **corindón**
Coruña, La Corunna
coruñes -ñesa *adj* (pertaining to) Corunna; *mf* native or inhabitant of Corunna
coruscación *f* flash of a meteor; (poet.) coruscation
coruscante *adj* flashing, sparkling
coruscar **§86** *vn* (poet.) to coruscate
corusco -ca *adj* (poet.) coruscating
corva *f* see **corvo**
corvadura *f* bend; curvature; (arch.) bend of an arch or vault
corvato *m* young crow, young rook
corvecito *m* little crow, little rook
corvejón *m* gambrel, hock; spur (*of a cock*); (orn.) cormorant
corvejos *mpl* gambrel, hock
corveta *f* curvet
corvetear *vn* to curvet
córvidos *mpl* (orn.) Corvidae
corvino -na *adj* corvine; *f* (ichth.) corvina; **corvina blanca** (ichth.) croaker; **corvina negra** (ichth.) black drum, drumfish
corvo -va *adj* arched, curved, bent; *m* pothook; (ichth.) corvina; *f* ham, bend or back of knee; (vet.) curb
corzo -za *mf* (zool.) roe deer
corzuelo *m* wheat left in the husk
cosa *f* thing; **a cosa hecha** as good as done, sure-fire; **como si tal cosa** (coll.) as if nothing had happened; **en cosa de** in a matter of; **no . . . alguna cosa** or **no . . . cosa** nothing; **no . . . gran cosa** not much, not very much; **no haber tal cosa** to be not so; **no ser gran cosa** to be of no importance, to not amount to much; **otra cosa** something else; **¿qué cosa?** what's new?; **¿qué es cosa y cosa?** what's the answer to this?; **cosa corta** pittance, trifle; **cosa de** a matter of; **cosa de cajón** matter of course; **cosa de entidad** something worth while; **cosa del otro jueves** (coll.) something unheard-of; (coll.) something out of date; **cosa de mieles** (coll.) something exquisite; **cosa de nunca acabar** bore, something tiresome; **cosa de oír** something worth hearing; **cosa de reír** laughing matter; **cosa de risa** something to laugh at; **cosa de ver** something worth seeing; **cosa en sí** (philos.) Ding an sich, thing-in-itself; **cosa nunca vista** (coll.) something unheard-of; **cosa perdida** hopeless or incorrigible person; **cosa rara** strange thing; strange to say; **cosas de** doings of, tricks of; **cosas del mundo** ups and downs; **cosas de viento** (coll.) frivolities; **cosa seria** serious matter; the real thing, a worthwhile proposition; **cosa y cosa** puzzle, riddle
cosaco -ca *adj & mf* Cossack; *m* brute
cosario -ria *adj* traveled, frequented; *m* carrier, messenger, deliveryman; hunter
coscar **§86** *vr* (coll.) to shrug one's shoulders, to give a shrug
coscarana *f* (dial.) cracknel
coscoja *f* (bot.) kermes, kermes oak; dry leaves of kermes oak
coscojal *m* or **coscojar** *m* field of kermes oak
coscojita *f* var. of **coxcojilla**
coscojo *m* kermes, kermes berry; **coscojos** *mpl* iron bosses of horse's bit
coscón -cona *adj* (coll.) sly, crafty
coscoroba *f* (orn.) coscoroba
coscorrón *m* bump on the head, contusion
cosecante *f* (trig.) cosecant
cosecha *f* harvest, crop; harvest time; (fig.) crop (*e.g., of lies*); **de su cosecha** (coll.) of one's own invention, out of one's own head; **cosecha de vino** vintage
cosechadora *f* harvester (*machine*)
cosechar *va* to harvest, reap, gather; (Am.) to grow; *vn* to harvest
cosechero -ra *mf* harvester, reaper; vintner
coselete *m* corselet (*armor*); pikeman; (zool.) corselet (*thorax of insect*)
coseno *m* (trig.) cosine; **coseno verso** (trig.) coversed sine
cose-papeles *m* (*pl:* **-les**) stapler
coser *va* to sew; to rivet together; to lace (*a belt*); to join, unite closely; to stab; **coser a preguntas** to riddle with questions; **coser a puñaladas** (coll.) to cut or slash to pieces; *vn* to sew; **ser coser y cantar** (coll.) to be a cinch; *vr* **coserse con** or **contra** (coll.) to become closely united or associated with
cosetada *f* quick step, run
cosicosa *f* var. of **quisicosa**
cosido *m* sewing; **cosido de cama** sheet, quilt, and blanket stitched together
cosidura *f* (naut.) lashing
cosignatario -ria *adj & mf* cosignatory
cosmético -ca *adj & m* cosmetic
cosmogonía *f* cosmogony
cosmogónico -ca *adj* cosmogonic or cosmogonical
cosmografía *f* cosmography
cosmográfico -ca *adj* cosmographic or cosmographical
cosmógrafo -fa *mf* cosmographer
cosmología *f* cosmology
cosmológico -ca *adj* cosmological
cosmólogo -ga *mf* cosmologist
cosmonauta *m* cosmonaut
cosmopolita *adj* cosmopolitan; *mf* cosmopolitan; cosmopolite
cosmopolitismo *m* cosmopolitanism
cosmorama *m* cosmorama
cosmos *m* cosmos (*universe*); (bot.) cosmos
coso *m* enclosure for bullfighting; main street; (ent.) wood borer
cospe *m* chop, hack
cospel *m* blank (*from which to stamp coin*)
cosque *m* (coll.) bump on the head, contusion
cosquilladizo -za *adj* peevish, touchy
cosquillar *va* (archaic) to tickle
cosquillas *fpl* ticklishness; **buscarle a uno las cosquillas** (coll.) to try to annoy someone; **hacerle a uno cosquillas** (coll.) to stir up someone's curiosity; (coll.) to worry or scare someone; **no sufrir cosquillas** or **tener malas cosquillas** (coll.) to be impatient, be touchy
cosquillear *va* to tickle; to tease; to arouse the curiosity of; to make apprehensive; *vr* to become curious; to become annoyed; to enjoy oneself, to have a good time
cosquillejas *fpl* ticklishness
cosquilleo *m* tickling, tickling sensation

cosquilloso -sa *adj* ticklish; (fig.) touchy, ticklish
costa *f* cost, price; board and wages; coast; shore, bank; edge iron (*of shoemaker*); **costas** *fpl* (law) costs; **a costa de** at the expense of; **a toda costa** at any price; **barajar la costa** to sail close to shore; **condenar en costas** (law) to sentence to pay the costs; **ir** or **navegar costa a costa** to sail along the coast; **Costa Brava** Mediterranean coast from Pals to Tordera in province of Gerona, Spain; **Costa del Atlántico** Atlantic Coast; **Costa de los Esclavos** Slave Coast; **Costa del Pacífico** Pacific Coast; **Costa de Marfil** Ivory Coast; **Costa de Oro** Gold Coast; Côte-d'Or (*in France*); **Costa Firme** Spanish Main; **costa marítima** seacoast
costado *m* side (*of human body, of a ship*); (mil.) flank; (Am.) station platform; (min.) side face (*of a gallery*); **costados** *mpl* stock, ancestors
costal *adj* (anat.) costal; *m* bag, sack; tamper, stamper; **estar hecho un costal de huesos** (coll.) to be nothing but skin and bones; **costal de los pecados** human body (*full of sin*)
costalada *f* or **costalazo** *m* blow on the back or side (*from a fall*)
costalejo *m* small sack
costalero *m* (prov.) public errand boy; bearer of image of saint in Easter procession in Seville
costanero -ra *adj* coastal; sloping; *f* slope; **costaneras** *fpl* rafters
costanilla *f* short steep street
costar §77 *va & vn* to cost; **costar trabajo** + *inf* to be hard to + *inf;* **cueste lo que cueste** cost what it may
costarricense *adj* Costa Rican
costarriqueño -ña *adj & mf* Costa Rican
coste *m* cost, price; **a coste y costas** at cost
costear *va* to defray the cost of; to sail along the coast of; *vn* to sail along the coast; *vr* to pay for itself; to pay one's way
costeño -ña *adj* coastal; coasting; *mf* (Am.) coast dweller
costero -ra *adj* coastal; *m* slab (*outside piece cut from log*); side wall (*of blast furnace*); *f* side of a bale or package; fishing season; coast; slope
costezuela *f* slight slope
costilla *f* rib; (anat., bot. & naut.) rib; (carp.) fur; (coll.) wealth, property; (coll.) rib (*wife, better half*); stave; rung; **costillas** *fpl* back, shoulders; **calentar** or **medir las costillas a** (coll.) to thrash, beat, cudgel; **costilla cervical** (anat.) cervical rib; **costillas falsas** (anat.) false ribs; **costillas flotantes** (anat.) floating ribs; **costillas verdaderas** (anat.) true ribs
costillaje *m* or **costillar** *m* (anat.) ribs; ribbing, framework; (carp.) furring; lagging (*of a tunnel*)
costilludo -da *adj* (coll.) broad-shouldered, heavy-set
costo *m* cost; (bot.) sawwort; costusroot; **a costo y costas** at cost; **costo de la vida** cost of living; **costo hortense** (bot.) costmary; **costo, seguro y flete** (com.) cost, insurance, and freight
costoso -sa *adj* costly, expensive; grievous
costra *f* scab, crust, scale; snuff (*of candle wick*); scab (*on a cut or wound*); **costra láctea** (path.) infantile impetigo
costrada *f* crumb pie
costroso -sa *adj* scabby, crusty, scaly
costumbre *f* custom; **de costumbre** usually; usual; **tener por costumbre** + *inf* to be in the habit of + *ger*
costumbrista *adj* (*novel, writer, painting, painter*) depicting regional manners, customs, scenes, etc.; *mf* writer who depicts regional manners and customs
costura *f* sewing, needlework; tailoring; seam; (mach.) seam, joint; (naut.) splice; **alta costura** fashion designing, haute couture; high fashion, high style; **de costura francesa** full-fashioned (*hose*); **sentar las costuras** to press the seams; **sentarle a uno las costuras** (coll.) to take someone to task
costurera *f* seamstress, dressmaker
costurero *m* sewing table; sewing room; sewing case
costurón *m* large seam; coarse seam; big scar
cota *f* coat of arms; coat of mail; quota, share; elevation; (top.) bench mark; (top.) datum level; **cota de armas** coat of arms, tabard; **cota de malla** coat of mail
cotana *f* mortise; mortise chisel
cotangente *f* (trig.) cotangent
cotanza *f* coutances (*fine linen*)
cotarra *f* side of a ravine
cotarrera *f* (coll.) gossip, gossipy woman; (slang) prostitute
cotarro *m* night lodging for beggars and tramps; side of a ravine; **alborotar el cotarro** (coll.) to stir up a row; **andar de cotarro en cotarro** (coll.) to fool around from one place to another
cotejar *va* to compare, collate
cotejo *m* comparison, collation
cotense *m* (Am.) coarse hemp
coterráneo -a *adj & mf* var. of **conterráneo**
cotí *m* (*pl:* **-tíes**) bedtick, ticking
cotidiano -na *adj* daily, everyday, quotidian
cótila *f* (anat.) cotyla, acetabulum
cotiledón *m* (bot. & embryol.) cotyledon
cotiledóneo -a *adj* (bot.) cotyledonous
cotiloideo -a *adj* (anat.) cotyloid
cotilla *mf* (coll.) tattletale; *f* (archaic) corselet, corset
cotillear *vn* to gossip
cotilleo *m* gossip
cotillo *m* face (*of a hammer*)
cotillón *m* cotillion
cotín *m* (sport) backstroke (*in returning a ball*)
cotiza *f* dent (*for the warp*); (her.) cotise; (Am.) Indian sandal
cotización *f* quotation (*of a price*); current price, price list; quota; dues
cotizante *adj* dues-paying; *mf* dues payer
cotizar §76 *va* to quote (*a price*); to prorate; to cry out (*prices*) in the stock exchange; *vn* to collect dues; to pay dues
coto *m* enclosed pasture; preserve; landmark; boundary; (ichth.) sculpin; (pharm.) coto, coto bark; (zool.) howling monkey; (slang) churchyard; (slang) hospital; (Am.) goiter; **poner coto a** to check, to put a stop to; **coto social** workers' benefit society
cotón *m* cotton (*fabric*)
cotona *f* (Am.) man's work shirt; (Am.) sleeveless shirt; (Am.) blouse; (Am.) chamois jacket
cotonada *f* calico, print
cotoncillo *m* (paint.) button of maulstick
cotonía *f* dimity
cotorra *f* (orn.) parrot; (orn.) parakeet; (orn.) magpie; (coll.) chatterbox; (Am.) overnight hangout
cotorrear *vn* (coll.) to chatter, to gossip, to gabble
cotorreo *m* (coll.) chattering, gossip, gabble
cotorrera *f* female parrot; (coll.) chatterbox
cotorrón -rrona *adj* trying to be young, affecting youth
cototo *m* (Am.) bump
cotral *m & f* var. of **cutral**
cotudo -da *adj* cottony, hairy; (Am.) goitrous
cotufa *f* Jerusalem artichoke (*tuber of the plant*); tidbit, delicacy; **hacer cotufas** (Am.) to be fastidious; **pedir cotufas en el golfo** (coll.) to ask for the moon
coturnado -da *adj* buskined
coturno *m* buskin; **calzar el coturno** to write in the sublime style; to write tragedies; **de alto coturno** lofty, elevated, sublime
cotutor *m* coguardian
covacha *f* small cave; (Am.) cubbyhole; (Am.) shanty
covachuela *f* small cave; (archaic) office of crown minister (*in vaulted basement corridors of Royal Palace in Madrid*)
covachuelista *m* or **covachuelo** *m* (coll.) clerk; (coll.) government clerk
covanilla *f* or **covanillo** *m* basket for gathering grapes
covezuela *f* small cave
coxa *f* (ent.) coxa

coxal *adj* coxal; *m* (anat.) coxa
coxalgia *f* (path.) coxalgia
coxálgico -ca *adj* coxalgic
coxcojilla or **coxcojita** *f* hopscotch; **a coxcojita** hippety-hoppety
coxcox; a coxcox hippety-hoppety
coxis *m* (*pl:* **-xis**) var. of **cóccix**
coxofemoral *adj* coxofemoral
coy *m* (naut.) hammock, cot
coyote *m* (zool.) coyote, prairie wolf
coyunda *f* strap for yoking oxen; marriage; tyranny; sandal string
coyuntero *m* var. of **acoyuntero**
coyuntura *f* conjuncture, juncture; turn, chance, opportunity; (anat.) joint, articulation; **en coyuntura** at the right time
coz *f* (*pl:* **coces**) kick; butt (*of gun*); kick, recoil (*of gun*); ebb, reflux; kickback; big end (*of pole or mast*); (coll.) insult, churlishness; **dar coces** to kick; **tirar coces** to kick; (coll.) to kick (*to resist, to complain*)
C.P.B. or **c.p.b.** abr. of **cuyos pies beso**
cps. abr. of **compañeros**
crabrón *m* (ent.) hornet
crac *m* crash; **hacer crac** to crash, to fail; **crac financiero** crash, failure in business
Cracovia *f* Cracow
crampón *m* crampon, calk, climbing iron
cramponado -da *adj* (her.) cramponee
cran *m* (print.) nick
craneal or **craneano -na** *adj* cranial
cráneo *m* (anat.) skull, cranium
craneología *f* craniology
craneometría *f* craniometry
craneotomía *f* (surg.) craniotomy
crápula *f* drunkenness; licentiousness
crapuloso -sa *adj* drunken; licentious
crascitar *vn* to crow, to croak
crasia *f* crasis, temperament, constitution
crasiento -ta *adj* greasy
crasis *f* (*pl:* **-sis**) crasis; (gram.) crasis
crasitud *f* fatness, corpulence
craso -sa *adj* thick, coarse; fat, greasy; gross, crass (*error, ignorance, etc.*); (*cap.*) *m* Crassus
crasuláceo -a *adj* (bot.) crassulaceous
cráter *m* crater; (elec. & mil.) crater; (*cap.*) *m* (astr.) Crater
crátera *f* crater (*vessel*)
craticula *f* wicket through which nuns receive communion
crea *f* crea (*linen fabric*)
creación *f* creation; **la Creación** the Creation
creacionismo *m* (philos. & theol.) creationism
creador -dora *adj* creative; *mf* creator; **el Creador** the Creator
crear *va* to create; *vr* to build up (*e.g., a clientele*); to trump up (*an excuse*)
creativo -va *adj* creative
crecedero -ra *adj* growing; large enough to allow for growth (*said of child's clothes*)
crecepelo *m* hair restorer
crecer §34 *vn* to grow, increase; to rise, to swell (*said of a stream or flood*); **crecer como la mala hierba** to grow wild; *vr* to assume more authority or importance; to get bolder and more daring
creces *fpl* increase, extra, excess; **con creces** in abundance, in excess; **de creces** growing (*said of a child*)
crecido -da *adj* large, big, grown; swollen; **crecidos** *mpl* wide stitches (*in knitting*); *f* freshet, flood
creciente *adj* crescent; growing, increasing; (phonet.) rising (*diphthong*); *m* (her.) crescent; **creciente de la luna** (astr.) crescent (*increasing moon*); *f* freshet, flood; **creciente del mar** (naut.) high tide, flood tide
crecimiento *m* growth, increase; rise (*in value*)
crec.te abr. of **creciente**
credencia *f* credence, sideboard; (eccl.) credence
credencial *adj* & *f* credential; **credenciales** *fpl* credentials
credibilidad *f* credibility
crediticio -cia *adj* (pertaining to) credit
crédito *m* credit; (com. & educ.) credit; **abrir crédito a** (com.) to give credit to; **a crédito** (com.) on credit; **dar crédito a** to give credence or credit to; to credit, to do credit to
credo *m* creed; credo; (mus.) credo; **con el credo en la boca** (coll.) with one's heart in one's mouth; **en un credo** (coll.) in a trice; **que canta el credo** (coll.) with an air of importance
credulidad *f* credulity
crédulo -la *adj* credulous
creedero -ra *adj* believable; **creederas** *fpl* (coll.) credulity; **tener buenas creederas** (coll.) to be too gullible
creedor -dora *adj* credulous
creencia *f* belief; credence; creed, persuasion
creer §35 *va* & *vn* to believe, to think; **¡ya lo creo!** (coll.) I should say so!; **creer en** to believe in (*e.g., God*); *vr* to believe; to believe oneself to be; **¡que te crees tú eso!** (iron.) you think so!
crehuela *f* crea (*linen fabric*)
creíble *adj* credible, believable
crema *f* cream; cold cream; shoe polish; (gram.) diaeresis; (fig.) cream (*e.g., of society*); **crema de afeitar** shaving cream; **crema de menta** crème de menthe; **crema desvanecedora** vanishing cream
cremación *f* cremation
cremallera *f* (mach.) rack; rack rail; zipper; **cremallera y piñón** rack and pinion
cremástico -ca *adj* chremastic, economic; *f* chremastics, economics
crematorio -ria *adj* & *m* crematory
cremera *f* creamer
cremería *f* (Am.) creamery
cremómetro *m* creamometer, cremometer
cremona *f* espagnolette, casement bolt; *m* Cremona (*violin*)
crémor *m* cream of tartar; **crémor tártaro** cream of tartar
cremoso -sa *adj* creamy
crena *f* (anat. & bot.) crenation
crenado -da *adj* (bot.) crenate
crencha *f* part (*of hair*); hair on each side of part
creosol *m* (chem.) creosol
creosota *f* creosote
creosotar *va* to creosote
crep *m* o **crepé** *m* crepe
crepitación *f* crepitation, crackling; (med.) crepitation
crepitante *adj* crepitant, crackling
crepitar *vn* to crepitate, to crackle
crepuscular *adj* crepuscular
crepusculino -na *adj* crepusculine, twilight
crepúsculo *m* twilight
cresa *f* egg of queen bee; maggot; flybow
crescendo *m* (mus.) crescendo
Creso *m* (biog. & fig.) Croesus
cresol *m* (chem.) cresol
crespilla *f* (bot.) morel
crespina *f* hair net
crespo -pa *adj* curled, crispy; curly; angry, vexed; turgid (*style*)
crespón *m* crape; **crespón de la China** crepe de Chine; **crespón fúnebre** crape; mourning band
cresta *f* crest (*of bird, of wave, of mountain, of helmet*); (anat., arch., bot., mach. & zool.) crest; **alzar** or **levantar la cresta a** (coll.) to cut short, to mortify; **cresta de gallo** cockscomb; (bot.) cockscomb, yellow rattle
crestado -da *adj* crested
crestería *f* (fort.) battlement; (arch.) openwork cornice, cresting
crestillo *m* (bot.) clematis
crestomatía *f* chrestomathy
crestón *m* large crest; crest (*of helmet*); (min.) outcrop
crestudo -da *adj* heavy-crested; haughty
creta *f* chalk; (*cap.*) *f* Crete
cretáceo -a *adj* cretaceous; (geol.) Cretaceous; *m* (geol.) Cretaceous
cretácico *m* (geol.) Cretaceous
cretense *adj* & *mf* Cretan
crético -ca *adj* Cretan, Cretic; *m* cretic (*metrical foot*)
cretinismo *m* (path.) cretinism
cretino -na *adj* cretinic; *mf* cretin
cretona *f* cretonne
creyente *adj* believing; *mf* believer
creyón *m* crayon

crezneja *f* var. of **crizneja**
cría *f* raising, rearing; breeding; keeping (*of bees*); brood, litter; suckling; nursing; fledgling; **cría caballar** horse breeding
criada *f* see **criado**
criadero -ra *adj* fruitful, prolific; *m* nursery, tree nursery; breeding place; fish hatchery; (min.) seam, vein; **criadero de ostras** oyster bed
criadilla *f* testicle (*of animal*); potato, tuber; small roll (*of bread*); **criadilla almizclada** (bot.) red truffle; **criadilla de tierra** (bot.) truffle
criado -da *adj* bred; **bien criado** well-bred; **mal criado** ill-bred; *mf* servant; *f* female servant, maid; wash bat; **criada de servir** housemaid
criador -dora *adj* creative; fruitful, abounding; nurturing; *mf* breeder, raiser; keeper (*of bees*); creator; *f* wet nurse
criaduelo -la *mf* little servant
criamiento *m* care, upkeep, maintenance
crianza *f* raising, rearing; nursing; lactation; breeding, manners; **buena crianza** good breeding; **mala crianza** bad breeding
criar §90 *va* to raise, rear, bring up; to breed, to grow; to nurse, nourish; to foster; to fatten (*an animal*); to create; **criar carnes** to put on fat, put on weight
criatura *f* creature; little creature (*child, baby*); creature (*person owing his position to another*)
criba *f* screen, sieve; (min.) jig
cribado *m* screening, sieving
cribador -dora *adj* screening, sieving; *mf* screener, siever, screen tender
cribar *va* to screen, to sieve
cribo *m* screen, sieve
criboso -sa *adj* sievelike
cric *m* (*pl:* **crics**) jack, lifting jack; **cric de cremallera** ratchet jack
cricoides *adj* (anat.) cricoid; *m* (*pl:* **-coides**) (anat.) cricoid
cricquet *m* (sport) cricket
Crimea *f* Crimea
crimen *m* crime; **crimen de guerra** war crime; **crimen de lesa majestad** lese majesty
criminación *f* crimination
criminal *adj* criminal; *mf* criminal; **criminal de guerra** war criminal
criminalidad *f* criminality
criminalista *mf* criminal lawyer; penologist, criminalist
criminar *va* to criminate
criminología *f* criminology
criminológico -ca *adj* criminological
criminólogo -ga *mf* criminologist
criminoso -sa *adj* criminal; *mf* criminal; (Am.) slanderer
crimno *m* wheat or spelt meal
crin *f* mane; horsehair; **crin vegetal** vegetable horsehair
crinado -da *adj* (poet.) long-haired
crinito -ta *adj* crinite (*comet*)
crinoideo -a *adj* (zool.) crinoid; *m* (zool.) crinoid, sea lily
crinolina *f* crinoline (*cloth*); (Am.) crinoline (*skirt*)
crío *m* (coll.) nursing infant; (coll.) infant
criogénico -ca *adj* cryogenic; *f* cryogenics
criógeno -na *adj* cryogenic; *m* cryogen
criohidrato *m* (chem.) cryohydrate
criolita *f* (mineral.) cryolite
criología *f* cryology
criollismo *m* (Am.) native character; (Am.) advocacy of native manners and customs and things in general
criollo -lla *adj & mf* Creole; native (*in Latin America*); hundred-per-cent Argentine, Colombian, Venezuelan, etc.
criómetro *m* cryometer
crioscopia *f* cryoscopy
crioscopio *m* cryoscope
crióstato *m* cryostat
crioterapia *f* (med.) cryotherapy
cripta *f* crypt; (anat.) crypt
criptogámico -ca *adj* cryptogamic
criptógamo -ma *adj* cryptogamous; *f* (bot.) cryptogam
criptografía *f* cryptography
criptográfico -ca *adj* cryptographic
criptógrafo -fa *mf* cryptographer (*person*); *m* cryptograph (*device*)
criptograma *m* cryptogram
criptón *m* (chem.) krypton
crique *m* var. of **cric**
cris *m* (*pl:* **crises**) creese (*dagger*)
crisálida *f* (ent.) chrysalis
crisantema *f* or **crisantemo** *m* (bot.) chrysanthemum
Criseida *f* (myth.) Chryseis; (myth.) Cressida (*in medieval redaction*)
crisis *f* (*pl:* **-sis**) crisis; depression (*economic*); mature judgment; **crisis de llanto** outburst of tears, fit of weeping; **crisis de vivienda** housing shortage; **crisis ministerial** cabinet crisis; **crisis nerviosa** nervous breakdown
crisma *m & f* (eccl.) chrism; *f* (slang) bean, head
crismal *adj & m* (eccl.) chrismal
crismera *f* chrismatory
crismón *m* chrismon
crisoberilo *m* (mineral.) chrysoberyl
crisol *m* crucible; (fig.) crucible
crisolada *f* charge of a crucible
crisólito *m* (mineral.) chrysolite
crisopacio *m* var. of **crisoprasa**
crisopeya *f* chrysopoeia (*transmuting into gold*)
crisoprasa *f* (mineral.) chrysoprase
Crisóstomo, San Juan Saint John Chrysostom
crisotilo *m* (mineral.) chrysotile
crispadura *f* or **crispamiento** *m* twitching
crispar *va* to cause to twitch; *vr* to twitch
crispatura *f* twitching
crispir *va* to grain, to marble
crista *f* (her.) crest
cristal *m* crystal (*glass; glass ornament*); (chem., mineral. & rad.) crystal; pane of glass; mirror, looking glass; crystal glass, flint glass; (poet.) crystal (*water*); **cristal cilindrado** plate glass; **cristal de patente** (naut.) bull's-eye (*glass in ship's side, deck, etc.*); **cristal de reloj** crystal, watch crystal; **cristal de roca** crystal, rock crystal; **cristal hilado** spun glass, glass wool; **cristal líquido** liquid crystal; liquid glass; **cristal tallado** cut glass
cristalera *f* China closet; sideboard; glass door
cristalería *f* glasswork; glassworks; glass store; glassware; closet of glassware
cristalino -na *adj* crystalline; *m* (anat.) crystalline lens
cristalito *m* (mineral.) crystallite
cristalización *f* crystallization
cristalizador *m* crystallizer (*vessel*)
cristalizar §76 *va & vr* to crystallize
cristalofísica *f* physics of crystalline substances
cristalografía *f* crystallography
cristalográfico -ca *adj* crystallographic or crystallographical
cristaloide *m* crystalloid
cristaloideo -a *adj* crystalloid
cristaloquímica *f* chemistry of crystalline substances
cristel *m* var. of **clister**
Cristián *m* Christian (*man's name*)
cristianamente *adv* Christianly, in a Christian manner
cristianar *va* (coll.) to christen, baptize
cristiandad *f* Christendom; Christianity (*conformity to Christian religion*); missionary's flock
cristianesco -ca *adj* Christian, imitating the Christian (*said of something Moorish*)
cristianísimo -ma *adj* Most Christian (*sovereign*)
cristianismo *m* Christianity; christening, baptism
cristianización *f* Christianization
cristianizar §76 *va* to Christianize
cristiano -na *adj* Christian; *mf* Christian; *m* soul, person; Spanish (*language*); (coll.) watered wine
cristino -na *mf* Cristino (*partisan of Maria Christina*); (*cap.*) *f* Christine

Cristo *m* Christ; crucifix; **donde Cristo dió las tres voces** (coll.) in the middle of nowhere; **poner como un cristo** (coll.) to abuse, to beat up
Cristóbal *m* Christopher
cristofué *m* (orn.) Venezuelan greenfinch
cristus *m* (*pl:* **-tus**) christcross; **no saber el cristus** (coll.) to be very ignorant
crisuela *f* drip pan (*of lamp*)
criterio *m* criterion; judgment, discernment
crítica *f* see **crítico**
criticador -dora *adj* criticizing, faultfinding; *mf* criticizer, faultfinder
criticar §86 *va* to criticize
criticastro *m* criticaster
criticismo *m* (philos.) criticism
crítico -ca *adj* critical; (Am.) faultfinding; *m* critic; (coll.) pedant; *f* criticism; critique; gossip; **alta crítica** high criticism; **crítica textual** textual criticism
criticón -cona *adj* (coll.) censorious, faultfinding; *mf* (coll.) critic, faultfinder
critiquizar §76 *va* (coll.) to overcriticize
crizneja *f* braid of hair; rope of osiers or rushes
Croacia *f* Croatia
croar *vn* to croak (*said of frogs*)
croata *adj* & *mf* Croatian; *m* Croatian (*language*)
crocante *m* almond brittle, peanut brittle
croceína *f* (chem.) crocein
crocino -na *adj* (pertaining to) saffron; *f* (chem.) crocin
crocitar *vn* to crow, to croak
croché *m* crochet, crochet work
crochet *m* (box.) hook
cromado -da *adj* chrome, chromium-plated; *m* chromium plating
cromañón *m* (anthrop.) Cro-Magnon
cromañonense *adj* (anthrop.) Cro-Magnon
cromar *va* to chrome (*to plate with chromium*)
cromático -ca *adj* chromatic; (mus.) chromatic; *f* chromatics
cromatina *f* (biol.) chromatin
cromatismo *m* chromatism
cromato *m* (chem.) chromate
cromatóforo *m* (biol.) chromatophore
crómico -ca *adj* (chem.) chromic
crominancia *f* (phys.) crominance
cromismo *m* (bot.) chromatism
cromita *f* (mineral.) chromite
cromito *m* (chem.) chromite
cromo *m* (chem.) chromium, chrome; chromo (*picture*)
cromóforo *m* (chem.) chromophore
cromógeno -na *adj* chromogenic; *m* (chem.) chromogen
cromolitografía *f* chromolithography; chromolithograph (*picture*)
cromolitografiar §90 *va* to chromolithograph
cromolitográfico -ca *adj* chromolithographic
cromolitógrafo -fa *mf* chromolithographer
cromoplasma *m* (biol.) chromoplasm
cromoplasto *m* (bot.) chromoplast
cromoscopio *m* (telv.) chromoscope, color tube
cromosfera *f* (astr.) chromosphere
cromoso -sa *adj* (chem.) chromous
cromosoma *m* (biol.) chromosome; **cromosoma sexual** (biol.) sex chromosome
cromotipia *f* chromotypy or chromotypography
cromotipografía *f* chromotypography
cromotipográfico -ca *adj* chromotypographic
crónica *f* see **crónico**
cronicidad *f* chronicity, chronic nature
crónico -ca *adj* chronic; inveterate (*vices*); long-standing; *f* chronicle; news, news chronicle, feature story; **Crónicas** *fpl* (Bib.) Chronicles
cronicón *m* brief chronicle
cronista *mf* chronicler; reporter, feature writer; **cronista de radio** newscaster, radio newscaster
cronístico -ca *adj* (pertaining to a) chronicle; chronicler's
cronógrafo -fa *mf* chronographer; *m* chronograph
cronología *f* chronology
cronológico -ca *adj* chronologic or chronological
cronologista *mf* or **cronólogo -ga** *mf* chronologist
cronometrador -dora *mf* (sport) timekeeper
cronometraje *m* (sport) clocking, timing
cronometrar *va* (sport) to clock, to time
cronometría *f* chronometry
cronómetro *m* chronometer; stop watch
Cronos *m* (myth.) Cronus
cronoscopio *m* chronoscope
croqueta *f* croquette
croquis *m* (*pl:* **-quis**) sketch
croscitar *vn* to crow, to croak
crosse *f* (sport) lacrosse; **jugar a la crosse** to play lacrosse
crótalo *m* (zool.) rattlesnake; castanet
crotón *m* (bot.) croton
crotorar *vn* to rattle (*said of a stork or crane*)
cruce *m* cross, crossing; crossroads; intersection; exchange (*e.g., of letters*); (elec.) crossed wires (*short*); **cruce a nivel** (rail.) grade crossing; **cruce de palabras** (philol.) blending; **cruce en trébol** cloverleaf, cloverleaf intersection (*in a highway*)
crucera *f* withers (*of horse*)
crucería *f* (arch.) boss (*in Gothic vaulting*)
crucero *m* (eccl.) crucifer, cross-bearer; crossroads; railroad crossing; timber; crosspiece; (nav.) cruiser; (naut. & aer.) cruise, cruising; (arch.) transept; (arch.) crossing (*where transept crosses nave*); (*cap.*) *m* (astr.) Southern Cross; **crucero a nivel** (rail.) grade crossing
cruceta *f* crosspiece (*e.g., of trelliswork*); (mach.) crosshead (*of connecting rod*); (naut.) crosstree
crucial *adj* crucial; (surg.) crucial
cruciata *f* (bot.) crosswort
cruciferario *m* (eccl.) crucifer, cross-bearer
crucífero -ra *adj* (bot.) cruciferous; *f* (bot.) crucifer
crucificado -da *adj* crucified; **el Crucificado** the Crucified (*Christ*)
crucificar §86 *va* to crucify; (coll.) to crucify (*to torture, torment*)
crucifijo *m* crucifix
crucifixión *f* crucifixion; (*cap.*) *f* Crucifixion
cruciforme *adj* cruciform, cross-shaped
crucigrama *m* crossword puzzle
crucigramista *mf* crossworder
crucillo *m* pushpin
cruda *f* see **crudo**
crudelísimo -ma *adj super* very or most cruel
crudeza *f* rawness, crudeness; unripeness; hardness (*of water*); roughness, severity, harshness; (coll.) blustering; **crudezas** *fpl* undigested food, indigestible food
crudo -da *adj* raw, crude; unripe; unbleached (*linen*); hard (*water*); raw (*weather*); **estar crudo** (Am.) to have a hangover; **medio crudo** rare (*meat*); *m* burlap; *f* (Am.) hangover
cruel *adj* cruel; intense (*cold*); fierce, bitter, bloody (*struggle, battle*)
crueldad *f* cruelty
cruento -ta *adj* bloody
crujía *f* corridor, hall; block, row of houses; ward, hospital ward; bay (*space between two walls*); (naut.) midship gangway; **pasar** or **sufrir una crujía** (coll.) to have a hard time of it; **crujía de piezas** suite of rooms
crujidero -ra *adj* crackling; creaking; chattering, clattering; rustling
crujido *m* crackle; creak; chatter, clatter; rustle
crujiente *adj* var. of **crujidero**
crujir *vn* to crackle; to creak; to chatter, clatter; to rustle
crúor *m* (physiol.) cruor; (poet.) blood
crup *m* (path.) croup
crupal *adj* croupous
cruposo -sa *adj* croupy
crural *adj* (anat.) crural
crustáceo -a *adj* crustaceous; (zool.) crustaceous, crustacean; *m* (zool.) crustacean
crústula *f* var. of **cortezuela**
cruz *f* (*pl:* **cruces**) cross; tails (*of a coin*); withers (*of quadruped*); (math.) plus sign; (naut.) crown (*of anchor*); (print.) dagger; top of trunk (*where horizontal branches begin*); (fig.) cross (*suffering, burden*); **de la cruz a la fecha** from beginning to end; **en cruz** crosswise; cross-shaped; in quarters; (her.)

quarterly; **Cruz del Sur** (astr.) Southern Cross; **cruz de Malta** Maltese cross; (bot.) scarlet lychnis; **cruz de San Andrés** Saint Andrew's cross; **cruz gamada** gammadion, fylfot, swastika; **cruz latina** Latin cross; **cruz potenzada** (her.) potent cross; **cruz roja** red cross; **Cruz Roja** Red Cross; **cruz trebolada** (her.) tréflé cross, botony cross; **cruz y raya** (coll.) I have my fill, that's enough
cruzado -da *adj* crossed; cross (*breed*); twilled; double-breasted; **con los brazos cruzados** with arms crossed, idle; *m* crusader; knight; *f* crusade; crossroads, intersection
cruzamiento *m* crossing; cross-breeding; (elec.) cross; **cruzamiento retrógrado** backcross
cruzar **§76** *va* to cross; to cut across; to honor with the cross, confer the cross on; to twill; to exchange (*correspondence*); (naut.) to cruise, cruise over; **cruzarle a uno la cara** to lash someone in the face; *vn* to cross; to fold over (*said of clothing when it is full*); to cruise; *vr* to cross in front; to cross each other; to cross one another's path; to take the cross (*to join a crusade*); **cruzarse con** to pass (*e.g., another automobile*); **cruzarse de brazos** to cross one's arms, remain idle, do nothing
cs. abr. of **céntimos** & **cuartos**
csardas *f* (mus.) czardas
c.ta abr. of **cuenta**
cte. abr. of **corriente**
ctetología *f* ctetology
c.to abr. of **cuarto**
cts. abr. of **céntimos** & **cuartos**
c/u abr. of **cada uno**
cuaba *f* (bot.) Jamaica rosewood; (Am.) gyp
cuaco *m* (Am.) yucca flour; (Am.) horse
cuad. abr. of **cuadrado**
cuaderna *f* (naut.) frame; **cuaderna de escuadra** (naut.) square frame; **cuaderna maestra** (naut.) midship frame; **cuaderna sesgada** (naut.) cant frame
cuadernal *m* double or triple block
cuadernillo *m* (eccl.) liturgical calendar; quinternion
cuaderno *m* notebook; folder; (print.) quarternion; **cuaderno de bitácora** (naut.) logbook; **cuaderno de hojas cambiables** or **sueltas** loose-leaf notebook
cuadra *f* see **cuadro**
cuadrada *f* see **cuadrado**
cuadradamente *adv* exactly, fully
cuadradillo *m* ruler; plotting paper; square iron bar; gusset (*of shirt*); lump (*of sugar*)
cuadrado -da *adj* square; quadrate; perfect, complete; square-shouldered; *m* (geom. & math.) square; quadrate; ruler; clock (*in stockings*); gusset (*of shirt*); die (*for making coins*); (print.) quadrat; **de cuadrado** perfectly; full-faced (*view*); **dejar de cuadrado** to sting to the quick; **cuadrado mágico** magic square; *f* (mus.) breve
cuadragenario -ria *adj* & *mf* quadragenarian
cuadragesimal *adj* Quadragesimal
cuadragésimo -ma *adj* & *m* fortieth; *f* (eccl.) Lent; (eccl.) Quadragesima
cuadral *m* (carp.) angle brace
cuadrangular *adj* quadrangular; *m* (baseball) home run
cuadrángulo -la *adj* quadrangular; *m* quadrangle
cuadrantal *m* quadrantal (*liquid measure*)
cuadrante *m* fourth part of an inheritance; dial, face (*of watch, clock, etc.*); (astr. & geom.) quadrant; (carp.) angle brace; **cuadrante de sintonía** (rad.) tuning dial; **cuadrante solar** sundial
cuadranura *f* radial crack in trees (*sign of rotting*)
cuadrar *va* to square; to form into a square; to please; (math.) to square; (math.) to determine the square of; (taur.) to line up, to square off (*the bull*); **cuadrar** + *inf* (Am.) to be pleasing to + *inf*; *vn* to square, to conform; *vr* to stand at attention, to square one's shoulders; (coll.) become solemn, to assume a serious air
cuadratín *m* (print.) quadrat
cuadratura *f* (astr., elec. & math.) quadrature; **cuadratura del círculo** (math.) quadrature of the circle; (coll.) impossibility
cuadrete *m* small square
cuadricenal *adj* done every forty years
cuadríceps *m* (anat.) quadriceps; *adj* quadricipital
cuadrícula *f* quadrille ruling
cuadricular *adj* squared, in squares; *va* to graticulate, to quadrille
cuadrienal *ajd* & *f* quadrennial
cuadrienio *m* quadrennium, period of four years
cuadrífido -da *adj* (bot.) quadrifid
cuadrifilar *adj* four-wire
cuadrifoliado -da *adj* four-leaf
cuadrifolio -lia *adj* four-leaf; *m* (arch.) quatrefoil
cuadriforme *adj* quadriform
cuadriga *f* (hist.) quadriga
cuadrilátero -ra *adj* quadrilateral; *m* quadrilateral; (box.) ring
cuadriliteral or **cuadrilítero -ra** *adj* quadriliteral, four-letter
cuadrilongo -ga *adj* oblong, rectangular; *m* oblong, rectangle; (mil.) rectangular formation
cuadrilla *f* group, party, crew, troup, gang, squad; quadrille; (taur.) cuadrilla, quadrille; **cuadrilla de demolición** demolition squad
cuadrillar *vn* (Am.) to quadrille
cuadrillazo *m* (Am.) surprise attack; **dar cuadrillazo a** (Am.) to gang up on
cuadrillero *m* chief, leader, foreman; (orn.) tanager
cuadrillo *m* bolt, quarrel (*arrow*)
cuadrimestre *adj* & *m* var. of **cuatrimestre**
cuadrimotor *m* (aer.) four-motor plane
cuadringentésimo -ma *adj* & *m* four-hundredth
cuadrinomio *m* (alg.) quadrinomial
cuadripartido -da *adj* quadripartite
cuadriplaza *m* (aer.) four-seater
cuadriplicar **§86** *va* var. of **cuadruplicar**
cuadrisílabo -ba *adj* & *m* var. of **cuatrisílabo**
cuadriviario -ria *adj* four-lane
cuadrivio *m* crossroads (*of four roads*); quadrivium (*four upper subjects of medieval seven liberal arts*)
cuadrivista *m* scholar trained in the quadrivium
cuadríyugo *m* four-horse chariot
cuadro -dra *adj* square ‖ *m* square; picture, painting; frame (*of picture, door, bicycle, etc.*); flower bed, patch; table, outline; staff, personnel; (lit.) picture; (mil.) square; (mil.) cadre; (print.) platen; (sport) team; (theat.) scene; (coll.) sight, mess; **a cuadros** checked; **en cuadro** square, e.g., **ocho pulgadas en cuadro** eight inches square; **en cuadro** (coll.) topsy-turvy; **estar** or **quedarse en cuadro** to be all alone in the world; to be on one's uppers; (mil.) to be skeletonized; **cuadro al óleo** oil painting; **cuadro conmutador** (elec. & telp.) switchboard; **cuadro de contador** (elec.) meter panel; **cuadro de costumbres** (lit.) sketch of manners and customs; **cuadro de distribución** (elec. & telp.) switchboard; **cuadro de mandos** panelboard; **cuadro de vidrio** pane of glass; **cuadro indicador** score board; (elec.) annunciator; **cuadro vivo** tableau ‖ *f* hall, large room; dormitory, ward; stable; croup, rump; (naut.) quarter; (Am.) block of houses, square
cuadrúmano -na *adj* (zool.) quadrumanous; *m* (zool.) quadrumane
cuadrupedal *adj* quadrupedal
cuadrúpedo -da *adj* quadruped; (coll.) doltish; *m* quadruped; (coll.) dolt
cuádruple *adj* & *m* quadruple
cuadrúplex *m* (telg.) quadruplex system
cuadruplicación *f* quadruplication
cuadruplicar **§86** *va* to quadruplicate, to quadruple; *vr* to quadruple
cuádruplo -pla *adj* & *m* var. of **cuádruple**
cuaga *f* (zool.) quagga
cuajada *f* see **cuajado**
cuajadillo *m* fancy work on silk
cuajado -da *adj* dumfounded; *m* mincemeat; *f* curd; cottage cheese
cuajadura *f* curdling, coagulation
cuajaleche *m* (bot.) bedstraw, cheese rennet

cuajamiento *m* var. of **cuajadura**
cuajar *m* (zool.) rennet bag; *va* to curd, to curdle, to coagulate; to thicken, to jelly; to overdeck; (coll.) to please, to suit; *vn* (coll.) to jell, take shape; (coll.) to take hold, catch on, succeed; (Am.) to prattle; *vr* to curd, to curdle, to coagulate; to thicken, to jelly; to sleep soundly; (coll.) to become crowded
cuajarón *m* clot, grume
cuajilote *m* (bot.) tropical American tree (*Parmentiera edulis*)
cuajo *m* rennet; curdle; rennet bag; thickening (*of cane juice*); idle chatting; recess (*in school*); **de cuajo** by the roots
cuakerismo *m* var. of **cuaquerismo**
cuákero -ra *adj & mf* var. of **cuáquero**
cual *adj & pron rel* as, such as; **el cual** which, who; **por lo cual** for which reason; **cual . . . tal** like . . . like, e.g., **cual el padre, tal el hijo** like father like son; just as . . . so, e.g., **cual es Pedro, tal es Juan** just as Peter is, so is John, John is like Peter; *adv* as; **cual si** as if; *prep* like
cuál *adj & pron interr* which, what, which one; how!; **cuál . . . cuál** some . . . some
cualicho *m* (Am.) evil spirit, demon
cualidad *f* quality; characteristic
cualímetro *m* qualimeter
cualitativo -va *adj* qualitative
cualquier *adj indef* (*pl:* **cualesquier**) apocopated form of **cualquiera,** used only before nouns and adjectives
cualquiera (*pl:* **cualesquiera**) *pron indef* anyone; *pron rel* whichever; whoever; *adj indef* any; *adj rel* whichever; *m* anybody, nobody (*person of no account*)
cuan *adv* as
cuán *adv* how, how much
cuando *conj* when; in case (that); although; since; **aún cuando** even though; **de cuando en cuando** from time to time; **cuando más** at most; **cuando menos** at least; **cuando mucho** at most; **cuando quiera** whenever; *prep* (coll.) at the time of
cuándo *adv* when?, e.g., **¿cuándo llegará?** when will he arrive?; when, e.g., **no sé cuándo llegará** I don't know when he will arrive; **¿de cuándo acá?** since when?; how come?; **cuándo . . . cuándo** sometimes . . . sometimes
cuandoquiera *adv* any time; **cuandoquiera que** whenever
cuantía *f* quantity; importance, distinction; **de mayor cuantía** first-rate; grave, serious; **de menor cuantía** second-rate; of minor seriousness
cuantiar **§90** *va* to estimate, to appraise
cuántico -ca *adj* (phys.) quantum
cuantidad *f* quantity
cuantificar **§86** *va* to quantify
cuantimás *adv* (coll.) at least
cuantímetro *m* quantimeter
cuantioso -sa *adj* numerous, large, substantial
cuantitativo -va *adj* quantitative
cuanto -ta *adj & pron rel* as much as, whatever; **unos cuantos** some few; **cuanto** as much as, all that (which); **cuantos** as many as, all those who, everybody who; **cuanto** *adv* as soon as; as long as; **en cuanto** as soon as; while; insofar as; **en cuanto a** as to, as for; **por cuanto** inasmuch as; **por cuanto . . . por tanto** inasmuch as . . . therefore; **cuanto antes** as soon as possible; **cuanto más . . . tanto más** the more . . . the more, e.g., **cuanto más tiene tanto más desea** the more he has the more he wants; **cuanto más** at least; **cuanto más que** all the more because; **cuanto y más** at least; **cuanto y más que** all the more because; *m* (*pl:* **-ta**) (phys.) quantum
cuánto -ta *adj & pron interr* how much; **cuántos** how many; **cuánto** *adv interr* how, how much; how long; how long ago; **cada cuánto** how often
cuaquerismo *m* Quakerism
cuáquero -ra *adj & mf* Quaker; *f* Quakeress
cuarcífero -ra *adj* quartziferous
cuarcita *f* (mineral.) quartzite
cuarenta *adj & m* forty; **acusarle a uno las cuarenta** (coll.) to give someone a piece of one's mind
cuarentavo -va *adj & m* fortieth
cuarentena *f* forty, two score; quarantine; Lent; forty days, months, years, etc.; suspension of approval
cuarentón -tona *adj* forty-year-old; *mf* person forty years old
cuaresma *f* Lent; Lenten sermons
cuaresmal *adj* Lenten
cuaresmario *m* Lenten sermons
cuarta *f* see **cuarto**
cuartago *m* nag, pony
cuartal *m* dry measure equal to 5.60 liters; dry measure equal to 17.50 liters; quarter loaf of bread
cuartán *m* dry measure equal to 18.08 liters; oil measure equal to 4.15 liters
cuartana *f* (path.) quartan
cuartanal *adj* quartan
cuartanario -ria *adj* suffering from quartan
cuartazos *m* (scornful) fat slob
cuartear *va* to quarter; to divide; to zigzag over (*a road*); to bid a fourth higher for; to take the fourth place in (*a game*); (Am.) to whip, to lash; (naut.) to box (*the compass*); *vn* (taur.) to step aside, to dodge; (Am.) to compromise; *vr* to crack, split; (taur.) to step aside, to dodge
cuartel *m* quarter; section, ward (*of a city*); lot (*of ground*); flower bed; (her.) quarter; (mil.) barracks; (mil.) quarter (*clemency to conquered enemy*); (naut.) hatch (*door over hatchway*); (coll.) house, home; **cuarteles** *mpl* (mil.) quarters; **no dar cuartel a** to give no quarter to; **cuartel de bomberos** engine house, firehouse; **cuartel de la salud** (coll.) refuge, haven; **cuartel general** (mil.) headquarters
cuartelada *f* mutiny, military uprising
cuartelar *va* (her.) to quarter
cuartelero -ra *adj* barrack, soldier; *m* soldier charged with policing the barracks
cuartelesco -ca *adj* barrack, soldier
cuartelillo *m* (mil.) barracks; police station
cuarteo *m* quartering; dividing; dodging; crack, split
cuartera *f* dry measure equal to about 70 liters; land measure equal to about 30 acres; log, piece of lumber
cuarterada *f* land measure equal to about 7 sq. mi.
cuarterola *f* quarter cask
cuarterón -rona *mf* quadroon; *m* quartern, fourth; quarter pound; panel (*of a door*); wicket (*small door in larger one*)
cuarteta *f* quatrain with the rhyme abba; quatrain with second and fourth lines rhymed
cuartete *m* or **cuarteto** *m* quatrain (*poem*); quartet (*group of four*); (mus.) quartet or quartette
cuartilla *f* pastern (*of horse*); quarter sheet of paper; sheet of paper; quarter arroba; dry measure equal to 13.87 liters; liquid measure equal to 4.033 liters
cuartillo *m* dry measure equal to 1.156 liters; liquid measure equal to 0.504 liters
cuartilludo -da *adj* long-pasterned (*horse*)
cuartizo *m* quartersawed timber
cuarto -ta *adj* fourth; quarter ‖ *m* fourth; quarter; quarter-hour; room, bedroom; **cuartos** *mpl* (coll.) money, cash; **de tres al cuarto** of little importance; **echar su cuarto a espadas** (coll.) to butt into the conversation; **en cuarto** quarto (*said of a volume*); **hacer cuartos a** to quarter; **no tener un cuarto** (coll.) to not have a cent; **por cuarto cuartos** (coll.) for a song, for practically nothing; **tener buenos cuartos** (coll.) to be strong and husky; **cuarto creciente** first quarter (*of moon*); **cuarto de aseo** lavatory; **cuarto de baño** bathroom; **cuarto de dormir** bedroom; **cuarto de estar** living room; **cuarto de huésped** spare room, guest room; **cuarto de juegos** playroom, nursery; **cuarto delantero** forequarter; **cuarto de luna** (astr.) quarter; **cuarto menguante** last quarter (*of*

moon); **cuarto obscuro** (phot.) darkroom; **cuarto trasero** (cook.) rump (*e.g., of a cow*) ‖ *f* fourth, fourth part, quarter; (mus.) fourth; (naut.) point, rhumb (*of compass card*); four of a kind (*in cards*); span (*of hand*); (Am.) horse whip
cuartón *m* quartersawed timber; square field
cuartucho *m* shack, hovel
cuarzo *m* (mineral.) quartz
cuarzoso -sa *adj* quartzose or quartzous
cuascle *m* (Am.) horse blanket
cuasi *adv* almost; quasi
cuasia *f* (bot. & pharm.) quassia; **cuasia de Jamaica** (bot. & pharm.) bitterwood, Jamaica quassia
cuasicontrato *m* (law) quasi contract
cuasidelito *m* (law) quasi delict
cuasimodo *m* (eccl.) Quasimodo
cuate -ta *adj* (Am.) twin; (Am.) chummy; *mf* (Am.) twin; (Am.) chum, pal
cuaternario -ria *adj* quaternary; (chem.) quaternary; (geol.) Quaternary; *m* (geol.) Quaternary
cuaterno -na *adj* quaternary
cuatí *m* (*pl:* **-tíes**) var. of **coatí**
cuatralbo -ba *adj* having four white feet
cuatrero *m* horse thief, cattle thief, rustler
cuatricromía *f* four-color reproduction, four-color process
cuatriduano -na *adj* four-day-long
cuatrienio *m* var. of **cuadrienio**
cuatrifilar *adj* four-wire
cuatrillizo -za *mf* quadruplet
cuatrillo *m* lansquenet (*card game*)
cuatrillón *m* British quadrillion; septillion (*in U.S.A.*)
cuatrimestre *adj* four-month; *m* four months
cuatrimotor *adj masc* four-motor
cuatrinca *f* foursome; four of a kind (*in cards*)
cuatripartito -ta *adj* var. of **cuadripartido**
cuatrirreactor *m* (aer.) four-engine jet plane
cuatrisílabo -ba *adj* quadrisyllabic; *m* quadrisyllable
cuatro *adj* four; **las cuatro** four o'clock; *m* four; fourth (*in dates*); (mus.) quartet (*of voices*); **más de cuatro** (coll.) quite a number (*of people*)
cuatrocentista *adj* fifteenth-century; *m* (f.a.) quattrocentist
cuatrocientos -tas *adj & m* four hundred
cuatrodoblar *va* to quadruplicate
cuatropea *f* sales tax on horses; quadruped; cattle market place
Cuatro Vientos Madrid airport
cuba *f* cask, barrel; tub, vat; stack (*of blast furnace*); bucket (*of turbine*); (coll.) tub (*fat person*); (coll.) toper; **estar hecho una cuba** (coll.) to be tanked up; **cuba del flotador** float chamber (*of carburetor*); **cuba de riego** street sprinkler
cubaje *m* (Am.) cubing
cubanismo *m* Cubanism
cubanizar §76 *va* to Cubanize
cubano -na *adj & mf* Cuban
cubeba *f* (bot. & pharm.) cubeb
cubera *f* (ichth.) snapper
cubería *f* cooperage; cooper's shop
cubero *m* cooper
cubertura *f* var. of **cobertura**
cubeta *f* keg, small cask or barrel; pail, small bucket; toilet bowl; cup or cistern (*of barometer*); (chem. & phot.) tray (*of glass, hard rubber, etc.*); (phot.) cuvette; (mus.) pedestal (*of harp*); (Am.) high hat; **cubeta de aceite** (mach.) oil well; **cubeta de goteo** drip pan
cubeto *m* small pail or bucket, small tub
cúbica *f* see **cúbico**
cubicación *f* cubing; cubic measure
cubicar §86 *va* to determine the volume of; (math.) to cube
cúbico -ca *adj* cubic, cubical; (cryst. & math.) cubic; (math.) cube (*root*); *f* cubica (*fabric*)
cubículo *m* cubicle
cubierta *f* see **cubierto**
cubiertamente *adv* secretly, under cover
cubierto -ta *pp of* **cubrir** ‖ *m* cover, roof, shelter; cover (*place for one person at table*); knife, fork, and spoon; tray with napkin for serving bread and cakes; meal (*at a fixed price*); table d'hôte; **a cubierto de** under cover of (*e.g., darkness*); protected from (*e.g., the rain*); **bajo cubierto** under cover, indoors ‖ *f* cover; envelope; casing; roof; paper cover (*of a book*); shoe (*of a tire*); hood (*of motor*); (naut.) deck; **bajo cubierta** under separate cover; **entre cubiertas** (naut.) between decks; **cubierta alta** (naut.) upper deck; **cubierta corrida** flush deck; **cubierta de aterrizaje** (nav.) flight deck; **cubierta de cama** bedcover; **cubierta de guindaste** (naut.) spar deck; **cubierta de mesa** table cover; **cubierta de paseo** (naut.) promenade deck; **cubierta de salón** (naut.) saloon deck; **cubierta de vuelo** (nav.) flight deck; **cubierta principal** (naut.) main deck
cubija *f* (Am.) blanket
cubijar *va* var. of **cobijar**
cubil *m* lair, den (*of wild animals*); bed (*of stream*)
cubilar *m* lair, den; sheepfold; *vn* to take shelter overnight (*said of sheep and shepherd*)
cubilete *m* (cook.) copper pan or mold; pannikin; juggler's goblet, dicebox; mince pie; (Am.) high hat; (bot.) yellow pond lily; intrigue, wirepulling
cubiletear *vn* to juggle; to scheme, to intrigue; (Am.) to dabble in politics
cubileteo *m* jugglery
cubiletero *m* juggler; copper pan or mold
cubilote *m* (found.) cupola
cubilla *f* (ent.) oil beetle
cubillo *m* (ent.) oil beetle; earthen water jug
cubismo *m* (f.a.) cubism
cubista *adj & mf* (f.a.) cubist
cubital *adj* cubital
cúbito *m* (anat.) cubitus
cubo *m* bucket; hub (*of wheel*); socket (*of a candelabrum; of a wrench*); bayonet socket; reserve water tank (*for mill*); cube; (arch.) dado; (mach.) barrel, drum; (math.) cube; (Am.) finger bowl
cuboides *adj* (anat.) cuboid; *m* (*pl:* **-boides**) (anat.) cuboid, cuboid bone
cubreasiento *m* (aut.) seat cover
cubrebandeja *f* tray cloth
cubrecabeza *f* helmet (*e.g., of aviator*)
cubrecadena *f* chain guard
cubrecama *f* counterpane, bedspread
cubrecorsé *m* corset cover, underbodice
cubrefuego *m* curfew
cubrejunta *f* (carp.) fish
cubremantel *m* fancy tablecloth
cubreneumático *m* (aut.) tire cover
cubrenuca *f* havelock; neckguard
cubreobjeto or **cubreobjetos** *m* (*pl:* **-tos**) cover glass, cover slip (*for microscopic preparations*)
cubrepantalones *mpl* overalls
cubreplatos *m* (*pl:* **-tos**) dish cover
cubrerrueda *f* mudguard
cubresexo *m* G string, cache-sexe
cubretablero *m* (aut.) cowl
cubretetera *f* cozy, tea cozy
cubrimiento *m* covering
cubrir §17, 9 *va* to cover, cover over, cover up; to cover (*a mare*); (mil.) to cover (*e.g., a retreat*); *vr* to cover oneself; to become covered; to put one's hat on; to cover (*to settle a debt*)
cuca *f* see **cuco**
cucamonas *fpl* (coll.) fawning, wheedling
cucaña *f* greased pole to be walked on or climbed (*as a game*); (coll.) cinch
cucañero -ra *mf* (coll.) parasite, hanger-on
cucar §86 *va* to wink; to make fun of; to sight (*game*); (Am.) to excite, stir up; *vn* to go off on a run (*said of cattle when bitten by flies*)
cucaracha *f* (ent.) cockroach, roach; (zool.) wood louse, pill bug
cucarachero -ra *adj* (Am.) amorous, lecherous; *f* cockroach trap
cucarda *f* cockade
cuclillas; ponerse en cuclillas to squat, to crouch
cuclillo *m* (orn.) cuckoo; (orn.) yellow-billed cuckoo; cuckold; **cuclillo de las lluvias** (orn.) yellow-billed cuckoo
cuco -ca *adj* crafty, sly; (coll.) nice, cute; *mf* crafty, sly person; *m* India berry; bogeyman;

(ent.) caterpillar; (orn.) cuckoo; (coll.) gambler; *f* (bot.) chufa; (ent.) caterpillar; (coll.) gambling woman; **mala cuca** (coll.) vicious, evil person
cucú *m* (*pl:* **-cúes**) cuckoo (*call of cuckoo*)
cuculado -da or **cuculiforme** *adj* cowled, cowl-like, cuculiate
cuculí *f* (*pl:* **-líes**) (Am.) wild pigeon (*Melopelia meloda*); **jugar la** or **hasta la cuculí** (Am.) to shoot the works
cuculla *f* cowl; hood
cucúrbita *f* (archaic) retort
cucurbitáceo -a *adj* (bot.) cucurbitaceous
cucurucho *m* paper cone, cornet; ice-cream cone
cucuy *m* or **cucuyo** *m* var. of **cocuyo**
cuchara *f* spoon; ladle; scoop; trowel; dipper (*of power shovel*); (Am.) pickpocket; **media cuchara** (coll.) mediocre person; **meter su cuchara** (coll.) to meddle, to butt in, to put in one's oar; **cuchara de café** teaspoon; **cuchara de sopa** tablespoon
cucharada *f* spoonful; ladleful; scooping; **meter su cucharada** (coll.) to meddle, to butt in; **cucharada de café** teaspoonful; **cucharada de sopa** tablespoonful
cucharadita *f* teaspoon; teaspoonful
cucharal *m* shepherd's goatskin spoon bag
cucharear *va* to spoon, to ladle out; (hort.) to sprinkle
cucharero -ra *mf* spoon maker or dealer; *m* spoon rack
cuchareta *f* small spoon; Andalusian wheat; (orn.) shoveler; (vet.) liver rot, sheep rot
cucharetear *vn* (coll.) to stir the pot; (coll.) to meddle
cucharetero -ra *mf* maker of wooden ladles; dealer in wooden ladles; *m* spoon rack; petticoat fringe
cucharilla *f* small spoon, teaspoon; ladle (*of tinsmith*); liver disease of hogs; (surg.) curette
cucharón *m* large spoon; soup ladle, dipper; scoop; (orn.) spoonbill; (mach.) bucket; **despacharse con el cucharón** (coll.) to take care of oneself, to look out for number one; **cucharón de quijadas** grab bucket, clamshell bucket
cucharro *m* (naut.) harpings, buttocks
cuchichear *va & vn* to whisper
cuchicheo *m* whispering
cuchichero -ra *mf* whisperer
cuchichiar *vn* to call or cry (*said of partridge*)
cuchilla *f* knife, cutting tool; large knife, cleaver; blade (*of razor, of sword*); hogback, mountain ridge, runner (*of skate, sled, sleigh*); (elec.) blade (*of switch*); (poet.) sword; (archaic) halberd; **cuchilla de carnicero** butcher knife
cuchillada *f* slash, hack, gash; **cuchilladas** *fpl* quarrel, fight; slashes (*ornamental slits in garment*); **dar cuchillada** (coll.) to be the hit of the town (*said of a show*)
cuchillar *adj* (pertaining to a) knife; knifelike
cuchilleja *f* small knife or blade
cuchillería *f* cutlery; cutler's shop
cuchillero *m* cutler; iron band or clasp
cuchillo *m* knife; knife edge; gore (*in garment*); lower tusk (*of wild boar*); (carp.) upright; (naut.) triangular sail; **pasar a cuchillo** to put to the sword, put to death; **cuchillo de armadura** (arch.) gable frame; **cuchillo de cocina** kitchen knife; **cuchillo de monte** hunting knife; **cuchillo de vidriero** putty knife; **cuchillo puñal** bowie knife
cuchipanda *f* (coll.) merry feast
cuchitril *m* hole, corner, den, hut
cuchuchear *vn* to whisper; (coll.) to gossip
cuchufleta *f* (coll.) joke, joking, fun
cuchufletear *vn* (coll.) to joke, make fun
cuchufletero -ra *adj* (coll.) joking, funmaking; *mf* (coll.) joker, funmaker
cuchumbo *m* (Am.) dicebox; (Am.) dice (*game*)
cudú *m* (*pl:* **-dúes**) (zool.) kudu
cuelga *f* bunch of fruit hung up for keeping; (coll.) birthday present
cuelgacapas *m* (*pl:* **-pas**) cloak hanger
cuelmo *m* candlewood
cuellicorto -ta *adj* short-necked
cuellierguido -da *adj* stiff, haughty
cuellilargo -ga *adj* long-necked
cuello *m* neck; collar; shirt collar; **levantar el cuello** (coll.) to be on one's feet again (*after poverty or misfortune*); **cuello blando** soft collar; **cuello de camisa** shirtband, neckband; **cuello de cisne** gooseneck; **cuello de pajarita** or **cuello doblado** wing collar; piccadilly; **cuello duro** stiff collar; **cuello postizo** detachable collar
cuenca *f* wooden bowl; socket (*of eye*); valley; basin, river basin, watershed; **cuenca de captación** catchment area or basin; **cuenca de polvo** dust bowl
cuencano -na *adj* (pertaining to) Cuenca; *mf* native or inhabitant of Cuenca, Ecuador
cuenco *m* earthen bowl; hollow
cuenda *f* end or tie of a skein
cuenta *f* count, calculation; account; bill; bead (*of rosary*); check (*in a restaurant*); **abonar en cuenta a** to credit to the account of; **a cuenta** or **a buena cuenta** on account; **adeudar en cuenta a** to charge with, to charge to the account of; **a fin de cuentas** after all, in the last analysis; **ajustar cuentas con** (coll.) to settle accounts with; **caer en la cuenta** (coll.) to see, get the point; to realize; **cargar en cuenta a** to charge with, charge to the account of; **correr por cuenta de** to be under, be under the administration of; **dar buena cuenta de sí** to give a good account of oneself; **dar cuenta de** to use up, destroy; **darle cuenta a uno de una cosa** to give an account of something to someone; **darse cuenta de** (coll.) to realize, become aware of; **de cuenta** of importance; **de cuenta y riesgo de** for the account and risk of; **echar la cuenta sin la huéspeda** (coll.) to reckon without one's host; **en cuenta con** in account with; **en resumidas cuentas** to sum up, in short; **hacer cuenta de** to count on; to esteem; **hacer cuenta que** (coll.) to suppose that, to assume that; **llevar cuentas** to keep accounts; **más de la cuenta** too long; too much; **no tener cuenta con** to have nothing to do with; **perder la cuenta de** to lose account of; **por la cuenta** apparently; **por mi cuenta** to my way of thinking; **tener en cuenta** to take into account, bear in mind; **tener cuenta** to be worth while; **tomar en cuenta** to take into account, give credit for; **tomar por su cuenta** to take upon oneself, assume responsibility for; **vamos a cuentas** (coll.) let's settle this; **cuenta corriente** current account; charge account; checking account; **cuenta de gastos** expense account; **cuenta de la vieja** (coll.) counting on one's fingers; **cuenta en participación** joint account; **cuentas a cobrar** accounts receivable; **cuentas del gran capitán** account overdrawn; **cuentas galanas** (coll.) illusions, idle dreams; **cuentas por pagar** accounts payable; *interj* careful!, look out!
cuentacorrentista *mf* depositor, person with a checking account
cuentadante *mf* trustee
cuentagotas *m* (*pl:* **-tas**) dropper, medicine dropper
cuentahilos *m* (*pl:* **-los**) cloth prover, yarn tester; (coll.) pedant, hairsplitter
cuentakilómetros *m* (*pl:* **-tros**) (aut.) speedometer, odometer
cuentamilla *f* (naut.) log (*chip and line*); speedometer, odometer
cuentapasos *m* (*pl:* **-sos**) pedometer, odometer
cuentero -ra *adj* (coll.) gossipy; *mf* (coll.) gossip
cuentezuela *f* small account
cuentista *adj* (coll.) gossipy; *mf* (coll.) gossip; storyteller; story writer, short-story writer
cuento *m* story, tale; short story; prop, support; tip, ferrule; count; (coll.) evil story, gossip; (coll.) trouble, disagreement; (archaic) million; **contar cuentos** to tell tales; **degollar el cuento a** (coll.) to cut into the story of; **dejarse de cuentos** (coll.) to come to the point; **despachurrar** or **destripar el cuento a** (coll.) to butt into and finish the

story of; (coll.) to thwart the plans of; **ése es el cuento** (coll.) that's the gist of the matter; **estar en el cuento** to be well-informed; **hablar en el cuento** to speak to the point; **¡puro cuento!** pure fiction!; **quitarse de cuentos** (coll.) to come to the point; **sin cuento** countless; **traer a cuento** to bring up (*a subject*); **venir a cuento** (coll.) to be opportune; **cuento de hadas** fairy tale; **cuento del tío** or **del tocomocho** (Am.) gyp, swindle; **cuento de nunca acabar** (coll.) endless story, endless affair; **cuento de penas** (coll.) hard-luck story; **cuento de viejas** (coll.) wild story, nonsense; old wives' tale; **cuento largo** (fig.) long story

cuentón -tona *adj* (coll.) gossipy; *mf* (coll.) gossip

cuera *f* (archaic) leather jacket

cuercíneo -a *adj* (bot.) quercine

cuercitrón *m* (bot.) black oak, quercitron

cuerda *f* see **cuerdo**

cuerdezuela *f* var. of **cordezuela**

cuerdo -da *adj* sane; wise, prudent; *f* cord, rope, string; watch spring; (act or effect of) winding a watch or clock; fishing line; string of galley slaves (*tied together*); hanging (*execution by hanging*); (anat.) cord, tendon; (aer., anat., eng. & geom.) chord; (mus.) string; (mus.) voice (*bass, tenor, contralto, soprano*); (path.) stricture (*of urethra*); **acabarse la cuerda** to run down, e.g., **se acabó la cuerda** the watch ran down; **aflojar la cuerda** to ease up; **apretar la cuerda** to tighten up, become more severe; **bajo cuerda** secretly; underhandedly; **dar cuerda a** to wind (*a watch or clock*); to give free rein to, to give rope to; **por debajo de cuerda** secretly; underhandedly; **sin cuerda** unwound, rundown; **cuerda de piano** piano wire; **cuerda de presos** chain gang; **cuerda de suspensión** shroud, shroud line (*of parachute*); **cuerda de tripa** (mus.) catgut; **cuerda de volatinero** acrobat's rope; **cuerda espinal** (anat.) spinal cord; **cuerda floja** slack rope; **cuerda freno** or **cuerda guía** (aer.) dragrope; **cuerdas vocales** (anat.) vocal cords; **cuerda tesa** tightrope

cuerezuelo *m* var. of **corezuelo**

cuerna *f* vessel made of a horn; trumpet made of a horn, huntinghorn; antler

cuernecillo *m* (bot.) bird's-foot trefoil, babies'-slippers

cuerno *m* horn (*curved and extended growth; material*); (anat.) cornu; (ent.) horn (*antenna*); (fig.) horn (*of moon*); (mil.) wing; (mus. & naut.) horn; (vet.) callosity; **en los cuernos del toro** (coll.) in great danger; **levantar hasta los cuernos de la luna** (coll.) to praise to the skies; **saber a cuerno quemado** (coll.) to be unpleasant, be distasteful; **cuerno de Amón** (anat. & pal.) cornu ammonis; **cuerno de caza** huntinghorn; **cuerno de ciervo** hartshorn; (pharm.) hartshorn; **cuerno de la abundancia** horn of plenty; **Cuerno de Oro** Golden Horn; **cuerno de yunque** horn of an anvil; **cuerno inglés** (mus.) English horn; *interj* upon my word!

cuero *m* pelt, rawhide; leather; wine bag, wineskin; (coll.) toper; (Am.) whip; **en cueros** or **en cueros vivos** stark naked; **cuero cabelludo** scalp; **cuero de suela** sole leather; **cuero en verde** rawhide

cuerpear *vn* (Am.) to duck, to dodge

cuerpecillo *m* small body; corselet

cuerpo *m* body; substance; bulk; volume (*book*); trunk; waist; build (*of a person*); corpus (*of writings, laws, etc.*); corps, staff; corpse; (mil.) corps; (print.) point; (racing) length; **a cuerpo descubierto** unprotected; manifestly; **dar con el cuerpo en tierra** (coll.) to fall flat on the ground; **de cuerpo entero** full-length (*picture*); **de medio cuerpo** half-length (*picture*); **descubrir el cuerpo** to drop one's guard; to stick one's neck out; **en cuerpo** or **en cuerpo de camisa** in shirt sleeves; **estar de cuerpo presente** to be on view, to lie in state; to be present in person; **falsear el cuerpo** to dodge, to duck; **hacer del cuerpo** (coll.) to have a movement of the bowels; **hurtar el cuerpo** to dodge, to duck; **sacar el cuerpo** (Am.) to dodge, to duck; **tomar cuerpo** to grow (*said, e.g., of a rumor*); **cuerpo a cuerpo** hand to hand; **cuerpo astral** (theosophy) astral body; **cuerpo calloso** (anat.) corpus callosum; **cuerpo celeste** heavenly body; **cuerpo compuesto** (chem.) compound; **cuerpo de administración militar** (mil.) quartermaster corps; **cuerpo de aviación** air corps; **cuerpo de baile** corps de ballet; **cuerpo de bomberos** fire brigade, fire company; **cuerpo de ejército** (mil.) army corps; **cuerpo de guardia** (mil.) guard; (mil.) post of the guard; **cuerpo de inclusión** (path.) inclusion body; **cuerpo del delito** (law) corpus delicti; **cuerpo de redacción** editorial staff; **cuerpo de sanidad** sanitary corps; **cuerpo diplomático** diplomatic corps; **cuerpo extraño** foreign matter (*in an organism*); **cuerpo lúteo** (embryol.) corpus luteum; **cuerpo simple** (chem.) simple substance, element; **cuerpo volante** (mil.) flying column

cuerudo -da *adj* (Am.) slow, sluggish; (Am.) heavy-skinned; (Am.) thick-skinned, long-suffering

cuerva *f* female rook

cuervo *m* (orn.) raven; (*cap.*) *m* (astr.) Raven; **cuervo marino** (orn.) cormorant; **cuervo merendero** (orn.) rook

cuesco *m* stone (*of fruit*); millstone (*of olive-oil mill*); (min.) dross, scoria; (coll.) noisy windiness; **cuesco de lobo** (bot.) puffball; **cuesco grande de lobo** (bot.) giant puffball

cuesta *f* hill, slope; charity solicitation, charity drive; **a cuestas** on one's back or shoulders; **hacérsele a uno cuesta arriba** to be repugnant to a person; **hacérsele a uno cuesta arriba** + *inf* to find it hard to + *inf;* **ir cuesta abajo** to go downhill, be on the decline; **cuesta abajo** downhill; **cuesta arriba** uphill

cuestación *f* charity solicitation, charity drive

cuestezuela *f* little hill or slope

cuestión *f* question; affair, matter; dispute, quarrel; **andar en cuestiones** to wrangle; **en cuestión de** in a matter of; **cuestión batallona** controversial question, moot question; **cuestión candente** burning question; **cuestión de tormento** torture; **cuestión palpitante** burning question

cuestionable *adj* questionable

cuestionar *va* to question, controvert, dispute

cuestionario *m* questionnaire

cuesto *m* hill

cuestor *m* quaestor; solicitor for charity

cuestuario -ria or **cuestuoso -sa** *adj* lucrative, profitable

cuestura *f* quaestorship

cuetear *vr* (Am.) to go off, to blow up; (Am.) to get drunk; (Am.) to croak, to kick the bucket

cueto *m* fortified eminence; peak, rocky peak

cueva *f* cave; cellar; den (*of thieves or wild animals*)

cuévano *m* hamper, pannier (*especially for grapes*)

cueza *f* or **cuezo** *m* mortar trough

cufifo -fa *adj* (Am.) tipsy, fuddled

cugujada *f* (orn.) crested lark

cugulla *f* cowl

cuicacoche *m* (orn.) long-billed thrasher

cuico -ca *adj* (Am.) outside, foreign, strange; *m* (Am.) cop

cuida *f* girl who takes care of a younger girl (*in school*)

cuidado *m* care; concern; worry; **correr al cuidado de** to be the concern of, to be the lookout of; **de cuidado** dangerously; **estar con cuidado** to be worried, to be afraid; **estar de cuidado** (coll.) to be dangerously ill; **pierda Vd. cuidado** don't worry, forget it; **salir de cuidado** to be delivered; **tener cuidado** to be careful; *interj* look out!, beware! **¡cuidado con . . . !** look out for . . . !, beware of . . . !; **¡cuidado me llamo!** (coll.) look out for me!, you'd better behave!

cuidadora *f* (Am.) chaperon, nurse, caretaker

cuidadoso -sa *adj* careful, watchful, anxious, concerned

cuidar *va* to care for, watch over, take care of, take good care of; *vn* **cuidar de** to take care of; **cuidar de** + *inf* to care to + *inf; vr* to take care of oneself (*i.e., one's health, comforts, etc.*); **cuidarse de** to care about (*e.g., what people say*); **cuidarse de** + *inf* to be careful to + *inf;* to be careful about + *ger*
cuido *m* care (*e.g., of the house, the garden*)
cuino *m* (Am.) short-legged pig
cuita *f* trouble, worry, sorrow
cuitado -da *adj* troubled, worried; timid, shy
cuitamiento *m* timidity, shyness
cuja *f* bedstead; lance bucket
cují *m* (bot.) huisache
cujón *m* var. of **cogujón**
culantrillo *m* (bot.) maidenhair; **culantrillo bastardo** or **menor** (bot.) maidenhair spleenwort; **culantrillo de pozo** (bot.) maidenhair, Venus's-hair
culantro *m* (bot.) coriander
culata *f* haunch, buttock; butt (*of gun*); breech (*of cannon*); (elec.) keeper, yoke (*of magnet*); (mach.) head (*of cylinder*)
culatada *f* kick, recoil (*of firearm*)
culatazo *m* kick, recoil (*of firearm*); blow with the butt of a gun
culcusido *m* rough darning, rough patch
culebra *f* (zool.) snake; coil (*of still*); (coll.) sudden disturbance; (coll.) joke, trick; **saber más que las culebras** (coll.) to be foxy; **culebra de anteojos** (zool.) cobra; **culebra de cascabel** (zool.) rattlesnake; **culebra de herradura** (zool.) horseshoe snake
culebrazo *m* joke, trick
culebrear *vn* to wiggle, to wriggle, to wriggle along; to wind, to meander; to zigzag
culebreo *m* wiggling, wriggling; winding, zigzagging
culebrilla *f* (path.) tetter; rocking staff (*of loom*); crack (*in barrel of gun*); (bot.) green dragon
culebrino -na *adj* snaky, snake-like; *f* (mil.) culverin
culebrón *m* large snake; (coll.) crafty fellow; (coll.) evil woman
culeco -ca *adj* (Am.) home-loving
culén *m* (bot.) basil
culero -ra *adj* lazy; *m* diaper; *f* dirt spot in child's underpants; patch on seat of pants or drawers
culí *m* (*pl:* **-líes**) coolie
culiblanco *m* (orn.) wheatear, stonechat
culinario -ria *adj* culinary
culinegro -gra *adj* (coll.) black-rumped
culipandear *vr* (Am.) to shrink, to draw back in fear
culminación *f* culmination; height; (astr.) culmination
culminante *adj* culminant, predominant, top
culminar *va* to finish; to round out; *vn* to culminate; (astr.) to culminate; **culminar con** to end with, to wind up with
culo *m* seat, behind; anus; buttocks (*of animal*); bottom (*e.g., of a jar*); **volver el culo** (coll.) to run away; **culo de mal asiento** (coll.) restless person, fidgety person; **culo de vaso** (coll.) imitation stone
culombio *m* (elec.) coulomb
culón -lona *adj* big-rumped; *m* (coll.) retired soldier
culote *m* base (*of a projectile*); base (*of vacuum tube or incandescent lamp*)
culpa *f* blame, guilt, fault; **echar la culpa a uno de una cosa** to put the blame on someone for something; **tener la culpa** to be wrong, to be to blame; **tener la culpa de** to be to blame for; **Vd. tiene la culpa** it's your fault
culpabilidad *f* culpability, guiltiness
culpabilísimo -ma *adj super* very or most culpable or guilty
culpable *adj* culpable, blamable, guilty; *mf* culprit
culpación *f* inculpation, blame
culpado -da *adj* guilty; *mf* culprit
culpar *va* to blame, censure, accuse; *vr* to take the blame
cultalatiniparla *f* (hum.) euphuistic speech, macaronic speech
cultedad *f* (hum.) affectation, fustian
culteranismo *m* euphuism, cultism
culterano -na *adj* euphuistic, Gongoristic; *mf* euphuist, cultist
cultero -ra *adj* (hum.) high-flown
cultiparlar *vn* to speak in a euphuistic manner
cultiparlista *adj* euphuistic in speech; *mf* euphuist in speech
cultipicaño -ña *adj* mock-euphuistic, burlesquely euphuistic
cultismo *m* cultism (*Gongorism*); learned word
cultivable *adj* cultivable
cultivación *f* cultivation, tilling
cultivador -dora *adj* cultivating, farming; *mf* cultivator, farmer; *f* cultivator (*implement*)
cultivar *va* to cultivate; (bact.) to culture
cultivo *m* cultivation; farming; (bact.) culture; **cultivo de secano** dry farming; **cultivo de tejidos** (bact.) tissue culture
culto -ta *adj* cultivated, cultured; euphuistic; (philol.) learned; *m* worship; cult; cultus; **culto a la personalidad** personality cult
cultor -tora *adj* worshipful; worshiping; *mf* worshiper
cultura *f* culture; cultivation; **cultura física** physical culture; **cultura taurina** training as a bullfighter
cultural *adj* cultural
culturar *va* to cultivate, to till
cumarú *m* (bot.) coumarou
Cumas *f* Cumae (*ancient city of Italy*)
cumbre *f* summit; (fig.) acme, pinnacle; (naut.) ridgepole; *adj* top, greatest, crowning
cumbrera *f* summit; ridgepole, ridgepiece; lintel, doorhead
cúmel *m* kümmel
cumiche *m* (Am.) baby (*youngest member of a family*)
cumínico -ca *adj* (chem.) cumic
cuminol *m* (chem.) cuminole, cumaldehyde
cumís *m* kumiss
cúmplase *m* approval; (Am.) decree
cumpleaños *m* (*pl:* **-ños**) birthday
cumplefaltas *m* (*pl:* **-tas**) substitute, replacement (*person*)
cumplidamente *adv* fully, completely
cumplidero -ra *adj* expiring (*by a certain date*); necessary
cumplido -da *adj* full, complete; full (*said of a garment*); courteous, correct; *m* attention, courtesy, correctness; compliment; present; **deshacerse en cumplidos** to be overobsequious
cumplidor -dora *adj* reliable, trustworthy
cumplimentar *va* to compliment, congratulate; to pay a complimentary visit to; to execute (*an order*); to fill out (*a form, a questionnaire*)
cumplimentero -ra *adj* (coll.) effusive, full of compliments
cumplimiento *m* fulfillment; perfection; compliment; courtesy, correctness; formality; **de** or **por cumplimiento** as a matter of pure formality
cumplir *va* to execute, perform, fulfill; to keep (*a promise*); **cumplir años** to have a birthday; **cumplir . . . años** to be . . . years old, to reach the age of . . .; **cumplir una condena** to serve a term; **cumplir a una persona** + *inf* to behoove someone to + *inf*, to be necessary or important for someone to + *inf*; *vn* to fall due; to expire; to finish one's military service; to keep one's promise, to fulfill one's obligation; **por cumplir** as a mere formality; **cumpla yo, y tiren ellos** do right and fear no man; **cumplir con** to fulfill (*an obligation*); to fulfill one's obligation to; **cumplir por** to act on behalf of; to pay the respects of, e.g., **cumpla Vd. por mí** pay my respects; *vr* to come true, be fulfilled; to fall due; **cúmplase** approved
cumquibus *m* (coll.) boodle, wherewithal
cumucho *m* (Am.) crowd, heap
cumular *va* to cumulate
cumulativo -va *adj* cumulative
cúmulo *m* heap, cumulus; lot, great many; (meteor.) cumulus, thunderhead
cumulocirro *m* (meteor.) cumulo-cirrus
cumuloestrato *m* (meteor.) cumulo-stratus
cúmulonimbo *m* (meteor.) cumulo-nimbus

cuna *f* cradle; foundling home or asylum; (naut. & constr.) cradle; (fig.) cradle (*place of birth or origin*); family, lineage, birth; **cunas** *fpl* cat's cradle
cunar *va* to cradle, rock in a cradle
cundido *m* provision of olive oil, vinegar, and salt given to shepherds; olive oil, cheese, and honey given to children to make them eat bread
cundir *vn* to spread; to swell, puff up; to increase, multiply
cuneado -da *adj* (bot.) cuneate
cunear *va* to cradle, rock in a cradle; *vr* (coll.) to rock, to swing, to sway
cuneco -ca *mf* (Am.) baby (*youngest member of a family*)
cuneiforme *adj* cuneiform; (anat.) cuneiform; *m* (anat.) cuneiform; (bot.) cuneate
cuneo *m* rocking, swinging; (naut.) rolling
cúneo *m* (hist.) cuneus; (mil.) wedge
cunero -ra *adj* (taur.) unknown, unpedigreed (*bull*); (pol.) outside (*candidate*); *mf* foundling; *f* cradle rocker (*in royal palace*)
cuneta *f* ditch, gutter; catch drain
cunicultor -tora *adj* rabbit-raising; *mf* rabbit raiser or breeder
cunicultura *f* rabbit raising, rabbit breeding
cuña *f* wedge; paving stone in the form of truncated pyramid; (anat.) cuneiform; (print.) quoin; (coll.) backing, support; (coll.) backer; **ser buena cuña** (coll.) to push one's way in, to take up a lot of room
cuñada *f* sister-in-law
cuñadía *f* affinity, relationship by marriage
cuñado *m* brother-in-law
cuñete *m* keg; firkin
cuño *m* die for stamping coins, medals, etc.; stamp (*made by die*); (mil.) wedge; (fig.) mark, stamp
cuociente *m* (archaic) var. of **cociente**
cuodlibético -ca *adj* quodlibetic or quodlibetical
cuodlibeto *m* quodlibet; (coll.) witticism, joke
cuota *f* quota; share; rate; fare; tuition, tuition fee; **cuota de inmigración** immigration quota
cuotidiano -na *adj* var. of **cotidiano**
cupe *1st sg pret ind of* **caber**
cupé *m* coupé (*automobile and carriage*); **cupé comercial** business coupé; **cupé deportivo** sport coupé
cupido *m* gallant lover; cupid (*winged baby, symbol of love*); (*cap.*) *m* (myth.) Cupid
cupla *f* coupling; (mech.) couple; **cupla motora** (mech.) torque
cuplé *m* popular song
cupletista *f* popular singer (*woman*)
cupo *m* quota, share; *3d sg pret ind of* **caber**
cupón *m* coupon
cupón-respuesta *m* reply coupon
cupresáceo -a or **cupresíneo -a** *adj* (bot.) cupressineous
cupresino -na *adj* (poet.) cypress
cúprico -ca *adj* coppery; (chem.) cupric
cuprífero -ra *adj* cupriferous
cuprita *f* (mineral.) cuprite
cuproníquel *m* cupronickel
cuproso -sa *adj* (chem.) cuprous
cúpula *f* (arch., anat. & nav.) cupola; (arch.) dome; (bot. & zool.) cupule; **cúpula de arena** (rail.) sand dome; **cúpula de toma de vapor** (rail.) steam dome
cupulífero -ra *adj* (bot.) cupuliferous
cupulino *m* (arch.) cupola (*lantern over dome*)
cuquería *f* craftiness, slyness; (coll.) niceness, cuteness
cuquillo *m* (orn.) cuckoo
cura *m* curate; parish priest; (coll.) priest; **este cura** (coll.) I; *f* cure; care, treatment (*of a wound*); **no tener cura** (coll.) to be hopeless, be incorrigible; **ponerse en cura** to undergo treatment; **primera cura** first aid; **tener cura** to be curable; **cura de aguas** water cure; **cura de almas** care of souls; **cura de reposo** rest cure; **cura de urgencia** first aid
curabilidad *f* curability
curable *adj* curable
curaca *m* (Am.) boss, chief
curación *f* treatment; healing; cure, curing
curadillo *m* (ichth.) codfish
curado -da *adj* dry, hardened
curador -dora *mf* caretaker, overseer; healer; curer; (law) guardian
curaduría *f* (law) guardianship
cúralotodo *m* (*pl:* **-do**) var. of **sánalotodo**
curalle *m* (falc.) casting
curandería *f* or **curanderismo** *m* quackery
curandero -ra *mf* quack, healer
curar *va* to treat (*a sick person*); to heal; to cure (*a disease, an evil, a sick person; meat, fish, hides, etc.*); to season (*wood*); to see (*someone*) through an illness; to dress (*a wound*); *vn* to cure; to recover; **curar de** to recover from; to take care of; to care about, to mind, to pay attention to; *vr* to take treatment; to cure oneself; to cure; to recover; to season; (Am.) to get drunk; **curarse de** to recover from, to get over; **curarse en salud** to be forewarned
curare *m* curare
curarizar **§76** *va* to curarize
curasao *m* curaçao (*liqueur*)
curatela *f* var. of **curaduría**
curativo -va *adj & f* curative
curato *m* curacy; parish
curazao *m* curaçao (*liqueur*); (*cap.*) *f* Curaçao
curbaril *m* (bot.) courbaril
cúrcuma *f* turmeric, curcuma root; curcumin
curcuncho -cha *adj* (Am.) stooped, hunchbacked; (Am.) annoyed, upset
curcusilla *f* var. of **rabadilla**
curda *f* see **curdo**
Curdistán, el Kurdistan
curdo -da *adj* Kurdish; *mf* Kurd; *m* Kurdish (*language*); *f* (coll.) drunkenness
cureña *f* gun carriage; gunstock in the rough; stay of crossbow; **a cureña rasa** (fort.) without a parapet, without breastwork; (coll.) without shelter
cureñaje *m* gun carriages
curesca *f* waste left after combing cloth
cureta *f* (surg.) curette
curetaje *m* (surg.) curettage
curia *f* (hist.) curia; care, carefulness; (law) bar; **Curia romana** Roman Curia
curial *adj* curial; *m* attorney; court clerk
curialesco -ca *adj* legalistic, hairsplitting (*style, etc.*)
curiana *f* (ent.) cockroach
curie *m* (phys.) curie
curiel *m* (Am.) guinea pig
curieterapia *f* curietherapy
Curiles *fpl* Kurile Islands
curio *m* (chem.) curium
curiosear *va* (coll.) to pry into; *vn* (coll.) to snoop, to pry around; (coll.) to browse around
curioseo *m* (coll.) snooping, prying; (coll.) browsing
curiosidad *f* curiosity; curio; neatness, cleanness; care, diligence
curioso -sa *adj* curious; odd, rare, quaint; neat, clean, tidy; careful, diligent; (Am.) cute; *mf* busybody
Curlandia *f* Courland
curricán *m* (fishing) spinning tackle; (Am.) plug
currinche *m* cub reporter; (coll.) hit playwright
curro -rra *adj* (coll.) sporty, flashy
curruca *f* (orn.) whitethroat; **curruca de cabeza negra** (orn.) blackcap; **curruca de los pantanos** (orn.) marsh warbler
currutaco -ca *adj* (coll.) dudish, sporty; *m* (coll.) dude, sport
cursado -da *adj* skilled, versed; taken (*as a course in school*)
cursante *adj* attending; *mf* student
cursar *va* to haunt, to frequent; to devote oneself to; to take, to attend; to study; to facilitate; to send, to circulate; to forward
cursería *f* cheapness, flashiness, vulgarity; (coll.) group of cheap flashy people
cursi *adj* (coll.) cheap, vulgar, flashy
cursilería *f* var. of **cursería**
cursillista *mf* student taking a short course
cursillo *m* short course (*in school*); short series of lectures
cursivo -va *adj* cursive; *f* cursive; italics
curso *m* course; price, quotation, current rate;

circulation, currency; program, series; textbook; **cursos** *mpl* loose bowels; **dar curso a** to forward; to give course to (*e.g., tears*); **en curso de impresión** in press; **curso académico** academic year; **curso legal** legal tender
cursor *m* (elec.) sliding contact; (mach.) slide; indicator (*of slide rule*); **cursor de procesiones** marshal
curtación *f* (astr.) curtation
curtido *m* tanning; tanning bark; **curtidos** *mpl* tanned leather; (Am.) pickles
curtidor *m* tanner
curtidura *f* tanning
curtiduría *f* tannery
curtiembre *f* (Am.) tannery
curtiente *adj* tanning; *m* tanning material
curtimiento *m* tanning; tan
curtir *va* to tan (*hides*); to tan, to sunburn; to harden, to inure; to season or harden by exposure to the weather; **estar curtido en** to be skilled or expert in; *vr* to become tanned, become sunburned; to become hardened, become inured; to become weather-beaten
curubu *m* (bot.) passionflower (*of Colombia*)
curuca *f* (orn.) barn owl, screech owl
curucú *m* (orn.) quetzal; (Am.) snake-bite poisoning
curucucú *m* (Am.) snake-bite poisoning
curuguá *m* (bot.) cassabanana
curuja *f* var. of **curuca**
curul *adj* curule
curupay *m* (bot.) curupay
cururú *m* (*pl:* **-rúes**) (zool.) Surinam toad
curva *f* see **curvo**
curvadura *f* (arch.) curvature of an arch or vault; (med.) painful exhaustion
curvatón *m* slight curve; (naut.) gusset, gusset stay
curvatubos *m* (*pl:* **-bos**) pipe bender
curvatura or **curvidad** *f* curvature
curvilíneo -a *adj* curvilinear; (coll.) curvaceous (*woman*)
curvímetro *m* curvometer
curvo -va *adj* curve, curved, bent; *f* curve, bend; (rail.) crossover; **curva de frecuencias** (statistics) frequency curve; **curva de nivel** contour line; **curva isobárica** (meteor.) isobar
cusca *f* (Am.) jag, drunk; (Am.) slattern, slut
cuscurro *m* end crust, crouton
cuscús *m* var. of **alcuzcuz**
cúscuta *f* (bot.) dodder
cusir *va* (coll.) var. of **corcusir**
cusita *adj* & *mf* (Bib.) Cushite
cusma *f* var. of **cuzma**
cúspide *f* peak (*of a mountain*); cusp, tip, apex; (anat.) cusp (*of a tooth*); (anat.) cuspid (*tooth*); (geom.) vertex (*of cone or pyramid*); (fig.) apex, top, extreme
cuspídeo -a *adj* cuspidate
custodia *f* custody, care; guard (*in charge of a prisoner*); shrine; (eccl.) monstrance; **custodia preventiva** protective custody
custodiar *va* to guard, watch over
custodio *m* guard, custodian
cusumbe *m* or **cusumbo** *m* var. of **coatí**
cususa *f* (Am.) rum
cutáneo -a *adj* cutaneous
cúter *m* (naut.) cutter (*sailboat with one mast*)
cutí *m* (*pl:* **-tíes**) bedtick, ticking
cuticolor *adj* cuticolor
cutícula *f* (anat. & bot.) cuticle
cuticular *adj* cuticular
cutina *f* (biochem.) cutin
cutinización *f* (bot.) cutinization
cutio *m* work, labor
cutir *va* to knock, to strike
cutirreacción *f* (med. & vet.) cutireaction
cutis *m* & *f* skin (*of human body, especially the face*); **cutis anserina** goose flesh
cutitis *f* (path.) dermatitis
cutización *f* (physiol.) cutization
cutral *m* old worn-out ox; *f* old cow that no longer bears
cutre *adj* miserly, stingy; *mf* miser, skinflint
cuy *m* (Am.) cavy
cuyo -ya *adj rel* whose; *m* (coll.) beau, lover
cuz *interj* here, here! (*to call a dog*)
cuzcuz *m* var. of **alcuzcuz**
cuzo *m* (prov.) doggie
cuzma *f* (Am.) sleeveless shirt or tunic of palm, cork, or wool fiber (*worn by South American Indians*)
cuzqueño -ña *adj* (pertaining to) Cuzco; *mf* native or inhabitant of Cuzco
CV abr. of **caballo de vapor**
c/v or **c/vta.** abr. of **cuenta de venta**
czar *m* var. of **zar**
czarevitz *m* var. of **zarevitz**
czariano -na *adj* var. of **zariano**
czarina *f* var. of **zarina**

Ch

Ch, ch *f* fourth letter of the Spanish alphabet
cha *m* (*pl:* **chaes**) (Am.) tea
chabacanada or **chabacanería** *f* crudeness, vulgarity
chabacano -na *adj* awkward, clumsy; crude, cheap; *m* (Am.) apricot
chabola *f* hut, shack, shanty
chacal *m* (zool.) jackal
chacanear *va* (Am.) to spur, to goad
chacarero -ra *mf* (Am.) farm laborer, field worker
chacarrachaca *f* (coll.) racket, wrangling, row, brawl
chacate *m* (bot.) chacate
chacina *f* dried beef; pork seasoned for sausages
chacó *m* (*pl:* **-cós**) shako
chacolí *m* (*pl:* **-líes**) chacolí (*sour wine of Vizcaya, Spain*)
chacolotear *vn* to clatter (*said of loose horseshoe*)
chacoloteo *m* clattering (*of loose horseshoe*)
chacona *f* (mus.) chaconne
chaconada *f* jaconet (*thin cotton fabric*)
chaconero -ra *mf* chaconne writer or dancer
chacota *f* fun, noisy laughter, racket; **echar a chacota** (coll.) to sneer at; **hacer chacota de** (coll.) to make fun of
chacotear *vn* to laugh and make a lot of noise
chacoteo *m* noisy laughter
chacotero -ra *adj* loud-laughing; *mf* loud or noisy laugher, noisemaker
chacra *f* (Am.) small farm; (Am.) field marked off for cultivation
chacuaco -ca *adj* (Am.) ugly, repugnant; (Am.) crude, boorish; *m* (Am.) silver-smelting furnace; (Am.) cigar butt
chacha *f* (coll.) lass; (coll.) nursemaid
chachalaca *f* (orn.) chachalaca; (Am.) chatterbox (*person*)
chachalaquero -ra *adj* (Am.) loquacious, talkative
cháchara *f* (coll.) chatter, idle talk; **cháchara**s *fpl* junk
chacharear *vn* (coll.) to chatter, to prate
chacharero -ra *adj* (coll.) chattering; *mf* (coll.) chatterbox
chacho *m* (coll.) boy, lad
chafaldete *m* (naut.) clew line
chafaldita *f* (coll.) jest, banter
chafalditero -ra *adj* (coll.) jesting, bantering
chafalmejas *mf* (*pl:* **-jas**) (coll.) dauber (*poor painter*)
chafalonía *f* old plate
chafallar *va* (coll.) to botch
chafallo *m* (coll.) botch, poor patch
chafallón -llona *adj* (coll.) botching; *mf* botcher
chafandín *m* pompous empty head
chafar *va* to flatten; to wrinkle, to rumple, to muss; (coll.) to cut short
chafariz *m* (*pl:* **-rices**) top of monumental fountain from which water spouts
chafarotazo *m* blow or stroke with a cutlass
chafarote *m* cutlass; (coll.) sword
chafarrinada *f* blot, stain, spot; daub (*poor painting*)
chafarrinar *va* to blot, stain, spot
chafarrinón *m* blot, stain, spot; **echar un chafarrinón a** (coll.) to be rude to; (coll.) to throw mud at
chaflán *m* chamfer; (arch.) cant
chaflanar *va* to chamfer
chagrén *m* or **chagrín** *m* shagreen
chah *m* shah
chaira *f* steel (*for sharpening knives*); shoemaker's blade
chajá *m* (*pl:* **-jaes**) (orn.) screamer, crested screamer
chal *m* shawl
chalado -da *adj* (coll.) addlebrained; (coll.) madly in love
chalán -lana *adj* horse-dealing; *mf* horse dealer; trader; (Am.) broncobuster, horsebreaker; *f* scow, flatboat, barge
chalanear *va* to drive (*deals*) shrewdly; (Am.) to break (*horses*); *vn* to dicker, to horse-trade
chalaneo *m* shrewd dealing, horse trading
chalanería *f* shrewdness in dealing, horse trading
chalanesco -ca *adj* horse-trading, sharp-dealing
chalar *vr* (dial.) to lose one's head; **chalarse por** (dial.) to become mad or crazy about
chalate *m* (Am.) skinny old nag
chalaza *f* (bot. & embryol.) chalaza
chaleco *m* vest, waistcoat; **chaleco salvavidas** life preserver
chalet *m* (*pl:* **chaletes**) chalet; villa
chalí *m* challie or challis
chalina *f* bow tie with long ends, scarf
chalón *m* shalloon
chalote *m* (bot.) shallot, scallion
chalupa *f* (naut.) shallop, small two-master; lifeboat; (Am.) corncake
chalupero *m* boatman, skipper; rower
chama *f* (slang) swapping, trading
chamaco -ca *mf* (Am.) urchin, youngster, kid
chamada *f* brushwood; (dial.) streak of bad luck
chamagoso -sa *adj* dirty, filthy; common, tawdry; (Am.) botched
chamal *m* (Am.) chiripá; (bot.) edible Dioön
chamán *m* shaman
chamar *va* (slang) to swap
chamara or **chamarasca** *f* brushwood; brush fire
chamarilear *va* var. of **chamar**
chamarilero -ra *mf* junk dealer, old-clothes dealer
chamarillero -ra *mf* junk dealer, old-clothes dealer; *m* gambler
chamarillón -llona *mf* poor player (*at cards*)
chamariz *m* (*pl:* **-rices**) (orn.) greenfinch
chamarón *m* (orn.) bottle tit, long-tailed titmouse
chamarra *f* sheepskin jacket
chamarreta *f* loose jacket
chamba *f* (coll.) fluke, scratch (*e.g., in billiards*)
chambelán *m* chamberlain; (Am.) atomizer, spray
chambergo -ga *adj* Schomberg (*regiment, uniform, etc., which existed in Madrid at time of Charles II*); *m* broad-brimmed soft hat; (orn.) reedbird; *f* narrow silk ribbon
chamberguilla *f* (dial.) narrow silk ribbon
chamberí *adj* (*pl:* **-ríes**) (Am.) showy, flashy
chamberinada *f* (Am.) ostentation, flashiness
chambilla *f* stone wall surmounted by iron grating
chambón -bona *adj* (coll.) clumsy, awkward (*in games*); unskillful; lucky; *mf* (coll.) foozler, bungler
chambonada *f* (coll.) clumsiness; (coll.) foozle; fluke, stroke of luck
chambonear *vn* to play awkwardly, to foozle
chamborote *adj* (Am.) long-nosed
chambra *f* house blouse or tunic, negligee
chambrana *f* trim (*around a door, window, etc.*); (Am.) shouting, uproar
chamburgo *m* (Am.) pool, stagnant water
chamburo *m* (bot.) papaw tree
chamicera *f* strip of burned woodland
chamico *m* (bot.) jimson weed, thorn apple; **dar chamico a** (Am.) to bewitch, seduce

chamiza *f* (bot.) chamiso; brush used as firewood
chamizo *m* half-burned tree; half-burned log or stick; chamiso-thatched hut; (coll.) hangout, joint
chamorra *f* see **chamorro**
chamorrar *va* (coll.) to shear (*the head*)
chamorro -rra *adj* (coll.) with head shorn, with hair cut; *f* (coll.) shorn head
champán *m* sampan; champagne (*wine*)
champaña *m* champagne (*wine*); **la Champaña** Champagne
champañizar §76 *va* to make sparkling, make effervescent, champagnize
champar *va* (coll.) to talk meanly to, to remind (*someone*) of a favor
champiñón *m* mushroom
champú *m* (*pl:* **-púes**) shampoo
champurrar *va* (coll.) to mix, mix in
chamuscado -da *adj* (coll.) touched, infected (*with a vice or passion*)
chamuscar §86 *va* to singe, to scorch; (Am.) to undersell
chamusco *m* singe, singeing
chamusquina *f* singe, singeing; (coll.) quarrel, row; **oler a chamusquina** (coll.) to look like a fight; (coll.) to be heresy
chanada *f* (coll.) trick, deceit
chanca *f* var. of **chancla**
chancar §86 *va* (Am.) to crush (*stones*)
chancear *vn & vr* to joke, to jest
chancero -ra *adj* joking, jesting, merry
chanciller *m* chancellor
chancillería *f* chancery (*court of equity*)
chancla *f* worn-out shoe, shoe worn down at the heel; slipper
chancleta *f* slipper; **en chancleta** in slippers, in shoes without heels; *mf* (coll.) good-for-nothing
chancletazo *m* blow with slipper
chancletear *vn* to go about in slippers, to go about clattering one's slippers
chancleteo *m* clatter of slippers
chanclo *m* clog (*shoe with wooden sole*); overshoe, rubber
chanco *m* stilt
chancro *m* (path.) chancre
chancroso -sa *adj* chancrous
cháncharras máncharras *fpl* (coll.) subterfuge; **andar en cháncharras máncharras** (coll.) to beat about the bush
chanchería *f* (Am.) pork butcher's shop
chancho -cha *adj* (Am.) dirty, piggish; *m* (Am.) pig
chanchullero -ra *adj* (coll.) crooked; *mf* (coll.) crooked person
chanchullo *m* (coll.) crookedness; **andar en chanchullos** (coll.) to be up to some crookedness
chanfaina *f* stew of chopped lungs
chanflón -flona *adj* misshapen, crude
changador *m* (Am.) public errand boy
changarro *m* (Am.) little shop
chango -ga *adj* (Am.) quick, skilful; (Am.) sporty; (Am.) dull, stupid; *mf* (Am.) house servant; (Am.) monkey
changote *m* (found.) bloom
changüí *m* (*pl:* **-güíes**) (coll.) trick, deception; (slang) idle talk; **dar changüí a** (coll.) to trick
chantaje *m* blackmail
chantajista *mf* blackmailer
chantar *va* to put on; to stick, push, or force on; (coll.) to tell (*someone something*) straight from the shoulder; *vr* to put on, to clap on (*e.g., one's hat*)
chantillón *m* pattern, templet
chanto *m* (prov.) flagstone
chantre *m* cantor, precentor
chantría *f* precentorship
chanza *f* joke, jest; **de chanza** jokingly, in fun
chanzoneta *f* chansonnette; (coll.) joke, jest
chanzonetero *m* chansonnier
chao *m* chow (*dog*)
chapa *f* sheet, plate; veneer; flush (*on cheek*); rouge; (coll.) judgment, good sense; (Am.) lock; **chapas** *fpl* (game of) tossing coins; **chapa de patente** or **chapa matrícula** (aut.) license plate
chapado -da *adj* lined or covered with sheets or sheeting (*of metal*); veneered; nice, fine; **chapado a la antigua** old-fashioned
chapalear *vn* to splash; to clatter (*said of loose horseshoe*)
chapaleo *m* splashing; clatter (*of loose horseshoe*)
chapaleta *f* (hyd.) clack valve
chapaleteo *m* splash, splashing (*of water on the shore*); patter (*of rain*)
chapapote *m* (Am.) tar; chapapote, Mexican asphalt
chapar *va* to cover or line with metal sheeting; to veneer; to let go, to smack down (*something disagreeable*); to plate (*with gold or silver*)
chaparra *f* (bot.) kermes oak; chaparral (*thicket*)
chaparrada *f* downpour
chaparral *m* chaparral
chaparrear *vn* to rain hard, to pour
chaparreras *fpl* (Am.) chaps (*cowboy trousers*)
chaparro *m* (bot.) chaparro; chaparral (*thicket*); short, chubby person
chaparrón *m* downpour; (Am.) shower (*e.g., of insults*)
chapatal *m* mudhole
chapeado -da *adj* lined or covered with sheets or sheeting (*of metal*); veneered; *m* veneer; plywood
chapear *va* to cover or line with metal sheeting; to veneer; *vn* to clatter (*said of a loose horseshoe*)
chapecar §86 *va* (Am.) to braid, to plait; (Am.) to string (*garlic, onions, etc.*)
chapeo *m* (coll.) hat
chapera *f* (mas.) board with wooden cleats (*for climbing*)
chapería *f* sheet metal; sheet-metal work
chaperón *m* (archaic) chaperon (*hood*)
chapeta *f* red spot on the cheek
chapetón -tona *adj* (Am.) awkward, green; *mf* (obs.) newly arrived and green Spanish soldier (*in Latin America*); (archaic) Spanish or European new arrival (*in Latin America*); *m* (Am.) silver disk (*on riding harness*)
chapetonada *f* (Am.) greenhornism (*of a foreigner*); (obs.) illness of Spanish or European new arrivals in Latin America (*from change of climate*)
chapín -pina *adj* (Am.) clubfooted; *m* chopine (*clog worn especially by women*); sandal, slipper, dance slipper; (bot.) lady's-slipper; (ichth.) trunkfish
chapinazo *m* blow with a clog
chápiro *m* (Am.) silver disk (*on riding harness*); **¡por vida del chápiro!**, **¡por vida del chápiro verde!** or **¡voto al chápiro!** (coll.) good grief!
chapista *mf* tinsmith; (aut.) body and fender repairman; **chapista carrocero** (aut.) body and fender repairman
chapistería *f* tinsmithing, sheet-metal work; body and fender repair shop
chapitel *m* (arch.) spire; (arch.) capital; (naut.) agate socket (*of needle*)
chapitón -tona *adj* (Am.) new (*in a job*); *mf* (Am.) novice; (Am.) newly arrived European in South America
chapitonada *f* (Am.) inexperience
chapó *m* (*pl:* **-pós**) four-hand pool or billiards; four-hand match
chapodar *va* to trim, to clear of branches
chapodo *m* branch trimmed from a tree
chapón *m* large blot (*of ink*)
chapona *f* house blouse or tunic
chapotear *va* to moisten, to sponge; *vn* to splash
chapoteo *m* sponging; splashing
chapucear *va* to botch, bungle
chapucería *f* botch, bungle, patchwork
chapucero -ra *adj* rough, crude; bungling, clumsy; cheating; *mf* bungler; amateur, dabster; *m* blacksmith; junk dealer
chapulín *m* (Am.) grasshopper
chapurrar *va* to jabber (*a language*); to jumble (*in conversation*); (coll.) to mix, to mix in
chapurrear *va* to jabber (*a language*); *vn* to jabber
chapurreo *m* jabbering

chapuz *m* (*pl:* **-puces**) duck, ducking (*sudden dip under water*); botch; bungling
chapuza *f* botch, bungle
chapuzar §76 *va, vn & vr* to duck
chapuzón *m* ducking (*sudden dip under water*)
chaqué *m* cutaway coat, morning coat
chaquehue *m* (Am.) corn grits
chaqueta *f* jacket
chaquete *m* backgammon
chaquetudo *m* (ent.) potato beetle
chaquira *f* (Am.) glass bead
charabán *m* char-à-banc
charada *f* charade
charadrio *m* var. of **alcaraván**
charamusca *f* (Am.) candy twist; **charamuscas** *fpl* (Am.) brushwood, firewood
charanga *f* (mus.) brass band
charango *m* (Am.) bandurria (*kind of lute*)
charanguero -ra *adj* rough, crude; bungling, clumsy; *mf* bungler; *m* (prov.) peddler; (prov.) small coast-trading boat
charca *f* pool
charcal *m* puddly spot
charco *m* puddle; **pasar el charco** (coll.) to cross the pond (*the ocean*)
charla *f* (coll.) chat, chatting; (coll.) talk, lecture; (coll.) chatter, prattle; (orn.) missel thrush; **charla de chimenea** fireside chat
charlador -dora *adj* (coll.) prattling, garrulous; (coll.) gossiping; *mf* (coll.) prattler, chatterbox; (coll.) gossip
charladuría *f* prattling, small talk; gossip
charlar *vn* (coll.) to chat; (coll.) to chatter, to prattle
charlatán -tana *adj* prattling, garrulous; gossiping; charlatan; *mf* prattler, chatterbox; gossip; charlatan
charlatanear *vn* (coll.) to chatter, to prattle; (coll.) to gossip
charlatanería *f* loquacity, garrulity
charlatanismo *m* loquacity, garrulity; charlatanism
charlotear *vn* (coll.) to chatter, to prattle; (coll.) to gossip
charloteo *m* (coll.) chatter, prattle; (coll.) gossip
charneca *f* (bot.) mastic tree
charnecal *m* growth of mastic trees
charnela *f* hinge; (mach.) knuckle; (zool.) hinge (*of bivalve shell*); **charnela de dirección** (aut.) steering knuckle
charneta *f* (coll.) var. of **charnela**
charol *m* varnish, polish; patent leather; (Am.) painted metal tray; **calzarse las de charol** (Am.) to hit the jack pot; **darse charol** (coll.) to brag, to blow one's own horn
charola *f* (Am.) painted metal tray; (Am.) large eye, ugly big eye
charolado -da *adj* shiny
charolar *va* to varnish, polish, enamel, japan
charolista *mf* varnisher, polisher, gilder
charpa *f* pistol belt; sling (*to support hurt arm*)
charquear *va* (Am.) to jerk (*beef*); (Am.) to slash, to cut to pieces; (Am.) to malign, vilify
charquetal *m* puddly spot
charqui *m* (Am.) jerked beef
charrada *f* boorishness; country dance; (coll.) overfancy work or adornment
charrán *m* rascal
charranada *f* piece of rascality
charranear *vn* to be a rascal
charranería *f* rascality
charrasca *f* (hum.) dangling or trailing sword; (coll.) folding knife
charrascal *m* var. of **carrascal**
charrasco *m* (hum.) dangling or trailing sword
charreada *f* (Am.) rodeo
charrería *f* overfancy work or adornment
charretera *f* epaulet; garter; buckle (*of garter*); (coll.) shoulder pad (*for carrying water*)
charro -rra *adj* coarse, ill-bred; of Salamanca; (coll.) showy, flashy, loud; (coll.) overfancy; **estar** or **ir bien charro** (coll.) to be flashily dressed; *mf* peasant, rustic; peasant of province of Salamanca; *m* (Am.) Mexican horseman in fancy riding costume
charrúa *f* (naut.) small tugboat
chartreuse *m* chartreuse
chasca *f* see **chasco**
chascar §86 *va* to click (*the tongue*); to crunch (*food*); to swallow; *vn* to crack (*to break with a sharp noise*)
chascarrillo *m* (coll.) snappy story
chascás *m* (mil.) schapska
chasco -ca *adj* (Am.) crinkly; crinkly-haired; *m* trick, joke; disappointment; **dar un chasco a** to play a trick on; **llevarse chasco** to be disappointed; *f* small branches cleaned from a tree
chascón -cona *adj* (Am.) disheveled; (Am.) bushy-haired
chasis *m* (*pl:* **-sis**) (aut. & rad.) chassis; (phot.) plateholder
chasponazo *m* scratch or dent made by a grazing bullet
chasquear *va* to crack (*e.g., a whip*); to play a trick on; to disappoint; to fail to keep (*a promise*); *vn* to crack (*to break with a sharp noise*); (Am.) to chatter (*said of teeth*); *vr* to come to naught; to become disappointed
chasqui *m* (Am.) Indian courier
chasquido *m* swish, crack of a whip; crack, cracking sound (*of something breaking*)
chata *f* see **chato**
chatarra *f* slag containing some iron; junk, scrap iron; **chatarra de acero** scrap steel
chatarraje *m* junk, scrap iron
chatarrería *f* junk yard
chatarrero -ra *mf* junk dealer, scrap-iron dealer
chatedad *f* (coll.) flatness
chato -ta *adj* flat; flat-nosed; blunt; (Am.) commonplace, humdrum; *m* (coll.) wine cup, wineglass; *f* scow, barge; bedpan; flatcar
chatón *m* large stone (*in its setting*)
chatre *adj* (Am.) all dressed up; *m* (Am.) short skirt
chau *interj* (Am.) so long!
chaucha *f* (Am.) small change, chicken feed; (Am.) bean; (Am.) early potato; (Am.) poverty; *adj* (Am.) poor, miserable
chauche *m* red-lead floor paint
chaul *m* blue Chinese silk
chauvinismo *m* chauvinism
chauvinista *adj* chauvinistic; *mf* chauvinist
chaval -vala *adj* (coll.) young; *m* (coll.) lad; *f* (coll.) lass
chavasca *f* var. of **chasca**
chaveta *f* (mach.) cotter, cotter pin, forelock; (mach.) key; **perder la chaveta (por)** (coll.) to go out of one's head (for)
chavetera *f* (mach.) keyway, key seat
chavo *m* (Am.) cent; (Am.) 350 sq. meters
chayote *m* (bot.) chayote (*plant and fruit*)
chayotera *f* (bot.) chayote (*plant*)
chaza *f* (sport) stopping the ball; (sport) mark where ball was stopped; **hacer chazas** to walk on the hind feet (*said of a horse*)
chazador *m* (sport) stop (*player*); (sport) marker
chazar §76 *va* (sport) to stop or interfere with (*the ball*); (sport) to mark (*the spot where ball was stopped*)
che *interj* (Am.) hey!, say!
checo -ca *adj & mf* Czech; *m* Czech (*language*); (*cap.*) *f* Checa (*Soviet secret police*)
checoeslovaco -ca *adj & mf* Czecho-Slovak or Czecho-Slovakian
Checoeslovaquia *f* Czecho-Slovakia
checoslovaco -ca *adj & mf* Czecho-Slovak or Czecho-Slovakian
Checoslovaquia *f* Czecho-Slovakia
chechén *m* (Am.) poison ivy
chécheres *mpl* (Am.) trinkets, junk
Chefú Chefoo
cheira *f* var. of **chaira**
chelín *m* shilling; schilling
chepa *f* (coll.) hunch, hump
cheque *m* check; **cheque certificado** certified check; **cheque de viajeros** traveler's check
Cherburgo *f* Cherbourg
cherna *f* or **cherno** *m* (ichth.) giant perch, dusky perch; (ichth.) grouper
cherva *f* (bot.) castor-oil plant
cheurón *m* (her.) chevron; (arch.) chevron molding
cheuronado -da *adj* (her.) chevrony

chía *f* (hist.) short mourning cloak; (hist.) cowl worn as a mark of nobility; (bot.) chia (*any of several species of Salvia of Mexico*); chia seed; chia (*beverage*)
chibalete *m* (print.) composing cabinet
chibuquí *m* (*pl:* **-quíes**) chibouk
chicada *f* herd of sickly and underdeveloped sheep; childishness, childish act
chicalote *m* (bot.) Mexican poppy
chicana *f* baffle plate; (Am.) chicanery; (Am.) quibbling
chicaneada *f* (Am.) piece of chicanery
chicaneo *m* (Am.) chicane, chicanery
chicanería *f* (Am.) chicanery
chicanero -ra *mf* (Am.) chicaner; (Am.) shyster lawyer
chicle *m* chicle (*gumlike substance*); chewing gum; **chicle de burbuja, chicle de globo,** or **chicle hinchable** bubble gum
chiclear *vn* to chew gum
chicloso -sa *adj* (Am.) gummy, sticky
chico -ca *adj* small, little; *mf* child, youngster; *m* lad, little fellow; (coll.) young fellow; (coll.) my boy, old man; *f* lass, little girl; (coll.) my dear
chicoco -ca *mf* (coll.) husky youngster; (Am.) dwarf
chicolear *vn* (coll.) to make compliments; *vr* (Am.) to enjoy oneself
chicoleo *m* (coll.) compliment (*to a woman*)
chicoria *f* (bot.) chicory
chicorro *m* (coll.) husky guy
chicorrotico -ca, chicorrotillo -lla or **chicorrotito -ta** *adj* (coll.) small, tiny
chicorrotín -tina *adj* (coll.) small, tiny; *mf* (coll.) tiny child, tot
chicotazo *m* (Am.) lash, blow with a whip
chicote -ta *mf* (coll.) husky youngster; *m* (coll.) cigar; (coll.) cigar stub; (Am.) whip; (naut.) piece of rope, end of rope
chicotear *va* (Am.) to lash, whip, flog; (Am.) to dispatch, to kill; (Am.) to splash stucco on (*a wall*)
chicozapote *m* (bot.) sapodilla
chicuelo -la *adj* small, little; *m* little boy; *f* little girl
chicha *f* chicha, corn liquor; (coll.) meat; **de chicha y nabo** (coll.) insignificant, worthless; **ni chicha ni limonada** (coll.) neither fish nor fowl
chícharo *m* pea; (Am.) poor cigar; (Am.) apprentice
chicharra *f* (ent.) locust, harvest fly; kazoo; (coll.) chatterbox; (Am.) buzzer, noisy tool; **cantar la chicharra** (coll.) to be hot and sultry
chicharrar *va* to scorch; to bother, to bedevil
chicharrear *vn* (Am.) to chirp (*said of a cicada*)
chicharrero *m* (coll.) hot place or region
chicharro *m* cracklings (*residue of hogs' fat*); (ichth.) caranx
chicharrón *m* cracklings (*residue of hogs' fat*); burned or scorched food; (coll.) person scorched by the sun
chiche *f* (Am.) infant's toy; (Am.) trinket; (Am.) breast; (Am.) wet nurse
chichear *va, vn & vr* to hiss
chicheo *m* hiss, hissing
chichigua *f* (Am.) wet nurse; (Am.) shade tree; (Am.) small change; (Am.) trifle
chichisbeo *m* ardent wooing; ardent suitor
chichón -chona *adj* (Am.) joking; (Am.) large-breasted; *m* bump or lump on the head
chichonera *f* (coll.) wadded hat (*to protect a child's head from bumps*)
chifla *f* hissing; whistling; whistle; paring knife; **estar de chifla** (Am.) to be in a bad humor
chifladera *f* whistle
chiflado -da *adj* (coll.) daffy; *mf* (coll.) nut; (coll.) crank
chifladura *f* hissing; whistling; (coll.) daffiness; (coll.) whim, craze, wild idea
chiflar *va* to hiss (*e.g., an actor*); to gulp down (*wine or liquor*); to pare (*leather*); *vn* to whistle; (Am.) to sing (*said of birds*); *vr* (coll.) to become unbalanced; **chiflarse con** (coll.) to be or get nutty about
chiflato *m* whistle
chifle *m* whistle; bird call (*instrument*); powder flask, powder horn; (Am.) horn used to carry water
chiflete *m* whistle
chiflido *m* whistle; whistling sound
chiflo *m* whistle
chiflón *m* (Am.) cold blast (*of air*); (Am.) rapids; (Am.) flume; (Am.) slide of loose stone (*in a mine*)
chigre *m* (naut.) winch; (dial.) cider shop
chilaba *f* jelab or jellaba
chilaquiles *mpl* (Am.) casserole of tortillas, tomatoes, and chili
chilar *m* field of chilies
chile *m* (bot.) chili (*plant and fruit*); **chile con carne** (Am.) chile con carne or chili con carne; (*cap.*) *m* Chile
chilenismo *m* Chileanism
chileno -na or **chileño -ña** *adj & mf* Chilean
chilindrina *f* (coll.) trifle; (coll.) joke, funny story; (coll.) jest, banter
chilindrinero -ra *adj* (coll.) joking, storytelling; *mf* (coll.) joker, storyteller
chilindrón *m* Pope Joan (*card game*)
chilipuca *f* Sieva bean (*seed or bean*)
chiltipiquín *m* (bot.) chili (*plant and fruit*)
chilla *f* (hunt.) fox call, hare call; clapboard; (Am.) small fox
chillado *m* clapboard roof
chillador -dora *adj* shrieking, squeaking, screaming, squealing; *mf* screamer, squealer
chillar *vn* to shriek; to screech; to creak, to squeak; to hiss, to sizzle; to scream (*said of colors*); (hunt.) to call (*with fox call, etc.*); (Am.) to squeal (*to turn informer*); **no chillar** (Am.) to not say a word; *vr* (Am.) to be piqued, be offended
chillería *f* shrieks, screams, outcries; screaming and scolding
chillido *m* shriek, scream
chillo *m* (hunt.) fox call, hare call
chillón -llona *adj* (coll.) shrieking, screaming; shrill, screechy; high-pitched; loud (*color*); *m* lath nail; **chillón real** large nail, spike
chimachima *m* (orn.) chimachima
chimango *m* (orn.) chimango
chimenea *f* chimney, smokestack; fireplace, hearth; stovepipe, stovepipe hat; vent (*of parachute*); (naut.) funnel; (min.) shaft; stove; **caer por la chimenea** (coll.) to come unexpectedly and without effort; **chimenea francesa** fireplace, fireplace and mantel
chimpancé *m* (zool.) chimpanzee
chimuelo -la *adj* (Am.) toothless; *mf* (Am.) toothless person
china *f*. see **chino**
chinampa *f* artificial garden reclaimed from a lake (*near Mexico city*)
chinanta *f* chinanta (*Philippine weight, equal to 13 pounds 12 ounces*)
chinarro *m* large pebble, stone
chinazo *m* blow with a stone
chincapino *m* (bot.) chinquapin
chinchar *va* (coll.) to bother, to annoy; (coll.) to kill
chincharrazo *m* blow with the flat of a sword
chincharrero *m* buggy place; fishing smack
chinche *m & f* (ent.) bedbug; (ent.) bug; thumbtack; (coll.) bore, tiresome person; (Am.) grouch; **caer** or **morir como chinches** (coll.) to die like flies
chincheta *f* thumbtack
chinchilla *f* (zool.) chinchilla (*animal and fur*)
chinchín *m* street music; ballyhoo; (bot.) bottle gourd; (Am.) drizzle
chinchorrería *f* (coll.) mischievous gossip, mischievous piece of gossip; (coll.) impertinence, bother; (coll.) hoax
chinchorrero -ra *adj* (coll.) mischievous, gossipy; (coll.) impertinent, importunate
chinchorro *m* sweep net; small rowboat; hammock; (Am.) flock, drove
chinchoso -sa *adj* (coll.) boring, tiresome
chiné *adj* Chiné (*fabric*)
chinela *f* slipper; clog
chinelón *m* big slipper, high slipper
chinero *m* china closet

chinesco -ca *adj* Chinese; **chinescos** *mpl* (mus.) bell tree
chingar §59 *va* (coll.) to tipple (*wine or liquor*); (Am.) to bother, harass; (Am.) to bob; *vn & vr* (coll.) to tipple; (Am.) to misfire; (Am.) to fail
chinguirito *m* (Am.) cheap rum; (Am.) swig (*of liquor*)
chinito -ta *mf* (Am.) dearie
chino -na *adj* Chinese; *mf* Chinese; (Am.) half-breed (*cross between non-white races*); *m* Chinaman; Chinese (*language*); (Am.) boy, newsboy; **me es chino** it's Greek to me; *f* Chinese woman; china, porcelain; China silk; pebble; game of guessing which hand holds a pebble; (bot.) chinaroot; (Am.) half-breed maidservant; (Am.) top, spinning top; **la China** China
chinoamericano -na *adj* Sino-American
chinuco *m* Chinook (*Indian; language*); chinook (*wind*)
chiolita *f* (mineral.) chiolite
chipé *f* truth, goodness; **de chipé** (coll.) first-class, excellent
chipén *m* activity, excitement; **de chipén** (coll.) first-class, excellent
chipichipi *m* (Am.) mist, drizzle
chipirón *m* (zool.) squid
Chipre *f* Cyprus
chipriota or **chipriote** *adj & mf* Cypriote or Cyprian
chiqueadores *mpl* (Am.) medicated paper disks stuck on the temples to cure headache; (Am.) paper or tortoise-shell spangles (*old female adornment in Mexico*)
chiquero *m* pigsty; bull pen; (theat.) dressing room
chiquichaque *m* sawyer; noise of chewing
chiquiguao *m* (zool.) snapper, snapping turtle
chiquigüite *m* or **chiquihuite** *m* (Am.) reed basket
chiquilicuatro *m* (coll.) meddler, schemer
chiquilín -lina *mf* (Am.) tot, little youngster
chiquillada *f* childish prank, mischievousness
chiquillería *f* (coll.) crowd of small fry, crowd of youngsters
chiquillo -lla *mf* child, youngster
chiquirritico -ca, chiquirritillo -lla or **chiquirritito -ta** *adj* (coll.) small, tiny
chiquirritín -tina or **chiquitín -tina** *adj* (coll.) tiny; *mf* (coll.) tiny child, tot
chiquito -ta *adj* small, tiny; **andarse en chiquitas** (coll.) to beat about the bush; *mf* little one
chiribita *f* spark; (bot.) daisy; **chiribitas** *fpl* (coll.) spots in front of the eyes; **echar chiribitas** (coll.) to blow up, hit the ceiling
chiribitil *m* garret; hovel; (coll.) crib, cubbyhole
chirigota *f* (coll.) joke, joking, fun
chirigotero -ra *adj* (coll.) joking, funmaking
chirimbolo *m* (coll.) utensil, tool, implement, vessel; **chirimbolos de cocina** (coll.) kitchenware
chirimía *f* (mus.) hornpipe; *mf* hornpipe player
chirimoya *f* cherimoya (*fruit*)
chirimoyo *m* (bot.) cherimoya; **chirimoyo del Senegal** (bot.) sweetsop
chirinola *f* boys' game of bowling; trifle; **estar de chirinola** (coll.) to be in good spirits
chiripa *f* fluke, scratch (*in billiards*); (coll.) lucky stroke, piece of luck, fluke
chiripá *m* (Am.) chiripá (*blanket wrapped around waist and hips and thighs*)
chiripear *va* to win (*points*) by a fluke
chiripero *m* winner by a fluke; (coll.) lucky fellow
chirivía *f* (bot.) parsnip (*plant and root*); (orn.) wagtail
chirla *f* (zool.) small clam
chirlador -dora *adj* ranting
chirlar *vn* (coll.) to rant
chirlata *f* (coll.) gambling joint (*where stakes are copper and small silver coins*)
chirle *adj* (coll.) tasteless, insipid; *m* sheep manure, goat manure
chirlo *m* slash in the face; long scar on the face
chirlomirlo *m* tidbit; (orn.) thrush
chirlota *f* (orn.) meadow lark, eastern meadow lark
chirona *f* (coll.) jug, jail
chirriadero -ra or **chirriador -dora** *adj* hissing; creaking, squeaking; shrieking (*bird*)
chirriante *adj* hissing; creaking, squeaky
chirriar §90 *vn* to hiss, sizzle; to creak, squeak; to shriek (*said of birds*); to chirp (*said of crickets*); (coll.) to sing out of tune; (coll.) to be out of tune, to play out of tune (*said of a musical instrument*); *vr* (Am.) to go on a spree; (Am.) to shiver
chirrido *m* hiss, sizzle; creak, squeak; shrieking (*of birds*); chirping (*of crickets*)
chirrío *m* (coll.) var. of **chirrido**
chirrión *m* squeaky tumbrel
chirrionero *m* tumbrel driver
chirula *f* (mus.) fipple flute or pipe
chirumen *m* (coll.) judgment, acumen, brains
chis *interj* sh-sh!, hush!; **¡chis, chis!** hey!, pst!
chiscón *m* (coll.) hut, hovel
chischás *m* clash of swords
chisgarabís *m* (coll.) meddler, schemer
chisguete *m* (coll.) drink or swallow of wine; (coll.) squirt; **echar un chisguete** (coll.) to take a swig
chisma *f* (archaic) gossip
chismar *vn* (archaic) var. of **chismear**
chisme *m* gossip, piece of gossip; (coll.) trinket, gadget, jigger; **chismes** *mpl* gossip; articles, equipment (*e.g., for writing, shaving, etc.*); **chisme de vecindad** (coll.) idle talker, chatterbox
chismear *vn* to gossip
chismería *f* gossip, gossiping; cattiness
chismero -ra *adj & mf* var. of **chismoso**
chismografía *f* (coll.) gossiping, fondness for gossip
chismorrear *vn* (coll.) to gossip
chismorreo *m* (coll.) gossip, gossiping
chismoso -sa *adj* gossipy; catty; *mf* gossip
chispa *f* see **chispo**
chispazo *m* flying spark; burn from a spark; straw (*token, indication*); (coll.) gossip, tale, piece of gossip
chispeante *adj* sparkling (*writing, imagination, person*); (Am.) drizzly
chispear *vn* to spark; to sparkle; to drizzle; (fig.) to sparkle
chispero -ra *adj* sparking, sparkling (*firecracker*); *m* blacksmith; junk dealer; (rail.) spark arrester; (coll.) denizen of the Madrid underworld
chispo -pa *adj* (coll.) tipsy; *m* (coll.) swallow, drink; *f* spark; sparkle (*tiny diamond*); drop (*small amount*); lightning; (fig.) sparkle, wit; (coll.) drunk, drunken spree; (Am.) false rumor (bot.) coreopsis; **chispas** *fpl* sprinkle (*of rain*), e.g., **caen chispas** it is sprinkling; **¡chispas!** blazes!; **coger una chispa** (coll.) to go on a drunk; **dar chispa** (Am.) to work, to click; **echar chispas** (coll.) to blow up, hit the ceiling; (Am.) to be all dressed up; **ser una chispa** (coll.) to be a little hustler; **chispa de entrehierro** (elec.) jump spark
chispoleto -ta *adj* lively, wide-awake
chisporrotear *vn* (coll.) to spark, to sputter
chisporroteo *m* (coll.) sparking, sputtering
chisposo -sa *adj* sparking, sputtering
chisquero *m* leather bag (*fastened to belt*); pocket lighter
chistar *vn* to speak, be about to speak; **no chistar** to not say a word; **sin chistar ni mistar** (coll.) without saying a word
chiste *m* witticism; joke, funny thing; **caer en el chiste** (coll.) to get wise, to get the point; **contar un chiste** to tell a joke; **dar en el chiste** (coll.) to guess right, to do the right thing
chistera *f* fish basket; top hat; (sport) cesta, wickerwork racket
chistoso -sa *adj* witty; funny; *mf* wit (*person*)
chistu *m* var. of **chirula**
chita *f* (anat.) anklebone; boys' quoits; **a la chita callando** (coll.) in silence; (coll.) stealthily, secretly; **dar en la chita** (coll.) to hit the nail on the head; **tirar a dos chitas** (coll.) to try to kill two birds with one stone

chitar *vn* var. of **chistar**
chiticalla *mf* (coll.) clam, tight-lipped person; *f* (coll.) secret
chiticallando *adv* (coll.) in silence; (coll.) stealthily, secretly; **a la chiticallando** (coll.) in silence; (coll.) stealthily, secretly
chito *m* piece of wood on which stakes or bets are placed; **irse a chitos** (coll.) to bum around; *interj* sh-sh!, hush!
chitón *m* (zool.) chiton; *interj* sh-sh!, hush!
chivarras *fpl* (Am.) shaggy kid breeches
chivatazo *m* (slang) squealing, peaching
chivateado -da *adj* (Am.) cash (*payment*)
chivatear *va* (Am.) to cheat, deceive; *vn* (Am.) to give the war cry; *vr* (Am.) to get scared
chivato *m* (zool.) kid; (slang) squealer; (Am.) helper, apprentice
chivetero or **chivital** *m* fold for kids
chivo -va *mf* (zool.) kid; *m* billy goat; tank for the lees of olive oil
cho *interj* whoa!
chocador -dora *adj* shocking; *mf* shocker
chocante *adj* shocking; scurrilous; (Am.) tiresome
chocar §86 *va* to shock; to aggravate, irritate; (slang) to please; **¡chóquela!** or **¡choque Vd. esos cinco!** (coll.) shake! (*i.e., shake hands!*); *vn* to shock; to collide; to clash, to fight; **chocar con** to collide with; to clash with
chocarrear *vn & vr* to tell coarse jokes
chocarrería *f* coarse joke; scurrility
chocarrero -ra *adj* coarse, scurrilous; *mf* coarse joker
choclar *vn* to drive the ball through the hoop (*in croquet*)
choclo *m* clog (*shoe with wooden sole*); (Am.) low shoe; (Am.) ear of corn
choclón *m* driving ball through the hoop (*in croquet*)
choco *m* small cuttlefish
chocolate *m* chocolate; **chocolate a la española** thick chocolate (*beverage*); **chocolate a la francesa** thin chocolate (*beverage*)
chocolatera *f* see **chocolatero**
chocolatería *f* chocolate factory; chocolate shop
chocolatero -ra *adj* fond of chocolate; *mf* chocolate maker; chocolate dealer; *f* chocolate pot; (orn.) spoonbill
chocolatín *m* cake of chocolate
chocha *f* see **chocho**
chochaperdiz *f* (*pl:* **-dices**) (orn.) woodcock
chochear *vn* to dote, become childish; (coll.) to dote, be infatuated
chochera *f* dotage; doting act or word; **ser la chochera de** (Am.) to be the choice of, be the foible of
chochez *f* (*pl:* **-checes**) dotage; doting act or word
chochín *m* young or baby woodcock; (orn.) wren
chochita *f* (orn.) wren
chocho -cha *adj* doddering; doting; *m* lupine (*seed*); cinnamon candy; **chochos** *mpl* candy to quiet a child; *f* (orn.) woodcock; **chocha de mar** (ichth.) shrimpfish
chofe *m* lung
chófer *m* chauffeur; driver
chofeta *f* fire pan (*for lighting cigars*)
cholo -la *adj* (Am.) Indian; (Am.) half-breed (*Indian and white*); (Am.) half-civilized (*Indian*); *mf* (Am.) Indian; (Am.) half-breed; (Am.) half-civilized Indian; (Am.) boor, rustic; (Am.) coward; (Am.) darling; *m* (Am.) black dog; *f* (coll.) noodle, head; (coll.) brains, ability
cholla *f* (coll.) noodle, head; (coll.) brains, ability; (bot.) cholla; (Am.) calm, apathy, dullness
chomite *m* (Am.) coarse wool; woolen skirt (*worn by Mexican Indian women*)
chompa *f* (Am.) sweater; (Am.) iron bar; (Am.) hand drill
chonta *f* (bot.) tucuma
chopa *f* (ichth.) chopa, rudder fish; (naut.) topgallant poop
chopal *m*, **chopalera** or **chopera** *f* grove of black poplars
chopo *m* (bot.) black poplar; (coll.) musket, gun; **chopo blanco** (bot.) white poplar; **chopo de Italia** (bot.) Lombardy poplar; **chopo de la Carolina** (bot.) Carolina poplar; **chopo del Canadá** o **de Virginia** (bot.) cottonwood; **chopo lombardo** (bot.) Lombardy poplar
chopontil *m* (zool.) snapper, snapping turtle
choque *m* shock; impact, collision; (elec., med. & fig.) shock; (elec.) choke, choke coil; (mil.) clash, skirmish; (naut.) chock; **choque de agua, choque de ariete** water hammer; **choque glótico** (phonet.) glottal stop
choquezuela *f* (anat.) kneepan
chorcha *f* (orn.) woodcock
chordón *m* var. of **churdón**
choricería *f* sausage shop
choricero -ra *mf* sausage maker or dealer; *f* (mach.) sausage filler
chorizo *m* smoked pork sausage; ropewalker's pole
chorla *f* (orn.) sand grouse
chorlito *m* (orn.) golden plover; (coll.) scatterbrains; **chorlito blanco** (orn.) sanderling; **chorlito de manchas acaneladas** (orn.) solitary sandpiper; **chorlito de mar** (orn.) red phalarope; **chorlito de mar apizarrado** (orn.) northern phalarope; **chorlito dorado** (orn.) American golden plover; **chorlito gris** (orn.) black-bellied plover; **chorlito gritón peleador** (orn.) killdeer; **chorlito palmeado de pico largo** (orn.) stilt sandpiper; **chorlito pardo mayor** or **patiamarilla** (orn.) lesser yellowlegs; **chorlito playero** (orn.) black-bellied plover; **chorlito playero manchado** (orn.) spotted sandpiper; **chorlito siberiano** (orn.) Pacific golden plover; **chorlito verde** (orn.) American golden plover
chorlo *m* (mineral.) schorl, tourmaline; (mineral.) aluminum silicate; (orn.) curlew; (orn.) spotted sandpiper; (Am.) great-great-great-grandchild; **chorlo blanco nadador** (orn.) Wilson's phalarope; **chorlo de las playas** (orn.) surfbird; **chorlo grande de patas amarillas** (orn.) greater yellowlegs; **chorlo gris pecho negro** (orn.) black-billed plover; **chorlo gris pico largo** (orn.) long-billed dowitcher; **chorlo manchado** (orn.) spotted sandpiper; **chorlo menor de patas amarillas** (orn.) lesser yellowlegs; **chorlo nadador de pies lobados** (orn.) red phalarope; **chorlo pampa** (orn.) American golden plover; **chorlo real** (orn.) greater yellowlegs; **chorlo rojizo** (orn.) knot (*Calidris canutus rufus*); **chorlo rojizo de mar** (orn.) red phalarope
chorrada *f* (coll.) extra dash (*of a liquid*)
chorreado -da *adj* with dark vertical stripes (*said of cattle*)
chorreadura *f* spurting, spouting, gushing; dripping; (coll.) trickling; stain from constant dripping
chorreante *adj* dripping
chorrear *vn* to spurt, to spout, to gush; to drip; (coll.) to trickle
chorreo *m* spurting, spouting, gushing; dripping; (coll.) trickling
chorreón *m* gushing; dripping; stain from dripping; trickle
chorrera *f* spout, channel; mark left by running water; cut, gulley; rapids (*in a stream*); jabot; knight's, magistrate's, or pilgrim's pendant; (Am.) string, stream (*of things*)
chorretada *f* (coll.) squirt, sudden gush; (coll.) extra dash (*of a liquid*); **hablar a chorretadas** (coll.) to pour forth words
chorrillo *m* (coll.) constant stream (*e.g., of money*); **irse por el chorrillo** (coll.) to follow the current (*to do what others do*); **sembrar a chorrillo** (agr.) to sow with a funnel; **tomar el chorrillo de** + *inf* (coll.) to get the habit of + *ger*
chorro *m* spurt, jet; stream, flow; **a chorros** in abundance; **chorro de arena** sandblast; **chorro de voz** fullness of voice
chorroborro *m* (coll.) flood
chorrón *m* dressed hemp
chortal *m* puddle from a surface spring
chotacabras *m* (*pl:* **-bras**) (orn.) goatsucker, nighthawk
chotear *va* (Am.) to make fun of

chotis *m* schottische (*dance and music*)
choto -ta *mf* sucking kid; lamb
chotuno -na *adj* sucking (*kid*); weak, sickly (*lamb*); **oler a chotuno** to smell like a goat
chova *f* (orn.) rook; (orn.) Cornish chough; **chova pinariega** (orn.) alpine chough
chovinismo *m* var. of **chauvinismo**
chovinista *adj & mf* var. of **chauvinista**
choz *f* blow, surprise; **dar** or **hacer choz a** to surprise
choza *f* hut, cabin, lodge
chozno -na *mf* great-great-great-great-grandchild
chozo *m* small hut, small cabin
chozpar *vn* to caper, to gambol (*said of small animals*)
chozpo *m* caper, gambol
chozpón -pona *adj* capering, gamboling, frisky
chozuela *f* small hut, small cabin, shanty
christmas *m* (*pl:* **-mas**) Christmas card
chubasco *m* squall, shower, storm; (naut.) threatening cloud; temporary upset (*in one's plans*); **aguantar el chubasco** to weather the storm; **chubasco de agua** (naut.) rainstorm; **chubasco de nieve** blizzard; **chubasco de viento** (naut.) windstorm
chubascoso -sa *adj* showery, squally
chubasquería *f* (naut.) mass of threatening clouds on the horizon
chubasquero *m* raincoat
chucero *m* (mil.) pikeman
chucrut *m* or **chucruta** *f* sauerkraut
chucha *f* (coll.) female dog, bitch; (coll.) drunk, spree; (coll.) idleness; (Am.) opossum
chuchaqui *m* (Am.) hangover
chuchear *va* to trap (*small game*); *vn* to whisper
chuchería *f* trinket, knickknack; tidbit, delicacy; (hunt.) trapping small game
chuchero -ra *adj* (hunt.) for trapping small game; *m* (Am.) switch tender
chucho *m* (coll.) dog; (*cap.*) *m* child Jesus; (*l.c.*) *interj* get out of here! (*said to a dog*); down! (*said to restrain a dog*)
chuchumeco -ca *adj* (Am.) stunted, dwarfish; *mf* (coll.) little runt
chueco -ca *adj* (Am.) crooked, bent; (Am.) bow-legged; *f* stump (*of tree*); head of bone; hockey; hockey ball; (coll.) joke, trick
chueta *mf* (Balearic Islands) Chueta (*descendant of Christianized Jews*)
chufa *f* (bot.) chufa (*plant and tuber*)
chufar *va* to scoff at; *vn & vr* to scoff
chufería *f* orgeat shop
chufero -ra *mf* orgeat vendor; chufa vendor
chufeta *f* fire pan (*for lighting cigars*); (coll.) joke, jest
chufleta *f* (coll.) joke, jest
chufletear *vn* (coll.) to joke, to jest
chufletero -ra *adj* (coll.) joking, jesting; *mf* (coll.) joker, jester
chula *f* see **chulo**
chulada *f* vulgarity; light-heartedness, light-hearted remark
chulama *f* (slang) girl
chulamo *m* (slang) boy
chulapo -pa or **chulapón -pona** *adj* (coll.) smart, pert; *mf* (coll.) sporty person (*in lower classes of Madrid*)
chulear *va* (Am.) to flirt with
chulería *f* ease, charm, sparkle; flashiness, snap; group of sporty people (*in lower classes of Madrid*)
chulesco -ca *adj* smart, pert, sporty
chuleta *f* chop, cutlet; (carp.) fill-in; (coll.) slap, smack; (coll.) crib, pony
chulo -la *adj* flashy, snappy; foxy; (Am.) pretty, good-looking; *m* sporty fellow (*in lower classes of Madrid*); pimp; (taur.) attendant on foot; butcher's helper; *f* flashy dame (*in lower classes of Madrid*)
chumacera *f* (mach.) pillow block, journal bearing; (naut.) strip of wood through which tholepins are driven and whose purpose is to protect the gunwale; (naut.) rowlock, oarlock
chumbera *f* (bot.) prickly pear
chunga *f* (coll.) jest, fun; **estar de chunga** (coll.) to be in a jesting mood
chungar §59 *vr* (coll.) to jest, to joke
chunguear *vr* (coll.) var. of **chungar**
chunguero -ra *adj* (coll.) joking, full of fun
chupa *f* (mil.) frock; **poner como chupa de dómine** (coll.) to upbraid, to abuse
chupada *f* see **chupado**
chupadero -ra *adj* sucking; *m* teething ring
chupado -da *adj* (coll.) lean, skinny; **chupado de cara** (coll.) lantern-jawed; *f* suck, sucking; pull (*on a cigar*)
chupador -dora *adj* sucking; absorbent; *mf* (Am.) smoker; (Am.) heavy drinker; *m* teething ring
chupadura *f* suck, sucking
chupaflor *m* (Am.) hummingbird
chupaleta *f* (Am.) lollipop
chupamieles *m* (bot.) bugloss
chupamirto *m* (orn.) hummingbird
chupar *va* to suck; to absorb; to milk, to sap (*someone's wealth*); (Am.) to smoke; (Am.) to guzzle, to drink; *vn* to suck; *vr* to lose strength, to decline; to smack (*one's lips*)
chuparrosa *m* (Am.) hummingbird
chupatintas *mf* (*pl:* **-tas**) (coll.) office drudge
chupeta *f* short frock; (naut.) roundhouse; **chupeta de escala** (naut.) companion
chupete *m* pacifier (*rubber nipple for a baby*); (Am.) lollipop; **de chupete** (coll.) splendid, fine
chupetear *va & vn* to keep sucking gently
chupeteo *m* gentle steady sucking
chupetín *m* jerkin, waistcoat
chupetón *m* hard suck
chupín *m* short suck
chupón -pona *adj* (coll.) sucking; (coll.) swindling; *mf* (coll.) swindler; *m* (bot.) sucker; (mach.) sucker (*piston*)
chupóptero *m* (hum.) parasite, sponger
chuquisa *f* (Am.) party girl
churdón *m* (bot.) raspberry (*plant and fruit*); raspberry jam
chureca *f* (bot.) sweet pea
churla *f* or **churlo** *m* seroon
churra *f* see **churro**
churrasco *m* (Am.) barbecue
churrasquear *va* (Am.) to barbecue
churre *m* (coll.) thick, dirty grease; (coll.) dirt, grease, filth
churretada *f* large dirty spot (*on hands or face*); mass of dirty spots (*on hands or face*)
churrete *m* dirty spot (*on hands or face*)
churretoso -sa *adj* full of dirty spots
churriana *f* (slang) prostitute
churriburri *m* (coll.) var. of **zurriburri**
churriento -ta *adj* greasy
churrigueresco -ca *adj* (arch.) churrigueresque; flashy, loud, tawdry
churriguerismo *m* (arch.) churriguerism (*excess of ornamentation*)
churriguerista *m* (arch.) churriguerist
churro -rra *adj* coarse (*wool*); coarse-wooled (*sheep*); *mf* coarse-wooled sheep; *m* cucumber-shaped fritter; (coll.) botch; *f* (orn.) sand grouse
churrullero -ra *adj* gossipy, loquacious; *mf* gossip, chatterbox
churruscar §86 *va* to burn (*food*); *vr* to burn, become burnt (*said of food*)
churrusco *m* burnt toast
churumbel *m* (coll.) child, youngster
churumbela *f* (mus.) flageolet; (Am.) maté cup
churumo *m* (coll.) juice, substance
chus *interj* here, here! (*to call a dog*); **no decir chus ni mus** to not say boo
chuscada *f* drollery, pleasantry
chusco -ca *adj* droll, funny; *m* (Am.) mongrel (*dog*)
chusma *f* galley slaves; mob, rabble
chuspa *f* (Am.) bag
chusquel *m* (slang) house dog
chutar or **chutear** *va* to kick (*a football*)
chuva *f* (zool.) spider monkey
chuza *f* (Am.) strike (*in bowling*)
chuzar §76 *va* (Am.) to prick, to wound
chuzo *m* pike; (Am.) whip; **echar chuzos** (coll.) to boast, to brag; (coll.) to storm, to rage; **llover chuzos** (coll.) to rain pitchforks
chuzón -zona *adj* sly, crafty; witty, clever, adroit (*in conversation*)
chuzonada *f* var. of **bufonada**
chuzonería *f* joke, trick

D

D, d *f* fifth letter of the Spanish alphabet
D. abr. of **don**
D.ª abr. of **doña**
dable *adj* possible, feasible
daca give me, hand over to me; **andar al daca y toma** (coll.) to be at cross purposes
dacio -cia *adj & mf* Dacian; **la Dacia** Dacia
dación *f* (law) yielding, handing over
dactilado -da *adj* finger-shaped
dactilar *adj* var. of **digital**
dactílico -ca *adj* dactylic
dactiliografía *f* dactyliography
dactiliología *f* dactyliology
dáctilo *m* dactyl
dactilográfico -ca *adj* typewriting
dactilógrafo -fa *mf* typist, typewriter; *m* typewriter (*machine*)
dactilograma *m* dactylogram, fingerprint
dactilología *f* dactylology, sign language
dactiloscopia *f* dactyloscopy
dactiloscópico -ca *adj* dactyloscopic
dadaísmo *m* Dadaism
dádiva *f* gift, present
dadivar *va* to give a present to, make gifts to
dadivosidad *f* generosity, liberality
dadivoso -sa generous, liberal
dado -da *adj* given; **dado que** given that; provided that, as long as; *m* die; (arch.) dado; (mach.) block; **dados** *mpl* dice; **el dado está tirado** (coll.) the die is cast; **cargar los dados** to load the dice; **correr el dado** (coll.) to be in luck; **dados cargados** loaded dice
dador -dora *adj* giving; *mf* giver, donor; bearer (*of a letter*); drawer (*of a bill of exchange*)
Dafne *f* (myth.) Daphne
daga *f* dagger; line of bricks in a kiln; **llegar a las dagas** (coll.) to get to the real difficulty
daguerrotipar *va* to daguerreotype
daguerrotipo *m* daguerreotype
dala *f* (naut.) pump dale
dalia *f* (bot.) dahlia
Dalila or **Dálila** *f* (Bib.) Delilah
Dalmacia *f* Dalmatia
dálmata *adj & mf* Dalmatian
dalmático -ca *adj* Dalmatian; *f* dalmatic (*vestment*)
daltonismo *m* (path.) Daltonism
dalla *f* scythe
dallador *m* mower, grass mower (*with scythe*)
dallar *va* to cut (*grass*) with the scythe
dalle *m* scythe
dama *f* lady, dame; lady of honor; king (*in checkers*); queen (*in chess and cards*); mistress, concubine; (found.) dam; (theat.) leading lady; **damas** *fpl* checkers; **muy dama** ladylike; **señalar dama** to crown a man (*in checkers*); **soplar la dama a** (checkers) to huff the king of; (coll.) to cut out (*a rival*); to beat (*someone*) to it; **dama cortesana** courtesan; **dama de noche** (bot.) night jasmine; **dama joven** (theat.) young lead
damado -da *adj* checkered
damajuana *f* demijohn
damascado -da *adj* damask; damascene
damasceno -na *adj & mf* Damascene
damasco *m* damask (*fabric*); (bot.) damson (*tree and fruit*); **Damasco** *f* Damascus
damasina *f* light damask, damassin
damasquillo *m* light damask, damassin; (dial.) apricot
damasquina *f* see **damasquino**
damasquinado -da *adj* damascene; *m* damascene (*steel or iron with water marking; incrustation of gold or silver wire and enamel in steel or copper*)
damasquinar *va* to damascene
damasquino -na *adj* Damascene; damascene; *f* (bot.) French marigold
damería *f* nicety, prudery; caution, circumspection
damero *m* checkerboard
damisela *f* young lady, damsel; courtesan
damnación *f* damnation
damnificar §86 *va* to damage, hurt, injure
Damocles *m* or **Dámocles** *m* (myth.) Damocles
Damón *m* (myth.) Damon
Dánae *f* (myth.) Danae
Danaides *fpl* (myth.) Danaides
Danao *m* (myth.) Danaus
danchado -da *adj* (her.) dentelated
dandismo *m* dandyism
danés -nesa *adj* Danish; *mf* Dane; *m* Danish (*language*)
dango *m* (orn.) gannet
dánico -ca *adj* Danish
Daniel *m* Daniel
danta *f* (zool.) tapir
dantelado -da *adj* (her.) dentelated
dantesco -ca *adj* Dantesque
danubiano -na *adj* Danubian
Danubio *m* Danube
danza *f* dance; dancing; habanera; mess, row; **armar una danza** (coll.) to start a row; **meter en la danza** (coll.) to drag into a deal or scheme, to involve; **baja danza** allemande; **danza de cintas** Maypole dance; **danza de espadas** sword dance; (coll.) quarrel, row; **danza de la muerte** dance of death; **danza macabra** danse macabre
danzador -dora *adj* dancing; *mf* dancer
danzante *adj* dancing; *mf* public dancer; (coll.) hustler; (coll.) scatterbrain, meddler
danzar §76 *va* to dance; *vn* to dance; (fig.) to dance; (coll.) to butt in
danzarín -rina *adj* dancing; *mf* dancer, fine dancer; (coll.) scatterbrain, meddler
danzón *m* danzón (*Cuban dance*)
dañable *adj* harmful; reprehensible
dañado -da *adj* bad, wicked; spoiled, tainted; damned; *mf* person damned
dañar *va* to hurt; to damage, to harm; to spoil; *vr* to become damaged; to spoil
dañino -na *adj* harmful, destructive; evil, wicked
daño *m* hurt; damage, harm; (Am.) witchcraft, enchantment; **a daño de** at the risk of; **en daño de** to the harm or detriment of; **hacerse daño** to hurt oneself
dañoso -sa *adj* harmful, injurious
dar §36 *va* to give; to cause; to yield; to hit, to strike; to strike, e.g., **el reloj da las tres** the clock is striking three; to deal (*cards*); to overtake, to attack (*said of fever, pain, etc.*); to wish (*e.g., good morning*); to take (*a walk, ride*); to promulgate; **dar a conocer** to make known; **dar de** to paint with (*e.g., varnish*); to smear with (*e.g., butter*); **dar de beber** to give something to drink; **dar de bofetones** to beat with a stick; **dar de comer a** to give something to eat to, to feed; **dar de palos** to slap in the face; **darle a uno por** + *inf* to get the idea of + *ger*, e.g., **a todos los niños de la vecindad les dió por jugar a la pelota** all the children in the neighborhood got the idea of playing ball; **dar por** to consider as; **dar prestado** to lend; **dar que decir** to give rise to complaint or criticism; **dar que hablar** to cause a lot of talk; to give rise to complaint or criticism; **dar que hacer** to cause annoyance or trouble; **dar que pensar** to set (*a person thinking*); to give rise to suspicion; **dar que sentir** to cause sorrow, to

cause harm; **dar, que van dando** (coll.) to hand it back, to return blow for blow, to return insult for insult; **dar y tomar** to discuss ‖ *vn* to fall; to occur, to arise; to strike, e.g., **dan las tres** it is striking three o'clock; **el reloj acaba de dar** the clock has just struck; to tell, intimate, e.g., **me da el corazón que** my heart tells me that; **dar a** to overlook, to face, to open on; **dar con** to meet, encounter, run into; to hit upon, to come upon; **dar de espaldas** to fall on one's back; **dar de sí** to stretch, to give; **dar en** to hit; to overlook; to fall into; to run into; to catch on to (*a joke*); to be bent on; **dar en** + *inf* to begin to + *inf;* to be bent on + *ger;* **dar en qué pensar** to give rise to suspicion; **dar sobre** to overlook; **dar tras** to pursue hotly; **dar y tomar sobre** to discuss, argue about ‖ *vr* to give oneself up; to yield, to give in; to occur, be found; **darse a** to give oneself over to, to devote oneself to; **darse a conocer** to make a name for oneself, to make oneself known; to get to know each other; **darse contra** to run into; **dárselas de** to pose as; **darse por** to be considered as; to consider oneself (or itself) as; **darse por aludido** to take the hint; **darse por entendido** to understand, to show an understanding; to be appreciative, to show appreciation; to be responsive; **darse por vencido** to give in, to give up

dardabasí *m* (*pl:* **-síes**) (orn.) kite, hawk

Dardanelos *mpl* Dardanelles

dardanio -nia *adj* Dardan, Dardanian

dárdano -na *adj & mf* Dardan, Dardanian; (*cap.*) *m* (myth.) Dardanus

dardo *m* dart; small lance; cutting remark; (arch.) dart; (ichth.) dace

dares y tomares *mpl* (coll.) give and take; (coll.) disputes, quarrels; **andar en dares y tomares con** (coll.) to quarrel with

Darío *m* Darius

dársena *f* inner harbor, dock

darviniano -na *adj* Darwinian, Darwinist

darvinismo *m* Darwinism

darvinista *mf* Darwinian, Darwinist

dasocracia *f* forestry

dasocrático -ca *adj* forest, forestry

dasonomía *f* forestry

dasonómico -ca *adj* forest, forestry

data *f* date; (com.) item; outlet of reservoir; **de larga data** of long standing; **estar de mala data** (coll.) to be in a bad humor

datación *f* dating

datar *va* to date; *vn* to date; **datar de** to date from

dataría *f* datary (*office*)

datario *m* datary (*cardinal*)

dátil *m* date (*fruit*); (zool.) date shell

datilado -da *adj* datelike

datilera *f* (bot.) date palm

datismo *m* (rhet.) excess of synonyms

dativo -va *adj & m* (gram.) dative

dato *m* datum; basis, fact

datura *f* (bot.) datura

daturina *f* (pharm.) stramonium

dauco *m* (bot.) wild carrot; (bot.) bishop's-weed

David *m* David

davídico -ca *adj* Davidic, Davidical

daza *f* (bot.) sorghum

D.D.T. *m* symbol of **diclorodifeniltricloroetano**

de *prep* (to express possession) of, -'s, e.g., **el coche de Juan** the car of John, John's car; **este coche es de Vd.** this car is yours; (to indicate membership) of, e.g., **la gente de la aldea** the people of the village; **los miembros de la academia** the members of the academy; (to express association), e.g., **gente de teatro** theater people; **médico de hospital** hospital physician; (to denote occupation or office) as, e.g., **trabaja de ingeniero** he works as an engineer; **está de presidente** he is acting as chairman, he is chairman now; (to express material) of, e.g., **un anillo de acero** a ring of steel; **medias de seda** silk stockings; (to indicate price), e.g., **el precio del sombrero es de seis dólares** the price of the hat is six dollars; (to express source or origin), e.g., **sal de mar** sea salt; **café de moca** Mocha coffee; (to express quality, characteristic, nature, or kind), e.g., **el señor de traje negro** the gentleman in the black suit; **casa de dos pisos** two-story house; **motor de cuatro cilindros** four-cylinder motor; **dolor de muelas** toothache; **discurso de elección** election speech; (to express dimension or size), e.g., **un viaje de cien kilómetros** a one-hundred-kilometer trip; **un buque de mil toneladas** a one-thousand-ton ship; (to express manner), e.g., **de buena gana** willingly; **de golpe** suddenly; (to express contents, what is contained) of, e.g., **un vaso de cerveza** a glass of beer; (to indicate the point of departure) from, e.g., **de París a Madrid** from Paris to Madrid; **salió de Londres esta mañana** he left London this morning; (to indicate time of occurrence) in, e.g., **de día** in the daytime; **de noche** in the nighttime; (to indicate the driving force), e.g., **máquina de vapor** steam engine; **bomba de hidrógeno** hydrogen bomb; (to indicate the purpose of an object), e.g., **banco de ahorros** savings bank; **máquina de coser** sewing machine; (to express cause) with, of, e.g., **temblar de miedo** to tremble with fear; **morir de hambre** to die of hunger; (to indicate the agent with the passive voice) by, e.g., **querido de todos** loved by everybody; **acompañado de un guía** accompanied by a guide; (between words in apposition), e.g., **la ciudad de Méjico** the city of Mexico; **el año de 1963** the year of 1963; **el pobre de mi hermano** my poor brother; (between words in apposition in interjectional phrases), e.g., **¡desgraciados de nosotros!** unhappy we!; (after **un millón, millones, un billón, billones,** etc.), e.g., **dos millones de habitantes** two million inhabitants; (after **hablar, opinar, pensar,** etc.) about, e.g., **no hemos hablado de ella** we did not speak about her; (with a following infinitive after certain verbs) to, e.g., **se alegró de vernos** he was glad to see us; (with a following infinitive after certain adjectives) to, e.g., **el ruso es difícil de aprender** Russian is hard to learn; **esta agua no es buena de beber** this water is not good to drink; (with a following infinitive to express condition) if, unless, e.g., **de haberlo sabido yo** if I had known it; **de no venir él** unless he comes; (after a comparative and before a numeral) than, e.g., **más de doscientos** more than two hundred; (to indicate the position of part of the body) on, e.g., **estar de rodillas** to be on one's (his, her, etc.) knees; **caer de cara** to fall on one's (his, her, etc.) face; **acostarse de lado** to lie on one's (his, her, etc.) side; (to form prepositional phrases with certain adverbs), e.g., **antes de las seis** before six o'clock; **cerca de la iglesia** near the church; **de a** (to express rate, value, weight, etc.), e.g., **un billete de a cinco dólares** a five-dollar bill; **un jamón de a veinte-cinco kilos** a twenty-five-kilogram ham; **de entre** from between; through, out of (*e.g., one's hands*)

dé *1st sg pres subj of* **dar**

dea *f* (poet.) goddess

deambular *vn* to ambulate, to stroll

deambulatorio *m* (arch.) ambulatory

deán *m* (eccl.) dean

deanato or **deanazgo** *m* (eccl.) deanship

debajo *adv* below, underneath; **debajo de** under, below, underneath

debate *m* debate; altercation, fight

debatir *va* to debate; to battle, to fight; *vn* to debate; *vr* to struggle

debe *m* (com.) debit

debelación *f* conquering, conquest

debelador -dora *adj* conquering; *mf* conqueror

debelar *va* to conquer, subdue

deber *m* duty; debt; school work, homework; **últimos deberes** last rites; *va* to owe; *v aux* must; **deber** + *inf* must, have to, ought to, should + *inf* (*to express necessity or obligation*); **deber de** + *inf* must + *inf* (*to express conjecture*); *vr* to be dedicated, be committed; **deberse a** to be due to

debidamente *adv* duly

debido -da *adj* just, reasonable, due, proper; **debido a** due to
débil *adj* weak; (gram.) weak (*vowel; verb*)
debilidad *f* weakness, debility; **debilidad mental** mental deficiency
debilitación *f* or **debilitamiento** *m* debilitation
debilitar *va* to debilitate; *vr* to weaken, become weak
debitar *va* (com.) to debit
débito *m* debit; **débito conyugal** conjugal obligation (to have offspring)
debó *m* (*pl:* **-boes**) scraper (*for skins*)
Débora *f* Deborah
debutante *m* debutant (*man*); *f* debutante (*woman*)
debutar *vn* to make one's debut
década *f* decade
decadencia *f* decadence
decadente *adj* decadent; *mf* (lit.) decadent
decadentismo *m* (lit.) decadence
decadentista *adj & mf* (lit.) decadent
decaedro *m* (geom.) decahedron
decaer §28 *vn* to decay; to fail, weaken, sink; (naut.) to drift from the course
decágono -na *adj & m* (geom.) decagon
decagramo *m* decagram
decaigo *1st sg pres ind of* **decaer**
decaimiento *m* decay; decline, weakness
decalaje *m* unwedging, unkeying; unscotching (*of a wheel*); shift; (elec.) phase shift; (aer.) stagger; **decalaje de escobillas** (elec.) brush shift
decalcomanía *f* decalcomania
decalescencia *f* (metal.) decalescence
decalitro *m* decaliter
decálogo *m* decalog
decalvante *adj* (med.) decalvant
decalvar *va* to shave the head of (*as punishment*)
decámetro *m* decameter
decampar *vn* to decamp
decanato *m* deanship; deanery; (eccl.) deanship
decano -na *adj* senior; *m* dean (*of a school*); (fig.) dean
decantación *f* decantation
decantar *va* to decant; to exaggerate, puff up; to exalt, to extol; *vn* **decantar por** to back up, support
decapar *va* to oxidize and clean the surface of (*a metal*)
decapitación *f* decapitation
decapitar *va* to decapitate
decápodo -da *adj & m* (zool.) decapod
decárea *f* decare
decasílabo -ba *adj* decasyllable, decasyllabic; *m* decasyllable
decastéreo *m* decastere
decatlo or **decatlón** *m* (sport) decathlon
deceleración *f* deceleration
decelerar *va, vn & vr* to decelerate
decembrino -na *adj* (pertaining to) December
decena *f* see **deceno**
decenal *adj* decennial
decenario -ria *adj* (pertaining to) ten; *m* decade; ten-bead rosary
decencia *f* decency, propriety; dignity; cleanliness, tidiness
decenio *m* decade
deceno -na *adj & m* tenth; *f* ten, about ten; (period of) ten days; (mus.) tenth (*interval and organ stop*); **las decenas** the tens (*the numbers 10, 20, 30, etc.*)
decentar §18 *va* to cut the first slice of; to begin to lose (*e.g., health*); *vr* to get bedsores
decente *adj* decent, proper; dignified; clean, decent-looking; respectable
decenvir *m* decemvir
decenviral *adj* decemviral
decenvirato *m* decemvirate
decenviro *m* decemvir
decepción *f* disappointment; deception
decepcionar *va* to disappoint
deceso *m* (obs.) decease, death
deciárea *f* deciare
decibel *m,* **decibelio** or **decíbelo** *m* (phys.) decibel
decible *adj* utterable, to be told
decidero -ra *adj* mentionable; **decideras** *fpl* (coll.) fluency
decidido -da *adj* decided; determined
decidir *va* to decide; to persuade; to decide on; **decidir a** + *inf* to persuade to + *inf; vn* to decide; **decidir** + *inf* to decide to + *inf; vr* to decide; **decidirse a** + *inf* to decide to + *inf*
decidor -dora *adj* facile, fluent, witty; *mf* pleasant talker, wit
deciduo -dua *adj* (bot. & zool.) deciduous
deciestéreo *m* decistere
decigramo *m* decigram
decilitro *m* deciliter
decillón *m* British decillion
décima *f* see **décimo**
decimación *f* decimation
décimacuarta *adj & f* var. of **décimocuarta**
decimal *adj & m* decimal
decimalizar §76 *va* to decimalize
décimanona *adj & f* var. of **décimonona**
décimanovena *adj & f* var. of **décimonovena**
décimaoctava *adj & f* var. of **décimoctava**
décimaquinta *adj & f* var. of **décimoquinta**
décimaséptima *adj & f* var. of **décimoséptima**
décimasexta *adj & f* var. of **décimosexta**
décimatercera *adj & f* var. of **décimotercera**
décimatercia *adj & f* var. of **décimotercia**
decímetro *m* decimeter
décimo -ma *adj* tenth; *m* tenth; tenth part of a lottery ticket; *f* tenth; (mus.) tenth; Spanish ten-line stanza of octosyllables with the following rhyme scheme: abba - accddc
décimoctavo -va *adj* eighteenth; *f* (mus.) eighteenth
décimocuarto -ta *adj* fourteenth; *f* (mus.) fourteenth
décimonono -na *adj* nineteenth; *f* (mus.) nineteenth (*interval and organ stop*)
décimonoveno -na *adj* nineteenth; *f* (mus.) nineteenth (*interval and organ stop*)
décimoquinto -ta *adj* fifteenth; *f* (mus.) fifteenth
décimoséptimo -ma *adj* seventeenth; *f* (mus.) seventeenth
décimosexto -ta *adj* sixteenth; *f* (mus.) sixteenth
décimotercero -ra *adj* thirteenth; *f* (mus.) thirteenth
décimotercio -cia *adj* thirteenth; *f* (mus.) thirteenth
decir *m* saying; say-so; **al decir de** according to; **decir de las gentes** talk (*unfavorable*) ‖ §37 *va* to say, to tell; to talk (*e.g., nonsense*); to speak (*the truth*); to show, reveal; to call; to read, e.g., **el artículo cuatro dice así ...** article four reads thus ...; **como quien dice** or **como si dijéramos** so to speak; **como quien no dice nada** and this is important; **como dijo el otro** as the fellow said; **ello dirá** we shall see; **el qué dirán** what people say; **es decir** that is to say; **mejor dicho** rather; **no hay más que decir** there is nothing more to do about it; **no decir ni malo ni bueno** to make no answer; **no digamos** as one might say; **por decirlo así** so to speak; **por decir mejor** rather, in other words; **¿qué dice?** what is it, e.g., **¡María! — ¿Qué dice, mamá?** Mary! What is it, mama?; **querer decir** to mean; **que digamos** to speak of, e.g., **no llueve que digamos** it isn't raining to speak of; what we might call, e.g., **no estaba muy limpio que digamos** he was not what we might call very clean; **decir entre sí** to say to oneself; **decir** + *inf* to say that + *ind*, e.g., **decía tener muchos amigos en Madrid** he said he had many friends in Madrid; **decirle a uno cuántas son cinco** (coll.) to tell a person what's what, to speak one's mind to a person; **decirle a uno que** + *subj* to tell someone to + *inf;* **decir misa** to say mass; **decir para sí** to say to oneself; **decir por decir** to talk for talk's sake; **decir que sí** to say yes; **decírselo a uno deletreado** (coll.) to spell it out to a person; **¡diga!** hello! (*on answering telephone*); **¡digo, digo!** say!, listen! ‖ *vn* to suit, to fit; **¿porqué dice?** why do you ask?, e.g., **Yo soy de Madrid. ¿Porqué dice?** I'm from Madrid. Why

do you ask?; **Vd. dirá** say when; **decir bien a** to suit, go well on; **decir con** to harmonize with; **decir mal a** to not suit, to not go well on ‖ *vr* to be said, to be told; to be called; to call oneself; **se dice** it is said, they say
decisión *f* decision
decisivo -va *adj* decisive
declamación *f* declamation
declamador -dora *adj* declaiming; *mf* declaimer
declamar *va & vn* to declaim
declamatorio -ria *adj* declamatory
declarable *adj* declarable
declaración *f* declaration; (bridge) bid
declaradamente *adv* manifestly, clearly
declarante *mf* declarant; (bridge) bidder
declarar *va* to declare; *vn* to declare; (law) to testify, to make a statement; *vr* to declare oneself; to arise, occur, take place, break out
declarativo -va *adj* declarative
declaratorio -ria *adj* declaratory
declinable *adj* declinable
declinación *f* declination; fall, decline; (astr. & magnetism) declination; (gram.) declension
declinar *va* to decline, refuse; (gram.) to decline; *vn* to decline, to turn down or away; to abate, diminish; to degenerate; (gram.) to decline
declinatoria *f* (law) declinatory plea
declinatorio *m* declinatory compass
declive *m* descent, declivity; slope (*amount of sloping*); **en declive** (fig.) on the decline
declividad *f* declivity
declivio *m* var. of **declive**
decocción *f* decoction; (pharm.) decoction
decoloración *f* decolorization, loss of color
decolorar *va* to decolorize; *vr* to lose color
decollaje *m* (aer.) take-off
decollar *vn* (aer.) to take off
decomisar *va* to confiscate, seize
decomiso *m* confiscation, seizure
decoración *f* decoration; memorizing, memorization; (theat.) set, scenery; **decoraciones** *fpl* (theat.) scenery; **decoración interior** interior decoration
decorado -da *adj* decorated; *m* decoration; (theat.) décor, scenery; memorizing
decorador -dora *mf* decorator
decorar *va* to decorate; to memorize
decorativo -va *adj* decorative
decoro *m* decorum; honor, respect
decoroso -sa *adj* decorous, decent; honorable, respectful
decrecer §34 *vn* to decrease, diminish
decreciente *adj* decreasing, diminishing; (phonet.) falling (*diphthong*)
decrecimiento *m* decrease, diminution
decremento *m* decrement, decrease; (rad.) decrement
decrémetro *m* (rad.) decremeter
decrepitación *f* crackling
decrepitar *vn* to crackle
decrépito -ta *adj* decrepit
decrepitud *f* decrepitude; decline; **en la decrepitud** on the decline
decrescendo *m* (mus.) decrescendo
decretal *adj* decretal; *f* decretal; **decretales** *fpl* decretals
decretalista *m* (theol.) decretalist
decretar *va* to decree
decretero *m* list of decrees
decretista *m* decretist
decreto *m* decree
decreto-ley *m* decree law
decretorio -ria *adj* (med.) critical
decúbito *m* (med.) decubitus; (path.) decubitus (*ulcer*)
decumbente *adj* decumbent; (bot.) decumbent
decuplar *va* to decuple
decuplicar §86 *va* to decuple
décuplo -pla *adj & m* decuple, tenfold
decuria *f* decury
decurrente *adj* (bot.) decurrent
decursas *fpl* arrears
decurso *m* course (*of time*)
decuso -sa or **decusado -da** *adj* decussate; (bot.) decussate
dechado *m* example, sample, model, standard; sampler (*embroidered cloth*)
dedada *f* touch (*small quantity, e.g., of honey, picked up on finger*); flip of finger; **dar una dedada de miel a** (coll.) to feed the hopes of
dedal *m* thimble; thimbleful; fingerstall
dedalera *f* (bot.) foxglove
Dédalo *m* (myth.) Daedalus; (*l.c.*) *m* labyrinth
dedeo *m* (mus.) finger dexterity
dedicación *f* dedication; dedicatory inscription on a building
dedicante *mf* dedicator
dedicar §86 *va* to dedicate (*e.g., a church, a monument, a book, one's life*); to autograph (*a book, a photograph*); to devote (*e.g., one's time*); *vr* to devote oneself
dedicativo -va *adj* dedicative
dedicatorio -ria *adj* dedicatory; *f* dedication (*e.g., of a book*); autograph, inscription (*in a book, on a photograph*)
dedil *m* fingerstall
dedillo *m* small finger; **jugar al dedillo** (coll.) to cheat in weighing; **saber al dedillo** (coll.) to have at one's finger tips
dedo *m* finger; toe; finger's breadth, finger; (coll.) bit; **alzar el dedo** (coll.) to raise one's hand (*in taking an oath, etc.*); **cogerse los dedos** to burn one's fingers; **el dedo de Dios** the hand of God; **estar a dos dedos de** + *inf* (coll.) to be within an ace of + *ger;* **irse de entre los dedos** (coll.) to slip between the fingers; **no tener dos dedos de frente** (coll.) to have no brains; **poner el dedo en la llaga** to put one's finger on the sore spot; **poner los cinco dedos en la cara a** (coll.) to slap in the face; **tener en la punta de los dedos** (coll.) to have at one's finger tips; **dedo anular** ring finger; **dedo auricular** little finger; **dedo cordial, de en medio,** or **del corazón** middle finger; **dedo gordo** thumb; big toe; **dedo índice** index finger, forefinger; **dedo mayor** middle finger; **dedo médico** ring finger; **dedo meñique** little finger; **dedo mostrador** index finger, forefinger; **dedo pulgar** thumb; big toe; **dedo saludador** index finger, forefinger
dedolación *f* (surg.) dedolation
dedolar §77 *va* (surg.) to cut (*skin*) obliquely
deducción *f* deduction; derivation; (mus.) diatonic scale
deducible *adj* deducible; deductible
deducir §38 *va* to deduce; to deduct; (law) to allege
deductivo -va *adj* deductive
deduje *1st sg pret ind of* **deducir**
deduzco *1st sg pres ind of* **deducir**
defalcar §86 *va* var. of **desfalcar**
defasar *va* (elec.) to dephase
defecación *f* defecation
defecar §86 *va* to defecate, purify, refine; *vn* to defecate
defección *f* defection; insurrection; mean quirk
defeccionar *vn & vr* (Am.) to defect, desert
defectible *adj* unsure; faulty, defective
defectivo -va *adj* defective; (gram.) defective
defecto *m* defect; shortage, lack, absence; **defectos** *mpl* (print.) sheets left over or sheets lacking (*after printing*); **en defecto de** for lack of, in default of; **defecto de masa** (phys.) mass defect
defectuosamente *adv* imperfectly
defectuoso -sa *adj* defective, faulty
defeminación *f* masculinization
defendedero -ra *adj* defensible
defendedor -dora *mf* defender
defender §66 *va* to defend; to protect; to delay, interfere with; (law) to defend; (archaic) to forbid, prohibit; *vr* to defend oneself; to get along
defendible *adj* defensible
defenestración *f* defenestration; violent dismissal or discharge
defensa *f* defense; (law & sport) defense; (naut.) skid; fender, guard; horn (*of bull*); tusk (*of elephant*); (Am.) bumper (*of automobile*); **defensa en profundidad** (mil.) defense in depth; *m* (football) back
defensión *f* defense, protection
defensivo -va *adj* defensive; *m* defense, protection; *f* defensive; **estar a la defensiva** to be on the defensive

defensor -sora *adj* defending; *mf* defender; (law) counsel for the defense
defensoría *f* (law) defense (*as a practice or service*)
defensorio *m* written defense
deferencia *f* deference
deferente *adj* deferential; (anat.) deferent
deferir §62 *va* (law) to refer, transfer, delegate; *vn* to defer; **deferir a** to defer to (*e.g., the wishes of someone*)
deficiencia *f* deficiency, defect
deficiente *adj* deficient, defective
déficit *m* (*pl:* **-cit**) deficit; lack, shortage
deficitario -ria *adj* (pertaining to a) deficit, deficiency; lacking
definible *adj* definable
definición *f* definition; outcome; decision, verdict; (opt.) definition
definido -da *adj* definite; defined, sharp
definidor -dora *adj* defining; *mf* definer; *m* (eccl.) definitor
definir *va* to define; to determine, to settle; (paint.) to finish, to complete; *vr* (Am.) to clarify one's political position
definitivo -va *adj* definitive; **en definitiva** definitively; in short
deflación *f* (econ.) deflation
deflagración *f* (chem.) deflagration
deflagrar *vn* (chem.) to deflagrate
deflector *m* deflector, baffle; (naut.) deflector
deflegmar *va* (chem.) to dephlegmate
deflexión *f* deflection
defoliación *f* defoliation
deformación *f* deformation; (mach.) strain; (rad.) distortion
deformado -da *adj* deformed; out of shape
deformar *va* to deform; *vr* to become deformed
deforme *adj* deformed
deformidad *f* deformity; crude error; great offense, enormity
defraudación *f* defrauding; robbing, cheating; defeat; interception (*e.g., of light*)
defraudador -dora *mf* defrauder
defraudar *va* to defraud, to cheat; to disappoint; to defeat (*e.g., one's hopes*); to cut off (*light*); **defraudar algo a uno** to cheat someone out of something
defuera *adv* outside; **por defuera** outside, on the outside
defunción *f* death, demise
degaullista *adj & mf* de Gaullist
degeneración *f* degeneration; degeneracy; **degeneración amiloidea** (path.) amyloid degeneration; **degeneración grasosa** (path.) fatty degeneration; **degeneración hialina** (path.) hyaline degeneration
degenerado -da *adj & mf* degenerate
degenerar *vn* to degenerate
degenerativo -va *adj* degenerative
deglución *f* swallowing, deglutition
deglutir *va & vn* to swallow
degollación *f* throat-cutting, massacre; décolletage; **degollación de los inocentes** slaughter of the innocents
degolladero *m* neck, throttle; slaughterhouse; scaffold (*for capital punishment*); décolletage
degollado *m* décolletage, low neck; (orn.) rose-breasted grosbeak
degollador -dora *adj* throat-cutting; *mf* executioner
degolladura *f* throat-cutting; décolletage; joint (*between bricks*)
degollante *mf* (coll.) bore, fool
degollar §19 *va* to cut in the throat, to cut in the neck; to kill, massacre; to cut (*a dress*) low in the neck; to spoil, to murder (*a performance, drama, etc.*); to bore, become obnoxious to
degollina *f* (coll.) slaughter, butchery
degradación *f* degradation (*demotion; depravity*); (geol.) degradation
degradante *adj* degrading
degradar *va* to degrade (*to demote, to demean; to deprave, to debase*); (geol.) to degrade; (mil.) to break
degüello *m* throat-cutting, massacre, slaughter; slender part, neck
degustación *f* tasting
degustar *va* to taste (*e.g., wines*); to savor
dehesa *f* pasture land, meadow; (taur.) range
dehesar *va* to convert into pasture
dehesero *m* keeper of pasture land
dehiscencia *f* (biol. & bot.) dehiscence
dehiscente *adj* dehiscent
deicida *adj* deicidal; *mf* deicide (*person*)
deicidio *m* deicide (*act*)
deidad *f* deity; (coll.) beauty
deificación *f* deification
deificar §86 *va* to deify; *vr* (theol.) to become deified (*by divine union*)
deífico -ca *adj* deific
deiforme *adj* (poet.) godlike
Deípara *adj* Deipara (*pertaining to the Virgin Mary*)
deísmo *m* deism
deísta *adj* deistic; *mf* deist
deja *f* jut, projection
dejación *f* abandonment, relinquishment; **hacer dejación de** to abandon
dejadez *f* laziness, negligence; untidiness, slovenliness; fatigue, low spirits
dejado -da *adj* lazy, negligent; untidy, slovenly; dejected, low-spirited, listless; **dejado de la mano de Dios** vile, infamous, beyond redemption; bungling; *f* (sport) easy short return (*of ball*)
dejamiento *m* abandonment, relinquishment; laziness; untidiness; dejection
dejar *va* to leave; to abandon; to yield, produce; to appoint; to lend; **dejar** + *inf* to let + *inf*, to permit + *inf;* to let be + *pp*, *e.g.,* **dejar oír la voz** to let one's voice be heard; **dejar caer** to drop, let fall; **dejar feo a** (coll.) to slight; **dejar fresco a** (coll.) to discomfit, leave in the lurch; **dejar por** to leave as, to consider as; **dejar por** or **que** + *inf* to leave to be + *pp*, e.g., **dejó mucho trabajo por hacer** he left a lot of work to be done; **dejar ver** to show, to make it plain ‖ *vn* to stop; **no dejar de** + *inf* to not fail to + *inf;* **dejar de** + *inf* to stop or cease + *ger;* to fail to + *inf* ‖ *vr* to be careless or slovenly; to grow (*a beard, a mustache*); **dejarse** + *inf* to allow oneself to + *inf;* to allow oneself to be + *pp;* **dejarse a** to give oneself over to, to be devoted to; to yield to; **dejarse de** to cut out (*talk, nonsense*); to stop asking (*questions*); to stop making (*compliments*); to put aside (*doubts*); **dejarse de** + *inf* to stop + *ger;* **dejarse decir** to let slip (*in conversation*); **dejarse ver** to show up; to be evident, be easily seen
dejillo *m* accent (*of a region*); aftertaste
dejo *m* abandonment; end, stop; accent (*of a region*); slovenliness, neglect; aftertaste; (fig.) touch, aftertaste; drop (*in voice*)
del contraction of **de** and **el**
delación *f* accusation, denunciation, information
delantal *m* apron; workman's apron
delante *adv* before, in front, ahead; **delante de** before, in front of, ahead of
delantero -ra *adj* front; head; first; *m* postilion; nosing (*of stair tread*); (sport) forward; *f* front, front part; fore skirt; front (*of garment*); front row; front edge (*of book*); lead, advantage; cowcatcher; (taur.) front row (*of tendido bajo, i.e., third row counting barrera and contrabarrera*); **coger la delantera a** or **tomar la delantera a** to get ahead of, to outstrip; to get a start on; **tomar la delantera** to take the lead; **delanteras** *fpl* overalls
delatable *adj* accusable
delatar *va* to accuse, denounce, inform on; to reveal, divulge
delator -tora *adj* accusing, informing; *mf* accuser, denouncer, informer
dele *m* (print.) dele
deleble *adj* eradicable
delectación *f* delectation
delegación *f* delegation; (com.) branch; (Am.) police station
delegado -da *mf* delegate; (com.) agent, representative
delegar §59 *va* to delegate
deleitabilísimo -ma *adj super* very or most delectable
deleitable *adj* delectable

deleitación *f* or **deleitamiento** *m* delectation, delight
deleitar *va* to delight; *vr* to delight, to take delight; **deleitarse con** or **en** to delight in, to take delight in; **deleitarse en** + *inf* to delight in or to take delight in + *ger*
deleite *m* delight
deleitoso -sa *adj* delightful, delicious
deletéreo -a *adj* deleterious, noxious
deletreador -dora *adj* spelling; *mf* speller
deletrear *va* to spell; to decipher; to interpret; *vn* to spell; to decipher
deletreo *m* spelling
deleznable *adj* perishable, fragile; crumbly; slippery; frail, unstable
deleznar *vr* to slip, slide
délfico -ca *adj* Delphian or Delphic
delfín *m* dauphin; (zool.) dolphin; (*cap.*) *m* (astr.) Dolphin
delfina *f* dauphiness
Delfos *f* Delphi
delga *f* (elec.) commutator bar
delgadez *f* thinness, leanness, slenderness; delicateness, tenuity, lightness; acuity, ingenuity
delgado -da *adj* thin, lean, slender, slim, lank; delicate, tenuous, light; acute, ingenious; (agr.) poor, exhausted; *m* flank (*of an animal*); (naut.) dead rise
delgaducho -cha *adj* thinnish, lanky
deliberación *f* deliberation
deliberadamente *adv* deliberately
deliberante *adj* deliberative
deliberar *va* to deliberate; **deliberar** + *inf* to come to a decision to + *inf; vn* to deliberate
deliberativo -va *adj* deliberative; (coll.) opinionated
delicadez *f* delicateness; touchiness; laziness
delicadeza *f* delicacy, delicateness; acuity, ingenuity; scrupulousness
delicado -da *adj* delicate; acute, ingenious; touchy, hard to please; cautious, scrupulous
delicia *f* delight
delicioso -sa *adj* delicious, delightful
delictivo -va or **delictuoso -sa** *adj* criminal
delicuescencia *f* deliquescence
delicuescente *adj* deliquescent
delimitación *f* delimitation
delimitar *va* to delimit
delincuencia *f* guilt, criminality, delinquency
delincuente *adj* guilty, criminal, delinquent; *mf* guilty person, criminal, delinquent
delineación *f* delineation
delineador -dora *adj* delineating; *mf* delineator, designer
delineamento or **delineamiento** *m* delineation
delineante *adj* delineating, drafting; *mf* delineator, draftsman
delinear *va* to delineate, to outline
delinquimiento *m* transgression, guilt, delinquency
delinquir §39 *vn* to transgress, be guilty, be delinquent
delio -lia *adj & mf* Delian
deliquio *m* swoon, faint
delirante *adj* delirious
delirar *vn* to be delirious, to rave, to rant; to talk nonsense
delirio *m* delirium; nonsense
delírium tremens *m* (path.) delirium tremens
delito *m* crime, transgression; **delito de incendio** arson; **delito de lesa majestad** lese majesty
Delos *f* Delos
delta *f* delta; *m & f* delta (*of a river*)
deltoides *adj* deltoid (*triangular*); (anat.) deltoid; *m* (anat.) deltoid, deltoid muscle
deludir *va* to delude
delusor -sora *adj* delusive; *mf* deluder
delusorio -ria *adj* delusive, delusory
demacración *f* emaciation
demacrar *va & vr* to waste away
demagogia *f* demagoguery or demagogy
demagógico -ca *adj* demagogic
demagogo -ga *mf* demagog
demanda *f* demand; petition; claim; complaint; undertaking; begging; charity box (*carried by beggars*); lawsuit; quest (*of the Holy Grail*); (elec.) load; **ir en demanda de** to go looking for; **tener demanda** to be in demand; **demanda máxima** (elec.) peak load
demandadero -ra *mf* messenger (*in convents and prisons*); outside errand boy or girl
demandado -da *mf* (law) defendant
demandador -dora *mf* claimant, solicitor; (law) complainant, plaintiff
demandante *mf* (law) plaintiff, complainant
demandar *va* to demand; (law) to sue, file a suit against
demarcación *f* demarcation
demarcador -dora *adj* demarcating; *mf* demarcator
demarcar §86 *va* to demarcate
demás *adj indef* other, rest of the, e.g., **la demás gente** the rest of the people; **estar demás** to be useless; to be in the way, be unwanted; **lo demás** the rest; **por lo demás** furthermore, besides; *pron indef* others; **los** or **las demás** the others, the rest; *adv* besides; **por demás** in vain; too, too much; **demás de** besides, in addition to
demasía *f* excess, superabundance, surplus; boldness, audacity; insolence, outrage; evil, guilt, wrong; **en demasía** too, too much, excessively
demasiadamente *adv* too, too much, excessively
demasiado -da *adj & pron indef* too much; **demasiados -das** *adj & pron indef pl* too many; **demasiado** *adv* too; too much, too hard
demasiar *vr* (coll.) to go too far, to exceed the bounds of reason
demediar *va* to divide in half; to reach the middle of; to use up half of; *vn* to be divided in half
demencia *f* dementia, insanity; **demencia precoz** (path.) dementia praecox
dementar *va* to drive crazy; *vr* to go crazy
demente *adj* demented, insane; *mf* lunatic, crazy person; *m* madman
demérito *m* demerit, unworthiness
demeritorio -ria *adj* undeserving
Deméter *f* or **Demetria** *f* (myth.) Demeter
demisión *f* yielding, submission, humility
demiurgo *m* (philos.) Demiurge
democracia *f* democracy
demócrata *adj* democratic; *mf* democrat
democrático -ca *adj* democratic
democratización *f* democratization
democratizar §76 *va & vr* to democratize
Demócrito *m* Democritus
Demogorgón *m* (myth.) Demogorgon
demografía *f* demography
demográfico -ca *adj* demographic or demographical
demoledor -dora *adj* demolishing, destructive; *mf* demolisher
demoler §63 *va* to demolish
demolición *f* demolition
demonche *m* (coll.) devil
demoníaco -ca *adj* demoniac or demoniacal; demonic; *mf* demoniac
demonio *m* demon; devil; **estar hecho un demonio** (coll.) to be wild, be crazy as the devil; **estudiar con el demonio** (coll.) to be full of devilishness
demonismo *m* demonism
demonolatría *f* demonolatry
demonología *f* demonology
demonomancia *f* demonomancy
demontre *m* (coll.) devil; *interj* the deuce!, the devil!
demora *f* delay; (naut.) bearing
demorar *va* to delay; *vn* to delay, tarry, linger; to be delayed; (naut.) to bear
Demóstenes *m* Demosthenes
demostrabilidad *f* demonstrability
demostrable *adj* demonstrable
demostración *f* demonstration
demostrador -dora *adj* demonstrating; *mf* demonstrator; *m* hand (*of clock*); gnomon (*of sundial*)
demostrar §77 *va* to demonstrate; **demostrar** + *inf* to demonstrate that + *ind*
demostrativo -va *adj* demonstrative; (gram.) demonstrative; *m* (gram.) demonstrative
demótico -ca *adj* demotic

demudación *f* change, alteration; change of countenance
demudar *va* to change, to alter; to cloak, to disguise; *vr* to change, be changed; to change countenance, to color suddenly
demulcente *adj & m* demulcent
demulsibilidad *f* (chem.) demulsibility
demulsionar *va* (chem.) demulsify
denario -ria *adj* denary; *m* denarius
dendriforme *adj* dendriform
dendrita *f* (anat., physiol. & mineral.) dendrite
dendrítico -ca *adj* dendritic or dendritical
dendrografía *f* dendrography
dendroide *adj* dendroid
dendrómetro *m* dendrometer
denegación *f* denial, refusal
denegar §29 *va* to deny, to refuse; (law) to deny, to refuse
denegrecer §34 *va* to blacken, to darken; *vr* to become black, to turn dark
denegrido -da *adj* blackish
dengoso -sa *adj* overnice, prudish, affected
dengue *m* overniceness, prudery; cape with long points; sardine boat; (path.) dengue
denguero -ra *adj* overnice, prudish
denigración *f* defamation, revilement; insult
denigrante *adj* defamatory; insulting; *mf* defamer; insulter
denigrar *va* to defame, revile, sully; to insult
denigrativo -va *adj* defamatory; insulting
denodado -da *adj* brave, daring, bold
denominación *f* denomination
denominadamente *adv* distinctly, markedly
denominador -dora *adj* denominating; *mf* denominator; *m* (math.) denominator
denominar *va* to name, to indicate, to denominate
denominativo -va *adj* denominative; (gram.) denominative; *m* (gram.) denominative
denostadamente *adv* insultingly, abusively
denostador -dora *adj* insulting; *mf* insulter, abuser
denostar §77 *va* to insult, abuse
denostoso -sa *adj* insulting
denotación *f* denotation
denotar *va* to denote
denotativo -va *adj* denotative
densidad *f* density; darkness; confusion; (fig.) solidity, fullness, substance; **densidad de flujo** (phys.) flux density
densimetría *f* densimetry
densímetro *m* densimeter
denso -sa *adj* dense; dark; confused; thick, crowded; (fig.) solid, full, rich
dentado -da *adj* toothed, dentate; (philately) perforated; *m* gear; teeth; (philately) perforation; **dentado de peine** (philately) comb perforation
dentadura *f* denture, set of teeth; **ablandarle a uno la dentadura** (coll.) to punch someone in the teeth, to knock someone's teeth out; **dentadura artificial** denture, set of artificial teeth
dental *adj* dental; (phonet.) dental; *m* tooth of threshing machine; moldboard (*of plow*); *f* (phonet.) dental
dentalización *f* (phonet.) dentalization
dentalizar §76 *va* (phonet.) to dentalize; *vr* (phonet.) to become dentalized
dentar §18 *va* to tooth, furnish with teeth; (philately) to perforate; **sin dentar** (philately) imperforate; *vn* to teethe
dentario -ria *adj* dental; *f* (bot.) toothwort
dentejón *m* yoke for oxen
dentelaria *f* (bot.) leadwort
dentellado -da *adj* denticulate; serrulate; bitten with the teeth; (arch.) denticulate; (her.) dentelated; *f* biting; bite; tooth mark; **a dentelladas** with the teeth
dentellar *vn* to chatter (*said of teeth*)
dentellear *va* to nibble, nibble at
dentellón *m* cam, tooth (*of lock*); (arch.) tooth (*of toothing*); (arch.) dentil
dentera *f* tooth edge; envy; eagerness, great desire; **dar dentera** to set the teeth on edge; to make eager or impatient
dentezuelo *m* little tooth
dentición *f* dentition, teething
denticulación *f* denticulation
denticulado -da *adj* denticulate
denticular *adj* denticular
dentículo *m* little tooth; (arch.) dentil; (bot. & zool.) dentation
dentífrico -ca *adj* tooth (*paste, etc.*); *m* dentifrice
dentilabial *adj & f* (phonet.) dentilabial
dentilingual *adj & f* (phonet.) dentilingual
dentina *f* (anat.) dentine
dentirrostro -tra *adj* dentirostral or dentirostrate; *m* (orn.) dentiroster
dentista *mf* dentist
dentistería *f* dentistry
dentística *f* (Am.) dentistry
dentivano -na *adj* (vet.) having long, wide teeth
dentón -tona *adj* having large, uneven teeth; *m* (ichth.) dentex
dentro *adv* inside, within; **por dentro** on the inside; **dentro de** inside, within; **dentro de poco** shortly; **dentro en** on the inside of; **dentro o fuera** (coll.) yes or no
dentudo -da *adj* having large, uneven teeth
denudación *f* denudation
denudar *va* to denude, lay bare; *vn* to be denuded; to be stripped of bark
denuedo *m* bravery, daring
denuesto *m* insult, abuse
denuncia *f* proclamation, announcement; foretelling; denunciation
denunciación *f* denunciation
denunciador -dora *mf* denouncer, denunciator
denunciante *mf* denouncer
denunciar *va* to proclaim; to foretell; to denounce, to denunciate, to squeal on; (dipl. & min.) to denounce
denunciatorio -ria *adj* denunciatory
denuncio *m* (min.) denouncement, denunciation
deontología *f* deontology; **deontología médica** medical ethics
deparar *va* to provide, furnish; to present
departamental *adj* departmental
departamento *m* department; compartment; naval district (*in Spain*); (rail.) compartment; apartment
departidor -dora *adj* conversing; *mf* converser, conversationalist
departir *vn* to chat, to converse
depauperación *f* impoverishment; weakening, exhaustion, depletion
depauperar *va* to pauperize, to impoverish; to weaken, exhaust, deplete; *vr* to become weakened, become exhausted
dependencia *f* dependence, dependency; branch, branch office; affair, charge, agency; relationship; friendship; employees, clerks; **dependencias** *fpl* accessories
depender *vn* to depend; **depender de** to depend on or upon
dependienta *f* female employee, clerk, store clerk
dependiente *adj* dependent; (pertaining to a) branch; *mf* dependent; employee, clerk, store clerk
depilación *f* depilation
depilar *va* to depilate
depilatorio -ria *adj & m* depilatory
deplorable *adj* deplorable
deplorar *va* to deplore
depondré *1st sg fut ind of* **deponer**
deponente *adj* (gram.) deponent; *mf* (law) deponent; *m* (gram.) deponent verb
deponer §69 *va* to set aside, to put aside, to remove, to take down; to remove from office, to depose; to lay down (*arms*); (law) to depose, to depone; *vn* to have a movement (*of bowels*); (law) to depose, to depone; (Am.) to vomit
depongo *1st sg pres ind of* **deponer**
depopulador -dora *adj* devastating; *mf* destroyer, plunderer
deportación *f* deportation
deportado -da *mf* deportee
deportante *mf* sport fan; sportsman
deportar *va* to deport
deporte *m* sport; outdoor recreation
deportismo *m* sport, sports; love of sport or sports; participation in sports

deportista *adj* (pertaining to) sport; sporting; *mf* sport fan; *m* sportsman; *f* sportswoman
deportivo -va *adj* (pertaining to) sport, sports
deposición *f* deposition, deposal; removal (*from office*); bowel movement; (law) deposition
depositador -dora *adj* depositing; *mf* depositor
depositante *mf* depositor
depositar *va* to deposit; to store; to entrust; to confide; to check (*baggage*); to bond (*merchandise*); to commit (*a person*); to place (*a corpse*) in a receiving vault; (law) to free (*a young person*) from parental restraint; *vr* to deposit, to settle
depositaría *f* depository; public treasury; trust
depositario -ria *adj* depository; (pertaining to a) deposit; *mf* depositary, repository; *m* public treasurer
depósito *m* depot, warehouse; deposit; stack (*of books in a library*); dump; reservoir; tank; well (*of a fountain pen*); (mil.) depot; **en depósito** on deposit; **depósito anatómico** morgue; **depósito comercial** bonded warehouse; **depósito de agua** reservoir; water tank; **depósito (judicial) de cadáveres** morgue; **depósito de cereales** grain elevator; **depósito de equipajes** (rail.) checkroom; **depósito de gasolina** (aut.) gas tank; **depósito de locomotoras** (rail.) roundhouse; **depósito de municiones** munition dump
depravación *f* depravation, depravity
depravado -da *adj* depraved
depravador -dora *adj* depraving; *mf* depraver
depravar *va* to deprave; *vr* to become depraved
deprecación *f* entreaty, prayer
deprecante *adj* entreating, imploring
deprecar §86 *va* to entreat, to implore
deprecativo -va *adj* deprecative; (gram.) imperative; *m* (gram.) imperative (*with supplication or entreaty*)
deprecatorio -ria *adj* deprecatory
depreciación *f* depreciation (*in value*)
depreciar *va & vn* to depreciate (*to diminish in value*)
depredación *f* depredation; embezzlement; (law) depredation
depredador -dora *adj* depredating; predatory; *mf* depredator; predator
depredar *va* to depredate; to embezzle
depresión *f* depression; drop, dip; (path.) depression; (meteor.) depression, low; recess, recession (*e.g., in a wall*)
depresivo -va *adj* depressive
depresor -sora *adj* depressing; *mf* depressor; *m* (anat., physiol. & surg.) depressor; **depresor de la lengua** (med.) tongue depressor
deprimente *adj* depressive; depressing; depressant; *m* (med.) depressant
deprimido -da *adj* depressed, flattened; weakened; receding (*e.g., forehead*)
deprimir *va* to depress, to compress; to push in; to belittle; to humiliate; to weaken; *vr* to be or become depressed or compressed; to be or become humiliated; to be weakened, to become weak; to recede
depuesto -ta *pp of* **deponer**
depuración *f* purification; purging
depurar *va* to purify, refine, cleanse; to purge; *vr* to be or become purified, to be cleansed
depurativo -va *adj & m* (med.) depurative
depuse *1st sg pret ind of* **deponer**
derecera *f* straight road, straight path
derecha *f* see **derecho**
derechamente *adv* directly, straight; wisely, justly; properly
derechazo *m* blow with the right (*hand*); (box.) right
derechero -ra *adj* right, just, sure; *m* tax collector; *f* straightaway, straight road
derechismo *m* rightism
derechista *adj & mf* rightist
derecho -cha *adj* right; right-hand; right-handed; straight; standing, upright; *m* law; right; grant, privilege, exemption; road, path; right side (*e.g., of cloth*); **derechos** *mpl* dues, duties, fees, taxes; **según derecho** by right, by rights; **derecho canónico** canon law; **derecho civil** civil law; **derecho consuetudinario** common law; **derecho de asilo** right of asylum; **derecho de gentes** international law; **derecho de reunión** right of assembly; **derecho de propiedad literaria** copyright; **derecho de subscripción** (com.) right; **derecho de visita** right of search; **derecho divino** divine right; **derecho internacional** international law; **derecho romano** Roman law; **derechos civiles** civil rights; **derechos consulares** consular fees; **derechos de aduana** customhouse duties; **derechos de almacenaje** storage (*costs*); **derechos de autor** royalty; **derechos del hombre** rights of man; **derechos naturales** natural rights; **derechos reservados** copyright; *f* right hand; right-hand side; (pol.) right; **a derechas** right, rightly; **a la derecha** right, on the right, to the right; **derecho** *adv* directly, straight; rightly, wisely; **todo derecho** straight ahead
derechura *f* rightness, rectitude; directness, straightness; servants' wages; **en derechura** directly, straight; right away, without delay; with determination, steadfastly
deriva *f* (aer. & naut.) drift; (gun.) drift compensation; **ir a la deriva** (naut.) to drift, to be adrift
derivación *f* derivation; (gram., math. & med.) derivation; (gun.) drift; (elec.) shunt, shunt connection; **en derivación** (elec.) shunt, shunted; **derivación regresiva** (philol.) back formation
derivado -da *adj* derived; derivative; (gram.) derivative; (elec.) shunt, derived; *m* derivative, by-product; **derivado regresivo** (philol.) back formation, *f* (math.) derivative
derivador *m* (elec.) graduator
derivar *va* to derive; to turn (*e.g., one's attention*); to guide, to lead; (elec.) to shunt; *vn & vr* to derive, to be derived; (aer. & naut.) to drift
derivativo -va *adj & m* (gram. & med.) derivative
derivo *m* derivation, origin
derivómetro *m* (aer. & naut.) drift meter
dermalgia *f* (path.) skin neuralgia
dermatitis *f* (path.) dermatitis
dermatoesqueleto *m* (zool.) exoskeleton
dermatografía *f* (path.) dermatographia; dermatography (*description of skin*)
dermatología *f* dermatology
dermatológico -ca *adj* dermatological
dermatólogo -ga *mf* dermatologist
dermatosis *f* (path.) dermatosis
dermesto *m* (ent.) larder beetle
dérmico -ca *adj* dermic, dermal
dermis *f* (anat.) dermis, cutis
dermografía *f* or **dermografismo** *m* (path.) dermographia or dermographism
-dero -ra *suffix adj* -able, e.g., **casadero** marriageable; **comedero** eatable; -ible, e.g., **hacedero** feasible; *suffix m* used to indicate the place where something is performed, e.g., **desembarcadero** landing place; **lavadero** washing place; **picadero** riding school
derogación *f* abolition, elimination; decrease, deterioration, derogation
derogar §59 *va* to destroy, abolish, modify, reform (*a law, custom, etc.*)
derogatorio -ria *adj* abolishing, modifying, repealing
derrabadura *f* cutting or pulling out the tail; wound left after cutting tail
derrabar *va* to cut or pull out the tail of, to dock
derrama *f* apportionment of a tax; special tax
derramadero *m* dumping ground, dumping place; weir, spillway
derramado -da *adj* extravagant, prodigal, lavish
derramamiento *m* pouring, spilling, shedding; spreading, scattering, publishing; lavishing, wasting; waterflow, dispersion
derramar *va* to pour out, to spill, to shed; to spread, scatter, publish; to lavish, to waste; to apportion (*e.g., taxes*); *vr* to run over, to overflow; to spread, spread out; to open, flow, empty (*said of a stream*)
derramasolaces *mf* (*pl:* **-ces**) wet blanket

derrame *m* pouring, spill, shed; spread, dispersion; lavishing, waste; overflow; leakage; (arch.) splay, chamfering; slope; outlet; (med.) discharge, effusion
derramo *m* (arch.) splay, chamfering, flare, flanging
derrapar *vn* to skid
derredor *m* circumference; **al** or **en derredor** around, round about; **al** or **en derredor de** around; **por todo el derredor** all around, in every direction
derrelicción *f* dereliction, abandonment
derrelicto *m* (naut.) derelict (*ship*)
derrelinquir §39 *va* to forsake, to abandon
derrenegar §29 *vn* (coll.) to be a hater; **derrenegar de** (coll.) to be a hater of, to hate, loathe, detest
derrengado -da *adj* twisted, bent, crooked; lame, crippled, out of shape
derrengadura *f* crookedness; lameness, sore back
derrengar §29 or §59 *va* to break the back of, to cripple; to bend, make crooked; (dial.) to knock (*fruit*) from tree with a stick
derrengo *m* (dial.) stick for knocking fruit from tree
derreniego *m* (coll.) curse, blasphemy
derretido -da *adj* madly in love; *m* concrete
derretimiento *m* melting, thawing; intense love, mad passion
derretir §94 *va* to melt, to thaw; to squander; (coll.) to change (*money*); *vr* to melt, to thaw; to be or fall madly in love; to be very susceptible, to fall in love easily; (coll.) to be worried, uneasy, or impatient
derribador -dora *adj* overthrowing; *mf* overthrower; *m* feller (*in abattoir*)
derribar *va* to demolish, destroy, tear down, knock down; to wreck; to fell; to overthrow; to subdue (*an emotion or passion*); to bring down, shoot down; to bring down, humiliate; *vr* to fall down, tumble down; to throw oneself on the ground
derribo *m* demolition, wrecking, overthrow; felling; bringing down (*of an enemy plane*); **derribos** *mpl* debris, rubble
derrocadero *m* rocky precipice
derrocamiento *m* flinging, throwing down, overthrow; demolition; ousting
derrocar §86 or §95 *va* to throw from a rock or precipice; to demolish, tear down, knock down; to overthrow, bring down, humble, oust
derrochador -dora *adj* squandering; *mf* squanderer, wastrel
derrochar *va* to waste, squander
derroche *m* waste, squandering, extravagance, profusion
derrota *f* rout, defeat; route, road, way; (naut.) course
derrotado -da *adj* threadbare, shabby
derrotar *va* to rout, put to flight; to defeat; to wear, wear out; to squander, waste; to ruin; *vr* (naut.) to drift from the course
derrote *m* upward thrust with the horns
derrotero *m* (naut.) ship's course, navigation route; route, course
derrotismo *m* defeatism
derrotista *adj & mf* defeatist
derrubiar *va & vr* to wash away, to wear away
derrubio *m* washout; alluvium
derruir §41 *va* to tear down, to raze, to destroy, to ruin
derrumbadero *m* precipice, crag; hazard, risky business
derrumbamiento *m* plunge, headlong plunge; collapse, cave-in; (eng.) wrecking; **derrumbamiento de tierra** landslide
derrumbar *va* to throw headlong; *vr* to plunge headlong; to crumble, collapse; to fall in, cave in
derrumbe *m* precipice; fall; landslide; cave-in; (eng.) wrecking
derrumbo *m* precipice
derviche *m* dervish
des- *prefix* de-, e.g., **descornar** dehorn; **destronar** dethrone; dis-, e.g., **desconfiar** distrust; **descubrir** discover; un-, e.g., **desgraciado** unfortunate; **desigual** unequal; **desabotonar** unbutton; **desenganchar** unhook; under-, e.g., **desnutrido** underfed
desabarrancar §86 *va* to pull out of a ditch; to extricate
desabastecer §34 *va* to deprive of supplies or provisions
desabejar *va* to remove the bees from
desabillé *m* deshabille
desabollador *m* dent remover (*tool*)
desabollar *va* to knock the dents out of, to straighten, to flatten; *vr* to flatten out
desabollonar *va* var. of **desabollar**
desabonar *vr* to drop one's subscription
desabono *m* cancellation of subscription, discontinuance of subscription; damage, harm (*through gossip*)
desabor *m* tastelessness, insipidity
desabordar *vr* (naut.) to get clear of a ship; (naut.) to get clear of each other (*said of two ships which have run afoul of each other*)
desaborido -da *adj* tasteless, insipid; flimsy, insignificant; (coll.) dull, witless; *mf* (coll.) dull, witless person
desabotonar *va* to unbutton; *vn* to blossom, to bloom
desabrido -da *adj* tasteless, insipid, unseasoned; rough, unpleasant, uneven; gruff, surly; unseasonable, inclement; kicking, hard-kicking (*said of a gun*)
desabrigado -da *adj* lightly dressed; unsheltered; uncovered, unprotected, defenseless
desabrigar §59 *va* to uncover, bare, undress; to deprive of shelter or protection; *vr* to uncover oneself, to undress, to take off clothing; to be deprived of shelter or protection
desabrigo *m* uncovering; lack of covering or clothing; lack of protection; unprotected place; abandonment, desertion
desabrillantar *va* to deprive of luster; *vr* to lose luster
desabrimiento *m* lack of seasoning, insipidity, flatness; bitterness, despondency; harshness; recoil (*of firearms*)
desabrir *va* to give a bad taste to; to embitter; *vr* to become embittered
desabrochar *va* to unsnap, to unbutton, to unfasten, to unclasp; to reveal; *vr* to become unfastened; (coll.) to unbosom oneself; **desabrocharse con** (coll.) to unbosom oneself to, to open up one's heart to
desacalorar *vr* to cool off; (fig.) to cool off (*from anger*)
desacatador -dora *adj* disrespectful, irreverent; *mf* disrespectful or irreverent person
desacatamiento *m* disrespect, irreverence
desacatar *va* to treat disrespectfully, to be disrespectful toward, to be irreverent toward
desacato *m* disrespect, irreverence, contempt
desacedar *va* to remove the roughness from
desaceitado -da *adj* unoiled
desaceitar *va* to remove the oil from
desaceleración *f* deceleration
desacelerar *va & vr* to decelerate
desacerar *va* to remove or wear away the steel from; *vr* to lose its steel surface or edge (*said, e.g., of a tool*)
desacertado -da *adj* wrong, unwise; wide of the mark
desacertar §18 *vn* to be wrong
desacidificar §86 *va* to remove the acidity from; to neutralize (*an acid*)
desacierto *m* error, mistake, blunder
desacobardar *va* to free of fear, to stiffen
desacomodado -da *adj* inconvenient; troublesome; out of service, unemployed; not well-to-do
desacomodamiento *m* inconvenience
desacomodar *va* to inconvenience, disturb; to discharge, dismiss; *vr* to lose one's job
desacomodo *m* discharge, dismissal
desacompañamiento *m* abandonment, lack of company
desacompañar *va* to abandon, leave the company of
desaconsejado -da *adj* ill-advised
desaconsejar *va* to dissuade, try to dissuade
desacoplar *va* to disconnect, to uncouple
desacordado -da *adj* discordant; (mus.) out of tune, inharmonious; (paint.) inharmonious (*in color*), out of proportion

desacordar §77 *va* to put out of tune; *vr* to get out of tune; to become forgetful
desacorde *adj* discordant, inharmonious, incongruous
desacorralar *va* to take out of a corral or inclosure; (taur.) to bring (*a bull*) out into the ring or into an open field; (coll.) to get (*someone*) out of a hole or jam
desacostumbrado -da *adj* unaccustomed, unusual
desacostumbrar *va* to break of a habit or custom, to wean away
desacotar *va* to lay open (*a pasture or field*); to refuse, reject; *vn* to withdraw from a conference or deal
desacoto *m* opening a pasture or field
desacreditar *va* to discredit, bring discredit on; *vn* to discredit, to bring discredit
desacuerdo *m* discord, disaccord, disagreement; error, mistake; forgetfulness, forgetting; derangement; unconsciousness
desaderezar §76 *va* to disarrange, to ruffle, to upset; *vr* to become disarranged, be put in disorder
desadeudar *va* to free from debt; *vr* to get out of debt
desadormecer §34 *va* to awaken; to free from numbness; *vr* to awaken, get awake; to get free of numbness
desadornar *va* to remove the ornaments or decorations from; *vr* to be unadorned
desadorno *m* lack of ornaments, lack of decoration
desadvertido -da *adj* inattentive; unnoticed
desadvertimiento *m* inadvertence
desadvertir §62 *va* to fail to notice, to not notice, to be unaware of
desafear *va* to make less ugly, to remove the ugliness of; *vr* to become less ugly, to lose one's or its ugliness
desafección *f* disaffection, dislike
desafectar *va* to dislike
desafecto -ta *adj* disaffected; opposed; *m* disaffection, dislike
desaferrar *va* to loosen, let go, unfasten; to make (*a person*) change his mind; (naut.) to raise (*the anchors*)
desafiadero *m* secret dueling ground
desafiador -dora *adj* challenging, defiant; *mf* challenger; duelist; feudist
desafiar §90 *va* to challenge, dare, defy; to oppose, to face, to rival, to compete with; **desafiar a** + *inf* to challenge to + *inf*; *vn* to feud; *vr* to challenge each other; to compete
desafición *f* disaffection, dislike
desaficionar *va* to cause to dislike; *vr* to become disliked; **desaficionarse de** to lose one's liking for
desafilar *va* to dull, make dull; *vr* to dull, become dull
desafinación *f* dissonance, being out of tune
desafinadamente *adv* out of tune
desafinado -da *adj* out of tune, flat
desafinar *va* to put out of tune; to play or sing out of tune; *vn* to get out of tune; to play or sing out of tune; (coll.) to speak indiscreetly; *vr* to get out of tune; to play or sing out of tune
desafío *m* challenge, dare; rivalry, competition
desaforado -da *adj* disorderly, outrageous, impudent; huge, colossal, enormous; *mf* rowdy
desaforar §77 *va* to encroach upon the rights of; *vr* to forget oneself, to act in an outrageous manner
desaforrar *va* to take the lining out of
desafortunadamente *adv* unfortunately
desafortunado -da *adj* unfortunate, unlucky
desafuero *m* excess, outrage, lawlessness
desagarrar *va* (coll.) to let go of, to loosen one's hold on
desagraciado -da *adj* graceless, ungraceful
desagraciar *va* to make ungraceful, to deprive of charm
desagradable *adj* disagreeable
desagradar *va* to displease; **desagradar** + *inf* to displease (*someone*) to + *inf*, to not like to + *inf*; *vn* to displease; *vr* to be displeased; **desagradarse de** to be displeased at
desagradecer §34 *va* to be ungrateful for, to be unappreciative of
desagradecido -da *adj* ungrateful; **desagradecido a** ungrateful for (*a kindness*); **desagradecido con** or **para con** ungrateful to (*a person*)
desagradecimiento *m* ungratefulness, ingratitude
desagrado *m* displeasure
desagraviar *va* to make amends to, to indemnify
desagravio *m* amends, compensation, indemnification
desagregación *f* disintegration; (geol.) disintegration
desagregar §59 *va* & *vr* to disintegrate
desaguadero *m* drain, outlet; (fig.) drain (*source of expense*)
desaguador *m* drain, outlet; irrigation drain
desaguar §23 *va* to drain, empty; to waste, squander; *vn* to flow, to empty; *vr* to drain, be drained; to vomit; to have a movement (*of bowels*)
desaguazar §76 *va* to drain, to empty
desagüe *m* drainage, sewerage; drain, outlet
desaguisado -da *adj* illegal, unreasonable; *m* wrong, offense, outrage
desaherrojar *va* to unshackle
desahijar *va* to separate young cattle from (*the dams*); *vr* to swarm
desahitar *vr* to get rid of indigestion
desahogado -da *adj* forward, brazen, impudent; clear, free, roomy; comfortable, in comfortable circumstances; (naut.) free-running, free-sailing
desahogar §59 *va* to relieve, give comfort to; to give rein to (*desires, passions, etc.*); *vr* to ease one's discomfort, to take it easy, to get comfortable; to get out of trouble or worry, to recover; to let oneself go; to unbosom oneself, to open up one's heart; **desahogarse de** to unbosom oneself of; **desahogarse en** to burst forth in (*e.g., insults*)
desahogo *m* brazenness, impudence; ample room; comfort; ease; comfortable circumstances; outlet, relief; recovery; unbosoming, unburdening
desahuciado -da *adj* hopeless
desahuciar *va* to deprive of hope, to give up hope for; to oust, evict, dispossess; *vr* to lose all hope
desahucio *m* ousting, eviction, dispossession
desahumado -da *adj* weak, vapid (*liquor*)
desahumar *va* to free of smoke
desainadura *f* (vet.) loss of fat from overwork
desainar §75 *va* to remove the fat from; to lessen the thickness or substance of; *vr* to lose fat
desairadamente *adv* ungracefully; scornfully
desairado -da *adj* slighted, snubbed; unattractive; unsuccessful
desairar *va* to slight, disregard, overlook, snub
desaire *m* ungracefulness, unattractiveness, lack of charm; slight, rebuff, disregard, snub
desaislar §75 *va* to join, connect; *vr* to be no longer separated or isolated; to come out of seclusion
desajustar *va* to put out of order; *vr* to get out of order; to disagree, to fail to agree
desajuste *m* being out of order, disorder; disagreement
desalabanza *f* belittling, disparagement
desalabar *va* to belittle, disparage
desalabear *va* to straighten (*a warped board*)
desalabeo *m* straightening
desalado -da *adj* hasty, anxious, eager
desalar *va* to desalt, remove the salt from; to clip the wings of; *vr* to hasten, to rush; **desalarse por** + *inf* to be eager to + *inf*, to yearn to + *inf*
desalazón *f* desalting, removal of salt
desalbardar *va* to remove the packsaddle from
desalentadamente *adv* with discouragement; faintly, feebly
desalentar §18 *va* to put out of breath; to discourage; *vr* to become discouraged
desalfombrar *va* to remove the rugs or carpets from
desalforjar *va* to take out of the saddlebags; *vr* (coll.) to loosen one's clothes (*because of heat*)

desalhajar *va* to remove the furniture from, to remove the appointments from (*a room*)
desaliento *m* discouragement; faintness, weakness
desalineación *f* disalignment, lack of alignment
desalinear *va* to put out of line or alignment, to disalign
desaliñado -da *adj* slovenly, dirty; careless, neglectful
desaliñar *va* to disarrange, to make slovenly, to dirty; *vr* to become disarranged, to become slovenly, become dirty
desaliño *m* slovenliness, dirtiness; carelessness, neglect; **desaliños** *mpl* long earrings
desalivar *vn & vr* to salivate
desalmado -da *adj* cruel, inhuman, merciless, soulless
desalmamiento *m* cruelty, inhumanity, soullessness
desalmar *va* to weaken; to disturb, upset; *vr* to become disturbed, to get upset; **desalmarse por** to have a longing for, to crave
desalmenado -da *adj* without merlons, stripped of merlons
desalmidonar *va* to remove the starch from
desalojamiento *m* dislodging, eviction, ejection
desalojar *va* to dislodge, to evict, to eject, to oust; to empty, to clear (*of people*); *vn* to leave, move out or away
desalojo *m* var. of **desalojamiento**
desalquilado -da *adj* unrented, vacant
desalquilar *va* to stop renting, to vacate; *vr* to be unrented, be vacant
desalterar *va* to calm, to quiet; *vr* to become calm, become quiet; to quench one's thirst
desalumbrado -da *adj* dazzled, dazed; unsure
desalumbramiento *m* blindness; loss of knack, unsureness
desamable *adj* unlovable
desamado -da *adj* unloved
desamador -dora *adj* hating; *mf* hater
desamar *va* to cease loving, to dislike, to hate, to detest
desamarrar *va* to untie, unlash; (naut.) to unmoor; to unbend (*a rope*); *vr* to part; to come loose, get loose
desamasado -da *adj* undone, detached
desamigado -da *adj* unfriendly, estranged
desamistar *vr* to fall out, to quarrel, to become estranged
desamoblar §77 *va* to remove the furniture from
desamoldar *va* to change the form of; to throw out of proportion
desamontonar *va* to take apart, take away (*things piled in a heap*); to squander
desamor *m* coldness, indifference; hatred
desamorado -da *adj* unloving, cold-hearted, loveless
desamorar *va* to alienate the affections of; *vr* to stop loving
desamoroso -sa *adj* loveless, cold, scornful
desamorrar *va* (coll.) to make (*a person*) talk, to cheer (*a person*) up
desamortajar *va* to unshroud
desamortización *f* freedom from mortmain
desamortizar §76 *va* to free from mortmain
desamotinar *vr* to withdraw from a mutiny
desamparadamente *adv* without protection, helplessly
desamparador -dora *adj* forsaking; *mf* forsaker, deserter
desamparar *va* to abandon, forsake, leave; (law) to give up, to release
desamparo *m* abandonment, helplessness, lack of protection
desamueblado -da *adj* unfurnished
desamueblar *va* to remove the furniture from
desanalfabetizar §76 *va* to teach (*a person*) to read and write
desanclar or **desancorar** *va* (naut.) to weigh the anchor of; *vn* (naut.) to weigh anchor
desandar §20 *va* to retrace, go back over (*the road traveled*)
desandrajado -da *adj* ragged, in tatters
desanduve *1st sg pret ind of* **desandar**
desangramiento *m* excessive bleeding; complete draining
desangrar *va* to bleed copiously; to drain, draw a large amount of water from; (fig.) to bleed, impoverish; *vr* to bleed copiously, lose a great amount of blood
desangre *m* bleeding; drain, draining
desanidar *va* to dislodge, to oust; *vn* to leave the nest
desanimación *f* discouragement, low spirits, downheartedness
desanimadamente *adv* with discouragement, downheartedly
desanimar *va* to discourage, dishearten; *vr* to become discouraged, become disheartened
desánimo *m* discouragement, low spirits
desanublar *va* to brighten; to clarify; *vr* to get bright, to clear up
desanudar *va* to untie; to disentangle, clear up
desaojadera *f* charmer, woman who cures the evil eye
desaojar *va* to dispel the evil eye for
desapacibilidad *f* unpleasantness, disagreeableness
desapacible *adj* unpleasant, disagreeable
desapadrinar *va* to disapprove, disavow
desaparear *va* to separate (*the two of a pair*)
desaparecer §34 *va* to cause to disappear; *vn & vr* to disappear
desaparecido -da *adj* missing; extinct; **desaparecidos** *mpl* missing persons
desaparecimiento *m* disappearance
desaparejar *va* to unharness, unhitch; (naut.) to unrig
desaparición *f* disappearance
desaparroquiar *va* to remove from a parish; to drive customers away from; *vr* to lose one's parish; to lose customers
desapasionado -da *adj* dispassionate
desapasionar *va* to free of passion, love, or fondness; *vr* to overcome one's passion; to become indifferent or unconcerned; **desapasionarse de** to overcome one's passion for
desapegar §59 *va* to unglue; to loosen, detach; *vr* to come loose; to become indifferent
desapego *m* coolness, indifference, dislike
desapercibidamente *adv* without notice, without warning
desapercibido -da *adj* unprovided, wanting; unnoticed
desapercibimiento *m* unpreparedness
desapestar *va* to disinfect (*a person contaminated with the plague*)
desapiadado -da *adj* merciless, pitiless
desaplacible *adj* disagreeable
desaplicación *f* lack of application; idleness, laziness
desaplicado -da *adj* lazy, idle
desaplicar §86 *va* to make lazy or idle; *vr* to become lazy or idle
desaplomar *va* to put out of plumb; *vr* to get out of plumb
desapoderado -da *adj* headlong, impetuous; wild, violent
desapoderamiento *m* dispossession; depriving of power or authority
desapoderar *va* to dispossess; to deprive of power or authority; *vr* to become dispossessed; **desapoderarse de** to lose possession of
desapolillar *va* to free of moths; *vr* (coll.) to go out in the cold, to go out after being long indoors
desaporcar §86 *va* to remove the piled-up earth from around (*a plant*)
desaposentar *va* to drive out of one's room or quarters; to cast aside; *vr* to give up one's room or quarters
desaposesionar *va* to dispossess
desapoyar *va* to deprive of support
desapreciar *va* to depreciate (*to lessen the value of; to belittle*)
desaprecio *m* depreciation (*drop in value; belittling*)
desaprender *va* to unlearn; *vn* to forget what one has learned
desaprensar *va* to remove the gloss from (*fabrics*); to ease, to free

desaprensión *f* freedom from worry or fear, unapprehensiveness; unscrupulousness
desaprensivo -va *adj* unapprehensive, unworried; unscrupulous
desapretar §18 *va* to loosen; to relieve; (print.) to unlock; *vr* to loosen one's clothing
desaprisionar *va* to free from jail, to free from shackles; *vr* to extricate oneself, to get free
desaprobación *f* disapproval, deprecation
desaprobar §77 *va* to disapprove, to deprecate; *vn* to disapprove
desapropiación *f* or **desapropiamiento** *m* divestment, surrender (*of property*)
desapropiar *va* to divest, deprive; **desapropiar a una persona de** to divest or deprive a person of; *vr* to divest oneself; **desapropiarse de** to divest oneself of, to surrender, to transfer (*property*)
desapropio *m* var. of **desapropiación**
desaprovechado -da *adj* unproductive; lazy, indifferent
desaprovechamiento *m* ill use, poor use; unimprovement
desaprovechar *va* to make no use of, to use to no advantage; *vn* to lose one's advantage, to slip back
desapuntalar *va* to remove the props, supports, or shoring from
desapuntar *va* to unstitch; to put (*a gun or cannon*) out of aim
desaquellar *vr* (coll.) to be or feel discouraged
desarbolar *va* (naut.) to unmast, to dismast; to clear of trees
desarbolo *m* (naut.) unmasting a ship
desarenar *va* to clear of sand
desareno *m* clearing of sand
desarmable *adj* demountable
desarmador *m* hammer (*of gun*); (Am.) screwdriver
desarmadura *f* or **desarmamiento** *m* disarmament
desarmar *va* to disarm; to dismount, take apart, undo; to calm, to temper, to dissipate; (naut.) to lay up, to decommission; *vn* to disarm
desarme *m* disarmament; dismounting, dismantling; (naut.) decommissioning
desarraigar §59 *va* to uproot, root out, dig up; to extirpate, exterminate; to evict, throw out; to make (*a person*) change his opinion
desarraigo *m* uprooting; extermination
desarrancar §86 *vr* to withdraw (*from a group or association*)
desarrapado -da *adj* var. of **desharrapado**
desarrebozadamente *adv* openly, frankly, without concealment
desarrebozar §76 *va* to unmuffle, to uncover, to reveal
desarrebujar *va* to disentangle; to clarify, elucidate; to unbundle (*a person*); *vr* to unbundle oneself
desarreglado -da *adj* intemperate; unruly, disorderly, slovenly; out of order
desarreglar *va* to disarrange, to put out of order; *vr* to become disarranged, to get out of order
desarreglo *m* disarrangement, disorder, confusion, bad order
desarrendamiento *m* discontinuance of rent; voiding of a lease
desarrendar §18 *va* to unbridle; to stop renting; *vr* to shake off the bridle; to be unrented
desarrimar *va* to separate, to remove; to dissuade
desarrimo *m* lack of support
desarrollable *adj* developable
desarrollar *va* to unroll, unfold, unwind, unfurl; to develop; (math. & phot.) to develop; *vn* to unroll, unfold, unwind; to develop; *vr* to unfold, to develop; to take place
desarrollo *m* unrolling, unfolding, unwinding; development; (math. & phot.) development
desarropar *va* to unclothe, undress; *vr* to take one's clothes off, to undress
desarrugadura *f* unwrinkling
desarrugar §59 *va & vr* to unwrinkle
desarrumar *va* (naut.) to break out, to unstow; (naut.) to unload (*in order to examine hull*)
desarticulación *f* disarticulation; (surg.) disarticulation
desarticular *va* to disarticulate; to take apart; to tear apart, to break up; (surg.) to disarticulate; *vr* to disarticulate
desartillar *va* to remove the gun from (*a boat or fort*)
desarzonar *va* to unsaddle, to unhorse
desasado -da *adj* without handles; with broken handles
desaseado -da *adj* dirty, unclean, untidy
desasear *va* to make dirty, to leave untidy
desasegurar *va* to make uncertain; to make unsteady, to remove the supports from; to cancel the insurance on
desasentar §18 *va* to remove, move away; *vn* to displease, be disliked; to be unbecoming; *vr* to stand up, get up from one's seat
desaseo *m* dirtiness, uncleanliness, untidiness
desasgo *1st sg pres ind of* **desasir**
desasimiento *m* loosening, releasing; detachment, disinterest
desasimilación *f* (physiol.) disassimilation
desasimilar *va* (physiol.) to disassimilate; *vr* to be disassimilated
desasir §22 *va* to let go; to loosen, unfasten; *vr* to let loose; to come loose; **desasirse de** to let go; to give up; to get rid of
desasistir *va* to abandon, forsake
desasnar *va* (coll.) to give good manners to, to polish; *vr* (coll.) to acquire good manners
desasociable *adj* unsociable
desasociar *va* to disassociate (*two or more persons*)
desasosegadamente *adv* uneasily, worriedly, anxiously
desasosegar §29 *va* to disquiet, worry, disturb; *vr* to become disquieted, to worry, to get upset
desasosiego *m* disquiet, worry, anxiety
desastado -da *adj* hornless
desastar *va* to dehorn
desastrado -da *adj* unfortunate, unlucky; shabby, ragged; *mf* shabby person, ragged person
desastre *m* disaster; **ir al desastre** to go to pieces, to fall apart (*said, e.g., of a business*)
desastroso -sa *adj* unfortunate, disastrous
desatacar §86 *va* to unfasten, undo, unbutton
desatadamente *adv* freely, without restraint
desatado -da *adj* loose; mad, wild; fierce, violent
desatadura *f* untying, unfastening, loosening; solving, resolving
desatancar §86 *va* to unclog, to open up; *vr* to get out of the mud, get out of a rut
desatar *va* to untie, undo, unfasten; to solve, unravel; *vr* to come untied; to break loose (*said, e.g., of a storm*); to lose all reserve or restraint; to go too far, to forget oneself; to talk without restraint; **desatarse en** to burst forth in (*e.g., insults*)
desatascar §86 *va* to pull out of the mud, to pull out of a rut; to unclog; to extricate, release from a tight spot or difficulty; *vr* to get out of the mud, get out of a rut
desataviar §90 *va* to strip of adornment or ornaments, to disarray
desatavío *m* slovenliness, uncleanliness, disarray
desate *m* unrestraint, unrestrained talk; flood (*e.g., of words*); **desate del vientre** loose bowels
desatención *f* inattention, disregard; disrespect, discourtesy
desatender §66 *va* to pay no attention to, take no notice of; to slight, disregard
desatentado -da *adj* injudicious, thoughtless, unwise; extreme, severe, out of proportion
desatentar §18 *va* to cause to lose the sense of touch; to confuse, to perplex; *vr* to lose one's sense of touch; to become confused or perplexed
desatento -ta *adj* inattentive, disregardful; impolite, unmannerly
desaterrar §18 *va* (min.) to clear of rubbish and debris; (Am.) to move away, to clear away (*earth or mud*)

desatesorar *va* to spend (*one's treasure or hoardings*)
desatiento *m* loss of sense of touch; confusion, perplexity, uneasiness, worry
desatierre *m* (min.) dumping ground; (Am.) removal of earth or mud
desatinado -da *adj* unwise, foolish; wild, crazy; unruly, in disorder, confused; *mf* fool, blunderer
desatinar *va* to confuse, bewilder; *vn* to act or talk foolishly; to lose one's bearings; *vr* to lose one's bearings
desatino *m* folly, foolishness, nonsense; tactlessness, awkwardness, irrelevancy
desatolondrar *va* to bring to; *vr* to come to
desatollar *va* to pull out of the mud, to pull out of a rut; *vr* to get out of the mud, get out of a rut
desatontar *vr* to recover from being stunned
desatorar *va* (naut.) to break out, to unstow; (min.) to clear of rubbish or debris
desatornillar *va* to unscrew
desatracar §86 *va* (naut.) to move away (*one boat from alongside another*); *vn* (naut.) to keep away from the coast; *vr* (naut.) to move away, to push off
desatraer §88 *va* to separate, detach
desatraigo *1st sg pres ind of* **desatraer**
desatraillar §75 *va & vr* var. of **destraillar**
desatraje *1st sg pret ind of* **desatraer**
desatrampar *va* to unclog
desatrancar §86 *va* to unbolt, unbar; to unclog
desatufar *vr* to get out of the close air (*e.g., of a crowded room*); (fig.) to cool off, to quiet down
desaturdir *va & vr* to rouse from a daze or stupor
desautoridad *f* want of authority
desautorización *f* withdrawal of authority
desautorizado -da *adj* unauthorized; discredited
desautorizar §76 *va* to deprive of authority or credit
desavahado -da *adj* free of clouds, mist, or steam; free, easy, calm
desavahamiento *m* airing; uncovering, cooling
desavahar *va* to air, ventilate; to let cool off, let the steam out of; *vr* to unburden oneself, to brighten up
desavecindado -da *adj* unoccupied, deserted
desavecindar *vr* to move, to move to another place
desavendré *1st sg fut ind of* **desavenir**
desavenencia *f* discord, disagreement, hostility
desavengo *1st sg pres ind of* **desavenir**
desavenido -da *adj* contrary, disagreeable; incompatible
desavenir §92 *va* to make hostile, bring disagreement among, sow discord among; *vr* to disagree; **desavenirse con** or **de** to disagree with
desaventajado -da *adj* disadvantageous
desaventura *f* misfortune
desaviar §90 *va* to mislead, lead astray; to deprive of needs or equipment; *vr* to be misled, to go astray; to be without necessary equipment
desavine *1st sg pret ind of* **desavenir**
desaviniendo *ger of* **desavenir**
desavío *m* leading astray, going astray; inconvenience, want of equipment
desavisado -da *adj* unadvised, uninformed
desavisar *va* to give different advice to, give new advice to
desayudar *va* to keep help from, to keep (*a person*) from being helped
desayunado -da *adj* with breakfast over; **estar desayunado** to have had breakfast
desayunar *vn* to breakfast; *vr* to breakfast; to receive the first news; **desayunarse con** to have breakfast on; **desayunarse de** to receive the first news of
desayuno *m* breakfast, light breakfast; breakfasting
desazogar §59 *va* to remove the quicksilver from
desazón *f* tastelessness, insipidity; displeasure, bitterness, annoyance; discomfort, indisposition; unfitness for cultivation
desazonado -da *adj* indisposed; displeased; unfit for cultivation
desazonar *va* to make tasteless; to displease, annoy, embitter; *vr* to be displeased, annoyed, or embittered; to be indisposed, to feel ill; to become tasteless
desazufrar *va* to desulfurize
desbabar *vn & vr* to drivel, to slobber
desbagar §59 *va* to extract (*flaxseed*) from the capsules
desbancar §86 *va* (naut.) to clear of benches; to win the bank from; to cut out, to supplant
desbandada *f* disbandment; **a la desbandada** helter-skelter, in confusion
desbandar *vr* to run away, to flee in disorder; to disband; (mil.) to desert the colors
desbarahustar *va* var. of **desbarajustar**
desbarahuste *m* var. of **desbarajuste**
desbarajustar *va* to throw into confusion or disorder; *vr* to get out of order, to break down
desbarajuste *m* confusion, disorder
desbaratadamente *adv* in confusion, in disorder
desbaratado -da *adj* (coll.) corrupt, debauched
desbaratador -dora *mf* destroyer
desbaratamiento *m* ruin, destruction, downfall, upset
desbaratar *va* to spoil, disrupt, ruin, destroy; to waste, squander; to debunk; (mil.) to rout, throw into confusion; *vn* to talk nonsense; *vr* to talk or act unreasonably, to be unbalanced
desbarate *m* disruption, ruin, destruction; debunking; loose bowels; **desbarate de vientre** loose bowels
desbarato *m* ruin, destruction
desbarbado -da *adj* beardless
desbarbar *va* to cut the roots, vanes, or filaments of, to trim; (coll.) to shave; *vr* (coll.) to shave, get shaved
desbarbillar *va* to cut off the rootlets of (*young vines*)
desbardar *va* to unthatch
desbarnizar §76 *va* to remove the varnish from
desbarrancadero *m* (Am.) precipice
desbarrancar §86 *va* to level (*uneven ground*); (Am.) to throw over a precipice; *vr* (Am.) to fall over a precipice
desbarrar *va* to unbar; (Am.) to clear of mud; *vn* (sport) to throw the bar with all one's might but without taking aim; to slip away; to steal away; to talk nonsense, to act foolishly
desbarretar *va* to unbar, unbolt; to remove the lining of (*shoes*)
desbarrigado -da *adj* small-bellied
desbarrigar §59 *va* (coll.) to slash in the belly, to rip open the belly of
desbarro *m* slip, blunder; slipping away; nonsense, folly
desbastador *m* dressing chisel
desbastadura *f* roughdressed effect
desbastar *va* to work or shape roughly, to roughdress, to scabble; to consume, waste, weaken; to polish, take off the rough edges of, educate; *vr* to take on polish
desbaste *m* roughdressing; roughdressed state
desbastecido -da *adj* without provisions or supplies
desbautizar §76 *va* to change the name of; *vr* (coll.) to lose one's temper, become very impatient or angry
desbazadero *m* wet, slippery place
desbeber *vn* (coll.) to urinate
desbecerrar *va* to wean calves from (*their mothers*)
desbloquear *va* to break the blockade of, to relieve the blockade of; (com.) to unfreeze
desbloqueo *m* relieving a blockade; (com.) unfreezing
desbocado -da *adj* wide-mouthed (*said of a gun*); nicked (*said of a tool*); neckless (*jug*); runaway (*horse*); loose, licentious; (coll.) foulmouthed; (coll.) loosemouthed; *mf* (coll.) foulmouthed person
desbocamiento *m* running away; licentiousness; (coll.) abusiveness, insulting language, obscenity

desbocar **§86** *va* to break the mouth or spout of; *vn* to empty (*said of a river*); to run, to open, to end (*said of a street*); *vr* to break loose, to run away (*said of a horse*); to burst forth in insults, to swear, to curse; to become debauched, to lead a life of violence
desbonetar *vr* (coll.) to take one's cap off
desboquillar *va* to remove or break the mouth, stem, or nozzle of
desbordamiento *m* overflowing, inundation; violence (*of conduct*)
desbordante *adj* overflowing
desbordar *vn* to overflow; *vr* to overflow; to lose one's self-control, to yield to evil
desborde *m* overflowing, inundation
desbornizar **§76** *va* to remove the cork from (*a tree*)
desborrar *va* to burl; (prov.) to strip of shoots
desbozalar *va* unmuzzle
desbragado -da *adj* (coll.) without pants; (scornful) ragged, shabby; *mf* (scornful) ragged person
desbravar *va* to break in, to tame; *vn & vr* to become less wild; to abate, to moderate; to cool off, calm down; to lose strength (*said of liquors*)
desbravecer **§34** *vn & vr* to become less wild; to abate, to moderate; to cool off, calm down; to lose strength (*said of liquors*)
desbrazar **§76** *vr* to wave the arms with violence
desbrevar *vr* to lose body and strength (*said of wine*)
desbridamiento *m* unbridling; (surg.) débridement, removal of lacerated or contaminated material
desbridar *va* to unbridle; (surg.) to débride
desbriznar *va* to cut or divide into small parts; to chop up, to mince (*meat*); to remove the strings from (*vegetables*); to pull the stamens from (*saffron*)
desbroce *m* var. of **desbrozo**
desbrozar **§76** *va* to clear of brush or underbrush, to clear of rubbish, to clean up
desbrozo *m* clearing of brush or underbrush, clearing of rubbish
desbrujar *va* to wear away, to destroy
desbuchar *va* to disgorge (*said of birds*); to tell (*secrets*); to remove the maw from (*a bird*); to remove the fat from
desbulla *f* oyster shell
desbullador -dora *mf* oyster opener, oyster vendor; *m* oyster fork
desbullar *va* to open (*an oyster*)
descabal *adj* incomplete, imperfect
descabalamiento *m* removal of parts, loss of parts, damage
descabalar *va* to make incomplete, to take away or lose parts of, to damage
descabalgadura *f* dismounting, alighting from a horse
descabalgar **§59** *va* to dismount (*a gun*); to knock (*a gun*) out by destroying the carriage; *vn* to dismount, to alight from a horse
descabellado -da *adj* disheveled; rash, preposterous, wild
descabellar *va* to dishevel, to muss, to rumple; (taur.) to kill (*the bull*) by piercing the base of its brain with the sword; *vr* to become disheveled, to become mussed
descabello *m* (taur.) killing the bull by piercing the base of its brair with the sword
descabestrar *va* to unhalter
descabezado -da *adj* rash, wild, crazy
descabezamiento *m* beheading; quandary
descabezar **§76** *va* to behead; to top (*e.g., a tree*); (coll.) to be about to get the best of (*e.g., a task*); **descabezar el sueño** to nod, to doze; *vn* to adjoin, to border; *vr* to shed the grain (*said of cereals*); to rack one's brain
descabritar *va* to wean goats from (*the mother*)
descabullir **§26** *vr* to slip away, to sneak away; to avoid facing a problem; to refuse to face realities; **descabullirse de** to wriggle out of (*e.g., a difficulty*)
descachar *va* (Am.) to dehorn
descacharrado -da *adj* (Am.) dirty, ragged
descachazar **§76** *va* (Am.) to skim froth from (*cane juice*)
descaderado -da *adj* narrow-hipped
descaderar *va* to injure the hips of; *vr* to injure one's hips
descadillar *va* to cut off the loose threads of (*the warp*)
descaecer **§34** *vn* to decline, fade away
descaecimiento *m* weakness, debility; despondency, dejection
descafilar *va* to clean and smooth (*old bricks and stones*)
descalabazar **§76** *vr* (coll.) to rack one's brain
descalabrado -da *adj* wounded in the head; worsted; **salir descalabrado** to come out the loser, to lose out
descalabradura *f* bump in the head; scab on the head
descalabrar *va* to hit, to hurt, to hit in the head; to damage, to ruin; *vr* to hurt one's head
descalabro *m* misfortune, damage, loss
descalandrajar *va* to tear to shreds
descalcador *m* (naut.) ravehook
descalcar **§86** *va* (naut.) to remove oakum from (*seams*)
descalce *m* undermining
descalcez *f* barefootedness
descalificación *f* disqualification; (sport) disqualification
descalificar **§86** *va* to disqualify (*to deprive of a right, etc.*); (sport) to disqualify
descalzar **§76** *va* to take off (*footwear*); to take the shoes or stockings off (*a person*); to remove wedges or chocks from; to dig under, to undermine; *vr* to take off one's shoes and stockings; to take off one's gloves; to take off (*shoes or gloves*); to lose a shoe (*said of a horse*); to become discalced (*said of a friar*); **descalzarse de risa** to split one's sides with laughter
descalzo -za *adj* barefoot, unshod; discalced (*said, e.g., of a friar*); seedy, down at the heel
descamación *f* desquamation
descamar *vr* to desquamate
descambiar *va* to exchange back again
descaminadamente *adv* off the road; mistakenly, wrongly
descaminado -da *adj* off the road; lost, misguided; ill-advised
descaminar *va* to lead astray, to mislead, to misguide; to declare contraband; to seize (*smuggled goods*); to punish for smuggling; (Am.) to waylay, to hold up; *vr* to go astray, to get lost; to run off the road
descamino *m* leading astray; going astray; running off the road; nonsense; lack of tact; seizure of smuggled goods; smuggled goods seized
descamisado -da *adj* shirtless, ragged; poor, wretched; *m* ragamuffin; poor person; wretch; **Descamisados** *mpl* Spanish liberals of 1820; (Am.) followers of General Perón around 1950
descamisar *va* to remove the shirt of, to strip; to hull, to husk; (found.) to remove the mold from; (Am.) to ruin
descampado -da *adj* free, open, clear; **en descampado** in the open country
descampar *va* to clear (*a piece of land*); *vn* to stop work; to stop raining
descanar *va* (Am.) to thin out the gray hairs from
descansadamente *adv* easily, without trouble; tranquilly, calmly, peacefully
descansadero *m* stage, stopping place, resting place
descansadillo *m* (aut.) footrest
descansado -da *adj* easy; rested, refreshed; tranquil, unworried
descansapié *m* or **descansapiés** *m* (*pl:* **-piés**) (aut.) footrest
descansar *va* to help, to give a hand to; to rest (*e.g., one's head*); to support, to hold up; *vn* to rest; to be quiet; to stop work; to lie down; to lie (*be buried*); to rest, to lean; to sleep; to not worry; to lie fallow; **descansar en** to trust in
descansillo *m* landing (*of stairs*)
descanso *m* rest, quiet, stillness, peace; ease, relief; aid, help; landing (*of stairs*); (mach.) seat, bench, support, bracket; (mil.) parade rest; (theat.) intermission; rest (*peace of*

death); (Am.) bridge; (Am.) water closet; **a discreción descanso** (mil.) at ease; **en su lugar descanso** (mil.) parade rest; **descanso dominical** Sunday observance
descantar *va* to clear of stones
descantear *va* to smooth the angles or corners of, to round off; to splay, to chamfer, to edge
descanterar *va* to remove the crust, corners, or ends of
descantillar *va* to break off, to pare off, to chip off; to deduct, to subtract; to speak ill of
descantillón *m* gauge, pattern, rule, templet; square
descantonar *va* to pare off, to chip off; to take off (*corners*); to subtract
descañonar *va* to pluck; to shave against the grain; (coll.) to fleece, to swindle; (coll.) to break, to win the pot from
descaperuzar §76 *va* to unhood, to uncowl; *vr* to take off one's hood, cowl, or hunting cap
descaperuzo *m* taking off one's hood, cowl, or hunting cap
descapillar *va* to take off the hood of
descapiruzar §76 *va* (Am.) to dishevel, to muss the hair of; (Am.) to rumple, to crumple; (Am.) to dull (*velvet*) by rubbing the wrong way
descapitalizar §76 *va* to deprive (*a town or city*) of its status as capital
descapotable *adj & m* (aut.) convertible
descapotar *va* to lower the top of (*an automobile*)
descapsulador *m* bottle opener
descarado -da *adj* impudent, shameless; saucy
descaramiento *m* impudence, shamelessness; sauciness
descarar *vr* to speak or behave in an impudent manner; to be saucy; **descararse a pedir** to have the nerve to ask for; **descararse con** to speak insolently to, to behave insolently towards
descarbonatar *va* to decarbonate, remove carbonic acid from
descarburación *f* decarbonization
descarburador -dora *adj* decarbonizing
descarburar *va* to decarbonize
descarga *f* unloading; discharge, firing (*of a gun, etc.*); clearing (*of a ship*); unburdening; (com.) discount; (elec.) discharge; **descarga de aduana** clearance through customhouse; **descarga superficial** (elec.) surface leakage
descargadero *m* unloading place, wharf
descargador *m* unloader; (naut.) lighterman; (ord.) wormer
descargadura *f* bone that a butcher takes out of a piece of meat
descargar §59 *va* to unload; to ease (*one's conscience*); to shoot, to fire, to discharge; to free; to dump; to take the flap and bones from (*loin*); to deal, to inflict (*e.g., blows*); to clear, to acquit; to free (*e.g., of a debt*); (com.) to take up (*a draft*); (elec.) to discharge; (naut.) to brace (*a lee*); (naut.) to clear (*the sails or yards*); **descargar un golpe en, contra,** or **sobre** to strike a blow at; *vn* to empty (*said of a river*); to open (*said of a hall, walk, street, etc.*); to burst (*said of a storm*); *vr* to unburden oneself; to resign; **descargarse de** to get rid of; to clear oneself of (*a charge*); to resign from; **descargarse con** or **en una persona de una cosa** to unload something on someone
descargo *m* unloading; discharge, acquittal; acquittance (*of a debt*); receipt, release; (law) deposition favorable to defendant
descargue *m* unloading
descariñar *vr* to become cool, become indifferent
descariño *m* coolness, indifference
descarnadamente *adv* plainly, frankly, to the point
descarnado -da *adj* lean, thin, spare; bare; bony, cadaverous; **la descarnada** Death
descarnador *m* (dent.) scraper
descarnadura *f* removal of flesh
descarnar *va* to remove the flesh from; to wear down, wear away; to chip; to detach from the things of this world; *vr* to lose flesh
descaro *m* effrontery, impudence
descarriamiento *m* var. of **descarrío**
descarriar §90 *va* to misguide, lead astray; to separate (*cattle*); *vr* to go astray; to go wrong
descarrilador -dora *adj* derailing; *mf* derailer; **descarrilador de trenes** train wrecker
descarriladura *f* or **descarrilamiento** *m* derailment
descarrilar *vn* to derail, to jump the track; (coll.) to get off the track, wander from the point; *vr* to derail, to jump the track
descarrío *m* going astray; ruin, damnation
descartar *va* to reject, cast aside; to discard; *vr* to discard; to shirk, evade; **descartarse de** to shirk, evade (*e.g., a commitment*)
descarte *m* rejection, casting aside; discarding; discard (*cards discarded*); shirking, evasion
descasado -da *adj* jumbled, mixed up
descasamiento *m* annulment (*of marriage*); divorce
descasar *va* to annul the marriage of; to disturb, to disturb the arrangement of; (print.) to change the arrangement of (*pages of a folio*); *vr* to separate by an annulment of marriage; to become disarranged
descascar §86 *va* to peel, to shell; *vr* to break to pieces; to chatter, to bluster
descascarar *va* to peel, to shell; *vr* to peel off, to shell off
descascarillado *m* hulling, shelling
descascarillar *va & vr* to hull, to shell
descaspar *va* to remove the dandruff from
descasque *m* decortication (*especially of cork tree*)
descastado -da *adj* ungrateful, ungrateful to one's own
descastamiento *m* ingratitude
descastar *va* to exterminate (*destructive animals and insects*); *vr* to become depraved, to turn ingrate
descatolizar §76 *va* to cause to give up Catholicism; *vr* to give up Catholicism
descaudalado -da *adj* ruined, penniless
descebar *va* to unprime (*a firearm*)
descendencia *f* descent (*family tree; issue*)
descendente *adj* descending, descendent, down
descender §66 *va* to lower, take down, bring down; to descend, go down (*e.g., stairs*); *vn* to descend, go down, get down; to run, to flow; to be derived; to decline; (mus.) to descend; **descender a** to descend to, to stoop to; **descender a** + *inf* to go or come down to + *inf;* **descender de** to descend from
descendiente *mf* descendant
descendimiento *m* descent, lowering
descensión *f* descent, descending
descenso *m* descent (*act of descending; downward course in station, value, etc.*); decline, falling off; drop (*in temperature*); (path.) hernia, rupture, prolapse (*of uterus*)
descentrado -da *adj* off center, out of plumb
descentralización *f* decentralization
descentralizador -dora *adj* decentralizing
descentralizar §76 *va* to decentralize
descentrar *va* to put off center; *vr* to get off center, to get out of line
desceñido -da *adj* loose, loose-fitting
desceñidura *f* unbelting, ungirding; loosening or removal of a belt, etc.
desceñir §74 *va* to unbelt, ungird; to take off (*a belt, etc.*)
descepar *va* to pull up by the roots; to exterminate; (naut.) to remove the stocks from (*an anchor*)
descerar *va* to cut away the dry combs from (*a beehive*)
descercar §86 *va* to destroy or tear down the wall or fence of; to raise the siege of; to force the enemy to raise the siege of
descerco *m* raising a siege
descerebrar *va* to brain, to dash out the brains of
descerezar §76 *va* to pulp (*coffee berry*)
descerrajado -da *adj* (coll.) wicked, evil, corrupt
descerrajadura *f* lock-breaking
descerrajar *va* to break or tear off the lock of; (coll.) to shoot, discharge (*a shot*)
descerrar §18 *va* to open

descerrumar *vr* to wrench its joints (*said of a horse*)
descervigar **§59** *va* to twist the neck of (*an animal*); *vr* to humble oneself
descifrable *adj* decipherable
descifrador *m* decipherer; decoder
descifrar *va* to decipher; to decode
descifre *m* deciphering; decoding
descimbramiento *m* (arch.) removal of centers
descimbrar *va* (arch.) to remove the center of (*e.g., an arch*)
descimentar *va* to demolish the foundations of
descinchar *va* to ungird
descivilizar **§76** *va* to uncivilize, to make uncivilized; *vr* to become uncivilized
desclasificación *f* (sport) disqualification
desclasificar **§86** *va* (sport) to disqualify
desclavador *m* nail puller
desclavar *va* to remove the nails from, to unnail; to take (*a precious stone*) out of its setting
desclorurar *va* to remove sodium chloride from; to remove salt from (*the diet*)
descoagular *va* to dissolve (*a clot*)
descobajar *va* to pull the stem from (*grapes*)
descobijar *va* to uncover, to open; to deprive of shelter
descocado -da *adj* forward, insolent
descocar **§86** *va* to clear (*trees*) of insects; *vr* to clean itself of fleas, etc. (*said of birds and other animals*); (coll.) to be impudent; (coll.) to act or speak insolently
descocer **§30** *va* to digest
descoco *m* (coll.) impudence, insolence
descochollado -da *adj* (Am.) ragged, in tatters
descodar *va* (dial.) to unstitch, to rip
descoger **§49** *va* to extend, spread, unfold
descogollar *va* to strip (*a tree*) of shoots; to take the heart out of (*vegetables*)
descogotado -da *adj* (coll.) low-necked
descogotar *va* to break the neck of; to dehorn (*a stag*)
descohesor *m* (rad.) decoherer
descolar *va* to dock, crop, or cut the tail off (*an animal*); to cut off the fag end of (*cloth*); (Am.) to slight; (Am.) to dismiss (*an employee*)
descolchar *va* (naut.) to untwist (*a cable*)
descolgar **§79** *va* to take down; to unhook; to take down the draperies, hangings, etc. in; *vr* to slip down; to come down; to come on suddenly, to show up unexpectedly; **descolgarse con** (coll.) to come out with suddenly, to blurt out; **descolgarse de** or **por** to slip down (*e.g., a wall*)
descoligado -da *adj* unattached, unfederated
descolmar *va* to strike (*with a strickle*); to level off; to diminish
descolmillar *va* to pull out the eyeteeth or the fangs of
descolocado -da *adj* out of place, in the wrong place
descolón *m* (coll.) slight
descoloración *f* decolorization, color removal
descoloramiento *m* discoloring, discoloration
descolorar *va & vr* to discolor
descolorido -da *adj* discolored, faded, off color
descolorimiento *m* discoloring, discoloration
descolorir *va & vr* to discolor
descollado -da *adj* haughty; outstanding
descollamiento *m* var. of **descuello**
descollante *adj* outstanding
descollar **§77** *vn* to stand out, excel
descombrar *va* to disencumber, to clear of obstacles
descombro *m* disencumbrance, clearing of obstacles
descomedido -da *adj* immoderate, excessive; rude, disrespectful, impolite
descomedimiento *m* rudeness, disrespect, impoliteness
descomedir **§94** *vr* to be rude, be disrespectful
descomer *vn* (coll.) to have a movement of the bowels
descomodidad *f* inconvenience
descompadrar *va* (coll.) to break up the friendship of; *vn* (coll.) to be no longer friends, to fall out
descompaginar *va* to disorganize, to upset
descompás *m* excess, immoderateness
descompasado -da *adj* extreme, immoderate, out of all reason
descompasar *vr* to be extreme, be immoderate
descompletar *va* to make incomplete, to break (*e.g., a set of dishes*)
descompondré *1st sg fut ind of* **descomponer**
descomponer **§69** *va* to decompose; to disturb, upset, discompose, disorganize; to put out of order; to alienate, set at odds; *vr* to decompose; to become distorted (*said of the face*); to fall to pieces (*with regard to health*); to get out of order; to lose one's temper; **descomponerse con** to fall out with
descompongo *1st sg pres ind of* **descomponer**
descomposición *f* decomposition; disturbance, disorder, disorganization; discomposure; discord
descompostura *f* decomposition; disorder, disorganization; untidiness; impudence, brazenness
descompresión *f* decompression
descompuesto -ta *adj* impudent, brazen, impolite; angry, exasperated; out of order; *pp of* **descomponer**
descompuse *1st sg pret ind of* **descomponer**
descomulgado -da *adj* wicked, perverse, evil
descomulgar **§59** *va* to excommunicate
descomunal *adj* extraordinary, enormous, monstrous
desconceptuar **§33** *va* to discredit; *vr* to become discredited
desconcertado -da *adj* unrestrained, wicked; out of order; disconcerted
desconcertador *m* disturber, tinkerer
desconcertar **§18** *va* to put out of order, to disturb; to dislocate; to surprise, to disconcert, to baffle; *vr* to get out of order; to become dislocated; to become disconcerted; to get upset; to become estranged
desconcierto *m* disrepair, disorder; disagreement; unrestraint, imprudence; mismanagement; looseness of bowels
desconcordia *f* discord, disunion, disagreement
desconchabar *vr* (Am.) to become dislocated, to get out of joint
desconchado *m* scaly wall; chip, chipped place (*e.g., in china*)
desconchar *va & vr* to scale off, to chip, to chip off
desconectar *va* to detach; (elec. & mach.) to disconnect; *vr* to become detached; (elec. & mach.) to become disconnected
desconexión *f* disconnection
desconfiado -da *adj* distrustful, suspicious
desconfianza *f* distrust
desconfiar **§90** *vn* to have no confidence; **desconfiar de** to have no confidence in, to distrust
desconformar *vn* to dissent, disagree; *vr* to disagree, to not go well together
desconforme *adj* disagreeing
desconformidad *f* nonconformity, unconformity, disconformity; disagreement
descongelación *f* melting, defrosting
descongelador *m* defroster
descongelar *va, vn & vr* to melt, to defrost; (com.) to unfreeze
descongestión *f* removal or lessening of congestion
descongestionar *va* to remove or lessen the congestion of; *vr* to become less congested
descongojar *va* to relieve, to console
desconocedor -dora *adj* ignorant
desconocer **§32** *va* to not know, be ignorant of; to not recognize; to disown, disavow, deny; to slight, overlook, pretend not to know, disregard, ignore; to have nothing to do with; to fail to see; *vr* to be or become unrecognizable, to be or become quite changed; to be unknown
desconocidamente *adv* unknowingly
desconocido -da *adj* unknown; unrecognizable; ungrateful; strange, unfamiliar; quite changed, quite different; *mf* unknown, unknown person

desconocimiento *m* ignorance; disregard; ingratitude
desconozco *1st sg pres ind of* **desconocer**
desconsentir §62 *va* to not consent to, to not acquiesce in
desconsideración *f* inconsiderateness
desconsiderado -da *adj* ill-considered; inconsiderate
desconsiderar *va* to be inconsiderate of; to fail to consider
desconsolación *f* grief, disconsolateness
desconsolado -da *adj* disconsolate, grief-stricken; disordered; weak (*said of the stomach*)
desconsolador -dora *adj* distressing
desconsolar §77 *va* to grieve, to distress; *vr* to grieve, be distressed
desconsuelo *m* grief, disconsolation, disconsolateness; neediness, helplessness; stomach disorder
descontable *adj* discountable
descontaminación *f* decontamination
descontaminar *va* to decontaminate
descontar §77 *va* to discount; to deduct; to rebate; to take for granted
descontentadizo -za *adj* hard to please, easily displeased
descontentamiento *m* discontentment, displeasure; disagreement, unfriendliness
descontentar *va* to dissatisfy, to displease; *vr* to be dissatisfied, to be displeased
descontento -ta *adj* discontent, discontented, displeased; *m* discontent, displeasure
descontinuación *f* discontinuation
descontinuar §33 *va* to discontinue
descontinuo -nua *adj* discontinuous
desconvendré *1st sg fut ind of* **desconvenir**
desconvengo *1st sg pres ind of* **desconvenir**
desconvenible *adj* incongruous, incompatible, discrepant
desconveniencia *f* unsuitableness; incongruity; inconvenience
desconveniente *adj* unsuitable; incongruous; inconvenient
desconvenir §92 *vn* to disagree; to be incongruous; to not match; *vr* to disagree; to be incongruous
desconversable *adj* unsociable, retiring
desconvidar *va* to cancel an invitation to; to take back (*something promised*)
desconvine *1st sg pret ind of* **desconvenir**
desconviniendo *ger of* **desconvenir**
descopar *va* to top (*a tree*)
descorazonamiento *m* broken-heartedness; discouragement, dejection
descorazonar *va* to tear out the heart of; to dishearten, discourage; *vr* to become disheartened or discouraged
descorchador *m* decorticator (*person or machine*); corkscrew
descorchar *va* to remove the bark or cork from (*cork oak*); to uncork; to break open (*a beehive*) in order to extract honey; to break open, to break into
descorche *m* removal of bark or cork
descordar §77 *va* to unstring (*e.g., a musical instrument*)
descorderar *va* to separate lambs from (*mother*) in order to form new flocks
descornamiento *m* dehorning
descornar §77 *va* to dehorn; *vr* (coll.) to rack one's brains in vain
descorrear *va* to shed or rub the velvet off (*the antlers*); *vn & vr* to shed or rub the velvet off the antlers (*said, e.g., of a young deer*)
descorrer *va* to run back over; to draw (*e.g., a curtain*); *vn & vr* to flow, to run off
descorrimiento *m* flow, flowing away
descortés *adj* discourteous, impolite
descortesía *f* discourtesy, impoliteness
descortezador *m* decorticator
descortezadura *f* removal of bark; bark removed
descortezamiento *m* removal of bark
descortezar §76 *va* to strip off the bark of; to take off the crust of; to hull, to shell; (coll.) to polish, to civilize; *vr* (coll.) to become polished
descortezo *m* removal of bark
descortinar *va* (mil.) to demolish (*a curtain*)
descosedura *f* rip, ripping
descoser *va* to unstitch, to rip; **descoser la boca** to reveal a secret; *vr* to loose one's tongue; (coll.) to break wind
descosido -da *adj* indiscreet, imprudent; unconnected, desultory; slovenly, disorderly, immoderate, wild; **como un descosido** (coll.) wildly; **reír como un descosido** to laugh like a wild man; *m* open seam, tear, rip
descostar *vr* to move away
descostillar *va* to beat in the ribs, to bruise the ribs of; *vr* to fall flat on one's back
descostrar *va* to remove the crust from
descotar *va* to cut low in the neck
descote *m* low neck, low cut (*around neck*)
descoyuntamiento *m* dislocation; great fatigue, exhaustion
descoyuntar *va* to dislocate; to annoy, to bore; *vr* to become dislocated, to get out of joint
descrecencia *f* decrease, decreasing
descrecer §34 *vn* to decrease, diminish
descrecimiento *m* decrease, diminution
descrédito *m* discredit
descreer §35 *va* to disbelieve, discredit; to deny due credit to; *vn* to disbelieve
descreído -da *adj* unbelieving; *mf* unbeliever, disbeliever
descreimiento *m* unbelief, disbelief
descremadora *f* cream separator
descremar *va* to skim (*milk*)
descrestar *va* to remove the crest or comb of
descrianza *f* incivility, coarseness, rudeness
descriar §90 *vr* to spoil, deteriorate, waste away
describir §17, 9 *va* to describe
descripción *f* description
descriptible *adj* describable
descriptivo -va *adj* descriptive
descriptor -tora *adj* descriptive; *mf* describer
descrismar *va* to remove the chrism from; (coll.) to wallop in the head, to break the skull of; *vr* (coll.) to lose one's temper; (coll.) to rack one's brain; (coll.) to break one's skull
descristianar *va* to remove the chrism from; (coll.) to wallop in the head, to break the skull of; *vr* (coll.) to break one's skull
descristianizar §76 *va* to dechristianize; *vr* to become dechristianized
descrito -ta *pp of* **describir**
descruce *m* uncrossing
descruzar §76 *va* to uncross, remove from a crossed position
descto. abr. of **descuento**
descuadernar *va* to unbind, take the binding off (*a book*); to undo, upset, put out of order; *vr* to get loose, come unbound
descuadrillado *m* (vet.) sprain in the haunch
descuadrillar *vr* to have a sprain in the haunches (*said of a horse*)
descuajar *va* to liquefy, to dissolve (*something clotted, coagulated, etc.*); to uproot, pull up by the roots; to eradicate (*a vice*); (coll.) to dishearten, discourage; *vr* to liquefy, be dissolved
descuajaringar §59 *vr* (coll.) to collapse, be broken down with fatigue; (Am.) to fall to pieces
descuaje *m* or **descuajo** *m* pulling up by the roots, grubbing, clearing away underbrush
descuartizamiento *m* quartering; dividing into pieces, carving; quartering (*punishment*)
descuartizar §76 *va* to quarter; to divide into pieces, to carve; to quarter (*as punishment*)
descubierta *f* see **descubierto**
descubiertamente *adv* clearly, openly, manifestly
descubierto -ta *pp of* **descubrir;** *adj* uncovered, bareheaded; under fire, under accusation; bare (*said, e.g., of a field*); *m* exposition of the holy sacrament; deficit, shortage; **al descubierto** (com.) short; openly; in the open; **en descubierto** (com.) overdrawn; **vender al descubierto** (com.) to sell short; *f* open pie, pie without top crust; (mil.) reconnoitering; (naut.) scanning horizon at sunrise and sunset; (naut.) morning and evening inspection of rigging; **a la descubierta** in the open; openly; reconnoitering

descubridero *m* lookout, eminence commanding a vast expanse
descubridor -dora *adj* discovering; *mf* discoverer; *m* (mil.) scout
descubrimiento *m* discovery; unveiling
descubrir §17, 9 *va* to discover, find out; to uncover, expose to view, lay open, reveal; to invent; to unveil (*a statue*); *vr* to take off one's hat, cap, etc.; to be discovered; to be uncovered; **descubrirse a** or **con** to open one's heart to
descuello *m* distinction, excellence; excessive height; haughtiness, loftiness
descuento *m* discount; deduction, rebate
descuerar *va* (Am.) to flay, to skin; (Am.) to flay, to criticize
descuernacabras *m* strong cold north wind
descuerno *m* (coll.) affront, slight
descuidado -da *adj* careless, negligent; dirty, slovenly; unaware, off guard
descuidar *va* to neglect, overlook; to free of worry; to distract, divert; *vn* to not bother, to not worry; *vr* to be distracted, be diverted; to not bother, to not worry; to become careless; **descuidarse de** to not bother about; **descuidarse de** + *inf* to neglect to + *inf;* **descuidarse de sí mismo** to neglect oneself
descuidero -ra *mf* sneak thief
descuido *m* carelessness, neglect, negligence; oversight, mistake, slip; thoughtlessness, faux pas, slight; **al descuido** with studied carelessness; **con descuido** without thinking
descuitado -da *adj* carefree
descular *va* to break the bottom of (*e.g., a bottle*)
descumbrado -da *adj* smooth, without a crest or peak; clean, free
deschavetar *vr* (Am.) to get rattled, to lose one's head
deschuponar *va* to strip (*a tree*) of shoots and suckers
desde *prep* since, from; after; **desde aquí** from here; **desde entonces** since then, ever since; **desde entonces a esta parte** since that time; **desde hace** for, e.g., **está aquí desde hace tres meses** he has been here for three months; **desde . . . hasta** from . . . to; **desde luego** at once; doubtless, of course; **desde que** since
desdecir §37 *vn* to degenerate, to slip back; to differ; to decline; *vr* to retract; **desdecirse de** to retract, take back (*something said*)
desdén *m* disdain, scorn, contempt; **al desdén** with studied carelessness, with studied neglect
desdentado -da *adj* toothless, edentate; *m* (zool.) edentate
desdentar §18 *va* to pull the teeth of
desdeñable *adj* despicable, contemptible
desdeñadamente *adv* scornfully, disdainfully
desdeñador -dora *adj* scornful, disdainful; *mf* scorner, disdainer
desdeñar *va* to scorn, to disdain; *vr* to be disdainful; **desdeñarse de** to loathe; **desdeñarse de** + *inf* to not deign to + *inf*
desdeñoso -sa *adj* scornful, disdainful
desdevanar *va* to unwind
desdibujado -da *adj* poorly drawn, badly outlined (*said of a drawing or a character in a book*)
desdibujar *vr* to become blurred, become clouded
desdicha *f* see **desdicho**
desdichado -da *adj* unfortunate, unlucky; miserable, unhappy, wretched; (coll.) backward, timid; *mf* wretch
desdicho -cha *pp of* **desdecir;** *f* misfortune; indigence, misery
desdigo *1st sg pres ind of* **desdecir**
desdije *1st sg pret ind of* **desdecir**
desdinerar *va* to impoverish
desdiré *1st sg fut ind of* **desdecir**
desdoblamiento *m* unfolding; splitting; elucidation; **desdoblamiento de la personalidad** disintegration of the personality
desdoblar *va & vr* to unfold, spread open; to split; to divide, break down
desdorar *va* to remove the gold from, remove the gilding from; to damage, sully (*e.g., reputation*); *vr* to lose its gold or gilding; to become damaged or sullied (*said, e.g., of reputation*)
desdoro *m* blemish, blot, stigma
desdoroso -sa *adj* damaging (*to reputation, etc.*)
deseabilidad *f* desirability
deseable *adj* desirable
deseador -dora *mf* desirer, wisher
desear *va* to desire, wish; **desear** + *inf* to desire to, to wish to + *inf*
desecación *f* drying, desiccation
desecador -dora *adj* desiccating; *m* drying room; dryer, desiccator
desecamiento *m* var. of **desecación**
desecante *adj* desiccant; *m* desiccant, drier
desecar §86 *va* to dry, drain, desiccate; *vr* to dry up, drain, desiccate
desecativo -va *adj* desiccative
desechable *adj* disposable
desechadamente *adv* contemptibly, despicably
desechar *va* to cast aside, throw out; to think little of, to underrate; to blame, to censure; to drop (*an employee*); to turn (*a key to open door*)
desecho *m* remainder, residue; débris, rubbish, offal; castoff; contempt, low opinion; **desecho de hierro** scrap iron
desedificación *f* bad example
desedificar §86 *va* to set a bad example for, to give a bad example to
desegregación *f* desegregation
desegregar §59 *va* to desegregate
deselectrización *f* (elec.) discharge, discharging
deselectrizar §76 *va* (elec.) to discharge (*a body*)
desellar *va* to unseal
desembalaje *m* unpacking
desembalar *va* to unpack
desembaldosar *va* to remove the bricks or paving tiles from (*a floor, a room, etc.*)
desembalse *m* loss of water in a dam
desembanastar *va* to take out of a basket; (coll.) to draw (*e.g., a sword*); to talk indiscreetly about; *vr* to break out, to break loose (*said of an animal*); (coll.) to alight from a carriage
desembarazado -da *adj* free, open; easy, unrestrained
desembarazar §76 *va* to disembarrass, to disengage; to clear (*a road*); to empty (*a room*); *vr* to free oneself; to be cleared; to be emptied; **desembarazarse de** to get rid of
desembarazo *m* freedom; ease, naturalness, lack of restraint; (Am.) delivery, accouchement; **con desembarazo** readily, comfortably; quickly
desembarcadero *m* wharf, pier, landing place
desembarcar §86 *va* to debark, disembark, unload; *vn* to debark, disembark, land, go ashore; to leave ship; (coll.) to alight; to end (*said of a staircase at landing*); *vr* to debark, disembark, land, go ashore
desembarco *m* debarkation, disembarkation, landing; landing (*of stairs*)
desembargar §59 *va* to free, to disengage; (law) to raise the attachment or seizure of
desembargo *m* (law) raising of an attachment or seizure
desembarque *m* debarkation, disembarkation, unloading
desembarrancar §86 *va & vn* to float (*said of a ship that ran aground*)
desembarrar *va* to clear of mud
desembaular §75 *va* to take out of a trunk; (coll.) to unburden oneself of
desembebecer §34 *vr* to come to, to recover one's senses
desembelesar *vr* to recover from one's amazement or stupefaction
desemblantado -da *adj* with changed countenance, with changed expression
desemblantar *vr* to change countenance, to color suddenly
desembocadero *m* exit, opening, outlet; mouth (*e.g., of river*)
desembocadura *f* mouth (*e.g., of river*); opening, outlet (*e.g., of street*); (Am.) channel (*between islands*)

desembocar §86 *vn* to flow, to empty; to end; **desembocar en** to flow or empty into; to end at (*said of a street*)
desembojar *va* to remove (*cocoons*) from rearing bushes
desembolsar *va* to empty out of a purse; to disburse, to pay out
desembolso *m* payment, expenditure; outlay; disbursement
desemboque *m* var. of **desembocadero**
desemborrachar *va & vr* to sober up
desemboscar §86 *va* to drive out of the woods; to bring out of ambush; *vr* to come out of the woods; to come out of ambush
desembotar *va* to remove the dullness from, to sharpen, to make sharp; *vr* to lose its dullness, to sharpen, to become sharp
desembozar §76 *va* to unmuffle, unmask; *vr* to unmuffle, unmask; to show one's true colors
desembozo *m* unmuffling, unmasking
desembragar §59 *va* (mach.) to disengage, to unclutch; (mach.) to disconnect (*e.g., a shaft*); *vn* to throw the clutch out
desembrague *m* (mach.) disengaging, disengagement
desembravecer §34 *va* to tame, domesticate; to calm, pacify; *vr* to become tame, to become domesticated
desembravecimiento *m* taming, domestication; calming
desembrazar §76 *va* to take (*something*) off the arm; to hurl (*a weapon*)
desembriagar §59 *va & vr* to sober up
desembridar *va* to unbridle
desembrollar *va* (coll.) to unravel, untangle
desembrozar §76 *va* var. of **desbrozar**
desembuchar *va* to disgorge (*said of birds*); to tell (*secrets*)
desemejante *adj* dissimilar, unlike; **desemejante de** unlike
desemejanza *f* dissimilarity, unlikeness, disagreement
desemejar *va* to disfigure, make look bad, change; *vn* to be unlike, to not look alike
desempacar §86 *va* to unpack, unwrap (*merchandise*); *vr* to cool off, calm down
desempachar *va* to relieve of indigestion; to free of timidity or bashfulness; *vr* to be relieved of indigestion; to get rid of one's timidity or bashfulness
desempacho *m* ease, calmness, unconcern
desempalagar §59 *va* to rid of nausea; *vr* to get rid of nausea
desempañar *va* to remove the blur, steam, smear, etc. from (*glass*); to remove the swaddling clothes from
desempapelar *va* to unwrap; to remove the paper from (*a wall, room, etc.*)
desempaque *m* unpacking, unwrapping
desempaquetar *va* to unpack, to unwrap
desemparejar *va* to unmatch, make unlike, uneven or unequal
desemparentado -da *adj* without relatives
desempastelar *va* (print.) to distribute (*mixed type*)
desempatar *va* to break the tie between, to break (*a tie vote*)
desempate *m* breaking the tie
desempedrar §18 *va* to remove the paving stones from, to unpave; (coll.) to pound (*the pavement*); **ir desempedrando la calle** (fig.) to dash down the street
desempegar §59 *va* to remove the pitch from
desempeñado -da *adj* clear, out of debt
desempeñar *va* to redeem, to recover, to take out of pawn or hock; to free from debt, to free from a commitment; to get (*a person*) out of a jam; to fulfill, carry out, accomplish; to fill (*a function*); to play (*a rôle*); *vr* to get out of a jam; to get out of debt
desempeño *m* redeeming a pledge; taking out of hock; payment (*of a debt*); discharge, fulfilment; performance, acting of a part
desempeorar *vr* to recover, to recover one's strength
desemperezar §76 *vn & vr* to shake off one's laziness
desempernar *va* to unbolt
desempleo *m* unemployment
desemplomar *va* to remove the lead from; to remove the seals from; (dent.) to take the filling out of; *vr* to come out (*said of a filling*)
desemplumar *va* to pluck, to take the feathers out of
desempolvadura *f* dusting, removal of dust or powder
desempolvar *va* to dust, to dust off; to renew; to brush up on; *vr* to brush up
desempolvoradura *f* var. of **desempolvadura**
desempolvorar *va* to dust, to dust off
desemponzoñar *va* to free from the effects of poison; to free of poison
desempotrar *va* to remove, take out (*something fixed or plugged in a wall*)
desempozar §76 *va* to remove from a well
desenalbardar *va* to remove the packsaddle from; to unharness
desenamorar *va* to destroy the love or affection of; *vr* to become cold or indifferent
desenastar *va* to take the handle or shaft off (*a tool, weapon, etc.*)
desencabalgar §59 *va* to dismount (*a gun*)
desencabestrar *va* to disentangle the feet of (*an animal*) from the halter
desencadenamiento *m* unchaining, unleashing; outbreak
desencadenar *va* to unchain, unleash, let loose; *vr* to be unchained, to break loose, to break out, to break forth
desencajamiento *m* dislocation; disjointedness; ricketiness, run-down appearance
desencajar *va* to dislocate; to throw out of joint, to disconnect; *vr* to get out of joint, become dislocated; to become contorted (*said of face or part of face*)
desencaje *m* var. of **desencajamiento**
desencajonamiento *m* unboxing, unpacking; (taur.) removal of bulls from box
desencajonar *va* to take out of a box, to unpack; to take (*bulls*) out of a box
desencalabrinar *va* to free of dizziness
desencalcar §86 *va* to loosen (*what was caked or packed*)
desencallar *va* to set (*a stranded ship*) afloat
desencaminar *va* to mislead, to lead astray
desencantamiento *m* disenchantment; disillusionment
desencantar *va* to disenchant; to disillusion; *vr* to become disenchanted; to become disillusioned
desencantaración *f* drawing lots
desencantarar *va* to draw (*lots*) from an urn; to exclude (*a name or names*) from balloting
desencanto *m* var. of **desencantamiento**
desencapillar *va* (naut.) to take the rigging from, to unrig
desencapotar *va* to take the cloak off (*a person*); to make (*a horse*) keep his head up; (coll.) to reveal, to manifest; *vr* to take off one's cloak; to keep its head up (*said of a horse*); to clear up (*said of sky*); to cool off, calm down
desencaprichar *va* to make (*a person*) give in; *vr* to give in, to give up a pet idea
desencarcelar *va* to free from jail, to set at liberty
desencarecer §34 *va* to lower the price of; *vn & vr* to come down (*in price*)
desencarnar *va* to keep (*dogs*) from eating game; to lose one's liking for; to disembody; *vr* to cast off the body, to die
desencastillar *va* to drive out of a castle; to reveal, make appear, show; to cause (*a person*) to fall from power, favor, etc.
desencerrar §18 *va* to unclose; to free from confinement; to reveal, to disclose
desencintar *va* to remove the ribbons from; to remove the curb of (*a sidewalk*)
desenclavar *va* to remove the nails from, to unnail; to expel or drive out forcibly
desenclavijar *va* to pull the pegs or pins out of; to let go, to disconnect
desencoger §49 *va* to spread out, to unfold; *vr* to lose one's timidity or bashfulness
desencogimiento *m* ease, naturalness
desencoladura *f* ungluing
desencolar *va* to unglue; *vr* to come unglued

desencolerizar §76 *va & vr* to calm down, to cool off
desenconar *va* to allay (*an inflammation*); to calm (*a person; a person's rancor or ill will*); *vr* to abate; to calm down; to soften up, get soft
desencono *m* allayment; calming, mitigation
desencordar §77 *va* to unstring (*e.g., a musical instrument*)
desencordelar *va* to unstring
desencorvar *va* to straighten
desencovar §77 *va* to get (*especially an animal*) out of a cave; to free of a risk or danger
desencrespar *va & vr* to uncurl, to unfrizzle
desencuadernado -da *adj* back on one's feet (*after fatigue or a beating*)
desencuadernar *va* to unbind, take the binding off (*a book*); *vr* to get loose, come unbound
desenchufar *va* to unplug, to disconnect
desendemoniar *va* to drive evil spirits out of; *vr* to be free of evil spirits
desendiablar *va* to drive evil spirits out of
desendiosar *va* to humble the vanity of, to bring down to earth
desenfadaderas *fpl* (coll.) resources, resourcefulness; **tener buenas desenfadaderas** (coll.) to be resourceful; (coll.) to be easygoing
desenfadado -da *adj* free, clear; ample, spacious; carefree, casual
desenfadar *va* to free of anger or annoyance; *vr* to cool off, calm down
desenfado *m* ease, freedom, naturalness; casualness; cheek, effrontery
desenfaldar *va* to untuck
desenfardar or **desenfardelar** *va* to unpack, to open
desenfilada *f* (mil.) defilade
desenfilar *va & vr* (fort. & mil.) to defilade
desenfocado -da *adj* out of focus
desenfoque *m* putting out of focus, distortion
desenfrailar *va* (prov.) to top (*a tree*); *vn* to leave the monastic life, become secularized; (coll.) to take a vacation; (coll.) to be freed, be emancipated; *vr* to leave the monastic life, become secularized
desenfrenado -da *adj* unbridled, licentious, wanton
desenfrenamiento *m* var. of **desenfreno**
desenfrenar *va* to unbridle, remove the bit from; *vr* to yield to vice and evil; to fly into a passion; to break loose (*said, e.g., of a storm*)
desenfreno *m* unruliness, licentiousness, wantonness; **desenfreno de vientre** loose bowels, diarrhea
desenfundar *va* to unsheathe
desenfurecer §34 *va* to quiet the anger of; *vr* to calm down, cool off
desenganchar *va* to unhook, unpin, unfasten; to uncouple; to unhitch, to unharness; *vr* to come unhooked, to come unfastened
desengañadamente *adv* openly, sincerely; (coll.) badly, poorly, carelessly
desengañador -dora *adj* disillusioning, disappointing
desengañar *va* to undeceive, disabuse; to disillusion; *vr* to become disillusioned
desengaño *m* disabusal; disillusionment; disappointment; plain fact, plain truth
desengarrafar *va* to release one's grip on
desengarzar §76 *va* to take out of a setting; to loosen, to disconnect
desengastar *va* to take (*e.g., a precious stone*) out of its setting
desengomar *va* to ungum; to unsize (*silk*)
desengoznar *va* to unhinge; to disconnect, upset, throw out of gear; *vr* to contort the body (*as in certain dances*)
desengranar *va & vr* to unmesh, disengage
desengrane *m* unmeshing, disengaging
desengrasar *va* to take the grease out of; *vn* (coll.) to get thin; (coll.) to take away the greasy taste by eating olives, fruit, etc.
desengrase *m* removal of grease
desengraso *m* (Am.) dessert
desengrosar §77 *va* to make thin, lean, or fine; *vr* to become thin, lean, or fine
desengrudar *va* to scrape or rub the paste off
desenhebrar *va* to unthread; (fig.) to unravel
desenhornar *va* to take out of the oven
desenjaezar §76 *va* to unharness, to take the trappings off (*a horse*)
desenjalmar *va* to take the packsaddle off (*a horse, mule, etc.*)
desenjaular *va* to take out of the cage; to take out of jail or out of confinement
desenlabonar *va* var. of **deseslabonar**
desenlace *m* outcome; denouement (*of drama*)
desenladrillar *va* to take up the bricks or tiles from (*floor*)
desenlazar §76 *va* to untie; to solve; to unravel (*plot of play*); *vr* to untie, come untied; to unfold (*said of plot of play*)
desenlodar *va* to clear of mud
desenlosar *va* to take up the flagstones in (*a room, patio, etc.*)
desenlutar *va* to make (*a person*) give up mourning; *vr* to give up mourning
desenmallar *va* to take (*fish*) out of the net
desenmarañar *va* to disentangle; to unravel
desenmascaradamente *adv* barefacedly
desenmascaramiento *m* unmasking; exposure, exposé
desenmascarar *va* to unmask; to expose; *vr* to unmask, take one's mask off
desenmohecer §34 *va* to clear of rust; *vr* to become clear of rust
desenmudecer §34 *va* to free of a speech impediment; *vn* to get rid of a speech impediment; to break a long silence
desenojar *va* to free of anger, to allay the anger of; *vr* to cool off, calm down; to amuse oneself
desenojo *m* coolness, calmness, freedom from anger
desenredar *va* to disentangle, resolve; to clear up, straighten out; *vr* to extricate oneself
desenredo *m* disentanglement; denouement (*of plot*)
desenrollar *va & vr* to unroll, unwind, unreel, unfurl
desenroscar §86 *va & vr* to untwine; to unscrew
desensamblar *va & vr* to disjoint
desensañar *va* to calm, to pacify; *vr* to calm down, to cool off
desensartar *va* to unstring, to unthread
desensebar *va* to strip of fat; *vn* to change one's pursuits to break the monotony; (coll.) to take away the greasy taste by eating olives, fruit, etc.
desenseñamiento *m* ignorance
desenseñar *va* to unteach (*something learned wrongly*)
desensibilización *f* desensitization
desensibilizar §76 *va* to desensitize; *vr* to become desensitized
desensillar *va* to unsaddle (*a horse*)
desensoberbecer §34 *va* to humble, to lessen the pride of; *vr* to become humbled, to lose one's pride
desensortijado -da *adj* uncurled; dislocated
desentablar *va* to rip the boards or planks from; to disturb, upset, confuse; to break off (*a friendship, bargain, etc.*)
desentalingar §59 *va* (naut.) to unbend (*a cable*)
desentarimar *va* to take up the inlaid floor or parquetry in
desentender §66 *vr* to not participate; to affect ignorance; **desentenderse de** to take no part in, to renounce; to detach oneself from, free oneself from; to pay no attention to; to affect ignorance of
desenterrador *m* exhumer
desenterramiento *m* unearthing, disinterment; (fig.) unearthing; (fig.) recall, recalling
desenterrar §18 *va* to unearth, disinter; to dig up; (fig.) to unearth, to dig up; (fig.) to remember, recall
desentierramuertos *mf* (*pl:* **-tos**) (coll.) defamer of the dead
desentoldar *va* to take the awning from; to strip of adornment
desentonación *f* var. of **desentono**
desentonadamente *adv* out of tune
desentonado -da *adj* out of tune, flat; inharmonious
desentonamiento *m* var. of **desentono**

desentonar *va* to humble the pride of; *vn* to be out of tune; to clash, to be out of harmony; *vr* to talk loud and disrespectfully
desentono *m* false note, dissonance; rude tone of voice
desentornillar *va* to unscrew
desentorpecer §34 *va* to free of numbness; to polish, give a polish to (*a person*); *vr* to get rid of numbness, be freed of numbness; to take on a polish
desentrampar *va* (coll.) to free of debts; *vr* (coll.) to get out of debt
desentrañamiento *m* disembowelment, evisceration; giving one's all for love
desentrañar *va* to disembowel, to eviscerate; to dig deeply into, to figure out; *vr* to give one's all to one's beloved
desentrenado -da *adj* (sport) out of training
desentrenamiento *m* (sport) lack of training
desentrenar *vr* (sport) to be out of training, to slip
desentristecer §34 *va* to cheer, comfort, banish the sadness of
desentronizar §76 *va* to dethrone; to deprive of power, favor, or standing
desentumecer §34 *va* to take out the numbness of, to relieve of numbness; *vr* to shake off the numbness
desentumecimiento *m* freedom from numbness
desentumir *va & vr* var. of **desentumecer**
desenvainar *va* to unsheathe; to stretch out (*the claws*); (coll.) to show, expose
desenvelejar *va* (naut.) to strip of sails
desenvendar *va* to unbandage
desenvergar §59 *va* (naut.) to unbend (*a sail*)
desenviolar *va* to bless or purify (*a holy place that was desecrated*)
desenvoltura *f* ease, free and easy manner; fluency; lewdness (*chiefly in women*)
desenvolvedor -dora *adj* scrutinizing, curious, prying; *mf* investigator, curious person
desenvolver §63 & §17, 9 *va* to unroll, unfold; to unwrap; to develop (*e.g., a theme, one's mind, an industry*); to disentangle, unravel, clear up; *vr* to be forward, be too bold; to extricate oneself; to unroll; to develop, to evolve; to be unraveled, be cleared up
desenvolvimiento *m* unfolding; elucidation; development
desenvuelto -ta *pp of* **desenvolver;** *adj* easy, free and easy; fluent; bold, daring; forward, brazen
desenzarzar §76 *va* to pull out of the brambles; (coll.) to separate and reconcile (*quarrelers*); (Am.) to clear (*a field*) of brambles
deseo *m* desire, wish; **coger a deseo** to succeed in gratifying one's desire for; **venir en deseo de** to desire, to want
deseoso -sa *adj* desirous
desequido -da *adj* very dry, too dry
desequilibrado -da *adj* unbalanced; (fig.) unbalanced
desequilibrar *va* to unbalance; *vr* to become unbalanced
desequilibrio *m* disequilibrium, imbalance, unbalanced condition; unbalanced mental condition
deserción *f* desertion; (law) forfeiture (*of right of appeal*)
deserrado -da *adj* free of error
desertar *va* to desert; (law) to forfeit (*right of appeal*); *vn* to desert; **desertar a** to go over to; **desertar de** to desert
desértico -ca *adj* desert
desertor *m* (mil. & fig.) deserter
deservicio *m* disservice
deservir §94 *va* to disserve, do an ill turn to
desescarchador *m* defroster
deseslabonar *va* to cut the links of, to unlink
desespaldar *va* to wrench the back of, break the back of; to take the back off or out of (*e.g., a chair*); *vr* to wrench one's back, to break one's back
desespañolizar §76 *va* to free of Spanish influence; *vr* to become free of Spanish influence; to give up one's Spanish nationality
desesperación *f* despair, desperation; **ser una desesperación** (coll.) to be unbearable
desesperado -da *adj* desperate, despairing; hopeless (*e.g., condition*); *mf* desperate person
desesperante *adj* despairing; exasperating, maddening
desesperanza *f* hopelessness
desesperanzado -da *adj* hopeless
desesperanzar §76 *va* to make hopeless, to deprive of hope; to discourage; *vr* to lose hope
desesperar *va* to make hopeless, to deprive of hope, to drive to despair; (coll.) to exasperate, to drive wild; *vn* to be hopeless, to lose hope, to be driven to despair, to despair; (coll.) to be exasperated, be driven wild
desespero *m* var. of **desesperación**
desestalinización *f* destalinization
desestalinizar §76 *va & vn* to destalinize
desestancar §86 *va* to open (*something stopped up*); (com.) to open the market to, to make free of duty, to raise the monopoly on
desestanco *m* opening, clearing
desestañado *m* untinning, detinning; unsoldering
desestañar *va* to untin, to detin; to unsolder; *vr* to detin; to come unsoldered
desesterar *va* to remove the mats from (*floor, stairs*)
desesterilizar §76 *va* to desterilize (*gold*)
desestero *m* removal of mats; season for removing mats
desestima or **desestimación** *f* low regard, disesteem; refusal, rejection
desestimar *va* to hold in low regard, to disesteem; to refuse, to reject
deséxito *m* failure
desexualizar §76 *va* to desexualize
desfachatado -da *adj* (coll.) impudent, brazen, shameless
desfachatez *f* (coll.) impudence, brazenness, shamelessness
desfajar *va* to ungird, to unbind
desfalcador -dora *mf* defaulter
desfalcar §86 *va* to remove part of, to lop off; to embezzle; to bring down in standing or favor; *vn* to embezzle, to defalcate
desfalco *m* removal, lopping off; embezzlement, defalcation
desfallecer §34 *va* to weaken, to debilitate; *vn* to fall away, grow weak; to faint, faint away; **desfallecer de ánimo** to lose courage
desfallecido -da *adj* faint, fainting, languid
desfalleciente *adj* languishing, failing
desfallecimiento *m* weakening, debilitation; languor; faint, fainting
desfasaje *m* (elec.) phase displacement
desfasar *vn* (elec.) to be out of phase; to be out of tune; to not fit
desfavorable *adj* unfavorable
desfavorecer §34 *va* to disfavor; to disfigure
desfibrar *va* to remove the fibers from
desfiguración *f* or **desfiguramiento** *m* disfigurement; deformation; alteration; distortion
desfigurar *va* to disfigure; to cloud, to darken; to disguise (*voice*); to change, to alter; to distort, misrepresent; *vr* to change countenance
desfijar *va* to pull off, to detach
desfiladero *m* defile, pass
desfilar *vn* to defile, march in review, parade; (coll.) to file by or out
desfile *m* defiling, marching in review, parade
desflecar §86 *va* to remove the flakes from (*wool*) or frettings of (*cloth*)
desflemar *va* (chem.) to dephlegmate; *vn* to expel phlegm
desflocar §95 *va* var. of **desflecar**
desfloración *f* or **desfloramiento** *m* defloration, deflowering
desflorar *va* to deflower; to treat superficially
desflorecer §34 *vn & vr* to lose flowers, to wither
desflorecimiento *m* loss of flowers, withering
desfogar §59 *va* to vent, make an opening in (*e.g., a furnace*); to slake (*lime*); (fig.) to vent (*e.g., one's anger*); to give loose rein to (*a horse*); *vn* (naut.) to break into rain and wind (*said of threatening clouds*); *vr* to vent one's anger, to blow off steam
desfogonar *va* to burst the vent of (*a gun*); *vr* to burst (*said of vent of gun*)

desfogue *m* vent; (Am.) drain hole (*in large aqueduct*); venting of emotions, venting of anger
desfollonar *va* to trim (*a plant*)
desfondamiento *m* (sport) collapse
desfondar *va* to break or remove the bottom of; to stave in; (naut.) to bilge, to knock in the bottom of (*a ship*); (agr.) to dig up (*the soil*) to a great depth; *vr* (naut.) to bilge; (sport) to collapse
desfonde *m* (agr.) digging the soil to a great depth
desforestación *f* deforestation
desforestar *va* to deforest
desformar *va* to deform
desforrar *va* to remove the lining of; to strip
desfortalecer §34 *va* to dismantle, to demolish (*a fort*); to deprive a fortress of (*its garrison*)
desfrenar *va* to unbridle; *vn* (aut.) to take the breaks off; *vr* to yield to one's emotions or passions; to break loose (*said, e.g., of a storm*)
desfruncir §50 *va* to unfold, to spread out
desgaire *m* slovenliness; affected carelessness; scornful attitude; **al desgaire** carelessly, with affected carelessness; scornfully
desgajadura *f* tearing, breaking; splitting of a branch from a tree
desgajar *va* to tear off, to break off; to split off (*a branch*); *vr* to come off, to come loose, to break off, to break away; **desgajarse el cielo** to become stormy, to rain hard
desgaje *m* tearing, breaking, splitting
desgalgadero *m* rocky slope; cliff, precipice
desgalgar §59 *va* to throw headlong; *vr* to fall headlong, to rush headlong
desgalichado -da *adj* (coll.) sloppy, ungainly
desgana *f* lack of appetite; indifference; boredom, disgust; unwillingness; **a desgana** unwillingly, reluctantly
desganado -da *adj* not hungry; indifferent
desganar *va* to make indifferent; *vr* to lose one's appetite; to become indifferent; to be bored
desganchar *va* to lop or tear the branches off (*a tree*)
desgano *m* var. of **desgana**
desgañitar *vr* (coll.) to struggle and scream; (coll.) to scream oneself hoarse
desgarbado -da *adj* graceless, ungainly, uncouth
desgargantar *vr* (coll.) to shout oneself hoarse
desgargolar *va* to ripple (*flax or hemp*); to remove (*a board*) from a groove or notch
desgaritar *vn* to lose the way, to go astray; *vr* to lose the way, to go astray; to get separated from the fold; to abandon an undertaking
desgarrado -da *adj* torn, ripped; tattered; shameless, barefaced, licentious
desgarradura *f* var. of **desgarrón**
desgarramiento *m* tearing, rending
desgarrar *va* to tear, to rend; to cough up; *vr* to withdraw, retire
desgarre *m* tear, rent
desgarro *m* tear, rent; outburst; boldness, barefacedness, effrontery; boasting, braggadocio
desgarrón *m* large tear or rip; shred, tatter
desgasificar §86 *va* to degas, to degasify
desgastar *va* to abrade, consume, wear away; to weaken, spoil, vitiate; *vr* to wear away, lose one's strength, decline
desgaste *m* abrasion, attrition, wear, wearing down, fray, fraying
desgausamiento *m* degaussing
desgausar *va* to degauss
desgaznatar *vr* (coll.) to shout oneself hoarse
desglazador *m* defroster
desglosar *va* to obliterate a note in (*a writing*); to set aside (*a question*); to detach (*a page or pages*); to break down, to analyse
desglose *m* obliteration of a note or gloss; separation; detachment; breakdown, analysis
desgobernado -da *adj* ungovernable, uncontrollable
desgobernar §18 *va* to upset the government of; to misgovern; to dislocate (*bones*); (naut.) to steer poorly; *vn* (naut.) to steer poorly; *vr* to go through contortions (*as in certain dances*)
desgobierno *m* mismanagement, maladministration, misgovernment; dislocation
desgolletar *va* to break the neck of (*e.g., a bottle*); to loosen or remove (*clothing around the neck*)
desgomar *va* to ungum; to unsize (*silk*)
desgonzar §76 *va* to unhinge; to disconnect, upset, throw out of gear; *vr* to be disconnected, upset, or thrown out of gear
desgoznar *va & vr* var. of **desengoznar**
desgracia *f* misfortune, bad luck; disfavor, disgrace; lack of charm or grace; unpleasantness, gruffness; **caer en desgracia** (coll.) to be in disfavor, to lose favor; **correr con desgracia** to have no luck; **por desgracia** unfortunately
desgraciado -da *adj* unfortunate; unhappy; graceless, ungraceful; ungracious, unpleasant, disagreeable; *mf* wretch, unfortunate
desgraciar *va* to displease; to spoil; *vr* to spoil; to decline, to degenerate; to fall out; to fail, to fall through
desgramar *va* to pull up the grass in (*a field*)
desgranador -dora *adj* shelling, threshing; *mf* sheller, thresher; *f* threshing machine
desgranar *va* to remove the grain from, to remove or pick the grapes from (*a bunch of grapes*), to shell (*e.g., peas*); to thresh; to sift (*powder*); *vr* to fall from the ear, to drop from the bunch; to shell, to seed; to come loose (*said of beads*); to wear away (*said of vent of firearms*)
desgrane *m* shelling, picking; coming loose (*of grain, grapes, beads, etc.*); threshing
desgranzar §76 *va* to separate the chaff from; (paint.) to give (*colors*) the first grinding
desgrasar *va* to remove the grease from (*e.g., wool*)
desgrase *m* removal of grease
desgravación *f* lowering of duties or taxes; removal of lien or mortgage
desgravar *va* to lower duties or taxes on; to remove a lien or mortgage on
desgreñar *va* to dishevel; *vr* to get disheveled; to pull each other's hair, to get into a fight
desguace *m* roughhewing, roughdressing; taking down, disassembling of a boat
desguarnecer §34 *va* to remove the ornaments from, to strip of trimmings; to strip down, to remove the accessories from; to unharness; to unman (*a fortress*); to disarm (*an opponent*)
desguarnecimiento *m* stripping; disarming
desguazar §76 *va* to roughhew or roughdress (*timber*); to take down, to break down (*a ship*)
desguince *m* knife for cutting rags in paper mills; dodge, dodging
desguindar *va* (naut.) to lower, bring down; *vr* to slide down
desguinzar §76 *va* to cut (*rags, in paper mills*)
deshabillé *m* deshabille or dishabille
deshabitado -da *adj* uninhabited, unoccupied
deshabitar *va* to move out of; to abandon, to desert (*a town or region*)
deshabituación *f* disuse, disusage
deshabituar §33 *va* to make unaccustomed, to disaccustom; *vr* to become unaccustomed, become disaccustomed
deshacedor -dora *adj* undoing; *mf* undoer; **deshacedor de agravios** righter of wrongs
deshacer §55 *va* to undo; to take apart; to untie, to open; to consume, diminish, destroy; to carve, cut up; to wear away; to put to flight, to rout; to melt, dissolve; to violate (*a treaty*); to right (*wrongs*); *vr* to get out of order, to break, to break to pieces; to go to pieces, to melt (*in the mouth*); to strive hard; to grow weak; to disappear; to be grieved, to be impatient; to bump, to bruise; **deshacerse de** to get rid of; **deshacerse en** to burst into (*tears*); to lavish (*praise, flattery*); **deshacerse por** + *inf* to strive hard to + *inf*
deshago *1st sg pres ind of* **deshacer**
deshaldo *m* spring trimming of honeycombs
deshambrido -da *adj* famished, starving
desharé *1st sg fut ind of* **deshacer**
desharrapado -da *adj* ragged, shabby
desharrapamiento *m* raggedness, shabbiness, poverty, indigence

deshebillar *va* to unbuckle
deshebrar *va* to ravel, to unthread; to tear to shreds
deshecha *f* see **deshecho**
deshechizar §76 *va* to take the spell or curse off (*a person*); to disappoint
deshechizo *m* breaking a spell or curse; disappointment
deshecho -cha *pp of* **deshacer;** *adj* strong, violent, hard; great, good (*luck*); *f* feint, simulation, sham, pretense; polite farewell; way-out; l'envoi (*of a poem*); **a la deshecha** with dissimulation; **hacer la deshecha** to feign, to pretend; (Am.) to pretend to be uninterested
deshelador *m* (aer.) deicer
deshelar §18 *va & vr* to melt, to thaw; to defrost; (aer.) to deice
desherbar §18 *va* to pull, pull up (*weeds*); to weed (*e.g., a field*)
desheredación *f* disinheritance
desheredado -da *adj* disinherited; underprivileged
desheredamiento *m* var. of **desheredación**
desheredar *va* to disinherit; *vr* to disgrace one's family, be a disgrace to one's family
deshermanar *va* to make unlike, to unmatch; *vr* to fail as a brother
desherrar §18 *va* to unchain, unshackle; to unshoe (*a horse*)
desherrumbrar *va* to clean of rust, to take the rust off; *vr* to get free of rust
deshice *1st sg pret ind of* **deshacer**
deshidratación *f* dehydration
deshidratar *va & vr* to dehydrate
deshielo *m* thaw, thawing; defrosting
deshierba *f* weeding
deshilachado *m* removal of ravels or frayings
deshilachar *va* to pull ravels or frayings from (*a fabric*); *vr* to fray
deshilado -da *adj* in a file; **a la deshilada** in file, in single file; clandestinely; *m* drawn work, openwork, hemstitching
deshiladura *f* unweaving; reduction of rags to a pulp (*in paper manufacturing*); pulp (*for manufacturing paper*)
deshilar *va* to unweave leaving a fringe; to shred (*meat*); to distract (*a swarm of bees*) to a new hive; *vn* to get thin
deshilo *m* distracting bees to new hive
deshilvanado -da *adj* disconnected, loose, incoherent, desultory
deshilvanar *va* (sew.) to unbaste, untack
deshincar §86 *va* to pull out, to pull up (*something driven in*)
deshinchar *va* to deflate (*a balloon, news, etc.*); to give vent to (*anger, annoyance, etc.*); *vr* to go down (*said of a swelling, tumor, etc.*); (coll.) to become deflated (*in self-esteem*)
deshinchazón *m* abatement of swelling
deshipnotizar §76 *va* to dehypnotize
deshipotecar §86 *va* to cancel the mortgage on, to free of mortgage
deshojador *m* stripper of leaves, defoliator
deshojadura *f* defoliation
deshojar *va* to defoliate, to strip the leaves off (*a plant or tree*); to tear the leaves out of (*a book*); *vr* to defoliate
deshoje *m* fall of leaves
deshollejar *va* to peel, pare, skin (*e.g., grapes*); to shell (*e.g., beans*)
deshollinadera *f* long-handled brush or broom
deshollinador -dora *adj* chimney-sweeping; *mf* chimney sweep, chimney sweeper; (coll.) scrutinizer; *m* long-handled brush or broom
deshollinar *va* to clean, to sweep (*a chimney*); to clean (*walls and ceiling*) with long-handled brush; (coll.) to scrutinize
deshonestar *vr* to act unbecomingly or indecently
deshonestidad *f* immodesty, indecency
deshonesto -ta *adj* immodest, indecent
deshonor *m* dishonor
deshonorar *va* to dishonor; to deprive of office or occupation; to deface, disfigure; *vr* to be dishonored
deshonra *f* dishonor, disgrace; dishonorable act; **tener a deshonra** to consider dishonorable
deshonrabuenos *mf* (*pl:* **-nos**) (coll.) slanderer; (coll.) black sheep
deshonradamente *adv* dishonorably, disgracefully
deshonrador -dora *adj* dishonorable, disgraceful; *mf* dishonorer, disgracer; *m* seducer
deshonrar *va* to dishonor, to disgrace; to violate, to seduce (*a woman*); to insult, defame; to scorn, despise
deshonrible *adj* (coll.) shameless, contemptible; *mf* (coll.) shameless person, contemptible person
deshonroso -sa *adj* dishonorable, ignominious, indecent
deshora *f* inopportune time, inconvenient time; **a deshora** or **a deshoras** inopportunely, at an inconvenient time; without preparation
deshornar *va* var. of **desenhornar**
deshospedamiento *m* refusal of lodging, inhospitality
deshospedar *va* to deprive of lodging, to refuse lodging to
deshuesadora *f* pitter (*device*)
deshuesar *va* to bone; to stone, to take the pits out of (*fruit*)
deshumanar *vr* to become dehumanized
deshumanización *f* dehumanization
deshumanizar §76 *va* to dehumanize
deshumedecedor -dora *adj* dehumidifying; *m* dehumidifier
deshumedecer §34 *va* to dehumidify, to dry up; *vr* to become dehumidified, to dry up
deshumidificar §86 *va* to dehumidify
desiderátum *m* (*pl:* **-rata**) desideratum
desidia *f* laziness, indolence
desidioso -sa *adj* lazy, indolent; *mf* lazy person
desierto -ta *adj* desert; deserted; *m* desert; wilderness; **predicar en desierto** (coll.) to preach to deaf ears; **Desierto Arábigo** *or* **de Arabia** Arabian Desert; **Desierto de Libia** Libyan Desert; **Desierto de Sahara** Sahara Desert
designación *f* designation, selection
designar *va* to plan (*a piece of work*); to designate, to appoint, to select
designio *m* design, purpose, plan
desigual *adj* unequal; rough, uneven, irregular, jerky; arduous, difficult; changeable, inconstant
desigualar *va* to make unequal; *vr* to become unequal; to get ahead
desigualdad *f* inequality; roughness, unevenness
desilusión *f* disillusion, disillusionment; disappointment
desilusionar *va* to disillusion; to disappoint; *vr* to be disillusioned; to be disappointed
desimanación *f* demagnetization
desimanar *va* to demagnetize; *vr* to become demagnetized
desimantación *f* var. of **desimanación**
desimantar *va & vr* var. of **desimanar**
desimpondré *1st sg fut ind of* **desimponer**
desimponer §69 *va* (print.) to break up the imposition of (*a form*)
desimpongo *1st sg pres ind of* **desimponer**
desimpresionar *va* to undeceive; to remove the impression of; *vr* to be undeceived; **desimpresionarse de** to free one's mind of
desimpuesto -ta *pp of* **desimponer**
desimpuse *1st sg pret ind of* **desimponer**
desinclinar *va* to disincline; *vr* to disincline, be disinclined
desincorporar *va & vr* to separate, to break up
desincrustante *m* disincrustant
desincrustar *va* to disincrust
desinencia *f* (gram.) termination, ending, desinence; **desinencia casual** (gram.) case ending
desinfección *f* disinfection
desinfectante *adj & m* disinfectant
desinfectar *va* to disinfect; *vr* to become disinfected
desinfestar *va* to disinfest
desinficionar *va & vr* var. of **desinfectar**
desinflación *f* or **desinflado** *m* deflation
desinflamación *f* decrease of inflammation, loss of inflammation

desinflamar *va* to remove the inflammation from; *vr* to lose its inflammation (*said of a wound, part of body, etc.*)
desinflar *va* to deflate; (coll.) to deflate (*a person*); *vr* to become deflated; (coll.) to be or become deflated
desinsacular *va* to draw lots on (*certain names*)
desinsectación *f* fumigation, freeing of insects
desinsectar *va* to fumigate, to free of insects
desintegración *f* disintegration
desintegrar *va & vr* to disintegrate
desinterés *m* disinterestedness
desinteresado -da *adj* disinterested, impartial; uninterested
desinteresar *vr* to lose interest
desintonizar §76 *va* (rad.) to put out of tune; (rad.) to tune out
desinvernar §18 *va* (mil.) to take out of winter quarters; *vn & vr* (mil.) to go out of or to leave winter quarters
desistencia *f* or **desistimiento** *m* desistence; (law) waiving a right
desistir *vn* to desist; (law) to waive a right; **desistir de** to desist from, to give up; **desistir de** + *inf* to stop, leave off + *ger*
desjarretadera *f* hooked knife for hamstringing or hocking animals
desjarretar *va* to hamstring, to hock; (coll.) to weaken, to bleed to excess
desjarrete *m* hamstringing, hocking
desjugar §59 *va* to draw the juice from
desjuiciado -da *adj* devoid of judgment, senseless
desjuntar *va & vr* to disjoin, to sever, to separate
deslabonar *va* to unlink; to disconnect; to destroy; *vr* to come unlinked; to be disconnected; to be destroyed; to retire, to withdraw
desladrillar *va* var. of **desenladrillar**
deslamar *va* to clear of mud, to remove silt from
deslastrar *va* (naut.) to unballast, to remove the ballast from
deslatar *va* to remove the laths from
deslavado -da *adj* barefaced; *mf* barefaced person
deslavadura *f* superficial washing; fading, weakening
deslavar *va* to wash superficially; to fade, weaken, take the life out of
deslavazar §76 *va* var. of **deslavar**
deslazar §76 *va & vr* var. of **desenlazar**
desleal *adj* disloyal
deslealtad *f* disloyalty
deslechugar §59 *va* to prune (*e.g., vines*); to strip leaves from; to trim off (*shoots*)
deslechuguillar *va* var. of **deslechugar**
desleidura *f* or **desleimiento** *m* dilution, thinning; dissolving
desleír §73 *va* to dilute, to diffuse; to dissolve; to thin (*paint*); to be diffuse or prolix in (*thought*); *vr* to become diluted; to dissolve
deslendrar §18 *va* to clean the nits out of (*hair*)
deslenguado -da *adj* shameless, foul-mouthed, scurrilous
deslenguamiento *m* (coll.) shamelessness, impudence, indecency
deslenguar §23 *va* to cut the tongue of, to cut out the tongue of; *vr* (coll.) to blab, talk too much; (coll.) to speak or act shamelessly or indecently
desliar §90 *va* to untie, unpack; to separate the refuse from (*the juice, in making wine*); (fig.) to unravel; *vr* to come untied
desligadura *f* untying, unbinding, loosening; unraveling, disentangling
desligar §59 *va* to untie, to unbind; to unravel, to disentangle; to excuse, to exempt; to absolve from ecclesiastical censure; (mus.) to play or sing (*something*) staccato; *vr* to come loose, to come untied; to become disentangled
deslindador *m* surveyor
deslindamiento *m* determination of boundaries, demarcation; explanation, defining
deslindar *va* to bound, to mark the boundaries of; to explain, to define
deslinde *m* var. of **deslindamiento**
deslingar §59 *va* (naut.) to unsling
desliñar *va* to clean (*fulled cloth, before sending it to the press*)
deslío *m* decanting new wine
desliz *m* (*pl:* **-lices**) sliding, slipping; slide (*smooth surface*); backslide; peccadillo, slip
deslizable *adj* sliding; weak, fragile, brittle
deslizadero -ra *adj* slippery; *m* slide, slippery spot; launching way; *f* (mach.) slide, guide
deslizadizo -za *adj* slippery
deslizador *m* (aer.) glider
deslizamiento *m* sliding, slipping; skid, skidding; **deslizamiento de tierra** landslide
deslizante *adj* sliding, gliding; slipping; skidding
deslizar §76 *va* to slide, make slide; to let slip (*a remark*); *vn* to slide, glide; to slip; *vr* to slide, glide; to slip; to skid; to slip out (*said of a remark*); to slip away, sneak away; to backslide, slide back (*e.g., into a vice*)
deslomadura *f* breaking the back; (vet.) aponeurositis of the loins
deslomar *va* to strain or break the back of; *vr* to strain or break one's back, to work oneself to death
deslucido -da *adj* quiet, unshowy; dull, undistinguished
deslucimiento *m* tarnishing, dulling; lack of brilliance, dullness; lack of charm, grace, distinction; ungracefulness, uncouthness, failure
deslucir §60 *va* to tarnish, to dull the luster of, to deprive of charm, grace, distinction; to discredit
deslumbrador -dora *adj* dazzling; bewildering, baffling
deslumbramiento *m* glare, dazzling; bewilderment, bafflement
deslumbrante *adj* dazzling; bewildering, baffling
deslumbrar *va* to dazzle; to bewilder, to baffle; *vr* to be dazzled; to be bewildered, be baffled
deslustrado -da *adj* dull, flat; frosted, ground (*glass*)
deslustrador -dora *adj* tarnishing, dulling; *mf* tarnisher
deslustrar *va* to tarnish, to dull, to dim; to frost (*glass*); to discredit; *vr* to tarnish, dull, dim
deslustre *m* tarnishing, dulling; dullness, dimness; dinginess; discredit, stain, stigma
deslustroso -sa *adj* ugly, unbecoming; disgraceful
desluzco *1st sg pres ind of* **deslucir**
desmadejamiento *m* enervation, weakness
desmadejar *va* to enervate, weaken; *vr* to become enervated, become weakened
desmadrado -da *adj* abandoned by the mother, motherless (*said of animals*)
desmadrar *va* to wean (*young cattle*)
desmagnetizar §76 *va* to demagnetize; *vr* to become demagnetized
desmajolar §77 *va* to pull up (*new vines*) by the root; to untie, to loosen (*shoes*)
desmalladura *f* undoing or cutting meshes
desmallar *va* to undo or cut the meshes of (*a net*)
desmamar *va* to wean
desmamonar *va* to cut the young shoots off (*a tree or vine*)
desmán *m* excess, misbehavior; mishap, misfortune; (zool.) desman
desmanar *vr* to stray from the flock or herd
desmanchar *va* (Am.) to clean of spots, to remove spots from (*clothing*)
desmandado -da *adj* disobedient, intractable, out of hand
desmandar *va* to cancel, countermand, revoke; to revoke (*a legacy, bequest*); *vr* to be impudent and ill-mannered; to go away, to keep apart; to stray from the flock or herd; to get out of hand
desmanear *va* to unfetter, to unshackle
desmangar §59 *va* to take off the handle of
desmanotado -da *adj* (coll.) shy, awkward, unhandy
desmantecar §86 *va* to take the butter out of
desmantelado -da *adj* dilapidated
desmantelamiento *m* dismantling; dilapidation

desmantelar *va* to dismantle; to dilapidate; (naut.) to unmast; (naut.) to unrig; *vr* to dilapidate (*to fall into disrepair or partial ruin*)
desmaña *f* clumsiness, awkwardness, laziness, bungling
desmañado -da *adj* clumsy, awkward, lazy; bungled
desmarrido -da *adj* languid, exhausted
desmarrir §53 *vr* to become exhausted; to grow sad
desmatar *va* to grub, dig up
desmayado -da *adj* languid, colorless, apathetic; dull (*color*)
desmayar *va* to dishearten, to depress; *vn* to lose heart; to falter; *vr* to faint
desmayo *m* depression; faltering; faint, fainting fit; (bot.) weeping willow; **sin desmayo** unfaltering; unfalteringly
desmazalado -da *adj* weak, weakened; downcast, dispirited
desmedido -da *adj* excessive; limitless, boundless
desmedir §94 *vr* to be impudent, to forget oneself
desmedrado -da *adj* run-down
desmedrar *va* to impair; *vn* to decline; *vr* to deteriorate
desmedro *m* impairment, deterioration, decline
desmejora *f* or **desmejoramiento** *m* impairment, deterioration, decline
desmejorar *va* to impair, to spoil; *vn* to decline, lose one's health; *vr* to be impaired, be spoiled; to decline, lose one's health; lose one's charm and attractiveness; (coll.) to grow thin, weak, old
desmelar §18 *va* to remove the honey from (*hive*)
desmelenar *va* to dishevel, to muss; *vr* to become disheveled, become mussed
desmembración *f* or **desmembramiento** *m* dismemberment
desmembrar §18 *va* to dismember; *vr* to become dismembered, to break up
desmemoria *f* forgetfulness, poor memory
desmemoriado -da *adj* forgetful, having a weak memory, having no memory
desmemoriar *vr* to become forgetful, to lose one's memory
desmenguar §23 *va* to lessen, to diminish, to break off
desmentida *f* contradiction, denial; **dar una desmentida a** to give the lie to
desmentido *m* (coll.) contradiction, denial
desmentir §62 *va* to belie; to give the lie to; to conceal (*e.g., evidence*); *vn* to be out of line, to be off level; *vr* to make an about-face, to contradict oneself
desmenudear *va & vn* (Am.) to sell at retail
desmenuzable *adj* crumbly
desmenuzamiento *m* crumbing, crumbling, shredding
desmenuzar §76 *va* to crumb, to crumble, to shred; to examine closely, to criticize severely; *vr* to crumb, to crumble, to shred
desmeollamiento *m* removal of marrow or pith
desmeollar *va* to take the marrow or pith from
desmerecedor -dora *adj* unworthy, undeserving
desmerecer §34 *va* to be or become unworthy of (*praise, reward, etc.*); to detract from, to spoil; *vn* to lose worth, to decline in value; to compare unfavorably; **desmerecer de** to compare unfavorably with
desmerecimiento *m* unworthiness
desmesura *f* immoderation, lack of restraint, excess
desmesurado -da *adj* disproportionate, extreme, excessive; insolent, impudent; *mf* insolent person, impudent person
desmesurar *va* to disturb, to put out of order; *vr* to be impudent, to be insolent, to go too far
desmigajar *va* to crumble, to grind up; to crumb; *vr* to crumble, to break up; to crumb
desmigar §59 *va* to crumble, to crumb (*bread*); *vr* to crumble, to crumb
desmilitarización *f* demilitarization
desmilitarizar §76 *va* to demilitarize
desmineralización *f* (med.) demineralization
desmirriado -da *adj* (coll.) lean, exhausted, emaciated, run-down
desmocha or **desmochadura** *f* topping; dehorning; cutting, excision
desmochar *va* to top (*a tree*); to dehorn (*a bull*); to cut (*a literary work, musical composition, etc.*)
desmoche *m* var. of **desmocha**
desmocho *m* toppings (*e.g., of trees*)
desmodular *va* (rad.) to demodulate
desmogar §59 *vn* to cast the horns (*said, e.g., of deer*)
desmogue *m* casting of horns
desmolado -da *adj* toothless
desmonetización *f* demonetization
desmonetizar §76 *va* to demonetize
desmontable *adj* demountable, detachable; *m* (aut.) tire iron
desmontadura *f* clearing; leveling; demounting; dismounting
desmontaje *m* (mach.) demounting, disassembling, takedown
desmontar *va* to clear (*land, woods*); to level (*ground*); to level off (*piles of earth, etc.*); to tear down; to dismount, take apart; to uncock (*a firearm*); to knock out (*enemy's guns*); to unhorse, to throw (*a rider*); *vn & vr* to dismount, to alight
desmonte *m* clearing; leveling; felling of trees; felled trees; brush; cut (*for a canal, highway, or railroad*)
desmoñar *va* to undo the hairknot of (*a woman*); *vr* to come loose, to get loose (*said of a hairknot*)
desmoralización *f* demoralization
desmoralizador -dora *adj* demoralizing
desmoralizar §76 *va* to demoralize; *vr* to become demoralized (*said of an army*)
desmorecer §34 *vr* to feel deeply or intensely; to stifle, to choke
desmoronadizo -za *adj* crumbly
desmoronamiento *m* wearing away; crumbling, decline, decay
desmoronar *va* to wear down, to wear away; *vr* to wear down, to wear away; to crumble, decline, decay
desmostar *vr* to lose must (*said of grapes*)
desmotadera *f* burler (*woman*); **desmotadera de algodón** cotton gin
desmotador -dora *mf* burler; *f* burling machine; **desmotadora de algodón** cotton gin
desmotar *va* to burl (*wool*); to gin (*cotton*)
desmovilización *f* demobilization
desmovilizar §76 *va* to demobilize
desmullir §26 *va* to undo, to spoil (*something soft or fluffy*)
desmurador *m* mouser (*cat*)
desnacionalización *f* denationalization
desnacionalizar §76 *va* to denationalize
desnarigado -da *adj* noseless; small-nosed
desnarigar §59 *va* to cut off the nose of; to punch or bang in the nose; *vr* to bump one's nose
desnatadora *f* cream separator
desnatar *va* to skim, to separate cream from; to cream, to take the choicest part of; to remove scum from; (found.) to remove the slag from
desnaturalización *f* denaturalization; (chem.) denaturation
desnaturalizado -da *adj* denaturalized; (chem.) denatured; unnatural (*parent, child*)
desnaturalizar §76 *va* to denaturalize; to denature, to pervert; (chem.) to denature; *vr* to become denaturalized; to lose one's citizenship
desnazificación *f* denazification
desnazificar §86 *va* to denazify
desnegar §29 *vr* to take back what one said, to retract
desnervar *va* to enervate
desnevado -da *adj* clear of snow
desnevar §18 *vn* to melt, to thaw
desnieve *m* melting, thaw
desnitrificación *f* denitrification
desnitrificar §86 *va* to denitrify
desnivel *m* unevenness, difference of level, drop

desnivelación *f* unleveling; unevenness, difference of level
desnivelar *va* to make uneven; *vr* to become uneven
desnortado -da *adj* (Am.) aimless
desnucar §86 *va* to dislocate or to break the back of the neck of; to kill (*an animal*) by a blow on the back of the neck; *vr* to dislocate one's neck, to break one's neck
desnudamente *adv* nakedly; clearly, openly, without concealment
desnudar *va* to undress; to lay bare, to denude, to strip; to draw (*the sword*); (coll.) to fleece; **desnudar a un santo para vestir a otro** (coll.) to rob Peter to pay Paul; *vr* to undress, to get undressed; to become evident, be revealed; **desnudarse de** to free oneself of, to cast aside (*e.g., bad habits*); to get rid of; to shed (*leaves, flowers, etc.*)
desnudez *f* nakedness, bareness, nudity
desnudismo *m* nudism
desnudista *mf* nudist; *f* stripteaser
desnudo -da *adj* naked, bare, nude; penniless; clear, evident; *m* (f.a.) nude
desnutrición *f* underfeeding, undernourishment, malnutrition
desnutrido -da *adj* underfed, undernourished
desnutrir *vr* to become undernourished, to suffer from undernourishment
desobedecer §34 *va & vn* to disobey
desobediencia *f* disobedience; **desobediencia civil** civil disobedience
desobediente *adj* disobedient
desobligar §59 *va* to free of an obligation; to antagonize, to alienate, to offend, to disoblige
desobstrucción *f* removal of obstructions or obstacles
desobstruir §41 *va* to free, to clear of obstructions, to clear of obstacles, to move obstacles out of the way of; *vr* to become free of obstructions, to open up
desobstruyente *adj & m* (med.) deobstruent
desocupación *f* unemployment; leisure
desocupado -da *adj* free, vacant, empty; unemployed; idle; free, not busy; *mf* unemployed, unemployed person
desocupar *va* to clear, to empty, vacate (*a place or space*); to take out, remove; to leave unoccupied; *vn* (coll.) to be delivered (*said of a woman*); *vr* to become clear, empty, vacated; to become unoccupied, become idle
desodorante *adj & m* deodorant
desodorar *va* to deodorize
desodorización *f* deodorization
desodorizar §76 *va* to deodorize
desoigo *1st sg pres ind of* **desoír**
desoír §64 *va* to not hear, to not heed, to be deaf to
desojar *va* to break the eye of (*e.g., of a needle*); *vr* to look hard, to strain one's eyes
desolación *f* desolation
desolado -da *adj* desolate; disconsolate
desolador -dora *adj* desolating; *mf* desolater
desolar §77 *va* to desolate, lay waste; *vr* to be desolate, be disconsolate
desoldar §77 *va* to unsolder; *vr* to come unsoldered
desolladero *m* slaughterhouse; (coll.) gyp store, gyp hotel; (coll.) gambling joint
desollado -da *adj* (coll.) brazen, impudent, shameless
desollador -dora *adj* skinning, flaying; fleecing; *mf* skinner, flayer; fleecer; *m* (orn.) butcher bird
desolladura *f* skinning, flaying; damage, hurt; scratch, bruise; fleecing, extortion
desollar §77 *va* to flay, to skin; to do great harm to; (fig.) to fleece; **desollar vivo** (coll.) to skin alive; (coll.) to flay (*to criticize severely*)
desollón *m* (coll.) scratch, bruise
desopilación *f* freeing or curing of obstructions, deoppilation
desopilante *adj* screamingly funny
desopilar *va* to free or cure of obstructions; to make howl with laughter; *vr* to become freed or cured of obstructions; to roar with laughter
desopilativo -va *adj & m* (med.) deoppilative, deobstruent
desopinado -da *adj* discredited
desopinar *va* to discredit, to defame
desopresión *f* freedom from oppression
desoprimir *va* to free from oppression
desorbitado -da *adj* out of proportion; popeyed (*from fear, terror, etc.*); crazy
desorden *m* disorder
desordenado -da *adj* disordered, disorderly, wild, unruly
desordenamiento *m* disorder, confusion
desordenar *va* to disorder, to throw into disorder, to put out of order; *vr* to get out of order; to be unruly or unmanageable; to go too far, to exceed all reason
desorejado -da *adj* (coll.) abject, infamous; (Am.) off tune (*said of a singer*); (Am.) brazen, shameless
desorejamiento *m* cutting off ears
desorejar *va* to cut off the ears of
desorganización *f* disorganization
desorganizadamente *adv* in a disorganized fashion
desorganizador -dora *adj* disorganizing; *mf* disorganizer
desorganizar §76 *va* to disorganize; *vr* to be or become disorganized
desorientación *f* leading astray, going astray; confusion; (psychopath.) disorientation
desorientar *va* to cause (*a person*) to lose his bearings or his way; to lead astray; to confuse; *vr* to lose one's bearings, to lose one's way; to go astray; to become confused
desorillar *va* to cut the selvage off, cut the border off, cut the edge off
desortijado -da *adj* (vet.) sprained, dislocated
desortijar *va* (agr.) to hoe or weed for the first time
desosar §40 *va* var. of **deshuesar**
desovar *vn* to spawn (*said of fish*); to oviposit (*said of insects*)
desove *m* spawning; spawning season; oviposition
desovillar *va* to unravel, disentangle; (fig.) to unravel, disentangle; to give heart to, to encourage; *vr* to become unraveled or disentangled, to be cleared up or solved
desoxidable *adj* deoxidizable
desoxidación *f* deoxidization
desoxidante *adj* deoxidizing; *m* deoxidizer
desoxidar *va* to deoxidize; *vr* to become deoxidized
desoxigenación *f* deoxygenation
desoxigenante *m* deoxidizer
desoxigenar *va* to deoxygenate, to deoxidize; *vr* to become deoxygenated, to become deoxidized
desozonizar §76 *va* to deozonize
despabiladeras *fpl* snuffers
despabilado -da *adj* wide-awake; (fig.) wide-awake
despabilador -dora *mf* snuffer; *m* snuffers
despabiladura *f* snuffing, snuff (*of a wick*)
despabilar *va* to trim, to snuff (*candle*); to snitch; (coll.) to dispatch (*a meal*); to dissipate (*a fortune*); (coll.) to dispatch, to kill; to brighten up, make alert; *vr* to brighten up, to become alert; to wake up; (Am.) to leave, go away
despacio *adv* slowly; at leisure; (Am.) in a low voice; *interj* easy there!; *m* (Am.) delay
despacioso -sa *adj* slow, sluggish
despacito *adv* (coll.) slowly, gently; *interj* easy!
despachaderas *fpl* (coll.) surly reply; (coll.) resourcefulness; **tener buenas despachaderas** (coll.) to not beat about the bush
despachado -da *adj* (coll.) brazen, impudent; ready, quick, resourceful
despachador -dora *adj* dispatching, shipping; *mf* dispatcher
despachante *m* (Am.) clerk, employee; **despachante de aduana** (Am.) customhouse broker
despachar *va* to dispatch, to expedite; to send, to ship; to decide, to settle; to dismiss, to discharge; to hurry; to sell; to wait on (*customers*); to attend to (*correspondence*); (coll.) to dispatch, to kill; *vn* to hurry, be expeditious; to come to a decision; to work, be employed; *vr* to hurry; (coll.) to be delivered (*said of a*

woman); **despacharse a su gusto** to speak one's mind

despacho *m* dispatch, expedition; shipping; dismissal; office, study, store, shop; dispatch, message; (law) mandamus; **estar al despacho** to be under consideration, to be pending; **tener buen despacho** to be capable and energetic; **despacho de aduana** clearance; **despacho de billetes** ticket office; **despacho de localidades** box office

despachurramiento *m* (coll.) smashing, squashing, crushing; (coll.) mangling, butchering; (coll.) squelching

despachurrar *va* (coll.) to smash, squash, crush; (coll.) to mangle, butcher, murder (*e.g., a speech*); (coll.) to squelch

despajadura *f* winnowing

despajar *va* to winnow (*grain*); (min.) to sift

despaldar *va* & *vr* var. of **desespaldar**

despaldilladura *f* breaking the back or shoulder of an animal

despaldillar *va* to break the back or shoulder of (*an animal*)

despaletillar *va* to break the back or shoulder of; (coll.) to pound in the back

despalillador -dora *mf* stripper (*of tobacco, etc.*)

despalilladura *f* stripping (*of tobacco, etc.*)

despalillar *va* to strip (*tobacco*); to separate (*grapes or raisins*) from the stalk, to stem

despalmador *m* (naut.) careenage, careening place; hoof-paring knife

despalmadura *f* (naut.) careenage (*cleaning and calking*); chamfering, beveling; paring a horse's hoof; parings (*of hoofs*)

despalmar *va* (naut.) to careen, to clean and calk (*bottom of a ship*); to chamfer, to bevel; to pare (*horse's hoof*); to pull up (*grass*)

despalme *m* paring a horse's hoof; cut or slash (*in tree trunk to bring down tree*)

despampanador -dora *mf* pruner of vines

despampanadura *f* pruning vines

despampanante *adj* (coll.) dumfounding, upsetting, disturbing; (coll.) stunning, terrific

despampanar *va* to prune (*vines*); to trim the suckers and shoots off (*vines*); (coll.) to astound, dumfound; *vn* (coll.) to open one's heart, to talk freely; *vr* (coll.) to give oneself a hard bump, to fall and hurt oneself

despampanillar *va* to prune (*vines*)

despamplonar *va* to thin the stems and shoots of; *vr* to sprain one's hand

despancación *f* (Am.) husking

despancar §86 *va* (Am.) to husk (*corn*)

despancijar *va* (coll.) to disembowel, to rip open the belly of; *vr* (coll.) to be disemboweled

despanzurrar *va* (coll.) to disembowel, to rip open the belly of; to smash; to slay, to kill; *vr* (coll.) to be disemboweled

despapar *vn* to raise its head too high (*said of a horse*)

desparecer §34 *vn* to disappear

desparedar *va* to remove the walls or partitions from

desparejar *va* to break the pair of

desparejo -ja *adj* rough, uneven; inconstant, fickle

desparpajar *va* to take apart in a bungling way, to take apart sloppily; *vn* & *vr* (coll.) to talk nonsense, to rave

desparpajo *m* (coll.) pertness, flippancy; (coll.) impudence, effrontery; (Am.) disorder

desparramado -da *adj* broad, open

desparramador -dora *adj* & *mf* spendthrift

desparramamiento *m* spreading, scattering, spilling; squandering, extravagance

desparramar *va* to spread, to scatter, to spill; to squander; *vr* to spread, to scatter, to spill, to be spilled; to make merry, to have a wild time

despartidor -dora *adj* separating; *mf* separator, divider

despartimiento *m* separation, division; reconciliation

despartir *va* to part, separate, divide, dispart; to reconcile, to make peace between; *vr* to separate, dispart

desparvar *va* (agr.) to pile up (*threshed grain*) for winnowing

despasar *va* & *vr* (naut.) to unreeve

despatarrada *f* (coll.) split (*in dancing*); **hacer la despatarrada** (coll.) to stretch out, feigning illness or death

despatarrar *va* (coll.) to make (*a person*) open his legs wide; to dumfound; *vr* (coll.) to open one's legs wide; (coll.) to fall to the ground or floor with legs widespread; to lie motionless

despatillado *m* (carp.) cut to make a tenon

despatillar *va* (carp.) to tenon; (naut.) to break off the fluke of (*an anchor*); to shave off the side whiskers of; *vr* to shave off one's side whiskers

despavesaderas *fpl* (Am.) snuffers

despavesadura *f* snuffing

despavesar *va* to snuff (*candle*); to blow the ashes off (*embers*)

despavonar *va* to remove the bluing from (*iron or steel*)

despavorido -da *adj* terrified, frightened

despavorir §53 *vn* & *vr* to be terrified, be aghast

despeado -da *adj* footsore

despeadura *f* or **despeamiento** *m* footsoreness

despear *vr* to bruise one's feet, to get one's feet sore

despectivo -va *adj* depreciatory, disparaging, contemptuous; (gram.) pejorative

despechadamente *adv* spitefully

despechar *va* to spite; to drive to despair; (coll.) to wean; *vr* to be spited; to despair

despecho *m* spite; despair; (Am.) weaning; **a despecho** unwillingly; **a despecho de** in spite of, despite; **por despecho** out of spite

despechugadura *f* carving the breast of a fowl; (coll.) baring one's breast

despechugar §59 *va* to carve the breast of (*a fowl*); *vr* (coll.) to uncover one's breast, to go with bare breast

despedazamiento *m* breaking to pieces, tearing to pieces, falling to pieces; abuse, ruination, destruction

despedazar §76 *va* to break to pieces, to tear to pieces; to ruin (*a reputation*); to break (*one's heart, the law*); *vr* to break or fall to pieces; **despedazarse de risa** to split one's sides laughing

despedida *f* farewell, leave-taking; leave, parting; dismissal, discharge; conclusion (*of a letter*); envoi (*to a poem*)

despedimiento *m* farewell; parting; dismissal

despedir §94 *va* to throw, to hurl; to emit, send forth, send out; to dismiss, to discharge; to see off; (fig.) to banish (*suspicion*); **despedir en la puerta** to see to the door; *vr* to take leave, say good-by; to give up one's job; **despedirse a la francesa** to take French leave; **despedirse de** to take leave of, say good-by to

despedregar §59 *va* to clear of stones

despegable *adj* detachable

despegado -da *adj* (coll.) harsh, unpleasant, gruff, surly

despegadura *f* loosening, detaching; opening

despegar §59 *va* to loosen (*something glued or sealed*); to detach; to open; *vn* (aer.) to take off; *vr* to get loose; to become alienated; **despegarse con** to not suit, to not go well with

despego *m* coolness, indifference; (coll.) gruffness; ingratitude

despegue *m* (aer.) take-off

despeinado -da *adj* uncombed, unkempt

despeinar *va* to take down the hair of; to muss the hair of; *vr* to take down one's hair; to muss one's hair

despejado -da *adj* clear, cloudless; unobstructed; easy, unconstrained; bright, sprightly, vivacious

despejar *va* to free, to clear; to clear up, to clarify, to explain; (math.) to find (*an unknown quantity*); *vr* to be free and easy, to be sprightly; to be amused; to clear up (*said of the weather*); to come out of a fever

despejo *m* clearing; grace, ease, sprightliness; talent, ability, understanding

despelotar *va* to dishevel; *vr* to get plump

despeluzar §76 *va* to muss the hair of; to make the hair of (*a person*) stand on end;

(Am.) to take everything from, to clean out; *vr* to be mussed; to stand on end (*said of the hair*)
despeluznante *adj* frightful, horrifying
despeluznar *va & vr* var. of **despeluzar**
despellejadura *f* skinning, flaying; scratch, bruise; (fig.) maligning, roasting
despellejar *va* to skin, flay; (fig.) to malign, to gossip about, to roast
despenar *va* to console; (coll.) to kill; (Am.) to make hopeless
despendedor -dora *adj & mf* spendthrift, prodigal
despender *va* to spend; to waste, squander, misspend
despensa *f* pantry, larder; (naut.) storeroom; provisions; daily marketing; office of steward, butlership
despensería *f* office of steward, butlership
despensero -ra *mf* steward, butler, dispenser; (naut.) storekeeper
despeñadamente *adv* hastily; audaciously, boldly
despeñadero -ra *adj* steep, precipitous; *m* crag, cliff, precipice; risk, danger
despeñadizo -za *adj* steep, precipitous
despeñamiento *m* var. of **despeño**
despeñar *va* to hurl over a cliff, to fling down a precipice; *vr* to hurl oneself over a cliff; to fall headlong; to plunge down; to plunge downward (*into vice, evil, etc.*); **despeñarse de un vicio a otro** to plunge downward from one vice to another
despeño *m* hurling over a cliff; plunge, plunge over a cliff; headlong fall; ruin, damnation; failure, collapse (*e.g., of a business*)
despepitado *m* (Am.) pitted preserved fruit
despepitadora *f* (Am.) cotton gin
despepitar *va* to seed, to remove the seeds from; (Am.) to stone (*fruit*); (Am.) to core (*an apple*); *vr* to scream in anger, to rush about screaming; (coll.) to strive, to struggle; **despepitarse por** (coll.) to be mad about
despercudir *va* to clean, to wash; *vr* (Am.) to brighten up
desperdiciado -da or **desperdiciador -dora** *adj & mf* spendthrift, prodigal
desperdiciar *va* to waste, squander; to fail to take advantage of, to miss
desperdicio *m* waste, squandering; leftover, residue; **desperdicios** *mpl* waste products; by-products; rubbish; **no tener desperdicio** (coll.) to be useful, to be fine; (iron.) to be fine
desperdigamiento *m* separation, scattering
desperdigar §59 *va* to separate, scatter
desperecer §34 *vr* to be extremely eager, to be burning
desperezar §76 *va* to shake off (*sleep*) by stretching; *vr* to stretch, to stretch one's arms and legs
desperezo *m* stretching, stretching the arms and legs
desperfeccionar *va* to impair, to damage
desperfecto *m* flaw, blemish, imperfection; slight damage
desperfilar *va* (paint.) to soften the lines of; (mil.) to camouflage the outlines of (*trenches, defenses, etc.*)
despernado -da *adj* weary, tired of walking
despernar §18 *va* to cut or injure the legs of; *vr* to cut or injure one's legs
despersonalización *f* depersonalization
despertador -dora *mf* awakener; *m* alarm clock; admonition, warning
despertamiento *m* awakening
despertar §18 *va* to awaken, to wake up; to arouse, to stir up; *vn & vr* to awaken, to wake up
despesar *m* displeasure, sorrow, regret
despestañar *va* to pluck the eyelashes of; *vr* to look hard, to strain one's eyes; (Am.) to go without sleep
despezar §31 *va* to taper (*a pipe or tube*); (arch.) to divide (*a stone wall, arch, vault, etc.*) into constituent parts
despezo *m* taper, tapering; (mas.) face of stone joining another; (arch.) division of stone wall, arch, or vault
despezonar *va* to take the umbo or nipple off (*a lemon, lime, etc.*); to divide, separate; *vr* to come off (*said of an umbo, nipple, end of an axle or spindle, etc.*)
despezuñar *vr* to become useless (*said of a horse's foot*); (Am.) to run, to rush; **despezuñarse por** to be eager about or for
despiadado -da *adj* unmerciful, merciless, ruthless
despicar §86 *va* to satisfy (*a person who was offended*); *vr* to be satisfied, to be requited
despichar *va* to squeeze dry; *vn* (slang) to croak, to die
despidiente *m* stick holding a hanging scaffold away from wall; **despidiente de agua** flashing
despido *m* dismissal, discharge, layoff
despierto -ta *adj* wide-awake; **soñar despierto** to daydream
despiezo *m* (arch.) division of stone wall, arch, or vault
despilaramiento *m* (Am.) removal of shoring (*in a mine*)
despilarar *va* (Am.) to remove the shoring from (*a mine*)
despilfarrado -da *adj* shabby, ragged; wasteful, prodigal; *mf* wasteful person, prodigal
despilfarrador -dora *adj* spendthrift, wasteful; *mf* spendthrift
despilfarrar *va* to squander, to squander recklessly, to waste; *vr* (coll.) to go on a spending spree
despilfarro *m* squandering, lavishness; waste, wastefulness, extravagance; shabbiness, slovenliness
despimpollar *va* to trim the useless shoots off (*a vine*)
despinces *mpl* burling tweezers
despinochar *va* to husk (*corn*)
despintar *va* to take the paint off (*e.g., a wall*); to distort, upset, reverse, disfigure, spoil; (Am.) to turn (*one's glance, one's eyes*) away; *vn* to slip back, to decline; **despintar de** to discredit (*e.g., one's ancestors*); *vr* to wash off, to fade; **no despintársele a uno** (coll.) to not fade from one's memory
despinte *m* (Am.) inferior ore
despinzadera *f* burler (*woman*); burling iron
despinzar §76 *va* to burl
despinzas *fpl* burling tweezers
despiojar *va* to delouse; (coll.) to free of misery; *vr* to be deloused
despioje *m* or **despiojo** *m* delousing
despique *m* satisfaction, requital
despistar *va* to throw off the scent, to throw off the track; *vr* to run off the track, run off the road
despiste *m* throwing off the scent; running off the track; losing one's way
despitonado -da or **despitorrado -da** *adj* (taur.) with a cracked or broken horn
despizcar §86 *va* to crush, break up, grind up; *vr* to be crushed, be broken up, be ground up; to bend all one's efforts
desplacer *m* displeasure; **§34** *va* to displease
desplanchar *va* to wrinkle, rumple, muss (*something that was ironed*); *vr* to wrinkle, rumple, muss
desplantación *f* uprooting, eradication
desplantador *m* trowel, garden trowel
desplantar *va* to uproot; to turn or move (*something*) from the vertical; *vr* to turn or move from the vertical; to lose one's upright posture (*in dancing or fencing*)
desplante *m* irregular posture (*in dancing and fencing*); (Am.) boldness, impudence, boasting
desplatar *va* to remove the silver from
desplate *m* separation or removal of silver
desplayado *m* (Am.) sandy beach
desplayar *vn* to recede, recede from the beach (*said of the sea*)
desplazado -da *adj* displaced (*person*); *mf* displaced person
desplazamiento *m* displacement (*of a volume of water*); motion, move; movement; shift
desplazar §76 *va* to displace (*a volume of water*); to take the place of; *vr* to move; to shift
desplegadura *f* spreading out, unfolding; explanation; unfurling

desplegar §29 *va* to spread, lay out, unfold; to display; to elucidate, explain; to unfurl; (mil.) to deploy; *vr* to spread out, open, unfold; (mil.) to deploy
despleguetear *va* to clip the tendrils from (*vines and runners*)
despliegue *m* spreading out, unfolding; display; unfurling; (mil.) deployment
desplomar *va* to put or knock out of plumb; *vr* to get out of plumb, to lean over; to topple over, to collapse; to fall over in a faint; (fig.) to crumble (*said, e.g., of a throne*); (aer.) to pancake
desplome *m* leaning; toppling, collapse; falling in a faint; crumbling, downfall; (arch.) overhang; (aer.) pancaking; **en desplome** (arch.) overhanging
desplomo *m* leaning
desplumadura *f* plucking, deplumation
desplumar *va* to pluck, deplume; (coll.) to fleece (*by deception or in gambling*); *vr* to molt
desplume *m* plucking; (coll.) fleecing
despoblación *f* depopulation
despoblado *m* deserted spot, wilderness; holding up, waylaying; **en despoblado** at a deserted spot, in the wilds
despoblar §77 *va* to depopulate, to dispeople; to despoil, lay waste; *vr* to become depopulated
despoetizar §76 *va* to divest of poetry, deprive of poetic qualities
despojador -dora *adj* despoiling, plundering; *mf* despoiler, plunderer
despojar *va* to strip, divest, despoil; to dispossess; *vr* to undress; **despojarse de** to take off (*a piece of clothing*); to give up, to relinquish, to divest oneself of
despojo *m* despoilment, despoliation; dispossession; plunder, spoils, booty; prey, victim; head, pluck, and feet of slaughtered animals; giblets; parts of wings, legs, head, and neck of fowl; **despojos** *mpl* leavings, scraps; mortal remains; second-hand building materials; (geol.) debris
despolarización *f* (chem. & phys.) depolarization
despolarizador -dora *adj* depolarizing; *m* (chem. & phys.) depolarizer
despolarizar §76 *va* (chem. & phys.) to depolarize
despoletar *va* to defuse (*a mine or bomb*)
despolvar *va* to dust, to remove the dust or powder from
despolvorear *va* to dust, dust off; to scatter, dissipate; (Am.) to dust, sprinkle
despopularización *f* loss of popularity
despopularizar §76 *va* to make unpopular; *vr* to become unpopular
desportilladura *f* chipping; chip, nick
desportillar *va* to chip, to chip the edge of, to chip the mouth or neck of (*a pitcher, bottle, etc.*); *vr* to chip, chip off
desposado -da *adj* handcuffed, manacled; recently married; *mf* newlywed
desposar *va* to marry (*to join as husband and wife*); *vr* to be betrothed, to get engaged; to get married
desposeer §35 *va* to dispossess, to divest; *vr* to give up one's property; **desposeerse de** to divest oneself of
desposeimiento *m* dispossession
desposorios *mpl* betrothal, engagement; nuptials, marriage
despostador *m* (Am.) carver (*of slaughtered animals*)
despostar *va* (Am.) to cut up, carve up (*slaughtered animals*)
desposte *m* (Am.) carving, quartering
déspota *m* despot
despótico -ca *adj* despotic
despotismo *m* despotism; **despotismo ilustrado** enlightened despotism
despotizar §76 *va & vn* to tyrannize
despotricar §86 *vn & vr* (coll.) to talk without restraint, to rant
despotrique *m* (coll.) wild talk, ranting
despreciable *adj* despicable, contemptible
despreciador -dora *adj* scornful, contemptuous
despreciar *va* to despise, to scorn; to rebuff, to slight; to forget, to forgive, to overlook; to cast aside, to reject; *vr* to not deign; **despreciarse de** + *inf* to not deign to + *inf*
despreciativo -va *adj* depreciative, contemptuous
desprecio *m* scorn, contempt; slight, rebuff
desprender *va* to loosen; to detach; to give off, send out, emit, release, liberate; *vr* to loosen, to come loose; to come forth, to issue; **desprenderse de** to give up; to be clear from, be deduced from
desprendido -da *adj* generous, disinterested
desprendimiento *m* loosening, coming loose, detachment; emission, release, liberation; landslide; generosity, disinterestedness
despreocupación *f* impartiality, lack of bias; relaxation, unconcernedness; unconventionality
despreocupado -da *adj* impartial, unbiased; relaxed, carefree, unconcerned, unworried; unconventional; (Am.) sloppy, slovenly
despreocupante *adj* relaxing
despreocupar *vr* to divert one's mind, to forget one's worries, to relax
desprestigiar *va* to run down, to disparage; *vr* to lose one's reputation or standing, to lose caste
desprestigio *m* disparagement; loss of reputation, unpopularity
desprevención *f* improvidence, unpreparedness
desprevenido -da *adj* unprepared, off one's guard; **coger a una persona desprevenida** to catch somebody unawares
desproporción *f* disproportion
desproporcionado -da *adj* disproportional or disproportionate
desproporcionar *va* to disproportion
despropositado -da *adj* nonsensical, absurd
despropósito *m* nonsense, absurdity
desproveer §35 & §17, 9 *va* to deprive of essentials, deprive of supplies
desprovisto -ta *pp of* **desproveer;** *adj* unprovided, deprived, devoid
despueble *m* or **despueblo** *m* depopulation
después *adv* after, afterwards; later; next; **después de** after; next to; **después de** + *inf* after + *ger;* **después (de) que** after
despulgar §59 *va* to remove the fleas from
despulido -da *adj* ground (*e.g., glass*)
despulir *va* to remove the polish from
despulpador *m* pulper (*machine*)
despulpar *va* to pulp (*to deprive of pulp*)
despulsar *va* to take the breath of, to lay low; *vr* to be eager
despumación *f* skimming
despumadera *f* skimmer
despumar *va* to skim
despuntado -da *adj* dull, blunt
despuntadura *f* dulling, blunting
despuntar *va* to dull, to blunt; to nip, nibble (*grass*); to cut away the dry combs of (*a beehive*); (naut.) to double (*e.g., a cape*); *vn* to begin to sprout or bud; to come on, to dawn (*said of the day, the morning, etc.*); to stand out; **despuntar en** or **por** to show an aptitude in or for; *vr* to become dull, be blunted
despunte *m* var. of **despuntadura**
desquejar *va* (hort.) to slip (*to take cuttings from*)
desqueje *m* (hort.) slipping
desquerer §70 *va* to stop caring for, to no longer want
desquerré *1st sg fut ind of* **desquerer**
desquiciamiento *m* unhinging; upsetting, unsettling
desquiciar *va* to unhinge; to upset, unsettle, turn upside down, perturb; (coll.) to undermine, overthrow, deprive of favor or standing; *vr* to come unhinged; to become upset, to collapse
desquicio *m* (Am.) confusion, disorder, anarchy, ruin, destruction
desquijaramiento *m* breaking the jaws
desquijarar *va* to break the jaws of; *vr* to break one's jaws; **desquijararse de risa** (coll.) to laugh uproariously
desquijerar *va* (carp.) to tenon

desquilatar *va* to reduce the fineness of (*a gold alloy*); to devaluate, lower the value of
desquise *1st sg pret ind of* **desquerer**
desquitar *va* to retrieve, to recoup; to avenge; *vr* to retrieve a loss, win back one's money; to take revenge, get even; **desquitarse con** to get back at
desquite *m* retrieving, recovery; avenging, revenge, retaliation; (sport) return game, return match
desrabotar *va* to cut off the tail of (*especially sheep*)
desramar *va* to strip of branches
desranchar *vr* to leave, to decamp; (mil.) to disperse, break up (*said of soldiers in the same barracks or mess*)
desraspadora *f* stemming machine (*in wine making*)
desraspar *va* to stem (*grapes*)
desrastrojar *va* to remove the stubble from
desratización *f* deratting
desratizar §76 *va* to derat
desrazonable *adj* (coll.) unreasonable
desreglar *va & vr* var. of **desarreglar**
desrelingar §59 *va* (naut.) to detach the boltropes from (*sails*)
desreputación *f* (coll.) dishonor, discredit
desrielar *vn* (Am.) to jump the track
desriñonar *va* to break the back of, to cripple
desrizar §76 *va* to uncurl; (naut.) to unfurl, to let out by means of the reef points; *vr* to uncurl
desroblar *va* to unclinch, to unrivet
destacado -da *adj* outstanding, distinguished
destacamento *m* (mil.) detachment
destacar §86 *va* to emphasize, to highlight, to point up; to make stand out (*in a painting*); (mil.) to detail; *vn* (fig.) to stand out, be distinguished; *vr* to stand out, to project; (fig.) to stand out, be distinguished
destaconar *va* to wear down the heels of (*shoes*)
destajador *m* forging hammer
destajar *va* to arrange for, to contract for; to cut (*cards*)
destajero -ra or **destajista** *mf* pieceworker, jobber
destajo *m* piecework; job, contract; **a destajo** by the piece, by the job, on contract; eagerly, diligently; **hablar a destajo** (coll.) to talk too much
destalinización *f* destalinization
destalinizar §76 *va & vn* to destalinize
destalonar *va* to remove the heels from, to wear down the heels of; to detach (*a coupon*); to detach the coupon from; to level (*the hoofs of a horse*)
destallar *va* to prune useless stems or shoots from
destapacorona *m* (Am.) bottle opener
destapada *f* open pie, pie without top crust
destapadero *m* (elec.) knockout
destapador *m* bottle opener
destapadura *f* uncovering; uncorking; revelation
destapar *va* to uncover, take the cover or lid off; to open; to unplug, uncork; to reveal; *vr* to get uncovered; to throw off one's covers (*in bed*); **destaparse con** to open one's heart to
destapiado *m* place where mud walls have been torn down
destapiar *va* to tear down the mud walls around
destapizar §76 *va* to remove the hangings or draperies from; to take up the carpet from; *vn* to remove the hangings or draperies; to take up the carpet
destaponar *va* to unstop, to uncork (*to remove the stopper or cork from; to open up*)
destarar *va* to deduct the tare on
destartalado -da *adj* shabby, disordered; poorly furnished, poorly equipped
destartalo *m* (coll.) shabbiness, disordered condition
destazador *m* carver (*of slaughtered animals*)
destazar §76 *va* to cut up, carve up (*slaughtered animals*)
destechadura *f* unroofing
destechar *va* to unroof
destejar *va* to remove the tiles from the roof of, to untile; to remove the tiles from the coping of (*a wall*)
destejer *va* to unweave, unknit, unbraid; to upset, undo, disturb
destellar *va* to flash (*light, sparks, etc.*); *vn* to sparkle, to flash, to beam, to twinkle
destello *m* sparkle, flash, beam; (fig.) flash (*e.g., of insight*)
destemplado -da *adj* irregular, agitated (*pulse*); disagreeable, unpleasant (*e.g., voice*); out of tune; (f.a.) inharmonious
destemplanza *f* intemperance; inclemency (*of weather*); irregularity, agitation (*of the pulse*); indisposition; lack of moderation, excess
destemplar *va* to disturb the order or harmony of; to untune, put (*a musical instrument*) out of tune; to untemper, deprive (*a metal*) of temper; to steep, to infuse; *vr* to get out of tune; to lose its temper (*said of metal*); to become irregular (*said of the pulse*); to get excited; (Am.) to be on edge (*said of teeth*)
destemple *m* dissonance; slight indisposition; upset, disturbance; untempering
destentar §18 *va* to remove temptation from, to lead away from temptation
desteñir §74 *va* to discolor; to fade (*a color*); *vn & vr* to fade
desternillar *vr* to break one's cartilage or gristle; **desternillarse de risa** to split one's sides with laughter
desterradero *m* wilderness, waste, desert
desterrado -da *adj* exiled, banished; *mf* exile
desterrar §18 *va* to exile; to banish (*e.g., sadness*); to remove earth from (*roots*); *vr* to go into exile; to withdraw from the world
desterronador *m* (agr.) roller harrow
desterronar *va* to crush, to crumble (*soil, earth*), to crush the lumps of earth of (*a field*), to harrow
destetadera *f* weaning device attached to teats of cows
destetar *va* to wean; to separate (*a child*) from the comforts of home; to deprive of affection; *vr* to be weaned; to be separated from the comforts of home; **destetarse con** to have been brought up on
destete *m* weaning
desteto *m* weaned cattle; stable of weaned mules
destiempo; a destiempo inopportunely, untimely, out of season
destiento *m* shock, surprise
destierre *m* removal of dirt from ore
destierro *m* exile; wilderness, waste
destilable *adj* distillable
destilación *f* distillation; (physiol.) flow of humors; **destilación fraccionada** (chem.) fractional distillation
destiladera *f* still, distiller; filter; scheme, stratagem; (Am.) water filter
destilado *m* distillate
destilador -dora *adj* distilling; to be distilled; *mf* distiller; *m* water filter; still, alembic
destilar *va* to distill; to filter; to exude; *vn* to distill; *vr* to filter; to exude
destilatorio -ria *adj* distilling; *m* distillery; still, alembic
destilería *f* distillery, distilling plant
destinación *f* destination (*act of destining; purpose*)
destinar *va* to destine; to assign; to designate; **destinar a** + *inf* to destine (*e.g., money*) to + *inf;* **destinar para** to destine for
destinatario -ria *mf* addressee; consignee; recipient (*e.g., of homage, applause*)
destino *m* destiny; destination (*place to which a person is going or a thing is being sent; setting apart for a purpose*); office, employment; place of employment; **con destino a** bound for; (*cap.*) *m* (myth.) Destiny
destiño *m* blackish empty part of honeycomb
destiranizado -da *adj* free from tyranny
destitución *f* destitution, depriving; dismissal
destituíble *adj* removable
destituir §41 *va* to deprive; to dismiss, dismiss from office
destocar §86 *va* to take the hat or cap off (*a person*); *vr* to take off one's hat or cap

destorcedura *f* untwisting
destorcer **§87** *va* to untwist; to straighten (*something bent*); *vr* to untwist, become untwisted; (naut.) to drift, get off the course
destornillado -da *adj* inconsiderate, rash, mad, out of one's head
destornillador *m* screwdriver; **destornillador de trinquete** ratchet screwdriver
destornillamiento *m* unscrewing
destornillar *va* to unscrew; *vr* to unscrew; (fig.) to lose one's head, to act or talk like a wild man
destoser *vr* to cough (*in getting ready to talk or to attract attention*)
destostar **§77** *vr* to turn white again (*after sunburn*)
destrabar *va* to detach, loosen, separate; to untie, unfetter
destraillar **§75** *va* to uncouple, to unleash (*hounds*); *vr* to be unleashed
destral *m* hatchet
destraleja *f* little hatchet
destralero *m* hatchet maker or vendor
destramar *va* to undo the warp of, to unweave
destrejar *vn* to proceed with skill or dexterity
destrenzar **§76** *va* to unbraid, to unplait
destreza *f* skill, dexterity
destrincar **§86** *va* (naut.) to unlash
destripacuentos *m* (*pl:* **-tos**) (coll.) interrupter, butter-in
destripamiento *m* disembowelment; crushing, mangling
destripar *va* to gut, disembowel; to take the insides out of (*e.g., a pillow*); to crush, to mangle; (coll.) to spoil (*a story, by interrupting and revealing its outcome*)
destripaterrones *m* (*pl:* **-nes**) (coll.) clodhopper
destrísimo -ma *adj super* very or most skilful
destriunfar *va* to force (*another player*) to play trumps
destrizar **§76** *va* to break to pieces, to tear to shreds; *vr* to get angry, to be greatly distressed
destrocar **§95** *va* to swap back again
destrón *m* blind man's guide
destronamiento *m* dethronement; overthrow
destronar *va* to dethrone; to overthrow
destroncadora *f* stump puller
destroncamiento *m* detruncation; chopping down; dislocation; ruination; exhaustion
destroncar **§86** *va* to detruncate; to chop off, to chop down; to lop off; to maim, dislocate; to ruin, to bring to ruin; to exhaust, wear out; to interrupt; *vr* to be exhausted, be worn out
destrozar **§76** *va* to break to pieces, to shatter, to destroy; to squander; to annihilate, wipe out (*e.g., an army*)
destrozo *m* destruction; havoc; annihilation, massacre
destrozón -zona *adj* hard on clothing
destrucción *f* destruction
destructibilidad *f* destructibility
destructible *adj* destructible
destructividad *f* destructiveness
destructivo -va *adj* destructive
destructor -tora *adj* destructive; *mf* destroyer; *m* (nav.) destroyer
destrueco or **destrueque** *m* return of an exchange; re-exchange
destruíble *adj* destructible
destruidor -dora *adj* destructive; *mf* destroyer
destruir **§41** *va* to destroy; *vr* (alg.) to cancel each other
desubstanciar *va* var. of **desustanciar**
desucación *f* extraction of juice
desucar **§86** *va* to extract the juice from
desudación *f* wiping off sweat
desudar *va* to wipe the sweat off
desuellacaras *m* (*pl:* **-ras**) (coll.) scraper (*unskilful barber*); (coll.) scamp, scalawag
desuello *m* skinning, flaying; fleecing; boldness, shamelessness; **ser un desuello** (coll.) to be highway robbery (*said of exorbitant prices*)
desuetud *f* desuetude
desulfuración *f* desulfurization
desulfurar *va* to desulfurize
desuncir **§50** *va & vr* to unyoke
desunión *f* disunion
desunir *va* to take apart; to separate; to disunite; *vr* to come apart; to separate; to disunite
desuñar *va* to tear out the nails, claws, or fangs of; to pull up the dead roots of (*a plant*); *vr* (coll.) to work one's fingers to the bone; (coll.) to work hard and skilfully with one's hands; (coll.) to plunge into vice, gambling, thievery, etc.
desurcar **§86** *va* to remove the furrows from, take out the furrows of
desurdir *va* to remove the warp from, to unweave; to frustrate, to nip (*a plot*) in the bud
desusado -da *adj* out of use, out of date, obsolete; uncommon; rusty (*out of practice*)
desusar *va* to disuse, to stop using; *vr* to be no longer used, to go out of date
desuso *m* disuse; desuetude; **caído en desuso** obsolete
desustanciar *va* to deprive of substance, deprive of strength, weaken
desvahar *va* (agr.) to clean out the dry and withered parts of (*a plant*)
desvaído -da *adj* gaunt, tall and lanky; dull (*said of colors*)
desvainar *va* to shell (*beans, peas, etc.*)
desvalido -da *adj* destitute, helpless
desvalijador *m* robber, highwayman
desvalijamiento *m* theft of contents of a valise, trunk, etc.; robbery, plunder
desvalijar *va* to steal the contents of (*a valise, trunk, etc.*); to rob, plunder
desvalijo *m* var. of **desvalijamiento**
desvalimiento *m* abandonment, helplessness, disfavor
desvalorar *va* to devalue
desvalorización *f* devaluation
desvalorizar **§76** *va* to devalue
desván *m* garret, loft; **desván gatero** cockloft
desvanecedor *m* (phot.) mask
desvanecer **§34** *va* to cause to disappear or vanish, to dispel, to dissipate (*e.g., smoke, doubt, suspicion*); to break up (*e.g., a conspiracy*); to banish, cast aside (*a thought, idea, recollection*); to mask (*part of a photographic print*); *vr* to disappear, vanish; to be dissipated, to evanesce; to evaporate; to faint, to swoon; (rad.) to fade
desvanecido -da *adj* faint; proud, haughty, vain
desvanecimiento *m* disappearance, evanescence, dissipation; pride, haughtiness, vanity; faintness, giddiness, dizziness; fainting spell; (rad.) fading, fade-out
desvarar *va* to slide, to slip; (naut.) to refloat, set afloat (*a grounded ship*)
desvariado -da *adj* raving, delirious, crazy; disordered, nonsensical; long and wild (*said of branches of trees*)
desvariar **§90** *vn* to rave, rant, be delirious
desvarío *m* delirium, craziness; nonsense, wild idea, extravagance; inconstancy; caprice, whim; monstrosity
desvedar *va* to permit, to allow, to remove the prohibition from
desvelado -da *adj* wakeful, awake, sleepless; watchful, vigilant; anxious, worried, fearful
desvelamiento *m* var. of **desvelo**
desvelar *va* to keep awake; to reveal; *vr* to keep or stay awake, to go without sleep, to pass a sleepless night; to be watchful or vigilant; **desvelarse por** to be anxious about, be greatly concerned about
desvelo *m* wakefulness, lack of sleep; watchfulness, vigilance; anxiety, concern
desvenar *va* to remove the vein or filaments from; to strip (*tobacco*); to extract (*the ore*) from the veins; to arch the cannon of (*a horse's bit*)
desvencijado -da *adj* rickety, falling apart
desvencijar *va* to break, loosen, take apart
desvendar *va* to unbandage; *vr* to come unbandaged
desveno *m* port, tongue groove (*of horse's bit*)
desventaja *f* disadvantage
desventajoso -sa *adj* disadvantageous

desventar §18 *va* to vent, let the air out of
desventura *f* misfortune
desventurado -da *adj* unfortunate; faint-hearted; stingy; *mf* faint-hearted person; miser
desvergonzado -da *adj* unabashed, impudent; shameless; *mf* shameless person
desvergonzar §98 *vr* to be impudent or insolent; **desvergonzarse con** to be impudent or insolent to
desvergüenza *f* impudence, insolence; shamelessness
desvestir §94 *va & vr* to undress
desvezar §76 *va* to make unaccustomed; *vr* to become unaccustomed
desviación *f* deflection, deviation; detour; (med.) extravasation; (rad. & telv.) drift
desviacionismo *m* deviationism
desviacionista *mf* deviationist (*communist who does not hew to the party line*)
desviadero *m* (rail.) siding, turnout
desviado -da *adj* astray; off the track; devious
desviar §90 *va* to turn aside, to turn away, to deviate, to deflect; to dissuade, to sway; (rail.) to switch; to parry, ward off (*in fencing*); *vr* to turn aside, be deflected, to deviate, to swerve, to branch off; to be dissuaded
desvío *m* deflection, deviation; coldness, indifference, dislike; detour, turnout; (rail.) siding, sidetrack; wall support (*for hanging scaffolding*)
desvirar *va* to pare off the edges of (*a sole*); to trim (*a book*); (naut.) to unwind (*a cable or rope, on a capstan*)
desvirgar §59 *va* to deflower, to ravish
desvirtuar §33 *va* to weaken, detract from, spoil; *vr* to decline; to spoil, to become spoiled
desvitalización *f* devitalization
desvitalizar §76 *va* to devitalize
desvitrificar §86 *va* to devitrify; *vr* to become devitrified
desvivir *vr* to be eager, be anxious; **desvivirse por** to long for, be crazy about; **desvivirse por** + *inf* to be eager to, be anxious to + *inf*
desvolvedor *m* wrench, screw key
desvolver §63 & §17, 9 *va* to change, change the form of; to turn up (*the soil*); to loosen, to unscrew (*a nut or screw*)
desvuelto -ta *pp of* **desvolver**
desyemar *va* to remove the buds from; to remove the yolk from
desyerba *f* weeding; weeding hoe
desyerbar *va* var. of **desherbar**
desyugar §59 *va* to unyoke
deszocar §86 *va* to put (*a foot*) out of commission; (arch.) to remove the socle from (*a column*); *vr* to put one's foot out of commission
deszumar *va* to squeeze the juice out of
detall *m* retail; **al detall** retail, at retail
detalladamente *adv* in detail
detallar *va* to detail, to particularize, to tell in detail; to retail, to sell at retail
detalle *m* detail, particular; detailed account; (f.a.) detail; (Am.) retail; **en detalle** in detail
detallista *mf* person fond of detail; painter or writer skilled in detail; retailer
detasa *f* (rail.) rebate
detección *f* detection; (elec. & rad.) detection
detectar *va* to detect; (elec. & rad.) to detect
detective *m* detective
detectivesco -ca *adj* detective
detector -tora *adj* detecting; *m* detector; (elec. & rad.) detector; **detector a** or **de cristal** (rad.) crystal detector; **detector a válvula** (rad. & telv.) vacuum-tube detector; **detector de galena** (rad.) galena detector; **detector de mentiras** lie detector; **detector de minas** mine detector; *f* (rad. & telv.) vacuum-tube detector
detén *2d sg impv of* **detener**
detención *f* detainment, detention; delay; care, thoroughness; **detención ilegal** (law) detainer
detendré *1st sg fut ind of* **detener**
detenedor -dora *adj* stopping; *mf* detainer, stopper; *m* (mach.) arrester, catch
detener §85 *va* to stop, to check, to hold, to hold back; to detain, to arrest; to dam, to dam up; to keep, retain, reserve; **detener el aliento** to hold one's breath; *vr* to stop; to delay, to tarry, to linger, to pause; **detenerse a** + *inf* to stop to + *inf*; **¡detente, bala!** stop, bullet! (*words on the breast patch of the Carlists*)
detengo *1st sg pres ind of* **detener**
detenidamente *adv* carefully, thoroughly
detenido -da *adj* lengthy; timid, hesitant; mean, stingy, niggardly; careful, thorough; slow, dilatory; *mf* prisoner
detenimiento *m* var. of **detención**
detentación *f* (law) deforcement
detentador *m* (law) deforciant
detentar *va* to hold (*a position, title, etc.*); (law) to deforce
detergente *adj & m* detergent
deterger §49 *va* to deterge
deterioración *f* var. of **deterioro**
deteriorar *va & vr* to deteriorate
deterioro *m* deterioration
determinabilidad *f* determinability
determinable *adj* determinable
determinación *f* determination
determinado -da *adj* determined, resolute; determinate; certain; (gram.) definite (*article*)
determinante *adj* determinant; *m* determinant; (biol., log. & math.) determinant
determinar *va* to determine; to cause, bring about; to lead; **determinar a (una persona) a** + *inf* to lead or induce (*a person*) to + *inf*; **determinar** + *inf* to decide to + *inf*; *vr* to determine, to decide; **determinarse a** + *inf* to decide to + *inf*
determinativo -va *adj* determinative; (gram.) determinative
determinismo *m* (philos.) determinism
determinista *adj & mf* (philos.) determinist
detersión *f* detersion
detersivo -va *adj & m* detersive
detersorio -ria *adj & m* var. of **detergente**
detestable *adj* detestable
detestación *f* cursing; detestation
detestar *va* to curse; to detest; **detestar** + *inf* to hate to + *inf*, e.g., **detesto salir con la lluvia** I hate to go out in the rain; *vn* to detest; **detestar de** to detest
detienebuey *m* (bot.) restharrow
detiento *m* start, shock, upset
detonación *f* detonation; knock (*of an internal-combustion engine*)
detonador *m* detonator
detonante *adj* detonating
detonar *vn* to detonate
detorsión *f* sprain, twisting of a ligament, muscle, limb, or joint
detracción *f* detraction
detractar *va* to defame, vilify
detractor -tora *adj* detractive, disparaging; *mf* detractor, disparager
detraer §88 *va* to detract, take away; to defame, vilify
detraigo *1st sg pres ind of* **detraer**
detraje *1st sg pret ind of* **detraer**
detrás *adv* behind; **por detrás de** behind the back of; **detrás de** behind, back of
detricción *f* detrition
detrimento *m* damage, harm, loss, detriment
detrítico -ca *adj* (geol.) detrital
detrito *m* detritus, debris, dirt; (geol.) detritus
detritus *m* (*pl:* **-tus**) var. of **detrito**
detuve *1st sg pret ind of* **detener**
Deucalión *m* (myth.) Deucalion
deudo -da *mf* relative; *m* relationship, kinship; duty, obligation; *f* debt; indebtedness; (Bib.) debt (*sin*); **llenarse de deudas** to get deeply in debt; **deuda activa** asset, credit; **deuda de honor** or **deuda de juego** debt of honor; **deuda flotante** floating debt; **deuda pasiva** liability, debit; **deuda pública** public debt
deudor -dora *adj* indebted; *mf* debtor; **deudor hipotecario** mortgagor; **deudor moroso** delinquent (*in payment*)
deuterio *m* (chem.) deuterium
deuterión *m* (chem.) deuteron
Deuteronomio *m* (Bib.) Deuteronomy
deutón *m* (chem.) deuton (*i.e., deuteron*)
deutoplasma *m* (biol.) deutoplasm
devalar *vn* (naut.) to drift, to drift from the course

devaluación *f* devaluation
devaluar §33 *va* to devalue
devanadera *f* winding frame
devanado *m* winding; (elec.) winding
devanador -dora *adj* winding; *m* core (*of a ball of yarn*); (Am.) winding frame
devanar *va* to wind, to spool, to roll; *vr* (Am.) to double up with laughter; (Am.) to writhe with pain
devanear *vn* to rave, talk nonsense; to fritter away one's time, to loaf around
devaneo *m* raving, nonsense, madness; loafing; flirtation
devastación *f* devastation
devastador -dora *adj* devastating; *mf* devastator
devastar *va* to devastate
develación *f* revelation, discovery; unveiling (*of, e.g., a statue*)
develar *va* to reveal, uncover; to unveil (*e.g., a statue*)
devendré *1st sg fut ind of* **devenir**
devengar §59 *va* to earn (*wages*); to draw (*interest*)
devengo *m* earning; amount earned, earnings; *1st sg pres ind of* **devenir**
devenir §92 *vn* to happen; (philos.) to become
deviación *f* var. of **desviación**
devine *1st sg pret ind of* **devenir**
devoción *f* devotion
devocionario *m* prayer book
devolución *f* return, restitution; (eccl.) devolution
devolutivo -va or **devolutorio -ria** *adj* (law) returnable
devolver §63 & §17, 9 *va* to return, give back, send back; to requite, to pay back; (coll.) to vomit; *vr* (Am.) to return, come back
devoniano -na *adj & mf* Devonian; (geol.) Devonian
devónico -ca *adj* (geol.) Devonic, Devonian
devorador -dora *adj* devouring; *mf* devourer
devorante *adj* devouring
devorar *va* to devour; (fig.) to devour
devotería *f* (coll.) sanctimony, sanctimoniousness
devoto -ta *adj* devout; devoted; devotional; *mf* devotee; *m* object of devotion or worship
devuelto -ta *pp of* **devolver**
dexiocardia *f* var. of **dextrocardia**
dextrina *f* (chem.) dextrin or dextrine
dextrocardia *f* (anat.) dextrocardia
dextrógiro -ra *adj* (phys.) dextrogyrous
dextrorrotatorio -ria *adj* (phys.) dextrorotatory
dextrorso -sa *adj* (bot.) dextrorse
dextrosa *f* (biochem.) dextrose
deyección *f* (physiol.) dejection; (geol.) ejecta, ejection
dezmable *adj* tithable
dezmatorio *m* tithing; place where tithes are collected
dezmeño -ña *adj* (pertaining to) tithe
dezmería *f* tithe land
dezmero -ra *adj* (pertaining to) tithe; *mf* tither
D.F. abr. of **Distrito Federal**
d/f abr. of **días fecha**
dg. abr. of **decigramo** or **decigramos**
Dg. abr. of **decagramo** or **decagramos**
dho. abr. of **dicho**
di *2d sg impv of* **decir**
dí *1st sg pret ind of* **dar**
día *m* day; daytime; daylight; **días** *mpl* birthday; **a días** once in a while; **al día** a day, per day; up to date; **alcanzar en días** (coll.) to survive (*another person*); **al otro día** on the following day; **buenos días** good morning; **¡cualquier día!** I should say not!; **dar los buenos días a** to pass the time of day with; **dar los días a** to wish (*someone*) many happy returns of the day; to congratulate (*someone*) on his saint's day; **de día** in the daytime, in the daylight; **el día menos pensado** (coll.) when least expected; **el mejor día** some fine day; **en cuatro días** in a few days; **en días de Dios, en días del mundo** or **en los días de la vida** never; **en el día** nowadays; the same day; **en pleno día** in broad daylight; **en su día** in due time; **entrado en días** advanced in years; **ocho días** a week; **poner al día** to bring up to date; **ponerse al día** to catch up (*in one's debts*); **quince días** two weeks, a fortnight; **tener sus días** to have one's day, to be up in years; **un día sí y otro no** every other day; **vivir al día** to live from hand to mouth; **día de acción de gracias** Thanksgiving, Thanksgiving Day (*in U.S.A.*); **día de años** birthday; **día de año nuevo** New Year or New Year's Day; **día de asueto** day off, time off; **día de ayuno** fast day; **día de carne** meat day; **día de ceniza** Ash Wednesday; **día de Colón** Columbus Day; **día de cutio** or **de hacienda** workday; **día de engañabobos** the 28th of December, celebrated like April Fools' Day; **día de gracias** Thanksgiving Day (*in U.S.A.*); **día de guardar** (eccl.) holyday, holyday of obligation; **día de hogar** or **de huelga** day off; **día de inauguración** (f.a.) private viewing; **día de joya** court day; **día del idioma** anniversary of death of Cervantes (*23d of April*); **día del juicio** Day of Judgment; **día de la raza** Columbus Day, Discovery Day; **día de los caídos** Memorial Day; **día de los (santos) inocentes** (eccl.) Holy Innocents' Day (*December 28, popularly celebrated like April Fools' Day*); **día de pescado** fish day; **día de precepto** (eccl.) holyday, holyday of obligation; **día de ramos** Palm Sunday; **día de Reyes** Twelfth-night; **día de San Martín** Martinmas; **día de todos los santos** All Saints' Day; **día de trabajo** workday, weekday; **día de vigilia** fast day; **día diado** fixed day; **día feriado** (law) court holiday; holiday, day off; **día festivo** holiday; **día hábil** working day, business day; (law) court day; **día laborable** workday, weekday; **día lectivo** school day; **día onomástico** saint's day, birthday; **día puente** day taken off because it falls between two holidays; **días de demora** or **de estadía** (naut.) lay days; **días de gracia** (coll.) days of grace; **día útil** workday
diabasa *f* (mineral.) diabase
diabetes *f* (path.) diabetes
diabético -ca *adj & mf* diabetic
diabetómetro *m* diabetometer
diabla *f* (coll.) she-devil; carding machine; **a la diabla** (coll.) carelessly, any old way
diablear *vn* (coll.) to play pranks
diablesa *f* (coll.) she-devil
diablesco -ca *adj* diabolical, devilish
diablillo *m* imp; person disguised as devil; (coll.) schemer; **diablillo de Descartes** Cartesian devil, diver, or imp
diablo *m* devil; (mach.) devil; (billiards & pool) bridge, rest, cue rest; **¡diablos!** the devil!; **ahí será el diablo** (coll.) there will be the devil to pay; **como el diablo** (coll.) like the devil; **darse al diablo** (coll.) to get angry, go wild; **del diablo, de los diablos, de mil diablos,** or **de todos los diablos** a hell of a; **llevarse el diablo** (coll.) to turn out badly; **pobre diablo** (coll.) poor devil; **diablo cojuelo** tricky devil; **diablo encarnado** devil incarnate; **diablo marino** (ichth.) scorpene; **diablo punzante** (zool.) moloch; **diablos azules** (Am.) blue devils (*delirium tremens*)
diablura *f* devilment, deviltry (*mischief; daring*)
diabólico -ca *adj* diabolic, diabolical, devilish; (coll.) devilish (*very bad; mischievous*)
diabolín *m* chocolate drop
diabolismo *m* diabolism (*doctrine*)
diábolo *m* yo-yo
diacatolicón *m* (pharm.) purgative electuary
diacitrón *m* candied citron, candied lemon peel
diacodión *m* (pharm.) diacodion
diaconado *m* deaconry, diaconate
diaconal *adj* deaconal, diaconal
diaconato *m* deaconry, diaconate
diaconía *f* diaconia; deacon's house
diaconisa *f* deaconess
diácono *m* deacon
diacrítico -ca *adj* (gram. & med.) diacritic or diacritical

diacronía *f* diachrony
diacrónico -ca *adj* diachronic
diadelfo -fa *adj* (bot.) diadelphous
diadema *f* diadem; tiara (*ornamental coronet worn by women*)
diademado -da *adj* (her.) diademed
diado -da *adj* fixed (*day*)
diafanidad *f* diaphanousness, translucency
diafanizar **§76** *va* to make diaphanous
diáfano -na *adj* diaphanous
diáfisis *f* (anat. & bot.) diaphysis
diaforesis *f* (med.) diaphoresis
diaforético -ca *adj* diaphoretic or diaphoretical; *m* diaphoretic
diafragma *m* diaphragm; **diafragma iris** (opt.) iris diaphragm
diafragmático -ca *adj* diaphragmatic
diagnosis *f* (*pl:* **-sis**) (bot., zool. & med.) diagnosis
diagnosticar **§86** *va* to diagnose
diagnóstico -ca *adj* diagnostic; *m* diagnostic; diagnosis
diagonal *adj* diagonal; *f* diagonal; diagonal cloth
diágrafo *m* diagraph
diagrama *m* diagram
diagramático -ca *adj* diagrammatic
diálaga *f* (mineral.) diallage
dialectal *adj* dialectal
dialectalismo *m* dialecticism
dialéctico -ca *adj* dialectic or dialectical; sophistical; *m* dialectic (*philosopher*); dialectician; *f* dialectic, dialectics; sophistry
dialecto *m* dialect
dialectología *f* dialectology
dialicarpelar *adj* (bot.) dialycarpous
diálisis *f* (*pl:* **-sis**) dialysis
dialítico -ca *adj* dialytic
dializador *m* (physical chem.) dialyzer
dializar **§76** *va* to dialyze
dialogal *adj* dialogic
dialogar **§59** *va* to write in the form of a dialogue; *vn* to talk, to converse
dialogismo *m* (rhet.) dialogism, Wellerism
dialogístico -ca *adj* interlocutory, dialogistic
dialogizar **§76** *vn* to dialogue, to converse
diálogo *m* dialogue; friendly relations
dialoguista *mf* dialogist (*writer*)
dialtea *f* (pharm.) marsh-mallow ointment
diamagnético -ca *adj & m* diamagnetic
diamagnetismo *m* diamagnetism
diamantado -da *adj* diamondlike
diamantar *va* to make shine or sparkle like diamonds
diamante *m* diamond; **diamante en bruto** diamond in the rough; (fig.) diamond in the rough; **diamante negro** black diamond (*carbon diamond*); **diamante rosa** rose diamond
diamantífero -ra *adj* diamantiferous
diamantino -na *adj* (pertaining to or like a) diamond; (poet.) hard, unshakable
diamantista *mf* diamond cutter; diamond merchant
diamela *f* (bot.) Arabian jasmine
diametral *adj* diametric, diametrical, diametral
diámetro *m* diameter
diana *f* (mil.) reveille; bull's-eye; (*cap.*) *f* (myth.) Diana; **hacer diana** to hit the bull's-eye or to score a bull's-eye
dianche *m* (coll.) devil; *interj* (coll.) the deuce!, the devil!
diandro -dra *adj* (bot.) diandrous
diantre *m* (coll.) devil; *interj* (coll.) the dickens!, the deuce!
diapalma *f* (pharm.) diapalma
diapasón *m* (mus.) diapason; (mus.) tuning fork; (mus.) pitch pipe; (mus.) finger board (*e.g., of violin*); **bajar el diapasón** (coll.) to lower one's voice, to change one's tune; **subir el diapasón** (coll.) to raise one's voice; **diapasón normal** (mus.) diapason normal
diapédesis *f* (physiol.) diapedesis
diapente *m* (ancient mus. & ancient pharm.) diapente
diapositiva *f* (phot.) diapositive; slide, lantern slide
diaprea *f* small round plum
diaquilón *m* (pharm.) diachylon
diario -ria *adj* daily; (Am.) street (*clothes*); **a diario** daily, everyday; *m* daily (*paper*); diary; daily household expenses, daily ration; day book; **diario de navegación** (naut.) log book; **diario hablado** (rad.) newscast
diarismo *m* (Am.) journalism
diarista *mf* diarist; *m* newspaperman
diarrea *f* (path.) diarrhea
diartrosis *f* (*pl:* **-sis**) (anat.) diarthrosis
diascordio *m* (pharm.) diascordium
diasén *m* (pharm.) senna purgative
diáspero *m* (mineral.) jasper
Diáspora *f* (Bib. & fig.) Diaspora
diásporo *m* (mineral.) diaspore
diaspro *m* var. of **diáspero**
diastasa *f* (biochem.) diastase
diastásico -ca *adj* (biochem. & surg.) diastasic
diastasis *f* (surg.) diastasis
diástilo *m* (arch.) diastyle
diástole *f* (physiol. & gram.) diastole
diastólico -ca *adj* diastolic
diastrofismo *m* (geol.) diastrophism
diatérmano -na *adj* (phys.) diathermanous
diatermia *f* (med.) diathermy
diatérmico -ca *adj* (med. & phys.) diathermic
diatesarón *m* (ancient mus., ancient pharm. & rel.) diatessaron
diatésico -ca *adj* diathetic
diátesis *f* (med.) diathesis
diatomáceo -a *adj* diatomaceous
diatomea *f* (bot.) diatom
diatónico -ca *adj* (mus.) diatonic
diatriba *f* diatribe
dibásico -ca *adj* (chem.) dibasic
dibujante *mf* sketcher, illustrator; *m* draftsman; *f* draftswoman
dibujar *va* to draw, to design; to sketch; to depict, to outline; *vr* to be outlined; to come to the surface (*said, e.g., of something concealed or hidden*)
dibujo *m* drawing; sketch; depiction; design; **no meterse en dibujos** (coll.) to attend to one's own business; **dibujo animado** animated cartoon
dicacidad *f* wittiness, sharpness, sarcasm
dicasio *m* (bot.) dichasium
dicaz *adj* (*pl:* **-caces**) witty, sharp, sarcastic
dicción *f* word; diction
diccionario *m* dictionary; **Diccionario de Autoridades** dictionary of Spanish Academy, whose first edition appeared from 1726 to 1739
diccionarista *mf* lexicographer
dic.e abr. of **diciembre**
dicentra *f* (bot.) dicentra, bleeding heart
diciembre *m* December
diciendo *ger of* **decir**
diclino -na *adj* (bot.) diclinous
diclorodifeniltricloroetano *m* (chem.) dichlorodiphenyl-trichloroethane
dicloruro *m* (chem.) dichloride, bichloride
dicotiledón *adj* (bot.) dicotyledonous; *m* (bot.) dicotyledon
dicotiledóneo -a *adj* (bot.) dicotyledonous
dicotomía *f* dichotomy; (astr., biol., bot. & log.) dichotomy; split fees (*among doctors*)
dicotómico -ca *adj* dichotomic
dicótomo -ma *adj* dichotomous
dicroico -ca *adj* dichroic
dicroísmo *m* dichroism
dicromático -ca *adj* dichromatic
dicromatismo *m* dichromatism
dicromato *m* (chem.) dichromate, bichromate
dictado *m* dictation; title of dignity or honor; **dictados** *mpl* dictates; **escribir al dictado** to take dictation; to take down (*something dictated*)
dictador *m* dictator
dictadora *f* dictaphone, dictating machine
dictadura *f* dictatorship
dictáfono *m* dictaphone
dictamen *m* dictum, opinion, judgment
dictaminar *va* to pass judgment on; *vn* to pass judgment
díctamo *m* (bot.) dittany; **díctamo blanco** (bot.) fraxinella
dictar *va* to dictate; to promulgate (*a law*); to inspire, to suggest; (Am.) to give (*a course*); (Am.) to deliver (*a lecture*); *vn* to dictate
dictatorial *adj* dictatorial (*pertaining to a dictator; imperious, overbearing*)

dictatorio -ria *adj* dictatorial (*pertaining to a dictator*)
dicterio *m* taunt, insult
dictógrafo *m* dictograph
dicha *f* see **dicho**
dicharachero -ra *adj* (coll.) vulgar, obscene, foul-mouthed
dicharacho *m* (coll.) vulgarity, obscenity
dichero -ra *adj* (coll.) witty; *mf* (coll.) wit
dicho -cha *adj* said; **mejor dicho** rather; *pp of* **decir; tener una cosa por dicha** to consider a matter settled; **dicho y hecho** no sooner said than done; *m* saying; pledge, promise of marriage; witticism, bright remark; (coll.) insulting remark; **dicho de las gentes** talk (*unfavorable*); *f* happiness, luck; **a dicha** or **por dicha** by chance
dichón -chona *adj* (Am.) sharp, sarcastic
dichoso -sa *adj* happy; fortunate, lucky; (coll.) annoying, tiresome; (iron.) lucky
didáctico -ca *adj* didactic or didactical; *f* didactics
didáctilo -la *adj* didactylous
didelfo -fa *adj & m* (zool.) didelphian
didimio *m* (chem.) didymium
dídimo -ma *adj* (bot. & zool.) didymous; *m* didymus (*testicle*)
Dido *f* (myth.) Dido
diecinueve *adj* nineteen; **las diecinueve** seven P.M.; *m* nineteen; nineteenth (*in dates*)
diecinueveavo -va *adj & m* nineteenth
dieciochavo -va *adj & m* eighteenth
diecioocheno -na *adj* eighteenth
dieciochesco -ca *adj* eighteenth-century
dieciochismo *m* eighteenth-century style or character
dieciochista *adj* eighteenth-century
dieciocho *adj* eighteen; **las dieciocho** six P.M.; *m* eighteen; eighteenth (*in dates*)
dieciséis *adj* sixteen; **las dieciséis** four P.M.; *m* sixteen; sixteenth (*in dates*)
dieciseisavo -va *adj* sixteenth; *m* sixteenth; **en dieciseisavo** sextodecimo (*book*)
dieciseiseno -na *adj* sixteenth
diecisiete *adj* seventeen; **las diecisiete** five P.M.; *m* seventeen; seventeenth (*in dates*)
diecisieteavo -va *adj & m* seventeenth
diedro *adj masc* (geom.) dihedral
Diego *m* James
dieléctrico -ca *adj & m* dielectric
diente *m* (anat.) tooth; tooth (*of saw, comb, rake, etc.*); tusk, fang; cog; **aguzar los dientes** to whet one's appetite; **apretar los dientes** to set one's teeth (*to prepare to resist*); **a regaña dientes** loathingly, with repugnance; **armado hasta los dientes** (coll.) armed to the teeth; **dar diente con diente** (coll.) to shake all over (*from fear or cold*); **decir entre dientes** (coll.) to mutter, to mumble; **de dientes afuera** (coll.) in bad faith; **enseñar los dientes** (coll.) to show one's teeth; **estar a diente** (coll.) to be famished; **hablar entre dientes** to chew one's words (*so as to be unintelligible*); (coll.) to mutter, to mumble; **mostrar los dientes** (coll.) to show one's teeth; **tener buen diente** to be a hearty eater; **tomar** or **traer entre dientes** (coll.) to have a grudge against; to speak ill of; **diente artificial** false tooth; **diente canino** (anat.) canine tooth, eye tooth; **diente de ajo** clove of garlic; (coll.) large, misshapen tooth; **diente de leche** milk tooth; **diente de león** (bot.) dandelion; **diente de lobo** burnisher; **diente de muerto** (bot.) grass pea; **diente de perro** sculptor's dented chisel; (arch.) dogtooth; (bot.) dogtooth violet; (sew.) featherstitch; (coll.) crude sewing; **diente incisivo** (anat.) incisor; **diente mamón** baby tooth; **diente molar** (anat.) molar, back tooth; **dientes de leche** baby teeth
dientimellado -da *adj* nick-toothed
dientudo -da *adj* var. of **dentudo**
diéresis *f* (*pl:* **-sis**) diaeresis
Diesel *m* Diesel engine or motor
dieseleléctrico -ca *adj* Diesel-electric
dieselización *f* equipment with Diesel engines, Dieselization
diesi *f* (mus.) diesis; (mus.) sharp
diestro -tra *adj* right; skilful, dexterous, handy; dexter; sagacious, shrewd; sly, artful; favorable, propitious; (her.) dexter; **a diestro y siniestro** right-and-left, wildly; *m* skilful fencer; bullfighter on foot; matador; bridle; *f* right hand; **juntar diestra con diestra** to join forces
dieta *f* diet (*regular food and drink; assembly*); (law) day's trip of ten leagues; **dietas** *fpl* per diem (*allowance*); pay, compensation (*e.g., of a legislator*); **estar a dieta** to be on a diet; **poner a dieta** to put on a diet; **dieta láctea** milk diet
dietar *va* to diet, to put on a diet
dietario *m* family budget; chronicler's record book
dietético -ca *adj* dietetic, dietary; *f* dietetics
dietista *mf* dietician or dietitian
diez *adj* ten; **las diez** ten o'clock; *m* (*pl:* **dieces**) ten; tenth (*in dates*); decade (*of Ave Marias*)
diezmal *adj* decimal
diezmar *va* to decimate; to tithe
diezmero -ra *mf* tither, collector of tithes
diezmesino -na *adj* ten-month
diezmilésimo -ma *adj & m* ten thousandth
diezmilímetro *m* tenth of a millimeter
diezmo *m* tithe
difamación *f* defamation
difamador -dora *adj* defaming; *mf* defamer
difamar *va* to defame
difamatorio -ria *adj* defamatory
difásico -ca *adj* (elec.) diphase, two-phase
diferencia *f* difference; (log.) differentia; **a diferencia de** unlike; **partir la diferencia** to split the difference; **diferencia de potencial** (phys.) difference of potential
diferenciación *f* differentiation
diferenciador -dora *adj* differentiating
diferencial *adj* differential; *m* (mach.) differential; *f* (math.) differential
diferenciar *va* to differentiate; (math.) to differentiate; *vn* to differ, to dissent; *vr* to differ, be different; to differentiate, become differentiated; to distinguish oneself; (bot.) to differentiate
diferendo *m* difference, disagreement
diferente *adj* different
diferir §62 *va* to defer, postpone, delay, put off; *vn* to differ, be different
difícil *adj* difficult, hard; **difícil de contentar** hard to please
dificílimo -ma *adj super* very or most difficult
difícilmente *adv* with difficulty
dificultad *f* difficulty; objection
dificultador -dora *adj* objecting, pessimistic; *mf* objector, pessimist
dificultar *va* to put obstacles in the way of, to make difficult; to consider difficult; **dificultar que** + *subj* to consider it difficult or unlikely that; *vn* to raise difficulties or objections; *vr* to become difficult
dificultosamente *adv* with difficulty
dificultoso -sa *adj* troublesome, difficult; (coll.) ugly, homely; (coll.) objecting, pessimistic
difidación *f* diffidation, declaration of war
difidencia *f* distrust
difidente *adj* distrustful
difilo -la *adj* (bot.) diphyllous
difluencia *f* diffluence
difluente *adj* diffluent
difluir §41 *vn* to flow away, to dissolve
difracción *f* diffraction
difractar *va* to diffract; *vr* to be diffracted
difractivo -va *adj* diffractive
difrangente *adj* diffractive
difteria *f* (path.) diphtheria
diftérico -ca *adj* diphtherial or diphtheritic
difteritis *f* (path.) diphtheritis
difteroide *adj* diphtheroid
difuminar *va* var. of **esfuminar**
difumino *m* var. of **esfumino**
difundido -da *adj* widespread, widely known
difundir *va* to diffuse, to disseminate, to spread; to divulge, to publish; (rad.) to broadcast; *vr* to spread
difuntear *va* to kill, to slay; *vr* to get killed, to die

difunto -ta *adj & mf* deceased; **difunto de taberna** dead-drunk; *m* corpse
difusibilidad *f* diffusibility
difusible *adj* diffusible
difusión *f* diffusion, dissemination, spread; diffuseness; (anthrop., chem. & phys.) diffusion; (rad.) broadcasting; **difusión normal** standard broadcasting
difusionismo *m* (anthrop.) diffusionist theory
difusivo -va *adj* diffusive
difuso -sa *adj* diffuse; broad, extended; prolix, wordy
difusor -sora *adj* diffusing; radiating; *m* diffuser
digerible *adj* digestible
digerir §62 *va* (physiol. & chem.) to digest; (fig.) to digest (*to think over, to try to understand; to bear, to put up with*); *vr* to digest
digestibilidad *f* digestibility
digestible *adj* digestible
digestión *f* digestion; **de mala digestión** indigestible
digestivo -va *adj & m* digestive
digesto *m* (law) digest
digestor *m* digester (*closed vessel*)
digitación *f* (mus.) fingering
digitado -da *adj* digitate; (bot.) digitate; (mus.) fingered
digital *adj* digital; *f* (bot. & pharm.) digitalis
digitalina *f* (chem. & pharm.) digitalin
digitígrado -da *adj & m* (zool.) digitigrade
dígito *m* (arith.) digit; (astr.) digit or point
dignación *f* condescension
dignar *vr* to deign, condescend; **dignarse** + *inf* to deign to + *inf*, to condescend to + *inf*
dignatario *m* dignitary, official
dignidad *f* dignity; dignitary
dignificación *f* dignification
dignificar §86 *va* to dignify; *vr* to become dignified
digno -na *adj* worthy, deserving; dignified; suitable, fitting; **digno de** + *inf* worthy of + *ger*
digo *1st sg pres ind of* **decir**
digrafía *f* or **dígrafo** *m* digraph
digrama *m* digram
digresión *f* digression; (astr.) digression
digresivo -va *adj* digressive
dije *1st sg pret ind of* **decir**; *m* amulet, charm, trinket; (coll.) jewel (*person*); (coll.) person all dressed-up; (coll.) handy person; **dijes** *mpl* boasting, bragging
dilaceración *f* dilaceration
dilacerar *va* to dilacerate, to tear to pieces; to damage (*honor, pride, etc.*)
dilación *f* delay
dilapidación *f* dilapidation, squandering
dilapidar *va* to dilapidate, to squander
dilatabilidad *f* dilatability
dilatable *adj* dilatable
dilatación *f* dilation, dilatation, expansion, distention; diffuseness, prolixity; calm, serenity, tranquility in sorrow or grief
dilatado -da *adj* vast, extensive, extended, numerous; diffuse, prolix
dilatador -dora *adj* dilating; *m* (anat. & surg.) dilator
dilatar *va* to dilate, expand; to defer, postpone; to spread (*e.g., fame*); (Am.) to delay; *vn* (Am.) to delay; *vr* to dilate, expand; to be deferred, be postponed; to spread; to be diffuse or prolix; (Am.) to delay
dilatativo -va *adj* dilative
dilatómetro *m* (phys.) dilatometer
dilatorio -ria *adj* (law) dilatory; *f* delay
dilección *f* true love
dilecto -ta *adj* dearly beloved
dilema *m* dilemma; (log.) dilemma
diletante *adj & mf* dilettante
diletantismo *m* dilettanteism
diligencia *f* diligence; stagecoach; caution, dispatch, speed; (coll.) errand; **hacer una diligencia** (coll.) to do an errand; (coll.) to have a bowel movement
diligenciar *va* to take steps to accomplish; to hasten
diligenciero *m* agent, representative
diligente *adj* diligent; prompt, quick
dilogía *f* ambiguity, double meaning
dilucidación *f* elucidation
dilucidador -dora *adj* elucidating; *mf* elucidator
dilucidar *va* to elucidate
dilucidario *m* commentary, exposition
dilución *f* dilution
diluente *m* thinner; (med.) diluent
diluído -da *adj* dilute
diluir §41 *va* to dilute; to thin; *vr* to dilute, become diluted
diluvial *adj* (geol.) Recent
diluviano -na *adj* diluvian, diluvial; (geol.) Recent
diluviar *vn* to rain hard, to pour
diluvio *m* deluge; (fig.) deluge; **el Diluvio** (Bib.) the Deluge, the Flood
dimanación *f* springing; origination
dimanar *vn* to spring, spring up; **dimanar de** to spring from, arise from, originate in
dimensión *f* dimension; **cuarta dimensión** (math.) fourth dimension
dimensional *adj* dimensional
dimensionar *va* to determine the proportions of, to determine the size of
dimes *mpl;* **andar en dimes y diretes con** (coll.) to bicker with
dimetría *f* (med.) dimetria
dímetro *m* (pros.) dimeter
diminución *f* diminution
diminuir §41 *va, vn, & vr* to diminish, to decrease
diminutamente *adv* sparingly; minutely
diminutivo -va *adj* diminishing; (gram.) diminutive; *m* (gram.) diminutive
diminuto -ta *adj* diminutive, tiny; defective, imperfect; (mus.) diminished
dimisión *f* demission, resignation
dimisionario -ria *adj* resigning; *mf* person resigning
dimisorias *fpl* (eccl.) dimissory letters; **dar dimisorias a** (coll.) to kick out, to fire; **llevar dimisorias** (coll.) to get kicked out, to get fired
dimitente *adj* resigning, retiring; *mf* person resigning
dimitir *va* to demit, to resign, to resign from; *vn* to demit, to resign
dimorfismo *m* dimorphism
dimorfo -fa *adj* dimorphous
din *m* (coll.) dough, money
dina *f* (phys.) dyne; (*cap.*) *f* Dinah
Dinamarca *f* Denmark
dinamarqués -quesa *adj* Danish; *mf* Dane; *m* Danish (*language*)
dinámico -ca *adj* dynamic; (fig.) dynamic; *f* dynamics
dinamismo *m* (philos.) dynamism
dinamista *adj* dynamistic; *mf* dynamist
dinamita *f* dynamite
dinamitar *va* to dynamite
dinamitazo *m* dynamite explosion
dinamitero -ra *adj* dynamiting; *m* dynamiter
dínamo *f* dynamo
dinamoeléctrico -ca *adj* dynamoelectric
dinamometría *f* (mech.) dynamometry
dinamométrico -ca *adj* dynamometric
dinamómetro *m* dynamometer
dinamotor *s* (elec.) dynamotor
dinasta *m* dynast
dinastía *f* dynasty
dinástico -ca *adj* dynastic or dynastical
dinastismo *m* loyalty to a dynasty
dinerada *f* or **dineral** *m* large amount of money
dinerario -ria *adj* monetary
dinerillo *m* (coll.) small amount of money
dinero *m* money; currency; wealth; **dinero contante** cash; **dinero contante y sonante** ready cash, spot cash; **dinero de bolsillo** pocket money; **dinero trocado** change
dineroso -sa *adj* rich, moneyed
dinga *f* dingey, dinghy
dingo *m* dingo (*wild dog*)
dinornis *m* (pal.) dinornis
dinosaurio *m* (pal.) dinosaur
dinoterio *m* (pal.) dinothere
dintel *m* (arch.) lintel, doorhead; threshold
dintelar *va* to provide with a lintel; to build in the form of a lintel

diocesano -na *adj & m* diocesan
diócesi *f* or **diócesis** *f* (*pl:* **-sis**) diocese
Diocleciano *m* Diocletian
diodo *m* (electron.) diode
Diógenes *m* Diogenes
dioico -ca *adj* (biol. & bot.) diecious or dioecious
Diomedes *m* (myth.) Diomedes
dionea *f* (bot.) Venus's-flytrap
dionisia *f* bloodstone; **Dionisias** *fpl* Dionysia (*festivals*)
dionisíaco -ca *adj* Dionysiac; **dionisíacas** *fpl* Dionysia (*festivals*)
Dionisio *m* Dionysius; Denis; **San Dionisio** Saint Denis
Dionisios *m* or **Dionisos** *m* (myth.) Dionysos or Dionysus
dioptra *f* sight (*of an instrument*); diopter, alidade
dioptria *f* (opt.) diopter (*unit*)
dióptrico -ca *adj* dioptric or dioptrical; *f* dioptrics
diorama *m* diorama
diorámico -ca *adj* dioramic
diorita *f* (mineral.) diorite
dios *m* god; (*cap.*) *m* God; **a la buena de Dios** (coll.) without cunning or malice; **estar con Dios** to be in heaven; **llamar a Dios de tú** to be wonderful, to be first-class; to be too familiar with everybody, to call everybody by his first name; **pasar las de Dios es Cristo** to go through fire and water; **permita Dios** God grant; **¡por Dios!** goodness!, for heaven's sake!; **¡válgame Dios!** bless me!, so help me God!; **¡vaya con Dios!** off with you!, be gone!; good-bye!; God's will be done!; **¡vive Dios!** by Jove!; **dios de los rebaños** or **de los pastores** shepherd god (*Pan*); **Dios mediante** God willing
diosa *f* goddess; (fig.) goddess (*very beautiful woman*)
dioscoreáceo -a *adj* (bot.) dioscoreaceous
Dioscuros or **Dióscuros** *mpl* (myth.) Dioscuri
diostedé *m* (orn.) toucan
dióxido *m* (chem.) dioxide; **dióxido de azufre** (chem.) sulfur dioxide
dipétalo -la *adj* (bot.) dipetalous
diplejía *f* (path.) diplegia; **diplejía espástica** (path.) cerebral palsy
diploclamídeo -a *adj* (bot.) diplochlamydeous
diplococo *m* (bact.) diplococcus
diplodoco *m* (pal.) diplodocus
diploma *m* diploma
diplomacia *f* diplomacy; **diplomacia del dólar** dollar diplomacy
diplomado -da *adj* having a diploma, graduate; *mf* diplomate, graduate
diplomático -ca *adj* diplomatic; *mf* diplomat, diplomatist; **diplomático de carrera** career diplomat; *f* diplomatics (*branch of paleography; diplomacy*)
diplopía *f* (med.) diplopia
dipolar *adj* dipolar
dipolo *m* (chem. & phys.) dipole
dipsomanía *f* (path.) dipsomania
dipsomaníaco -ca *adj* dipsomaniacal; *mf* dipsomaniac
dipsómano -na *adj & mf* dipsomaniac
díptero -ra *adj* (zool.) dipterous, dipteran, dipteral; (arch.) dipteral; *m* (zool.) dipteran; (arch.) dipteros (*building*)
díptica *f* diptych (*tablet*)
díptico *m* diptych (*picture*)
diptongación *f* diphthongization
diptongar §59 *va & vr* to diphthongize
diptongo *m* diphthong
diputación *f* deputation; congress
diputado -da *mf* deputy; **diputado** *f* deputy, congresswoman
diputador -dora *adj & mf* constituent
diputar *va* to delegate, commission, depute; to deputize; to designate
dique *m* dike, dam, mole, jetty; dry dock; (dent.) dam; (geol.) dike; (fig.) check, stop, bar; **dique de carena** dry dock; **dique de caucho** or **goma** (dent.) rubber dam
Dirce *f* (myth.) Dirce
dirceo -a *adj* Dircaean
diré *1st sg fut ind of* **decir**
dirección *f* direction; course, trend, tendency; management, administration; address; directorship; office, administration office; guidance; (aut.) steering; **perder la dirección** to lose control of the car; **dirección de tiro** (nav.) fire control; **dirección obligatoria** or **única** one way
direccional *adj* directional
directivo -va *adj* directive, managing; *mf* director, manager; *f* board of directors, management
directo -ta *adj* direct; straight; (gram.) direct
director -tora *adj* guiding, directing, leading; managing, governing; *mf* director, manager; editor (*of a paper*); principal (*of a school*); (mus.) conductor; **director de escena** stage manager; **director de funeraria** funeral director; **director espiritual** spiritual director; **director general** director-general; *f* directress
directorial *adj* directorial
directorio -ria *adj* directory, directive; directorial; *m* directory (*body of directors; book of names*); directorate, directorship, board of directors; directive; (*cap.*) *m* Directoire
directriz *f* (*pl:* **-trices**) directive; (geom.) directrix
dirigente *mf* leader, head, director, executive
dirigible *adj & m* dirigible
dirigir §42 *va* to direct, to manage; to turn; to steer (*an automobile*); to dedicate (*a work*); to address (*a letter; one's words, a speech, etc.*); *vr* to go, to betake oneself; to turn; **dirigirse a** to address oneself to, to address (*a person*); to apply to
dirigismo *m* state planning, state control
dirimente *adj* annulling
dirimible *adj* annullable
dirimir *va* to dissolve, annul; to solve (*a difficulty*); to settle (*a controversy*)
disanto *m* holy day, religious feastday
discantar *va* (mus.) to descant; *vn* to descant, to comment at length; (mus.) to descant
discante *m* descant; (mus.) descant; (coll.) folly
discar §86 *va & vn* (telp.) to dial
disceptación *f* disceptation, debate, discussion
disceptar *vn* to discept, debate, discuss
discernible *adj* discernible, perceptible
discernidor -dora *adj* discerning; *mf* discerner
discerniente *adj* discerning; discriminating
discernimiento *m* discernment; (law) commitment
discernir §43 *va* to discern, distinguish; (law) to entrust, to commit; *vn* to discern, distinguish
disciplina *f* discipline; teaching, instruction; whip, scourge
disciplinable *adj* disciplinable; pliant, teachable
disciplinado -da *adj* disciplined; many-colored (*said of flowers*)
disciplinal *adj* disciplinal
disciplinar *va* to discipline; to teach, instruct; to whip, to scourge
disciplinario -ria *adj* disciplinary
disciplinazo *m* lash
discipulado *m* discipleship; teaching, instruction; disciples, pupils
discipular *adj* discipular
discípulo -la *mf* pupil, student; disciple
disco *m* disk; record (*of phonograph*); (sport) discus; (astr., bot. & zool.) disk; (coll.) same old record, same old song; **disco de cola** (rail.) tail light; **disco de goma** washer (*e.g., for a spigot*); **disco de identificación** (mil.) identification tag; **disco de larga duración** long-playing record; **disco de Petri** Petri dish; **disco de señales** (rail.) semaphore; **disco explorador** (telv.) scanning disk; **disco rayado** (Am.) fixed idea; **disco selector** (telp.) dial
discóbolo *m* discus thrower
discófilo -la *mf* discophile, record lover
discoidal *adj* discoidal, disk-shaped
díscolo -la *adj* wayward, ungovernable, intractable; mischievous
discoloro -ra *adj* (bot.) discolor
discómano -na *mf* (coll.) var. of **discófilo**
disconforme *adj* disagreeing

disconformidad *f* nonconformity, unconformity, disconformity; disagreement
discontinuación *f* discontinuation
discontinuar §33 *va* to discontinue
discontinuidad *f* discontinuity
discontinuo -nua *adj* discontinuous
disconvendré *1st sg fut ind of* **disconvenir**
disconvengo *1st sg pres ind of* **disconvenir**
disconveniencia *f* unsuitableness; incongruity; inconvenience
disconveniente *adj* unsuitable; incongruous; inconvenient
disconvenir §92 *vn* to disagree; to be incongruous; to not match; *vr* to disagree; to be incongruous
disconvine *1st sg pret ind of* **disconvenir**
discordancia *f* discordance; (geol.) discordance
discordante *adj* discordant; (geol.) discordant
discordar §77 *vn* to disaccord; to be out of tune; to discord, to disagree; **discordar de** to disagree with
discorde *adj* discordant, opposed, in disagreement; (mus.) discordant, dissonant, out of tune
discordia *f* discord, disagreement
discoteca *f* (phonograph) record cabinet; record library
discrasia *f* (path.) dyscrasia
discreción *f* discretion; wit, sagacity; witticism; **a discreción** at discretion; (mil.) unconditionally (*at the mercy of an opponent*)
discrecional *adj* discretionary
discrepancia *f* discrepancy; dissent, disagreement; (mus.) discord
discrepante *adj* discrepant; dissenting, disagreeing; (mus.) discordant
discrepar *vn* to differ, disagree
discretear *vn* to try to be clever
discreteo *m* attempt at cleverness, attempted cleverness
discreto -ta *adj* discreet (*circumspect, cautious*); witty, sagacious; discrete (*separate; composed of distinct parts; marked by discretion*); (math. & med.) discrete
discretorio *m* (eccl.) council of seniors; (eccl.) council chamber
discrimen *m* hazard, risk, peril; difference
discriminación *f* discrimination; **discriminación racial** racial discrimination
discriminante *adj* discriminant, discriminating; *f* (math.) discriminant
discriminar *va* to discriminate, to distinguish; (Am.) to discriminate against; *vn* to discriminate
discriminativo -va *adj* discriminative
discromatopsia *f* (path.) dyschromatopsia
discromía *f* (path.) dyschroa
disculpa *f* excuse, apology
disculpable *adj* excusable; pardonable
disculpadamente *adv* pardonably
disculpar *va* to excuse; to offer as an excuse; (coll.) to pardon, to overlook; *vr* to excuse oneself, to apologize; **disculparse con** to make excuses to, to apologize to; **disculparse de** to make excuses for, to apologize for
discurrir *va* to invent, contrive; to infer, conjecture; *vn* to ramble, roam; to flow; to occur, take place; to think, reason; to discourse
discursear *vn* (coll.) to make a speech, to harangue
discursista *mf* great talker, idle talker
discursivo -va *adj* meditative
discurso *m* discourse, speech; course (*of time*); (gram.) speech; **discurso de la corona** King's Speech, Queen's Speech; **discurso de sobremesa** after-dinner speech
discusión *f* discussion; argument; **discusión de mesa redonda** round-table discussion
discutible *adj* disputable, debatable
discutidor -dora *adj* argumentative; *mf* arguer
discutir *va* to discuss; to argue about or over; to contradict, oppose; *vn* to discuss; to argue; **discutir sobre** to argue about or over
disecable *adj* dissectible
disecación *f* var. of **disección**
disecado -da *adj* (bot.) dissected (*leaf*)
disecador -dora *mf* var. of **disector**
disecar §86 *va* to dissect; to stuff (*dead animal*); to mount (*dead plant*); (fig.) to dissect
disección *f* dissection; anatomy; stuffing (*of dead animals*); mounting (*of dead plants*); (fig.) dissection (*critical analysis*)
disector -tora *mf* dissector
diseminación *f* dissemination; scattering
diseminador -dora *adj* disseminating, spreading; *mf* disseminator, spreader
diseminar *va* to disseminate; to scatter; *vr* to scatter
disensión *f* dissension; dissent
disenso *m* dissent, disagreement
disentería *f* (path.) dysentery; **disentería amibiana** (path.) amoebic dysentery
disentérico -ca *adj* dysenteric
disentimiento *m* dissent, disagreement
disentir §62 *vn* to dissent
diseñador -dora *mf* designer, sketcher
diseñar *va* to draw, design, sketch, outline
diseño *m* drawing, design, sketch, outline
disépalo -la *adj* (bot.) disepalous
disertación *f* dissertation, disquisition
disertador -dora *adj* disquisitive
disertante *adj* disquisitive, inquisitive; *mf* disquisitor, investigator; speaker
disertar *vn* to discourse in detail; **disertar acerca de** or **sobre** to discourse in detail on
diserto -ta *adj* fluent, eloquent
disestesia *f* (path.) dysesthesia
disfagia or **disfagía** *f* (path.) dysphagia
disfasia *f* (med.) dysphasia
disfavor *m* disfavor
disformar *va & vr* var. of **deformar**
disforme *adj* deformed; huge, monstrous
disformidad *f* deformity; hugeness, monstrousness
disforzar §52 *vr* (Am.) to be affected, prudish, finical
disfraz *m* (*pl:* **-fraces**) disguise
disfrazar §76 *va* to disguise
disfrutar *va* to enjoy, to have the benefit of, to take advantage of, to use; *vn* **disfrutar de** to enjoy, to have the use of; **disfrutar con** to enjoy, take enjoyment in (*e.g., music*)
disfrute *m* enjoyment, benefit, use
disfumar *va* var. of **esfumar**
disfumino *m* var. of **esfumino**
disfunción *f* (med.) dysfunction
disgregación *f* disintegration
disgregador -dora *adj* disintegrating; *mf* disintegrator
disgregar §59 *va* to disintegrate; *vr* to disintegrate; to disperse, break up
disgregativo -va *adj* disintegrating, disintegrative
disgustado -da *adj* tasteless, insipid, disagreeable; sad, sorrowful; displeased
disgustar *va* to displease; **disgustar** + *inf* to displease (*someone*) to + *inf*, to not like to + *inf; vr* to be displeased; to fall out; **disgustarse con** to be displeased at or with; to fall out with; **disgustarse de** to be displeased at or with; to be bored with, to be tired of
disgusto *m* disgust; annoyance, bother; worry, sorrow, grief; unpleasantness, quarrel, difference; **a disgusto** against one's will
disgustoso -sa *adj* unpleasant, disagreeable; tasteless
disidencia *f* dissidence; opposition; (eccl.) dissent
disidente *adj* dissident, dissentient; *mf* dissenter, dissident, dissentient; opponent
disidir *vn* to dissent; (eccl.) to dissent
disilábico -ca *adj* dissyllabic
disílabo -ba *adj* dissyllabic; *m* dissyllable
disimetría *f* dissymmetry
disimétrico -ca *adj* dissymmetric, dissymmetrical, unsymmetrical
disímil *adj* dissimilar
disimilación *f* dissimilation
disimilar *adj* dissimilar; *va & vr* to dissimilate
disimilitud *f* dissimilitude, dissimilarity
disimulación *f* dissimulation, dissembling
disimulado -da *adj* furtive, underhand, hypocritical; **a lo disimulado** or **a la disimulada** underhandedly; **hacer la disimulada** (coll.) to feign ignorance

disimular *va* to dissimulate, to dissemble; to disguise; to pardon, excuse; *vn* to dissimulate, to dissemble
disimulo *m* dissimulation, dissembling; tolerance, indulgence
disipación *f* dissipation; (fig.) dissipation (*dissolute way of life*)
disipado -da *adj* dissipated; spendthrift, prodigal; *mf* dissipated person, debauchee; spendthrift
disipador -dora *adj & mf* spendthrift
disipar *va* to dissipate; *vr* to dissipate, be dissipated, evanesce, disappear; to dissipate one's energies
dislalia *f* (med.) dyslalia
dislate *m* nonsense, absurdity
dislocación *f* dislocation; (geol.) dislocation, slip
dislocadura *f* dislocation
dislocar §86 *va* to dislocate; to displace; *vr* to dislocate
disloque *m* (coll.) top notch, tops
dismenorrea *f* (path.) dysmenorrhea
disminución *f* diminution
disminuir §41 *va, vn, & vr* to diminish, to decrease
disnea *f* (path.) dyspnea
disociación *f* dissociation
disociador -dora *adj* dissociative
disociar *va & vr* to dissociate
disolubilidad *f* dissolubility
disoluble *adj* dissoluble
disolución *f* dissolution; (fig.) dissolution (*e.g., of a family, partnership, government, treaty, contract*); dissoluteness, dissipation
disolutivo -va *adj* dissolutive
disoluto -ta *adj* dissolute; *mf* debauchee
disolvente *adj* dissolvent; demoralizing; *m* dissolvent, solvent
disolver §63 & §17, 9 *va* to dissolve; (law) to dissolve; to ruin, destroy; *vn* to dissolve; *vr* to dissolve
disón *m* (mus.) dissonance, discord
disonancia *f* dissonance; **hacer disonancia** to be out of harmony
disonante *adj* dissonant; *m* dissonant tone
disonar §77 *vn* to be discordant, to lack harmony, to disagree; to sound bad; to be objectionable, to cause surprise
dísono -na *adj* dissonant
dispar *adj* unlike, unequal, different, disparate; odd (*that does not match*)
disparada *f* (Am.) sudden flight; **a la disparada** (Am.) at full speed, like a shot; (Am.) in mad haste; **de una disparada** (Am.) at once, right away; **tomar la disparada** (Am.) to take to one's heels, to run away
disparadamente *adv* hastily; absurdly, nonsensically
disparadero *m* trigger; **poner en el disparadero** (coll.) to drive mad, to drive to distraction
disparador *m* shooter; trigger; escapement (*of watch*); release (*on a camera*); (naut.) anchor tripper; **poner en el disparador** (coll.) to drive mad, to drive to distraction; **disparador de bombas** (aer.) bomb release
disparar *va* to shoot; to throw, to hurl; *vn* to talk nonsense; *vr* to dash away, dash off, rush away; to go off (*said, e.g., of a gun*); to be beside oneself
disparatado -da *adj* absurd, nonsensical; frightful, awful
disparatador -dora *adj* idle, nonsensical; *mf* idle talker
disparatar *vn* to talk nonsense, to blunder
disparate *m* foolish remark; crazy idea; piece of foolishness; blunder, mistake; (coll.) outrage
disparatorio *m* lot of nonsense, lot of hot air
disparejo -ja *adj* uneven, unequal, different, disparate; rough, broken
disparidad *f* disparity
disparo *m* shot, discharge, firing; absurdity, nonsense; (mach.) release, trip, start; **cambiar disparos** to exchange shots
dispendio *m* waste, squandering
dispendioso -sa *adj* expensive
dispensa *f* dispensation
dispensable *adj* dispensable
dispensación *f* dispensation
dispensador -dora *adj* dispensing; *mf* dispenser
dispensar *va* to dispense; to dispense with; to exempt, excuse; to pardon, absolve; **dispensar de** + *inf* to excuse from + *ger;* **dispensar que** + *subj* to excuse for + *ger*, e.g., **dispénseme que le detenga** excuse me for keeping you
dispensaría *f* (Am.) dispensary
dispensario *m* dispensary; **dispensario de alimentos** soup kitchen
dispensatorio *m* dispensatory (*book on medicines; dispensary*)
dispepsia *f* (path.) dyspepsia; **dispepsia ácida** (path.) acid dyspepsia; **dispepsia atónica** (path.) atonic dyspepsia; **dispepsia catarral** (path.) catarrhal dyspepsia; **dispepsia fermentativa** (path.) fermentative dyspepsia; **dispepsia flatulenta** (path.) flatulent dyspepsia; **dispepsia nerviosa** (path.) nervous dyspepsia
dispépsico -ca or **dispéptico -ca** *adj & mf* dyspeptic
dispermia *f* (biol.) dispermy
dispersar *va & vr* to disperse
dispersión *f* dispersion, dispersal; (phys.) dispersion
dispersivo -va *adj* dispersive
disperso -sa *adj* dispersed, scattered, separated; preoccupied
dispirema *f* (biol.) dispireme
displacer §34 *va* (obs.) to displease
displicencia *f* coolness, indifference; discouragement; ill humor; contemptuousness
displicente *adj* disagreeable; peevish, fretful, ill-humored
dispnea *f* var. of **disnea**
dispondré *1st sg fut ind of* **disponer**
disponer §69 *va* to dispose, arrange, line up, prepare; to direct, order, decree; **disponer** + *inf* to arrange to + *inf*, to provide for + *ger; vn* to dispose; **disponer de** to dispose of, to assign for a use; to make use of, make use of the services of, have at one's disposal; *vr* to prepare oneself, get ready; to line up; to get ready to die, to make one's will; **disponerse a** or **para** + *inf* to get ready to + *inf*
dispongo *1st sg pres ind of* **disponer**
disponibilidad *f* availability; **disponibilidades** *fpl* quick assets, available assets
disponible *adj* available, disposable
disposición *f* disposition, arrangement; layout; disposal; inclination, aptitude; preparation; elegance; predisposition; state of health; **a la disposición de** at the disposal of, at the service of; **estar en disposición de** + *inf* to be ready to + *inf*; to be in the mood to + *inf;* **última disposición** last will and testament
dispositivo -va *adj* dispositive; *m* device, apparatus
disprosio *m* (chem.) dysprosium
dispuesto -ta *pp of* **disponer;** *adj* comely, graceful; skilful, sprightly; ready, prepared; **bien dispuesto** well, in good health; well-disposed, favorable; **mal dispuesto** ill, indisposed; ill-disposed, unfavorable
dispuse *1st sg pret ind of* **disponer**
disputa *f* dispute, disputation; fight, struggle; contest; **sin disputa** beyond dispute
disputador -dora *adj* disputant; disputatious; *mf* disputant, disputer
disputable *adj* disputable, debatable
disputar *va* to dispute, to question; to debate, to argue over; to fight for; *vn* to dispute; to debate, to argue; to fight, to struggle
disquero -ra *mf* phonograph record dealer
disquiria *f* (path.) dyschiria
disquisición *f* disquisition
disruptivo -va *adj* (elec.) disruptive
distal *adj* (anat.) distal
distancia *f* distance; (fig.) distance (*coldness, unfriendliness*); **a distancia** at a distance; **distancia focal** (opt.) focal distance, focal length
distanciar *va* to place at a distance, to put further apart; to distance, to outdistance
distante *adj* distant

distar *vn* to be far, be distant; to be different; **distar de** + *inf* to be far from + *ger*
distender §66 *va* to distend; *vr* to distend; to unwind, to run down; to relax
distensibilidad *f* distensibility
distensible *adj* distensible
distensión *f* distension; relaxation of tension
dístico -ca *adj* (bot.) distichous; *m* distich
distinción *f* distinction; distinctness; **a distinción de** in distinction from or to
distingo *m* distinction; qualification, reservation
distinguible *adj* distinguishable
distinguido -da *adj* distinguished; polished, refined, urbane
distinguir §44 *va* to distinguish
distintivo -va *adj* distinctive; *m* badge, insignia; distinctive mark; distinction
distinto -ta *adj* distinct; different
distocia *f* (med.) dystocia
dístomo -ma *adj* (zool.) distomatous
distorsión *f* distortion; (rad. & fig.) distortion
distorsionar *va* to distort, twist, turn
distracción *f* distraction; diversion, amusement; seduction; embezzlement, misappropriation
distraer §88 *va* to distract (*e.g., the attention*); to divert, amuse, entertain; to divert, to draw off; to lead astray, to seduce; to embezzle
distraído -da *adj* distracted, absent-minded; dissolute, licentious; (Am.) careless, slovenly
distraigo *1st sg pres ind of* **distraer**
distraimiento *m* var. of **distracción**
distraje *1st sg pret ind of* **distraer**
distribución *f* distribution; electric supply system; (mach.) timing gears; (mach.) valve gears; **distribución de frecuencias** (statistics) frequency distribution
distribuidor -dora *adj* distributing; *mf* distributor; *m* (aut.) distributor; (mach.) slide valve; (print.) ink roller; **distribuidor automático** vending machine, slot machine; *f* (agr.) spreader (*e.g., of fertilizer*)
distribuir §41 *va* to distribute
distributivo -va *adj & m* distributive
distrito *m* district; (rail.) section; **distrito federal** federal district; **distrito postal** postal zone
distrofía *f* (path.) dystrophy; **distrofía muscular progresiva** (path.) muscular dystrophy
distrófico -ca *adj* dystrophic
disturbar *va* to disturb
disturbio *m* disturbance
disuadir *va* to dissuade; **disuadir de** + *inf* to dissuade from + *ger*
disuasión *f* dissuasion
disuasivo -va *adj* dissuasive
disuelto -ta *pp of* **disolver**
disulfato *m* (chem.) disulfate
disulfuro *m* (chem.) disulfide
disuria *f* (path.) dysuria
disvulnerabilidad *f* disvulnerability
disyunción *f* disjunction; (log.) disjunction
disyunta *f* (mus.) disjunct motion
disyuntivo -va *adj* disjunctive; *f* dilemma, disjunctive
disyuntor *m* (elec.) circuit breaker
dita *f* surety, bondsman; security, bond
ditá *m* (bot.) dita (*tree and bark*)
ditaína *f* (chem.) ditamin or ditamine
diteísmo *m* ditheism
diteísta *adj* ditheistic; *mf* ditheist
diterpeno *m* (chem.) diterpene
ditirámbico -ca *adj* dithyrambic
ditirambo *m* dithyramb
ditisco *m* (ent.) water beetle
dítono *m* (mus.) ditone
diuca *f* (orn.) South American sparrow (*Fringilla diuca*); *m* (Am.) teacher's pet
diuresis *f* (path.) diuresis
diurético -ca *adj & m* (med.) diuretic
diurno -na *adj* day, diurnal; *m* (eccl.) diurnal; **diurnos** *mpl* (ent.) butterflies (*as distinct from moths*); **diurnas** *fpl* (orn.) diurnal birds of prey
diuturnidad *f* diuturnity, long duration
diuturno -na *adj* diuturnal, lasting
diva *f* see **divo**
divagación *f* rambling, wandering, digression, divagation
divagador -dora *adj* rambling, wandering; discursive; *mf* rambler, wanderer
divagar §59 *vn* to ramble, wander, digress, divagate
diván *m* divan (*Turkish council and room where it meets; low sofa; collection of poems*); **diván arca** box couch; **diván cama** day bed
divaricación *f* divarication
divaricado -da *adj* (bot.) divaricate
divergencia *f* divergence or divergency
divergente *adj* divergent
divergir §42 *vn* to diverge
diversidad *f* diversity; plenty, abundance
diversificación *f* diversification
diversificar §86 *va* to diversify; *vr* to diversify, produce diversity
diversiforme *adj* diversiform
diversión *f* diversion; (mil.) diversion
diverso -sa *adj* diverse, different; **diversos -sas** *adj pl* several, various, many
diverticular *adj* diverticular
diverticulitis *f* (path.) diverticulitis
divertículo *m* (anat. & path.) diverticulum
diverticulosis *f* (path.) diverticulosis
divertido -da *adj* amusing, funny; (Am.) tipsy
divertimiento *m* diversion; distraction; (mus.) divertissement
divertir §62 *va* to divert, to amuse; (mil.) to divert; *vr* to be amused, to have a good time, to enjoy oneself, to celebrate; **divertirse en** + *inf* to amuse oneself + *ger*, to enjoy + *ger*
dividendo *m* (math. & com.) dividend
divididero -ra *adj* divisible
dividir *va* to divide; *vr* to divide; to separate, part company
divieso *m* (path.) boil
divinal *adj* (poet.) divine
divinatorio -ria *adj* divining, divinatory
divinidad *f* divinity; beauty (*person*)
divinizar §76 *va* to divinize, deify; to sanctify; to extol, to exalt
divino -na *adj* divine; (fig.) divine; **a lo divino** written or revised in sacred form
divisa *f* emblem; badge; heraldic device; motto; hope, goal, ideal; monetary standard; divisional coin; currency, foreign exchange; (taur.) colored bow to distinguish bull of each owner
divisar *va* to descry, to espy; (her.) to vary
divisibilidad *f* divisibility
divisible *adj* divisible
división *f* division; (math. & mil.) division
divisional *adj* divisional
divisionario -ria *adj* divisional
divisivo -va *adj* divisive
divisor -sora *adj* dividing; *mf* divider; *m* (math.) divisor; **común divisor** (math.) common divisor; **máximo común divisor** (math.) greatest common divisor; **divisor de fase** (elec.) phase splitter; **divisor de voltaje** (rad.) voltage divider
divisorio -ria *adj* dividing; *m* (print.) copyholder; *f* dividing line; (geog.) divide; (mus.) bar, bar line; **divisoria continental** continental divide
divo -va *adj* (poet.) divine, godlike; *m* (poet.) god; (mus.) opera star; *f* (poet.) goddess; (mus.) diva
divorciar *va* to divorce (*a married couple*); (fig.) to divorce; *vr* to divorce, get divorced; **divorciarse de** to divorce, to get a divorce from
divorcio *m* divorce; divergency (*in opinions*)
divulgable *adj* revealable
divulgación *f* disclosure; divulgation, publicity; popularization
divulgador -dora *adj* divulging; *mf* divulger, revealer
divulgar §59 *va* to divulge, to disclose, to publish abroad
diyambo *m* diiamb
dizque (Am.) probably, probably not, e.g., **él dizque lo hizo** (Am.) he probably did it; *m* (coll.) gossip, piece of gossip
dl. abr. of **decilitro** or **decilitros**
Dl. abr. of **decalitro** or **decalitros**
dm. abr. of **decímetro** or **decímetros**
Dm. abr. of **decámetro** or **decámetros**

D.ⁿ abr. of **don**
dna. abr. of **docena**
do *adv & conj* (archaic) where
dobla *f* doubling; old Spanish gold coin
dobladillar *va* to hem, to border
dobladillo *m* hem, border; heavy knitting thread
doblado -da *adj* thickset, stocky; uneven, rough; double-dealing, deceitful; *m* (mov.) dubbing
doblador *m* (mach.) bender (*of a pipe, rail, etc.*)
doblaje *m* (mov.) dubbing
doblamiento *m* doubling, folding, creasing, bending
doblar *va* to double, to fold, to crease, to bend; (naut.) to double (*a cape*); to turn, to round (*a corner*); to cause (*a person*) to change his opinion or intentions; (mov.) to dub (*a film in another language*); (Am.) to shoot down; (bridge) to double; *vn* to turn (*e.g., to the right or left*); to toll; (theat. & mov.) to double, to stand in; (bridge) to double; *vr* to double, to fold, to crease, to bend; to bow, to stoop; to yield, give in; to become uneven or rough
doble *adj* double, two-fold; thick, heavy; thickset, stocky; two-faced, deceitful; *adv* double, doubly, e.g., **doble culpable** doubly guilty; *mf* (theat. & mov.) double, stand-in; *m* fold, crease; toll, knell; margin (*in stock market*); beer glass (*of a quarter liter*); **al doble** doubly
doblegable *adj* easily folded; pliant, pliable
doblegadizo -za *adj* easily folded, easily bent
doblegar §59 *va* to fold, to bend; to brandish, flourish; to sway, dominate, force to yield; to force (*a person*) to change his plans; *vr* to fold, to bend; to yield, to give in
doblemente *adv* doubly; deceitfully
doblero *m* (prov.) pretzel
doblete *adj* medium; *m* doublet (*false stone*); (philol.) doublet; (bridge) doubleton; (baseball) two-bagger, two-base hit
doblez *m* (*pl:* **-bleces**) fold, crease; cuff (*of trousers*); *m & f* double-dealing, duplicity
doblón *m* doubloon; **escupir doblones** (coll.) to make a vain display of wealth; **doblón de a ocho** piece of eight; **doblón de vaca** tripe
doblonada *f* pile of money; **echar doblonadas** (coll.) to exaggerate one's wealth
doboquera *f* blowgun, blowpipe
dócar *m* dogcart (*two-wheeled vehicle with two transverse seats back to back*)
doce *adj* twelve; **las doce** twelve o'clock; *m* twelve; twelfth (*in dates*)
doceañista *m* maker or follower of the Spanish Constitution of 1812
doceavo -va *adj & m* var. of **dozavo**
docena *f* see **doceno**
docenal *adj* sold by the dozen
docenario -ria *adj* made of twelve
docencia *f* teaching; (Am.) teaching staff
doceno -na *adj* twelfth, dozenth; *f* dozen; **docena del fraile** baker's dozen (*thirteen*)
docente *adj* educational, instructional, teaching
docetismo *m* Docetism
dócil *adj* docile; ductile, soft
docilidad *f* docility; ductility
docimasia *f* docimasy
docimástico -ca *adj* docimastic; *f* docimastic art
Doct. abr. of **Doctor**
docto -ta *adj* learned; (philol.) learned; *mf* scholar
doctor -tora *mf* doctor; **doctor angélico** Angelic Doctor (*Thomas Aquinas*); *f* (coll.) woman doctor; (coll.) doctor's wife; (coll.) bluestocking
doctorado *m* doctorate; doctorship (*learning*); studies leading to the doctorate
doctoral *adj* doctoral
doctoramiento *m* conferring the doctor's degree; taking the doctor's degree
doctorando -da *mf* candidate for the doctor's degree
doctorar *va* to give the doctor's degree to; (taur.) to authorize (*a novice*) to kill the bull, making him a full-fledged matador; *vr* to get the doctor's degree, to graduate as a doctor; (taur.) to become a full-fledged matador
doctrina *f* doctrine; teaching, instruction; wisdom, learning; preaching the Gospel; catechism; **doctrina cristiana** Christian doctrine; Institute of the Brothers of the Christian Schools; **doctrina de Monroe** Monroe Doctrine
doctrinador -dora *adj* teaching; *mf* teacher
doctrinal *adj* doctrinal; *m* manual of rules and precepts
doctrinar *va* to indoctrinate, to teach, to instruct
doctrinario -ria *adj & mf* doctrinaire
doctrinarismo *m* doctrinairism
doctrinero *m* teacher of Christian doctrine; (Am.) curate, parish priest
doctrino *m* orphan (*being raised in an asylum*); **parecer un doctrino** (coll.) to have a scared look
documentación *f* documentation; **documentación del buque** ship's papers
documentado -da *adj* documented, well-documented; well-informed; vouched-for
documental *adj* documental or documentary; *m* (mov.) documentary (*film*)
documentalista *mf* producer of documentary films
documentar *va* to document
documento *m* document; **documento de prueba** (law) exhibit
docum.ᵗᵒ abr. of **documento**
dodecaédrico -ca *adj* (geom.) dodecahedral
dodecaedro *m* (geom.) dodecahedron
dodecágono -na *adj* (geom.) dodecagonal; *m* (geom.) dodecagon
Dodecaneso, el the Dodecanese Islands
dodecasílabo -ba *adj* dodecasyllabic; *m* dodecasyllabic verse
dodó *m* (*pl:* **-does**) (orn.) dodo
dogal *m* halter, noose, hangman's rope; oppression, tyranny; **estar con el dogal a la garganta** or **al cuello** to be in a jam, to be in a tight spot
dogaresa *f* dogaressa, doge's wife
dogma *m* dogma
dogmático -ca *adj* dogmatic or dogmatical
dogmatismo *m* dogmatism
dogmatista *mf* propounder of heretical doctrines
dogmatizador *m* or **dogmatizante** *m* dogmatist
dogmatizar §76 *va & vn* to dogmatize
dogo -ga *mf* bulldog
dogre *m* dogger (*fishing boat*)
doladera *f* chip ax, broad ax; cooper's adze
dolador *m* hewer; stonecutter
doladura *f* shavings; chips
dolaje *m* wine absorbed by the cask
dolamas *fpl* or **dolames** *mpl* (vet.) hidden defects (*of a horse*); (Am.) complaint, indisposition (*of a person*)
dolar §77 *va* to hew (*wood or stone*)
dólar *m* dollar
dolencia *f* ailment, complaint, indisposition
doler §63 *va* to ache, to hurt, to pain; to grieve, to distress; to concern, be of concern to; **dolerle a uno el dinero** (coll.) to hate to spend money; **dolerle a uno** + *inf* to pain or grieve a person to + *inf; vn* to ache, to hurt, to pain; *vr* to complain; **dolerse con** to complain or lament to; **dolerse de** to complain about or of; to feel sorry for; to repent (*e.g., one's sins*)
dolicocéfalo -la *adj* (anthrop.) dolichocephalic
dolido -da *adj* complaining; grieved, hurt
doliente *adj* suffering, aching; ill, sick; sorrowful, sad; *mf* sufferer, sick person; mourner
dolmen *m* dolmen
dolménico -ca *adj* dolmenic
dolo *m* guile, deceit, fraud
dolobre *m* stone hammer
dolomía or **dolomita** *f* (mineral.) dolomite
dolomítico -ca *adj* dolomitic
dolor *m* ache, pain; grief, sorrow; regret, repentance; **Nuestra Señora de los Dolores** Mary of the Sorrows; **Dolores** *f* Dolores (*woman's name*); **dolor de cabeza** headache; **dolor de costado** pneumonia; **dolor de muelas** toothache; **dolor de oído** earache; **dolor de viudo** o **viuda** passing sorrow; **dolores**

de Nuestra Señora (eccl.) Dolors of Mary, sorrows of the Virgin Mary; **dolores del parto** labor pains
dolora *f* short sentimental and philosophic ballad, invented by Campoamor about 1846
dolorido -da *adj* sore, aching, painful; heartsick, grieving, disconsolate; *m* (dial.) chief mourner
doloroso -sa *adj* painful; pitiful, dolorous; **Dolorosa** *f* (f.a.) Sorrowing Mary; (coll.) weeping woman
doloso -sa *adj* guileful, deceitful, fraudulent
doma *f* taming, breaking; check, restraint
domable *adj* tamable, controllable
domador -dora *adj* taming; *mf* tamer; horsebreaker
domadura *f* taming; mastering, subduing
domar *va* to tame, to break, to break in; to master, to conquer, to subdue
dombo *m* dome
domeñable *adj* tamable, controllable, governable
domeñar *va* to tame, domesticate; to master, to subdue
domesticable *adj* domesticable
domesticación *f* domestication
domesticar §86 *va & vr* to domesticate
domesticidad *f* domesticity
doméstico -ca *adj* domestic; household; *mf* domestic (*servant*)
domestiquez *f* tameness
Domiciano *m* Domitian
domiciliar *va & vr* to domicile; to domiciliate
domiciliario -ria *adj* domiciliary; *mf* resident
domicilio *m* domicile; dwelling; **adquirir** or **contraer domicilio** to take up one's abode; **domicilio social** (com.) home office, company office
dominación *f* domination, dominance; (mil.) eminence, high ground; (sport) chinning; **dominaciones** *fpl* dominations (*high order of angels*)
dominador -dora *adj* dominating, controlling; domineering; *mf* dominator, ruler
dominancia *f* (biol.) dominance
dominante *adj* dominant; domineering; (astrol., biol. & mus.) dominant; *f* (mus.) dominant
dominar *va* to dominate; to domineer; to check, refrain, subdue, control; to handle perfectly (*a language*); to have a thorough knowledge of; *vn* to dominate; to domineer; *vr* to control oneself
dominativo -va *adj* dominating
dómine *m* Latin teacher; pedant; dominie, pedagogue
domingada *f* Sunday celebration, Sunday festival
domingo *m* Sunday; **guardar el domingo** to keep the Sabbath; **Santo Domingo** Saint Dominic; Santo Domingo (*city*); **domingo de adviento** Advent Sunday; **domingo de carnaval** Shrove Sunday; **domingo de cuasimodo** Quasimodo, Low Sunday; **domingo de la santísima trinidad** Trinity Sunday; **domingo de lázaro** or **de pasión** Passion Sunday; **domingo de ramos** Palm Sunday; **domingo de resurrección** Easter Sunday
dominguero -ra *adj* (coll.) Sunday
dominguillo *m* tumbler (*toy figure*)
dominguito *m* (orn.) yellowbird
dominica *f* see **dominico**
domínica *f* Sunday, Sabbath
dominical *adj* (pertaining to) Sunday; (pertaining to the) Sabbath; feudal (*fees*)
dominicano -na *adj* Dominican (*pertaining to Saint Dominic and to the Dominican Republic*); *mf* Dominican
dominico -ca *adj* Dominican (*pertaining to Saint Dominic*); *mf* Dominican; *f* (bot.) red periwinkle; **la Dominica** Dominica (*one of Lesser Antilles*)
dominio *m* dominion; domain; mastery (*e.g., of a foreign language*); (law) fee (*ownership*); **dominio absoluto** (law) fee simple; **dominio del aire** air supremacy; **dominio directo** (law) dominium directum; **dominio eminente** (law) eminent domain; **dominio público** (law) public domain; **dominio útil** (law) dominium utile
dominó *m* (*pl:* **-nós**) domino (*cloak with mask*); dominoes (*game*); set of dominoes
dómino *m* dominoes (*game*); set of dominoes
dom.º abr. of **domingo**
domo *m* (arch.) dome
dompedro *m* (bot.) four-o'clock, marvel-of-Peru
don *m* gift, present; natural gift, talent, faculty; Don (*Spanish title used before masculine Christian names, formerly given only to noblemen, now more widely used*); **don de acierto** tact, knack for doing the right thing; **don de errar** knack for doing the wrong thing; **don de gentes** charm, magnetism, winning manners; **don de lenguas** linguistic facility; **don de mando** ability to command; **Don Juan** Don Juan (*legendary Spanish nobleman; seducer of women*)
dona *f* (Am.) gift, legacy; **donas** *fpl* wedding presents given to the bride by the bridegroom
donación *f* donation; foundation, endowment
donada *f* lay sister
donado *m* lay brother
donador -dora *mf* giver, donor; **donador de sangre** blood donor
donaire *m* cleverness; bon mot, witticism; nimbleness, gracefulness
donairoso -sa *adj* clever; witty; nimble, graceful
Donaldo *m* Donald
donante *mf* donor; **donante de sangre** blood donor
donar *va* to give, donate
donatario *m* donee, donatory
donatismo *m* Donatism
donatista *adj & m* Donatist
donativo *m* gift, donation
doncel *m* bachelor (*young knight*); virgin (*man*); *adj* mild, mellow (*said, e.g., of wine*)
doncella *f* maiden, virgin; maid of honor; housemaid; lady's maid; (bot.) sensitive plant; (Am.) felon, whitlow; **Doncella del Lago** Lady of the Lake (*of Arthurian legend*); **Doncella de Orleáns** Maid of Orleans
doncellez *f* maidenhood, virginity
doncellona or **doncellueca** *f* maiden lady, spinster
donde *conj* where; wherein, in which; wherever; **por donde** whereby; **por donde quiera** anywhere, everywhere; **donde no** otherwise, if you don't; *prep* (Am.) at or to the house, store, office of
dónde *adv* where?, e.g., **¿dónde vive?** where does he live?; where, e.g., **dígame dónde vive** tell me where he lives; **¿a dónde?** where?, whither? **a dónde** where, whither; **¿de dónde?** whence?, from where?; **de dónde** whence, from where; **¿por dónde?** for what cause?, for what reason?; which way?
dondequiera *adv* anywhere; **dondequiera que** wherever
dondiego *m* fop, dandy, sport; (bot.) four-o'clock, marvel-of-Peru; **dondiego de día** (bot.) morning-glory; **dondiego de noche** (bot.) four-o'clock, marvel-of-Peru
donillero *m* sharper, smooth cheat
donjonado -da *adj* (her.) turreted
donjuán *m* (bot.) four-o'clock, marvel-of-Peru
donjuanesco -ca *adj* like Don Juan, philandering
donjuanismo *m* Don Juanism
donosidad *f* grace, wit, witticism
donoso -sa *adj* graceful, witty; (iron.) fine
donostiarra *adj* (pertaining to) San Sebastián; *mf* native or inhabitant of San Sebastián
donosura *f* gracefulness, wittiness, elegance
doña *f* doña (*Spanish title used before Christian names of married women or widows*)
doñear *vn* (coll.) to chase skirts, hang around women
dopa *f* (biochem.) dopa; **dopa oxidasa** (biochem.) dopaoxidase
doquier or **doquiera** *conj* wherever; **por doquier** on all sides, everywhere
dorada *f* see **dorado**
doradilla *f* (bot.) scale fern
doradillo *m* fine brass wire; (orn.) wagtail; satinwood

dorado -da *adj* gilt; golden; *m* gilt, gilding; (ichth.) dorado; (*cap.*) *m* (astr.) Dorado; **dorados** *mpl* gold or gilt trimmings (*on furniture*); **dorado de altura** (ichth.) dolphin; *f* (ichth.) gilthead
dorador *m* gilder
doradura *f* gilding
doral *m* (orn.) flycatcher
dorar *va* to cover with gold, to gild; to gold-plate; (cook.) to brown; (fig.) to sugar-coat; *vr* to become golden (*said, e.g., of horizon*); (cook) to turn brown
Dorcas *f* (Bib.) Dorcas
Dordoña *f* Dordogne
dórico -ca *adj* Doric; *m* Doric (*dialect*)
Dóride, la Doris
dorio -ria *adj & mf* Dorian
dormán *m* dolman (*of Turks, hussars, etc.*)
dormida *f* see **dormido**
dormidero -ra *adj* soporific; *m* sleeping place of cattle; *f* (bot.) opium poppy; **dormideras** *fpl* (coll.) sleepiness; **tener buenas dormideras** (coll.) to be a ready sleeper, to go to sleep easily
dormido -da *adj* asleep; dormant; slow, dull; **dormido sobre** relying on, confident in; *f* sleeping period (*of silkworm*); night's resting place (*of animals and birds*); night's sleep; (Am.) lodging for the night
dormidor -dora *adj* sleepy; *mf* sleeper
dormilón -lona *adj* (coll.) sleepy; *mf* (coll.) sleepyhead; *f* earring; armchair for napping; (bot.) mimosa, sensitive plant
dormir §45 *va* to put to sleep; (coll.) to sleep off (*e.g., wine*); *vn* to sleep; to stay overnight; **dormir sobre** to sleep over; *vr* to sleep; to go to sleep, to fall asleep; to go to sleep (*to become numb*)
dormirlas *m* hide-and-seek
dormitar *vn* to doze, to nap
dormitivo -va *adj & m* (med.) dormitive
dormitorio *m* dormitory; bedroom suit
dornajo *m* small round trough
dornillo *m* small trough; wooden bowl; wooden spittoon
Dorotea *f* Dorothy
dorsal *adj* dorsal; *m* (sport) number (*worn on front or back of shirt*)
dorsiflexión *f* dorsiflexion
dorso *m* back, dorsum
dorsolumbar *adj* dorsolumbar
dorsoventral *adj* dorsoventral
dos *adj* two; **las dos** two o'clock; *m* two; second (*in dates*); **en un dos por tres** (coll.) in a flash, in a second; **para entre los dos** between the two of us; **dos de mayo** national holiday of Spain, in commemoration of May 2, 1808, when the War of Independence against Napoleon I was begun
dosalbo -ba *adj* with two white feet (*said of a horse*)
dosañal *adj* biennial, two-year
doscientos -tas *adj & m* two hundred
dosel *m* canopy, dais
doselera *f* valance, drapery (*of canopy*)
doselete *m* (arch.) canopy (*over statue, tomb, etc.*)
dosificación *f* dosing, dosage; proportioning
dosificador *m* proportioner, mixing apparatus
dosificar §86 *va* to dose (*a medicine*); to proportion (*ingredients*)
dosimetría *f* dosimetry
dosimétrico -ca *adj* dosimetric
dosímetro *m* dosimeter
dosis *f* (*pl:* **-sis**) dose; **dosis de paciencia** dose of patience
dotación *f* dowry; endowment; (aer.) crew; (sport) crew (*of oarsmen*); (naut.) complement; staff, personnel; equipment
dotal *adj* dotal; (pertaining to) endowment
dotar *va* to dower, give a dowry to; to endow; to equip; to man (*e.g., a ship*); to staff (*e.g., an office*); to fix the wages of; (fig.) to endow
dote *m & f* dowry, marriage portion; *m* stock of counters (*for playing cards*); *f* endowment, talent, gift; **dotes de mando** leadership, ability to command
dovela *f* (arch.) voussoir
dovelaje *m* (arch.) voussoirs of an arch

doxología *f* doxology; **gran doxología** greater doxology; **pequeña doxología** lesser doxology
doy *1st sg pres ind of* **dar**
dozavado -da *adj* twelve-sided, twelvefold
dozavo -va *adj & m* twelfth; **en dozavo** duodecimo, twelvemo
d/p abr. of **días plazo**
draba *f* (bot.) whitlow grass
dracma *f* drachm, drachma; (pharm.) dram, drachm
Dracón *m* Draco
draconiano -na *adj* Draconian; (fig.) Draconian; draconian
draga *f* dredge, dredging machine; dredger (*boat*)
dragado *m* dredging
dragadora *f* dredge
dragaje *m* var. of **dragado**
dragaminas *m* (*pl:* **-nas**) (nav.) mine sweeper
dragar §59 *va* to dredge
drago *m* (bot.) dragon tree
dragomán *m* dragoman, interpreter
dragón *m* dragon (*fabulous animal*); (bot.) snapdragon; (ichth.) greater weever; (mil.) dragoon; (her.) wivern; (zool.) dragon, flying dragon; (vet.) dragon (*in horse's eye*); feed hole in reverberatory furnace; **dragón marino** (ichth.) greater weever; **dragón verde** (bot.) green dragon; **dragón volador** (zool.) flying dragon
dragona *f* dragoness; (mil.) shoulder knot; sword tassel
dragonado -da *adj* (her.) dragonné; *f* dragonnade
dragonal *m* var. of **drago**
dragoncillo *m* (mil.) dragon (*musket*); (bot.) tarragon
dragonear *vn* (Am.) to boast; (Am.) to flirt; **dragonear de** (Am.) to pass oneself off as; (Am.) to boast of being
dragontea *f* (bot.) green dragon
dragontino -na *adj* (pertaining to a) dragon
drama *m* drama (*play; genre; event or events in real life*)
dramamina *f* (pharm.) dramamine
dramático -ca *adj* dramatic; *mf* dramatist; actor; *f* dramatic art; drama (*genre*)
dramatismo *m* drama, dramatic effect
dramatizable *adj* dramatizable
dramatización *f* dramatization
dramatizar §76 *va* to dramatize
dramaturgia *f* dramaturgy
dramaturgo *m* dramaturgist
drapear *va* to drape
drástico -ca *adj* drastic; (med.) drastic
dravidiano -na *adj & mf* Dravidian; *m* Dravidian (*language*)
dren *m* drain (*ditch, pipe, etc.*); (surg.) drain; **dren en cigarrillo** (surg.) cigarette drain
drenaje *m* drainage; (surg.) drainage
drenar *va* to drain
Dresde *f* Dresden
dríada or **dríade** *f* (myth.) dryad
driblar *va & vn* (sport) to dribble
dril *m* drill, denim; (zool.) drill (*baboon*)
drino *m* (zool.) long-nosed tree snake
driza *f* (naut.) halyard
drizar §76 *va* (naut.) to hoist (*the yards*)
dro. abr. of **derecho**
droga *f* drug, medicine; trick, deceit; bother, annoyance; (Am.) bad debt; (Am.) drug on the market; **drogas mágicas, milagrosas** or **prodigiosas** wonder drugs
drogmán *m* var. of **dragomán**
droguería *f* drysaltery; drug business; drug store
droguero -ra *mf* drysalter; druggist
droguete *m* drugget
droguista *mf* drysalter; druggist; cheat, impostor
drolático -ca *adj* spicy, ribald
dromedario *m* dromedary; heavy animal; (coll.) brute (*person*)
dromógrafo *m* dromograph
dromomanía *f* (psychopath.) dromomania
dromotrópico -ca *adj* (physiol.) dromotropic
drope *m* (coll.) cur (*contemptible fellow*)
drosera *f* (bot.) sundew; (pharm.) drosera

droseráceo -a *adj* (bot.) droseraceous
drosófila *f* (ent.) drosophila
drosómetro *m* drosometer
druida *m* druid
druidesa *f* druidess
druídico -ca *adj* druidic or druidical
druidismo *m* druidism
drupa *f* (bot.) drupe, stone fruit
drupáceo -a *adj* (bot.) drupaceous
druso -sa *adj* Drusean; *mf* Druse; *f* (bot. & mineral.) druse
dúa *f* (min.) gang of workmen
dual *adj* dual; (gram.) dual; *m* (gram.) dual
dualidad *f* duality
dualismo *m* dualism
dualista *adj* dualistic; *mf* dualist
duba *f* earthen wall or enclosure
dubio *m* (law) doubtful point, doubt
dubitable *adj* doubtful, dubious
dubitación *f* dubitation, doubt
dubitativo -va *adj* dubitative
ducado *m* duchy, dukedom; ducat; **gran ducado** grand duchy
ducal *adj* ducal
ducentésimo -ma *adj & m* two-hundredth
dúctil *adj* ductile; (fig.) ductile, manageable, easy to handle
ductilidad *f* ductility
ductivo -va *adj* conducive
ducha *f* see **ducho**
duchar *va* to douche; to give a shower bath to; *vr* to douche; to take a shower bath
ducho -cha *adj* skilful, expert, experienced; *f* douche; shower bath; stripe; (med.) irrigation; **ducha en alfileres** needle bath
duda *f* doubt; **sin duda** beyond doubt; no doubt; without doubt
dudable *adj* doubtable, doubtful
dudar *va & vn* to doubt; **dudar de** to doubt; **dudar en** + *inf* to hesitate in + *ger*, to hesitate to + *inf*; **dudar haber** + *pp* to doubt having + *pp*
dudoso -sa *adj* doubtful, dubious
duela *f* stave (*of barrel*); **duela del hígado** (zool.) fluke, liver fluke
duelaje *m* var. of **dolaje**
duelista *m* duelist
duelo *m* grief, sorrow, affliction; mourning, bereavement; mourners; effort, strain; duel; **sin duelo** with abundance; **duelo judiciario** (hist.) judicial duel, trial or ordeal by battle
duende *m* elf, goblin, ghost; gold and silver cloth
duendo -da *adj* tame, gentle
dueñesco -ca *adj* (coll.) duennalike
dueño -ña *mf* owner, proprietor; **¡mi adorado dueño!** my beloved mistress! (*addressed to the woman one loves*); **ser dueño de** to own, to be master of; **ser dueño de** + *inf* to be free to, be at liberty to + *inf*; **hacerse dueño de** to take possession of; to master; **dueño de sí mismo** self-controlled; *m* landlord, master; *f* landlady, housekeeper, mistress; duenna; matron; (Am.) sweetheart; **dueña de casa** housewife
duermevela *m* (coll.) doze, light sleep; (coll.) fitful sleep; **a duermevela** (coll.) dozing, half-asleep
duerna *f* trough
duerno *m* (print.) double sheet (*folded together*)
duetista *mf* (mus.) duettist
dueto *m* (mus.) short duet
dugón *m* or **dugongo** *m* (zool.) dugong
dula *f* land irrigated from common ditch; common pasture land
dulcamara *f* (bot.) bittersweet
dulce *adj* sweet; rich; fresh (*water*); soft, ductile (*metal*); mild, gentle, pleasant; *m* candy, piece of candy; preserves; **dulces** *mpl* candy; **dulce de almíbar** preserved fruit; **un dulce** a piece of candy
dulcedumbre *f* sweetness
dulcémele *m* (mus.) dulcimer
dulcería *f* candy store, confectionery shop
dulcero -ra *adj* (coll.) sweet-toothed; *mf* confectioner; *f* candy dish, preserve dish
dulcificacion *f* sweetening; dulcification, mollification
dulcificante *m* (cook.) sweetening, sweetener
dulcificar §86 *va* to sweeten; to dulcify, mollify, appease; *vr* to sweeten, turn sweet
dulcinea *f* (coll.) sweetheart; ideal; (*cap.*) *f* Dulcinea (*peasant girl, Don Quijote's ideal*)
dulcísono -na *adj* (poet.) sweet-toned
dulía *f* dulia, worship of angels and saints
dulzaina *f* see **dulzaino**
dulzainero *m* flageolet player
dulzaino -na *adj* (coll.) too sweet, too rich; *f* (mus.) flageolet; (coll.) mess of sweets, mess of sweet food
dulzamara *f* var. of **dulcamara**
dulzarrón -rrona or **dulzón -zona** *adj* (coll.) too sweet, sickening, cloying
dulzor *m* sweetness; sweetness, pleasantness, gentleness
dulzura *f* sweetness; mildness (*e.g., of the weather*); sweetness, pleasantness, gentleness
duma *f* duma; (bot.) doom palm, doum palm
dumdum *f* dumdum, dumdum bullet
duna *f* dune
Dunquerque *m & f* Dunkirk
dúo *m* pair; (mus.) duet
duodecenal *adj* duodecennial
duodecimal *adj & m* duodecimal
duodécimo -ma *adj & m* twelfth
duodécuplo -pla *adj* duodecuple
duodenal *adj* duodenal
duodenectomía *f* (surg.) duodenectomy
duodeno -na *adj* twelfth; *m* (anat.) duodenum
duomesino -na *adj* two-month
dup.do abr. of **duplicado**
dúplex *m* duplex telegraphy; (metal.) duplex process
dúplica *f* (law) defendant's answer
duplicación *f* duplication, doubling
duplicadamente *adv* doubly
duplicado *m* duplicate; **por duplicado** in duplicate
duplicador -dora *adj* duplicating; *m* duplicator
duplicar §86 *va* to duplicate; to double; to repeat; (law) to answer (*plaintiff's reply*); *vr* to double
duplicata *f* duplicate
dúplice *adj* (obs.) double, duplex
duplicidad *f* duplicity; doubleness
duplo -pla *adj & m* double
duque *m* duke; (coll.) fold in mantilla; **gran duque** grand duke; (orn.) eagle owl; **duque de alba** (naut.) cluster of piles
duquesa *f* duchess; **gran duquesa** grand duchess; **duquesa viuda** dowager duchess
dura *f* see **duro**
durabilidad *f* durability
durable *adj* durable, lasting
duración *f* duration; endurance
duradero -ra *adj* lasting, serviceable
duraluminio *m* duralumin
duramadre *f* or **duramáter** *f* (anat.) dura mater
duramen *m* (bot.) duramen
durante *prep* during
duraplastia *f* (surg.) duraplasty
durar *vn* to last; to continue, to remain; to wear (*said of clothes*)
durativo -va *adj* durative; (gram.) durative, progressive
duraznero *m* (bot.) peach tree
duraznilla *f* peach (*fruit*)
duraznillo *m* (bot.) persicary, lady's-thumb
durazno *m* (bot.) peach tree; peach (*fruit*)
durbar *m* durbar
durdo *m* (ichth.) ballan, ballan wrasse
dureno *m* (chem.) durene
Durero, Alberto Albrecht or Albert Dürer
dureza *f* hardness; roughness; harshness; dullness (*in understanding*); (phys.) hardness (*of vacuum tube*); (med.) callosity; **dureza de corazón** hardheartedness; **dureza de oído** tone deafness; loss of hearing; **dureza de vientre** costiveness
durián *m* durian or durion (*fruit of Durio zibethinus*)
durillo *m* (bot.) laurustine; (bot.) dogwood
durina *f* (vet.) dourine
durmiente *adj* sleeping; *mf* sleeper; **dormir más que los siete durmientes** (coll.) to sleep all the time, to be a sleepyhead; **la**

Bella durmiente Sleeping Beauty; *m* girder, stringer, sleeper; (Am.) tie, crosstie; (Am.) steel bar (*to fasten a door*)
duro -ra *adj* hard; hard-boiled (*egg*); harsh, rough; unbearable; indifferent, cruel; stubborn, obstinate; stingy; inclement, stormy; (phys.) hard (*ray; vacuum tube*); (Am.) drunk; **estar muy duro con** to be hard on; **ser duro de pelar** (coll.) to be hard to deal with; (coll.) to be hard to get, to be hard to put across; **duro de corazón** hard-hearted; **duro de oído** tone-deaf; hard of hearing; **duro de oreja** hard of hearing; **duro** *adv* hard; *m* dollar (*Spanish coin worth 5 pesetas*); *f* (coll.) durability; **de mucha dura** (coll.) strong, durable (*cloth, clothing, etc.*)
durra *f* (bot.) durra
duruculi *m* (zool.) night ape
duunvir *m* duumvir
duunviral *adj* duumviral
duunvirato *m* duumvirate
duunviro *m* duumvir
dux *m* (*pl:* **dux**) doge
d/v abr. of **días vista**

E

E, e *f* sixth letter of the Spanish alphabet
E. abr. of **este** (*oriente*)
e *conj* (used for **y** before a word beginning with the vowel sound **i**) and
ea *interj* hey!
ebanista *m* cabinetmaker
ebanistería *f* cabinetwork, cabinetmaking; cabinetmaker's shop
ébano *m* (bot.) ebony (*tree and wood*)
ebenáceo -a *adj* (bot.) ebenaceous
ebonita *f* ebonite
ebriedad *f* inebriety
ebrio -bria *adj* drunk; (fig.) blind (*e.g., with anger*); *mf* drunk
ebrioso -sa *adj* drinking; tipsy; *mf* drinker
ebulición *f* or **ebullición** *f* boiling, ebullition; bubbling; **en ebulición** in ferment
ebullómetro *m* ebulliometer
ebulloscopio *m* ebullioscope
eburnación *f* (path.) eburnation
ebúrneo -a *adj* (pertaining to) ivory
eccehomo *m* eccehomo; wretch, wreck (*person*)
ec.[co] abr. of **eclesiástico**
Ecequiel *m* (Bib.) Ezekiel (*prophet and book*)
-ecer *suffix v* -ish, e.g., **empobrecer** impoverish; **establecer** establish; **perecer** perish; and many other verbs, e.g., **entristecer** sadden; **parecer** appear
-ecillo -lla *suffix dim* var. of **-illo** and attached to monosyllables ending in a consonant, e.g., **panecillo** roll; **pececillo** little fish; to dissyllables with radical **ie** or **ue** and ending in **o** or **a**, e.g., **muestrecilla** small sample; **piedrecilla** little rock; and to dissyllables ending in **ia, io,** and **ua,** e.g., **gloriecilla** touch of glory; **fragüecilla** little forge
-ecito -ta *suffix dim* var. of **-ito** and attached to monosyllables ending in a consonant (including **y**), e.g., **florecita** little flower; **bueyecito** little ox; to dissyllables with radical **ie** or **ue** and ending in **o** or **a**, e.g., **piedrecita** little rock; **cuerpecito** little body; and to dissyllables ending in **ia, io,** and **ua,** e.g., **biestecita** little beast; **lengüecita** little tongue
eclampsia *f* (path.) eclampsia
eclecticismo *m* eclecticism
ecléctico -ca *adj & mf* eclectic
Eclesiastés, el (Bib.) Ecclesiastes
eclesiástico -ca *adj* ecclesiastic or ecclesiastical; *m* ecclesiastic; **el Eclesiástico** (Bib.) Ecclesiasticus
eclesiastizar §76 *va* to transfer to ecclesiastical use or possession
eclímetro *m* clinometer
eclipsar *va* (astr. & fig.) to eclipse; (fig.) to outshine; *vr* (astr. & fig.) to be eclipsed; (fig.) to disappear
eclipse *m* (astr. & fig.) eclipse; **eclipse de Luna** lunar eclipse; **eclipse de Sol** solar eclipse; **eclipse parcial** partial eclipse; **eclipse total** total eclipse
eclipsis *f* (*pl:* **-sis**) (gram.) ellipsis
eclíptico -ca *adj* ecliptic or ecliptical; *f* ecliptic
eclisa *f* (rail.) fishplate
eclisar *va* (rail.) to fish
écloga *f* var. of **égloga**
eclosión *f* opening, blossoming, birth
eco *m* echo; rumbling; (*cap.*) *f* (myth.) Echo; **hacer eco** to correspond, be proportional; to attract attention; **tener eco** to spread, catch on, get popular
ecoico -ca *adj* echoic
ecolalia *f* (psychol.) echolalia
ecología *f* ecology
ecólogo *m* ecologist
economato *m* stewardship, guardianship; commissary (*store*)
economía *f* economy; want, misery; **economías** *fpl* savings; **economía dirigida** or **planificada** planned economy; **economía doméstica** home economics; **economía política** political economy, economics
económico -ca *adj* economic or economical; thrifty, saving; miserly, niggardly
economista *mf* economist
economizador *m* (mach.) economizer
economizar §76 *va & vn* to economize; to save
ecónomo *m* supply priest; ecclesiastical administrator; guardian; steward
ecrán *m* (mov.) screen; (phot.) filter
ectasia *f* (path.) ectasia
éctasis *f* (pros.) ectasis
ectoblasto *m* (embryol.) ectoblast
ectodermo *m* (embryol.) ectoderm
ectoparásito *m* (zool.) ectoparasite
ectopia *f* (path.) ectopia
ectoplasma *m* (biol. & spiritualism) ectoplasm
ectropión *m* (path.) ectropion
ecuación *f* (math., astr. & chem.) equation; **ecuación cuadrática** (alg.) quadratic equation; **ecuación de primer grado** (alg.) linear equation; **ecuación de segundo grado** (alg.) quadratic equation; **ecuación diferencial** (math.) differential equation; **ecuación personal** personal equation; **ecuación simultánea** (alg.) simultaneous equation
ecuador *m* equator; **el Ecuador** Ecuador
ecuánime *adj* calm, composed, equanimous; impartial
ecuanimidad *f* equanimity; impartiality
ecuatorial *adj* equatorial; *m* (astr.) equatorial (*instrument*)
ecuatorianismo *m* Ecuadorianism
ecuatoriano -na *adj & mf* Ecuadoran, Ecuadorian
ecuestre *adj* equestrian
ecuménico -ca *adj* ecumenic or ecumenical
ecúmeno *m* inhabited part of the earth
ecuóreo -a *adj* (poet.) of the sea, aequorial
eczema *m & f* (path.) eczema
eczematoso -sa *adj* eczematous
echacantos *m* (*pl:* **-tos**) (coll.) empty-headed fellow
echacorvear *vn* (coll.) to pimp, to procure
echacorvería *f* (coll.) pimpery, procuring
echacuervos *m* (*pl:* **-vos**) (coll.) pimp, procurer; (coll.) cheat, gyp
echada *f* see **echado**
echadera *f* wooden shovel (*for putting bread in oven*)
echadero *m* place to rest, place to stretch out
echadillo -lla *adj & mf* (coll.) foundling
echadizo -za *adj* waste, discarded; spread around secretly; sent to spy; *mf* foundling; spy
echado -da *adj* lying down; (Am.) lazy, indolent, idle; *m* (min.) dip in vein; *f* throw; man's length (*stretched out on ground*); (Am.) boast, falsehood
echador -dora *adj* throwing, hurling; (Am.) boastful, bragging; *mf* (Am.) braggart; *m* waiter who pours coffee
echadura *f* setting (*of hens*); **echadura de pollos** brood of chicks
echalumbre *m* (orn.) junco
echamiento *m* throwing, hurling, throwing away
echapellas *m* (*pl:* **-llas**) wool soaker
echaperros *m* (*pl:* **-rros**) beadle who keeps dogs out of church
echar *va* to throw, cast, fling, throw away, throw out; to discharge, dismiss; to pour; to give out, issue, send forth, emit, publish; to

swallow, to take; to smoke (*cigar, cigaret*); to attribute, ascribe; to turn (*key*); to deliver (*speech, sermon, etc.*); to utter (*curses*); to put on (*a play*); to put forth, to begin to have or grow (*hair, teeth, shoots, etc.*); to impose, levy (*tax*); to acquire (*a stomach, bad disposition, etc.*); to deal (*cards*); to tell (*a fortune*); to mate, to couple (*male and female animals*); to cast (*a glance*); to shed (*blood*); to lay (*blame*); **echar abajo** to overthrow, demolish, ruin, destroy; to break down; **echar a pasear** (coll.) to dismiss harshly, to dismiss without ceremony; **echar a perder** to spoil, to ruin; **echar de menos** to miss; **echarla de** (coll.) to claim to be, to boast of being; **echarlo todo a rodar** (coll.) to upset everything, to spoil everything; (coll.) to fly off the handle; **echar menos** to miss ‖ *vn* to sprout; **echar a** + *inf* to begin to + *inf;* to burst out + *ger;* **echar a perder** to spoil, to ruin; **echar de ver** to notice; **echar por** to take up, go into (*a profession*); to turn toward (*the right or left*); to go down (*a road*) ‖ *vr* to throw or hurl oneself; to lie down, stretch out; to fall (*said of the wind*); to set (*said of a hen*); to throw on (*a wrap*); **echarse a** + *inf* to begin to + *inf;* to burst out + *ger;* **echarse a morir** (coll.) to give up in despair; **echarse a perder** to spoil, to be ruined; **echarse atrás** to back out; **echarse de ver** to be noticeable, to be easy to see; **echárselas de** to claim to be, to boast of being; **echarse sobre** to rush at, to fall upon

echarpe *m & f* sash

echazón *f* throwing; (naut.) jettison

echiquier *m* Exchequer

echona *f* (Am.) sickle

edad *f* age; **corta edad** youth, youthfulness; **de edad** older, e.g., **una señora de edad** an older woman; **en edad de quintas** of draft age; **mayor edad** majority; **menor edad** minority; **¿qué edad le echa Vd.?** how old do you think he is?; **¿qué edad tiene Vd.?** how old are you?; **edad antigua** ancient times; **edad crítica** change of life (*in women*); **edad de bronce** (myth.) bronze age; **edad de discreción** age of discretion; **edad de la máquina** machine age; **edad del bronce** (archeol.) Bronze Age; **edad del hielo** (geol.) ice age; **edad del hierro** (archeol.) Iron Age; **edad de oro** (myth.) golden age; **edad de piedra** (archeol.) Stone Age; **edad de plata** (myth.) silver age; **edad escolar** school age; **Edad Media** Middle Ages; **edad mental** (psychol.) mental age; **edad viril** prime of life

edafología *f* edaphology, soil science

edda *f* (lit.) Edda

edecán *m* aide-de-camp

edelweiss *f* (bot.) edelweiss

edema *m* (path.) edema

edematoso -sa *adj* edematous

edén *m* (Bib. & fig.) Eden

edénico -ca *adj* Edenic

edición *f* publication; edition; **la segunda edición de** the spit and image of; **edición crítica** critical edition; **edición diamante** (print.) diamond edition; **edición diplomática** diplomatic edition; **edición príncipe** first edition, editio princeps

edicional *adj* publishing

edicto *m* edict

edificación *f* building, construction; buildings; edification

edificador -dora *adj* building; edifying; *mf* builder

edificante *adj* edifying

edificar §86 *va* to build, construct, erect; to edify

edificativo -va *adj* edifying

edificatorio -ria *adj* building, constructing

edificio *m* building, edifice

edil *m* aedile, edile; councilman

Edimburgo *f* Edinburgh

Edipo *m* (myth.) Oedipus

Edita *f* Edith

editar *va* to publish

editor -tora *adj* publishing; *mf* publisher; editor (*writer of editorials*)

editorial *adj* publishing; editorial; *m* editorial; *f* publishing house

editorialista *mf* editor, editorial writer

editorializar §76 *vn* (Am.) to editorialize

Edmundo *m* Edmund

-edor -dora *suffix adj* -ing, e.g., **aprendedor** learning; **bebedor** drinking; *suffix mf* -er, e.g., **aprendedor** learner; **bebedor** drinker

edrar *va* (agr.) to dig (*vineyards*) the second time

edredón *m* eider down; quilt; feather pillow

eduardiano -na *adj* Edwardian

Eduardo *m* Edward

educable *adj* educable

educación *f* education; breeding; good manners; **educación de adultos** adult education; **educación física** physical education

educacional *adj* educational

educador -dora *adj* educating, training; *mf* educator

educando -da *adj & mf* student, pupil

educar §86 *va* to educate, to train; to rear, bring up

educativo -va *adj* educative

educción *f* eduction; exhaust (*of steam engine*)

educir §38 *va* to educe, bring out

eductor *m* steam ejector

eduje *1st sg pret ind of* **educir**

edulcoración *f* (pharm.) sweetening; (Am.) softening of water

edulcorar *va* (pharm.) to sweeten; (Am.) to soften (*water*)

eduzco *1st sg pres ind of* **educir**

Eetes *m* (myth.) Aeëtes

EE.UU. abr. of **Estados Unidos**

efectismo *m* striving for effect, sensationalism

efectista *adj* sensational, theatrical; *mf* sensationalist

efectivamente *adv* really, actually; effectively; sure enough

efectividad *f* effectiveness; (mil.) permanent status

efectivo -va *adj* real, actual; regular, permanent (*employment*); effective; **hacer efectivo** to carry out; to cash (*a check*); *m* cash; **efectivos** *mpl* (mil.) effectives, troops; **en efectivo** in cash; **efectivo en caja** cash in hand

efecto *m* effect; end, purpose; commercial document; article; (billiards) English; **efectos** *mpl* effects, property, merchandise; assets; **a efectos de** for the purpose of; **a efectos de** + *inf* for the purpose of + *ger;* **a ese** or **tal efecto** for that purpose; **al efecto** for the purpose; **de doble efecto** (mach.) double-acting; **de simple efecto** (mach.) single-acting; **en efecto** sure enough; **llevar a efecto** or **poner en efecto** to carry out, to put into effect; **por efecto de** as a result of; **surtir efecto** to have the desired effect, to work; **efecto de Doppler** (phys.) Doppler effect; **efecto de empaquetamiento** (phys.) packing effect; **efectos a pagar** bills payable; **efectos a recibir** bills receivable; **efectos de consumo** consumers' goods; **efectos sanitarios** plumbing fixtures; **efectos sonoros** (mov. & rad.) sound effects; **efecto útil** (mech.) efficiency, output

efectuación *f* accomplishment

efectuar §33 *va* to effect, carry out; *vr* to be carried out, to take place

efedrina *f* (pharm.) ephedrine

efélide *f* freckle, ephelis

efeméride *f* anniversary; **efemérides** *fsg* event, date; **efemérides** *fpl* ephemerides; diary, journal, record; **efemérides astronómicas** ephemerides

efemérido *m* (ent.) ephemerid

efémero *m* (bot.) stinking iris

efendi *m* effendi

eferente *adj* (physiol.) efferent

efervescencia *f* effervescence

efervescente *adj* effervescent

efesino -na or **efesio -sia** *adj & mf* Ephesian

Éfeso *f* Ephesus

eficacia *f* effectiveness, efficacy

eficaz *adj* (*pl:* **-caces**) effective, effectual, efficacious

eficiencia *f* efficiency; (mech.) efficiency

eficiente *adj* efficient

efigie *f* effigy; **ahorcar en efigie** to hang in effigy; **quemar en efigie** to burn in effigy
efímero -ra *adj* ephemeral; *f* (ent.) May fly
eflorecer §34 *vr* (chem.) to effloresce
eflorescencia *f* (bot. & chem.) efflorescence
eflorescente *adj* (bot. & chem.) efflorescent
efluvio *m* effluvium; **efluvio eléctrico** luminous discharge, brush discharge
Efraín *m* (Bib.) Ephraim
efugio *m* evasion, subterfuge
efusión *f* effusion; (fig.) warmth, effusion; **efusión de sangre** bloodshed
efusivo -va *adj* effusive; (geol. & fig.) effusive
egida or **égida** *f* (myth. & fig.) aegis
egílope *m* (bot.) egilops, wild grass; (bot.) European wild oat; (path.) egilops
egipcíaco -ca or **egipciano -na** *adj & mf* Egyptian
egipcio -cia *adj & mf* Egyptian; *m* Egyptian (*language*)
egiptano -na *adj & mf* Egyptian; (obs.) gypsy
Egipto *m* Egypt; (myth.) Aegyptus
egiptología *f* Egyptology
egiptológico -ca *adj* Egyptological
egiptólogo -ga *mf* Egyptologist
égira *f* var. of **hégira**
Egisto *m* (myth.) Aegisthus
eglantina *f* (bot.) eglantine, sweetbrier
eglefino *m* (ichth.) haddock
égloga *f* eclogue
egocéntrico -ca *adj & mf* egocentric
egoísmo *m* egoism
egoísta *adj* egoistic; *mf* egoist
ególatra *adj* self-worshiping
egolatría *f* self-worship
Egospótamos *m* (hist.) Aegospotami
egotismo *m* egotism
egotista *adj* egotistic or egotistical; *mf* egotist
egregio -gia *adj* distinguished, eminent
egresar *va* (Am.) to withdraw (*money*); *vn* (Am.) to leave, go away; (Am.) to graduate
egreso *m* debit; (Am.) departure; (Am.) graduation
egrisar *va* to polish (*diamonds*)
eh *interj* eh!
eíder *m* (orn.) eider, eider duck
einsteinio *m* (chem.) einsteinium
eje *m* axis; axle, shaft; axletree; (math.) axis; (fig.) core, crux, main point; (*cap.*) *m* Axis (*Fascist bloc*); **eje de apoyo** knife edge (*of scale beam*); **eje de balancín** (mach.) rocker, rockershaft; **eje de carretón** axletree; **eje delantero** front axle; **eje de levas** (mach.) camshaft; **eje flotante** (mach.) floating axle; **eje óptico** (opt. & cryst.) optical axis; **eje principal** major axis; main shaft; **eje Roma-Berlín** Rome-Berlin axis; **eje trasero** rear axle
ejecución *f* execution; carrying out; (law) attachment, distraint
ejecutable *adj* feasible, practicable; (law) suable for debt, distrainable
ejecutante *adj* executing; *mf* performer, executant; (law) distrainor
ejecutar *va* to execute; to perform; to carry out; (law) to distrain
ejecutivamente *adv* promptly, with dispatch
ejecutivo -va *adj* executive; insistent, imperative; *m* (Am.) executive
ejecutor -tora *adj* executive; *mf* executive; executor; distrainor; **ejecutor de la justicia** executioner; **ejecutor testamentario** executor (*of a will*); **ejecutora testamentaria** executrix
ejecutoria *f* see **ejecutorio**
ejecutoría *f* (law) office of distrainor
ejecutoriar *va* to confirm; (law) to obtain (*a judgment*) in one's favor
ejecutorio -ria *adj* (law) executory; *f* pedigree, letters patent of nobility; decree
ejemplar *adj* exemplary; *m* exemplar; pattern; model; sample; example; precedent; copy (*of a book or magazine*); example (*warning to others*); **sin ejemplar** without precedent; as a special case; **ejemplar de cortesía** complimentary copy; **ejemplar muestra** sample copy
ejemplaridad *f* exemplary behavior, exemplary quality or character
ejemplarizar §76 *va* (Am.) to set an example to; (Am.) to illustrate with an example
ejemplificación *f* exemplification, illustration
ejemplificar §86 *va* to exemplify, illustrate
ejemplo *m* example, instance; **dar ejemplo** to set an example; **por ejemplo** for example, for instance; **seguir el ejemplo de** to follow the example of; **sin ejemplo** unexampled
ejercer §91 *va* to practice, exercise; to exert; *vn* to practice; to hold office; **ejercer de** to practice as (*e.g., a lawyer*), to work as (*e.g., a newspaperman*)
ejercicio *m* exercise, drill; exertion; practice; tenure (*of office*); fiscal year; balance sheet; **hacer ejercicio** to take exercise; (mil.) to drill; **ejercicio antiaéreo** air-raid drill; **ejercicio económico** budget period; **ejercicios espirituales** spiritual retreat
ejercitación *f* exercise, practice
ejercitante *adj* exercising; *mf* incumbent; exercitant (*in a spiritual retreat*)
ejercitar *va* to exercise; to practice; to drill, to train; *vr* to exercise; to practice
ejército *m* army; (fig.) army; arm (*of national defense*); **los tres ejércitos** the three arms of the service; **ejército del aire** air force; **ejército de Salvación** Salvation Army; **ejército permanente** standing army
ejidatario -ra *mf* (Am.) squatter, settler on public land
ejido *m* commons, public land, communal farm
ejión *m* (arch.) corbel piece, purlin
-ejo -ja *suffix dim & pej* e.g., **caballejo** little horse, nag; **librejo** cheap book, poor book; **medianejo** fair to middling
ejote *m* (Am.) tender bean pod
el *art def masc* (*pl:* **los**) the; *pron dem masc* the one, that, e.g., **el de mi hermano** that of my brother
él *pron pers masc* he, him, it
elaboración *f* elaboration; working; development
elaborado -da *adj* elaborate, high-wrought; finished (*product*)
elaborar *va* to elaborate; (physiol.) to elaborate; to work (*e.g., wood*)
elación *f* haughtiness; magnanimity, nobility; pomposity (*of style*)
elasmobranquio *m* (ichth.) elasmobranch
elástica *f* see **elástico**
elasticidad *f* elasticity
elástico -ca *adj* elastic; *m* elastic; *f* knit undershirt; **elásticas** *fpl* (Am.) suspenders
elastificar §86 *va* to make elastic, to elasticize
elastina *f* (biochem.) elastin
elaterina *f* (chem.) elaterin
elaterio *m* (bot.) squirting cucumber
elayómetro *m* oleometer, elaeometer
elche *m* apostate, renegade
Eldorado *m* El Dorado
eleagnáceo -a *adj* (bot.) elaeagnaceous
eleático -ca *adj & mf* Eleatic
eleborastro *m* (bot.) helleboraster
eléboro *m* (bot. & pharm.) hellebore; **eléboro negro** (bot.) Christmas rose, winter rose
elección *f* election; choice, free election; (theol.) election
eleccionario -ria *adj* (Am.) (pertaining to an) election, electoral
electivo -va *adj* elective
electo -ta *adj & m* elect
elector -tora *adj* electing; *mf* elector; *m* elector (*German prince*)
electorado *m* electorate
electoral *adj* electoral
electorero *m* heeler, henchman
Electra *f* (myth.) Electra
electricidad *f* electricity; **electricidad estática** static electricity; **electricidad vítrea** vitreous electricity
electricista *mf* electrician
eléctrico -ca *adj* electric or electrical
electrificación *f* electrification
electrificar §86 *va* to electrify
electriz *f* (*pl:* **-trices**) electress (*wife or widow of an elector of old German Empire*)
electrizable *adj* electrifiable
electrización *f* electrification
electrizador -dora *adj* electrifying

electrizar §76 *va* to electrify; (fig.) to electrify; *vr* to become electrified
electro *m* amber; electromagnet; electrum (*alloy*)
electroafeitadora *f* electric shaver
electrobomba *f* motor-driven pump
electrocardiógrafo *m* electrocardiograph
electrocardiograma *m* electrocardiogram
electrocirugía *f* electrosurgery
electrocución *f* electrocution
electrocutar *va* to electrocute
electrochoque *m* electroshock
electrodinámico -ca *adj* electrodynamic; *f* electrodynamics
electrodo or **eléctrodo** *m* electrode; **electrodo de calomel** (physical chem.) calomel electrode
electrodoméstico -ca *adj* household-electric
electrofónico -ca *adj* electrophonic
electróforo *m* (phys.) electrophorus
electrógeno -na *adj* generating electricity; *m* electric generator
electroimán *m* electromagnet
electrólisis *f* electrolysis
electrolítico -ca *adj* electrolytic
electrólito *m* electrolyte
electrolización *f* electrolyzation
electrolizar §76 *va* to electrolyze
electrología *f* science or study of electricity
electromagnético -ca *adj* electromagnetic
electromagnetismo *m* electromagnetism
electrometalurgia *f* electrometallurgy
electrometría *f* electrometry
electrométrico -ca *adj* electrometric
electrómetro *m* electrometer
electromotor -tora or **-triz** (*pl:* **-trices**) *adj* electromotive; *m* electromotor, electric motor
electrón *m* (phys. & chem.) electron; **electrón voltio** (*pl:* **electrones voltios**) (phys.) electron volt
electronegativo -va *adj* electronegative
electroneumático -ca *adj* (mus.) electropneumatic
electrónico -ca *adj* electronic; *f* electronics
electrón-voltio *m* (*pl:* **electrones-voltios** or **electrón-voltios**) (phys.) electron volt
electropositivo -va *adj* electropositive
electroquímico -ca *adj* electrochemical; *f* electrochemistry
electroscopio *m* (phys.) electroscope
electroshockterapia *f* (med.) electro-convulsive treatment
electrostático -ca *adj* electrostatic; *f* electrostatics
electrotecnia *f* electrical engineering, electrotechnics
electrotécnico -ca *adj* electrotechnical
electroterapia *f* electrotherapy
electrotipar *va* to electrotype
electrotipia *f* electrotypy
electrotipo *m* electrotype
electrotrén *m* electric train
electuario *m* electuary
elefancía *f* (path.) elephantiasis
elefancíaco -ca *adj & mf* elephantiac
elefanta *f* female elephant
elefante *m* elephant; (coll.) jumbo; **elefante blanco** (fig.) white elephant; **elefante de mar** (zool.) walrus; **elefante marino** (zool.) sea elephant, elephant seal
elefantiasis *f* or **elefantíasis** *f* (path.) elephantiasis
elefantino -na *adj* elephantine
elegancia *f* elegance; style
elegante *adj* elegant; stylish; *mf* fashion plate (*person*)
elegantizar §76 *va* to make elegant, to give style to
elegía *f* elegy
elegíaco -ca *adj* elegiac
elegibilidad *f* eligibility
elegible *adj* eligible
elegido -da *adj & mf* elect, chosen
elegir §72 *va* to elect; to choose, select; **elegir** + *inf* to choose to + *inf*
élego -ga *adj* elegiac
elemental *adj* elemental; elementary
elemento *m* element; member; (anat. & biol.) element; (chem.) element, simple substance; (elec.) cell (*of a battery*); **los cuatro elementos** the four elements (*fire, air, water, and earth*); **los elementos** the elements (*first principles; atmospheric forces*); means, resources; **estar en su elemento** to be in one's element; **elemento calentador** (elec.) heating element; **elemento de caldeo** (rad.) heating element; **elemento de compuestos** (gram.) combining form, word element; **elemento primario** (elec.) primary cell; **elemento secundario** (elec.) secondary cell; **elemento trazador** (phys.) tracer element
elemí *m* (*pl:* **-míes**) elemi
Elena *f* Helen, Elaine; **Santa Elena** Saint Helena (*British island and colony in South Atlantic*)
elenco *m* list, table, catalogue; personnel; (theat.) cast
eleómetro *m* oleometer, elaeometer
eleusino -na *adj & mf* Eleusinian
elevación *f* elevation; (arch. & astr.) elevation; (eccl.) Elevation; **elevación a potencias** (math.) involution
elevacristales *m* (*pl:* **-les**) (aut.) window regulator
elevado -da *adj* high, elevated; lofty, sublime
elevador -dora *adj* elevating; *m* elevator; **elevador de granos** grain elevator; **elevador de tensión** (elec.) booster
elevaje *m* raising, rearing
elevamiento *m* elevation, exaltation
elevar *va* to elevate; (math.) to raise (*to a power*); **elevar hasta las nubes** to praise to the skies; *vr* to rise, ascend; to be elevated or exalted; to become vain or conceited
elfino -na *adj* elfin
elfo *m* elf
Elí *m* (Bib.) Eli
Elías *m* (Bib.) Elijah; Ellis, Eliot, Elliot
elidir *va* to strike out, nullify; to elide (*a sound*)
elijación *f* (pharm.) seething
elijar *va* (pharm.) to seethe
eliminación *f* elimination; (physiol.) elimination
eliminador -dora *adj* eliminating; *mf* eliminator; **eliminador de baterías** (rad.) battery eliminator
eliminar *va* to eliminate; (math. & physiol.) to eliminate
eliminatoria *f* (sport) elimination match, race, etc.
elipse *f* (geom.) ellipse
elipsis *f* (*pl:* **-sis**) (gram.) ellipsis
elipsógrafo *m* ellipsograph
elipsoide *m & f* (geom.) ellipsoid
elíptico -ca *adj* (geom. & gram.) elliptic or elliptical
elíseo -a *adj* Elysian; (*cap.*) *m* (Bib.) Elisha; (myth. & fig.) Elysium
elisio -sia *adj* Elysian; *m* (myth. & fig.) Elysium
elisión *f* elision
élitro *m* elytrum, shard (*of beetle*)
elixir or **elíxir** *m* elixir; **elixir paregórico** (pharm.) paregoric
elocución *f* elocution; diction, style
elocuencia *f* eloquence
elocuente *adj* eloquent
elogiable *adj* praiseworthy
elogiador -dora *adj* eulogistic; *mf* eulogist
elogiar *va* to praise, laud, eulogize
elogio *m* praise, eulogy; **elogios** *mpl* praise
elogioso -sa *adj* eulogistic
Eloísa *f* Eloise, Héloïse
elongación *f* (astr.) elongation
elote *m* (Am.) ear of green corn, ear of roasting corn
elucidación *f* elucidation
elucidar *va* to elucidate
eludible *adj* avoidable, escapable
eludir *va* to elude, evade; **eludir** + *inf* to avoid + *ger*
elzevir *m* (bibliog. & print.) Elzevir
elzeviriano -na *adj* Elzevir, Elzevirian
elzevirio *m* var. of **elzevir**
ella *pron pers fem* she, her, it; (coll.) trouble, e.g., **aquí fué ella** here's where the trouble was; **mañana será ella** the trouble will come tomorrow

ello *pron pers neut* it; (coll.) trouble, e.g., **aquí fué ello** here's where the trouble was; **ello es que** the fact is that; *adv* really, indeed; **ello no** by no means, not at all; **ello sí** most certainly; *m* (psychoanal.) id
ellos, ellas *pron pers pl* they, them
E.M. abr. of **Estado Mayor**
Em.ª abr. of **Eminencia**
Ema *f* Emma
emaciación *f* emaciation
emanación *f* emanation; **emanación del radio** (chem.) radium emanation
emanar *vn* emanate
emancipación *f* emancipation
emancipador -dora *adj* emancipating; *mf* emancipator
emancipar *va* to emancipate; *vr* to become emancipated; (coll.) to take too much liberty, to go too far
Emanuel *m* (Bib.) Immanuel
emasculación *f* emasculation
emascular *va* to emasculate
embabiamiento *m* (coll.) fascination, amazement, stupefaction
embabucar §86 *va* var. of **embaucar**
embachar *va* to pen (*sheep for shearing*)
embadurnador -dora *adj* daubing; *mf* dauber
embadurnamiento *m* daub, daubing
embadurnar *va* to daub, to bedaub, to besmear; *vn* to daub
embaidor -dora *adj* tricky, deceptive; *mf* trickster, deceiver, cheat
embaimiento *m* trickery, deception
embaír §53 *va* to trick, to deceive
embajada *f* embassy; ambassadorship; diplomatic message; (coll.) errand, mission; **buena embajada** (iron.) fine proposition
embajador *m* ambassador; **embajadores** *mpl* ambassador and wife
embajadora *f* ambassadress; ambassador's wife
embajatorio -ria *adj* ambassadorial
embalador *m* packer
embalaje *m* packing; package; (sport) sprint
embalamiento *m* packing; (sport) sprint
embalar *va* to pack; *vn* to beat the sea with oars to scare fish into the nets; (sport) to sprint; (aut.) to step on the gas; *vr* to race (*said of a motor*)
embaldosado *m* tile paving
embaldosar *va* to pave with tile
embalsadero *m* swamp, marsh
embalsamador -dora *adj* embalming; *mf* embalmer
embalsamamiento *m* embalming, embalmment
embalsamar *va* to embalm (*a corpse; to perfume the air*); *vr* to be or become perfumed; (Am.) to get full of pus
embalsar *va* to dam, to dam up; to put on a raft; (naut.) to sling, to hoist; *vr* to dam up
embalse *m* dam; damming; water dammed up; (naut.) slinging
embalumar *va* to load down, to overload; *vr* to take on too much, to overload oneself with work
emballenado *m* whalebone framework
emballenar *va* to bone, to stiffen with whalebones or stays
emballestado -da *adj* (vet.) foundered; *m* (vet.) founder
embanastar *va* to put into a basket; to overcrowd; *vr* to be overcrowded
embancar §86 *vn* to sail over the shoals; *vr* (found.) to stick to the walls of the furnace; (Am.) to silt up, to become dammed up
embanderar *va* to bedeck with flags or banners
embanquetar *va* (Am.) to put sidewalks on (*streets*)
embarazada *adj fem* pregnant; *f* pregnant woman
embarazadamente *adv* with difficulty
embarazador -dora *adj* embarrassing, disturbing
embarazar §76 *va* to embarrass, interfere with, hold up; to make pregnant; *vr* to be obstructed; to become pregnant
embarazo *m* embarrassment, interference, obstruction; timidity, awkwardness; pregnancy; indigestion
embarazoso -sa *adj* embarrassing; inconvenient, harmful; complicated, hard to solve
embarbar *va* (taur.) to throw (*the bull*) by seizing both horns
embarbascar §86 *vr* to become entangled in roots (*said of a plow*); to become entangled or confused
embarbecer §34 *vn* to grow a beard
embarbillado *m* (carp.) rabbet, rabbeting
embarbillar *va* (carp.) to rabbet
embarcación *f* boat, ship, vessel; embarkation (*of people*); **embarcación de alijo** tender
embarcadero *m* pier, wharf; (rail.) platform
embarcador *m* shipper
embarcar §86 *va* to embark; to ship; (fig.) to embark, to launch (*in an enterprise*); **embarcar agua** to ship water; *vn* to entrain; *vr* to embark, to go aboard; (naut.) to sign up, to ship; (fig.) to embark, become entangled (*in an enterprise*)
embarco *m* embarkation (*of people*)
embardar *va* to thatch
embargar §59 *va* to embargo; to paralyze; (law) to seize, to attach
embargo *m* indigestion; embargo; (law) seizure, attachment; **sin embargo** nevertheless, however
embarnecer §34 *vn* to get fat
embarnecimiento *m* fattening
embarnizadura *f* varnish, varnishing
embarnizar §76 *va* to varnish
embarque *m* shipment (*of goods*)
embarrada *f* (Am.) blunder
embarrador -dora *adj* cheating, scheming; *mf* cheat, schemer
embarradura *f* mud splash; smear, stain; (dial.) plastering; (Am.) vilification
embarrancar §86 *va* to run aground; to run into a ditch; to tie up, entangle, compromise; *vn* to run aground; to run into a ditch; *vr* to run into a ditch; to get tied up, get stuck
embarrar *va* to splash with mud; to smear, stain, bedaub; to pry up, lift with a bar; (dial.) to plaster; (Am.) to vilify; (Am.) to involve; **embarrarla** (Am.) to spoil everything; *vr* to take refuge in the trees (*said of partridges*)
embarrilador *m* packer of barrels
embarrilar *va* to barrel, to put in barrels
embarrotar *va* to bar, to fasten with bars
embarullador -dora *adj* (coll.) muddling; *mf* (coll.) muddler
embarullar *va* (coll.) to mix up, make a mess of; (coll.) to do carelessly, to do in a disorderly way
embasamiento *m* (arch.) foundation
embastar *va* to baste, to stitch; to put (*cloth*) in embroidering frame
embaste *m* basting, stitching
embastecer §34 *vn* to become fat; *vr* to become coarse
embate *m* blow, sudden attack; surf, dashing (*of waves*); gust (*of wind*); fresh summer sea breeze; impact; **embates de la fortuna** sudden changes of fortune
embaucador -dora *adj* deceptive, tricky; *mf* deceiver, trickster, swindler
embaucamiento *m* deception, trickery
embaucar §86 *va* to deceive, to trick, to bamboozle
embaulado -da *adj* crowded, packed, jammed
embaular §75 *va* to put into a trunk; (coll.) to gulp down
embausamiento *m* amazement, stupefaction
embayar *vr* (Am.) to get wrought up over nothing
embazadura *f* brown dye; astonishment, wonder
embazar §76 *va* to dye brown; to embrown; to astound; to embarrass, hinder; *vn* to be dumfounded; *vr* to get bored; to become surfeited
embebecer §34 *va* to entertain, to amuse, to enchant; *vr* to be enchanted; to be astounded
embebecimiento *m* enchantment; astonishment
embebedor -dora *adj* absorbent
embeber *va* to absorb, to soak up; to saturate, to soak; to take up, shorten; to fit, fit in; to insert; to imbed; to include; to contain; *vn* to shrink, contract; *vr* to be enchanted; to be

astounded; to become absorbed or immersed; to become well versed
embebido -da *adj* contracted, elided (*vowel*); (arch.) engaged (*column*)
embecadura *f* (arch.) spandrel
embelecador -dora *adj* deceiving, cheating; *mf* imposter, cheat
embelecar §86 *va* to deceive, cheat, bamboozle
embeleco *m* fraud, imposition; bore; **embelecos** *mpl* cuteness
embeleñar *va* to dope, to stupefy; to charm, to fascinate
embelesador -dora *adj* charming, fascinating, entrancing
embelesamiento *m* charm, fascination, rapture, enchantment
embelesar *va* to charm, fascinate, enrapture; *vr* to be charmed, be fascinated, be enraptured
embeleso *m* delight, charming thing; entrancement
embellaquecer §34 *vr* to become sly, to get deceitful
embellecedor -dora *adj* embellishing, beautifying; *m* (aut.) hubcap
embellecer §34 *va* to embellish, to beautify
embellecimiento *m* embellishment, beautification
embermejar or **embermejecer §34** *va* to dye red, make red; to make blush; *vn* to turn red or reddish; *vr* to blush
emberrenchinar or **emberrinchar** *vr* (coll.) to fly into a rage, to become raving mad
embestida *f* attack, assault; (coll.) touch (*for loan or handout*)
embestidor -dora *adj* attacking; *m* (coll.) beat, sponger
embestidura *f* attack, assault
embestir §94 *va* to attack, to assail; to hit, to strike; (coll.) to touch, to accost for a loan or handout; (coll.) to charge; *vn* (coll.) to rush forth, to charge, to attack; **embestir con** or **contra** to rush upon; to crash into
embetunar *va* to black, blacken; to bituminize; to cover with tar
embicar §86 *va* (naut.) to top (*a yard*); (Am.) to tilt, to turn over (*in order to empty*); (Am.) to fit, insert; *vn* (Am.) to run aground
embijar *va* to paint vermilion; (Am.) to dirty, to smear
embisagrar *va* to hinge
embizcar §86 *vn & vr* to be or to become cross-eyed
emblandecer §34 *va* to soften, placate, mollify; *vr* to soften, yield; to be moved to pity
emblanquecer §34 *va* to bleach, to whiten; *vr* to turn white
emblanquecimiento *m* bleaching, whitening
emblema *m* emblem
emblemático -ca *adj* emblematic or emblematical
embobamiento *m* fascination, amazement
embobar *va* to fascinate, hold in suspense; *vr* to be fascinated, to stand gaping; **embobarse con, de** or **en** to be fascinated at, to gape at
embobecer §34 *va* to make foolish, to make silly; *vr* to become foolish, to get silly
embocadero *m* mouth, outlet, narrow channel
embocado -da *adj* mild, smooth (*said of wine*)
embocadura *f* nozzle; mouthpiece (*of musical instrument*); skill in playing wind instrument; tip (*of cigarette*); bit (*of bridle*); taste (*of wine*); passage, narrows (*from sea into a river*); stage entrance; (arch.) proscenium arch
embocar §86 *va* to put in the mouth; to put (*into or through a narrow passage*); to undertake, to take on; (coll.) to gulp down; (coll.) to try to put over (*something false*); **embocarle algo a uno** (coll.) to force something on someone; (coll.) to spring something on someone; *vn & vr* to go or enter (*into or through a narrow passage*)
embocinado -da *adj* trumpet-shaped
embodegar §59 *va* to store, store away (*wine, olive oil, etc.*)
embojar *va* to place bushes in (*shelves for silkworm rearing*)
embojo *m* bush (*of southernwood, scrub oak, etc., for silk worms*)
embolada *f* stroke (*of piston*)
embolado *m* (theat.) minor rôle; bull with wooden balls on horns; (coll.) trick, deception
embolador -dora *mf* (Am.) shoeblack, shoeshine
embolar *va* to fit or equip (*bull's horns*) with wooden balls; to size (*for gilding*); to shine, polish (*shoes*)
embolectomía *f* (surg.) embolectomy
embolia *f* (path.) embolus, clot; (path.) embolism; **embolia aérea** (path.) air bends
embolismal *adj* embolismic
embolismar *va* (coll.) to gossip about, carry tales about; (Am.) to stir up, incite
embolismático -ca *adj* confused, muddled, incomprehensible
embolísmico -ca *adj* embolismic
embolismo *m* embolism (*to regularize calendar*); confusion, complication; mess, entanglement; (coll.) gossip, lie, fraud
émbolo *m* (mach.) piston; (path.) embolus, clot; **émbolo buzo** (mach.) plunger
embolsar *va* to pocket, to take in
embolso *m* pocketing
embonada *f* (naut.) sheathing
embonar *va* to improve; (naut.) to sheathe; (Am.) to fertilize
embono *m* (naut.) sheathing
emboñigar §59 *va* to smear with cow dung
emboque *m* passage through a small opening; (coll.) cheat, deception, hoax; (coll.) fooling, trifling, idle talk
emboquillar *va* to put a tip on (*a cigarette*); to prepare (*a hole*) for blasting; to cut an entrance in (*a shaft or tunnel*); (Am.) to point or chink (*joints*)
embornal *m* (naut.) scupper
emborrachador -dora *adj* intoxicating
emborrachamiento *m* (coll.) drunkenness
emborrachar *va* to intoxicate; *vr* to become intoxicated, to get drunk; to be blinded (*by passion*); to run, to run together (*said of colors*); **emborracharse con** or **de** to get drunk on (*e.g., gin*)
emborrar *va* to stuff, to pad; to card a second time; (coll.) to gulp down
emborrascar §86 *va* to stir up, to aggravate; *vr* to get stormy; to fail (*said of a business*); (Am.) to peter out (*said of a mine*)
emborrazamiento *m* larding a fowl
emborrazar §76 *va* to lard (*a fowl*)
emborricar §86 *vr* (coll.) to get all confused; (coll.) to fall madly in love
emborrizar §76 *va* to give first combing to (*wool*); (prov.) to bread (*food for frying*); (prov.) to sugar-coat (*cake*)
emborronador -dora *adj* blotting, scribbling; *mf* scribbler
emborronar *va* to blot, to cover with blots, to scribble; *vr* to blot, to become blotted
emborrullar *vr* (coll.) to squabble or wrangle loudly
emboscada *f* ambush, ambuscade; **caer en una emboscada** to fall into an ambush; to fall into a trap
emboscado *m* draft dodger
emboscadura *f* var. of **emboscada**
emboscar §86 *va* to ambush, put in hiding for surprise attack; *vr* to ambush, lie in ambush; to hide in the woods, go deep into the woods; to dodge work, to dodge responsibilities by taking an easy job
embosquecer §34 *vn* to become wooded
embostar *va* to fertilize with manure; (Am.) to plaster (*walls*) with a mixture of earth and manure
embotado -da *adj* blunt, dull; (Am.) black-pawed
embotadura *f* bluntness, dullness
embotamiento *m* dulling; dullness
embotar *va* to blunt, to dull; (fig.) to dull, stupefy, enervate, weaken; to put (*tobacco*) in a jar; (Am.) to put leather sheathes on (*the spurs of a game cock*); *vr* to get dull; (coll.) to put on boots
embotellado -da *adj* prepared (*speech*); *m* bottling; bottleneck
embotellador -dora *adj* bottling; *mf* bottler; *f* bottling machine

embotellamiento *m* bottling; bottling up; traffic jam
embotellar *va* to bottle; to tie up; (nav.) to bottle up
emboticar §86 *vr* (Am.) to stuff oneself with medicine
embotijar *va* to put or keep in jugs; (mas.) to pave (*a surface*) with a layer of jugs to support a tile floor; *vr* (coll.) to swell, to puff up; (coll.) to get angry
embovedar *va* to arch, to vault; to enclose in a vault
embozadamente *adv* cautiously, equivocally
embozado -da *adj* wrapped up, disguised; obscure, puzzling, equivocal; *mf* person with muffled or concealed face
embozalar *va* to muzzle
embozar §76 *va* to cover (*the face*) with cloak or muffler; to muffle; to muzzle; to dissemble, to disguise; *vr* to muffle oneself up, to pull one's cloak over one's face
embozo *m* muffler, part of cloak held over the face; folded part of sheet touching the face; cunning, slyness, faked concern; **con embozo** with caution, with concealment; **de embozo** disguised; **quitarse el embozo** (coll.) to remove one's mask, to lay one's cards on the table; **sin embozo** openly, frankly
embrace *m* curtain clasp
embracilado -da *adj* constantly carried around in someone's arms (*said of a child*)
embragar §59 *va* to engage by means of the clutch; (mach.) to connect (*e.g., a shaft*); (naut.) to sling; *vn* to throw the clutch in
embrague *m* clutch; throwing in the clutch; **embrague de cono** cone clutch; **embrague de mordaza** dog clutch, jaw clutch
embravecer §34 *va* to enrage, infuriate; *vn* to get strong, gather strength (*said of plants*); *vr* to get angry; to swell, get rough (*said of sea*); **embravecerse con** o **contra** to get angry at or with
embravecido -da *adj* angry, furious; wild, rough
embravecimiento *m* anger, fury, rage
embrazadura *f* grasp, clasping; clasp of shield
embrazar §76 *va* to fasten (*shield*) to left arm; *vn* (mach.) to mesh, engage (*said of gears*)
embreadura *f* tarring; caulking with tar or pitch
embrear *va* to cover or soak with tar or pitch; to caulk with tar or pitch
embregar §59 *vr* to quarrel, to wrangle
embreñar *vr* to hide in the brambles
embriagador -dora *adj* intoxicating
embriagar §59 *va* to intoxicate; to transport, to enrapture; *vr* to get drunk
embriaguez *f* intoxication, drunkenness; rapture
embridar *va* to bridle; to govern, check, restrain
embriogenia *f* (biol.) embryogeny
embriogénico -ca *adj* embryogenic
embriología *f* embryology
embriológico -ca *adj* embryologic or embryological
embriólogo -ga *mf* embryologist
embrión *m* (biol., bot. & fig.) embryo; **en embrión** in embryo
embrional *adj* embryonal
embrionario -ria *adj* embryonic
embroca *f* poultice
embrocación *f* (med.) embrocation
embrocar §86 *va* to turn over to empty; to place upside down; to wind on a bobbin; to tack (*soles of shoes*) to the last; (taur.) to catch between the horns; *vr* (Am.) to put (*a garment*) on over the head; (Am.) to fall on one's face
embrochalado *m* header, header beam
embrochalar *va* to support with a crossbeam, to frame with a header beam
embrolla *f* (coll.) var. of **embrollo**
embrollador -dora *adj* embroiling, confusing; *mf* embroiler, troublemaker
embrollar *va* to embroil
embrollo *m* embroilment; imbroglio; lie, trick, deception; impasse, muddle, awkward situation
embrollón -llona *adj & mf* (coll.) var. of **embrollador**
embrolloso -sa *adj* (coll.) tangled, confusing
embromado -da *adj* annoyed; misty, hazy; (Am.) sick, ill; (Am.) in trouble
embromador -dora *mf* jokester; trickster; tease
embromar *va* to joke with, to make fun of; to tease; to cheat, deceive; to delay, hold up; *vr* (Am.) to dally, loiter; (Am.) to be bored
embroquelar *vr* to shield oneself, to defend oneself
embroquetar *va* to skewer the legs of (*fowl*)
embrujado -da *adj* bewitching
embrujamiento *m* bewitchment
embrujar *va* to bewitch
embrujo *m* spell, charm; charmer
embrutecedor -dora *adj* brutalizing, stupefying
embrutecer §34 *va* to brutalize, to stupefy
embrutecimiento *m* brutalization, stupefaction
embuchacar §86 *va* (Am.) to wound (*a fighting cock*) in the craw; (Am. slang) to make pregnant; (Am.) to keep (*a secret*)
embuchado *m* pork sausage; blind, subterfuge; fraudulent voting
embuchar *va* to stuff (*an animal*) with minced meat, to cram the maw of (*an animal*); (coll.) to gulp down
embudador -dora *mf* funneler
embudar *va* to put a funnel in; to trick; to snare, ensnare
embudista *adj* tricky, scheming; *mf* trickster, schemer
embudo *m* funnel; trick, fraud; (mil.) shell hole; **embudo de bomba** (mil.) bomb crater
embullamiento *m* (Am.) var. of **embullo**
embullar *va* to key up, excite; *vr* to become keyed up, become excited
embullo *m* (Am.) excitement, revelry
emburriar *va* (dial.) to push
emburujar *va* to make lumpy; to pile up, to jumble; *vr* to get lumpy; (Am.) to wrap oneself up, to be wrapped up
embuste *m* lie, trick, fraud; **embustes** *mpl* trinkets, baubles
embustear *vn* to be always lying, to be tricky all the time
embustería *f* (coll.) trick, imposture, deceit
embustero -ra *adj* lying; tricky; *mf* liar; trickster
embutidera *f* rivet set
embutido -da *adj* recessed, flush; *m* inlay, marquetry; sausage; (Am.) lace embroidery
embutidor *m* nail set; rivet set
embutir *va* to insert; to stuff, pack tight; to shrink, condense; to inlay; to set flush; to hammer, to fashion (*sheet metal*); to countersink; (naut.) to worm; (coll.) to gulp down, to cram; *vr* to squeeze in; (coll.) to stuff oneself
emelga *f* var. of **amelga**
emenagogo -ga *adj & m* (med.) emmenagogue
emergencia *f* emergence; emergency; happening, incident; (bot.) emergence
emergente *adj* emergent
emerger §49 *vn* to emerge; to surface (*said of a submarine*)
emeritense *adj* (pertaining to) Mérida; *mf* native or inhabitant of Mérida
emérito -ta *adj* emeritus, retired
emersión *f* emersion; surfacing (*of a submarine*); (astr.) emersion
emético -ca *adj* emetic; *m* emetic; tartar emetic
emétrope *mf* emmetrope
emetropía *f* emmetropia
E.M.G. abr. of **Estado Mayor General**
emigración *f* emigration; migration
emigrado -da *mf* émigré
emigrante *adj & mf* emigrant
emigrar *vn* to emigrate; to migrate
emigratorio -ria *adj* (pertaining to) emigration; migratory
Emilia *f* Emily
eminencia *f* eminence; (eccl.) Eminence
eminente *adj* eminent
emir *m* emeer, emir

emisario -ria *mf* emissary
emisión *f* emission; issuance; broadcast; (com.) issue; **emisión seriada** (rad.) serial
emisionario -ria *adj* (com.) issuing
emisivo -va *adj* emissive
emisor -sora *adj* emitting; broadcasting; *m* radio transmitter; wireless transmitter; *f* broadcasting station
emitir *va* to emit, send forth; to broadcast; to utter, express; to issue, give out; (com.) to issue
Em.mo abr. of **Eminentísimo**
emoción *f* emotion
emocionadamente *adv* with emotion, with feeling
emocional *adj* emotional
emocionalismo *m* emotionalism
emocionante *adj* moving, stirring, touching; thrilling
emocionar *va* to move, to stir, to touch, to stir the heart of; *vr* to be moved, be moved to pity
emoliente *adj & m* emollient
emolumento *m* emolument
emotividad *f* emotion, expression of emotion
emotivo -va *adj* emotive; emotional
empacadizo -za *adj* (Am.) touchy, easily angered
empacado -da *adj* (Am.) grim, gruff; (Am.) stubborn
empacador -dora *adj* packing, crating; (Am.) balky, stubborn; *f* packing machine, baling machine
empacar §86 *va* to pack, to crate; (Am.) to anger; *vr* to balk, get balky; to be stubborn; to get rattled, become confused; (Am.) to get angry
empacón -cona *adj* (Am.) stubborn; (Am.) balky
empachado -da *adj* awkward, backward, fumbling; surfeited, upset; (naut.) cluttered (*said of deck*)
empachar *va* to hinder, impede; to disguise; to overload, surfeit, upset, give indigestion to; *vr* to be embarrassed, to blush; to be upset, have indigestion
empacho *m* hindrance, obstacle; surfeit, indigestion; embarrassment, bashfulness
empachoso -sa *adj* surfeiting, sickening; shameful
empadrar *vr* to be too attached to one's father or one's parents (*said of a child*)
empadronador *m* census taker
empadronamiento *m* census; taking of census; registration
empadronar *va* to register, take the census of (*inhabitants for police, taxes, voting, etc.*); *vr* to register, be counted in the census
empajada *f* straw and bran soaked together for horses
empajar *va* to fill or cover with straw; to pack with straw; to bottom (*a chair*) with straw or rush; (Am.) to roof with straw; *vr* (coll.) to feather one's nest; (Am.) to get more than enough
empajolar §77 *va* to fumigate with a sulphur match (*the inside of jugs, casks, etc., that have been washed*)
empalagamiento *m* var. of **empalago**
empalagar §59 *va* to surfeit, pall, cloy; to bore, weary, annoy
empalago *m* surfeit, cloying; bore, annoyance
empalagoso -sa *adj* sickening, sickeningly sweet; mawkish; fawning; *mf* fawning bore
empalamiento *m* impalement
empalar *va* to impale
empaliada *f* bunting
empaliar *va* to decorate with bunting
empalizada *f* stockade, fence, palisade
empalizar §76 *va* to stockade, to fence, to fence in
empalmadura *f* var. of **empalme**
empalmar *va* to join, connect, couple, splice; to combine; to palm (*a card*); *vn* to connect, make connections; to bisect; **empalmar con** to follow, to succeed; *vr* to hold a knife hidden between one's palm and sleeve
empalme *m* joint, connection, coupling, splice; combination; palming; (elec.) joint; (rail.) junction, connection
empalmillar *va* to welt (*a shoe*)
empalmo *m* (arch.) lintel
empalomado *m* loose-stone dam, dam of dry masonry
empalomar *va* (naut.) to sew (*boltrope and sail*)
empalletado *m* (naut.) mattress barricade
empampar *vr* (Am.) to get lost on the pampas
empanada *f* see **empanado**
empanadilla *f* pie; folding carriage step
empanado -da *adj* without windows or openings, unlighted, unventilated; breaded; *f* pie, meat pie, vegetable pie; fraud, concealment
empanar *va* (cook.) to bread; to sow with wheat; *vr* (agr.) to be choked with too much seed
empandar *va* to bend, to make sag; *vr* to bend, to sag
empandillar *va* to slip (*two or more cards together*) in order to cheat; to dupe, to hoax
empanizado *m* (Am.) bread crumbs
empanizar §76 *va* (Am.) to bread (*e.g., a cutlet*)
empantanar *va* to flood, to swamp; to hold up, obstruct; *vr* to become flooded, become swamped
empañado -da *adj* misty; flat (*said, e.g., of voice*)
empañadura *f* swaddling, swaddling clothes
empañar *va* to swaddle; to dim, dull, blur, fog; to tarnish, to sully; *vr* to dim, dull, blur, fog; to film, to mist; to become sad or gloomy
empañetar *va* (Am.) to plaster
empañicar §86 *va* (naut.) to hand, to furl
empapagayar *vr* to act like a parrot; to curve one's nose like the beak of a parrot
empapamiento *m* soaking, saturation; ecstasy, trance
empapar *va* to soak, saturate; to soak up; to drench, soak in, penetrate; *vr* to soak; to be soaked; (coll.) to be surfeited; **empaparse en** to soak in, to soak up, to saturate; to be imbued with
empapelado *m* paper, papering, paper hanging; paper lining
empapelador -dora *mf* paper hanger
empapelar *va* to wrap up in paper; to paper; to line with paper; to wallpaper
empapirotar *va & vr* to dress up, to dress elaborately
empapuciar or **empapujar** *va* (coll.) to stuff, to feed too much
empaque *m* packing; (coll.) look, appearance, mien; solemnness, stiffness; (Am.) nerve, brazenness
empaquetado -da *adj* snappily dressed; *m* (mach.) packing
empaquetador -dora *mf* packer; *f* packing machine
empaquetadura *f* packing; gasket
empaquetar *va* to pack; to jam, stuff, pack; to dress up; (mach.) to pack
emparamentar *va* to adorn, bedeck
emparchar *va* to apply plaster to; (naut.) to stop up (*a leak*) with rope mat
emparedado -da *mf* recluse; *m* sandwich
emparedamiento *m* immurement, confinement; prison; cloister
emparedar *va* to wall in, to immure, to confine
emparejadura *f* equaling, evening, matching
emparejamiento *m* matching; smoothing, leveling; evening up
emparejar *va* to pair, to match; to even, make even; to smooth, to level off; to close (*a door*) flush; *vn* to come up, catch up, come abreast; **emparejar con** to catch up with; to be even with; *vr* to pair, to match
emparentado -da *adj* related by marriage; related
emparentar §18 *vn* to become related by marriage; **emparentar con** to marry into (*e.g., a rich family*)
emparrado *m* arbor, bower
emparrar *va* to embower
emparrillado *m* grate, grating, grillage, grid
emparrillar *va* to grill; *vr* (Am.) to go to bed
emparvar *va* to heap (*grain*) for thrashing
empastador -dora *mf* (Am.) bookbinder; *m* paste brush

empastadura *f* filling (*of a tooth*); (Am.) binding (*of a book*)
empastar *va* to cover or fill with paste; to bind (*a book*) with stiff covers; to fill (*a tooth*); (f.a.) to impaste; *vr* (Am.) to be covered with underbrush
empaste *m* filling (*of a tooth*); binding in stiff boards; (paint.) harmony of colors
empastelamiento *m* (print.) pieing
empastelar *va* (coll.) to settle in a hurry without regard to right or wrong; (coll.) to botch (*a word or words in typing*); (print.) to pie
empatar *va, vn & vr* to tie (*in games and elections*); **empatársela a uno** to tie someone (*in games and elections*)
empate *m* tie, draw; (Am.) penholder
empatía *f* (psychol.) empathy
empavar *va* (Am.) to kid, to razz
empavesada *f* (naut.) armings, waistcloths
empavesado *m* soldier provided with a shield; dressing of a ship, bunting
empavesar *va* to bedeck with flags or bunting; to dress (*a ship*); to veil (*a monument for ceremony of unveiling*)
empavón -vona *adj* (Am.) easily kidded
empavonar *va* to blue (*iron or steel*); (Am.) to grease; *vr* (Am.) to dress up
empecatado -da *adj* incorrigible, evil-minded, devilish; ill-starred, unlucky
empecer **§34** *va* (archaic) to damage, hurt; *vn* to stand in the way
empecimiento *m* (archaic) damage; obstacle
empecinado -da *adj* stubborn; *m* pitch maker
empecinamiento *m* stubbornness
empecinar *va* to dip in pitch; to fill with mud; *vr* (Am.) to be stubborn, to persist
empedernido -da *adj* hardened, hard-hearted; inveterate
empedernir **§53** *va* to harden; *vr* to harden, get hard; to become hard-hearted
Empédocles *m* Empedocles
empedrado -da *adj* cloud-flecked; pock-marked; (Am.) black-spotted (*horse*); *m* paving; stone paving
empedrador *m* stone paver
empedramiento *m* stone paving; pile of stones at base of bridge pier
empedrar **§18** *va* to pave with stones; to sprinkle, to bespatter
empega *f* pitch; mark made with pitch on sheep
empegado *m* tarpaulin
empegadura *f* coat of pitch; coating with pitch
empegar **§59** *va* to cover or coat with pitch; to mark (*sheep*) with pitch
empego *m* marking sheep with pitch
empeguntar *va* to mark (*sheep*) with pitch
empeine *m* pubes; instep; vamp; (bot.) cotton flower; (bot.) liverwort; (path.) tetter
empeinoso -sa *adj* tetterous
empelar *vn* to grow hair; to have like coats (*said of two or more horses*)
empelazgar **§59** *vn* (coll.) to get into a quarrel
empelechar *va* to cover or line with marble; to lay (*slabs of marble*)
empelotar *vr* (coll.) to get all tangled up or confused; to get involved in a row; (Am.) to strip, to take all one's clothes off
empeltre *m* (hort.) side graft
empella *f* vamp, upper
empellar *va* to push, shove, jostle
empellejar *va* to cover with skins, to line with skins
empeller **§46** *va* var. of **empellar**
empellón *m* push, shove; **a empellones** roughly, violently
empenachar *va* to adorn with plumes, to plume
empenaje *m* (aer.) empennage
empenta *f* prop, stay, shoring
empentar *va* (min.) to wall, wall up; (dial.) to push, shove
empeñado -da *adj* bitter, heated (*dispute*); persistent, determined
empeñar *va* to pawn; to pledge; to involve; to force, engage, compel; to begin (*a battle, dispute, etc.*); *vr* to bind oneself; to insist; to go in debt; to start (*said of a battle, dispute, etc.*); (naut.) to risk running aground; **empeñarse en** to engage in (*e.g., a battle, dispute*); to persist in, to insist on; to go in debt to the amount of; **empeñarse en** + *inf* to insist on + *ger;* **empeñarse por** to intercede for or in behalf of
empeñero -ra *mf* (Am.) pawnbroker
empeño *m* pledge, obligation, engagement; pawn; pawnshop; persistence, insistence; perseverance; eagerness, determination; endeavor, effort; favor, protection; pledge, backer, patron; **con empeño** eagerly, with determination
empeñoso -sa *adj* (Am.) eager, determined; (Am.) diligent
empeoramiento *m* impairment, worsening
empeorar *va* to make worse, impair; *vn & vr* to get worse
empequeñecer **§34** *va* to dwarf, to make smaller, to diminish; to belittle
empequeñecimiento *m* diminution, lessening; belittling
emperador *m* emperor; **emperadores** *mpl* emperor and empress
emperatriz *f* (*pl:* **-trices**) empress
emperchar *va* to hang on a clothes rack; *vr* to be caught in a snare
emperdigar **§59** *va* to prepare; to brown (*meat*); to broil (*partridges*)
emperejilar *va & vr* (coll.) to dress up, to dress fancily
emperezar **§76** *va* to make lazy; to delay, to slow down; *vr* to be or become lazy
empergaminar *va* to bind with parchment
empericar **§86** *vr* (Am.) to get drunk
emperifollar *va & vr* to dress up gaudily, to spruce up
empernar *va* to bolt, to bolt together
empero *conj* but; however
emperrada *f* tresillo (*card game*)
emperramiento *m* obstinacy, stubbornness
emperrar *vr* (coll.) to be or get obstinate or stubborn; (Am.) to cry, to burst out crying
empetro *m* (bot.) samphire
empezar **§31** *va & vn* to begin; **empezar a** + *inf* to begin to + *inf*, to begin + *ger;* **empezar por** + *inf* to begin by + *ger*
empicar **§86** *vr* to become too fond, to become infatuated, to be taken in
empicotadura *f* pillorying
empicotar *va* to pillory
empiece *m* (coll.) beginning
empiema *m* (path.) empyema; (surg.) operation to drain empyema
empilar *va* to pile, pile up
empilonar *va* (Am.) to pile up (*dried tobacco leaves*)
empinado -da *adj* high, lofty; stiff, stuck-up; (her.) saltant, salient; *f* (aer.) zooming; **irse a la empinada** to rear (*said, e.g., of a horse*)
empinadura *f* or **empinamiento** *m* elevation, raising; rising, towering
empinar *va* to raise, lift; to raise and tip over; (coll.) to crook (*the elbow*); (aer.) to zoom; *vn* (coll.) to drink, be a toper; *vr* to stand on tiptoe; to rear (*said, e.g., of a horse*); to rise high, to tower; (aer.) to zoom; (Am.) to overeat
empingorotado -da *adj* of high and influential social standing; proud, haughty
empingorotar *va* (coll.) to put on top; *vr* (coll.) to get up, to climb up (*e.g., on a table or chair*); (coll.) to be proud, be haughty
empino *m* (arch.) vertex of a cross vault
empiñonado *m* candied pine-nut kernel
empíreo -a *adj* empyrean or empyreal; *m* empyrean
empireuma *m* (chem.) empyreuma
empírico -ca *adj* empiric or empirical; *mf* empiricist
empirismo *m* empiricism
empirista *mf* empiricist
empitonar *va* (taur.) to catch with the horns
empizarrado *m* slate roof
empizarrar *va* to slate, to roof with slate
emplastadura *f* or **emplastamiento** *m* application of plasters; application of make-up or paint; make-up
emplastar *va* to apply a plaster to; to put make-up on; to smear up; (coll.) to tie up (*a deal*); *vr* to put on make-up; to smear oneself up

emplastecer §34 *va* (paint.) to smooth with filler
emplástico -ca *adj* sticky
emplasto *m* plaster, poultice; unsatisfactory compromise or settlement; (coll.) splotch (*on clothing or body*); (coll.) weakling; (coll.) misfit (*person*); patch, tire patch
emplástrico -ca *adj* var. of **emplástico**
emplazamiento *m* summoning; (law) summons; emplacement, location, site
emplazar §76 *va* to summons; (law) to summon; to place, locate
empleado -da *mf* clerk; employee
emplear *va* to employ, to engage; to use, use up; **estarle a uno bien empleado** (coll.) to serve someone right; *vr* to be employed; to busy oneself; **empleársele bien a uno** (coll.) to serve someone right
empleita *f* plaited strand of esparto grass; (Am.) straw hat
empleitero -ra *mf* plaiter and vender of esparto grass
emplenta *f* section of mud wall made in one form; wall plastered on only one side; masonry with rubble between the facings
empleo *m* employ, employment; use; public office; (mil.) rank
empleomanía *f* (coll.) zeal or eagerness to hold public office; (Am.) excessive number of people eager to hold public office
emplomado *m* lead roof
emplomador *m* leadworker
emplomadura *f* leadwork, leading; lead covering, lead lining; (Am.) plumbing
emplomar *va* to lead; to cover or roof with lead; to line with lead; to place a lead seal on (*e.g., a bale*); (Am.) to fill (*a tooth*)
emplumar *va* to put a feather or feathers on; to tar and feather; to thrash; **emplumarlas** (Am.) to flee, beat it; *vn* to fledge, to get feathers
emplumecer §34 *vn* to fledge, to get feathers
empobrecedor -dora *adj* impoverishing
empobrecer §34 *va* to impoverish; to weaken; *vn & vr* to become poor or impoverished
empobrecimiento *m* impoverishment
empodrecer §34 *vn & vr* to rot
empolvado -da *adj* (Am.) rusty (*out of practice*)
empolvar *va* to cover with dust; to powder, to put powder on; *vr* to become covered with dust; to become covered with powder; (Am.) to get rusty (*in knowledge or skill*)
empolvoramiento *m* covering with dust; powdering
empolvorar *va* var. of **empolvar**
empolvorizar §76 *va* var. of **empolvar**
empollado -da *adj* (coll.) shut-in; **ir bien empollado** (coll.) to be primed for an examination
empolladura *f* brooding; brood; brood of bees
empollar *va* to brood, hatch (*eggs*); (coll.) to bone up on; *vn* to breed (*said of insects*); (coll.) to grind, to study hard; **empollar sobre** (coll.) to bone up on
empollón -llona *mf* (scornful) grind (*student*)
emponchado -da *adj* (Am.) poncho-wearing; (Am.) suspicious-looking
emponzoñador -dora *adj* poisoning; *mf* poisoner
emponzoñamiento *m* poisoning
emponzoñar *va* to poison; to corrupt
empopar *va* (naut.) to turn (*the stern*) toward the wind; *vn* (naut.) to be down by the stern; (naut.) to sail before the wind
emporcar §95 *va* to soil, to dirty; *vn* to get soiled, get dirty
emporio *m* emporium; center of culture
empotrado -da *adj* built-in; set-in, recessed
empotramiento *m* planting, embedding, fastening; interlocking; (carp.) abutment, abutting joint
empotrar *va* to plant, embed, recess, fix in a wall; to scarf, to splice; *vn & vr* to interlock
empozar §76 *va* to throw or put into a well; to soak (*flax*); *vn* to form into puddles; *vr* (coll.) to fail to be carried out
empradizar §76 *va* to convert into pasture land
emprendedor -dora *adj* enterprising
emprender *va* to undertake; **emprenderla con** (coll.) to pester, to squabble with, to have it out with; **emprenderla para** (coll.) to set out for
empreñar *va* to impregnate, make pregnant; *vr* to become pregnant
empresa *f* enterprise, undertaking; motto, device; concern, company, firm; **la empresa** management (*as distinguished from labor*); **empresa anunciadora** advertising agency; **empresa constructora** building concern; **empresa de tranvías** traction company
empresario -ria *mf* contractor; industrialist, business leader; manager; theatrical manager; impresario; **empresario de circo** showman; **empresario de pompas fúnebres** undertaker; **empresario de publicidad** advertising man
emprestar *va* to borrow; (slang) to lend
empréstito *m* loan, government loan
emprima *f* first fruits
emprimado *m* second combing of wool
emprimar *va* to give a second combing to (*wool*); (paint.) to prime; (coll.) to hoodwink, to dupe, to defraud
empringar §59 *va & vr* var. of **pringar**
empuchar *va* to buck (*skeins of thread*)
empujador -dora *adj* pushing; *m & f* pusher; **empujadora niveladora** bulldozer
empujar *va* to push, to shove; to dismiss; to replace; *vn* to push, to shove; **empujad** or **empujar** push (*word on public door*)
empujatierra *f* bulldozer
empuje *m* push; thrust; (fig.) push, energy, enterprise; (phys.) thrust
empujón *m* push, hard shove; rapid progress; **a empujones** (coll.) roughly, violently; (coll.) by fits and starts; **tratar a empujones** (coll.) to push around
empulgadura *f* bending the bow of a crossbow; tenseness of string of crossbow
empulgar §59 *va* to bend the bow of (*a crossbow*); to fill with fleas
empulguera *f* wing of crossbow; **empulgueras** *fpl* thumbscrew (*instrument of torture*)
empuntar *va* to put a point on; **empuntarlas** (Am.) to beat it, run away
empuñadura *f* hilt (*of sword*); first words of a story; (Am.) handle (*e.g., of an umbrella*)
empuñar *va* to clutch, to grasp; to obtain (*a job*); **empuñar el cetro** to start to reign, to ascend the throne
empuñidura *f* (naut.) earing
empurpurar *va* to empurple
emú *m* (*pl:* **emúes**) (orn.) emu
emulación *f* emulation
emulador -dora *adj* emulative, emulating; *mf* emulator
emular *va & vn* to emulate; **emular con** to emulate, vie with
emulgente *adj* emulgent
émulo -la *adj* emulous; *mf* rival, emulator
emulsión *f* emulsion
emulsionamiento *m* emulsification
emulsionar *va* to emulsify
emulsivo -va *adj* emulsive
emulsor *m* emulsor, emulsifier
emunción *f* excretion
emuntorio -ria *adj & m* emunctory
en *prep* at, e.g., **estuvo en el teatro anoche** he was at the theater last night; in, e.g., **está en Madrid ahora** he is now in Madrid; **escribió la carta en francés** he wrote the letter in French; into, e.g., **entró en el cuarto silenciosamente** he came quietly into the room; by, e.g., **le conocí en el andar** I knew him by his walk; of, e.g., **pensaba en mis dos hermanos** I was thinking of my two brothers; on, e.g., **puso el libro en la mesa** he put the book on the table
enaceitar *va* to oil, grease; to spot with oil; *vr* to become oily or rancid
enacerar *va* to steel, make steely, harden
enagua *f* petticoat, underskirt; **enaguas** *fpl* petticoat
enaguachar *va* to spill water over, to soak with water, to flood; to upset the stomach of; *vr* to become upset (*from excessive eating or drinking*)

enaguar §23 *va* to spill water over, to flood
enaguazar §76 *va* to flood; *vr* to flood, become flooded
enagüillas *fpl* short skirt, kilt
enajenable *adj* alienable
enajenación *f* alienation; rapture; distraction, absence of mind; **enajenación mental** mental derangement
enajenamiento *m* var. of **enajenación**
enajenar *va* to transport, enrapture; to alienate, dispose of (*property*); to alienate (*a friend*); *vr* to be transported, enraptured; **enajenarse de** to get rid of (*property*); to become alienated from (*a friend*)
enálage *f* (gram.) enallage
enalbar *va* to make white-hot in a forge
enalbardar *va* to saddle, to put a packsaddle on; to dip in a batter; to lard (*a fowl*)
enalmagrado -da *adj* vile, despicable
enalmagrar *va* to color with red ocher
enaltecer §34 to exalt, extol; *vr* to be exalted, be extolled
enaltecimiento *m* exaltation, exalting, extolling
enamarillecer §34 *vn* & *vr* to become or to turn yellow
enamoradamente *adv* lovingly
enamoradizo -za *adj* susceptible (*to love*)
enamorado -da *adj* in love, lovesick; susceptible (*to love*); *mf* sweetheart; *m* lover
enamorador -dora *adj* wooing, love-making; *mf* wooer, love-maker, suitor
enamoramiento *m* love, love-making; falling in love
enamorar *va* to enamor, to inspire love in; to make love to; *vr* to fall in love; **enamorarse de** to fall in love with
enamoricar §86 *vr* (coll.) to trifle in love, to be slightly in love
enamoriscar §86 *vr* (dial. & Am.) var. of **enamoricar**
enanchar *va* (coll.) to widen
enangostar *va* & *vr* to narrow
enanismo *m* dwarfism, nanism
enano -na *adj* dwarfish; *mf* dwarf
enante *f* (bot.) water fennel
enarbolar *va* to hoist, raise on high, hang out (*e.g., a flag*); to brandish (*e.g., a sword*); *vr* to get angry; to rear
enarcar §86 *va* to arch; to hoop (*barrels*)
enardecer §34 *va* to inflame, to fire, to excite; *vr* to get excited; to become inflamed (*said, e.g., of a sore*)
enardecimiento *m* inflaming; excitement; inflammation (*e.g., of a sore*)
enarenación *f* sanding; coat of plaster (*in final preparation for painting a wall*)
enarenar *va* to sand, throw sand on; (min.) to mix fine sand with (*silver ore*) to speed amalgamation; *vn* (naut.) to run aground
enarmonar *va* to stand up; *vr* to rear
enarmónico -ca *adj* (mus.) enharmonic
enartrosis *f* (anat.) enarthrosis
enastado -da *adj* horned; antlered
enastar *va* to put a handle on, to put a shaft on
enastillar *va* to put a handle on
encabalgamiento *m* gun carriage; (pros.) enjambement
encabalgar §59 *va* to provide with horses; *vn* to rest, to lean
encaballado *m* (print.) pieing, jumbling (*of type and lines*)
encaballar *va* to overlap; (print.) to pi; *vn* to rest, to lean; *vr* to overlap; (print.) to be pied
encabellecer §34 *vr* to grow hair
encabestradura *f* (vet.) halter sore (*on pastern*)
encabestrar *va* to put (*a halter*) on; to lead by a halter; to subdue, to win over; *vr* to get a front leg entangled in the halter
encabezado *m* process of fortifying wines
encabezamiento *m* census, tax list, tax rate; heading, headline, title; caption; opening words (*of a document*); **encabezamiento de factura** billhead
encabezar §76 *va* to draw up (*a tax list*); to head, to lead; to put a heading or title to; to fortify (*wine*); (carp.) to scarf, to join; *vr* to compromise, to settle
encabillar *va* to dowel, to pin
encabrahigar §59 *va* var. of **cabrahigar**
encabriar *va* to put in the rafters for (*the roof*)
encabritar *vr* to rear (*said of a horse*); (aer. & naut.) to shoot up, to nose up
encachado *m* stone or concrete lining of bed of stream or sewer, riprap
encachar *va* to line with stones or concrete (*the bed of a stream, trench, or sewer*), to riprap
encadar *vr* to get scared, become intimidated
encadenación *f* chaining; connecting, connection; concatenation
encadenado *m* (arch.) buttress
encadenadura *f* or **encadenamiento** *m* var. of **encadenación**
encadenar *va* to chain, to enchain, to put in chains; to brace, to buttress; (mas.) to bond; to connect, tie together, bind; to tie down, immobilize; *vr* to be linked together, to hang together
encajador *m* enchaser; enchasing tool
encajadura *f* inserting, insertion, fitting; recess, groove, socket
encajar *va* to put, to insert; to enchase; to fit, make fit; to put in (*a joke or remark*); to put in (*a joke or remark*) inopportunely; to tell (*a story*) at the wrong time; to put away (*money*); to give, let go (*e.g., a blow*); (coll.) to throw, to hurl; **encajar una cosa a uno** (coll.) to force something on someone, to palm off something on someone; (coll.) to force someone to listen to something; *vn* to fit, to close right (*said, e.g., of a door*); to be fitting or appropriate; **encajar con** or **en** to fit into, to fit, to match; *vr* (coll.) to put on (*a garment*); to squeeze, to squeeze one's way; (coll.) to intrude, butt in
encaje *m* insertion; fitting, matching; recess, groove, socket; lace; inlay, mosaic; fit, look, appearance; **encaje de bolillos** bobbin lace, bone lace, pillow lace; **encaje de Malinas** malines, Mechlin lace
encajero -ra *mf* lacemaker; lace dealer
encajetillar *va* to put (*cigarettes or tobacco*) in packages or packs
encajonado *m* cofferdam; (mas.) coffer
encajonamiento *m* boxing, crating; narrowing (*of a stream or river*)
encajonar *va* to box, to case, to crate; to squeeze in or through; to dovetail; to coffer; to buttress; *vr* to narrow, to run through a narrow channel or ravine; to squeeze in or through
encalabozar §76 *va* (coll.) to throw into jail
encalabrinar *va* to make dizzy (*said, e.g., of an odor*); to rattle, to fluster; *vr* (coll.) to get stubborn, to get a fixed idea in one's mind
encalada *f* metal ornament on harness
encalado *m* var. of **encaladura**
encalador -dora *mf* whitewasher; *m* lime pit, lime vat
encaladura *f* whitewashing; (agr.) liming
encalar *va* to whitewash; to lime (*hides*); (agr.) to lime; to sprinkle with lime, to treat with lime
encalmado -da *adj* (naut.) becalmed; (com.) quiet (*market*)
encalmadura *f* (vet.) overheating
encalmar *vr* (vet.) to be overheated; (naut.) to be becalmed
encalostrar *vr* to be sick with colostration, to get sick from the first milk
encalvecer §34 *vn* to become bald
encalladero *m* (naut.) shoal, sand bank
encalladura *f* running aground
encallar *vn* to run aground; to fail; to get entangled in a deal
encallecer §34 *vn* to get corns, get calluses; *vr* to get corns, get calluses; to become callous, become hardened
encallejonar *va* & *vr* to run down an alley or narrow passage
encamación *f* (min.) shoring, support
encamar *va* to stretch out on the ground or the floor; *vr* (coll.) to take to bed; to lie down, to hide (*said of game*); to bend over, to droop (*said of grain*)

encamarar *va* to store (*grain or fruit*)
encambijar *va* to store and distribute (*water*)
encambrar *va* var. of **encamarar**
encambronar *va* to hedge with brambles; to reinforce with iron
encaminadura *f* or **encaminamiento** *m* directing, forwarding
encaminar *va* to set on the way, to show the way to; to forward; to direct (*e.g., one's energies, one's attention*); **encaminar a** + *inf* to guide or direct (*someone*) to + *inf; vr* to set out, to be on one's way
encamisada *f* (mil.) camisade, night attack; night masquerade
encamisar *va* to put a shirt on (*a person*); to put slip covers on; to hide, conceal, disguise; *vr* to put one's shirt on; (mil.) to make a camisade or night attack
encamo *m* hiding place (*of game*)
encampanado -da *adj* bell-shaped
encanalar *va* to pipe, to channel
encanalizar §76 *va* var. of **encanalar**
encanallamiento *m* corruption, depravity
encanallar *va* to corrupt, to deprave; *vr* to become corrupt, to get depraved; to associate with low company, to keep bad company
encanar *vr* to stiffen with anger (*said of an infant*)
encanastar *va* to put in a basket
encancerar *vr* to have cancer; to become cancerous
encandecer §34 *va* to make white-hot, to make incandescent
encandelar *vn* to blossom with catkin
encandiladera *f* (coll.) procuress, bawd
encandilado -da *adj* (coll.) stiff, erect; (coll.) cocked (*hat*)
encandiladora *f* (coll.) var. of **encandiladera**
encandilamiento *m* glare
encandilante *adj* sparkling; dazzling
encandilar *va* to dazzle; (fig.) to dazzle, bewilder; (coll.) to stir (*a fire*); *vr* to sparkle, to flash (*said of eyes*)
encanecer §34 *va* (poet.) to turn white; *vn & vr* to become gray or gray-haired; to become old; to become moldy
encanijamiento *m* weakening, emaciation
encanijar *va* to make sick or weak; *vr* to get sickly, become emaciated
encanillar *va* to wind on a spool
encantación *f* var. of **encantamento**
encantado -da *adj* satisfied, delighted; (coll.) absent-minded, in a trance; (coll.) empty and spacious, rambling (*said of a house*); *mf* (coll.) person on whom a spell has been cast
encantador -dora *adj* enchanting, charming, delightful; *mf* charmer; **encantador de serpientes** snake charmer; *m* enchanter; *f* enchantress
encantamento or **encantamiento** *m* spell; enchantment, charm, delight
encantar *va* to cast a spell on, to bewitch; to enchant, charm, delight; **encantar a uno** + *inf* to enchant, charm, delight someone to + *inf*
encantarar *va* to put into a jar or ballot box
encante *m* auction, public sale; auction house
encanto *m* var. of **encantamento**
encantorio *m* (coll.) var. of **encantamento**
encantusar *va* (coll.) to wheedle, to coax
encanutar *va* to shape like a tube; to put in a tube; to put (*a cigarette*) in a holder
encañada *f* gorge, ravine
encañado *m* water pipe; trellis of reeds
encañador -dora *mf* silk winder
encañar *va* to pipe; to drain with pipes; to prop up (*plants*) with reeds; to wind on a spool; *vn & vr* to form stalks (*said of cereals*)
encañizada *f* reed fence; reed fence to catch fish, weir
encañizar §76 *va* to set up frame for (*silkworms*); to line (*a vault*) with a web of reeds and rope
encañonar *va* to pipe; to wind on a spool; to plait, to fold; to tip in (*a sheet of paper in a book*); *vn* to fledge out
encapachadura *f* pile of bags full of olives for pressing
encapachar *va* to put (*e.g., olives*) in bags for pressing
encapar *va* to put a cloak on; *vr* to put on one's cloak
encapazar §76 *va* var. of **encapachar**
encaperuzar §76 *va* to put a hood on; *vr* to put on one's hood
encapillar *va* to put a hood or cowl on; to hood (*a falcon*); (naut.) to rig (*the yards*); (min.) to start a new gallery in; **lo encapillado** (coll.) what one has on; *vr* (coll.) to put on (*a garment, especially over the head*)
encapirotar *va* to put a hood on; *vr* to put on one's hood
encapotado -da *adj* overcast, overclouded
encapotadura *f* or **encapotamiento** *m* grim look, frown
encapotar *va* to cloak; *vr* to put on one's cloak; to look grim, to frown; to become overcast, become overclouded; to pull the mouth down too close to the chest (*said of a horse*)
encaprichar *vr* to persist in one's whims; **encapricharse con** or **en** to whimsically set one's mind upon; **encapricharse por** (coll.) to be or become infatuated with
encapuchar *va* to put a cowl or hood on; *vr* to put one's cowl or hood on
encapuzar §76 *va* to put a cowl on; *vr* to put on one's cowl
encaracolado *m* spiral adornment
encaracolar *va* to give a spiral shape or form to
encarado -da *adj* faced, featured, favored; **bien encarado** well-featured, well-favored; **mal encarado** ill-featured, ill-favored
encaramar *va* to raise, lift up, elevate; to praise, extol; (coll.) to elevate, dignify, exalt; *vr* to climb; to get on top; to rise, rise up; (Am.) to blush
encaramiento *m* aiming, pointing; facing, encounter
encarar *va* to aim, to point; to face (*a problem, question, etc.*); *vn & vr* to come face to face; **encararse a** or **con** to face, confront, stand up to
encaratular *vr* to put on a mask, to mask oneself
encarcavinar *va* to put in a grave, to bury; to suffocate, asphyxiate; to choke with a foul odor
encarcelación *f* or **encarcelamiento** *m* incarceration, imprisonment
encarcelar *va* to jail, incarcerate, imprison; (carp.) to clamp (*glued parts*); to plaster in, to imbed in mortar; (naut.) to woold; *vr* to stay indoors
encare *m* aiming
encarecer §34 *va* to raise the price of; to raise (*the price or cost*); to extol; to overrate; to urge; **encarecer que** + *subj* to urge to + *inf; vn & vr* to rise in price
encarecidamente *adv* insistently, eagerly
encarecimiento *m* increase; extolling, overrating; **con encarecimiento** insistently, eagerly
encargado -da *mf* representative, person in charge, agent; **encargado de negocios** chargé d'affaires; **encargado de vía** (rail.) roadmaster, supervisor
encargamiento *m* duty, obligation
encargar §59 *va* to entrust; to urge, to warn; to order (*goods*); to summon; to ask for, to request; **encargar algo a uno** to entrust someone with something, to put someone in charge of something; **encargar que** + *subj* to entrust with + *ger;* to urge to + *inf; vr* to take charge; **encargarse de** to be in charge of, to take charge of, to undertake; **encargarse de** + *inf* to take charge of + *ger*, to undertake to + *inf*
encargo *m* charge, commission, job, assignment, responsibility; warning; order; request; employment, office; **ni de encargo** (coll.) as if made to order
encariñamiento *m* endearment
encariñar *va* to awaken love or affection in; *vr* to become fond; **encariñarse con** to become fond of, become attached to
encarna *f* feeding entrails to hunting dogs
encarnación *f* incarnation; (theol.) Incarnation; (f.a.) flesh color, incarnadine
encarnadino -na *adj* reddish, pink
encarnado -da *adj* incarnate; red; flesh-colored, incarnadine; *m* flesh color, incarnadine

encarnadura *f* (surg.) healing characteristics of flesh; slash, cut (*of weapon*); feeding on entrails of game
encarnamiento *m* (med.) incarnation
encarnar *va* to incarnate, to embody; to bait (*fishhook*); to flesh (*hunting dog*); to mix, incorporate; to represent, to play; (f.a.) to give color of flesh to (*a statue*); *vn* to become incarnate; to incarn, heal over; to leave a strong impression; to be thrust into the flesh; to eat the entrails of game (*said of hunting dogs*)
encarne *m* first entrails given to hunting dogs
encarnecer **§34** *vn* to grow fat, put on flesh
encarnizadamente *adv* cruelly; fiercely, bitterly
encarnizado -da *adj* bloody, blood-shot; fierce, bitter, hard-fought
encarnizamiento *m* anger, fury; cruelty; fierceness, bitterness (*e.g., of a combat*)
encarnizar **§76** *va* to flesh (*a hunting dog*); to anger, infuriate; *vr* to be greedy for flesh (*said of animals*); to get angry, be infuriated; to fight bitterly; **encarnizarse con** or **en** to be merciless to, to treat inhumanly
encaro *m* stare, staring; aim, aiming; blunderbuss; rest for cheek (*on gunstock*)
encarpetar *va* to put in a portfolio, to file away; to table, to pigeonhole
encarrilar or **encarrillar** *va* to put back on the rails; to put on the right track, to set right; to guide, direct; *vr* to get stuck and slip off the pulley
encarroñar *va & vr* to rot
encarrujado -da *adj* curled, kinky; fluted; *m* fluting, shirring, gathering
encarrujar *vr* to curl, coil, kink
encartar *va* to outlaw, proscribe; to enroll, register; to register for taxes; to insert, slip in (*a card*); (cards) to lead (*a suit that can or must be followed*); *vr* (cards) to be unable to discard
encarte *m* leading a suit that can or must be followed; order of cards at end of hand
encartonador *m* bookbinder
encartonar *va* to put cardboard on, to cover or protect with cardboard; to bind (*books*) in boards
encasamento or **encasamiento** *m* (arch.) fascia
encasar *va* to set (*broken bone*)
encascabelar *va* to adorn with bells
encascotar *va* to fill with rubble, to mix with rubble
encasillado *m* set of pigeonholes; pattern of squares; list of government candidates
encasillar *va* to pigeonhole; to classify, sort out; to assign (*a candidate*) to a voting district
encasquetar *va* to stick (*a hat, cap, etc.*) on the head; to put (*an idea*) in someone's mind; to put in (*a remark*); *vr* to stick (*a hat, cap, etc.*) on one's head; to get (*an idea*) deeply rooted in one's mind
encasquillador *m* (Am.) horseshoer
encasquillar *va* to put a tip on; (mach.) to bush; (Am.) to shoe (*a horse*); *vr* to stick, get stuck (*said of a gun or a bullet in a gun*)
encastar *va* to improve (*breed*) by crossing; *vn* to breed
encastillado -da *adj* castellated; haughty, proud
encastillamiento *m* fortification with castles; withdrawal to a castle; scaffolding; stubborn adherence to one's opinion
encastillar *va* to fortify with castles; to pile up; to assemble a scaffold in order to build (*a building or other structure*); to build queen cells in (*beehives*); *vn* to build queen cells; *vr* to stick, to get stuck; to shut oneself up in a castle; to take to the hills; to proudly ensconce oneself; to stick to one's opinion, to refuse to give in
encastrar *va* (mach.) to engage, to mesh
encastre *m* (mach.) engaging, meshing; socket; groove; insert
encatusar *va* var. of **engatusar**
encauchado *m* (Am.) rubber-lined fabric; (Am.) rubber-lined poncho
encauchar *va* to cover with rubber
encausar *va* to prosecute, to sue
encauste *m* var. of **encausto**
encausticar **§86** *va* to wax (*a floor*)
encáustico -ca *adj* (f.a.) encaustic; *m* furniture polish, floor polish
encausto *m* (f.a.) encaustic
encauzamiento *m* channeling; guiding, directing; direction
encauzar **§76** *va* to channel (*a stream*); to guide, direct
encavar *vr* to hide, to hide in a cave, burrow, etc. (*said of game*)
encebadamiento *m* surfeit (*of an animal*)
encebadar *va* to surfeit (*an animal*); *vr* to surfeit
encebollado *m* beef stew with onions
encebollar *va* to season heavily with onions
encefálico -ca *adj* encephalic
encefalitis *f* (path.) encephalitis
encéfalo *m* (anat.) encephalon
encefalomielitis *f* (path.) encephalomyelitis
encefalopatía *f* (path.) encephalopathy
enceguecer **§34** *va* (Am.) to blind; *vn & vr* (Am.) to go blind
encelado -da *adj* (Am.) madly in love
encelajar *vr* to be covered with bright-colored clouds
encelamiento *m* jealousy
encelar *va* to make jealous; *vr* to become jealous; to be in rut
enceldar *va* to put in a cell
encella *f* cheese mold; basket
encellar *va* to mold (*cheese*)
encenagado -da *adj* mixed with mud
encenagamiento *m* getting muddied; wallowing in vice
encenagar **§59** *vr* to get into the mud; to become muddied; to wallow in vice
encencerrado -da *adj* wearing a bell (*said of an animal*)
encencerrar *va* to bell, put a bell on (*cattle*)
encendaja *f* dried brush, kindling
encendedor -dora *adj* lighting, kindling; *m* lighter; sparker, igniter; (elec.) starter (*of fluorescent light*); **encendedor automático** cigarette lighter, cigar lighter
encender **§66** *va* to light, kindle, set fire to, ignite; to turn on (*lights, radio, etc.*); to burn (*e.g., the tongue*); to instigate, stir up, excite; *vr* to be kindled, catch fire, ignite; to burn; to be stirred up, become excited; to blush
encendidamente *adv* ardently, keenly, eagerly
encendido -da *adj* bright, high-colored, inflamed; red, flushed; keen, enthusiastic; *m* (aut.) ignition
encendimiento *m* lighting, kindling, ignition; burning; glow, incandescence; ardor, intensity
encenizar **§76** *va* to cover with ashes; *vr* to get covered with ashes
encentador -dora *adj* beginning
encentadura *f* or **encentamiento** *m* beginning, start
encentar **§18** *va* to begin; to cut the first slice of; *vr* to get bedsores
encentrar *va* to center
encepador *m* stocker (*of a gun*)
encepadura *f* stocking; (carp.) tie joint
encepar *va* to put in the stocks; to stock (*a gun*); (naut.) to stock (*the anchor*); (carp.) to fasten or join with ties; *vn* to take deep root; *vr* to take deep root; (naut.) to be fouled on the anchor (*said of a cable*)
encepe *m* taking deep root
encerado -da *adj* waxy, wax-colored; hard (*said of a boiled egg*); *m* oilcloth; tarpaulin; wax sticking plaster; blackboard; waxing (*of floors and furniture*)
encerador -dora *mf* floor waxer (*person*); *f* floor-waxing machine
enceramiento *m* waxing
encerar *va* to wax; to smear with wax; to stiffen with wax; to thicken (*lime*); *vn & vr* to turn yellow, to ripen (*said of grain*)
encernadar *va* to cover with ashes, to plaster with ashes
encerotar *va* to wax (*thread*)
encerradero *m* sheepfold; pen for bulls before fight

encerradura *f* or **encerramiento** *m* locking up, confinement; encirclement; jail, lockup; retreat, retirement
encerrar §18 *va* to shut in, lock in, lock up, confine; to encircle; to contain, to include; to involve, imply; *vr* to stay in the house; to lock oneself in; to go into seclusion
encerrona *f* (coll.) voluntary confinement; (coll.) trap; **dar una encerrona a** (coll.) to gang up on (*in gambling*); **hacer la encerrona** (coll.) to go into brief voluntary confinement
encespedar *va* to sod, to cover with sod
encestar *va* to put in a basket; (basketball) to put (*the ball*) through the basket
encía *f* (anat.) gum
encíclica *f* encyclical
enciclopedia *f* encyclopedia; **enciclopedia ambulante** or **viviente** walking encyclopedia
enciclopédico -ca *adj* encyclopedic
enciclopedismo *m* encyclopedism
enciclopedista *mf* encyclopedist
encierro *m* locking up, confinement; encirclement; inclusion; inclosure; prison, lockup; solitary confinement; (taur.) pen for bulls before fight; (taur.) driving bulls into pen before fight; retreat, retirement
encima *adv* above, overhead, at the top; besides, in addition; at hand, upon us; with you, e.g., **¿Tiene Vd. encima diez pesetas?** Do you have ten pesetas with you?; **de encima** (Am.) in the bargain; **echarse encima** to take upon oneself; **pasar por encima** to push right through; to push one's way to the top; **por encima** hastily, superficially; **por encima de** above, over; in spite of, against the will of; **quitar de encima a uno** to free one from, to take off one's shoulders; **quitarse de encima a** to shake off, get rid of; **encima de** on, upon; above, over
encimar *va* to put on top, to raise high; (Am.) to throw in; *vr* to rise above
encimero -ra *adj* top; superficial
encina *f* (bot.) holm oak, evergreen oak
encinal *m* or **encinar** *m* woods of oak, oak grove
encinilla *f* (bot.) germander
encino *m* (Am.) var. of **encina**
encinta *adj* pregnant, enceinte
encintado -da *adj* beribboned; *m* curb, curbing
encintar *va* to ribbon, beribbon; to install curbs in (*a street*)
encismar *va* to sow discord among
encizañador -dora *mf* var. of **cizañador**
encizañamiento *m* var. of **cizañamiento**
encizañar *va* var. of **cizañar**
enclaustrar *va* to cloister; to hide away
enclavación *f* nailing
enclavadura *f* pricking a horse's foot; groove, mortise; nails, nailing
enclavamiento *m* lock, locking; (med.) enclavement; (rail.) interlocking system (*of signals*)
enclavar *va* to nail; to prick (*a horse's foot*); to pierce, transfix; to lock; to enclave; (coll.) to deceive, cheat
enclave *m* (geog.) enclave
enclavijar *va* to pin, to dowel; to peg (*a string instrument*)
enclenque *adj* weak, feeble, sickly; *mf* sickly person
enclítico -ca *adj* (gram. & obstet.) enclitic; *m* (gram.) enclitic
enclocar §95 *vn & vr* to brood
encloquecer §34 *vn* var. of **enclocar**
encobar *vn & vr* to brood
encobertado -da *adj* (coll.) covered with a bedspread
encobijar *va* var. of **cobijar**
encobrado -da *adj* coppery
encobrar *va* to coat with copper
encoclar §77 *vn & vr* var. of **enclocar**
encocorar *va* (coll.) to annoy greatly; *vr* (coll.) to be greatly annoyed
encochado -da *adj* coach-riding
encodillar *vr* to hole up in a bend of the burrow (*said of a ferret or hare*)
encofrado *m* (min.) planking, timbering; (min.) planked gallery; form (*for concrete*)
encofrar *va* (min.) to plank, to timber; to build a form for (*concrete*)
encoger §49 *va* to shrink, contract; to intimidate, discourage; to let (*one's shoulders*) droop; *vn* to shrink, shrivel; *vr* to shrink, contract; to be bashful or timid; to cringe; **encogerse de hombros** to shrug one's shoulders
encogido -da *adj* timid, bashful
encogimiento *m* shrinking, shrinkage; timidity, bashfulness; crouch, crouching; **encogimiento de hombros** shrug, shrug of the shoulders
encogollar *vr* to climb to the treetops (*said of game*); to be proud, be haughty
encohetar *va* to harass (*an animal*) with firecrackers; *vr* (Am.) to get raving mad; (Am.) to get drunk
encojar *va* to cripple, to lame; *vr* to become lame; (coll.) to fall ill, to feign illness
encolado *m*, **encoladura** *f* or **encolamiento** *m* gluing; sizing; clarification (*of wine*)
encolar *va* to glue; to size; to throw out of reach; to clarify (*wine*); *vr* to be thrown out of reach, to be out of reach
encolerizar §76 *va* to anger, irritate; *vr* to become angry
encomendado *m* vassal of a knight commander
encomendamiento *m* charge, commission
encomendar §18 *va* to entrust, commend, commit; to knight; *vn* to hold a knight commandery or encomienda; *vr* to commend oneself, to commit oneself; to send regards
encomendero *m* encomendero (*holder of an encomienda*)
encomiable *adj* praiseworthy
encomiador -dora *adj* praising; *mf* encomiast
encomiar *va* to praise, to eulogize
encomiasta *m* encomiast
encomiástico -ca *adj* encomiastic
encomienda *f* charge, commission; praise, commendation; protection, favor; (eccl.) commendam; encomienda (*a Spanish dignity and estate; land in America and inhabiting Indians granted to Spanish colonists*); knight's cross (*of military orders*); (Am.) parcel-post package; **encomiendas** *fpl* regards, compliments; **en encomienda** (eccl.) in commendam
encomio *m* encomium
encompadrar *vn* (coll.) to become related as godfather and father; (coll.) to become close friends
enconado -da *adj* bitter, unfriendly
enconamiento *m* soreness, sore spot; rancor, ill will
enconar *va* to make sore, inflame; to poison (*someone's mind*); to irritate, aggravate, provoke; to rankle; *vr* to get sore, become inflamed; to become irritated or provoked; to rankle; (Am.) to filch, to snitch; **enconarse con** to be provoked at or with
enconchado -da *adj* (Am.) inlaid with pearl or mother-of-pearl
enconchar *vr* (Am.) to draw back into one's shell, to keep aloof
encongar §59 *vr* (Am.) to get furious
encono *m* rancor, ill will
enconoso -sa *adj* sore, sensitive; harmful; rancorous, malevolent
encontradizo -za *adj* bobbing up all the time; **hacerse el encontradizo** to try to be met (seemingly) by chance
encontrado -da *adj* opposite; opposing, contrary; hostile; **estar encontrado con** to be at odds with; **estar encontrados** to be at odds
encontrar §77 *va* to meet, to encounter; to find; *vn* to collide; *vr* to meet, to meet each other; to find oneself, to be found, to be situated, to be; to conflict; **encontrarse con** to meet, run into, run across, encounter; **encontrarse con que** to find to one's surprise that
encontrón *m* or **encontronazo** *m* jolt, collision
encopetado -da *adj* conceited, boastful; of noble descent, aristocratic; (Am.) drunk
encopetar *va* to raise (*the hair*) high over the forehead; *vr* to rise high over the forehead; to be conceited, to boast
encorachar *va* to put in a leather bag
encorajar *va* to give courage to; *vr* to fly into a rage
encorajinar *vr* (coll.) to get angry, fly into a rage

encorar **§77** *va* to cover with leather, to wrap in leather; to grow new skin over (*a sore*); *vn & vr* to grow new skin, to heal
encorazado -da *adj* covered with a cuirass; covered with leather
encorchar *va* to hive (*bees*); to cork (*bottles*)
encorchetar *va* to put hooks or clasps on; to fasten with hooks or clasps; to clamp
encordadura *f* strings (*of a musical instrument*)
encordaje *m* stringing (*of musical instrument or tennis racket*)
encordar **§77** *va* to string (*musical instrument, tennis racket, etc.*); to bind, to wrap (*with ropes, etc.*)
encordelar *va* to string; to tie with strings or cords
encordonar *va* to cord, to tie with cords
encorecer **§34** *va* to grow new skin over (*a sore*); *vn* to grow new skin, to heal
encoriación *f* healing (*of a sore or wound*)
encornado -da *adj* horned; **bien encornado** with good horns; **mal encornado** with poor horns
encornadura *f* horns, set of horns
encornudar *va* to cuckold, to make a cuckold of; *vn* to grow horns
encorozar **§76** *va* (Am.) to smooth up (*a wall*)
encorralar *va* to corral (*cattle*)
encorrear *va* to strap, to tie with a strap or straps
encorsetar *va & vr* to put a corset on, to lace a corset on tight
encortinar *va* to put curtains on; to provide with curtains
encorvada *f* stoop, bending; buck, bucking; cancan (*dance*); (bot.) hatchet vetch; **hacer la encorvada** (coll.) to malinger
encorvadura *f* or **encorvamiento** *m* bending, curving, curvature
encorvar *va* to bend, to curve; *vr* to bend over, to stoop; to buck; to be biased, be partial
encostalar *va* to bag, put in bags
encostillado *m* lagging (*in a mine or tunnel*)
encostradura *f* crust; (arch.) incrustation (*e.g., of marble*); whitewashing
encostrar *va* to cover with crust, to put crust on; to incrust (*e.g., marble*); *vr* to crust; to form a scab
encovadura *f* placing in the cellar; locking away, hiding
encovar **§77** *va* to put in the cellar; to keep, to lock away, to hide away; *vr* to hole up, to hide away
encrasar *va* to thicken; to fertilize
encrespado -da *adj* curly; rough, choppy; *m* curling the hair
encrespador *m* curling iron; hair curler
encrespadura *f* curling the hair
encrespamiento *m* curling; standing on end (*of hair*); roughness (*of waves*)
encrespar *va* to curl; to set (*the hair*) on end; to ruffle (*feathers*); to stir up (*the waves*); to anger; *vr* to curl; to stand on end; to become rough (*said of waves*); to become entangled; to bristle, to get angry
encrestado -da *adj* haughty, arrogant
encrestar *vr* to stiffen the crest or comb; to be haughty
encrucijada *f* crossroads; street intersection; ambush; chance to do harm
encrudecer **§34** *va* to make raw or sore; to irritate, exasperate; *vr* to get raw
encruelecer **§34** *va* to excite to cruelty, make cruel; *vr* to become cruel; to get furious
encuadernación *f* (b.b.) binding; bookbinding; bindery; **encuadernación a la holandesa** half binding; **encuadernación en pasta** cardboard binding
encuadernador -dora *mf* bookbinder; *m* clip, pin
encuadernar *va* to bind (*a book*); **sin encuadernar** unbound
encuadramiento *m* framing; encompassment
encuadrar *va* to frame; to fit in, to insert; to include; to encompass; (Am.) to summarize; *vn* to fit
encuadre *m* film adaptation (*of play, novel, etc.*); (mov. & telv.) frame; (telv.) vertical hold
encuarte *m* extra draft horse
encubar *va* to cask, to vat (*wine, etc.*); (min.) to shore up (*a shaft*)
encubertar **§18** *va* to trap, to caparison; to trap in mourning; to trap for war
encubierta *f* see **encubierto**
encubiertamente *adv* secretly; slyly, deceitfully; cautiously
encubierto -ta *pp of* **encubrir**; *f* fraud, deceit
encubridizo -za *adj* easily hidden, easily concealed
encubridor -dora *mf* concealer; (law) accessory after the fact
encubrimiento *m* concealment; (law) complicity
encubrir **§17,** 9 *va* to hide, conceal; to keep under cover; to feign, pretend; to include, comprise, involve; (law) to harbor, screen, conceal; *vr* to hide; to conceal one's identity, to disguise oneself
encuentro *m* meeting, encounter; clash, collision; find; joint; game, match; (print.) space, blank (*for insertion of letter of different color*); (mil.) encounter; **llevarse de encuentro** (Am.) to knock down, run over; (Am.) to drag down to ruin; **mal encuentro** unlucky encounter, foul play; **salir al encuentro a** to go to meet; to oppose, take a stand against; to get ahead of; **encuentro fronterizo** border clash
encuerar *va* (Am.) to strip, to undress; (Am.) to fleece
encuesta *f* inquiry; poll; survey (*e.g., of public opinion*)
encuevar *va & vr* var. of **encovar**
encuitar *vr* to grieve
enculatar *va* to cover (*a beehive*)
encumbrado -da *adj* high, lofty; stately, sublime; mighty, influential
encumbramiento *m* elevation, height, eminence; exaltation
encumbrar *va* to raise, elevate; to exalt, to honor, to dignify; to extol; to climb to the top of; *vr* to rise; to be highly honored; to be proud, be haughty; to tower; to be magniloquent
encunar *va* to put in the cradle; to catch between the horns
encureñar *va* to put on the gun carriage
encurtido *m* pickle
encurtir *va* to pickle (*fruit and vegetables*)
enchancletar *va* to put slippers on; to drag (*one's shoes*) like slippers
enchapado *m* veneer, overlay, plating
enchapar *va* to veneer, to overlay, to plate
encharcada *f* pool, puddle
encharcamiento *m* pooling, puddling
encharcar **§86** *va* to turn into a pool or puddle; to upset (*the stomach*); *vr* to turn into a pool or puddle; to wallow in vice
enchavetar *va* (mach.) to key
enchilada *f* (tresillo) stake in the pot; (Am.) corn cake seasoned with chili
enchilado *m* (Am.) shellfish stew with chili sauce; (bot.) chanterelle; (orn.) western meadow lark
enchilar *va* (Am.) to season with chili; (Am.) to anger; (Am.) to disappoint
enchinar *va* to pave with pebbles; (Am.) to curl (*hair*); *vr* to be covered with goose flesh
enchinarrar *va* to pave with cobbles
enchiquerar *va* to shut in the bull pen; (coll.) to jail
enchironar *va* (coll.) to jail
enchivar *vr* (Am.) to fly into a rage
enchufable *adj* fitting; plug-in
enchufamiento *m* fitting; connecting; merging
enchufar *va* to fit (*a pipe*); to connect (*two pipes*) together; (elec.) to connect, to plug in; to fit together; to merge (*two businesses*); *vn* to fit (*said of a pipe*); *vr* to merge
enchufe *m* fitting; male end (*of pipe*); joint (*of two pipes*); (elec.) connector, plug and jack, plug and receptacle; (elec.) plug; (elec.) receptacle; (coll.) political sinecure; **tener enchufe** (coll.) to have a drag, to have pull; **tener un enchufe** (coll.) to have a sinecure

enchufismo *m* (coll.) political sinecurism, holding an extra job through political influence
enchufista *mf* (coll.) political sinecurist, holder of an extra job through political influence
enchuletar *va* (carp.) to fill in
ende; por ende therefore
endeble *adj* feeble, weak; worthless; fragile, flimsy
endeblez *f* feebleness, weakness; worthlessness; fragility, flimsiness
endécada *f* eleven years
endecágono -na *adj* (geom.) hendecagonal; *m* (geom.) hendecagon, undecagon
endecasílabo -ba *adj* hendecasyllabic; *m* hendecasyllable
endecha *f* dirge; assonanced seven-syllabled quatrain; **endecha real** assonanced seven-syllabled quatrain whose last line is hendecasyllabic
endechadera *f* weeper, professional mourner
endechar *va* to sing a dirge to; *vr* to grieve, to mourn
endehesar *va* to put to pasture
endejas *fpl* (mas.) toothing
endemia *f* endemic
endémico -ca *adj* endemic
endemoniado -da *adj* possessed of the devil; furious, violent, wild; (coll.) devilish, fiendish; *mf* person possessed
endemoniar *va* to possess with the devil; (coll.) to anger, irritate; *vr* (coll.) to be angered or irritated
endentado -da *adj* (her.) serrated, indented
endentar §18 *va* to mesh, to engage; to tooth, furnish with teeth; to key; *vn* to mesh, to engage
endentecer §34 *vn* to teethe
enderezadamente *adv* straight, honestly
enderezado -da *adj* favorable, fitting, opportune; straight; fair, right
enderezador -dora *mf* good manager, person who knows how to straighten things out; *m* straightener (*tool*)
enderezamiento *m* straightening; standing
enderezar §76 *va* to straighten; to stand up; to cock; to put in order, to regulate; to fix, to punish; to direct; to dedicate; (aer.) to flatten out; *vn* to go straight; *vr* to straighten; to stand up, to straighten up; to get back on a sound footing; to go straight; to go, to make one's way, to head; (aer.) to flatten out; **enderezarse a** + *inf* to take steps to + *inf*
enderrotar *va & vn* (naut.) to head
endeudar *vr* to run into debt; to acknowledge indebtedness
endevotado -da *adj* pious, devout; fond, devoted
endiablada *f* see **endiablado**
endiabladamente *adv* horribly
endiablado -da *adj* devilish; ugly, deformed; annoying, pestiferous; (Am.) complicated, difficult; (Am.) dangerous, risky; *f* noisy masquerade
endiablar *va* to entangle, confuse; to bewitch; (coll.) to pervert, to corrupt; *vr* to be furious, be in a rage; (coll.) to be perverted or corrupted
endíadis *f* (rhet.) hendiadys
endibia *f* (bot.) endive
endilgar §59 *va* (coll.) to direct, send; (coll.) to help, to guide; (coll.) to hasten, expedite; (coll.) to spring, let go, unload (*something unpleasant*); *vr* (coll.) to slip away, slip out
Endimión *m* (myth.) Endymion
endino -na *adj* (coll.) wicked, vile
endiosamiento *m* pride, conceit, vanity; absorption, abstraction
endiosar *va* to deify; *vr* to be stuck-up; to be absorbed (*e.g., in reading*)
endocardio *m* (anat.) endocardium
endocarditis *f* (path.) endocarditis
endocarpio *m* (bot.) endocarp
endocrino -na *adj & f* (physiol.) endocrine
endocrinología *f* endocrinology
endodermo *m* (bot.) endodermis
endoesqueleto *m* (zool.) endoskeleton
endogamia *f* endogamy, inbreeding; (biol.) endogamy
endogénesis *f* (biol.) endogeny
endógeno -na *adj* endogenous
endolinfa *f* (anat.) endolymph
endomingado -da *adj* (worn on) Sunday; dressed in one's Sunday clothes
endomingar §59 *vr* to dress up in one's Sunday clothes
endomisio *m* (anat.) endomysium
endoparásito *m* (zool.) endoparasite
endoplasma *m* (biol.) endoplasm
endorsar *va* var. of **endosar**
endorso *m* var. of **endoso**
endosante *mf* indorser
endosar *va* to indorse; to unload (*a task or something unpleasant*)
endosatario -ria *mf* indorsee
endoscopio *m* (med.) endoscope
endose *m* (Am.) var. of **endoso**
endoselar *va* to hang with a canopy or dais
endosmosis *f* or **endósmosis** *f* (phys., chem. & physiol.) endosmosis
endoso *m* indorsement
endospermo *m* (bot.) endosperm
endospora *f* (bot. & bact.) endospore
endotecio *m* (bot.) endothecium
endotelio *m* (anat.) endothelium
endotérmico -ca *adj* (chem.) endothermic
endriago *m* fabulous monster
endrino -na *adj* sloe-colored; *m* (bot.) sloe, blackthorn; *f* sloe (*fruit*)
endrogar §59 *vr* (Am.) to run into debt
endulzadura *f* sweetening; mitigation
endulzar §76 *va* to sweeten; to soften, mitigate, make bearable
endurador -dora *adj* saving, stingy
endurancia *f* (sport) endurance
endurar *va* to harden; to suffer, endure; to delay, put off; to save; *vr* to harden, get hard
endurecer §34 *va* to harden; to inure; *vr* to harden; to become inured; to become hardened or cruel
endurecido -da *adj* hard, strong; inured, experienced; hard-hearted; tenacious, obstinate; (phys.) hard (*ray*)
endurecimiento *m* hardening; hardness; hardheartedness; tenacity, obstinacy; **endurecimiento arterial** (path.) hardening of the arteries
enea *f* var. of **anea**
eneágono *m* (geom.) nonagon
Eneas *m* (myth.) Aeneas
enebral *m* growth of juniper trees
enebrina *f* juniper berry
enebro *m* (bot.) juniper; **enebro de la miera** (bot.) cade
enechado -da *adj & mf* foundling
Eneida *f* Aeneid
enejar *va* to put an axle or axles on; to fasten to the axle
eneldo *m* (bot.) dill
enema *f* (med.) enema; **enema de bario** or **enema opaca** (med.) barium enema
enemigo -ga *adj* enemy; inimical, hostile; *mf* enemy, foe; **el enemigo malo** the Evil One; **el enemigo número uno** the enemy number one; **enemigo jurado** sworn enemy; **enemigo público** public enemy; *f* enmity, ill will, hatred
enemistad *f* enmity
enemistar *va* to estrange, to make enemies of; *vr* to become enemies; **enemistarse con** to become estranged from
éneo -a *adj* (poet.) bronze, aënean
energético -ca *adj* (phys.) (pertaining to) energy; (elec.) (pertaining to) power; *f* energetics
energía *f* energy; **energía actual** (phys.) kinetic energy; **energía atómica** (phys.) atomic energy; **energía blanca** water power; **energía cinética** (phys.) kinetic energy; **energía eléctrica** electric power; **energía hidráulica** water power; **energía libre** (phys.) free energy; **energía potencial** (phys.) potential energy; **energía radiante** (phys.) radiant energy; **energía térmica** steam-generated power; **energía viva** (phys.) kinetic energy
enérgico -ca *adj* energetic
energúmeno -na *mf* energumen; wild person, crazy person
enero *m* January

enervación *f* enervation; weakening; effemination, effeminacy
enervador -dora *adj* enervating
enervamiento *m* enervation
enervar *va* to enervate; to weaken; to effeminate
enésimo -ma *adj* (math.) nth
enfadadizo -za *adj* irritable, peevish
enfadar *va* to annoy, to anger, to bother; *vr* to be annoyed, get angry
enfado *m* annoyance; anger, irritation; trouble, bother
enfadoso -sa *adj* annoying, bothersome
enfaldador *m* large pin for tucking up or fastening skirt
enfaldar *va* to lop off the lower branches of; *vr* to tuck up one's skirt
enfaldo *m* tucked-up skirt; hollow made by holding up skirt to carry something
enfangar §59 *va* to muddy, cover with mud; *vr* to sink in the mud; to get involved in dirty business; to be sunk in vice
enfardar *va* to bale, to pack
enfardelador -dora *mf* packer
enfardeladura *f* bundling; packing
enfardelar *va* to bundle; to bale, to pack
énfasis (*pl:* **-sis**) *m & f* emphasis; *m* bombast, affectation
enfático -ca *adj* emphatic
enfermar *va* to sicken, make sick; *vn* to sicken, get sick; **enfermar del corazón** to have heart trouble
enfermedad *f* sickness, illness, disease; **enfermedad bronceada** or **enfermedad de Addison** (path.) Addison's disease; **enfermedad carencial** deficiency disease; **enfermedad del mosaico** (plant path.) mosaic disease; **enfermedad del sueño** (path.) sleeping sickness; **enfermedad de Parkinson** (path.) Parkinson's disease; **enfermedad de pecho** (path.) tuberculosis, consumption; **enfermedad de radiación** (path.) radiation sickness; **enfermedad mental** mental disease; **enfermedad por carencia** (med.) deficiency disease; **enfermedad profesional** occupational disease; **enfermedad venérea** veneral disease
enfermera *f* see **enfermero**
enfermería *f* infirmary; sanitarium; (naut.) sick bay; patients, sufferers
enfermero -ra *mf* nurse; **enfermera ambulante** visiting nurse
enfermizo -za *adj* sickly; unhealthy (*e.g., climate*)
enfermo -ma *adj* sick, ill; sickly; **caer enfermo** to take sick; **enfermo de amor** lovesick; *mf* patient; **el enfermo de Europa** the Sick Man of Europe (*Turkey*)
enfermoso -sa *adj* (Am.) sickish, sickly
enfermucho -cha *adj* (coll.) sickish
enfervorizador -dora *adj* inspiring, encouraging
enfervorizar §76 *va* to inspire, encourage
enfeudación *f* (law) enfeoffment (*act and instrument*)
enfeudar *va* (law) to enfeoff (*to give as a fief*)
enfielar *va* to balance (*scales*)
enfiestar *vr* (Am.) to have a good time, to be on a lark
enfilado -da *adj* (her.) enfiled; *f* (mil.) enfilade
enfilamiento *m* enfilade, alignment
enfilar *va* to enfilade, to line up; to string (*e.g., pearls*); to aim; to go down, go up (*e.g., the street*); (mil.) to enfilade
enfisema *m* (path.) emphysema
enfistolar *va & vr* to turn into a fistula
enfiteusis *m & f* (law) emphyteusis
enfiteuta *mf* emphyteuta
enfitéutico -ca *adj* emphyteutic
enflacar §86 *vn* to get thin
enflaquecer §34 *va* to make thin; to weaken; *vn* to get thin; to flag, grow spiritless; *vr* to get thin, lose weight
enflaquecimiento *m* loss of flesh, loss of weight; weakening
enflautado -da *adj* (coll.) inflated, pompous
enflautador -dora *mf* (coll.) procurer, bawd
enflautar *va* to blow up, inflate; (coll.) to cheat, deceive; (coll.) to procure
enflechado -da *adj* with the arrow ready to shoot (*said of a bow*)
enfloración *f* enfleurage
enflorar *va* to flower, adorn with flowers
enfocamiento *m* focusing
enfocar §86 *va* to focus; (fig.) to size up; *vr* to focus; **enfocarse a** + *inf* to focus one's attention on + *ger*
enfoque *m* focus, focusing; approach (*to a problem*)
enfosado *m* var. of **encebadamiento**
enfoscar §86 *va* (mas.) to patch or fill with mortar; to trim with mortar; *vr* to become grumpy; to become immersed in business; to get cloudy
enfrailado -da *adj* cloistered; monkish
enfrailar *va* to make a monk or friar of; *vn & vr* to become a monk or friar
enfranque *m* shank (*of the sole of a shoe*)
enfranquecer §34 *va* to enfranchise, to set free
enfrascamiento *m* entanglement, involvement
enfrascar §86 *va* to bottle; *vr* to become entangled, become involved; to be overloaded with work; to be having a lot of fun
enfrenador -dora *mf* bridler
enfrenamiento *m* bridling; checking, restraining; (mach.) braking
enfrenar *va* to bridle; to check with the bit or bridle; (mach.) to brake; to check, restrain
enfrentamiento *m* confrontation; opposition; alignment
enfrentar *va* to confront, to put face to face; to face; to meet (*opposition*); *vn* to be opposite each other, to be facing; **enfrentar con** to be opposite, to be across from; *vr* to meet face to face; **enfrentarse con** to confront; to face, to stand up to, to cope with
enfrente *adv* in front, opposite; **enfrente de** in front of, opposite; against, opposed to
enfriadera *f* bottle cooler, wine cooler, ice pail
enfriadero *m* cooling place; cold storage
enfriador -dora *adj* cooling; *m* cooling place
enfriamiento *m* cooling, refrigeration; (path.) cold
enfriar §90 *va* to cool, to make cold, to chill; to temper; (Am.) to kill; *vn* to cool off, to turn cold; *vr* to cool off, to turn cold; to be tempered
enfroscar §86 *vr* to become entangled, become involved
enfullar *va* (coll.) to make (*a game*) crooked
enfundadura *f* casing, sheathing
enfundar *va* to sheathe, to put (*e.g., a pillow*) in its case; to stuff, to fill; to contain; to muffle (*a drum*)
enfurción *f* var. of **infurción**
enfurecer §34 *va* to infuriate, enrage; *vr* to rage, become infuriated
enfurecimiento *m* infuriation
enfurruñamiento *m* sulk, sulkiness
enfurruñar *vr* (coll.) to sulk; (dial.) to get cloudy
enfurtir *va* to full (*cloth*); to felt
engabanado -da *adj* overcoated, wearing an overcoat
engace *m* union, connection
engafar *va* to bend (*crossbow*); to hook; to half-cock (*a gun*)
engaitador -dora *adj* (coll.) beguiling, deluding, cozening, humbugging
engaitar *va* (coll.) to beguile, delude, cozen, humbug
engalanar *va* to adorn, bedeck; (naut.) to dress
engalgar §59 *va* to scotch (*a wheel*); (naut.) to back (*an anchor*)
engallado -da *adj* straight, erect; haughty
engallador *m* checkrein
engalladura *f* var. of **galladura**
engallar *va* to stand up straight and haughty; *vr* to stand up straight and haughty; to raise the head held close to the chest (*said of a horse*)
enganchador *m* (rail.) brakeman; recruiting officer
enganchamiento *m* hooking, coupling; inveigling; recruiting
enganchar *va* to hook; to couple; to hang or catch on a hook; to hitch; (coll.) to inveigle; to inveigle into enlisting, to recruit; *vn* to be

hooked; to get caught (*e.g., on a hook*); *vr* to be hooked; to get caught (*e.g., on a hook*); to enlist
enganche *m* hooking; hook; inveigling; enlisting; recruiting of labor; (rail.) coupler, coupling
engañabobos (*pl:* **-bos**) *mf* (coll.) bamboozler; *m* (coll.) bamboozle
engañadizo -za *adj* easily deceived, deceivable
engañador -dora *adj* deceptive; winsome; *mf* cheat
engañapastores *m* (*pl:* **-res**) (orn.) goatsucker
engañar *va* to deceive, fool, cheat; to while away (*time*); to ward off (*hunger, sleep*); to make appetizing; *vr* to deceive oneself; to be mistaken
engañifa *f* (coll.) trick, cheat; (coll.) catchpenny
engaño *m* deceit, fraud; falsehood; mistake, misunderstanding; **llamarse a engaño** (coll.) to claim deception, to back out because of misrepresentation
engañoso -sa *adj* deceitful; deceptive
engarabatar *va* to hook; to make crooked; *vr* to get crooked
engarabitar *vn* (coll.) to climb; *vr* (coll.) to climb; to get stiff or numb (*from cold*)
engarbar *vr* to perch high (*said of birds*)
engarbullar *va* (coll.) to mix up, entangle
engarce *m* linking; enchasing; setting
engargantadura *f* meshing (*of gears*)
engargantar *va* to put into the throat; *vn* to mesh, to engage; *vr* to mesh, to engage; to put one's foot in the stirrup up to the instep
engargante *m* meshing (*of gears*)
engargolado *m* groove for sliding door; tongue-and-groove joint
engargolar *va* to groove, to mortise; to fit (*pipes*)
engaritar *va* to equip with sentry boxes; (coll.) to trick
engarnio *m* (coll.) var. of **plepa**
engarrafar *va* (coll.) to grapple, to seize tightly
engarrar *va* to seize
engarro *m* seizing, seizure
engarzadura *f* var. of **engarce**
engarzar §76 *va* to link, to wire (*jewels*); to enchase; to curl
engastador -dora *mf* enchaser, setter
engastar *va* to enchase, to set, to mount
engaste *m* enchasing; setting, mounting; flat pearl
engatado -da *adj* thievish
engatar *va* (coll.) to cheat, to take in
engatillado -da *adj* having a high, thick neck (*said of a horse or bull*); *m* (mach.) flat-lock seaming, grooved seaming
engatillar *va* to clamp, to cramp; to fit (*floor beams*); to joint (*sheets of metal*) with flat-lock seams
engatusador -dora *adj* (coll.) wheedling, coaxing; *mf* (coll.) wheedler, coaxer
engatusamiento *m* (coll.) wheedling, coaxing, blandishment
engatusar *va* (coll.) to wheedle, to coax, to blandish; **engatusar para que** + *subj* to inveigle into + *ger*
engavetar *va* (Am.) to pigeonhole
engavillar *va* var. of **agavillar**
engazar §76 *va* to link, to wire (*jewels*); to enchase; to curl; to dye in the cloth; (naut.) to strap (*blocks*)
engendrador -dora *adj* engendering, begetting, generating; *mf* begetter, generator
engendramiento *m* engendering, generation, begetting
engendrar *va* to engender, beget; (geom.) to generate
engendro *m* foetus; stunt (*animal or plant*); botch, bungle; (coll.) runt; (coll.) clownish person; **mal engendro** (coll.) unruly youth, young tough
engeridor *m* (hort.) grafter; grafting knife
engibar *va* to make humpbacked
englandado -da or **englantado -da** *adj* (her.) acorned
englobar *va* to include, lump together
engolado -da *adj* (her.) engouled
engolfar *vn* to go far out on the ocean; *vr* to go far out on the ocean; to become deeply absorbed, to be lost in thought; to let oneself go
engolillado -da *adj* wearing a ruff; wearing a lawyer's collar; (coll.) proud of observing old styles
engolondrinar *va* (coll.) to make vain or conceited; *vr* (coll.) to be or get vain or conceited; (coll.) to have a trifling love affair
engolosinador -dora *adj* alluring, tempting
engolosinar *va* to allure, to tempt; *vr* to take a liking; **engolosinarse con** to take a liking for
engollamiento *m* presumption, vanity
engolletar *vr* (coll.) to be vain or conceited
engomado -da *adj* starchy; (Am.) spruce, all dressed up; *m* gumming (*of a postage stamp*); gummy paste
engomadura *f* gumming; first coat which bees give to their hives
engomar *va* to gum (*fabrics, papers, etc.*)
engorar §19 *va* to addle
engorda *f* (Am.) fattening; (Am.) animals being fattened
engordadero *m* fattening sty; fattening time; fodder for fattening
engordador -dora *adj* fattening; *mf* fattener
engordar *va* to fatten; *vn* to get fat; (coll.) to fatten, get fat (*rich*)
engorde *m* fattening
engorro *m* obstacle, nuisance, bother
engorroso -sa *adj* annoying, bothersome
engoznar *va* to hinge, to fasten with hinges
Engracia *f* Grace
engranaje *m* gearing, gears, gear; (fig.) bond, connection; **engranaje de distribución** (aut.) timing gears; **engranaje de marcha atrás** (aut.) reverse gear; **engranaje de tornillo sin fin** worm gear; **engranaje diferencial** differential gear
engranar *va* to gear; to unite, to interlock; *vn* to gear
engrandar *va* var. of **agrandar**
engrandecer §34 *va* to enlarge, amplify, magnify; to enhance; to extol; to elevate, to exalt; *vr* to be exalted
engrandecimiento *m* enlargement, amplification; enhancement; praise; exaltation
engrane *m* gear, gearing; mesh, meshing
engranerar *va* to store (*grain*)
engranujar *vr* to become pimply; (coll.) to go to the bad
engrapador -dora *m & f* stapler
engrapar *va* to clamp, to cramp
engrasación *f* greasing, lubrication
engrasadera *f* grease cup
engrasado *m* var. of **engrase**
engrasador -dora *adj* grease, greasing; *mf* greaser; *m* grease cup; oiler (*of wool*)
engrasamiento *m* var. of **engrasación**
engrasar *va* to grease, lubricate; to smear or stain with grease; to foul; to dress (*cloth*); to fertilize; *vr* to get smeared or stained with grease; to foul
engrase *m* greasing, lubrication; grease
engravar *va* to gravel, to spread gravel over
engravecer §34 *va* to make heavy; *vr* to get heavy
engredar *va* to clay, to chalk
engreído -da *adj* vain, conceited
engreimiento *m* vanity, conceit
engreír §73 *va* to make vain or conceited; *vr* to become vain or conceited
engreñado -da *adj* disheveled
engrescar §86 *va* to goad into fighting; to stir to merriment; *vr* to pick a fight; to be stirred to merriment, to join the merriment
engrifar *va* to curl, to crisp, to crimp; to make (*hair*) stand on end; *vr* to curl up; to stand on end; to rear
engrillar *va* to shackle, to put in irons; *vr* to shoot, sprout (*said of potatoes*)
engrilletar *va* to shackle, to fetter; (naut.) to shackle (*two lengths of chain*)
engringar §59 *vr* to imitate the ways of foreigners (*especially Americans and Englishmen*)
engrosamiento *m* broadening; increase, enlargement

engrosar §77 *va* to thicken, broaden; to enlarge; *vn* to get fat; *vr* to thicken, broaden; to become enlarged, to swell
engrudador -dora *mf* paster; *m* pasting brush or tool
engrudamiento *m* pasting
engrudar *va* to paste
engrudo *m* paste; belt dressing
engruesar *vn* to get fat
engrumecer §34 *vr* to clot, to curdle
engualdrapar *va* to caparison
enguantar *va & vr* to put gloves on
enguatar *va* to line or interline with raw cotton
enguedejado -da *adj* in long locks; wearing long locks; (coll.) proud of one's long locks
enguijarrado *m* cobblestone paving
enguijarrar *va* to pave with cobblestones
enguillar *va* (naut.) to wind (*a heavy rope*) with a thin rope
enguillotar *vr* to rush in eagerly, to get involved
enguirnaldar *va* to enwreathe, to garland; to trim, bedeck
enguizgar §59 *va* to incite, stimulate
engullidor -dora *mf* gulper, gobbler
engullir §26 *va* to gulp down; (fig.) to swallow (*nonsense*)
engurrio *m* sadness, melancholy
enhacinar *va* var. of **hacinar**
enharinar *va* to cover with flour, to smear with flour
enhastiar §90 *va* to cloy; to annoy, to bore
enhastillar *va* to put arrows in (*a quiver*)
enhatijar *va* to close or shut (*a beehive*) with esparto netting
enhebillar *va* to put a buckle on (*a strap*)
enhebrar *va* to thread (*a needle*); to string (*e.g., pearls*); (coll.) to rattle off (*e.g., lies*)
enhenar *va* to cover with hay
enherbolar *va* to poison (*arrows, etc.*) with herbs
enhestador *m* raiser, hoister
enhestadura *f* or **enhestamiento** *m* erection, raising, hoisting
enhestar §18 *va* to erect, stand straight; to hoist, raise high; *vr* to stand straight or upright; to rise high
enhielar *va* to mix with gall, to make bitter
enhiesto -ta *adj* erect, straight, upright, raised
enhilar *va* to thread; to arrange in order, to marshal (*ideas*); to line up; to direct; *vn* to move
enhorabuena *adv* safely, luckily; all right, O.K.; **enhorabuena que** + *subj* it is all right that . . . ; *f* congratulations; **dar la enhorabuena a** to congratulate
enhoramala *adv* in an evil hour, under an unlucky star, unluckily; **enviar** or **mandar enhoramala** to send to the devil; **nacer enhoramala** to be born to an unhappy fate; **vete enhoramala** go to the devil
enhorcar §86 *va* to string (*onions or garlic*)
enhornar *va* to put into an oven
enhuecar §86 *va* var. of **ahuecar**
enhuerar *va, vn, & vr* to addle; (fig.) to addle
enigma *m* enigma, puzzle, riddle
enigmático -ca *adj* enigmatic or enigmatical
enigmatista *mf* person who talks in enigmas or riddles
enjablar *va* to insert (*barrelhead*) in croze
enjabonado *m* or **enjabonadura** *f* soaping, washing
enjabonar *va* to soap; to lather; (coll.) to soft-soap; (coll.) to abuse, upbraid
enjaezar §76 *va* to trap, to put trappings on, to harness
enjaguadura *f* var. of **enjuagadura**
enjaguar §23 *va* var. of **enjuagar**
enjalbegado *m* whitewashing
enjalbegador -dora *adj* whitewashing; *mf* whitewasher
enjalbegadura *f* whitewashing
enjalbegar §59 *va* to whitewash; to paint (*the face*); *vr* to paint one's face
enjalma *f* light packsaddle
enjalmar *va* to put (*a packsaddle*) on; *vn* to make packsaddles
enjalmero *m* packsaddle maker or dealer
enjambradera *f* cell of queen bee; bee which hums as signal for swarming
enjambradero *m* swarmer (*place where bees swarm*)
enjambrar *va* to swarm (*bees*); to empty (*a hive*); *vn* to swarm (*in order to form new colony*); to increase greatly, to multiply abundantly
enjambrazón *f* swarming (*of bees*)
enjambre *m* swarm; (fig.) swarm
enjaquimar *va* to put the headstall on (*an animal*)
enjarciar *va* (naut.) to rig
enjardinar *va* to arrange (*trees or flowers*) as in a garden; to turn or convert into a garden; *vr* to spend the day in the garden
enjaretado *m* grating, lattice work
enjaretar *va* to run (*a string, cord, ribbon, etc.*) through a casing or hem; to coerce; (coll.) to put across, to spring (*something unpleasant*); (coll.) to rush headlong through; *vr* (coll.) to insinuate oneself
enjarrar *vr* (Am.) to stand akimbo
enjaular *va* to cage; to jail, imprison; (min.) to load in the cage
enjebar *va* to steep (*cloth*) in lye before dyeing; to whiten with a thin coat of plaster; (Am.) to soap
enjebe *m* alum; lye; plaster whitening
enjergar §59 *va* (coll.) to launch, to manage to get (*something*) started, to start (*something*) on a shoestring; (coll.) to string along (*words*) without rhyme or reason
enjertación *f* var. of **injertación**
enjertar *va* var. of **injertar**
enjerto *m* grafted plant; mixture, conglomeration
enjimelgar §59 *va* (naut.) to fish (*a mast, beam, etc.*)
enjoyar *va* to bejewel; to embellish; to set with precious stones
enjoyelado -da *adj* wrought into jewels; bejeweled
enjoyelador *m* setter, jeweler
enjuagadientes *m* (*pl:* **-tes**) mouthwash
enjuagadura *f* rinse, rinsing; wash
enjuagar §59 *va* to rinse, rinse out (*mouth, kettle, etc.*)
enjuagatorio *m* rinse, rinsing; wash, rinsing water; washbowl; mouthwash
enjuague *m* rinse, rinsing; wash, rinsing water; washbowl; mouthwash; plot, scheme
enjugador *m* drier; clotheshorse
enjugamanos *m* (*pl:* **-nos**) towel
enjugaparabrisas *m* (*pl:* **-sas**) windshield wiper
enjugar §59 *va* to dry; to wipe, to wipe off; (fig.) to wipe out (*e.g., a debt*); *vr* to get thin, lose weight
enjuiciamiento *m* examining, judging; (law) suit; (law) trial; (law) sentence
enjuiciar *va* to examine, take under advisement, pass judgment on; (law) to sue; (law) to try; (law) to sentence
enjulio or **enjullo** *m* cloth beam, warp rod (*of loom*)
enjuncar §86 *va* to cover with rush; to tie with rush ropes
enjundia *f* axunge; substance; force, vigor
enjundioso -sa *adj* fatty, greasy; substantial; (dial.) annoying, boring
enjunque *m* (naut.) heavy ballast, pig-iron ballast, kentledge
enjuta *f* see **enjuto**
enjutar *va* to dry (*e.g., plaster*)
enjutez *f* dryness
enjuto -ta *adj* lean, skinny; dry (*eyes; weather*); reserved, quiet, stolid; **enjutos** *mpl* brushwood; crackers, tidbits (*to excite thirst*); *f* (arch.) spandrel; (arch.) pendentive
enlabiador -dora *mf* humbug, bamboozler
enlabiar *va* to humbug, to bamboozle, to take in; to bring one's lips to, to press one's lips against
enlabio *m* humbug, bamboozle
enlace *m* lacing, linking, connection; liaison; relationship; marriage; engagement, betrothal; (chem.) linkage; (rail.) connection; (rail.)

crossover; **enlace domiciliario** (Am.) house service
enlaciar *va, vn & vr* to wither; to rumple
enladrillado *m* brick paving, brick pavement; bricklaying; brickwork
enladrillador *m* brick paver, bricklayer
enladrilladura *f* var. of **enladrillado**
enladrillar *va* to pave with bricks; to brick
enlagunar *va & vr* to flood
enlajado *m* (Am.) flagstone
enlajar *va* (Am.) to pave with flagstones
enlamar *va* to cover with silt
enlanado -da *adj* woolly
enlardar *va* (cook.) to baste
enlatado *m* canning
enlatar *va* to can; (dial. & Am.) to put a tin roof on, to roof with tin
enlazador -dora *adj* linking, connecting; *mf* connecter
enlazadura *f* or **enlazamiento** *m* var. of **enlace**
enlazar §76 *va* to lace, to enlace, to link, to connect; to lasso; *vn* to connect (*said, e.g., of two trains*); *vr* to be linked, be connected; to connect, to interlock; to get married; to become related by marriage
enlechar *va* to grout
enlegajar *va* to arrange (*papers*) in a file; to file (*papers*)
enlegamar *va* to cover with mud; *vr* to get covered with mud; to silt up
enlejiar §90 *va* to put (*clothes*) in lye; (chem.) to dissolve (*an alkaline substance*) in water
enlenzar §31 *va* to strengthen (*woodwork, especially, wood carvings*) with adhesive tape
enlerdar *va* to slow down, to dull
enlevaje *m* (rowing) spurt
enligar §59 *va* to smear with birdlime; *vr* to be caught with birdlime
enlistonado *m* laths, lathing
enlistonar *va* to lath, to batten
enlizar §76 *va* to add leashes to (*a loom*)
enlobreguecer §34 *va* to make dark; *vr* to get dark
enlodadura *f* or **enlodamiento** *m* muddying; muddiness
enlodar *va* to muddy, soil with mud; to plaster with mud; (chem.) to lute (*a joint, porous surface, etc.*); to seal with mud; to vilify, defame; *vr* to get muddied, be soiled with mud
enlodazar §76 *va* to muddy, bemire; *vr* to mire, mire up
enloquecedor -dora *adj* maddening
enloquecer §34 *va* to drive crazy, to madden, to distract; *vn* to go crazy; to become barren (*said of trees*)
enloquecimiento *m* madness, insanity
enlosado *m* flagstone paving
enlosador *m* flagstone paver
enlosar *va* to pave with flagstone
enlozado -da *adj* (Am.) enameled; *m* (Am.) enameling; (Am.) enamelware
enlozanar *vr* to be fresh, be luxuriant
enlozar §76 *va* (Am.) to enamel (*especially iron*)
enlucido *m* plaster, coat of plaster; plastering
enlucidor *m* plasterer
enlucimiento *m* plastering; polishing
enlucir §60 *va* to plaster (*walls*); to polish (*metal*)
enlustrecer §34 *va* to brighten, to shine
enlutado -da *mf* person dressed in mourning; *m* mourning (*especially drapery*)
enlutar *va* to put in mourning, to dress in mourning; to darken; to sadden; *vr* to be in mourning, to dress in mourning
enllantar *va* to put a rim or tire on (*a wheel*)
enllentecer §34 *va & vr* to soften
enllocar §95 *vn & vr* var. of **enclocar**
enmaderación *f* wood construction, timber work; shoring
enmaderado *m* wood construction, timber work; timber
enmaderamiento *m* wood construction, timber work
enmaderar *va* to cover with boards or timber
enmadrar *vr* to become excessively fond of one's mother
enmagrecer §34 *va* to make thin or skinny; *vn & vr* to get thin or skinny
enmalecer §34 *va* to harm, spoil, corrupt
enmalezar §76 *vr* to become overgrown with brush
enmallar *vr* to get caught in the meshes of the net (*said of a fish*)
enmangar §59 *va* to put a handle on
enmantar *va* to put a blanket on, to cover with a blanket; to cover up, to wrap up; *vr* to be melancholy
enmantecado *m* (orn.) cowbird
enmarañador -dora *adj* entangling
enmarañamiento *m* tangle; entanglement, confusion
enmarañar *va* to tangle; to entangle, confuse, mix up; *vr* to get tangled; to become entangled or confused; to fall out, become enemies; to turn dark, turn cloudy
enmarar *vr* (naut.) to reach the high sea, to get out of sight of land
enmarcar §86 *va* to frame
enmaridar *vn & vr* to marry, to take a husband
enmarillecer §34 *vr* to turn pale, to turn yellow
enmaromar *va* to tie with a rope
enmasar *va* to mass (*troops*)
enmascarado *m* mask, person wearing a mask
enmascaramiento *m* camouflage
enmascarar *va* to mask; (fig.) to mask, disguise; *vr* to put on a mask, to masquerade
enmasillar *va* to putty
enmatar *vr* to hide in the bushes (*said of game*)
enmelar §18 *va* to add honey to, to smear with honey; to sweeten; *vn* to make honey
enmendación *f* emendation, correction
enmendador -dora *mf* corrector, emender
enmendadura *f* emendation, correction
enmendar §18 *va* to emend, to correct; to amend; to make amends for; *vr* to amend, to reform, to go straight
enmienda *f* emendation, correction; amendment; amends; **enmiendas** *fpl* (agr.) amendment
enmohecer §34 *va* to make moldy; to rust; to cast aside, neglect; to dull (*e.g., the memory*); *vr* to get moldy; to rust; to fade away, disappear
enmohecimiento *m* getting moldy, moldiness; rusting; disappearance
enmollecer §34 *va & vr* to soften
enmondar *va* var. of **desliñar**
enmontar *vr* (Am.) to be overgrown with weeds and brush
enmordazar §76 *va* var. of **amordazar**
enmostar *va* to stain with grape juice; *vn* to become stained with grape juice
enmudecer §34 *va* to hush, to silence; *vr* to be silent, to keep silent; to lose the power of speech
enmuescar §86 *va* to notch; to mortise
enmugrecer §34 *va* to soil, to cover with dirt
enmustiar *va & vr* to wither
enneciar *vr* to become foolish, get stupid
ennegrecer §34 *va* to dye black, to blacken; *vn* to turn black; *vr* to turn black; to be dark or black (*said, e.g., of the future*)
ennegrecimiento *m* blackening, turning black
ennoblecedor -dora *adj* ennobling
ennoblecer §34 *va* to ennoble; to adorn, embellish; *vr* to become ennobled
ennoblecimiento *m* ennoblement; nobility; fame, glory
ennudecer §34 *vn* to stop growing, to wither
en.º abr. of **enero**
enodio *m* fawn, young deer
enojada *f* (Am.) anger, fit of anger
enojadizo -za *adj* ill-tempered, irritable
enojar *va* to anger, make angry; to annoy, vex; *vr* to get angry; **enojarse con** or **contra** to become angry with (*a person*); **enojarse de** to become angry at (*a thing*)
enojo *m* anger; annoyance, bother; **enojos** *mpl* annoyance, bother
enojón -jona *adj* (Am.) irritable, touchy
enojoso -sa *adj* annoying, bothersome, vexatious
enología *f* oenology
enológico -ca *adj* oenological
enómetro *m* oenometer
Enona *f* (myth.) Oenone

enorgullecer §34 *va* to make proud, to fill with pride; *vr* to be proud, to swell with pride; **enorgullecerse de** to pride oneself on or upon; **enorgullecerse de** + *inf* to pride oneself on + *ger*, to boast of + *ger*
enorgullecimiento *m* pride
enorme *adj* enormous; (coll.) terrific
enormidad *f* enormity
enotecnia *f* wine making; oenology
enotécnico -ca *adj* wine-making
enquiciar *va* to hang (*a door or window*); to put in order; to fasten, make firm
enquillotrar *vr* (coll.) to fall in love
enquiridión *m* handbook, manual, enchiridion
enquistamiento *m* encystment
enquistar *va & vr* to encyst
enrabiar *va* to enrage; *vn* to get or have rabies; *vr* to become enraged
enraizar §97 *vn* to take root
enramada *f* arbor, bower; decoration made of branches; shelter made of branches
enramado *m* (min.) lining made of branches; (naut.) frames (*of a ship*)
enramar *va* to intertwine (*branches*); to adorn with branches; to spread branches, flowers over (*a room, street, etc.*); (naut.) to set up (*the frames of a ship under construction*); *vn* to sprout branches; *vr* to hide in the branches
enramblar *va* to tenter (*cloth*)
enrame *m* intertwining or adorning with branches; **de enrame** climbing
enranciar *va* to make rancid; *vr* to become rancid
enrarecer §34 *va* to rarefy, make less dense; to make scarce; *vn* to become scarce; *vr* to rarefy, become less dense; to become scarce
enrarecimiento *m* rarefaction; scarceness, scarcity
enrasado -da *adj* plain; flush
enrasamiento *m* leveling, grading
enrasar *va* to make even or flush; to level, to grade; *vn* to be even or flush
enrase *m* leveling, grading; (mas.) leveling course
enratonar *vr* (coll.) to get sick from eating mice (*said of cats*)
enrayar *va* to put spokes in (*a wheel*); to scotch (*a wheel*) with a spoke
enredadera *adj fem* (bot.) climbing; *f* (bot.) vine, climbing plant; (bot.) bindweed
enredador -dora *mf* (coll.) gossip, tattler; (coll.) meddler, busybody
enredar *va* to catch in a net; to set (*snares, nets, or traps*); to tangle up; to involve, entangle; to start (*e.g., a fight*); to interweave, intertwine; to compromise, endanger; to alienate; *vn* to be frisky, to romp around; *vr* to get tangled up; to get involved or entangled; (coll.) to have an affair
enredijo *m* (coll.) tangle
enredista *mf* (Am.) var. of **enredador**
enredo *m* tangle; entanglement, complication; mischievous lie; restlessness, friskiness; plot (*e.g., of a play*)
enredón -dona *adj* scheming; *mf* schemer
enredoso -sa *adj* tangled, entangled, full of difficulties
enrejado *m* grating, lattice, trellis; lacing; bamboo curtain; openwork embroidery; **enrejado de alambre** wire netting
enrejalar *va* to pile (*bricks, boards, etc.*) alternately crisscross
enrejar *va* to put grates or grating on (*e.g., a window*); to grate, to lattice; to fence or surround with a grating; to share, fasten the share on (*a plow*); to cut (*feet of oxen or horses*) with plowshare; to pile (*bricks, boards, etc.*) alternately crisscross
enrevesado -da *adj* var. of **revesado**
enriado *m* retting
enriador -dora *mf* retter
enriamiento *m* retting
enriar §90 *va* to ret
enrieladura *f* laying rails; rails, tracks
enrielar *va* to make into ingots; to pour into the ingot mold; (Am.) to lay rails on (*a road*); to put on the rails; (fig.) to put on the right track
enripiar *va* to fill with rubble, to riprap
Enrique *m* Henry
enriquecedor -dora *adj* enriching, fertilizing
enriquecer §34 *va* to enrich; to enhance; to adorn; *vn* to get rich, to prosper; *vr* to become enriched; to get rich, to prosper
enriquecimiento *m* enrichment
enriqueño -ña *adj* of or like Henry II of Castile
Enriqueta *f* Henrietta, Harriet
Enriquito *m* Harry
enriscado -da *adj* craggy, full of cliffs
enriscar §86 *va* to raise; *vr* to rise; to hide or take refuge among the rocks
enristrar *va* to couch (*the lance*); to string (*e.g., onions*); to go straight to; to straighten out (*a difficulty*); (Am.) to recruit
enristre *m* couching the lance
enrizamiento *m* curling
enrizar §76 *va & vr* to curl
enrocamiento *m* rock fill, riprap
enrocar §95 *va* to put (*flax, hemp, wool, etc.*) on the distaff; §86 *va & vn* (chess) to castle; (croquet) to roquet
enroco *m* (Am.) var. of **enroque**
enrodar §77 *va* to subject to torture by the wheel
enrodelado -da *adj* armed with a buckler or shield
enrodrigar §59 *va* to prop, prop up (*plants*)
enrodrigonar *va* to prop up, to tie up (*plants*)
enrojar *va* to redden, make red; to heat (*furnace or oven*); *vr* to redden, turn red
enrojecer §34 *va* to redden, make red; to make red-hot; to make blush; *vn* to blush; *vr* to redden, turn red; to get red-hot; to flush; to get sore
enrojecido -da *adj* reddened; flushed; sore
enrolar *va* to enroll
enrollado *m* volute; (elec.) winding
enrollar *va* to wind, coil, reel, roll up, enroll; to pave with cylindrical stones
enromar *va* to blunt, to dull; *vr* to become blunt, get dull
enronquecer §34 *va* to make hoarse; *vn & vr* to grow hoarse
enronquecimiento *m* hoarseness
enroñar *va* to cover with scabs; to touch with filth; to rust, make rusty; *vr* to rust, get rusty
enroque *m* (chess) castling
enroscadamente *adv* twisting, coiling
enroscadura *f* twisting, coiling; twist, coil, convolution
enroscar §86 *va* to twist, to coil; to twist in, to screw in; *vr* to twist, to coil, to curl
enrubiador -dora *adj* bleaching
enrubiar *va* to make blond, to bleach (*hair*); *vr* to turn blond, to bleach
enrubio *m* bleaching; bleaching lotion
enrudecer §34 *va* to make rough or crude; to make dull or stupid
enruinecer §34 *vn* to become debased, to get worse and worse
enrular *va* (Am.) to curl (*hair*)
ensabanada *f* var. of **encamisada**
ensabanado *m* first coat of plaster
ensabanar *va* to wrap up in a sheet; (mas.) to apply the first coat of plaster to
ensacador -dora *mf* bagger; *m* bagging machine
ensacar §86 *va* to bag, to put in a bag
ensaimada *f* twisted coffee cake
ensalada *f* salad; hodgepodge; **ensalada de frutas** fruit salad; **ensalada repelada** mixed salad
ensaladera *f* salad bowl
ensaladilla *f* assorted candy; setting of varicolored jewels; hodgepodge
ensalmador -dora *mf* bonesetter; powwow (*person*)
ensalmar *va* to set (*a bone*); to powwow, to heal by incantation
ensalmista *m* powwow (*person*)
ensalmo *m* powwow, incantation (*for curing*); **por ensalmo** as if by magic
ensalobrar *vr* to turn salty or briny
ensalzamiento *m* extolling; exaltation
ensalzar §76 *va* to extol; to exalt, elevate
ensambenitar *va* to put the sanbenito on (*a person*)

ensamblador *m* joiner, assembler
ensambladora *f* (carp.) jointer
ensambladura *f* joining, assembling; joint; **ensambladura a cola de milano** dovetail joint; **ensambladura a media madera** halved joint; **ensambladura de caja y espiga** mortise-and-tenon joint; **ensambladura de inglete** miter joint; **ensambladura de lengüeta y ranura** tongue-and-groove joint; **ensambladura de pasador** pin-connected joint; **ensambladura enrasada** flush joint; **ensambladura francesa** scarf, scarf joint
ensamblaje *m* joining, assembling; joint, union; stolen fragments of another author's works
ensamblar *va* to join, connect, assemble, fit together; (carp.) to joint; **ensamblar a caja y espiga** to mortise; **ensamblar a cola de milano** to dovetail
ensamble *m* var. of **ensambladura**
ensanchador -dora *adj* widening, expanding, stretching; *m* expander, stretcher; reamer; glove stretcher; **ensanchador de neumáticos** tire spreader
ensanchamiento *m* extension, expansion
ensanchar *va* to widen, enlarge, extend; to ease, let out (*close-fitting garment*); to unburden (*one's heart*); *vn* to be high and mighty; to get fat; *vr* to widen, to expand; to be high and mighty
ensanche *m* widening, extension; extent; fold in seam (*for subsequent enlargement of garment*); extension (*e.g., of a street*); suburban development; **ensanche de banda** (rad.) band spread
ensandecer §34 *vn* to get silly, to get simple, become feeble-minded
ensangostar *va* var. of **angostar**
ensangrentado -da *adj* bloody, blood-stained, gory
ensangrentamiento *m* staining with blood; bathing in blood
ensangrentar §18 *va* to stain with blood; to bathe in blood; *vr* to rage, get furious, go wild; to rise up in sanguinary factions; **ensangrentarse con** or **contra** to be cruel to, to try to hurt
ensañado -da *adj* angry, irritated; merciless, vengeful; cruel, ferocious
ensañamiento *m* extreme cruelty, barbarity, brutality; (law) aggravation
ensañar *va* to anger, enrage; *vr* to exult in cruelty; to rage (*said, e.g., of a disease*); **ensañarse en** to exult in hurting (*a defenseless person*)
ensarnecer §34 *vn* to get the itch
ensartar *va* to string (*e.g., beads*); to thread; (coll.) to pierce, to run through, e.g., **el toro le ensartó el cuerno** the bull ran its horn through him; to rattle off (*e.g., lies*); *vr* to squeeze in
ensay *m* (*pl:* **-sayes**) var. of **ensaye**
ensayador *m* assayer; rehearser
ensayalar *vr* to wear sackcloth
ensayar *va* to try, try on, try out; to test; to assay; to rehearse; **ensayar a** + *inf* to teach to + *inf*, to train to + *inf*; *vr* to practice; **ensayarse a** + *inf* to practice + *ger*, to rehearse + *ger*
ensaye *m* assay (*of metals*)
ensayismo *m* essay (*literary genre*)
ensayista *mf* essayist; (Am.) assayer
ensayo *m* trying, testing; trial, test; (lit.) essay; assay; practice, exercise; rehearsal; (chem.) analysis; **ensayo de coro** choir practice; **ensayo general** (theat.) dress rehearsal
ensebar *va* to tallow, to rub or smear with tallow; (coll.) to grease
enseguida *adv* at once, immediately
enselvado -da *adj* wooded
enselvar *va* to place in the woods; *vr* to hide in the woods; to become wooded
ensenada *f* inlet, cove
ensenar *va* to embosom; (naut.) to run (*a boat*) into an inlet or cove
enseña *f* standard, ensign, colors
enseñable *adj* teachable
enseñado -da *adj* trained, educated, informed; housebroken (*dog, cat*); trained (*hunting dog*)
enseñamiento *m* teaching; education, instruction; (archaic) teaching, precept
enseñante *adj* teaching
enseñanza *f* teaching; education, instruction; lesson (*instructive event or warning example*); **segunda enseñanza** or **enseñanza media** secondary education (*education in high school or liceo*); **enseñanza objetiva** object teaching; **enseñanza primaria** or **primera** primary education; **enseñanza secundaria** secondary education; **enseñanza superior** higher education
enseñar *va* to teach, to train; to show, to point out; **enseñar a** + *inf* to teach to + *inf*, to teach how to + *inf*; **enseñar algo a alguien** to teach someone something; *vn* to teach
enseñoreamiento *m* seizure, possession
enseñorear *va* to put in possession; *vr* to take possession; to control oneself; **enseñorearse de** to take possession of
enserar *va* to cover with matweed
enseres *mpl* household goods, implements, utensils, equipment
enseriar *vr* (Am.) to become serious
ensiforme *adj* sword-shaped; (anat., bot. & zool.) ensiform
ensilaje *m* ensilage, silage
ensilar *va* to ensilage
ensillado -da *adj* saddle-backed; *f* saddleback (*hill*)
ensilladura *f* saddling; back of horse where saddle fits; curve of the back
ensillar *va* to saddle
ensimismamiento *m* engrossment, self-absorption, deep thought
ensimismar *vr* to lose oneself, to become absorbed in thought; (Am.) to be proud, be boastful
ensoberbecer §34 *va* to make proud; *vr* to become proud; to become insolent; to swell, get rough (*said of the sea*)
ensoberbecimiento *m* pride, haughtiness
ensogar §59 *va* to fasten or bind with a rope; to wrap (*a bottle*) in ropework
ensolerar *va* to fix stools to (*beehives*)
ensolver §63 & §17, 9 *va* to include, contain; to shorten, contract; (med.) to resolve, clear up
ensombrecer §34 *va* to darken, cloud; *vr* to become sad and gloomy
ensombrerado -da *adj* (coll.) wearing a hat, with hat on
ensopar *va* to dip, to dunk; to steep, to soak
ensordecedor -dora *adj* deafening
ensordecer §34 *va* to deafen, make deaf; (phonet.) to unvoice; *vn* to become deaf; to play deaf, to not answer; *vr* (phonet.) to unvoice
ensordecimiento *m* (act of) deafening; deafness
ensortijamiento *m* curling; curls, ringlets, kinks
ensortijar *va* to curl, to kink; to clasp (*one's hands*); to ring (*e.g., a swine's snout*); *vr* to curl, to kink
ensotar *vr* to go into a thicket, to hide in the bush
ensuciador -dora *adj* staining, soiling; defiling
ensuciamiento *m* staining, soiling; defilement
ensuciar *va* to dirty, stain, soil, smear; to sully, defile; *vn* to soil; **ensuciar en** to soil (*one's bed or one's clothes*); *vr* to soil oneself; (coll.) to take bribes; **ensuciarse en** to soil (*one's bed or one's clothes*)
ensuelto -ta *pp of* **ensolver**
ensueño *m* dream; daydream
ensullo *m* var. of **enjulio**
entablación *f* boarding, planking; flooring; church register
entablado *m* wooden framework; flooring (*of boards*)
entabladura *f* boarding, planking
entablamento *m* board roof
entablar *va* to board, board up; (surg.) to splint; to start (*e.g., a conversation*); to bring (*e.g., a suit or action*); to set up (*the men on checkerboard or chessboard*); *vr* to settle (*said of wind*)

entable *m* boarding, planking; position of men (*on checkerboard or chessboard*); (Am.) business, undertaking; (Am.) circumstances, setting
entablerar *vr* (taur.) to hug the fence, to stick close to the barrier (*said of bull*)
entablillar *va* (surg.) to splint; (Am.) to cut (*chocolate*) into blocks or tablets
entablón -blona *adj* (Am.) blustering, browbeating; *mf* (Am.) bully
entablonado *m* planking
entado -da *adj* (her.) enté; **entado en punta** (her.) enté en point
entalamadura *f* arched cover (*of cart or wagon*)
entalamar *va* to cover (*a wagon*) with an arched canvas cover
entalegar §59 *va* to bag, put in a bag; to hoard (*money*)
entalingadura *f* (naut.) clinch
entalingar §59 *va* (naut.) to clinch (*cable*) to the anchor
entallador *m* sculptor, carver; engraver; fitter
entalladura *f* or **entallamiento** *m* sculpture, carving; engraving; slot, groove, mortise; gash, slash
entallar *va* to sculpture, to carve; to engrave; to notch, make a cut in; to slot, to groove, to mortise; to tailor, to fit (*a garment*); *vn* to fit (*said of clothing*); to take shape, to fill out; (coll.) to fit, go well, be appropriate
entallecer §34 *vn & vr* to shoot, to sprout
entallo *m* intaglio
entapizada *f* rug, carpet; (fig.) carpet (*e.g., of daisies*)
entapizar §76 *va* to tapestry; to hang (*e.g., with tapestry*); to cover (*walls, chairs, etc.*) with a fabric; to overgrow (*said of weeds, etc.*)
entarascar §86 *va & vr* to dress up too fancily
entarimando *m* hardwood floor, inlaid floor
entarimar *va* to put a hardwood floor or inlaid floor on or over; *vr* (coll.) to put on airs
entarquinamiento *m* (agr.) reclamation by siltation
entarquinar *va* to fertilize with silt; to smear or soil with mud or slime; to reclaim (*a swamp*) with silt
entarugado *m* paving of wooden blocks
entarugar §59 *va* to pave with wooden blocks
entasia *f* (path.) entasia
éntasis *f* (arch.) entasis
ente *m* being; (coll.) guy, queer duck
entecado -da or **enteco -ca** *adj* sickly, weakly
entejar *va* to tile, to cover with tile
entelarañado -da *adj* cobwebby, full of cobwebs
entelequia *f* (philos.) entelechy
entelerido -da *adj* shaking with cold or fright; (Am.) frail, sickly
entelo *m* (zool.) entellus
entena *f* (naut.) lateen yard
entenado -da *mf* stepchild
entenallas *fpl* small vise, hand vise
entendederas *fpl* (coll.) brains; **tener malas entendederas** (coll.) to have no brains
entendedor -dora *adj* understanding, intelligent; *mf* understanding person; **al buen entendedor, pocas palabras** a word to the wise is enough
entender *m* opinion, understanding; **a mi entender** or **según mi entender** in my opinion, according to my understanding; **§66** *va* to understand; to intend, to mean; to believe; *vn* to understand; **entender de** to be experienced as (*e.g., a carpenter*); to have authority to pass on, to be a judge of; **entender de razones** to listen to reason; **entender en** to be familiar with; to deal with, take care of; to have authority to pass on; *vr* to be understood; to be meant; to understand each other; to have a secret understanding; to know what one is up to; **entenderse con** to get along with; to have an understanding with; to concern
entendidamente *adv* skilfully, knowingly
entendido -da *adj* expert, skilled, trained, learned; **los entendidos** well-informed persons, informed sources; **no darse por entendido** to pay no attention, to pretend not to understand
entendimiento *m* understanding; (philos.) understanding
entenebrecer §34 *va* to darken, make dark; *vr* to get dark
entente *f* (dipl.) entente
enterado -da *adj* informed, fully informed; (Am.) conceited, haughty; *m* insider
enteralgia *f* (path.) enteralgia
enterar *va* to inform, acquaint; *vn* (Am.) to get better, recover; *vr* to understand; to find out; **enterarse de** to find out about, learn about, become aware of; to understand
entercar §86 *vr* to get stubborn
enterectomía *f* (surg.) enterectomy
entereza *f* entirety, completeness; perfection; integrity, fairness; firmness, constancy, fortitude; strictness, rigor; **entereza virginal** virginity
entérico -ca *adj* enteric
enterísimo -ma *adj super* most complete; (bot.) entire
enteritis *f* (path.) enteritis
enterizo -za *adj* solid, in one piece
enternecedor -dora *adj* affecting, touching, moving
enternecer §34 *va* to touch, to move to pity; *vr* to be touched, to be moved to pity
enternecidamente *adv* compassionately, tenderly
enternecimiento *m* pity, compassion
entero -ra *adj* whole, entire, complete; honest, upright; sound, vigorous; firm, energetic; (coll.) strong, heavy (*fabric*); not castrated; (arith.) whole, integral; (bot.) entire; *m* (arith.) integer; **por entero** wholly, entirely, completely
enterohepatitis *f* (path.) enterohepatitis; **enterohepatitis infecciosa** (vet.) blackhead, infectious enterohepatitis
enterología *f* enterology
enterostomía *f* (surg.) enterostomy
enterotomía *f* (surg.) enterotomy
enterrador *m* gravedigger; (ent.) burying beetle
enterramiento *m* interment, burial; grave; tomb
enterrar §18 *va* to inter, bury; (fig.) to bury (*to conceal by covering; to abandon, to forget*); to outlive, to survive; *vr* (fig.) to be buried, to hide away
enterronar *va* to cover with clumps of earth
entesamiento *m* stretching, tightness, tautness
entesar §18 *va* to stretch, tighten, make taut
entestado -da *adj* stubborn, obstinate
entestecer §34 *va & vr* to stiffen
entibación *f* shoring, timbering
entibador *m* (min.) timberman
entibar *va* (min.) to prop up, shore up; *vn* to rest, lean
entibiadero *m* cooling room, cooling bath
entibiar *va* to make lukewarm; to temper, moderate; *vr* to become lukewarm; to cool down, cool off
entibo *m* (min.) timber, timbering; foundation, support; (arch.) abutment
entidad *f* entity; organization; consequence, importance, moment
entierramuertos *m* (*pl:* **-tos**) gravedigger
entierro *m* interment, burial; grave; tomb; funeral; buried treasure
entiesar *va* to stiffen
entigrecer §34 *vr* to get mad, to fly into a rage
entimema *m* (log.) enthymeme
entinar *va* to put into a vat; to put (*wool*) in the degreasing bath
entintado *m* (print.) inking
entintar *va* to ink; to ink in; to stain with ink; to dye
entinte *m* (print.) inking
entizar §76 *va* to chalk (*billiard cue*)
entiznar *va* to soil with soot; to stain, to spot; to defame
entoldado *m* covering with awnings; tent, group of tents (*on beach front*)
entoldamiento *m* covering with awnings
entoldar *va* to cover with an awning; to adorn with hangings; *vr* to become overcast, get cloudy; to be proud and haughty

entomizar §76 *va* to tie esparto cord on (*boards to be plastered*)
entomología *f* entomology
entomológico -ca *adj* entomologic or entomological
entomólogo -ga *mf* entomologist
entonación *f* intoning; intonation; blowing of bellows; (phonet.) intonation
entonadera *f* bellows lever (*of an organ*)
entonado -da *adj* haughty, arrogant; (mus.) harmonious, in tune; *m* (phonet.) toning
entonador -dora *mf* bellows blower (*person*)
entonamiento *m* var. of **entonación**
entonar *va* to intone; to intonate; to sing (*something*) in tune; to blow (*an organ*) with bellows; to harmonize (*colors*); (mus., paint. & phot.) to tone; to tone up (*the body*); *vn* to sing in tune; *vr* to put on airs, be puffed up with pride
entonces *adv* then; and so; **de entonces acá** since then, since that time; **en aquel entonces** at that time; **pues entonces** well then
entonelar *va* to put in casks, to put in barrels
entongar §59 *va* (Am.) to pile up (*boxes and packing cases*); (Am.) to pile up in rows
entono *m* intoning; haughtiness, arrogance
entontecer §34 *va* to make foolish or silly; *vn & vr* to become foolish or silly
entontecimiento *m* foolishness, silliness
entorchado -da *adj* (arch.) wreathed; *m* wreathed cord; bullion (*twisted fringe of uniform*); **ganar los entorchados** to win one's stripes
entorchar *va* to twist (*candles*) to make a torch; to wreathe or twine (*a string or cord*) with silk or wire
entorilar *va* to drive (*a bull*) into the pen
entornado -da *adj* half-closed, on the jar
entornar *va* to upset; to half-close (*door; eyes*); *vr* to upset, to be upset
entornillar *va* to twist, to twist into a spiral; to screw, to screw on, to screw up
entorpecer §34 *va* to stupefy; to dull, benumb; to obstruct, delay, slow up; to make (*e.g., a piece of machinery*) stick; *vr* to stick, get stuck
entorpecimiento *m* stupefaction; dulling, benumbing; obstruction, delay; sticking, jamming
entortadura *f* or **entortamiento** *m* bending; crookedness
entortar §77 *va* to bend, make crooked; to make blind in one eye; *vr* to bend, get crooked
entosigar §59 *va* to poison
entozoario *m* (zool.) entozoan
entrado -da *adj* (Am.) meddling, self-assertive; **entrado en años** advanced in years; *f* entry, entrance; accession; entree; admission; arrival; beginning; hand (*at cards*); receipts; income; entry, entrance hall; (com.) entry; (cook.) entree; admission ticket; (elec.) input; (theat.) house (*audience; size of audience*); gate (*number of people paying admission; amount they pay*); (coll.) short call; (Am.) onslaught, rain (*e.g., of blows*); (Am.) down payment; **dar entrada a** to admit; to give an opening or chance to; (naut.) to give right of entry to (*a ship*); **mucha entrada** good house, good turnout; **entrada de explotación** operating revenue; **entrada de pavana** (coll.) twaddle, bombast; **entrada de taquilla** gate (*number of people paying admission; amount they pay*); **entrada general** (theat.) top gallery; **entrada llena** full house
entradón *m* (sport) big gate (*large attendance*)
entrador -dora *adj* (Am.) energetic, lively, hustling; (Am.) intruding, self-assertive
entramado -da *adj* half-timbered; *m* timber framework
entramar *va* to build the framework for, to make half-timbered
entrambos -bas *adj & pron indef* both
entrampar *va* to trap; to trick; (coll.) to entangle; (coll.) to burden with debt; *vr* to get trapped; (coll.) to become entangled; (coll.) to run into debt
entrante *adj* entering; incoming, inbound; next, coming; (math. & mil.) re-entering; *mf* entrant; **entrantes y salientes** (coll.) hangers-on; *m* (naut.) flood tide
entraña *f* internal part; heart, center; **entrañas** *fpl* entrails; (fig.) entrails (*e.g., of the earth*); heart, feeling, will; (fig.) temper, disposition
entrañable *adj* close, intimate; deep-felt
entrañar *va* to bury deep, to enwomb; to contain, involve; *vr* to be buried deep, be enwombed; to become very close or intimate
entrañoso -sa *adj* intimate, inmost
entrapada *f* crimson cloth (*for hangings and upholstery*)
entrapajar *va* to wrap up with rags, to bandage with rags
entrapar *va* to powder (*the hair*) to remove grease and dirt; to puff up (*the hair*) with powder and grease; (agr.) to fertilize (*a root*) with old rags; *vr* to get full of dust and dirt; to be dulled by grit
entrapazar §76 *va* to cheat, swindle
entrar *va* to bring in, to show in; to attack; to invade, take by force; to influence, to impress; (naut.) to overtake; *vn* to enter, go in, come in; to attack; to empty (*said of a river*); to have entree; to begin; to begin to be felt; to rise (*said of wind, tide, etc.*); to be understandable; **entrar a** + *inf* to go in to + *inf;* to begin to + *inf;* **entrar a matar** (taur.) to go in for the kill; **entrar bien** to be suitable; **entrar en** to enter; to enter into; to fit in or into; to take up, adopt; **entrar en el número de** to be counted among; **entrar por** to follow (*e.g., a custom, fashion*)
entre *prep* between; among; in the course of; **entre manos** at hand, in hand; **entre mí** to myself; **entre que** while; **entre tanto** meanwhile, in the meantime; **entre tú y yo** between you and me
entreabierto -ta *adj* half-open, ajar; *pp of* **entreabrir**
entreabrir §17, 9 *va* to half-open (*door; eyes*)
entreacto *m* entr'acte; small cigar
entreancho -cha *adj* neither broad nor narrow
entrecalle *f* (arch.) space between moldings
entrecanal *f* (arch.) fillet (*between two flutings*)
entrecano -na *adj* graying (*hair; person*)
entrecarril *m* (Am.) gage (*of rails*)
entrecasco *m* var. of **entrecorteza**
entrecavar *va* to loosen the earth around (*e.g., root of vine*); (dial.) to clear of weeds, to weed
entrecejo *m* space between eyebrows; frown; **con entrecejo** with a frown; **arrugar el entrecejo, fruncir el entrecejo** or **ponerse de entrecejo** to knit or to wrinkle one's brow, to frown
entrecierre *m* interlock; (elec.) interlocking connector
entrecinta *f* (arch.) collar beam
entreclaro -ra *adj* lightish, clearish
entrecogedura *f* catching, seizing; squeezing, overcoming
entrecoger §49 *va* to catch, seize; to press hard, to put down, to silence
entrecomar *va* to set off between commas, to set off between quotation marks
entrecoro *m* (eccl.) chancel
entrecortado -da *adj* intermittent, broken
entrecortadura *f* partial cut; intermittent interruption
entrecortar *va* to cut here and there; to break into now and then, to cut off from time to time
entrecorteza *f* ingrown bark (*defect in timber resulting from growing together of two branches*)
entrecruzar §76 *va & vr* to intercross; to interlace, interweave; to interbreed
entrecubierta *f* or **entrecubiertas** *fpl* (naut.) between-decks
entrecuesto *m* loin, sirloin; backbone (*of an animal*)
entrechocar §86 *vr* to collide, to clash
entrechoque *m* collision, clash
entredicho *m* interdiction, prohibition; (law) injunction; **estar en entredicho** to be under suspicion; **poner en entredicho** to cast doubt on
entredoble *adj* of medium thickness or weight

entredós *m* (sew.) insertion; entre-deux, console placed between two windows; (print.) long primer
entrefilete *m* short feature, special item (*in a newspaper*)
entrefino -na *adj* medium, of medium quality
entreforro *m* (naut.) parceling
entrega *f* delivery; surrender; fascicle, instalment, issue, number (*of a magazine, etc.*); abandon; (mas.) tailing; **por entregas** in instalments
entregamiento *m* delivery
entregar **§59** *va* to deliver; to surrender, hand over; to betray; to fit, insert, embed; **entregarla** (coll.) to die; *vr* to give in, to surrender; to devote oneself; to abandon oneself, to yield; **entregarse de** to take charge of, take possession of
entreguismo *m* (Am.) political defeatism
entrehierro *m* (phys.) air gap; (phys.) pole gap (*of cyclotron*); (elec.) spark gap; **entrehierro de chispa amortiguada** (elec.) quenched gap
entrelargo -ga *adj* fairly long
entrelazado da *adj* (her.) interlaced, interfretted; *m* interlace, interlacery
entrelazar **§76** *va* to interlace, interweave, entwine
entrelínea *f* writing between the lines, interlineation; (print.) space, lead
entrelinear *va* to write between the lines
entreliño *m* space between rows of trees or vines
entrelistado -da *adj* with colored stripes
entreluces *mpl* twilight; dawn
entrelucir **§60** *vn* to show through; to shine dimly
entreluzco *1st sg pres ind of* **entrelucir**
entremediar *va* to put between or in the midst of
entremedias *adv* in between; in the meantime; **entremedias de** between; among, in the midst of
entremés *m* side dish, hors d'oeuvre; interlude; (theat.) interlude (*inserted in a mystery*); (theat.) short scene or farce (*inserted in an auto or between two acts of a comedia*)
entremesear *va* to enliven (*a conversation*); *vn* to play in an entremés
entremesil *adj* (pertaining to an) entremés
entremesista *mf* writer or actor of entremeses
entremeter *va* to put in, insert; to fold (*a diaper*); *vr* to butt in, intrude, meddle
entremetido -da *adj* meddlesome; *mf* meddler, intruder
entremetimiento *m* interposition, insertion; meddlesomeness, intrusion
entremezcladura *f* intermingling, intermixing, intermixture
entremezclar *va & vr* to intermingle, to intermix
entremiche *m* (naut.) carling
entremiso *m* cheese vat, cheese shelf
entremorir **§45 & §17,** 9 *vn* to flicker, die out, burn out
entrenador *m* (sport) trainer, coach
entrenamiento *m* (sport) training, coaching
entrenar *va & vr* (sport) to train, to coach
entrencar **§86** *va* to put rods or crosstrees in (*beehive*)
entreno *m* (sport) training
entrenudo *m* (bot.) internode
entrenzar **§76** *va* to plait, braid (*hair*)
entreoído -da *pp of* **entreoír;** *adj* half-heard; **saber de** or **por entreoídas** (coll.) to know from having heard some talk about
entreoigo *1st sg pres ind of* **entreoír**
entreoír **§64** *va* to hear vaguely, to hear something said about
entreordinario -ria *adj* middling
entrepalmadura *f* (vet.) ulcerous sore (*on horse's hoof*)
entrepanes *mpl* unsown ground (*amidst sown areas*)
entrepañado -da *adj* paneled
entrepaño *m* panel (*e.g., of door*); shelf; (arch.) pier (*wall between two openings*)
entreparecer **§34** *vr* to show through; to have some resemblance
entrepaso *m* rack pace (*of horse*)
entrepeines *mpl* comb wool
entrepelado -da *adj* pied, parti-colored (*said of a horse*)
entrepelar *va* to pluck irregularly; *vn* to be pied or parti-colored (*said of horses*)
entrepernar **§18** *vn* to intertwine the legs
entrepierna *f* or **entrepiernas** *fpl* (anat.) side of thigh between the legs; crotch; patches in the crotch of trousers or drawers; (Am.) bathing trunks
entrepiso *m* mezzanine, entresol; (min.) intermediate gallery
entreplanos *m* (*pl:* **-nos**) (aer.) gap
entreplanta *f* mezzanine
entrepuente *m* or **entrepuentes** *mpl* (naut.) between-decks
entrepunzadura *f* dull shooting pains
entrepunzar **§76** *vn* to have dull shooting pains
entrerraído -da *adj* worn in spots, threadbare in spots
entrerrenglón *m* space between lines, interline; (print.) space, lead
entrerrenglonadura *f* writing between the lines, interlineation
entrerrenglonar *va* to write between the lines
entrerriel *m* gage (*of railroad*)
entrerrosca *f* (mach.) nipple
entresaca or **entresacadura** *f* picking out, selection; sifting; thinning, pruning
entresacar **§86** *va* to pick out, select; to sift, cull; to thin out (*e.g., trees*); to prune (*branches*)
entresijo *m* (anat. & zool.) mesentery; arcanum, secret; obstacle; **tener muchos entresijos** to be complicated, be hard to figure out; to be cautious, be mysterious
entresuelo *m* mezzanine, entresol; (theat.) first balcony
entresurco *m* space between furrows
entretalla or **entretalladura** *f* bas-relief
entretallar *va* to carve, engrave; to carve or cut in bas-relief; to make openwork in; to intercept, obstruct; *vr* to fit together
entretanto *adv* meanwhile; *m* meanwhile, meantime; **por entretanto** in the meantime
entretecho *m* (Am.) attic, garret
entretejedor -dora *adj* interweaving
entretejedura *f* interweaving
entretejer *va* to interweave
entretejimiento *m* var. of **entretejedura**
entretela *f* (sew.) interlining; **entretelas** *fpl* (coll.) heartstrings, inmost being
entretelar *va* (sew.) to interline
entretelones *mpl* events behind the scenes, persons behind the scenes
entretén *2d sg impv of* **entretener**
entretención *f* (Am.) entertainment, amusement
entretendré *1st sg fut ind of* **entretener**
entretenedor -dora *adj* entertaining; *mf* entertainer
entretener **§85** *va* to entertain, amuse; to keep amused; to delay, put off; to make bearable, to allay (*pain*); to while away (*the time*); to deceive; to maintain, to keep up; **entretener el hambre** (coll.) to take a bite in order to stave off hunger till mealtime; (coll.) to try to forget one's hunger; *vr* to be amused, to amuse oneself; **entretenerse con** or **en** + *inf* to amuse oneself + *ger*
entretengo *1st sg pres ind of* **entretener**
entretenido -da *adj* entertaining, amusing; (rad.) undamped, continuous (*waves*); *f* entertainment; kept woman; **dar la entretenida a** or **dar con la entretenida a** to keep talking in order to avoid granting a request
entretenimiento *m* entertainment, amusement; maintenance, upkeep
entretiempo *m* spring or autumn (*the season between the seasons, i.e., between summer and winter*); **de entretiempo** lightweight (*coat*)
entretuve *1st sg pret ind of* **entretener**
entreuntar **§75** *va* to oil on the surface, oil lightly
entreveía *1st sg imperf ind of* **entrever**
entrevenar *vr* to spread through the veins
entreventana *f* (arch.) pier (*wall between two windows*)

entreveo *1st sg pres ind of* **entrever**
entrever **§93** *va* to glimpse, descry; to guess, divine, suspect
entreverar *va* to mix in, to intermingle; *vr* to be intermixed, to intermingle; (Am.) to get mixed together without order; (Am.) to clash in hand-to-hand combat (*said of two forces of cavalry*)
entrevero *m* (Am.) intermingling; (Am.) jumble, confusion; (Am.) hand-to-hand combat between two forces of cavalry
entrevía *f* (rail.) gage
entrevista *f* see **entrevisto**
entrevistar *vr* to have an interview; **entrevistarse con** to interview, to talk with
entrevisto -ta *pp of* **entrever;** *f* interview
entripado -da *adj* in the belly; not cleaned (*said of a dead animal*); *m* bellyache; (coll.) anger, veiled displeasure
entristecedor -dora *adj* saddening
entristecer **§34** *va* to sadden; to make gloomy; *vr* to sadden, become sad
entristecimiento *m* sadness, gloominess
entrojar *va* to garner (*grain*)
entrometer *va & vr* var. of **entremeter**
entrometido -da *adj & mf* var. of **entremetido**
entrometimiento *m* var. of **entremetimiento**
entronar *va* to enthrone
entroncamiento *m* relationship, connection; connection, junction (*of rail lines*)
entroncar **§86** *va* to show or prove the relationship between; *vn* to be related, be connected; to connect (*said of two or more rail lines*); **entroncar con** to be or become related to
entronerar *va* (billiards) to pocket (*a ball*); *vr* to be pocketed, to fall into a pocket
entronización *f* enthronement; exaltation; popularization
entronizar **§76** *va* to enthrone; to exalt; to promote, popularize; *vr* to be enthroned; to seize power; to become the vogue; to be puffed up with pride
entronque *m* var. of **entroncamiento**
entropía *f* (thermodynamics) entropy
entruchada *f* or **entruchado** *m* (coll.) decoy, trick, intrigue
entruchar *va* (coll.) to decoy, to trick
entruchón -chona *mf* (coll.) decoy, trickster
entrujar *va* to store (*especially olives*); (coll.) to pocket
entubar *va* to pipe; to install new tubes in (*a boiler*); (min.) to case, to line (*a shaft*)
entuerto *m* wrong, injustice, insult; **entuertos** *mpl* afterpains
entullecer **§34** *va* to stop, check; *vn & vr* to become crippled, become paralyzed
entumecer **§34** *va* to benumb, make numb; *vr* to become numb, to go to sleep (*said of limbs*); to swell, to surge
entumecimiento *m* numbness, deadness, torpor; swell, swelling
entumir *vr* to become numb, to go to sleep (*said of a limb*)
entunicar **§86** *va* (paint.) to plaster for frescoing
entupir *va* to block, clog, stop up; to compress; *vr* to become blocked, clogged, or stopped up
enturbiamiento *m* muddiness; confusion, disorder
enturbiar *va* to stir up, to muddy; to obscure, to confuse, to derange; *vr* to get muddy; to become deranged or disordered
entusiasmar *va* to enthuse, enrapture; *vr* to enthuse, be enthusiastic
entusiasmo *m* enthusiasm
entusiasta *adj* enthusiastic; *mf* enthusiast
entusiástico -ca *adj* enthusiastic
enucleación *f* (surg.) enucleation
enuclear *va* to enucleate
énula campana *f* (bot.) elecampane
enumeración *f* enumeration
enumerador -dora *mf* enumerator; **enumerador censal** census taker
enumerar *va* to enumerate
enumerativo -va *adj* enumerative
enunciación *f* enunciation
enunciado *m* enunciation, statement
enunciar *va* to enounce, enunciate
enunciativo -va *adj* enunciative; (gram.) declarative
enuresis *f* (path.) enuresis
envainador -dora *adj* sheathing
envainar *va* to sheathe
envalentonamiento *m* boldness, daring; encouragement
envalentonar *va* to embolden, to encourage; *vr* to pluck up
envalijar *va* to put or pack in a valise
envanecer **§34** *va* to make vain; *vr* to become vain; **envanecerse con, de, en,** or **por** to swell with pride at
envanecimiento *m* vanity, conceit
envaramiento *m* numbness, stiffness
envarar *va* to benumb, stiffen
envarbascar **§86** *va* to infect (*water*) with mullein to stun the fish
envasado *m* packing, bottling, canning
envasador -dora *adj* packing; *mf* packer, filler; *m* large funnel
envasar *va* to pack, to package, to bottle, to can; to sack (*grain*); to insert; to thrust, push, poke (*a sword*); to drink (*e.g., wine*) to excess; *vn* to drink to excess; *vr* to stab oneself; to stab each other
envase *m* packing, bottling, canning; package, container, bottle, jar, can; **envase de hojalata** tin can
envedijar *vr* to get tangled; (coll.) to get into a fist fight
envejecer **§34** *va* to age, make old; *vn* to age, grow old; to go out-of-date; to last a long time; *vr* to age, grow old; to go out-of-date
envejecido -da *adj* old, aged; tried, experienced
envejecimiento *m* aging; age
envenenador -dora *adj* poisoning; *mf* poisoner
envenenamiento *m* poisoning; **envenenamiento plúmbico** lead poisoning
envenenar *va* to poison; (fig.) to put an evil interpretation on (*someone's words or deeds*); (fig.) to envenom, to embitter; *vr* to take poison
enverar *vn* to turn golden-red (*said of ripening fruit*)
enverdecer **§34** *vn & vr* to turn green, be covered with verdure
enverdecimiento *m* turning green; verdure
envergadura *f* breadth (*of sails*); (aer.) span, wingspread; spread (*of wings of bird*); (fig.) spread, compass, reach
envergar **§59** *va* (naut.) to bend (*the sails*)
envergue *m* (naut.) sail rope, roband
enverjado *m* lattice, trellis, grillwork, grating
envero *m* golden red (*of ripening fruit*); golden-red grape
envés *m* wrong side; (coll.) back, shoulders
envesado -da *adj* showing the back side; *m* fleshy side of hide or skin
envestir **§94** *va* var. of **investir**
enviada *f* fishing scow
enviadizo -za *adj* sent, regularly sent
enviado *m* messenger; envoy; **enviado extraordinario** envoy extraordinary
enviajado -da *adj* sloping, oblique
enviar **§90** *va* to send; to ship; **enviar a** + *inf* to send to + *inf*
enviciamiento *m* corruption, vitiation; addiction
enviciar *va* to corrupt, vitiate, spoil; *vn* to have abundant leaves and little fruit; *vr* to become addicted, to become overfond; **enviciarse con** or **en** to become addicted to, to become overfond of
envidador -dora *mf* bidder, bettor (*at cards*)
envidar *va* to bid against, to bet against; *vn* to bid, to bet
envidia *f* envy; desire
envidiable *adj* enviable
envidiar *va* to envy, to begrudge; to desire
envidioso -sa *adj* envious; covetous, greedy
envigado *m* beams, joists
envigar **§59** *va* to install the beams in (*a building*); *vn* to install the beams
envilecedor -dora *adj* debasing, degrading
envilecer **§34** *va* to vilify, debase; *vr* to be debased, to degrade oneself; to cringe, grovel
envilecimiento *m* vilification, debasement, degradation; cringing, groveling

envinado -da *adj* (Am.) wine-colored
envinagrar *va* to put vinegar in or on; *vr* to sour, to turn sour
envinar *va* to put wine in (*water*)
envío *m* sending, shipment, remittance; autograph, inscription (*in a book*)
envión *m* push, shove
envirotado -da *adj* stiff, stuck-up
enviscamiento *m* smearing with birdlime
enviscar §86 *va* to incite, provoke, stir up; to smear (*branches*) with birdlime; *vr* to be caught or stuck with birdlime
envite *m* stake; side bet; offer, invitation; push, shove; (bridge) bid; **al primer envite** at the start, right off
enviudar *vn* to become widowed, to become a widow or widower
envoltorio *m* bundle; wrapping; knot (*in cloth from mixture of different kind of wool*)
envoltura *f* cover, wrapper, envelope; swaddling clothes; (aer. & bot.) envelope
envolvedor -dora *mf* wrapping clerk, wrapper; *m* wrapping, cover; bed, cot, or table used for swaddling children
envolvente *adj* (mil.) encircling; *f* cover, housing
envolver §63 & §17, 9 *va* to wrap, wrap up; to swaddle; to wind; to imply, mean; to involve; to floor (*an opponent*); to surround; (mil.) to encircle; *vr* to wrap up; to become involved; to have an affair
envolvimiento *m* wrapping, envelopment; involvement; winding; wallowing place (*for animals*); (mil.) encirclement
envuelto -ta *pp of* **envolver**
enyerbar *vr* (Am.) to be overgrown with grass, be covered with grass
enyesado *m* plastering; treatment of wine with gypsum; treatment of soil with gypsum
enyesadura *f* plastering
enyesar *va* to plaster; to mix plaster with; (surg.) to put in a plaster cast; to treat (*wine or soils*) with gypsum
enyugar §59 *va* to yoke
enzainar *vr* (coll.) to look askance, to look sidewise; (coll.) to become untrustworthy, to turn traitor
enzalamar *va* (coll.) to provoke, to incite
enzamarrado -da *adj* wearing an undressed sheepskin jacket
enzarzar §76 *va* to throw into the brambles, to cover with brambles; to involve, involve in a dispute; to set hurdles for (*silkworms*); *vr* to get entangled in brambles; to get involved, get involved in a dispute
enzima *f* (biochem.) enzyme
enzímico -ca *adj* enzymatic
enzootia *f* (vet.) enzoötic
enzunchar *va* to bind with hoops or iron bands
enzurdecer §34 *vn* to become left-handed
enzurizar §76 *va* to sow discord among
enzurronar *va* to bag; (coll.) to put inside
eoceno -na *adj & m* (geol.) Eocene
eoliano -na *adj* (geol.) aeolian
eólico -ca *adj* Aeolian; (geol.) aeolian; *m* Aeolic (*dialect*)
Eólide, la Aeolis
eolio -lia *adj & mf* Aeolian; *adj & m* Aeolic (*dialect*)
eolítico -ca *adj* (archeol.) eolithic
Éolo *m* (myth.) Aeolus
eón *m* aeon; (Gnosticism) aeon
Eos *f* (myth.) Eos
eosina *f* (chem.) eosin
epacta *f* epact
epactilla *f* liturgical calendar
epazote *m* (bot.) Mexican tea
E.P.D. abr. of **en paz descanse**
epéndimo *m* (anat.) ependyma
epéntesis *f* (*pl:* **-sis**) (gram.) epenthesis
epentético -ca *adj* epenthetic
eperlano *m* (ichth.) smelt
épica *f* see **épico**
epicáliz *m* (*pl:* **-lices**) (bot.) epicalyx
epicarpio *m* (bot.) epicarp
epicedio *m* epicedium
epiceno -na *adj* (gram.) epicene
epicentro *m* epicenter
epicíclico -ca *adj* epicyclic
epiciclo *m* (astr. & geom.) epicycle
epicicloide *f* (geom.) epicycloid
épico -ca *adj* epic or epical; (fig.) epic, heroic, sublime; *m* epic poet; *f* epic poetry
epicotilo *m* (bot.) epicotyl
Epicteto *m* Epictetus
epicureísmo *m* Epicureanism
epicúreo -a *adj* Epicurean; epicurean; *mf* Epicurean; epicurean, epicure
Epicuro *m* Epicurus
epidemia *f* epidemic
epidemial *adj* var. of **epidémico**
epidemicidad *f* epidemicity
epidémico -ca *adj* epidemic or epidemical
epidemiología *f* epidemiology
epidemiólogo -ga *mf* epidemiologist
epidérmico -ca *adj* epidermal
epidermis *f* (anat.) epidermis
epidota *f* (mineral.) epidote
Epifanía *f* (eccl.) Epiphany; (*l.c.*) *f* epiphany (*apparition*)
epífisis *f* (*pl:* **-sis**) (anat.) epiphysis
epífito -ta *adj* epiphytic; *f* (bot.) epiphyte
epifonema *f* (rhet.) epiphonema
epífora *f* (path.) epiphora
epigástrico -ca *adj* epigastric
epigastrio *m* (anat. & zool.) epigastrium
epigea *f* (bot.) epigaea; **epigea rastrera** (bot.) trailing arbutus
epigénico -ca *adj* (geol.) epigene
epiglotis *f* (anat.) epiglottis
epígono *m* follower, disciple
epígrafe *m* epigraph; inscription; motto, device; title; headline
epigrafía *f* epigraphy
epigráfico -ca *adj* epigraphic
epigrafista *mf* epigrapher
epigrama *m* epigram
epigramatario -ria *adj* epigrammatic; *mf* epigrammatist; *m* collection of epigrams
epigramático -ca *adj* epigrammatic
epilepsia *f* (path.) epilepsy
epiléptico -ca *adj & mf* epileptic
epilogación *f* epilogue
epilogal *adj* epilogic; compendious
epilogar §59 *va* to recapitulate, sum up
epilogismo *m* (astr.) computation
epílogo *m* epilogue; (rhet.) peroration
epinicio *m* song of victory
epiplón *m* (anat. & zool.) epiploön, omentum
Epiro, el Epirus
episcopado *m* episcopacy, episcopate
episcopal *adj* episcopal; Episcopal
episcopalismo *m* (eccl.) episcopalism; Episcopalianism
episcopalista *adj & mf* Episcopalian
episcopologio *m* catalogue of bishops
episódico -ca *adj* episodic or episodical
episodio *m* episode
epispástico -ca *adj & m* (med.) epispastic
epistaxis *f* (path.) epistaxis
epistemología *f* epistemology
epistemológico -ca *adj* epistemological
epistilo *m* (arch.) epistyle
epístola *f* epistle; (eccl.) Epistle
epistolar *adj* epistolary
epistolario *m* volume of letters; (eccl.) epistolary
epistolero *m* (eccl.) epistler
epitafio *m* epitaph
epitalamio *m* epithalamium
epitelial *adj* epithelial
epitelio *m* (anat.) epithelium
epitelioma *m* (path.) epithelioma
epítema *m* (med.) epithem
epíteto *m* epithet
epítimo *m* (bot.) clover dodder
epitomar *va* to epitomize
epítome *m* epitome
epizootia *f* epizoötic
epizoótico -ca *adj* epizoötic
E.P.M. abr. of **en propia mano**
época *f* epoch, age, time; (astr. & geol.) epoch; **formar** or **hacer época** to be epoch-making; **época glacial** (geol.) ice age; **época victoriana** Victorian age
epoda *f* or **epodo** *m* epode
epónimo -ma *adj* eponymous
epopeya *f* epic, epic poem; (fig.) epic

épsilon *f* epsilon
epsomita *f* (mineral.) epsomite
equiángulo -la *adj* (geom.) equiangular
equidad *f* equity; (law) equity; equableness (*of disposition*); reasonableness (*in prices or other terms*)
equidistancia *f* equidistance
equidistante *adj* equidistant
equidistar *vn* to be equidistant
equidna *f* (zool.) echidna
équido *m* (zool.) equid
equilátero -ra *adj* equilateral
equilibración *f* equilibration
equilibrado -da *adj* sensible, prudent
equilibrar *va* to balance, equilibrate; to balance (*the budget*); *vr* to balance, equilibrate
equilibrio *m* equilibrium, balance, equipoise; balancing (*of the budget*); **equilibrio europeo** or **equilibrio político** (dipl.) balance of power
equilibrista *adj* equilibristic; *mf* equilibrist, balancer, ropedancer
equimosis *f* (*pl:* **-sis**) black-and-blue mark, ecchymosis
equino -na *adj* equine; *m* equine; (arch. & zool.) echinus
equinoccial *adj* equinoctial; *f* equinoctial (*line*)
equinoccio *m* (astr.) equinox; **equinoccio otoñal** or **de otoño** (astr.) autumnal equinox; **equinoccio vernal** or **de primavera** (astr.) vernal equinox
equinococo *m* (zool.) echinococcus
equinodermo *m* (zool.) echinoderm
equipaje *m* baggage; piece of baggage; equipment; (naut.) crew; (mil.) baggage train; **equipaje de mano** hand baggage
equipar *va* to equip, fit out; to equip and provision (*a ship*)
equiparación *f* comparison; equalization
equiparar *va* to compare; to equalize, make equal or like
equipier *m* (*pl:* **-piers**) teammate
equipo *m* equipment, outfit; set; unit; crew; (sport) team; **equipo de novia** trousseau; **equipo de radio** radio set; **equipo de urgencia** first-aid kit
equiponderancia *f* equality in weight
equiponderar *vn* to be equal in weight
equipotencial *adj* (phys.) equipotential
equisetáceo -a *adj* (bot.) equisetaceous
equiseto *m* (bot.) equisetum, horsetail; **equiseto menor** (bot.) bottle brush, field horsetail
equitación *f* equitation, horsemanship
equitativo -va *adj* equitable
equivaldré *1st sg fut ind of* **equivaler**
equivalencia *f* equivalence
equivalente *adj & m* equivalent
equivaler §89 *va* to be equivalent to, to be equal to; *vn* to be equivalent, to be equal
equivalgo *1st sg pres ind of* **equivaler**
equivocación *f* mistakenness; mistake
equivocadamente *adv* mistakenly, by mistake
equivocado -da *adj* mistaken, wrong
equivocar §86 *va* to mistake; to mix (*to confuse completely*); *vr* to be mistaken, to make a mistake; to miss one's calling; **equivocarse con** to be mistaken for; **equivocarse de** to be mistaken in; **me equivoqué de camino** I took the wrong road; **se equivocó de casa** he went to the wrong house
equívoco -ca *adj* equivocal; *m* equivocation, ambiguity; pun; mix-up
equivoquista *mf* punster; equivocator
-era *suffix f* see **-ero**
era *f* era, age, period; (geol.) era; threshing floor; vegetable patch, garden bed; mixing board; **era arqueozoica** (geol.) Archeozoic era; **era atómica** atomic age; **era común** Common Era; **era cristiana** or **era de Cristo** Christian Era; **era de hortalizas** vegetable garden; **era vulgar** Vulgar Era; *1st sg imperf ind of* **ser**
eral *m* two-year-old bull
erar *va* to lay out patches or beds in (*a garden*)
erario *m* state treasury
erasmiano -na *adj & mf* Erasmian
Erasmo *m* Erasmus
Erato *f* (myth.) Erato
erbio *m* (chem.) erbium
Erebo *m* (myth.) Erebus (*underworld*)
erección *f* erection; establishment; tension; (physiol.) erection
eréctil *adj* erectile
erectilidad *f* erectility
erector -tora *adj* erecting; *mf* erector, builder
eremita *m* eremite, hermit
eremítico -ca *adj* eremitic; solitary
eremitorio *m* location of a hermitage or hermitages
erepsina *f* (biochem.) erepsin
eres *2d sg pres ind of* **ser**
eretismo *m* (physiol.) erethism
ergástula *f* or **ergástulo** *m* (hist.) slave prison
ergio *m* (phys.) erg
ergosterol *m* (pharm.) ergosterol
ergotina *f* (pharm.) ergotin
ergotismo *m* ergotism (*sophistry*); (plant path.) ergot; (path.) ergotism
ergotizar §76 *vn* to ergotize, argue sophistically
erguen *m* (bot.) argan tree
erguimiento *m* raising, straightening
erguir §47 *va* to raise, lift up, straighten; *vr* to swell with pride
-ería *suffix f* -ery, e.g., **cervecería** brewery; **tontería** foolery; **mojigatería** priggery; -ry, e.g., **carpintería** carpentry; **joyería** jewelry; **pedantería** pedantry; -ing, e.g., **barbería** barbering; **ingeniería** engineering; -ness, e.g., **niñería** childishness; **tontería** foolishness; and many other words, without a corresponding suffix in English, indicating a place where something is made or sold, e.g., **librería** bookstore; **zapatería** shoemaker's shop; shoe store
erial or **eriazo -za** *adj* unplowed, uncultivated; *m* unplowed land, uncultivated land
erica *f* (bot.) heath, heather
ericáceo -a *adj* (bot.) ericaceous
Erico *m* Eric
erigir §42 *va* to erect, build; to establish; to elevate; *vr* to be elevated; **erigirse en** to be elevated to; to set oneself up as, to pose as
Erín *f;* **la Verde Erín** (poet.) Erin
erina *f* (surg.) tenaculum
eringe *f* (bot.) field eryngo
Erinia *f* (myth.) Erinys
erío -a *adj & m* var. of **erial**
erisipela *f* (path.) erysipelas
erisipeloide *f* (path.) erysipeloid
erístico -ca *adj* eristic; *f* eristic (*art of disputation*)
eritema *m* (path.) erythema
eritreo -a *adj & mf* Eritrean; Erythraean; (*cap.*) *f* Eritrea
eritrina *f* (chem.) erythrin
eritrita *f* (mineral.) erythrite
eritroblasto *m* (anat.) erythroblast
eritrocito *m* (anat.) erythrocyte
eritroxiláceo -a *adj* (bot.) erythroxylaceous
erizado -da *adj* spiny, bristly, bristling; **erizado de** bristling with
erizar §76 *va* to set on end, make bristle; **estar erizado de** to bristle with (*e.g., difficulties*); *vr* to stand on end, to bristle
erizo *m* (zool.) hedgehog; (bot.) thistle; bur (*prickly involucre, e.g., of chestnut*); (mach.) pinwheel; (mach.) urchin (*of weaving machine*); cheval-de-frise (*along top of wall*); (coll.) harsh, unruly person; **erizo de mar** or **erizo marino** (zool.) sea urchin
erizón *m* (bot.) blue genista; **erizones** *mpl* (bot.) spiny yellow genista (*Genista horrida*)
ermit. abr. of **ermitaño**
ermita *f* hermitage
ermitaño -ña *mf* hermit; *m* eremite; (zool.) hermit crab
ermitorio *m* var. of **eremitorio**
Ernesto *m* Ernest
-ero -ra *suffix adj* e.g., **aduanero** customhouse; **guerrero** warlike; *suffix mf* -er, e.g., **carcelero** jailer; **extranjero** foreigner; **molinero** miller; *suffix m* -eer, e.g., **bucanero** buccaneer; **cañonero** cannoneer; **ingeniero** engineer; -ier, e.g., **alabardero** halberdier; **bombardero** bombardier; **cajero** cashier; **gondolero** gondolier; -ary, e.g., **granero** granary; and in many other words, without a

corresponding suffix in English, indicating the place where something is kept, e.g., **azucarero** sugar bowl; **tintero** inkwell; *suffix f* -ary, e.g., **abejera** apiary; **pajarera** aviary; and in many other words, without a corresponding suffix in English indicating the place where something is kept, e.g., **ensaladera** salad bowl; **sombrerera** hat box
erogación *f* distribution (*of property or wealth*); (Am.) gift, charity
erogar §59 *va* to distribute (*property, wealth*); to cause, give rise to
Eros *m* (myth.) Eros
erosión *f* erosion; (geol.) erosion
erosionar *va & vr* to erode
erosivo -va *adj* erosive; *m* erosive substance or agent
erotema *f* (rhet.) rhetorical question
erótico -ca *adj* erotic; *f* erotic poetry
erotismo *m* erotism
erotomanía *f* (path.) erotomania
erotómano -na *adj & mf* erotic
errabundo -da *adj* wandering
erradicable *adj* eradicable
erradicación *f* eradication
erradicar §86 *va* to eradicate
erradizo -za *adj* wandering; stumbling, fumbling
errado -da *adj* mistaken; unwise, unbecoming
erraj *m* fine coal made of crushed olive stones
errante *adj* wandering, roving; nomadic
errar §48 *va* to miss (*a target, one's calling*); (archaic) to fail; *vn* to wander; to err, be wrong or mistaken; *vr* to err, be wrong or mistaken
errata *f* erratum; printer's error
errático -ca *adj* wandering; (geol.) erratic
errátil *adj* wavering, fallible
erróneo -a *adj* erroneous
erronía *f* grudge, dislike; (archaic) incredulity; (archaic) stubbornness
error *m* error, mistake; **salvo error u omisión** barring error or omission; **error craso** blunder, break
erso -sa *adj & m* Erse
erubescencia *f* modesty, blushing; erubescence
erubescente *adj* red, blushing; erubescent
eructación *f* var. of **eructo**
eructar *vn* to belch, eruct; (coll.) to brag
eructo *m* belch, belching, eructation
erudición *f* erudition, learning
erudito -ta *adj* erudite, learned, scholarly; *mf* scholar, savant; **erudito a la violeta** highbrow, intellectual fourflusher
eruginoso -sa *adj* rusty
erumpir *vn* to erupt (*said of volcano*)
erupción *f* eruption; bursting forth, outburst; (path. & dent.) eruption
eruptivo -va *adj* eruptive
erutar *vn* var. of **eructar**
eruto *m* var. of **eructo**
ervato *m* var. of **servato**
ervilla *f* var. of **arveja**
es *3d sg pres ind of* **ser**
Esaú *m* (Bib.) Esau
esbatimentar *va* (paint.) to draw or paint a shadow in; *vn* to cause a shadow
esbatimento *m* (paint.) shade or shadow
esbeltez *f* or **esbelteza** *f* gracefulness, slenderness, elegance, litheness
esbelto -ta *adj* graceful, slender, well-built, svelte
esbirro *m* bailiff, constable; myrmidon, minion of the law
esbozar §76 *va* to sketch, outline
esbozo *m* sketch, outline
escabechado -da *adj* (coll.) with dyed hair; (coll.) painted, with painted face
escabechar *va* to pickle; (coll.) to flunk; (coll.) to kill, to slay, to stab to death; to dye (*the hair*); *vr* to dye one's hair; **escabecharse las canas** to dye one's hair
escabeche *m* pickle; pickled fish; hair dye
escabechina *f* (coll.) ravage, destruction
escabel *m* stool; footstool; (fig.) stepping stone (*means of advancement*)
escabiosa *f* see **escabioso**
escabiosis *f* (path.) scabies
escabioso -sa *adj* scabious, mangy; *f* (bot.) scabious; **escabiosa de Indias** (bot.) sweet scabious; **escabiosa mordida** (bot.) blue scabious
escabro *m* (vet.) scabs (*on sheep*); (plant path.) scaly bark
escabrosidad *f* scabrousness; harshness, roughness
escabroso -sa *adj* scabrous, risqué; harsh, rough, bumpy
escabuche *f* weeding hoe
escabullimiento *m* slipping or sneaking away, escape
escabullir §26 *vr* to slip away, to clear out, to sneak away, to escape
escacado -da *adj* (her.) checky
escachar *va* to squash, crush
escacharrar *va* to break (*an earthen pot*); to spoil, damage, ruin
escachifollar *va* var. of **cachifollar**
escafandra *f* or **escafandro** *m* diving suit, diving outfit; **escafandra espacial** space helmet
escafandrista *mf* diver
escafilar *va* var. of **descafilar**
escafoides *m* (anat.) scaphoid
Escafusa *f* Schaffhausen
escajo *m* var. of **escalio**
escala *f* ladder, stepladder; scale (*graduated line*); call (*of a boat*); port of call; stop (*of airplane*); (mus.) scale; **en escala de** on a scale of (*e.g., an inch to a mile*); **en grande escala** on a large scale; **en pequeña escala** on a small scale; **hacer escala en** (naut.) to call at; **escala cromática** (mus.) chromatic scale; **escala de cuerda** rope ladder; **escala de Jacob** (Bib.) Jacob's ladder; (bot.) Jacob's-ladder; **escala de jarcia** (naut.) Jacob's ladder; **escala de los vientos** wind scale; **escala de travesaños** peg ladder; **escala de viento** (naut.) rope ladder; **escala diatónica** (mus.) diatonic scale; **escala mayor** (mus.) major scale; **escala menor** (mus.) minor scale; **escala móvil** (econ.) sliding scale (*e.g., of salaries*)
escalabrar *va & vr* var. of **descalabrar**
escalada *f* escalade, scaling; climbing
escalador -dora *adj* burglarious; *mf* scaler, climber; burglar, housebreaker
escalafón *m* roster, register (*showing position, seniority, merits, etc.*)
escalamera *f* (naut.) rowlock, oarlock
escalamiento *m* scaling (*ascent by or as by ladder; measurement by a scale*); burglary
escálamo *m* (naut.) thole, tholepin
escalar *va* to escalade, to scale (*a wall*); to enter by scaling; to break in, to break through (*e.g., a wall*); to burglarize; to climb; to open the gates of (*a sluice, trench, channel, etc.*); to slit and clean (*a fish or other animal*) for curing or salting; *vn* to climb; (fig.) to make one's way up by fair means or foul; (naut.) to call; *vr* to escalate
escalatorres *mf* (*pl:* **-rres**) steeplejack, human fly
Escalda *m* Scheldt (*river*)
escaldado -da *adj* (coll.) cautious, wary, scared; (coll.) loose, lewd (*woman*)
escaldadura *f* scald, scalding
escaldar *va* to scald; to make red-hot; *vr* to be scalded; to chafe
escaldo *m* skald (*ancient Scandinavian bard*)
escaleno -na *adj* (geom. & anat.) scalene; *m* (anat.) scalenus
escalenoedro *m* (cryst.) scalenohedron
escalentamiento *m* (vet.) sorefoot
escalera *f* stairs, stairway; ladder; (cards) sequence; (poker) straight; **de escalera abajo** of the servants, from below stairs; **por la escalera abajo** down the stairs; **escalera ascensora** (Am.) moving stairway, escalator; **escalera automática** escalator; **escalera de caracol** winding stairs; **escalera de escape** fire escape; **escalera de ganchos** hook ladder; **escalera de gato** cat ladder; **escalera de husillo** winding stairs; **escalera de incendio** fire ladder; **escalera de mano** ladder; **escalera de papagayo** peg ladder; **escalera de salvamento** fire escape; **escalera de**

servicio service stairs, back stairs; **escalera de tijera** or **escalera doble** stepladder; **escalera espiral** spiral staircase; **escalera excusada** or **falsa** private stairs (*to bedrooms and apartments*); **escalera extensible** extension ladder; **escalera hurtada** secret stairway; **escalera interior** back stairs; **escalera mecánica** escalator; **escalera movible** ladder; **escalera móvil** or **rodante** moving stairway, escalator
escalerilla *f* low step; car step; short ladder; sequence of three or five (*in cards*); rack (*for pinion*); (vet.) mouth prop, jaw lever (*for exploring horse's mouth*)
escalerista *m* (Am.) stairbuilder
escalerón *m* large stairway; peg ladder
escaleta *f* frame for lifting carriages
escalfado -da *adj* blistered (*said of plastered wall*); poached (*egg*)
escalfador *m* barber's metal pitcher (*for heating water*); chafing dish; painter's torch
escalfar *va* to poach (*eggs*); to burn, to bake (*bread*) brown
escalfarote *m* hair-lined or hay-lined shoe or boot
escalfeta *f* var. of **chofeta**
escalinata *f* stone step, front step
escalio *m* wasteland to be cultivated
escalmo *m* (naut.) thole; heavy wedge
escalo *m* burglary, breaking in; digging for escape, digging for forcible entry
escalofriado -da *adj* chilly, chilled
escalofriante *adj* chilling; frightening, hair-raising
escalofriar **§90** *va* to cause (*someone*) to shudder
escalofrío *m* chill
escalón *m* step, rung; tread (*of step*); (fig.) echelon, step, stage, grade; (fig.) stepping stone (*to fulfill an ambition*); (mil.) echelon; (rad.) stage; **en escalones** irregularly, unevenly (*made or cut*)
escalona *f* (bot.) scallion
escalonar *va* to place at intervals, to space out, to spread out; to stagger (*e.g., working hours*); to mark off (*at intervals*); (mil.) to echelon
escalonia or **escaloña** *f* var. of **escalona**
escalpar *va* to scalp
escalpelo *m* (surg.) scalpel
escama *f* (zool. & bot.) scale; resentment, grudge; fear, suspicion
escamado -da *adj* (coll.) fearful, distrustful; *m* scalework; *f* embroidery in scalework
escamadura *f* scaling
escamar *va* to scale; (coll.) to frighten, to shake the confidence of; *vr* to scale; (coll.) to be scared, to lose confidence
escamel *m* sword-maker's anvil
escamocho *m* leavings (*of food and drink*)
escamón -mona *adj* fearful, apprehensive
escamonda *f* pruning
escamondadura *f* pruned branches
escamondar *va* to prune (*a tree*); (fig.) to trim, to prune
escamondo *m* var. of **escamonda**
escamonea *f* (bot. & pharm.) scammony
escamonear *vr* (coll.) to lose confidence, become suspicious
escamoso -sa *adj* scaly, squamous
escamotar *va* to make disappear by sleight of hand; to palm (*a card*); to whisk out of sight, to cause to vanish; to snitch, to swipe; *vr* to disappear
escamoteable *adj* retractable
escamoteador -dora *mf* prestidigitator; thief, swindler
escamotear *va & vr* var. of **escamotar**
escamoteo *m* sleight of hand; palming; snitching, swiping
escampado -da *adj* free, open, clear; *f* break in rain, clear spell
escampar *va* to clear out; *vn* to stop raining; to ease up, to stop
escampavía *f* (naut.) scout; (naut.) revenue cutter, coast guard cutter
escampo *m* emptying, clearing out; end of rain
escamudo -da *adj* scaly
escamujar *va* to prune (*especially olive trees*); to clear out (*branches*)
escamujo *m* pruning, clearing out of branches
escancia *f* pouring, serving, or drinking wine
escanciador -dora *mf* one who passes the wines or other drinks
escanciar *va* to pour, to serve, to drink (*wine*); *vn* to drink wine
escanda *f* (bot.) spelt (*wheat*)
escandalar *m* (naut.) compass room (*in a galley*)
escandalera *f* (coll.) commotion, excitement
escandalizador -dora *adj* scandalizing; *mf* scandalizer
escandalizar **§76** *va* to scandalize; to outrage; *vr* to be scandalized; to be angered or irritated
escandalizativo -va *adj* scandalous
escándalo *m* scandal; shameful conduct, bad example; commotion, uproar; surprise, wonder; **causar escándalo** to make a scene
escandaloso -sa *adj* scandalous; turbulent, violent, restless; *f* (naut.) gafftopsail; **echar la escandalosa** (coll.) to use harsh words, to scold abusively
escandallar *va* (naut.) to sound; to sample (*a product*)
escandallo *m* (naut.) sounding lead; sampling (*of a product*); (com.) cost accounting; **echar el escandallo** (naut.) to take soundings
escandelar *m* var. of **escandalar**
escandia *f* (bot.) emmer
Escandinavia *f* Scandinavia
escandinavo -va *adj & mf* Scandinavian
escandio *m* (chem.) scandium
escandir *va* to scan (*verse*)
escansión *f* scansion
escantillar *va* to measure off, to lay off
escantillón *m* pattern, templet; rule, gage
escaña *f* var. of **escanda**
escaño *m* settle, bench with back for two or more people; seat (*in parliament*); (Am.) park bench
escañuelo *m* footstool
escapada *f* escape, flight; escapade; run, quick trip; **en una escapada** at full speed
escapadita *f* quick getaway; flying trip
escapamiento *m* var. of **escapada**
escapar *va* to save, preserve, to free; to drive (*a horse*) hard; *vn* to escape; to slip away, to flee, to run away; **escapar a** to escape (*e.g., death*); *vr* to escape; to slip away, to flee, to run away; to escape, to leak (*said of gas, water, etc.*); **escaparse a** to escape from (*a person*); to escape (*death*); **escaparse de** to escape from (*e.g., jail*); **escapársele a uno** to let slip, to say inadvertently; to miss, to not notice; to escape one's notice
escaparate *m* show window; cabinet (*for displaying curios or specimens*)
escaparatista *mf* window dresser
escapatoria *f* escape, getaway; (coll.) subterfuge, evasion; (fig.) escape (*from responsibilities, duties, etc.*)
escape *m* escape; flight; leak; exhaust; exhaust valve; escapement (*of a watch*); **a escape** at full speed, on the run; **escape de áncora** (horl.) anchor escapement; **escape de rejilla** (rad.) grid leak; **escape libre** (mach.) cutout
escapismo *m* escapism
escapista *adj & mf* escapist
escapo *m* (arch., bot. & zool.) scape
escápula *f* (anat.) scapula, shoulder blade
escapular *adj* scapular; *va* (naut.) to double or to round (*a cape*)
escapulario *m* scapular, scapulary
escaque *m* square (*of checkerboard or chessboard*); (her.) square; **escaques** *mpl* chess
escaqueado -da *adj* checkered
escara *f* see **escaro**
escarabajear *va* (coll.) to harass, to worry; *vn* to crawl around, to swarm; to scrawl, to scribble
escarabajeo *m* (coll.) harassment, worry
escarabajo *m* (ent.) scarab, black beetle; (f.a.) scarabaeus; flaw (*in fabric or casting*); (coll.) runt; **escarabajos** *mpl* (coll.) scribbling, scrawl; **escarabajo de agua** (ent.) water beetle; **escarabajo enterrador** (ent.) burying beetle; **escarabajo estercolero** (ent.) dor, dorbeetle; **escarabajo patatero** (ent.)

potato beetle or bug; **escarabajo pelotero** (ent.) tumblebug; **escarabajo sepulturero** (ent.) burying beetle
escarabajuelo *m* (ent.) vine beetle
escaramucear *vn* var. of **escaramuzar**
escaramujo *m* (bot.) dog rose (*plant and fruit*); (zool.) barnacle (*Pollicipes cornucopia*)
escaramuza *f* skirmish
escaramuzador *m* skirmisher
escaramuzar **§76** *vn* to skirmish
escarapela *f* cockade; quarrel ending in hair pulling or fisticuffs
escarapelar *vn & vr* to quarrel, to wrangle (*said of women*); **escarapelársele a uno el cuerpo** to have goose flesh
escaravia *f* (bot.) skirret
escarbadientes *m* (*pl:* **-tes**) toothpick
escarbador *m* scraper, scratcher; pryer; plugging chisel
escarbadura *f* scraping, scratching
escarbaorejas *m* (*pl:* **-jas**) earpick
escarbar *va* to scratch, to scratch up (*the ground*); to dig into; to poke (*the fire*); to pick (*teeth, ears, etc.*); to pry into
escarbo *m* scraping, scratching
escarcela *f* large pouch; game bag; cuisse or cuish (*of armor*)
escarceo *m* evasion, digression; (naut.) small bubbling waves (*due to currents*); **escarceos** *mpl* prancing
escarcina *f* cutlass
escarcha *f* frost, hoarfrost
escarchado -da *adj* frosted; *m* frost-like embroidery of gold or silver; *f* (bot.) ice plant
escarchar *va* to frost, to put frosting on (*e.g., a cake*); to dilute (*potter's clay*); to spangle; *vn* to be frost, e.g., **esta noche ha escarchado** last night there was frost
escarche *m* frost-like embroidery of gold and silver
escarcho *m* (ichth.) red surmullet
escarda *f* weeding; weeding time; weeding hoe
escardadera *f* weeder (*woman*); weeding hoe
escardador -dora *mf* weeder (*person*); *m* weeding hoe
escardadura *f* weeding
escardar or **escardillar** *va* to weed, to weed out
escardillo *m* dibble, weeding hoe; flicker in the dark
escariador *m* reamer
escariar *va* to ream
escarificación *f* (agr. & surg.) scarification
escarificador *m* (agr.) scarifier, cultivator, harrow; (surg.) scarifier, scarificator
escarificar **§86** *va* (agr. & surg.) to scarify; (surg.) to remove the dead skin from
escarioso -sa *adj* (bot.) scarious
escarizar **§76** *va* (surg.) to remove the dead skin from
escarlador *m* comb polisher
escarlata *adj* scarlet; *f* scarlet (*color and cloth*); (path.) scarlet fever
escarlatina *f* (path.) scarlatina, scarlet fever; crimson woolen fabric
escarmenar *va* to comb (*wool, silk, etc.*); to take away (*money or something else*) as punishment; to cheat a little at a time
escarmentar **§18** *va* to punish severely; *vn* to learn by experience, to learn one's lesson; **escarmentar en cabeza ajena** to learn by another person's mistakes; **escarmentar en cabeza propia** to learn by one's own mistakes
escarmiento *m* punishment, penalty; lesson, example, warning; caution, wisdom
escarnecedor -dora *adj* scoffing, ridiculing; *mf* scoffer
escarnecer **§34** *va* to scoff at, to make fun of, to ridicule
escarnecidamente *adv* scoffingly, mockingly
escarnecimiento or **escarnio** *m* scoffing, derision, gibe
escaro -ra *adj* duck-toed; *m* (ichth.) scarus, parrot fish; *f* (path.) slough
escarola *f* (bot.) endive; head of endive; (archaic) ruff, frill
escarolado -da *adj* ruffled, frilled, curled
escarolar *va* var. of **alechugar**
escarótico -ca *adj & m* (med.) escharotic
escarpa *f* scarp, escarpment; (fort.) scarp, escarpment
escarpado -da *adj* steep; rough, rugged, craggy
escarpadura *f* scarp, escarpment; cliff, bluff; solleret (*of armor*)
escarpar *va* to scarp, to escarp; to rasp (*sculpture*)
escarpe *m* var. of **escarpadura**
escarpelo *m* rasp; (surg.) scalpel
escarpia *f* tenterhook; meat hook; spike
escarpiador *m* clamp, staple (*to fasten a pipe to a wall*)
escarpidor *m* large-toothed comb
escarpín *m* pump (*slipperlike shoe*); sock (*worn over stocking or other sock*)
escarpión; en escarpión in the form of a tenterhook
escartivana *f* var. of **cartivana**
escarza *f* (vet.) sore hoof (*from nail*)
escarzano *adj masc* segmental (*arch*)
escarzar **§76** *va* to clear (*a hive*) of black combs; to bend (*a stick*) into an arc by means of cords
escarzo *m* black comb without honey; removal of honey from hive; floss silk; punk
escasear *va* to give sparingly; to save, to spare, to avoid; to bevel, to cut at an angle; *vn* to be scarce, to become scarce
escasero -ra *adj* (coll.) sparing; (coll.) saving, frugal; (coll.) stingy; *mf* (coll.) skinflint
escasez *f* scarcity, shortness; want, need; stinginess
escaso -sa *adj* scarce; little, slight; scanty; parsimonious, frugal; stingy; scant, e.g., **media hora escasa** a scant half-hour; **escaso de** scant of, short of
escatimar *va* to scrimp; **escatimar a uno la comida** to scrimp someone for food; *vn* to scrimp
escatimoso -sa *adj* sly, scrimpy, mean
escatología *f* scatology; (theol.) eschatology
escatológico -ca *adj* scatological; eschatological
escavanar *va* to loosen and weed (*the ground*)
escayola *f* scagliola; stucco
escayolar *va* to overlay with scagliola; to stucco; (surg.) to put in a plaster cast
escena *f* scene; stage; incident, episode; **poner en escena** to stage (*a play*)
escenario *m* stage; setting; background
escénico -ca *adj* scenic (*pertaining to a stage or to stage effects*)
escenificación *f* staging, portrayal; adaptation for the stage
escenificar **§86** *va* to stage, to portray; to adapt for the stage
escenografía *f* scenography
escenográfico -ca *adj* scenographic or scenographical
escenógrafo -fa *adj* scenographic; *mf* scenographer
escepticismo *m* scepticism
escéptico -ca *adj* sceptic or sceptical; *mf* sceptic
esciente *adj* knowing
escila *f* (bot.) squill; (*cap.*) *f* (geog. & myth.) Scylla; **estar entre Escila y Caribdis** to be between Scylla and Charybdis
escinco *m* (zool.) skink
escindible *adj* fissionable
escindir *va* to split
Escipión *m* Scipio
escirro *m* (path.) scirrhus
escirroso -sa *adj* scirrhous
escisión *f* scission, fission; splitting; schism; (biol.) fission; (surg.) excision
escita *adj & mf* Scythian
Escitia, la Scythia
escítico -ca *adj* Scythian
esclarea *f* (bot.) clary
esclarecedor -dora *adj* enlightening; ennobling
esclarecer **§34** *va* to brighten, to light up; to explain, to elucidate; to enlighten; to ennoble; *vn* to dawn
esclarecidamente *adv* illustriously, nobly; brilliantly
esclarecido -da *adj* illustrious, noble; manifest, obvious

esclarecimiento *m* illumination; explanation, elucidation; enlightenment; ennoblement
esclavina *f* pelerine; tippet; pilgrim's cloak
esclavista *adj* proslavery; *mf* advocate of slavery
esclavitud *f* slavery
esclavización *f* enslavement
esclavizar **§76** *va* to enslave
esclavo -va *adj* enslaved; **esclavo de su palabra** faithful to one's word; *mf* slave; (fig.) slave, drudge
esclavón -vona *adj & mf* var. of **eslavón**
esclavonio -nia *adj & mf* var. of **eslavonio;** (*cap.*) *f* var. of **Eslavonia**
esclerénquima *m* (bot.) sclerenchyma
esclerocio *m* (bot.) sclerotium
esclerodermia *f* (path.) scleroderma
escleroma *m* (path.) scleroma
esclerómetro *m* sclerometer
esclerosis *f* (*pl:* **-sis**) (path. & bot.) sclerosis; **esclerosis en placas** or **esclerosis múltiple** (path.) multiple sclerosis
escleroso -sa *adj* sclerous; (path.) sclerotic
esclerótico -ca *adj & f* (anat.) sclerotic
esclerotitis *f* (path.) sclerotitis
esclerotomía *f* (surg.) sclerotomy
esclusa *f* lock, floodgate, sluice; **esclusa de aire** (eng.) caisson
esclusada *f* lockful; flood of water released to swell a river
esclusero *m* lock tender
esc.º abr. of **escudo**
escoa *f* (naut.) point of greatest curvature (*of a ship's rib*)
escoba *f* broom; (bot.) broom
escobada *f* sweep; quick sweeping
escobadera *f* woman sweeper
escobajo *m* old broom; grape stem (*with grapes removed*)
escobar *m* field of broom; *va* to sweep with a broom
escobazar **§76** *va* to sprinkle with a wet broom
escobazo *m* blow with a broom; sweep
escobén *m* (naut.) hawsehole
escobera *f* see **escobero**
escobería *f* broom factory; broom store
escobero -ra *mf* broom maker or vendor; *f* (bot.) Spanish broom
escobeta *f* brush, small broom
escobilla *f* brush, whisk, small broom; sweepings of gold or silver (*e.g., in a mint*); (bot.) teasel (*plant and bur*); (elec.) brush; **escobilla de afeitar** or **de barba** shaving brush; **escobilla de carbón** (elec.) carbon brush
escobillado *m* (Am.) brush (*in dancing*)
escobillar *va* to brush
escobillón *m* push broom; boiler-flue cleaner; (gun.) swab
escobina *f* chips from drilling; filings
escobo *m* broom thicket, brushwood
escobón *m* long-handled broom; short-handled broom; scrubbing brush; (bot.) broom
escocedura *f* chafing, chafed skin
escocer **§30** *va* to chafe; to annoy, to displease; *vn* to smart, to sting; *vr* to feel sorry; to chafe, become chafed
escocés -cesa *adj* Scotch; *mf* Scot; *m* Scotchman; Scotch (*dialect; whiskey*); *f* (mus.) écossaise
escocia *f* (arch.) scotia; codfish; (*cap.*) *f* Scotland; **la Nueva Escocia** Nova Scotia
escocimiento *m* smarting or stinging sensation; chafed skin
escoda *f* bushhammer
escodadero *m* place where deer rub the velvet off their antlers
escodar *va* to bushhammer, to carve or trim (*stone*) with bushhammer; to shake or rub (*the antlers*) to free them of velvet; (prov.) to cut off the tail of
escofieta *f* hair net
escofina *f* rasp
escofinar *va* to rasp
escofión *m* net headpiece
escogedor -dora *adj* choosing, selecting; *mf* chooser, selector
escoger **§49** *va* to choose, to select
escogidamente *adv* cleverly, wisely; completely, in an excellent manner; carefully
escogido -da *adj* selected; choice, select; **los escogidos** (theol.) the elect
escogimiento *m* choosing, selecting
escolanía *f* choirboys' school or association (*in Catalonia*)
escolano *m* choirboy (*pupil*)
escolapio -pia *adj* pertaining to the Scuole Pie (*religious schools founded in Rome in the seventeenth century*); *m* Escolapio, Piarist
escolar *adj* (pertaining to) school, scholastic; *m* pupil, scholar; **§77** *vn & vr* to squeeze one's way
escolástica *f* see **escolástico**
escolasticismo *m* scholasticism; (philos.) scholasticism
escolástico -ca *adj & mf* scholastic; *f* scholasticism
escólex *m* (*pl:* **escólex**) (zool.) scolex
escoliador *m* scholiast
escoliar *va* to comment, to gloss (*a text*)
escoliasta *m* scholiast
escolimado -da *adj* (coll.) weak, sickly
escolimoso -sa *adj* (coll.) impatient, restless
escolio *m* scholium
escoliosis *f* (path.) scoliosis
escolopendra *f* (zool.) scolopendra, centipede; (bot.) hart's-tongue
escolta *f* escort; attendant; (aer. & nav.) escort
escoltar *va* to escort, to attend
escollar *vn* (Am.) to hit a reef, to run aground on a reef; (Am.) to fail
escollera *f* rock fill; jetty, breakwater; row of rocks jutting out of the sea
escollo *m* reef, rock; (fig.) pitfall; (fig.) stumbling block
escolloso -sa *adj* dangerous, risky; thorny (*problem*)
escombra *f* clearing, clearing out
escombrar *va* to clear, to clear out
escombrera *f* dump, spoil bank
escombro *m* rubbish, debris; (ichth.) mackerel; **escombros** *spl* rubbish, debris; (min.) deads
escomer *vr* to wear away
esconce *m* corner, angle
escondedero *m* hiding place
esconder *m* hide-and-seek; *va* to hide; to harbor, to contain; *vr* to hide; to lurk
escondidamente *adv* secretly, hiddenly
escondido -da *adj* hidden, out of the way; **a escondidas** secretly, on the sly; **a escondidas de** without the knowledge of; **en escondido** secretly, on the sly
escondillas; a escondillas hiddenly, on the sly
escondimiento *m* hiding, concealment
escondite *m* hiding place; hide-and-seek; **jugar al escondite** to play hide-and-seek
escondrijo *m* hiding place; nook
esconzado -da *adj* angular
escopeta *f* shotgun; **aquí te quiero, escopeta** (coll.) now or never; **escopeta blanca** gentleman hunter; **escopeta de aire comprimido** air rifle; **escopeta de dos cañones** double-barreled shotgun; **escopeta de viento** air rifle; **escopeta negra** professional hunter
escopetar *va* (min.) to clear the earth from (*a gold mine*)
escopetazo *m* gunshot; gunshot wound; sudden bad news; (Am.) sarcasm, insult
escopetear *va* to shoot at with a shotgun; *vr* to shoot at each other with shotguns; **escopetearse a** (coll.) to shower each other with, e.g., **se escopeteaban a lisonjas** they showered each other with flattery; **se escopeteaban a improperios** they showered each other with insults
escopeteo *m* firing a shotgun; gunfire
escopetería *f* soldiers armed with shotguns; gunfire
escopetero *m* soldier armed with a shotgun, musketeer; gunner; armed guard; gunsmith
escopladura *f* chisel cut, notch, mortise
escopleadora *f* mortising machine
escopleadura *f* var. of **escopladura**
escoplear *va* to chisel
escoplo *m* turning chisel, woodworking chisel
escopolamina *f* (chem.) scopolamine
escora *f* (naut.) level line; (naut.) shore; (naut.) list

escorar *va* (naut.) to shore; *vn* (naut.) to list; (naut.) to reach low tide
escorbútico -ca *adj & mf* scorbutic
escorbuto *m* (path.) scorbutus, scurvy
escorchar *va* to flay, to skin
escordio *m* (bot.) water germander
escoria *f* scoria, dross, slag; (fig.) trash, dregs; (petrog.) scoria
escoriáceo -a *adj* scoriaceous
escorial *m* slag dump; lava bed; abandoned mine; **El Escorial** El Escorial (*town in central Spain*); the Escorial or the Escurial (*monastery, palace, and royal mausoleum at El Escorial, built in sixteenth century*)
escoriar *va* var. of **excoriar**
escorificar §86 *va* to scorify
escorpena or **escorpina** *f* (ichth.) scorpene
Escorpio *m* (astr.) Scorpio
escorpioide *f* (bot.) scorpion grass
escorpión *m* (ent.) scorpion; scorpion (*scourge; ancient catapult*); (ichth.) scorpion fish; (*cap.*) *m* (astr.) Scorpio; **tener lengua de escorpión** to have a biting tongue
escorrozo *m* (coll.) pleasure, enjoyment
escorzado *m* var. of **escorzo**
escorzar §76 *va* (f.a.) to foreshorten
escorzo *m* (f.a) foreshortening
escorzón *m* (zool.) toad
escorzonera *f* (bot.) viper's-grass
escoscar §86 *va* to remove the dandruff from; to hull, to shell; *vr* to shrug one's shoulders
escota *f* (naut.) sheet; **escota mayor** (naut.) mainsheet
escotado -da *adj* sharp, pointed; low-necked; *m* low neck (*in a dress*); armhole (*in armor*); (theat.) large trap door; notch, recess
escotadura *f* low neck (*in dress*); armhole (*in armor*); (theat.) large trap door; notch, recess
escotar *va* to cut (*something*) to fit; to draw water from (*e.g., a river*) through a drain or trench; *vn* to club together, to go Dutch
escote *m* low neck; tucker; share, quota, scot; **ir a escote** or **pagar a escote** to go Dutch
escotero -ra *adj* traveling light (*i.e., without baggage*); *f* (naut.) sheet hole; (naut.) chock
escotilla *f* (naut.) hatchway
escotillón *m* hatchway, bulkhead, trap door (*e.g., to a cellar*); (theat.) trap door; (naut.) small hatchway
escotín *m* (naut.) topsail sheet
escotismo *m* Scotism
escozor *m* smarting or stinging sensation; sorrow, grief
escriba *m* scribe (*teacher of Jewish law*)
escribanía *f* court clerkship; court clerk's office; portable writing desk; writing materials
escribano *m* court clerk; lawyer's clerk; clerk; (archaic) scrivener; (archaic) notary; **escribano del agua** (ent.) whirligig beetle
escribido -da *pp of* **escribir,** used only in expression **leído y escribido** (coll.) posing as learned
escribidor *m* (coll.) poor writer
escribiente *mf* clerk, office clerk; writer; **escribiente a máquina** typist
escribir *m* writing; **§17,** 9 *va & vn* to write; *vr* to enroll, to enlist; to write to each other; **no escribirse** to be impossible to describe, to be impossible to say
escriño *m* straw hamper; jewel case; hiding place; (prov.) cup of acorn
escrit.ª abr. of **escritura**
escrita *f* see **escrito**
escritilla *f* lamb's fry
escrito -ta *pp of* **escribir;** *adj* streaked; *m* writing; document, manuscript; (law) writ, brief; **por escrito** in writing; *f* (ichth.) spotted skate
escritor -tora *mf* writer
escritorcillo -lla *mf* writer of no account
escritorio *m* writing desk, escritoire; (print.) desk with sloping top; office; **escritorio ministro** office desk; **escritorio norteamericano** roll-top desk
escritura *f* writing; handwriting, script; (law) indenture, instrument; (law) sworn statement; (law) deed; **escritura al tacto** touch typewriting; **escritura a máquina** typewriting; **escritura de riesgo** (naut.) marine-insurance policy; (*cap.*) *f* Scripture; **Sagrada Escritura** Holy Scripture
escriturar *va* (law) to establish by affidavit, to execute (*e.g., a sale*) by means of a deed; to book (*e.g., an actor for a play*)
escriturario -ria *adj* (law) notarial; *m* Scripturist
escrnía. abr. of **escribanía**
escrno. abr. de **escribano**
escrófula *f* (path.) scrofula
escrofularia *f* (bot.) figwort
escrofuloso -sa *adj* scrofulous
escrotal *adj* scrotal
escroto *m* (anat.) scrotum
escrupulillo *m* slight scruple; jinglet
escrupulizar §76 *vn* to scruple, have scruples; to be overcautious
escrúpulo *m* scruple; (pharm.) scruple
escrupulosidad *f* scrupulosity, scrupulousness
escrupuloso -sa *adj* scrupulous
escrutación *f* scrutiny, examination
escrutador -dora *adj* searching; *mf* examiner, inspector; teller of votes, inspector of election returns
escrutar *va* to scrutinize; to count (*votes*)
escrutinio *m* scrutiny; inspection of election returns, counting of votes
escrutiñador -dora *mf* examiner, inspector, censor
escuadra *f* (carp.) square; triangle (*of draftsman*); bracket; angle iron, angle brace, gusset; squad, gang; (mil.) squad; (nav.) squadron; **a escuadra** square, at right angles; **falsa escuadra** bevel square; **fuera de escuadra** out of square; **escuadra de agrimensor** cross-staff; **escuadra falsa** bevel square
escuadración *f* squaring
escuadrar *va* (carp.) to square
escuadreo *m* squaring, quadrature
escuadría *f* dimensions of cross section
escuadrilla *f* (nav. & aer.) escadrille
escuadrón *m* flock, swarm; (mil.) squadron (*of cavalry*)
escuadronista *m* (mil.) cavalry tactician
escualidez *f* squalor; paleness, emaciation
escuálido -da *adj* squalid; pale, emaciated, thin
escualo *m* (ichth.) spiny dogfish
escualor *m* squalor
escucha *f* listening; chaperon (*in convents*); (mil.) scout, vedette; **estar de escucha** (coll.) to eavesdrop; *mf* listener
escuchador -dora *adj* listening
escuchar *va* to listen to; to heed, to mind; *vn* to listen; *vr* to speak with pompous deliberation, to be pleased at the sound of one's own voice
escuchimizado -da *adj* feeble, exhausted
escudar *va* to shield
escuderaje *m* shield service
escuderear *va* to wait on, to attend
escudero *m* shield-bearer, esquire; nobleman; lady's page; shield maker
escuderón *m* (coll.) fourflusher
escudete *m* escutcheon; (sew.) gusset; (carp.) escutcheon, escutcheon plate (*around keyhole*); (bot.) white water lily
escudilla *f* bowl
escudo *m* shield, buckler; (bot., her. & fig.) shield; (zool.) shield, scute, scutum; coat of arms; escutcheon, escutcheon plate (*around keyhole*); (naut.) backboard; **escudo de armas** coat of arms; **escudo térmico** heat shield (*of space capsule*)
escudriñador -dora *adj* scrutinizing, prying; *mf* scrutinizer, prier
escudriñamiento *m* scrutinizing, scrutiny
escudriñar *va* to scrutinize, to pry into
escuela *f* school; **hacer escuela** to start or found a school; to set a fashion; **escuela comercial** business college; **escuela de artes y oficios** trade school; **escuela de graduados** graduate school; **escuela de ingenieros de montes** forestry school; **escuela del hogar y profesional de la mujer** school of home economics; **escuela de párvulos** kindergarten; **escuela de verano** summer school; **escuela dominical** Sunday school; **Escuela Naval Militar** Naval Academy

(U.S.A.); Royal Naval College (Brit.); **escuela normal** normal school; **escuela para enfermeras** school of nursing; **escuela parroquial** parochial school; **escuela preparatoria** preparatory school
escuelante *m* (Am.) schoolboy; *f* (Am.) schoolgirl; *mf* (Am.) teacher
escuelero -ra *mf* (Am.) pupil; (Am.) teacher
escuerzo *m* (zool.) toad; (coll.) sickly-looking person
escueto -ta *adj* free, unencumbered; plain, bare, unadorned
escuintle *m* (Am.) mutt; (Am.) brat
Esculapio *m* (myth.) Aesculapius; (fig.) Aesculapian (*any physician*)
esculcar §86 *va* (Am.) to search, to frisk
esculpidor *m* sculptor; engraver
esculpir *va* to sculpture, to carve; to engrave
escultismo *m* scoutcraft, outdoor activities
escultista *mf* scout, athlete; *m* outdoorsman
escultor *m* sculptor
escultora *f* sculptress
escultórico -ca *adj* sculptural
escultura *f* sculpture
escultural *adj* sculptural, sculpturesque, statuesque
escuna *f* (naut.) schooner
escupetina *f* var. of **escupitina**
escupidera *f* cuspidor, spittoon; (prov. & Am.) chamber pot
escupidero *m* spitting place, place full of spit; (fig.) seat of scorn, embarrassing position
escupido -da *adj* the spit and image of, e.g., **María es escupida la madre** Mary is the spit and image of her mother; *m* spit, spittle
escupidor -dora *adj* spitting all the time; *mf* great spitter; *m* (prov. & Am.) cuspidor, spittoon; (Am.) round mat
escupidura *f* spit, spittle; fever blister or sore
escupir *va* to spit; to cast aside with scorn; to throw off; (fig.) to spit, to spit forth; *vn* to spit; **escupir a** to scoff at
escupitajo *m* (coll.) spit, spittle
escupitina *f* (coll.) spit, spittle; (coll.) spitting, constant spitting
escupitinajo *m* (coll.) var. of **escupitajo**
escupo *m* spit, spittle
escurar *va* to scour (*cloth*) before fulling
escurialense *adj* pertaining to El Escorial (*town*) and to the Escorial (*building*)
escurra *m* scoundrel, rascal
escurreplatos *m* (*pl:* **-tos**) dish rack, draining rack
escurribanda *f* (coll.) subterfuge, evasion; (coll.) looseness of bowels; (coll.) running (*of a sore*); (coll.) scuffle
escurridero *m* drainpipe, drain hole, outlet; drainboard; slippery place; (phot.) rack for drying plates
escurridizo -za *adj* slippery
escurrido -da *adj* narrow-hipped; wearing tight-fitting skirts; (Am.) abashed, ashamed
escurridor *m* colander; dish rack, draining rack; (phot.) rack for drying plates
escurriduras or **escurrimbres** *fpl* lees, dregs
escurrimiento *m* draining; dripping; (elec.) creepage; (fig.) slip
escurrir *va* to drain (*a vessel; a liquid; dishes*); to wring, to wring out; to slip; *vn* to drip, to ooze, to trickle; to slip, to slide; to be slippery; *vr* to drip, to ooze, to trickle; to slip, to slide; to escape, to slip away; to slip out (*said of a remark*); **escurrirse de entre las manos** to slip out of or through one's hands
escusalí *m* (*pl:* **-líes**) little apron
Escútari *m* Scutari
escutelado -da *adj* (bot., zool. & orn.) scutellate
escutelo *m* (bot. & zool.) scutellum
escutiforme *adj* scutiform, scutate
Esdras *m* (Bib.) Esdras
esdrujulear *vn* to use proparoxytones all the time
esdrujulizar §76 *va* to give a proparoxytonic accent to
esdrújulo -la *adj* (gram.) proparoxytonic; (*verse*) whose last word is accented on antepenult; *m* (gram.) proparoxytone
ese, esa *adj dem* (*pl:* **esos, esas**) that; **ese** *f* s (*letter*); S-shaped link (*of chain*); sound hole (*in violins*); **hacer eses** to zigzag, to reel (*from too much drink*)
ése, ésa *pron dem* (*pl:* **ésos, ésas**) that one; *f* your city
esecilla *f* little link
esencia *f* essence; gasoline; (chem.) essence; **en esencia** in essence; **quinta esencia** quintessence; **esencia de pera** banana oil
esencial *adj & m* essential
esfacelar *vr* (path.) to sphacelate
esfacelo *m* (path.) sphacelus
esfágnea *f* (bot.) sphagnum
esfena *f* or **esfeno** *m* (mineral.) sphene
esfenoidal *adj* sphenoidal
esfenoides *m* (anat.) sphenoid, sphenoid bone
esfera *f* (geom.) sphere; (fig.) sphere (*range, surroundings*); (poet.) sphere (*sky, heavens*); dial (*e.g., of clock*); **esfera armilar** armillary sphere; **esfera celeste** sphere, celestial sphere; **esfera de actividad** sphere of action; **esfera de influencia** (dipl.) sphere of influence
esferal *adj* var. of **esférico**
esfericidad *f* sphericity
esférico -ca *adj* sperical; *m* (sport) ball
esferilla *f* little sphere, little ball
esferoidal *adj* spheroidal
esferoide *m* (geom.) spheroid
esferómetro *m* spherometer
esférula *f* spherule
esfigmógrafo *m* (physiol.) sphygmograph
esfinge *f* sphinx; (fig.) sphinx (*mysterious person*); (fig.) sly, vengeful woman; (ent.) hawk moth
esfínter *m* (anat.) sphincter
esforrocinar *va* to trim runners from (*trunk of vine*)
esforrocino *m* (bot.) sarmentum or runner growing from trunk of vine
esforzado -da *adj* vigorous, courageous, enterprising
esforzador -dora *adj* encouraging
esforzar §52 *va* to strengthen, to invigorate; to encourage; *vr* to exert oneself; **esforzarse a, en** or **por** + *inf* to strive to + *inf*
esfragístico -ca *adj* sphragistic; *f* sphragistics
esfuerzo *m* effort; vigor, spirit, courage; stress
esfumado -da *adj* (paint.) sfumato
esfumar *va* (f.a.) to stump; (paint.) to tone down, to soften; *vr* to disappear, to fade away
esfuminar *va* (f.a.) to stump
esfumino *m* (f.a.) stump
esgarrar *va* to try to cough up (*phlegm*); to tear, rend; *vn* to clear one's throat
esgrafiado *m* (f.a.) sgrafitto
esgrafiar *va* (f.a.) to decorate with sgraffito
esgrima *f* fencing (*art*)
esgrimidor *m* fencer
esgrimidura *f* fencing (*act*)
esgrimir *va* to wield; to brandish; to swing (*e.g., a new argument*); *vn* to fence
esgrimista *mf* (Am.) fencer; (Am.) gyp, panhandler
esguazable *adj* fordable
esguazar §76 *va* to ford
esguazo *m* fording; ford
esgucio *m* (arch.) cavetto
esguín *m* (ichth.) samlet, parr
esguince *m* dodge, duck; feint; frown, scornful look; sprain, twist (*of a joint*)
esguízaro -ra *adj & mf* Swiss; **pobre esguízaro** (coll.) wretch, ragamuffin
eslabón *m* link (*of chain*); (fig.) link; steel (*for striking fire from flint; for sharpening knives*); **eslabón perdido** missing link (*between man and monkey*)
eslabonador -dora *adj* linking, interlinking
eslabonamiento *m* linkage, linking; interlinking, stringing together, sequence
eslabonar *va* to link; to interlink, to string together; *vr* to link
eslalom *m* slalom
eslavo -va *adj* Slav; Slavic; *mf* Slav; *m* Slavic (*language*)
eslavoeclesiástico *m* Church Slavic or Slavonic (*language*)
eslavón -vona *adj & mf* Slav

eslavonio -nia *adj & mf* Slavonian; (*cap.*) *f* Slavonia
eslinga *f* (naut.) sling
eslingar §59 *va* (naut.) to sling
eslizón *m* (zool.) seps
eslora *f* (naut.) length; **esloras** *fpl* (naut.) binding strakes (*of deck*)
eslovaco -ca *adj & mf* Slovak or Slovakian; *m* Slovak (*language*)
Eslovaquia *f* Slovakia
Eslovenia *f* Slovenia
esloveno -na *adj & mf* Slovene or Slovenian; *m* Slovenian (*language*)
esmaltado *m* enameling
esmaltador -dora *mf* enameler
esmaltadura *f* var. of **esmaltado**
esmaltar *va* to enamel; to adorn with bright colors; to adorn, to embellish
esmalte *m* enamel; enamel work; (anat.) enamel; smalt (*pigment and color*); (her.) tincture; **esmalte alveolado** or **tabicado** cloisonné; **esmalte campeado** or **vaciado** champlevé; **esmalte de uñas** or **esmalte para las uñas** nail polish
esmaltín *m* smalt
esmaltina *f* (mineral.) smaltite
esméctico -ca *adj* smectic
esmerado -da *adj* careful, painstaking
esmeralda *f* emerald
esmeraldino -na *adj* emerald (*in color*)
esmerar *va* to polish, to brighten; *vr* to take pains, to use great care; to get results; **esmerarse en** or **por** + *inf* to strive to + *inf*, to take pains to + *inf*
esmerejón *m* (orn.) goshawk; (orn.) merlin; small-caliber gun
esmeril *m* emery; small-caliber gun
esmerilador *m* grinder (*workman*)
esmeriladora *f* emery wheel, grinder
esmerilar *va* to grind, to polish with emery
esmerillón *m* swivel
esmero *m* great care; cleanliness, neatness
Esmirna *f* Smyrna
esmirriado -da *adj* var. of **desmirriado**
esmoladera *f* grindstone
esmoquin *m* var. of **smoking**
esnob *adj* snobbish; *mf* (*pl:* **esnobs**) snob
esnobismo *m* snobbery, snobbishness
esnordeste *m* east-northeast
eso *pron dem neut* that; **a eso de** about (*e.g., six o'clock*); **por eso** therefore, for that reason; **eso es** that's it; that is
esófago *m* (anat.) esophagus
esópico -ca *adj* Aesopian or Aesopic
Esopo *m* Aesop
esotérico -ca *adj* esoteric
esotro -tra *adj & pron dem* (archaic) that other
esotropia *f* (path.) esotropia
espabiladeras *fpl* snuffers
espabilar *va* to trim, to snuff (*candle*)
espaciado -da *adj* scattered; *m* (print.) spacing
espaciador *m* space bar
espacial *adj* spatial; (pertaining to) space
espaciamiento *m* spacing; expatiation
espaciar §90 (Am.) & **regular** *va* to space; to scatter, to spread; (print.) to space; (print.) to lead; *vr* to enlarge, to expatiate; to relax, to amuse oneself
espacio *m* space; room; period, interval; (mus.) interval; (print.) space; delay, slowness; **por espacio de** in the space of (*e.g., a year*); **espacio de almacenaje** storage space; **espacio de chispa** (elec.) spark gap (*of spark plug*); **espacio de pelo** (print.) hair space; **espacio euclidiano** (geom.) Euclidean space; **espacio exterior** outer space; **espacio vital** Lebensraum
espaciosidad *f* spaciousness
espacioso -sa *adj* spacious, roomy; slow, deliberate
espachurrar *va* var. of **despachurrar**
espada *f* sword; playing card (*representing a sword*) equivalent to spade; (ichth.) swordfish; **espadas** *fpl* card suit corresponding to spades; **entre la espada y la pared** between the devil and the deep blue sea; **envainar la espada** to sheathe the sword; **medir las espadas** to measure swords; **espada de Damocles** sword of Damocles; **espada de dos filos** two-edged sword; *m* swordsman; (taur.) matador
espadachín *m* swordsman, skilled swordsman; bully
espadador -dora *mf* scutcher, hemp or flax beater
espadaña *f* (bot.) cattail, bulrush, reed mace (*Typha latifolia*); bell gable; **espadaña fina** (bot.) flagon
espadañada *f* spewing of blood; abundance, large number
espadañal *m* meadow full of cattail
espadañar *va* to spread out (*the tail feathers*)
espadar *va* to swingle, to scutch
espadarte *m* (ichth.) swordfish
espadería *f* sword cutlery, sword shop
espadero *m* swordmaker, swordsmith, sword dealer
espádice *m* (bot.) spadix
espadilla *f* scull (*oar*); swingle; ace of spades; bodkin (*for lady's hair*); red insignia of order of Santiago
espadillar *va* to swingle
espadín *m* rapier
espadón *m* (coll.) brass hat (*in army and elsewhere*); (coll.) braggart soldier; eunuch
espadrapo *m* var. of **esparadrapo**
espagírico -ca *adj* metallurgic; spagyric, iatrochemical; *f* metallurgy; spagyric, iatrochemistry
espahí *m* (*pl:* **-híes**) spahi
espalar *va* to shovel (*e.g., snow*)
espalda *f* back; **espaldas** *fpl* back, shoulders; (mil.) rearguard; **a espaldas** or **a espaldas vueltas** treacherously; **a espaldas de** behind, back of (*a building*); **cargado de espaldas** round-shouldered; **dar de espaldas** to fall on one's back; **echarse a las espaldas** to forget about (*a worry, duty, etc.*); **echarse sobre las espaldas** to take on, to assume as a responsibility; **hablar por las espaldas de** to talk behind the back of; **no sacarle espaldas al trabajo** to keep one's shoulder to the wheel; **tener buenas espaldas** (coll.) to have broad shoulders; **volver las espaldas a** to turn a cold shoulder to
espaldar *m* back; backplate (*of armor*); back (*of chair*); shell, shield (*of turtle*); espalier, trellis; **espaldares** *mpl* wall hangings
espaldarazo *m* accolade; slap on the back; **dar el espaldarazo a** to approve, to validate, to recognize
espaldarcete *m* épaulière (*of armor*)
espaldarón *m* backplate (*of armor*)
espaldear *va* (naut.) to dash against the stern of (*a ship*)
espalder *m* stern rower (*in galley*)
espaldera *f* espalier, trellis; trellised wall
espaldilla *f* (anat.) scapula, shoulder blade; back (*of jacket*)
espalditendido -da *adj* (coll.) stretched out on one's back
espaldón *m* (carp.) mortise; (fort.) intrenchment
espaldonar *vr* (mil.) to hide from enemy fire
espaldudo -da *adj* broad-shouldered, heavy-set
espalera *f* espalier, trellis
espalmadura *f* parings (*of hoofs*)
espalmar *va* var. of **despalmar**
espalto *m* (paint.) dark glaze
espantable *adj* frightful, terrible
espantada *f* stampede (*flight*); cold feet
espantadizo -za *adj* shy, scary
espantador -dora *adj* frightening
espantajo *m* scarecrow (*figure; person*); (fig.) scarecrow, bugaboo
espantalobos *m* (*pl:* **-bos**) (bot.) bladder senna
espantamoscas *m* (*pl:* **-cas**) fly chaser; flytrap; fly net
espantapájaros *m* (*pl:* **-ros**) scarecrow (*figure*)
espantar *va* to scare, to frighten; to frighten away, to chase away; *vr* to become scared, to become frightened; to marvel, to wonder
espanto *m* fright, terror, consternation; threat; (Am.) ghost, spook
espantoso -sa *adj* frightful; awful, fearful, astounding

España *f* Spain; **la Nueva España** New Spain (*Mexico in colonial period*); **las Españas** Spain and the countries of Spanish America
español -ñola *adj* Spanish; **a la española** in the Spanish fashion or manner; *mf* Spaniard; *m* Spanish (*language*); **los españoles** the Spanish (*people*); *f* Spanish woman; **La Española** Hispaniola (*Santo Domingo*)
españolado -da *adj* Spanish-looking; *f* Spanish sort of remark, Spanish mannerism; (scornful) Spanish take-off (*by foreigners*)
españolar *va & vr* (coll.) var. of **españolizar**
españolería *f* var. of **españolada**
españoleta *f* ancient Spanish dance; (Am.) espagnolette
españolismo *m* love of Spain, Spanish patriotism; Spanish nature or essence; Hispanicism
españolización *f* Hispaniolization
españolizar §76 *va* to make Spanish or like Spanish; to make (*a word*) Spanish; *vr* to become Spanish, to adopt Spanish customs
esparadrapo *m* court plaster, sticking plaster
esparaván *m* (vet.) spavin; (orn.) sparrow hawk
esparavel *m* mortarboard, hawk; casting net
esparceta *f* (bot.) sainfoin
esparciata *adj & mf* Spartan
esparcidamente *adv* separately; here and there; merrily, freely
esparcido -da *adj* merry, gay, open, candid
esparcidor -dora *adj* scattering, spreading; relaxing, diverting; *mf* scatterer, spreader
esparcilla *f* (bot.) spurry, corn spurry; (bot.) sainfoin
esparcimiento *m* scattering, spreading; spreading abroad, dissemination; relaxation, diversion; joviality, openness, frankness; **esparcimiento de banda** (rad.) band spread
esparcir §50 *va* to scatter, to spread; to spread abroad; to relax, to divert; *vr* to scatter, to spread; to spread abroad; to disperse; to relax, to take it easy
esparragado *m* dish of asparagus
esparragador -dora *mf* asparagus grower
esparragar §59 *vn* to grow asparagus
espárrago *m* (bot.) asparagus (*plant and its shoots*); tent or awning pole; peg ladder; stud bolt; **espárragos** *mpl* asparagus (*for eating*)
esparragón *m* double-thread silk cloth
esparraguero -ra *mf* asparagus grower or dealer; *f* (bot.) asparagus (*plant*); asparagus bed; asparagus dish
esparrancado -da *adj* with one's legs wide apart; too wide apart or open
esparrancar §86 *vr* (coll.) to spread one's legs wide apart
Esparta *f* Sparta
Espártaco *m* Spartacus
espartal *m* esparto field
espartano -na *adj & mf* Spartan; (fig.) Spartan
esparteña *f* matweed sandal
espartería *f* esparto wear (*cordage, shoes, baskets, mats*); esparto-wear shop or business
espartero -ra *mf* esparto-wear maker or dealer
espartilla *f* horsebrush of esparto grass
espartizal *m* esparto field
esparto *m* (bot.) esparto or esparto grass
esparver *m* (orn.) sparrow hawk
espasmo *m* (path.) spasm; **espasmo cínico** (path.) cynic spasm
espasmódico -ca *adj* spasmodic, convulsive
espasticidad *f* (path.) spasticity
espástico -ca *adj* spastic
espata *f* (bot.) spathe
espatarrada *f* (coll.) var. of **despatarrada**
espático -ca *adj* (mineral.) spathic
espato *m* (mineral.) spar; **espato calizo** (mineral.) calcspar; **espato de Islandia** (mineral.) Iceland spar; **espato flúor** (mineral.) fluor spar; **espato pesado** (mineral.) heavy spar, barite
espátula *f* spatula; palette knife; putty knife; (orn.) shoveler, spoonbill; (bot.) stinking iris, gladdon
espatulado -da *adj* spatulate
espatulomancía *f* spatulamancy
espaviento *m* fuss, excitement
espavorido -da *adj* terrified, frightened
especia *f* spice
especiado -da *adj* spicy
especial *adj* special, especial; **en especial** especially
especialidad *f* specialty, speciality
especialista *adj & mf* specialist
especialización *f* specialization
especializar §76 *va, vn & vr* to specialize
especiar *va* to spice
especie *f* species; kind, sort; matter; objection, pretext, show, appearance; news, rumor; **en especie** in kind (*in goods or produce*); **escapársele a uno una especie** to be indiscreet, to talk too much; **la especie** the species (*mankind*); **soltar una especie** to try to draw a person out; **especies sacramentales** (eccl.) species
especiería *f* spice store; spicery (*spices*); spice business; grocery store
especiero -ra *mf* spice dealer; *m* spice box
especificación *f* specification
especificar §86 *va* to specify; to itemize
especificativo -va *adj* specificative; (gram.) restrictive
específico -ca *adj* specific; *m* specific (*medicine*); patent medicine
espécimen *m* (*pl:* **especímenes**) specimen
especiosidad *f* neatness, beauty; speciosity, speciousness
especioso -sa *adj* neat, beautiful; specious
especiota *f* (coll.) crazy idea; (coll.) hoax, fake news
espectacular *adj* spectacular
espectáculo *m* spectacle; **dar un espectáculo** to create a scene, to make a scene
espectador -dora *adj* watching; *mf* spectator
espectral *adj* spectral, ghostly; (phys.) spectral, spectrum
espectro *m* specter, phantom, ghost; (phys.) spectrum; **espectro de radio** radio spectrum; **espectro magnético** magnetic curves
espectrógrafo *m* spectrograph; **espectrógrafo de masa** or **de masas** (phys.) mass spectrograph
espectroscopia *f* spectroscopy
espectroscópico -ca *adj* spectroscopic
espectroscopio *m* spectroscope
especulación *f* contemplation; speculation; (com.) speculation; report, account, statement
especulador -dora *adj* speculating; *mf* speculator
especular *adj* specular; *va* to view, inspect, contemplate; to speculate about or on; *vn* to speculate; (com.) to speculate; (coll.) to manage to improve one's lot
especulativo -va *adj* speculative; *f* (philos.) faculty of speculation or reason
espéculo *m* (med. & surg.) speculum
espejado -da *adj* mirrorlike, smooth or bright (*as a mirror*); mirrored
espejar *va* var. of **despejar**
espejear *vn* to shine, to sparkle
espejeo *m* var. of **espejismo**
espejería *f* mirror shop
espejero *m* mirror maker or dealer
espejismo *m* (opt. & fig.) mirage
espejo *m* mirror, looking glass; (fig.) mirror; model; **espejo de cuerpo entero** pier glass, full-length mirror; **espejo de falla** (geol.) slickenside; **espejo de los incas** (mineral.) obsidian; **espejo de retrovisión** (aut.) rear-view mirror; **espejo de Venus** (bot.) Venus's-looking-glass; **espejo de vestir** pier glass, full-length mirror; **espejo retrovisor** (aut.) rear-view mirror; **espejo ustorio** burning glass
espejuelo *m* small looking glass; (mineral.) selenite; candied citron or pumpkin; (arch.) rose window with openings filled with selenite; (vet.) chestnut; (fig.) mirage; **espejuelos** *mpl* spectacles; lenses of spectacles
espeleología *f* speleology
espeleólogo -ga *mf* speleologist
espelta *f* (bot.) spelt
espélteo -a *adj* (pertaining to) spelt
espelunca *f* cave, cavern
espeluzar §76 *va & vr* var. of **despeluzar**

espeluznante *adj* hair-raising
espeluznar *va & vr* var. of **despeluzar**
espeluzno *m* (coll.) chill, terror
espeque *m* prop, support; lever, handspike
espera *f* wait, waiting; restraint, composure; respite; delay; (law) stay; (carp.) notch; (hunt.) blind, hunter's blind; **en espera** waiting; **en espera de** waiting for, while waiting for; **no tener espera** to be of the greatest urgency, to be unpostponable
esperador -dora *adj* expectant
esperantista *adj & mf* Esperantist
esperanto *m* Esperanto
esperanza *f* hope; hopefulness; **tener puesta su esperanza en** to pin one's faith on; **esperanza de vida** life expectancy
esperanzado -da *adj* hopeful (*having hope*)
esperanzador -dora *adj* hopeful (*causing or giving hope*)
esperanzar **§76** *va* to give hope to, to make hopeful
esperanzoso -sa *adj* hopeful (*having great hope*)
esperar *va* to hope for; to hope; to expect; to await, to wait for; **ir a esperar** to go to meet; *vn* to hope; to wait; **esperar** + *inf* to hope to + *inf;* **esperar a que** + *subj* to wait until + *ind;* **esperar desesperando** to hope against hope; **esperar en** to put one's hope or trust in; **esperar que** + *fut ind* or *pres subj* to hope that + *fut ind;* **esperar sentado** to have a good wait, to wait for nothing; *vr* to expect
esperezar **§76** *vr* to stretch, to stretch one's arms and legs
esperezo *m* stretching, stretching the arms and legs
esperinque *m* (ichth.) smelt
esperma *f* sperm; **esperma de ballena** spermaceti
espermaceti *m* spermaceti
espermático -ca *adj* spermatic
espermatofita *f* (bot.) spermatophyte
espermatorrea *f* (path.) spermatorrhea
espermatozoide *m* or **espermatozoo** *m* (zool.) spermatozoön
espermófita *f* var. of **espermatofita**
espermogonio *m* (bot.) spermogonium
espernada *f* open link (*at end of chain*)
esperón *m* (naut.) spur (*ram of war vessel*); (Am.) long wait
esperonte *m* (fort.) spur
esperpento *m* (coll.) fright (*ugly person or thing*); nonsense, absurdity
espesador *m* thickener
espesamiento *m* thickening (*act*)
espesante *m* thickening (*substance*)
espesar *m* thickness, depth (*of woods*); *va* to thicken; to make closer, to weave tighter; *vr* to thicken, to become thick or thicker
espesativo -va *adj* thickening
espeso -sa *adj* thick; heavy (*liquid*); dirty, greasy, untidy
espesor *m* thickness; (coll.) thickness (*of a liquid or gas*)
espesura *f* thickness; shock of hair; thicket; dirtiness, greasiness, untidiness
espetaperro; a espetaperro or **a espetaperros** (coll.) at full speed
espetar *va* to spit, to skewer; to pierce, to pierce through, to transfix; **espetarle a uno una cosa** (coll.) to spring something on someone; *vr* to be stiff and solemn; (coll.) to steady oneself, to settle, to settle down
espetera *f* scullery, kitchen rack
espetón *m* poker; iron pin; large pin; spit; poke, jab; (ichth.) needlefish
espía *mf* spy; tattletale, squealer; *m* (coll.) cop (*policeman*); *f* (naut.) warping; (naut.) warp
espiar **§90** *va* to spy on; *vn* to spy; (naut.) to warp a ship; *vr* (naut.) to warp a ship
espibia *f*, **espibio** *m* or **espibión** *m* (vet.) sprain in the neck (*of horse*)
espicanardi *f* or **espicanardo** *m* (bot.) spikenard
espiciforme *adj* (bot.) spiciform
espícula *f* (anat., bot. & zool.) spicule
espicular *adj* spicular or spiculate
espichar *va* to prick; *vn* (coll.) to die; *vr* (Am.) to get thin
espiche *m* prick (*pointed weapon or instrument*); (naut.) peg, spigot
espichón *m* prick, stab (*wound*)
espiga *f* (bot.) spike, ear; (archeol. & surg.) spica; (carp.) tenon, pin, peg; (mach.) tongue; brad; clapper (*of bell*); stem (*of a key*); shank (*e.g., of a rivet*); fuse (*of a bomb*); (naut.) masthead; **espiga de la Virgen** (astr.) Spica; **espigas comprobadoras** (elec.) testing prongs
espigadera *f* gleaner
espigado -da *adj* spiky; ripe, seeded; spindly; tall, grown-up; (bot.) spicate
espigador -dora *mf* gleaner
espigadura *f* gleaning
espigar **§59** *va* to glean; (fig.) to glean; to tenon, to pin, to dowel; *vn* to ear, to form ears (*said of cereals*); *vr* to grow tall
espigo *m* stem, shank
espigón *m* sting; point of a sharp tool or nail; sharp ear or spike; ear of corn; peak; breakwater
espigueo *m* gleaning; gleaning time
espiguilla *f* (bot.) spikelet; tape, fringe; (bot.) meadow grass
espina *f* thorn, spine; fishbone; (anat., bot. & zool.) spine; (fig.) thorn; doubt, uncertainty; **dar mala espina a** (coll.) to worry, to make anxious; **estar en espinas** (coll.) to be on pins and needles; **sacarse la espina** (coll.) to get even, make up a loss; **espina blanca** (bot.) cotton thistle; **espina de pescado** herringbone (*in fabrics*); **espina de pez** fishbone; **espina dorsal** (anat.) spinal column; **espina santa** or **vera** (bot.) Christ's-thorn, Jerusalem thorn
espinaca *f* (bot.) spinach; **espinacas** *fpl* spinach (*for eating*)
espinadura *f* prick, pricking
espinal *adj* spinal
espinapez *m* herringbone (*in hardwood or tile floor*); thorny matter, difficulty
espinar *m* thorny spot; (fig.) thorny matter; *va* to prick (*said of thorns*); to protect (*trees*) with thorn bushes; (fig.) to sting, to provoke; *vn* to prick
espinazo *m* (anat.) backbone; (arch.) keystone
espinel *m* trawl, trawl line
espinela *f* (mineral.) spinel
espíneo -a *adj* made of thorns; thornlike
espinera *f* (bot.) hawthorn
espineta *f* (mus.) spinet
espingarda *f* small cannon; long Moorish shotgun; (coll.) tall ungainly woman
espinilla *f* (anat.) shinbone; (path.) blackhead
espinillera *f* (sport) shin guard; greave, jambe
espinillo *m* (bot.) Jerusalem thorn, horse bean; (bot.) huisache
espino *m* (bot.) hawthorn; **espino artificial** barbed wire; **espino albar** or **blanco** (bot.) hawthorn; **espino cerval** or **hediondo** (bot.) buckthorn; **espino negro** (bot.) blackthorn
espinochar *va* to husk (*e.g., corn*)
espinosismo *m* Spinozism
espinosista *adj* Spinozistic; *mf* Spinozist
espinoso -sa *adj* thorny; bony (*fish*); spinous, spinose; (fig.) thorny; *m* (ichth.) stickleback
espínula *f* spinule
espiocha *f* pickaxe
espión *m* spy
espionaje *m* spying, espial; espionage
espira *f* turn (*of helix or spiral*); (elec.) turn (*of a winding*); (geom. & zool.) spire; (arch.) surbase (*of a pedestal*)
espiración *f* breathing; exhalation, expiration
espiráculo *m* (zool.) spiracle
espirador -dora *adj* (physiol.) expiratory
espiral *adj* spiral; *f* spiral spring; (horol.) hairspring; (geom.) spiral
espirante *adj & f* (phonet.) spirant
espirar *va* to breathe, to breathe out (*an odor*); to encourage; *vn* to breathe; to exhale; (poet.) to blow gently
espirea *f* (bot.) spiraea
espirilo *m* (bact.) spirillum
espiritado -da *adj* (coll.) ghostlike (*extremely thin*)

espiritar *va* to possess with the devil; (coll.) to stir, to disturb, to upset; to waste away; *vr* to be possessed with the devil; (coll.) to be stirred, disturbed, or upset; to waste away
espiritismo *m* spiritualism, spiritism
espiritista *adj* spiritualistic, spiritistic; *mf* spiritualist, spiritist
espiritoso -sa *adj* spirited; spirituous
espiritrompa *f* (zool.) proboscis (*of insects*)
espíritu *m* spirit; mind; ghost; (gram.) breathing (*in ancient Greek*); **espíritus** *mpl* spirits, demons; **espíritu de cuerpo** esprit de corps; **espíritu de equipo** spirit of teamwork; **Espíritu Santo** Holy Ghost, Holy Spirit; **dar, despedir** or **exhalar el espíritu** to breathe one's last
espiritual *adj* spiritual; energetic, lively; keen, susceptible, soulful; *f* spiritual (*religious song*)
espiritualidad *f* spirituality; energy, liveliness; keenness, susceptibility, soulfulness
espiritualismo *m* spiritualism (*as opposed to materialism*)
espiritualista *adj* spiritualistic; *mf* spiritualist
espiritualización *f* spiritualization
espiritualizar §76 *va* to spiritualize
espirituoso -sa *adj* var. of **espiritoso**
espirogira *f* (bot.) spirogyra
espirómetro *m* spirometer
espiroqueta *f* (bact.) spirochete
espita *f* tap, cock (*for a cask*); (coll.) tippler
espitar *va* to tap (*a cask or barrel*)
espito *m* peel (*hanger used for drying paper*)
esplácnico -ca *adj* splanchnic
esplendente *adj* (poet.) splendent
esplender *vn* (poet.) to shine
esplendidez *f* splendor; abundance; magnificence, show, pomp; generosity, lavishness; resplendence
espléndido -da *adj* splendid; abundant; magnificent; generous, lavish; resplendent
esplendor *m* splendor
esplendoroso -sa *adj* resplendent, magnificent; (poet.) brilliant, shining
esplenectomía *f* (surg.) splenectomy
esplénico -ca *adj* (anat.) splenetic, splenic
esplenio *m* (anat.) splenium; (anat.) splenius; bandage, compress
esplenitis *f* (path.) splenitis
espliego *m* (bot.) lavender (*plant and dried flowers and leaves*)
esplín *m* melancholy, hypochondria
esplique *m* bird snare
espodumeno *m* (mineral.) spodumene
espolada *f* prick with spur; **espolada de vino** (coll.) shot of wine
espolazo *m* var. of **espolada**
espoleadura *f* spurgall
espolear *va* to spur; (fig.) to spur on
espoleta *f* fuse (*of a bomb*); wishbone; **espoleta de explosión retardada** delayed-action fuse; **espoleta de percusión** percussion fuse; **espoleta de proximidad** proximity fuse; **espoleta de tiempos** time fuse
espolín *m* spur (*fastened with pin instead of straps*); shuttle for brocading flowers on silk; flowered brocade; (bot.) feather grass
espolinar *va* to brocade with flowers
espolio *m* despoliation; (eccl.) spolium
espolique *m* or **espolista** *m* groom who walks in front of master's horse
espolón *m* spur (*on leg of cock; of range of mountains*); fetlock (*projection on back of horse's leg*); spur, beak (*ram of war vessel*); mole, dike; jetty; cutwater (*of ship or bridge*); (arch.) buttress; (arti.) trail spade; (carp.) spur; (naut.) stem (*of bow*); (coll.) chilblain
espolonada *f* violent onslaught of horsemen
espolvorear *va* to dust (*to remove dust from; to sprinkle dust on*); to sprinkle (*e.g., sugar*); *vr* to dust off, come off (*said of dust*)
espolvorizar §76 *va* to dust, sprinkle with dust
espondaico -ca *adj* spondaic
espondeo *m* spondee
espóndil *m* (anat.) spondyl
espondilitis *f* (path.) spondylitis
espóndilo *m* var. of **espóndil**
espongina *f* (biochem.) spongin
esponja *f* sponge; (coll.) sponge, sponger; **beber como una esponja** to drink like a fish; **tirar la esponja** (coll.) to throw up (or in) or to toss up (or in) the sponge (*to acknowledge defeat*); **esponja de baño** bath sponge
esponjado -da *adj* proud, puffed up; (coll.) fresh, healthy; *m* brittle sugar bar (*made of white of egg and sugar, used to sweeten water*)
esponjadura *f* puffing up, fluffiness; conceit; (found.) flaw in casting
esponjar *va* to puff up, to make fluffy; *vr* to puff up, to become fluffy; (fig.) to be puffed up, be conceited; (coll.) to look fresh, to glow with health
esponjera *f* sponge tray, sponge rack
esponjosidad *f* sponginess
esponjoso -sa *adj* spongy
esponsales *mpl* betrothal, engagement
esponsalicio -cia *adj* (pertaining to a) betrothal, engagement
espontanear *vr* to own up; to open one's heart
espontaneidad *f* spontaneity
espontáneo -a *adj* spontaneous; (bot. & biol.) spontaneous; *m* (taur.) spectator who jumps into the ring to fight the bull
espontón *m* spontoon
espontonada *f* salute with a spontoon, blow with a spontoon
espora *f* (biol.) spore
esporádico -ca *adj* sporadic
esporangio *m* (bot.) sporangium
esporidio *m* (bot.) sporidium
esporo *m* var. of **espora**
esporocarpo *m* (bot.) sporocarp
esporofila *f* (bot.) sporophyll
esporofito *m* (bot.) sporophyte
esporozoo -a *adj & m* (zool.) sporozoan
esportada *f* basketful
esportilla *f* small two-handled basket
esportillero *m* carrier (*workman*); errand boy, street porter
esportillo *m* basket made of esparto grass; **coger el esportillo a** (coll.) to catch the attention of
espórula *f* (bot.) sporule
esporulación *f* (biol.) sporulation
esposa *f* see **esposo**
esposado -da *adj & mf* var. of **desposado**
esposar *va* to handcuff
esposo -sa *mf* spouse; *m* husband; *f* wife; **esposas** *fpl* manacles, handcuffs
esprue *m & f* (path.) sprue
espuela *f* spur; (fig.) spur (*incitement, stimulus*); **calzar espuela** to be a knight; **calzar la espuela a** to knight; **echar la espuela** (coll.) to take a nightcap together; **espuela de caballero** (bot.) delphinium, rocket larkspur; **espuela de galán** (bot.) Indian cress, garden nasturtium
espuerta *f* two-handled basket (*for carrying earth, rubble, etc.*); **a espuertas** in abundance
espulgabueyes *m* (*pl:* **-yes**) (orn.) oxpecker, beefeater
espulgadero *m* place where beggars clean themselves of lice or fleas
espulgar §59 *va* to delouse, to clean of lice or fleas; to examine closely, to scrutinize
espulgo *m* removal of lice or fleas; close examination, scrutiny; choice, careful selection
espuma *f* foam, spume, froth; scum; (fig.) cream; **crecer como (la) espuma** (coll.) to grow like weeds; (coll.) to have a meteoric rise; **espuma de caucho** foam rubber; **espuma de jabón** lather; **espuma de mar** (mineral.) meerschaum; **espuma de nitro** wall saltpeter
espumadera *f* skimmer; spray nozzle
espumador -dora *mf* skimmer
espumaje *m* foaminess, frothiness; scumminess
espumajear *vn* to froth at the mouth
espumajo *m* var. of **espumarajo**
espumajoso -sa *adj* foamy, frothy
espumante *adj* foaming, frothing; sparkling (*wine*)
espumar *va* to skim; *vn* to foam, to froth; to sparkle (*said of wine*); to grow or increase rapidly
espumarajear *vn* var. of **espumajear**
espumarajo *m* froth, frothing at the mouth; **echar espumarajos por la boca** (coll.) to froth at the mouth

espúmeo -a *adj* var. of **espumoso**
espumero *m* salina (*deposit of crystallized salt*)
espumilla *f* voile; (Am.) meringue
espumillón *m* heavy silk fabric
espumoso -sa *adj* foamy, frothy; scummy; lathery; sparkling (*wine*)
espundia *f* (path.) leishmaniasis; (vet.) cancerous ulcer (*of horses*)
espurio -ria *adj* spurious
espurrear or **espurriar** *va* to sprinkle with water by squirting from the mouth
esputar *va & vn* to spit
esputazo *m* splotch of spit
esputo *m* spit, saliva; sputum
esq. abr. of **esquina**
esquebrajar *va & vr* var. of **resquebrajar**
esqueje *m* (hort.) cutting, slip
esquela *f* note; announcement; death note; death notice; **esquela de defunción** or **esquela mortuoria** death note; death notice
esquelético -ca *adj* skeletal; thin, wasted
esqueleto *m* skeleton; (fig.) skeleton (*thin person; sketch, outline*); (Am.) blank form; **en esqueleto** incomplete, unfinished
esquema *m* scheme, schema, diagram; (philos.) schema
esquemático -ca *adj* schematic
esquematismo *m* schematism
esquematizar §76 *va* to sketch, to outline, to diagram
esquena *f* backbone; spine (*of a fish*)
esquenanto *m* (bot.) camel grass
esquero *m* leather bag (*fastened to belt*)
esquí *m* (*pl:* **esquís**) ski; skiing; (aer.) skid; **esquí acuático** water ski; water skiing; **esquí remolcado** skijoring
esquiador -dora *adj* ski; *mf* skier
esquiar §90 *vn* to ski
esquíbala *f* (path.) scybalum
esquiciar *va* to sketch
esquicio *m* sketch
esquifada *f* skiffload, boatload
esquifar *va* (naut.) to fit out, to man
esquifazón *f* (naut.) outfit, boat's crew
esquife *m* skiff; small boat, jolly boat; (arch.) cylindrical vault, barrel arch
esquiismo *m* skiing
esquila *f* hand bell; sacring bell, squilla; cowbell; sheepshearing; (bot.) squill; (ent.) whirligig beetle; (zool.) squill, mantis crab
esquilador -dora *mf* sheepshearer (*person*); *f* sheepshearer (*machine*)
esquilar *va* to shear, to fleece
esquileo *m* shearing, sheepshearing
esquilimoso -sa *adj* (coll.) fastidious, squeamish
esquilmar *va* to harvest; to impoverish; to drain, to exhaust (*the soil*); to steal, carry away; (fig.) to drain (*a source of wealth*)
esquilmo *m* harvest, farm produce; (fig.) harvest
Esquilo *m* Aeschylus
esquilón *m* large hand bell
esquimal *adj* Eskimoan; *mf* Eskimo
esquina *f* corner; (Am.) country store; **a la vuelta de la esquina** around the corner; **hacer esquina** to be on a corner (*said of a building*)
esquinado -da *adj* having a corner or corners; sharp-cornered; unsociable, intractable; piqued; angry
esquinal *m* angle iron, knee brace, gusset
esquinancia *f* var. of **esquinencia**
esquinante *m* or **esquinanto** *m* var. of **esquenanto**
esquinar *va* to be on the corner of, to form a corner with; *vn* **esquinar con** to be on the corner of, to form a corner with; *vr* to quarrel, to fall out; **esquinarse con** to quarrel with, to fall out with
esquinazo *m* (coll.) corner; (Am.) serenade; **dar esquinazo a** (coll.) to shake off; (coll.) to leave in the lurch
esquinco *m* var. of **escinco**
esquinela *f* greave, jambe
esquinencia *f* (path.) quinsy
esquinera *f* corner piece (*of furniture*)
Esquines *m* Aeschines
esquinudo -da *adj* sharp-cornered
esquinzar §76 *va* var. of **desguinzar**
esquirla *f* splinter (*of stone, glass; of bone*)
esquirol *m* scab, strikebreaker; (dial.) squirrel
esquisto *m* (geol.) schist; **esquisto aluminoso** alum schist
esquistoso -sa *adj* schistose or schistous
esquitar *va* to remit, to cancel (*a debt*)
esquite *m* (Am.) popcorn
esquivada *f* evasion, dodge; **esquivada lateral** (box.) side step
esquivar *va* to avoid, to shun, to evade; to dodge, to side-step; *vr* to withdraw, to shy away; to dodge, to side-step
esquivez *f* aloofness, gruffness, scorn
esquivo -va *adj* aloof, gruff, scornful; fleeting, elusive
esquizado -da *adj* mottled (*marble*)
esquizocarpio *m* (bot.) schizocarp
esquizofrenia *f* (path.) schizophrenia
esquizofrénico -ca *adj & mf* schizophrenic
esquizomiceto *m* (bot.) schizomycete
essudeste or **essueste** *m* east-southeast
estabilidad *f* stability
estabilísimo -ma *adj super* very or most stable
estabilización *f* stabilization
estabilizador -dora *adj* stabilizing; *mf* stabilizer (*person*); *m* stabilizer (*device*)
estabilizar §76 *va* to stabilize; *vr* to become stabilized
estable *adj* stable; *mf* steady or permanent guest (*e.g., at a boarding house*)
establear *va* to accustom to the stable; *vr* to become accustomed to the stable
establecedor -dora *adj* founding; *mf* founder
establecer §34 *va* to establish; to institute; *vr* to become a resident, to take up residence; to set up in business
establecimiento *m* establishment; place of business; settlement; ordinance, decree, statute; **Establecimientos de los Estrechos** Straits Settlements (*in Malay Peninsula*)
establero *m* stableman, groom
establo *m* stable; **establos de Augías** (myth.) Augean Stables
estabulación *f* stabling
estabular *va* to stable, to raise in a stable
estaca *f* stake, pale, picket; (hort.) cutting, stem cutting; club, cudgel; spike; (min.) claim
estacada *f* stockade, palisade; lists (*tilting field*); dueling ground; (fig.) predicament; **dejar en la estacada** to leave in the lurch; **quedar** or **quedarse en la estacada** to succumb in a duel, on the field of battle, etc.; to lose out; to fail hopelessly
estacar §86 *va* to tie (*an animal*) to a stake; to stake off; *vr* to stand stiff as a pole
estacazo *m* blow with a stake or a club; reverse, setback
estación *f* station; season; stop; resort; (astr. & eccl.) station; **vestir con la estación** to dress according to the season; **estación balnearia** bathing resort; **estación central** (elec.) power plant; **estación de aparcamiento** (aut.) parking station, parking lot; **estación de bandera** (rail.) flag station; **estación de cabeza** (rail.) terminal station; **estación de carga** freight station; **estación de clasificación** (rail.) classification yard; **estación de empalme** or **enlace** (rail.) junction; **estación de fin de línea** (rail.) terminal; **estación de fuerza** (elec.) power plant; **estación de gasolina** gas station, filling station; **estación de la seca** dry season; **estación de las lluvias** rainy season; **estación de paso** (rail.) way station; **estación de radiodifusión** (rad.) broadcasting station; **estación de servicio** (aut.) service station; **estación difusora** or **emisora** (rad.) broadcasting station; **estación elevadora** pumping station; **estaciones de la cruz** (eccl.) stations of the cross; **estación extrema** (rail.) terminal station; **estación gasolinera** gas station, filling station; **estación telefónica** telephone exchange; **estación termoeléctrica** steam power plant
estacional *adj* seasonal; stationary
estacionalidad *f* seasonal characteristic, seasonal demand

estacionamiento *m* stationing; (aut.) parking
estacionar *va* to station; (aut.) to park; *vn* (aut.) to park; *vr* to station oneself; to be stationed; to remain stationary; (aut.) to park; **se prohibe estacionarse** (aut.) no parking
estacionario -ria *adj* stationary; *mf* (archaic) stationer (*bookseller*)
estacionero -ra *mf* visitor to shrines in search of indulgences
estacte *f* oil of myrrh
estacha *f* (naut.) hawser; towline, harpoon rope
estada *f* stop, stay
estadal *m* linear measure of about 3.3 meters; blessed ribbon worn about the neck; **estadal cuadrado** square measure of about 11.2 square meters
estadia *f* (surv.) stadia
estadía *f* sitting (*e.g., before a painter*); (com.) demurrage; (Am.) stay
estadillo *m* register, roll, roster; (mil.) muster roll
estadio *m* stadium; stage, phase; furlong
estadista *m* statesman; statistician
estadístico -ca *adj* statistical; *m* statistician; *f* statistics
estadiunense *adj & mf* var. of **estadounidense**
estadizo -za *adj* stagnant (*water*); heavy, stifling (*air*)
estado *m* state, condition, station; status; state, government, country; statement, report; staff; **en estado (interesante)** or **en estado de buena esperanza** in the family way, pregnant; **los tres estados** the three estates (*noblemen, clergymen, and common people*); **Estados Unidos** *msg* or **los Estados Unidos** *mpl* the United States *ssg;* **mudar de estado** or **tomar estado** to take a wife; to go into the church; **estado civil** marital status; **estado de ánimo** state of mind; **estado de cosas** state of affairs; **estado de cuenta** (com.) statement; **estado de guerra** martial law; **estado de sitio** state of siege; **estado honesto** spinsterhood; **estado libre asociado** commonwealth; **Estado Libre de Irlanda** Irish Free State; **Estado Libre del Congo** Congo Free State; **Estado Libre de Orange** Orange Free State; **estado llano** commons, common people; **estado mayor** (mil.) staff; **estado mayor conjunto** (mil.) joint chiefs of staff; **estado mayor general** (mil.) general staff; **estados bálticos** Baltic States; **Estados Berberiscos** Barbary States; **estados generales** (hist.) States-General (*in France*); **Estados Malayos** Malay States; **Estados Malayos Federados** Federated Malay States; **estado sólido** (phys.) solid state; **estado tapón** buffer state
estado-policía *m* (*pl:* **estados-policías**) police state
estadounidense or **estadunidense** *adj* American, United States; *mf* American (*native or inhabitant of the United States*)
estafa *f* trick, swindle; swindling; stirrup
estafador -dora *mf* cheat, swindler
estafar *va* to defraud, to swindle; to overcharge
estafermo *m* revolving figure of an armed man, used as target in a game; dumfounded person; (coll.) simpleton
estafeta *f* post, courier; post office; branch post office; diplomatic mail; messenger
estafetero *m* postmaster; post-office clerk
estafetil *adj* post, courier; post-office
estafilococo *m* (bact.) staphylococcus
estafiloma *m* (path.) staphyloma
estafisagria *f* (bot.) stavesacre
estagnación *f* var. of **estancamiento**
estagnar *va* var. of **estancar**
estajanovismo *m* var. of **stajanovismo**
estala *f* (naut.) call, stop
estalación *f* class, category
estalactita *f* stalactite
estalagmita *f* stalagmite
estalladura *f* blowout
estallar *vn* to burst, to explode; to break out (*said, e.g., of a fire, a revolution, a war*); to break forth (*said of anger*); to burst with anger
estallido *m* report, explosion; crack, crash; outbreak (*e.g., of war*); **dar un estallido** to crash, to explode
estambrar *va* to spin or weave (*wool*) into worsted
estambre *m* worsted, woolen yarn; (bot.) stamen; (fig.) thread, course (*of life*)
Estambul *f* Stambul, Istanbul
estamento *m* estate (*each of four represented in Cortes of Aragon*)
estameña *f* tammy cloth, estamene
estameñete *m* light tammy cloth
estaminado -da *adj* (bot.) staminate (*having stamens and no pistils*)
estamíneo -a *adj* worsted; (bot.) stamineous
estaminífero -ra *adj* (bot.) staminate, staminiferous
estaminodio or **estaminodo** *m* (bot.) staminode or staminodium
estampa *f* print, stamp, engraving; swage; press, printing; track, footstep; aspect; **la propia estampa de** the very image of; **parecer la estampa de la herejía** (coll.) to be a sight, to be a mess (*to be ugly, to be shabbily dressed*); **estampa de Navidad** Christmas card
estampación *f* printing, stamping, engraving; swaging; embossing; (b.b.) tooling; **estampación en seco** (b.b.) blind tooling
estampado *m* printing, stamping, engraving; swaging; print, cotton print
estampador *m* stamper, engraver
estampar *va* to print, to stamp, to engrave; to swage; to sink (*e.g., one's foot in the mud*); to fix, to engrave (*on the mind*); (b.b.) to tool; (coll.) to dash, to slam; **estampar en seco** (b.b.) to blind-tool
estampería *f* stamp or print shop or business
estampero -ra *mf* stamp or print maker or dealer
estampía; de estampía suddenly, unexpectedly
estampida *f* crash, explosion, report (*of a gun*); (Am.) stampede
estampido *m* crash, explosion, report (*of a gun*)
estampilla *f* stamp, seal; rubber stamp (*of signature*); (Am.) stamp (*postage or revenue*)
estampillado *m* stamping; rubber-stamping
estampillar *va* to stamp; to rubber-stamp
estancación *f* stagnation; deadlock; state monopoly
estancamiento *m* stagnation; (fig.) stagnation, deadlock
estancar §86 *va* to stanch, to stem, to check; to hold up, to stall, to suspend (*a deal*); to deadlock; to corner (*a product*); to monopolize (*said particularly of the state*); *vr* to stagnate; to be a state monopoly
estancia *f* stay; room; dwelling; day in hospital; cost of day in hospital; stanza; (Am.) country place; (Am.) cattle ranch; (Am.) truck farm
estanciero *m* (Am.) farmer, rancher
estanco -ca *adj* stanch, watertight; **estanco al aire** airtight; *m* monopoly, state monopoly; cigar store, government store (*for sale of stamps, tobacco, matches, etc.*); archives; (Am.) liquor store
estándar *m* (Am.) standard
estandardización *f* standardization
estandardizar §76 *va* to standardize
estandarización *f* var. of **estandardización**
estandarizar §76 *va* var. of **estandardizar**
estandarte *m* standard, banner
estandartización *f* var. of **estandardización**
estandartizar §76 *va* var. of **estandardizar**
estangurria *f* (path.) strangury; catheter
estannato *m* (chem.) stannate
estánnico -ca *adj* (chem.) stannic
estannoso -sa *adj* (chem.) stannous
estanque *m* reservoir, basin; pond, pool
estanquero -ra *mf* storekeeper (*in store of government monopolies*); tobacconist; *m* reservoir attendant
estanquidad *f* watertightness
estanquillero -ra *mf* storekeeper (*in store of government monopolies*); tobacconist

estanquillo *m* government store, cigar store; (Am.) small shop; (Am.) tavern
estantal *m* (mas.) abutment
estantalar *va* to brace, to prop, to support
estante *adj* being, residing; fixed, permanent; *m* shelf; shelving; open bookcase; post, upright
estantería *f* shelving; book stacks
estantigua *f* phantom, hobgoblin; (coll.) lank, dirty and ragged person, big scarecrow
estantío -a *adj* inactive, stationary; slow, dull, lukewarm
estañado *m* tinning
estañador *m* tinman, tinner; soldering iron
estañadura *f* tinning; tinwork
estañar *va* to tin; to tin-plate; to solder
estañero *m* tinsmith; tinman (*dealer*)
estaño *m* (chem.) tin
estapedio *m* (anat.) stapedius
estaquero *m* year-old buck or doe
estaquilla *f* peg, pin, dowel; brad; spike
estaquillador *m* pegging awl
estaquillar *va* to peg, to fasten with pegs
estar §51 *v aux* (used with gerund to form the progressive form) to be, e.g., **le estoy escribiendo una carta** I am writing him a letter ‖ *vn* to be; to be in; to be ready; **¿a cuántos estamos?** what day of the month is it today?; **¿dónde estamos?** what have we come to?, can you imagine it?; **¡está bien!** all right!; **estamos a** today is (*a certain day of the month*); **estar a** to cost (*a certain amount*); **estar a dos velas** (coll.) to be hard up; **estar al caer** (coll.) to be about to happen; (coll.) to be about to strike (*the hour*); **estar a la que salta** (coll.) to be always ready to make the most of things; **estar a matar** (coll.) to be bitter enemies; **estar a obscuras** (coll.) to be in the dark (*ignorant*); **estar bien** to be well; **estar bien con** to be on good terms with; **estar con** to have an interview with; to agree with; to have (*a disease*); **estar con ánimo de** + *inf* to have a mind to, to have a notion to + *inf;* **estar de** to be (*for the time being*); **estar de caza** to be hunting, to be on a hunting trip; **estar de más** (coll.) to be de trop, to be in the way; (coll.) to be unnecessary; (coll.) to be idle; **estar de prisa** to be in a hurry; **estar de viaje** to be on a trip, to be traveling; **estar en** to understand, to be on to; to cost (*a certain amount*); **estar en ánimo de** + *inf* to have a mind to, to have a notion to + *inf;* **estar en grande** to have one's way in everything; to live in luxury; **estar en que** to be sure that; **estar en todo** to have a finger in everything; **estar mal** to be ill; **estar mal con** to be on bad terms with; **estar para** + *inf* to be about to + *inf;* **estar por** to be for, to be in favor of; **estar por** + *inf* to be in favor of + *ger;* to remain to be + *pp*, e.g., **la carta está por escribir** the letter remains to be written; to be about to (*e.g., happen*); to have a mind to, to have a notion to + *inf;* **estar que** + *ind* to be fairly + *ger*, e.g., **estaba que brincaba** he was fairly leaping (*e.g., with enthusiasm*); **estar sobre sí** to be wary, to be cautious; **¿está Vd.?** do you understand? ‖ *vr* to stay (*e.g., home*); to keep (*quiet*); **estarse de charla** to linger to chat; **estarse de más** (coll.) to be idle
estarcido *m* stencil (*letters and designs*)
estarcir §50 *va* to stencil
estarna *f* (orn.) gray partridge
estatal *adj* (pertaining to the) state
estátice *m* (bot.) thrift, sea pink
estático -ca *adj* static; dumfounded, speechless; *f* (mech.) statics
estatidad *f* statehood
estatificación *f* nationalization (*of property*)
estatificar §86 *va* to nationalize (*property*)
estatismo *m* static state; statism
estatista *adj & mf* statist
estatización *f* (Am.) nationalization (*of property*)
estatizar §76 *va* (Am.) to nationalize (*property*)
estatocisto *m* (zool.) statocyst
estatolito *m* (zool.) statolith
estator *m* (mach. & elec.) stator
estatorreactor *m* (aer.) ram-jet engine
estatoscopio or **estatóscopo** *m* (phys.) statoscope
estatua *f* statue; **ahorcar en estatua** to hang in effigy; **quedarse hecho una estatua** (coll.) to stand aghast, to be struck with amazement; **estatua de la Libertad** Statue of Liberty; **estatua orante** (sculp.) orant statue; **estatua yacente** (sculp.) jacent statue
estatuar §33 *va* to statue, to make a statue of; to adorn with statues
estatuario -ria *adj* statuary; *m* statuary (*person*); *f* statuary (*art*)
estatúder *m* stadholder
estatuderato *m* stadholderate or stadholdership
estatuilla *f* statuette
estatuir §41 *va* to establish, arrange, prove
estatuita *f* statuette
estatura *f* stature
estatutario -ria *adj* statutory
estatuto *m* statute
estaurolita *f* (mineral.) staurolite
estay *m* (naut.) stay; **estay mayor** (naut.) mainstay
este, esta *adj dem* (*pl:* **estos, estas**) this; *m* east; east wind
éste, ésta *pron dem* (*pl:* **éstos, éstas**) this one; *f* this city (*where I am*)
esté *1st sg pres subj of* **estar**
esteapsina *f* (biochem.) steapsin
estearato *m* (chem.) stearate
esteárico -ca *adj* (chem.) stearic
estearina *f* (chem.) stearin
estearopteno *m* (chem.) stearoptene
esteatita *f* (mineral.) steatite
esteatitoso -sa *adj* (mineral.) steatitic
esteatopigia *f* (anthrop.) steatopygia
esteba *f* (naut.) steeve (*used for stowing bales of wool*); (bot.) meadow spear grass
Esteban *m* Stephen
estebar *va* to pack (*cloth*) in the dye kettle
estefanita *f* (mineral.) stephanite
estegomía *f* (ent.) stegomyia
estegosauro *m* (pal.) stegosaurus
estela *f* wake (*of a ship*); trail (*of a heavenly body, rocket, etc.*); (arch. & bot.) stele; (bot.) lady's-mantle
estelar *adj* stellar, sidereal; star
estelario -ria *adj* stellar; *f* (bot.) lady's-mantle
estelífero -ra *adj* (poet.) starry
estelión *m* (zool.) tarente; toadstone
estelón *m* toadstone
estema *m* (zool.) stemma (*simple eye of insect*)
estemple *m* (min.) stemple
esténico -ca *adj* (med.) sthenic
estenocardia *f* (path.) stenocardia
estenografía *f* stenography
estenográfico -ca *adj* stenographic
estenógrafo -fa *mf* stenographer
estenosis *f* (path.) stenosis, stricture
estenotipia *f* stenotypy; stenotype (*letter or group of letters*)
estenotipiadora *f* stenotype (*machine*)
Estentor *m* (myth.) Stentor
estentóreo -a *adj* stentorian
estepa *f* steppe, barren plain; (bot.) rockrose
estepar *m* field of rockroses
estepilla *f* (bot.) white-leaved rockrose
estequiología *f* stoichiology
estequiometría *f* stoichiometry
éster *m* or **ester** *m* (chem.) ester
Ester *f* Esther
estera *f* mat, matting; (mach.) apron; **esteras** *fpl* caterpillar tread; **cargado de esteras** (coll.) out of patience
esterar *va* to cover with a mat or mats; *vn* (coll.) to dress for winter ahead of time
estercoladura *f* or **estercolamiento** *m* dunging, manuring
estercolar *m* dunghill; §77 *va & vn* to dung, to manure
estercolero *m* dung collector; dunghill
estercolizo -za *adj* dungy, mucky
estercóreo -a *adj* stercoraceous
estercuelo *m* manuring, fertilizing
esterculiáceo -a *adj* (bot.) sterculiaceous
estéreo *m* stere
estereóbato *m* (arch.) stereobate

estereocinema *m* (mov.) three-D
estereocromía *f* stereochromy
estereofonía *f* stereophony
estereofónico -ca *adj* stereophonic
estereofotografía *f* stereophotography
estereografía *f* stereography
estereográfico -ca *adj* stereographic or stereographical
estereograma *m* stereogram
estereoisomería *f* (chem.) stereoisomerism
estereometría *f* stereometry
estereopsis *f* stereopsis
estereóptico *m* stereopticon
estereoquímico -ca *adj* stereochemical; *f* stereochemistry
estereoscopia *f* stereoscopy
estereoscópico -ca *adj* stereoscopic
estereoscopio *m* stereoscope
estereotipar *va* to stereotype; (fig.) to stereotype
estereotipia *f* stereotype; stereotypy
estereotipo *m* stereotype
estereotomía *f* stereotomy, stonecutting
estereotropismo *m* (biol.) stereotropism
estereovisión *f* stereovision
estereria *f* mat shop; mat business
esterero -ra *mf* mat maker or dealer; mat repairer, mat layer
estéril *adj* sterile; futile
esterilidad *f* sterility; futility
esterilización *f* sterilization
esterilizador -dora *mf* sterilizer; *m* sterilizer (*apparatus*)
esterilizar §76 *va* to sterilize; *vr* to become sterile
esterilla *f* small mat; straw mat; gold or silver plait; canvas; **esterilla de alambre** wire mesh
esterlín *m* bocasine, colored buckram
esterlina *adj fem* sterling (*pound*)
esternal *adj* (anat.) sternal
esternón *m* (anat.) sternum, breastbone
estero *m* matting; time for laying matting; estuary; tideland; (Am.) stream; (Am.) swamp
esterquero or **esterquilinio** *m* dunghill
estertor *m* stertor, râle, rhonchus; death rattle; **estertor agónico** death rattle
estertoroso -sa *adj* stertorous
estesiómetro *m* esthesiometer
esteta *mf* aesthete
estético -ca *adj* aesthetic, aesthetical; *mf* aesthetician; *f* aesthetics
estetoscopia *f* (med.) stethoscopy; stethoscopic findings
estetoscópico -ca *adj* stethoscopic
estetoscopio *m* (med.) stethoscope
esteva *f* plow handle, stilt
estevado -da *adj* bowlegged
estevón *m* var. of **esteva**
estezado *m* var. of **correal**
estiaje *m* low water
estiba *f* rammer; place for packing wool in bags; (naut.) stowage
estibador *m* (naut.) stevedore, longshoreman
estibar *va* to pack, to stuff; (naut.) to stow
estibia *f* var. of **espibia**
estibina *f* (chem.) stibine
estibio *m* (chem.) stibium
estibonio *m* (chem.) stibonium
estiércol *m* dung, manure
estigio -gia *adj* Stygian; (*cap.*) *f* (myth.) Styx
estigioso -sa *adj* Stygian, gloomy, mysterious
estigma *m* (bot., hist., path., zool. & fig.) stigma; **estigmas** *mpl* stigmata (*marks resembling the wounds on the body of Christ*)
estigmatismo *m* (opt. & path.) stigmatism
estigmatización *f* stigmatization
estigmatizado *m* (eccl.) stigmatic (*person bearing marks suggesting the wounds of Christ*)
estigmatizador -dora *adj* stigmatizing; *mf* stigmatizer
estigmatizar §76 *va* to stigmatize
estilar *va* to draw up (*a document*); to affect, to be given to; *vn & vr* to be in style; **estilarse** + *inf* to be the style to + *inf*
estilete *m* stiletto; stylet; style (*of a recording instrument*); (surg.) stylet

estilicidio *m* stillicide, dripping; (med.) stillicidium
estilismo *m* (lit.) excessive attention to style
estilista *mf* stylist; designer
estilístico -ca *adj* stylistic; *f* stylistics
estilita *adj* (eccl. hist.) stylitic; *m* (eccl. hist.) stylite
estilización *f* stylization; designing
estilizar §76 *va* to stylize; to design
estilo *m* style; stylus; gnomon; (bot. & print.) style; **al estilo de** in the style of; **de estilo** period (*chair, furniture, etc.*); **por el estilo** like that, of the kind; **por el estilo de** like; **estilo antiguo** (chron.) Old Style; **estilo culto** (lit.) euphuistic style; **estilo directo** (gram.) direct discourse; **estilo imperio** (f.a.) Empire; **estilo indirecto** (gram.) indirect discourse; **estilo llano** (lit.) simple style; **estilo nuevo** (chron.) New Style
estilográfico -ca *adj* stylographic; fountain-pen (*e.g., ink*); *f* fountain pen
estilógrafo *m* stylograph
estiloides *adj* (anat.) styloid
estima *f* esteem; (naut.) dead reckoning
estimabilidad *f* estimableness
estimabilísimo -ma *adj super* very or most estimable
estimable *adj* estimable, highly esteemed; appreciable
estimación *f* estimation, esteem; estimate
estimador -dora *adj* appreciative; estimating
estimar *va* to esteem; to estimate; to think, to believe; (coll.) to like, to be fond of; **estimar en poco** to hold in low esteem; *vr* to have great esteem for oneself; to esteem each other
estimativo -va *adj* respectful; *f* judgment; moral perception; instinct
estimulación *f* stimulation
estimulante *adj* stimulating, stimulant; *m* stimulant
estimular *va & vn* to stimulate; **estimular a** + *inf* to stimulate to + *inf*
estímulo *m* stimulus
estinco *m* var. of **escinco**
estío *m* summer
estipe *m* (bot. & zool.) stipe
estipendiar *va* to stipend, to give a stipend to
estipendiario -ria *adj & mf* stipendiary
estipendio *m* stipend; salary, wages
estípite *m* (arch.) pedestal in form of inverted truncated rectangular pyramid; (bot.) stipe
estipticar §86 *va* (med.) to constrict
estipticidad *f* stypticity, astringency
estíptico -ca *adj* styptic; constipated; mean, stingy; *m* styptic
estípula *f* (bot.) stipule
estipulación *f* stipulation
estipulado -da *adj* (bot.) stipulate
estipular *adj* (bot.) stipular; *va* to stipulate
estipulilla *f* (bot.) stipel
estira *f* currier's knife
estirable *adj* stretchy, stretchable
estiracáceo -a *adj* (bot.) styracaceous
estiradamente *adv* scarcely, hardly; violently; tensely
estirado -da *adj* stuck-up; soberly dressed; prim; (coll.) closefisted, pennypinching; **estirado en frío** (metal.) hard-drawn
estirador *m* stretcher
estirajar *va* (coll.) var. of **estirar**
estirajón *m* (coll.) var. of **estirón**
estiramiento *m* stretching; drawing (*of metals*)
estirar *va* to stretch; to draw (*metal or wire*); to iron lightly; (fig.) to stretch (*money*); (fig.) to stretch out (*a speech, job, appointment, etc.*); *vr* to stretch; to put on airs
estirazar §76 *va* (coll.) var. of **estirar**
estireno *m* (chem.) styrene
Estiria *f* Styria
estirón *m* jerk, tug; **dar un estirón** (coll.) to grow up quickly
estirpe *f* stock, race, family; pedigree; strain (*of a family*)
estítico -ca *adj* var. of **estíptico**
estivación *f* (bot. & zool.) aestivation
estivada *f* brushland turned up and burned in preparation for cultivation
estival *adj* aestival, summer
estivo -va *adj* (poet.) var. of **estival**

esto *pron dem neut* this; **en esto** at this point
estocada *f* thrust, stab, lunge; stab wound; deathblow; (fig.) blow (*something which causes suffering*); **estocada caída** (taur.) stab on the side
estocafís *m* unsplit smoked codfish
Estocolmo *f* Stockholm
estofa *f* quilted material; quality, class
estofado -da *adj* ornamented; *m* stew
estofador -dora *mf* quilter
estofar *va* to quilt; to size (*wood carvings*) for gilding; to distemper (*burnished gold*); to stew
estoicismo *m* stoicism; Stoicism
estoico -ca *adj* stoic, stoical; Stoic, Stoical; *mf* stoic; Stoic
estola *f* stole
estolidez *f* stupidity, imbecility
estólido -da *adj* stupid, imbecile
estolón *m* (eccl.) deacon's stole; (bot. & zool.) stolon
estoma *m* (anat., bot. & zool.) stoma
estomacal *adj* stomachic; (pertaining to the) stomach; *m* (med.) stomachic
estomagar §59 *va* to upset, give indigestion; to pall, to cloy; (coll.) to annoy, to vex
estómago *m* stomach; **revolver el estómago** to turn the stomach; **tener buen estómago** or **mucho estómago** (coll.) to be thick-skinned; (coll.) to have an easy conscience; **estómago de avestruz** (coll.) cast-iron stomach, iron digestion
estomatical *adj* stomachic
estomático -ca *adj* stomatic (*pertaining to the mouth*)
estomaticón *m* stomach plaster
estomatitis *f* (path.) stomatitis
estomatología *f* stomatology
estomatoplastia *f* (surg.) stomatoplasty
estonio -nia *adj* & *mf* Estonian; *m* Estonian (*language*); (*cap.*) *f* Estonia
estopa *f* tow; burlap; (mach.) packing; (naut.) oakum; **estopa de acero** steel wool; **estopa de algodón** cotton waste
estopada *f* tow for spinning
estopear *va* (naut.) to calk with oakum
estopeño -ña *adj* (pertaining to or made of) tow
estoperol *m* tow wick; (naut.) clout nail; (Am.) brass-headed tack
estopilla *f* fine part of flax or hemp; lawn, cambric; cheesecloth
estopín *m* blasting cap, exploder
estopón *m* coarse tow
estopor *m* (naut.) stopper
estoposo -sa *adj* (pertaining to) tow; towlike
estoque *m* rapier; tip of a sword; (bot.) sword lily, corn flag, gladiolus
estoqueador *m* swordsman; matador
estoquear *va* to stab with sword or rapier
estoqueo *m* thrusting, stabbing
estor *m* blind, shade, window shade
estoraque *m* (bot.) storax (*tree and balsam*)
estorbador -dora *adj* hindering, obstructing; annoying
estorbar *va* to hinder, to obstruct; to annoy, to inconvenience; **estorbarle a uno lo negro** (coll.) to dislike reading, to be illiterate; *vn* (coll.) to be in the way; **estorbar** + *inf* to prevent one from + *ger*
estorbo *m* hindrance, obstruction; annoyance
estorboso -sa *adj* hindering, obstructing; annoying
estornija *f* washer (*under linchpin*)
estornino *m* (orn.) starling; **estornino de los pastores** (orn.) grackle, myna
estornudar *vn* to sneeze
estornudo *m* sneeze, sneezing
estornutativo -va or **estornutatorio -ria** *adj* sternutative
estotro -tra *adj* & *pron dem* (archaic) this other
estovar *va* var. of **rehogar**
estoy *1st sg pres ind of* **estar**
estrábico -ca *adj* strabismal or strabismic
estrabismo *m* (path.) strabismus; **estrabismo convergente** (path.) cross-eye
Estrabón *m* Strabo
estrabotomía *f* (surg.) strabotomy
estracilla *f* rag; brown paper
estrada *f* road, highway; **batir la estrada** (mil.) to reconnoiter; **estrada encubierta** (fort.) covert way
Estradivario *m* Stradivarius; (*l.c.*) *m* Stradivarius (*violin*)
estrado *m* dais; stage, lecture platform; podium (*of orchestra conductor*); drawing room; drawing-room furniture; baker's table; **estrados** *mpl* court rooms; **citar para estrados** (law) to subpoena
estrafalario -ria *adj* (coll.) slovenly, sloppy; (coll.) wild, extravagant, outlandish; *mf* (coll.) screwball
estragado -da *adj* corrupt, depraved
estragador -dora *adj* corrupting, depraving
estragamiento *m* corruption, depravation
estragar §59 *va* to corrupt, to deprave, to vitiate, to spoil
estrago *m* damage, ruin, havoc; destruction, devastation; corruption; **estragos** *mpl* damage, ruin, havoc
estragón *m* (bot.) tarragon
estrambote *m* couplet, triplet, etc. (*at end of poem, especially a sonnet*)
estrambótico -ca adj (coll.) odd, queer, freakish
estramonio *m* (bot.) stramonium
estrangol *m* (vet.) strangullion
estrangul *m* (mus.) mouthpiece, reed
estrangulación *f* strangulation; (path. & surg.) strangulation; (mach.) choke, choking
estrangulador *m* throttle; (aut.) choke
estrangular *va* to strangle; (path. & surg.) to strangulate; (mach.) to choke; (mach.) to throttle; *vr* to strangle
estranguria *f* (path.) strangury
estrapalucio *m* (coll.) breakage, crash; (coll.) rumpus, fracas
estraperlear *vn* to deal in the black market, to be a black-market dealer
estraperlismo *m* black-market dealing; black marketeers
estraperlista *adj* black-market; *mf* black marketeer
estraperlo *m* black market
estrapontín *m* folding seat, flap seat (*in automobile, train, theater, etc.*); (aut.) jump seat
Estrasburgo *f* Strasbourg
estratagema *f* stratagem; craftiness
estratega *m* strategist
estrategia *f* strategy, strategics; **alta estrategia** (mil.) grand strategy
estratégico -ca *adj* strategic or strategical; *m* strategist, militarist
estratego *m* var. of **estratega**
estratificación *f* stratification
estratificar §86 *va* & *vr* to stratify
estratigrafía *f* stratigraphy
estratigráfico -ca *adj* stratigraphic
estrato *m* layer; (meteor.) stratus; (anat. & geol.) stratum
estratocúmulo *m* (meteor.) strato-cumulus
estratosfera *f* stratosphere
estratosférico -ca *adj* stratospheric
estratovisión *f* stratovision
estrave *m* (naut.) stem knee
estraza *f* rag
estrechamiento *m* narrowing; tightening; closer relations; rapprochement
estrechar *va* to narrow; to tighten; to hem in; to press, to pursue; to bring closer together; to force, to compel; to hug, to embrace; **estrechar la mano a** to grasp the hand of, to shake hands with; *vr* to contract; to squeeze; to come closer together; to hug, to embrace; to retrench; **estrecharse con** to persuade by friendly entreaty; **estrecharse en** to squeeze into; **estrecharse en los gastos** to cut down expenses; **estrecharse la mano** to shake hands
estrechez *f* narrowness; tightness; closeness, intimacy; strictness, austerity; want, poverty; urgency; trouble, jam; **hallarse en gran estrechez** to be in a jam, to be in dire straits; **estrechez de miras** (fig.) narrowness, narrow outlook
estrecho -cha *adj* narrow; tight; close, intimate; stingy; strict, rigid, austere; exact, punctual, conscientious; poor, indigent; mean-

spirited; **estrecho de conciencia** strict, austere, strait-laced; **estrecho de medios** in straitened circumstances; *m* fix, predicament; strait; channel; **poner en estrecho de** + *inf* to force to + *inf;* **estrecho de Gibraltar** Strait of Gibraltar; **estrecho de la Florida** Florida Strait; **estrecho de la Sonda** Sunda Strait; **estrecho de Magallanes** Strait of Magellan

estrechón *m* flapping (*of sails*); (coll.) handclasp, handshake

estrechura *f* narrowness, narrow passage; closeness, intimacy; strictness, austerity; trouble, jam

estregadera *f* scrubbing brush; scraper, foot scraper

estregadero *m* place on which animals rub themselves (*as deer rub their antlers*); place for washing and scrubbing clothes

estregadura *f* or **estregamiento** *m* rubbing, scrubbing, scouring

estregar §29 *va* to rub hard, to scrub, to scour

estregón *m* hard rub, rough rub

estrella *f* star; (elec.) star; (mov.) star (*man or woman*); (print.) star, asterisk; (fig.) star (*person who stands out; destiny, fortune; white spot on forehead of horse*); **con estrellas** after sunset, before sunrise; **nacer con estrella** to be favored by fortune; **poner sobre las estrellas** to praise to the skies; **tener estrella** to be favored by fortune; **tener buena estrella** to be lucky; **tener mala estrella** to be unlucky; **ver las estrellas** (coll.) to see stars; **estrella de Belén** Star of Bethlehem; (bot.) Star-of-Bethlehem; **estrella de los Alpes** (bot.) edelweiss; **estrella de mar** (zool.) starfish; (bot.) aster, China aster; **estrella de rabo** comet; **estrella doble** (astr.) double star; **estrella enana** (astr.) dwarf star; **estrella fija** (astr.) fixed star; **estrella filante** or **fugaz** shooting star; **estrella polar** (astr.) polestar; **estrella poligonal** (geom.) star polygon; **estrellas y listas** Stars and Stripes; **estrella vespertina** evening star

estrelladera *f* (cook.) slice, turnover

estrelladero *m* egg pan (*of pastry cooks*)

estrellado -da *adj* starred, star-spangled; star-shaped; fried (*said of eggs*); star-faced (*said of horses*)

estrellamar *f* (zool.) starfish

estrellar *adj* star, starry; *va* to star, to spangle with stars; to fry (*eggs*); (coll.) to shatter, to dash to pieces; *vr* to be spangled with stars; to crash; (fig.) to crash

estrellato *m* (theat.) stardom

estrellero -ra *adj* holding its head high (*said of a horse*)

estrellizar §76 *va* to beautify with stars

estrellón *m* large star; star (*kind of fireworks*); (coll.) stroke of luck; (Am.) collision, shock

estremecer §34 *va* to shake; to rend (*the air*); (fig.) to shake, to perturb; *vr* to shake, to shiver, to shudder

estremecimiento *m* shaking, shiver, shivering, shuddering

estrena *f* gift of appreciation; (archaic) first use; (archaic) wedding, marriage

estrenar *va* to use or wear for the first time; to perform (*a play*) for the first time; to show (*a movie*) for the first time; to try out (*something new*); *vr* to make one's start, to appear for the first time; to make the day's first transaction; to open (*said of a play or movie*)

entrenista *mf* (theat.) first-nighter

estreno *m* beginning, debut; first performance, première; **estreno de una casa** housewarming

estrenque *m* heavy esparto rope

estrenuidad *f* strenuousness, activity; vigor, enterprise

estrenuo -nua *adj* strenuous, active, vigorous

estreñido -da *adj* constipated; stingy

estreñimiento *m* constipation

estreñir §74 *va* to bind, to constipate; **estreñir el bolsillo** (coll.) to be tight, to be stingy; *vr* to become constipated

estrepada *f* pull, pull in unison (*on a rope; on the oars*)

estrépito *m* noise, racket, uproar, crash; show, ostentation, fuss

estrepitoso -sa *adj* noisy, boisterous, deafening; notorious; shocking

estreptococia *f* (path.) streptococcic infection

estreptocócico -ca *adj* streptococcic

estreptococo *m* (bact.) streptococcus

estreptomicina *f* (pharm.) streptomycin

estreptotricina *f* (pharm.) streptotrichin

estría *f* stria, flute, groove; (arch. & med.) stria

estriación *f* striation

estriado -da *adj* striated, grooved, fluted

estriadura *f* fluting, striation

estriar §90 *va* to striate, to flute, to groove; *vr* to become fluted or grooved

estribación *f* (geog.) spur, counterfort

estribadero *m* prop, support

estribar *va* to rest on, to press down on; to fasten; *vn* to rest, to lean; to be based; **estribar en** + *inf* to be based on + *inf*

estribera *f* stirrup

estribería *f* stirrup factory or shop

estriberón *m* stepping stone; (mil.) temporary road

estribillo *m* burden, refrain, chorus; initial theme (*of a poem*); pet word or phrase

estribo *m* stirrup; (arch.) abutment, buttress; footboard; (aut.) running board; (mach.) brace, stay, stirrup; (carp.) joist hanger, cross prop; (geog.) spur, counterfort; (anat.) stapes; (taur.) white stirrup board at base of fence (*used to help a man escape over the fence*); (fig.) support, foundation; **perder los estribos** to talk nonsense; to lose one's head, fly off the handle; **tenerse en los estribos** to keep a steady head

estribor *m* (naut.) starboard

estricnina *f* (chem.) strychnine

estricote; al estricote hither and thither, from pillar to post

estricto -ta *adj* strict, severe; narrow (*meaning of a word*)

estrictura *f* (path.) stricture

estridencia *f* stridence

estridente *adj* strident

estridor *m* stridence; (path.) stridor

estridulación *f* stridulation; (zool.) stridulation

estridular *vn* to stridulate

estriduloso -sa *adj* stridulant, stridulous; (path.) stridulous

estrige *f* (orn.) barn owl; (orn.) little owl

estrinque *m* var. of **estrenque**

estro *m* inspiration (*of poet or artist*); rut, heat; orgasm; (ent.) botfly

estróbilo *m* (bot.) strobile; (zool.) strobile, strobila

estrobo *m* (naut.) grommet, becket

estroboscopio *m* stroboscope

estrobotrón *m* (electron.) strobotron

estrofa *f* strophe

estrófico -ca *adj* strophic

estrógeno *m* (biochem.) estrogen

estroma *m* (anat., biol. & bot.) stroma

Estrómboli *m* Stromboli

estrona *f* (biochem.) estrone

estronciana *f* (chem.) strontia

estroncianita *f* (mineral.) strontianite

estroncio *m* (chem.) strontium

estropada *f* var. of **estrepada**

estropajear *va* (mas.) to rub down or to scour (*a plastered wall*) in order to remove loose particles or dust

estropajeo *m* (mas.) rubbing or scrubbing a plastered wall

estropajo *m* esparto scrubbing brush; rag for scrubbing, mop, dishcloth; (bot.) luffa, dishcloth gourd; **servir de estropajo** (coll.) to do the dirty work, to be treated with indifference

estropajoso -sa *adj* (coll.) ragged, slovenly; (coll.) tough, leathery (*said, e.g., of meat*); (coll.) stammering

estropear *va* to abuse, to mistreat; to spoil, to ruin; to cripple, to maim; (mas.) to stir (*mortar*) a second time; *vr* to spoil, go to ruin; to fail

estropeo *m* abuse, mistreatment; damage; crippling

estropicio *m* (coll.) breakage, crash; (coll.) havoc, ruin; (coll.) rumpus, fracas
estructura *f* structure
estructuración *f* construction, organization
estructural *adj* structural
estructurar *va* to construct, to organize
estruendo *m* crash; confusion, uproar; (coll.) pomp; (Am.) detonating rocket
estrujador -dora *adj* squeezing; *f* squeezer; wine press
estrujadura *f* or **estrujamiento** *m* squeezing, pressing, crushing; mashing, bruising; (metal.) extrusion
estrujar *va* to squeeze, to press, to crush; to mash, to rumple, to bruise; (coll.) to drain, to exhaust; (metal.) to extrude
estrujón *m* squeezing, pressing, crushing; last pressing of grapes; (coll.) crush, jam
estruma *f* (path.) struma (*scrofula; goiter*)
estrumoso -sa *adj* strumous
estuación *f* flow of tide, flood tide
estuante *adj* hot, burning
Estuardo, María Mary Stuart
estuario *m* estuary; tideland
estucador *m* stucco plasterer
estucar §86 *va* to stucco
estuco *m* stucco
estuche *m* box, case; casket, jewel case; slipcase; sheath (*for scissors*); (coll.) handy fellow; **estuche de afeites** vanity case, compact
estudiado -da *adj* affected, mannered, studied
estudiador -dora *adj* (coll.) very studious
estudiantado *m* student body
estudiante *mf* student
estudiantil *adj* (coll.) (pertaining to a) student, college
estudiantino -na *adj* (coll.) student; **a la estudiantina** (coll.) like a student, like students; *f* group of students; student serenade; carnival masquerade in student disguise
estudiantón *m* (scornful) dull grind
estudiar *va* to study; to hear (*someone's lesson; an actor recite his lines*); to design; (f.a.) to copy (*nature or a model*); *vn* to study; **estudiar para médico** to study to become a doctor
estudio *m* study; studio; (mov. & rad.) studio; designing, planning; survey; (mus.) étude; **altos estudios** advanced studies
estudiosidad *f* studiousness
estudioso -sa *adj* studious; *m* student, scholar
estufa *f* stove; heater; foot stove; steam cabinet, steam room; hothouse; dryer; **estufa de desinfección** sterilizer
estufador *m* stewing pan
estufero *m* var. of **estufista**
estufilla *f* hand muff; foot stove; chafing dish
estufista *m* stovemaker; stove or heater repairman or dealer
estulticia *f* silliness, foolishness
estulto -ta *adj* silly, foolish
estuoso -sa *adj* hot, burning
estupefacción *f* stupefaction (*daze*); (coll.) stupefaction (*great amazement*)
estupefaciente *adj & m* (med.) narcotic, stupefacient
estupefactivo -va *adj* stupefying
estupefacto -ta *adj* stupefied, dumfounded
estupendo -da *adj* stupendous, wonderful; (coll.) famous, distinguished
estupidez *f* (*pl:* **-deces**) stupidity
estúpido -da *adj & mf* stupid
estupor *m* stupor; amazement, surprise
estuprador *m* rapist, violator
estuprar *va* to rape, to violate
estupro *m* rape, violation
estuque *m* var. of **estuco**
estuquería *f* stuccoing; stucco work
estuquista *m* stucco plasterer, stuccoist
esturar *va & vr* to burn, to parch, to scorch
esturgar §59 *va* to smooth off and finish (*pottery*)
esturión *m* (ichth.) sturgeon; **esturión blanco** (ichth.) white sturgeon, beluga
estuve *1st sg pret ind of* **estar**
ésula *f* (bot.) spurge
esvarar *vn & vr* to slide, to slip
esvarón *m* slide, slip
esvástica *f* var. of **svástica**
esviaje *m* skew
-eta *suffix dim* e.g., **aleta** fin; **historieta** anecdote; **placeta** small public square
etalaje *m* bosh (*of blast furnace*)
etamín *m* or **etamine** *m* etamine (*fabric*)
etano *m* (chem.) ethane
etapa *f* stage; (mil.) campaign or marching ration; (mil.) stage (*of journey*); (rad.) stage; **a pequeñas etapas** by easy stages; **de etapa única** single-stage
etcétera *f* the character &, which means **y lo demás; hacer por etcéteras** (coll.) to dash off
-ete *suffix dim & pej* e.g., **caballerete** dude; **lugarete** hamlet; **vejete** little old fellow
Etelredo *m* Ethelred
éter *m* aether or ether (*heavens; upper regions*); (phys.) aether or ether (*hypothetical medium*); (chem.) ether (R_2O)
etéreo -a *adj* aethereal or ethereal; (phys.) aethereal or ethereal; (chem.) ethereal
eterificación *f* (chem.) etherification
eterificar §86 *va* (chem.) etherify
eterización *f* (med.) etherization
eterizar §76 *va* to etherize
eternal *adj* eternal
eternidad *f* eternity
eternizable *adj* worthy of being immortalized
eternizar §76 *va* to eternize; to make endless, to prolong endlessly; *vr* to be endless or interminable; to never finish
eterno -na *adj* eternal
etesio -sia *adj & m* etesian
ético -ca *adj* ethic or ethical; (path.) consumptive; *mf* (path.) consumptive; *m* ethicist, moralist; *f* ethics
etileno *m* (chem.) ethylene
etílico -ca *adj* ethylic
etilo *m* (chem.) ethyl
étimo *m* var. of **étimon**
etimología *f* etymology, **etimología popular** folk etymology, popular etymology
etimológico -ca *adj* etymological
etimologista *mf* etymologist
etimologizar §76 *va* to etymologize (*a word*); *vn* to etymologize; (coll.) to pose as an etymologist
etimólogo -ga *mf* etymologist
étimon *m* (philol.) etymon
etiología *f* aetiology
etíope *adj & mf* Ethiopian; *m* (old chem.) ethiops
Etiopía *f* Ethiopia
etiópico -ca *adj* Ethiopic, Ethiopian; *m* Ethiopic (*language*)
etiopio -pia *adj & mf* Ethiopian
etiqueta *f* etiquette; formality; tag, label; formal dress, formal clothes; **de etiqueta** full-dress, formal; **estar de etiqueta** to have become cool toward each other; **etiqueta menor** semiformal dress
etiquetar *va* to tag, to label
etiquetero -ra *adj* ceremonious, formal; full of compliments
etiquez *f* (path.) consumption
etites *f* (mineral.) eaglestone
etmoides *adj & m* (anat.) ethmoid
Etna, el Mount Etna
étneo -nea *adj* Etnean
étnico -ca *adj* ethnic or ethnical; (gram.) gentilic
etnografía *f* ethnography
etnográfico -ca *adj* ethnographic or ethnographical
etnógrafo -fa *mf* ethnographer
etnología *f* ethnology
etnológico -ca *adj* ethnologic or ethnological
etnólogo -ga *mf* ethnologist
Etolia, la Aetolia
etopea or **etopeya** *f* (rhet.) ethopoeia
etrurio -ria *adj & mf* Etrurian
etrusco -ca *adj & mf* Etruscan; *m* Etruscan (*language*)
etusa *f* (bot.) fool's-parsley
E.U. abr. of **Estados Unidos**
E.U.A. abr. of **Estados Unidos de América**
Eubea *f* Euboea
eucaína *f* (pharm.) eucaine
eucalipto *m* (bot.) eucalyptus

eucaliptol *m* eucalyptol
Eucaristía *f* (eccl.) Eucharist
eucarístico -ca *adj* Eucharistic
Euclides *m* Euclid
euclidiano -na *adj* Euclidean; **no euclidiano** non-Euclidean
eucologio *m* (eccl.) euchology
eucrasia *f* (med.) eucrasia
eudemonismo *m* eudaemonism
eudiómetro *m* eudiometer
eufémico -ca *adj* euphemistic
eufemismo *m* euphemism
eufemístico -ca *adj* euphemistic
eufonía *f* euphony
eufónico -ca *adj* euphonic
eufono -na *adj* euphonious
euforbiáceo -a *adj* (bot.) euphorbiaceous
euforbio *m* (bot.) euphorbia, spurge; (pharm.) euphorbia (*dried herb*); (pharm.) euphorbium (*gum resin*)
euforia *f* (psychol.) euphoria; moment of glory; endurance, fortitude
eufórico -ca *adj* euphoric
eufrasia *f* (bot.) eyebright, euphrasy
Éufrates *m* Euphrates
Eufrosina *f* (myth.) Euphrosyne
eufuísmo *m* euphuism
eufuísta *adj* euphuistic; *mf* euphuist
eufuístico -ca *adj* euphuistic
eugenesia *f* eugenics
eugenésico -ca *adj* eugenic
Eugenia *f* Eugenia
Eugenio *m* Eugene
Euménides *fpl* (myth.) Eumenides
eunuco *m* eunuch
eupatorio *m* (bot.) eupatorium, boneset
eupepsia *f* (med.) eupepsia
eupéptico -ca *adj* eupeptic
Eurasia *f* Eurasia
eurasiano -na *adj & mf* Eurasian
eureka *interj* eureka!
Eurídice *f* (myth.) Eurydice
Eurípides *m* Euripides
euritmia *f* (f.a.) eurhythmy; (med.) normal rhythm of pulse
eurítmico -ca *adj* (f.a.) eurhythmic; (med.) normal, regular
euro *m* east wind
Europa *f* Europe; (myth.) Europa
europeidad *f* or **europeísmo** *m* Europeanism
europeizante *adj* Europeanizing; *mf* (Am.) advocate of European manners and customs
europeizar §76 *va* to Europeanize; *vr* to become Europeanized
europeo -a *adj & mf* European
europio *m* (chem.) europium
éuscaro -ra or **eusquero -ra** *adj & m* Basque (*language*)
Eustaquio *m* Eustace
éustilo *m* (arch.) eustyle
eutanasia *f* euthanasia; (med.) euthanasia, mercy killing
euténica *f* euthenics
Euterpe *f* (myth.) Euterpe
eutiquiano -na *adj & mf* Eutychian
eutrapelia *f* moderation (*in one's diversions*); simple pastime; lightheartedness
eutrapélico -ca *adj* moderate, simple; lighthearted
eutropelia *f* var. of **eutrapelia**
Eva *f* Eve
evacuación *f* evacuation; **evacuación de basuras** garbage disposal
evacuado -da *mf* evacuee
evacuante *adj & m* (med.) evacuant
evacuar *va* to evacuate; (mil.) to evacuate; to transact (*a deal*), to do (*an errand*); to drain (*a sore or humor*); to make (*a visit*); to carry out, to execute; **evacuar el vientre** to have a movement of the bowels; *vn* (mil.) to evacuate; to have a movement of the bowels
evacuativo -va *adj & m* (med.) evacuant
evacuatorio -ria *adj* evacuant; *m* public urinal
evadido -da *adj* escaped; *mf* escapee
evadir *va* to avoid; to evade; *vr* to evade; to flee, to escape
evagación *f* distraction; digression
evaluación *f* evaluation
evaluador -dora *adj* evaluating
evaluar §33 *va* to evaluate
evanescente *adj* evanescent; (bot.) evanescent
evangélico -ca *adj* evangelic or evangelical
Evangelio *m* gospel; Gospel, Evangel; (*l.c.*) *m* (coll.) gospel, gospel truth; **evangelios** *mpl* Gospel booklet with relics, worn around the neck of children; **decir** or **hablar el evangelio** to speak the gospel truth
evangelismo *m* evangelism
evangelista *m* gospeler, singer of the Gospel; (Am.) penman, scrivener, public writer; (*cap.*) *m* Evangelist
evangelistero *m* singer of Gospel in High Masses
evangelización *f* evangelization
evangelizador -dora *adj* evangelizing; *mf* evangelizer, evangelist
evangelizar §76 *va & vn* to evangelize
Evang.º abr. of **Evangelio**
Evang.ta abr. of **Evangelista**
evaporable *adj* evaporable
evaporación *f* evaporation
evaporado -da *adj* scatterbrained
evaporador -dora *adj* evaporating; *m* evaporator (*apparatus*)
evaporar *va* to evaporate; *vr* to evaporate (*change into vapor; vanish, disappear*)
evaporizar §76 *va, vn & vr* to vaporize
evasión *f* escape; evasion
evasivo -va *adj* evasive; *f* evasion
evección *f* (astr.) evection
evento *m* chance event, happening; **a todo evento** for any eventuality
eventual *adj* eventual, contingent
eventualidad *f* eventuality, contingency
eversión *f* destruction, ruin, desolation; (med.) eversion
evicción *f* (law) eviction, dispossession in virtue of an antecedent right
evidencia *f* evidence; obviousness; **en evidencia** in evidence; (coll.) in the open
evidenciar *va* to evidence, to make evident
evidente *adj* evident
evisceración *f* (surg.) evisceration
evitable *adj* avoidable, preventable
evitación *f* avoidance
evitar *va* to avoid, to shun; to keep off (*e.g., dust*); to prevent; **evitar** + *inf* to avoid + *ger*
eviterno -na *adj* unending, imperishable
evo *m* (poet.) age, aeon; (theol.) eternity
evocación *f* evocation
evocador -dora *adj* evoking; evocative
evocar §86 *va* to evoke
evolución *f* evolution; (biol., philos., mil. & nav.) evolution; change (*in attitude, plans, conduct, etc.*)
evolucionar *vn* to evolve; (mil. & nav.) to perform evolutions or maneuvers; to change (*in attitude, plans, conduct, etc.*)
evolucionismo *m* (biol.) evolution, evolutionism
evolucionista *adj* evolutionist, evolutionistic, evolutionary; *mf* evolutionist
evolutivo -va *adj* evolutionary
evónimo *m* (bot.) spindle tree, wahoo
ex *adj* ex- (*former*), e.g., **ex ministro** ex-minister; **su ex mujer** his ex-wife
ex abrupto (Lat.) abruptly, brashly; *m* abruptness, brash remark
exacción *f* exaction, requirement, demand; levy
exacerbación *f* exacerbation
exacerbar *va* to exacerbate; *vr* to become exacerbated
exactitud *f* exactness; punctuality
exacto -ta *adj* exact; punctual, faithful; complete
exactor *m* taxgatherer
exageración *f* exaggeration
exagerado -da *adj* exaggerated; exaggerating
exagerador -dora *adj* exaggerating; *mf* exaggerator
exagerar *va* to exaggerate
exaltación *f* exaltation
exaltado -da *adj* exalted; hot-headed, extreme
exaltar *va* to exalt; *vr* to become excited or wrought-up
examen *m* examination; **sufrir un examen** to take an examination
examinador -dora *mf* examiner

examinando -da *mf* examinee
examinar *va* to examine; to inspect; *vr* to take an examination; **examinarse de** to take an examination in; **examinarse de ingreso** to take entrance examinations
exangüe *adj* bloodless, anemic; exhausted, worn-out; dead
exanimación *f* exanimation
exánime *adj* exanimate, lifeless, in a faint
exantema *m* (path.) exanthema
exantemático -ca *adj* exanthematic
exasperación *f* exasperation
exasperar *va* to exasperate
Exc.ª abr. of **Excelencia**
excandecencia *f* anger, exasperation
excandecer §34 *va* to enrage, to incense; *vr* to become enraged
excarcelación *f* release from custody
excarcelar *va* to release (*a prisoner*)
excava *f* (agr.) removal of soil around a plant
excavación *f* excavation
excavador -dora *adj* excavating; *mf* excavator (*person*); *m* (dent. & surg.) excavator; *f* excavator, power shovel
excavar *va* to excavate; (agr.) to remove soil from around (*a plant*)
excave *m* digging, excavation
excedencia *f* excess; leave; leave pay
excedente *adj* excessive; excess, in excess; on leave; *m* excess, surplus; government employee on leave; **excedentes** *mpl* surplus property
exceder *va* & *vn* to exceed, to excel; **exceder de** to exceed; *vr* to exceed; to go too far, to go to extremes; **excederse a sí mismo** (coll.) to outdo oneself
excelencia *f* excellence or excellency; **por excelencia** par excellence; (*cap.*) *f* Excellency (*title*)
excelente *adj* excellent
excelsitud *f* loftiness, sublimity
excelso -sa *adj* lofty, elevated, sublime; **el Excelso** the Most High
excéntrica *f* see **excéntrico**
excentricidad *f* eccentricity; (coll.) eccentricity (*oddity, peculiarity*)
excéntrico -ca *adj* eccentric; erratic; (coll.) eccentric (*odd, peculiar*); *mf* (coll.) eccentric; *f* (mach.) eccentric
excepción *f* exception; **a excepción de** with the exception of
excepcional *adj* exceptional
excepcionar *va* (law) to protest against, to deny the validity of
excepto *prep* except
exceptuar §33 *va* to except; to exempt
excerpta or **excerta** *f* excerpt
excesivo -va *adj* excessive
exceso *m* excess; (fig.) excess (*abuse; eating or drinking too much*); **en** or **por exceso** to excess (*too much*); **exceso de equipaje** excess baggage; **exceso de peso** excess weight; **exceso de velocidad** speeding
excipiente *m* (pharm.) excipient
excisión *f* (surg.) excision
excitabilidad *f* excitability
excitable *adj* excitable
excitación *f* excitation, excitement; (phys. & physiol.) excitation
excitador -dora *adj* exciting; *m* (elec.) exciter (*for producing jump sparks*)
excitante *adj* exciting; stimulating; *m* (physiol.) excitant; (med.) stimulant
excitar *va* to excite; (elec. & physiol.) to excite; *vr* to become excited
excitativo -va *adj* excitative
excitatriz *f* (*pl:* **-trices**) (elec.) exciter (*for producing a magnetic field*)
exclamación *f* exclamation
exclamar *va* & *vn* to exclaim
exclamativo -va or **exclamatorio -ria** *adj* exclamatory
exclaustración *f* secularization
exclaustrado -da *mf* secularized ecclesiastic
exclaustrar *va* to secularize (*a monk*)
excluir §41 *va* to exclude
exclusión *f* exclusion; **con exclusión de** to the exclusion of
exclusiva *f* see **exclusivo**
exclusive *adv* exclusively
exclusividad *f* exclusive feature; exclusiveness; **con exclusividad** exclusively
exclusivismo *m* exclusivism
exclusivista *adj* exclusive, clannish; *mf* exclusivist
exclusivo -va *adj* exclusive; *f* turndown, rejection; sole right, special privilege; exclusive news release
Exc.ᵐᵒ abr. of **Excelentísimo**
excogitar *va* to excogitate, to think out
ex combatiente *m* ex-serviceman, veteran
excomulgado -da *adj* excommunicated; (coll.) pert, saucy; *mf* excommunicant, excommunicated person
excomulgador *m* excommunicator
excomulgar §59 *va* to excommunicate; to anathematize; (coll.) to proscribe, to ostracize; (coll.) to flay, to treat harshly
excomunión *f* excommunication
excoriación *f* excoriation, skinning
excoriar *va* to excoriate, to skin; *vr* to be excoriated; to skin oneself (*e.g., on the arm*)
excrecencia *f* excrescence
excrecente *adj* excrescent
excreción *f* (physiol.) excretion; evacuation
excremental *adj* excremental
excrementar *vn* to have an evacuation
excrementicio -cia *adj* excremental; (physiol.) waste (*matter*)
excremento *m* excrement
excrescencia *f* var. of **excrecencia**
excreta *f* (physiol.) excreta
excretar *va* (physiol.) to excrete; *vn* to eject the excrements
excretorio -ria *adj* (physiol.) excretory; *m* toilet
exculpación *f* exculpation, exoneration
exculpar *va* to exculpate, to exonerate
excursión *f* incursion; excursion
excursionismo *m* excursioning; touring
excursionista *adj* (pertaining to an) excursion; *mf* excursionist
excusa *f* excuse; basket with lid; **buscar excusa** to look for an excuse; **excusa es decir** it is unnecessary to say
excusabaraja *f* basket with lid
excusable *adj* excusable; avoidable
excusadamente *adv* unnecessarily
excusado -da *adj* exempt; unnecessary; reserved, set apart; *m* water closet, toilet
excusador -dora *adj* excusing; *m* substitute, vicar
excusalí *m* (*pl:* **-líes**) little apron
excusapecados *mf* (*pl:* **-dos**) indulgent person
excusar *va* to excuse; to avoid, to shun, to prevent; to exempt; to make unnecessary, to replace; **excusarle a uno de algo** to excuse someone for something; **excusar** + *inf* to not have to + *inf; vr* to excuse oneself; to apologize; **excusarse de** + *inf* to decline to + *inf*
excusión *f* (civil law) discussion
execrable *adj* execrable
execración *f* anathematization; execration
execrador -dora *adj* execrating; *mf* execrator
execrando -da *adj* execrable
execrar *va* to anathematize; to execrate
execratorio -ria *adj* execratory
exedra *f* (arch.) exedra
exégesis *f* (*pl:* **-sis**) exegesis
exegético -ca *adj* exegetic or exegetical
exención *f* exemption
exencionar *va* to exempt
exentamente *adv* freely; frankly, simply
exentar *va* to exempt
exento -ta *adj* exempt; clear, open, unobstructed; free, disengaged; deprived
exequátur *m* (*pl:* **-tur**) exequatur
exequias *fpl* obsequies, exequies
exequible *adj* attainable, feasible
exergo *m* exergue
éxeunt (Lat.) exeunt (*they go out*)
exfoliación *f* exfoliation
exfoliador -dora *adj* tear-off
exfoliar *va* & *vr* to exfoliate
exhalación *f* exhalation; shooting star; flash of lightning; fume, vapor
exhalar *va* to exhale, to emit (*gases, odors*); to breathe forth (*sighs, complaints*); **exhalar el**

último suspiro to breathe one's last; *vr* to exhale; to breathe hard (*from overexertion*); to hurry; to have a craving
exhaustivo -va *adj* exhaustive
exhaustizar §76 *vr* to become exhausted
exhausto -ta *adj* exhausted; (coll.) wasted away
exheredación *f* disinheritance
exheredar *va* to disinherit
exhibición *f* exhibition; exhibit
exhibicionismo *m* (psychol.) exhibitionism
exhibicionista *mf* exhibitionist
exhibir *va* to exhibit; (law) to exhibit (*a document*); *vr* (coll.) to show oneself, to like to be seen
exhilarante *adj* exhilarating; laughing (*gas*)
exhortación *f* exhortation
exhortador -dora *adj* exhorting; *mf* exhorter
exhortar *va* to exhort; **exhortar a** + *inf* to exhort to + *inf*
exhortativo -va *adj* exhortative
exhortatorio -ria *adj* exhortatory
exhorto *m* (law) letters rogatory
exhumación *f* exhumation
exhumador -dora *mf* exhumer
exhumar *va* to exhume
exigencia *f* exigency, requirement, demand
exigente *adj* exacting, exigent, demanding
exigible or **exigidero -ra** *adj* exigible, requirable; payable on demand
exigir §42 *va* to exact, to require, to demand, to call for; **exigir** + *inf* to require (*something*) to be + *pp*
exigüidad *f* exiguity, exiguousness; meagreness, smallness, scantiness
exiguo -gua *adj* exiguous; meagre, small, scanty
exilado -da *adj* & *mf* exile
exilar *va* to exile
exilio *m* exile
eximente *adj* (law) exempting
eximio -mia *adj* select, choice, superior, distinguished
eximir *va* to exempt; **eximir de** + *inf* to exempt from + *ger*
exina *f* (bot.) extine (*of pollen*)
exinanición *f* inanition, exinanition
exinánido -da *adj* exhausted, debilitated
existencia *f* existence; **existencias** *fpl* (com.) stock; **en existencia** (com.) in stock
existencial *adj* existentialist
existencialismo *m* (philos.) existentialism
existencialista *adj* & *mf* existentialist
existente *adj* existing, existent, extant
existimación *f* judgment, opinion
existimar *va* to judge, to deem, to esteem
existimativo -va *adj* putative
existir *vn* to exist
existista *adj* (Am.) me-too; *mf* (Am.) me-tooer
éxit (Lat.) exit (*he or she goes out*)
éxito *m* outcome, result; success; hit (*successful stroke, performance, etc.*); **éxito de librería** best seller (*book*); **éxito de taquilla** box-office hit, good box office; **éxito de venta** best seller; **éxito rotundo** smash hit
exitoso -sa *adj* (Am.) successful
ex libris *m* (*pl:* **-bris**) ex libris, bookplate
exobiología *f* exobiology
éxodo *m* exodus; (*cap.*) *m* (Bib.) Exodus
exodoncia or **exodontología** *f* exodontia
exoftalmía *f* (path.) exophthalmos or exophthalmia
exoftálmico -ca *adj* exophthalmic
exoftalmos *m* var. of **exoftalmía**
exogamia *f* exogamy; (biol.) exogamy
exógeno -na *adj* exogenous
exoneración *f* exoneration; discharge, dismissal; defecation
exonerar *va* to exonerate (*to relieve of an obligation*); to discharge; *vn* to defecate
exónfalo *m* (path.) exomphalos
exorable *adj* exorable
exorar *va* to beg, to entreat
exorbitancia *f* exorbitance or exorbitancy
exorbitante *adj* exorbitant
exorcismo *m* exorcism
exorcista *mf* exorcist; *m* exorcist (*priest*)
exorcistado *m* (eccl.) third minor order
exorcizar §76 *va* to exorcise
exordio *m* exordium
exornación *f* adornment, embellishment
exornar *va* to adorn, to embellish
exorno *m* adornment, embellishment
exosfera *f* exosphere
exósmosis *f* (physical chem. & physiol.) exosmosis
exospora *f* (bot.) exospore
exosqueleto *m* (zool.) exoskeleton
exostoma *m* (bot.) exostome
exostósico -ca *adj* exostotic
exostosis *f* (*pl:* **-sis**) (bot. & path.) exostosis
exoteca *f* (zool.) exotheca
exotecio *m* (bot.) exothecium
exotérico -ca *adj* exoteric
exotérmico -ca *adj* (chem.) exothermic
exoticidad *f* exoticity
exótico -ca *adj* exotic; striking, stunning
exotiquez *f* exoticalness, exoticism
exotismo *m* exoticism
exotospora *f* (biol.) exotospore
exotoxina *f* (biochem.) exotoxin
exotropía *f* (path.) exotropia
expandir *va* & *vr* to spread, extend, expand
expansibilidad *f* expansibility
expansible *adj* expansible
expansión *f* expansion; expansiveness; relief, recreation, rest
expansionar *va* to expand (*e.g., production*); *vr* to expand; to open one's heart; to enjoy oneself, to relax, to take it easy
expansionismo *m* expansionism
expansionista *adj* & *mf* expansionist
expansivo -va *adj* expansive; (fig.) expansive
expatriación *f* expatriation
expatriado -da *adj* expatriate; *mf* expatriate, displaced person
expatriar §90 & **regular** *va* to expatriate; *vr* to expatriate, to leave one's country
expectación *f* expectancy; (med.) expectation; **expectación de vida** life expectancy
expectante *adj* expectant
expectativa *f* expectation, expectancy; **estar en la expectativa de** to be expecting, to be on the lookout for; **expectativa de vida** expectation of life
expectoración *f* expectoration
expectorante *adj* & *m* expectorant
expectorar *va* & *vn* to expectorate
expedición *f* expedition; shipment; issuance; (fig.) expedition
expedicionario -ria *adj* expeditionary; *mf* expeditionist, member of an expedition
expedidor -dora *mf* sender, shipper; *m* dispenser (*device*)
expediente *m* expedient; expedition; (law) action, proceedings; dossier; record; reason, motive; supply, provision; **formar** or **instruir expediente a** to impeach (*a public official*); **expediente académico** (educ.) record
expedienteo *m* red tape; (law) execution (*of papers, etc.*)
expedir §94 *va* to send, to ship, to remit; to issue; to expedite
expeditar *va* (Am.) to expedite
expeditivo -va *adj* expeditious
expedito -ta *adj* free, easy, ready, expeditious; clear, open
expeler *va* to expel, to eject
expendedor -dora *adj* spending; dealing, trading; vending; *mf* dealer, agent, retailer; ticket agent; distributer of counterfeit money
expendeduría *f* cigar store, retail store (*for sale of state-monopolized articles*); **expendeduría de billetes** (Am.) ticket office
expender *va* to expend; to sell on a commission; to sell at retail; to circulate (*counterfeit money*)
expendición *f* commission selling; retailing
expendio *m* expense; (Am.) shop, store; (Am.) ticket office; (Am.) retailing
expensar *va* (Am.) to defray (*expenses*)
expensas *fpl* expenses; **a expensas de** at the expense of
experiencia *f* experience (*practical knowledge gained by doing or living through things; something experienced, event participated in*); experiment; **aprender con su propria experiencia** to learn by experience
experimentación *f* experimentation

experimentado -da *adj* experienced
experimentador -dora *adj* experimenting; *mf* experimenter
experimental *adj* experimental
experimentalismo *m* experimentalism
experimentar *va* to test, to try, to try out; to experience, undergo, feel; *vn* to experiment
experimentativo -va *adj* experimental
experimento *m* experience; experiment
experto -ta *adj & m* expert
expiable *adj* expiable
expiación *f* expiation, atonement; cleansing, purification
expiar §90 *va* to expiate, to atone for; to cleanse, to purify
expiativo -va *adj* expiative, expiatory
expiatorio -ria *adj* expiatory
expilar *va* to rob, to despoil
expillo *m* (bot.) feverfew
expiración *f* expiration
expirante *adj* expiring
expirar *vn* to expire (*to emit the breath; to die; to come to an end*)
explanación *f* leveling, grading; explanation, elucidation
explanada *f* esplanade; (fort.) esplanade
explanar *va* to level, to grade; to explain, to elucidate
explantación *f* (biol.) explantation
explayar *va* to extend, to enlarge; *vr* to extend, to spread out; to discourse at large; **explayarse con** to unbosom oneself to
expletivo -va *adj* expletive
explicable *adj* explicable, explainable
explicación *f* explanation, explication; **pedir explicaciones** to demand an explanation
explicaderas *fpl* (coll.) way of explaining; **tener buenas explicaderas** (coll.) to have a way of explaining things
explicador -dora *mf* explainer, commentator
explicar §86 *va* to explain; to expound; *vr* to explain oneself; to understand, e.g., **ahora me lo explico** now I understand it
explicativo -va *adj* explanatory, explicative
explicatorio -ria *adj* explanatory, explicatory
explícito -ta *adj* explicit
exploración *f* exploration; (mil.) scouting; (telv.) scanning
explorador -dora *adj* exploring; exploratory; (telv.) scanning; *mf* explorer; *m* (mil.) scout; boy scout; (med.) explorer (*instrument*); (telv.) scanning disk
exploramiento *m* exploration
explorar *va & vn* to explore; (telv.) to scan; (mil.) to scout
explorativo -va *adj* explorative
exploratorio -ria *adj* exploratory
explosímetro *m* explosimeter
explosión *f* explosion; combustion (*e.g., of gasoline in a motor*); (phonet.) explosion
explosivo -va *adj* explosive; (phonet.) explosive; *m* explosive; *f* (phonet.) explosive
explosor *m* exploder, blasting machine
explotable *adj* workable; exploitable
explotación *f* running, operation; working; exploitation
explotador -dora *adj* running, operating; exploiting; *mf* operator; exploiter
explotar *va* to run, to operate (*e.g., a railroad*); to work (*a mine*); to exploit; *vn* to explode
expoliación *f* spoliation; (rhet.) repetition, elaboration
expoliador -dora *adj* spoliating; *mf* spoliator
expoliar *va* to spoliate, to despoil
expolio *m* spoliation
expondré *1st sg fut ind of* **exponer**
exponencial *adj* (math.) exponential
exponente *adj* explaining, expounding; *m* exponent; (alg.) exponent
exponer §69 *va* to expose; to abandon (*a child*); to expound; to show; to put (*a corpse*) on view; (eccl.) to expose (*the Host*); *vn* (eccl.) to expose the Host; *vr* to expose oneself (*e.g., to a danger*)
expongo *1st sg pres ind of* **exponer**
exportación *f* export, exportation; exports
exportador -dora *adj* exporting; *mf* exporter
exportar *va & vn* to export
exposición *f* exposition; exposure (*exposing or being exposed; position as to points of compass*); (rhet.) exposition; (phot.) exposure; show, fair, exposition; **exposición universal** world's fair
exposímetro *m* (phot.) exposure meter, light meter
expositivo -va *adj* expositive
expósito -ta *adj* exposed or abandoned (*child*); *mf* foundling
expositor -tora *adj* expository; *mf* exponent; expositor, expounder, commentator; exhibitor
expremijo *m* cheese vat, cheese shelf
exprés *adj* express (*train*); *m* express train; caffè espresso; (Am.) express company
expresable *adj* (Am.) expressible
expresado -da *adj* above-mentioned
expresamente *adv* expressly
expresar *va* to express; to specify; *vr* to express oneself
expresión *f* expression; squeezing; (math.) expression; **expresiones** *fpl* regards
expresionismo *m* (f.a.) expressionism
expresionista *adj & mf* expressionist
expresividad *f* expressiveness
expresivo -va *adj* expressive; kind, affectionate
expreso -sa *adj* expressed; express (*clear, definite; for a particular purpose; train, car, elevator, etc.*); *m* express (*train; fast shipment*); (Am.) express company
exprimible *adj* expressible
exprimidamente *adv* stiffly; primly, prudishly; with affectation; grudgingly
exprimidera *f* or **exprimidero** *m* squeezer; **exprimidera de naranjas** orange squeezer
exprimido -da *adj* lean, skinny; stiff, stuck-up; prim, prudish; affected, overprecise
exprimidor *m* wringer; squeezer
exprimir *va* to express, to squeeze, to press out; to wring, wring out; to express vividly; (Am.) to empty (*a firearm*)
ex profeso *adv* on purpose, expressly
expropiación *f* expropriation
expropiador -dora *mf* expropriator
expropiar *va* to expropriate
expuesto -ta *adj* dangerous, hazardous; *pp of* **exponer**
expugnable *adj* expugnable, pregnable
expugnación *f* taking by storm
expugnar *va* to take by storm
expulsador -dora *mf* ejector
expulsanieves *m* (*pl:* **-ves**) snowplow
expulsar *va* to expel, to expulse, to drive out
expulsión *f* expulsion
expulsivo -va *adj* expulsive
expulsor *m* ejector (*of firearm*)
expurgación *f* expurgation
expurgar §59 *va* to expurgate
expurgatorio -ria *adj* expurgatory
expurgo *m* expurgation; expurgated parts (*of a book*); elimination of green and damaged grapes before pressing
expuse *1st sg pret ind of* **exponer**
exquisitez *f* exquisiteness; excellence; affectation
exquisito -ta *adj* exquisite; consummate, excellent; genteel; affected
exsicación *f* exsiccation
exsomático -ca *adj* exsomatic
exstrofia *f* (path.) exstrophy
éxtasi *m* var. of **éxtasis**
extasiar §90 & regular *va* to delight, to enrapture; *vr* to go into ecstasies, to become enraptured
éxtasis *m* (*pl:* **-sis**) ecstasy
extático -ca *adj* ecstatic
extemporal *adj* unseasonable
extemporaneidad *f* unseasonableness; untimeliness
extemporáneo -a *adj* unseasonable; untimely, inopportune; (pharm.) magistral
extender §66 *va* to extend, to stretch out, to spread, to spread out; to draw up (*a document*); *vr* to extend, to stretch out, to spread, to spread out; to go on and on (*talking, explaining, etc.*); (coll.) to be puffed up; **extenderse a** or **hasta** to reach, to amount to
extendidamente *adv* in detail, at great length
extensible *adj* stretchy, extensible

extensión *f* extension, extent, extensity; expanse; range; (psychol.) extensity; (telp.) extension
extensivo -va *adj* extensive; (agr.) extensive; **hacer extensivos a** to extend (*congratulations, good wishes, etc.*) to; **hacerse extensivo a** to extend to
extenso -sa *adj* extended, vast, extensive; **por extenso** in detail, at great length
extensor -sora *adj* extending; extensile; *m* (anat.) extensor; chest or muscle exerciser; **extensor de cubiertas** (Am.) tire spreader
extenuación *f* extenuation, emaciation, weakening
extenuante *adj* weakening, debilitating
extenuar §33 *va* to extenuate, to emaciate, to weaken
extenuativo -va *adj* emaciating, weakening
exterior *adj* exterior, external, outer, outside, outward; foreign; *m* exterior, outside; appearance, bearing; **al exterior** or **a lo exterior** on the outside; outwardly; **del exterior** from abroad; **en el exterior** on the outside; abroad; **en exteriores** (mov.) on location
exterioridad *f* exteriority, externality; externals, outward appearance, outward show; **exterioridades** *fpl* show, pomp
exteriorista *adj* outgoing, outgiving (*e.g., nature, personality*); *mf* extrovert
exteriorización *f* revelation, manifestation; (surg.) temporary removal (*of an internal organ*); (psychol.) doubling of personality
exteriorizar §76 *va* to reveal, to make manifest; *vr* to unbosom one's heart
exteriormente *adv* on the outside; outwardly, seemingly
exterminable *adj* exterminable
exterminador -dora *adj* exterminating; *mf* exterminator (*person*); *m* exterminator (*apparatus*)
exterminar *va* to exterminate
exterminio *m* extermination
externado *m* day school
externo -na *adj* external, outside; (anat.) external; *mf* day scholar, day pupil; day-school pupil
extima *f* (anat.) extima
extina *f* (bot.) extine
extinción *f* extinction; elimination, obliteration
extinguible *adj* extinguishable
extinguir §44 *va* to extinguish, to quench, to put out, to wipe out; to carry out, to fulfil; to spend, to serve (*a period of time*); *vr* to go out, to be extinguished; to become extinct
extintivo -va *adj* extinctive; (law) extinctive
extinto -ta *adj* extinguished; extinct; (Am.) dead, deceased
extintor -tora *adj* extinguishing; *m* fire extinguisher; **extintor de espuma** foam extinguisher; **extintor de granada** fire grenade
extirpación *f* extirpation
extirpador -dora *adj* extirpating; *mf* extirpator; *m* (agr.) cultivator
extirpar *va* to extirpate
extorno *m* (ins.) premium adjustment (*based on modification of policy*)
extorsión *f* extortion; damage, harm
extorsionar *va* to extort; to damage, harm
extra *adj* extra; **extra de** (coll.) besides, in addition to; *mf* (theat.) extra; *m* extra (*of a newspaper*); (coll.) extra (*gratuity*)
extrabronquial *adj* extrabronchial
extrabucal *adj* extrabuccal
extrabulbar *adj* extrabulbar
extracapsular *adj* extracapsular
extracardíaco -ca *adj* extracardial
extracción *f* extraction; number drawing (*in lottery*); **extracción de raíces** (math.) extraction of roots, evolution
extracelular *adj* extracellular
extracístico -ca *adj* extracystic
extracorriente *f* (elec.) extra current
extracorto -ta *adj* (rad.) ultrashort
extractador -dora *mf* abstractor
extractar *va* to abstract (*a writing*)
extractivo -va *adj* extractive; extractable
extracto *m* abstract (*of a writing*); (pharm.) extract; **extracto de índigo** indigo extract; **extracto de malta** malt extract
extractor -tora *mf* extractor; *m* extractor (*apparatus*); **extractor de aire** ventilator; **extractor de rueda** (aut.) wheel puller
extracurricular *adj* extracurricular
extradición *f* extradition
extraditable *adj* extraditable
extradós *m* (arch.) extrados
extraelevado -da *adj* (rad.) ultrahigh
extraembrionario -ria *adj* extraembryonic
extraente *adj* extracting; *mf* extractor
extraer §88 *va* to extract; to pull; (math.) to extract (*a root*)
extraeuropeo -a *adj* outside of Europe, non-European
extrafino -na *adj* extrafine
extrafuerte *adj* heavy-duty
extragenital *adj* extragenital
extrahepático -ca *adj* extrahepatic
extraigo *1st sg pres ind of* **extraer**
extraje *1st sg pret ind of* **extraer**
extrajudicial *adj* extrajudicial
extralegal *adj* extralegal
extralimitación *f* overstepping, taking advantage
extralimitar *vr* to overstep, to go too far
extramedular *adj* extramedullary
extrameridiano -na *adj* extrameridional
extramural *adj* extramural
extramuros *adv* beyond the walls, outside the town or city
extranjería *f* alienism, alienship
extranjerismo *m* xenomania; borrowing, foreignism
extranjerizar §76 *va* to mix foreign customs with; *vr* to become mixed with foreign customs
extranjero -ra *adj* foreign; *mf* foreigner; **extranjero enemigo** enemy alien; *m* foreign land; **del extranjero** from abroad; **en el extranjero, por el extranjero** abroad
extranjía *f* (coll.) alienship; **de extranjía** (coll.) foreign; (coll.) strange, unexpected
extranjis; de extranjis (coll.) foreign; (coll.) strange, unexpected; (coll.) secretly
extraña *f* see **extraño**
extrañación *f* or **extrañamiento** *m* banishment, expatriation
extrañar *va* to banish, to expatriate; to surprise; to find strange, to be surprised at; (dial. & Am.) to miss; **extrañar** + *inf* to surprise to + *inf*, e.g., **me extrañó encontrar a Vd. aquí** it surprised me to find you here; *vn* to be strange; *vr* to be surprised; to wonder; to refuse; **extrañarse de** + *inf* to be surprised to + *inf*
extrañez *f* or **extrañeza** *f* strangeness, peculiarity; estrangement; wonder
extraño -ña *adj* foreign; strange; extraneous; **extraño a** unconnected with; *mf* foreigner; stranger; *f* (bot.) China aster
extraoficial *adj* unofficial
extraordinario -ria *adj* extraordinary; extra; *m* extra dish; extra number (*of a periodical*); special mail
extrapélvico -ca *adj* extrapelvic
extrapiramidal *adj* extrapyramidal
extraplacentario -ria *adj* extraplacental
extraplano -na *adj* extra-flat
extrapolación *f* (math.) extrapolation
extrapolar *adj* extrapolar; *va & vn* (math.) to extrapolate
extrapulmonar *adj* extrapulmonary
extrarradio *m* outer edge of town
extrarrápido -da *adj* (phot.) extra-fast
extrasensorial *adj* extrasensory
extraseroso -sa *adj* extraserous
extrasístole *f* (med.) extrasystole
extraterreno -na *adj* extramundane
extraterrestre *adj* extraterrestrial; (astr.) extraterrestrial
extraterritorial *adj* extraterritorial
extraterritorialidad *f* extraterritoriality
extrauterino -na *adj* extrauterine
extravagancia *f* extravagance, folly, wildness, nonsense
extravagante *adj* extravagant, foolish, wild, nonsensical; in transit (*said of mail in post office*); **extravagantes** *fpl* (canon law) Extravagants or Extravagantes
extravagar §59 *vn* to ramble, to talk nonsense

extravaginal *adj* (anat. & bot.) extravaginal
extravasación *f* extravasation
extravasar *va* to extravasate; *vr* (physiol.) to extravasate
extravascular *adj* extravascular
extravenar *va & vr* to exude through the veins
extraventricular *adj* extraventricular
extraversión *f* (psychol.) extroversion or extraversion
extraviadamente *adv* astray; beside oneself; at random, wandering
extraviar **§90** *va* to lead astray; to mislead; to mislay, to misplace; *vr* to go astray; to wander; to get lost; to be wrong; to get out of line or out of alignment
extravío *m* misleading; misplacement; going astray; loss; misconduct; error, wrong; (coll.) annoyance
extrema *f* see **extremo**
extremadamente *adv* extremely
extremado -da *adj* extreme, excessive; consummate
extremar *va* to carry far, carry to the limit; *vr* to exert oneself to the utmost; **extremarse en** + *inf* to strive hard to + *inf*
extremaunción *f* (eccl.) extreme unction
extremeño -ña *adj* frontier; Estremenian; *mf* frontier dweller; Estremenian
extremidad *f* extremity; end, tip; **la última extremidad** one's last moment (*death*); **extremidades** *fpl* extremities (*hands and feet*)
extremismo *m* extremism
extremista *mf* extremist
extremo -ma *adj* extreme; ultimate; utmost; critical, desperate; *m* end, extremity, tip; extreme; point (*of a conversation, letter, etc.*); great care; winter pasture, winter grazing; (football) end; **al extremo de** to the point of; **con, de, en** or **por extremo** extremely; **de extremo a extremo** from one end to the other; **hacer extremos** to gush, be demonstrative; **pasar de un extremo a otro** to go from one extreme to the other; **extremo muerto** dead end; *f* (coll.) extremity (*extreme need*); (coll.) end, final moment (*of life*); (coll.) extreme unction
extremosidad *f* effusiveness, gushiness
extremoso -sa *adj* extreme; demonstrative, effusive; forthright
extrínseco -ca *adj* extrinsic
extrofia *f* var. of **exstrofia**
extrorso -sa *adj* (bot.) extrorse
extroversión *f* (path.) extroversion
extrovertido -da *mf* extrovert
extrusión *f* (metal.) extrusion
exuberancia *f* exuberance
exuberante *adj* exuberant
exuberar *vn* to exuberate
exudación *f* exudation
exudado *m* exudate
exudar *va & vn* to exude
exulceración *f* chafing, slight ulceration
exulcerar *va & vn* to chafe, to ulcerate lightly
exultación *f* exultation
exultar *vn* to exult
exutorio *m* (med.) issue, artificial ulcer (*for discharge of pus*)
exvoto *m* ex-voto, votive offering
eyaculación *f* (physiol.) ejaculation
eyaculador -dora *adj* (physiol.) ejaculatory
eyacular *va & vn* (physiol.) to ejaculate
eyector *m* (mach.) ejector
-ez *suffix f* -hood, e.g., **niñez** childhood; **viudez** widowhood; -ness, e.g., **altivez** haughtiness; **madurez** ripeness; **pequeñez** smallness; -ty, e.g., **aridez** aridity; **fluidez** fluidity; **rapidez** rapidity
-eza *suffix f* -ness, e.g., **grandeza** bigness; greatness; **ligereza** lightness; **limpieza** cleanliness; -ty, e.g., **certeza** certainty; **pureza** purity
Ezequías *m* (Bib.) Hezekiah
Ezequiel *m* (Bib.) Ezekiel (*prophet and book*)

F

F, f *f* seventh letter of the Spanish alphabet
F. abr. of **fulano**
fab. abr. of **fabricante**
f.a.b. abr. of **franco a bordo**
fabada *f* Asturian bean soup with pork and sausage
Fabián *m* Fabian
fabiano -na *adj & mf* Fabian
fabla *f* imitation of Old Spanish
fabordón *m* (mus.) faux-bourdon
fábrica *f* manufacture; factory, plant, mill; building; fabric; masonry; invention; church rate; church funds; vestry, church board; **de fábrica** (pertaining to or made of) masonry; **fábrica de la moneda** mint; **fábrica de montaje** assembly plant
fabricación *f* fabrication, manufacture; **fabricación en serie** mass production
fabricador -dora *mf* fabricator, inventor, schemer
fabricante *mf* manufacturer; *m* factory owner, plant owner, mill owner
fabricar **§86** *va* to fabricate, to manufacture; to devise, invent, bring about, forge
fabricoide *m* fabricoid
fabril *adj* manufacturing
fabriquero *m* manufacturer, factory owner; charcoal burner (*person*); churchwarden
fabuco *m* beechnut, mast (*food for animals*)
fábula *f* fable; rumor, gossip; talk (*e.g., of the town*); story, lie; plot, story, tale; **la Fábula** mythology; **fábulas milesias** Milesian tales
fabulador *m* var. of **fabulista**
fabulario *m* collection of fables, book of fables
fabulista *mf* fabulist
fabuloso -sa *adj* fabulous
faca *f* cutlass, falchion
facción *f* faction; feature; factious group; battle; **facciones** *fpl* features (*face*); **estar de facción** (mil.) to be on duty
faccionar *va* to incite to rebellion; *vr* to rebel
faccionario -ria *adj* factional; *mf* partisan, factionalist
faccioso -sa *adj* factious; rebellious; *mf* partisan; rebel
faceto -ta *adj* (Am.) affected, smart; (Am.) finicky; *f* facet; (arch., zool. & fig.) facet
facial *adj* facial; face; intuitive
facie *f* (cryst.) face
facies *f* (med.) face (*indicating a certain disease*); (biol.) facies
fácil *adj* easy; facile; pliant, yielding, docile; probable, likely; loose, wanton; **poco fácil a** not given to
facilidad *f* ease, easiness, facility; **facilidades** *fpl* facilities (*conveniences, means*); **facilidades de pago** easy payments
facílimo -ma *adj super* very or most easy
facilitación *f* facilitation; furnishing, providing
facilitar *va* to facilitate, to expedite; to furnish, to provide; (coll.) to oversimplify
facilitón -tona *adj* (coll.) brash, bumbling; *mf* (coll.) bumbler
facineroso -sa *adj* wicked, villainous; *mf* villain, rascal; criminal
facistol *m* lectern, choir desk
facón *m* (Am.) dagger; **pelar el facón** (Am.) to pull a knife
faconazo *m* (Am.) stab
facóquero *m* (zool.) wart hog
facsímil *m* var. of **facsímile**
facsimilar *adj* facsimile; *va* to facsimile, to make a facsimile of
facsímile *m* facsimile; **a facsímile** in facsimile

fact.ª abr. of **factura**
factaje *m* carriage, conveyance, delivery
factible *adj* feasible, doable
facticio -cia *adj* factitious
factitivo -va *adj* (gram.) causative
factor *m* commission merchant; baggageman; freight agent; factor (*element that helps to bring about a result*); (biochem., biol., law, math. & physiol.) factor; **factor de potencia** (elec.) power factor; **factor Rh** (biochem.) Rh factor
factoraje *m* factorage (*business of commission merchant*)
factoría *f* factory (*trading post in a foreign country*); factorage (*business of commission merchant*); (Am.) factory; (Am.) foundry
factorial *f* (math.) factorial
factótum *m* (coll.) factotum; (coll.) busybody; (coll.) confidant
factura *f* form, execution, workmanship; manufacture; invoice, bill; **según factura** as per invoice; **factura consular** consular invoice; **factura simulada** pro forma invoice
facturación *f* invoicing, billing; checking (*of baggage*)
facturar *va* (com.) to invoice, to bill; to check (*baggage*)
fácula *f* (astr.) facula
facultad *f* faculty; power; permission; option; knowledge, skill; school (*of a university*); (med.) strength, resistance; **facultad de altos estudios** school of advanced studies, graduate school
facultar *va* to empower, to authorize
facultativo -va *adj* (pertaining to a) faculty; of a doctor; facultative, optional; (biol.) facultative; *m* doctor (*physician or surgeon*)
facundia *f* eloquence, fluency; gift of gab
facundo -da *adj* eloquent, fluent; talkative
facha *f* (coll.) appearance, look; **ponerse en facha** (coll.) to get ready, be prepared; (naut.) to lie to; **facha a facha** face to face; *m & f* (coll.) ridiculous figure
fachado -da *adj*; **bien fachado** (coll.) good-looking; **mal fachado** (coll.) bad-looking; *f* façade; frontage; title page; (coll.) front, presence; **hacer fachada con** to face, overlook
fachear *vn* (naut.) to lie to
fachenda *f* (coll.) boasting, ostentation; *m* (coll.) boaster, show-off
fachendear *vn* (coll.) to boast, to show off
fachendista, fachendón -dona or **fachendoso -sa** *adj* (coll.) boastful, ostentatious; *mf* (coll.) boaster, show-off
fachinal *m* (Am.) marsh, marshland
fachoso -sa or **fachudo -da** *adj* ill-favored, funny-looking; boastful, ostentatious
fada *f* fairy, witch
faena *f* task, job, chore; work, toil; stunt; (taur.) windup; (taur.) stunt, skill, trick (*of bullfighters on a cattle-raising farm*); (mil.) fatigue, fatigue duty; (Am.) extra work, overtime; (Am.) morning work in the field; (Am.) gang of laborers
faenero *m* (Am.) farm hand
faenza *f* faïence
faetón *m* phaeton; (*cap.*) *m* (myth.) Phaethon
fagáceo -a *adj* (bot.) fagaceous
fagocito *m* (physiol.) phagocyte
fagocitosis *f* phagocytosis
fagot *m* (*pl:* **-gotes**) (mus.) bassoon; bassoonist
fagotista *m* (mus.) bassoonist
faisán *m* (orn.) pheasant; **faisán de Mogolia** (orn.) Mongolian pheasant; **faisán dorado** (orn.) golden pheasant; **faisán plateado** (orn.) silver pheasant

faisana *f* hen pheasant
faisanería *f* pheasant preserve, pheasantry
faisanero -ra *mf* pheasant raiser
faja *f* sash, girdle, belt; bandage; strip, band; sheet; zone; newspaper wrapper; plaster border (*of door or window*); lane (*of highway*); strip (*of landing field*); (arch. & surg.) fascia; (her.) fesse; (naut.) reef band; (rad.) channel; **faja abdominal** abdominal supporter; **faja de desgarre** (aer.) rip panel; **faja divisora** parting strip (*of a road*); **faja medical** supporter
fajado *m* mine timber
fajadura *f* wrapping; bandaging; swaddling; (naut.) parceling
fajamiento *m* wrapping; bandaging; swaddling
fajar *va* to wrap; to bandage; to swaddle; to put a wrapper on (*a newspaper or magazine*); (Am.) to beat, to thrash; (Am.) to give (*a slap, a whipping*); (Am.) to attack, jump on; *vr* to put on a sash or belt
fajardo *m* meat pie, mince pie
fajeado -da *adj* striped, banded, fasciated
fajero *m* knitted swaddling band; dealer in sashes, belts, etc.; clerk who wraps newspapers for mailing
fajín *m* sash (*badge of distinction*)
fajina *f* fagot, fascine; shock, rick; toil, task, chore; (fort.) fascine; (mil.) call to mess; (archaic) call to quarters; **meter fajina** to blab, to jabber
fajinada *f* (fort.) fascine work
fajo *m* bundle; **fajos** *mpl* swaddling clothes
fajol *m* (bot.) buckwheat
fajón *m* large sash; large strip or band; plaster border (*of door or window*)
fakir *m* var. of **faquir**
falacia *f* deceit; perfidy; (log.) fallacy
falange *f* phalanx; (anat. & zool.) phalanx; (iron.) array (*of people*); (poet.) army; (*cap.*) *f* (pol.) Falange
falangero *m* (zool.) phalanger
falangeta *f* (anat.) phalangette
falangia *f* (ent.) daddy longlegs
falangiano -na *adj* phalangeal
falangio *m* var. of **falangia**
falangista *adj & mf* Falangist
falansterio *m* phalanstery
falaris *f* (orn.) coot
falárope *m* (orn.) phalarope
falaz *adj* (*pl:* **-laces**) deceitful; perfidious; fallacious, deceptive, misleading
falbalá *m* (*pl:* **-laes**) (archaic) square flap sewed in the rear slit of the skirt of a coat; ruffle, flounce
falca *f* warp (*in a board*); (naut.) washboard; (dial.) wedge; (Am.) small still
falcado -da *adj* falcate
falce *f* sickle; curved knife; (anat.) falx
falciforme *adj* falciform
falcinelo *m* (orn.) glossy ibis
falcón *m* (arti.) falcon
falconete *m* (arti.) falconet
falda *f* skirt, dress; flap, fold; lap; loin (*e.g., of beef*); brim (*of hat*); foothill, lower slope (*of a mountain*); (arm.) skirt; (coll.) skirt (*woman*); **cosido** or **pegado a las faldas de** tied to the apron strings of
faldamenta *f* or **faldamento** *m* skirt; ugly, long skirt
faldar *m* (arm.) skirt (*of tasses*)
faldear *va* to climb (*a hill*); (Am.) to wind one's way up (*a hill*)
faldellín *m* short skirt; underskirt
faldero -ra *adj* skirt; lap; lady-loving; *m* lap dog; *f* skirt maker
faldeta *f* small skirt; (theat.) stage screen
faldicorto -ta *adj* short-skirted
faldilla *f* flap of a saddle; **faldillas** *fpl* skirts, coattails; (Am.) petticoat
faldistorio *m* faldstool
faldón *m* coattail; shirttail; skirt, tail; flap; saddle flap; top millstone; triangular slope (*of a hip roof*)
faldriquera *f* var. of **faltriquera**
faldulario *m* or **faldumenta** *f* trailing clothing
falena *f* (ent.) geometrid
falencia *f* fallacy, mistake; falsehood; (Am.) failure, bankruptcy
falencioso -sa *adj* fallacious, erroneous; false
falibilidad *f* fallibility
falible *adj* fallible
fálico -ca *adj* phallic
falina *f* (biochem.) phallin
falismo *m* phallicism or phallism
falo *m* phallus
falsabraga *f* (fort.) low outer rampart
falsada *f* swoop (*of bird of prey*)
falsario -ria *adj* falsifying; lying; *mf* falsifier, crook; liar
falsarregla *f* bevel square; guide lines (*for writing*)
falsarrienda *f* checkrein
falseamiento *m* falsification; counterfeit; forgery
falsear *va* to falsify; to misrepresent, to fake; to counterfeit; to forge; to pick (*a lock*); to bevel; to pierce (*armor*); *vn* to sag, buckle; to give, give way; to flag; to be out of tune
falsedad *f* falsehood; falsity
falseo *m* bevel; beveling
falsete *m* plug, tap; small door; falsetto (*voice*)
falsetista *m* falsetto (*person*)
falsía *f* falsity, treachery, duplicity
falsificación *f* falsification; counterfeit; forgery; fake
falsificador -dora *mf* falsifier; counterfeiter; forger; faker
falsificar §86 *va & vn* to falsify; to counterfeit; to forge; to fake
falsilla *f* guide lines (*for writing*)
falso -sa *adj* false; counterfeit; vicious (*horse*); *m* patch, reinforcement; (philately) forgery (*forged stamp*); **coger en falso** to catch in a lie; **de falso** or **en falso** without proper support; **envidar de falso** or **en falso** to bluff (*in betting*); (fig.) to invite half-heartedly; **sobre falso** without proper support
falta *f* see **falto**
faltante *adj* wanting, missing
faltar *va* to offend, to insult; *vn* to be missing; to be lacking, be wanting; to be short, fall short; to run out; to fail; to be absent; to be unfaithful; to die; to be impudent; to slip; to lack, need, be in need of, e.g., **me falta dinero** I lack money, I need money; **¡no faltaba más!** the very idea!, that's the last straw!; **faltar a** to go back on (*e.g., a promise*); **faltar a la clase** to cut class, be absent from class; **faltar a la verdad** to fail to tell the truth; **faltar a una cita** to break an appointment; **faltar . . . para** to be . . . to, e.g., **faltan diez minutos para las dos** it is ten minutes to two; **falta un cuarto para la una** it is a quarter to one; **faltar poco para** + *inf* to be near + *ger*, e.g., **falta poco para terminarse el año** the year is near ending; **faltar poco para que** + *subj* to come near + *ger*, e.g., **poco faltó para que cayese en el estanque** he came near falling into the pool; **faltar por** + *inf* to remain to be + *pp*, e.g., **faltan por escribir tres cartas** three letters remain to be written
falto -ta *adj* short, lacking, wanting; mean, lowly; short (*weight or measure*); (Am.) dull, stupid; **falto de** short of, lacking ‖ *f* lack, want; shortage; fault, mistake; misdemeanor, misdeed; flaw, defect; absence, cut; (sport) fault; **a falta de** for want of; **echar en falta** to miss; **hacer buena falta** to be badly needed; **hacer falta** to be needed, be necessary; to be lacking, be missing; to fail, to miss; to need, e.g., **me hacían falta esos papeles** I needed those papers; to miss, e.g., **Vd. me ha hecho mucha falta** I have missed you very much; **hacer falta** + *inf* to be necessary to + *inf;* **sin falta** without fail; **falta de ortografía** misspelling; **falta de pie** (tennis) foot fault
faltón -tona *adj* (coll.) dilatory, remiss
faltoso -sa *adj* (coll.) non compos mentis; (Am.) quarrelsome
faltriquera *f* pocket; handbag; **rascar** or **rascarse la faltriquera** (coll.) to cough up
falúa *f* (naut.) harbor felucca, tender
falucho *m* (naut.) felucca
falla *f* see **fallo**
fallada *f* (cards) ruff

fallar *va* to ruff, to trump; (law) to judge, pass judgment on; *vn* to fail, to miss; to sag, weaken; to miss fire; to break down; (law) to judge, pass judgment
falleba *f* espagnolette, door bolt
fallecer **§34** *vn* to decease, die; to fail, expire, run out
fallecido -da *adj* deceased, late
fallecimiento *m* decease, death; failure, expiration
fallero -ra *adj & mf* absentee (*worker or employee*); *f* queen of the falla (*in Valencia, Spain*)
fallido -da *adj* unsuccessful, sterile; uncollectible; without standing; bankrupt
fallo -lla *adj* (dial.) weak, faint; (Am.) silly, simple; **estar fallo a** to be out of (*cards of a certain suit*); *m* decision; short suit; (law) judgment, verdict; **tener fallo a** or **de** to be out of (*cards of a certain suit*); *f* defect; failure, breakdown; (geol. & min.) fault; (archaic) faille (*woman's scarflike headdress*); spectacular bonfire in Valencia on the eve of Saint Joseph's Day (*March 19th*)
fama *f* fame; reputation; rumor; (Am.) bull's-eye (*center of target and shot which hits it*); **correr fama** to be rumored; **es fama** it is rumored, it is said
famélico -ca *adj* famished, hungry, starving
familia *f* family; **en familia** en famille, in the family circle
familiar *adj* familiar; (pertaining to the) family, e.g., **lazos familiares** family ties; colloquial; **ser familiar a** to be familiar to; *m* familiar; member of the family; member of the household; household servant; acquaintance; familiar spirit; (eccl.) familiar; **familiar dependiente** dependent
familiaridad *f* familiarity
familiarización *f* familiarization
familiarizar **§76** *va* to familiarize; *vr* to become familiar; to become too familiar; **familiarizarse con** to familiarize oneself with, to become familiar with
famoso -sa *adj* famous; (coll.) famous (*excellent, first-rate*); (coll.) some, e.g., **famoso tarambana** (coll.) some crackpot
fámula *f* (coll.) maidservant
fámulo *m* famulus; (coll.) servant
fanal *m* beacon, lighthouse; lantern; bell glass, bell jar, glass cover; lamp shade; (fig.) torch, guide
fanático -ca *adj* fanatic or fanatical; *mf* fanatic; (sport) fan
fanatismo *m* fanaticism; (sport) fans
fanatizador -dora *mf* spreader of fanaticism
fanatizar **§76** *va* to make fanatical
fandango *m* fandango; disorder, topsy-turvy; (coll.) dance; (Am.) carousal
fandanguear *vn* (coll.) to carouse around
fandulario *m* var. of **faldulario**
faneca *f* (ichth.) bib
fanega *f* fanega (*1.58 bu. in Spain*); **fanega de tierra** fanegada (*1.59 acres in Spain*)
fanegada *f* fanegada (*1.59 acres in Spain*); **a fanegadas** (*coll.*) in great abundance
fanerógamo -ma *adj* (bot.) phanerogamous; *f* (bot.) phanerogam
fanfarrear *vn* var. of **fanfarronear**
fanfarria *f* (coll.) bluster, bragging; fanfare (*loud show; flourish of trumpets or hunting horns*); (mus.) fanfare; *m* (coll.) blusterer, braggart
fanfarrón -rrona *adj* (coll.) blustering, bragging; (coll.) flashy, trashy; *mf* (coll.) blusterer, braggart, sword rattler
fanfarronada *f* bluster, bravado, fanfaronade
fanfarronear *vn* to bluster, to brag
fanfarronería *f* (coll.) blustering, bragging, fanfaronading, sword rattling
fanfurriña *f* (coll.) pet, fit of peevishness
fangal *m* or **fangar** *m* quagmire, mudhole
fango *m* mud, mire; (fig.) mud; **llenar de fango** (fig.) to sling mud at
fangoso -sa *adj* muddy, miry; soft and sticky
fanón *m* (eccl.) fanon
fantaseador -dora *adj* daydreaming; *mf* daydreamer, dreamer
fantasear *va* to dream of; *vn* to fancy, to daydream; **fantasear de** to boast of being
fantasía *f* fantasy; fancy; imagery; (coll.) vanity, conceit; (naut.) dead reckoning; (mus.) fantasy, fantasia; **fantasías** *fpl* pearls, string of pearls; **de fantasía** fancy, colored; fancy, imitation (*e.g., jewelry*); **tocar por fantasía** (Am.) to play by ear
fantasioso -sa *adj* (coll.) vain, conceited
fantasma *m* phantom; stuffed shirt; (telv.) ghost; **fantasma magnético** magnetic curves; *f* scarecrow, hobgoblin
fantasmagoría *f* phantasmagoria
fantasmagórico -ca *adj* phantasmagorial or phantasmagoric
fantasmal *adj* phantasmal
fantasmón -mona *adj* (coll.) conceited; *mf* (coll.) stuffed shirt; *m* scarecrow
fantástico -ca *adj* fantastic; fanciful; conceited
fantoche *m* marionette, puppet; (coll.) nincompoop; (coll.) whippersnapper; (fig.) puppet
fañado -da *adj* one-year-old (*animal*)
faquín *m* porter, errand boy
faquir *m* fakir
farachar *va* to swingle, to scutch
farádico -ca *adj* faradic
faradímetro *m* faradmeter
faradio *m* (elec.) farad
faradismo *m* faradism; (med.) faradism
faradización *f* (med.) faradization
faradizar **§76** *va* (med.) to faradize
faralá *m* (*pl:* **-laes**) ruffle, flounce; (coll.) frill
farallón *m* cliff, headland; (min.) outcrop
faramalla *f* (coll.) claptrap; (coll.) sham, fake; (Am.) trash, rubbish; *mf* (coll.) gossip, schemer, cheat
faramallero -ra or **faramallón -llona** *adj* (coll.) gossiping, scheming, cheating; *mf* (coll.) gossip, schemer, cheat
farándola *f* farandole (*dance*); (dial.) ruffle, flounce
farándula *f* farandole (*dance*); confusion, web of lies; (coll.) wicked gossip; (Am.) jam (*of people*), buzz (*of voices*); (archaic) acting; company of actors, company of barnstormers
farandulear *vn* (coll.) to boast, to brag, to show off
farandulero -ra *adj* (coll.) gossiping, scheming; cheating; (pertaining to the) theater; *mf* (coll.) gossip, schemer, cheat; comedian, player
Faraón *m* Pharaoh; (*l.c.*) *m* faro (*card game*)
faraónico -ca *adj* Pharaonic
faraute *m* herald, messenger; prologue (*actor*); (coll.) busybody
farda *f* tax levied on Jews and Moors (*in Spain*); bundle of clothing; notch, mortise
fardacho *m* (zool.) lizard
fardaje *m* var. of **fardería**
fardar *va* to supply with clothes
fardel *m* bag (*carried over shoulder*); bundle; (coll.) slob
fardela *f* (orn.) shearwater; **fardela del Atlántico** (orn.) Manx shearwater
fardería *f* pile of bundles
fardo *m* bundle
farellón *m* cliff, headland
farfalá *m* (*pl:* **-laes**) ruffle, flounce
farfallear *vn* (dial.) to stammer, stutter
farfallón -llona *adj* (coll.) jabbering, spluttering; (coll.) hasty, bungling
farfalloso -sa *adj* (dial.) stammering, stuttering
fárfara *f* (bot.) coltsfoot; pellicle (*of eggshell*); **en fárfara** immature; half done
farfolla *f* husk, cornhusk; (coll.) sham, fake
farfulla *f* (coll.) sputtering; *mf* (coll.) sputterer; *adj* (coll.) sputtering
farfulladamente *adv* (coll.) sputteringly
farfullador -dora *adj* (coll.) sputtering; *mf* (coll.) sputterer
farfullamiento *m* (coll.) sputtering, gibbering
farfullar *va* (coll.) to sputter through (*e.g., a lesson*); (coll.) to stumble through (*a task*); *vn* (coll.) to sputter, to gibber
farfullero -ra *adj & mf* (coll.) var. of **farfullador**
fargallón -llona *adj* (coll.) hasty, bungling; (coll.) slovenly, untidy; *mf* (coll.) botcher, bungler

farillón *m* var. of **farallón**
farináceo -a *adj* (bot.) farinaceous
faringe *f* (anat.) pharynx
faríngeo -a *adj* pharyngeal
faringitis *f* (path.) pharyngitis
faringoscopia *f* pharyngoscopy
faringoscopio *m* pharyngoscope
farinoso -sa *adj* var. of **harinoso**
farisaico -ca *adj* pharisaic or pharisaical; Pharisaic
farisaísmo *m* pharisaism; Pharisaism
fariseo *m* pharisee; Pharisee; (coll.) tall, lanky good-for-nothing
farmacéutico -ca *adj* pharmaceutic or pharmaceutical; *mf* pharmacist, druggist; *f* pharmaceutics
farmacia *f* pharmacy, drug store; **farmacia de guardia** drug store open overtime, drug store open all night
fármaco *m* drug, medicine
farmacognosia *f* pharmacognosy
farmacología *f* pharmacology
farmacólogo -ga *mf* pharmacologist
farmacopea *f* pharmacopoeia
farmacopola *m* pharmacist, pharmacopolist
farmacopólico -ca *adj* pharmaceutical
faro *m* lighthouse, beacon; floodlight; lantern; (aut.) headlight, headlamp; (fig.) beacon; **faro aéreo** air beacon; **faro piloto** (aut.) spotlight; **faros de carretera** (aut.) bright lights; **faros de cruce** (aut.) dimmers; **faros de población** or **de situación** (aut.) parking lights
farol *m* lantern; lamp, light; street lamp; (rail.) headlight; (taur.) farol (*pase in which bullfighter swirls cape over his shoulders*); (coll.) conceited fellow; **farol de tope** (naut.) headlight
farola *f* street light, lamppost; beacon, lighthouse
farolazo *m* blow with a lantern; (Am.) swig, drink
farolear *vn* (coll.) to boast, to brag
faroleo *m* (coll.) boasting, bragging
farolería *f* (coll.) boasting, bragging; lamp or lantern shop
farolero -ra *adj* (coll.) boasting, bragging; *mf* (coll.) boaster, braggart; *m* lamp or lantern maker or dealer; lamplighter
farolillo *m* (bot.) Canterbury bell; (bot.) balloon vine, heartseed
farolito *m* small lantern; (bot.) winter cherry; **farolito de enredadera** (bot.) balloon vine, heartseed
farolón -lona *adj* (coll.) boasting, bragging; (coll.) *mf* boaster, bragger; *m* (coll.) large lamp or lantern
farota *f* (coll.) minx, vixen
farotón -tona *adj* (coll.) cheeky, brazen; *mf* (coll.) cheeky person
farpa *f* point of a scallop
farpado -da *adj* scalloped
farra *f* (ichth.) salmon trout; (Am.) revelry, spree
fárrago *m* farrago, hodgepodge
farragoso -sa *adj* confused, disordered
farraguista *mf* muddlehead
farro *m* peeled barley; spelt wheat
farruco -ca *adj* (coll.) bold, fearless; *mf* (coll.) Galician abroad, Asturian abroad; *f* farruca (*Spanish gypsy dance*)
farruto -ta *adj* (Am.) sickly
farsa *f* (theat.) farce; company of players; crude play, grotesque play; (fig.) farce, absurdity; (fig.) humbug
farsanta *f* (archaic) farce actress
farsante *adj* & *mf* (coll.) fake, humbug; *m* (archaic) farce actor
farseto *m* quilted jacket (*worn under armor*)
farsista *mf* author of farces
fas; por fas o por nefas rightly or wrongly, in any event
fasces *fpl* fasces
fascia *f* (anat. & surg.) fascia
fascial *adj* fascial
fasciculado -da *adj* fascicled
fascículo *m* fascicle or fasciculus (*of printed book*); (anat.) fascicle or fasciculus; (bot.) fascicle
fascinación *f* fascination; bewitchment, spell
fascinador -dora *adj* fascinating; *mf* fascinator
fascinante *adj* fascinating
fascinar *va* to fascinate; to bewitch; to cast a spell on, by a look, to cast the evil eye on
fascismo *m* fascism; (*cap.*) *m* Fascism
fascista *adj* & *mf* fascist; (*cap.*) *adj* & *mf* Fascist
fascólomo *m* (zool.) wombat
fase *f* phase; (astr., biol., elec. & phys.) phase; **en fase** (elec.) in phase; **fuera de fase** (elec.) out of phase; **fase partida** (elec.) split phase
faseolina *f* (biochem.) phaseolin
fásoles *mpl* (bot.) beans, string beans
fastidiar *va* to cloy, to sicken; to annoy, to bore; to disappoint; *vr* to get bored; to make a fool of oneself
fastidio *m* squeamishness; annoyance, boredom; profound dislike
fastidioso -sa *adj* cloying, sickening; annoying, boring; annoyed, displeased
fastigio *m* apex, tip, summit; (anat.) fastigium; (arch.) pediment, fastigium
fasto -ta *adj* happy, fortunate; *m* pomp, magnificence, show; **fastos** *mpl* fasti
fastoso -sa or **fastuoso -sa** *adj* vain, pompous; magnificent
fatal *adj* fatal; unfortunate; inevitable; bad, evil
fatalidad *f* fatality; fate; misfortune
fatalismo *m* fatalism
fatalista *adj* fatalistic; *mf* fatalist
fatalmente *adv* fatally; inevitably; badly, poorly
Fata Morgana *f* (meteor.) Fata Morgana
fatídico -ca *adj* fatidic; fateful
fatiga *f* fatigue; hardship; hard breathing; (mech. & physiol.) fatigue; **fatigas** *fpl* nausea
fatigador -dora or **fatigante** *adj* var. of **fatigoso**
fatigar §59 *va* to fatigue, to tire, to weary; to annoy, to harass; to rack (*one's brains*); *vr* to tire, get tired, tire oneself out
fatigoso -sa *adj* fatiguing, tiring; (coll.) trying, tedious
fatuidad *f* fatuity; conceit
fatuo -tua *adj* fatuous; conceited
faucal *adj* faucal
fauces *fpl* (anat.) fauces
fauna *f* fauna; (*cap.*) *f* (myth.) Fauna
fáunico -ca *adj* faunal
fauno *m* (myth.) faun
fáustico -ca *adj* Faustian
fausto -ta *adj* happy, fortunate; *m* pomp, magnificence, show; (*cap.*) *m* Faust
faustoso -sa *adj* magnificent
fautor -tora *mf* abetter, accomplice, instigator
favila *f* (poet.) ember, spark
favo *m* (path.) favus
favonio *m* (poet.) zephyr
favor *m* favor; (fig.) favor (*gift, token, ribbon*); **favores** *mpl* favors (*of a woman*); **a favor de** under cover of; with the aid of, by means of; in favor of; in behalf of; **estar en favor** to be in favor; **hágame Vd. el favor de** + *inf* do me the favor of + *ger;* **por favor** please; **tener a su favor** to have under one's wing; **vender favores** to peddle influence
favorable *adj* favorable
favorecedor -dora *adj* favoring; *mf* favorer; customer
favorecer §34 *va* to favor
favoritismo *m* favoritism
favorito -ta *adj* & *mf* favorite
favoso -sa *adj* favose
faya *f* faille (*silk cloth*)
fayanca *f* unstable posture; **de fayanca** carelessly
faz *f* (*pl:* **faces**) face; aspect; obverse; **faz a faz** face to face
F.C. or **f.c.** abr. of **ferrocarril**
fe *f* faith; fidelity; certificate; testimony, witness; **¡a fe mía!** upon my faith!; **a la buena fe** with simplicity, guilelessly; **dar fe de** to attest, to certify; **de buena fe** in good faith; **de mala fe** in bad faith; **hacer fe** to be valid, have validity; **la fe del carbonero** simple faith; **¡por mi fe!** upon my faith!; **tener fe en** to have faith in; **fe de bautismo** certificate of baptism; **fe de erratas** errata, list

of errata; **fe de nacimiento** birth certificate; **fe de óbito** death certificate
fealdad *f* ugliness
Febe *f* (myth.) Phoebe; (poet.) Phoebe (*moon*)
febeo -a *adj* (poet.) Phoebean
feble *adj* weak, feeble; lacking in weight or fineness (*said of a coin or alloy*); *m* foible, weak point
feb.º abr. of **febrero**
Febo *m* (myth.) Phoebus; (poet.) Phoebus (*sun*)
febrero *m* February
febricitante *adj* feverish
febrífugo -ga *adj* & *m* febrifuge
febrígeno -na *adj* fever-producing
febril *adj* febrile, feverish
fecal *adj* fecal
fecalito *m* (path.) fecalith
fécula *f* starch; fecula; dregs; **fécula de maranta** arrowroot (*starch*)
feculento -ta *adj* feculent (*foul, fecal*); starchy
feculoso -sa *adj* starchy
fecundación *f* fecundation; (biol.) fecundation
fecundador -dora *adj* fecundating
fecundar *va* to fecundate; (biol.) to fecundate
fecundativo -va *adj* fecundative
fecundidad *f* fecundity
fecundizar **§76** *va* to fecundate, to fertilize
fecundo -da *adj* fecund
fecha *f* see **fecho**
fechación *f* dating
fechador *m* (Am.) canceling stamp
fechar *va* to date
fecho -cha *adj* issued, executed; *f* date; day; **con fecha de** under date of; **¿cuál es la fecha de hoy?** what is the date?; **de antigua fecha** or **de larga fecha** of long standing; **hasta la fecha** to date
fechoría *f* misdeed, villainy
federación *f* federation
federal *adj* & *mf* federal
federalismo *m* federalism
federalista *adj* & *mf* federalist
federar *va* to federate; to federalize
federativo -va *adj* federative
Federica *f* Frederica
Federico *m* Frederick
Fedra *f* (myth.) Phaedra
feérico -ca *adj* fairy, fairylike
fehaciente *adj* authentic
felá *m* (*pl:* **-laes**) fellah
felandrio *m* (bot.) water fennel
feldespático -ca *adj* feldspathic or feldspathose
feldespato *m* (mineral.) feldspar
felice *adj* (poet.) happy
felicidad *f* felicity, happiness; luck, good luck
felicísimo -ma *adj super* very or most happy
felicitación *f* felicitation, congratulation
felicitar *va* to felicitate, congratulate; to wish happiness to
félido -da *adj* feline; *m* (zool.) felid
feligrés -gresa *mf* parishioner, church member
feligresía *f* parish (*members of parish*); country parish
felino -na *adj* (zool. & fig.) feline; *m* (zool.) feline
Felipe *m* Philip
feliz *adj* (*pl:* **-lices**) happy; lucky; felicitous
felodermo *m* (bot.) phelloderm
felógeno *m* (bot.) phellogen
felón -lona *adj* perfidious, treacherous, felonious; *mf* wicked person, felon
felonía *f* perfidy, treachery; (feud.) felony
felpa *f* plush; (coll.) drubbing; (coll.) sharp reprimand
felpado -da *adj* plushy, velvety
felpar *va* to cover with plush; (poet.) to carpet (*e.g., with grass or flowers*)
felpilla *f* chenille
felpón *m* (prov.) coarse velvet; (prov.) hard beating
felposo -sa *adj* felted; plushy
felpudo -da *adj* plushy, velvety, downy; *m* mat, plush mat
felsita *f* (mineral.) felsite
f.e.m. abr. of **fuerza electromotriz**
femenil *adj* feminine, womanly
femenino -na *adj* feminine; (bot.) female; (gram.) feminine; *m* (gram.) feminine; **el eterno femenino** (lit.) the eternal feminine
fementido -da *adj* false, treacherous, unfaithful
feminidad *f* femininity
feminismo *m* feminism
feminista *adj* feminist, feministic; *mf* feminist
femoral *adj* femoral
fémur *m* (anat.) femur, thighbone; (ent.) femur
fenacetina *f* (pharm.) phenacetin
fenaquistiscopio *m* phenakistoscope
fenda *f* crack, split
fenecer **§34** *va* to finish, to close; *vn* to die; to come to an end
fenecimiento *m* finish, termination; death
fenianismo *m* Fenianism
feniano -na *adj* & *m* Fenian
fenice *adj* & *mf* Phoenician
fenicio -cia *adj* & *mf* Phoenician; (*cap.*) *f* Phoenicia
fénico -ca *adj* (chem.) carbolic, phenic
fenileno *m* (chem.) phenylene
fenilo *m* (chem.) phenyl
fénix *m* (*pl:* **-nix** or **-nices**) (myth. & fig.) phoenix; **el fénix de los ingenios** Lope de Vega
fenobarbital *m* (pharm.) phenobarbital
fenocristal *m* (geol.) phenocryst
fenogreco *m* (bot.) fenugreek
fenol *m* (chem.) phenol
fenolftaleína *f* (chem.) phenolphthalein
fenología *f* phenology
fenomenal *adj* phenomenal; (fig.) phenomenal
fenomenalismo *m* (philos.) phenomenalism
fenómeno *m* phenomenon; (philos.) phenomenon; (coll.) monster, freak
fenomenología *f* (philos.) phenomenology
fenotiacina *f* (chem.) phenothiazine
fenotipo *m* (biol.) phenotype
feo -a *adj* ugly; **feo** *adv* (Am.) bad, e.g., **oler feo** to smell bad; *m* (coll.) slight; **dejar feo a** or **hacer un feo a** (coll.) to slight
feote -ta *adj* very ugly, hideous
feracidad *f* fertility, feracity
feral *adj* cruel, bloody, feral
feraz *adj* (*pl:* **-races**) fertile, feracious
féretro *m* bier, coffin
feria *f* fair; market; market-day crowd; deal, agreement; weekday; rest, repose; day off, holiday; (Am.) change; (Am.) tip; **ferias** *fpl* holiday gift to servants or the poor; **revolver la feria** (coll.) to upset the applecart
feriado -da *adj* see **día**
ferial *adj* week (*day*); *m* market; market place
feriante *adj* fairgoing; *mf* fairgoer
feriar *va* to buy, to sell, to exchange; to buy at the fair; to make a gift to; *vn* to take off, take a few days off
ferino -na *adj* wild, savage, ferine
fermata *f* (mus.) pause
fermentable *adj* fermentable
fermentación *f* fermentation; (fig.) fermentation
fermentador -dora *adj* fermenting
fermentante *adj* fermentive
fermentar *va* & *vn* to ferment; (fig.) to ferment
fermentativo -va *adj* fermentative
fermento *m* ferment
fermio *m* (chem.) fermium
fernandina *f* (archaic) farandine (*fabric*)
Fernando *m* Ferdinand
Fern.do abr. of **Fernando**
feroce *adj* (poet.) var. of **feroz**
ferocidad *f* ferocity
ferocísimo -ma *adj super* very or most ferocious
feróstico -ca *adj* (coll.) irritable, unruly; (coll.) very ugly
feroz *adj* (*pl:* **-roces**) ferocious
ferrar **§18** *va* to trim with iron, to cover with iron; to stamp or punch
ferrato *m* (chem.) ferrate
férreo -a *adj* ferreous; iron; tough, strong
ferrería *f* ironworks, foundry
ferrete *m* sulfate of copper; iron stamp or punch

ferretear *va* to trim with iron, to cover with iron; to stamp or punch; to work with iron
ferretería *f* ironworks; hardware; hardware store
ferretero -ra *mf* hardware dealer
férrico -ca *adj* (chem.) ferric
ferrificar §86 *vr* to turn into iron
ferrizo -za *adj* iron
ferro *m* (naut.) anchor
ferroaluminio *m* ferroaluminum
ferrocarril *m* railroad, railway; **ferrocarril aéreo** elevated railway; **ferrocarril de circunvalación** belt line; **ferrocarril de cremallera** rack railway; **ferrocarril de sangre** animal-drawn railway; **ferrocarril de vapor** steam railroad; **ferrocarril de vía angosta** narrow-gauge railway; **ferrocarril de vía normal** standard-gauge railway; **ferrocarril elevado** elevated railway; **ferrocarril funicular** funicular railway; **ferrocarril subterráneo** subway; **ferrocarril urbano** street railway
ferrocarrilero -ra *adj & m* (Am.) var. of **ferroviario**
ferrocerio *m* ferrocerium
ferrocianuro *m* (chem.) ferrocyanide
ferroconcreto *m* ferroconcrete
ferrocromo *m* ferrochrome or ferrochromium
ferrohormigón *m* ferroconcrete
ferromagnético -ca *adj* (phys.) ferromagnetic
ferromanganeso *m* ferromanganese
ferrón *m* ironworker
ferroníquel *m* ferronickel
ferroprusiato *m* (chem.) ferroprussiate
ferroso -sa *adj* ferrous; (chem.) ferrous
ferrotipia *f* (phot.) ferrotype (*process*)
ferrotipo *m* (phot.) ferrotype, tintype
ferrotungsteno *m* ferrotungsten
ferrovía *f* railway
ferrovial *adj* (pertaining to the) railroad, railway
ferroviario -ria *adj* (pertaining to the) railroad, railway, rail; *m* railroader
ferrugiento -ta *adj* iron, irony
ferruginoso -sa *adj* ferruginous; iron (*water*)
fértil *adj* fertile; (fig.) fertile
fertilidad *f* fertility
fertilizable *adj* fertilizable
fertilización *f* fertilization; **fertilización cruzada** (bot. & biol.) cross-fertilization
fertilizador -dora *adj* fertilizing; *mf* fertilizer
fertilizante *adj* fertilizing; *mf* fertilizer; *m* fertilizer (*e.g., manure*)
fertilizar §76 *va* to fertilize; *vr* to become fertile, become fertile again
férula *f* ferule; authority, rule; (bot.) giant fennel; (surg.) splint; **estar bajo la férula de** to be under the thumb of
feruláceo -a *adj* (bot.) ferulaceous
ferventísimo -ma *adj super* very or most fervent
férvido -da *adj* fervid (*hot, boiling; vehement*); burning (*thirst, fever*)
ferviente *adj* fervent
fervor *m* fervor
fervorín *m* short prayer
fervorizar §76 *va* to incite, inflame, inspire
fervoroso -sa *adj* fervent, fervid
festejar *va* to fete, entertain, honor; to court, woo; to celebrate; (Am.) to beat, thrash; *vr* to enjoy oneself, have a good time
festejo *m* feast, entertainment; courting, wooing; ovation, celebration; (Am.) revelry; **festejos** *mpl* public festivities
festín *m* feast, banquet
festinación *f* (Am.) hurry, haste
festinar *va* (Am.) to hurry, hasten
festival *m* festival, music festival
festividad *f* witticism; festivity; holiday
festivo -va *adj* witty; humorous; festive; festal, festival; (lit.) burlesque
festón *m* festoon
festonar or **festonear** *va* to festoon
fetal *adj* fetal
feticida *adj* feticidal; *mf* killer of a fetus
feticidio *m* feticide (*act*)
fetiche *m* fetish
fetichismo *m* fetishism
fetichista *adj* fetishistic; *mf* fetishist
fetidez *f* fetidity, foulness
fétido -da *adj* fetid, foul
fetiquismo *m* var. of **fetichismo**
feto *m* (embryol.) fetus
fetor *m* var. of **hedor**
feúco -ca or **feúcho -cha** *adj* very ugly, repulsive
feudado -da *adj* feudatory (*held as a fief*)
feudal *adj* feudal; feudalistic
feudalidad *f* feudality; feudalism
feudalismo *m* feudalism
feudatario -ria *adj & m* feudatory
feudista *m* (law) feudist
feudo *m* (law) feud; (law) fief; **feudos** *mpl* (hum.) bailiwick; **feudo franco** (law) freehold
fez *m* fez
fiable *adj* trustworthy, reliable
fiado -da *adj* trusting; **al fiado** on credit, on trust; **en fiado** on bail
fiador -dora *mf* bail (*person*); bondsman; **salir fiador por** to go bail for; *m* fastener; trigger; catch, pawl, stop; tumbler (*of a lock*); (Am.) chin strap
fiambrar *va* to prepare (*food*) for serving cold
fiambre *adj* cold, cold-served (*food*); (coll.) old, stale, out-of-date (*e.g., news*); *m* cold lunch, cold food; (coll.) stale news; **fiambres** *mpl* cold cuts; **de fiambre** (coll.) on credit, borrowed
fiambrera *f* lunch basket; dinner pail, lunch pail; portable food warmer
fiambrería *f* (Am.) delicatessen store; (Am.) grillroom
fianza *f* guarantee, surety; bond; bail (*guarantee and person giving guarantee*); **fianza carcelera** bail (*guarantee*)
fiar §90 *va* to guarantee, go surety for; to give credit to; to entrust, confide; to sell on credit; *vn* to trust; **fiar en** to trust in, put one's trust in; *vr* to trust; **fiarse a** or **de** to trust in, rely on
fiasco *m* fiasco
fíat *m* fiat
fibra *f* fiber; grain (*of wood*); (bot.) fibril (*root hair*); (min.) vein; (fig.) fiber, strength, vigor; **fibras del corazón** heartstrings (*deepest feelings*); **fibras de vidrio** fiberglas
fibravidrio *m* fiberglas
fibrilación *f* (path.) fibrillation
fibrilla *f* (anat. & bot.) fibril
fibrina *f* (bot. & physiol.) fibrin
fibrinógeno *m* (physiol.) fibrinogen
fibrinoso -sa *adj* fibrinous
fibrocartílago *m* (anat.) fibrocartilage
fibroide *adj* fibroid; *m* (path.) fibroid
fibroideo -a *adj* fibroid
fibroína *f* (biochem.) fibroin
fibroma *m* (path.) fibroma
fibroso -sa *adj* fibrous
fíbula *f* (anat. & archeol.) fibula
fibular *adj* fibular
ficción *f* fiction; (law) fiction
ficcionario -ria *adj* fictional
fice *m* (ichth.) hake
ficología *f* phycology
ficticio -cia *adj* fictitious
ficha *f* chip; domino (*piece*); slug; counter; token; filing card; record; police record; (elec.) plug; (Am.) check; (Am.) bad actor; **llevar ficha** to have a police record; **ser una buena ficha** (Am.) to be a sly fox; **ficha antropométrica** anthropometric chart; **ficha catalográfica** card, index card (*of a library*)
fichador -dora *mf* file clerk
fichar *va* to play (*a domino*); to file (*e.g., cards*); to make the anthropometric chart of; (coll.) to black-list
fichero *m* card index, filing cabinet, file case
fidecomiso *m* var. of **fideicomiso**
fidedigno -na *adj* reliable, trustworthy
fideero -ra *mf* vermicelli maker or dealer, spaghetti maker or dealer
fideicomisario -ria *adj & mf* (law) fideicommissary
fideicomiso *m* (law) fideicommissum; trusteeship (*of the UN*)
fideicomitente *mf* (law) fideicommissioner

fidelería *f* (Am.) vermicelli factory, spaghetti factory
fidelidad *f* fidelity; punctiliousness; **alta fidelidad** (rad.) high fidelity
fidelísimo -ma *adj super* very or most faithful
fideo *m* (coll.) skinny person; **fideos** *mpl* vermicelli
Fidias *m* Phidias
fiduciario -ria *adj & mf* fiduciary
fiebre *f* (path. & fig.) fever; **fiebre aftosa** (vet.) aphthous fever; **fiebre amarilla** (path.) yellow fever; **fiebre cerebral** (path.) brain fever; **fiebre continua** (path.) continued fever; **fiebre de garrapatas** (path.) tick fever; **fiebre de las Montañas Rocosas** (path.) Rocky Mountain spotted fever; **fiebre del heno** (path.) hay fever; **fiebre de Tejas** (vet.) Texas fever; **fiebre entérica** (path.) enteric fever; **fiebre láctea** (path.) milk fever; **fiebre ondulante** (path.) undulant fever; **fiebre paratifoidea** (path.) paratyphoid fever; **fiebre puerperal** (path.) puerperal fever; **fiebre reumática** (path.) rheumatic fever; **fiebre sextana** (path.) sextan; **fiebre tifoidea** (path.) typhoid fever; **fiebre tifoidea ambulante** or **ambulatoria** (path.) walking typhoid fever
fiel *adj* faithful; honest, trustworthy; exact; punctilious; sincere; *m* public inspector, inspector of weights and measures; pointer (*of scales*); pin (*of scissors*); **en fiel** balanced, in balance; **los fieles** the faithful; **fiel de romana** inspector of weights in a slaughterhouse
fielato *m* inspector's office; octroi (*office*)
fieltrar *va* to felt
fieltro *m* felt; felt hat, felt coat, felt rug
fiemo *m* (prov.) dung, manure
fiera *f* see **fiero**
fierabrás *m* (coll.) bully, spitfire; (coll.) little terror, brat
fierecilla *f* shrew
fiereza *f* fierceness, ferocity; cruelty; ugliness, deformity
fiero -ra *adj* fierce; terrible; cruel; ugly; tremendous; proud, haughty; **fieros** *mpl* boasts, threats; **echar** or **hacer fieros** to bluster; *f* wild animal; (taur.) bull; fiend (*person*); **ser una fiera para** (coll.) to be a fiend for (*e.g., work*)
fierro *m* (Am.) var. of **hierro**
fiesta *f* feast, holy day; holiday; festivity, celebration, party; **fiestas** *fpl* holidays, vacation; **aguar la fiesta** (coll.) to be a kill-joy; **estar de fiesta** (coll.) to be in a good mood, to be in a holiday mood; **hacer fiesta** to take off (*from work*); **hacer fiestas (a)** to fawn (on); **la fiesta brava** the fierce sport (*bullfighting*); **no estar para fiestas** (coll.) to be in no mood for joking; **por fin de fiesta** to top it off; **se acabó la fiesta** (coll.) let's drop it, that'll do; **tengamos la fiesta en paz** (coll.) cut it out; **fiesta de guardar** holy day; **fiesta de la hispanidad** or **fiesta de la raza** Columbus Day, Discovery Day; **fiesta del árbol** Arbor Day; **fiesta de precepto** holy day; **fiesta de todos los santos** All Saints' Day; **fiesta fija** or **inmoble** (eccl.) immovable feast; **fiesta movible** (eccl.) movable feast; **fiesta nacional** national holiday; national sport (*bullfighting*); **fiesta onomástica** saint's day, birthday; **fiesta simple** (eccl.) simple; **fiestas navideñas** Christmas holidays; **fiestas nemeas** Nemean games; **fiestas órficas** Orphic mysteries
fiestero -ra *adj* gay, merry, jolly; *mf* jolly person, merrymaker; party-goer
fígaro *m* barber; short jacket; (coll.) meddler, schemer
figle *m* (mus.) ophicleide; ophicleidist
figón *m* cheap eating house
figonero -ra *mf* keeper of a cheap eating house
figulino -na *adj* figuline
figura *f* figure; face, countenance; face card; (arith., geom., log. & rhet.) figure; (mus.) note (*showing length of sound*); (theat.) character; **hacer figura** to cut a figure; *m* (coll.) pompous fellow; *mf* sorry figure
figuración *f* figuration; representation; (mus.) figuration; (theat.) supers, extras; (Am.) role in society, distinguished role in society
figurado -da *adj* figurative (*language, style, etc.*); imaginary, illusory
figuranta *f* (theat.) figurante
figurante *m* (theat.) figurant
figurar *va* to figure, depict, trace; to represent; to feign; *vn* to figure (*to participate, appear, be conspicuous*); to be in the limelight; *vr* to figure, to imagine
figurativo -va *adj* figurative
figurería *f* grimace, face
figurero -ra *adj* (coll.) grimacing, fond of grimacing; *mf* (coll.) grimacer; maker or seller of small figures or statuettes
figurilla or **figurita** *f* figurine; marionette; *mf* (coll.) silly little runt
figurín *m* dummy, model, lay figure; fashion plate (*design; person*)
figurina *f* figurine
figurón *m* (coll.) stuffed shirt, pretentious nobody; **figurón de proa** (naut.) figurehead
fija *f* see **fijo**
fijacarteles *m* (*pl:* **-les**) billposter
fijación *f* fixation; fixing, fastening; posting; (chem., phot., psychoanal. & psychol.) fixation; **fijación del complemento** (bact.) complement fixation; **fijación del nitrógeno** (chem.) nitrogen fixation; **fijación de precios** price fixing
fijado *m* (phot.) fixing
fijador -dora *adj* fixing; *m* carpenter who hangs doors and windows; (mas.) pointer; (phot.) fixing bath; sprayer; hair set, hair spray
fijamárgenes *m* (*pl:* **-nes**) marginal stop (*of typewriter*)
fijapeinados *m* (*pl:* **-dos**) hair set, hair spray
fijar *va* to fix; to fasten; to paste, to glue; to drive (*a stake*); to post (*bills*); to set (*a date; the hair*); to establish (*e.g., residence*); (phot.) to fix; *vr* to become fixed, to settle; to notice; **fijarse en** to notice, to pay attention to; to imagine; **fijarse en** + *inf* to be intent on + *ger*
fijativo -va *adj & m* fixative
fijeza *f* firmness, solidity; steadfastness; fixity; **mirar con fijeza** to stare at
Fiji *m* Fiji (*islands*)
fijiano -na *adj & mf* Fijian
fijo -ja *adj* fixed; agreed upon; firm, solid, secure; fast; permanent; stationary; sure; determined; **de fijo** surely, without doubt; *f* hinge; trowel; **a la fija** (Am.) surely, without doubt; **ésa es la fija** (coll.) it is a sure thing; **ésta es la fija** this is it (*i.e., what is feared or hoped for*)
fil *m* (archaic) inspector of weights in a slaughter house; **estar en fil** or **en un fil** to be equally balanced, be alike; **fil derecho** leapfrog
fila *f* row, line, tier; file; rank; (coll.) hatred, dislike; **cerrar las filas** (mil.) to close ranks; **en fila** in a row; in single file; **en filas** (mil.) in active service; **llamar a filas** (mil.) to call to the colors; **pasarse a las filas de** to go over to; **ponerse en fila** to line up; **romper filas** (mil.) to break ranks; **salirse de la fila** to get out of line; **fila india** single file, Indian file
filacteria *f* phylactery; (f.a.) phylactery
Filadelfia *f* Philadelphia
filadelfiano -na *adj & mf* Philadelphian
filadiz *m* floss silk
filamento *m* filament; (bot. & elec.) filament
filamentoso -sa *adj* filamentous
filandria *f* (zool.) filander
filandro *m* (zool.) philander
filantropía *f* philanthropy
filantrópico -ca *adj* philanthropic or philanthropical
filántropo -pa *mf* philanthropist
filar *va* (naut.) to ease out, pay out slowly (*a cable*)
filaria *f* (zool.) filaria
filariasis *f* or **filariosis** *f* (path.) filariasis
filarmonía *f* love of harmony or music
filarmónico -ca *adj & mf* philharmonic
filástica *f* (naut.) rope yarn

filatelia *f* philately
filatélico -ca *adj* philatelic; *mf* philatelist
filatelista *mf* philatelist
filatería *f* fast talking (*to deceive*); prolixity
filatero -ra *adj* fast-talking (*to deceive*); prolix; *mf* fast talker; great talker
filatura *f* spinning; spinning mill
Filemón *m* (myth. & Bib.) Philemon
fileno -na *adj* (coll.) delicate, tiny
filete *m* filet or fillet (*of meat or fish*); narrow hem; small spit; snaffle bit; welt (*of shoe*); edge, rim; thread (*of screw*); (arch. & b.b.) fillet; (print.) ornamental bar or line
fileteado *m* threads (*of a screw*); (b.b.) tooling
filetear *va* to fillet; (b.b.) to tool; to thread (*e.g., a screw*)
fileteo *m* threading
filetón *m* heavy bullion (*for embroidering*)
filfa *f* (coll.) hoax, fake
filheleno -na *adj & mf* philhellene
filiación *f* filiation; description, characteristics; (mil.) regimental register
filial *adj* filial; *f* (com.) affiliate, subsidiary
filiar *va* to register; *vr* to enroll; to enlist
filibote *m* (naut.) flyboat
filibustear *vn* to filibuster (*to act as a military freebooter or buccaneer*)
filibusterismo *m* filibusterism
filibustero *m* filibuster (*freebooter, buccaneer*)
filicida *adj* filicidal; *mf* filicide (*person*)
filicidio *m* filicide (*act*)
filiforme *adj* filiform
filigrana *f* filigree; watermark (*in paper*); delicacy; cutie (*attractive child or young girl*); (bot.) lantana; (fig.) fancy work
filigranado -da *adj* var. of **afiligranado**
fililí *m* (*pl:* **-líes**) (coll.) peach, honey (*fine person or thing*)
filio *m* (ent.) phyllium
filipéndula *f* (bot.) spirea filipendula, dropwort
filipense *adj & mf* Philippian
filípico -ca *adj* (poet.) Philippic; *f* philippic; (*cap.*) *f* (hist.) Philippic (*of Demosthenes; of Cicero*)
filipichín *m* moreen
filipino -na *adj* Filipine, Filipino, or Philippine; *mf* Filipino; **Filipinas** *fpl* Philippines (*islands*)
Filipo *m* Philip (*e.g., of Macedonia*); (poet.) Philip
Filipos *f* Philippi
Filis *f* Phyllis; (*l.c.*) *f* (poet.) charm, grace, delicacy; trinket, charm
filisteísmo *m* Philistinism
filisteo -a *adj* (Bib. & fig.) Philistine; *m* (Bib. & fig.) Philistine; tall, heavy fellow
filita *f* (mineral.) phyllite
film *m* (*pl:* **films**) film, moving picture; **film de bulto** or **film en relieve** three-dimensional film
filmación *f* filming
filmar *va & vr* to film
fílmico -ca *adj* (mov.) (pertaining to) film
filmoteca *f* film library
filo *m* edge, cutting edge; dividing line; ridge; (biol.) phylum; **al filo de** at, about (*e.g., sunset, ten o'clock*); **dar filo a, dar un filo a** or **sacar el filo a** to sharpen; **pasar al filo de la espada** to put to the sword; **por filo** exactly; **filo del viento** (naut.) direction of the wind
filobús *m* trolley bus, trackless trolley
filocladio *m* var. of **cladodio**
filocomunista *adj & mf* procommunist
filodio *m* (bot.) phyllode
filófago -ga *adj* phyllophagous
filogénesis *f* (biol.) phylogenesis
filogenia *f* (biol.) phylogeny
filogénico -ca *adj* phylogenic, phylogenetic
filología *f* philology
filológico -ca *adj* philological; *f* philology
filólogo -ga *mf* philologian, philologist
filolumenista *mf* matchbox collector
filomanía *f* (bot.) phyllomania
filomela *f* (poet.) philomela, philomel, or Philomel (*nightingale*); (*cap.*) *f* (myth.) Philomela
filomena *f* (poet.) philomela, philomel, or Philomel (*nightingale*)
filomeno *m* (orn.) cedarbird
filón *m* vein, seam, lode; (fig.) gold mine; **filón ramal** (min.) feeder
filópodo -da *adj & m* (zool.) phyllopod
filosa *f* see **filoso**
filoseda *f* silk and woolen cloth, silk and cotton cloth; schappe
filoso -sa *adj* (Am.) sharp, sharp-edged; *f* (bot.) hypocist
filosofador -dora *adj* philosophizing; *mf* philosophizer
filosofar *vn* to philosophize
filosofastro *m* philosophaster
filosofear *vn* var. of **filosofar**
filosofía *f* philosophy; **filosofía moral** moral philosophy
filosófico -ca *adj* philosophic or philosophical
filósofo -fa *mf* philosopher
filotaxia *f* (bot.) phyllotaxis
filote *m* (Am.) corn silk
filoxera *f* (ent.) phylloxera
filtrable *adj* filterable
filtración *f* filtration; leak, leakage; (fig.) leak (*of funds*)
filtrado *m* filtering; filtrate
filtrador -dora *adj* filtering; *mf* filterer; *m* filter
filtraje *m* filtering
filtrar *va* to filter, to filtrate; *vn* to leak (*said, e.g., of water or of roof*); *vr* to filter, to filtrate; (fig.) to disappear, to leak away (*said of money*)
filtro *m* filter; seaside fresh-water spring; philter, love potion; (elec. & opt.) filter; **filtro de bandas** (elec.) band filter, band-pass filter; **filtro de paso alto** (elec.) high-pass filter; **filtro de paso bajo** (elec.) low-pass filter; **filtro de paso de banda** (elec.) band filter, band-pass filter; **filtro paso inferior** (elec.) low-pass filter; **filtro paso superior** (elec.) high-pass filter
filtrónico -ca *adj* (pertaining to a) filter
filtro-prensa *m* (*pl:* **filtros-prensas**) filter press
filudo -da *adj* (Am.) sharp
filum *m* (biol.) phylum
filván *m* featheredge (*on sharpened tool*)
fillós *mpl* fritter
fimbria *f* border (*of a skirt*); fringe
fimo *m* dung, manure
fimosis *f* (path.) phimosis
fin *m* (*& f*) end; end, purpose; **a fin de** + *inf* in order to + *inf;* **a fin de cuentas** after all; **a fin de que** in order that, so that; **a fines de** at the end of, toward the end of, late in (*a period of time*); **al fin** finally; **al fin del mundo** far, far away; **al fin y a la postre** or **al fin y al cabo** after all, in the end; **dar fin a** to put an end to, to stop; **dar fin de** to put an end to, to destroy, to wipe out; **en fin** finally, in a word, in short; well; **poner fin a** to put an end to, to stop; **por fin** finally, in a word, in short; **sin fin** endless; endlessly; **un sin fin de** no end of; **fin de semana** weekend
finado -da *adj* deceased, late; *mf* deceased
final *adj* final; *m* end; (mus.) finale; **por final** finally; *f* (sport) finals; **final de partida** windup (*of a game*)
finalidad *f* end, purpose
finalismo *m* (philos.) finalism
finalista *mf* (philos. & sport) finalist
finalizar §76 *va* to end, terminate; (law) to execute (*a deed, contract, etc.*); *vn* to end, terminate
finamiento *m* end, conclusion; decease
financiación *f* financing
financiamiento *m* (Am.) financing
financiar *va* to finance
financiero -ra *adj* financial; *mf* financier
finanzas *fpl* finances
finar *vn* to die; *vr* to long, to yearn
finca *f* property, piece of real estate; (Am.) farm, ranch; **buena finca** (coll.) sly fellow, bad egg; **finca cafetera** coffee plantation
fincabilidad *f* real estate
fincar §86 *vn* to buy up real estate; (Am.) to reside, rest, be found; *vr* to buy up real estate
finchado -da *adj* (coll.) conceited, vain
finchar *vr* (coll.) to be conceited
finear *va* to pole (*a boat*)

Fineas *m* Phineas
finés -nesa *adj* Finnic; Finnish; *mf* Finn (*member of any Finnic-speaking people; native of Finland*); *m* Finnic language
fineza *f* fineness; favor, kindness; little gift; (bridge) finesse
fingido -da *adj* false, deceptive; fake, sham; affected
fingidor -dora *adj* false, fake; *mf* faker
fingimiento *m* feigning, faking, pretense
fingir §42 *va* to feign, pretend, fake; *vn* to feign, pretend; **fingir** + *inf* to feign to, to pretend to + *inf; vr* to feign to be, to pretend to be
finible *adj* endable, terminable
finiquitar *va* to settle, to close (*an account*); (coll.) to finish, wind up
finiquito *m* settlement, closing (*of an account*); **dar finiquito a** to settle, close out; (coll.) to finish, wind up
finir *vn* (archaic & Am.) to end
finisecular *adj* fin-de-siècle
finítimo -ma *adj* bordering, neighboring
finito -ta *adj* finite
Finlandia *f* Finland
finlandés -desa *adj* Finnish; *mf* Finn, Finlander; *m* Finnish (*language*)
fino -na *adj* fine; sheer; thin, slender; thin (*cloth, paper, sole of shoe, etc.*); pure (*water*); courteous, polite; cunning, shrewd; fond, true
finoúgrio -gria *adj* Finno-Ugric
finta *f* feint (*fake threat*)
fintar *vn* to feint
finura *f* fineness, excellence; courtesy, politeness; (aer.) fineness ratio
finústico -ca *adj* (coll.) overpolite, obsequious
finustiquería *f* (coll.) overpoliteness, obsequiousness
fiñana *m* black-bearded wheat
fiord *m* or **fiordo** *m* fiord
fioritura *f* trimming, adornment
firma *f* signature; (act of) signing; firm; **con mi firma** under my hand; **firma en blanco** blank signature
firmal *m* brooch
firmamento *m* firmament
firmán *m* firman
firmante *adj* signatory; *mf* signer, signatory
firmar *va & vn* to sign
firme *adj* firm, steady; hard, solid; staunch, unswerving; (com.) steady (*market*); **¡firmes!** (mil.) attention!; *adv* firmly, steadily; *m* roadbed; **de firme** hard; steadily; **en firme** (com.) firm; **en lo firme** in the right
firmeza *f* firmness; steadiness, constancy
firmón *m* shyster who will sign anything
firuletes *mpl* (Am.) finery, frippery
fiscal *adj* fiscal, (pertaining to a) treasury; *m* treasurer; district attorney, public prosecutor; busybody, informer
fiscalía *f* office of treasurer; office of district attorney
fiscalización *f* control, inspection; prosecution; prying, informing
fiscalizar §76 *va* to control, to inspect; to oversee, superintend; to prosecute; to pry into, to talk about (*somebody's conduct*)
fisco *m* state treasury, exchequer
fisga *f* fishgig, fish spear; snooping; banter, raillery; (dial.) grain of spelt; (dial.) spelt bread; **hacer fisga a** to make fun of
fisgador -dora *adj* mocking, scoffing; *mf* mocker, scoffer
fisgar §59 *va* to fish with a spear, to harpoon; to pry into, to spy on; *vn* to snoop; to mock, to scoff; *vr* to mock, to scoff
fisgón -gona *mf* (coll.) jester; (coll.) busybody
fisgonear *va* (coll.) to keep prying into (*other people's business*)
fisgoneo *m* (coll.) constant prying, constant nosiness
fisible *adj* fissionable
físico -ca *adj* physical; (Am.) finicky, prudish; *mf* physicist; *m* physique, look, appearance; (archaic & dial.) physician; *f* physics; **física nuclear** nuclear physics
físicoquímico -ca *adj* physicochemical; *mf* physicochemist; *f* physicochemisty
físil *adj* fissile, fissionable
fisiocracia *f* physiocracy
fisiócrata *adj* physiocratic; *mf* physiocrat
fisiocrático -ca *adj* physiocratic
fisiografía *f* physiography
fisiográfico -ca *adj* physiographic
fisiógrafo -fa *mf* physiographer
fisiología *f* physiology; **fisiología vegetal** plant physiology
fisiológico -ca *adj* physiological
fisiólogo -ga *mf* physiologist
fisión *f* (phys.) fission
fisionable *adj* fissionable
fisionar *va & vr* to split
fisionomía *f* physiognomy
fisioterapia *f* physiotherapy
fisíparo -ra *adj* (biol.) fissiparous
fisípedo -da *adj & m* (zool.) fissiped
fisirrostro -tra *adj* (orn.) fissirostral
fisonomía *f* physiognomy
fisonómico -ca *adj* physiognomic or physiognomical
fisonomista *mf* physiognomist
fisónomo -ma *mf* physiognomist
fisostigmina *f* (chem.) physostigmine
fistol *m* sly fellow; (Am.) necktie pin
fistra *f* (bot.) bishop's-weed
fístula *f* fistula; (path.) fistula; (mus.) reed
fistular *adj* fistular; *va* to make fistulous
fistuloso -sa *adj* fistulous
fisura *f* (anat., path. & min.) fissure; **fisura del paladar** cleft palate
fita *f* sketch, drawing (*of animated cartoon*)
fitina *f* (chem.) phytin
fitófago -ga *adj* (zool.) phytophagous
fitogeografía *f* phytogeography
fitografía *f* phytography
fitográfico -ca *adj* phytographic or phytographical
fitógrafo -fa *mf* phytographer
fitolacáceo -a *adj* (bot.) phytolaccaceous
fitología *f* botany, phytology
fitopatología *f* (bot. & med.) phytopathology
fitoplancton *m* (*biol.*) phytoplankton
fitotomía *f* phytotomy
flabelado -da *adj* flabellate
flabeliforme *adj* flabelliform
flabelo *m* (eccl., bot., & zool.) flabellum
flaccidez *f* flaccidity; softness
fláccido -da *adj* flaccid; soft
flaco -ca *adj* thin, skinny; weak; **flaco de cabeza** befuddled, confused; *m* weak spot, foible
flacucho -cha *adj* (coll.) thinnish
flacura *f* thinness, skinniness; weakness
flagelación *f* flagellation
flagelado -da *adj* (bot. & biol.) flagellate; *m* (bot.) flagellate
flagelador -dora *adj* flagellant; *mf* flagellator
flagelante *adj & mf* flagellant; *m* Flagellant
flagelar *va* to scourge, to whip, to flagellate; to flay, criticize severely
flagelo *m* scourge, whip; (biol.) flagellum; (fig.) scourge, calamity
flagrancia *f* (poet.) blazing, flaming
flagrante *adj* (poet.) blazing, flaming; occurring; **en flagrante** in the act
flagrar *vn* (poet.) to blaze, flame
flama *f* flame; reverberation
flamante *adj* bright, flaming; brand-new, spick-and-span
flamberga *f* (archaic) rapier, flamberg
flameante *adj* flamboyant; (arch.) flamboyant
flamear *va* to flame (*to sterilize with flame*); *vn* to flame; to flame with anger; to wave, flutter
flamen *m* (*pl:* **flámines**) (hist.) flamen
flamenco -ca *adj* Flemish; buxom; Andalusian gypsy (*dance, song, etc.*); (coll.) gypsyish, flashy, snappy; *mf* Fleming; *m* Flemish (*language*); Andalusian gypsy dance, song, or music; (orn.) flamingo; **los flamencos** the Flemish (*people*)
flamenquilla *f* small platter; (bot.) marigold
flámeo -a *adj* flamelike
flamero *m* torch holder, torch stand
flamígero -ra *adj* (poet.) flaming, flamelike; (arch.) flamboyant
flámula *f* streamer; (bot.) banewort
flan *m* custard, soufflé; blank (*from which to stamp coin*)

flanco *m* flank, side; (fort., mach., mil. & nav.) flank; (aut.) sidewall (*of tire*); **coger por el flanco** (coll.) to catch off guard; **conocerle** or **saberle a uno el flanco** to know someone's weak side
Flandes *f* Flanders
flanear *vn* to loaf, loaf around
flanqueador -dora *adj* flanking; *mf* flanker; *m* (mil.) flanker
flanqueamiento *m* var. of **flanqueo**
flanquear *va* to flank
flanqueo *m* flanking
flaquear *vn* to weaken, to flag, to give way; to become faint; to lose heart
flaqueza *f* thinness, skinniness; weakness, lack of strength; weakness, failing
flato *m* flatus, gas; (Am.) gloominess, melancholy
flatoso -sa *adj* flatulent, windy; (Am.) gloomy, melancholy
flatulencia *f* flatulence
flatulento -ta *adj* flatulent
flatuosidad *f* flatulence, windiness
flatuoso -sa *adj* var. of **flatoso**
flauta *f* (mus.) flute; **flauta del dios Pan** or **flauta de Pan** (mus.) Panpipe, Pan's pipes; *m* flautist, flutist
flautado -da *adj* flutelike; *m* (mus.) flute (*organ stop*)
flauteado -da *adj* flutelike, sweet
flautear *vn* to flute, play a flute
flautero -ra *mf* flute maker
flautillo *m* (mus.) shawm
flautín *m* (mus.) piccolo
flautista *mf* flautist, flutist
flavo -va *adj* fallow
flébil *adj* (poet.) sad, tearful, plaintive
flebitis *f* (path.) phlebitis
flebosclerosis *f* (path.) phlebosclerosis
flebotomía *f* phlebotomy, bloodletting
flebotomiano *m* phlebotomist
fleco *m* fringe; ragged edge; bangs; **flecos** *mpl* gossamer
flecha *f* arrow; sag, dip (*of cable*); (aer.) sweepback; (fort.) flèche; (mach.) shaft; **la flecha del parto** Parthian shot; **flecha de mar** (zool.) squid
flechador *m* archer, bowman
flechadura *f* (naut.) ratlines
flechar *va* to draw or stretch (*the bow*); to wound with an arrow; to kill with an arrow; (coll.) to infatuate; *vn* to be bent or stretched (*said of a bow in position to shoot an arrow*)
flechaste *m* (naut.) ratline
flechazo *m* arrow shot; arrow wound; (coll.) sudden passion, love at first sight
flechería *f* stock of arrows; shower of arrows
flechero -ra *adj* lovable, winsome; (Am.) tenacious, persevering; *mf* archer; arrow maker; *m* bowman; quiver
flegmonoso -sa *adj* var. of **flemonoso**
fleje *m* iron hoop or strap
flema *f* (physiol. & fig.) phlegm; **gastar flema** to be phlegmatic; to be slow to anger
flemático -ca *adj* phlegmatic or phlegmatical
fleme *m* veterinarian's fleam
flemón *m* (path.) phlegmon; (path.) gumboil
flemonoso -sa *adj* phlegmonous
flemoso -sa *adj* phlegmy
flemudo -da *adj* phlegmatic, lazy
fleo *m* (bot.) timothy
flequillo *m* bangs
Flesinga *f* Flushing
fletador *m* (naut.) charterer
fletamento *m* (naut.) chartering; (naut.) charter party
fletante *mf* shipowner
fletar *va* (naut.) to charter (*a ship*); (naut.) to load (*e.g., cattle*); (Am.) to hire (*a horse, carriage, etc.*); *vr* (Am.) to beat it, get out
fletcherismo *m* Fletcherism
flete *m* (naut.) freight, cargo; (naut.) freightage; (Am.) freight (*carried on land*); **falso flete** (naut.) dead freight
flexibilidad *f* flexibility
flexible *adj* flexible; soft (*hat*); *m* (elec.) cord, flexible cord; soft hat
flexión *f* flection; (gram.) flection, inflection
flexional *adj* (gram.) flectional, inflectional
flexo *m* gooseneck (*of a lamp*)
flexor -xora *adj* bending, flexing; *m* (anat.) flexor
flexuoso -sa *adj* flexuous
flictena *f* (path.) phlyctena, bulla
flinflanear *vn* to tinkle
flinflaneo *m* tinkling
flirt *m* flirting
flirtación *f* flirtation
flirteador -dora *adj* flirtatious; *mf* flirt (*person*)
flirtear *vn* to flirt
flirteo *m* flirting, flirtation
flocadura *f* fringe trimming
floculento -ta *adj* (chem.) flocculent
floema *m* (bot.) phloem
flogístico -ca *adj* (path. & old chem.) phlogistic
flogisto *m* (old chem.) phlogiston
flogopita *f* (mineral.) phlogopite
flojear *vn* to slacken, ease up, idle; to weaken
flojedad *f* looseness, slackness; limpness; laxity, laziness; weakness
flojel *m* nap (*of cloth*); down, soft feathers
flojera *f* (coll.) var. of **flojedad**
flojo -ja *adj* loose, slack; limp; lax, lazy, dilatory, languid; weak; light (*wind*); sagging, unsupported (*prices*); thin, poor (*writing*); (Am.) fearful, timid; **flojo de muelles** (coll.) incontinent (*unable to restrain natural evacuation*)
floqueado -da *adj* trimmed with fringe
flor *f* flower; blossom; flowers of wine; grain (*of leather*); (chem.) flowers; (fig.) bouquet, compliment; (fig.) flower (*choicest part*); **a flor de** at or near the surface of; even with; **a flor de agua** at water level; **andarse a la flor del berro** (coll.) to lead a life of pleasure; **dar en la flor** to get the knack; **decir flores a** to say pretty things to, to flirt with; **de mi flor** (coll.) excellent, magnificent; **echar flores a** to say pretty things to, to flirt with; **en flor** in flower, in blossom; **la flor de la canela** (coll.) the tops; **la flor y nata de** the flower of, the cream of; **flor de amor** (bot.) amaranth; **flor de antimonio** (chem.) flowers of antimony; **flor de azufre** (chem.) flowers of sulphur; **flor de calentura** (bot.) milkweed; **flor de embudo** (bot.) calla; **flor de harina** flour; **flor de la cera** (bot.) wax plant (*Hoya carnosa*); **flor de la edad** flower of life, bloom of youth; **flor de la maravilla** (bot.) tigerflower; (coll.) delicate convalescent; **flor de la oreja** sacred ear or sacred earflower; **flor de la Pascua** (bot.) poinsettia; **flor de la Trinidad** (bot.) pansy; **flor de la vida** flower of life, prime of life; (bot.) cotton rose; **flor de lazo** (bot.) tiger lily; **flor del campo** wild flower; **flor de lis** fleur-de-lis (*royal coat of arms of France*); (her.) fleur-de-lis; (bot.) jacobean lily; **flor de lis florenzada** (f.a.) fleur-de-lis; **flor del sol** (bot.) sunflower; **flor de mano** paper flower, artificial flower; **flor de príncipe** (bot.) red periwinkle; **flor de un día** (bot.) tigerflower; **flor de una hora** (bot.) flower of an hour; **flores cordiales** sudorific flowers; **flores de cantueso** (coll.) triviality
flora *f* flora; (*cap.*) *f* (myth.) Flora
floración *f* flowering, florescence
florado -da *adj* flowered; *f* (dial.) blossom time (*for beekeepers*)
floral *adj* floral
florar *vn* to flower, blossom, bloom
florcita *f* (Am.) little flower; **andar de florcita** (Am.) to stroll around with a flower in one's buttonhole, to loaf around
flordelisado -da *adj* (her.) fleury
floreado -da *adj* flowered; floury
florear *va* to flower, to decorate with flowers; to embellish with florid language; to stack (*cards*); to bolt (*flour*); to sort out; *vn* to quiver (*said of the tip of a sword*); to twang away (*on a guitar*); (coll.) to throw bouquets, to pay compliments
florecer §34 *vn* to flower, blossom, bloom; to flourish; *vr* to become moldy
florecido -da *adj* moldy; blooming
floreciente *adj* florescent, inflorescent, flowering; flourishing
florecimiento *m* flowering, blossoming, blooming; continued prosperity

Florencia *f* Florence (*Italian city; feminine given name*)
florentino -na *adj & mf* Florentine
florentísimo -ma *adj super* very or most flourishing
floreo *m* idle talk; bright remark; quivering (*of tip of sword*); steady twanging (*of a guitar*); (mus.) flourish; **andarse con floreos** (coll.) to beat about the bush
florería *f* (Am.) florist's shop
florero -ra *adj* flattering, jesting; *mf* flatterer, jester; florist; *m* vase; flowerpot; potted flower; flower stand, jardiniere; (f.a.) flower piece; *f* flower girl
florescencia *f* (bot.) florescence, inflorescence
floresta *f* woods, grove; rural scene, rural setting; anthology
florestero *m* forest guard or warden
floreta *f* border or reinforcement on the edge of a girth
floretazo *m* stroke with a foil
florete *adj* first-class, superfine; *m* foil, fencing foil; medium-grade cotton fabric
floretear *va* to flower, to decorate with flowers; *vn* to fence
floretista *m* fencer
floricina *f* (chem.) phlorizin
floricultor -tora *mf* floriculturist, florist
floricultura *f* floriculture
Florida, la see **florido**
floridano -na *adj & mf* Floridan or Floridian
floridez *f* wealth of flowers, abundance of flowers; floweriness (*e.g., of style*)
florido -da *adj* flowery, florid, full of flowers; choice, select; (lit.) flowery, florid; **la Florida** Florida
florífero -ra *adj* floriferous
florilegio *m* anthology
florín *m* florin (*coin*)
floripondio *m* (bot.) floripondio; splotchy floral adornment; (lit.) floweriness, flowery style or language
florista *mf* florist; maker or seller of artificial flowers
floristería *f* flower shop
florón *m* large flower; (arch. & f.a.) finial; (arch.) rosette; (print.) tailpiece, vignette
floronado -da *adj* (her.) fleury (*said of a cross*)
flósculo *m* (bot.) floscule, floret
flosculoso -sa *adj* flosculous
flota *f* (naut., nav. & aer.) fleet; (fig.) fleet (*of cars, trucks, etc.*); **flota de guerra** navy; **flota en naftalina** (naut.) moth-ball fleet
flotabilidad *f* floatability; buoyancy
flotable *adj* floatable; navigable for rafts and logs
flotación *f* flotation; buoyancy; (metal.) flotation
flotador -dora *adj* floating; *mf* floater; *m* float (*e.g., of fish line*); (aer., bot. & mach.) float
flotadura *f* floating, flotation
flotaje *m* log driving
flotamiento *m* floating, flotation; log driving
flotante *adj* floating; flowing (*e.g., beard*)
flotar *vn* to float; to wave (*said, e.g., of a flag*)
flote *m* floating; **a flote** afloat; (fig.) on one's feet; **poner a flote** to float; **ponerse a flote** to get out of a jam
flotilla *f* flotilla
flox *m* (bot.) phlox
fluctuación *f* fluctuation; wavering, hesitation; (biol. & med.) fluctuation
fluctuante *adj* fluctuant
fluctuar **§33** *vn* to fluctuate; to bob up and down; to wave; to waver; to be in danger
fluctuoso -sa *adj* fluctuating, wavering
fluencia *f* flowing, running; source, spring; fluency; (elec.) creepage
fluente *adj* fluid, flowing; bleeding (*hemorrhoids*)
fluidez *f* fluidity; fluency (*of language or style*)
flúido -da *adj* fluid; fluent (*language, style*); *m* fluid
fluir **§41** *vn* to flow
flujo *m* flow, discharge, flux; looseness (*of bowels*); (chem., metal., phys. & path.) flux; (naut.) flow, rising tide; **flujo blanco** (path.) whites; **flujo de reír** constant laughing; **flujo de risa** fit of noisy laughter; **flujo de vientre** loose bowels; **flujo magnético** magnetic flux; **flujo y reflujo** ebb and flow
flujómetro *m* (phys.) fluxmeter
fluminense *adj* (pertaining to) Rio de Janeiro; *mf* native or inhabitant of Rio de Janeiro
flúor *m* (chem.) fluorin or fluorine; (chem.) flux
fluoresceína *f* (chem.) fluorescein
fluorescencia *f* fluorescence
fluorescente *adj* fluorescent
fluorhídrico -ca *adj* (chem.) hydrofluoric
fluórico -ca *adj* fluoric
fluorina or **fluorita** *f* (mineral.) fluorite, fluor, fluor spar
fluorización *f* fluoridation (*of drinking water*); (geol.) fluoridation
fluorizar **§76** *va* to fluoridate
fluoroscopia *f* fluoroscopy
fluoroscópico -ca *adj* fluoroscopic
fluoroscopio *m* fluoroscope
fluoruro *m* (chem.) fluoride
fluvial *adj* fluvial
flux *m* flush (*e.g., in poker*); (Am.) suit of clothes; **estar a flux** (Am.) to be penniless; **hacer flux** (coll.) to blow in everything without settling accounts; **tener flux** (Am.) to be lucky; **flux real** royal flush
fluxión *f* (math. & path.) fluxion; (path.) congestion; (path.) cold in the head; **fluxión de muelas** (path.) swollen cheek, abscessed tooth; **fluxión de pecho** (path.) inflammation of the lungs, pneumonia
fluyente *adj* fluid, flowing; fleeting
f.º abr. of **folio**
fo *interj* pew!
fobia *f* phobia
foca *f* (zool.) seal; **foca de trompa** (zool.) sea elephant; **foca fraile** (zool.) monk seal
focal *adj* focal
focalización *f* focalization
focense *adj & mf* Phocian
Fócida, la Phocis
focino *m* goad used to drive an elephant
foco *m* (math., med., phys., opt., seismol. & fig.) focus; center (*e.g., of vice*); core (*of an abscess*); source of light; (coll.) electric light, electric-light bulb; **fuera de foco** out of focus
fóculo *m* small hearth
focha *f* (orn.) European coot
fodolí *adj* (*pl:* **-líes**) meddlesome
foena *f* fish spear
fofo -fa *adj* fluffy, soft, spongy
fofoque *m* (naut.) middle jib
fogaje *m* fumage, hearth money (*tax*); (Am.) blush, flush; (Am.) fire, blaze
fogarada *f* blaze, fire, bonfire; (dial.) rash, eruption
fogaril *m* cresset
fogarizar **§76** *va* to start fires or bonfires in
fogata *f* blaze, bonfire; (mil.) mine, fougasse
fogón *m* firebox; cooking stove; (arti.) vent; (naut.) cookhouse; (Am.) gathering of soldiers and civilians around a fire; **fogón eléctrico** electric burner
fogonadura *f* (naut.) mast hole
fogonazo *m* powder flash
fogonero or **fogonista** *m* fireman (*of furnace, boiler, locomotive, etc.*)
fogosidad *f* fire, dash, spirit
fogoso -sa *adj* fiery, impetuous, spirited, vehement
foguear *va* to scale (*a gun*); to accustom to the smell of gunpowder; to inure; (coll.) to look daggers at
fogueo *m* target practice
foguezuelo *m* little fire
foja *f* (orn.) European coot; (law) leaf, sheet
fol. abr. of **folio**
folgo *m* foot-warming bag
folía *f* light music, popular music
foliáceo -a *adj* foliaceous
foliación *f* foliation (*of the leaves of a book*); (bot. & geol.) foliation
foliado -da *adj* (bot.) foliate
foliar *adj* foliar; *va* to foliate, to folio (*the leaves of a book*)
foliatura *f* foliature; foliation
folicular *adj* follicular
foliculario *m* (coll.) pamphleteer, news writer
foliculina *f* (biochem.) folliculin

folículo *m* (anat. & bot.) follicle
folio *m* folio (*leaf of a book*); (bookkeeping) folio; (print.) running head; **al primer folio** right off the bat; **de a folio** (coll.) enormous, tremendous; **en folio** in folio; **folio atlántico** atlas folio
folíolo *m* (bot.) foliole
folklore *m* folklore
folklórico -ca *adj* folkloric, (pertaining to) folklore
folklorista *mf* folklorist
folla *f* mixture, hodgepodge; (theat.) medley
follada *f* puff-paste pie
follaje *m* foliage; gaudy ornament; fustian; (arch.) foliage
follajería *f* (arch. & f.a.) foliation
follar *va* to foliate (*to shape like a leaf*); **§77** *va* to blow with bellows; *vr* to break wind without making a noise
follero or **folletero** *m* bellows maker or dealer
folletín *m* newspaper serial (*usually printed at bottom of page*)
folletinesco -ca *adj* serial; serial-like; exciting, intriguing
folletinista *mf* serial writer
folletista *mf* pamphleteer
folleto *m* pamphlet, brochure, tract, booklet
folletón *m* var. of **folletín**
follón -llona *adj* lazy, careless, indolent; arrogant, blustering, cowardly, worthless; *mf* lazy loafer; good-for-nothing; *m* noiseless rocket
fomentación *f* (med.) fomentation
fomentador -dora *adj* fomenting; promoting; *mf* fomenter; promoter
fomentar *va* to foment (*e.g., hatred*); to promote, encourage, foster; to warm; to enliven; (med.) to foment
fomento *m* fomentation; promotion, encouragement, fostering; improvement, development; warmth; (med.) fomentation
fon *m* (phonet.) phone
fonda *f* inn, restaurant
fondable *adj* (naut.) fit for anchoring
fondado -da *adj* reinforced in the heads (*said of a barrel*); (Am.) heeled, well-heeled
fondeadero *m* (naut.) anchorage (*place*)
fondeado -da *adj* (Am.) heeled, well-heeled
fondear *va* (naut.) to sound; to search (*a ship*); to scrutinize, examine closely; *vn* (naut.) to cast anchor; *vr* (Am.) to save up for a rainy day
fondeo *m* (naut.) search; (naut.) anchorage, casting anchor
fondero -ra *mf* (Am.) innkeeper
fondillón *m* dregs of a refilled cask; old Alicante wine
fondillos *mpl* seat (*of trousers*)
fondista *mf* innkeeper, restaurant keeper
fondo *m* bottom; back, rear; background; ground (*of a piece of cloth*); head (*of a barrel, boiler, etc.*); depth (*e.g., of a house*); fund; (anat.) fundus; (sport) distance, endurance; (fig.) bottom (*essence*); (fig.) fund, reservoir (*great amount*); **fondos** *mpl* funds (*money*); **a fondo** thoroughly; **a fondo perdido** without expecting to get the money back; **bajos fondos sociales** scum of the earth; underworld; **colar a fondo** (naut.) to sink; **dar fondo** (naut.) to cast anchor; **doble fondo** (naut.) double bottom; **echar a fondo** (naut.) to sink; **en el fondo** at bottom; **entrar en el fondo de** to get to the bottom of; **estar en fondos** to have funds available; **irse a fondo** (naut.) to founder; to fail (*said of a business venture*); **tener buen fondo** to be good-natured; **tener mal fondo** to be ill-natured; **fondo de amortización** sinking fund; **fondo falso** false bottom; **fondo rotativo** revolving fund; **fondo vitalicio** life annuity
fondón -dona *adj* (coll.) flabby, pursy
fonducho *m* cheap eating house
fonema *m* (phonet.) phoneme
fonémico -ca *adj* phonemic; *f* phonemics
fonético -ca *adj* phonetic; *f* phonetics
fonetista *mf* phonetician
fónico -ca *adj* phonic; *f* phonics
fonil *m* (naut.) large wooden funnel
fonje *adj* soft, fluffy
fono *m* earphone; phone
fonocaptor *m* (elec.) pickup
fonografía *f* phonography
fonográfico -ca *adj* phonographic
fonógrafo *m* phonograph
fonograma *m* phonogram
fonolita *f* (mineral.) phonolite
fonología *f* phonology
fonológico -ca *adj* phonologic or phonological
fonólogo -ga *mf* phonologist
fonoscopio *m* phonoscope
fontal *adj* fontal
fontana *f* (dial. & poet.) fountain
fontanal *adj* fontal; *m* spring; place abounding in springs
fontanar *m* spring
fontanela *f* (anat.) fontanel
fontanería *f* pipelaying; plumbing; water supply system, water department
fontanero -ra *adj* (pertaining to a) fountain; *m* pipelayer; plumber and electrician
fontículo *m* (med.) var. of **exutorio**
foque *m* (naut.) jib; (coll.) piccadilly (*collar*)
foquillo *m* flashlight bulb
foquito *m* flashlight bulb; dial light
forajido -da *adj* fugitive; *mf* fugitive, outlaw; bandit, malefactor
foral *adj* statutory
foramen *m* foramen; hole in nether millstone; (anat. & bot.) foramen
foraminíferos *mpl* (zool.) foraminifera
foráneo -a *adj* strange, foreign; *mf* stranger, outsider
forastero -ra *adj* outside, strange; *mf* outsider, stranger
forbante *m* pirate, freebooter
forcejar or **forcejear** *vn* to struggle; to contend
forcejeo or **forcejo** *m* struggle, struggling; resistance, opposition
forcejón *m* violent effort, violent tug
forcejudo -da *adj* husky, robust
fórceps *m* (*pl:* **-ceps**) (obstet. & zool.) forceps
forcipresión *f* or **forcipresura** *f* (surg.) forcipressure
forense *adj* forensic, legal
forero -ra *adj* statutory; *m* leaseholder
forestal *adj* (pertaining to a) forest
forestería *f* (Am.) forestry
forillo *m* (theat.) small back cloth (*seen through opening in backdrop*)
forja *f* forge; forging; concocting; ironworks, foundry; silversmith's forge; mortar; **forja a la catalana** Catalan forge or furnace
forjador -dora *adj* forging; *mf* forger; maker; smith, blacksmith
forjadura *f* forging
forjar *va* to forge; to build (*with stone and mortar*); (fig.) to forge (*e.g., lies*); **forjar a martinete** to drop-forge; *vr* to think up, to dream up
forma *f* form; shape; way; format; **de esta forma** in this way, in this wise; **de forma** of distinction; **de forma que** so that, with the result that; **en debida forma** in due form; **en forma** in form; (sport) in form
formación *f* formation; training; bullion, twisted fringe; (elec., geol. & mil.) formation; **formación de palabras** word formation; **formación en masa** (mil.) mass formation
formador -dora or **-triz** (*pl:* **-trices**) *adj* forming; *mf* former
formaje *m* cheese mold or vat
formal *adj* formal; serious (*matter*); sedate, settled; reliable; express, definite
formaldehido *m* (chem.) formaldehyde
formalidad *f* formality; seriousness; reliability
formalina *f* (chem.) formalin
formalismo *m* formalism; red tape
formalista *adj* formalistic; *mf* formalist
formalizar §76 *va* to formalize; to formulate; to put in final form; to legalize; *vr* to become serious; to take offense
formar *va* to form; to train, educate; (elec.) to form (*plates of storage battery*); *vn* to form; to form a line; to embroider with chenille; *vr* to form; to form a line, stand in line, fall in; to take form; to grow, develop
formativo -va *adj* formative
formato *m* format

formatriz *adj fem* see **formador**
formejar *va* (naut.) to tie up (*a ship*); (naut.) to clear the decks of (*a ship*)
formero *m* (arch.) formeret, wall rib
formiato *m* (chem.) formate
fórmico -ca *adj* formic
formidable *adj* formidable; terrific
formidoloso -sa *adj* timorous; frightful, horrible
formillón *m* hat block
formol *m* (chem.) formol
formón *m* chisel; punch
fórmula *f* formula; prescription; recipe; **por fórmula** as a matter of form
formulación *f* formulation
formulador -dora *mf* formulator
formular *adj* formulary; *va* to formulate
formulario -ria *adj* formulary; formal; *m* formulary; form; (pharm.) formulary; **formulario de pedido** order blank
fornicación *f* fornication
fornicador -dora *adj* fornicating; *mf* fornicator
fornicar §86 *vn* to fornicate
fornicario -ria *adj* fornicating; *mf* fornicator
fornicio *m* fornication
fornido -da *adj* robust, husky
fornitura *f* (print.) type melted down to complete a font; **fornituras** *fpl* (mil.) cartridge belt
foro *m* (hist. & law) forum; (law) emphyteusis; bar (*legal profession*); back, rear (*of stage*); **por tal foro** on such condition
forragatear *va* (coll.) to scribble, to scribble all over
forraje *m* forage; (coll.) hodgepodge
forrajeador -dora *adj* foraging; *m* forager
forrajear *va & vn* to forage
forrajero -ra *adj* forage; *f* forage rope; aiglet, lanyard; shoulder braid
forrar *va* to line; to cover (*book, umbrella, etc.*); (paint.) to stretch (*a canvas*); *vr* (Am.) to stuff oneself
forro *m* lining; cover; (her.) fur; (naut.) planking, sheathing; **no conocer ni por el forro** (coll.) to not know in the slightest; **no haber visto ni por el forro** (coll.) to have seen neither hide nor hair of; **ni por el forro** (coll.) not by a long shot; **forro de freno** (aut.) brake lining
forsitia *f* (bot.) forsythia
fortachón -chona *adj* (coll.) burly, husky, tough
fortalecedor -dora *adj* fortifying, strengthening
fortalecer §34 *va* to fortify, to strengthen
fortalecimiento *m* fortification, strengthening; fortifications; tonic, fortifier
fortaleza *f* fortitude; strength, vigor; firmness; fortress, stronghold; **fortaleza volante** (aer.) flying fortress
forte *interj* (naut.) avast!
fortepiano *m* (mus.) pianoforte
fortificación *f* fortification
fortificador -dora *adj* fortifying
fortificante *adj* fortifying; *m* fortifier, tonic
fortificar §86 *va & vn* to fortify
fortín *m* small fort; bunker
fortísimo -ma *adj super* very or most strong
fortuitez *f* fortuity
fortuito -ta *adj* fortuitous
fortuna *f* fortune; storm, tempest; **de fortuna** makeshift; **por fortuna** fortunately
fortunón *m* (coll.) windfall, great piece of luck
forúnculo *m* var. of **furúnculo**
forzado -da *adj* forced; forcible (*e.g., entry*); (fig.) forced (*e.g., smile*); hard (*labor*); *m* galley slave, convict
forzador *m* forcer; ravisher, violator
forzal *m* back (*of a comb*)
forzamiento *m* forcing
forzar §52 *va* to force; (agr.) to force; **forzar a** + *inf* or **forzar a que** + *subj* to force to + *inf*
forzosamente *adv* necessarily; violently, by force
forzoso -sa *adj* inescapable, unavoidable; strong, husky, robust; hard (*labor*); forced (*e.g., landing, march*); *f* (coll.) squeeze (*pressure to do something*); **hacer la forzosa a** (coll.) to put the squeeze on
forzudo -da *adj* strong, husky, robust
fosa *f* grave; (anat.) fossa; (aut.) pit; **fosa de los leones** (Bib.) lions' den; **fosa séptica** septic tank
fosal *m* cemetery; (prov.) grave
fosar *va* to dig a ditch around; to moat
fosco -ca *adj* cross, sullen; dark; (naut.) threatening; *f* haze; (dial.) thicket, jungle
fosfatar *va* to phosphatize
fosfático -ca *adj* phosphatic
fosfato *m* (chem. & agr.) phosphate; **fosfato cálcico** (chem.) calcium phosphate
fosfaturia *f* (path.) phosphaturia
fosfeno *m* (physiol.) phosfene
fosfina *f* (chem.) phosphine
fosfito *m* (chem.) phosphite
fosfonio *m* (chem.) phosphonium
fosforar *va* to phosphorate
fosforecer §34 *vn* to phosphoresce
fosforero -ra *mf* match vendor; *m* matchbox holder; *f* matchbox
fosforescencia *f* phosphorescence
fosforescente *adj* phosphorescent
fosfórico -ca *adj* (chem.) phosphoric
fosforita *f* (mineral.) phosphorite
fósforo *m* (chem.) phosphorus; match; (coll.) brilliance, talent; (*cap.*) *m* (poet.) Phosphor (*morning star*); **fósforo de seguridad** safety match
fosforoscopio *m* phosphoroscope
fosforoso -sa *adj* (chem.) phosphorous
fosfurado -da *adj* (chem.) phosphureted
fosfuro *m* (chem.) phosphide
fosgeno *m* (chem.) phosgene
fósil *adj & m* fossil; (fig.) fossil
fosilífero -ra *adj* fossiliferous
fosilización *f* fossilization
fosilizar §76 *vr* to fossilize
foso *m* fosse, pit, hole; (fort.) fosse, moat; (theat.) pit
fótico -ca *adj* photic
fotingo *m* (coll.) jalopy, low-price car
fotio *m* (phys.) phot
foto *f* photo
fotoactínico -ca *adj* photoactinic
fotocalco *m* photoprint
fotocelda or **fotocélula** *f* (elec.) photocell
fotocincografía *f* photozincography
fotocinesis *f* (physiol.) photokinesis
fotocinético -ca *adj* photokinetic
fotoconductividad *f* (elec.) photoconductivity
fotocopia *f* photocopy
fotocromía *f* photochromy, color photography
fotocromo *m* photochrome
fotodesintegración *f* (phys.) photodisintegration
fotodinámico -ca *adj* photodynamic; *f* photodynamics
fotodrama *m* photoplay
fotoeléctrico -ca *adj* photoelectric
fotoelectrón *m* (physical chem.) photoelectron
fotoesfera *f* var. of **fotosfera**
fotofija *m* (sport) photo-finish camera
fotofobia *f* (path.) photophobia
fotogénico -ca *adj* (biol. & phot.) photogenic
fotógeno -na *adj* (biol.) photogenic; *m* (chem.) photogen
fotograbado *m* photoengraving
fotograbador -dora *mf* photoengraver
fotograbar *va* to photoengrave
fotografía *f* photograph (*picture*); photography (*art or process*); photograph gallery; **fotografía al magnesio** flashlight photograph; **fotografía en colores** color photography; **fotografía en relieve** photorelief
fotografiar §90 *va* to photograph; to depict in photographic detail; *vn* to photograph
fotográfico -ca *adj* photographic
fotógrafo -fa *mf* photographer
fotogrametría *f* photogrammetry
fotogramétrico -ca *adj* photogrammetric or photogrammetrical
fotolaboratorio *m* photographic laboratory
fotólisis *f* photolysis
fotolitografía *f* photolithography; photolithograph
fotolitografiar §90 *va* to photolithograph

fotomecánico -ca *adj* photomechanical
fotometría *f* photometry
fotómetro *m* photometer; light meter
fotomicrografía *f* photomicrography
fotomontaje *m* photomontage
fotón *m* (phys.) photon
fotoperiodismo *m* photojournalism
fotopila *f* (elec.) photovoltaic cell
fotoquímico -ca *adj* photochemical; *f* photochemistry
fotorreconocimiento *m* photoreconnaissance
fotorrelieve *m* photorelief
fotosensible or **fotosensitivo -va** *adj* photosensitive
fotosfera *f* (astr.) photosphere
fotosíntesis *f* (bot. & chem.) photosynthesis
fotospectroscopio *m* photospectroscope
fotostatar *va & vn* to photostat
fotostático -ca *adj* photostatic
fotóstato *m* photostat
fototactismo *m* or **fototaxis** *f* (biol.) phototaxis
fototelegrafía *f* phototelegraphy
fototelegrafiar §90 *va & vn* to phototelegraph
fototelégrafo *m* phototelegraph
fototerapia *f* phototherapeutics or phototherapy
fototipia *f* phototypy
fototipo *m* phototype
fototipografía *f* phototypography
fototropismo *m* (biol.) phototropism
fototubo *m* (elec.) phototube
fotovoltaico -ca *adj* photovoltaic
fóvea *f* fovea; (bot.) fovea; **fóvea central** (anat.) fovea centralis, central depression (*of retina*)
Fr. abr. of **Fray**
fra. abr. of **factura**
frac *m* (*pl:* **fraques**) swallow-tailed coat, full-dress coat, tails
fracasar *vn* to fail; to break to pieces
fracaso *m* failure; collapse, crash
fracción *f* fraction; faction, party; (math.) fraction; **fracción compleja** (math.) complex fraction; **fracción compuesta** (math.) compound fraction; **fracción continua** (math.) continued fraction; **fracción decimal** (math.) decimal fraction; **fracción impropia** (math.) improper fraction; **fracción periódica** (math.) periodic fraction; **fracción propia** (math.) proper fraction
fraccionado -da *adj* fractional
fraccionador -dora *adj* fractionating
fraccionamiento *m* breaking up, dismemberment; fractionization; (chem.) fractionation
fraccionar *va* to break up; to fractionize; (chem.) to fractionate
fraccionario -ria *adj* fractionary; fractional; fractional (*currency*)
fractura *f* fracture; breaking in, housebreaking; (geol. & surg.) fracture; **fractura complicada** (surg.) compound fracture; **fractura conminuta** (surg.) comminution, comminuted fracture
fracturar *va & vr* to fracture; to break open
fraga *f* (bot.) raspberry; thicket of brambles
fragancia *f* fragrance; good name
fragante *adj* fragrant; occurring; **en fragante** in the act
fragaria *f* (bot.) strawberry (*plant and fruit*)
fragata *f* (naut.) frigate; (orn.) frigate bird; **fragata ligera** (naut.) corvette
frágil *adj* fragile; frail; loose (*morally*); (Am.) poor, in want
fragilidad *f* fragility; frailty; looseness; lapse, moral lapse
fragmentación *f* fragmentation; (biol.) fragmentation
fragmentar *va* to break into fragments; *vr* to fragment
fragmentario -ria *adj* fragmentary
fragmento *m* fragment
fragor *m* crash, din, uproar
fragoroso -sa *adj* noisy, thundering
fragosidad *f* roughness, unevenness; thickness, denseness (*of a forest*); rough road; brambly path
fragoso -sa *adj* rough, uneven; brambly; noisy, thundering
fragua *f* forge; (fig.) hotbed; (fig.) fuel (*that feeds a passion*)
fraguado *m* setting, hardening
fraguador -dora *adj* scheming; *mf* schemer
fraguar §23 *va* to forge; (fig.) to forge (*e.g., lies*); (fig.) to hatch, brew, scheme; *vn* to set (*said, e.g., of cement*)
fragura *f* var. of **fragosidad**
fraile *m* friar; tuck (*at bottom of robe or skirt*); (print.) friar; (Am.) priest, cleric; (Am.) bagasse; **fraile de misa y olla** (coll.) friarling; **fraile negro** Black Friar (*Dominican*); **fraile rezador** (ent.) mantis, praying mantis
frailear *va* (dial.) to trim close to the trunk
frailecillo *m* little friar; (orn.) puffin
frailengo -ga or **fraileño -ña** *adj* (coll.) friary, monkish; priestlike
frailería *f* (coll.) friars
frailero -ra *adj* of a friar; (coll.) fond of priests, pious
frailesco -ca *adj* (coll.) var. of **frailengo**
frailía *f* priesthood
fraililIos *mpl* (bot.) wake-robin
frailuco *m* (coll.) wretched little friar
frailuno -na *adj* (coll.) friarish; (Am.) priest-loving, clerical-minded
frambesia *f* (path.) yaws, frambesia
frambuesa *f* raspberry (*fruit*)
frambueso *m* (bot.) raspberry, raspberry bush
frámea *f* dart, javelin
francachela *f* (coll.) feast, spread; (coll.) carousal, high time; (Am.) excessive familiarity
francachón -chona *adj* (Am.) overfamiliar
francalete *m* strap with buckle
francés -cesa *adj* French; **a la francesa** in the French fashion or manner; **despedirse, irse** or **marcharse a la francesa** (coll.) to take French leave; *m* Frenchman; French (*language*); **el francés antiguo** Old French; **los franceses** the French (*people*); *f* Frenchwoman
francesada *f* typical French remark; French invasion of Spain in 1808
francesilla *f* French roll; (bot.) turban buttercup
Francfort del Main Frankfurt am Main
Francfort del Oder Frankfurt an der Oder
Francia *f* France
franciano *m* French (*dialect of Île de France*)
francio *m* (chem.) francium
Francisca *f* see **francisco**
franciscano -na *adj & mf* Franciscan
francisco -ca *adj & mf* Franciscan; (*cap.*) *m* Francis; *f* Frances
francmasón *m* Freemason
francmasonería *f* Freemasonry
francmasónico -ca *adj* Freemasonic
Fran.co abr. of **Francisco**
franco -ca *adj* frank; liberal, generous; free, open (*road*); gratis; loamy, rich (*soil*); Frankish; **franco a bordo** free on board; **franco de porte** postpaid; *mf* Frank; *m* franc; Frankish (*language*); tax-free days (*in a fair*)
francoalemán -mana *adj* Franco-German
francobordo *m* (naut.) freeboard
francocanadiense *adj* French-Canadian; *mf* French Canadian
Franco Condado, el Franche-Comté
francófilo -la *adj & mf* Francophile
francófobo -ba *adj & mf* Francophobe
francolín *m* (orn.) black partridge, francolin
francoprovenzal *adj & m* Franco-Provençal
francote -ta *adj* (coll.) frank, open-hearted, wholehearted
francotirador *m* franc-tireur; sniper
Francho *m* Frank
franchote -ta or **franchute -ta** *mf* (coll.) Frenchy
franela *f* flannel; **franela de algodón** cotton flannel
frangente *m* accident, mishap
frangible *adj* frangible
frangir §42 *va* to break up, to break to pieces
frangollar *va* (coll.) to bungle, dash off
frangollo *m* porridge, stew, mash; (coll.) mess, botch
frangollón -llona *adj* (Am.) bungling; *mf* (Am.) bungler
frángula *f* (bot.) alder buckthorn

franja *f* fringe; strip, band
franjar or **franjear** *va* to fringe
franqueamiento *m* var. of **franqueo**
franquear *va* to exempt; to grant; to enfranchise; to open, to clear (*the way*); to cross, get over; to free (*a slave*); to frank (*a letter*); *vr* to yield; to unbosom oneself; **franquearse a** or **con** to open one's heart to
franqueo *m* freeing, liberation; postage; franking (*of a letter*); **franqueo concertado** postal permit
franqueza *f* frankness; liberality, generosity; freedom
franquía *f* (naut.) sea room; **estar en franquía** (naut. & coll.) to be in the open; **ponerse en franquía** (naut. & coll.) to get in the open
franquicia *f* franchise; exemption, tax exemption; **franquicia postal** franking privilege
franquista *mf* supporter of General Franco
fraque *m* var. of **frac**
frasca *f* twigs, brushwood; (Am.) rumpus, excitement
frasco *m* bottle, flask; jar (*e.g., of olives*)
frase *f* phrase; sentence; idiom; **gastar frases** (coll.) to talk all around the subject, to talk without coming to the point; **frase compleja** (gram.) complex sentence; **frase hecha** saying, proverb; fixed or set expression, cliché; **frase musical** (mus.) phrase
frasear *va* to phrase; (mus.) to phrase; (coll.) to adorn with phrases; *vn* (coll.) to talk without saying anything
fraseo *m* phrasing; (mus.) phrasing
fraseología *f* phraseology; verbosity
frasquera *f* bottle carrier, bottle frame, cellaret
frasqueta *f* (print.) frisket
fratás *m* plastering trowel
fratasar *va* to smooth with plastering trowel
fraterna *f* see **fraterno**
fraternal *adj* fraternal, brotherly
fraternar *va* to reprimand sharply
fraternidad *f* fraternity, brotherhood
fraternización *f* fraternization
fraternizar §76 *vn* to fraternize
fraterno -na *adj* fraternal, brotherly; *f* sharp reprimand
fratría *f* phratry
fratricida *adj* fratricidal; *mf* fratricide (*person*)
fratricidio *m* fratricide (*act*)
fraude *m* fraud
fraudulencia *f* fraudulence or fraudulency
fraudulento -ta *adj* fraudulent
fray *m* Fra
frazada *f* blanket
freático -ca *adj* phreatic
frecuencia *f* frequency; **alta frecuencia** high frequency; **baja frecuencia** low frequency; **con frecuencia** frequently; **frecuencia intermedia** (rad.) intermediate frequency; **frecuencia modulada** (rad.) frequency modulation; **frecuencia muy alta** (rad. & telv.) very high frequency; **frecuencia ultraalta** or **ultraelevada** (*rad.*) ultrahigh frequency
frecuencímetro *m* (elec.) frequency meter
frecuentación *f* frequentation
frecuentador -dora *mf* frequenter
frecuentar *va* to repeat, do over and over again; to frequent
frecuentativo -va *adj & m* (gram.) frequentative
frecuente *adj* frequent; common
fregadero *m* sink, kitchen sink
fregado -da *adj* (Am.) annoying, bothersome; (Am.) bold, daring; (Am.) stubborn; *m* rubbing; scrubbing; mopping; (coll.) mess; (coll.) rumpus, row
fregador -dora *mf* dishwasher; *m* sink; dishcloth; mop
fregadura *f* or **fregamiento** *m* rubbing; scrubbing; scouring; mopping; dishwashing
fregar §29 *va* to rub; to scrub; to scour; to mop; to wash (*dishes*); (Am.) to annoy, bother; *vr* (Am.) to be bad off, be in a bad way
fregatriz *f* (*pl:* **-trices**) var. of **fregona**
fregazón *f* var. of **fregadura**
fregona *f* kitchenmaid, dishwasher
fregonil *adj* (coll.) (pertaining to a) kitchenmaid, dishwasher
freidura *f* frying
freiduría *f* fried-fish store
freila *f* nun of a military order; (archaic) lay sister
freile *m* knight of a military order; priest of a military order
freimiento *m* var. of **freidura**
freír §73 & §17, 9 *va* to fry; (coll.) to bore to death; *vn* to fry; **al freír será el reír** he laughs best who laughs last; **dejarle a uno freír en su aceite** (coll.) to let someone stew in his own juice; *vr* to fry; (coll.) to be bored to death; **freírsela a uno** (coll.) to scheme to deceive someone
fréjol *m* var. of **frijol**
frémito *m* roar
frenada *f* or **frenado** *m* braking
frenaje *m* braking; **frenaje de regeneración** (elec.) regenerative braking
frenar *va* to check, hold back, restrain; to brake
frenazo *m* sudden braking
frenería *f* bridle making; harness shop
frenero *m* bridle maker or dealer; (rail.) brakeman
frenesí *m* (*pl:* **-síes**) frenzy
frenético -ca *adj* phrenetic; fanatic; mad, frantic
frénico -ca *adj* phrenic; (anat.) phrenic
frenillar *va* var. of **afrenillar**
frenillo *m* (anat.) frenum; muzzle; (naut.) tarred rope; (naut.) bobstay; **no tener frenillo** or **no tener frenillo en la lengua** (coll.) to not mince one's words, to be too outspoken
frenitis *f* (path.) phrenitis
freno *m* bit; bridle; brake; (fig.) brake, curb, check, restraint; **hablar sin freno** to rave, to talk like a wild man; **morder el freno** to champ the bit; **tascar el freno** to champ the bit; (fig.) to bear with impatience; **freno de aire** air brake; **freno de cinta** band brake; **freno de cono** cone brake; **freno de contrapedal** coaster brake; **freno de estacionamiento** (aut.) parking brake; **freno de mano** hand brake; **freno de pedal** or **freno de pie** foot brake; **freno de puerta** door check; **freno hidráulico** hydraulic brake; **freno neumático** air brake
frenología *f* phrenology
frenológico -ca *adj* phrenological
frenologista *mf* or **frenólogo -ga** *mf* phrenologist
frenopatía *f* (path.) phrenopathy
frental *adj* frontal
frente *m & f* front (*e.g., of a building*); *m* obverse; (fort., mil. & pol.) front; (mil.) front rank, front line; *f* brow, forehead, face, head, front; **a frente** straight ahead; **al frente** in front; (com.) carried forward (*to opposite page*); **al frente de** in charge of; **arrugar la frente** to knit the brow, to frown; **con la frente levantada** (coll.) calmly; (coll.) brazenly; **de frente** forward; straight ahead; abreast; **del frente** (com.) carried forward (*from opposite page*); **en frente** in front, opposite; **en frente de** in front of, opposite; against, opposed to; **hacer frente a** to face; **llevar de frente** to carry forward, go right ahead with; **frente a** in front of; **frente a frente** face to face; **frente caliente** (meteor.) warm front; **frente de ondas** (phys.) wave front; **frente frío** (meteor.) cold front; **frente por frente de** right opposite
frentón -tona *adj* var. of **frontudo**
freo *m* channel, strait
freón *m* freon
fres *m* fringe
fresa *f* (bot.) strawberry (*plant and fruit*); ruff, fraise; countersinking bit; cutter (*of milling machine*); reamer; (dent.) burr
fresado *m* countersinking; milling; reaming
fresadora *f* milling machine
fresal *m* strawberry patch
fresar *va* to adorn or trim with friezes; to countersink, to mill, to ream
fresca *f* see **fresco**
frescachón -chona *adj* bouncing, buxom; (naut.) brisk (*wind*), moderate (*gale*)

frescal *adj* slightly salted; **frescales** *mf* (coll.) forward sort of person
frescamente *adv* recently, of late; offhand; brazenly
frescar §86 *vn* (naut.) to blow up (*said of the wind*)
fresco -ca *adj* fresh; cool; buxom, ruddy; calm, unruffled; light (*cloth or clothing*); wet (*paint*); (naut.) strong (*breeze*); (coll.) fresh, cheeky ‖ *m* coolness, fresh air; fresh fish; fresh bacon; (f.a.) fresco (*art; picture*); (Am.) cool drink; **al fresco** in the night air; in the open air; (f.a.) in fresco; **dejar fresco** (coll.) to leave in the lurch; **estar fresco** (coll.) to be in a fine pinch; **hacer fresco** to be cool (*said of the weather*); **pintar al fresco** (f.a.) to fresco; **quedar fresco** (coll.) to be in a fine pinch; **quedarse tan fresco** (coll.) to show no offense, to be unconcerned; **tomar el fresco** to get some fresh air ‖ *f* fresh air; cool time of the day (*early morning or evening*); (coll.) blunt remark, piece of one's mind; **tomar la fresca** to get some fresh air; **salir con la fresca** to go out in the cool of the morning
frescor *m* freshness; cool, coolness; (paint.) flesh color
frescote -ta *adj* (coll.) buxom, plump and rosy
frescura *f* freshness; cool, coolness; greenness (*of a spot or region*); calmness, coolness; unconcern, offhand manner; sharp reply; (coll.) cheek
fresero -ra *mf* strawberry seller; *f* (bot.) strawberry (*plant*)
fresnal *adj* ash, ashen
fresneda *f* growth of ash trees
fresnillo *m* (bot.) fraxinella
fresno *m* (bot.) ash, ash tree; ash (*wood*)
fresón *m* Chilean strawberry (*fruit*); large strawberry
fresquedal *m* cool, damp, green spot
fresquera *f* see **fresquero**
fresquería *f* (Am.) ice-cream parlor
fresquero -ra *mf* fresh-fish peddler; *f* food cabinet, meat closet; icebox
fresquilla *f* flat-shaped peach
fresquísimo -ma *adj super* very or most fresh
fresquista *mf* frescoer
freteado -da *adj* (her.) fretted
freudiano -na *adj & mf* Freudian
freudismo *m* Freudianism
frey *m* Fra
frez *f* dung
freza *f* dung; spawning; spawning season; spawn, roe; feeding season of silkworms; hole dug by an animal
frezada *f* blanket
frezar §76 *vn* to dung; to spawn; to feed (*said of silkworms*); to root or scratch
friabilidad *f* friability
friable *adj* friable
frialdad *f* coldness, frigidity; nonsense, stupidity; carelessness, laxity; (path.) impotence; (path.) frigidity (*abnormal sexual indifference*); (fig.) coldness, frigidity; (fig.) coolness
friático -ca *adj* chilly; awkward, stupid
fricación *f* rubbing; (phonet.) fricative sound
fricandó *m* fricandeau
fricar §86 *va* to rub
fricasé *m* fricassee; **guisar a la fricasé** to fricassee
fricativo -va *adj & f* (phonet.) fricative
fricción *f* rub, rubbing; massage; (mech.) friction; (pharm.) rubbing liniment; (fig.) friction
friccional *adj* frictional
friccionar *va* to rub; to massage
friega *f* rubbing, massage; (Am.) annoyance, bother; (Am.) beating, whipping
friera *f* chilblain on the heel
frígano *m* (ent.) caddis fly
Frigia *f* see **frigio**
frigidez *f* frigidity; (path.) frigidity (*abnormal sexual indifference*)
frígido -da *adj* (poet.) cold, frigid
frigio -gia *adj & mf* Phrygian; (*cap.*) *f* Phrygia
frigorífero *m* freezing chamber
frigorífico -ca *adj* refrigerating; cold-storage; *m* refrigerator; (Am.) packing house, cold-storage plant
frigorizar §76 *va* to freeze
frijol *m* or **fríjol** *m* (bot.) kidney bean; **frijol caballero** or **de Antibo** (bot.) hyacinth bean; **frijol de media luna** (bot.) Lima bean; **frijol de ojos negros** (bot.) black-eyed bean; **frijol iztagapa** (bot.) civet bean, Sieva bean
frijolear *va* (Am.) to bother, annoy
frijolizar §76 *va* (Am.) to bewitch
fringilago *m* (orn.) great titmouse
fringílido -da *adj* (orn.) fringilloid; *m* (orn.) fringillid
frío -a *adj* cold, frigid; colorless, dull, weak; (fig.) cold, frigid; (fig.) cool; (fig.) cold (*remote from what one is looking for*); *m* cold, coldness; **fríos** *mpl* chills and fever; **no darle a una persona frío ni calentura** (coll.) to leave a person indifferent; **hacer frío** to be cold (*said of the weather*); **tener frío** to be cold (*said of a person*); **tomar frío** to catch cold
friolento -ta *adj* chilly
friolero -ra *adj* chilly; *f* trifle, trinket; snack, bite
frisa *f* frieze (*woolen cloth*); (fort.) fraise
frisador -dora *mf* friezer (*of cloth*)
frisadura *f* friezing (*of cloth*)
frisar *va* to frieze, to frizz (*cloth*); to rub; to pack, to line; to fit, to fasten; (naut.) to calk; *vn* to get along, to agree; to approach; **frisar con** or **en** to border on
frisio -sia *adj & mf* Frisian; *m* Frisian (*language*); (*cap.*) *f* Friesland
friso *m* (arch.) frieze; wainscot, dado
frísol *m* var. of **frijol**
frisón -sona *adj & mf* Frisian; *m* Frisian (*language*)
frisuelo *m* fritter; (bot.) kidney bean
frita *f* see **frito**
fritada *f* fry
fritado *m* fritting (*of materials for glass*)
fritanga *f* fry
fritar *va* to frit (*materials for glass*)
fritilaria *f* (bot. & ent.) fritillary
frito -ta *pp of* **freír**; *adj* fried; (coll.) bored to death, worried to death; *m* fry; *f* frit
fritura *f* var. of **fritada**
frivolidad *f* frivolity
frivolité *f* (sew.) tatting; **hacer frivolité** (sew.) to tat
frívolo -la *adj* frivolous
friz *f* flower of beech tree
fronda *f* (bot.) frond; (surg.) sling-shaped bandage; **frondas** *fpl* frondage
fronde *m* (bot.) frond (*of a fern*)
frondescencia *f* (bot.) frondescence
frondescente *adj* frondescent
frondosidad *f* frondage
frondoso -sa *adj* leafy; woodsy; shady; luxuriant
frontal *adj* frontal; *m* frontal; (anat., arch. & eccl.) frontal
frontalera *f* front (*of a bridle*); yoke pad (*for oxen*)
frontera *f* see **frontero**
fronterizo -za *adj* frontier, border; bordering; opposite
frontero -ra *adj* front; frontier, border; facing, opposite; *m* child's frontlet or brow pad; frontier commander; *f* frontier, border; frontage; front wall; binder of frail basket
frontil *m* yoke pad (*for oxen*)
frontín *m* (Am.) front (*of bridle*); (Am.) fillip
frontino -na *adj* marked in the face (*said of an animal*)
frontis *m* (*pl:* **-tis**) façade, front
frontispicio *m* frontispiece (*of a book*); (arch.) frontispiece; (coll.) face
frontón *m* gable (*over door or window*); (arch.) pediment; (sport) wall used in pelota; (sport) frontón, pelota court or building
frontudo -da *adj* big-browed; broad-faced
frotación *f* rubbing
frotador -dora *adj* rubbing; *mf* rubber; *m* (elec.) brush
frotadura *f* rubbing
frotamiento *m* rubbing; (mech.) friction
frotar *va & vr* to rub
frote *m* var. of **frotadura**
frotis *m* (*pl:* **-tis**) (bact.) smear
fructífero -ra *adj* fructiferous; fruitful
fructificación *f* fructification

fructificar §86 *vn* to fructify
fructosa *f* (chem.) fructose
fructuosidad *f* fruitfulness
fructuoso -sa *adj* fruitful, fructuous
frufrú *m* frou-frou, swishing, rustling (*of silk*)
frugal *adj* temperate (*in eating and drinking*)
frugalidad *f* temperance, sobriety
frugívoro -ra *adj* frugivorous
fruición *f* enjoyment, gratification, fruition; wicked joy, evil satisfaction (*in another's sorrow or trouble*)
fruir §41 *vn* to enjoy oneself, be gratified
fruitivo -va *adj* enjoyable
frunce *m* pleat; (sew.) shirr, shirring, gathering
fruncido -da *adj* frowning; stern, grim, gruff; *m* pleat; (sew.) shirr, shirring, gathering
fruncimiento *m* wrinkling; deceit, cheating; (sew.) shirring, gathering
fruncir §50 *va* to wrinkle, contract, pucker, pleat; to knit (*eyebrows*); to curl, purse (*lips*); to conceal, disguise (*truth*); (sew.) to shirr, to gather; *vr* to be shocked, to affect modesty
fruslera *f* see **fruslero**
fruslería *f* trifle, trinket; (coll.) futility, triviality
fruslero -ra *adj* frivolous, futile, trifling; *f* brass or copper turnings or chips
frustración *f* frustration
frustráneo -a *adj* unprofitable, vain
frustrar *va* to frustrate, to thwart; *vr* to be frustrated
frústula *f* (bot.) frustule
fruta *f* fruit (*e.g., apple, pear, strawberry*); (coll.) fruit (*result*); **frutas** *fpl* fruit, e.g., **me gustan las frutas** I like fruit; **fruta de hueso** stone fruit; **fruta del tiempo** fruit in season; **fruta de sartén** fritter, pancake; **fruta nueva** novelty; **fruta prohibida** forbidden fruit
frutaje *m* (paint.) fruit piece
frutal *adj* fruit (*tree*); *m* fruit tree
frutar *vn* to bear fruit
frutecer §34 *vn* (poet.) to bear fruit
frutera *f* see **frutero**
frutería *f* fruit store
frutero -ra *adj* fruit (*boat, dish, etc.*); *mf* fruiterer, fruit vendor; *m* fruit dish; doily for covering fruit; tray of imitation fruit; fruit cabinet; tilt-top fruit table; (paint.) fruit piece; *f* fruitwoman
frutescente *adj* frutescent
frútice *m* (bot.) shrub, frutex
fruticoso -sa *adj* fruticose
fruticultura *f* fruitgrowing, cultivation of fruit trees
frutilla *f* India berry (*used as bead for rosaries*); Chilean strawberry; (Am.) trichinosis
frutillar *m* (Am.) strawberry patch
frutillero *m* (Am.) strawberry grower; (Am.) strawberry hawker
fruto *m* (bot.) fruit (*part containing seeds*); (fig.) fruit (*result; product*), e.g., **el fruto de mucho trabajo** the fruit of much effort; **los frutos de la tierra** the fruits of the earth; **frutos** *mpl* produce, commodities; **sacar fruto** to derive benefit; **sin fruto** (coll.) fruitlessly, in vain; **fruto de bendición** legitimate offspring; **fruto del pan** breadfruit
ftaleína *f* (chem.) phthalein
ftálico -ca *adj* (chem.) phthalic
ftalina *f* (chem.) phthalin
ftiocol *m* (biochem.) phthiocol
fu *interj* spit! (*of cat*); faugh!, fie!; **ni fu ni fa** (coll.) neither one thing nor the other
FUA abr. of **frecuencia ultraalta**
fucáceo -a *adj* (bot.) fucaceous
fúcar *m* nabob, tycoon
fucilar *vn* to flash with sheet lightning; to flash, to shine
fucilazo *m* heat lightning, sheet lightning
fuco *m* (bot.) rockweed
fucsia *f* (bot.) fuchsia
fucsina *f* (chem.) fuchsin
fucha *interj* (Am.) ugh!, pew!
fué *3d sg pret ind of* **ir** *and* **ser**
fuego *m* fire; light (*to light a cigar, cigaret, etc.*); firing; light, beacon, lighthouse; hearth, home; burning sensation; rash, skin eruption; cold sore, fever blister; **a fuego y hierro** or **a fuego y sangre** without mercy, without quarter; violently, sweeping straight ahead; **abrir fuego** to open fire; **apagar los fuegos** (mil.) to quiet the enemy's fire; (coll.) to upset or get the best of an opponent; **dar fuego a** to give a light to; (naut.) to bream (*a ship's bottom*); **echar fuego** (coll.) to blow up, hit the ceiling; **echar fuego por los ojos** to look daggers; **entre dos fuegos** between two fires; **estar hecho un fuego** to be all stirred up; to be burning with anger; **hacer fuego** to fire, to shoot; **jugar con fuego** to play with fire; **levantar fuego** to stir up a row; **marcar a fuego** to brand; **meter a fuego y sangre** to lay waste; **pegar fuego a** to set fire to, to set on fire; **poner a fuego y sangre** to lay waste; **prender fuego a** to set fire to, to set on fire; **prenderse fuego** to catch fire, to catch on fire; **romper el fuego** to open fire; to stir up a row; **fuego de contacto** (arti.) contact firing; **fuego de San Antón** or **fuego de San Marcial** (path.) Saint Anthony's fire; **fuego de Santelmo** St. Elmo's fire; **fuego fatuo** ignis fatuus; **fuego graneado** drumfire; **fuego griego** Greek fire; **fuego nutrido** drumfire; **fuegos artificiales** fireworks; **fuegos en los labios** cold sore, fever blister; *interj* (mil.) fire!; **¡fuego de Dios!** or **¡fuego de Cristo!** confound it!
fueguino -na *adj & mf* Fuegian
fuelle *m* bellows; pucker, wrinkle, fold; folding carriage top; clouds over mountaintop, wind clouds; (phot.) bellows (*of folding camera*); (rail.) flexible cover (*between two cars of a vestibule train*); (coll.) gossip, talebearer
fuente *f* fountain; spring; running water (*in the house*); public hydrant; font, baptismal font; platter, tray; (fig.) source; **beber en buenas fuentes** (coll.) to be well-informed, to be well supplied with information; **fuente de alimentación** (elec.) source of current; (rad.) power pack; **fuente de beber** drinking fountain; **fuente de gasolina** gasoline pump; **Fuente de la juventud** Fountain of Youth; **fuente de poder** (elec.) source of current; (rad.) power pack; **fuente de sodas** soda fountain; **fuente luminosa** or **mágica** illuminated fountain; **fuente pieria** Pierian spring; **fuentes bien informadas** well-informed sources; **fuentes fidedignas** reliable sources; **fuentes termales** hot springs; **fuente surtidora** (elec.) source of current; (rad.) power pack
fuer; a fuer de as a, on the score of, by way of
fuera *adv* out, outside; away, out of town; **de fuera** outside; **desde fuera** from the outside; **por fuera** on the outside; **fuera de** outside, outside of; away from, out of; aside from; in addition to; **fuera de que** aside from the fact that; **fuera de sí** beside oneself
fuereño -ña *mf* (Am.) stranger, hick, yokel
fuero *m* law, statute; power, jurisdiction; code of laws; exemption, privilege; **fueros** *mpl* (coll.) pride, arrogance; **fuero interior** or **interno** conscience, inmost heart
fuerte *adj* strong; bad, severe; intense; rough; harsh; loud; hard; heavy; (gram.) strong (*vowel; verb*); **hacerse fuerte** to stick to one's guns; (mil.) to hole up, to dig in; *adv* loud; hard; heavily; *m* fort; forte, strong point
fuerza *f* force; strength; power; main body (*e.g., of an army*); literal meaning; **fuerzas** *fpl* (mil. & nav.) forces; **a fuerza de** by dint of, by force of; **a fuerza de brazos** or **de puños** (coll.) by hard work; **a la fuerza** by force, forcibly; **a viva fuerza** by main strength; **cobrar fuerzas** to recover one's strength; **en fuerza de** because of, on account of; **hacer fuerza** to strain, struggle; to be strained; to convince, persuade; **hacer fuerza de remos** to pull hard on the oars; **hacer fuerza de vela** (naut.) to crowd on sail; **mandar fuerza** to have great influence; **por fuerza** perforce, necessarily; by force; **ser fuerza** + *inf* to be necessary to + *inf;* **fuerza aérea** air force; **fuerza animal** animal power; **fuerza centrífuga** centrifugal force; **fuerza centrípeta** centripetal force; **fuerza**

coercitiva (phys.) coercive force; **fuerza contraelectromotriz** (elec.) back electromotive force, counter electromotive force; **fuerza de agua** water power; **fuerza de las señales** (rad.) signal strength; **fuerza de sangre** animal power; **fuerza electromotriz** electromotive force; **fuerza hidráulica** water power; **fuerza mayor** (law) force majeure, act of God; **fuerza motriz** motive power; **fuerza pública** police; **fuerza vital** vital force, vital principle; **fuerza viva** (phys.) kinetic energy
fuetazo *m* (Am.) lash
fuete *m* (Am.) whip, horsewhip
fufar *vn* to spit (*said of a cat*)
fuga *f* flight; leak; ardor, vigor; (mus.) fugue; **apelar a la fuga** or **darse a la fuga** to take flight, to run away, to be on the run; **poner en fuga** to put to flight; **ponerse en fuga** to take to flight
fugacidad *f* fugacity, evanescence
fugada *f* gust of wind
fugar §59 *vr* to flee, run away, escape
fugaz *adj* (*pl:* **-gaces**) fleeting, transitory, fugacious; (bot.) fugacious
fugitivo -va *adj & mf* fugitive
fuguillas *m* (*pl:* **-llas**) (coll.) hustler
fui *1st sg pret ind of* **ir** *and* **ser**
fuina *f* (zool.) stone marten, beech marten
ful *adj* (slang) bogus, sham
fulano -na *mf* so-and-so; **fulano de tal** John Doe; **fulano, sutano y mengano** Tom, Dick, and Harry; **fulano y mengano** John Doe and Richard Roe
fular *m* foulard
fulcro *m* (bot., ent., ichth. & mach.) fulcrum
fulero -ra *adj* (coll.) useless, unsatisfactory
fulgente *adj* fulgent, resplendent
fúlgido -da *adj* bright, resplendent; *m* (chem.) fulgide
fulgor *m* splendor, brilliance
fulgurante *adj* shining, dazzling, fulgurant
fulgurar *vn* to flash, to fulgurate
fulgurita *f* fulgurite
fulguroso -sa *adj* fulgurous
fúlica *f* (orn.) coot; **fúlica negra** (orn.) European coot
fuliginoso -sa *adj* fuliginous
fulmicotón *m* guncotton
fulminación *f* fulmination
fulminante *adj* fulminant; sudden; (med.) fulminant
fulminar *va* to strike with lighting; to strike dead; to fulminate, to thunder (*censure, threats, etc.*); to hurl, hurl forth; to brandish; *vn* to fulminate
fulminato *m* (chem.) fulminate; **fulminato mercúrico** (chem.) mercury fulminate
fulmíneo -a *adj* fulminous
fulmínico -ca *adj* fulminic
fulminoso -sa *adj* fulminous
fullear *vn* (coll.) to cheat
fulleresco -ca *adj* of crooks
fullería *f* cheating; trick, trickery
fullero -ra *adj* cheating, crooked; tricky; *mf* cheat, crook; tricky person; **fullero de naipes** cardsharp
fullona *f* (coll.) row, quarrel, wrangle
fumable *adj* smokable; (Am.) acceptable
fumada *f* puff (*of smoke*); Am. smoking
fumadero *m* smoking room; **fumadero de opio** opium den
fumador -dora *adj* smoking; *mf* smoker; **fumador de opio** opium smoker
fumagina *f* (plant path.) fumagine
fumar *va* to smoke (*e.g., a cigar*); *vn* to smoke; **se prohibe fumar** no smoking; **fumar en pipa** to smoke a pipe; *vr* (coll.) to squander; (coll.) to cut (*class*)
fumarada *f* puff, blast (*of smoke*); pipeful (*of tobacco*)
fumaria *f* (bot.) fumitory
fumariáceo -a *adj* (bot.) fumariaceous
fumarina *f* (chem. & pharm.) fumarine
fumarola *f* fumarole
fumífero -ra *adj* (poet.) smoking, smoke-producing
fumífugo -ga *adj* smokeless, smoke-dispersing
fumigación *f* fumigation; **fumigación aérea** crop dusting
fumigador -dora *mf* fumigator (*person*); *m* fumigator (*apparatus*)
fumigante *m* fumigant (*substance used for fumigation*)
fumigar §59 *va* to fumigate
fumígeno -na *adj* smoke-producing; *m* smoke producer (*apparatus*)
fumista *m* stove or heater repairman or dealer
fumistería *f* stove or heater shop
fumívoro -ra *adj* smokeless, smoke-consuming
fumorola *f* var. of **fumarola**
fumosidad *f* smokiness
fumoso -sa *adj* smoky
funambulesco -ca *adj* funambulatory; fantastic, extravagant
funambulía *f* ropewalking, ropedancing
funámbulo -la *mf* ropewalker, ropedancer
función *f* function; operation; duty, office, position; show, performance; **entrar en funciones** (coll.) to take office, to take up one's duties; **estar en funciones** (coll.) to be in office; (coll.) to be in session; **función de aficionados** amateur theatricals; **función de títeres** puppet show; **función potencial** (math.) potential function; **función secundaria** side show; **función trigonométrica** trigonometric function
funcional *adj* functional
funcionalismo *m* functionalism
funcionamiento *m* functioning; working, running, performance
funcionar *vn* to function; to work, to run
funcionario *m* functionary, official, public official, civil servant
funcionarismo *m* bureaucracy; job seeking
funcionero -ra *adj* (coll.) officious, self-important; (coll.) fussy
fund. abr. of **fundador**
funda *f* case, sheath, envelope, cover, slip; slip cover; holdall; **funda de almohada** pillowcase; **funda de asientos** seat cover; **funda de gafas** spectacle case; **funda de neumático** tire cover; **funda de pistolas** pistol case, holster
fundación *f* foundation
fundadamente *adv* with good reason; on good authority
fundador -dora *adj* founding; *mf* founder
fundamental *adj* fundamental; foundation
fundamentalismo *m* (rel.) fundamentalism
fundamentalista *mf* (rel.) fundamentalist
fundamentar *va* to lay the foundations of or for; to found, establish
fundamento *m* foundation; basis; grounds, reason; seriousness, reliability, trustworthiness; weft, woof
fundar *va* to found; to base; **fundar en** or **sobre** to found on or upon; to base on or upon; *vr* to be founded; to be based; **fundarse en** to base one's opinion on
fundente *adj* fusing; melting, molten; *m* (chem. & metal.) flux; (med.) dissolvent
fundería *f* smelter; foundry
fundible *adj* fusible
fundición *f* founding; smelting; fusion; smelter; foundry; forge; cast iron; (print.) font; **fundición gris** gray iron
fundidor *m* founder, smelter, foundryman
fundillo *m* (Am.) behind; (Am.) knockout (*beautiful woman*); **fundillos** *mpl* (Am.) seat (*of trousers*)
fundilludo -da *adj* (Am.) big-seated (*trousers*); (Am.) big-rumped; *m* (Am.) man, male; (Am.) easy mark, simp
fundir *va* to found (*a metal; a statue*); to smelt; to fuse; to melt; to mix (*paint*); to burn out (*an electric filament*); (Am.) to ruin; *vr* to smelt; to fuse; to melt; (fig.) to fuse, merge, blend; (Am.) to ruin oneself; (Am.) to be or become ruined
fundo *m* (law) country property
fundón *m* (Am.) long case or sheath; (Am.) riding habit
fúnebre *adj* funeral; funereal, gloomy
funeral *adj* funeral; funereal; *m* funeral (*often without the corpse*); **funerales** *mpl* funeral; **funeral de corpore insepulto** funeral (*with corpse present*)

funerala; a la funerala (mil.) with arms inverted (*as a token of mourning*)
funerario -ria *adj* funerary; funeral; *m* funeral director, mortician; *f* undertaking establishment; funeral parlor
funéreo -a *adj* (poet.) funereal
funestar *va* to soil, tarnish, profane, violate
funestidad *f* (Am.) calamity
funesto -ta *adj* fatal, ill-fated; sad, sorrowful; baneful (*e.g., influence*)
fungible *adj* expendable, consumable; (law) fungible
fungicida *adj* fungicidal; *m* fungicide
fungir §42 *vn* (Am.) to act, function; (Am.) to loiter, to loaf; (Am.) to pinch hit
fungo *m* (path.) fungus
fungoideo -a *adj* fungoid
fungología *f* fungology
fungosidad *f* fungosity; (path.) fungosity
fungoso -sa *adj* fungous
funiculado -da *adj* (bot.) funiculate
funicular *adj* & *m* funicular
funículo *m* (anat., bot. & zool.) funiculus; (arch.) cable molding
fuñique *adj* slow, shy; dull, heavy
furente *adj* wild, raging
furcífero -ra *adj* forked; (zool.) furciferous
fúrfura *f* (path.) furfur
furfuráceo -a *adj* furfuraceous; (bot.) furfuraceous
furgón *m* van, wagon; (rail.) baggage car, freight car, boxcar; (rail.) caboose
furgoneta *f* light truck, delivery truck
furia *f* fury (*anger; violence; haste; angry person*); (*cap.*) *f* Fury; **a toda furia** like fury; **estar dado a las furias** to be in a fury
furibundo -da *adj* furious, enraged, frenzied
furiente *adj* var. of **furente**
furierismo *m* Fourierism
furioso -sa *adj* furious; tremendous; (her.) charging, leaping
furo -ra *adj* shy, diffident; (dial.) wild, untamed; *m* orifice (*in sugar mold*)
furor *m* furor, rage; **entrar** or **montar en furor** to fly into a rage; **hacer furor** to be the rage; **furor uterino** (path.) nymphomania
furriel *m* or **furrier** *m* fourrier (*quartermaster*); manager of the royal stables
furtivo -va *adj* furtive; clandestine, sneaky
furúnculo *m* (path.) boil, furuncle
furunculoso -sa *adj* furunculous
fusa *f* (mus.) demisemiquaver, thirty-second note
fusca *f* see **fusco**
fuscina *f* (biochem.) fuscin
fusco -ca *adj* fuscous, dark brownish-gray; *f* (orn.) black scoter
fusé *m* (horol.) fusee
fuselado -da *adj* streamlined; *m* streamlining
fuselaje *m* (aer.) fuselage
fuselar *va* (aer.) to streamline
fusente *adj* receding (*tide*)
fusibilidad *f* fusibility
fusible *adj* fusible; *m* (elec.) fuse; **fusible de cartucho** (elec.) cartridge fuse
fusiforme *adj* fusiform, spindle-shaped
fusil *m* gun, rifle; **fusil ametrallador** automatic rifle; **fusil de aguja** needle gun (*of Dreyse*); **fusil de chispa** flintlock (*musket*)
fúsil *adj* fusible
fusilamiento *m* shooting, execution
fusilar *va* to shoot, to execute; (coll.) to plagiarize
fusilazo *m* gunshot, rifle shot; heat lightning, sheet lightning
fusilería *f* guns, rifles; body of fusileers; fusillade
fusilero -ra *adj* (pertaining to a) gun, rifle; *m* fusileer; **fusilero de montaña** (mil.) chasseur
fusión *f* fusion; melting; (fig.) fusion; **fusión de empresas** (com.) merger; **fusión de voces** (philol.) blending
fusionar *va* & *vr* to fuse, to merge
fusionismo *m* (pol.) fusionism
fusionista *adj* & *mf* fusionist
fusique *m* bottle-shaped snuffbox; (coll.) tight-fitting garment
fuslina *f* smelter
fusor *m* smelting ladle
fusta *f* brushwood, twigs; coachman's whip; riding whip; (naut.) lateen-rigged vedette
fustal *m*, **fustán** *m* or **fustaño** *m* fustian (*coarse cloth*)
fustazo *m* lash
fuste *m* wood, timber; stem, shaft; saddletree; shank (*of bolt or rivet*); importance, substance, character; **fuste delantero** saddlebow
fustete *m* (bot.) fustic (*Cotinus coggygria; Chlorophora tinctoria and its wood*); (bot.) smoke tree, Venetian sumac (*Cotinus coggygria*)
fustigación *f* lashing, whipping; severe censure
fustigar §59 *va* to lash, to whip; to censure severely
fustina *f* smelter; (chem.) fustin
fut. abr. of **futuro**
fútbol *m* football; **fútbol asociación** association football, soccer
futbolista *m* football player; soccer player
futbolístico -ca *adj* (pertaining to) football
futesa *f* trifle, triviality
fútil *adj* futile (*unimportant*); trifling, inconsequential, frivolous
futileza *f* (Am.) futility
futilidad *f* futility (*unimportance*); frivolousness
futre *m* (Am.) dude, dandy
futura *f* see **futuro**
futurismo *m* futurism
futurista *adj* futuristic; *mf* futurist
futuro -ra *adj* future; *m* future; (gram.) future; (coll.) fiancé; **futuros** *mpl* (com.) futures; *f* (law) reversion (*right of succeeding to an estate*); (coll.) fiancée
Fz. abr. of **Fernández**

G

G, g *f* eighth letter of the Spanish alphabet
g. abr. of **gramo** or **gramos**
G. abr. of **gracia**
gabacho -cha *adj & mf* Pyrenean; (coll.) Frenchy; (Am.) gringo; *m* (coll.) Frenchified Spanish
gabán *m* overcoat, greatcoat
gabardina *f* gabardine; raincoat (*generally with belt*)
gabarra *f* barge; lighter; fishing sloop
gabarrero *m* bargeman; lighterman
gabarro *m* flaw, defect (*in a fabric*); filling, badigeon; pip (*disease of fowl*); bother; mistake (*in calculating*); (geol.) nodule
gabazo *m* var. of **bagazo**
gabela *f* tax; burden
gabinete *m* office (*of doctor, dentist, lawyer*); studio, study; boudoir; laboratory; cabinet (*of government; collection, display; private room*); **de gabinete** parlor, theoretical (*person*); **gabinete de aseo** washroom, lavatory, toilet; **gabinete de lectura** reading room
gabinetero *m* laboratory caretaker
gablete *m* gable (*over door or window*)
Gabriel *m* Gabriel
gacel *m* male gazelle
gacela *f* (zool.) gazelle
gaceta *f* gazette; sagger (*fire-clay box*); (Am.) newspaper; **mentir más que la gaceta** (coll.) to lie like a trooper
gacetero -ra *mf* news vendor, seller of newspapers; *m* gazeteer; newspaper man
gacetilla *f* gossip column, town talk (*in a newspaper*); short news item; (coll.) gossip (*person*)
gacetillero *m* gossip columnist
gacetín *m* (Am.) box (*of type-holding tray*)
gacetista *mf* newspaper reader; newsmonger
gacha *f* see **gacho**
gacheta *f* spring catch (*of lock*); paste
gacho -cha *adj* turned down; drooping, flopping; slouch (*hat*); with horns curved downward; *f* watery mass or mush; (Am.) earthenware bowl; **gachas** *fpl* pap, mush, porridge; (coll.) mud; (prov.) caresses; **a gachas** on all fours; **hacerse unas gachas** (coll.) to be mushy; **gachas de avena** oatmeal
gachón -chona *adj* (coll.) nice, cute; (prov.) spoiled, pampered
gachonada *f* (coll.) cuteness, charm
gachonear *va* (coll.) to flirt with; *vn* (coll.) to be cute
gachonería *f* (coll.) var. of **gachonada**
gachumbo *m* (Am.) fruit shell (*used to make cups and other vessels*)
gachupín -pina, gachupo -pa or **gachuzo -za** *mf* Spanish settler in America
gádido *m* (ichth.) gadid
gaditano -na *adj* (pertaining to) Cádiz; *mf* native or inhabitant of Cádiz
gadolinio *m* (chem.) gadolinium
gaélico -ca *adj* Gaelic; *mf* Gael; *m* Gaelic (*language*)
gafa *f* see **gafo**
gafar *va* to hook, to snatch with a hook, the claws, etc.
gafe *m* (coll.) hoodoo, jinx
gafedad *f* (path.) claw hand; (path.) anesthetic leprosy
gafete *m* hook and eye
gafo -fa *adj* claw-handed; (Am.) footsore; *f* hook (*for bending crossbow*); clamp, cramp; temple (*sidepiece of a pair of spectacles*); **gafas** *fpl* can hooks; spectacles, glasses; **unas gafas** a pair of glasses; **gafas de sol, gafas para sol, gafas parasoles** sunglasses
gago -ga *adj* (Am.) stuttering
gaguear *vn* (Am.) to stutter
gaguera *f* (Am.) stuttering
gaicano *m* (ichth.) remora
gaita *f* hornpipe; bagpipe; silly answer; chore, hard task; (coll.) neck; **estar de gaita** (coll.) to be in a gay mood; **templar gaitas a** (coll.) to humor; **gaita gallega** bagpipe
gaitería *f* flashy dress, gaudy dress
gaitero -ra *adj* (coll.) flashy, gaudy, showy; (coll.) garrulous; *m* bagpipe player
gaje *m* (archaic) gage (*e.g., of battle*); **gajes** *mpl* wages, salary; **gajes del oficio** (hum.) cares of office, unpleasant part of a job
gajo *m* branch of tree (*especially when broken off*); small stem (*of bunch of grapes*); bunch; kernel; slice (*e.g., of orange*); prong, tine (*e.g., of pitchfork*); spur (*of hills*); (bot.) lobe (*of leaf*); **gajo de nuez** nutmeat
gajoso -sa *adj* branched, branchy; stemmed; pronged
gala *f* festive dress or array; charm, elegance; choice, favorite; (poet.) pomp, show, splendor; (Am.) fee, tip; **galas** *fpl* finery, regalia; wedding presents; gifts, talents; beauties (*of diction, style, etc.*); **de gala** gala; full-dress; **hacer gala de** or **tener a gala** to make a show of; to take pride in, to glory in
Galaad *m* (Bib.) Gilead; Galahad (*of Round Table*)
galabardera *f* (bot.) dog rose (*plant and fruit*)
Galacia *f* Galatia
galactagogo -ga *adj & m* (med. & vet.) galactagogue
galáctico -ca *adj* (astr.) galactic
galactita or **galactites** *f* (mineral.) galactite
galactómetro *m* galactometer
galactosa *f* (chem.) galactose
galafate *m* slick thief; slicker; laborer; constable
galaico -ca *adj* Galician
galaicoportugués -guesa *adj & m* Galician-Portuguese
galán *m* fine-looking fellow; gallant, lover, suitor, ladies' man; (theat.) principal character; **primer galán** (theat.) leading man; **segundo galán** (theat.) second lead; **galán de noche** (bot.) night jasmine; **galán joven** (theat.) juvenile
galancete *m* (theat.) juvenile
galanga *f* (bot.) taro; (bot.) galingale (*Alpinia officinarum and rhizome*)
galano -na *adj* spruce, smartly dressed; graceful, elegant; rich, tasteful; (Am.) mottled
galante *adj* gallant, attentive to women; coquettish (*woman*); loose (*woman*)
galanteador -dora *adj* love-making; *m* gallant, lover, love-maker, flirt
galantear *va* to court, woo, make love to, flirt with
galanteo *m* courting, wooing, flirting
galantería *f* gallantry; charm, elegance; liberality, generosity
galantina *f* (cook.) galantine
galanura *f* charm, elegance
galapagar *m* place full of tortoises; breeding place for tortoises
galápago *m* (zool.) tortoise (*of genera Clemmys and Emys*); moldboard (*of plow*); centering arch; ingot (*of copper, lead, or tin*); hatch batten; brick mold; light saddle; (mil.) testudo, galapago; (coll.) sly fellow; **las Galápagos** the Galápagos Islands
galapaguera *f* tortoise pond
galapo *m* top, laying top (*used in making rope*)
galardón *m* reward, prize
galardonador -dora *adj* rewarding; *mf* rewarder

galardonar *va* to reward
gálata *adj & mf* Galatian
Galatea *f* (myth.) Galatea
galaxia *f* (mineral.) galactite; (astr.) galaxy
galayo *m* peak, cliff
galbana *f* (coll.) laziness, shiftlessness
galbanado -da *adj* galbanum-colored, yellowish
galbanero -ra *adj* (coll.) var. of **galbanoso**
gálbano *m* galbanum; **dar gálbano a** (coll.) to lead on, to deceive
galbanoso -sa *adj* (coll.) lazy, shiftless, indolent
gálbula *f* (bot.) galbulus, cone of cypress
galdrufa *f* (dial.) top, spinning top
galeato *adj masc* defensive (*preface*)
galeaza *f* (naut.) galleass
galega *f* (bot.) goat's-rue
galena *f* see **galeno**
galénico -ca *adj* Galenic
galenismo *m* Galenism
galeno -na *adj* (naut.) gentle, soft (*breeze*); (*cap.*) *m* Galen; (coll.) Galen (*physician*); (*l.c.*) *f* (mineral.) galena
gáleo *m* (ichth.) dogfish; (ichth.) swordfish
galeón *m* (naut.) galleon
galeota *f* (naut.) galiot
galeote *m* galley slave
galera *f* covered wagon; ward (*of hospital*); women's jail; row of reverberatory furnaces; line (*dividing two parts of fraction*); (carp.) jack plane; (naut. & print.) galley; (zool.) squilla, mantis crab; **galeras** *fpl* rowing on a galley (*as punishment*)
galerada *f* wagonload; (print.) galley, full galley; (print.) galley proof
galerero *m* driver of a covered wagon
galería *f* gallery; back porch; bay window; (ent.) bee moth; (fort., min., naut. & theat.) gallery; **hablar para la galería** (coll.) to play to the gallery; **galería de pinturas** picture gallery; **galería de popa** (naut.) stern gallery; **galería de tiro** shooting gallery; **galería fotográfica** photographic gallery; **galería visitable** manhole
galerín *m* (print.) galley
galerita *f* (orn.) crested lark
galerna *f* or **galerno** *m* stormy blast from the northwest (*on northern coast of Spain*)
Gales *f* Wales; **el país de Gales** Wales; **la Nueva Gales del Sur** New South Wales
galés -lesa *adj* Welsh; *m* Welshman; Welsh (*language*); **los galeses** the Welsh (*people*); *f* Welsh woman
galfarro *m* bum, loafer
galgo -ga *adj* (Am.) sweet-toothed; *mf* (coll.) gadabout; *m* greyhound; (fig.) greyhound (*ocean liner*); **galgo ruso** Russian wolfhound; *f* greyhound bitch; rolling stone; rash, mange; ankle ribbon; stretcher on which the poor are carried to the cemetery; hub brake (*on a wagon*); millstone for grinding olives; (Am.) gage (*of wire, sheet metal, etc.*)
galgueño -ña or **galguesco -ca** *adj* (pertaining to a) greyhound
gálgulo *m* (orn.) blue magpie
Galia, la Gaul
galibar *va* to fashion (*part of ship*) according to a template
gálibo *m* pattern, template; (naut.) template; (rail.) gabarit; (fig.) elegance
galicado -da *adj* Gallic, full of Gallicisms
galicanismo *m* (eccl.) Gallicanism
galicano -na *adj* (eccl.) Gallican; Gallic
Galicia *f* Galicia (*of Poland and of Spain*)
galiciano -na *adj & mf* Galician (*of Poland and of Spain*)
galicismo *m* Gallicism
galicista *adj* French, gallicizing; *mf* gallicizer, user of gallicisms
gálico -ca *adj* Gallic; (chem.) gallic; *m* (path.) syphilis
galicoso -sa *adj & mf* syphilitic
galileo -a *adj & mf* Galilean; **el Galileo** the Galilean, the Man of Galilee; *f* galilee (*porch*); (*cap.*) *f* Galilee
galillo *m* (anat.) uvula
galimatías *m* rigmarole, gibberish
galináceo -a *adj* var. of **gallináceo**
galio *m* (chem.) gallium; (bot.) bedstraw
galiparla *f* Frenchified Spanish
galiparlista *m* var. of **galicista**
galipodio *m* galipot or gallipot (*oleoresin*)
galo -la *adj* Gallic; *mf* Gaul; *m* Gaulish (*language*)
galocha *f* clog, wooden shoe
galomanía *f* Gallomania
galón *m* gallon; galloon; braid, stripe; (mil.) chevron
galoneadura *f* galloons, trimming
galonear *va* to trim with galloons or braid
galonero -ra *mf* galloon or braid maker or dealer
galonista *m* (coll.) student of a military academy who is allowed to wear the chevrons of corporal or sergeant as a reward
galop *m* or **galopa** *f* galop (*dance*)
galopante *adj* galloping
galopar *va* (Am.) to gallop (*a horse*); *vn* to gallop; to galop
galope *m* gallop; **a galope** or **de galope** at a gallop; in great haste; **a galope tendido** at full speed, on the run
galopeado -da *adj* hasty, sketchy; *m* (coll.) buffeting, punching, beating
galopear *vn* to gallop
galopillo *m* kitchen boy, scullion
galopín *m* ragamuffin; scoundrel; scullion; wise guy; (naut.) cabin boy; (coll.) loafer
galopo *m* scoundrel
galorromano -na *adj* Gallo-Roman
Galván *m* Gawain (*of Round Table and the Amadis of Gaul*)
galvánico -ca *adj* galvanic
galvanismo *m* galvanism
galvanización *f* galvanization
galvanizar §76 *va* to galvanize; (fig.) to galvanize
galvano *m* (print.) electroplate
galvanocauterio *m* (med.) galvanocautery
galvanometría *f* galvanometry
galvanométrico -ca *adj* galvanometric
galvanómetro *m* galvanometer
galvanoplastia *f* galvanoplasty; electroplating
galvanoplástico -ca *adj* galvanoplastic; *f* galvanoplastics
galvanoscopio *m* galvanoscope
galvanotropismo *m* (biol.) galvanotropism
galladura *f* tread (*of an egg*)
gallarda *f* see **gallardo**
gallardear *vn & vr* to be graceful, elegant, gallant
gallardete *m* pennant, streamer; **gallardete azul** (naut.) blue ribbon (*prize*)
gallardetón *m* broad pennant with two tails
gallardía *f* gracefulness, elegance, gallantry, bravery; generosity; nobility
gallardo -da *adj* graceful, elegant, gallant, brave; generous; noble; fierce (*storm*); *f* galliard (*dance*)
gallareta *f* (orn.) European coot; **gallareta de pico blanco** (orn.) North American coot
gallarito *m* (bot.) lousewort (*Pedicularis sylvatica*)
gallarón *m* (orn.) little bustard
gallaruza *f* (archaic) hooded cloak
gallear *va* to tread (*said of a cock*); *vn* to stand out, excel; (coll.) to yell and threaten
gallegada *f* Galicians; Galicianism; Galician dance
gallego -ga *adj & mf* Galician (*of Spain*); *m* Galician (*dialect*)
gallegoportugués -guesa *adj & m* var. of **galaicoportugués**
galleguismo *m* Galicianism (*of Galicia, Spain*)
galleo *m* rough spot in a casting (*from rapid cooling*)
gallero -ra *adj* (Am.) cockfighting; *m* breeder of gamecocks; *f* cockpit
galleta *f* hardtack, ship biscuit, ship bread; cracker; biscuit; little pitcher; briquet (*of anthracite*); (coll.) slap
gallina *f* hen; **acostarse con las gallinas** (coll.) to go to bed with the chickens; **estar como gallina en corral ajeno** (coll.) to be like a fish out of water; **gallina brahma** brahma (*chicken*); **gallina ciega** blindman's buff; **gallina de agua** (orn.) coot; **gallina de Guinea** guinea hen; **gallina de río** (orn.)

coot; **gallina Guinea** or **pintada** guinea hen; **gallina sorda** (orn.) woodcock; *mf* chicken-hearted person; *adj* chicken-hearted
gallináceo -a *adj* (orn.) gallinaceous
gallinazo -za *mf* (orn.) turkey buzzard; *f* hen dung
gallinería *f* flock of hens; chicken market; cowardice
gallinero -ra *mf* chicken dealer, poultry dealer; *m* hencoop, henhouse; paradise, top gallery; poultry basket; madhouse
gallineta *f* (orn.) European coot; (orn.) woodcock; (Am.) guinea hen
gallipato *m* (zool.) Spanish newt, European salamandrid (*Pleurodeles waltlii*)
gallipava *f* large hen
gallipavo *m* (orn.) turkey; (coll.) sour note
gallipollo *m* cockerel
gallipuente *m* bridge without railing
gallístico -ca *adj* (pertaining to a) cock
gallito *m* somebody (*person of importance*); **gallito del lugar** cock of the walk; **gallito del rey** (ichth.) peacock fish
gallo *m* cock, rooster; false note, sour note; (coll.) boss; (box.) bantam weight; (ichth.) dory; **tener mucho gallo** (coll.) to be cocky; **gallo de bosque** (orn.) wood grouse; **gallo del corral** cock of the walk; **gallo de pelea** or **de riña** fighting cock, gamecock; **gallo de roca** (orn.) cock of the rock; **gallo en la garganta** frog in the throat; **gallo silvestre** (orn.) capercaillie, wood grouse
gallocresta *f* (bot.) wild sage, vervain sage
gallofa *f* food for pilgrims; alms, charity; vegetables for salad or soup; French roll; liturgical calendar; talk, gossip
gallofar or **gallofear** *vn* to bum, beg, loaf around
gallofero -ra or **gallofo -fa** *adj* bumming, begging, loafing; *mf* bum, beggar, loafer
gallón *m* sod, turf; (arch.) echinus
gallote -ta *adj* (dial. & Am.) cocky
gama *f* gamma; doe, female fallow deer; (mus. & fig.) gamut
gamado -da *adj* formed with four capital gammas; see **cruz**
gamarra *f* martingale
gamarza *f* (bot.) African rue
gamba *f* (zool.) prawn (*Pandalus*)
gámbaro *m* var. of **cámaro**
gambax *m* (*pl:* **gambax**) acton
gamberrada *f* hooliganism
gamberrismo *m* hooliganism, rowdyism; hooligans, rowdies
gamberro -rra *adj & mf* libertine; *m* hooligan, rowdy, hoodlum, roughneck; *f* (dial.) prostitute
gambesina *f* or **gambesón** *m* acton
gambeta *f* crosscaper; caper, prance
gambetear *vn* to caper, to prance
gambeto *m* cloak, mantle; cap used to keep baby's head straight
gambir *m* (pharm.) gambier
gambito *m* gambit
gamboa *f* (bot.) quince
gambota *f* (naut.) counter timber
gambusino -na *mf* (Am.) prospector; (Am.) adventurer, fortune hunter
gamella *f* bow (*of yoke*); feed trough; camlet (*cloth*); (min.) pan
gamellón *m* trough for treading grapes; long ridge
gametangio *m* (bot.) gametangium
gameto *m* (biol.) gamete
gametofita *f* or **gametofito** *m* (bot.) gametophyte
gametogénesis *f* (biol.) gametogenesis
gamo *m* buck, male fallow deer
gamofilo -la *adj* (bot.) gamophyllous
gamogénesis *f* (biol.) gamogenesis
gamón *m* (bot.) asphodel
gamonal *m* field of asphodel; (Am) landlord; (Am.) powerful and abusive landlord; (Am.) political boss
gamonalismo *m* (Am.) bossism
gamonito *m* shoot, sucker
gamopétalo -la *adj* (bot.) gamopetalous
gamosépalo -la *adj* (bot.) gamosepalous
gamuno -na *adj* buck (*skin*)
gamuza *f* (zool.) chamois; chamois (*leather*); vici, vici kid (*leather*)
gamuzado -da *adj* chamois-colored
gana *f* desire; **darle a uno la (real) gana de** + *inf* (coll.) to feel like + *ger*, e.g., **me da la gana de comer** I feel like eating; **de buena gana** willingly; **de gana** in earnest; willingly; **de mala gana** unwillingly; **tener gana** or **ganas de** + *inf* to feel like + *ger*, to have a mind to + *inf;* **tener ganas a** (coll.) to pick a fight with; **venir en gana a** to come into the head of, e.g., **dice lo que le venga en gana** he says whatever comes into his head
ganadería *f* cattle; cattle ranch; cattle raising, animal husbandry; livestock; brand, stock; (taur.) breeding ranch
ganadero -ra *adj* (pertaining to) cattle, livestock; *mf* cattle dealer; cattle breeder; *m* cattleman
ganado *m* cattle, livestock; stock of bees; (coll.) flock or mob of people; **ganado caballar** horses; **ganado cabrío** goats; **ganado de cerda** swine; **ganado de cría** cattle for breeding; **ganado lanar** sheep; **ganado mayor** cows, bulls, horses, and mules; **ganado menor** sheep, goats, etc.; **ganado menudo** young cattle; **ganado merino** merino sheep; **ganado moreno** swine; **ganado ovejuno** sheep; **ganado porcino** swine; **ganado vacuno** cattle, bovine cattle
ganador -dora *adj* winning; hard-working; *mf* winner; earner
ganancia *f* gain, profit; (elec.) gain; (Am.) extra, bonus; **ganancias y pérdidas** (com.) profit and loss
ganancial *adj* (pertaining to) profit
ganancioso -sa *adj* gainful, profitable; winning; *mf* winner
ganapán *m* errand boy, messenger; drudge; penniless fellow; (coll.) coarse fellow
ganapanería *f* drudgery
ganapierde *m & f* giveaway (*game of checkers*); **jugar al** or **a la ganapierde** to play giveaway
ganar *va* to earn; to gain; to win; to reach; to cross; to beat, defeat; to outstrip, win out over; to take over, to win over; **ganar algo a alguien** to win something from someone; **ganar de comer** to earn a living; *vn* to earn; to improve; *vr* to earn (*e.g., a livelihood*); to win over; (Am.) to hide, take refuge; (Am.) to slip away, disappear
ganchada *f* (Am.) favor
ganchero *m* log driver; gentle mount; (Am.) odd-jobber
ganchete *m* small hook; **a medio ganchete** (coll.) half, half-done; **de medio ganchete** carelessly, sloppily
ganchillo *m* crochet, crochet work; crochet needle; **hacer ganchillo** to crochet
gancho *m* hook; fishhook; coaxer, enticer; pimp; (Am.) hairpin; (Am.) lady's saddle; **echar el gancho a** (coll.) to hook in, to land; **tener gancho** (coll.) to have a way with the men; **gancho de botalones** (naut.) gooseneck
ganchoso -sa or **ganchudo -da** *adj* hooked
gándara *f* low wasteland
gandaya *f* (coll.) bumming, loafing, idleness; netting; **andar a la gandaya, buscar** or **correr la gandaya** or **ir por la gandaya** (coll.) to bum one's way, to be a tramp
gandinga *f* (min.) concentrate, washed fine ore
gandujado *m* accordion pleating
gandujar *va* to pleat, shirr, fold
gandul -dula *adj* (coll.) loafing, idling; (coll.) sly, crafty; *mf* (coll.) loafer, idler
gandulear *vn* to loaf, to idle
gandulería *f* (coll.) loafing, idleness
ganeta *f* (zool.) genet
ganforro -rra *mf* (coll.) scoundrel
ganga *f* (min.) gangue; (orn.) pin-tailed sand grouse; (orn.) upland plover; bargain; cinch, snap
ganglio *m* (anat. & path.) ganglion; **ganglio linfático** (anat.) lymph gland or node
ganglionar *adj* ganglionic
gangocho *m* (Am.) burlap
gangosidad *f* snuffliness, nasality
gangoso -sa *adj* snuffling, nasal

gangrena *f* (path.) gangrene
gangrenar *va & vr* to gangrene
gangrenoso -sa *adj* gangrenous
gangsterismo *m* gangsterism
ganguear *vn* to snuffle, to talk through the nose
gangueo *m* snuffle, talking through the nose
ganguero -ra *adj & mf* var. of **ganguista**
gánguil *m* (naut.) dump scow; (naut.) fishing sailboat with sweep net; sweep net
ganguista *adj* (coll.) bargain-hunting; (coll.) self-seeking; *mf* (coll.) bargain hunter; (coll.) self-seeker; *m* (coll.) lucky fellow
Ganimedes *m* (myth.) Ganymede
ganoideo -a *adj & m* (ichth.) ganoid
ganoso -sa *adj* desirous; (Am.) spirited (*horse*)
gansa *f* see **ganso**
gansada *f* (coll.) stupidity
gansarón *m* (orn.) goose; tall, lanky fellow
ganso -sa *mf* slob, dope, dullard, rube; *m* (orn.) goose; gander; **ganso bravo** wild goose; **ganso de corbata** (orn.) Canada goose; **ganso monjita** (orn.) barnacle goose; **ganso monjita atlántico** (orn.) American brant (*Branta bernicla hrota*); *f* goose (*female*)
Gante *f* Ghent
gantés -tesa *adj* (pertaining to) Ghent; *mf* native or inhabitant of Ghent
ganzúa *f* picklock (*hook; thief*); (coll.) pumper (*of secrets*)
ganzuar §33 *va* to open with a picklock; (coll.) to pump (*secrets*)
gañán *m* farm hand; rough, husky fellow
gañanía *f* gang of farm hands; lodge for farm hands
gañido *m* yelp, yelping; croak, croaking
gañiles *mpl* (zool.) larynx (*of animal*); gills of tunny fish
gañir §25 *vn* to yelp; to croak; (coll.) to wheeze
gañón *m* or **gañote** *m* (coll.) throat, gullet; (dial.) fritter
garabatada *f* hooking; hookful
garabatear *va* to scribble; *vn* to hook; to beat about the bush; to scribble
garabateo *m* hooking; scribbling
garabato *m* hook; pothook (*hooked rod; scrawl*); dibble, weeding hoe; (coll.) charm, winsomeness; **garabatos** *mpl* awkward movements of hands and fingers; **garabato de carnicero** meathook
garabatoso -sa *adj* full of scribbling; winsome
garabito *m* stall in market place; hook
garage *m* or **garaje** *m* garage
garajista *m* garage man
garambaina *f* gaudy trimming; (coll.) trinket; **garambainas** *fpl* simpering, smirking; scribbling
garante *adj* responsible; *mf* guarantor
garantía *f* guarantee, guaranty
garantir §53 *va* to guarantee
garantizar §76 *va* to guarantee
garañón *m* stud jackass; stud camel; libertine; (Am.) stallion
garapacho *m* carapace; wooden or cork bowl
garapiña *f* sugar-coating, icing; embroidered braid or galloon; (Am.) iced pineapple juice
garapiñar *va* to candy; to sugar-coat, to ice (*e.g., a cake*)
garapiñera *f* ice-cream freezer; cooler (*for wine and other drinks*)
garapita *f* net to catch small fish
garapito *m* (ent.) water bug, back swimmer
garapullo *m* paper dart
garatura *f* scraper (*used in tanning*)
garatusa *f* (coll.) coaxing, wheedling
garbancero -ra *adj* (pertaining to the) chickpea; *mf* chickpea dealer
garbanzal *m* chickpea patch
garbanzo *m* (bot.) chickpea (*plant and seed*); **garbanzo negro** (fig.) black sheep
garbanzuelo *m* (vet.) spavin
garbar *va* to sheaf or sheave
garbear *va* (dial.) to sheaf or sheave; *vn* to put on airs, to be full of pretense
garbera *f* (agr.) shock
garbías *mpl* fried cake made of herbs, cheese, eggs, and flour
garbillador -dora *adj* sieving, screening, riddling; *mf* siever, screener, riddler
garbillar *va* to sieve, to screen, to riddle
garbillo *m* sieve, screen, riddle; screened ore, riddled ore
garbino *m* southwest wind
garbo *m* fine bearing, jaunty air; grace, elegance; gallantry, magnanimity
garbón *m* male partridge
garboso -sa *adj* spruce, natty, sprightly, jaunty; generous
garbullo *m* noise, confusion
garcero *m* (Am.) heronry
garceta *f* (orn.) lesser egret (*Egretta garzetta*); side lock (*of hair*)
gardenia *f* (bot.) gardenia
garduño -ña *mf* (coll.) sneak thief; *f* (zool.) stone marten, beech marten
garete; al garete (naut. & fig.) adrift
garfa *f* claw
garfada *f* clawing
garfear *vn* to hook
garfio *m* hook; gaff; **garfios de trepar** climbing irons
gargajeada *f* var. of **gargajeo**
gargajear *vn* to spit phlegm
gargajeo *m* spitting or ejection of phlegm
gargajiento -ta *adj & mf* var. of **gargajoso**
gargajo *m* phlegm
gargajoso -sa *adj* hawking; *mf* hawker (*of phlegm*)
garganta *f* throat; instep; neck, throat (*e.g., of a river, vase*); gorge, ravine; sheath (*of plow*); (arch.) shaft; (arch.) gorge; (bot.) throat; (mach.) groove (*of a sheave*); **tener buena garganta** to have a good voice, to sing well
gargantada *f* throatful (*e.g., of blood*); (coll.) throatful (*swallow*)
gargantear *va* (naut.) to strap; *vn* to warble
garganteo *m* warble, warbling
gargantilla *f* necklace
gárgara *f* gargling; **gárgaras** *fpl* (Am.) gargle (*liquid*); **hacer gárgaras** to gargle
gargarear *vn* (Am.) var. of **gargarizar**
gargarismo *m* gargling; gargle (*liquid*)
gargarizar §76 *vn* to gargle
gárgol *adj* addle (*egg*); *m* gain, croze (*groove*)
gárgola *f* head of flax; (arch.) gargoyle
garguero or **gargüero** *m* gullet; windpipe
garifo -fa *adj* natty, spruce, showy
gariofilea *f* (bot.) wild carnation
garita *f* watchtower; sentry box; porter's lodge; water closet, privy (*with one seat*); cab (*of truck, power shovel, etc.*); railroad-crossing box; hut, hovel; (Am.) octroi; (Am.) city gate; **garita de centinela** sentry box; **garita de señales** (rail.) signal tower
garitear *vn* (coll.) to frequent gambling houses, to hang around gambling joints
garitero *m* owner of a gambling house; gambler
garito *m* gambling den; gambling profits
garla *f* (coll.) talk, chatter, prattle
garlador -dora *adj* (coll.) chattering, prattling; *mf* (coll.) chatterer, prattler
garlar *vn* (coll.) to talk, chatter, prattle
garlito *m* fish trap; (coll.) trap, snare; **caer en el garlito** (coll.) to fall into the trap; **coger en el garlito** (coll.) to catch in the act
garlocha *f* goad, goad stick
garlopa *f* (carp.) jointer plane, trying plane
garlopar *va* (carp.) to plane
garlopín *m* (carp.) jack plane, fore plane
garma *f* (dial.) steep slope
garnacha *f* gown, robe (*e.g., of a judge*); company of strolling players; grenache (*grape; wine*)
garniel *m* muleteer's leather bag; muleteer's girdle
Garona *m* Garonne
garra *f* claw, talon; catch, claw, hook; (fig.) claw (*hand*); **caer en las garras de** (coll.) to fall into the clutches of; **echar la garra a** (coll.) to get one's hands on, to arrest; **sacar de las garras de** (coll.) to free from
garrafa *f* carafe, decanter
garrafal *adj* awful, terrific
garrafiñar *va* (coll.) to snatch, snatch away
garrafón *m* carboy, demijohn
garrama *f* (coll.) filching, stealing
garramar *va* (coll.) to filch, to steal
garrancha *f* (bot.) spadix; (coll.) sword

garranchada *f* or **garranchazo** *m* slash, gash
garrancho *m* broken branch
garranchuelo *m* (bot.) crab grass
garrapata *f* (ent.) chigger, cattle tick, sheep tick; (mil.) disabled horse
garrapatear *vn* to scrawl, scribble
garrapatero *m* (orn.) cowbird, buffalo bird
garrapato *m* pothook, scrawl
garrapiñar *va* var. of **garapiñar**
garrapiñera *f* var. of **garapiñera**
garrar or **garrear** *vn* (naut.) to drag the anchor
garrido -da *adj* handsome, spruce, elegant
garroba *f* carob bean
garrobal *m* growth of carob trees
garrobilla *f* chips of carob wood used for staining
garrocha *f* goad, goad stick; (sport) pole (*used in pole vault*)
garrochear *va* var. of **agarrochar**
garrochón *m* (taur.) lance
garrofa *f* carob bean
garrón *m* spur, talon; paw
garrotal *m* plantation of slips or cuttings of olive trees
garrotazo *m* blow with a cudgel
garrote *m* club, cudgel; garrote (*method of execution; iron collar used for this*); (hort.) olive cutting; (Am.) brake; **dar garrote a** to garrote
garrotero -ra *adj* (Am.) stingy; *m* (Am.) brakeman
garrotillo *m* (path.) croup
garrubia *f* (bot.) black-eyed bean; carob bean
garrucha *f* pulley, sheave
garrucho *m* (naut.) cringle
garrudo -da *adj* big-clawed; (Am.) brawny, husky
garrulador -dora *adj* var. of **gárrulo**
garrulería *f* chatter, prattle
garrulidad *f* garrulity, garrulousness
gárrulo -la *adj* chirping; garrulous; noisy (*said of the wind*); *m* (orn.) jay
garúa *f* (Am.) drizzle
garuar §33 *vn* (Am.) to drizzle
garujo *m* concrete
garulla *f* loose grapes; (coll.) mob, rabble
garullada *f* (coll.) mob, rabble
garzo -za *adj* blue; *m* (bot.) agaric; *f* (orn.) heron; (orn.) crane, blue crane; **garza real** (orn.) heron, gray heron (*Ardea cinerea*)
garzón *m* boy; youth, stripling; (orn.) blue crane, great blue heron
garzota *f* (orn.) night heron; plumage, crest
gas *m* gas; **gas amoníaco** (chem.) ammonia gas; **gas carbónico** (chem.) carbonic-acid gas, carbon dioxide; **gas cloacal** sewer gas; **gas combustible natural** natural gas; **gas de aceite** oil gas; **gas de agua** water gas; **gas de alumbrado** illuminating gas; **gas de carbón** or **de hulla** coal gas; **gas de guerra** (mil.) poison gas; **gas de los pantanos** marsh gas; **gas exhilarante** or **hilarante** laughing gas; **gas inerte** (chem.) inert gas; **gas lacrimógeno** tear gas; **gas mostaza** mustard gas; **gas natural** natural gas; **gas pobre** producer gas; **gas raro** (chem.) rare gas; **gas tóxico** (mil.) poison gas; **gas vesicante** blister gas
gasa *f* gauze, chiffon; crepe (*token of mourning*); **gasa antiséptica** antiseptic gauze; **gasa de alambre** wire gauze
gascón -cona *adj* Gascon; boastful; *mf* Gascon
gasconada *f* gasconade
gasconés -nesa *adj* & *mf* Gascon
gasconismo *m* Gasconism
Gascuña *f* Gascony
gaseamiento *m* gassing
gasear *va* to gas (*to attack, poison, or asphyxiate with gas*); (chem.) to gas
gaseiforme *adj* gasiform
gaseoso -sa *adj* gaseous, gassy; *f* soda water, carbonated water
gasificación *f* gasification
gasificar §59 *va* to gasify; to elate, exalt; *vr* to gasify
gasiforme *adj* var. of **gaseiforme**
gasista *m* gas fitter; gasworker
gasoducto *m* gas pipe line
gasógeno *m* gas generator, gas producer; mixture of benzine and alcohol used for lighting and for removal of spots
gas-oil *m* diesel oil
gasoleno *m* or **gasolina** *f* gasolene or gasoline
gasolinera *f* powerboat, gasoline motor boat; gas station, filling station
gasómetro *m* gasometer; gasholder, gas tank
Gaspar *m* Jasper
gastable *adj* expendable
gastadero *m* (coll.) waster (*way of wasting time, money, patience, etc.*)
gastado -da *adj* used up; worn-out; spent; crummy (*joke*)
gastador -dora *adj* & *mf* spendthrift; *m* convict; (mil.) sapper, pioneer, axeman
gastadura *f* rub, wear, worn spot
gastamiento *m* waste; wear; consumption
gastar *va* to spend; to waste; to wear; to wear out; to be hard on (*e.g., shoes*); to use up; to lay waste; to always show; to wear (*e.g., a beard*); to keep (*e.g., a carriage*); to play (*a joke*); **gastarlas** (coll.) to act, to behave; *vn* to spend; **gastar de** to spend; *vr* to waste away; to wear; to wear out; to become used up
gasterópodo -da *adj* & *m* var. of **gastrópodo**
gasto *m* cost, expense; wear; flow, rate of flow; **cubrir gastos** to cover expenses; **hacer el gasto** (coll.) to do most of the talking; (coll.) to be the subject of conversation; **pagar los gastos** to foot the bill; **gastos de conservación** or **de entretenimiento** upkeep, maintenance; **gastos de explotación** operating expenses; **gastos de primer establecimiento** initial expenses, initial costs; **gastos de representación** incidental expenses, allowances; **gastos de sostenimiento** upkeep, maintenance; **gastos menudos** petty expenses
gastoso -sa *adj* spendthrift, extravagant
gastralgia *f* (path.) gastralgia
gastrectomía *f* (surg.) gastrectomy
gástrico -ca *adj* gastric
gastritis *f* (path.) gastritis
gastroenteritis *f* (path.) gastroenteritis
gastroenterología *f* gastroenterology
gastrointestinal *adj* gastrointestinal
gastronomía *f* gastronomy
gastronómico -ca *adj* gastronomic or gastronomical
gastrónomo -ma *mf* gastronome or gastronomer, gourmet
gastrópodo -da *adj* & *m* (zool.) gastropod
gastrovascular *adj* gastrovascular
gástrula *f* (embryol.) gastrula
gata *f* she-cat; low-hanging cloud on mountainside; (bot.) restharrow; (coll.) woman of Madrid; (Am.) working girl; **a gatas** on all fours; **gata parida** (coll.) skeleton (*skinny person*)
gatada *f* catlike act; cats; litter of cats; sudden turn of a hare when pursued; (coll.) sly trick
gatallón -llona *adj* (coll.) scoundrelly; *mf* (coll.) scoundrel
gatatumba *f* (coll.) fake respect, fake emotion, fake pain
gatazo *m* (coll.) gyp; **dar gatazo a** (coll.) to gyp
gateado -da *adj* catlike; cat-colored; grained; striped; *m* creeping, crawling, climbing; (coll.) scratching, clawing; gateado (*tropical American cabinet wood*)
gateamiento *m* creeping, crawling, climbing; (coll.) scratching, clawing
gatear *va* (coll.) to scratch, to claw; (coll.) to snitch; *vn* to creep, crawl, climb, go on all fours
gatera *f* see **gatero**
gatería *f* (coll.) cats; (coll.) gang of roughnecks; (coll.) hypocrisy, fake humility
gatero -ra *adj* full of cats; *mf* cat dealer; cat lover; *f* cathole; hiding place; (naut.) hawsehole
gatesco -ca *adj* (coll.) catlike, feline
gatillazo *m* click of trigger; **dar gatillazo** (coll.) to be disappointing, to be a flop
gatillo *m* trigger; hammer, cock (*of firearm*); dentist's forceps; clamp; nape (*of bull*); (coll.) little pickpocket

gato *m* (zool.) cat; tomcat; jack, lifting jack; hooking tongs; moneybag; clamp; sly fellow; sneak thief; (coll.) native of Madrid; (Am.) outdoor market; (Am.) hot-water bottle; **dar** or **vender gato por liebre** (coll.) to cheat, to gyp; **gato cazador** mouser; **gato de algalia** (zool.) civet cat; **gato de Angora** Angora cat; **gato de cremallera** rack-and-pinion jack, ratchet jack; **gato de nueve colas** cat-o'-nine-tails; **gato desmurador** mouser; **gato de tornillo** screw jack, jackscrew; **gato encerrado** something fishy **(coll.)**; **gato hidráulico** hydraulic jack; **gato maltés** Maltese cat; **gato manés** Manx cat; **gato montés** (zool.) wildcat; **gato rodante** dolly; **gato volador** or **volante** (zool.) flying cat, flying lemur
gatuno -na *adj* cat, catlike; *f* (bot.) restharrow
gatuña *f* (bot.) restharrow
gatuperio *m* hodgepodge; (coll.) trick, scheme, intrigue
gauchada *f* (Am.) Gaucho stunt, sly trick; (Am.) kindness, favor
gauchaje *m* (Am.) gathering of Gauchos, gang of Gauchos
gauchesco -ca *adj* Gaucho
gaucho -cha *adj* warped, uneven; sly, crafty; coarse, rude; (Am.) Gaucho; *m* (Am.) Gaucho; (Am.) good horseman; *f* (Am.) mannish woman; (Am.) loose woman
gaudeamus *m* (*pl:* **-mus**) (coll.) feasting, celebrating, merrymaking
gaulteria *f* (bot.) gaultheria, wintergreen
gausio *m* (phys.) gauss
gavaje *m* gavage
gavanza *f* dog rose (*flower*)
gavanzo *m* (bot.) dog rose
gaveta *f* drawer, till; (aut.) glove compartment
gavetero *m* furniture maker
gavia *f* ditch, drain; (naut.) topsail; (naut.) maintopsail; (orn.) gull; (min.) gang of basket passers
gavial *m* (zool.) gavial
gaviero *m* (naut.) topman, mastman
gavieta *f* (naut.) mizzenmast crow's-nest, bowsprit crow's-nest
gaviete *m* (naut.) cathead
gavilán *m* (orn.) sparrow hawk; nib (*of pen*); quillon (*of cross guard of sword*); hair stroke (*in writing*); pappus; metal tip (*of a goad*); (Am.) ingrowing nail
gavilla *f* sheaf, bundle; gang of thugs
gavillero *m* row of sheaves
gavina *f* var. of **gaviota**
gavión *m* (fort. & hyd.) gabion; (coll.) big wide hat
gaviota *f* (orn.) gull, herring gull; **gaviota salteadora** (orn.) jaeger
gaviotín *m* (orn.) tern (*Sterna hirundo*)
gavota *f* gavotte (*dance and music*)
gaya *f* see **gayo**
gayadura *f* colored stripes, colored striping
gayar *va* to trim with colored stripes
gayo -ya *adj* gay, bright, showy; *m* (orn.) bluejay; *f* colored stripe; (orn.) magpie
gayola *f* cage; (coll.) jail; (prov.) raised lookout in a vineyard
gayomba *f* (bot.) Spanish broom; (bot.) yellow lupine
gayuba *f* (bot.) bearberry
gayubal *m* bearberry field
gaza *f* (naut.) loop, bend
gazafatón *m* (coll.) var. of **gazapatón**
gazapa *f* (coll.) lie
gazapatón *m* (coll.) bloomer (*in speech*)
gazapera *f* rabbit warren; (coll.) gang, gang of thugs; (coll.) brawl, row; (vet.) distemper (*of cats*)
gazapina *f* (coll.) gang, gang of thugs; (coll.) brawl, row
gazapo *m* young rabbit; sly fellow; slip, error; squatty person; (coll.) big lie
gazmiar *vn* to nibble all the time; *vr* (coll.) to complain
gazmoñada or **gazmoñería** *f* priggishness
gazmoñero -ra or **gazmoño -ña** *adj* priggish, strait-laced, demure; *mf* prig
gaznápiro -ra *mf* gawk, boob
gaznar *vn* var. of **graznar**
gaznatada *f* or **gaznatazo** *m* punch in the gullet
gaznate *m* gullet, throttle; fritter
gaznatón *m* punch in the gullet; fritter
gazné *m* (Am.) large colored kerchief
gazpacho *m* cold vegetable soup, gazpacho
gazuza *f* (coll.) hunger
gea *f* description of the minerals of a region; (*cap.*) *f* (myth.) Gaea
geco *m* (zool.) gecko, tarente
Gedeón *m* (Bib.) Gideon
gedeonada *f* (coll.) platitude, commonplace
gehena *m* (Bib.) Gehenna
géiser *m* geyser
geisha *f* geisha
gel *m* (chem. & phys.) gel
gelación *f* gelation
gelatina *f* gelatin
gelatinificar §86 *va* to gelatinize
gelatinoso -sa *adj* gelatinous
gélido -da *adj* gelid, frigid
gelsemio *m* (bot.) yellow jasmine; (pharm.) gelsemium
gema *f* gem, precious stone; (bot.) bud, gemma; wane (*of board or plank*)
gemación *f* (bot. & zool.) gemmation
gemebundo -da *adj* full of groans
gemelo -la *adj* & *mf* twin; *m* (anat.) gemellus; **gemelos** *mpl* twins; binoculars; cuff links, set of buttons; **Gemelos** *mpl* (astr.) Gemini (*constellation*); **gemelos de campo** field glasses; **gemelos de teatro** opera glasses; **gemelos fraternos** fraternal twins; **gemelos homólogos** or **idénticos** identical twins; **gemelos heterólogos** fraternal twins; *f* (bot.) Arabian jasmine
gemido *m* moan, groan; wail, whine; howl, roar, whistle; (poet.) sigh
gemidor -dora *adj* moaning, groaning; wailing, whining; howling, roaring, whistling
gemífero -ra *adj* gemmiferous, full of gems or precious stones; (bot.) gemmate; (bot. & zool.) gemmiferous
gemificar §86 *vn* (bot.) to gemmate
geminación *f* gemination; (phonet. & rhet.) gemination
geminado -da *adj* geminate
geminar *va* & *vr* to geminate
Géminis *m* (astr.) Gemini (*constellation and sign of zodiac*); (*l.c.*) *m* (pharm.) plaster (*of ceruse and wax*)
gemíparo -ra *adj* (biol.) gemmiparous
gemiquear *vn* (dial. & Am.) to whine
gemiqueo *m* (dial. & Am.) whining
gemir §94 *vn* to moan, groan; to wail, whine; to howl, roar, whistle; to pine away, to grieve
gémula *f* (bot., zool. & biol.) gemmule
gen *m* (biol.) gene
genciana *f* (bot.) gentian (*plant and root*); **genciana amarilla** (bot.) bitterwort
gencianáceo -a *adj* (bot.) gentianaceous
gencianilla *f* (bot.) bitterwort
gendarme *m* gendarme
gendarmería *f* gendarmerie
genealogía *f* genealogy
genealógico -ca *adj* genealogical
genealogista *mf* genealogist
generación *f* generation; **generación espontánea** (biol.) spontaneous generation
generador -dora *adj* generating; *mf* generator; *m* (elec.) generator (*dynamo*); (mach.) generator (*steam boiler, etc.*); **generador de barrido** (telv.) sweep generator
general *adj* general; vast, enormous; widely informed; *m* (mil.) general, general officer; (rel.) general; **en general** or **por lo general** in general; **general de brigada** (mil.) brigadier general; **general de división** (mil.) major general; **general en jefe** (mil.) general in chief; **generales** *fpl* personal data (*such as name, age, nationality*)
generala *f* general's wife; call to arms
generalato *m* generalship; generals of an army
generalero *m* (prov.) customhouse officer
generalidad *f* generality; bulk, majority; Catalan legislative assembly; (prov.) custom duties
generalísimo *m* generalissimo
generalización *f* generalization
generalizador -dora *adj* generalizing

generalizar §76 *va & vn* to generalize; *vr* to become generalized
generar *va* to generate; (elec.) to generate
generativo -va *adj* generative
generatriz *f* (*pl:* **-trices**) (elec. & geom.) generatrix
genérico -ca *adj* generic; (gram.) indefinite (*article*); (gram.) common (*noun*); (gram.) indicating gender (*said of an ending*)
género *m* kind, sort; manner, way; material (*textile fabric*); (biol. & log.) genus; (f.a. & lit.) genre; (gram.) gender; **géneros** *mpl* material, goods, merchandise; **de género** (f.a.) genre, e.g., **pintor de género** genre painter; **género chico** (theat.) one-act comedy; **género de punto** knit goods, knitwear; **género humano** humankind, human race; **género ínfimo** (theat.) light vaudeville; **género novelístico** fiction; **género picaresco** (theat.) burlesque; **género tipo** (biol.) type genus
generosidad *f* generosity
generoso -sa *adj* generous; highborn; brave; excellent, superb; warm (*heart*); generous, rich (*wine*)
genésico -ca *adj* genesic
génesis *f* (*pl:* **-sis**) genesis; **el Génesis** (Bib.) Genesis
geneticista *mf* geneticist
genético -ca *adj* genetic; *f* genetics
genetista *mf* geneticist
geniado -da *adj* tempered; **bien geniado** well-tempered, good-natured; **mal geniado** ill-tempered
genial *adj* inspired, brilliant, genius-like; cheerful, pleasant; temperamental
genialidad *f* peculiarity; genius
geniano -na *adj* (anat. & zool.) genial
geniazo *m* (coll.) strong temper
genicida *adj & mf* var. of **genocida**
genicidio *m* var. of **genocidio**
geniculación *f* geniculation
geniculado -da *adj* geniculate
geniecillo *m* (coll.) strong temper; (f.a.) cupid
genio *m* temper; disposition, temperament; genius; character, force; (myth.) genie, jinni; (coll.) fire, spirit
genioso -sa *adj* ill-natured
genipa *f* (bot.) genipap
genista *f* (bot.) Spanish broom; (bot.) genista
genital *adj* genital; **genitales** *mpl* (anat.) testicles; (anat.) genitals
genitivo -va *adj & m* (gram.) genitive
génitourinario -ria *adj* genitourinary
genízaro -ra *adj & m* var. of **jenízaro**
Genl abr. of **general**
genocida *adj* genocidal; *mf* genocide (*person*)
genocidio *m* genocide (*act*)
genol *m* (naut.) futtock
genoma *m* (biol.) genom
genotipo *m* (biol.) genotype
Génova *f* Genoa
genovés -vesa *adj & mf* Genoese
Genoveva *f* Genevieve, Winifred
gente *f* people; troops; (naut.) complement; (coll.) folks (*relatives*); **de gente en gente** from generation to generation; **hacer gente** to recruit; (coll.) to draw a crowd; **la gente chic** the smart set; **ser gente** (Am.) to be somebody; **gente baja** lower classes, rabble; **gente bien** (coll.) nice people; **gente de alpargata** simple folk; **gente de barrio** loafers; **gente de bien** decent people; **gente de blusa** working people; **gente be bronce** gypsies; **gente de capa negra** (coll.) decent citizens; **gente de capa parda** (coll.) countryfolk; **gente de carda** or **de la carda** (coll.) scoundrels, bullies; **gente de coleta** (coll.) bullfighters; **gente de color** colored people; **gente de escalera abajo** (coll.) underdogs; **gente de gallaruza** (coll.) countryfolk; **gente de gavilla** crooks, thugs; **gente de la cuchilla** (coll.) butchers; **gente de la garra** (coll.) thieves; **gente de la vida airada** bullies, libertines; **gente del bronce** (coll.) lively people; **gente del gordillo** common people, plebeians; **gente del polvillo** (coll.) masons; **gente de pardillo** or **del pardillo** country people, peasants; **gente del rey** convicts; **gente de mal vivir** thugs, underworld; **gente de mar** seafaring people; **gente de medio pelo** people of limited means; **gente de paz** friend (*in answer to "Who is there?"*); **gente de pelo** or **de pelusa** (coll.) well-to-do people; **gente de pluma** (coll.) clerks; **gente de poco más o menos** (coll.) nincompoop, nobody; **gente de razón** (Am.) white people; **gente de seguida** gangsters, bandits; **gente de su majestad** convicts; **gente de toda broza** (coll.) loafers, bums; **gente de trato** tradespeople; **gente de traza** responsible people; **gente forzada** convicts; **gente gorda** (coll.) people of standing; **gente menuda** (coll.) small fry; (coll.) common people; **gente perdida** bums; **gente principal** outstanding people
gentecilla *f* mob, rabble
gentil *adj* gentile, heathen; genteel, elegant; strange, wondrous; terrific; *mf* gentile, heathen
gentileza *f* gentility, elegance, politeness; gallantry; show, splendor; ease, smoothness; **gentilezas** *fpl* beauties, adornments (*of language, style, etc.*)
gentilhombre *m* (*pl:* **gentileshombres**) gentleman (*attendant to person of high rank*); messenger to the king; kind sir, my good man; **gentilhombre de cámara** gentleman in waiting
gentilicio -cia *adj* national; family; (gram.) gentile; *m* (gram.) gentile
gentílico -ca *adj* heathenish
gentilidad *f* or **gentilismo** *m* heathendom
gentilizar §76 *va* to heathenize; *vn* to observe heathen rites
gentío *m* crowd, throng, mob
gentualla or **gentuza** *f* rabble, scum of society
genuflexión *f* genuflection or genuflexion
genuino -na *adj* genuine
geocéntrico -ca *adj* geocentric or geocentrical
geoda *f* (geol.) geode
geodesia *f* geodesy
geodésico -ca *adj* geodesic, geodetic
geodesta *mf* geodesist
geofagía *f* geophagy
geofísico -ca *adj* geophysical; *mf* geophysicist; *f* geophysics
geófita *f* (bot.) geophyte
Geofredo *m* Geoffrey
geognosia *f* geognosy
geografía *f* geography; **geografía física** physical geography; **geografía lingüística** linguistic geography
geográfico -ca *adj* geographic or geographical
geógrafo -fa *mf* geographer
geoide *m* geoid
geología *f* geology
geológico -ca *adj* geologic or geological
geólogo -ga *mf* geologist
geomagnético -ca *adj* geomagnetic
geomancía *f* geomancy
geomántico -ca *adj* geomantic; *mf* geomancer
geómetra *mf* geometer, geometrician; *m* (zool.) geometer, inchworm, measuring worm
geometral *adj* var. of **geométrico**
geometría *f* geometry; **geometría analítica** analytic geometry; **geometría del** or **en el espacio** solid geometry; **geometría euclidiana** Euclidian geometry; **geometría no euclidiana** non-Euclidian geometry; **geometría plana** plane geometry; **geometría proyectiva** projective geometry
geométrico -ca *adj* geometric or geometrical
geométrido *m* (ent.) geometrid
geometrizar §76 *va* to geometrize; *vn* to geometrize; (coll.) to pretend to be a geometrician
geomorfología *f* geomorphology
geopolítico -ca *adj* geopolitical; *f* geopolitics
geoponía *f* geoponics
geopónico -ca *adj* geoponic; *f* geoponics
geoquímica *f* geochemistry
georama *m* georama
georgiano -na *adj & mf* Georgian
geórgica *f* georgic (*poem*)
Georgina *f* Georgiana, Georgina (*woman's name*)
geosinclinal *adj & m* (geol.) geosynclinal
geotactismo *m* or **geotaxia** *f* geotaxis
geotectónico -ca *adj* geotectonic; *f* geotectonics

geotérmico -ca *adj* geothermal
geotrópico -ca *adj* geotropic
geotropismo *m* (biol.) geotropism
geraniáceo -a *adj* (bot.) geraniaceous
geranio *m* (bot.) geranium; **geranio de rosa** (bot.) rose geranium; **geranio malva** (bot.) nutmeg geranium
Gerardo *m* Gerald, Gerard
gerbo *m* var. of **jerbo**
gerencia *f* management; managership, directorship; manager's office
gerente *m* manager, director; **gerente de publicidad** advertising manager; **gerente de ventas** sales manager
geriatría *f* geriatrics
geriatra *adj* geriatrical; *mf* geriatrician, geriatrist
geriátrico -ca *adj* geriatrical
gerifalte *m* (orn.) gerfalcon; (slang) thief; **como un gerifalte** superbly
germandrina *f* (bot.) germander, wall germander
germanesco -ca *adj* slang, gypsy
Germania *f* (hist. & fig.) Germania
germanía *f* slang or jargon of gypsies and thieves
germánico -ca *adj* Germanic; *m* Germanic (*group of languages*)
germanio *m* (chem.) germanium
germanismo *m* Germanism
germanista *mf* Germanist
germanización *f* Germanization
germanizar §76 *va & vr* to Germanize
germano -na *adj* Germanic, Teutonic; *mf* German, Teuton; *m* brother-german
germanófilo -la *adj & mf* Germanophile
germanófobo -ba *adj & mf* Germanophobe
germen *m* (bact., biol., embryol. & fig.) germ; **germen plasma** germ plasm
germicida *adj* germicidal; *m* germicide
germinación *f* germination
germinador -dora *adj* germinating; *m* germinator
germinal *adj* germinal; germ
germinante *adj* germinant
germinar *vn* to germinate
germinativo -va *adj* germinative
germón *m* (ichth.) albacore (*Germo alalunga*)
gerontología *f* gerontology
Gertrudis *f* Gertrude
gerundense *adj* (pertaining to) Gerona; *mf* native or inhabitant of Gerona
gerundiada *f* (coll.) bombastic expression
gerundiano -na *adj* (coll.) bombastic
gerundino *m* gerundive (*in Latin grammar*)
gerundio *m* gerund, present participle; (coll.) bombastic writer or speaker
gesta *f* (archaic) gest (*metrical romance; feat, exploit*)
gestación *f* gestation; (fig.) gestation
gestaltismo *m* Gestalt psychology
gestapo *f* Gestapo (*Nazi secret police*)
gestatorio -ria *adj* gestatory; gestatorial (*chair*)
gestear *vn* var. of **gesticular**
gestería *f* crudity, vulgarity
gesticulación *f* face; grimace
gesticular *vn* to make a face, to make faces; to gesture
gestión *f* step, measure; management
gestionar *va* to pursue, prosecute, strive for; to manage; to take steps to attain or to accomplish
gesto *m* face; grimace, wry face; look, appearance; gesture; **estar de buen gesto** to be in a good humor; **estar de mal gesto** to be in a bad humor; **hacer gestos** to make faces; to gesture; **hacer gestos a** to make faces at; to look askance at; **poner gesto** to look annoyed; **gesto de manos** gesture
gestor -tora *adj* managing; *m* manager
gestoría *f* management
gestudo -da *adj* (coll.) cross-looking
Getsemaní *m* (Bib.) Gethsemane
ghetto *m* ghetto
giba *f* hump; (coll.) annoyance, inconvenience
gibado -da *adj* humped, hunchbacked
gibar *va* to hump, to hunch; (coll.) to annoy, bother
gibelino -na *adj & m* Ghibelline
gibón *m* (zool.) gibbon
gibosidad *f* gibbosity
giboso -sa *adj* gibbous, humped
Gibraltar Gibraltar
gibraltareño -ña *adj* (pertaining to) Gibraltar; *mf* native or inhabitant of Gibraltar
giga *f* jig (*dance and music*)
giganta *f* giantess; (bot.) sunflower
gigante *adj* giant, gigantic; *m* giant; giant figure (*in a procession*); (slang) middle finger; **gigante en tierra de enanos** (coll.) little runt; (coll.) big fish in a little pond
giganteo -a *adj* gigantean; *f* (bot.) sunflower
gigantesco -ca *adj* gigantic
gigantez *f* giantism; gigantic size
gigantilla *f* little giantess; big-headed masked figure; little fat girl; little fat woman
gigantismo *m* (path.) giantism or gigantism
gigantón -tona *mf* huge giant; *m* giant figure (*in a procession*); **echar los gigantones a** (coll.) to rake over the coals
gigote *m* chopped-meat stew; **hacer gigote** (coll.) to chop into small pieces
gijonense or **gijonés -nesa** *adj* (pertaining to) Gijón; *mf* native or inhabitant of Gijón
Gil *m* Giles
gilbertio *m* (phys.) gilbert
Gilberto *m* Gilbert
gilí *adj* (*pl:* **-líes**) (coll.) foolish, stupid
gilvo -va *adj* honey-colored
gimnasia *f* gymnastics; **gimnasia sueca** calisthenics, light gymnastics, setting-up exercise
gimnasio *m* gymnasium
gimnasta *mf* gymnast
gimnástico -ca *adj* gymnastic; *f* gymnastics
gímnico -ca *adj* athletic, gymnastic
gimnospermo -ma *adj* gymnospermous; *f* (bot.) gymnosperm
gimnoto *m* (ichth.) electric eel
gimotear *vn* (coll.) to whine
gimoteo *m* (coll.) whining
ginandro -dra *adj* (bot.) gynandrous
ginebra *f* gin (*drink*); bedlam; din; (mus.) xylophone; (*cap.*) *f* Geneva; (myth.) Guinevere; **ginebra holandesa** Holland gin
ginebrada *f* puff-paste pie
ginebrés -bresa or **ginebrino -na** *adj & mf* Genevan or Genevese
gineceo *m* (bot.) gynoecium, gynaeceum; (hist.) gynaeceum (*women's apartments*)
ginecología *f* gynecology
ginecológico -ca *adj* gynecological
ginecólogo -ga *mf* gynecologist
ginesta *f* (bot.) Spanish broom
gineta *f* (zool.) genet
gingidio *m* (bot.) bishop's-weed
gingival *adj* gingival
gingivitis *f* (path.) gingivitis
gínglimo *m* (anat.) ginglymus, hinge joint
gingo *m* (bot.) gingko
giniatría *f* gyniatrics
ginóforo *m* (bot.) gynophore
ginsén *m* (bot.) ginseng (*plant and root*)
gipsófila *f* (bot.) gypsophila, babies'-breath
gira *f* var. of **jira**
girado -da *mf* (com.) drawee
girador -dora *mf* (com.) drawer
giralda *f* weathercock (*in form of person or animal*); **la Giralda** the Giralda (*square tower of cathedral of Seville, Spain, surmounted by bronze statue of Faith, which turns in the wind*)
giraldete *m* (eccl.) sleeveless rochet
giraldilla *f* small weathercock
giramachos *m* (*pl:* **-chos**) tap wrench
girándula *f* girandole
girante *adj* revolving
girar *va* to pay (*a visit*); (com.) to draw; *vn* to turn; to gyrate, to rotate; to revolve; to trade; (com.) to draw
girasol *m* (bot.) sunflower; sycophant
giratorio -ria *adj* revolving; gyratory; *f* revolving bookcase
giravión *m* gyroplane
girino *m* (ent.) whirligig; (obs.) tadpole
giro -ra *adj* (Am.) black-and-white (*cock*); yellow (*cock*); (Am.) cocky; *m* turn; gyration, rotation; revolution; turn, trend, course;

threat, boast; gash, slash; expression; turn (*of phrase*); line (*of business*); trade; (com.) draft; **giro a la vista** (com.) sight draft; **giro electrónico** (phys.) spin, electron spin; **giro postal** money order; *f* var. of **jira**
giroaleta *f* (naut.) gyrofin
girocompás *m* gyrocompass
giroestabilizador *m* (aer. & naut.) gyrostabilizer
giroflé *m* (bot.) clove
girola *f* (arch.) apse aisle
girómetro *m* gyrometer
girón *m* var. of **jirón**
girondino -na *adj & m* (hist.) Girondist
giropiloto *m* (aer.) gyropilot
giroplano *m* (aer.) gyroplane
giroscópico -ca *adj* gyroscopic
giroscopio or **giróscopo** *m* gyroscope
girostático -ca *adj* gyrostatic; *f* gyrostatics
giróstato *m* gyrostat
gis *m* (archaic) chalk; (Am.) slate pencil
giste *m* var. of **jiste**
gitanada *f* gypsylike trick; fawning, flattery
gitanear *vn* to lead the life of a gypsy; to fawn, to flatter
gitanería *f* fawning, flattery; band of gypsies; gypsy life; gypsyism
gitanesco -ca *adj* gypsy, gypsyish
gitanismo *m* gypsies; gypsy life, gypsy lore; gypsyism
gitano -na *adj* gypsy; sly, tricky; flattering, honey-mouthed; *mf* gypsy; *m* Gypsy (*language*)
glabro -bra *adj* (bot. & zool.) glabrous
glaciación *f* glaciation, freezing
glacial *adj* glacial; frigid (*zone*); (chem.) glacial; (fig.) cold, indifferent
glaciar *m* glacier
glaciario -ria *adj* glacial
glacis *m* (*pl:* **-cis**) glacis; (fort.) glacis
gladiador *m* or **gladiator** *m* gladiator
gladiatorio -ria *adj* gladiatorial
gladio *m* (bot.) cattail, reed mace; (zool.) gladius
gladíolo *m* (bot.) cattail, reed mace; (bot.) gladiolus; (anat.) gladiolus (*mesosternum*)
glande *m* (anat.) glans penis
glándula *f* (anat. & bot.) gland; **glándula carótida** (anat.) carotid gland; **glándula cerrada** (anat.) ductless gland; **glándula endocrina** (anat.) endocrine gland; **glándula lagrimal** (anat.) lachrymal gland; **glándula mamaria** (anat.) mammary gland; **glándula paratiroides** (anat.) parathyroid gland; **glándula pineal** (anat.) pineal gland; **glándula pituitaria** (anat.) pituitary gland; **glándula prostática** (anat.) prostate gland; **glándula salival** (anat.) salivary gland; **glándula sebácea** (anat.) sebaceous gland; **glándula submaxilar** (anat.) submaxillary gland; **glándula sudorípara** (anat.) sweat gland; **glándula suprarrenal** (anat.) adrenal gland, suprarenal gland; **glándula tiroides** (anat.) thyroid gland
glandular *adj* glandular
glanduloso -sa *adj* glandulous
glasé *m* glacé silk
glaseado -da *adj* glacé; glossy, shiny
glasear *va* to calender, to satin; to glacé (*fruit, leather, etc.*); (paint.) to glaze
glasto *m* (bot.) woad
glauberita *f* (chem.) glauberite
glaucio *m* (bot.) horn poppy
glauco -ca *adj* glaucous; (bot.) glaucous; *m* (zool.) glaucus, sea slug
glaucoma *m* (path.) glaucoma
glaucomatoso -sa *adj* glaucomatous; *mf* sufferer from glaucoma
gleba *f* clod or lump of earth turned over by plow; estate, landed property
glena *f* (anat.) glenoid cavity
glenoideo -a *adj* glenoid
glera *f* gravel pit
glicérico *adj* (chem.) glyceric
glicérido *m* (chem.) glyceride
glicerilo *m* (chem.) glyceryl
glicerina *f* glycerin
glicerol *m* (chem.) glycerol
glicina *f* (bot.) Chinese wistaria; (chem.) glycine
glicogénico -ca *adj* glycogenic
glicógeno *m* (biochem.) glycogen
glicol *m* (chem.) glycol
glifo *m* (arch.) glyph
glioma *m* (path.) glioma
gliptografía *f* glyptography
global *adj* total; global, world-wide
globo *m* globe; balloon; globe, lamp shade; cell (*of dirigible*); **en globo** as a whole; in broad outlines; in bulk; **globo aerostático** balloon; **globo barrera** (mil.) barrage balloon; **globo cautivo** captive balloon; **globo celeste** (astr.) celestial globe; **globo cometa** kite balloon; **globo de fuego** (astr.) bolide; **globo del ojo** (anat.) eyeball; **globo de observación** observation balloon; **globo libre** free balloon; **globo piloto** pilot balloon; **globo sonda** sounding balloon, trial balloon; (fig.) trial balloon (*statement made to test public opinion*); **globo terráqueo** or **terrestre** globe (*earth; map of earth in form of sphere*)
globoso -sa *adj* globose, globate
globular *adj* globular; *va* to make round, to shape like a globe
globulina *f* (biochem.) globulin; **globulina gama** (physiol.) gamma globulin
glóbulo *m* globule; (bot.) globule; (physiol.) corpuscle; **glóbulo blanco** (physiol.) white corpuscle; **glóbulo rojo** (physiol.) red corpuscle
globuloso -sa *adj* globulose
glogló *m* var. of **gluglú**
glomérula *f* (bot.) glomerule
glomérulo *m* (anat.) glomerulus
gloria *f* glory; gloria (*fabric; halo*); ladylock (*pastry*); **estar en sus glorias** (coll.) to be in one's glory; **ganar la gloria** to go to glory (*to die*); **oler a gloria** (coll.) to smell heavenly; **saber a gloria** (coll.) to taste heavenly; (*cap.*) *m* (eccl.) Gloria
gloriar §90 *va* to glory, to glorify; *vr* to glory; **gloriarse de** to glory in (*e.g., one's achievements*); **gloriarse en** to glory in (*e.g., the Lord*)
glorieta *f* arbor, bower, summerhouse; square, public square; traffic circle
glorificable *adj* glorifiable
glorificación *f* glorification
glorificar §86 *va* to glorify; *vr* to be covered with glory; to glory
glorioso -sa *adj* glorious; proud, boastful; *f* (bot.) glory lily; **echar de la gloriosa** to boast of one's exploits, to show off; **la Gloriosa** the Virgin
glosa *f* gloss; gloss (*form of poem*); (mus.) variation
glosador -dora *adj* glossing; glossatorial; *mf* glosser; *m* glossator
glosar *va* to gloss; (Am.) to scold; *vn* to gloss; to find fault
glosario *m* glossary
glose *m* glossing, commenting
glosectomía *f* (surg.) glossectomy
glosis *f* (zool.) glossa
glositis *f* (path.) glossitis
glosopeda *f* (vet.) foot-and-mouth disease
glótico -ca *adj* glottal
glotis *f* (*pl:* **-tis**) (anat.) glottis
glotón -tona *adj* gluttonous; *mf* glutton; *m* (zool.) glutton (*Gulo gulo*)
glotonear *vn* to be gluttonous, to gormandize
glotonería *f* gluttony
gloxínea *f* (bot.) gloxinia
glucina *f* (chem.) glucina
glucinio *m* (chem.) glucinium or glucinum
glucoproteína *f* (biochem.) glycoprotein
glucosa *f* (biochem.) glucose
glucósido *m* (chem.) glucoside
glucosuria *f* (path.) glycosuria
gluglú *m* gurgle, glug; gobble (*of turkey*); **hacer gluglú** to gurgle, to glug
gluglutear *vn* to gobble (*said of a turkey*)
gluma *f* (bot.) glume
gluten *m* gluten
glutenoso -sa *adj* glutenous
glúteo -a *adj* (anat.) gluteal
glutinoso -sa *adj* glutinous
gnatión *m* (anat.) gnathion
gneis *m* (geol.) gneiss

gnéisico -ca *adj* gneissic
gnómico -ca *adj* gnomic
gnomo *m* gnome; (myth.) gnome
gnomon *m* gnomon
gnosticismo *m* Gnosticism
gnóstico -ca *adj & mf* Gnostic
gnu *m* var. of **ñu**
goa *f* (metal.) pig, bloom
gob. abr. of **gobierno**
gobelino *m* goblin
gobernable *adj* governable
gobernación *f* governing; government; interior, department of the interior; (Am.) territory
gobernador -dora *adj* governing; *m* governor; *f* woman governor; governor's wife
gobernalle *m* rudder, helm
gobernante *adj* ruling; *mf* ruler; *m* (coll.) self-appointed head
gobernar §18 *va* to govern; to guide, direct; to control, rule; to steer; *vn* to govern; to steer, e.g., **este buque no gobierna bien** this boat does not steer well
gobernoso -sa *adj* (coll.) orderly
gobierna *f* weather vane
gobierno *m* government; governor's office, governor's residence; governership; management, control, rule; guidance; navigability (*of a ship*); **de buen gobierno** navigable (*ship*); **para su gobierno** for your guidance; **servir de gobierno** (coll.) to serve as guide; **gobierno de monigotes** puppet government; **gobierno doméstico** housekeeping; **gobierno exilado** government in exile; **gobierno local** local government; **gobierno títere** puppet government
gobio *m* (ichth.) gudgeon; (ichth.) goby
gob.no or **gob.o** abr. of **gobierno**
gob.r abr. of **gobernador**
goce *m* enjoyment
gocete *m* (archaic) collar of mail; (archaic) shield of mail for armpit
gocho -cha *mf* (coll.) hog
godesco -ca *adj* gay, merry
godo -da *adj* Gothic; *mf* Goth; Spanish noble; (Am. scornful) Spaniard
Godofredo *m* Godfrey
goecia *f* black magic
gofo -fa *adj* stupid, crude; (paint.) dwarf (*figure*)
gol *m* (football) goal
gola *f* gullet; (arm.) gorget; (fort.) gorge; (mil.) gorget (*military badge*); (arch.) cyma, ogee
goldre *m* quiver (*for arrows*)
goleta *f* (naut.) schooner
golf *m* (sport) golf
golfán *m* (bot.) white water lily
golfear *vn* (coll.) to live the life of a ragamuffin
golfería *f* mob of ragamuffins; knavery
golfín *m* (zool.) dolphin
golfista *mf* (sport) golfer
golfo -fa *mf* little scoundrel, ragamuffin (*of Madrid*); *m* gulf; open sea, main; faro (*game*); chaos, confusion; great number, multitude; (coll.) tramp, bum; **golfo Arábigo** Red Sea; **golfo de Adén** Gulf of Aden; **golfo de Bengala** Bay of Bengal; **golfo de Botnia** Gulf of Bothnia; **golfo de Corinto** Gulf of Corinth; **golfo de Gascuña** Bay of Biscay; **golfo de Méjico** Gulf of Mexico; **golfo de Panamá** Gulf of Panama; **golfo de San Lorenzo** Gulf of St. Lawrence; **golfo de Valencia** Gulf of Valencia; **golfo de Venecia** Gulf of Venice; **golfo de Vizcaya** Bay of Biscay; **golfo Pérsico** Persian Gulf
Gólgota, el (Bib.) Golgotha
Goliat *m* (Bib.) Goliath
golilla *f* gorget, ruff; magistrate's collar; sleeve, collar (*of terra-cotta pipe*); pipe flange; (Am.) necktie; (Am.) erectile bristles (*of fowl*); **ajustar** or **apretar la golilla a** (coll.) to bring to reason; (coll.) to hang, to garrote; *m* (archaic) magistrate; (archaic) civilian
golondrina *f* wanderer; (orn.) swallow; (ichth.) swallow fish; **golondrina cola tijera** (orn.) barn swallow (*Hirundo erythrogastra*); **golondrina de mar** (orn.) tern (*Hydrocheli-don*); **golondrina purpúrea** (orn.) purple martin
golondrinera *f* (bot.) swallowwort, celandine
golondrino *m* male swallow; vagabond; deserter; (path.) tumor under armpit
golondro *m* desire, whim; (coll.) sponger; **andar de golondro** (coll.) to have a lot of wild ideas; **campar de golondro** (coll.) to be a sponger, live by one's wits
golosear *vn* var. of **golosinar**
golosina *f* sweet, delicacy, tidbit; eagerness, appetite, greediness; trifle; attraction
golosinar or **golosinear** *vn* to go around nibbling on sweets, to be always indulging in sweets
golosmear *vn* to sniff the cooking
goloso -sa *adj* sweet-toothed; gluttonous; greedy; *mf* gourmand
golpazo *m* bang, heavy blow, stroke, or knock; hard slap; pounding
golpe *m* blow, hit, beat, knock; stroke; bruise, bump; heartbeat; crowd, throng; flap (*of pocket*); trimming; mass, abundance; blow (*misfortune*); surprise, wonder; witticism; high spot; **a golpe seguro** with certainty; **caer de golpe** to collapse; **dar golpe** to make a hit, to be a sensation; **dar golpe a** to taste; **dar golpe en bola** to come off with flying colors; **de golpe** suddenly, all at once; **de golpe y porrazo** or **zumbido** (coll.) slam-bang; **de un golpe** at one stroke, at one time; **matar a golpes** to beat to death; **no dar golpe** to not do a stroke of work; **golpe de agua** water hammer; **golpe de arco** (mus.) bowing; **golpe de ariete** water hammer; **golpe de estado** coup d'état; **golpe de fortuna** lucky hit, stroke of luck; **golpe de gancho** (box.) hook; **golpe de gracia** coup de grâce, finishing stroke; **golpe de mano** (mil.) surprise attack; **golpe de mar** surge, heavy sea; **golpe de ojo** insight; glance; **golpe de pechos** beating one's bosom or breast; **golpe de teatro** dramatic turn of events; **golpe de tijera** scissors kick (*in swimming*); **golpe de tos** coughing spell, fit of coughing; **golpe de viento** (naut.) gust of wind; **golpe de vista** glance, look; **golpe en vago** miss; flop, failure; (baseball) strike; **golpe inverso** (box.) jab; **golpe lateral** (box.) swing; **golpe mortal** deathblow; **golpe teatral** dramatic turn of events
golpeadero *m* spot worn from beating; place struck by falling water; beating sound
golpeador -dora *adj* striking, beating, knocking; *mf* striker, beater, knocker; *m* (Am.) door knocker
golpeadura *f* striking, hitting, beating, knocking
golpear *va* to strike, hit, beat, knock; to bruise, bump; *vn* to beat, to knock; to tick; to knock (*said of an automobile motor*)
golpeo *m* var. of **golpeadura**
golpete *m* door catch, window catch (*to hold door or window open*); **jugar de golpete** (coll.) to cheat in weighing
golpetear *va & vn* to beat, knock, hammer, pound; to rattle
golpeteo *m* beating, knocking, hammering, pounding; rattling
gollería *f* dainty, delicacy; (coll.) favor, extra
golletazo *m* blow on the neck of a bottle (*to open it*); sudden termination of negotiations; (taur.) stab in the lungs
gollete *m* throat, neck; neck (*e.g., of bottle*); neckband (*of religious habit*); **estar hasta el gollete** (coll.) to have enough, to be out of patience; to be full (*of food*); to be stuck
gollizno or **gollizo** *m* gully, ravine
golloría *f* var. of **gollería**
goma *f* gum, rubber; eraser, rubber; elastic, rubber band; tire; mucilage; (path.) gumma; (plant path.) gumming disease; (Am.) hangover; **goma adragante** tragacanth; **goma arábiga** gum arabic; **goma de borrar** eraser, rubber; **goma de mascar** chewing gum; **goma elástica** gum elastic; **goma espumosa** foam rubber; **goma guta** gamboge; **goma laca** shellac; **goma para pegar** mucilage; **goma quino** kino gum

gomaguta *f* gamboge
gomecillo *m* (coll.) blind man's guide
gomero -ra *adj* (pertaining to) gum, rubber; *m* rubber man, rubber producer; rubber-plantation worker; (bot.) gum tree
gomia *f* dragon (*in Corpus Christi procession*); bugaboo, bugbear; (coll.) glutton; waster, destroyer (*agent, cause*)
gomífero -ra *adj* gummiferous, gum-bearing
gomista *mf* dealer in rubber goods
Gomorra *f* (Bib.) Gomorrah or Gomorrha
gomorresina *f* gum resin
gomosería *f* dudishness
gomosidad *f* gumminess; stickiness
gomosis *f* (plant path.) gummosis
gomoso -sa *adj* gummy; (pertaining to) gum; *m* dude, dandy
gónada *f* (anat.) gonad
gonce *m* var. of **gozne**
góndola *f* gondola; (rail.) gondola
gondolero *m* gondolier
gonfalón *m* var. of **confalón**
gonfaloniero *m* var. of **confaloniero**
gongo *m* gong
gongorino -na *adj* Gongoristic; *mf* Gongorist
gongorismo *m* Gongorism
gongorizar §76 *vn* to be Gongoristic, to use Gongorisms
gonia *f* (biol.) gonium
gonidio *m* (bot.) gonidium
goniometría *f* goniometry
goniómetro *m* goniometer; **goniómetro de aplicación** contact goniometer
gonococo *m* (bact.) gonococcus
gonóforo *m* (bot. & zool.) gonophore
gonorrea *f* (path.) gonorrhea
gonorreico -ca *adj* gonorrheal
gorbión *m* var. of **gurbión**
gordal *adj* big, large-size
gordana *f* animal fat
gordiano -na *adj* Gordian
gordiflón -flona or **gordinflón -flona** *adj* (coll.) chubby, pudgy
gordo -da *adj* fat, stout, corpulent, plump; fatty, greasy, oily; big, large; coarse; whopping big; hard (*water*); **hablar gordo** (coll.) to talk big; **se armó la gorda** (coll.) there was a big hullabaloo; *m* fat, suet; (coll.) first prize (*in lottery*)
gordolobo *m* (bot.) mullein, great mullein
gordura *f* fatness, stoutness, corpulence; fat, grease
gorfe *m* deep whirlpool
gorga *f* hawk's meal; whirlpool
gorgojar *vr* var. of **agorgojar**
gorgojo *m* (ent.) grub, weevil; (coll.) dwarf, tiny person
gorgojoso -sa *adj* grubby, weevily
gorgón *m* (Am.) concrete
Gorgona *f* (myth.) Gorgon
gorgonear *vn* to gobble (*said of a turkey*)
gorgóneo -a *adj* Gorgon, Gorgonian
gorgonzola *m* Gorgonzola (*cheese*)
gorgorán *m* grogram
gorgorita *f* little bubble; (coll.) trill
gorgoritear *vn* (coll.) to trill
gorgorito *m* (coll.) trill; **hacer gorgoritos** (coll.) to trill
gorgorotada *f* gulp
gorgotear *vn* to gurgle, burble
gorgoteo *m* gurgle, burble, burbling
gorgotero *m* peddler, hawker
gorguera *f* ruff; (arch.) gorgerin; (arm.) gorget
gorguz *m* (*pl:* **-guces**) javelin; pole used for removing pine cones
gorigori *m* (coll.) mournful singing at a funeral
gorila *m* (zool.) gorilla
gorja *f* gorge, throat; **estar de gorja** (coll.) to be full of joy
gorjal *m* (arm.) gorget; (eccl.) scarf
gorjear *vn* to warble, to trill; *vr* to gurgle (*said of a baby*)
gorjeo *m* warble, trill; warbling; gurgle (*of a baby*)
gorjerete *m* (surg.) gorget
gorra *f* cap; busby; sponging, bumming; **andar de gorra** to sponge; **colarse de gorra** (coll.) to crash the gate; **comer de gorra** to eat at the expense of other people; **hablarse de gorra** (coll.) to bow without speaking, to greet each other without speaking; **vivir de gorra** to live on other people; **gorra de pelo** (mil.) bearskin cap; **gorra de visera** cap
gorrada *f* tipping the hat
gorrear *vn* (Am.) to sponge
gorrero -ra *mf* maker of caps and headwear, dealer in caps and headware; (coll.) sponger
gorretada *f* tipping the hat
gorrilla *f* small cap; peasant's hat
gorrín *m* var. of **gorrino**
gorrinada *f* pigs, drove of pigs; (coll.) piggishness
gorrinera *f* pigpen, pigsty; (coll.) pigpen (*filthy place*)
gorrinería *f* dirt, filth; piggishness
gorrino -na *mf* sucking pig; hog; (fig.) pig
gorrión *m* (orn.) sparrow; **gorrión triguero** (orn.) bunting
gorriona *f* female sparrow
gorrionera *f* (coll.) den of thugs, den of vice
gorrista *adj* sponging; *mf* sponger
gorro *m* cap, bonnet; baby's bonnet; **aguantar el gorro** to give in; **apretarse el gorro** (coll.) to beat it, to duck out; **gorro de dormir** nightcap; **gorro frigio** liberty cap
gorrón -rrona *adj* sponging; *mf* sponger, dead beat; *m* pebble; lazy silkworm; tailings; pivot; (mach.) gudgeon, journal; *f* prostitute
gorronal *m* pebbly spot
gorronear *vn* to sponge
gorullo *m* ball, lump (*e.g., of wool*)
gorupo *m* granny knot
gosipino -na *adj* cotton, cottony
gota *f* drop; (path.) gout; **gotas** *fpl* drops (*medicine*); touch of rum or brandy dropped in coffee; **llover a gotas espaciadas** to sprinkle, to rain in scattered drops; **sudar la gota gorda** (coll.) to work one's head off; **gota a gota** drop by drop
goteado -da *adj* splattered, speckled
gotear *vn* to drip; to dribble; to sprinkle (*to rain in scattered drops*)
goteo *m* dripping; dribbling
gotera *f* leak; drip, dripping; mark left by dripping water; valance; (plant path.) tree disease caused by infiltration of water into trunk; **goteras** *fpl* (coll.) aches, pains; **estar lleno de goteras** (coll.) to be full of aches and pains
goterón *m* big raindrop; (arch.) throat
gótica *f* see **gótico**
goticismo *m* Gothicism
gótico -ca *adj* Gothic; (f.a.) Gothic; (print.) black-letter; noble, illustrious; *m* Gothic (*language*); (f.a.) Gothic; *f* (print.) black letter, Old English
Gotinga *f* Göttingen
gotón -tona *adj* & *mf* Goth
gotoso -sa *adj* gouty; *mf* gout sufferer
goyesco -ca *adj* (pertaining to) Goya; in the style of Goya
gozar §76 *va* to enjoy, possess; *vn* to enjoy oneself; **gozar de** to enjoy, possess; *vr* to enjoy oneself; to rejoice; **gozarse en** + *inf* to enjoy + *ger*
gozne *m* hinge
gozo *m* joy, rejoicing; blaze from dry chips of wood; **gozos** *mpl* couplets in praise of the Virgin; **brincar** or **saltar de gozo** (coll.) to leap with joy; **no caber en sí de gozo** (coll.) to be beside oneself with joy
gozoso -sa *adj* joyful; **gozoso con** or **de** joyful over
gozque *m* or **gozquejo** *m* little yapper (*dog*)
gr. abr. of **gramo**
Graal *m* var. of **Grial**
grabación *f* engraving; recording (*of phonograph record*); **grabación de alambre** wire recording; **grabación sobre cinta** tape recording
grabado *m* engraving (*act, art, plate, and picture*); picture, print, cut; recording (*of phonograph record*)
grabador -dora *adj* recording; *mf* engraver; *f* recorder; **grabadora de alambre** wire recorder; **grabadora de cinta** tape recorder
grabadura *f* engraving

grabar *va* to engrave; to record (*a sound, a song, a phonograph record, etc.*); (fig.) to engrave (*e.g., on the memory*); **grabar en** or **sobre cinta** to tape-record; *vr* to become engraved (*on the memory*)
grabazón *f* carved onlays
gracejada *f* (Am.) clownishness, cheap comedy
gracejar *vn* to be engaging, be fascinating (*in what one says*); to have a light touch, be witty
gracejo *m* charm, winsome manner; lightness, wit; (Am.) clown
gracia *f* grace (*gracefulness, charm; favor; pardon*); joke, witticism, witty remark; point (*of a joke*); (theol.) grace; (coll.) name, e.g., **¿cuál es su gracia de Vd.?** what is your name?; **gracias** *fpl* thanks; **caer de la gracia de** to get into the bad graces of; **caer en gracia a** to please, be pleasing to; **dar en la gracia de decir** (coll.) to harp on; **de gracia** gratis, gratuitously; **decir dos gracias a uno** (coll.) to tell someone a thing or two; **en gracia a** because of; **estar en gracia cerca de** to be in the good graces of; **hacer gracia** to please, be pleasing; **hacer gracia de algo a uno** to exempt or free someone from something; **hacerle a uno gracia** to strike someone as funny; **las Gracias** (myth.) the Graces; **¡linda gracia!** nonsense!; **no estar de gracia** or **para gracias** to be in no mood for joking; **no verle la gracia a uno** to not think that someone is funny; **pedir una gracia** to ask a favor; **tener gracia** to be funny, be astounding; **gracia de Dios** air and sunshine; daily bread; **gracia de niño** cuteness, brightness (*of a child*); **gracias a** thanks to (*because of; owing to*); **¡gracias!** thanks!; **¡gracias a Dios!** thank heavens!
graciable *adj* gracious, kindly; easy to grant
grácil *adj* gracile, thin, slender; tiny
graciola *f* (bot.) hedge hyssop
graciosamente *adv* gracefully; graciously; wittily; gratis
graciosidad *f* gracefulness; graciousness; wit, wittiness
gracioso -sa *adj* graceful; attractive; gracious; witty; free, gratis, gratuitous; strange; *mf* (theat.) comic, clown; *m* (theat.) gracioso (*gay, comic character in Spanish comedy*)
Graco *m* Gracchus
grada *f* step; row of seats, gradin; grandstand, tiers of seats; grille or wicket in the parlor of a convent; step in front of altar; (agr.) harrow; slip (*inclined plane on which ship is built*); (min.) stope; **gradas** *fpl* stone steps (*in front of building*); **grada de discos** (agr.) disk harrow
gradación *f* gradation; (gram.) comparison (*of adjective*)
gradado -da *adj* stepped
gradar *va* (agr.) to harrow
gradeo *m* (agr.) harrowing
gradería *f* rows of seats (*in an amphitheater or stadium*); bleachers; stone steps (*in front of building, in garden, etc.*); **gradería cubierta** grandstand
gradiente *m* (math. & meteor.) gradient; (Am.) gradient (*slope*)
gradilla *f* small stepladder; tile mold, brick mold; (chem.) tube rack; (eccl.) gradin
gradina *f* gradine
gradinar *va* to carve with a gradine
gradíolo *m* var. of **gladíolo**
grado *m* step; grade, degree; grade (*class in school*); (educ.) degree (*e.g., of bachelor*); (gram., math. & mus.) degree; (mil.) rank; **grados** *mpl* (eccl.) minor orders; **a mal de mi grado** against my wishes, unwillingly; **de buen grado** willingly, gladly; **de grado** willingly, gladly; **de grado en grado** by degrees; **de grado o por fuerza** willy-nilly; **de mal grado** unwillingly; **de su grado** willingly; **en alto grado** to a great extent; **en grado superlativo** or **en sumo grado** in the highest degree; **mal de mi grado** against my wishes, unwillingly; **¡grado a Dios!** thank heavens!
graduable *adj* adjustable
graduación *f* graduation; grading; standing; strength (*of spirituous liquor*); (mil.) rank
graduador *m* (elec.) graduator
gradual *adj* gradual; *m* (eccl.) gradual
graduando -da *adj* graduating; *mf* graduate, candidate for a degree
graduar §33 *va* to graduate; to grade; to regulate (*e.g., a spigot, valve, potentiometer*); to estimate, evaluate, appraise; to graduate (*a student*); **graduar de** to graduate (*a student*) as (*e.g., a bachelor*); (mil.) to give the rank of (*e.g., captain*) to; **graduar de** or **por** to grade as (*good, bad, etc.*); *vr* to graduate, be graduated; **graduarse de** to receive the degree of (*e.g., bachelor*)
grafía *f* spelling; (gram.) graph
gráfico -ca *adj* graphic or graphical; printing; illustrated; picture, camera; *m* diagram; *f* graph; picture
grafila or **gráfila** *f* knurl, milled edge of coin
grafioles *mpl* S-shaped cakes or biscuits
grafito *m* graphite; (archeol.) graffito
grafología *f* graphology
grafomanía *f* graphomania
grafómetro *m* graphometer
grafospasmo *m* writer's cramp
gragea *f* small colored candy; sugar-coated pill
grajear *vn* to caw; to chatter; to gurgle (*said of a baby*)
grajero -ra *adj* (pertaining to the) rook or crow; full of or haunted by rooks or crows
grajiento -ta *adj* (Am.) foul, noisome
grajo -ja *mf* (orn.) rook, crow; **grajo de pico amarillo** (orn.) chough, alpine chough
gral. abr. of **general**
grama *f* (bot.) Bermuda grass; **grama del norte** (bot.) couch grass, quitch; **grama de olor** or **de los prados** (bot.) vernal grass
gramaje *m* weight (*in grams of a sheet of paper one meter square*)
gramal *m* field of Bermuda grass, quitch field
gramalote *m* (bot.) guinea grass
gramalla *f* coat of mail
gramática *f* see **gramático**
gramatical *adj* grammatical
gramático -ca *adj* grammatical; *mf* grammarian; *f* grammar; **gramática parda** (coll.) shrewdness, craftiness
gramatiquear *vn* (coll.) to bore with questions of grammar, to be always correcting someone's grammar
gramatiquería *f* (coll.) grammatical hairsplitting
gramil *m* gauge, marking gauge, joiner's gauge
gramilla *f* scutching board; (bot.) joint grass
gramíneo -a *adj* gramineous
graminívoro -ra *adj* graminivorous
gramión *m* (chem.) gram ion
gramo *m* gram
gramofónico -ca *adj* phonograph
gramófono *m* gramophone
gramola *f* console phonograph; portable phonograph
gramoso -sa *adj* Bermuda-grass
grampa *f* clamp
gran *adj* apocopated form of **grande**, used before nouns of both genders in the singular
grana *f* seeding; seeding time; seed; (ent.) cochineal; kermes (*dyestuff*); red; fine scarlet cloth; **dar en grana** to go to seed; **grana del paraíso** (bot.) cardamon; **grana encarnada** (bot.) pokeberry
granada & **Granada** *f* see **granado**
granadera *f* grenadier's pouch
granadero *m* grenadier
granadilla *f* (bot.) passionflower (*plant and flower*); passion fruit
granadino -na *adj* (pertaining to) Granada; *mf* native or inhabitant of Granada; *m* pomegranate flower; *f* grenadine (*fabric; syrup*)
granado -da *adj* choice, select, distinguished; mature, expert; tall, lanky; *m* (bot.) pomegranate; **granado blanco** (bot.) rose of Sharon; *f* pomegranate (*fruit*); grenade; (*cap.*) *f* Granada; **la Nueva Granada** New Granada; **granada de mano** hand grenade; **granada de metralla** shrapnel; **granada extintora** fire grenade
granalla *f* granulated metal; filings; **granalla de carbón** carbon granules
granangular *adj* (opt.) wide-angle

granar *va* to grain (*powder*); *vn* to seed
granate *m* garnet (*stone and color*); **granate almandino** deep-red garnet; *adj invar* garnet
granazón *f* seeding; **no llegar a granazón** to fall by the wayside
Gran Bretaña, la Great Britain
grande *adj* big, large; great; *m* grandee; **en grande** as a whole; on a grand scale; in a big way; **grande de España** grandee, Spanish grandee
grandevo -va *adj* (poet.) aged, hoary
grandeza *f* bigness, largeness; greatness; grandeur; size; grandeeship; grandees
grandilocuencia *f* grandiloquence
grandilocuente or **grandílocuo -cua** *adj* grandiloquent
grandillón -llona *adj* (coll.) oversize, overgrown
grandiosidad *f* grandeur, magnificence
grandioso -sa *adj* grandiose, grand
grandísono -na *adj* (poet.) high-sounding, resounding
grandor *m* size
grandote -ta *adj* (coll.) pretty big, biggish
grandullón -llona *adj* (coll.) var. of **grandillón**
graneado -da *adj* ground; spattered; heavy and continuous (*firing*)
graneador *m* stipple graver
granear *va* to sow; to grain (*powder; a lithographic stone*); to stipple
granel; a granel at random; loose, in bulk; lavishly, in abundance
granelar *va* to grain (*leather*)
graneo *m* sowing; stippling
granero -ra *adj* (pertaining to) grain; *mf* grain dealer; *m* granary; (fig.) granary (*region*)
granetazo *m* blow with a punch; punch mark
granete *m* center punch
granetear *va* to punch, mark with a punch
granetería *f* grain business
granetero -ra *mf* grain dealer
granévano *m* (bot.) goat's-thorn, tragacanth
granguardia *f* (mil.) grand guard
granífugo -ga *adj* hail-dispersing
granilla *f* grape seed
granillo *m* fine grain; profit, gain
granilloso -sa *adj* granular
granítico -ca *adj* granite; granitic
granito *m* granite; **echar un granito de sal** (coll.) to add spice to what one says
granívoro -ra *adj* granivorous
granizada *f* hailstorm; (fig.) hailstorm; (Am.) ice drink
granizado *m* water ice
granizal *m* (Am.) hailstorm
granizar §76 *va* to hail; to sprinkle; *vn* to hail
granizo *m* hail; (fig.) hail (*abundance*)
granja *f* grange, farm; dairy; country place; **granja escuela** farm school
granjeador -dora *adj* (Am.) ingratiating; *mf* (Am.) ingratiating person
granjear *va* to gain, to earn; to win, win over; *vr* to win, win over; to draw (*applause*)
granjeo *m* gain, profit; winning
granjería *f* farming, husbandry; gain, profit
granjero -ra *mf* farmer; *m* husbandman
grano *m* grain; grape, berry; (path.) pimple; grain (*weight*); **granos** *mpl* grain; **con un grano de sal** with a grain of salt; **ir al grano** (coll.) to come to the point; **grano de belleza** beauty spot; **grano de café** coffee bean; **granos de amor** (bot.) gromwell
granoso -sa *adj* granular (*surface*)
granuja *f* loose grape; grapestone, grapeseed; *m* scoundrel; (coll.) waif, little waif
granujada *f* rascality, deviltry
granujería *f* gang of scalawags; rascality
granujo *m* (coll.) pimple, pustule
granujoso -sa *adj* pimpled, pimply, pustular
granulación *f* granulation
granular *adj* granular; pimply; *va* to granulate; *vr* to granulate; (path.) to granulate
granulita *f* or **granulito** *m* (geol.) granulite
gránulo *m* granule; (bot. & pharm.) granule
granuloso -sa *adj* granular; (path.) granular; *f* (chem.) granulose
granza *f* (bot.) madder; pea coal; **granzas** *fpl* chaff; screenings, siftings; dross
granzón *m* piece of ore that won't pass through sieve; **granzones** *mpl* knots of hay that won't pass through sieve and that are left uneaten by cattle
grañón *m* boiled wheat grains
grao *m* beach, shore
grapa *f* staple; clip, clamp
grasa *f* see **graso**
grasera *f* vessel for fat or grease; (cook.) dripping pan
grasería *f* tallow chandler's shop
grasero *m* slag dump
graseza *f* fattiness, greasiness
grasiento -ta *adj* greasy
grasilla *f* pounce (*fine powder*)
graso -sa *adj* fatty, greasy; (chem.) fatty; *m* fattiness, greasiness; *f* fat, grease; pounce (*fine powder*); (chem.) fat; (Am.) shoe polish, shoe shine; **grasas** *fpl* slag; **grasa de ballena** blubber
grasones *mpl* porridge, wheat porridge
grasoso -sa *adj* fatty, greasy
grasura *f* var. of **grosura**
grata *f* see **grato**
gratar *va* to clean or burnish with a wire brush
gratificación *f* gratification, reward, fee; bonus
gratificador -dora *adj* gratifying; rewarding; tipping; *mf* gratifier; rewarder; tipper
gratificar §86 *va* to gratify; to reward; to tip, to fee
gratil *m* or **grátil** *m* (naut.) leech; (naut.) slings (*middle part of yard*)
gratín *m*; **al gratín** (cook.) au gratin
gratis *adv* gratis
gratisdato -ta *adj* gratis, free
gratitud *f* gratitude
grato -ta *adj* pleasing; free; (Am.) grateful; *f* favor (*letter*); wire brush
gratonada *f* chicken stew
gratuitamente *adv* gratuitously; free, gratis
gratuito -ta *adj* gratuitous
gratulación *f* gratulation
gratular *va* to congratulate; *vr* to rejoice
gratulatorio -ria *adj* gratulatory, congratulatory
grauvaca *f* (geol.) graywacke
grava *f* gravel; crushed stone; **grava provechosa** (min.) pay dirt
gravamen *m* burden, obligation; encumbrance; assessment
gravar *va* to burden, to encumber; to assess (*property*)
gravativo -va *adj* burdensome, heavy; dragging, heavy (*pain*)
grave *adj* heavy (*having weight*); grave, serious, solemn; hard, difficult; annoying; ill, sick; grave, deep, low (*sound*); noble, majestic (*music*); (gram.) paroxytone; (gram.) grave (*accent*)
gravear *vn* to rest, press, weigh
gravedad *f* gravity; (phys. & mus.) gravity; **de gravedad** seriously; **gravedad nula** weightlessness
gravedoso -sa *adj* heavy, pompous
gravela *f* (path.) gravel
grávida *f* see **grávido**
gravidez *f* gravidity
grávido -da *adj* gravid; (poet.) full, loaded, abundant; *f* pregnant woman
gravimetría *f* gravimetry
gravimétrico -ca *adj* gravimetric or gravimetrical
gravitación *f* (phys.) gravitation
gravitacional *adj* gravitational
gravitar *vn* to gravitate; to rest, press; **gravitar sobre** to be a burden to; to encumber; to live on (*another person*)
gravoso -sa *adj* onerous, burdensome, costly; boring, tiresome
graznador -dora *adj* cawing, croaking; cackling
graznar *vn* to caw, to croak; to cackle; to not know what one is talking about; to cackle (*in singing*)
graznido *m* caw, croak; cackle; chatter, jabber; cackle, cackling (*of a singer*)
greba *f* greave
greca *f* see **greco**
Grecia *f* Greece

greciano -na or **grecisco -ca** *adj* Grecian
grecismo *m* Grecism
grecizar §76 *va & vn* to Grecize
greco -ca *adj & mf* Grecian, Greek; *f* Grecian fret
grecolatino -na *adj* Greco-Latin
grecorromano -na *adj* Greco-Roman
greda *f* clay, fuller's earth
gredal *adj* clayey; *m* clay pit
gredoso -sa *adj* clayey
gregal *adj* gregarious; *m* northeast wind (*in Mediterranean*)
gregario -ria *adj* gregarious; slavish
gregoriano -na *adj* Gregorian
Gregorio *m* Gregory
greguería *f* shouting, hubbub; **greguerías** *fpl* (lit.) impressionistic imagery in epigrammatic prose
gregüescos *mpl* pantaloons, wide breeches (*worn in sixteenth and seventeenth centuries*)
greguisco -ca *adj* Grecian
greguizar §76 *va* to Grecize
gremial *adj* (pertaining to a) union; *m* guildsman; union man, union member; (eccl.) gremial
gremio *m* guild, corporation; society, association; union, trade union; lap; **gremio solteril** single blessedness
grenchudo -da *adj* long-haired, long-maned
greña *f* shock, tangled mop (*of hair*); entanglement; (prov.) heap of grain to be thrashed; (prov.) first leaves of new shoot; **andar a la greña** (coll.) to pull each other's hair; (coll.) to get into a hot argument
greñudo -da *adj* shock-headed; dishevelled; *m* shy horse
gres *m* sandstone; siliceous clay; stoneware
gresca *f* clamor, uproar; quarrel, row
grey *f* flock; group, party; people, nation; congregation (*of faithful*)
Grial *m* Grail; **Santo Grial** Holy Grail
griego -ga *adj* Greek; *mf* Greek; (coll.) greek (*cheat, sharper*); *m* Greek (*language*); **hablar en griego** (coll.) to talk unintelligibly
grieta *f* crack, crevice, fissure; chap (*in skin*)
grietado -da *adj* crackled; *m* (f.a.) crackle (*cracked surface*); (f.a.) crackleware
grietar *vr* to crack, to split; to become chapped
grietoso -sa *adj* cracky, cracked
grifa *f* see **grifo**
grifería *f* faucets, spigots; spigot shop
grifo -fa *adj* curly, tangled; (Am.) bristly, bristling; (Am.) haughty, arrogant; (Am.) drunk; (Am.) colored; **ponerse grifo** (Am.) to stand on end (*said of hair*); *mf* (Am.) mulatto; (Am.) drug addict; *m* faucet, spigot, cock; (myth.) griffin; (Am.) **gas station**; *f* hashish, marijuana
grifón *m* large faucet or spigot
grigallo *m* (orn.) capercaillie
grilla *f* female cricket; (rad.) grid; (coll.) lie; **¡ésa es grilla!** (coll.) you expect me to believe that!
grillar *vr* to shoot, sprout
grillera *f* cricket hole; cricket cage
grillero *m* jailer (*who shackles prisoners*); cricket dealer
grillete *m* fetter, shackle
grillo *m* (ent.) cricket; shoot, sprout; drag, obstacle; gyve; **grillos** *mpl* fetters, shackles; **andar a grillos** (coll.) to trifle away one's time; **grillo cebollero** or **real** (ent.) mole cricket
grillotalpa *f* (ent.) mole cricket
grima *f* annoyance, horror; **dar grima a** to annoy, horrify, grate on the nerves of
grimoso -sa *adj* annoying, horrifying
grímpola *f* (naut.) pennant, streamer
gringo -ga *mf* (scornful) foreigner; (Am.) gringo (*Anglo-Saxon*); *m* (coll.) gibberish
griñolera *f* (bot.) rose box
griñón *m* wimple; nectarine
gripal *adj* of grippe, grippal
gripe *f* (path.) grippe
gris *adj* gray; dull, gloomy; *m* gray; (zool.) miniver, Siberian squirrel; (coll.) cold, cold wind; **hacer gris** (coll.) to be sharp, be brisk (*said of weather*)
grisáceo -a *adj* grayish
grisalla *f* (f.a.) grisaille
grisar *va* to polish (*diamonds*)
griseta *f* flowered silk; grisette; (plant path.) tree disease caused by infiltration of water into trunk
grisiento -ta *adj* (Am.) grayish
grisú *m* (*pl:* **-súes**) (min.) firedamp
grita *f* outcry, shout; tumult, hubbub; **dar grita a** (coll.) to hoot at
gritador -dora *adj* crying, shouting, screaming; *mf* crier, shouter, screamer
gritar *vn* to cry out, to shout
gritería *f* or **griterío** *m* outcry, shouting, uproar
grito *m* cry, shout; scream, shriek; **a grito herido** or **pelado** in a loud shriek; **alzar el grito** (coll.) to raise one's voice brazenly; **asparse a gritos** (coll.) to scream wildly (*said of a child*); (coll.) to shout at the top of one's voice; **estar en un grito** to moan in constant pain; **el último grito** (coll.) the latest thing, all the rage; **poner el grito en el cielo** (coll.) to raise the roof, to complain loudly; **poner el grito en el cielo contra** (coll.) to cry out against
gritón -tona *adj* (coll.) shouting, screaming; *mf* (coll.) shouter, screamer
griva *f* (orn.) missel thrush
gro. abr. of **género**
gro *m* grosgrain
groar *vn* to croak (*said of frogs*)
Grocio *m* Grotius
groelandés -desa *adj & mf* var. of **groenlandés**
Groelandia *f* var. of **Groenlandia**
groenlandés -desa *adj* Greenlandic; *mf* Greenlander
Groenlandia *f* Greenland
groera *f* (naut.) rope hole
gromo *m* bud
grosella *f* currant (*fruit*); **grosella silvestre** gooseberry (*fruit*)
grosellero *m* (bot.) currant (*plant*); **grosellero silvestre** (bot.) gooseberry (*plant*)
grosería *f* grossness, coarseness, crudeness; churlishness, rudeness; stupidity; vulgarity
grosero -ra *adj* gross, coarse, rough, crude; churlish, rude; stupid; vulgar; *mf* churl, boor, mucker
grosísimo -ma *adj super* very or most thick or bulky; very coarse; very stout
grosor *m* thickness, bulk
grosulariáceo -a *adj* (bot.) grossulariaceous
grosura *f* fat, suet, tallow; meat, meat diet; parts of animals (*head, legs, intestines, etc.*); coarseness; ordinariness, vulgarity; (obs.) Saturday
grotesco -ca *adj* grotesque (*ridiculous*); (f.a.) grotesque; *m* (f.a.) grotesque
grúa *f* crane, derrick; **grúa corredera** or **corrediza** traveling crane; **grúa de auxilio** wrecking crane; **grúa de caballete** gantry crane; **grúa de tijera** shears (*hoisting device*)
grúa-remolque *m* tow truck
grueso -sa *adj* thick, bulky, heavy, big, gross; coarse, ordinary; stout; rough, heavy (*seas*); heavy (*line; rug, carpet*); *m* thickness; bulk; heavy stroke (*in writing*); **en grueso** in gross or in the gross; *f* gross (*twelve dozen*)
gruir §41 *vn* to crunk (*said of a crane*)
grujidor *m* glazier's nippers; glass cutter
grujir *va* to trim (*glass*) with nippers
grulla *f* (orn.) crane; **grulla de Numidia** (orn.) Numidian crane, demoiselle crane
grullada *f* flock of cranes; (coll.) gang of loafers; (coll.) platitude
grumete *m* (naut.) cabin boy, ship's boy
grumo *m* clot; curd; bunch, cluster; bud; wing tip (*of bird*); (arch.) Gothic finial
grumoso -sa *adj* clotty; curdly; bunchy, clustered
gruñente *adj* grunting; growling; *m* (slang) grunter (*hog*)
gruñido *m* grunt; growl; grumble; creak; (coll.) scolding
gruñidor -dora *adj* grunting; growling; (coll.) grumbling, discontent; *mf* grunter; growler; (coll.) grumbler

gruñimiento *m* grunting; growling; grumbling
gruñir **§25** *vn* to grunt; to growl; to grumble; to creak (*said, e.g., of a door*)
gruñón -ñona *adj* (coll.) grumbly, grumpy
grupa *f* croup, rump (*of horse*)
grupada *f* squall
grupera *f* crupper; pillion, cushion back of saddle for baggage
grupeto *m* (mus.) turn, grupetto
grupo *m* group; (mach. & elec.) unit, set; granny knot; **grupo carboxilo** (chem.) carboxyl group; **grupo de carga** (elec.) battery-charging unit or set; **grupo de motor y generador** (elec.) motor generator set; **grupo electrógeno** (elec.) generator unit, generating unit; **grupo motopropulsor** (elec.) electric drive, motor drive; (aer.) power plant; **grupo motor** (aut.) power plant; **grupo sanguíneo** blood group, blood type
gruta *f* grotto; **gruta Coriciana** Corycian Cave
grutesco -ca *adj & m* (f.a.) grotesque
gruyère *m* Gruyère, Swiss cheese
gte. abr. of **gerente**
guaca *f* (Am.) Indian tomb; (Am.) hidden treasure; (Am.) Indian altar
guacal *m* (Am.) crate
guacamayo -ya *adj* (Am.) flashy, sporty; *m* (orn.) macaw
guacamole *m* (Am.) avocado salad
guacia *f* (bot.) acacia (*plant and gum*)
guaco *m* (bot.) guaco; (orn.) curassow
guachapear *va* (coll.) to splash with the feet; (coll.) to botch, bungle; *vn* to clatter, to clank
guacharaca *f* (orn.) chachalaca
guácharo -ra *adj* sickly, dropsical; *m* (orn.) oilbird
guachinango -ga *adj* (Am.) cunning, flattering; *mf* (offensive term used by Cubans) Mexican; *m* (ichth.) red snapper; *f* (Am.) wooden bar (*across a door or window*)
guacho -cha *adj* (Am.) homeless, motherless, orphan; (Am.) odd, unmatched (*e.g., shoe*)
guadafiones *mpl* fetterlock (*shackle*)
guadal *m* bog, swamp; (Am.) bamboo grass; (Am.) dune, sand hill
Guadalupe *f* Guadeloupe
guadamací *m* (*pl:* **-cíes**) embossed leather, stamped leather; **guadamací brocado** gold or silver embossed leather
guadamacil *m* var. of **guadamací**
guadamacilería *f* embossed-leather business; embossed-leather shop
guadamacilero *m* embossed-leather maker or dealer
guadamecí *m* (*pl:* **-cíes**) var. of **guadamací**
guadamecil *m* var. of **guadamací**
guadaña *f* scythe
guadañador -dora *adj* mowing; *f* mowing machine
guadañar *va* to scythe, to mow
guadañero *m* scytheman, mower
guadañeta *f* squid-jigger
guadañil *m* var. of **guadañero**
guadaño *m* harbor boat
guadapero *m* (bot.) wild pear (*tree*); boy who carries food out to the harvestmen
guadarnés *m* harness room; harness keeper
guadijeño -ña *adj* (pertaining to) Guadix; *mf* native or inhabitant of Guadix; *m* poniard
guadua *f* (bot.) guadua (*Guadua latifolia and stems*)
guadual *m* growth of guaduas
guagua *f* trifle, triviality; (Am.) bus; (Am.) paca (*rodent*); (Am.) orange scale (*insect*); **de guagua** (coll.) free, gratis; *mf* (Am.) baby
guagüero -ra *adj* (Am.) paca-hunting (*e.g., dog*); *mf* (Am.) sponger; (Am.) bus driver
guaicán *m* (ichth.) remora
guaira *f* (naut.) leg-of-mutton sail; (Am.) smelting furnace (*of Indians*)
guairabo *m* (orn.) night heron
guairo *m* small vessel with two leg-of-mutton sails
guaita *f* (archaic) night watch, night sentinel
guajada *f* (Am.) nonsense, folly
guajalote *m* (Am.) turkey (*fowl*)
guájar *m & f* or **guájaras** *fpl* craggy section of mountains
guaje *adj* (Am.) foolish, crazy; (Am.) knavish; *m* (Am.) calabash, gourd; (Am.) junk, trinket; (Am.) nobody, good-for-nothing; (Am.) fool; **hacer guaje** (Am.) to deceive
guajear *vn* (Am.) to play stupid
guájete; guájete por guájete (coll.) tit for tat
guajiro -ra *adj* (Am.) rustic, boorish; *mf* white peasant of Cuba; (Am.) peasant, stranger; *f* Cuban peasant song
guajolote *m* (Am.) turkey (*fowl*); (Am.) simpleton
gualda *f* see **gualdo**
gualdado -da *adj* yellow-dyed
gualdera *f* (carp.) bridgeboard, horse; (arti.) trail
gualdo -da *adj* yellow; *f* (bot.) weld, dyer's rocket
gualdrapa *f* housing, trappings; (coll.) dirty rag hanging from clothing
gualdrapazo *m* flap or flapping sound of sail (*against rigging*)
gualdrapear *va* to alternate, to line up in alternation; *vn* to flap (*said of sails*)
gualdrapeo *m* flapping of sails
gualdrapero *m* raggedy fellow
Gualterio *m* Walter
guamá *m* or **guamo** *m* (bot.) guamá
guanábana *f* soursop (*fruit*)
guanábano *m* (bot.) soursop (*tree*)
guanaco *m* (zool.) guanaco
Guanahaní *f* Watling
guanajo -ja *adj* (Am.) dull, stupid; *m* (Am.) turkey
guanana *f* (orn.) blue goose; **guanana blanca** (orn.) lesser snow goose; **guanana prieta** (orn.) tule goose
guando *m* (Am.) handbarrow
guanero -ra *adj* (pertaining to) guano; *m* guano ship; (coll.) guano tycoon; *f* guano deposit; **guaneras** *fpl* guano islands
guango *m* (Am.) pigtail (*of Indian women*)
guanidina *f* (chem.) guanidine
guanín *m* (Am.) base gold
guanina *f* (bot.) stinking weed; (chem.) guanine
guano *m* guano; (bot.) palm tree
guantada *f* or **guantazo** *m* slap
guante *m* glove; **guantes** *mpl* tip, fee; **adobar los guantes a** (coll.) to treat, to tip; **arrojar el guante** to throw down the gauntlet; **echar el guante a** (coll.) to grasp, seize; **echar un guante** to collect for charity; **recoger el guante** to take up the gauntlet; **salvo el guante** (coll.) excuse my glove (*in shaking hands*)
guantelete *m* gauntlet; (surg.) gauntlet
guantera *f* see **guantero**
guantería *f* glove business; glove shop
guantero -ra *mf* glover, glove maker or dealer; *m & f* glove compartment
guañín *m* var. of **guanín**
guañir **§25** *vn* (prov.) to squeal (*said of pigs*)
guao *m* (bot.) guao (*Comocladia*); (bot.) sumac; **ser como la sombra del guao** or **tener peor sombra que un guao** (Am.) to be a jinx
guapamente *adv* (coll.) showily; (coll.) boldly; (coll.) very well, fine
guapear *vn* (coll.) to bluster, to act tough; (coll.) to dress in a showy manner, to be sporty
guapetón -tona *adj* (coll.) big and handsome; (coll.) flashy, sporty; (coll.) fearless, dauntless; *m* (coll.) bully, toughy
guapeza *f* (coll.) good looks; (coll.) showiness, flashiness; (coll.) boldness, daring; (coll.) bravado
guapo -pa *adj* (coll.) handsome, good-looking; (coll.) showy, flashy; (Am.) bold, daring; *m* bully; gallant, lady's man; **guapos** *mpl* (dial.) trinkets; **echarla de guapo** (coll.) to bluster, to act tough
guapote -ta *adj* (coll.) kindly, good-natured; (coll.) pretty, nice
guapura *f* (coll.) good looks
guaracha *f* guaracha (*old Spanish dance and music*)
guarache *m* (Am.) sandal; (Am.) tire patch

guaraní (*pl:* **-níes**) *adj & mf* Guarani; *m* Guarani (*language*)
guarapo *m* juice of sugar cane; guarapo (*fermented juice of sugar cane*)
guarda *mf* guard, keeper, custodian; (Am.) trolley-car conductor; *m* guard; caretaker **guarda de la aduana** customhouse officer; **guarda forestal** forest ranger; *f* guard, custody; observance (*of a law*); guard (*e.g., of sword*); ward (*of lock or key*); (b.b.) flyleaf; **guardas** *fpl* (b.b.) end paper
guardabarrera *mf* (rail.) gatekeeper
guardabarros *m* (*pl:* **-rros**) splashboard; (aut.) fender, mudguard
guardabosque *m* forest keeper, gamekeeper; (Am.) shortstop
guardabrazo *m* (arm.) brassard
guardabrisa *m* (aut.) windshield; (naut.) glass lamp shade (*for candles*)
guardacabo *m* (naut.) thimble
guardacabras *mf* (*pl:* **-bras**) goatherd
guardacadena *m* chain guard
guardacalor *m* asbestos insulation (*e.g., of a boiler*)
guardacantón *m* spur stone, corner spur stone
guardacarril *m* var. of **contracarril**
guardacartas *m* (*pl:* **-tas**) letter file
guardacartuchos *m* (*pl:* **-chos**) cartridge box
guardacenizas *m* (*pl:* **-zas**) ashpan
guardacoches *m* (*pl:* **-ches**) car watcher
guardacostas *m* (*pl:* **-tas**) revenue cutter, coast guard cutter; **guardacostas** *mpl* coast guard (*service*)
guardador -dora *adj* guarding, protecting; keeping, preserving; observant, regardful, mindful; stingy; *m* guardian; keeper; observer (*e.g., of laws*); (archaic) guardian of the spoils of war
guardaespaldas *m* (*pl:* **-das**) bodyguard
guardaesquinas *m* (*pl:* **-nas**) (coll.) corner loafer
guardafango *m* (aut.) mudguard, fender
guardafrenos *m* (*pl:* **-nos**) (rail.) brakeman, flagman
guardafuego *m* fender, fireguard (*of fireplace*); (naut.) breaming board
guardaguas *m* (*pl:* **-guas**) (naut.) batten to keep water out of portholes
guardagujas *m* (*pl:* **-jas**) switchman
guardainfante *m* farthingale; (naut.) whelps (*of capstan*)
guardajoyas *m* (*pl:* **-yas**) jewel case
guardalado *m* rail, railing (*e.g., of a bridge*)
guardalmacén *mf* storekeeper; warehouseman; (Am.) station master
guardalobo *m* (bot.) poet's cassia
guardalodos *m* (*pl:* **-dos**) (Am.) mudguard
guardamalleta *f* lambrequin, valance; (arch.) bargeboard
guardamancebo *m* (naut.) manrope
guardamano *m* guard of a sword
guardameta *m* (sport) goalkeeper
guardamonte *m* trigger guard; forest keeper; poncho
guardamozo *m* var. of **guardamancebo**
guardamuebles *m* (*pl:* **-bles**) warehouse (*for furniture*); furniture storeroom; palace guard or keeper of furniture
guardamujer *f* (archaic) lady in waiting
guardanieve *m* snowshed
guardapelo *m* locket
guardapesca *m* (naut.) fish warden's boat
guardapolvo *m* cover, cloth (*to protect from dust*); duster (*lightweight coat*); inner lid (*of watch*); flashing, hood (*over door or window*)
guardapuente *m* bridge guard
guardapuerta *f* storm door; portière
guardar *va* to guard; to keep; to preserve, protect; to watch, watch over; to show (*consideration*); to save, e.g., **¡Dios guarde a la Reina!** God save the Queen!; *vn* to keep, to save; **¡guarda!** look out!, watch out!; *vr* to be on one's guard; to keep (*affection, hate, etc.*) for each other; **guardarse de** to guard against, watch out for, look out for; **guardarse de** + *inf* to guard against + *ger*, to take care not to + *inf;* **guardársele a uno** to store up vengeance against someone
guardarraya *f* (Am.) boundary line
guardarriel *m* var. of **contracarril**
guardarrío *m* (orn.) kingfisher
guardarropa *mf* wardrober, keeper of the wardrobe; *m* wardrobe (*room, closet, etc.*); checkroom, cloakroom; (bot.) lavender cotton; check boy; *f* check girl, hat girl
guardarropía *f* (theat.) wardrobe
guardarruedas *m* (*pl:* **-das**) spur stone, corner spur stone; (rail.) wheel guard
guardasilla *f* chair rail
guardatimón *m* (naut.) stern chaser
guardaventana *f* storm window
guardavía *m* (rail.) trackwalker, flagman, lineman
guardavientos *m* (*pl:* **-tos**) chimney pot; windbreak
guardavivo or **guardavivos** *m* (*pl:* **-vos**) bead, corner bead
guardería *f* guard, guardship; **guardería infantil** day nursery
guardesa *f* woman guard; guard's wife
guardia *f* care, protection; guard (*body of armed men; position in fencing*); (naut.) watch; **de guardia** on duty; on guard; **en guardia** on guard; (fencing) on guard; **montar la guardia** to mount guard; **guardia civil** rural police; **guardia de asalto** shock corps; **guardia de corps** bodyguard (*group of guards*); **guardia nacional** national guard; **guardia suiza** Swiss guards; *m* guard, guardsman; **guardia civil** rural policeman; **guardia de corps** bodyguard (*single guard*); **guardia marina** *m* midshipman; **guardia municipal** or **guardia urbano** policeman
guardiacivil *m* rural policeman
guardián -diana *mf* guardian; *m* (eccl.) guardian; (naut.) heavy hawser
guardianía *f* (eccl.) guardianship (*of Franciscans*)
guardilla *f* attic; attic room; end tooth (*of a comb*); (sew.) guard
guardillón *m* loft, attic; top attic
guardín *m* (naut.) tiller cable, tiller chain
guardoso -sa *adj* careful, tidy; thrifty; stingy
guarecer §34 *va* to take in, give shelter or protection to; to keep, preserve; to treat (*a sick person*); *vr* to take refuge, take shelter
guariao *m* (orn.) limpkin
guarida *f* den, lair (*of animals*); shelter; cover, hide-out; haunt, hangout; stamping grounds
guarín *m* sucking pig
guarismo *m* cipher, figure, number
guarne *m* (naut.) turn (*of a cable*)
guarnecedor -dora *adj* trimming; binding; plastering; *mf* trimmer; binder; plasterer
guarnecer §34 *va* to trim; to bind, to edge; to equip, to provide; to stucco, to plaster; to harness; to set (*jewels*); to garrison; to line (*brakes*); to bush (*a bearing*); (cook.) to garnish
guarnecido *m* stucco, plaster
guarnés *m* var. of **guadarnés**
guarnición *f* trimming; binding, edging; provision; stuccoing, plastering; setting (*of jewels*); flounce; garrison (*troops*); guard (*of sword*); lining (*of brakes, clutch, etc.*); packing (*of piston*); (cook.) garnish; **guarniciones** *fpl* harness; fittings, fixtures; **guarniciones de alumbrado eléctrico** electric-light fixtures; **guarniciones de gas** gas fixtures
guarnicionar *va* to garrison
guarnicionería *f* harness making; harness maker's shop
guarnicionero -ra *mf* harness maker or dealer
guarniel *m* muleteer's leather bag
guarnigón *m* young quail
guarnir §53 *va* to trim; (naut.) to reeve, to rig
guaro *m* small parrot; (Am.) rum
guarro -rra *mf* hog
guarte *interj* look out!
guasa *f* see **guaso**
guasca *f* (Am.) rawhide
guasear *vr* (coll.) to joke, jest, kid; **guasearse de** (coll.) to poke fun at
guasería *f* (Am.) dullness, heaviness, timidity; (Am.) coarseness, crudity
guaso -sa *adj* (Am.) coarse, crude, uncouth; *mf* (Am.) peasant; *f* (coll.) dullness, heaviness, churlishness; (coll.) joking, kidding; (ichth.) West Indian jewfish

guasón -sona *adj* (coll.) dull, heavy, churlish; (coll.) funny, comical, humorous; *mf* (coll.) dullard, dolt; (coll.) joker, kidder
guasquear *va* (Am.) to rawhide, to flog
guata *f* wad, padding, raw cotton; (Am.) padded cotton blanket; (Am.) belly, paunch; (Am.) warping, bulging; **echar guata** (Am.) to get fat; (Am.) to become prosperous
guataca *f* (Am.) spade; (Am.) big ear; *m* (Am.) big-eared fellow
guatacudo -da *adj* (Am.) big-eared
Guatemala *f* Guatemala
guatemalteco -ca *adj & mf* Guatemalan
guatemaltequismo *m* Guatemalanism
guateque *m* Cuban shindig; party; afternoon party
guatil *m* (bot.) genipap
guau *m* (bot.) woodbine, Virginia creeper; bowwow (*of dog*); *interj* bowwow!
guay *interj* (poet.) woe!; **tener muchos guayes** to be full of woes; to be full of aches and pains; **¡guay de . . . !** (poet.) woe to . . . !; **¡guay de mí!** (poet.) woe is me!
guaya *f* lament, complaint
guayaba *f* guava, guava apple (*fruit*); guava jelly; (Am.) lie, fake; **guayabas** *fpl* (Am.) bulging eyes
guayabera *f* man's short blouse
guayabo *m* (bot.) guava (*tree*)
guayacán *m* or **guayaco** *m* (bot.) guaiacum, lignum vitae
guayacol *m* (chem.) guaiacol
Guayana *f* Guiana; **la Guayana Francesa** French Guiana; **la Guayana Holandesa** Dutch Guiana; **la Guayana Inglesa** British Guiana
guayanés -nesa *adj & mf* Guianan or Guianese
guayín *m* (Am.) light covered carriage
guayina *f* (Am.) station wagon
guayule *m* (bot.) guayule (*shrub and rubber*)
gubarte *m* (zool.) humpback (*whale*)
gubernamental *adj* governmental; government; strong-government (*e.g., advocate*)
gubernativo -va *adj* governmental
gubia *f* (carp.) gouge
guedeja *f* long hair; lion's mane; **guedejas** *fpl* shaggy coat (*of animal*)
guedejón -jona, guedejoso -sa or **guedejudo -da** *adj* long-haired; heavy-maned
güeldo *m* bait consisting of shrimps and other crustaceans
Güeldres Gelderland
güelfo -fa *adj* Guelfic or Guelphic; *m* Guelf or Guelph
güemul *m* (zool.) guemal or guemul (*South American deer: Hippocamelus bisulcus*)
Guepeu *f* Ogpu (*Soviet secret police*)
güero -ra *adj & mf* (Am.) blond
guerra *f* war, warfare; conflict, struggle; billiards; **armar en guerra** (nav.) to commission; **dar guerra** (coll.) to annoy, harass, be troublesome; **entrar en guerra** to go to war; **Gran Guerra** Great War; **guerra a muerte** war to the death; **guerra atómica** atomic war; **guerra bacilar, bacteriana** or **bacteriológica** germ war, germ warfare; **guerra biológica** biological warfare; **guerra blanca** cold war; **guerra civil** civil war; **guerra de Crimea** Crimean War; **guerra de guerrillas** guerrilla warfare; **guerra de la Independencia** War of Independence; **guerra de las dos Rosas** War of the Roses; **guerra del opio** Opium War; **guerra de los Cien Años** Hundred Years' War; **guerra de los Siete Años** Seven Years' War; **guerra de los Treinta Años** Thirty Years' War; **guerra del Peloponeso** Peloponnesian War; **guerra del Transvaal** Boer War; **guerra de nervios** war of nerves; **guerra de ondas** radio jamming; **guerra de precios** price war; **guerra de Troya** (myth.) Trojan War; **guerra entre Norte y Sur** Civil War, War between the States (*in the United States*); **guerra Francoprusiana** Franco-Prussian War; **guerra fría** cold war; **guerra hispanoamericana** Spanish-American War; **Guerra Mundial** World War; **guerra psicológica** psychological warfare; **guerra química** chemical warfare; **guerra relámpago** blitzkrieg; **guerra santa** holy war; **guerra sin cuartel** war without quarter; **guerras púnicas** Punic Wars; **guerra total** total war
guerreador -dora *adj* warlike; warring; *mf* warrior, fighter
guerrear *vn* to war, wage war, fight; to resist, put up an argument
guerrero -ra *adj* (pertaining to) war; warlike; warring; mischievous; *mf* fighter; *m* warrior, fighting man, soldier; *f* tight-fitting military jacket
guerrilla *f* band of skirmishers; band of guerrillas; guerrilla warfare
guerrillear *vn* to skirmish; to fight guerrilla warfare
guerrillero *m* guerrilla; guerrilla leader
guía *mf* guide; leader; adviser, mentor; *m* (mil.) guide; *f* guide; guidance; guidebook, directory; leader (*horse*); road marker (*for snowstorms*); marker (*for river navigation*); handle bar; young shoot (*left on vine for training others*); shoot, sprout; fence (*of a saw*); turned-up end of mustache; customhouse permit; (mach.) guide; (min.) leader; (naut.) guy; (rail.) timetable; (Am.) tip (*of stock, branch, etc.*); **guías** *fpl* reins for driving leader horses; **a guías** driving four-in-hand; **echarse con las guías** or **con guías y todo** to ride roughshod; **guía oficial de España** Spanish government yearbook; **guía sonora** sound track (*of film*); **guía telefónica** telephone directory; **guía vocacional** vocational guidance
guiadera *f* (mach.) guide
guiador -dora *adj* guiding; *mf* guide, leader
guiar §90 *va* to guide, to lead; to steer, to drive; to pilot; to train (*a plant*); *vn* to shoot, to sprout; *vr* to be guided; **guiarse de** or **por** to be guided by, to go by
Guido *m* Guy
guiguí *m* (*pl:* **-guíes**) (zool.) flying squirrel
guija *f* pebble; (bot.) grass pea
guijarral *m* place full of large pebbles and cobbles
guijarreño -ña *adj* full of cobbles, cobbly; hard; flint-hearted; hefty, robust
guijarro *m* large pebble, cobble
guijarroso -sa *adj* full of cobbles, cobbly, rocky
guijeño -ña *adj* gravelly, pebbly; hard-hearted
guijo *m* gravel; (mach.) gudgeon
guijón *m* caries, tooth decay
guijoso -sa *adj* pebbly, gravelly
guileña *f* (bot.) columbine
güilogis *m* (f.a.) guilloche
guilla *f* rich harvest
guillado -da *adj* (coll.) daffy
guilladura *f* (coll.) daffiness, craziness
guillame *m* (carp.) rabbet plane
guillar *vr* to leave, to flee; to become unbalanced
Guillermina *f* Wilhelmina
Guillermo *m* William
güillín *m* var. of **huillín**
Guill.° abr. of **Guillermo**
guillomo *m* (bot.) Juneberry, shadberry, serviceberry
guillote *adj* lazy, idle; simple, credulous; *m* harvester; iron pin
guillotina *f* guillotine; paper cutter; (surg. & law) guillotine; **de guillotina** sash (*window*)
guillotinar *va* to guillotine
guimbalete *m* pump handle
guimbarda *f* (carp.) grooving plane
guinchar *va* to goad, prod, prick
guincho *m* goad, prod; (orn.) American osprey
guinda *f* sour cherry (*fruit*); (naut.) height of masts; **guinda garrafal** sweet cherry (*fruit*)
guindal *m* (bot.) sour cherry (*tree*); (naut.) hawser; (naut.) crane
guindalera *f* sour-cherry orchard
guindaleta *f* (naut.) rope, hempen rope
guindaleza *f* (naut.) hawser
guindamaina *f* (naut.) dipping the colors (*as a salute*)
guindar *va* to hoist, to hang up; (coll.) to win; (coll.) to hang, to string up
guindaste *m* (naut.) jib crane
guindilla *f* small sour cherry; Guinea pepper (*fruit*); *m* (coll.) cop, policeman

guindillo *m* small sour cherry tree; **guindillo de Indias** (bot.) Guinea pepper (*plant*)
guindo *m* (bot.) sour cherry (*tree*); **guindo griego** (bot.) sweet cherry (*tree*)
guindola *f* (naut.) boatswain's chair; (naut.) life buoy; (naut.) log chip
guineo -a *adj* Guinea; Guinean; *m* Guineaman; banana; *f* guinea (*coin*); (*cap.*) *f* Guinea; **la Guinea Española** Spanish Guinea; **la Guinea Francesa** French Guinea; **la Guinea Portuguesa** Portuguese Guinea; **la Nueva Guinea** New Guinea
guinga *f* gingham
guinja *f* jujube
guinjo *m* (bot.) jujube tree
guínjol *m* var. of **guinja**
guinjolero *m* var. of **guinjo**
guiñada *f* wink; (naut.) yaw
guiñador -dora *adj* winking; *mf* winker
guiñadura *f* var. of **guiñada**
guiñapiento -ta *adj* ragged, raggedy
guiñapo *m* rag, tatter; tatterdemalion; reprobate
guiñaposo -sa *adj* var. of **guiñapiento**
guiñar *va* to wink (*an eye*); *vn* to wink; (naut.) to yaw; *vr* to wink at each other
guiño *m* wink; face, grimace; **hacerse guiños** to make faces at each other
guión *m* cross (*carried before prelate in procession*); royal standard; leader (*in a dance; among animals*); hyphen; dash; (mil.) guidon; outline; (mov. & theat.) scenario; (mus.) repeat sign; (rad. & telv.) script; **guión de las codornices** (orn.) corn crake; **guión de montaje** (mov.) cutter's script; **guión de rodaje** (mov.) shooting script
guionista *mf* (mov.) scenarist; (mov.) person who writes titles for a movie in a foreign language; scriptwriter
guipur *m* guipure
güira *f* (bot.) calabash tree
guirigay *m* (coll.) gibberish; hubbub, confusion
guirindola *f* jabot, frill
guirlache *m* almond brittle, peanut brittle
guirnalda *f* garland, wreath; (bot.) globe amaranth
güiro *m* (bot.) bottle gourd; (Am.) musical instrument made of a gourd; (Am.) green corn stalk
guiropa *f* meat stew
guisa *f* manner, wise, way; **a guisa de** like, in the manner of; by way of
guisado *m* stew; meat stew
guisador -dora or **guisandero -ra** *mf* cook
guisante *m* (bot.) pea (*plant and seed*); **guisante de olor** (bot.) sweet pea
guisar *va* to stew, to cook; to arrange, put in order; *vn* to cook
guiso *m* dish; seasoning
guisote *m* hash, poor dish
guita *f* twine; (coll.) money
guitarra *f* (mus.) guitar
guitarrazo *m* blow with a guitar
guitarrear *vn* to play the guitar
guitarreo *m* strumming on the guitar
guitarrería *f* guitar shop, string-instrument shop
guitarrero -ra *mf* guitar maker or dealer; guitarist; guitar enthusiast
guitarresco -ca *adj* (coll.) (pertaining to the) guitar
guitarrillo *m* small four-string guitar
guitarrista *mf* guitarist
guitarro *m* small four-string guitar; (coll.) little runt
guitarrón *m* big guitar; (coll.) sly rascal
guitero -ra *mf* twine maker or dealer
guitón -tona *mf* tramp, bum; (coll.) little scamp, rascal
guitonear *vn* to loaf, to bum around
guitonería *f* loafing, bumming, vagabondage; gang of bums
guizacillo *m* (bot.) hedgehog grass
guizgar §59 *va* var. of **enguizgar**
guizque *m* pole with a hook for reaching things
gula *f* gorging, guzzling; gluttony
gules *mpl* (her.) gules
gulosidad *f* gluttony
guloso -sa *adj* gorging, guzzling; gluttonous
gulusmear *vn* to sniff the cooking
gullería *f* var. of **gollería**
gullоría *f* favor, extra; (orn.) calander
gúmena *f* (naut.) heavy cable
gumía *f* Moorish dagger or poniard
gumífero -ra *adj* var. of **gomífero**
gura *f* (orn.) crowned pigeon
gurbio -bia *adj* curved
gurbión *m* (pharm.) euphorbium; coarse twisted silk
guripa *m* (slang) soldier
guro *m* (slang) bailiff, alguazil
gurriato *m* young sparrow
gurrufero *m* (coll.) ugly old nag
gurrumino -na *adj* weak, run-down; *m* (coll.) doting husband, henpecked husband; *f* uxoriousness
gurrupié *m* croupier; gamester's assistant
gurullada *f* (coll.) gang of loafers
gurullo *m* lump, knot
gurvio -via *adj* var. of **gurbio**
gusanear *vn* to swarm, to teem
gusanera *f* nest of worms; worm pit (*compost heap for breeding worms as food for chickens*); (coll.) ruling passion
gusaniento -ta *adj* wormy, grubby, maggoty
gusanillo *m* small worm; twist of gold, silver, or silk; twist stitch; spur (*of gimlet or bit*); **matar el gusanillo** (coll.) to take a shot of liquor before breakfast
gusano *m* worm; maggot; (fig.) worm (*poor soul, contemptible person*); **matar el gusano** (coll.) to take a shot of liquor before breakfast; **gusano de la conciencia** worm of conscience (*remorse*); **gusano de la manzana** apple worm; **gusano del queso** cheese skipper, cheese hopper; **gusano de luz** glowworm; **gusano de San Antón** wood louse; **gusano de seda** or **de la seda** silkworm; **gusano de tierra** earthworm; **gusano plano** flatworm; **gusano rojo** gapeworm
gusanoso -sa *adj* wormy, grubby
gusarapiento -ta *adj* wormy; dirty, filthy
gusarapo *m* waterworm, vinegar worm
gustable *adj* worth being tasted
gustación *f* tasting; taste
gustadura *f* tasting, sampling
gustar *va* to taste; to try, test, sample; to please, be pleasing to; to like, e.g., **no le gustaron a Juan estas manzanas** John did not like these apples; **gustar** + *inf* to like to + *inf*, e.g., **me gusta viajar** I like to travel; *vn* to like, e.g., **como Vd. guste** as you like; **gustar de** to like, e.g., **gusto de la música** I like music; **gustar de** + *inf* to like to + *inf*, e.g., **gusto de leer** I like to read
gustativo -va *adj* gustative
gustatorio -ria *adj* gustatory
Gustavo *m* Gustavus; **Gustavo Adolfo** Gustavus Adolphus
gustazo *m* (coll.) great pleasure, fiendish pleasure
gustillo *m* slight taste, touch
gusto *m* taste; flavor; liking; pleasure; caprice, whim; **a gusto** at will; as you like it; in comfort; **a gusto de** to the taste of, to the liking of; **con mucho gusto** with pleasure, gladly; **dar gusto a** to please; **encontrarse a gusto** or **estar a gusto** to be comfortable; to like it (*e.g., in the country*); **ser del gusto de** to be to the liking of; **tanto gusto** I was so glad to see you; glad to meet you; **tener gusto en** + *inf* to be glad to + *inf;* **tomar (el) gusto a** to take a liking for
gustoso -sa *adj* tasty; pleasant, agreeable; ready, willing, glad
gutagamba *f* (bot.) garcinia (*Garcinia morella*); gamboge, Ceylon gamboge
gutapercha *f* gutta-percha
gutífero -ra *adj* (bot.) guttiferous
gutural *adj* guttural; (phonet.) guttural
guzla *f* (mus.) gusla (*kind of rebec*)

H

H, h *f* ninth letter of the Spanish alphabet
ha *3d sg pres ind of* **haber;** *interj* ha!
haba *f* (bot.) bean, broad bean; bean (*of coffee, cocoa, etc.*); kernel; voting ball; (vet.) tumor on horse's palate; **son habas contadas** it's a sure thing; **haba caballuna** (bot.) horse bean; **haba de Egipto** (bot.) taro; **haba de las Indias** (bot.) sweet pea; **haba de San Ignacio** St.-Ignatius's-bean; **haba panosa** (bot.) horse bean; **haba tonca** tonka bean
Habacuc *m* (Bib.) Habakkuk
habado -da *adj* having a tumor on the palate (*said of a horse*); dappled (*horse*); mottled (*fowl*)
Habana, La see **habano**
habanero -ra *adj & mf* Havanese; *f* habanera (*dance and music*)
habano -na *adj* Havana (*tobacco; brown*); *m* Havana cigar; **La Habana** Havana
habar *m* bean patch
hábeas corpus *m* (law) habeas corpus
haber *m* salary, wages; (com.) credit, credit side; **haberes** *mpl* property, wealth ‖ §54 *va* to get hold of, to lay hands on; (archaic) to have, to get; **habido -da** taking place, held, e.g., **una conferencia habida en París** a conference held in Paris ‖ *v impers* ago, e.g., **cinco años ha** five years ago; (*3d sg pres ind:* **hay**) there to be, e.g., **mañana habrá función** there will be a show tomorrow; **¿cuánta distancia hay de aquí a . . .?** or **¿cuánto hay de aquí a . . .?** how far is it to . . .?; **no haber que** + *inf* to be unnecessary to + *inf;* to be useless to + *inf;* one should not + *inf;* **no hay de qué** you're welcome, don't mention it; **haber que** + *inf* to be necessary to + *inf* ‖ *v aux* to have, e.g., **he leído la carta** I have read the letter; **haber de** + *inf* must, to be to + *inf*, e.g., **ha de llegar antes de las seis** he is to arrive before six o'clock ‖ *vr* to behave oneself, conduct oneself; **habérselas con** to deal with, to have it out with
haberío *m* beast of burden; cattle
habichuela *f* (bot.) kidney bean, string bean; **habichuela verde** string bean
habiente *adj* (law) having, possessing
hábil *adj* skilful; capable; work (*day*); (law) competent
habilidad *f* skill; ability, capability; feat; scheme, trick
habilidoso -sa *adj* skilful
habilitación *f* qualification; financing; equipment; paymastership; **habilitaciones** *fpl* fixtures (*e.g., of a store*); **habilitación de la bandera** permission (*to a foreign vessel*) to engage in coasting trade
habilitado -da *adj* entitled, qualified; (philately) authorized, legalized; *m* paymaster
habilitador -dora *mf* outfitter, equipper
habilitar *va* to enable, to entitle, to qualify; to pass (*in an examination*); to finance (*a person*); to provide; to equip, fit out; to set up
habitabilidad *f* inhabitability
habitable *adj* inhabitable, habitable
habitación *f* habitation; house, dwelling; room; (biol.) habitat; **habitación del forastero** spare room; **habitación doble** double room; **habitación individual** single room; **habitación para los niños** nursery; **habitación popular** low-cost housing; **habitación salón** suite (*in a hotel*)
habitáculo *m* house, dwelling; hovel
habitador -dora *adj* inhabiting; *mf* inhabitant
habitante *mf* inhabitant
habitar *va* to inhabit, live in; to occupy (*e.g., an apartment*); *vn* to live
habitat *m* (biol.) habitat
hábito *m* habit (*custom; disposition acquired by repetition; dress*); **ahorcar** or **colgar el hábito** (coll.) to leave the priesthood, to doff the cassock, **tener por hábito** + *inf* to be in the habit of + *ger*; **tomar el hábito** to enter religion
habituación *f* habituation
habituado -da *mf* habitué
habitual *adj* habitual; usual, regular
habituar §33 *va* to habituate, accustom; **habituar a** + *inf* to accustom to + *inf; vr* to become habituated, become accustomed; **habituarse a** + *inf* to become accustomed to + *inf*
habitud *f* connection, relation
habla *f* speech (*faculty of speaking; manner of speaking; language, dialect; talk or address to a group of people*); **al habla** speaking; in contact, in communication; (naut.) within hailing distance; **¡al habla!** speaking! (*in answer to call of one's name on telephone*); **de habla latina** Romance-language-speaking; **negar** or **quitar el habla a** to not speak to (*because of a quarrel*); **perder el habla** to lose one's speech
hablado -da *adj* spoken; **bien hablado** well-tongued; well-spoken; **mal hablado** ill-tongued
hablador -dora *adj* talkative; gossipy; *mf* talker, chatterbox; gossip
habladuría *f* idle rumor; cut, sarcasm; gossip, piece of gossip
hablanchín -china *adj & mf* (coll.) var. of **hablador**
hablante *adj* speaking; *mf* speaker
hablantín -tina *adj & mf* (coll.) var. of **hablador**
hablar *va* to speak, to talk (*a language*); to talk (*e.g., nonsense*); **hablarlo todo** to spill everything; *vn* to speak, to talk; **dar que hablar** to cause talk; **es hablar por demás** it's wasted talk; **estar hablando** to be almost alive (*said of painting or sculpture*); **no hablar con** to not speak to (*because of a quarrel*); **hablar alto** to speak up; **hablar claro** to talk straight from the shoulder; *vr* to talk to each other; **hablárselo todo** to let nobody get a word in edgewise; to contradict oneself all the time
hablilla *f* story, gossip, piece of gossip
hablista *mf* speaker, good speaker
habón *m* wheal
habré *1st sg fut ind of* **haber**
hacanea *f* sturdy little horse
hacedero -ra *adj* feasible, practicable
hacedor *m* steward, manager; (*cap.*) *m* Maker (*God*)
hacendado -da *adj* landed, property-owning; *mf* property-owner; (Am.) rancher, cattle rancher
hacendar §18 *va* to transfer; **hacendarle a uno con** to transfer (*property*) to someone; *vr* to acquire property
hacendero -ra *adj* sedulous, thrifty; *f* community project or undertaking
hacendista *m* economist; fiscal expert; man of private means
hacendoso -sa *adj* diligent, industrious; thrifty
hacer §55 *va* to make; to do; to pack (*a trunk*); to give (*an order*); to cause; to accustom; to play (*a part*); to play the part of; to act, perform (*a play*); to pretend to be; to imagine (*someone*) to be; to hold, to contain; to have made; to ask (*a question*); **desde hace** for, e.g., **estoy aquí desde hace diez días** I have been here (for) ten days; **estaba allí**

desde hacía dos meses I had been there (for) two months; **hace** ago, e.g., **hace dos semanas** two weeks ago; **hacer con** to provide with; **hacer mucho (tiempo) que** to be a long time since; **hacer . . . que** to be . . . since, e.g., **hace un mes que Juan estuvo aquí** it is a month since John was here; **hacía un mes que Juan había estado aquí** it was a month since John had been here; **mañana hará un mes que Juan estuvo aquí** it will be a month tomorrow since John was here; **hacer** + *inf* to have + *inf*, e.g., **le haré llamar a su puerta** I shall have him knock at your door; to make + *inf*, e.g., **me hizo estudiar** he made me study; to have + *pp*, e.g., **haremos construir una casa** we shall have a house built; for expressions like **hacer calor** to be warm, to be hot (*said of weather*), see the noun ‖ *vn* to act; to matter; **hacer a** to fit; **hacer como que** + *ind* to pretend to + *inf;* **hacer de** to act as, work as; **hacer por** + *inf* to try to + *inf;* **hacer que** + *ind* to pretend to + *inf;* **hacer que** + *subj* to see to it that; to cause to + *inf* ‖ *vr* to make oneself; to become, get to be; to grow; to turn into; to imagine; **hacerse a** + *inf* to become accustomed to + *inf;* **hacerse a una parte** or **a un lado** to step aside, to withdraw; **hacerse con** to seize, get hold of, to make off with; **hacerse chiquito** or **el chiquito** (coll.) to sing small; **hacérsele a uno** + *adj* to strike or impress one as + *adj*, e.g., **lo que Vd. dijo se me hizo difícil de creer** what you said struck me as hard to believe; **hacerse viejo** (coll.) to kill time

hacera *f* var. of **acera**

hacia *prep* toward; near, about; **hacia abajo** downwards; **hacia adelante** forwards; **hacia arriba** upwards; **hacia atrás** backwards; (coll.) the wrong way; **hacia dentro** inwards; **hacia fuera** outwards

hacienda *f* farm, farmstead, country property; property, fortune, possessions; treasury; (Am.) ranch; (Am.) cattle, livestock; **haciendas** *fpl* household chores; **hacienda pública** public finance

hacina *f* (agr.) shock, stack; pile, heap

hacinador -dora *mf* stacker

hacinamiento *m* piling, heaping, stacking

hacinar *va* to pile, heap, stack

hacha *f* heavy wax candle with four wicks, torch, firebrand; axe; battle-axe; thatch; (coll.) expert

hachar *va* to hew with an axe; (Am.) to get the better of (*in an argument*)

hachazo *m* blow or stroke with an axe

hachear *va* to hew with an axe; *vn* to hack with an axe

hachero *m* torch stand; torchbearer; woodcutter; (mil.) sapper

hachich *m* or **hachís** *m* hashish

hacho *m* bunch of resinous wood or of tow and pitch (*for a torch*); beacon (*hill overlooking sea*)

hachón *m* large torch; cresset

hachote *m* (naut.) short, thick candle

hachuela *f* small axe; (Am.) hatchet

hada *f* fairy; (fig.) charmer (*fascinating woman*); (obs.) fate, destiny; **Hadas** *fpl* (myth.) Fates; **hada madrina** fairy godmother

hadado -da *adj* fateful; magic, wonder-working; **bien hadado** lucky; **mal hadado** ill-fated

hadar *va* to foretell; to predestine; to charm, cast a spell on

Hades *m* (myth. & Bib.) Hades

hado *m* fate, destiny

hafiz *m* (*pl:* **-fices**) warden

hafnio *m* (chem.) hafnium

hagiografía *f* hagiography

hagiográfico -ca *adj* hagiographic or hagiographical

hagiógrafo *m* hagiographer

hagiología *f* hagiology

hago *1st sg pres ind of* **hacer**

haiga *m* (slang) sporty-looking car; (slang) sporty-looking person

Haití *m* Haiti

haitiano -na *adj & mf* Haitian

hala *interj* get going!; come, come!, here, here!

halagador -dora *adj* flattering

halagar §59 *va* to cajole, fawn on; to gratify, to attract; to flatter

halago *m* cajolery; gratification; flattery; **halagos** *mpl* flattery, flattering words

halagüeño -ña *adj* attractive, charming; bright, rosy, promising; flattering

halar *va* (naut.) to haul, pull; *vn* (naut.) to pull ahead

halazona *f* (pharm.) halazone

halcón *m* (orn.) falcon; **halcón montano** haggard hawk; **halcón niego** eyas; **halcón palumbario** (orn.) pigeon hawk, merlin; **halcón peregrino** (orn.) peregrine falcon; **halcón peregrino patero** (orn.) duck hawk

halconear *vn* to act and dress brazenly in order to attract men

halconera *f* mew, place for falcons

halconería *f* hawking, falconry

halconero *m* hawker, falconer

halda *f* skirt; packing burlap; **de haldas o de mangas** (coll.) one way or another, right or wrong; **poner haldas en cinta** (coll.) to pull up one's skirts to run; (coll.) to roll up one's sleeves (*for work*)

haldada *f* skirtful

haldear *vn* to dash along with skirts flying

haldeta *f* flap

haldudo -da *adj* full-skirted

hale *interj* get going!

haleche *m* (ichth.) anchovy

Halicarnaso *f* Halicarnassus

halieto *m* (orn.) osprey, fish hawk

halita *f* (mineral.) halite (*rock salt*); (mineral.) websterite (*aluminite*); (petrog.) websterite

hálito *m* halitus, breath, vapor; (poet.) gentle breeze

halitosis *f* halitosis

halo *m* (meteor, f.a. & fig.) halo

halófilo -la *adj* (bot.) halophilous

halófito -ta *adj* (bot.) halophytic; *f* (bot.) halophyte

halogenación *f* halogenation

halógeno *m* (chem.) halogen

haloideo -a *adj & m* (chem.) haloid

halón *m* (meteor.) halo

halozono *m* var. of **halazona**

halterio *m* dumbbell; halter (*of insect*)

haluro *m* (chem.) halide

hallaca *f* var. of **hayaca**

hallado -da *adj* found; **bien hallado** unconstrained; **mal hallado** uneasy, constrained; *f* finding, discovery

hallador -dora *mf* finder

hallar *va* to find; *vr* to find oneself; to be; **no hallarse** to not like it, be annoyed; **hallarse bien con** to be satisfied with; **hallarse en todo** to butt in everywhere; to have one's hand in everything, to be mixed up in everything; **hallárselo todo hecho** to never have to turn a hand

hallazgo *m* finding, discovery; find; reward (*for finding something*), e.g., **cinco dólares de hallazgo** five dollars reward

hallulla *f* or **hallullo** *m* bread baked on embers or hot stones; (Am.) fine bread

hamaca *f* hammock

hamacar §86 *va* (Am.) to swing, to rock

hamadríada *f* (myth.) hamadryad

hámago *m* beebread; nausea, loathing, disgust

hamamelidáceo -a *adj* (bot.) hamamelidaceous

hamamelina *f* (pharm.) witch hazel

hamaquear *va & vr* (Am.) to swing, to rock

hamaquero *m* hammock maker; hammock bearer; hammock hook

hambre *f* hunger; famine; starvation; **entretener el hambre** (coll.) to take a bite to stave off hunger till mealtime; (coll.) to try to forget one's hunger; **matar de hambre** to starve (*a person*) to death; **morir de hambre** to starve to death, to die of starvation; **pasar hambre** to go hungry; **tener hambre** to be hungry; **tener hambre de** to be hungry for, to hunger for

hambreador *m* (Am.) food profiteer

hambrear *va* to starve, to famish; *vn* to starve, to famish, to hunger

hambriento -ta *adj* hungry; **hambriento de** hungry for (*e.g., wealth*)

hambrón -brona *adj* (coll.) starving; *mf* (coll.) starveling
hambruna *f* (Am.) mad hunger
Hamburgo *f* Hamburg
hamburgués -guesa *adj* (pertaining to) Hamburg; *mf* native or inhabitant of Hamburg; *f* hamburger (*sandwich*)
hamita *mf* Hamite
hamo *m* fishhook
hampa *f* vagrancy, rowdyism; (coll.) rowdies
hampesco -ca *adj* vagabond, rowdyish
hampón *m* rowdy, bully, tough
han *3d pl pres ind of* **haber**
hangar *m* (aer.) hangar
hanoveriano -na *adj & mf* Hanoverian
hansa *f* var. of **ansa**
hanseático -ca *adj* var. of **anseático**
hanumán *m* (zool.) langur
haploide *adj & m* (biol.) haploid
haplología *f* (philol.) haplology
haragán -gana *adj* idling, loafing, lazy; *mf* idler, loafer, good-for-nothing
haraganear *vn* to idle, to loaf, to hang around
haraganería *f* idleness, loafing, laziness
harakiri *m* hari-kari
harambel *m* var. of **arambel**
harapiento -ta *adj* ragged
harapo *m* rag, tatter; **andar** or **estar hecho un harapo** (coll.) to be in rags
haraposo -sa *adj* ragged
haré *1st sg fut ind of* **hacer**
harem *m* or **harén** *m* harem
harfango *m* (orn.) snowy owl
harija *f* mill dust, stive
harina *f* flour; **donde no hay harina, todo es mohina** poverty parts good company; **estar metido en harina** (coll.) to be deeply absorbed; (coll.) to be fat, be heavy; **ser harina de otro costal** (coll.) to be a horse of another color; **harina de maíz** corn meal
harinero -ra *adj* (pertaining to) flour; *m* flour dealer; flour bin or chest
harinoso -sa *adj* floury, mealy; farinaceous
harma *f* var. of **alárgama**
harmonía *f* var. of **armonía**
harnero *m* sieve; **estar hecho un harnero** to be riddled with wounds
Haroldo *m* Harold
harón -rona *adj* lazy; balky; *mf* lazy loafer
haronear *vn* to be slow, be lazy, idle around, to dawdle
haronero *m* sieve, sifter
haronía *f* laziness
harpa *f* var. of **arpa**
harpía *f* (coll.) ugly shrew, jade; (coll.) harpy (*rapacious person*); (zool.) harpy bat (*Nyctimene*); (myth.) Harpy
harpillera *f* burlap, bagging, sackcloth
harre *m & interj* var. of **arre**
hartar *va* to stuff, satiate; to satisfy, gratify; to tire, bore; **hartar de** to overwhelm with, deluge with; *vn* to stuff, be satiated; *vr* to stuff, be satiated; to tire, be bored
hartazgo *m* or **hartazón** *m* fill, bellyful; **darse un hartazgo** (coll.) to eat one's fill; **darse un hartazgo de** (coll.) to have or to get one's fill of (*e.g., peanuts, reading, eating*)
harto -ta *adj* full, satiated, fed up; much, very much; **harto de** full of, sick of, fed up with; **harto** *adv* quite, very; enough
hartura *f* fill, satiety; abundance; full satisfaction; **con hartura** in abundance, on a large scale
has *2d sg pres ind of* **haber**
hasta *adv* even; *prep* until, till; to, as far as, up to, down to; as much as; **hasta aquí** so far; **hasta después** good-by, so long; **hasta después de** until after; **hasta la vista** or **hasta luego** good-by, so long; **hasta mañana** see you tomorrow; **hasta no más** to the utmost; **hasta que** until, till; **hasta tanto que** until, till
hastial *m* gable end; (min.) side wall; bumpkin
hastiar **§90** *va* to sicken, cloy, surfeit; to annoy, bore
hastío *m* nausea, disgust, surfeit; annoyance, boredom
hastioso -sa *adj* sickening; annoying, boresome
hataca *f* large wooden ladle; rolling pin
hatajar *va & vn* to divide into small herds or flocks; to separate from the herd or flock
hatajo *m* small herd, small flock; (coll.) lot, flock (*e.g., of nonsense*)
hatear *va* (coll.) to pack up; *vn* to get one's outfit together; to bring provisions to shepherds
hatería *f* provisions, supplies, or equipment for several days (*for shepherds, farm hands, miners, etc.*)
hatero -ra *adj* pack (*animal*); *mf* (Am.) rancher; *m* pack carrier
hatijo *m* straw for beehives
hato *m* herd (*of cattle*); flock (*of sheep*); shepherds' hut; provisions for shepherds; everyday outfit; pack, bundle (*of clothes*); ring, clique; gang (*of thugs*); lot, flock (*of nonsense*); (Am.) cattle ranch; **liar el hato** (coll.) to pack, pack up, pack one's baggage; **menear el hato a** (coll.) to beat up; **revolver el hato** (coll.) to stir up trouble
hawaiano -na *adj & mf* Hawaiian; *m* Hawaiian (*language*)
haxix *m* var. of **hachich**
hay *3d sg pres ind of* **haber**
haya *1st sg pres subj of* **haber;** *f* (bot.) beech, beech tree; **La Haya** The Hague
hayaca *f* (Am.) mince pie
hayal *m* or **hayedo** *m* beech forest
hayo *m* (bot.) coca; (Am.) coca leaves prepared for chewing
hayuco *m* beechnut, mast (*food for hogs*)
haz *m* (*pl:* **haces**) bunch, bundle, fagot; sheaf; pencil, beam (*of rays*); (arch.) clustered column; (bot.) fascicle; (mil.) file of soldiers; (mil.) troops drawn up in divisions; *f* (*pl:* **haces**) face; surface (*of the earth*); right side (*e.g., of cloth*); **a sobre haz** on the surface; **en haz y en paz** by common consent; **hacer haz** to be in line, be flush; **ser de dos haces** to be two-faced; *2d sg impv of* **hacer**
haza *f* field (*for crops*)
hazaleja *f* towel
hazaña *f* deed, feat, exploit
hazañería *f* fuss (*trivial perturbation*)
hazañero -ra *adj* fussy, fluttery
hazañoso -sa *adj* gallant, courageous, heroic
hazmerreír *m* (coll.) butt, laughingstock
he *adv* lo, lo and behold; **he aquí** here is, here are, e.g., **he aquí a su hermano** here is your brother; **he allí** there is, there are, e.g., **helos allí** there they are; *1st sg pres ind of* **haber**
hé *2d sg impv of* **haber**
hebdómada *f* week, hebdomad; seven years
hebdomadario -ria *adj* hebdomadal or hebdomadary
Hebe *f* (myth.) Hebe
hebilla *f* buckle; **no faltar hebilla a** (coll.) to be tiptop, to be perfect
hebillaje *m* buckles, set of buckles
hebillero -ra *mf* buckle maker or dealer
hebra *f* thread, fiber; vein; grain (*in wood*); (fig.) thread (*of conversation*); **hebras** *fpl* (poet.) hair; **de una hebra** (Am.) all at once; **estar** or **ser de buena hebra** (coll.) to be strong and husky; **pegar la hebra** (coll.) to strike up a conversation; (coll.) to talk on and on
hebraico -ca *adj* Hebraic
hebraísmo *m* Hebraism
hebraísta *mf* Hebraist (*scholar skilled in Hebrew language and literature*)
hebraizante *adj* Hebraizing; *mf* Hebraist
hebraizar **§97** *vn* to Hebraize
hebreo -a *adj & mf* Hebrew; *m* Hebrew (*language*); (coll.) usurer
Hébridas, las the Hebrides; **Nuevas Hébridas** New Hebrides
hebroso -sa *adj* fibrous, stringy
Hécate *f* (myth.) Hecate
hecatombe *f* hecatomb
hect. abr. of **hectárea**
hectárea *f* hectare
héctico -ca *adj & mf* var. of **hético**
hectiquez *f* var. of **hetiquez**
hectocótilo *m* (zool.) hectocotylus
hectógrafo *m* hectograph
hectogramo *m* hectogram
hectólitro *m* hectoliter
hectómetro *m* hectometer

Héctor *m* (myth.) Hector
Hécuba *f* (myth.) Hecuba
hechiceresco -ca *adj* magical
hechicería *f* sorcery, wizardry, witchcraft; (fig.) charm, fascination
hechicero -ra *adj* magic; bewitching, charming, enchanting; *mf* magician, sorcerer; charmer, enchanter; *m* wizard, sorcerer; *f* witch, sorceress
hechizar §76 *va* to bewitch, cast a spell on; (fig.) to bewitch, charm, enchant, delight; *vn* to be charming, to enchant; to practice sorcery
hechizo -za *adj* fake, deceptive; detachable; made, manufactured; fit, suitable; skilful (*work*); (Am.) local, home (*product*); *m* spell, charm; magic, sorcery; (fig.) magic, sorcery, glamour; (fig.) charmer; **hechizos** *mpl* charms (*of a woman*)
hecho -cha *pp of* **hacer;** *adj* accustomed, inured; finished, perfect; ready-made; full-grown; **a lo hecho pecho** make the best out of a bad situation; **estar hecho** to be turned into, to be, to look like; **hecho y derecho** finished, complete; *m* fact; deed, act; matter; event; **de hecho** in fact; (law) de facto; **en hecho de verdad** as a matter of fact; **estar en el hecho de** to catch on to, to get the point of; **hecho consumado** fait accompli; **hecho de armas** feat of arms; **Hechos de los Apóstoles** (Bib.) Acts of the Apostles; **¡hecho!** O.K.!, all right!
hechura *f* make, making; creation, creature; form, shape, cut, build; workmanship; (Am.) drink, treat; **hechuras** *fpl* cost of making; **no tener hechura** to be impracticable
hedentina *f* stench, stink
heder §66 *va* to bore, annoy; *vn* to stink
hediondez *f* stench, stink
hediondo -da *adj* stinking; smelly; annoying, boring; filthy, dirty, obscene; *m* (bot.) bean trefoil; (zool.) skunk
hedonismo *m* hedonism
hedonista *mf* hedonist
hedor *m* stench, stink
Hefestos *m* (myth.) Hephaestus
hegelianismo *m* Hegelianism
hegeliano -na *adj & mf* Hegelian
hegemonía *f* hegemony
hégira *f* var. of **héjira**
heguemonía *f* var. of **hegemonía**
héjira *f* hegira (*Mohammedan era*)
helada *f* see **helado**
Hélade *f* Hellas (*Greece*)
heladería *f* (Am.) ice-cream parlor
heladero -ra *mf* (Am.) ice-cream maker or dealer; *f* (Am.) freezer, refrigerator; (Am.) ice-cream tray
heladizo -za *adj* easily frozen
helado -da *adj* cold; icy; (fig.) frozen (*with fear, surprise, etc.*); (fig.) cold, chilly; *m* cold drink; water ice; ice cream; **helado al corte** brick ice cream; **helado de barquillo** ice-cream cone; *f* freeze, freezing; frost (*freezing condition*); **helada blanca** hoarfrost
helador -dora *adj* freezing; *f* ice-cream freezer
heladura *f* crack in trunk of tree caused by cold
helamiento *m* freeze, freezing
helar §18 *va* to freeze; to congeal, harden; to astonish, dumfound; to discourage; *vn* to freeze; *vr* to freeze; to congeal, harden, set; to become frostbitten
helechal *m* fernland, fernery
helecho *m* (bot.) fern; **helecho acuático** (bot.) water fern, osmunda; **helecho arbóreo** (bot.) tree fern; **helecho florido** (bot.) flowering fern; **helecho macho** (bot.) male fern; **helecho real** (bot.) royal fern
helena & **Helena** *f* see **heleno**
helénico -ca *adj* Hellenic
helenio *m* (bot.) elecampane
helenismo *m* Hellenism
helenista *mf* Hellenist
helenístico -ca *adj* Hellenistic
helenización *f* Hellenization
helenizar §76 *va & vr* to Hellenize
heleno -na *adj* Hellenic; *mf* Hellene; *f* jack-o'-lantern, St. Elmo's fire; (*cap.*) *f* Helen of Troy
helero *m* glacier
Helesponto *m* Hellespont
helgado -da *adj* jag-toothed, snaggle-toothed
helgadura *f* gaps in teeth, uneven teeth
heliaco -ca *adj* (astr.) heliacal
heliantemo *m* (bot.) helianthemum
heliantina *f* helianthin
helianto *m* (bot.) helianthus
hélice *f* helix (*spiral*); (anat., elec. & geom.) helix; screw propeller; screw or propeller (*of boat*); propeller (*of airplane*); (mach.) fly
hélico -ca *adj* helical
helicoidal *adj* helicoidal
helicoide *adj* helicoid; *m* (geom.) helicoid
helicoideo -a *adj* (bot. & zool.) helicoid
Helicón *m* (hist., myth. & fig.) Helicon; (*l.c.*) *m* (mus.) helicon
Helicónides *fpl* (myth.) Muses
heliconio -nia or **-na** *adj* Heliconian; Muses'
helicóptero *m* (aer.) helicopter
helio *m* (chem.) helium
heliocéntrico -ca *adj* heliocentric
heliograbado *m* helioengraving
heliografía *f* heliography
heliógrafo *m* heliograph
Helios *m* (myth.) Helios
helioscopio *m* helioscope
helióstato *m* heliostat
helioterapia *f* heliotherapy
heliotipia *f* heliotype, heliotypy
heliotropio *m* var. of **heliotropo**
heliotropismo *m* (biol.) heliotropism
heliotropo *m* (bot. & mineral.) heliotrope
helipuerto *m* heliport
helmintiasis *f* (path.) helminthiasis
helminto *m* (zool.) helminth
helmintología *f* helminthology
helvecio -cia *adj & mf* Helvetian; **la Helvecia** Helvetia
helvético -ca *adj* Helvetic; *mf* Helvetian
hemático -ca *adj* hematic
hematíe *m* (physiol.) red cell
hematina *f* (physiol.) hematin
hematita or **hematites** *f* (mineral.) hematite
hematocele *m* (path.) hematocele
hematócrito *m* hematocrit
hematopoyesis *f* (physiol.) hematopoiesis
hematosis *f* (physiol.) hematosis
hematoxilina *f* (chem.) hematoxylin
hembra *adj* female, e.g., **un pez hembra** a female fish; (bot. & mach.) female; weak, thin, delicate; *f* female (*human or animal*); eye (*of hook and eye*); nut; strike (*of a lock*); (bot.) female; **hembra de terraja** (mach.) die; **hembra del timón** (naut.) rudder gudgeon; **hembras de la familia** distaff side
hembraje *m* (Am.) female flock or herd
hembrear *vn* to be drawn to the female (*said of animals*); to produce only females, to produce more females than males
hembrilla *f* eyebolt; (mach.) female
hemélitro -tra *adj* hemelytral; *m* (ent.) hemelytron or hemelytrum
hemeralopía *f* (path.) hemeralopia
hemeroteca *f* newspaper and magazine library, periodical library
hemicelulosa *f* (chem.) hemicellulose
hemiciclo *m* hemicycle (*half circle; semicircular structure*); floor (*of legislative body*)
hemicránea *f* (path.) hemicrania
hemiédrico -ca or **hemiedro -dra** *adj* (cryst.) hemihedral
hemiesfera *f* var. of **hemisferio**
hemina *f* (biochem.) hemin; (hist.) hemina
hemíono *m* (zool.) hemionus, kiang
hemiplejía *f* (path.) hemiplegia
hemíptero -ra *adj* (ent.) hemipterous
hemisférico -ca *adj* hemispherical
hemisferio *m* hemisphere; **hemisferios de Magdeburgo** (phys.) Magdeburg hemispheres
hemisferoide *m* (geom.) hemispheroid
hemistiquio *m* hemistich
hemiterpeno *m* (chem.) hemiterpene
hemocianina *f* (biochem.) hemocyanin
hemofilia *f* (path.) hemophilia
hemofílico -ca *adj* hemophilic; *mf* hemophiliac
hemoglobina *f* (biochem.) hemoglobin
hemoleucocito *m* (anat.) hemoleucocyte
hemolisina *f* (immun.) hemolysin

hemólisis *f* (immun.) hemolysis
hemoptisis *f* (path.) hemoptysis
hemorragia *f* (path.) hemorrhage
hemorrágico -ca *adj* hemorrhagic
hemorroidal *adj* hemorrhoidal
hemorroidectomía *f* (surg.) hemorrhoidectomy
hemorroides *fpl* (path.) hemorrhoids
hemorroo *m* (zool.) cerastes, horned viper
hemos *1st pl pres ind of* **haber**
hemostático -ca *adj & m* (med.) hemostatic
hemostato or **hemóstato** *m* hemostat
henaje *m* tedding
henal *m* hayloft
henar *m* hayfield
henchidor -dora *adj* filling; *mf* filler
henchidura *f* filling, stuffing; heave, swell (*of waves*)
henchimiento *m* filling, stuffing; (naut.) piece of wood used to fill in
henchir §94 *va* to fill; to stuff; to heap (*e.g., with favors, insults*); *vr* to be filled; to stuff, stuff oneself
hendedor -dora *adj* cleaving, cracking, splitting
hendedura *f* cleft, crack, split
hender §66 *va* to cleave, crack, split; to cleave (*the air, the water, the clouds, etc.*); to force one's way through; *vr* to cleave, crack, split
hendible *adj* cleavable; fissionable
hendidura *f* var. of **hendedura**
hendiente *m* downstroke of a sword
hendimiento *m* cleaving, cracking, splitting; fission
heneador -dora *adj* tedding; *mf* tedder, haymaker; *m* tedder (*machine*)
henear *va* to ted, to hay
henequén *m* (bot.) henequen (*plant and fiber*)
henificación *f* tedding, haying
henificar §86 *va* to ted, to hay
henil *m* hayloft, haymow
henna *f* henna (*dye*)
heno *m* hay; (bot.) crimson clover; **heno blanco** (bot.) velvet grass
henojil *m* garter
henoteísmo *m* henotheism
henrio *m* (elec.) henry
heñir §74 *va* to knead; **hay mucho que heñir** (coll.) there's still a lot to do
heparina *f* (pharm.) heparin
hepático -ca *adj* hepatic; *f* (bot.) hepatica, liverwort; **hepática estrellada** (bot.) woodruff
hepatitis *f* (path.) hepatitis
hepatización *f* (path.) hepatization
heptaedro *m* (geom.) heptahedron
heptagonal *adj* heptagonal
heptágono -na *adj* heptagonal; *m* (geom.) heptagon
heptámetro *m* heptameter
heptangular *adj* heptangular
heptano *m* (chem.) heptane
heptarquía *f* heptarchy; **la Heptarquía anglosajona** the Heptarchy
heptasilábico -ca *adj* heptasyllabic
heptasílabo -ba *adj* heptasyllabic; *m* heptasyllable
Heptateuco *m* (Bib.) Heptateuch
Hera *f* (myth.) Hera or Here
Heracles *m* (myth.) Heracles
Heráclito *m* Heraclitus
heraldía *f* heraldry (*office or duty of herald*)
heráldico -ca *adj* heraldic; *mf* heraldist; *f* heraldry
heraldo *m* herald
herbáceo -a *adj* herbaceous
herbajar *va* to graze, put to graze; *vn* to graze
herbaje *m* herbage; grazing fee; coarse woolen cloth
herbajear *va & vn* var. of **herbajar**
herbajero *m* renter of pasture
herbar §18 *va* to dress (*hides*) with herbs
herbario -ria *adj* herbal; *m* herbarium (*treatise; room or building*); herbalist, botanist; rumen (*of ruminant*)
herbazal *m* grassland
herbecer §34 *vn* to sprout; to turn green (*with grass*)
herbero *m* gullet (*of ruminants*)
herbicida *m* weed killer
herbífero -ra *adj* herbiferous
herbívoro -ra *adj* herbivorous
herbolario -ria *adj & mf* (coll.) scatterbrain; *m* herbalist (*botanist; herbman*); herb store
herboristería *f* herb store
herborizar §76 *vn* to gather herbs
herboso -sa *adj* herby, grassy
herciano -na *adj* (elec.) Hertzian
Herculano *f* Herculaneum
hercúleo -a *adj* Herculean (*pertaining to Hercules*); herculean (*strong, courageous*)
Hércules *m* (astr. & myth.) Hercules; (*l.c.*) *m* strong man
heredable *adj* inheritable, hereditable
heredad *f* country property, country estate
heredamiento *m* inheritance; landed estate; (law) endowment
heredar *va & vn* to inherit
heredero -ra *adj* inheritable, inheriting; *mf* heir, inheritor; landowner, owner of a country estate; **heredero forzoso** (law) heir apparent; **heredero presuntivo** (law) heir presumptive; *m* heir; *f* heiress
hereditario -ria *adj* hereditary
hereje *mf* heretic
herejía *f* heresy; insult, outrage; (coll.) outrageous price
herén *f* var. of **yero**
herencia *f* inheritance, heritage; estate; (biol.) heredity; **herencia ligada al sexo** (biol.) sex-linkage
heresiarca *m* heresiarch
herético -ca *adj* heretic or heretical
herido -da *adj* hurt (*injured; offended*); wounded; **mal herido** seriously injured, seriously wounded; *mf* injured person, wounded person; **los heridos** the injured, the wounded; *m* wounded soldier; *f* injury, wound; insult, outrage; **renovar la herida** to open an old sore; **tocar en la herida** to sting to the quick
herir §62 *va* to hurt, injure; to wound; to strike; to beat down upon; to play (*a stringed instrument*); to pluck (*a string*); to touch, to move; to offend
herma *m* (hist.) herma
hermafrodismo *m* var. of **hermafroditismo**
hermafrodita *adj* hermaphrodite, hermaphroditic; *m* hermaphrodite
hermafroditismo *m* (biol.) hermaphroditism
hermafrodito *adj & m* var. of **hermafrodita**
hermana *f* see **hermano**
hermanable *adj* brotherly, fraternal; compatible
hermanado -da *adj* like, mated, matched
hermanamiento *m* matching, mating; harmonizing; brotherly union
hermanar *va* to match, to mate; to join, combine; to harmonize (*e.g., opinions*); *vr* to match; to become brothers (*in spirit*)
hermanastra *f* stepsister
hermanastro *m* stepbrother
hermanazgo *m* or **hermandad** *f* brotherhood; sisterhood; sorority; close friendship; conformity, close relationship
hermanear *va* to call (*someone*) brother
hermano -na *adj* sister (*e.g., language*); *mf* mate, twin, companion; *m* brother; **hermanos** *mpl* brother and sister; **medio hermano** half brother; **primo hermano** first cousin; **hermano carnal** blood brother; **hermano de leche** foster brother; **hermano de madre** half brother by the same mother; **hermano de padre** half brother by the same father; **hermano político** brother-in-law; **hermanos de la doctrina (cristiana)** Christian Brothers; **hermanos siameses** Siamese twins; *f* sister; **media hermana** half sister; **prima hermana** first cousin; **ser prima hermana de** (coll.) to be much like; **hermana carnal** blood sister; **hermana de la caridad** Sister of Charity, Sister of Mercy; **hermana de leche** foster sister; **hermana de madre** half sister by the same mother; **hermana de padre** half sister by the same father; **hermana política** sister-in-law
hermenéutico -ca *adj* hermeneutic; *f* hermeneutics
Hermes *m* (myth.) Hermes

hermeticidad *f* airtightness; impenetrability
hermético -ca *adj* hermetic, airtight; impenetrable (*person, secret, etc.*); tight-lipped, tight-mouthed
hermetismo *m* secretiveness, secrecy
Hermíone *f* (myth.) Hermione
hermoseador -dora *adj* beautifying; *mf* beautifier
hermoseamiento *m* beautification, embellishment
hermosear *va* to beautify, embellish
hermosilla *f* (bot.) throatwort
hermoso -sa *adj* beautiful; handsome
hermosura *f* beauty; belle, beauty (*beautiful woman*)
hernia *f* (path.) hernia; **hernia estrangulada** (path.) strangulated hernia
herniado -da *adj* suffering from hernia; *mf* person suffering from hernia
herniar *vr* to herniate; to protrude
herniario -ria *adj* hernial; *f* (bot.) burstwort
hernioso -sa *adj & mf* var. of **herniado**
hernista *m* hernia surgeon
Hero *f* (myth.) Hero
Herodes *m* (Bib.) Herod; **andar** or **ir de Herodes a Pilatos** (coll.) to go from pillar to post, to be driven from pillar to post
herodiano -na *adj* Herodian
Herodías *f* (Bib.) Herodias
Heródoto *m* Herodotus
héroe *m* hero
heroicidad *f* heroicity, heroism; heroic deed
heroico -ca *adj* heroic; (med.) heroic; **a la heroica** in the heroic manner
heroicocómico -ca *adj* heroicomic, mock-heroic
heroína *f* heroine; (pharm.) heroin
heroísmo *m* heroism
herpe *m & f* (path.) herpes
herpético -ca *adj* herpetic
herpetología *f* herpetology
herpil *m* esparto net (*for carrying straw, melons, etc.*)
herrada *f* bucket
herradero *m* branding of cattle; place for branding cattle; (taur.) topsy-turvy bullring
herrador *m* horseshoer, farrier
herradora *f* (coll.) horseshoer's wife
herradura *f* horseshoe; **mostrar las herraduras** to kick; (coll.) to show one's heels
herraj *m* var. of **erraj**
herraje *m* iron fittings, iron trimmings, ironwork, hardware; fine coal made of crushed olive stones
herramental *adj* tool; *m* tool bag, toolbox
herramienta *f* tool; tools, set of tools; (coll.) horns (*of bull*); (coll.) grinders (*teeth*); **herramienta motriz** power tool; **herramientas de dotación** (aut.) tools that come with the car
herrar §18 *va* to shoe (*a horse*); to brand (*cattle*); to trim with ironwork; to hoop (*a barrel*)
herrén *m* mixed fodder (*oats, rye, barley, etc.*)
herrenal *m* or **herreñal** *m* field of mixed grain
herrería *f* blacksmith shop; blacksmithing; ironworks; disturbance, uproar
herrerillo *m* (orn.) blue titmouse; (orn.) great titmouse
herrero *m* blacksmith; iron forger; **herrero de grueso** ironworker; **herrero de obra** steelworker, structural ironworker
herreruelo *m* (orn.) coal titmouse
herrete *m* tip (*of metal*)
herretear *va* to tip, put a metal tip on
herrezuelo *m* small piece of iron
herrín *m* rust
herrón *m* quoit; washer; iron bar (*used in planting*); (Am.) tip (*of spinning top*)
herronada *f* blow with iron bar; hard peck (*with bird's beak*)
herrumbrar *va & vr* var. of **aherrumbrar**
herrumbre *f* rust; taste of iron; (bot.) rust, plant rot
herrumbroso -sa *adj* rusty; (bot.) rusty
hertziano -na *adj* (elec.) Hertzian
herventar §18 *va* to boil
hervidero *m* boiling; boiling spring, bubbling spring; rattle (*e.g., in the chest*); swarm (*of worms, of people, etc.*)
hervidor *m* cooker, boiler
herviente *adj* var. of **hirviente**
hervir §62 *vn* to boil; to boil, to seethe (*said of the sea; of an angry person*); to swarm, to teem
hervor *m* boil, boiling; force, vigor, determination; fire, restlessness (*of youth*); **alzar** or **levantar el hervor** to begin to boil; **hervor de la sangre** skin rash
hervoroso -sa *adj* ardent, fiery, impetuous
hesiense *adj & mf* Hessian
Hesíodo *m* Hesiod
hesitación *f* hesitation
hesitar *vn* to hesitate
Hesperia *f* see **hesperio**
Hespérides *fpl* (myth.) Hesperides (*four nymphs*)
hesperidina *f* (chem.) hesperidin
hesperidio *m* (bot.) hesperidium
hespérido -da *adj* Hesperian (*western*)
hesperio -ria *adj* Hesperian (*of Spain or Italy*); (*cap.*) *f* Hesperia (*Spain or Italy*)
héspero -ra *adj* var. of **hesperio**; (*cap.*) *m* Hesperus (*evening star*)
heteo -a *adj & mf* var. of **hitita**
hetera *f* (hist.) hetaera; courtesan, prostitute
heterocerco -ca *adj* (ichth.) heterocercal
heterocíclico -ca *adj* (chem.) heterocyclic
heteroclamídeo -a *adj* (bot.) heterochlamydeous
heteróclito -ta *adj* heteroclite
heterodinaje *m* (rad.) heterodyning
heterodinar *va & vn* (rad.) to heterodyne
heterodino -na *adj* (rad.) heterodyne; *f* (rad.) heterodyne (*auxiliary oscillator*)
heterodoxia *f* heterodoxy
heterodoxo -xa *adj* heterodox; *mf* heterodox person
heteroecia *f* (biol.) heteroecism
heterofilia *f* (bot.) heterophylly
heterofilo -la *adj* (bot.) heterophyllous
heterogamia *f* heterogamy
heterógamo -ma *adj* (bot.) heterogamous
heterogeneidad *f* heterogeneity
heterogéneo -a *adj* heterogeneous
heterónimo -ma *adj* heteronymous; *m* heteronym
heteroplastia *f* (surg.) heteroplasty
heterótrofo -fa *adj* (biol.) heterotrophic
hético -ca *adj & mf* hectic
hetiquez *f* (path.) consumption
hetmán *m* hetman (*cossack chief*)
heurístico -ca *adj* heuristic
hexacordo *m* (mus.) hexachord
hexaédrico -ca *adj* hexahedral
hexaedro *m* (geom.) hexahedron
hexafluoruro *m* (chem.) hexafluoride
hexagonal *adj* hexagonal
hexágono -na *adj* hexagonal; *m* (geom.) hexagon
hexagrama *m* hexagram
hexametilenotetramina *f* (chem.) hexamethylenetetramine
hexámetro -tra *adj & m* hexameter
hexángulo -la *adj* hexangular
hexano *m* (chem.) hexane
hexapétalo -la *adj* (bot.) hexapetalous
hexápodo -da *adj* hexapod; *m* (ent.) hexapod
Hexateuco *m* (Bib.) Hexateuch
hexosa *f* (chem.) hexose
hez *f* (*pl:* **heces**) (fig.) scum, dregs; **heces** *fpl* lee, sediment, dregs; feces, excrement; (fig.) dregs
Hg. abr. of **hectogramo**
hi *interj* var. of **ji**
Híadas or **Híades** *fpl* (astr. & myth.) Hyades or Hyads
hialino -na *adj* hyaline (*glassy*); *f* (biochem.) hyaline
hialita *f* (mineral.) hyalite
hialitis *f* (path.) hyalitis
hialoideo -a *adj* hyaloid
hialoides *f* (anat.) hyaloid
hialoplasma *m* (biol.) hyaloplasm
hialotecnia or **hialurgia** *f* glass work
hiante *adj* (pros.) having hiatus
hiato *m* hiatus (*in a text*); (anat., gram. & pros.) hiatus
hibernación *f* (biol.) hibernation
hibernal *adj* hibernal

hibernar *vn* (biol.) to hibernate
hibernés -nesa or **hiberniano -na** *adj & mf* Hibernian
hibérnico -ca *adj* Hibernian
hibisco *m* (bot.) hibiscus
hibridación *f* hybridization
hibridar *va & vn* to hybridize
hibridismo *m* hybridism
híbrido -da *adj & m* hybrid
hicaco *m* (bot.) coco plum (*tree and fruit*)
hice *1st sg pret ind of* **hacer**
Hicsos *mpl* (hist.) Hyksos
hidalgo -ga *adj* noble, illustrious, imperious; *m* nobleman; *f* noblewoman
hidalguete -ta *mf* (coll.) impecunious noble
hidalguez *f* or **hidalguía** *f* nobility
hidalguito -ta *mf* cute little noble
hidantoína *f* (chem.) hydantoin
hidátide *f* (path.) hydatid
hidatídico -ca *adj* hydatid
hidno *m* (bot.) hydnum
hidra *f* hydra (*persistent evil*); (zool.) hydra (*polyp*); (zool.) poisonous sea snake (*Hydrus bicolor*); (*cap.*) *f* (astr. & myth.) Hydra
hidracida *f* (chem.) hydrazide
hidrácido *m* (chem.) hydracid
hidracina *f* (chem.) hydrazine
hidrangea *f* (bot.) hydrangea
hidrargirismo *m* (path.) hydrargyriasis
hidrargiro *m* (chem.) hydrargyrum
hidratación *f* (chem.) hydration
hidratado -da *adj* hydrous
hidratar *va & vr* (chem.) to hydrate
hidrato *m* (chem.) hydrate; **hidrato amónico** (chem.) ammonium hydroxide; **hidrato de carbono** (chem.) carbohydrate; **hidrato de cloral** (chem.) chloral hydrate
hidráulico -ca *adj* hydraulic; *m* hydraulician, hydraulic engineer; *f* hydraulics
hídrico -ca *adj* (chem.) hydric
hidro *m* (aer.) hydroplane
hidroavión *m* (aer.) hydroplane
hidrocarburo *m* (chem.) hydrocarbon
hidrocefalía *f* (path.) hydrocephalus
hidrocéfalo -la *adj* hydrocephalous
hidrocele *m* (path.) hydrocele
hidrodeslizador *m* gliding boat
hidrodinámico -ca *adj* hydrodynamic; *f* hydrodynamics
hidroelectricidad *f* hydroelectricity
hidroeléctrico -ca *adj* hydroelectric
hidrófana *f* or **hidrófano** *m* (mineral.) hydrophane
hidrófido *m* (zool.) sea serpent, sea snake, hydrophid
hidrófilo -la *adj* (chem.) hydrophile or hydrophilic; absorbent; *m* (ent.) water beetle
hidrófita *f* (bot.) hydrophyte
hidrofobia *f* (path.) hydrophobia
hidrofóbico -ca *adj* hydrophobic
hidrófobo -ba *adj* hydrophobic (*suffering from hydrophobia*); *mf* hydrophobe
hidrófono *m* hydrophone
hidrófugo -ga *adj* waterproof
hidrogel *m* (chem.) hydrogel
hidrogenación *f* (chem.) hydrogenation
hidrogenar *va* (chem.) to hydrogenate
hidrogenión *m* (chem.) hydrogen ion
hidrógeno *m* (chem.) hydrogen; **hidrógeno pesado** (chem.) heavy hydrogen
hidrografía *f* hydrography
hidrográfico -ca *adj* hydrographic
hidrógrafo -fa *mf* hydrographer
hidroide *m* (zool.) hydroid
hidrólisis *f* (chem.) hydrolysis
hidrolítico -ca *adj* hydrolytic
hidrolizar §76 *va & vr* (chem.) to hydrolize
hidrología *f* hydrology
hidrólogo -ga *mf* hydrologist
hidromancía *f* hydromancy
hidromántico -ca *adj* hydromantic
hidromecánico -ca *adj* hydromechanical; *f* hydromechanics
hidromedusa *f* (zool.) hydromedusa
hidromel *m* hydromel
hidrometeoro *m* (meteor.) hydrometeor
hidrometría *f* mechanics of water flow
hidrómetro *m* current gauge, water meter
hidromiel *m* var. of **hidromel**
hidrópata *mf* hydropath or hydropathist
hidropatía *f* hydropathy
hidropático -ca *adj* hydropathic
hidropesía *f* (path.) dropsy; (path.) hydrops
hidrópico -ca *adj* dropsical, hydropic; very thirsty; insatiable
hidroplano *m* hydroplane (*boat*); (aer.) hydroplane
hidroponía *f* hydroponics
hidropónico -ca *adj* hydroponic
hidroquinona *f* (chem.) hydroquinone
hidrosfera *f* hydrosphere
hidrosis *f* (path.) hidrosis
hidrosol *m* (chem.) hydrosol
hidrostático -ca *adj* hydrostatic; *f* hydrostatics
hidrostato or **hidróstato** *m* hydrostat
hidrosulfito *m* (chem.) hydrosulfite; **hidrosulfito sódico** (chem.) hydrosulfite, sodium hydrosulfite (*reducing agent*)
hidrosulfuro *m* (chem.) hydrosulfide
hidrotecnia *f* hydrotechny
hidroterapia *f* hydrotherapeutics or hydrotherapy
hidroterápico -ca *adj* hydrotherapeutic
hidrotérmico -ca *adj* hydrothermal
hidrotórax *m* (path.) hydrothorax
hidrotropismo *m* hydrotropism
hidróxido *m* (chem.) hydroxide; **hidróxido de calcio** (chem.) calcium hydroxide; **hidróxido de potasio** (chem.) potassium hydroxide; **hidróxido de sodio** (chem.) sodium hydroxide
hidroxilamina *f* (chem.) hydroxylamine
hidroxilo *m* (chem.) hydroxyl
hidrozoico -ca *adj* hydrozoic, hydrozoan
hidrozoo *m* (zool.) hydrozoan
hidruro *m* (chem.) hydride; **hidruro de litio** (chem.) lithium hydride
hiedra *f* (bot.) ivy; **hiedra terrestre** (bot.) ground ivy; **hiedra venenosa** (bot.) poison ivy
hiel *f* gall, bile; (fig.) bitterness, sorrow; **echar la hiel** (coll.) to strain, to overwork; **hiel de la tierra** (bot.) lesser centaury
hielo *m* ice; frost, cold; astonishment; **romper el hielo** (fig.) to break the ice; **hielo carbónico** dry ice; **hielo flotante** ice pack; **hielo seco** dry ice
hiemación *f* wintering; (bot.) winter blooming
hiemal *adj* winter, hiemal
hiena *f* (zool.) hyena; **hiena manchada** (zool.) spotted hyena; **hiena parda** (zool.) brown hyena; **hiena rayada** (zool.) striped hyena
hienda *f* dung
hierático -ca *adj* hieratic or hieratical
hierba *f* grass; herb; **hierbas** *fpl* grass, pasture; herb poison; vegetable soup (*for monks*); years of age (*said of animals*); **mala hierba** weed; (coll.) wayward young man; **y otras hierbas** (hum.) and many other things; **hierba amargosa** (bot.) ragweed; **hierba amarilla** (bot.) oxeye, oxeye daisy (*Heliopsis*); **hierba artética** (bot.) ground pine; **hierba ballestera** (bot.) white hellebore; **hierba belida** (bot.) buttercup, blisterflower; **hierba buena** (bot.) mint; **hierba callera** (bot.) sedum, orpine; **hierba cana** (bot.) groundsel; **hierba carmín** (bot.) pokeberry, pokeweed; **hierba centella** (bot.) marsh marigold; **hierba de ballesteros** (bot.) white hellebore; **hierba de clavo** (bot.) primrose willow; **hierba de Guinea** (bot.) Guinea grass; **hierba de hechiceros** (bot.) nightshade, black nightshade; **hierba de la culebra** (bot.) green dragon; **hierba de la golondrina** (bot.) celandine; **hierba del ala** (bot.) elecampane; **hierba de la madre** (bot.) toothwort; **hierba de la moneda** (bot.) moneywort; **hierba de la paciencia** (bot.) herb patience, spinach dock; **hierba de la plata** (bot.) honesty; **hierba de la rabia** (bot.) madwort; **hierba de las calenturas** (bot.) hedge hyssop; **hierba de las coyunturas** (bot.) joint fir; **hierba de las cucharas** (bot.) scurvy grass; **hierba de la segur** (bot.) hatchet vetch; **hierba de las golondrinas** (bot.) celandine; **hierba de las heridas** (bot.) selfheal; **hierba del asno** (bot.) evening primrose; **hierba de las quemaduras** (bot.)

groundsel; **hierba de las serpientes** (bot.) star thistle; **hierba de la tos** (bot.) rosette ramonda; **hierba de la Trinidad** (bot.) liverwort; **hierba del burro** (bot.) fireweed (*a wild lettuce*); **hierba del cáncer** (bot.) leadwort; **hierba del hígado** (bot.) liverwort; **hierba del maná** (bot.) manna grass, gloating fescue; **hierba del moro** (bot.) elecampane; **hierba de los canarios** (bot.) chickweed; **hierba de los canónigos** (bot.) corn salad; **hierba de los gatos** (bot.) rosette ramonda; **hierba de los indios** (bot.) comfrey; **hierba de los tiñosos** (bot.) burdock; **hierba del papa** (bot.) cat thyme; **hierba del Paraguay** (bot.) Paraguay tea; **hierba del pobre** (bot.) hedge hyssop; **hierba del Sudán** (bot.) Sudan grass; **hierba del toro** (bot.) hyssop loosestrife; **hierba de París** (bot.) herb Paris, truelove; **hierba de pordioseros** (bot.) traveler's-joy; **hierba de San Benito** (bot.) herb bennet; **hierba de San Cristóbal** (bot.) baneberry; **hierba de San Gerardo** (bot.) goutweed; **hierba de San Juan** (bot.) Saint-John's-wort; **hierba de San Lorenzo** (bot.) wood sanicle; **hierba de San Pablo** (bot.) cowslip, primrose; **hierba de San Pablo mayor** (bot.) oxlip, polyanthus; **hierba de San Roberto** (bot.) red shanks, fox geranium; **hierba de Santa Catalina** (bot.) touch-me-not; **hierba de Santa María** (bot.) costmary; **hierba de Santiago** (bot.) tansy ragwort; **hierba doncella** (bot.) large periwinkle, cut-finger; **hierba elefante** (bot.) elephant grass; **hierba estañera** (bot.) scouring grass, Dutch grass; **hierba fina** (bot.) Rhode Island bent; **hierba fuerte** (bot.) cat thyme; **hierba gatera** (bot.) catmint, catnip; **hierba hedionda** (bot.) jimson weed, thorn apple; **hierba lombriguera** (bot.) tansy; **hierba mate** (bot.) maté, Brazilian holly; **hierba medicinal** herb, medicinal herb; **hierba moli** (myth.) moly; **hierba mora** (bot.) nightshade, black nightshade; **hierba pajarera** (bot.) chickweed; **hierba pastel** (bot.) woad; **hierba peluda** (bot.) rosette ramonda; (bot.) rice cut-grass; **hierba piojera** (bot.) stavesacre; **hierba pulguera** (bot.) fleawort; **hierba puntera** (bot.) houseleek; **hierba Rhodes** (bot.) Rhodes grass; **hierba romana** (bot.) costmary; **hierba sagrada** (bot.) vervain; **hierba santa** (bot.) mint; **hierba sarracena** (bot.) costmary; **hierbas finas** fines herbes (*garnish made of chopped mushrooms, shallots, parsley, etc.*); **hierba tosera** (bot.) rosette ramonda; **hierba turca** (bot.) burstwort; **hierba velluda** (bot.) bulbous buttercup, meadow crowfoot

hierbabuena *f* (bot.) mint

hiero *m* var. of **yero**

hierofanta *m* or **hierofante** *m* hierophant

hieroglífico -ca *adj & m* var. of **jeroglífico**

hierosolimitano -na *adj & mf* var. of **jerosolimitano**

hierro *m* iron; brand (*stamped with hot iron*); **hierros** *mpl* irons (*chains, fetters, etc.*); **a hierro y fuego** without mercy, without quarter; violently, sweeping straight ahead; **llevar hierro a Vizcaya** to carry coals to Newcastle; **machacar en hierro frío** (coll.) to waste one's time (*in trying to change a person's nature*); **marcar con hierro** to brand; **hierro acanalado** corrugated iron; **hierro colado** cast iron; **hierro colado en barras** pig iron; **hierro de desecho** scrap iron; **hierro de marcar** branding iron; **hierro dulce** wrought iron; **hierro especular** (mineral.) specular iron; **hierro fundido** cast iron; **hierro galvanizado** galvanized iron; **hierro ondulado** corrugated iron

hifa *f* (bot.) hypha

higa *f* baby's fist-shaped amulet; scorn, contempt; **dar higa** to miss fire (*said of a gun*); **no dar dos higas por** (coll.) to not care a rap for

higadilla *f* or **higadillo** *m* liver (*of birds, fish, and other small animals*)

hígado *m* (anat.) liver; **hígados** *mpl* (coll.) guts, courage; **echar los hígados** (coll.) to strain, to overwork; **hasta los hígados** (coll.) from the bottom of one's heart; **malos hígados** ill will, hatred; **moler los hígados a** (coll.) to pester; **querer comer los hígados a** (coll.) to have a deep grudge against; **hígado de bacalao** cod liver

Higea or **Higía** *f* (myth.) Hygeia

higiene *f* hygiene; **higiene mental** mental hygiene; **higiene sexual** sex hygiene; **higiene social** social hygiene

higiénico -ca *adj* hygienic

higienista *adj & mf* hygienist; *m* public health doctor

higienización *f* hygienization

higienizar §76 *va* to hygienize, make hygienic

higo *m* fig (*fruit*); (vet.) thrush; **de higos a brevas** (coll.) once in a while; **no dársele a uno un higo de, no dar un higo por, no estimar en un higo** to not care a rap for; **no valer un higo** (coll.) to be not worth a continental; **higo chumbo** or **higo de tuna** prickly pear (*fruit*); **higo zafarí** sweet fig

higrometría *f* hygrometry

higrométrico -ca *adj* hygrometric

higrómetro *m* hygrometer

higroscópico -ca *adj* hygroscopic

higroscopio *m* hygroscope

higuana *f* var. of **iguana**

higuera *f* (bot.) fig tree; **higuera chumba** (bot.) prickly pear; **higuera de Bengala** (bot.) banyan; **higuera de Egipto** (bot.) caprifig, wild fig; **higuera del diablo, del infierno** or **infernal** (bot.) castor-oil plant; **higuera de Indias, de pala** or **de tuna** (bot.) prickly pear; **higuera loca** (bot.) jimson weed

higuereta or **higuerilla** *f* (bot.) castor-oil plant

hija *f* see **hijo**

hijadalgo *f* (*pl:* **hijasdalgo**) var. of **hidalga**

hijastro -tra *mf* stepchild; *m* stepson; *f* stepdaughter

hijo -ja *mf* child; young (*of an animal*); (fig.) child, fruit, result; **cada hijo de vecino** (coll.) every man Jack, every mother's son; **hijo de bendición** legitimate child; good child; **hijo de la cuna** foundling; **hijo del amor** love child; **hijo de leche** foster child; *m* son; native son; **hijos** *mpl* children, descendants; **Hijo de Dios** Son of God; **hijo del agua** good sailor; good swimmer; **Hijo del Hombre** Son of Man (*Jesus*); **hijo de su padre** (coll.) chip off the old block; **hijo de sus propias obras** self-made man; **hijo natural** love child; **hijo político** son-in-law; **hijo pródigo** prodigal son; *f* daughter; native daughter; **hija de Eva** daughter of Eve; **hija política** daughter-in-law

hijodalgo *m* (*pl:* **hijosdalgo**) var. of **hidalgo**

hijuela *f* see **hijuelo**

hijuelero *m* rural postman

hijuelo -la *mf* offspring; *m* little son, little child; (bot.) shoot, sucker; *f* little daughter, little girl; accessory; extra strip (*used to widen a garment*); extra little mattress placed under mattress to fill a hollow; branch drain; branch sewer; side path, crosspath; rural mail service (*off the main highway*); estate (*of decedent*); palm seed; (eccl.) pall (*to cover chalice*)

hila *f* row, line; thin gut; spinning; **hilas** *fpl* lint (*for dressing wounds*); (Am.) cotton waste; **a la hila** in single file

hilable *adj* spinnable, spinning, fit for spinning

hilacha *f* shred, raveling, fraying; **hilachas** *fpl* lint; **mostrar la hilacha** (Am.) to show one's worst side; **hilacha de acero** steel wool; **hilacha de algodón** cotton waste; **hilacha de vidrio** spun glass

hilacho *m* var. of **hilacha; hilachos** *mpl* (Am.) rags, tatters

hilachoso -sa *adj* shreddy, frayed, raveled

hilada *f* row, line; (mas.) course; **hilada atizonada** or **de cabezal** (mas.) header course; **hilada de coronación** (mas.) coping; **hilada de faja** (mas.) stretcher course; **hilada voladiza** (mas.) corbel course

hiladillo *m* braid

hiladizo -za *adj* spinnable

hilado *m* spinning; yarn, thread
hilador -dora *mf* spinner; *f* spinning machine
hilandería *f* spinning (*art*); spinning frame; spinning mill
hilandero -ra *mf* spinner; *m* spinning shop, spinning mill
hilar *va* to spin (*wool, thread, a cocoon, etc.*); to infer, conjecture; *vn* to spin; **hilar delgado** or **fino** (coll.) to hew close to the line; **hilar largo** (coll.) to drag on
hilaracha *f* var. of **hilacha**
hilarante *adj* mirthful, sprightful; laughing (*gas*)
hilaridad *f* hilarity
Hilario *m* Hilary
hilatura *f* spinning
hilaza *f* yarn, thread; uneven thread; coarse thread; **descubrir la hilaza** to show one's true nature
hilera *f* row, line; fine thread, fine yarn; ridgepole; (mach.) drawplate; (mas.) course; (mil.) file; (zool.) spinneret
hilero *m* ripple (*caused by two opposing currents*); stream, current
hilio *m* (anat.) hilum
hilo *m* thread; yarn; filament; string (*e.g., of pearls*); linen, linen fabric; light or thin wire; thin stream (*e.g., of water*); beam (*of light*); edge (*of razor, sword, etc.*); (bot.) hilum; (elec.) wire; (opt.) cross hair, cross wire; (zool.) thread (*of spider*); (fig.) thread (*of a speech, of life, etc.*); **a hilo** uninterruptedly; in line, parallel; **al hilo** along the thread, with the thread; **estar colgado de un hilo** (coll.) to hang by a thread; **irse al hilo** or **tras el hilo de la gente** to follow the crowd (*to do what others do*); **manejar los hilos** to pull strings; **perder el hilo de** to lose the thread of; **tomar el hilo** to pick up the thread (*e.g., of the conversation*); **vivir al hilo del mundo** (coll.) to follow the crowd; **hilo bramante** twine; **hilo cruzado** (opt.) cross hair, cross wire; **hilo de la muerte** end of life; **hilo de masa** (aut.) ground wire; **hilo de medianoche** midnight sharp; **hilo de mediodía** twelve noon sharp; **hilo dental** dental floss; **hilo de retorno** (elec.) return, return wire; **hilo de salmar** twine; **hilo de tierra** (rad.) ground wire; **hilos taquimétricos** (surv.) stadia hairs
hilozoísmo *m* (philos.) hylozoism
hilván *m* (sew.) tacking, basting; basting stitch; (Am.) hem; (Am.) basting thread; **hablar de hilván** (coll.) to jabber along
hilvanar *va* (sew.) to tack, to baste; to outline, to sketch; (coll.) to hurry (*a job*); (Am.) to hem; *vn* (sew.) to tack, to baste
himalayo -ya *adj* Himalayan; **el Himalaya** The Himalaya, The Himalayas
himen *m* (anat.) hymen
himeneo *m* marriage; hymeneal (*wedding song*); (bot.) courbaril; (*cap.*) *m* (myth.) Hymen
himenio *m* (bot.) hymenium
himenóptero -ra *adj* (zool.) hymenopterous; *m* (zool.) hymenopter
Himeto *m* Hymettus
himnario *m* hymnal, hymn book
himno *m* hymn; **himno nacional** national anthem
himnología *f* hymnology
himplar *vn* to roar, to bellow
hin *m* neigh, whinny
hincadura *f* driving, thrusting, sinking
hincapié *m* firm footing; foot stamping; emphasis; **hacer hincapié** (coll.) to take a firm stand; **hacer hincapié en** (coll.) to lay great stress on
hincar §86 *va* to stick, to drive, to thrust, to sink; to go down on, to fall on (*one's knee or knees*); *vr* to kneel, kneel down
hinco *m* post, pole (*sunk in the ground*)
hincón *m* boat post (*for fastening a boat to the shore*)
hincha *f* (coll.) grudge, ill will; *mf* (sport) rooter, fan
hinchable *adj* bubble (*chewing gum*)
hinchado -da *adj* swollen; swollen with pride; pompous, high-flown (*style, language*); *m* inflation (*of a tire*); *f* (sport) rooters, fans
hinchar *va* to swell; to inflate; to pump up; to embroider, exaggerate; *vr* to swell; to swell up, become puffed up (*with pride*)
hinchazón *f* swelling; conceit, vanity; bombast
hinchismo *m* (sport) rooters, fans
hindí *m* Hindi
hindú -dúa *adj & mf* (*pl:* **-dúes -dúas**) Hindu or Hindoo
hinduísmo *m* Hinduism
Hindustán, el var. of **el Indostán**
hindustaní *m* var. of **indostaní**
hiniesta *f* (bot.) Spanish broom
hinojal *m* fennel bed, fennel field
hinojo *m* (bot.) fennel; **de hinojos** kneeling, on one's knees; **hinojo acuático** (bot.) water fennel; **hinojo hediondo** (bot.) dill; **hinojo marino** or **marítimo** (bot.) samphire
hintero *m* kneading table (*of baker*)
hioideo -a *adj* hyoid
hioides *adj* hyoid; *m* (anat.) hyoid or hyoides
hiosciamina *f* (chem.) hyoscyamine
hioscina *f* (chem.) hyoscine
hipabisal *adj* (geol.) hypabyssal
hipálage *f* (rhet.) hypallage
hipar *vn* to hiccough; to pant; to whine; to be worn out; **hipar por** to long for, to want badly
Hiparco *m* Hipparchus
Hipatia *f* Hypatia
hiperacidez *f* hyperacidity
hiperacusia or **hiperacusis** *f* (path.) hyperacusis
hiperbático -ca *adj* hyperbatic
hipérbaton *m* (gram.) hyperbaton
hipérbola *f* (geom.) hyperbola
hipérbole *f* (rhet.) hyperbole
hiperbólico -ca *adj* (geom. & rhet.) hyperbolic
hiperbolismo *m* (rhet.) hyperbolism
hiperbolizar §76 *vn* to hyperbolize
hiperboloide *m* (geom.) hyperboloid
hiperbóreo -a *adj* hyperborean; *mf* hyperborean; (myth.) Hyperborean
hipercinesia *f* (path.) hyperkinesia
hiperclorhidria *f* (path.) hyperchlorhydria
hipercrisis *f* (med.) extreme crisis
hipercrítico -ca *adj* hypercritical; *m* severe critic, captious censor; *f* severe criticism
hiperdulía *f* (theol.) hyperdulia
hiperemia *f* (path.) hyperemia
hiperestesia *f* (path.) hyperesthesia
Hiperión *m* (myth.) Hyperion
hipermetropía *f* (path.) hypermetropia
Hipermnestra *f* (myth.) Hypermnestra
hiperopía *f* (path.) hyperopia
hiperópico -ca *adj* hyperopic
hiperpirexia *f* (path.) hyperpyrexia
hiperpituitarismo *m* (path.) hyperpituitarism
hiperpnea *f* (path.) hyperpnea
hipersensibilidad *f* (path.) hypersensitivity
hipersensible *adj* (path.) hypersensitive
hipertensión *f* (path.) hypertension, high blood pressure
hipertenso -sa *mf* person with high blood pressure
hipertiroidismo *m* (path.) hyperthyroidism
hipertónico -ca *adj* (chem. & physiol.) hypertonic
hipertrofia *f* (biol. & path.) hypertrophy
hipertrofiar *vr* to hypertrophy
hipertrófico -ca *adj* hypertrophic
hípico -ca *adj* hippic, equine, horse
hipido *m* whining
hipismo *m* horse breeding; horse racing
hipnal *m* (chem.) hypnale; (obs.) hypnale (*adder*)
Hipnos *m* (myth.) Hypnos
hipnosis *f* hypnosis
hipnótico -ca *adj & mf* hypnotic; *m* (med.) hypnotic (*sedative*)
hipnotismo *m* hypnotism
hipnotista *mf* hypnotist
hipnotización *f* hypnotization
hipnotizador -dora *adj* hypnotizing; *mf* hypnotizer
hipnotizar §76 *va* to hypnotize
hipo *m* hiccough; longing, keen desire; grudge; (phot.) hypo (*sodium hyposulfite*); **tener hipo contra** to have a grudge against; **tener hipo por** to crave

hipoblasto *m* (embryol.) hypoblast; (bot.) cotyledon of a grass
hipobosco *m* (ent.) horse tick
hipocampo *m* (anat., ichth. & myth.) hippocampus
hipocausto *m* (archeol.) hypocaust
hipocicloide *f* (geom.) hypocycloid
hipoclorito *m* (chem.) hypochlorite
hipocloroso -sa *adj* (chem.) hypochlorous
hipocondría *f* (path.) hypochondria
hipocondríaco -ca *adj & mf* hypochondriac
hipocondrio *m* (anat.) hypochondrium
hipocorístico -ca *adj* hypocoristic
hipocotíleo *m* (bot.) hypocotyl
hipocrás *m* hippocras
Hipócrates *m* Hippocrates
hipocrático -ca *adj* Hippocratic
Hipocrene *f* (myth.) Hippocrene
hipocresía *f* hypocrisy
hipócrita *adj* hypocritical; *mf* hypocrite
hipodérmico -ca *adj* hypodermic
hipodermo -ma *adj* (bot.) hypodermal
hipódromo *m* hippodrome
hipófisis *f* (*pl:* **-sis**) (anat.) hypophysis
hipofosfito *m* (chem.) hypophosphite
hipofosfórico -ca *adj* (chem.) hypophosphoric
hipofosforoso -sa *adj* (chem.) hypophosphorous
hipogástrico -ca *adj* hypogastric
hipogastrio *m* (anat. & zool.) hypogastrium
hipogénico -ca *adj* (geol.) hypogene
hipogeo -a *adj* (bot. & zool.) hypogeous; *m* (arch.) hypogeum
hipogloso -sa *adj* (anat.) hypoglossal; *m* (anat.) hypoglossal; (ichth.) halibut (*Hippoglossus*)
hipogrifo *m* (myth.) hippogriff
hipoide *adj* (mach.) hypoid
Hipólito *m* (myth.) Hippolytus
hipopótamo *m* (zool.) hippopotamus
hiposo -sa *adj* having hiccoughs
hipóstasis *f* (*pl:* **-sis**) (philos. & theol.) hypostasis
hipostático -ca *adj* hypostatic
hipóstilo -la *adj & m* (arch.) hypostyle
hiposulfito *m* (chem.) hyposulfite (*thiosulfate; salt of hyposulfurous acid*); **hiposulfito de sodio** (chem.) sodium hyposulfite ($Na_2S_2O_4$); (chem. & phot.) sodium hyposulfite ($Na_2S_2O_3$)
hiposulfuroso -sa *adj* (chem.) hyposulfurous
hipotálamo *m* (anat.) hypothalamus
hipoteca *f* mortgage; (law) hypothec; **¡buena hipoteca!** or **¡vaya una hipoteca!** (iron.) you can believe it, if you want to!
hipotecación *f* hypothecation
hipotecar §86 *va* to hypothecate, to mortgage
hipotenusa *f* (geom.) hypotenuse
hipotermia *f* (med.) hypothermia
hipótesis *f* (*pl:* **-sis**) hypothesis; **hipótesis nebular** (astr.) nebular hypothesis
hipotético -ca *adj* hypothetic or hypothetical
hipotiroidismo *m* (path.) hypothyroidism
hipotónico -ca *adj* (chem. & physiol.) hypotonic
hipoxantina *f* (chem.) hypoxanthine
hipsometría *f* hypsometry
hipsómetro *m* hypsometer
hircino -na *adj* hircine
hirco *m* (zool.) wild goat
hircocervo *m* (myth.) hircocervus
hiriente *adj* stinging, cutting, offensive
hirma *f* list, selvage
hirsuto -ta *adj* hirsute, bristly; (fig.) harsh, brusque, gruff
hirviendo *adj invar* boiling
hirviente *adj* boiling, seething
hisca *f* birdlime
hiscal *m* three-strand esparto rope
hisopada *f* sprinkling with holy water
hisopar *va* var. of **hisopear**
hisopazo *m* blow with an aspergillum
hisopear *va* to sprinkle with an aspergillum, to asperse
hisopillo *m* mouth swab; (bot.) winter savory
hisopo *m* (bot.) hyssop; (eccl.) aspergillum, hyssop; (Am.) brush, paint brush, shaving brush; **hisopo húmedo** wool fat, wool grease
hispalense *adj & mf* Sevillian
Hispania *f* Hispania
hispánico -ca *adj* Hispanic
hispanidad *f* Spanish nature, essence or spirit; Spanish solidarity, Spanish union
Hispaniola *f* former name of Santo Domingo
hispanismo *m* Hispanicism; Spanish studies, interest in Spanish language and literature
hispanista *mf* Hispanist
hispanizar §76 *va* to Hispanicize
hispano -na *adj* Hispanic, Spanish; Spanish American; *mf* Spaniard; Spanish American
hispanoamericanizar §76 *va* to make Spanish American; *vr* to become Spanish American
hispanoamericano -na *adj* Spanish American (*of America where Spanish is spoken*); Spanish-American (*of Spain and America or of Spain and the United States*); *mf* Spanish American (*native or inhabitant of America where Spanish is spoken*)
hispanoárabe *adj* Spanish-Arab or Spanish-Arabic; Hispano-Moresque
hispanófilo -la *adj & mf* Hispanophile
hispanófobo -ba *adj & mf* Hispanophobe
hispanohablante or **hispanoparlante** *adj* Spanish-speaking; *mf* speaker of Spanish
hispanomarroquí *adj* (*pl:* **-quíes**) Spanish-Moroccan
híspido -da *adj* hispid, bristly, spiny
hispir *va* to puff up, make fluffy; *vn & vr* to puff up, become fluffy
histamina *f* (chem.) histamine
histerectomía *f* (surg.) hysterectomy
histéresis *f* (phys.) hysteresis
histeria *f* (path.) hysteria
histérico -ca *adj* (path.) hysteric or hysterical
histerismo *m* (path.) hysteria
histerotomía *f* (surg.) hysterotomy
histidina *f* (chem.) histidine
histólisis *f* (biol.) histolysis
histología *f* histology
histólogo -ga *mf* histologist
histona *f* (biochem.) histone
historia *f* history; story, tale; painting of a historical subject; **historias** *fpl* (coll.) gossip, meddling; **armar historias** (Am.) to make trouble; **de historia** notorious; **dejarse de historias** (coll.) to come to the point; **la historia antigua** ancient history; **la historia contemporánea** contemporary history; **la historia medieval** or **media** medieval history; **la historia moderna** modern history; **la historia natural** natural history; **pasar a la historia** to become a thing of the past; **picar en historia** to turn out to be serious; **historia de lagrimitas** (coll.) sob story
historiado -da *adj* (arch.) historiated; (f.a.) richly adorned; (f.a.) storied (*painting, tapestry*); (coll.) overadorned
historiador -dora *mf* historian
historial *adj* historical; *m* record, dossier
historiar §90 & regular *va* to tell the history of; to tell the story of; (f.a.) to depict (*a historical event*)
historicidad *f* historicity
histórico -ca *adj* historic, historical
historieta *f* anecdote, brief account; **historieta gráfica** comic strip
historiografía *f* historiography
historiógrafo -fa *mf* historiographer
histrión *m* actor, histrion; juggler, clown, buffoon; fake, humbug
histriónico -ca *adj* histrionic
histrionisa *f* (archaic) actress, ballet dancer
histrionismo *m* histrionics; actors
hita *f* see **hito**
híter *m* (biol.) hyther
hitita *adj & mf* Hittite; *m* Hittite (*language*)
hitleriano -na *mf* Hitlerite
hitlerismo *m* Hitlerism
hito -ta *adj* fixed, firm; adjoining (*house, street*); black (*horse*); *m* landmark, milestone; peg, hob; quoits; aim, goal; **dar en el hito** to hit the nail on the head; **mirar de hito en hito** to eye up and down, to stare at; **mudar de hito** to not be able to keep still; (coll.) to keep trying new ways or methods; *f* brad, small headless cut nail; landmark, milestone
hitón *m* large headless cut nail
hizo *3d sg pret ind of* **hacer**
hizono *m* (chem.) hyzone

Hl. abr. of **hectolitro**
Hm. abr. of **hectómetro**
Hno. abr. of **Hermano**
Hnos. abr. of **Hermanos**
hoazín *m* (orn.) hoatzin
hobachón -chona *adj* (coll.) lumpish (*fat and sluggish*)
hobachonería *f* (coll.) lumpishness
hobo *m* var. of **jobo**
hocicada *f* blow with the snout; blow in the snout
hocicar §86 *va* to nuzzle; (slang) to keep on kissing; *vn* to nuzzle, to grub; to run into a snag; (naut.) to dip (*said of the bow of a ship*)
hocico *m* snout; (coll.) snout (*of person*); (coll.) face, sour face; **caer de hocicos** (coll.) to fall on one's face; **meter el hocico en todo** (coll.) to poke or put one's nose in everything; **poner hocico** (coll.) to make a face
hocicón -cona or **hocicudo -da** *adj* snouty, big-snouted
hocino *m* sickle; dale, glen; gorge, narrows
hociquear *va & vn* var. of **hocicar**
hodómetro *m* var. of **odómetro**
hogaño *adv* (coll.) this year; (coll.) nowadays, at the present time
hogar *m* fireplace, hearth; furnace; bowl (*of tobacco pipe*); home; household; home life; bonfire; **hogar substituto** (Am.) foster home
hogareño -ña *adj* home-loving; *mf* homebody, stay-at-home
hogaza *f* large loaf of bread; cobloaf
hoguera *f* bonfire
hoja *f* leaf (*of plant, book, door, folding door, spring, table, etc.; petal*); pad (*of aquatic plant*); sheet; blank (*sheet of paper*); foil; blade (*of knife, saw, sword, etc.*); runner (*of skates*); pane (*of glass*); veneer; side (*of hog*); sword; slat (*e.g., of Venetian blind*); land cultivated every other year; **desdoblar la hoja** (coll.) to open the subject again; **doblar la hoja** to close the subject for the time being; to change the subject, to digress; **poner como hoja de perejil** (coll.) to give a tongue lashing to; **tener hoja** to be counterfeit; **hoja batiente** casement sash; **hoja clínica** clinical chart; **hoja de afeitar** razor blade; **hoja de embalaje** packing slip; **hoja de encuadernador** (b.b.) end paper; **hoja de estaño** tin foil; **hoja de estudios** (educ.) transcript; **hoja de guarda** (b.b.) flyleaf; **hoja del anunciante** tear sheet; **hoja de lata** tin, tin plate; **hoja de nenúfar** lily pad; **hoja de paga** pay roll; **hoja de parra** fig leaf (*on a statue*); **hoja de pedidos** (com.) order blank; **hoja de plata** silver foil, silver leaf; **hoja de rodaje** (mov.) shooting record or report; **hoja de ruta** waybill; **hoja de servicios** record of service; (mil.) service record; **hoja de trébol** cloverleaf (*intersection*); **hoja maestra** master blade (*of spring*); **hojas alternas** (bot.) alternate leaves; **hojas del autor** (print.) advance sheets; **hoja suelta** leaflet, handbill; (b.b.) flyleaf; **hoja volante** leaflet, handbill
hoja-bloque *f* (*pl:* **hojas-bloque**) (philately) souvenir sheet
hojalata *f* tin, tin plate
hajalatería *f* tinwork; tinsmith's shop; sheet-metal work
hojalatero *m* tinsmith; sheet-metal worker
hojaldrado -da *adj* flaky
hojaldrar *va* to make into puff paste
hojaldre *m & f* puff paste
hojaldrero -ra or **hojaldrista** *mf* puff-paste baker
hojaranzo *m* (bot.) hornbeam; (bot.) oleander, rosebay
hojarasca *f* fallen leaves, dead leaves; excess foliage; vain show, bluff; trash, rubbish; (arch.) foliage
hojaseca *f* (ent.) leaf insect
hojear *va* to leaf through (*a book, a batch of papers*); *vn* to scale off; to flutter (*said of leaves of trees*)
hojilla *f* (Am.) cigaret paper; **hojilla magnética** (phys.) magnetic tracing, magnetic curves
hojoso -sa or **hojudo -da** *adj* leafy
hojuela *f* leaflet; pancake; foil; gold or silver braid; pressed-olive skins; **hojuela de estaño** tin foil
hol. abr. of **holandés**
hola *interj* hey!, ho!; hello!
Holanda *f* Holland; (*l.c.*) *f* fine chambray
holandés -desa *adj* Dutch; **a la holandesa** or **en holandesa** (b.b.) half-bound; *mf* Hollander; *m* Dutchman; Dutch (*language*); **el Holandés errante** the Flying Dutchman; **los holandeses** the Dutch (*people*); *f* Dutch woman
holandeta or **holandilla** *f* linen lining
holgachón -chona *adj* (coll.) ease-loving, idling; *mf* idler, loafer
holgadero *m* hangout
holgado -da *adj* idle, unoccupied; loose, full, roomy; comfortable; free; fairly well-off
holganza *f* idleness; ease, leisure; pleasure, enjoyment
holgar §79 *vn* to idle, to not work; to ease up, rest up; to be of no use, to be unnecessary; to be too loose, to not fit; to be glad; **holgar** + *inf* to be needless to + *inf;* **holgar con** or **de** to be glad at; *vr* to be glad; to be amused; **holgarse con** or **de** to be glad at; **holgarse de** + *inf* to be glad to + *inf*
holgazán -zana *adj* loafing, lazy; *mf* loafer, bum
holgazanear *vn* to loaf, to bum around
holgazanería *f* loafing, bumming, laziness
holgón -gona *adj* pleasure-loving; *mf* lizard, lounge lizard
holgorio *m* (coll.) gaiety, merriment, hilariousness
holgueta *f* (coll.) enjoyment, merriment
holgura *f* enjoyment, merriment; ease, comfort; looseness, fullness; (mach.) play
holmio *m* (chem.) holmium
holocaína *f* (pharm.) holocaine
holocausto *m* holocaust (*burnt offering; complete destruction by fire; wholesale destruction*); sacrifice, offering
holoceno -na *adj* (geol.) Holocene, Recent
holoédrico -ca *adj* (cryst.) holohedral
Holofernes *m* (Bib.) Holofernes
hológrafo -fa *adj & m* var. of **ológrafo**
holoturia *f* (zool.) holothurian, sea cucumber
holladero -ra *adj* traveled, trodden (*part of road*)
holladura *f* treading, trampling
hollar §77 *va* to tread, tread upon; (fig.) to tread under foot, to trample upon
hollejo *m* skin, peel, hull
hollín *m* soot
hollinar *va* (Am.) to make sooty, to soil with soot
holliniento -ta *adj* sooty
hombracho *m* husky big fellow
hombrada *f* manly thing; piece of folly; bravado
hombradía *f* manliness; courage
hombre *m* man; omber (*card game*); (coll.) my boy, old chap; (slang) husband, man; **buen hombre** good-natured fellow; **ser mucho hombre** to be a well-versed man; **ser muy hombre** to be a he-man; **ser todo un hombre** to be a full-grown man; **¡hombre al agua!** or **¡hombre a la mar!** man overboard!; **hombre bueno** man of legal age in good standing; (law) referee, arbiter; **hombre de armas** man-at-arms (*heavily armed soldier on horseback*); **hombre de bien** honest man, honorable man; **hombre de cabeza** man of talent; **hombre de campo** or **del campo** countryman; **hombre de criazón** or **hombre de remensa** serf; **hombre de dinero** man of means; **hombre de distinción** man of distinction; **hombre de estado** statesman; **hombre de fama** man of repute; **hombre de fondo** man of brains, man of great ability; **hombre de fondos** man of property; **hombre de guerra** man-at-arms (*military man*); **hombre de iglesia** man of the church, man of God; **hombre de la calle** man in the street (*average citizen*); **hombre de la situación** (Am.) man of the hour; **hombre del destino** Man of Destiny (*Napoleon*); **hombre de letras** man of letters; **Hombre de los Dolores** Man of Sorrows (*Jesus*); **hombre de mundo**

man of the world; **hombre de paja** straw man (*nonentity*); cat's-paw; **hombre de palabra** man of his word; **hombre de pelo en pecho** brave man; **hombre de prendas** man of parts; **hombre de suposición** man of straw; **hombre de veras** matter-of-fact fellow; serious fellow; **hombre hecho** grown man; well-educated man; **hombre mono** missing link; **hombre rana** (*pl:* **hombres rana**) frogman; **hombre viejo** (theol.) old man; *interj* upon my word!, man alive!

hombrear *vn* to try to act full-grown (*said of a boy*); to try to be somebody; to shoulder, push with the shoulder; to be mannish (*said of a woman*); to be a bully; **hombrear con** to strive to equal; *vr* **hombrearse con** to strive to equal

hombrecillo *m* homunculus, little man; (bot.) hop

hombrera *f* shoulder (*of garment*); shoulder padding; (arm.) pauldron; epaulet

hombría *f* manliness; **hombría de bien** honesty, honorableness

hombrillo *m* yoke (*of a shirt*); shoulder piece

hombrituerto -ta *adj* with shoulder raised (*in attitude of boasting*)

hombro *m* shoulder; (print.) shoulder; **a hombros de** on the shoulders of; **arrimar el hombro** to lend a hand, to put one's shoulder to the wheel; **echar al hombro** to take upon oneself; **encoger los hombros** to droop one's shoulders, to let one's shoulders droop (*in patience or resignation*); **encogerse de hombros** to shrug one's shoulders; to droop one's shoulders, to let one's shoulders droop (*in patience or resignation*); to crouch, to shrink with fear; to not answer; **escurrir el hombro** to shirk; **mirar por encima del hombro** to look down upon; **salir en hombros** to be carried off on the shoulders of the crowd; **hombro a hombro** (coll.) shoulder to shoulder

hombrón *m* (coll.) man of parts; (coll.) husky fellow

hombruno -na *adj* (coll.) mannish

homenaje *m* homage (*respect*); testimonial; gift; (feud.) homage; **en homenaje a** in honor of; **rendir homenaje a** to swear allegiance to; **homenaje de boca** lip service

homenajear *va* to honor, to fete

homeópata *adj* homeopathic; *mf* homeopath or homeopathist

homeopatía *f* homeopathy

homeopático -ca *adj* homeopathic

homérico -ca *adj* Homeric

Homero *m* Homer

homicida *adj* homicidal; cruel, inhuman; **homicida de sí mismo** (coll.) suicidal (*destructive of one's own health*); *mf* homicide (*person*)

homicidio *m* homicide (*act*); **homicidio intencional** voluntary manslaughter

homilética *f* homiletics; study of sacred authors

homilía *f* homily

homiliario *m* homiliarium

homilista *m* homilist

hominal *adj* human

hominicaco *m* (coll.) poor sap, nincompoop

homocerco -ca *adj* (ichth.) homocercal

homoclamídeo -a *adj* (bot.) homochlamydeous

homocromía *f* (zool.) protective coloration

homofonía *f* (phonet. & mus.) homophony

homófono -na *adj* (phonet.) homophonous; (mus.) homophonic

homogeneidad *f* homogeneity

homogeneización *f* homogenization

homogeneizar §76 *va* to homogenize

homogéneo -a *adj* homogeneous

homogenización *f* var. of **homogeneización**

homogenizar §76 *va* var. of **homogeneizar**

homógrafo -fa *adj* homographic; *m* homograph

homologación *f* equalization; (law) homologation; (sport) validation

homologar §59 *va* to make equal; (law) to homologate; (sport) to validate (*a record*)

homología *f* homology

homólogo -ga *adj* homologous

homonimia *f* homonymy

homónimo -ma *adj* homonymous; of the same name; *mf* namesake; *m* homonym

homóptero -ra *adj* (ent.) homopterous

homosexual *adj & mf* homosexual

homosexualidad *f* homosexuality

homúnculo *m* (coll.) homunculus; (coll.) guy, fellow

honda *f* see **hondo**

hondazo *m* blow with a sling

hondear *va* (naut.) to sound; (naut.) to unload

hondero *m* (hist.) slinger (*soldier*)

hondigo *m* sling

hondillos *mpl* patches in the crotch of trousers

hondo -da *adj* deep; low; *m* depth; bottom; *f* sling (*for hurling missiles; rope used for hoisting*); slingshot; **hondo** *adv* deep

hondón *m* bottom (*e.,g, of a tumbler*); eye (*of needle*); foot piece (*of stirrup*); lowland

hondonada *f* lowland, bottom land

hondura *f* depth, profundity; **meterse en honduras** (coll.) to go beyond one's depth

Honduras *f* Honduras; **la Honduras Británica** British Honduras

hondureñismo *m* Honduranism

hondureño -ña *adj & mf* Honduran

honestar *va* to honor; to palliate, to excuse

honestidad *f* decency, decorum; honesty, uprightness; purity, chastity; modesty; fairness

honesto -ta *adj* decent, proper; honest, upright; pure, chaste; modest; fair, reasonable (*price*)

hongo *m* (bot.) mushroom; derby, bowler

honor *m* honor; honesty; **honores** *mpl* honors; honorary status or position; **en honor a la verdad** to tell the truth; **en honor de** in honor of; **hacer honor a** (coll.) to do or show honor to; (coll.) to honor (*one's signature*); **hacer los honores** to do the honors; **honores de la guerra** honors of war

honorable *adj* honorable (*worthy of honor*); (*cap.*) *adj* Honorable (*title*)

honorario -ria *adj* honorary; *m* honorarium, fee

honorífico -ca *adj* honorific, honorable

honra *f* honor; dignity; **honras** *fpl* memorial service; **tener a mucha honra** to be proud of

honradez *f* honesty

honrado -da *adj* honest, honorable; **honrado a carta cabal** fair and square

honrador -dora *adj* honoring; *mf* honorer

honramiento *m* honoring

honrar *va* to honor; *vr* to be honored; **honrarse de** + *inf* to deem it an honor to + *inf*

honrilla *f* concern (*at what people will say*); **por la negra honrilla** out of concern for what people will say

honroso -sa *adj* honorable (*behavior, position, etc.*)

hopa *f* long cassock; sack in which an executed criminal is placed

hopalanda *f* houppelande

hopear *va* (coll.) to throw out, to kick out; *vn* to wag the tail; to romp, race around

hoplita *m* hoplite

hopo *m* tuft, shock (*of hair*); bushy tail; **seguir el hopo a** ((coll.) to keep right after; **sudar el hopo** (coll.) to work hard, to sweat; **volver el hopo** (coll.) to beat it; *interj* get out of here!

hoque *m* var. of **alboroque**

hora *f* hour; time, e.g., **hora de acostarse** time to go to bed; time (*to die*), e.g., **ya le llegó la hora** or **la última hora** his time has come; **Horas** *fpl* (myth.) Hours; **a buena hora** (coll.) in good time, opportunely; (iron.) too late; **a la hora** on time; **a la hora de ahora** or **a la hora de ésta** (coll.) right now; **a la hora horada** on the dot; **a las pocas horas** within a few hours; **a las pocas horas de** + *inf* a few hours after + *ger;* **dar hora** to fix a time; **dar la hora** to strike (*said of a clock*); to be just right; (coll.) to be a knockout (*said of a beautiful woman*); **de última hora** late (*news*); up-to-date; latest, most up-to-date; **en buen** or **buena hora** or **en hora buena** safely, luckily; all right, O.K.; **en mal** or **mala hora** or **en hora mala** in an evil hour, unluckily; **fuera de horas** after

hours; **hasta altas horas** until late into the night; **las cuarenta horas** (eccl.) forty hours' devotion; **no ver la hora de** (coll.) to be hardly able to wait for; **por horas** by the hour; **¿qué hora es?** what time is it?; **hora cero** (mil.) zero hour; **hora de aglomeración** rush hour; **hora de clase** (educ.) class hour; **hora de comer** mealtime; **hora deshorada** (coll.) fatal hour; **hora de verano** daylight-saving time; **hora de verdad** (taur.) kill; **hora legal** or **oficial** standard time; **horas canónicas** canonical hours; **horas de consulta** office hours (*of a doctor*); **horas de ocio** leisure hours; **hora semestral** semester hour; **horas extraordinarias de trabajo** overtime; **horas menores** (eccl.) little hours; *adv* now
horaciano -na *adj* Horatian
Horacio *m* Horace
horadación *f* drilling, boring, piercing
horadador -dora *adj* drilling, boring, piercing; *mf* driller, borer
horadar *va* to drill, bore, pierce
horado *m* hole; cave, cavern
hora-hombre *f* (*pl:* **horas-hombre**) man-hour
horario -ria *adj* (pertaining to the) hour; *m* hour hand; timetable; clock; face (*of clock or watch*); **horario escolar** roster
horca *f* pitchfork; gallows, gibbet; forked prop (*for plants and trees*); string (*of onions or garlic*); **tener horca y cuchillo** (hist.) to have life-and-death power; (coll.) to be absolute boss, to be a tyrant; **Horcas Caudinas** Caudine Forks
horcado -da *adj* forked, forklike
horcadura *f* upper part of tree trunk; fork (*made by two branches*)
horcajadas; a horcajadas astride, astraddle
horcajadillas; a horcajadillas var. of **a horcajadas**
horcajadura *f* crotch (*formed by two legs or by two branches*)
horcajo *m* fork (*made by two streams*); yoke (*for mules*)
horcate *m* hames (*of harness*)
horco *m* string (*of onions or garlic*)
horcón *m* pitchfork; forked prop
horchata *f* orgeat
horchatería *f* orgeat shop or store
horchatero -ra *mf* orgeat maker or dealer
horda *f* horde
hordiate *m* pearl barley; barley water
horizontal *adj* horizontal; *f* horizontal; **buscar** or **tomar la horizontal** (Am.) to lie down
horizonte *m* horizon; (fig.) horizon
horma *f* form, mold; shoe tree, shoe last; block, hat block; dry wall; **hallar la horma de su zapato** (coll.) to find just the thing; (coll.) to meet one's match; **horma de bota** shoe tree, boot tree
hormaza *f* dry wall
hormazo *m* blow with a block or last; pile of stones
hormiga *f* (ent.) ant; itch; **ser una hormiga** to be very thrifty; **hormiga blanca** (ent.) white ant; **hormiga león** (ent.) ant lion; **hormiga roja** or **silvestre** (ent.) red ant (*Formica rufa*)
hormigo *m* sifted ashes used in smelting quicksilver; **hormigos** *mpl* dessert made of bread crumbs, crushed almonds, and honey; coarse parts of ground wheat
hormigón *m* concrete; **hormigón armado** reinforced concrete; **hormigón hidráulico** hydraulic mortar
hormigonera *f* concrete mixer
hormigoso -sa *adj* (pertaining to the) ant; full of ants; ant-eaten; itchy
hormigueamiento *m* var. of **hormigueo**
hormigueante *adj* swarming; crawly, creepy; teeming
hormiguear *vn* to swarm; to crawl, to creep (*with a sensation of insects*); to teem, to abound
hormigueo *m* swarming; crawling sensation; (coll.) worry, unrest
hormiguero *m* anthill; swarm, mob (*of people*); place swarming with people; pile of burned compost; (orn.) wryneck
hormiguesco -ca *adj* (pertaining to the) ant
hormiguilla *f* itch
hormiguillo *m* line of workmen passing material from one to the other; (vet.) founder
hormilla *f* buttonmold
hormillón *m* hat block
hormón *m* or **hormona** *f* (physiol.) hormone
hormonal *adj* hormonal
hornabeque *m* (fort.) hornwork
hornablenda *f* (mineral.) hornblende
hornacina *f* (arch.) niche
hornacho *m* (min.) horizontal opening; furnace for casting statues
hornachuela *f* hut, cabin
hornada *f* batch, bake (*of bread, bricks, etc.*); (coll.) crop (*of appointments, promotions, etc.*)
hornaguear *va* to dig (*the earth*) for coal
hornaguero -ra *adj* coal; wide, spacious; *f* coal
hornaza *f* jeweler's furnace; (f.a.) glazing yellow
hornazo *m* Easter cake filled with hard-boiled eggs; Easter present to Lenten preacher
hornear *va* (Am.) to bake; *vn* to bake; to be a baker
hornería *f* baking (*trade*); bakery
hornero -ra *mf* baker; *m* (orn.) baker, ovenbird
hornija *f* brushwood
hornijero *m* carrier of brushwood
hornilla *f* kitchen charcoal grate; pigeonhole (*recess for pigeons to nest*)
hornillo *m* small furnace; kitchen stove; fire pot; hot plate; bowl (*of tobacco pipe*); (mil.) fougasse; (min.) blast hole; **hornillo de atenor** athenor (*self-feeding furnace of alchemists*)
horno *m* furnace; kiln; oven; **alto horno** blast furnace; **horno de cal** limekiln; **horno de coque** coke oven; **horno de coquizar** coking oven; **horno de cuba** shaft furnace; **horno de fundición** smelting furnace; **horno de hogar abierto** open-hearth furnace; **horno de ladrillos** brickkiln; **horno de mufla** muffle furnace; **horno de pudelar** puddling furnace; **horno de regeneración** regenerative furnace; **horno de reverbero** or **de tostadillo** reverberatory furnace; **horno Siemens-Martin** open-hearth furnace
horología *f* horology
horologio *m* (eccl.) horologe
horón *m* large round hamper or frail
horondo -da *adj* var. of **orondo**
horópter *m* (opt.) horopter
horoptérico -ca *adj* horopteric
horóptero *m* var. of **horópter**
horoscopar *vn* to make horoscopes
horoscopia *f* horoscopy
horoscopizar §76 *vn* var. of **horoscopar**
horóscopo *m* (astrol.) horoscope; **sacar un horóscopo** (astrol.) to cast a horoscope
horqueta *f* fork, pitchfork; fork (*made by two branches*); (Am.) fork (*in river, road, etc.*)
horquilla *f* fork, pitchfork; forked pole; hairpin; fork (*of bicycle*); cradle (*of French telephone*); step or tread (*of stilts*); (aut.) clutch lever; (mach.) yoke
horrendo -da *adj* horrendous
hórreo *m* granary; (prov.) granary or barn raised on pillars (*for protection from mice and dampness*)
horrero *m* granary keeper or tender
horribilísimo -ma *adj super* very or most horrible
horrible *adj* horrible
horridez *f* horribleness
hórrido -da or **horrífico -ca** *adj* horrible, horrendous
horripilación *f* bristling of the hair; (path.) horripilation
horripilante *adj* hair-raising, terrifying
horripilar *va* to make the hair of (*someone*) stand on end; to terrify; *vn* to terrify; *vr* to be or become terrified
horrisonante or **horrísono -na** *adj* horrisonant
horro -rra *adj* enfranchised; free, untrammeled
horror *m* horror; horrid thing; atrocity; **¡qué horror!** how terrible!; horrors!; **tener en horror** to abhor, hate, detest; **tener horror a** to have a horror of

horrorizar §76 *va* to horrify; *vr* to be horrified
horroroso -sa *adj* horrid, horrible; (coll.) hideous, ugly
horrura *f* filth, dirt, dross
hortaliza *f* vegetable
hortatorio -ria *adj* hortatory
hortelano -na *adj* (pertaining to a) garden; *m* gardener; orchardman; (orn.) ortolan; *f* gardener's wife
hortense *adj* (pertaining to a) garden
hortensia *f* (bot.) hydrangea; (bot.) hortensia; (*cap.*) *f* Hortense
hortera *f* wooden bowl; *m* (coll.) store clerk
hortícola *adj* horticultural; *m* horticulturist
horticultor -tora *mf* horticulturist
horticultura *f* horticulture
Hos. abr. of **Hermanos**
hosanna *m & interj* hosanna
hosco -ca *adj* dark; sullen, gloomy; proud, arrogant
hoscoso -sa *adj* rough, bristly
hospedador -dora *mf* host, one who provides lodging
hospedaje *m* lodging; cost of lodging
hospedamiento *m* lodging
hospedar *va* to lodge; *vr* to lodge, stop, put up
hospedería *f* hospice (*maintained by a religious order*); lodging; inn, hostelry
hospedero -ra *mf* host, innkeeper
hospiciano -na *mf* inmate of a poorhouse
hospicio *m* hospice; orphan asylum; poorhouse
hospital *m* hospital; **estar hecho un hospital** (coll.) to be full of aches and pains; (coll.) to be turned into a hospital (*said of a house full of sick people*); **hospital ambulante** (mil.) field hospital; **hospital de aislamiento** isolation hospital; **hospital de campaña** (mil.) field hospital; **hospital de la sangre** poor relations; **hospital de primera sangre** or **de sangre** (mil.) field hospital; **hospital robado** (coll.) bare house (*without furniture or adornments*)
hospitalario -ria *adj* hospitable; *mf* (hist.) hospitaler; (hist.) Hospitaler
hospitalero -ra *mf* hospital manager; hospitaler; hospitable person
hospitalidad *f* hospitality; hospitalization (*stay in a hospital*)
hospitalización *f* hospitalization
hospitalizar §76 *va* to hospitalize
hosquedad *f* darkness; sullenness, gloominess; arrogance
hostal *m* var. of **hostería**
hostelería *f* hotel business; association of hotel keepers
hostelero -ra *mf* innkeeper; hotel keeper
hostería *f* inn, hostelry
hostia *f* sacrificial victim; wafer; (eccl.) wafer, Host
hostiario *m* wafer box; wafer mold
hostiero -ra *mf* wafer maker; *m* wafer box
hostigamiento *m* lashing, scourging; harassment; pestering
hostigar §59 *va* to lash, scourge; to drive, harass; to pester, plague; (Am.) to cloy
hostigo *m* lash; weather-beaten wall; beating of wind and rain
hostigoso -sa *adj* (Am.) cloying, sickening
hostil *adj* hostile
hostilidad *f* hostility; **hostilidades** *fpl* hostilities (*warfare*); **cesar en las hostilidades** to cease hostilities; **romper las hostilidades** to start hostilities
hostilizar §76 *va* to harry, to harass (*an enemy*); to make it hot for, to antagonize
hotel *m* hotel; mansion, villa
hotelero -ra *adj* (pertaining to a) hotel; *mf* hotelkeeper
hotentote -ta *adj & mf* Hottentot
hovero -ra *adj* blossom-colored (*horse*); egg-colored
hoy *adv & m* today; **de hoy a mañana** any time now; **de hoy en adelante** or **de hoy más** from now on, henceforth; **por hoy** for the present; **hoy día** nowadays; **hoy por hoy** at the present time, as of today
hoya *f* hole, pit, ditch; grave; valley; whirlpool; seedbed; (Am.) basin (*of river*); **tener un pie en la hoya** to have one foot in the grave
hoyada *f* low spot, depression
hoyanca *f* (coll.) potter's field, common grave for the poor
hoyo *m* hole; pockmark; grave
hoyoso -sa *adj* holey, full of holes
hoyuela *f* fonticulus, hollow at front of neck
hoyuelo *m* dimple; pitching pennies (*boy's game*); fonticulus, hollow at front of neck
hoz *f* (*pl:* **hoces**) sickle; defile, ravine; narrow pass; (anat.) falx; **de hoz y de coz** (coll.) headlong, recklessly; **la hoz y el martillo** the hammer and sickle; **meter la hoz en mies ajena** to mind other people's business; **hoz del cerebelo** (anat.) falx cerebelli; **hoz del cerebro** (anat.) falx cerebri
hozada *f* stroke with a sickle; grass (or other grain) cut with one stroke of sickle
hozadero *m* place where hogs root up the earth
hozadura *f* hole made by a rooting hog
hozar §76 *va & vn* to root, to nuzzle
hta. abr. of **hasta**
huacal *m* (Am.) var. of **guacal**
huachinango *m* (ichth.) red snapper
huanca *f* (Am.) Indian reed horn
huando *m* (Am.) var. of **guando**
huango *m* (Am.) var. of **guango**
huarache *m* (Am.) var. of **guarache**
huauzontli *m* (Am.) goosefoot
hube *1st sg pret ind of* **haber**
hucha *f* large sheet; chest (*that can be used as a seat*); money box, toy bank; savings, nest egg
huchear *vn* to cry, shout, yelp
huebra *f* day's plowing of a yoke of oxen; pair of mules and plowman hired for a day; fallow
huebrero *m* plowman hired with pair of mules; owner of pair of mules who rents them out by the day
hueca *f* see **hueco**
huecadal *m* var. of **oquedal**
hueco -ca *adj* hollow; soft, fluffy, spongy; vain, conceited; deep, resounding (*voice*); affected, pompous (*style, language*); *m* hollow; interval; opening (*in wall for window, in a row of parked cars, etc.*); socket (*of a bone*); (coll.) opening (*vacancy*); **hueco de la axila** armpit; **hueco de la mano** hollow of the hand; **hueco del ascensor** elevator shaft; **hueco de escalera** stair well; *f* hollow; spiral groove in spindle (*to keep thread from slipping*)
huecograbado *m* photogravure
huélfago *m* (vet.) heaves
huelga *f* rest, leisure, idleness; sport, merriment; pleasant spot; strike (*of workmen*); (mach.) play (*between two parts*); (agr.) fallow (*period of being fallow*); **ir a la huelga** or **ponerse en huelga** to go on strike; **huelga de brazos caídos** sit-down strike; slowdown (*strike*); **huelga de hambre** hunger strike; **huelga de ocupación** sit-down strike; **huelga patronal** lockout; **huelga sentada** sit-down strike
huelgo *m* breath; room, space; play, allowance
huelguista *mf* striker
huelguístico -ca *adj* (pertaining to a) strike
huelveño -ña *adj* (pertaining) to Huelva; *mf* native or inhabitant of Huelva
huella *f* tread, treading; track, footprint; trace, mark; rut; tread (*of stairs*); (aut.) tread (*of tire*); **seguir las huellas de** to follow in the footsteps of; **huella dactilar** or **digital** fingerprint; **huella de sonido** (mov.) sound track
huello *m* walking (*condition of road for walking*); tread, hoofbeat; bottom of hoof
huemul *m* var. of **güemul**
huérfago *m* var. of **huélfago**
huerfanato *m* orphanage
huérfano -na *adj* orphan, orphaned; alone, deserted; *mf* orphan
huero -ra *adj* addle; (fig.) addle; (Am.) blond; **salir huero** (coll.) to turn out bad, to flop; *mf* (Am.) blond
huerta *f* garden, vegetable garden; fruit garden; irrigated region
huertano -na *adj* (pertaining to a) garden; *mf* gardener
huertero -ra *adj* (Am.) (pertaining to a) garden; *mf* (Am.) gardener

huerto *m* orchard; garden, kitchen garden
huesa *f* grave; **tener un pie en la huesa** to have one foot in the grave
huesillo *m* (Am.) dried peach
hueso *m* bone; stone, pit (*of fruit*); (fig.) hard job, drudgery; (Am.) junk, piece of junk; (Am.) good-for-nothing; **huesos** *mpl* bones (*mortal remains*); (coll.) hand; **desenterrar los huesos de uno** to drag someone's skeleton out of the closet; **calarse hasta los huesos** to get soaked to the skin; **estar en los huesos** to be nothing but skin and bones; **la sin hueso** (coll.) the tongue; **no dejarle a uno un hueso sano** (coll.) to pick someone to pieces; (coll.) to beat someone up, to give someone a good thrashing; **no poder con sus huesos** (coll.) to be all in; **soltar la sin hueso** (coll.) to wag one's tongue, to talk too much; (coll.) to pour forth insults; **tener los huesos molidos** to be fagged out; **hueso de la alegría** crazy bone, funny bone; **hueso de la suerte** wishbone; **hueso duro de roer** (coll.) a hard nut to crack; **hueso occipital** (anat.) occipital bone; **hueso temporal** (anat.) temporal bone
huesoso -sa *adj* bony
huésped -peda *mf* guest; lodger; stranger; host; (bot. & zool.) host; (archaic) innkeeper; **echar la cuenta sin la huéspeda** or **no contar con la huéspeda** (coll.) to reckon without one's host; **huésped de honor** guest of honor; *f* hostess
hueste *f* host (*army*); followers
huesudo -da *adj* big-boned
hueva *f* roe (*fish eggs*)
huevar *vn* to begin to lay (*said of birds*)
huevera *f* see **huevero**
huevería *f* egg store
huevero -ra *mf* egg dealer; *m* egg dish; *f* egg-cup; oviduct (*of birds*)
huevo *m* egg; (biol.) ovum; **huevo a la plancha** fried egg; **huevo al plato** shirred egg; **huevo de Colón** or **de Juanelo** something that looks hard at first but turns out to be easy; **huevo del té** tea ball; **huevo de zurcir** darning egg or gourd; **huevo de faltriquera** candied egg; **huevo duro** hard-boiled egg; **huevo en agua** soft-boiled egg; **huevo en cáscara** soft-boiled egg; **huevo escalfado** poached egg; **huevo estrellado** or **frito** fried egg; **huevo pasado por agua** soft-boiled egg; **huevos pericos** (Am.) scrambled eggs; **huevos revueltos** scrambled eggs; **huevo tibio** (Am.) soft-boiled egg
huf *interj* var. of **uf**
Hugo *m* Hugh
hugonote -ta *adj* Huguenotic; *mf* Huguenot
huída *f* flight; escape; leak; putlog hole; splay, flare (*at opening of a hole*); shying (*of a horse*)
huidero -ra *adj* fugitive; *m* cover, shelter (*of animals*)
huidizo -za *adj* fugitive; evasive
huilota *f* (orn.) mourning dove
huillín *m* (zool.) Chilean otter
huir §41 *va* to flee, avoid, shun; to duck; *vn* to flee; to fly (*said, e.g., of time*); to slip (*from the memory*); *vr* to flee
huisache *m* (bot.) sponge tree
hujier *m* var. of **ujier**
hule *m* oilcloth, oilskin; rubber; (taur.) blood, goring
hulear *vn* (Am.) to gather rubber
hulero -ra *adj* (Am.) (pertaining to) rubber; *mf* rubber gatherer, rubber worker
hulla *f* coal, soft coal; **hulla azul** tide power; wind power; **hulla blanca** white coal, water power; **hulla grasa** soft coal; **hulla magra** hard coal; **hulla negra** short-flame coal; **hulla seca** hard coal
hullero -ra *adj* (pertaining to) coal; *f* colliery, coal mine
humada *f* smoke signal
humanal *adj* human
humanar *va* to humanize; *vr* to become more human; to become man (*said of Jesus Christ*); **humanarse a** + *inf* (Am.) to condescend to + *inf*
humanidad *f* humanity; (coll.) fatness, corpulence; **las humanidades** the humanities
humanismo *m* humanism
humanista *adj & mf* humanist
humanístico -ca *adj* humanistic
humanitario -ria *adj & mf* humanitarian
humanitarismo *m* humanitarianism
humanizar §76 *va & vr* to humanize; to soften, to cool off, to calm down
humano -na *adj* human (*pertaining to man*); humane (*kind, merciful; civilizing*); *m* human
humarada *f* var. of **humareda**
humarazo *m* var. of **humazo**
humareda *f* cloud of smoke
humazo *m* dense smoke; poison smoke (*to drive rats from a ship*); **dar humazo a** (coll.) to smoke out
Humberto *m* Humbert
humeada *f* (Am.) puff of smoke
humeante *adj* smoky, smoking; steamy, steaming; reeking
humear *va* (Am.) to smoke, to fumigate; *vn* to smoke, give off smoke; to steam; to reek; to last, to persist (*said of traces of a quarrel, disturbance, etc.*); to be conceited, to be puffed up; *vr* to smoke, give off smoke
humectación *f* humidification
humectador *m* humidifier; humidor (*in textile mills*); moistener (*e.g., of stamps*)
humectar *va & vr* var. of **humedecer**
humectativo -va *adj* moistening, humectant
humedad *f* humidity, moisture, dampness; **humedad relativa** (meteor.) relative humidity
humedal *m* moist ground
humedecer §34 *va* to humidify, moisten, dampen; to wet; to soak; *vr* to become moist, become damp; to become wet
húmedo -da *adj* humid, moist, damp; wet
humera *f* (coll.) drunk, spree
humeral *adj* (anat.) humeral; *m* (eccl.) humeral veil
humero *m* smokestack, chimney; (dial.) smokehouse
húmero *m* (anat.) humerus
húmico -ca *adj* (chem.) humic
humifuso -sa *adj* (bot.) humifuse
humildad *f* humility; humbleness
humilde *adj* humble
humillación *f* humiliation; (act of) humbling
humilladero *m* boundary crucifix, calvary, road shrine; prie-dieu
humillador -dora *adj* humiliating; *mf* humiliator
humillante *adj* humiliating
humillar *va* to humiliate; to humble; to bow (*one's head*); to bend (*one's body, knees, etc.*); *vr* to be humble; to humble oneself; to cringe, grovel
humillo *m* (vet.) pig fever; **humillos** *mpl* airs, conceit
humina *f* (biochem.) humin
humo *m* smoke; fume, steam; gauze; **humos** *mpl* airs, conceit; hearths, homes; **a humo de pajas** (coll.) lightly, thoughtlessly; **bajar los humos a** (coll.) to take down a peg; **echar más humo que una chimenea** to smoke like a chimney; **hacer humo** (coll.) to cook; (coll.) to stick around; (coll.) to smoke (*said, e.g., of a fireplace*); **irse todo en humo** to go up in smoke; **parar el humo** (coll.) to split hairs; **subírsele a uno el humo a las narices** (coll.) to get angry, be annoyed; **tragar el humo** to inhale (*in smoking*); **vender humos** (coll.) to scheme by claiming to have the inside track, to peddle influence
humor *m* humor; **buen humor** good humor; **mal humor** bad humor; **seguirle el humor a una persona** to humor a person; **humor ácueo** or **acuoso** (anat.) aqueous humor; **humor vítreo** (anat.) vitreous humor
humorado -da *adj;* **bien humorado** good-humored; **mal humorado** bad-humored; *f* sally, bit of humor, pleasantry; whim
humorismo *m* humor, humorousness
humorista *adj* humorous; *mf* humorist (*writer*)
humorístico -ca *adj* humorous (*writer, cartoon*)
humoroso -sa *adj* full of humor, watery
humoso -sa *adj* smoky; smoking; steamy
humus *m* humus
hundible *adj* sinkable

hundimiento *m* sinking; collapse; settling, cave-in; undoing; destruction; crash; disappearance
hundir *va* to sink; to plunge; to overwhelm; to confound, confute; to undo; to destroy, ruin; to crash, shatter; *vr* to sink, collapse; to settle, cave in; to come to ruin, be wiped out; to be turned upside down; to sink (*below the horizon*); (coll.) to vanish, disappear; **aunque se hunda el mundo** (coll.) let the heavens fall, come what may
Hunfredo *m* Humphrey
húngaro -ra *adj & mf* Hungarian; *m* Hungarian (*language*)
Hungría *f* Hungary
húnico -ca *adj* Hunnic
huno -na *adj* Hunnic; *mf* Hun
hupe *f* punk
hura *f* hole, burrow; coarse brush; carbuncle; (bot.) sandbox tree; **hura ruidosa** (bot.) sandbox tree
huracán *m* hurricane; (naut.) hurricane
huracanado -da *adj* hurricane-like, tempestuous
huracanar *vr* to hurricane, to blow like a hurricane
hurañía *f* shyness, diffidence
huraño -ña *adj* shy, diffident, retiring
hurgar §59 *va* to poke; (fig.) to stir up, incite; **peor es hurgallo** (*i.e.*, **hurgarlo**) (coll.) better let it alone, the less said the better; *vn* to poke; **hurgar en** to poke into
hurgón *m* poker; (coll.) thrust, stab
hurgonada *f* poke, poking; (coll.) thrust, stab
hurgonazo *m* thrust with a poker; (coll.) jab, thrust, stab
hurgonear *va* to poke (*the fire*); (coll.) to jab, to stab at
hurgonero *m* poker (*metal rod for stirring fire*)
hurí *f* (*pl:* **-ríes**) houri (*of Mohammedan paradise*)
hurón -rona *adj* (coll.) shy, diffident; *mf* (coll.) prier, snooper; (coll.) shy or diffident person; *m* (zool.) ferret; **hurón menor** (zool.) grison; *f* female ferret
huronear *va & vn* to ferret, hunt with a ferret; (coll.) to ferret, to pry
huronera *f* ferret hole; (coll.) lair, hiding place
huronero *m* ferreter
huroniense *adj & m* (geol.) Huronian
hurra *interj* hurrah!
hurraca *f* var. of **urraca**
hurtacuerpo *m* (Am.) cold shoulder, slight
hurtadillas; a hurtadillas stealthily, on the sly; **a hurtadillas de** unbeknown to
hurtadineros *m* (*pl:* **-nos**) (prov.) bank, toy bank
hurtador -dora *adj* thieving; *mf* thief
hurtar *va* to steal, filch; to cheat (*in weights or measures*); to wear away (*the soil*); to plagiarize; to move away, withdraw; **hurtar a** to steal from; **hurtar el cuerpo** to dodge, to duck; *vr* to withdraw, to hide; **hurtarse a** to hide from, to avoid, to duck
hurto *m* thieving; theft; (min.) driftway; **a hurto** stealthily, on the sly; **coger con el hurto en las manos** to catch with the goods
husada *f* spindleful
húsar *m* (mil.) hussar
husero *m* brow antler (*of a yearling deer*)
husillo *m* screw, worm (*of a press*); spindle; drain, overflow
husita *adj & mf* Hussite
husitismo *m* Hussitism
husma *f* (coll.) snooping; **andar a la husma** (coll.) to go snooping around
husmeador -dora *adj* scenting; (coll.) prying; *mf* scenter; (coll.) prier
husmear *va* to scent, to smell out; (coll.) to pry into; *vn* to become gamy or high, to smell bad (*said of meat*)
husmeo *m* scenting; (coll.) prying
husmo *m* high odor, gaminess; **andarse al husmo** to be on the scent; **estar al husmo** (coll.) to wait for a chance
huso *m* spindle; bobbin; drum (*of windlass*); **ser más derecho que un huso** (coll.) to be as straight as a ramrod; **huso esférico** (geom.) lune; **huso horario** time zone (*between two meridians*)
huta *f* hunter's blind
hutía *f* (zool.) hutia
huy *interj* ouch!
huyente *adj* receding (*forehead*); shifty (*glance*)

I

I, i *f* tenth letter of the Spanish alphabet
-ía *suffix f* see **-ío**
ib. abr. of **ibídem**
iba *1st sg imperf ind of* **ir**
Iberia *f* Iberia
ibérico -ca or **iberio -ria** *adj* Iberian
iberismo *m* Iberism
ibero -ra *adj & mf* Iberian
Iberoamérica *f* Ibero-America
iberoamericano -na *adj & mf* Ibero-American
íbice *m* (zool.) ibex
ibicenco -ca *adj* (pertaining to) Iviza; *mf* native or inhabitant of Iviza
ibídem *adv* (Lat.) ibidem (*in the same place*)
ibis *f* (*pl:* **ibis**) (orn.) ibis
Ibiza *f* Iviza (*Balearic island*)
ibón *m* lake on slopes of Pyrenees
ibseniano -na *adj & mf* Ibsenian
icaco or **icaquero** *m* (bot.) coco plum (*tree and fruit*)
icáreo -a *adj* Icarian
icario -ria *adj* Icarian; (*cap.*) *m* (myth.) Icarius
Ícaro *m* (myth.) Icarus
icástico -ca *adj* natural, plain
iceberg *m* (*pl:* **-bergs**) iceberg
icneumón *m* (zool.) ichneumon; (ent.) ichneumon, ichneumon fly
icnografía *f* (arch.) ichnography
-ico -ca *suffix adj* -ic, e.g., **metálico** metallic; **público** public; **volcánico** volcanic; -ical, e.g., **crítico** critical; **lógico** logical; **músico** musical; para la comparación de **-ic** e **-ical**, véase **-ic** en la parte de inglés-español; (chem.) -ic, e.g., **cúprico** cupric; **sulfúrico** sulfuric; *suffix mf* -ic, e.g., **doméstico** domestic; -ician, e.g., **lógico** logician; **músico** musician; -ist, e.g., **botánico** botanist; **químico** chemist; *suffix m* -ic, e.g., **crítico** critic; **mecánico** mechanic; *suffix f* -ic, e.g., **aritmética** arithmetic; **música** music; -ics, e.g., **física** physics; **política** politics; **-ico -ca** (accented on penult) *suffix adj & m* Aragonese equivalent of **-ito**, sometimes with a touch of sarcasm, e.g., **elegantica** nice and stylish; **inocentico** kind of innocent; **angelico** imp of an angel
icón *m* (eccl.) icon
icono *m* icon (*image, picture*)
iconoclasia *f* or **iconoclasmo** *m* iconoclasm
iconoclasta *adj* iconoclastic; *mf* iconoclast
iconógeno *m* (phot.) developer (*chemical bath or reagent*)
iconografía *f* iconography
iconográfico -ca *adj* iconographic or iconographical
iconólatra *adj* iconolatrous; *mf* iconolater
iconolatría *f* iconolatry
iconología *f* iconology
iconomanía *f* iconomania
iconoscópico -ca *adj* (pertaining to the) iconoscope
iconoscopio *m* (telv.) iconoscope
iconostasio *m* (eccl.) iconostasion
icor *m* (path.) ichor (*from ulcer*)
icoroso -sa *adj* ichorous
icosaedro *m* (geom.) icosahedron
ictericia *f* (path.) icterus, jaundice
ictericiado -da *adj* jaundiced; *mf* person with jaundice
ictérico -ca *adj* icteric; jaundiced; *mf* person with jaundice
ictíneo -a *adj* fish-shaped; *m* submarine boat
ictiófago -ga *adj* ichthyophagous; *mf* ichthyophagist
ictiol *m* (pharm.) ichthyol
ictiología *f* ichthyology
ictiológico -ca *adj* ichthyologic or ichthyological
ictiólogo -ga *mf* ichthyologist
ictiosauro *m* (pal.) ichthyosaur or ichthyosaurus
ictiosis *f* (path.) ichthyosis
ictiosismo *m* (vet.) ichthyosism
ichal *m* field of ichu
icho or **ichú** *m* (bot.) ichu
íd. abr. of **ídem**
ida *f* see **ido**
idea *f* idea; **mudar de idea** to change one's mind; **idea fija** fixed idea
ideación *f* ideation
ideal *adj & m* ideal
idealidad *f* ideality
idealismo *m* idealism
idealista *adj* idealist, idealistic; *mf* idealist
idealístico -ca *adj* (philos.) idealistic
idealización *f* idealization
idealizar §76 *va* to idealize
idear *va* to think up, plan, devise
ideario *m* body of ideas or concepts
ídem *adj & pron* (Lat.) idem
idemista *adj* yes-saying; *mf* yes sayer
idéntico -ca *adj* identic or identical; very similar
identidad *f* identity, sameness
identificación *f* identification
identificar §86 *va* to identify
ideografía *f* ideograph
ideográfico -ca *adj* ideographic or ideographical
ideograma *m* ideogram
ideología *f* ideology
ideológico -ca *adj* ideologic or ideological
ideólogo -ga *mf* ideologist
idílico -ca *adj* idyllic
idilio *m* idyl
idioeléctrico -ca *adj* idioelectric or idioelectrical
idioma *m* language; speech, jargon; **idioma hablado** spoken language
idiomático -ca *adj* idiomatic; linguistic
idiosincrasia *f* idiosyncrasy
idiosincrásico -ca *adj* idiosyncratic
idiota *adj* idiotic; *mf* idiot
idiotez *f* idiocy; **idiotez mogólica** Mongolian idiocy
idiótico *m* idioticon
idiotismo *m* ignorance; idiom; idiocy
idiotizar §76 *va* to drive crazy; *vr* to go crazy
ido -da *adj* wild, scatterbrained; **los idos** the dead; *pp of* **ir**; *f* going; departure; sally; rashness; trail; **de ida y vuelta** round-trip; **idas y venidas** comings and goings
idólatra *adj* idolatrous; *m* idolater; *f* idolatress
idolatrar *va & vn* to idolize; **idolatrar en** to idolize
idolatría *f* idolatry; idolization
idolátrico -ca *adj* idolatrous
ídolo *m* idol; (fig.) idol
idolología *f* science dealing with idols
Idomeneo *m* (myth.) Idomeneus
idoneidad *f* fitness; suitability
idóneo -a *adj* fit; suitable
-idor -dora *suffix adj* -ing, e.g., **seguidor** following; **vividor** living; *suffix mf* -er, e.g., **seguidor** follower; **vividor** liver
idumeo -a *adj & mf* Idumaean or Idumean; (*cap.*) *f* (Bib.) Idumaea
idus *mpl* ides
i.e. abr. of **id est** (Lat.) **esto es, es decir**
-iento -ta *suffix adj* -y, e.g., **hambriento** hungry; **polvoriento** dusty; powdery; **sediento** thirsty; **sudoriento** sweaty

Ifigenia *f* (myth.) Iphigenia
igl.ª abr. of **iglesia**
iglesia *f* church; **entrar en la iglesia** to go into the church (*clerical profession*); **ir a la iglesia** to go to church; **llevar a la iglesia** to lead (*a woman*) to the altar; **iglesia colegial** collegiate church; **Iglesia de Inglaterra** Church of England; **Iglesia griega ortodoxa** Greek Orthodox Church; **Iglesia latina** Latin Church; **iglesia militante** church militant; **Iglesia ortodoxa** Orthodox Church; **iglesia triunfante** church triumphant
iglesiero -ra *adj* (Am.) churchgoing; *mf* (Am.) churchgoer
iglú *m* (*pl:* **-glúes**) igloo
ignaciano -na *adj & m* Ignatian, Jesuit
Ignacio *m* Ignatius
ignaro -ra *adj* ignorant
ignavia *f* laziness
ignavo -va *adj* lazy
ígneo -a *adj* igneous
ignición *f* ignition
ignícola *adj* fire-worshiping; *mf* fire worshiper
ignífero -ra *adj* igniferous
ignífugo -ga *adj & m* ignifuge
ignito -ta *adj* ignited, inflamed
ignívomo -ma *adj* (poet.) ignivomous
ignominia *f* ignominy
ignominioso -sa *adj* ignominious
ignorancia *f* ignorance
ignorante *adj* ignorant; *mf* ignoramus
ignorar *va* not to know, to be ignorant of
ignoto -ta *adj* unknown
igorrote *adj* Igorot; *m* Igorot or Igorrote
igual *adj* equal; smooth, level, even, uniform; equable, firm, constant; unchanging; indifferent; **me es igual** it is all the same to me, it makes no difference to me; *m* equal; sign of equality; **al igual de** like, after the fashion of; **al igual que** as; like; while, whereas; **en igual de** instead of; **sin igual** matchless, unrivaled; **igual que** as well as
iguala *f* equalization; agreement; annual fee; level
igualación *f* equalization; agreement
igualado -da *adj* with even plumage
igualador -dora *adj* equalizing; leveling; *mf* equalizer; leveler; **igualador de caminos** road planer; **igualador de dientes** jointer (*of saws*)
igualamiento *m* equalization
igualar *va* to equalize; to smooth, to level, to even, to smooth off; to match; to deem equal; to adjust, to face, to fit; (math.) to equate; to joint (*saws*); to set (*a clock or watch*); *vn & vr* to be equal; **igualar a** or **con** or **igualarse a** or **con** to equal, to be equal to
igualdad *f* equality, sameness; smoothness, evenness; **igualdad de ánimo** equability, equanimity
igualitario -ria *adj & mf* equalitarian
igualmente *adv* equally; likewise; (coll.) the same to you
iguana *f* (zool.) iguana
iguanodonte *m* (pal.) iguanodont
igüedo *m* (zool.) buck
ijada *f* flank (*of animal*); loin; stitch (*pain in the side*); **tener su ijada** to have its weak point
ijadear *vn* to pant, to quiver (*from fatigue*)
ijar *m* flank (*of animal*); loin
ilación *f* illation; order, connection
ilapso *m* trance, ecstatic trance
ilativo -va *adj* inferential, illative; *f* illative
Il.ᵉ abr. of **Ilustre**
ilegal *adj* illegal
ilegalidad *f* illegality
ilegibilidad *f* illegibility
ilegible *adj* illegible
ilegitimar *va* to make or prove illegitimate, to illegitimate
ilegitimidad *f* illegitimacy
ilegítimo -ma *adj* illegitimate
íleo *m* (path.) ileus
ileocecal *adj* ileocaecal
íleon *m* (anat.) ileum; (anat.) ilium
ileso -sa *adj* unharmed, unscathed; whole, untouched
iletrado -da *adj* unlettered, uncultured
ilíaco -ca *adj* (anat. & path.) ileac; (anat.) iliac; (myth.) Iliac
Ilíada *f* Iliad
iliberal *adj* illiberal
iliberalidad *f* illiberality
ilicáceo -a *adj* (bot.) ilicaceous
ilíceo -a *adj* oak
ilicíneo -a *adj* (bot.) ilicaceous
ilicitano -na *adj* (pertaining to) Elche; *mf* native or inhabitant of Elche
ilícito -ta *adj* illicit; unlawful; unjust
ilicitud *f* illicitness; unlawfulness; unjustness
iliense *adj* Ilian
ilimitable *adj* illimitable
ilimitado -da *adj* limitless, unlimited
ilinio *m* (chem.) illinium
ilion *m* (anat.) ilium; (anat.) ileum
Ilión *m* (myth.) Ilium or Ilion
ilíquido -da *adj* unliquidated
Iliria *f* see **ilirio**
ilírico -ca *adj* Illyric
ilirio -ria *adj & mf* Illyrian; (*cap.*) *f* Illyria
iliterato -ta *adj* illiterate
Il.ᵐᵒ abr. of **Ilustrísimo**
ilógico -ca *adj* illogical
ilota *mf* Helot; (fig.) helot
ilotismo *m* helotism
iludir *va* to elude, evade
iluminación *f* illumination; (f.a.) illumination; (f.a.) painting in distemper; **iluminación indirecta** indirect lighting
iluminado -da *adj* illuminated; **iluminados** *mpl* Illuminated, Illuminati
iluminador -dora *adj* illuminating; *mf* illuminator
iluminar *va* to illuminate; (f.a.) to illuminate
iluminativo -va *adj* illuminative
iluminismo *m* Illuminism
ilusión *f* illusion; delusion; zeal, enthusiasm, fanaticism; dream; **forjarse** or **hacerse ilusiones** to indulge in wishful thinking, to kid oneself; **ilusión óptica** optical illusion
ilusionar *va* to delude, to beguile; *vr* to be deluded, to have illusions, to indulge in wishful thinking
ilusionismo *m* prestidigitation
ilusionista *mf* illusionist, prestidigitator
ilusivo -va *adj* illusive
iluso -sa *adj* deluded; misguided; visionary
ilusorio -ria *adj* illusory
ilustración *f* illustration; learning; enlightenment; elucidation; illustrated magazine
ilustrado -da *adj* informed, learned; illustrated; enlightened
ilustrador -dora *adj* illustrative; enlightening; explicatory; *mf* illustrator
ilustrar *va* to illustrate; to make famous or illustrious; to shed glory on, to cause to shine; to enlighten; to elucidate; (theol.) to inspire; *vr* to be enlightened; to become famous
ilustrativo -va *adj* illustrative
ilustre *adj* illustrious
ilustrísimo -ma *adj super* very or most illustrious; (eccl.) Most Reverend (*bishop*)
illicitano -na *adj & mf* var. of **ilicitano**
Illmo. abr. of **Ilustrísimo**
-illo -lla *suffix dim* has the force of little, somewhat, rather and often indicates an attitude of indifference or depreciation, e.g., **cigarrillo** cigaret; **coquetilla** little coquette; **cucharilla** small spoon, teaspoon; **chiquillo** youngster; **abatidillo** somewhat downcast
imagen *f* image; picture; **a su imagen** in his own image; **imagen de bulto** statue, image in high relief; **imagen fantasma** (telv.) ghost image; **imagen real** (phys.) real image; **imagen virtual** (phys.) virtual image
imaginable *adj* imaginable
imaginación *f* imagination
imaginar *va, vn & vr* to imagine; **imaginarse** + *inf* to imagine + *ger*
imaginario -ria *adj* imaginary; *mf* painter or sculptor of religious images; *f* (mil.) reserve guard
imaginativo -va *adj* imaginative; *f* imagination; understanding
imaginería *f* fancy colored embroidery; carving or painting of religious images

imaginero *m* painter or sculptor of religious images
imago *m* (zool.) imago
imán *m* (mineral., phys. & fig.) magnet; (fig.) magnetism; imam; **imán de herradura** horseshoe magnet; **imán inductor** (elec.) field magnet
imanación *f* magnetization
imanar *va* to magnetize; *vr* to become magnetized
imantación *f* var. of **imanación**
imantar *va & vr* var. of **imanar**
imbatible *adj* unbeatable
imbatido -da *adj* unbeaten
imbécil *adj & mf* imbecile
imbecilidad *f* imbecility
imbele *adj* weak, feeble; defenseless, unfit to fight
imberbe *adj* beardless
imbibición *f* imbibition
imbornal *m* scupper, drain hole; (naut.) scupper
imborrable *adj* ineffaceable, ineradicable
imbricación *f* imbrication
imbricado -da *adj* imbricate or imbricated
imbuir §41 *va* to imbue; **imbuir de** or **en** to imbue with
imitable *adj* imitable; worthy of imitation
imitación *f* imitation; **a imitación de** in imitation of; **de imitación** imitation, e.g., **joyas de imitación** imitation jewelry; *adj* imitation, e.g., **joyas imitación** imitation jewelry
imitado -da *adj* imitated, copied; like; mock, sham; imitation, e.g., **perlas imitadas** imitation pearls
imitador -dora *adj* imitating, imitative; *mf* imitator
imitar *va* to imitate
imitativo -va *adj* imitative
imoscapo *m* (arch.) apophyge
impacción *f* impact; (dent. & med.) impaction
impaciencia *f* impatience; act or show of impatience
impacientar *va* to make impatient; *vr* to grow impatient
impaciente *adj* impatient
impactado -da *adj* (dent.) impacted
impacto *m* impact; hit; blow; mark (*left by a projectile*); (fig.) impact; **impacto de bala** bullet mark; **impacto directo** direct hit
impagable *adj* unpayable; priceless
impalpabilidad *f* impalpability
impalpable *adj* impalpable
impanación *f* (theol.) impanation
impar *adj* unmatched; (math.) odd, uneven; *m* (math.) odd number
imparcial *adj* impartial; nonpartisan
imparcialidad *f* impartiality; **extremar la imparcialidad** to lean over backward
imparidad *f* oddness, unevenness
imparidígito -ta *adj* (zool.) imparidigitate
imparipinado -da *adj* (bot.) imparipinnate
imparisílabo -ba or **imparisilábico -ca** *adj* (gram.) imparisyllabic
impartible *adj* indivisible
impartir *va* to distribute, transmit; (law) to seek, solicit
impás *m* (bridge) finesse
impasibilidad *f* impassibility, impassivity
impasible *adj* impassible, impassive
impavidez *f* intrepidity, fearlessness
impávido -da *adj* intrepid, fearless, dauntless
impecabilidad *f* impeccability
impecable *adj* impeccable
impedancia *f* (elec.) impedance
impedido -da *adj* crippled, paralytic
impedimenta *f* (mil.) impedimenta
impedimento *m* impediment, obstacle, hindrance; (law) impediment, disability
impedir §94 *va* to prevent; **impedir algo a uno** to prevent someone from doing something; **impedir** + *inf* or **impedir que** + *subj* to prevent or keep from + *ger*
impeditivo -va *adj* preventive, hindering
impeler *va* to impel; **impeler a** + *inf* to impel to + *inf*
impender *va* to spend, to invest
impenetrabilidad *f* impenetrability
impenetrable *adj* impenetrable
impenitencia *f* impenitence
impenitente *adj* impenitent; hardened, inveterate; *mf* impenitent
impensa *f* (law) expense, upkeep expense
impensable *adj* unthinkable
impensado -da *adj* unexpected
imperador -dora *adj* ruling, commanding
imperante *adj* ruling; prevailing; (astrol.) dominant
imperar *vn* to rule, reign, hold sway, prevail
imperativo -va *adj* imperative; imperious, dictatorial; (gram.) imperative; *m* imperative; (gram.) imperative; **imperativo categórico** (philos.) categorical imperative; *f* tone of command, commanding manner
imperatoria *f* (bot.) masterwort
imperceptibilidad *f* imperceptibility
imperceptible *adj* imperceptible
imperdible *adj* unlosable; *m* safety pin
imperdonable *adj* unforgivable, unpardonable
imperecedero -ra *adj* imperishable, undying
imperfección *f* imperfection
imperfectivo -va *adj* (gram.) imperfective
imperfecto -ta *adj* imperfect; (gram.) imperfect; *m* (gram.) imperfect
imperforable *adj* imperforable; (aut.) puncture-proof
imperforación *f* imperforation
imperforado -da *adj* imperforate
imperial *adj* imperial; *f* imperial, upper deck (*of diligence, bus, or trolley car*)
imperialismo *m* imperialism
imperialista *adj* imperialist, imperialistic; *mf* imperialist
impericia *f* inexpertness, unskilfulness
imperio *m* empire; dominion, sway; imperium; **celeste imperio** or **imperio celeste** Celestial Empire (*China*); **estilo imperio** (f.a.) Empire; **Sacro Imperio Romano-Germánico** Holy Roman Empire; **Imperio del sol naciente** Empire of the Rising Sun (*Japan*); **Imperio romano** Roman Empire
imperioso -sa *adj* imperious; imperative
imperito -ta *adj* inexpert, unskilled
impermanencia *f* impermanence
impermanente *adj* impermanent
impermeabilidad *f* impermeability
impermeabilización *f* waterproofing (*action*)
impermeabilizante *m* waterproofing (*material*)
impermeabilizar §76 *va* to make waterproof, to waterproof
impermeable *adj* impermeable; waterproof; impervious; *m* raincoat
impermutable *adj* impermutable; unexchangeable
imperscrutabilidad *f* inscrutability
imperscrutable *adj* inscrutable
impersonal *adj* impersonal; (gram.) impersonal
impersonalidad *f* impersonality
impersonalizar §76 *va* (gram.) to use (*a verb*) impersonally
impersuasible *adj* unpersuadable
impersuasión *f* unpersuadableness
impertérrito -ta *adj* dauntless, intrepid
impertinencia *f* irrelevance; impertinence
impertinente *adj* irrelevant; impertinent; fussy; **impertinentes** *mpl* lorgnette
imperturbabilidad *f* imperturbability
imperturbable *adj* imperturbable, unperturbable, unshakable
imperturbado -da *adj* unperturbed, undisturbed
impétigo *m* (path.) impetigo
impetra *f* permission, allowance
impetración *f* begging, petition; obtaining by entreaty
impetrador -dora *mf* impetrator
impetrar *va* to beg for; to obtain by entreaty
ímpetu *m* impetus; haste, violence; impetuousness
impetuosidad *f* impetuosity
impetuoso -sa *adj* impetuous
impiedad *f* pitilessness; impiety
impiedoso -sa *adj* pitiless
impío -a *adj* pitiless, cruel; impious
impla *f* wimple; material for making wimples
implacabilidad *f* implacability
implacable *adj* implacable

implantación *f* implantation; introduction
implantar *va* to implant; to introduce
implaticable *adj* unmentionable, not for conversation
implicación *f* contradiction; implication, complicity
implicar §86 *va* to implicate; to imply; *vn* to stand in the way, to imply contradiction
implícitamente *adv* implicitly, impliedly
implícito -ta *adj* implicit, implied
imploración *f* imploration, supplication, entreaty
implorar *va* to implore
implosión *f* implosion; (phonet.) implosion
implosivo -va *adj & f* (phonet.) implosive
implotar *vn* to burst inwards
implume *adj* featherless, unfeathered; unfledged
impluvio *m* impluvium
impolarizable *adj* impolarizable
impolítico -ca *adj* impolite, discourteous; *f* impoliteness, discourtesy
impoluto -ta *adj* unpolluted
imponderabilidad *f* imponderability, imponderableness
imponderable *adj & m* imponderable
impondré *1st sg fut ind of* **imponer**
imponente *adj* imposing; *mf* depositor
imponer §69 *va* to impose (*one's will, taxes, silence, etc.*); (print.) to impose; (eccl.) to impose (*the hands*); to instruct; to invest; to deposit (*money*); to impute falsely; *vn* to dominate, command respect; *vr* to assume (*e.g., an obligation*); to become trained; to command attention, impel recognition; **imponerse a** to dominate, command respect from; to get the best of; **imponerse de** to learn, find out
impongo *1st sg pres ind of* **imponer**
imponible *adj* taxable
impopular *adj* unpopular
impopularidad *f* unpopularity
impopularizar §76 *va* to make unpopular; *vr* to become unpopular
importación *f* import, importation; imports
importador -dora *adj* importing; *mf* importer
importancia *f* importance; size; concern, seriousness; **ser de la importancia de** to concern
importante *adj* important; large, considerable
importar *va* to import; to be worth, be valued at, amount to; to involve, imply; to concern; *vn* to import; to be important; to matter, make a difference
importe *m* amount
importunación *f* importuning, pestering
importunar *va* to importune
importunidad *f* importunity, annoyance; inopportunity, untimeliness
importuno -na *adj* importunate; inopportune
imposibilidad *f* impossibility
imposibilitar *va* to make unable; to make impossible, to prevent; *vr* to become unable; to become impossible; to become paralyzed
imposible *adj* impossible
imposición *f* imposition (*e.g., of one's will*); investiture; deposit (*of money*); (print.) make-up, imposition; (eccl.) imposition, laying on of hands; **imposición de manos** (eccl.) laying on of hands
impositivo -va *adj* (pertaining to) tax
imposta *f* (arch.) impost; (arch.) fascia; sill
impostor -tora *adj* cheating; slandering; *m* impostor; slanderer; *f* impostress; slanderer
impostura *f* imposture; slander
impotable *adj* undrinkable
impotencia *f* impotence; (path.) impotence
impotente *adj* impotent; (path.) impotent
impracticabilidad *f* impracticability, impassability
impracticable *adj* impracticable, impassable; impractical
impráctico -ca *adj* unpractical, impractical
imprecación *f* imprecation
imprecar §86 *va* to imprecate
imprecatorio -ria *adj* imprecatory
imprecisión *f* imprecision
impreciso -sa *adj* imprecise; vague, indefinite; inexact, inaccurate
impregnación *f* (phys.) impregnation
impregnar *va* (phys.) to impregnate, saturate; *vr* (phys.) to become impregnated, become saturated
impremeditación *f* unpremeditation
impremeditado -da *adj* unpremeditated
imprenta *f* printing; printing shop, printing house; press; printed matter; letterpress; **en imprenta** in press
imprentar *va* (Am.) to press, iron; (Am.) to mark
imprescindible *adj* essential, indispensable
imprescriptible *adj* imprescriptible, inalienable
impresentable *adj* unpresentable
impresión *f* printing; print, edition, issue; presswork; stamp, stamping; impression, impress, footprint; (phot.) print; (fig.) impression; **impresión dactilar** or **digital** fingerprint
impresionabilidad *f* impressionability, impressibility, susceptibility
impresionable *adj* impressionable, impressible
impresionante *adj* impressive; sensational
impresionar *va* to impress; to record (*a phonograph wire, tape or disk*); (phot.) to expose; *vn* to make an impression; *vr* to be impressed
impresionismo *m* (paint., lit. & mus.) impressionism
impresionista *adj* impressionistic; *mf* impressionist
impreso -sa *pp of* **imprimir;** *m* printed paper or book; **impresos** *mpl* printed matter
impresor -sora *adj* printing; *mf* printer (*workman or owner*); *f* wife of printer
imprestable *adj* unlendable
imprevisible *adj* unforeseeable
imprevisión *f* improvidence; oversight
imprevisor -sora *adj* improvident
imprevisto -ta *adj* unforeseen, unexpected; **imprevistos** *mpl* unforeseen expenses, emergencies
imprimación *f* priming; priming material
imprimadera *f* priming tool
imprimador *m* primer
imprimar *va* to prime
imprimátur *m* (*pl:* **-tur**) imprimatur
imprimible *adj* printable
imprimir *va* to impart (*fear, respect, etc.; motion*); §17, 9 *va* to print; to stamp, imprint, impress; to press (*a phonograph record*); to leave (*footprints*); (print.) to print
improbabilidad *f* improbability, unlikelihood
improbable *adj* improbable, unlikely
improbar §77 *va* to disapprove
improbidad *f* dishonesty, improbity
ímprobo -ba *adj* dishonest; arduous
improcedencia *f* lack of rightness; unfitness, untimeliness
improcedente *adj* not right; unfit, untimely
improductivo -va *adj* unproductive; unemployed
impronta *f* stamp, impress, impression; (fig.) stamp, mark
impronunciable *adj* unpronounceable
improperar *va* to insult, to revile
improperio *m* insult, indignity
impropicio -cia *adj* unpropitious, inauspicious
impropiedad *f* impropriety (*especially in language*)
impropio -pia *adj* improper, unsuited; foreign; (math.) improper
improporción *f* disproportion
improporcionado -da *adj* disproportionate
improrrogable *adj* unextendible
impróspero -ra *adj* unsuccessful
impróvido -da *adj* unprepared, improvident
improvisación *f* improvisation, extemporization; meteoric rise, undeserved success; (mus.) impromptu
improvisadamente *adv* unexpectedly, suddenly; extempore
improvisado -da *adj* unexpected, sudden
improvisador -dora *adj* improvising; *mf* improviser
improvisamente *adv* var. of **improvisadamente**
improvisar *va* to improvise, to extemporize; to utter extemporaneously; *vn* to improvise, to extemporize

improviso -sa *adj* unexpected, unforeseen; **al improviso** or **de improviso** unexpectedly, suddenly
improvisto -ta *adj* unexpected, unforeseen; **a la improvista** unexpectedly, suddenly
imprudencia *f* imprudence; **imprudencia temeraria** criminal negligence
imprudente *adj* imprudent
impúber -bera or **impúbero -ra** *adj* impuberate
impublicable *adj* unpublishable
impudencia *f* impudence; shamelessness
impudente *adj* impudent; shameless
impudicia or **impudicicia** *f* immodesty, impudicity
impúdico -ca *adj* immodest
impudor *m* immodesty, shamelessness
impuesto -ta *pp of* **imponer; estar** or **quedar impuesto de** to be informed of or about; *m* tax, impost
impugnable *adj* assailable, vulnerable
impugnación *f* opposition, impugnation
impugnar *va* to oppose, impugn, contest
impulsar *va* to impel; to drive; **impulsar a** + *inf* to impel to + *inf*
impulsión *f* impulsion; impulse, drive
impulsividad *f* impulsiveness
impulsivo -va *adj* impulsive
impulso *m* impulse; (mech.) impulse
impulsor -sora *adj* impelling; *mf* impeller
impune *adj* unpunished
impunemente *adv* with impunity
impunidad *f* impunity
impureza *f* impurity
impurificación *f* defilement
impurificar §86 *va* to make impure, to defile
impuro -ra *adj* impure
impuse *1st sg pret ind of* **imponer**
imputable *adj* imputable
imputación *f* imputation; assignment
imputador -dora *mf* imputer
imputar *va* to impute; to assign; (com.) to credit on account
in- *prefix* in-, e.g., **inconstante** inconstant; **inacción** inaction; **invadir** invade; (*before* **m**) im-, e.g., **inmediato** immediate; un-, e.g., **infeliz** unhappy; **inaudito** unheard-of
inabarcable *adj* unembraceable; that cannot be taken in or encompassed
inabordable *adj* unapproachable
inabrogable *adj* indefeasible
inacabable *adj* interminable
inaccesibilidad *f* inaccessibility
inaccesible *adj* inaccessible
inacción *f* inaction
inacentuado -da *adj* unaccented
inaceptable *adj* unacceptable
inactividad *f* inactivity
inactivo -va *adj* inactive
inadaptabilidad *f* unadaptability, inadaptability
inadaptable *adj* unadaptable, inadaptable
inadaptado -da *adj* unsuited, unsuitable; maladjusted
inadecuación *f* unsuitability; inadequacy
inadecuado -da *adj* unsuited, ill-suited; inadequate
inadmisibilidad *f* inadmissibility
inadmisible *adj* inadmissible; unallowable
inadoptable *adj* unadoptable
inadvertencia *f* inadvertence, oversight
inadvertidamente *adv* inadvertently; carelessly
inadvertido -da *adj* inadvertent, unwitting, inattentive; thoughtless, careless; unseen, unnoticed, unobserved
inafectado -da *adj* unaffected
inagotable *adj* inexhaustible, exhaustless
inaguantable *adj* intolerable, unsufferable
inajenable *adj* inalienable
inalámbrico -ca *adj* (elec.) wireless
inalcanzable *adj* unattainable, unreachable
inalienabilidad *f* inalienability
inalienable *adj* inalienable
inalterabilidad *f* unalterability
inalterable *adj* unalterable
inalterado -da *adj* unaltered
inameno -na *adj* unpleasant, disagreeable
inamisible *adj* unlosable
inamistoso -sa *adj* unfriendly
inamovible *adj* undetachable; built-in; unremovable, irremovable
inamovilidad *f* irremovability; tenure, permanent tenure
inanalizable *adj* unanalyzable
inane *adj* inane
inanición *f* inanition
inanidad *f* inanity
inanimado -da *adj* inanimate
inánime *adj* weak, spiritless, lifeless
inapagable *adj* unextinguishable
inapeable *adj* incomprehensible, inconceivable; stubborn, obstinate
inapelable *adj* unappealable; inevitable, unavoidable
inapercibido -da *adj* unnoticed
inapetencia *f* lack or loss of appetite
inapetente *adj* having no appetite, inappetent
inaplazable *adj* undeferrable
inaplicable *adj* inapplicable
inaplicación *f* inapplication, lack of application; inapplicability
inaplicado -da *adj* lazy, indolent, careless
inapolillable *adj* moth-free, moth-resisting
inapreciable *adj* inestimable; imperceptible; inappreciable
inapto -ta *adj* inapt
inarmónico -ca *adj* unharmonious; unharmonic, inharmonic
inarrugable *adj* wrinkle-free (*fabric*)
inarticulado -da *adj* inarticulate
inartístico -ca *adj* inartistic
inasequibilidad *f* inaccessibility
inasequible *adj* unattainable, inaccessible
inasimilable *adj* unassimilable
inasistencia *f* absence
inastillable *adj* nonshatterable, unshatterable, shatterproof
inatacable *adj* unattackable; unchallengeable, unquestionable; **inatacable por** resistant to, resisting
inatención *f* inattention
inatento -ta *adj* inattentive
inaudible *adj* inaudible
inaudito -ta *adj* unheard-of; astounding, extraordinary; outrageous, monstrous
inauguración *f* inauguration; unveiling
inaugural *adj* inaugural
inaugurar *va* to inaugurate; to unveil (*e.g., a statue*)
inavenible *adj* uncompromising, disagreeable
inaveriguable *adj* unascertainable
inaveriguado -da *adj* not ascertained, not checked
inca *mf* Inca; *m* Inca (*ruler*)
incaico -ca *adj* Inca, Incan
incalculable *adj* incalculable
incalificable *adj* unqualifiable; unspeakable
incalmable *adj* unsubduable
incambiable *adj* unchangeable; unexchangeable
incandescencia *f* incandescence
incandescente *adj* incandescent
incansable *adj* indefatigable, untiring
incantable *adj* unsingable
incapacidad *f* incapacity, inability, incapability
incapacitar *va* to incapacitate; to declare incompetent
incapaz *adj* (*pl:* **-paces**) incapable, unable; incompetent; not large enough; simple, stupid; crude, ignorant; (coll.) impossible, unbearable, frightful
incarceración *f* (path.) incarceration
incasable *adj* unmarriageable; unmarriable; opposed to getting married
incásico -ca *adj* var. of **incaico**
incasto -ta *adj* unchaste
incautación *f* (law) seizure, attachment
incautar *vr;* **incautarse de** to hold (*until claimed*); (law) to seize, to attach
incauto -ta *adj* unwary, heedless, incautious
incendaja *f* kindling
incendiar *va* to set on fire; *vr* to catch fire
incendiario -ria *adj* incendiary; *mf* incendiary, firebug
incendio *m* fire (*conflagration*); consuming passion
incensación *f* (act of) incensing or burning incense
incensada *f* swing of incense burner; flattery

incensar §18 *va* to incense, perfume with incense; (fig.) to incense, to flatter
incensario *m* incensory, censer, incense burner
incensurable *adj* unblamable
incentivo -va *adj & m* incentive
inceremonioso -sa *adj* unceremonious
incertidumbre *f* uncertainty, incertitude
incertísimo -ma *adj super* very or most uncertain
incesable *adj* unceasing
incesante *adj* incessant
incesto *m* incest
incestuoso -sa *adj* incestuous; *mf* incestuous person
incidencia *f* incidence; incident; (geom. & phys.) incidence; **por incidencia** by chance
incidental *adj* incidental
incidente *adj* incident; incidental; *m* incident
incidir *va* to cut, make an incision in; *vn* to fall; to fall into error; **incidir en** or **sobre** to impinge on, to strike
incienso *m* incense; frankincense; (bot.) southernwood; (fig.) incense
incierto -ta *adj* uncertain
incindir *va* to cut, make an incision in
incinerable *adj* incinerable; to be withdrawn from circulation and burned (*said of bank notes*)
incineración *f* incineration; **incineración de cadáveres** cremation
incinerador *m* incinerator
incinerar *va* to incinerate, to cremate
incipiente *adj* incipient
incircunciso -sa *adj* uncircumcised
incircunscripto -ta *adj* uncircumscribed
incisión *f* incision; caesura; incisiveness, sarcasm
incisivo -va *adj* incisive; barbed, caustic; (anat.) incisive; *m* (anat.) incisor
inciso -sa *adj* choppy (*style of writing*); (bot.) incised; *m* sentence; clause; comma
incisorio -ria *adj* incisory
incitación *f* incitation
incitamento or **incitamiento** *m* incitement
incitar *va* to incite; **incitar a** + *inf* to incite to + *inf*
incivil *adj* uncivil
incivilidad *f* incivility
incivilizado -da *adj* uncivilized
inclasificable *adj* unclassifiable
inclaustración *f* entry into a convent or monastery
inclemencia *f* inclemency; **a la inclemencia** exposed, shelterless
inclemente *adj* inclement
inclinación *f* inclination; bent, leaning; bow
inclinado -da *adj* inclined; **bien inclinado** well-disposed, good-natured; **mal inclinado** ill-disposed, ill-natured
inclinar *va* to incline, to bend, to bow; to move, impel, turn; *vn* to incline, bend, bow; **inclinar a** to resemble; *vr* to incline, be inclined, tend; to bow; **inclinarse a** to resemble; to be inclined to; **inclinarse a** + *inf* to be inclined to + *inf*
inclinómetro *m* inclinometer
ínclito -ta *adj* illustrious, distinguished
incluir §41 *va* to include; to inclose
inclusa *f* see **incluso**
inclusero -ra *adj* (coll.) raised as a foundling; *mf* (coll.) foundling
inclusión *f* inclusion; friendship
inclusive *adv* inclusively; *prep* including
inclusivo -va *adj* inclusive, including
incluso -sa *adj* inclosed; *f* foundling home or asylum; **incluso** *adv* inclusively; even; *prep* including
incoación *f* (law) initiation
incoagulable *adj* uncoagulable
incoar *va* (law) to initiate
incoativo -va *adj* (gram.) inchoative
incobrable *adj* irrecoverable; uncollectible
incoercible *adj* incoercible
incógnito -ta *adj* unknown; incognito; *mf* incognito (*person*); *m* incognito (*state*); **de incógnito** incognito; *f* (math. & fig.) unknown quantity
incognoscible *adj* unknowable
incoherencia *f* incoherence
incoherente *adj* incoherent
íncola *m* inhabitant
incoloro -ra *adj* colorless
incólume *adj* unharmed, sound, safe, untouched
incolumidad *f* safeness, security; preservation
incombustibilidad *f* incombustibility
incombustibilización *f* fireproofing
incombustible *adj* incombustible; fireproof; (fig.) cold, indifferent
incombusto -ta *adj* unburned
incomerciable *adj* unsalable, unmarketable; unnegotiable (*that cannot be got past*)
incomible *adj* (coll.) uneatable, inedible
incomodar *va* to incommode, inconvenience; *vr* to become vexed, get annoyed; to inconvenience oneself, to be inconvenienced
incomodidad *f* inconvenience; discomfort, uncomfortableness; anger, annoyance
incómodo -da *adj* inconvenient; uncomfortable; *m* inconvenience; discomfort
incomparable or **incomparado -da** *adj* incomparable
incomparencia *f* failure to appear
incompartible *adj* indivisible; unsharable
incompasivo -va *adj* pitiless, unsympathetic
incompatibilidad *f* incompatibility
incompatible *adj* incompatible; conflicting
incompetencia *f* incompetence or incompetency
incompetente *adj* incompetent
incompetible *adj* unmatchable (*price*)
incomplejo -ja *adj* incomplex, simple
incompleto -ta *adj* incomplete
incomplexo -xa *adj* incomplex, simple
incomponible *adj* unmendable, unrepairable
incomportable *adj* unbearable, intolerable
incomposibilidad *f* unmendable condition; incompatibility
incomposible *adj* unmendable; incompatible
incomprable *adj* unpurchasable
incomprehensibilidad *f* incomprehensibility
incomprehensible *adj* incomprehensible
incomprendido -da *adj* misunderstood
incomprensibilidad *f* incomprehensibility
incomprensible *adj* incomprehensible
incomprensivo -va *adj* unintelligent, ignorant
incompresibilidad *f* incompressibility
incompresible *adj* incompressible
incomunicabilidad *f* incommunicability
incomunicable *adj* incommunicable
incomunicación *f* isolation, solitary confinement
incomunicado -da *adj* incommunicado
incomunicar §86 *va* to isolate, put in solitary confinement; to close, shut off; *vr* to isolate oneself, become isolated
inconcebibilidad *f* inconceivability
inconcebible *adj* inconceivable
inconciliable *adj* irreconcilable
inconcino -na *adj* disarranged, disordered
inconcluso -sa *adj* unfinished
inconcluyente *adj* inconclusive
inconcuso -sa *adj* undeniable, unquestionable
incondicional *adj* unconditional
inconducente *adj* unconducive
inconel *m* inconel
inconexión *f* disconnection; irrelevance
inconexo -xa *adj* unconnected, disconnected; irrelevant
inconfeso -sa *adj* unconfessed
inconfidencia *f* distrust
inconfidente *adj* distrustful
inconforme *adj* in disagreement, out of sympathy
inconfundible *adj* unmistakable
incongelable *adj* uncongealable
incongelado -da *adj* uncongealed, unfrozen
incongruencia *f* incongruity
incongruente *adj* incongruent, incongruous
incongruo -grua *adj* incongruous
inconmensurabilidad *f* incommensurability
inconmensurable *adj* incommensurable, incommensurate
inconmovible *adj* firm, lasting; unyielding, inexorable
inconmutable *adj* immutable; unexchangeable
inconocible *adj* unknowable
inconquistable *adj* unconquerable; unbending

inconsciencia *f* unconsciousness; unawareness, insensibility; inattention, inadvertence
inconsciente *adj* unconscious; unaware, insensible; oblivious; **lo inconsciente** the unconscious
inconsecuencia *f* inconsequence; inconsistency
inconsecuente *adj* inconsequent, inconsequential; inconsistent
inconsideración *f* inconsiderateness
inconsiderado -da *adj* inconsiderate
inconsiguiente *adj* inconsistent
inconsistencia *f* inconsistency
inconsistente *adj* inconsistent
inconsolable *adj* inconsolable
inconsonante *adj* inconsonant
inconstancia *f* inconstancy
inconstante *adj* inconstant
inconstitucional *adj* unconstitutional
inconstitucionalidad *f* unconstitutionality
inconstruíble *adj* unbuildable
inconsútil *adj* seamless
incontable *adj* uncountable, countless
incontaminado -da *adj* uncontaminated
incontenible *adj* irrepressible
incontestable *adj* incontestable, unanswerable, unquestionable
incontestado -da *adj* unquestioned
incontinencia *f* incontinence; (path.) incontinence
incontinente *adj* incontinent; *adv* at once, instantly
incontinenti *adv* at once, instantly
incontrastable *adj* invincible; inconvincible
incontratable *adj* unruly; unsociable; undeniable
incontrolado -da *adj* uncontrolled
incontrovertibilidad *f* incontrovertibility
incontrovertible *adj* incontrovertible
inconvencible *adj* inconvincible
inconvenible *adj* intractable, uncompromising
inconveniencia *f* inconvenience; unsuitability; impoliteness, impropriety; absurdity, nonsense
inconveniente *adj* inconvenient; unsuitable; impolite; *m* obstacle, difficulty; damage
inconversable *adj* unsociable, uncommunicative, surly
inconvertibilidad *f* inconvertibility
inconvertible *adj* inconvertible
incoordinación *f* incoördination
incordio *m* (path.) bubo; (slang) nuisance, boor
incorporación *f* incorporation, embodiment; association, participation
incorporadero *m* (metal.) patio
incorporado -da *adj* sitting up (*from reclining position*); built-in
incorporal *adj* incorporeal, intangible
incorporar *va* to incorporate, to embody; *vr* to incorporate; to sit up (*from reclining position*); to associate, participate; **incorporarse a** to join (*a society*)
incorporeidad *f* incorporealness, incorporeity
incorpóreo -a *adj* incorporeal, bodiless
incorrección *f* incorrectness
incorrecto -ta *adj* incorrect
incorregibilidad *f* incorrigibility
incorregible *adj* incorrigible
incorrupción *f* incorruptness, purity
incorruptibilidad *f* incorruptibility
incorruptible *adj* incorruptible
incorrupto -ta *adj* uncorrupted, incorrupt; pure, chaste
increado -da *adj* uncreated
incredibilidad *f* incredibility
incredulidad *f* incredulity; disbelief
incrédulo -la *adj* incredulous; unbelieving; *mf* unbeliever, disbeliever
increíble *adj* incredible
incrementar *va* to increase
incremento *m* increase, increment; (math.) increment
increpación *f* chiding, rebuke
increpador -dora *adj* chiding; *mf* chider, rebuker
increpar *va* to chide, rebuke
incriminación *f* incrimination; exaggeration of guilt
incriminar *va* to incriminate; to exaggerate the gravity of (*a defect, weakness, misdeed, etc.*)
incristalizable *adj* uncrystallizable
incruento -ta *adj* bloodless
incrustación *f* incrustation; inlay
incrustante *adj* incrustive
incrustar *va* to incrust; to inlay; *vr* to incrust; to become engraved (*in the memory*)
incubación *f* incubation
incubadora *f* incubator
incubar *va & vn* to incubate; *vr* to brew, be brewing
íncubo *m* incubus; (med.) incubus
incuestionable *adj* unquestionable
inculcación *f* inculcation; (print.) locking
inculcar §86 *va* to inculcate; (print.) to lock up; *vr* to be obstinate
inculpabilidad *f* inculpability, blamelessness, guiltlessness
inculpable *adj* inculpable, blameless, guiltless
inculpación *f* inculpation
inculpadamente *adv* faultlessly
inculpado -da *adj* faultless, innocent; accused, charged with guilt
inculpar *va* to blame, accuse, inculpate
incultivable *adj* untillable
inculto -ta *adj* uncultivated; untilled; uncultured; uncivilized
incultura *f* lack of cultivation; lack of culture
incumbencia *f* incumbency; duty, obligation; **ser de la incumbencia de** to be within the province of
incumbente *adj* incumbent; (bot. & zool.) incumbent
incumbir *vn* to be incumbent; **incumbir a** to be incumbent on; **incumbir a uno** + *inf* to become incumbent on one to + *inf*
incumplido -da *adj* unfulfilled; unpunctual
incumplimiento *m* nonfulfillment, unfulfillment, breach
incumplir *va* to not fulfill, to fail to fulfill
incunable *adj* incunabular; *m* incunabulum
incurabilidad *f* incurability
incurable *adj & mf* incurable
incuria *f* carelessness, negligence
incurioso -sa *adj* careless, negligent
incurrimiento *m* incurring
incurrir *vn* to become liable; **incurrir en** to incur
incursión *f* incursion, inroad, attack, raid
incusar *va* to accuse
incuso -sa *adj* incuse
indagación *f* investigation
indagador -dora *adj* investigating; *mf* investigator
indagar §59 *va* to investigate
indagatorio -ria *adj* (law) investigatory
indebido -da *adj* undue; illegal, unlawful; improper
indecencia *f* indecency
indecentada *f* shame, infamy
indecente *adj* indecent
indecible *adj* unspeakable, unutterable
indecisión *f* indecision
indeciso -sa *adj* undecided; indecisive
indeclinable *adj* undeclinable; undeniable; (gram.) undeclinable, indeclinable
indecoro *m* indecorum
indecoroso -sa *adj* indecorous, improper
indefectible *adj* unfailing, indefectible
indefendible or **indefensible** *adj* indefensible
indefensión *f* defenselessness
indefenso -sa *adj* undefended, unguarded, defenseless
indefinible *adj* indefinable or undefinable; unexpressible; incomprehensible
indefinido -da *adj* indefinite, vague; limitless
indehiscencia *f* (bot.) indehiscence
indehiscente *adj* (bot.) indehiscent
indelebilidad *f* indelibility
indeleble *adj* indelible
indeliberación *f* lack of deliberation, indeliberation
indeliberado -da *adj* unpremeditated, indeliberate
indelicadeza *f* indelicacy
indelicado -da *adj* indelicate
indemne *adj* undamaged
indemnidad *f* indemnity (*security against damage or loss*)

indemnización *f* indemnification; indemnity; **indemnización por despido** severance pay
indemnizar §76 *va* to indemnify; to reimburse
indemostrable *adj* undemonstrable, indemonstrable
independencia *f* independence
independiente *adj* independent; **independiente de** independent of; **independientes entre sí** independent of each other; *mf* independent
independista *adj* (pertaining to) independence; *mf* advocate of independence
independizar §76 *va* to free, emancipate; *vr* to make oneself independent, become independent
indescifrable *adj* indecipherable
indescriptible *adj* undescribable, indescribable
indeseable *adj* undesirable
indeseado -da *adj* unwanted
indesignable *adj* undeterminable
indesmallable *adj* run-proof, hole-proof (*mesh or net*)
indestructibilidad *f* indestructibility
indestructible *adj* indestructible
indeterminabilidad *f* indeterminability
indeterminable *adj* undeterminable, indeterminable
indeterminación *f* indetermination
indeterminado -da *adj* indeterminate
indeterminismo *m* indeterminism
indeterminista *adj* indeterminist, indeterministic; *mf* indeterminist
indevoción *f* indevotion, impiety
indevoto -ta *adj* undevout; not fond, not devoted
indezuelo -la *mf* little Indian
india *f* & **la India** see **indio**
indiada *f* (Am.) gang of Indians
indiana *f* see **indiano**
indianismo *m* Indianism
indianista *mf* Indianist
indiano -na *adj* Spanish American; East Indian; West Indian; *mf* Spanish American; East Indian; West Indian; person back from America with great wealth; **indiano de hilo negro** (coll.) skinflint; *f* printed calico
indicación *f* indication; **por indicación de** at the direction of
indicado -da *adj* set, appointed; obvious, appropriate; **muy indicado** just the thing
indicador -dora *adj* indicating; indicatory; *mf* indicator; *m* indicator; (chem.) indicator; **indicadores de dirección** (aut.) turn signals
indicán *m* (chem. & biochem.) indican
indicante *adj* & *m* indicant
indicanuria *f* (path.) indicanuria
indicar §86 *va* to indicate
indicativo -va *adj* indicative; (gram.) indicative; *m* (gram.) indicative; **indicativo de llamada** (telg.) call letters
indicción *f* indiction
índice *m* index; (math.) index; **índice de compresión** (mach.) compression index; **índice de libros prohibidos** (eccl.) Index; **índice de materias** table of contents; **índice de octano** (chem.) octane number or rating; **índice de oro** (chem.) gold number; **índice de refracción** (phys.) index of refraction; **índice en el corte** thumb index; **índice expurgatorio** (eccl.) Index Expurgatorius; **índice onomástico** index of proper names
indiciar *va* to suspect, surmise; to betoken, indicate
indicio *m* sign, token, indication; **indicios** *mpl* (chem.) traces; (law) evidence; **indicios vehementes** (law) circumstantial evidence
índico -ca *adj* East Indian
indiferencia *f* indifference
indiferente *adj* indifferent
indiferentismo *m* indifferentism
indígena *adj* indigenous; *mf* native
indigencia *f* indigence
indigente *adj* indigent; **los indigentes** the indigent
indigerible *adj* indigestible
indigestar *va* to make (*food*) indigestible; *vr* to have indigestion; to cause indigestion, to be indigestible; to be disliked, be unbearable
indigestibilidad *f* indigestibility
indigestible *adj* indigestible
indigestión *f* indigestion
indigesto -ta *adj* undigested
indignación *f* indignation
indignado -da *adj* indignant
indignar *va* to anger, irritate, make indignant; *vr* to get indignant; **indignarse con** or **contra** to become indignant at (*a person*); **indignarse de** or **por** to become indignant at (*a mean act*); **indignarse de** + *inf* to be or become indignant at + *ger*
indignidad *f* unworthiness; indignity
indigno -na *adj* unworthy; low, contemptible
índigo *m* (bot. & chem.) indigo; indigo (*of the solar spectrum*)
indiligencia *f* negligence, laziness
indino -na *adj* (coll.) saucy, mischievous
indio -dia *adj* Indian; blue; *mf* Indian (*of America or Asia*); *m* (chem.) indium; *f* wealth, riches; **la India** India; **Indias Occidentales** West Indies; **Indias Occidentales Holandesas** Dutch West Indies; **Indias Orientales** East Indies; **Indias Orientales Holandesas** Dutch East Indies
indirecto -ta *adj* indirect; *f* hint, innuendo; **indirecta del padre Cobos** broad hint
indiscernibilidad *f* indiscernibility
indiscernible *adj* indiscernible
indisciplina *f* indiscipline, lack of discipline
indisciplinable *adj* indisciplinable
indisciplinado -da *adj* undisciplined; insubordinate
indisciplinar *va* to disturb the discipline of; *vr* to disregard discipline, become undisciplined
indiscreción *f* indiscretion
indiscreto -ta *adj* indiscreet
indisculpable *adj* inexcusable
indiscutible *adj* unquestionable, indisputable, undeniable
indisolubilidad *f* indissolubility
indisoluble *adj* indissoluble
indispensabilidad *f* indispensability
indispensable *adj* indispensable; unpardonable
indispondré *1st sg fut ind of* **indisponer**
indisponer §69 *va* to upset (*e.g., a plan*); to indispose; **indisponer a una persona con** to prejudice or set a person against; *vr* to become indisposed; **indisponerse con** to fall out with
indispongo *1st sg pres ind of* **indisponer**
indisposición *f* unpreparedness; indisposition; disagreement, unpleasantness
indispuesto -ta *pp* of **indisponer;** *adj* indisposed (*slightly ill*)
indispuse *1st sg pret ind of* **indisponer**
indisputabilidad *f* indisputability
indisputable *adj* indisputable
indistinción *f* indistinctness; identity; lack of distinction
indistinguible *adj* indistinguishable
indistinto -ta *adj* indistinct
individuación *f* individuation
individual *adj* individual; single (*e.g., room*)
individualidad *f* individuality
individualismo *m* individualism
individualista *adj* individualistic; *mf* individualist
individualizar §76 *va* to individualize
individualmente *adv* individually
individuamente *adv* indivisibly, inseparately
individuo -dua *adj* individual; indivisible, inseparable; *mf* (coll.) individual (*person*); *m* individual; member, fellow (*of a society, etc.*); (biol.) individual; **su individuo** one's own self
indivisibilidad *f* indivisibility
indivisible *adj* indivisible
indivisión *f* indivision, entirety, oneness
indiviso -sa *adj* undivided; joint (*property*)
indo -da *adj* & *mf* Hindu; (*cap.*) *m* Indus (*river*)
indoblegable *adj* inflexible, unyielding
indócil *adj* indocile, unteachable
indocilidad *f* indocility, unteachableness
indocto -ta *adj* unlearned, ignorant
indocumentado -da *adj* unidentified, without identifying documents; *mf* nobody (*person of no account*)
indochino -na *adj* & *mf* Indochinese; **la Indochina** Indochina; **la Indochina Francesa** French Indochina
indoeuropeo -a *adj* & *m* Indo-European
indofenol *m* (chem.) indophenol

indogermánico -ca *adj & m* Indo-Germanic
indol *m* (chem.) indole
índole *f* temper, disposition; class, kind
indolencia *f* indolence; absence of pain or suffering
indolente *adj* indolent; (med.) indolent
indoloro -ra *adj* painless
indomable *adj* indomitable; uncontrollable
indomado -da *adj* untamed
indomalayo -ya *adj* Indo-Malayan
indomeñable *adj* var. of **indomable**
indomesticable *adj* untamable
indomesticado -da *adj* undomesticated
indoméstico -ca *adj* untamed; wild, undomesticated
indómito -ta *adj* untamable, indomitable; unruly
indonesio -sia *adj & mf* Indonesian; **la Indonesia** Indonesia
Indostán, el Hindustan
indostanés -nesa *adj* Hindustani; *mf* native or inhabitant of Hindustan
indostaní *m* Hindustani (*language*)
indostánico -ca *adj* Hindustani
indostano -na *adj & mf* var. of **indostanés**
indotación *f* lack of dowry
indotado -da *adj* without a dowry
indoxilo *m* (chem.) indoxyl
indubitable *adj* indubitable, doubtless
indubitado -da *adj* undoubted, certain
inducción *f* (log. & elec.) induction; **inducción electromagnética** (elec.) electromagnetic induction; **inducción mutua** (elec.) mutual induction
inducido *m* (elec.) armature (*of motor or dynamo*); **inducido de tambor** (elec.) drum armature
inducir §38 *va* to induce; (log.) to induce, to infer; (elec.) to induce; **inducir a** + *inf* to induce to + *inf;* **inducir en error** to lead into error
inductancia *f* (elec.) inductance; **inductancia mutua** (elec.) mutual inductance
inductividad *f* inductivity
inductivo -va *adj* inductive
inductor -tora or **-triz** (*pl:* **-trices**) *adj* inducing; inductive; *m* instigator; (elec.) inductor, field
indudable *adj* indubitable, certain, doubtless
induje *1st sg pret ind of* **inducir**
indulgencia *f* indulgence; **indulgencia plenaria** (eccl.) plenary indulgence
indulgenciar *va* to indulge, grant an indulgence to
indulgente *adj* indulgent
indultar *va* to pardon; to free, to exempt
indulto *m* pardon; exemption
indumentario -ria *adj* (pertaining to) clothing; *f* historical study of clothing; garb, clothing, dress
indumento *m* clothing; (bot.) indumentum
induración *f* induration; (med.) induration
indurar *va* (med.) to indurate
indusio *m* (bot.) indusium
industria *f* industry; effort, ingenuity; profession; **de industria** on purpose
industrial *adj* industrial; *m* industrialist
industrialismo *m* industrialism
industrialización *f* industrialization
industrializar §76 *va* to industrialize; *vr* to become industrialized
industriar *va* to train, teach, instruct; *vr* to manage, to get along
industrioso -sa *adj* industrious; hard-working; clever, skilful
induzco *1st sg pres ind of* **inducir**
inedia *f* fasting; inanition
inédito -ta *adj* unpublished; new, unknown
ineducable *adj* uneducable
ineducación *f* lack of education; unmannerliness
ineducado -da *adj* uneducated; ill-bred
inefabilidad *f* ineffability
inefable *adj* ineffable
ineficacia *f* inefficacy
ineficaz *adj* (*pl:* **-caces**) ineffective, ineffectual
ineficiencia *f* inefficiency
ineficiente *adj* inefficient
inelasticidad *f* inelasticity
inelástico -ca *adj* inelastic
inelegancia *f* inelegance or inelegancy
inelegante *adj* inelegant
inelegibilidad *f* ineligibility
inelegible *adj* ineligible
ineluctable *adj* ineluctable
ineludible *adj* inescapable, inevitable
inenarrable *adj* inexpressible, untold
inencogible *adj* unshrinkable
inencontrable *adj* unfindable
inepcia *f* silliness; ineptitude
ineptitud *f* inaptitude, ineptitude; gaucherie
inepto -ta *adj* inapt, inept; gauche
inequidad *f* inequity
inequívoco -ca *adj* unequivocal, unmistakable, unambiguous
inercia *f* inertia; (mech.) inertia; **inercia de la matriz** (med.) inertia
inercial *adj* inertial
inerme *adj* unarmed; (biol.) unarmed
inerte *adj* inert; slow, sluggish; inactive
inerudito -ta *adj* unscholarly
inervación *f* innervation
Inés *f* Agnes
inescrutabilidad *f* inscrutability
inescrutable or **inescudriñable** *adj* inscrutable
inesperable *adj* not to be hoped for, not to be expected
inesperado -da *adj* unexpected, unforeseen
inestabilidad *f* instability
inestable *adj* unstable, instable
inestimabilidad *f* inestimability
inestimable *adj* inestimable
inestimado -da *adj* unestimated; underestimated
inestorbado -da *adj* unchecked; undisturbed
inevitabilidad *f* inevitability
inevitable *adj* inevitable, unavoidable
inexactitud *f* inexactness
inexacto -ta *adj* inexact
inexcusable *adj* inexcusable; indispensable; inescapable, indefeasible
inexhausto -ta *adj* unexhausted
inexistencia *f* inexistence, nonexistence
inexistente *adj* inexistent, nonexistent
inexorabilidad *f* inexorability
inexorable *adj* inexorable
inexperiencia *f* inexperience
inexperto -ta *adj* inexperienced, inexpert
inexpiable *adj* inexpiable
inexplicable *adj* inexplicable, unexplainable
inexplicado -da *adj* unexplained
inexplorado -da *adj* unexplored
inexplosible *adj* unexplosive
inexplotado -da *adj* unexploited
inexpresable *adj* inexpressible
inexpresivo -va *adj* inexpressive
inexpuesto -ta *adj* (phot.) unexposed
inexpugnabilidad *f* inexpugnability, impregnability
inexpugnable *adj* inexpugnable, impregnable; firm, unpersuadable
inextensible *adj* unextendible, unstretchable
inextenso -sa *adj* unextended
inextinguible *adj* inextinguishable, unextinguishable; lasting, perpetual
inextinto -ta *adj* unextinguished
inextirpable *adj* ineradicable
inextricabilidad *f* inextricability
inextricable *adj* inextricable
infacundo -da *adj* ineloquent, not fluent
infalibilidad *f* infallibility
infalible *adj* infallible
infamación *f* defamation
infamador -dora *adj* defaming, slanderous; *mf* defamer
infamante *adj* opprobrious; (law) infamous (*punishment*)
infamar *va* to defame, discredit
infamativo -va *adj* defaming, slanderous
infamatorio -ria *adj* defamatory, libelous
infame *adj* infamous; (coll.) frightful; *mf* scoundrel
infamia *f* infamy
infancia *f* infancy; (fig.) infancy
infando -da *adj* frightful, unmentionable
infanta *f* female infant; infanta
infantado *m* appanage

infante *m* infant; infante; (mil.) infantryman; **infante de coro** (eccl.) choirboy; **infante de marina** (mil.) marine
infantería *f* infantry; **infantería de marina** marines, marine corps
infanticida *adj* infanticidal; *mf* infanticide (*person*)
infanticidio *m* infanticide (*act*)
infantil *adj* infantile, infant; innocent; infantile, childlike; children's
infantilismo *m* childishness; infantilism
infanzón *m* nobleman of limited rights
infanzona *f* noblewoman of limited rights
infartación *f* (path.) infarction
infartar *va* (path.) to produce an infarct in
infarto *m* (path.) infarct
infatigabilidad *f* indefatigability
infatigable *adj* indefatigable
infatuación *f* vanity, conceit
infatuar **§33** *va* to make vain or conceited; *vr* to become vain or conceited
infausto -ta *adj* unlucky, fatal
infebril *adj* feverless
infección *f* infection; **infección focal** (path.) focal infection
infeccionar *va* to infect
infeccioso -sa *adj* infectious
infectar *va* to infect; *vr* to become infected
infectividad *f* infectivity
infectivo -va *adj* infective
infecto -ta *adj* infected; foul, corrupt
infecundidad *f* sterility, infecundity
infecundo -da *adj* sterile, infecund
infelice *adj* (poet.) var. of **infeliz**
infelicidad *f* infelicity; misfortune
infeliz (*pl:* **-lices**) *adj* unhappy; (coll.) simple, good-hearted; *m* wretch, poor soul
inferencia *f* inference
inferior *adj* inferior; lower; **inferior a** inferior to; lower than; less than, smaller than; *m* inferior
inferioridad *f* inferiority
inferir **§62** *va* to infer; to entail, lead to; to cause, inflict; to offer (*e.g., an insult*)
infernáculo *m* hopscotch
infernal *adj* infernal; (coll.) infernal (*very bad, detestable*)
infernar **§18** *va* to damn; to vex, irritate
infernillo *m* chafing dish
inferno -na *adj* (poet.) infernal
ínfero -ra *adj* (bot.) inferior, lower, under
infestación *f* infestation
infestar *va* to infest; *vr* to become infested
infesto -ta *adj* (poet.) harmful
inficionamiento *m* infection
inficionar *va* to infect; *vr* to become infected
infidelidad *f* infidelity; unbelievers
infidelísimo -ma *adj super* very or most unfaithful
infidencia *f* faithlessness; treason
infidente *adj* faithless, disloyal; treasonable
ínfido -da *adj* faithless, disloyal
infiel *adj* unfaithful; inaccurate, inexact; infidel; *mf* infidel
infiernillo *m* chafing dish
infierno *m* hell; inferno; hades; chafing dish; **en el quinto infierno** or **en los quintos infiernos** (coll.) far, far away
infigurable *adj* incorporeal; unimaginable
infiltración *f* infiltration
infiltrar *va & vr* to infiltrate
ínfimo -ma *adj* lowest; least; humblest, most abject; meanest, vilest
infinible *adj* interminable
infinidad *f* infinity
infinitesimal *adj* infinitesimal
infinitésimo *m* (math.) infinitesimal
infinitivo -va *adj & m* (gram.) infinitive
infinito -ta *adj* infinite; *m* infinite; (math.) infinity; **a lo infinito** or **hasta lo infinito** ad infinitum; **el infinito** the Infinite (*God*); **infinito** *adv* infinitely, extremely, immensely
infinitud *f* infinitude
infirmar *va* (law) to invalidate
inflación *f* inflation; vanity, conceit
inflacionismo *m* inflationism
inflacionista *adj* inflationary; *mf* inflationist
inflado *m* inflation (*e.g., of a tire*)
inflamabilidad *f* inflammability
inflamable *adj* inflammable, flamable
inflamación *f* inflammation, ignition; enthusiasm, ardor; (path.) inflammation; **inflamación espontánea** spontaneous combustion
inflamado -da *adj* sore, inflamed
inflamar *va* to inflame; to set on fire; *vr* to inflame, become inflamed; to catch fire
inflamatorio -ria *adj* inflammatory
inflamiento *m* var. of **inflación**
inflar *va* to inflate; to exaggerate; to puff up with pride; *vn* to inflate; to be puffed up with pride
inflativo -va *adj* inflating
inflatorio -ria *adj* inflationary
inflexibilidad *f* inflexibility
inflexible *adj* inflexible; unbending, unyielding
inflexión *f* inflection; (geom. & gram.) inflection
infligir **§42** *va* to inflict; **infligir a** to inflict on
inflorescencia *f* (bot.) inflorescence (*arrangement*)
influencia *f* influence; (theol.) divine grace
influenciar *va* to influence
influenza *f* (path.) influenza
influir **§41** *vn* to influence, to have influence; to have great weight; **influir sobre** or **en** to influence, to have an influence on
influjo *m* influence; (naut.) rising tide
influyente *adj* influential
infolio *m* folio (*book*)
inforciado *m* infortiate
información *f* information; testimonial; (law) brief; (law) investigation, judicial inquiry; **abrir una información** (law) to begin legal proceedings; **a título de información** unofficially
informador -dora *adj* informing; *mf* informer; reporter
informal *adj* informal; unreliable; *m* unreliable fellow
informalidad *f* informality; unreliability
informante *mf* informant
informar *va* to inform; to shape, fill, give form to; *vn* to inform; (law) to plead; **informar contra** to inform against; *vr* to inquire, find out; **informarse de** to inquire into, find out about, investigate
informativo -va *adj* informational, informative; (pertaining to) news
informe *adj* shapeless, formless; *m* information; item of information, piece of information; notice; report; **informes** *mpl* information
informidad *f* shapelessness, formlessness
infortificable *adj* unfortifiable
infortuna *f* (astrol.) adverse influence of stars
infortunado -da *adj* unfortunate, unlucky
infortunio *m* misfortune; mishap
infosura *f* (vet.) founder
infracción *f* infraction, infringement, violation
infraconsumo *m* underconsumption
infracto -ta *adj* firm, steady, unshakable
infractor -tora *adj* violating; *mf* violator, transgressor
infraestructura *f* var. of **infrastructura**
infrahumano -na *adj* subhuman
inframundo *m* underworld
infrangible *adj* infrangible, unbreakable
infranqueable *adj* impassable
infrarrojo -ja *adj & m* infrared
infrascripto -ta or **infrascrito -ta** *adj* undersigned; hereinafter mentioned
infrastructura *f* (rail.) roadbed
infrecuencia *f* infrequence or infrequency
infrecuente *adj* infrequent
infringir **§42** *va* to infringe
infructífero -ra *adj* unfruitful; unprofitable
infructuosidad *f* unfruitfulness
infructuoso -sa *adj* fruitless, unfruitful
ínfula *f* infula; **ínfulas** *spl* conceit, airs; **darse ínfulas** to put on airs
infumable *adj* unsmokable; (coll.) unbearable
infundado -da *adj* unfounded, ungrounded, baseless
infundible *adj* infusible
infundio *m* (coll.) story, lie, fib
infundioso -sa *adj* (coll.) lying
infundir *va* to infuse; to instil

infurción *f* ground lease or rent
infurtir *va* to full (*cloth*); to felt
infusibilidad *f* infusibility
infusible *adj* infusible
infusión *f* infusion; sprinkling (*to baptize*); **estar en infusión para** (coll.) to be all set for
infuso -sa *adj* inspired, given (*by God*)
infusorio -ria *adj* & *m* (zool.) infusorian
ingenerable *adj* ingenerable
ingeniar *va* to think up, conceive, contrive; *vr* to manage; **ingeniarse a** or **para** + *inf* to manage to + *inf;* **ingeniarse a vivir** or **para ir viviendo** to manage to get along
ingeniatura *f* (coll.) ingenuity, cleverness
ingeniería *f* engineering
ingenieril *adj* engineering
ingeniero *m* engineer; **ingeniero de caminos, canales y puertos** government civil engineer; **ingeniero civil** civil engineer; **ingeniero del ejército** army engineer; **ingeniero de minas** mining engineer; **ingeniero de montes** forestry engineer; **ingeniero electricista** electrical engineer; **ingeniero mécanico** mechanical engineer; **ingeniero militar** army engineer; **ingeniero paisajista** landscape engineer; **ingeniero químico** chemical engineer
ingenio *m* talent, creative faculty; skill, wit, cleverness; talented person; apparatus, engine, machine; paper cutter; engine of war; (Am.) sugar mill, sugar plantation; **afilar** or **aguzar el ingenio** to sharpen one's wits
ingeniosidad *f* ingeniousness, ingenuity; wittiness
ingenioso -sa *adj* ingenious; witty
ingénito -ta *adj* unbegotten; innate, inborn
ingente *adj* huge, enormous
ingenuidad *f* ingenuousness
ingenuo -nua *adj* ingenuous; (archaic) freeborn
ingerencia *f* var. of **injerencia**
ingeridura *f* var. of **injeridura**
ingerir §62 *va* & *vr* var. of **injerir**
ingestión *f* ingestion
Inglaterra *f* England; **la Nueva Inglaterra** New England
ingle *f* (anat.) groin
inglés -glesa *adj* English; **a la inglesa** in the English fashion or manner; *m* Englishman; English (*language*); **el inglés antiguo** Old English; **el inglés básico** Basic English; **el inglés medio** Middle English; **los ingleses** the English (*people*); *f* Englishwoman
inglesar *va* to Anglicize
inglesismo *m* Anglicism
inglete *m* angle of 45°; miter
inglosable *adj* unglossable
ingobernable *adj* ungovernable, uncontrollable, unruly
ingramatical *adj* ungrammatical
ingratitud *f* ingratitude, ungratefulness
ingrato -ta *adj* thankless (*ungrateful; not appreciated; unrewarding*); harsh, unpleasant; hard, cruel; sterile, unproductive (*soil*); *mf* ingrate
ingravidez *f* lightness, tenuousness; weightlessness
ingrávido -da *adj* light, tenuous; weightless
ingrediente *m* ingredient
ingresado -da *mf* admittee, new student
ingresar *va* to enter (*e.g., a child in an orphanage*); to deposit, transfer (*money*); *vn* to enter, become a member; to come in (*said of profits, etc.*); *vr* (Am.) to enlist
ingreso *m* entrance; ingress; admission; entry, receipts; **ingresos** *mpl* income, revenue
íngrimo -ma *adj* (Am.) solitary, alone
inguinal or **inguinario -ria** *adj* inguinal
ingurgitación *f* ingurgitation
ingurgitar *va* to ingurgitate, swallow greedily
ingustable *adj* unpalatable, unsavory
inhábil *adj* unable; unskilful; unqualified, incompetent; unfit
inhabilidad *f* inability, disability; unskilfulness; unfitness
inhabilitación *f* disqualification, incapacitation
inhabilitar *va* to disqualify, to disable, to incapacitate
inhabitable *adj* uninhabitable
inhabitado -da *adj* uninhabited
inhacedero -ra *adj* unfeasible
inhalación *f* (med.) inhalation
inhalador *m* (med.) inhaler
inhalar *va* (med.) to inhale
inherencia *f* inherence
inherente *adj* inherent
inhestar §18 *va* & *vr* var. of **enhestar**
inhibición *f* inhibition
inhibir *va* to inhibit; (law) to stay (*a judge from further proceedings*); *vr* to stay out, stay on the side lines
inhibitivo -va *adj* inhibitive
inhibitorio -ria *adj* inhibitory
inhiesto -ta *adj* raised, upright
inhonestidad *f* immodesty, indecency
inhonesto -ta *adj* immodest, indecent
inhospedable, inhospitable, inhospital or **inhospitalario -ria** *adj* inhospitable
inhospitalidad *f* inhospitality
inhóspito -ta *adj* inhospitable (*affording no shelter or protection*)
inhumación *f* inhumation
inhumanidad *f* inhumanity
inhumanitario -ria *adj* unphilanthropic
inhumano -na *adj* inhuman, inhumane; (Am.) dirty, filthy
inhumar *va* to inhume
iniciación *f* initiation
iniciado -da *adj* & *mf* initiate
iniciador -dora *adj* initiating; *mf* initiator
inicial *adj* & *f* initial
iniciar *va* to initiate; *vr* to be initiated; (eccl.) to receive first orders
iniciativo -va *adj* initiative, initiating; *f* initiative; **tomar la iniciativa** to take the initiative
inicio *m* start, beginning, initiation
inicuo -cua *adj* iniquitous
inigualado -da *adj* unequaled; (math.) uneven
inimaginable *adj* unimaginable, inconceivable
inimicísimo -ma *adj super* very or most inimical or hostile
inimitable *adj* inimitable
ininflamable *adj* uninflammable
ininteligente *adj* unintelligent
ininteligible *adj* unintelligible
ininterrumpido -da *adj* uninterrupted
iniquidad *f* iniquity
iniquísimo -ma *adj super* very or most iniquitous
injerencia *f* interference, meddling
injeridura *f* (agr.) graft, stock of graft
injerir §62 *va* (hort.) to graft; to insert, introduce; to ingest; (Am.) to swallow, take in; *vr* to interfere, to meddle
injertación *f* (hort. & surg.) grafting
injertador *m* (hort.) grafter
injertar *va* (hort. & surg.) to engraft, ingraft, graft
injertera *f* orchard of transplanted seedlings
injerto *m* (hort. & surg.) graft; **injerto cutáneo** (surg.) skin grafting
injuria *f* offense, insult; wrong, abuse; harm, damage
injuriador -dora *adj* offensive, insulting; abusive; *mf* offender, insulter
injuriante *adj* offending, insulting
injuriar *va* to offend, insult; to wrong, abuse; to harm, damage, injure
injurioso -sa *adj* offensive, insulting; abusive; harmful; profane (*language*)
injusticia *f* injustice
injustificable *adj* unjustifiable, unwarrantable
injustificado -da *adj* unjustified
injusto -ta *adj* unjust
inllevable *adj* unbearable, insupportable
inmaculado -da *adj* immaculate; **Inmaculada Concepción** Immaculate Conception
inmadurez *f* immaturity; flightiness
inmanejable *adj* unmanageable, unruly; unwieldy
inmanencia *f* immanence
inmanente *adj* immanent
inmarcesible or **inmarchitable** *adj* unfading; unwithering
inmaterial *adj* immaterial
inmaterialidad *f* immateriality

inmaterialismo *m* immaterialism
inmaturo -ra *adj* unripe; immature
inmediación *f* immediacy, immediateness; proximity, nearness; contact; **inmediaciones** *fpl* environs, neighborhood
inmediatamente *adv* immediately
inmediato -ta *adj* immediate; adjoining, close, next; next below; next above; **llegar** or **venir a las inmediatas** (coll.) to get down to brass tacks; **inmediato a** right next to; immediately preceding; immediately following
inmedicable *adj* immedicable, incurable
inmejorable *adj* unimprovable, unsurpassable, superb
inmemorable or **inmemorial** *adj* immemorial
inmensidad *f* immensity
inmenso -sa *adj* immense
inmensurable *adj* immensurable; unmeasurable
inmerecido -da *adj* unmerited, undeserved, unearned
inmergir §42 *va* to immerse; *vr* to be immersed; to immerge
inmérito -ta *adj* unmerited; unjust
inmeritorio -ria *adj* not meritorious, undeserving
inmersión *f* immersion; dip; (surg.) immersion
inmerso -sa *adj* immersed
inmigración *f* immigration
inmigrado -da or **inmigrante** *adj & mf* immigrant
inmigrar *vn* to immigrate
inminencia *f* imminence or imminency
inminente *adj* imminent; early
inmiscible *adj* immiscible
inmiscuir §41 & regular *va* to mix; *vr* to meddle, interfere
inmobiliario -ria *adj* real-estate
inmoble *adj* immovable, unmovable; motionless; firm, constant
inmoderación *f* immoderation
inmoderado -da *adj* immoderate
inmodestia *f* immodesty
inmodesto -ta *adj* immodest
inmódico -ca *adj* excessive
inmolación *f* immolation
inmolador -dora *adj* immolating; *mf* immolator
inmolar *va* to immolate
inmoral *adj* immoral
inmoralidad *f* immorality
inmortal *adj* immortal, deathless; *mf* immortal
inmortalidad *f* immortality
inmortalizar §76 *va* to immortalize
inmortificación *f* immortification, unrestraint, license
inmortificado -da *adj* immortified, unrestrained
inmotivado -da *adj* unmotivated, ungrounded
inmoto -ta *adj* unmoved
inmovible or **inmóvil** *adj* var. of **inmoble**
inmovilidad *f* immovability; immobility
inmovilización *f* immobilization
inmovilizar §76 *va* to immobilize; to bring to a standstill; to tie up (*capital*) in merchandise of slow turnover
inmudable *adj* immutable
inmueble *adj* (law) immovable; *m* property, piece of real estate; **inmuebles** *mpl* immovables, real estate
inmundicia *f* dirt, filth; impurity, indecency
inmundo -da *adj* dirty, filthy; impure, indecent
inmune *adj* free, exempt; immune; **inmune contra** immune to
inmunidad *f* immunity; **inmunidad pasiva** (immun.) passive immunity
inmunización *f* immunization
inmunizar §76 *va* to immunize
inmunología *f* immunology
inmunólogo -ga *mf* immunologist
inmutabilidad *f* immutability
inmutable *adj* immutable
inmutación *f* change, alteration
inmutar *va* to change, to alter; to disturb, upset; *vr* to change, to alter; to change countenance, to be out of countenance; **sin inmutarse** without batting an eye
innatismo *m* innatism
innato -ta *adj* innate, born, inborn; natural
innatural *adj* unnatural
innavegable *adj* unnavigable; unseaworthy
innecesario -ria *adj* unnecessary
innegable *adj* undeniable
innegociable *adj* unnegotiable
innoble *adj* ignoble
innocuo -cua *adj* innocuous
innominable *adj* unnameable
innominado -da *adj* unnamed; anonymous; (anat.) innominate
innovación *f* innovation
innovador -dora *adj* innovating; *mf* innovator
innovamiento *m* innovation
innovar *va* to innovate
innumerabilidad *f* innumerability
innumerable *adj* innumerable
innúmero -ra *adj* numberless, countless
inobediencia *f* inobedience
inobediente *adj* inobedient
inobservable *adj* inobservable, unobservable
inobservancia *f* inobservance, nonobservance
inobservante *adj* unobservant
inocencia *f* innocence
Inocencio *m* Innocent
inocentada *f* (coll.) simple remark, simple thing; (coll.) good-natured blunder; (coll.) practical joke; (coll.) April Fools' joke
inocente *adj & mf* innocent; **coger por inocente** to make an April fool of
inocentón -tona *adj* (coll.) simple, credulous; *mf* (coll.) simple, credulous person, dupe
inocuidad *f* innocuousness
inoculable *adj* inoculable
inoculación *f* inoculation
inoculante *adj* inoculating
inocular *va* to inoculate; (fig.) to contaminate, pervert; *vn* to inoculate; *vr* to be or become inoculated; (fig.) to be contaminated or perverted
inocuo -cua *adj* innocuous
inodoro -ra *adj* inodorous, odorless; *m* deodorizer; water closet, toilet
inofensivo -va *adj* inoffensive
inoficioso -sa *adj* inofficious, inoperative; (law) inofficious
inolvidable *adj* unforgettable
inope *adj* impecunious
inoperable *adj* (surg.) inoperable
inoperancia *f* inactivity, disuse
inoperante *adj* inoperative, ineffectual
inopia *f* poverty
inopinable *adj* indisputable
inopinado -da *adj* unexpected
inoportunidad *f* untimeliness, inopportuneness
inoportuno -na *adj* untimely, inopportune
inordenado -da *adj* disordered, in disorder
inorgánico -ca *adj* inorganic
inorganizado -da *adj* unorganized
inoxidable *adj* inoxidable, inoxidizable; stainless (*steel*)
inquebrantable *adj* unbreakable; unyielding; irrevocable
inquietador -dora *adj* disquieting; *mf* disturber
inquietante *adj* disquieting, disturbing
inquietar *va* to disquiet, to disturb, to worry; to stir up, harass, excite; *vr* to become disquieted, to worry; **inquietarse con, de** or **por** to get upset about, to worry about
inquieto -ta *adj* anxious, worried, restless
inquietud *f* disquiet, disquietude, inquietude, uneasiness, restlessness; concern
inquilinato *m* rent, lease; (Am.) rooming house
inquilino -na *mf* tenant, renter, lessee
inquina *f* aversion, dislike, ill will
inquinamiento *m* contamination
inquinar *va* to contaminate
inquiridor -dora *adj* inquiring; *mf* inquirer
inquirir §56 *va* to inquire, inquire into, investigate; *vn* to inquire
inquisición *f* inquisition; (*cap.*) *f* Inquisition
inquisidor -dora *adj* inquiring; *mf* inquirer, inquisitor; (*cap.*) *m* (eccl.) Inquisitor
inquisitivo -va *adj* investigative
inquisitoriado -da *adj* condemned by the Inquisition
inquisitorial *adj* inquisitorial

inquisitorio -ria *adj* var. of **inquisitivo**
inri *m* I.N.R.I. (*initials of Iesus Nazarenus, Rex Iudaeorum, i.e., Jesus of Nazareth, King of the Jews*); (fig.) brand, stigma, insult
insabible *adj* unknowable
insaciable *adj* insatiable
insaculación *f* balloting by drawing lots
insacular *va* to cast (*ballots*) by drawing lots
insalivación *f* (physiol.) insalivation
insalivar *va* (physiol.) to insalivate
insalubre *adj* unhealthful, insalubrious, unsanitary, insanitary
insalubridad *f* unhealthfulness, unsanitary condition
insalvable *adj* insurmountable
insanable *adj* incurable
insania *f* insanity
insano -na *adj* insane; mad, wild
insatisfecho -cha *adj* unsatisfied
inscribir §17, 9 *va* to inscribe; (geom. & fig.) to inscribe; (law) to record; *vr* to enroll, register
inscripción *f* inscription; enrolment, registration
inscrito -ta *adj* (geom.) inscribed; *pp of* **inscribir**
insecable *adj* indivisible; (coll.) undryable, undrying
insecticida *adj* insecticide, insecticidal; *m* insecticide
insectil *adj* insectile
insectívoro -ra *adj* insectivorous; *m* (zool.) insectivore; *f* (bot.) insectivore
insecto *m* insect
inseguridad *f* insecurity, unsafeness; uncertainty
inseguro -ra *adj* insecure, unsafe; uncertain
inseminación *f* insemination; **inseminación artificial** artificial insemination
inseminar *va* to inseminate
insenescencia *f* agelessness
insensatez *f* insensateness, folly, brainlessness
insensato -ta *adj* insensate (*foolish, blind*)
insensibilidad *f* insensibility; hardheartedness
insensibilizador *m* deadener (*of pain*)
insensibilizar §76 *va* to make insensible; *vr* to become insensible
insensible *adj* insensible; insentient; imperceptible; insensitive; hardhearted
inseparabilidad *f* inseparability
inseparable *adj* inseparable; indetachable; *mf* inseparable; *m* (orn.) lovebird
insepulto -ta *adj* unburied
inserción *f* insertion; (bot. & zool.) insertion
inserir §62 *va* to insert; to graft; to ingest
insertar *va* to insert; *vr* (bot. & zool.) to be inserted
inserto -ta *adj* inserted
inservible *adj* useless
insidia *f* ambush; plotting
insidiador -dora *adj* waylaying; plotting; *mf* waylayer; plotter
insidiar *va* to ambush, waylay; to plot against
insidioso -sa *adj* insidious
insigne *adj* famous, noted, renowned
insignia *f* decoration, badge, device; standard; (naut.) pennant; **insignias** *fpl* insignia
insignificancia *f* insignificance
insignificante *adj* insignificant
insinceridad *f* insincerity
insincero -ra *adj* insincere
insinuación *f* insinuation, intimation, hint
insinuante *adj* insinuating, slick, crafty, engaging
insinuar §33 *va* to insinuate; to suggest, hint at; *vr* to insinuate oneself; to work one's way; to flow, to run; to slip in, to creep in; to ingratiate oneself
insinuativo -va *adj* insinuative
insipidez *f* insipidity
insípido -da *adj* insipid
insipiencia *f* ignorance; lack of wisdom
insipiente *adj* ignorant; unwise
insistencia *f* insistence
insistente *adj* insistent
insistir *vn* to insist; **insistir en** or **sobre** to insist on or upon; **insistir en** + *inf* to insist on + *ger;* **insistir en que** + *subj* to insist that

ínsito -ta *adj* inbred, innate, inherent
insociabilidad *f* unsociability
insociable or **insocial** *adj* unsociable
insolación *f* insolation; (meteor.) insolation; (path.) sunstroke, insolation
insolar *va* to insolate; to expose, to expose to the sun; *vr* to take a sun bath; to get sunstruck
insoldable *adj* incapable of being soldered; irremediable; unmendable
insolencia *f* insolence
insolentar *va* to make insolent; *vr* to become insolent
insolente *adj* insolent; *mf* insolent person
insólito -ta *adj* unusual, unaccustomed
insolubilidad *f* insolubility
insoluble *adj* insoluble; insolvable
insoluto -ta *adj* unpaid
insolvencia *f* insolvency
insolvente *adj* insolvent
insomne *adj* sleepless
insomnio *m* insomnia, sleeplessness
insondable *adj* unfathomable, inscrutable
insonorizar §76 *va* to soundproof
insonoro -ra *adj* soundproof, soundless
insoportable *adj* insupportable, unbearable; extremely annoying
insoslayable *adj* unavoidable
insospechado -da *adj* unsuspected
insostenible *adj* untenable, indefensible; unsustainable
inspección *f* inspection; inspectorship; inspector's office
inspeccionar *va* to inspect
inspector -tora *adj* inspecting; *mf* inspector
inspiración *f* inhalation; inspiration
inspiradamente *adv* inspiredly, with inspiration
inspirador -dora *adj* inspiring; (anat.) inspiratory; *mf* inspirer
inspirante *adj* inspiring
inspirar *va & vn* to inhale, breathe in; to inspire; **inspirar a** + *inf* to inspire to + *inf; vr* to be inspired; **inspirarse en** to be inspired by
inspirativo -va *adj* inspirational
inspiratorio -ria *adj* (anat.) inspiratory
instabilidad *f* var. of **inestabilidad**
instable *adj* var. of **inestable**
instalación *f* installation, instalment; plant, factory; equipment, outfit; arrangements, appointments; fittings; **instalaciones hoteleras** hotel facilities, hotel accommodations; **instalación sanitaria** plumbing
instalador -dora *mf* installer; **instalador de cañería** plumber; **instalador de líneas** lineman; **instalador sanitario** plumber
instalar *va* to install; *vr* to become installed; to settle
instancia *f* instance, request, entreaty; memorial; (law) instance; **a instancia de** at the instance of
instantáneo -a *adj* instantaneous; instant; *f* snapshot
instante *m* instant, moment; **a cada instante** all the time, at every moment; **al instante** right away, immediately; **en un instante** quickly, soon; **por instantes** uninterruptedly; any time
instantemente *adv* insistently, urgently
instar *va* to press, urge; **instar a** + *inf* or **instar a que** + *subj* to urge to + *inf; vn* to insist; to be urgent; **instar para, por** or **sobre** to insist on
instauración *f* restoration; reëstablishment
instaurar *va* to restore; to reëstablish
instaurativo -va *adj* restorative
instigación *f* instigation; **a instigación de** at the instigation of
instigador -dora *adj* instigating; *mf* instigator
instigar §59 *va* to instigate
instilación *f* instillation
instilar *va* to instill
instintivo -va *adj* instinctive
instinto *m* instinct; **instinto de rebaño** herd instinct
institución *f* institution; (law) institution; **instituciones** *fpl* constitution (*of a government*); principles (*of an art or science*)

institucional *adj* institutional
instituidor -dora *adj* founding; *mf* founder
instituir §41 *va* to institute, found, establish; to teach, instruct
instituta *f* (law) institutes
instituto *m* constitution, rule (*e.g., of a religious order*); institute; high school; **instituto de segunda enseñanza** or **de enseñanza media** high school
institutor -tora *adj* founding; *mf* founder; teacher, instructor
institutriz *f* (*pl:* **-trices**) governess
instridente *adj* var. of **estridente**
instrucción *f* instruction, education; **instrucción pública** education, educational system; **instrucciones** *fpl* instructions, directions
instructivo -va *adj* instructive
instructor -tora *adj* instructing; *mf* teacher, instructor; *f* instructress
instruído -da *adj* well-educated, well-posted
instruir §41 *va* to instruct; to draw up; **instruir de, en,** or **sobre** to instruct about or on
instrumentación *f* instrumentation
instrumental *adj* instrumental; *m* instruments (*of music, surgery, etc.*); kit of instruments
instrumentar *va* (mus.) to instrument
instrumentista *mf* instrumentalist; instrument maker or dealer
instrumento *m* instrument; (mus.) instrument; (fig.) tool, cat's-paw; **instrumento de boquilla** (mus.) brass wind, brass-wind instrument; **instrumento de cuerda** (mus.) stringed instrument; **instrumento de lengüeta** (mus.) reed, reed instrument; **instrumento de percusión** (mus.) percussion instrument; **instrumento de precisión** precision instrument; **instrumento de punteo** (mus.) plucked instrument (*e.g., harp*); **instrumento de viento** (mus.) wind instrument
insuave *adj* rough; unpleasant, disagreeable
insuavidad *f* roughness; unpleasantness
insubordinación *f* insubordination
insubordinado -da *adj* insubordinate
insubordinar *va* to make insubordinate, incite to insubordination; *vr* to become insubordinate, to rebel
insubsanable *adj* irreparable
insubsistencia *f* impermanence, instability; lack of subsistence; groundlessness
insubsistente *adj* impermanent, unstable; lacking in subsistence; groundless
insubstancial *adj* unsubstantial, insubstantial
insubstancialidad *f* insubstantiality
insubstituíble *adj* irreplaceable
insudar *vn* to toil, to drudge, strive hard
insuficiencia *f* insufficiency, inadequacy; **insuficiencia mitral** (path.) mitral insufficiency
insuficiente *adj* insufficient, inadequate
insuflación *f* insufflation; blowing
insuflador *m* (med.) syringe
insuflar *va* to insufflate; to blow, to blow air in (*e.g., an organ*)
insufrible *adj* insufferable
ínsula *f* island; unimportant place
insulano -na *adj* (archaic) insular; *mf* (archaic) islander
insular *adj* insular; *mf* islander
insularidad *f* insularity
insulina *f* (med.) insulin
Insulindia, la Indonesia
insulínico -ca *adj* (pertaining to) insulin
insulismo *m* (path.) insulin shock
insulsez *f* tastelessness; dullness, heaviness
insulso -sa *adj* tasteless; dull, heavy
insultante *adj* insulting
insultar *va* to insult; to attack unexpectedly and with violence; *vr* to faint
insulto *m* insult; sudden attack; fainting spell; **insulto a superiores** (mil.) insubordination
insumable *adj* exorbitant
insume *adj* expensive
insumergible *adj* unsinkable
insumir *va* (Am.) to consume, use up (*money*); *vn* (Am.) to ooze
insumiso -sa *adj* unsubmissive
insuperable *adj* insuperable
insuperado -da *adj* unbeaten
insurgente *adj & mf* insurgent
insurrección *f* insurrection; (coll.) lack of deference
insurreccional *adj* insurrectionary
insurreccionar *va* to incite to rebellion; *vr* to rise up, to rebel
insurrecto -ta *adj* rebellious; *mf* insurrectionist
insusceptibilidad *f* insusceptibility
insusceptible *adj* insusceptible
insustancial *adj* var. of **insubstancial**
insustancialidad *f* var. of **insubstancialidad**
insustituíble *adj* var. of **insubstituíble**
intacto -ta *adj* intact, undamaged, unbroken
intachable *adj* irreproachable
intangibilidad *f* intangibility, untouchableness
intangible *adj* intangible, untouchable
integérrimo -ma *adj super* very or most complete, honorable, or irreproachable
integrable *adj* (math.) integrable
integración *f* integration
integrado -da *adj* in one piece
integrador *m* integrator
integral *adj* integral; (math.) integral; *f* (math.) integral; (math.) integral sign, sign of integration
integrante *adj* integrant, integral; constituent; *mf* member
integrar *va* to integrate; to form, make up; to reimburse; (math.) to integrate
integridad *f* integrity; virginity
íntegro -gra *adj* integral, whole, complete; honest, upright
integumento *m* integument; mask, disguise
intelección *f* understanding
intelectivo -va *adj* intellective; *f* understanding (*faculty*)
intelecto *m* intellect
intelectual *adj & mf* intellectual
intelectualidad *f* intellectuality; intelligentsia
intelectualismo *m* intellectualism
intelectualoide *m* (coll.) egghead, highbrow
inteligencia *f* intelligence, understanding; collusion; **estar en inteligencia con** to be in collusion with
inteligenciado -da *adj* well-informed
inteligente *adj* intelligent; trained, skilled
inteligibilidad *f* intelligibility
inteligible *adj* intelligible
intemperancia *f* intemperance
intemperante *adj* intemperate
intemperie *f* inclemency (*of weather*); **a la intemperie** in the open air, unsheltered
intemperizar §76 *va* to weather
intempestivo -va *adj* unseasonable, untimely, ill-timed
intemporal *adj* timeless
intención *f* intention; viciousness (*of an animal*); caution; **intenciones** *fpl* intentions (*with respect to marrying*); **con intención** deliberately, knowingly; **de intención** on purpose; **primera intención** (coll.) openness, readiness; (surg.) first intention; **segunda intención** underhandedness; (surg.) second intention
intencionadamente *adv* intentionally
intencionado -da *adj* intentioned, disposed; intentional; picaresque; **bien intencionado** well-intentioned; **mal intencionado** ill-intentioned, ill-disposed
intencional *adj* intentional; inner
intendencia *f* intendance; intendancy; (Am.) mayoralty
intendenta *f* intendant's wife; (Am.) mayor's wife
intendente *m* intendant; **intendente municipal** (Am.) mayor
intensar *va & vr* to intensify
intensidad *f* intensity
intensificación *f* intensification
intensificar §86 *va & vr* to intensify
intensión *f* intensity, intenseness
intensivo -va *adj* intensive
intenso -sa *adj* intense
intentar *va* to try, to attempt; to try out; to intend; (law) to initiate (*e.g., a suit*); **intentar** + *inf* to try to + *inf*
intento *m* intent, purpose; **de intento** on purpose

intentona *f* (coll.) foolhardiness, rash attempt
interacción *f* interaction, interplay
interaliado -da *adj* interallied
interamericanismo *m* inter-Americanism
interamericano -na *adj* inter-American
interandino -na *adj* inter-Andean
intercadencia *f* unevenness, irregularity; harshness; (med.) intercadence
intercalación *f* intercalation
intercalar *adj* intercalary; *va* to intercalate
intercambiable *adj* interchangeable
intercambiar *va & vr* to interchange
intercambio *m* interchange
interceder *vn* intercede
intercelular *adj* intercellular
intercepción *f* or **interceptación** *f* interception
interceptar *va* to intercept
interceptor -tora *adj* intercepting; *mf* interceptor; *m* separator; trap; (aer.) interceptor
intercesión *f* intercession
intercesor -sora *adj* interceding; *mf* intercessor
intercesorio -ria *adj* intercessory
interciso -sa *adj* cut into pieces (*said of a martyr*); **día interciso** (archaic) half holiday (*in the morning*)
intercolonial *adj* intercolonial
intercolumnio *m* (arch.) intercolumniation
intercomunicación *f* intercommunication
intercomunicador *m* intercom
intercomunicar §86 *vr* to intercommunicate
interconectar *va* to interconnect
interconexión *f* interconnection
interconfesional *adj* interdenominational
intercontinental *adj* intercontinental
intercostal *adj* (anat.) intercostal
intercurrente *adj* (path.) intercurrent
intercutáneo -a *adj* intercutaneous
interdecir §37 *va* to interdict
interdental *adj & f* (phonet.) interdental
interdepartamental *adj* interdepartmental
interdependencia *f* interdependence
interdependiente *adj* interdependent
interdicción *f* interdiction
interdicto *m* interdict
interdicho -cha *pp of* **interdecir**
interdigital *adj* interdigital
interdigo *1st sg pres ind of* **interdecir**
interdije *1st sg pret ind of* **interdecir**
interdiré *1st sg fut ind of* **interdecir**
intereje *m* (aut.) wheel base
interés *m* interest; **poner a interés** to put out at interest; **interés compuesto** compound interest; **intereses creados** vested interests; **interés simple** simple interest
interesable *adj* selfish, mercenary
interesado -da *adj* interested; selfish; *mf* interested person, interested party
interesante *adj* interesting
interesar *va* to interest; to give an interest to; to involve; **interesarle a uno** + *inf* to interest someone to + *inf; vn* to be interesting; *vr* to be interested; **interesarse en** or **por** to be interested in, to take an interest in
interescolar *adj* intercollegiate, interscholastic
interesencia *f* attendance
interesente *adj* present
interestadal *adj* interstate
interestelar *adj* interstellar
inter-etapa *adj invar* (rad.) interstage
interfecto -ta *adj* (law) murdered; *mf* (law) murdered person, victim of murder
interferencia *f* interference; (phys. & rad.) interference; **no interferencia** noninterference
interferencial *adj* (phys.) interferential
interferir §62 *va* to interfere with; *vn* to interfere; (phys.) to interfere
interferómetro *m* (phys.) interferometer
interfoliar *va* to interfoliate, to interleave
interfono *m* intercom
intergubernamental *adj* intergovernmental
ínterin *m* (*pl:* **intérines**) temporary incumbency; (eccl.) Interim; *adv* meanwhile; *conj* (coll.) while, until, as long as
interinamente *adv* in the meantime; temporarily
interinar *va* to fill (*a post*) temporarily, to fill in an acting capacity
interinidad *f* temporariness; temporary incumbency
interino -na *adj* temporary, acting, interim
interior *adj* interior; inner, inside; (pertaining to) home; domestic; *m* interior; mind, soul; **interiores** *mpl* entrails, insides; **Interior** City (*word written on an envelope to indicate that the letter is to go to the city in which it is mailed*)
interioridad *f* inwardness; inside; **interioridades** *fpl* family secrets, private matters, inside story
interiorizar §76 *va* to keep well informed, to give inside information to; *vr* to keep well informed; **interiorizarse de** to find out about
interiormente *adv* on the inside; inwardly
interjección *f* (gram.) interjection
interjectivo -va *adj* (gram.) interjectional
interlínea *f* interline; (print.) space, lead
interlineación *f* interlineation
interlineal *adj* interlinear
interlinear *va* to interline; (print.) to space, to lead
interlocutor -tora *mf* interlocutor; speaker, party
interlocutorio -ria *adj* (law) interlocutory
intérlope *adj* interloping (*said of commerce and ships*)
interludio *m* (mus.) interlude
interlunar *adj* interlunar
interlunio *m* (astr.) interlunation
intermaxilar *adj* intermaxillary
intermediar *vn* to stand in the middle; to intermediate
intermediario -ria *adj* intermediary; mediating; *mf* intermediary; mediator; *m* (com.) middleman
intermedio -dia *adj* intermediate, intervening; (phonet.) medial; *m* interval, interim; (theat.) entr'acte, interlude, intermission; (mus.) intermezzo; **por intermedio de** (Am.) by means of
interminable *adj* interminable
intermisión *f* intermission; (path.) intermission
intermiso -sa *adj* interrupted, suspended
intermitencia *f* intermittence or intermittency; (path.) intermission
intermitente *adj* intermittent
intermitir *va* to intermit
internación *f* commitment, internment; penetration, moving inland
internacional *adj* international; (*cap.*) *f* International (*association*); Internationale (*hymn*); **Internacional Comunista** Communist International
internacionalidad *f* internationality
internacionalismo *m* internationalism
internacionalista *mf* internationalist
internacionalización *f* internationalization
internacionalizar §76 *va* to internationalize
internado -da *mf* (mil.) internee; *m* student boarding; boarding students; boarding school
internamiento *m* sending inland; commitment, internment; bedding (*of sick people*)
internar *va* to send inland; to commit, to intern; *vn* to move inland; *vr* to move inland; to worm one's way into another's confidence; to study deeply; to take refuge, hide
internista *mf* (med.) internist
interno -na *adj* internal; inward; inside; boarding; *mf* boarding-school student; **interno de hospital** intern
internodio *m* internode
internuncio *m* internuncio
interoceánico -ca *adj* interoceanic
interocular *adj* interocular
interóseo -a *adj* interosseous
interpaginar *va* to interpage
interparietal *adj* (anat.) interparietal
interparlamentario -ria *adj* interparliamentary
interpelación *f* beseeching; interpellation
interpelar *va* to ask aid or protection of; to ask for explanations; to interpellate
interpenetración *f* interpenetration
interplanetario -ria *adj* interplanetary

interpolación *f* interpolation; brief stop (*e.g., in a speech*)
interpolar *adj* interpolar; *va* to interpolate; to stop or interrupt for a moment; (math.) to interpolate
interpondré *1st sg fut ind of* **interponer**
interponer §69 *va* to interpose; to appoint as mediator; *vr* to interpose, stand between, intercede
interpongo *1st sg pres ind of* **interponer**
interposición *f* interposition
interprender *va* to take by surprise
interpresa *f* taking by surprise, surprise action, surprise attack
interpretable *adj* interpretable
interpretación *f* interpretation
interpretador -dora *adj* interpreting; *mf* interpreter
interpretar *va* to interpret
interpretativo -va *adj* interpretative or interpretive
intérprete *mf* interpreter
interpuesto -ta *pp of* **interponer**
interpuse *1st sg pret ind of* **interponer**
interracial *adj* interracial
interregno *m* interregnum
interrogación *f* interrogation; (gram.) question mark, interrogation mark
interrogado -da *adj* questioned; *mf* person questioned, party questioned
interrogante *adj* questioning; interrogative; question (*mark*); *mf* questioner, interrogator; *m* question mark
interrogar §59 *va & vn* to question, to interrogate
interrogativo -va *adj* interrogative; *m* (gram.) interrogative
interrogatorio *m* interrogatory
interrumpidamente *adv* interruptedly
interrumpir *va* to interrupt
interrupción *f* interruption
interruptor -tora *adj* interrupting; *m* (elec.) switch; **interruptor a palanca** (elec.) toggle switch; **interruptor automático** (elec.) circuit breaker; **interruptor de cuchilla** (elec.) knife switch; **interruptor del encendido** (aut.) ignition switch; **interruptor de reloj** (elec.) time switch; **interruptor de rótula** (elec.) toggle switch; **interruptor de una caída** (elec.) single-throw switch; **interruptor de volquete** (elec.) tumbler switch
intersecar §86 *va & vr* to intersect
intersección *f* (geom.) intersection
intersideral *adj* intersidereal
intersticial *adj* interstitial
intersticio *m* interstice; interval
intertrigo *m* (path.) intertrigo
intertropical *adj* intertropical
interuniversitario -ria *adj* interuniversity, intercollegiate
interurbano -na *adj* interurban
intervalo *m* interval; (mus.) interval; **claro intervalo** lucid interval
intervención *f* intervention; supervision, inspection; participation; auditing; (surg.) operation; **no intervención** (dipl.) nonintervention; **intervención de los precios** price control
intervencionista *adj & mf* interventionist
intervendré *1st sg fut ind of* **intervenir**
intervengo *1st sg pres ind of* **intervenir**
intervenir §92 *va* to take up, to work on; to inspect, to supervise; to audit; to offer to pay (*a draft*); to tap (*a telephone line*); (surg.) to operate on; *vn* to intervene; to intercede; to happen; to participate; *vr* to be found (*as a result of inspection*); **intervenírsele a uno** to be found on someone, e.g., **se le intervino una carta secreta** a secret letter was found on him, they found a secret letter on him
interventor *m* election supervisor; (com.) auditor
interviev *m & f* (*pl:* **-vievs**) interview
interviuvador -dora *mf* interviewer
intervievar *va* to interview
intervine *1st sg pret ind of* **intervenir**
interviniendo *ger of* **intervenir**
intervistar *vr* var. of **entrevistar**
interviú *m & f* interview
intervocálico -ca *adj* intervocalic
interyacente *adj* interjacent
interzonal *adj* interzonal or interzone
intestado -da *adj & mf* intestate
intestinal *adj* intestinal
intestino -na *adj* intestine (*internal; domestic*); *m* (anat.) intestine, intestines; **intestino ciego** (anat.) caecum; **intestino delgado** (anat.) small intestine; **intestino grueso** (anat.) large intestine; **intestinos** *mpl* (anat.) intestines
intimación *f* announcement, declaration; intimation (*announcement*)
íntimamente *adv* intimately; deeply
intimar *va* to intimate, to notify, to order; *vn* to become intimate or well-acquainted; *vr* to soak in; to become intimate or well-acquainted
intimidación *f* intimidation
intimidad *f* intimacy; homeyness; privacy
intimidar *va* to intimidate; *vr* to become intimidated
íntimo -ma *adj* intimate; innermost; homey; private
intina *f* (bot.) intine
intitular *va* to entitle; to give a title to; *vr* to give oneself a title, use a title; to be called
intocable *mf* untouchable (*person of lowest caste in India*)
intocado -da *adj* intact, untouched
intolerabilidad *f* intolerability
intolerable *adj* intolerable
intolerancia *f* intolerance
intolerante *adj & mf* intolerant
intonso -sa *adj* unshorn; ignorant, rustic; uncut (*said of a book or magazine*); *mf* ignorant person, rustic
intoxicación *f* (med.) poisoning, intoxication
intoxicar §86 *va* (med.) to poison, intoxicate
intracruce *m* or **intracruzamiento** *m* inbreeding
intradós *m* (arch.) intrados
intraducible *adj* untranslatable
intramolecular *adj* intramolecular
intramural *adj* (anat.) intramural
intramuros *adv* intra muros, within the walls
intramuscular *adj* intramuscular
intranquilidad *f* worry, uneasiness; unrest
intranquilizar §76 *va* to disquiet, to worry; *vr* to become disquieted, to worry
intranquilo -la *adj* worried, uneasy; restless
intransferible *adj* untransferable
intransigencia *f* intransigence or intransigency
intransigente *adj & mf* intransigent, irreconcilable, die-hard
intransitable *adj* impassable
intransitivo -va *adj* (gram.) intransitive
intransmisible *adj* untransmissible
intransmutable *adj* intransmutable
intratabilidad *f* intractability; unsociability
intratable *adj* intractable; unsociable; impassable
intravenoso -sa *adj* intravenous
intrepidez *f* intrepidity
intrépido -da *adj* intrepid
intriga *f* intrigue
intrigante *adj* intriguing, scheming; *mf* intriguer
intrigar §59 *va* to intrigue, to excite the curiosity of; *vn* to intrigue; *vr* to be intrigued
intrincación *f* intricacy
intrincado -da *adj* intricate
intrincamiento *m* intricacy
intrincar §86 *va* to confuse, entangle, complicate
intríngulis *m* (*pl:* **-lis**) (coll.) ulterior motive; (coll.) enigma, conundrum, mystery
intrínseco -ca *adj* intrinsic or intrinsical
introducción *f* introduction; insertion
introducir §38 *va* to introduce; to insert, put in; *vr* to gain access; to interfere, intrude, meddle
introductivo -va *adj* introductory
introductor -tora *adj* introductory; *mf* introducer
introduje *1st sg pret ind of* **introducir**
introduzco *1st sg pres ind of* **introducir**
introito *m* (theat.) prologue; (eccl.) Introit
intromisión *f* insertion; meddling

introrso -sa *adj* (bot.) introrse
introspección *f* introspection
introspectivo -va *adj* introspective
introversión *f* introversion
introverso -sa *adj* introvert
introvertido -da *mf* introvert
intrusar *vr* to seize unlawfully
intrusión *f* intrusion; charlatanry, quackery
intrusismo *m* intrusion; practice of a profession without authority
intruso -sa *adj* intrusive; *mf* intruder, interloper; dishonest practitioner
intubación *f* (med.) intubation
intuición *f* intuition
intuicionismo *m* intuitionism
intuir §41 *va* to intuit; to divine, to guess, to sense
intuitivo -va *adj* intuitive, intuitional
intuito *m* view, glance, look; **por intuito de** in view of
intumescencia *f* swelling, intumescence
intumescente *adj* swelling, intumescent
intususcepción *f* (biol. & path.) intussusception
inulasa *f* (biochem.) inulase
inulina *f* (chem.) inulin
inulto -ta *adj* (poet.) unavenged
inundación *f* inundation, flood
inundar *va* to inundate, to flood
inurbanidad *f* incivility, discourtesy
inurbano -na *adj* uncivil, discourteous
inusitado -da *adj* unusual; out of use
inusual *adj* unusual
inútil *adj* useless
inutilidad *f* uselessness, inutility; incapacity
inutilizado -da *adj* unused, unemployed
inutilizar §76 *va* to make useless; *vr* to become useless; to be disabled
invadeable *adj* unfordable
invadir *va* to invade
invaginación *f* invagination
invaginar *va & vr* to invaginate
invalidación *f* invalidation
invalidar *va* to invalidate; to weaken, make helpless
invalidez *f* invalidity
inválido -da *adj & mf* invalid
invar *m* invar (*alloy*)
invariabilidad *f* invariability
invariable *adj* invariable
invariante *adj & f* invariant
invasión *f* invasion
invasor -sora *adj* invading; *mf* invader
invectiva *f* invective
invectivar *va* to inveigh against
invencibilidad *f* invincibility
invencible *adj* invincible
invención *f* finding; invention; **Invención de la Santa Cruz** (eccl.) Invention of the Cross
invencionero -ra *adj* inventive; cheating; *mf* inventor; cheat
invendible *adj* unsalable
invendido -da *adj* unsold
inventar *va* to invent
inventariar §90 & regular *va* to inventory
inventario *m* inventory
inventivo -va *adj* inventive; *f* inventiveness
invento *m* invention
inventor -tora *adj* inventive; *mf* inventor
inverecundia *f* shamelessness, insolence
inverecundo -da *adj* shameless, insolent
inverisímil *adj* improbable, unlikely
inverisimilitud *f* improbability, inverisimilitude
invernación *f* wintering; hibernation
invernáculo *m* hothouse, conservatory
invernada *f* wintertime; wintering; (Am.) pasture, pasturing, pasture land
invernadero *m* hothouse, conservatory; winter resort; winter pasture
invernal *adj* (pertaining to) winter; *m* (Am.) large winter stable (*in the Andes*)
invernante *mf* winter vacationist
invernar §18 *vn* to winter; to be winter
invernazo *m* rainy season (*in Tropics*)
inverne *m* (Am.) winter pasture (*time*); (Am.) winter fattening
invernizo -za *adj* (pertaining to) winter; wintery
inverosímil *adj* improbable, unlikely
inverosimilitud *f* improbability, inverisimilitude
inversión *f* inversion; investment; subversion, overthrow; (gram.) inverted order
inversionista *adj* (pertaining to) investment; *mf* investor
inverso -sa *adj* inverse, opposite; **a** or **por la inversa** on the contrary; *m* (box.) jab
inversor -sora *adj* inverting, reversing; *m* reversing mechanism; (elec.) reverser
invertasa *f* (biochem.) invertase
invertebrado -da *adj & m* invertebrate
invertido -da *adj* inverted; *mf* (psychiatry) invert
invertina *f* (biochem.) invertase
invertir §62 *va* to invert; to reverse; to invest; to spend
investidura *f* investiture; station, position
investigación *f* investigation
investigador -dora *adj* investigating; *mf* investigator
investigar §59 *va* to investigate
investir §94 *va* to invest (*to vest, install*); **investir de** or **con** to invest with
inveterado -da *adj* inveterate, confirmed
inveterar *vr* to become old; to become chronic
invicto -ta *adj* unconquered
invidente *adj* blind; *mf* blind person
invierno *m* winter; (Am.) rainy season
invigilar *vn* to watch with concern
inviolabilidad *f* inviolability
inviolable *adj* inviolable
inviolado -da *adj* inviolate
invisibilidad *f* invisibility
invisible *adj* invisible; (coll.) hiding; *m* (Am.) hair net; (Am.) invisible hairpin; **en un invisible** in less than no time
invitación *f* invitation
invitado -da *mf* person invited, guest
invitar *va* to invite; **invitar a** + *inf* to invite to + *inf*
invocación *f* invocation
invocador -dora *adj* invoking; *mf* invoker
invocar §86 *va* to invoke
invocatorio -ria *adj* invocatory
involución *f* involution; (biol. & med.) involution; (math.) involution (*assemblage of pairs of collinear conjugate points*)
involucrado -da (bot.) involucrate
involucrar *va* to jumble; to introduce irrelevantly; *vr* to get jumbled
involucro *m* (bot.) involucre
involuntariedad *f* involuntariness
involuntario -ria *adj* involuntary
involuta *f* (arch.) volute; (geom.) involute
invulnerabilidad *f* invulnerability
invulnerable *adj* invulnerable
inyección *f* injection; **inyección hipodérmica** hypodermic injection
inyectable *adj* injectable
inyectado -da *adj* congested, inflamed
inyectar *va* to inject; *vr* to become congested
inyector *m* (mach.) injector
iñiguista *adj* Jesuitic; *mf* Jesuit
-ío -ía *suffix adj* e.g., **bravío** fierce; **cabrío** goatish; *suffix m* indicates a group or collection, e.g., **caserío** group of houses; **gentío** crowd of people; *suffix f* -y, e.g., **filosofía** philosophy; **geología** geology
Ío *f* (myth.) Io
ion *m* (chem. & phys.) ion; **ion hidrógeno** (*pl:* **iones hidrógeno**) (chem.) hydrogen ion
iónico -ca *adj* (chem. & phys.) ionic
ionio *m* (chem.) ionium
ionización *f* ionization
ionizar §76 *va & vr* to ionize
ionosfera *f* ionosphere
iota *f* iota (*Greek letter*)
iotacismo *m* iotacism
ipecacuana *f* (bot.) ipecac or ipecacuanha (*plant, root, and medicine*)
ir §57 *vn* to go; to come, e.g., **ya voy** I'm coming; to move, to walk; to be becoming, to fit, to suit; to be; to be at stake; to involve; **lo que va de** so far (as), e.g., **lo que va de este mes** so far this month; **lo que va de rodaje** so far as the filming has gone; **¡qué va!** of course not!; **¡vaya!** the deuce!; what a . . . !,

e.g., **¡vaya un hombre!** what a man!; **ir a** + *inf* to go to + *inf;* to be going to + *inf* (*expressing futurity*); **ir a buscar** to call for, to go get; **ir a parar en** to end up in; **ir con cuidado** to be careful; **ir con miedo** to be afraid; **ir con tiento** to be watchful; **ir de caza** to go hunting; **ir de pesca** to go fishing; **ir por** to go for, to go after; to follow (*a career*); **ir** + *pp* to be + *pp; vr* to go away; to ooze, to leak; to slip; to wear away; to get old; to break to pieces; to break wind; to lose control of natural evacuations; **la de vámonos** (slang) death; **irse de** to discard; **irse haciendo** to make one's way
ira *f* ire, wrath; **¡ira de Dios!** Lord help us!
iraca *f* (bot.) jipijapa; (Am.) Panama hat
iracundia *f* anger, angriness, wrath
iracundo -da *adj* angry, wrathful, ireful
Irak, el Irak or Iraq
Irán, el Iran
iranés -nesa or **iranio -nia** *adj & mf* Iranian; *m* Iranian (*language*)
iraqués -quesa or **iraquiano -na** *adj & mf* Iraqi; *m* Iraqi (*dialect*)
irascibilidad *f* irascibility
irascible *adj* irascible
Irene *f* Irene
iridáceo -a *adj* (bot.) iridaceous
íride *f* (bot.) gladdon, stinking iris
iridescencia *f* var. of **iridiscencia**
iridescente *adj* var. of **iridiscente**
iridio *m* (chem.) iridium
iridiscencia *f* iridescence
iridiscente *adj* iridescent
iris *m* (*pl:* **iris**) iris, rainbow; (anat. & opt.) iris; (mineral.) noble opal; **iris amarillo** (bot.) sweet flag; **iris de paz** peacemaker; (*cap.*) *f* (myth.) Iris
irisación *f* iridescence
irisado -da *adj* rainbow, rainbow-hued
irisar *va* to iris; *vn* to iridesce
iritis *f* (path.) iritis
irlanda *f* cotton cloth, woolen cloth; Irish linen; (*cap.*) *f* Ireland; **la Irlanda del Norte** or **la Irlanda Septentrional** Northern Ireland
irlandés -desa *adj* Irish; *m* Irishman; Irish (*language*); **los irlandeses** the Irish (*people*); *f* Irishwoman
ironía *f* irony
irónico -ca *adj* ironic, ironical
ironizar §76 *va* to ridicule
iroqués -quesa *adj* Iroquoian; *mf* Iroquoian or Iroquois
irracional *adj* irrational, unreasoning; (math.) irrational
irracionalidad *f* irrationality
irradiación *f* irradiation; influence; (med.) irradiation; (rad.) broadcast
irradiar *va* to radiate; to irradiate; (rad.) to broadcast; *vn* to radiate
irrazonable *adj* unreasonable
irreal *adj* unreal
irrealidad *f* unreality
irrealizable *adj* unrealizable, unattainable
irrebatible *adj* irrefutable
irreconciliable *adj* unreconcilable, irreconcilable
irreconciliado -da *adj* unreconciled
irreconocible *adj* unrecognizable
irrecuperable *adj* irrecoverable, irretrievable
irrecusable *adj* unimpeachable
irredentista *mf* Irredentist
irredento -ta *adj* unredeemed (*region*)
irredimible *adj* irredeemable
irreducible or **irreductible** *adj* irreducible
irreembolsable *adj* not refunded
irreemplazable *adj* unreplaceable, irreplaceable
irreflexión *f* irreflection, rashness
irreflexivo -va *adj* unreflecting, thoughtless
irreformable *adj* irreformable, incorrigible
irrefragable *adj* irrefragable
irrefrenable *adj* unbridled, uncontrollable, irrepressible
irrefutable *adj* irrefutable
irregenerado -da *adj* unregenerate
irregular *adj* irregular; (bot., geom., gram. & mil.) irregular; *m* (mil.) irregular
irregularidad *f* irregularity; (coll.) embezzlement, irregularity
irreligión *f* irreligion
irreligiosidad *f* irreligiousness
irreligioso -sa *adj* unreligious; irreligious
irrellenable *adj* nonrefillable
irremediable *adj* irremediable
irremisible *adj* irremissible, unpardonable
irremovible *adj* irremovable
irremunerado -da *adj* unremunerated
irrenovable *adj* unrenewable
irrenunciable *adj* unrenounceable
irreparable *adj* irreparable
irreprensible *adj* irreprehensible, unexceptionable
irrepresentable *adj* unplayable
irreprimible *adj* irrepressible
irreprochable *adj* irreproachable, faultless
irrescindible *adj* unrescindable
irresistible *adj* irresistible
irresoluble *adj* unsolvable, unworkable
irresolución *f* irresolution, indecision
irresoluto -ta *adj* irresolute
irrespeto *m* (Am.) disrespect
irrespetuoso -sa *adj* disrespectful
irrespirable *adj* unbreathable
irresponsabilidad *f* irresponsibility
irresponsable *adj* irresponsible
irrestañable *adj* unstaunchable
irresuelto -ta *adj* irresolute, wavering, hesitant
irreverencia *f* irreverence
irreverenciar *va* to treat irreverently, to profane
irreverente *adj* irreverent
irreversible *adj* irreversible
irrevocabilidad *f* irrevocability
irrevocable *adj* irrevocable
irrevocado -da *adj* unrevoked
irrigable *adj* irrigable
irrigación *f* irrigation; (med.) irrigation
irrigador *m* irrigator; sprinkler
irrigar §59 *va* to irrigate; (med.) to irrigate
irrisible *adj* laughable, ridiculous
irrisión *f* derision, ridicule; (coll.) butt, laughingstock
irrisorio -ria *adj* ridiculous, derisory; insignificant, ridiculously small
irritabilidad *f* irritability
irritable *adj* irritable
irritación *f* irritation; nullification
irritadamente *adv* angrily, vexedly
irritador -dora *adj* irritating
irritamiento *m* anger, irritation
irritante *adj & m* irritant
irritar *va* to irritate; (law) to irritate, to render null and void; to stir up; *vr* to become irritated, to be exasperated
írrito -ta *adj* (law) null and void
irrogar §59 *va* to cause (*harm or damage*)
irrompible *adj* unbreakable
irruir §41 *va* to raid, to invade; to assault
irrumpir *vn* to burst in, to irrupt; to invade; **irrumpir en** to burst into (*e.g., a room*)
irrupción *f* irruption; invasion
irruptor -tora *adj* irruptive
irunés -nesa *adj* (pertaining to) Irún; *mf* native or inhabitant of Irún
-isa *suffix f* -ess, e.g., **poetisa** poetess; **sacerdotisa** priestess
Isaac *m* Isaac
Isabel *f* Isabella, Elizabeth; **Isabel la Católica** Isabella I, queen of Castile and León
isabelino -na *adj* Isabelline; Elizabethan; light-bay; *mf* Isabelline; Elizabethan; *m* light-bay horse
isabelita *f* (ichth.) isabelita
isagoge *f* isagoge, introduction
Isaías m (Bib.) Isaiah
isalóbara *f* (meteor.) isallobar
iscariote *adj* traitorous; bold, brazen
isíaco -ca *adj* Isiac
isidoriano -na *adj* Isidorian
Isidoro *m* Isidore
isidro -dra *mf* (coll.) hick, yokel, jake
Isis *f* (myth.) Isis
isla *f* island; block (*of houses*); (fig.) island (*hill, grove of trees*); **las Mil Islas** the Thousand Islands; **la Isla de la Reunión** Reunion; **la**

Isla del cabo Bretón Cape Breton Island; **la Isla del Diablo** Devil's Island; **la Isla del Norte** North Island; **la Isla del Príncipe Eduardo** Prince Edward Island; **la Isla del Sur** South Island; **Isla de Man** Isle of Man; **la Isla de Pascua** Easter Island; **Isla de Pinos** Isle of Pines; **isla de seguridad** safety island, safety zone; **islas Afortunadas** (myth.) Fortunate Islands; **islas Aleutas, Aleutianas** or **Aleutinas** Aleutian Islands; **islas Almirantes** Admiralty Islands; **islas Anglonormandas** Channel Islands; **islas Bahamas** Bahama Islands; **islas Baleares** Balearic Islands; **islas Bisayas** Visayan Islands; **Islas Británicas** British Isles; **islas Canarias** Canary Islands; **islas Curiles** Kurile Islands; **islas de Barlovento** Windward Islands; **islas Carolinas** Caroline Islands; **islas de Cabo Verde** Cape Verde Islands; **islas de las Especias** Spice Islands; **islas de la Sociedad** Society Islands; **islas de la Sonda** Sunda Islands; **islas del Canal** Channel Islands; **islas del Dodecaneso** Dodecanese Islands; **islas de los Amigos** Friendly Islands; **islas de (los) Galápagos** Galápagos Islands; **islas de Sotavento** Leeward Islands; **Islas Filipinas** Philippine Islands; **islas Jonias** Ionian Islands; **islas Malvinas** Falkland Islands; **islas Normandas** Channel Islands; **islas Salomón** Solomon Islands; **islas Vírgenes** Virgin Islands; **islas Visayas** Visayan Islands

Islam, el Islam

islámico -ca *adj* Islamic

islamismo *m* Islamism

islamista *adj* Islamistic; *m* Islamist, Islamite

islamita *adj & m* Islamite

islamizar §76 *va, vn & vr* to Islamize

islandés -desa *adj* Icelandic; *mf* Icelander; *m* Icelandic (*language*)

Islandia *f* Iceland

islándico -ca *adj* Icelandic

islario *m* description of islands; map of islands

isleño -ña *adj* (pertaining to an) island; *mf* islander; (in Cuba) Canarian

isleo *m* island; island of ground (*surrounded by other ground of different nature*)

isleta *f* isle, islet

islilla *f* (anat.) collar bone

islote *m* small barren island; large jutting rock (*in sea*)

Ismael *m* (Bib.) Ishmael

ismaelita *mf* Ishmaelite

ismo *m* ism; isthmus

isobárico -ca *adj* isobaric

isobaro -ra *adj* isobaric; *m* (chem.) isobar; *f* (meteor.) isobar

isoclino -na *adj* isoclinal; *f* isoclinal line

Isócrates *m* Isocrates

isocromático -ca *adj* isochromatic

isócrono -na *adj* isochronal, isochronous

isodáctilo -la *adj* isodactylous

isodinámico -ca *adj* isodynamic

isoete *m* (bot.) quillwort

isogloso -sa *adj* isoglossal; *f* isogloss

isogónico -ca *adj* isogonic

isógono -na *adj* isogonic; *f* isogonic line

Isolda *f* (myth.) Iseult

isomería *f* (chem.) isomerism

isomérico -ca *adj* (chem.) isomeric, isomerical

isomerismo *m* (chem.) isomerism

isómero -ra *adj* (chem.) isomeric, isomerical; *m* (chem.) isomer

isométrico -ca *adj* isometric or isometrical

isomorfismo *m* (biol., chem. & mineral.) isomorphism

isomorfo -fa *adj* (biol., chem. & mineral.) isomorphic

isoniacida *f* (pharm.) isoniazid

isoperímetro -tra *adj* isoperimetric or isoperimetrical

isópodo -da *adj & m* (zool.) isopod

isopreno *m* (chem.) isoprene

isoquímeno -na *adj* (meteor.) isocheimenal; *f* (meteor.) isocheim

isósceles *adj* (geom.) isosceles

isotermo -ma *adj* isothermal; *f* isotherm

isótero -ra *adj* isotheral; *f* isothere

isotopia *f* isotopy

isotópico -ca *adj* isotopic

isótopo *m* (chem.) isotope

isotropía *f* (biol. & phys.) isotropy

isotrópico -ca *adj* (biol. & phys.) isotropic

isotropo -pa *adj* (biol. & phys.) isotropic, isotropous

isquiático -ca *adj* (anat.) ischial

isquión *m* (anat.) ischium

Israel *m* Israel

israelí (*pl* **-líes**) *adj & mf* Israeli

israelita *adj & mf* Israelite

israelítico -ca *adj* Israelitish

Istambul *f* Istanbul

istmeño -ña *adj & mf* isthmian

ístmico -ca *adj* isthmian, isthmic

istmo *m* isthmus; (anat.) isthmus; **istmo de Corinto** Isthmus of Corinth; **istmo de Panamá** Isthmus of Panama; **istmo de Suez** Isthmus of Suez

istriar §90 *va & vr* var. of **estriar**

-ita *suffix* see **-ito**

Ítaca *f* Ithaca (*island west of Greece*)

Italia *f* Italy

italianismo *m* Italianism

italianizar §76 *va* to Italianize; *vr* to become Italianized

italiano -na *adj & mf* Italian; **a la italiana** in the Italian fashion or manner; *m* Italian (*language*)

itálico -ca *adj* Italic; (print.) italic; *f* (print.) italic, italics

ítalo -la *adj & mf* (poet.) Italian

itea *f* (bot.) itea

ítem *m* item, article, section; addition

iterable *adj* repeatable

iteración *f* iteration

iterar *va* iterate

iterativo -va *adj* iterative

iterbia *f* (chem.) ytterbia

itérbico -ca *adj* ytterbic

iterbio *m* (chem.) ytterbium

itinerario -ria *adj & m* itinerary

-ito -ta *suffix dim* has the force of little, nice and . . . , cute, dear, humble, somewhat, rather, etc. and is sometimes equivalent to English **-y** or -ie, e.g., **un poquito** a little bit; **hijita** little daughter; **tempranito** nice and early; **subidito** rather high; **perrito** doggie; **Juanito** Johnny; **Anita** Annie; is often added to adverbs, interjections, etc., e.g., **ahorita** right now; **¡adiosito!** bye-bye!; *suffix adj* -ite, e.g., **bipartito** bipartite; **finito** finite; *suffix adj & mf* **favorito** favorite; *suffix m* (chem.) -ite, e.g., **sulfito** sulfite; *suffix f* (com., explosives, mineral. & pal.) -ite, e.g., **vulcanita** vulcanite; **cordita** cordite; **dolomita** dolomite; **amonita** ammonite; **-ita** *adj & mf* -ite, e.g., **israelita** Israelite; **moscovita** Muscovite

itria *f* (chem.) yttria

ítrico -ca *adj* yttric

itrio *m* (chem.) yttrium

Ixión *m* (myth.) Ixion

ixtle *m* istle (*fiber*)

izado *m* hoisting

izaga *f* land full of rushes or reeds

izaje *m* (Am.) hoisting

izar §76 *va* (naut.) to hoist, haul up; **¡iza!** yo-heave-ho!

-izo -za *suffix adj* expresses the idea of tendency or susceptibility, e.g., **bermejizo** reddish; **enfermizo** sickly; **heladizo** easily frozen; **-y**, e.g., **cobrizo** coppery; **pajizo** strawy; *suffix m* e.g., **vaquerizo** cattle tender; *suffix f* e.g., **caballeriza** stable

izote *m* (bot.) Adam's-needle, bear grass; (bot.) Spanish dagger

izq.º abr. of **izquierdo**

izquierda *f* see **izquierdo**

izquierdear *vn* to go awry, to go wild, to go astray

izquierdismo *m* leftism

izquierdista *adj & mf* leftist

izquierdizante *adj* leftish; *mf* leftish person

izquierdo -da *adj* left; left-hand; left-handed; crooked; **a la izquierda** left, on the left, to the left; **levantarse del izquierdo** to get out of bed on the wrong side; *f* left hand; left-hand side; (pol.) left

J

J, j *f* eleventh letter of the Spanish alphabet
ja *interj* ha!
jabalcón *m* strut, brace
jabalconar *va* to support with struts, to brace
jabalí *m* (*pl:* **-líes**) (zool.) wild boar; **jabalí de Erimanto** (myth.) Erymanthian boar; **jabalí de verrugas** (zool.) wart hog
jabalina *f* (hist. & sport) javelin; wild sow
jabardear *vn* to swarm (*said of bees*)
jabardillo *m* noisy swarm (*of insects or birds*); (coll.) noisy swarm (*of people*)
jabardo *m* afterswarm; poor swarm, small swarm; (coll.) noisy swarm (*of people*)
jabato *m* young wild boar
jábega *f* sweep net; fishing smack
jabegote *m* sweep-net fisherman
jabeguero -ra *adj* sweep-net; *m* sweep-net fisherman
jabeque *m* (naut.) xebec; (coll.) gash in the face
jabí *m* (*pl:* **-bíes**) (bot.) brasiletto (*tree and wood*); small wild apple; small grape of Granada
jabillo *m* (bot.) sandbox tree
jabladera *f* croze, crozing saw
jable *m* croze (*groove*)
jabón *m* soap; cake of soap; **dar jabón a** (coll.) to softsoap; **dar un jabón a** (coll.) to upbraid, rake over the coals; **jabón blando** soft soap; **jabón de afeitar** shaving soap; **jabón de Castilla** Castile soap; **jabón de tocador** or **de olor** toilet soap; **jabón de piedra** hard soap; **jabón de sastre** French chalk, soapstone; **jabón duro** hard soap; **jabón en polvo** soap powder; **jabón graso** soft soap; **jabón para la barba** shaving soap
jabonado *m* soaping; wash (*clothes washed or to be washed*)
jabonadura *f* soaping; **jabonaduras** *fpl* soapy water; soapsuds; **dar una jabonadura a** (coll.) to upbraid, to rake over the coals, to lambaste
jabonar *va* to soap; (coll.) to upbraid, to rake over the coals
jaboncillo *m* cake of toilet soap; French chalk; (bot.) soapberry, soapberry tree; **jaboncillo de sastre** French chalk
jabonera *f* see **jabonero**
jabonería *f* soap factory; soap store
jabonero -ra *adj* (pertaining to) soap; yellowish, dirty-white (*bull*); *mf* soapmaker; soap dealer; **jabonero de las Antillas** (bot.) chinaberry, wild China tree; *f* soap dish; (bot.) soapwort
jaboneta *f* or **jabonete** *m* cake of toilet soap
jabonoso -sa *adj* soapy
jaca *f* cob, jennet; gamecock
jacal *m* (Am.) hut, shack; (zool.) jackal
jacalero -ra *adj* (Am.) hut-dwelling; *mf* (Am.) hut dweller; **andar de jacalero** (Am.) to go on a spree
jácara *f* see **jácaro**
jacarandá *m* (bot.) jacaranda
jacarandoso -sa *adj* (coll.) gay, carefree; (coll.) sporty
jacarear *vn* to sing merry ballads; (coll.) to go serenading, to go singing in the street; (coll.) to be disagreeable, be offensive
jacarero -ra *adj* serenading; (coll.) gay, merry, witty; *mf* serenader; (coll.) jester, wag, wit
jácaro -ra *adj* braggart; *m* braggart, bully; *f* merry ballad; merry dance or tune; serenaders, night revelers; (coll.) story, argument; (coll.) lie, fake; (coll.) annoyance
jácena *f* girder; header beam
jacerina *f* coat of mail
jacilla *f* mark on the ground (*left by a thing that has stood for a long time*)
jacintino -na *adj* hyacinthine, violet
jacinto *m* (bot.) hyacinth; (mineral.) hyacinth, jacinth; (*cap.*) *m* (myth.) Hyacinthus; **jacinto de penacho** (bot.) tassel hyacinth; **jacinto estrellado** (bot.) Cuban lily, hyacinth of Peru; **jacinto racimoso silvestre** (bot.) grape hyacinth
jaco *m* nag, jade; (orn.) gray parrot; (obs.) coat of mail; (obs.) goatskin jacket
Jacob *m* (Bib.) Jacob
jacobeo -a *adj* of St. James
jacobínico -ca *adj* Jacobinic or Jacobinical
jacobinismo *m* Jacobinism
jacobinizar §76 *va* to Jacobinize; *vn* to boast of or make a show of Jacobinism
jacobino -na *adj & mf* Jacobin
jacobita *mf* pilgrim to Santiago de Compostela; *m* Jacobite
Jacobo *m* James; Jacob
jactancia *f* boasting, bragging; boastfulness
jactancioso -sa *adj* boastful, bragging
jactar *vr* to boast, to brag; **jactarse de** + *inf* to boast of + *ger*
jaculatorio -ria *adj* ejaculatory; *f* ejaculation (*short, sudden prayer*)
jade *m* (mineral.) jade
jadeante *adj* panting, out of breath
jadear *vn* to pant
jadeo *m* panting
jaecero -ra *mf* harness maker
jaez *m* (*pl:* **jaeces**) harness, piece of harness; kind, stripe, quality, character; **jaeces** *mpl* trappings
jaezar §76 *va* var. of **enjaezar**
jafético -ca *adj* Japhetic
jagua *f* (bot.) genipap
jaguar *m* (zool.) jaguar
jaguarzo *m* (bot.) rockrose
jagüey *m* (Am.) reservoir; (Am.) tiny mosquito; (bot.) Indian fig
jaharrar *va* to plaster
jaharro *m* plaster, plastering
Jahel *f* (Bib.) Jael
jai alai *m* jai alai (*Spanish game like rackets*)
jaibería *f* (Am.) slyness, trickiness
Jaime *m* James
jaique *m* hooded cape
jairar *va* to bevel (*leather*)
jaire *m* bevel cut
jalapa *f* (bot.) jalap
jalar *va* (coll.) to pull, to haul; (Am.) to flirt with; *vr* (Am.) to get drunk; (Am.) to beat it, get out
jalbegador -dora *adj & mf* var. of **enjalbegador**
jalbegar §59 *va & vr* var. of **enjalbegar**
jalbegue *m* whitewash; whitewashing; paint, make-up
jaldado -da, jalde or **jaldo -da** *adj* bright-yellow
jalea *f* jelly; **hacerse una jalea** (coll.) to be madly in love
jaleador -dora *adj* cheering; *mf* cheerer
jalear *va* to cheer (*hounds; dancers*); to flirt with; (Am.) to bother, tease; *vn* to dance the jaleo; *vr* to dance the jaleo; to have a noisy time; to dance and sway
jaleo *m* cheering; noisy time, jamboree; jaleo (*vivacious Spanish solo dance*)
jaletina *f* gelatine; calf's foot jelly
jalifa *m* Spanish Moroccan caliph
jalifato *m* Spanish Moroccan caliphate
jalisco -ca *adj* (Am.) drunk; *m* (Am.) straw hat
jalma *f* light packsaddle
jalmería *f* packsaddle work
jalmero *m* packsaddle maker or dealer

jalón *m* stage; (surv.) flagpole, range pole; (Am.) jerk, tug; (Am.) swig, drink; **jalón de mira** (surv.) leveling rod
jalonamiento *m* staking, marking, laying out
jalonar *va* to lay out, stake out, mark out
jalonero *m* (surv.) rodman
jaloque *m* southeast wind
jallullo *m* (prov.) bread baked on embers or hot stones
jamaica *m* Jamaica, Jamaica rum; *f* (bot.) roselle, Jamaica sorrel; (Am.) charity fair; (*cap.*) *f* Jamaica
jamaicano -na *adj & mf* Jamaican
jamar *va* (coll.) to eat
jamás *adv* never; **jamás por jamás** never more
jamba *f* (arch.) jamb; (slang) loose woman; sweetheart
jambaje *m* (arch.) doorframe, window frame
jámbico -ca *adj* var. of **yámbico**
jamelgo *m* (coll.) jade, nag
jamerdana *f* sewer of an abattoir
jamerdar *va* to clean the guts of (*a slaughtered animal*); (coll.) to wash with a lick and a promise
jamete *m* samite
jámila *f* var. of **alpechín**
jamón *m* ham
jamona *adj fem* fat and middle-aged (*woman*); *f* fat and middle-aged woman
jámparo *m* (Am.) canoe, rowboat
jamuga *f* or **jamugas** *fpl* sidesaddle (*in form of folding chair*); **ir en jamugas** to ride sidesaddle
jamurar *va* to scoop out, bail out
jándalo -la *adj & mf* (coll.) Andalusian
jangada *f* (coll.) piece of folly; (coll.) dirty trick; raft; life-saving raft or float
Janículo *m* Janiculum
Jano *m* (myth.) Janus
Jansenio *m* Jansen
jansenismo *m* Jansenism
jansenista *adj* Jansenist, Jansenistic; *mf* Jansenist
Jantipa or **Jantipe** *f* Xanthippe
japón -pona *adj & mf* var. of **japonés; el Japón** Japan
japonense *adj & mf* var. of **japonés**
japonés -nesa *adj & mf* Japanese; *m* Japanese (*language*)
japuta *f* (ichth.) pomfret
jaque *m* check (*in chess*); saddlebag; (coll.) bully; (obs.) smooth hairdo; **dar jaque a** to check (*in chess*); **dar jaque mate a** to checkmate (*in chess*); **en jaque** in check (*in chess*); **estar muy jaque** (coll.) to be full of pep; **tener en jaque** to hold a threat over the head of; **jaque mate** checkmate (*in chess*); *interj* check! (*in chess*); **¡jaque de aquí!** get out of here!
jaquear *va* to check (*in chess*); to harass (*an enemy*); *vn* (coll.) to be a bully
jaqueca *f* headache, sick headache; **dar jaqueca a** (coll.) to bore to death
jaquecoso -sa *adj* boring, tiresome
jaquel *adj* (Am.) blood (*orange*); *m* (her.) square
jaquelado -da *adj* (her.) checky; square-faceted
jaquemar *m* jack (*figure of man which strikes time in a clock*)
jaqueta *f* (archaic & prov.) blouse, jacket
jaquetilla *f* small short loose coat
jaquetón *m* (zool.) man-eater (*shark*); (coll.) bully
jáquima *f* rope headstall
jaquimazo *m* blow with a headstall; (coll.) great disappointment
jara *f* see **jaro**
jarabe *m* syrup; sweet drink; **jarabe de pico** (coll.) empty talk, idle promise, lip service
jarabear *va* to prescribe syrups or potions for; *vr* to take syrups or potions, to take laxatives
jaraíz *m* (*pl:* **-íces**) wine press
jaral *m* growth of rockrose; puzzle, complication
jaramago *m* (bot.) wall rocket
jaramugo *m* tiny fish (*used as bait*)
jarana *f* (coll.) fun, merrymaking; (coll.) rumpus; (coll.) trick, deceit; (Am.) jest, joke; (Am.) small guitar; **ir de jarana** (coll.) to go on a spree, to go merrymaking
jaranear *vn* (coll.) to go on a spree, to go merrymaking; (coll.) to raise a rumpus
jaranero -ra *adj* merrymaking; fun-loving, gay, merry; *m* reveler
jaranista *adj* (Am.) var. of **jaranero**
jarano *m* sombrero
jarazo *m* arrow shot, arrow wound
jarcia *f* bundle; fishing tackle; (coll.) mess, jumble; **jarcias** *fpl* tackle, rigging; **jarcia de firme** or **jarcia muerta** (naut.) standing rigging; **jarcia trozada** junk (*old cable*)
jarciar *va* var. of **enjarciar**
jardín *m* garden, flower garden; park; flaw in an emerald; (baseball) field, outfield; (naut.) privy, latrine; **jardín botánico** botanical garden; **jardín central** (baseball) center field; **jardín de la infancia** kindergarten; **jardín del Edén** (Bib.) Garden of Eden; **jardín derecho** (baseball) right field; **jardín izquierdo** (baseball) left field; **jardín zoológico** zoölogical garden
jardinaje *m* (Am.) gardening
jardinera *f* see **jardinero**
jardinería *f* gardening, landscape gardening
jardinero -ra *mf* gardener; **jardinero adornista** landscape gardener; *m* (baseball) fielder, outfielder; *f* jardiniere; basket carriage; summer trolley car, open trolley car
jardinista *mf* garden expert
jarear *vr* (Am.) to flee, run away; (Am.) to swing, to sway; (Am.) to die of starvation
jareta *f* (sew.) casing
jaretón *m* broad hem
jarife *m* var. of **jerife**
jarifo -fa *adj* natty, spruce, showy
jaripeo *m* (Am.) rodeo
jaro -ra *adj* carroty; red (*hog or boar*); *m* thicket; small oak; (bot.) arum; *f* sharp-pointed arrow; (bot.) rockrose (*Cistus ladaniferus*); **jara blanca** (bot.) white-leaved rockrose
jarocho -cha *adj* brusque, bluff; *mf* brusque, insulting person; (Am.) peasant of Veracruz
jaropar *va* (coll.) to overdose with syrups and drugs; (coll.) to fix up a dose for
jarope *m* syrup; (coll.) nasty potion
jaropear *va* (coll.) to overdose with syrups and drugs; *vr* (coll.) to overdose oneself, take too much medicine
jaropeo *m* (coll.) overdosing oneself, abuse of medicine
jarra *f* pitcher, water pitcher; jug; **en jarras** or **de jarras** with arms akimbo
jarrazo *m* blow with a jar, jug, or pitcher
jarrear *va* to plaster; *vn* (coll.) to draw water or wine with a jug or pitcher; (prov.) to pour, to rain hard
jarrero *m* maker or seller of jars, jugs, etc.
jarrete *m* hock; gambrel; ham
jarretera *f* garter; (*cap.*) *f* Garter (*order; badge of the order*)
jarro *m* pitcher; **echar un jarro de agua (fría) a** (coll.) to pour cold water on
jarrón *m* vase; (arch.) urn
Jartum *f* Khartoum or Khartum
Jasón *m* (myth.) Jason
jaspe *m* (mineral.) jasper
jaspeado -da *adj* marbled, speckled, jaspered; jaspery; *m* marbling, speckling
jaspeadura *f* marbling, speckling
jaspear *va* to marble, to speckle
jaspeo *m* var. of **jaspeadura**
jastial *m* (prov.) var. of **hastial**
jateo -a *adj* fox-hunting; *mf* foxhound
jato -ta *mf* calf
Jauja *f* Cockaigne, Shangrila; **¿estamos aquí o en Jauja?** (coll.) where do you think you are?; **vivir en Jauja** (coll.) to live in the lap of luxury
jaula *f* cage; crate; (elec., mach. & min.) cage; (Am.) open freight car; **jaula de locos** insane asylum; (fig.) madhouse (*place of confusion*)
jauría *f* pack (*of hounds*)
javanés -nesa *adj & mf* Javanese; *m* Javanese (*language*)
Javier *m* Xavier
jayán -yana *mf* big brute of a person
jazarán *m* coat of mail

jazmín *m* (bot.) jasmine; **jazmín de Arabia** (bot.) Arabian jasmine; **jazmín de la India** (bot.) gardenia; **jazmín del Cabo** (bot.) Cape jasmine; **jazmín silvestre** (bot.) yellow jasmine
jazz *m* (mus.) jazz
jazz-band *m* jazz band
J.C. abr. of **Jesucristo**
je *interj* var. of **ji**
jebe *m* rock alum; India rubber; (bot.) rubber plant (*Hevea brasiliensis*)
jedive *m* khedive
jefa *f* female head or leader; **jefa de ruta** hostess (*on a bus*)
jefatura *f* chieftaincy, chieftainship; leadership; headquarters
jefe *m* chief, leader, head; boss; (her.) chief; (mil.) field officer; **en jefe** in chief; **mandar en jefe** (mil.) to be commander in chief; **quedar jefe** (Am.) to gamble away everything; **jefe de cocina** chef; **jefe de coro** choirmaster; **jefe de día** (mil.) officer of the day; **jefe de equipajes** (rail.) baggage master; **jefe de estación** (rail.) station agent, stationmaster; **jefe del estado** or **jefe del ejecutivo** chief executive; **jefe de meseros** (Am.) headwaiter; **jefe de redacción** editor in chief; **jefe de ruta** guide; hostess (*on a bus*); **jefe de tren** (rail.) conductor; **jefe supremo** commander in chief
Jefté *m* (Bib.) Jephthah
Jehová *m* Jehovah
jehovismo *m* Jehovism
Jehú *m* (Bib.) Jehu
jeito *m* anchovy net, sardine net
jeja *f* white wheat
jején *m* (ent.) gnat, mosquito
jemal *adj* as long as the distance between tip of thumb and tip of forefinger
jeme *m* space between tip of thumb and tip of forefinger when extended; (coll.) face (*of a woman*)
jenabe *m* or **jenable** *m* mustard
jengibre *m* (bot.) ginger (*plant, root, and spice*)
jeniquén *m* (Am.) henequen
jenízaro -ra *adj* mixed, hybrid; *m* Janizary
Jenofonte *m* Xenophon
jeque *m* sheik
jerapellina *f* old raggedy and torn garment
jerarca *m* hierarch; ruler
jerarquía *f* hierarchy; **de jerarquía** of importance, prominent
jerárquico -ca *adj* hierarchic or hierarchical
jerarquizar **§76** *va* to hierarchize
jerbo *m* (zool.) jerboa
jeremíaco -ca *adj* Jeremian or Jeremianic
jeremiada *f* (coll.) jeremiad
Jeremías *m* (Bib.) Jeremiah; (*l.c.*) *mf* (*pl:* **-as**) (coll.) constant complainer
jerez *m* sherry
jerezano -na *adj* (pertaining to) Jerez; *mf* native or inhabitant of Jerez
jerga *f* coarse cloth; straw mattress; corduroy; jargon (*of a trade or special group; gibberish*); **en jerga** (coll.) unfinished
jergal *adj* of a trade, of a profession (*said, e.g., of a word or idiom*)
jergón *m* straw mattress; (mineral.) jargon; (coll.) ill-fitting clothes; (coll.) lummox
Jericó *f* Jericho
jerifalte *m* var. of **gerifalte**
jerife *m* shereef
jerifiano -na *adj* sherifian
jerigonza *f* slang; jargon (*of a trade or special group*); (coll.) gibberish, jargon; (coll.) folly, piece of folly
jeringa *f* syringe; enema; gun (*for projecting grease, etc.*); (coll.) plague, annoyance; **jeringa de engrase** or **grasa** grease gun; **jeringa hipodérmica** hypodermic syringe
jeringación *f* syringing; injection; (coll.) plague, annoyance
jeringador -dora *adj* (coll.) plaguing, pestering; *mf* (coll.) plague, pest
jeringar **§59** *va* to syringe; to inject; to give an enema to; (coll.) to annoy, bore, molest; *vr* to give oneself an enema; (coll.) to be annoyed
jeringazo *m* injection, shot
jeringuear *va* (Am.) to plague, pester
jeringuilla *f* syringe (*for injecting fluids into body*); (bot.) syringa, mock orange
Jerjes *m* Xerxes
jerofante *m* var. of **hierofanta**
jeroglífico -ca *adj* hieroglyphic or hieroglyphical; *m* hieroglyphic; rebus
jerónimo -ma *adj & m* Hieronymite; (*cap.*) *m* Jerome
jerosolimitano -na *adj* (pertaining to) Jerusalem; *mf* native or inhabitant of Jerusalem
jerpa *f* (hort.) sterile shoot (*of vine*)
jersey *m* jersey (*sweater*)
Jerusalén *f* Jerusalem
Jesé *m* (Bib.) Jesse
Jesucristo *m* Jesus Christ
jesuíta *adj & m* Jesuit; (coll.) Jesuit (*intriguer*)
jesuítico -ca *adj* Jesuitic or Jesuitical; (coll.) Jesuitic or Jesuitical (*crafty*)
jesuitisa *f* Jesuitess
jesuitismo *m* Jesuitism; (coll.) jesuitism (*casuistry*)
Jesús *m* Jesus; bambino (*image of baby Jesus*); **en un decir Jesús** or **en un Jesús** in an instant; **hasta verte, Jesús mío** to the last drop; **¡Jesús, María y José!** my gracious!
jeta *f* pig face; pouched mouth; hog's snout; (coll.) phiz, mug; **estar con tanta jeta** (coll.) to make a long face; **poner jeta** (coll.) to pouch one's lips
jetón -tona or **jetudo -da** *adj* snouted; grim, gruff
Jetró *m* (Bib.) Jethro
Jezabel *f* (Bib.) Jezebel
Jhs. abr. of **Jesús**
ji *interj* he!; **¡ji, ji!** te-hee!; **¡ji, ji, ji!** he, he, he!
jíbaro -ra *adj & mf* (Am.) peasant
jibia *f* (zool.) cuttlefish
jibión *m* cuttlebone
Jibraltar var. of **Gibraltar**
jibraltareño -ña *adj & mf* var. of **gibraltareño**
jícara *f* chocolate cup; (Am.) calabash (*used as cup*)
jicarazo *m* blow with a chocolate cup; poisoning
jícaro *m* (Am.) calabash tree
jicotea *f* (zool.) mud turtle
jifa *f* offal (*of slaughtered animal*)
jiferada *f* blow with a slaughtering knife
jifería *f* slaughtering
jifero -ra *adj* (pertaining to the) slaughterhouse; (coll.) dirty, filthy, vile; *m* slaughtering knife; slaughterer, butcher
jifia *f* (ichth.) swordfish
jifosuro *m* (zool.) xiphosuran
jiga *f* var. of **giga**
jigote *m* var. of **gigote**
jiguilete *m* var. of **jiquilete**
jijallar *m* thicket of saltwort
jijallo *m* (bot.) saltwort
jilguero *m* (orn.) goldfinch, linnet
jimagua *adj & mf* (Am.) twin
jimelga *f* (naut.) fish (*of a mast*)
jimenzar **§31** *va* (prov.) to ripple (*flax*)
jimio *m* var. of **simio**
jinestada *f* sauce made of milk, rice flour, dates, spices, etc.
jineta *f* riding with stirrups high and legs bent; sergeant's shoulder knot; (zool.) genet; **tener los cascos a la jineta** (coll.) to be a scatterbrain, to be a harum-scarum
jinete *m* horseman, rider; cavalryman; purebred horse; *f* horsewoman
jineteada *f* (Am.) horsebreaking
jinetear *va* (Am.) to break in (*a horse*); *vn* to ride around on horseback, to show off one's horsemanship; *vr* (Am.) to be puffed up
jinglar *vn* to swing, to rock
jingoísmo *m* jingoism
jingoísta *adj* jingo, jingoist, jingoistic; *mf* jingo, jingoist
jínjol *m* var. of **azufaifa**
jinjolero *m* var. of **azufaifo**
jipato -ta *adj* (Am.) pale, wan; (Am.) insipid
jipi *m* (coll.) Panama hat
jipijapa *f* (bot.) jipijapa; strip of jipijapa straw; *m* jipijapa, Panama hat
jiquilete *m* (Am.) indigo plant

jira *f* slip, strip; picnic, outing; tour; trip; swing, political trip
jirafa *f* (zool.) giraffe
jirel *m* rich caparison
jíride *f* (bot.) gladdon, stinking iris
jirón *m* shred, tatter, tear; pennant; (sew.) facing (*of skirt*); (her.) gyron; (fig.) shred, drop, bit; **hacer jirones** to tear to shreds
jironado -da *adj* shredded, tattered, torn
jiste *m* barm, froth, foam (*of beer*)
jitomate *m* (Am.) tomato
jo *interj* whoa!
Joaquín *m* Joachim
Job *m* (Bib.) Job; (*l.c.*) *m* (*pl:* **jobs**) (fig.) Job (*very patient man*)
jobo *m* (bot.) hog plum, yellow mombin
jocoserio -ria *adj* seriocomic, jocoserious
jocosidad *f* jocosity; jocularity; joke, witticism
jocoso -sa *adj* jocose; jocular
jocotal *m* (bot.) Spanish plum (*tree*)
jocote *m* Spanish plum (*fruit*)
jocoyote *m* (Am.) var. of **socoyote**
jocundidad *f* jocundity
jocundo -da *adj* jocund
jofaina *f* washbowl, basin
jolgorio *m* (coll.) var. of **holgorio**
jolito *m* rest, calm; **en jolito** disappointed
joloano -na *adj* Suluan; *mf* Sulu, Suluan
jollín *m* (coll.) merriment, jollification, uproar
Jonás *m* (Bib.) Jonah
Jonatás *m* Jonathan
Jonia *f* see **jonio**
jónico -ca *adj* Ionian, Ionic; (arch.) Ionic; *mf* Ionian
jonio -nia *adj* Ionian, Ionic; *mf* Ionian; (*cap.*) *f* Ionia
jonrón *m* (baseball) home run
Jordán *m* Jordan (*river*); (fig.) fountain of youth; (fig.) rebirth, regeneration; **ir al Jordán** (coll.) to be rejuvenated, to be born again
Jordania *f* Jordan (*country*)
jordano -na *adj* & *mf* Jordanian
jorfe *m* sustaining wall; cliff, precipice
Jorja *f* Georgia (*woman's name*)
Jorge *m* George
jorguín *m* wizard, sorcerer
jorguina *f* witch, sorceress
jorguinería *f* witchcraft, sorcery
jornada *f* day's journey; journey, trip, stage; workday (*number of hours of work*); day; session; battle; lifetime, span of life; passing (*death*); summer residence (*of diplomat or diplomatic corps*); undertaking; occasion, circumstance, event; (mil.) expedition; (archaic) act (*of a play*); **a grandes** or **a largas jornadas** by forced marches; **al fin de la jornada** in the end, at the wind-up; **caminar por sus jornadas** to proceed with circumspection; **echar** or **hacer mala jornada** to get nowhere, to make little or no progress; **jornada ordinaria** full time
jornal *m* salary, wage; day's wages; day's work; **a jornal** by the day; **jornal mínimo** minimum wage
jornalar *va* to hire by the day
jornalero *m* day laborer
joroba *f* hump; (coll.) annoyance, bother
jorobado -da *adj* humpbacked, hunchbacked; (coll.) annoyed, bothered, in a jam; *mf* humpback, hunchback
jorobadura *f* (coll.) annoyance, bother
jorobar *va* (coll.) to annoy, bother
jorongo *m* (Am.) poncho; (Am.) woolen blanket
jorrar *va* (archaic) to tow; see **red**
jorro *adj masc* (Am.) poor (*tobacco*); see **red**
jos *mpl* josses (*Chinese household divinities*)
josa *f* unfenced orchard
Josafat *m* (Bib.) Jehoshaphat
José *m* Joseph; **José de Arimatea** (Bib.) Joseph of Arimathea
Josefa or **Josefina** *f* Josephine
Josefo *m* Josephus
Josías *m* (Bib.) Josiah
jostrado -da *adj* banded and round-headed (*shaft*)
Josué *m* (Bib.) Joshua
jota *f* j (*letter*); jota (*Spanish dance*); jot, iota, tittle; vegetable soup; **no entender** or **no saber jota** or **una jota** (coll.) to be completely ignorant, to not know what is going on; **sin faltar una jota** (coll.) in minutest detail
jotacismo *m* use of **j** instead of **g** before **e** and **i**
jovada *f* (prov.) daywork (*of a pair of mules*)
Jove *m* (myth.) Jove
joven *adj* young; **ser joven de esperanzas** (coll.) to have a bright future; *mf* youth, young person; **de joven** as a youth, as a young man (or woman)
jovencísimo -ma *adj super* very young
jovial *adj* jovial; Jovian, Jovelike
jovialidad *f* joviality
joviano -na or **jovio -via** *adj* Jovian
joya *f* jewel, piece of jewelry; diamond brooch; gift, present; (arch. & arti.) astragal; (fig.) jewel (*person or thing*); **joyas** *fpl* trousseau; **joya de familia** heirloom; **joyas de fantasía** costume jewelry
joyante *adj* glossy (*silk*)
joyel *m* small jewel
joyelero *m* jewel case, casket
joyería *f* jewelry; jewelry shop; jewelry business
joyero -ra *mf* jeweler; *m* jewel case, casket; *f* (archaic) embroideress
joyo *m* (bot.) cockle
joyón *m* big, ugly jewel
joyuyo *m* (orn.) wood duck
juaguarzo *m* var. of **jaguarzo**
Juan *m* John; **Buen Juan** (coll.) sap, easy mark; **Juan de Gante** John of Gaunt; **Juan de las viñas** (fig.) puppet; **Juan Español** the Spanish people; the typical Spaniard; **Juan Lanas** (coll.) simpleton, poor devil; **Juan Palomo** (coll.) good-for-nothing
Juana *f* Jane, Jean, Joan; **juanas** *fpl* glove stretcher; **Juana de Arco** Joan of Arc, Jeanne d'Arc; **Juana la papisa** Pope Joan
juanete *m* bunion; high cheekbone; (naut.) topgallant; (naut.) topgallant sail; **juanete de proa** (naut.) foretopgallant sail; **juanete de sobremesana** (naut.) mizzen-topgallant sail; **juanete mayor** (naut.) main-topgallant sail
juanetero *m* (naut.) topman (*in charge of topgallants*)
juanetudo -da *adj* full of bunions
Juanillo *m* Jack, Johnny
Juanita *f* Jenny, Jeannette
Juanito *m* var. of **Juanillo**
juarda *f* stain, spot
juardoso -sa *adj* stained, spotted
jube *m* (arch.) jube, rood screen
jubete *m* mail-covered doublet
jubilación *f* retirement; pension
jubilado -da *adj* retired; *mf* pensioner
jubilamiento *m* var. of **jubilación**
jubilar *adj* jubilee (*e.g., indulgence*); *va* to retire; to pension; (coll.) to throw out, cast off; *vn* to rejoice; to retire; to be pensioned; *vr* to rejoice; to retire; to be pensioned; (Am.) to decline, go to pieces; (Am.) to play truant; (Am.) to be a past master (*in a game, vice, etc.*)
jubilate *m* Jubilate (*third Sunday after Easter*)
jubileo *m* (hist. & eccl.) jubilee; (coll.) great doings, much going and coming; **por jubileo** (coll.) once in a long while
júbilo *m* jubilation
jubiloso -sa *adj* jubilant
jubón *m* jerkin, tight-fitting jacket; **jubón de azotes** (coll.) public whipping
júcaro *m* tropical hardwood tree and its wood (*genus: Terminalia*)
Judá *m* (Bib.) Judah (*son of Jacob; kingdom; tribe*)
judaico -ca *adj* Judaic, Jewish; *f* spine of fossil sea urchin
judaísmo *m* Judaism
judaíta *mf* Judahite; Israelite
judaizante *adj* Judaizing; *mf* Judaizer, Judaist
judaizar §97 *vn* to Judaize; to boast of being a Jew (*said of a person born a Christian*)
Judas *m* (*pl:* **-das**) (Bib. & fig.) Judas; effigy of Judas burned during Holy Week; **estar hecho** or **parecer un Judas** (coll.) to be sloppy, to go around in rags; **Judas Iscariote** (Bib.) Judas Iscariot
Judea *f* Judea

judeo-español -ñola *adj* Judaeo-Spanish; *mf* Judaeo-Spaniard; *m* Judaeo-Spanish (*dialect*)
judería *f* Jewry (*ghetto; race, people*)
judía *f* see **judío**
judiada *f* Jewish act; (coll.) cruelty; (coll.) usury
judiar *m* bean patch
judicatura *f* judicature; judgeship
judicial *adj* judicial (*pertaining to courts, judges, etc.*)
judiciario -ria *adj* astrological; *m* astrologer
judío -a *adj* Jewish; Judean; usurious; *mf* Jew; Judean; usurer; **judío de señal** (hist.) converted Jew wearing distinguishing badge on shoulder; *m* (orn.) common ani; **Judío errante** Wandering Jew; *f* Jewess; (bot.) kidney bean, string bean, haricot; **judía de careta** (bot.) black-eyed bean; **judía de España** or **judía escarlata** (bot.) scarlet runner, kidney bean; **judía de la peladilla** (bot.) Lima bean
Judit *f* Judith
judo *m* judo
juego *m* play, playing; game; gambling; cards (*game*); set; suit, suite; movement, works; motion; play (*of water, light, colors, etc.*); hand (*quota of cards of one player*); (mach.) play; (sport) field, court, alley, etc. (*according to sport*); (sport) game (*certain number of points won*); (fig.) game (*e.g., diplomacy*); **a juego** to match, e.g., **un pañuelo a juego** a handkerchief to match; **conocerle a uno el juego** to be on to someone; **descubrir su juego** (cards & fig.) to show one's hand; **en juego** at stake; **hacer el juego a** to play into the hands of; **hacer juego** to match; **hacer juego con** to match, to go with; **hacer su juego** to have one's way; **no ser cosa de juego** to be no laughing matter; **por juego** in fun, for fun; **verle a uno el juego** to be on to someone; **juego carteado** card game not played for money; **juego de ajedrez** chess, game of chess; **juego de alcoba** bedroom suit; **juego de azar** game of chance; **juego de bolas** (mach.) ball bearing; **juego de bolos** bowling; **juego de comedor** dining-room suit; **juego de compadres** (coll.) collusion; **juego de damas** checkers, game of checkers; **juego de envite** game played for money, gambling game; **juego de escritorio** desk set; **juego de la cuna** cat's cradle; **juego de la pulga** tiddlywinks; **juego del salto** leapfrog; **juego del tres en raya** game similar to tick-tack-toe, which is played with movable pebbles or counters instead of written ciphers and crosses; **juego de manos** juggling, legerdemain, sleight of hand; **juego de naipes** cards, card game; **juego de niños** child's play (*something easy*); **juego de palabras** pun, play on words; **juego de pelota** ball (*game*); pelota; **juego de piernas** footwork (*in sports and dancing*); **juego de por ver** (Am.) game played for fun (*not for money*); **juego de prendas** forfeits, game of forfeits; **juego de suerte** game of chance; **juego de tejo** shuffleboard; **juego de timbres** (mus.) glockenspiel; **juego de vocablos** or **voces** pun, play on words; **juego limpio** fair play; **juego público** gambling house; **juegos de sociedad** parlor games; **juegos ístmicos** Isthmian games; **juegos malabares** juggling, jugglery; flimflam; **juegos olímpicos** (hist.) Olympian games, Olympic games; Olympic games (*of modern times*); **juegos pitios** Pythian games; **juego sucio** (sport) foul play
juerga *f* (coll.) carousal, spree; **ir de juerga** (coll.) to go on a spree; **juerga de borrachera** (coll.) drinking bout, binge
juerguista *adj* (coll.) carousing, roistering; *mf* (coll.) carouser, roisterer
juev. abr. of **jueves**
jueves *m* (*pl:* **-ves**) Thursday; **Jueves gordo** or **lardero** Thursday before Shrove Tuesday; **Jueves santo** Maundy Thursday, Holy Thursday
juez *m* (*pl:* **jueces**) judge; **juez arbitrador** or **árbitro** (law) umpire; **juez de guardia** coroner; **juez de instrucción** examining magistrate; **juez de línea** (football) field judge; **juez de llegada** (sport) goal judge; **juez de palo** (coll.) ignorant judge; **juez de paz** justice of the peace; **juez de salida** (sport) starter; **juez de tiempo** (sport) timekeeper
jugada *f* play; throw, stroke; **mala jugada** mean trick, dirty trick
jugador -dora *mf* player; gambler; **jugador de manos** juggler
jugar §58 *va* to play (*e.g., a card, a knight, a game of chess*); to gamble; to stake, to risk; to gamble away; to wield (*a sword*); to work; to move (*e.g., hands, toes*); to match for, e.g., **jugar a uno las bebidas** to match someone for the drinks; *vn* to play; to gamble; to work; to match; to figure; to come into action (*said of weapons and firearms*); **jugar a** to play (*cards, tennis, etc.*); **jugar con** to toy with (*a person, a person's affections*); to match; **jugar en** to have a hand in; **jugar fuerte** or **grueso** to gamble heavily; *vr* to gamble, to risk (*one's salary, one's life*); to be at stake; **jugarse el todo por el todo** to stake all, to shoot the works
jugarreta *f* (coll.) bad play, poor play; (coll.) mean trick, dirty trick
juglandáceo -a or **juglándeo -a** *adj* (bot.) juglandaceous
juglar *m* (archaic) minstrel, jongleur; (archaic) juggler (*jester, buffoon*)
juglaresco -ca *adj* of minstrels, of jongleurs
jugo *m* juice; gravy; sauce; (fig.) gist, essence, substance; **en su jugo** (cook.) au jus; **sacar el jugo a** (fig.) to get the substance out of; **jugo de muñeca** (coll.) elbow grease; **jugo gástrico** (physiol.) gastric juice; **jugo pancreático** (physiol.) pancreatic juice
jugosidad *f* juiciness; substance, importance
jugoso -sa *adj* juicy; substantial, important
juguete *m* toy, plaything; joke, jest; gay song; (theat.) skit; (fig.) plaything, sport (*e.g., of fortune, passion, wind*); **de juguete** toy, e.g., **soldado de juguete** toy soldier; **por juguete** for fun, in fun; **juguete de movimiento** mechanical toy
juguetear *vn* to play, frolic, romp; (poet.) to blow lightly
jugueteo *m* playing, frolicking, romping
juguetería *f* toy business; toyshop; toys
juguetero -ra *adj* toy (*e.g., industry*); *mf* toy dealer; *m* whatnot, étagère
juguete-sorpresa *m* (*pl:* **juguetes-sorpresa**) jack-in-the-box
juguetón -tona *adj* playful, frisky
juicio *m* judgment; (law) trial; (log. & theol.) judgment; **asentar el juicio** to settle down, to come to one's senses; **el juicio final** or **universal** the Judgment or the Last Judgment; **estar en su cabal juicio** to be in one's right mind; **estar fuera de juicio** to be out of one's mind; **pedir en juicio** (law) to sue; **perder el juicio** to lose one's mind; **juicio de Dios** (hist.) ordeal (*to test guilt or innocence*)
juicioso -sa *adj* judicious, wise
Jul. abr. of **julio**
julán *m* (zool.) piddock
julepe *m* julep; mint julep; (coll.) scolding; (Am.) scare
Julián *m* Julian
juliano -na *adj* Julian; (*cap.*) *m* Julian; **Juliano el Apóstata** Julian the Apostate; *f* Juliana; (*l.c.*) *f* (bot.) damewort
Julieta *f* Juliet
julio *m* July; (phys.) joule; (*cap.*) *m* Julius
julo *m* lead cow, lead mule
juma *f* (Am.) drunk, spree
jumento -ta *mf* ass, donkey; *m* (coll.) ass, fool
jumera *f* (coll.) drunk, spree
Jun. abr. of **junio**
juncáceo -a *adj* (bot.) juncaceous
juncada *f* cylindrical fritter
juncal *adj* willowy, rushy; willowy (*form, body*); (prov.) handsome, elegant; *m* growth of rushes
juncar *m* clump of rushes, growth of rushes
júnceo -a *adj* rushy, rushlike
juncia *f* (bot.) sedge; **vender juncia** (coll.) to boast, to brag
juncial *m* growth of sedge
junciana *f* (coll.) vain show, bluff

juncino -na *adj* rushy
junco *m* junk (*Chinese ship*); rattan (*cane*); (bot.) rush, bulrush (*Juncus effusus*); **junco de esteras** (bot.) rush, bulrush (*Juncus effusus*); **junco de Indias** (bot.) rattan; **junco de laguna** (bot.) bulrush, tule; **junco florido** (bot.) flowering rush; **junco marinero, marino** or **marítimo** (bot.) bulrush, tule; **junco oloroso** (bot.) camel grass
juncoso -sa *adj* rushy
jungla *f* jungle
junio *m* June
júnior *m* (sport) novice
junípero *m* var. of **enebro**
Juno *f* (myth.) Juno
junquera *f* (bot.) rush, bulrush (*Juncus effusus*)
junqueral *m* growth of rushes
junquillo *m* (bot.) jonquil; (bot.) rattan palm; (arch.) bead; (carp.) strip of wood, reglet (*to fill or cover joints*); **junquillo amarillo** (bot.) jonquil; **junquillo de noche** (bot.) gladiolus (*Gladiolus tristis*); **junquillo oloroso** (bot.) jonquil
junquito *m* (orn.) junco
junta *f* see **junto**
juntamente *adv* together; at the same time
juntar *va* to join, unite; to gather, to gather together; to half-close; *vr* to gather, to gather together; to associate closely; to copulate
juntera *f* (carp.) jointer
junterilla *f* (carp.) rabbet plane
junto -ta *adj* joined, united; **juntos -tas** *adj pl* together; *f* meeting, conference; board, council; session; union, junction; seam; joint; washer, gasket; (arch.) joint; (Am.) junction (*of two rivers*); **junta a inglete** (carp.) miter, miter joint; **junta de cardán** (aut.) universal joint; **junta de comercio** board of trade; **junta de sanidad** board of health; **junta universal** (aut.) universal joint; **junto** *adv* together, at the same time; **en** or **por junto** all together, all told; **todo junto** at the same time, all at once; **junto a** near, close to; **junto con** along with, together with
juntura *f* joint, junction, seam; coupling; (anat.) joint
Júpiter *m* (astr. & myth.) Jupiter; **Júpiter tonante** or **tronante** (myth.) the Thunderer, Jupiter Tonans
jura *f* oath; pledge of allegiance
jurado -da *adj* sworn; **tenérsela jurada a** (coll.) to have it in for; *m* jury; juror, juryman
jurador -dora *mf* swearer
juramentar *va* to swear in; *vr* to take an oath, to be sworn in
juramento *m* oath; curse, swearword; **prestar juramento** to take oath; **prestar juramento a** to administer an oath to; **juramento de Hipócrates** Hippocratic oath
jurar *va* to swear; to swear allegiance to; to swear in; *vn* to swear (*to take an oath; to curse*); **jurar** + *inf* to swear to + *inf*, e.g., **juró decir la verdad** he swore to tell the truth; *vr* to swear; **jurársela a uno** or **jurárselas a uno** (coll.) to have it in for someone, to swear to get even with someone
jurásico -ca *adj & m* (geol.) Jurassic
jurel *m* (ichth.) caranx, saurel, yellow jack; (Am.) fear, terror; (Am.) drunk, drunkenness
jurero *m* (Am.) false witness
jurídico -ca *adj* juridical
jurisconsulto *m* jurisconsult
jurisdicción *f* jurisdiction
jurisdiccional *adj* jurisdictional
jurisperito *m* legal expert
jurisprudencia *f* jurisprudence
jurista *mf* jurist
juro *m* right of perpetual ownership; **de juro** with certainty, inevitably
jusbarba *f* (bot.) butcher's-broom
justa *f* see **justo**
justador *m* jouster, tilter
justamente *adv* justly; tightly; just; just at that time
justar *vn* to joust, to tilt
justicia *f* justice; rightness; (coll.) execution (*putting to death*); **de justicia** justly, deservedly; **hacer justicia a** to do justice to; **ir por justicia** to go to court, to bring suit; *m* judge, justice; (archaic) bailiff
justiciable *adj* actionable; justiciable
justiciazgo *m* judgeship, justiceship
justiciero -ra *adj* just, fair; stern, righteous
justificable *adj* justifiable
justificación *f* justification; (print.) justification
justificado -da *adj* just, right (*act*); just, upright (*person*)
justificante *m* written proof
justificar §86 *va* to justify; (print.) to justify
justificativo -va *adj* justificatory
justillo *m* waist, underwaist
Justiniano *m* Justinian
justipreciar *va* to estimate with precision
justiprecio *m* precise estimation
justo -ta *adj* just; exact, correct; tight; *mf* righteous person; **los justos** the just; *f* joust; contest; **justo** *adv* just; tight; right, in tune; in straitened circumstances
Jutlandia *f* Jutland
juto -ta *mf* Jute
Juvenal *m* Juvenal
juvenil *adj* juvenile, youthful
juventud *f* youth (*early period of life; early period; young people*)
juvia *f* (bot.) Brazil-nut tree
juzgado *m* court, tribunal
juzgamundos *m* (*pl:* **-dos**) (coll.) faultfinder
juzgar §59 *va & vn* to judge; **a juzgar por** judging by or from; **juzgar de** to judge, pass judgment on

K

K, k *f* twelfth letter of the Spanish alphabet
kan *m* khan (*title; caravansary*)
kanato *m* khanate
kantiano -na *adj & mf* Kantian
kantismo *m* Kantianism
kantista *adj & mf* var. of **kantiano**
kc. abr. of **kilociclo**
kepis *m* (*pl:* **-pis**) var. of **quepis**
keratina *f* var. of **queratina**
kermes *m* (*pl:* **-mes**) var. of **quermes**
kermesse *f* var. of **quermese**
keroseno *m* kerosene, coal oil
kg. abr. of **kilogramo**
kgm. abr. of **kilográmetro**
kilate *m* var. of **quilate**
kiliárea *f* kiliare
kilo *m* kilo (*kilogram*)
kiloamperio *m* kiloampere
kilocaloría *f* (phys.) kilogram calorie, kilocalorie
kilociclo *m* kilocycle
kilográmetro *m* kilogrammeter
kilogramo *m* kilogram or kilogramme
kilolitro *m* kiloliter
kilometraje *m* kilometrage, distance in kilometers
kilométrico -ca *adj* kilometric
kilómetro *m* kilometer
kilotonelada *f* kiloton
kilovatio *m* kilowatt
kilovatio-hora *m* (*pl:* **kilovatios-hora**) kilowatt-hour
kilovoltio *m* kilovolt
kimógrafo *m* var. of **quimógrafo**
kimono *m* var. of **quimono**
kindergarten *m* kindergarten
kinescopio *m* (telv.) kinescope
kino *m* var. of **quino**
kiosko *m* var. of **quiosco**
kirguís *m* Kirghiz
Kirie *m* (eccl.) Kyrie
kiwi *m* (orn.) kiwi
kl. abr. of **kilolitro**
klistrón *m* (phys.) klystron
km. abr. of **kilómetro**
kodak *m & f* kodak
kph. abr. of **kilómetros por hora**
krach *m* var. of **crac**
Kremlín *m* Kremlin
kulak *m* kulak (*well-to-do Russian peasant*)
kurdo -da *adj & mf* var. of **curdo**
kv. abr. of **kilovatio**

L

L, l *f* thirteenth letter of the Spanish alphabet
la *art def fem* the; *pron pers fem* her, it; you; *pron dem fem* the one, that, e.g., **la de mi hermano** that of my brother
Labán *m* (Bib.) Laban
lábaro *m* labarum; (hist.) labarum
labela *f* (ent.) labellum
labelo *m* (bot.) labellum
laberíntico -ca *adj* labyrinthine, mazy
laberinto *m* labyrinth, maze; (anat. & mach.) labyrinth; **el laberinto de Creta** (myth.) the Labyrinth
labia *f* (coll.) fluency, smoothness (*in speech*)
labiado -da *adj* (anat., zool. & bot.) labiate; *f* (bot.) labiate
labial *adj* & *f* labial
labializar §76 *va* (phonet.) to labialize
labiérnago *m* (bot.) phillyrea, mock privet
labihendido -da *adj* harelipped
lábil *adj* liable to slip; unstable; (chem.) labile
labilidad *f* lability
labio *m* lip; lip, brim (*of glass or tumbler*); (anat., bot. & zool.) labium; (mach.) lip; (surg.) lip (*of wound*); (fig.) lips (*words, speech*); **labios** *mpl* (fig.) lips (*words, speech*); **chuparse los labios** to smack one's lips; **lamerse los labios** to lick one's lips; **leer en los labios** to lip-read; **morderse los labios** (coll.) to bite one's tongue; **no morderse los labios** (coll.) to speak out, to be outspoken; **labio inferior** lower lip; **labio leporino** harelip; **labio superior** upper lip
labiodental *adj* & *f* (phonet.) labiodental
labiolectura *f* lip reading
labioso -sa *adj* (Am.) fluent, smooth
labor *f* labor, work; farm work, farming, tilling; needlework, embroidery, fancywork; sewing school for little girls; thousand tiles, thousand bricks; **labores** *fpl* (min.) workings; **labor blanca** linen work, linen embroidery; **labor de ganchillo** crocheting
laborable *adj* workable; arable, tillable; work (*day*)
laboral *adj* (pertaining to) labor
laborante *adj* working; *m* political henchman
laborar *va* to work; *vn* to work; to scheme
laboratorio *m* laboratory
laborear *va* to work; (min.) to work (*a mine*); *vn* (naut.) to reeve
laboreo *m* working; tilling; (min.) working, exploitation; (naut.) reeving
laboriosidad *f* laboriousness
laborioso -sa *adj* laborious
laborismo *m* British Labour Party
laborista *adj* Labor (*party*); *mf* Laborite
labra *f* working, carving
labrada *f* see **labrado**
labradero -ra *adj* workable; arable, tillable
labradío -a *adj* arable, tillable; *m* tillable soil
labrado -da *adj* worked, wrought, fashioned; carved; figured, embroidered; *m* working, carving; cultivated field; **labrado de madera** wood carving; *f* fallow ground (*to be sown the following year*)
labrador -dora *adj* work; farm; *mf* farmer; peasant; *m* plowman; **el Labrador** Labrador (*in Newfoundland*); *f* (slang) hand
labradoresco -ca *adj* farm, peasant
labradorita *f* (mineral.) labradorite
labrantín *m* small farmer, poor farmer
labrantío -a *adj* & *m* var. of **labradío**
labranza *f* farming; farm, farm land; work
labrar *va* to work, to fashion; to carve; to till; to plow; to build; to cause, bring about; **sin labrar** crude, unfinished; *vn* to make a lasting impression; *vr* to carve out (*e.g., a future, a fortune*)
labriego -ga *mf* peasant
labro *m* (ichth.) wrasse; (zool.) labrum
labrusca *f* wild grapevine; (bot.) fox grape; (bot.) ivy vine (*Ampelopsis cordata*)
laca *f* lac (*resinous substance; color*); lacquer (*varnish and object coated with lacquer*); **laca de uñas** nail polish; **laca en grano** grained lac, seed-lac; **laco en palo** or **en rama** stick-lac
lacayo *m* lackey, footman, groom; knot of ribbons
lacayuno -na *adj* lackey, servile
lacear *va* to trim or bedeck with bows; to tie with a bow; to drive (*game*) within shot; to trap or snare (*small game*)
lacedemón *adj masc* & *m* Lacedaemonian
Lacedemonia, la see **lacedemonio**
lacedemónico -ca *adj* Lacedaemonian
lacedemonio -nia *adj* & *mf* Lacedaemonian; **la Lacedemonia** Lacedaemon
laceración *f* laceration
lacerar *va* to lacerate; (fig.) to damage (*honor, reputation, etc.*); *vn* to have lots of trouble, to be in want
laceria *f* trouble, bother, worry; poverty, want
lacería *f* bows, ornamental bows; (arch.) interlacery
lacerioso -sa *adj* troubled, worried; poor, needy
lacero *m* lassoer, roper; dogcatcher; poacher
lacinia *f* (bot.) lacinia
laciniado -da *adj* (bot.) laciniate
lacio -cia *adj* withered, faded; flaccid, languid; straight, lank (*hair*); **el Lacio** Latium
lacón *m* picnic (*shoulder of pork*)
Laconia *f* see **laconio**
lacónico -ca *adj* laconic
laconio -nia *adj* & *mf* Laconian; (*cap.*) *f* Laconia
laconismo *m* laconism
lacra *f* mark (*left by illness*), fault, defect; (Am.) sore, ulcer; (Am.) scab
lacrar *va* to lay low, to strike down; to damage, hurt; to seal (*with sealing wax*); *vr* to be stricken
lacre *m* sealing wax
lácrima *f* (archaic) tear; **lácrima cristi** Lachryma Christi (*wine*)
lacrimal *adj* lachrymal, tearful
lacrimatorio -ria *adj* & *m* lachrymatory
lacrimógeno -na *adj* tear, tear-producing
lacrimoso -sa *adj* lachrymose, tearful
lactación *f* var. of **lactancia**
lactama *f* (biochem.) lactam
lactancia *f* lactation
lactar *va* & *vn* to suckle
lactasa *f* (biochem.) lactase
lactato *m* (chem.) lactate
lácteo -a *adj* lacteous, milky
lactescencia *f* lactescence
lactescente *adj* lactescent; (bot.) lactescent
lacticinio *m* milk, milk food
lacticinoso -sa *adj* milky
láctico -ca *adj* lactic
lactífero -ra *adj* lactiferous
lactobacilina *f* acidophilus milk
lactoflavina *f* lactoflavin
lactómetro *m* lactometer
lactona *f* (chem.) lactone
lactosa *f* (chem.) lactose
lactumen *m* (path.) milk crust
lacunario *m* var. of **lagunar**
lacustre *adj* lacustrine; (geol.) lacustrine
lacha *f* (ichth.) anchovy; (ichth.) herring; (slang) shame; (dial.) ugly look; **ser de poca lacha** (coll.) to not amount to much
lada *f* (bot.) rockrose
ládano *m* labdanum

ladear *va* to tip, to tilt; to bend, to lean; *vn* to tip, to tilt; to bend, to lean; to go down; to turn away, to turn off; to deviate (*said of compass needle*); *vr* to tip, to tilt; to bend, to lean; to be even, be equal; (fig.) to lean (*to an opinion, party, etc.*); (Am.) to fall in love; **ladearse con** (coll.) to go at or to the side of; (coll.) to fall out with
ladeo *m* tipping, tilting; bending, leaning; bent, inclination
ladera *f* see **ladero**
ladería *f* (archaic) small plain on mountainside
ladero -ra *adj* side, lateral; *f* slope, hillside
ladierno *m* var. of **aladierna**
ladilla *f* (ent.) crab louse; **pegarse como ladilla** (coll.) to stick like a leech
ladillo *m* (print.) sidenote
ladino -na *adj* sly, cunning, crafty; fluent; foreign-language-speaking; (Am.) Ladino; *m* Ladin (*Romansh*); Ladino (*mixed Spanish and Hebrew*); (Am.) Ladino
lado *m* side; direction; room, space; mat (*used as side of cart*); favor, protection; (geom.) side; **lados** *mpl* advisers, backers; **al lado de** by the side of; **dejar a un lado** to skip, to leave aside; **de lado** tilted; square, e.g., **ocho pulgadas de lado** eight inches square; **de otro lado** on the other hand; **de un lado** on the one hand; **echar a un lado** to cast aside, to neglect; to wind up, bring to an end; **hacer lado** to make room; **hacerse a un lado** to step aside; **mirar de lado** or **de medio lado** to look askance at; to sneak a look at; **ponerse al lado de** to take sides with; **por el lado de** in the direction of; **por todos lados** on all sides; **tener lado izquierdo** (coll.) to have a lot of courage; **tirar por su lado** to pull for oneself; **lado débil** weak side, weak point; **lado de la epístola** (eccl.) Epistle side; **lado del evangelio** (eccl.) Gospel side
ladón *m* var. of **lada**
ladra *f* barking
ladrador -dora *adj* barking; (coll.) scowling
ladrar *va* to bark (*insults, orders, etc.*); *vn* to bark; (coll.) to bark (*to threaten idly*)
ladrear *vn* to keep on barking
ladrería *f* (path.) leprosy; (vet.) swine cysticercosis
ladrido *m* bark, barking; (coll.) blame, slander
ladrillado *m* brick floor, tile floor
ladrillal *m* brickyard
ladrillar *m* brickyard; *va* to pave with bricks; to brick
ladrillazo *m* blow with a brick
ladrillero -ra *mf* brickmaker; brick dealer; *f* brick mold
ladrillo *m* brick; tile; cake (*e.g., of chocolate*); **ladrillo de fuego** or **ladrillo refractario** firebrick
ladrilloso -sa *adj* brick; brick-red
ladrón -drona *adj* thieving, thievish; *mf* thief; *m* sluice gate; run (*on side of candle*); **ladrón de corazones** lady-killer
ladronear *vn* to go about thieving
ladronera *f* den of thieves; theft, robbery; bank, child's bank; sluice gate; (fort.) machicolation
ladronería *f* thievery; den of thieves; gang of thieves
ladronerío *m* (Am.) gang of thieves; (Am.) wave of thievery
ladronesco -ca *adj* (coll.) thieves'; *f* (coll.) gang of thieves
ladronicio *m* var. of **latrocinio**
ladronzuelo -la *mf* petty thief
lagaña *f* var. of **legaña**
lagar *m* wine press, olive press, apple press; winery; olive farm
lagarada *f* pressing of wine
lagarejo *m* trough for pressing wine; **hacer lagarejos a** (coll.) to squirt grape juice in the face of; **hacerse lagarejo** (coll.) to become bruised or crushed (*said of grapes*); (coll.) to roughhouse
lagarero *m* wine presser, olive presser
lagareta *f* trough for pressing wine; pool, puddle
lagarta *f* female lizard; (ent.) gypsy moth; (coll.) sly woman
lagartado -da *adj* var. of **alagartado**
lagartero -ra *adj* lizard-hunting; *f* lizard hole
lagartija *f* (zool.) green lizard; (zool.) wall lizard
lagartijero -ra *adj* lizard-hunting
lagarto *m* (zool.) lizard; (coll.) sly fellow; **lagarto cornudo** (zool.) horned toad; **lagarto de Indias** (zool.) alligator
lagena *f* (zool.) lagena
lago *m* lake; **el lago de Constanza** Lake of Constance; **Grandes Lagos** Great Lakes; **Gran Lago Salado** Great Salt Lake; **lago de amor** (her.) wake knot; **lago de Aral** Lake Aral; **lago de leones** (archaic) cave or den of lions; **lago de Tiberíades** Sea of Tiberias, Sea of Galilee
lagotear *va & vn* (coll.) to flatter
lagotería *f* (coll.) flattery
lagotero -ra *adj* (coll.) flattering; *mf* (coll.) flatterer
lágrima *f* tear; drop; tear (*of sap or juice*); juice exuded by ripe grapes; **beberse las lágrimas** (coll.) to hold back one's tears; **deshacerse en lágrimas** to weep bitterly; **llorar a lágrima viva** to shed bitter tears; **mover a lágrimas** to move to tears; **lágrima de Salomón** (bot.) lily of the valley; **lágrimas de cocodrilo** crocodile tears; **lágrimas de David** or **de Job** (bot.) Job's-tears
lagrimable *adj* tearful, deplorable
lagrimal *adj* lachrymal; (anat.) lachrymal; *m* (anat.) lachrymal caruncle
lagrimar *vn* to weep
lagrimear *vn* to weep easily, to be tearful; to run (*said of the eyes*)
lagrimeo *m* weeping; flow of tears (*from an illness*)
lagrimón *m* (iron.) tear, big tear
lagrimoso -sa *adj* tearful; watery (*eyes*)
laguna *f* lagoon; lacuna, gap; (anat., bot. & zool.) lacuna
lagunajo *m* puddle, pool
lagunar *m* (arch.) lacunar
lagunero -ra *adj* (pertaining to a) lagoon
lagunoso -sa *adj* full of lagoons
laical *adj* lay, laic
laicismo *m* secularism
laicista *adj & mf* secularist
laicización *f* laicization
laicizar §76 *va* to laicize
laico -ca *adj*, lay, laic; *mf* lay person, laic
laísmo *m* use of **la** and **las** as indirect objects
laísta *mf* user of **la** and **las** as indirect objects
laja *f* slab, flagstone; (naut.) stone flat
lakistas *mpl* Lake poets (*Wordsworth, Coleridge, and Southey*)
lama *m* lama (*Buddhist priest in Tibet*); *f* mud, slime, ooze; surface film; lamé (*fabric*); (bot.) sea lettuce
lamaísmo *m* Lamaism
lamaísta *adj & mf* Lamaist
lamarquismo *m* Lamarckianism or Lamarckism
lamarquista *adj & mf* Lamarckian
lamasería *f* lamasery
lambel *m* (her.) label, lambel
Lamberto *m* Lambert
lambrequín *m* lambrequin; (her.) lambrequin
lambrija *f* worm; (coll.) skinny person
lameculos *mf* (*pl:* **-los**) (coll.) bootlicker
lamedal *m* mudhole
lamedero *m* salt lick
lamedor -dora *adj* licking; *mf* licker; *m* syrup; ruse, chicanery; **dar lamedor** (coll.) to lose at the beginning in order to take in one's opponent
lamedura *f* (act of) licking
lamelar *adj* lamellar
lamelibranquio -quia *adj & m* (zool.) lamellibranch
lamentable *adj* lamentable
lamentación *f* lamentation; **Lamentaciones de Jeremías** (Bib.) Lamentations
lamentador -dora *adj* lamenting, mourning; *mf* lamenter, mourner
lamentar *va, vn & vr* to lament, to mourn; **lamentar** + *inf* to be sorry to + *inf;* **lamentarse de** or **por** to lament, to mourn
lamento *m* lament

lamentoso -sa *adj* lamentable; plaintive, lamenting
lameplatos *mf* (*pl:* **-tos**) (coll.) glutton; (coll.) eater of scraps and leavings
lamer *va* to lick; to lap, lap against; to lick (*said of flames*); *vr* to lick (*e.g., one's lips*)
lamerón -rona *adj* (coll.) sweet-toothed
lametada *f* lick, lap
lametón *m* greedy lick
lamia *f* (ichth. & myth.) lamia
lamiáceo -a *adj* (bot.) lamiaceous
lamido -da *adj* scrawny, wan; prim; worn, frayed; smooth, sleek, glossy; (f.a.) fine; *f* (Am.) lick, licking
lamiente *adj* licking; lambent
lamiero *m* (bot.) dead nettle
lámina *f* lamina, sheet, plate, strip; engraving; copper plate; cut, picture; (anat., bot., geol. & zool.) lamina
laminación *f* lamination
laminadero *m* rolling mill (*factory*)
laminado -da *adj* laminate; laminated; *m* lamination; (metal.) rolling
laminador -dora *adj* laminating; rolling; *m* rolling-mill worker; rolling mill
laminar *adj* laminar; *va* to laminate; to roll (*iron or steel*); (dial.) to guzzle (*sweets*)
laminilla *f* lamella; (bot.) lamella
laminoso -sa *adj* laminose
lamiscar §86 *va* (coll.) to lick greedily
lamoso -sa *adj* muddy, slimy
lampacear *va* (naut.) to swab, to mop
lampadario *m* (eccl.) lampadary (*priest; lamppost*); floor lamp
lampante *adj* lamp (*oil*)
lampar *vr* var. of **alampar**
lámpara *f* lamp, light; grease spot, oil spot (*on clothing*); bough placed at door as love token; (rad.) vacuum tube; **atizar las lámparas** (coll.) to fill up the glasses again; **lámpara astral** astral lamp; **lámpara de Aladino** Aladdin's lamp; **lámpara de alcohol** spirit lamp; **lámpara de alto** stop light; **lámpara de arco** arc lamp, arc light; **lámpara de bolsillo** flashlight; **lámpara de carretera** (aut.) bright light; **lámpara de cruce** (aut.) dimmer; **lámpara de parada** stop light; **lámpara de pie** floor lamp; **lámpara de seguridad** safety lamp; **lámpara de sobremesa** table lamp; **lámpara de soldar** blowtorch; **lámpara de techo** ceiling light; (aut.) dome light; **lámpara de vapor de mercurio** (elec.) mercury-vapor lamp; **lámpara indicadora** pilot light; **lámpara inundante** floodlight; **lámpara piloto** or **lámpara testigo** pilot light
lamparería *f* lamp shop; lampistry
lamparero -ra *mf* lampmaker, lamp dealer; lampist, lamplighter
lamparilla *f* small lamp; rush candle; night light; (bot.) aspen; (coll.) glass of brandy
lamparín *m* lamp bracket (*used in churches*)
lamparista *mf* var. of **lamparero**
lamparón *m* big lamp; big grease spot; **lamparones** *mpl* (path.) king's evil; (vet.) streptothricosis
lampatán *m* (bot.) chinaroot
lampazo *m* (bot.) burdock; (bot.) toad lily, white water lily; (naut.) swab, mop; **lampazos** *mpl* (path.) rash
lampiño -ña *adj* hairless; beardless
lampista *mf* lampist, lamplighter; *m* plumber, tinsmith, electrician, glazier
lampistería *f* lampistry; shop of plumber, tinsmith, electrician, glazier, etc.
lampo *m* (poet.) flash of light
lamprea *f* (ichth.) lamprey; **lamprea glutinosa** (ichth.) hagfish
lamprear *va* to season with wine, honey, and sour gravy
lampreazo *m* (coll.) lashing, whipping
lamprehuela or **lampreílla** *f* (ichth.) sand pride, mud lamprey
lámpsana *f* (bot.) nipplewort
lana *f* wool; **lana de acero** steel wool; **lana de ceiba** kapok; **lana de escorias** mineral wool, rock wool; **lana de vidrio** glass wool; **lana mineral** mineral wool, rock wool
lanado -da *adj* lanate; *f* (arti.) sponge
lanaje *m* wool (*material and cloth made from it*)
lanar *adj* (pertaining to) wool; wool-bearing
lanaria *f* (bot.) soapwort
lancasteriano -na *adj & mf* Lancastrian
lance *m* cast, throw; catch, haul (*in a net*); play, move, turn, stroke; pass, chance, juncture; incident, event, episode; affair; row, quarrel; (taur.) move with cape; **de lance** cheap, at a bargain; second-hand; **echar buen lance** (coll.) to have a break; **tener pocos lances** (coll.) to be dull and uninteresting; **lance apretado** tight pinch, tight corner; **lance de fortuna** chance, accident; **lance de honor** affair of honor, challenge, duel
lanceado -da *adj* var. of **alanceado**
lancear *va* var. of **alancear**
lancéola *f* (bot.) ribwort
lanceolado -da *adj* (bot.) lanceolate
lancera *f* rack for lances
lancería *f* lances; troop of lancers
lancero *m* lancer, pikeman, spearman; **lanceros** *mpl* lancers (*dance and music*)
lanceta *f* (surg.) lancet
lancetada *f* or **lancetazo** *m* (surg.) lancing
lancetero *m* lancet case
lancinante *adj* piercing (*pain*)
lancinar *va* to lancinate, lacerate, pierce
lancurdia *f* small trout
lancha *f* barge, lighter; cutter; (naut.) longboat; (nav.) launch; snare for partridges; slab, flagstone; (Am.) mist, fog; (Am.) frost; **lancha automóvil** launch, motor launch; **lancha bombardera** or **cañonera** (nav.) gunboat; **lancha de auxilio** lifeboat (*stationed on shore*); **lancha de carreras** speedboat, race boat; **lancha de desembarco** (nav.) landing craft (*LCP*); **lancha de pesca** fishing smack; **lancha obusera** (nav.) gunboat; **lancha salvavidas** lifeboat (*on shipboard*); **lancha torpedera** (nav.) torpedo boat
lanchada *f* boatload
lanchaje *m* lighterage
lanchar *m* flagstone quarry; *vn* (Am.) to freeze
lanchazo *m* blow with a flat stone
lanchero *m* boatman, bargeman, lighterman
lanchón *m* lighter, flatboat
landa *f* swampland, moor
landgrave *m* landgrave
landgraviato *m* landgraviate
landó *m* (*pl:* **-dós**) landau
landre *f* small tumor (*in glands of neck, armpit, groin, etc.*); hidden pocket
landrilla *f* (vet.) tongue worm
lanería *f* wool shop; **lanerías** *fpl* woolens, woolen goods
lanero -ra *adj* (pertaining to) wool; *m* wool stapler; wool warehouse; (orn.) lanner
langarucho -cha *adj* (Am.) var. of **larguirucho**
langaruto -ta *adj* (coll.) var. of **larguirucho**
langosta *f* (ent.) locust; (zool.) spiny lobster; (coll.) scourge; (coll.) wastrel; **langosta a la Termidor** (cook.) lobster thermidor
langostera *f* lobster pot
langostín *m* or **langostino** *m* (zool.) prawn (*Peneus*)
langostón *m* (ent.) green grasshopper
langrave *m* var. of **landgrave**
languedociano -na *adj & mf* Languedocian
languescente *adj* languishing
languidecer §34 *vn* to languish
languidez *f* languor
lánguido -da *adj* languid, languorous
lanífero -ra *adj* (poet.) woolly; (bot.) downy
lanificación *f* or **lanificio** *m* woolwork
lanilla *f* nap; swanskin, canton flannel
lanolina *f* lanolin
lanosidad *f* (bot.) pubescence
lanoso -sa *adj* woolly
lansquenete *m* lansquenet (*foot soldier; card game*)
lantano *m* (chem.) lanthanum
lanudo -da *adj* woolly, fleecy
lanuginoso -sa *adj* lanuginous, downy
lanza *f* lance, pike; lancer, pikeman; wagon pole; nozzle; **medir lanzas** to cross swords; **romper lanzas** to intercede; to clear the way
lanzabombas *m* (*pl:* **-bas**) (aer.) bomb release; (mil.) trench mortar

lanzacabos *adj invar* line-throwing, life-saving
lanzacohetes *m* (*pl:* **-tes**) (mil.) rocket launcher
lanzada *f* see **lanzado**
lanzadera *f* shuttle; **parecer una lanzadera** (coll.) to buzz around, to hustle back and forth
lanzadero *m* log path, dragging road
lanzadiscos *m* (*pl:* **-cos**) var. of **lanzaplatos**
lanzado -da *adj* (sport) running (*start*); (naut.) raking, sloping (*mast*); *f* thrust or stroke with a lance
lanzador -dora *mf* thrower, hurler, slinger; **lanzador de lodo** (fig.) mudslinger; *m* (aer.) jettison gear; (baseball) pitcher
lanzaespumas *m* foam extinguisher
lanzafuego *m* linstock, match staff
lanzahélices *m* (*pl:* **-ces**) var. of **lanzaplatos**
lanzahidroplanos *m* (*pl:* **-nos**) (aer.) catapult
lanzallamas *m* (*pl:* **-mas**) (mil.) flame thrower
lanzamiento *m* launch, hurl, throw, fling; launching (*of a boat*); launching, shot (*of a rocket into space*); (law) dispossession; (naut.) steeve; (aer.) jump; (aer.) airdrop; (aer.) release
lanzaminas *m* (*pl:* **-nas**) (mil.) mine thrower; (nav.) mine layer
lanzaplatos *m* (*pl:* **-tos**) (sport) trap (*for throwing clay pigeons into the air*)
lanzar **§76** *va* to launch (*an arrow, curses, an offensive, a new product, a boat*); to hurl, to throw, to fling; to cast (*a glance*); to throw up, vomit; to put forth (*flowers, leaves*); to throw (*e.g., the javelin*); to toss, to toss out (*e.g., a remark*); (aer.) to airdrop; (aer.) to release (*a bomb*); (law) to dispossess; *vr* to launch; to hurl oneself, to throw oneself, to rush, to dash; to jump; (sport) to sprint; (aer.) to jump
Lanzarote *m* Lancelot (*of Round Table*)
lanzatorpedos *adj invar* (mil. & nav.) torpedo-launching; *m* (*pl:* **-dos**) (nav.) torpedo tube
lanzazo *m* thrust or stroke with a lance
lanzón *m* short and thick dagger
laña *f* clamp; rivet; green coconut
lañador *m* clamper; riveter (*of chinaware*)
lañar *va* to clamp; to rivet (*chinaware*); (prov.) to split (*a fish*) for salting
laocio -cia *adj & mf* Laotian
Laocoonte *m* (myth.) Laocoön
laosiano -na *adj & mf* var. of **laocio**
lapa *f* vegetable film (*produced by ferns, moss, etc.*); (bot.) burdock; (zool.) limpet
lapachar *m* swamp, marsh
lápade *f* (zool.) limpet
lapicero *m* pencil holder; mechanical pencil
lápida *f* tablet (*slab of stone for an inscription*); **lápida sepulcral** gravestone
lapidación *f* stoning to death, lapidation
lapidar *va* to stone to death, to lapidate
lapidario -ria *adj & m* lapidary
lapídeo -a *adj* stony, lapideous
lapidificación *f* lapidification
lapidificar **§86** *va & vr* to lapidify
lapilla *f* (bot.) hound's-tongue
lapislázuli *m* (mineral.) lapis lazuli
lápiz *m* (*pl:* **-pices**) black lead; pencil, lead pencil; **lápiz de labios** lipstick; **lápiz de pizarra** slate pencil; **lápiz de plomo** graphite; **lápiz encarnado** red ocher; **lápiz estíptico** styptic pencil; **lápiz labial** lipstick; **lápiz plomo** graphite; **lápiz rojo** red ocher; **lápiz tinta** indelible lead pencil
lapizar *m* black-lead mine, graphite mine; **§76** *va* to pencil
lapo *m* (coll.) blow with the flat of a sword, blow with a cane or stick; (Am.) drink, swig
lapón -pona *adj* Lappish; *mf* Lapp, Laplander (*native or inhabitant*); *m* Lappish (*language*)
Laponia *f* Lapland
lapso *m* lapse (*passing of time; slipping into guilt or error*)
laqueado -da *adj* lacquered; *m* lacquering
laquear *va* to lacquer
Laquesis *f* (myth.) Lachesis
lardar or **lardear** *va* (cook.) to baste; (cook.) to lard
lardo *m* back fat, lard fat
lardón *m* (print.) bite (*white spot*); marginal addition
lardoso -sa *adj* fatty, greasy
lares *mpl* home; **lares y penates** lares and penates (*household gods of Romans*)
larga *f* see **largo**
largada *f* (Am.) start, starting signal (*in a race*)
largamente *adv* at length, at large; at ease, in comfort; generously; long, for a long time
largar **§59** *va* to release, let go; to ease, slack, let up on; (coll.) to utter, let out; (naut.) to unfurl; (Am.) to throw; (Am.) to give, strike (*a hard blow*); *vr* to move away; (coll.) to beat it, sneak away; (naut.) to take to sea; (naut.) to come loose (*said of anchor*)
largo -ga *adj* long; generous, liberal; abundant; quick, ready; (coll.) shrewd, cunning; (phonet.) long; (naut.) loose, slack; **largos -gas** *adj pl* long, many (*e.g., years*); **a la larga** lengthwise; in the long run; in the end; at great length; **a lo más largo** at the most; **a lo largo** lengthwise; at great length; far away; **a lo largo de** along; along with; throughout; in the course of; far out in (*e.g., the sea*); **de largo** in a gown, in long robes; **hacerse a lo largo** (naut.) to get in the open sea; **ir para largo** to take a long time; **pasar de largo** to pass along, pass by, pass without stopping; to take a quick look, to be indifferent; to miss; **ponerse de largo** to come out, to make one's debut; **vestir de largo** to wear long clothes; **largo de lengua** loose-tongued; **largo de manos** ready-fisted; **largo de uñas** (coll.) light-fingered; **largo** *adv* abundantly; *m* length; (mus.) largo; **¡largo de aquí!** get out of here!; *f* long billiard cue; **dar largas a** to postpone, put off
largor *m* length
larguero *m* stringer; bolster; (aer.) longeron
largueza *f* length; largess, generosity
larguirucho -cha *adj* (coll.) gangling, lanky
larguísimo -ma *adj super* very long
largura *f* length
largurucho -cha *adj* (coll.) var. of **larguirucho**
lárice *m* (bot.) larch tree
laricino -na *adj* (pertaining to the) larch
laricio *m* var. of **lárice**
laringe *f* (anat.) larynx
laríngeo -a *adj* laryngeal
laringitis *f* (path.) laryngitis
laringología *f* laryngology
laringólogo -ga *mf* laryngologist
laringoscopia *f* laryngoscopy
laringoscópico -ca *adj* laryngoscopic
laringoscopio *m* laryngoscope
larva *f* (ent.) larva; mask; hobgoblin
larvado -da *adj* (path.) larval
larval *adj* larval
las *art def fem pl & pron pers & dem fem pl* see **los**
lasca *f* chip of stone; (dial.) slice
lascar *m* lascar (*East Indian sailor*); **§86** *va* to slacken, to pay out; (Am.) to bruise, to fray; *vr* (Am.) to bruise, to fray
lascivia *f* lasciviousness
lascivo -va *adj* lascivious; merry, playful, frisky
laserpicio *m* (bot.) laserwort
lasitud *f* lassitude
laso -sa *adj* tired, weary, exhausted; weak, wan, languid; untwisted (*silk thread*)
lastar *va* to pay up (*money*) for someone else; to suffer (*a punishment*) for someone else
lástima *f* pity; complaint; **dar, hacer** or **poner lástima** to be pitiful; **estar hecho una lástima** to be a sorry sight; **es lástima (que)** it is a pity (that); **¡qué lástima!** what a shame!, what a pity!; **¡qué lástima de saliva!** (coll.) what a waste of breath!
lastimador -dora *adj* hurtful, injurious
lastimadura *f* hurt, injury; bruise
lastimar *va* to hurt, injure; to bruise; to offend, to hurt; to pity; to move to pity; *vr* to hurt oneself; to bruise oneself; **lastimarse de** to complain about; to feel sorry for
lastimero -ra *adj* hurtful, injurious; pitiful, doleful
lastimoso -sa *adj* pitiful
lastón *m* (bot.) fescue grass
lastra *f* slab, flagstone
lastrado or **lastraje** *m* ballasting

lastrar *va* (naut. & aer.) to ballast
lastre *m* rock face; (naut. & aer.) ballast; (fig.) ballast (*steadiness*); (coll.) snack (*before drinking wine*); **lastre de agua** (naut. & aer.) water ballast
lasún *m* var. of **locha**
lat. abr. of **latín** & **latitud**
lata *f* see **lato**
latamente *adv* at great length; broadly
latastro *m* (arch.) plinth
lataz *m* (*pl:* **-taces**) (zool.) sea otter
latebra *f* den, hiding place
latebroso -sa *adj* furtive, secretive
latencia *f* (path.) latent period
latente *adj* latent
lateral *adj* lateral
lateranense *adj* Lateran
látex *m* (*pl:* **-tex**) (bot.) latex
latido *m* bark, yelp; beat, throb
latiente *adj* beating, throbbing
latifundio *m* large, run-down landed estate
latifundista *mf* large landowner
latigazo *m* lash; whipping (*of a cable*); lashing (*severe scolding*); crack of whip; (coll.) drink, swallow
látigo *m* whip, horsewhip; cinch strap; rope used in weighing with a steelyard; long plume around a hat; (coll.) bean pole (*person*)
latigudo -da *adj* (Am.) leathery
latiguear *va* (Am.) to lash; *vn* to crack a whip
latigueo *m* cracking a whip
latiguera *f* cinch strap
latiguillo *m* small whip; (bot.) stolon; (coll.) claptrap (*of an actor*); **de latiguillo** (coll.) claptrap
latín *m* Latin (*language*); (coll.) Latin word or phrase; **bajo latín** Low Latin; **decir** or **echar los latines a** (coll.) to marry, to officiate at the marriage of; (coll.) to bless; **saber latín** or **mucho latín** (coll.) to be very shrewd; **latín clásico** Classical Latin; **latín de cocina** dog Latin, hog Latin; **latín rústico** or **vulgar** Vulgar Latin
latinajo *m* (coll.) dog Latin; (coll.) Latin word or phrase
latinamente *adv* in Latin; in the Latin manner
latinar *vn* to speak or write Latin
latinear *vn* to speak or write Latin; (coll.) to use Latin words and phrases
latinidad *f* Latinity; Latin (*language*); **alta latinidad** period of Classical Latin; **baja** or **ínfima latinidad** Low Latin
latiniparla *f* excessive use of Latin words and phrases
latinismo *m* Latinism
latinista *mf* Latinist
latinización *f* Latinization
latinizar §76 *va* to Latinize; *vn* (coll.) to use Latin words or phrases; *vr* to Latinize
latino -na *adj* Latin; (naut.) lateen; *mf* Latin (*person*)
Latinoamérica *f* Latin America
latinoamericano -na *adj* Latin-American; *mf* Latin American
latir *va* (Am.) to annoy, bore; *vn* to bark, yelp; to beat, throb
latitud *f* latitude; (fig.) latitude (*freedom, scope; climate, region*)
latitudinal *adj* latitudinal
latitudinario -ria *adj & mf* latitudinarian
latitudinarismo *m* latitudinarianism
lato -ta *adj* broad; (fig.) broad (*meaning of a word*); *f* log; batten, lath; tin plate; tin, tin can; (coll.) annoyance, bore; **estar en la lata** (Am.) to be penniless
latón *m* brass; (dial.) hackberry (*fruit*); **latón en hojas** or **planchas** latten; **latón rojo** red brass
latonería *f* brasswork; brassworks; brassware
latonero *m* brassworker, brazier; (dial.) hackberry, nettle tree
latoso -sa *adj* (coll.) annoying, boring
latría *f* (theol.) latria
latrocinio *m* thievery; thievishness
latvio -via *adj & mf* Latvian; (*cap.*) *f* Latvia
laucha *f* (Am.) mouse
laúd *m* (mus.) lute; (naut.) catboat; (zool.) leatherback
laudabilidad *f* laudability
laudable *adj* laudable
láudano *m* (pharm.) laudanum
laudar *va* (law) to render (*a decision*), to make (*an award*)
laudatorio -ria *adj* laudatory; *f* eulogy
laude *f* (archeol.) tombstone; **laudes** *fpl* (eccl.) lauds; **tocar a laudes** (coll.) to sing one's own praises
laudo *m* (law) decision, award, finding
launa *f* sheet of metal; slate clay; splint (*of ancient armor*)
lauráceo -a *adj* (bot.) lauraceous
láurea *f* see **láureo**
laureado -da *adj* laureate; laureled; *mf* laureate; (*cap.*) *f* military cross of Saint Ferdinand
laureando *m* graduate, candidate for a degree
laurear *va* to crown with laurel; to trim or adorn with laurel; to reward, honor, decorate
lauredal *m* growth of laurels
laurel *m* (bot.) laurel; (fig.) laurels (*of fame or victory*); **dormirse sobre sus laureles** to rest or sleep on one's laurels; **laurel cerezo** or **real** (bot.) cherry laurel; **laurel rosa** (bot.) oleander, rosebay
laurentino -na *adj* Laurentian; (geol.) Laurentian; *m* (geol.) Laurentian
láureo -a *adj* (pertaining to) laurel; *f* laurel wreath
lauréola *f* crown of laurel, laurel wreath; halo; (bot.) spurge laurel, daphne; **lauréola hembra** (bot.) mezereon
lauro *m* (bot.) laurel; (fig.) laurels (*fame*)
lauroceraso *m* (bot.) cherry laurel
lauto -ta *adj* rich, sumptuous
lava *f* lava; (min.) washing
lavable *adj* washable
lavabo *m* washstand (*bowl with faucets*); washroom, lavatory; (eccl. & hist.) lavabo; (eccl.) Lavabo (*towel*)
lavacaras *mf* (*pl:* **-ras**) (coll.) fawner, flatterer
lavación *f* wash
lavacoches *m* (*pl:* **-ches**) car washer
lavadedos *m* (*pl:* **-dos**) finger bowl
lavadero *m* laundry; washing place (*by a stream*); washboard; washtub; (min.) buddle; (Am.) placer
lavado -da *adj* (coll.) brazen, impudent; *m* wash, washing; laundry; (med.) lavage; (paint.) wash; **lavado a seco** or **lavado químico** dry cleaning; **lavado cerebral** or **de cerebro** brain washing
lavador -dora *adj* washing; *m* (phot.) washer; *f* washing machine; **lavadora de platos** or **de vajilla** dishwasher; **lavadora mecánica** automatic washer, automatic washing machine
lavadura *f* washing; washings (*dirty water; abraded material*); glove-leather dressing
lavafrutas *m* (*pl:* **-tas**) finger bowl
lavaje *m* wool washing; (surg.) swabbing
lavajo *m* water hole
lavamanos *m* (*pl:* **-nos**) washstand (*stand with basin and pitcher; bowl with faucets*); washbowl
lavamiento *m* wash, washing; enema
lavanco *m* wild duck; (orn.) widgeon (*Anas americana*)
lavanda *f* (bot.) lavender; lavender water
lavandera *f* laundress, laundrywoman, washwoman; (orn.) wagtail; (orn.) sandpiper (*Tringoides hypoleucus*)
lavandería *f* laundry
lavandero *m* launderer, laundryman
lavándula *f* (bot.) lavender
lavaojos *m* (*pl:* **-jos**) eyecup
lavaparabrisas *m* (*pl:* **-sas**) windshield washer
lavaplatos *mf* (*pl:* **-tos**) (coll.) dishwasher in a restaurant; *m* dishwasher (*machine*)
lavar *va* to wash; (mas., min., paint. & fig.) to wash; *vr* to wash
lavativa *f* enema (*liquid and apparatus*); (coll.) bore, bother, annoyance
lavatorio *m* wash; lavatory, washroom; (med.) wash, lotion; (eccl.) Maundy; (eccl.) lavatory
lavazas *fpl* dirty water, wash water
lave *m* (min.) washing
lavotear *va & vr* (coll.) to wash in a hurry
lavoteo *m* (coll.) quick wash

laxación *f* laxation, slackening, easing
laxamiento *m* laxation, slackening; laxness
laxante *adj & m* (med.) laxative
laxar *va* to slack, to ease; to loosen (*the bowels*); *vr* to slack, to ease
laxativo -va *adj & m* var. of **laxante**
laxidad or **laxitud** *f* slackness, laxity
laxo -xa *adj* lax (*slack; loose in morals*)
lay *m* lay (*poem*)
laya *f* spade; kind, quality
layador *m* spader, spademan
layar *va* to spade, dig with a spade
Layo *m* (myth.) Laius
lazada *f* bowknot
lazar §76 *va* to lasso
lazareto *m* lazaretto
lazarillo *m* blind man's guide
lazarino -na *adj* leprous; *mf* leper
lázaro *m* raggedy beggar; (*cap.*) *m* Lazarus; **estar hecho un lázaro** to be full of sores
lazaroso -sa *adj & mf* var. of **lazarino**
lazo *m* bow, knot, tie; bow tie; loop; bowknot; lasso, lariat; snare, trap; bond, tie; angle iron, tie bar; topiary design; **armar lazo a** (coll.) to set a trap for; **caer en el lazo** (coll.) to fall into the trap; **tender un lazo a** to lead into a trap; **lazo corredizo** running knot; **lazo de amor** truelove knot; **lazo de unión** (fig.) bond
lazulita *f* (mineral.) lazulite; (mineral.) lapis lazuli
lb. abr. of **libra**
Ldo. abr. of **Licenciado**
le *pron pers* to him, to her, to it; to you; him; you
leal *adj* loyal, faithful; devoted; reliable, trustworthy; *m* loyalist
lealtad *f* loyalty, fidelity; devotion; reliability, trustworthiness
Leandro *m* (myth.) Leander
lebeche *m* (naut.) southwest wind
leberquisa *f* (mineral.) magnetic pyrites
lebrada *f* rabbit fricassee
lebrato or **lebratón** *m* young hare, leveret
lebrel -brela *mf* whippet
lebrero -ra *adj* hare-hunting
lebrillo *m* tub, washtub
lebrón *m* large hare; (coll.) coward; (Am.) wise guy
lebroncillo *m* var. of **lebrato**
lebruno -na *adj* leporine, harelike
lección *f* lesson; reading (*interpretation of a passage*); (eccl.) lection; **dar una lección a** to give or teach a lesson to (*to reprove*); **dar la lección** to recite one's lesson; **echar lección** to assign the lesson; **tomar una lección a** to hear the lesson of
leccionario *m* (eccl.) lectionary
leccionista *mf* private tutor, coach
lecitina *f* (biochem.) lecithin
lectivo -va *adj* school (*day, year, etc.*)
lector -tora *adj* reading; *mf* reader; *m* lector; foreign-language instructor; meter reader; **lector mental** mind reader
lectorado *m* (eccl.) lectorate (*order*); modern-language instruction; professorship
lectoría *f* (eccl.) lectorate (*office*)
lectura *f* reading; public lecture; subject; culture; reading (*interpretation of a passage*); (elec.) playback; **ir con lectura** to know what one is about, to be purposive; **lectura chica** (print.) small pica; **lectura de la mente** mind reading; **lectura gorda** (print.) pica
lecha *f* (ichth.) milt (*secretion and gland*)
lechada *f* grout; slurry; pulp (*for making paper*); whitewash; **lechada de cal** milk of lime
lechal *adj* sucking; milky (*plant*); *m* milk (*of plant*)
lechar *adj* sucking; milky (*plant*); milk (*cow, plant, etc.*); *va* (Am.) to milk; (Am.) to whitewash
lechaza *f* var. of **lecha**
lechazo *m* suckling (*animal*); weaned lamb
leche *f* milk; **como una leche** (coll.) tender (*e.g., meat*); **dar a leche** to farm out (*sheep*); **estar con la leche en los labios** to lack experience; **estar en leche** to be still green or undeveloped (*said of plants and fruit*); (naut.) to be calm; **mamar en la leche** (coll.) to soak up as a child, to learn in childhood; **pedir leche a las cabrillas** to ask for the impossible; **leche condensada** condensed milk; **leche de coco** coconut milk; **leche de gallina** (bot.) star-of-Bethlehem; **leche de magnesia** (pharm.) milk of magnesia; **leche de manteca** buttermilk; **leche desnatada** skim milk; **leche en polvo** milk powder, powdered milk; **leche evaporada** evaporated milk; **leche homogeneizada** homogenized milk; **leche pasterizada** pasteurized milk
lechecillas *fpl* sweatbread; entrails
lechera *f* see **lechero**
lechería *f* dairy, creamery
lechero -ra *adj* milk; milch; (coll.) stingy, grasping; *m* milkman, dairyman; *f* milkmaid, dairymaid; milk can; milk pitcher; **lechera amarga** (bot.) milkwort
lecheruela or **lechetrezna** *f* (bot.) sun spurge
lechigada *f* brood, litter; (coll.) crew, gang, lot
lechillo *m* (bot.) hornbeam, American hornbeam
lechín *m* Andalusian olive (*tree and fruit*); (vet.) watery boil
lechino *m* (surg.) tent; (vet.) watery boil
lecho *m* bed; couch; (mas.) bed; (min.) floor; bed (*of river, road, etc.; base; layer, stratum*); **abandonar el lecho** to get up (*from illness*); **lecho de plumas** (fig.) feather bed (*comfortable situation*); **lecho de roca** bedrock
lecho-litera *m* (*pl:* **lechos-literas**) double-decker (*bed*)
lechón -chona *adj* (coll.) filthy, sloppy; *mf* sucking pig; (coll.) pig (*dirty person*); *m* pig; *f* sow
lechoso -sa *adj* milky; *m* (bot.) papaya (*tree*); *f* papaya (*fruit*)
lechuga *f* (bot.) lettuce; head of lettuce; frill; **lechugas** *fpl* lettuce (*leaves used in salad*); **lechuga romana** (bot.) romaine, romaine lettuce
lechugado -da *adj* lettuce-shaped
lechuguero -ra *mf* lettuce dealer
lechuguilla *f* wild lettuce; frill, ruff; (bot.) corn sow thistle; (bot.) lechuguilla
lechuguino -na *adj* fashionable, stylish; *mf* fashion plate; *m* small lettuce (*before transplanting*); (coll.) young flirt
lechuzo -za *adj* sucking (*mule*); owlish; *m* bill collector; summons server; (coll.) owl-faced fellow; *f* (orn.) barn owl, screech owl; (coll.) owl-faced woman; **lechuza blanca** (orn.) snowy owl
ledo -da *adj* (poet.) gay, merry, cheerful; (*cap.*) *f* (myth.) Leda
leer §35 *va* to read; *vn* to read; to lecture; **leer en** to read (*someone's thoughts*); **leer entre líneas** to read between the lines; *vr* to read, e.g., **este libro se lee con facilidad** this book reads easily
leg. abr. of **legal & legislatura**
lega *f* see **lego**
legacía *f* legateship; commission, message (*entrusted to a legate*)
legación *f* legation
legado *m* legacy; legate
legajar *va* (Am.) var. of **enlegajar**
legajo *m* file, dossier, docket, bundle of papers
legal *adj* legal; right, correct
legalidad *f* legality; rightness, correctness
legalista *adj* legalistic
legalización *f* legalization; authentication
legalizar §76 *va* to legalize; to authenticate (*a document, signature, etc.*)
legamente *adv* as a layman
légamo *m* slime, ooze
legamoso -sa *adj* slimy, oozy
leganal *m* pool of mud, mudhole
légano *m* var. of **légamo**
legaña *f* (path.) bleareye, rheum
legañoso -sa *adj* blear-eyed
legar §59 *va* to send as a legate or deputy; (law & fig.) to bequeath
legatario -ria *mf* (law) legatee, devisee
legenda *f* legend (*saint's life*)
legendario -ria *adj* legendary
legibilidad *f* legibility

legible *adj* legible
legión *f* legion; **constituir legión** to be legion; **legión de Honor** Legion of Honor; **legión extranjera** (mil.) foreign legion
legionario -ria *adj* legionary; *m* legionary; legionnaire
legislación *f* legislation
legislador -dora *adj* legislating, legislative; *mf* legislator
legislar *vn* to legislate
legislativo -va *adj* legislative
legislatura *f* session, term of a legislature; (Am.) legislature
legisperito *m* legalist, legal expert
legista *m* legalist, legal expert; law professor
legítima *f* see **legítimo**
legitimación *f* legitimation
legitimar *va* to legitimate; to establish or prove legally
legitimidad *f* legitimacy; rightness, justice
legitimismo *m* legitimism
legitimista *adj & mf* legitimist
legítimo -ma *adj* legitimate; fair, equitable; genuine; *f* (law) legitim
lego -ga *adj* lay; of a layman, uninformed; *m* layman; lay brother; *f* lay sister
legón *m* (agr.) hoe
legra *f* (surg.) bone scraper, periosteotome
legración *f* (surg.) periosteotomy
legrado *m* scraping of hides
legradura *f* var. of **legración**
legrar *va* to scrape (*hides*); (surg.) to scrape (*a bone*)
legrón *m* (surg.) large bone scraper or periosteotome (*of veterinarian*)
legua *f* league (*measure*); **a la legua, a legua, a leguas, de cien leguas, de mil leguas, de muchas leguas** or **de media legua** far, far away
leguleyo *m* pettifogger
legumbre *f* (bot.) legume; (bot.) vegetable
legumina *f* (biochem.) legumin
leguminoso -sa *adj* leguminous
leíble *adj* legible
leído -da *adj* well-read; **leído y escribido** (coll.) posing as learned; *f* reading
leila *f* Moorish dance
leishmaniosis *f* (path.) leishmaniasis or leishmaniosis
leísmo *m* use of **le** to the exclusion of **lo** and **la**
leísta *mf* user of **le** to the exclusion of **lo** and **la**
leitmotiv *m* (*pl:* **-tivs**) (mus.) leitmotiv; (Am.) fixed idea
lejanía *f* distance, remoteness; distant place
lejano -na *adj* distant, remote
lejas *adj fem pl* distant; **de lejas tierras** from distant lands
lejía *f* lye; (coll.) dressing-down, rebuke
lejiadora *f* washing machine
lejío *m* dyers' lye
lejísimo or **lejísimos** *adv* very far away
lejitos *adv* pretty far, rather far
lejos *adv* far; **a lo lejos** at a distance, in the distance; **de lejos, de muy lejos** or **desde lejos** from a distance; **estar lejos de** + *inf* to be far from + *ger;* **ir lejos** to go far; **lejos de** far from (*e.g., the city, one's mind*); *m* appearance at a distance; glimpse; distant point or spot (*in a painting*); **tener buen lejos** to look good at a distance
lejuelos *adv* var. of **lejitos**
lelilí *m* (*pl:* **-líes**) Moorish war cry
lelo -la *adj* stupid, dull; *mf* simpleton, dolt
lema *m* motto, slogan; theme, lemma
lemnáceo -a *adj* (bot.) lemnaceous
lemniscata *f* (geom.) lemniscate
lemnisco *m* lemniscus; ribbon, fillet; (anat.) lemniscus
lempira *m* lempira (*monetary unit of Honduras*)
lémur *m* (zool.) lemur; **lémures** *mpl* ghosts, apparitions; (myth.) lemures
len *adj* soft, untwisted (*silk or thread*)
lena *f* spirit, vigor
lencería *f* linen goods, dry goods; linen room, linen closet; linen shop, drygoods store; drygoods section (*of a city*)
lencero -ra *mf* linen dealer, drygoods dealer
lendel *m* gin race, gin ring
lendrera *f* fine comb, comb for removing nits or lice; (coll.) head full of lice
lendrero *m* place full of nits or lice
lendroso -sa *adj* nitty, lousy
lene *adj* soft; light; kind, agreeable
lengua *f* (anat.) tongue; (fig.) tongue (*language; bell clapper; animal's tongue used as food*); (fig.) tongue (*of land, of fire, of a shoe*); **andar en lenguas** (coll.) to be gossiped about; **buscar la lengua a** (coll.) to pick a fight with; **con la lengua de un palmo** (coll.) with great eagerness; **dar la lengua** (coll.) to chew the rag; **de lengua en lengua** from mouth to mouth; **echar la lengua por** or **echar la lengua de un palmo por** (coll.) to be eager for, to crave; (coll.) to strive for; **hacerse lenguas de** (coll.) to rave about; **irse** or **írsele a uno la lengua** (coll.) to blab; **mala lengua** (coll.) gossip, evil tongue; **malas lenguas** (coll.) gossips; (coll.) people; **morderse la lengua** to hold one's tongue; **sacar la lengua a** (coll.) to stick one's tongue out at; **soltar la lengua** to blow off steam; **tener en la lengua** (coll.) to have on the tip of one's tongue; **tener la lengua gorda** (coll.) to talk thick; (coll.) to be drunk; **tirar de la lengua a** (coll.) to draw out (*to persuade to talk*); **tomar en lenguas a** (coll.) to gossip about; **tomar lengua** or **lenguas** to pick up news; **trabársele** or **trastrabársele la lengua a uno** to become tongue-tied; **lengua canina** (bot.) hound's-tongue; **lengua cerval** or **cervina** (bot.) hart's-tongue; **lengua de buey** (bot.) ox-tongue; **lengua de ciervo** (bot.) hart's-tongue; **lengua de cordero** (bot.) plantain; **lengua de estropajo** (coll.) jabberer; **lengua de oc** langue d'oc; **lengua de oíl** langue d'oïl; **lengua de perro** (bot.) hound's-tongue; **lengua de trapo** (coll.) jabberer; **lengua franca** lingua franca; **lengua madre** or **matriz** mother tongue (*language from which another language is derived*); **lengua materna** mother tongue (*language naturally acquired by reason of nationality*); **lengua muerta** dead language; **lenguas aglutinantes** agglutinative languages; **lengua santa** Hebrew language; **lenguas modernas** modern languages; **lenguas vivas** living languages, modern languages; **lengua universal** universal language; **lengua vulgar** vernacular
lenguadeta *f* (ichth.) small sole
lenguado *m* (ichth.) sole; (ichth.) flounder (*Paralichthys brasiliensis*)
lenguadoque *m* langue d'oc
lenguaje *m* language; **lenguaje de los signos** sign language
lenguarada *f* var. of **lengüetada**
lenguaraz (*pl:* **-races**) *adj* foul-mouthed, scurrilous; garrulous, loquacious; accomplished in languages; *mf* linguist; (Am.) interpreter
lenguaz *adj* (*pl:* **-guaces**) garrulous
lenguaza *f* (bot.) bugloss
lengüeta *f* large bit; pointer (*of scales*); tongue (*of shoe*); ladyfinger; (anat.) epiglottis; (arch.) buttress; (carp. & mus.) tongue; (mus.) reed (*of reed instrument*); (mach.) feather, wedge; (Am.) paper cutter; (Am.) petticoat fringe; **a lengüeta y ranura** tongue-and-groove
lengüetada *f* licking, lapping
lengüetear *vn* to stick one's tongue out; to flicker, to flutter; (Am.) to jabber
lengüetería *f* (mus.) reedwork, reed stops (*of an organ*)
lengüicorto -ta *adj* (coll.) timid, reserved
lengüilargo -ga *adj* (coll.) foul-mouthed, scurrilous
lengüita *f* (ichth.) tongue-fish
lenidad *f* lenity, lenience
lenificar §86 *va* to soften; to soothe
lenificativo -va *adj* soothing
Leningrado *f* Leningrad
leninismo *m* Leninism
leninista *adj & mf* Leninist or Leninite
lenitivo -va *adj & m* lenitive
lenocinio *m* pandering, procuring
lente *m & f* (opt. & geol.) lens; magnifying glass; **lentes** *mpl* nose glasses; **lente de aumento** magnifying glass; **lente de contacto** or **len-**

te invisible contact lens; **lentes de náriz** or **de pinzas** pince-nez; **lentes polarizantes** polaroid lenses; **lente telefotográfico** telephoto lens; **lente tórica** or **toral** toric lens
lentecer §34 *vn & vr* to soften
lenteja *f* (bot.) lentil (*plant and seed*); pendulum bob, disk; **lenteja acuática** or **de agua** (bot.) lesser duckweed
lentejar *m* field of lentils
lentejuela *f* spangle, sequin; (bot.) lenticel
lenticular *adj* lenticular
lentiscal *m* thicket of mastic trees
lentisco *m* (bot.) mastic tree
lentitud *f* slowness; (fig.) slowness, sluggishness
lento -ta *adj* slow; sticky; low (*fire*)
lenzuelo *m* (agr.) sheet for carrying straw
leña *f* firewood, kindling wood; (coll.) beating, drubbing; **cargar de leña** (coll.) to beat, give a drubbing to; **echar leña al fuego** to make things worse, to stir up trouble; **llevar leña al monte** to carry coals to Newcastle
leñador -dora *mf* dealer in kindling wood; woodcutter; *m* woodman, woodsman
leñame *m* wood; stock or provision of firewood
leñatero *m* woodman, woodsman
leñazo *m* (coll.) blow with a cudgel
leñera *f* woodshed
leñero *m* wood dealer; wood purchaser; woodshed
leño *m* log; wood; (coll.) sap, dullard; (poet.) ship, vessel; **dormir como un leño** to sleep like a log; **leño hediondo** (bot.) bean trefoil
leñoso -sa *adj* woody, ligneous
Leo *m* (astr.) Leo
león *m* (zool.) lion; (ent.) ant lion; (fig.) lion (*very brave or strong man*); (*cap.*) *m* Leo (*man's name*); (astr.) Leo; **león de América** (zool.) mountain lion; **león de Nemea** (myth.) Nemean lion; **león marino** (zool.) sea lion
leona *f* lioness; brave, haughty woman
leonado -da *adj* tawny, fulvous
Leonardo *m* Leonard
leonera *f* cage or den of lions; (coll.) dive, gambling joint; attic, lumber room, junk room
leonería *f* boldness, fierceness
leonero *m* keeper of lions; (coll.) keeper of a gambling house
leonés -nesa *adj & mf* Leonese; *m* Leonese (*dialect*)
leónica *f* (anat.) ranine vein
leónida *f* (astr.) Leonid
Leónidas *m* Leonidas
leonino -na *adj* leonine; (law) one-sided (*contract*); *f* (path.) leontiasis
Leonor *f* Eleanor, Leonora, Leonore
leontíasis *f* (path.) leontiasis
leontina *f* watch chain
leopardo *m* (zool.) leopard
leopoldina *f* fob (*short chain*); (mil.) Spanish shako
Leopoldo *m* Leopold
lepe *m* (Am.) flip in the ear; **¡por vida de Lepe!** upon my soul!; **saber más que Lepe** to be very keen and wide-awake
leperada *f* (Am.) foulness, coarseness, vulgarity
lépero -ra *mf* (Am.) coarse person; (Am.) hoodlum
lepidio *m* (bot.) pepper cress
Lépido *m* Lepidus
lepidolita *f* (mineral.) lepidolite
lepidóptero -ra *adj* (ent.) lepidopterous; *m* (ent.) lepidopteron
lepidosirena *f* (ichth.) lepidosiren
lepisma *f* (ent.) bristletail, silverfish
leporino -na *adj* leporine, harelike
lepra *f* (path.) leprosy
leprosería *f* leprosarium
leproso -sa *adj* leprous; *mf* leper
leptofilo -la *adj* (bot.) leptophyllous
leptorrino -na *adj* (anthrop.) leptorrhine
lercha *f* reed on which fish and birds are strung and carried
lerdo -da *adj* slow, sluggish, dull, heavy; coarse, crude; *f* (vet.) tumor in pastern
lerdón *m* (vet.) tumor in pastern
les *pron pers* to them, to you; them, you
lesbianismo *m* Lesbianism
lesbiano -na or **lesbio -bia** *adj & mf* Lesbian; *f* Lesbian (*homosexual woman*)
lésbico -ca *adj* Lesbian
lesión *f* lesion; harm, injury; (path. & law) lesion
lesionar *va* to hurt, injure
lesivo -va *adj* harmful, injurious
lesna *f* awl
lesnordeste *m* east-northeast; east-northeast wind
leso -sa *adj* hurt, damaged, wounded; harmed, injured, offended; perverted; (Am.) simple, foolish
lessueste *m* east-southeast; east-southeast wind
leste *m* (naut.) east
lesueste *m* var. of **lessueste**
letal *adj* lethal
letame *m* manure
letanía *f* litany; (coll.) litany (*repeated series*)
letárgico -ca *adj* lethargic
letargo *m* lethargy
letargoso -sa *adj* lethargic (*producing lethargy*)
Lete *m* (myth.) Lethe (*river*)
leteo -a *adj* Lethean; (*cap.*) *m* (myth.) Lethe (*river*)
lético -ca *adj* Lettish
letificar §86 *va* to cheer, to enliven
letón -tona *adj* Lettish; *mf* Lett; *m* Lettish or Lett (*language*)
Letonia *f* Latvia
letra *f* letter (*of alphabet*); handwriting (*manner of writing*); words (*of a song*); (com.) draft; (print.) type (*character used in printing; such pieces collectively*); (fig.) letter (*literal meaning*); **letras** *fpl* letters (*literature*); (coll.) word, a line (*news, note*); **aceptar una letra** (com.) to accept a bill of exchange; **a la letra** to the letter (*literally*); **a letra vista** (com.) at sight; **bellas letras** belles lettres; **cuatro letras** or **dos letras** (coll.) a line (*short letter or note*); **en letras de molde** in print; **escribir en letra de molde** to print (*to write in letters resembling printed letters*); **las letras y las armas** the pen and the sword; **primeras letras** elementary education, three R's; **tener mucha letra** (coll.) to know one's way around; **letra a la vista** (com.) sight draft; **letra alemana** German script; **letra canina** dog's letter (*trilled r, i.e., rr*); **letra capital** capital letter; **letra de cambio** (com.) bill of exchange, draft; **letra de curia** court hand; **letra de imprenta** (print.) type; **letra de mano** handwriting; **letra de molde** printed letter; **letra futura** (print.) futura, Gothic; **letra gótica** (print.) black letter, Old English; **letra mayúscula** capital letter; **letra menuda** fine print; smartness, cunning; **letra minúscula** small letter; **letra muerta** dead letter (*unenforced law*); **letra negrilla** (print.) boldface; **letra redonda** (print.) roman
letrado -da *adj* lettered (*learned*); (coll.) pedantic; *m* lawyer; *f* (coll.) lawyer's wife
Letrán, San Juan de St. John Lateran (*church*)
letrero *m* label; sign, placard, poster
letrilla *f* short-line verse with a refrain at end of each strophe; (mus.) rondelet
letrina *f* latrine, privy, toilet; (fig.) cesspool (*filthy place*)
letrista *mf* writer of lyrics (*i.e., words of a song*); engrosser, calligrapher
leucemia *f* (path.) leukemia
leucina *f* (biochem.) leucine
leucisco *m* (ichth.) dace, roach
leucita *f* (mineral.) leucite
leucobase *f* (chem.) leuco base
leucocitemia *f* (path.) leucocythemia
leucocito *m* (physiol.) leucocyte
leucocitosis *f* (path.) leucocytosis
leucoma *m* (path.) leucoma
leucomaína *f* (biochem.) leucomaine
leucón *m* (zool.) leucon
leucopenia *f* (path.) leucopenia
leucoplasto *m* (bot.) leucoplast
leucorrea *f* (path.) leucorrhea
leudar *va* to leaven, to ferment with yeast; *vr* to rise, become fermented
leudo -da *adj* leavened, fermented

leva *f* weighing anchor; (mil.) levy; (naut.) swell; vane (*of water wheel*); (mach.) cam
levada *f* portion of silkworms moved from one place to another; flourish (*of sword, foil, etc.*); stroke (*of piston*); rise (*of sun, moon, stars*)
levadero -ra *adj* collectible, leviable
levadizo -za *adj* lift (*bridge*)
levador *m* piler (*in paper mill*); tricky thief; (mach.) cam
levadura *f* leaven; leavening; yeast; board; **levadura comprimida** yeast cake; **levadura de cerveza** brewer's yeast, beer yeast; **levadura química** baking soda
levantacarril *m* (rail.) track jack
levantacoches *m* (*pl:* **-ches**) auto jack
levantado -da *adj* elevated, lofty, sublime; proud, haughty; *f* getting up (*from bed*)
levantador -dora *adj* lifting, elevating; *mf* lifter, elevator; insurrectionist, rebel; (coll.) slanderer
levantamiento *m* rise, lift, elevation; insurrection, uprising, revolt; elevation, sublimity; survey; (geol.) upheaval; (mach.) exhaust port; (prov.) settlement (*of an account*); **levantamiento del cadáver** inquest; **levantamiento del censo** or **de los censos** census taking; **levantamiento de planos** or **levantamiento topográfico** surveying
levantar *va* to raise; to lift; to elevate; to straighten; to stir up, rouse, agitate; to adjourn; to clear (*the table*); to break (*camp*); to break up (*housekeeping*); to make (*a survey*); to start (*game*); to bear (*false witness*); to raise (*troops; a siege*); to weigh (*anchor*); *vr* to rise; to get up; to stand up; to straighten up; to rebel, rise up
levantaválvulas *m* (*pl:* **-las**) valve lifter
levantaventana *m* sash lift
levante *m* levanter (*wind*); East, Orient; (*cap.*) *m* Levant; northeastern Mediterranean shores of Spain; region around Valencia, Alicante, and Murcia; **de levante** ready to leave
levantino -na *adj* Levantine; of the northeastern Mediterranean shores of Spain; *mf* Levantine; native or inhabitant of the northeastern Mediterranean shores of Spain
levantisco -ca *adj* (archaic) Levantine; turbulent, restless; *mf* (archaic) Levantine
levar *va* (naut.) to weigh (*anchor*); *vr* (naut.) to set sail
leve *adj* light; slight, trivial, trifling
levedad *f* lightness; trivialness, levity
Leví *m* (Bib.) Levi
leviatán *m* (Bib. & fig.) leviathan
levigación *f* levigation
levigar §59 *va* to levigate (*to mix with water so as to separate finer particles*)
levirato *m* (hist.) levirate
levita *m* (Bib.) Levite; deacon; *f* frock coat
levitación *f* levitation
levítico -ca *adj* Levitical; (*cap.*) *m* (Bib.) Leviticus
levitón *m* heavy frock coat
levógiro -ra *adj* (chem. & opt.) levorotatory
levoglucosa *f* (chem.) levoglucose
levulina *f* (chem.) levuline
levulínico -ca *adj* levulinic
levulosa *f* (chem.) levulose
lewisita *f* (mil.) lewisite
léxico -ca *adj* lexical; m lexicon; wordstock; vocabulary (*e.g., of an author*)
lexicografía *f* lexicography
lexicográfico -ca *adj* lexicographic
lexicógrafo -fa *mf* lexicographer
lexicología *f* lexicology
lexicológico -ca *adj* lexicologic or lexicological
lexicólogo -ga *mf* lexicologist
lexicón *m* lexicon
ley *f* law; loyalty, devotion; norm, standard; fineness (*of a metal*); **a ley de caballero** on the word of a gentleman; **a toda ley** according to principle; with the utmost sincerity; **dar la ley** to set an example; to set the pace, to impose one's will; **de buena ley** sterling, genuine; **tener** or **tomar ley a** to be or become devoted to; **venir contra una ley** to break a law; **ley antigua** Mosaic law; **ley de la selva** law of the jungle; **ley de las fases** (physical chem.) phase rule; **ley del embudo** (coll.) one-sided law; **ley del menor esfuerzo** line of least resistance; **ley de Moisés** law of Moses; **ley del talión** law of retaliation; **leyes suntuarias** sumptuary laws; **ley marcial** martial law; **ley mosaica** Mosaic law; **ley natural** natural law; **ley no escrita** unwritten law; **ley periódica** (chem.) periodic law; **ley sálica** Salic law; **ley seca** dry law
leyenda *f* legend; reading
leyendario -ria *adj* legendary
leyente *adj* reading; *mf* reader
lezna *f* awl
Lía *f* (Bib.) Leah; (*l.c.*) *f* plaited esparto rope; **lías** *fpl* lee, dregs; **estar hecho una lía** (coll.) to be drunk
liana *f* (bot.) liana or liane
lianza *f* (Am.) account, credit (*in a store*)
liar §90 *va* to tie, bind; to tie up, wrap up; to roll (*a cigaret*); (coll.) to embroil, involve; **liarlas** (coll.) to beat it, to duck out; (coll.) to kick the bucket; *vr* to join together, be associated; to have a liaison; (coll.) to become embroiled, become involved; **liárselos** to roll one's own (*i.e., cigarets*)
liara *f* var. of **aliara**
liásico -ca *adj & m* (geol.) Liassic
liatón *m* esparto rope
libación *f* libation; (hum.) libation (*alcoholic drink*)
libanés -nesa *adj & mf* Lebanese
Líbano, el Lebanon (*republic at east end of Mediterranean*); the Lebanon Mountains
libar *va* to suck; to taste; *vn* to pour out a libation; to imbibe
libelista *m* libeler, lampoonist
libelo *m* libel, lampoon; (law) petition
libélula *f* (ent.) dragonfly
líber *m* (bot.) bast, liber
liberación *f* liberation; quittance; redemption (*e.g., of a mortgage*)
liberador -dora *adj* liberating; *mf* liberator
liberal *adj* liberal; quick, ready; (pol.) liberal; (Am.) liberal (*broad-minded*); *mf* (pol.) liberal
liberalidad *f* liberality
liberalismo *m* liberalism
liberalización *f* liberalization
liberalizar §76 *va & vr* to liberalize
liberar *va* to free
liberiano -na *adj & mf* Liberian
libérrimo -ma *adj super* very or most free
liberta *f* freedwoman
libertad *f* liberty, freedom; **en libertad** at liberty, at large; **tomarse la libertad de** + *inf* to take the liberty to + *inf;* **tomarse libertades** to take liberties (*to be too familiar*); **libertad de comercio** free trade; **libertad de cultos** freedom of worship; **libertad de empresa** free enterprise; **libertad de enseñanza** academic freedom; **libertad de imprenta** freedom of the press; **libertad de los mares** freedom of the seas; **libertad de palabra** freedom of speech, free speech; **libertad de prensa** freedom of the press; **libertad de reunión** freedom of assembly
libertadamente *adv* brashly, wantonly, impudently
libertado -da *adj* free; bold, daring
libertador -dora *adj* liberating; *mf* liberator
libertar *va* to liberate, to set free; to free; to save, preserve (*from death, jail, etc.*)
libertario -ria *adj* anarchistic; *mf* anarchist
liberticida *adj* liberticidal; *mf* liberticide, destroyer of liberty
libertinaje *m* libertinism
libertino -na *adj & mf* libertine
liberto *m* freedman; probationer (*convicted delinquent on probation*)
Libia *f* see **libio**
líbico -ca *adj* Libyan
libídine *f* (psychol.) libido; lust, lewdness
libidinoso -sa *adj* libidinous
libido *f* (psychol.) libido
libio -bia *adj & mf* Libyan; **la Libia** Libya
libón *m* bubbling spring; pool
libra *f* pound (*weight, coin*); (*cap.*) *f* (astr.) Libra; **libra esterlina** pound sterling
libración *f* libration; (astr.) libration

libraco or **libracho** *m* cheap book, poor book
librado -da *adj* finished, ruined; **bien librado** successful; **mal librado** unsuccessful; *mf* (com.) drawee
librador -dora *mf* deliverer; *m* grocer's scoop; (com.) drawer
libramiento *m* deliverance, exemption; warrant (*for payment of money*)
librancista *m* (com.) holder of a draft
libranza *f* (com.) draft, bill of exchange; **libranza postal** money order
librapié *m* (mech.) foot-pound
librar *va* to free; to save, spare, deliver; to place (*e.g., one's hope*); to pass (*sentence*); to give, to join (*battle*); to decide; (com.) to draw; *vn* to be delivered, to give birth; to expel the placenta; to receive a visitor in the locutory (*said of a nun*); (com.) to draw; **a bien** or **a buen librar** as well as could be expected; **librar bien** to come off well, to succeed; **librar mal** to come off badly, to fail; *vr* to free oneself; to escape; **librarse de buena** (coll.) to get out of a jam, to have a close shave
libratorio *m* locutory
librazo *m* big book; blow with a book
libre *adj* free; single, unmarried; free, outspoken, brash; free, loose, licentious; guiltless, innocent; **libre de porte** postage prepaid, freight prepaid
librea *f* livery (*uniform*); coat (*of deer and other animals*); (coll.) servants; (fig.) livery (*outward appearance*); **llevar librea** to be a servant
librear *va* to sell by the pound
librecambio *m* free trade
librecambista *adj* free-trading; *mf* freetrader
librejo *m* var. of **libraco**
librepensador -dora *adj* freethinking; *mf* freethinker
librepensamiento *m* free thought, freethinking
librería *f* bookstore, bookshop; book business; bookshelf; library; **librería de viejo** second-hand bookshop
libreril *adj* book (*e.g., trade*)
librero *m* bookseller; (Am.) bookshelf, bookcase
libresco -ca *adj* book, bookish
libreta *f* loaf of bread; notebook; **libreta de banco** bankbook
librete *m* foot stove, foot brasier; booklet
libretín *m* booklet
libretista *mf* librettist
libreto *m* (mus.) libretto
librillo *m* tub, washtub; book (*of postage stamps, gold leaf, cigaret paper, etc.*); omasum (*of ruminant*); **librillo de cera** folded wax taper
libro *m* book; omasum (*of ruminant*); **ahorcar los libros** (coll.) to give up studying, to leave school; **a libro abierto** at sight; **el libro de Mormón** the book of Mormon; **hacer libro nuevo** (coll.) to turn over a new leaf; **libro a la rústica** paperbound book; **libro de actas** minute book; **libro de caballerías** romance of chivalry; **libro de caja** cashbook; **libro de cocina** cookbook; **libro de cheques** checkbook; **libro de chistes** joke book; **libro de lance** second-hand book; **libro de mayor venta** best seller; **libro de memoria** memo book; **libro de oro** Golden Book (*of Venetian nobility*); **libro de recuerdos** scrapbook; **libro de teléfonos** telephone book; **libro de texto** textbook; **libro diario** day book; **libro en folio** folio (*book*); **libro en rústica** paperbound book; **libro mayor** ledger; **libro procesional** or **procesionario** processional; **Libros sibilinos** Sibylline Books; **libro talonario** checkbook, stub book
libro-registro *m* (com.) book (*of a company*)
licantropía *f* lycanthropy
licántropo *m* lycanthrope
licencia *f* license (*permission; document showing such permission; abuse of liberty; licentiousness*); licentiate; master's degree; (mil.) furlough; **licencia absoluta** (mil.) discharge; **licencia de matrimonio** marriage license; **licencia poética** poetic license
licenciado -da *adj* licensed; free; pedantic; *mf* licenciate (*person who has a permit to practice a profession; holder of a licentiate or master's degree*); lawyer; (coll.) university student; (mil.) discharged soldier; **licenciado de presidio** freed prisoner; **Licenciado Vidriera** (coll.) namby-pamby
licenciamiento *m* graduation with a licentiate or master's degree; discharge of soldiers
licenciar *va* to license; to confer the degree of master on; (mil.) to discharge; *vr* to receive the master's degree; to be lewd; (mil.) to be discharged
licenciatura *f* licentiate, master's degree; graduation with a licentiate or master's degree; work leading to a licentiate or master's degree
licencioso -sa *adj* licentious
liceo *m* lyceum; lycée
licio -cia *adj & mf* Lycian; (*cap.*) *f* Lycia
licitación *f* bidding
licitador -dora *mf* bidder
licitar *va* to bid on; (Am.) to buy at auction, to sell at auction; *vn* to bid
lícito -ta *adj* licit; just, right; as prescribed
licitud *f* lawfulness; rightness
lícnide *f* or **licnis** *m* (bot.) lychnis
licopodio *m* (bot.) ground pine, lycopodium
licor *m* liquor (*spirituous beverage; any liquid*); liqueur (*spirituous liquor sweetened and flavored with aromatic substances*); (pharm.) liquor; **licores espiritosos** or **espirituosos** ardent spirits, spirituous liquors
licorero -ra *mf* (Am.) distiller; (Am.) liquor dealer; *f* cellaret
licorista *mf* distiller; liquor dealer
licoroso -sa *adj* spirituous, alcoholic; generous, rich (*wine*)
lictor *m* (hist.) lictor
licuable *adj* liquefiable
licuación *f* liquefaction; melting; (metal.) liquation
licuador *m* mechanical juice squeezer
licuar *va* to liquefy; to melt; (metal.) to liquate; *vr* to melt
licuefacción *f* liquefaction
licuefacer §55 *va & vr* to liquefy
licuefactible *adj* liquefiable
licuefacto -ta *adj* liquefied
licuescencia *f* liquescence
licuescente *adj* liquescent
licurgo -ga *adj* smart, keen; *m* lawmaker; (*cap.*) *m* Lycurgus
lichera *f* bedcover
lid *f* fight, combat; dispute, argument; **en buena lid** fairly, by fair means
líder *m* leader
lidia *f* & **Lidia** *f* see **lidio**
lidiadero -ra *adj* fighting, fit for fighting; *f* (Am.) quarreling, bickering
lidiador -dora *mf* fighter; *m* bullfighter
lidiar *va* to fight (*bulls*); *vn* to fight, to battle; to face up, to resist; **lidiar con** to contend with, to have to put up with
lidio -dia *adj* Lydian; (mus.) Lydian; *mf* Lydian; *f* fight; bullfight; (*cap.*) *f* Lydia
lidita *f* lyddite (*explosive*); (mineral.) Lydian stone
liebratón *m* var. of **lebrato**
liebre *f* (zool.) hare; coward; **coger una liebre** (coll.) to fall without hurting oneself; **levantar la liebre** (coll.) to do something to attract attention; **liebre de mar** or **liebre marina** (zool.) sea hare; (zool.) porcelain crab
liebrecilla *f* (bot.) bluebottle
Lieja *f* Liége
liendre *f* nit; **cascar** or **machacar las liendres a** (coll.) to beat up, to thrash; (coll.) to rake over the coals
lientera or **lientería** *f* (path.) lientery
lientérico -ca *adj* lienteric
liento -ta *adj* damp, dank
lienza *f* strip of cloth
lienzo *m* linen, linen cloth; linen handkerchief; face or front (*of a wall or building*); (fort.) curtain; (paint.) canvas; **lienzo de la Verónica** veronica (*representing Christ's face*)
liga *f* garter; league; alloy; birdlime; band, rubber band; bond, union; (bot.) mistletoe; **Liga anseática** Hanseatic League; **liga de goma** rubber band
ligación *f* ligation, binding, bond

ligada *f* ligature, tie, bond; (naut.) seizing, lashing
ligado *m* (mus. & print.) ligature
ligador *m* (surg.) ligator
ligadura *f* ligature, tie, bond; (mus. & surg.) ligature; (naut.) seizing, lashing
ligamaza *f* birdlime
ligamen *m* spell said to cause impotency
ligamento *m* ligament; (anat. & zool.) ligament
ligamentoso -sa *adj* ligamentous
ligamiento *m* tie, bond; union, harmony
ligapierna *f* garter
ligar §59 *va* to tie, bind; to alloy; to join, combine; (surg.) to ligate; (fig.) to bind, commit; *vn* (coll.) to flirt, to have an affair; *vr* to league together; (fig.) to become bound or committed
ligazón *f* bond, union; (naut.) futtock
ligereza *f* lightness; speed, rapidity, swiftness; fickleness, flightiness; indiscretion, tactlessness; **ligereza de mano** light touch, skill
ligero -ra *adj* light (*in weight; in arms or equipment; slight, delicate; agile, nimble; unimportant; superficial; flippant; fickle, flighty; cheerful; said also of food, wine, sleep*); weak (*e.g., tea*); **a la ligera** lightly; quickly; simply, unceremoniously; **de ligero** thoughtlessly; rashly; **ligero de cascos** scatterbrained, light-headed; **ligero de lengua** loose-tongued; **ligero de pies** light-footed; **ligero de ropa** scantily clad; **ligero** *adv* (Am.) fast, quickly, rapidly
lignario -ria *adj* ligneous
lignificar §86 *vr* to lignify
lignina *f* (bot.) lignin
lignito *m* (mineral.) lignite
lignocelulosa *f* lignocellulose
ligón *m* hoe
ligroína *f* (chem.) ligroin
lígula *f* (anat.) ligula; (bot. & zool.) ligula or ligule
ligulado -da *adj* ligulate
ligur or **ligurino -na** *adj & mf* Ligurian
ligustre *m* flower of privet
ligustrino -na *adj* (pertaining to) privet
ligustro *m* (bot.) privet
lija *f* (ichth.) dogfish; dogfish skin; sandpaper
lijado *m* sanding, sandpapering
lijar *va* to sand, to sandpaper
lila *f* (bot.) lilac (*shrub and flower*); *m* lilac (*color*); (*cap.*) *f* Lille
lilac *f* (*pl:* **lilaques**) (bot.) lilac (*shrub and flower*)
lilaila *f* (coll.) trickiness, cunning; Moorish war cry; (archaic) Berber fabric of silk and wool
lilao *m* (coll.) vain show
liliáceo -a *adj* (bot.) liliaceous
liliputiense *adj & mf* Lilliputian
lima *f* file (*tool*); sweet lime; (arch.) hip; (arch.) hip rafter; (bot.) sweet-lime tree; **lima de cola de rata** rattail file; **lima de doble picadura** double-cut file, cross-cut file; **lima delgada** slim file; **lima de mediacaña** half-round file; **lima de picadura sencilla** single-cut file; **lima de uñas** nail file; **lima hoya** (arch.) valley (*of a roof*); **lima muza** smooth file; **lima sorda** dead-smooth file; **lima tesa** (arch.) hip; **lima triangular** three-square file
limador -dora *mf* filer; *f* (mach.) shaper; power-file
limadura *f* filing; **limaduras** *fpl* filings
limalla *f* filings
limar *va* to file; to file down; to polish, touch up; to curtail, cut down; to smooth, smooth over
limatón *m* coarse round file
limaza *f* (zool.) slug
limazo *m* sliminess
limbo *m* edge; (astr., bot. & surv.) limb; (theol.) limbo; (coll.) distraction, diversion; **estar en el limbo** (coll.) to be distraught
Limburgo Limburg
limen *m* threshold; (psychol., physiol. & fig.) threshold
limenso *m* (Am.) honeydew melon
limeño -ña *adj & mf* Limean
limero -ra *mf* lime dealer; *m* (bot.) sweet-lime tree; *f* (naut.) rudderhole
limeta *f* long-necked bottle or flask
liminal *adj* (psychol.) liminal
limitación *f* limitation
limitacorrientes *m* (*pl:* **-tes**) (elec.) var. of **limitador de corriente**
limitado -da *adj* limited; dull-witted
limitador *m* limiter; **limitador de corriente** (elec.) clock meter; (elec.) slot meter, coin-operated meter; (elec.) current limiter
limitáneo -a *adj* limitary
limitar *va* to limit; to bound; to cut down, to reduce; **limitar a** + *inf* to limit to + *ger*; *vn* to be contiguous; **limitar con** to border on
limitativo -va *adj* limitative
límite *m* limit; **no tener límites** to know no limit
limítrofe *adj* bordering
limnología *f* limnology
limo *m* slime, mud
limón *m* shaft (*of wagon*); lemon; (arch.) string; (bot.) lemon, lemon tree; (Am.) lime (*fruit of Citrus aurantifolia*); **limón silvestre** May apple (*fruit*)
limonado -da *adj* lemon, lemon-colored; *f* lemonade
limonar *m* lemon grove
limoncillo *m* (bot.) citronella
limoncito *m* (bot.) limeberry, bergamot lime, orangeberry
limoneno *m* (chem.) limonene
limonero -ra *adj* shaft (*horse*); *mf* shaft horse; lemon seller or vendor; *m* (bot.) lemon, lemon tree; (Am.) lime tree (*Citrus aurantifolia*); *f* shaft (*of wagon*); shafts
limonita *f* (mineral.) limonite
limosidad *f* sliminess, muddiness
limosina *f* (aut.) limousine
limosna *f* alms
limosnear *vn* to beg
limosnero -ra *adj* almsgiving, charitable; *m* almsgiver, almoner; alms box; (Am.) beggar; *f* nun who collects alms; alms bag
limoso -sa *adj* slimy, muddy
limpia *f* see **limpio**
limpiabarros *m* (*pl:* **-rros**) scraper, foot scraper
limpiabotas *m* (*pl:* **-tas**) bootblack
limpiacristales *m* (*pl:* **-les**) windshield washer
limpiachimeneas *m* (*pl:* **-as**) chimney sweep
limpiadera *f* brush; plowstaff
limpiadientes *m* (*pl:* **-tes**) toothpick
limpiador -dora *adj* cleaning; *mf* cleaner
limpiadura *f* cleaning; **limpiaduras** *fpl* cleanings
limpiaduría *f* (Am.) dry-cleaning establishment
limpialimas *m* (*pl:* **-mas**) file card (*brush*)
limpiamente *adv* cleanly, in a clean manner; neatly; skillfully, with ease; simply, sincerely; honestly, unselfishly
limpiametales *m* (*pl:* **-les**) metal polish
limpiamiento *m* cleaning
limpianieve *m* snowplow
limpiaoídos *m* (*pl:* **-dos**) earpick
limpiaparabrisas *m* (*pl:* **-sas**) windshield wiper
limpiaparrilla *m* slice bar
limpiapiés *m* (*pl:* **-piés**) (Am.) door mat
limpiapipas *m* (*pl:* **-pas**) pipe cleaner
limpiaplumas *m* (*pl:* **-mas**) penwiper
limpiapozos *mf* (*pl:* **-zos**) cesspool cleaner
limpiar *va* to clean; to cleanse; to exonerate; to clean out, to prune (*a tree*); to shine (*shoes*); (coll.) to snitch; (coll.) to clean out (*someone in gambling*); (coll.) to clean up (*money in gambling*); (mil.) to mop up; **limpiarle a uno cierta cantidad** (coll.) to clean someone out of a certain amount of money; *vr* to clean, to clean oneself
limpiatubos *m* (*pl:* **-bos**) tube cleaner, flue scraper; swab, bailer
limpiaúñas *m* (*pl:* **-ñas**) orange stick, nail cleaner
limpiavía *f* (rail.) pilot, cowcatcher; **limpiavías** *m* (*pl:* **-as**) track cleaner
limpiavidrio *m* windshield wiper
limpidez *f* (poet.) limpidity
límpido -da *adj* (poet.) limpid

limpieza *f* cleaning; cleanness; cleanliness; neatness; ease, skill; chastity; honesty, disinterestedness; fair play; (fig.) house cleaning; **limpieza de bolsa** (coll.) lack of funds; **limpieza en seco** dry cleaning
limpio -pia *adj* clean; cleanly; neat, tidy; pure; chaste; clear, free; **dejar limpio** (coll.) to clean out (*of money*); **en limpio** net; **poner en limpio** to recopy clearly, to make a clear copy of; **quedar limpio** (coll.) to be cleaned out (*of money*); **sacar en limpio** to deduce, understand; to recopy clearly, to make a clear copy of; **limpio de polvo y paja** (coll.) free, for nothing; (coll.) net, after deducting expenses; *f* cleaning; **limpio** *adv* cleanly, in a clean manner; fair; **jugar limpio** to play fair
limpión *m* lick, quick cleaning; (coll.) cleaner; (Am.) dishcloth
lín. abr. of **línea**
lina *f* (Am.) coarse wool
linaje *m* lineage; class, description; **linajes** *mpl* people of high lineage; **linaje humano** humankind; **linaje puro** (biol.) pure line
linajista *m* genealogist
linajudo -da *adj* of high lineage, highborn; *mf* person of high lineage
lináloe *m* (bot.) aloe
linalol *m* (chem.) linaloöl
linar *m* flax field
linaria *f* (bot.) toadflax, snapdragon
linaza *f* flaxseed, linseed
lince *m* (zool.) lynx; keen, shrewd, or discerning person; (*cap.*) *m* (astr.) Lynx; **lince de las estepas** (zool.) caracal; *adj* keen (*sight, eyes*); keen, shrewd, discerning
lincear *va* (coll.) to see into, to see through
linceo -a *adj* lyncean; (poet.) keen (*sight, eyes*)
linchamiento *m* lynching
linchar *va* to lynch
lindante *adj* adjoining, bordering
lindar *vn* to be contiguous; **lindar con** to border on
lindazo *m* boundary
linde *m & f* limit, boundary
lindero -ra *adj* adjoining, bordering; *m* limit, edge; *f* limit, boundary
lindeza *f* prettiness, niceness; harmony, proportion, elegance; funny remark, witticism; (coll.) flirting; **lindezas** *fpl* (coll.) insults
lindo -da *adj* pretty, nice; fine, wonderful; **de lo lindo** a great deal; wonderfully; *m* (coll.) dude, sissy
lindura *f* prettiness, niceness; beauty (*beautiful woman*)
línea *f* line; lines (*outline of a figure, dress, etc.*); figure, waistline; **conservar la línea** to keep one's figure; **en toda la línea** all along the line; **la línea** (geog.) the line (*the equator*); **leer entre líneas** to read between the lines; **línea aclínica** (phys.) aclinic line; **línea agónica** (phys.) agonic line; **línea alámbrica** (elec.) line, wire; **línea de agua** water line; **línea de base** base line; **línea de batalla** line of battle; **línea de circunvalación** (rail.) belt line; (fort.) line of circumvallation; **línea de colimación** line of collimation; **línea de combate** line of battle; **línea de demarcación** (hist.) Line of Demarcation; **línea de empalme** (rail.) branch line; **línea de flotación** water line; **línea de fondo** (tennis) base line; (tennis) service line; **línea de fuego** (mil.) firing line; **línea de fuerza** (phys.) line of force; (elec.) power line; **línea de incidencia** line of incidence; **línea del lado** (tennis) side line; **línea del fuerte** (naut.) level line; **línea del partido** party line (*especially of Communist party*); **línea de media red** or **de mitad** (tennis) center service line; **línea de mira** (arti. & surv.) line of sight; **línea de montaje** assembly line; **línea de puntos** dotted line; **línea de respeto** limit of the marine belt; **línea de saque** or **de servicio** (tennis) service line; **línea de tierra** ground line; **línea de tiro** (mil.) line of fire; **línea férrea** railway; **línea geodésica** (math.) geodesic line; **línea internacional de cambio de fecha** international date line; **línea principal** (telp.) trunk line; **línea punteada** dotted line; **línea suplementaria** (mus.) ledger line, added line; **línea transversal** (geom.) transversal; **línea troncal** (rail.) trunk line
lineal *adj* lineal, linear
lineamento *m* lineament; **lineamentos** *mpl* lineaments (*especially of the face*)
lineamiento *m* lineament; **lineamientos** *mpl* (Am.) general outline, broad outline
linear *adj* linear (*leaf*); *va* to line; to sketch, outline; to delimit; to mark off, mark out
linearidad *f* linearity
linfa *f* (anat. & physiol.) lymph; (poet.) water
linfadenitis *f* (path.) lymphadenitis
linfangitis *f* (path.) lymphangitis
linfático -ca *adj* lymphatic; (fig.) lymphatic
linfocito *m* (anat.) lymphocyte
lingote *m* ingot; slug; (print.) slug; **lingote de hierro** pig iron
linguado -da *adj* (her.) langued
lingual *adj* lingual; (phonet.) lingual; *f* (phonet.) lingual
linguete *m* pawl, dog, ratchet
lingüista *mf* linguist (*person who studies linguistic phenomena*)
lingüístico -ca *adj* linguistic; *f* linguistics
linimento *m* liniment
linina *f* (biol. & chem.) linin
linneano -na *adj* Linnaean or Linnean
lino *m* (bot.) flax; flax fiber; linen; canvas; (poet.) sail
linóleo *m* linoleum
linón *m* lawn (*fabric*)
linotipia *f* linotype
linotipista *mf* linotyper or linotypist
lintel *m* var. of **dintel**
linterna *f* lantern; (arch. & mach.) lantern; (naut.) lantern (*of lighthouse*); **linterna de Aristóteles** (zool.) Aristotle's lantern; **linterna china** Japanese lantern; **linterna eléctrica** flashlight; **linterna mágica** magic lantern; **linterna sorda** dark lantern; **linterna veneciana** Japanese lantern
linternazo *m* blow with a lantern; (coll.) blow, smack
linternero -ra *mf* lantern maker or dealer
linternón *m* big lantern; (naut.) poop lantern
liño *m* row of trees, shrubs, or other plants
liñuelo *m* strand (*of a rope or cable*)
lío *m* bundle, package; batch (*of papers*); (coll.) muddle, mess; (coll.) liaison; **armar un lío** (coll.) to raise a row, stir up trouble; **hacerse un lío** (coll.) to get in a jam; **traer un lío con** (coll.) to have an affair with
lionés -nesa *adj & mf* Lyonese; **a la lionesa** (cook.) lyonnaise (*potatoes*)
liorna *f* (coll.) uproar, hubbub, confusion; (*cap.*) *f* Leghorn (*city*)
lioso -sa *adj* (coll.) scheming, trouble-making; (coll.) knotty, troublesome
lipasa *f* (biochem.) lipase
lipoma *m* (path.) lipoma
liq.ⁿ abr. of **liquidación**
líq.º abr. of **líquido**
liquefacción *f* liquefaction
liquefacer §55 *va & vr* to liquefy
liquefactible *adj* liquefiable
liquefacto -ta *adj* liquefied
liquen *m* (bot. & path.) lichen
liquenina *f* (chem.) lichenin
liquenología *f* lichenology
liquenoso -sa *adj* lichenous
liquidable *adj* liquefiable
liquidación *f* liquefaction; liquidation
liquidador -dora *adj* liquidating; *mf* liquidator; **liquidador de averías** insurance adjuster
liquidámbar *m* (bot.) liquidambar (*tree and liquid*)
liquidar *va & vr* to liquefy; to liquidate
liquidez *f* liquidity
líquido -da *adj* liquid; (com.) net; (phonet.) liquid; *m* liquid; (com.) net; **líquido amoniacal** ammoniacal liquor, ammonia liquor; **líquido imponible** taxable net; *f* (phonet.) liquid
lira *f* (mus.) lyre; inspiration, poetry (*of a given poet*); (*cap.*) *f* (astr.) Lyre or Lyra
lirado -da *adj* lyre-shaped; (bot.) lyrate

liria *f* birdlime
lírico -ca *adj* lyric, lyrical; (theat.) lyric (*musical, operatic*); (Am.) fantastic, utopian; *m* lyric poet; (Am.) visionary, utopian; *f* lyric poetry
lirio *m* (bot.) iris; **lirio amarillo** (bot.) yellow flag; **lirio blanco** (bot.) lily; **lirio de agua** (bot.) calla, calla lily; **lirio de Florencia** (bot.) fleur-de-lis, orris, Florentine iris; **lirio de los valles** (bot.) lily of the valley; **lirio de mar** (zool.) sea lily (*crinoid*); **lirio hediondo** (bot.) stinking iris, gladdon; **lirio tricolor** (bot.) red jasmine
liriodendro *m* (bot.) tulip tree, yellow pine
lirismo *m* lyricism
lirón *m* (zool.) dormouse; (bot.) water plantain; (fig.) sleepyhead
lis *f* (bot.) iris; (bot.) lily
lisa *f* see **liso**
Lisandro *m* Lysander
Lisboa *f* Lisbon
lisboeta, lisbonense or **lisbonés -nesa** *adj* (pertaining to) Lisbon; *mf* native or inhabitant of Lisbon
lisencoísmo *m* Lysenkoism
lisera *f* (fort.) berm
lisiado -da *adj* hurt, abused; crippled; eager, wild (*about something*); *mf* cripple
lisiar *va* to hurt, abuse; to cripple; *vr* to become crippled
lisimaquia *f* (bot.) loosestrife; **lisimaquia roja** (bot.) purple loosestrife, willow herb
lisina *f* (biochem.) lysin or lysine
Lisipo *m* Lysippus
liso -sa *adj* smooth, even; plain, unadorned (*clothes*); simple, plain-dealing; **liso y llano** simple, easy; *m* (min.) smooth face (*of a rock*); *f* (ichth.) spiny loach; (ichth.) gray mullet; (ichth.) striped mullet
lisofobia *f* (psycopath.) lyssophobia
lisol *m* lysol
lisonja *f* flattery; (her.) lozenge
lisonjeador -dora *adj* flattering; pleasing; *mf* flatterer
lisonjear *va & vn* to flatter; to please, delight; *vr* to flatter oneself
lisonjero -ra *adj* flattering; pleasing; *mf* flatterer
lista *f* see **listo**
listado -da *adj* striped
listar *va* to list
listeado -da *adj* var. of **listado**
listel *m* (arch.) listel, fillet; milled edge of coin
listerina *f* listerine
listero *m* timekeeper; roll taker, roll keeper
listeza *f* (coll.) readiness, quickness, alertness, craftiness
listo -ta *adj* ready, prepared; ready, quick, prompt; alert, wide-awake; **estar listo** to be finished (*with a task*); **pasarse de listo** (coll.) to bubble over, to go out on a limb; **más listo que Cardona** (coll.) as quick as lightning; **listo de manos** (coll.) light-fingered ‖ *f* list; roll; strip; colored stripe (*in a fabric*); roll call; **pasar lista** to call the roll; **lista de bajas** casualty list; **lista de comidas** bill of fare; **lista de correos** general delivery; **lista de espera** waiting list; **lista de frecuencia** frequency list (*of words*); **lista de pagos** pay roll; **lista de revista** (mil.) roll call; **lista negra** black list, black book
listón -tona *adj* white-striped, light-striped (*bull*); *m* tape, ribbon; strip (*of wood*); lath; (arch.) listel, fillet
listonado *m* lath, lathing
listonar *va* to build or construct with strips of wood
listoncillo *m* (carp.) bead
lisura *f* smoothness, evenness; candor, simplicity; (Am.) piece of impudence; (Am.) obscenity
lit. abr. of **literalmente**
lita *f* (vet.) tongue worm (*especially in a dog*)
litargirio *m* (chem.) litharge
lite *f* lawsuit
litera *f* litter; berth (*in boat or train*); **litera alta** upper berth; **litera baja** lower berth
literal *adj* literal
literalidad *f* literalness, literality
literalismo *m* literalism
literalista *adj* literalist, literalistic; *mf* literalist
literario -ria *adj* literary
literato -ta *adj* literary (*person*); *mf* literary person, writer
literatura *f* literature; **literatura de escape** escape literature
litiasis *f* (path.) lithiasis
lítico -ca *adj* lithic; (chem.) lithic
litigación *f* litigation
litigante *adj & mf* litigant
litigar §59 *va & vn* litigate
litigio *m* lawsuit, litigation; dispute, argument
litigioso -sa *adj* litigious
litina *f* (chem.) lithia
litio *m* (chem.) lithium
litis *f* (*pl:* **-tis**) lawsuit
litisconsorte *mf* (law) joint litigant
litiscontestación *f* (law) answer to an allegation; (law) litiscontestation
litisexpensas *fpl* (law) costs of a suit
litispendencia *f* (law) pending litigation
litoclasa *f* (geol.) lithoclase
litófago -ga *adj* (zool.) lithophagous
litofotografía *f* lithophotography
litografía *f* lithograph; lithography
litografiar §90 *va* to lithograph
litográfico -ca *adj* lithographic
litógrafo -fa *mf* lithographer
litoideo -a *adj* lithoid
litología *f* (geol. & med.) lithology
litológico -ca *adj* lithologic or lithological
litomarga *f* (mineral.) lithomarge
litopón *m* lithopone
litoral *adj* littoral, coastal; *m* littoral, coast, shore
litorina *f* (zool.) periwinkle
litosfera *f* lithosphere
lítote *f* (rhet.) litotes
litotomía *f* (surg.) lithotomy
litotricia *f* (surg.) lithotrity
litotritor *m* (surg.) lithotrite
litráceo -a *adj* (bot.) lythraceous
litre *m* (bot.) lithi
litro *m* liter
Lituania *f* Lithuania
lituano -na *adj & mf* Lithuanian; *m* Lithuanian (*language*)
lituo *m* (hist.) lituus (*augur's staff; trumpet*)
liturgia *f* liturgy
litúrgico -ca *adj* liturgic or liturgical
liturgista *m* liturgist
liviandad *f* lightness; fickleness; triviality; lewdness
liviano -na *adj* light; fickle; trivial; lewd; *m* leading donkey; **livianos** *mpl* lights, lungs
lividez *f* lividity
lívido -da *adj* livid
Livio *m* Livy
livor *m* lividness; evil, envy, hate; disorder
lixiviador *m* leach (*vessel*)
lixiviar *va & vr* to leach
liza *f* lists (*place of combat*); combat, contest; (ichth.) mullet; **entrar en liza** to enter the lists
lizarol *m* harness shaft (*of loom*)
lizo *m* warp; heddle, leash
Lm. abr. of **lumen**
lo *art def neut* (followed by masc form of adj) the, e.g., **lo hermoso** the beautiful; (the adj can often be translated by corresponding noun ending in -ness), e.g., **lo rápido de sus movimientos** the rapidness of his movements; (followed by adv or inflected adj) how, e.g., **me sorprende ver lo bien que habla Vd. el español** I am surprised to see how well you speak Spanish; **perdieron cuanto tenían a pesar de lo tacaños que eran** they lost all they had in spite of how stingy they were; **lo más** as . . . as, e.g., **lo más temprano posible** as early as possible; *pron pers* him, it; you; (with verb **estar, ser, parecer,** etc., it represents an adj or noun understood and is either not translated or is translated by 'so'), e.g., **estoy cansado pero ella no lo está** I am tired but she is not; **aunque no es rico, quiere parecerlo** although he is not rich, he wants to appear so; *pron dem* that; **de lo que** + *verb* more than + *verb*, e.g., **escri-**

be mejor de lo que habla he writes better than he speaks; **todo lo que** all that, e.g., **he perdido todo lo que tenía** I lost all I had; **lo de** the question of, the matter of, e.g., **lo de la guerra fría** the question of the cold war; **lo de que** the fact that, the statement that; **lo de siempre** the same old story; **lo que** what, e.g., **lo que Vd. necesita es ejercicio** what you need is exercise
loa *f* praise; prologue (*of medieval play*); short dramatic poem
loable *adj* laudable, praiseworthy
loador -dora *adj* eulogistic; *mf* eulogizer, eulogist
loar *va* to praise
loba *f* see **lobo**
lobado -da *adj* lobate
lobagante *m* (zool.) lobster (*Homarus*)
lobanillo *m* wen, cyst; gall
lobato *m* wolf cub
lobelia *f* (bot.) lobelia
lobeliáceo -a *adj* (bot.) lobeliaceous
lobero -ra *adj* (pertaining to the) wolf; *m* wolf hunter; *f* thicket infested with wolves
lobezno *m* wolf cub; wolfkin, little wolf
lobina *f* (ichth.) bass, sea bass
lobo -ba *adj & mf* (Am.) half-breed; *m* (zool.) wolf; (ichth.) loach; lobe; (coll.) drunk; **coger** or **pillar un lobo** (coll.) to get a jag on; **desollar** or **dormir un lobo** (coll.) to sleep off a drunk; **lobo cerval** or **cervario** (zool.) lynx; **lobo de mar** (ichth.) sea wolf, wolf fish; (coll.) old salt, sea dog (*experienced sailor*); **lobo marino** (zool.) seal; **lobo marsupial** (zool.) thylacine, Tasmanian wolf; **lobo solitario** (fig.) lone wolf; *f* she-wolf; ridge between furrows; soutane, cassock
loboso -sa *adj* full of wolves, infested with wolves
lobotomía *f* (surg.) lobotomy
lóbrego -ga *adj* gloomy (*dark; sad, melancholy*)
lobreguecer §34 *va* to make dark, make gloomy; *vn* to grow dark
lobreguez *f* darkness; gloominess
lobulado -da *adj* lobate, lobed; lobulate; (arch.) foliated
lobular *adj* lobular; lobar
lobulillo *m* lobule
lóbulo *m* lobe; (arch.) foil
lobuno -na *adj* (pertaining to the) wolf, wolfish
locación *f* lease
local *adj* local; (med.) local; *m* rooms, quarters, premises: **local de negocios** place of business; **local prohibido** disorderly house
localidad *f* locality; accommodations (*e.g., on a train*); (theat.) seat
localismo *m* localism
localización *f* localization; location; **localización de averías** trouble shooting
localizar §76 *va* to localize; to locate; to shoot (*trouble*); to limit, to limit the spread of; *vr* to be or become localized; to be located; (coll.) to become acclimated
locatario -ria *mf* renter, tenant
locativo -va *adj* (pertaining to a) lease; (gram.) locative; *m* (gram.) locative
locería *f* (Am.) chinaware; (Am.) set of china dishes; (Am.) pottery
locero -ra *mf* (coll.) var. of **ollero**
loción *f* wash, ablution; (pharm.) lotion
loco -ca *adj* crazy, mad, insane; wild, harum-scarum; awry; wonderful (*luck*); huge (*crop*); loose (*pulley*); (naut.) wild; **estar loco por** (coll.) to be crazy or mad about; **volver loco** to drive crazy; **loco de amor** madly in love; **loco de atar** (coll.) crazy as a bedbug, raving mad; **loco de contento** (coll.) mad with joy; **loco perenne** permanently mad; (coll.) full of fun; **loco rematado** (coll.) crazy as a bedbug, raving mad; *mf* insane person, lunatic, maniac; *m* fool (*jester*)
locoísmo *m* (vet.) loco disease
locomoción *f* locomotion
locomotivo -va *adj* locomotive
locomotor -tora or **-triz** (*pl:* **-trices**) *adj* locomotor; locomotive; **locomotora** *f* (rail.) engine, locomotive; **locomotora de empuje** (rail.) pusher engine; **locomotora de maniobras** (rail.) shifting engine; **locomotora de mercancías** (rail.) freight engine; **locomotora de viajeros** (rail.) passenger engine
locomotora-ténder *f* (*pl:* **locomotoras-ténder**) (rail.) tank engine, tank locomotive
locomóvil *adj* locomobile; *f* locomobile, tractor
locro *m* (Am.) meat and vegetable stew
locuacidad *f* loquacity
locuaz *adj* (*pl:* **-cuaces**) loquacious
locución *f* locution, expression; idiomatic phrase
locuelo -la *adj* (coll.) wild, frisky (*youngster*); *f* speech, way of speaking (*of an individual*)
loculado -da *adj* (bot.) loculate
locular *adj* locular
loculicida *adj* loculicidal
lóculo *m* (bot. & hist.) loculus
locura *f* madness, insanity; madness, folly; **locura de doble forma** (psychopath.) manic-depressive insanity
locutor -tora *mf* (rad.) announcer, commentator
locutorio *m* parlor, locutory (*in a nunnery*); telephone booth
locha *f* or **loche** *m* (ichth.) loach
lodachar *m*, **lodazal** *m* or **lodazar** *m* mudhole
lodo *m* mud; (chem.) lute (*substance used to close or seal a joint, porous surface, etc.*)
lodoñero *m* (bot.) guaiacum, lignum vitae
lodoso -sa *adj* muddy
lofobranquio -quia *adj & m* (ichth.) lophobranch
loganiáceo -a *adj* (bot.) loganiaceous
logarítmico -ca *adj* logarithmic or logarithmical
logaritmo *m* (math.) logarithm; **logaritmo vulgar** (math.) common logarithm
logia *f* lodge (*e.g., of Masons*); (arch.) loggia
lógico -ca *adj* logical; *mf* logician; *f* logic
logístico -ca *adj* (mil.) logistic or logistical; *f* (mil.) logistics
logogrifo *m* logogriph
logomaquia *f* logomachy
logotipo *m* (print.) logotype
logrado -da *adj* successful
lograr *va* to get, obtain; to attain; to produce, manage to produce; **lograr** + *inf* to succeed in + *ger; vr* to succeed, turn out well
logrear *vn* to be a moneylender; to profiteer
logrería *f* moneylending, usury; profiteering
logrerismo *m* (Am.) peculation
logrero -ra *adj* moneylending, usurious; profiteering; grasping; *mf* moneylender, usurer; profiteer; (Am.) sponger
logro *m* attainment; gain, profit; success; usury; **dar** or **prestar a logro** to lend at usurious rates
loica *f* (orn.) tanager
Loira *m* Loire
loísmo *m* use of **lo** for the accusative, instead of **le**
loísta *mf* user of **lo** for the accusative, instead of **le**
lolardo *m* Lollard
loma *f* long, low hill; **la loma de San Juan** San Juan Hill
lombarda *f* see **lombardo**
Lombardía *f* Lombardy
lombardo -da *adj & mf* Lombard; *f* (bot.) drumhead cabbage
lombriguera *f* hole in the ground made by a worm; wormy place; (bot.) tansy
lombriz *f* (*pl:* **-brices**) (zool.) worm, earthworm; (coll.) beanpole (*tall, skinny person*); **lombrices** *fpl* (path.) worms; **lombriz de los niños** (zool.) pinworm, threadworm; **lombriz de tierra** (zool.) earthworm; **lombriz intestinal** (zool.) intestinal worm; **lombriz solitaria** (zool.) tapeworm
lombrosiano -na *adj* Lombrosian
lomear *vn* to arch the back (*said of a horse*)
lomentáceo -a *adj* (bot.) lomentaceous
lomento *m* (bot.) loment
lomera *f* backstrap (*of harness*); ridgepole; (b.b.) backing
lometa *f* hill
lomienhiesto -ta *adj* var. of **lominhiesto**
lomillería *f* (Am.) harness maker's shop
lomillo *m* (sew.) cross-stitch; **lomillos** *spl* pads of packsaddle

lominhiesto -ta *adj* high-backed, high-cropped; (coll.) vain, conceited
lomo *m* back (*of animal, of book, of knife*); ridge between furrows; crease; loin; **lomos** *mpl* ribs; **lomo de asno** (rail.) hump
lomudo -da *adj* broad-backed
lona *f* canvas; (naut.) sailcloth; (poet.) sail; (Am.) burlap
loncha *f* slab, flagstone; slice, strip
londinense or **londonense** *adj* (pertaining to) London; *mf* Londoner
Londres *m* London; **el Gran Londres** Greater London
long. abr. of **longitud**
longanimidad *f* long-suffering, forbearance, magnanimity
longánimo -ma *adj* long-suffering, magnanimous
longaniza *f* pork sausage; (coll.) beanpole (*tall, skinny person*)
longevidad *f* longevity
longevo -va *adj* longevous, aged, very old
longílocuo -cua *adj* long-tongued, talkative
longiloquio *m* long, tiresome conversation
longincuidad *f* remoteness, distance; length (*of time*); length, extension
longincuo -cua *adj* remote, distant
Longino *m* Longinus
longirrostro -tra *adj* longirostral; (pal.) longirostrine
longísimo -ma *adj super* very long
longitud *f* longitude; length; **longitud de onda** (phys.) wave length
longitudinal *adj* longitudinal
longividente *adj* far-seeing, far-sighted
longobardo -da *adj & mf* Longobard
longorón *m* (zool.) piddock
longuera *f* long strip of land
longuetas *fpl* (surg.) bandages
longuísimo -ma *adj super* very long
lonja *f* exchange, market; grocery store; wool warehouse; slice; strap; stone step (*in front of church*); gallery, passageway
lonjear *va* (Am.) to cut (*hide*) into strips
lonjeta *f* bower, summerhouse
lonjista *mf* grocer
lontananza *f* far horizon; (paint.) background; **en lontananza** far away
loor *m* praise
lopiano -na *adj* (pertaining to) Lope de Vega
lopista *mf* authority on Lope de Vega
loquear *vn* to talk nonsense, to act like a fool; to have a high time, to carry on
loquera *f* see **loquero**
loquería *f* (Am.) madhouse, insane asylum
loquero -ra *mf* guard in an insane asylum; *m* (Am.) confusion, pandemonium; (Am.) madhouse (*place of confusion*); *f* insane asylum; (Am.) madness, insanity
loquesco -ca *adj* funny, jolly
loquial *adj* lochial
loquios *mpl* (obstet.) lochia
lorán *m* (naut.) loran
lorantáceo -a *adj* (bot.) loranthaceous
loranto *m* (bot.) mistletoe (*Loranthus*)
lord *m* (*pl:* **lores**) lord; Lord (*title*)
lordosis *f* (path.) lordosis
loredo *m* var. of **lauredal**
Lorena, la Lorraine
lorenés -nesa *adj* Lorrainese; *mf* Lorrainer
Lorenzo *m* Laurence or Lawrence
loriga *f* (arm. & zool.) lorica
loriguillo *m* (bot.) mezereon
loris *m* (*pl:* **-ris**) (zool.) loris; **loris cenceño** (zool.) slow loris
loro -ra *adj* dark-brown; blond; *m* (orn.) parrot; (bot.) cherry laurel; (ichth.) scarus; glass bedpan; (Am.) spy; **loro de mar** (ichth.) peacock fish
lorza *f* pleat, tuck
Lor.zo abr. of **Lorenzo**
los, las *art def pl* the; *pron pers pl* you, them; *pron dem* those, e.g., **los de mi hermano** those of my brother
losa *f* slab, flagstone; grave; **echar** or **poner una losa encima** to shut tight (*so that no news will leak out*)
losado *m* var. of **enlosado**
Losana *f* Lausanne
losange *m* lozenge, diamond; (geom. & her.) lozenge; (baseball) diamond
losangeado -da *adj* lozenged, lozenge-shaped; (her.) lozengy
losanjado -da *adj* (her.) lozengy
losar *va* var. of **enlosar**
loseta *f* small flagstone; **coger en la loseta** (coll.) to trick
lota *f* (ichth.) burbot
lote *m* lot, share, portion; lottery prize; (Am.) lot (*of ground*); (Am.) remnant; (Am.) swallow, swig; (Am.) dunce
lotear *va* (Am.) to divide into lots
lotería *f* lottery; lottery office; lotto (*game*); (fig.) gamble (*risk, chance*); **echar a la lotería** to put up (*money*) on the lottery
lotero -ra *mf* dealer in lottery tickets
lotificar §86 *va* (Am.) to divide into lots
lotiforme *adj* lotiform
lotización *f* (Am.) division into lots, development of new lots
lotizar §76 *va* (Am.) to divide into lots
loto *m* (bot., arch. & myth.) lotus; (bot.) lotus tree; **loto azul** (bot.) blue lotus, Egyptian lotus
lotófago -ga *adj* lotus-eating; *mf* lotus-eater
Lovaina *f* Louvain
lovaniense *adj* (pertaining to) Louvain; *mf* native or inhabitant of Louvain
loxocosmo *m* loxocosm
loxodromia *f* (naut.) loxodrome, rhumb line
loxodrómico -ca *adj* (naut.) loxodromic or loxodromical
loxodromismo *m* loxodromism
loxoftalmía *f* (path.) loxophthalmus
loxótico -ca *adj* loxotic
loxotomía *f* (surg.) loxotomy
loyo *m* (bot.) boletus
loza *f* crockery, earthenware; **loza fina** china, chinaware
lozanear *vn* to be luxuriant; to be full of life; to grow wild; *vr* to be luxuriant; to be full of life; to luxuriate, to take great delight
lozanía *f* verdure, luxuriance; vigor, exuberance; pride, haughtiness
lozano -na *adj* verdant, luxuriant; vigorous, exuberant; proud, haughty
L.S. abr. of **Locus Sigilli** (Lat.) **lugar del sello**
lúa *f* currying mitt; (prov.) saffron bag
lubigante *m* (zool.) lobster (*Homarus*)
lubina *f* var. of **lobina**
lubricación *f* lubrication
lubricador -dora *adj* lubricating; *mf* lubricator; *m* lubricator (*device*)
lubricán *m* dawn
lubricante *adj & m* lubricant
lubricar §86 *va* to lubricate
lubricidad *f* lubricity
lúbrico -ca *adj* lubricous (*slippery; lewd*)
lubrificar §86 *va* to lubricate
Lucano *m* Lucan
Lucas *m* Luke
lucentísimo -ma *adj super* very or most bright or shining
lucera *f* skylight, transom
lucerna *f* chandelier; loophole; (ichth.) flying gurnard; (*cap.*) *f* Lucerne
lucérnula *f* (bot.) corn cockle
lucero *m* Venus (*as morning or evening star*); bright star; light (*in a wall*); star (*in forehead of animal*); brilliance, splendor; **luceros** *mpl* (poet.) eyes; **lucero del alba** or **de la mañana** morning star (*Venus*); **lucero de la tarde** evening star (*Venus*)
Lucía *f* Lucy, Lucia
Luciano *m* Lucian
lucidez *f* lucidity; keenness; (psychol.) lucidity
lucido -da *adj* gracious, generous, magnificent; brilliant, successful; sumptuous, gorgeous
lúcido -da *adj* lucid (*clear, easy to understand*); (med.) lucid
lucidor -dora *adj* shining
lucidura *f* whitewash
luciente *adj* bright, shining, lucent
luciérnaga *f* (ent.) glowworm, firefly
Lucifer *m* Lucifer (*chief rebel angel; Venus as the morning star*); (*l.c.*) *m* overbearing fellow
luciferasa *f* (biochem.) luciferase

luciferino -na *adj* Luciferian; *f* (biochem.) luciferin
lucífero -ra *adj* (poet.) shining, dazzling; (*cap.*) *m* Lucifer (*Venus as the morning star*)
lucífugo -ga *adj* (biol.) lucifugous
lucillo *m* tomb, sepulcher
lucimiento *m* brilliancy, luster; show, display, dash; success; **quedar** or **salir con lucimiento** to come off with great success, to come off with flying colors
lucio -cia *adj* bright, shiny; *m* salt pool; (ichth.) pike, luce
lución *m* (zool.) blindworm, slowworm
lucir §60 *va* to illuminate, light up; to show, to display, to put on; to help, benefit; to plaster; to sport (*e.g., a new suit*); *vn* to shine; (fig.) to shine (*to be brilliant, to excel*); *vr* to dress up; to come off well; (fig.) to shine (*to be brilliant, to excel*); (iron.) to flop
lucrar *va* to get, obtain; *vn & vr* to profit; **lucrar de** to profit from, make money on
lucrativo -va *adj* lucrative
Lucrecia *f* Lucrece or Lucretia
Lucrecio *m* Lucretius
lucro *m* gain, profit; **lucros y daños** profit and loss
lucroso -sa *adj* lucrative, profitable
luctuoso -sa *adj* sad, gloomy
lucubración *f* lucubration
lucubrar *va & vn* lucubrate
Lúculo *m* Lucullus
lúcuma *f* canistel (*fruit*)
lucha *f* fight; struggle; wrestling; wrestling match; quarrel; **lucha de clases** class struggle; **lucha de la cuerda** (sport) tug of war; **lucha por la vida** struggle for existence
luchador -dora *mf* fighter; struggler; wrestler
luchar *vn* to fight; to struggle; to wrestle; to quarrel; **luchar por** + *inf* to struggle to + *inf*
lucharniego -ga *adj* night-hunting (*dog*)
ludibrio *m* mockery, scorn, derision
ludimiento *m* rubbing
ludión *m* (phys.) Cartesian devil
ludir *va, vn & vr* to rub, rub together
lúe *f* var. of **lúes**
luego *adv* soon; at once; then; therefore, then; **con tres luegos** (coll.) in a hurry; **desde luego** right away; of course; **hasta luego** good-bye, so long; **luego como** as soon as; **luego de** after, right after; **luego de** + *inf* after + *ger;* **luego que** as soon as
luengo -ga *adj* long
lúes *f* (path.) pestilence; (path.) lues (*syphilis*); **lúes canina** (vet.) distemper
luético -ca *adj* luetic
lugano *m* (orn.) linnet (*Acanthis spinus*)
lugar *m* place, position; site, spot; seat; room, space; village, hamlet; (geom.) locus; **dar lugar** to make room; **dar lugar a** to give rise to; **dar lugar a que** + *subj* to give reason for + *ger;* to give rise to + *ger;* **en lugar de** instead of, in place of; **en primer lugar** in the first place; **hacer lugar** to make room; **hacerse lugar** to make a place for oneself; **no ha lugar** (law) petition refused; **tener lugar** to fit; to take place; **tener lugar de** to take the place of, to serve as; **lugar ciego** (rad.) blind spot; **lugar común** toilet, water closet; commonplace; **lugar de cita** tryst; **lugares estrechos** close quarters; **lugar geométrico** (geom.) locus; **lugar seguro** safe place
lugarejo *m* hamlet
lugareño -na *adj* (pertaining to a) village; *mf* villager
lugarete *m* hamlet
lugarón *m* dull country town
lugartenencia *f* lieutenancy
lugarteniente *m* lieutenant
luge *m* sled
lugre *m* (naut.) lugger
lúgubre *adj* dismal, gloomy, lugubrious
luir §41 *va* (Am.) to rumple, to muss; (Am.) to polish (*pottery*); (naut.) to gall, to wear; *vr* (Am.) to rub, to wear away
Luis *m* Louis; Lewis; **Luis Felipe** Louis Philippe; **Luis Napoleón** Louis Napoleon
luisa *f* (bot.) lemon verbena; (*cap.*) *f* Louisa or Louise
Luisiana, La Louisiana
luisianense *adj & mf* Louisianan
lujación *f* var. of **luxación**
lujar *va* (Am.) to shine, to polish; (Am.) to rub; (Am.) to shine (*shoes*); *vr* to be dislocated
lujo *m* luxury; **de lujo** de luxe; **gastar mucho lujo** to live in high style; **lujo de** excess of, too much, too many
lujoso -sa *adj* luxurious; ostentatious; magnificent
lujuria *f* lust, lechery, luxury
lujuriante *adj* lustful; luxuriant
lujuriar *vn* to lust, to be lustful or lecherous; to couple, to pair (*said of animals*)
lujurioso -sa *adj* lustful, lecherous, lewd; *mf* lecher
lula *f* see **lulo**
luliano -na *adj* Lullian; *mf* Lullianist or Lullist
lulismo *m* philosophy of Raymond Lully
lulista *adj* Lullian; *mf* Lullianist or Lullist
lulo -la *adj* (Am.) lank, slender; *m* (Am.) bundle; *f* (prov.) squid
lulú *m* (*pl:* **-lúes**) spitz dog, Pomeranian
lumaquela *f* (petrog.) lumachel or lumachella
lumbago *m* (path.) lumbago
lumbán *m* (bot.) lumbang
lumbar *adj* lumbar
lumbarización *f* (path.) lumbarization
lumbodinia *f* (path.) lumbodynia
lumbosacro -cra *adj* lumbosacral
lumbrada *f* large fire, blaze
lumbral *m* var. of **umbral**
lumbrarada *f* var. of **lumbrada**
lumbre *f* fire, light; opening, light (*in a wall*); light (*to light a cigar or cigaret*); brightness, brilliance; knowledge, learning; (fig.) light (*of a countenance*); **lumbres** *fpl* tinder box; **a lumbre de pajas** (coll.) in a flash, like a flash; **a lumbre mansa** with slow flame; **echar lumbre** (coll.) to blow one's top; **ni por lumbre** (coll.) not for love or money; **ser la lumbre de los ojos de** to be the apple of the eye of; **lumbre del agua** surface of the water
lumbrera *f* light, source of light; louver (*opening to let in air and light*); skylight; dormer window; (carp.) slit (*in face of plane*); (mach.) port; (min.) ventilating shaft; (naut.) air duct; (fig.) light (*example, shining figure*); **lumbreras** *fpl* eyes; **lumbrera de admisión** (mach.) intake port; **lumbrera de escape** (mach.) exhaust port
lumbrerada *f* var. of **lumbrada**
lumbrical *adj* (anat.) lumbrical
lumbricosis *f* (path.) lumbricosis
lumen *m* (anat., bot. & phys.) lumen; **lumen hora** (*pl:* **lúmenes hora**) (phys.) lumen-hour
luminal *m* (pharm.) luminal
luminar *m* luminary; (fig.) luminary (*person*)
luminaria *f* (eccl.) altar lights; **luminarias** *fpl* lights, illumination (*for decoration*)
lumínico -ca *adj* photic; (pertaining to) light; lighting (*e.g., fixture*)
luminífero -ra *adj* luminiferous
luminiscencia *f* luminescence
luminiscente *adj* luminescent
luminosidad *f* luminosity
luminoso -sa *adj* luminous; (fig.) bright (*e.g., idea*)
luminotecnia *f* lighting engineering
luminotécnico -ca *adj* lighting; *m* lighting engineer
lun. abr. of **lunes**
luna *f* moon; moonlight; plate glass; mirror; lens, glass (*of spectacles*); (coll.) caprice, whim, wild idea; (ichth.) sunfish, moonfish; **dejar a la luna de Valencia** (coll.) to disappoint; **estar de buena luna** to be in a good humor; **estar de mala luna** to be in a bad humor; **ladrar a la luna** (coll.) to bark at the moon; **media luna** half moon; crescent (*shape of moon in first or last quarter; Mohammedanism; Turkish Empire*); **quedarse a la luna de Valencia** (coll.) to be disappointed; **luna creciente** crescent moon; **luna de agua** (bot.) white water lily; **luna de miel** honeymoon; **luna llena** full moon; **luna menguante** waning moon; **luna nueva** new moon
lunación *f* (astr.) lunation
lunado -da *adj* lunate; *f* (Am.) moonlight party

lunanco -ca *adj* with one quarter higher than the other (*said, e.g., of a horse*)
lunar *adj* lunar; *m* mole; polka dot; (fig.) stain, blot; (fig.) stigma; **lunar postizo** beauty spot
lunaria *f* (bot.) lunary; **lunaria menor** (bot.) moonwort
lunático -ca *adj* lunatic; temporarily unbalanced; *mf* lunatic; person temporarily unbalanced; moonstruck person
lunecilla *f* crescent-shaped jewel
lunes *m* (*pl:* **-nes**) Monday; **hacer san lunes** (Am.) to knock off on Monday; (Am.) to knock off on Monday because of a hangover; **lunes de carnaval** Shrove Monday
luneta *f* lens, glass (*of spectacles*); orchestra seat; front tile; lunette (*crescent-shaped ornament*); (arch. & fort.) lunette; (mach.) rest (*of a lathe*); (aut.) rear window
lunetario *m* (Am.) orchestra, parquet
luneto *m* (arch.) lunette
lunfardo *m* (Am.) thief; (Am.) underworld slang, thieves' Latin
lunisolar *adj* (astr.) lunisolar
lúnula *f* (anat. & zool.) lunule; (astr.) moon (*of other planets than the earth*); (geom.) lune; (opt.) meniscus
lupa *f* magnifying glass
lupanar *m* bawdyhouse, brothel
lupanario -ria *adj* (pertaining to a) bawdyhouse
lupercales *fpl* (hist.) Lupercalia
lupia *f* wen, cyst; (metal.) bloom; (Am.) bit, trifle; (Am.) witch doctor, quack; **lupias** *fpl* (Am.) small change
lupino -na *adj* lupine; *m* (bot.) lupine
lupulina *f* (bot.) black medic
lúpulo *m* (bot.) hop, hop vine; hops (*dried flowers of hop vine*)
lupus *m* (path.) lupus
luquete *m* slice of orange or lemon used to flavor wine; spot, hole (*in clothing*); bald spot; sulfur match or fuse; (arch.) dome (*of a Byzantine vault*); (Am.) unplowed patch in a fallow
Lurdes *f* Lourdes
lúrida *f* (orn.) golden oriole
lurio -ria *adj* (Am.) mad, crazy; (Am.) madly in love
lurte *m* (prov.) avalanche
lusitanismo *m* Lusitanism
lusitano -na *adj & mf* Lusitanian; Portuguese
lustrabotas *m* (*pl:* **-tas**) (Am.) bootblack
lustración *f* lustration
lustral *adj* lustral
lustrar *va* to shine, polish; to lustrate; *vn* to wander, roam
lustre *m* luster, gloss, shine, polish; shoe polish; (fig.) luster (*fame, glory*)
lustrina *f* lustrine; lustring; (Am.) shoe polish
lustro *m* lustrum (*five years*); chandelier; (hist.) lustrum
lustroso -sa *adj* shining, bright, lustrous
lútea *f* see **lúteo**
lutecio *m* (chem.) lutecium
luteína *f* (biochem. & physiol.) lutein
lúteo -a *adj* luteous; muddy, miry; mean, low, vile; *f* (orn.) golden oriole
luteolina *f* (chem.) luteolin
luteoma *m* (path.) luteoma
luteranismo *m* Lutheranism
luterano -na *adj & mf* Lutheran
Lutero *m* Luther
lutidina *f* (chem.) lutidine
luto *m* mourning; sorrow, bereavement; **lutos** *mpl* crape, mourning draperies; **aliviar el luto** to go out of deep mourning; **estar de luto** to be in mourning; **medio luto** half mourning; **luto riguroso** deep mourning
lutocaro *m* (Am.) trash cart
lutria *f* (zool.) otter
Luvre *m* Louvre (*museum*)
lux *m* (*pl:* **lux**) (phys.) lux
luxación *f* luxation, dislocation
luxar *va* to luxate, dislocate
Luxemburgo *m* Luxemburg
luxemburgués -guesa *adj* Luxemburgian; *mf* Luxemburger
luz *f* (*pl:* **luces**) light; window, opening, light; guiding light; (coll.) money; **luces** *fpl* enlightenment, culture; **a la luz de** in the light of; **a primera luz** at dawn; **a toda luz** or **a todas luces** everywhere; by all means; **dar a luz** to have a child; to give birth to; to bring out, publish; **echar luz** (coll.) to recover, get stronger; **echar luz sobre** to cast, shed, or throw light on; **entre dos luces** at twilight; (coll.) half-seas over, half drunk; **sacar a luz** to bring to light; **salir a luz** to come to light; to come out, be published; to take place; **ver la luz** to see the light, see the light of day; **luces de Bengala** (aer.) flares; **luces de carretera** (aut.) bright lights; **luces de cruce** (aut.) dimmers; **luz de balizaje** (aer.) marker light; **luz de Bengala** Bengal light; **luz de calcio** calcium light; **luz de frenado** brake light; **luz de magnesio** magnesium light; (phot.) flash bulb, flashlight; **luz de matrícula** license-plate light; **luz del mundo** (theol.) light of the World; **luz de parada** or **paro** stop light; **luz fría** cold light; **luz indicadora** pilot light; **luz negra** (phys.) black light; **luz trasera** tail light
Luzbel *m* Lucifer (*chief rebel angel, Satan*)
luzco *1st sg pres ind of* **lucir**
Lx. abr. of **lux**

Ll

Ll, ll *f* fourteenth letter of the Spanish alphabet
llaga *f* ulcer; sore; torment, cause of pain or sorrow; (mas.) seam
llagar §59 *va* to make sore; to hurt, to wound
llagua *f* var. of **yagua**
llama *f* flame, blaze; marsh, swamp; fiery passion; (zool.) llama; **salir de las llamas y caer en las brasas** to jump out of the frying pan into the fire; **llama manométrica** (phys.) manometric flame; **llama oxidante** (chem.) oxidizing flame; **llama reductora** (chem.) reducing flame
llamada *f* see **llamado**
llamadera *f* goad
llamado -da *adj* so-called; *m* call; *f* call; sign, signal (*to call someone*); knock, ring; reference, reference mark; (mil.) call, call to arms; **tocar** or **batir llamada** (mil.) to sound the call to arms; **llamada a filas** (mil.) call to the colors; **llamada a quintas** draft call
llamador -dora *mf* caller; *m* messenger; knocker; push button
llamamiento *m* call; divine inspiration
llamar *va* to call; to name; to summon; to call upon, to invoke; to attract; **estar llamado a** to have a natural aptitude for; *vn* to knock, to ring; *vr* to be called; (naut.) to veer; **¿cómo se llama Vd.?** what is your name?
llamarada *f* flare-up; flush; (fig.) flare-up, outburst
llamargo *m* marsh, swamp
llamarón *m* (Am.) var. of **llamarada**
llamativo -va *adj* thirst-raising; showy, flashy, gaudy
llamazar *m* marsh, swamp
llambria *f* steep rocky surface, steep face of a rock
llame *m* (Am.) bird net, bird trap
llameante *adj* flaming, blazing, flashing
llamear *vn* to flame, blaze, flash
llampo *m* (Am.) ore; (Am.) stone quarry
llana *f* see **llano**
llanada *f* plain, level ground
llanero *m* plainsman
llaneza *f* plainness, simplicity
llano -na *adj* smooth, even, level; plane; plain, simple; clear, evident; (phonet.) paroxytone; *m* plain; llano (*broad treeless plain*); landing (*of stairs*); side of a sheet of paper; *f* trowel; plain; **a la llana** simply; in the open; **de llano** plainly, openly
llanque *m* (Am.) rawhide sandal
llanta *f* felloe; rim (*of wheel*); tire; (bot.) kale; **llanta de goma** rubber tire; **llanta de oruga** track (*band of caterpillar tractor*)
llantén *m* (bot.) plantain; **llantén menor** (bot.) ribwort
llantera *f* (coll.) blubber, yammer
llantería *f* or **llanterío** *m* (Am.) weeping, wailing
llantina *f* (coll.) var. of **llantera**
llanto *m* weeping, crying; **en llanto** in tears
llanura *f* smoothness, evenness, level; plain; **llanura aluvial** flood plain
llapa *f* var. of **yapa**
llapango -ga *adj* (Am.) barefooted (*Indian*)
llares *fpl* pothanger
llatar *m* (prov.) rail fence
llaupangue *m* (bot.) pink francoa
llauquear *vr* (Am.) to fall to pieces, to come to ruin
llave *f* key; wrench, key; faucet, spigot; (elec.) switch; (print.) bracket; (mus.) key; (fig.) key (*means of solving a problem, secret, etc.; place controlling entrance to a sea, country, etc.*); **debajo de llave** under lock and key; **echar la llave a** to lock; **llave de afinar** (mus.) tuning key or hammer; **llave de cadena** chain tongs or wrench; **llave de caja** socket wrench; **llave de cambio** shift key; **llave de caño** pipe wrench; **llave de cubo** socket wrench; **llave de estufa** damper (*to control draft*); **llave de la mano** span of the hand; **llave del pie** distance from heel to instep; **llave de mandíbulas** or **llave dentada** alligator wrench; **llave de paso** stopcock; passkey; **llave de percusión** or **de pistón** percussion lock; **llave de purga** drain cock; **llave de salto** margin release, margin release key; **llave de tiempo atrasado** (elec.) delayed-time switch; **llave de trinquete** ratchet wrench; **llave espacial** space bar or key; **llave falsa** false key, picklock; **llave inglesa** monkey wrench; **llave maestra** master key, skeleton key; **llave para embutir** (elec.) flush switch, flushmounted switch; **llave para tubos** pipe wrench; **llaves de la iglesia** (eccl.) power of the keys; *adj* key
llavero -ra *mf* keeper of the keys; turnkey; *m* key ring
llavín *m* latchkey
lleco -ca *adj* virgin (*soil*)
llegada *f* arrival
llegar §59 *va* to push, bring up; *vn* to arrive; to happen; to reach; to amount; to be equal; **llegar a** to arrive at; **llegar a** + *inf* to come to, to get to + *inf;* to succeed in + *ger;* **llegar a ser** to become; *vr* to move close, come near; to get, to go
llena *f* see **lleno**
llenado *m* filling
llenador -dora *adj* (Am.) filling (*food*)
llenar *va* to fill; to fill out; to fulfill; to satisfy; to overwhelm; to annoy, bother; *vn* to be full (*said of moon*); *vr* to fill, fill up, become full; (coll.) to stuff oneself; (coll.) to become annoyed; **llenarse a rebosar** to be filled to overflowing; **llenarse de** to get covered with; to be overwhelmed with; to be deeply in (*e.g., debt*)
llenero -ra *adj* full, entire, complete
lleno -na *adj* full; solid; **lleno a rebosar** full to overflowing; *m* fill, plenty; fulness, full enjoyment; perfection, completeness; full moon; full house (*e.g., in a theater*); **de lleno** fully, entirely; squarely; **lleno de la luna** full of the moon; *f* flood
llenura *f* fulness, abundance
llera *f* gravel pit
lleta *f* (bot.) sprout
lleudar *va & vr* var. of **leudar**
lleuque *m* (bot.) plum fir
lleva or **llevada** *f* carrying, conveying; ride; **lleva gratuita** free ride
llevadero -ra *adj* bearable, tolerable
llevar *va* to carry, to take, to lead; to carry away, take away; to yield; to keep (*accounts, books, etc.*); to carry on, to conduct (*correspondence*); to put (*a play on the screen, a program on the air*); to be in charge of, to manage; to lead (*a certain kind of life*); to bear (*arms*); to bear, to stand for; to suffer (*punishment*); to charge (*a certain price*); to take off, sever; to get, obtain; to win; to wear (*clothes*); to have been, e.g., **llevo mucho tiempo aquí** I have been here a long time; **lleva cinco días ausente** he has been absent five days; **llevo dos años de estudiar el español** I have been studying Spanish for two years; (arith.) to carry; **a todo llevar** for all kinds of wear (*said of clothing*); **llevar a** to exceed; to be ahead of (*by a certain distance*), e.g., **este vapor lleva cinco millas al otro** this

steamer is five miles ahead of the other one; to be heavier than (*by a certain weight*), e.g., **este muchacho lleva tres kilogramos a aquél** this boy is three kilograms heavier than that one; to be older than (*by a certain number of days, months, years, etc.*), e.g., **mi hijo lleva al suyo un año** my son is a year older than yours; **llevar a alguien a** + *inf* to take someone to + *inf;* to lead someone to + *inf;* **llevarla hecha** (coll.) to have it all figured out; **llevar las de perder** (coll.) to be in a bad way; **llevar puesto** to wear, to have on (*a garment*); **llevar** + *pp* to have + *pp*, e.g.,**lleva conseguidas muchas victorias** he has won many victories; **no llevarlas todas consigo** (coll.) to be scared ‖ *vn* to lead; to charge; **llevar y traer** (coll.) to go around gossiping ‖ *vr* to carry away; to take, take away; to seize; to carry off; to win, carry off; to get along; **llevarse algo a alguien** to take something away from someone, to steal something from someone; **llevarse bien** to get along together; **llevarse bien con** to get along with, to fit in with; **llevarse mal con** to be on bad terms with

lloradera *f* (coll.) blubbering, yammering

llorador -dora *adj* weeping; *mf* weeper

lloraduelos *mf* (*pl:* **-los**) (coll.) sobber, sniveler, crybaby

lloralástimas *mf* (*pl:* **-mas**) (coll.) sniveling skinflint, poverty-crying penny pincher

lloramico *m* weeping; **lloramicos** *mf* (*pl:* **-cos**) (coll.) crybaby

lloranduelos *m* (*pl:* **-los**) (coll.) var. of **lloraduelos**

llorante *adj* weeping

llorar *va* to weep; to weep over; to mourn; *vn* to weep, to cry; to drip; to water, to run (*said of the eyes*); (plant path.) to weep

lloredo *m* growth of laurels

llorera *f* (coll.) blubber, yammer

llorica *mf* whiner, crybaby

lloriquear *vn* to whimper, to whine

lloriqueo *m* whimper, whimpering, whining

llorisquear *vn* (Am.) var. of **lloriquear**

llorisqueo *m* (Am.) var. of **lloriqueo**

lloro *m* weeping, crying; tears

llorón -rona *adj* weeping, whining; (bot.) weeping; *mf* weeper, whiner; crybaby; *m* (bot.) weeping willow; pendulous plume; *f* weeper, hired mourner

lloroso -sa *adj* weeping, weepy; tearful, sad

llovedero *m* (coll.) rainy spell

llovedizo -za *adj* leaky (*roof*); rain (*water*)

llover §63 *va* to rain (*to send like rain*); *vn* to rain; **como llovido** unexpectedly; **como llovido del cielo** like manna from heaven; **llueva o no** rain or shine; **llueve** it is raining; *vr* to leak (*said of a roof*)

llovido -da *mf* stowaway

llovioso -sa *adj* var. of **lluvioso**

llovizna *f* drizzle

lloviznar *vn* to drizzle

lloviznoso -sa *adj* drizzled, wet from drizzle; (Am.) drizzly

llueca *f* brooding hen

lluvia *f* rain; rain water; (fig.) rain; (fig.) heap, mass, flock; **lluvia de estrellas** star shower; **lluvia de oro** heap of gold, great wealth; (bot.) golden chain, laburnum; (bot.) goldenrod; **lluvia radiactiva** fallout, radioactive fallout

lluviosidad *f* raininess

lluvioso -sa *adj* rainy

M

M, m *f* fifteenth letter of the Spanish alphabet
m. abr. of **mañana, masculino, meridiano, metro** or **metros, milla, minuto** or **minutos** & **muerto**
M. abr. of **Madre (religiosa), Maestro, Majestad, mediano** & **Merced**
m/ abr. of **mi** & **mes**
m² abr. of **metro cuadrado** & **metros cuadrados**
M.ª abr. of **María**
maca *f* flaw, blemish; spot, stain; bruise (*on fruit*); fraud, deceit
Macabeo *m* (Bib.) Maccabaeus; **macabeos** *mpl* (Bib.) Maccabees
macábrico -ca or **macabro -bra** *adj* macabre
macaco -ca *adj* (Am.) ugly, misshapen; *mf* (zool.) macaque; **macaco de la India** (zool.) rhesus; *f* (Am.) drunk, jag
macadam *m* macadam
macadamizar §76 *va* to macadamize
macadán *m* var. of **macadam**
macana *f* (Am.) macana (*wooden sword or club*); trick, lie; drug on the market; (Am.) nonsense; (Am.) botch
macanazo *m* (Am.) blow with a macana; (Am.) great nonsense
macanear *vn* (Am.) to exaggerate, boast, joke
macanudo -da *adj* (coll.) stunning, terrific; (Am.) strong, husky; (Am.) swell, grand; (Am.) nonsensical
macar §86 *vr* to rot from bruises (*said of fruit*)
macareo *m* tide rip in a river
macarrón *m* macaroon; (naut.) bulwark; **macarrones** *mpl* macaroni; (naut.) stanchions
macarronea *f* macaronic (*poem*)
macarrónico -ca *adj* macaronic
macasar *m* antimacassar
macear *va* to mace, to hammer, to pound; *vn* to be insistent, to bore
macedón -dona *adj* & *mf* Macedonian
macedonia *f* & **Macedonia** *f* see **macedonio**
macedónico -ca *adj* Macedonian
macedonio -nia *adj* & *mf* Macedonian; *f* macédoine (*salad; medley*); (*cap.*) *f* Macedonia; **macedonia de frutas** fruit salad
macelo *m* slaughterhouse
maceo *m* macing, hammering
maceración *f* maceration
macerador -dora *adj* macerating; *mf* macerater
maceramiento *m* var. of **maceración**
macerar *va* & *vr* to macerate
macerina *f* (Am.) saucer with device to hold chocolate cup
macero *m* macer, macebearer
maceta *f* tool handle; stone hammer, mason's hammer; flowerpot; vase for artificial flowers; (bot.) corymb; **maceta de aforrar** (naut.) serving mallet; **maceta de hojalatero** tinner's hammer
macetero *m* flowerpot stand
macfarlán *m* or **macferlán** *m* inverness, inverness cape
macia *f* var. of **macis**
macicez *f* solidity; massiveness
macilento -ta *adj* wan
macillo *m* hammer (*of piano*)
macis *f* mace (*spice*)
macito *m* tapper (*of a bell, decoherer, etc.*)
macizar §76 *va* to fill in, make solid
macizo -za *adj* solid; massive; (fig.) solid, sound; *m* solid; flower bed; wall space; clump, mass; mountain mass, massif; (aut.) solid tire
macla *f* wooden flail; (mineral.) macle
macle *m* (her.) mascle
maclura *f* (bot.) Osage orange (*plant and fruit*)
macolla *f* cluster, bunch
macollar *vn* & *vr* var. of **amacollar**
macón *m* dry, brown honeycomb
macramé *m* macramé
macrobiótico -ca *adj* macrobiotic; *f* macrobiotics
macrocito *m* (path.) macrocyte
macrocosmo *m* macrocosm
macrofísica *f* macrophysics
macrogameto *m* (biol.) macrogamete
macromolécula *f* macromolecule
macrosmático -ca *adj* (zool.) macrosmatic
macruro -ra *adj* & *m* (zool.) macruran
macsura *f* area reserved in a mosque for caliph and imam
macuache *m* (Am.) ignorant Mexican Indian
macuba *f* maccaboy (*perfumed snuff*); (ent.) musk beetle
macuco -ca *adj* (Am.) strong, husky; (Am.) sly, cunning; (Am.) notable, important; *m* (Am.) overgrown boy
mácula *f* spot; stain, blemish; (anat., astr. & path.) macula; (coll.) deception, trick; **mácula solar** sunspot
macular *va* to spot; (print.) to mackle; *vr* (print.) to mackle
maculatura *f* (print.) mackle; (print.) mackled sheet of paper
macuquero *m* bootleg miner
macuto *m* (Am.) alms basket; (mil.) knapsack
macha *f* (zool.) tellina; (Am.) drunk, drunkenness; (Am.) joke, jest; (Am.) mannish woman
machaca *f* crusher; *mf* (coll.) bore; **¡dale, machaca!** (coll.) cut it out!
machacadera *f* crusher
machacador -dora *adj* crushing; *mf* crusher; *f* crusher (*machine*); **machacadora de martillos** hammer mill
machacamiento *m* crushing, pounding
machacante *m* (mil.) sergeant's aid
machacar §86 *va* to crush, to mash, to pound; *vn* to be insistent, to bore
machacón -cona *adj* boring, tiresome; *mf* bore
machaconería *f* boresomeness, tiresomeness
machada *f* flock of billy goats; (coll.) stupidity
machado *m* hatchet
machamartillo; a machamartillo (coll.) firmly, tightly; blindly, with blind faith
machaqueo *m* crushing, pounding
machaquería *f* tiresomeness, dullness
machaquero -ra *adj* (coll.) boring; *mf* (coll.) bore
machar *va* to crush, grind; *vr* (Am.) to get drunk
mache *m* (phys.) Mache unit
macheta *f* cleaver
machetazo *m* blow or hack with a machete
machete *m* machete; cane knife
machetear *va* var. of **amachetear**
machetero *m* man who clears ground with a machete; cane cutter; (Am.) revolutionary; (Am.) grind (*student*); **machetero de salón** (Am.) parlor revolutionary
machi *m* or **machí** *m* (Am.) medicine man
machihembradora *f* (carp.) machine for cutting tongue and groove; (carp.) mortiser (*machine*)
machihembrar *va* (carp.) to feather; (carp.) to mortise
machina *f* derrick, crane; pile driver
macho *adj* male, e.g., **la comadreja macho** the male weasel; **la flor macho** the male flower; strong, tough; stupid; (bot. & mach.) male; *m* sledge hammer; square anvil; anvil block; abutment, pillar; male (*animal*); hemule; hook (*of hook and eye*); stupid fellow;

foreigner, Anglo-Saxon; (coll.) blond; pin, peg; (coll.) he-man; (mach.) male piece or part; **macho cabrío** he-goat, billy goat; **macho de aterrajar** (mach.) tap, screw tap; **macho de cabrío** he-goat, billy goat; **macho de terraja** (mach.) tap, screw tap
machón *m* pillar, buttress
machona *adj fem* mannish (*woman*)
machorro -rra *adj* barren, sterile; *f* barren female
machota *f* hammer, mallet; (coll.) mannish woman; **a la machota** (Am.) carelessly, any old way
machote *m* hammer, mallet; rough draft
machucadura *f* or **machucamiento** *m* crushing, pounding; bruise, contusion
machucar **§86** *va* to crush, to pound, to bruise
machucón *m* (Am.) crushing; (Am.) bruise
machucho -cha *adj* thoughtful, judicious; elderly
machuelo *m* small he-mule; germ; clove (*of garlic*); (Am.) tap
madama *f* madame; (coll.) missus; (bot.) garden balsam
madamisela *f* young lady, damsel; mademoiselle
madamita *m* (coll.) sissy
madapolán *m* madapollam
madeja *f* skein, hank; mass of hair; (coll.) listless fellow; **hacer madeja** to rope, become ropy; **madeja sin cuenda** (coll.) hopeless tangle; (coll.) muddlehead; (coll.) sloppy fellow
madera *f* wood; piece of wood; lumber, timber; horny part (*of hoof*); (coll.) knack, flair, makings, qualities; **no holgar la madera** (coll.) to work all the time; **saber a la madera** (coll.) to be a chip off the old block; **ser de mala madera** or **tener mala madera** (coll.) to be a lazy loafer; **madera alburente** sapwood; **madera aserradiza** lumber (*cut for use*); **madera contrachapada** plywood; **madera de corazón** heartwood; **madera de raja** split timber; **madera de sierra** lumber (*cut for use*); **madera fósil** lignite; **madera laminada** plywood; **madera plástica** plastic wood; **madera serradiza** lumber (*cut for use*); **maderas preciosas** fancy woods; *m* Madeira, Madeira wine
maderable *adj* timber-yielding
maderada *f* raft, float
maderaje *m* or **maderamen** *m* lumber, woodwork
maderar *va* var. of **enmaderar**
maderería *f* lumberyard
maderero -ra *adj* (pertaining to) lumber; *m* lumberman; carpenter
maderista *m* (Am.) lumberman
madero *m* log, beam; (coll.) dolt; ship, vessel
madianita *mf* (Bib.) Midianite
Madona *f* Madonna; (f.a.) Madonna
mador *m* moisture, slight sweat
madoroso -sa *adj* moist
madrás *m* madras
madrastra *f* stepmother; callous mother; nuisance; (bot.) apple mint
madraza *f* (coll.) doting mother
madre *f* mother; matron; womb; bed (*of river*); main sewer; main irrigation ditch; mother (*of vinegar*); sediment, dregs; (fig.) mother; **futura madre** expectant mother; **sacar de madre a** (coll.) to upset, disturb; **ser la madre del cordero** to be the real cause; **madre adoptiva** foster mother; **madre de Dios** (eccl.) Mother of God; **madre del clavo** clove; **madre de leche** wet nurse; **madre de perlas** (zool.) pearl oyster; **madre patria** mother country, old country; **madre política** mother-in-law; stepmother; **madre tierra** mother earth; *adj* mother, e.g., **lengua madre** mother tongue; **leona madre** mother lioness
madrear *vn* to look like one's mother; (coll.) to keep saying ma (*said of a child*); *vr* to turn, grow sour
madrecilla *f* ovary (*of a bird*)
madreclavo *m* clove of two-year growth
madreña *f* wooden shoe
madreperla *f* (zool.) pearl oyster; mother-of-pearl
madrépora *f* (zool.) madrepore
madrepórico -ca *adj* madreporic
madrero -ra *adj* mother-loving
madreselva *f* (bot.) honeysuckle, trumpet honeysuckle; **madreselva de jardín** (bot.) yellow honeysuckle
madrigado -da *adj* that has sired (*said of a bull*); twice-married (*said of a woman*); (coll.) experienced
madrigal *m* madrigal; (mus.) madrigal
madrigalesco -ca *adj* madrigalian; elegant, overnice
madriguera *f* burrow, den, lair; (fig.) den (*e.g., of thieves*)
madrileño -ña *adj* Madrid, Madrilenian; *mf* Madrilenian
madrina *f* godmother; patroness; protectress; prop, stanchion; shore, brace; strap for yoking two horses; (Am.) leading mare; (Am.) tame herd used to gather and lead untamed cattle; **madrina de bodas** bridesmaid; **madrina de guerra** war mother (*soldier's correspondent*)
madrinazgo *m* godmothership; sponsorship
madrona *f* main sewer; (bot.) toothwort; (coll.) doting mother
madroncillo *m* strawberry (*fruit*)
madroñal *m* growth of arbutus or strawberry trees
madroñera *f* (bot.) arbutus, strawberry tree; growth of arbutus or strawberry trees
madroño *m* (bot.) arbutus, strawberry tree; (bot.) madroño; madroño apple; fruit of strawberry tree; berry-shaped tassel
madrugada *f* dawn; early morning (*before sunrise*); early rising; **de madrugada** early, at the break of day
madrugador -dora *adj* early-rising; *mf* early riser
madrugar **§59** *vn* to get up early; to be ahead, to be out in front
madrugón -gona *adj* early-rising; *m* (coll.) very early rising, getting up very early; **dar madrugón** (coll.) to get up very early
maduración *f* ripening; maturation
maduradero *m* place for ripening fruit
madurar *va* to ripen; to mature; to maturate; to think out; *vn* to ripen; to mature; to maturate
madurez *f* ripeness; maturity
maduro -ra *adj* ripe; mature
maese *m* (obs.) messer, master; (obs.) journeyman; **maese coral** prestidigitation, sleight of hand
maestra *f* see **maestro**
maestral *m* northwest wind; queen cell
maestralizar **§76** *vn* (naut.) to decline to the northwest (*said of compass*)
maestramente *adv* masterly, in a masterly fashion, skilfully
maestrante *m* member of riding club
maestranza *f* riding club of noblemen; arsenal, armory; navy yard; (Am.) machine shop
maestrazgo *m* mastership (*of a military order*)
maestre *m* master (*of a military order*); (naut.) master; **gran maestre** grand master
maestrear *va* to direct, manage, take over; to cut back slightly (*a grapevine*); (mas.) to screed; *vn* to domineer, to be domineering
maestresala *m* (archaic) chief waiter, taster (*for a nobleman*)
maestría *f* mastery; mastership; trick, deceit; cure; master's degree
maestril *m* queen cell
maestro -tra *adj* masterful, masterly; main, principal; trained, e.g., **perro maestro** trained dog; master, e.g., **llave maestra** master key; **maestro mecánico** master mechanic; **maestros cantores** mastersingers; *m* master; teacher; maestro (*in music, painting, etc.*); (educ.) master; (naut.) mainmast; **gran maestro** grand master (*of Masons*); **maestro aguañón** master builder of water works; **maestro de armas** fencing master; **maestro de capilla** choirmaster; **maestro de ceremonias** master of ceremonies; **maestro de cocina** chef; **maestro de equitación** riding master; **maestro de escuela** elementary schoolteacher; **maestro de esgrima** fencing master; **maestro de obra prima** shoemaker

(*who makes shoes*); **maestro de obras** builder, master builder; **maestro de ribera** ship carpenter, shipwright; **maestro de taller** (Am.) master mechanic; *f* teacher; schoolmistress; teacher's wife; elementary school; (mas.) screed, guide line; (fig.) teacher (*such as adversity*); **maestra de escuela** schoolmistress
Magallanes *m* Magellan
magallánico -ca *adj* Magellanic
magancear *vn* (Am.) to bum, to loaf around
magancería *f* cheat, deceit
magancés *adj* evil, treacherous
maganel *m* (archaic) battering ram
maganto -ta *adj* wan, languid, spiritless
maganza *f* (Am.) bumming, loafing
magaña *f* trick, deceit; flaw (*in bore of a gun*)
magarza *f* (bot.) feverfew
magarzuela *f* (bot.) mayweed, stinking camomile
Magdalena *f* Magdalen, Madeleine; (*l.c.*) *f* (fig.) magdalene (*repentant prostitute*); oval-shaped biscuit; **estar hecha una magdalena** (coll.) to be inconsolable; **Santa María Magdalena** (Bib.) Mary Magdalene
magdaleniense *adj* (geol.) Magdalenian
magdaleón *m* (pharm.) cylindrical plaster or poultice
magenta *m* magenta
magia *f* magic; **magia blanca** white magic; **magia negra** black magic
magiar *adj & mf* Magyar; *m* Magyar (*language*)
mágico -ca *adj* magic or magical; *mf* magician; *f* magic
magín *m* (coll.) fancy, imagination; (coll.) keenness, ability
magisterial *adj* teaching
magisterio *m* teaching; teachers; teaching profession; guidance, leadership; solemnity, pomposity
magistrado *m* magistrate
magistral *adj* magistral, magisterial; master; masterly; (fort. & pharm.) magistral; *m* (metal.) magistral
magistratura *f* magistracy
magma *m* magma; (geol. & pharm.) magma
magnanimidad *f* magnanimity
magnánimo -ma *adj* magnanimous
magnate *m* magnate
magnesia *f* (chem.) magnesia
magnesiano -na *adj* magnesian
magnésico -ca *adj* magnesic
magnesio *m* (chem.) magnesium; (phot.) flashlight (*light; photograph*)
magnesita *f* (mineral.) magnesite
magnético -ca *adj* magnetic
magnetismo *m* magnetism; **magnetismo animal** animal magnetism; **magnetismo permanente** (phys.) permanent magnetism; **magnetismo remanente** (phys.) remanent magnetism; **magnetismo terrestre** terrestrial magnetism
magnetita *f* (mineral.) magnetite
magnetización *f* magnetization
magnetizador -dora *adj* magnetizing; *mf* magnetizer
magnetizar §76 *va* to magnetize
magneto *m & f* magneto
magnetoeléctrico -ca *adj* magnetoelectric
magnetofón *m* var. of **magnetófono**
magnetofónico -ca *adj* recording (*tape or wire*)
magnetófono *m* (phys.) magnetophone; wire recorder, tape recorder
magnetómetro *m* magnetometer
magnetón *m* (phys.) magneton
magnetosfera *f* magnetosphere
magnetrón *m* (rad.) magnetron
magnicidio *m* assassination of a great man
magnificación *f* (opt.) magnification; exaltation
magnificador -dora *adj* magnifying; extolling, exalting
magnificar §86 *va* (opt.) to magnify; to extol, to exalt
magníficat *m* Magnificat
magnificencia *f* magnificence
magnificente *adj* magnificent
magnificentísimo -ma *adj super* very or most magnificent
magnífico -ca *adj* magnificent; liberal, lavish
magnitud *f* magnitude; (astr. & math.) magnitude
magno -na *adj* great, e.g., **Alejandro Magno** Alexander the Great
magnolia *f* (bot.) magnolia
mago -ga *adj* magian, magical; Magian; *mf* magian, magician; *m* wizard; Magus, Magian; (zool.) tarsier; **magos de Oriente** Magi, Wise Men of the East
magostar *va* to roast (*chestnuts*) at a picnic
magosto *m* chestnut roast; roast chestnuts; picnic fire for roasting chestnuts
magra *f* see **magro**
magrez *f* thinness, leanness, meagerness
magro -gra *adj* thin, lean, meager; mean, paltry; *m* (coll.) loin of pork; *f* slice of ham; **¡magras!** *interj* (coll.) absolutely no!
magrura *f* var. of **magrez**
maguar *vr* (Am.) to be disappointed
maguer *conj* (obs.) although
magüeta *f* heifer
magüeto *m* young bull
maguey *m* (bot.) maguey
maguillo *m* (bot.) crab apple
magujo *m* (naut.) ravehook
magulladura *f* or **magullamiento** *m* bruise, bruising
magullar *va & vr* to bruise
Maguncia *f* Mainz
magyar *adj & mf* var. of **magiar**
maharajá *m* (*pl:* **-jaes**) maharaja
mahatma *m* mahatma; (theosophy) mahatma
Mahoma *m* Mohammed
mahometano -na *adj & mf* Mohammedan
mahometismo *m* Mohammedanism
mahometista *adj* Mohammedan; *mf* Mohammedan; Christianized Mohammedan who returns to Mohammedanism
mahometizar §76 *va* to Mohammedanize; *vn* to profess Mohammedanism
mahón *m* nankeen
mahona *f* mahone (*Turkish vessel*)
mahonesa *f* mayonnaise; (bot.) Mahon stock, Virginia stock
maicena *f* fine corn flour
maicillo *m* (bot.) gama grass; (Am.) gravel
maído *m* meow
maillechort *m* var. of **melchor**
maimón *m* monkey; **maimones** *mpl* Andalusian soup made with olive oil
Maimónides *m* Maimonides
mainel *m* railing, handrail
maitinada *f* dawn
maitines *mpl* (eccl.) matins
maíz *m* (bot.) maize, Indian corn; **maíz de Guinea** or **maíz morocho** (bot.) Guinea corn, durra; **maíz en la mazorca** corn on the cob
maizal *m* cornfield
majada *f* sheepfold; dung, manure
majadal *m* richly manured land
majadear *vn* to take shelter for the night (*said of sheep*); to manure
majaderear *va* (Am.) to pester, annoy
majadería *f* (coll.) folly, annoyance
majaderillo *m* bobbin for making lace
majadero -ra *adj* stupid, annoying; *mf* dolt, bore; *m* pestle, pounder; bobbin for making lace
majador -dora *adj* crushing, pounding, grinding; *mf* crusher, pounder, grinder
majadura *f* crushing, pounding, grinding
majagranzas *m* (*pl:* **-zas**) (coll.) stupid bore; (coll.) churl, peasant
majagua *f* (bot.) majagua, corkwood
majal *m* school of fish
majamiento *m* var. of **majadura**
majano *m* heap of loose stones (*in a field or at crossroads*)
majar *va* to crush, pound, mash, grind; (coll.) to annoy, harass
majear *va* (Am.) to cheat, deceive; *vn* to be a bully
majenza *f* (coll.) var. of **majeza**
majestad *f* majesty; (*cap.*) *f* Majesty (*title*)
majestoso -sa *adj* majestic
majestuosidad *f* majesty
majestuoso -sa *adj* majestic

majeza *f* (coll.) sportiness, gaudiness; insolence
majo -ja *adj* sporty, gaudy; pretty, nice; insolent; (coll.) all dressed up; *mf* sport (*flashy person*); *m* (coll.) bully
majolar *m* field of English hawthorn
majoleta *f* var. of **marjoleta**
majoleto *m* var. of **marjoleto**
majorca *f* var. of **mazorca**
majuela *f* haw or berry (*of Crataegus monogyna*); shoestring
majuelo *m* (bot.) English hawthorn (*Crataegus monogyna*); young fruit-yielding grapevine
mal *adj* apocopated form of **malo,** used only before masculine singular nouns; *adv* badly, poorly; wrong, wrongly; hardly, scarcely; with difficulty; **mal de fondos** short of money; **mal que bien** any old way; **mal que le pese** in spite of him; *m* evil; harm, damage; wrong; misfortune; disease, sickness; **de mal en peor** from bad to worse; **echar a mal** to scorn, have a poor opinion of; **estar mal** to be ill; **estar mal con** to be on the outs with; **parar en mal** to come to an evil end; **por mal de mis pecados** to my sorrow, unfortunately for me; **tener a mal** to be displeased with, to object to; **mal ardiente** (path.) St. Anthony's fire; **mal caduco** or **mal comicial** (path.) falling sickness; **mal de corazón** (path.) epilepsy; (path.) nausea; **mal de la puna** mountain sickness; **mal de las montañas** mountain sickness; **mal de la tierra** homesickness; **mal de los ardientes** (path.) St. Anthony's fire; **mal de mar** seasickness; **mal de ojo** evil eye; **mal de piedra** (path.) stone, urinary calculi; **mal de rayos** radiation sickness; **mal de vuelo** airsickness; **¡mal haya . . . !** curses on . . . !
mala *f* see **malo**
malabar *adj & mf* Malabarese; see **juego**
malabárico -ca *adj* Malabarese
malabarismo *m* juggling
malabarista *mf* juggler
malacate *m* (min.) whim (*hoisting machine*); (Am.) bobbin, spindle
malacia *f* (path.) depraved appetite
malacitano -na *adj & mf* var. of **malagueño**
malacología *f* malacology
malacondicionado -da *adj* evil, gruff, surly
malaconsejado -da *adj* ill-advised
malacopterigio -gia *adj & m* (zool.) malacopterygian
malacostráceo -a *adj & m* (zool.) malacostracan
malacostumbrado -da *adj* of bad habits; spoiled, pampered
malacuenda *f* burlap; oakum, tow
málaga *m* Malaga wine
malagradecido -da *adj* (Am.) ungrateful
malagueño -ña *adj* (pertaining to) Malaga; *mf* native or inhabitant of Malaga; *f* malaguena (*song and dance*)
malagueta *f* grains of paradise, melegueta pepper; (bot.) bayberry (*Pimenta acris*)
malamente *adv* badly, poorly; wrong, wrongly
malandante *adj* unfortunate, unlucky
malandanza *f* misfortune, bad luck
malandar *m* home-fed hog
malandrín -drina *adj* evil, wicked; *mf* scoundrel
malanga *f* (bot.) caladium
Malaquías *m* (Bib.) Malachi
malaquita *f* (mineral.) malachite
malar *adj & m* (anat.) malar
malaria *f* (path.) malaria
malasio -sia *adj & mf* Malaysian; **la Malasia** Malaysia
malavenido -da *adj* in disagreement
malaventura *f* misfortune
malaventurado -da *adj* unfortunate
malaventuranza *f* misfortune
malayo -ya *adj & mf* Malay, Malayan; *m* Malay (*language*); (*cap.*) *f* Malaya
malbaratador -dora *adj* underselling; squandering; *mf* underseller; squanderer
malbaratamiento *m* var. of **malbarato**
malbaratar *va* to undersell (*an article*); to squander
malbaratillo *m* second-hand shop
malbarato *m* underselling; squandering
malcarado -da *adj* evil-faced
malcasado -da *adj* mismated; undutiful (*spouse*)
malcasar *va* to mismate; *vn & vr* to be mismated
malcaso *m* treachery, perfidy
malcocinado *m* entrails; butcher shop (*where entrails are sold*)
malcomer *va & vn* to eat poorly, to eat lightly
malcomido -da *adj* underfed
malcontento -ta *adj* discontent; malcontent; *mf* malcontent
malcoraje *m* (bot.) herb mercury
malcorte *m* illegal cutting of timber
malcriado -da *adj* ill-bred
malcriar §90 *va* (coll.) to spoil, pamper
maldad *f* badness, evil, wickedness
maldecidor -dora *adj* slanderous; *mf* detractor, slanderer
maldecir §24 *va* to curse; *vn* to damn, to curse; to detract; **maldecir de** to slander, speak ill of, vilify
maldiciente *adj* cursing; slanderous; *mf* detractor, slanderer
maldición *f* malediction, curse; (coll.) curse, oath
maldigo *1st sg pres ind of* **maldecir**
maldije *1st sg pret ind of* **maldecir**
maldispuesto -ta *adj* indisposed; ill-disposed, unwilling
maldito -ta *adj* wicked; damned, accursed; **no saber maldita la cosa de** (coll.) to not know a single thing about; **maldito lo que me importa** (coll.) I don't give a damn about it; *m* Evil One (*Devil*); **los malditos** the damned; *f* (coll.) tongue; **soltar la maldita** (coll.) to talk without restraint, to talk freely; to pour forth a flood of curses
maleabilidad *f* malleability
maleabilizar §76 *va* to make malleable
maleable *adj* malleable; (coll.) easily spoiled; (coll.) easily led astray
maleante *adj* corrupting; evil, wicked; (coll.) scoffing, malicious; *mf* hoodlum, rowdy; (coll.) scoffer
malear *va* to damage, spoil; to corrupt; *vr* to spoil; to become spoiled; to become corrupt; to sour, turn sour (*said of soil*)
malecón *m* levee, dike; sea wall
maledicencia *f* slander, scandal, evil talk
maleficencia *f* maleficence
maleficiar *va* to damage, harm; to curse, cast a spell on
maleficio *m* curse, spell; witchcraft, black magic
maléfico -ca *adj* maleficent; malevolent; spellcasting; *m* sorcerer
malencarado -da *adj* ill-featured, ill-favored, ugly
malentendido *m* misunderstanding
maleolar *adj* hammer-shaped; (anat.) malleolar
maléolo *m* (anat.) malleolus
malestar *m* malaise, indisposition
maleta *f* valise; **hacer la maleta** to pack up, to get ready for a trip; *m* (coll.) bungler, ham bullfighter
maletero *m* valise maker or dealer; porter, station porter
maletín *m* small bag, satchel; **maletín de grupa** (mil.) saddlebag
malevolencia *f* malevolence
malévolo -la *adj & mf* malevolent
maleza *f* weeds; thicket, underbrush
malformación *f* malformation
malfuncionamiento *m* malfunction
malgastado -da *adj* ill-spent
malgastador -dora *mf* wastrel, squanderer, spendthrift
malgastar *va* to waste, squander
malhablado -da *adj* foul-mouthed, foul-spoken
malhadado -da *adj* ill-starred, unfortunate
malhecho -cha *adj* malformed, deformed; *m* evil deed, misdeed
malhechor -chora *adj* malefactory; *mf* malefactor; *f* malefactress
malherir §62 *va* to injure badly, to wound badly
malhojo *m* vegetable refuse
malhumorado -da *adj* ill-humored
malicia *f* evil; malice; slyness, trickiness; insidiousness; (coll.) suspicion

maliciar *va* to suspect; to spoil; *vr* to suspect; to become spoiled
malicioso -sa *adj* evil; malicious; sly, tricky; insidious; suspicious
málico -ca *adj* malic
malignar *va* to vitiate, corrupt; to spoil; *vr* to become vitiated; to spoil
malignidad *f* malignity, malignance
maligno -na *adj* malign, malignant, evil, unkind; (path.) malign, malignant
malilla *f* manilla (*second-best trump*)
Malinas *f* Mechlin or Malines
malintencionado -da *adj* ill-disposed, evil-disposed
malmandado -da *adj* unwilling, disobedient
malmaridada *adj fem* faithless (*wife*); *f* faithless wife
malmeter *va* to waste, squander; to alienate; to lead astray, to misguide
malmirado -da *adj* inconsiderate; disliked
malo -la *adj* bad; poor; evil; naughty, mischievous; sick; in bad shape; wrong; **a malas** on bad terms; **estar de malas** to be out of luck; **lo malo es que** the trouble is that; **por malas o por buenas** willingly or unwillingly; **ser malo de engañar** (coll.) to be hard to trick; **venir de malas** to have bad intentions; **malo con** or **para con** mean to; **malo de** +*inf* hard to+*inf; m* wicked person; **el Malo** the Evil One (*the Devil*); *f* mailbag; mail
malogrado -da *adj* late, ill-fated
malogramiento *m* var. of **malogro**
malograr *va* to miss, to waste; to spoil; *vr* to fail; to turn out badly; to come to an untimely end
malogro *m* failure; loss, waste (*e.g., of time*); disappointment; untimely death
maloliente *adj* malodorous, ill-smelling
malón *m* mean trick; (Am.) surprise attack; (Am.) Indian raid; (Am.) surprise party
malparado -da *adj* hurt, damaged; **salir malparado de** to come out worsted in
malparar *va* to mistreat, put in a bad way
malparir *vn* to miscarry
malparto *m* miscarriage
malpigiáceo -a *adj* (bot.) malpighiaceous
malpraxis *f* malpractice
malquerencia *f* dislike
malquerer §70 *va* to dislike
malquerré *1st sg fut ind of* **malquerer**
malquise *1st sg pret ind of* **malquerer**
malquistar *va* to alienate; *vr* to become alienated
malquisto -ta *adj* estranged; disliked, unpopular
malrotar *va* to squander
malsano -na *adj* unhealthy
malsín *m* evil gossip; troublemaker
malsonante *adj* offensive, obnoxious
malsufrido -da *adj* impatient, unforbearing
malta *m* malt; *f* pitch, tar; (Am.) quality beer; (Am.) jug
maltasa *f* (biochem.) maltase
maltés -tesa *adj & mf* Maltese; *m* Maltese (*language*)
maltosa *f* (chem.) maltose
maltrabaja *mf* (coll.) lazy loafer
maltrapillo *m* (coll.) ragamuffin
maltratamiento *m* maltreatment, ill treatment, abuse
maltratar *va* to maltreat, ill-treat, abuse; to damage, harm, spoil
maltrato *m* var. of **maltratamiento**
maltrecho -cha *adj* battered, damaged, abused
maltusianismo *m* Malthusianism
maltusiano -na *adj & mf* Malthusian
maluco -ca or **malucho -cha** *adj* (coll.) slightly ill, sickish
malva *f* (bot.) mallow; **haber nacido con** or **en las malvas** (coll.) to be of humble birth; **ser una malva** or **como una malva** (coll.) to be meek and mild, to be as gentle as a lamb; **malva arbórea** (bot.) rose mallow, hollyhock; **malva común** (bot.) cheeseflower; **malva de hoja redonda** (bot.) dwarf mallow; **malva de olor** (bot.) nutmeg geranium; **malva loca, real** or **rósea** (bot.) rose mallow, hollyhock
malváceo -a *adj* (bot.) malvaceous
malvado -da *adj* evil, wicked; *mf* evildoer
malvar *m* growth of mallows; *va* to corrupt, to deprave
malvarrosa *f* (bot.) rose mallow, hollyhock
malvasía *f* malmsey (*wine*); malvasia grape
malvavisco *m* (bot.) marsh mallow
malvender *va* to sell at a loss, to undersell
malversación *f* malversation, graft, embezzlement
malversador -dora *mf* grafter, embezzler
malversar *va & vn* to graft, to embezzle
malvezar §76 *va* to give bad habits to; *vr* to get bad habits
malvís *m* (orn.) song thrush, redwing
malviz *m* (*pl:* **-vices**) var. of **malvís**
malla *f* mesh; meshwork, network; mail (*of armor*); meshed or netted fabric; tights; bathing suit; (rad.) grid; **malla de alambre** wire mesh, wire netting
mallar *vn* to make meshing or network; to get caught in the meshes of a net (*said of a fish*)
mallero *m* mesh maker
malletazo *m* (sport) blow or stroke with a mallet
mallete *m* mallet; (naut.) partner; (sport) mallet (*in croquet and polo*)
malleto *m* beating maul (*used in paper mills*)
mallo *m* mallet; pall-mall (*game and alley*)
Mallorca *f* Majorca
mallorquín -quina *adj & mf* Majorcan; *m* Majorcan (*dialect*)
mama *f* (anat.) mamma; (coll.) mama or mamma (*mother*)
mamá *f* (*pl:* **-más**) (coll.) mama or mamma (*mother*)
mamacallos *m* (*pl:* **-llos**) simpleton, fool
mamada *f* sucking; sucking time; suck; (Am.) cinch
mamadera *f* breast pump; (Am.) nipple; (Am.) nursing bottle
mamador -dora *adj* sucking; *mf* sucker; (Am.) souse, drunk
mamalón -lona *adj* (Am.) loafing, sponging
mamama or **mamamama** *f* (Am.) granny, grandmother
mamandurria *f* (Am.) sinecure
mamantón -tona *adj* sucking (*animal*)
mamar *va* to suck; to take in or absorb as a child; (coll.) to swallow; (coll.) to wangle; **mamóla** (coll.) he was taken in; *vn* to suck; *vr* to get drunk; to have (*a scare*); (coll.) to swallow; (coll.) to wangle; **mamarse a uno** (coll.) to get the best of someone; (coll.) to take someone in; (coll.) to do away with someone; **mamarse el dedo** (coll.) to be taken in
mamario -ria *adj* mammary
mamarrachada *f* (coll.) collection of junk; (coll.) piece of folly; (coll.) daub
mamarrachero -ra or **mamarrachista** *mf* (coll.) botcher, dauber
mamarracho *m* (coll.) botch, mess, piece of junk, daub, scarecrow; (coll.) fellow, guy, milksop
mambla *f* mound, knoll
mambrú *m* (*pl:* **-brúes**) (naut.) kitchen funnel or stack
mamelón *m* mound, knoll, hillock; (anat. & bot.) mammilla
mameluco -ca *mf* mameluco, mestizo (*in Brazil*); *m* mameluke (*slave*); Mameluke (*soldier*); dolt, boob; *f* (Am.) prostitute
mamella *f* mammilla (*in neck of a goat*)
mamey *m* (bot.) mammee
mamífero -ra *adj* (zool.) mammalian; *m* (zool.) mammal, mammalian
mamila *f* breast; teat (*of a man*)
mamilar *adj* mammillary
mammón *m* (Bib.) Mammon
mamola *f* chuck (*under the chin*); **hacer la mamola a** to chuck under the chin; (coll.) to make a fool of
mamón -mona *adj* sucking; fond of sucking; *mf* suckling; *m* (bot.) shoot, sucker; (bot.) genip; *f* chuck (*under the chin*)
mamoso -sa *adj* sucking
mamotreto *m* notebook, memo book; (coll.) bulky book, bulky batch of papers; (coll.) piece of junk
mampara *f* screen; folding screen; small door

mamparo *m* (naut.) bulkhead
mamperlán *m* temporary railing
mamporro *m* bump, contusion
mampostear *va* to make or build of rubble
mampostería *f* rubblework
mampostero *m* rubble mason
mampuesto -ta *adj* rubble; *m* rough stone; parapet; (Am.) support for a gun in taking aim; **de mampuesto** spare; emergency; under cover, from a parapet; *f* (mas.) course
mamujar *va & vn* to suck intermittently
mamullar *va* to chew as if sucking; (coll.) to mumble, to mutter
mamut *m* (*pl:* **-muts**) (pal.) mammoth
maná *m* (Bib.) manna; (bot.) manna (*exudate of Fraxinus ornus and other plants*); godsend, salvation (*in form of cheap and abundant food*)
manada *f* flock, herd, pack, drove; handful; (coll.) crowd, mob
manadero -ra *adj* flowing, running; *m* source, spring; shepherd, herdsman
manantial *adj* flowing, running; *m* source, spring; (fig.) source, origin; **manantial de energía** (elec.) source of current
manantío -a *adj* flowing, running
manar *va* to pour forth, to run with; *vn* to pour forth, to run; (fig.) to abound, to run
Manasés *m* (Bib.) Manasseh
manatí *m* (*pl:* **-tíes**) (zool.) manatee, sea cow
manato *m* var. of **manatí**
manaza *f* big hand
mancamiento *m* maiming; lack, want
mancar §86 *va* to maim (*especially in the hand*); *vn* (naut.) to abate, to slack (*said of wind*)
manceba *f* concubine
mancebía *f* brothel; wild oats; licentious living
mancebo *m* youth, young man; bachelor; clerk; helper (*e.g., in drug store or barbershop*)
mancera *f* plow handle
mancerina *f* var. of **macerina**
mancilla *f* spot, blemish
mancillar *va* to spot, blemish; (fig.) to spot, blemish
mancipación *f* enslavement; (law) conveyance, transfer
mancipar *va* to enslave; (law) to convey, transfer
manco -ca *adj* one-handed; one-armed; maimed; defective, faulty; *mf* one-handed person, one-armed person; **el manco de Lepanto** Cervantes; *m* (Am.) old nag
mancome *m* (bot.) sassy or sassywood
mancomún; de mancomún jointly, in agreement
mancomunadamente *adv* jointly, in agreement
mancomunar *va* to unite, combine; to pool; (law) to require joint payment or execution of; *vr* to unite, combine
mancomunidad *f* union, association; commonwealth
mancornar §77 *va* to down (*a young bull*) and hold his horns on the ground; to tie a horn and a front leg of (*a steer*) with a rope; to tie (*two beasts*) together by the horns; (coll.) to join, bring together
mancuerda *f* rack (*torture*)
mancuerna *f* pair tied together; yoke fastened by the horns; **mancuernas** *fpl* (Am.) cuff links
mancha *f* spot, stain; speckle; patch; sketch; (fig.) stain, blot; (Am.) flock, school; **mancha amarilla** (anat.) yellow spot; **mancha ocular** (zool.) eyespot; **mancha solar** sun spot
manchadizo -za *adj* easily spotted or stained
manchar *va* to spot, stain; to speckle; (fig.) to stain, blot; **¡mancha!** wet paint!
manchego -ga *adj* (pertaining to) La Mancha; *mf* native or inhabitant of La Mancha
manchón *m* big spot; patch of heavy growth (*in a field*)
manchoso -sa *adj* (prov.) var. of **manchadizo**
manchú -chúa (*pl:* **-chúes** or **-chús** & **-chúas**) *adj & mf* Manchu; *m* Manchu (*language*)
manchuriano -na *adj & mf* Manchurian
manda *f* offer, gift; bequest, legacy
mandadero -ra *mf* messenger; *m* errand boy; office boy; *f* errand girl
mandado *m* order, command; errand; **hacer un mandado** to run an errand
mandamás *m* (slang) head man, big boss
mandamiento *m* order, command; (Bib.) commandment; (law) writ; **los cinco mandamientos** (coll.) the five fingers of the hand; **los diez mandamientos** (Bib.) the Ten Commandments; **mandamiento de arresto** or **prisión** (law) warrant of arrest
mandante *m* (law) mandator
mandar *va* to order; to command; to send; to bequeath; (Am.) to overlook, to dominate (*e.g., the countryside*); **mandar** + *inf* to order to + *inf*, to have + *inf*, e.g., **me mandó entrar** he had me come in; to order or have + *pp*, e.g., **mandó componer el reloj** he had the watch repaired; **mandar llamar** to send for; *vn* to command, be in command; to be the boss; **mandar decir que** to send word that; **mandar por** to send for; **mande Vd.** I beg your pardon; *vr* to get around (*said of a convalescent*); to be communicating (*said of rooms*); **mandarse con** to communicate with (*another room*); **mandarse por** to use (*e.g., a door, stairway*)
mandarín -rina *adj* mandarin; *m* mandarin; (coll.) official held in low esteem; *f* mandarin or tangerine (*fruit*); Mandarin (*language*)
mandarino *m* (bot.) mandarin (*tree*)
mandarria *f* (naut.) iron maul, sledge hammer
mandatario *m* agent; (law & dipl.) mandatary, mandatory; (Am.) chief executive; **primer mandatario** (Am.) chief executive (*of the country*)
mandato *m* mandate; (law & dipl.) mandate; (eccl.) maundy; (Am.) term (*of office*)
mandíbula *f* jaw; (anat. & zool.) mandible; **reír a mandíbula batiente** to roar with laughter
mandibular *adj* mandibular
mandil *m* apron; leather apron; cleaning rag; apron (*of Freemasons*)
mandilar *va* to wipe or clean (*a horse*) with a rag
mandilete *m* (fort.) cover of a loophole
mandilón *m* (coll.) coward
mandinga *m* (Am.) imp, little rogue
mandioca *f* (bot.) manioc (*plant and starch*)
mando *m* command; drive, control; **mandos** *mpl* controls; **alto mando** high command; **estar al mando** to be in command; **tener el mando y el palo** (coll.) to rule the roost, to be the boss; **tomar el mando** to take command; **mando a distancia** remote control; **mando a mano** hand control; **mando a punta de dedo** finger-tip control; **mando de las válvulas** (mach.) timing gears; **mando doble** (aut.) dual drive; **mando por botón** push-button control; **mando único** (rad.) single control
mandoble *m* two-handed slash or blow (*e.g., with a sword*); sharp reproof
mandolina *f* (mus.) mandolin
mandón -dona *adj* bossy; *mf* bossy person; *m* (Am.) boss, foreman (*in a mine*); (Am.) starter (*in horse race*)
mandrachero *m* keeper of a gambling house
mandracho *m* gambling house
mandrágora *f* (bot.) mandragora or mandrake
mandrágula *f* (coll.) mandragora or mandrake; (coll.) phantom, ghost
mandria *adj* cowardly; trifling, worthless
mandril *m* (mach.) mandrel or mandril; chuck; reamer; punch; (zool.) mandrill; **mandril de ensanchar** (mach.) driftpin
mandrilado *m* boring; reaming; (mach.) drifting
mandrilar *va* to bore (*a cylinder*); to ream; (mach.) to drift (*a hole*)
mandrín *m* (mach.) driftpin
mandrinar *va* var. of **mandrilar**
mandrón *m* stone or wood ball (*used as a missile*); mangonel (*catapult*)
manducación *f* (coll.) eating
manducar §86 *va & vn* (coll.) to eat
manducatoria *f* (coll.) food, sustenance
manea *f* hopple (*rope or chain*)
manear *va* to hobble or hopple (*an animal*); to handle, to wield; (Am.) to trip with a rope

manecilla *f* small hand; hand (*of clock or watch*); clasp, book clasp; (print.) index, fist; (bot.) tendril
manejabilidad *f* manageability
manejable *adj* manageable
manejado -da *adj* managed, handled; **bien manejado** (paint.) loose; **mal manejado** (paint.) tight
manejar *va* to manage; to handle, to wield; (equit.) to manage (*a horse*); to drive (*an automobile*); *vr* to manage; to behave; to get around, move about
manejo *m* handling; management; scheming, intrigue; (equit.) manège; (Am.) driving; **manejo a distancia** remote control; **manejo doméstico** housekeeping; **manejos de corte** court intrigues
maneota *f* var. of **manea**
manera *f* see **manero**
manerismo *m* var. of **manierismo**
manero -ra *adj* tame (*falcon*); *f* manner; way; flap; slit (*in skirt*); (f.a. & lit.) manner (*e.g., of Raphael*); **maneras** *fpl* manners; **a la manera de** in the manner of; like; **de manera que** so that; **de ninguna manera** by no manner of means; **en gran manera** to a great degree; extremely; **sobre manera** exceedingly, beyond measure
manes *mpl* manes
manés -nesa *adj* Manx; *m* Manxman; Manx (*language*); **maneses** *mpl* Manx
manezuela *f* small hand; clasp; handle
manga *f* sleeve; hose; portmanteau (*laced together at the ends*); conical cloth strainer; scoop net; air shaft; wind scoop; waterspout; band of armed men; (bridge) game; (eccl.) manga; (naut.) beam (*widest part*); (Am.) crowd, mob; (Am.) cattle chute; (Am.) manga (*poncho*); **mangas** *fpl* profits, extras; **andar manga con hombro** (coll.) to be upside down, to be topsy-turvy; **en mangas de camisa** in shirt sleeves; **estar de manga** (coll.) to be in cahoots; **estar mangas por hombro** (coll.) to be topsy-turvy; **hacer mangas y capirotes** (coll.) to rush ahead without bothering about details; **hacerse** or **ir de manga** (coll.) to be in cahoots; **ser de manga ancha** or **tener manga ancha** to be indulgent, be easy-going; **manga de agua** waterspout, cloudburst; **manga de ángel** angel sleeve; **manga de camisa** shirt sleeve; **manga de jamón** leg-of-mutton sleeve; **manga de riego** watering hose; **manga de viento** whirlwind; **manga marina** waterspout; **manga perdida** sleeve with slit through which the arm projects
mangajarro *m* long, dirty sleeve
mangaje *m* length of hose
mangana *f* lasso
manganear *va* to lasso; (Am.) to vex, annoy
manganeo *m* lassoing
manganesa or **manganesia** *f* (mineral.) manganese dioxide, pyrolusite
manganeso *m* (chem.) manganese
mangánico -ca *adj* manganic
manganilla *f* trick, scheme, deceit
manganita *f* (chem.) manganite
mangano *m* (archaic) mangonel
manganoso -sa *adj* manganous
mangante *m* (coll.) cheat, loafer, good-for-nothing
manglar *m* mangrove swamp
mangle *m* (bot.) mangrove; *f* (mach.) mangle
mango *m* handle; (bot.) mango; **mango de cuchillo** (zool.) razor clam; **mango de escoba** broomstick; (aer.) stick, control stick
mangón *m* retailer; (Am.) corral
mangonada *f* blow or shove with the arm
mangonear *vn* (coll.) to loiter, to loaf around; (coll.) to meddle; (coll.) to dabble; **mangonear en** (coll.) to meddle in; (coll.) to dabble in
mangoneo *m* (coll.) meddling; (coll.) dabbling
mangonero -ra *adj* (coll.) meddlesome
mangorrero -ra *adj* rough, crude (*knife*); (coll.) handled; (coll.) worthless, useless; (coll.) idle, unemployed
mangorrillo *m* plow handle
mangosta *f* (zool.) mongoose
mangostán *m* (bot.) mangosteen (*tree*)
mangosto *m* mangosteen (*fruit*)
mangote *m* (coll.) long, wide sleeve; sleeve protector, cuffette
mangual *m* (mil.) flail, morning star
manguardia *f* wing wall, buttress (*of bridge*)
manguera *f* hose; waterspout; (naut.) funnel, air duct; (naut.) wind sail; **manguera contra incendios** fire hose
manguero *m* hoseman
mangueta *f* fountain syringe; door jamb; lever; neck (*of water-flushed toilet*); (aut.) stub axle
manguita *f* small sleeve; case, sheath
manguitería *f* furriery; fur shop
manguitero *m* furrier
manguito *m* muff; lace half sleeve; sleeve guard or protector; mantle (*of gaslight*); coffee cake; (mach.) sleeve; (mach.) coupling; **manguito para la muñeca** wristlet
maní *m* (*pl:* **-níes** or **-nises**) (bot.) peanut
manía *f* mania; (psychopath.) mania; **manía de grandezas** folie de grandeur, megalomania
maniabierto -ta *adj* open-handed, lavish
maníaco -ca *adj* maniac or maniacal; (psychopath.) manic; *mf* maniac
manialbo -ba *adj* white-footed (*horse*)
manía-melancolía *f* (psychopath.) manic-depressive insanity
maniatar *va* to tie the hands of, to manacle
maniático -ca *adj* maniacal; stubborn; queer; crazy (*enthusiastic*); *mf* maniac
manicomio *m* insane asylum, madhouse
manicordio *m* (mus.) manichord
manicorto -ta *adj* short-handed; (coll.) close-fisted, stingy; *mf* (coll.) skinflint
manicuro -ra *mf* manicure, manicurist; *f* manicure; manicuring
manido -da *adj* worn, stale; hackneyed; hidden, concealed; (Am.) full, swarming; (cook.) high; *f* haunt, hangout, den
manierismo *m* (f.a. & lit.) mannerism
manifacero -ra *adj* (coll.) scheming, meddlesome; *mf* (coll.) schemer, meddler
manifactura *f* manufacture; form, shape
manifestación *f* manifestation; demonstration (*public gathering to exhibit sympathy or opinion*)
manifestante *mf* manifestant; demonstrator
manifestar §18 *va* to manifest, make manifest; (eccl.) to expose (*the Host*); *vn* to demonstrate; *vr* to be or become manifest
manifiesto -ta *adj* manifest; *m* manifesto; (naut.) manifest; (eccl.) exhibition of the Host; **estar de manifiesto** to be manifest; **poner de manifiesto** to make manifest
manigero *m* boss of a gang of farmhands
manigua *f* Cuban jungle or thicket; **coger manigua** (Am.) to blush; **irse a la manigua** (Am.) to revolt
manija *f* handle; crank; clamp, collar; (rail.) coupling
manilargo -ga *adj* long-handed; ready-fisted; generous
manilense or **manileño -ña** *adj* Manila; *mf* native or inhabitant of Manila
maniluvio *m* (med.) hand bath
manilla *f* bracelet; handcuff, manacle; hand (*e.g., of watch*)
manillar *m* handle bar
maniobra *f* handling, operation; maneuver; (fig.) maneuver; (naut.) gear, tackle; **maniobras** *fpl* (rail.) shifting
maniobrabilidad *f* maneuverability
maniobrable *adj* maneuverable
maniobrar *vn* to work with the hands; to maneuver; (rail.) to shift; (fig.) to maneuver
maniobrero -ra *adj* (mil.) maneuvering; (mil.) skilled in maneuvering
maniobrista *adj* (naut.) skilled in maneuvering; *m* (naut.) skilful maneuverer
maniota *f* var. of **manea**
manipodio *m* (coll.) var. of **monipodio**
manipulación *f* manipulation
manipulador -dora *adj* manipulating; *mf* manipulator; *m* (telg.) key, telegraph key
manipular *va* to manipulate; (coll.) to manipulate (*to one's own purpose or advantage*)
manipuleo *m* (coll.) manipulation, maneuvering
manípulo *m* (hist. & eccl.) maniple

maniqueísmo *m* Manicheanism or Manicheism
maniqueo -a *adj & mf* Manichean
maniquete *m* black lace mitten
maniquí (*pl:* **-quíes**) *m* manikin, mannequin; dress form; (fig.) puppet; *f* mannequin, model
manir §53 *va* to keep (*game*) until it is high
manirroto -ta *adj* lavish, prodigal, spendthrift
manita *f* (chem.) mannitol, manna sugar
manivacío -a *adj* (coll.) empty-handed
manivela *f* crank; **manivela de arranque** starting crank
manjar *m* food, dish; tidbit, delicacy; pastime that gives a lift; **manjar blanco** blancmange; creamed chicken
manjorrada *f* (coll.) mess of food
Man.[1] abr. of **Manuel**
mano *f* hand; forefoot; coat (*e.g. of paint*); hand, round (*of a game*); hand (*of clock or watch*); turn; pestle, masher; trunk (*of elephant*); quire (*of paper*); mano, cylindrical grindstone (*for cocoa*); reprimand; **manos** *fpl* labor (*as distinguished from materials*); **abrir la mano** to accept gifts; to be generous; to be more lenient; **a la mano** at hand, on hand; within reach; easy to understand; **a mano** by hand; at hand; artificially; **a mano abierta** open-handedly; **a mano airada** violently; **a mano armada** armed (*e.g., attack*); insistently; **a manos llenas** generously; abundantly; **asentar la mano a** to give a beating; to reprimand; **asidos de la mano** hand in hand; **bajar la mano** to come down (*in price*); **bajo mano** underhandedly; **buenas manos** skill, dexterity; **caer en manos de** to fall into the hands of; **cerrar la mano** to be stingy; **¡dame esa mano!** (coll.) put it here!; **dar de manos** to fall flat on one's face; **dar la mano** to lend a hand; **darse las manos** to join hands; to shake hands (with each other); **de la mano** by hand, by the hand; **de las manos** hand in hand; **de manos a boca** suddenly, unexpectedly; **de primera mano** at first hand; first-hand; **de segunda mano** second-hand; **echar mano a** to seize; **echar mano a la bolsa** to take money out of one's purse; **echar mano de** to resort to; **echar una mano** to lend a hand; to play a game; **en buena mano está** (coll.) after you, you drink first; **escribir a la mano** to take dictation; **escribir a manos de** to write in care of; **estrecharse la mano** to shake hands; **ganarle a uno por la mano** to steal a march on someone; **imponer las manos** (eccl.) to lay hands on; **lavarse las manos de** to wash one's hands of; **llegar a las manos** to come to blows; **malas manos** awkwardness, lack of skill; **mudar de manos** to change hands; **probar la mano** to try one's hand; **salir a mano** (Am.) to come out even; **tener mano con** to have a pull with; **tener mano izquierda** (coll.) to have one's wits about one; **tomar la mano** to begin, to start in; to start the discussion; **untar la mano a** (coll.) to grease the palm of; **venir a las manos** to come to blows; **vivir de la mano a la boca** to live from hand to mouth; **mano a mano** face to face; on an equal footing; **mano de gato** cat's-paw; master hand, master touch (*of a person who has polished or edited the work of another person*); (coll.) make-up; **mano de obra** labor; **mano derecha** right-hand man; **mano de santo** (coll.) sure cure; **mano negra** Black Hand; **manos aguadas** butterfingers; **¡manos a la obra!** to work!, let's get to work!; **manos libres** outside earnings; **manos limpias** (coll.) clean hands; extras, perquisites; **manos muertas** (law) dead hand, mortmain; **mano sobre mano** idly; **manos puercas** (coll.) graft; *m* first to play, e.g., **soy mano** I'm first, I lead
manobre *m* (prov.) hod carrier
manobrero *m* keeper of irrigating ditches
manojo *m* handful, bunch, bundle; (Am.) hand (*of tobacco*); **a manojos** in abundance
manojuelo *m* small bunch or bundle
manolesco -ca *adj* loud, flashy, coarse
manolo -la *mf* Madrid sport; fast liver; (*cap.*) *m* Mannie
manométrico -ca *adj* manometric
manómetro *m* manometer
manopla *f* gauntlet; postilion's whip; (coll.) big hand; (Am.) brass knuckles
manosa *f* (chem.) mannose
manosear *va* to handle, finger; to fiddle with; to muss, rumple; (Am.) to pet, to fondle
manoseo *m* handling, fingering; fiddling; mussing, rumpling; (Am.) petting, fondling
manota *f* big hand
manotada *f* or **manotazo** *m* slap
manoteado *m* var. of **manoteo**
manotear *va* to slap, to smack; *vn* to gesticulate
manoteo *m* slapping; gesticulation
manotón *m* slap
manquear *vn* to be handless; to be one-handed; to be crippled; to pretend to be handless; to act crippled
manquedad *f* or **manquera** *f* lack of one or both hands or arms; crippled condition; defect
mansalva; a mansalva without danger, without running any risk; **a mansalva de** safe from
mansarda *f* mansard, mansard roof
mansedumbre *f* gentleness, mildness, meekness; tameness
mansejón -jona *adj* very gentle or tame
mansera *f* (Am.) vat for cane juice
mansión *f* stay; dwelling, abode; **hacer mansión** to stop, stay, put up; **mansión celestial** heavenly home
mansito *adv* (coll.) softly, quietly
manso -sa *adj* gentle, mild, meek; tame; *m* bellwether; farmhouse; (eccl.) manse
mansurrón -rrona *adj* extremely gentle, extremely meek; extremely tame
manta *f* blanket; large shawl; muffler; (mil.) mantelet; (coll.) beating; (Am.) coarse cotton cloth; (Am.) poncho; **a manta de Dios** copiously; **dar una manta a** (coll.) to toss in a blanket; **tirar de la manta** (coll.) to let the cat out of the bag; **manta de coche** lap robe; **manta de viaje** robe, rug, steamer rug
mantaterilla *f* coarse hempen blanketing
manteador -dora *adj* tossing; *mf* tosser
manteamiento *m* tossing in a blanket
mantear *va* to toss in a blanket; (Am.) to abuse, mistreat; *vn* (prov.) to gad (*said of a woman*)
manteca *f* lard; pomade; butter; (slang) dough (*money*); **como manteca** smooth as butter; **manteca de cacahuete** peanut butter; **manteca de cacao** cocoa butter; **manteca de cerdo** lard; **manteca de coco** coconut butter; **manteca de codo** (coll.) elbow grease; **manteca de puerco** lard; **manteca de vaca** butter
mantecada *f* slice of buttered bread; butter bun
mantecado *m* biscuit; custard ice cream, French ice cream
mantecón *m* (coll.) pampered fellow, mollycoddle
mantecoso -sa *adj* buttery
manteísta *m* student; day student
mantel *m* tablecloth; altar cloth; **levantar el mantel** or **los manteles** to clear the table
mantelería *f* table linen
manteleta *f* mantelet, lady's cape
mantelete *m* (mil.) mantelet; (eccl.) mantelletta; (her.) mantling
mantelillo *m* centerpiece (*of embroidery*)
mantelito *m* lunch cloth
mantelo *m* wide apron
mantellina *f* mantilla (*head scarf*)
mantención *f* (coll.) maintenance
mantendré *1st sg fut ind of* **mantener**
mantenedor *m* presiding officer of a contest
mantener §85 *va* to maintain, to keep; to keep up; *vr* to maintain oneself; to keep, to stay; to remain firm
mantengo *1st sg pres ind of* **mantener**
mantenida *f* (Am.) kept woman
mantenido *m* (Am.) gigolo (*man supported by a woman*)
manteniente; a manteniente with all one's might; with both hands
mantenimiento *m* maintenance; sustenance, food; living
manteo *m* tossing in a blanket; mantle, cloak

mantequera *f* see **mantequero**
mantequería *f* creamery
mantequero -ra *adj* (pertaining to) butter; *mf* butter maker or dealer; *f* churn, butter churn; butter dish
mantequilla *f* butter; butterfat; hard sauce; **mantequilla azucarada** hard sauce; **mantequilla derretida** drawn butter
mantequillera *f* (Am.) butter dish
mantequillero *m* (Am.) butter maker or dealer
mantero -ra *mf* blanket maker or dealer
mantés -tesa *adj* (coll.) scoundrely; *mf* (coll.) scoundrel
mantilla *f* mantilla (*head scarf*); horsecloth; (print.) blanket; **mantillas** *fpl* swaddling clothes; **estar en mantillas** (coll.) to be in its infancy (*said of an undertaking*)
mantillo *m* humus, vegetable mold; manure
mantis *f* (ent.) mantis; **mantis religiosa** (ent.) mantis, praying mantis
mantisa *f* (math.) mantissa
manto *m* mantle, cloak; large plain mantilla; mantel (*of fireplace*); robe, gown (*of priest, professor, etc.*); (geol.) stratum; (zool.) mantle; (fig.) cloak
mantón -tona *adj* with drooping wings; *m* shawl; **mantón de Manila** (coll.) embroidered silk shawl
mantuano -na *adj & mf* Mantuan
mantudo -da *adj* with drooping wings
mantuve *1st sg pret ind of* **mantener**
manuable *adj* handy, easy to handle, workable
manual *adj* manual, hand; handy; home; easy; easy-going; *m* manual, handbook; notebook
manubrio *m* handle; crank; (anat., bot. & zool.) manubrium
manucodiata *f* (orn.) bird of paradise
manuela *f* open hack (*used in Madrid*)
manuella *f* (naut.) capstan bar
manufactura *f* manufactory; manufacture
manufacturar *va* to manufacture
manufacturero -ra *adj* manufacturing
manumisión *f* (law) manumission
manumiso -sa *adj* free, emancipated
manumisor *m* manumitter
manumitir *va* (law) manumit
manuscribir §17, 9 *va & vn* to write by hand
manuscrito -ta *adj* manuscript, written by hand; *m* manuscript; *pp of* **manuscribir**
manutención *f* maintenance; board; protection, shelter
manutendré *1st sg fut ind of* **manutener**
manutener §85 *va* (law) to maintain, support
manutengo *1st sg pres ind of* **manutener**
manutisa *f* var. of **minutisa**
manutuve *1st sg pret ind of* **manutener**
manvacío -a *adj* (coll.) var. of **manivacío**
manzana *f* apple (*fruit*); city block, block of houses; knob of a sword; knob (*on furniture*); **manzana asperiega** or **esperiega** cider apple; **manzana de Adán** Adam's apple; **manzana de la discordia** apple of discord, bone of contention; **manzana espinosa** (bot.) thorn apple
manzanal *m* apple tree; apple orchard
manzanar *m* apple orchard
manzanera *f* var. of **maguillo**
manzanil *adj* (pertaining to the) apple
manzanilla *f* (bot. & pharm.) camomile; manzanilla (*small round olive; pale dry sherry*); knob (*on furniture*); tip of chin; pad, cushion (*of foot of clawed animal*); **manzanilla de Indias** manchineel apple (*fruit*); **manzanilla fétida** or **hedionda** (bot.) stinking camomile; **manzanilla loca** (bot.) ringflower, oxeye; (bot.) Spanish or yellow camomile
manzanillo *m* (bot.) manchineel
manzanita *f* little apple; (bot.) manzanita; **manzanita de dama** Neapolitan medlar (*fruit*)
manzano *m* (bot.) apple, apple tree; **manzano enano de San Juan** or **del paraíso** (hort.) paradise, paradise apple
maña *f* see **maño**
mañana *f* morning; **de mañana** early in the morning; **en la mañana** in the morning; **muy de mañana** very early in the morning; **por la mañana** in the morning; **tomar la mañana** to get up early; (coll.) to take a shot of liquor before breakfast; *m* tomorrow; morrow (*future time*); *adv* tomorrow; **¡hasta mañana!** so long until tomorrow!; **pasado mañana** the day after tomorrow
mañanero -ra *adj* morning; early-rising
mañanica or **mañanita** *f* break of day, early morning; woman's knitted bed jacket
mañear *va & vn* to manage craftily
mañerear *vn* (Am.) to dawdle, to dillydally
mañería *f* sterility; feudal right of inheritance from one who dies without legitimate heirs
mañero -ra *adj* clever, shrewd; easy; (Am.) balky, mulish; (Am.) shy, scary
maño -ña *adj* (coll.) Aragonese; (dial. & Am.) dear, darling; *m* (dial. & Am.) brother; *f* skill, dexterity, cleverness; craftiness, cunning; vice, bad habit; bunch (*of flax, hemp, etc.*); (dial.) sauciness; (dial. & Am.) sister; **darse maña** to take care of oneself, to manage; **darse maña para** + *inf* to manage to, to contrive to + *inf*
mañoco *m* tapioca; (Am.) Indian corn meal
mañoso -sa *adj* skilful, clever; crafty, tricky; vicious
mañuela *f* craftiness, trickiness, meanness; **mañuelas** *mf* (*pl:* **-las**) (coll.) tricky person
maorí (*pl:* **-rís** or **-ríes**) *adj & mf* Maori
mapa *m* map; **mapa itinerario** road map; **mapa mundi** world map, map of the world; *f* (coll.) top (*finest of its lot or kind*); **llevarse la mapa** (coll.) to take the prize
mapache *m* (zool.) coon, raccoon
mapamundi *m* world map, map of the world
mapanare *f* (zool.) fer-de-lance; (zool.) bushmaster
mapurite *m* or **mapurito** *m* (zool.) skunk
maque *m* lacquer; (bot.) tree of heaven
maquear *va* to lacquer; (Am.) to varnish
maqueta *f* maquette; mock-up; (print.) dummy (*of a book*)
maquí *m* (*pl:* **-quíes**) (zool.) macaco; (bot.) maqui
maquiavélico -ca *adj* Machiavellian (*pertaining to Machiavelli; crafty, astute*)
maquiavelismo *m* Machiavellianism
maquiavelista *adj & mf* Machiavellian
maquiavelizar §76 *vn* to be Machiavellian
Maquiavelo *m* Machiavelli
maquila *f* multure, miller's toll
maquilar *va* to exact toll for (*a grinding*)
maquilero -ra *mf* collector of miller's toll
maquillador *m* make-up man
maquillaje *m* (theat.) make-up
maquillar *va & vr* to make up
máquina *f* machine; engine; locomotive; edifice, mansion; plan, project; clippers; (lit. & theat.) machine; (fig.) machinery; (coll.) pile, heap, lot; (coll.) bike; **escribir a** or **con máquina** to typewrite; **máquina apisonadora** road roller; **máquina calculadora** computer; **máquina de afeitar** safety razor; **máquina de apostar** betting machine, gambling machine; **máquina de componer** (print.) typesetter; **máquina de coser** sewing machine; **máquina de dictar** dictating machine; **máquina de escribir** typewriter; **máquina de lavar** washing machine; **máquina de sumar** adding machine; **máquina de vapor** steam engine; **máquina de volar** flying machine; **máquina Diesel** Diesel engine; **máquina electrostática** (elec.) static machine; **máquina estenotipiadora** stenotype; **máquina fotográfica** camera; **máquina hiladora** spinning machine; **máquina infernal** infernal machine; **máquina parlante** talking machine; **máquina piloto** (rail.) pilot engine; **máquina sacaperras, tragamonedas** or **tragaperras** slot machine
maquinación *f* machination, scheming, plotting
maquinador -dora *adj* machinating, scheming, plotting; *mf* machinator, schemer, plotter
máquina-herramienta *f* (*pl:* **máquinas-herramientas**) machine tool
maquinal *adj* mechanical; (fig.) mechanical
maquinar *va & vn* to machinate, scheme, plot
maquinaria *f* machinery; applied mechanics; (fig.) machinery

maquinilla *f* winch; clippers; **maquinilla cortapelos** hair clippers; **maquinilla de afeitar** safety razor; **maquinilla de rizar** curling iron
maquinismo *m* (econ.) mechanization
maquinista *mf* machinist; engineer (*who runs an engine*); **primer maquinista** (naut.) engineer officer; **segundo maquinista** (naut.) machinist
mar *m & f* sea; tide, flood; (fig.) sea, e.g., **mar de lágrimas** sea of tears; (fig.) oceans, e.g., **la mar de trabajo** oceans of work; **alta mar** high seas; **a mares** copiously; **arrojarse a la mar** to plunge, take great risks; **baja mar** low tide; **correr los mares** to follow the sea; **de mar a mar** from one end to the other; (coll.) all dressed-up; **echar a la mar** (naut.) to launch; **hablar de la mar** (coll.) to talk wildly; to take up an endless subject; **hacerse a la mar** to put to sea; **la mar de** a lot of, lots of; **meter la mar en un pozo** to attempt the impossible; **meterse mar adentro** to go beyond one's depth; **mar alta** rough sea; **mar Amarillo** Yellow Sea; **mar ancha** high seas; **mar Arábigo** Arabian Sea; **mar Aral** Aral Sea; **mar Báltico** Baltic Sea; **mar Blanco** White Sea; **mar bonanza** calm sea; **mar Cantábrico** Bay of Biscay; **mar Caribe** Caribbean Sea; **mar Caspio** Caspian Sea; **mar de costado** beam sea; **mar de fondo** ground swell; **mar de Galilea** Sea of Galilee; **mar de Irlanda** Irish Sea; **mar de la China** China Sea; **mar de la China Meridional** South China Sea; **mar de la China Oriental** East China Sea; **mar de las Antillas** Caribbean Sea; **mar de las Indias** Indian Ocean; **mar del Coral** Coral Sea; **mar de leva** ground swell; **mar del Japón** Inland Sea, Sea of Japan; **mar del Norte** North Sea; **mar de los Sargazos** Sargasso Sea; **mar del sur** South Seas (*south of the equator*); **mar de Mármara** Sea of Marmara or Marmora; **mar de nubes** cloud bank; **mar de Omán** Gulf of Oman; **mar de Sargazos** Sargasso Sea; **mar Egeo** Aegean Sea (*of ancient times*); **mar Jonio** Ionian Sea; **mar larga** high sea; **mar Latino** Mediterranean Sea; **mar llena** high tide; **mar Mediterráneo** Mediterranean Sea; **mar Muerto** Dead Sea; **mar Negro** Black Sea; **mar Rojo** Red Sea; **mar tendida** swell (*of sea*); **mar Tirreno** Tyrrhenian Sea
marabú *m* (*pl:* **-búes**) (orn.) marabou (*bird and trimming*); (bot.) Cuban weed (*Diegrostachys nutans*)
marabuto *m* Mohammedan hermitage
maraca *f* (Am.) maraca (*dried gourd filled with seeds or pebbles and used for marking rhythm*); (Am.) game played with three dice marked with sun, gold coin (diamond), bowl (heart), star, moon, and anchor; (Am.) harlot
maracá *m* (Am.) maraca (*dried gourd used for marking rhythm*)
maragato -ta *adj* Maragato; *mf* Maragato (*descendant of Celtiberian inhabitants in León, Spain*)
maraña *f* thicket, jungle; silk waste; poor silk cloth; tangle (*of thread, hair, etc.*); complexity, puzzle; trick, scheme; (bot.) kermes oak
marañal *m* field of kermes oak
marañar *va* to tangle; to entangle; *vr* to get tangled; to become entangled
marañero -ra or **marañoso -sa** *adj* intriguing, scheming; *mf* intriguer, schemer; cheat
marañón *m* (bot.) cashew
maraquiana *f* (bot.) marijuana (*Nicotiana glauca*)
marasmo *m* (path.) marasmus; (fig.) depression, stagnation
Maratón *m* Marathon; (l.c.) *m* (sport) marathon
maravedí *m* (*pl:* **-dís, -dises** or **-díes**) maravedi
maravilla *f* wonder, marvel; (bot.) marigold, calendula; (bot.) four-o'clock, marvel-of-Peru; (bot.) ivy-leaved morning-glory; **a las maravillas** or **a las mil maravillas** magnificently; **a maravilla** wonderfully well; **hacer maravillas con** to do wonders with; **por maravilla** rarely, seldom, on occasion
maravillar *va* to astonish, amaze; *vr* to wonder, to marvel; **maravillarse con** or **de** to wonder at, to marvel at
maravilloso -sa *adj* wonderful, marvelous; **lo maravilloso** (lit.) the marvelous, the supernatural
marbete *m* stamp, label; baggage check; edge, border; rope, binding; **marbete engomado** sticker
marca *f* mark; stamp; sign; make; brand; score; height-measuring bar; march (*frontier; territory*); shipping mark; record (*e.g., of endurance*); (naut.) seamark, landmark; **de marca** outstanding; **de marca mayor** or **de más de marca** most outstanding; **marca de agua** watermark (*in paper*); **marca de fábrica** trademark; **marca de máximo calado** (naut.) Plimsoll line; **marca depositada** trademark; **marca de reconocimiento** (naut.) seamark, landmark; **marca de taquilla** box-office record; **marca privativa** trademark; **marca registrada** registered trademark
marcación *f* (naut.) relative bearing; (naut.) taking a ship's bearing
marcado -da *adj* marked, pronounced; *m* (print.) feeding
marcador -dora *adj* marking; branding; *mf* marker; brander; *m* marker; sampler (*embroidered cloth*); (sport) marker (*device for marking, e.g., a tennis court*); (sport) marker, scoreboard; (print.) feeder; (print.) feedboard
marcaje *m* (telp.) dialing; (sport) scoring
marcapaso *m* (med.) pacemaker (*to regulate heartbeat*)
marcar §86 *va* to mark; to stamp; to brand; to embroider; to initial (*e.g., a handkerchief*); to designate; to lay out (*a task*); to point out, to stress; to show (*the hour*); to make (*a score*); to score (*a point*); to dial (*a telephone number*); *vr* to take its bearings (*said of a ship*)
marcasita *f* (mineral.) marcasite
marceador -dora *adj* shearing; *mf* shearer
marcear *va* to shear (*e.g., sheep*); *vn* to be Marchlike, to be rough as March (*said of weather*)
Marcela *f* Marcella
Marcelo *m* Marcellus
marceño -ña *adj* (pertaining to) March
marceo *m* springtime cleaning of honeycombs
marcero -ra *adj* shearing
marcescencia *f* (bot.) marcescence
marcescente *adj* (bot.) marcescent
marcial *adj* martial; plain, simple; (*cap.*) *m* Martial
marcialidad *f* martiality, martialness
marciano -na *adj & mf* Martian
marco *m* frame; standard (*of weights and measures*); framework; size stick (*for measuring foot*); mark (*coin; weight*); (*cap.*) *m* Mark, Marcus; **marco de imprimir** (phot.) printing frame
márcola *f* pruning hook
marconigrama *m* marconigram
Marcos *m* Mark
marcha *f* march; running, functioning; operation; rate of speed; course, path (*e.g., of rays of light*); departure; (mil. & mus.) march; (aut.) speed (*in relation to gears*); (fig.) march, course, progress; (dial.) bonfire; **a toda marcha** at full speed; **batir la marcha** or **batir marcha** (mus.) to strike up a march; **cambiar de marcha** to shift gears; **en marcha** under way; on the march; in motion; **poner en marcha** to start, to launch (*a project*); **ponerse en marcha** to start, to strike out; **primera marcha** (mach.) low gear; **segunda marcha** second (gear); **sobre la marcha** at once, right away; **marcha a rueda libre** (mach.) freewheeling; **marcha atrás** (mach.) reverse; **marcha de ensayo** trial run; **marcha del hambre** hunger march; **marcha directa** (mach.) high gear; **marcha en ralentí** or **en vacío** idling; **marcha forzada** (mil.) forced march; **marcha fúnebre** (mus.) dead march, funeral march; **marcha nupcial** (mus.) wedding march
marchamar *va* to mark at the customhouse
marchamero *m* customhouse marker

marchamo *m* customhouse mark; lead seal
marchante *adj* commercial; *m* dealer, merchant; (Am.) customer
marchapié *m* (naut.) footrope; running board (*of a carriage*)
marchar *vn* to march; to run; to work; to go; to go away, leave; to proceed, come along, progress; (mil.) to march; **marchar en ralentí** or **en vacío** to idle; *vr* to go away, leave
marchitable *adj* easily withered, perishable
marchitamiento *m* withering; languishing
marchitar *va* to wilt, to wither; *vr* to wilt, to wither; (fig.) to wilt, to languish
marchitez *f* withered state; languor
marchito -ta *adj* withered; languid
marchoso -sa *adj* (slang) breezy, jaunty; (prov.) sporty; (prov.) roisterous
Mardoqueo *m* (Bib.) Mordecai
marea *f* (naut.) tide; gentle sea breeze; dew, drizzle; street dirt washed away; **marea alta** high tide; **marea baja** low tide; **marea creciente** or **entrante** flood tide; **marea menguante, saliente** or **vaciante** ebb tide; **marea muerta** neap tide; **marea viva** spring tide
mareado -da *adj* nauseated, seasick, lightheaded
mareaje *m* navigation, seamanship; course (*of a ship*)
mareamiento *m* var. of **mareo**
mareamotor -triz (*pl:* **-trices**) *adj* tide-driven
marear *va* to navigate, sail; to hoist (*sails*); (coll.) to annoy; *vn* (coll.) to be annoying; *vr* to become nauseated, to become seasick; to get giddy; to become damaged at sea (*said of merchandise*)
mareca *f* (orn.) baldpate
marecanita *f* (mineral.) marekanite
marejada *f* ground swell; stirring, undercurrent (*of unrest*); **marejada de fondo** ground swell
maremagno or **mare mágnum** *m* (coll.) mess, confusion; (coll.) omnium-gatherum
maremoto *m* earthquake at sea; bore, tidal bore
mare nóstrum *m* mare nostrum (*our sea, i.e., the Mediterranean*)
mareo *m* nausea; seasickness; plane sickness; (coll.) annoyance
mareógrafo *m* marigraph
marero *adj masc* sea (*breeze or wind*)
mareta *f* surge; rumbling (*of a mob*); agitation, disturbance
maretazo *m* billow
márfaga *f* ticking
marfil *m* ivory; **marfil vegetal** ivory nut
marfileño -ña *adj* (pertaining to) ivory
marfilino -na *adj* (pertaining to) ivory; *f* imitation ivory
marfuz -fuza *adj* (*pl:* **-fuces** & **-fuzas**) rejected, cast aside; false, deceptive
marga *f* marl; ticking
margal *m* marlpit, marly ground
margallón *m* (bot.) dwarf fan palm
margar §59 *va* to marl
margarita *f* pearl; (bot.) daisy, marguerite; (mineral.) margarite; (naut.) sheepshank (*knot*); (zool.) periwinkle; (*cap.*) *f* Margaret, Marguerite; **echar margaritas a los cerdos** or **a los puercos** to cast pearls before swine; **margarita de los prados** (bot.) English daisy, bachelor's-button; **margarita mayor** (bot.) oxeye daisy
margen *m & f* margin; border, edge; note, marginal note; occasion; **al margen de** aside from; aloof from; outside of; independent of; **andarse por los márgenes** to beat about the bush; **dar margen para** to give occasion for; **dejar al margen** to leave out; **quedar al margen de** to be left on the outside of; **margen de seguridad** margin of safety
marginado -da *adj* (bot.) marginal
marginador *m* marginal stop (*of typewriter*)
marginal *adj* marginal
marginar *va* to write marginal notes in (*a text*); to leave a margin on (*a printed or written sheet*); (Am.) to line (*e.g., the bank of a river*)
marginoso -sa *adj* wide-margined
margoso -sa *adj* marly
margrave *m* margrave
margraviato *m* margraviate
margravina *f* margravine
Marg.ta abr. of **Margarita**
marguera *f* marlpit
marhojo *m* var. of **malhojo**
maría *f* (coll.) white wax taper; (*cap.*) *f* Mary
mariache *m* or **mariachi** *m* rousing type of Mexican popular music; musician who plays this music
mariano -na *adj* Marian; *m* Marion (*man's name*); *f* Marion, Marian, or Marianne
marica *f* (orn.) magpie; jack of diamonds; *m* (coll.) sissy, milksop
maricangalla *f* (naut.) ringtail
Maricastaña; en tiempo or **en tiempos de Maricastaña** in times of yore
maricón *m* (coll.) sissy; sodomite
maridable *adj* conjugal, matrimonial
maridaje *m* married life; (fig.) marriage, union
maridar *va* to combine, join, unite; *vn* to get married; to live as man and wife
maridazo *m* (coll.) doting husband, henpecked husband
maridillo *m* ridiculous little husband; foot stove
marido *m* husband
mariguana *f* (bot.) marijuana (*Cannabis sativa*); **mariguana falsa** (bot.) marijuana (*Nicotiana glauca*)
mariguano *m* (Am.) marihuana addict
mariguanza *f* (Am.) hocus-pocus; (Am.) pirouette; **mariguanzas** *fpl* (Am.) quackery, powwowing; (Am.) clowning
marihuana *f* var. of **mariguana**
marimacho *m* (coll.) mannish woman
marimandona *f* (prov.) bossy woman
marimanta *f* (coll.) hobgoblin, bugaboo
marimarica *m* (coll.) sissy, milksop
marimba *f* (mus.) marimba; (Am.) beating, flogging
marimbero -ra *mf* marimba player
marimoña *f* (bot.) turban buttercup
marimorena *f* (coll.) fight, row
marina *f* see **marino**
marinaje *m* var. of **marinería**
marinar *va* to salt, to marinate (*fish*); to man, to put a new crew on (*a ship*); *vn* to be a sailor
marinear *vn* to be a sailor; to get one's sea legs
marinera *f* see **marinero**
marinería *f* seamanship, sailoring; sailors, ship's crew
marinero -ra *adj* seaworthy, navigable; marine, sea; *m* mariner, seaman, sailor; (zool.) paper nautilus; **a la marinera** or **a lo marinero** sailor-fashion; **marinero de agua dulce** landlubber; **marinero matalote** lubber, landlubber; *f* sailor blouse; middy, middy blouse
marinesco -ca *adj* (pertaining to the) sailor; sailorly; **a la marinesca** sailor-fashion
marinista *mf* seascapist
marino -na *adj* marine, sea; *m* mariner, seaman, sailor; *f* navy (*personnel*); seascape, marine; seaside, shore; fleet; sailing, navigation; **marina de guerra** navy; **marina mercante** merchant marine
Mario *m* Marius
marión *m* (ichth.) sturgeon
marioneta *f* marionette
maripérez *f* hook to fasten frying pan to trivet
mariposa f (ent. & fig.) butterfly; (ichth.) butterfly fish; wing nut; butterfly valve; rushlight; prostitute; (Am.) blindman's buff; **mariposa nocturna** (ent.) moth
mariposear *vn* to be capricious, to be fickle; to flutter around
mariposón *m* (coll.) fickle flirt
mariquita *m* (coll.) sissy, milksop; *f* (ent.) ladybird; (*cap.*) *f* Molly, Polly
marisabidilla *f* (coll.) bluestocking, know-it-all
mariscador -dora *mf* gatherer of shellfish
mariscal *m* (mil.) marshal; veterinarian; blacksmith; **mariscal de campo** (mil.) field marshal; (archaic) major general
mariscala *f* marshaless
mariscalato *m* or **mariscalía** *f* marshalate

mariscar §86 *vn* to gather shellfish
marisco *m* shellfish; **mariscos** *mpl* seafood
marisma *f* marsh, swamp; salt marsh
marismeño -ña *adj* marsh, swamp; marshy, swampy
marismo *m* (bot.) orach
marisqueo *m* shellfishery
marisquería *f* seafood store
marisquero -ra *adj* shellfish; seafood; *mf* catcher of shellfish; shellfish dealer; seafood dealer
marista *adj & mf* (eccl.) Marist
marital *adj* marital
marítimo -ma *adj* maritime; marine, sea
maritornes *f* (*pl:* **-nes**) (coll.) ugly, mannish maidservant, wench
marizápalos *m* (*pl:* **-los**) (coll.) fight, row
marjal *m* marsh, moor, fen
marjoleta *f* haw or berry (*of Crataegus monogyna and C. oxyacantha*)
marjoleto *m* (bot.) English hawthorn (*Crataegus monogyna and C. oxyacantha*)
marlota *f* close-fitting Moorish gown
marlotar *va* to tie, pinch, squeeze; to cut, tear away; (archaic) to squander
marmella *f* var. of **mamella**
marmita *f* pot, boiler; **marmita de gigante** (geol.) pothole
marmitón *m* scullion, kitchen scullion
mármol *m* marble; marver (*for rolling hot glass*)
marmolejo *m* small marble column
marmoleño -ña *adj* (pertaining to) marble
marmolería *f* marble work; marble works
marmolillo *m* spur stone; dolt
marmolista *m* marble worker; marble dealer
marmolización *f* marbling
marmolizar §76 *va & vr* to marble
marmoración *f* stucco
marmóreo -a *adj* marmoreal
marmoroso -sa *adj* marble, marmoreal
marmosete *m* vignette
marmota *f* (zool.) marmot; worsted cap; sleepyhead; sleepy-headed woman; ugly wench; **marmota de Alemania** (zool.) hamster; **marmota de América** (zool.) ground hog, woodchuck
maro *m* (bot.) cat thyme; (bot.) clary
marojal *m* growth of red-berried mistletoes; growth of pubescent oak trees
marojo *m* (bot.) red-berried mistletoe (*Viscum cruciatum*); (bot.) pubescent oak, durmast
maroma *f* rope of hemp or esparto; (Am.) acrobatics
maromear *vn* (Am.) to walk a tightrope, to stunt; (Am.) to sway (*toward one party or the other*)
maromero -ra *mf* (Am.) tightrope walker
marón *m* (ichth.) sturgeon; ram, male sheep
marquear *va* to sow or plant in straight lines
marqueo *m* layout for planting trees
marqués *m* marquis; (coll.) one-eyed fellow; **marqueses** *mpl* marquis and marchioness
marquesa *f* marquise, marchioness; marquee (*over an entrance*); (coll.) one-eyed woman
marquesado *m* marquisate
marquesina *f* marquee (*over an entrance*); locomotive cab
marquesita *f* var. of **marcasita**
marquesota *f* (archaic) high stiff collar
marqueta *f* cake of crude wax
marqueteador *m* worker in marquetry
marquetería *f* marquetry (*inlaid work*); cabinetwork, woodwork
marquiana *f* var. of **maraquiana**
marra *f* gap (*in a row, e.g., of trees*); stone hammer, spalling hammer
márraga *f* ticking
marrajo -ja *adj* malicious, wicked (*bull*); sly, tricky; *m* (ichth.) shark
marramao or **marramáu** *m* caterwaul
marramizar §76 *vn* to caterwaul
marrana *f* see **marrano**
marranada *f* (coll.) piggishness, filthiness
marranalla *f* (coll.) rabble, riffraff
marranchón -chona *mf* pig
marranería *f* (coll.) var. of **marranada**
marranillo *m* little pig; sucking pig
marrano -na *adj* (coll.) dirty, sloppy; base, vile; *mf* hog; *m* male hog, boar; drum (*of water wheel*); timber (*of shaft or well*); (fig.) hog; axle (*of bucket wheel*); (fig.) cur; *f* sow; (coll.) slut
marrar *vn* to miss, fail; to go astray
marras *adv* (coll.) long ago, a long time ago; **de marras** (coll.) of a long time ago; (coll.) well-known; **hacer marras de** (Am.) to be a long time since
marrasquino *m* maraschino
marrazo *m* mattock
marrear *va* to strike with a stone hammer
marrillo *m* short, thick stick
marro *m* quoits (*played with a stone*); dodge, duck; slip, miss; tag (*game*); cat (*used in tipcat*)
marrón *adj invar* maroon (*very dark red*); tan (*shoes*); **marrón -rrona** *adj* (Am.) fugitive, runaway (*slave*); *m* maroon (*very dark red*); stone (*used as sort of quoit*); (Am.) maroon (*fugitive slave, descendant of fugitive Negro slaves in West Indies and Dutch Guiana; explosive*); **marrones** *mpl* marrons (*chestnuts preserved in syrup*)
marronaje *m* (Am.) fugitive slaves
marroquí (*pl:* **-quíes**) *adj & mf* Moroccan; *m* morocco, morocco leather
marroquín -quina *adj, mf & m* var. of **marroquí**
marroquinería *f* morocco-leather dressing; morocco-leather shop
marrubial *m* field of horehound
marrubio *m* (bot.) horehound; **marrubio acuático** (bot.) water horehound; **marrubio blanco** (bot.) white horehound
marrueco -ca *adj & mf* Moroccan; **Marruecos** *m* Morocco; **el Marruecos Español** Spanish Morocco; **el Marruecos Francés** French Morocco
marrullería *f* cajolery, wheedling
marrullero -ra *adj* cajoling, wheedling; *mf* cajoler, wheedler
Marsella *f* Marseilles
marsellés -llesa *adj* (pertaining to) Marseilles; *mf* native or inhabitant of Marseilles; *m* coarse jacket; (*cap.*) *f* Marseillaise (*French national song*)
Marsias *m* (myth.) Marsyas
marsopa or **marsopla** *f* (zool.) porpoise, harbor porpoise, sea hog
marsupial *adj & m* (zool.) marsupial
mart. abr. of **martes**
marta *f* (zool.) pine marten; (*cap.*) *f* Martha; **marta cebellina** (zool.) sable, Siberian sable; sable (*fur*); **marta del Canadá** (zool.) fisher
martagón -gona *mf* (coll.) crafty person; *m* (bot.) Turk's-cap lily
Marte *m* (astr. & myth.) Mars
martellina *f* marteline
martes *m* (*pl:* **-tes**) Tuesday; **martes de carnaval** Shrove Tuesday
martillada *f* blow or stroke with a hammer
martillado *m* (action of) hammering
martillador -dora *adj* hammering; *mf* hammerer
martillar *va* to hammer; to worry, torment
martillazo *m* hard blow with a hammer; (box.) chop
martillear *va* var. of **martillar**
martilleo *m* hammering; (fig.) hammering
martillero *m* (Am.) auctioneer
martillete *m* tinner's hammer
martillo *m* hammer; (anat.) hammer, malleus; (mus.) tuning hammer; auction house; scourge (*person*); **a macha martillo** strongly but crudely (*constructed*); **a martillo** by hammering, with a hammer; **de martillo** wrought, hammered (*metal*); **martillo de agua** (phys.) water hammer (*glass tube*); **martillo de caída** or **martillo pilón** drop hammer; **martillo percusor** or **percutor** (med.) percussion hammer; **martillo perforador** jackhammer; **martillo picador** (*pl:* **martillos picadores**) hammer drill, jackhammer; **martillo sacaclavos** claw hammer
Martín *m* Martin; **llegarle** or **venirle a uno su San Martín** (coll.) to pay for one's wild oats; **San Martín** (coll.) season for killing hogs; **martín cazador** (*pl:* **martín caza-**

dores) (orn.) laughing jackass; **martín del río** (orn.) night heron; **martín pescador** (*pl:* **martín pescadores**) (orn.) kingfisher
martina *f* (ichth.) sand cusk, cusk eel
martinete *m* drop hammer; pile driver; hammer (*of piano*); (orn.) night heron; **martinete de báscula** tilt hammer
martingala *f* trick, cunning; **martingalas** *fpl* breeches worn under armor
Martinica, la Martinique
martinico *m* (coll.) goblin, ghost
mártir *mf* martyr
martirio *m* martyrdom
martirizar §76 *va* to martyrize, to martyr
martirologio *m* martyrology
márts. abr. of **mártires**
martucha *f* (zool.) kinkajou
Maruja *f* (coll.) Mary
marullo *m* surge, swell
marxismo *m* Marxism
marxista *adj* & *mf* Marxian or Marxist
marzal *adj* (pertaining to) March
marzo *m* March
marzoleta *f* var. of **marjoleta**
marzoleto *m* var. of **marjoleto**
mas *conj* but
más *adv* more; most; longer; faster; rather; **a lo más** at most, at the most; **a más** besides, in addition; **a más de** besides, in addition to; **a más y mejor** hard, copiously; to one's heart's content; **como el que más** as the next one (*i.e., as any or anybody*); **cuando más** at the most; **de más** extra; too much, too many; **en más de** at more than + *numeral;* **en más que** more highly than; for more than; **estar de más** to be unnecessary, be superfluous, to be in the way; **los más de** most of, the majority of; **ni más ni menos** neither more nor less; **no . . . más** no longer; **no . . . más nada** nothing more; **no . . . más que** only; **poco más o menos** little more or less, practically; **por más que** however much, no matter how much; **más bien** rather; **más de** more than + *numeral;* **más que** more than; better than; although; **más y más** more and more, harder and harder; **sin más ni más** (coll.) suddenly, in a rush, just like that, without more ado; *prep* plus; *m* more; plus (*sign*); **tener sus más y sus menos** (coll.) to have one's (or its) good points and bad points
masa *f* mass; dough; mash; nature, disposition; (phys.) mass; (elec.) ground (*e.g., of an automobile*); (Am.) flesh (*e.g., of fruit*); **en masa** in the mass; en masse; mass, e.g., **la inoculación en masa** mass inoculation; **las masas** the masses; **masa crítica** (phys.) critical mass
masacre *m* massacre
masada *f* farmhouse
masadero *m* farmer
masaje *m* massage
masajear *va* to massage
masajista *m* masseur; *f* masseuse
masar *va* to knead; to massage
mascabado -da *adj* & *m* muscovado
mascada *f* chew; chewing; (Am.) silk handkerchief
mascador -dora *adj* chewing; *mf* chewer, masticator
mascadura *f* chewing; chew; (naut.) fretting, galling (*of a cable*)
mascar §86 *va* to chew; (coll.) to mumble, to mutter; *vr* (naut.) to fret, to gall
máscara *f* mask; masquerade (*costume*); (fig.) mask; **máscaras** *fpl* masque, masquerade; **arrancar** or **quitar la máscara a** (fig.) to unmask; **quitarse la máscara** (fig.) to take off one's mask; **máscara antigás, máscara contra gases** or **máscara de gases** gas mask; **máscara de cabeza** head shield (*of welder*); **máscara de seguridad** safety mask; **máscara respiratoria** respirator; *mf* (coll.) mask, masquerader, mummer
mascarada *f* masquerade; party of masqueraders
mascarero -ra *mf* costumer
mascareta *f* little mask
mascarilla *f* little mask; half mask; false face (*funny*); death mask; **mascarilla contra gases asfixiantes** gas mask
mascarón *m* large mask; false face; fright (*ugly person*); (arch.) mask; **mascarón de proa** (naut.) figurehead
mascota *f* mascot
mascujada *f* (coll.) mumbling
mascujar *va* & *vn* (coll.) to chew poorly or hurriedly; (coll.) to mumble, to mutter
masculinidad *f* masculinity
masculinizar §76 *va* (gram.) to make masculine
masculino -na *adj* masculine; (bot.) male; (gram.) masculine; *m* (gram.) masculine
mascullar *va* & *vn* (coll.) to mumble, to mutter; (coll.) to chew hurriedly
masecoral *m* or **masejicomar** *m* sleight of hand
masera *f* kneading trough; cover for kneading trough
masería *f* var. of **masada**
masetero *m* (anat.) masseter
masía *f* (prov.) farmhouse; (prov.) farm
másico -ca *adj* (phys.) (pertaining to) mass
masicoral *m* var. of **masecoral**
masicote *m* massicot
masiliense *adj* (pertaining to) Marseilles; *mf* native or inhabitant of Marseilles
masilla *f* putty
masita *f* (mil.) pittance withheld for shoes and clothes; (Am.) cake
maslo *m* root (*of the tail of a quadruped*); stem
masón *m* mess of dough for fowls; Mason
masonería *f* Masonry
masónico -ca *adj* Masonic
masonita *f* (mineral.) masonite; masonite (*fiberboard*)
masoquismo *m* (path.) masochism
masoquista *adj* masochistic; *mf* masochist
mastelerillo *m* (naut.) topgallant mast; **mastelerillo de juanete** (naut.) foretopgallant mast; **mastelerillo de mayor** (naut.) maintopgallant mast
mastelero *m* (naut.) topmast; **mastelero de mayor** (naut.) maintopmast; **mastelero de proa** or **de velacho** (naut.) foretopmast
masticación *f* mastication; (tech.) mastication
masticador *m* masticator (*machine*); salivant bit
masticar §86 *va* to masticate; to meditate upon; to mumble; to cover with mastic; (tech.) to masticate (*e.g., rubber*)
masticatorio -ria *adj* & *m* masticatory
mástico *m* var. of **mástique**
mastigador *m* salivant bit
mástil *m* (naut.) mast; (mus.) neck (*of violin*); upright; stalk; stanchion; stem, shaft (*of feather*)
mastín -tina *mf* mastiff; (coll.) dolt, ignoramus; **mastín danés** Great Dane
mástique *m* mastic
mastitis *f* (path.) mastitis
masto *m* (prov.) stock (*on which a graft is made*); male animal, cock
mastodonte *m* (pal.) mastodon
mastoidectomía *f* (surg.) mastoidectomy
mastoideo -a *adj* (anat.) mastoid
mastoides *adj* & *f* (anat.) mastoid
mastoiditis *f* (path.) mastoiditis
mastranto or **mastranzo** *m* (bot.) horse mint, apple mint
mastuerzo *m* (bot.) cress, peppercress, peppergrass; simpleton, dolt
masturbación *f* masturbation
masturbar *vr* to masturbate
masurio *m* (chem.) masurium
masvale *m* var. of **malvasía**
mat. abr. of **matemática**
mata *f* bush, shrub; blade, sprig; head of hair, crop of hair; brush, underbrush; (bot.) mastic tree; (metal.) matte; **saltar de la mata** (coll.) to come out of hiding; **mata parda** (bot.) chaparro (*oak*); **mata rubia** (bot.) kermes, kermes oak
matabuey *m* (bot.) shrubby hare's-ear
matacabras *m* (*pl:* **-bras**) cold blast from the north
matacán *m* dog poison; nux vomica; cobblestone; (fort.) machicolation
matacandelas *m* (*pl:* **-las**) candle extinguisher

matacandil *m* (bot.) London rocket; (prov.) spiny lobster
matacandiles *m* (*pl:* **-les**) (bot.) star-of-Bethlehem
matachín *m* merry-andrew; dance of merry-andrews; slaughterman; (coll.) bully
matachinada *f* merry-andrewism, clowning; (coll.) concern
matadero *m* abattoir, slaughter house; danger spot; (coll.) drudgery
matador -dora *mf* killer; *m* (taur. & cards) matador; **matador de mujeres** lady-killer
matadura *f* sore, gall
matafuego *m* fire extinguisher; fireman
matagallos *m* (*pl:* **-llos**) (bot.) Jerusalem sage
matajudío *m* (ichth.) striped mullet
matalahuga or **matalahuva** *f* var. of **anís**
mátalas callando *mf* (coll.) schemer
matalobos *m* (*pl:* **-bos**) (bot.) wolf's-bane
matalón -lona *adj* skinny and full of sores (*said of a horse*); *mf* skinny old nag
matalotaje *m* (naut.) ship stores; (coll.) mess, jumble
matalote *adj & mf* var. of **matalón;** *m* (naut.) next ship (*forward or astern, in a column of ships*)
matamalezas *m* (*pl:* **-zas**) weed killer
matamoros *m* (*pl:* **-ros**) (coll.) bully, braggart
matamoscas *m* (*pl:* **-cas**) fly swatter; fly-paper, piece of flypaper
matanza *f* slaughter, slaughtering, butchering; massacre; slaughtering season; pork products; (coll.) concern
mataperrada *f* (coll.) prank of a street urchin
mataperros *m* (*pl:* **-rros**) (coll.) street urchin; (Am.) harum-scarum
matapiojos *m* (*pl:* **-jos**) (ent.) dragonfly
matapolvo *m* light rain, sprinkling
matapulgas *f* (*pl:* **-gas**) (bot.) horse mint, apple mint
matar *va* to kill; to butcher (*animals for food*); to put out (*a fire, a light*); to slack (*lime*); to lay (*dust*); to dull; to mat (*metal*); to tone down (*a color*); to round off (*e.g., rough edges*); to gall (*a horse*); to spot (*a card*); to play a card higher than; to ruin, to wreck; to slay, to bore to death; (fig.) to kill (*time, hunger, etc.*); *vn* to kill; **estar a matar con** to be very much annoyed at; to be on the outs with; *vr* to kill oneself; to be killed; to drudge, overwork; to be grieved, be disappointed; **matarse con** to quarrel with; **matarse por** to struggle for; **matarse por** + *inf* to struggle to + *inf*
matarife *m* butcher, slaughterman
matarratas *m* rat poison; (coll.) rotgut
matarrubia *f* (bot.) kermes, kermes oak
matasanos *m* (*pl:* **-nos**) (coll.) quack doctor
matasellar *va* to cancel (*stamps*); to postmark
matasellos *m* (*pl:* **-llos**) canceler (*of postage stamps*); postmark
matasiete *m* (*pl:* **-te**) (coll.) bully, braggart
matatías *m* (*pl:* **-as**) (coll.) moneylender, pawnbroker
matazarzas *m* (*pl:* **-zas**) weed killer
mate *adj* dull, flat; *m* checkmate; (bot.) maté (*plant, leaves, and tea*); maté gourd; **dar mate ahogado a** (chess) to stalemate; **mate ahogado** (chess) stalemate; **mate amargo** or **cimarrón** black or bitter maté; **dar mate a** to checkmate; to make fun of, laugh at
matear *va* to plant at regular intervals; to make dull; (Am.) to checkmate; *vr* to sprout (*said of wheat*); to hunt through the bushes (*said of a hunting dog*); (Am.) to drink maté
matemático -ca *adj* mathematical; (coll.) obvious, unquestionable, *mf* mathematician; *f* mathematics; **matemáticas** *fpl* mathematics
Mateo *m* Matthew
materia *f* matter; stuff, material; subject; (path.) matter (*pus*); **en materia de** in the matter of, as regards; **entrar en materia** to go into the matter; **primera materia** raw material; **materia colorante** dyestuff; **materia médica** materia medica (*remedial substances; branch of medicine*); **materia prima** raw material
material *adj* material; physical (*effort*); crude; *m* material; equipment, matériel; (mil.) matériel; (print.) matter, copy; **ser material** (coll.) to be immaterial; **material fijo** (rail.) permanent way; **material móvil** or **rodante** (rail.) rolling stock
materialidad *f* materiality, corporeity; outward appearance; literal meaning; crudeness, coarseness; literalness
materialismo *m* materialism
materialista *adj* materialistic; *mf* materialist; *m* dealer in building material
materialización *f* materialization (*e.g., of thought*)
materializar **§76** *va* to materialize (*e.g., thought*); to realize (*profit*); *vr* to become materialistic
maternal *adj* maternal, mother (*e.g., love*)
maternidad *f* maternity; motherhood; maternity (*maternity hospital*)
materno -na *adj* maternal, mother (*e.g., tongue*)
Matías *m* Matthias
matidez *f* dullness, flatness
matihuelo *m* tumbler (*toy figure*)
Matilde *f* Matilda
matinal *adj* matinal, morning
matinée *m & f* matinée (*afternoon performance*); dressing gown, wrapper
matitez *f* flatness (*of a sound*)
matiz *m* (*pl:* **-tices**) hue, shade, nuance; (fig.) shade
matizar **§76** *va* to blend; to match (*in color*); to shade (*colors, sounds, etc.*); to adorn, bedeck (*e.g., a speech*)
mato *m* var. of **matorral**
matojo *m* (bot.) salsolaceous shrub (*Haloxylon articulatum*)
matón *m* (coll.) bully, browbeater; **matón sopista** (coll.) poverty-stricken bully
matonismo *m* (coll.) bullying, browbeating
matorral *m* thicket, underbrush
matoso -sa *adj* dense, thick, brushy
matraca *f* noisemaker (*wooden rattle*); pestering, harassment; pest, bore; **dar matraca a** (coll.) to jeer at, to taunt
matracalada *f* mob
matracar **§86** *vn* (Am.) to pester, be a pest
matraquear *vn* (coll.) to make a racket; (coll.) to jeer, to taunt
matraqueo *m* (coll.) racket; (coll.) jeering, taunting
matraquista *mf* (coll.) jeerer, taunter
matraz *m* (*pl:* **-traces**) flask, matrass; **matraz de lavado** (chem.) wash bottle
matrería *f* cunning, shrewdness
matrero -ra *adj* cunning, shrewd
matriarca *f* matriarch
matriarcado *m* matriarchy
matriarcal *adj* matriarchal
matricaria *f* (bot.) feverfew
matricida *adj* matricidal; *mf* matricide (*person*)
matricidio *m* matricide (*act*)
matrícula *f* register, roll, roster; license; registry; matriculation, registration
matriculado -da *adj & mf* matriculate
matricular *va & vr* to register, enroll; to matriculate
matrimonesco -ca *adj* (hum.) matrimonial
matrimonial *adj* matrimonial
matrimonialmente *adv* as husband and wife
matrimoniar *vn* to marry, get married
matrimonio *m* matrimony; marriage; married couple; **matrimonio de compañerismo** companionate marriage; **matrimonio de la mano izquierda** left-handed marriage; **matrimonio civil** civil marriage; **matrimonio consensual** common-law marriage; **matrimonio morganático** morganatic marriage; **matrimonio putativo** (canon law) putative marriage; **matrimonio rato** unconsummated marriage
matritense *adj & mf* var. of **madrileño**
matriz (*pl:* **-trices**) *adj* main, mother, first; *f* matrix (*womb; mold; impression of phonograph record*); screw nut; original draft; stub (*e.g., of checkbook*); (anat., biol., geol. & math.) matrix
matrona *f* matron; midwife; (coll.) matronly lady; matron (*in jail, custom house, etc.*)
matronal *adj* matronal, matronly
matronaza *f* matron

maturrango -ga *adj* (Am.) clumsy, rough; *mf* poor rider; *f* cajolery, trickery; (coll.) prostitute
Matusalén *m* (Bib. & fig.) Methuselah; **vivir más años que Matusalén** to be as old as Methuselah
matute *m* smuggling; smuggled goods; gambling den
matutear *vn* to smuggle
matutero -ra *mf* smuggler
matutinal or **matutino -na** *adj* matutinal, morning
maula *f* junk, trash; remnant; trick, trickery; *mf* (coll.) tricky person, poor pay, lazy loafer
maulería *f* remnant shop; trickery, trickiness
maulero -ra *mf* remnant dealer; trickster, cheat
maullador -dora *adj* meowing
maullar §75 *vn* to meow
maullido or **maúllo** *m* meow
Mauricio *m* Maurice or Morris; **la isla Mauricio** or **la isla de Mauricio** Mauritius
máuser *m* Mauser
mausoleo *m* mausoleum
maxila *f* (anat. & zool.) maxilla
maxilar *adj & m* (anat.) maxillary
máxima *f* see **máximo**
máxime *adv* chiefly, principally, especially
Maximiliano *m* Maximilian
máximo -ma *adj* maximum; top; superlative, superb; *m* maximum; *f* maxim; principle
máximum *m* maximum
maxvelio *m* (elec.) maxwell
may. abr. of **mayúscula**
maya *adj & mf* Maya or Mayan; *f* May queen; clown; (bot.) English daisy; (bot.) pinguin
mayador -dora *adj* meowing
mayal *m* flail; horse-drawn shaft of conical stone (*of olive-oil mill*)
mayar *vn* var. of **maullar**
mayear *vn* to be like May (*said of weather*)
mayestático -ca *adj* of majesty, royal
mayido *m* meow
may.mo abr. of **mayordomo**
mayo *m* May; Maypole; **mayos** *mpl* serenading on the eve of May day
mayólica *f* majolica
mayonesa *f* mayonnaise
mayor *adj* greater; larger; older, elder; greatest; largest; oldest, eldest; elderly; major; main (*e.g., street*); high (*altar, mass*); (log. & mus.) major; **ser mayor de edad** to be of age; *m* superior, chief, head; **mayores** *mpl* elders; ancestors, forefathers; (eccl.) major orders; **al por mayor** wholesale; **por mayor** wholesale; summarily; **mayor de edad** major (*person of legal age*); **mayor general** staff officer; *f* (log.) major premise
mayoral *m* foreman, boss; head shepherd; stagecoach driver; (Am.) trolley-car conductor
mayoralía *f* flock, herd; shepherd's wages
mayorana *f* var. of **mejorana**
mayorazga *f* female owner of an entailed estate; heiress to an entailed estate
mayorazgo *m* primogeniture; right of primogeniture; entailed estate descending by primogeniture; heir to an entailed estate; first-born son
mayordoma *f* stewardess, housekeeper; wife of major-domo or steward
mayordomear *va* to manage, administer (*a household or estate*)
mayordomía *f* major-domoship, stewardship
mayordomo *m* major-domo, steward, butler
mayoría *f* superiority; majority (*being of full age; larger number or part*); **alcanzar su mayoría de edad** to come of age; **mayoría de edad** majority
mayoridad *f* superiority; majority (*full age*)
mayorista *adj* wholesale; *m* wholesaler
mayoritario -ria *adj* (pertaining to the) majority
mayormente *adv* chiefly, mainly
mayúsculo -la *adj* capital (*letter*); large; (coll.) tremendous, awful; *f* capital letter
maza *f* mace (*weapon; staff*); maul; hemp brake; drop hammer; pile driver; tup (*of drop hammer or pile driver*); heavy drumstick; hub; thick end of billiard cue; rag tied as a joke on a person's clothes; stick tied to a dog's tail; astounding pronouncement; (coll.) bore; (coll.) oracle; **la maza y la mona** constant companions; **maza de fraga** drop hammer; **maza de gimnasia** Indian club; **maza sorda** (bot.) reed mace
mazacote *m* barilla, kali; concrete; crude piece of work; (coll.) tough, doughy food; (coll.) bore
mazada *f* blow with a mace or club; **dar mazada a** (coll.) to hurt, injure
mazado *m* churning
mazagatos *m* (coll.) rumpus, row, wrangle
mazagrán *m* cold coffee and rum
mazamorra *f* crumbs; thick corn soup; (naut.) mess of broken hardtack
mazapán *m* marchpane or marzipan
mazar §76 *va* to churn (*milk*)
mazarí *m* (*pl:* **-ríes**) floor brick or tile
mazarota *f* (found.) deadhead
mazazo *m* var. of **mazada**
mazdeísmo *m* Mazdaism
mazdeísta *adj* Mazdean; *mf* Mazdaist
mazmorra *f* dungeon, underground dungeon
maznar *va* to knead; to beat (*hot iron*)
mazo *m* mallet, maul; bunch; clapper (*of bell*); stack (*e.g., of cards*); bore
mazonado -da *adj* (her.) masoned
mazonería *f* stone masonry; relief
mazonero *m* stone mason
mazorca *f* spindleful; ear of corn; cocoa bean; (carp.) spindle (*in a baluster*); **comer maíz en** or **de la mazorca** to eat corn on the cob
mazorquera *f* (bot.) selfheal
mazorral *adj* coarse, crude, rough
mazurca *f* (mus.) mazourka or mazurka
m/c abr. of **mi cargo, mi cuenta & moneda corriente**
m/cta abr. of **mi cuenta**
m/cte abr. of **moneda corriente**
M.e abr. of **Madre**
me *pron pers & reflex* (used as object of verb) me, to me; myself, to myself
meada *f* urination, water; spot made by urine
meadero *m* urinal
meados *mpl* urine
meaja *f* crumb; **meaja de huevo** tread (*of an egg*)
meajuela *f* slavering chain (*of bit*)
meándrico -ca *adj* meandrous, meandering
meandro *m* meander; (f.a.) meander; wandering speech or writing
mear *va* to urinate on; *vn & vr* to urinate
meato *m* (anat.) meatus
meauca *f* (orn.) shearwater
Meca *f* mecca or Mecca (*place sought by many people*); **La Meca** Mecca (*city*); **la Meca del cine** movieland
mecachis *interj* var. of **caramba**
mecánica *f* see **mecánico**
mecanicismo *m* (biol. & philos.) mechanism
mecanicista *adj* (biol. & philos.) mechanistic; *mf* (biol. & philos.) mechanist
mecánico -ca *adj* mechanical; (coll.) low, mean; *m* mechanic; machinist; workman, repairman; driver, chauffeur; *f* mechanics; machinery, works; (coll.) meanness; (coll.) contemptible thing; **mecánicas** *fpl* (coll.) chores, household chores; **mecánica celeste** (astr.) celestial mechanics; **mecánica cuántica** (phys.) quantum mechanics
mecanismo *m* mechanism; **mecanismo de disparo** or **mecanismo gatillo** trigger mechanism
mecanización *f* mechanization
mecanizar §76 *va* to mechanize
mecano -na *adj & mf* Meccan; *m* Erector set
mecanografía *f* typewriting; **mecanografía al tacto** touch typewriting
mecanografiar §90 *va & vn* to type, to typewrite
mecanográfico -ca *adj* typewriting
mecanógrafo -fa *mf* typist, typewriter
mecanoterapia *f* mechanotherapy
mecapal *m* (Am.) strap of fiber, bark, or leather
mecapalero -ra *mf* (Am.) porter, messenger
mecate *m* (Am.) packthread; (Am.) boor
mecedero *m* stirrer, shaker
mecedor -dora *adj* swinging, rocking; *m* stirrer, shaker; swing; *f* rocker, rocking chair

mecedura *f* swinging, rocking
Mecenas *m* Maecenas; (*l.c.*) *m* (*pl:* **-nas**) (fig.) Maecenas
mecenazgo *m* Maecenasship, patronage
mecer §61 *va* to stir, to shake; to swing, to rock; *vr* to swing, to rock
meconio *m* meconium; poppy juice
mecha *f* wick; fuse, match; tinder; lock of hair; interlarding of bacon; bundle (*of threads*)
mechar *va* (cook.) to lard, to interlard
mechazo *m* (min.) fizzle (*of a blast fuse*); **dar mechazo** to fizzle
mechera *f* shoplifter (*woman*); larding pin
mechero *m* burner; socket (*of candlestick*); pocket lighter; jet; **mechero de gas** gas burner; **mechero de mariposa** fantail (*burner*); **mechero encendedor** pilot, pilot light (*e.g., of a gas stove*)
mechinal *m* putlog hole; (coll.) hovel
mechón *m* shock of hair; tuft, mop, shock
mechoso -sa *adj* thready, towy; shockheaded
medalla *f* medal; medallion
medallero *m* medal cabinet
medallista *mf* medalist (*engraver of medals*)
medallón *m* medallion; locket
médano *m* sandbank, dune
medanoso -sa *adj* sandy, duny
medaño *m* var. of **médano**
media *f* see **medio**
mediacaña *f* trochilus, scotia; gouge; half-round file; curling tongs (*for hair*); (print.) double rule
mediación *f* mediation; (astr., dipl. & mus.) mediation
mediado -da *adj* half-full; half over, e.g., **iba mediada la tarde** the afternoon was half over; **a mediados de** about the middle of
mediador -dora *adj* mediating, mediatorial; *mf* mediator; **mediador de cambio** medium of exchange
medial *adj* (bot. & zool.) median; (phonet.) medial
mediana *f* see **mediano**
medianejo -ja *adj* (coll.) fair to middling
medianería *f* party wall; party-line fence or hedge
medianero -ra *adj* middle, dividing; mediating; *mf* mediator; *m* owner of an adjoining house
medianía *f* halfway; moderate circumstances; mediocrity (*person*); (Am.) partition wall
medianidad *f* var. of **medianía**
medianil *m* sloping land or field; party wall
mediano -na *adj* middling, medium; average, fair, fairly good; (bot. & zool.) median; (coll.) mediocre; *m* (anat.) median; *f* long billiard cue; (geom.) median
medianoche *f* midnight; (*pl:* **mediasnoches**) *f* meat pie
mediante *adj* intervening; **Dios mediante** God willing; *prep* by means of, through
mediar *va* to make half-full; *vn* to be or get halfway; to be half over; to be in the middle; to mediate, to intervene; to elapse; to take place
mediastino *m* (anat.) mediastinum
mediatamente *adv* mediately, indirectly
mediatinta *f* (paint. & phot.) half-tone
mediatizar §76 *va* to control, get control of; to make a puppet of (*a government*)
mediato -ta *adj* mediate
mediator *m* ombre (*card game*)
medible *adj* measurable
médica *f* see **médico**
medicable *adj* medicable
medicación *f* medication
medical *adj* medical
medicamento *m* medicament, medicine; **medicamentos sulfas** (pharm.) sulfa drugs
medicamentoso -sa *adj* medicinal
medicar §86 *va* (archaic) to treat, to medicate (*a patient*); *vr* (archaic) to treat oneself, to doctor oneself
medicastro *m* (coll.) medicaster, quack
medicina *f* medicine (*science and art; remedy*); **medicina del espacio** space medicine; **medicina doméstica** home remedies; **medicina interna** internal medicine; **medicina preventiva** or **profiláctica** preventive medicine; **medicina social** socialized medicine; **medicina veterinaria** veterinary medicine
medicinal *adj* medicinal
medicinamiento *m* treatment, medication
medicinante *m* quack, healer; medical student who treats patients
medicinar *va* to treat (*a sick person*)
medición *f* measuring, measurement; metering
médico -ca *adj* medical; *m* doctor, physician; **médico de cabecera** family physician; **médico de plaza** bullring physician; **médico general** general practitioner; **médico partero** obstetrician; *f* woman doctor; doctor's wife
médicolegal *adj* medicolegal
médicoquirúrgico -ca *adj* medicochirurgical
medicucho *m* (coll.) var. of **medicastro**
medida *f* measurement; measure; step; moderation; (pros.) measure; **a medida de** in proportion to; according to; **a medida que** in proportion as; **en la medida que** to the extent that; **hecho a la medida** custom-made; **llenarse la medida** to drain the cup of sorrow; **tomarle a uno las medidas** to take one's measure; **tomar sus medidas** to size up a situation; **medida para áridos** dry measure; **medida para líquidos** liquid measure
medidamente *adv* with moderation
medidor -dora *adj* measuring; *mf* measurer; *m* gauge; (Am.) meter
mediero -ra *mf* hosier, stocking maker or dealer; stocking knitter; partner (*in farming or stock raising*); (Am.) partner (*in business*)
medieval *adj* medieval
medievalidad *f* medievalism (*medieval quality or nature*)
medievalismo *m* medievalism
medievalista *mf* medievalist
medievo *m* Middle Ages
medina *f* (Arab.) large city, metropolis
medio -dia *adj* half, half a, e.g., **media manzana** half an apple; a half, e.g., **media libra** a half pound; middle, intermediate; medium; medieval (*times*); mean, average; mid, e.g., **a media tarde** in mid afternoon; in the middle of, e.g., **a media comida** in the middle of the meal; **a medias** half-and-half, e.g., **dinero adquirido a medias por dos personas** money acquired half-and-half by two persons; half, e.g., **dueño a medias** half owner; **dormido a medias** half asleep; **ir a medias** to go halves, to go fifty-fifty ‖ **medio** *adv* half, e.g., **medio muerto** half dead; **medio . . . medio** half . . . half ‖ *m* (arith.) half; middle; medium, environment; step, measure; means; medium, spiritualistic medium; (bot. & bact.) medium; (baseball) shortstop; **medios** *mpl* means; (taur.) center (*of ring*); **a medio** half, e.g., **a medio vestir** half dressed; **de medio a medio** half-and-half; smack, plump; completely; **de por medio** half; in between, halfway; **desde en medio de** from the middle of; **echar por en medio** (coll.) to take the bull by the horns; **en medio** in the middle; in the meantime; **en medio de** in the middle of; in the midst of; in spite of; **entrar de por medio** to intercede; **estar de por medio** to mediate; **justo medio** happy medium, golden mean; **meterse de por medio** to intercede; **por medio de** by means of, through; **quitar de en medio** (coll.) to do away with, to get out of the way, to put out of the way; **quitarse de en medio** (coll.) to get out, get out of the way, duck; **tomar los medios** to take measures ‖ *f* stocking; half past, e.g., **las tres y media** half past three; (math.) mean; **dar la media** to strike half past; **media diferencial** (math.) arithmetical mean; **media media** or **media corta** (Am.) sock; **media proporcional** (math.) mean proportional, geometric mean; **medias de cristal** nylons, nylon stockings
mediocre *adj* mediocre, medium
mediocridad *f* mediocrity; mediocre circumstances
mediodía *m* noon, midday; south; (naut.) south wind; **en pleno mediodía** at broad noon; **hacer mediodía** to stop for the noon meal; **mediodía medio** (astr.) mean noon
medioeval *adj* var. of **medieval**

medioevo *m* Middle Ages
mediooeste *m* Middle West (*of the U.S.A.*)
medio-oriental *adj* Middle Eastern
mediopaño *m* light wool cloth
mediquillo *m* (coll.) medicaster, quack; Philippine Indian quack
medir §94 *va* to measure; to scan (*verse*); *vn* to measure; *vr* to be moderate, act with moderation
meditabundo -da *adj* meditative
meditación *f* meditation
meditador -dora *adj* meditating, meditative
meditar *va* to meditate; to contemplate, to plan (*e.g., an escape*); *vn* to meditate
meditativo -va *adj* meditative
Mediterráneo -a *adj & m* Mediterranean
médium *mf* (*pl:* **-dium** or **-diums**) medium, spiritualistic medium
mediúmnico -ca *adj* mediumistic
mediumnismo *m* spiritualism
medo -da *adj* Median; *mf* Mede, Median
medra *f* growth, thriving, prosperity
medrador -dora *mf* schemer, person who is on the make
medrana *f* (coll.) fear
medrar *vn* to grow, thrive, prosper; **¡medrados estamos!** now look what's happened!
medregal *m* (ichth.) amberfish, pilot fish
medriñaque *m* medrinaque (*cloth used as padding for women's garments*); short peasant skirt
medro *m* growth, thriving; **medros** *mpl* progress, improvement
medroso -sa *adj* fearful, timid; dreadful, terrible
medula or **médula** *f* (anat.) medulla, marrow; (bot.) medulla, pith; (fig.) marrow, essence, gist; **medula espinal** (anat.) spinal cord; **medula oblonga** or **oblongada** (anat.) medulla oblongata
medular *adj* medullary; (fig.) pithy, marrowy
meduloso -sa *adj* marrowy; (bot.) pithy
medusa *f* (zool.) medusa, jellyfish; (*cap.*) *f* (myth.) Medusa
medusar *va* to frighten, scare
Mefistófeles *m* Mephistopheles
mefistofélico -ca *adj* Mephistophelian
mefítico -ca *adj* mephitic
mefitis *f* mephitis
megaciclo *m* (rad.) megacycle
megáfono *m* megaphone
megalítico -ca *adj* megalithic
megalito *m* (archeol.) megalith
megalocéfalo -la *adj* megalocephalous
megalomanía *f* (psychopath.) megalomania
megalómano -na *adj* megalomaniacal; *mf* megalomaniac
megalosaurio *m* (pal.) megalosaur
mégano *m* var. of **médano**
megaterio *m* (pal.) megathere
megatón *m* or **megatonelada** *f* megaton
mego -ga *adj* meek, gentle
megohmio *m* (elec.) megohm
mehara *m* or **mehari** *m* var. of **meharí**
meharí *m* (*pl:* **-ríes**) mehari (*swift African dromedary*)
mehedí *m* (*pl:* **-díes**) Mahdi
Mej. abr. of **Méjico**
mejana *f* islet (*in a river*)
mejicanismo *m* Mexicanism
mejicano -na *adj & mf* Mexican
Méjico *m* Mexico; **Nuevo Méjico** New Mexico; *f* Mexico City
mejido -da *adj* beaten with sugar and milk (*said of eggs*)
mejilla *f* cheek
mejillón *m* (zool.) mussel
mejor *adj* better; best; highest (*bidder*); *adv* better; best; rather; **a lo mejor** (coll.) like as not; (coll.) worse luck; **mejor dicho** rather; **mejor que** rather than; **mejor que mejor** all the better; **tanto mejor** so much the better
mejora *f* growth, improvement; alteration, renovation; higher bid; additional bequests
mejorable *adj* ameliorable, improvable
mejoramiento *m* amelioration, improvement
mejorana *f* (bot.) sweet marjoram
mejorante *m* ameliorant, improver
mejorar *va* to make better, to improve; to mend; to raise (*a bid*); to leave an additional bequest to; *vn & vr* to get better, to recover; to mend; to clear up (*said of weather*); to get along, to progress
mejoría *f* improvement (*in success, health, etc.*)
mejunje *m* mess, mixture, brew
melado -da *adj* honey-colored; *m* (Am.) thick cane syrup; honey cake sprinkled with seeds; *f* toast dipped in honey; dried marmalade
meladora *f* (Am.) last sugar-boiling pan
meladucha *f* coarse, mealy apple
meladura *f* concentrated cane syrup
meláfido or **meláfiro** *m* (geol.) melaphyre
melámpiro *m* (bot.) cowwheat
melampo *m* (theat.) prompter's candle or light
melancolía *f* melancholy; (path.) melancholia
melancólico -ca *adj* melancholy, melancholic; (path.) melancholic
melancolizar §76 *va* to sadden, to give a melancholy aspect to; *vr* to become sad, become melancholy
melanesio -sia *adj & mf* Melanesian; **la Melanesia** Melanesia
melanita *f* (mineral.) melanite
melanoma *m* (path.) melanoma
melanosis *f* (path.) melanosis
melapia *f* pippin, pearmain
melar *adj* honey-sweet; **§18** *va* to fill (*combs*) with honey; *vn* to become filled with honey; to boil sugar-cane juice clear
melaza *f* molasses
Melburna *f* Melbourne
melca *f* (bot.) sorghum
melcocha *f* taffy, molasses candy
melcochero -ra *mf* maker or seller of molasses candy
melchor *m* German silver, nickel silver; (*cap.*) *m* Melchior
melducha *f* coarse mealy apple
meleagrina *f* (zool.) pearl oyster
Meleagro *m* (myth.) Meleager
melena *f* long lock of hair (*falling over face or eyes*); long hair (*falling over shoulders*); loose hair (*unbound*); mane (*of lion*); forelock (*of horse*); (path.) melena; **andar a la melena** (coll.) to pull each other's hair; (coll.) to get into a hot argument; **estar en melena** (coll.) to have one's hair down; **hacer venir** or **traer a la melena** (coll.) to put the screws on; **venir a la melena** (coll.) to yield, to give in
melenera *f* forehead of an ox; yoke pad
meleno *m* (coll.) peasant, rustic
melenudo -da *adj* shockheaded, bushy-headed
melero -ra *adj* honeyed; *mf* dealer in honey; *m* storage place for honey; *f* damage or rot of melons from rain or hail; (bot.) oxtongue
melgacho *m* (ichth.) spotted dogfish
melgar *m* field of medic or lucerne
melgo -ga *adj* twin
meliáceo -a *adj* meliaceous
mélico -ca *adj* melic
melificado -da *adj* var. of **melifluo**
melificar §86 *va* to make or draw honey from (*flowers*); *vn* to make honey
melifluencia *f* mellifluence
melifluidad *f* mellifluence, mellifluousness
melifluo -flua *adj* mellifluent or mellifluous
meliloto -ta *adj* simple, stupid; *mf* simpleton, dolt; *m* (bot.) melilot, sweet clover
melindre *m* honey fritter; ladyfinger; tape, narrow ribbon; **melindres** *mpl* finickiness, prudery
melindrear *vn* to be finicky, be prudish
melindrería *f* finickiness, prudery
melindrero -ra *adj* var. of **melindroso**
melindrizar §76 *vn* var. of **melindrear**
melindroso -sa *adj* finicky, prudish
melinita *f* melinite
melisa *f* (bot.) lemon balm, garden balm
melito *m* (pharm.) hydromel
melocotón *m* (bot.) peach, peach tree; peach (*fruit*); **melocotón en almíbar** canned peaches
melocotonar *m* peach orchard
melocotonero *m* (bot.) peach tree
melodía *f* melody

melódico -ca *adj* melodic
melodión *m* (mus.) melodeon
melodioso -sa *adj* melodious
melodista *mf* melodist
melodrama *m* melodrama
melodramático -ca *adj* melodramatic
meloe *m* (ent.) oil beetle
melografía *f* art of writing music
meloja *f* honey water
melojar *m* growth of pubescent oak trees
melojo *m* (bot.) pubescent oak, durmast
melolonta *m* (ent.) cockchafer
melomanía *f* melomania, love of music
melómano -na *mf* melomane, melomaniac, music lover
melón *m* (bot.) muskmelon; melon (*fruit*); dolt, ignoramus; (coll.) bald head; (zool.) ichneumon; **catar el melón** (coll.) to sound a person out; (coll.) to see what something is like; **decentar el melón** (coll.) to take a big risk; **melón de agua** watermelon; **melón de costa** (bot.) Turk's-head
melonar *m* melon patch
meloncillo *m* (zool.) ichneumon
melonero -ra *mf* melon raiser or dealer
melonzapote *m* (bot.) papaya, papaw
melopeya *f* (mus.) melopoeia
melosa *f* see **meloso**
melosidad *f* mildness, sweetness, mellowness
melosilla *f* oak blight
meloso -sa *adj* honeyed; mild, sweet, mellow; *f* (bot.) Chilean tarweed
Melpómene *f* (myth.) Melpomene
melsa *f* sloth, phlegm
meltón *m* melton
mella *f* nick, dent, notch; gap, hollow; harm, injury; **hacer mella a** to have an effect on; **hacer mella en** to harm, injure (*e.g., a reputation*)
mellado -da *adj* snaggle-toothed
mellar *va* to nick, dent, notch; to harm, injure (*honor, credit, etc.*); *vr* to nick, dent; to be harmed, be injured
mellizo -za *adj & mf* twin; *f* honey sausage
mellón *m* straw torch
memada *f* (coll.) piece of folly
membrado -da *adj* (her.) membered
membrana *f* (bot. & zool.) membrane; (telp. & rad.) diaphragm; **membrana fónica** (telp.) diaphragm; **membrana mucosa** (anat.) mucous membrane; **membrana pituitaria** (anat.) pituitary membrane; **membrana serosa** (anat.) serous membrane; **membrana timpánica** (anat.) tympanic membrane
membranáceo -a *adj* membranaceous
membranoso -sa *adj* membranous
membrete *m* letterhead; heading; address; invitation; note, memo
membrillar *m* quince-tree orchard; (bot.) quince tree
membrillate *m* quince preserves
membrillero *m* (bot.) quince tree
membrillo *m* (bot.) quince (*tree and fruit*)
membrudo -da *adj* burly, husky
memeches; a memeches (Am.) astride, on horseback
memela *f* (Am.) corn-meal pancake
memento *m* (eccl.) Memento
memez *f* (dial.) folly, nonsense
memiso *m* (bot.) calabur tree
Memnón *m* (myth.) Memnon
memo -ma *adj* simple, foolish; *mf* simpleton, fool
memorable *adj* memorable
memoráculo *m* memorial (*e.g., a monument*)
memorando -da *adj* var. of **memorable**
memorándum *m* (*pl:* **-dum**) memorandum; letterhead (*paper with letterhead*); professional services (*section of newspaper advertisements*); (Am.) certificate of deposit
memorar *va & vr* to remember
memoratísimo -ma *adj super* eternally remembered
memoria *f* memory; memoir; account, record; **memorias** *fpl* memoirs; regards; **de memoria** by heart; (prov.) with one's mouth wide-open; **encomendar a la memoria** to commit to memory; **en memoria de** in memory of; **hablar de memoria** (coll.) to say the first thing that comes to one's mind; **hacer memoria de** to bring up
memorial *m* memorandum book; memorial (*written statement making a petition*); (law) brief; **haber perdido los memoriales** (coll.) to have forgotten, to have lost the thread
memorialista *m* amanuensis
memorión *m* (coll.) terrific memory
memorioso -sa *adj* retentive, of retentive memory
memorístico -ca *adj* (pertaining to) memory
memorizar §76 *va* to memorize
mena *f* (ichth.) picarel; (min.) ore; (naut.) size or thickness of cordage
ménade *f* (hist. & fig.) maenad
menaje *m* household furniture; school supplies
Mencio *m* Mencius
mención *f* mention; **en mención** in question, under discussion; **hacer mención de** to make mention of; **mención honorífica** honorable mention
mencionar *va* to mention
menchevique *m* Menshevik
mendacidad *f* mendacity
mendaz (*pl:* **-daces**) *adj* mendacious; *mf* liar
mendelevio *m* (chem.) mendelevium
mendeliano -na *adj* Mendelian
mendelismo *m* Mendelism, Mendelianism
mendicación *f* begging
mendicante *adj & mf* mendicant
mendicidad *f* mendicancy, mendicity
mendiganta *f* woman beggar
mendigante *adj* begging, mendicant; *mf* beggar, mendicant
mendigar §59 *va* to beg, to beg for; *vn* to beg
mendigo -ga *mf* beggar
mendiguez *f* begging, beggary
mendoso -sa *adj* false, lying; mistaken, wrong
mendrugo *m* crust, crumb (*especially that given to beggars*)
menear *va* to stir; to shake; to wag; to wiggle; to manage; **peor es meneallo** (*i.e.,* **menearlo**) (coll.) better let it alone, the less said the better; *vr* to shake; to wag; to wiggle; (coll.) to hustle, bestir oneself
menegilda *f* (coll.) servant, housemaid
Menelao *m* (myth.) Menelaus
meneo *m* stirring; shaking; wagging; wiggling; hustling; (coll.) drubbing, flogging
menester *m* want, lack; need; job, occupation; **menesteres** *mpl* bodily needs; property; (coll.) tools, implements; **haber menester** to need; **ser menester** to be necessary; **ser menester** + *inf* to be necessary to + *inf*
menesteroso -sa *adj* needy; *mf* needy person
menestra *f* vegetable soup, vegetable stew; (coll.) hodgepodge; **menestras** *fpl* dried vegetables
menestral -trala *mf* artisan, mechanic
menestralería *f* artisanship
menestralía *f* artisans, mechanics (*as a group or class*)
menestrete *m* (naut.) nail puller
Menfis *f* Memphis
meng. abr. of **menguante**
mengano -na *mf* (coll.) so-and-so
mengua *f* diminution; decline, decay; want, lack; poverty; discredit; **en mengua de** to the discredit of; to the detriment of
menguado -da *adj* timid, cowardly; silly, foolish; mean, stingy; fatal; *m* drop stitch
menguamiento *m* var. of **mengua**
menguante *adj* diminishing; declining; waning; *f* decay, decline; low water; ebb tide; **menguante de la luna** waning of the moon
menguar §23 *va* to lessen, diminish; to defame; *vn* to lessen, diminish; to decline, decay; to drop-stitch; to wane (*said of the moon*); to fall (*said of the tide*)
mengue *m* (coll.) devil
menhir *m* (archeol.) menhir
menina *f* young lady in waiting, maid of honor
meníngeo -a *adj* meningeal
meninges *fpl* (anat.) meninges
meningitis *f* (path.) meningitis; **meningitis cerebroespinal** (path.) cerebrospinal meningitis
meningococo *m* (bact.) meningococcus
menino *m* noble page of the royal family

menique *adj & m* (archaic) var. of **meñique**
menisco *m* (anat., opt. & phys.) meniscus
menispermáceo -a *adj* (bot.) menispermaceous
menjuí *m* var. of **benjuí**
menjunje *m* or **menjurje** *m* var. of **mejunje**
menonita *adj & mf* Mennonite
menopausia *f* (physiol.) menopause
menor *adj* less, lesser; smaller; younger; least; smallest; youngest; minor; (log. & mus.) minor; **menor de edad** minor; *m* minor; (eccl.) Minorite; **al por menor** retail; **por menor** retail; in detail, minutely; **menor de edad** minor; *f* (log.) minor premise
Menorca *f* Minorca
menorete; al menorete or **por el menorete** (coll.) at least
menoría *f* inferiority, subordination; minority (*time of being under age*)
menorista *mf* (Am.) retailer, retail dealer
menorquín -quina *adj & mf* Minorcan; *m* Minorcan (*dialect*)
menorragia *f* (path.) menorrhagia
menos *adv* less; fewer; lower; least; fewest; lowest; rather not; **al menos** at least; **a menos que** unless; **a lo menos** at least; **de menos** less, e.g., **un dólar de menos** a dollar less; **echar de menos** or **echar menos** to miss; **en menos que** at less than; **ir a menos** to be scarce; **lo menos** at least; **los** (or **las**) **menos** the fewest; **no poder menos de** + *inf* to not be able to help + *ger;* **no ser para menos** to be good cause, to be good reason, to not be surprising; **por lo menos** at least; **tener a menos** or **en menos** + *inf* to deem it beneath one to + *inf;* **tener en menos** to think little of; **venir a menos** to decay, to decline; **menos de** less than + *numeral;* **¡menos mal!** lucky you!, lucky break!, it might be worse!; **menos mal que** it's a good thing that; **menos que** less than ‖ *prep* less, minus; except; of or to (*in telling time*), e.g., **las dos menos cuarto** a quarter of two ‖ *m* minus (*sign*)
menoscabar *va* to lessen, reduce; to damage, spoil; to discredit
menoscabo *m* lessening, reduction; damage, loss; detriment, discredit
menoscuenta *f* part payment (*of a debt*)
menospreciable *adj* despicable, contemptible
menospreciador -dora *adj* scornful, contemptuous; *mf* scorner, despiser
menospreciar *va* to underestimate, undervalue; to scorn, despise
menospreciativo -va *adj* scornful, contemptuous
menosprecio *m* underestimation, undervaluation; scorn, contempt
mensaje *m* message; errand; **mensaje cifrado** cipher message
mensajería *f* stagecoach, public conveyance; **mensajerías** *fpl* transportation company; express service; express; shipping line; shipping office; **mensajerías** *msg* freight train
mensajero -ra *mf* messenger; *m* harbinger; freight train
menso -sa *adj* (Am.) silly, disagreeable
menstruación *f* menstruation
menstrual *adj* (physiol.) menstrual
menstruar §33 *vn* to menstruate
menstruo -trua *adj* menstruous; *m* menstruation; menses; (chem.) menstruum
menstruoso -sa *adj* menstruous
mensual *adj* menstrual, monthly; *f* monthly, monthly periodical
mensualidad *f* monthly pay, monthly allowance, monthly instalment
ménsula *f* brace, bracket; elbow rest; (arch.) corbel
mensurabilidad *f* mensurability
mensurable *adj* mensurable
mensuración *f* mensuration
mensural *adj* mensural
mensurar *va* to measure
menta *f* (bot.) mint; **menta romana** or **verde** (bot.) spearmint
mentado -da *adj* famed, renowned
mental *adj* mental
mentalidad *f* mentality, psychology
mentalismo *m* mind reading, clairvoyance
mentalista *mf* mind reader, clairvoyant
mentar §18 *va* to name, to mention
mentastro *m* (bot.) horse mint, apple mint
mente *f* mind; **leer mentes** to read minds; **tener en la mente** to have in mind
mentecatería or **mentecatez** *f* simpleness, folly
mentecato -ta *adj* simple, foolish; *mf* simpleton, fool
mentidero *m* (coll.) gathering place to talk and loaf
mentido -da *adj* false, deceptive
mentidor -dora *adj* false, lying; *mf* liar
mentir §62 *va* to disappoint, to fail to keep (*a promise*); *vn* to lie; to be false, be deceptive; to clash (*said of a color*); **¡miento!** my mistake!, my error!
mentira *f* lie; story, fiction; illusion, vanity; mistake, error; (coll.) white spot (*on fingernails*); (Am.) cracking of knuckles; **coger en una mentira** to catch in a lie; **de mentiras** in jest; **parece mentira** it's hard to believe; **mentira inocente** or **oficiosa** white lie
mentirijillas; de mentirijillas in fun, in jest; for fun (*not for money*)
mentirilla *f* fib, white lie; **de mentirillas** in fun, in jest; for fun (*not for money*)
mentirón *m* whopper, big lie
mentiroso -sa *adj* lying; full of mistakes; *mf* liar
mentís *m* (*pl:* **-tís**) insult; lie, flat denial; **dar un mentís a** to give the lie to
mentol *m* (chem.) menthol
mentolado -da *adj* mentholated
mentón *m* chin
mentor *m* mentor; (*cap.*) *m* (myth.) Mentor
menú *m* (*pl:* **-nús**) menu
menuceles *mpl* tithe of minor fruits
menudamente *adv* minutely, in detail; at retail
menudear *va* to do frequently, to repeat frequently; to tell in detail; (Am.) to sell at retail; *vn* to be frequent, to happen frequently; to rain, come down in abundance; to go into detail
menudencia *f* smallness; minuteness; meticulousness; trifle; **menudencias** *fpl* pork products; (Am.) giblets
menudeo *m* constant repetition; detailed account; retail; **al menudeo** at retail
menudero -ra *mf* retailer
menudillo *m* fetlock joint; **menudillos** *mpl* giblets
menudo -da *adj* small, slight; minute; common, vulgar; petty; futile, worthless; meticulous; *m* small change; rice coal; blood and entrails of beef; edible portions of fowl; tithe of minor fruits; **menudos** *mpl* small change; **a menudo** often; **por menudo** in detail; at retail
menuzo *m* bit, fragment, small piece
meñique *adj* little (*finger*); (coll.) little, tiny; *m* little finger
meollar *m* (naut.) spun yarn
meollo *m* (anat.) marrow; (bot.) pith; brain; brains, intelligence; marrow, gist, essence
meolludo -da *adj* marrowy; brainy, intelligent
meón -ona *adj* urinating, constantly urinating; dripping (*e.g., fog*); *f* newborn female infant
meque *m* slap, rap (*with the knuckles*)
mequetrefe *m* (coll.) whippersnapper, jackanapes
merar *va* to mix, to blend
merca *f* (coll.) purchase
mercachifle *m* peddler; small dealer
mercachiflear *vn* (coll.) to deal on a shoestring
mercadear *vn* to deal, to trade
mercader -dera *mf* merchant, dealer; **mercader de grueso** wholesale merchant; *f* tradeswoman; merchant's wife
mercadería *f* commodity; **mercaderías** *fpl* goods, merchandise; ledger
mercado *m* market; market place; **lanzar al mercado** to put on the market; **mercado bursátil** or **de valores** stock market; **Mercado Común Europeo** European Common Market; **mercado negro** black market
mercadotecnia *f* marketing
mercaduría *f* commodity
mercal *m* (Am.) tequila (*liquor*)

mercancía *f* trade, dealing; merchandise; piece of merchandise; **mercancías** *fpl* goods, merchandise; **mercancías** *msg* freight train
mercante *adj* merchant; *m* merchant; (naut.) merchantman
mercantil *adj* mercantile; mercenary
mercantilismo *m* mercantilism
mercantilista *adj & mf* mercantilist
mercar §86 *va* to buy, purchase
merced *f* favor, grace; mercy (*power, discretion*); **a merced** or **a mercedes** without pay, voluntarily; **estar a la merced de** to be at the mercy of; **muchas mercedes** many thanks; **vuestra merced** your grace, your honor, your worship; **merced a** thanks to; **merced de agua** free distribution of irrigating water
mercedario -ria *adj* of the Mercedarians; *mf* Mercedarian
Mercedes *f* Mercedes (*feminine name*)
mercenario -ria *adj* (mil. & fig.) mercenary; *mf* Mercedarian; *m* (mil.) mercenary; day laborer; salaried employee
mercería *f* haberdashery (*notions; notions store*); (Am.) dry-goods store; (Am.) hardware store
mercerizar §76 *va* to mercerize
mercero *m* haberdasher, notions dealer or clerk; (Am.) dry-goods merchant; (Am.) hardware merchant
merciano -na *adj & mf* Mercian
mercología *f* marketing (*transaction of business; study of the phenomena of the transaction of business*)
mercológico -ca *adj* (pertaining to) marketing
merc.[s] abr. of **mercaderías**
mercurial *adj* mercurial; (astr. & myth.) Mercurial; *m* (pharm.) mercurial; *f* (bot.) herb mercury
mercurialismo *m* (path.) mercurialism
mercúrico -ca *adj* (chem.) mercuric
mercurio *m* (chem.) mercury; (*cap.*) *m* (astr. & myth.) Mercury
mercurioso -sa *adj* (chem.) mercurous
mercurocromo *m* mercurochrome
merdellón -llona *mf* (coll.) sloppy servant
merdoso -sa *adj* (coll.) dirty, filthy
merecedor -dora *adj* deserving
merecer §34 *va* to deserve, to merit; to be worth; to win (*praise*); to attain (*one's goal*); **merecer** + *inf* to deserve to + *inf;* **merecer la pena** to be worth while; *vn* to deserve, be deserving; **merecer bien de** to deserve the gratitude of; *vr* to be fertile (*said of sheep*)
merecido -da *adj* deserved; *m* just deserts; **llevar su merecido** to get what's coming to one
mereciente *adj* deserving
merecimiento *m* desert, merit
merendar §18 *va* to lunch on, to have for lunch; to keep an eye on, to peep at; *vn* to lunch, to have lunch; *vr* to manage to get
merendero *m* lunchroom; summerhouse; picnic grounds
merendilla *f* light lunch
merendona *f* fine layout, fine spread
merengar §59 *va* to whip (*cream*)
merengue *m* meringue
meretriz *f* (*pl:* **-trices**) prostitute, harlot
merey *m* (bot.) cashew
mergánsar *m* or **mergo** *m* (orn.) cormorant
mericarpo *m* (bot.) mericarp
meridiano -na *adj* meridian; bright, dazzling; *m* meridian; **primer meridiano** prime meridian; *f* couch; afternoon nap; meridian, meridian line; **a la meridiana** at noon
meridional *adj* meridional, southern; *mf* meridional, southerner
merienda *f* lunch, light meal, afternoon snack; (coll.) hunchback; **merienda de negros** (coll.) bedlam; **juntar meriendas** (coll.) to join forces; (coll.) to make up
merindad *f* (archaic) royal judgeship of sheepwalks
merino -na *adj* merino; thick and curly (*hair*); *mf* merino (*sheep*); *m* shepherd of merinos; merino (*wool; fabric*); (archaic) royal judge of sheepwalks
meristemo *m* (bot.) meristem
mérito *m* merit, desert; worth, value; **méritos** *mpl* (law) merit; **hacer mérito de** to make mention of; **hacer méritos** to put one's best foot forward
meritorio -ria *adj* meritorious; *m* volunteer worker; learner (*without pay*)
merla *f* (orn.) blackbird
merleta *f* (her.) martlet
merlín *m* (naut.) marline; (*cap.*) *m* Merlin; **saber más que Merlín** to be very smart, to be a wizard
merlo *m* (ichth.) black wrasse; (Am.) simpleton, boob
merlón *m* (fort.) merlon
merluza *f* (ichth.) hake; (coll.) drunk, spree, jag
merma *f* decrease, reduction; (com.) leakage
mermar *va* to decrease, lessen, reduce; *vn* to decrease, diminish, shrink, dwindle
mermelada *f* marmalade
mero -ra *adj* mere; *m* (ichth.) hind, grouper, jewfish; (ichth.) giant perch
merodeador -dora *adj* marauding; *mf* marauder
merodear *vn* to maraud
merodeo *m* marauding
merodista *mf* marauder
merovingio -gia *adj & m* Merovingian
merquén *m* (Am.) mixed salt and chili
mer.[s] abr. of **mercancías**
meruéndano *m* (prov.) bilberry
mes *m* month; menses; monthly pay; **caer en el mes del obispo** (coll.) to come at the right time; **mes anomalístico** (astr.) anomalistic month; **meses mayores** months preceding harvest; last months of pregnancy; **mes lunar** lunar month
mesa *f* table; desk; counter; food, fare; tableland; landing (*of staircase*); facet; flat side (*of blade or tool*); game (*e.g., of billiards*); court, playing surface; board (*group of officers*); desk (*section of office*); mesa (*flat-topped hill*); **¡a la mesa!** let's eat!; **alzar la mesa** (coll.) to clear the table; **a mesa puesta** with no cost or worry; **estar a mesa y mantel de** to live on, live at the expense of; **hacer mesa gallega** or **limpia** to clean up (*in gambling*); **levantar la mesa** to clear the table; **media mesa** low-price table (*in a restaurant*); **poner la mesa** to set or lay the table; **quitar la mesa** (Am.) to clear the table; **tener a mesa y mantel** to feed, to support; **tener mesa** to keep open house; **mesa de altar** altar; **mesa de batalla** sorting table (*in post office*); **mesa de billar** billiard table; **mesa de cambios** commercial bank; **mesa de consola** console table; **mesa de extensión** extension table; **mesa de guarnición** (naut.) channel; **mesa de juego** gambling table, gaming table; **mesa de milanos** (coll.) scanty fare; **mesa de trucos** pool table; **mesa de té** coffee table, tea table; **mesa franca** open table; **mesa operatoria** (surg.) operating table; **mesa parlante** planchette; **mesa perezosa** drop table; **mesa redonda** common table; table d'hôte, ordinary; **Mesa Redonda** (myth.) Round Table (*at which King Arthur and knights sat*)
mesada *f* monthly pay, monthly allowance
mesadura *f* tearing the hair, pulling hair
mesalina *f* dissolute woman
mesana *f* (naut.) mizzen (*sail; mast*)
mesar *va* to tear, to pull out (*hair*); *vr* to pull each other's hair
mescal *m* (bot.) mescal (*plant and liquor*)
mescolanza *f* (coll.) var. of **mezcolanza**
meseguería *f* harvest watch; assessment to pay for harvest watch
meseguero -ra *adj* (pertaining to the) harvest; *m* harvest watchman; (prov.) vineyard watchman
mesencéfalo *m* (anat.) mesencephalon, midbrain
mesénquima *m* (embryol.) mesenchyme
mesentérico -ca *adj* mesenteric
mesenterio *m* (anat.) mesentery
mesenteritis *f* (path.) mesenteritis
mesera *f* (Am.) waitress
meseraico -ca *adj* var. of **mesentérico**

mesero *m* journeyman on monthly wages; (Am.) waiter
meseta *f* landing (*of staircase*); plateau; **meseta de guarnición** (naut.) channel
mesiado *m* var. of **mesiazgo**
mesiánico -ca *adj* Messianic
mesianismo *m* Messianism
Mesías *m* (Bib. & fig.) Messiah
mesiazgo *m* Messiahship
mesilla *f* landing (*of staircase*); sideboard; window sill; mantel, mantelpiece; night table; half-joking scolding
mesillo *m* first menses after childbirth
mesita *f* small table; **mesita portateléfono** telephone table
mesitileno *m* (chem.) mesitylene
mesmedad *f*; **por su misma mesmedad** (coll.) without outside help, all by oneself, all by itself
mesmeriano -na *adj* mesmerian; mesmeric; *mf* mesmerian
mesmerismo *m* mesmerism
mesmerista *mf* mesmerist
mesnada *f* armed retinue; company, band
mesnadero *m* member of an armed retinue
mesoblasto *m* (embryol.) mesoblast
mesocarpio *m* (bot.) mesocarp
mesocéfalo -la *adj* (anthrop.) mesocephalic
mesodermo *m* (bot.) mesoderm
mesofilo *m* (bot.) mesophyll
mesófita *f* (bot.) mesophyte
mesogastrio *m* (anat. & zool.) mesogastrium
mesón *m* inn, tavern; (phys.) meson; (Am.) showcase
mesonaje *m* street or quarter full of taverns
mesonero -ra *adj* (pertaining to an) inn, tavern; *mf* innkeeper, tavern keeper
mesonista *adj* (pertaining to an) inn, tavern
mesorrino -na *adj* (anthrop.) mesorrhine
mesosfera *f* mesosphere
mesotórax *m* (*pl:* **-rax**) (zool.) mesothorax
mesotorio *m* (chem.) mesothorium
mesotrón *m* (phys.) mesotron
mesozoico -ca *adj & m* (geol.) Mesozoic
mesquite *m* var. of **mezquite**
mesta *f* (archaic) association of cattle raisers; **mestas** *fpl* confluence (*of two streams*)
mestal *m* growth of shrubs
mesteño -ña *adj* stray; (Am.) wild, untamed (*animal*)
mester *m* (archaic) trade, craft, mystery; (archaic) genre, literary genre; **mester de clerecía** (archaic) clerical verse (*of Spanish literature of thirteenth and fourteenth centuries*); **mester de juglaría** (archaic) minstrelsy, verse of jongleurs (*of Spanish literature beginning with tenth century*)
mesticia *f* sadness
mestizaje *m* crossbreeding
mestizar §76 *va* to crossbreed
mestizo -za *adj* mixed, mongrel; half-blooded; hybrid; *mf* half-breed, half-blood; mestizo; mongrel; hybrid; *m & f* (Am.) bran bread
mesto *m* (bot.) false cork oak, bastard cork tree; (bot.) Turkey oak; (bot.) mock privet
mestura *f* maslin
mesura *f* gravity, dignity; politeness, reverence; calm, circumspection, restraint
mesurado -da *adj* grave, dignified; polite, respectful; calm, circumspect, restrained; moderate, temperate
mesurar *va* to moderate, to temper; *vr* to restrain oneself, act with restraint
meta *f* (sport & fig.) goal
metabólico -ca *adj* (physiol. & zool.) metabolic
metabolismo *m* (physiol.) metabolism; **metabolismo basal** (physiol.) basal metabolism
metacarpiano -na *adj & m* (anat.) metacarpal
metacarpo *m* (anat.) metacarpus
metacentro *m* metacenter
metacrilato *m* (chem.) methacrylate
metacrílico -ca *adj* methacrylic
metacromatismo *m* (physical chem.) metachromatism
metacronismo *m* metachronism
metafase *f* (biol.) metaphase
metafísico -ca *adj* metaphysical; *m* metaphysician; *f* metaphysics
metafonía *f* (phonet.) metaphony, umlaut
metáfora *f* metaphor; **mezclar las metáforas** to mix metaphors
metafórico -ca *adj* metaphorical
metaforizar §76 *va* to express metaphorically; *vn* to use metaphors
metafrasis *f* (*pl:* **-sis**) metaphrase
metagénesis *f* (biol.) metagenesis
metal *m* metal; brass, latten; quality, condition; timbre (*of voice*); money; (her.) metal; (mus.) brass; **el vil metal** (coll.) filthy lucre; **metal antifricción** antifriction metal; **metal blanco** nickel silver; **metal britannia** Britannia metal; **metal bruto** base metal; **metal campanil** bell metal; **metal común** base metal; **metal de babbitt** Babbitt metal; **metal de campana** bell metal; **metal de imprenta** type metal; **metal desplegado** expanded metal; **metal dúctil** soft metal; **metales alcalinotérreos** (chem.) alkaline-earth metals; **metal inglés** Britannia metal; **metal monel** Monel metal; **metal noble** noble metal
metalado -da *adj* alloyed, impure
metalario *m* metalist, metalworker
metalepsis *f* (*pl:* **-sis**) (rhet.) metalepsis
metalero -ra *adj* (Am.) (pertaining to) metal; *m* (Am.) metalworker
metálico -ca *adj* metallic; *m* metalist, metalworker; hard cash, coin; *f* metallurgy
metalífero -ra *adj* metal-bearing, metalliferous
metalina *f* metaline (*alloy*)
metalista *m* metalist, metalworker
metalistería *f* metalwork
metalización *f* metalization
metalizado -da *adj* (coll.) moneyed, rich; (coll.) money-mad
metalizar §76 *va* to metalize; *vr* to become metalized; to become mercenary; to become rich and hard-hearted
metalografía *f* metallography
metalográfico -ca *adj* metallographic
metaloide *m* nonmetal
metaloideo -a *adj* nonmetallic
metaloterapia *f* metallotherapy
metalurgia *f* metallurgy
metalúrgico -ca *adj* metallurgic; *m* metallurgist; metalworker
metalurgista *m* metallurgist; metalworker
metalla *f* scraps of gold leaf for mending
metámero -ra *adj* (chem. & zool.) metameric; *m* (zool.) metamere
metamórfico -ca *adj* metamorphic
metamorfismo *m* metamorphism
metamorfosear *va & vr* to metamorphose
metamorfosis *f* (*pl:* **-sis**) metamorphosis
metano *m* (chem.) methane
metanol *m* (chem.) methanol
metaplasma *m* (biol.) metaplasm
metaplasmo *m* (gram.) metaplasm
metaproteína *f* (biochem.) metaprotein
metasomatismo *m* (geol.) metasomatism
metástasis *f* (*pl:* **-sis**) (path.) metastasis
metatarsiano -na *adj & m* (anat.) metatarsal
metatarso *m* (anat. & zool.) metatarsus
metate *m* (Am.) stone on which corn and chocolate are ground
metátesis *f* (*pl:* **-sis**) (philol.) metathesis
metatórax *m* (*pl:* **-rax**) (zool.) metathorax
metazoo *m* (zool.) metazoan
meteco -ca *adj* strange; *mf* stranger, outsider
metedor -dora *mf* smuggler; *m* diaper
meteduría *f* smuggling
metempsicosis *f* or **metempsícosis** *f* (*pl:* **-sis**) metempsychosis
metemuertos *m* (*pl:* **-tos**) stagehand; busybody
metencéfalo *m* (anat.) metencephalon, hindbrain
meteo *m* weather broadcast
meteórico -ca *adj* meteoric; (fig.) meteoric
meteorismo *m* (path.) meteorism, tympanites
meteorito *m* meteorite
meteorizar §76 *va* (path.) to meteorize; *vr* to be affected by the weather (*said of the soil*); (path.) to become meteorized
meteoro or **metéoro** *m* meteor (*atmospheric phenomenon*); weather, kind of weather (*rain, snow, hail, etc.*)

meteorología *f* meteorology
meteorológico -ca *adj* meteorologic or meteorological
meteorologista *mf* or **meteorólogo -ga** *mf* meteorologist
meter *va* to put, to place, to insert; to take in (*a seam*); to smuggle; to make (*noise, trouble*); to cause (*fear*); to start (*a rumor, a row*); to tell (*lies*); to stake (*money*); to pocket (*a pool ball*); to hole (*a golf ball*); (Am.) to strike (*a blow*); *vr* to project, to extend; to butt in, to meddle; to become (*e.g., a soldier*); **meterse a** to set oneself up as; **meterse a** + *inf* to take it upon oneself to + *inf;* **meterse con** to pick a quarrel or fight with; **meterse en** to get into; to plunge into; to empty into (*said of a river*); **meterse en sí mismo** to keep one's own counsel
metesillas *m* (*pl:* **-llas**) stagehand
meticulosidad *f* shyness, fear; meticulousness
meticuloso -sa *adj* shy, fearful; meticulous, scrupulous
metida *f* see **metido**
metidillo *m* diaper
metido -da *adj* full, rich; close, tight; **estar muy metido con** to be on very close terms with; **estar muy metido en** to be deeply involved in; *m* punch, push; strong lye; diaper; loose leaf; (sew.) seam (*edges left after making a seam*); (coll.) harsh dressing-down; *f* pocketing a pool ball; holing a golf ball; (naut.) setting (*of sun, star, etc.*)
metilamina *f* (chem.) methylamine
metilato *m* (chem.) methylate
metileno *m* (chem.) methylene
metílico -ca *adj* (chem.) methylic
metilo *m* (chem.) methyl
metimiento *m* insertion; influence, upper hand
metionina *f* (biochem.) methionine
metódico -ca *adj* methodic or methodical
metodismo *m* Methodism
metodista *adj* & *mf* Methodist
metodizar §76 *va* to methodize
método *m* method
metodología *f* methodology
metol *m* (chem.) metol
métomentodo *mf* (coll.) meddler, intruder
metonimia *f* (rhet.) metonymy
metonímico -ca *adj* metonymic or metonymical
métopa *f* (arch.) metope
metraje *m* distance in meters; meterage, measuring; (mov.) length of film in meters (*en inglés se usa* footage, *es decir, longitud de película en pies*); **de corto metraje** short (*movie*); **de largo metraje** full-length (*movie*)
metralla *f* grapeshot; shrapnel balls; shrapnel; scrap iron
metrallar *va* var. of **ametrallar**
metrallazo *m* discharge of grapeshot; discharge of shrapnel
metralleta *f* machine gun
metrar *va* to meter, to measure
métrico -ca *adj* metric, metrical; *f* metrics, art of metrical composition
metrificación *f* versification
metrificador -dora *mf* versifier
metrificar §86 *va* to put into verse; *vn* to versify
metrista *mf* metrist, versifier
metritis *f* (path.) metritis
metro *m* meter (*unit; verse*); ruler; tape measure; subway; **metro patrón** standard meter; **metro plegadizo** folding rule
metrología *f* metrology
metronómico -ca *adj* metronomic
metrónomo *m* (mus.) metronome
metrópoli *f* metropolis; mother country; (eccl.) metropolis
metropolitano -na *adj* metropolitan; *m* subway; (eccl.) metropolitan
metrorragia *f* (path.) metrorrhagia
Méx. abr. of **México**
mexicanidad *f* Mexicanism, Mexican spirit
mexicano -na *adj* & *mf* (Am.) Mexican
México *m* (Am.) Mexico; **Nuevo México** New Mexico; *f* Mexico City
meya *f* (zool.) spider crab
mezcal *m* var. of **mescal**
mezcla *f* mixture; mortar; tweed; **mezcla pobre** (aut.) lean mixture; **mezcla rica** (aut.) rich mixture
mezclable *adj* mixable
mezcladizo *m* maslin
mezclador -dora *mf* mixer; **mezclador automático** combination faucet; *f* concrete mixer
mezcladura *f* or **mezclamiento** *m* mixture
mezclar *va* to mix; to blend; *vr* to mix; to mingle; to take part; to meddle; to intermarry
mezclilla *f* light tweed; (orn.) black-and-white warbler
mezcolanza *f* (coll.) mixture, hodgepodge, medley, jumble
mezquinar *va* (Am.) to be stingy with; *vn* (Am.) to be stingy
mezquindad *f* meanness, stinginess; poverty, need; smallness, tininess; wretchedness
mezquino -na *adj* mean, stingy; poor, needy; small, tiny; wretched, unlucky
mezquita *f* mosque
mezquite *m* (bot.) mesquite
mezzo-soprano *m* mezzo-soprano (*voice*); *f* mezzo-soprano (*woman*)
mg. abr. of **miligramo** or **miligramos**
mho *m* (elec.) mho
mi *adj poss* my; *m* (mus.) mi
mí (used as object of prepositions) *pron pers* me; *pron reflex* me, myself
miaja *f* crumb
mialgia *f* (path.) myalgia
mialmas; como unas mialmas (coll.) with the greatest pleasure
miar §90 *vn* to meow
miasma *m* miasma
miasmático -ca *adj* miasmal or miasmatic
miastenia *f* (path.) myasthenia
miau *m* meow
mica *f* (mineral.) mica
micáceo -a *adj* micaceous
micacita *f* (mineral.) mica schist
micado *m* mikado
micasquisto *m* (mineral.) mica schist
micción *f* micturition
micela *f* (biol. & chem.) micelle
micelar *adj* micellar
micelio *m* (bot.) mycelium
Micenas *f* Mycenae
micénico -ca *adj* Mycenaean
mico *m* long-tailed monkey; (coll.) skinny fellow; (coll.) hoodlum; **dar** or **hacer mico** (coll.) to miss a date, to not keep a date; **dejar hecho un mico** (coll.) to abash, ruffle, upset; **quedarse hecho un mico** (coll.) to be abashed, ruffled, upset
micología *f* mycology
micológico -ca *adj* mycologic or mycological
micólogo -ga *mf* mycologist
micosis *f* (path.) mycosis
micra *f* micron
microanálisis *m* (chem.) microanalysis
microbarógrafo *m* microbarograph
microbiano -na *adj* microbial
micróbico -ca *adj* microbic
microbio *m* microbe
microbiología *f* microbiology
microbiológico -ca *adj* microbiological
microbiólogo -ga *mf* microbiologist
microcéfalo -la *adj* (anthrop. & path.) microcephalic
microcito *m* (path.) microcyte
microclina *f* (mineral.) microcline
micrococo *m* (bact.) micrococcus
microcopia *f* microcopy
microcosmo *m* microcosm
microdisección *f* microdissection
microdonte *adj* & *m* microdont
microfaradio *m* (elec.) microfarad
microficha *f* microcard
microfilm *m* microfilm
microfilmación *f* or **microfilmaje** *m* microfilming
microfilmar *va* to microfilm
microfísica *f* microphysics
micrófito *m* (bot.) microphyte
microfónico -ca *adj* microphonic
micrófono *m* microphone
microfoto *f* microphotograph

microfotografía *f* microphotography; microphotograph
microgameto *m* (biol.) microgamete
micrografía *f* micrography
microgramo *m* microgram
micrometría *f* micrometry
micrométrico -ca *adj* micrometric or micrometrical
micrómetro *m* micrometer
micromilímetro *m* micromillimeter
micromovimiento *m* micromotion
micrón *m* micron
micronesio -sia *adj & mf* Micronesian; **la Micronesia** Micronesia
microonda *f* (phys.) microwave
microorganismo *m* (bact.) microörganism
micropelícula *f* microfilm
micrópilo *m* (bot. & zool.) micropyle
microquímica *f* microchemistry
microscopia *f* microscopy
microscópico -ca *adj* microscopic or microscopical
microscopio *m* microscope; **microscopio electrónico** electron microscope
microscopista *mf* microscopist
microsismo *m* microseism
microsoma *m* (biol.) microsome
microsporangio *m* (bot.) microsporangium
microsporo -ra *adj* microsporous; *f* (bot.) microspore
microsurco *m* microgroove; *adj invar* microgroove
microteléfono *m* (telp.) handset (*telephone with receiver and mouthpiece on same handle*)
micrótomo *m* microtome
micturición *f* micturition
Michigán *m* Michigan
michito *m* (coll.) pussy, pussy cat
micho -cha *mf* (coll.) cat, puss
mida *f* (ent.) plant louse
Midas *m* (myth.) Midas
midriasis *f* (path.) mydriasis
midriático -ca *adj & m* mydriatic
miedo *m* fear; dread; **dar miedo a** to frighten; **de miedo** terrifically; **tener miedo (a)** to be afraid (of); **miedo cerval** intense fear
miedoso -sa *adj* (coll.) afraid, scared
miel *f* honey; molasses; (Am.) syrup; **dejar a media miel** or **con la miel en los labios** (coll.) to spoil the fun for; **hacerse de miel** to be peaches and cream; **miel rosada** (pharm.) honey of rose
mielencéfalo *m* (anat.) myelencephalon
mielgo -ga *adj & mf* twin; *f* plot of ground marked for planting; winnowing fork; (bot.) medic, lucerne; (ichth.) fox shark
mielina *f* (anat.) myelin
mielitis *f* (path.) myelitis
miembro *m* member; limb; **miembro de honor** honorary member; **miembro viril** (anat.) virile member; **miembro** *f* member, female member
mientes *fpl* mind, thought; **caer en mientes** or **en las mientes** to come to mind; **parar** or **poner mientes en** to consider, to reflect on; **traer a las mientes** to bring or to call to mind; **venírsele a uno a las mientes** to come to one's mind, to occur to one
mientras *conj* while; whereas; **mientras más** (or **menos**) **. . . más** (or **menos**) the more (or the less) . . . the more (or the less), e.g., **mientras más tiene más desea** the more he has the more he wants; **mientras que** while; whereas; **mientras tanto** meanwhile, in the meantime
miera *f* juniper oil; pine turpentine
miérc. abr. of **miércoles**
miércoles *m* (*pl:* **-les**) Wednesday; **miércoles corvillo** (coll.) Ash Wednesday; **miércoles de ceniza** Ash Wednesday
mierra *f* sled, stone drag
mies *f* grain, cereal; harvest time; (fig.) harvest (*of converts to Christianity*); **mieses** *fpl* grain fields
miga *f* bit; crumb (*soft part of bread*); substance; **migas** *fpl* fried crumbs; **hacer buenas migas (con)** to get along well (with); **hacer malas migas (con)** to get along badly (with); **hacerse migas** to be smashed to bits; **tener miga** (coll.) to have a point, to have something to it
migaja *f* crumb; bit; smattering; **migajas** *fpl* crumbs, leavings, offals; **reparar en migajas** (coll.) to bother about trifles
migajón *m* crumb; (coll.) substance
migala *f* (ent.) bird spider
migar §59 *va* to crumb (*bread*); to put crumbs in (*a liquid*)
Mig.[1] abr. of **Miguel**
migración *f* migration
migraña *f* (path.) migraine
migrador -dora or **migratorio -ria** *adj* migratory
Miguel *m* Michael; **Miguel Ángel** Michelangelo
miguelear *va* (Am.) to make love to, to court
migueleño -ña *adj* (Am.) impolite, discourteous
miguelete *m* var. of **miquelete**
Miguelito *m* Mike, Micky
mihrab *m* (*pl:* **mihrabs**) mihrab
mijar *m* field of millet
mijo *m* (bot.) broomcorn millet; **mijo de sol agreste** (bot.) corn gromwell; **mijo gris** (bot.) gromwell
mil *adj & m* thousand, a thousand, one thousand; **a las mil y quinientas** (coll.) at an unearthly hour; **las mil y quinientas** (coll.) a mess of lentils; **las Mil y una noches** the Thousand and One Nights; **mil en grano** (bot.) burstwort
miladi *f* milady
milagrear *vn* to perform miracles
milagrería *f* tale of miracles
milagrero -ra *adj* superstitious; miracle-faking; miracle-working
milagro *m* miracle, wonder; votive offering; (theat.) miracle, miracle play; **colgar el milagro a** to put the blame on; **hacer milagros** to do wonders; **por milagro** for a wonder; **vivir de milagro** to have a hard time getting along; to have had a narrow escape
milagrón *m* (coll.) fuss, excitement
milagroso -sa *adj* miraculous; marvelous, wonderful
milamores *f* (bot.) red valerian
Milán *f* Milan
milanés -nesa *adj & mf* Milanese
milano *m* burr or down of thistle; (orn.) kite; (ichth.) flying gurnard
Milcíades *m* Miltiades
mildeu *m* or **mildiú** *m* (agr.) mildew; **mildeu de la patata** potato mildew or mold
milefolio *m* (bot.) milfoil
milenario -ria *adj* millenial; millenarian; *mf* millenarian; *m* millenium
milenio *m* millenium
milenrama *f* (bot.) yarrow
milenta *adj & m* (coll.) thousand, a thousand
milépora *f* (zool.) millepore
milésimo -ma *adj & m* thousandth, millesimal; *f* mill (*thousandth of monetary unit*)
milesio -sia *adj & mf* Milesian
milés.[s] abr. of **milésimas**
Mileto *f* Miletus
milgranar *m* field of burstwort
milgranos *m* (*pl:* **-nos**) (bot.) burstwort
milhojas *m* (*pl:* **-jas**) var. of **milenrama**
mili *f* (coll.) militia, army
miliamperímetro *m* (elec.) milliammeter
miliamperio *m* (elec.) milliampere
miliar *adj* miliary; (pertaining to a) mile; (path.) miliary
miliario -ria *adj* milliary; (pertaining to a) mile
milibar *m* millibar
milicia *f* militia; soldiery; art of warfare; military service; **milicia nacional** national guard
miliciano -na *adj* military; *m* militiaman
miligramo *m* milligram
mililitro *m* milliliter
milímetro *m* millimeter
milimicrón *m* millimicron
milípedo *m* (zool.) millepede
milipulgada *f* mil (*0.001 inch*)
militante *adj & mf* militant

militar *adj* military; (pertaining to the) army; *m* military man, soldier; *vn* to serve in the army; to go to war, to fight; to struggle; to militate (*for or against*)
militara *f* wife, daughter, or widow of a soldier
militarismo *m* militarism
militarista *adj & mf* militarist
militarización *f* militarization
militarizar §76 *va* militarize
militarón *m* (coll.) old campaigner; (coll.) militarist
militarote *m* (coll.) swashbuckler
mílite *m* soldier
milivoltio *m* (elec.) millivolt
milmillonésimo -ma *adj & m* billionth
miloca *f* (orn.) Tengmalm's owl
milocha *f* kite
milor *m* or **milord** *m* (*pl:* **-lores**) milord
milpa *f* (Am.) cornfield
milpiés *m* (*pl:* **-piés**) (ent.) centipede; (zool.) wood louse
miltoniano -na *adj* Miltonian or Miltonic
milla *f* mile; **milla marina** (naut.) nautical mile, geographical mile
millar *m* thousand; **a millares** by the thousand
millarada *f* thousand, about a thousand; **a millaradas** by the thousand, thousandfold; **echar millaradas** to boast of great wealth
millo *m* (bot.) millet; **millo de escoba** (bot.) broom millet, broomcorn millet
millón *m* million
millonada *f* million, about a million
millonario -ria *adj* millionaire; of a million or more inhabitants; *mf* millionaire
millonésimo -ma *adj & m* millionth
mimar *va* to pet, fondle; to pamper, indulge
mimbar *m* mimbar, Moslem pulpit
mimbral *m* osiery
mimbrar *va* to humble, to overwhelm
mimbre *m & f* osier, wicker, withe; (bot.) osier
mimbrear *vn & vr* to sway
mimbreño -ña *adj* willowy, withy
mimbrera *f* (bot.) osier, osier willow
mimbreral *m* osiery
mimbrón *m* var. of **mimbrera**
mimbroso -sa *adj* wicker
mimeografiar §90 *va* to mimeograph
mimeógrafo *m* mimeograph
mímesis *f* (rhet., biol. & path.) mimesis
mimético -ca *adj* (biol. & mineral.) mimetic
mimetismo *m* (biol.) protective coloration, mimetism
mímico -ca *adj* of mimes; mimic; *m* author of mimes; *f* mimicry; gesticulations; sign language
mimicria *f* (biol.) mimicry
mimo *m* mime; pampering, indulgence; finickiness, fussiness
mimosa *f* see **mimoso**
mimosáceo -a *adj* (bot.) mimosaceous
mimoso -sa *adj* pampered, spoiled; finicky, fussy; *f* (bot.) mimosa; **mimosa púdica** or **vergonzosa** (bot.) mimosa, sensitive plant
mina *f* mine; (min.) seam, vein, lode; lead (*of pencil*); (mil. & nav.) mine; (fig.) mine, storehouse, gold mine; (fig.) sinecure; (Am.) moll; **beneficiar una mina** to work a mine; **encontrar una mina** (fig.) to strike a gold mine; **volar la mina** to break one's silence; **voló la mina** the truth is out; **mina de carbón** coal mine; **mina de oro** gold mine; **mina hullera** coal mine
minado *m* mine working; (nav.) mining (*e.g., of a harbor*)
minador -dora *adj* mining; (nav.) mine-laying; *m* mining engineer; (mil.) miner; (nav.) mine layer
minal *adj* (pertaining to a) mine
minar *va* to mine; to undermine; to consume; to plug away at; (mil. & nav.) to mine; *vn* to mine
minarete *m* minaret
mineraje *m* mining; **mineraje a tajo abierto** strip mining
mineral *adj* mineral; *m* mineral; ore; fountainhead; mine; source, origin
mineralización *f* mineralization
mineralizar §76 *va* to mineralize; *vr* to become mineralized
mineralogía *f* mineralogy
mineralógico -ca *adj* mineralogical
mineralogista *mf* mineralogist
minería *f* mining; mines; miners; mine operators
minero -ra *adj* mining; *m* miner; mine operator; (fig.) source, origin
mineromedicinal *adj* mineral (*water*)
Minerva *f* (myth.) Minerva; (*l.c.*) *f* (eccl.) procession; (print.) small press; **de propia minerva** out of one's own head
mingitorio *m* upright urinal
mingo *m* object ball; **poner el mingo** (coll.) to stand out, excel, distinguish oneself; **tomar el mingo a** (coll.) to tease, to taunt
mingón -gona *adj* (Am.) spoiled (*child*)
miniar *va* to miniate, to illuminate (*a manuscript*); to paint in miniature
miniatura *f* miniature; **en miniatura** in miniature; *adj invar* miniature; toy (*e.g., dog*)
miniaturesco -ca *adj* miniature
miniaturista *mf* miniaturist
miniaturización *f* miniaturization
miniaturizar §76 *va* to miniaturize
minifundio *m* small farm
minim *m* (pharm.) minim
mínima *f* see **mínimo**
minimización *f* diminution, reduction; minimization; minimizing
minimizar §76 *va* to diminish, reduce; to minimize
mínimo -ma *adj* minimum; minimal; tiny, minute; least, smallest; *m* minimum; *f* tiny bit; minim; (mus.) minim
mínimum *m* minimum
minino -na *mf* (coll.) cat, kitty
minio *m* (chem.) minium
ministerial *adj* ministerial; *m* minister
ministerio *m* ministry; cabinet; government; **formar ministerio** to form a government; **ministerio de asuntos exteriores** foreign office; **ministerio de Asuntos Exteriores** Department of State (U.S.A.); Foreign Office (Brit.); **ministerio de Defensa Nacional** Department of Defense (U.S.A.); **ministerio de Hacienda** Treasury Department (U.S.A.); Treasury (Brit.); **ministerio de Justicia** Department of Justice (U.S.A.); Department of the Lord Chancellor (Brit.); **ministerio de la Gobernación** Department of the Interior (U.S.A.); Home Office (Brit.); **ministerio del Aire** Department of the Air Force (U.S.A.); Air Ministry (Brit.); **ministerio del Ejército** Department of the Army (U.S.A.); War Office (Brit.); **ministerio de Marina** Department of the Navy (U.S.A.); Board of Admiralty (Brit.)
ministra *f* woman minister; minister's wife
ministrador -dora *adj & mf* ministrant
ministrante *adj* ministrant; *mf* ministrant; trained nurse
ministrar *va* to administer; to supply; to minister; *vn* to minister
ministril *m* tipstaff; musician; wind instrument; minstrel (*retainer who sang and played for his lord*)
ministro *m* minister; bailiff, constable; (pol., dipl. & eccl.) minister; **primer ministro** prime minister, premier; **ministro de asuntos exteriores** foreign minister; **ministro de Asuntos Exteriores** Secretary of State (U.S.A.); Minister of Foreign Affairs (Brit.); **ministro de Gobernación** Home Secretary (Brit.); **ministro de Hacienda** Chancellor of the Exchequer (Brit.); **ministro de Justicia** Attorney General (U.S.A.); **ministro plenipotenciario** minister plenipotentiary; **ministro sin cartera** minister without portfolio; **ministro** *f* minister (*woman*)
min.º abr. of **ministro**
mino *interj* here, pussy!
minoico -ca *adj* Minoan
minoración *f* lessening, diminution; weakening
minorar *va* to lessen, diminish; to weaken
minorativo -va *adj* lessening, diminishing; laxative; *m* laxative

minoría *f* minority (*condition and time of being under age; smaller number or part*)
minoridad *f* minority (*being under age*)
minorista *adj* retail; *m* retailer; cleric holding minor orders
minoritario -ria *adj* (pertaining to the) minority
Minos *m* (myth.) Minos
Minotauro *m* (myth.) Minotaur
minucia *f* trifle; **minucias** *fpl* minutiae; (archaic) minor tithes
minuciosidad *f* minuteness; meticulousness; fussiness
minucioso -sa *adj* minute; meticulous; fussy
minué *m* minuet (*dance and music*)
minuendo *m* (math.) minuend
minuete *m* var. of **minué**
minúsculo -la *adj* small (*letter*); small, tiny; *f* small letter
minuta *f* see **minuto**
minutar *va* to make a draft of, to minute
minutario *m* notary's ledger
minutería *f* minute marks (*on face of clock or watch*); (elec.) automatic time switch (*used in hotel hallways*)
minutero *m* minute hand
minutisa *f* (bot.) sweet william
minuto -ta *adj* minute; *m* minute (*of an hour; of a degree*); *f* first draft, rough draft; memorandum; lawyer's bill; roll, list; bill of fare
miñón *m* border guard, forest guard; (prov.) slag; (prov.) iron ore
miñona *f* (print.) minion
miñoneta *f* (bot.) mignonette
miñosa *f* (zool.) earthworm
mio *interj* pussy, pussy!
mío -a *adj poss* mine, of mine; *pron poss* mine; **de mío** on my own accord; by myself
miocardio *m* (anat.) myocardium
miocarditis *f* (path.) myocarditis
mioceno -na *adj & m* (geol.) Miocene
mioglobina *f* (biochem.) myoglobin
miógrafo *m* myograph
miología *f* myology
mioma *m* (path.) myoma
miope *adj* myopic, near-sighted; (fig.) myopic; *mf* myope
miopía *f* (path.) myopia, near-sightedness
miosis *f* (path.) myosis
miosota *f* (bot.) German madwort
miosotis *m* (bot.) myosotis, forget-me-not; (bot.) German madwort
Miqueas *m* (Bib.) Micah
miquelete *m* miquelet
mira *f* sight; target; object, aim, purpose; level rod; **estar a la mira** to be on the lookout; **estar a la mira de que** to be on the lookout to see that; **poner la mira en** or **tener miras sobre** to have designs on; **mira esférica** globe sight
mirabel *m* (bot.) mock cypress; (bot.) sunflower
mirabolano or **mirabolanos** *m* (bot.) var. of **mirobálano**
mirada *f* see **mirado**
miradero *m* cynosure; concern, thing most watched; lookout, observatory
mirado -da *adj* thoughtful, cautious, circumspect; **bien mirado** well-thought-of; **mal mirado** little liked, looked on with disfavor; *f* glance, look; **apuñalar con la mirada** to look daggers at; **echar una mirada a** to take a look at
mirador -dora *adj* looking, overlooking; *m* watchtower; mirador; bay window, closed porch
miradura *f* glance, look
miraguano *m* (bot.) fan palm, thatch palm; (Am.) kapok
miraje *m* mirage
miramelindos *m* (*pl:* **-dos**) (bot.) balsam
miramiento *m* look; considerateness, regard; care, caution, circumspection; misgiving; **miramientos** *mpl* fuss, bother, worry
miranda *f* belvedere; eminence, vantage point
mirar *va* to look at; to watch; to contemplate, consider; to consider carefully, to be careful about; to esteem, have regard for; **mirar bien** to look with favor on, to like; **mirar mal** to look with disfavor on, to dislike; **mirar por encima** to glance at ‖ *vn* to look; to glance; **¡mira!** look!; look out!; **mirar a** to look at; to glance at; to aim at; to face, overlook; to concern; **mirar a** + *inf* to aim to + *inf;* **mirar por** to look after, to look out for ‖ *vr* to look at oneself; to look at each other; **mirar a sí** to know one's place; **mirarse en ello** to watch one's step; **mirarse en una persona** to be all wrapped up in a person; **mirarse unos a otros** to stand dumbfounded looking at each other
mirasol *m* (bot.) sunflower
miríada *f* myriad (*ten thousand; very great number*)
miriámetro *m* ten thousand meters
miriápodo -da *adj & m* var. of **miriópodo**
miricáceo -a *adj* (bot.) myricaceous
mirificar §86 *va* to exalt, extol
mirífico -ca *adj* marvelous, wonderful
mirilla *f* peephole; (surv.) target; (phot.) finder
miriñaque *m* crinoline; hoop skirt; bauble, trinket; (Am.) cowcatcher
miriópodo -da *adj & m* (zool.) myriapod
mirística *f* (bot.) nutmeg (*tree*)
miristicáceo -a *adj* (bot.) myristicaceous
mirla *f* (orn.) blackbird
mirlamiento *m* self-importance, airs
mirlar *vr* (coll.) to act important, to put on airs
mirlo *m* (orn.) blackbird; (coll.) affected expression of solemnity; **aguantar el mirlo** (coll.) to keep quiet, refuse to answer; **soltar el mirlo** (coll.) to jabber, to scold; **mirlo blanco** (coll.) rare bird; **mirlo de agua** (orn.) water ouzel
mirmecófago -ga *adj* myrmecophagous
mirmecófilo -la *adj* myrmecophilous; *m* (ent.) myrmecophile
mirmecología *f* myrmecology
mirmecólogo -ga *mf* myrmecologist
Mirmidón *m* (myth.) Myrmidon; (*l.c.*) *m* dwarf, tiny fellow
mirobálano *m* (bot.) myrobalan (*tree and fruit*)
mirón -rona *adj* onlooking; nosy, inquisitive; *mf* onlooker; kibitzer; busybody
mirra *f* myrrh
mirrado -da *adj* myrrhed
mirrino -na *adj* myrrhic
mirtáceo -a *adj* (bot.) myrtaceous
mirtino -na *adj* myrtiform
mirto *m* (bot.) myrtle; **mirto de Brabante** (bot.) gale, sweet gale
misa *f* (eccl. & mus.) mass; **cantar misa** to say mass; **como en misa** in dead silence; **decir misa** to say mass; **no saber de la misa la media** (coll.) to not know what it's all about; **oír misa** to hear mass; **misa cantada** High Mass; **misa de campaña** (mil.) mass in the field; outdoor mass; **misa del gallo** Christmas-eve mass; **misa de prima** early mass; **misa de réquiem** requiem mass; **misa mayor** High Mass; **misa rezada** Low Mass
misacantano *m* officiant at Mass, priest who says Mass for the first time
misal *m* (eccl.) missal, Mass book
misantropía *f* misanthropy
misantrópico -ca *adj* misanthropic
misantropismo *m* var. of **misantropía**
misántropo *m* misanthrope
misar *vn* (coll.) to say mass; (coll.) to hear mass
misario *m* (eccl.) acolyte
miscegenación *f* miscegenation
misceláneo -a *adj* miscellaneous; *f* miscellany; miscellanies
miscible *adj* miscible
miserabilísimo -ma *adj super* very or most miserable; very or most stingy
miserable *adj* miserable, wretched; mean, stingy; vile, wicked, despicable; *mf* wretch; cur, cad
miseración *f* pity, mercy
miserando -da *adj* pitiful
miserear *va* (coll.) to scrimp, to begrudge; *vn* (coll.) to be stingy
miserere *m* (eccl. & mus.) Miserere; (path.) ileus
miseria *f* misery, wretchedness; poverty; stinginess; (coll.) trifle, pittance; (slang) lice; **comerse de miseria** (coll.) to live in great poverty

misericordia *f* mercy, compassion; misericord (*dagger*); (arch.) miserere, misericord; (eccl.) misericord (*hall; dispensation*)
misericordioso -sa *adj* merciful
misero -ra *adj* (coll.) mass-loving, church-going
mísero -ra *adj* miserable, wretched; miserly, stingy
misérrimo -ma *adj super* very or most miserable or wretched; very or most miserly
misión *f* mission; food for harvesters; **misiones** *fpl* (eccl.) foreign missions; **ir a misiones** to go away as a missionary
misional *adj* missionary
misionar *va* to spread (*e.g., faith*); to spread the faith to; *vn* to conduct a mission, do missionary work
misionario *m* envoy, missionary; (eccl.) missionary
misionero -ra *adj* missionary; *m* (eccl.) missionary
Misisipí *m* Mississippi (*river and state*)
misivo -va *adj & f* missive
mismamente *adv* (coll.) exactly
mismísimo -ma *adj super* selfsame, very same
mismo -ma *adj & pron indef* same; own, very; self, e.g., **ella misma** herself; myself, yourself, himself, itself, e.g., **yo mismo** I myself; **su padre mismo** his father himself; **en España misma** in Spain itself; **así mismo** in like manner, likewise, also; **casi lo mismo** much the same; **lo mismo** the same thing; just the same; **lo mismo me da** (coll.) it's all the same to me; **por lo mismo** for the same reason, for that very reason; **mismo . . . que** same . . . as; **mismo** *adv* right, e.g., **ahora mismo** right now; **aquí mismo** right here; **en España mismo** right in Spain; **desde Sevilla mismo** right from Seville
misogamia *f* misogamy
misógamo -ma *adj* misogamic; *mf* misogamist
misoginia *f* misogyny
misógino -na *adj* misogynous; *mf* misogynist
misoneísmo *m* misoneism
misoneísta *mf* misoneist
mispíquel *m* (mineral.) mispickel
mistagogo *m* (hist.) mystagogue
mistar *vn* to mumble
mistela *f* flavored brandy; sweet wine
misterio *m* mystery; (theat.) mystery, mystery play; **misterios de Eleusis** Eleusinian mysteries
misterioso -sa *adj* mysterious
mística *f* see **místico**
misticismo *m* mysticism
místico -ca *adj* mystic, mystical; *mf* mystic; *m* (naut.) mistic; *f* mystical theology; literary mysticism
misticón -cona *adj* pietistic; *mf* pietist
mistificación *f* var. of **mixtificación**
mistificar §86 *va* var. of **mixtificar**
mistifori *m* (coll.) var. of **mixtifori**
mistilíneo -a *adj* var. of **mixtilíneo**
mistral *m* mistral (*wind*)
mistura *f* var. of **mixtura**
Misurí *m* Missouri (*river and state*)
mita *f* (zool.) mite, cheese mite; (Am.) Indian slave labor
mitad *f* half; middle; **a (la) mitad de** halfway through; **cara mitad** (coll.) better half (*husband and especially wife*); **en la mitad de** in the middle of; **la mitad de** half the, e.g., **la mitad del dinero** half the money; **mentir por la mitad de la barba** (coll.) to tell fish stories; **por la mitad** in the middle, in half; **mitad y mitad** half-and-half
mítico -ca *adj* mythic or mythical
mitigación *f* mitigation
mitigador -dora *adj* mitigating; *mf* mitigator
mitigar §59 *va* to mitigate, allay, appease; *vr* to mitigate
mitigativo -va *adj* mitigative
Mitilene *f* Mytilene
mitin *m* (*pl:* **mitins** or **mítines**) meeting, rally
mito *m* myth
mitología *f* mythology; **mitología nórdica** Norse mythology
mitológico -ca *adj* mythological; *mf* mythologist
mitologista *mf* or **mitólogo -ga** *mf* mythologist
mitón *m* mitt (*glove which leaves the fingers uncovered*)
mitósico -ca *adj* mitotic
mitosis *f* (biol.) mitosis
mitra *f* miter (*e.g., of a bishop; episcopal office or dignity*); chimney pot; (*cap.*) *m* (myth.) Mithras
mitrado -da *adj* mitered; *m* bishop, archbishop; (bot.) miter mushroom
mitral *adj* mitral; (anat.) mitral
mitrar *vn* (coll.) to be mitered, to become a bishop
Mitridates *m* Mithridates
mítulo *m* (zool.) mussel
mixedema *f* (path.) myxedema
mixomatosis *f* (vet.) myxomatosis
mixomiceto *m* (bot.) myxomycete
mixtela *f* var. of **mistela**
mixtificación *f* hoax, mystification
mixtificar §86 *va* to hoax, to mystify
mixtifori *m* (coll.) hodgepodge
mixtilíneo -a *adj* mixtilineal
mixtión *f* mixture
mixto -ta *adj* mixed; *m* compound; match; explosive compound
mixtura *f* mixture; maslin
mixturar *va* to mix
mixturero -ra *adj* mixing; *mf* mixer; *f* (Am.) flower girl
miz *interj* pussy, pussy!
mízcalo *m* (bot.) edible milk mushroom (*Lactarius deliciosus*)
mizo -za *mf* (coll.) cat
m/l abr. of **mi letra**
mm. abr. of **milímetro** or **milímetros**
m/m abr. of **más o menos**
Mm. abr. of **miriámetro** or **miriámetros**
m/n abr. of **moneda nacional**
mnemónico -ca *adj* mnemonic; *f* mnemonics
Mnemosina or **Mnemósine** *f* (myth.) Mnemosyne
mnemotecnia *f* mnemotechny
mnemotécnico -ca *adj* mnemotechnic or mnemotechnical; *f* mnemotechnics
moabita *adj & mf* Moabite
moaré *m* var. of **muaré**
mobiliario -ria *adj* personal (*property*); *m* suit of furniture
moblaje *m* furniture, suit of furniture
moblar §77 *va* to furnish
moca *f* (Am.) mudhole; (Am.) wineglass; *m* Mocha coffee
mocador *m* handkerchief
mocar §86 *va* to blow the nose of; *vr* to blow one's nose
mocarro *m* (coll.) snot
mocasín *m* moccasin; (zool.) moccasin, cottonmouth; **mocasín de agua** (zool.) water moccasin
mocasina *f* moccasin
mocear *vn* to act young; to run around, to sow one's wild oats; to grow up; to run around after women
mocedad *f* youth; wild oats; licentious living
mocejón *m* (zool.) mussel
moceril *adj* youthful
mocerío *m* young people, crowd of young people
mocero *adj masc* woman-crazy; fast-living
mocetón *m* strapping young fellow
mocetona *f* buxom young woman
mocil *adj* youthful
moción *f* motion, movement; inclination, leaning; divine inspiration; motion (*in a deliberative assembly*); **hacer** or **presentar una moción** to make a motion
mocionante *mf* (Am.) mover (*of a proposition*)
mocionar *va* (Am.) to move (*to propose in a deliberative assembly*); *vn* (Am.) to move, make a motion
mocito -ta *adj* quite young; *mf* youngster
moco *m* mucus; snot; candle drippings; snuff (*of candlewick*); slag; **a moco de candil** by candle light; **llorar a moco tendido** (coll.) to cry like a baby; **quitar los mocos a** (coll.) to slap in the face; **moco del bauprés** (naut.)

dolphin striker, martingale; **moco de pavo** crest of a turkey; (bot.) cockscomb; (coll.) trifle
mocoso -sa *adj* snively, snotty; ill-bred, rude; saucy, flip; mean, good-for-nothing; *mf* brat
mocosuelo -la *mf* (coll.) brat; (coll.) meddler, schemer; (coll.) greenhorn
mocosuena; **traducir mocosuena** (coll.) to translate with cognates, to translate word for word
mochada *f* butt (*with the head*)
mochales; **estar mochales** (coll.) to be madly in love
mochar *va* to butt; (Am.) to dehorn
mochazo *m* blow with the butt of a gun
mocheta *f* thick or flat edge (*of a tool*); frame (*of door or window*); reëntering angle; (carp.) rabbet
mochete *m* (orn.) sparrow hawk
mochil *m* errand boy for farmers in the field
mochila *f* (mil.) knapsack; haversack; (mil.) ration (*for soldier or his horse*); tool bag; **de mochila** knapsack (*spray, pump, etc.*)
mochín *m* executioner
mocho -cha *adj* blunt, flat; stub-pointed; stub-horned; topped (*tree*); (coll.) cropped, shorn; *m* butt end
mochuelo *m* (orn.) little owl (*Athene noctua*); (print.) omission; **echarle a uno el mochuelo** (coll.) to give someone the worst of a deal; **cargar con el mochuelo** or **tocarle a uno el mochuelo** (coll.) to get the worst of a deal; **mochuelo de los bosques** (orn.) tawny owl
moda *f* fashion, mode, style; **a la moda** fashionable; **a la moda de** after the fashion of, in the style of; **de moda** in fashion, fashionable, popular; **fuera de moda** out of fashion; **pasar de moda** to go out of fashion
modado -da *adj*; **bien modado** (Am.) well-mannered; **mal modado** (Am.) ill-mannered
modal *adj* modal; **modales** *mpl* manners
modalidad *f* modality, way, manner, method; nature; kind
modelación *f* or **modelado** *m* modeling; molding
modelaje *m* modeling; molding; patternmaking
modelar *va* to model; to form, shape; to mold; *vr* to model; **modelarse sobre** to pattern oneself after
modélico -ca *adj* model
modelismo *m* patternmaking; molding
modelista *mf* patternmaker; molder
modelo *m* model; pattern; equal, peer; form, blank; style, e.g., **último modelo** latest style; **modelo vivo** live model; *mf* model, fashion model, mannequin; *adj invar* model, e.g., **una ciudad modelo** a model city
moderación *f* moderation
moderador -dora *adj* moderating; *mf* moderator; *m* (mach., phys. & chem.) moderator
moderante *m* (educ.) moderator
moderantismo *m* moderation; (pol.) conservatism
moderar *va* to moderate; to control, restrain; *vr* to moderate; to control onself, restrain oneself
modernidad *f* modernity
modernismo *m* modernism; neologism
modernista *adj* modernist, modernistic; *mf* modernist
modernización *f* modernization
modernizar §76 *va & vr* to modernize
moderno -na *adj & m* modern
modestia *f* modesty
modesto -ta *adj* modest
modicidad *f* moderateness, reasonableness
módico -ca *adj* moderate, reasonable
modificable *adj* modifiable
modificación *f* modification
modificador -dora *adj* modifying; *mf* modifier
modificante *adj* modifying; *m* (gram.) modifier
modificar §86 *va & vr* to modify
modillón *m* (arch.) modillion
modismo *m* idiom
modista *mf* dressmaker, modiste; **modista de sombreros** milliner
modistería *f* dressmaking; (Am.) ladies' dress shop
modistilla *f* (coll.) poor or unskilled dressmaker; seamstress, dressmaker's helper
modisto *m* ladies' tailor
modo *m* mode, manner, way, method; (gram.) mood or mode; (mus.) mode; **al modo** or **a modo de** like, in the manner of, on the order of; **al modo español** in the Spanish manner; **a mi modo** in my own way; **de buen modo** politely; **de ese modo** at that rate; **del mismo modo que** in the same way as; **de mal modo** impolitely, rudely; **de modo que** so that; so, and so; **de ningún modo** by no means; **de todos modos** at any rate, anyhow; **de un modo u otro** in one way or another, somehow; **en cierto modo** after or in a fashion; **por modo de** as, by way of; **sobre modo** extremely; **uno a modo de** a sort of, a kind of; **modo conjuntivo** (gram.) compound conjunction; **modo de ser** nature, disposition; **modo imperativo** (gram.) imperative mood; **modo indicativo** (gram.) indicative mood; **modo potencial** (gram.) potential mood; **modo subjuntivo** (gram.) subjunctive mood
modorra *f* see **modorro**
modorrar *va* to make drowsy, make heavy; *vr* to get drowsy, fall asleep; to become flabby (*said of fruit*)
modorrilla *f* (coll.) third night watch
modorro -rra *adj* drowsy, heavy; dull, stupid; flabby (*fruit*); poisoned by mercury (*in a mine*); (vet.) giddy; *f* drowsiness, heaviness; (vet.) gid, staggers
modoso -sa *adj* quiet, well-behaved
modrego *m* (coll.) awkward fellow, clumsy fellow
modulación *f* modulation; **modulación de altura** or **de amplitud** (rad.) amplitude modulation; **modulación de fase** (rad.) phase modulation; **modulación de frecuencia** (rad.) frequency modulation
modulado -da *adj* well-modulated; sweet, harmonious
modulador -dora *adj* modulating; *mf* modulator; *m* (rad.) modulator
modular *adj* modular; *va & vn* to modulate
módulo *m* modulus (*standard, norm*); module (*of a coin or medal*); (arch., hyd. & mach.) module; (phys.) modulus; (mus.) modulation
moduloso -sa *adj* harmonious
moer *m* moire; mohair
mofa *f* scoffing, jeering, mocking; **hacer mofa de** to scoff at, jeer at, make fun of
mofador -dora *adj* scoffing, jeering, mocking; *mf* scoffer, jeerer, mocker
mofadura *f* var. of **mofa**
mofar *vn & vr* to scoff, jeer, mock; **mofarse de** to scoff at, jeer at, make fun of
mofeta *f* (min.) blackdamp; mofette (*from a mine or from past volcanic activity*); (zool.) skunk, polecat
moflete *m* (coll.) jowl
mofletudo -da *adj* big-jowled, chubby-cheeked
mogate *m* glaze; **a** or **de medio mogate** carelessly
mogato -ta *adj & mf* var. of **mojigato**
mogol -gola *adj & mf* Mongol, Mongolian; **el gran Mogol** the Great Mogul; *m* Mongolian (*language*)
Mogolia, la Mongolia; **la Mogolia Exterior** Outer Mongolia; **la Mogolia Interior** Inner Mongolia
mogólico -ca *adj* Mongolian
mogolismo *m* Mongolism
mogoloide *adj & mf* Mongoloid
mogollón *m* sponging; **comer de mogollón** (coll.) to sponge
mogón -gona *adj* one-horned, single-horned; broken-horned
mogote *m* hummock, knoll; pile of faggots, stack of sheaves; budding antler
mogrollo *m* sponger; (coll.) roughneck
moharra *f* tip (*of lance, mast, etc.*); (Am.) spear (*for bullfighting*)
moharrache *m* or **moharracho** *m* clown
mohatra *f* fake sale; cheat
mohecer §34 *va & vr* var. of **enmohecer**
moheda *f* or **mohedal** *m* bramblewood, jungle
mohicano -na *adj & mf* Mohican

mohiento -ta *adj* moldy, musty, mildewed
mohín *m* face, grimace, pouting
mohíno -na *adj* sad, gloomy; annoyed, peeved; black, black-nosed (*horse, cow, etc.*); *mf* hinny; *m* lone player (*against whom the rest gang up*); (orn.) blue magpie; *f* annoyance, displeasure
moho *m* (bot.) mold; rust, verdigris; laziness, sloth; **no criar moho** (coll.) to get no chance to grow stale; **moho del pan** bread mold
mohoso -sa *adj* moldy, musty, mildewed; rusty; stale (*joke*)
Moisés *m* Moses; (*l.c.*) *m* basket used as cradle
mojado -da *adj* wet; drenched, soaked; moist; (phonet.) liquid, mouillé; *m* (Am.) wetback; *f* wetting; drenching, soaking; stab
mojador -dora *adj* wetting; moistening; *mf* wetter; moistener; *m* moistener (*for fingers, stamps, etc.*)
mojadura *f* wetting; drenching, soaking; moistening
mojama *f* dry, salted tuna
mojar *va* to wet; to drench, soak; to dampen, moisten; (coll.) to stab; *vn* to dunk; **mojar en** (coll.) to get mixed up in; *vr* to get wet; to get drenched or soaked
mojarra *f* (ichth.) mojarra; (Am.) broad dagger
mojarrilla *mf* (coll.) jolly person
moje *m* gravy, sauce
mojel *m* (naut.) braided cord or cable
mojera *f* (bot.) whitebeam
mojí *m* (*pl:* **-jíes**) var. of **mojicón**
mojicón *m* muffin, bun; (coll.) punch in the face
mojiganga *f* mummery, masquerade, morris dance; clowning; (coll.) hypocrisy
mojigatería or **mojigatez** *f* hypocrisy; prudishness, sanctimoniousness
mojigato -ta *adj* hypocritical; prudish, sanctimonious; *mf* hypocrite; prude
mojinete *m* coping; ridge (*of roof*); caress, tap on the cheek; (Am.) gable
mojo *m* var. of **moje**
mojón *m* boundary stone, landmark, monument; pile, heap; turd; winetaster; quoits
mojona or **mojonación** *f* var. of **amojonamiento**
mojonar *va* var. of **amojonar**
mojonera *f* boundary, marked boundary; line of boundary stones or landmarks
mojonero *m* gauger
mol *m* (chem.) mol
mola *f* (path.) mole; (hist.) mole (*sacrificial cake*)
molada *f* batch of ground pigment
molal *adj* (chem.) molal
molar *adj* (anat., phys. & path.) molar; *m* (anat.) molar (*tooth*)
molcajete *m* stone mortar standing on a tripod
moldar *va* to mold; to put molding on
moldavo -va *adj & mf* Moldavian
molde *m* mold; matrix, cast, stamp; form, frame; pattern; model, ideal; (print.) form; **de molde** printed; fitting, to the purpose; **venir de molde** to be just right
moldeado *m* molding, casting
moldeador -dora *adj* molding; *m* molder; (carp.) molding machine; *f* (found.) molding machine
moldear *va* to mold; to cast; to put molding on
moldeo *m* molding; casting
moldería *f* molding (*preparation of molds*)
moldura *f* molding (*shaped strip of wood*)
moldurar *va* to put molding on
moldurista *m* molding maker
mole *adj* soft; *m* Mexican dish of meat or turkey cooked with chili and sesame sauce; *f* mass, bulk, heap
molécula *f* (chem. & phys.) molecule
molécula-gramo *f* (*pl:* **moléculas-gramos**) (chem.) gram molecule
molecular *adj* molecular
molecular-gramo *adj* gram-molecular
moledero -ra *adj* for grinding, to be ground; *f* grindstone; (coll.) bother, annoyance
moledor -dora *adj* grinding; (coll.) boring; *mf* grinder; (coll.) bore; *m* grinder, mill, crusher; roller (*of sugar mill*); *f* grinder, crusher
moledura *f* grinding, milling; fatigue, weariness
molejón *m* grindstone
molendero -ra *mf* miller, grinder; *m* chocolate grinder (*person*)
moleño -ña *adj* millstone (*rock*); *f* flint
moler §63 *va* to grind, to mill; to annoy, harass; to tire out, to weary; to wear out, to spoil; (coll.) to chew; **a todo moler** wholeheartedly; **moler a palos** to beat up; *vr* to wear oneself out
molero *m* millstone maker or dealer
molesquina *f* moleskin
molestador -dora *adj* disturbing, annoying; *mf* disturber, annoyer
molestar *va* to molest, disturb; to annoy, bother; to tire, weary; *vr* to be annoyed; to bother; **molestarse con** to bother about or with; **molestarse en** + *inf* to bother to + *inf*, to take the trouble to + *inf*
molestia *f* molestation, annoyance, bother; discomfort, disturbance; unpleasantness, quarrel
molesto -ta *adj* annoying, bothersome; annoyed, bothered; uncomfortable
molestoso -sa *adj* (dial. & Am.) annoying, troublesome
moleta *f* muller; glass polisher; stamp, punch; roller; (print.) ink grinder
moleteado *m* knurl
moletear *va* to knurl
moletón *m* outing flannel, flannelet
molibdato *m* (chem.) molybdate
molibdenita *f* (mineral.) molybdenite
molibdeno *m* (chem.) molybdenum
molibdenoso -sa *adj* (chem.) molybdenous
molíbdico -ca *adj* (chem.) molybdic
molicie *f* softness; flabbiness; fondness for luxury, effeminacy; sensual pleasures
molido -da *adj* worn out, exhausted; see **oro**
molienda *f* grinding, milling; grist; mill; grinding season (*for sugar cane and olives*); (coll.) fatigue, weariness; (coll.) annoyance, bore, bother
molificación *f* softening
molificar §86 *va & vr* to soften
molimiento *m* grinding; fatigue, weariness; discouragement
molinar *m* row of windmills
molinería *f* milling; milling industry; group of mills
molinero -ra *adj* (pertaining to a) mill; for grinding, to be ground; *mf* miller; *f* miller's wife
molinete *m* little mill; ventilating fan; windmill (*paper toy*); turnstile; twirl (*of cane*); brandish, flourish (*of sword*); (hyd.) current meter; (naut.) winch; drum (*of winch*)
molinillo *m* hand mill; chocolate beater; **molinillo de café** coffee grinder
molino *m* mill; grinder; restless person; **luchar con los molinos de viento** to tilt at windmills; **molino harinero** gristmill, flour mill; **molino de sangre** animal-driven mill; hand mill; **molino de viento** windmill (*machine; paper toy*); **molinos de viento** (fig.) windmills (*imaginary enemy*)
Moloc *m* (Bib.) Moloch; (*l.c.*) *m* (zool.) moloch
móloc *m* (Am.) mashed potatoes
molondro or **molondrón** *m* (coll.) lazy lummox
moltura *f* grinding
molusco *m* (zool.) mollusk
molla *f* lean meat; (prov.) soft part of bread
mollar *adj* soft, tender; easily shelled; mushy, pulpy; right, ripe; lean (*meat*); productive, easy; (coll.) gullible, easily taken in
mollear *vn* to give, to yield; to bend
molledo *m* fleshy part (*of leg, arm, etc.*); soft part of bread
molleja *f* gizzard; sweetbread; **criar molleja** (coll.) to grow lazy
mollejón *m* grindstone; (coll.) big fat loafer; (coll.) good-natured fellow
mollera *f* crown (*of head*); brains, sense; head, mind; **tener buena mollera** (coll.) to have a good head on one's shoulders; **cerrado de mollera** stupid; **duro de mollera** (coll.) stubborn, dull
mollero *m* (coll.) lean meat

molleta *f* biscuit; brown bread; **molletas** *fpl* snuffers
mollete *m* muffin, French roll; chubby cheek; fleshy part (*of arm*)
molletudo -da *adj* var. of **mofletudo**
mollificar §86 *va* var. of **molificar**
mollino -na *adj* drizzly; *f* drizzle
mollizna *f* drizzle
molliznar or **molliznear** *vn* to drizzle
momentáneo -a *adj* momentary
momento *m* moment; (mech.) moment; **a cada momento** at every moment, all the time; **al momento** at once; **de momento** present; suddenly; for the present; **de un momento a otro** at any moment; **en un momento** in a moment; **por momentos** continuously; any moment, presently; **momento angular** (mech.) angular momentum; **momento de inercia** (mech.) moment of inertia; **momento magnético** (phys.) magnetic moment; **momento psicológico** psychological moment
momería *f* clowning
momero -ra *adj* clowning; *mf* clown
momia *f* see **momio**
momificación *f* mummification
momificar §86 *va* & *vr* to mummify
momio -mia *adj* lean, skinny; *m* extra; bargain; **de momio** free, gratis; *f* mummy
momista *mf* bargain hunter
Momo *m* (myth.) Momus; (*l.c.*) *m* face, grimace, clowning; (coll.) caress, fondling; **hacer momos a** (coll.) to make eyes at (*a woman*)
momórdiga *f* (bot.) balsam apple
mona *f* see **mono**
monacal *adj* monachal
monacato *m* monkhood, monasticism
monacillo *m* altar boy, acolyte
monacita *f* (mineral.) monazite
monacordio *m* (mus.) manichord
monada *f* monkeyshine; monkey face, grimace; darling, cute little thing; cuteness; flattery; piece of foolishness; triviality, childishness
mónada *f* (biol., chem., philos. & zool.) monad
monadélfico -ca *adj* (bot.) monadelphous
monadismo *m* (philos.) monadism
monago *m* (coll.) altar boy, acolyte; **llenar el monago** (coll.) to eat
monaguillo *m* var. of **monacillo**
monandria *f* monandry; (bot.) monandry
monándrico -ca *adj* monandrous
monandro -dra *adj* (bot.) monandrous
monaquismo *m* monachism, monasticism
monarca *m* monarch; **los Monarcas de Oriente** the Wise Men of the East
monarquía *f* monarchy; **monarquía absoluta** absolute monarchy; **monarquía constitucional** constitutional monarchy
monárquico -ca *adj* monarchic or monarchical; *mf* monarchist
monarquismo *m* monarchism
monarquista *adj* monarchist, monarchistic; *mf* monarchist
monasterial *adj* monasterial
monasterio *m* monastery
monasticismo *m* var. of **monacato**
monástico -ca *adj* monastic or monastical
monast.º abr. of **monasterio**
Moncenisio *m* Mont Cenis
monda *f* see **mondo**
mondadientes *m* (*pl:* **-tes**) toothpick
mondador -dora *adj* cleaning; peeling, paring; *mf* cleaner; peeler, parer; *f* peeler, peeling machine
mondadura *f* pruning, trimming; **mondaduras** *fpl* peelings, parings
mondaoídos *m* (*pl:* **-dos**) earpick
mondaorejas *m* (*pl:* **-jas**) var. of **mondaoídos**
mondar *va* to clean; to prune, to trim; to peel, to pare, to hull, to husk; to cut the hair of; (coll.) to fleece; *vr* to lose one's hair (*e.g., after an illness*); to pick (*one's teeth*)
mondarajas *fpl* (coll.) peelings
mondejo *m* stuffed tripe
mondo -da *adj* clean, clear, pure; **mondo y lirondo** (coll.) pure, unadulterated; *f* pruning, trimming; parings, peelings; pruning season; clearing of a cemetery for further burials
mondón *m* stripped tree trunk
mondonga *f* (coll.) kitchen wench
mondongo *m* tripe; (coll.) guts
mondonguería *f* tripe shop
mondonguero -ra *mf* tripe dealer
mondonguil *adj* (coll.) (pertaining to) tripe
monear *vn* (coll.) to be a monkey, to make faces; (Am.) to boast
moneda *f* money; coin; mint; **la Moneda** Santiago, the government of Chile; **pagar en la misma moneda** to pay back in one's own coin; **moneda corriente** currency; (coll.) everyday matter, common knowledge; **moneda falsa** counterfeit; **moneda imaginaria** money of account; **moneda menuda** change; **moneda metálica** or **sonante** metal money, specie; **moneda suelta** change
monedaje *m* coining, minting; seigniorage
monedar or **monedear** *va* to coin, to mint
monedero *m* moneyer; moneybag; change purse; **monedero falso** counterfeiter
monegasco -ca *adj* & *mf* Monegasque
monería *f* monkeyshine; cuteness; triviality, childishness
monesco -ca *adj* (coll.) apish
monetario -ria *adj* monetary
monetización *f* monetization
monetizar §76 *va* to monetize
monfí *m* (*pl:* **-fíes**) (hist.) Moorish highwayman (*in Andalusia*)
mongol -gola *adj* & *mf* var. of **mogol**
mongólico -ca *adj* var. of **mogólico**
mongolismo *m* var. of **mogolismo**
moniato *m* var. of **buniato**
monicaco *m* (coll.) whippersnapper
monición *f* monition; remonstrance
monigote *m* lay brother; rag figure, stuffed form; botched painting, botched statue; (coll.) boob, sap; (fig.) puppet
moniliforme *adj* moniliform; (bot. & zool.) moniliform
monillo *m* waist, bodice
monipodio *m* (coll.) illegal deal, collusion, cabal
monís *f* trinket; **monises** *mpl* (coll.) money, dough
monismo *m* (philos.) monism
monista *adj* monist, monistic; *mf* monist
mónita *f* (coll.) smoothness, slickness
monitor *m* monitor; (hyd., naut. & rad.) monitor; (zool.) monitor, monitor lizard
monitorio -ria *adj* monitorial; monitory; *m* monitory; threat of excommunication; *f* monitory
monja *f* nun; **monjas** *fpl* lingering sparks in a burned piece of paper
monje *m* monk; recluse, anchorite; (orn.) great titmouse; **monje negro** Black Monk (*Benedictine*)
monjía *f* monkhood
monjil *adj* nunnish, nun's; *m* nun's dress; (archaic) mourning dress; angel sleeve
monjío *m* nunhood; taking the veil
mono -na *adj* (coll.) cute, cute little, nice; (Am.) red (*hair*); *m* (zool.) monkey, ape; mimic; (fig.) monkey (*in gestures*); squirt, whippersnapper; coveralls; (taur.) attendant on foot; (Am.) pile of fruit or vegetables (*in a store or market*); **estar de monos** (coll.) to be on the outs; **meter los monos a** (Am.) to scare the life out of; **mono araña** (zool.) spider monkey; **mono aullador, mono chillón** (zool.) howling monkey; **mono de Gibraltar** (zool.) Barbary ape; *f* (zool.) Barbary ape; female monkey; (coll.) copycat, ape; (taur.) guard for right leg; (coll.) drunk (*person*); (coll.) drunkenness; (coll.) hangover; **dormir la mona** (coll.) to sleep it off, to sleep off a drunk; **pillar una mona** (coll.) to go on a jag; **pintar la mona** (coll.) to act important; **quedarse como** or **quedarse hecho una mona** (coll.) to be disconcerted, to lose countenance
monoatómico -ca *adj* monoatomic
monobásico -ca *adj* (chem.) monobasic
monocarpelar *adj* monocarpellary
monocarril *m* var. of **monorriel**
monócero -ra *adj* monocerous; (*cap.*) *m* (astr.) Monoceros
monoceronte *m* or **monocerote** *m* (myth.) unicorn

monocilíndrico -ca *adj* single-cylinder
monoclínico -ca *adj* (cryst.) monoclinic
monocordio *m* (mus.) monochord
monocotiledón *m* (bot.) monocotyledon
monocroico -ca *adj* monochroic
monocromático -ca *adj* monochromatic
monocromía *f* monochromy
monocromo -ma *adj & m* monochrome
monocular *adj* monocular
monóculo -la *adj* monocular (*having only one eye*); *m* monocle; (surg.) monoculus
monocultura *f* (agr.) monoculture, cultivation of a single crop
monodia *f* (mus.) monody
monódico -ca *adj* monodic
monofásico -ca *adj* (elec.) monophase, single-phase
monofilo -la *adj* (bot.) monophyllous
monofisita *mf* (rel.) Monophysite
monofónico -ca *adj* monophonic
monogamia *f* monogamy; (zool.) monogamy
monogámico -ca *adj* monogamic
monogamista *adj* monogamist, monogamistic; *mf* monogamist
monógamo -ma *adj* monogamous; monogamistic; *mf* monogamist
monogenismo *m* (anthrop.) monogenism
monogenista *mf* monogenist
monógino -na *adj* (bot.) monogynous
monografía *f* monograph
monográfico -ca *adj* monographic; special (*course, theme, subject*)
monografista *mf* monographer
monograma *m* monogram
monoico -ca *adj* (bot.) monoecious
monolítico -ca *adj* monolithic
monolito *m* monolith
monologar §59 *vn* to engage in a monologue, to soliloquize
monólogo *m* monologue
monologuista *mf* monologuist
monomanía *f* monomania; **monomanía de grandezas** folie des grandeurs, megalomania
monomaníaco -ca or **monómano -na** *adj* monomaniacal; *mf* monomaniac
monometálico -ca *adj* (chem.) monometallic
monometalismo *m* monometallism
monometalista *adj & mf* monometallist
monomio *m* (alg.) monomial
monono -na *adj* (coll.) sweet, darling, cute
monopastos *m* (*pl:* **-tos**) sheave
monopatín *m* scooter (*child's vehicle*)
monopétalo -la *adj* (bot.) monopetalous
monoplano *m* (aer.) monoplane
monoplaza *m* (aer.) single-seater
monoplejía *f* (path.) monoplegia
monopolio *m* monopoly
monopolista *mf* monopolist
monopolización *f* monopolization
monopolizador -dora *adj* monopolizing; monopolistic; *mf* monopolizer
monopolizar §76 *va* to monopolize
monóptero -ra *adj* (arch.) monopteral
monorriel *m* monorail
monorrimo -ma *adj* monorhymed
monosabio *m* (taur.) costumed ring servant of picador
monosacárido *m* (chem.) monosaccharide
monosépalo -la *adj* (bot.) monosepalous
monosilábico -ca *adj* monosyllabic
monosílabo -ba *adj* monosyllabic; *m* monosyllable
monospastos *m* (*pl:* **-tos**) var. of **monopastos**
monospermo -ma *adj* (bot.) monospermous
monóstrofe *f* monostrophe
monote *m* (coll.) person transfixed (*with amazement, terror, etc.*); (coll.) pedant; (prov.) disturbance, riot
monoteico -ca *adj* monotheistic
monoteísmo *m* monotheism
monoteísta *adj* monotheist, monotheistic; *mf* monotheist
monotipia *f* (print.) monotype (*machine; method*)
monotipista *mf* monotyper
monotipo *m* (print.) monotype (*machine*)
monotonía *f* monotony
monótono -na *adj* monotonous
monotrema *adj & m* (zool.) monotreme
monovalente *adj* (chem. & bact.) monovalent
monóxido *m* (chem.) monoxide
monroísmo *m* Monroeism, Monroe Doctrine
Mons. abr. of **Monseñor**
monseñor *m* monseigneur; (eccl.) monsignor
monserga *f* (coll.) gibberish
monstruo *m* monster; **el monstruo de la naturaleza** Lope de Vega; **monstruo de Gila** (zool.) Gila monster
monstruosidad *f* monstrosity
monstruoso -sa *adj* monstrous
monta *f* mounting; sum, total; stud farm; account, e.g., **de poca monta** of little account, of little importance; (mil.) call to horse
montacargas *m* (*pl:* **-gas**) freight elevator, hoist
montacarros *m* (*pl:* **-rros**) automobile dealer
montada *f* see **montado**
montadero *m* horse block
montado -da *adj* mounted (*on horseback; in position for use; in a setting*); *m* horseman, trooper; *f* port, tongue groove (*of horse's bit*)
montador *m* mounter; horse block; fitter, erector, installer; (mov.) cutter
montadura *f* mounting; harness (*of a riding horse*); setting (*of a precious stone*)
montaje *m* montage; setting up; (mach.) mounting, assembly; (rad.) hookup; **montajes** *mpl* (arti.) mount
montanear *vn* to eat acorns and mast (*said of hogs*)
montanera *f* oak forest, acorn pasture for hogs; feeding of hogs on acorns; acorn-feeding season
montanero *m* forest ranger
montano -na *adj* (pertaining to a) mountain; montane
montantada *f* boasting; crowd, multitude
montante *m* post, upright; strut; transom; broadsword; amount; (arch.) mullion; *f* flood tide
montantear *vn* to wield the broadsword; to boast, to meddle
montantero *m* (archaic) fighter with a broadsword
montaña *f* mountain; forested region; **la Montaña** the province of Santander, Spain; **montaña de hielo** iceberg; **montaña rusa** roller coaster, switchback; **Montañas Rocosas** or **Roqueñas** Rocky Mountains, Rockies
montañero -ra *adj* mountaineering; *mf* mountain climber
montañés -ñesa *adj* (pertaining to a) mountain, highland; mountain-dwelling; (pertaining to) la Montaña; *mf* mountaineer, highlander; native or inhabitant of la Montaña; *m* dialect of la Montaña
montañesismo *m* fondness for mountains
montañeta *f* hill, small mountain
montañismo *m* mountaineering, mountain climbing
montañoso -sa *adj* mountainous
montañuela *f* var. of **montañeta**
montaplatos *m* (*pl:* **-tos**) dumbwaiter
montar *va* to mount; to get on; to ride (*a horse, a bicycle, a person's shoulders, etc.*); to set up, establish (*a service*); to amount to; to cock (*a gun*); to set (*a precious stone*); to cover (*a mare*); to wind (*a clock*); to fine (*for trespassing of cattle, etc.*); (mach.) to mount, to assemble; (elec.) to hook up; (mil.) to mount (*guard*); (naut.) to mount (*a certain number of cannon*); (naut.) to command (*a ship*); (naut.) to round (*a cape*); *vn* to mount; to get on top; to ride; to weigh, be important; **tanto monta** it's all the same; **¡montas!** (coll.) come now!; *vr* to mount; to get on top
montaraz (*pl:* **-races**) *adj* backwoods; wild, untamed; *m* warden, forester
montazgar §59 *va* to collect cattle toll from
montazgo *m* toll for passage of cattle
monte *m* mount, mountain; woods, woodland; obstruction, interference; backwoods, brush, wild country; bank, kitty; monte (*card game*); widow (*in card playing*); (coll.) dirty mop of hair; **andar a monte** (coll.) to take to the woods; (coll.) to be out of circulation; **el monte Ábila** Jebel Musa (*opposite Gibraltar*); **el**

monte Blanco Mont Blanc; **el monte Carmelo** Mount Carmel; **el monte de los Olivos** Mount Olive; **el monte Etna** Mount Aetna; **el monte Olivete** Mount Olivet; **el monte Palatino** the Palatine Hill; **el monte Parnaso** Mount Parnassus; **el monte Pelado** Mount Pelée; **el monte Sinaí** Mount Sinai; **monte alto** forest; **monte bajo** thicket, brushwood; **monte de piedad** pawnshop; **monte de Venus** (anat.) mons Veneris; **monte pío** pension fund (*for widows and orphans*); mutual benefit society; **montes Apalaches** Appalachian Mountains; **montes Balcanes** Balkan Mountains; **montes Grampianos** Grampian Hills; **montes Himalaya** Himalaya Mountains; **montes Laurentinos** Laurentian Mountains; **montes Urales** Ural Mountains

montea *f* hunting, beating the wood (*to rouse game*); stonecutting; (arch.) rise (*of an arch*); working drawing

montear *va* to hunt, to track down; to make a working drawing of; to arch, to vault

montecillo *m* mount, hillock

montenegrino -na *adj & mf* Montenegrin

montepío *m* pension fund (*for widows and orphans*); mutual benefit society

montera *f* cloth cap; skylight; head (*of boiler of a still*); huntress, huntswoman; bullfighter's hat; (naut.) moonsail

monterería *f* cap shop

monterero -ra *mf* cap maker or dealer

montería *f* hunt; hunting; big-game hunting; hunting party; (paint.) hunting scene; **andar de montería** to go hunting

monterilla *f* (naut.) moonsail

montero *m* hunter, huntsman

montés or **montesino -na** *adj* wild (*cat, goat, etc.*)

montículo *m* var. of **montecillo**

montilla *m* montilla (*a pale dry sherry*)

monto *m* sum, total

montón *m* pile, heap; crowd; (coll.) lot, great deal, great many; **a montones** (coll.) in abundance; **a, de** or **en montón** (coll.) together, taken together; **ser del montón** (coll.) to be quite ordinary; **montón de robo** widow (*at cards*); **montón de tierra** (coll.) feeble old person

montonera *f* (Am.) squad of mounted insurgents

montuno -na *adj* wooded; (Am.) rustic; (Am.) wild, untamed

montuoso -sa *adj* woody, wooded; rugged; hilly

montura *f* mount (*riding horse*); seat, saddle; harness (*of a riding horse*); mounting (*of precious stone, gun, telescope, etc*); frame (*of spectacles*); (mach.) mounting, assembly

monumental *adj* monumental

monumento *m* monument

monzón *m & f* monsoon

monzónico -ca *adj* monsoonal

moña *f* doll; mannequin (*lay figure*); ribbon, hair ribbon; bow of ribbons; (coll.) drunk

moño *m* topknot (*of hair, of ribbons; of feathers of certain birds*); top, crest; (Am.) forelock (*of horse*); (Am.) whim, caprice; **moños** *mpl* frippery; **ponerse moños** (coll.) to put on airs

moñón -ñona or **moñudo -da** *adj* topped, crested

moquear *vn* to snivel, to have a runny nose

moqueo *m* sniveling, runny nose

moquero *m* pocket handkerchief

moqueta *f* moquette

moquete *m* punch in the face, punch in the nose

moquetear *va* to punch in the nose; *vn* (coll.) to snivel all the time

moquillo *m* watery discharge (*from nose in cold weather*); (vet.) distemper; (vet.) pip

moquita *f* watery nose

mor *m* love; **por mor de** for love of; because of

mora *f* see **moro**

morabito *m* Mohammedan hermit; Mohammedan hermitage

moráceo -a *adj* (bot.) moraceous

moracho -cha *adj & m* light mulberry (*color*)

morado -da *adj & m* mulberry (*color*); *f* abode, house, dwelling; stay, sojourn

morador -dora *adj* dwelling, living; *mf* dweller, resident

moradux *m* var. of **almoraduj**

moraga *f* sheaf, bundle; fish fry

moral *adj* moral; *m* (bot.) black mulberry (*tree*); *f* morals (*ethics; conduct*); morale (*e.g., of soldiers*); (coll.) moral (*e.g., of a fable*)

moraleja *f* moral (*e.g., of a fable*)

moralidad *f* morality; moral (*e.g., of a fable*); morality play

moralista *m* moralist (*teacher or writer*)

moralizador -dora *adj* moralizing; *mf* moralizer

moralizar §76 *va & vn* to moralize

morapio *m* (coll.) red wine

morar *vn* to live, dwell

moratorio -ria *adj* moratory; *f* moratorium

moravo -va *adj & mf* Moravian

morbidez *f* (paint.) morbidezza

morbididad *f* morbidity (*sick rate*)

mórbido -da *adj* (paint.) soft, delicate, mellow; morbid

morbífico -ca *adj* morbific or morbifical

morbilidad *f* var. of **morbididad**

morbo *m* disease, illness; **morbo comicial** (path.) epilepsy; **morbo gálico** (path.) syphilis; **morbo regio** (path.) jaundice

morbosidad *f* morbidity

morboso -sa *adj* morbid, diseased

morcajo *m* maslin, mixture of wheat and rye

morcella *f* spark from a candle

morciguillo *m* var. of **murciélago**

morcilla *f* see **morcillo**

morcillero -ra *mf* maker or seller of blood puddings; (coll.) gagging actor, adlibber

morcillo -lla *adj* reddish-black (*horse*); *m* fleshy part of arm; *f* black pudding, blood pudding; (coll.) gag (*interpolation by an actor*)

morcón *m* large blood pudding; (coll.) short stocky person; (coll.) sloppy person

mordacidad *f* mordacity; mordancy

mordaga *f* (coll.) drunk, drunkenness

mordaz *adj* (*pl:* **-daces**) mordacious; burning, corrosive; mordant; (fig.) mordacious, mordant, sarcastic

mordaza *f* gag; clamp, jaw; pincers, tongs; pipe vise; (fig.) gag; **poner la mordaza a** to gag (*to silence*); **mordaza dental** (surg.) gag

mordedor -dora *adj* biting; (fig.) biting, sarcastic; *mf* biter

mordedura *f* bite

mordelón *m* (Am.) bribe-taking officer, crooked cop

mordente *m* mordant; (mus.) mordent

morder §63 *va* to bite; to nibble; to snatch; to wear away, wear down; to eat away; to gossip about, to ridicule; (Am.) to graft; *vn* to bite; to take hold; (Am.) to graft

mordicación *f* biting, stinging

mordicante *adj* burning, corrosive; mordant, sarcastic

mordicar §86 *va & vn* to bite, to sting

mordicativo -va *adj* biting, corrosive

mordido -da *adj* wasted, worn; *m* (coll.) nibble, bite; *f* (Am.) bite; (Am.) petty graft, racket

mordiente *m* mordant

mordihuí *m* (*pl:* **-huíes**) (ent.) grub, weevil

mordimiento *m* var. of **mordedura**

mordiscar §86 *va* to nibble at, to gnaw at; to champ; *vn* to nibble, to gnaw away; to champ

mordisco *m* nibble, bite

mordisquear *va & vn* var. of **mordiscar**

moreda *f* (bot.) black mulberry tree; growth of white mulberries

morena *f* see **moreno**

morenez *f* brownness, darkness

morenillo *m* paste of powdered charcoal and vinegar used by sheepshearer to treat cuts

moreno -na *adj* brown, dark brown; dark, dark-complexioned; (coll.) colored; (Am.) mulatto; *mf* (coll.) colored person; (Am.) mulatto; *m* brunet; *f* brunette; brown bread; rick (*of new-mown hay*); (geol.) moraine; (ichth.) moray; (path.) piles

morenote -ta *adj* very dark

morera *f* (bot.) white mulberry (*tree*)

moreral *m* growth of white mulberry trees
morería *f* Moorish quarter; Moorish land
moretón *m* (coll.) bruise, black-and-blue mark
morfa *f* (plant path.) citrus scab
morfea *f* (path.) morphea
Morfeo *m* (myth.) Morpheus
morfema *m* (gram.) morpheme
morfina *f* (chem.) morphine
morfinismo *m* (path.) morphinism
morfinomanía *f* drug habit
morfinómano -na *adj* addicted to drugs; *mf* drug addict
morfogénesis *f* morphogenesis
morfógeno -na *adj* (embryol.) morphogenic
morfología *f* (biol. & gram.) morphology
morfológico -ca *adj* morphologic or morphological
morga *f* foul-smelling juice that oozes from a heap of olives; (bot.) India berry tree
Morgana *f* (myth.) Fata Morgana, Morgan le Fay
morganático -ca *adj* morganatic
moribundo -da *adj* moribund, dying; *mf* moribund, dying person
moriche *m* (bot.) mirity palm
moridero *m* (Am.) unhealthy spot
moriego -ga *adj* Moorish
morigeración *f* moderation, temperance
morigerado -da *adj* moderate, temperate
morigerar *va* to moderate, restrain
morilla *f* (bot.) morel
morillero *m* var. of **mochil**
morillo *m* firedog, andiron
morina *f* (chem.) morin
morir §45 & §17, 9 *va* to die (*e.g., a painful death*); *vn* to die; to die away; **morir ahogado** to drown, to die by drowning; **morir de risa** to die laughing; **morir de viejo** to die of old age; **morir helado** to freeze to death; **morir por** to be crazy about, to pine for; **morir quemado** to burn to death; **morir vestido** (coll.) to die a violent death; *vr* to die; to be dying; to die out; to go to sleep (*said of a leg or arm*); **morirse por** to be crazy about, to pine for; **morirse por** + *inf* to be dying to + *inf*
morisco -ca *adj* Morisco, Moorish; *mf* Moor converted to Christianity (*after the Reconquest*); (Am.) Morisco (*offspring of mulatto and Spaniard*)
morisma *f* Mohammedanism; Moors, crowd of Moors
morisqueta *f* Moorish trick; mean trick; unsalted boiled rice
morito *m* (orn.) glossy ibis
morlaco -ca *adj* acting silly or ignorant; *m* (taur.) bull, big bull; **morlacos** *mpl* (Am.) dough, cash
morlón -lona *adj* acting silly or ignorant
mormón -mona *mf* Mormon; *m* (zool.) mormon, mandrill
mormónico -ca *adj* Mormon
mormonismo *m* Mormonism
moro -ra *adj* Moorish; Moslem; unbaptized; (coll.) unwatered (*wine*); dappled, spotted (*horse*); *mf* Moor; Moslem; Moro (*Mohammedan Malay of Philippine Islands*); **moro de paz** peaceful person; **moros en la costa** (coll.) trouble in the offing; *f* black mulberry (*fruit*); white mulberry (*fruit*); blackberry, brambleberry (*fruit*); (law) delay
morocada *f* butt of a ram
morocho -cha *adj* (Am.) strong, robust; (Am.) dark
morojo *m* fruit of strawberry tree
morón *m* mound, knoll; moron
moroncho -cha *adj* var. of **morondo**
morondanga *f* (coll.) hodgepodge
morondo -da *adj* stripped, bare (*of hair, leaves, etc.*)
morónico -ca *adj* moronic
moronismo *m* moronism
morosidad *f* slowness, tardiness; delinquency
moroso -sa *adj* slow, tardy, dilatory; delinquent
morquera *f* (bot.) winter savory
morra *f* top, crown (*of head*); mora (*game*); purr (*of cat*); **andar a la morra** (coll.) to come to blows; *interj* here pussy!
morrada *f* butt, butting; punch, slap
morral *m* nose bag; knapsack; game bag; wallet (*bag for traveling*); (coll.) boor, rustic
morralla *f* small fish; rabble, trash
morrillo *m* boulder; fat of neck (*of an animal*); (coll.) thick neck
morriña *f* (vet.) dropsy; (coll.) blues, melancholy, loneliness; **morriña de la tierra** (coll.) homesickness; **morriña negra** (vet.) blackleg
morriñoso -sa *adj* rachitic, sickly; (coll.) blue, melancholy, lonely
morrión *m* morion; helmet
morrionera *f* (bot.) wayfaring tree
morro *m* knob; knoll; pebble; snout; bulwark; ward (*of a lock*); **estar de morro** or **morros** (coll.) to be on the outs; **poner morro** to pucker one's lips, make a snout
morrocotudo -da *adj* (coll.) strong, heavy, thick; (coll.) weighty (*matter, business*); (Am.) rich; (Am.) big, enormous; (Am.) monotonous (*writing or work of art*)
morrón *adj* knotted (*flag*); *m* (coll.) crash, collision
morroncho -cha *adj* (prov.) mild, gentle
morrongo -ga or **morroño -ña** *mf* (coll.) cat
morrudo -da *adj* snouted; thick-lipped
morsa *f* (zool.) walrus; (Am.) vise
morsana *f* (bot.) bean caper
mortadela *f* Bologna sausage
mortaja *f* shroud, winding sheet; (carp.) mortise; (Am.) cigarette paper
mortal *adj* mortal; hard, killing, deadly; sure, definitive, conclusive; deathly pale; mortally ill, at death's door; *m* mortal
mortalidad *f* mortality (*mortal nature; death rate*)
mortandad *f* mortality, massacre, butchery
mortecino -na *adj* dead; dying; weak, failing; **hacer la mortecina** (coll.) to play dead, play possum
morterada *f* bowlful, batch (*mixed at one time in a mortar*); discharge of a mortar
morterete *m* small mortar (*used for salvos and public festivities*); floating candle
mortero *m* mortar (*bowl; mixture of lime, etc.*); (arti.) mortar; **mortero de trinchera** (arti.) trench gun or mortar
morteruelo *m* noise-making hemisphere (*toy*); fricassee of hog's liver
mortífero -ra *adj* deadly
mortificación *f* mortification
mortificador -dora or **mortificante** *adj* mortifying
mortificar §86 *va & vr* to mortify
mortuorio -ria *adj* mortuary; funeral; *m* funeral
morucho *m* (taur.) young bull with wooden balls on horns
morueco *m* tup, ram
mórula *f* (embryol.) morula
moruno -na *adj* Moorish
morusa *f* (coll.) cash, money
Mosa *m* Meuse
mosaico -ca *adj* Mosaic (*of Moses*); (f.a.) mosaic; *m* tile; paving tile; (aer., f.a., & telv.) mosaic; **mosaico del tabaco** (plant path.) tobacco mosaic; **mosaico de madera** (f.a.) marquetry
mosaísmo *m* Mosaism
mosca *f* (ent.) fly; fly (*used in fishing*); imperial (*beard*); (coll.) cash, dough; (coll.) bore, nuisance; (coll.) disappointment; (Am.) sponger, parasite; **moscas** *fpl* sparks; **aflojar la mosca** (coll.) to shell out, to fork out; **papar moscas** (coll.) to gape, to gawk; **soltar la mosca** (coll.) to shell out, to fork out; **mosca abeja** (ent.) bee fly; **mosca borriquera** (ent.) horse tick; **mosca de burro** or **de caballo** (ent.) horsefly; **mosca de España** (ent.) Spanish fly; **mosca de la aceituna** (ent.) olive fly; **mosca de la carne** (ent.) flesh fly, meat fly; **mosca de las cerezas** (ent.) cherry fruit fly; **mosca de las frutas** (ent.) fruit fly; **mosca del olivo** (ent.) olive fly; **mosca del queso** (ent.) cheese fly; **mosca del vinagre** (ent.) vinegar fly, fruit fly; **mosca de mayo** (ent.) May fly; **mosca de sierra** (ent.) sawfly; **mosca de un día** (ent.) May fly; **mosca mediterránea** (ent.) fruit fly; **mosca muer-**

ta (coll.) hypocrite; **mosca picadora de los establos** (ent.) stable fly; **moscas blancas** snowflakes; **moscas volantes** muscae volitantes, spots before the eyes; *m* (box.) flyweight
moscabado -da *adj & m* var. of **mascabado**
moscarda *f* (ent.) flesh fly; (ent.) blowfly, bluebottle; egg of queen bee
moscardear *vn* to lay eggs (*said of queen bee*)
moscardino *m* (zool.) dormouse
moscardón *m* (ent.) botfly; (ent.) flesh fly; (ent.) hornet; (coll.) bore, annoyance (*person*)
moscareta *f* (orn.) flycatcher
moscarrón *m* var. of **moscardón**
moscatel *m* muscatel (*grape or wine*); (coll.) bore, nuisance
moscella *f* var. of **morcella**
mosco *m* (ent.) mosquito
moscón *m* large fly; (ent.) bluebottle; (ent.) flesh fly; (bot.) maple; (coll.) sly fellow
moscona *f* brazen woman, hussy
mosconear *va* to bore, bother, annoy; *vn* to make a nuisance of oneself
Moscovia *f* Muscovy
moscovita *adj & mf* Muscovite; *f* (mineral.) muscovite
moscovítico -ca *adj* Muscovitic
Moscú *f* Moscow
Mosela *m* Moselle
mosén *m* (prov.) father (*priest*); (obs.) sir (*title given to member of lesser nobility in Aragon*)
mosqueador *m* flyflap; (coll.) tail (*of horse or other animal*)
mosquear *va* to shoo (*flies*); to answer sharply; to beat, to whip; *vr* to shake off annoyances; to take offense
mosqueo *m* chasing flies; resentment
mosquero *m* flyflap, flytrap; fly swatter; flypaper
mosquerola or **mosqueruela** *f* (hort.) muscadine (*pear*)
mosqueta *f* (bot.) Japan globeflower; **mosqueta silvestre** (bot.) dog rose
mosquetazo *m* musket shot, musket wound
mosquete *m* musket
mosquetería *f* musketry (*troops; shooting*)
mosquetero *m* musketeer; (theat.) spectator with standing room in pit
mosquetón *m* snap hook, spring hook
mosquil or **mosquino -na** *adj* (pertaining to a) fly
mosquitera *f* or **mosquitero** *m* mosquito net or netting; fly net
mosquito *m* (ent.) mosquito; gnat; (coll.) tippler
mostacera *f* or **mostacero** *m* mustard pot
mostacilla *f* mustard-seed shot; tiny bead
mostacho *m* mustache; (coll.) spot on the face; (naut.) shroud (*of bowsprit*)
mostachón *m* macaroon
mostachoso -sa *adj* mustachioed
mostagán *m* (coll.) wine
mostajo *m* (bot.) whitebeam
mostaza *f* (bot.) mustard; mustard seed (*seed; dust shot*); mustard (*powder or paste*); **hacer la mostaza** (coll.) to give a bloody nose to each other (*said of boys*); **subírsele la mostaza a las narices** (coll.) to fly into a rage; **mostaza blanca** (bot.) white mustard; **mostaza de los alemanes** horseradish; **mostaza silvestre** (bot.) charlock
mostazal *m* mustard patch
mostazo *m* (bot.) mustard; strong, sticky must
mostear *vn* to yield must; to put must into vats; to mix must with old wine
mostela *f* (agr.) sheaf
mostelera *f* place where sheaves are stacked
mostellar *m* (bot.) whitebeam
mostillo *m* mustard sauce (*made of must and mustard*)
mosto *m* must (*unfermented juice*); **mosto de cerveza** wort
mostrado -da *adj* accustomed, inured
mostrador -dora *adj* showing, pointing; *mf* shower, pointer; *m* counter (*in a store*); bar; dial (*of clock*)
mostrar §77 *va* to show; *vr* to show; to show oneself to be
mostrear *va* to spot, to splash
mostrenco -ca *adj* unclaimed, ownerless; (coll.) homeless; (coll.) stray (*animal*); (coll.) slow, dull; (coll.) fat, heavy; *mf* (coll.) dolt, dullard
mota *f* speck, mote; burl, knot; hill, rise; fault; (Am.) powder puff
motacila *f* (orn.) wagtail
mote *m* riddle, enigma; device, emblem; nickname; (Am.) stewed corn
motear *va* to speck, speckle; to dapple, mottle
motejador -dora *adj* name-calling; scoffing; *mf* name-caller; scoffer
motejar *va* to call (*someone*) names; to scoff at, to ridicule; **motejar de** to brand as
motejo *m* name-calling; scoffing
motel *m* motel (*roadside hotel for motorists*)
motete *m* (mus.) motet
motil *m* var. of **mochil**
motilar *va* to shear (*the head*)
motilidad *f* (biol.) motility
motilón -lona *adj* hairless; short-haired; *m* (coll.) lay brother
motín *m* mutiny, uprising
motivación *f* motivation; rationalization
motivar *va* to motivate; to explain, to rationalize
motivo -va *adj* motive; *m* motive, reason; (f.a. & mus.) motif, motive; **con motivo de** because of; on the occasion of; **de su motivo** on his own accord; **motivo conductor** (mus.) leitmotif
moto *m* guidepost, landmark; *f* (coll.) motorcycle
motobomba *f* power pump; fire engine, fire truck
motocamión *m* motor truck
motocicleta *f* motorcycle
motociclismo *m* motorcycling
motociclista *mf* motorcyclist
motociclo *m* motorcycle
motocultivo *m* mechanical farming
motocultor *m* power cultivator
motocultura *f* var. of **motocultivo**
motódromo *m* motordrome
motogrúa *f* truck crane
motolito -ta *adj* simple, stupid; **vivir de motolito** to live on others, be a sponger; *f* (orn.) wagtail
motón *m* (naut.) block, pulley; **a rechina motón** stretched to the breaking point (*said of a cable*)
motonáutico -ca *adj* (pertaining to the) motorboat; *f* (art and science of) motorboating
motonautismo *m* (sport) motorboating
motonave *f* motor ship
motonería *f* (naut.) tackle, set of blocks or pulleys
motoneta *f* scooter, motor scooter; light three-wheel truck
motoniveladora *f* motor grader
motopropulsor -sora *adj* (elec.) motor-driven; (aer.) motor-and-propeller (*e.g., unit*)
motor -tora or **-triz** (*pl:* **-trices**) *adj* motor, motive; (anat.) motor; *m* motor; engine; **primer motor** (philos.) prime mover; **motor a chorro** or **a retropropulsión** (aer.) jet engine; **motor cohete** rocket motor; **motor de arranque** (aut.) starter, starting motor; **motor de combustión** combustion engine; **motor de combustión interna** or **motor de explosión** internal-combustion engine; **motor de cuatro tiempos** four-cycle engine; **motor de dos tiempos** two-cycle engine; **motor de gas** gas engine; **motor de inducción** (elec.) induction motor; **motor de jaula de ardilla** (elec.) squirrel-cage motor; **motor Diesel** Diesel engine or motor; **motor fuera de borda** outboard motor; **motor sincrónico** (elec.) synchronous motor; **motor térmico** heat engine; **motora** *f* small motorboat
motor-convertidor *m* (*pl:* **motores-convertidores**) (elec.) motor converter
motor-generador *m* (*pl:* **motores-generadores**) (elec.) motor generator
motorismo *m* motoring; motorcycling; motorcycle racing
motorista *mf* motorist; motorcyclist; motorcycle racer; *m* highway motorcycle policeman; (Am.) motorman, trolley motorman

motorización *f* motorization
motorizar §76 *va* to motorize
motosegadora *f* power mower
motosierra *f* power saw
motovelero *m* (naut.) motor sailer
motril *m* errand boy
mousse *f* (cook.) mousse
movedizo -za *adj* moving; shaky, unsteady; quick, shifting; fickle, inconstant
movedor -dora *adj* moving; *mf* mover
mover §63 *va* to move; to stir; to wag (*tail*); to stir up; to use (*influence, pull*); to abort; **mover a alguien a** + *inf* to move someone to + *inf*, to prompt someone to + *inf*; *vn* to abort, miscarry; to bud, sprout; (arch.) to spring (*said of an arch or vault*); *vr* to move; to be moved
movible *adj* movable; changeable, fickle; (astr.) movable
móvil *adj* movable; mobile; moving; changeable, fickle; *m* moving body; cause, motive, incentive
movilidad *f* mobility; fickleness; susceptibility; transportation
movilización *f* mobilization
movilizar §76 *va, vn & vr* to mobilize
movimiento *m* movement; motion; moving; (f.a. & lit.) movement; (mus.) movement (*tempo*); **en movimiento** in motion; **movimiento browniano** (phys.) brownian movement; **movimiento continuo** perpetual motion; **movimiento de resistencia** resistance movement; **movimiento de vaivén** alternating motion; **movimiento ondulatorio** (phys.) wave motion; **movimiento paralelo** (mus.) parallel motion; **movimiento perdido** lost motion; **movimiento periódico** (phys.) periodic motion; **movimiento perpetuo** perpetual motion
moyana *f* bran biscuit for sheep dogs; (coll.) lie
moyuelo *m* fine bran
moza *f* see **mozo**
mozalbete *m* lad, young fellow
mozallón *m* strapping young workman
mozancón *m* strapping young fellow
mozancona *f* tall buxom lass
mozárabe *adj* Mozarabic; *mf* Mozarab (*Christian in Moslem Spain*)
moznado -da *adj* (her.) disarmed
mozo -za *adj* young, youthful; single, unmarried; *m* youth, lad; servant, waiter; porter; cloak hanger; **buen mozo** or **real mozo** good-looking, good-looking fellow; **mozo de caballerías** o **caballos** stable boy, hostler; **mozo de café** waiter; **mozo de cámara** (naut.) cabin boy; **mozo de campo y plaza** farm-and-house boy; **mozo de ciego** blind man's guide; **mozo de cocina** kitchen hand; **mozo de cordel** public errand boy; **mozo de cuadra** stable boy; **mozo de cuerda** public errand boy; **mozo de espada** bullfighter's servant; **mozo de espuelas** groom who walks in front of master's horse; **mozo de esquina** public errand boy; **mozo de estación** station porter; **mozo de estoques** (taur.) sword handler (*of matador*); **mozo de hotel** bellboy, bellhop; **mozo de paja y cebada** hostler at an inn; **mozo de restaurante** waiter; *f* girl, lass; wench, kitchen wench; mistress; wash bat; last hand, last game; **buena moza** or **real moza** good-looking, good-looking girl or woman; **moza de taberna** barmaid
mozo-faquín *m* (*pl:* **mozos-faquines**) porter
mozuelo -la *mf* youngster; *m* young fellow; *f* young girl
m/p abr. of **mi pagaré**
M.P.S. abr. of **Muy Poderoso Señor**
mr. abr. of **mártir**
m/r abr. of **mi remesa**
mrd. abr. of **merced**
Mro. abr. of **Maestro**
mrs. abr. of **maravedises** & **mártires**
M.S. abr. of **manuscrito**
m.s a.s abr. of **muchos años**
M.SS. abr. of **manuscritos**
mtd. abr. of **mitad**
mu *m* moo (*of cow*); *f* bye-bye (*sleep*); **ir a la mu** to go bye-bye

muaré *m* moire or moiré; *adj invar* moiré
mucamo -ma *mf* (Am.) servant, house servant
múcara *f* (naut.) shoal; (naut.) foul waters
muceta *f* hood (*e.g., of one holding a doctor's degree*); (eccl.) mozzetta
mucilaginoso -sa *adj* mucilaginous
mucilago or **mucílago** *m* mucilage
mucina *f* (biochem.) mucin
mucoide *m* (biochem.) mucoid
mucosa *f* see **mucoso**
mucosidad *f* mucosity; mucus
mucoso -sa *adj* mucous; *f* (anat.) mucosa
mucronato -ta *adj* mucronate
múcura *f* (Am.) water pitcher; (Am.) dolt, thickhead; (Am.) opossum
mucus *m* mucus
muchacha *f* see **muchacho**
muchachada *f* boyish prank, girlish prank; group of boys, group of girls; noisy crowd of youngsters
muchachear *vn* to act like a boy, act like a girl
muchachería *f* boyish prank, girlish prank; noisy crowd of youngsters
muchachez *f* boyishness, girlishness
muchachil *adj* boyish, girlish
muchacho -cha *adj* (coll.) boyish, girlish, youthful; *mf* (coll.) youth, young person; servant; *m* boy; *f* girl; maid; **muchacha de servir** servant girl
muchachón *m* overgrown boy
muchedumbre *f* crowd, multitude; flock (*of persons or things*); mob, rabble
mucho -cha *adj & pron* (*comp & super:* **más**) much, a lot of, a great deal of; a long (*time*); **muchos -chas** *adj & pron pl* (*comp & super:* **más**) many; **mucho** *adv* (*comp & super:* **más**) much, a lot, a great deal; hard; often; a long time; (coll.) yes, indeed; **con mucho** by far; **ni con mucho** or **ni mucho menos** not by a long shot, not by any means; **por mucho que** however much, no matter how much; **sentir mucho** to be very sorry; **ser mucho que no** + *subj* to be unlikely that... not, e.g., **mucho será que no llueva esta mañana** it is unlikely that it will not rain this morning; **mucho más** much more; **mucho que sí** (coll.) yes, indeed, *m* much; **tener en mucho** to hold in high esteem, to make much of; **tener mucho de** to take after
muda *f* see **mudo**
mudable *adj* changeable; fickle, inconstant
mudada *f* (Am.) change of clothes
mudadizo -za *adj* var. of **mudable**
mudanza *f* change; moving; inconstancy, fickleness; figure (*in a dance*); **estar de mudanza** to be moving (*from one house to another*); **hacer mudanza** or **mudanzas** to be changeable; to be fickle (*especially in love*)
mudar *m* (bot.) giant calotropis; *va* to change; to move; to shed, to molt; to change (*one's voice; said of a boy*); *vn* to change; **mudar de** to change (*clothing, location, one's mind, opinion*); *vr* to change; to change clothing or underclothing; to move; to move away; to have a movement of the bowels; **mudarse de** to change (*clothing, location, one's mind, one's opinion, etc.*)
mudéjar *adj* Mudejar; (arch.) Mudejar; *mf* Mudejar (*Mohammedan living under Spanish Christian king*)
mudez *f* dumbness, muteness; prolonged silence
mudo -da *adj* dumb, silent, mute; (gram.) mute (*letter*); (phonet.) voiceless, surd; *mf* mute (*person*); *f* change; change of voice; change of clothes; molt, molting; molting season; cosmetic; nest of birds of prey; **estar de muda** to be changing one's voice (*said of a boy*); **estar en muda** (coll.) to keep mum
mueblaje *m* var. of **moblaje**
mueble *adj* movable; *m* piece of furniture; cabinet (*e.g., of a radio*); **muebles** *mpl* furniture; **muebles de estilo** period furniture
mueblería *f* furniture factory, furniture store
mueblero -ra *adj* (pertaining to) furniture
mueblista *adj* (pertaining to) furniture; *mf* furniture maker, furniture dealer
mueca *f* face, grimace; **hacer muecas** to make faces

muecín *m* var. of **almuecín**
muela *f* millstone; grindstone; water for running a mill; mound, knoll; (anat.) back tooth, grinder; (bot.) grass pea; **haberle salido a uno la muela del juicio** to have cut one's wisdom teeth (*to be shrewd*); **muela cordal** wisdom tooth; **muela de esmeril** emery grinder, emery wheel; **muela del juicio** wisdom tooth; **muela de molino** millstone
muelo *m* stack of grain
muellaje *m* wharfage
muelle *adj* soft; easy, luxurious; *m* spring; pier, wharf, dock; chatelaine (*clasp worn at woman's waist*); (rail.) freight platform; **muelle de válvula** valve spring; **muelle real** (horol.) mainspring
muérdago *m* (bot.) mistletoe (*Viscum album*)
muerdo *m* (coll.) bite; (coll.) bit
muergo *m* (zool.) razon clam; wheat smut
muermo *m* (vet.) glanders; (bot.) muermo (*tree and wood*)
muermoso -sa *adj* glanderous
muerte *f* death; murder; Death (*skeleton with scythe*); **a muerte** to death, to the death; **dar la muerte a** to put to death; **de mala muerte** crummy, not much of a; **de muerte** implacably; hopelessly (*e.g., ill*); **estar a la muerte** to be at death's door; **tomarse la muerte por su mano** to take one's life in one's hands; **muerte civil** civil death, loss of rights; **muerte chiquita** (coll.) nervous shudder
muerto -ta *pp of* **morir** and **matar;** *adj* dead; flat, dull; slaked (*lime*); (elec.) dead; (rad.) dead-end; **estar muerto por** (coll.) to be crazy about; **muerto de** dying of (*e.g., hunger*); *mf* dead person, corpse; *m* dummy (*at cards*); **muertos** *mpl* (coll.) piles (*driven in ground*); **cargar con el muerto** (coll.) to be left holding the bag; **echar el muerto a** to put the blame on; **hacer** or **hacerse el muerto** to play possum; (coll.) to play deaf, to affect ignorance; **levantar un muerto** to vote using the name of a dead person; **tocar a muerto** to toll
muesca *f* notch, nick; (carp.) mortise
muestra *f* sample; sign (*in front of shop, hotel, etc.*); model, specimen; face, dial (*of watch or clock*); sampler; bearing; fag end of cloth (*with name of manufacturer*); set (*of dog in presence of game*); show, sign, indication; (mil.) review; (philately) specimen; **dar muestras de** to show signs of; **estar de muestra** to set (*said of a hunting dog*); **pasar muestra** to check carefully; (mil.) to review
muestrario *m* sample book, collection of samples
muestreo *m* (statistics) sampling
muévedo *m* abortion (*aborted fetus*)
muezín *m* var. of **almuecín**
mufla *f* muffle (*of a furnace*)
muftí *m* (*pl:* **-tíes**) mufti (*Mohammedan legal expounder*)
muga *f* landmark, boundary; spawning; fecundation of roe
mugido *m* moo, low; bellow; roar
mugidor -dora *adj* mooing, lowing; bellowing; roaring
múgil *m* var. of **mójol**
mugir §42 *vn* to moo, to low; to bellow; to roar
mugre *f* dirt, filth
mugriento -ta *adj* dirty, filthy
mugrón *m* (hort.) layer (*of vine*); shoot, sprig, sucker
mugronar *va* (hort.) var. of **amugronar**
mugroso -sa *adj* var. of **mugriento**
muguete *m* (bot.) lily of the valley
muharra *f* var. of **moharra**
mujer *f* woman; wife; **ser mujer** to be a grown woman; **tomar mujer** to take a wife; **mujer de digo y hago** husky woman; **mujer de gobierno** housekeeper; **mujer del arte** or **de mal vivir** prostitute; **mujer de su casa** good manager (*of household*); **mujer fatal** vamp, vampire; **mujer mundana, perdida** or **pública** prostitute; **mujer policía** (*pl:* **mujeres policías**) policewoman
mujercilla *f* woman of no account; sissy
mujeriego -ga *adj* womanly; womanish; fond of women; **ir** or **montar a la mujeriega** or **a mujeriegas** to ride sidesaddle; *m* skirts, flock of women
mujeril *adj* womanly; womanish
mujerío *m* skirts, flock of women
mujerona *f* big strapping woman; matron
mujerzuela *f* woman of no account
mújol *m* (ichth.) mullet, striped mullet
mula *f* mule, she-mule; trash, junk; (Am.) ingrate, traitor; **en mula de San Francisco** on shank's mare; **hacer la mula** (coll.) to shirk, to back down, to back out
mulada *f* drove of mules
muladar *m* dungheap; trash heap; filth, corruption
muladí *m* (*pl:* **-díes**) Spaniard who embraced Mohammedanism
mular *adj* (pertaining to the) mule
mulata *f* see **mulato**
mulatero *m* mule hirer; muleteer
mulato -ta *adj & mf* mulatto; *f* (zool.) grapsoid
mulero *m* mule boy
muleta *f* crutch; prop, support; light lunch; (taur.) muleta (*staff with red flag*); (zool.) unio; **tener muletas** (coll.) to be as old as the hills
muletada *f* drove of mules
muletero *m* var. of **mulatero**
muletilla *f* cross-handle cane; braid frog; pet word, pet phrase; (taur.) muleta (*staff with red flag*)
muletillero -ra *mf* person always using pet words or phrases
muleto *m* young mule
muletón *m* swan's-down
mulilla *f* small mule; (zool.) eleven-banded armadillo; **mulillas de arrastre** (taur.) team of mules that drags dead bull from the arena
mulo *m* mule or hinny; **mulo castellano** mule (*offspring of male ass and mare*)
mulso -sa *adj* honeyed
multa *f* fine
multar *va* to fine
multicelular *adj* multicellular
multicolor *adj* many-colored, multicolored
multicopista *adj* duplicating, copying; *m* duplicator, copying machine
multidentado -da *adj* multidentate
multiempleo *m* (coll.) moonlighting
multifacético -ca *adj* many-sided
multifásico -ca *adj* var. of **polifásico**
multifilar *adj* multiple-wire
multifloro -ra *adj* (bot.) multiflorous, many-flowered
multiforme *adj* multiform
multigrafiar §90 to multigraph
multígrafo *m* multigraph
multigrávida *adj fem* multiparous
multilateral *adj* multilateral (*participated in by more than two nations*)
multilátero -ra *adj* multilateral (*many-sided*)
multimillonario -ria *mf* multimillionaire
multípara *adj fem* multiparous; *f* multipara
múltiple *adj* multiple, manifold; *m* (mach.) manifold; **múltiple de admisión** intake manifold; **múltiple de escape** exhaust manifold
multiplete *m* (phys.) multiplet
múltiplex *adj* (rad. & telg.) multiplex
multiplicable *adj* multipliable
multiplicación *f* multiplication
multiplicador -dora *adj* multiplying; *mf* multiplier; *m* (math.) multiplier
multiplicando *m* (math.) multiplicand
multiplicar §86 *va, vn & vr* to multiply
multíplice *adj* multiple, manifold
multiplicidad *f* multiplicity
múltiplo -pla *adj* multiple, manifold; (elec. & math.) multiple; *m* (elec. & math.) multiple; **mínimo común múltiplo** (math.) least common multiple; **en múltiplo** (elec.) in multiple
multipolar *adj* (anat. & elec.) multipolar or multipole
multiseccional *adj* multisectional, multistage
multitud *f* multitude
multivalvo -va *adj* multivalve
mullido -da *adj* fluffy, soft; ready, all set; *m* soft filling or stuffing (*for cushions, etc.*)

mullir §26 *va* to fluff, to soften; to beat up, to shake up (*a bed*); to ready, to get into shape; (agr.) to loosen (*the earth*) around a stalk; *vr* to become fluffy; to be beaten up or shaken up; **mullírselas a una persona** (coll.) to punish a person; (coll.) to be wise to a person
mullo *m* (ichth.) red mullet; (Am.) glass bead
mundanal *adj* var. of **mundano**
mundanalidad *f* worldliness
mundanear *vn* to be worldly-minded
mundanería *f* worldliness, sophistication; worldly behavior
mundanesco -ca *adj* worldly; *f* worldliness; worldly people
mundanidad *f* worldliness
mundanismo *m* worldliness; cosmopolitanism
mundanista *adj* worldly; cosmopolitan; *mf* worldly person; cosmopolitan
mundano -na *adj* mundane, worldly; loose (*woman*)
mundial *adj* world-wide, world
mundialmente *adv* throughout the world
mundicia *f* cleanness, cleanliness
mundificación *f* cleansing, purification
mundificar §86 *va* to cleanse, purify
mundificativo -va *adj* (med.) cleansing
mundillo *m* arched clotheshorse; cushion for making lace; warming pan; (bot.) cranberry tree, guelder-rose, snowball; world (*e.g., of politics, scholars, etc.*)
mundinovi *m* var. of **mundonuevo**
mundo *m* world; Saratoga trunk; savoir-vivre; (coll.) flock; (bot.) guelder-rose, snowball; **así va el mundo** so it goes; **correr mundo** to travel, go traveling; **desde que el mundo es mundo** (coll.) since the world began; **echar al mundo** to bring into the world; to bring forth, to create; **echarse al mundo** to debauch oneself; to become a prostitute; **el otro mundo** the other world (*future life*); **gran mundo** high society; **medio mundo** (coll.) half the world (*a lot of people*); **morir para el mundo** to give up the world, to go into seclusion; **Nuevo Mundo** New World; **tener mundo** or **mucho mundo** (coll.) to be experienced, be sophisticated; **todo el mundo** everybody; **ver mundo** to travel, to see the world; **mundo elegante** society, high society; **Mundo novísimo** Oceania
mundología *f* worldly experience, worldliness
mundonuevo *m* peep show, portable cosmorama
munición *f* munition, ammunition; supplies; load, charge (*of a gun*); buckshot; **de munición** (mil.) G.I., government issue; (coll.) done hurriedly; **municiones de boca** (mil.) food, provisions; **municiones de guerra** (mil.) war supplies; **munición menuda** bird shot
municionamiento *m* military supplies, ordnance stores
municionar *va* to munition, to supply with ammunition
municionero -ra *mf* supplier; *f* pouch for shot
municipal *adj* municipal; *m* policeman
municipalidad *f* municipality
municipalización *f* municipalization
municipalizar §76 *va* to municipalize
munícipe *m* citizen; councilman
municipio *m* municipality; council, town council
munidad *f* susceptibility (*to infection*)
munificencia *f* munificence
munificente or **munífico -ca** *adj* munificent
muniquense or **muniqués -quesa** *adj* (pertaining to) Munich; *mf* native or inhabitant of Munich
munitoria *f* art of fortification
muñeca *f* (anat.) wrist; doll; (coll.) doll (*tiny woman; pretty but silly girl*); manikin, dress form; stone marker; pounce bag; tea bag; (mach.) puppet; **menear las muñecas** (coll.) to hustle at a job; **muñeca de trapo** rag baby, rag doll; **muñeca parlante** talking doll
muñeco *m* doll (*toy puppet representing a male child or small animal*); puppet, manikin, dummy; effeminate fellow; (coll.) lad, little fellow; (fig.) puppet; **tener muñecos en la cabeza** to have an exaggerated opinion of oneself, to build castles in Spain
muñequear *vn* to fence from the wrist
muñequera *f* bracelet or strap (*for wrist watch*)
muñequería *f* (coll.) overdressing, exaggerated finery; (coll.) flock of youngsters
muñequilla *f* rubbing or polishing rag or bag; (mach.) pin; (mach.) chuck; (Am.) young ear of corn
muñidor *m* beadle; heeler, henchman; author, maker
muñir §25 *va* to summon; (pol.) to fix, to rig
muñón *m* stump (*of amputated limb*); (arti.) trunnion; (carp.) dowel; (mach.) gudgeon, journal; **muñón de dirección** (aut.) steering knuckle
muñonera *f* (arti.) trunnion plate; journal box, bearing
muradal *m* var. of **muladar**
murajes *mpl* (bot.) pimpernel
mural *adj* mural
muralla *f* wall, rampart; **Gran muralla** or **muralla de la China** Chinese Wall
murallón *m* large wall, heavy wall
murar *va* to wall, surround with a wall
murceguillo or **murciégalo** *m* var. of **murciélago**
murciélago *m* (zool.) bat; (ichth.) gurnard
murecillo *m* (anat.) muscle
murena *f* (ichth.) moray
murga *f* foul-smelling juice coming from a heap of olives; (coll.) band of street musicians; (coll.) tin-pan band; **dar murga a** (coll.) to bother, annoy
murgón *m* (ichth.) samlet, parr
múrgula *f* (bot.) morel
muriático -ca *adj* muriatic
muriato *m* (chem.) muriate
múrice *m* (zool.) murex; (poet.) murex, purple
muriente *adj* dying; faint (*e.g., light*)
murino -na *adj & m* (zool.) murine
murmujear *va & vn* (coll.) to murmur
murmullar *vn* to murmur
murmullo *m* murmur; whisper; ripple; rustle; (med.) murmur (*e.g., of heart*)
murmuración *f* gossip, gossiping
murmurador -dora *adj* murmuring; gossiping; *mf* murmurer; gossip
murmurante *adj* murmuring, rippling
murmurar *va* to murmur, to mutter; to murmur at; *vn* to murmur, to mutter; to whisper; to purl, to ripple; to rustle; (coll.) to gossip
murmureo *m* murmuring sound
murmurio *m* murmur; ripple; rustle
muro *m* wall; rampart; **muro de contención** dam; **muro de los lamentos** Wailing Wall; **muro supersónico** sonic barrier
murria *f* see **murrio**
múrrino -na *adj* murrhine
murrio -rria *adj* sad, dejected, sullen, morose; *f* (coll.) sadness, dejection, sullenness
murta *f* (bot.) myrtle; myrtle berry
murtal *m* or **murtela** *f* growth of myrtles
murtón *m* myrtle berry
murucuyá *f* (*pl:* **-yaes**) (bot.) passionflower
murueco *m* var. of **morueco**
musa *f* muse; (*cap.*) *f* (myth.) Muse; **soplarle a uno la musa** (coll.) to be inspired to write verse; (coll.) to be lucky at gambling
musáceo -a *adj* (bot.) musaceous
musaraña *f* (zool.) shrew, shrewmouse; bug, worm; floating speck in the eye; (coll.) misshapen figure; **mirar a las musarañas** (coll.) to stare vacantly; **pensar en las musarañas** (coll.) to be absent-minded; **musaraña de agua** (zool.) water shrew
muscardina *f* (zool.) muscardine
muscaria *f* (orn.) flycatcher
muscarina *f* (chem.) muscarine
muscícapa *f* var. of **muscaria**
muscínea *f* (bot.) bryophyte
musco -ca *adj* dark-brown; *m* (bot.) moss
muscular *adj* muscular
musculatura *f* musculature; muscularity
músculo *m* (anat.) muscle; (zool.) finback, razorback
musculoso -sa *adj* muscular
muselina *f* muslin
museo *m* museum; **museo de cera** waxworks
muserola *f* noseband
musgaño *m* (zool.) white-toothed shrew

musgo -ga *adj* dark-brown; *m* (bot.) moss; **musgo de Irlanda** (bot.) Irish moss; **musgo de Islandia** (bot.) Iceland moss; **musgo de roble** (bot.) oak moss; **musgo marino** (bot.) coralline; **musgo terrestre** (bot.) club moss
musgoso -sa *adj* mossy; moss-covered
música *f* see **músico**
musical *adj* musical
musicalidad *f* musicianship
music-hall *m* cabaret, burlesque show
músico -ca *adj* musical; *mf* musician; **músico mayor** bandmaster; *f* music; band; (coll.) noise, racket; **con buena música se viene** (coll.) that's a fine how-de-do; **con la música a otra parte** (coll.) get out, don't bother me; **música celestial** (coll.) nonsense, moonshine, piffle; **música clásica** classical music; **música coreada** choral music; **música de baile** dance music; **música de cámara** chamber music; **música de campanas** chimes; **música de danza** dance music; **música de fondo** background music; **música de iglesia** church music; **música de programa** program music; **música de salón** chamber music; **música instrumental** instrumental music; **música mundana** music of the spheres; **música negra** jazz music; **música popular** popular music; **música rítmica** music of stringed instruments; **música sacra** or **sagrada** sacred music; **música vocal** vocal music
musicógrafo -fa *mf* musicographer
musicología *f* musicology
musicológico -ca *adj* musicological
musicólogo -ga *mf* musicologist
musiquero *m* music cabinet
musitar *va & vn* to mumble, whisper
musivo *adj masc* mosaic (*gold*)
muslera *f* (arm.) cuisse or cuish
muslim or **muslime** *adj & mf* Moslem, Muslem or Muslim
muslímico -ca *adj* Moslemic, Mussulmanic
muslo *m* (anat.) thigh; drumstick (*of cooked chicken, turkey, etc.*)
musmón *m* (zool.) mouflon
musola *f* (ichth.) smooth hound
musquerola *f* var. of **mosquerola**
mustaco *m* cake made with must
mustango *m* (Am.) mustang
mustela *f* (ichth.) dog shark (*Mustelus vulgaris*); (zool.) weasel
mustio -tia *adj.* sad, gloomy; withered; (Am.) hypocritical
musulmán -mana *adj & mf* Mussulman
muta *f* pack of hounds
mutabilidad *f* mutability
mutación *f* mutation; change of weather, unsettled weather; (theat.) change of scene; (biol. & phonet.) mutation
mutacional *adj* mutational
mutante *m* (biol.) mutant
mutarrotación *f* (chem.) mutarotation
mutilación *f* mutilation
mutilado -da *adj* crippled; *mf* cripple; **mutilado de guerra** war cripple
mutilador -dora *adj* mutilating; *mf* mutilator
mutilar *va* to mutilate; to cripple
mútilo -la *adj* mutilated, armless; incomplete
mutis *m* (theat.) exit; **hacer mutis** (theat.) to exit; to say nothing, to keep quiet
mutismo *m* mutism; silence
mutual *adj* mutual
mutualidad *f* mutuality; mutual aid; mutual benefit society
mutualismo *m* mutualism
mutualista *adj* mutualistic; mutual-benefit-society; *mf* mutualist; member of a mutual benefit society
mutuante *mf* lender
mutuario -ria or **mutuatario -ria** *mf* borrower
mútulo *m* (arch.) mutule
mutuo -tua *adj* mutual; *m* (law) mutuum
muy *adv* very; very much, frequently; too, e.g., **está muy ocupado para poder dedicarse a los deportes** he is too busy to be able to devote himself to sports; very much of a, e.g., **muy mujer** very much of a woman; **muy de noche** late at night; **muy señor mío** Dear Sir
muz *m* (*pl:* **muces**) (naut.) upper extremity of cutwater
muza *f* see **muzo**
muzárabe *adj & mf* var. of **mozárabe**
muzo -za *adj* dead-smooth; *f* dead-smooth file

N

N, n *f* sixteenth letter of the Spanish alphabet; (*l.c.*) *f* (alg.) n (*indefinite number*)
n. abr. of **nacido** & **noche**
n/ abr. of **nuestro**
N. abr. of **Norte**
naba *f* (bot.) rape, cole
nabab *m* or **nababo** *m* nabob
nabal or **nabar** *adj* (pertaining to the) turnip; *m* turnip field
nabería *f* heap of turnips; turnip soup; turnip stand (*e.g., in a market*)
nabí *m* (*pl:* **-bíes**) Moorish prophet
nabicol *m* (bot.) turnip
nabina *f* rapeseed, turnip seed
nabiza *f* rape rootlets; rape oil; **nabizas** *fpl* turnip greens, turnip leaves
nabo *m* (bot.) turnip (*plant and root*); newel (*of winding stairs*); (naut.) mast; root of tail (*of quadrupeds*); **tener la cabeza más pelada que un nabo** to be as bald as a billiard ball; **nabo del diablo** (bot.) water fennel, water dropwort; **nabo de Suecia** (bot.) Swedish turnip; **nabo gallego, gordo** or **redondo** (bot.) rape, cole
Nabot *m* (Bib.) Naboth
Nabucodonosor *m* (Bib.) Nebuchadnezzar
nácar *m* mother-of-pearl, nacre
nácara *f* (Am.) kettle-drum
nacarado -da *adj* mother-of-pearl (*in material or appearance*)
nacáreo -a or **nacarino -na** *adj* mother-of-pearl (*in nature or appearance*)
nacatamal *m* (Am.) meat-filled tamale
nacela *f* (aer.) nacelle; (arch.) scotia; (anat.) fossa navicularis
nacencia *f* growth, tumor
nacer §34 *vn* to be born; to bud, to begin to grow; to arise, take rise, originate, spring up, appear; to dawn; *vr* to bud, to shoot; to split (*said of seams*)
nacido -da *adj* natural, innate; apt, proper, fit; **bien nacido** of noble birth; **mal nacido** lowborn; **nacida** *adj fem* née or nee; *m* human being, offspring; growth, boil
naciente *adj* nascent; incipient, recent; resurgent; rising (*sun*); (chem.) nascent; *m* east; **nacientes** *fpl* source, headwaters
nacimiento *m* birth; origin, growth, beginning; lineage, descent; crèche (*Nativity scene*); spring (*of water*); **de nacimiento** from birth
nación *f* nation; **de nación** by birth; from birth; **la nación más favorecida** (dipl.) most favored nation; **naciones del Eje** Axis nations; **Naciones Unidas** United Nations; **nación miembro** (*pl:* **naciones miembros**) member nation
nacional *adj* national; domestic (*product*); *mf* national; *m* militiaman
nacionalidad *f* nationality
nacionalismo *m* nationalism
nacionalista *adj* nationalist, nationalistic; *mf* nationalist
nacionalización *f* nationalization
nacionalizar §76 *va* to nationalize; to naturalize
nacionalsocialismo *m* National Socialism
nacionalsocialista *adj* & *mf* National Socialist
nacista *adj* & *mf* Nazi
naco *m* (Am.) rolled leaf of tobacco
nacrita *f* (mineral.) kaolinite
nacho -cha *adj* snub-nosed
nada *f* nothingness; *pron indef* nothing, not anything; very little; **de nada** don't mention it, you're welcome; **en nada** almost; *adv* not at all; well then; **nada más** only; **nada menos que** not less than
nadada *f* (Am.) swim
nadaderas *fpl* water bladder, water wings
nadadero *m* swimming place
nadador -dora *adj* swimming, floating; *mf* swimmer; *m* (Am.) float (*to hold up fishing nets*)
nadar *vn* to swim; to float; to fit loosely or too loosely; **nadar en** to revel in; **nadar en riqueza** to be rolling in wealth; **nadar en suspiros** to be full of sighs; **nadar entre dos aguas** to swim under water, to float under the surface; to carry water on both shoulders
nadear *va* to destroy, wipe out
nadería *f* trifle
nadie *m* nobody (*person of no importance*); **ser un don nadie** (coll.) to be a nonentity; *pron indef* nobody, not anybody, no one
nadir *m* (astr. & fig.) nadir
nado; a nado swimming, floating; **pasar a nado** to swim across
nafa *f* orange flower
nafta *f* naphtha; (Am.) gasoline
Naftalí *m* (Bib.) Naphtali
naftaleno *m* or **naftalina** *f* (chem.) naphthalene or naphthaline
naftol *m* (chem.) naphthol
nagual *m* (Am.) sorcerer, wizard; (Am.) inseparable companion (*said of an animal*)
naguas *fpl* petticoat
Nahúm *m* (Bib.) Nahum
naife *m* diamond of the first water
naipe *m* playing card; deck of cards; **naipes** *mpl* cards (*game*); **cortar el naipe** to cut the cards; **darle a uno el naipe** (coll.) to have good luck, to be a lucky player; **darle a uno el naipe por** (coll.) to have a knack for, e.g., **no le da el naipe por el tenis** he does not have a knack for tennis; **jugar a los naipes** to play cards; **pandillar el naipe** (slang) to stack the cards; **tener buen naipe** to be lucky (*in gambling*); **tener mal naipe** to be unlucky (*in gambling*); **naipe de figura** face card
naipesco -ca *adj* card, pertaining to cards
naire *m* mahout, elephant keeper
naja *f* (zool.) naja; **salir de naja** (slang) to scram, to beat it
nalga *f* buttock, rump
nalgada *f* shoulder, ham; blow on the buttocks, blow with the buttocks
nalgar *adj* gluteal, pertaining to the buttocks
nalgatorio *m* (coll.) posterior, buttocks
nalgudo -da *adj* with a big posterior
nana *f* (coll.) grandma; (Am.) child's nurse; lullaby, cradlesong
nanear *vn* to waddle
nanquín *m* nankeen or nankin
nansa *f* bow net, bag net; fish pond
nansú *m* nainsook
nao *f* ship, vessel
naonato -ta *adj* born on shipboard
napa *f* (Am.) sheet of underground water
napea *f* (myth.) wood nymph
napelo *m* (bot.) monkshood, wolf's-bane
Napoleón *m* Napoleon; (*l.c.*) *m* napoleon (*coin*)
napoleónico -ca *adj* Napoleonic
Nápoles *f* Naples
napolitano -na *adj* Neapolitan; *mf* Neapolitan (*person*); *m* Neapolitan (*dialect*)
naque *m* pair of strolling comedians
naranja *f* orange; **media naranja** (arch.) cupola; (coll.) sidekick; (coll.) better half; **naranja cajel** Seville or sour orange; **naranja de ombligo** navel orange; **naranja mandarina** mandarin orange; **naranja roja** or **sanguínea** blood orange; **naranja tangerina** tangerine

naranjado -da *adj* orange, orange-colored; *f* orangeade; orange juice; orange marmalade; coarse act or remark, vulgarity
naranjal *m* orange grove
naranjero -ra *adj* orange; orange-sized; *mf* orange vender; *m* (prov.) orange tree
naranjilla *f* green orange for preserving
naranjo *m* (bot.) orange tree; (coll.) boob
Narbona *f* Narbonne
narbonense or **narbonés -nesa** *adj* (pertaining to) Narbonne; *mf* native or inhabitant of Narbonne
narceína *f* (chem.) narceine
narcisismo *m* (psychoanal.) narcissism
narciso *m* (bot.) narcissus; fop, dandy; (*cap.*) *m* (myth.) Narcissus; **narciso trompón** (bot.) daffodil
narcosis *f* narcosis
narcótico -ca *adj* & *m* narcotic
narcotina *f* (chem.) narcotine
narcotismo *m* narcotism
narcotizar §76 *va* to narcotize, to dope
nardo *m* (bot. & pharm.) nard; (bot.) tuberose; spikenard (*of the ancients*); **nardo marítimo** (bot.) sea daffodil
narguile *m* hookah, narghile
narigada *f* (Am.) pinch of snuff
narigón -gona *adj* big-nosed; *mf* big-nosed person; *m* big nose
narigudo -da *adj* big-nosed; nose-shaped; *mf* big-nosed person
nariguera *f* nose ring
nariz *f* (*pl:* **-rices**) nose; nostril; sense of smell; bouquet (*of wine*); **hablar por las narices** to talk through the nose; **sonarse las narices** to blow one's nose; **tabicarse las narices** to hold one's nose; **tener agarrado por las narices** to lead by the nose; **nariz aguileña** aquiline nose; **nariz helénica** Grecian nose
narizón -zona *adj* (coll.) big-nosed
narizota *f* big ugly nose
narrable *adj* narratable
narración *f* narration
narrador -dora *adj* narrating; *mf* narrator
narrar *va* to narrate
narrativo -va *adj* narrative; *f* narrative (*story; skill in storytelling*)
narria *f* sled, sledge; drag (*sledge for conveying heavy bodies*); (coll.) big heavy woman
narval *m* (zool.) narwhal
N.ª S.ª abr. of **Nuestra Señora**
nasa *f* bow net, bag net; fish basket; bread basket; flour box
nasal *adj* & *f* nasal
nasalidad *f* nasality
nasalización *f* nasalization
nasalizar §76 *va* to nasalize
nasardo *m* (mus.) nasard
nasica *f* (zool.) proboscis monkey
naso *m* (coll.) big nose
nástico -ca *adj* (plant physiol.) nastic
nata *f* see **nato**
natación *f* swimming
natal *adj* natal; native; *m* birth; birthday
natalicio -cia *adj* natal; *m* birthday; birth
natalidad *f* natality, birth rate; **natalidad dirigida** planned parenthood
Natán *m* (Bib.) Nathan
Natanael *m* (Bib.) Nathanael
natátil *adj* natant; (bot.) natant, aquatic
natatorio -ria *adj* natatorial
naterón *m* cottage cheese
natillas *fpl* custard
natío -a *adj* natural, native; *m* birth; nature; **de su natío** naturally
natividad *f* birth, nativity; Christmas; Nativity (*festival commemorating birth of Christ, the Virgin Mary, or John the Baptist*)
nativo -va *adj* native; natural; natural-born; innate
nato -ta *adj* born, e.g., **criminal nato** born criminal; *f* cream; élite, best part; skim, scum; **natas** *fpl* whipped cream with sugar; **nata y flor** cream (*e.g., of society*)
natrolita *f* (mineral.) natrolite
natrón *m* (mineral.) natron
natura *f* genital organs; (archaic) nature
natural *adj* natural; native; (mus.) natural; *mf* native; *m* temper, disposition, nature; **al natural** au naturel; rough, unfinished; live (*e.g., program*); **del natural** (f.a.) from life, from nature
naturaleza *f* nature; nationality; genitals, female genitals; temperament, disposition; **segunda naturaleza** second nature; **naturaleza muerta** (f.a.) still life
naturalidad *f* naturalness; nationality
naturalismo *m* naturalism
naturalista *adj* naturalist, naturalistic; *mf* naturalist
naturalización *f* naturalization
naturalizar §76 *va* to naturalize; *vr* to become naturalized; to naturalize (*to live like the natives in a foreign country*)
naturalmente *adv* naturally; of course
naturopatía *f* naturopathy
naufragar §59 *vn* to be wrecked, to sink, to be shipwrecked; to fail
naufragio *m* shipwreck; failure, ruin
náufrago -ga *adj* shipwrecked; *mf* shipwrecked person; *m* (ichth.) shark
náusea *f* nausea, sickness, disgust; **dar náuseas a** to sicken, to disgust; **tener náuseas** to be nauseated, to be sick at one's stomach
nauseabundo -da *adj* nauseous, nauseating, loathsome, sickening
nauseado -da *adj* nauseated, sick
nausear *vn* to nauseate, to sicken, to become disgusted
nauseativo -va or **nauseoso -sa** *adj* var. of **nauseabundo**
Nausica or **Nausícaa** *f* (myth.) Nausicaä
nauta *m* mariner, sailor
náutico -ca *adj* nautical; *f* nautics
nautilo *m* (zool.) nautilus
nava *f* hollow plain between mountains
navacero -ra *mf* gardener in sandy marshland
navaja *f* folding knife; razor; tusk of wild boar; pocketknife, penknife; (zool.) razor clam; (coll.) evil tongue; **navaja de afeitar** razor; **navaja de injertar** grafter, grafting knife, grafting instrument; **navaja de seguridad** safety razor
navajada *f* or **navajazo** *m* slash, gash (*made with folding knife or razor*)
navajero *m* razor case; cloth for cleaning razor; cup for cleaning razor; knife wielder; razor wielder
navajo *m* pool of rain water
naval *adj* nautical; naval; **naval militar** naval
navarro -rra *adj* & *mf* Navarrese; *m* Navarrese (*dialect*); (*cap.*) *f* Navarre
navazo *m* pool of rain water; garden in sandy marshland
nave *f* ship, vessel; aisle (*of a shop, factory, store, etc.*); commercial ground floor; hall, shed, bay, building; **quemar las naves** to burn one's boats; **nave central** (arch.) nave; **nave del desierto** ship of the desert (*camel*); **Nave de San Pedro** Roman Catholic Church; **nave lateral** (arch.) aisle (*of nave*); **nave principal** (arch.) nave
navecilla *f* small ship; (eccl.) navicula (*censer*)
navegabilidad *f* navigability
navegable *adj* navigable (*said of a river, canal, etc.*)
navegación *f* navigation; sea voyage; **navegación a vela** sailing
navegador -dora or **navegante** *adj* navigating; *mf* navigator
navegar §59 *va* to navigate, to sail; *vn* to navigate, to sail; to move about
navegatorio -ria *adj* navigational
navel *f* (*pl:* **-vels**) navel orange
naveta *f* small ship; (eccl.) navicula (*censer*); small drawer
navícula *f* small ship; (bot.) navicula
navicular *adj* navicular, boat-shaped; *m* (anat.) navicular
Navidad *f* Christmas; Christmas time; **contar** or **tener muchas Navidades** to be pretty old; **¡Felices Navidades!** Merry Christmas!
navidal *m* Christmas card
navideño -ña *adj* Christmas, of Christmas
naviero -ra *adj* ship, shipping; *m* shipowner; outfitter

navío *m* ship, vessel; **Navío Argo** (astr.) Argo Navis; **navío de alto bordo** ship of the line; **navío de guerra** warship, ship of war; **navío de línea** ship of the line
náyade *f* (myth.) naiad
nazareno -na *adj* Nazarene; *mf* Nazarene; *m* penitent in Passion Week processions; **el Nazareno** or **el Divino Nazareno** the Nazarene
nazareo -a *adj & mf* Nazarene
Nazaret Nazareth
nazi *adj & mf* Nazi
nazificar §86 *va* to Nazify
nazismo *m* Nazism or Naziism
názula *f* cottage cheese
N.B. abr. of **nota bene**
nébeda *f* (bot.) catnip, catmint
nebí *m* (*pl:* **-bíes**) var. of **neblí**
nebladura *f* (agr.) damage from fog; (vet.) gid
neblí *m* (*pl:* **-blíes**) (orn.) stone falcon, merlin (*Falco aesalon*)
neblina *f* fog, mist
neblinoso -sa *adj* foggy, misty
nebreda *f* juniper plantation
nebrina *f* juniper berry
nebrisense *adj* pertaining to Lebrija; *mf* native or inhabitant of Lebrija
nebular *adj* (astr.) nebular
nebulización *f* nebulization
nebulizar §76 *va & vn* to nebulize
nebulón *m* scheming hypocrite
nebulosa *f* see **nebuloso**
nebulosidad *f* nebulosity, nebulousness; cloudiness; cloud, shadow; gloominess, sullenness
nebuloso -sa *adj* nebulous, cloudy, misty, hazy, vague; gloomy, sullen; (astr.) nebulous, nebular; *f* (astr.) nebula; **nebulosa espiral** (astr.) spiral nebula
necear *vn* to talk nonsense; to foolishly persist
necedad *f* foolishness, stupidity, folly
necesario -ria *adj* necessary; *f* water closet, privy
neceser *m* toilet case; sewing kit; **neceser de belleza** vanity, vanity case; **neceser de costura** workbasket
necesidad *f* necessity; need, want, starvation; urination, defecation; **de** or **por necesidad** of necessity
necesitado -da *adj* necessitous, poor, needy; **estar necesitado de** to be in need of; *mf* poor or needy person
necesitar *va* to require, necessitate; to need; **necesitar** + *inf* to have to, to need to + *inf; vn* to be in need; **necesitar de** to need, be in need of; *vr* to be needed, be necessary
necio -cia *adj* foolish, stupid, crazy; unwise, rash; stubborn, bullheaded; (Am.) touchy; *mf* fool; bullheaded person
necrocomio *m* morgue
necrología *f* necrology
necromancia or **necromancía** *f* necromancy
necromántico -ca necromantic; *m* necromancer
necrópolis *f* (*pl:* **-lis**) necropolis
necropsia or **necroscopia** *f* var. of **autopsia**
necrosis *f* (*pl:* **-sis**) (path. & bot.) necrosis
néctar *m* (myth., bot. & fig.) nectar
nectáreo -a *adj* nectareous
nectarino -na *adj* nectarine; *f* (orn.) honey creeper
nectario *m* (bot.) nectary
necturo *m* (zool.) mud puppy
neerlandés -desa *adj* Netherlandish, Dutch; *mf* Netherlander; *m* Dutchman; Netherlandish or Dutch (*language*); *f* Dutchwoman
nefando -da *adj* infamous, abominable
nefario -ria *adj* nefarious, heinous
nefasto -ta *adj* ominous, fatal, tragic
nefoscopio *m* nephoscope
nefralgia *f* (path.) nephralgia
nefrectomía *f* (surg.) nephrectomy
nefridio *m* (embryol.) nephridium
nefrita *f* (mineral.) nephrite
nefrítico -ca *adj* nephritic
nefritis *f* (path.) nephritis
nefrolito *m* (path.) nephrolith
nefrotomía *f* (surg.) nephrotomy
negable *adj* deniable
negación *f* negation; denial; refusal
negado -da *adj* unfit, incompetent; dull, indifferent
negador -dora *adj* denying; refusing; *mf* denier; refuser
negar §29 *va* to deny; to refuse; to prohibit; to disown, disclaim; to conceal; **negar haber** + *pp* to deny having + *pp; vn* to deny; (Am.) to misfire (*said of firearms*); *vr* to avoid; to refuse; to deny oneself to callers; **negarse a** to refuse (*something*); **negarse a** + *inf* to refuse to + *inf;* **negarse a sí mismo** to deny oneself, to practice self-denial
negativa *f* see **negativo**
negativismo *m* negativism
negativo -va *adj* negative; *m* (phot.) negative; *f* negative; denial; refusal; (phot.) negative
negatrón *m* (chem.) negatron
negligencia *f* negligence
negligente *adj* negligent
negociabilidad *f* negotiability
negociable *adj* negotiable
negociación *f* negotiation; matter, subject
negociado *m* department, bureau; business, affair
negociador -dora *adj* negotiating; *mf* negotiator
negociante *m* dealer, trader, businessman
negociar *va* to negotiate; to dicker for; *vn* to negotiate, to trade, to deal
negocio *m* business; affair, transaction, deal; job, work; profit; (Am.) store; (Am.) kitchen; **evacuar un negocio** to conclude a deal; **hacer su negocio** to look out for oneself
negocioso -sa *adj* businesslike
negondo *m* (bot.) box elder
negra *f* see **negro**
negral *adj* blackish
negrear *vn* to turn black, to be blackish
negrecer §34 *vn* to become black
negrería *f* Negroes, group of Negroes
negrero -ra *adj* slave-trading; (fig.) slave-driving; *mf* slave trader, slave driver; (fig.) slave driver; (Am.) friend of Negroes; *m* slave-trading vessel
negreta *f* (orn.) black scoter; (print.) boldface
negrilla *f* (zool.) black conger eel; (print.) boldface; (plant path.) fumagine
negrillera *f* plantation of elms, elm grove
negrillo *m* (bot.) elm tree; (prov.) blight; (Am.) black silver ore; (Am.) linnet
negrito -ta *mf* Negrito (*member of certain dwarfish Negroid peoples*); *f* (print.) blackface
negro -gra *adj* black; dark; gloomy, dismal; unhappy, fatal, evil, wicked; Negro; (coll.) broke, without means; **pasar las negras** (coll.) to be having a terrible time; *mf* (Am.) dear, darling; *m* black (*color, person*); **negro animal** boneblack; **negro de humo** lampblack; **negro de marfil** ivory black; **negro de platino** platinum black; *f* black (*woman or girl*); (mus.) quarter note; (Am.) honey, sweetheart
negroide or **negroideo -a** *adj* Negroid
negror *m* or **negrura** *f* blackness
negruzco -ca *adj* blackish, dark
neguijón *m* caries, tooth decay
neguilla *f* (bot.) corn cockle; corn cockle seed; (bot.) love-in-a-mist; age mark (*in horse's mouth*); cunning, rascality
neguillón *m* (bot.) corn cockle
negundo *m* (bot.) box elder
Negus *m* (*pl:* **-gus**) Negus (*emperor of Ethiopia*)
Nehemías *m* (Bib.) Nehemiah
neis *m* (geol.) gneiss
nelumbio *m* (bot.) nelumbo
nema *f* seal (*of a letter*)
nematelminto *m* (zool.) nemathelminth
nematocisto *m* (bot.) nematocyst
nematoda *m* (zool.) nematode
neme *m* (Am.) asphalt
nemeo -a *adj* Nemean
Némesis *f* (myth.) Nemesis
nemoroso -sa *adj* woody; sylvan; leafy
Nemrod *m* (Bib. & fig.) Nimrod
nena *f* (coll.) baby (*girl*)
nene *m* (coll.) baby (*boy*); villain
neneque *mf* (Am.) wretch, weakling
nenúfar *m* (bot.) white water lily; **nenúfar amarillo** (bot.) spatterdock, yellow water lily

neo *m* (chem.) neon
neocatolicismo *m* Neo-Catholicism
neocatólico -ca *adj & mf* Neo-Catholic
neocelandés -desa *adj* New Zealand; *mf* New Zealander
neoclasicismo *m* neoclassicism
neoclásico -ca *adj* neoclassic; *mf* neoclassicist
neodimio *m* (chem.) neodymium
neoescocés -cesa *adj & mf* Nova Scotian
neoescolasticismo *m* Neo-Scholasticism
neófito -ta *mf* neophyte
neofobia *f* aversion to the new
neogranadino -na *adj* pertaining to New Granada (*formerly Colombia and Panama*); *mf* native or inhabitant of New Granada
neoguineano -na *adj & mf* New Guinean
neoiterbio *m* (chem.) neoytterbium
neolatino -na *adj* Neo-Latin
neolítico -ca *adj* neolithic
neología *f* neology
neologismo *m* neologism
neologista or **neólogo -ga** *mf* neologist
neomejicano -na *adj & mf* New Mexican
neomenia *f* new moon; first day of the new moon
neomicina *f* (pharm.) neomycin
neón *m* (chem.) neon
neoplasia *f* or **neoplasma** *m* (path.) neoplasm
neoplatonicismo *m* Neo-Platonism
neopreno *m* neoprene
neosalvarsán *m* neosalvarsan
neotenia *f* (biol.) neoteny
neotomismo *m* Neo-Thomism
neoyorquino -na *adj* New York; *mf* New Yorker
neozoico -ca *adj* Neozoic
Nepal, el Nepal
nepalés -lesa *adj & mf* Nepalese; *m* Nepali (*language*)
nepalí *m* Nepali (*language*)
nepente *m* or **nepenta** *f* nepenthe (*magic potion*); (bot.) nepenthe
neperiano -na *adj* Napierian
nepote *m* relative and favorite of the Pope; (*cap.*) *m* Nepos
nepotismo *m* nepotism
neptúneo -a *adj* (poet.) Neptunian
neptúnico -ca *adj* (geol.) Neptunian
neptunio *m* (chem.) neptunium
Neptuno *m* (myth. & astr.) Neptune
nequicia *f* iniquity, perversity
nereida *f* (myth.) Nereid
Nereo *m* (myth.) Nereus
nerol *m* (chem.) nerol
Nerón *m* Nero
nervadura *f* nervation, ribbing; (bot. & ent.) nervure
nerval *adj* nerval
nérveo -a *adj* nerve, nerval
nerviación *f* nervation, nervure
nervino -na *adj & m* nervine
nervio *m* (anat. & bot.) nerve; rib (*of insect's wing*); (fig.) nerve (*physical and mental vigor*); string (*of musical instrument*); (arch.) rib in intrados of a vault; fillet (*rib in back of binding of a book*); (naut.) stay, span rope; **tener nervio** to be steadfast; **nervio auditivo** (anat.) auditory nerve; **nervio ciático** (anat.) sciatic nerve; **nervio medial** (bot.) midrib; **nervio olfativo** (anat.) olfactory nerve; **nervio óptico** (anat.) optic nerve
nerviosidad *f* nervosity; nervousness
nerviosismo *m* nervousness
nervioso -sa *adj* nervous; vigorous, energetic, sinewy; nerve (*tonic; tissue; disease*)
nervosidad *f* nervosity; flexibility, ductility; (bot.) nervation; potency (*of an argument*)
nervoso -sa *adj* var. of **nervioso**
nervudo -da *adj* strong-nerved, vigorous, energetic, sinewy
nervura *f* ribbing, backbone (*of book*); (bot.) nervation
nesciencia *f* nescience
nesga *f* (sew.) gore
nesgar §59 *va* to gore, to cut (*cloth*) on the bias
Neso *m* (myth.) Nessus
néspera *f* (bot.) medlar tree
Néstor *m* (myth.) Nestor
nestoriano -na *adj & mf* Nestorian
neto -ta *adj* pure, clean, neat; (com.) net; *m* (arch.) dado
neuma *m* (mus.) neume; *m & f* (rhet.) expression by nods, signs, or interjections
neumático -ca *adj* pneumatic; *m* tire, pneumatic tire; **neumático acordonado** cord tire; **neumático balón** balloon tire; **neumático de cordones** or **de cuerdas** cord tire; **neumático de recambio** or **de repuesto** spare tire; *f* pneumatics
neumococo *m* (bact.) pneumococcus
neumonía *f* (path.) pneumonia; **neumonía doble** (path.) double pneumonia
neumónico -ca *adj* pneumonic
neumotórax *m* (path. & med.) pneumothorax
neuralgia *f* (path.) neuralgia
neurastenia *f* (path.) neurasthenia
neurasténico -ca *adj & mf* neurasthenic
neurectomía *f* (surg.) neurectomy
neuritis *f* (path.) neuritis
neurocirugía *f* neurosurgery
neuroglia *f* (anat.) neuroglia
neurología *f* neurology
neurológico -ca *adj* neurological
neurólogo -ga *mf* neurologist
neurona *f* (anat.) neuron or neurone
neurópata *mf* neuropath
neuropatía *f* neuropathy
neuropático -ca *adj* neuropathic
neuropsiquiatría *f* neuropsychiatry
neuroquirúrgico -ca *adj* neurosurgical
neurosis *f* (*pl:* **-sis**) (path.) neurosis; **neurosis de ansiedad** (psychoanal.) anxiety neurosis; **neurosis de guerra** (path.) shell shock
neurótico -ca *adj & mf* neurotic
neutoniano -na or **neutónico -ca** *adj* Newtonian
neutral *adj & mf* neutral
neutralidad *f* neutrality
neutralismo *m* neutralism
neutralista *adj & mf* neutralist
neutralización *f* neutralization
neutralizar §76 *va* neutralize
neutrino *m* (phys.) neutrino
neutro -tra *adj* neuter; neutral (*e.g., in color*); (bot., chem., elec., phonet. & zool.) neutral; (gram.) neuter; (gram.) intransitive
neutrón *m* (phys.) neutron
nevada *f* see **nevado**
nevadilla *f* (bot.) whitlowwort
nevado -da *adj* snow-covered; snow-white; *f* snow, snowfall
nevar §18 *va* to make snow-white; *vn* to snow
nevasca *f* snowfall; snowstorm, blizzard
nevatilla *f* (orn.) wagtail
nevazo *m* snowfall
nevazón *f* (Am.) snowfall
nevera *f* see **nevero**
nevería *f* ice-cream parlor
nevero -ra *mf* ice dealer; ice-cream storekeeper; *m* place of perpetual snow; perpetual snow; *f* icebox, refrigerator; icehouse; **nevera eléctrica** electric refrigerator
nevisca *f* light snowfall, flurry; sleet
neviscar §86 *vn* to snow lightly; to sleet
nevoso -sa *adj* snowy
nexo *m* nexus; *adv* (slang) nix (*no*)
ni *conj* neither, nor; **ni . . . ni** neither . . . nor; **ni . . . siquiera** not even
niacina *f* (chem.) niacin
niara *f* straw rick
nibelungo *m* (myth.) Nibelung
Nicaragua *f* Nicaragua; (*l.c.*) *f* (bot.) balsam apple
nicaragüense or **nicaragüeño -ña** *adj & mf* Nicaraguan
Nicea *f* Nicaea
niceno -na *adj & mf* Nicene
Nicolás *m* Nicholas; **San Nicolás** Saint Nicholas; Santa Claus
nicotina *f* nicotine
nicotínico -ca *adj* nicotinic
nicromo *m* nichrome
nictalopía *f* nyctalopia
nicho *m* niche
nidada *f* nest (*of eggs*); brood, hatch
nidal *m* nest (*where hen lays eggs*); nest egg; haunt; source, basis, foundation
nidificar §86 *vn* to nest, to build a nest or nests

nido *m* nest; haunt; home; source; (fig.) nest (*of thieves, machine guns, etc.*); **caerse de un nido** (coll.) to be an easy mark; **de nido de abeja** honeycomb (*coil, radiator, etc.*)
niebla *f* fog, mist, haze; mildew; (fig.) fog, confusion; **hay niebla** it is foggy; **niebla artificial** smoke screen; **niebla meona** dripping fog
niel *m* niello
nielado *m* nielloing
nielar *va* to niello
nieto -ta *mf* grandchild; *m* grandson; **nietos** *mpl* grandchildren; *f* granddaughter
nietzscheano -na *adj & mf* Nietzschean
nietzschismo *m* Nietzscheism or Nietzscheanism
nieve *f* snow; (telv.) snow (*snowlike pattern*); (poet.) snow (*pure whiteness*); (slang) snow (*cocaine, heroin*); (Am.) water ice; **nieve carbónica** (chem.) carbon dioxide snow
Níger *m* Niger
Nigeria *f* Nigeria
nigola *f* (naut.) ratlin
nigromancia or **nigromancía** *f* necromancy
nigromante *m* necromancer
nigromántico -ca *adj* necromantic; *mf* necromancer
nigua *f* (ent.) chigoe, sand flea
nihilismo *m* nihilism
nihilista *adj* nihilistic; *mf* nihilist
Nilo *m* Nile; **Nilo Azul** Blue Nile
nilón *m* nylon
nimbar *va* to encircle with a halo
nimbo *m* nimbus, halo; (meteor.) nimbus
nimboso -sa *adj* cloudy, stormy, rainy
nimiamente *adv* excessively
nimiedad *f* excess, superfluity; fussiness, fastidiousness; trifle; (coll.) timidity
nimio -mia *adj* excessive; fussy, fastidious; stingy; small, negligible, worthless; (coll.) timid
ninfa *f* (myth., ent. & fig.) nymph; **ninfa marina** mermaid (*expert woman swimmer*)
ninfea *f* (bot.) white water lily
ninfo *m* (coll.) fop, dandy
ninfomanía *f* (path.) nymphomania
ningún *adj indef* apocopated form of **ninguno,** used only before masculine singular nouns and adjectives
ninguno -na *adj indef* no, not any; **de ninguna manera** by no means; *pron indef masc & fem* none, not any; neither, e.g., **ninguna de estas dos formas** neither of these forms; **ninguno** *pron indef* nobody, no one
Nínive *f* Nineveh
ninivita *adj* Ninevitical or Ninevitish; *mf* Ninevite
niña *f* see **niño**
niñada *f* childishness
niñato *m* unborn calf (*of butchered cow*)
niñear *vn* to act like a child
niñera *f* see **niñero**
niñería *f* childishness; trifle
niñero -ra *adj* child-loving, fond of children; *mf* dandler; *f* nursemaid, dry nurse
niñeta *f* pupil (*of the eye*)
niñez *f* childhood; childishness; (fig.) infancy; **segunda niñez** second childhood
niño -ña *adj* young, inexperienced; childlike, childish; *mf* child; **desde niño** from childhood; **niño azul** blue baby; **niño de la piedra** foundling; **niño expósito** foundling; **niño prodigio** infant prodigy; **niño travieso** imp; *m* child, boy; **niño bonito** fop, dandy, playboy; **niño de coro** (eccl.) choirboy; **niño de la bola** child Jesus, bambino; (coll.) lucky fellow; **niño de teta** suckling, babe in arms; **niño explorador** boy scout; **niño Jesús** child Jesus; bambino (*image of baby Jesus*); **niño gótico** fop, dandy, playboy; **niño zangolotino** (coll.) grown boy who passes as a child; *f* child, girl; (anat.) pupil (*of the eye*); **niña exploradora** girl scout; **niña del ojo** (coll.) apple of one's eye
Níobe *f* (myth.) Niobe
niobio *m* (chem.) niobium
nipa *f* (bot.) nipa palm
nipón -pona *adj & mf* Nipponese
níquel *m* (chem.) nickel
niquelado *m* or **niqueladura** *f* nickel plate
niquelar *va* to nickel-plate
niquelina *f* (mineral.) niccolite
niquiscocio *m* (coll.) trifle
nirvana, el nirvana or Nirvana
níscalo *m* (bot.) var. of **mízcalo**
níspero *m* (bot.) medlar (*tree and fruit*); (bot.) sapodilla; **níspero del Canadá** (bot.) shadberry, shadbush; **níspero del Japón** (bot.) loquat
níspola *f* medlar (*fruit*)
nistagmo *m* (path.) nystagmus
nitidez *f* brightness, clearness; sharpness
nítido -da *adj* bright, clear; sharp (*said of a photograph*)
nitón *m* (chem.) niton
nitración *f* (chem.) nitration
nitral *m* niter or saltpeter bed
nitrar *va* to nitrate, to nitrify
nitrato *m* (chem.) nitrate; **nitrato amónico** (chem.) ammonium nitrate; **nitrato de Chile** Chile saltpeter; **nitrato de plata** (chem.) silver nitrate; **nitrato de potasio** (chem.) potassium nitrate
nitrería *f* saltpeter works
nítrico -ca *adj* (chem.) nitric
nitrificación *f* nitrification
nitrificar §86 *va* to nitrify
nitrilo *m* (chem.) nitrile
nitrito *m* (chem.) nitrite
nitro *m* saltpeter, niter (*potassium nitrate*); **nitro de Chile** saltpeter, niter, Chile saltpeter (*sodium nitrate*)
nitrobacterias *fpl* (agr.) nitrobacteria
nitrobenceno *m* or **nitrobencina** *f* (chem.) nitrobenzene
nitrocal *f* nitrolime
nitrocelulosa *f* nitrocellulose
nitrogenado -da *adj* nitrogenous
nitrógeno *m* (chem.) nitrogen
nitroglicerina *f* nitroglycerine
nitrólico -ca *adj* (chem.) nitrolic
nitrómetro *m* nitrometer
nitrosilo *m* (chem.) nitrosyl
nitroso -sa *adj* (chem.) nitrous
nitruro *m* (chem.) nitride
nivel *m* level; **a nivel** at grade; **estar a un nivel** to be on the same footing; **nivel de aire** or **de burbuja** spirit level; **nivel del mar** sea level; **nivel de vida** standard of living
nivelación *f* leveling
nivelada *f* (surv.) sight
nivelador -dora *adj* leveling; *mf* leveler; *f* grader, road scraper
nivelar *va* to level; to even, to make even; to grade; to take the level of, to survey; to balance (*the budget*); *vr* to become level
níveo -a *adj* (poet.) snowy
nivoso -sa *adj* snowy
nixtamal *m* (Am.) corn steeped in lime water to make tortillas
Niza *f* Nice
nizardo -da *adj* (pertaining to) Nice; *mf* native or inhabitant of Nice
N.º abr. of **número**
no *adv* not; no; **¿no?** is it not so?; **¿cómo no?** why not?; of course, certainly; **creer que no** to think not, to believe not; **ya no** no longer; **no bien** no sooner; **no más que** not more than; only; **no sea que** lest; **no . . . sino** only; **no . . . ya** no longer
nobabia *f* (aer.) dope
nobelio *m* (chem.) nobelium
nobiliario -ria *adj* nobiliary; *m* peerage book, peerage list
nobilísimamente *adv super* very or most nobly
nobilísimo -ma *adj super* very or most noble
noble *adj* noble; *m* noble, nobleman; noble (*Spanish and English coin*)
nobleza *f* nobility
noblote -ta *adj* noble, generous
noca *f* (zool.) spider crab
nocaut *m* (box.) knockout
nocedal *m* var. of **noguera1**
nocente *adj* harmful; guilty
noción *f* notion, rudiment
nocivo -va *adj* noxious, harmful
noctambulación *f* noctambulation
noctambulismo *m* noctambulism

noctámbulo -la *adj* nighttime; night-wandering; *mf* nighthawk, night owl; nightwalker
nocturno -na *adj* night, nocturnal; lonely, sad, melancholy; *m* (mus.) nocturne
nocharniego -ga *adj* night-hunting (*dog*)
noche *f* night, nighttime; darkness; **a buenas noches** (coll.) in the dark; **a prima noche** or **a primera noche** shortly after dark; **buenas noches** good evening; good night; **de noche** at night, in the nighttime; **de la noche a la mañana** overnight; unexpectedly, suddenly; **esta noche** tonight; **hacer noche en** to spend the night in; **hacerse de noche** to grow dark; **muy de noche** late at night; **por la noche** at night, in the nighttime; **noche buena** Christmas Eve; **noche de bodas** wedding night; **noche de estreno** (theat.) first night; **noche de uvas** New Year's Eve; **noche intempestiva** (poet.) far into the night; **noche toledana** sleepless night; **noche vieja** New Year's Eve; watch night
nochebuena *f* Christmas Eve; (bot.) poinsettia
nochebueno *m* Christmas cake; Yule log
nocherniego -ga *adj* night-wandering
nochizo *m* (bot.) wild hazel
nodal *adj* nodal
nodo *m* (astr., med. & phys.) node
No-Do *m* (mov.) abr. of **Noticiario y Documentales** newsreel; newsreel theater
nodriza *f* wet nurse; (aut.) vacuum tank; (naut.) tender
nodular *adj* nodular
nódulo *m* nodule; (anat., geol. & min.) nodule
Noé *m* (Bib.) Noah
Noemí *f* Naomi
nogada *f* sauce of ground walnuts and spice for fish
nogal *m* (bot.) English walnut; walnut (*wood*); **nogal ceniciento** or **nogal de Cuba** (bot.) butternut; **nogal de la brujería** (bot.) witch hazel; **nogal negro** (bot.) black walnut
nogalina *f* walnut stain
noguera *f* (bot.) English walnut
noguerado -da *adj* walnut-colored
nogueral *m* walnut grove
nogueruela *f* (bot.) spurge
nómada or **nómade** *adj* nomad, nomadic; *mf* nomad
nomadismo *m* nomadism
nombradamente *adv* expressly
nombradía *f* fame, renown, reputation
nombrado -da *adj* famous, well-known
nombramiento *m* naming; appointment; (mil.) commission
nombrar *va* to name; to appoint; (mil.) to commission
nombre *m* name; fame, reputation; nickname; watchword; (gram.) noun; **dar el nombre** to give the watchword; **del mismo nombre** (elec.) like (*poles of a magnet*); **de nombres contrarios** (elec.) unlike (*poles of a magnet*); **en nombre de** in the name of; **hacerse un nombre** to make a name for oneself; **mal nombre** nickname; **no tener nombre** to be unspeakable; **poner nombre a** to give a name to; to set a price on; **por nombre de** by the name of; **nombre apelativo** or **común** (gram.) common noun; **nombre colectivo** (gram.) collective noun; **nombre comercial** firm name; **nombre de lugar** place name; **nombre de pila** first name, Christian name; **nombre de soltera** maiden name; **nombre postizo** alias; **nombre propio** (gram.) proper noun; **nombre substantivo** (gram.) noun; **nombre supuesto** alias; **nombre y apellido** full name
nomenclador *m* or **nomenclátor** *m* catalogue of names; technical glossary; nomenclator
nomenclatura *f* nomenclature
nomeolvides *f* (*pl:* **-des**) (bot.) forget-me-not; (bot.) German madwort
nómina *f* list, roll; pay roll; **nómina de sueldos** pay roll
nominación *f* naming, nomination; appointment
nominador -dora *adj* nominating; *mf* nominator
nominal *adj* nominal; noun, substantive
nominalismo *m* nominalism
nominalista *mf* nominalist
nominar *va* to name; to appoint
nominativo -va *adj* nominative (*having person's name*); (gram.) nominative; *m* (gram.) nominative
nominilla *f* voucher
nómino *m* nominee
nomparell *m* (print.) nonpareil
non *adj* (math.) odd, uneven; *m* (math.) odd number; **andar de nones** (coll.) to be idle; **estar de non** (coll.) to be unmatched; to be useless; **quedar de non** (coll.) to be alone, to be without a companion
nona *f* see **nono**
nonada *f* trifle, nothing
nonagenario -ria *adj* & *mf* nonagenarian
nonagésimo -ma *adj* & *m* ninetieth
nonágono *m* (geom.) nonagon
nonato -ta *adj* unborn, still nonexistent; ill-born; born by Caesarean operation
noningentésimo -ma *adj* & *m* nine hundredth
nonio *m* vernier; slide rule
nono -na *adj* & *m* ninth; *f* (eccl.) nones; **nonas** *fpl* (hist.) nones
non séquitur *m* non sequitur (*unfounded conclusion*)
nopal *m* (bot.) prickly pear; **nopal castellano** (bot.) Indian fig; **nopal de la cochinilla** (bot.) cochineal fig
noque *m* tanning vat
noquear *va* (box.) to knock out
noquero *m* tanner, leather dresser
norabuena *f* congratulation; *adv* fortunately
Noráfrica *f* North Africa
noramala *adv* var. of **enhoramala**
noray *m* (naut.) bollard, mooring
norcoreano -na *adj* & *mf* North Korean
nordestada *f* northeaster
nordestal *adj* northeast; northeastern; northeasterly
nordeste *m* northeast; northeaster; *adj* northeast; northeastern
nordestear *vn* (naut.) to turn from north toward east (*said of compass*)
nórdico -ca *adj* Nordic; Norse (*e.g., mythology*); *mf* Nordic; *m* Norse (*old Scandinavian language*)
nordista *m* Northerner (*in U.S. Civil War*)
nordoccidental *adj* northwestern
noria *f* chain pump, Persian wheel; Ferris wheel; (coll.) treadmill (*futile drudgery*)
norma *f* norm, standard; rule, regulation, method; (carp. & mas.) square
normal *adj* normal, standard; perpendicular, *f* normal school; perpendicular
normalidad *f* normality, normalcy
normalista *mf* normal-school student
normalización *f* normalization, standardization; regulation
normalizar §76 *va* to normalize, standardize; to regulate
normalmente *adv* normally; perpendicularly
Normandía *f* Normandy
normando -da *adj* Norman; (arch.) Normanesque; *mf* Norman; *m* Norman French (*dialect*); Norseman, Northman
normánico *m* Norman French (*dialect*)
normano -na *adj* & *mf* var. of **normando**
Norna *f* (myth.) Norn
nornordeste *m* or **nornoreste** *m* north-northeast
nornoroeste *m* or **nornorueste** *m* north-northwest
noroccidental *adj* northwestern
noroeste *m* northwest; northwester; *adj* northwest; northwestern
noroestear *vn* (naut.) to turn from north toward west (*said of compass*)
nortada *f* norther, north wind
norte *m* north; north wind; North Pole; North Star; (fig.) lodestar, polestar (*guide*)
norteafricano -na *adj* & *mf* North African
Norteamérica *f* North America
norteamericano -na *adj* & *mf* North American; American (*i.e., of the U.S.A.*)
nortear *vn* (naut.) to steer to the north; (naut.) to turn northerly (*said of the wind*)
norteño -ña *adj* northern
nórtico -ca *adj* northern

noruego -ga *adj & mf* Norwegian; *m* Norwegian (*language*); (*cap.*) *f* Norway
norueste *m & adj* var. of **noroeste**
noruestar *vn* var. of **noroestear**
nos *pron pers & reflex* (used as object of verb) us, to us; ourselves, to ourselves; each other, to each other; *pron pers* (used as object of preposition in Biblical language) us; (fictitious plural, used as subject of verb or object of preposition, by high dignitaries of church and court) we; us
nosocomial *adj* (Am.) (pertaining to a) hospital
nosocomio *m* (Am.) hospital, public-health center
nosotros -tras *pron pers* (used as subject of verb and object of preposition; plural of modesty sometimes used by writers) we; us
nostalgia *f* nostalgia, homesickness
nostálgico -ca *adj* nostalgic, homesick
nota *f* see **noto**
notabilidad *f* notability (*quality; person*)
notabilísimo -ma *adj super* very or most notable
notable *adj* notable, noteworthy; *mf* notable, worthy
notación *f* notation
notar *va* to note, to notice, to annotate; to dictate; to criticize; to discredit
notaría *f* profession of notary; notary's office
notariado -da *adj* notarized; *m* profession of notary
notarial *adj* notarial
notariato *m* title of notary; practice of a notary
notario *m* notary, notary public
noticia *f* news; notice, information; knowledge; notion, rudiment; **una noticia** a news item; **noticia remota** vague notion, vague recollection; **noticias de actualidad** news of the day; **noticias de última hora** late news
noticiar *va* to notify, give notice to; to give notice of
noticiario -ria *adj* (pertaining to) news; *m* up-to-the-minute news; newsreel; (rad.) newscast; **noticiario cinematográfico** newsreel; **noticiario deportivo** sports news; **noticiario gráfico** picture page (*in a newspaper*); **noticiario teatral** theater news, theater page
noticiero -ra *adj* (pertaining to) news; *m* newsman; late news
notición *m* (coll.) big news, wild or fantastic story
noticioso -sa *adj* informed; learned, widely informed; (Am.) (pertaining to) news; (Am.) newsy; *m* (Am.) news item; (Am.) news report
notificación *f* notification
notificar §86 *va* to notify (*to give notice of or to*); to report on; **notificar a una persona una cosa** to notify a person of something
noto -ta *adj* well-known; illegitimate; *m* south wind; *f* note; mark, grade (*in school*); check (*e.g., in a restaurant*); (mus.) note; **caer en nota** to get talked about, to cause a scandal; **tomar nota de** to take note of; **nota de adorno** (mus.) grace note; **nota marginal** marginal note; **nota tónica** (mus.) keynote
notocordio *m* (biol.) notochord
notoriedad *f* notoriety (*being well known or famous*)
notorio -ria *adj* notorious (*well-known*); evident, manifest
nóumeno *m* (philos.) noumenon
nov. abr. of **noviembre**
nova *f* (astr.) nova
novación *f* (law) novation
novador -dora *adj* innovating; *mf* innovator
noval *adj* newly broken (*said of land*)
novar *va* (law) to novate
novatada *f* hazing; beginner's blunder
novato -ta *adj* beginning; *mf* beginner; freshman
novator -tora *mf* innovator
novecientos -tas *adj & m* nine hundred
novedad *f* newness, novelty; surprise; happening; news; change; inconstancy; failing health; **novedades** *fpl* fashions; **hacer novedad** to unexpectedly cause great surprise; to make drastic changes; **sin novedad** as usual; without anything happening; safe; well
novedoso -sa *adj* novel; innovating; (Am.) fictional
novel *adj* new, inexperienced, beginning; *m* beginner
novela *f* novel, romance; story, lie; **novela caballista** cowboy story, novel of western life; **novela de clave** roman à clef; **novela policíaca** or **policial** detective story; **novela por entregas** serial
novelador -dora *mf* novelist
novelar *va* to novelize; *vn* to write novels; to tell stories
novelería *f* curiosity; fondness for fiction; worthless fiction
novelero -ra *adj* curious, fond of novelty; fond of fiction; gossipy; inconstant, fickle
novelesco -ca *adj* novelistic; fictional; like a novel, romantic, fantastic
novelista *mf* novelist
novelístico -ca *adj* fictional, (pertaining to the) novel; *f* fiction, novel; treatise on the novel
novelizar §76 *va* to novelize, to fictionalize
novembrino -na *adj* (pertaining to) November
noveno -na *adj & m* ninth; *f* (eccl.) novena
noventa *adj & m* ninety
noventavo -va *adj & m* ninetieth
noventón -tona *adj & mf* nonagenarian
novia *f* fiancée; bride; **novia de guerra** war bride
noviazgo *m* engagement, courtship
noviciado *m* novitiate, apprenticeship; (eccl.) novitiate
novicio -cia *adj* inexperienced, beginning; *mf* novice, beginner, apprentice; (eccl.) novice
noviembre *m* November
novilunio *m* new moon
novilla *f* heifer
novillada *f* drove of young cattle; fight with young bulls
novillero *m* herdsman who cares for young cattle; stable for young cattle; pasture ground for young cattle; (taur.) aspiring fighter, untrained fighter; (coll.) truant
novillo *m* young bull; (coll.) cuckold; **novillos** fight with young bulls; **hacer novillos** to play truant
novio *m* suitor; fiancé; bridegroom; **novios** *mpl* engaged couple; bride and groom
novísimo -ma *adj super* newest, latest, most recent; *m* each of the last stages of man: death, judgment, hell, and heaven; **Novísima** *f* revised code of Spanish law (*1805*)
novocaína *f* novocaine
noyó *m* (*pl:* **-yoes**) noyau (*a cordial*)
nro. abr. of **nuestro**
N.S. abr. of **Nuestro Señor**
N.S.J.C. abr. of **Nuestro Señor Jesucristo**
ntro. abr. of **nuestro**
nubado -da *adj* clouded; cloud-shaped; *f* local shower; abundance, plenty
nubarrada *f* var. of **nubada**
nubarrón *m* large black cloud, storm cloud
nube *f* cloud (*fog suspended in air; crowd, multitude, flock; shadow in precious stones; sorrow, gloom*); light lace head scarf; white spot on cornea; **andar** or **estar por las nubes** to be sky-high (*in price*); **poner a uno por las nubes, subir a uno a las nubes** or **hasta las nubes** to praise someone to the skies; **subir a las nubes** to go sky-high (*in price*); **nube correo** scud; **nube de lluvia** rain cloud; **nube de polvo** dust cloud; **nube de verano** summer shower; (fig.) passing annoyance
nubiense *adj & mf* Nubian
núbil *adj* nubile, marriageable
nubilidad *f* nubility, marriageability
nublado -da *adj* cloudy; **está nublado** it is cloudy; *m* storm cloud; impending danger; multitude; abundance; **aguantar el nublado** to suffer resignedly, to take a disappointment resignedly; **descargar el nublado** to rain, snow, or hail hard; to unburden one's anger in explosive words
nublar *va & vr* var. of **anublar**
nublo -bla *adj* cloudy; *m* storm cloud; bunt, wheat smut
nubloso -sa *adj* cloudy; adverse, unfortunate

nubosidad *f* cloudiness; (meteor.) percentage of cloudiness (*at a given time*); (meteor.) cloud rate (*in a given period*)
nuboso -sa *adj* var. of **nubloso**
nuca *f* nape
nucifraga or **nucífraga** *f* (orn.) nutcracker
nucleado -da *adj* (bot.) nucleate
nuclear *adj* (phys.) nuclear
nucleario -ria *adj* nuclear, nucleate
nucleasa *f* (biochem.) nuclease
nucleico -ca *adj* nucleic
nucleína *f* (biochem.) nuclein
nucleínico -ca *adj* nucleic
núcleo *m* core, nucleus; kernel (*of nut*); stone (*of fruit*); (chem.) ring, nucleus; (elec.) core (*of an electromagnet*); (anat., biol. & phys.) nucleus; **núcleo bencénico** (chem.) benzene ring or nucleus
nucléolo *m* (biol.) nucleolus
nucleón *m* (phys.) nucleon
nucleónico -ca *adj* nucleonic; *f* nucleonics
nudillo *m* knuckle; knot in stockings; dowel, plug (*e.g., in a wall*); **dar con la badila en los nudillos a** to rap the knuckles of
nudismo *m* nudism
nudista *mf* nudist
nudo -da *adj* nude, naked; *m* knot; tie, union, bond; crux; node, plot, tangle; difficulty; crisis (*in drama*); juncture, center, point of crossing; (bot.) node; (naut.) knot; **cortar el nudo gordiano** (myth. & fig.) to cut the Gordian knot; **hacérsele a uno un nudo en la garganta** to get a knot in one's throat; **nudo corredizo** slip knot
nudosidad *f* knottiness; knot
nudoso -sa *adj* knotted, knotty
nuecero -ra *mf* walnut vender, nut vender
nuégado *m* nougat
nuera *f* daughter-in-law
nuestrama *f* mistress
nuestramo *m* master
nuestro -tra *adj poss* our; *pron poss* ours; **los nuestros** our friends, our men, our side
nueva *f* see **nuevo**
Nueva Delhi *f* New Delhi
nuevamente *adv* newly, recently; again
Nueva Orleáns *f* New Orleans
Nueva York *m & f* New York; **el Gran Nueva York** Greater New York
Nueva Zelanda *f* New Zealand
nueve *adj* nine; **las nueve** nine o'clock; *m* nine; ninth (*in dates*)
nuevo -va *adj* new; **de nuevo** again, anew; **¿qué hay de nuevo?** what's new?; **nuevo flamante** brand-new; *mf* novice; freshman; *f* news, fresh news
nuevomejicano -na *adj & mf* New Mexican
Nuevo Méjico *m* New Mexico
nuez *f* (*pl:* **nueces**) walnut; nut; Adam's apple; nut or frog (*of violin bow*); **apretar a uno la nuez** (coll.) to choke someone to death; **nuez de agallas** oak gall; **nuez de betel** betel nut; **nuez de cola** kola nut; (pharm.) kola; **nuez de especia** (bot.) nutmeg; **nuez de la garganta** Adam's apple; **nuez de marfil** ivory nut; **nuez dura** (bot.) hickory; hickory nut; **nuez encarcelada** (bot.) pecan (*tree and fruit*); **nuez moscada** (bot.) nutmeg; **nuez vómica** (bot.) nux vomica (*tree and seed*)
nueza *f* (bot.) bryony
nulamente *adv* with no effect
nulidad *f* nullity; incapacity; (coll.) nobody, person of no importance
nulo -la *adj* null, void, worthless
núm. abr. of **número**
Numancia *f* Numantia
numantino -na *adj & mf* Numantine or Numantian
numen *m* deity; inspiration
numerable *adj* numerable
numeración *f* numeration
numerador -dora *adj* numbering; *m* numerator; numbering; (math.) numerator; *f* numbering machine
numeral *adj* numeral
numerar *va* to numerate; to number; to calculate
numerario -ria *adj* numerary; *m* cash, coin, specie
numérico -ca *adj* numerical
número *m* number; lottery ticket; size (*e.g., of shoes*); (gram.) number; **números** *mpl* (poet. & mus.) numbers; **los Números** (Bib.) Numbers; **de número** regular (*said of members of an association*); **el mayor número** most, the majority; **los números centenares** the hundreds (*100, 200, 300, etc.*); **mirar por el número uno** to look out for number one (*oneself*); **sin número** without number, countless; **número arábigo** Arabic numeral; **número atómico** (chem.) atomic number; **número atrasado** back number (*of a newspaper, magazine*); **número cardinal** cardinal number; **número concreto** concrete number; **número de cetano** (chem.) cetane number; **número de guarismo** Arabic numeral; **número de masa** (phys.) mass number **número entero** whole number; **número equivocado** (telp.) wrong number; **número fraccionario** fractional number; **número impar** or **número non** odd number; **número másico** (phys.) mass number; **número mixto** mixed number; **número ordinal** ordinal number; **número par** even number; **número quebrado** fractional number; **número redondo** round number; **número romano** Roman numeral
numeroso -sa *adj* numerous
númida *adj & mf* Numidian
numídico -ca *adj* Numidian
numisma *m* coin, money
numismático -ca *adj* numismatic; *mf* numismatist; *f* numismatics
numulario *m* money broker
nunca *adv* never; **nunca jamás** never more
nunciatura *f* nunciature
nuncio *m* messenger; forerunner, harbinger; nuncio; **nuncio apostólico** nuncio, papal nuncio
nupcial *adj* nuptial
nupcialidad *f* marriage rate, nuptiality
nupcias *fpl* nuptials, marriage; **casarse en segundas nupcias** to marry the second time
nutación *f* (astr. & bot.) nutation
nutra or **nutria** *f* (zool.) otter
nutricio -cia *adj* nutritious, nutritive
nutrición *f* nutrition; (biol.) nutrition
nutrido -da *adj* great, intense, robust, vigorous, steady; full, abounding, rich, heavy
nutrimento or **nutrimiento** *m* nutriment, nourishment
nutrir *va* to nourish, to feed; to fill to overflowing; to supply, to stock; *vr* to be enriched
nutritivo -va *adj* nutritive, nutritious
nutriz *f* (*pl:* **-trices**) wet nurse

Ñ, ñ *f* seventeenth letter of the Spanish alphabet
ñagaza *f* var. of **añagaza**
ñajú *m* (bot.) okra or gumbo
ñámbar *m* (bot.) Jamaica rosewood
ñame *m* (bot.) yam (*vine and root*)
ñandú *m* (*pl:* **-dúes**) (orn.) nandu, American ostrich
ñandutí *m* (Am.) fine Paraguayan linenware
ñangotar *vr* (Am.) to squat, to squat down
ñaño -ña *adj* (Am.) close, intimate; (Am.) spoiled, overindulged; *m* (Am.) elder brother; *f* (Am.) elder sister; (Am.) nursemaid; (Am.) dear
ñapa *f* (Am.) lagniappe, something thrown in; **de ñapa** (Am.) in the bargain
ñaque *m* junk, pile of junk
ñaruso -sa *adj* (Am.) pock-marked
ñeque *adj* (Am.) drooping (*eyes*); (Am.) strong, vigorous; *m* (Am.) energy, pep; (Am.) slap, blow; **tener mucho ñeque** (Am.) to be full of pep
ñilhue *m* (Am.) sow thistle
ñiquiñaque *m* (coll.) trash (*person or thing*)
ñisca or **ñizca** *f* (Am.) bit, fragment
ñoclo *m* macaroon
ñolombre *m* (Am.) old peasant; **¡viene ñolombre!** (Am.) here comes the bogeyman!
ñongo -ga *adj* (Am.) slow, lazy, timid; (Am.) shapeless
ñoñería *f* timid act, whiny remark
ñoñez *f* timid act, whiny remark; timidity, whininess
ñoño -ña *adj* (coll.) timid and whiny; *mf* timid and whiny person
ñorbo *m* (Am.) passionflower
ñu *m* (zool.) brindled gnu, blue wildebeest
ñudillo *m* var. of **nudillo**
ñudo *m* knot
ñudoso -sa *adj* var. of **nudoso**
ñufla *mf* (Am.) good-for-nothing; *m* (Am.) worthless object
ñuñu *m* (bot.) blue-eyed grass
ñuto -ta *adj* (Am.) ground to dust or powder

O, o *f* eighteenth letter of the Spanish alphabet
o *conj* or; **o . . . o** either . . . or
oasis *m* (*pl:* **-sis**) oasis
ob. abr. of **obispo**
obcecación *f* obfuscation
obcecar §86 *va* to obfuscate, blind
obduración *f* obduracy
obedecedor -dora *adj* obeying, obedient; *mf* obeyer
obedecer §34 *va & vn* to obey; **obedecer a** to yield to, be due to, be in keeping with, arise from
obediencia *f* obedience; **a la obediencia** your obedient servant; **dar la obediencia a** to be submissive to
obediente *adj* obedient
obelisco *m* obelisk; (print.) dagger
obencadura *f* (naut.) shrouds
obenque *m* guy; **obenques** *mpl* (naut.) shrouds
obertura *f* (mus.) overture
obesidad *f* obesity
obeso -sa *adj* obese
óbice *m* hindrance, obstacle
obispado *m* bishopric
obispal *adj* episcopal
obispalía *f* palace of a bishop; bishopric
obispar *vn* to become a bishop, to be appointed bishop; to get married (*said of a woman*); *vr* to be disappointed; (coll.) to die
obispillo *m* boy bishop (*boy dressed as a bishop*); rump, croup (*of a fowl*); large pork sausage
obispo *m* bishop; **obispo sufragáneo** suffragan bishop; **obispo universal** Universal Bishop
óbito *m* decease, demise
obituario *m* obituary; (eccl.) obituary
objeción *f* objection
objetante *adj* objecting; *mf* objector; **objetante de conciencia** conscientious objector
objetar *va* to object; to raise (*difficulties, objections, etc.*); to set up, offer, present (*an opposing argument*); **no tener nada que objetar** to have no objections to make
objetividad *f* objectivity
objetivo -va *adj* objective; (gram.) objective; *m* objective (*end, aim*); (opt.) objective
objeto *m* object; subject matter; (gram.) object; **al objeto de** with the object of; **objetos de cotillón** favors (*small gifts such as streamers, noisemakers, hats, toy balloons*)
oblación *f* oblation
oblada *f* offering of bread on the occasion of a requiem
oblato -ta *adj & mf* (eccl.) oblate; *f* (eccl.) oblation
oblea *f* wafer; pill, tablet; **estar hecho una oblea** (coll.) to be nothing but skin and bones
obleera *f* wafer holder or box
oblicuángulo -la *adj* oblique-angled
oblicuar *va* to cant, to slant; *vn* to oblique; (mil.) to oblique
oblicuidad *f* obliquity; **oblicuidad de la eclíptica** (astr.) obliquity of the ecliptic
oblicuo -cua *adj* oblique
obligación *f* obligation; bond; debenture; **obligaciones** *fpl* family responsibilities; **correr obligación a** to be under obligation to
obligacionista *mf* bondholder
obligado -da *adj* obliged, grateful; submissive; (mus.) obbligato; *m* city or town contractor or supplier; (mus.) obbligato
obligar §59 *va* to obligate; to oblige; to force; **obligar a** + *inf* to obligate to + *inf;* to oblige to + *inf*; to force to + *inf;* **obligar a que** or **para que** + *subj* to oblige to + *inf;* to force to + *inf; vr* to obligate oneself, to bind oneself; **obligarse a** + *inf* to obligate oneself to + *inf*
obligatorio -ria *adj* obligatory
obliteración *f* lack of memory; cancellation (*of postage stamps*); (med.) obliteration
obliterar *va* to cancel, to obliterate (*a postage stamp*); (med.) to obliterate
oblongo -ga *adj* oblong
ob.º abr. of **obispo**
oboe *m* (mus.) oboe; (mus.) oboist
oboísta *mf* (mus.) oboist
óbolo *m* mite (*small contribution*)
obpo. abr. of **obispo**
obra *f* work; building, construction; repair work; hearth (*of blast furnace*); **obras** *fpl* construction; repairs, alterations; **buena obra** charity, good works; **meter en obra** or **poner por obra** to undertake, to set to work on; **obra de** a matter of (*e.g., ten minutes*); **obra de consulta** reference work; **obra de El Escorial** (coll.) endless undertaking; **obra de manos** handwork; **obra de romanos** herculean task, Trojan task; immense, lasting piece of work; **obra maestra** masterpiece; **obra muerta** (naut.) rail, freeboard, upper works; **obra pía** charity; religious foundation; (coll.) profit, useful effort; **obra prima** shoemaking; **obras de campo** (fort.) fieldwork; **obra segunda** shoe repairing; **obras públicas** public works; **obra viva** (naut.) quickwork (*submerged part of ship when loaded*)
obrada *f* day's labor, day's plowing; land measure (*varying between 39 and 54 ares*)
obrador -dora *adj* working; *mf* worker; *m* workman; shop, workshop; *f* working woman
obradura *f* charge or pressing of an olive-oil mill
obraje *m* manufacture; mill, woolen mill
obrajero *m* foreman, superintendent
obrar *va* to build; to work, perform; to work (*e.g., wood*); *vn* to work; to act, operate, proceed; to be; to have a movement of the bowels; **obra en mi poder** I have at hand, I have in my possession; **obrar en contra de** to work against
obrepción *f* (law) concealment of the truth
obrepticio -cia *adj* obreptitious
obrera *f* see **obrero**
obrería *f* status of workman; money for church repairs; churchwarden's office or warehouse
obrerismo *m* laborism; labor; labor movement
obrerista *adj* (pertaining to) labor; *mf* laborist, laborite
obrero -ra *adj* working; (pertaining to) labor; *m* workman; worker; churchwarden; **los obreros** labor (*as distinguished from management*); *f* working woman; (ent.) worker
obrero-patronal *adj* labor-management
obrizo -za *adj* pure, refined (*gold*)
obscenidad *f* obscenity
obsceno -na *adj* obscene
obscuración *f* darkness, obscurity
obscurantismo *m* obscurantism
obscurantista *adj & mf* obscurantist
obscurecer §34 *va* to darken; to dim, becloud; to discredit, to dim; to cloud, confuse; (paint.) to shade; *vn* to grow dark; *vr* to grow cloudy, to cloud over; to become dimmed; (coll.) to fade away, fade out
obscurecimiento *m* darkening, obscuration; clouding; fading; (paint.) shading
obscuridad *f* obscurity; darkness; gloominess
obscuro -ra *adj* obscure; dark; gloomy; uncertain, dangerous; (paint.) dark, shaded; **a obscuras** in the dark; (fig.) in the dark; *m* dark; (paint.) dark, shading; **hacer obscuro** to be dark (*because of night or clouds*)
obsecración *f* obsecration
obsecuencia *f* obedience, submissiveness

obsecuente *adj* obedient, submissive
obseder *va* to obsess
obsequiado -da *mf* recipient; guest of honor
obsequiador -dora *adj* fawning; *mf* fawner, flatterer
obsequiante *adj* fawning; *mf* fawner, flatterer; *m* suitor
obsequiar *va* to fawn over, flatter, pay attentions to; to present; to give; to court, to woo
obsequio *m* fawning, flattery, obsequiousness; gift; attention, courtesy; **en obsequio de** in honor of; out of consideration for
obsequiosidad *f* obsequiousness; kindness, courtesy
obsequioso -sa *adj* obsequious; obliging, courteous
observable *adj* observable
observación *f* observation
observador -dora *adj* observant; *mf* observer
observancia *f* observance; deference, respectfulness (*toward elders or superiors*); **poner en observancia** to enforce in a most conscientious fashion
observante *adj* observant
observar *va* to observe
observatorio *m* observatory
obsesión *f* obsession
obsesionante *adj* obsessing, haunting, harassing
obsesionar *va* to obsess
obsesivo -va *adj* obsessive
obseso -sa *adj* obsessed, possessed
obsidiana *f* (mineral.) obsidian
obsidional *adj* (pertaining to a) siege; obsidional (*coins; crown*)
obstaculizar §76 *va* to prevent; to obstruct
obstáculo *m* obstacle
obstante *adj* standing in the way; **no obstante** however, nevertheless; in spite of; **no obstante** + *inf* in spite of + *ger*
obstar *vn* to stand in the way; **obstar a** or **para** to hinder, check, oppose
obstetricia *f* obstetrics
obstétrico -ca *adj* obstetrical; *m* obstetrician; *f* obstetrics
obstinación *f* obstinacy
obstinado -da *adj* obstinate
obstinar *vr* to be obstinate; **obstinarse en** + *inf* to be obstinate in + *ger*, to persist in + *ger*
obstrucción *f* obstruction; (path.) stoppage
obstruccionismo *m* obstructionism
obstruccionista *adj* & *mf* obstructionist
obstructivo -va *adj* obstructive
obstructor -tora *adj* obstructing, obstructive
obstruir §41 *va* to obstruct, to interfere with; to block (*e.g., a doorway*); to stop up (*e.g., a pipe*)
obtemperar *va* to obey, yield to
obtención *f* (act of) obtaining, obtainment, obtention
obtendré *1st sg fut ind of* **obtener**
obtener §85 *va* to obtain; to keep, preserve
obtengo *1st sg pres ind of* **obtener**
obtenible *adj* obtainable
obturación *f* obturation, stopping, plugging
obturador -triz (*pl:* **-dores -trices**) *adj* stopping, plugging; *m* stopper, plug; (aut.) choke; (aut.) throttle; (phot.) shutter, obturator; (surg.) obturator; **obturador de guillotina** (phot.) drop shutter
obturar *va* to obturate, to plug, to stop up; (aut.) to throttle
obtusángulo -la *adj* obtuse-angled
obtuso -sa *adj* obtuse; (fig.) obtuse
obtuve *1st sg pret ind of* **obtener**
obué *m* var. of **oboe**
obús *m* howitzer; shell; plunger (*of tire valve*)
obvención *f* extra, bonus
obvencional *adj* incidental
obverso -sa *adj* obverse
obviar §90 & **regular** *va* to obviate; to remove (*e.g., doubts*); *vn* to stand in the way
obvio -via *adj* obvious; unnecessary
obyecto *m* objection
obyurgación *f* objurgation
oca *f* (orn.) goose; (bot.) oca; royal goose (*game*)
ocarina *f* (mus.) ocarina
ocasión *f* occasion, opportunity, chance; bargain; **aprovechar la ocasión** to improve the occasion; **asir, coger** or **tomar la ocasión por el copete, por la melena** or **por los cabellos** (coll.) to take time by the forelock; **con ocasión de** on the occasion of; **de ocasión** second-hand; **en varias ocasiones** on several occasions
ocasionado -da *adj* dangerous; exposed, subject, liable; annoying, provocative
ocasional *adj* occasional; causal; causing; responsible (*cause*); accidental, incidental
ocasionar *va* to cause, to occasion; to stir up; to endanger
ocaso *m* west; setting (*of a heavenly body*); sunset; decline; end, death
occidental *adj* occidental; western; Occidental; *mf* Occidental
occidentalización *f* westernization
occidentalizar §76 *va* to westernize; to Occidentalize
occidente *m* occident; (*cap.*) *m* Occident
occipital *adj* occipital; *m* (anat.) occipital, occipital bone
occipucio *m* (anat.) occiput
occisión *f* violent death
occiso -sa *adj* killed; *mf* person killed, victim
Oceanía, la Oceania
oceánico -ca *adj* oceanic; *mf* South Sea Islander
Oceánidas *fpl* (myth.) Oceanids
océano or **oceano** *m* ocean; (fig.) ocean (*vast expanse of anything*); (*cap.*) *m* (myth.) Oceanus; **gran Océano** Pacific Ocean; **océano Antártico** Antarctic Ocean; **océano Ártico** Arctic Ocean; **océano Atlántico** Atlantic Ocean; **océano Austral** Antarctic Ocean; **océano Glacial del Norte** Arctic Ocean; **océano Glacial del Sur** Antarctic Ocean; **océano Índico** Indian Ocean; **océano Pacífico** Pacific Ocean
oceanografía *f* oceanography
oceanográfico -ca *adj* oceanographic or oceanographical
oceanógrafo -fa *mf* oceanographer
ocelado -da *adj* ocellate
ocelo *m* (zool.) ocellus (*simple eye of some invertebrates; eyelike spot on wings of certain birds*)
ocelote *m* (zool.) ocelot
ocena *f* (path.) ozena
ociar *vn* & *vr* to idle, to loiter
ocio *m* idleness, leisure; distraction, pastime
ociosidad *f* idleness
ocioso -sa *adj* idle; useless; *mf* idler
oclocracia *f* mob rule, ochlocracy
ocluir §41 *va* (chem. & dent.) to occlude; *vr* (dent.) to occlude
oclusal *adj* (anat. & dent.) occlusal
oclusión *f* (chem., dent., med. & phonet.) occlusion
oclusivo -va *adj* occlusive; *f* (phonet.) occlusive
ocotal *m* (Am.) pine grove
ocote *m* (Am.) ocote pine, torch pine; (Am.) ocote torch
ocozol *m* (bot.) sweet gum
ocre *m* (mineral.) ocher; **ocre amarillo** yellow ocher; **ocre rojo** red ocher
ocroso -sa *adj* ocherous
octaédrico -ca *adj* octahedral
octaedro *m* (geom.) octahedron
octagonal *adj* octagonal
octágono -na *adj* octagonal; *m* octagon
octanaje *m* (chem.) octane number; **de alto octanaje** high-octane
octano *m* (chem.) octane
octava *f* see **octavo**
Octaviano *m* Octavian
octavilla *f* handbill; eight-syllable verse
octavín *m* (mus.) piccolo
Octavio *m* Octavius
octavo -va *adj* eighth; *mf* octoroon; *m* eighth; **en octavo** octavo (*said of a volume*); *f* (mus., pros. & eccl.) octave; (pros.) hendecasyllabic octave, rhymed abababcc
oct.e abr. of **octubre**
octeto *m* (mus.) octet or octette
octillón *m* British octillion
octingentésimo -ma *adj* & *m* eight hundredth
octobrino -na *adj* (pertaining to) October

octogenario -ria *adj & mf* octogenarian
octogésimo -ma *adj & m* eightieth
octogonal *adj* var. of **octagonal**
octógono -na *adj & m* var. of **octágono**
octosilábico -ca *adj* octosyllabic
octosílabo -ba *adj* octosyllabic; *m* octosyllable (*verse*)
octóstilo -la *adj* (arch.) octastyle
octubre *m* October
óctuple *adj & m* octuple
octuplicar §86 *va & vr* to octuple
óctuplo -pla *adj & m* var. of **óctuple**
oculado -da *adj* big-eyed
ocular *adj* ocular; *m* (opt.) eyeglass, eyepiece, ocular
oculista *mf* oculist
oculística *f* ophthalmology
óculo *m* (arch.) oculus, œil-de-bœuf
ocultación *f* occultation; hiding, concealment; (astr.) occultation
ocultante *adj* blinding (*e.g., smoke*)
ocultar *va* to hide, conceal; **ocultar una cosa a** or **de una persona** to hide a thing from a person; *vr* to hide; **ocultársele a uno** to be hidden from one
ocultismo *m* occultism
ocultista *mf* occultist
oculto -ta *adj* hidden, concealed; occult; **de oculto** incognito; stealthily; **en oculto** secretly
ocupación *f* occupation; occupancy; employment
ocupacional *adj* occupational
ocupado -da *adj* busy; occupied; pregnant
ocupador -dora *adj* occupying; *mf* occupier
ocupante *adj* occupying; *mf* occupant; **ocupantes** *mpl* occupying forces
ocupar *va* to occupy; to busy, keep busy; to employ; to bother, annoy; to attract the attention of; *vr* to become occupied; to be busy; to become preoccupied; **ocuparse con, de** or **en** to be busy with, be engaged in; to pay attention to; **ocuparse de** + *inf* to bother to + *inf*, to take the trouble to + *inf*
ocurrencia *f* occurrence; witticism; bright idea; **ocurrencia de acreedores** (law) meeting of creditors
ocurrente *adj* witty
ocurrir *vn* to occur, to happen; to come; to occur (*to come to mind*); **ocurrir a** to have recourse to; **ocurrírsele a uno** + *inf* to occur to one to + *inf*
ochavado -da *adj* eight-sided
ochavar *va* to make eight-sided, to make octagonal
ochavear *vn* (coll.) to be stingy
ochavo *m* octagon, octagonal building
ochavón -vona *mf* (Am.) octoroon
ochenta *adj & m* eighty
ochentavo -va *adj & m* eightieth
ochenteno -na *adj* eightieth; *f* eighty
ochentón -tona *adj & mf* (coll.) octogenarian
ocho *adj* eight; **las ocho** eight o'clock; *m* eight; eighth (*in dates*)
ochocientos -tas *adj & m* eight hundred; **el Ochocientos** the Nineteenth Century
ochotona *f* (zool.) pika
oda *f* ode
odalisca *f* odalisque
odeón *m* odeum
Odesa *f* Odessa
odiable *adj* hateful
odiar *va* to hate
Odín *m* (myth.) Odin
odio *m* hatred; **tener odio a** to hate
odiosidad *f* odiousness, hatefulness; hatred
odioso -sa *adj* odious, hateful
Odisea *f* (myth.) Odyssey; (*l.c.*) *f* (fig.) odyssey
Odiseo *m* (myth.) Odysseus
Odoacro *m* Odoacer
odómetro *m* odometer, taximeter; pedometer
odontalgia *f* (path.) odontalgia, toothache
odontálgico -ca *adj* odontalgic
odontoblasto *m* (anat.) odontoblast
odontoceto -ta *adj & m* (zool.) odontocete
odontología *f* odontology
odontológico -ca *adj* odontological
odontólogo -ga *mf* odontologist
odorante *adj* odorous, fragrant
odorífero -ra *adj* odoriferous
odre *m* goatskin wine bag; (coll.) drunk, drunkard
odrería *f* wineskin shop
odrero *m* wineskin maker or dealer
odrezuelo *m* small wineskin
odrina *f* oxskin wine bag
OEA *f* OAS (*Organization of American States*)
oerstedio *m* (elec.) oersted
oesnoroeste *m* or **oesnorueste** *m* west-northwest
oessudoeste *m* or **oessudueste** *m* west-southwest
oeste *m* west; west wind
Ofelia *f* Ophelia
ofendedor -dora *adj* offending; *mf* offender
ofender *va & vn* to offend; to harm; *vr* to take offense
ofensa *f* offense
ofensivo -va *adj* offensive; *f* offensive; **en la ofensiva** on the offensive; **tomar la ofensiva** to take the offensive; **ofensiva de paz** peace offensive
ofensor -sora *adj* offending; *mf* offender
oferente *adj* offering; *mf* offerer
oferta *f* offer; gift, present; **oferta y demanda** supply and demand
ofertorio *m* (eccl.) offertory
oficial *adj* official; *m* official, officer; skilled workman; clerk, office worker; journeyman; (mil. & nav.) commissioned officer; **oficial de complemento** (mil.) reserve officer; **oficial general** (mil.) general officer
oficiala *f* craftswoman, skilled working woman
oficialía *f* clerkship; status of journeyman
oficialidad *f* officers, body of officers; official nature
oficiante *m* (eccl.) officiant
oficiar *va* to announce officially in writing; to celebrate (*mass*); to officiate at; *vn* (eccl.) to officiate; **oficiar de** (coll.) to act as, behave as
oficina *f* office; pharmacist's laboratory; shop; (fig.) factory (*e.g., of lies*); **oficinas** *fpl* offices (*parts of house devoted to household work*); **oficina de objetos perdidos** lost-and-found department; **oficina matriz** home office
oficinal *adj* (pharm.) officinal
oficinesco -ca *adj* office, clerical; bureaucratic
oficinista *mf* clerk, office worker
oficio *m* office, occupation; rôle, function; craft, trade; memo, official note; (eccl.) office; **buenos oficios** (dipl.) good offices; **de oficio** officially; professional; (sport) professional; **desempeñar el oficio de** to play the rôle of; **Santo Oficio** Holy Office, Inquisition; **tomar por oficio** (coll.) to take to, to keep at; **oficio de difuntos** (eccl.) office of the dead; **oficio público** public office; **oficio servil** common labor
oficiosidad *f* diligence; complaisance, obligingness; officiousness
oficioso -sa *adj* diligent; obliging; officious, meddlesome; profitable; unofficial; (dipl.) officious
ofidio -dia *adj & m* (zool.) ophidian
Ofir *m* (Bib.) Ophir
ofita *f* (mineral.) ophite
Ofiuco *m* (astr.) Ophiucus
ofrecedor -dora *mf* offerer
ofrecer §34 *va* to offer; *vn* to offer; **ofrecer** + *inf* to offer to + *inf; vr* to offer; to offer oneself; to happen; **ofrecerse a** + *inf* to offer to + *inf*
ofreciente *adj & mf* var. of **oferente**
ofrecimiento *m* offer, offering; **ofrecimiento de presentación** introductory offer
ofrenda *f* offering; gift
ofrendar *va* to make offerings of; to contribute, make a contribution of
oftalmía *f* (path.) ophthalmia
oftálmico -ca *adj* ophthalmic
oftalmología *f* ophthalmology
oftalmológico -ca *adj* ophthalmological
oftalmólogo -ga *mf* ophthalmologist
oftalmoscopia *f* ophthalmoscopy
oftalmoscopio *m* ophthalmoscope
ofuscación *f* or **ofuscamiento** *m* obfuscation, blindness, bewilderment, confusion
ofuscar §86 *va* to obfuscate, dazzle, confuse

ogaño *adv* var. of **hogaño**
ogro *m* ogre; (coll.) ogre (*person*)
Oh *interj* O!, Oh!
óhmetro *m* var. of **ohmímetro**
óhmico -ca *adj* ohmic
ohmímetro *m* (elec.) ohmmeter
ohmio *m* (elec.) ohm
oíble *adj* audible
oída *f* hearing; **de** or **por oídas** by hearsay
oídio *m* (bot. & plant path.) oïdium, powdery mildew
oído *m* hearing (*sense*); (anat.) ear; (arti.) vent, priming hole; **abrir los oídos** to lend an ear; **abrir tanto oído** or **tanto el oído** to be all ears; **aguzar los oídos** to prick up one's ears; **al oído** by listening; confidentially; **dar oídos** to lend an ear, to listen favorably; **decir al oído** to whisper; **de oído** by ear; **entrar por un oído y salir por el otro** to go in one ear and out the other; **hacer oídos de mercader** to turn a deaf ear; **pegarse al oído** to stick in one's ears (*said, e.g., of a song*); **prestar el oído** or **los oídos** (coll.) to lend an ear; **prestar oído a** (coll.) to give ear to; **regalar el oído a** (coll.) to tickle the ear of, to flatter; **ser todo oídos** (coll.) to be all ears; **tener oído** or **buen oído** to have a good ear (*for music*); **tener oído para la música** to have an ear for music; **oído medio** (anat.) middle ear
oidor -dora *mf* hearer; *m* (archaic) judge
oidoría *f* (archaic) judgeship
oigo *1st sg pres ind of* **oír**
oír §64 *va* to hear; to listen to; to attend (*lectures*); **¡ahora lo oigo!** the first I've heard about it!; **oír** + *inf* to hear + *inf*, e.g., **oí entrar a mi hermano** I heard my brother come in; to hear + *ger*, e.g., **oí cantar a la muchacha** I heard the girl singing; to hear + *pp*, e.g., **oí tocar la campana** I heard the bell rung; **oír decir que** to hear that, to hear it said that; **oír hablar de** to hear about, to hear tell of; *vn* to hear; to listen; **¡oiga!** the idea!, the very idea!; *vr* to like to hear oneself talk
oíslo *mf* (coll.) darling; *f* (coll.) beloved wife
ojada *f* (Am.) skylight; (Am.) putlog hole
ojal *m* buttonhole; eyelet; grommet
ojalá *interj* God grant!, would to God!
ojaladera *f* buttonhole maker
ojalador -dora *mf* buttonhole maker
ojaladura *f* set of buttonholes
ojalar *va* to sew buttonholes in
ojalatero *m* (coll.) armchair partisan, stay-at-home well-wisher (*in a civil war*)
ojaranzo *m* (bot.) hornbeam
ojeada *f* glance; **echar una ojeada a** to cast a glance at; **buena ojeada** eyeful
ojeador *m* (hunt.) beater of game
ojear *va* to eye, stare at; to hoodoo, cast the evil eye upon; to start, to rouse (*game*); to frighten, to startle
ojén *m* anisette
ojeo *m* (hunt.) beating for game
ojera *f* eyecup, eyeglass; **ojeras** *fpl* rings under the eyes
ojeriza *f* grudge, ill will
ojeroso -sa *adj* with rings under the eyes
ojerudo -da *adj* with heavy rings or dark circles under the eyes
ojete *m* eyelet, eyehole; (coll.) behind
ojetear *va* to make eyelets in
ojetera *f* strip of eyelets (*for lacing, e.g., a corset*); stamp or punch to make metal eyelets
ojialegre *adj* (coll.) bright-eyed
ojienjuto -ta *adj* (coll.) dry-eyed, tearless
ojigallo *m* (Am.) wine spiked with brandy
ojigarzo -za *adj* (coll.) var. of **ojizarco**
ojillo *m* eyelet, grommet
ojimel *m* or **ojimiel** *m* (pharm.) oxymel
ojimoreno -na *adj* (coll.) brown-eyed
ojinegro -gra or **ojiprieto -ta** *adj* (coll.) black-eyed
ojirrisueño -ña *adj* (coll.) bright-eyed
ojituerto -ta *adj* cross-eyed
ojiva *f* (arch.) ogive; **ojiva de lanceta** (arch.) lancet, lancet arch
ojival *adj* ogival; (arch.) ogival
ojizaino -na *adj* (coll.) squint-eyed, squinty
ojizarco -ca *adj* (coll.) blue-eyed
ojo *m* (anat.) eye; (fig.) eye (*e.g., of needle, cheese, tools; center of flower; round window; glance, look; watchful look; way of thinking, appreciation*); bow (*of key*); opening, well (*of stairs*); span, bay (*of bridge*); spring (*of water*); speck of grease (*in soup*); size (*of type*); face (*of type*); scrubbing (*with soap*); **abrir el ojo** to keep one's eyes open; **abrirle los ojos a uno** to open someone's eyes (*to disabuse someone*); **abrir los ojos** to open one's eyes (*to become disillusioned*); to have an eye to the main chance; **a cierra ojos** half-asleep; recklessly, rashly; **a los ojos de** in the eyes of; **a ojo** by sight, by guess; **a ojos vistas** visibly, openly; **con buenos ojos** favorably; **costar un ojo de la cara** to cost a mint, to cost a gold mine; **dar en los ojos** to be self-evident; **delante de los ojos de uno** before one's eyes; **de ojos almendrados** almond-eyed; **echar el ojo a** (coll.) to have an eye on (*to regard with desire*); **hacer del ojo** to wink at each other (*to indicate a secret understanding*); **hacerse ojos** to look sharply; **hasta los ojos** up to one's ears (*e.g., in love, in work*); **más ven cuatro ojos que dos** two heads are better than one; **mirar con ojos de carnero degollado** to make sheep's eyes (at); **no pegar el ojo** (coll.) to not sleep a wink all night; **no quitar los ojos de** to not take one's eyes off; **poner los ojos en blanco** to roll one's eyes; **saltar a los ojos** to be self-evident; **tener los ojos en** to have an eye on, to keep an eye on; **valer un ojo de la cara** to be worth a mint; **ojo avizor** eagle eye; **ojo clínico** or **médico** medical aptitude, ability to diagnose; **ojo de buey** (arch.) bull's-eye; (bot.) oxeye; **ojo de gato** tiger-eye (*gem*); (mineral.) cat's-eye; **ojo de la cerradura** keyhole; **Ojo del Toro** (astr.) Bull's-eye; **ojo de pavo real** (ent.) peacock butterfly (*Vanessa io*); **ojo de poeta** or **de Venus** (bot.) black-eyed Susan (*Thunbergia alata*); **ojo eléctrico** electric eye; **ojo mágico** (rad.) magic eye; **ojo por ojo** an eye for an eye; **ojos saltones** or **reventones** bulging eyes; *interj* beware!; look out!; attention!; **¡mucho ojo!** be careful!, watch out!; **¡ojo con . . . !** beware of . . . !; look out for . . . !; **¡ojo, mancha!** fresh paint!
ojoso -sa *adj* eyey, full of eyes, full of holes
ojuelos *mpl* sparkling eyes; spectacles
ola *f* wave, billow; surge, swell (*e.g., of a crowd of people*); **ola de calor** heat wave; **ola de frío** cold wave; **ola de marea** tidal wave
olaje *m* var. of **oleaje**
ole *m* or **olé** *m* bravo; *interj* bravo!
oleáceo -a *adj* (bot.) oleaceous
oleada *f* big wave; beating of the waves; surge, swell (*of a crowd of people*); wave (*e.g., of strikes*); big crop of olive oil
oleaginosidad *f* oiliness
oleaginoso -sa *adj* oily, oleaginous
oleaje *m* surge, rush of waves; rough sea
olear *va* to administer extreme unction to; *vn* to surge, to swell (*said of the sea*); *vr* to grease oneself (*for wrestling*)
oleario -ria *adj* oily
oleastro *m* (bot.) wild olive
oleato *m* (chem.) oleate
oleaza *f* watery dregs in olive-oil mill
olécranon *m* (anat.) olecranon
oledero -ra *adj* odorous
oledor -dora *adj* smelling; (Am.) fawning
oleico -ca *adj* (chem.) oleic
oleícola *adj* olive-growing, olive-oil-producing
oleicultor -tora *mf* olive grower, olive-oil producer
oleicultura *f* olive growing, production of olive oil
oleífero -ra *adj* (bot.) oleiferous
oleína *f* (chem.) olein
óleo *m* oil; holy oil; oil, oil painting
oleoducto *m* pipe line
oleografía *f* oleograph
oleomargarina *f* oleomargarin or oleomargarine
oleómetro *m* oleometer
oleorresina *f* oleoresin
oleosidad *f* oiliness
oleoso -sa *adj* oily

oler §65 *va* to smell; to look into, pry into; to sniff, sniff out (*e.g., a secret*); *vn* to smell, to be fragrant, to smell bad; **no oler bien** (coll.) to look suspicious; **oler a** to smell of, smell like; to reek with; to smack of; **oler donde guisan** (coll.) to know one's way around, to have an eye on the main chance
olfacción *f* olfaction
olfatear *va* to smell, scent, sniff; (coll.) to scent (*trouble, a good deal, etc.*)
olfateo *m* smell, smelling, scent
olfativo -va *adj* olfactory
olfato *m* smell, sense of smell; scent (*smell left in passing*); keenness, keen insight
olfatorio -ria *adj* olfactory
olíbano *m* frankincense
oliente *adj* smelling, odorous
oliera *f* (eccl.) chrismal (*vessel*)
oligarca *m* oligarch
oligarquía *f* oligarchy
oligárquico -ca *adj* oligarchic or oligarchical
oligisto *m* (mineral.) oligist
oligoceno -na *adj & m* (geol.) Oligocene
Olimpia *f* (geog.) Olympia
Olimpíada *f* Olympiad
olímpicamente *adv* haughtily, boastfully
olímpico -ca *adj* Olympian; Olympic; haughty, boastful
olimpiónico *m* winner in the Olympian games
Olimpo, el (geog., myth. & fig.) Mount Olympus
Olinto *f* Olynthus
oliscar §86 *va* to smell, scent, sniff; to investigate; *vn* to smell bad (*said of spoiled meat*)
olisquear *va* (coll.) to smell, scent, sniff; (coll.) to investigate
oliva *f* (bot.) olive (*tree and fruit*); olive (*color*); (anat.) olive; (orn.) barn owl; (fig.) olive branch, peace
oliváceo -a *adj* olivaceous
olivar *adj* olive; *m* olive grove; *va* to trim off the lower branches of; *vr* to bubble in baking (*said of bread*)
olivarda *f* (orn.) green goshawk; (bot.) elecampane
olivarero -ra *adj* olive (*growing, industry, etc.*); *mf* olive grower
olivastro *m* (bot.) wild olive; **olivastro de Rodas** (bot.) aloe
olivera *f* (bot.) olive tree
Oliverio *m* Oliver
olivero *m* olive storage
olivífero -ra *adj* (poet.) grown with olive trees
olivillo *m* (bot.) phillyrea, mock privet
olivino *m* (mineral.) olivine
olivo *m* (bot.) olive (*tree*); **tomar el olivo** (taur.) to duck behind the barrier; (slang) to beat it; **olivo silvestre** (bot.) wild olive
olmeda *f* or **olmedo** *m* elm grove
olmo *m* (bot.) elm
ológrafo -fa *adj & m* holograph
olomina *f* (ichth.) minnow
olor *m* odor; promise, hope; **estar al olor** (coll.) to be on the scent; **tener en mal olor** to hold in bad odor; **olor de santidad** odor of sanctity
olorizar §76 *va* to perfume
oloroso -sa *adj* odorous, fragrant
olote *m* (Am.) cob, corncob
olvidadizo -za *adj* forgetful; ungrateful; **hacerse olvidadizo** or **el olvidadizo** to pretend to be forgetful
olvidado -da *adj* forgetful; ungrateful; **estar olvidado** (coll.) to be ancient history
olvidar *va & vn* to forget; **olvidar** + *inf* to forget to + *inf; vr* to forget oneself; **olvidarse de** to forget; **olvidarse de** + *inf* to forget to + *inf;* **olvidársele a uno** to forget, e.g., **se me olvidó mi pasaporte** I forgot my passport; **olvidársele a uno** + *inf* to forget to + *inf*, e.g., **se me olvidó cerrar la ventana** I forgot to close the window
olvido *m* forgetfulness; oblivion; **enterrar en el olvido** to cast into oblivion
olla *f* pot, kettle; stew; eddy, whirlpool; (coll.) stomach; **recordar las ollas de Egipto** to remember happier days; **olla carnicera** large kettle, boiler; **olla de fuego** (mil.) incendiary grenade; **olla de grillos** (coll.) pandemonium; **olla de** or **a presión** pressure cooker; **olla podrida** Spanish stew (*made of meat, fowl, sausage, vegetables, etc.*)
ollao *m* (naut.) eyelet hole (*of sail*)
ollar *adj* soft (*stone*); *m* horse's nostril
ollería *f* pottery; earthenware shop
ollero -ra *mf* potter; dealer in earthenware
olluco *m* var. of **ulluco**
olluela *f* small pot or kettle
omaso *m* (zool.) omasum
omatidio *m* (zool.) ommatidium
ombligo *m* navel, umbilicus; umbilical cord; (fig.) center, heart; **ombligo de Venus** (bot.) Venus's-navelwort
ombliguero *m* navel bandage for infants
ombliguismo *m* belly dancing
ombría *f* shade, shady place
ombú *m* (*pl:* **-búes**) (bot.) umbra tree
omega *f* omega
omental *adj* omental
omento *m* (anat.) omentum
ómicron *f* (*pl:* **omícrones**) omicron
ominar *va* to omen, to presage
ominoso -sa *adj* ominous
omisión *f* omission; neglect
omiso -sa *adj* neglectful, remiss, careless
omitir *va* to omit; to overlook, neglect; **no omitir esfuerzos** to spare no efforts; **omitir** + *inf* to omit + *ger*
ómnibus *m* (*pl:* **-bus**) bus, omnibus; **ómnibus de dos pisos** double-decker; *adj* accommodation (*train*)
omnímodo -da *adj* all-embracing, all-inclusive
omnipotencia *f* omnipotence
omnipotente *adj* omnipotent
omnipresencia *f* omnipresence
omnipresente *adj* omnipresent
omnisapiente *adj* omniscient
omnisciencia *f* omniscience
omnisciente or **omniscio -cia** *adj* omniscient
omnívoro -ra *adj* omnivorous; *m* omnivore
omóplato *m* (anat.) shoulder blade
-ón -ona *suffix aug & pej* e.g., **cortinón** big heavy curtain; **hombrón** husky fellow; **mujerona** strapping big woman; **solterona** old maid; *suffix pej* e.g., **mandón** bossy; **respondón** saucy; **tragón** gluttonous; *suffix m* used to form nouns which denote result of action expressed by verb, e.g., **empujón** push; **resbalón** slide, slip; **salpicón** splash; *suffix dim* e.g., **callejón** lane, alley; **plumón** down; **ratón** mouse; **volantón** fledgling
onagra *f* (bot.) evening primrose
onagro *m* (zool.) onager
Onán *m* (Bib.) Onan
onanismo *m* onanism
once *adj* eleven; **las once** eleven o'clock; **estar a las once** (coll.) to be crooked (*said, e.g., of a part of clothing*); **hacer** or **tomar las once** (coll.) to take a bite or snack in the forenoon; *m* eleven; eleventh (*in dates*); (football) eleven (*team*)
oncear *va* to weigh out by ounces
onceavo -va *adj & m* var. of **onzavo**
oncejera *f* snare to catch birds
oncejo *m* (orn.) black martin, European swift
onceno -na *adj & m* eleventh
oncijera *f* var. of **oncejera**
oncología *f* oncology
onda *f* wave; flicker; curl, wave (*in hair*); (phys.) wave; (sew.) scallop; **de toda onda** (rad.) all-wave; **onda amortiguada** (elec.) damped wave; **onda corta** (rad.) short wave; **onda de choque** (aer.) shock wave; blast wave (*of a nuclear explosion*); **onda electromagnética** (phys.) electromagnetic wave; **onda herciana** or **hertziana** (elec.) Hertzian wave; **onda larga** (rad.) long wave; **onda luminosa** (phys.) light wave; **onda media** or **normal** (rad.) standard broadcast wave; **onda portadora** or **portante** (rad.) carrier wave; **ondas cerebrales** (med.) brain waves; **ondas continuas** or **ondas entretenidas** (rad.) continuous waves; **ondas encefálicas** (med.) brain waves; **onda sonora** (phys.) sound wave
ondatra *m* (zool.) muskrat
ondeado -da *adj* wavy; *m* waving, waviness
ondeante *adj* waving, undulating; flowing

ondear *va* to wave (*e.g., the hair*); *vn* to wave; to ripple; to flow; to flicker; to be wavy; *vr* to wave, to sway, to swing

ondeo *m* waving, rippling; flickering; swaying

ondina *f* (myth.) undine

ondisonante *adj* (poet.) babbling, rippling

ondógrafo *m* ondograph

ondoso -sa *adj* wavy

ondulación *f* undulation; wave; wave motion; **ondulación al agua** water wave; **ondulación permanente** permanent wave

ondulado -da *adj* undulate, rippled, wavy; rolling (*e.g., country*); corrugated; *m* wave (*in hair*); **ondulado al agua** finger wave

ondulante *adj* undulant; waving

ondular *va* to wave (*the hair*); *vn* to undulate; to wriggle

ondulatorio -ria *adj* undulatory

oneroso -sa *adj* onerous; (law) onerous

Onfala *f* (myth.) Omphale

ónice *m* or **ónique** *m* (mineral.) onyx

oniromancia or **oniromancía** *f* oneiromancy

ónix *m* (mineral.) onyx

onomancia or **onomancía** *f* onomancy

onomástico -ca *adj* onomastic; of proper names; *m* saint's day, birthday; *f* onomasticon, list of proper names; study of proper names

onomatología *f* onomatology

onomatopeya *f* onomatopoeia

onomatopéyico -ca *adj* onomatopeic or onomatopoetic

onomatopeyismo *m* (Am.) onomatopoeia

onoquiles *f* (bot.) alkanet, dyer's alkanet

ontina *f* (bot.) white sage

ontogenia *f* ontogeny

ontología *f* ontology

ontológico -ca *adj* ontological

ontologismo *m* (theol.) ontologism

ONU *f* UN (*United Nations*)

onubense *adj* (pertaining to) Huelva; *mf* native or inhabitant of Huelva

onz. abr. of **onza**

onza *f* ounce; (zool.) ounce; **onza de oro** Spanish doubloon

onzavo -va *adj & m* eleventh

oocito *m* (biol.) oöcyte

ooforectomía *f* (surg.) oöphorectomy

ooforitis *f* (path.) oöphoritis

oogonio *m* (bot.) oögonium

oolítico -ca *adj* oölitic

oolito *m* (mineral.) oölite

oología *f* oölogy

oosfera *f* (bot.) oösphere

oósporo -ra *adj* (bot.) oösporous; *m* (bot.) oöspore

opacar §86 *va* (Am.) to cloud, darken; *vr* (Am.) to become cloudy, to become obscure

opacidad *f* opacity; sadness, gloominess

opaco -ca *adj* opaque; sad, gloomy

opado -da *adj* swollen, puffed

opalescencia *f* opalescence

opalescente *adj* opalescent

opalino -na *adj* opaline

ópalo *m* (mineral.) opal

opción *f* option; (com.) option

ópera *f* (mus.) opera; **ópera bufa** (mus.) opera buffa; (mus.) opéra bouffe, comic opera; **ópera cómica** (mus.) comic opera; **ópera espiritual** (mus.) oratorio; **ópera semiseria** (mus.) light opera; **ópera seria** (mus.) grand opera

operable *adj* operable; practical, feasible; (surg.) operable

operación *f* operation; **operación cesárea** (surg.) Caesarean operation

operacional *adj* operational

operado -da *mf* patient operated on

operador -dora *adj* operating, operative; *mf* operator; (surg.) operator, operative surgeon; (telg. & telp.) operator

operante *adj* operating, active

operar *va* (surg.) to operate on (*a person or a part of body*); **operar a uno de una cosa** (surg.) to operate on someone for something; *vn* to work; to operate (*said, e.g., of a drug or medicine*); (com., mil., nav. & surg.) to operate; *vr* (surg.) to be operated on

operario -ria *mf* operative (*worker; laborer*); *m* workman; *f* working woman

operativo -va *adj* operative

operatorio -ria *adj* operating, working; (surg.) operating, operative

opérculo *m* (bot. & zool.) operculum

opereta *f* (mus.) operetta

operista *mf* opera singer; (Am.) composer of operas

operístico -ca *adj* operatic

operoso -sa *adj* laborious

opiáceo -a *adj* opiate (*containing opium; bringing sleep; quieting*)

opiado -da *adj & m* opiate

opiático -ca *adj* var. of **opiáceo**

opiato -ta *adj, m & f* opiate

opilación *f* (path.) obstruction; (path.) amenorrhea; (path.) dropsy

opilar *va* to obstruct; *vr* to have amenorrhea

opilativo -va *adj* obstructive, constipating

opimo -ma *adj* rich, fruitful, abundant

opinable *adj* moot

opinar *vn* to opine; to judge, pass judgment

opinión *f* opinion, view, judgment; reputation, public image; **cambiar** or **mudar de opinión** to change one's mind; **casarse con su opinión** (coll.) to stick to one's opinion; **ser de opinión que** to be of the opinion that; **opinión pública** public opinion

opio *m* (pharm.) opium

opíparo -ra *adj* sumptuous, magnificent (*banquet*)

oploteca *f* museum of ancient weapons, museum of arms

opobálsamo *m* balm of Gilead (*resin*)

opondré *1st sg fut ind of* **oponer**

oponente *adj* (anat.) opponent

oponer §69 *va* to put up, to offer (*e.g., resistance*); to juxtapose; **oponer una cosa a otra** to oppose something to something else, to set up something against something else; *vr* to oppose each other; to face each other, be juxtaposed; **oponerse a** to oppose, be opposed to; to be against, to resist; to compete for (*e.g., a professorship*)

opongo *1st sg pres ind of* **oponer**

oponible *adj* opposable

opopónace *f* (bot.) Hercules' allheal

opopónaco *m* (pharm.) opopanax

oporto *m* port (*wine*)

oportunidad *f* opportuneness; opportunity; occasion; **oportunidades** *fpl* opportune remarks, witticisms; **aprovechar la oportunidad** to seize the opportunity; **con toda oportunidad** in due time, in ample time

oportunismo *m* opportunism

oportunista *adj* opportunistic; *mf* opportunist

oportuno -na *adj* opportune; witty

oposición *f* opposition; competitive examinations

oposicionista *adj & mf* (pol.) oppositionist

opositor -tora *adj* rivaling, competing; *mf* opponent; competitor (*for a position*)

opoterapia *f* organotherapy

opresión *f* oppression; pressure

opresivo -va *adj* oppressive

opresor -sora *adj* oppressive; *mf* oppressor

oprimir *va* to oppress; to squeeze, to press

oprobiar *va* to defame, to revile

oprobio *m* opprobrium

oprobioso -sa *adj* opprobrious

opsonina *f* (bact.) opsonin

optar *va* to assume (*an office*); *vn* to opt; **optar a** or **por** to opt or decide in favor of, to choose; **optar a** or **por** + *inf* to decide to + *inf*, to choose to + *inf*

optativo -va *adj* optative, optional; (gram.) optative; *m* (gram.) optative (*mood*)

óptico -ca *adj* optic, optical; *mf* optician; *f* optics; optician's office; optical store; stereoscope

óptimamente *adv* to perfection

optimates *mpl* worthies, grandees

optimismo *m* optimism

optimista *adj* optimistic; *mf* optimist

óptimo -ma *adj super* very good, best, optimum

optometría *f* optometry

optometrista *mf* optometrist

optómetro *m* optometer

opuesto -ta *pp of* **oponer;** *adj* opposite, contrary; (bot.) opposite

opugnación *f* attack, assault; refutation

opugnador -dora *adj* attacking, assaulting; *mf* attacker
opugnar *va* to attack, to lay siege to; to oppugn
opulencia *f* opulence
opulento -ta *adj* opulent
opúsculo *m* short work, opuscule
opuse *1st sg pret ind of* **oponer**
oque; de oque (coll.) gratis
oquedad *f* hollow; (fig.) hollowness
oquedal *m* growth of tall trees without underbrush
oqueruela *f* kink in thread
ora; *conj* **ora . . . ora** now . . . then, now . . . now
oración *f* oration; speech; prayer; hour of prayer; (gram.) sentence; (gram.) clause; **oraciones** *fpl* prayers, call to prayer; **hacer oración** to pray; **oración compuesta** (gram.) compound sentence; **oración dependiente** (gram.) clause; (gram.) dependent clause; **oración dominical** Lord's prayer; **oración fúnebre** funeral oration; **oración principal** (gram.) main sentence; **oración simple** (gram.) simple sentence; **oración subordinada** (gram.) dependent clause, subordinate clause
oracional *adj* (gram.) sentential, (pertaining to the) sentence; *m* prayer book
oráculo *m* oracle; (fig.) oracle (*wise person; wise answer*); **oráculo délfico** Delphic oracle
orador -dora *mf* orator, speaker; petitioner; **orador de plazuela** soapbox orator; **orador de sobremesa** after-dinner speaker; *m* preacher
oraje *m* rough weather
oral *adj* oral
orangista *m* Orangeman
orangután *m* (zool.) orang-outang
orante *adj* (f.a.) orant, in the posture of prayer
orar *vn* to pray; to speak, make a speech; **orar por** to pray for
orate *mf* lunatic; (coll.) crazy person, wild person
oratorio -ria *adj* oratorical; *m* oratory (*small chapel*); (mus.) oratorio; *f* oratory
orbe *m* orb; world; (ichth.) globefish
orbicular *adj* orbicular
órbita *f* (anat., astr., phys. & fig.) orbit; **fuera de sus órbitas** (coll.) out of one's head
orbital *adj* orbital
orca *f* (zool.) killer whale
Órcadas *fpl* Orkney Islands
orcaneta *f* (bot.) alkanet, dyer's alkanet; **orcaneta roja** (bot.) alkanet, dyer's alkanet
orco *m* (zool.) killer whale; (poet.) Hades, the lower world; (*cap.*) *m* (myth.) Orcus
orchilla *f* (bot. & chem.) archil
órdago; de órdago (coll.) swell, real, e.g., **un discurso de órdago** a swell speech; **una bofetada de órdago** a real smack on the face
ordalías *fpl* (hist.) ordeal (*trial by fire, water, etc.*)
orden *m* order (*way one thing follows another; formal or methodical arrangement; peace, quiet; class, category*); (arch., biol., gram. & math.) order; (eccl.) order (*sixth sacrament*); (mil.) order (*formation*); **en orden** in order; **en orden a** with regard to; **llamar al orden** to call to order; **poner en orden** to put in order; **por su orden** in order (*of succession*); **orden de batalla** (mil.) order of battle, battle array; **orden de colocación** (gram.) word order; **orden de la misa, orden del culto** (eccl.) ordinal; **orden del día** order of the day (*in a legislative body*); **orden de marcha** working order; **Orden Nuevo** (pol.) New Order ‖ *f* order (*command; honor society; fraternal organization*); (eccl.) order (*monastic brotherhood; grade or rank of Christian ministry*); (mil.) order (*command*); (theol.) order (*any of nine grades of angels*); **a la orden de** (com.) to the order of; **estar a la orden del día** to be the order of the day (*i.e., the prevailing custom*); **estar a las órdenes de** to be at the service of; **sagradas órdenes** (eccl.) holy orders; **por orden de** by order of; **orden de allanamiento** (law) search warrant; **orden de caballería** order of knighthood; **orden de la Jarretera** (Brit.) Order of the Garter; **orden del Cister** Cistercian Order; **orden del día** (mil.) order of the day; **orden de San Agustín** Augustinian Order; **órdenes mayores** (eccl.) major orders; **órdenes menores** (eccl.) minor orders; **órdenes sagradas** (eccl.) holy orders
ordenación *f* order; ordering; auditor's office; (arch. & paint.) ordinance, balance; (eccl.) ordination; **ordenación de montes** forestry; **ordenación urbana** city planning
ordenado -da *adj* orderly; *f* (geom.) ordinate
ordenador *m* chief auditor; computer
ordenamiento *m* ordering, arrangement; law, decree; set of laws
ordenancista *adj* strict, rigid; *mf* martinet
ordenando or **ordenante** *m* (eccl.) ordinand
ordenanza *f* ordinance (*law, decree*); order, system; command; (arch. & paint.) ordinance; **ser de ordenanza** (coll.) to be the rule; *m* errand boy; (mil.) orderly
ordenar *va* to arrange; to order; (eccl.) to ordain; **ordenar** + *inf* to order to + *inf; vr* (eccl.) to become ordained, to take orders; **ordenarse de sacerdote** to become ordained as priest
ordeña *f* (Am.) milking
ordeñadero *m* milk pail
ordeñador -dora *adj* milking; *mf* milker; *f* milk maid; milking machine
ordeñar *va* to milk; to strip (*e.g., olives*) from a branch by a milking motion
ordeño *m* milking; **a ordeño** with milking motion; stripping olives from the branch
ordiate *m* barley water
ordinal *adj* orderly; ordinal; *m* ordinal
ordinariez *f* (coll.) coarseness, crudeness
ordinario -ria *adj* ordinary; daily (*expenses*); *m* ordinary (*judge; bishop*); daily household expenses; delivery man; **de ordinario** ordinarily; **ordinario de la misa** (eccl.) ordinary, Ordinary of the Mass
ordo *m* (eccl.) ordinal
ordoviciense *adj & m* (geol.) Ordovician
oréada or **oréade** *f* (myth.) Oread
orear *va* to air; *vr* to become aired, to dry in the air; to take an airing
oreas *m* (*pl:* **-as**) (zool.) eland
orégano *m* (bot.) wild marjoram
oreja *f* (anat.) ear, outer ear; flap (*of shoe*); flatterer; gossip; (mach.) lug, flange, ear; **aguzar las orejas** to prick up one's ears; **apearse por las orejas** (coll.) to take a tumble (*from a horse*); (coll.) to give a stupid answer; **bajar las orejas** (coll.) to come down from one's perch; **calentar a uno las orejas** (coll.) to dress someone down; **con las orejas caídas** or **gachas** (coll.) crestfallen; **con las orejas tan largas** all ears; **descubrir** or **enseñar las orejas** (coll.) to show the cloven hoof, to give oneself away; **mojar la oreja** to be looking for a fight; **tirar la oreja** or **las orejas, tirar de la oreja a Jorge** (coll.) to play cards for money; **ver las orejas al lobo** to be in great danger; **oreja de fraile** (bot.) asarabacca; **oreja de mercader** deaf ears; **oreja de monje** (bot.) Venus's-navelwort; **oreja de oso** (bot.) auricula, bear's-ear; **oreja de ratón** (bot.) snowberry; **oreja marina** (zool.) abalone
orejano -na *adj* unbranded (*cattle*)
orejeado -da *adj* (coll.) listening, ready to answer
orejear *vn* to shake or wiggle the ears; to act reluctantly; to whisper
orejera *f* earflap, earcap, earlap; earmuff; earthboard (*of plow*)
orejeta *f* lug
orejón *m* strip of dried peach; pull on the ear; dog's-ear (*of page of book*); (fort.) orillion
orejudo -da *adj* long-eared, big-eared
orejuela *f* little ear; handle (*of tray*)
orenga *f* (naut.) floor timber; (naut.) frame
oreo *m* breeze, fresh air; airing
oreoselino *m* (bot.) mountain parsley
Orestes *m* (myth.) Orestes
orfanato *m* orphanage
orfanatorio *m* (Am.) orphanage

orfandad *f* orphanage, orphanhood; abandonment, neglect
orfebre *m* goldsmith, silversmith
orfebrería *f* gold or silver work
orfelinato *m* (Am.) orphanage
Orfeo *m* (myth.) Orpheus
orfeón *m* glee club, choral society
orfeonista *mf* member of a glee club or choral society
órfico -ca *adj* Orphean, Orphic; **órficas** *fpl* Orphic mysteries
orfo *m* (ichth.) sea bream
organdí *m* (*pl:* **-díes**) organdy
organero *m* organ maker, organ builder
organicismo *m* (biol., med. & philos.) organicism
organicista *adj & mf* organicist
orgánico -ca *adj* organic
organillero -ra *mf* organ-grinder
organillo *m* barrel organ, hand organ, hurdy-gurdy
organismo *m* organism; agency, organization; (biol.) organism; **organismo cimógeno** (biol.) zymogenic organism; **organismo patógeno** (biol.) pathogenic organism
organista *mf* (mus.) organist
organización *f* organization; **organización científica del trabajo** scientific management
organizador -dora *adj* organizing; *mf* organizer
organizar §76 *va & vr* to organize
órgano *m* (mus. & physiol.) organ; part (*of a machine*); (bot.) organ-pipe cactus; organ (*means, instrument; medium*); **órgano de campanas** (mus.) carillon, glockenspiel; **órgano de cilindro** (mus.) barrel organ; **órgano de la voz** (anat.) vocal organ; **órgano de lengüetas** (mus.) reed organ; **órgano de los sentidos** (physiol.) sense organ; **órgano de manubrio** hand organ, street organ; **órgano móvil** (mach.) moving part; **órgano sensorio** (physiol.) sense organ; **órganos genitales** (anat.) genital organs
organografía *f* organography
organología *f* organology
organoterapia *f* organotherapy
orgánulo *m* (biol.) tiny organism
orgasmo *m* (physiol.) orgasm
orgástico -ca *adj* orgasmic or orgastic
orgia or **orgía** *f* orgy; **orgias** or **orgías** *fpl* orgies (*of ancient Greece*)
orgiástico -ca *adj* orgiastic
orgullo *m* haughtiness; pride
orgulloso -sa *adj* haughty, conceited; proud
oribe *m* goldsmith
orientable *adj* adjustable
orientación *f* orientation; prospect, exposure; bearings; (naut.) trimming the sails
orientador -dora *adj* leading; *mf* leader
oriental *adj* oriental; eastern; Oriental; *mf* Oriental
orientalismo *m* Orientalism
orientalista *mf* Orientalist
orientalizar §76 *va* to Orientalize
orientar *va* to orient, to orientate; to guide, direct; (naut.) to trim (*a sail*); *vr* to orient oneself, to find one's bearings
oriente *m* east; source, origin; youth; east wind; orient (*luster of the pearl*); (*cap.*) *m* Orient; **Cercano Oriente** Near East; **Extremo Oriente** or **Lejano Oriente** Far East; **gran oriente** grand lodge (*of Masons*); **Próximo Oriente** Near East; **Oriente Medio** Middle East
orificación *f* (dent.) gold filling
orificador *m* (dent.) plugger
orificar §86 *va* (dent.) to fill with gold
orífice *m* goldsmith
orificio *m* orifice, hole
oriflama *f* oriflamme
orifrés *m* orphrey
origen *m* origin; extraction, descent; **en el origen** at the beginning
Orígenes *m* Origen
original *adj* original; queer, odd, quaint; *m* original; character, queer duck; **de buen original** on good authority; **original de imprenta** (print.) copy
originalidad *f* originality; queerness, oddness, quaintness
originar *va & vr* to originate, to start
originario -ria *adj* originating, native; original
orilla *f* border, edge; margin; bank, shore; sidewalk; fresh breeze; shoulder (*of road*); **orillas** *fpl* (Am.) outskirts; **a la orilla** near, on the brink; **salir a la orilla** to manage to get through
orillar *va* to put a border or edge on; to trim; to settle, to arrange; *vn & vr* to skirt the edge, come up to the shore
orillo *m* list, selvage
orín *m* rust; **orines** *mpl* urine; **tomarse de orín** to get rusty
orina *f* urine
orinal *m* chamber pot, urinal; **orinal del cielo** (coll.) rainy place, rainy region
orinar *va* to pass, to urinate (*e.g., blood*); *vn & vr* to urinate
oriniento -ta *adj* rusty
orinque *m* (naut.) buoy rope
oriol *m* (orn.) oriole
Orión *m* (astr.) Orion
oriundez *f* origin
oriundo -da *adj & mf* native; **ser oriundo de** to come from, to hail from
orla *f* border, edge, margin; fringe, trimming; (her.) orle
orlador -dora *mf* borderer, edger
orladura *f* border, edge, trimming
orlar *va* to border, to put an edge on; to trim, trim with a fringe
Orleanista *adj & mf* Orleanist
orlo *m* Alpine horn; (arch.) plinth; (mus.) horn stop (*of an organ*)
ormesí *m* (*pl:* **-síes**) watered silk fabric
ormino *m* (bot.) wild sage
orn. abr. of **orden**
ornado -da *adj* ornate
ornamentación *f* ornamentation
ornamental *adj* ornamental
ornamentar *va* to ornament, adorn, decorate
ornamento *m* ornament; adornment; **ornamentos** *mpl* (eccl.) ornaments
ornato *m* adornment, show
ornitodelfo -fa *adj & m* (*zool.*) monotreme, ornithodelphian
ornitología *f* ornithology
ornitológico -ca *adj* ornithological
ornitólogo -ga *mf* ornithologist
ornitomancia or **ornitomancía** *f* ornithomancy
ornitorrinco *m* (zool.) duckbill, ornithorhyncus
orno *m* (bot.) manna ash
oro *m* gold; playing card (*representing a gold coin*) equivalent to diamond; **oros** *mpl* card suit corresponding to diamonds; **de oro y azul** (coll.) all dressed up; **poner de oro y azul** (coll.) to rake over the coals; **ponerle colores al oro** to gild the lily; **oro batido** gold foil, gold leaf; **oro coronario** fine gold; **oro de ley** standard gold; **oro en barras** bullion; **oro en libritos** gold leaf; **oro molido** ormolu; **oro mosaico** or **musivo** mosaic gold
orobanca *f* (bot.) broomrape
orobancáceo -a *adj* (bot.) orobanchaceous
orobias *m* fine incense
orogenia *f* orogeny
orogénico -ca *adj* orogenic
orografía *f* orography
orográfico -ca *adj* orographic or orographical
orología *f* orology
orómetro *m* orometer
orondo -da *adj* big-bellied (*bottle*); hollow, puffed up; (coll.) pompous; (Am.) calm, unflustered
oropel *m* tinsel; brass foil; accomplishment (*in some social art or grace*); flowery speech; (fig.) tinsel; **gastar mucho oropel** (coll.) to put on a front
oropelar *va* to tinsel, to trim with tinsel; to fake
oropelero -ra *mf* tinsel maker or dealer; flamboyant orator
oropelesco -ca *adj* tinselly, tawdry
oropéndola *f* (orn.) golden oriole
oropimente *m* (mineral.) orpiment

oroya *f* basket of rope railway
orozuz *m* (bot.) licorice
orquesta *f* (mus.) orchestra; (theat.) orchestra (*space occupied by musicians*); **orquesta de cámara** chamber orchestra; **orquesta de cuerda** string orchestra; **orquesta típica** regional orchestra (*which plays music typical of its place of origin*)
orquestación *f* orchestration
orquestal *adj* orchestral
orquestar *va* to orchestrate
orquestina *f* small orchestra
orquidáceo -a *adj* (bot.) orchidaceous
órquide *f* (bot.) orchis
orquídea *f* (bot.) orchid
orquitis *f* (path.) orchitis
orre; en orre loose, in bulk
ortega *f* (orn.) sand grouse
orticón *m* (telv.) orthicon
ortiga *f* (bot.) nettle; **ser como unas ortigas** (coll.) to be a grouch; **ortiga de mar** (zool.) sea nettle, jellyfish; **ortiga hedionda** (bot.) hedge nettle
ortigal *m* nettle field
ortivo -va *adj* (astr.) ortive
orto *m* rise (*of sun or star*)
ortoclasa *f* var. of **ortosa**
ortocromático -ca *adj* (phot.) orthochromatic
ortodoncia *f* orthodontia
ortodoxia *f* orthodoxy
ortodoxo -xa *adj* orthodox
ortoepia *f* orthoëpy
ortoépico -ca *adj* orthoëpic
ortofonía *f* orthophony
ortogénesis *f* (biol.) orthogenesis
ortognato -ta *adj* orthognathous
ortogonal *adj* orthogonal
ortografía *f* (gram. & geom.) orthography
ortografiar §90 *va & vn* to spell
ortográfico -ca *adj* orthographic or orthographical
ortógrafo -fa *mf* orthographer
ortología *f* orthoëpy
ortológico -ca *adj* orthoëpic
ortólogo -ga *mf* orthoëpist
ortopedia *f* orthopedics
ortopédico -ca *adj* orthopedic; *mf* orthopedist
ortopedista *mf* orthopedist
ortóptero -ra *adj* (ent.) orthopterous; *m* (ent.) orthopteran
ortorrómbico -ca *adj* (cryst.) orthorhombic
ortosa *f* (mineral.) orthoclase
ortotropismo *m* (bot.) orthotropism
ortótropo -pa *adj* (bot.) orthotropous
oruga *f* (bot.) rocket; rocket sauce; (ent.) caterpillar; (mach.) caterpillar (*device moving on endless belts*)
orujo *m* bagasse of grapes or olives
orvallar *vn* (dial.) to drizzle
orvalle *m* (bot.) wild sage
orvallo *m* (dial.) drizzle, dew
orza *f* gallipot, crock; (naut.) luffing; (naut.) luff; **orza central de deriva** (naut.) centerboard
orzaga *f* (bot.) orach
orzar §76 *vn* (naut.) to luff, to round to
orzaya *f* nursemaid
orzuelo *m* (path.) sty; snare (*to catch birds*); trap (*to catch wild animals*)
orzura *f* (chem.) minium
os *pron pers & reflex* (used as object of verb and corresponds to **vos** and **vosotros**); you, to you; yourself, to yourself; yourselves, to yourselves; each other, to each other; *interj* shoo!
osa *f* (zool.) she-bear; **Osa mayor** (astr.) Great Bear, Ursa Major; **Osa menor** (astr.) Little Bear, Ursa Minor; **el Osa** Ossa, Mount Ossa
osadía *f* boldness, daring
osado -da *adj* bold, daring
osambre *m* or **osamenta** *f* skeleton; bones
osar *m* ossuary, charnel house; *vn* to dare; **osar** + *inf* to dare + *inf*, to dare to + *inf*
osario *m* ossuary, charnel house
oscense *adj* (pertaining to) Huesca; *mf* native or inhabitant of Huesca
oscilación *f* oscillation; fluctuation; wavering, hesitation
oscilador -dora *adj* oscillating; *m* oscillator; (rad.) oscillator; **oscilador de relajación** (elec.) relaxation oscillator
oscilante *adj* oscillating, oscillatory
oscilar *vn* to oscillate; to waver, hesitate; (phys.) to oscillate
oscilatorio -ria *adj* oscillatory
oscilógrafo *m* (phys.) oscillograph
oscilograma *m* (phys.) oscillogram
osciloscopio *m* (phys.) oscilloscope
oscino -na *adj & f* (orn.) oscine
oscitación *f* gaping, yawning, oscitancy
oscitancia *f* careless oversight
osco -ca *adj & mf* Oscan; *m* Oscan (*language*)
osculación *f* (geom.) osculation
osculador -dora *adj* (geom.) osculatory
osculatorio -ria *adj* osculatory
osculatriz *f* (*pl:* **-trices**) (geom.) osculatrix
ósculo *m* osculation, kiss; (zool.) osculum (*of a sponge*)
oscurantismo *m* var. of **obscurantismo**
oscurantista *adj & mf* var. of **obscurantista**
oscurecer §34 *va, vn & vr* var. of **obscurecer**
oscurecimiento *m* var. of **obscurecimiento**
oscuridad *f* var. of **obscuridad**
oscuro -ra *adj & m* var. of **obscuro**
osear *va* var. of **oxear**
Oseas *m* (Bib.) Hosea
osecico, osecillo or **osecito** *m* little bone
óseo -a *adj* osseous, bony
osera *f* bear's den
osero *m* ossuary
osezno *m* cub or whelp of a bear
osezuelo *m* little bone
Osián *m* Ossian
osiánico -ca *adj* Ossianic
osianismo *m* Ossianism
osículo *m* (anat.) ossicle
osificación *f* ossification
osificar §86 *va & vr* to ossify
osífraga *f* or **osífrago** *m* (orn.) ossifrage
Osiris *m* (myth.) Osiris
osmanlí (*pl:* **-líes**) *adj & m* Osmanli
osmio *m* (chem.) osmium
ósmosis *f* (chem. & physiol.) osmosis
osmótico -ca *adj* osmotic
-oso -sa *suffix adj* -ous, e.g., **famoso** famous; **maravilloso** marvelous; -ful, e.g., **doloroso** painful; **espantoso** frightful; -y e.g., **jugoso** juicy; **rocoso** rocky; (chem.) -ous, e.g., **nitroso** nitrous; **sulfuroso** sulfurous
oso *m* (zool.) bear; **hacer el oso** (coll.) to make a fool of oneself; (coll.) to be overdemonstrative (*in love*); **oso bezudo** (zool.) sloth bear; **oso blanco** (zool.) polar bear; **oso colmenero** (zool.) honey badger; **oso del Tibet** (zool.) black bear; **oso gris** (zool.) grizzly bear; **oso hormiguero** (zool.) ant bear, anteater; **oso lavador** (zool.) coon, raccoon; **oso marino** (zool.) fur seal (*Callorhinus alascanus*); **oso marítimo** (zool.) polar bear; **oso negro** (zool.) black bear; **oso pardo** (zool.) brown bear
ososo -sa *adj* bony, osseous
osta *f* (naut.) guy, vang
ostaga *f* (naut.) tie
oste *interj* var. of **oxte**
osteítis *f* (path.) osteitis
ostensible *adj* visible, manifest
ostensión *f* show, manifestation; (eccl.) ostension
ostensivo -va *adj* ostensive; clear, obvious
ostensorio *m* (eccl.) monstrance
ostentación *f* showing; ostentation
ostentador -dora *adj* ostentatious; *mf* ostentatious person
ostentar *va* to show; to display, make a show of; *vr* to show off; to boast
ostentativo -va *adj* ostentatious
ostento *m* portent, prodigy
ostentoso -sa *adj* ostentatious
osteoblasto *m* (anat.) osteoblast
osteolita *f* (mineral.) osteolite
osteología *f* osteology
osteológico -ca *adj* osteological
osteólogo -ga *mf* osteologist
osteoma *m* (path.) osteoma
osteomalacia *f* (path.) osteomalacia
osteomielitis *f* (path.) osteomyelitis

osteópata *mf* osteopath, osteopathist
osteopatía *f* osteopathy
osteopático -ca *adj* osteopathic
osteotomía *f* (surg.) osteotomy
ostial *m* mouth of a harbor; pearl-growing shell; pearl fishery
ostiario *m* (eccl.) ostiary
ostión *m* large oyster
ostra *f* (zool.) oyster; **ostra perlera** (zool.) pearl oyster
ostráceo -a *adj* oyster; (zool.) ostraceous
ostracismo *m* ostracism
ostral *m* oyster bed, oyster farm
ostrera *f* see **ostrero**
ostrería *f* oysterhouse
ostrero -ra *adj* (pertaining to the) oyster; *m* oysterman; oyster bed, oyster farm; (orn.) oyster bird; *f* oysterwoman; (dial.) oyster bed
ostrícola *adj* oyster-raising, oyster-growing
ostricultura *f* oyster culture
ostro *m* large oyster; south; south wind; (zool.) purple (*mollusk and purple dye*)
ostrogodo -da *adj* & *mf* Ostrogoth
ostugo *m* corner; bit, whit
osudo -da *adj* bony
osuno -na *adj* bearish, bearlike
otacústico -ca *adj* otacoustic
otalgia *f* (path.) otalgia
otálgico -ca *adj* otalgic
O.T.A.N., la Nato (*North Atlantic Treaty Organization*)
otáñez *m* (coll.) old nobleman or esquire who served and accompanied a lady
O.T.A.S.E., la Seato (*Southeast Asia Treaty Organization*)
-ote -ta *suffix aug* e.g., **animalote** big animal; **grandote** biggish; **terminote** big word; **manota** big hand; *suffix dim* e.g., **camarote** stateroom, cabin; **islote** small barren island
oteador -dora *adj* watchful, spying; *mf* watcher, spy, lookout
otear *va* to survey, look down upon or over; to watch, keep an eye on
Otelo *m* Othello
otero *m* hillock, knoll
oteruelo *m* mound, hummock
otitis *f* (path.) otitis
oto *m* (orn.) tawny owl
otocisto *m* (zool.) otocyst
otoesclerosis *f* var. of **otosclerosis**
otolaringología *f* otolaryngology
otología *f* otology
otólogo -ga *mf* otologist
otomán *m* ottoman (*corded silk fabric*)
otomano -na *adj* & *mf* Ottoman; *f* ottoman (*sofa*)
Otón *m* Otto
otoñada *f* autumn time; autumn pasturage
otoñal *adj* autumnal, autumn, fall
otoñar *vn* to spend the autumn; to grow in autumn; *vr* (agr.) to soften up from autumn rains (*said of the ground*)
otoñizo -za *adj* autumnal
otoño *m* autumn, fall; fall crop of hay
otorgadero -ra *adj* grantable
otorgador -dora *adj* granting; *mf* grantor
otorgamiento *m* consent; grant; granting, conferring; approval; (law) execution of a document
otorgante *mf* grantor; (law) maker (*of a deed*)
otorgar §59 *va* to agree to; to grant, to confer; (law) to execute (*e.g., a deed*)
otorrea *f* (path.) catarrh of the ear
otorrinolaringología *f* otorhinolaryngology
otorrinolaringólogo -ga *mf* otorhinolaryngologist
otosclerosis *f* (path.) otosclerosis
otoscopia *f* otoscopy
otoscopio *m* otoscope
otramente *adv* otherwise; in a different way
otro -tra *adj indef* other, another; *pron indef* other one, another one; **algún otro** someone else, somebody else; **al otro día** on the next day; **al otro día de** + *inf* on the day after + *ger;* **como dijo el otro** as someone said; **el otro día** the other day; the next day; **¡ésa es otra!** (coll.) that's a fine thing!; **ser muy otro** (coll.) to be quite changed; **¡otra!** (theat.) encore; **otro tanto** as much, the same thing

otrora *adv* formerly, of yore
otrosí *adv* furthermore
ova *f* (bot.) sea lettuce; (arch.) egg (*in egg-and-dart ornaments*); **ovas** *fpl* roe
ovación *f* ovation
ovacionar *va* to give an ovation to
ovado -da *adj* ovate; oval; impregnated (*fowl*)
oval or **ovalado -da** *adj* oval
ovalar *va* to make oval
oválico -ca *adj* oval, oval-shaped
óvalo *m* oval; (arch.) egg (*in egg-and-dart ornaments*)
ovante *adj* victorious, triumphant
ovar *vn* to lay eggs
ovárico -ca *adj* ovarian
ovario *m* (anat. & bot.) ovary; (arch.) egg-ornamented molding
ovariotomía *f* (surg.) ovariotomy
ovaritis *f* (path.) ovaritis
ovecico, ovecillo or **ovecito** *m* small egg
oveja *f* ewe, female sheep; **oveja negra** (fig.) black sheep; **oveja perdida** (fig.) lost sheep
ovejero -ra *adj* (pertaining to) sheep; *mf* sheep raiser; *m* shepherd; *f* shepherdess
ovejuela *f* young ewe
ovejuno -na *adj* (pertaining to) sheep
overo -ra *adj* blossom-colored (*horse*); egg-colored; *f* ovary of a bird
ovetense *adj* (pertaining to) Oviedo; *mf* native or inhabitant of Oviedo
ovezuelo *m* small egg
ovículo *m* (arch.) oviculum
Ovidio *m* Ovid
óvido -da *adj* & *m* ovine; **óvidos** *mpl* (zool.) Ovidae
oviducto *m* (anat.) oviduct
oviforme *adj* oviform
ovil *m* sheepcote
ovillar *va* to wind up (*e.g., wool*); to sum up; *vn* to form into a ball; *vr* to curl up into a ball
ovillo *m* ball of yarn; ball, heap; tangled ball; **hacerse un ovillo** (coll.) to cower, to recoil; (coll.) to get all tangled up (*in speech*)
ovino -na *adj* & *m* ovine
ovio -via *adj* var. of **obvio**
ovíparo -ra *adj* oviparous
oviscapto *m* (zool.) ovipositor
ovoide or **ovoideo -a** *adj* ovoid
óvolo *m* (arch.) ovolo
ovoso -sa *adj* full of roe
ovovivíparo -ra *adj* ovoviviparous
ovulación *f* (biol.) ovulation
ovular *adj* ovular
óvulo *m* (biol. & bot.) ovule
ox *interj* shoo! (*to scare away fowl*)
oxalato *m* (chem.) oxalate
oxalidáceo -a *adj* (bot.) oxalidaceous
oxálico -ca *adj* oxalic
oxalme *m* brine mixed with vinegar
oxe *interj* var. of **ox**
oxear *va* & *vn* to shoo
oxfordiano -na *adj* & *mf* Oxfordian
oxfordiense *adj* & *m* (geol.) Oxfordian
oxhídrico -ca *adj* (chem.) oxyhydrogen
oxhidrilo *m* (chem.) hydroxyl
oxiacanto -ta *adj* thorny; *f* (bot.) hawthorn, whitethorn
oxiacetilénico -ca *adj* oxyacetylene
oxidable *adj* oxidizable
oxidación *f* oxidation
oxidante *adj* oxidizing; *m* (chem.) oxidizer
oxidar *va* to oxidize; *vr* to oxidize; to get rusty; (fig.) to get rusty (*said of one's knowledge of a subject*)
óxido *m* (chem.) oxide; **óxido amarillo** yellow oxide; **óxido de aluminio** (chem.) aluminum oxide; **óxido de carbono** (chem.) carbon monoxide; **óxido de cinc** (chem.) zinc oxide; **óxido de hierro** (chem.) iron oxide; **óxido de mercurio** (chem.) mercuric oxide; **óxido nitroso** (chem.) nitrous oxide
oxigenación *f* oxygenation
oxigenar *va* oxygenate; *vr* (chem.) to become oxygenated; to take the air, to go out for fresh air
oxígeno *m* (chem.) oxygen
oxigonio -nia *adj* (geom.) acute-angled
oxihemoglobina *f* (biochem.) oxyhemoglobin

oximel *m* or **oximiel** *m* (pharm.) oxymel
oxirrino -na *adj* (zool.) oxyrhine
oxítono -na *adj & m* (phonet.) oxytone
oxizacre *m* bittersweet drink
oxoniense *adj & mf* Oxonian
oxozono *m* (chem.) oxozone
oxte *interj* get out!, beat it!; **sin decir oxte ni moxte** (coll.) without opening one's mouth
oye *3d sg pres ind & 2d sg impv of* **oír**
oyente *mf* hearer; listener (*to radio*); auditor (*in school*)
oyes *2d sg pres ind of* **oír**
ozona *f* var. of **ozono**
ozonizar **§76** *va & vr* to ozonize
ozono *m* (chem.) ozone
ozonosfera *f* ozonosphere, ozone layer
ozonuro *m* (chem.) ozonide
ozostomía *f* (path.) ozostomia

P

P, p *f* nineteenth letter of the Spanish alphabet
P. abr. of **Padre, Papa** & **Pregunta**
p.ª abr. of **para**
P.A. abr. of **Por ausencia** & **Por autorización**
pabellón *m* pavilion; bell tent; flag, banner; stack (*of guns*); building (*e.g., of an exposition*); canopy (*over bed, throne, altar*); summerhouse; (anat. & arch.) pavilion; (mus.) bell (*of wind instrument*); (naut.) flag, colors; protection; **pabellón de conveniencia** (naut.) flag of convenience; **pabellón nacional** national flag
pabilo or **pábilo** *m* wick; snuff (*of candle*)
pabilón *m* flax or wool hanging from distaff
pablar *vn* (hum.) to jabber
Pablo *m* Paul; **¡guarda, Pablo!** (coll.) careful there!
pábulo *m* pabulum; (fig.) support, encouragement, fuel
paca *f* (zool.) spotted cavy; bale
pacana *f* (bot.) pecan (*tree and fruit*)
pacanero *m* (bot.) pecan (*tree*)
pacatería or **pacatez** *f* mildness, gentleness
pacato -ta *adj* mild, gentle
pacay *m* (*pl:* **-cayes** or **-caes**) (bot.) pacay (*tree and fruit*)
pacedero -ra *adj* pasturable
pacedura *f* pasture
pacense *adj* (pertaining to) Badajoz; *mf* native or inhabitant of Badajoz
paceño -ña *adj* (pertaining to) La Paz (*Bolivia*); *mf* native or inhabitant of La Paz
pacer §34 *va* to pasture, graze; to gnaw, eat away; *vn* to pasture, graze
paciencia *f* patience; almond cooky
paciente *adj & mf* patient; *m* (gram.) patient, recipient of an action
pacienzudo -da *adj* patient, long-suffering
pacificación *f* pacification; peace, calm, quiet
pacificador -dora *adj* pacifying; *mf* pacifier, peace-maker
pacificar §86 *va* to pacify; *vn* to sue for peace; *vr* to calm down
pacífico -ca *adj* pacific; (*cap.*) *adj & m* Pacific (*ocean*)
pacifismo *m* pacifism
pacifista *adj* pacifist, pacifistic; *mf* pacifist
paco *m* (zool.) paco, alpaca; (mineral.) paco; Moorish sniper; sniper; (*cap.*) *m* Frank
pacón *m* (bot.) soap tree
pacotilla *f* goods carried by seamen or officers free of freight; merchandise; bother, annoyance; deal, venture; trash, junk; **hacer la pacotilla** (coll.) to pack up; **hacer su pacotilla** (coll.) to make a cleanup; **ser de pacotilla** to be shoddy, to be poorly made
pacotillero -ra *mf* (Am.) peddler
pactar *va* to agree to, to agree upon; *vn* to come to an agreement; to temporize
pacto *m* pact, covenant
pachá *m* (*pl:* **-chaes**) var. of **bajá**
pachón -chona *adj* (Am.) woolly, shaggy; *m* pointer (*dog*); phlegmatic fellow, sluggard
pachorra *f* (coll.) sluggishness, indolence
pachorrudo -da *adj* (coll.) sluggish, indolent
pachucho -cha *adj* overripe; weak, drooping
pachulí *m* (*pl:* **-líes**) (bot.) patchouli
padecer §34 *va* to suffer; to endure; to be victim of (*a mistake, illusion, etc.*); *vn* to suffer; **padecer con** or **de** to suffer from
padecimiento *m* suffering
padilla *f* small frying pan; bread oven
padrastro *m* stepfather; bad father; obstacle; hangnail; (mil.) eminence, high ground
padrazo *m* (coll.) indulgent father
padre *m* father; stallion, sire; (eccl.) father; **padres** *mpl* parents; ancestors; **de padre y muy señor mío** (coll.) hard, terrific (*e.g., beating*); **santos padres** fathers of the church; **padre de la patria** Father of his Country; (hum.) Solon (*legislator*); **padre de pila** godfather; **padre político** father-in-law; step-father; **Padre Santo** Holy Father; **Padres apostólicos** Apostolic Fathers; **padres conscriptos** conscript father; **padres de la iglesia** fathers of the church; *adj* (Am.) swell, grand
padrear *vn* to resemble one's father; to breed (*said of a male animal*)
padrenuestro *m* (*pl:* **padrenuestros**) Lord's Prayer; paternoster (*prayer and bead*)
padrillo *m* (Am.) stallion
padrina *f* godmother
padrinazgo *m* godfathership; sponsorship, patronage
padrino *m* godfather; sponsor; second (*in a duel*); **padrinos** *mpl* godfather and godmother; **padrino de boda** best man, groomsman
padrón *m* poll, census; pattern, model; memorial column; note of infamy; (coll.) indulgent father; (Am.) stallion
padrote *m* (Am.) pimp, procurer; (Am.) gigolo
paella *f* saffron-flavored stew of chicken, seafood, and rice with vegetables
paf *interj* bang!
pañón *m* (arch.) soffit
pág. abr. of **página**
paga *f* pay, payment; wages, salary; fine; requital; **buena paga** good pay (*person*); **mala paga** poor pay (*person*)
pagable *adj* payable
pagadero -ra *adj* payable; *m* time of payment, term, grace
pagado -da *adj* pleased, cheerful; **estamos pagados** we're quits; **pagado de sí mismo** self-satisfied, conceited
pagador -dora *adj* paying; *mf* payer; paymaster; paying teller
pagaduría *f* disbursement office, paymaster's office
pagamento or **pagamiento** *m* payment
paganismo *m* paganism
paganizar *va & vn* to paganize
pagano -na *adj & mf* pagan; *m* (coll.) easy mark, scapegoat
pagar §59 *va* to pay; to pay for; to return (*e.g., a kindness, a visit*); **pagarla** or **pagarlas** (coll.) to pay for it; *vn* to pay; **a luego pagar** cash, for cash; *vr* to become fond, become enamored; to yield to flattery; to boast, make a show; to be satisfied
pagaré *m* promissory note, I.O.U.
pagd.º abr. of **pagado**
pagel *m* (ichth.) red surmullet
página *f* page; (fig.) page (*of history*)
paginación *f* pagination
paginar *va* to page
pago *adj* (coll.) paid; *m* payment; district, region (*especially of vineyards or olive groves*); **en pago de** in payment of or for; **pago a la entrega** cash on delivery; **pago a plazos** installment payment, installment plan
pagoda *f* pagoda
pagote *m* (coll.) easy mark, scapegoat
pagro *m* (ichth.) porgy
paguro *m* (zool.) hermit crab
paila *f* large pan
pailebote *m* (naut.) small sleek schooner
painel *m* panel
pairar *vn* (naut.) to lie to
pairo *m* (naut.) lying to

país *m* country, land; back of fan; (f.a.) landscape; **el país de Gales** Wales; **el País Vasco** the Basque Country; **los Países Bajos** the Low Countries (*Belgium, The Netherlands, and Luxemburg*); The Netherlands (*Holland*); **país satélite** satellite country
paisaje *m* landscape; (f.a.) landscape
paisajista *mf* landscape painter, landscapist
paisajístico -ca *adj* (pertaining to) landscape
paisana *f* see **paisano**
paisanaje *m* peasantry; civilians; fellow citizenship
paisano -na *adj* of the same country; (Am.) rustic, boorish; *mf* peasant; *m* countryman; civilian; (orn.) road runner; **de paisano** in civies; *f* countrywoman
paisista *mf* landscape painter
paja *f* straw; chaff (*husk of wheat, oats, rye, etc.*); trash, rubbish, chaff, deadwood; **en un quítame allá esas pajas** (coll.) in a jiffy; **no dormirse en las pajas** (coll.) to not let the grass grow under one's feet; **no importar una paja** to be of no utter use or importance; **no levantar paja del suelo** to not lift a hand, to not do a stroke of work; **paja centenaza** rye straw; **paja de madera** excelsior; **paja pelaza** beaten barley straw; **¡pajas!** no less so!
pajado -da *adj* straw-colored; *f* chaff (*to be used as fodder*)
pajar *m* haystack, hayrick, straw loft
pájara *f* paper kite; paper rooster; bird; crafty female; **pájara pinta** game of forfeits
pajarear *vn* to go out to catch birds; to loaf around; (Am.) to shy (*said of a horse*)
pajarel *m* (orn.) redpoll
pajarera *f* see **pajarero**
pajarería *f* flock of birds, large number of birds; bird store; pet shop
pajarero -ra *adj* (coll.) bright, cheerful; (coll.) bright-colored, gaudy; *m* bird dealer, bird fancier; *f* aviary; large bird cage
pajarilla *f* (bot.) columbine; paper kite; paper rooster; milt, spleen (*of hog*)
pajarita *f* paper kite; paper rooster; bow tie; wing collar, piccadilly; (bot.) toadflax, snapdragon; **pajarita de las nieves** (orn.) wagtail
pájaro *m* bird; crafty fellow; expert; **matar dos pájaros de una pedrada** to kill two birds with one stone; **pájaro bobo** (orn.) penguin; **pájaro carpintero** (orn.) woodpecker; **pájaro de cuenta** (coll.) big shot; **pájaro gato** (orn.) catbird; **pájaro gordo** (coll.) big shot; **pájaro mosca** (*pl:* **pájaros moscas**) (orn.) hummingbird; **pájaro polilla** (orn.) kingfisher; **pájaro sastre** (orn.) tailorbird; **pájaro trompeta** (orn.) trumpeter; **pájaro verdugo** (orn.) butcherbird
pajarota or **pajarotada** *f* hoax, canard
pajarote *m* large bird
pajarraco or **pajaruco** *m* ugly big bird; (coll.) sly fellow, sneaky fellow
pajaza *f* fodder refuse
pajazo *m* (vet.) spot or scar on cornea of horse
paje *m* page; valet; dressing table; (naut.) cabin boy; **paje de hacha** linkboy
pajear *vn* to feed well on straw; (coll.) to act, behave
pajecillo *m* washstand
pajel *m* var. of **pagel**
pajera *f* see **pajero**
pajería *f* straw store; (coll.) bore, annoyance
pajero -ra *mf* straw dealer; *f* straw loft
pajil *adj* (pertaining to a) page (*boy*)
pajilla *f* cigarette; cigarette rolled in corn husk; lock spring
pajita *f* straw, drinking straw
pajizo -za *adj* straw, strawy; straw-colored
pajolero -ra *adj* annoying, pestiferous; voluble, convivial
pajón *m* coarse straw
pajoso -sa *adj* strawy, full of straw
pajote *m* straw mat for covering plants
pajuela *f* short straw; sulphur match or fuse; (Am.) match; (Am.) gold or silver toothpick
pajuncio *m* (scornful) page (*boy*)
pajuno -na *adj* var. of **pajil**
pajuz *m* or **pajuzo** *m* rotted straw used for manure
Pakistán, el Pakistan
pakistanés -nesa *adj* Pakistani
pakistaní (*pl:* **-níes**) *adj & mf* var. of **pakistano**
pakistano -na *adj & mf* Pakistani
pal *m* (her.) pale
pala *f* shovel; blade (*of hoe, spade, oar, etc.*); scoop; racket; upper (*of shoe*); scraper; setting (*of precious stones*); flat surface (*of tooth*); leaf (*of hinge*); paddle; peel (*of baker*); cake turner; (mil. & nav.) shoulder strap; (coll.) cunning, craftiness; bucket (*of power shovel*); **meter la pala** (coll.) to be slick, to be crooked; **pala de doble concha** clamshell bucket, grab bucket; **pala mecánica** power shovel
palabra *f* word; speech; words (*of a song*); (*cap.*) *f* (theol.) Word (*second person of Trinity*); **bajo su palabra** on one's word; **cruzar palabras con** to exchange words with; to have words with; **cuatro palabras** a word, a few words; **dar la palabra a** to give the floor to; **dar palabra y mano** to give one's word; to give one's word in marriage; **dar su palabra** to give one's word; **decir a medias palabras** to hint at; **de palabra** by word of mouth; **dirigir la palabra a** to address; to direct one's words to; **dos palabras** a word, a few words; **en una palabra** in a word; **pedir la palabra** to ask for the floor; **remojar la palabra** (coll.) to wet one's whistle; **sobre su palabra** on one's word; **tener la palabra** to have the floor; **tener palabras** to have words, to have words with each other; **tomar la palabra** to take the floor; **tomarle a una persona la palabra** to take a person at his word; **trabarse de palabras** to have words, get into an argument; **última palabra** last word; (fig.) last word (*most up-to-date style; thing that cannot be improved*); **usar de la palabra** to speak, make a speech; **venir contra su palabra** to go against one's word; **palabra clave** key word; **palabra de Dios** Word of God; **palabra de enchufamiento** portmanteau word; **palabra de matrimonio** promise of marriage; **palabra esdrújula** (phonet.) proparoxytone; **palabra llana** (phonet.) paroxytone; **palabras al aire** (coll.) hot air; **palabras cruzadas** word square; crossword puzzle; **palabras mayores** words (*angry words, quarrel*); *interj* hey!, say!; word of honor!
palabrada *f* wordiness, flow of words; vulgarity (*word*)
palabreja *f* minor word, incidental word
palabreo *m* (coll.) chatter
palabrería *f* (coll.) wordiness; (coll.) empty promises
palabrerío *m* (Am.) wordiness, windiness, hot air
palabrero -ra *adj* wordy, windy; *mf* windbag
palabrimujer *adj masc* (coll.) female-voiced; *m* (coll.) fellow with a female voice
palabrista *adj & mf* var. of **palabrero**
palabrita *f* pointed word; **palabritas mansas** *mf* honey-tongued schemer
palabrón -brona *adj* wordy, windy
palabrota *f* vulgarity (*word*)
palaciano -na *adj* (pertaining to the) palace, court
palaciego -ga *adj* (pertaining to the) palace, court; *m* courtier
palacio *m* palace; mansion; building; **Palacio de la Alborada** official residence of the chief executive of Brazil, in Brasilia; **Palacio de la Moneda** official residence of the chief executive of Chile, in Santiago; **palacio municipal** city hall
palacra or **palacrana** *f* gold nugget
palada *f* shovelful; stroke (*of an oar*)
paladar *m* (anat.) palate; (fig.) palate (*taste; gourmet*); **paladar blando** (anat.) soft palate; **paladar duro** (anat.) hard palate
paladear *va* to taste, to relish; to clean the mouth or palate of (*an animal*); to rub the palate of (*a baby*) with something sweet; to take a liking for; *vn* to show a desire for suck-

ing (*said of a baby*); *vr* to taste; **paladearse con** to taste, to relish
paladeo *m* tasting, relishing
paladial *adj & f* (phonet.) palatal
paladín *m* paladin
paladino -na *adj* public, open; *m* paladin
paladio *m* (chem.) palladium
paladión *m* palladium (*protection*); (*cap.*) *m* (myth.) Palladium
palado -da *adj* (her.) paly
palafito *m* (archeol.) palafitte, lake dwelling
palafrén *m* palfrey; groom's horse
palafrenero *m* groom, stableboy; equerry
palahierro *m* shaft socket of a millstone
palamallo *m* pall-mall (*game*)
palamedea *f* (orn.) screamer
palamenta *f* (naut.) oarage, set of oars
palanca *f* (mach. & mech.) lever; pole (*for carrying a weight*); crowbar; (fort.) outwork made of stakes and earth; (fig.) soul, prime mover; (Am.) friend with pull; **palanca de cambio** (aut.) gearshift lever; **palanca de gancho** cant hook; **palanca de mando** (aer.) control stick; **palanca de mayúsculas** shift key (*of typewriter*); **palanca portatipos** type bar (*of typewriter*)
palancada *f* move made with a lever, leverage
palancana or **palangana** *f* washbowl
palanganero *m* washstand (*stand with basin and pitcher*)
palangre *m* boulter, trawl, trotline
palangrero *m* boulterer, trawler
palanquera *f* stockade; (fort.) log rampart
palanquero *m* leverman; (archaic) blower of bellows; (Am.) brakeman; (Am.) timberman
palanqueta *f* jimmy; dumbbell; lever; (nav.) bar shot; (Am.) honeyed popcorn
palanquilla *f* billet (*square iron rod*)
palanquín *m* errand boy, porter; palankeen or palanquin; (naut.) double tackle
Palas *f* (myth.) Pallas; **Palas Atenea** (myth.) Pallas Athene
palasán *m* (bot.) rattan, rotang
palastro *m* sheet iron, plate steel; plate of lock
palatal *adj* palatal; (phonet.) palatal; *f* (phonet.) palatal
palatalización *f* palatalization
palatalizar §76 *va & vr* to palatalize
palatina *f* see **palatino**
palatinado *m* palatinate; (*cap.*) *m* Palatinate
palatino -na *adj* (anat.) palatal; palatine; Palatine; *m* Palatine; **el Palatino** the Palatine; *f* tippet (*scarf*)
palatizar §76 *va* to palatalize
palatosquisis *f* cleft palate
palay *m* paddy (*rice in husk*)
palazo *m* blow with a shovel
palazón *m* woodwork, timber
palco *m* (theat.) box; (theat.) bench, row of seats; **palco de platea** (theat.) parquet box; **palco escénico** (theat.) stage
paleador *m* shoveler; stoker
palear *va* to beat, to pound; to shovel
palenque *m* paling, palisade; arena; (fig.) arena; **tener la vida en un palenque** (coll.) to be in great danger
palentino -na *adj* (pertaining to) Palencia; *mf* native or inhabitant of Palencia
paleobotánica *f* paleobotany
paleografía *f* paleography
paleográfico -ca *adj* paleographic
paleógrafo -fa *mf* paleographer
paleolítico -ca *adj* paleolithic
paleontología *f* paleontology
paleontólogo -ga *mf* paleontologist
paleoterio *m* (pal.) palaeothere
paleozoico -ca *adj & m* Paleozoic
palería *f* draining, drainage
palero *m* shovel maker or dealer; drainer; shoveler; (mil.) pioneer, sapper
palestino -na *adj & mf* Palestinian; (*cap.*) *f* Palestine
palestra *f* palaestra; wrestling; struggle, dispute
paléstrico -ca *adj* palaestric
palestrita *m* wrestler
paleta *f* small shovel; fire shovel; trowel; paddle; blade, bucket, vane; (anat.) shoulder blade; (paint.) palette, pallet; (Am.) lollipop; **de paleta** ready, at hand; **en dos paletas** (coll.) in a jiffy
paletada *f* trowelful; blow with a shovel; **en dos paletadas** (coll.) in a jiffy
paletazo *m* blow with a shovel or trowel; side thrust with the horn
paletear *va* to beat (*hides*); *vn* to row without advancing; to go around without advancing (*said of paddle wheel*)
paletero *m* two-year-old fallow deer
paletilla *f* (anat.) shoulder blade; sternum cartilage; **poner la paletilla en su lugar a** (coll.) to rake over the coals
paleto *m* fallow deer; rustic, yokel
paletó *m* (*pl:* **-toes**) (archaic) overcoat, paletot
paletón *m* bit or web (*of key*)
paletoque *m* man's doublet or jacket
pali *adj & m* Pali
palia *f* (eccl.) altar cloth; (eccl.) pall, pallium
paliacate *m* (Am.) bandanna
paliación *f* palliation
paliadamente *adv* secretly, hiddenly
paliar §90 & regular *va* to palliate
paliativo -va *adj & m* palliative
paliatorio -ria *adj* concealing, veiling
palidecer §34 *vn* to pale, turn pale
palidez *f* paleness, pallor
pálido -da *adj* pale, pallid
paliducho -cha *adj* palish
palillero -ra *mf* toothpick maker or dealer; *m* toothpick holder
palillo *m* knitting-needle holder; toothpick; drumstick; tobacco stem; bobbin (*for making lace*); **palillos** *mpl* pins (*sometimes used in billiards*); chopsticks; castanets; (coll.) rudiments; (coll.) trifles
palimpsesto *m* palimpsest
palíndromo -ma *adj* palindromic; *m* palindrome
palingenesia *f* palingenesis
palingenésico -ca *adj* palingenetic
palinodia *f* backdown, recantation, palinode; **cantar la palinodia** to eat crow
palio *m* (anat., eccl. & hist.) pallium; cloak, mantle; baldachin, dais, canopy; (hist.) prize (*silk cloth*) for winning a horse race
palique *m* (coll.) chit-chat, small talk
paliquear *vn* (coll.) to chat, gossip
palisandro *m* (bot.) palisander, Brazilian rosewood
palitroque *m* stick
paliza *f* beating
palizada *f* fenced-in enclosure; stockade; embankment
palma *f* palm (*of hand*); (bot.) palm (*tree and leaf*); sole (*of hoof*); (fig.) palm; **palmas** *fpl* clapping, applause; **andar en palmas** to be highly esteemed; **batir palmas** to clap, applaud; **llevarse la palma** to bear the palm, to carry off the palm; **palma brava** (bot.) fan palm (*Corypha minor*); **palma de cera** (bot.) wax palm; **palma indiana** (bot.) coconut palm; **palma loca** (bot.) yucca; **palma real** (bot.) royal palm
palmáceo -a *adj* (bot.) palmaceous
palmacristi *f* (bot.) palma Christi
palmado -da *adj* palmate; (bot. & zool.) palmate; (slang) broke; *f* slap; hand, applause, clapping; **dar palmadas** to clap hands
palmar *adj* (anat.) palmar; clear, evident; *m* palm grove; fuller's thistle; *vn* (coll.) to die
palmario -ria *adj* clear, evident
palmatoria *f* ferule; candlestick
palmeado -da *adj* palmate; (bot. & zool.) palmate
palmear *va* (print.) to level (*a form*); (Am.) to pat, to slap; *vn* to clap; *vr* (naut.) to go aloft hand over hand
palmense *adj* (pertaining to) Las Palmas; *mf* native or inhabitant of Las Palmas, Canary Islands
palmeo *m* measuring by spans or palms
pálmer *m* micrometer caliper
palmera *f* elephant's ear (*cake*); (bot.) date palm; **palmera de betel** (bot.) betel palm; **palmera de las Antillas** (bot.) royal palm; **palmera de sombrilla** (bot.) talipot; **palmera enana** or **de abanico** (bot.) dwarf fan palm

palmeral *m* grove of date palms
palmero *m* palmer (*pilgrim from Holy Land*); caretaker of palm trees
palmesano -na *adj* (pertaining to) Palma; *mf* native or inhabitant of Palma, Majorca
palmeta *f* ferule; blow with a ferule
palmetazo *m* blow with a ferule; severe scolding
palmiche *m* (bot.) royal palm; nut of royal palm; (Am.) Palm Beach (*fabric*)
palmífero -ra *adj* (poet.) palmiferous
palmilla *f* blue woolen cloth; inner sole
palmípedo -da *adj* & *f* (zool.) palmiped
palmitato *m* (chem.) palmitate
palmitieso -sa *adj* flat-hoofed (*horse*)
palmito *m* (bot.) palmetto, dwarf fan palm; sprout (*of palm*); (coll.) face (*of a woman*); (coll.) slender figure (*of a woman*)
palmo *m* span, palm; **crecer a palmos** (coll.) to grow by leaps and bounds; **dejar con un palmo de narices** (coll.) to disappoint; **tener medido a palmos** to know every inch of
palmotear *vn* to clap
palmoteo *m* clapping; striking with a ferule
palo *m* stick; whack, blow with a stick; staff; handle; (naut.) mast; wood; execution on gallows; suit (*at cards*); (print.) hook or stroke (*of an ascender or descender*); (her.) pale; **dar palos de ciego** to lay about, to swing wildly; **de tal palo tal astilla** like father like son; **servir del palo** to follow suit; **palo áloe** aloes, aloes wood; **palo brasil** brazilwood; **palo campeche** logwood; **palo de áloe** aloes, aloes wood; **palo de barranco** (bot.) American hornbeam; **palo de Campeche** logwood; **palo de Cuba** (bot.) fustic; **palo de escoba** broomstick; **palo de hierro** (bot.) ironwood; **palo de jabón** soapbark, quillai bark; **palo de hule** (bot.) rubber tree; **palo de lanza** (bot.) lancewood; **palo de las Indias** lignum vitae (*wood*); **palo del Brasil** brazilwood; **palo de mesana** (naut.) mizzenmast; **palo de planchar** ironing board; **palo de rosa** (bot.) tulipwood (*tree and wood*); **palo de trinquete** (naut.) foremast; **palo dulce** licorice root; **palo en alto** big stick (*military or political coercive power*); **palo mayor** (naut.) mainmast; **palo santo** lignum vitae (*wood*)
paloma *f* (orn.) pigeon, dove; (fig.) dove, meek person, easy-going person; prostitute; (naut.) sling of yard; (slang) high collar; (slang) brandy and soda; **palomas** *fpl* whitecaps; **paloma brava** (orn.) stock dove; **paloma buchona** pouter (*pigeon*); **paloma capuchina** (orn.) capuchin (*pigeon*); **paloma colipava** (orn.) fantail; **paloma de pitahaya** (orn.) white-winged dove; **paloma emigrante** (orn.) passenger pigeon; **paloma mensajera** homing pigeon; **paloma silvestre** (orn.) stock dove; **paloma torcaz** (orn.) ringdove, wood pigeon; **paloma triste** (orn.) mourning dove; **paloma volcanera** (orn.) wood pigeon (*Columba fasciata*); **paloma zorita, zura, zurana** or **zurita** (orn.) rock dove
palomadura *f* (naut.) boltrope tie
palomar *adj* hard-twisted (*twine*); *m* pigeon house, dovecot
palomariego -ga *adj* domestic (*pigeon*)
palomear *vn* to hunt pigeons, to shoot pigeons; to breed pigeons
palomera *f* see **palomero**
palomería *f* pigeon shooting
palomero -ra *mf* pigeon breeder or fancier, pigeon seller; *f* small pigeon house; bleak spot
palometa *f* (mach.) pillow block; (ichth.) pomfret; (ichth.) weever; (ichth.) palometa (*Parona signata*)
palomilla *f* doveling; small butterfly; white horse; back (*of horse*); wall bracket; (bot.) alkanet (*Alkanna tinctoria*); (bot.) fumitory; (ent.) grain moth; (mach.) pillow block, journal bearing; (print.) galley rack; **palomillas** *fpl* whitecaps
palomina *f* pigeon droppings; (bot.) fumitory
palomino *m* young stock dove; palomino (*horse*); (coll.) dirty spot on shirttail
palomita *f* doveling; (Am.) piece of popcorn; (Am.) darling; **palomitas** *fpl* (Am.) popcorn
palomo *m* cock pigeon; (orn.) ringdove
palor *m* pallor
palotada *f* stroke with a drumstick; **no dar palotada** (coll.) to not do or say the right thing; (coll.) to be dilatory
palote *m* stick, drumstick; scribbled downstroke
paloteado *m* stick dance; (coll.) noisy scuffle
palotear *vn* to knock sticks together; to wrangle
paloteo *m* noise of sticks knocking together; (coll.) noisy scuffle
palpabilidad *f* palpability
palpable *adj* palpable
palpación *f* touching, feeling; groping; (med.) palpation
palpadura *f* or **palpamiento** *m* touching, feeling; groping
palpar *va* to touch, to feel; to grope through; to find self-evident; (med.) to palpate; *vn* to grope
pálpebra *f* eyelid
palpebral *adj* palpebral
palpitación *f* palpitation
palpitante *adj* palpitating; throbbing; thrilling; burning, of the moment (*said of an event, issue, etc.*)
palpitar *vn* to palpitate, to throb; to flash, to break forth (*said of an emotion*)
pálpito *m* thrill, excitement; (Am.) presentiment
palpo *m* palpus, feeler
palta *f* (Am.) avocado (*fruit*)
palto *m* (Am.) avocado tree
palúdico -ca *adj* marshy; marsh, malarial
paludismo *m* (path.) malaria
palurdo -da *adj* rustic, boorish; *mf* rustic, boor
palustre *adj* marshy, boggy; *m* trowel
pallador *m* (Am.) wandering minstrel
pallaquear *va* (Am.) var. of **pallar**
pallar *va* to extract (*metal*) from ore
pallete *m* (naut.) fender mat, cargo mat
pallón *m* assay button (*of gold or silver*)
pamela *f* woman's wide-brimmed straw hat; picture hat; (*cap.*) *f* Pamela (*woman's name*)
pamema *f* (coll.) trifle, bagatelle; (coll.) bunkum, humbug; (coll.) flattery
pampa *f* pampa; **La Pampa** the Pampas
pámpana *f* vine leaf; **tocar** or **zurrar la pámpana a** (coll.) to drub, to thrash
pampanada *f* juice of vine shoots
pampanaje *m* large growth of tendrils or shoots; froth, bluff; show, tinsel
pampanilla *f* loincloth; kilt worn by Indians
pampanito *m* (ichth.) pompano
pámpano *m* tendril; vine leaf; (ichth.) gilthead
pampanoso -sa *adj* full of tendrils
pampelmusa *f* var. of **pamplemusa**
pampero -ra *adj* & *mf* (Am.) pampean; *m* (Am.) pampero (*southwest wind from the Andes over the pampas*)
pampirolada *f* garlic sauce; (coll.) nonsense, simpleness
pamplemusa *f* (bot.) shaddock (*tree and fruit*); (bot.) grapefruit (*tree and fruit*)
pamplina *f* (bot.) chickweed; (bot.) large-flowered hypecoum; (coll.) nonsense, trifle, silly remark; **pamplina de agua** (bot.) brookweed; **pamplina de canarios** (bot.) chickweed
pamplinada *f* (coll.) nonsense, trifle
pamplinero -ra or **pamplinoso -sa** *adj* simple, silly
pamporcino *m* (bot.) cyclamen, sowbread
pamposado -da *adj* (coll.) idle, lazy
pampringada *f* toast dipped in gravy; (coll.) nonsense, triviality
pan *m* bread; loaf, loaf of bread; wheat; food; pie dough; cake (*e.g., of soap, wax*); gold foil or leaf, silver foil or leaf; (*cap.*) *m* (myth.) Pan; **panes** *mpl* grain, breadstuff; **a pan y agua** on bread and water; **buscar pan de trastrigo** (coll.) to be looking for trouble; **como el pan bendito** (coll.) as easy as pie; **de pan llevar** arable, tillable (*land*); **ganarse el pan** to earn one's livelihood; **llamar al pan pan y al vino vino** to call a spade a spade; **venderse como pan bendito** (coll.) to sell like hot cakes; **pan ázimo** unleavened bread; **pan bazo** brown bread; **pan candeal** white bread; **pan casero** homemade bread;

pan de azúcar sugar loaf (*mass of sugar; hat; hill*); **pan de cuco** (bot.) stonecrop; **pan de gluten** gluten bread; **pan del día** fresh bread; **pan de munición** army bread; prison bread; **pan de oro** gold leaf, gold foil; **panes de la proposición** (Bib.) shewbread; **pan porcino** (bot.) sowbread; **pan negro** black bread; **pan rallado** bread crumbs; **pan tierno** fresh bread; **pan y quesillo** (bot.) shepherd's-purse
pana *f* plush, velveteen, corduroy; (naut.) flooring board; (aut.) breakdown; **pana abordonada** or **acanillada** corduroy
pánace *f* (bot.) Hercules' allheal
panacea *f* panacea
panadear *va* to make (*flour*) into bread; *vn* to make bread, to be in the bread business
panadeo *m* making bread
panadería *f* bakery; baking business
panadero -ra *mf* baker; **panaderos** *mpl* clog dance
panadizo *m* (path.) felon, whitlow; (coll.) sickly person
panado -da *adj* breaded, bread-crumbed; flavored with toast
panal *m* honeycomb; hornet comb; lemon-flavored meringue
panamá *m* (*pl:* **-maes**) panama, panama hat; (*cap.*) *m* Panama (*country*); *f* Panama, Panama City
panameño -ña *adj & mf* Panamanian
panamericanismo *m* Pan-Americanism
panamericanista *mf* Pan-Americanist
panamericano -na *adj* Pan-American
panarábico -ca *adj* Pan-Arabian
panario -ria *adj* (pertaining to) bread
panarizo *m* var. of **panadizo**
panarra *m* (coll.) lazy simpleton
panatela *f* long thin spongecake
Panateneas *fpl* (hist.) Panathenaea
panática *f* (naut.) store of bread
panatier *m* var. of **panetero**
panca *f* (Am.) cornhusk
pancada *f* contract for lump sale
pancarpia *f* garland of flowers
pancarta *f* placard, poster
pancellar *m* or **pancera** *f* (arm.) belly plate
pancista *adj* weaseling, non-committal; *mf* weaseler
pancrático -ca *adj* var. of **pancreático**
páncreas *m* (*pl:* **-creas**) (anat.) pancreas
pancreático -ca *adj* pancreatic
pancreatina *f* (biochem.) pancreatin
pancromático -ca *adj* panchromatic
pancho *m* (ichth.) spawn of sea bream; (coll.) paunch, belly; (*cap.*) *m* (Am.) Frank
panda *m* see **pando**; *f* see **pando**
pandanáceo -a *adj* (bot.) pandanaceous
pandear *vn & vr* to warp, to bulge, to buckle, to sag, to bend
pandectas *fpl* (com.) index book; (*cap.*) *fpl* Pandects
pandemia *f* pandemic
pandémico -ca *adj* pandemic
pandemonio o **pandemónium** *m* pandemonium (*place*)
pandeo *m* warping, bulging, buckling, sagging, bending
pandera *f* (mus.) tambourine
panderada *f* tambourines; tambourine players; (coll.) nonsense
panderazo *m* blow with a tambourine
pandereta *f* (mus.) tambourine
panderete *m* (mus.) tambourine; brick wall in which bricks are laid on edge
panderetear *vn* to celebrate playing the tambourine, to sing and dance and play the tambourine
pandereteo *m* celebrating and playing the tambourine, singing and dancing and playing the tambourine
panderetero -ra *mf* tambourine player; tambourine maker or dealer
pandero *m* (mus.) tambourine; paper kite; (coll.) jabberer, silly chatterbox
pandiculación *f* stretching, pandiculation
pandilla *f* party, faction; gang, band; picnic, excursion; stacking cards
pandillaje *m* banding together; leaguing, intriguing
pandillar *va* to form into bands or gangs; **pandillar el naipe** (slang) to stack the cards
pandillero or **pandillista** *m* gang leader
pando -da *adj* bulging; slow-moving; slow, deliberate; *m* plain between two mountains; *f* gallery of a cloister; **panda** *m* (zool.) panda; **panda gigante** (zool.) giant panda
pandorada *f* evil, misfortune
pandorga *f* kite; (coll.) fat, lazy woman
panecillo *m* roll, manchet, crescent; crescent (*crescent-shaped object*)
panegírico -ca *adj* panegyrical; *m* panegyric
panegirista *mf* panegyrist
panegirizar §76 *va* to panegyrize, to eulogize
panel *m* panel; (elec.) panel; (naut.) removable floor board
panela *f* prism-shaped cake; corncake; (her.) poplar leaf (*on a shield*)
panenteísmo *m* (theol.) panentheism
panera *f* granary; bread basket; (dial.) bread tray
panero *m* baker's basket; round mat
paneslavismo *m* Pan-Slavism
paneslavista *adj* Pan-Slav or Pan-Slavic; *mf* Pan-Slavist
panetela *f* (cook.) panada; panetella (*cigar*)
panetería *f* pantry of royal palace
panetero -ra *mf* pantler
Panfilia *f* Pamphylia
panfilismo *m* extreme gentleness, great mildness
pánfilo -la *adj* slow, sluggish; discouraged; *mf* sluggard
panfletista *mf* pamphleteer
panfleto *m* pamphlet
pangelín *m* (bot.) angelin
pangénesis *f* (biol.) pangenesis
pangermanismo *m* Pan-Germanism
pangermanista *adj* Pan-German, Pan-Germanic; *mf* Pan-German
pangolín *m* (zool.) pangolin
panhelénico -ca *adj* Panhellenic
panhelenismo *m* Panhellenism
paniaguado *m* (archaic) servant, minion; (coll.) protégé, favorite
pánico -ca *adj* panic, panicky; *m* panic
panícula *f* (bot.) panicle
paniculado -da *adj* (bot.) paniculate
panicular *adj* pannicular
panículo *m* (anat.) panniculus; **panículo adiposo** (anat.) panniculus adiposus
paniego -ga *adj* bread-eating; wheat-bearing; *m* (dial.) charcoal bag
panificación *f* panification, making bread
panificar §86 *va* to make (*flour*) into bread; to convert (*pasture land*) into wheat fields
panique *m* (zool.) flying fox
panislamismo *m* Pan-Islamism
panislamista *adj* Pan-Islamic; *mf* Pan-Islamist
panizal *m* field of foxtail millet; (dial.) foam on cider
panizo *m* (bot.) Italian millet, foxtail millet; (Am.) gangue; **panizo de las Indias** (bot.) Indian corn; **panizo negro** (bot.) sorghum
panjí *m* (*pl:* **-jíes**) (bot.) China tree
panocha *f* ear of grain; ear of corn; (bot.) panicle; bunch of small fish fried with tails sticking together; bunch of fruit hung up for keeping; (Am.) panocha (*brown sugar; candy made from it*)
panoja *f* ear of grain; ear of corn; (bot.) panicle; bunch of small fish fried with tails sticking together; bunch of fruit hung up for keeping
panol *m* var. of **pañol**
panoli *m* (slang) simpleton
panoplia *f* panoply; wall trophy; study of ancient weapons
panorama *m* panorama
panorámico -ca *adj* panoramic
panoso -sa *adj* mealy
panqué *m* or **panqueque** *m* pancake
pantagruélico -ca *adj* Pantagruelian or Pantagruelic
pantalón *m* trousers; **pantalones** *mpl* trousers, pants, pantaloons; **calzarse** or **ponerse los pantalones** (coll.) to wear the pants, to

wear the trousers (*said of a wife*); **pantalón de agua** (aer.) emergency water ballast bag (*built in two sections and resembling a pair of trousers suspended at the waist, each leg being full of water and the valve being at the lower end of each leg*); **pantalón de salvamento** (naut.) breeches buoy; **pantalones de equitación** riding breeches; **pantalones de golf** golf trousers, knickerbockers; **pantalón rana** coveralls

pantalla *f* lamp shade; fire screen; motion-picture screen; television screen; person standing in front of another, person standing in the way; blind (*person concealing another's actions*); (phys.) screen; (fig.) screen (*moving pictures*); (Am.) fan; **llevar a la pantalla** to put (*a play*) on the screen; **servir de pantalla a** to be a blind for (*someone*); **pantalla acústica** (rad.) baffle; **pantalla de chimenea** fire screen; **pantalla fluorescente** (phys.) fluorescent screen; **pantalla plateada** silver screen (*movies*); **pantalla televisora** television screen

pantanal *m* swampland

pantanizar **§76** *vr* to become marshy or swampy; to dam up

pantano *m* bog, marsh, swamp; dam, reservoir; trouble, obstacle, morass; **Pantanos Pontinos** Pontine Marshes

pantanoso -sa *adj* marshy, swampy; muddy; knotty, difficult

pantasana *f* seine

panteísmo *m* pantheism

panteísta *adj* pantheistic; *mf* pantheist

panteístico -ca *adj* pantheistic

panteón *m* pantheon; mausoleum; cemetery

pantera *f* (zool.) panther (*Panthera pardus*)

pantógrafo *m* pantograph; (elec.) pantograph

pantómetra *f* pantometer

pantomima *f* pantomime

pantomímico -ca *adj* pantomimic

pantomimo *m* pantomimist

pantoque *m* (naut.) bilge

pantorrilla *f* calf (*of leg*)

pantorrillera *f* padded stocking

pantorrilludo -da *adj* thick-calved

pantoténico -ca *adj* pantothenic

pantufla *f* slipper, house slipper

pantuflazo *m* blow with a slipper, slippering

pantuflo *m* var. of **pantufla**

panza *f* paunch; belly (*e.g., of a vase*); (zool.) paunch, rumen (*of ruminant*); **panza de burra** (coll.) dark overcast (*sky*)

panzada *f* push with the belly; (coll.) bellyful

panzón -zona *adj* big-bellied; *m* big belly

panzudo -da *adj* big-bellied, paunchy

pañal *m* diaper; shirttail; **pañales** *mpl* swaddling clothes; infancy; early stages

pañalón *m* (coll.) sloppy-looking person

pañería *f* dry goods; cloths; dry-goods store, dry-goods department (*of a store*); cloth store, cloth department

pañero -ra *adj* dry-goods, cloth; *mf* dry-goods dealer, clothier

pañete *m* light, thin cloth; **pañetes** *mpl* trunks (*worn by fishermen*); breechcloth (*of crucifix*)

pañito *m* small cloth; **pañito de adorno** doily

pañizuelo *m* var. of **pañuelo**

paño *m* cloth; paper (*e.g., of needles*); breadth (*of cloth*); spot (*on face*); growth over eye; blur (*in mirror, precious stone, etc.*); hanging, drapery; (naut.) sailcloth, canvas; (Am.) shawl, kerchief; **al paño** (theat.) off-stage; **conocer el paño** (coll.) to know one's business, to know what one is up to; **poner el paño al púlpito** (coll.) to hold forth, to speak ex cathedra; **paño de adorno** antimacassar; **paño de altar** altar cloth; **paño de arrás** arras; **paño de cáliz** (eccl.) chalice veil; **paño de cocina** washrag, dishcloth; **paño de lágrimas** recourse, stand-by, helping hand; **paño de limpiar** cleaning rag; **paño de manos** towel; **paño de mesa** tablecloth; **paño de tumba** crape; **paño mortuorio** pall, hearsecloth; **paño pardillo** sacking, cheap coarse cloth; **paños calientes** (coll.) half measures; **paños menores** underclothing

pañol *m* (naut.) storeroom

pañolería *f* handkerchief shop; handkerchief business

pañolero -ra *mf* handkerchief maker or seller; *m* (naut.) storekeeper, yeoman

pañoleta *f* fichu; triangular plot of ground

pañolón *m* large shawl, scarf

pañoso -sa *adj* ragged, in rags; *f* (coll.) cloak, cloth cape

pañuelo *m* handkerchief; shawl; **pañuelo de bolsillo** or **de la mano** pocket handkerchief; **pañuelo de hierbas** bandana; **pañuelo para el cuello** scarf

papa *f* potato; (coll.) fake, hoax; (coll.) food, grub; (Am.) snap, cinch; **papas** (coll.) pap; **echar papas** (Am.) to fib, to lie; **no saber ni papa** (Am.) to not know a thing; **papa de caña** (bot.) Jerusalem artichoke; *m* pope; (coll.) papa; **papa negro** black pope

papá *m* (*pl:* **-pás**) (coll.) papa; **papás** *mpl* papa and mama

papable *adj* papable; eligible

papacito *m* (Am.) papa, daddy

papada *f* double chin; dewlap

papadilla *f* flesh under the chin

papado *m* papacy

papafigo *m* (orn.) figpecker; (orn.) golden oriole

papagaya *f* female parrot

papagayo *m* (orn.) parrot; (bot.) Joseph's-coat; (bot.) caladium; (ichth.) wrasse, peacock fish; (ichth.) roosterfish, papagallo; chatterbox; **papagayo de noche** (orn.) oilbird

papahigo *m* winter cap (*covering head, ears, and neck*)

papahuevos *m* (*pl:* **-vos**) (coll.) simpleton; (Am.) big-headed dwarf (*in a procession*)

papaína *f* (biochem.) papain

papal *adj* papal; *m* (Am.) potato field

papalino -na *adj* papal; *f* sunbonnet; (coll.) drunk (*spell of drinking*)

papamoscas *m* (*pl:* **-cas**) (orn.) flycatcher; (coll.) simpleton

papanatas *m* (*pl:* **-tas**) (coll.) simpleton, gawk

papandujo -ja *adj* (coll.) too soft, overripe

papar *va* to eat without chewing; (coll.) to eat; (coll.) to pay little attention to, to pass over hurriedly

páparo *m* gawk, gump

paparote -ta *mf* simpleton, boob

paparrabias *mf* (*pl:* **-bias**) (coll.) grouch, crab

paparrasolla *f* hobgoblin

paparrucha *f* (coll.) hoax; (coll.) trifle, inconsequentiality

paparruchada *f* (Am.) triviality, bagatelle

papasal *m* trifle, pastime

papatoste *m* var. of **papanatas**

papaveráceo -a *adj* (bot.) papaveraceous

papavientos *m* (*pl:* **-tos**) (orn.) goatsucker

papaya *f* papaya (*fruit*)

papayo *m* (bot.) papaya (*tree*)

pápaz *m* (used by African Moors) Christian priest

papazgo *m* papacy

papel *m* paper; piece of paper; rôle, part; character, figure; **desempeñar** or **hacer un papel** to play a rôle; **hacer papel** to cut a figure, to be somebody; **hacer buen papel** to make a good showing, to come out all right; **hacer el papel de** to play the rôle of; **hacer gran papel** to splurge, to cut a wide swath; **hacer mal papel** to come out badly, to fail; **tener buenos papeles** to have good backing; to be in the right; **traer los papeles mojados** (coll.) to bear false news; **papel alquitranado** tar paper; **papel biblia** Bible paper; **papel buscapolos** (elec.) pole-determining paper; **papel carbón** carbon paper; **papel cebolla** onionskin; **papel continuo** paper in rolls; **papel corrugado** corrugated paper; **papel cuché** art paper; **papel de barba** (theat.) rôle of an old man; **papel de barbas** untrimmed paper; **papel de calcar** tracing paper; **papel de cartas** letter paper; **papel de China** India paper; **papel de cúrcuma** (chem.) curcuma paper, turmeric paper; **papel de empapelar** or **de entapizar** wall-paper; **papel de escribir** writing paper; **papel de esmeril** emery paper; **papel de estaño** tin foil; **papel de estraza** brown wrapping paper; **papel de excusado** toilet paper;

papel de filtro filter paper; **papel de fumar** cigarette paper; **papel de lija** sandpaper; **papel de luto** mourning paper; **papel de marquilla** drawing paper; **papel de música** music paper; **papel de oficio** foolscap; **papel de ozono** (chem.) ozone paper; **papel de periódico** newsprint; **papel de seda** onionskin; tissue paper; **papel de segundón** second fiddle; **papel de tornasol** litmus paper; **papel higiénico** toilet paper; **papel mojado** scrap of paper; (coll.) trifle, triviality; **papel moneda** paper money; **papel pergamino** parchment paper; **papel pintado** wallpaper; **papel rayado** ruled paper; **papel satinado** glazed paper; **papel secante** blotting paper; **papel sepia** (phot.) sepia paper; **papel viejo** waste paper; **papel vitela** vellum paper; **papel volante** printed leaflet, handbill

papelear *vn* to look through papers; (coll.) to cut a figure, make a show

papelejo *m* scrap of paper

papeleo *m* looking through papers; red tape

papelera *f* see **papelero**

papelería *f* stationery store; scattered paper, mess of papers

papelerío *m* lot of paper; scattered paper, mess of papers

papelero -ra *adj* boastful, showy; (pertaining to) paper; *mf* paper manufacturer, paper dealer, stationer; *m* (bot.) paper mulberry; (Am.) paper boy; *f* paper case; writing desk; lot of papers; wastebasket

papeleta *f* slip of paper; card, file card; pawn ticket; examination paper; ballot; (coll.) tough problem; **no saberse la papeleta** to not know one's business; **papeleta de empeño** or **del monte** pawn ticket; **papeleta de fichero** filing card

papeletizar **§76** *va* to abstract on slips of paper or cards

papelillo *m* cigarette; paper (*of powdered medicine*)

papelina *f* tall drinking glass; poplin

papelista *m* papermaker, paper manufacturer; paper dealer, stationer; paper hanger; archivist

papelón -lona *adj* (coll.) bluffing, four-flushing; *mf* (coll.) bluffer, fourflusher; *m* worthless piece of paper; thin cardboard; (Am.) crystallized cane syrup

papelonear *vn* (coll.) to bluff, to four-flush

papelorio *m* mess of paper or papers

papelote *m* worthless paper, worthless piece of paper; (Am.) kite, child's kite

papel-prensa *m* newsprint

papelucho *m* var. of **papelote**

papera *f* goiter; mumps; **paperas** *fpl* scrofula

papero *m* pap pot; pap

papialbillo *m* (zool.) genet

papiamento *m* Curaçao Creole (*language of Curaçao and other Netherlands colonies of South America*)

papila *f* (anat. & bot.) papilla; **papila del gusto** (anat.) taste bud

papilar *adj* papillary

papilionáceo -a *adj* (bot.) papilionaceous

papiloma *m* (path.) papilloma

papilla *f* pap; guile, deceit

papillote *m* hair twisted in curlpaper; *f* (cook.) papillote, paper wrapper

papín *m* homemade sweet cake

papión *m* (zool.) papion

papiráceo -a *adj* papyraceous

papiro *m* (bot.) papyrus; papyrus (*strip of pith of this plant; record written on papyrus*)

papirolada *f* var. of **pampirolada**

papirotada *f* fillip; (coll.) folly, piece of stupidity

papirotazo *m* fillip

papirote *m* fillip; (coll.) nincompoop

papisa *f* popess; **Juana la papisa, la papisa Juana** Pope Joan

papismo *m* papistry, popery

papista *adj & mf* papist

papístico -ca *adj* papistic or papistical

papo *m* craw, maw; dewlap; puff (*in a dress*); (bot.) pappus; **papo de viento** (naut.) pocket in partly opened sail

papón *m* bogeyman

paporrear *va* to whip, to flog

papú -púa (*pl:* **-púes** & **-púas**) *adj & mf* Papuan

Papuasia, la Papua

papudo -da *adj* big-crawed; goitery

papujado -da *adj* full-gorged; swollen, puffed up

pápula *f* (path.) papule

papuloso -sa *adj* papulose

paq. abr. of **paquete**

paquear *va* to snipe at; *vn* to snipe

paquebote *m* packet boat

paqueo *m* sniping

paquete -ta *adj* (coll.) chic, dolled up; (Am.) insincere, self-important; *m* package, parcel, bundle, bale; packet boat; (coll.) sport, dandy; **en paquete aparte** under separate cover, in a separate package; **paquete de planchas fotográficas** film pack; **paquete regalo** (*pl:* **paquetes regalos**) gift package; **paquetes postales** parcel post (*service*)

paquetería *f* smallwares, notions

paquetero -ra *adj* packing, wrapping; *mf* parcel maker, wrapper; general distributor of bundles of newspapers; *m* (dial.) smuggler

paquidermo -ma *adj* (zool.) pachydermous; *m* (zool.) pachyderm

paquisandra *f* (bot.) pachysandra

Paquistán, el Pakistan

Paquita *f* Fanny

par *adj* like, similar, equal; (math.) even ‖ *m* pair, couple; principal rafter; peer (*equal; nobleman*); (elec. & mech.) couple; (math.) even number; **a pares** in twos; **al par** equally; jointly; at the same time; **de par en par** wide-open; completely; overtly; **en par de** on par with, equal to; **sin par** peerless, matchless, unequaled; **par de fuerzas** (mech.) couple; **¿pares o nones?** odd or even? (*guessing game*); **par motor** (mech.) torque; **par térmico** (elec.) thermocouple; **par termoeléctrico** (elec.) thermoelectric couple ‖ *f* par; **a la par** equally; jointly; at the same time; (com.) at par; **a la par con** abreast with; **a la par que** as well as; while, at the same time that; **bajo la par** (com.) below par or under par; **sobre la par** (com.) above par

para *prep* to, for; towards; compared to; by (*a certain time*); **para** + *inf* in order to + *inf;* about to + *inf;* **para con** towards; **para mí** for me; to myself; **para que** in order that, so that; **¿para qué?** for what reason?

pára *3d sg pres ind of* **parar**

parabién *m* congratulation; **dar el parabién a** to congratulate

parábola *f* parable; (geom.) parabola

parabólico -ca *adj* parabolic; (geom.) parabolic

paraboloide *m* (geom.) paraboloid

parabrisa *m* or **parabrisas** *m* (*pl:* **-sas**) windshield; **parabrisas panorámico** (aut.) wraparound windshield

paracaídas *m* (*pl:* **-das**) parachute; **salvarse en paracaídas** to parachute to safety; **paracaídas piloto** pilot chute

paracaidismo *m* parachute jumping

paracaidista *mf* parachutist; *m* (mil.) paratrooper

Paracelso *m* Paracelsus

paracentesis *f* paracentesis

paracleto or **paráclito** *m* Paraclete

paracronismo *m* parachronism

parachispas *m* (*pl:* **-pas**) spark arrester; (elec.) spark arrester

parachoques *m* (*pl:* **-ques**) (rail.) bumper, bumping post; (aut.) bumper

parada *f* see **parado**

paradera *f* sluice gate, floodgate; fishing seine

paradero *m* end; whereabouts; stopping place; (Am.) railroad station

paradiclorobenceno *m* (chem.) paradichlorobenzene

paradigma *m* (gram. & fig.) paradigm

paradina *f* scrub pasture with sheep pens

paradisíaco -ca *adj* paradisiacal

paradislero *m* hunter on the watch; newsmonger

parado -da *adj* slow, spiritless, witless; idle, out of work, unemployed; stopped; closed; (Am.) straight, standing; (Am.) proud, stiff; **salir mejor parado** to come off better ‖ *f* stop; end; stay, suspension; shutdown; stake (*in gambling*); dam; stall (*for cattle*); stud farm; parry (*in fencing*); relay (*of horses*); post (*for keeping horses for relays*); (mil.) parade, dress parade, review; (mus.) pause; **doblar la parada** to double the stakes; to double one's bid; **salir a la parada a** to go to meet; **parada de taxi** taxi stand; **parada en cuarta** (fencing) parry of or in carte or quarte; **parada en primera** (fencing) parry of or in prime; **parada en segunda** (fencing) parry of or in seconde; **parada en tercera** (fencing) parry of or in tierce
paradoja *f* see **paradojo**
paradójico -ca *adj* paradoxical
paradojo -ja *adj* paradoxical; *f* paradox
parador -dora *adj* stopping; heavy-betting; *mf* heavy bettor; *m* inn, wayside inn, hostelry; **parador de turismo** motel
paraestatal *adj* government-coöperating, government-affiliated (*e.g., agency*)
parafina *f* paraffin
parafraseador -dora *adj* paraphrasing; *mf* paraphraser
parafrasear *va* to paraphrase
paráfrasis *f* (*pl:* **-sis**) paraphrase
parafraste *m* paraphrast
parafrástico -ca *adj* paraphrastic
paragoge *f* (gram.) paragoge
paragógico -ca *adj* paragogic
paragolpes *m* (*pl:* **-pes**) (rail.) buffer, bumper
paragrafía *f* (path.) paragraphia
parágrafo *m* paragraph
paragranizo *m* canvas cover to protect crops from hail
paraguas *m* (*pl:* **-guas**) umbrella
paraguatán *m* (bot.) Central American madder (*Sickingia tinctoria*)
Paraguay, el Paraguay
paraguaya *f* see **paraguayo**
paraguayano -na *adj & mf* Paraguayan
paraguayo -ya *adj & mf* Paraguayan; *f* flat-shaped peach
paragüería *f* umbrella store
paragüero -ra *mf* umbrella maker; umbrella vendor; *m* umbrella stand
parahuso *m* pump drill
paraíso *m* paradise; paradise (*top gallery of theater*); **paraíso de los bobos** (coll.) air castles; **paraíso terrenal** paradise, garden of Eden
paraje *m* place, spot; state, condition
parajismero -ra *adj* grimacing
parajismo *m* face, grimace
paral *m* putlog; (naut.) ground ways
paraláctico -ca *adj* parallactic
paralaje *f* parallax
paralar *va* to putlog
paralasis *f* (*pl:* **-sis**) var. of **paralaje**
paralaxi *f* var. of **paralaje**
paraldehido *m* (chem.) paraldehyde
paralela *f* see **paralelo**
paralelar *va* to parallel, to compare
paralelepípedo *m* (geom.) parallelepiped or parallelepipedon
paralelismo *m* parallelism
paralelizar §76 *va* to parallel, to compare
paralelo -la *adj* parallel; *m* (geog. & fig.) parallel; **en paralelo** (elec.) in parallel; *f* (geom. & fort.) parallel; **paralelas** *fpl* (sport) parallel bars
paralelogramo *m* (geom.) parallelogram
paralipómenos *mpl* (Bib.) Paralipomena
paralipsis *f* (*pl:* **-sis**) (rhet.) paralipsis
parálisis *f* (*pl:* **-sis**) paralysis; **parálisis agitante** (path.) paralysis agitans; **parálisis cerebral infantil** (path.) cerebral palsy; **parálisis infantil** (path.) infantile paralysis
paraliticar §86 *vr* to become paralyzed
paralítico -ca *adj & mf* paralytic
paralización *f* paralization
paralizador -dora *adj* paralyzing
paralizar §76 *va* to paralyze; (fig.) to paralyze; *vr* to become paralyzed

paralogismo *m* (log.) paralogism
paralogizar §76 *va* to try to convince with specious arguments; *vr* to paralogize
paramagnético -ca *adj* paramagnetic
paramagnetismo *m* paramagnetism
paramecio *m* (zool.) paramecium
paramentar *va* to adorn, bedeck; to caparison; to face, to surface
paramento *m* adornment, ornament; hangings; caparison; face, surface; **paramentos sacerdotales** (eccl.) liturgical vestments
paramera *f* bleak, barren country
parámetro *m* (math.) parameter
páramo *m* high barren plain; bleak windy spot; (Am.) cold drizzle
parancero *m* birdcatcher
parangón *m* comparison
parangona *f* (print.) paragon
parangonar *va* to compare
paranieves *m* (*pl:* **-ves**) snow fence
paraninfo *m* assembly hall, auditorium; speaker at opening exercises (*of a university*); bringer of joy; (poet.) best man, groomsman
paranoia *f* (path.) paranoia
paranoico -ca *adj & mf* paranoiac
paranoya *f* var. of **paranoia**
paranza *f* hunter's hut or blind
parapetar *va* to fortify with parapets; *vr* to fortify oneself with parapets; to protect oneself
parapeto *m* parapet; (fort.) parapet
paraplejía *f* (path.) paraplegia
parapléjico -ca *adj & mf* paraplegic
parapoco *mf* (*pl:* **parapoco**) (coll.) numskull
parapsicología *f* parapsychology
parar *m* lansquenet (*card game*); *va* to stop; to check; to change; to prepare; to put up, to stake; to parry; to order; to get, acquire; to fix (*attention*); (hunt.) to point (*game*); (print.) to set; (Am.) to prick up (*ears*); *vn* to stop; to put up (*e.g., in a hotel*); **sin parar** right away; **parar en** to become; to run to (*said of a train or rail line*); **parar a las manos de** or **en poder de** to come into the hands of; *vr* to stop; to stop work; to turn, to become; to be ready for danger; to stand up on end (*said, e.g., of hair*); (Am.) to stand up; **pararse a** + *inf* to stop to + *inf*, to pause to + *inf;* **pararse en** to pay attention to
pararrayo or **pararrayos** *m* (*pl:* **-yos**) lightning rod; lightning arrester; **pararrayo de cuernos** horn lightning arrester
parasanga *f* parasang
parasceve *m* parasceve
paraselene *f* (meteor.) paraselene
parasicología *f* var. of **parapsicología**
parasimpático -ca *adj & m* (anat. & physiol.) parasympathetic
parasíntesis *f* (gram.) parasynthesis
parasismo *m* var. of **paroxismo**
parasitario -ria *adj* parasitic
parasiticida *adj & m* parasiticide
parasítico -ca *adj* parasitic
parasitismo *m* parasitism
parásito -ta *adj* parasitic; (elec.) stray; *m* (biol. & fig.) parasite; **parásitos atmosféricos** (rad.) atmospherics, static
parasito -ta *adj & m* var. of **parásito**
parasitología *f* parasitology
parasitológico -ca *adj* parasitological
parasitólogo -ga *mf* parasitologist
parasol *m* parasol; (bot.) umbel
parata *f* step terrace
paratífico -ca or **paratifoide** *adj* paratyphoid
paratifoidea *f* (path.) paratyphoid fever
paratiroideo -a *adj* parathyroid
paratiroides *adj & m* parathyroid
paratopes *m* (*pl:* **-pes**) (rail.) bumper, bumping post
paraulata *f* (orn.) Venezuelan thrush
paraván *m* screen
paraviento *m* screen; bicycle windshield (*of celluloid*)
parca *f* & **Parcas** *fpl* see **parco**
parce *m* reward card (*in school*)
parcela *f* plot, piece of ground; particle
parcelación *f* or **parcelamiento** *m* parceling (*of land*)
parcelar *va* to parcel, to divide into lots
parcial *adj* partial; partisan; *mf* partisan

parcialidad *f* partiality; faction, party; clique; partisanship; sociability, friendliness
parcidad *f* var. of **parquedad**
parcimonia *f* var. of **parsimonia**
parcionero -ra *adj* participant; *mf* participant; accomplice
parcísimo -ma *adj super* very or most frugal; very or most moderate
parco -ca *adj* frugal, sparing; moderate; *f* (poet.) death; **Parcas** *fpl* (myth.) Parcae, Fates
parcha *f* (bot.) passionflower
parchar *va* (Am.) to mend, to patch
parchazo *m* large plaster; (naut.) bang of a sail against mast or yard; (coll.) gyp, swindle; **pegar un parchazo a** (coll.) to gyp, to swindle
parche *m* plaster, sticking plaster; patch; drum; drumhead; daub, botch, splotch; **pegar un parche a** (coll.) to gyp, to swindle; **parche poroso** porous plaster
parchesí *m* parcheesi
parchista *m* (coll.) sponger
pardal *adj* rustic; *m* (orn.) linnet; (orn.) swallow; (zool.) leopard; (zool.) camelopard; (bot.) wolfsbane; (coll.) sly fellow
pardear *vn* to be drabbish, to appear drab
pardejón -jona *adj* (Am.) drabbish
pardela *f* (orn.) small sea gull
pardiez *interj* (coll.) by Jove!
pardillo -lla *adj* drab; *m* (orn.) redpoll, linnet; (coll.) sly fellow
pardisco -ca *adj* var. of **pardusco**
pardo -da *adj* brown; drab; dark; cloudy; dull, flat (*voice*); dark (*beer*); (Am.) mulatto; *mf* (Am.) mulatto; *m* brown; drab; (zool.) leopard
pardusco -ca *adj* drabbish, grayish
pareado -da *adj* in the form of a couplet, rhymed; *m* couplet
parear *va* to pair; to match; (taur.) to thrust banderillas in; *vr* to pair off
parecencia *f* resemblance, likeness
parecer *m* opinion; look, mien, countenance; **a mi parecer** to my mind, in my opinion; **por el bien parecer** for appearance, to save appearances; §34 *vn* to appear; to show up; to look, to seem; **a lo que parece** or **al parecer** apparently; **cambiar** or **mudar de parecer** to change one's mind; **me parece que sí** I guess so, so it seems to me; **¿qué le parece?** what do you think?, what is your opinion?; **según parece** apparently; **parecer** + *inf* to seem to + *inf*; *vr* to look alike, to resemble each other; **parecerse a** to look like
parecido -da *adj* like, similar; **parecidos -das** *adj pl* alike, e.g., **estas casas son parecidas** these houses are alike; **bien parecido** good-looking; **mal parecido** ill-favored, hard-looking; **parecido a** like, e.g., **esta casa es parecida a la otra** this house is like the other one; *m* similarity, resemblance, likeness
pared *f* wall; **dejar pegado a la pared** (coll.) to nonplus; **entre cuatro paredes** shut in, withdrawn; **hasta la pared de enfrente** (coll.) to the limit, with all one's might; **pared maestra** main wall; **pared medianera** partition wall, party wall; **pared por medio** partition wall; next door; **pared supersónica** sonic barrier
paredaño -ña *adj* adjoining, separated by a wall
paredón *m* wall standing amid ruins; thick wall
paregórico -ca *adj & m* paregoric
pareja *f* see **parejo**
parejero -ra *adj* even, equal; (Am.) servile, cringing; *m* (Am.) steed, race horse
parejo -ja *adj* equal, like; even, smooth; **por parejo** or **por un parejo** alike, on a par; *f* pair, couple; dancing partner (*male or female*); **parejas** *fpl* pair (*of cards*); **correr parejas** or **a las parejas** to be abreast, arrive together; to go together, match, be equal; **correr parejas con** to keep up with, to keep abreast of
parejura *f* equality, similarity; evenness, smoothness
paremia *f* paroemia, proverb
paremiología *f* paroemiology
paremiólogo -ga *mf* paroemiologist
parénesis *f* (*pl:* **-sis**) admonition, exhortation
parenético -ca *adj* admonitory
parénquima *m* (anat. & bot.) parenchyma
parenquimatoso -sa *adj* parenchymatous
parental *adj* parental
parentela *f* kinsfolk, relations
parenteral *adj* parenteral
parentesco *m* relationship; bond, tie
paréntesis *m* (*pl:* **-sis**) (gram.) parenthesis; (fig.) parenthesis, break, interval; **dentro de un paréntesis** or **entre paréntesis** in parentheses; **entre paréntesis** or **por paréntesis** parenthetically; by the way
parentético -ca *adj* parenthetic or parenthetical
pareo *m* pairing; matching
paresa *f* peeress
paresia or **paresis** *f* (path.) paresis
parético -ca *adj & mf* paretic
pargo *m* (ichth.) porgy; **pargo colorado** (ichth.) dog snapper; **pargo criollo** or **guachinango** (ichth.) red snapper, muttonfish, mutton snapper
parhelia *f* var. of **parhelio**
parhélico -ca *adj* parheliacal or parhelic
parhelio *m* (meteor.) parhelion
parhilera *f* ridgepole
paria *mf* & **parias** *fpl* see **pario**
paría *f* peerage
parián *m* (Am.) market
parición *f* parturition time of cattle
parida *adj fem* recently delivered; *f* woman recently delivered
paridad *f* parity; comparison
paridera *adj* prolific (*female*); *f* parturition; parturition time; parturition place
paridora *adj* prolific (*female*)
pariente -ta *adj* related; *mf* relative; (coll.) spouse
parietal *adj* parietal; (anat., bot. & zool.) parietal; *m* (anat.) parietal
parificación *f* exemplification
parificar §86 *va* to exemplify, to show by comparison
parigual *adj & m* like, equal
parihuela *f* or **parihuelas** *fpl* handbarrow; stretcher
pario -ria *adj & mf* Parian; **paria** *mf* pariah (*of low caste of India and Burma*); outcast, pariah; **parias** *fpl* tribute, homage; (anat.) placenta
paripé *m* (slang) arrogance, haughtiness; **dar el paripé a** (slang) to cajole, deceive; **hacer el paripé** (slang) to put on airs
paripinado -da *adj* (bot.) paripinnate
parir *va* to bear, to give birth to, to bring forth; *vn* to give birth; to lay eggs; to come forth, to come to light; to express oneself, to talk well
Paris *m* (myth.) Paris
París *m* Paris
parisiense *adj & mf* Parisian
parisilábico -ca or **parisílabo -ba** *adj* parisyllabic
parisino -na *adj* (coll.) Parisian
paritario -ria *adj* labor-management (*board*)
parla *f* ease, facility in speaking; chatter, gossip
parlador -dora *adj* chattering, gossiping; *mf* chatterbox, gossip
parladuría *f* chatter, gossip, talk
parlaembalde *mf* (*pl:* **parlaembalde**) (coll.) chatterbox
parlamentar *vn* to talk, chat; to parley
parlamentario -ria *adj* parliamentary; *mf* parliamentarian
parlamentarismo *m* parliamentarism
parlamento *m* parliament; parley; speech; (theat.) speech; **Parlamento Largo** (hist.) Long Parliament
parlanchín -china *adj* (coll.) chattering, jabbering; *mf* (coll.) chatterer, jabberer; *m* (orn.) garden warbler
parlante *adj* talking
parlar *vn* to speak with facility; to chatter, to gossip, to talk too much; to talk (*said, e.g., of a parrot*)
parlatorio *m* talk, chat; parlor
parlería *f* loquacity, garrulity; gossip; (poet.) song of birds; (poet.) babbling of brooks

parlero -ra *adj* loquacious, garrulous; gossipy; singing, song (*bird*); expressive (*eyes*); babbling (*brook or spring*)
parleta *f* (coll.) chat, idle talk, gabble
parlón -lona *adj* (coll.) talkative; *mf* (coll.) talker
parlotear *vn* (coll.) to prattle, jabber
parloteo *m* (coll.) prattle, jabber
Parménides *m* Parmenides
parmesano -na *adj & mf* Parmesan; *m* Parmesan (*cheese*)
parnasiano -na *adj* Parnassian
parnaso *m* Parnassus (*collection of poems*); **el Parnaso** Mount Parnassus
parné *m* (slang) dough, cash
paro *m* shutdown, work stoppage; lockout; (orn.) titmouse; (Am.) throw (*of dice*); **paro carbonero** (orn.) great titmouse; **paro forzoso** layoff, unemployment
parodia *f* parody, travesty
parodiar *va* to parody, to travesty
paródico -ca *adj* parodical
parodista *mf* parodist
parola *f* (coll.) fluency, volubility; (coll.) chat, idle talk
parolero -ra *adj* (coll.) chattering, jabbering
pároli *m* paroli, leaving one's stake and winnings in the pot
parolina *f* (coll.) var. of **parola**
paronimia *f* paronymy
parónimo -ma *adj* paronymous; *m* paronym
paronomasia *f* paronomasia
parótida *f* (anat.) parotid; **parótidas** *fpl* (path.) mumps
parotideo -a *adj* (anat.) parotid, parotidean; (path.) parotitic
paroxismal *adj* paroxysmal
paroxismo *m* paroxysm; (path.) paroxysm
paroxítono -na *adj & m* (phonet.) paroxytone
parpadear *vn* to blink, to wink; to flicker
parpadeo *m* blinking, winking; flicker
párpado *m* eyelid
parpar *vn* to quack
parque *m* park; parking; parking space; parking lot; park, garden (*for wild animals*); equipment, outfit; (mil.) park; **parque de atracciones** amusement park; **parque de incendios** fire station; **parque de recreo** pleasure ground; amusement park; **parque para caballos** paddock; **parque zoológico** zoölogical garden
parquear *va* var. of **aparquear**
parquedad *f* frugality; moderation
parqueo *m* (Am.) parking
parquet *m* market, stock market
parra *f* (bot.) grapevine; earthen jar; **subirse a la parra** (coll.) to blow up, to hit the ceiling
parrado -da *adj* spreading
parrafada *f* (coll.) confidential interview
parrafeada *f* (Am.) confidential chat
parrafear *vn* to chat confidentially
parrafeo *m* confidential chat
párrafo *m* paragraph; (coll.) chat; **echar párrafos** (coll.) to gossip away; **echar un párrafo** (coll.) to chat, have a chat; **párrafo aparte** (coll.) changing the subject
parragón *m* assayer's standard silver bar
parral *m* vine arbor, grape arbor; place full of vine arbors; wild, untrimmed vineyard; large earthen jar for honey
parranda *f* (coll.) spree, party; **andar de parranda** (coll.) to go out on a spree, to go out to celebrate
parrandear *vn* (coll.) to go out on a spree, to go out to celebrate
parrandero -ra *adj* (coll.) reveling; *mf* (coll.) reveler
parrandista *mf* (coll.) reveler, carouser
parrar *vn* to spread out (*said of trees and plants*)
parricida *adj* patricidal; parricidal; *mf* patricide (*person*); parricide (*person*)
parricidio *m* patricide (*act*); parricide (*act*)
parrilla *f* grill, gridiron, broiler; grate, grating; earthen jug; grille (*e.g., of auto*); grill, grillroom; **asar a la parrilla** to broil
parriza *f* wild grapevine
parro *m* (orn.) duck
párroco *m* parson, parish priest
parrocha *f* (ichth.) small sardine; canned sardine
parrón *m* wild grapevine
parroquia *f* parish; parochial church; clientele, customers
parroquial *adj* parochial
parroquialidad *f* parochialism
parroquiano -na *adj* parochial, parish; *mf* parishioner; customer
parsi *adj* Parsic; *mf* Parsee or Parsi; *m* Parsee or Parsi (*dialect*)
parsimonia *f* parsimony; moderation
parsimonioso -sa *adj* parsimonious; moderate
parsismo *m* Parseeism
parte *f* part; share; party; side; direction; (theat. & mus.) part; (law) party; **partes** *fpl* parts, gifts, talent; faction; parts, genitals; **a parte de** apart from; **de buena parte** on good authority; **de la parte de** on the part of; **de un mes a esta parte** for about a month (*past*); **de parte a parte** from one end to the other, through and through; from one to the other; **de parte de** on the side of; on behalf of; **echar a mala parte** to look upon with disapproval; to use (*a word or phrase*) improperly; **en buena parte** in good part (*without taking offense*); **en ninguna parte** nowhere; **en parte** in part; **hacer las partes de** to act on behalf of; **la mayor parte** most, the majority; **por la mayor parte** for the most part; **por mi (su) parte** for or on my (his) part; **por otra parte** in another direction; elsewhere; on the other hand; **por todas partes** everywhere; **salva sea la parte** (coll.) excuse me for not mentioning where (*i.e., in what part of the body*); **tener parte con una mujer** to have intercourse with a woman; **tomar a mala parte** to look upon with disapproval; to use (*a word or phrase*) improperly; **tomar parte en** to take part in; **parte actora** (law) prosecution; plaintiff; **parte alicuanta** (math.) aliquant part; **parte alícuota** (math.) aliquot part; **parte de la oración** or **parte del discurso** (gram.) part of speech; **parte del león** lion's share; **parte de por medio** small-part actor; **partes contratantes** (dipl.) contracting parties; **parte por parte** in full; **partes naturales, pudendas** or **vergonzosas** privates, private parts; *m* dispatch, communiqué; **dar parte a** to inform; *adv* part, partly
parteaguas *m* (*pl:* **-guas**) divide, ridge; **parteaguas continental** continental divide
partear *va* to assist (*a woman*) in childbirth
parteluz *m* (*pl:* **-luces**) (arch.) mullion, sash bar
partencia *f* departure
partenogénesis *f* (biol.) parthenogenesis
partenogenético -ca *adj* parthenogenetic
Partenón *m* Parthenon
partenueces *m* (*pl:* **-ces**) nutcracker
partera *f* midwife
partería *f* midwifery
partero *m* accoucheur, man midwife
parterre *m* flower bed
partesana *f* (archaic) halberd
Partia *f* Parthia
partible *adj* divisible, separable
partición *f* partition, division
particionero -ra *adj & mf* participant
participación *f* communication, notification; participation; share (*in a lottery ticket*)
participante *adj* notifying; participant; *mf* notifier; participant; accomplice
participar *va* to communicate; to inform; **participar una cosa a una persona** to notify or inform a person of something; *vn* to participate; **participar de** to partake of; **participar en** to partake in, to participate in
partícipe *adj & mf* participant
participial *adj* participial
participio *m* (gram.) participle; **participio activo** or **de presente** (gram.) present participle; **participio pasivo** or **de pretérito** (gram.) past participle, perfect participle
pártico -ca *adj* Parthian
partícula *f* particle; (eccl., gram. & phys.) particle; **partícula nobiliaria** nobiliary particle; **partícula prepositiva** (gram.) prefix

particular *adj* particular; peculiar; private, personal; *m* particular (*item, point*); matter, subject; individual; private individual; **en particular** in particular; in private
particularidad *f* particularity; intimacy
particularización *f* particularization; specialization
particularizar §76 *va & vn* to particularize; *vr* to be distinguished, to stand out; **particularizarse en** + *inf* to specialize in + *ger*
partida *f* see **partido**
partidamente *adv* separately
partidario -ria *adj* partisan; *mf* partisan, supporter
partidismo *m* partisanship
partidista *adj & mf* partisan
partido -da *adj* generous, open-handed; (her.) party ‖ *m* (pol.) party; decision; profit, advantage; step, measure; deal, agreement; protection, support; match (*prospective partner in marriage*); district, county; area or circuit under care of a physician or surgeon; (sport) team; (sport) game, match; (sport) handicap, odds; (dial.) room; (Am.) part (*in hair*); **sacar partido de** to derive profit from; **tomar partido** to make up one's mind, take a stand, take sides; **partido conservador** (pol.) conservative party; **partido de desempate** (sport) play-off ‖ *f* departure; entry, item; certificate; party, group, band, gang; band of guerrillas; game; hand (*of cards*); set (*of tennis*); lot, shipment; (fig.) departure (*death*); (coll.) behavior; (Am.) part (*in hair*); **buena partida** (coll.) good turn; **echar una partida** to play a game (*e.g., of cards*); **mala partida** (coll.) mean trick; **partida de bautismo** certificate of baptism; **partida de campo** picnic; **partida de caza** hunting party; **partida de defunción** death certificate; **partida de matrimonio** marriage certificate; **partida de nacimiento** birth certificate; **partida de pesca** fishing party; **partida doble** (com.) double entry; **partida serrana** (coll.) dirty trick, double cross; **partida sencilla** or **simple** (com.) single entry
partidor *m* divider, separator, cleaver, splitter; (math.) divisor; **partidor de tensión** (rad.) voltage divider
partidura *f* part (*in hair*)
partija *f* small part; partition
partil *adj* (astrol.) partile
partimento or **partimiento** *m* partition, division
partiquino -na *mf* (mus.) singer of small parts
partir *va* to divide; to distribute; to share; to split, split open; to break, crack; to gash; (math.) to divide; (coll.) to upset, disconcert; *vn* to start, depart, leave, set out; to make up one's mind; **a partir de** beginning with; **partir a** + *inf* to start out to, to depart to + *inf;* **partir de** to reckon from; *vr* to become divided or split; to crack, to split
partisano -na *mf* (mil.) partisan
partitivo -va *adj* partitive; (gram.) partitive
partitura *f* (mus.) score
parto -ta *adj & mf* Parthian; *m* childbirth, delivery, labor; newborn child; product, offspring; prospect; brain child; **el parto de los montes** a great cry, but little wool; **estar de parto** to be in labor; **parto del ingenio** brain child
parturición *f* parturition
parturienta or **-te** *adj* parturient (*woman*); *f* woman in confinement
párulis *m* (*pl:* **-lis**) (path.) gumboil; (path.) phlegmon
parva *f* see **parvo**
parvada *f* heaps of unthreshed grain; flock, covey
parvedad *f* smallness, minuteness; light breakfast (*on fast days*)
parvero *m* long pile of grain for winnowing
parvidad *f* var. of **parvedad**
parvificar §86 *va* to make small; to diminish, lessen
parvo -va *adj* small, little; *f* light breakfast (*on fast days*); heap of unthreshed grain; heap, pile
parvulez *f* smallness; simpleness, innocence
parvulista *mf* kindergartner, kindergarten teacher
párvulo -la *adj* small, tiny; simple, innocent; humble, timid; *mf* child, tot; kindergartner (*child*)
pasa *f* see **paso**
pasable *adj* passable, fair
pasacalle *m* quickstep; (mus.) lively march; (mus.) passacaglia
pasacaminos *m* (*pl:* **-nos**) runner (*of carpet*)
pasacólica *f* (path.) upset stomach
pasada *f* see **pasado**
pasadero -ra *adj* passable; fair, good enough; *f* stepping stone; colander; walkway, catwalk; (naut.) spun yarn
pasadía *f* subsistence, fair subsistence; (Am.) picnic in the country
pasadillo *m* two-face embroidery
pasadizo *m* passage, corridor, hallway, alley; catwalk
pasado -da *adj* past; gone by; overripe, spoiled; stale; overdone; burned out; out-of-date, antiquated; (gram.) past; **lo pasado, pasado** let bygones be bygones; **pasado de maduro** overripe; *m* past; (mil.) deserter; (gram.) past; **pasados** *mpl* ancestors; **pasado próximo** recent past; *f* passage, passing; weft thread; **de pasada** in passing, hastily; **mala pasada** (coll.) mean trick
pasador -dora *adj* smuggling; *mf* smuggler; *m* door bolt; bolt, pin (*e.g., of hinge*); hatpin; brooch; stickpin; safety pin; strainer; colander; (naut.) marlinspike; **pasador de enganche** (rail.) coupling pin; **pasador de horquilla** cotter pin
pasadura *f* passage, transit; convulsive sobbing (*of a child*)
pasagonzalo *m* (coll.) tap, slight tap, flick
pasaje *m* passage; fare; fares; passengers; (mus.) passage; (naut.) strait; **cobrar el pasaje** to collect fares; **de pasaje** passenger
pasajero -ra *adj* passing, fleeting; common, frequented (*road, street, etc.*); migratory (*bird*); *mf* passenger; **pasajero no presentado** no-show (*passenger who fails to notify the company that he is not going to use his reservation*)
pasajuego *m* (sport) return of a serve
pasamanar *va* to passement, to trim with lace
pasamanería *f* passementerie, lace; passementerie or lace shop; lacemaking
pasamanero -ra *mf* passementerie maker or dealer
pasamano *m* passement, lace; handrail; (naut.) gangway
pasamiento *m* passage, transit
pasamontaña *m* or **pasamontañas** *m* (*pl:* **-ñas**) balaclava helmet, cap comforter, ski mask
pasante *adj* (her.) passant; *m* tutor; docent; assistant (*of a teacher, lawyer, or doctor*); **pasante de pluma** barrister's clerk
pasantía *f* tutorage, tutorship; docentship; assistantship
pasapán *m* (coll.) gullet
pasapasa *m* legerdemain
pasaportar *va* to issue a passport to
pasaporte *m* passport; (mil.) transportation (*for a soldier*); (fig.) passport
pasar *m* livelihood; **un buen pasar** enough to get along on ‖ *va* to pass; to cross, go through or over; to take across; to send, transfer, transmit; to slip in (*contraband*); to spend; to swallow; to excel; to stand, stand for, overlook; to undergo, to suffer; to go through (*a book*); to dry in the sun; to tutor, give private lessons in; to study with and assist (*a doctor or lawyer*); **pasar en blanco, en claro** or **por alto** to disregard; to omit, leave out, skip; **pasarlo** to be (*said of health*); to get along; to live; **pasarlo bien** to enjoy oneself, to have a good time ‖ *vn* to pass; to go; to pass away; to pass over (*said, e.g., of a fit of anger*); to happen; to last, to do; to spread; to get along; to yield; to come in, e.g., **pase Vd.** come in; **ir pasando** to manage to get along; **pasar a** + *inf* to go on to + *inf;* to stop by to + *inf;* **pasar a ser** to become; **pasar de** to go beyond, to exceed; to go above; to get beyond being;

pasar de + *inf* to go beyond + *ger;* **pasar de . . . años** to be more than . . . years old; **pasar por** to pass by, down, through, over, etc.; to pass as, to pass for; to stop or call at; **pasar por encima** to push right through; to push one's way to the top; **pasar sin** to do without; **pasar y traspasar** to pass back and forth ‖ *vr* to pass; to go; to excel; to pass over (*said, e.g., of a fit of anger*); to get along; to pass away; to take an examination; to leak; to be porous; to go too far; to become overripe, become overcooked, become tainted; to rot; to melt; to burn out; to not fit, to be loose (*said of a key, of a screw, etc.*); **pasarse al enemigo** to go over to the enemy; **pasarse de** + *adj* to be too + *adj;* **pasarse de** + *noun* to become + *noun;* **pasársele a uno** to forget, e.g., **se me pasó lo que me dijo Vd.** I forgot what you told me; **pasársele a uno** + *inf* to forget to + *inf,* e.g., **se me pasó abrir la ventana** I forgot to open the window; **pasarse por** to stop or call at; **pasarse sin** to to do without

pasarela *f* footbridge; catwalk; gangplank

pasarríos *m* (*pl:* **-rríos**) (zool.) basilisk, lizard

pasatapas *m* (*pl:* **-pas**) (elec.) bushing (*of a transformer*)

pasatiempo *m* pastime

pasavante *m* (nav.) safe-conduct

pasavolante *m* hasty act, thoughtlessness

pascua *f* Passover; Easter; Twelfth-night; Pentecost; Christmas; **pascuas** *fpl* Christmas holiday (*from Christmas to Twelfth-night*); **dar las pascuas** to wish a Happy New Year; **estar como una pascua** or **unas pascuas** (coll.) to be bubbling over with joy; **¡Felices Pascuas!** Merry Christmas!; **santas pascuas** (coll.) there's no choice, I give up; **Pascua de flores** Easter; **Pascua del Espíritu Santo** Pentecost; **Pascua de Navidad** Christmas; **Pascua de Resurrección** or **Pascua florida** Easter; **Pascuas navideñas** Christmas holiday (*from Christmas to Twelfth-night*)

pascual *adj* paschal

pascueta *f* (bot.) fireweed (*a wild lettuce*)

pascuilla *f* first Sunday after Easter

pase *m* pass (*permit; manipulation of mesmerist; free ticket*); exequatur; feint (*in fencing*); (taur.) pass (*move in which bullfighter, after inciting bull with muleta, allows him to pass by*); **pase de cortesía** complimentary ticket

paseante *adj* strolling; *mf* stroller; **paseante en corte** (coll.) loafer

pasear *va* to walk (*a child, a horse*); to promenade, show off; to cast (*a glance*); *vn* to take a walk; to go for a ride; **enviar** or **mandar a uno a pasear** (coll.) to send someone on his way, to dismiss a person without ceremony; *vr* to take a walk; to go for a ride; to wander, ramble; to take it easy; **pasearse a caballo** to go horseback riding; **pasearse en automóvil** to take an automobile ride; **pasearse en bicicleta** to go bicycling; **pasearse en canoa** to go boating; **pasearse en coche** to go for a ride

paseata *f* (coll.) walk, ride

paseíllo *m* processional entrance of the bullfighters

paseo *m* walk, stroll, promenade; ride; drive; avenue; **dar un paseo** to take a walk; to take a ride; **echar, enviar** or **mandar a uno a paseo** (coll.) to send someone on his way, to dismiss a person without ceremony; **ir de paseo** to go walking, to go out for a walk; to go for a ride; **sacar a paseo** to take out for a walk; to take out for a ride; **paseo de caballos** bridle path; **paseo de la cuadrilla** (taur.) processional entrance of the bullfighters

pasero -ra *adj* pacing, walking (*horse*); *mf* raisin seller; *f* drying of fruit; drying hurdle, drying room

pasibilidad *f* passibility, sensibility

pasible *adj* passible, sensible; deserving

pasicorto -ta *adj* making short steps

pasiega *f* nurse

pasiflora *f* (bot.) passionflower

pasifloráceo -a *adj* (bot.) passifloraceous

pasilargo -ga *adj* making long steps

pasillo *m* short step; passage, corridor; (sew.) basting stitch; (theat.) short piece, sketch

pasión *f* passion; (*cap.*) *f* (rel. & f.a.) Passion; **tener pasión por** to have a passion for

pasional *adj* passional

pasionaria *f* (bot.) passionflower (*plant and flower*)

pasionario *m* (eccl.) Passion songbook

pasioncilla *f* passing emotion; ugly grudge

pasionero *m* (eccl.) Passion singer; priest assigned to a hospital

pasionista *m* (eccl.) Passion singer

pasitamente *adv* gently, softly

pasito *m* short step; *adv* gently, softly

pasitrote *m* short trot

pasividad *f* passivity, passiveness

pasivo -va *adj* passive; retirement (*pension*); (gram.) passive; *m* (com.) liabilities; (com.) debit side (*of an account*)

pasmar *va* to chill; to frostbite; to stun, benumb; to dumfound, astound; *vr* to chill; to become frostbitten; to be astounded; to get lockjaw; to become dull or flat (*said, e.g., of colors*)

pasmarota or **pasmarotada** *f* (coll.) feigned spasm; (coll.) exaggerated show of surprise

pasmarote *m* (coll.) flabbergasted person

pasmo *m* (path.) cold; (path.) lockjaw, tetanus; astonishment; wonder, prodigy; **de pasmo** astonishingly

pasmón -mona *adj* open-mouthed, gawky; *mf* gawk

pasmoso -sa *adj* astounding; awesome

paso -sa *adj* dried (*fruit*) ‖ *m* step, pace; step (*of stairs*); gait, walk; go (*in traffic*); passing; passage; step, measure, démarche; permit, pass; strait; footstep, footprint; incident, happening; basting stitch; exequatur; pitch (*of propeller, nut, screw*); (elec.) pitch; (rad.) stage; (theat.) short piece, sketch, skit; **abrir paso** to open a path or way; to clear the way; **abrirse paso** to make one's way; **a buen paso** at a good pace or rate, hurriedly; **a cada paso** at every step, at every turn; **a dos pasos de** a short distance from; **a ese paso** at that rate; **aflojar el paso** (coll.) to slow down; **alargar el paso** (coll.) to hasten one's steps; **al paso** in passing, on the way; (chess) en passant; **al paso que** while, whereas; **al paso que vamos** at the rate we are going; **a paso de caracol** at a snail's pace; **a paso de carga** with leaps and bounds; **a paso de tortuga** at a snail's pace; **apretar** or **avivar el paso** (coll.) to hasten one's steps; **avanzar a grandes pasos** to make great or rapid strides; **buen paso** high living; **caminar a paso fino** to single, to single-foot; **ceder el paso** to step aside, to make way, to stay back, to keep clear, to let pass; **dar paso a** to give rise to; **dar pasos** to take steps; **dar un paso** to take a step; **de paso** in passing; at the same time; **de paso para** on the way to; **estar de paso** to be passing through; **llevar el paso** to keep step; **marcar el paso** (mil.) to mark time; (Am.) to obey humbly; **por sus pasos contados** in the usual way; **romper paso** to break step; **salir al paso a** to run into, to waylay; to buck, oppose; to confront; **salir del paso** (coll.) to get out of a jam, get out of a difficulty; **seguir los pasos a** to keep an eye on, to check; **seguir los pasos de** (fig.) to follow the footsteps of; **volver sobre sus pasos** to retrace one's steps; **paso a nivel** (rail.) grade crossing; **paso a paso** step by step; **paso de ambladura** or **andadura** amble; **paso de ganado** cattle crossing; **paso de ganso** (mil.) goose step; **pasa doble** (mil.) military march, quickstep; **paso en falso** slip, false step; **paso fino** single-foot (*of a horse*); **paso ligero** pitapat; (mil.) double time, double-quick; **paso polar** (elec.) pole pitch; **pasos de gigante** (sport) giant's stride; **paso único** (aut.) one line, single line ‖ *f* raisin; kink (*of Negro's hair*); (naut.) channel; **estar hecho una pasa** (coll.) to be all dried up, to be full of wrinkles; **pasa de Corinto** currant ‖ **paso** *adv* gently, softly; **¡paso!** easy there!

pasodoble *m* (mil.) military march, quickstep

pasoso -sa *adj* (Am.) porous; (Am.) sweaty

pasote *m* var. of **pazote**

paspa *f* (Am.) crack in the lips (*from cold and wind*)
paspié *m* (mus.) passepied (*music and dance*)
pasquín *m* pasquinade, lampoon; billboard
pasquinada *f* squib, lampoon
pasquinar *va* to pasquinade, to lampoon
pasta *f* paste, dough, pie crust, soup paste; mash; pulp (*for making paper*); cardboard; (b.b.) board binding; filling (*of a tooth*); (mineral. & ceramics) paste; (coll.) dough (*money*); cookie; **pastas** *fpl* noodles, macaroni, spaghetti, etc.; **de buena pasta** kindly, well-disposed; **media pasta** (b.b.) half binding; **pasta de hígado de ganso** pâté de foie gras; **pasta dentífrica** tooth paste; **pasta española** (b.b.) marbled leather binding, tree calf; **pasta seca** cookie
pastadero *m* pasture land
pastaflora *f* sponge cake
pastar *va* to lead to the pasture; *vn* to graze
pasteca *f* (naut.) snatch block
pastel *m* pie; pastry roll; meat pie; pastel (*drawing; crayon*); pastil or pastille (*pastel for crayons; crayon*); settlement, pacification; cheat, trick (*in shuffling cards*); (coll.) plot, deal; (bot.) woad; (print.) pi; (print.) smear
pastelear *vn* to temporize, to weasel
pastelejo *m* small pie
pastelería *f* pastry; pastry shop; pastry cooking
pastelero -ra *mf* pastry cook; (coll.) easy-going person, weaseler
pastelillo *m* tart, cake; pat (*e.g., of butter*); **pastelillo de hígado de ganso** pâté de foie gras
pastelista *mf* pastelist
pastelito *m* patty
pastelón *m* meat pie
pastenco -ca *adj* newly weaned (*cattle*)
pasterización *f* pasteurization
pasterizar §76 *va* to pasteurize
pastero *m* workman who throws crushed olives into pressing bags
pasteurizar §76 *va* var. of **pasterizar**
pastilla *f* tablet, lozenge, drop; dab (*soft mass*); cake (*of soap, chocolate, etc.*)
pastinaca *f* (bot.) parsnip; (ichth.) sting ray
pastizal *m* pasture for horses
pasto *m* pasture; grass; food, nourishment; (fig.) food (*e.g., for thought, gossip*); **a pasto** to excess; in abundance; **a todo pasto** freely, without restriction; **de pasto** ordinary, everyday
pastor *m* shepherd; **el Buen Pastor** (Bib.) the Good Shepherd; **pastor protestante** pastor, protestant minister
pastora *f* shepherdess; (bot.) poinsettia
pastoral *adj* pastoral; *f* (eccl. & lit.) pastoral; (mus.) pastoral or pastorale
pastorear *va* to shepherd (*flocks or souls*)
pastorela *f* shepherd's song; pastoral (*lyric poem*); (lit.) pastourelle
pastoreo *m* shepherding, pasturing
pastoría *f* shepherding; shepherds
pastoricio -cia or **pastoril** *adj* pastoral
pastosidad *f* pastiness, doughiness; mellowness
pastoso -sa *adj* pasty, doughy; mellow (*voice*); (paint.) pastose
pastura *f* pasture; fodder
pasturaje *m* pasturage, pasture land; pasturing fee
pata *f* paw, foot, leg; pocket flap; leg (*of furniture*); (hum.) leg (*of human being*); (orn.) duck (*female of drake*); **a cuatro patas** (coll.) on all fours; **a la pata llana** plainly, frankly; **enseñar la pata** (coll.) to show the cloven hoof, to give oneself away; **estirar la pata** (coll.) to kick the bucket; **meter la pata** (coll.) to butt in, to upset everything, to put one's foot in it; **sacar la pata** (coll.) to show the cloven hoof, to give oneself away; **salir** or **ser pata** or **patas** to be a tie; to be tied; **saltar a la pata coja** to hop; **tener mala pata** to be unlucky; **pata de araña** (mach.) oil groove; **pata de cabra** crowbar; **pata de gallina** radial crack in trees (*sign of rot*); **pata de gallo** crow's-foot (*at corner of eye*); (coll.) bull, blunder; (coll.) absurdity, piece of nonsense; **pata de palo** peg leg (*leg and person*); **pata es la traviesa** tit for tat; **pata galana** (coll.) game leg; (coll.) lame person; **pata hendida** cloven hoof; **patas arriba** (coll.) on one's back, upside down; (coll.) topsy-turvy; **patas** *m* (*pl:* **-tas**) (coll.) devil
pataco -ca *adj* churlish; *mf* churl; *f* (bot.) Jerusalem artichoke
patada *f* kick; stamp, stamping (*of foot*); (coll.) step; (coll.) footstep, track; **a patadas** (coll.) on all sides; **dar la patada a** to kick out
patagio *m* (zool.) patagium
patagón -gona *adj* Patagonian; (coll.) big-footed; *mf* Patagonian
patagónico -ca *adj* Patagonian
patagorrilla *f* or **patagorrillo** *m* haslet (*dish*)
patalear *vn* to kick; to stamp the feet
pataleo *m* kicking; stamping
pataleta *f* (coll.) feigned fit or convulsion
patán *adj masc* (coll.) churlish, boorish, loutish; *m* (coll.) churl, boor, lout; (coll.) villager, peasant
patanería *f* (coll.) churlishness, boorishness, loutishness
pataplún *interj* ker-plunk!
patarata *f* foolishness, simpleness; affectation; overpoliteness
pataratero -ra *adj* simple; affected; overpolite
patarráez *m* (*pl:* **-rraíces**) (naut.) preventer shroud
patata *f* (bot.) potato; **patata de caña** (bot.) Jerusalem artichoke; **patatas fritas** fried potatoes; **patatas majadas** mashed potatoes
patatal *m* or **patatar** *m* potato patch
patatear *vr* to flunk
patatero -ra *adj* (pertaining to the) potato; potato-eating; (coll.) up from the ranks; *mf* potato seller
patatús *m* (coll.) fainting fit
pateadura *f* or **pateamiento** *m* kicking, stamping; noisy protest; (coll.) severe dressing down
patear *va* (coll.) to kick; (coll.) to trample on, tread on; (coll.) to treat roughly; *vn* (coll.) to stamp one's foot (*in anger*); (coll.) to bustle around, to make a fuss; (Am.) to kick (*said of a gun*)
patela *f* (anat., archeol. & zool.) patela; (zool.) limpet
patelar *adj* (anat.) patellar
patélula *f* (bot.) patella
patena *f* large medal worn around the neck by peasant women; (eccl.) paten
patentar *va* to patent
patente *adj* patent, clear, evident; *f* grant, privilege, warrant; **de patente** (Am.) excellent, first-class; **patente de circulación** (aut.) owner's license; **patente de corso** (naut.) letters of marque; **patente de invención** patent; **patente de sanidad** (naut.) bill of health
patentizar §76 *va* to make evident, to reveal
pateo *m* (coll.) kicking, stamping
páter *m* (mil.) padre; **páter familias** (Roman law) paterfamilias
paternal *adj* paternal; fatherly; paternalistic
paternalismo *m* paternalism
paternidad *f* paternity; fatherhood; **paternidad literaria** authorship
paterno -na *adj* paternal
paternóster *m* (*pl:* **paternóster**) paternoster; big tight knot
pateta *m* (coll.) devil; (coll.) cripple (*in feet or legs*)
patético -ca *adj* pathetic
patetismo *m* pathos
patiabierto -ta *adj* (coll.) bowlegged
patialbillo *m* (zool.) genet
patialbo -ba or **patiblanco -ca** *adj* white-footed
patibulario -ria *adj* of the scaffold; horrifying, hair-raising
patíbulo *m* scaffold (*for executions*)
paticojo -ja *adj* (coll.) lame, crippled
patidifuso -sa *adj* (hum.) silly, stunned, agape, flabbergasted
patiecillo *m* small patio
patiestevado -da *adj* bandy-legged, bowlegged
patihendido -da *adj* cloven-footed, cloven-hoofed

patilla *f* small paw or foot; chape (*of buckle*); pocket flap; (naut.) compass; (elec.) connecting lead (*of a vacuum tube*); (Am.) watermelon; **patillas** *fpl* sideburns, side whiskers; **patillas** *m* (coll.) the devil
patilludo -da *adj* bewhiskered
patín *m* small patio; (orn.) petrel; skate; skid, slide, runner; (aer.) skid; (elec.) contact shoe; (rail.) base (*of rail*); (naut.) skiff; **patín de cola** (aer.) tail skid; **patín de cuchilla** or **de hielo** ice skate; **patín de ruedas** roller skate
pátina *f* patina
patinadero *m* skating rink
patinador -dora *mf* skater; **patinador de fantasía** fancy skater; **patinador de figura** figure skater
patinaje *m* skidding; skating; **patinaje artístico** figure skating; **patinaje de fantasía** fancy skating; **patinaje de figura** figure skating
patinar *va* to patinate, give an artificial patina to; *vn* to skate; to skid; to slip, to spin
patinazo *m* skid, sudden skid; slipping, spinning
patinejo *m* small patio
patinete *m* scooter (*child's vehicle*)
patinillo *m* small patio
patio *m* patio, court, yard; campus; (metal.) patio; (rail.) yard, switchyard; (theat.) orchestra; **patio de carga** (rail.) freight yard; **patio de maniobras** (rail.) switchyard; **patio de recreo** playground
patipollo *m* duckling
patiquebrar §18 *va* to break the leg of (*an animal*); *vr* to break a leg
patita *f* small paw or foot; **poner de patitas en la calle** (coll.) to throw out, to bounce
patitieso -sa *adj* (coll.) paralyzed (*in feet or legs*); (coll.) dumfounded; stiff, haughty; lifeless, dead
patito *m* duckling, young duck; **el Patito Feo** the Ugly Duckling
patituerto -ta *adj* crooked-legged; (coll.) crooked, lopsided, misshapen
patizambo -ba *adj* knock-kneed
pato *m* (orn.) duck, drake; **el pato Donaldo** Donald Duck; **pagar el pato** (coll.) to be the goat; **pato almizclado** (orn.) Muscovy duck; **pato bobo** (orn.) booby; **pato canelo** (orn.) sheldrake; **pato cuchareta** (orn.) shoveler (*Spatula clypeata*); **pato chiquito** (orn.) teal, blue-winged teal; **pato de flojel** (orn.) eider, eider duck; **pato mandarín** (orn.) mandarin duck; **pato marrueco** (orn.) widgeon; **pato negro** (orn.) black scoter; **pato pelucón** (orn.) canvasback; **pato picazo** (orn.) widgeon; **pato real** (orn.) mallard; **pato sierra** (orn.) goosander, merganser; **pato silbador** (orn.) widgeon; **pato silvestre** (orn.) mallard; **pato zarcel** (orn.) blue-winged teal
patochada *f* (coll.) blunder, stupidity
patogénesis *f* or **patogenia** *f* pathogenesis or pathogeny
patogénico -ca *adj* pathogenic
patógeno -na *adj* pathogenic (*producing disease*)
patojo -ja *adj* crooked-legged, waddling (*like a duck*); *mf* (Am.) young person
patología *f* pathology; **patología vegetal** plant pathology
patológico -ca *adj* pathologic or pathological
patólogo -ga *mf* pathologist
patón -tona *adj* (coll.) big-footed, big-pawed
patoso -sa *adj* smart-alecky
patota *f* (Am.) gang of young thugs
Patr. abr. of **Patriarca**
patraña *f* (coll.) fake, humbug, hoax
patrañero -ra *mf* (coll.) fake, humbug (*person*)
patrañoso -sa *adj* (coll.) fake
patria *f* see **patrio**
patriarca *m* patriarch
patriarcado *m* patriarchate; patriarchy
patriarcal *adj* patriarchal; *f* patriarch's church; patriarchate (*territory*)
patriciado *m* patriciate
patricio -cia *adj* patrician; (Am.) American-born; *m* patrician
patrimonial *adj* patrimonial
patrimonialidad *f* (eccl.) birthright
patrimonio *m* patrimony
patrio -tria *adj* native, home; paternal; *f* country (*land where one is a citizen*); mother country, fatherland, native land; birthplace; (fig.) home (*e.g., of the arts*); **patria celestial** heavenly home; **patria chica** native heath
patriota *mf* patriot
patriotería *f* (coll.) spread-eagleism, exaggerated patriotism
patriotero -ra *adj* (coll.) spread-eagle, exaggeratedly patriotic; *mf* (coll.) spread-eagleist
patriótico -ca *adj* patriotic
patriotismo *m* patriotism
patrístico -ca *adj* patristic; *f* patristics
patrocinador -dora *adj* sponsoring; *mf* sponsor, patron; (rad. & telv.) sponsor
patrocinar *va* to favor, sponsor, patronize; (rad. & telv.) to sponsor
patrocinio *m* favor, sponsorship, patronage; (rad. & telv.) sponsorship
Patroclo *m* (myth.) Patroclus
patrología *f* patrology
patrón -trona *mf* sponsor, protector; patron saint; *m* patron; landlord; owner, master; boss, foreman; host; skipper (*of a boat*); pattern; standard (*of measure, of money*); stock (*on which a graft is made*); **patrón oro** gold standard; **patrón picado** stencil (*sheet to make letters and designs*); *f* patroness; landlady; owner, mistress; hostess; (naut.) galleon ranking next to flagship
patronal *adj* patronal; employers'
patronar *va* var. of **patronear**
patronato *m* employers' association; foundation; board of trustees; patronage; **patronato de turismo** organization to encourage touring
patronazgo *m* var. of **patronato**
patronear *va* to skipper
patronía *f* skippership
patronímico -ca *adj & m* patronymic
patrono -na *mf* sponsor, protector; employer; *m* patron; landlord; boss, foreman; lord of the manor; **los patronos** management; *f* patroness; landlady
patrulla *f* (aer., mil. & nav.) patrol; gang, band
patrullaje *m* (aer., mil. & nav.) patrolling
patrullar *va & vn* (aer., mil. & nav.) to patrol
patrullero -ra *adj* (pertaining to) patrol; *m* (naut.) patrol ship
patuá *m* (*pl:* **-tuaes**) patois
patudo -da *adj* (coll.) big-footed, big-pawed
patués *m* patois
patulea *f* (coll.) disorderly soldiers; (coll.) mob, gang of roughnecks; (coll.) group of noisy brats
patullar *vn* to stamp around; (coll.) to make a fuss, to hustle around; (coll.) to chat
paují *m* (*pl:* **-jíes**) (orn.) cashew bird
paujil *m* var. of **paují**
paúl *m* bog, marsh
paular *m* bog, marsh; *vn* (coll.) to talk, chat; **ni paula ni maula** doesn't even open his mouth; **sin paular ni maular** without saying boo
paulatino -na *adj* slow, gradual
paulilla *f* (ent.) grain moth
paulina *f* & **Paulina** *f* see **paulino**
paulinista *adj & mf* Paulinist
paulino -na *adj* Pauline; *f* decree of excommunication; (coll.) censure, reproof; (coll.) poison-pen letter; (*cap.*) *f* Pauline
paulonia *f* (bot.) paulownia
pauperismo *m* pauperism
paupérrimo -ma *adj super* very or most poor
pausa *f* pause; slowness, delay; (gram.) pause; (mus.) rest
pausado -da *adj* slow, calm, deliberate; **pausado** *adv* slowly, calmly, deliberately
pausar *va & vn* to slow down
pauta *f* ruler; guide lines (*for writing*); guideline, rule, guide, standard, model; (mus.) ruled staff; **marcar la pauta a** to set the pace for
pautada *f* (mus.) musical staff
pautador *m* paper ruler (*person*)
pautar *va* to rule (*paper*); to give directions for

pava *f* (orn.) turkey hen; furnace bellows; Paul Jones (*dance*); (coll.) dull, colorless woman; **pelar la pava** (coll.) to make love at a window; **pava real** (orn.) peahen
pavada *f* flock of turkeys; (coll.) dullness, inanity
pavana *f* pavan (*dance and music*)
pavear *vn* (Am.) to talk nonsense; (Am.) to make love at a window
pavero -ra *mf* turkey raiser and dealer; *m* Andalusian broad-brimmed hat
pavés *m* pavis, large shield; **alzar** or **levantar sobre el pavés** to elevate to leadership, to glorify
pavesa *f* ember, spark; **estar hecho una pavesa** (coll.) to be weak and exhausted; **ser una pavesa** (coll.) to be meek and mild
pavesada *f* var. of **empavesada**
pavezno *m* young turkey
pavía *f* (bot.) pavy, clingstone peach (*tree and fruit*)
pávido -da *adj* (poet.) timid, fearful
pavimentación *f* paving
pavimentar *va* to pave
pavimento *m* paving, pavement
paviota *f* (orn.) sea gull
pavipollo *m* young turkey
pavisoso -sa *adj* dull, graceless
pavita *f* (orn.) sunbird, sun bittern
pavitonto -ta *adj* stupid, foolish
pavo *m* (orn.) turkey; turkey cock; (coll.) dull, colorless fellow; **comer pavo** (coll.) to be a wallflower; **ponerse hecho un pavo** (slang) to blush; **pavo de matorral** (orn.) brush turkey; **pavo real** (orn.) peacock
pavón *m* bluing, browning, bronzing (*of iron or steel*); (orn.) peacock; (ent.) peacock butterfly; (*cap.*) *m* (astr.) Peacock
pavonado -da *adj* dark-blue; gun-metal; *m* bluing, browning, bronzing (*of iron or steel*); *f* (coll.) stroll, short walk; (coll.) show, vain display
pavonar *va* to blue, to brown, to bronze (*iron or steel*)
pavonear *vn & vr* to strut, swagger, show off
pavoneo *m* strutting, swaggering
pavor *m* fear, terror
pavorde *m* (eccl.) provost
pavordear *vn* to swarm (*said of bees*)
pavordía *f* (eccl.) provostship
pavoroso -sa *adj* frightful, terrible
pavura *f* var. of **pavor**
paya *f* (Am.) improvised song, accompanied on the guitar
payasada *f* clownishness, clownish stunt, clownish remark
payasear *vn* (Am.) to be clownish
payasería *f* (Am.) clownishness; (Am.) clown's life
payaso *m* clown; laughingstock
payés -yesa *mf* Catalan peasant
payo -ya *adj* rustic, peasant; *m* churl, gump
payuelas *fpl* (path.) chicken pox
paz *f* (*pl:* **paces**) peace; peacefulness; (eccl.) pax (*ceremony and tablet*); **¡a la paz de Dios!** (coll.) God be with you!; **dejar en paz** to leave alone; **descansar en paz** to rest in peace; **estar en paz** to be even; to be quits; **hacer las paces con** to make peace with, to come to terms with; **no dar paz a** to give no rest to; **poner en paz** or **poner paz entre** to reconcile; **salir en paz** (coll.) to break even (*in gambling*); *interj* peace!, quiet!
pazguatería *f* simpleness, doltishness
pazguato -ta *adj* simple, doltish; *mf* simpleton, dolt
pazote *m* (bot.) wormseed, Mexican tea
pazpuerca *adj fem* (coll.) sluttish; *f* (coll.) slut
pbro. abr. of **presbítero**
pche or **pchs** *interj* pshaw!
P.D. abr. of **posdata**
P.e abr. of **Padre**
pea *f* drunkenness, drunken spree
peaje *m* toll
peajero *m* toll collector, tollkeeper
peal *m* foot (*of stocking*); knitted legging; (coll.) good-for-nothing
peán *m* (hist.) paean
peana or **peaña** *f* base, pedestal, stand; hat block; window sill; altar step
peatón *m* walker, pedestrian; rural postman
pebete *m* punk, joss stick; fuse; (coll.) stinker (*thing*)
pebetero *m* perfume censer
pebrada *f* sauce of pepper, garlic, parsley, and vinegar
pebre *m & f* sauce of pepper, garlic, parsley, and vinegar; pepper; (Am.) mashed potatoes
peca *f* freckle
pecable *adj* peccable
pecado *m* sin; (coll.) devil; **de mis pecados** of mine; **por mal de mis pecados** to my sorrow, unfortunately for me; **siete pecados capitales** seven deadly sins; **pecado capital** capital sin; **pecado mortal** mortal sin; **pecado original** (theol.) original sin; **pecado venial** venial sin
pecador -dora *adj* sinning, sinful; *mf* sinner; *f* (coll.) prostitute
pecaminoso -sa *adj* sinful
pecante *adj* sinning; excessive
pecar §86 *vn* to sin; to go astray; **pecar de** + *adj* to be too + *adj*
pecarí *m* (*pl:* **-ríes**) (zool.) peccary
pécari *m* var. of **pecarí**
pecblenda *f* var. of **pechblenda**
pece *m* ridge between furrows; *f* mud or mortar for walls or other building
pececico, pececillo or **pececito** *m* little fish
peceño -ña *adj* pitchy
pecera *f* fish globe, fish bowl
pecezuela *f* small piece
pecezuelo *m* little foot; little fish
peciento -ta *adj* pitchy (*in color*)
peciluengo -ga *adj* long-stalked
pecina *f* fishpool; slime
pecinal *m* slime hole, swamp
pecinoso -sa *adj* slimy
pecio *m* (naut.) flotsam
peciolado -da *adj* petiolate
pecíolo *m* (bot. & zool.) petiole
pécora *f* head of sheep; **buena pécora** or **mala pécora** (coll.) schemer (*generally a woman*)
pecorea *f* cattle stealing; marauding, looting; hanging around, staying out
pecorear *va* to steal (*cattle*); *vn* to maraud, to loot
pecoso -sa *adj* freckly, freckle-faced
pecten *m* (zool.) pecten
pectina *f* (chem.) pectin
pectinado -da *adj* pectinate
pectíneo -a *adj* pectinate; (anat.) pectineal; *m* (anat.) pectineus
pectinibranquio -quia *adj* (zool.) pectinibranchian
pectoral *adj* pectoral; *m* pectoral; breastplate (*of Jewish high priest*); (pharm.) pectoral; (eccl.) pectoral cross
pecuario -ria *adj* (pertaining to) cattle
peculado *m* peculation
peculiar *adj* peculiar
peculiaridad *f* peculiarity
peculio *m* (law) peculium; small fund, small savings
pecunia *f* (coll.) cash, dough
pecuniario -ria *adj* pecuniary
pechar *va* to pay as a tax; to fulfill; to take on (*a disagreeable burden or responsibility*); (Am.) to bump or push with the chest; (Am.) to drive one's horse against; (Am.) to strike for a loan; *vn* **pechar con** to take on (*a disagreeable burden or responsibility*)
pechblenda *f* (mineral.) pitchblende
peche *m* pilgrim's scallop; *adj* (Am.) thin, sickly
pechera *f* see **pechero**
pechería *f* taxes; tax roll
pechero -ra *adj* taxable; *mf* taxpayer; commoner, plebeian; *m* bib; *f* shirt front, shirt bosom; vestee; chest protector; bib (*of apron*); breast strap (*of harness*); (coll.) bosom
pechiblanco -ca *adj* white-breasted
pechicolorado *m* (orn.) redpoll, linnet
pechina *f* pilgrim's scallop; (arch.) pendentive
pechirrojo *m* (orn.) redpoll
pechisacado -da *adj* (coll.) vain, arrogant
pecho *m* (anat.) chest; breast, bosom; teat; heart, courage; slope, hill; voice, strength of

voice; tax, tribute; **abrir el pecho** to unbosom oneself; **a pecho abierto** frankly; **a pecho descubierto** unprotected, unarmed; openly, frankly; **dar el pecho** to nurse, to suckle; (coll.) to face it out; **de dos pechos** double-breasted; **descubrir el pecho** to unbosom oneself; **de un solo pecho** single-breasted; **echar el pecho al agua** (coll.) to put one's shoulder to the wheel; (coll.) to speak out; **en pechos de camisa** (Am.) in shirt sleeves; **entre pecho y espalda** deep, in the heart; **tomar a pecho** to take to heart; **tomarse a pechos** (Am.) to take seriously, to make an issue of; (Am.) to take offense at; **¡pecho al agua!** take heart!, put your shoulder to the wheel!; **pecho amarillo** (orn.) yellowthroat, Maryland yellowthroat; **pecho de pichón** (path.) pigeon breast
pechuelo *m* small breast
pechuga *f* breast (*of fowl*); (coll.) breast, bosom; (coll.) slope, hill; (Am.) brass, cheek; (Am.) treachery, perfidy
pechugón -gona *adj* (coll.) big-chested; (Am.) brazen, forward; *mf* (Am.) sponger; *m* slap or blow on the chest; fall on the chest; hard push, strong effort
pechuguera *f* deep cough
pedagogía *f* pedagogy
pedagógico -ca *adj* pedagogic or pedagogical
pedagogo -ga *mf* pedagogue; mentor
pedaje *m* toll
pedal *m* pedal, treadle; (mus.) pedal; **pedal de freno** (aut.) brake pedal; **pedal suave** or **celeste** (mus.) soft pedal
pedalear *vn* to pedal
pedalero *m* (mus.) pedal board, pedal keyboard
pedáneo -a *adj* (law) petty, puisne
pedanía *f* district
pedante *adj* pedantic; *mf* pedant; *m* (archaic) home tutor
pedantear *vn* to be pedantic
pedantería *f* pedantry
pedantesco -ca *adj* pedantic
pedantismo *m* pedantry
pedato -ta *adj* (bot.) pedate
pedazo *m* piece; **a pedazos** in pieces; **caerse a pedazos** to fall apart; (coll.) to be broken-down, to let oneself go to pieces; (coll.) to be kindly, be unsuspecting; (coll.) to be fagged out; (coll.) to be stumbly, to be awkward; **hacer pedazos** (coll.) to break to pieces; **hacerse pedazos** (coll.) to fall to pieces; (coll.) to strain, wear oneself out, overexercise; **morirse por sus pedazos** (coll.) to be madly in love; **ser un pedazo de pan** (coll.) to be kindly, be the quintessence of kindness; **pedazo de alcornoque, de animal** or **de bruto** (coll.) dolt, imbecile, good-for-nothing; **pedazo del alma, de las entrañas** or **del corazón** (coll.) darling, apple of one's eye (*child*); **pedazo de pan** crumb (*small amount*); song (*small price*)
pedazuelo *m* small piece, bit
pederasta *m* pederast
pederastia *f* pederasty
pedernal *m* flint (*variety of quartz; piece used for striking fire*); flintiness; flint-hearted person
pedernalino -na *adj* flinty; (fig.) flinty
pedestal *m* pedestal
pedestre *adj* pedestrian; (fig.) pedestrian
pedestremente *adv* on foot; (fig.) in a pedestrian manner
pedestrismo *m* pedestrianism; walking; foot racing; cross-country racing
pedestrista *mf* walker; foot racer; cross-country racer
pediatra *mf* pediatrician
pediatría *f* pediatrics
pediátrico -ca *adj* pediatric
pedicelo *m* (bot. & zool.) pedicel
pedicoj *m* jump, hop (*on one foot*)
pedicular *adj* pedicular
pedículo *m* (bot.) pedicle
pedicuro -ra *mf* pedicure (*person*)
pedido *m* request; (com.) order; **a pedido** on request; **pedido de ensayo** (com.) trial order
pedidor -dora *adj* insistent, importunate
pedidura *f* asking, begging
pedigón -gona *adj* (coll.) insistent, importunate
pedigüeño -ña *adj* insistent, demanding, bothersome
pediluvio *m* foot bath
pedimento *m* petition; (law) claim, bill
pedio -dia *adj* (anat.) (pertaining to the) foot
pedipalpo *m* (zool.) pedipalpus
pedir §94 *va* to ask, to ask for; to request; to demand, require; to need; to ask for the hand of, to ask for in marriage; to order (*merchandise*); (gram.) to govern; **pedir algo a alguien** to ask someone for something; **pedir prestado a** to borrow from; *vn* to ask; to beg; (law) to bring claim, bring suit; **a pedir de boca** opportunely; as desired; **venir a pedir de boca** to be just the thing; to come at the right time
pedo *m* wind, flatulence; **andar pedo** (Am.) to be drunk
pedorrero -ra *adj* flatulent; *f* flatulence; **pedorreras** *fpl* tights
pedorreta *f* sound made to imitate the breaking of wind
pedorro -rra *adj* flatulent
pedrada *f* stoning; hit or blow with a stone; mark or bruise made by a stone; rosette, bow (*for hair or hat*); (coll.) hint, taunt; **como pedrada en ojo de boticario** (coll.) apropos, just in time; **matar a pedradas** to stone to death
pedral *m* (naut.) stone used to hold a net or cable in place
pedrea *f* stoning; fight with stones; hailing
pedregal *m* stony ground
pedregoso -sa *adj* stony, rocky; suffering from gallstones; *mf* sufferer from gallstones
pedrejón *m* boulder
pedreñal *m* flintlock, firelock
pedrera *f* quarry, stone quarry
pedreral *m* packsaddle for carrying stones
pedrería *f* precious stones, jewelry
pedrero *m* stonecutter; slinger
pedreta or **pedrezuela** *f* small stone
pedrisca *f* var. of **pedrisco**
pedriscal *m* stony ground
pedrisco *m* shower of stones, stoning; heap of loose stones; hailstones; hailstorm
pedrisquero *m* hailstorm
pedriza *f* stony spot; stone fence
Pedro *m* Peter; **Pedro el Ermitaño** Peter the Hermit; **Pedro el Grande** Peter the Great
pedroche *m* stony ground
pedrusco *m* rough stone, boulder
pedunculado -da *adj* pedunculate
peduncular *adj* peduncular
pedúnculo *m* (anat., bot. & zool.) peduncle, stalk
peer §35 *vn & vr* to break wind
pega *f* sticking; pitch varnish; drubbing; catch question (*in an examination*); (coll.) trick, joke; (ichth.) remora; (min.) firing a blast; (orn.) magpie; **de pega** (slang) fake; **pega reborda** (orn.) shrike
pegadillo *m* little patch, little plaster; (Am.) lace; **pegadillo de mal de madre** (coll.) bore, nuisance
pegadizo -za *adj* sticky; contagious; sponging, parasitic; false, imitation
pegado *m* patch, sticking plaster
pegador *m* paper hanger; billposter; (min.) blaster
pegadura *f* sticking
pegajosa *f* see **pegajoso**
pegajosidad *f* stickiness
pegajoso -sa *adj* sticky; catching, contagious; alluring, tempting; (coll.) soft, gentle, mellow; (coll.) mushy; *f* (bot.) marvel-of-Peru
pegamento or **pegamiento** *m* sticking, joining; glue, cement
pegamoscas *m* (*pl:* **-cas**) (bot.) catchfly
pegapega *f* (bot.) bedstraw
pegar §59 *va* to stick, to paste; to fasten, attach, tie; to post (*bills*); to set (*fire*); to transmit, communicate (*a disease*); to beat; to let go (*a blow, slap, etc.*); to let out (*a cry*); to take (*a jump, a run*); to sew on (*a button*); **no pegar el ojo** (coll.) to not sleep a wink all night; **pegar un tiro a** to shoot; *vn* to stick, to catch;

to take root, take hold; to cling; to join, be contiguous; to make an impression; to fit, to match; to be fitting; to pass, be accepted; to beat; to knock; to stumble; *vr* to stick, to catch; to take root, take hold; to burn to the bottom of the pan; to hang on, stick around; to be catching (*said of a disease*); **pegársela a uno** (coll.) to make a fool of someone

pegarropa *m* (bot.) beggar's-lice

pegásides *fpl* (myth.) Muses

Pegaso *m* (myth. & astr.) Pegasus

pegata *f* (coll.) cheat, swindle, fraud

pegmatita *f* (petrog.) pegmatite

pego *m* cheating by sticking two cards together; **dar** o **tirar el pego** to make two cards stick together; (coll.) to dazzle, to cheat

pegote *m* pitch plaster; sticking plaster; (coll.) sticky mess; (coll.) hanger-on, sponger; (coll.) crude addition (*to a writing or a work of art*)

pegotear *vn* (coll.) to hang around, to sponge

pegotería *f* (coll.) hanging around, sponging

pegual *m* (Am.) saddle strap with ring at each end

peguera *f* pitch pit (*in which pine wood is burned to yield pitch*); place for heating pitch for marking sheep

peguero *m* pitch maker or dealer

pegujal *m* small fund; small holdings; fund of knowledge

pegujalejo *m* tiny holdings

pegujalero *m* small farmer

pegujar *m* var. of **pegujal**

pegujarero *m* var. of **pegujalero**

pegujón *m* or **pegullón** *m* lump or ball of wool or hair

pegunta *f* pitch mark on sheep

peguntar *va* to mark (*sheep*) with pitch

pehuén *m* (bot.) monkey puzzle

peina *f* var. of **peineta**

peinado -da *adj* combed; groomed; effeminate; (lit.) overnice; *m* hairdo, coiffure; **peinado al agua** finger wave; *f* combing

peinador -dora *mf* hairdresser; *m* wrapper, dressing gown, peignoir; *f* combing machine

peinadura *f* combing; combings

peinar *va* to comb; to riffle (*cards*); *vr* to comb one's hair

peinazo *m* (carp.) rail (*e.g., of a door*)

peine *m* comb; instep; reed (*of a loom*); (coll.) sly fellow, tricky fellow; (zool.) pecten; **a sobre peine** lightly, slightly; **peine de balas** cartridge clip; **peine de pastor** or **de Venus** (bot.) lady's-comb

peinera *f* see **peinero**

peinería *f* comb factory or shop

peinero -ra *mf* comb maker or dealer; *f* comb case

peineta *f* ornamental comb, back comb

peinetero -ra *mf* comb maker or dealer

Peipín *m* Peiping

p.ej. abr. of **por ejemplo**

peje *m* fish; (coll.) slicker, slick guy; **peje ángel** (ichth.) angelfish; **peje araña** (ichth.) scorpion fish; **peje diablo** (ichth.) scorpene

pejebuey *m* (zool.) manatee

pejegallo *m* (ichth.) roosterfish

pejemuller *m* (zool.) manatee

pejepalo *m* unsplit smoked codfish

pejerrey *m* (ichth.) atherine

pejesapo *m* (ichth.) angler

pejiguera *f* (coll.) bother, nuisance

p.ejm. abr. of **por ejemplo**

pekinés -nesa *adj & mf* var. of **pequinés**

pela *f* barking (*e.g., of a cork oak*)

pelada *f* see **pelado**

peladero *m* place for scalding slaughtered hogs or fowl; (coll.) den of cardsharps; (Am.) wasteland

peladilla *f* sugar almond; pebble

peladillo *m* (bot.) clingstone peach (*tree and fruit*); **peladillos** *mpl* wool stripped from the pelt

pelado -da *adj* bare; bald; barren; peeled; poor, penniless; even (*ten, twenty, hundred, etc.*); (Am.) ill-bred; *f* pelt, sheepskin (*stripped of wool*)

pelador -dora *adj* peeling; *mf* peeler

peladura *f* peeling, barking

pelafustán -tana *mf* (coll.) good-for-nothing

pelagallos *m* (*pl:* **-llos**) (coll.) tramp, bum

pelagatos *m* (*pl:* **-tos**) (coll.) wretch, outcast, ragamuffin

pelágico -ca *adj* pelagic

pelagra *f* (path.) pellagra

pelagroso -sa *adj* pellagrous

pelaire *m* wool carder

pelairía *f* wool carding

pelaje *m* coat, fur, pelage; (coll.) stripe (*sort, type*)

pelambrar *va* var. of **apelambrar**

pelambre *m* batch of hides to be fleshed; steeping liquid; hair; hair scraped from skins; lack of hair, bare spots

pelambrera *f* fleshing room; bushiness, hairiness; (path.) alopecia

pelambrero *m* flesher, steeper

pelamen *m* (coll.) var. of **pelambre**

pelamesa *f* scuffle, hair-pulling scuffle; bunch of hair

pelandusca *f* (coll.) prostitute, whore

pelantrín *m* small farmer; (Am.) pauper

pelar *va* to cut (*hair*); to pluck, pull out (*hair, feathers*); to peel, skin, husk, hull, shell, bark; to show (*the teeth*); (coll.) to clean out (*in gambling*); (Am.) to beat, to thrash; (Am.) to slander; *vr* to peel off; to lose one's hair; to get a haircut; (Am.) to clear out, make a getaway; **pelárselas** (coll.) to be efficient, expeditious, enthusiastic; (coll.) to kick the bucket (*to die*); **pelárselas por** (coll.) to crave; **pelárselas por** + *inf* to crave to + *inf*

pelarela *f* (path.) alopecia

pelarruecas *f* (*pl:* **-cas**) (coll.) woman who makes a living spinning

pelasgo -ga *adj & mf* Pelasgian

pelaza or **pelazga** *f* (coll.) quarrel, row

peldaño *m* step (*of stairs*)

pelea *f* fight; quarrel; struggle; **pelea de gallos** cockfight

peleador -dora *adj* fighting; quarrelsome; *mf* fighter

pelear *vn* to fight; to quarrel; to struggle; *vr* to fight, fight each other; to part company

pelechar *va* (coll.) to keep in food and clothing; *vn* to shed (*said of animals*); to get new hair; to fledge; (coll.) to be better off, to take a turn for the better

pelele *m* stuffed figure (*of straw and rags*); baby's knitted sleeping suit; (coll.) simpleton, laughingstock, lightweight

Peleo *m* (myth.) Peleus

peleón -ona *adj* (coll.) pugnacious, quarrelsome; (coll.) cheap, ordinary (*wine*); *m* (coll.) cheap wine; *f* (coll.) row, scuffle, altercation, fracas

pelerina *f* pelerine

pelete *m* punter (*in gambling*); (coll.) poor fellow, nobody; **en pelete** naked

peletería *f* furriery; fur shop; (Am.) shoe store

peletero -ra *mf* furrier; (Am.) shoe dealer, shoe merchant; *m* (Am.) shoe salesman

pelgar *m* (coll.) var. of **pelagallos**

peliagudo -da *adj* furry, long-haired; (coll.) arduous, ticklish; (coll.) tricky

peliblanco -ca *adj* white-haired

peliblando -da *adj* soft-haired

pelicano -na *adj* gray-haired

pelícano *m* (orn.) pelican

pelicorto -ta *adj* short-haired

película *f* pellicle; film; (phot. & mov.) film; motion picture; (Am.) blunder, break; **película de dibujo** (mov.) animated cartoon; **película de largo metraje** (mov.) full-length film; **película de seguridad** (phot.) safety film; **película en carretes** (phot.) roll film; **película en colores** (phot. & mov.) color film; **película en paquetes** (phot.) film pack; **película hablada** (mov.) talking film; **película sonora** (mov.) sound film

pelicular *adj* pellicular, filmy

peliculero -ra *adj* moving-picture; *mf* scenario writer; *m* movie actor; *f* movie actress

peligrar *vn* to be in danger

peligro *m* danger, peril, risk; **correr peligro** to be in danger; **fuera de peligro** out of danger; **ponerse en peligro de paz** to be alerted for war; **peligro amarillo** yellow peril

peligrosidad *f* dangerousness
peligroso -sa *adj* dangerous, perilous
pelilargo -ga *adj* long-haired
pelillo *m* (coll.) trifle, trifling difference; **echar pelillos a la mar** (coll.) to bury the hatchet; **no pararse en pelillos** (coll.) to not bother about trifles, to pay no attention to small matters; **no tener pelillos en la lengua** (coll.) to speak right out
pelilloso -sa *adj* (coll.) touchy
pelinegro -gra *adj* black-haired
Pelión, el Pelion; **levantar el Pelión sobre el Osa** to heap Pelion upon Ossa
pelirrojo -ja *adj* red-haired, redheaded; *mf* redhead
pelirrubio -bia *adj* fair-haired, blond; *m* blond; *f* blonde
pelitieso -sa *adj* straight-haired, stiff-haired
pelitre *m* (bot.) bertram, pellitory of Spain
pelitrique *m* (coll.) trifle, trinket
pelma *m* (coll.) flat mass; undigested food; *mf* (coll.) lump, poke, sluggard; (slang) easy mark
pelmacería *f* slowness, heaviness, pokiness
pelmazo *m* flat mass; undigested food; (coll.) lump, poke, sluggard
pelo *m* hair; down (*on skin, fruit, etc.*); nap (*of cloth*); grain (*in wood*); fiber, filament; coat (*of animal*); flaw (*in precious stones*); raw silk; color (*of horse*); kiss (*in billiards*); split (*in hoof*); hair or thread (*caught on tip of a pen*); cross hair (*of optical instrument*); hair trigger; hairspring (*of watch*); trifle; **al pelo** with the hair, with the nap; (coll.) perfectly, to the point; **a medios pelos** (coll.) tipsy; **a pelo** with the hair, with the nap; (coll.) timely, in good time; **con todos sus pelos y señales** chapter and verse; **contra pelo** backwards; against the hair or nap; (coll.) inopportunely; **cortar un pelo en el aire** to be sharp, be keen; **de medio pelo** (coll.) four-flushing; (coll.) trifling; **echar pelos a la mar** (coll.) to bury the hatchet; **en pelo** bareback; **escapar por un pelo** to escape by a hairbreadth, to have a narrow escape; **estar hasta por encima de los pelos** (coll.) to have one's fill, to be fed up; **hacer el pelo a** to do the hair of; to fix the hair of; **hacerse el pelo** to do one's hair; to fix one's hair; to have one's hair cut; **no tener pelo de tonto** (coll.) to be wide-awake; **no tener pelos en la lengua** (coll.) to be outspoken, to not mince words; **ponerle a uno los pelos de punta** to make one's hair stand on end; **relucirle a uno el pelo** (coll.) to be sleek, be well fed; **tomar el pelo a** (coll.) to make fun of, to make a fool of; **venir a pelo** to come in handy; **venir al pelo a** to suit perfectly; **pelo a la garçonne** shingle; **pelo arriba** against the hair; **pelo de camello** camel's hair; **pelo de cofre** or **de Judas** red hair; redhead (*person*); **pelos absorbentes** (bot.) root hair; **pelos de la estadia** (surv.) stadia hairs; **pelos y señales** (coll.) minutest details
pelón -lona *adj* bald, hairless; (coll.) dull, stupid; (coll.) poor, penniless; *m* (Am.) dried peach; *f* (path.) alopecia; (Am.) prostitute; (Am.) death
pelonería *f* (coll.) want, poverty
pelonía *f* (path.) alopecia
Pélope *m* (myth.) Pelops
peloponense *adj & mf* Peloponnesian
peloponesíaco -ca *adj* Peloponnesian
Peloponeso *m* Peloponnesus
pelosilla *f* (bot.) mouse-ear
peloso -sa *adj* hairy
pelota *f* ball; ball game; handball; (Am.) boat made of cowhide; **dejar en pelota** (coll.) to strip; (coll.) to clean out, leave penniless; **en pelota** stripped, naked; **estar la pelota en el tejado** (coll.) to be up in the air, to be of uncertain outcome; **no tocar pelota** (coll.) to not get to the root of the difficulty; **pelota acuática** (sport) water polo; **pelota de viento** football, basketball (*inflated with air*); **pelota medicinal** medicine ball; **pelota rodada** (baseball) grounder; **pelota vasca** (sport) pelota
pelota-base *f* baseball
pelotari *mf* pelota player
pelotazo *m* blow or hit with a ball
pelote *m* goat's hair
pelotear *va* to audit (*an account*); *vn* to knock a ball around (*without playing a game*); to wrangle, to argue; **pelotear con** to play ball with (*e.g., a pillow*)
pelotera *f* (coll.) brawl, row
pelotería *f* heap of balls; pile of goat's hair
pelotero *m* ball maker; ballplayer; (coll.) brawl, row
pelotilla *f* pellet; ball of wax and broken glass attached to end of scourge; **hacer la pelotilla a** (coll.) to soft-soap
pelotillero -ra *adj* fawning, cringing
pelotón *m* large ball; ball of hair; gang, crowd; (mil.) platoon; **pelotón de fusilamiento** firing squad; **pelotón de los torpes** (mil.) awkward squad
peltraba *f* (slang) game bag
peltre *m* spelter, pewter
peltrería *f* pewter factory; pewter business
peltrero *m* pewterer, pewter worker or dealer
peluca *f* wig; (coll.) wig (*one who wears a wig; severe reprimand*)
pelucón -cona *adj* wig-wearing; bewigged; (Am.) conservative; *m* big bushy wig; *f* gold doubloon
peluche *m* plush
peludo -da *adj* hairy, shaggy, furry; *m* bast mat
peluquería *f* hairdresser's (shop), barbershop
peluquero -ra *mf* hairdresser, barber; wigmaker
peluquín *m* scratchwig; peruke
pelusa *f* down; fuzz, nap; (coll.) jealousy, envy (*of a child*)
pelusilla *f* fuzz; (bot.) mouse-ear
pelviano -na *adj* pelvic
pelvímetro *m* pelvimeter
pelvis *f* (*pl:* **-vis**) (anat.) pelvis
pella *f* pellet; puff (*of pastry*); rough casting; tender head of cauliflower; raw lard; (orn.) gray heron; (coll.) sum of money, debt, theft; **hacer pella** (slang) to play hooky
pellada *f* pellet; batch of mortar or plaster
pelleja *f* hide; skin; undressed sheepskin; (coll.) prostitute
pellejería *f* leather dressing; skinnery; skins, hides; (Am.) jam, trouble
pellejero -ra *mf* leather dresser; skinner
pellejina *f* small skin
pellejo *m* skin; pelt, rawhide; peel, rind; wineskin; (fig.) hide, skin (*life*); (coll.) sot, drunkard; **dar, dejar** or **perder el pellejo** (coll.) to die; **estar** or **hallarse en el pellejo de otro** to be in somebody else's shoes; **no tener más que el pellejo** (coll.) to be nothing but skin and bones; **salvar el pellejo** (coll.) to save one's skin
pellejudo -da *adj* flabby, baggy
pelleta *f* var. of **pelleja**
pelletería *f* var. of **pellejería**
pelletero *m* var. of **pellejero**
pellica *f* robe or coverlet of fine furs; small dressed skin; jacket of fine skins
pellico *m* shepherd's jacket (*made of skins*)
pellijero *m* var. of **pellejero**
pellín *m* (bot.) antarctic or mountain beach
pelliquero *m* maker of shepherd's jackets
pelliza *f* pelisse; (mil.) dolman
pellizcar **§86** *va* to pinch; to nip; to take a pinch of; *vr* (coll.) to long, to pine
pellizco *m* pinch; nip; bit, pinch; **pellizco de monja** cookie
pello *m* fine fur jacket
pellón *m* or **pellote** *m* fur cloak or robe
pelluzgón *m* bunch or tuft of hair
pena *f* see **peno**
penable *adj* penal, punishable
penachera *f* crest; plume, panache
penacho *m* crest; plume, panache; arrogance, haughtiness; (bot.) tassel
penachudo -da *adj* crested, plumed
penachuelo *m* small crest; small plume
penadamente *adv* painfully, with great effort
penadilla *f* narrow-mouthed drinking vessel
penado -da *adj* afflicted, grieved; arduous, difficult; narrow-mouthed (*vessel*); *mf* convict
penal *adj* penal; *m* penitentiary

penalidad *f* trouble, hardship; punishability; (law) penalty
penalista *mf* penologist
penante *adj* suffering, afflicted; *m* (coll.) suitor
penar *va* to penalize; to punish; *vn* to suffer; to linger (*although suffering or dying*); to suffer, to be tormented (*in Hell*); **penar por** to pine for, to long for; *vr* to grieve, to sorrow
penates *mpl* penates
penca *f* pulpy leaf (*e.g., of cactus*); pulpy part (*of leaf*); cowhide (*used for flogging*); **coger una penca** (Am.) to get drunk; **hacerse de pencas** (coll.) to let oneself be coaxed
pencazo *m* lash with a cowhide
penco *m* (bot.) Indian fig; (coll.) jade, hack, nag; (Am.) boor
pencudo -da *adj* having pulpy leaves
pendanga *f* jack of diamonds; (coll.) prostitute
pendejo *m* pubes (*hair*); (coll.) coward; (Am.) fool
pendencia *f* dispute, quarrel, fight; (law) pending litigation
pendenciar *vn* to dispute, quarrel, fight, wrangle
pendenciero -ra *adj* quarrelsome; *mf* wrangler
pendenzuela *f* little dispute or quarrel
pender *vn* to hang, dangle; to depend; to be pending
pendiente *adj* pendent, hanging, dangling; pending; under way; awaiting, expecting; **estar pendiente de** to depend on; to hang on (*e.g., someone's words*); to be in process of; *m* earring, pendant; watch chain; *f* slope, grade; dip, pitch; curve (*of a graph*)
pendil *m* woman's mantle; **tomar el pendil** (coll.) to leave, go away
péndol *m* (naut.) boot-topping
péndola *f* pendulum (*of clock*); clock (*with pendulum*); queen post; bridging brace; feather; pen, quill
pendolaje *m* (naut.) right of seizure
pendolario *m* penman
pendolear *vn & vr* to dangle, to swing
pendolero -ra *adj* (coll.) loose, dangling, sloppy
pendolista *mf* copyist, calligrapher; *m* penman
pendolón *m* large pendulum; king post
pendón *m* banner, standard, pennon; (bot.) shoot, tiller; (coll.) slattern
pendonear *vn* (coll.) var. of **pindonguear**
pendular *adj* of a pendulum
péndulo -la *adj* pendent, hanging; *m* pendulum; clock; **péndulo compensado** or **de compensación** compensation pendulum; **péndulo de segundos** seconds pendulum; **péndulo de torsión** torsion pendulum; **péndulo matemático** mathematical pendulum
pene *m* (anat.) penis
peneca *mf* (Am.) first-grade pupil; *f* (Am.) first grade (*in school*)
penela *f* flatboat, canal boat
Penélope *f* (myth.) Penelope
peneque *adj* (coll.) drunk
penetrabilidad *f* penetrability
penetrable *adj* penetrable
penetración *f* penetration; (fig.) penetration, insight; **penetración pacífica** (pol.) peaceful penetration
penetrador -dora *adj* keen, penetrating
penetrante *adj* penetrating; (fig.) penetrating
penetrar *va* to penetrate; to pierce; to grasp, fathom; to see through (*someone's intentions*); *vn* to penetrate; **penetrar en, entre** or **por entre** to penetrate into; *vr* to grasp, fathom; to realize; to become convinced; **penetrarse de** to become impregnated with; to become imbued with
penetrativo -va *adj* penetrative
pénfigo *m* (path.) pemphigus
penicilina *f* (pharm.) penicillin
penígero -ra *adj* (poet.) winged, feathered
penillanura *f* (geol.) peneplain
península *f* peninsula; **Península Balcánica** or **de los Balcanes** Balkan Peninsula; **península del Labrador** Labrador; **Península Ibérica** Iberian Peninsula; **península Malaya** or **de Malaca** Malay Peninsula
peninsular *adj & mf* peninsular
penique *m* penny
penisla *f* var. of **península**

penit. abr. of **penitente**
penitencia *f* penitence; penance; **hacer penitencia** to do penance; to eat sparingly; to take potluck
penitenciado -da *adj* punished by the Inquisition; punished; *mf* (Am.) convict
penitencial *adj* penitential; *m* (eccl.) penitential, penitential book
penitenciar *va* to impose penance on; to punish
penitenciaría *f* penitentiary; (eccl.) penitentiary
penitenciario -ria *adj* penitentiary; *m* (eccl.) penitentiary (*officer*)
penitenta *f* penitent woman; female confessant
penitente *adj & mf* penitent
pennado -da *adj* pennate
penninervio -via *adj* (bot.) penninervate
peno -na *adj & mf* Carthaginian ‖ *f* punishment; penalty; pain; hardship, toil; sorrow, grief; effort, trouble; choker (*jeweled collar*); (orn.) penna; **penas** *fpl* (Am.) ghosts; **a penas** hardly; **a duras penas** with great difficuty; **merecer la pena** to be worth while; **¡qué pena!** what a pity!; **so pena de** under penalty of; **última pena de la vida** death; **valer la pena** to be worth while; **valer la pena** + *inf* to be worth while to + *inf*, e.g., **no vale la pena ir al teatro esta noche** it isn't worth while to go to the theater this evening; **valer la pena de** + *inf* to be worth + *ger*, e.g., **aquella ciudad no vale la pena de visitarse** that city is not worth visiting; **pena capital** capital punishment; **pena infamante** loss of civil rights, banishment; **pena de muerte** death penalty, capital punishment; **pena de la vida** capital punishment
penol *m* (naut.) yardarm, peak
penología *f* penology
penológico -ca *adj* penological
penologista *mf* **penólogo -ga** *mf* penologist
penoso -sa *adj* arduous, difficult; suffering, afflicted; (coll.) conceited; (Am.) shy, timid
pensado -da *adj* deliberate, thought-out; **bien pensado** advised, wise; **de pensado** on purpose; **mal pensado** evil-minded; foolish, unwise
pensador -dora *adj* thinking; *m* thinker
pensamiento *m* thought; suspicion; (bot.) pansy; **en un pensamiento** in a twinkling, in a jiffy; **ni por pensamiento** not even in thought
pensar §18 *va* to think; to think over; to think of (*a card, a number, etc.*); to feed (*animals*); **pensar** + *inf* to intend to + *inf;* to almost + *inf;* **pensar de** to think of (*to have a certain opinion of*); *vn* to think; **sin pensar** unexpectedly; **pensar en** to think of (*to direct one's thoughts to*); **pensar en** + *inf* to think of + *ger*; *vr* to think; **pensárselo mejor** to think better of it, to change one's mind
pensativo -va *adj* pensive, thoughtful
pensel *m* (bot.) turnsole
penseque *m* (coll.) oversight, inadvertence
pensil *adj* pensile; *m* enchanted garden
Pensilvania *f* Pennsylvania
pensilvano -na *adj & mf* Pennsylvanian
pensión *f* pension, annuity; allowance; boarding house; board; fellowship (*for study*); grant-in-aid; bother, disadvantage; burden; **pensión completa** room and board
pensionado -da *mf* pensioner; fellow; *m* dormitory; boarding school
pensionar *va* to pension; to burden
pensionario *m* pensionary, magistrate
pensionista *mf* pensioner; boarder; pupil of a boarding school; **medio pensionista** day boarder (*in a school*)
pentaclo *m* pentacle
pentadáctilo -la *adj* pentadactyl
pentaedro *m* (geom.) pentahedron
pentagonal *adj* pentagonal
pentágono -na *adj* pentagonal; *m* (geom.) pentagon; **el Pentágono** the Pentagon (*building of U.S. Department of Defense in Washington*)
pentágrama or **pentagrama** *m* (mus.) staff, musical staff
pentámero -ra *adj* (bot. & zool.) pentamerous
pentámetro -tra *adj & m* pentameter
pentano *m* (chem.) pentane

pentarquía *f* pentarchy
pentasílabo -ba *adj* pentasyllabic; *m* pentasyllable
Pentateuco *m* (Bib.) Pentateuch
pentatlo *m* (sport) pentathlon
pentatónico -ca *adj* pentatonic
pentavalente *adj* (chem.) pentavalent
Pentecostés *f* Pentecost
pentodo or **péntodo** *m* (elec.) pentode
pentosa *f* (chem.) pentose
pentosana *f* (chem.) pentosan
penúltimo -ma *adj* penultimate; next to last; *f* (phonet.) penult
penumbra *f* penumbra; semidarkness, half-light
penuria *f* penury (*dearth*)
Penyab *m* Punjab
peña *f* rock, boulder; cliff; peen (*of hammer*); club, group, circle; **durar por peñas** to last a long time
peñascal *m* spiry terrain, rocky country
peñasco *m* spire of rock, pinnacle, crag; strong silk; (zool.) murex; (anat.) petrous portion (*of temporal bone*)
peñascoso -sa *adj* rocky, craggy
peño *m* (dial.) foundling
peñol *m* var. of **peñón**
péñola *f* pen, quill
peñón *m* rock, spire; **peñón de Gibraltar** Rock of Gibraltar
peón *m* pedestrian; foot soldier; laborer; pawn (*in chess*); man (*in checkers*); top, peg top; spindle, axle; hive; (taur.) attendant, assistant; (Am.) farm hand; **peón caminero** road laborer; **peón de albañil** or **de mano** hod carrier; **peón ferrocarrilero** (rail.) section hand
peonada *f* day's work of a laborer; gang of laborers
peonaje *m* gang of laborers; squad of foot soldiers
peonería *f* day's plowing
peonía *f* (bot.) peony; (bot.) rosary pea; (obs.) land in conquered territory given to an infantryman to settle on
peonza *f* whip top, whipping top; (coll.) noisy little squirt; **a peonza** (coll.) on foot
peor *adj & adv* worse; worst; **peor que peor** worse and worse
peoría *f* worseness; worsening
pepa *f* (Am.) seed (*e.g., of apple*); (Am.) marble; (*cap.*) *f* Jo, Jozy
Pepe *m* Joe
pepián *m* var. of **pipián**
Pepillo or **Pepín** *m* Joe
pepinar *m* cucumber patch
pepinillo *m* (bot.) gherkin (*Cucumis anguria and fruit; small cucumber used for pickles*); **pepinillo del diablo** (bot.) squirting cucumber
pepino *m* (bot.) cucumber; **no dársele a uno un pepino de** or **por** (coll.) to not care about, to not give a fig for
pepita *f* pip (*small seed*); melon seed; nugget; (vet.) pip; **no tener pepita en la lengua** (coll.) to speak freely, to speak without restraint; (*cap.*) *f* Jozy
Pepito *m* Joe
pepitoria *f* giblet fricassee with egg sauce; medley, hodgepodge
pepitoso -sa *adj* pippy (*full of pips*); suffering from pip
peplo *m* (hist.) peplum
pepón *m* (bot.) watermelon
pepona *f* large paper doll
pepónide *f* (bot.) pepo
pepsina *f* (biochem.) pepsin
péptico -ca *adj* peptic
péptido *m* (biochem.) peptide
peptizar §76 *va* (chem.) to peptize
peptona *f* (biochem.) peptone
pequén *m* (orn.) burrowing owl (*of Chile*)
pequeñez *f* (*pl:* **-ñeces**) smallness; infancy; trifle; (fig.) smallness
pequeñín *m* little one, baby, child
pequeño -ña *adj* little, small; young; low, humble; **en pequeño** briefly, in a word; on a small scale
pequeñuelo -la *adj* very small, tiny; very young; *mf* baby, tot
pequín *m* pekin; (*cap.*) *m* Pekin
pequinés -nesa *adj* Pekinese; *mf* Pekinese (*native of Pekin; dog*)
pera *f* pear (*fruit*); goatee, imperial; cinch, sinecure; pear-shaped bulb (*of camera shutter, auto horn, etc.*); (elec.) pear-shaped switch; **partir peras con** (coll.) to be on intimate terms with; **ponerle a uno las peras a cuatro** or **a ocho** (coll.) to put the squeeze on someone
perada *f* pear jam; pear brandy
peral *m* (bot.) pear, pear tree
peraleda *f* orchard of pear trees
peraltar *va* (arch.) to stilt; (rail.) to bank, to superelevate
peralte *m* (arch.) stilt; (arch.) height, rise; (rail.) superelevation
peralto *m* (geom.) height
perantón *m* (bot.) mock cypress; large fan; (coll.) tall person
perborato *m* (chem.) perborate
perca *f* (ichth.) perch; **perca de mar** (ichth.) sea bass
percal *m* percale
percalina *f* percaline
percance *m* mischance, misfortune; **percances** *mpl* perquisites
percatar *vr* to be on one's guard; **percatarse de** to notice, to become aware of, to suspect; to beware of, to guard against
percebe *m* (zool.) barnacle (*Pollicipes cornucopia*); (coll.) fool, ignoramus
percebimiento *m* var. of **apercibimiento**
percentil *m* percentile
percepción *f* perception; percept; collection
perceptibilidad *f* perceptibility; collectability
perceptible *adj* perceptible; collectable
perceptivo -va *adj* perceptive (*having the faculty of perceiving*); perceptual (*pertaining to perception*)
perceptor -tora *adj* percipient; *mf* percipient; collector (*e.g., of taxes*)
Perceval *m* Percival
percibidero -ra *adj* perceptible
percibir *va* to perceive; to collect
percibo *m* collecting, collection
perclorato *m* (chem.) perchlorate
percloruro *m* (chem.) perchloride
percocería *f* small piece of hammered silverware
percuciente *adj* percutient, percussive
percudir *va* to tarnish, to dull; to spread through; *vr* to spot with mildew (*said of clean wash*)
percusión *f* percussion; (med.) percussion
percusor *m* (med.) percussor (*person who strikes; percussion hammer*); firing pin
percutir *va* to percuss
percutor *m* firing pin
percha *f* perch, pole, roost; clothes tree; coat hanger; coat hook; barber pole; napping (*of cloth*); snare (*to catch birds*); perch for a falcon; (naut.) spar, rough log; (ichth.) perch; **estar en percha** to be in the bag
perchar *va* to nap (*cloth*)
perchero *m* rack, clothes rack
percherón -rona *adj & mf* Percheron
perchón *m* poorly pruned shoot (*of vine*)
perchonar *vn* to leave poorly pruned shoots on the vine; to lay snares for game
perdedero *m* cause of loss; gambling den; den of vice; rabbit's burrow
perdedor -dora *adj* losing; *mf* loser
perder §66 *va* to lose; to waste, squander; to miss (*e.g., a train, an opportunity*); to flunk (*a course*); to ruin; to spoil; *vn* to lose; to fade; *vr* to lose one's way, get lost, go astray; to miscarry; to sink, go to the bottom; to become ruined; to spoil, get spoiled; to fall into disuse; to lose one's virtue (*said of a woman*); **perderse en** to fall all over oneself in (*e.g., excuses*); **perderse por** to be madly in love with
perdición *f* perdition; loss; unbridled passion; outrage; ruination
pérdida *f* loss; waste; damage, ruination; **estar** or **ir a pérdidas y ganancias** to share profit and loss; **no tener pérdida** (coll.) to be easy to find; **pérdidas blancas** (path.) whites
perdidamente *adv* madly, wildly; uselessly

perdidizo -za *adj* supposed to be lost; **hacer perdidizo** (coll.) to hide; (coll.) to drop, to lose (*on purpose*); **hacerse perdidizo** (coll.) to lose on purpose (*in a game*); **hacerse el perdidizo** (coll.) to make oneself scarce
perdido -da *adj* stray, wild (*bullet*); wide, loose (*sleeve*); countersunk; fruitless, unsuccessful; dissolute; off, spare, idle (*hours*); absent, distracted; confirmed, inveterate; **perdido por** mad about; *m* profligate, rake; (print.) extra printing (*to make up for spoiled sheets*); **al perdido** carelessly, sloppily
perdidoso -sa *adj* losing, unlucky; easily lost
perdigar §59 *va* to brown, to broil slightly; (coll.) to make ready, prepare
perdigón *m* young partridge; decoy partridge; shot; (coll.) profligate; (coll.) heavy loser (*in gambling*); (coll.) failure (*student who failed*); **perdigón zorrero** buckshot
perdigonada *f* shot with bird shot; wound caused by bird shot
perdigonera *f* pouch for shot
perdiguero -ra *adj* partridge-hunting; *m* pointer, setter; game dealer
perdimiento *m* loss, waste, ruin
perdis *m* (*pl:* **-dis**) (coll.) rake, good-for-nothing
perditancia *f* (elec.) leakage conductance, leakance
perdiz *f* (*pl:* **-dices**) (orn.) partridge; **perdiz blanca** (orn.) rock ptarmigan; **perdiz, o no comerla** (coll.) whole hog or none; **perdiz pardilla** (orn.) gray partridge; **perdiz real** or **roja** (orn.) red-legged partridge
perdón *m* pardon, forgiveness; (coll.) burning drop of oil, wax, etc.; **con perdón** by your leave
perdonable *adj* pardonable
perdonador -dora *adj* forgiving; *mf* pardoner; *m* (eccl.) pardoner
perdonar *va* to pardon, forgive, excuse; **no perdonar** to not miss, to not omit
perdonavidas *m* (*pl:* **-das**) (coll.) bully
perdulario -ria *adj* careless, sloppy; vicious, incorrigible
perdurable *adj* lasting, long-lasting; everlasting; *f* durance, everlasting (*a material*)
perdurar *vn* to last, last a long time, survive
perecear *va* (coll.) to put off, delay (*out of laziness, indifference, etc.*)
perecedero -ra *adj* perishable; mortal; *m* (coll.) misery, extreme want; danger spot
perecer §34 *vn* to perish; to suffer, become exhausted; to be in great want; **perecer ahogado** to drown; *vr* to pine; **perecerse de risa** to be dying of laughter; **perecerse por** to pine for, to be dying for; to be mad about (*e.g., a woman*)
perecimiento *m* perishing, end, death
pereda *f* orchard of pear trees
peregrinación *f* or **peregrinaje** *m* peregrination; pilgrimage
peregrinar *vn* to peregrinate; to go as a pilgrim; to journey through life
peregrinidad *f* rareness, strangeness
peregrino -na *adj* wandering, traveling; peregrine, foreign; rare, strange; singular; beautiful, excellent; mortal; migratory (*bird*); *mf* pilgrim
perejil *m* (bot.) parsley; (coll.) frippery, tawdry dress or ornaments; **perejiles** *mpl* (naut.) pennants and banners hoisted to bedeck a ship; (coll.) handles (*titles, etc.*); (coll.) frippery; **perejil de mar** (bot.) samphire; **perejil de monte** (bot.) mountain parsley; **perejil de perro** (bot.) fool's-parsley; **perejil marino** (bot.) samphire
perenal *adj* var. of **perenne**
perencejo *m* var. of **perengano**
perendeca *f* (coll.) prostitute
perendengue *m* earring; trinket, cheap ornament
perene *adj* var. of **perenne**
perengano -na *mf* so-and-so
perenne *adj* perennial; (bot.) perennial
perennidad *f* perenniality
perentoriedad *f* peremptoriness; urgency
perentorio -ria *adj* peremptory; urgent
perero *m* fruit parer
pereza *f* laziness; slowness
perezoso -sa *adj* lazy; slow, dull, heavy; *mf* lazybones; sleepyhead; *m* (zool.) sloth
perfección *f* perfection; **a la perfección** to perfection
perfeccionamiento *m* perfection, improvement
perfeccionar *va* to perfect, improve
perfeccionista *mf* perfectionist
perfectibilidad *f* perfectibility
perfectible *adj* perfectible
perfectivo -va *adj* perfective
perfecto -ta *adj* perfect; (gram.) perfect; *m* (gram.) perfect
perfidia *f* perfidy
pérfido -da *adj* perfidious
perfil *m* profile; side view; cross section; thin stroke (*in writing*); trimming; outline, sketch; skyline; (iron mfg.) shape; **perfiles** *mpl* finishing touches; courtesies; **perfil aerodinámico** (aer.) streamlining
perfilado -da *adj* long and thin (*face*); well-formed (*nose*); delicate (*features*); streamlined
perfiladura *f* profiling, outlining; outline
perfilar *va* to profile, to outline; to perfect, to polish, to finish; *vr* to be outlined; to show one's profile, to stand sideways; (coll.) to dress up
perfoliado -da *adj* (bot.) perfoliate; *f* (bot.) hare's-ear
perfoliata *f* (bot.) hare's-ear
perfolla *f* cornhusk
perforación *f* perforation; drilling, boring; puncture; punch
perforador -dora *adj* perforating; drilling; *mf* perforator; *m* (telg.) perforator; *f* pneumatic drill, compressed-air drill, rock drill; (mach.) perforator
perforante *adj* perforating; armor-piercing
perforar *va* to perforate; to drill, to bore; to puncture; to punch (*e.g., card*)
perforista *mf* keypuncher
performance *f* (sport) performance
perfumadero *m* perfuming pan
perfumador -dora *mf* perfumer; *m* perfuming pan; perfume atomizer
perfumar *va* to perfume
perfume *m* perfume
perfumear *va* var. of **perfumar**
perfumería *f* perfumery
perfumero -ra or **perfumista** *mf* perfumer
perfunctorio -ria *adj* perfunctory
perg. abr. of **pergamino**
pergal *m* leather paring for sandal thongs
pergaminero *m* parchment-maker, parchment seller
pergamino *m* parchment
Pérgamo *f* Pergamum
pergeniar *va* to comprehend, to know thoroughly
pergenio *m* (coll.) appearance, looks
pergeñar *va* to execute; to perform with skill; to grasp thoroughly
pergeño *m* (coll.) appearance, looks
pérgola *f* pergola; roof garden
peri *f* (myth.) peri
periantio *m* (bot.) perianth
pericardíaco -ca *adj* pericardiac
pericardio *m* (anat.) pericardium
pericarditis *f* (path.) pericarditis
pericarpio *m* (bot.) pericarp, seedcase, seed vessel
pericia *f* skill, expertness
pericial *adj* expert; *m* expert; customhouse officer
Pericles *m* Pericles
periclitar *vn* to be in jeopardy, to be unsound or shaky
perico *m* periwig; large asparagus; large fan; queen of clubs; (naut.) mizzen-topgallant sail; (orn.) parakeet; (slang) chamber pot; (*cap.*) *m* Pete; **perico de los palotes** anybody, so-and-so; **perico entre ellas** (coll.) lady's man; **perico ligero** (zool.) sloth
pericón -cona *adj* fit for all uses (*said of a horse or mule*); *m* large fan; queen of clubs
pericráneo *m* (anat.) pericranium
peridoto *m* (mineral.) chrysolite, peridot
perieco -ca *adj* perioecic; **periecos** *mpl* perioeci

periferia *f* periphery; surroundings
periférico -ca *adj* peripheral
perifollo *m* (bot.) chervil; **perifollos** *mpl* (coll.) finery, frippery; **perifollo oloroso** (bot.) sweet cicely, sweet fern
perifonear *va* to broadcast
perifonía *f* broadcasting
perífono *m* broadcasting apparatus
perifrasear *vn* to periphrase
perífrasi *f* or **perífrasis** *f* (*pl:* **-sis**) periphrase or periphrasis
perifrástico -ca *adj* periphrastic
perigallo *m* loose skin under the chin; bright-colored hair ribbon; sling made of twine; (coll.) tall, lanky person; (naut.) topping lift
perigeo *m* (astr.) perigee
periginia *f* perigyny
perihelio *m* (astr.) perihelion
perilustre *adj* very illustrious
perilla *f* pear-shaped figure or ornament; goatee, imperial; pommel (*of saddlebow*); knob; lobe (*of ear*); **de perilla** or **de perillas** (coll.) apropos, to the point
perillán -llana *adj* rascally, crafty; *m* rascal, crafty fellow
perillo *m* scalloped cookie
perímetro *m* perimeter
perimisio *m* (anat.) perimysium
períncIito -ta *adj* illustrious, heroic
perineal *adj* perineal
perineo *m* (anat.) perineum
perineurio *m* (anat.) perineurium
perinola *f* teetotum; pear-shaped figure or ornament; (coll.) pert little woman
perioca *f* argument, summary
periodicidad *f* periodicity; regularity
periódico -ca *adj* periodic; periodical; *m* periodical; newspaper
periodismo *m* newspaper work, journalism
periodista *mf* journalist; *m* newspaperman; *f* newspaperwoman
periodístico -ca *adj* (pertaining to the) newspaper, journalistic
periodización *f* division into periods
período *m* period; (gram.) compound sentence; (phys.) cycle; **período de incubación** (path.) incubation period; **período glacial** (geol.) glacial period; **período lectivo** term (*in school*); **período medio** (phys.) half life (*of radioactive substance*)
periodontal *adj* periodontal
periostio *m* (anat.) periosteum
periostitis *f* (path.) periostitis
peripatético -ca *adj* Peripatetic; (coll.) ridiculous, wild (*in one's opinions*); *m* Peripatetic
peripato *m* Peripateticism; Peripatetics
peripecia *f* peripeteia, vicissitude
periplo *m* periplus (*voyage around coast or island; account of such voyage*); trip, journey
períptero -ra *adj* (arch.) peripteral
peripuesto -ta *adj* (coll.) dudish, all spruced up, sporty
periquear *vn* to be too free, take too much liberty (*said of a woman*)
periquete *m* (coll.) jiffy; **en un periquete** (coll.) in a jiffy
periquillo *m* sugarplum
periquito *m* (orn.) parakeet; (naut.) skysail; **periquito de Australia** (orn.) budgerigar, zebra parakeet
periscio -cia *adj* periscian; **periscios** *mpl* periscii
periscópico -ca *adj* periscopic
periscopio *m* periscope
perisodáctilo -la *adj* & *m* (zool.) perissodactyl
perisología *f* pleonasm, verbiage
peristalsis *f* (*pl:* **-sis**) (physiol.) peristalsis
peristáltico -ca *adj* peristaltic
peristaltismo *m* var. of **peristalsis**
peristilo *m* (arch.) peristyle
perístole *f* (physiol.) peristole, peristalsis
perístoma *m* (bot.) peristome
peritación *f* work of an expert
peritaje *m* work of an expert; expert's fee; training course for experts
perito -ta *adj* skilled, skilful; expert; *m* expert
peritoneal *adj* peritoneal
peritoneo *m* (anat.) peritoneum
peritonitis *f* (path.) peritonitis
perjudicador -dora *adj* harmful, injurious; *mf* harmer, injurer
perjudicar §86 *va* to harm, damage, impair, prejudice
perjudicial *adj* harmful, injurious, prejudicial
perjuicio *m* harm, injury, damage, prejudice; **en perjuicio de** to the detriment of; **sin perjuicio de** without affecting
perjurador -dora *adj* perjured; *mf* perjurer
perjurar *vn* to commit perjury; to swear, be profane; *vr* to commit perjury; to perjure oneself
perjurio *m* perjury
perjuro -ra *adj* perjured; *mf* perjurer; *m* perjury
perla *f* pearl; (fig.) pearl, jewel (*person or thing*); (pharm.) pearl, capsule; (f.a.) pearl; **de perlas** perfectly; **perla de ampolla** blister pearl
perlado -da *adj* pearled; pearly
perlático -ca *adj* palsied, paralyzed; *mf* paralytic
perlería *f* collection of pearls
perlero -ra *adj* (pertaining to the) pearl
perlesía *f* (path.) palsy, paralysis
perlífero -ra *adj* pearl-bearing
perlino -na *adj* pearl, pearl-colored
perlita *f* (metal. & petrog.) perlite; (mineral.) phonolite
perlongar §59 *va* to sail along; *vn* to sail along the coast; (naut.) to pay out a cable
permaloy *m* permalloy
permanecer §34 *vn* to stay, remain
permaneciente *adj* staying; permanent
permanencia *f* permanence; stay, sojourn; **permanencias** *fpl* (educ.) study hours
permanente *adj* permanent; *f* permanent (*wave*); **permanente en frío** cold wave (*in hair*)
permanganato *m* (chem.) permanganate; **permanganato de potasio** (chem.) potassium permanganate
permangánico -ca *adj* permanganic
permansión *f* var. of **permanencia**
permeabilidad *f* permeability
permeable *adj* permeable
permeancia *f* (elec.) permeance
pérmico -ca *adj* & *m* (geol.) Permian
permisible *adj* permissible
permisión *f* permission
permisivo -va *adj* permissive
permiso *m* permission; permit; time off; tolerance (*in coinage*); leave; **con permiso** on leave; excuse me; **de permiso** on leave; **permiso de circulación** (aut.) owner's license; **permiso de conducir** (aut.) driver's license
permisor -sora *adj* var. of **permitidor**
permistión *f* mixture, concoction
permitidero -ra *adj* permissible
permitidor -dora *adj* permitting
permitir *va* to permit, to allow; **permitir** + *inf* to permit or allow to + *inf;* to enable to + *inf;* **permitir que** + *subj* to permit or allow to + *inf; vr* to be permitted; to allow oneself (*e.g., a criticism*); **no se permite fumar** no smoking; **permitirse** + *inf* to take the liberty to + *inf*
permuta *f* barter, exchange
permutable *adj* exchangeable; permutable
permutación *f* interchange, exchange; permutation; (math.) permutation
permutar *va* to interchange; to barter; to permute
pernada *f* kick; leg (*of some object*)
pernaza *f* big leg, thick leg
perneador -dora *adj* strong-legged
pernear *vn* to kick, shake the legs; (coll.) to fuss, to hustle, to fret
perneo *m* (dial.) hog market
pernera *f* leg (*of trousers*)
pernería *f* (naut.) stock of bolts
perneta *f* small leg; **en pernetas** barelegged
pernete *m* small bolt, pin, peg
perniabierto -ta *adj* bowlegged
pernicioso -sa *adj* pernicious
pernil *m* thigh (*of animal*); leg (*of trousers*)
pernio *m* hinge
perniquebrar §18 *va* to break the leg or legs of; *vr* to break one's leg or legs

pernituerto -ta *adj* crooked-legged
perno *m* bolt; eye (*of hook-and-eye hinge*); **perno de expansión** expansion bolt; **perno roscado** screw bolt
pernoctar *vn* to spend the night, to spend the night away from home
pernotar *va* to note, observe
pero *conj* but, yet; *m* (bot.) permain; (coll.) but, objection; (coll.) fault, defect; **poner pero a** (coll.) to find fault with
perogrullada *f* (coll.) platitude, inanity
perol *m* kettle (*in form of hemisphere*)
perón *m* (Am.) pear-shaped apple
peroné *m* (anat.) fibula
peroneo -a *adj* fibular
peroración *f* peroration; (coll.) harangue
perorar *vn* to perorate; (coll.) to orate
perorata *f* harangue, declamation, tiresome speech
peroxiácido *m* (chem.) peroxyacid
peróxido *m* (chem.) peroxide; **peróxido de hidrógeno** (chem.) hydrogen peroxide; **peróxido de plomo** (chem.) lead dioxide (O_2Pb)
perpendicular *adj & f* perpendicular
perpendicularidad *f* perpendicularity
perpendículo *m* plumb bob; pendulum; (geom.) altitude of a triangle
perpetración *f* perpetration
perpetrador -dora *mf* perpetrator
perpetrar *va* to perpetrate
perpetua *f* see **perpetuo**
perpetuación *f* perpetuation
perpetuar **§33** *va* to perpetuate; *vr* to be perpetuated
perpetuidad *f* perpetuity
perpetuo -tua *adj* perpetual; life; *f* (bot.) globe amaranth; **perpetua amarilla** (bot.) everlasting flower; **perpetua encarnada** (bot.) globe amaranth
perpiaño *m* (mas.) bondstone, perpend
Perpiñán *f* Perpignan
perplejidad *f* perplexity; worry, anxiety
perplejo -ja *adj* perplexed; worried, anxious; baffling, perplexing
perpunte *m* pourpoint (*quilted doublet*)
perquirir **§56** *va* to seek out, investigate
perra *f* see **perro**
perrada *f* pack of dogs; drudgery; (coll.) dirty trick, meanness, treachery
perrengue *m* (coll.) irascible fellow, grouch; (coll.) Negro
perrera *f* doghouse, kennel; tantrum; drudgery; (coll.) poor pay (*person*)
perrería *f* pack of dogs; gang of thieves; angry word; (coll.) dirty trick, meanness, treachery
perrero *m* beadle who keeps dogs out of church; master of the hounds; dog fancier; dogcatcher
perrezno *m* puppy
perrillo -lla *mf* puppy; *m* trigger
perrito *m* doggie
perro -rra *adj* (coll.) wicked, mean; (coll.) hard, bitter, troublesome; (Am.) rash, stubborn; (Am.) selfish, stingy; *m* dog; (mach.) dog, pawl; **a otro perro con ese hueso** tell that to the marines; **el perro del hortelano** dog in the manger; **perro ardero** squirrel dog; **perro caliente** (slang) hot dog; **perro cobrador** retriever; **perro chico** (coll.) copper coin (*five centimes*); **perro dalmático** coach dog; **perro de aguas** spaniel; **perro de ajeo** bird dog, retriever; **perro de lanas** poodle; **perro de muestra** pointer, setter; **perro de pastor** sheep dog, shepherd dog; **perro de San Bernardo** Saint Bernard; **perro faldero** lap dog; **perro hiena** (zool.) Cape hunting dog; **perro jabalinero** boarhound; **perro lebrel** whippet; **perro lebrero** rabbit dog; **perro lobero** wolf dog; **perro lulú** spitz dog; **perro maestro** trained dog; **perro marino** (ichth.) dogfish, shark; **perro ovejero** sheep dog, shepherd dog; **perro pastor alemán** German shepherd dog; **perro policía** police dog; **perro pomerano** Pomeranian (*dog*); **perro raposero** foxhound; **perro rastrero** trackhound; **perro viejo** (coll.) wise old owl; *f* bitch; tantrum; (coll.) drunk, drunkenness
perro-lazarillo *m* (*pl:* **perros-lazarillo**) Seeing Eye dog
perroquete *m* (naut.) topgallant mast
perruno -na *adj* canine, dog; *f* dog bread, dog cake
persa *adj & mf* Persian; *m* Persian (*language*)
persecución *f* pursuit; persecution; annoyance, harassment
persecutorio -ria *adj* (pertaining to) persecution; persecutional
Perséfone *f* (myth.) Persephone
perseguidor -dora *mf* pursuer; persecutor; *f* (Am.) hangover
perseguimiento *m* var. of **persecución**
perseguir **§82** *va* to pursue; to persecute; to annoy, harass
Perseida *f* (astr.) Perseid
Perseo *m* (myth. & astr.) Perseus
persevante *m* pursuivant, pursuivant of arms
perseverancia *f* perseverance
perseverante *adj* persevering
perseverar *vn* to persevere; **perseverar en** + *inf* to persevere in + *ger*
persiano -na *adj & mf* Persian; *f* flowered silk; slatted shutter; (aut.) louver; **persiana de tiro** or **persiana interior americana** Venetian blind
persicaria *f* (bot.) persicary, lady's-thumb; (bot.) prince's-feather
pérsico -ca *adj* Persian; *m* (bot.) peach (*tree and fruit*)
persignar *vr* to cross oneself, make the sign of the cross; to make the first sale of the day; (coll.) to cross oneself in surprise
pérsigo *m* (bot.) peach (*tree and fruit*)
persistencia *f* persistence or persistency
persistente *adj* persistent
persistir *vn* to persist; **persistir en** + *inf* to persist in + *ger*
persona *f* person; personage; (gram. & theol.) person; **personas** *fpl* people; **conjunta persona** spouse (*man or wife*); **de persona a persona** tête à tête, man to man; **en persona** in person; **en la persona de** in the person of; **hacer de su persona** (coll.) to have a bowel movement; **por persona** per capita; **por su persona** in person; **primera persona** (gram.) first person; **segunda persona** (gram.) second person; **tercera persona** (gram.) third person; **persona agente** (gram.) agent; **persona desplazada** displaced person; **persona grata** persona grata; **persona jurídica** (law) juristic person; **persona paciente** (gram.) recipient of the action
personada *adj* (bot.) personate (*corolla*)
personado *m* (eccl.) benefice without jurisdiction; (eccl.) incumbent of a benefice without jurisdiction
personaje *m* personage; (theat.) personage, character; somebody (*person of importance*)
personal *adj* personal; *m* personnel, staff, force; staff expenses (*of an office*)
personalidad *f* personality; (law) personality; **personalidad desdoblada** split personality
personalismo *m* selfishness; personality
personalista *adj* selfish, self-seeking
personalización *f* personalization
personalizar **§76** *va* to personalize; to make personal remarks about; (gram.) to make (*an impersonal verb*) personal; *vr* to become personal
personar *vr* var. of **apersonar**
personería *f* solicitorship; (law) personality
personero *m* solicitor; delegate
personificación *f* personification
personificar **§86** *va* to personify
personilla *f* (coll.) queer little person
personudo -da *adj* husky
perspectivo -va *adj* perspective; *m* expert in perspective; *f* perspective; outlook, prospect; appearance; deceptive appearance; **perspectiva lineal** linear perspective
perspicacia or **perspicacidad** *f* perspicacity, discernment; keen sight
perspicaz *adj* (*pl:* **-caces**) perspicacious, discerning; keen-sighted
perspicuidad *f* perspicuity
perspicuo -cua *adj* perspicuous
perspiración *f* perspiration
perspirar *vn* to perspire
persuadidor -dora *mf* persuader

persuadir *va* to persuade; **persuadir a** + *inf* to persuade to + *inf;* **persuadir a que** + *subj* to persuade to + *inf; vr* to become persuaded or convinced
persuasible *adj* credible, plausible
persuasión *f* persuasion
persuasivo -va *adj* persuasive; *f* persuasion, persuasiveness
persuasor -sora *mf* persuader
pertenecer §34 *vn* to belong; to pertain, to concern; *vr* to be independent
pertenecido *m* property
perteneciente *adj* pertaining
pertenencia *f* property; ownership; appurtenance, accessory; province, domain; **ser de la pertenencia de** to be under the ownership of; to be in the bailiwick or province of
pértiga *f* pole, rod, staff; (sport) pole (*used in pole vault*)
pertigal *m* pole, rod, staff
pértigo *m* tongue (*of wagon*)
pertiguería *f* office of verger
pertiguero *m* verger
pertinacia *f* pertinacity; persistence (*e.g., of a disease*)
pertinaz *adj* (*pl:* **-naces**) pertinacious; persistent (*e.g., headache*)
pertinencia *f* pertinence, relevance
pertinente *adj* pertinent, relevant
pertrechar *va* to supply, provide, equip; to prepare, to implement
pertrechos *mpl* supplies, provisions, equipment; tools; **pertrechos de guerra** ordnance
perturbación *f* perturbation; disturbance; upset
perturbadamente *adv* in confusion
perturbado -da *adj* insane; *mf* insane person
perturbador -dora *adj* perturbing; disturbing; *mf* perturber; disturber
perturbar *va* to perturb; to disturb; to upset, disconcert; to confuse, interrupt
Perú, el Peru
peruanismo *m* Peruvianism
peruano -na *adj & mf* Peruvian
peruétano *m* (bot.) wild pear; end, tip, projection
perulero -ra *adj & mf* Peruvian; *mf* person who has returned wealthy from Peru; *m* round earthen jug with small mouth
Perusa *f* Perugia
peruviano -na *adj & mf* Peruvian
perversidad *f* perversity
perversión *f* perversion; (psycopath.) perversion
perverso -sa *adj* perverse; profligate, depraved; *mf* profligate
pervertido -da *adj* (psychopath.) perverse; *mf* (psychopath.) pervert
pervertidor -dora *adj* perverting, depraving; *mf* perverter
pervertimiento *m* perversion, corruption
pervertir §62 *va* to pervert; *vr* to become perverted
pervigilio *m* sleeplessness, wakefulness
pervinca *f* (bot.) periwinkle
pervivencia *f* persistence, survival
pervulgar §59 *va* to divulge, proclaim
peryódico -ca *adj* (chem.) periodic
peryoduro *m* (chem.) periodide
pesa *f* weight (*of scales, clock, gymnasium, etc.*); **tirar la pesa** (sport) to put the shot; **pesas y medidas** weights and measures
pesacartas *m* (*pl:* **-tas**) letter scales
pesada *f* see **pesado**
pesadez *f* heaviness; clumsiness, slowness; annoyance; tiresomeness, dullness; harshness; (phys.) gravity
pesadilla *f* nightmare; (fig.) nightmare
pesado -da *adj* heavy; clumsy, sluggish, slow; tiresome, dull; harsh; *f* quantity weighed at one time
pesador -dora *mf* weigher
pesadumbre *f* sorrow, grief; trouble; weight, heaviness
pesaje *m* weighing; paddock
pesalicores *m* (*pl:* **-res**) hydrometer
pésame *m* condolence; **dar el pésame por** to present one's condolences for, to extend one's sympathy for or on
pesante *adj* having weight
pesantez *f* (phys.) gravity
pesar *m* sorrow, regret; **a pesar de** in spite of; *va* to weigh; to grieve, to make sorry; (fig.) to weigh; **mal que me (le, etc.) pese** whether I (you, etc.) like it or not; **pesar** + *inf* or **pesar de** + *inf* to be sorry that + *ind*, e.g., **me pesa haber firmado esa protesta** I am sorry that I signed that protest; **pesar sus palabras** to weigh one's words; **pese a** in spite of; **pese a que** in spite of the fact that; **pese a quien pese** regardless, whether they like it or not; *vn* to weigh; to have weight; to be heavy; to cause sorrow, cause regret; (fig.) to weigh (*to have influence, be important*)
pesario *m* (med.) pessary
pesaroso -sa *adj* sorrowful, regretful
pesca *f* fishing; catch (*of fish*); **ir de pesca** to go fishing; **llevar de pesca** to take (*someone*) fishing; **pesca de bajura** offshore fishing; **pesca de gran altura** deep-sea fishing
pescada *f* (ichth.) hake; dried and cured fish
pescadería *f* fish market; fish store; fish stand
pescadero -ra *mf* fish dealer; fishmonger; *f* fishwoman
pescadilla *f* (ichth.) codling; (ichth.) weakfish; **pescadilla de red** or **pescadilla real** (ichth.) pescadilla (*Sagenichthys ancylodon*)
pescado *m* fish (*that has been caught*); salted codfish
pescador -dora *adj* fishing; *mf* fisher; *m* fisherman; (ichth.) angler; *f* fisherwoman
pescante *m* coach box; (aut.) front seat; jib (*of derrick*); (naut.) davit; (theat.) trap door
pescar §86 *va* to fish; to catch (*fish*); to fish for; to fish out; (elec.) to fish; (coll.) to manage to get; (coll.) to catch, catch up (*e.g., in a lie*); *vn* to fish
pescozada *f* or **pescozón** *m* slap in the neck, slap on the head
pescozudo -da *adj* thick-necked
pescuezo *m* neck; haughtiness
pescuño *m* colter wedge (*of plow*)
pese see **pesar**
pesebre *m* crib, rack; manger; (Am.) crèche
pesebrera *f* row of mangers; mangers
pesebrón *m* boot (*of a coach*)
peseta *f* peseta (*Spanish monetary unit*); **cambiar la peseta** (coll.) to get sick and vomit
pésete *m* curse
pesetero -ra *adj* greedy, grasping; (costing a) peseta
pesia *interj* confound it!
pesiar *vn* to curse
pesillo *m* small scales (*for weighing coins*)
pesimismo *m* pessimism
pesimista *adj* pessimistic; *mf* pessimist
pésimo -ma *adj super* very bad, abominable, miserable
peso *m* weight; scale, balance; burden, load; judgment, good sense; (fig.) weight (*importance; burden*); peso (*Spanish American monetary unit*); **a peso de dinero, oro** or **plata** at a very high price; **caerse de su peso** to be self-evident; **de peso** of due weight; of sound judgment, serious, important; **en peso** in the air; entirely; on the fence; **llevar el peso de la batalla** to bear the brunt of the battle; **reducir peso** to reduce (*to lose weight, e.g., by exercising*); **peso atómico** (phys.) atomic weight; **peso en vivo** live weight; **peso específico** (phys.) specific gravity; **peso fuerte** (box.) heavyweight; **peso gallo** (box.) bantamweight; **peso ligero** or **liviano** (box.) lightweight; **peso mediano** or **medio** (box.) middleweight; **peso mediano fuerte** or **peso medio fuerte** (box.) light heavyweight; **peso mediano ligero** or **peso medio ligero** (box.) welterweight; **peso molecular** (phys.) molecular weight; **peso mosca** (box.) flyweight; **peso muerto** dead weight; (aer.) dead load; **peso pesado** (box.) heavyweight; **peso pesado ligero** (box.) light heavyweight; **peso pluma** (box.) featherweight
pésol *m* pea
pesón *m* balance, scales
pesor *m* (prov. & Am.) weight, gravity
pespuntador -dora *mf* backstitcher

pespuntar *va & vn* to backstitch
pespunte *m* backstitch, backstitching
pespuntear *va & vn* var. of **pespuntar**
pesquera *f* see **pesquero**
pesquería *f* fishery (*business; place*); fishing
pesquero -ra *adj* fishing (*boat, industry, etc.*); *m* fishing boat; *f* fishery; fishing ground; weir, garth
pesquis *m* acumen, keenness
pesquisa *f* inquiry, investigation; *m* (Am.) cop, policeman
pesquisador -dora *mf* investigator
pesquisante *adj* investigating, investigative
pesquisar *va* to inquire into, to investigate
pestalociano -na *adj* (educ.) Pestalozzian
pestaña *f* eyelash; flange; fluke (*of anchor*); edging (*lace*); index tab; (aut.) tire rim; **pestañas** *fpl* (bot.) cilia; **no mover pestaña** to not bat an eye; **no pegar pestaña** (coll.) to not sleep a wink; **pestañas vibrátiles** (biol.) cilia
pestañear *vn* to wink, to blink; **no pestañear ante un peligro** to not flinch in the face of a danger; **sin pestañear** without batting an eye
pestañeo *m* winking, blinking
pestañoso -sa *adj* with long eyelashes; (biol.) ciliate
peste *f* pest, plague; epidemic; stink, stench; corruption, depravity; evil; (coll.) wealth, abundance; (Am.) head cold; (Am.) smallpox; **decir** or **hablar pestes de** (coll.) to talk against, to criticize; **echar pestes (contra)** (coll.) to fume (at); **peste blanca** white plague (*tuberculosis*); **peste bubónica** (path.) bubonic plague
pestífero -ra *adj* pestiferous; stinking, noxious
pestilencia *f* pestilence
pestilencial *adj* pestilential, pestiferous
pestilencioso -sa *adj* pestilential (*having to do with pestilence*)
pestilente *adj* pestilent, pestiferous
pestillo *m* bolt (*of a lock*); door latch; **pestillo de golpe** night bolt, spring bolt
pestiño *m* honey fritter
pestorejazo *m* var. of **pestorejón**
pestorejo *m* var. of **cerviguillo**
pestorejón *m* blow on the back of the neck
pesuña *f* hoof; dry dirt stuck on a person's feet
pesuño *m* toe, digit (*half of cloven hoof*); **pesuño falso** dewclaw
petaca *f* cigar case; tobacco pouch; leather-covered chest; leather-covered hamper; (Am.) trunk; **petacas** *fpl* (Am.) big hips (*of a woman*)
pétalo *m* (bot.) petal
petanque *m* silver ore
petar *va* (coll.) to please
petardear *va* to blow open with petards; to swindle, to take in; *vn* (aut.) to backfire
petardeo *m* swindling; (aut.) backfire
petardero *m* petardeer; swindler
petardista *mf* swindler, cheat
petardo *m* petard; bomb; swindle, cheat; **pedir un petardo a** (coll.) to swindle
petate *m* sleeping mat; bedding (*of service man or prisoner*); (coll.) luggage; (coll.) cheat; (coll.) poor soul; **liar el petate** (coll.) to pack up and get out; (coll.) to kick the bucket
petenera *f* Andalusian popular song
petequia *f* (path.) petechia
petera *f* (coll.) brawl, row; stubbornness, temper
peteretes *mpl* (coll.) sweets, tidbits
peterrear *vn* (coll.) to crackle
peticano or **peticanon** *m* (print.) double pica
petición *f* petition; plea; request; (law) claim, bill; **petición de mano** formal betrothal; **petición de principio** (log.) petitio principii
peticionar *va* (Am.) to petition
peticionario -ria *mf* petitioner
petifoque *m* (naut.) flying jib
petigrís *m* squirrel (*fur*)
petillo *m* stomacher
petimetra *f* showy or gaudy woman
petimetre *m* dude, sport, dandy
petirrojo *m* (orn.) redbreast
petitorio -ria *adj* petitionary; *m* (coll.) tiresome and repeated demand; drug catalogue; *f* (coll.) petition
peto *m* breastplate; plastron; peen; (zool.) plastron; (taur.) mattress covering (*to protect horses*); (ichth.) wahoo
petral *m* breastband, breast collar
Petrarca *m* Petrarch
petraria *f* petrary, ballista
petrarquesco -ca *adj* Petrarchan, Petrarchian
petrarquismo *m* Petrarchism
petrel *m* (orn.) petrel; **petrel de la tempestad** (orn.) stormy petrel; **petrel gigante** (orn.) giant fulmar
pétreo -a *adj* stony; rocky
petrificación *f* petrifaction or petrification
petrificar §86 *va & vr* to petrify
petrífico -ca *adj* petrifactive, petrifying
Petrogrado *f* Petrograd
petrografía *f* petrography
petrolato *m* (pharm.) petrolatum
petróleo *m* petroleum; **petróleo combustible** fuel oil; **petróleo crudo** crude oil; **petróleo de alumbrado** kerosene; **petróleo de hogar** or **de horno** furnace oil; **petróleo lampante** kerosene
petrolero -ra *adj* (pertaining to) oil, petroleum; incendiary; radical; *mf* oil dealer, kerosene dealer; incendiary; radical; *m* oil man; (naut.) oil tanker; pétroleur; *f* pétroleuse
petrolífero -ra *adj* petroliferous
petrología *f* petrology
petroquímico -ca *adj* petrochemical
petroso -sa *adj* petrous; (anat.) petrous
petulancia *f* flippancy, pertness, insolence
petulante *adj* flippant, pert, insolent
petunia *f* (bot.) petunia
peucédano *m* (bot.) hog's-fennel
peyorativo -va *adj* depreciatory; (gram.) pejorative
pez *m* (*pl:* **peces**) fish; long heap (*e.g., of wheat*); (coll.) reward, just desert; (rel.) fish (*symbol*); (fig.) fish (*good swimmer*); **como un pez en el agua** (coll.) snug as a bug in a rug; **salga pez o salga rana** (coll.) blindly, hit or miss; **pez aguja** (ichth.) garfish; **pez ballesta** (ichth.) triggerfish; **pez caimán** (ichth.) garfish, alligator gar; **pez cofre** (ichth.) cowfish; **pez de color** goldfish; **pez de plata** (ent.) silverfish; **pez de rey** (ichth.) atherine; **pez de San Pedro** (ichth.) dory; **pez eléctrico** (ichth.) electric ray; **pez elefante** (ichth.) elephant fish, **pez espada** (ichth.) swordfish; **pez gallo** (ichth.) elephant fish; **pez gordo** (coll.) big shot, tycoon; **pez hoja** (ichth.) paddle fish; **pez limón** (ichth.) amber jack (*Seriola lalandi*); **pez luna** (ichth.) sunfish, moonfish; **pez martillo** (ichth.) hammerhead; **pez mujer** (zool.) manatee; **pez palo** dried codfish; **pez saltador** (ichth.) skipjack; **pez sierra** (ichth.) sawfish; **pez vela** (ichth.) sailfish; **pez víbora** (ichth.) stingbull; **pez volador** flying fish; (ichth.) flying gurnard; **pez zorro** (ichth.) tiger shark ‖ *f* pitch, tar; meconium; **pez griega** or **rubia** rosin
pezolada *f* fag end
pezón *m* stem; nipple, teat; pivot; pin (*of key*); point (*of land*); umbo (*of lemon, lime, etc.*)
pezonera *f* nipple shield; linchpin
pezpalo *m* var. of **pejepalo**
pez-papagayo *m* (*pl:* **peces-papagayos**) (ichth.) parrot fish
pezpita *f* or **pezpítalo** *m* (orn.) wagtail
pezuelo *m* fringe at end of cloth
pezuña *f* hoof
P.G.M. abr. of **Primera Guerra Mundial**
pi *f* (math.) pi
piache; tarde piache (coll.) too late
piada *f* peeping, chirping; (coll.) mimic phrase or expression
piador -dora *adj* peeping, chirping; (coll.) begging
piadoso -sa *adj* merciful; pitiful; pious, devout
piafar *vn* to paw, to stamp (*said of a horse*)
piale *m* (Am.) throwing a lasso
piamadre *f* or **piamáter** *f* (anat.) pia mater
Piamonte, el Piedmont
piamontés -tesa *adj & mf* Piedmontese

pian *m* (path.) pian
pianino *m* upright piano
pianista *mf* pianist; piano manufacturer; piano dealer
pianístico -ca *adj* pianistic; (pertaining to the) piano
piano *m* piano; **gran piano** grand piano; **piano cuadrado** square piano; **piano de cola** grand piano; **piano de manubrio** piano organ, street piano; **piano de media cola** baby grand; **piano de mesa** square piano; **piano recto** or **vertical** upright piano
pianoforte *m* (mus.) pianoforte
pianola *f* pianola
piar §90 *vn* to peep, to chirp; (coll.) to cry, whine
piara *f* herd (*of swine*); drove (*of mules, etc.*)
piariego -ga *adj* herd-owning
piastra *f* piaster
pica *f* pike; pikeman; (taur.) goad; stonecutter's hammer; (path. & vet.) pica, vitiated appetite; (Am.) pique, resentment
picabueyes *m* (*pl:* **-yes**) (orn.) oxpecker, beefeater
picacero -ra *adj* magpie-chasing (*said of a hawk*)
picacho *m* sharp peak
picada *f* see **picado**
picadero *m* riding school; (taur.) training field (*for picadors*); boat skid, boat block
picadillo *m* hash; minced pork (*for sausages*)
picado -da *adj* perforated; traced in perforations; pitted; cut (*tobacco*); cracked (*ice*); piqued; choppy (*sea*); *m* mincemeat; (aer.) dive; *f* peck; bite (*of insect or fish*); (surv.) line of stakes; staking out; (Am.) path, trail; (Am.) narrow ford; (Am.) dive; (Am.) knock (*at door*); **echar una picada a** (Am.) to hit for a loan
picador *m* horsebreaker; picador (*mounted bullfighter who thrusts a goad into bull*); worker with a pick; operator of pneumatic tool; chopping block; (slang) picklock (*thief*); **picador de limas** (mach.) file cutter
picadora *f* tobacco-shredding machine; **picadora de carne** meat chopper
picadura *f* bite, prick, sting; nick, cut; puncture; cut tobacco; (dent.) slight cavity
picafigo *m* (orn.) figpecker
picaflor *m* or **picaflores** *m* (*pl:* **-flores**) (orn.) hummingbird
picagallina *f* (bot.) chickweed
picagrega *f* (orn.) shrike
picahielos *m* (*pl:* **-los**) ice pick
picajón -jona or **picajoso -sa** *adj* (coll.) touchy, peevish
pical *m* crossroads
picamaderos *m* (*pl:* **-ros**) (orn.) green woodpecker
picana *f* (Am.) goad
picanear *va* (Am.) to goad; (Am.) to stir up, goad on
picante *adj* biting, pricking, stinging; piquant; racy; (Am.) highly seasoned; *m* acrimony, mordancy; piquancy; (Am.) highly seasoned sauce
picaño -ña *adj* lazy, shameless, ragged; *m* patch (*on shoe*)
picapedrero *m* stonecutter, quarrier
picapica *f* itch-producing vegetable powder, leaves, etc.
picapinos *m* (*pl:* **-nos**) (orn.) great spotted woodpecker
picapleitos *m* (*pl:* **-tos**) (coll.) quarrelsome fellow; (coll.) pettifogger, shyster
picaporte *m* latch; latchkey; knocker, door knocker
picaposte *m* (orn.) woodpecker
picapuerco *m* (orn.) spotted woodpecker (*Dryobates medius*)
picar §86 *va* to prick, pierce, puncture; to punch (*a ticket*); to sting; to bite; to burn; to peck; to nibble, pick at; to pit, to pock; to mince, chop up, cut up; to stick, to poke; to spur; to goad; (sew.) to pink; to perforate; to harass, pursue; to itch; to tame; to stipple; to roughen; to pique, annoy; (taur.) to goad ‖ *vn* to itch; to burn (*said of sun*); to nibble; to have a smattering; to put on the finishing touches; to catch, be catching; to pick up (*said of business*); (coll.) to bite (*to be caught, as by a trick*); (coll.) to move along; (aer.) to dive; **picar en** to nibble at; to be somewhat of a; to dabble in; **picar muy alto** (coll.) to aim high, to expect too much ‖ *vr* to become moth-eaten; to prick, to begin to turn sour; to begin to rot; to become decayed (*said of a tooth*); to become ripply (*said of surface of sea*); to swoop down; to become piqued, to take offense; **picarse de** to boast of being
picaraza *f* (orn.) magpie
picardear *va* to train in knavishness; *vn* to be a knave or rascal; to play tricks; to be mischievous; *vr* to go bad, to acquire bad habits
picardía *f* knavery, crookedness; scheming, trickiness; mischief; vileness, lewdness; gang of crooks; **la Picardía** Picardy; **picardías** *fpl* insults
picardihuela *f* prank, mischievousness
picardo -da *adj & mf* Picard; *m* Picard (*dialect*)
picaresco -ca *adj* roguish, rascally; picaresque; rough, coarse, crude; (coll.) witty, humorous, gay; *f* gang of rogues; rascality
picaril *adj* roguish, rascally
pícaro -ra *adj* roguish, crooked; scheming, tricky; low, vile; mischievous; *mf* rogue, crook; schemer; *m* (lit.) picaro; **pícaro de cocina** scullion, kitchen boy
picarón -rona *adj* (coll.) roguish, mischievous; *mf* rogue, picaroon; *m* (Am.) cruller
picarrelincho *m* (orn.) green woodpecker
picatoste *m* buttered toast; fried bread
picazo -za *adj* piebald; *m* piebald (*horse*); jab, jab with a pike or spear; (coll.) peck; (orn.) young magpie; *f* (orn.) magpie; **picaza chillona** or **manchada** (orn.) shrike; **picaza marina** (orn.) flamingo
picazón *f* itch; itching; (coll.) annoyance, displeasure
píceo -a *adj* piceous, pitchy; *f* (bot.) spruce, spruce tree
Picio *m;* **más feo que Picio** ugly as the devil
pick-up *m* pickup; phonograph
picnóstilo *m* (arch.) pycnostyle
pico *m* beak, bill; spout (*of pitcher*); beak (*of anvil*); corner (*e.g., of handkerchief*); nib, tip, sharp point; peak; pick, pickax; talkativeness; pile, lot (*of money*); (coll.) mouth; (elec.) peak; (naut.) bill (*of anchor*); (naut.) peak (*of a sail*); (naut.) bow, prow; (orn.) woodpecker; **andar a picos pardos** (coll.) to loaf around; **callar el pico** (coll.) to shut up, to keep one's mouth shut; **darse el pico** to bill (*said, e.g., of doves*); **hincar el pico** (coll.) to kick the bucket; **perder por el pico** (coll.) to talk too much for one's good; **tener mucho pico** (coll.) to talk too much, to tell all one knows; **y pico** odd, e.g., **doscientos y pico** two hundred odd; a little after, e.g., **a las dos y pico** a little after two o'clock; **pico barreno** or **carpintero** (orn.) woodpecker; **pico cangrejo** or **pico de cangreja** (naut.) gaff, spanker gaff; **pico de cigüeña** (bot.) stork's bill, heron's-bill; **pico de marfil** (orn.) ivorybill; **pico de oro** (fig.) silver-tongue; **pico duro** (orn.) grosbeak, pine grosbeak; **pico gordo** (orn.) hawfinch, grosbeak; **pico tijera** (orn.) skimmer, shearwater; **pico verde** (orn.) green woodpecker
picocarpintero *m* (orn.) woodpecker
picón -cona *adj* with upper teeth projecting (*said of a horse*); (Am.) touchy, sensitive; *m* kidding, teasing; charcoal for brasiers; broken rice
picor *m* smarting of the palate (*from something eaten*); itch, itching
picoso -sa *adj* pock-marked
picota *f* pillar or column on which heads of executed criminals were displayed; pillory; peak, point, spire; (naut.) cheek (*of pump*); **poner en picota** to hold up to public scorn
picotada *f* or **picotazo** *m* peck; sting
picote *m* goat's-hair cloth; glossy silk
picotear *va* to peck; *vn* to toss the head (*said of a horse*); (coll.) to chatter, jabber, gab; *vr* (coll.) to wrangle (*said of women*)
picotella *f* (orn.) nuthatch
picotería *f* (coll.) chattering, jabbering
picotero -ra *adj* (coll.) chattering, jabbering; *mf* chatterer, jabberer; *m* (orn.) waxwing

picotijera *m* (orn.) skimmer, shearwater
picotillo *m* rough goat's-hair cloth
picozapato *m* (orn.) shoebill
picrato *m* (chem.) picrate
pícrico -ca *adj* picric
picto -ta *adj* Pictish; *mf* Pict
pictografía *f* pictograph, picture writing
pictográfico -ca *adj* pictographic
pictórico -ca *adj* pictorial
picuda *f* see **picudo**
picudilla *f* crescent olive; (orn.) rail; (ichth.) picudilla
picudo -da *adj* beaked; pointed; long-snouted; (coll.) jabbering; *m* poker, rapier; (ent.) boll weevil; *f* (ichth.) barracuda
pichana *f* (Am.) broom
pichel *m* pewter tankard
pichihuén *m* (ichth.) walking fish
pichincha *f* (Am.) bargain, lucky break
pichón -chona *mf* (coll.) darling; *m* young pigeon; **pichón de paso** (Am.) passenger pigeon
pidientero *m* beggar
pidón -dona *adj* (coll.) var. of **pedigüeño**
pie *m* foot; footing; foothold; base, stand; stem (*of goblet*); foot (*unit of length; measure of verse*); footboard; trunk; young tree; sediment; foundation; origin; cause, reason; last player; foot, bottom (*of page*); caption; (theat.) cue; **a cuatro pies** on all fours; **al pie de** near; about, almost; **al pie de fábrica** (com.) at the factory; **al pie de la letra** literally; **al pie de la obra** (com.) delivered; **andar, caminar** or **ir con pie** or **pies de plomo** (coll.) to move with caution; **a pie** on foot, walking; **a pie enjuto** dryshod; without risk; without effort; **a pie juntillas, a pie juntillo,** or **a pies juntillos** with feet together; firmly, steadfastly; **buscar cinco** (or **tres**) **pies al gato** (coll.) to be looking for trouble; **dar pie a** to give cause for; **de a pie** foot (*soldier*); **del pie a la mano** at any moment; **de pie** or **de pies** standing; up and about; firm, steady; firmly, steadily; permanently; **de pies a cabeza** from head to foot; **en pie** standing; up and about; firm, steady; firmly, steadily; permanently; on the hoof; **en pie de guerra** on a war footing; **hacer pie** to have a good footing; **ir a pie** to go on foot, to walk; **írsele a uno los pies** to slip (*e.g., on the ice*); (fig.) to slip, to blunder; **irse por pies** or **por sus pies** to get away (*from another person*); **morir al pie del cañón** to die in the harness, to die with one's boots on; **nacer de pie** or **de pies** to be born with a silver spoon in one's mouth; **no dar pie con bola** (coll.) to keep on making mistakes, to make one mistake after another; **perder pie** to lose one's footing; **poner pies con cabeza** (coll.) to turn upside down; **ponerse de pie** or **en pie** to rise, to stand up; **tenerse en pie** to stay on one's feet, to remain standing; **volver pies atrás** to retrace one's steps; **pie calcáneo** (path.) clubfoot; **pie contrahecho** (path.) splayfoot; **pie de amigo** prop, support; **pie de atleta** (path.) athlete's foot; **pie de banco** silly remark; **pie de cabra** crowbar; (zool.) barnacle (*Pollicipes cornucopia*); **pie de carnero** (naut.) Samson post; **pie de guerra** war footing, war-time footing; **pie de imprenta** (print.) imprint, printer's mark; **pie de león** (bot.) lion's-foot; (bot.) edelweiss; **pie derecho** upright, stanchion; **pie de rey** caliper square, slide caliper; **pie de tabla** board foot; **pie de trinchera** (path.) trench foot; **pie marino** sea legs; **pie plano** (path.) flatfoot; **pie quebrado** (poet.) short line; **pie talo** (path.) clubfoot; **pie zambo** (path.) splayfoot
pie-bujía *f* (*pl:* **pies-bujías**) foot-candle
piececillo or **piececito** *m* little foot
piecezuela *f* little piece
piecezuelo *m* little foot
piedad *f* piety; pity, mercy
piedra *f* stone; rock; block; footstone; flint; heavy hailstone; (path.) stone; **a piedra y lodo** tight-shut; **de piedra en seco** dry-stone; **lanzar la primera piedra** to cast the first stone; **no dejar piedra por mover** to leave no stone unturned; **no dejar piedra sobre piedra** to raze to the ground, to wipe out; **poner la primera piedra** to lay the corner stone; **piedra angular** cornerstone; (fig.) cornerstone, keystone; **piedra arenisca** sandstone; **piedra azul** (chem.) bluestone; **piedra berroqueña** milestone; **piedra calaminar** (mineral.) calamine; **piedra caliza** limestone; **piedra de afilar** grindstone; **piedra de albardilla** copestone; **piedra de alumbre** (mineral.) alum rock, alum stone; **piedra de amolar** grindstone; **piedra de chispa** flint; **piedra de escándalo** bone of contention, object of indignation; **piedra de granizo** hailstone; **piedra de la luna** (mineral.) moonstone; **piedra de molino** millstone; **piedra de pipas** (mineral.) meerschaum; **piedra de toque** (mineral. & fig.) touchstone; **piedra filosofal** philosopher's stone; **piedra fina** precious stone; **piedra franca** freestone; **piedra fundamental** foundation stone; **piedra imán** loadstone; **piedra infernal** lunar caustic (*silver nitrate*); **piedra lipis** copper sulfate; **piedra melodreña** whetstone; **piedra meteórica** meteoric stone; **piedra miliar** or **miliaria** milestone; (fig.) milestone; **piedra pómez** pumice, pumice stone; **piedra preciosa** precious stone; **piedra viva** solid rock; **piedra voladora** millstone for grinding olives
piedrezuela *f* little stone
piel *f* skin; hide, pelt; fur; leather; peel, skin (*of fruit*); leather (*e.g., used to bind books*); **dar** or **soltar la piel** (coll.) to die; **ser de la piel del diablo** (coll.) to be a limb of the devil or of Satan, to be a harum-scarum; **piel de cabra** goatskin; **piel de foca** sealskin; **piel de gallina** goose flesh; **piel roja** *m* (*pl:* **pieles rojas**) redskin (*American Indian*)
piélago *m* sea; high sea; countless number
pie-libra *f* (*pl:* **pies-libras**) (mech.) foot-pound
piemia *f* var. of **pioemia**
pienso *m* feed, feeding (*in the stable*); **ni por pienso** by no means, don't think of it
pie-poundal *m* (mech.) foot-poundal
piérides *fpl* (myth.) Muses
pierio -ria *adj* Pierian
pierna *f* leg; post, upright; branch or leg (*of a compass*); downstroke (*of a letter*); (mach.) fork, shank; **a pierna suelta** or **tendida** (coll.) at ease, carefree; **dormir a pierna suelta** or **tendida** (coll.) to sleep soundly; **en piernas** barelegged; **estirar la pierna** (coll.) to lie down on the job; (coll.) to kick the bucket; **estirar** or **extender las piernas** to stretch one's legs, to go for a walk; **ser una buena pierna** (Am.) to be good-natured, be a good fellow
piernitendido -da *adj* with legs extended
piesgo *m* var. of **piezgo**
pietismo *m* Pietism
pietista *mf* Pietist
pieza *f* piece (*part, e.g., of a machine; single musical composition; play, drama; gun, cannon; man in checkers, chess, etc.; coin*); piece or article (*of clothing, of furniture*); space (*in time or place*); room; disappointment; **buena pieza** hussy; sly fox; **de una pieza** in one piece, solid; (Am.) honest, upright; **quedarse en una pieza** or **hecho una pieza** (coll.) to stand motionless, to be dumfounded; **pieza de recambio** spare part, extra; **pieza de recibo** reception room; **pieza de repuesto** spare part, extra; **pieza de respeto** special room, spare room; **pieza de tesis** thesis play; **pieza polar** (elec.) pole piece
piezgo *m* foot of a hide (*used to carry a liquid*); wineskin
piezoelectricidad *f* piezoelectricity
piezoeléctrico -ca *adj* piezoelectric
piezómetro *m* piezometer
pífano *m* fife; fifer
pifia *f* (billiards) miscue; (coll.) miscue, slip; **hacer pifia** to wheeze (*said of a voice or wind instrument*)
pifiar *va* (billiards) to make a miscue of (*a stroke*); *vn* (billiards) to miscue; to wheeze in playing the flute
pigargo *m* (orn.) fish hawk
Pigmalión *m* (myth.) Pygmalion
pigmentación *f* (biol.) pigmentation

pigmentar *va* to pigment; *vr* to pigment, become pigmented
pigmentario -ria *adj* pigmentary
pigmento *m* pigment
pigmeo -a *adj & mf* pygmy
pignoración *f* pledge, pledging; pawning; security
pignorar *va* to pledge; to pawn; to put up as security
pigre *adj* slothful, lazy
pigricia *f* sloth, laziness
pigro -gra *adj* var. of **pigre**
pihua *f* sandal
pihuela *f* jess (*on hawk's leg*); obstacle, hindrance; **pihuelas** *fpl* shackles, fetters
pijama *m* pajamas
pijota *f* var. of **pescadilla**
pila *f* basin; trough; sink; font, holy-water font; pile, heap; (elec., her. & phys.) pile; (elec.) battery, cell; **sacar de pila a** to stand godfather for; **pila atómica** (phys.) atomic pile; **pila de bicromato** (elec.) bichromate cell; **pila de gravedad** (elec.) gravity cell; **pila de linterna** flashlight battery; **pila húmeda** or **líquida** (elec.) wet cell, wet battery; **pila seca** (elec.) dry cell, dry battery; **pila voltaica** (elec.) voltaic battery, voltaic pile
pilada *f* batch of mortar; cloth fulled at one time; pile, heap
pilar *m* basin, bowl (*of fountain*); pillar; stone post, milestone; (fig.) pillar (*person*); *va* to pound, crush (*grain*)
pilastra *f* (arch.) pilaster
pilatero *m* fuller (*of cloth*)
Pilatos *m* Pilate
píldora *f* pill; (coll.) bad news; **dorar la píldora** (coll.) to gild the pill
pildorero *m* pill roller (*device*)
píleo *m* cardinal's biretta
pilero *m* workman who kneads potter's clay with his feet
pileta *f* basin, bowl (*of sink*); sink; small font or stoup; **pileta de natación** swimming pool
pilocarpina *f* (chem.) pilocarpine
pilón *m* pylon; water basin, drinking trough; loaf of sugar; mortar, pestle; counterpoise (*in olive press*); drop hammer; drop or ball (*of steelyard*); **pilón abrevadero** watering trough
piloncillo *m* (Am.) brown sugar
pilonero -ra *adj* (coll.) newsmongering; *mf* (coll.) newsmonger
pilongo -ga *adj* thin, lean; peeled and dried (*chestnut*)
pílori *m* pillory, stocks
pilórico -ca *adj* pyloric
píloro *m* (anat.) pylorus
pilosidad *f* pilosity
piloso -sa *adj* pilose, hairy, of hair
pilotaje *m* piling, pilework; (naut. & aer.) pilotage
pilotar *va* to pilot
pilote *m* pile (*for building*)
pilotear *va* to pilot; (Am.) to back, support
piloto *m* (aer., naut. & fig.) pilot; (naut.) mate, first mate; (ichth.) pilot fish; (Am.) hail fellow well met; **piloto de prueba** (aer.) test pilot; **piloto de puerto** harbor pilot
piltraca or **piltrafa** *f* skinny flesh; loot; **piltracas** or **piltrafas** *fpl* scraps, scraps of food; (Am.) rags, old clothes
pillada *f* (coll.) rascality
pillador -dora *adj* pillaging, plundering; thieving; *mf* pillager, plunderer; thief
pillaje *m* pillage, plunder
pillar *va* to pillage, plunder; to catch; (coll.) to catch (*e.g., in a lie*)
pillastre *m* or **pillastrón** *m* (coll.) rogue, rascal, big rascal
pillear *vn* (coll.) to be a rascal, act like a rascal
pillería *f* (coll.) rascality; (coll.) gang of scalawags
pillete *m* (coll.) little scamp
pillín *m* (coll.) little scamp; **pillín de aúpa** (coll.) sporty little devil
pillo -lla *adj* (coll.) roguish, rascally; (coll.) sly, crafty; (coll.) licentious; *m* (coll.) rogue, rascal, scalawag; (coll.) crafty fellow; (orn.) ibis
pilluelo *m* (coll.) scamp, little scamp
pimental *m* pepper patch
pimentero -ra *mf* pepper seller; *m* (bot.) pepper, black pepper; pepperbox; **pimentero falso** (bot.) pepper tree or shrub
pimentón *m* large pepper; cayenne pepper, red pepper; paprika
pimienta *f* pepper, black pepper; allspice, pimento; (bot.) allspice tree; **comer pimienta** (coll.) to get angry; **ser como una pimienta** (coll.) to be alert, be wide-awake; **tener mucha pimienta** (coll.) to be away up (*in price*); **pimienta de agua** (bot.) smartweed; **pimienta de Chiapas** or **de Tabasco** grains of paradise; **pimienta inglesa** allspice, pimento; **pimienta loca** or **silvestre** (bot.) chaste tree; **pimienta negra** black pepper
pimiento *m* (bot.) pepper, black pepper; (bot.) Guinea pepper; **pimiento de cornetilla** (bot.) chili; hot pepper, chili
pimpante *adj* smart, spruce
pimpido *m* (ichth.) dogfish
pimpín *m* boys' pinching game
pimpina *f* (Am.) earthen water jug with long spout
pimpinela *f* (bot.) salad burnet
pimplar *va* (coll.) to drink (*wine*)
pimpleo -a *adj* of the Muses
pimpollada *f* or **pimpollar** *m* grove or planting of young trees
pimpollear *vn* to sprout, to bud
pimpollecer §34 *vn* var. of **pimpollear**
pimpollejo *m* small sucker, shoot, or sprout
pimpollo *m* sucker, shoot, sprout; rosebud; young tree; (coll.) handsome child; (coll.) handsome young person
pimpolludo -da *adj* full of suckers, shoots, or buds
pina *f* see **pino**
pinabete *m* (bot.) fir tree
pinacoide *m* (cryst.) pinacoid
pinacoteca *f* picture gallery
pináculo *m* pinnacle; (arch. & fig.) pinnacle
pinado -da *adj* (bot.) pinnate
pinar *m* pine grove, pinery
pinarejo *m* small pine grove
pinariego -ga *adj* (pertaining to the) pine
pinastro *m* (bot.) pinaster, cluster pine
pinatar *m* growth of young pines
pinatífido -da *adj* (bot.) pinnatifid
pinatisecto -ta *adj* (bot.) pinnatisected
pinaza *f* (naut.) pinnace
pincarrasca *f* (bot.) Aleppo pine
pincarrascal *m* grove of Aleppo pines
pincarrasco *m* var. of **pincarrasca**
pincel *m* brush; (fig.) brush (*painter; style of painting*); painting; pencil, beam (*of light, etc.*); **pincel aéreo** air brush; **pincel de pelo de camello** camel's-hair brush
pincelación *f* (med.) penciling
pincelada *f* stroke (*with a brush*); touch, finish, flourish
pincelar *va* to paint; to paint a portrait of; to picture; (med.) to pencil
pincelero -ra *mf* maker of brushes, dealer in brushes, seller of brushes; *m* brush case
pincelote *m* coarse brush
pincerna *mf* cupbearer, server of drinks
pinciano -na *adj* (pertaining to) Valladolid; *mf* native or inhabitant of Valladolid
pincha *f* kitchenmaid
pinchadura *f* or **pinchamiento** *m* prick, puncture
pinchar *va* to prick, jab, pierce, puncture; to stir up, provoke; **no pinchar ni cortar** to have no influence, be of no account
pinchaúvas *m* (*pl:* **-vas**) (coll.) grape thief (*at market*); (coll.) cur, contemptible fellow; (slang) necktie pin, stickpin
pinchazo *m* prick, jab; puncture; prodding, provocation; **a prueba de pinchazos** (aut.) puncture-proof
pinche *m* scullion, kitchen boy; helper, apprentice
pincho *m* thorn, prick; prod (*pointed object*)
pinchón *m* (orn.) chaffinch
pinchudo -da *adj* thorny, prickly
pindárico -ca *adj* Pindaric
Píndaro *m* Pindar

Pindo *m* Pindus
pindonga *f* (coll.) gadabout (*woman*)
pindonguear *vn* (coll.) to gad about (*said of a woman*)
pineal *adj* pineal
pineda *f* pine grove; braid for garters
pingajo *m* (coll.) rag, tatter
pingajoso -sa *adj* ragged, tattered
pinganello *m* icicle
pinganitos; en pinganitos (coll.) in prosperity, in a high place
pingar §59 *vn* to drip; to jump
pingo *m* (coll.) rag, tatter; (coll.) ragamuffin; (coll.) horse; (Am.) nag; **pingos** *mpl* (coll.) cheap duds (*of female*); **andar, estar** or **ir de pingo** (coll.) to gad about (*said of a woman*)
pingorota *f* summit, pinnacle
pingorote *m* (coll.) end, tip, projection
pingorotudo -da *adj* (coll.) high, lofty, elevated
pingotear *vn* (Am.) to frolic, gambol
pingue *m* (naut.) turret steamer, pinkie
pingüe *adj* oily, greasy, fat; rich, abundant, fertile, profitable
pingüedinoso -sa *adj* fatty; juicy, greasy
pingüica *f* (bot.) manzanita (*Arctostaphylus pungens*)
pingüino *m* (orn.) penguin
pinguosidad *f* fat, fattiness, greasiness
pinífero -ra *adj* (poet.) full of pines, pine-bearing
pinillo *m* (bot.) ground pine; (bot.) mock cypress; **pinillo oloroso** (bot.) ground pine
pinino *m* (Am.) var. of **pinito**
pinito *m* first step; **hacer pinitos** to begin to walk; (fig.) to take the first steps
pinjante *m* pendant (*jewel*); (arch.) pendant
pinnado -da *adj* var. of **pinado**
pinnípedo -da *adj* & *m* (zool.) pinniped
pino -na *adj* steep; *m* (bot.) pine, pine tree; first step; **en pino** standing; **hacer pinos** to begin to walk; (fig.) to take the first steps; **pino albar** (bot.) Scotch pine; **pino araucano** (bot.) monkey puzzle; **pino carrasco** or **carrasqueño** (bot.) Aleppo pine; **pino cembro** (bot.) Swiss pine; **pino doncel** (bot.) Italian stone pine; **pino marítimo** (bot.) cluster pine, pinaster; **pino negral** (bot.) larch, Corsican pine; **pino negro** (bot.) Swiss mountain pine; **pino piñón** (bot.) piñon; **pino piñonero** (bot.) stone pine (*Pinus pinea*); **pino pudio** (bot.) larch; **pino rodeno** (bot.) cluster pine, pinaster; **pino salgareño** (bot.) larch, Corsican pine; **pino tea** (bot.) pitch pine ‖ *f* felloe (*section of rim of wheel*); pointed or conical mound
pinocha *f* pine needle
Pinocho *m* Pinocchio
pinole *m* pinole (*powder used in making chocolate*)
pinoso -sa *adj* piny
pinsapal *m* grove of Spanish firs
pinsapo *m* (bot.) Spanish fir
pinta *m* see **pinto**; *f* see **pinto**
pintacilgo *m* var. of **jilguero**
pintada *f* see **pintado**
pintadera *f* pastry tube
pintadillo *m* var. of **jilguero**
pintado -da *adj* spotted, mottled; tipsy; accented (*with a written accent*); (dial.) pockmarked; **estar** or **venir pintado** or **como pintado** to be just the thing; **el más pintado** (coll.) the aptest one, the shrewdest one; (coll.) the best one; *m* painting (*act*); *f* (orn.) guinea hen; (ichth.) sierra
pintamonas *mf* (*pl:* **-nas**) (coll.) dauber (*poor painter*)
pintar *va* to paint; to draw (*a letter, an accent mark, etc.*); to picture, depict; to exaggerate; to amount to; to put a written accent on; to spread icing or a design on (*a cake*) with pastry tube; **pintarla** (coll.) to put it on, to put on airs; *vn* to paint; to begin to turn red, begin to ripen; (coll.) to show, to turn out; **pintar como querer** to indulge in wishful thinking; *vr* to paint, to paint oneself, put on make-up; to begin to turn red, begin to ripen; to imagine; **pintarse solo para** (coll.) to show great aptitude for
pintarrajar or **pintarrajear** *va* (coll.) to daub; *vr* (coll.) to be daubed
pintarrajo *m* (coll.) daub (*badly painted picture*)
pintarroja *f* (ichth.) dogfish
pintear *vn* to drizzle
pintiparado -da *adj* similar; **pintiparado a** similar to, like, just like; **pintiparado para** just the thing for
pintiparar *va* to liken, make like; (coll.) to compare
pinto -ta *adj* (Am.) pinto; *m* (Am.) pinto (*bean*); **estar entre Pinto y Valdemoro** (coll.) to be half-seas over; *f* spot, mark, sign; dot; pint; lines near edge of Spanish playing card showing suit; **pinta** *m* (coll.) scoundrel
pintojo -ja *adj* spotted, mottled
pintón -tona *adj* ripening (*said of grapes*); medium-baked (*brick*); *m* (ent.) corn borer
pintor -tora *mf* painter (*artist; artisan*); **pintor de brocha gorda** painter, house painter; (coll.) dauber; **pintor de mala muerte** (coll.) dauber; **pintor paisajista** landscape painter
pintoresco -ca *adj* picturesque
pintoresquismo *m* picturesqueness
pintorrear *va* (coll.) to daub; *vr* (coll.) to be daubed
pintura *f* painting; paint; **hacer pinturas** (coll.) to prance; **no poder ver ni en pintura** to not be able to stand the sight of; **pintura a la aguada** (f.a.) water color; **pintura al agua** cold-water paint; **pintura al encausto** (f.a.) encaustic painting; **pintura al fresco** (f.a.) fresco; **pintura al óleo** (f.a.) oil painting; **pintura al pastel** (f.a.) pastel (*drawing*); **pintura al temple** (f.a.) tempera; **pintura alumínica** aluminum paint; **pintura bronceada** bronze paint; **pintura de aceite** oil paint; **pintura de aluminio** aluminum paint
pinturero -ra *adj* (coll.) showy, conceited; *mf* (coll.) show-off
pínula *f* (opt.) sight
pinza *f* clothespin; spring clamp; **pinzas** *fpl* pincers (*tool; claws of crab, etc.*); tweezers; (dent. & surg.) forceps; **pinza hemostática** hemostat
pinzón *m* (orn.) finch; (orn.) chaffinch; pump handle; **pinzón real** (orn.) bullfinch
pinzote *m* (naut.) whipstaff; (naut.) pintle
piña *f* fir cone, pine cone; knob; plug; cluster, knot; (bot.) pineapple; (metal.) pina or piña (*residuary cone of silver*); (naut.) wall knot; **piña de ratón** (bot.) pinguin
piñal *m* (Am.) pineapple plantation, pinery
piñata *f* pot; hanging pot of candy which is broken by blindfolded children with a stick at a masked ball the first Sunday of Lent
piñón *m* (mach. & orn.) pinion; piñon (*seed*); (bot.) physic nut; **piñón de Indias** (bot.) physic nut; **piñón de linterna** (mach.) lantern pinion; **piñón diferencial** (aut.) pinion gear
piñonata *f* shredded-almond preserves
piñonate *m* pine-kernel candy
piñoncillo *m* (orn.) pinion (*of wing*)
piñonear *vn* to click (*said of a gun being cocked*); (coll.) to become a young man, to reach the age of puberty; (coll.) to become an old fool, to become flirtatious (*said of a mature man*)
piñoneo *m* click (*of a gun being cocked*)
piñonero *m* (orn.) bullfinch
piñuela *f* figured silk; cypress nut; (bot.) pinguin
piñuelo *m* var. of **erraj**
pío -a *adj* pious; merciful, compassionate; pied, dappled (*horse*); *m* peeping, chirping (*of chickens*); (coll.) intense desire; (*cap.*) *m* Pius; **no decir ni pío** to not breathe a word, to say absolutely nothing
piocha *f* jeweled head adornment; artificial flower made of feathers; pick, pickax
pioemia *f* (path.) pyaemia
piogenia *f* (path.) formation of pus
piogénico -ca or **piógeno -na** *adj* pyogenic
piojento -ta *adj* lousy
piojería *f* lousiness; lousy place; (coll.) misery, poverty

piojillo *m* bird louse, plant louse; **matar el piojillo** (coll.) to carry on an underhanded business
piojo *m* (ent.) louse; bird louse; **como piojos en costura** (coll.) packed in like sardines; **piojo de mar** (zool.) whale louse; **piojo pegadizo** (ent.) crab louse; (coll.) hanger-on, pest, parasite; **piojo resucitado** (coll.) upstart, parvenu
piojoso -sa *adj* lousy; mean, stingy
piojuelo *m* little louse; green fly, plant louse
piola *f* (naut.) houseline
pión, piona *adj* peeping, chirping
pionero -ra *adj* pioneering; *mf* pioneer
pionía *f* seed of coral tree, bucare beans
piornal *m* or **piorneda** *f* growth of Spanish broom
piorno *m* (bot.) Spanish broom; (bot.) cytisus
piorrea *f* (path.) pyorrhea
pipa *f* pipe (*for smoking tobacco*); wine cask, hogshead; butt (*liquid measure*); pip (*of orange, melon, etc.*); (arti.) fusee; (mus.) pipe, reed; **fumar en pipa** to smoke a pipe; **pipa de espuma de mar** meerschaum pipe; **pipa de paz** pipe of peace; **pipa de riego** watering cart; **pipa de tierra** clay pipe
pipar *vn* to smoke a pipe
piperáceo -a *adj* (bot.) piperaceous
pipería *f* casks, hogsheads; (naut.) water barrels, supply barrels
piperina *f* (chem.) piperine
pipeta *f* pipette
pipí *m* (*pl:* **-píes**) (orn.) honey creeper, pitpit
pipián *m* ragout of chicken and mutton with bacon and crushed almonds
pipiar **§90** *vn* to peep, to chirp
pipiolo *m* (coll.) novice, greenhorn; (coll.) brat, urchin
pipirigallo *m* (bot.) sainfoin
pipirijaina *f* (coll.) company of strolling players
pipiripao *m* (coll.) sumptuous party
pipiritaña or **pipitaña** *f* boy's flute made of green cane
pipistrela *f* (zool.) bat
pipo *m* (orn.) lesser spotted woodpecker
piporro *m* (coll.) bassoon
pipote *m* keg
pique *m* pique, resentment; zeal, eagerness; (ent.) chigger; (naut.) crotch; spade (*playing card*); (Am.) shaft (*of mine*); **piques** *mpl* spades (*suit of playing cards*); **a pique** steep, jagged; (naut.) apeak; **a pique de** + *inf* in danger of + *ger;* on the verge of + *ger;* **echar a pique** (naut.) to sink (*a ship*); (fig.) to ruin, destroy; **irse a pique** (naut.) to sink; (fig.) to become ruined or destroyed; **tener un pique con** to be piqued at
piqué *m* piqué (*fabric*)
piquera *f* bung, bunghole; taphole; outlet or iron runner (*of blast furnace*); burner
piquería *f* troop of pikemen
piquero *m* pikeman; (orn.) booby
piqueta *f* pick, pickax; mason's hammer
piquetaje *m* staking out
piquete *m* sharp jab; small hole; survey pole; stake, picket; (mil.) picket; (Am.) pen, yard (*for animals*); (Am.) edge (*of scissors*); **piquete de ejecución** firing squad; **piquete de huelguistas** picket; **piquete de salvas** firing squad
piquetero *m* (min.) tool boy
piquetilla *f* gad, wedge; mason's pickaxe
piquillo *m* small beak or bill; picot
piquituerto *m* (orn.) crossbill
pira *f* pyre
piragón *m* var. of **pirausta**
piragua *f* pirogue; (sport) shell, single shell; (Am.) tailflower; (Am.) aroid
piragüero -ra *mf* person who steers a pirogue
piragüista *m* (sport) oarsman
piral *m* fabulous butterfly which lived in fire; (ent.) moth; **piral de la vid** (ent.) vine moth
piramidal *adj* pyramidal
pirámide *f* pyramid; **la gran Pirámide** the Great Pyramid; **las Pirámides** the Pyramids
Píramo *m* (myth.) Pyramus
piranga *f* (orn.) redbird, scarlet tanager
pirano *m* (chem.) pyran
pirata *m* pirate; hard-hearted wretch; *adj* piratical
piratear *vn* to pirate, to practice piracy
piratería *f* piracy; robbery; cruelty
pirático -ca *adj* piratical
pirausta *f* fabulous butterfly which lived in fire
pirca *f* (Am.) dry-stone wall
pirco *m* (Am.) succotash
pirenaico -ca *adj* Pyrenean
Pireo, el Peiraeus, Piraeus
pirético -ca *adj* pyretic
piretología *f* pyretology
pirexia *f* (path.) pyrexia
piribenzamina *f* (pharm.) pyribenzamine
pírico -ca *adj* (pertaining to) fire or fireworks
piridina *f* (chem.) pyridine
piriforme *adj* pyriform, pear-shaped
pirinaico -ca *adj* var. of **pirenaico**
pirineo -a *adj* Pyrenean; **Pirineos** *mpl* Pyrenees
pirita *f* (mineral.) pyrites; **pirita de cobre** (mineral.) copper pyrites; **pirita de hierro** or **pirita marcial** (mineral.) iron pyrites
piritoso -sa *adj* pyritic, pyritous
pirlitero *m* (bot.) English hawthorn (*Crataegus monogyna*)
pirobolista *m* (mil.) mine builder
piroelectricidad *f* pyroelectricity
pirófago -ga *adj* fire-eating; *mf* fire-eater
piróforo *m* (chem.) pyrophorus
pirogálico -ca *adj* pyrogallic
pirogalol *m* (chem.) pyrogallol
pirograbado *m* pyrography, pyrogravure
pirolusita *f* (mineral.) pyrolusite
piromancia or **piromancía** *f* pyromancy
piromanía *f* pyromania
pirómetro *m* pyrometer
piropear *va* (coll.) to flatter, to compliment, to flirt with
piropeo *m* (coll.) flattery, flirtation
piropo *m* garnet, carbuncle; (coll.) flattery, compliment, flirtatious remark
piróscafo *m* steamship
piroscopio *m* (phys.) pyroscope
pirosfera *f* pyrosphere
pirosis *f* (path.) pyrosis
pirotecnia *f* pyrotechnics
pirotécnico -ca *adj* pyrotechnic or pyrotechnical; *m* pyrotechnist, powder maker, fireworks manufacturer
piroxena *f* or **piroxeno** *m* (mineral.) pyroxene
piroxilina *f* pyroxylin
Pirra *f* (myth.) Pyrrha
pirrar *vr* (coll.) to long, to be eager; **pirrarse por** (coll.) to long for, to be eager for
pírrico -ca *adj* pyrrhic; Pyrrhic
Pirro *m* Pyrrhus
pirrol *m* (chem.) pyrrole
pirrónico -ca *adj* Pyrrhonistic; *mf* Pyrrhonist
pirronismo *m* Pyrrhonism
pirueta *f* pirouette
piruétano *m* (bot.) wild pear
piruetear *vn* to pirouette
piruja *f* flip young woman
pirul *m* (Am.) pepper tree
pirulí *m* (*pl:* **-líes**) candy on a stick, lollipop
pisa *f* tread, trampling, stamping; pressing of olives or grapes; volley of kicks
pisada *f* tread; footstep (*sound or mark*); footprint; trampling; **seguir las pisadas de** to walk in the steps of, to follow in the footsteps of
pisadera *f* (Am.) tread (*of stairs*)
pisador -dora *adj* high-stepping, prancing; *m* grape-treader
pisadura *f* treading; footstep
pisapapeles *m* (*pl:* **-les**) paperweight
pisar *va* to trample, tread on, step on, stamp on; to tamp, pack down; to tread, to press with the feet; to lie on or over, to cover part of; to ram; to infringe on; to cover (*a female bird*); (fig.) to tread all over, to abuse; (mus.) to pluck (*strings*); to strike (*keys*); *vn* to be right above (*said of one floor with respect to another*); **pisar firme** (Am.) to step high, be out on top; *vr* (Am.) to fail, to be disappointed
pisasfalto *m* pissasphalt, mineral tar
pisaúvas *m* (*pl:* **-vas**) grape-treader

pisaverde *m* (coll.) fop, coxcomb, dandy
piscator *m* almanac
piscatorio -ria *adj* piscatorial
piscicultor -tora *mf* pisciculturist, fish breeder
piscicultura *f* pisciculture, fish culture, fish breeding
piscifactoría *f* fish hatchery
pisciforme *adj* pisciform, fish-shaped
piscina *f* fishpool, fishpond; swimming pool; (eccl.) piscina; **revolver la piscina** (Am.) to stir up trouble
Piscis *m* (astr.) Pisces
piscívoro -ra *adj* piscivorous, fish-eating
pisco *m* Peruvian brandy; (Am.) brandy jug; (Am.) turkey
piscolabis *m* (*pl:* **-bis**) (coll.) snack, bite, treat
pisicorre *f* (Am.) station wagon
pisiforme *adj* pisiform, pea-shaped; (anat.) pisiform
Pisístrato *m* Pisistratus
piso *m* tread, treading; floor, flooring; floor, story; surface (*e.g., of a road*); apartment, flat; rent; (aut.) tread (*of tire*); (geol.) stage; (min.) level; **buscar piso** to look for a place to live; **piso alto** upper floor, top floor; **piso bajo** ground floor, first floor; **piso principal** main floor, second floor
pisón *m* tamper, rammer
pisonear *va* var. of **apisonar**
pisotear *va* to trample, to tramp on, to tread under foot; (fig.) to tread all over, to abuse
pisoteo *m* trampling; abuse
pisotón *m* heavy tread on someone's foot
pista *f* track; trace, trail; clew; race track; alley (*of bowling alley*); (aer.) runway; **estar sobre una pista** to be on the scent; **seguir la pista a** (coll.) to be on the trail of; **pista de aterrizaje** (aer.) landing field; **pista de despegue** (aer.) takeoff field; **pista de patinar** skating rink; **pista sonora** sound track
pistachero *m* (bot.) pistachio (*tree*)
pistacho *m* pistachio (*nut*)
pistadero *m* pestle, crusher, squeezer
pistar *va* to crush, to squeeze
pistero *m* drinking cup (*for invalids*)
pistilado -da *adj* (bot.) pistillate
pistilo *m* (bot.) pistil
pisto *m* chicken broth (*for the sick*); vegetable cutlet; jumbled speech or writing; mess (*unpleasant state of affairs*); **a pistos** (coll.) sparingly, scantily; **darse pisto** (coll.) to put on airs
pistola *f* pistol; sprayer, gun, nozzle; rock drill; pistole (*coin*); **pistola ametralladora** submachine gun; **pistola de arzón** horse pistol; **pistola engrasadora** grease gun
pistolera *f* holster
pistolerismo *m* gangsterism
pistolero *m* pistol-shooting gangster; operator of a rock drill
pistoletazo *m* pistol shot
pistolete *m* pistolet, pocket pistol
pistón *m* (mach. & mus.) piston; percussion cap
pistonear *vn* to knock (*said of an internal-combustion engine*)
pistoneo *m* knock, knocking (*of an internal-combustion engine*)
pistonudo -da *adj* (coll.) stunning, grand
pistoresa *f* poniard, short dagger
pistraje *m* or **pistraque** *m* slops
pistura *f* crushing, squeezing
pita *f* (bot.) American aloe, century plant; pita, pita fiber, pita thread; hiss, hissing; glass marble; hen
pitaco *m* stem of century plant
pitada *f* whistle, sound of a whistle; impropriety; whistling, hissing; (Am.) puff (*on a cigar, etc.*)
Pitágoras *m* Pythagoras
pitagórico -ca *adj & mf* Pythagorean
pitahaya *f* (bot.) cereus, night-blooming cereus
pitancería *f* distribution of doles or rations; place of distribution of doles or rations
pitancero *m* distributor of doles or rations; choir superintendent; (eccl.) steward
pitanga *f* (bot.) Surinam cherry (*Eugenia uniflora*)
pitanza *f* dole, ration; price; (coll.) daily bread
pitaña *f* var. of **legaña**
pitañoso -sa *adj* var. of **legañoso**
pitar *va* to distribute the dole to; to pay, pay off; to whistle disapproval of (*a bullfighter*); *vn* to blow a whistle, to whistle; to blow the horn, to honk; (coll.) to talk nonsense; **no pitar** (coll.) to not be in vogue, to not be popular
pitarra *f* var. of **legaña**
pitarroso -sa *adj* var. of **legañoso**
pitazo *m* whistle, whistling; honk (*of horn*)
pitecántropo *m* (anthrop.) pithecanthropus
pitezna *f* trigger (*of a trap*)
Pitias *m* (myth.) Pythias
pitido *m* whistle, whistling
pitillera *f* cigarette maker (*woman*); cigarette case
pitillo *m* cigarette
pítima *f* saffron poultice; (coll.) drunk, drunkenness
pitio -tia *adj* Pythian
pitío *m* var. of **pitido**
pitipié *m* scale (*with graduated spaces*)
pitiriasis *f* (path.) pityriasis
pitirre *m* (orn.) kingbird
pito *m* whistle; horn, auto horn; fife; fifer; cigarette; jackstone; (ent.) tick; (orn.) woodpecker; earthen vessel containing water which produces a whistling sound when air is blown into spout; **hacer un pito catalán a** (Am.) to thumb one's nose at; **no dársele a uno un pito de** (coll.) to not care or to not give a damn for, e.g., **no se me da un pito de lo que dice** I don't care a damn for what he says; **no tocar pito en** (coll.) to have no hand in; **no valer un pito** (coll.) to be not worth a damn; **pito real** (orn.) green woodpecker; **pitos flautos** (coll.) foolery, folly
pitoflero -ra *mf* (coll.) punk musician; (coll.) gossip, busybody
pitómetro *m* (hyd.) pitometer
pitón *m* lump, protuberance; sprig, young shoot; tenderling, budding horn; tip (*of horn*); nozzle, spout; (zool.) python; (*cap.*) *m* (myth.) Python
pitonisa *f* pythoness; witch, siren
pitorra *f* (orn.) woodcock
pitorrear *vr* (coll.) to jeer, scoff
pitorreo *m* (coll.) jeering, scoffing
pitorro *m* nozzle, spout
pitpit *m* (orn.) pitpit
pitreo *m* var. of **pitaco**
Pitsburgo *f* Pittsburgh
pituco -ca *adj* (Am.) thin, weak, feeble; (Am.) dandyish; *m* (Am.) dandy, dude
pituita *f* pituite, mucus, phlegm
pituitario -ria *adj* pituitary
pituitoso -sa *adj* pituitous
pituso -sa *adj* tiny, cute; *mf* tot
piular *vn* to peep, chirp
piulido *m* peeping, chirping
piune *m* (bot.) Chilean medicinal tree (*Lomatia ferruginea*)
piuquén *m* (orn.) Chilean wild brant
piuria *f* (path.) pyuria
pivotar *vn* to pivot
pivote *m* pivot
píxide *f* (eccl.) pyx
pixidio *m* (bot.) pyxidium
piyama *m* var. of **pijama**
pizarra *f* shale, slate; slate (*for roofs; for writing on*); blackboard (*of any material*)
pizarral *m* shale bed
pizarreño -ña *adj* slaty, slate-colored; shaly
pizarrería *f* slate quarry, shale quarry
pizarrero *m* slater
pizarrín *m* slate pencil
pizarrón *m* large slate; **pizarrón anotador** score board
pizarroso -sa *adj* slate-colored; full of slate
pizate *m* var. of **pazote**
pizca *f* (coll.) mite, whit, jot; **ni pizca** (coll.) not a bit
pizcar §86 *va* (coll.) to pinch
pizco *m* (coll.) pinch, pinching
pizmiento -ta *adj* pitch-colored
pizpereta or **pizpireta** *adj* brisk, lively, smart (*woman*)
pizpirigaña *f* boys' pinching game

pizpita *f* or **pizpitillo** *m* (orn.) wagtail
placa *f* plaque (*badge of an order*); plaque, tablet; plate, slab, sheet; (anat., elec., phot., rad. & zool.) plate; (Am.) spot, scab; **placa acribillada** (bot.) sieve plate; **placa de cuarzo** (elec.) quartz plate; **placa de matrícula** (aut.) license plate; **placa giratoria** turntable (*for locomotives, etc.; of phonograph*)
placabilidad *f* placability
placable *adj* placable
placaminero *m* (bot.) persimmon
placativo -va *adj* placatory
placear *va* to retail (*foodstuffs*); to reveal, make known
placebo *m* (eccl. & med.) placebo
placel *m* (naut.) sandbank, reef; pearl-fishery
pláceme *m* congratulation; **dar el pláceme a** to congratulate; **estar de plácemes** to be in luck
placenta *f* (anat., bot. & zool.) placenta
placentario -ria *adj* placental; *m* (zool.) placental
placentero -ra *adj* pleasant, agreeable
placer *m* (min.) placer; (naut.) sandbank, reef; pearl-fishery; pleasure; **a placer** at one's convenience; §67 *va* to please; **que me place** willingly, with pleasure
placero -ra *adj* public, market-place; *mf* market vendor; loafer, town gossip
placeta or **placetuela** *f* small public square
placibilidad *f* agreeableness
placible *adj* agreeable
placidez *f* placidity
plácido -da *adj* placid
placiente *adj* pleasing, agreeable
plácito *m* opinion, judgment
plafón *m* (arch.) soffit
plaga *f* plague; pest; scourge, calamity; abundance; sore, ulcer; clime, region; point (*of compass*)
plagado -da *adj* plagued, infested; smitten
plagar §59 *va* to plague, infest; **plagar de minas** to sow with mines; *vr* to become plagued or infested
plagiar *va* to plagiarize; (Am.) to abduct, kidnap
plagiario -ria *adj* plagiaristic; *mf* plagiarist
plagio *m* plagiarism; (Am.) abduction, kidnaping
plagioclasa *f* (mineral.) plagioclase
plagiostomo -ma *adj & m* (ichth.) plagiostome
plagiotropismo *m* (bot.) plagiotropism
plagiotropo -pa *adj* (bot.) plagiotropic
plaid *m* plaid
plan *m* plan; level, height; (med.) régime; (min.) mine floor; (naut.) floor timber; **plan de estudios** or **plan escolar** curriculum; **plan quinquenal** five-year plan
plana *f* see **plano**
planada *f* plain, level ground
planador *m* planisher
planco *m* (orn.) gannet, solan
plancton *m* (biol.) plankton
plancha *f* plate, sheet (*of metal*); gangplank; iron, flatiron; ironing; horizontal suspension (*in gymnastics*); (print.) plate; (coll.) blunder, break; (Am.) flatcar; (Am.) dental plate; **a la plancha** grilled; **tirarse una plancha** to make a break, to put one's foot in it; **plancha de blindaje** armor plate; **plancha de caldera** boiler plate; **plancha de sastre** tailor's goose; **plancha portainstrumentos** (aut.) instrument panel
planchada *f* gangplank; (arti.) apron
planchado *m* ironing, pressing
planchador -dora *mf* ironer; *f* ironer (*machine*)
planchar *va* to iron, to press (*clothing*); *vn* (Am.) to be a wallflower
planchear *va* to plate, to cover with metal plates or sheets
plancheta *f* (surv.) plane table
planchón *m* large or heavy plate (*of metal*); (Am.) glacier
planeación *f* planning; planing
planeador *m* (aer.) glider
planear *va* to plan, to outline; to plane (*a board*); *vn* (aer.) to volplane, to glide
planeo *m* planning; (aer.) volplane, gliding
planera *f* (bot.) planer tree
planeta *m* (astr. & astrol.) planet
planetario -ria *adj* planetary; (mach.) planetary; *m* planetarium
planetesimal *adj & m* planetesimal
planetícola *mf* dweller on another planet
planetista *m* astrologer
planetoide *m* (astr.) planetoid
planga *f* (orn.) gannet, solan
planicidad *f* flatness
planicie *f* level ground, plain
planificar §86 *va* to plan
planilla *f* (Am.) list, roll, schedule; (Am.) panel (*of candidates for office*); (Am.) ballot; (Am.) commutation ticket (*for trolleys and busses*)
planimetría *f* planimetry
planimétrico -ca *adj* planimetric or planimetrical
planímetro *m* planimeter
planisferio *m* planisphere
plankton *m* var. of **plancton**
plano -na *adj* plane; level; smooth, even; flat ‖ *m* plan; map; plane; (aer.) plane, wing; (b.b.) board; **caer de plano** to fall flat; **cantar de plano** (coll.) to make a clean breast of it; **de plano** clearly, plainly, flatly; flat; **levantar un plano** (surv.) to make a survey; **primer plano** foreground; **plano acotado** contour map; **plano de cola** (aer.) tail plane; **plano de deriva** (aer.) tail fin; **plano de dirección** (aer.) vertical stabilizer; **plano de incidencia** (opt.) plane of incidence; **plano de nivel** datum plane, datum level; **plano de profundidad** (aer.) horizontal stabilizer; **plano de prueba** (phys.) proof plane; **plano focal** (opt.) focal plane; **plano inclinado** (mech.) inclined plane; cable railway ‖ *f* flat country, plain; trowel; cooper's plane; handwriting (*of a beginner*); (print.) page; **a plana renglón** or **a plana y renglón** line for line; just right; **corregir** or **enmendar la plana a** to find fault with; to excel; **primera plana** first page; **plana curvada** drawknife; **plana mayor** (mil.) staff
planocóncavo -va *adj* plano-concave
planoconvexo -xa *adj* plano-convex
planta *f* (bot.) plant; sole (*of foot*); foot; planting; plan; project; floor; floor plan, ground plan; roster (*of an office staff*); stance (*in fencing and dancing*); plant, factory; **de planta** from the ground up; **echar plantas** to swagger, to bully; **tener buena planta** (coll.) to make a fine appearance; **planta baja** ground floor; **planta del sortilegio** (bot.) witch hazel; **planta de maceta** or **de tiesto** potted plant; **planta noble** ground floor; **plantas de adorno** (hort.) ornamental plants; **planta siempre verde** (bot.) evergreen
plantación *f* planting; plantation
plantador -dora *mf* planter; (Am.) planter (*colonist*); *m* dibble; *f* planter (*machine*)
plantagináceo -a *adj* (bot.) plantaginaceous
plantaina *f* var. of **llantén**
plantaje *m* plants, planting
plantar *adj* (anat.) plantar; *va* to plant; to establish, to found; (coll.) to plant (*a blow*); (coll.) to jilt; (coll.) to throw (*into the street, into prison*); to leave dumfounded; *vr* to stand, take a stand; (coll.) to balk (*said of an animal*); (coll.) to land, to get, to arrive; to gang together
plantario *m* seedbed
plante *m* ganging together
planteamiento *m* planning; establishment, execution; statement, exposition; framing (*of a question*)
plantear *va* to plan, to outline (*e.g., a deal*); to establish, to execute, to carry out; to state, to set up, to expound, to pose; to raise (*a question*); *vn* (archaic) to weep, sob, whine
plantel *m* nursery, nursery garden; establishment, plant (*educational institution*); group, gathering
plantificación *f* planning; (coll.) planting a blow; throwing, hurling (*e.g., into the street, jail, etc.*)

plantificar §86 *va* to plan, to outline; (coll.) to plant (*a blow*); (coll.) to throw (*into the street, into prison*); *vr* (coll.) to get, to arrive
plantígrado -da *adj & m* (zool.) plantigrade
plantilla *f* plantlet, young plant; insole; reinforced sole (*of stocking or sock*); model, pattern, template; staff (*e.g., of employees*); roster (*of office force*); plan, design; ladyfinger (*cake*); **echar plantillas al calzado** to half-sole shoes; **ser de plantilla** to be on the regular staff
plantillar *va* to put insoles in (*shoes*); to reinforce the sole of (*a stocking or sock*)
plantillero -ra *adj* swaggering; *mf* swaggerer, bully
plantío -a *adj* planted; ready to be planted; *m* planting, growth, patch
plantista *m* landscape gardener; (coll.) swaggerer, bully
plantón *m* shoot (*to be transplanted*); graft, cion; guard, watchman; soldier punished with extra guard duty; waiting, standing around; **dar un plantón** to be long in coming, to keep someone waiting; **estar de** or **en plantón** (coll.) to stand around (*for a long time*); **llevarse un plantón** (coll.) to be kept standing
planudo -da *adj* flat-bottomed
plañidero -ra *adj* weeping, mournful; *f* weeper, professional mourner, hired mourner
plañido or **plañimiento** *m* lamentation, wailing, weeping
plañir §25 *va* to lament, grieve over; *vn* to lament, grieve, bewail
plaqué *m* plate, plating (*of gold or silver*)
plaquear *va* to plate, to silver-plate
plaqueta *f* (anat.) plaquette, blood platelet
plaquín *m* hauberk, coat of mail
plasma *m* (anat., phys. & physiol.) plasma; **plasma sanguíneo** blood plasma; *f* (mineral.) plasm
plasmación *f* molding, shaping
plasmador -dora *adj* creative; *mf* molder, creator; (*cap.*) *m* Creator
plasmar *va* to mold, shape
plasmático -ca *adj* plasmatic
plasmodio *m* (biol.) plasmodium
plasmólisis *f* (physiol.) plasmolysis
plasmoquina *f* (pharm.) plasmochin
plasmosoma *m* (pharm.) plasmosome
plasta *f* paste, soft mass; flattened object, flattened mass; (coll.) poor job, bungle
plaste *m* sizing, filler
plastecer §34 *va* to size, to fill
plastecido *m* sizing, filling
plástica *f* see **plástico**
plasticidad *f* plasticity
plástico -ca *adj* plastic; *m* plastic (*substance*); *f* plastic (*art of modeling*); plastic arts
plastificar §86 *va & vr* to plasticize
plastilina *f* plasticine
plastrón *m* (fencing) plastron
plata *f* (chem.) silver; silver (*coin or coins*); wealth; money; **como una plata** (coll.) clean, shining; **en plata** (coll.) briefly, to the point; (coll.) plainly; (coll.) in sum; **quedarse sin plata** to be broke; **plata agria** (mineral.) stephanite; **plata alemana** German silver; **plata córnea** (mineral.) horn silver; **plata de piña** spongy silver; **plata dorada** silver gilt; **plata labrada** silverware; **plata roja** ruby silver
platabanda *f* border, edge; flower bed; (arch.) flat molding; splice plate, fishplate
plataforma *f* platform; (rail.) platform car, flatcar; (rail.) roadbed; (rail.) turntable; (geog.) platform; (mach.) index plate; (fig.) platform (*statement of policy of political party*); **plataforma giratoria** (rail.) turntable
platal *m* (coll.) lot of money
platalea *f* (orn.) pelican
platanáceo -a *adj* (bot.) platanaceous
platanal *m* or **platanar** *m* plantation of plantains
platanero -ra *adj* (pertaining to the) banana; *m* (bot.) plantain, banana
plátano *m* (bot.) plantain, banana (*Musa paradisiaca and fruit*); (bot.) plane tree; **plátano de occidente** (bot.) American plane tree; **plátano de oriente** (bot.) plane tree; **plátano falso** (bot.) sycamore maple; **plátano guineo** (bot.) banana
platea *f* (theat.) orchestra, parquet
plateado -da *adj* silver-plated; silver (*in color*); *m* silver plating; silver (*color*)
plateador *m* silver plater
plateadura *f* silver plating; silver (*used in plating*)
platear *va* to coat or plate with silver
platel *m* platter, tray
platelminto *m* (zool.) platyhelminth
platén *m* platen (*of typewriter*)
plateresco -ca *adj* (arch.) plateresque
platería *f* silversmith's shop; trade of silversmith
platero *m* silversmith; jeweller; **platero de oro** goldsmith
plática *f* talk, chat; talk, informal lecture; sermon; **libre plática** (naut.) pratique
platicar §86 *va* to talk over (*a matter*); to discuss; to preach; *vn* to talk, to chat; to discuss; to preach
platija *f* (ichth.) plaice
platilla *f* thin middling linen
platillo *m* plate; saucer; pan (*of scales*); stew; extra dish (*in a monastery*); subject of gossip; (mus.) cymbal; **platillo volador** or **volante** flying saucer
platina *f* platen; stage (*for microscope*); (chem.) platinum; (print.) imposing table
platinar *va* to platinize
platiniridio *m* platiniridium
platino *m* (chem.) platinum
platinocianuro *m* (chem.) platinocyanide
platinoide *m* platinoid
platinotipia *f* (phot.) platinotype
platirrino -na *adj & m* (zool.) platyrrhine
plato *m* dish; plate; course (*at meals*); daily fare; pan (*of scales*); subject of gossip; (arch.) ornamented metope; (mach.) plate, disk; (mach.) chuck; (poker) pot; **comer en un mismo plato** (coll.) to be close friends; **entre dos platos** with much bowing and bending; **hacer plato** to pass the food; **nada entre dos platos** (coll.) much ado about nothing; **ser plato de segunda mano** (coll.) to feel neglected, to be left out in the cold; **plato de segunda mano** (coll.) discard, castoff; **plato frutero** fruit dish; **plato fuerte** main course; **plato giratorio** turntable (*of phonograph*); **plato sopero** soup dish; **plato trinchero** trencher (*wooden platter*); dish
plató *m* (*pl:* **-tós**) (mov.) set
platón *m* large plate; (Am.) washbowl, basin; (Am.) platter; (*cap.*) *m* Plato
platónico -ca *adj* Platonic
platonismo *m* Platonism
platonista *mf* Platonist
platudo -da *adj* (Am.) rich, well-to-do
platuja *f* var. of **platija**
plausibilidad *f* praiseworthiness; acceptability, agreeableness
plausible *adj* praiseworthy; acceptable, agreeable, pleasing
plausivo -va *adj* applauding
plauso *m* var. of **aplauso**
plaustro *m* (poet.) cart, wagon
plautino -na *adj* Plautine
Plauto *m* Plautus
playa *f* beach, shore, strand; **playa de baños** bathing beach; **playa infantil** sand pile (*for children to play in*)
playado -da *adj* beach-lined
playazo *m* long, wide beach
playero -ra (pertaining to the) beach; *mf* fishmonger; **playero turco** (orn.) ruddy turnstone; *f* fishwoman; Andalusian song; beach shoe
playón *m* large beach
playuela *f* small beach
plaza *f* plaza, square; market, market place; town, city; fortified town or city; space, room; yard; office, employment; character, reputation; place, seat; **sacar a plaza** (coll.) to bring out into the open; **sentar plaza** (mil.) to enlist; **un cuatro plazas** a four-seater; **plaza de armas** (mil.) parade ground; (Am.)

public square; **plaza de gallos** cockpit (*for cockfights*); **plaza de toros** bull ring; **plaza fuerte** (fort.) stronghold, fortress, garrison; **plaza mayor** main square; **plaza montada** mounted soldier
plazco or **plazgo** *1st sg pres ind of* **placer**
plazo *m* term, time, extension; time limit; date of payment; instalment; **a largo plazo** long-range; (com.) long-term; **a plazo** on credit, on time; in instalments; **en breve plazo** within a short time; **vender a plazo** to sell on credit; to sell short
plazoleta *f* small square; small square or plaza in a public walk or garden
plazuela *f* small square
ple *m* handball
pleamar *f* (naut.) high tide, high water
plébano *m* parish priest
plebe *f* plebs, common people; (hist.) plebs
plebeísmo *m* plebeianism
plebeyez *f* (coll.) plebeianism
plebeyo -ya *adj & mf* plebeian
plebiscitario -ria *adj* (pertaining to a) plebiscite, plebiscitary
plebiscito *m* plebiscite
pleca *f* (print.) thin line or rule
plectognato -ta *adj & m* (zool.) plectognath
plectro *m* (mus.) plectrum; (poet.) inspiration
plegable *adj* folding; pliable
plegadamente *adv* in folds; confusedly; wholesale
plegadera *f* paper folder, paper knife
plegadizo -za *adj* folding; pliable
plegado *m* var. of **plegadura**
plegador -dora *adj* folding; *mf* folder; *m* folder, folding machine
plegadura *f* fold; plait, pleat, crease
plegamiento *m* fold; plait, pleat, crease; (geol.) fold
plegar §29 *va* to fold; to plait, to pleat, to crease; to fold over; *vr* to yield, give in
plegaria *f* prayer; noon call to prayer
pleguería *f* folds, plaits
pleguete *m* (bot.) tendril
pleistoceno -na *adj & m* (geol.) Pleistocene
pleita *f* plaited strand of esparto grass
pleiteador -dora *mf* pleader, litigant
pleitear *va & vn* (law) to plead, to litigate
pleitista *adj* litigious; *mf* litigious person
pleito *m* litigation, lawsuit; dispute, quarrel; fight, battle; **pleito de acreedores** bankruptcy proceedings; **pleito homenaje** (feud.) homage
plenamar *f* var. of **pleamar**
plenario -ria *adj* plenary
plenilunio *m* full moon
plenipotencia *f* full powers
plenipotenciario -ria *adj & mf* plenipotentiary
plenitud *f* plenitude, fullness; **plenitud de los tiempos** fullness of time
pleno -na *adj* full; joint (*session*); **en plena bahía** out in the bay, in the open bay; **en plena calle** in the middle of the street, right in the street; **en plena cara** right in the face, smack in the face; **en plena carrera** in the middle of the race; in full career; **en plena ciudad** in the heart of the city; **en plena cosecha** in the middle of the harvest; **en plena faena** in the midst of his (her, your, etc.) task; **en plena guerra** in the midst of war; **en plena intriga** in the midst of plotting; **en plena juventud** in the flower of youth; **en plena marcha** in full swing; **en plena noche** in the depth of night; **en plena retirada** in full retreat; **en plena temporada** at the height of the season; **en plena urbe** in the heart of the city; **en plena vista** in plain sight, in full view; **en pleno bloqueo** at the height of the blockade; **en pleno campo** in the open country; **en pleno día** in broad daylight; **en pleno invierno** in the deep (or depth) of winter, in midwinter; **en pleno mar** in the open sea; **en pleno mediodía** at broad noon, at high noon; **en pleno río** in midstream; **en pleno trabajo** in the thick of work; **en pleno verano** at the height of summer, in midsummer; **en pleno viento** in the full force of the wind; exposed to the wind on all sides; **en pleno vigor** in full vigor; in full swing; *m* plenum; full meeting (or session); (bowling) strike
pleocroísmo *m* (cryst.) pleochroism
pleonasmo *m* pleonasm
pleonástico -ca *adj* pleonastic
pleópodo *m* (zool.) swimmeret, pleopod
plepa *f* (coll.) mess (*person or thing full of defects*)
plesiosauro *m* (pal.) plesiosaur
pletina *f* iron plate, flange, shim
pletismógrafo *m* (physiol.) plethysmograph
plétora *f* plethora; superabundance; (path.) plethora
pletórico -ca *adj* plethoric; **pletórico de** overflowing with
pleura *f* (anat. & zool.) pleura
pleural *adj* pleural
pleuresía *f* (path.) pleurisy
pleurítico -ca *adj* pleuritic
pleuritis *f* (path.) pleuritis
pleurodinia *f* (path.) pain in the side
pleurodonto -ta *adj* (zool.) pleurodont
pleuronecto -ta *adj & m* (ichth.) pleuronectid
pleuroneumonía *f* (path.) pleuropneumonia
plexiglás *m* plexiglass
plexo *m* (anat. & zool.) plexus; **plexo solar** (anat.) solar plexus
Pléyade *f* Pleiad; **Pléyades** *fpl* (myth & astr.) Pleiades
plica *f* (law) escrow; (mus. & path.) plica
pliego *m* sheet (*of paper*); folder; cover, envelope; sealed letter or document; bid, specifications; **pliego cerrado** (naut.) sealed orders; **pliego de comprobar** (print.) proof; **pliego de condiciones** bid, specifications; **pliego de prensa** (print.) page proof; **pliego de principios** (print.) proof of front matter
pliegue *m* fold, pleat, crease; (geol.) fold; **pliegue acordeonado** or **en acordeón** (sew.) accordion pleat; **pliegue de tabla** (sew.) box pleat
plieguecillo *m* small sheet; small fold; small folder
Plinio *m* Pliny; **Plinio el Antiguo** Pliny the Elder; **Plinio el Joven** Pliny the Younger
plinto *m* (arch.) plinth; baseboard
pliocénico -ca or **plioceno -na** *adj & m* (geol.) Pliocene
plisado *m* pleat; pleating
plisar *va* to pleat
plomada *f* carpenter's lead pencil; plummet; plumb bob; sinker or sinkers (*of a fishing net*); scourge tipped with lead balls; (naut.) sounding lead
plomar *va* to seal with lead
plomazo *m* shot, gunshot
plomazón *f* cushion (*of goldsmith or silversmith*)
plombagina *f* plumbago, graphite
plomería *f* lead roofing; leadwork; plumbing
plomero *m* lead worker; plumber
plomífero -ra *adj* plumbiferous; *mf* (coll.) bore, nuisance
plomizo -za *adj* leaden; lead-colored
plomo *m* (chem.) lead; lead (*piece of lead; plumb bob, plummet; bullet*); sinker; (elec.) fuse; (coll.) bore; **a plomo** plumb, perpendicularly; (coll.) just right; **caer a plomo** to fall flat; **plomo azul** blue lead (*pigment*)
plomoso -sa *adj* var. of **plomizo**
Plotino *m* Plotinus
plugo *3d sg pret ind of* **placer**
pluma *f* feather; feathers; quill; plume; pen; penmanship; writer; (fig.) pen; (Am.) faucet; **dejar correr la pluma** to write away, to write for dear life; **escribir a vuela pluma** to write freely, to let onself go (*in writing*); **vivir de la pluma** to live by one's pen; **pluma esferográfica** (Am.) ball point pen; **pluma estilográfica** or **pluma fuente** (*pl:* **plumas fuente**) fountain pen; **pluma secundaria** (orn.) secondary feather
plumado -da *adj* feathered; *f* flourish, stroke (*of pen*); penful
plumafuente *f* fountain pen
plumaje *m* plumage; plumes, crest
plumajería *f* abundance of plumes
plumajero *m* plumist, feather dresser

plumazo *m* feather pillow, feather mattress; stroke (*of pen*); **de un plumazo** (coll.) with one fell stroke
plumazón *m* plumage, abundance of plumes; crest
plumbado -da *adj* sealed with a lead seal
plumbagina *f* var. of **plombagina**
plumbagináceo -a *adj* (bot.) plumbaginaceous
plúmbeo -a *adj* lead; heavy as lead
plúmbico -ca *adj* lead; (chem.) plumbic
plumeado *m* (f.a.) hatching
plumear *va* (f.a.) to hatch
plumeo *m* (f.a.) hatching
plúmeo -a *adj* feathery
plumería *f* or **plumerío** *m* feathers, wealth of feathers
plumerillo *m* (bot.) milkweed
plumero *m* penholder (*rack*); duster, feather duster; school companion (*box for pens and pencils*); **plumeros** *mpl* (bot.) goldenrod
plumífero -ra *adj* (poet.) feathered
plumilla *f* small feather, plumelet; point (*of fountain pen*); (bot.) plumule; **plumilla inglesa** (print.) script
plumión *m* (orn.) plumule
plumista *m* scrivener, clerk; feather or plume maker or dealer
plumón *m* (orn.) plumule; down; feather bed
plumoso -sa *adj* downy, feathery, plumose
plúmula *f* (bot.) plumule
plural *adj* (gram.) plural; manifold; *m* (gram.) plural; **plural de modestia** (gram.) editorial plural; **plural mayestático** (gram.) royal plural
pluralidad *f* plurality; **a pluralidad de votos** by a majority of votes
pluralizar §76 *va* to pluralize
plus *m* extra, bonus; **plus marca** *f* (sport) record
pluscuamperfecto -ta *adj & m* (gram.) pluperfect
plusmarca *f* (sport) record
plusmarquista *adj* (sport) record-breaking; *mf* (sport) record breaker
plusvalía *f* increased value, appreciation
Plutarco *m* Plutarch
plúteo *m* shelf, bookshelf; (hist.) pluteus
Pluto *m* (myth.) Plutus
plutocracia *f* plutocracy
plutócrata *mf* plutocrat
plutocrático -ca *adj* plutocratic
Plutón *m* (myth. & astr.) Pluto
plutoniano -na *adj* Plutonian
plutónico -ca *adj* (geol.) plutonic; (myth. & geol.) Plutonic
plutonio *m* (chem.) plutonium
Plutos *m* (myth.) Pluto
pluvial *adj* pluvial; rain
pluviómetro *m* pluviometer, rain gauge
pluviosidad *f* rainfall; raininess
pluvioso -sa *adj* pluvious, rainy
pneumático -ca *adj* var. of **neumático**
pno. abr. of **pergamino**
p.º abr. of **pero**
P.º abr. of **Pedro**
poa *f* (naut.) bridle
pobeda *f* white-poplar grove
población *f* population; village, town, city
poblacho *m* shabby old town or village
poblado -da *adj* populated; thick, bushy; *m* community
poblador -dora *adj* founding, settling; *mf* founder, settler
poblano -na *mf* (Am.) townsman, villager
poblar §77 *va* to people, populate; to found, settle, colonize; to stock (*a farm, a fishpond, a beehive*); to plant (*e.g., with trees*); *vn* to settle, colonize; to multiply, be prolific; *vr* to become full, covered, or crowded
poblazo *m* var. of **poblacho**
poblezuelo *m* small village
pobo *m* (bot.) white poplar
pobre *adj* poor; **más pobre que las ratas** or **una rata** (coll.) poor as a church mouse; **pobre de espíritu** poor in spirit; **¡pobre de mí!** poor me!; **pobre de solemnidad** poor as a church mouse; *mf* beggar, pauper; *m* poor man; poor devil
pobrería *f* var. of **pobretería**
pobrero *m* distributor of alms
pobrete -ta *adj* poor; wretched; (coll.) sorry-looking; *mf* wretch, unfortunate; *f* (coll.) prostitute
pobretear *vn* (coll.) to play poor, to act poor
pobretería *f* poor, poor people; beggars; poverty, wretchedness
pobreto *m* wretch, unfortunate
pobretón -tona *adj* poor, needy; *m* poor man
pobreza *f* poverty, want; poorness; vow of poverty
pobrezuelo -la *adj* poorish
pobrismo *m* poor, poor people; beggars
pócar *m* poker
pocero *m* well digger, well driller; cesspool cleaner
poceta *f* (Am.) basin, bowl
pocilga *f* pigpen; (fig.) pigpen
pocillo *m* sump, catch basin; chocolate cup
pócima *f* potion, concoction
poción *f* potion, dose
poco -ca *adj* little; few, e.g., **hay poca gente aquí** there are few people here; **pocos -cas** *adj pl* few; **poco** *adv* little; **poco** + *adj* un-, e.g., **poco inteligente** unintelligent; **a poco** shortly, shortly afterwards; **a poco de** + *inf* shortly after + *ger;* **dentro de poco** shortly; **en poco** almost; **estar en poco que** + *subj* to come near + *ger;* **otro poco** a little more; **por poco** almost, nearly; **tener en poco** to hold in low esteem, be scornful of; **un poco** a little; **un poco de** a little; **unos pocos** a few; **poco a poco** little by little; **¡poco a poco!** easy there!
póculo *m* drinking cup or glass
pocha *f* see **pocho**
pochi *adj* (Am.) short, too short
pocho -cha *adj* faded, discolored; overripe; rotten; (Am.) chubby; *mf* (Am.) U.S.-born Mexican; *f* (Am.) lie, trick, cheat
poda *f* pruning; pruning season
podadera *f* pruning knife or hook, billhook
podador -dora *adj* pruning; *mf* pruner
podagra *f* (path.) gout, podagra
podar *va* to prune
podazón *f* pruning season
podenco *m* hound
podenquero *m* keeper of the hounds
poder *m* power; hands; (law) power of attorney, proxy; **a poder de** by dint of; **caer en poder de** (mil.) to fall to; **de poder a poder** hand to hand; **el cuarto poder** the fourth estate (*the press, journalism*); **en poder de** in the power of; in the hands of; **obra en mi poder** I have at hand, I have in my possession; **plenos poderes** full powers; **por poderes** by proxy; **poder adquisitivo** or **poder de adquisición** purchasing power; **poder aéreo** air power; **poder aéreo atómico** atomic air power ‖ §68 *vn* to be possible; to be able, to have power or strength; **a más no poder** as hard as possible; **hasta más no poder** to the utmost; **no poder con** to not be able to stand, to not be able to manage; **no poder más** to be exhausted, to be all in; **no poder menos de** + *inf* to not be able to help + *ger;* **poder mucho** to have power or influence; **poder poco** to have little power or influence ‖ *v aux* **poder** + *inf* to be able to + *inf*, may, can, might, could + *inf;* **no poder ver** to not be able to stand
poderdante *mf* (law) constituent
poderhabiente *mf* (law) attorney, proxy
poderío *m* power, might; wealth, riches; sway, jurisdiction
poderoso -sa *adj* powerful, mighty; wealthy, rich
podíatra *mf* podiatrist
podiatría *f* podiatry
podio *m* (arch.) podium
podódromo *m* race track (*for foot races*)
podofilino *m* (pharm.) podophyllin
podofilo *m* podophyllum
podofilotoxina *f* (chem.) podophyllotoxin
podómetro *m* pedometer
podón *m* large pruning hook, large billhook
podre *m & f* pus, corruption
podré *1st sg fut ind of* **poder**
podrecer §34 *va, vn & vr* to rot
podrecimiento *m* var. of **podredura**

podredumbre *f* corruption, putrefaction; pus; gnawing sorrow
podredura or **podrición** *f* corruption, putrefaction
podridero *m* var. of **pudridero**
podrido -da *adj* rotten, putrid
podrigorio *m* (coll.) person full of aches and pains
podrimiento *m* var. of **pudrimiento**
podrir *va, vn & vr* var. of **pudrir** and used only in the *inf* & *pp*
poema *m* poem; **poema en prosa** prose poem; **poema sinfónico** (mus.) symphonic poem
poemático -ca *adj* poetic
poesía *f* poetry; poem; **bella poesía** (fig.) fairy tale (*untrue story*); **poesías órficas** Orphic hymns
poeta *m* poet
poetastro *m* poetaster
poético -ca *adj* poetic or poetical; *f* poetics
poetisa *f* poetess
poetizar §76 *va & vn* to poetize
poíno *m* gantry, barrelstand
poiquilotermo -ma *adj* (zool.) poikilothermal
polaco -ca *adj* Polish; *mf* Pole; **los polacos** the Polish; *m* Polish (*language*); *f* Polish dance
polacra *f* (naut.) polacre
polaina *f* legging
polar *adj* pole; polar; *f* polestar
polaridad *f* polarity
polarímetro *m* polarimeter
polariscopio *m* polariscope
polarización *f* polarization; **polarización de rejilla** (rad.) grid bias
polarizador -dora *adj* polarizing; *m* (opt.) polarizer
polarizar §76 *va* to polarize; *vr* to become polarized; to concentrate
polaroide *m* polaroid
polca *f* (mus.) polka
polcar §86 *vn* to polka, dance the polka
polea *f* pulley; (naut.) tackle
poleadas *fpl* porridge
poleame *m* (naut.) set of pulleys, tackle
polémico -ca *adj* polemic or polemical; *f* polemic (*controversy*); polemics (*art*)
polemista *mf* polemist
polemizar §76 *vn* to start a polemic
polemoniáceo -a *adj* (bot.) polemoniaceous
polemonio *m* (bot.) Greek valerian, Jacob's-ladder
polen *m* (bot.) pollen
polenta *f* polenta
poleo *m* cold wind, cold blast; (bot.) pennyroyal; (coll.) bombast, strutting
poleví *m* (*pl:* **-víes**) var. of **ponleví**
poliandria *f* polyandry; (bot.) polyandry
poliándrico -ca *adj* polyandrous
poliandro -dra *adj* (bot.) polyandrous
poliarquía *f* polyarchy
polibásico -ca *adj* (chem.) polybasic
polibasita *f* (mineral.) polybasite
policárpico -ca *adj* (bot.) polycarpic or polycarpous
pólice *m* thumb
policía *f* police; policing; politeness; cleanliness, neatness; body of ordinances regarding public order; **policía militar** military police; **policía secreta** secret police; **policía urbana** street cleaning; *m* policeman
policíaco -ca *adj* (pertaining to the) police; detective (*story*)
policial *adj* (pertaining to the) police; detective (*story*); *m* policeman
Policiano *m* Politian
policitación *f* unaccepted promise or offer
policlínica *f* polyclinic
policopia *f* multigraph
policromar *va* to polychrome
policromía *f* polichromy
policromo -ma *adj* polychrome
polichinela *m* punchinello; (*cap.*) *m* Punch
polidipsia *f* (path.) excessive thirst
Polidoro *m* (myth.) Polydorus
polidrupa *f* (bot.) berry (*of strawberry, blackberry, etc.*)
poliédrico -ca *adj* polyhedral
poliedro *m* (geom.) polyhedron
polietileno *m* (chem.) polyethylene
polifacético -ca *adj* (fig.) many-sided
polifagia or **polifagía** *f* (path.) polyphagia
polifásico -ca *adj* (elec.) polyphase, multiphase
Polifemo *m* (myth.) Polyphemus
polifilético -ca *adj* polyphyletic
polifonía *f* (mus. & phonet.) polyphony
polifónico -ca or **polífono -na** *adj* polyphonic
polígala *f* (bot.) milkwort; **polígala de Virginia** (bot.) snakeroot
poligamia *f* polygamy
poligámico -ca *adj* polygamic
polígamo -ma *adj* polygamous; *mf* polygamist
poligenismo *m* polygenism
poliglota *f* see **poligloto**
poliglotía *f* knowledge of many languages
poligloto -ta *adj & mf* polyglot; *f* polyglot Bible
poligonal *adj* polygonal
polígono -na *adj* polygonal; *m* (geom.) polygon
poligrafía *f* polygraphy
polígrafo *m* polygraph (*prolific writer; copying machine*); ball point pen; (med.) polygraph
polilla *f* (ent.) moth, clothes moth; (ent.) carpet moth; moths; (fig.) ravager, destroyer; **polilla de los museos de historia natural** (ent.) museum beetle; **polilla de los paños** (ent.) carpet moth; **polilla de los tapices** (ent.) carpet beetle
polillera *f* (bot.) moth mullein
polimatía *f* wide learning
polimería *f* polymerism
polimerización *f* polymerization
polimerizar §76 *va & vr* to polymerize
polímero -ra *adj* polymeric; *m* (chem.) polymer
Polimnia *f* (myth.) Polyhymnia
polimorfismo *m* polymorphism
polimorfo -fa *adj* polymorphous
polín *m* roller; skid
polinesio -sia *adj & mf* Polynesian; **la Polinesia** Polynesia
polineuritis *f* (path.) polyneuritis
polínico -ca *adj* pollinic or pollinical
polinífero -ra *adj* polliniferous
polinio *m* (bot.) pollinium
polinización *f* (bot.) pollination; **polinización cruzada** (bot.) cross-pollination
polinizar §76 *va* to pollinate
polinómico -ca *adj* polynomial
polinomio *m* (alg.) polynomial
polinosis *f* (path.) pollinosis, hay fever
polinuclear *adj* polynuclear
polio *m* (bot.) poly; *f* (path.) polio
poliomielitis *f* (path.) poliomyelitis
polipasto *m* tackle
polipero *m* (zool.) polypary
polipétalo -la *adj* (bot.) polypetalous
pólipo *m* (zool.) polyp; (path.) polyp or polypus
polipodio *m* (bot.) polypody, sweet fern
polisarcia *f* (path.) polysarcia, obesity
polisemia *f* polysemy
polisémico -ca or **polisemo -ma** *adj* polysemous
polisilábico -ca *adj* polysyllabic
polisílabo -ba *adj* polysyllabic; *m* polysyllable
polisíndeton *m* (rhet.) polysyndeton
polisintético -ca *adj* polysynthetic
polisón *m* bustle (*of woman's dress*)
polispasto *m* var. of **polipasto**
polista *adj* polo-playing; *mf* poloist, polo player
polistilo -la *adj* (arch.) polystyle; (bot.) polystylous; *m* (arch.) polystyle
polistireno *m* (chem.) polystyrene
Politburó *m* Politburo
politécnico -ca *adj* polytechnic
politeísmo *m* polytheism
politeísta *adj* polytheistic; *mf* polytheist
política *f* see **político**
politicastro *m* petty politician, corrupt politician
político -ca *adj* political; tactful; polite, courteous; -in-law, e.g., **padre político** father-in-law; *mf* politician; *f* politics; policy; manners, politeness, courtesy; **política de acorralamiento** policy of encirclement; **política de café** parlor politics; **política de campanario** (coll.) petty politics; **política de cerco** policy of encirclement; **política de la**

buena vecindad Good Neighbor Policy; **política del palo en alto** policy of the big stick; **política de partido** party politics; **política de poder** power politics; **política exterior** foreign policy
politicón -cona *adj* overpolite, obsequious; fond of politics
politiquear *vn* (coll.) to dabble in politics, to play politics; (coll.) to chatter politics
politiqueo *m* (coll.) dabbling in politics; (coll.) political chatter
politiquería *f* political chicanery
politiquero -ra *mf* political schemer
politiquilla *f* parlor politics
politiquillo *m* parlor politician
politonal *adj* polytonal
politonalidad *f* (mus.) polytonality
poliuria *f* (path.) polyuria
polivalencia *f* (bact. & chem.) polyvalence, multivalence
polivalente *adj* (bact. & chem.) polyvalent, multivalent
póliza *f* check, draft; contract, policy; tax stamp; custom-house permit; admission ticket; lampoon; **póliza de seguro** insurance policy; **póliza dotal** endowment policy
polizón *m* bum, tramp; stowaway
polizonte *m* (coll.) cop, policeman
polo *m* support, foundation; water ice on a stick, popsicle; polo (*Andalusian dance*); (hist.) polo (*corvée exacted from Philippine natives by Spanish*); (astr., geog., biol., elec. & math.) pole; (sport) polo; **polo acuático** or **de agua** (sport) water polo; **polo norte magnético** North Magnetic Pole; **polo sur magnético** South Magnetic Pole
polonés -nesa *adj* Polish; *mf* Pole; *m* Polish (*language*); *f* polonaise (*overdress*); (mus.) polonaise
Polonia *f* Poland
polonio *m* (chem.) polonium
poltrón -trona *adj* idle, lazy, comfort-loving; *f* easy chair; (fig.) sinecure
poltronería *f* idleness, laziness
poltronizar **§76** *vr* to idle, loaf, get lazy
polución *f* (path.) pollution; **polución voluntaria** self-polution
poluto -ta *adj* dirty, filthy
Pólux *m* (myth. & astr.) Pollux
polvareda *f* cloud of dust; rumpus
polvera *f* compact, powder case
polvificar **§86** *va* to pulverize
polvillo *m* fine dust
polvo *m* dust; powder; pinch (*e.g., of snuff*); **polvos** *mpl* dust; powder; **en polvo** powdered; **hacer polvo a** (coll.) to overcome, destroy, wipe out; **morder el polvo** to bite or lick the dust; **sacudir el polvo a** (coll.) to give a beating to, to beat up; (coll.) to show up, refute; **tomar el polvo** (Am.) to beat it, disappear; **tomar un polvo** to take a pinch of snuff; **polvo de cantárida** (pharm.) cantharides; **polvo dentífrico** tooth powder; **polvos blancos faciales** face powder; **polvos calmantes** sleeping powder; **polvos de arroz** rice powder; **polvos de baño** bath powder; **polvos de estaño** putty powder; **polvos de gas** bleaching powder; **polvos de la madre Celestina** (coll.) hocus-pocus; prestidigitation; **polvos de Seidlitz** Seidlitz powder; **polvos de talco** talcum powder
pólvora *f* powder, gunpowder; fireworks; bad humor; briskness, liveliness; **correr como pólvora en reguero** to spread like wildfire; **gastar la pólvora en salvas** to fuss around for nothing; **ser una pólvora** (coll.) to be a live wire; **pólvora de algodón** guncotton; **pólvora gigante** giant powder; **pólvora sin humo** smokeless powder; **pólvora sorda** noiseless powder; (fig.) sneak, underhanded fellow
polvoreamiento *m* dusting, sprinkling
polvorear *va* to dust, sprinkle with dust or powder
polvoriento -ta *adj* dusty; powdery
polvorín *m* fine powder; powder magazine; powder flask; (Am.) spitfire; (Am.) tick
polvorista *m* powder maker; fireworks manufacturer
polvorizable *adj* var. of **pulverizable**
polvorización *f* pulverization
polvorizar **§76** *va* to dust, sprinkle with dust or powder; to pulverize
polvoroso -sa *adj* dusty; **poner pies en polvorosa** (coll.) to take to one's heels, to beat it
polla *f* pullet; (orn.) coot; (orn.) water hen, moor hen, gallinule; (coll.) lassie; stake, kitty; **polla de agua** (orn.) corn crake
pollada *f* hatch, covey; broadside
pollancón -cona *mf* large chicken; *m* (coll.) overgrown boy
pollastre *m* (coll.) sly fellow
pollastro -tra *mf* grown chicken; *m* (coll.) sly fellow
pollazón *f* hatch, brood
pollera *f* see **pollero**
pollería *f* poultry shop, poultry market; poultry business; poultry; young people, younger set
pollero -ra *mf* poulterer; *m* poultry yard; *f* poultry yard; chicken coop; gocart; (Am.) skirt
pollino -na *mf* ass, donkey; (fig.) jackass
pollito -ta *mf* chick; (coll.) chick, chicken (*young person*); **pollito unicolor** (orn.) Baird's sandpiper
pollo *m* chicken; young bee; (fig.) chicken (*young person*); sly fellow
polluelo -la *mf* chick; *m* (bot.) saltwort
poma *f* apple; smelling bottle; pomander
pomáceo -a *adj* (bot.) pomaceous
pomada *f* pomade
pomar *m* orchard, apple orchard
pomarada *f* apple orchard
pomarrosa *f* (bot.) rose apple
pomelo *m* (bot.) pomelo, shaddock; (bot.) grapefruit (*tree and fruit*)
pomeranio -nia or **pomerano -na** *adj & mf* Pomeranian
pómez *f* pumice stone
pomífero -ra *adj* (poet.) pomiferous
pomo *m* (bot.) pome; pommel (*of hilt of sword*); flacon; pomander; (dial.) bouquet; **pomo de puerta** doorknob
pomología *f* pomology
pompa *f* see **pompo**
pompático -ca *adj* pompous
pompear *vn* to make a show, be pompous; *vr* (coll.) to strut; (coll.) to move with pomp and ceremony
Pompeya *f* Pompeii
pompeyano -na *adj & mf* Pompeian
Pompeyo *m* Pompey
pompo -pa *adj* (Am.) dull; *f* pomp; soap bubble; swell, bulge; billowing or ballooning (*of clothes*); spread (*of peacock's tail*); (naut.) pump; **pompa de jabón** soap bubble; **pompa fúnebre** funeral; **pompas térmicas** (aer.) rising air currents
pompón *m* pompon
pomponear *vr* (coll.) to strut; (coll.) to move with pomp and ceremony
pomposidad *f* pomposity
pomposo -sa *adj* pompous; high-flown, highfalutin
pómulo *m* (anat.) cheekbone
pon *2d sg impv of* **poner**
poncí *m* (*pl:* **-cíes**) var. of **poncidre**
poncidre *m* or **poncil** *m* (bot.) citron (*tree and fruit*)
Poncio *m* Pontius
ponchada *f* bowlful of punch; (Am.) contents of a poncho (*held together by its four corners*); (Am.) portion, batch
ponchadura *f* (Am.) blowout; (Am.) strike-out
ponchar *va & vr* (Am.) to puncture, to blow out; (Am.) to strike out (*in baseball*)
ponche *m* punch (*drink*); **ponche de huevo** eggnog
ponchera *f* punch bowl
poncho -cha *adj* lazy, careless, easy-going; (Am.) chubby; *m* poncho; greatcoat
ponderable *adj* ponderable; (fig.) ponderable
ponderación *f* weighing; pondering; circumspection; balance, equilibrium; exaggeration; **sin ponderación** without the slightest exaggeration
ponderado -da *adj* tactful, prudent

ponderador -dora *adj* pondering; balancing; exaggerating
ponderal *adj* in weight, ponderal
ponderar *va* to weigh; to ponder, ponder over; to balance; to exaggerate; to praise to the skies; to weight (*statistically*)
ponderativo -va *adj* exaggerating
ponderosidad *f* ponderosity; gravity, seriousness, circumspection
ponderoso -sa *adj* ponderous, heavy; grave, serious, circumspect
pondré *1st sg fut ind of* **poner**
ponedero -ra *adj* placeable; egg-laying; *m* nest; nest egg
ponedor -dora *adj* egg-laying; trained to rear on hind legs (*said of a horse*); *m* bidder
ponencia *f* paper, report; (law) report; (law) post of reporter
ponente *m* (law) reporter, referee
ponentino -na or **ponentisco -ca** *adj* occidental, western; *mf* occidental, westerner
poner §69 *va* to put, place, lay, set; to arrange, dispose; to put in (*a remark*); to put on (*a play*); to set (*a table*); to assume, suppose; to impose (*a law, tax, etc.*); to wager, to stake; to lay (*eggs*); to set down, put down (*in writing*); to take (*time*); to cause (*e.g., fear*); to make, to turn; (aut.) to go in (*e.g., high gear*); **poner a** + *inf* to set (*someone*) to + *inf;* **poner a uno de** to treat someone as a; to set someone up as a; **poner en claro** to clear up, explain; **poner en limpio** to make a clean copy of, to recopy; **poner por encima** to prefer, to put ahead ‖ *vr* to put oneself; to become, to get, to turn; to set (*said of sun, stars, etc.*); to dress, dress up; to get spotted; to get, reach, arrive; to put on (*hat, coat, etc.*); **ponerse a** + *inf* to set out to, to begin to + *inf;* **ponerse al tanto de** to catch on to; **ponerse bien** to get along, become successful; **ponerse bien con** to get in with, get on the good side of; **ponerse tan alto** to take offense, to become hoity-toity
pongo *m* (zool.) orang-outang; (Am.) Indian servant; (Am.) gully, ravine; *1st sg pres ind of* **poner**
ponientada *f* steady west wind
poniente *m* west; west wind
ponimiento *m* placing, laying, setting
ponleví *m* (*pl:* **-víes**) shoe with high wooden heel
ponqué *m* (Am.) poundcake
pontaje *m* bridge toll, pontage
pontana *f* slab or flagstone on the bed of a stream
pontazgo *m* bridge toll
pontear *va* to build a bridge over; *vn* to build bridges
pontederiáceo -a *adj* (bot.) pontederiaceous
pontezuela *f* or **pontezuelo** *m* small bridge
póntico -ca *adj* Pontic
pontificado *m* pontificate; papacy
pontifical *adj* pontifical; **de pontifical** (coll.) in full dress; *m* pontifical (*book*); **pontificales** *mpl* pontificals
pontificar §86 *vn* (coll.) to pontificate
pontífice *m* (hist. & eccl.) pontiff, pontifex; **el Sumo Pontífice** or **el Pontífice Romano** (eccl.) the Sovereign Pontiff, the Supreme Pontiff (*the Pope*)
pontificio -cia *adj* pontifical
pontil *m* punty
pontín *m* pontin (*Philippine coasting vessel*)
pontino -na *adj* between two holidays
ponto *m* (poet.) sea; (*cap.*) *m* (myth.) Pontus; **el Ponto** Pontus (*country*); **Ponto Euxino** Euxine Sea, Pontus Euxinus (*ancient name of Black Sea*)
pontocón *m* kick
pontón *m* pontoon; pontoon bridge; log bridge; old ship tied up at a wharf and used as warehouse, hospital, or prison; hulk (*old ship used as prison*); **pontón flotante** pontoon bridge, floating bridge
pontonero *m* (mil.) pontonier
ponzoña *f* poison; (fig.) poison
ponzoñoso -sa *adj* poisonous
popa *f* (naut.) poop, stern; **a popa, en popa** (naut.) abaft
popamiento *m* scorn; fondling, caressing
popar *va* to scorn, despise; to fondle, caress
pope *m* pope (*of Greek Orthodox Church*)
popel *adj* (naut.) sternmost
popelina *f* poplin
poplíteo -a *adj* (anat.) popliteal
popote *m* (Am.) straw for brooms; (Am.) straw or tube (*for drinking*)
populachería *f* cheap popularity, appeal to the mob; rabble rousing
populachero -ra *adj* of the people, people's, popular; cheap, vulgar; rabble-rousing; *mf* rabble rouser
populacho *m* populace, mob, rabble
popular *adj* popular
popularidad *f* popularity
popularización *f* popularization
popularizar §76 *va* to popularize; *vr* to become popular
populazo *m* var. of **populacho**
populeón *m* poplar ointment
populismo *m* Populism
populista *m* Populist
populoso -sa *adj* populous
popurrí *m* (*pl:* **-rríes**) (mus.) potpourri, medley
poquedad *f* paucity, slightness, scantiness; scarcity; timidity; trifle
póquer *m* poker
poquísimo -ma *adj super* very little; **poquísimos -mas** *adj super pl* few, very few
poquito -ta *adj* very little; timid, shy; diminutive, slight; **a poquito** little by little; **a poquitos** in small quantities; **de poquito** (coll.) timid, inept; **un poquito (de)** a little bit (of)
por *prep* by; through, over; by way of, via; in (*e.g., the morning; Spain*); for; for the sake of, on account of; in exchange for, in place of; as; about (*e.g., Christmastime*); out of (*e.g., ignorance*); times, e.g., **tres por cuatro** four times three; **estar por** + *inf* to be on the point of + *ger*, be ready to + *inf;* to be still to be + *pp*, e.g., **la carta está por escribir** the letter is still to be written; **ir por** to go for, to go after; to follow (*a career*); **por ciento** per cent; **por entre** among, between; **por que** because; in order that; **por qué** why; **por** + *adj* + **que** however + *adj*, e.g., **por rico que sea** however rich he may be; **por** + *inf* in order to + *inf;* because of + *ger*
porcachón -chona or **porcallón -llona** *adj* (coll.) dirty, hoggish; *mf* (coll.) big hog; (coll.) fat slob
porcelana *f* porcelain; **porcelana mandarina** mandarin porcelain; **porcelana paria** Parian, Parian porcelain
porcentaje *m* percentage
porcentual *adj* percentage
Porcia *f* Portia
porcino -na *adj* porcine; *m* little pig; bruise, bump
porción *f* portion
porcionero -ra *adj & mf* participant
porcionista *mf* shareholder, participant; boarding-school pupil
porcipelo *m* (coll.) bristle
porciúncula *f* Franciscan jubilee (*celebrated August second*)
porcuno -na *adj* porcine; hoggish
porche *m* porch, portico
pordiosear *vn* to beg, to go begging
pordioseo *m* begging
pordiosería *f* begging, beggary
pordiosero -ra *adj* begging, mendicant; *mf* beggar
porfía *f* persistence, stubbornness, obstinacy; **a porfía** in emulation, in competition
porfiado -da *adj* persistent, stubborn, obstinate; opinionated
porfiador -dora *adj* persistent; *mf* persistent person, fighter
porfiar §90 *vn* to persist; to argue stubbornly; **porfiar en** + *inf* to persist in + *ger*
porfídico -ca *adj* porphyritic
pórfido *m* porphyry
porfioso -sa *adj* var. of **porfiado**
porfolio *m* picture folder
poricida *adj* (bot.) poricidal
pormenor *m* detail, particular
pormenorizar §76 *va* to detail, tell in detail; to itemize

pornografía *f* pornography
pornográfico -ca *adj* pornographic
pornógrafo -fa *mf* pornographer
poro *m* pore
pororó *m* (Am.) popcorn
pororoca *f* (Am.) tide rip (*in Río de la Plata*)
porosidad *f* porosity
poroso -sa *adj* porous
poroto *m* (Am.) bean, string bean; (Am.) runt, little runt; **tomar los porotos** (Am.) to eat, have something to eat
porque *conj* because; in order that
porqué *m* (coll.) why, reason, motive; (coll.) quantity, amount, share; (coll.) dough, money, wherewithal
porquecilla *f* small sow
porquera *f* wild boar's lair
porquería *f* (coll.) dirt, filth; (coll.) crudity; (coll.) trifle; (coll.) botch; (coll.) junk (*poor or harmful food*)
porqueriza *f* pigsty, pigpen
porquerizo or **porquero** *m* swineherd
porquerón *m* (coll.) catchpole
porqueta *f* (zool.) wood louse
porquezuelo -la *mf* piglet, little pig
porra *f* see **porro**
porráceo -a *adj* porraceous, leek-green
porrada *f* blow, bump; thwack, slap; (coll.) stupidity; pile, heap
porrazo *m* clubbing; blow; bump
porrear *vn* (coll.) to be importunate, make a nuisance of oneself
porrería *f* (coll.) folly, stupidity; (coll.) dullness, slowness
porreta *f* green leaves of leeks, garlic, or onions; **en porreta** (coll.) naked
porretada *f* pile, heap
porrilla *f* forge hammer; (vet.) osseous tumor in the joints
porrillo *m* mason's hammer; **a porrillo** (coll.) in abundance
porrina *f* small, green crop; green leaves of leeks
porrino *m* leek seed; leek ready for transplanting
porro -rra *adj* (coll.) dull, stupid; *m* (bot.) leek; *f* club, bludgeon; maul; (coll.) bore, nuisance; (coll.) boasting; (Am.) knot, entanglement (*of hair*); (Am.) rooters, backers; **mandar a la porra** (coll.) to send (*someone*) on his way, to dismiss without ceremony
porrón -rrona *adj* (coll.) slow, heavy, sluggish; *m* earthen jug; wine bottle with a long side spout
porta- *combining form* bearer, e.g., **portaestandarte** color bearer; handle, e.g., **portalimas** file handle; hanger, e.g., **portacaño** pipe hanger; -holder or holder, e.g., **portaplacas** plateholder; **portapapeles** paper holder; rack, e.g., **portabotellas** bottle rack; socket, e.g., **portalámparas** lamp socket; -stand or stand, e.g., **portatintero** inkstand; **portarretorta** retort stand
porta *f* (naut.) porthole; (fort.) cover of a loophole; (football) goal
portaalmizcle *m* (zool.) musk deer
portaaviones *m* (*pl:* **-nes**) aircraft carrier, airplane carrier, flattop
portabandera *f* (mil.) socket for flagpole
portabombas *m* (*pl:* **-bas**) (aer.) bomb carrier
portabotellas *m* (*pl:* **-llas**) bottle rack, bottle carrier
portabrocas *m* (*pl:* **-cas**) drill chuck, drill holder
portacaja *f* drum strap
portacandado *m* hasp
portacaño *m* pipe hanger
portacartas *m* (*pl:* **-tas**) pouch, mailbag
portacojinete *m* diestock
portachuelo *m* mountain pass
portada *f* see **portado**
portadilla *f* (print.) bastard title, half title
portadiscos *m* (*pl:* **-cos**) turntable
portado -da *adj;* **bien portado** well-dressed; well-behaved; **mal portado** poorly dressed; badly behaved; *f* front, façade; portal; title page; cover (*of magazine*); **falsa portada** (print.) half title
portador -dora *adj* (rad.) carrier (*wave*); *mf* carrier, bearer; (com.) bearer; **portador de gérmenes** (med.) carrier; *m* waiter's tray; *f* pannier or box (*carried on each side of beast's back*)
portaequipaje *m* (aut.) trunk
portaequipajes *m* (*pl:* **-jes**) baggage rack
portaescobillas *m* (*pl:* **-llas**) (elec.) brush holder
portaestandarte *m* (coll.) color bearer
portaféretro *m* pallbearer
portafusible *m* (elec.) cutout, cutout base
portafusil *m* sling (*of a rifle*)
portaguantes *m* (*pl:* **-tes**) (aut.) glove compartment
portaguión *m* (mil.) guidon
portahachón *m* torchbearer
portaherramienta *m* (mach.) chuck
portaherramientas *m* (*pl:* **-tas**) toolholder
portainstrumentos *adj* see **plancha**
portaje *m* var. of **portazgo**
portal *m* vestibule, entrance hall; porch, portico; arcade; town or city gate; portal (*of a tunnel*); (Am.) crèche
portalada *f* portal; large gate
portalámparas *m* (*pl:* **-ras**) (elec.) socket, lamp holder; **portalámparas de bayoneta** bayonet socket; **portalámparas de cadena** pull socket, chain-pull socket; **portalámparas de llave giratoria** key socket; **portalámparas de rosca** screw socket
portalápiz *m* (*pl:* **-pices**) pencil holder
portaleña *f* door board; (naut.) porthole
portalero *m* tax collector (*at city gates*)
portalibros *m* (*pl:* **-bros**) book straps (*for schoolbooks*)
portalón *m* gate; (naut.) gangway (*opening in side of ship*)
portamantas *m* (*pl:* **-tas**) blanket straps, blanket holder
portamanteo *m* portmanteau
portaminas *m* (*pl:* **-nas**) mechanical pencil
portamira *m* (surv.) rodman
portamonedas *m* (*pl:* **-das**) pocketbook, purse
portaneumático *m* (aut.) tire rack
portante *adj* (rad.) carrier (*wave*); *m* pace (*in which feet on same side are lifted and put down together*); **tomar el portante** (coll.) to leave, get out
portantillo *m* easy pace
portanuevas *mf* (*pl:* **-vas**) newsmonger
portañola *f* (naut.) porthole
portañuela *f* fly (*of trousers*); (Am.) carriage door
portaobjetivo *m* nosepiece (*of microscope*)
portaobjeto *m* slide (*for microscope*); stage (*of microscope*)
portaollas *m* (*pl:* **-llas**) potholder
portapapeles *m* (*pl:* **-les**) brief case; paper holder, paper stand
portapaz *m & f* (eccl.) pax
portapechos *m* (*pl:* **-chos**) (Am.) brassière
portaplacas *m* (*pl:* **-cas**) (phot.) plateholder
portapliegos *m* (*pl:* **-gos**) brief case
portaplumas *m* (*pl:* **-mas**) penholder (*handle*)
portar *va* (Am.) to carry, to bear; (hunt.) to retrieve; *vn* (naut.) to fill (*said of a sail*); *vr* to behave, to conduct oneself
portarremos *m* (*pl:* **-mos**) oarlock, rowlock; **portarremos exterior** outrigger (*of a racing shell*)
portarretorta *f* retort stand
portarriendas *m* (*pl:* **-das**) terret
portasenos *m* (*pl:* **-nos**) brassière
portateléfono *adj* see **mesita**
portátil *adj* portable
portatintero *m* inkstand
portatipos *adj* see **palanca**
portatostadas *m* (*pl:* **-das**) toast rack
portaútil *m* toolholder
portaválvula *m* (rad.) socket
portavasos *m* (*pl:* **-sos**) glass stand, glass rack
portaventanero *m* door and window maker
portaviandas *m* (*pl:* **-das**) dinner pail
portaviento *m* bustle pipe
portaviones *m* (*pl:* **-nes**) var. of **portaaviones**
portavoz *m* (*pl:* **-voces**) megaphone; (fig.) mouthpiece (*person, newspaper, etc.*)

portazgar §59 *va* to collect toll from
portazgo *m* toll, road toll
portazguero *m* tollkeeper
portazo *m* bang or slam (*of door*)
porte *m* carrying, portage; carrying charge, freight; postage; behavior, conduct; dress, bearing; nobility; size, capacity; (Am.) birthday present; **porte concertado** mailing permit; **porte pagado** postage prepaid, freight prepaid
porteador *m* carrier
portear *va* to carry, to transport (*for a price*); *vn* to slam; *vr* to migrate (*said especially of birds*)
portento *m* prodigy, wonder
portentoso -sa *adj* portentous, extraordinary
porteño -ña *adj* (pertaining to) Buenos Aires; (pertaining to) Valparaíso; pertaining to any large South American city with a port; *mf* native or inhabitant of Buenos Aires, Valparaíso, or any large South American city with a port
porteo *m* carrying, portage
portera *f* see **portero**
portería *f* porter's lodge; job of porter; main door (*of a convent*); (naut.) portholes
portero -ra *mf* doorkeeper; gatekeeper; (sport) goalkeeper; *m* porter, janitor; doorman; *f* portress, janitress
portezuela *f* little door; door (*of carriage, automobile, etc.*); pocket flap
pórtico *m* portico, porch; little gate; (arch.) portico, piazza
portier *m* (*pl:* **-tiers**) portiere, door curtain
portilla *f* (naut.) porthole; private cart road, private cattle pass; fly (*of trousers*)
portillera *f* private cart road, private cattle pass
portillo *m* gap, breach, opening; notch, nick; wicket (*of larger door or gate*); gate (*in fence or wall; of bird cage*); narrow pass (*between hills*); private or side entrance; (fort.) postern
portón *m* large door or gate; vestibule door, inner door
portorriqueño -ña *adj & mf* var. of **puertorriqueño**
portuario -ria *adj* (pertaining to a) port, harbor, dock; *m* dock hand, dock worker
Portugal *m* Portugal
portugués -guesa *adj & mf* Portuguese; **los portugueses** the Portuguese (*people*); *m* Portugese (*language*)
portuguesada *f* (coll.) exaggeration
portuguesismo *m* Lusitanism
portulano *m* collection of harbor charts
porvenir *m* future; (fig.) promise
porvida *interj* by the living God! (*to express threat or anger*)
pos; en pos de after, behind; in pursuit of
posa *f* knell, toll; pause during burial for singing responsory; **posas** *fpl* buttocks
posada *f* home, dwelling; inn, wayside inn; lodging; boarding house; camp; traveling case containing knife, fork, and spoon
posadero -ra *mf* innkeeper; *m* reed or esparto-grass mat (*used as a seat*); **posaderas** *fpl* buttocks
posante *adj* smooth-sailing (*boat*)
posar *va* to put down (*a load or burden*) in order to rest or catch one's breath; *vn* to put up, to lodge; to alight, to perch; to pose (*for a photograph; as a model*); *vr* to alight, to perch; to settle (*said of sediment, dust, etc.*); to rest
posaverga *f* (naut.) yard prop
posbélico -ca *adj* postwar
poscafé *m* after-dinner cordial
poscombustión *f* (aer.) afterburning
poscomunión *f* Postcommunion
posdata *f* postscript
posdatar *va* (coll.) to add a postscript to (*a letter*)
pose *f* pose (*position of body; affectation*); (phot.) exposure, time exposure
poseedor -dora *mf* owner, possessor; holder (*e.g., of a record*)
poseer §35 *va* to own, to possess, to hold; to have a mastery of (*e.g., a foreign language*); *vr* to control oneself
poseído -da *adj* possessed; *mf* person possessed; *m* private farm land
Poseidón *m* (myth.) Poseidon
posesión *f* possession; **tomar posesión de** to take up (*a post, an assignment*)
posesionar *va* to give possession to; *vr* to take possession
posesionero *m* pasture-owning cattleman
posesivo -va *adj* possessive; (gram.) possessive; *m* (gram.) possessive
poseso -sa *adj* possessed; *mf* person possessed
posesor -sora *mf* owner, possessor
posesorio -ria *adj* possessory
posfecha *f* postdate
posfechar *va* to postdate
posfijo *m* (gram.) postfix
posgraduado -da *adj & mf* var. of **postgraduado**
posguerra *f* postwar period
posibilidad *f* possibility; means, property; aptitude, ability
posibilitar *va* to make possible
posible *adj* possible; **hacer todo lo posible** to do one's best; **posibles** *mpl* means, income, property
posición *f* position; standing; (law) deposition; (mil.) fortified position
positiva *f* see **positivo**
positivar *va* (phot.) to make a positive of
positivismo *m* positivism
positivista *adj* positivistic; *mf* positivist
positivo -va *adj* positive; **de positivo** positively, beyond a doubt; *m* (gram.) positive; *f* (phot.) positive
pósito *m* public granary; cooperative; **pósito pío** public granary run for charity
positrón *m* (phys.) positron
positura *f* position, state, disposition
posliminio *m* var. of **postliminio**
posma *f* (coll.) dullness, sloth; *mf* (coll.) snail (*person*); *adj* (coll.) dull, slothful, sluggish
posmeridiano -na *adj* var. of **postmeridiano**
poso *m* sediment, dregs; grounds; rest, quiet, calm
posología *f* posology
posón *m* reed or esparto-grass mat (*used as a seat*)
pospalatal *adj & f* var. of **postpalatal**
pospelo; a pospelo against the lay of the hair, against the nap; (coll.) violently, forcibly
pospierna *f* thigh (*of an animal*)
pospondré *1st sg fut ind of* **posponer**
posponer §69 *va* to subordinate; to think less of, to hold in less esteem
pospongo *1st sg pres ind of* **posponer**
posposición *f* subordination
pospuesto -ta *pp of* **posponer**
pospuse *1st sg pret ind of* **posponer**
posquemador *m* (aer.) afterburner
posta *f* relay (*of post horses*); posthouse; stage; stake, wager (*at cards*); slice (*of meat or fish*); commemorative poster; (arch.) Vitruvian scroll; (archaic) post, military post; **a posta** (coll.) on purpose; **correr la posta** to ride post; **por la posta** riding post; (coll.) posthaste; *m* postrider, courier
postal *adj* postal; *f* postal, postal card
postcomunión *f* var. of **poscomunión**
postdata *f* var. of **posdata**
postdiluviano -na *adj* postdiluvian
poste *m* post, pole, pillar; punishment in school consisting in standing for a time on a given spot; (sport) starting or finishing marker (*of a race*); **dar poste a** (coll.) to keep (*someone*) waiting; **llevar poste** (coll.) to be kept waiting; (coll.) to stand for hours in front of one's sweetheart's house; **oler el poste** (coll.) to smell a rat; **ser un poste** (coll.) to be lumpish; (coll.) to be very deaf; **poste de alumbrado** lamppost; **poste de amarre** (aer.) mooring mast; **poste de llegada** (sport) winning post; **poste de partida** (sport) starting post; **poste de teléfonos** telephone post; **poste de telégrafo** telegraph pole; (fig.) beanpole (*tall, thin person*); **poste distribuidor de gasolina** gasoline pump; **poste indicador** road sign; **poste telegráfico** telegraph pole
postelero *m* (naut.) skid, fender

postema *f* abscess; bore, tiresome person; (coll.) grudge
postemero *m* (surg.) lancet
postergación *f* delay, postponement; holding back, passing over
postergar §59 *va* to delay, postpone; to hold back, to pass over
postería *f* or **posterío** *m* (Am.) posts, poles, row of posts
posteridad *f* posterity; posthumous fame
posterior *adj* posterior, back, rear; back (*tooth*); later, subsequent; (phonet.) back; **posterior a** later than
posterioridad *f* posteriority; **con posterioridad** subsequently, later on; **con posterioridad a** subsequent to, later than
posteta *f* sheets of paper used for packing books; (b.b.) signature, section
postgraduado -da *adj & mf* postgraduate
postguerra *f* postwar period
posthipnótico -ca *adj* posthypnotic
postigo *m* wicket (*small door in larger one*); shutter; postern (*small or back door or gate*)
postila *f* note, comment
postilar *va* to annotate (*a text*)
postilla *f* scab
postillón *m* postilion, postboy
postilloso -sa *adj* scabby, full of scabs
postimagen *f* (psychol.) afterimage
postimpresionismo *m* postimpressionism
postimpresionista *mf* postimpressionist
postín *m* (coll.) show, vanity, arrogance; **darse postín** (coll.) to put on airs
postizo -za *adj* false, artificial; detachable (*collar*); *m* switch, false hair; *f* castanet
postliminio *m* (law) postliminy
postludio *m* (mus.) postlude
postmeridiano -na *adj* postmeridian
postnatal *adj* postnatal
postónico -ca *adj* (phonet.) posttonic
postoperatorio -ria *adj* postoperative
postor *m* bidder (*at an auction*); **mayor** or **mejor postor** highest bidder
postorbital *adj* postorbital
postpalatal *adj & f* (phonet.) postpalatal
postprandial *adj* postprandial
postración *f* prostration; **postración nerviosa** nervous prostration
postrador -dora *adj* prostrative; *m* kneeling stool
postrar *va* to prostrate; to weaken, exhaust; *vr* to prostrate oneself; to be prostrated
postre *adj* last, final; **a la postre** or **al postre** at last, finally; **a la postre de** after; *m* dessert; last to play; **postres** *mpl* dessert; **llegar a los postres** to arrive late or too late
postremero -ra or **postremo -ma** *adj* last
postrer *adj* apocopated form of **postrero,** used only before masculine singular nouns and adjectives
postrero -ra *adj* last; *mf* last, last one
postrimer *adj* apocopated form of **postrimero,** used only before masculine singular nouns and adjectives
postrimerías *fpl* latter part; last stages of man: death, judgment, hell, and heaven
postrimero -ra *adj* last
póstula or **postulación** *f* postulation, petition; nomination; (eccl.) postulation
postulado *m* postulate; **postulado de las paralelas** (math.) parallel postulate
postulador *m* (eccl.) postulator
postulanta *f* (rel.) postulant
postulante *mf* petitioner; *m* (rel.) postulant
postular *va* to postulate, seek, demand, claim; to nominate; (eccl.) to postulate
póstumo -ma *adj* posthumous
postura *f* posture; stand, attitude; stake, wager; bid; pact, agreement; egg; eggs; egg-laying; transplanting; transplanted plant; **postura del sol** sunset
potabilidad *f* potability, potableness
potabilizar §76 *va* (Am.) to make potable or drinkable
potable *adj* potable, drinkable
potación *f* potation
potaje *m* pottage; mixture (*drink*); mixture, jumble; jumbled speech; **potajes** *mpl* vegetables
potajería *f* garden vegetables; storeroom for garden vegetables
potala *f* anchor stone; tub (*clumsy boat*)
potar *va* to correct and mark (*weights and measures*); to drink
potasa *f* (chem.) potash; **potasa cáustica** (chem.) caustic potash
potásico -ca *adj* potassic, potassium
potasio *m* (chem.) potassium
pote *m* pot; jug; flowerpot; **a pote** in abundance; **pote de la cola** glue pot
potencia *f* potency; power; (math., mech., opt. & phys.) power; (arti.) reach; (min.) thickness of a vein; **lo último de potencia** to the best of one's power; **potencia de choque** striking power; **potencia de fuego** (mil.) fire power; **potencia de salida sin distorsión** (elec.) undistorted output; **potencias A B C** A.B.C. powers (*Argentina, Brazil, and Chile*); **Potencias centrales** or **centroeuropeas** Central Powers; **potencia motora** or **motriz** motive power; **potencia mundial** world power
potenciación *f* (math.) involution
potencial *adj* potential; (gram.) potential; *m* potential; (elec., gram., math. & phys.) potential; **potencial humano** man power
potencialidad *f* potentiality
potenciar *va* to harness (*water power; a person's energy, interest, enthusiasm*); (math.) to raise (*to a power*)
potenciómetro *m* (elec.) potentiometer
potentado *m* potentate
potente *adj* potent, powerful; (coll.) big, huge
potentila *f* (bot.) potentilla
potenza *f* (her.) tau cross
potera *f* pulldevil
poterna *f* (fort.) postern
potestad *f* power; potentate; (math.) power; **potestades** *fpl* Powers (*sixth order of angels*); **patria potestad** (law) patria potestas
potestativo -va *adj* (law) facultative, optional
potingue *m* (hum.) dose, concoction
potísimo -ma *adj* very powerful
potista *mf* (coll.) toper, hard drinker, soak
potosí *m* pile of money; gold mine (*source of great wealth*)
potra *f* filly; (path.) scrotal hernia; (coll.) rupture; **tener potra** (coll.) to be lucky
potrada *f* herd of colts
potranca *f* young mare
potrear *va* (coll.) to bother, harass
potrero -ra *adj* of or for a colt or colts; *m* colt tender; pasture for colts; (coll.) rupture specialist; (Am.) cattle ranch
potril *m* pasture for colts
potrilla *f* filly; *m* (coll.) chipper old fellow
potrillo *m* (Am.) colt
potro *m* colt; wooden horse (*punishment*); obstetrical chair; stocks (*to sling a horse for shoeing*); pit for dividing a beehive; pest, great annoyance; **potro de madera** horse, vaulting horse
potroso -sa *adj* ruptured; (coll.) fortunate, lucky
poundal *m* (phys.) poundal
poya *f* fee for baking in public oven; hemp bagasse
poyar *vn* to pay the baking fee
poyata *f* shelf, bracket; cupboard, closet
poyo *m* stone bench built against the wall at the front door; judge's fee
poza *f* puddle; pool for breaking hemp
pozal *m* pail, bucket; coping or curbstone of a well; sump, catch basin
pozanco *m* puddle or pool along a river after a flood
pozar §76 *vn* to dig, to grub
pozo *m* well; pit; eddy, whirlpool; fish tank (*on a boat*); (min.) shaft; (naut.) hold; (Am.) pool, puddle; (Am.) spring, fountain; **pozo abisinio** driven well, drivewell; **pozo airón** bottomless pit; **pozo artesiano** artesian well; **pozo de aire** (aer.) air pocket; **pozo de ciencia** fountain of knowledge (*person*); **pozo de lanzamiento** launching silo; **pozo de lobo** (mil.) foxhole; **pozo negro** cesspool; **pozo séptico** septic tank
pozuela *f* small puddle

pozuelo *m* small well; sump, catch basin
PP. abr. of **Padres**
P.P. abr. of **porte pagado & por poder**
p.p.do abr. of **próximo pasado**
prácrito or **pracrito** *m* Prakrit
práctica *f* see **práctico**
practicable *adj* practicable
practicaje *m* pilotage
practicanta *f* prescription clerk; nurse
practicante *mf* prescription clerk; hospital nurse, hospital intern; *m* intern; surgeon (*for minor surgery*)
practicar §86 *va* to practice; to bring about; to make, to cut (*a hole*); *vn & vr* to practice
práctico -ca *adj* practical; skilful, practiced; practicing (*e.g., churchman*); *m* practitioner, medical practitioner; (naut.) pilot; **práctico de puerto** harbor pilot; *f* practice; skill; **prácticas** *fpl* studies, apprenticeship, training
practicón -cona *mf* (coll.) old hand, practician
pradal *m* meadow, pasture
pradejón *m* small meadow
pradeño -ña *adj* (pertaining to a) meadow
pradera *f* meadowland; large meadow; prairie
pradería *f* meadowland
praderoso -sa *adj* (pertaining to a) meadow
prado *m* meadow, pasture; mall, walk, promenade; **a prado** grazing in the field; **prado de guadaña** meadow mowed annually
Praga *f* Prague
pragmático -ca *adj* pragmatic or pragmatical; *f* pragmatic sanction
pragmatismo *m* (philos.) pragmatism
pragmatista *adj & mf* (philos.) pragmatist
pral. abr. of **principal**
pralte. abr. of **principalmente**
prandial *adj* prandial
prao *m* proa (*Malay sailing boat*)
praseodimio *m* (chem.) praseodymium
prasio *m* (mineral.) prase
prasma *m* prasine, dark green agate
pratense *adj* pratal, living or growing in meadows
pravedad *f* depravity, wickedness
pravo -va *adj* depraved, wicked
Praxiteles *m* Praxiteles
pre *m* (mil.) daily pay
preadamita *m* preadamite
preadamítico -ca *adj* preadamic
preadaptación *f* (biol.) preadaptation
preámbulo *m* preamble; evasion; **no andarse** or **no detenerse en preámbulos** (coll.) to come to the point
preamplificador *m* (rad.) preamplifier
prebélico -ca *adj* prewar
prebenda *f* prebend; (coll.) sinecure; **prebendas** *fpl* patronage, political patronage
prebendado *m* prebend, prebendary
prebendar *va* to confer a prebend on
prebostal *adj* provostal, provost's
prebostazgo *m* provostship
preboste *m* provost
precalentar §18 *va* to preheat
precámbrico -ca *adj & m* (geol.) Pre-Cambrian
precariedad *f* precariousness
precario -ria *adj* precarious
precaución *f* precaution; **precauciones contra accidentes** accident prevention
precaucionado -da *adj* precautionary
precaucionar *vr* to be cautious, take precautions
precautelar *va* to guard against, take precautions against
precaver *va* to try to prevent; to protect, to save; *vn & vr* to be on one's guard; **precaverse contra** or **de** to provide against, to guard against
precavido -da *adj* cautious, precautious
precedencia *f* precedence or precedency
precedente *adj* preceding, precedent; *m* precedent
preceder *va & vn* to precede
precelente *adj* most excellent
preceptista *adj* preceptive; *mf* preceptist
preceptivo -va *adj* preceptive, mandatory; *f* rules, principles; **preceptiva literaria** rules of composition, principles of writing
precepto *m* precept; order, injunction
preceptor -tora *mf* teacher, Latin teacher; *m* preceptor; *f* preceptress
preceptoral *adj* preceptorial
preceptoril *adj* (scornful) preceptorial
preceptuar §33 *va* to lay down as a precept, to prescribe
preces *fpl* prayers, supplications
precesión *f* (mech.) precession; (rhet.) reticence; **precesión de los equinoccios** (astr.) precession of the equinoxes
preciado -da *adj* valued, esteemed; precious, valuable; proud, boastful
preciador -dora *mf* appraiser
preciar *va* to appraise, estimate; *vr* to boast; **preciarse de** to boast of being; **preciarse de** + *inf* to boast of + *ger*
precinta *f* strap, band; seal; corner patch or reinforcement; (naut.) parceling
precintar *va* to strap, bind; to seal
precinto *m* strapping, binding; seal; sealing strap; strap, band
precio *m* price; value, worth; esteem, credit; **al precio de** at the cost of; **a precio de coste** at cost; **a precios regalados** dirt-cheap; **no tener precio** to be priceless; **poner a precio** to offer a reward for; **poner precio a** to fix a price for; **precio de factura** invoice price; **precio de mercado** market price; **precio de situación** (Am.) cut price; **precio mínimo fijado** upset price; **precio tope** ceiling price
preciosidad *f* preciousness; beauty, charming thing
preciosismo *m* (lit.) preciosity
precioso -sa *adj* precious; valuable; witty, keen; (coll.) pretty
preciosura *f* (Am.) beauty, charming thing
precipicio *m* precipice; violent fall; ruin, destruction
precipitación *f* precipitation; (chem. & meteor.) precipitation; (fig.) precipitation, precipitance; **precipitación acuosa** rainfall
precipitadamente *adv* hastily, headlong
precipitadero *m* precipice, cliff
precipitado -da *adj* precipitant, precipitous; *m* (chem.) precipitate
precipitante *adj* precipitating; *m* (chem.) precipitant
precipitar *va* to precipitate; to rush, throw headlong, hurl; to hasten; (chem.) to precipitate; *vr* to rush, throw oneself headlong; (chem.) to precipitate
precípite *adj* teetering, about to fall
precipitina *f* (immun.) precipitin
precipitoso -sa *adj* risky, dangerous; precipitous, rash, reckless
precipitrón *m* (elec.) precipitron
precipuo -pua *adj* chief, principal
precisar *va* to state precisely, to specify; to fix, determine with precision; to need; **precisar a** + *inf* to force or oblige to + *inf; vn* to be necessary, be important; to be urgent; **precisar de** to need
precisión *f* necessity, obligation; precision; **precisiones** *fpl* data
preciso -sa *adj* necessary; precise
precitado -da *adj* aforesaid, above-mentioned
precito -ta *adj & mf* damned
preclaro -ra *adj* illustrious, famous
precocidad *f* precocity, precociousness
precognición *f* precognition
precolombino -na *adj* pre-Columbian
preconcebir §94 *va* to preconceive
preconcepción *f* preconception
preconfeccionado -da *adj* ready-made
preconización *f* preconization; (eccl.) preconization
preconizar §76 *va* to preconize, to commend publicly, to proclaim; (eccl.) to preconize
preconocer §32 *va* to know in advance, to foreknow
preconozco *1st sg pres ind of* **preconocer**
precordial *adj* (anat.) precordial
precoz *adj* (*pl:* **-coces**) precocious; untimely
precursor -sora *adj* precursory, preceding, preliminary; *mf* precursor, forerunner; **el precursor de Cristo** the Forerunner (*John the Baptist*)

predador -dora or **predator -tora** *adj* predacious, predatory
predecesor -sora *mf* predecessor
predecir §37 *va* to predict, foretell
predefinición *f* (theol.) predetermination
predefinir *va* (theol.) to predetermine
predestinaciano -na *adj & mf* predestinarian
predestinación *f* predestination; (theol.) predestination
predestinado -da *adj* predestined; *mf* (theol.) predestinate
predestinador -dora *adj & mf* predestinarian
predestinar *va* to predestine, to predestinate
predeterminación *f* predetermination
predeterminar *va* to predetermine
predial *adj* predial, real, landed; attached to the land
prédica *f* sermon, protestant sermon; harangue
predicable *adj* preachable; predicable; *m* (log.) predicable
predicación *f* preaching, preachment
predicaderas *fpl* (coll.) gift of preaching
predicado *m* predicate
predicador -dora *adj* preaching; *mf* preacher; *m* pulpit orator; (ent.) praying mantis; (coll.) sermonizer
predicamento *m* (log.) predicament, category; esteem, reputation
predicante *adj & mf* predicant
predicar §86 *va* to preach; to praise to the skies; to scold, to preach to; to predicate; *vn* to preach; to predicate
predicativo -va *adj* predicative
predicción *f* prediction; **predicción del tiempo** weather forecasting
predictor *m* predictor; (aer.) predictor
predicho -cha *pp de* **predecir**
predifunto -ta *adj* predeceased
predigerir §62 *va* to predigest
predigestión *f* predigestion
predigo *1st sg pres ind of* **predecir**
predije *1st sg pret ind of* **predecir**
predilección *f* predilection
predilecto -ta *adj* favorite, preferred
predio *m* property, estate; **predio rústico** farmstead; **predio urbano** town property; country dwelling
prediré *1st sg fut ind of* **predecir**
predispondré *1st sg fut ind of* **predisponer**
predisponer §69 *va* to predispose
predispongo *1st sg pres ind of* **predisponer**
predisposición *f* predisposition
predispuesto -ta *adj* predisposed, biased, prejudiced; *pp of* **predisponer**
predispuse *1st sg pret ind of* **predisponer**
predominación *f* predomination
predominancia *f* predominance
predominante *adj* predominant
predominar *va* to predominate; *vn* to predominate; to stand out; **predominar a** or **sobre** to tower over
predominio *m* predominance, superiority
preelección *f* preëlection
preelectoral *adj* preëlectoral; preëlection
preelegir §72 *va* to elect beforehand; (theol.) to predestine
preemción *f* var. of **preempción**
preeminencia *f* preëminence
preeminente *adj* preëminent
preempción *f* preëmption
preenfriar §90 *va* to precool
preescolar *adj* preschool
preestablecer §34 *va* to preestablish
preestreno *m* (mov.) preview
preexcelso -sa *adj* most high, most sublime
preexistencia *f* preëxistence
preexistente *adj* preëxistent
preexistir *vn* to preëxist
prefabricar §86 *va* to prefabricate
prefacio *m* preface
prefación *f* prologue, introduction
prefecto *m* prefect; mayor; governor
prefectura *f* prefecture
preferencia *f* preference; **de preferencia** preferably
preferencial *adj* (econ.) preferential
preferente *adj* preferential; preferable, preferred
preferentemente *adv* chiefly; preferably
preferible *adj* preferable
preferir §62 *va* to prefer; **preferir** + *inf* to prefer to + *inf*
prefiguración *f* prefiguration, foreshadowing
prefigurar *va* to prefigure, to foreshadow
prefijación *f* prefixing
prefijar *va* to prefix, to prearrange, to predetermine; (gram.) to prefix
prefijo -ja *adj* (gram.) prefixed; *m* (gram.) prefix
prefinición *f* setting a time limit
prefinir *va* to set a time limit for
prefloración *f* (bot.) praefloration
prefoliación *f* (bot.) praefoliation
preformación *f* preformation
prefulgente *adj* brilliant, resplendent
pregón *m* proclamation, public announcement
pregonar *va* to proclaim, to announce publicly; to hawk (*merchandise; news; a secret*); to praise openly; to outlaw, proscribe
pregonería *f* office of common crier or town crier
pregonero -ra *adj* proclaiming, divulging; *mf* divulger; auctioneer; *m* common crier, town crier
preguerra *f* prewar period
pregunta *f* question; **andar, estar** or **quedar a la cuarta pregunta** (coll.) to be penniless; **coser a preguntas** to riddle with questions; **dejarse de preguntas** to stop asking questions; **hacer una pregunta** to ask a question
preguntador -dora *adj* questioning; inquisitive; *mf* questioner
preguntar *va* to ask, to question; *vn* to ask, to inquire; **preguntar por** to ask after or for; *vr* to ask oneself; to wonder
preguntón -tona *adj* (coll.) inquisitive; *mf* (coll.) inquisitive person
pregustador *m* taster, king's taster
pregustar *va* to taste (*food and drink before it is served to a king*)
prehistoria *f* prehistory
prehistórico -ca *adj* prehistoric or prehistorical
preignición *f* preignition
preinsertar *va* to preinsert
prejudicio or **prejuicio** *m* prejudgment; prejudice
prejuzgar §59 *va* to prejudge
prelacía *f* prelacy
prelación *f* preference
prelada *f* prelatess
prelado *m* prelate
prelaticio -cia *adj* prelatic, prelatish
prelatura *f* prelature
preliminar *adj & m* preliminary; **preliminares** *mpl* front matter (*of a book*)
prelucir §60 *vn* to shine ahead, to shine forth
preludiar *va* to prelude; (mus.) to try out (*an instrument or the voice*); *vn* to prelude; (mus.) to prelude; (mus.) to run over the scales
preludio *m* prelude; (mus.) prelude
prelusión *f* introduction, prelusion
preluzco *1st sg pres ind of* **prelucir**
premarital *adj* premarital
prematuro -ra *adj* premature; (law) impubic
premédico -ca *adj* premedical
premeditación *f* premeditation
premeditado -da *adj* premeditated
premeditar *va* to premeditate
premiador -dora *adj* rewarding; *mf* rewarder
premiar *va* to reward; to give an award to
premidera *f* treadle of a loom
premio *m* reward; prize; premium; **a premio** at a premium, with interest; **premio gordo** (coll.) first prize (*especially in Christmas lottery*); **premio Nóbel** Nobel prize; Nobel prize winner
premiosidad *f* tightness, closeness; bothersomeness; strictness; slowness, heaviness
premioso -sa *adj* tight, close; troublesome, bothersome; strict, rigid; slow, heavy, dull
premiso -sa *adj* presupposed, anticipated; sent in advance; (law) preceding; *f* (law & log.) premise; mark, token, clue; **premisa mayor** (log.) major premise; **premisa menor** (log.) minor premise
premolar *adj & m* (anat.) premolar
premonitorio -ria *adj* premonitory

premonstratense *adj & m* (eccl.) Premonstratensian
premoriencia *f* (law) predecease
premoriente *adj & mf* (law) predeceased
premorir §45 & §17, 9 *vn* (law) to die first, to predecease
premostratense *adj & m* var. of **premonstratense**
premuerto -ta *pp of* **premorir;** *adj* predeceased
premura *f* pressure, haste, urgency
premuroso -sa *adj* pressing, urgent
prenatal *adj* prenatal
prenda *f* pledge; security; pawn; jewel, household article (*especially if offered for sale*); garment, article of clothing; gift, talent; darling, loved one; **prendas** *fpl* forfeits (*game*); **dar en prenda** to pawn; **en prenda** in pawn; **en prenda de** as a pledge of, as proof of; **prenda de vestir** garment, article of clothing
prendador -dora *adj* pawning, pledging; *mf* pawner, pledger
prendamiento *m* pawning, pledging; fancy
prendar *va* to pawn, to pledge; to charm, to captivate; *vr* to take a liking, fall in love; **prendarse de** to take a liking to or for, to fall in love with; **prendarse de amor** to fall in love
prendedero *m* fillet, brooch, bandeau; stickpin
prendedor *m* catcher; fillet, brooch, bandeau; stickpin
prendedura *f* tread (*of an egg*)
prender *va* to seize, grasp; to catch, imprison; to catch (*e.g., on a hook*); to dress up; to pin, pin together; to fasten; *vn* to catch; to take root; to catch fire; to turn out well; **prender en** to catch on (*e.g., a hook*); *vr* to dress up; to be fastened; **prenderse en** to catch hold of
prendería *f* second-hand shop
prendero -ra *mf* second-hand dealer
prendido -da *adj* dressed up; (Am.) constipated; (Am.) drunk; **bien prendido** well dressed, well gotten up; **ir prendido en** (Am.) to be involved in; **mal prendido** poorly dressed; *m* adornment, woman's headdress; pattern pricked on parchment for bobbin lace; piece of bobbin lace; **prendido de flores** bouquet
prendimiento *m* seizure, capture; catching; rooting, taking root
prenombre *m* praenomen
prenotar *va* to note in advance
prensa *f* press; printing press; vise; (fig.) press, newspapers; (phot.) printing frame; **dar a la prensa** to publish; **entrar en prensa** to go to press; **meter en prensa a uno** to put the squeeze on someone; **tener buena** (or **mala**) **prensa** to have a good (or bad) press; **prensa de filtrar** filter press; **prensa de imprenta** printing press; **prensa de vino** wine press; **prensa estopa** (mach.) stuffing box; **prensa hidráulica** hydraulic press; **prensa rotativa** (print.) rotary press; **prensa taladradora** drill press
prensado *m* pressing; luster, gloss (*from pressing*)
prensador -dora *adj* pressing; *mf* presser, press operator
prensadura *f* pressing, pressure
prensaestopas *m* (*pl:* **-pas**) (mach.) stuffing box
prensalimones *m* (*pl:* **-nes**) lemon squeezer
prensar *va* to press
prensil *adj* prehensile
prensión *f* prehension
prensista *m* (print.) pressman
prensor -sora *adj & f* (orn.) psittacine
prenunciar *va* to announce in advance, to presage
prenuncio *m* advance announcement, presage
preñado -da *adj* pregnant; sagging, bulging (*wall*); (fig.) pregnant; *m* pregnancy; fetus
preñar *va* (Am.) to make pregnant, to impregnate
preñez *f* pregnancy; fullness; threat, impending danger; inherent confusion
preocupación *f* preoccupation; preoccupancy; prejudice
preocupadamente *adv* with preoccupation; with prejudice
preocupante *adj* worrisome
preocupar *va* to preoccupy; *vr* to become preoccupied; to be prejudiced; **preocuparse con** or **por** to become preoccupied with; **preocuparse de** + *inf* to be concerned with + *ger*
preopinante *mf* previous speaker, first speaker
preopinar *vn* to give one's opinion earlier, to give one's opinion first
preordinación *f* preordination
preordinar *va* to preordain
prep. abr. of **preposición**
prepalatal *adj & f* (phonet.) prepalatal
preparación *f* preparation
preparado *m* (pharm.) preparation
preparador -dora *mf* preparer; preparator
preparamento or **preparamiento** *m* preparation
preparar *va* to prepare; **preparar a** or **para** + *inf* to prepare (*someone*) to + *inf; vr* to prepare, to get ready; **prepararse a** or **para** + *inf* to prepare to + *inf*, to get ready to + *inf*
preparativo -va *adj* preparative; *m* preparative, preparation
preparatorio -ria *adj* preparatory
preponderancia *f* preponderance
preponderante *adj* preponderant
preponderar *vn* to preponderate; to prevail
prepondré *1st sg fut ind of* **preponer**
preponer §69 *va* to put before, to prefer
prepongo *1st sg pres ind of* **preponer**
preposición *f* preposition
preposicional *adj* prepositional
prepositivo -va *adj* prepositive
prepósito *m* chairman, president; (eccl.) provost
prepositura *f* chairmanship, presidency; (eccl.) provostship
preposteración *f* reversal, upset
preposterar *va* to reverse, upset
prepóstero -ra *adj* reversed, upset, out of order, inopportune
prepotencia *f* prepotency; haughtiness, pride
prepotente *adj* prepotent; haughty, overbearing
prepucio *m* (anat.) prepuce, foreskin
prepuesto -ta *pp de* **preponer**
prepuse *1st sg pret ind of* **preponer**
prerrafaelismo *m* Pre-Raphaelitism
prerrafaelista *adj & m* Pre-Raphaelite
prerrogativa *f* prerogative
prerromanticismo *m* preromanticism
presa *f* see **preso**
presado -da *adj* pale-green; *f* reservoir
presagiar *va* to presage, forebode, betoken
presagio *m* presage, omen, token
presagioso -sa, presago -ga or **présago -ga** *adj* foreboding, betokening
presb. abr. of **presbítero**
presbicia *f* (path.) presbytia, far-sightedness
presbiope *adj* presbyopic; *mf* presbyope
presbiopía *f* (path.) presbyopia
présbita or **présbite** *adj* presbytic, far-sighted; *mf* presbyte
presbiterado *m* priesthood
presbiteral *adj* sacerdotal, priestly
presbiterato *m* var. of **presbiterado**
presbiterianismo *m* Presbyterianism
presbiteriano -na *adj & mf* Presbyterian
presbiterio *m* presbytery
presbítero *m* presbyter; priest
presciencia *f* prescience, foreknowledge; **presciencia divina** (theol.) foreknowledge
presciente *adj* prescient
prescindible *adj* dispensable
prescindir *vn;* **prescindir de** to leave aside, leave out, disregard; to do without, dispense with; **prescindir de** + *inf* to avoid + *ger;* to do without + *ger*
prescribir §17, 9 *va* to prescribe; (law) to acquire by uninterrupted possession; *vn* to prescribe; to become invalid by default
prescripción *f* prescription; (law & med.) prescription; **prescripción adquisitiva** (law) acquisitive prescription
prescriptible *adj* prescriptible
prescripto -ta or **prescrito -ta** *pp of* **prescribir**
presea *f* gem, jewel
preselector *m* (telp.) preselector

presencia *f* presence; show, display; **en presencia de** in the presence of; **presencia de ánimo** presence of mind
presencial *adj* actual, in person
presenciar *va* to witness, be present at
presentable *adj* presentable
presentación *f* presentation; introduction; appearance (*e.g., of a new automobile, book*); **a presentación** (com.) on presentation
presentado -da *mf* presentee; *m* (eccl.) presentee
presentador -dora *mf* presenter; bearer
presentalla *f* votive offering
presentáneo -a *adj* quick-acting
presentar *va* to present; to introduce (*one person to another*); **presentar armas** (mil.) to present arms; *vr* to present oneself; to appear; to introduce oneself
presente *adj* present; **al presente** or **de presente** at present; **hacer presente** to notify of, to remind of; **la presente** this letter; **mejorando lo presente** present company excepted; **por el, la** or **lo presente** for the present; **tener presente** to bear or keep in mind; *m* present, gift; person present; (gram.) present; *interj* here!, present! (*in answering roll call*)
presentemente *adv* at present, now
presentero *m* (eccl.) sponsor
presentimiento *m* presentiment
presentir §62 *va* to have a presentiment of
presepio *m* manger; stable
presera *f* (bot.) bedstraw
presero *m* keeper or tender of an irrigation ditch
preservación *f* preservation
preservador -dora *adj* preserving; *mf* preserver
preservar *va* to preserve, protect
preservativo -va *adj & m* preservative; preventive
presidario *m* var. of **presidiario**
presidencia *f* presidency; chairmanship; president's residence; president's office
presidencial *adj* presidential
presidencialista *adj* presidential
presidenta *f* president's wife; president (*woman*); chairwoman
presidente *m* president; chairman; **presidente electo** president-elect
presidiar *va* to garrison
presidiario *m* convict
presidio *m* garrison; penitentiary; citadel, fortress; prisoners, convicts; imprisonment; hard labor; aid, help; presidium
presidir *va* to preside over; to dominate; *vn* to preside
presilla *f* loop, fastener; clip; buttonhole stitching; shoulder strap (*of lady's garment*)
presión *f* pressure; **a presión** on draught (*beer*); **presión arterial** blood pressure; **presión atmosférica** atmospheric pressure, air pressure; **presión de inflado** tire pressure; **presión osmótica** osmotic pressure; **presión sanguínea** blood pressure
presionar *va* to press (*a button*); to put pressure on (*a person*)
preso -sa *adj* imprisoned; *mf* prisoner; convict; **coger preso a** or **poner preso a** to take prisoner; *f* seizure, capture; catch, prey; booty, spoils; dam; trench, ditch, flume; bit, morsel; talon, fang, tusk, claw; fishweir; (sport) hold, grip, grapple; **hacer presa** to seize, to hold tight; to take hold; to seize (*a chance, advantage, etc.*); **ser presa de** to be a victim of; to be a prey to; **presa de caldo** chicken broth
prest *m* var. of **pre**
prestación *f* lending; loan; service; (feudal law) service
prestadizo -za *adj* lendable
prestado -da *adj* lent, loaned; **dar prestado** to lend; **pedir** or **tomar prestado** to borrow
prestador -dora *adj* lending; *mf* lender
prestamera *f* (eccl.) benefice, church living
prestamero *m* (eccl.) incumbent of a benefice or church living
prestamista *mf* moneylender, pawnbroker
préstamo *m* lending; borrowing; loan; borrow, borrow pit; **dar a préstamo** to loan; **recibir en préstamo** or **tomar a préstamo** to borrow; **préstamo lingüístico** loan word, borrowing
prestancia *f* excellence, elegance, noble bearing
prestante *adj* excellent, elegant, noble
prestar *va* to lend, to loan; to give (*ear; help; news*); to pay (*attention*); to do (*a favor*); to render (*a service*); to take (*oath*); to keep (*silence*); to show (*patience*); *vn* to be useful; to give (*said, e.g., of a piece of cloth*); *vr* to lend oneself, to lend itself
prestatario -ria *adj* borrowing; *mf* borrower
preste *m* celebrant of high mass; (obs.) priest; **el Preste Juan** or **el Preste Juan de las Indias** Prester John
presteza *f* celerity, quickness
prestidigitación *f* prestidigitation
prestidigitador -dora *mf* prestidigitator
prestigiador -dora *adj* fascinating, captivating; *mf* faker, impostor
prestigiar *va* to accredit, sanction, glorify, lend luster to
prestigio *m* prestige; good standing; spell, fascination; illusion (*of sleight of hand*)
prestigioso -sa *adj* captivating, spellbinding; deceptive, illusory; famous, renowned
prestimonio *m* loan
prestiño *m* var. of **pestiño**
presto -ta *adj* quick, prompt, ready; nimble; **presto** *adv* right away
presumible *adj* presumable
presumido -da *adj* assuming, conceited, vain; *mf* vain pretender, would-be
presumir *va* to presume; *vn* to be conceited, to boast; **presumir de** + *adj* to boast of being + *adj*
presunción *f* presumption; conceit, vanity; (law) presumption
presuntivo -va *adj* presumptive
presunto -ta *adj* supposed, presumptive
presuntuosidad *f* conceit, vanity, priggery
presuntuoso -sa *adj* conceited, vain, priggish; *mf* conceited person, prig
presupondré *1st sg fut ind of* **presuponer**
presuponer §69 *va* to presuppose; to budget
presupongo *1st sg pres ind of* **presuponer**
presuposición *f* presupposition
presupuestal *adj* budgetary
presupuestar *va* to budget
presupuestario -ria *adj* budgetary
presupuesto -ta *adj* presupposed, estimated; *pp of* **presuponer;** *m* reason, motive; supposition; budget; estimate
presupuse *1st sg pret ind of* **presuponer**
presura *f* anxiety, worry; speed, quickness; zeal, ardor, persistence
presurizar §76 *va* (aer.) to pressurize
presuroso -sa *adj* speedy, quick, hasty; zealous, persistent
pretal *m* breastband, breast collar
pretencioso -sa *adj* conceited, vain; pretentious, showy
pretender *va* to pretend to, to claim; to try to do, to try for; **pretender** + *inf* to try to + *inf;* to claim to + *inf*
pretendido -da *adj* pretended
pretendienta *f* pretender, claimant (*woman*)
pretendiente *mf* pretender, claimant; office seeker; *m* suitor
pretensión *f* pretension; presumption; pursuit, effort
pretensioso -sa *adj* var. of **pretencioso**
pretenso -sa *adj* var. of **pretendido**
pretensor -sora *mf* pretender, claimant
preterición *f* preterition; (law & rhet.) preterition; **con preterición de** omitting, passing over
preterir §62 *va* to overlook, disregard; (law) to not mention (*an heir in a will*)
pretérito -ta *adj* past; (gram.) past, preterit; *m* past; (gram.) past, preterit; **pretérito imperfecto** (gram.) imperfect; **pretérito indefinido** (gram.) preterit, past absolute; **pretérito perfecto** (gram.) present perfect; **pretérito anterior** (gram.) past anterior, second pluperfect
pretermisión *f* pretermission
pretermitir *va* to pretermit
preternatural *adj* preternatural

pretextar *va* to pretext, to use as a pretext
pretexto *m* pretext
pretil *m* parapet, railing (*of stone, brick, metal*); walk or road along a parapet; (Am.) ledge
pretina *f* girdle, belt; waistband
pretinazo *m* blow with a girdle
pretinero -ra *mf* maker of girdles, belts, or waistbands
pretónico -ca *adj* (gram.) pretonic
pretor *m* praetor; black water in places where tunnies are found
pretorial *adj* praetorian
pretorianismo *m* praetorianism, military interference in politics
pretoriano -na *adj & m* praetorian
pretorio -ria *adj* praetorian; *m* (hist.) praetorium; (Am.) front steps
preuniversitario -ria *adj* preuniversity
prevaldré *1st sg fut ind of* **prevaler**
prevalecer §34 *vn* to prevail; to take root; to thrive; **prevalecer sobre** to prevail against or over
prevaleciente *adj* prevailing
prevaler §89 *vn* (archaic) to prevail; *vr* **prevalerse de** to avail oneself of, to take advantage of
prevalezco *1st sg pres ind of* **prevalecer**
prevalgo *1st sg pres ind of* **prevaler**
prevaricación *f* collusion, connivance; transgression; (law) prevarication
prevaricador -dora *mf* transgressor; (law) prevaricator
prevaricar §86 *vn* to collude, connive; to play false; to transgress; (law) to prevaricate; (coll.) to rave, to be delirious
prevaricato *m* corrupt practice; (law) prevarication
prevención *f* preparation; prevention; foresight; warning; prejudice; stock, supply; jail, lockup; (mil.) guardhouse; **a prevención** in case of emergency; **a prevención de que** ready in case that; **a** or **de prevención** spare; emergency
prevendré *1st sg fut ind of* **prevenir**
prevengo *1st sg pres ind of* **prevenir**
prevenidamente *adv* in advance, beforehand
prevenido -da *adj* prepared, ready; foresighted, forewarned; stocked, full
prevenir §92 *va* to prepare, make ready; to forestall, prevent, anticipate; to overcome; to warn; to prejudice, predispose; *vn* to come up (*said, e.g., of a storm*); *vr* to get prepared, get ready; to come to mind; **prevenirse a** or **contra** to prepare against or for (*e.g., danger*); **prevenirse con** or **de** to provide oneself with; **prevenírsele a uno** to come to someone's mind
preventivo -va *adj* preventive; warning
prever §93 *va* to foresee
previne *1st sg pret ind of* **prevenir**
previniendo *ger of* **prevenir**
previo -via *adj* previous, foregoing, preceding; preliminary; after, with previous, subject to, e.g., **previo acuerdo** subject to agreement
previsible *adj* foreseeable
previsión *f* prevision, foresight; foresightedness; forecast; **previsión del tiempo** weather forecasting; **previsión social** social security
previsor -sora *adj* far-seeing, foresighted, previsional
previsto -ta *pp of* **prever**
prez *m & f* honor, glory, worth
Príamo *m* (myth.) Priam
priapismo *m* (path.) priapism
Príapo *m* (myth.) Priapus
priesa *f* (archaic) var. of **prisa**
prieto -ta *adj* darking, black; stingy, mean; tight; compact; (Am.) dark-complexioned
prima *f* see **primo**
primacía *f* primacy; primateship; **detener la primacía** to hold the top place
primacial *adj* primatial; superior, supreme
primado -da *adj* primatial; *m* (eccl.) primate; primacy; *f* (coll.) gypping, rooking
primal -mala *adj & mf* yearling; *m* silk cord or braid
primario -ria *adj* primary; *m* (elec.) primary (*coil or winding*)
primate *m* worthy; (zool.) primate
primavera *f* spring, springtime; flowered silk; (bot.) cowslip, primrose; (orn.) robin (*Turdus migratorius*); (fig.) prime; **primavera de la China** (bot.) primrose, Chinese primrose
primaveral *adj* (pertaining to) spring
primazgo *m* cousinship; primacy
primear *vr* (coll.) to call each other cousin (*said of kings and noblemen*)
primer *adj* apocopated form of **primero**, used only before masculine singular nouns and adjectives
primerísimo -ma *adj super* very first
primerizo -za *adj* beginning; *mf* beginner, novice; *f* primipara
primero -ra *adj* first; former; early; primary; prime; raw (*material*); (arith.) prime; **de primero** at the outset; **primero** *adv* first (*in the first place; rather*); *m* first; **a primeros de** around the beginning of (*e.g., the month*)
primevo -va *adj* oldest
primicerio -ria *adj* first, top (*in rank or order*); *m* cantor, precentor
primicia *f* first fruits; **primicias** *fpl* (fig.) first fruits, beginnings
primicial *adj* primitial
primichón *m* silk skein
primigenio -nia *adj* original, primitive
primilla *f* pardon for the first offense
primípara *f* (obstet.) primipara
primista *m* small trader (*in stock market*)
primitivo -va *adj* primitive; *m* (f.a.) primitive
primo -ma *adj* first; prime (*excellent*); skillful; raw (*material*); (arith.) prime; **primo** *adv* in the first place; *mf* cousin; (coll.) booby, sucker, dupe; **primo carnal** or **primo hermano** first cousin, cousin-german; *f* early morning; bonus, bounty, subsidy; (eccl.) prime; (eccl.) first tonsure; (ins.) premium; (mil.) first quarter of the night; (mus.) treble (*string*)
primogénito -ta *adj & mf* first-born
primogenitura *f* primogeniture; birthright
primor *m* care, skill, elegance; beauty
primordial *adj* primordial
primorear *vn* to do a beautiful job, to perform with elegance
primoroso -sa *adj* careful, skillful, elegant; fine, exquisite
primuláceo -a *adj* (bot.) primulaceous
princesa *f* princess; princess royal; princesse dress; **princesa viuda** dowager princess
principada *f* (coll.) abuse of authority, petty tyranny
principado *m* princedom; principality; **principados** *mpl* (rel.) principalities
principal *adj* principal, main, chief; first, foremost; essential, important; famous, illustrious; (mus.) first; *m* principal, head, chief; main floor, second floor; (com. & law) principal; (mil.) main guard; (theat.) second balcony
principalidad *f* primacy, superiority, supremacy
principalmente *adv* above all else; principally
príncipe *m* prince; prince royal; **príncipes** *mpl* prince and princess; **portarse como un príncipe** to live like a prince; **príncipe consorte** prince consort; **príncipe de Asturias** heir apparent of the King of Spain; **príncipe de Gales** Prince of Wales; **príncipe de la Iglesia** Prince of the Church (*cardinal*); **príncipe de la paz** Prince of Peace (*Manuel de Godoy*); **príncipe de la sangre** prince of the blood; **príncipe de las tinieblas** Prince of Darkness; **príncipe de los ingenios** Cervantes; **príncipe negro** Black Prince; *adj* princeps, first (*edition*)
principela *f* (archaic) fine woolen fabric
principesco -ca *adj* princely
principiador -dora *adj* beginning; *mf* beginner
principianta *f* apprentice (*woman*)
principiante *adj* beginning; *mf* beginner, apprentice; novice, greenhorn
principiar *va, vn & vr* to begin; **principiar a** + *inf* to begin to + *inf*
principio *m* start, beginning; principle; source, origin; (chem.) principle; (cook.) entree; **principios** *mpl* front matter (*of a book*); **a principios de** around the beginning of (*e.g., the month*); **al principio** or **a los principios** in

the beginning, at first; **en principio** in principle; **en un principio** at the beginning; **por principio** on principle; **tener, tomar** or **traer principio de** to come or arise from; **principio de admiración** (gram.) inverted exclamation point; **principio de interrogación** (gram.) inverted question mark
principote *m* (coll.) upstart, parvenu
pringada *f* slice of bread dipped in gravy; grease spot
pringamoza *f* (bot.) nettle
pringar §59 *va* to dip or soak in grease; to dip in boiling fat (*as punishment*); to spot or stain with grease; (coll.) to wound, make bleed; (coll.) to slander, run down; (Am.) to splash, spatter; *vn* (coll.) to participate, meddle; (Am.) to drizzle; *vr* to peculate
pringón -gona *adj* (coll.) greasy; *m* (coll.) smearing oneself with grease; (coll.) grease spot
pringoso -sa *adj* greasy
pringote *m* hodgepodge
pringue *m & f* grease, fat; grease spot
pringuera *f* dripping pan
priodonte *m* or **prionodonte** *m* (zool.) giant armadillo
prior *m* prior; curate
priora *f* prioress
prioral *adj* of a prior or prioress
priorato or **priorazgo** *m* priorate; priory
prioridad *f* priority
prioste *m* steward (*of a brotherhood*)
prisa *f* hurry, haste; urgency; fight; crush, crowd; **a prisa** or **de prisa** quickly, hurriedly; **a toda prisa** with the greatest speed; **correr** or **dar prisa** to be urgent; **correrle prisa a uno** + *inf* to be in a hurry to + *inf*, e.g., **no le corre prisa cumplir su cometido** he is not in a hurry to do his job; **dar prisa a** to rush, to hurry; **darse prisa** to hurry, make haste; **estar de prisa** or **tener prisa** to be in a hurry; **tener prisa en** or **por** + *inf* to be in a hurry to + *inf*
priscal *m* night shelter for cattle
prisión *f* seizure, capture; arrest; imprisonment; prison; bond, union; **prisiones** *fpl* chains, shackles, fetters; **reducir a prisión** to incarcerate
prisionero -ra *mf* (mil.) prisoner (*soldier or civilian*); (fig.) captive (*of love or passion*); **prisionero de guerra** prisoner of war; *m* setscrew; stud bolt
prisma *m* (geom., opt. & cryst.) prism; (fig.) mirage; **prisma de Nicol** (opt.) Nicol prism
prismático -ca *adj* prismatic; **prismáticos** *mpl* prism binocular
priste *m* (ichth.) sawfish
prístino -na *adj* pristine; primeval; pure, clear, transparent
prisuelo *m* muzzle for ferrets
priv. abr. of **privilegio**
privación *f* privation
privada *f* see **privado**
privadamente *adv* privily, privately
privadero *m* cesspool cleaner
privado -da *adj* private; *m* favorite (*at court*); *f* privy, cesspool; pile of dirt
privanza *f* favor at court
privar *va* to deprive; to forbid, prohibit; *vn* to be in vogue; to prevail; to be in favor (*especially at court*); *vr* to deprive oneself; **privarse de** to give up; **privarse de** + *inf* to give up + *ger*
privativo -va *adj* privative; private, personal, peculiar; (gram.) privative; **privativo de** peculiar to
privilegiadamente *adv* in a privileged way, with special consideration
privilegiar *va* to privilege, to grant a privilege to
privilegio *m* privilege; **privilegio de invención** patent
pro *m & f* profit, advantage; **¡buena pro!** good appetite!; **de pro** of note, of worth; **el pro y el contra** the pros and the cons; **en pro de** pro, in behalf of
proa *f* (naut.) prow; (aer.) nose
proal *adj* forward, (pertaining to the) prow
pro-alemán -mana *adj & mf* pro-German
probabilidad *f* probability, likelihood
probabilismo *m* (philos.) probabilism
probable *adj* probable, likely
probación *f* probation
probado -da *adj* tried, tested; sorely tried; proved
probador -dora *mf* tester; taster; sampler; fitter; *m* tester (*device*); **probador de baterías** (elec.) battery tester; **probador de válvulas** (rad.) tube tester
probadura *f* sampling, tasting
probanza *f* (law) inquiry; (law) proof, evidence
probar §77 *va* to prove; to test; to try; to try on; to try out; to taste; to sample (*e.g., wine*) to fit; to suit, to agree with; **no probar** to not touch, to keep away from (*liquor*); *vn* **probar a** + *inf* to try to + *inf;* **probar de** to taste, take a taste of; *vr* to try on (*a suit of clothes*)
probatorio -ria *adj* probatory, probative; probational; *f* (law) time allowed for producing evidence
probatura *f* (coll.) trial, test
probeta *f* test tube; pressure gauge; beaker; powder prover
probidad *f* probity
problema *m* problem
problemático -ca *adj* problematic or problematical
probo -ba *adj* honest; fair, just
probóscide *f* (zool. & ent.) proboscis
proboscidio -dia *adj & m* (zool.) proboscidian
proc. abr. of **procesión**
procacidad *f* impudence, boldness
procaz *adj* (*pl:* **-caces**) impudent, bold
procedencia *f* origin, source; point of origin, point of departure; propriety
procedente *adj* coming, originating; proper
proceder *m* conduct, behavior; *vn* to proceed; to originate; to behave; to be proper; **proceder** + *inf* to be proper to + *inf;* **proceder a** + *inf* to proceed to + *inf;* **proceder contra** to proceed against, take action against; **proceder de** to proceed from, come from
procedimiento *m* procedure; proceeding; process; (law) proceedings; **procedimiento tricromo** three-color process
procela *f* (poet.) storm, tempest
proceloso -sa *adj* stormy, tempestuous
prócer *adj* high, lofty; *m* hero, leader, dignitary
procerato *m* heroic rôle, leadership
proceridad *f* height, loftiness; vigor, growth
prócero -ra or **procero -ra** *adj* high, lofty
proceroso -sa *adj* imposing, solemn, big and impressive-looking
procesable *adj* actionable, indictable
procesado -da *adj* legal; accused; *mf* accused, defendant
procesal *adj* legal
procesamiento *m* (law) prosecution; (law) indictment
procesar *va* (law) to sue, to prosecute; (law) to indict
procesión *f* procession; parade
procesional *adj & m* processional
procesionaria *f* (ent.) processional or processionary moth
procesionario *m* processional
procesionista *adj* (coll.) parade-loving; *mf* (coll.) parade lover, parade fan
proceso *m* process (*of time*); progress; (anat. & biol.) process; (law) suit, lawsuit; (law) trial; (med.) course, development (*of a disease*); **proceso verbal** (Am.) minutes, proceedings
procio *m* (chem.) protium
Proción *m* (astr.) Procyon
proclama *f* proclamation, manifesto; marriage banns
proclamación *f* proclamation; acclamation
proclamar *va* to proclaim; to acclaim
proclítico -ca *adj & m* (gram.) proclitic
proclive *adj* inclined, disposed, evil-disposed
proclividad *f* proclivity, evil proclivity
Procne *f* var. of **Progne**
procomún *m* or **procomunal** *m* public welfare, social welfare
procónsul *m* proconsul
proconsulado *m* proconsulate
proconsular *adj* proconsular
procrastinar *va* to procrastinate

procreación *f* procreation
procreador -dora *adj* procreative; *mf* procreator
procreante *adj* procreative
procrear *va* to procreate
proctología *f* proctology
proctoscopio *m* proctoscope
procumbente *adj* (bot.) procumbent
procura *f* power of attorney; attorneyship; business acumen
procuración *f* careful management; power of attorney; proxy; law office; attorneyship, solicitorship
procurador *m* solicitor, attorney; proxy; procurator (*for a monastery*)
procuradora *f* procuratrix (*especially for a nunnery*)
procuraduría *f* law office; proctorship; attorneyship, solicitorship
procurar *va* to strive for; to manage (*e.g., real estate*) as attorney; to yield, to produce; **procurar** + *inf* to try to, strive to + *inf*
procurrente *m* large peninsula
Procustes *m* or **Procusto** *m* (myth.) Procrustes
prodición *f* treachery
prodigalidad *f* prodigality
prodigar §59 *va* to lavish; to squander, to waste; to spread widely; *vr* to be a show-off
prodigio *m* prodigy
prodigiosidad *f* prodigiousness; excellence
prodigioso -sa *adj* prodigious, marvelous; fine, excellent
pródigo -ga *adj* lavish; prodigal; *mf* prodigal; (law) prodigal
prodrómico -ca *adj* prodromal
pródromo *m* (path.) prodrome
producción *f* production; crop, yield, produce; **producción en masa** or **en serie** mass production
producente *adj* productive; producing
producir §38 *va* to produce; to yield, to bear; to cause, bring about; *vr* to explain oneself; (Am.) to take place, happen
productividad *f* productivity
productivo -va *adj* productive
producto *m* product; proceeds; (chem. & math.) product; **producto alimenticio** foodstuff
productor -tora *adj* producing; *mf* producer
produje *1st sg pret ind of* **producir**
produzco *1st sg pres ind of* **producir**
proejar *vn* to resist with all one's might; to row against the current or the wind
proel *adj* (naut.) (pertaining to the) bow; *m* (naut.) bow oar, bowman
proemial *adj* proemial, prefatory, introductory
proemio *m* proem, preface, introduction
proeza *f* prowess; feat, stunt
prof. abr. of **profeta**
profanación *f* profanation
profanador -dora *adj* profanatory; *mf* profaner
profanamiento *m* var. of **profanación**
profanar *va* to profane
profanidad *f* profanity; indecency, immodesty
profano -na *adj* profane; worldly; indecent, immodest; lay; *mf* profane; worldly person; layman
profecía *f* prophecy; **las Profecías** (Bib.) the Prophets
proferir §62 *va* to utter
profesar *va & vn* to profess
profesión *f* profession
profesional *adj* professional; *mf* professional; practitioner
profesionalismo *m* professionalism
profeso -sa *adj & mf* (rel.) professed
profesor -sora *mf* teacher; professor; **profesor adjunto** associate professor; **profesor agregado** assistant professor; **profesor de intercambio** exchange professor; **profesor honorario** emeritus professor; **profesor numerario** or **titular** full professor; **profesor visitante** visiting professor
profesorado *m* professorship; professorate; faculty; teaching staff; teaching profession
profesoral *adj* professorial
profeta *m* prophet; **el Profeta** the Prophet (*Mohammed*)
profetal or **profético -ca** *adj* prophetic
profetisa *f* prophetess
profetizador -dora *adj* prophesying; *mf* prophesier
profetizar §76 *va & vn* to prophesy
proficiente *adj* progressing
proficuo -cua *adj* profitable, useful
profiláctico -ca *adj & m* prophylactic; preventive; *f* hygiene
profilaxis *f* prophylaxis
prófugo -ga *adj & mf* fugitive; *m* (mil.) slacker, draft dodger
profundidad *f* depth; profundity; (geom.) altitude, height
profundizar §76 *va* to deepen, make deeper; to fathom, go deep into, get to the bottom of; *vn* to go deep into things; *vr* to deepen, become deep
profundo -da *adj* profound; deep; *m* profundity; (poet.) sea, deep; hell, underworld
profusión *f* profusion
profuso -sa *adj* profuse
progenerado -da *adj* illustrious, distinguished; ahead of the times
progenie *f* lineage, descent, parentage
progenitor *m* progenitor
progenitura *f* lineage, descent; primogeniture; right of primogeniture
progesterona *f* (biochem.) progesterone
progimnasma *m* (rhet.) preparatory exercise
proglótide *f* or **proglotis** *f* (zool.) proglottid
prognatismo *m* prognathism
prognato -ta *adj* prognathous
Progne *f* (myth.) Procne; (*l.c.*) *f* (poet.) swallow
prognosis *f* (*pl:* **-sis**) forecast (*especially of weather*); prognosis
programa *m* program; **programa continuo** (mov.) continuous showing; **programa de estudios** curriculum; **programa doble** (mov.) double feature; **programa vivo** (rad.) live program
programación *f* programing
programar *va* to program
programático -ca *adj* (pertaining to a) program
progresar *vn* to progress
progresión *f* progression; (math.) progression; **progresión aritmética** arithmetical progression; **progresión geométrica** geometric progression
progresista *adj & mf* (pol.) progressive
progresivo -va *adj* progressive
progreso *m* progress; **progresos** *mpl* progress (*of a disease, of a pupil, etc.*); **hacer progresos** to make progress
prohibición *f* prohibition; **prohibición de virar a la derecha** (aut.) no right-hand turn
prohibicionista *adj & mf* prohibitionist
prohibir §99 *va* to prohibit, to forbid; **se prohíbe escupir** no spitting; **se prohíbe fijar carteles** post no bills; **se prohíbe fumar** no smoking; **se prohíbe el paso** no thoroughfare; **se prohíbe la entrada** keep out; **prohibir** + *inf* to forbid to + *inf*
prohibitivo -va *adj* prohibitive
prohibitorio -ria *adj* prohibitory
prohijación *f* adoption
prohijador -dora *mf* adopter
prohijamiento *m* var. of **prohijación**
prohijar §99 *va* to adopt
prohombre *m* master (*of a guild*); leader; top man (*of a group*); (coll.) big shot
prois *m* (naut.) stone or post (*for fastening a boat*); (naut.) cable (*for tying up a boat*)
prójima *f* (coll.) slut, jade
prójimo *m* fellow man, fellow creature, neighbor; (coll.) fellow
pról. abr. of **prólogo**
prolán *m* (biochem.) prolan
prolapso *m* (path.) prolapse
prole *f* offspring, progeny
prolegómeno *m* prolegomenon
prolepsis *f* (*pl:* **-sis**) (rhet.) prolepsis
proletariado *m* proletariat
proletario -ria *adj & m* proletarian
proletarizar §76 *va* to proletarianize; *vr* to become proletarianized
proliferación *f* proliferation
prolífero -ra *adj* (bot.) proliferous

prolificación *f* prolificacy
proliferante *adj* proliferating
proliferar *vn* (biol.) to proliferate; to proliferate
prolífico -ca *adj* prolific
prolijidad *f* tediousness; fussiness, fastidiousness; dullness, tiresomeness, rudeness
prolijo -ja *adj* too long, tedious; overcareful, fussy, fastidious; dull, tiresome, rude
prolina *f* (biochem.) proline
prologar §59 *va* to write a preface to or for; *vn* to prologuize
prólogo *m* prologue; preface
prologuista *mf* writer of prologues
prolonga *f* (arti.) prolonge
prolongación *f* prolongation, extension
prolongadamente *adv* at great length
prolongado -da *adj* prolonged; long
prolongamiento *m* var. of **prolongación**
prolongar §59 *va* to prolong, to extend; (geom.) to produce; *vr* to extend
proloquio *m* maxim, aphorism
prolusión *f* var. of **prelusión**
promanar *vn* to arise, originate
promecio *m* var. of **prometio**
promediar *va* to divide into two equal parts; to average; *vn* to mediate; to be half over
promedio *m* average, mean; middle
promesa *f* promise; pious offering; (fig.) promise (*something giving hope of success*)
prometedor -dora *adj* promising; *mf* promiser
Prometeo *m* (myth.) Prometheus
prometer *va* to promise; **prometer** + *inf* to promise to + *inf*; *vn* to promise; to give promise; *vr* to expect; to become engaged; **prometérselas felices** or **muy buenas** (coll.) to be too hopeful, to be overconfident
prometido -da *adj* engaged, betrothed; *m* fiancé; promise; *f* fiancée
prometiente *adj* promising
prometimiento *m* promise
prometio *m* (chem.) promethium
prominencia *f* prominence
prominente *adj* prominent, outstanding
promiscuar *vn* to eat meat and fish in the same meal during Lent and other fast days; to act inconsistently
promiscuidad *f* promiscuity; promiscuous intercourse; ambiguity
promiscuo -cua *adj* promiscuous; ambiguous
promisión *f* promise
promisorio -ria *adj* promissory
promoción *f* promotion; advancement; class, year, crop (*of persons promoted*)
promontorio *m* height, elevation; promontory, headland; bulky, unwieldly thing; (anat.) promontory
promotor -tora or **promovedor -dora** *adj* promotive; *mf* promoter
promover §63 *va* to promote; to further, to advance
promulgación *f* promulgation; publication, open declaration
promulgador -dora *adj* promulgating; *mf* promulgator; announcer
promulgar §59 *va* to promulgate; to proclaim, to publish abroad
pronación *f* (physiol.) pronation
pronador *m* (anat.) pronator
pronefros *m* (embryol.) pronephros
proneidad *f* proneness
prono -na *adj* prone
pronombre *m* pronoun; **pronombre complementario** object pronoun; **pronombre demostrativo** demonstrative pronoun; **pronombre indefinido** or **indeterminado** indefinite pronoun; **pronombre interrogativo** interrogative pronoun; **pronombre personal** personal pronoun; **pronombre posesivo** possessive pronoun; **pronombre relativo** relative pronoun; **pronombre sujeto** subject pronoun
pronominado -da *adj* (gram.) reflexive (*verb*)
pronominal *adj* (gram.) pronominal; (gram.) reflexive (*verb*)
pronosticable *adj* foretellable, predictable
pronosticación *f* prognostication
pronosticador -dora *adj* prognostic, prognosticating; *mf* prognosticator
pronosticar §86 *va* to prognosticate, to foretell
pronóstico *m* prognostic; almanac; (med.) prognosis; **de pronóstico gravísimo** in a serious condition; **de pronóstico reservado** in a critical condition
prontitud *f* promptness, promptitude; keenness, wittiness
pronto -ta *adj* quick, speedy; prompt; ready; **pronto** *adv* right away, soon; promptly; early; **lo más pronto posible** as soon as possible; **tan pronto como** as soon as; *m* jerk; (coll.) impulse, sudden impulse, fit of anger; **al pronto** right off; **de pronto** suddenly; hastily, without thinking; down (*payment*); **por de pronto** or **por lo pronto** for the present, provisionally
prontuario *m* notebook; compendium, handbook
prónuba *f* (poet.) bridesmaid
pronunciable *adj* pronounceable
pronunciación *f* pronunciation
pronunciado -da *adj* marked, pronounced; sharp (*curve*); steep (*hill*); bulky; *mf* rebel, insurgent
pronunciador -dora *adj* pronouncing; *mf* pronouncer
pronunciamiento *m* insurrection, uprising; (law) decree
pronunciar *va* to pronounce; to utter; to deliver, make (*a speech*); to decide on; *vr* to rebel; to declare oneself
propagación *f* propagation
propagador -dora *adj* propagating; *mf* propagator
propaganda *f* propaganda; advertising
propagandismo *m* propagandism
propagandista *adj & mf* propagandist
propagandístico -ca *adj* (pertaining to) propaganda
propagar §59 *va* to propagate; to spread, to extend; to broadcast; *vr* to propagate; to spread, to extend
propagativo -va *adj* propagative
propalación *f* spreading (*e.g., of rumors*)
propalador -dora *mf* divulger
propalar *va* to divulge, to spread
propano *m* (chem.) propane
propao *m* (naut.) breastwork
proparoxítono -na *adj & m* (phonet.) proparoxytone
propasar *vr* to go too far, to take undue liberty
propender *vn* to incline, tend, be inclined; **propender a** + *inf* to tend to + *inf*, to be inclined to + *inf*
propensión *f* propensity, liking; predisposition, susceptibility
propenso -sa *adj* inclined, prone, disposed
propi *f* (slang) tip
propiciación *f* propitiation
propiciador -dora *adj* propitiating; *mf* propitiator
propiciar *va* to propitiate; (Am.) to support, favor, sponsor
propiciatorio -ria *adj* propitiatory; *m* mercy seat; prie-dieu
propicio -cia *adj* propitious
propiedad *f* property; ownership; proprietorship; (f.a.) naturalness, likeness; **es propiedad** copyrighted; **propiedad horizontal** one-floor ownership in an apartment house; **propiedad literaria** copyright
propienda *f* listing attached to cheeks of an embroidery frame
propietario -ria *adj* proprietary; *m* proprietor; *f* proprietress
propilo *m* (chem.) propyl
propina *f* tip, fee; **de propina** (coll.) in the bargain
propinación *f* treat, invitation to drink; prescription or administration of medicine
propinar *va* to offer (*a drink*); to prescribe or administer (*medicine*); (coll.) to give (*e.g., a beating, a hard time*); *vr* to treat oneself to (*a drink*)
propincuidad *f* propinquity
propincuo -cua *adj* near, contiguous
propio -pia *adj* proper, suitable; peculiar, characteristic; natural; same; himself, herself, etc., e.g., **el propio capitán** the captain himself;

own, e.g., **mi propio hermano** my own brother; **el suyo propio** his very own; proper, e.g., **China propia** China proper; *m* messenger; native; **propios** *mpl* public lands, public property
propóleos *m* propolis, bee glue
propón *2d sg impv of* **proponer**
propondré *1st sg fut ind of* **proponer**
proponedor -dora *adj* proposing, propounding; *mf* proponent, propounder
proponente *adj* proposing, propounding
proponer §69 *va* to propose; to propound; to name, to present (*a candidate*); *vr* to plan; **proponerse** + *inf* to propose to + *inf*
propongo *1st sg pres ind of* **proponer**
proporción *f* proportion; opportunity; (math.) proportion; **proporciones** *fpl* proportions (*size; dimensions*)
proporcionable *adj* proportionable
proporcionado -da *adj* proportionate; proportioned; fit, suitable
proporcional *adj* proportional
proporcionalidad *f* proportionality
proporcionar *va* to proportion; to furnish, provide, supply, give; to adapt, adjust
proposición *f* proposition; **proposición dominante** (gram.) main clause, principal clause
propósito *m* aim, purpose, intention; subject matter; **a propósito** by the way; apropos, fitting; in place; **a propósito de** apropos of; **de propósito** on purpose; **fuera de propósito** irrelevant, beside the point, out of place
propuesto -ta *pp of* **proponer;** *adj* proposed; *f* proposal, proposition
propugnáculo *m* fortress; (fig.) bulwark
propugnar *va* to defend; to protect; to advocate
propulsa *f* repulse
propulsante *m* propellant
propulsar *va* to repulse; to propel, to drive; to promote
propulsión *f* repulse; propulsion; **propulsión a chorro** or **de chorro, propulsión a escape** or **de escape, propulsión por reacción** jet propulsion; **propulsión a cohete** rocket propulsion
propulsor -sora *adj* propellent, propulsive; *m* propellent; (rail. & fig.) booster; propeller
propuse *1st sg pret ind of* **proponer**
pror. abr. of **procurador**
prora *f* (poet.) prow
prorrata *f* prorate, quota; **a prorrata** pro rata
prorratear *va* to prorate, to apportion
prorrateo *m* apportionment; **a prorrateo** pro rata
prórroga or **prorrogación** *f* prorogation
prorrogar §59 *va* to prorogue; to defer, postpone
prorrumpir *vn* to spurt, shoot forth; to break forth, burst out
prosa *f* prose; (coll.) chatter, idle talk
prosado -da *adj* prose, in prose
prosador -dora *mf* prose writer; (coll.) chatterbox
prosaico -ca *adj* prose, prosaic; (fig.) prosaic, prosy
prosaísmo *m* prosaism, prosiness
prosapia *f* ancestry, lineage
proscenio *m* proscenium
proscribir §17, 9 *va* to proscribe, to outlaw
proscripción *f* proscription, exile, outlawry
proscripto -ta *pp of* **proscribir;** *mf* exile, outlaw
proscriptor -tora *adj* proscriptive; *mf* proscriber
proscrito -ta *pp & mf* var. of **proscripto**
prosector *m* prosector
prosecución *f* continuation, prosecution; pursuit
proseguir §82 *va* to continue, carry on; *vn* to continue
proselitismo *m* proselytism
prosélito *m* proselyte
prosénquima *f* (bot.) prosenchyma
Proserpina *f* (myth.) Proserpina or Proserpine
prosificación *f* prosification
prosificar §86 *va* to prosify, put into prose
prosimiano -na *adj & m* (zool.) prosimian
prosista *mf* prose writer; (coll.) chatterbox
prosístico -ca *adj* (pertaining to) prose
prosita *f* short piece of prose
prosodia *f* orthoëpy; prosody (*study of quantity in Greek and Latin verse*)
prosódico -ca *adj* orthoëpic; prosodic; stress (*accent*)
prosodista *mf* orthoëpist, phonologist
prosopopeya *f* (rhet.) prosopopoeia; (coll.) airs, pomposity, solemnity
prospección *f* prospecting (*for gold, oil, etc.*)
prospectar *va & vn* to prospect
prospecto *m* prospectus
prospector -tora *mf* prospector
prosperado -da *adj* prosperous (*rich*)
prosperar *va* to prosper, make prosper; *vn* to prosper, to thrive
prosperidad *f* prosperity
próspero -ra *adj* prosperous, thriving
próstata *f* (anat.) prostate
prostatectomía *f* (surg.) prostatectomy
prostático -ca *adj* prostatic, (pertaining to the) prostate; *m* prostate sufferer
prosternar *vr* to prostrate oneself
próstesis *f* (gram.) prosthesis
prostético -ca *adj* (gram.) prosthetic
prostíbulo *m* brothel
próstilo *m* (arch.) prostyle
prostitución *f* prostitution
prostituir §41 *va* to prostitute; *vr* to prostitute oneself; to become a prostitute
prostituta *f* prostitute
prosudo -da *adj* (Am.) pompous, solemn, formal; (Am.) domineering
protactinio *m* var. of **protoactinio**
protagonista *mf* protagonist
protagonizar §76 *va* to play the leading role of
Protágoras *m* Protagoras
protalo or **prótalo** *m* (bot.) prothallium
prótasis *f* (*pl:* **-sis**) (gram.) protasis
protección *f* protection; **protección aduanera** protective tariff; **protección civil** civil defense
proteccionismo *m* protectionism; protection of animals and plants
proteccionista *adj & mf* protectionist
protector -tora or **-triz** (*pl:* **-trices**) *adj* protective; *m* protector; *f* protectress
protectorado *m* protectorate
protectoría *f* protectorship, protectorate
protectorio -ria *adj* protective
proteger §49 *va* to protect
protegida *f* protégée
protegido *m* protégé
proteico -ca *adj* (biochem.) proteid, protein; (fig.) protean; (myth.) Protean
proteido *m* (biochem.) proteid
proteína *f* (biochem.) protein
Proteo *m* (myth. & fig.) Proteus
proterozoico -ca *adj & m* Proterozoic
protervia or **protervidad** *f* perversity
protervo -va *adj* perverse
prótesis *f* (gram. & surg.) prothesis or prosthesis
protesta *f* protest; protestation; promise, pledge; (law) protest
protestación *f* protestation; profession (*e.g., of faith*)
protestante *adj & mf* protestant; Protestant
protestantismo *m* Protestantism
protestar *va* to protest, asseverate; to profess (*one's faith*); (com.) to protest; *vn* to protest; **protestar de, contra** or **por** to protest (*to object to*)
protesto *m* (com.) protest
protético -ca *adj* (gram. & surg.) prothetic or prosthetic
protio *m* var. of **procio**
protoactinio *m* (chem.) protoactinium
protocolar *adj* protocolary; *va* to protocol
protocolizar §76 *va* to protocol
protocolo *m* protocol
protógina *f* (geol.) protogine
protomártir *m* protomartyr
protón *m* (phys. & chem.) proton
protonema *m* (bot.) protonema
protonotario *m* (eccl.) prothonotary
protoplasma *m* (biol.) protoplasm
protoplásmico -ca *adj* protoplasmic
protórax *m* (*pl:* **-rax**) (ent.) prothorax

prototipo *m* prototype
protozoario -ria or **protozoo -a** *adj* protozoan; *m* (zool.) protozoan, protozoön
protozoología *f* protozoölogy
protráctil *adj* protractile
protuberancia *f* protuberance; **protuberancias solares** (astr.) solar protuberances
protuberante *adj* protuberant
protutor *m* (law) guardian
prov.ª abr. of **provincia**
provecto -ta *adj* old, ripe
provecho *m* advantage, benefit; profit, gain; advance, progress; **¡buen provecho!** good luck!; good appetite!; **de provecho** useful, just right; decent
provechoso -sa *adj* advantageous, beneficial; profitable; useful
proveedor -dora *mf* supplier, provider, purveyor; steward
proveeduría *f* stewardship; storehouse
proveer §35 & §17, 9 *va* to provide, furnish; to supply; to resolve, settle; to confer, bestow; (law) to decree; *vn* to provide; **proveer a** to provide for; *vr* to have a movement of the bowels; **proveerse de** to provide oneself with
proveído *m* (law) interlocutory decree
proveimiento *m* provisioning
provena *f* (hort.) layer (*of vine*)
provendré *1st sg fut ind of* **provenir**
provengo *1st sg pres ind of* **provenir**
proveniente *adj* coming, originating, arising
provenir §92 *vn* to come, originate, arise
provento *m* product, yield
Provenza, la Provence
provenzal *adj & mf* Provençal; *m* Provençal (*language*)
proverbiador *m* book of proverbs
proverbial *adj* proverbial
proverbiar *vn* (coll.) to use proverbs
proverbio *m* proverb; **Proverbios** *mpl* (Bib.) Proverbs
proverbista *mf* (coll.) proverbialist
provicero *m* prophet, diviner
providencia *f* providence, foresight; (*cap.*) *f* Providence
providencial *adj* providential
providenciar *va* to make provision for; to settle, arrange
providente *adj* provident; prudent
próvido -da *adj* provident, watchful; favorable, propitious
provincia *f* province; **en provincias** in the provinces (*not in Madrid*); **las Provincias Vascongadas** the Basque Provinces; **Provincias Marítimas** Maritime Provinces (*of Canada*)
provincial *adj* provincial; *m* (eccl.) provincial
provincialismo *m* provincialism
provincianismo *m* provinciality
provinciano -na *adj & mf* provincial
provine *1st sg pret ind of* **provenir**
proviniendo *ger of* **provenir**
provisión *f* provision; **provisiones** *fpl* provisions
provisional *adj* provisional
proviso; al proviso right away, at once
provisor *m* provider; (eccl.) vicar general
provisora *f* stewardess (*in a convent*)
provisorato *m* stewardship
provisoría *f* stewardship; storeroom, pantry (*in a convent*)
provisorio -ria *adj* provisory, provisional
provisto -ta *pp of* **proveer**
provitamina *f* (biochem.) provitamin
provocación *f* provocation
provocador -dora *adj* provoking; provocative; *mf* provoker
provocante *adj* provocative
provocar §86 *va* to provoke; to forward, promote; to move, to incite, to tempt; **provocar a** + *inf* to provoke to + *inf;* to move to + *inf*, to tempt to + *inf; vn* to provoke; (coll.) to vomit
provocativo -va *adj* provocative
proxeneta *mf* go-between
proximal *adj* (anat.) proximal
próximamente *adv* soon, in the near future; proximately; approximately
proximidad *f* proximity; **proximidades** *fpl* neighborhood
próximo -ma *adj* next; near, neighboring; proximate, close; early; **próximo pasado** last (*month*)
proyección *f* projection; influence, distinction; **proyección cónica** conic projection; **proyección de Mercátor** (geog.) Mercator's projection
proyectar *va* to project (*a bullet; a film; a scheme*); to plan; to design (*e.g., a building*); (geom.) to project; **proyectar** + *inf* to plan to + *inf; vr* to project, stick out; to be projected, to fall (*said of a shadow*)
proyectil *m* projectile, missile; **proyectil buscador del blanco** homing missile; **proyectil dirigido** or **teleguiado** guided missile
proyectista *mf* projector, designer, planner; project administrator
proyectivo -va *adj* projective
proyecto *m* project; **proyecto de ley** bill (*in a legislative body*)
proyector *m* projector, searchlight; (mov.) projection machine
proyectura *f* (arch.) projection
prudencia *f* prudence
prudencial *adj* prudential
prudenciar *vr* (Am.) to be restrained, to hold oneself in
prudente *adj* prudent
prueba *f* proof; trial, test; examination; fitting (*e.g., of a suit of clothes*); sample (*of food or drink*); (math., phot. & print.) proof; (law) evidence, proof; (Am.) acrobatic stunt; (Am.) sleight of hand; **a prueba** on approval, on trial; perfect; **a prueba de** proof against; -proof, e.g., **a prueba de ácidos** acidproof; **a prueba de calor** heatproof; **poner a prueba** to put to the proof, to put to the test; **prueba de aptitud** aptitude test; **prueba de consolación** (sport) consolation match; **prueba de indicios** (law) circumstantial evidence; **prueba de inteligencia** intelligence test; **prueba directa** (law) direct evidence; **prueba indiciaria** (law) circumstantial evidence; **prueba indirecta** (law) indirect evidence; **prueba mental** mental test; **prueba plena** (law) convincing proof; **pruebas de planas** (print.) page proof; **pruebas de primeras** (print.) first proof; **pruebas de segundas** (print.) galley proof; **prueba semiplena** (law) imperfect proof
pruebista *mf* (Am.) acrobat
pruriginoso -sa *adj* pruriginous
prurigo *m* (path.) prurigo
prurito *m* itch; (path.) pruritus; (fig.) eagerness, urge, itch (*to do something*); **sentir el prurito de** + *inf* to itch to + *inf*
Prusia *f* Prussia
prusianismo *m* Prussianism
prusiano -na *adj & mf* Prussian
prusiato *m* (chem.) prussiate
prúsico -ca *adj* prussic
ps. abr. of **pesos**
P.S. abr. of **Post Scriptum** (Lat.) **posdata**
pseudohermafroditismo *m* var. of **seudohermafroditismo**
pseudomorfismo *m* (mineral.) pseudomorphism
pseudónimo *m* var. of **seudónimo**
psicastenia *f* (path.) psychasthenia
psicoanálisis *m* psychoanalysis
psicoanalista *mf* psychoanalyst
psicoanalítico -ca *adj* psychoanalytic or psychoanalytical
psicoanalizar §76 *va* to psychoanalyze
psicodinámico -ca *adj* psychodynamic; *f* psychodynamics
psicofísica *f* psychophysics
psicognostia *f* psychognosis
psicología *f* psychology; **psicología experimental** experimental psychology; **psicología infantil** child psychology
psicológico -ca *adj* psychologic or psychological
psicólogo -ga *mf* psychologist
psicometría *f* psychometry
psicométrico -ca *adj* psychometric
psiconeurosis *f* (*pl:* **-sis**) (path.) psychoneurosis

psicópata *mf* psychopath
psicopatía *f* psychopathy
psicopático -ca *adj* psychopathic
psicopatología *f* psychopathology
psicosis *f* (*pl:* **-sis**) (path.) psychosis; **psicosis de guerra** war psychosis, war scare; **psicosis maníacodepresiva** (psychopath.) manic-depressive insanity
psicosomático -ca *adj* psychosomatic
psicotecnia or **psicotécnica** *f* psychotechnology
psicoterapia *f* psychotherapy
psicrómetro *m* psychrometer
psilosis *f* (path.) psilosis (*fall of hair; sprue*)
psique *f* or **psiquis** *f* cheval glass; psyche (*soul, mind*); (*cap.*) *f* (myth.) Psyche
psiquiatra *mf* or **psiquíatra** *mf* psychiatrist
psiquiatría *f* psychiatry
psiquiátrico -ca *adj* psychiatric
psiquiatro *m* var. of **psiquiatra**
psíquico -ca *adj* psychic or psychical
psitacismo *m* psittacism
psitacosis *f* (path.) psittacosis, parrot disease
P.S.M. abr. of **por su mandato**
psoas *m* (anat.) psoas
psoríasis *f* (path.) psoriasis
pta. abr. of **pasta** & **peseta**
pte. abr. of **parte** & **presente**
pteridófita *f* (bot.) pteridophyte
pterodáctilo *m* (pal.) pterodactyl
ptialina *f* (path.) ptyalin
ptialismo *m* (path.) ptyalism
ptolemaico -ca *adj* Ptolemaic
Ptolomeo *m* var. of **Tolomeo**
ptomaína *f* (biochem.) ptomaine
Pto. Rico abr. of **Puerto Rico**
pu *interj* ugh!
púa *f* point, sharp point, prick, barb; tine, prong; needle (*of phonograph*); tooth (*of comb*); thorn; spine or quill (*of porcupine*); sting (*of pain or remorse*); (hort.) graft; (mus.) plectrum; (coll.) tricky person
puado *m* (set of) teeth, prongs
puar §33 *va* to put teeth on (*e.g., a comb*)
púber -bera or **púbero -ra** *adj* pubescent; *mf* person who has attained puberty
pubertad *f* puberty
pubes *m* (*pl:* **-bes**) var. of **pubis**
pubescencia *f* pubescence
pubescente *adj* pubescent
pubescer §34 *vn* to reach the age of puberty
pubiano -na or **púbico -ca** *adj* pubic
pubis *m* (*pl:* **-bis**) (anat.) pubes (*lower part of abdomen; hair covering it*); (anat.) pubis (*part of innominate bone*)
publicación *f* publication
publicano *m* (hist.) publican
publicar §86 *va* to publish; to publicize; (eccl.) to publish
publicata *f* certificate of publication
publicidad *f* publicity; advertising; **en publicidad** publicly; **publicidad de lanzamiento** advance publicity
publicista *mf* publicist
publicitario -ria *adj* (pertaining to) publicity, advertising; publishing
público -ca *adj* public; *m* public; audience; **en público** in public; *f* public examination or defense of thesis
pucha *f* (Am.) small bouquet
puchada *f* flour poultice; hogwash; thin mortar
puchera *f* (coll.) stew
pucherazo *m* blow with a pot or kettle; **dar pucherazo** (coll.) to count votes that weren't cast
puchero *m* pot, kettle; stew; (coll.) daily bread; (coll.) pout, pouting; **hacer pucheros** (coll.) to pout, to screw up one's face (*in crying or weeping*); **volcar el puchero** (coll.) to count votes that weren't cast
puches *mpl & fpl* porridge, gruel, pap
pucho *m* (Am.) fag end, remnant; (Am.) stump (*of cigar*); (Am.) trifle, trinket; (Am.) baby (*youngest member of a family*)
pude *1st sg pret ind of* **poder**
pudelación *f* (found.) puddling
pudelador *m* (found.) puddler
pudelaje *m* (found.) puddling
pudelar *va* (found.) to puddle
pudendo -da *adj* ugly, shameful, obscene; private (*parts*)
pudibundez *f* affected modesty
pudibundo -da *adj* modest, shy
pudicicia *f* chastity; modesty
púdico -ca *adj* modest, shy, chaste
pudiendo *ger of* **poder**
pudiente *adj* powerful; well-off, well-to-do; **poco pudiente** not so well-off, poorer; *mf* person of means; **los pudientes** the well-to-do
pudín *m* pudding
pudinga *f* (geol.) pudding stone
pudor *m* modesty, shyness; virtue, chastity
pudoroso -sa *adj* modest, shy
pudrición *f* rot, rotting; **pudrición roja** plant rot
pudridero *m* place of decomposition; compost heap; temporary vault (*for a corpse*)
pudrigorio *m* (coll.) var. of **podrigorio**
pudrimiento *m* rot, rotting
pudrir (*pp:* **podrido**) *va* to rot, putrefy; to worry; *vn* to be dead and buried; *vr* to rot, putrefy; to be worried, be harassed; to languish (*e.g., in jail*)
puebla *f* planting the seed of a vegetable
pueble *m* (min.) gang of workmen
pueblerino -na *adj* rustic, village, plebeian
pueblo *m* town, village; people, nation; common people; **pueblo de Dios** or **de Israel** children of Israel
puente *m* bridge; (aut.) rear axle; (naut.) deck; (mus. & naut.) bridge; (mus.) tailpiece; (cards) bender, bridge; **hacer un puente de plata a** (coll.) to smooth the way for, make it easy for; **hacer puente** to take the intervening day off; **puente aéreo** airlift, air bridge; **puente basculante** bascule bridge; **puente cantilever** cantilever bridge; **puente colgante** suspension bridge; **puente de barcas** boat bridge, pontoon bridge; **puente de engrase** (aut.) grease lift, grease rack; **puente delantero** (aut.) front axle, front-axle assembly; **puente de los suspiros** Bridge of Sighs; **puente de suspensión** suspension bridge; **puente flotante** (aut.) floating axle, **puente giratorio** swing drawbridge; **puente levadizo** drawbridge, lift drawbridge; **puente suspendido** hanging scaffold; **puente transbordador** transporter bridge; **puente trasero** (aut.) rear axle, rear-axle assembly; **puente voladizo** cantilever bridge
puentecilla *f* (mus.) bridge; (mus.) tailpiece
puentezuela *f* small bridge
puerco -ca *adj* dirty, filthy; piggish, hoggish; coarse, mean; lewd; slovenly; *m* (zool.) hog; **puerco de mar** (zool.) sea hog; **puerco espín** or **espino** (zool.) porcupine; **puerco jabalí, montés** or **salvaje** (zool.) wild boar; **puerco marino** (zool.) dolphin; *f* (zool.) sow; (zool.) wood louse; (path.) scrofula; (fig.) slattern; (fig.) slut; (fig.) selfish woman; **puerca montés** or **salvaje** sow of wild boar
puericia *f* childhood
puericultura *f* puericulture; child care
pueril *adj* puerile
puerilidad *f* puerility, childishness
puérpera *f* puerpera, woman who has just given birth to a child
puerperal *adj* puerperal
puerperio *m* (obstet.) puerperium
puerro *m* (bot.) leek, scallion
puerta *f* door, doorway; gate, gateway; (*cap.*) *f* Porte (*Turkey*); **puertas** *fpl* (coll.) octroi, tax on provisions (*entering a town*); **a puerta cerrada** or **a puertas cerradas** behind closed doors; **dar a uno con la puerta en la cara** or **las narices** (coll.) to slam the door in someone's face; **de puerta en puerta** from door to door; **de puertas para adentro** indoors; **fuera de puertas** outdoors, out of doors; **Sublime Puerta** Sublime Porte (*Turkey*); **tomar la puerta** to leave, go away; **puerta abierta** (dipl.) open door; **puerta cochera** porte-cochere; **puerta de corredera** sliding door; **puerta excusada** or **puerta falsa** back door, side door; **puerta giratoria** revolving door; **puerta plegadiza** folding

door; **Puertas de Hierro** Iron Gates (*on the Danube*); **puerta trasera** back door; **puerta vidriera** glass door
puertaventana *f* window shutter
puertezuela *f* little door
puertezuelo *m* small port or harbor
puerto *m* port, harbor, haven; mountain pass; (fig.) haven, refuge; **puerto aéreo** airport; **Puerto Arturo** Port Arthur; **puerto brigantino** Corunna; **puerto de arribada** (naut.) port of call; **puerto de depósito** bonded port; **Puerto de España** Port of Spain (*in Trinidad*); **puerto de matrícula** port of registry; **puerto franco** free port; **puerto marítimo** harbor, port; **Puerto Príncipe** Port-au-Prince; **puerto seco** frontier customhouse
puertorriqueño -ña *adj & mf* Puerto Rican
pues *adv* then, well; yes, certainly; why; anyhow; **pues que** since; *conj* for, since, because, inasmuch as; *interj* (coll.) well!, then!
puesta *f* see **puesto**
puestero -ra *mf* vendor, seller (*at a booth or stand*); *m* (Am.) tender of livestock (*on a ranch*)
puesto -ta *pp of* **poner; puesto que** since, inasmuch as; (archaic) although ‖ *adj* placed, put, set; dressed ‖ *m* place; booth, stand; post, position; office; station; barracks; blind (*for hunters*); **puesto de socorros** first-aid station; ‖ *f* setting; laying; putting; stake (*at cards*); **a puesta del sol, a puestas del sol** at sunset; **primera puesta** (mil.) new outfit (*given to a recruit*); **puesta a masa** (aut.) grounding (*of a wire*); **puesta a punto** completion, carrying out, perfection; adjustment; keeping in shape; **puesta a tierra** (elec.) grounding; **puesta de largo** coming out, social debut; **puesta en libertad** liberation, setting free; **puesta en marcha** starting; launching
puf *m* pouf (*circular ottoman*); *interj* ugh!
pufino *m* (orn.) shearwater
púgil *m* pugilist
pugilar *adj* pugilistic; *m* Hebrew manual of the Scriptures
pugilato or **pugilismo** *m* pugilism
pugilista *m* pugilist
pugilístico -ca *adj* pugilistic
pugna *f* fight, battle; struggle, conflict; **en pugna** at issue; **en pugna con** at odds with
pugnacidad *f* pugnacity
pugnante *adj* fighting, hostile; struggling
pugnar *vn* to fight; to struggle; to strive, persist; **pugnar para** or **por** + *inf* to struggle to + *inf*
pugnaz *adj* (*pl:* **-naces**) pugnacious
puja *f* push, effort; bid; **sacar de la puja** (coll.) to beat, get ahead of; (coll.) to get (*someone*) out of a jam; **vender a la puja** to auction
pujador -dora *mf* bidder
pujame *m* or **pujamen** *m* (naut.) foot (*of a sail*)
pujamiento *m* flow of humors or blood
pujante *adj* mighty, puissant, vigorous
pujanza *f* might, puissance, vigor
pujar *va* to push (*e.g., a project*); to raise, bid up (*a price*); *vn* to struggle, to strain; to falter; to grope (*for words*); (coll.) to snivel
pujavante *m* butteris, hoof parer
pujo *m* (path.) tenesmus; straining; irresistible impulse (*to laugh or cry*); eagerness, strong desire; (coll.) attempt
pulcritud *f* neatness, tidiness; circumspection
pulcro -cra *adj* neat, tidy, trim; circumspect
pulchinela *m* punchinello; (*cap.*) *m* Punch
pulga *f* flea; small top (*toy*); **de malas pulgas** peppery, hot-tempered, hot-headed; **hacer de una pulga un camello** or **un elefante** (coll.) to make a mountain out of a molehill; **no aguantar pulgas** (coll.) to stand for no nonsense; **pulga de mar** (zool.) beach flea, sand hopper
pulgada *f* inch
pulgar *m* thumb; shoot left on vine; **menear los pulgares** to uncover one's cards gradually; (coll.) to do fast fingerwork; **por sus pulgares** (coll.) on one's own hook, all by oneself
pulgarada *f* fillip (*with thumb*); pinch (*of salt, tobacco, etc.*); inch
pulgarcito *m* little thumb; (*cap.*) *m* Tom Thumb
pulgón *m* (ent.) plant louse
pulgoso -sa *adj* full of fleas
pulguera *f* place full of fleas; wing of crossbow; (bot.) fleawort
pulguillas *m* (*pl:* **-llas**) (coll.) touchy fellow
pulicán *m* dentist's forceps
pulidez *f* neatness; polish
pulido -da *adj* pretty; neat; polished; clean, spotless
pulidor -dora *adj* polishing; finishing; *mf* polisher; *f* polishing machine
pulimentar *va* to polish
pulimento *m* polish; **pulimento para muebles** furniture polish
pulir *va* to polish; to finish; (fig.) to give a polish to; *vr* to polish; to dress up, get dressed; (fig.) to take on a polish
pulmón *m* (anat.) lung; **pulmón de acero** or **pulmón de hierro** iron lung; **pulmón marino** (zool.) jellyfish
pulmonado -da *adj* pulmonate
pulmonar *adj* pulmonary
pulmonaria *f* (bot.) lungwort
pulmonía *f* (path.) pneumonia; case or attack of pneumonia; **coger una pulmonía** to get pneumonia
pulmoníaco -ca *adj* pneumonic; *mf* person sick with pneumonia
pulmotor *m* pulmotor
pulpa *f* pulp
pulpejo *m* soft flesh (*of finger, ear, etc.*)
pulpería *f* (Am.) grocery store, general store
pulpero *m* octopus fisher; (Am.) grocer, storekeeper
pulpeta *f* slice of meat
púlpito *m* pulpit; (fig.) pulpit
pulpo *m* (zool.) octopus
pulposo -sa *adj* pulpy
pulque *m* (Am.) pulque
pulquería *f* (Am.) pulque tavern or bar; (Am.) pulque still
pulquero -ra *mf* (Am.) pulque dealer
pulquérrimo -ma *adj super* very or most neat or tidy; very or most circumspect
pulsación *f* pulsation, throb, beat; strike, striking; touch (*of pianist or typist*); (phys. & physiol.) pulsation
pulsada *f* pulsation, beat (*of pulse*)
pulsador -dora *adj* pulsating; push (*key, pedal, etc.*); *m* push button
pulsar *va* to play (*piano, harp, guitar*); to strike (*a key*); to feel or take the pulse of; to sound out, examine; (Am.) to feel the weight of (*by lifting*); *vn* to pulsate, throb, beat
pulsátil *adj* pulsatile
pulsatila *f* (bot.) pasqueflower
pulsativo -va *adj* pulsative
pulsear *vn* to hand-wrestle
pulsera *f* bracelet; wristlet, watch strap; side lock (*of hair*); (surg.) wrist bandage; **pulsera de pedida** engagement bracelet
pulsímetro *m* pulsimeter
pulsista *adj* expert on the pulse; *mf* pulse expert (*physician*)
pulso *m* pulse; steadiness, steady hand; tact, care, caution; (Am.) bracelet; (Am.) wrist watch; **a pulso** with hand and wrist; by main strength, the hard way; freehand (*drawing*); (Am.) straight, at one gulp; **de pulso** tactful; **sacar a pulsos** (coll.) to carry out against odds; **sin pulso** lifeless; **tomar a pulso** (Am.) to drink (*something*) straight, to drink (*something*) with one swig; **tomar el pulso a** to feel or take the pulse of; (fig.) to look into, to scrutinize
pulsómetro *m* pulsometer
pulsorreactor *m* (aer.) ram-jet engine
pultáceo -a *adj* pultaceous; (med.) gangrened
pulular *vn* to pullulate
pulverizable *adj* pulverizable
pulverización *f* pulverization; atomizing; spraying
pulverizador -dora *adj* pulverizing; *mf* sprayer (*person*); *m* spray, sprayer
pulverizar §76 *va* to pulverize; to atomize; to spray; *vr* to pulverize

pulverulento -ta *adj* dusty; powdery
pulla *f* dig, cutting remark; indecency, filthy remark; (orn.) gannet
pullista *mf* scoffer, giber; foul-mouthed person
pum *interj* bang!
puma *m* (zool.) puma, cougar, panther
pumita *f* pumice stone
puna *f* (Am.) bleak tableland in Andes; (Am.) mountain sickness
punción *f* (surg.) puncture
puncionar *va* (surg.) to puncture
puncha *f* prickle, thorn, sharp point
punchar *va* to prick, puncture
punches *mpl* (Am.) popcorn
pundonor *m* point of honor; dignity, face
pundonoroso -sa *adj* punctilious, scrupulous; haughty, dignified
pungimiento *m* prick; sting
pungir §42 *va* to prick; to sting
pungitivo -va *adj* pricking; stinging
punible *adj* punishable
punición *f* punishment
púnico -ca *adj* Punic; (fig.) Punic
punitivo -va *adj* punitive
punta *f* point (*sharp end*); tip, end; butt (*of cigar*); nail; point, cape, headland; horn (*of bull*); tine, prong (*of antlers*); tip (*of tongue*); touch, tinge, trace; souring (*of wine*); (hunt.) pointing; style, graver; **puntas** *fpl* point lace; **de punta** on end; on tiptoe; **de punta en blanco** in full armor; (coll.) in full regalia; **estar de punta (con)** to be at odds (with); **hacer punta** to be or go first; to be opposed; to stand out; to knit; **sacar punta a** to put a point on, to sharpen; (coll.) to give a malicious twist to; **tener en la punta de los dedos** to have at one's finger tips; **punta de combate** war head (*of a torpedo*); **punta de chispa** (elec.) spark point; **punta de diamante** diamond point (*for cutting*); **punta de Europa** Europa Point; **punta de lanza** spearhead; (fig.) spearhead; **punta de París** wire nail; **punta de vidriar** glazier's point
puntación *f* pointing (*of Hebrew and Arabic letters*)
puntada *f* (sew.) stitch; hint; (Am.) stitch (*in the side*)
puntal *m* prop, support; stay, stanchion; elevation; (naut.) depth of hold; (fig.) backing, support; (Am.) bite, snack
puntapié *m* kick; **echar a puntapiés** (coll.) to kick out; **mandar a puntapiés** (coll.) to have an ascendancy over
puntar *va* to mark with dots or points; to point (*Hebrew or Arabic letters*)
puntazo *m* (Am.) jab, stab
punteado -da *adj* dotted; *m* dotting; dotted line; plucking the guitar; *f* dotting
puntear *va* to dot, to mark with dots or points; to pluck, to play (*a guitar*); to engrave or paint with dots; (sew.) to stitch; *vn* (naut.) to tack
puntel *m* pontil, punty
punteo *m* emphasis, great stress (*to drive home a point*); dots; (mus.) plucking
puntera *f* see **puntero**
puntería *f* aim, aiming; markmanship
puntero -ra *adj* sharpshooting; *m* pointer; stonecutter's chisel; hand (*of watch, clock, etc.*); punch; head, leader (*of a parade*); (mus.) finger pipe, chanter (*of bagpipe*); *f* toe, toe patch (*on shoe or stocking*); leather tip (*on shoe*); (coll.) kick
punterola *f* (min.) miner's pick, poll pick
puntiagudo -da *adj* sharp-pointed
puntilla *f* brad, finishing nail; narrow lace edging; point (*of fountain pen*); (carp.) tracing point; dagger; **dar la puntilla a** to stick the dagger in; (coll.) to finish off, destroy, ruin; **de** or **en puntillas** on tiptoe; **ponerse de puntillas** (coll.) to stick to one's opinion; **puntilla francesa** finishing nail
puntillazo *m* (coll.) kick
puntillero *m* puntillero, dagger man (*bullfighter who gives coup de grâce with dagger*)
puntillo *m* small point; punctilio; (mus.) dot, point
puntillón *m* (coll.) kick
puntilloso -sa *adj* punctilious, scrupulous
puntiseco -ca *adj* dry at the tips (*said of a plant*)
puntizón *m* (print.) frisket hole or mark
punto *m* point, dot; stitch, loop (*in knitting*); mesh; jot, mote; cabstand, hackstand; gun sight; hole (*in a belt*); break (*in mesh or net*); punctilio, point of honor; (gram.) period; (math., print. & sport) point; (fig.) point (*place; moment; feature; main idea; purpose; mark or quality*); **a buen punto** opportunely; **al punto** at once, instantly; **a punto** opportunely; ready; **a punto de** on the point of; **a punto fijo** precisely, with certainty; **a punto largo** roughly; **a punto que** just as, just when; **bajar de punto** to decline; **dar en el punto** to hit the nail on the head, find the trouble; **de medio punto** (arch.) semi-circular; **de punto** knitted; by the minute; **de todo punto** completely, entirely; **dos puntos** (gram.) colon; **en buen punto** fortunately; **en punto** sharp, on the dot, exactly, e.g., **son las dos en punto** it is two o'clock sharp; **en punto a** with regard to; **hasta el punto que** to the extent that; **poner los puntos sobre las íes** (coll.) to dot one's i's; **poner punto final a** to wind up, to bring to an end; **subir de punto** to grow, increase; to get worse; **tener a punto** to have ready; **punto capital** crux; **punto ciego** (anat.) blind spot; **punto de admiración** exclamation mark or point; **punto de aguja** knitting, knitwork; **punto de cadeneta** lock stitch; **punto de congelación** freezing point; **punto de costado** sharp pain across the heart; **punto de ebulición** or **ebullición** boiling point; **punto de encaje** lace; **punto de fuga** vanishing point; **punto de fusión** melting point; **punto de ganchillo** crocheting; **punto de gracia** funny side; **punto de honor** point of honor; **punto de la vista** (perspective) vanishing point; **punto de Hungría** herringbone (*in hardwood or tile floor*); **punto de malla** netting, netted fabric; **punto de media** knitwork, stockinet; **punto de mira** aim; center of attraction; **punto de partida** starting point, point of departure; **punto de rocío** (physical chem.) dew point; **punto de saturación** saturation point; **punto de vista** point of view; **¡punto en boca!** mum's the word!; **punto focal** (math.) focal point; **punto interrogante** question mark; **punto menos** almost; **punto menos que** almost; **punto muerto** dead center; (rad.) dead end; (fig.) stalemate, deadlock; **punto por punto** in detail; **puntos cardinales** cardinal points; **puntos suspensivos** suspension points; **puntos y rayas** (telg.) dots and dashes; **punto y coma** (construed as a masculine singular noun in Spanish) semicolon
puntoso -sa *adj* full of points; punctilious, scrupulous; haughty, dignified
puntuación *f* punctuation; mark, grade (*in school*); (sport) points, scoring
puntual *adj* punctual; certain, sure; exact; suitable
puntualidad *f* punctuality; certainty, sureness; exactness; suitability
puntualizado -da *adj* detailed, circumstantial
puntualizar §76 *va* to fix in the memory, to fix in one's mind; to detail, to give a detailed account of; to finish, to perfect; to draw up
puntualmente *adv* punctually; with precision; in detail
puntuar §33 *va & vn* to punctuate; (sport) to score
puntuoso -sa *adj* punctilious, scrupulous; haughty, dignified
puntura *f* puncture, prick; (print.) register point
punzada *f* prick; shooting pain; pang (*e.g., of remorse*)
punzador -dora *mf* puncher; *f* punching machine
punzadura *f* prick, puncture
punzante *adj* sharp, pricking; barbed, biting, caustic
punzaorejas *m* (*pl:* **-jas**) (ent.) earwig
punzar §76 *va* to prick, puncture, punch; to sting; to grieve; *vn* to sting
punzó *adj invar & m* poppy-red, flaming red

punzón *m* punch; pick; graver, burin; budding horn, tenderling; tip (*of horn*); **punzón de trazar** scriber
puñada *f* punch; **dar de puñadas a** to strike with the fist, to punch
puñado *m* handful; (fig.) handful; **a puñados** in abundance, by handfuls
puñal *m* poniard, dagger; deep grief
puñalada *f* stab (*with a dagger*); blow, sudden sorrow; **coser a puñaladas** (coll.) to cut to pieces; **puñalada de misericordia** coup de grâce; **puñalada por la espalda** or **puñalada trapera** stab in the back
puñalejo *m* small poniard or dagger
puñalero *m* maker or seller of poniards or daggers
puñera *f* double handful
puñetazo *m* punch; bang with the fist; **a puñetazos** with the fists
puñete *m* punch; bracelet
puño *m* fist; grasp; fistful, handful; handle (*e.g., of umbrella*); hilt; head (*of cane*); punch; cuff; wristband; (naut.) corner (*of sail*); **a puño cerrado** with the fist; firmly; **como un puño** (coll.) whopping big; (coll.) tiny, microscopic; **de puños** strong, valiant; **de su propio puño** or **de su puño y letra** in his own hand; **meter en un puño** (coll.) to flabbergast; **por sus puños** by oneself, on one's own; **ser como un puño** (coll.) to be close-fisted; (coll.) to be small (*in stature*); **tener en un puño** to have (*someone*) scared; **un puño de casa** (coll.) a little bit of a house, a tiny house; **puño de bastón** head of a cane
puoso -sa *adj* jagged; rough
pupa *f* pimple, pustule; fever blister; (ent.) pupa; child's word to express pain; **pupa coartada** (ent.) coarctate pupa; **pupa libre** (ent.) incomplete pupa; **pupa obtecta** (ent.) true pupa
pupal *adj* (ent.) pupal
pupario *m* (ent.) puparium
pupila *f* see **pupilo**
pupilaje *m* pupilage, wardship; boarding house; board (*cost*); boarding (*e.g., of a dog*); (aut.) storage
pupilar *adj* pupillary (*pertaining to a ward*); (anat.) pupillary
pupilero -ra *mf* boarding-house keeper
pupilo -la *mf* boarder; orphan, ward; pupil; *f* (anat.) pupil; **tener pupila** (coll.) to be quick, to be smart
pupinización *f* (elec.) Pupin system
pupitre *m* writing desk
puposo -sa *adj* pimply, pustulous
pupuso -sa *adj* (Am.) stubby, chubby; (Am.) swollen; (Am.) proud, haughty; (Am.) rich, wealthy
puque *adj* rotten (*egg*); (Am.) sickly
puquio *m* (Am.) spring or pool of fresh, clear water
puré *m* purée; **puré de patatas** mashed potatoes; **puré de tomates** stewed tomatoes
purear *vn* (coll.) to smoke cigars
pureza *f* purity
purga *f* purge; purgative, physic; drainings; drain valve
purgación *f* purge, purgation; **purgaciones** *fpl* (path.) gonorrhea
purgador -dora *adj* purging; *mf* purger
purgante *adj & m* purgative
purgar §59 *va* to purge; to physic; to drain; to purify, refine; to expiate; to control, to check (*passions*); to clear away (*suspicion*); *vn* to drain; to atone; *vr* to take a physic; to drain; to unburden oneself
purgativo -va *adj* purgative
purgatorio -ria *adj* purgatorial; *m* (theol. & fig.) purgatory; **tener en el purgatorio** to torture, to torment
puridad *f* purity; secrecy; **en puridad** openly, frankly; in secret
purificación *f* purification
purificadero -ra *adj* purifying, cleansing
purificador -dora *adj* purifying; *m* (eccl.) purificator; (eccl.) altar napkin
purificar §86 *va* to purify; *vr* to purify; to become purified
Purim *m* (rel.) Purim
purina *f* (chem.) purine
Purísima *f* Virgin Mary
purismo *m* purism
purista *adj* purist, puristic; *mf* purist
puritanismo *m* Puritanism
puritano -na *adj* puritan; puritanic; Puritan; *mf* puritan; Puritan
puro -ra *adj* pure; sheer; clear (*sky*); solid (*gold*); out-and-out, outright; **de puro** completely, totally; **de puro** + *adj* because of being + *adj*; *m* cigar
púrpura *f* purple; (poet.) blood; **púrpura de Tiro** Tyrian purple; **púrpura visual** (biochem.) visual purple
purpurado -da *adj* purple; *m* (eccl.) cardinal
purpurar *va* to purple; to dress in purple
purpúrea *f* see **purpúreo**
purpurear *vn* to purple, to have a purple tinge
purpúreo -a *adj* purple; *f* (bot.) burdock
purpurino -na *adj* purple; *f* (chem.) purpurin; bronze powder
purrela *f* poor wine, small wine
purriela *f* (coll.) junk, piece of junk
purulencia *f* purulence or purulency
purulento -ta *adj* purulent
pus *adj invar* (Am.) puce (*color*); *m* pus
puse *1st sg pret ind of* **poner**
pusilánime *adj* pusillanimous
pusilanimidad *f* pusillanimity
pústula *f* (bot. & path.) pustule
pustulación *f* pustulation
pustuloso -sa *adj* pustular
puta *f* whore, harlot
putaísmo *m* whoredom, harlotry; brothel
putañear *vn* (coll.) to whore around, to chase after lewd women
putañero *adj masc* (coll.) whoring, lewd
putativo -va *adj* spurious; putative
putear *vn* (coll.) var. of **putañear**
putero *adj masc* (coll.) var. of **putañero**
putesco -ca *adj* (coll.) whorish
putpurri *m* (mus.) potpourri, medley
putrefacción *f* putrefaction
putrefactivo -va *adj* putrefactive
putrefacto -ta *adj* rotten, putrid
putrescente *adj* putrescent
putrescible *adj* putrescible
putrescina *f* (biochem.) putrescine
putridez *f* putridity, rottenness
pútrido -da *adj* putrid, rotten
puya *f* goad, steel point; spur (*of cock*); (bot.) puya
puyazo *m* jab or wound with a goad; (fig.) jab, dig
puyo *m* (Am.) woolen poncho
puzol *m* or **puzolana** *f* (geol.) pozzolana

Q

Q, q *f* twentieth letter of the Spanish alphabet
q. abr. of **que**
q.b.s.m. abr. of **que besa su mano**
q.b.s.p. abr. of **que besa sus pies**
q.d.D.g. abr. of **que de Dios goce**
q.D.g. abr. of **que Dios guarde**
q.D. tenga en s.g. abr. of **que Dios tenga en su gracia**
q.e abr. of **que**
q.e.g.e. abr. of **que en gloria esté**
q.e.p.d. abr. of **que en paz descanse**
q.e.s.m. abr. of **que estrecha su mano**
q.n abr. of **quien**
qq. abr. of **quintales**
q.s.g.h. abr. of **que santa gloria haya**
quántum *m* (*pl:* **quanta**) (phys.) quantum
que *pron rel* that, which; who, whom; **el que** he who; which, the one which; who, the one who; *adv* than; *conj* that; for, because; let, e.g., **que entre** let him come in; **a que** (coll.) I bet that; **que no** and not; **que no** + *subj* without + *ger;* **que . . . que** whether . . . or
qué *adj & pron interr* what, which; what!; what a!; how!; **¿a qué?** why?; **sin qué ni para qué** without rhyme or reason; **¡qué de!** how much!, how many!; **¿qué más da?** what's the difference?; **¿qué tal?** how?; hello, how's everything?
quebracho *m* (bot.) quebracho, breakax
quebrada *f* see **quebrado**
quebradero *m* (obs.) breaker; **quebradero de cabeza** (coll.) worry, concern
quebradizo -za *adj* brittle, fragile; frail, delicate
quebrado -da *adj* weakened; bankrupt; ruptured; rough, winding; fractional; *mf* bankrupt; *m* (math.) fraction; (Am.) tobacco leaf full of holes; *f* gorge, ravine, gap; failure, bankruptcy; (Am.) brook
quebrador -dora *adj* breaking; *mf* breaker; lawbreaker
quebradura *f* breaking; fissure, slit; (path.) rupture
quebraja *f* crack, slit, fissure
quebrajar *va* to crack, to slit, to split
quebrajoso -sa *adj* brittle, fragile; full of cracks, splintery
quebramiento *m* var. of **quebrantamiento**
quebrantable *adj* breakable
quebrantador -dora *adj* breaking; crushing; *mf* breaker, crusher; *f* crusher (*machine*)
quebrantadura *f* var. of **quebrantamiento**
quebrantahuesos *m* (*pl:* **-sos**) (orn.) osprey, sea eagle; (orn.) lammergeier, bearded vulture; (coll.) bore, pest
quebrantamiento *m* breaking, breach; fracture, rupture; exhaustion, fatigue
quebrantaolas *m* (*pl:* **-las**) old ship used as a breakwater
quebrantapiedras *m* (*pl:* **-dras**) (bot.) burstwort
quebrantar *va* to break; to break in (*a colt*); to break open; to break out of; to grind, crush; to soften, mollify; (fig.) to break (*a contract, a will, the law, someone's heart*); *vr* to break; to become broken
quebrantaterrones *m* (*pl:* **-nes**) (coll.) clodhopper
quebranto *m* break, breaking; heavy loss; great sorrow; discouragement
quebrar §18 *va* to break; to bend, to twist; to crush; to overcome; to temper, soften; to dull, darken (*the countenance*); *vn* to break; to fail; to weaken, give in; **quebrar con** to break with (*e.g., a friend*); *vr* to break; to become broken; to weaken; to become ruptured
quebrazas *fpl* flaws or tiny cracks in the blade of a sword
queche *m* smack, ketch
quechemarín *m* (naut.) coasting lugger
quechua *adj & mf* var. of **quichua**
queda *f* see **quedo**
quedada *f* stay, sojourn; (naut.) lull
quedar *vn* to remain; to stay; to be left; to be left over; to stop, leave off; to turn out; to be; to be found, to be located; **quedar a** + *inf* to remain + *ger*, e.g., **quedar a deber** to remain owing; **quedar bien** or **mal** to acquit oneself well or badly; **quedar en** to agree on; **quedar en** + *inf* to agree to + *inf;* **quedar en que** to agree that; **quedar por** or **sin** + *inf* to remain to be + *pp*, e.g., **aún queda más de la mitad del ferrocarril por construir** more than half of the railroad still remains to be built; *vr* to remain; to stay; to stop; to be; to be left; to put up (*e.g., at a hotel*); **quedarse con** to keep, to take; **quedarse tan fresco** (coll.) to show no offense, to be unconcerned
quedito *adv* softly, gently
quedo -da *adj* quiet, still; gentle; *f* curfew; **quedo** *adv* softly, in a low voice; gropingly; **a quedo** or **de quedo** easy, slowly
quehacer *m* work, task, chore
queja *f* complaint, lament; whine, moan; (law) complaint
quejar *vr* to complain, lament; to whine, moan; **quejarse de** to complain about or of; **quejarse de** + *inf* to complain of + *ger;* **quejarse de haber** + *pp* to complain of having + *pp*
quejicoso -sa *adj* complaining, whining, whiny
quejido *m* complaint, whine, moan
quejigal *m* or **quejigar** *m* grove of gall oaks
quejigo *m* (bot.) gall oak
quejigueta *f* (bot.) dwarf oak of Morocco and southern Spain (*Quercus humilis*)
quejilloso -sa *adj* complaining, whining
quejoso -sa *adj* complaining, querulous
quejumbre *f* complaining, whine, moan
quejumbroso -sa *adj* complaining, whining, whiny
quela *f* (zool.) chela
quelícero *m* (ent.) chelicera
quelite *m* (bot.) pigweed
quelonio -nia *adj & m* (zool.) chelonian
quelpo *m* (bot.) kelp
quema *f* fire, burning; **a quema ropa** pointblank; **de quema** distilled; **hacer quema** (Am.) to hit the mark; **huir de la quema** to get out of danger; to dodge responsibility
quemada *f* see **quemado**
quemadero -ra *adj* for burning, to be burned; *m* stake (*for burning convicts*); incinerator (*for burning dead animals or damaged food*)
quemado -da *adj* burned; burnt out; (Am.) angry; (Am.) colored, dark; *m* burnt brush, burnt thicket; (coll.) fire, something burning, something burnt; **oler a quemado** (coll.) to smell of fire; *f* burnt brush, burnt thicket; (Am.) fire
quemador -dora *adj* burning; incendiary; *mf* burner; *m* burner; **quemador de gas** gas burner; **quemador de petróleo** oil burner
quemadura *f* burning; burn; sunburn; scald; smut (*plant disease*)
quemajoso -sa *adj* burning, smarting
quemar *va* to burn; to scald; to kindle, set on fire; to parch, scorch; to frostbite; to sell too cheap; *vn* to burn, be hot; *vr* to burn; to be burning up; (coll.) to fret, become impatient; (coll.) to be warm, be hot (*to be about to find something sought for*)
quemarropa; a quemarropa point-blank

quemazón *f* burning; burn; intense heat; (coll.) itch, smarting; (coll.) cutting remark; (coll.) pique, anger; (hum.) bargain sale; (Am.) mirage on the pampas
quenopodiáceo -a *adj* (bot.) chenopodiaceous
quenopodio *m* (bot.) chenopod, goosefoot
quepis *m* (*pl:* **-pis**) (mil.) kepi
quepo *1st sg pres ind of* **caber**
querargirita *f* (mineral.) cerargyrite
queratina *f* (zool.) keratin
queratógeno -na *adj* keratogenous
querella *f* complaint; quarrel, dispute; (law) complaint
querellado -da *mf* (law) defendant
querellador -dora or **querellante** *adj & mf* (law) complainant
querellar *vr* to complain; to whine; (law) to file a complaint, bring suit
querelloso -sa *adj* querulous; quarrelsome
querencia *f* fondness, liking; attraction; love of home; haunt (*of animals*); (taur.) favorite spot or refuge (*of a bull in the arena*); (coll.) favorite spot, perch
querencioso -sa *adj* homing, home-returning; favorite (*haunt or spot*); (coll.) affectionate
querendón -dona *adj* (Am.) affectionate
querer *m* love, affection; liking, fondness; **§70** *va* to wish, want, desire; to like; to love; **como quiera** anyhow, anyway; **como quiera que** whereas; since, inasmuch as; no matter how; **cuando quiera** any time; **donde quiera** anywhere; **que quiera, que no quiera** whether he wishes to or not; **sin querer** unwillingly; unintentionally; **querer bien** to love; **querer más** to prefer; *v aux* **querer** + *inf* to wish, want or desire to + *inf;* will + *inf;* to be about to, to be trying to + *inf*, e.g., **quiere llover** it is trying to rain; **querer decir** to mean; **querer más** + *inf* to prefer to + *inf*, would rather + *inf*
queresa *f* var. of **cresa**
querido -da *adj* dear; *mf* lover; paramour; (coll.) dearie; *f* mistress
quermes *m* (*pl:* **-mes**) (ent.) kermes insect; kermes (*dyestuff*); **quermes mineral** (chem.) kermes mineral
quermés *f* or **quermese** *f* bazaar (*for some charitable purpose*); village or country fair
querocha *f* var. of **cresa**
querochar *vn* to lay eggs (*said of bees and other insects*)
Queronea *f* Chaeronea
queroseno *m* var. of **keroseno**
querré *1st sg fut ind of* **querer**
quersoneso *m* chersonese; **el quersoneso de Tracia** the Chersonese (*Gallipoli Peninsula*)
querub *m* or **querube** *m* (poet.) cherub
querúbico -ca *adj* cherubic
querubín *m* (Bib., f.a. & theol.) cherub
querva *f* var. of **cherva**
quesadilla *f* cheese cake; sweet pastry
quesear *vn* to make cheese
quesera *f* see **quesero**
quesería *f* cheese-making season; cheese factory; cheese shop or store
quesero -ra *adj* caseous, cheesy; *mf* cheesemonger; cheesemaker; *f* cheese board; cheese mold; cheese tub; cheese dish; cheese factory
quesillo *m* heart of artichoke; **quesillo helado** brick ice cream
quesiqués *m* var. of **quisicosa**
queso *m* cheese; **queso de bola** Edam cheese; **queso de cerdo** headcheese; **queso de Edam** Edam cheese; **queso de Gruyère** Swiss cheese; **queso de higos** (Am.) fig paste; **queso de Holanda** Dutch cheese; **queso de Limburgo** Limburger; **queso de Roquefort** Roquefort cheese; **queso helado** brick ice cream; **queso parmesano** Parmesan cheese
queteno *m* (chem.) ketene
quetona *f* (chem.) ketone
quetosa *f* (chem.) ketose
quetzal *m* or **quetzale** *m* (orn.) quetzal; quetzal (*monetary unit of Guatemala*)
quevedos *mpl* pince-nez
quezal *m* (orn.) quetzal
quiá *interj* oh, no!
quianti *m* Chianti (*wine*)
quiasma *m* (rhet.) chiasmus; (anat. & biol.) chiasma
quicial *m* hinge-pole; hanging stile; pivot hole (*for hinge-pole*)
quicialera *f* hinge-pole; hanging stile
quicio *m* pivot hole (*for hinge-pole*); doorjamb; (Am.) front steps (*of a house*); **fuera de quicio** out of order; **sacar de quicio** to put out of order; **sacar de quicio** to unhinge (*a person*)
quichua *adj* Quechuan; *mf* Quechua; *m* Quechuan (*language*)
quid *m* quiddity, gist, core
quídam *m* (coll.) so-and-so; (coll.) nobody
quiebra *f* break; crack, fissure; damage, loss; bankruptcy
quiebrahacha *f* (bot.) breakax
quiebro *m* bending back at the waist; (mus.) trill; (taur.) dodge
quien *pron rel* who, whom; he who, she who; someone who, anyone who
quién *pron interr* who, whom; **¿Quién es quién?** Who's Who (*book of biographies*); **quién . . . quién** one . . . another
quienquiera *pron indef* anyone, anybody; **quienquiera que** whoever, whomever
quién vive *m* (mil.) challenge
quiescencia *f* (gram.) quiescence
quiescente *adj* (gram.) quiescent
quietación *f* quieting
quietador -dora *adj* quieting, calming; *mf* quieter
quietar *va & vr* var. of **aquietar**
quiete *f* hour of recreation (*after eating*)
quietismo *m* quietism
quietista *adj & mf* quietist
quieto -ta *adj* quiet, still, calm; virtuous
quietud *f* quiet, stillness, calm
quijada *f* (anat.) jaw, jawbone; (mach.) jaw
quijal *m* or **quijar** *m* (anat.) jaw; (anat.) grinder, molar tooth
quijarudo -da *adj* big-jawed
quijera *f* cheek strap; cheek of crossbow
quijo *m* (min.) quartz (*gold or silver ore*)
quijones *m* (*pl:* **-nes**) (bot.) aromatic herb (*Scandix australis*)
quijotada *f* (coll.) quixotism, quixotic deed
quijote *m* (arm.) cuisse; croup (*of horse*); (fig.) Quixote (*quixotic person*)
quijotear *vn* to act quixotically
quijotería *f* quixotry, quixotism
quijotesco -ca *adj* quixotic
quijotil *adj* of the Quixote (*the romance*)
quijotismo *m* quixotism; ridiculous pride or vanity
quilatador *m* assayer
quilatar *va* var. of **aquilatar**
quilate *m* carat; **quilates** *mpl* (fig.) weight in gold; **por quilates** (coll.) in small amounts, sparingly
quilatera *f* pearl gauge
quilífero -ra *adj* chyliferous
quilificación *f* (physiol.) chylification
quilificar **§86** *va & vr* (physiol.) to chylify
quilma *f* sack, bag
quilo *m* (physiol.) chyle; kilo (*kilogram*); **sudar el quilo** (coll.) to slave, to be a drudge
quilográmetro *m* var. of **kilográmetro**
quilogramo *m* var. of **kilogramo**
quilolitro *m* var. of **kilolitro**
quilométrico -ca *adj* var. of **kilométrico**
quilómetro *m* var. of **kilómetro**
quiloso -sa *adj* chylous
quilla *f* (aer., naut. & bot.) keel; (orn.) breastbone; **dar de quilla** (naut.) to keel over; **falsa quilla** (naut.) false keel; **poner en quilla** (naut.) to put on the stocks
quillay *m* (bot.) soapbark tree (*of Chile*)
quillotranza *f* (coll.) sorrow, bitterness
quillotrar *va* (coll.) to incite, stir up; (coll.) to make love to; (coll.) to charm, captivate; (coll.) to consider, think over; (coll.) to adorn, deck; *vr* (coll.) to fall in love; (coll.) to deck oneself out; (coll.) to complain
quillotro *m* (coll.) incitement; (coll.) sign, token; (coll.) love making, love affair; (coll.) problem, puzzler; (coll.) adornment, finery; (coll.) friend, favorite
quimafila *f* (bot.) pipsissewa

quimbombó *m* (*pl:* **-boes**) var. of **quingombó**
quimera *f* (myth., f.a. & fig.) chimera; quarrel, dispute
quimérico -ca or **quimerino -na** *adj* chimeric or chimerical
quimerista *adj* visionary; quarrelsome; *mf* visionary; wrangler
quimerizar §76 *vn* to indulge in chimeras
quimiatría *f* chemiatry
químico -ca *adj* chemical; *mf* chemist; *f* chemistry; **química del carbono** organic chemistry; **química física** physical chemistry; **química fisiológica** physiological chemistry; **química inorgánica** inorganic chemistry; **química mineral** or **orgánica** organic chemistry
quimicultura *f* tank farming
quimificación *f* (physiol.) chymification
quimificar §86 *va* (physiol.) chymify
quimiocirugía *f* chemosurgery
quimiosfera *f* chemosphere
quimiosíntesis *f* chemosynthesis
quimiotaxis *f* (biol.) chemotaxis
quimioterapia *f* chemotherapy
quimismo *m* chemism
quimista *m* var. of **alquimista**
quimo *m* (physiol.) chyme
quimógrafo *m* kymograph
quimoso -sa *adj* chymous
quimón *m* kimono cotton
quimono *m* kimono
quimosina *f* (biochem.) rennin
quina *f* (pharm.) cinchona, Peruvian bark; keno (*in lotto*); **quinas** *fpl* quinas (*arms of Portugal*); double fives (*in dice*)
quinal *m* (naut.) preventer shroud
quinaquina *f* var. of **quina**
quinario -ra *adj* quinary; *m* quinary; five-day devotion
quincajú *m* (*pl:* **-júes**) var. of **quincayú**
quincalla *f* hardware; costume jewelry
quincallería *f* hardware business; hardware store; hardware factory; gift shop
quincallero -ra *mf* hardware merchant; hardware maker
quincayú *m* (*pl:* **-yúes**) (zool.) kinkajou
quince *adj* fifteen; **las quince** three P.M.; *m* fifteen; fifteenth (*in dates*); **dar quince y falta a, dar quince y raya a** (coll.) to be a thousand times better than or superior to
quinceañero -ra *adj* fifteen-year-old; *mf* fifteen-year-old person
quinceavo -va *adj* & *m* var. of **quinzavo**
quincena *f* see **quinceno**
quincenal *adj* biweekly, fortnightly
quincenario -ria *adj* biweekly, fortnightly; *mf* person who spends one fortnight after another in jail
quinceno -na *adj* fifteenth; *mf* fifteen-month-old mule; *f* two weeks, fortnight; two weeks' pay; (mus.) fifteenth (*interval and organ stop*)
quincineta *f* (orn.) lapwing
quinconce *m* (Am.) var. of **quincunce**
quincuagena *f* fifty
quincuagenario -ria *adj* & *mf* quinquagenarian
quincuagésimo -ma *adj* & *m* fiftieth; *f* (eccl.) Quinquagesima
quincunce *m* (hort.) quincunx
quindécimo -ma *adj* & *m* fifteenth
quindenial *adj* fifteen-year
quindenio *m* fifteen-year period, fifteen years
quinescopio *m* var. of **kinescopio**
quingentésimo -ma *adj* & *m* five-hundredth
quingo *m* (Am.) zigzag, twist, turn
quingombó *m* (*pl:* **-boes**) (bot.) okra or gumbo (*plant and fruit*)
quiniela *f* pelota game of five; soccer lottery; numbers game; daily double
quinientos -tas *adj* & *m* five hundred
quinina *f* (chem.) quinine
quinismo *m* (path.) cinchonism
quino *m* kino; (bot.) cinchona; (pharm.) cinchona, Peruvian bark
quínoa *f* (bot.) South American pigweed (*Chenopodium quinoa*)
quínola *f* four of a kind (*at cards*); **quínolas** *fpl* reversi (*old card game*)
quinolillas *fpl* var. of **quínolas**
quinqué *m* student lamp, oil lamp, Argand lamp; (coll.) insight, perspicacity
quinquefolio *m* (bot.) cinquefoil
quinquenal *adj* quinquennial, five-year
quinquenervia *f* (bot.) ribwort
quinquenio *m* quinquennium, five-year period
quinquerreme *f* quinquereme
quinquillería *f* var. of **quincallería**
quinquillero -ra *mf* var. of **quincallero**
quinta *f* see **quinto**
quintacolumnista *mf* fifth columnist
quintador *m* draft or induction official
quintaesencia *f* quintessence
quintaesenciar *va* to refine, purify; to extract the quintessence of
quintal *m* quintal (*46 kg.*); **quintal métrico** quintal (*100 kg.*)
quintalada *f* (naut.) primage, hat money
quintaleño -ña *adj* capable of holding a quintal
quintalero -ra *adj* weighing a quintal
quintana *f* villa, country house
quintante *m* (astr.) quintant
quintañón -ñona *adj* & *mf* (coll.) centenarian
quintar *va* to draw (*one*) out of five; (mil.) to draft, to induct; to plow for the fifth time; *vn* to reach the fifth day (*said, especially, of the moon*); to bid a fifth higher (*at an auction*)
quintería *f* farmhouse, grange
quinterna *f* keno (*in lotto*)
quinterno *m* quinternion (*section of five sheets of paper*); keno (*in lotto*)
quintero *m* farmer; farm hand
quinteto *m* (mus.) quintet; quintet (*group of five*)
Quintiliano *m* Quintilian
quintilo *m* quintile
quintilla *f* five-line stanza of eight syllables and two rhymes; any five-line stanza with two rhymes
quintillizo -za *mf* (coll.) quint, quintuplet
quintillo *m* game of ombre played by five players
quintillón *m* British quintillion
quintín *m* quintin (*fine fabric*); **armar la de San Quintín** to raise a rumpus
quinto -ta *adj* fifth; *m* fifth; lot (*of ground*); pasture; (mil.) draftee; *f* villa, country house; (mil.) draft, induction; five of a kind (*at cards*); (mus.) fifth; **ir a quintas** to be drafted; **redimirse de las quintas** to be exempted from the draft
quintuplicación *f* quintuplication
quintuplicar §86 *va* & *vr* to quintuple
quíntuplo -pla *adj* & *m* quintuple, fivefold
quinua *f* var. of **quínoa**
quinzavo -va *adj* & *m* fifteenth
quiñón *m* share; lot, plot (*of arable land*)
quiñonero *m* part owner
quío -a *adj* & *mf* Chian; **Quío** *f* Chios (*island*)
quiosco *m* kiosk, summerhouse; stand; **quiosco de periódicos** newsstand; **quiosco de música** bandstand; **quiosco de necesidad** public toilet, comfort station
quiosquero *m* newsstand man
quipos *mpl* quipu (*colored cords and knots used by ancient Peruvians instead of writing*)
quiquiriquí *m* (*pl:* **-quíes**) cock-a-doodle-doo; (coll.) cock of the walk
quiragra *f* (path.) gout in the hand
quirinal *adj* Quirinal; (*cap.*) *m* Quirinal
quirófano *m* operating room
quirografía *f* chirography
quirográfico -ca *adj* chirographic
quirógrafo -fa *mf* chirographer; *m* chirograph
quiromancia or **quiromancía** *f* chiromancy, palmistry
quiromántico -ca *adj* chiromantic or chiromantical, of palmistry, of palmists; *mf* chiromancer, palmist
Quirón *m* (myth.) Chiron
quiropodia *f* chiropody
quiropodista *mf* chiropodist
quiropráctico -ca *adj* chiropractic; *mf* chiropractic, chiropractor; *f* chiropractic (*method of treatment*)
quiropractor *m* chiropractor
quiropraxia *f* chiropractic (*method of treatment*)

quiróptero -ra *adj & m* (zool.) chiropteran
quiroteca *f* glove
quirúrgico -ca *adj* surgical
quirurgo *m* surgeon
quiscal *m* (orn.) grackle
quiscamote *m* (bot.) cuckoopint
quise *1st sg pret ind of* **querer**
quisicosa *f* (coll.) puzzler (*thing which puzzles*)
quisquilla *f* trifle, triviality, quibble; (zool.) shrimp; **quisquillas** *fpl* hairsplitting; **dejarse de quisquillas** to stop fussing; **pararse en quisquillas** to bicker, to make a fuss over nothing
quisquillosidad *f* triviality; touchiness; fastidiousness; hairsplitting
quisquilloso -sa *adj* trifling; touchy; fastidious; hairsplitting
quistar *vr* to get along well, to be well liked
quiste *m* (bot., path. & zool.) cyst
quístico -ca *adj* (path.) cystic
quisto -ta *adj* liked; **bien quisto** well-liked; well-received; **mal quisto** disliked; unwelcome
quita *f* see **quito**
quitación *f* salary, income; (law) acquittance, release
quitador -dora *adj* removing; *mf* remover
quitaguas *m* (*pl:* **-guas**) umbrella
quitaipón *m* var. of **quitapón**
quitalodos *m* (*pl:* **-dos**) scraper, foot scraper
quitamanchas *mf* (*pl:* **-chas**) clothes cleaner, spot remover (*person*); *m* clothes cleaner, spot remover (*material*)
quitameriendas *f* (*pl:* **-das**) (bot.) meadow saffron, autumn crocus
quitamiedos *m* (*pl:* **-dos**) handrail, railing, rope
quitamotas *mf* (coll.) fawner, flatterer, bootlicker
quitanieve *m* or **quitanieves** *m* (*pl:* **-ves**) snowplow
quitanza *f* quittance
quitapelillos *mf* (*pl:* **-llos**) (coll.) fawner, flatterer, lickspittle
quitapesares *m* (*pl:* **-res**) (coll.) solace, comfort; (coll.) outdoor relaxation
quitapiedras *m* (*pl:* **-dras**) pilot, cowcatcher
quitapintura *f* paint remover
quitapón *m* headstall ornament for mules; **de quitapón** detachable, removable
quitar *va* to remove; to take away; to dispel; to clear (*the table*); to free; to save (*work or effort*); to take (*time*); to parry (*in fencing*); to prevent; **quitar** + *inf* to keep (*someone*) from + *ger;* **quitar algo a algo** to take something off something, to remove something from something, e.g., **quitaron dos carros al tren en Medina del Campo** they took two cars off the train at Medina del Campo; **quitar algo a uno** to remove something from someone; to take something away from someone; *vr* to take off (*hat, article of clothing, etc.*); to tip (*one's hat*); to come out (*said of a spot or stain*); to give up (*a vice*); to withdraw; **de quita y pon** detachable, removable; **¡quita allá!** or **¡quite allá!** don't tell me!
quitasol *m* parasol
quitasolillo or **quitasolillos** *m* (*pl:* **-llos**) (bot.) marsh pennywort
quitasueño *m* (coll.) worry, anxiety (*that dispels sleep*)
quite *m* removal; hindrance; dodge, dodging; parry (*in fencing*); (taur.) attracting the bull from a man in danger
quiteño -ña *adj* (pertaining to) Quito; *mf* native or inhabitant of Quito
quitina *f* (chem.) chitin
quitinoso -sa *adj* chitinous
quito -ta *adj* free, exempt; *f* (law) acquittance, release
quitón *m* (hist. & zool.) chiton
quitrín *m* (Am.) two-wheel carriage
quizá or **quizás** *adv* maybe, perhaps
quórum *m* (*pl:* **-rum**) quorum

R

R, r *f* twenty-first letter of the Spanish alphabet
R. abr. of **reprobado** (*en examen*), **respuesta, Reverencia** & **Reverendo**
raba *f* cod roe used as bait
rabada *f* hind quarter, rump
rabadán *m* head shepherd
rabadilla *f* (anat.) coccyx; (orn.) uropygium
rabanal *m* radish patch
rabanero -ra *adj* (coll.) short (*skirt*); (coll.) shameless, indecent; *mf* radish seller; *f* shameless woman, indecent woman; hors d'oeuvre dish, small oval dish
rabanete *m* small radish
rabanillo *m* sharpness (*of turning wine*); (bot.) jointed charlock; (coll.) sullenness; (coll.) eagerness, keenness
rabaniza *f* radish seed
rábano *m* (bot.) radish; **tomar el rábano por las hojas** (coll.) to be entirely wrong, to be on the wrong track; **rábano picante** or **rusticano** (bot.) horseradish; **rábano silvestre** (bot.) jointed charlock
rabárbaro *m* var. of **ruibarbo**
rabazuz *m* licorice extract
rabear *vn* to wag the tail; (naut.) to vibrate at the stern
rabel *m* (mus.) rebec; (hum.) backside
rabelesiano -na *adj* & *mf* Rabelaisian
rabeo *m* wagging the tail
rabera *f* tail end, breech; tang (*of a utensil*); handle (*of crossbow*); chaff
raberón *m* topped part of tree trunk
rabí *m* (*pl:* **-bíes**) rabbi
rabia *f* anger, rage; (path.) rabies; **tener rabia a** (coll.) to have a grudge against
rabiacana *f* (bot.) wake-robin
rabiar *vn* to rage, to rave; to get mad; to moan with pain; to have rabies; **a rabiar** like the deuce; **picar que rabia** to sting like the deuce; **rabiar por** to be dying for; **rabiar por** + *inf* to be dying to + *inf*
rabiatar *va* to tie together by the tail
rabiazorras *m* (coll.) east wind
rabicán apocopated form of **rabicano**
rabicano -na *adj* white-tailed
rábico -ca *adj* (med. & vet.) rabic
rabicorto -ta *adj* short-tailed; wearing a short dress
rábido -da *adj* var. of **rabioso;** *f* Moroccan monastery
rabieta *f* (coll.) tantrum, conniption
rabihorcado *m* (orn.) frigate bird
rabijunco *m* (orn.) tropic bird
rabilargo -ga *adj* long-tailed; *m* (orn.) blue magpie
rabillo *m* (bot.) leafstalk; (bot.) flower stalk; mildew spots (*on cereals*); (bot.) bearded darnel; tip; **con el rabillo del ojo** out of the corner of one's eye
rabínico -ca *adj* rabbinic or rabbinical
rabinismo *m* rabbinism
rabinista *mf* rabbinist
rabino *m* rabbi
rabioles *mpl* (cook.) ravioli
rabión *m* rapids (*in a river*)
rabioso -sa *adj* rabid, mad
rabisalsera *adj fem* (coll.) pert, flippant
rabiza *f* tip of fishing rod; (naut.) short piece of rope, end of rope
rabo *m* tail; (bot.) flower stalk; (fig.) tail, train; **con el rabo del ojo** out of the corner of one's eye; **rabo de junco** (orn.) red-billed tropic bird; **rabo de zorra** foxtail; (bot.) foxtail; **rabos de gallo** (meteor.) cocktail, mare's-tail (*cirrous clouds*); **rabo verde** (Am.) old rake
rabón -bona *adj* bobtail; *f* (Am.) canteen woman; **hacer rabona** (coll.) to play hooky
rabopelado *m* (zool.) opossum
raboseada or **raboseadura** *f* mussing, fretting, fraying, tampering
rabosear *va* to muss, fret, fray, tamper with
raboso -sa *adj* raggedy, frayed
rabotada *f* swish of the tail; (coll.) coarse remark, coarseness
rabotear *va* to cut off the tail of
raboteo *m* cropping of sheep's tails; tail-cropping time
rabudo -da *adj* long-tailed, large-tailed
rábula *m* pettifogger
racamenta *f* or **racamento** *m* (naut.) parral or parrel
racel *m* (naut.) run
racial *adj* racial
racima *f* grapes left on vines (*at vintage*)
racimal *adj* in bunches, in clusters
racimar *va* to pick (*a vine*) of grapes left after vintage; *vr* to cluster, to bunch
racimo *m* bunch; cluster; (bot.) raceme
racimoso -sa *adj* bunchy, full of bunches; (bot.) racemose
racimudo -da *adj* with large bunches
raciocinación *f* ratiocination
raciocinar *vn* to ratiocinate
raciocinio *m* reason; argument; ratiocination
ración *f* ration; portion; allowance; (mil.) ration; (eccl.) cathedral prebend; **ración de hambre** starvation wages, pittance
racionabilidad *f* reason, intelligence
racional *adj* rational; (math.) rational; *m* (eccl.) rational
racionalidad *f* rationality
racionalismo *m* rationalism
racionalista *adj* rationalistic; *mf* rationalist
racionalización *f* (com. & math.) rationalization
racionalizar **§76** *va* (math.) to rationalize
racionamiento *m* rationing
racionar *va* to ration; (mil.) to ration
racionero *m* distributor of rations; (eccl.) prebendary
racionista *mf* person who lives on an allowance or ration; *m* (theat.) utility man
racismo *m* racism
racista *adj* & *mf* racist
racha *f* (naut.) squall, gust of wind; (coll.) streak, streak of luck; split, crack; large chip (*of wood*)
rada *f* (naut.) road, roadstead
Radamanto *m* (myth.) Rhadamanthus
radar *m* (elec.) radar
radaroscopio or **radarscopio** *m* radarscope
radiación *f* radiation
radiactividad *f* radioactivity
radiactivo -va *adj* radioactive
radiado -da *adj* radiate; (bot. & zool.) radiate; *m* (zool.) radiate
radiador -dora *adj* radiating; *m* radiator
radial *adj* radial; (Am.) (pertaining to) radio; *m* (math.) radian
radián *m* (math.) radian
radiante *adj* radiant; (phys.) radiant; (fig.) radiant (*joyful, smiling*); *m* (astr.) radiant; (math.) radian
radiar *va* to radio; to broadcast; to irradiate; *vn* to radiate
radicación *f* (math.) evolution; taking root
radical *adj* radical; (bot., chem., math., philol. & pol.) radical; *mf* (pol.) radical; *m* (chem., math. & philol.) radical; **radical hidroxilo** (chem.) hydroxyl radical
radicalismo *m* radicalism

radicante *adj* rooted; situated; **radicante en** (mil.) based on
radicar §86 *vn* to take root; to be located; *vr* to take root; to settle, settle down
radicícola *adj* (zool.) radicolous, radicicolous
radicoso -sa *adj* radicular, rooty
radícula *f* (bot.) radicle
radiestesia *f* dowsing
radiestesista *adj* dowsing; *mf* dowser
radio *m* edge, outskirts; radius (*e.g., of action*); spoke, rung (*of wheel*); (anat. & geom.) radius; (chem.) radium; *m & f* radio (*broadcasting; set; message*); **en la radio** on the radio
radío -a *adj* wandering
radioactividad *f* var. of **radiactividad**
radioactivo -va *adj* var. of **radiactivo**
radioaficionado -da *mf* radio amateur, radio fan, radio ham
radioastronomía *f* radioastronomy
radiobiología *f* radiobiology
radiobrújula *f* radio compass
radiocarbono *m* (phys.) radioactive carbon
radiocomunicación *f* radio communication
radiodiagnosis *f* or **radiodiagnóstico** *m* X-ray diagnosis
radiodifundir *va & vn* to broadcast, to radiobroadcast
radiodifusión *f* broadcasting, radiobroadcasting
radiodifusor -sora *adj* radiobroadcasting; *f* radiobroadcasting station
radiodirigido -da *adj* radio-controlled
radioelemento *m* (chem.) radioactive element, radioelement; **radioelemento indicador** (phys.) tracer element
radioemisora *f* radiobroadcasting station
radioescucha *mf* radio listener; radio monitor
radioestación *f* radio station
radiofaro *m* radio beacon
radiofonema *m* (rad. & telv.) commercial (*paid advertisement*)
radiofonía *f* (phys. & rad.) radiophony
radiofónico -ca *adj* radiophonic
radiófono *m* (phys. & rad.) radiophone
radiofonógrafo *m* radiophonograph
radiofoto *f* radiophoto
radiofrecuencia *f* (rad.) radio frequency
radiofusión *f* (Am.) broadcasting, radiobroadcasting
radiogoniometría *f* radiogoniometry
radiogoniómetro *m* radiogoniometer
radiografía *f* radiograph; radiography
radiografiar §90 *va* to radiograph; to wireless
radiográfico -ca *adj* radiographic
radiograma *m* radiogram
radiogramófono *m* radiophonograph
radiogramola *f* radiophonograph
radioguía *f* radio range beacon
radioisótopo *m* radioisotope
radiolario *m* (zool.) radiolarian
radiolocalización *f* radiolocation
radiología *f* radiology
radiólogo -ga *mf* radiologist
radiómano -na *mf* (coll.) radio fan
radiomecánico *m* radio serviceman
radiomensaje *m* radio message
radiometría *f* radiometry
radiómetro *m* radiometer
radioonda *f* radio wave
radiopaco -ca *adj* radiopaque
radioperturbación *f* (rad.) jamming
radioquímica *f* radiochemistry
radiorrecepción *f* reception, radio reception
radiorreceptor -tora *adj* receiving, radio-receiving; *m & f* radio receiver, receiving set
radiorreparaciones *fpl* radio repairs
radiorreparador *m* radio repairman
radioscopia *f* radioscopy
radiosensitivo -va *adj* radiosensitive
radioseñal *f* radio signal
radioso -sa *adj* radiant
radiosonda *m & f* (meteor.) radiosonde
radioteatro *m* theater of the air
radiotecnia *f* radiotechnology
radiotécnico *m* radiotechnician
radiotelefonear *va* to radiotelephone
radiotelefonía *f* radiotelephony
radioteléfono *m* radiotelephone
radiotelegrafía *f* radiotelegraphy, wireless
radiotelegrafiar §90 *va* to radiotelegraph, to wireless
radiotelegrafista *mf* wireless operator
radiotelégrafo *m* radiotelegraph
radiotelescopio *m* radio telescope
radioterapia *f* radiotherapy
radiotermia *f* radiothermy
radiotorio *m* (chem.) radiothorium
radiotransmisión *f* radio transmission
radiotransmisor *m* radio transmitter
radiotrón *f* radiotron
radiovisión *f* radiovision, television
radioyente *mf* radio listener
radón *m* (chem.) radon
rádula *f* (zool.) radula
raedera *f* scraper (*tool*)
raedizo -za *adj* easily scraped or scratched
raedor -dora *adj* scraping; *mf* scraper; *m* strickle
raedura *f* scraping; **raeduras** *fpl* scrapings
raer §71 *va* to scrape, scrape off; to smooth, to level; to wipe out, to extirpate; *vr* to become worn, become frayed, wear away
rafa *f* (arch.) buttress; irrigation ditch; (vet.) crack in hoof; (min.) skewback (*cut in rock*)
Rafael *m* Raphael
rafaelesco -ca *adj* Raphaelesque
ráfaga *f* gust, puff; gust of wind; burst (*e.g., of machine-gun fire*); light cloud (*indicating a change in the weather*); flash of light; (rad.) jingle
rafania *f* (path.) raphania
rafe *m* (arch.) eaves; (anat. & bot.) raphe
rafear *va* to reinforce with buttresses
rafia *f* (bot.) raffia (*palm and fiber*)
Raf.[1] abr. of **Rafael**
raglán *m* raglan
ragua *f* top of sugar cane
rahez *adj* (*pl:* **-heces**) low, vile, contemptible
raiceja *f* rootlet
raicilla *f* (bot.) radicle; rootlet
raicita *f* (bot.) radicle
raído -da *adj* threadbare; barefaced
raigal *adj* (pertaining to a) root
raigambre *f* intertwined roots; (fig.) deep-rootedness
raigo *1st sg pres ind of* **raer**
raigón *m* large root; (anat.) root (*of tooth*); **raigón del Canadá** (bot.) Kentucky coffee tree
rail *m* (*pl:* **raíles**) rail (*of a track*)
raimiento *m* scraping; barefacedness, brazenness
Raimundo *m* Raymond
raíz *f* (*pl:* **-íces**) root; (bot., gram. & math.) root; **a raíz de** close to the root of; even with; right after, hard upon; **cortar de raíz** to nip in the bud; **de raíz** by the root; completely; **echar raíces** to take root; **raíz cuadrada** (math.) square root; **raíz cúbica** (math.) cube root; **raíz de remolacha** beet root
raja *f* crack, split; splinter, chip; slice; coarse cloth; **hacer rajas** to divide up; **hacerse rajas** (coll.) to break to pieces
rajá *m* (*pl:* **-jaes**) rajah
rajabroqueles *m* (*pl:* **-les**) (coll.) bully
rajadera *f* cleaver
rajadillo *m* sliced sugared almonds
rajadizo -za *adj* easily split
rajadura *f* crack, split
rajar *va* to split, to cleave; to crack; to slice; *vn* (coll.) to boast, to lie about one's feats; (coll.) to chatter, to jabber; *vr* to split, to cleave; to crack; (slang) to give up, to back down, to break one's promise
rajatabla; a rajatabla (coll.) at any cost, regardless; (Am.) promptly, vigorously
rajeta *f* varicolored light cloth
rajuela *f* small crack; rough stone
ralea *f* kind, quality; (coll.) breed, ilk; prey (*of birds of prey*)
ralear *vn* to become sparse, become thin; to yield thin bunches (*said of grapevines*); to show one's real make-up or nature, to be true to form
raleón -ona *adj* predatory, raptorial
raleza *f* sparsity, thinness
ralo -la *adj* sparse, thin; *m* (orn.) rail
ralladera *f* or **rallador** *m* (cook.) grater
ralladura *f* mark left by grater; gratings

rallar *va* to grate; (coll.) to grate on, annoy
rallo *m* grater; scraper; rasp; sprinkling nozzle (*of water pot*); unglazed porous jug (*for cooling water by evaporation*)
rallón *m* arrow with a cutting crosshead (*to be shot from a crossbow*)
rama *f* branch, bough; (fig.) branch (*e.g., of a family, of learning*); (print.) chase; **andarse por las ramas** (coll.) to beat about the bush; **en rama** crude, raw; in the grain; (b.b.) in sheets, unbound
ramada *f* foliage, branches; arbor; (Am.) covering, shed
Ramadán, el Ramadan
ramaje *m* foliage, branches
ramal *m* strand (*e.g., of a rope*); branch; (rail.) branch line; halter
ramalazo *m* lash; mark left by a lash; mark left by a blow in the face; mark or spot (*caused by disease or sickness*); sharp pain; blow, sudden sorrow
ramalear *vn* to be easily led by the halter
ramazón *f* cut branches, pile of branches
rambla *f* dry ravine; tenter, tentering machine; boulevard, avenue
ramblar *m* confluence of dry ravines
ramblazo or **ramblizo** *m* bed of a torrent
rameado -da *adj* branched, flowered (*design*)
rameal or **rámeo -a** *adj* ramal, rameal
ramera *f* whore, harlot
ramería *f* brothel; whoredom
ramial *m* ramie patch, ramie field
ramificación *f* ramification
ramificar **§86** *va & vr* to ramify
ramilla *f* sprig, twig; (fig.) small help, slight boost
ramillete *m* bouquet; (bot.) cluster; epergne, centerpiece; flower piece; pretty dish of sweets; collection; **ramillete de Constantinopla** (bot.) sweet william
ramilletero -ra *mf* maker or seller of bouquets; *m* flower vase; potted flower; *f* flower girl
ramina *f* ramie (*fiber*)
ramio *m* (bot.) ramie
ramito *m* small branch
ramiza *f* cut branches; work made of branches
ramnáceo -a *adj* (bot.) rhamnaceous
ramo *m* branch, limb; cluster, bouquet; string of onions; line (*of goods, business, etc.*); branch (*e.g., of a science*); touch, slight attack (*of a disease*); **ramo de olivo** olive branch
ramojo *m* brushwood, small wood, dead wood
ramón *m* browse; trimmed twigs; (bot.) hackberry; (*cap.*) *m* Raymond
ramonear *vn* to trim twigs; to browse
ramoneo *m* trimming twigs; trimming time; browsing
ramoso -sa *adj* ramous, branchy
rampa *f* ramp; cramp; (aer.) apron
rampante *adj* (her.) rampant
rampiñete *m* (arti.) vent drill or gimlet
ramplón -plona *adj* heavy, coarse (*said of shoes*); vulgar, common; *m* calk (*of horseshoe*)
ramplonería *f* coarseness; vulgarity
rampojo *m* grape stem (*with grapes removed*)
rampollo *m* (hort.) cutting
Ramsés *m* Rameses
ramulla *f* small branches cleaned from a tree; brushwood, small wood, dead wood
rana *f* (zool. & rail.) frog; **ranas** *fpl* (path.) ranula; **no ser rana** (coll.) to be adept, to be a past master; **rana arbórea** (zool.) tree frog; **rana de zarzal** (zool.) peeper; **rana marina** or **pescadora** (ichth.) angler; **rana toro** (zool.) bullfrog; **rana voladora** (zool.) flying frog
ranacuajo *m* var. of **renacuajo**
rancajada *f* uprooting
rancajo *m* splinter in the flesh
ranciar *va & vr* var. of **enranciar**
rancidez *f* or **ranciedad** *f* rankness, rancidity, staleness; oldness, antiquity
rancio -cia *adj* rank, rancid, stale; old (*wine*); old, ancient; (fig.) old, old-fashioned; *m* rancidness; rancid bacon; greasiness of cloth
rancioso -sa *adj* var. of **rancio**
rancheadero *m* settlement of huts
ranchear *va* (Am.) to sack, pillage; *vn & vr* to build huts, form a settlement
rancheo *m* (Am.) sacking, pillage
ranchería *f* settlement, hamlet
ranchero *m* messman; (Am.) rancher, ranchman
rancho *m* mess; messmates; camp; meeting, gathering; thatched hut; (Am.) ranch; (naut.) stock of provisions; **hacer rancho** (coll.) to make room; **hacer rancho aparte** (coll.) to go one's own way, to be a lone wolf; **rancho de Santa Bárbara** (naut.) rudder chamber
randa *f* lace trimming, netting; *m* (coll.) pickpocket
randado -da *adj* trimmed with lace
randera *f* lacemaker, lacewoman
Randolfo *m* Randolph
ranero *m* frogland, frog pond
rangífero *m* (zool.) reindeer
rango *m* rank; class, nature; (Am.) quality (*high social standing*); (Am.) pomp, splendor
rangua *f* socket, pivot bearing
Rangún *f* Rangoon
raní *f* (*pl:* **-níes**) ranee, rani
ranilla *f* frog (*of hoof*)
ránula *f* (path. & vet.) ranula
ranunculáceo -a *adj* (bot.) ranunculaceous
ranúnculo *m* (bot.) ranunculus, crowfoot; (bot.) field buttercup, blister plant
ranura *f* groove, slot; **a ranura y lengüeta** groove-and-tongue
ranurador -dora *adj* grooving; *f* grooving machine, slotting machine
ranurar *va* to groove, to slot
ranzón *m* ransom money
raña *f* thicket, copse; hook for catching octopuses and mollusks
raño *m* oyster rake; (ichth.) hogfish, scorpion fish
rapa *f* olive blossom
rapabarbas *m* (*pl:* **-bas**) (coll.) barber
rapabolsas *m* (*pl:* **-sas**) (coll.) pickpocket
rapaceja *f* lassie
rapacejo *m* laddie; flounce, edging
rapacería *f* rapacity; childishness, childish prank
rapacidad *f* rapacity
rapado *m* (Am.) shave, close haircut
rapador -dora *adj* scraping; *mf* scraper; *m* (coll.) barber
rapadura *f* shave, close haircut
rapagón *m* stripling, beardless young fellow
rapamiento *m* var. of **rapadura**
rapante *adj* thieving; (her.) rampant
rapapiés *m* (*pl:* **-piés**) snake, serpent (*kind of firecracker*)
rapapolvo *m* (coll.) dressing-down, sharp reprimand
rapar *va* to shave; to shave close, to crop; to scrape; (coll.) to snatch, filch; *vr* to shave; (Am.) to lead (*e.g., an easy life*)
rapavelas *m* (*pl:* **-las**) (slang) sexton, altar boy
rapaz (*pl:* **-paces**) *adj* thievish; rapacious; raptorial; *m* young boy, lad; **rapaces** *fpl* (zool.) Raptores
rapaza *f* young girl, lass
rapazada *f* childishness, childish prank
rapazuelo -la *mf* urchin, youngster
rape *m* (coll.) quick shave, quick haircut; (ichth.) angler; **al rape** cut very close
rapé *m* snuff (*tobacco*)
rapidez *f* rapidity
rápido -da *adj* rapid; *m* (rail.) express; **rápidos** *mpl* rapids (*in a river*)
rapiego -ga *adj* of prey (*said of a bird*)
rapingacho *m* (Am.) cheese omelet
rapiña *f* rapine; robbery, thievery
rapiñador -dora *adj* stealing, plundering; *mf* robber, plunderer
rapiñar *va* (coll.) to steal, to plunder
rapista *m* (coll.) barber
rapo *m* turnip (*root*)
rapónchigo *m* (bot.) rampion
rapóntico *m* var. of **ruipóntico**
raposa *f* (zool.) fox; female fox; (coll.) fox (*person*); **raposa de mar** (ichth.) thresher, thresher shark
raposear *vn* to be foxy, to be sly as a fox

raposeo *m* foxiness, cunning
raposera *f* fox hole, fox burrow
raposería *f* foxiness, cunning
raposino -na *adj* (pertaining to the) fox, foxy
raposo *m* male fox; (coll.) fox, foxy fellow; (coll.) easy-going, slipshod fellow; **raposo ferrero** (zool.) blue fox
raposuno -na *adj* var. of **raposino**
rapsoda *m* (hist.) rhapsodist
rapsodia *f* (mus. & lit.) rhapsody
rapsódico -ca *adj* rhapsodic or rhapsodical
rapsodista *m* (lit.) rhapsodist
raptar *va* to abduct; to kidnap
rapto *m* rapture; abduction; kidnaping; faint, swoon
raptor -tora *mf* kidnaper; *m* abductor, ravisher
rapuzar §76 *va* to trim, prune
raque *m* beachcombing; arrack (*liquor*); **andar** or **ir al raque** to go beachcombing
raquear *vn* to beachcomb
Raquel *f* Rachel
raqueo *m* beachcombing
raqueril *adj* beachcombing
raquero -ra *adj* piratical; *m* pirate; beachcomber; dock rat
raqueta *f* (sport) racket; (sport) battledore; (sport) battledore and shuttlecock, badminton; racket, snowshoe; rake (*of croupier*); (bot.) wall rocket
raquetazo *m* stroke (*with a racket*)
raquetero -ra *mf* racket maker or seller
raquetón *m* (sport) crosse (*racket used in lacrosse*)
raquialgia *f* (path.) rachialgia
raquídeo -a *adj* rachidian
raquis *m* (*pl:* **-quis**) (anat. & bot.) rachis
raquítico *adj* (path.) rachitic, rickety; rickety, flimsy, weak, miserable
raquitis *f* (path.) rachitis, rickets
raquitismo *m* (path.) rickets
raquitomía *f* (surg.) rachitomy
raquítomo *m* (surg.) rachitome
rara *f* see **raro**
raramente *adv* rarely, seldom; oddly, strangely
rarefacción *f* rarefaction
rarefacer §55 (has no compound tenses) *va & vr* to rarefy
rarefacto -ta *adj* rarefied, thin
rareza *f* rarity; rareness; queerness, funniness, oddness, strangeness; curiosity; peculiarity
raridad *f* rarity; (phys.) rarity, thinness, tenuity
rarificar §86 *va & vr* to rarefy
raro -ra *adj* rare; odd, strange; thin, sparse; *f* (orn.) South American passerine (*Phytotoma rara*)
ras *m* evenness; **a ras** close, even, flush; **a ras de** even with, flush with; **ras con ras** or **ras en ras** flush, on a level; grazing
rasa *f* see **raso**
rasadura *f* leveling with a strickle
rasamente *adv* clearly, openly
rasante *adj* grazing; flush; *f* grade line
rasar *va* to strickle, to smooth off with a strickle; to graze, to skim; *vr* to clear up
rascacielos *m* (*pl:* **-los**) skyscraper
rascacio *m* (ichth.) scorpene
rascadera *f* scraper; (coll.) currycomb
rascador *m* scraper; rasp; huller, sheller; ornamental hairpin
rascadora *f* street sweeper
rascadura *f* scraping; scratching, scratch
rascalino *m* (bot.) dodder
rascamiento *m* var. of **rascadura**
rascamoño *m* ornamental hairpin; (bot.) zinnia
rascapiés *m* (*pl:* **-piés**) scraper, foot scraper
rascar §86 *va* to scrape; to scuff; to scratch; to scrape clean; **llevar** or **tener con que rascar** (coll.) to be sorely hurt; *vn* (Am.) to itch; *vr* to pick (*a sore*); (Am.) to get drunk
rascatripas *mf* (*pl:* **-pas**) (coll.) scraper (*fiddler*)
rascazón *f* itch, itching
rascle *m* coral-fishing gear
rascón -cona *adj* sharp, acrid; *m* (orn.) rail; **rascón de agua** (orn.) crake
rascuñar *va* var. of **rasguñar**
rascuño *m* var. of **rasguño**
rasera *f* strike, strickle; (carp.) small plane; (cook.) spatula, turner
rasero *m* strike, strickle; **medir por un rasero** to treat with strict impartiality
rasete *m* satinet
rasgado -da *adj* wide-open, bright (*window*); wide-open (*mouth*); large (*eyes*); (Am.) outspoken; (Am.) generous; *m* tear, rip, rent
rasgador -dora *adj* tearing, ripping
rasgadura *f* tearing, tear, rip
rasgar §59 *va* to tear; to rip; *vr* to become torn
rasgo *m* flourish, stroke (*of pen*); trait, characteristic; feat, deed; flash of wit, bright remark; **rasgos** *mpl* features; **a grandes rasgos** in bold strokes
rasgón *m* tear, rip, rent
rasgueado *m* var. of **rasgueo**
rasguear *va* to thrum, to twang (*e.g., a guitar*); *vn* to make flourishes (*with a pen*)
rasgueo *m* thrumming, twanging (*e.g., on a guitar*)
rasguñar *va* to scratch; to sketch, outline
rasguño *m* scratch; sketch, outline
rasguñuelo *m* slight scratch
rasilla *f* camleteen; floor tile
rasión *f* shaving; grating
raso -sa *adj* smooth, flat, level, even; clear, cloudless; common, plain (*e.g., soldier*); backless (*chair*); skimming the ground; (coll.) brazen, shameless; *m* flat country; satin; **al raso** in the open air, in the open country; *f* thinness, thin spot (*in a fabric*); tableland; satin
rasoliso *m* satin
raspa *f* beard (*of ear of corn*); stalk, stem (*e.g., of a bunch of grapes*); spine, backbone (*of a fish*); cob (*with kernels removed*); shell, rind; hair or thread (*caught on tip of a pen*)
raspador *m* scraper
raspadora *f* street sweeper
raspadura *f* scraping; erasure; (Am.) pan sugar; **raspaduras** *fpl* scrapings
raspaje *m* (surg.) scraping
raspajo *m* grape stem (*with grapes removed*)
raspamiento *m* scraping
raspante *adj* abrasive; sharp (*wine*)
raspar *va* to scrape, scrape off; to scratch, scratch out; to graze; to bite (*said, e.g., of wine*); to take away, steal
raspear *vn* to scratch (*said of a pen*)
raspilla *f* (bot.) madwort, German madwort
raspón *m* (Am.) scratch, bruise; (Am.) scolding; (Am. coll.) involvement, complicity; (Am.) peasant's straw hat; **de raspón** askance
rasposo -sa *adj* rough; (Am.) stingy
rasqueta *f* scraper, wall scraper, shave hook; (Am.) currycomb
rasquetear *va* (Am.) to currycomb
rastacueril *adj* upstart
rastel *m* railing
rastillador -dora *mf* var. of **rastrillador**
rastillar *va* var. of **rastrillar**
rastra *f* rake; harrow; drag (*sledge for conveying heavy bodies*); string of dried fruit, string of onions; something trailing; track, trail; outcome entailing a penalty; shadow (*inseparable companion*); (naut.) drag, grapnel; **a rastra, a rastras** or **a la rastra** dragging; unwillingly; **caminar a rastras** to crawl; **llevar a rastra** to drag, to drag along; **pescar a la rastra** to trawl
rastracueros *m* (*pl:* **-ros**) big hide operator; upstart; boaster, show-off; sharper, adventurer
rastrallar *vn* var. of **restallar**
rastreador -dora *adj* tracking; *m* dredge; (nav.) mine sweeper
rastrear *va* to trail, to track, to trace; to scent; to drag; to dredge; to check into; to sell (*meat*) at the wholesale market; (nav.) to sweep (*e.g., a harbor for mines*); *vn* to rake; to skim the ground, to fly low
rastrel *m* var. of **ristrel**
rastreo *m* dragging, dredging; tracking (*e.g., of a satellite*)
rastrero -ra *adj* dragging, trailing; low-flying; low-hanging; abject, groveling, cringing; base, low; (bot.) creeping; *m* slaughterhouse employee; *f* (naut.) lower studding sail
rastrillada *f* rakeful; (Am.) track, footprint
rastrillador -dora *mf* raker; *f* rake (*on wheels*)
rastrillaje *m* raking

rastrillar *va* to rake; to hatchel, to comb (*flax, hemp, etc.*)
rastrillo *m* rake; hatchel, hackle, flax comb; battery (*of flintlock*); ward (*of key or lock*); rack (*of manger*); grating, iron gate; (fort.) portcullis; (rail.) cowcatcher
rastro *m* rake; harrow; trace, vestige; track, trail; scent; slaughterhouse; wholesale meat market; **el Rastro** the rag fair (*of Madrid*); **rastro de condensación** (aer.) contrail, vapor trail
rastrojal *m* stubble field
rastrojar *va* (agr.) to stubble, to clear of stubble
rastrojera *f* stubble field; stubble pasture; stubble-pasturing time or season
rastrojo *m* (agr.) stubble
rasura *f* shaving; scraping; **rasuras** *fpl* argol, crude tartar
rasuración *f* shaving; scraping
rasurar *va & vr* to shave
rata *f* (zool.) rat; female rat; female mouse; **rata blanca** (zool.) white rat; **rata de agua** (zool.) water rat; **rata de alcantarilla** (zool.) brown rat; **rata de campo** (zool.) meadow rat; **rata del trigo** (zool.) hamster; **rata de monte** or **rata silvestre** (zool.) vesper mouse; *m* (coll.) sneak thief
ratafía *f* ratafia or ratafee
ratania *f* (bot.) rhatany (*plant and root*)
rataplán *m* rub-a-dub
rata por cantidad *adv* pro rata
ratear *va* to decrease proportionately; to apportion, to distribute proportionately; to filch, to snitch; *vn* to crawl, to creep
ratel *m* (zool.) ratel
rateo *m* apportionment
rateramente *adv* basely, vilely
ratería *f* baseness, vileness, meanness; petty theft; petty thievery
ratero -ra *adj* thievish; dragging, trailing; low-flying; base, vile; *mf* sneak thief, pickpocket
ratificación *f* ratification
ratificar §86 *va* to ratify
ratigar §59 *va* to fasten the load in (*a cart*) with a rope
rátigo *m* cartload
ratina *f* ratiné (*fabric*)
Ratisbona *f* Ratisbon
rato *m* short time, short while, little while; nice time; long time; male rat; **a ratos** from time to time; **a ratos perdidos** in spare time, in one's leisure hours; **buen rato** pleasant time; (coll.) large amount; **de rato en rato** from time to time; **largo rato** a long time, a long while; **pasar el rato** (coll.) to waste one's time; **pasar un mal rato** to have a wretched time; **un rato** awhile
ratón *m* (zool.) mouse; (naut.) rock that rubs and cuts cables; **el ratón Miguelito** Mickey Mouse; **ratón almizclero** (zool.) muskrat; **ratón casero** (zool.) house mouse; **ratón de archivo** or **ratón de biblioteca** (coll.) bookworm (*person*); **ratón de campo** (zool.) field mouse
ratona *f* female mouse
ratonar *va* to eat (*e.g., cheese, bread*) full of holes (*said of a mouse*); *vr* to get sick from eating mice (*said of a cat*)
ratonero -ra *adj* (pertaining to a) mouse, mousy; *f* mousetrap; mousehole; nest of mice; **caer en la ratonera** (fig.) to fall into the trap
ratonesco -ca or **ratonil** *adj* (pertaining to a) mouse, mousy
rauco -ca *adj* (poet.) raucous, harsh, rough
raudal *m* stream, torrent; sudden abundance, plenty
raudo -da *adj* rapid, swift, impetuous; (poet.) whistling (*wind*)
ravenala *f* (bot.) traveler's tree
ravioles *mpl* var. of **rabioles**
raya *f* stripe; ray (*fine line*); stroke; dash (*in printing, writing, and telegraphy*); crease (*of trousers*); part (*in hair*); boundary line, limit; firebreak; mark, score; (arti.) rifle groove, spiral groove; (ichth.) ray; (phys.) line (*of spectrum*); **a rayas** striped; **doble raya vertical** (print.) parallels; **hacerse la raya** to part one's hair; **pasar de la raya** or **de raya** (fig.) to go too far; **tener a raya** to keep within bounds; **tres en raya** see **juego del tres en raya; raya espinosa** (ichth.) thornback; **rayas de Fraunhofer** (phys.) Fraunhofer lines
rayadillo *m* striped cotton duck
rayado -da *adj* striped; *m* ruling (*of paper*); rifling
rayador *m* (orn.) skimmer; (Am.) umpire; (Am.) storekeeper of company store
rayano -na *adj* bordering; borderline
rayar *va* to rule, to line (*paper*); to stripe; to scratch, score, mark; to cross out; to underscore; to rifle; *vn* to border; to stand out; to begin, arise, come forth (*said of the dawn, day, sun, light*); **rayar con** to border on; to be equal to, to match; **rayar en** to border on
rayo *m* ray, beam; lightning, flash of lightning; thunderbolt; spoke (*of wheel*); (fig.) thunderbolt, stroke of lightning; (fig.) wit (*person*); (fig.) live wire (*person*); (slang) eye; **echar rayos** (coll.) to blow up, hit the ceiling; **rayo lunar** moonbeam; **rayos alfa** (phys.) alpha rays; **rayos beta** (phys.) beta rays; **rayos canales** (phys.) canal rays; **rayos catódicos** (phys.) cathode rays; **rayos cósmicos** (phys.) cosmic rays; **rayos gama** (phys.) gamma rays; **rayos infrarrojos** (phys.) infrared rays; **rayo solar** or **rayo de sol** sunbeam; **rayos ultravioletas** (phys.) ultraviolet rays; **rayos X** X rays; **rayos y truenos** thunder and lightning; **rayo textorio** weaver's shuttle; **rayo violeta** violet ray; *1st sg pres ind of* **raer**
rayón *m* rayon
rayoso -sa *adj* striped
rayuela *f* pitching pennies
rayuelo *m* (orn.) snipe
raza *f* race; breed, strain; quality; crack, slit; ray of light (*coming through a crack*); light stripe (*in a fabric*); cleft in horse's hoof; **de raza** thoroughbred; **raza amarilla** yellow race; **raza blanca** white race; **raza cobriza** brown race; **raza negra** black race; **raza roja** red race
razado -da *adj* woven with light stripes
rázago *m* burlap, sackcloth
razón *f* reason; right, justice; account, story; rate (*quantity measured in proportion to something else*); (math.) ratio; **a razón de** at the rate of; **con razón o sin ella** right or wrong; rightly or wrongly; **dar la razón a** to agree with, to approve; **dar razón** to give information; **dar razón de** to give an account of; **en razón a** or **de** with regard to; **hacer la razón** to answer or return a toast; to join at table; **meter en razón** to bring to reason; **meterse en razón** to listen to reason; **no tener razón** to be wrong; **perder la razón** to lose one's reason, go out of one's mind; to hurt one's cause; **tener razón** to be right; **tomar razón de** to enter in the ledger, to record; **razón de estado** reason of state; **razón de masas** mass ratio; **razón de pie de banco** silly reason; **razón de ser** raison d'être; **razón directa** (math.) direct ratio; **razón geométrica** geometric ratio; **razón inversa** (math.) inverse ratio; **razón social** firm, firm name, trade name
razonable *adj* reasonable; fair, fair-sized
razonablejo -ja *adj* (coll.) reasonable, fair, moderate
razonado -da *adj* reasoned, reasoned out; itemized
razonador -dora *adj* reasoning; *mf* reasoner
razonamiento *m* reasoning
razonar *va* to reason, reason out; to itemize; *vn* to reason
razzia *f* razzia
R.bí abr. of **recibí**
R.D. abr. of **Real Decreto**
Rda. M. abr. of **Reverenda Madre**
Rdo. P. abr. of **Reverendo Padre**
R.e abr. of **récipe**
re- *prefix* (coll.) very, extremely, e.g., **rebién** very well; **redifícil** very difficult
rea *f* & **Rea** *f* see **reo**
reabierto -ta *pp of* **reabrir**
reabrir §17, 9 *va & vr* to reopen

reacción *f* reaction; (rad.) regeneration; **reacción en cadena** (phys.) chain reaction; **reacción reversible** (chem.) reversible reaction
reaccionar *vn* to react
reaccionario -ria *adj & mf* reactionary
reacio -cia *adj* obstinate, stubborn, fractious
reacomodo *m* readjustment
reacondicionamiento *m* reconditioning, overhauling
reacondicionar *va* to recondition, to overhaul
reactancia *f* (elec.) reactance
reactivación *f* reactivation
reactivar *va* to reactivate
reactivo -va *adj* reactive; *m* (chem.) reagent
reactor *m* (elec. & phys.) reactor; **reactor atómico** (phys.) atomic reactor; **reactor de cría** (phys.) breeder reactor; **reactor generador de energía** (phys.) power reactor; **reactor nuclear** (phys.) nuclear reactor
reactor-generador *m* (phys.) breeder reactor
reactualizar §76 *va* to revive, to revitalize
readaptar *va* to readapt
readmitir *va* to readmit
reafilar *va* to resharpen, to regrind
reafirmación *f* reaffirmation
reafirmar *va* to reaffirm
reagravación *f* renewed worsening, worsening anew
reagravar *va* to make worse again; *vr* to get worse again
reagrupar *va & vr* to regroup
reagudo -da *adj* very sharp, keen, acute
reajuste *m* readjustment
real *adj* real; royal; fine, beautiful, handsome, splendid, first-class; royalist; *m* king's tent, general's tent (*in the field*); camp, army camp; fairground; real (*old Spanish coin; Spanish money of account equal to a quarter of a peseta*); **alzar el real** or **los reales** to break camp; **asentar los reales** to encamp; **sentar el real** or **los reales** to settle; to become entrenched
reala *f* var. of **rehala**
realce *m* embossment, raised work, relief; enhancement, lustre, splendor; emphasis; (paint.) high light; **bordar de realce** to embroider in relief; (fig.) to embroider, to exaggerate
realegrar *vr* to be overjoyed
realejo *m* hand organ
realengo -ga *adj* (feud.) royal; unappropriated (*land*)
realera *f* queen cell
realeza *f* royalty
realidad *f* reality; truth, sincerity; **en realidad** actually, in reality; **en realidad de verdad** truly, in truth; **hecho realidad** come true, e.g., **un sueño hecho realidad** a dream come true
realimentación *f* (elec.) feedback
realismo *m* realism; royalism
realista *adj* realistic; royalistic; (coll.) realistic (*practical*); *mf* realist; royalist; (coll.) realist (*practical person*)
realizable *adj* realizable, attainable; salable
realización *f* fulfillment, realization; accomplishment, achievement; production; sale, sellout
realizador *m* (mov.) producer
realizar §76 *va* to fulfill; to carry out, accomplish; to sell, sell out; *vn* to realize (*to sell property for ready money*); *vr* to become fulfilled; to be carried out
realquilar *va & vn* to sublet
realzar §76 *va* to raise, elevate; to emboss; to heighten, set off, enhance; to emphasize; (paint.) to make stand out, to brighten up
reamar *va* to love dearly
reanimar *va* to reanimate, revive, restore; *vr* to reanimate, revive, recover one's spirits
reanudación *f* renewal, resumption
reanudar *va* to renew, to resume; *vr* to be or become renewed or resumed
reaparecer §34 *vn* to reappear
reaparición *f* reappearance
reapertura *f* reopening
reapretar §18 *va* to press or squeeze again; to press hard, to squeeze hard
reaprovisionar *va* to resupply, to replenish
rearar *va* to plow over, plow again
rearmamento *m* var. of **rearme**
rearmar *va & vr* to rearm
rearme *m* rearmament
reasegurar *va* to reinsure
reaseguro *m* reinsurance
reasentamiento *m* resettlement
reasentar §18 *va* to resettle
reasumir *va* to reassume, to resume
reasunción *f* reassumption, resumption
reata *f* rope or strap used to keep animals in single file; single file; front mule; (naut.) woolding; (Am.) rope, lasso; **de reata** in single file; (coll.) in blind submission; (coll.) right away
reatadura *f* tying again; tying tight; tying in single file
reatar *va* to tie again, to rebind; to reattach; to tie tight; to tie in single file
reato *m* (theol.) remaining sin (*after pardon*)
reaventar §18 *va* to winnow again
reavituallar *va & vr* to revictual
reavivar *va* to revive
rebaba *f* burr, fin, rough seam, rough edge; flange, border
rebabar *vr* to ooze out
rebaja *f* rebate; lowering; diminution
rebajado *m* soldier on inactive service
rebajador *m* rabbeting plane; (phot.) bath used to tone down contrasts; **rebajador de rayos** spokeshave
rebajamiento *m* lowering; diminution, reduction; deduction; deflation (*of a person's opinion of himself*)
rebajar *va* to lower; to diminish, reduce; to underbid; to rebate, discount; to deflate (*a person; a person's pride*); (paint.) to tone down; (arch.) to depress (*an arch*); (carp.) to rabbet; (carp.) to scarf, shave down; *vr* to stoop; to humble oneself; to become deflated; to be relieved of military service; (paint.) to become toned down; **rebajarse a** + *inf* to stoop to + *inf*, to condescend to + *inf*
rebajo *m* rabbet, groove; offset, recess
rebalaje *m* stream, current
rebalsa *f* pool, puddle; (path.) stagnated humor
rebalsar *va* to dam, dam back; *vn* to become dammed; *vr* to become dammed; to be held up, become checked; to pile up, accumulate
rebalse *m* damming; stagnation
rebanada *f* slice
rebanador -dora *adj* slicing; *mf* slicer; *f* slicing machine
rebanar *va* to slice; to slice off; to cut (*something*) through
rebanco *m* (arch.) upper socle
rebanear *va* (coll.) to slice
rebañadera *f* grapnel
rebañadura *f* var. of **arrebañadura**
rebañar *va* to gather up; to eat up
rebañego -ga *adj* gregarious, herd
rebaño *m* flock; (fig.) flock
rebañuelo *m* small flock
rebarbativo -va *adj* surly, crabbed, forbidding
rebasadero *m* place for passing; (naut.) safe place for passing
rebasar *va* to exceed, go beyond; to overflow; (naut.) to sail past; *vn* (Am.) to escape, avoid danger; **rebasar de** (naut.) to sail past, sail beyond
rebate *m* fight, encounter
rebatible *adj* refutable; vulnerable
rebatimiento *m* beating; repulsion; resistance; rebuttal, refutation; rebate
rebatiña *f* grabbing, scramble; **andar a la rebatiña** (coll.) to scramble
rebatir *va* to beat again, beat hard; to repel, drive back; to check; to resist; to strengthen, reinforce; to rebut, refute; to rebate, deduct; to parry (*in fencing*)
rebato *m* alarm, call to arms; (fig.) alarm, excitement; (mil.) surprise attack
rebautizar §76 *va* to rebaptize; (coll.) to rebaptize (*to give a new name to*)
Rebeca *f* Rebecca; (*l.c.*) *f* cardigan
rebeco *m* (zool.) chamois
rebelar *vr* to revolt, rebel; to resist; to break away
rebelde *adj* rebellious; stubborn; *m* rebel; (law) defaulter

rebeldía *f* rebelliousness; defiance, stubbornness; (law) default
rebelión *f* rebellion, revolt
rebelón -lona *adj* balky, restive
rebellín *m* var. of **revellín**
rebencazo *m* lash, blow with a whip
rebenque *m* whip (*for flogging galley slaves*); (naut.) ratline; (Am.) riding whip
rebién *adv* (coll.) very well
rebina *f* (agr.) third earthing-up
rebinar *va* (agr.) to earth up for the third time; *vn* (prov.) to meditate
rebisabuela *f* great-great-grandmother
rebisabuelo *m* great-great-grandfather
rebisnieta *f* great-great-granddaughter
rebisnieto *m* great-great-grandson
reblandecer **§34** *va & vr* to soften
reblandecimiento *m* softening; **reblandecimiento cerebral** (path.) softening of the brain
rebobinar *va* to rewind
rebocillo or **rebociño** *m* mantilla; shawl
rebollar *m* or **rebolledo** *m* growth of Turkey oaks
rebollidura *f* flaw in the bore of a gun
rebollo *m* (bot.) Turkey oak; (dial.) tree trunk
rebolludo -da *adj* thick-set; shapeless, irregular
rebombar *vn* to resound
reboño *m* mud stopped up in tailrace
reborde *m* flange, rim, collar
rebosadero *m* overflow, overflow pipe; spillway
rebosadura *f* or **rebosamiento** *m* overflow, overflowing
rebosante *adj* overflowing
rebosar *va* to overflow with, burst with (*e.g., joy*); to cause to overflow; *vn* to overflow, run over; to abound, be in abundance; **rebosar de** or **en** to overflow with, burst with (*e.g., joy*); to be rich in (*e.g., oil*); to have an abundance of (*e.g., money*); *vr* to overflow, run over
rebotación *f* (coll.) annoyance, worry, perturbation
rebotadera *f* nap-raising comb
rebotadura *f* bouncing; rebounding
rebotar *va* to bend (*the end or point of something*) back or over; to repel; to teasel; to change or alter in color or quality; (coll.) to annoy, worry, upset; *vn* to bounce; to bounce back, to rebound; *vr* to change in color or quality; to become annoyed, worried, upset
rebote *m* bounce; rebound; bump (*of airplane in rough weather*); **de rebote** indirectly
rebotica *f* back room (*of a drugstore; of any store*)
rebotín *m* second growth of mulberry leaves
rebozar **§76** *va* to muffle up (*one's face*); to cover with batter; to disguise (*bad news; evil intentions*); *vr* to muffle up, muffle oneself up
rebozo *m* muffling; muffler; shawl; disguise; **de rebozo** secretly, hiddenly; **sin rebozo** openly, frankly
rebramar *vn* to bellow again, to bellow loudly; to bellow back, answer with a bellow
rebramo *m* answering bellow
rebrotar *vn* to sprout, to shoot
rebrote *m* sprout, shoot, sucker
rebudiar *vn* (hunt.) to grunt (*as a wild boar at bay*)
rebudio *m* grunt (*of a wild boar*)
rebufar *vn* to snort again, to snort loudly
rebufe *m* snort, snorting
rebufo *m* expansion of air around muzzle of a gun
rebujado -da *adj* jumbled, entangled
rebujal *m* cattle in excess of fifty or a multiple of fifty; poor piece of land
rebujar *va* to jumble together; (naut.) to countersink; *vr* to wrap oneself all up
rebujina or **rebujiña** *f* (coll.) bustle, scuffle, mob
rebujo *m* woman's heavy veil or muffler (*for disguise*); clumsy bundle or package
rebultado -da *adj* bulky, massive
rebullicio *m* great bustle, loud uproar
rebullir **§26** *vn* to stir, begin to move; to give signs of life; *vr* to stir, begin to move
rebumbar *vn* to whistle, to whistle by (*said of a cannon ball*)
rebumbio *m* (coll.) noise, uproar
reburujar *va* (coll.) to wrap up in a bundle
reburujón *m* clumsy bundle or package
rebusca *f* searching, careful search; gleaning; leavings, refuse
rebuscado -da *adj* affected, unnatural, recherché
rebuscador -dora *adj* searching; gleaning; *mf* searcher; gleaner; dealer in gleanings
rebuscamiento *m* searching, careful searching; excessive elegance, affectation (*in language, bearing, etc.*)
rebuscar **§86** *va* to search into; to seek after; to glean
rebusco *m* var. of **rebusca**
rebutir *va* to stuff, to pack; to insert
rebuznador -dora *adj* braying
rebuznar *vn* to bray; (coll.) to talk nonsense
rebuzno *m* braying; (coll.) nonsense
recabar *va* to succeed in getting
recadero -ra or **recadista** *mf* messenger; *m* errand boy, deliveryman; *f* errand girl, delivery woman
recado *m* message; errand; gift, present; daily marketing; compliments, regards; safety, security, precaution; equipment, outfit; **a recado** or **a buen recado** in safety; **dar recados** to send regards; **enviar a un recado** to send on an errand; **mandar recado** to send word; **recado de escribir** writing materials
recaer **§28** *vn* to fall again, fall back; to relapse; to backslide; **recaer en** to come to, to fall to (*said, e.g., of an inheritance, an election*); **recaer sobre** to fall upon, devolve upon
recaída *f* relapse; backsliding
recaigo *1st sg pres ind of* **recaer**
recalada *f* (naut.) landfall (*sighting land*); (aer.) homing
recalar *va* to soak, saturate; *vn* (naut.) to sight land
recalcada *f* (naut.) listing, heeling
recalcadamente *adv* close, tight
recalcadura *f* packing, cramming, stuffing
recalcar **§86** *va* to press down, to squeeze; to pack, cram, stuff; to stress (*one's words*); *vn* (naut.) to list, to heel; **recalcar en** to stress, lay stress on; *vr* (coll.) to harp on the same string; (coll.) to sprawl; (coll.) to sprain (*e.g., one's wrist*)
recalce *m* hilling; extra felloe used instead of iron tire; underpinning
recalcitrante *adj* recalcitrant
recalcitrar *vn* to wince, back up; to balk, resist
recalentador -dora *adj* superheating; *m* superheater; **recalentador de vapor** superheater
recalentamiento *m* reheating; overheating; superheating
recalentar **§18** *va* to reheat, to warm over; to overheat; to superheat; to excite sexually; *vr* to overheat; to become spoiled by the heat (*said of fruit*)
recalescencia *f* (metal.) recalescence
recalmón *m* (naut.) lull (*in wind or sea*)
recalvastro -tra *adj* (coll.) baldpate, baldpated
recalzar **§76** *va* to hill (*plants*); to underpin, reinforce; to color (*a drawing or sketch*)
recalzo *m* extra felloe used instead of iron tire; underpinning
recalzón *m* extra felloe used instead of iron tire
recamado *m* raised embroidery
recamador -dora *mf* embroiderer
recamar *va* to embroider in relief
recámara *f* dressing room, wardrobe; equipage, stock of furnishings (*of house of a wealthy person*); chamber, breech (*of a gun*); (min.) blast hole; (coll.) reserve, caution; (Am.) bedroom; (Am.) bedroom furniture
recamarera *f* (Am.) maid, chambermaid
recambiar *va* to exchange again; (com.) to redraw
recambio *m* re-exchange; (com.) re-exchange, redraft; **de recambio** spare (*part, wheel, etc.*)
recamo *m* raised embroidery; frog (*button and loop on garments*)
recancamusa *f* (coll.) ruse, artifice, fraud

recancanilla *f* (coll.) hippety-hop, feigned limping of a child; (coll.) emphasis, stress; (coll.) subterfuge, evasion
recantación *f* recantation
recantar *va* to sing again; *vr* to recant
recantón *m* spurstone, checkstone
recapacitar *va* to run over in one's mind; *vn* to refresh one's memory; to think things over; **recapacitar sobre** to run over in one's mind
recapitalización *f* recapitalization
recapitalizar §76 *va* to recapitalize
recapitulación *f* recapitulation
recapitular *va & vn* to recapitulate
recarga *f* new charge, new tax; (elec.) recharge (*of battery*)
recargado -da *adj* overdone, overwrought
recargar §59 *va* to reload; to overload; to recharge; to overcharge; to resurface (*a road*); to increase (*e.g., tax rate*); to overadorn; (elec.) to recharge; (ins.) to load (*a premium*); *vr* (med.) to have a higher fever
recargo *m* new burden, increased burden; extra charge, new charge; increase (*e.g., of taxes*); penalty (*for late payment of taxes*); (med.) increased fever; **recargo al premio** (ins.) loading, margin
recata *f* retasting
recatado -da *adj* cautious, circumspect; modest, decent
recatar *va* to hide, conceal; to taste again; *vr* to hide; to be reserved, be afraid to take a stand; **recatarse de** + *inf* to be cautious about + *ger*
recatear *va* to haggle over; to sell at retail; (coll.) to avoid, to evade; *vn* to haggle
recatería *f* var. of **regatonería**
recato *m* reserve, caution; modesty, decency
recatón -tona *adj, mf & m* var. of **regatón**
recatonazo *m* blow with the tip of a lance
recatonear *va* var. of **regatonear**
recatonería *f* var. of **regatonería**
recauchaje *m* retreading (*of a tire*)
recauchar *va* to retread, to recap (*a tire*)
recauchutaje *m* var. of **recauchaje**
recauchutar *va* var. of **recauchar**
recaudación *f* tax collecting; sum collected; tax collector's office
recaudador -dora *adj* tax-collecting; *mf* collector, tax collector
recaudamiento *m* tax collecting; job of collector or tax collector; tax collector's district
recaudar *va* to gather, collect (*e.g., taxes*); to hold, guard, watch over
recaudo *m* tax collecting; care, precaution; bail, surety; **a recaudo** or **a buen recaudo** in safety, under guard
recavar *va* to dig again
recazo *m* guard (*of sword*); back (*of knife*)
recebar *va* to gravel, spread gravel over
recebo *m* gravel; liquid added to fill a cask or barrel
recechar *va* var. of **acechar**
rececho *m* var. of **acecho**
recejar *vn* to back up
recelamiento *m* var. of **recelo**
recelar *va* to fear, distrust; to get (*a mare*) in heat; *vn & vr* to fear, be afraid; **recelar de** or **recelarse de** to fear, be afraid of, distrust; **recelarse** + *inf* to be afraid of + *ger*
recelo *m* fear, distrust
receloso -sa *adj* fearful, distrustful
recensión *f* recension; review, book review
recentadura *f* leaven, leavening
recental *adj* sucking (*calf or lamb*)
recentar §18 *va* to leaven (*dough*); *vr* to become renewed
recentín *adj* var. of **recental**
recentísimo -ma *adj super* very or most recent
receñir §74 *va* to regird; to reëncircle; to fasten or tie again
recepción *f* reception; receipt; admission; (law) examination of witnesses; **recepción heterodina** (rad.) heterodyne reception; **recepción por batido** (rad.) beat reception
receptáculo *m* receptacle; shelter, refuge; (bot. & elec.) receptacle
receptador -dora *mf* receptor (*of a fugitive from justice*); receiver (*of stolen goods*)
receptar *va* to receive, welcome; to hide, conceal (*a fugitive from justice*); to hide, conceal, receive (*stolen goods*)
receptividad *f* receptivity; susceptibility (*to disease*)
receptivo -va *adj* receptive; susceptible (*to disease*)
recepto *m* shelter, place of refuge
receptor -tora *adj* receiving; *m* receiver; (telg., telp. & rad.) receiver, receiving set; (law & physiol.) receiver; **receptor de cabeza** headphone; **receptor de toda onda** (rad.) all-wave receiver; **receptor telefónico** (telp.) receiver (*part of phone held to ear*)
receptoría *f* receiver's office; (law) receivership
recercar §86 *va* to fence in, to fence in again; to reëncircle
recésit *m* rest from choir duty
recesivo -va *adj* (biol.) recessive
receso *m* separation, withdrawal; (Am.) recess (*of a legislative body*)
receta *f* recipe; (pharm.) prescription; (com.) order memo; (com.) amount carried forward
recetador *m* (pharm.) prescriptionist
recetar *va & vn* (pharm.) to prescribe; (coll.) to request, beg
recetario *m* prescription book or record; druggist's file; pharmacopoeia; recipe book
recetor *m* public treasurer; (law) receiver
recetoría *f* public treasury
Recia, la see **recio**
recial *m* rapids (*in a river*)
reciario *m* (hist.) retiarius
recibí *m* receipt; received payment
recibidero -ra *adj* receivable
recibidor -dora *adj* receiving; *mf* receiver; receiving teller; ticket collector; *m* anteroom; at-home
recibimiento *m* reception; welcome; anteroom; reception room; hall; parlor, salon; at-home
recibir *va* to receive; to welcome, to go to meet; *vn* to receive, entertain; (rad.) to receive; *vr* to be received, be admitted; **recibirse de** to graduate as, to be admitted to practice as
recibo *m* reception; receipt; anteroom; hall; parlor, salon; at-home; **acusar recibo de** to acknowledge receipt of; **estar de recibo** to be at home (*to callers*); **ser de recibo** to be acceptable
recidiva *f* relapse
recidivismo *m* recidivism
recidivista *mf* recidivist
reciedumbre *f* strength, vigor, endurance
recién *adv* (to be used only before past participles) recently, just, newly, e.g., **recién llegado** newly arrived; (Am.) recently, just now, a little while ago; (Am.) only then; *conj* (Am.) as soon as
reciente *adj* recent
recientemente *adv* recently
recinto *m* area, enclosure, place; (fort.) enceinte
recio -cia *adj* strong, robust; thick, coarse, heavy; harsh, rude; hard, bitter, arduous; severe (*weather*); swift, impetuous; **la Recia** Rhaetia; **recio** *adv* strongly; swiftly; hard; loud
récipe *m* (coll.) prescription; (coll.) scolding, dressing-down
recipiendario *m* newly inducted member
recipiente *adj* receiving, recipient; *m* recipient, vessel, container; receiver or bell glass (*of an air pump*)
recíproca *f* see **recíproco**
reciprocación *f* reciprocation
reciprocar §86 *va & vr* to reciprocate, to match
reciprocidad *f* reciprocity; (com.) reciprocity (*between two countries*)
recíproco -ca *adj* reciprocal; (gram.) reciprocal; *m* (gram.) reciprocal verb; *f* (math.) reciprocal
recitación *f* recitation
recitado *m* (mus.) recitative
recitador -dora *mf* reciter, elocutionist
recital *m* recital; (mus.) recital
recitar *va* to recite; to deliver (*a speech*)
recitativo -va *adj* recitative; (mus.) recitative
reciura *f* strength, vigor; severity (*of weather*)

reclamación *f* claim, demand; objection, remonstrance; complaint; reclamation (*protest*); (law) reclamation
reclamante *mf* complainer, objector, protester
reclamar *va* to keep calling; to claim, demand, reclaim; to decoy, lure (*a bird*); (law) to reclaim; **a reclamar** (naut.) atrip; *vn* to cry out, protest, reclaim; (poet.) to resound; *vr* to call to each other (*said of birds*)
reclame *m* (naut.) sheave hole; (naut.) tie block
reclamo *m* decoy bird; lure (*for birds*); bird call; call; allurement, attraction; ad; puff, blurb; reference; (law) reclamation; (naut.) tie block; (print.) catchword
reclavar *va* to nail again
recle *m* rest from choir duty
reclinación *f* reclining, recumbency; leaning
reclinable *adj* reclining (*seat*)
reclinar *va & vr* to recline; to lean
reclinatorio *m* prie-dieu; couch, lounge
recluir §41 *va* to seclude, shut in; to imprison, intern; *vr* to go into seclusion; to be interned
reclusión *f* reclusion, seclusion; imprisonment, internment; prison, penitentiary
recluso -sa *adj* secluded; confined, imprisoned; *mf* prisoner; inmate
reclusorio *m* place of retirement
recluta *f* recruiting; (Am.) roundup; *m* recruit
reclutador -dora *adj* recruiting; *mf* recruiter
reclutamiento *m* recruiting, recruitment; year's recruits
reclutar *va* to recruit; (Am.) to round up (*cattle*)
recobrar *va* to recover; *vr* to recover; to come to
recobro *m* recovery, retrieval; pickup (*of a motor*)
recocer §30 *va* to boil or cook again; to boil or cook to excess; to anneal; *vr* to boil or cook to excess; (fig.) to be burning up inside
recocido -da *adj* expert; *m & f* annealing
recocina *f* back kitchen
recocho -cha *adj* overcooked, overdone; hard-burned (*brick*)
recodadero *m* elbowboard, elbowchair
recodar *vn* to lean, lean with the elbows; to wind, twist, turn; *vr* to lean, lean on the elbows
recodo *m* bend, twist, turn, hook
recogedero *m* collector; collecting basin, drainage area
recogedor -dora *mf* gatherer, collector; harvester; protector, shelterer; *m* rake, scraper; collector, pan, trap
recogegotas *m* (*pl:* **-tas**) drip pan
recogemigas *m* (*pl:* **-gas**) crumb brush
recoger §49 *va* to pick up; to gather, collect; to gather together; to harvest; to suspend; to shorten, tighten, draw in; to withdraw; to put in a safe place, to keep; to take in, to welcome; to confine, to lock up; *vr* to take shelter, take refuge; to withdraw; to retire (*to go to bed*); to go home; to retrench, cut down expenses; **recogerse en sí mismo** to withdraw within oneself
recogido -da *adj* cloistered, recluse; modest, bashful; moderate, temperate; *mf* inmate (*e.g., of poorhouse*); *f* harvest; collection; withdrawal; suspension; inmate of a house of correction for women; **recogida de basuras** trash collection
recogimiento *m* gathering, collection; harvesting; suspension; protection, sheltering; confinement; self-communion; house of correction for women
recolar §77 *va* to strain again
recolección *f* compilation, summary; collection; harvest; retreat; house of retreat; recollection, spiritual meditation
recolectar *va* to gather, gather in; to pick (*cotton*)
recolector *m* collector, tax collector
recolegir §72 *va* to gather, collect
recoleto -ta *adj* self-communing; cloistered, recluse; simple, plain (*in dress*); of retreat (*said, e.g., of a monastery*); *m* (eccl.) Recollect
recomendable *adj* commendable
recomendación *f* recommendation; **recomendación del alma** prayers for the dying
recomendante *mf* recommender
recomendar §18 *va* to recommend; **recomendar** + *inf* to urge to + *inf*
recomendatorio -ria *adj* recommendatory
recomenzar §31 *va* to recommence, to begin again
recompensa *f* recompense, reward
recompensable *adj* recompensable; worthy of reward
recompensación *f* var. of **recompensa**
recompensar *va* to recompense, reward
recompondré *1st sg fut ind of* **recomponer**
recomponer §69 *va* to mend, repair; to recompose
recompongo *1st sg pres ind of* **recomponer**
recomposición *f* mending, repair; recomposition
recompra *f* repurchase
recomprar *va* to repurchase, to buy back
recompuesto -ta *pp of* **recomponer**
recompuse *1st sg pret ind of* **recomponer**
reconcentración *f* or **reconcentramiento** *m* concentration, gathering; concealment; deep thought, absorption
reconcentrar *va* to concentrate, bring together; to conceal; *vr* to gather together; to become absorbed in thought
reconciliable *adj* reconcilable
reconciliación *f* reconcilement or reconciliation
reconciliador -dora *adj* reconciliatory; *mf* reconciler
reconciliar *va* to reconcile; to confess (*a sinner*) summarily; (eccl.) to reconcile; *vr* to become reconciled; to make a slight extra confession
reconcomer *vr* (coll.) var. of **concomer**
reconcomio *m* (coll.) shrug, shrug of the shoulders; (coll.) fear, misgiving
reconditez *f* (*pl:* **-teces**) (coll.) obscurity, mystery
recóndito -ta *adj* recondite
reconducir §38 *va* to lead back; (law) to renew (*a lease*)
reconduje *1st sg pret ind of* **reconducir**
reconduzco *1st sg pres ind of* **reconducir**
reconfortar *va* to comfort again; to comfort, cheer, refresh
reconocedor -dora *mf* examiner, inspector
reconocer §32 *va* to recognize; to admit, to acknowledge; to examine, scrutinize; (mil.) to reconnoiter; *vn* (mil.) to reconnoiter; *vr* to be clear; to confess; to know oneself
reconocible *adj* recognizable
reconocidamente *adv* avowedly, confessedly; gratefully
reconocido -da *adj* recognized; grateful
reconocimiento *m* recognition; gratitude; admission, acknowledgment; examination; (dipl.) recognition; (mil.) reconnaissance; **reconocimiento médico** inquest
reconozco *1st sg pres ind of* **reconocer**
reconquista *f* reconquest
reconquistar *va* to reconquer, to reconquest; to recover
reconsideración *f* reconsideration
reconsiderar *va* to reconsider
reconstitución *f* reconstitution
reconstituir §41 *va* to reconstitute
reconstituyente *adj & m* reconstituent, tonic
reconstrucción *f* reconstruction
reconstructivo -va *adj* reconstructive
reconstructor -tora *adj* reconstructive
reconstruir §41 *va* to rebuild, to reconstruct, to recast
recontamiento *m* recounting, relating
recontar §77 *va* to re-count; to recount, relate
recontento -ta *adj* greatly pleased; *m* great satisfaction
reconvalecer §34 *vn* to convalesce again
reconvención *f* expostulation, remonstrance; (law) reconvention
reconvendré *1st sg fut ind of* **reconvenir**
reconvengo *1st sg pres ind of* **reconvenir**
reconvenir §92 *va* to expostulate with, to remonstrate with; (law) to countercharge; **reconvenirle a uno con, de, por** or **sobre algo** to expostulate or remonstrate with someone about, for, on or upon something
reconversión *f* reconversion
reconvertir §62 *va* to reconvert
reconvine *1st sg pret ind of* **reconvenir**

reconviniendo *ger of* **reconvenir**
recopilación *f* abridgment, summary; compilation; **Novísima Recopilación** revised code of Spanish law (1805)
recopilador -dora *mf* compiler
recopilar *va* to compile
recoquín *m* (coll.) chubby little fellow
record *m* (*pl:* **-cords**) (sport) record; **batir un record** to break a record; **establecer un record** to make a record
recordable *adj* memorable
recordación *f* recollection, remembrance
recordar **§77** *va* to remember; to remind; **recordar algo a uno** to remind someone of something; **recordar** + *inf* to remember to + *inf*, e.g., **recordó hacerlo** he remembered to do it; **recordar** + *perf inf* to remember + *ger*, e.g., **recordaba haberlo hecho** he remembered doing it; **recordar que** + *subj* to remind to + *inf*, e.g., **recuérdele Vd. que escriba** remind him to write; *vn* to remember; to get awake; to come to; **si mal no recuerdo** (coll.) if I remember correctly
recordativo -va *adj* reminding, reminiscent; *m* reminder
recordatorio *m* reminder; memento
recordman *m* (*pl:* **-men**) (sport) record holder
recorredor -dora *mf* traveler; **recorredor de la línea** (elec.) lineman; **recorredor de vía** (rail.) trackwalker
recorrer *va* to cross, to traverse, to go over or through; to run over; to look over, look through; to run through (*a book*); to overhaul; (print.) to justify
recorrido *m* trip, run, path, route; stroke (*of piston*); repair; scolding, dressing-down; **de gran recorrido** heavily traveled
recortado -da *adj* (bot.) notched; *m* cutout
recortadura *f* cutting; **recortaduras** *fpl* cuttings, trimmings
recortar *va* to trim, cut off, cut away; to pare off; to cut out (*figures*); to outline; *vr* to stand out, be outlined
recorte *m* cutting; clipping (*from a newspaper*); dodge, duck; (taur.) dodge to avoid the bull's charge; **recortes** *mpl* cuttings, trimmings; **recortes de periódico** or **de prensa** newspaper clippings
recorvar *va & vr* to bend, to bend over; to recurve
recorvo -va *adj* arched, curved, bent
recoser *va* to sew again; to mend
recosido *m* mending
recostadero *m* couch, lounge
recostar **§77** *va* to recline; to lean; *vr* to recline; to lean, to lean back, to sit back
recova *f* poultry business; poultry stand; (Am.) shed; (Am.) market; (hunt.) pack of hounds
recovar *va* to buy (*poultry and eggs*) for resale
recoveco *m* turn, bend, twist; subterfuge, trick
recovero -ra *mf* poultry dealer
recre *m* var. of **recle**
recreable *adj* recreative, entertaining
recreación *f* recreation; recess (*in school*)
recrear *va* to re-create; to recreate, amuse; *vr* to recreate, take recreation, amuse oneself
recreativo -va *adj* recreative
recrecer **§34** *va* to increase; *vn* to increase; to recur; *vr* to recover one's spirits
recrecimiento *m* increase, growth; recurrence; recovery
recremento *m* (physiol.) recrement
recreo *m* recreation; place of amusement; (Am.) open-air restaurant; (Am.) daytime outdoor band concert
recría *f* breeding in new pastures; reanimation; redemption
recriar **§90** *va* to improve (*horses, cattle, etc.*) with new pastures; to fatten away from home; to reanimate, regenerate; to redeem
recriminación *f* recrimination
recriminador -dora *mf* recriminator
recriminar *va* to recriminate (*an accusation*); *vn* to recriminate; **recriminar contra** to recriminate (*an accuser*); *vr* to exchange recriminations
recriminatorio -ria *adj* recriminatory
recrudecer **§34** *vn & vr* to break out again, flare up, get worse
recrudecimiento *m* or **recrudescencia** *f* recrudescence
recrudescente *adj* recrudescent
recrujir *vn* to squeak
recruzar **§76** *va & vr* to recross
recta *f* see **recto**
rectal *adj* rectal
rectangular *adj* rectangular
rectángulo -la *adj* right, right-angled; *m* (geom.) rectangle
rectificación *f* rectification; reboring
rectificador -dora *adj* rectifying; *mf* rectifier; *m* (chem. & elec.) rectifier; **rectificador de selenio** (elec.) selenium rectifier; *f* grinder
rectificar **§86** *va* to rectify; (chem. & elec.) to rectify; to rebore (*a cylinder*); to true up; *vr* to mend one's ways
rectificativo -va *adj* rectifying
rectilíneo -a *adj* rectilinear
rectinervio -via *adj* (bot.) rectinerved
rectitud *f* rectitude, righteousness, correctness; straightness
recto -ta *adj* straight; right (*angle*); right, just, righteous; literal (*meaning*); *m* (anat.) rectum; (anat.) rectus (*muscle*); *f* straight line; (rail.) straightaway; **recta de llegada** (sport) home stretch
rectocele *m* (path.) rectocele
rector -tora *adj* governing, directing, managing; *mf* principal, superior; *m* rector; rector or president (*of a university*)
rectorado *m* principalship; rectorate
rectoral *adj* rectorial
rectorar *vn* to become a rector
rectoría *f* principal's office; rector's office; rectorate; rectory; president's house; leadership
rectriz *f* (*pl:* **-trices**) (orn.) rectrix
recua *f* drove; multitude
recuadrar *va* to graticulate; to print in a box
recuadro *m* (arch.) square, panel; box (*section of printing enclosed in borders*)
recubierto -ta *pp of* **recubrir**
recubrimiento *m* cover, covering; capping, coating; surfacing
recubrir **§17**, 9 *va* to re-cover; to cover, to cap, to coat; to recap (*a tire*); to surface
recudimiento *m* (law) power to collect rents
recudir *va* to pay (*what is due*); *vn* to come back, to revert
recuelo *m* strong lye; warmed-over coffee
recuento *m* re-count; count; inventory; **recuento de vocabulario** word count; **recuento sanguíneo** (med.) blood count
recuentro *m* var. of **reencuentro**
recuerdo *m* memory, remembrance; souvenir, memento, keepsake; **recuerdos** *mpl* regards
recuero *m* muleteer
recuesta *f* request
recuestar *va* to request
recuesto *m* slope
reculada *f* backing, falling back, recoil; (coll.) backing down
recular *vn* to back up, to fall back; to recoil (*said of a firearm*); (coll.) to back down
reculo -la *adj* tailless (*fowl*)
reculones; a reculones (coll.) backwards, backing up
recuñar *va* (min.) to dig by wedging
recuperable *adj* recoverable
recuperación *f* recuperation, recovery
recuperador -dora *adj* recuperative; *m* (mach.) recuperator; **recuperador de Cowper** (metal.) hot-blast stove
recuperar *va & vr* to recuperate, to recover
recuperativo -va *adj* recuperative
recura *f* comb saw
recurar *va* to tooth (*a comb*)
recurrente *adj* (anat., math. & path.) recurrent; *mf* complainant
recurrir *vn* to resort, have recourse; to revert
recurso *m* recourse; resource, resort; (law) appeal; **recursos** *mpl* resources, means; **recursos naturales** natural resources
recusación *f* refusal, rejection; (law) recusation, challenge
recusar *va* to refuse, reject; (law) to recuse, to challenge
rechazador -dora *adj* repelling; *mf* repeller

rechazamiento *m* repulsion; rejection
rechazar §76 *va* to repel, repulse, drive back; to reject
rechazo *m* rebound, recoil; rejection
rechifla *f* catcall, hissing, hooting; (coll.) ridicule, derision
rechiflar *va & vn* to catcall, to hiss; *vr* to ridicule, make fun
rechinador -dora *adj* creaking, squeaking, grating
rechinamiento *m* creaking, squeaking, grating
rechinar *vn* to creak, squeak, grate; to gnash; to balk, be sour, act with bad grace
rechinido or **rechino** *m* var. of **rechinamiento**
rechistar *vn* to speak; **no rechistar** to not say a word
rechoncho -cha *adj* (coll.) chubby, tubby
rechupete; de rechupete (coll.) splendid, fine
red *f* net; netting; network, system (*of railroads, telephones, streets, etc.*); baggage rack; (opt.) grating; (fig.) net, snare; **a red barredera** (fig.) with a clean sweep; **caer en la red** (coll.) to fall into the trap; **red barredera** seine, dragnet; (fig.) dragnet; **red de alimentación** (elec.) feed line, power line; **red de araña** cobweb; **red de canalización** (elec.) distribution main, local supply circuit; **red de difracción** (opt.) diffraction grating; **red de distribución** water main, city water main; (elec.) power line, house current; **red de emisoras** radio network; **red de jorrar** or **de jorro** seine, dragnet; **red radiotransmisora** radio network; **red de salvamento** life net
redacción *f* redaction; writing; editing; editorial staff; newspaper office
redactar *va* to write up, to word; to edit, be the editor of
redactor -tora *mf* writer; editor, newspaper editor
redada *f* casting a net; catch, netful (*of fish*); (coll.) catch, haul, roundup (*e.g., of criminals*)
redaño *m* caul (*the great omentum*); **redaños** *mpl* strength, courage, spirit
redar *va* to net, to haul in
redargución *f* retort; (law) impugnation
redargüir §21 *va* to retort (*an argument*); (law) to impugn
redaya *f* river fishing net
redecilla *f* small net; netting; hair net; (zool.) reticulum, honeycomb stomach
redecir §37 *va* to say over and over again
rededor *m* surroundings; **al rededor** or **en rededor (de)** around
redejón *m* large netting
redel *m* (naut.) loof frame
redención *f* redemption; support, assistance
redendija *f* var. of **rendija**
redentor -tora *adj* redeeming, redemptive; *mf* redeemer; (*cap.*) *m* Redeemer
redeña *f* scoop net, dip net
redero -ra *adj* (pertaining to a) net, reticular; *mf* netmaker; birdcatcher who uses nets; fisherman who uses nets
redescontar §77 *va* to rediscount
redescubierto -ta *pp of* **redescubrir**
redescubrimiento *m* rediscovery
redescubrir §17, 9 *va* to rediscover
redescuento *m* rediscount
redevanar *va* to rewind
redhibición *f* redhibition, cancellation of a purchase because of misrepresentation
redhibir *va* to cancel (*a purchase*) because of misrepresentation
redhibitorio -ria *adj* redhibitory
redición *f* repetition, constant repetition
redicho -cha *adj* (coll.) affected, overprecise (*in speech*); *pp of* **redecir**
rediente *m* (fort.) redan; (arch.) foliated cusp
rediezmar *va* to tithe a second time
rediezmo *m* extra tithe
redifusión *f* rebroadcasting
redigo *1st sg pres ind of* **redecir**
redije *1st sg pret ind of* **redecir**
redil *m* sheepfold
redilar or **redilear** *va* var. of **amajadar**
redimible *adj* redeemable
redimir *va* to redeem; to exempt; to buy back
redingote *m* redingote
rediré *1st sg fut ind of* **redecir**
redistribución *f* redistribution
redistribuir §41 *va* to redistribute
rédito *m* income, revenue, yield
redituable or **reditual** *adj* income-producing
redituar §33 *va* to yield, produce
redivivo -va *adj* resuscitated, revived; *mf* ghost
redoblado -da *adj* stocky, heavy-built; strong, heavy; (mil.) double-quick
redobladura *f* or **redoblamiento** *m* doubling; clinching; repeating, repetition
redoblante *m* (mil.) snare drum; (mil.) snare drummer
redoblar *va* to double; to clinch, bend back or over; to repeat, do over again; *vn* to roll a drum
redoble *m* doubling; clinching; repeating; roll of a drum
redoblegar §59 *va* to double, to bend
redoblón *m* clinch nail, rivet
redolente *adj* aching, paining
redoler §63 *vn* (coll.) to ache, to keep aching
redolor *m* dull pain, dull afterpain
redoma *f* phial, flask, balloon
redomado -da *adj* sly, canny; (coll.) crooked
redonda *f* see **redondo**
redondamente *adv* roundly; around; clearly, plainly, decidedly
redondeamiento *m* rounding; (phonet.) rounding
redondear *va* to round, make round; to round off; to round out; to clear (*an estate*); (phonet.) to round; *vr* to be or become well-off; to be in the clear
redondel *m* (coll.) circle; round cloak; ring (*arena of bull ring*)
redondela *f* (coll.) circle; (Am.) round mat
redondete -ta *adj* roundish
redondez *f* roundness
redondillo -lla *adj* (print.) roman; *f* eight-syllable quatrain with rhyme abba or abab
redondo -da *adj* round; clear, straightforward; definitive; pasture (*land*); (print.) roman; *m* round, ring, circle; (coll.) cash; **caer redondo** to fall senseless; **en redondo** around; clearly, plainly; *f* district, region; pasture; (mus.) whole note, semibreve; (naut.) square sail; **a la redonda** around, roundabout
redondón *m* large circle or sphere
redopelo *m* rubbing the wrong way; (coll.) row, scuffle; **a** or **al redopelo** the wrong way; (coll.) against all reason, violently; **traer al redopelo** (coll.) to ride roughshod over
redova *f* redowa
redro *m* annual ring of the horn (*of sheep or goat*); *adv* (coll.) back, behind
redrojo *m* small bunch of grapes remaining after vintage; late fruit, late blossom; (coll.) little runt, puny child
redropelo *m* var. of **redopelo**
redroviento *m* (hunt.) wind blowing from position of hunter in direction of the game
redruejo *m* var. of **redrojo**
reducción *f* reduction; (mach.) reducer (*to join two pipes or shafts of different sizes*); (Am.) settlement of converted Indians; **reducción al absurdo** reductio ad absurdum
reducible *adj* reducible
reducido -da *adj* reduced, diminished; small; compact; abridged
reducimiento *m* reduction
reducir §38 *va* to reduce; (chem., math., surg. & phot.) to reduce; *vr* to reduce; to confine oneself, to cut down; **reducirse a** to come to, to amount to; **reducirse a** + *inf* to find oneself forced to + *inf*
reductasa *f* (biochem.) reductase
reducto *m* (fort.) redoubt
reductor -tora *adj* reducing; *m* reducer; (chem. & phot.) reducer
reduje *1st sg pret ind of* **reducir**
redundancia *f* redundance or redundancy
redundante *adj* redundant
redundar *vn* to overflow; to redound; **redundar en** to redound to
reduplicación *f* reduplication; (gram.) reduplication

reduplicado -da *adj* reduplicate; (bot.) reduplicate
reduplicar §86 *va* to reduplicate
reduvio *m* (ent.) assassin bug
reduzco *1st sg pres ind of* **reducir**
reedificación *f* rebuilding
reedificador -dora *mf* rebuilder
reedificar §86 *va* to rebuild
reeditar *va* to republish, to reprint
reeducación *f* reëducation
reeducar §86 *va* to reëducate
reelección *f* reëlection
reelecto -ta *adj* reëlected
reelegible *adj* reëligible
reelegir §72 *va* to reëlect
reembalar *va* to repack
reembarcar §86 *va, vn & vr* to reëmbark, to reship
reembarco *m* reëmbarkation
reembarque *m* reshipment
reembolsar *va* to reimburse; to refund; *vr* to collect, to collect a debt
reembolso *m* reimbursement; refund; **contra reembolso** cash on delivery, collect on delivery
reempacar §86 *va* to repack
reempaquetar *va* (mach.) to repack
reemplazable *adj* replaceable
reemplazante *m* replacement (*person*)
reemplazar §76 *va* to replace
reemplazo *m* replacement; (mil.) substitute; (mil.) replacements
reencaminar *va* to reroute
reencarnación *f* reincarnation
reencarnar *va* to reincarnate; *vn & vr* to become reincarnated
reencender §66 *va* to relight, to rekindle; to reignite
reencuadernación *f* (b.b.) rebinding
reencuadernar *va* (b.b.) to rebind
reencuentro *m* new meeting; collision; clash (*of troops*)
reenganchamiento *m* var. of **reenganche**
reenganchar *va & vr* to reënlist
reenganche *m* reënlistment; bounty for reënlisting
reengendrador -dora *adj* regenerating; *mf* regenerator
reengendrar *va* to regenerate
reensayar *va* to test again, to try out again; to assay again
reensaye *m* second assay
reensayo *m* second test, second tryout, retrial; new rehearsal
reentrar *vn* to reënter
reenviar §90 *va* to forward; to send back
reenvidar *va* to raise (*the bid*)
reenvite *m* raised bid
reescribir §17, 9 *va* to rewrite
reestrenar *va* (theat.) to revive
reestreno *m* (theat.) revival
reexamen *m* or **reexaminación** *f* reëxamination
reexaminar *va* to reëxamine
reexpedición *f* forwarding, reshipment
reexpedir §94 *va* to forward, to reship
reexportación *f* reëxport; reëxportation
reexportar *va* to reëxport
refacción *f* refection, refreshment; repair, repairs; allowance; (coll.) extra, bonus; (Am.) upkeep; (Am.) spare part
refaccionar *va* (Am.) to repair; (Am.) to finance
refaccionario -nia *adj* (com.) accruing from profits that have been plowed back
refaccionista *adj* (Am.) finance; *mf* (Am.) financial backer
refajo *m* skirt; underskirt, slip
refalsado -da *adj* false, deceptive
refección *f* refection, refreshment; repair, repairs
refectorio *m* refectory
referencia *f* reference; account, narration, report; **de referencia** in question
referendario *m* var. of **refrendario**
referéndum *m* (*pl:* **-dums**) referendum
referente *adj* referring; **en lo referente a** with regard to
referible *adj* narratable, tellable
referido -da *adj* said, in question, above-mentioned; **el referido** or **la referida** the said person, the person in question
referir §62 *va* to refer; to tell, narrate, report; *vr* to refer
refertero -ra *adj* quarrelsome
refigurar *va* to imagine anew
refilón; de refilón askance; in passing
refinación *f* refining, refinement
refinadera *f* stone roller for kneading chocolate
refinado -da *adj* refined; fine, distinguished; sly, slick
refinador *m* refiner
refinadura *f* refining
refinamiento *m* refinement (*act of refining; elegance; improvement on something else; exaggerated sense of perfection*); refinement of cruelty
refinar *va* to refine; to polish (*e.g., a writing*)
refinería *f* refinery
refino -na *adj* very fine, extra fine; *m* refining; coffee, cocoa, and sugar exchange; (Am.) brandy
refirmar *va* to support, hold up; to ratify
refitolero -ra *mf* refectioner; (coll.) busybody, meddler; (Am.) fawner
reflectar *va* to reflect
reflector -tora *adj* reflecting; *m* reflector; searchlight
refleja *f* see **reflejo**
reflejar *va* to reflect; to show, reveal; to reflect on; *vn* to reflect; *vr* to be reflected
reflejo -ja *adj* reflected; (gram.) reflexive; (physiol.) reflex; *m* glare; reflection; reflex; (physiol.) reflex; **reflejo condicionado** (psychol.) conditioned reflex or response; **reflejo patelar** or **rotuliano** (med.) patellar reflex, knee jerk; *f* reflexion
reflexible *adj* reflexible
reflexión *f* reflection
reflexionar *va* to reflect on or upon; *vn* to reflect; **reflexionar en** or **sobre** to reflect on or upon
reflexivo -va *adj* reflective; (fig.) reflective; (gram.) reflexive; *m* (gram.) reflexive (*pronoun or verb*)
reflexología *f* study of conditioned reflexes, reflexology
reflorecer §34 *vn* to blossom or flower again; to flourish again, to reflourish
reflorecimiento *m* new blossoming, new flowering; reflourishment
refluente *adj* refluent
refluir §41 *vn* to flow back; to redound
reflujo *m* ebb, reflux
refocilación *f* cheer, exhilaration
refocilar *va* to cheer, exhilarate; to strengthen, fortify; *vr* to be cheered, be exhilarated; to take it easy; to abandon oneself to voluptuous living
refocilo *m* var. of **refocilación**
reforestación *f* reforestation
reforma *f* reform; reformation; renovation, alteration; (*cap.*) *f* (hist.) Reformation; **reforma penitenciaria** prison reform
reformación *f* reformation; re-formation
reformado -da *adj* reformed; Reformed; (archaic) retired (*soldier*); *mf* Reformed
reformador -dora *adj* reforming; *mf* reformer
reformar *va* to reform; to re-form; to mend, repair; to renovate; to revise; to reorganize; to disband (*an organization*); to drop (*an employee*); *vr* to reform; to restrain oneself, to hold oneself in check
reformativo -va *adj* reformative
reformatorio -ria *adj & m* reformatory
reformista *adj & mf* reformist
reforrar *va* to reline
reforzado -da *adj* reinforced; *m* tape, ribbon; braid
reforzador *m* (phot.) intensifier
reforzamiento *m* reinforcing
reforzar §52 *va* to reinforce; to strengthen; to cheer up, encourage; (elec.) to boost; (phot.) to intensify
refracción *f* (phys. & opt.) refraction
refractar *va* to refract
refractario -ria *adj* refractory; rebellious

refractivo -va *adj* refractive
refracto -ta *adj* refracted
refractómetro *m* refractometer
refractor -tora *adj* refractive; *m* (opt.) refractor
refrán *m* proverb, saying
refranero *m* collection of proverbs
refranesco -ca *adj* proverbial (*phrases, notions, etc.*)
refrangibilidad *f* refrangibility
refrangible *adj* refrangible
refranista *mf* proverbialist, user of proverbs
refregadura *f* rubbing; rub (*mark*)
refregamiento *m* rubbing
refregar §29 *va* to rub; (coll.) to upbraid, reprove
refregón *m* (coll.) rubbing; (coll.) rub (*mark*); gust of wind
refreír §73 & §17, 9 *va* to fry again, fry well, fry too much; (coll.) to bore stiff
refrenada *f* var. of **sofrenada**
refrenamiento *m* check, restraint
refrenar *va* to rein, curb; to check, restrain
refrendación *f* countersigning; legalization, authentication; visé; (coll.) repetition
refrendar *va* to countersign; to legalize, to authenticate; to visé; (coll.) to repeat, to take again
refrendario *m* countersigner
refrendata *f* countersignature
refrendo *m* countersigning; countersignature
refrentado *m* facing, milling
refrentar *va* to face, grind, mill
refrescador -dora *adj* refreshing; cooling
refrescadura *f* refreshing, refreshment; cooling
refrescamiento *m* var. of **refresco**
refrescante *adj* refreshing; cooling; refrigerant; *m* refrigerant
refrescar §86 *va* to refresh; to renew; to cool, to refrigerate; **refrescar la memoria** to refresh the memory; *vn* to refresh; to rest up; to refresh oneself; to go out for fresh air; (naut.) to blow up (*said of the wind*); *vr* to refresh; to cool off, get cooler; to refresh oneself; to go out for fresh air; (naut.) to blow up (*said of the wind*)
refresco *m* refreshment; soft drink, cold drink; refreshments; **de refresco** anew; fresh (*troops*)
refresquería *f* (Am.) refreshment stand
refriante *m* refrigerant
refriega *f* scuffle, affray, fray
refrigeración *f* refrigeration; cooling; **refrigeración con aire frío** air-cooling; **refrigeración por agua** water-cooling; **refrigeración por aire** air-cooling
refrigerador -dora *adj* refrigerating; *m* refrigerator; ice bucket, cooler
refrigerante *adj* cooling, refrigerant; *m* refrigerant; refrigerator; cooler, cooling bath (*of a still*); cool drink
refrigerar *va* to cool; to refrigerate; to refresh; to air-condition; *vr* to cool off, become cooler
refrigerativo -va *adj* refrigerative
refrigerio *m* cool feeling; relief; refreshment, pick-me-up
refringencia *f* refringency
refringente *adj* refringent
refringir §42 *va* to refract
refrito -ta *pp of* **refreír;** *m* rehash (*especially of a play*)
refucilar *vn* (Am.) to lighten
refuerzo *m* reinforcement; strengthening; bracing; aid, support; **refuerzos** *mpl* (mil.) reinforcements
refugiado -da *mf* refugee
refugiar *va* to shelter; *vr* to take refuge
refugio *m* refuge; hospice; shelter; haunt, retreat; safety zone (*in traffic*); **refugio antiaéreo** air-raid shelter, bomb shelter; **refugio antiatómico** fallout shelter; **refugio a prueba de bombas** bombproof shelter
refulgencia *f* refulgence
refulgente *adj* refulgent
refulgir §42 *vn* to be refulgent, to shine
refundición *f* recast, recasting; revision; adaptation (*e.g., of a play*)
refundidor -dora *mf* recaster, adapter (*e.g., of a play*); reviser
refundir *va* to recast (*metals*); to recast, to adapt (*a play, a novel*); to revise (*a book*); *vn* to redound
refunfuñador -dora *adj* grumbling, growling
refunfuñadura *f* grumbling, growling
refunfuñar *vn* to grumble, to growl
refunfuño *m* var. of **refunfuñadura**
refutación *f* refutation
refutar *va* to refute
regacear *va* to tuck up
regadera *f* watering pot, watering can; irrigating ditch; sprinkler head; street sprinkler
regadero *m* irrigating ditch
regadío -a *adj* irrigable; *m* irrigable land; irrigated land
regadizo -za *adj* irrigable
regador -dora *adj* irrigating; *mf* irrigator; *f* sprinkler
regadura *f* irrigation; sprinkling
regaifa *f* cake; grooved stone of an olive-oil mill
regajal *m* or **regajo** *m* puddle or pool left by a stream; stream, creek
regala *f* (naut.) plank-sheer, gunwale
regalado -da *adj* delicate, dainty; pleasing, delicious; pleasant; *f* royal stable; king's horses
regalador -dora *adj* regaling, entertaining; *mf* regaler, entertainer
regalamiento *m* regalement
regalar *va* to give, to present; to regale; to treat; to caress, to fondle; to give away; to melt; *vr* to regale oneself; to melt
regalejo *m* small gift, little treat
regalero *m* royal purveyor of fruit and flowers
regalía *f* privilege, exemption, perquisite; bonus; (Am.) muff; **regalías** *fpl* regalia (*rights and privileges of king*)
regalicia *f* var. of **regaliz**
regalillo *m* small gift; fur muff
regalismo *m* regalism
regalista *mf* regalist
regaliz *m* or **regaliza** *f* (bot.) licorice; licorice (*candy*)
regalo *m* gift, present; joy, pleasure; regalement; treat, delicacy
regalón -lona *adj* (coll.) comfort-loving, spoiled, pampered; (coll.) soft, easy (*life*)
regante *m* irrigation subscriber; irrigation workman
regañada *f* (dial.) cookie; (Am.) growl, snarl
regañadientes; a regañadientes grumbling, unwillingly
regañamiento *m* growling, snarling; grumbling; (coll.) scolding
regañar *va* (coll.) to scold; *vn* to growl, snarl; to grumble; to quarrel; to split, crack open (*said, e.g., of cherries, chestnuts, bread*)
regañir §25 *vn* to yelp, to yowl
regaño *m* growl, snarl; grumble; burst crust (*of a loaf of bread*); (coll.) scolding
regañón -ñona *adj* (coll.) grumbling, scolding; northeast (*wind*); *mf* (coll.) grumbler, scold
regar §29 *va* to water, sprinkle; to irrigate; to strew, spread, sprinkle; to water (*a region or territory*)
regata *f* irrigating ditch; regatta, boat race
regate *m* dodge, duck; (sport) dribbling; (coll.) subterfuge
regatear *va* to haggle over; to begrudge; to sell at retail; (sport) to dribble; (coll.) to avoid, to evade; *vn* to haggle, to bargain; (sport) to dribble; (coll.) to duck, to dodge; (naut.) to race
regateo *m* haggling, bargaining
regatería *f* retail
regatero -ra *adj* retailing; (coll.) haggling; *mf* retailer
regato *m* var. of **regajal**
regatón -tona *adj* retailing; (coll.) haggling; *mf* retailer; *m* tip, ferrule
regatonear *va* to sell at retail
regatonería *f* retail; retail business
regazar §76 *va* to tuck up
regazo *m* lap; (fig.) lap
regencia *f* regency; regentship
regeneración *f* regeneration; (elec.) feedback
regenerador -dora *adj* regenerating; *mf* regenerator; *m* (mach.) regenerator
regenerar *va & vr* to regenerate

regenerativo -va *adj* regenerative
regenta *f* wife of regent; directress, manageress; woman professor
regentar *va* to direct, to manage; to preside over; to boss
regente *adj* ruling, governing; regent; *mf* regent; *m* director, manager; registered pharmacist; (print.) foreman; professor
regentear *va* to boss, boss over
regicida *adj* regicidal; *mf* regicide (*person*)
regicidio *m* regicide (*act*)
regidor -dora *adj* ruling, governing; *m* alderman, councilman; *f* alderman's wife, councilman's wife; councilwoman
regidoría or **regiduría** *f* office or post of alderman or councilman
régimen *m* (*pl:* **regímenes**) regime, regimen; rate; normal rate; system, regulations, rules; flow; performance; conditions, normal operation; period (*e.g., of bad weather*); (gram.) government; **de régimen** normal, rated; **en régimen de** on the basis of; **régimen alimenticio** diet; **régimen desclorurado** salt-free diet; **régimen lácteo** milk diet; **régimen permanente** (phys.) steady state; **régimen títere** puppet regime
regimentación *f* regimentation
regimental *adj* regimental
regimentar §18 *va* to regiment
regimiento *m* rule, government; aldermen, councilmen; office of alderman or councilman; (mil.) regiment; (naut.) pilot's book of rules
Reginaldo *m* Reginald
regio -gia *adj* royal, regal
regiomontano -na *adj* (pertaining to) Monterrey; *mf* native or inhabitant of Monterrey
región *f* region; **región sombra** (astr.) umbra
regional *adj* regional
regionalismo *m* regionalism
regionalista *adj* regionalistic, regionalist; *mf* regionalist
regionario -ria *adj* regionary
regir §72 *va* to rule, govern; to control; to manage; to guide, steer; to keep (*the bowels*) open; (gram.) to govern; *vn* to prevail, be in force; to work; (naut.) to steer, steer well
registrador -dora *adj* registering; recording; *m* registrar, recorder; inspector; **registrador de la propiedad** recorder of deeds; **registrador de vuelo** (aer.) flight recorder; *f* cash register
registrar *va* to examine, to inspect, to search; to register; to record; to mark with a bookmark; (print.) to register; *vr* to register; to be recorded
registro *m* examination, inspection; registration, registry; recording; entry, record; bookmark; regulator (*of a watch*); inspection box; manhole; damper (*of a stove*); (mus.) stop, organ stop; (mus.) pedal; (print.) register
regla *f* rule; ruler; order; moderation; menstruation; **en regla** in order, in due form; **falsa regla** guide lines (*for writing*); **por regla general** as a general rule; **salir de regla** to go too far; **regla áurea** (arith.) golden rule; **regla de cálculo** slide rule; **regla del paralelogramo** (mech.) parallelogram law; **regla de oro, regla de proporción** or **regla de tres** (arith.) golden rule, rule of proportion, or rule of three
reglable *adj* adjustable
reglado -da *adj* moderate, temperate; regulated
reglamentación *f* regulation; rules
reglamentar *va* to regulate
reglamentario -ria *adj* regular, statutory, prescribed, (pertaining to a) regulation
reglamento *m* regulation; regulations
reglar *adj* (eccl.) regular; *va* to rule (*paper*); to regulate; *vr* to guide oneself, be guided
regleta *f* (print.) lead, leading
regletear *va* (print.) to lead, to space (*lines*)
reglilla *f* slide (*of slide rule*)
reglón *m* level (*of a mason*)
regnícola *adj* native; *mf* native; native writer
regocijado -da *adj* cheering; glad, happy, cheerful
regocijador -dora *adj* cheering
regocijar *va* to cheer, delight, rejoice; *vr* to rejoice
regocijo *m* cheer, joy, gladness, rejoicing
regodear *vr* (coll.) to take delight; (coll.) to joke, to jest
regodeo *m* (coll.) delight; (coll.) diversion, amusement; (coll.) joking, jesting
regojo *m* piece of bread left on table; little runt
regolaje *m* good humor, gentle nature
regoldano -na *adj* wild (*chestnut*)
regoldar §19 *vn* (vulg.) to belch
regoldo *m* (bot.) wild chestnut
regolfar *vn* to flow back, surge back; *vr* to flow back, surge back; to turn, be deflected (*said of the wind*)
regolfo *m* eddy, whirlpool; bay, inlet
regomar *va* (aut.) to retread
regona *f* irrigation canal
regordete -ta *adj* chubby, plump, dumpy
regostar *vr* var. of **arregostar**
regosto *m* var. of **arregosto**
regraciación *f* gratitude
regraciar *va* to show gratitude for
regresar *vn* to return; **regresar a** + *inf* to return to + *inf*
regresión *f* regression
regresivo -va *adj* regressive
regreso *m* return; (eccl.) regress; **de regreso** back
regruñir §25 *vn* to growl, to snarl
reguardar *va* (coll.) to take good care of
regüeldo *m* (vulg.) belch, belching
reguera *f* irrigating ditch
reguero *m* trickle, drip; track, furrow (*left by running water*); irrigating ditch; **ser un reguero de pólvora** to spread like wildfire
reguilete *m* var. of **rehilero**
regulable *adj* adjustable
regulación *f* regulation; control; **regulación del tono** (rad.) tone control; **regulación del volumen sonoro** (rad.) volume control
regulado -da *adj* regular
regulador -dora *adj* regulating; *mf* regulator; *m* throttle (*of locomotive*); (mach. & elec.) regulator; (mach.) governor; **reguladores** *mpl* (mus.) swell; **regulador de bolas** or **de fuerza centrífuga** (mach.) ball governor; **regulador de tensión** (elec.) voltage regulator; **regulador de volumen** (rad.) volume control
regular *adj* regular; fair, moderate, medium; (bot., eccl., geom., gram. & mil.) regular; **por lo regular** as a rule; *m* (eccl. & mil.) regular; *va* to regulate; to put in order; to throttle
regularidad *f* regularity; (rel.) strict observance of the rule
regularización *f* regularization; regulation
regularizar §76 to regularize; to regulate
regularmente *adv* regularly; fairly, moderately
regulativo -va *adj* regulative
régulo *m* regulus; (chem. & metal.) regulus; (orn.) kinglet; (*cap.*) *m* (astr.) Regulus
regurgitación *f* regurgitation
regurgitar *vn* to regurgitate
rehabilitación *f* rehabilitation
rehabilitar *va* to rehabilitate; to renovate, to overhaul; *vr* to become rehabilitated; to get overhauled
rehacer §55 *va* to do over, make over, remake; to rehash; to repair, renovate; *vr* to recover, to rally; to recover oneself
rehacimiento *m* remaking; rehash; repair, renovation
rehago *1st sg pres ind of* **rehacer**
rehala *f* flock of sheep of different owners under the care of one shepherd
rehalero *m* shepherd of a flock of sheep of different owners
reharé *1st sg fut ind of* **rehacer**
rehartar *va* to satiate, to cloy
rehecho -cha *pp of* **rehacer**; *adj* squat, broad-shouldered
rehelear *vn* to taste bitter
reheleo *m* bitterness
rehén *m* hostage; **llevarse en rehenes** to carry off as a hostage; **retener como rehén** to hold as a hostage; **quedar en rehenes** to be held as a hostage
rehenchido *m* filler, filling
rehenchimiento *m* refilling; stuffing, filling
rehenchir §94&§99 *va* to refill; to stuff, to fill

rehendija *f* var. of **rendija**
reherimiento *m* repulse
reherir §62 *va* to repulse, repel; to wound again
reherrar §18 *va* to reshoe (*a horse*)
rehervir §62 *va* to boil again; *vn* to boil again, to boil up; to be madly in love; to be blinded by passion; *vr* to ferment, to turn sour
rehíce *1st sg pret ind of* **rehacer**
rehiladillo *m* narrow ribbon
rehilandera *f* pinwheel (*toy*)
rehilar §99 *va* to twist too hard: *vn* to quiver; to whiz, whiz by
rehilero or **rehilete** *m* dart (*used in game of darts*); shuttlecock; (taur.) banderilla; dig, cutting remark
rehílo *m* quiver, shake
rehogar §59 *va* to cook with a slow fire in butter or oil
rehollar §77 *va* to trample under foot; to tread again
rehoya *f* deep hole
rehoyar *vn* to hollow out an old hole for planting a tree
rehoyo *m* var. of **rehoya**
rehuída *f* fleeing, flight; backtracking (*of game*)
rehuir §41 *va* to flee, to shrink from; to avoid, to decline; to dislike; **rehuir** + *inf* to decline to + *inf;* to dislike to + *inf; vn* to flee, to shrink; to backtrack (*said of game*); *vr* to flee, to shrink
rehumedecer §34 *va* to wet through and through, to soak
rehundir §99 *va* to sink; to deepen; to recast (*a metal*); to squander; *vr* to sink
rehurtar §99 *vr* to flee in an unexpected direction (*said of game*)
rehusar §99 *va* to refuse, turn down; **rehusar** + *inf* to refuse to + *inf*
reidero -ra *adj* (coll.) laughable; **reideras** *fpl* (coll.) laughing mood, spell of laughing
reidor -dora *adj* laughing; *mf* laugher
reimportación *f* reimportation, reimport
reimportar *va* to reimport
reimpresión *f* reprint, reimpression
reimpreso -sa *pp of* **reimprimir**
reimprimir §17, 9 *va* to reprint
reina *f* queen; queen bee; (chess & fig.) queen; **reina claudia** greengage; **reina de belleza** beauty queen; **reina de los ángeles** (ichth.) angelfish (*Angelichthys ciliaris*); **reina de los bosques** (bot.) woodruff (*Asperula odorata*); **reina de los prados** (bot.) meadowsweet; **reina de Sabá** Queen of Sheba; **reina luisa** (bot.) lemon verbena; **reina madre** queen mother; **reina Margarita** (bot.) aster, China aster; **reina mora** hopscotch; **reina regente** queen regent (*in place of absent king*); **reina reinante** queen regent, queen regnant; **reina viuda** dowager queen, queen dowager
reinado *m* reign; **durante el reinado de** in the reign of
reinador -dora *mf* ruler
reinal *m* twisted hemp cord
reinante *adj* reigning; prevailing
reinar *vn* to reign; to prevail
reincidencia *f* backsliding; repetition of an offense; relapse
reincidente *adj* backsliding; *mf* backslider
reincidir *vn* to backslide; to repeat an offense; to relapse
reineta *f* reinette (*type of apple*)
reinfección *f* reinfection
reinfectar *va* to reinfect
reinflar *va* to reinflate
reingresar *vn* to reënter
reingreso *m* reëntry
reinita *f* (orn.) honey creeper; (bot.) pot marigold; (Am.) glowworm, firefly; **reinita cabeza negra** (orn.) blackpoll; **reinita trepadora** (orn.) black-and-white creeper or warbler
reino *m* kingdom; **reino animal** animal kingdom; **reino de los cielos** kingdom of heaven; **reino mineral** mineral kingdom; **Reino Unido** United Kingdom; **reino vegetal** vegetable kingdom
reinoculación *f* reinoculation
reinocular *va & vr* to reinoculate
reinstalación *f* reinstatement, reinstallation
reinstalar *va* to reinstate, reinstall
reintegrable *adj* repayable
reintegración *f* redintegration, restoration, recovery
reintegrar *va* to redintegrate; to restore; to pay back; *vr* to redintegrate; to recover; to return, go back
reintegro *m* restoration, recovery; payment
reinversión *f* reinvestment
reinvertir §62 *va* to reinvest
reír §73 *va* to laugh at or over; *vn* to laugh; (fig.) to laugh (*said of a brook or fountain*); **reír de** to laugh at; *vr* to laugh; (coll.) to tear (*from wear or flimsiness*); **reírse de** to laugh at
reiteración *f* reiteration
reiteradamente *adv* repeatedly
reiterar *va* to reiterate, to repeat
reiterativo -va *adj* reiterative
reivindicable *adj* (law) repleviable
reivindicación *f* (law) replevin; claim, demand; recovery
reivindicar §86 *va* (law) to replevy; to claim, demand (*e.g., one's rights*); to recover, to reclaim; to lay hold of or on
reja *f* grate, grating, grille; plowshare, colter; plowing; (phys.) lattice; **entre rejas** behind bars
rejacar §86 *va* var. of **arrejacar**
rejada *f* var. of **arrejada**
rejado *m* grating
rejal *m* pile of bricks laid on edge and crisscross
rejalgar *m* (mineral.) realgar; noisome material
rejera *f* (naut.) mooring line, painter
rejería *f* ornamental ironwork
rejero *m* ornamental ironworker
rejilla *f* screen; grating; lattice, latticework; latticed window; cane, cane upholstery; (aut.) grille; (rail.) baggage netting; foot stove, foot brasier; fire grate; (rad.) grid; (elec.) grid (*of storage battery*)
rejo *m* sharp point; goad; hob (*for quoits*); iron frame (*of a door*); strength, vigor; (bot.) radicle
rejón *m* spear; dagger; (taur.) lance
rejonazo *m* (taur.) thrust with lance that breaks off in bull's neck
rejoncillo *m* (taur.) small lance
rejoneador *m* (taur.) rejoneador (*mounted bullfighter who breaks lance in neck of bull*)
rejoneadora *f* (taur.) lady rejoneador
rejonear *va* (taur.) to jab (*the bull*) with a lance made to break off in the bull's neck
rejoneo *m* (taur.) jabbing with a lance
rejuela *f* small grate; foot stove, foot brasier
rejuntado *m* (mas.) pointing
rejuntar *va* (mas.) to point
rejuvenecer §34 *va* to rejuvenate; *vn & vr* to rejuvenate, become rejuvenated
rejuvenecimiento *m* rejuvenation
relabra *f* new carving
relabrar *va* to carve again
relación *f* relation; speech, long passage (*in a play*); account; list; (law) report; **relaciones** *fpl* betrothal, engagement; **en relación con** commensurate with; **falsa relación** (mus.) false relation; **relación de ciego** blind man's ballad; **relaciones públicas** public relations
relacionado -da *adj* related
relacionar *va* to relate; *vr* to relate, to be or become related
relai *m* or **relais** *m* (elec.) relay
relajación *f* relaxation; slackening, letup; laxity; rupture, hernia
relajado -da *adj* ruptured; debauched, dissolute, lax, loose
relajador -dora *adj* relaxative; *mf* relaxer
relajadura *f* (Am.) hernia
relajamiento *m* var. of **relajación**
relajante *adj & m* relaxative
relajar *va* to relax; to slacken; to debauch; *vn* to relax; *vr* to relax; to become relaxed; to become debauched; to become ruptured
relajo -ja *adj* (Am.) shy, aloof, gruff; (Am.) fiery, spirited; *m* (Am.) disorder, commotion; (Am.) baseness, vileness, lewdness; (Am.) joke, scorn; **echar a relajo** (Am.) to make fun of
relamer *va* to lick again; *vr* to lick one's lips; to gloat; to relish; to slick oneself up
relamido -da *adj* prim, overnice

relámpago *m* lightning; flash; flash of lightning; flash of wit; **relámpagos** *mpl* lightning; **relámpago de calor** heat lightning; **relámpago difuso** sheet lightning; **relámpago fotogénico** (phot.) flash bulb, flashlight
relampagueante *adj* lightening; flashing
relampaguear *vn* to lighten; to flash, to sparkle
relampagueo *m* lightning; flashing
relance *m* chance, uncertainty; second choice or lot; **de relance** by chance, unexpectedly
relanzar **§76** *va* to throw again, to throw hard; to repel, to repulse; to cast (*ballots*) again
relapso -sa *adj* backsliding; *mf* backslider; *m* relapse
relatador -dora *adj* relating, narrating; *mf* relater, narrator
relatar *va* to relate, to report; (law) to report (*a trial*)
relatividad *f* relativity; (phys.) relativity
relativismo *m* relativism
relativo -va *adj* relative; (gram.) relative; *m* (gram.) relative
relato *m* story; statement, report
relator -tora *adj* narrating, reporting; *mf* relator, reporter; *m* (law) court reporter
relatoría *f* (law) office of court reporter
relavar *va* to wash again
relave *m* second washing; **relaves** *mpl* washings (*of ore*)
relazar **§76** *va* to tie up
relé *m* var. of **relai**
releer **§35** *va* to reread
relegación *f* relegation; banishment, exile; postponement
relegar **§59** *va* to relegate; to banish, exile; to postpone, to shelve, to lay aside
relej *m* var. of **releje**
relejar *vn* to batter (*said of a wall*)
releje *m* rut, track; batter (*of a wall*); (path.) sordes
relente *m* night dew, light drizzle; (coll.) impudence, assurance
relentecer **§34** *vn & vr* to soften
relevación *f* relief; absolution; emphasis, enhancement, reinforcement; (law) relief
relevante *adj* outstanding
relevar *va* to emboss, make stand out in relief, make stand out; to relieve; to release; to absolve; to replace, to substitute; (mil.) to relieve; *vn* to stand out in relief
relevo *m* (mil.) relief; **relevos** *mpl* (sport) relay race; **relevo de mandos** (mil.) change of command
relicario *m* reliquary; shrine; (Am. & prov.) locket
relicto -ta *adj* (law) left at one's death (*said of an estate*); (biol.) relict
relieve *m* relief (*design standing out from surface*); prominence; (fort.) relief; **relieves** *mpl* leavings, offals; **alto relieve** high relief; **bajo relieve** bas-relief, low relief; **en relieve** in relief; **medio relieve** half relief; **poner de relieve** to point out, to emphasize, to make stand out
religa *f* metal added to an alloy (*to change proportion*)
religar **§59** *va* to tie again; to bind more tightly; to alloy again
religión *f* religion; **entrar en religión** to go into the church; **religión natural** natural religion; **religión revelada** revealed religion
religionario -ria *mf* Protestant
religiosidad *f* religiosity, religiousness
religioso -sa *adj & mf* religious
relimar *va* to file again
relimpiar *va* to clean again; to clean thoroughly
relimpio -pia *adj* (coll.) very clean, spick-and-span
relinchador -dora *adj* loud-neighing, neighing frequently
relinchar *vn* to neigh
relinchido or **relincho** *m* neigh, neighing; cry of joy
relindo -da *adj* very pretty
relinga *f* (naut.) boltrope; lead rope (*of fishing net*)
relingar **§59** *va* (naut.) to rope (*a sail*); to fasten the lead rope to (*a fishing net*); *vn* (naut.) to rustle
reliquia *f* relic; trace, vestige; ailment; (biol.) relict; **reliquia de familia** heirloom
reló *m* (coll.) var. of **reloj**
reloco -ca *adj* (coll.) downright crazy
reloj *m* watch; clock; meter; **relojes** *mpl* (bot.) stork's-bill; **aprender a conocer el reloj** to learn how to tell time; **como un reloj** like clockwork; **conocer el reloj** to know how to tell time; **estar como un reloj** to be in good shape; **reloj de agua** water clock; **reloj de antesala** grandfather's clock; **reloj de arena** sandglass, hourglass; **reloj de autocuerda** self-winding watch; **reloj de caja** grandfather's clock; **reloj de campana** striking clock; **reloj de carillón** chime clock; **reloj de cuclillo** or **cuco** cuckoo clock; **reloj de cuerda automática** self-winding watch or clock; **reloj de bolsillo** watch, pocket watch; **reloj de estacionamiento** parking meter; **reloj de la muerte** (ent.) deathwatch; **reloj de longitudes** box chronometer; **reloj de ocho días cuerda** eight-day clock; **reloj de péndola** pendulum clock; **reloj de pesas** weight-driven clock; **reloj de pulsera** wrist watch; **reloj de repetición** repeater, repeating watch; **reloj de segundos muertos** stop watch; **reloj de sobremesa** desk clock; **reloj de sol** sundial; **reloj despertador** alarm clock; **reloj de torre** tower clock; **reloj magistral** master clock; **reloj marino** marine chronometer; **reloj para vigilantes** watchman's clock; **reloj registrador** time clock; **reloj registrador de tarjetas** punch clock
relojera *f* see **relojero**
relojería *f* watchmaking, clockmaking; watchmaker's shop or store
relojero -ra *adj* (pertaining to a) watch, clock; watchmaking; *mf* watchmaker, clockmaker; *f* watchcase; watch stand; watch pocket
reluciente *adj* shining, flashing, brilliant
relucir **§60** *vn* to shine; (fig.) to shine
reluctancia *f* (elec.) reluctance
reluctante *adj* unruly, unmanageable
reluctividad *f* (elec.) reluctivity
reluchar *vn* to struggle
relujar *va* (Am.) to shine (*shoes*)
relumbrante *adj* dazzling, resplendent
relumbrar *vn* to shine brightly, to dazzle, to glare
relumbre *m* beam, sparkle; flash of bright light; taste of copper or iron (*from having been kept or cooked in copper or iron vessels*)
relumbro *m* var. of **relumbrón**
relumbrón *m* flash of bright light, dazzling brightness, glare; tinsel; **de relumbrón** showy, tawdry; flashily
relumbroso -sa *adj* var. of **relumbrante**
reluzco *1st sg pres ind of* **relucir**
rellanar *va* to level, smooth, or flatten again; *vr* to sprawl in one's seat
rellano *m* landing (*of stairs*); level stretch (*in sloping country*)
rellenable *adj* refillable
rellenar *va* to refill; to fill up; to fill, to stuff; to pad; to point (*e.g., bricks*); to fill out; (coll.) to cram, stuff; *vr* to fill up; (coll.) to cram, stuff, stuff oneself
relleno -na *adj* very full, packed; stuffed; *m* filling, stuffing; forcemeat; padding, wadding; (mach.) packing; (fig.) padding (*of a writing or speech*)
remachado *m* riveting
remachador -dora *adj* riveting; *mf* riveter; *f* riveting machine
remachadura *f* riveting
remachar *va* to clinch (*a driven nail*); to rivet; to confirm, to stress
remache *m* clinching; riveting; rivet
remador -dora *mf* rower
remadura *f* rowing
remallar *va* to mend (*a net or netting; a stocking or run in a stocking*)
remalladora *f* stocking mender (*woman or machine*)
remamiento *m* var. of **remadura**

remandar *va* to order over and over again
remanecer §34 *vn* to show up again unexpectedly
remanente *adj* remanent; remnant; *m* remains, remnant, leftover
remanga *f* shrimp trap
remangar §59 *va & vr* var. of **arremangar**
remango *m* var. of **arremango**
remansar *vn & vr* to dam up, to back up
remanso *m* dead water, backwater; still water; sluggishness
remante *adj* rowing; *mf* rower
remar *vn* to row; to toil, struggle
remarcar §86 *va* to mark again
rematadamente *adv* totally, absolutely
rematado -da *adj* bad off, hopeless; **loco rematado** (coll.) crazy as a bedbug, raving mad
rematamiento *m* var. of **remate**
rematante *m* highest bidder
rematar *va* to finish off, kill off; to finish, put an end to; to put the last stitch in; to knock down (*in an auction*); *vn* to end; *vr* to come to ruin; (Am.) to get worse
remate *m* end; closing (*e.g., of an account*); crest, top, finial; highest bid; sale (*at an auction*); (Am.) edge, selvage; **de remate** absolutely, completely, hopelessly; **por remate** finally, in the end
remecedor -dora *adj* shaking, swinging; *m* worker who beats or shakes down olives from the tree
remecer §61 *va & vr* to shake, to swing
remedable *adj* imitable
remedador -dora *adj* imitative; *mf* imitator, mimic
remedar *va* to imitate, copy; to ape, mimic; to mock
remediable *adj* remediable
remediador -dora *adj* remedial
remédialotodo *m* (*pl:* **-dos**) var. of **sánalotodo**
remediar *va* to remedy; to free, to save (*from danger*); to help; to prevent
remediavagos *m* (*pl:* **-gos**) short cut
remedición *f* remeasuring; remeasurement
remedio *m* remedy; help; recourse; amendment, correction; (law) appeal; **no hay remedio** or **más remedio** it can't be helped; **no tener más remedio que** + *inf* to not be able to help + *ger;* **no tener para un remedio** to be penniless; **no tener remedio** to be unavoidable, to be unable to be helped; **sin remedio** inevitable; **remedio heroico** desperate remedy
remedión *m* (theat.) substitute performance
remedir §94 *va* to remeasure
remedo *m* imitation, copy; poor imitation
remellado -da *adj* jagged, dented; ectropic (*eye or lip*); harelipped; *mf* harelipped person
remellar *va* to unhair (*hides*)
remellón -llona *adj & mf* (coll.) var. of **remellado**
remembranza *f* remembrance, recollection
remembrar *va* var. of **rememorar**
rememoración *f* remembering
rememorar *va* to remember, recall
rememorativo -va *adj* commemorative
remendado -da *adj* spotted, patchy
remendar §18 *va* to patch, mend, repair; to darn; to emend, correct; to touch up
remendón -dona *adj* mending, repairing; *mf* mender, repairer; tailor (*who does mending*); shoe mender, shoemaker
rementir §62 *vn* to tell barefaced lies
remero -ra *mf* rower, paddler; *m* oarsman; *f* (orn.) flight feather
remesa *f* remittance; shipment
remesar *va* to remit; to ship; to pluck, pull out (*hair*)
remesón *m* plucking of hair; tuft of hair plucked out; stopping a horse in full gallop
remeter *va* to put back; to put in further; to tuck in (*e.g., the bedclothes*)
remezón *m* (Am.) tremor (*slight earthquake*)
remiel *m* second extraction of sugar from the cane
remiendo *m* patch; repair, mending; retouching; spot; emendation, correction; (print.) job printing, job work; **a remiendos** (coll.) piecemeal; **echar un remiendo a** to put a patch on; **echar un remiendo a la vida** (coll.) to take a bite to eat
rémiges *fpl* (orn.) remiges
remilgado -da *adj* prim and finicky, affected, smirking
remilgar §59 *vr* to be prim and finicky, to smirk
remilgo *m* primness, overniceness, affectation
rémington *m* Remington gun
reminiscencia *f* reminiscence; (philos.) reminiscence
remirado -da *adj* circumspect, discreet
remirar *va* to look at again, to look over again, to review; to look at hard; *vr* to take great pains; to enjoy looking over; to contemplate with pleasure; **remirarse en** to take great pains with
remisible *adj* remissible
remisión *f* remission; reference; **remisión de los pecados** remission of sins
remisivo -va *adj* (pertaining to a) reference
remiso -sa *adj* lazy, indolent, sluggish
remisor -sora *mf* sender, shipper
remitente *adj* remittent; *mf* sender, shipper
remitido *m* personal (*in a newspaper*)
remitir *va* to remit; to forward, send, ship; to refer; to defer, postpone, put off; to pardon, forgive; *vn* to remit, let up; to refer *vr* to remit, let up; to defer, yield
remo *m* oar; leg, arm, wing; toil, labor; (sport) rowing; (sport) crew (*rowing in races*); **al remo** rowing; at hard labor; (*cap.*) *m* (myth.) Remus
remoción *f* removal; dismissal; modification
remodelar *va* (Am.) to remodel
remojadero *m* steeping tub, soaking vat
remojar *va* to soak, to steep, to dip; to celebrate with a drink
remojo *m* soaking, steeping, dipping; **echar en remojo** (coll.) to put off till a more opportune time
remolacha *f* (bot.) beet (*plant and root*); **remolacha azucarera** (bot.) sugar beet; **remolacha forrajera** (bot.) mangel-wurzel
remolar *m* oar maker; oar shop
remolcador -dora *adj* towing; *m* tug, tugboat, towboat
remolcar §86 *va* to tow; to take in tow; to draw or take (*someone*) in
remoler §63 *va* to grind up; (coll.) to bore; *vn* (Am.) to run around with women
remolido *m* (mineral.) ground ore
remolienda *f* (Am.) carousing
remolimiento *m* grinding
remolinar *vn & vr* to whirl about, to eddy
remolinear *va, vn & vr* to whirl about, to eddy
remolino *m* eddy, whirlpool; swirl, whirl; whirlwind; disturbance, commotion; press, throng; cowlick
remolón -lona *adj* soft, lazy, shirky; *mf* quitter, shirker; **hacerse el remolón** to shirk, to back down, to back out; *m* upper tusk of wild boar; point (*of horse's tooth*)
remolonear *vn & vr* to refuse to move, to stand still, to duck work or effort
remolque *m* tow (*act; what is towed; rope, chain*); (aut.) trailer; **tomar a remolque** to take in tow
remondar *va* to clean out, to prune again
remonta *f* shoe repair; patch (*on riding breeches*); restuffing of a saddle; remount cavalry; remount (*supply of horses*); remount-cavalry headquarters
remontamiento *m* (act of) remounting cavalry
remontar *va* to frighten away; to mend, repair (*a saddle, shoes, pants*); to go up (*e.g., a river*); (mil.) to remount; to elevate, raise up; *vn* to go back (*in time*); *vr* to rise, rise up; to soar; to go back (*in time*); to take to the woods (*said of a slave*)
remonte *m* repair, repairing; remounting; rising; soaring
remontista *m* (mil.) remount commissioner
remontuar *m* stem-winder
remoque *m* (coll.) gibe, cut
remoquete *m* punch; nickname; witticism, sarcasm; (coll.) flirting, love-making; **dar remoquete a** (coll.) to embarrass

rémora *f* (ichth.) remora; hindrance, obstacle, obstruction
remordedor -dora *adj* disturbing, causing remorse
remorder §63 *va* to bite again; to sting, prick, cause remorse to; *vr* to show one's worry or trouble
remordimiento *m* remorse
remosquear *vr* (coll.) to become suspicious, become upset; (print.) to become blurred or smeared
remostar *va* to put must into (*old wine*); *vr* to rot (*said of fruit*); to taste sweet (*said of wine*)
remostecer §34 *vr* to rot (*said of fruit*)
remosto *m* adding must to old wine; sweetening, sweetness (*of wine*)
remotamente *adv* remotely; unlikely; vaguely
remoto -ta *adj* remote; unlikely; **estar remoto** to be rusty (*about something once known*)
remover §63 *va* to remove; to disturb, upset; to shake; to stir; to dismiss, discharge; *vr* to remove, move away
removimiento *m* var. of **remoción**
remozamiento *m* rejuvenation
remozar §76 *va* to rejuvenate; *vr* to rejuvenate, become rejuvenated
rempujar *va* (coll.) to push, jostle; (coll.) to push (*e.g., an idea, plan*) through; (hunt.) to drive in a corner
rempujo *m* (coll.) push, jostle; (naut.) sailmaker's palm
rempujón *m* (coll.) push, shove
remuda *f* change, replacement; change of clothes
remudamiento *m* change, replacement
remudar *va* to change again; to change, replace; to transplant
remugar §59 *va* var. of **rumiar**
remullir §26 *va* to fluff, beat up (*e.g., a pillow*)
remuneración *f* remuneration; **remuneración por rendimiento** piece wage
remunerador -dora *adj* remunerating; *mf* remunerator
remunerar *va* to remunerate
remunerativo -va *adj* remunerative
remusgar §59 *va* to guess, suspect
remusgo *m* guess, suspicion; sharp, cold breeze
renacentista *adj* (pertaining to the) Renaissance; *mf* Renaissancist
renacer §34 *vn* to be reborn, to be born again; to bloom again; to recover
renaciente *adj* renascent
renacimiento *m* rebirth; renaissance; (*cap.*) *m* Renaissance
renacuajo *m* (zool.) tadpole, polliwog; (elec.) frog; (coll.) shrimp (*little fellow*)
renadío *m* new crop after haying
renal *adj* renal
Renania *f* Rhineland
renano -na *adj* Rhenish
Renato *m* René
rencilla *f* bicker, feud, quarrel
rencilloso -sa *adj* bickering, feuding, quarrelsome
renco -ca *adj* hipshot, lame
rencor *m* rancor
rencoroso -sa *adj* rancorous
rendaje *m* set of reins and bridles
rendajo *m* var. of **arrendajo**
rendar *va* to plow the second time; (prov.) to weed; (prov.) to imitate
rendibú *m* (*pl:* **-búes**) (archaic) bow, reverence, attention
rendición *f* surrender; submission; fatigue, exhaustion; yield; rendering (*e.g., of justice*)
rendido -da *adj* tired, worn out; attentive, submissive, obsequious; overcome, beaten
rendija *f* crack, split, slit
rendimiento *m* submission; obsequiousness; fatigue, exhaustion; yield; output, performance; (mech.) efficiency
rendir §94 *va* to conquer; to subdue, to overcome; to surrender; to exhaust, wear out; to return, give back; to hand over; to yield, produce; to throw up, vomit; to render, give (*e.g., thanks*); to do (*homage*); *vn* to yield; *vr* to surrender; to yield, give in; to become exhausted, become worn out
rene *f* (anat.) kidney
renegado -da *adj* renegade; (coll.) harsh, gruff, profane; *mf* renegade; *m* ombre (*card game*)
renegador -dora *adj* profane; *mf* swearer
renegar §29 *va* to deny vigorously; to abhor, to detest; *vn* to curse; to apostatize, to become a Mohammedan; (coll.) to utter insults; **renegar de** to deny; to curse; to abhor, to detest
renegociación *f* renegotiation
renegón -gona *adj* (coll.) profane; *mf* (coll.) swearer, inveterate swearer
renegrear *vn* to turn very black
renegrido -da *adj* black-and-blue
RENFE *f* abr. of **Red Nacional de los Ferrocarriles Españoles**
rengífero *m* var. of **rangífero**
rengle *m* or **renglera** *f* row, file, line
renglón *m* line (*of writing or print; of business*); **a renglón seguido** below, right after; **leer entre renglones** to read between the lines
renglonadura *f* ruling, ruled lines
rengo -ga *adj* var. of **renco**
renguear *vn* (Am.) to limp
reniego *m* curse
reniforme *adj* reniform
renil *adj* barren or spayed (*sheep*)
renio *m* (chem.) rhenium
renitencia *f* reluctance, renitency; resistance
renitente *adj* reluctant, renitent; resistant
reno *m* (zool.) reindeer
renombrado -da *adj* renowned, famous
renombre *m* renown; surname, family name
renovable *adj* renewable
renovación *f* renovation; renewal; transformation, restoration; remodeling
renovador -dora *adj* renewing, reviving; *mf* renovator
renoval *m* growth of new sprouts in a clearing
renovar §77 *va* to renovate; to renew; to transform, to restore; to remodel; *vr* to renew, become new again
renovero -ra *mf* usurer, money lender
renquear *vn* to limp
renta *f* rent; annuity; income; private income; public debt; government bonds; **renta nacional** gross national product; **rentas patrimoniales** endowment income; **renta vitalicia** life annuity
rentabilidad *f* (econ.) yield
rentable *adj* income-yielding; *m* income-yielding investment
rentado -da *adj* enjoying an income
rentar *va* to produce, yield (*an income or profit*)
rentero -ra *adj* tributary, tax-paying; *mf* rural tenant, tenant farmer
rentilla *f* game played with six dice, each marked 1, 2, 3, 4, 5, or 6, on only one side
rentista *mf* financier; bondholder; person of independent means
rentístico -ca *adj* financial
rento *m* annual rent; farm
rentoso -sa *adj* income-yielding
renuencia *f* reluctance, unwillingness
renuente *adj* reluctant, unwilling
renuevo *m* sprout, shoot; renewal
renuncia *f* renunciation; resignation; (law) waiver; **hacer renuncia de** to resign (*a post*)
renunciable *adj* renounceable
renunciación *f* renunciation, renouncement
renunciamiento *m* renunciation
renunciar *va* to renounce; to resign; to renege; **renunciar una cosa en otra persona** to renounce something in favor of another person; *vn* to resign; to renege; **renunciar a** to give up (*a plan; the world*); *vr* to give up; **renunciarse a** + *inf* to give up + *ger;* **renunciarse a sí mismo** to deny oneself
renuncio *m* renege; slip, mistake; (coll.) lie; **coger en un renuncio** (coll.) to catch in a lie
renvalsar *va* to rabbet; to shave off, to plane down (*a door or window*)
renvalso *m* rabbet; shaving a door or window to make it fit
reñidamente *adv* bitterly
reñidero *m* cockpit, fighting pit
reñido -da *adj* at variance, on bad terms; bitter, hard-fought
reñidor -dora *adj* quarrelsome; scolding

reñidura *f* (coll.) scolding
reñir §74 *va* to scold; to fight; to fight for; *vn* to quarrel, fight; to fall out, be at odds
reo -a *adj* guilty, criminal; **reo** *mf* offender, criminal; (law) defendant; *m* (ichth.) sea trout; **rea** *f* (law) defendant; (Am.) slattern; (*cap.*) *f* (myth.) Rhea
reóforo *m* (elec.) rheophore
reojo; de reojo askance, out of the corner of one's eye; over one's shoulder; (coll.) hostilely, scornfully
reómetro *m* rheometer
reorganización *f* reorganization
reorganizar §76 *va & vr* to reorganize
reorientar *va* to reorient
reóstato *m* (elec.) rheostat
repacer §34 *va* to eat up (*all the pasture*)
repagar §59 *va* to pay too much for
repajo *m* field enclosed with a hedge
repajolero -ra *adj* var. of **pajolero**
repanchigar or **repantigar §59** *vr* to loll, to sprawl out in a chair
repapilar *vr* to glut, to stuff
reparable *adj* reparable; noteworthy; noticeable
reparación *f* repairing, repairs; reparation
reparado -da *adj* strengthened, supplied; squint-eyed; *f* sudden start, sudden shying away (*of a horse*)
reparador -dora *adj* repairing, (pertaining to) repair; restorative; faultfinding; *mf* repairer; restorative; faultfinder; *m* repairman; restorative
reparamiento *m* var. of **reparación** & **reparo**
reparar *va* to repair, to mend; to make amends for; to restore; to notice, observe; to parry; *vn* to stop; **reparar en** to notice, pay attention to; *vr* to stop; to check oneself, to refrain; (Am.) to rear
reparativo -va *adj* reparative
reparista *adj* (Am.) faultfinding
reparo *m* repairing, repairs; restorative; notice, observation; doubt, objection; shelter, protection; bashfulness; parry; **no tener reparos en** + *inf* to have no hesitation in + *ger;* **poner reparo a** to raise an objection to
reparón -rona *adj* (coll.) faultfinding; *mf* (coll.) faultfinder
repartible *adj* distributable
repartición *f* distribution; deal, dealing
repartidamente *adv* distributively
repartidero -ra *adj* to be distributed, for distribution
repartidor -dora *adj* distributing; *mf* distributor; assessor; dealer
repartimiento *m* distribution; repartition; assessment; dealing
repartir *va* to distribute; to assess; to deal (*cards*)
reparto *m* distribution; delivery; assessment; deal; (theat.) cast; (Am.) real-estate development
repasadera *f* (carp.) finishing plane
repasadora *f* wool comber (*woman*)
repasar *va* to repass; to retrace; to pass by or over again; to revise; to review; to mend (*clothing*); to comb (*dyed wool*); to amalgamate (*silver ore*)
repasata *f* (coll.) reprimand, dressing-down
repaso *m* review; (coll.) reprimand, dressing-down
repastar *va* to feed again; to have fed again; to mix again, to add more flour or water to
repasto *m* extra feeding
repatriación *f* repatriation; return home
repatriado -da *adj* repatriated; sent home; *mf* repatriate
repatriar §90 *va* to repatriate; to send home; *vn & vr* to be repatriated; to go or come home
repavimentar *va* to repave
repechar *vn* to climb, to go up hill
repeche *adj* (Am.) fine, swell, excellent
repecho *m* short steep incline; **a repecho** uphill
repeinado -da *adj* all slicked up
repeinar *va* to comb again; *vr* to do one's hair, to groom one's hair
repeladura *f* second shearing or clipping
repelar *va* to pull out (*hair*); to pull out the hair of; to nibble, to nip; to clip (*e.g., the nails*); (Am.) to scold; (Am.) to anger, irritate; *vr* to feel sorry, to repent
repelente *adj* repellent; (Am.) grim, gruff
repeler *va* to repel, to repulse
repelo *m* twist, turn (*against the grain, nap, etc.*); crooked grain; (coll.) spat, scuffle; (coll.) aversion; (Am.) rag; **repelo de frío** chill
repelón *m* pull on the hair; kink (*in a stocking*); snatch; spurt; **a repelones** (coll.) little by little, with effort; **de repelón** (coll.) swiftly
repeloso -sa *adj* crooked-grained; (coll.) touchy, grouchy
repeluzno *m* (coll.) chill
repellar *va* to splash plaster on (*a wall*)
repensar §18 *va* to think over again
repente *m* (coll.) start, sudden movement; **de repente** suddenly
repentino -na *adj* sudden, unexpected
repentista *mf* (mus.) improviser; (mus.) sight reader; improviser, extemporizer
repentización *f* (mus.) sight reading; improvisation, extemporization
repentizar §76 *vn* (mus.) to perform at sight, to sight-read; to improvise
repentón *m* (coll.) violent start or movement
repeor *adj & adv* (coll.) much worse
repercudida *f* rebound; repercussion
repercudir *va, vn & vr* var. of **repercutir**
repercusión *f* repercussion; reflection (*of light*)
repercusivo -va *adj & m* (med.) repellent
repercutir *va* (med.) to repel; *vn* to rebound; to reëcho, reverberate; **repercutir en** to have a repercussion on; *vr* to reverberate
repertorio *m* repertory; repertoire
repesar *va* to reweigh; to weigh with great care
repeso *m* reweighing; weight office; reweighing charge
repetición *f* repetition; repeating mechanism (*of a watch*); repeating watch; (mus.) repeat
repetidamente *adv* repeatedly
repetidor -dora *adj* repeating; *m* (telp.) repeater
repetir §94 *va* to repeat; *vn* to repeat; (path.) to repeat; *vr* to repeat oneself; (paint. & sculp.) to copy oneself
repicar §86 *va* to chop up, to mince; to ring, to sound; to prick again, sting again; to repique (*in piquet*); *vn* to peal, ring out, resound; *vr* to boast, be conceited
repicotear *va* to adorn with a jagged or wavy edge
repinaldo *m* (hort.) delicious (*large apple*)
repinar *vr* to rise, to soar
repintar *va* to repaint; (print.) to mackle, to blur; *vn* to repaint; *vr* to paint, to use rouge; (print.) to mackle, to blur
repinte *m* repaint
repique *m* chopping, mincing; peal, ringing; repique (*in piquet*); (coll.) squabble
repiquete *m* lively pealing (*of bells*); brisk rapping; clash, skirmish; (naut.) short tack
repiquetear *va* to ring gayly; to beat away at; *vn* to resound, to peal; (mach.) to chatter, clatter; *vr* (coll.) to wrangle, to insult each other
repiqueteo *m* gay ringing or pealing; beating, rapping; (mach.) chatter, clatter
repisa *f* shelf, ledge; console, bracket; **repisa de chimenea** mantelpiece; **repisa de ventana** window sill
repisar *va* to tread again; to tamp, pack down; to cram, to grind into one's head
repiso *m* thin wine
repizcar §86 *va* to pinch
repizco *m* pinch
replantación *f* replanting
replantar *va* to replant
replantear *va* to plan or outline again; to restate; to lay out (*a plan*)
replanteo *m* new plan, new outline; new layout; restatement
repleción *f* repletion, fullness
replegable *adj* folding; (aer.) retractable
replegar §29 *va* to fold over and over; *vr* to fold, fold up; (mil.) to fall back
repletar *va & vr* to stuff, to cram
repleto -ta *adj* replete, full, loaded; fat, chubby

réplica *f* answer, argument, retort; (f.a.) replica; (law) replication
replicador -dora *adj* argumentative; *mf* arguer
replicar §86 *va* to argue against (*e.g., an order*); *vn* to argue back, answer back, retort
replicato *m* answer, argument
replicón -cona *adj* (coll.) saucy, flip
repliegue *m* fold, crease; (mil.) falling back, retirement
repoblación *f* repopulation; restocking; afforestation
repoblar §77 *va* to repopulate; to restock (*e.g., an aquarium*); to afforest
repodar *va* to prune again
repodrir *va & vr* var. of **repudrir** only in the *inf*
repollar *vn & vr* to head (*said, e.g., of a cabbage*)
repollo *m* (bot.) cabbage; head (*e.g., of cabbage*)
repolludo -da *adj* cabbage-headed, round-headed; headed (*e.g., cabbage*); chubby
repolluelo *m* little cabbage; little head (*of cabbage*)
repondré *1st sg fut ind of* **reponer**
reponer §69 *va* to replace, to put back; to restore; to revive (*a play*); to reply, retort; *vr* to recover; to calm down
repongo *1st sg pres ind of* **reponer**
reportación *f* calm, moderation
reportaje *m* reporting; report, news report; **reportaje gráfico** story in pictures; **reportaje radiofónico** (rad.) newscast
reportamiento *m* check, restraint
reportar *va* to check, restrain; to get, obtain; to bring, carry; to transfer (*a drawing to a lithographic stone*); to report; *vr* to restrain or control oneself
reporte *m* report, news report; gossip; transfer (*drawing in lithographic crayon*)
repórter *m* reporter
reporteril *adj* reportorial
reporterismo *m* reporting, news reporting
reportero -ra *mf* reporter; **reportero gráfico** news photographer; **reportero radiofónico** (rad.) newscaster
reportista *mf* transferrer (*of a drawing to a lithographic stone*)
reportorio *m* calendar, almanac
reposadero *m* (metal.) iron runner
reposado -da *adj* reposeful; solemn, grave
reposar *va* to let (*food, a drink, etc.*) settle; **reposar la comida** to rest or take a nap after eating; *vn & vr* to rest; to take a nap; to lie, be at rest (*in the grave*); to settle
reposición *f* replacement; recovery (*e.g., of health*); (theat.) revival
repositorio *m* repository
reposo *m* rest, repose
repostada *f* (prov. & Am.) sharp reply, piece of abuse
repostaje *m* refueling
repostar *va, vn & vr* to stock up; to refuel
repostería *f* pastry shop; pastry-shop equipment; confectionery, pastry making, pastry cooking; pastry-shop employees; pantry
repostero *m* confectioner, pastry cook; king's butler; square cloth or cover ornamented with coat of arms
repregunta *f* (law) cross-examination
repreguntar *va* (law) to cross-examine
reprendedor -dora *adj & mf* var. of **reprensor**
reprender *va* to reprehend, to scold
reprensible *adj* reprehensible
reprensión *f* reprehension, scolding
reprensivo -va *adj* reproachful
reprensor -sora *adj* reproachful; *mf* reprehender, reproacher
represa *f* dam; damming; check, repression; recapture (*of a ship*)
represalia *f* reprisal; retaliation; **represalias** *fpl* reprisal; **tomar represalias** to make reprisals
represaliar *va* to make reprisals on, to retaliate on
represar *va* to dam; to check, repress; to recapture (*a ship*); *vr* to become dammed
representable *adj* representable; performable (*play*)
representación *f* representation; dignity, standing; performance; production; representatives; **en representación de** representing; **representación proporcional** (pol.) proportional representation
representador -dora *adj* representing; *mf* actor, player
representanta *f* actress
representante *adj* representing; *mf* representative; actor, player; (com.) agent, representative
representar *va* to represent; to show, express; to state, declare; to act, perform, play; to appear to be (*so many years old*); *vr* to imagine
representativo -va *adj* representative
represión *f* damming; repression; (psychoanal.) repression
represivo -va *adj* repressive
represor -sora *adj* repressive; *mf* represser
reprimenda *f* reprimand
reprimible *adj* repressible
reprimir *va* to repress
reprobable *adj* reprovable
reprobación *f* reprobation, reproval, reproof; flunk, failure
reprobado -da *adj* failed (*in an exam*); *mf* person who has failed; *adj & mf* var. of **réprobo**
reprobador -dora *adj* reproving; *mf* reprover
reprobar §77 *va* to reprove, to reprobate; to flunk, to fail
reprobatorio -ria *adj* reprobative
réprobo -ba *adj & mf* (theol.) reprobate
reprochable *adj* reproachable
reprochador -dora *adj* reproachful; *mf* reproacher
reprochar *va* to reproach; **reprochar algo a alguien** to reproach someone for something
reproche *m* reproach
reproducción *f* reproduction; breeding
reproducir §38 *va & vr* to reproduce
reproductible *adj* reproducible
reproductivo -va *adj* productive
reproductor -tora *adj* reproductive; reproducing; *mf* reproducer; breeder (*animal*); *m* (mach. & elec.) reproducer
reproduje *1st sg pret ind of* **reproducir**
reproduzco *1st sg pres ind of* **reproducir**
repromisión *f* renewed promise
repropiar *vr* to get balky (*said of a horse*)
repropio -pia *adj* balky (*horse*)
reprueba *f* new proof
reps *m* rep or repp (*fabric*)
reptación *f* crawl, crawling
reptar *vn* to crawl; to be craven, to cringe
reptil *adj & m* (zool. & fig.) reptile
república *f* republic; **la República de Platón** The Republic, The Republic of Plato; **República Árabe Unida** United Arab Republic; **república de las letras** republic of letters; **República Dominicana** Dominican Republic; **república literaria** republic of letters
republicanismo *m* republicanism
republicano -na *adj & mf* republican; *m* patriot
repúblico *m* prominent citizen; statesman; patriot
repudiación *f* repudiation
repudiar *va* to repudiate
repudio *m* repudiation (*of a wife*)
repudrir (*pp:* **repodrido**) *va* to rot completely; (coll.) to irritate, vex; *vr* to rot completely; (coll.) to languish, to pine away
repuesto -ta *pp of* **reponer;** *adj* secluded; spare, extra; *m* stock, supply; serving table; pantry; spare part; **de repuesto** spare, extra
repugnancia *f* repugnance or repugnancy
repugnante *adj* repugnant
repugnar *va* to conflict with; to contradict; to object to, to avoid (*e.g., work*); to revolt, to be repugnant to; *vn* to be repugnant; *vr* to conflict
repujado -da *adj* repoussé; *m* repoussage; repoussé
repujar *va* to do repoussé work on (*metal sheets*); to emboss (*e.g., leather*)
repulgado -da *adj* affected
repulgar §59 *va* (sew.) to hem, to border

repulgo *m* (sew.) hem, border; (cook.) fancy edging (*e.g., of a pie or cake*); **repulgo de empanada** trifle, ridiculous scruple
repulido -da *adj* highly polished; all dolled up
repulir *va* to repolish; to dress up, doll up; *vr* to dress up, doll up
repulsa *f* rejection, refusal; reprimand
repulsar *va* to reject, to refuse
repulsión *f* repulsion; rejection, refusal; (phys.) repulsion; (fig.) repulsion (*strong dislike*)
repulsivo -va *adj* (phys. & fig.) repulsive
repullo *m* dart; start, jump
repunta *f* point, cape; touch, sign; (coll.) quarrel, dispute
repuntar *va* (Am.) to round up (*scattered animals*); *vn* to begin to appear; (naut.) to begin to rise; (naut.) to begin to ebb; *vr* to begin to turn sour; (coll.) to fall out
repunte *m* (naut.) rise of tide, ebb of tide
repurgar §59 *va* to repurge
repuse *1st sg pret ind of* **reponer**
reputación *f* reputation, repute
reputado -da *adj;* **bien reputado** highly reputed; **mal reputado** of low repute
reputar *va* to repute; to esteem
requebrador -dora *adj* flirtatious; *mf* flirt
requebrajo *m* cheap flattery; brazen flirtation
requebrar §18 *va* to break more, to recrush; to flatter; to say flattering things to, to flirt with
requemado -da *adj* burnt; tanned, sunburned; *m* black crepe
requemamiento *m* bite, sting
requemar *va* to burn again; to parch; to overcook; to inflame; to bite, sting (*the mouth*); *vr* to become tanned or sunburned; to smolder, to burn within
requemazón *f* bite, sting
requerer §70 *va* (coll.) to love dearly
requerimiento *m* notification; request; summons; urging; checking, examination; requirement; seeking; (law) injunction
requerir §62 *va* to notify; to request; to summon; to urge; to check, examine; to require; to seek, to look for; to reach for; to court, woo, make love to
requesón *m* cottage cheese, pot cheese; curd
requeté *m* Carlist volunteer; Carlist volunteer militia
requete- *prefix* (coll.) very, extremely, e.g., **requetebién** very well, fine; **requetesabroso** extremely tasty
requiebro *m* recrushing; crushed ore; flattery; flattering remarks, flirtation
réquiem *m* (*pl:* **réquiems**) requiem (*mass and music*)
requilorios *mpl* (coll.) waste of time, beating about the bush
requintador -dora *mf* outbidder
requintar *va* to outbid by a fifth; to exceed, surpass; (mus.) to raise or lower by five points
requinto *m* second fifth to be removed; advance of a fifth in bidding; (mus.) fife; (mus.) fifer; (mus.) small guitar
requisa *f* inspection; round of inspection; round (*made by jailer*); (mil.) requisition
requisar *va* to inspect; (mil.) to requisition
requisición *f* (mil.) requisition
requisito -ta *adj* requisite; *m* requisite, requirement; accomplishment (*in some social art or grace*); **requisito previo** prerequisite
requives *mpl* var. of **arrequives**
res *f* head of cattle; beast; **res de vientre** breeding female (*animal*)
resaber §80 *va* to know thoroughly
resabiado -da *adj* wicked, sly, crafty; spoiled, ill-bred (*child*)
resabiar *va* to give a vice or bad habits to; *vr* to contract a vice or bad habits; to relish; to become displeased; to become tasteless
resabido -da *adj* well-known, notorious; pedantic
resabio *m* unpleasant aftertaste; vice, bad habit
resabioso -sa *adj* (Am.) sly, crafty; (Am.) wicked, vicious (*horse*)
resabré *1st sg fut ind of* **resaber**
resaca *f* surge, surf, undertow; (com.) redraft; (slang) hangover; **traer una resaca** (slang) to have a hangover
resacar §86 *va* (naut.) to underrun; (hunt.) to flush out; (com.) to redraw; (coll.) to take out again, to take right out
resalado -da *adj* (coll.) charming, witty
resalar *va* to salt again
resaldré *1st sg fut ind of* **resalir**
resalga *f* brine
resalgo *1st sg pres ind of* **resalir**
resalir §81 *vn* to jut out, project
resalsero *m* rough stretch of sea
resaltar *va* to emphasize; *vn* to bounce, rebound; to jut out, project; to stand out
resalte *m* projection
resalto *m* bounce, rebound; projection
resaludar *va* to return a greeting or salute to
resalutación *f* return greeting or salute
resalvo *m* sapling or staddle (*left in stubbing*)
resallar *va* to weed again
resanar *va* to retouch with gold or gilt; to repair; to patch (*a chipped wall*)
resarcible *adj* indemnifiable
resarcimiento *m* compensation, indemnification, repayment
resarcir §50 *va* to make amends to (*a person*); to repay (*a harm, an insult*); to make up for, to make good (*a loss*); to mend, repair; *vr;* **resarcirse de** to make up for
resbaladero -ra *adj* slippery; *m* slippery place; chute; *f* slide
resbaladizo -za *adj* slippery; skiddy; risky; shaky, treacherous (*memory*)
resbalador -dora *adj* sliding; skiddy
resbaladura *f* mark left from sliding or slipping
resbalamiento *m* slide, slip; skid
resbalar *vn* to slide; to skid; *vr* to slide, to slip; (fig.) to slip, to misstep
resbalera *f* slippery place
resbalón *m* slide, slip; skid, skidding; misstep
resbaloso -sa *adj* slippery
rescaldar *va* var. of **escaldar**
rescatar *va* to ransom, redeem; to rescue; to make up for (*lost time*); to relieve; to atone for; to trade valuables for (*ordinary goods*)
rescate *m* ransom, redemption; rescue; salvage; ransom money; prisoner's base (*children's game*)
rescaza *f* (ichth.) scorpene
rescindir *va* to rescind
rescisión *f* rescission
rescoldera *f* (path.) heartburn
rescoldo *m* embers; smoldering; scruple, doubt; **arder en rescoldo** to smolder
rescontrar §77 *va* (com.) to set off, to offset, to balance
rescripto *m* rescript
rescuentro *m* (com.) offset, balance
resé *1st sg pres ind of* **resaber**
resecación *f* thorough drying, desiccation
resecar §86 *va* to dry up, to dry out; (surg.) to resect; *vr* to dry up, to dry out
resección *f* resection
reseco -ca *adj* very dry, too dry; very lean; *m* dry part (*of a tree; of a honeycomb*)
reseda *f* (bot.) mignonette; (bot.) dyer's rocket
resedáceo -a *adj* (bot.) resedaceous
resegar §29 *va* to mow again
reseguir §82 *va* to edge (*a sword*)
resellar *va* to reseal; to restamp; to recoin; to surcharge; *vr* to become a turncoat
resembrar §18 *va* to resow, to replant
resentido -da *adj* resentful
resentimiento *m* resentment; sorrow, disappointment
resentir §62 *vr* to become weakened, begin to give way; to be resentful; **resentirse de** to begin to feel the bad effects of; to resent; to suffer from; **resentirse por** to resent
reseña *f* sketch, outline; review (*of a book*); newspaper account; (mil.) review
reseñar *va* to sketch, outline; to review (*a book*); to check; (mil.) to review
resepa *1st sg pres subj of* **resaber**
resequido -da *adj* parched, dried up
resero *m* (Am.) cowboy, herdsman; (Am.) livestock dealer
reserpina *f* (pharm.) reserpine
reserva *f* reserve; reservation; (com. & mil.) reserve; **a reserva de** with the intention of;

con or **bajo la mayor reserva** in strictest confidence; **sin reserva** without reservation; **reserva de indios** (U.S.A.) Indian reservation; **reserva mental** mental reservation
reservación *f* reservation
reservado -da *adj* reserved; *m* reservation, reserved place; (rail.) reserved compartment
reservar *va* to reserve; to postpone; to put aside; to exempt; to conceal, keep secret; *vr* to save oneself, to bide one's time; to beware, to be distrustful
reservista *adj* (mil.) reserve; *mf* (mil.) reservist
reservón -vona *adj* (coll.) reserved, retiring, distant
reservorio *m* reservoir
resfriado *m* cold (*e.g., in the head*); watering before plowing; **resfriado común** common cold
resfriador -dora *adj* cooling
resfriadura *f* (vet.) cold
resfriamiento *m* cooling, refrigeration
resfriante *adj* cooling; *m* cooler of a still
resfriar §90 *va* to cool, to chill; to cool off (*e.g., enthusiasm*); *vn* to turn cold; *vr* to catch cold; to cool, to chill; (fig.) to cool off, grow cold
resfrío *m* cold
resguardar *va* to defend; to protect, to shield; *vr* to take shelter; to protect oneself
resguardo *m* defense; protection; guard; guarantee; check, voucher; frontier guard; (naut.) wide berth, sea room
residencia *f* residence, residency; (educ.) residence; (law) impeachment
residencial *adj* residential; residentiary
residenciar *va* to call to account; (law) to impeach
residente *adj* resident, residing; *mf* resident
residir *vn* to reside
residual *adj* residual, residuary
residuo *m* remains, residue; residuum; (math.) remainder
resiembra *f* resowing, replanting
resigna *f* (eccl.) resignation
resignación *f* resignation
resignadamente *adv* resignedly
resignar *va* to resign; **resignar el mando en otra persona** to resign command to another person; *vr* to resign oneself; to become resigned; **resignarse a** + *inf* to resign oneself to + *inf*
resiliencia *f* (mech.) resilience
resina *f* resin, rosin; **resina acaroide** acaroide gum or resin
resinación *f* extraction of resin
resinar *va* to draw resin from
resinato *m* (chem.) resinate
resinero -ra *adj* (pertaining to) resin; *m* resin extractor
resinífero -ra *adj* resiniferous
resinoide *adj & m* resinoid
resinoideo -a *adj* resinoid
resinoso -sa *adj* resinous
resistencia *f* resistance; strength; (elec.) resistance; **oponer resistencia** to offer resistance; **resistencia al avance** (aer.) drag; **resistencia de rejilla** (rad.) grid leak; **resistencia pasiva** passive resistance
resistente *adj* resistant; strong, firm
resistero *m* hottest time of the day; heat from glare of sun; spot made hot by glare of sun
resistibilidad *f* resistibility
resistible *adj* resistible
resistidero *m* var. of **resistero**
resistidor -dora *adj* resistant
resistir *va* to resist (*temptation*); to bear, to stand, to withstand; *vn* to resist; **resistir a** to resist (*a contrary force, a desire to laugh*); **resistir a** + *inf* to refuse to + *inf;* to resist + *ger; vr* to resist; to struggle; to bear up; **resistirse a** + *inf* to refuse to + *inf;* to resist + *ger*
resistividad *f* (elec.) resistivity
resistivo -va *adj* resistive
resistor *m* (elec.) resistor
resma *f* ream (*of paper*)
resmilla *f* package of a hundred sheets of letter paper
resnatrón *m* (elec.) resnatron
resobado -da *adj* threadbare, hackneyed
resobrar *vn* to be greatly in excess
resobrina *f* grandniece, great-niece
resobrino *m* grandnephew, great-nephew
resol *m* sun's glare
resolano -na *adj* sunny and sheltered (*from wind*); *f* sunny and sheltered spot
resoluble *adj* resoluble, resolvable
resolución *f* resolution; **en resolución** in sum, in a word
resolutivo -va *adj & m* (med.) resolutive
resoluto -ta *adj* resolute; brief, compendious; expert, skillful
resolvente *adj & m* resolvent
resolver §63 & §17, 9 *va* to resolve; to decide on; to solve; to dissolve; to analyze, divide; to sum up; **resolver** + *inf* to resolve to + *inf; vr* to resolve; **resolverse a** + *inf* to resolve to + *inf;* **resolverse en** to turn into; **resolverse por** to resolve on or upon
resollar §77 *vn* to breathe; to breathe hard, to pant; to breathe again, breathe freely; to stop for a rest; (coll.) to show up; **no resollar** to not say a word
resonación *f* resounding
resonador *m* resonator; (telg.) sounder
resonancia *f* resonance; echo; (fig.) repercussion; **tener resonancia** to be bruited abroad, to be headlined
resonante *adj* resonant; resounding, echoing
resonar §77 *vn* to resonate; to resound, to echo
resoplar *vn* to puff, to breathe hard; to snort
resoplido or **resoplo** *m* puffing, hard breathing; snort
resorber *va* to resorb
resorcina *f* (chem.) resorcin or resorcinol
resorción *f* resorption
resorte *m* spring; springiness; means; motive; province, scope; (Am.) rubber band; **ser del resorte de** (Am.) to be within the province of; **tocar resortes** to pull wires; **resorte espiral** coil spring
respailar *vn* (coll.) to scurry; **ir respailando** (coll.) to scurry along
respaldar *m* back (*of a seat*); *va* to indorse; (fig.) to indorse; (fig.) to back; *vr* to lean back; to sprawl, sprawl out
respaldo *m* back (*of a seat; of a sheet of paper*); indorsement; backing; (min.) wall of a vein
respectar *va* to concern; **por lo que respecta a** as far as . . . is concerned
respectivo -va *adj* respective
respecto *m* respect, reference, relation; **al respecto** in the matter; **bajo ese respecto** in that respect; **con respecto a** or **de, respecto a** or **de** with respect to, with regard to
respeluzar §76 *va & vr* var. of **despeluzar**
respetabilidad *f* respectability
respetable *adj* respectable; **a respetable distancia** at a respectable distance; **el más respetable** the oldest
respetador -dora *adj* respectful
respetar *va* to respect
respeto *m* respect; consideration; spare; **campar por su respeto** or **sus respetos** to be self-centered, to be inconsiderate; **de respeto** spare, extra; **estar de respeto** to be all decked out; **ofrecer sus respetos a** to pay one's respects to
respetuosidad *f* respectfulness; awesomeness; humility, obedience
respetuoso -sa *adj* respectful; impressive, awesome; humble, obedient
réspice *m* (coll.) sharp reply; (coll.) sharp reproof
respigador -dora *mf* gleaner
respigar §59 *va* to glean
respigón *m* hangnail; (vet.) sore on heel (*of horse*)
respingado -da *adj* upturned, turned up (*nose*)
respingar §59 *vn* to balk, to shy; (coll.) to curl up (*said of edge of poorly made garment*); (coll.) to resist, to give in unwillingly
respingo *m* balking, shying; wincing; violent shaking; (coll.) gesture of revolt, gesture of revulsion
respingón -gona *adj* (Am.) surly, churlish; upturned, turned up (*nose*)

respingoso -sa *adj* balky; (coll.) gruff, sour
respirable *adj* breathable
respiración *f* respiration, breathing; ventilation
respiradero *m* vent, venthole (*in a barrel*); air valve; ventilation shaft; louver; breather, respite; snorkel; (coll.) organ of respiration
respirador -dora *adj* breathing; respiratory; *m* respirator
respirar *va* to breathe; (fig.) to breathe (*e.g., love, kindness*); *vn* to breathe; to leak; to breathe again, breathe freely; to breathe a sigh of relief; to catch one's breath, to stop for a rest; (coll.) to show up; to smell; **no respirar** (coll.) to not breathe a word; **sin respirar** without respite, without letup; **respirar a** to smell of
respiratorio -ria *adj* respiratory
respiro *m* breathing; respite, breather, breathing spell; reprieve, relief; extension of time (*for payment*)
resplandecer §34 *vn* to shine; to flash, to glitter; (fig.) to shine, stand out
resplandeciente *adj* brilliant, radiant; resplendent
resplandecimiento *m* brilliance, radiance
resplandina *f* (coll.) sharp reproof
resplandor *m* brilliance, radiance; glare; resplendence; cosmetic
respondedor -dora *adj & mf* respondent
responder *va* to answer; to clear up, explain away; to answer with (*e.g., an insult*); *vn* to answer; to respond; to reëcho; to correspond, harmonize; to yield, produce; to face; to answer back, be saucy; **responder a** to answer; to match; **responder de** to answer for (*a thing*); **responder por** to answer for (*a person*)
respondón -dona *adj* (coll.) saucy
responsabilidad *f* responsibility
responsabilizar §76 *va* to make responsible; *vr* to take the responsibility
responsable *adj* responsible; **responsable de** responsible for
responsar *va* (coll.) to scold; *vn* to say prayers for the dead
responsear *vn* (coll.) to say prayers for the dead
responsivo -va *adj* responsive
responso *m* (eccl.) prayer for the dead; (coll.) reprimand, scolding
responsorio *m* (eccl.) responsory
respuesta *f* answer, response; (rad.) response; **respuesta comercial** business-reply card
resquebradura *f* crack, split
resquebrajadizo -za *adj* easily cracked or split
resquebrajadura *f* var. of **resquebradura**
resquebrajar *va & vr* to crack, to split
resquebrajo *m* var. of **resquebradura**
resquebrajoso -sa *adj* var. of **resquebrajadizo**
resquebrar §18 *va & vr* to begin to crack or split
resquemar *va* to bite, sting (*the tongue*); to parch; to burn (*food*); *vn* to bite, sting; *vr* to become parched; to become burned; to smolder (*to be furious without showing it*)
resquemazón *f* or **resquemo** *m* bite, sting (*of food*); burnt taste (*of food*); parching; burning
resquemor *m* sorrow, grief; bite, sting (*of food*)
resquicio *m* crack, chink; chance, opportunity, occasion
resta *f* (math.) subtraction; (math.) remainder
restablecer §34 *va* to reëstablish, to restore; *vr* to recover
restablecimiento *m* reëstablishment, restoration; recovery
restallar *vn* to crack (*like a whip*); to crackle
restampar *va* to reprint, to restamp, to reëngrave
restante *adj* remaining; *m* rest, remainder
restañar *va* to stanch (*blood*); to retin; *vn* to crack (*like a whip*); to crackle; to stanch, be stanched; *vr* to stanch, be stanched
restañasangre *f* bloodstone
restaño *m* stanching, stopping; stagnation; gold cloth, silver cloth
restar *va* to deduct; to return (*a ball*); to reduce, take away; (math.) to subtract; **restar a** to take from; *vn* to remain, be left
restauración *f* restoration
restaurador -dora *mf* reviver; restorer
restaurán *m* restaurant
restaurante *adj* restoring; *mf* restorer; *m* restaurant; **restaurante automático** automat
restaurar *va* to restore; to recover
restaurativo -va *adj & m* restorative
restinga *f* (naut.) shoal, bar
restingar *m* (naut.) shoaly spot
restitución *f* restitution, return
restituíble *adj* returnable; restorable
restituidor -dora *adj* restoring; *mf* restorer
restituir §41 *va* to return, give back; to restore; *vr* to return, come back
restitutorio -ria *adj* restitutory
resto *m* rest, remainder, residue; stakes (*at cards*); return (*of ball*); player who returns ball; (math.) remainder; **restos** *mpl* remains, mortal remains; **a resto abierto** (coll.) without limit; **echar** or **envidar el resto** to stake all, to shoot the works; (coll.) to spread oneself, to make the greatest effort; **restos de serie** remnants; **restos mortales** remains, mortal remains
restorán *m* restaurant
restregadura *f* hard rubbing or scrubbing; rub (*mark*)
restregamiento *m* hard rubbing or scrubbing
restregar §29 *va* to rub or scrub hard; *vr* to rub hard
restregón *m* hard rub, rough rub
restribar *vn* to rest heavily, lean heavily
restricción *f* restriction, restraint; **restricción mental** mental reservation
restrictivo -va *adj* restrictive; (gram.) restrictive
restricto -ta *adj* restricted, limited
restringa *f* var. of **restinga**
restringente *adj & m* restringent
restringir §42 *va* to restrict; to constrict, contract
restriñimiento *m* constriction, contraction
restriñir §25 *va* to constrict, contract
resucitación *f* resuscitation
resucitador -dora *adj* resuscitative; *mf* resuscitator
resucitar *va* to resuscitate; to resurrect; (coll.) to resuscitate, revive; *vn* to resuscitate; to resurrect; (coll.) to revive
resudación *f* light sweat, slight perspiration; oozing
resudamiento *m* sweating; seepage
resudar *vn* to sweat or perspire slightly; to dry out; to ooze; *vr* to ooze
resudor *m* light sweat, slight perspiration
resuelto -ta *pp of* **resolver;** *adj* resolute, determined, resolved; quick, prompt
resuello *m* breathing; hard breathing
resulta *f* result; outcome; vacancy; **de resultas de** as a result of
resultado *m* result
resultancia *f* result
resultando *m* (law) finding
resultante *adj* resultant; *f* (mech.) resultant
resultar *vn* to result; to prove to be, to turn out to be; to become; (coll.) to please; **resultar de** to result from; to arise from; **resultar ser** to turn out to be
resumbruno -na *adj* yellowish black (*hawk*)
resumen *m* summary, recapitulation, résumé; **en resumen** in a word, to sum up
resumidamente *adv* in a word, to sum up
resumidero *m* (Am.) drain, sewer
resumir *va* to sum up, summarize; *vr* to be reduced, be transformed
resupe *1st sg pret ind of* **resaber**
resurgimiento *m* resurgence
resurgir §42 *vn* to resurge; to revive; to result
resurrección *f* resurrection; (*cap.*) *f* (theol.) Resurrection
resurtida *f* rebound
resurtir *vn* to rebound, bounce back
retablo *m* series of historical paintings or carvings; (eccl.) altarpiece, retable, reredos
retacar §86 *va* (billiards) to hit (*the ball*) twice
retacería *f* odds and ends (*of cloth*)

retaco *m* short fowling piece; short cue; (coll.) chubby fellow
retacón -cona *adj* (Am.) chubby
retador -dora *adj* challenging; *m* challenger
retaguardia *f* rear guard; **a retaguardia** in the rear; **picar la retaguardia** to pursue the rear guard hotly
retahila *f* string, line
retajar *va* to cut round; to trim the nib of (*a quill pen*)
retal *m* remnant, piece; piece of hide (*for making glue*)
retaladrar *va* to rebore
retallar *va* to retouch (*an engraving*); (arch.) to build ledges or projections in (*a wall*)
retallecer §34 *vn* to sprout again
retallo *m* new sprout; (arch.) ledge, projection
retama *f* (bot.) Spanish broom; **retama de China** (bot.) Spanish broom; **retama de escoba** (bot.) furze; **retama de olor** (bot.) Spanish broom; **retama de tintes** or **de tintoreros** (bot.) dyeweed, woodwaxen; **retama macho** (bot.) Spanish broom; **retama negra** (bot.) furze
retamal *m* or **retamar** *m* growth of Spanish broom; growth of furze
retamero -ra *adj* broomy; furzy
retar *va* to challenge, to dare; (coll.) to blame, find fault with
retardación *f* retardation, delay; deceleration
retardador -dora or **-triz** (*pl:* **-trices**) *adj* retarding, delaying
retardar *va & vr* to retard, to slow down; to decelerate
retardo *m* retard, retardation, delay
retartalillas *fpl* flow of words, garrulity
retasa or **retasación** *f* reappraisement
retasar *va* to reappraise; to reduce the appraisement of (*an object left unsold in an auction*)
retazar §76 *va* to tear to pieces; to separate into small flocks
retazo *m* remnant, piece; scrap; portion, fragment (*e.g., of a speech*)
rete- *prefix* (coll.) very, extremely, e.g., **retebién** very well
retecho *m* eaves
retejar *va* to repair (*a tile roof*), to retile (*a roof*); (coll.) to provide with clothing and footwear
retejer *va* to weave closely or tightly
retejo *m* roof repairing, retiling
retel *m* fishing net
retemblar §18 *vn* to shake, quiver
retén *m* store, stock, reserve; pawl, catch; (mil.) reserve, reserve corps; *2d sg impv of* **retener**
retención *f* retention; stoppage (*of payment of wages, etc.*); amount withheld; (law) retainer
retendré *1st sg fut ind of* **retener**
retener §85 *va* to retain, keep, withhold; to stop (*payment*); to detain, arrest
retengo *1st sg pres ind of* **retener**
retenida *f* guy; (naut.) preventer rope; (naut.) fast
retenimiento *m* retention
retentar §18 *va* to threaten with a relapse
retentiva *f* see **retentivo**
retentividad *f* (phys.) retentivity
retentivo -va *adj* retentive; *f* retentiveness, memory
reteñir §74 *va* to redye; *vn* to ding-dong, to jingle; to ring (*said of the ears*)
retesamiento *m* tightening
retesar *va* to draw or stretch tighter
reteso *m* tightening; breast, slight rise
reticencia *f* half-truth; evasiveness; (rhet.) reticence
reticente *adj* deceptive, misleading; noncommittal
rético -ca *adj & mf* Rhaetian; *m* Rhaetian (*language*)
retícula *f* reticule (*small handbag*); half-tone screen; (opt.) reticule; (*cap.*) *f* (astr.) Reticule
reticulación *f* reticulation
reticulado -da *adj* reticulate
reticular *adj* reticular
retículo *m* reticulum, network; (anat., bot. & zool.) reticulum; (opt.) reticle, spider lines

retienta *f* (taur.) second testing of mettle of young bull
retina *f* (anat.) retina
retiniano -na *adj* retinal
retinitis *f* (path.) retinitis
retinte *m* second dyeing; ding-dong, jingle; (coll.) tone of reproach
retintín *m* ding-dong, jingle; ringing (*in the ears*); (coll.) tone of reproach
retinto -ta *adj* dark-chestnut (*horse*)
retiñir §25 *vn* to ding-dong, to jingle; to ring (*said of the ears*)
retiración *f* withdrawal; (print.) (act of) backing; (print.) form for backing
retirada *f* see **retirado**
retiradamente *adv* secretly; in seclusion
retirado -da *adj* far, distant; retired; *m* (mil.) retired officer; *f* retirement, withdrawal; place of refuge; dry bed (*left by changed course of stream*); (mil.) retreat, retirement; (mil.) retreat (*signal at sunset*); **emprender la retirada, batirse en retirada** or **marchar en retirada** (mil.) to beat a retreat; **en plena retirada** in full retreat
retiramiento *m* retirement
retirar *va* to retire, to withdraw; to take away; to force out; (print.) to back; *vr* to retire, to withdraw; (mil.) to retire
retiro *m* retirement; withdrawal; (eccl.) retreat; (mil.) retirement, pension; **retiro obrero** social security
reto *m* challenge, dare; threat; (Am.) insult
retobado -da *adj* (Am.) saucy; (Am.) stubborn; (Am.) sly, crafty
retobar *va* (Am.) to cover or line with hide; (Am.) to wrap in burlap, leather, or oilcloth; *vr* (Am.) to stand aloof, be unpleasant
retocador -dora *mf* (phot.) retoucher
retocamiento *m* retouching
retocar §86 *va* to retouch; to touch up; to finish, give the finishing touch to; to play back (*a phonograph record*); (phot.) to retouch
retoñar *vn* to sprout, to shoot; to reappear, revive
retoñecer §34 *vn* var. of **retoñar**
retoño *m* sprout, shoot, sucker
retoque *m* retouching; finishing touch; touch (*of sickness*)
retor *m* twilled cotton fabric
rétor *m* rhetor
retorcedura *f* twisting; wringing; writhing
retorcer §87 *va* to twist; to twist together; to wring (*the hands*); (fig.) to twist, misconstrue; *vr* to twist; to writhe
retorcido *m* tutti-frutti
retorcimiento *m* var. of **retorcedura**
retórica *f* see **retórico**
retoricar §86 *va* (coll.) to treat with sophistry or subtleties; *vn* to speak rhetorically; (coll.) to use sophistry or subtleties
retórico -ca *adj* rhetorical; *mf* rhetorician; *f* rhetoric; **retóricas** *fpl* (coll.) sophistries, subtleties
retornamiento *m* return
retornar *va* to return, give back; to back, back up; to twist again; *vn & vr* to return, go back
retornelo *m* (mus.) ritornello
retorno *m* return; barter, exchange; reward, requital; return carriage, return horse, return donkey; (naut.) leading block; **retorno eterno** (philos.) eternal recurrence; **retorno por masa** (elec.) ground return (*e.g., in an automobile or radio*); **retorno por tierra** (elec.) ground return; **retorno terrestre** (elec.) ground
retorromano -na *adj & m* Rhaeto-Romanic
retorsión *f* retorsion; retaliation; twist, misconstruction; (law) retorsion
retorta *f* (chem.) retort
retortero *m* twist, turn; **andar al retortero** (coll.) to bustle around, to worry around; **traer al retortero** (coll.) to push around, to harass; (coll.) to string along, to mislead with false promises and flattery
retortijar *va* to curl up, twist up
retortijón *m* curling up, twisting up; **retortijón de tripas** bellyache, cramps
retostado -da *adj* dark-brown
retostar §77 *va* to toast again; to toast brown

retozador -dora *adj* var. of **retozón**
retozadura *f* frolicking, gamboling, romping
retozar §76 *vn* to frolic, gambol, romp; to become aroused or inflamed
retozo *m* frolic, gambol, romping; **retozo de la risa** giggle, titter
retozón -zona *adj* frolicsome, frisky, playful
retracción *f* retraction
retractable *adj* retractable; revocable
retractación *f* retraction, retractation
retractar *va* to retract; (law) to redeem; *vr* to retract; **retractarse de** to retract, take back (*something said*)
retráctil *adj* retractile; (aer.) retractable
retracto *m* (law) prior right to purchase
retractor -tora *adj* retractive; *m* (surg.) retractor
retraducir §38 *va* to retranslate
retraduje *1st sg pret ind of* **retraducir**
retraduzco *1st sg pres ind of* **retraducir**
retraer §88 *va* to bring again, bring back; to dissuade; (law) to redeem; *vr* to withdraw, retire; to keep or stay in retirement; to take refuge; **retraerse a sagrado** to take sanctuary; **retraerse de** to withdraw from, give up, abandon
retraído -da *adj* solitary; reserved, shy; *mf* person who has taken sanctuary
retraigo *1st sg pres ind of* **retraer**
retraimiento *m* withdrawal, retirement; solitude; reserve, shyness; asylum, refuge; sanctum, retreat
retraje *1st sg pret ind of* **retraer**
retranca *f* breeching; (Am.) brake
retranquear *va* to hoist and put (*building stones*) in place
retranqueo *m* hoisting and placing building stones
retranquero *m* (Am.) brakeman
retransmisión *f* rebroadcasting
retransmitir *va* to rebroadcast
retraqueo *m* (arch.) setback
retrasar *va* to delay, retard; to put off; to set or turn back (*a watch or clock*); to slow down (*a watch or clock*); *vn* to be too slow; to be or fall behind (*e.g., in one's studies*); *vr* to delay, be late, be slow, be behind time; to be too slow; to go or be slow (*said of a watch or clock*); **retrasarse en** + *inf* to be late or slow in + *ger*
retraso *m* delay, slowness; lag; **tener retraso** to be late; **retraso de fase** (elec.) phase lag
retratador -dora *mf* var. of **retratista**
retratar *va* to portray; to photograph; to imitate; (fig.) to portray; *vr* to sit for a portrait or photograph; to be photographed
retratería *f* (Am.) photography
retratista *mf* portraitist, portrait painter
retrato *m* portrait; photograph; copy, imitation; portraiture, description; (fig.) picture; **ser el vivo retrato de** to be the living image of
retrechar *vn* to back, back up (*said of a horse*)
retrechería *f* (coll.) slyness, cunning, evasiveness
retrechero -ra *adj* (coll.) sly, cunning, evasive; (coll.) attractive; (Am.) shy (*horse*)
retrepado -da *adj* leaning backward; slanting backward
retrepar *vr* to lean back; to lean back in a chair
retreta *f* (mil.) retreat, tattoo; tattoo (*military parade and celebration after dark*); (Am.) nighttime outdoor band concert
retrete *m* toilet, water closet
retretero *m* lavatory man
retribución *f* repayment, reward; compensation, pay; fee
retribuir §41 *va* to repay, reward, pay back; to pay for
retributivo -va *adj* rewarding
retroactividad *f* retroactivity
retroactivo -va *adj* retroactive
retrocarga; de retrocarga breech-loading
retroceder *vn* to retrocede; to back away; to back out, back down
retrocesión *f* retrocession
retroceso *m* retrocession, backing; recoil (*of a gun*); flare-up (*of a disease*)
retrocohete *m* retrorocket
retrodisparo *m* retrofiring
retroflexión *f* retroflexion; (path.) retroflexion
retrogradación *f* retrogradation; (astr.) retrogradation
retrogradar *vn* (astr.) to retrograde
retrógrado -da *adj* retrograde; (pol.) reactionary; *mf* (pol.) reactionary
retrogresión *f* retrogression
retromarcha *f* (aut.) reverse
retronar §77 *vn* to thunder, to rumble
retropilastra *f* (arch.) pilaster back of a column
retropropulsión *f* (aer.) jet propulsion
retropulsión *f* (obstet. & path.) retropulsion
retrospección *f* retrospect, retrospection
retrospectivo -va *adj* retrospective
retrotracción *f* (law) antedating
retrotraer §88 *va* (law) to antedate, to date back
retrotraigo *1st sg pres ind of* **retrotraer**
retrotraje *1st sg pret ind of* **retrotraer**
retrovender *va* (law) to sell back
retrovendición *f* or **retroventa** *f* (law) selling back
retroversión *f* (path.) retroversion
retrovisor *m* (aut.) rear-view mirror
retrucar §86 *vn* to answer, to reply; (billiards) to kiss
retruco *m* (billiards) kiss
retruécano *m* pun, play on words
retruque *m* var. of **retruco**
retumbante *adj* resounding, rumbling; bombastic, high-flown
retumbar *vn* to resound, to rumble
retumbo *m* resounding, rumble, echo
retundir *va* to even (*the face of a wall*)
retuso -sa *adj* (bot.) retuse
retuve *1st sg pret ind of* **retener**
reuma *m & f* (path.) rheumatism; (path.) rheum
reumático -ca *adj & mf* rheumatic
reumátide *f* (path.) rheumatic dermatosis
reumatismo *m* (path.) rheumatism
reumatoideo -a *adj* rheumatoid
reunificación *f* reunification
reunificar §86 *va* to reunify
reunión *f* reunion, gathering, meeting; assemblage (*of persons or things*)
reunir §75 *va* to join, unite; to assemble, gather together, bring together; to reunite; to combine; to raise (*money*); *vr* to unite; to assemble, gather together, meet, come together; to reunite; to concur, conspire
reuntar §75 *va* to oil again, grease again
revacunación *f* revaccination
revacunar *va* to revaccinate
reválida *f* final examination (*for a degree*)
revalidación *f* ratification, revalidation
revalidar *va* to ratify, revalidate; *vr* to take an examination for a degree
revaloración *f* (econ.) revaluation
revalorar *va* to revalue
revalorización *f* revaluation; reclamation
revalorizar §76 *va* to revalue; to reclaim
revancha *f* revenge, reprisal
revanchista *adj & mf* revanchist
revecero -ra *adj* shifting; *mf* farmhand in charge of relays of oxen
reveedor *m* revisor, inspector
revejecer §34 *vn & vr* to age before one's time
revejido -da *adj* aged before one's time
revelación *f* revelation
revelado -da *adj* revealed; *m* (phot.) development
revelador -dora *adj* revealing; *mf* revealer; *m* (phot.) developer
revelamiento *m* revealment
revelandero -ra *mf* fake who lays claim to divine revelation
revelar *va* to reveal; (phot.) to develop
reveler *va* (med.) to bring about revulsion in
revellín *m* (fort.) ravelin
revenar *vn* to sprout (*after a trimming, topping, or grafting*)
revendedera *f* var. of **revendedora**
revendedor -dora *mf* reseller; retailer; scalper, ticket speculator
revender *va* to resell; to retail
revendré *1st sg fut ind of* **revenir**
revengo *1st sg pres ind of* **revenir**
revenido *m* annealing

revenimiento *m* return (*to a previous state*); shrinking, drying out; souring; (min.) cave-in
revenir §92 *vn* to come back; *vr* to shrink, dry out; to turn sour; to weaken, back down; (min.) to cave in
reveno *m* sprout (*that grows after a trimming, topping, or grafting*)
reventa *f* resale
reventadero *m* rough ground; (coll.) chore, hard task
reventador *m* (theat.) paid hisser
reventar §18 *va* to smash, crush; to burst, explode, blow out; to ruin; to annoy, bore; to work (*a person*) to death; to run (*a horse*) to death; *vn* to burst, explode, blow out; to break (*said of waves*); (coll.) to burst out (*said, e.g., of anger*); (coll.) to die a violent death; (coll.) to croak (*to die*); **reventar por** + *inf* to be bursting to + *inf; vr* to burst, explode, blow out; to be worked to death; to be run to death (*said of a horse*)
reventazón *f* burst, bursting; blowout; dashing of waves
reventón *adj masc* bursting; bulging; *m* burst; steep hill; difficulty, jam; jog; (aut.) blowout
rever §93 *va* to revise, review, inspect; (law) to retry
reverar *va* (naut.) to drive (*a ship*) off the sand (*said of a strong current*)
reverberación *f* reverberation
reverberante *adj* reverberant
reverberar *vn* to reverberate
reverberatorio -ria *adj* reverberatory
reverbero *m* reverberation; reflector; reflecting lamp; street lamp; (Am.) chafing dish
reverdecer §34 *va* to turn green again; *vn* to turn or grow green again; to come to life again, acquire new vigor
reverdeciente *adj* green, turning green; fresh, renewed
reverencia *f* reverence; bow, curtsy; (*cap.*) *f* Reverence (*title*)
reverenciable *adj* worthy of reverence, worshipful
reverenciador -dora *adj* revering
reverencial *adj* reverential
reverenciar *va* to revere, reverence; *vn* to bow, curtsy
reverendísimo -ma *adj super* most reverend
reverendo -da *adj* reverend; (coll.) solemn, serious; **reverendas** *fpl* (eccl.) dimissory letter; fine qualities, sterling qualities
reverente *adj* reverent
reversibilidad *f* reversibility
reversible *adj* reversible
reversión *f* reversion; (biol. & law) reversion
reverso *m* back; wrong side; reverse (*of coin or medal*); **el reverso de la medalla** the entire opposite, the opposite in every respect
reverter §66 *vn* to overflow
revertir §62 *vn* to revert; (law) to revert
revés *m* back, reverse; backhand (*stroke*); counterstroke; wrong side; (fig.) reverse, setback; change of mood; **al revés** wrong side out, inside out; backwards, in the opposite way; **de revés** wrong side out, inside out; backwards, in the opposite way; from left to right; **el revés de la medalla** the entire opposite, the opposite in every respect
revesa *f* (naut.) back water, eddy
revesado -da *adj* complex, intricate; wild, unmanageable
revesar *va* to vomit
revesino *m* reversi (*game of cards*)
revestimiento *m* covering, coating, facing, lining, surfacing
revestir §94 *va* to put on, to don; to cover, coat, face, line, surface, revet; to adorn (*a story*); to disguise; to assume, take on; **revestir con** or **de** to invest with; *vr* to put on vestments; to be haughty or proud; to be carried along; **revestirse con** or **de** to be invested with; to gird oneself with (*e.g., patience*)
reveza *f* var. of **revesa**
revezar §76 *va* to replace, to spell; *vn* to alternate, work in shifts
revezo *m* shifting; shift; relay of a yoke of oxen, mules, etc.
reviejo -ja *adj* very old; *m* withered branch
revientabuey *m* (ent.) buprestid beetle
reviernes *m* Friday after Easter (*each of the first seven*)
revine *1st sg pret ind of* **revenir**
reviniendo *ger of* **revenir**
revirado -da *adj* twisted (*wood*)
revirar *va* to turn, twist; to turn over; (naut.) to veer again; *vn* (naut.) to veer again
revisador -dora *adj* revisory
revisar *va* to revise, review, check; to audit
revisión *f* revision, review, check
revisionismo *m* revisionism
revisionista *adj & mf* revisionist
revisita *f* reinspection
revisor -sora *adj* revisory; *mf* reviewer, examiner; (rail.) conductor, ticket collector; **revisor de cuentas** auditor
revista *f* see **revisto**
revistar *va* (mil.) to review
revistero -ra *mf* reviewer (*of books*); contributor, magazine writer; (Am.) editor of a review or magazine
revisto -ta *pp of* **rever;** *f* review (*reëxamination; survey; magazine; criticism*); (mil. & theat.) review; (law) retrial, new trial; **pasar revista a** to review, go over carefully; (mil.) to review; **suplicar en revista** (law) to appeal
revitalizar §76 *va* to revitalize
revividero *m* silkworm incubator
revivificación *f* revivification
revivificar §86 *va* to revivify
revivir *va* to revive; *vn* to revive, to be revived, to live again
revocable *adj* revocable
revocación *f* revocation
revocador -dora *adj* revoking; *m* plasterer
revocadura *f* plastering, stuccoing; (paint.) edge of canvas covered by frame
revocar §86 *va* to revoke; to dissuade; to drive back, drive away; to plaster, to stucco; *vn* to be driven back or away
revocatorio -ria *adj* revocatory
revoco *m* plastering, stucco; driving back or away; furze cover of a charcoal basket
revolar §77 *vn & vr* to flutter, flutter around; to fly again
revolcadero *m* wallowing place (*of animals*)
revolcar §95 *va* to knock down, to roll over; (coll.) to floor; (coll.) to flunk, to fail; *vr* to wallow; to roll around; to be stubborn
revolcón *m* (coll.) upset, tumble
revolear *vn* to fly around and around
revolotear *va* to fling in the air; *vn* to flutter, flutter around, flit
revoloteo *m* flutter, fluttering
revoltijo or **revoltillo** *m* mass, mess, jumble; twisted mass of guts; confusion
revoltina *f* disturbance, uprising
revoltón *m* vine grub; (arch.) vault; (arch.) turn in a molding
revoltoso -sa *adj* mischievous; winding; complicated; riotous, rebellious; *mf* rioter, rebel
revolución *f* revolution
revolucionar *va* to incite to rebellion; to revolutionize; *vr* to revolt
revolucionario -ria *adj* revolutionary; *mf* revolutionist, revolutionary
revoluto -ta *adj* (coll.) upset; *m* (Am.) panic
revolvedero *m* var. of **revolcadero**
revolvedora *f* (Am.) mixer (*e.g., of concrete*)
revolver §63 & §17, 9 *va* to shake; to stir; to turn upside down; to turn around; to wrap up; to disarrange, mess up, mix up; to disturb, upset; to alienate; to retrace (*one's steps*); to swing (*a horse*) around; to revolve, turn over (*in one's mind*) ‖ *vn* to retrace one's steps; to swing around (*said, e.g., of a horseman*) ‖ *vr* to turn around; to retrace one's steps; to toss and turn; to swing around (*said, e.g., of a horseman*); to turn around; (astr.) to revolve (*in an orbit*); to turn stormy; to get rough (*said of the sea*); **revolverse a, contra** or **sobre** to turn and face (*the enemy*); to turn against
revólver *m* revolver
revolvimiento *m* revolving, revolution
revoque *m* plastering, stucco
revotar *vr* to reverse one's vote
revuelco *m* upset, tumble; wallowing

revuelo *m* second flight; flying around and around; disturbance; excitement; **de revuelo** lightly, incidentally
revuelto -ta *pp of* **revolver;** *adj* scrambled; easily turned (*horse*); mischievous; complicated; confused, disordered; changeable (*weather*); *f* second turn; fight, row; revolution, revolt; disturbance; turn; turning point; change
revuelvepiedras *m* (*pl:* **-dras**) (orn.) turnstone
revulsar *vn* (Am.) to vomit
revulsión *f* (med.) revulsion
revulsivo -va or **revulsorio -ria** *adj & m* revulsive
rey *m* king; queen bee; (cards, chess & fig.) king; (coll.) swineherd; **reyes** *mpl* king and queen; **el rey intruso** Joseph Bonaparte; **no temer rey ni roque** (coll.) to not be afraid of anything or anybody; **servir al rey** to fight for king and country; **rey de armas** earl marshal; (her.) king of arms; **rey de codornices** (orn.) corn crake; **rey de las aves** king of birds (*eagle*); **rey de los animales** king of beasts (*lion*); **rey de zarza** (orn.) wren; **Reyes Católicos** Catholic Sovereigns (*Ferdinand and Isabella*); **Reyes Magos** Magi, Three Wise Men, Wise Men of the East (*they play the rôle of Santa Claus in Latin countries*); **reyes pastores** Shepherd kings
reyerta *f* quarrel, wrangle
reyezuelo *m* kinglet; (orn.) kinglet, wren; **reyezuelo moñudo** (orn.) goldcrest
rezado *m* prayer; divine service
rezador -dora *adj* praying; *mf* prayer (*person*); *f* (ent.) praying mantis
rezaga *f* rear guard
rezagado -da *mf* straggler, laggard
rezagar §59 *va* to outstrip, leave behind; to put off, postpone; *vr* to stay behind, fall behind
rezago *m* residue, remainder
rezar §76 *va* to pray (*a prayer*); to say (*a prayer, mass, etc.*); (coll.) to say, read; (coll.) to call for, e.g., **el periódico reza agua** the newspaper calls for rain; *vn* to pray; (coll.) to grumble; (coll.) to say, read, e.g., **esta página reza así** this page reads thus; **rezar con** (coll.) to concern, to have to do with
rezno *m* (ent.) bot; (bot.) castor-oil plant
rezo *m* prayer; daily prayer; devotions
rezón *m* grapnel
rezongador -dora *adj* grumbling, growling; *mf* grumbler, growler
rezongar §59 *vn* to grumble, growl
rezonglón -glona *adj & mf* (coll.) var. of **rezongador**
rezongo *m* grumbling, growling
rezongón -gona *adj & mf* (coll.) var. of **rezongador**
rezumadero *m* spot where a vessel oozes; oozing, seepage
rezumar *va* to ooze (*moisture*); *vn* to ooze, to seep; *vr* to ooze, to seep; to leak; (coll.) to seep out, leak out (*said, e.g., of a piece of gossip*)
ría *f* narrow inlet, estuary, fiord
riacho or **riachuelo** *m* rivulet, streamlet
riada *f* flood, freshet; (fig.) flood
riba *f* slope, embankment
ribaldería *f* (archaic) knavery, rascality
ribaldo -da *adj* (archaic) knavish, rascally; *m* (archaic) knave, rascal; bawd, procurer
ribazo *m* slope, embankment
ribazón *f* var. of **arribazón**
ribera *f* bank, shore, beach; riverside; dike, levee; **volar la ribera** (coll.) to be fond of wandering and adventure
ribereño -ña *adj* riverside, riparian; *mf* riversider, riparian
riberiego -ga *adj* sedentary (*sheep*); riparian
ribero *m* dike, levee
ribete *m* edge, trimming, border; addition; embellishment (*to a story*); **ribetes** *mpl* strain, streak, touch
ribeteado -da *adj* irritated (*eyes or eyelids*)
ribetear *va* to edge, trim, border, bind
riboflavina *f* (biochem.) riboflavin
ricacho -cha or **ricachón -chona** *mf* (coll.) vulgar rich person
ricadueña *f* (*pl:* **ricasdueñas**) (archaic) noblewoman, peeress
ricahembra *f* (*pl:* **ricashembras**) (archaic) var. of **ricadueña**
Ricardo *m* Richard
ricial *adj* green (*stubble field*); fresh-grown (*pasture*)
ricino *m* (bot.) castor-oil plant
rico -ca *adj* rich; dear, darling; *mf* rich person; **nuevo rico** nouveau riche
ricohombre *m* (*pl:* **ricoshombres**) (archaic) grandee, nobleman
rictus *m* (*pl:* **-tus**) convulsive grin
ricura *f* (coll.) richness; (coll.) excellence; (coll.) darling, sweetheart
ridiculez *f* ridiculousness, absurdity; touchiness
ridiculizar §76 *va* to ridicule
ridículo -la *adj* ridiculous; touchy; *m* ridiculous situation; reticule; **poner en ridículo** to make a fool of, to expose to ridicule; **ponerse en ridículo** to make a fool of oneself
riego *m* irrigation; watering, sprinkling; irrigation water
riel *m* ingot; curtain rod; (rail.) rail
rielar *vn* to shimmer, to gleam; (poet.) to twinkle
rielera *f* ingot mold
rienda *f* rein; **a rienda suelta** swiftly, violently; with free rein; **aflojar las riendas a** to give rein to; **dar rienda suelta a** to give free rein to; **falsa rienda** checkrein; **soltar las riendas** to let go, to let down the bars; **tener las riendas** to draw rein; **tomar las riendas** to take the reins
riente *adj* laughing; bright, cheerful
riesgo *m* risk, danger; **a riesgo de** + *inf* at the risk of + *ger;* **correr riesgo** to run or take a risk
riesgoso -sa *adj* (Am.) risky
Rif, El Er Rif
rifa *f* raffle; fight, quarrel
rifador *m* raffler; raffle vendor; fighter
rifadura *f* (naut.) splitting (*of a sail*)
rifar *va* to raffle, to raffle off; *vn* to raffle; to fight, quarrel; *vr* (naut.) to split (*said of a sail*)
rifeño -ña *adj* Riffian; *mf* Riff, Riffian
rifirrafe *m* (coll.) squabble, row
rifle *m* rifle
riflero *m* (Am.) rifleman (*soldier*)
rigente *adj* (poet.) rigid
rigidez *f* rigidity; **rigidez cadavérica** rigor mortis
rígido -da *adj* rigid
rigodón *m* rigadoon (*dance and music*)
rigor *m* rigor; (path. & physiol.) rigor; **de rigor** de rigueur; **en rigor** as a matter of fact; **rigor de la muerte** rigor mortis
rigorismo *m* rigorism
rigorista *adj* rigoristic; *mf* rigorist; stickler
rigoroso -sa *adj* var. of **riguroso**
rigurosidad *f* rigorousness; severity
riguroso -sa *adj* rigorous; severe
rija *f* (path.) lachrymal fistula; fight, quarrel
rijador -dora *adj* var. of **rijoso**
rijo *m* lust, sensuality
rijoso -sa *adj* lustful, sensual; quarrelsome
rilar *vn* to shiver; *vr* to shake
rima *f* rhyme; heap, pile; **rimas** *fpl* poems, poetry; **octava rima** (pros.) ottava rima; **tercia rima** (pros.) terza rima; **rima femenina** (pros.) feminine rhyme; **rima masculina** (pros.) masculine rhyme; **rima perfecta** perfect rhyme
rimador -dora *adj* rhyming; *mf* rhymer; rhymester (*maker of poor rhymes or verse*)
rimar *va & vn* to rhyme
rimbombancia *f* resonance, echo; showiness, flashiness
rimbombante *adj* resounding; showy, flashy
rimbombar *vn* to resound, to echo
rimbombe *m* or **rimbombo** *m* resonance, echo; high-sounding word
rimero *m* heap, pile
Rin *m* Rhine; (*l.c.*) *m* Rhine wine
rinal *adj* rhinal
rinanto *m* (bot.) wild sage, vervain sage
rincocéfalo -la *adj & m* (zool.) rhynchocephalian

rincón *m* corner; nook, angle; patch, small piece (*e.g., of land*); bit, end; (coll.) home; **rincón de chimenea** chimney corner
rinconada *f* corner
rinconera *f* corner piece (*of furniture*); corner table; (arch.) wall between corner and window
rinencéfalo *m* (anat.) rhinencephalon
ringla *f* or **ringle** *m* (coll.) var. of **ringlera**
ringlera *f* row, line, tier
ringlero *m* ruled line (*for writing exercise*)
ringorrango *m* (coll.) curlicue (*in writing*); (coll.) frill, frippery
rinitis *f* (path.) rhinitis
rinoceronte *m* (zool.) rhinoceros
rinoplastia *f* (surg.) rhinoplasty
rinoscopia *f* rhinoscopy
rinoscopio *m* rhinoscope
riña *f* fight, scuffle, fray, brawl; **riña de campanario** petty local row; **riña de gallos** cockfight; **riña tumultuaria** free-for-all
riñón *m* (anat.) kidney; (min.) kidney ore; (cook.) kidney; (fig.) heart, center; **riñones** *mpl* back, loins; **tener recubierto** or **bien cubierto el riñón** (coll.) to be well-heeled; **riñón flotante** (path.) floating kidney
riñonada *f* (anat.) cortical tissue (*of kidney*); loins; kidney stew
río *m* river; (fig.) river (*e.g., of blood*); great flow, stream (*of people or things*); **a río revuelto** in confusion, in disorder; **pescar en río revuelto** to fish in troubled waters
riolada *f* (coll.) great flow, stream (*of people or things*)
riolita *f* (mineral.) rhyolite
rioplatense *adj* Platine; *mf* native or inhabitant of the Basin of the River Plate
riostra *f* brace, stay; guy, guy wire
riostrar *va* to brace, to stay
ripia *f* shingle; slab (*outside cut of log*)
ripiar *va* to fill with rubble, to riprap; *vn* to shingle
ripio *m* refuse, debris; rubble, debris; padding (*in writing, speech, or verse*); **no perder ripio** to not miss a word; (coll.) to not miss a trick
ripioso -sa *adj* rubbly; padded (*e.g., verse*)
riqueza *f* wealth, riches; richness; **riquezas** *fpl* wealth, riches; precious objects
riquísimo -ma *adj super* very or most rich
risa *f* laugh, laughter; **caerse** or **desternillarse de risa** to split one's sides with laughter; **dar risa a uno** to make someone laugh; **morirse de risa** to die laughing; **perderse de risas** to be convulsed with laughter; **reventar de risa** to burst with laughter; **tener la risa** to keep from laughing; **risa falsa** feigned laugh; **risa sardesca** or **sardónica** (path.) sardonic grin
risada *f* var. of **risotada**
riscal *m* cragged region
risco *m* cliff, crag; honey fritter
riscoso -sa *adj* cragged
risibilidad *f* risibility
risible *adj* risible, laughable
risica, risilla or **risita** *f* giggle, titter; feigned laugh, false laugh
risol *m* (cook.) rissole
risotada *f* guffaw, horse laugh, boisterous laugh
risotear *vn* to guffaw, to laugh boisterously
risoteo *m* var. of **risotada**
ríspido -da *adj* harsh, gruff
rispo -pa *adj* harsh, gruff; unruly
ristra *f* string of onions, string of garlic; (coll.) string, row, file
ristre *m* lance rest
ristrel *m* rail, heavy rail (*of wood*)
risueño -ña *adj* smiling; (fig.) smiling
rítmico -ca *adj* rhythmic or rhythmical; *f* rhythmics
ritmo *m* rhythm
rito *m* rite; **rito romano** Roman rite
ritón *m* (archeol.) rhyton
ritornello *m* var. of **retornelo**
ritual *adj & m* ritual; **ser de ritual** to be ordained by custom
ritualidad *f* observance of formalities
ritualismo *m* ritualism
ritualista *adj* ritualistic, ritualist; *mf* ritualist
rival *adj & mf* rival
rivalidad *f* rivalry; enmity
rivalizar **§76** *vn* to vie, to compete; **rivalizar con** to rival
rivera *f* creek, brook
riza *f* see **rizo**
rizado -da *adj* curly; ripply; *m* curling; curliness; curls; pleats
rizador *m* curling iron; hair curler
rizal *m* var. of **ricial**
rizar **§76** *va* to curl; to crimple; to ripple; *vr* to curl, be curly; to ripple
rizo -za *adj* curly; *m* curl, ringlet; ripple; (aer.) loop; (naut.) reef point; **hacer** or **rizar el rizo** (aer.) to loop the loop; **largar rizos** (naut.) to let out the reef; **tomar rizos** (naut.) to take in the reef; *f* barley stubble; stubbly hay left in rack (*by horses*); ravage, destruction
rizófago -ga *adj* (zool.) rhizophagous
rizoforáceo -a *adj* (bot.) rhizophoraceous
rizoide *adj* rhizoid; *m* (bot.) rhizoid
rizoma *m* (bot.) rhizome
rizópodo *m* (zool.) rhizopod
rizoso -sa *adj* curly
rizotomía *f* (surg.) rhizotomy
r.[1] abr. of **real** (*moneda*)
R.[1] abr. of **Real** (*del rey*)
R.M. abr. of **Reverenda Madre**
Rmrz. abr. of **Ramírez**
R.O. abr. of **Real Orden**
ro *interj* **¡ro ro!** bye-bye!, hushaby! (*lullaby word*); *m* (slang) husband
roa *f* (naut.) stem
roano -na *adj* roan
rob *m* fruit jelly
robadera *f* (agr.) harrow
robador -dora *adj* robbing, thieving; *mf* robber, thief
róbalo or **robalo** *m* (ichth.) bass, sea bass; (ichth.) snook
robar *va* to rob, to steal; to abduct; to sweep away, carry away; to make round, to round off; to draw (*a card or domino*); to win over; **robarle algo a alguien** to rob someone of something, to rob or steal something from someone; *vn & vr* to steal
robellón *m* (bot.) field mushroom
Roberto *m* Robert
robezo *m* (zool.) chamois
robín *m* rust
robinete *m* spigot, faucet, cock, valve
robinia *f* (bot.) locust
robinsonismo *m* isolation, independence, self-sufficiency
robladero -ra *adj* made to be clinched or riveted
robladura *f* clinching, riveting
roblar *va* to clinch, to rivet
roble *m* (bot.) British oak; husky person; strong thing or object; strength, bulwark; **roble ahumado** fumed oak; **roble ahorquillado** (bot.) turkey oak (*Quercus catesbaei*); **roble albero** (bot.) British oak, durmast (*Quercus sessiflora*); **roble blanco de América** (bot.) white oak (*Quercus alba*); **roble blanco de California** (bot.) valley or California oak, swamp oak; **roble borne** (bot.) pubescent oak, durmast; **roble carrasqueño** (bot.) gall oak; **roble de fruto grande** (bot.) bur oak, mossy-cup oak; **roble de hojas aliradas** (bot.) overcup oak; **roble de los pantanos** (bot.) pin oak, swamp oak; **roble escarlata** (bot.) scarlet oak; **roble negral, negro** or **villano** (bot.) pubescent oak, durmast; **roble rojo** (bot.) red oak
robleda *f*, **robledal** *m* or **robledo** *m* woods of oak trees
roblizo -za *adj* strong, hard, robust
roblón *m* rivet; ridge (*of tiles*)
roblonar *va & vn* to rivet
robo *m* robbery, theft; draw (*card or cards drawn*); **robo con escalo** burglary
roboración *f* strengthening; corroboration
roborar *va* to strengthen; to corroborate
roborativo -va *adj* strengthening; corroborative
robot *m* (*pl:* **-bots**) robot; (fig.) robot (*person*)
robra *f* var. of **alboroque**
robustecedor -dora *adj* strengthening

robustecer §76 *va* to make strong, to strengthen; *vr* to become strong
robustez *f* or **robusteza** *f* robustness
robusto -ta *adj* robust
roca *f* rock; **la Roca** the Rock (*Gibraltar*); **roca de respaldo** (geol. & min.) wall rock; **roca Tarpeya** Tarpeian Rock
rocada *f* rock (*wool or flax on distaff*)
rocadero *m* knob or head (*of a distaff*); conical paper hat worn as a mark of infamy
rocador *m* knob or head (*of a distaff*)
rocalla *f* pebbles; stone chips; large glass bead; (f.a.) rocaille
rocalloso -sa *adj* pebbly, stony
rocambola *f* (bot.) giant garlic, rocambole
roce *m* rubbing; contact, frequent contact
rocero -ra *adj* (dial.) too familiar (*with inferiors*); brush (*wood*)
rociada *f* see **rociado**
rociadera *f* watering can, sprinkling can, sprinkler
rociado -da *adj* dewy; bedewed; *m* spraying; *f* sprinkling; dew; dew-drenched grass given to a horse as medicine; shower (*of stones, bullets*); volley (*of rebukes*)
rociador *m* clothes sprinkler; sprayer; **rociador automático** spray bomb
rociadura *f* or **rociamiento** *m* sprinkling; spraying
rociar §90 *va* to sprinkle (*e.g., water; flowers with water*); to spray; to bedew; to scatter; *vn* to drizzle; to be dew, e.g., **rocía esta mañana** there is dew this morning
rocín *m* hack, nag; draft horse, work horse; (coll.) coarse, stupid fellow; (Am.) draft ox; (Am.) riding horse; **rocín matalón** thin, worn-out horse
rocinante *m* worn-out horse
rocino *m* var. of **rocín**
rocío *m* dew; drizzle; sprinkling; (naut.) spindrift; **rocío de sol** (bot.) sundew
roción *m* splash of waves
rococó *adj & m* (f.a.) rococo
rocoso -sa *adj* rocky
rocha *f* clearing
rochela *f* (Am.) noise, racket; **La Rochela** La Rochelle (*city*)
rocho *m* (myth) roc (*bird*)
roda *f* (naut.) stem
rodaballo *m* (ichth.) turbot; (ichth.) brill; (coll.) sly fellow; **rodaballo menor** (ichth.) brill (*Rhombus laevis*)
rodada *f* see **rodado**
rodadero -ra *adj* shaped to roll, ready to roll; easy-rolling, smooth-rolling
rodadizo -za *adj* easy-rolling, smooth-rolling
rodado -da *adj* dapple; rounded, fluent (*period*); scattered (*fragments of ore*); on wheels, rolling; *m* boulder; stray piece of ore; *f* rut, track (*left by wheel*)
rodador -dora *adj* rolling; *m* (ent.) mosquito; (ichth.) sunfish
rodadura *f* rolling; rut; tread
rodaja *f* disk, small wheel, caster; round slice; rowel
rodaje *m* wheels, set of wheels; shooting, filming (*of a moving picture, of a scene, etc.*); **en rodaje** (aut.) being broken in, being run in; (mov.) being filmed
rodal *m* place, spot, patch; cart with solid wheels
rodamiento *m* bearing; tread (*of a tire*); **rodamientos** *mpl* running gear; **rodamiento a bolas** ball bearing; **rodamiento a rodillos** roller bearing
rodánico -ca *adj* (pertaining to the) Rhone
rodano -na *adj & mf* Rhodian
Ródano *m* Rhone
rodante *adj* rolling
rodapelo *m* var. of **redopelo**
rodapié *m* baseboard; drapery around the bottom of a bed, table, etc.
rodaplancha *f* ward (*of a key*)
rodar §77 *va* to roll; to take, to shoot (*a moving picture*); to film; to screen, to project; to drag along; to roll down (*e.g., the stairs*); to turn (*a key*); (Am.) to knock down; *vn* to roll, roll along; to run (*on wheels*); to roll down; to rotate, to revolve; to tumble; to roam, wander about; to prowl; to abound; (aer.) to taxi; **echarlo todo a rodar** (coll.) to upset everything, to spoil everything; (coll.) to fly off the handle; **ir rodando** to come along all right; **rodar por** to go around through (*e.g., stores*) in vain; (coll.) to be at the beck and call of
Rodas *f* Rhodes
rodeabrazo; a rodeabrazo winding up, swinging the arm for a throw
rodeador -dora *adj* surrounding
rodear *va* to surround, go around; to turn around; (Am.) to round up; *vn* to go around; to go a roundabout way; to beat about the bush; *vr* to turn, twist, toss about
rodela *f* buckler, target
rodenal *m* growth of cluster pine trees
rodeno -na *adj* red, reddish; see **pino**
rodeo *m* surrounding; detour, roundabout way; dodge, duck; evasion, subterfuge; roundup; rodeo (*roundup; cowboy exhibition*); **andar con rodeos** to beat about the bush; **dejarse de rodeos** to stop beating about the bush
rodero -ra *adj* (pertaining to a) wheel; *f* track, rut (*left by a wheel*); cart or wagon road across a field
Rodesia, la Rhodesia
rodete *m* knot (*of hair*); padded ring (*for carrying an object on the head*); fifth wheel; belt pulley, band pulley; ward (*of a lock*); (hyd.) drum wheel
rodezno *m* horizontal water wheel; gear that meshes with millstone gear
rodezuela *f* small wheel
rodilla *f* (anat.) knee; padded ring (*for carrying an object on the head*); ward (*of a lock*); floor rag, kitchen rag, mop; **a media rodilla** on one knee; **de rodillas** kneeling, on one's knees; **doblar la rodilla** to get down on one knee; to yield, give in; **hincar la rodilla** to kneel down; to bow one's head, to humble oneself; **hincarse de rodillas** or **ponerse de rodillas** to kneel, kneel down; **rodilla de fregona** (path.) housemaid's knee
rodillada *f* push or blow with the knee; blow on the knee; (act of) kneeling
rodillar *va* to roll
rodillazo *m* push or blow with the knee
rodillero -ra *adj* (pertaining to the) knee; *f* kneepiece, genouillère (*of armor*); knee (*of garment*); kneecap, kneepad (*cover*); baggy knee (*of trousers*); knee injury (*of a horse caused by fall*); (mus.) knee swell (*of organ*)
rodillo *m* roller; rolling pin; road roller; inking roller; platen (*of typewriter*); **rodillo de vapor** steam roller
rodilludo -da *adj* big-kneed
rodio -dia *adj & mf* Rhodian; *m* (chem.) rhodium
rodiota *adj & mf* Rhodian
rodo *m* roller; **a rodo** in abundance
rododafne *f* (bot.) rosebay
rododendro *m* (bot.) rhododendron
rodofíceo -a *adj* (bot.) rhodophyceous
Rodolfo *m* Rudolph; Ralph
rodomiel *m* (pharm.) honey of rose
rodomontada *f* rodomontade
rodopsina *f* (physiol.) rhodopsin
rodora *f* (bot.) rhodora
rodriga *f* prop, stake (*for plants*)
rodrigar §59 *va* to prop, prop up, stake (*plants*)
rodrigazón *f* season for propping plants
Rodrigo *m* Roderick
rodrigón *m* prop, stake (*for plants*); (coll.) old retainer who escorts ladies
roedor -dora *adj* gnawing; (fig.) biting, stinging, consuming; (zool.) rodent; *m* (zool.) rodent
roedura *f* gnawing; nibble; place that has been nibbled
roel *m* (her.) bezant
roela *f* disk of crude gold or silver
roentgenograma *m* roentgenogram
roentgenología *f* roentgenology
roentgenólogo -ga *mf* roentgenologist
roentgenoterapia *f* roentgenotherapy
roer §78 *va* to gnaw, gnaw away at; to pick (*a bone*); to wear away, to wear down
roete *m* (pharm.) pomegranate wine

rogación *f* petition, request; (hist.) rogation; **rogaciones** *fpl* (eccl.) rogations
rogado -da *adj* fond of being coaxed
rogante *adj* suppliant
rogar §79 *va & vn* to beg; to pray; **hacerse de rogar** to like to be coaxed; **rogar por** to plead for; to pray for
rogativo -va *adj* supplicatory; *f* (eccl.) rogation; **rogativas** *fpl* (eccl.) rogations
rogatorio -ria *adj* rogatory
Rogelio or **Rogerio** *m* Roger
rogo *m* (poet.) pyre
roído -da *adj* (coll.) miserly, stingy
roigo *1st sg pres ind of* **roer**
rojal *adj* reddish; *m* reddish earth
rojear *vn* to redden; to become reddish
rojete *m* rouge (*for face*)
rojez *f* redness
rojizo -za *adj* reddish
rojo -ja *adj* red; ruddy; red-haired; Red (*communist*); *mf* Red (*communist*); *m* red; **al rojo** to a red heat; **rojo cereza** cherry red (*of incandescence*); **rojo de Burdeos** Bordeaux red; **rojo de plomo** red lead; **rojo de rubia** (chem.) madder; **rojo turco** Turkey red
rojura *f* redness
rol *m* roll, list; (naut.) muster roll
Rolando *m* Roland
rolar *vn* (naut.) to veer around; (Am.) to associate
Roldán *m* Roland
roldana *f* sheave
rolde *m* circle, ring (*of people*)
rolla *f* collar of a draft horse; child's nurse
rollar *va* to roll, roll up
rollizo -za *adj* round, cylindrical; plump, stocky, stodgy, sturdy; *m* round log
rollo *m* roll; roller, rolling pin; round log; cylindrical stone; cylindrical pillar (*in main square of town*); yoke pad; rôle
rollón *m* mixed bran and flour
rollona *f* (coll.) nurse, child's nurse
Roma *f* see **romo**
romadizar §76 *vr* to catch cold, to have a cold in the head
romadizo *m* cold, cold in the head
romaico -ca *adj & m* Romaic
romana *f* see **romano**
romanador *m* weighmaster
romanar *va* to weigh with a steelyard
romance *adj* Romance (*language*); *m* Romance language; Spanish language; romance of chivalry; octosyllabic verse with alternate lines in assonance; narrative poem in octosyllabic verse; **romances** *mpl* prattle, excuses; **en buen romance** in plain language; **hablar en romance** to speak plainly, to come to the point; **romance de ciego** ballad sung and sold on the streets by a blind man; **romance heroico** or **real** hendecasyllabic verse with alternate lines in assonance
romancear *va* to translate into the vernacular, to translate into Spanish
romanceresco -ca *adj* romantic (*event, story, imagination*)
romancerista *mf* romancist
romancero -ra *mf* romancer, romancist; *m* collection of Old Spanish romances
romancesco -ca *adj* novelistic; romantic
romancillo *m* verse of less than eight syllables with alternate lines in assonance
romancista *mf* romancer; writer in Spanish, writer in the vernacular (*not in Latin*)
romanche *m* Romansh
romanear *va* to weigh with a steelyard; (naut.) to balance; *vn* to weigh more
romaneo *m* weighing with a steelyard
romanero *m* weighmaster
romanesco -ca *adj* Roman; novelistic; romantic
romanía; de romanía (coll.) crestfallen
románico -ca *adj* Romance, Romanic (*language*); (arch.) Romanesque; *m* (arch.) Romanesque
romanillo -lla *adj* round-hand; (print.) roman; *f* (Am.) dining-room screen
romanismo *m* Romanism; Romance philology; Romance-language phenomenon (*root, idiom, characteristic*); (offensive) Romanism (*Catholic religion*)
romanista *mf* Romanist; (offensive) Romanist (*member of the Roman Catholic Church*)
romanística *f* Romance scholarship
romanización *f* Romanization
romanizar §76 *va & vr* to Romanize
romano -na *adj* Roman; romaine (*lettuce*); *mf* Roman; *f* steelyard
romanticismo *m* romanticism; (*cap.*) *m* Romantic Movement
romántico -ca *adj* romantic; *mf* romanticist; romantic
romanza *f* (mus.) romance, romanza
romanzar §76 *va* var. of **romancear**
romaza *f* (bot.) dock, sorrel
rombal *adj* (geom.) rhombic
rombencéfalo *m* (anat.) rhombencephalon, hindbrain
rómbico -ca *adj* (cryst.) rhombic
rombo *m* (geom.) rhomb or rhombus; diamond (*in cards*)
romboedro *m* (geom.) rhombohedron
romboidal *adj* rhomboid, rhomboidal
romboide *m* (geom.) rhomboid
romeo -a *adj* Romaean (*Byzantine Greek*)
romeraje *m* pilgrimage
romeral *m* growth of rosemary
romería *f* pilgrimage; gathering at a shrine on saint's day; crowd, gathering
romeriego -ga *adj* fond of pilgrimages
romero -ra *mf* pilgrim; *m* (bot.) rosemary
romí *adj* (*pl:* **-míes**) see **azafrán**
romo -ma *adj* blunt, dull; flat-nosed; (*cap.*) *f* Rome
rompeátomos *m* (*pl:* **-mos**) (phys.) atom smasher
rompecabezas *m* (*pl:* **-zas**) slung shot; riddle, puzzle; jigsaw puzzle
rompecoches *m* (*pl:* **-ches**) durance, everlasting (*material*)
rompedero -ra *adj* fragile, breakable; *f* iron punch, blacksmith's punch; powder screen
rompedura *f* breaking, breakage
rompeesquinas *m* (*pl:* **-nas**) (coll.) var. of **rompesquinas**
rompegalas *mf* (*pl:* **-las**) (coll.) shabby-looking person
rompehielos *m* (*pl:* **-los**) icebreaker, iceboat
rompehuelgas *mf* (*pl:* **-gas**) strikebreaker
rompenueces *m* (*pl:* **-ces**) nutcracker
rompeolas *m* (*pl:* **-las**) breakwater, mole
romper §17, 9 *va* to break; to tear; to break through; to plow for the first time; **romper el hielo** (fig.) to break the ice; *vn* to break (*said of waves, of the dawn*); to break or burst open (*said of flowers*); to break down; **de rompe y rasga** (coll.) determined; **romper a** + *inf* to suddenly start to + *inf*, to burst out + *ger*, e.g., **romper a llorar** to burst out crying; **romper con** to break with
rompesacos *m* (*pl:* **-cos**) (bot.) goat grass; (bot.) lyme grass
rompesquinas *m* (*pl:* **-nas**) (coll.) corner loafer, corner bully
rompible *adj* breakable
rompido *m* newly broken ground
rompiente *m* reef, rock, shoal
rompimiento *m* break, breakage; breach, crack; (paint.) opening in background; (theat.) open drop scene; (min.) breakthrough
Rómulo *m* (myth.) Romulus
ron *m* (*pl:* **rones**) rum; **ron de laurel** or **de malagueta** bay rum
ronca *f* see **ronco**
roncador -dora *adj* snoring; *mf* snorer; *m* (ichth.) roncador, croaker
roncar §86 *vn* to snore; to roar (*said of wind or sea*); to cry in rutting season; (coll.) to bully, threaten
ronce *m* (coll.) coaxing, cajoling
roncear *vn* to kill time, to fool around; (coll.) to coax, cajole; (naut.) to sail slowly
roncería *f* killing time, fooling around; (coll.) coaxing, cajoling; (naut.) slow sailing
roncero -ra *adj* poky; grouchy; (coll.) coaxing, cajoling; (naut.) slow-sailing
ronco -ca *adj* hoarse, raucous; *m* (ichth.) grunt; *f* rut (*season*); cry of buck in rutting season; halberd; (coll.) bullying; **echar roncas** (coll.) to bully

roncón *m* drone of a bagpipe
roncha *f* welt; black-and-blue mark; (coll.) gyp; round slice
ronchar *va* to crunch; *vn* to make a crunching sound (*said, e.g., of raw potatoes*); to raise welts
ronda *f* night patrol or round; night serenaders; round (*of visits*); (coll.) round (*of cigars or wine*); (Am.) ring-around-a-rosy; **coger la ronda a** to catch in the act; **ronda de matrícula** (nav.) press gang
rondador *m* night watchman; serenader; rounder; prowler
rondalla *f* story, tale; (dial.) serenaders
rondar *va* to go around, fly around; to patrol; (coll.) to hang over, threaten; (coll.) to hang around, to hound; (coll.) to court; (coll.) to go serenading (*young women*); (coll.) to go up to around, e.g., **las temperaturas rondarán los 40 grados** the temperature will go up to around forty degrees; *vn* to patrol by night, go the rounds in the night; to gad about at nighttime; to go serenading; to prowl; (mil.) to make the rounds
rondel *m* rondel
rondeño -ña *adj* (pertaining to) Ronda; *mf* native or inhabitant of Ronda; *f* (mus.) fandango of Ronda
rondín *m* corporal's round (*to visit sentinels*); watchman in a naval arsenal
rondís *m* or **rondiz** *m* face of a precious stone
rondó *m* (*pl:* **-dós**) rondeau; (mus.) rondo
rondón; de rondón brashly
ronquear *vn* to be hoarse
ronquedad *f* raucousness, harshness, hoarseness
ronquera *f* hoarseness (*from a cold*)
ronquido *m* snore, snoring; rasp, rasping sound
ronronear *vn* to purr (*said of a cat or airplane*)
ronroneo *m* purr, purring
ronza; ir a la ronza (naut.) to fall to leeward
ronzal *m* halter; (naut.) double tackle, purchase rope
ronzar **§76** *va* to crunch; (naut.) to move with a lever
roña *f* scab, mange; sticky dirt; pine bark; (bot.) rust; stinginess; stingy person; trickiness; moral infection; **jugar a roña** or **a la roña** (Am.) to play for fun (*not for money*)
roñada *f* (naut.) garland, grommet
roñería *f* (coll.) stinginess
roñica *mf* (coll.) skinflint
roñoso -sa *adj* scabby, mangy; dirty, filthy; rusty; (coll.) stingy
ropa *f* clothing, clothes; dry goods; **a quema ropa** point-blank; **a toca ropa** at close range; **ropa blanca** linen (*tablecloths, napkins, sheets, towels, shirts, etc.*); **ropa de cama** bed linen (*sheets, pillowcases, etc.*); bedclothes (*blankets, quilts, etc.*); **ropa de cámara** or **de levantar** dressing gown, wrapper, bath robe; **ropa dominguera** Sunday best; **ropa hecha** ready-made clothes; **ropa interior** underwear; **ropas menores** underwear; **ropa sucia** laundry (*clothes to be washed*); **ropa vieja** old clothes; stew made from leftovers
ropaje *m* clothes, clothing; robe, gown; drapery; language
ropálico -ca *adj* (pros.) rhopalic
ropavejería *f* old-clothes shop
ropavejero -ra *mf* old-clothes dealer; *m* old-clothesman
ropería *f* clothing business; clothing store; **ropería de viejo** old-clothes shop
ropero -ra *mf* ready-made clothier; wardrobe keeper; *m* wardrobe, clothes closet; charitable organization for the distribution of old clothes
ropeta *f* var. of **ropilla**
ropilla *f* doublet; **dar una ropilla a** (coll.) to scold mildly, to reprove gently
ropón *m* loose coat; double quilting; (Am.) woman's riding habit
roque *m* rook (*in chess*)
roqueda *f* or **roquedal** *m* rocky place or region
roqueño -ña *adj* rocky; hard as rock
roquería *f* (Am.) rookery (*of seals*)
roquero -ra *adj* rocky, built on rock
roqueta *f* (bot.) roquette, rocket salad
roquete *m* barbed spearhead; ramrod, rammer; (eccl.) rochet
rorcual *m* (zool.) rorqual, finback, razorback
rorro *m* (coll.) baby; (Am.) doll
ros *m* (mil.) Spanish shako
rosa *f* see **roso**
rosáceo -a *adj* rosaceous; (bot.) rosaceous
rosacruz (*pl:* **-cruces**) *adj & mf* Rosicrucian
rosada *f* see **rosado**
rosadelfa *f* (bot.) azalea
rosado -da *adj* rose; rose-colored, rosy; *f* frost
rosal *m* (bot.) rosebush; **rosal de China** or **rosal japonés** (bot.) japonica; **rosal de pitiminí** (bot.) crimson rambler (*plant*); **rosal perruno** or **silvestre** (bot.) dog rose
rosaleda or **rosalera** *f* rosary, rose garden
Rosalía *f* Rosalie
rosar *vr* to turn red, to blush
rosariera *f* (bot.) bead tree
rosariero *m* dealer in rosaries; (coll.) hypocrite
rosario *m* rosary; string (*e.g., of misfortunes*); chain pump; (coll.) backbone; group reciting the rosary; reciting the rosary
rosbif *m* (*pl:* **-bifs**) roast beef
rosca *f* coil, spiral; turn (*of a spiral*); twist, twisted roll; (mach.) thread; nut and bolt, screw and nut; fleshiness; arch ring; (Am.) padded ring (*for carrying an object on the head*); **hacer la rosca a** (coll.) to hound (*a person*); (coll.) to play up to; **hacer la rosca** or **hacer la rosca del galgo** (coll.) to curl up and go to sleep anywhere; **pasarse de rosca** to be or become stripped, to not fit (*said of a screw or nut*); to go too far, to take too much liberty; **rosca de Arquímedes** Archimedes' screw
roscadero *m* (dial.) large hamper
roscado -da *adj* threaded; spiral; *m* threading
roscar **§86** *va* to thread
rosco or **roscón** *m* twisted roll (*of bread*)
Rosellón, el the Roussillon
róseo -a *adj* rose, rosy
roséola *f* (path.) roseola, rose rash; (path.) roseola, German measles
rosero -ra *mf* gatherer of saffron flowers
roseta *f* red spot on the cheek; sprinkling nozzle (*of water pot*); (metal.) rosette; metal tip of steelyard; **rosetas** *fpl* popcorn
rosetón *m* (arch.) rosette; (arch.) rose window, wheel window
rosicler *m* pink of dawn; ruby silver
rosicruciano -na *adj & mf* Rosicrucian
rosillo -lla *adj* light red, pink; roan
rosita *f* little rose; **rositas** *fpl* popcorn; **de rositas** (coll.) free, for nothing
rosmarino -na *adj* light red, pink; *m* (bot.) rosemary
rosmaro *m* var. of **manatí**
roso -sa *adj* red; threadbare; **a roso y velludo** completely, without exception ‖ *f* rose (*flower*); (Am.) rosebush; rose (*rose-shaped ribbon; precious stone; perfume*); red spot (*on skin*); rose diamond; (arch.) rose, rose window; **rosas** *fpl* popcorn; **verlo todo de color de rosa** to see everything through rose-colored glasses; **rosa albardera** (bot.) peony; **rosa de China** (bot.) China rose; **rosa de Damasco** (bot.) damask rose; **rosa de güeldres** (bot.) guelder-rose; **rosa de Jericó** (bot.) rose of Jericho; **rosa de los vientos** (naut.) compass card; **rosa de pitiminí** (hort.) crimson rambler; **rosa de rejalgar** (bot.) peony; **rosa de Siria** (bot.) rose of Sharon; **rosa náutica** (naut.) compass card; **rosa montés** (bot.) peony ‖ *m* rose, pink
rosoli *m* rosolio (*a drink*)
rosolí *m* (bot.) sundew
rosón *m* (ent.) bot
rosqueado -da *adj* spiral, twisted
rosquete *m* coffeecake
rosquilla *f* coffeecake, doughnut, cruller; (ent.) grub; **saber a rosquillas** (coll.) to be gratifying, to be satisfying
rostrado -da *adj* rostrate
rostral *adj* rostral
rostritorcido -da or **rostrituerto -ta** *adj* (coll.) sullen, gruff, morose
rostro *m* beak; face; snout; (anat., naut. & zool.) rostrum; **hacer rostro a** to face up to; to face, to accept; **rostro a rostro** face to face
rostropálido -da *mf* paleface (*white person; so called by American Indians*)

rota *f* see **roto**
rotación *f* rotation; **rotación de cosechas** or **de cultivos** rotation of crops
rotacismo *m* rhotacism
rotador -dora *adj* rotatory; *m* (anat.) rotator
rotar *vn* var. of **rodar**
rotario -ria *adj & m* Rotarian
rotativo -va *adj* rotary; revolving; *m* metropolitan newspaper; *f* (print.) rotary press
rotatorio -ria *adj* rotatory
roten *m* or **rotén** *m* (bot.) rattan; rattan (*cane or staff*)
rotífero -ra *adj* rotiferous; *m* (zool.) rotifer
roto -ta *pp of* **romper;** *adj* broken, shattered; torn; ragged; debauched, licentious; *mf* (in Argentina and Peru) Chilean, poor Chilean; *f* rout, defeat; (bot.) rattan, rattan palm; (naut.) route, course; **de rota** or **de rota batida** with complete loss or destruction; all of a sudden
rotocosido *m* patched clothing
rotograbado *m* rotogravure
rotonda *f* rear of stagecoach; rotunda; (Am.) roundhouse
rotor *m* (mach. & elec.) rotor
rótula *f* lozenge; (anat.) kneecap, kneepan; hinge joint; knuckle
rotulación *f* labeling, lettering; hinge joint
rotular *adj* rotular; *va* to label, to title, to letter
rotulata *f* collection of labels or posters; (coll.) label, title, mark
rotuliano -na *adj* rotulian
rotulista *m* letterer, sign maker, sign painter
rótulo *m* label, title, lettering; show bill, poster
rotunda *f* see **rotundo**
rotundamente *adv* roundly, categorically
rotundidad *f* roundness; rotundity
rotundo -da *adj* round; rotund, full, sonorous; round, peremptory; *f* rotunda
rotura *f* breaking, breakage; breach, opening; (vet.) plaster, poultice
roturación *f* plowing untilled ground; newly plowed untilled ground
roturar *va* to plow, to break (*untilled ground*)
roya *f* (bot.) rust, mildew, plant rot; coir, coconut fiber
royo *1st sg pres ind of* **roer**
roza *f* grubbing, stubbing; clearing
rozadera *f* var. of **rozón**
rozador -dora *mf* stubber
rozadura *f* rubbing; chafing; abrasion; (bot.) punkwood
rozagante *adj* showy, pompous; elegant, magnificent; flowing, sweeping (*gown, robe*)
rozamiento *m* rubbing, friction; (mech. & fig.) friction
rozar §76 *va* to grub, to stub; to clear (*land*); to nibble (*grass*); to cut and gather (*small branches or grass*); to scrape; to graze; to border on; *vn* to graze, graze by; *vr* to interfere (*to strike one foot against another*); to hobnob, to be close, be on close terms; to falter, stammer; to be alike; (naut.) to fret, to gall
roznar *va* to crunch; *vn* to bray
roznido *m* crunch, crunching noise; bray, braying
rozno *m* small donkey
rozo *m* grubbing, stubbing; chips, brush; **ser de buen rozo** (coll.) to have a good appetite
rozón *m* short, broad scythe or sickle
R.P. abr. of **Reverendo Padre**
rs. or **r.[s]** abr. of **reales** (*moneda*)
R.S. abr. of **Real Servicio**
Rte. abr. of **Remite**
rúa *f* village street; wagon road; **hacer la rúa** to walk or ride around town
Ruán *f* Rouen
ruano -na *adj* roan; *f* woolen fabric
rubefacción *f* rubefaction
rubefaciente *adj & m* (med.) rubefacient
Rubén *m* (Bib.) Reuben
rúbeo -a *adj* reddish
rubéola *f* (path.) German measles
ruberoide *m* rubberoid
rubescente *adj* rubescent
rubeta *f* (zool.) peeper, tree toad
rubí *m* (*pl:* **-bíes**) ruby; (horol.) ruby, jewel; (orn.) vermilion flycatcher; **rubí balaje** (mineral.) balas ruby; **rubí de Bohemia** (mineral.) rose quartz; **rubí espinela** (mineral.) ruby spinel; **rubí oriental** (mineral.) Oriental or true ruby
rubia *f* see **rubio**
rubiáceo -a *adj* (bot.) rubiaceous
rubial *adj* reddish (*soil or plant*); *m* madder field
rubiales *mf* (*pl:* **-les**) (coll.) goldilocks
rubicán -cana *adj* rubican
rubicela *f* (mineral.) rubicel
Rubicón *m* Rubicon; **pasar el Rubicón** to cross the Rubicon
rubicundez *f* rubicundity; reddishness
rubicundo -da *adj* rubicund; reddish
rubidio *m* (chem.) rubidium
rubificar §86 *va* to redden, to dye red; (med.) to make (*the skin*) red
rubilla *f* (bot.) woodruff
rubín *m* ruby; rust
rubinejo *m* little ruby
rubio -bia *adj* golden, blond, fair; *m* blond (*man or boy*); (ichth.) red gurnard; **rubio volador** (ichth.) sea robin; *f* blonde (*girl or woman*); station wagon; (coll.) peseta; (bot.) madder (*plant and root*); **rubia platino** platinum blonde; **rubia oxigenada** peroxide blonde
rublo *m* ruble
rubor *m* bright red; flush, blush; bashfulness
ruborizar §76 *va* to make flush, make blush; *vr* to flush, to blush
ruboroso -sa *adj* blushing, bashful
rúbrica *f* rubric; title, heading; flourish (*to a signature*); **ser de rúbrica** (coll.) to be in accordance with ritual or custom
rubricar §86 *va* to add one's flourish to (*a document, with or without one's signature*); to sign and seal; to certify to, to attest
rubrificar §86 *va* to rubricate, make red
rubriquista *m* rubrician
rubro -bra *adj* red; *m* (Am.) title, heading
ruc *m* var. of **rocho**
ruca *f* (bot.) rocket salad
rucio -cia *adj* silver-gray; (coll.) gray-haired
ruche *m* or **rucho** *m* (coll.) donkey
ruda *f* see **rudo**
rudeza *f* coarseness, roughness; rudeness, crudeness; dullness, stupidity; severity
rudimental *adj* rudimental
rudimentario -ria *adj* rudimentary
rudimento *m* rudiment
rudo -da *adj* coarse, rough; rude, crude; dull, stupid; hard, severe; (phonet.) rough (*breathing*); *f* (bot.) rue; **ruda cabruna** (bot.) goat's-rue; **ruda de muros** (bot.) wall rue
rueca *f* distaff; twist, turn; (fig.) distaff, female sex, women
rueda *f* wheel; caster, roller; ring, circle (*of people*); rack (*for torture*); round slice; pinwheel; turn, time; spread (*of peacock's tail*); (ichth.) sunfish; **hacer la rueda** to spread its tail (*said of a peacock*); **hacer la rueda a** (coll.) to keep after; (coll.) to flatter, play up to; **quinta rueda** fifth wheel (*superfluous person or thing*); **rueda catalina** (horol.) escapement wheel; **rueda de alfarero** potter's wheel; **rueda de andar** treadmill; **rueda de cadena** sprocket, sprocket wheel; **rueda de carro** cart wheel; **rueda de corriente media** or **de costado** breast wheel; **rueda de escape** (horol.) escapement wheel; **rueda de esmeril** emery wheel; **rueda de feria** Ferris wheel; **rueda de fuego** pinwheel; **rueda de linterna** (mach.) lantern wheel; **rueda de molino** mill wheel; **rueda dentada** gearwheel; **rueda de paletas** paddle wheel; **rueda de pecho** breast wheel; **rueda de prensa** press conference; **rueda de presos** line-up (*of suspects or criminals*); **rueda de recambio** spare wheel; **rueda de Santa Catalina** (horol.) escapement wheel; **rueda de tornillo sin fin** worm wheel; **rueda de trinquete** (mach.) ratchet wheel; **rueda directriz** (aut.) steering wheel; **rueda hidráulica** water wheel; **rueda inferior** undershot water wheel; **rueda libre** (mach.) freewheel; **rueda loca** idler wheel; **rueda motriz** (mach.) drive wheel, driving wheel, driver; **rueda superior** overshot water wheel

ruedecilla *f* caster, roller
ruedero *m* wheelwright
ruedo *m* turn, rotation; edge (*of something round*); round mat; skirt lining; selvage; ring (*arena of bull ring*); (box.) ring; **a todo ruedo** at all events
ruego *m* request, petition, entreaty; prayer
ruezno *m* walnut burr
rufián -fiana *mf* bawd, go-between; *m* pimp; scoundrel; (archaic) hired killer
rufianear *vn* to pander
rufianería *f* pandering
rufianesco -ca *adj* scoundrelly; *f* gang of scoundrels; scoundrelly conduct
rufo -fa *adj* sandy, sandy-haired, rufous; curly, curly-haired; rough, tough
rugar §59 *va & vr* var. of **arrugar**
rugido *m* roar; bellow; rumble (*of intestines*)
ruginoso -sa *adj* rusty
rugir §42 *vn* to roar; to bellow; to rumble; to be said, to come out
rugosidad *f* ruggedness, corrugation, rugosity
rugoso -sa *adj* rugged, corrugated, wrinkled, ridged
ruibarbo *m* (bot. & pharm.) rhubarb (*Rheum palmatum and Rheum officinale*)
ruido *m* noise; repercussion; row, rumpus; **hacer** or **meter ruido** to start a row; to create a stir or a sensation; **querer ruido** to be looking for a fight; **quitarse de ruidos** (coll.) to stay out of trouble; **ruidos de fondo** background noise
ruidoso -sa *adj* noisy, loud; sensational
ruin *adj* base, mean, vile; puny; small, petty, stingy; vicious (*animal*); *m* scoundrel; tip of tail of cat; **en nombrando al ruin de Roma, luego asoma** talk of the Devil and he will appear; **un ruin ido, otro venido** out of the frying pan into the fire
ruina *f* ruin; **estar hecho una ruina** to be a wreck (*said of a person*); **batir en ruina** (mil.) to breach, break through; **amenazar ruina** to begin to fall to pieces
ruinar *va & vr* var. of **arruinar**
ruindad *f* baseness, meanness, vileness; pettiness, stinginess; viciousness
ruinoso -sa *adj* ruinous; tottery, tottering; rundown, useless
ruiponce *m* (bot.) rampion
ruipóntico *m* (bot. & pharm.) rhubarb (*Rheum rhaponticum*)
ruiseñor *m* (orn.) nightingale
rujada *f* (dial.) heavy shower
rular *va & vn* to roll
ruleta *f* roulette (*game; wheel with sharp teeth*); (Am.) tape measure
ruleteo *m* (Am.) cruising (*in search of fares*)
ruletero *m* (Am.) cruiser (*taxi driver cruising in search of fares*)
rulo *m* ball; roller; conical stone (*of olive-oil mill*)
rumanche *m* Romansh
Rumania *f* Rumania
rumano -na *adj & mf* Rumanian; *m* Rumanian (*language*)
rumazón *f* (naut.) overcast horizon
rumba *f* rumba (*dance and music*)
rumbadas *fpl* var. of **arrumbadas**
rumbático -ca *adj* pompous, showy
rumbo *m* bearing, course, direction; (coll.) pomp, show; (coll.) generosity; (her.) rustre; **abatir el rumbo** (naut.) to fall to leeward; **con rumbo a** bound for, in the direction of; **hacer rumbo a** to head for, to sail for; **ir al rumbo** (Am.) to be on the right track; **tener mucho rumbo** to be showy, to be pompous; **rumbo a** bound for; **rumbo de la aguja** (naut.) rhumb; **rumbo verdadero** (naut.) true course
rumbón -bona *adj* (coll.) generous
rumboso -sa *adj* pompous, magnificent; (coll.) generous
rumen *m* (zool.) rumen
rumí *m* (*pl:* **-míes**) (Arab.) Christian
rumia or **rumiación** *f* rumination
rumiador -dora *adj* ruminating; *mf* ruminator
rumiadura *f* rumination
rumiante *adj* (zool. & fig.) ruminant; *m* (zool.) ruminant
rumiar *va & vn* to ruminate; (coll.) to ruminate, meditate
rumión -miona *adj* (coll.) ruminative, brooding; *mf* (coll.) brooder
rumo *m* first hoop of a cask or barrel
rumor *m* rumor; murmur, buzz (*of voices*); rumble
rumorear *va* to rumor, to spread by rumor; *vn* to murmur, buzz, rumble; *vr* to be rumored
rumoroso -sa *adj* noisy, loud, rumbling
runa *f* rune
runcinado -da *adj* (bot.) runcinate
runfla or **runflada** *f* (coll.) string, row; sequence (*of cards*); **echar runflas** (coll.) to bluster
rúnico -ca or **runo -na** *adj* runic
runrún *m* (coll.) rumor; (coll.) murmur, rumble; (coll.) purr; (coll.) rustle
runrunear *vr* to be whispered about, be bruited about; (coll.) to purr; (coll.) to rustle
runruneo *m* rumor, whispering; (coll.) purring; (coll.) rustling
ruñar *va* to croze (*a stave*)
Ruperto *m* Rupert
rupestre *adj* rupestrian
rupia *f* (path.) rupia; rupee
rupicabra or **rupicapra** *f* (zool.) chamois
rupícola *adj* rupicolous, growing or living on rocks; *m* (orn.) cock of the rock
ruptor *m* (elec.) contact breaker
ruptura *f* rupture, break; crack, split; fission; (fig.) rupture, break (*in friendly relations*)
ruqueta *f* (bot.) rocket; (bot.) hedge mustard
rural *adj* rural; small-town, country
rurícola *mf* ruralist
rus *m* (bot.) sumach
rusco *m* (bot.) butcher's-broom
rusel *m* woolen serge
Rusia *f* Russia; **la Rusia Soviética** Soviet Russia; **la Rusia Blanca** White Russia
rusiente *adj* candent
rusificación *f* Russianization
rusificar §86 *va* to Russianize; *vr* to become Russianized
ruso -sa *adj & mf* Russian; *m* Russian (*language*); ulster; **gran ruso** Great Russian; **pequeño ruso** Little Russian; **ruso blanco** White Russian
rusófilo -la *adj & mf* Russophile
rusofobia *f* Russophobia
rusófobo -ba *adj & mf* Russophobe
rusojaponés -nesa *adj* Russo-Japanese
rúst. abr. of **rústica**
rusticación *f* rustication
rustical *adj* rustic, rural
rusticano -na *adj* wild (*plant*)
rusticar §86 *vn* to rusticate
rusticidad *f* rusticity; coarseness, crudeness, clumsiness
rústico -ca *adj* rustic; coarse, crude, clumsy; Vulgar (*Latin*); **a la rústica** or **en rústica** paper-bound; *m* rustic, peasant
rustiquez *f* or **rustiqueza** *f* var. of **rusticidad**
rustro *m* (her.) rustre
Rut *f* Ruth
ruta *f* route; (Am.) spree; **ruta de Birmania** Burma Road
rutabaga *f* (bot.) rutabaga
rutáceo -a *adj* (bot.) rutaceous
Rutenia *f* Ruthenia
rutenio *m* (chem.) ruthenium
ruteno -na *adj & mf* Ruthenian; *m* Ruthenian (*language*)
rutero -ra *mf* var. of **rutista**
rutilante *adj* (poet.) shining, sparkling
rutilar *vn* (poet.) to shine, sparkle
rutilo *m* (mineral.) rutile
rútilo -la *adj* bright, shining, dazzling
rutina *f* routine; (chem.) rutin
rutinario -ria *adj* routine (*method; worker*); *mf* routinist
rutinero -ra *adj* routine (*e.g., method*); *mf* routinist
rutista *mf* experienced driver, driver who knows the roads; *m* long-distance teamster; road bicycle racer
ruzafa *f* garden, park

S

S, s *f* twenty-second letter of the Spanish alphabet
S. abr. of **San, Santo, sobresaliente, & sur**
S.ª abr. of **Señora**
s. a. abr. of **sin año**
sáb. abr. of **sábado**
Sabá Sheba; **reina de Sabá** Queen of Sheba
sábado *m* Saturday; Sabbath (*of the Jews*); witches' Sabbath; **hacer sábado** to do the weekly Saturday housecleaning; **sábado de gloria** or **sábado santo** Holy Saturday
sabalar *m* shad net
sabalera *f* fire grate (*of reverberatory furnace*)
sabalero *m* shad fisherman
sábalo *m* (ichth.) shad; (Am.) tarpon
sabana *f* savanna or savannah
sábana *f* sheet; altar cloth; **pegársele a uno las sábanas** (coll.) to stay in bed late
sabandija *f* bug, insect, worm; (fig.) vermin (*person*); **sabandijas** *fpl* vermin
sabanero -ra *adj* (pertaining to a) savanna; *mf* savanna dweller; *m* (orn.) meadow lark
sabanilla *f* small sheet; woollen spread; napkin, kerchief, hand towel; outer altar cloth; communion cloth
sabañón *m* chilblain; **comer como un sabañón** (coll.) to eat like a pig
sabatario -ria *adj* Sabbatarian; *mf* Sabbatarian (*one who observes Saturday as Sabbath*)
sabático -ca *adj* (pertaining to) Saturday; (pertaining to the) Sabbath; (Jewish hist.) sabbatical
sabatino -na *adj* (pertaining to) Saturday; *f* Saturday mass; Saturday review, Saturday theme (*in schools*)
sabatismo *m* Sabbatarianism
sabatizar §76 *vn* to rest on Saturday, to not work on Saturday
sabedor -dora *adj* informed
sabeísmo *m* Sabaeanism
sabela *f* (zool.) sabella
sabelección *m & f* (bot.) peppergrass
sábelotodo *m* (*pl:* **sábelotodo**) (coll.) know-it-all, wiseacre, wise guy
sabeo -a *adj & mf* Sabaean
saber *m* knowledge, learning; **según mi leal saber y entender** to the best of my knowledge; §80 *va & vn* to know (*by reasoning or by learning*); to find out; to taste; **a saber** namely, to wit; **hacer saber** to inform, to let know; **no saber cuántas son cinco** or **no saber cuántas son dos y dos** (coll.) to not know what it's all about; **no saber cómo** + *inf* to not know how to, to be at a loss to + *inf;* **no saber dónde meterse** to not know which way to turn; **no sé cuántos** so-and-so, what's his name; **(un) no sé qué** a certain (*something*); **que yo sepa** to my knowledge, as far as I know; **¡y qué sé yo!, ¡y qué sé yo qué más!** and what not, and so forth; **saber a** to taste of, to taste like; to smack of; to know how to get to (*e.g., a person's house*); **saber a poco** to be just a taste, to taste like more; **saber cuántas son cinco** (coll.) to know a thing or two, to know what's what; **saber de** to know, know of, know about, hear of, hear from; to be aware of; **saber lo que es bueno** (coll.) to know the ropes; **saber** + *inf* to know how to, to be able to + *inf; vr* to know; **sabérselo todo** (coll.) to know it all
sabicú *m* (bot.) horseflesh mahogany
sabidillo -lla *adj & mf* (scornful) know-it-all
sabido -da *adj* well-informed; learned; **de sabido** certainly, surely
sabiduría *f* wisdom; knowledge, learning; information; **Sabiduría de Salomón** (Bib.) Wisdom of Solomon (*book of the Apocrypha*)
sabiendas; a sabiendas knowingly, consciously; **a sabiendas de que** knowing that
sabihondez *f* (coll.) affected learning, pretension to wisdom
sabihondo -da *adj* (coll.) know-it-all, wiseacred; *mf* (coll.) know-it-all, wiseacre
sabina *f* see **sabino**
sabinar *m* growth of savins
sabino -na *adj* Sabine; roan (*horse*); *mf* Sabine; *f* (bot. & pharm.) savin
sabio -bia *adj* wise; learned; trained (*animal*); *mf* wise person, scholar, scientist; *m* wise man, sage
sabiondez *f* (coll.) var. of **sabihondez**
sabiondo -da *adj & mf* (coll.) var. of **sabihondo**
sablazo *m* stroke with a saber, wound from a saber; (coll.) sponging; **dar un sablazo a** (coll.) to hit for a loan
sable *m* saber, cutlass; (her.) sable; (coll.) sponging
sableador -dora *mf* sponger; *m* saber wielder; rough soldier
sablear *va* (coll.) to hit for a loan, to sponge on; *vn* (coll.) to try to borrow money, to go around sponging
sablista *mf* (coll.) sponger
sablón *m* coarse sand
saboga *f* (ichth.) small shad
saboneta *f* hunting watch
sabor *m* taste, flavor; (fig.) flavor; **sabores** *mpl* beads on bit (*of bridle*); **a sabor** to one's taste, to one's liking
saborcillo *m* slight taste, touch
saboreamiento *m* flavoring, flavor; tasting, taste; relish, relishing
saborear *va* to flavor; to taste; to savor; to allure, entice; *vr* to smack one's lips; **saborearse con** to taste; to savor
saboreo *m* flavoring; tasting; savoring
saborete *m* slight flavor; slight taste
sabotaje *m* sabotage
saboteador -dora *mf* saboteur
sabotear *va & vn* to sabotage
Saboya, la Savoy
saboyano -na *adj & mf* Savoyard; *f* open skirt; plum pudding
sabré *1st sg fut ind of* **saber**
sabroso -sa *adj* tasty, savory, delicious; (coll.) saltish
sabucal *m* grove of elders
sabuco *m* (bot.) elder
sabueso *m* bloodhound, beagle; (fig.) bloodhound (*detective, sleuth*)
sabugal *m* var. of **sabucal**
sabugo *m* var. of **sabuco**
sábulo *m* coarse sand
sabuloso -sa *adj* sandy, gritty, sabulous
saburra *f* saburra; coat on tongue
saburral *adj* saburral
saburrar *va* to ballast with rocks and sand
saburroso -sa *adj* foul (*mouth or stomach*); coated (*tongue*)
saca *f* extraction; exportation; coarse sack; first draft, first copy; **de saca** (Am.) at full speed; **estar de saca** to be on sale; (coll.) to be marriageable
sacabala *f* (surg.) bullet-extracting forceps; **sacabalas** *m* (*pl:* **-las**) (arti.) bullet screw
sacabocado or **sacabocados** *m* (*pl:* **-dos**) ticket punch; punch; sure thing
sacabolsas *m* (*pl:* **-sas**) swindle
sacabotas *m* (*pl:* **-tas**) bootjack
sacabrocas *m* (*pl:* **-cas**) tack puller, nail puller
sacabuche *m* (bot.) strawberry tomato; (mus.) sackbut (*instrument or player*); (coll.) nincompoop; (naut.) hand pump

sacaclavos *m* (*pl:* **-vos**) nail puller; **sacaclavos de horquilla** claw bar
sacacorchos *m* (*pl:* **-chos**) corkscrew
sacacuartos *m* (*pl:* **-tos**) (coll.) catchpenny, bamboozle
sacadinero or **sacadineros** *m* (*pl:* **-ros**) (coll.) catchpenny, bamboozle; (coll.) bamboozler
sacador -dora *mf* (tennis) server; *m* (print.) delivery table
sacadura *f* (sew.) sloping cut
sacafilásticas *f* (*pl:* **-cas**) priming wire
sacaliña *f* stick, goad stick; trick, cunning
sacamanchas *mf* (*pl:* **-chas**) clothes cleaner, spot remover; dry cleaner; dyer
sacamantas *m* (*pl:* **-tas**) (coll.) delinquent-tax collector
sacamantecas *m* (*pl:* **-cas**) (coll.) Jack the Ripper
sacamiento *m* extraction; removal
sacamolero *m* (coll.) dentist
sacamuelas *mf* (*pl:* **-las**) (coll.) tooth puller; (coll.) charlatan, quack
sacamuertos *m* (*pl:* **-tos**) stagehand
sacanete *m* lansquenet (*card game*)
sacapelotas *m* (*pl:* **-tas**) bullet screw; (fig.) cur
sacaperras *m* (*pl:* **-rras**) (coll.) gambling machine
sacapintura *m* paint remover
sacapotras *m* (*pl:* **-tras**) (coll.) butcher (*surgeon*)
sacapuntas *m* (*pl:* **-tas**) pencil sharpener
sacar §86 *va* to draw, draw out, pull out; to pull up; to take out, get out; to extract, to remove; to stick out (*e.g., one's chest*); to show, bring out, publish; to find out, to solve; to elicit, draw out (*a secret*); to determine; to copy; to take (*a photograph*); to except, to exclude; to quote; to win (*a prize*); to get, obtain; to produce, invent, imitate; to serve (*a ball*); **sacar a bailar** (coll.) to drag in; **sacar adelante** to nurture, rear; **sacar a relucir** (coll.) to bring up unexpectedly; **sacar a volar** to bring out (*especially a bashful person*); **sacar de espesor** to pare down, make thin; **sacar de pobre** to lift out of poverty; **sacar de sí** to drive mad, to make crazy; **sacar en claro** or **en limpio** to deduce, to conclude clearly; to recopy clearly; **sacar mentiroso** to give the lie to
sacarificación *f* saccharification
sacarificar §86 *va* to saccharify
sacarimetría *f* saccharimetry
sacarímetro *m* saccharimeter
sacarino -na *adj* saccharine; *f* (chem.) saccharine
sacaroideo -a *adj* saccharoid
sacarosa *f* (chem.) saccharose, sucrose
sacarruedas *m* (*pl:* **-das**) (aut.) wheel puller
sacasillas *m* (*pl:* **-llas**) (coll.) stagehand
sacatapón *m* corkscrew
sacate *m* var. of **zacate**
sacatrapos *m* (*pl:* **-pos**) (arti.) wad hook, wormer
sacerdocio *m* priesthood
sacerdotal *adj* sacerdotal, priestly
sacerdote *m* priest; **sumo sacerdote** high priest
sacerdotisa *f* priestess
sácere *m* (bot.) maple
saciable *adj* satiable
saciar *va* to satiate
saciedad *f* satiety, satiation
saciña *f* (bot.) white willow
sacio -cia *adj* satiated
saco *m* sack, bag; sackful, bagful; pack (*e.g., of lies*); (mil.) sack, plunder, pillage; serve (*in ball games*); (anat., bot. & zool.) sac; coat; (sew.) sacque; **no echar en saco roto** (coll.) to not forget, to not overlook; **poner a saco** to plunder, to loot; **saco de noche** satchel, handbag, overnight bag; **saco terrero** (fort.) sandbag
sacra *f* see **sacro**
sacramentación *f* administration of sacraments; (theol.) transubstantiation
sacramental *adj* sacramental; *m* sacramental; member of an association devoted to the worship of the sacrament; *f* association devoted to the worship of the sacrament
sacramentar *va* to administer the sacraments to; (theol.) to transubstantiate; (coll.) to conceal, to hide; *vr* (theol.) to transubstantiate
sacramentario -ria *adj* & *mf* Sacramentarian
sacramento *m* sacrament; **santísimo sacramento** Holy Sacrament; **sacramento del altar** sacrament (*Eucharist*)
sacratísimo -ma *adj super* very or most sacred or holy
sacre *m* (orn. & arti.) saker; thief
sacrificadero *m* place for sacrifice
sacrificador -dora *adj* sacrificing; *mf* sacrificer
sacrificar §86 *va* to sacrifice; to slaughter; *vn* to sacrifice; *vr* to sacrifice, to sacrifice oneself; to devote oneself to God
sacrificatorio -ria *adj* sacrificial
sacrificio *m* sacrifice; **santo sacrificio** mass; **sacrificio del altar** Sacrifice of the Mass
sacrilegio *m* sacrilege
sacrílego -ga *adj* sacrilegious
sacrismoche *m* or **sacrismocho** *m* (coll.) fellow dressed in shabby black clothes
sacrista *m* sexton
sacristán *m* sacristan; sexton; hoops (*for skirt*); **ser gran sacristán** (coll.) to be crafty, to be wily; **sacristán de amén** (coll.) yes man
sacristana *f* sacristan's wife; sexton's wife; nun in charge of sacristy
sacristanía *f* office of sacristan or sexton
sacristía *f* sacristy; office of sacristan or sexton
sacro -cra *adj* sacred; (anat.) sacral; *m* (anat.) sacrum; *f* (eccl.) sacring tablet
sacroilíaco -ca *adj* (anat.) sacroiliac
sacrosanto -ta *adj* sacrosanct
sacudido -da *adj* indocile, intractable; determined, resolute; *f* shake, jar, jolt, jerk, bump; (elec.) shock
sacudidor -dora *adj* shaking, beating; *m* shaker, beater; duster; **sacudidor de alfombras** carpetbeater
sacudidura *f* shake (*especially to remove dust*)
sacudimiento *m* shaking, shake, jolt, jerk
sacudión *m* jolt, jerk
sacudir *va* to shake; to jar, jolt; to rock; to shake off, to throw off; to beat; *vr* to shake, shake oneself; to rock; to shake off; to manage to get along, to wangle through
sacudón *m* (Am.) jolt, jerk
sáculo *m* (anat.) saccule
sachadura *f* weeding
sachar *va* to weed
sacho *m* weeder, weeding tool
sádico -ca *adj* sadistic; *mf* sadist
sadismo *m* sadism
saduceísmo *m* Sadduceeism
saduceo -a *adj* Sadducean; *mf* Sadducee, Sadducean
saeta *f* arrow, dart; hand (*of clock or watch*); gnomon; magnetic needle; bud of vine; sacred song; (*cap.*) *f* (astr.) Sagitta
saetada *f* or **saetazo** *m* arrow shot; arrow wound
saetear *va* var. of **asaetear**
saetero -ra *adj* (pertaining to an) arrow; *m* archer, bowman; *f* (fort.) loophole; narrow window
saetilla *f* small arrow; hand (*of watch or clock*); magnetic needle; sacred song, devotional verse; (bot.) arrowhead; (arch.) dart (*in egg-and-dart ornaments*)
saetín *m* millrace, flume; brad; sateen
safari *m* safari
safeno -na *adj* (anat.) saphenous
sáfico -ca *adj* & *m* Sapphic
Safira *f* (Bib.) Sapphira
Safo *f* Sappho
saga *f* saga; witch, sorceress
sagacidad *f* sagacity
sagapeno *m* sagapenum
sagatí *m* sagathy, sayette
sagaz *adj* (*pl:* **-gaces**) sagacious; keen-scented
sagita *f* (arch.) rise (*of an arch*)
sagitado -da *adj* (bot.) sagittate
sagital *adj* sagittal; (anat. & zool.) sagittal
sagitaria *f* (bot.) arrowhead
sagitario *m* bowman; (*cap.*) *m* (astr.) Sagittarius

ságoma *f* (arch.) pattern, templet
sagrado -da *adj* sacred; *m* asylum, haven, place of refuge; **acogerse a sagrado** to take sanctuary
sagrario *m* sacrarium, sanctuary, shrine; (eccl.) ciborium
sagú *m* (*pl:* **-gúes**) sago (*starch*); (bot.) sago, sago palm
saguaro *m* (bot.) saguaro, giant cactus
saguino *m* (zool.) tamarin
ságula *f* small frock
saguntino -na *adj* (pertaining to) Sagunto; *mf* native or inhabitant of Sagunto
Sahara *m* Sahara
sahariano -na *adj* (pertaining to the) Sahara; *f* tight-fitting military jacket
sahína *f* var. of **zahína**
sahornar *vr* to skin oneself, to scrape or scratch oneself
sahorno *m* skin abrasion, scratch
sahuaro *m* var. of **saguaro**
sahumado -da *adj* bettered, improved; (Am.) drunk
sahumador *m* perfuming pot, incense pot; stretcher, clothes drier
sahumadura *f* smoking, perfuming with smoke or incense
sahumar §99 *va* to smoke, to perfume with smoke or incense
sahumerio or **sahúmo** *m* smoking, perfuming; incense, aromatic smoke
saica *f* saic (*ketch used in the Levant*)
saicar *m* sidecar
saín *m* grease, fat; fish oil; greasiness, grease spot
sainar §75 *va* to fatten
sainete *m* flavor, relish, spice, zest; sauce, seasoning; tidbit, delicacy; elegance; one-act farce
sainetear *vn* to act in a farce
sainetero *m* farce writer
sainetesco -ca *adj* farcical, burlesque
saíno *m* (zool.) peccary
saja *f* incision; leaf stalk of Manila hemp
sajador *m* bleeder; (surg.) scarifier (*instrument*)
sajadura *f* incision; slit, crack
sajar *va* to cut, make an incision in, tap
sajelar *va* to sift and clean (*clay*)
sajía *f* incision
sajón -jona *adj & mf* Saxon
Sajonia *f* Saxony
Sajonia-Coburgo-Gotha *f* Saxe-Coburg-Gotha
sal *f* salt; charm, grace; wit, wittiness; (Am.) bad luck, misfortune; **echar en sal** (coll.) to keep back; **estar hecho de sal** to be full of life, be in a good mood; **sal amoníaca, sal amoníaco** sal ammoniac; **sal ática** Attic salt; **sal común** common salt; **sal de acederas** salt of sorrel; **sal de compás** rock salt; **sal de Epsom** Epsom salt; **sal de la Higuera** Epsom salt; **sales aromáticas** smelling salts; **sal gema** rock salt; **sal marina** sea salt; **sal volátil** sal volatile; *2d sg impv of* **salir**
sala *f* hall; drawing room, living room, sitting room, salon, parlor; (law) bench; **hacer sala** to form a quorum (*in court*); **sala de batalla** sorting room (*in postoffice*); **sala de clase** classroom; **sala de equipajes** baggage room; **sala de enfermos** infirmary; **sala de espectáculos** auditorium; **sala de espera** waiting room; **sala de estar** living room, sitting room; **sala de fiestas** night club; **sala de gálibos** (naut.) mold loft; **sala de hospital** hospital ward; **sala de justicia** court of justice, courtroom; **sala del cine** moving-picture house; **sala de lectura** reading room; **sala de máquinas** engine room; **sala de muestras** showroom; **sala de recepción** or **recibo** reception hall; **sala de recreo** amusement parlor
salabardo *m* scoop net, dip net
salacidad *f* salacity, salaciousness
saladar *m* salt marsh; barren brine-soaked land
saladero *m* salting room, salting house
saladillo -lla *adj* half-salted; *m* half-salted bacon; salted peanut; *f* (bot.) saltbush
Saladino *m* Saladin
salado -da *adj* salt; salty; brine-soaked; witty, facetious; (Am.) expensive; (Am.) unfortunate; *m* (bot.) saltwort
salador -dora *mf* salter (*of meat, fish*); *m* salting room, salting house
saladura *f* salting
salamandra *f* salamander (*stove*); (zool. & myth.) salamander; **salamandra acuática** or **salamandra de agua** (zool.) newt, triton; **salamandra gigante** (zool.) giant salamander, hellbender
salamandria *f* (zool.) gecko, tarente
salamandrino -na *adj* (pertaining to or like the) salamander
salamanqués -quesa *adj* (pertaining to) Salamanca; *mf* native or inhabitant of Salamanca; *f* (zool.) gecko, tarente
salamanquino -na *adj* (pertaining to) Salamanca; *mf* native or inhabitant of Salamanca
Salamina *f* Salamis
salangana *f* (orn.) swift (*Collocalia esculenta*)
salar *va* to salt, to season or preserve with salt; to put too much salt on
salariado *m* payment by means of wages, remuneration in wages
salariar *va* to fix a salary or wages for
salario *m* wages, pay; **salario anual garantizado** guaranteed annual wage; **salario de hambre** starvation wages
salaz *adj* (*pl:* **-laces**) salacious
salazón *f* salting; salt meat, salt fish; salt-meat and salt-fish business
salazonero -ra *adj* salt-meat, salt-fish
salbanda *f* (min.) selvage
salce *m* (bot.) willow
salceda *f* or **salcedo** *m* willow grove, salicetum
salcereta *f* dicebox
salcochar *va* to boil in salt water
salcocho *m* (Am.) food boiled in salt water
salchicha *f* sausage; (fort.) saucisson, large fascine; (mil.) saucisson (*fuse*)
salchichería *f* sausage shop
salchichero -ra *mf* sausage maker or seller
salchichón *m* large sausage; (fort.) saucisson, large fascine
saldar *va* to settle, liquidate; to sell out, to sell out at reduced prices
saldista *m* liquidation broker; remnant salesman
saldo *m* settlement, liquidation; (com.) balance; remnant, leftover; bargain; **saldo acreedor** credit balance; **saldo deudor** debit balance
saldré *1st sg fut ind of* **salir**
saledizo -za *adj* projecting; *m* projection, ledge
salega *f* lick, salt lick
salegar *m* lick, salt lick; §59 *vn* to lick salt
salema *f* (ichth.) gilthead, sheepshead
salep *m* salep
salera *f* stone or block on which salt is placed for cattle
salero *m* saltcellar, saltshaker; salt lick; salthouse, salt storage; (coll.) charm, grace, wit; wit (*person*)
saleroso -sa *adj* (coll.) salty, witty; charming, winsome, lively
salesa *adj & f* Salesian (*of Order of the Visitation*)
salesiano -na *adj & mf* Salesian (*of orders founded by Don Bosco and of Order of the Visitation*)
saleta *f* little hall; royal antechamber; court of appeal
salgada or **salgadera** *f* (bot.) orach, mountain spinach
salgar §59 *va* to salt (*cattle*)
salgareño *adj* see **pino**
salgo *1st sg pres ind of* **salir**
salguera *f* or **salguero** *m* (bot.) willow
salicáceo -a *adj* (bot.) salicaceous
salicaria *f* (bot.) loosestrife, purple loosestrife
salicilato *m* (chem.) salicylate
salicílico -ca *adj* (chem.) salicylic
salicina *f* (chem.) salicin
sálico -ca *adj* Salic
salicor *m* (bot.) saltwort (*Salsola soda*)
salida *f* see **salido**
salidero -ra *adj* gadabout, on the go; *m* way-out, exit
salidizo *m* projection, ledge

salido -da *adj* bulging, projecting; in heat (*said of a female*); *f* start; going out, coming out, leaving; departure; way out, exit; check (*to return to theater after intermission*); outlet; recourse, issue, outcome, result; loophole, subterfuge; pretext; outlay, expenditure; projection; outlying fields (*near city gate*); (bridge) lead; (sport) start; (mil.) sally, sortie; (naut.) sudden jerk in starting; (naut.) headway; (coll.) witticism; (com. & fig.) outlet; (elec.) output; **dar la salida** (theat.) to give the cue; **tener buenas salidas** (coll.) to be full of witty remarks; **tener salida** to sell well; to be popular with the boys (*said of young ladies*); **salida de auxilio** or **de socorro** emergency exit; **salida de baño** bathrobe, bathing wrap; **salida de pie de banco** (coll.) nonsense, piece of folly; **salida de sol** sunrise; **salida de teatro** evening wrap; **salida de teatros** after-theater party, after-theater supper; **salida de tono** (coll.) irrelevancy, impropriety; **salida lanzada** (sport) running start
saliente *adj* salient, projecting; outgoing, outbound; rising (*e.g., sun*); *m* east; *f* projection; shoulder (*of a bastion; of a road*)
salífero -ra *adj* saliferous
salificable *adj* (chem.) salifiable
salificación *f* (chem.) salification
salificar §86 *va* (chem.) to salify
salimiento *m* departure
salín *m* salthouse
salina *f* see **salino**
salinero -ra *adj* spotted red and white (*said of a bull*); *mf* saltmaker, salter
salinidad *f* salinity
salino -na *adj* saline; *f* salt mine; salt marsh; salt works
salio -lia *adj & mf* Salian
salir §81 *vn* to go out, come out; to leave, go away; to sail; to get out; to run out, come to an end, be over; to appear, to show, to show up; to come out, come off (*said, e.g., of a stain*); to rise (*said, e.g., of the sun*); to shoot, spring, come up; to project, stand out, stick out; to make the first move, be the first to play; to result, turn out; to be drawn (*in a lottery*); to be elected; to happen, occur; to check, come out right; (bridge) to lead; (theat.) to enter, appear; (naut.) to get ahead (*said of one boat with respect to another*); **salga lo que saliere** (coll.) come what may; **salir a** to come to, to amount to; to resemble, look like; to open into; **salir a** + *inf* to go or come out to + *inf;* **salir adelante** or **avante** to be successful, to win out; **salir al encuentro a** to go to meet; to oppose, take a stand against; to get ahead of; **salir bien en un examen** to pass an examination; **salir con** to come out with (*e.g., an unexpected remark, a claim*); **salir con bien** to be successful; **salir contra** to come out against; **salir de** to cease being; to depart from; to get rid of, to dispose of; to lose one's (*head, judgment, consciousness*); **salir disparado** to start like a shot; **salir pitando** (coll.) to start off on a mad run; (coll.) to blow up, get suddenly angry; *vr* to slip out, to escape; to slip off, to run off; to leak (*said of a liquid or its container*); to boil over; **salirse con la suya** to come out ahead, to have one's way; to carry one's point
salitrado -da *adj* saltpetrous
salitral *adj* saltpetrous; *m* saltpeter bed; saltpeter works
salitre *m* saltpeter (*potassium nitrate*)
salitrera *f* see **salitrero**
salitrería *f* saltpeter works
salitrero -ra *adj* (pertaining to) saltpeter; *mf* saltpeter refiner, saltpeter dealer; *f* saltpeter bed
salitroso -sa *adj* saltpetrous
saliva *f* saliva; **gastar saliva** (coll.) to talk in vain; to prattle; **tragar saliva** (coll.) to suffer an offense or disappointment in silence; (coll.) to be speechless
salivación *f* salivation
salivajo *m* (coll.) spit, expectoration
salival *adj* salivary
salivar *vn* to salivate
salivazo *m* (coll.) spit, expectoration
saliveras *fpl* round knobs on bits of a bridle
salivoso -sa *adj* salivous
salma *f* ton (*in reckoning displacement of vessels*); salma (*Italian, Sicilian, and Maltese measure*); light packsaddle
salmanticense or **salmantino -na** *adj* (pertaining to) Salamanca; *mf* native or inhabitant of Salamanca
salmear *vn* to sing psalms
salmer *m* (arch.) skewback
salmista *m* psalmist (*composer or cantor*); **el Salmista** (Bib.) the Psalmist
salmo *m* psalm; **los Salmos** (Bib.) the Psalms; **salmos penitenciales** (Bib.) penitential psalms
salmodia *f* psalmody; (coll.) singsong, monotonous song
salmodiar *va* to singsong, to sing monotonously; *vn* to sing psalms; to singsong
salmón *m* salmon (*color*); (ichth.) salmon; **salmón zancado** (ichth.) kelt
salmonado -da *adj* salmon-like; salmon (*in color*)
salmoncillo *m* (ichth.) samlet, parr
salmonera *f* salmon net
salmonete *m* (ichth.) red mullet
salmorear *va* (Am.) to lecture, to scold
salmorejo *m* rabbit sauce; salmi
salmuera *f* brine, pickle; briny moisture; salty food or drink
salmuerar *vr* to get sick from too much salt (*said of cattle*)
salobral *adj* saline (*ground*); *m* saline ground
salobre *adj* brackish, saltish
salobreño -na *adj & m* var. of **salobral**
salobridad *f* brackishness, saltiness
salol *m* (chem.) salol
saloma *f* (naut.) chantey
salomador *m* (naut.) chanteyman
salomar *vn* (naut.) to sing chanteys
Salomé *f* (Bib.) Salome
Salomón *m* Solomon; (fig.) Solomon
salomónico -ca *adj* Solomonic; (arch.) twisted (*column*)
salón *m* salon; drawing room; saloon (*e.g., of a steamship*); meeting room; **salón de actos** auditorium, assembly hall; **salón de baile** ballroom; **salón de belleza** beauty parlor; **salón del automóvil** automobile show; **salón del trono** throne room; **salón de pinturas** picture gallery; **salón de recreo** recreation hall; **salón de refrescos** ice-cream parlor; **salón de sesiones** assembly hall; **salón de tertulia** lounge; **salón de ventas** salesroom; **salón social** lounge
saloncillo *m* rest room (*e.g., of a theater*)
salpa *f* (ichth.) gilthead; (zool.) salpa
salpicadero *m* splasher, splashguard
salpicadura *f* splash, splashing, spattering; **salpicaduras** *fpl* indirect results
salpicar §86 *va* to splash, bespatter; to sprinkle; to skip through; *vn* to splash
salpicón *m* salmagundi; (coll.) splash, splashing; (coll.) hash, chopped mixture, hodgepodge; (Am.) cold fruit juice
salpimentar §18 *va* to salt and pepper; (fig.) to sweeten (*to make pleasant and agreeable*)
salpimienta *f* mixture of salt and pepper
salpique *m* splash, spatter
salpresamiento *m* preservation with salt
salpresar *va* to preserve with salt
salpreso -sa *adj* preserved with salt
salpullido *m* rash, eruption; flea bites
salpullir §26 *va* to cause a rash in; to splotch; *vr* to break out
salsa *f* sauce, dressing, gravy; **cocer en su propia salsa** to stew in one's own juice; **salsa blanca** white sauce; **salsa de ají** chili sauce; **salsa de San Bernardo** (coll.) hunger; **salsa de tomate** catsup, ketchup; **salsa francesa** French dressing; **salsa holandesa** hollandaise sauce; **salsa inglesa** Worcestershire sauce; **salsa mahonesa** or **mayonesa** mayonnaise; **salsa tártara** tartare sauce
salsedumbre *f* saltiness
salsera *f* gravy dish, gravy boat; small saucer (*to mix paints*)
salsereta, salserilla or **salseruela** *f* small saucer (*used especially to mix paints*)

salsifí *m* (*pl:* **-fíes**) (bot.) salsify; **salsifí de España** (bot.) viper's-grass; **salsifí de los prados** (bot.) yellow goatsbeard; **salsifí negro** (bot.) viper's-grass
saltabanco or **saltabancos** *m* (*pl:* **-cos**) quack, mountebank; prestidigitator; (coll.) trifler, nuisance
saltabardales *mf* (*pl:* **-les**) (coll.) wild youngster
saltabarrancos *mf* (*pl:* **-cos**) (coll.) jumping jack (*person*)
saltacaballo *m* (arch.) crossette
saltación *f* jumping, leaping; dance, dancing
saltacharquillos *mf* (*pl:* **-llos**) (coll.) youngster who goes jumping and tiptoeing about for effect
saltadero *m* jumping place; fountain, jet
saltadizo -za *adj* brittle, shattery
saltador -dora *adj* jumping, leaping; *mf* jumper, leaper; *m* skipping rope; **saltador del margen** margin release
saltadura *f* chip (*in surface of a stone*)
saltaembanco *m* var. of **saltabanco**
saltamimbres *m* (*pl:* **-bres**) (orn.) sedge warbler
saltamontes *m* (*pl:* **-tes**) (ent.) grasshopper
saltante *adj* saltant
saltaojos *m* (*pl:* **-jos**) (bot.) peony
saltaparedes *mf* (*pl:* **-des**) (coll.) var. of **saltabardales**
saltaperico *m* (bot.) manyroot; (Am.) snake, serpent (*kind of firework*)
saltar *va* to jump, jump over, leap; to skip, skip over; (naut.) to lower (*a cable*); to cover (*a female*); *vn* to jump, leap, hop, skip; to bounce, bound, fly; to shoot up, to spurt; to come loose, to come off, to slip off; to crack, break, burst; to chip; to stick out, to project; to skip a rank (*in being promoted*); to flash in the mind or memory; **saltar a la vista** or **los ojos** to be self-evident; **saltar con** to come out with (*e.g., an irrelevant remark*); **saltar de** to be kicked out of (*a job*); **saltar por** to jump over; *vr* to skip (*in reading or copying*)
saltarelo *m* old Spanish dance based on Italian saltarello
saltarén *m* guitar dance tune; (ent.) grasshopper
saltarín -rina *adj* dancing; *mf* dancer; *m* wild youth, restless young fellow
saltarregla *f* bevel square
saltaterandate *m* long-stitch embroidery
saltatrás *mf* (*pl:* **-trás**) var. of **tornatrás**
saltatriz *f* (*pl:* **-trices**) ballet girl, ballerina
saltatumbas *m* (*pl:* **-bas**) (coll.) burying parson
salteador *m* highwayman, holdup man
salteadora *f* female companion of highwaymen, moll; female robber
salteamiento *m* assault, holdup, highway robbery
saltear *va* to attack, to hold up, to waylay; to overtake suddenly, to take by surprise; to do in fits and starts, to leave for something else; to sauté
salteo *m* var. of **salteamiento**
salterio *m* (mus.) psaltery; rosary; (*cap.*) *m* Psalter
saltero -ra *adj* highland
saltígrado -da *adj* jumping (*said of animals*)
saltimbanco or **saltimbanqui** *m* (coll.) var. of **saltabanco**
salto *m* jump, leap, spring, bound; dive; skip; fall, waterfall; omission (*in reading or copying*); leapfrog; leap (*in promotion or advancement*); palpitation (*of heart*); **a saltos** by leaps; skipping; **de un salto** at one jump; **en un salto** quickly; **ir de un salto a** (Am.) to hurry over to; **por salto** (coll.) skipping, jumping around; **salto a ciegas** leap in the dark; **salto con garrocha** or **salto con pértiga** (sport) pole vault; **salto de altura** (sport) high jump; **salto de ángel** swan dive; **salto de cama** morning wrap, dressing gown; **salto de carnero** bucking; **salto de carpa** jackknife; **salto de esquí** or **con esquí** ski jump; **salto de longitud** (sport) broad jump; **salto de mal año** (coll.) sudden rise in fortune; **salto de mata** flight for fear of punishment; **salto de trucha** tumbling; **salto de vallas** (sport) leaping or clearing a hurdle; **salto de viento** (naut.) sudden shift in the wind; **salto en paracaídas** parachute jump; **salto mortal** somersault; **salto ornamental** fancy dive
saltón -tona *adj* jumping, hopping; projecting; bulging; *m* (ent.) grasshopper; (ent.) maggot
salubérrimo -ma *adj super* very or most salubrious or healthful
salubre *adj* salubrious, healthful
salubridad *f* salubrity; health, public health
salud *f* health; welfare; salvation; **saludes** *fpl* greetings, compliments; **¡a su salud!** to your health!; **beber a la salud de** to drink to the health of; **estar bien de salud** to be in good health; **estar mal de salud** to be in bad health; **gastar salud** to enjoy wonderful health; **vender** or **verter salud** (coll.) to radiate health; *interj* (coll.) greetings!
saludable *adj* healthful, wholesome; salutary
saludador -dora *mf* greeter, saluter; *m* quack, medicine man
saludar *va* to greet, salute, hail, bow to; (mil.) to salute; (mil.) to fire a salute for; (naut.) to dip the flag to; (coll.) to get a smattering of; to treat by incantation of magic; *vn* to salute; to bow
saludo *m* greeting, salute, bow, salutation; (mil.) salute; **saludo final** conclusion (*of a letter*)
salumbre *f* flower of salt
Salustio *m* Sallust
salutación *f* salutation, greeting, bow; **salutación angélica** Angelic Salutation
salutífero -ra *adj* var. of **saludable**
salutista *mf* Salvationist, member of the Salvation Army
salva *f* see **salvo**
salvabarros *m* (*pl:* **-rros**) mudguard
salvable *adj* savable, salvable
salvación *f* salvation
salvadera *f* sandbox (*for sprinkling sand on ink*)
salvado *m* bran
salvador -dora *adj* saving; *mf* savior, saver; lifesaver; rescuer; (*cap.*) *m* Saviour; **El Salvador** El Salvador (*country in Central America*)
salvadoreño -ña *adj & mf* Salvadoran
salvaguardar *va* to safeguard
salvaguardia *f* safeguard, safe-conduct; protection, shelter; *m* bodyguard, safeguard, escort; mark of protection (*on a building in wartime*)
salvajada *f* savagery, brutality
salvaje *adj* wild, uncultivated; savage; stupid; *mf* savage; dolt
salvajería *f* savagery
salvajino -na *adj* wild; savage; gamy (*said of meat*); *f* wild animal; wild animals; game (*flesh of wild animal*); wild-animal skins
salvajismo *m* savagery, savageness
salvamano; a salvamano without danger, without running any risk
salvamanteles *m* (*pl:* **-les**) coaster (*small tray placed under a tumbler*)
salvamento *m* salvation; lifesaving; rescue; rescue work; salvage; safety, place of safety
salvamiento *m* (archaic) var. of **salvamento**
salvante *adj* saving; *prep* saving, except
salvar *va* to save (*shipwrecked person, drowning person, lost soul, etc.*); to salvage; to avoid (*difficulty, inconvenience, etc.*); to clear (*obstacle*); to get around, to overcome (*difficulty*); to go over, to jump over; to cover, get over (*a distance*); to rise above; to except, make an exception of; to notarize (*alterations, emendations, etc.*); to prove legally the innocence of; **salvar las apariencias** to save face, to keep up appearances; *vn* to taste (*in order to prove that food or drink is not poisoned*); *vr* to save oneself; to be saved; **sálvese el que pueda** everyone for himself
salvarsán *m* salvarsan
salvavidas *m* (*pl:* **-das**) life preserver; lifeboat; fender, guard (*in front of electric cars*)
salvedad *f* reservation, qualification
salvia *f* (bot.) sage, salvia

salvilla *f* tray with depressions into which cups and glasses fit; (Am.) cruet stand
salvo -va *adj* safe; omitted, unmentioned; **a salvo** out of danger; **a salvo de** safe from; **dejar a salvo** to set aside, make an exception of; **en salvo** at liberty; out of danger; **poner a salvo** to put in a safe place; **ponerse a salvo** to seek safety, to reach safety; **quedar a salvo** to be safe, be out of danger; to be an exception; **sentirse a salvo** to feel safe ‖ **salvo** *prep* save, except for; **salvo que** unless ‖ *f* greeting, welcome; salvo; oath, solemn promise; salver, tray; ordeal (*test of innocence*); tasting (*of food before serving it, e.g., to a king*); **salva de aplausos** round or burst of applause
salvoconducto *m* safe-conduct
salladura *f* weeding
sallar *va* to weed; to store (*planks*) on skidding
sallete *m* weeder, weeding tool
sámago *m* sapwood
sámara *f* (bot.) samara
samarilla *f* (bot.) ironwort
samario *m* (chem.) samarium
samarita *adj & mf* Samaritan
samaritano -na *adj & mf* Samaritan; **el buen samaritano** (Bib.) the Good Samaritan; *m* Samaritan (*language*)
samaruguera *f* small-mesh fishing net
sambenitar *va* to put the sanbenito on (*a person*); to mark with a note of infamy; to disgrace
sambenito *m* sanbenito; note of infamy; disgrace
samblaje *m* joint, joining
sambuca *f* (mus.) sambuke
samio -mia *adj & mf* Samian
samisén *m* (mus.) samisen
samoano -na *adj & mf* Samoan
Samos *f* Samos
samotracio -cia *adj & mf* Samothracian; (*cap.*) *f* Samothrace
samovar *m* samovar
sampaguita *f* (bot.) Arabian jasmine
sampán *m* sampan
sampsuco *m* (bot.) marjoram
Samuel *m* Samuel
samuga *f* var. of **jamuga**
samurai *m* samurai
san *adj* apocopated form of **santo**, used before masculine names of saints, except Tomás, Tomé, Toribio, and Domingo
sanable *adj* curable
sanador -dora *adj* healing; *mf* healer
sánalotodo *m* (*pl:* **-do**) cure-all
sanapudio *m* (bot.) alder buckthorn; **sanapudio blanco** (bot.) cornel, red dogwood
sanar *va* to cure, to heal; *vn* to heal; to recover
sanativo -va *adj* sanative, curative
sanatorio *m* sanatorium, sanitarium, hospital
sanción *f* sanction; penalty; evil consequence; **pragmática sanción** or **sanción pragmática** pragmatic sanction
sancionar *va* to sanction; to penalize
sancochado *m* parboiling
sancochar *va* to parboil
sancocho *m* parboiled meat; (Am.) stew
sancta *m* fore part of tabernacle; **non sancta** *adj fem* wicked, depraved
sanctasanctórum *m* (*pl:* **-rum**) sanctum sanctorum; arcanum; something highly cherished
Sanctus *m* (*pl:* **-tus**) (eccl. & mus.) Sanctus
sanchopancesco -ca *adj* like Sancho Panza; credulous but shrewd and realistic
sandalia *f* sandal
sandalino -na *adj* (pertaining to) sandalwood
sándalo *m* (bot.) yellow sandalwood; (bot.) bergamot (*a mint*); sandalwood oil; **sándalo blanco** (bot.) sandalwood, white sandalwood; **sándalo rojo** (bot.) red sandalwood
sandáraca *f* sandarac (*resin; realgar*)
sandez *f* (*pl:* **-deces**) folly, nonsense; piece of nonsense
sandía *f* (bot.) watermelon (*plant and fruit*)
sandiar *m* watermelon patch
sandio -dia *adj* foolish, nonsensical, silly
sandunga *f* (coll.) geniality, charm
sandunguero -ra *adj* (coll.) genial, charming
saneado -da *adj* clear, unencumbered
saneamiento *m* guarantee; indemnification; adjustment; sanitation, drainage
sanear *va* to guarantee (*amends or satisfaction*); to make amends for, to indemnify; to make an adjustment for (*damages resulting from defect in thing purchased*); to make sanitary, to drain, to dry up
sanedrín *m* Sanhedrim
sanfrancia *f* (coll.) row, quarrel, dispute
San Gotardo *m* St. Gotthard
sangradera *f* (surg.) lancet; basin for blood; overflow sluice; irrigation ditch
sangrador *m* bloodletter; drain, outlet
sangradura *f* bleeding, bloodletting; inner pit of arm opposite elbow; vein incision; outlet, draining
sangrar *va* to bleed; to drain; to tap (*a furnace; a tree*); to draw resin from; (print.) to indent; (coll.) to filch from; (Am.) to bleed (*to draw or extort money from*); *vn* to bleed; **estar sangrando** to be new or recent; to be plain or evident; *vr* to have oneself bled; to run (*said of colors*)
sangraza *f* contaminated blood
sangre *f* blood; spirit, fire; **a sangre** by animal power, by horsepower; **a sangre caliente** impulsively; **a sangre fría** in cold blood; **a sangre y fuego** without mercy, without quarter; violently, sweeping straight ahead; **bajársele a uno la sangre a los talones** or **helársele a uno la sangre** (coll.) to have one's blood run cold; **pura sangre** *m* thoroughbred; **sangre azul** blue blood; **sangre fría** sang-froid, cold-bloodedness; **sangre torera** bullfighting in the blood
sangría *f* bleeding, bloodletting; outlet, draining; ditch, trench; sangaree; tap (*in a tree*); tapping (*of a furnace*); inner pit of arm opposite elbow; resin cut; pilfering; (print.) indentation; **sangría suelta** free bleeding; constant drain (*on one's resources*)
sangriento -ta *adj* bleeding, bloody; sanguinary; savage (*e.g., insult*); (poet.) blood-red
sanguaza *f* contaminated blood; red vegetable fluid
sangüesa *f* raspberry (*fruit*)
sangüeso *m* (bot.) raspberry, raspberry bush
sanguificación *f* (physiol.) hematosis
sanguificar §86 *va* to produce blood from
sanguijolero -ra *mf* leecher
sanguijuela *f* (zool.) leech; (coll.) leech (*person*); **sanguijuela borriquera** (ent.) horseleech
sanguijuelero -ra *mf* leecher
sanguina *f* see **sanguino**
sanguinario -ria *adj* sanguinary, bloodthirsty; *f* (bot.) bloodroot; (mineral.) bloodstone; **La Sanguinaria** Bloody Mary (*Queen of England*); **sanguinaria del Canadá** (bot.) puccoon; **sanguinaria mayor** (bot.) knotgrass; **sanguinaria menor** (bot.) whitlowwort
sanguíneo -a *adj* sanguineous
sanguino -na *adj* blood; bloody; sanguineous; blood-red; *m* (bot.) mock privet; (bot.) red dogwood; *f* sanguine (*red crayon; drawing in red crayon*)
sanguinolencia *f* bloodiness, sanguinolence
sanguinolento -ta *adj* bloody, sanguinolent
sanguinoso -sa *adj* sanguinous; sanguinary
sanguiñuelo *m* (bot.) red dogwood
sanguisorba *f* (bot.) burnet
sanguisuela or **sanguja** *f* var. of **sanguijuela**
sanícula *f* (bot.) sanicle, self-heal
sanidad *f* healthiness; healthfulness; health; sanitation; **en sanidad** in health, in good health; **sanidad pública** health department
sanidina *f* (mineral.) sanidine
sanie *f* or **sanies** *f* (path.) sanies
sanioso -sa *adj* (path.) sanious
sanitario -ria *adj* sanitary; *m* military health officer
sanjacado *m* sanjak
sanjaco *m* sanjakbeg
sanjuanada *f* picnic on Saint John's day
sanjuanero -ra *adj* ripe by Saint John's day
sanjuanista *m* knight of Saint John of Jerusalem
San Lorenzo *m* St. Lawrence (*river*)

sanmiguelada *f* Michaelmastide
sanmigueleño -ña *adj* ripe by Michaelmas
sano -na *adj* healthy, hale; healthful, salutary; sound; right, correct, sane; earnest, sincere; safe, sure; (coll.) whole, untouched, unharmed, unbroken; **cortar por lo sano** (coll.) to use desperate remedies; **sano de Castilla** (slang) thief in disguise; **sano y salvo** safe and sound
San Petersburgo St. Petersburg
sanrafael *m* (bot.) zinnia
San Salvador *f* San Salvador (*island of Bahamas; capital of El Salvador*)
sanscritista *mf* Sanskritist
sánscrito -ta *adj & m* Sanskrit
sanseacabó *interj* (coll.) finished!, O.K.!
sanseviera *f* (bot.) sansevieria
sansimoniano -na *adj* Saint-Simonian; *mf* Saint-Simonian, Saint-Simonist
sansimonismo *m* Saint-Simonianism
sansirolé *mf* (coll.) nincompoop, simpleton
Sansón *m* (Bib. & fig.) Samson
santabárbara *f* (naut.) powder magazine
Santa Elena St. Helena (*British island and colony in South Atlantic*)
santaláceo -a *adj* (bot.) santalaceous
santanderino -na *adj* (pertaining to) Santander; *mf* native or inhabitant of Santander
santelmo *m* St. Elmo's fire
santero -ra *adj* image-worshipping; *mf* caretaker of a sanctuary; beggar carrying saint's image; guard, watcher; (slang) friend of thieves
Santiago *m* James; (Bib.) Saint James; **Santiago el Mayor** (Bib.) Saint James the Greater; **Santiago el Menor** (Bib.) Saint James the Less; *interj* war cry of medieval Spaniards
santiagueño -ña *adj* ripe by St. James's day
santiaguero -ra *adj* (pertaining to) Santiago de Cuba; *mf* native or inhabitant of Santiago de Cuba
santiagués -guesa *adj* (pertaining to) Santiago de Compostela; *mf* native or inhabitant of Santiago de Compostela
santiaguino -na *adj* (pertaining to) Santiago de Chile; *mf* native or inhabitant of Santiago de Chile
santiaguista *adj* pertaining to the Order of St. James; *m* knight of St. James
santiamén *m* (coll.) jiffy, instant, twinkling of an eye; **en un santiamén** (coll.) in a jiffy
santidad *f* sanctity, saintliness, holiness; **su Santidad** his Holiness
santificación *f* sanctification
santificador -dora *adj* sanctifying; *mf* sanctifier
santificar §86 *va* to sanctify, to consecrate, to hallow; to keep (*holy days*); (coll.) to excuse, to justify; *vr* (coll.) to excuse oneself, to justify oneself
santiguada *f* crossing oneself, sign of the cross; (coll.) rough treatment, slap, abuse; **¡para** or **por mi santiguada!** by the rood!, upon my faith!
santiguadero -ra *mf* powwower, quack; *f* powwow, healing with passes and prayers
santiguador -dora *mf* powwower, quack
santiguamiento *m* var. of **santiguada**
santiguar §23 *va* to bless, to make the sign of the cross over; to powwow, to make passes and say prayers over; (coll.) to punish, to slap, to abuse; *vr* to make the sign of the cross, to cross oneself; (Am.) to cross oneself to express surprise
santimonia *f* holiness, sanctity; (bot.) chrysanthemum
santiscario *m* invention; **de mi santiscario** (coll.) of my own invention
santísimo -ma *adj super* very or most holy; livelong (*e.g., day*); *m* Holy Sacrament
santito *m* (coll.) sissy
santo -ta *adj* saint, saintly, holy, blessed; livelong (*e.g., day*); (coll.) simple, artless; **su santa voluntad** his own sweet will; **santa bofetada** fine smack in the face; **santo y bueno** well and good; *mf* saint; *m* image of a saint; saint's day (*celebrated as one's anniversary*); (coll.) picture or engraving of a saint; picture; password, watchword; **a santo de** because of; **alzarse con el santo y la limosna** (coll.) to take the pot, to walk away with the whole thing, to make a clean sweep; **dar el santo** to give the watchword; **desnudar a un santo para vestir a otro** to rob Peter to pay Paul; **írsele a uno el santo al cielo** (coll.) to forget what one was up to; **no es santo de mi devoción** (coll.) I'm not very keen on him; **tener el santo de espaldas** (taur.) to do nothing right, to have a streak of bad luck; **tener santos en la corte** to have a friend at court; **santo titular** patron saint; **santo y seña** password, watchword
Santo Domingo Hispaniola (*island on which are situated Haiti and the Dominican Republic*)
santón *m* pagan ascetic, Mohammedan ascetic, dervish; hypocrite; tycoon; sage
santónico *m* (bot.) santonica
santonina *f* (pharm.) santonin
santoral *m* lives of saints; choir book; calendar of saints' days
santuario *m* sanctuary; shrine; (Am.) buried treasure
santucho -cha *adj & mf* (coll.) var. of **santurrón**
santulón -lona *adj & mf* (Am.) var. of **santurrón**
santurrón -rrona *adj* sanctimonious; *mf* sanctimonious person
santurronería *f* sanctimony, sanctimoniousness
saña *f* rage, fury; cruelty
sañoso -sa or **sañudo -da** *adj* enraged, furious; choleric
sao *m* (bot.) phillyrea; (Am.) small savannah with clusters of trees and bushes
Saona *m* Saône
sapidez *f* sapidity
sápido -da *adj* sapid, savory
sapiencia *f* sapience, wisdom; (*cap.*) *f* (Bib.) Wisdom of Solomon
sapiente *adj* sapient, wise; *mf* wise person
sapillo *m* little toad; (path.) ranula
sapina *f* var. of **salicor**
sapindáceo -a *adj* (bot.) sapindaceous
sapindo *m* (bot.) soapberry
sapino *m* (bot.) fir; (bot.) savin
sapo *m* (zool.) toad; (ichth.) toadfish; (coll.) stuffed shirt; (coll.) beast, pest; **echar sapos y culebras** (coll.) to talk nonsense, to utter angry abuses; **sapo marino** (ichth.) angler
saponáceo -a *adj* saponaceous
saponaria *f* (bot.) soapwort, bouncing Bet
saponificable *adj* saponifiable
saponificación *f* saponification
saponificar §86 *va & vr* to saponify
saponina *f* (chem.) saponin
saponita *f* (mineral.) saponite
saporífero -ra *adj* saporific
sapotáceo -a *adj* (bot.) sapotaceous
sapote *m* var. of **zapote**
sapotear *va* (Am.) to finger, touch, feel
sapotillo *m* var. of **zapotillo**
saprófago -ga *adj* (zool.) saprophagous
saprófito -ta *adj* (bot.) saprophytic; *m* (biol.) saprophyte
saque *m* serve, service (*e.g., in tennis*); service line; server; (Am.) distillery; **tener buen saque** (coll.) to be a heavy eater and drinker
saqueador -dora *adj* sacking, plundering; *mf* sacker, plunderer
saqueamiento *m* sacking, plunder, pillage, loot
saquear *va* to sack, to plunder, to pillage, to pilfer, to loot
saqueo *m* var. of **saqueamiento**
saquería *f* manufacture of sacks; collection of sacks
saquerío *m* collection of sacks
saquero -ra *adj* packing (*needle*); *mf* maker or vendor of sacks or bags
saquete *m* small sack; (arti.) cartridge bag
saquilada *f* contents of a bag that is not full
S.A.R. abr. of **Su Alteza Real**
Sara *f* Sarah, Sally
saragüete *m* (coll.) soirée at home, informal evening party

sarampión *m* (path.) measles; **sarampión alemán** (path.) German measles; **sarampión negro** (path.) black measles
sarampioso -sa *adj* measly
sarao *m* soirée, evening party
sarape *m* (Am.) serape
sarapia *f* (bot.) tonka bean (*tree and fruit*)
sarapico *m* (orn.) curlew; (orn.) tattler, yellowlegs; (bot.) shooting star
sarcasmo *m* sarcasm
sarcástico -ca *adj* sarcastic
sarcia *f* load, burden
sarcina *f* (bact.) sarcina
sarcocarpio *m* (bot.) sarcocarp
sarcocele *m* (path.) sarcocele
sarcocola *f* sarcocolla (*gum*)
sarcófago *m* sarcophagus
sarcolema *m* (anat.) sarcolemma
sarcología *f* sarcology
sarcoma *m* (path.) sarcoma
sarda *f* see **sardo**
sardana *f* sardana (*Catalonian dance and music*)
sardanapalesco -ca *adj* Sardanapalian
Sardanápalo *m* Sardanapalus
sardesco -ca *adj* small (*said of ass, horse, etc.*); (coll.) coarse, brazen; *m* small ass, pony
sardina *f* (ichth.) sardine; **como sardinas en banasta** or **en lata** (coll.) packed like sardines
sardinal *m* sardine net
sardinel *m* (mas.) rowlock
sardinero -ra *adj* (pertaining to the) sardine; *mf* sardine dealer
sardineta *f* small sardine; pointed two-stripe chevron; cheese extending beyond mold
sardio *m* sard
sardo -da *adj* Sardinian; black, white, and red (*said of cattle*); *mf* Sardinian; *m* Sardinian (*language*); *f* (ichth.) horse mackerel
sardonia *f* (bot.) Sardinian herb
sardónica *f* see **sardónico**
sardónice *f* (mineral.) sardonyx
sardónico -ca *adj* sardonic (*laugh*); (Am.) sardonic, sarcastic; *f* (mineral.) sardonyx
sardonio *m* or **sardónique** *f* var. of **sardónica**
sarga *f* serge; painted wall fabric; (bot.) willow
sargadilla *f* (bot.) saltbush (*Suaeda splendens*)
sargado -da *adj* twilled, serge
sargal *m* willow grove
sargatilla *f* or **sargatillo** *m* (bot.) white willow
sargazo *m* (bot.) sargasso, gulfweed
sargenta *f* sergeant's wife; sergeant's halberd; big coarse woman
sargentear *va* to command as a sergeant; to boss, to manage; *vn* (coll.) to be bossy
sargentería *f* sergeant's drill
sargentía *f* sergeancy
sargento *m* sergeant
sargentona *f* big coarse woman
sargo m (ichth.) sargo; (ichth.) Bermuda bream, silvery porgy
sarguero -ra *adj* (pertaining to the) willow; *mf* painter of wall fabrics
sarilla *f* (bot.) marjoram
sarmentador -dora *mf* gatherer of vine shoots
sarmentar §18 *vn* to gather pruned vine shoots
sarmentazo *m* large vine shoot; blow with a vine shoot
sarmentera *f* gathering vine shoots; storage of vine shoots
sarmentillo *m* slender vine shoot
sarmentoso -sa *adj* running, twining, sarmentous
sarmiento *m* (bot.) vine shoot, running stem, sarmentum
sarna *f* itch, mange, scabies; **más viejo que la sarna** (coll.) old as Methuselah; **sarna de los barberos** barber's itch
sarnoso -sa *adj* itchy, mangy, scabious
sarpullido *m* var. of **salpullido**
sarpullir §26 *va & vr* var. of **salpullir**
sarracénico -ca *adj* Saracenic
sarraceno -na *adj & mf* Saracen
sarracina *f* scuffle, free fight, free-for-all; bloody brawl
Sarre *m* Saar (*river*); Saar or Saarland
sarrés -rresa *adj* (pertaining to the) Saar; *mf* Saarlander
sarria *f* coarse net for carrying straw
sarrieta *f* deep feed bag
sarrillo *m* death rattle; (bot.) arum
sarro *m* incrustation, crust; fur (*e.g., on tongue*); tartar (*on teeth*); (path.) sordes; (bot.) rust, mildew
sarroso -sa *adj* incrusted, crusty; full of tartar
sarta *f* string (*e.g., of beads*); line, file, series
sartal *m* string (*e.g., of beads*)
sartén *f* frying pan; contents of frying pan, frying panful; **saltar de la sartén y dar en las brasas** (coll.) to jump out of the frying pan into the fire; **tener la sartén por el mango** (coll.) to be in control, to have the upper hand
sartenada *f* contents of frying pan, frying panful
sartenazo *m* blow with a frying pan; (coll.) hard blow
sartorio -ria *adj* (anat.) sartorial
sasafrás *m* (bot.) sassafras (*tree and dried root bark*)
sastra *f* female tailor; tailor's wife
sastre *m* tailor
sastrería *f* tailoring; tailor shop
sastresa *f* (dial.) female tailor
Satán *m* or **Satanás** *m* Satan
satánico -ca *adj* satanic or Satanic
satelitario -ria *adj* (pertaining to a) satellite
satélite *m* (astr. & fig.) satellite; (mach.) satellite pinion; (coll.) sheriff, bailiff, constable; *adj* satellite; suburban
satelizar §76 *va* to put into orbit; *vr* to go into orbit, to become a satellite
satén *m* sateen
satinar *va* to satin (*e.g., paper*)
sátira *f* satire
satírico -ca *adj* satiric or satirical; *mf* satirist
satirio *m* (zool.) water rat
satirión *m* (bot.) male orchis; (zool.) water rat
satirizar §76 *va & vn* to satirize
sátiro *m* (myth.) satyr; satyr (*lewd man*)
satisdación *f* (law) bail, surety, security
satisfacción *f* satisfaction; **a satisfacción** satisfactorily; **a satisfacción de** to the satisfaction of
satisfacer §55 *va & vn* to satisfy; *vr* to satisfy oneself, be satisfied, take satisfaction
satisfaciente *adj* satisfying
satisfactorio -ria *adj* satisfactory
satisfago *1st sg pres ind of* **satisfacer**
satisfaré *1st sg fut ind of* **satisfacer**
satisfaz *2d sg impv of* **satisfacer**
satisfecho -cha satisfied; conceited; *pp of* **satisfacer**
satisfice *1st sg pret ind of* **satisfacer**
sativo -va *adj* sown, cultivated
sátrapa *m* satrap; (coll.) crafty fellow; *adj* (coll.) crafty
satrapía *f* satrapy
saturable *adj* saturable
saturación *f* saturation; satiation
saturador -dora *adj* saturating; *mf* saturator; *m* saturator (*apparatus*)
saturar *va* to saturate; to satiate
saturnal *adj* Saturnian; Saturnalian; *f* saturnalia (*orgy*); **saturnales** *fpl* Saturnalia (*festival of Saturn*)
saturniano -na *adj* Saturnian (*pertaining to Saturn; pertaining to a Latin verse*); saturnine
saturnino -na *adj* saturnine
saturnismo *m* (path.) saturnism
Saturno *m* (myth. & astr.) Saturn
sauce *m* (bot.) willow; **sauce blanco** (bot.) white willow; **sauce cabruno** (bot.) sallow, goat willow; **sauce de Babilonia** or **sauce llorón** (bot.) weeping willow
sauceda *f*, **saucedal** *m*, or **saucera** *f* willow grove
saucillo *m* (bot.) knotgrass
saúco *m* (bot.) elder, elderberry; second hoof (*of horses*)
Saúl *m* (Bib.) Saul
Saulo *m* (Bib.) Saul (*original name of apostle Paul*)

sauquillo *m* (bot.) snowball, guelder-rose, cranberry tree
saurio -ria *adj & m* (zool.) saurian
sausería *f* palace larder
sausier *m* chief of palace larder
sautor *m* (her.) saltier
sauz *m* (*pl:* **sauces**) var. of **sauce**
sauzal *m* willow grove
sauzgatillo *m* (bot.) agnus castus, chaste tree
savia *f* sap (*of a plant*); (fig.) sap
sáxeo -a *adj* rocky, stony
saxífraga *f* (bot.) saxifrage
saxifragáceo -a *adj* (bot.) saxifragaceous
saxifragia *f* var. of **saxífraga**
saxofonista *mf* saxophonist
saxofón *m* or **saxófono** *m* (mus.) saxophone
saya *f* skirt; petticoat
sayal *m* sackcloth, coarse woolen cloth; skirt
sayalería *f* weaving of sackcloth
sayalero -ra *mf* weaver of sackcloth
sayalesco -ca *adj* sackcloth
sayalete *m* light flannel for undergarments
sayete *m* short smock
sayo *m* smock frock, tunic; (coll.) garment; **cortar un sayo a** (coll.) to talk behind the back of; **decir para su sayo** (coll.) to say to oneself, to say in one's sleeve
sayón *m* executioner; fierce-looking fellow
sayuela *f* serge shirt
sazón *f* ripeness, maturity; season; time, occasion; taste, relish, seasoning; **a la sazón** at that time; **en sazón** on time, opportunely; ripe, in season
sazonado -da *adj* tasty, seasoned; expressive, witty; *m* seasoning
sazonar *va* to ripen, to mature; to season; *vr* to ripen, to mature
s/c abr. of **su cuenta**
S.C. or **s.c.** abr. of **su casa**
Scherezada *f* Scheherazade
S.D. abr. of **se despide**
SE abr. of **sudeste**
S.E. abr. of **Su Excelencia**
se *pron reflex* himself, to himself; herself, to herself; itself, to itself; themselves, to themselves; yourself, to yourself; yourselves, to yourselves; oneself, to oneself; each other, to each other; *pron pers* (used before the pronouns **lo, la, los,** or **las**) to him, to her, to it, to them, to you
sé *1st sg pres ind of* **saber;** *2d sg impv of* **ser**
sea *1st sg pres subj of* **ser**
s.e., autor abr. of **sin editor, autor** privately printed
sebáceo -a *adj* sebaceous
Sebastián *m* Sebastian
sebastiano *m* var. of **sebestén**
sebe *f* wattle, stockade
sebestén *m* (bot.) sebesten (*tree and fruit*)
sebillo *m* light tallow
sebo *m* tallow; grease, fat, suet
seboso -sa *adj* tallowy; greasy, fatty, suety
seca *f* see **seco**
secácul *m* parsnip (*root*)
secadal *m* dry, barren soil; dry sand bank
secadero -ra *adj* dry, easily kept dry; *m* drying place, drying room
secadillo *m* almond meringue
sacadío -a *adj* capable of drying up, exhaustible
secador -dora *adj* drying; *m* dryer; drying place; hair dryer; *f* clothes dryer
secamente *adv* dryly, curtly; gruffly, harshly, sharply
secamiento *m* drying; drying up, withering
secano *m* unwatered land, dry land; dry sand bank; dryness; **cultivo de secano** dry farming
secansa *f* sequence (*in cards*)
secante *adj* drying, siccative; blotting; (geom. & trig.) secant; *m* siccative; blotting paper; *f* (geom. & trig.) secant
secar §86 *va* to dry, to dry up, to wipe dry; to annoy, bore, vex, tease; *vr* to dry, to get dry; to dry oneself; to get thin; to wither; to be dry, be thirsty; to run dry (*said, e.g., of a well*)
secaral *m* var. of **sequeral**
secarropa *f* clothes drier; **secarropa de travesaños** clotheshorse
secatón -tona *adj* (coll.) dull, inane
secatura *f* dullness, inanity, tiresomeness
sección *f* section; cross section; department (*e.g., of a store*); (arch., geom. & mil.) section; **sección cesárea** (surg.) Caesarean section; **sección cónica** (math.) conic section; **sección de captura** (phys.) capture cross section; **sección de fondo** editorial section (*of a paper*); **secciones cónicas** conic sections (*branch of geometry*); **sección transversal** cross section
seccional *adj* sectional (*e.g., bookcase*)
seccionamiento *m* sectioning
seccionar *va* to section
secesión *f* secession
secesionismo *m* secessionism
secesionista *adj & mf* secessionist
seceso *m* stool, excrement
seco -ca *adj* dry; dried, dried up, withered, dead; arid; lean, lank; plain, unadorned; cold, lukewarm, indifferent; sharp, harsh; straight (*drink*); *m* (Am.) blow, bump; **en seco** high and dry; without cause or reason; without resources; suddenly; *f* drought; dry season; (med.) desquamation; infarction (*of a gland*); dry sand bank; **a secas** merely, simply; **a secas y sin llover** (coll.) without a word of warning
secoya *f* (bot.) sequoia
secreción *f* segregation; (physiol.) secretion
secreta *f* see **secreto**
secretar *va* (physiol.) to secrete
secretaría *f* or **secretariado** *m* secretariat, secretaryship, office of secretary
secretario -ria *adj* confidential, trusted; *mf* secretary; *m* (orn.) secretary bird; *f* secretary's wife
secretear *vn* (coll.) to whisper, to talk confidentially
secreteo *m* (coll.) whispering, confidential talk
secreter *m* secretary (*writing desk*)
secretina *f* (biochem.) secretin
secretista *mf* naturalist; (coll.) whisperer
secret.° abr. of **secretario**
secreto -ta *adj* secret; secretive; *m* secret; secrecy; key (*combination for opening a lock*); soundboard (*of musical instrument*); hiding place, secret drawer or compartment; **en el secreto de las cosas** on the inside; **en secreto** in secret; **secreto a voces** open secret; **secreto de estado** state secret; **secreto de Pulchinela** (coll.) open secret; *f* licentiate's examination; secret investigation; (eccl.) secret (*prayer*); secret police; privy, water closet
secretor -tora or **secretorio -ria** *adj* (physiol.) secretory
secta *f* sect
sectador -dora *adj & mf* var. of **sectario**
sectario -ria *adj* sectarian, denominational; sectary; *mf* sectarian; sectary
sectarismo *m* sectarianism, denominationalism
sectil *adj* sectile
sectilio *m* sectile mosaic
sector *m* sector; (geom., math. & mil.) sector; **sector de distribución** (elec.) house current, power line
secuacidad *f* partisanship
secuaz (*pl:* **-cuaces**) *adj* partisan; *mf* partisan, follower
secuela *f* sequel, result; (med.) sequela, aftermath
secuencia *f* (eccl., mov. & mus.) sequence
secuestración *f* (law) sequestration
secuestrador -dora *adj* kidnaping; *mf* kidnaper
secuestrar *va* to kidnap; (law) to sequester
secuestro *m* kidnaping; (law) sequestration, sequestered property; (med.) sequestrum; umpire, referee
secular *adj* secular; centesimal, e.g., **los años seculares** the centesimal years (*1800, 1900, 2000, etc.*)
secularidad *f* secularity
secularismo *m* secularism
secularista *mf* secularist
secularización *f* secularization
secularizar §76 *va* to secularize; *vr* to become or to be secularized
secundante *mf* seconder; *m* second (*in boxing*)

secundar *va* to second, to back
secundario -ria *adj* secondary; *m* (elec.) secondary (*coil or winding*)
secundinas *fpl* afterbirth, secundines
secundípara *adj fem* secundiparous; *f* secundipara
sed *f* thirst; drought, dryness, need for water; (fig.) thirst; **apagar la sed, matar la sed** to quench the thirst; **tener sed** to be thirsty; **tener sed de** to be thirsty for, to thirst for
seda *f* silk; wild boar's bristles; **como una seda** (coll.) smooth as silk; sweet-natured; easy as pie; **de media seda** half-silk; **de toda seda** all silk; **seda conchal** choice silk; **seda encerada** dental floss; **seda floja** floss silk, untwisted silk; **seda joyante** glossy silk
sedación *f* soothing; (med.) sedation
sedadera *f* hackle for dressing flax
sedal *m* fish line, fishing line; (vet.) rowel
sedalino -na *adj* silk; silky; *f* silkaline; schappe; half-silk fabric
sedán *m* (aut.) sedan; **sedán de reparto** delivery truck
sedante *adj & m* sedative
sedar *va* to soothe, quiet, allay
sedativo -va *adj & m* (med.) sedative
sede *f* seat; headquarters; (eccl.) see; **Santa Sede** Holy See; **Sede apostólica** Apostolic See; **sede social** (com.) main office, headquarters
sedear *va* to clean with a bristle brush
Sedecías *m* (Bib.) Zedekiah
sedentario -ria *adj* sedentary
sedente *adj* sitting, seated
sedeño -ña *adj* (pertaining to) silk; bristly; *f* fine tow of flax; fine linen; fiber; horsehair fishing line
sedera *f* see **sedero**
sedería *f* silk stuff, silks; silk business; silk store
sedero -ra *adj* (pertaining to) silk; *mf* silk weaver; silk dealer; *f* bristle brush
sedicente or **sediciente** *adj* so-called, self-styled
sedición *f* sedition
sedicioso -sa *adj* seditious; *mf* seditionary
sediento -ta *adj* thirsty; dry (*land*); anxious, eager
sedimentación *f* sedimentation
sedimentar *va & vr* to sediment, to settle
sedimentario -ria *adj* sedimental or sedimentary; (geol.) sedimentary
sedimento *m* sediment
sedoso -sa *adj* silky
seducción *f* temptation; seduction; bribery; charm, captivation
seducible *adj* seducible
seducir §38 *va* to tempt, lead astray; to seduce; to captivate
seductivo -va *adj* tempting; seductive; captivating
seductor -tora *adj* tempting; seductive; captivating; *mf* tempter; seducer; charmer, captivator
seduje *1st sg pret ind of* **seducir**
seduzco *1st sg pres ind of* **seducir**
sefardí (*pl:* **-díes**) *adj* Sephardic; *mf* Sephardi; **sefardíes** *mpl* Sephardim; *m* language of the Sephardim
sefardita *adj* Sephardic; *mf* Sephardi
segable *adj* ready to be harvested
segada *f* harvest
segadero -ra *adj* ready to be harvested; *f* sickle
segador -dora *adj* harvesting; mowing; *m* harvester, harvestman; (ent.) harvestman, daddy longlegs; *f* harvester (*woman; machine*); mowing machine; **segadora de césped** lawn mower; **segadora trilladora** harvester-thresher, combine
segar §29 *va* to reap, to mow, to harvest; to cut off, to mow down; *vn* to reap, to mow, to harvest
segazón *f* harvest; harvest time
seglar *adj* secular, lay; *m* layman; *f* laywoman
segmentación *f* segmentation
segmental *adj* segmental; (arch. & zool.) segmental
segmentario -ria *adj* segmentary
segmento *m* segment; **segmento de émbolo** piston ring
segoviano -na or **segoviense** *adj* (pertaining to) Segovia; *mf* native or inhabitant of Segovia
segregación *f* segregation; (physiol.) secretion
segregacionista *mf* segregationist
segregar §59 *va* to segregate; to excommunicate; (physiol.) to secrete
segregativo -va *adj* segregative
segrí *m* heavy silk fabric
segueta *f* buhl saw, marquetry saw; hacksaw
seguetear *vn* to saw with a buhl saw
seguida *f* see **seguido**
seguidamente *adv* without interruption, successively; at once, immediately; next, next in order
seguidero *m* guide lines for writing
seguidilla *f* Spanish stanza made up of a quatrain of alternating seven-syllable and five-syllable verses, with the second and fourth verses in assonance, and of three final verses, the first and third of which are five-syllable in assonance and the second seven-syllable; **seguidillas** *fpl* (mus.) seguidillas (*air and dance*)
seguido -da *adj* continued, successive; straight, direct; in a row, running, e.g., **cuatro días seguidos** four days in a row, four days running; **todo seguido** straight ahead; *m* drop stitch in a stocking foot; *f* series, succession, continuation; **de seguida** without interruption, continuously; at once, immediately; in a row, e.g., **cuatro días de seguida** four days in a row; **en seguida** at once, immediately
seguidor -dora *adj* following; homing (*e.g., torpedo*); *mf* follower; *m* guide lines for writing
seguimiento *m* following, pursuit, chase, hunt; continuation
seguir §82 *va* to follow; to pursue; to dog, to hound; to prosecute; to continue; to bring, to institute (*e.g., a suit*); *vn* to go on, to continue; to still be, to be now; **como sigue** as follows; **seguir adelante** to go ahead; **seguir** + *ger* to keep, to continue + *ger; vr* to follow, to ensue; to issue, to spring
según *adv* depending on circumstances; **según que** according as; *prep* according to, as per; *conj* as, according as; **según y como, según y conforme** that depends, depending on circumstances; according as
segunda *f* see **segundo**
segundar *va* to repeat at once; *vn* to come next, to be second; to do it again
segundario -ria *adj* var. of **secundario**
segundero -ra *adj* second (*said of a crop in the same season*); *m* second hand; **segundero central** sweep second hand, sweep-second, center-second
segundilla *f* call bell (*in convents*)
segundillo *m* second serving of bread (*in a convent*)
segundo -da *adj* second; **de segunda mano** second-hand; **segunda intención** double meaning; double dealing; *m* second; **sin segundo** unequaled; *f* double turn (*of lock*); double meaning; (mus.) second (*part; interval*); (aut.) second
segundogénito -ta *adj & mf* second-born
segundogenitura *f* secundogeniture
segundón *m* second son; younger son
seguntino -na *adj* (pertaining to) Sigüenza; *mf* native or inhabitant of Sigüenza
segur *f* axe; sickle
segurador *m* security, bondsman
segureja *f* small hatchet
seguridad *f* security; surety; safety; certainty; sureness; confidence; assurance, guarantee; surety bond; **seguridad colectiva** collective security; **seguridad social** social security
seguro -ra *adj* sure, certain; secure, safe; reliable, dependable; firm, constant; steady, unfailing; **seguro** *adv* surely; *m* assurance, certainty; safety; confidence; insurance; pawl, dog, latch, stop; safety lock (*of breech mechanism*); **a buen seguro, al seguro,** or **de seguro** surely, truly; **en seguro** in safety; **irse del seguro** (coll.) to forget oneself, to cast

prudence aside; **sobre seguro** without risk; **seguro contra accidentes** accident insurance; **seguro de desocupación** unemployment insurance; **seguro de enfermedad** health insurance; **seguro de incendios** fire insurance; **seguro mutuo** mutual insurance; **seguro sobre la vida** life insurance
segurón *m* large axe
seis *adj* six; **las seis** six o'clock; *m* six; sixth (*in dates*)
seisavado -da *adj* hexagonal
seisavar *va* to make hexagonal
seisavo -va *adj* sixth; *m* sixth; hexagon
seiscientos -tas *adj & m* six hundred; **el Seiscientos** the Seventeenth Century
seise *m* singing and dancing choir boy (*six in all*) in Seville cathedral in certain festivals
seiseno -na *adj* sixth
seisillo *m* (mus.) sextuplet
seísmico -ca *adj* var. of **sísmico**
seísmo *m* var. of **sismo**
selacio -cia *adj & m* (ichth.) selachian
selección *f* selection; **selección natural** (biol.) natural selection
seleccionamiento *m* selecting, choosing
seleccionar *va* to select
selecta *f* see **selecto**
selectividad *f* (rad.) selectivity
selectivo -va *adj* selective; (rad.) selective
selecto -ta *adj* select, choice; *f* selection (*of works of different authors*); **selectas** *fpl* analects
selector -tora *adj* selective; selecting, selector; *m* (telp.) selector (*mechanism of dial telephone*)
Selene *f* (myth.) Selene
selenio *m* (chem.) selenium
selenita *mf* moon dweller; *f* (mineral.) selenite
seleniuro *m* (chem.) selenide
selenografía *f* selenography
selenógrafo -fa *mf* selenographer
selenosis *f* (*pl:* **-sis**) white spots on nails
self *f* (elec.) coil, self-induction coil
selfactina *f* self-acting mule (*spinning machine*)
selva *f* forest, woods; jungle; (Am.) selva; **Selva Negra** Black Forest (*in Germany*)
selvático -ca *adj* woodsy; rustic, wild
selvatiquez *f* woodsiness; rusticity, wildness
selvicultura *f* forestry
selvoso -sa *adj* woody, wooded, sylvan
sellador -dora *mf* sealer; stamper
selladura *f* sealing; stamping; stamp, impress
sellaje *m* sealing
sellaporos *m* (*pl:* **-ros**) (paint.) filler
sellar *va* to seal; to stamp; to cover, to close; to finish up
sello *m* seal; stamp; signet; stamp office; wafer; (fig.) seal; **echar** or **poner el sello a** to bring to perfection; **gran sello** great seal; **sello adherido** adhesive stamp; **sello aéreo** air-mail stamp; **sello de correo** postage stamp; **sello de goma** rubber stamp; **sello de Salomón** Solomon's seal; (bot.) Solomon's-seal; **sello de urgencia** special-delivery stamp; **sello fiscal** revenue stamp
semafórico -ca *adj* semaphoric
semaforista *m* (rail.) signalman
semáforo *m* semaphore; traffic light
semana *f* week; week's pay; septenary (*period of seven months, years, etc.*); **entre semana** during the week (*but not on the first or last days*); **semana de pasión** Passion Week; **semana inglesa** working week of five and a half days, working week ending Saturday noon; **semana grande, semana mayor,** or **semana santa** Holy Week; **Semana Santa** book containing Holy Week services and prayers
semanal *adj* weekly
semanalmente *adv* weekly
semanario -ria *adj* weekly; *m* weekly (*publication*)
semanería *f* week work
semanero -ra *adj* engaged by the week; *mf* week worker
semanilla *f* book containing Holy Week services and prayers
semántico -ca *adj* semantic; *f* semantics
semantista *mf* semanticist
semasiología *f* semasiology
semasiológico -ca *adj* semasiological
semblante *m* face, mien, countenance; look, appearance; **componer el semblante** to take on a sober look; to put on a calm appearance; **estar de mal semblante** to frown, to look grouchy; **mudar de semblante** to change color; to take on a different aspect
semblantear *va* (Am.) to look straight in the face
semblanza *f* (biographical) sketch, portrait
sembrada *f* sown ground
sembradera *f* seeder, seeding machine; sowing machine
sembradío -a *adj* ready for sowing, suitable for sowing
sembrado *m* cultivated field, sown ground; **sembrados** *mpl* grain fields
sembrador -dora *adj* seeding, sowing; *mf* seeder, sower; *f* seeder, seeding machine; sowing machine
sembradura *f* seeding, sowing
sembrar **§18** *va* to seed; to sow; to spread, to scatter; to sprinkle; *vn* to seed; to sow
semeja *f* similarity, likeness, resemblance; sign, mark
semejable *adj* like, resembling
semejado -da *adj* like
semejante *adj* like, similar; such; (math.) like, similar; **semejantes** *adj pl* alike, e.g., **estos libros son semejantes** these books are alike; **semejante a** like, e.g., **este libro es semejante al otro** this book is like the other one; *m* resemblance, likeness; fellow, fellow man
semejanza *f* similarity, resemblance; simile; **a semejanza de** like, as
semejar *va* to resemble, to be like; *vn & vr* to be alike; **semejar a** or **semejarse a** to resemble, to be like
Semele *f* or **Sémele** *f* (myth.) Semele
semen *m* (bot. & physiol.) semen
semencera *f* seeding, sowing
semencontra *m* (pharm.) santonica
semental *adj* (pertaining to) seed, sowing; stud, breeding (*animal*); *m* sire; stock bull; stallion
sementar **§18** *va* to seed, to sow
sementera *f* seeding, sowing; sown land; seedtime, sowing time; (fig.) hotbed
sementero *m* seed bag; seeding, sowing
sementino -na *adj* (pertaining to) seed
semestral *adj* (pertaining to a) semester; six-month
semestre *adj* semestral; six-month; *m* semester; period of six months
semianual *adj* semiannual
semiárido -da *adj* semiarid
semiautomático -ca *adj* semiautomatic
semibola *f* (bridge) little slam
semibreve *f* (mus.) whole note, semibreve
semicabrón *m* satyr
semicadencia *f* (mus.) semicadence
semicapro *m* var. of **semicabrón**
semicilíndrico -ca *adj* semicylindrical
semicircular *adj* semicircular
semicírculo *m* semicircle
semicivilizado -da *adj* semicivilized
semiconductor -tora *adj* (elec.) semiconducting; *m* (elec.) semiconductor
semiconsciente *adj* semiconscious
semiconsonante *adj* semiconsonantal; *f* semiconsonant
semicoque *m* semicoke
semicorchea *f* (mus.) semiquaver, sixteenth note
semiculto -ta *adj* (philol.) semilearned
semidea *f* (poet.) var. of **semidiosa**
semideo *m* (poet.) var. of **semidiós**
semideponente *adj* (gram.) semideponent
semidiámetro *m* (astr. & geom.) semidiameter
semidiesel *m* semi-Diesel engine
semidifunto -ta *adj* half-dead
semidiós *m* demigod
semidiosa *f* demigoddess
semidivino -na *adj* semidivine
semidormido -da *adj* half-asleep
semieje *m* semiaxis
semielíptico -ca *adj* semielliptical

semiesfera *f* hemisphere
semiesférico -ca *adj* hemispherical
semiesquina *f* place near the corner; **semiesquina a** around the corner from
semifinal *adj & f* (sport) semifinal
semifluido -da *adj & m* semifluid
semifusa *f* (mus.) sixty-fourth note
semigola *f* (fort.) demigorge
semihombre *m* half-man; pigmy
semilíquido -da *adj & m* semiliquid
semilunar *adj* semilunar
semilunio *m* (astr.) half a lunation
semilla *f* seed; **semilla brincadora** jumping bean; **semilla de césped** grass seed
semillero *m* seed, seed plot; nursery; (fig.) hotbed
seminal *adj* seminal
seminario *m* seminary; seminar; seed plot; nursery; **seminario conciliar** seminary, theological seminary
seminarista *m* seminarist
seminífero -ra *adj* seminiferous
semínima *f* (mus.) crotchet; **semínimas** *fpl* trifles
semínola *adj & mf* Seminole
semioficial *adj* semiofficial
semiología *f* semeiology
semiótico -ca *adj* semeiotic; *f* semeiotics
semipedal *adj* semipedal
semipelagianismo *m* Semi-Pelagianism
semipelagiano -na *adj & m* Semi-Pelagian
semipermeable *adj* semipermeable
semipleno -na *adj* (law) incomplete, imperfect
semipopular *adj* semipopular
Semíramis *f* Semiramis
semi-remolque *m* semitrailer
semirrecto -ta *adj* (geom.) of 45 degrees
semirrígido -da *adj* (aer.) semirigid
semirrubio -bia *adj* rather blond, somewhat blond
semisalvaje *adj* half-savage; *mf* half savage
semisecular *adj* half-century
semiseda *f* half silk
semiseparado -da *adj* semidetached
semisólido -da *adj & m* semisolid
semisuma *f* half
semita *adj* Semitic; *mf* Semite, Semitic
semítico -ca *adj* Semitic; *m* Semitic (*group of languages*)
semitismo *m* Semitism
semitista *mf* Semitist
semitono *m* (mus.) semitone, half tone
semitropical *adj* semitropical
semivivo -va *adj* half-alive
semivocal *adj* semivocalic; *f* semivowel
sémola *f* semolina, groats
semoviente *adj* self-moving; **semovientes** *mpl* stock (*horses, cattle, etc.*)
sempiterno -na *adj* sempiternal, everlasting; *f* durance, everlasting (*a material*); (bot.) globe amaranth
sen *m* (bot. & pharm.) senna
sena *f* six (*in dice*); (bot. & pharm.) senna; **senas** *fpl* double sixes; (*cap.*) *m* Seine
senado *m* senate
senadoconsulto *m* senatus consultum
senador -dora *mf* senator
senaduría *f* senatorship
Senaquerib *m* Sennacherib
senara *f* land allowed to be worked as part wages; yield of such land; commons
senario -ria *adj* senary, sextuple
senatorial or **senatorio -ria** *adj* senatorial
sencillez *f* simplicity, simpleness, plainness, candor
sencillo -lla *adj* simple, plain, unaffected; (bot.) single; *m* change, loose change; (baseball) single
senda *f* path, footpath
senderar or **senderear** *va* to guide or lead by a path; to cut or open a path through; *vn* to take extraordinary measures
sendero *m* path, footpath, byway
sendos -das *adj pl* one each, one to each, e.g., **les dió sendos libros** he gave one book to each of them, he gave each of them a book; **hay tres circuitos recorridos por sendas corrientes** there are three circuits traversed by one current each
séneca *m* wise man, man of wisdom; (*cap.*) *m* Seneca
senectud *f* age, old age
Senegal, el Senegal
senegalés -lesa *adj & mf* Senegalese
senescal *m* seneschal
senescalado *m* seneschalsy (*territory; office*)
senescalía *f* seneschalsy (*office of seneschal*)
senescencia *f* senescence, aging
senescente *adj* senescent, aging
senil *adj* senile
senilidad *f* senility
senilismo *m* premature senility
sénior *m* (sport) star
seno *m* bosom, breast; heart; womb; lap; bay, gulf; trough (*between two waves*); cavity, hollow, recess; asylum, refuge; slack; curvature of slack sail or rope; (anat., bot., zool. & path.) sinus; (arch.) spandrel; (trig.) sine; **en el seno de** in the bosom of, in the heart of; in the midst of, in the presence of; **seno de Abrahán** Abraham's bosom; **seno verso** (trig.) versed sine
sensación *f* sensation; **hacer sensación** to cause a sensation
sensacional *adj* sensational
sensacionalismo *m* sensationalism; (philos.) sensationalism
sensacionalista *mf* (philos.) sensationalist
sensacionismo *m* (philos.) sensationalism
sensacionista *mf* (philos.) sensationalist
sensatez *f* good sense
sensato -ta *adj* sensible
sensibilidad *f* sensibility; sensitivity; (phot. & rad.) sensitiveness, sensitivity
sensibilización *f* sensitization
sensibilizar §76 *va* to sensitize (*e.g., the ear to music*); (phot.) to sensitize
sensible *adj* sensible; perceptible, noticeable, appreciable; sensitive; deplorable, lamentable; (phot. & rad.) sensitive
sensiblería *f* sentimentality, mawkishness
sensiblero -ra *adj* sentimental, mawkish
sensitivo -va *adj* sensitive, sense; sentient; stimulating; *f* (bot.) sensitive plant
sensorio -ria *adj* sensorial, sensory; *m* sensorium
sensual *adj* sensual, sensuous; *mf* sensualist
sensualidad *f* sensuality
sensualismo *m* sensualism; (philos.) sensualism
sensualista *adj & mf* sensualist; (philos.) sensualist
sentada *f* see **sentado**
sentadero *m* place to sit (*stone, board, log, etc.*)
sentadillas; a sentadillas sidesaddle
sentado -da *adj* seated; established, settled; stable, permanent; sedate, judicious; raw; (bot.) sessile; **dar por sentado** to take for granted, to consider as settled; *f* sitting; **de una sentada** at one sitting
sentamiento *m* settling
sentar §18 *va* to seat; to set, to establish; to suit, fit, become, to agree with; *vr* to sit, to sit down; to settle, to settle down; **sentarse a** (coll.) to mark the flesh of, to leave a mark on the skin of, e.g., **se me ha sentado una costura** (coll.) a seam left a mark on my skin
sentencia *f* sentence; (law) sentence
sentenciador -dora *adj* sentencing; *mf* sentencer
sentenciar *va* to sentence; to declare sententiously; to consign (*e.g., to the wastebasket*)
sentencioso -sa *adj* sententious
senticar *m* thicket, brambles
sentido -da *adj* felt, experienced; deep-felt, full of feeling, sensitive; eloquent, convincing; **darse por sentido** to show resentment, to take offense; *m* sense; meaning; direction; (geom. & mech.) sense; **aguzar el sentido** (coll.) to prick up one's ears; **con todos mis cinco sentidos** (coll.) with all my heart and soul; **costar un sentido** (coll.) to cost a fortune; **doble sentido** double-entendre; **en tal sentido** to this effect; **perder el sentido** to faint, to lose consciousness; **poner sus cinco sentidos en** (coll.) to be all eyes and ears for, to be mad about; **recobrar el sentido** to regain consciousness; **sin sentido** meaning-

less; unconscious; **tener puestos sus cinco sentidos en** (coll.) to be all eyes and ears for, to be mad about; **valer un sentido** (coll.) to be worth a fortune; **sentido común** common sense
sentimental *adj* sentimental
sentimentalismo *m* sentimentalism, sentimentality
sentimentalista *adj* sentimental; *mf* sentimentalist
sentimiento *m* sentiment; feeling; sorrow, regret
sentina *f* (naut.) bilge; foul, filthy place; hotbed of vice
sentir *m* feeling; opinion, judgment ‖ §62 *va* to feel; to hear; to regret, to be or feel sorry for; to sense; to recite (*e.g., verse*) with appropriate gestures; **dar que sentir** to give cause for regret; **sentir** + *inf* to regret to, to be or feel sorry to + *inf;* to hear + *inf*, e.g., **le sentí entrar esta mañana** I heard you come in this morning ‖ *vn* to feel; to be sorry, to feel sorry; **sin sentir** inadvertently, without being aware ‖ *vr* to feel, e.g., **me siento enfermo** I feel sick; to feel oneself to be, e.g., **me siento poeta** I feel myself to be a poet; to complain, to be resentful; to crack, be cracked; to begin to decay or rot; (naut.) to spring; **sentirse con** to feel, e.g., **me siento con mucho frío** I feel very cold; **sentirse de** to feel (*e.g., a blow*); to have a pain in, to feel sick in; to resent
seña *f* sign, mark, token; (mil.) password, watchword; **señas** *fpl* address; description; **dar señas de** to show signs of (*e.g., fatigue*); to describe; **hablar por señas** to talk by signs; **hacer señas** to motion; **por las señas** (coll.) to all appearances; **por señas** or **por más señas** (coll.) as a greater proof, specifically; **señas mortales** strong proof; **señas personales** personal description
señá *f* colloquial contraction of **señora,** commonly used before first names
señal *f* sign, mark, token; landmark; bookmark; trace, vestige; scar; signal; signal flag; light, traffic light; image, representation; reminder; pledge; earnest money; mark of distinction; brand; (rad.) signal; **en señal de** in proof of, in token of, as a token of; **ni señal** not a trace left; **señal de alto** stop signal; **señal de brazos** (naut.) arm signal; **señal de carretera** road sign; **señal de disco, señal de guitarra** (rail.) banjo signal; **señal de la cruz** sign of the cross; **señal del código** (naut.) code flag, code pennant; **señal de nieblas** fog signal; **señal de ocupado** (telp.) busy signal; **señal de parada** stop signal; **señal de peligro** danger signal, distress signal; **señal de tráfico** traffic sign; **señal de tramo** (rail.) block signal; **señal digital** fingerprint; **señales de dirección** (aut.) turn signals; **señales de ruta** highway signals; **señales marítimas** flags of the international code of signals; **señal horaria** time signal; **señal luminosa** traffic light; **señal para marcar** (telp.) dial tone; **señal urbana** traffic signal
señaladamente *adv* signally; especially
señalado -da *adj* signal, noted, distinguished
señalamiento *m* designation, pointing out; appointment, date
señalar *va* to mark; to show, indicate; to signal; to point at, to point out; to brand; to designate, determine, fix; to appoint; to sign and seal; to mark down (*points of score in card games*); to scar; to threaten (*a thing*); **señalar con el dedo** to point at, to point out; *vr* to distinguish oneself, to excel
señalero *m* signalman
señalización *f* (rail.) signaling; equipping with signals
señalizar §76 *va* to signal; to equip with signals
señero -ra *adj* solitary; unique
señolear *vn* to hunt with a decoy
señor -ñora *adj* ruling, master, controlling; (coll.) lordly, magnificent; (coll.) fine ‖ *m* sir, mister; gentleman; lord, master, owner; seignior; seigneur (*feudal*); (coll.) father-in-law; **señores** *mpl* Mr. and Mrs.; ladies and gentlemen: **descansar en el Señor** to rest in the Lord; **dormir en el Señor** to sleep in the Lord; **el gran señor** the Grand Turk; **el Señor** the Lord; **morir en el Señor** to die in the Lord; **muy señor mío** Dear Sir; **nuestro Señor** our Lord; **pues señor** well sir (*in telling a story*); **señor de horca y cuchillo** absolute lord, absolute master; (coll.) big shot; **Señor de los ejércitos** Lord of hosts; **señor eminentísimo** (eccl.) Eminence ‖ *f* madam, missus; lady, dame; mistress, owner; wife; (coll.) mother-in-law; **muy señora mía** Dear Madam; **Nuestra Señora** our Lady; **Nuestra Señora de los Dolores** Our Lady of Sorrows, Mary of the Sorrows; **señora de compañía** chaperon; **señora mayor** old lady, dowager
señorada *f* gentlemanly act, ladylike act
señoraje *m* seigniorage
señoreador -dora *adj* ruling; domineering, overbearing; *mf* ruler, master; domineering person
señoreaje *m* seigniorage
señoreamiento *m* domination, rule; mastery; seizure
señorear *va* to dominate, to rule; to master, to control (*e.g., passions*); to lord it over; to seize, take control of; to tower over; to excel; (coll.) to keep calling (*someone*) lord; *vn* to strut, to swagger; *vr* to control oneself; to strut, to swagger; **señorearse de** to seize, take control of
señoría *f* lordship, ladyship (*title and person*); rule, sway; signory (*governing body of medieval Italian city; Italian republic*)
señorial *adj* seigniorial, lordly; noble, majestic; feudal (*fees*)
señoril *adj* seignorial, lordly; majestic, haughty
señorío *m* seigniory; dominion, sway, rule; mastery (*e.g., of passions*); lordliness, majesty, arrogance; nobility, gentry, bon ton
señorita *f* young lady; miss; (coll.) mistress of the house
señorita-torera *f* lady bullfighter
señoritingo *m* (scornful) lordling
señorito *m* master, young gentleman, lordling; (coll.) master of the house; (scornful) playboy
señorón -rona *mf* (coll.) big shot, bigwig
señuelo *m* decoy, lure; bait; enticement
seó *m* (coll.) var. of **seor**
seo *f* (dial.) cathedral
seor *m* contraction of **señor**
seora *f* contraction of **señora**
sepa *1st sg pres subj of* **saber**
sépalo *m* (bot.) sepal
sepancuantos *m* (*pl:* **-tos**) (coll.) punishment, beating, scolding
separable *adj* separable, detachable
separación *f* separation
separado -da *adj* separate; apart; separated; **por separado** separately; under separate cover
separador -dora *adj* separating; *mf* separator; *m* separator (*machine; partition in storage battery*)
separar *va* to separate; to dismiss, discharge; *vr* to separate; to resign; (law) to waive a right
separata *f* offprint
separatismo *m* separatism
separatista *adj & mf* separatist
separativo -va *adj* separative
sepedón *m* (zool.) seps
sepelio *m* burial, interment
sepia *f* (zool.) sepia (*mollusk, secretion, pigment*); *m* sepia (*color; print*)
sepsis *f* (path.) sepsis
septal *adj* septal
sept.e abr. of **septiembre**
septembrino -na *adj* (pertaining to) September
septena *f* see **septeno**
septenario -ria *adj* septenary; *m* seven days
septenio *m* septennate, septennium, septenary
septeno -na *adj* seventh; *f* seven
Septentrión *m* North; (astr.) Great Bear
septentrional *adj* septentrional, northern
septeto *m* (mus.) septet
septicemia *f* (path.) septicemia; **septicemia hemorrágica** (vet.) hemorrhagic septicemia

septicida *adj* (bot.) septicidal
séptico -ca *adj* septic
septiembre *m* September
septífrago -ga *adj* (bot.) septifragal
septillo *m* (mus.) septimole
septillón *m* British septillion
séptimo -ma *adj & m* seventh; *f* sequence of seven (*in cards*); (mus.) seventh
septingentésimo -ma *adj & m* seven hundredth
septisílabo -ba *adj* seven-syllable
septo *m* (anat.) septum
septuagenario -ria *adj & mf* septuagenarian or septuagenary
septuagésimo ma *adj & m* seventieth; *f* (eccl.) Septuagesima, Septuagesima Sunday
septuplicación *f* septuplication
septuplicar §86 *va* to septuple
séptuplo -pla *adj & m* septuple, sevenfold
sepulcral *adj* sepulchral; (fig.) sepulchral
sepulcro *m* sepulcher, tomb, grave; (arch.) sepulcher; **santo sepulcro** Holy Sepulcher; **ser un sepulcro** to be good at keeping a secret; **sepulcro blanqueado** whited sepulcher (*hypocrite*)
sepultar *va* to bury, entomb; (fig.) to bury, hide away; (fig.) to bury, overwhelm, sink; *vr* to be buried (*e.g., in deep thought*)
sepulto -ta *adj* buried
sepultura *f* sepulture (*act and place*); **dar sepultura a** to bury; **estar con un pie en la sepultura** to have one foot in the grave
sepulturera *f* gravedigger's wife
sepulturero *m* gravedigger
sequedad *f* drought, dryness; gruffness, surliness
sequedal *m* or **sequeral** *m* dry, barren soil
sequero *m* unirrigated land; dryness; drying place
sequeroso -sa *adj* dried out; dry, barren
sequete *m* hard biscuit, hardtack; blow, bump; (coll.) gruffness, gruffness in answering
sequía *f* drought
sequillo *m* sweet biscuit
sequío *m* unwatered land; dryness
séquito *m* retinue, entourage, suite, personnel; following, popularity
sequizo -za *adj* dryish
ser *m* being; essence; life; **seres sensitivos** sentient beings; **ser humano** human being; **Ser Supremo** Supreme Being ‖ §83 *v aux* (used with past participle to form passive voice) to be, e.g., **el discurso fué aplaudido por todos** the speech was applauded by everybody ‖ *vn* to be; **a no ser por** if it were not for; **a no ser que** unless; **¡cómo es eso!** what are you up to? (*as a reproof*); **¡cómo ha de ser!** what can you expect? (*to express resignation*); **érase que se era** (coll.) once upon a time; **es a saber** to wit, namely; **es decir** that is to say; **es de creer que** it is to be believed that; **es de esperar que** it is to be hoped that; **no sea que** lest; **o sea** that is to say; **sea lo que sea** or **sea lo que fuere** be that as it may; **si yo fuera Vd.** if I were you; **un sí es, no es** a whit, a jot; **ser de** to belong to; to become of, e.g., **¿qué ha sido de él?** what has become of him; to be (*said of price, material, origin*), e.g., **el precio del sombrero es de seis dólares** the price of the hat is six dollars; **el reloj es de oro** the watch is gold; **ser de** + *inf* to be enough to + *inf;* to be to be + *pp*, e.g., **es de sentir(se) que** it is to be regretted that; **ser de lo que hay** (coll.) to be unequaled, to be among the worst; **ser de ver** to be worth seeing; **ser para** to suit, to be fitting for, to be fit for; **ser para poco** to not amount to much; **soy con Vd.** I'll be right with you; **soy yo** it is I
sera *f* frail, pannier without handles
serado *m* var. of **seraje**
seráfico -ca *adj* seraphic; **hacer la seráfica** to affect modesty
serafín *m* (Bib. & theol.) seraph; person of great beauty
serafina *f* fine baize
seraje *m* frails, panniers
serapino *m* sagapenum
serba *f* serviceberry, sorb (*fruit*)
serbal *m* (bot.) service tree, serviceberry (*tree*); **serbal de los cazadores** (bot.) rowan, mountain ash
Serbia *f* var. of **Servia**
serbo *m* (bot.) service tree
serena *f* see **sereno**
serenar *va* to calm; to pacify; to cool; to settle; *vn* to become calm; *vr* to become calm; to cool; to settle
serenata *f* serenade
serenero *m* woman's headpiece for protection against night air; (Am.) bandanna
serenidad *f* serenity, calm; (*cap.*) *f* Serenity (*title*); **serenidad del espíritu** peace of mind
serenísimo -ma *adj super* very or most serene, calm, or clear; serenissimo (*title of honor*)
sereno -na *adj* serene, calm; clear, cloudless; *m* night watchman (*who polices streets and carries keys to houses on his beat*); night dew, night air; **al sereno** in the night air; *f* serena, night love song; (coll.) night dew, night air; **a la serena** (coll.) in the night air
serete *m* small frail
sergas *fpl* deeds, exploits
sergenta *f* lay sister of the order of Santiago
seriado -da *adj* (rad.) serial
serial *adj* serial, seriate; *m* (rad.) serial; serial lacrimógeno
sérico -ca *adj* silken, seric; serous
sericultor -tora *mf* sericulturist
sericultura *f* sericulture, silk culture
serie *f* series; **de serie** stock, e.g., **coche de serie** stock car; **en serie** mass (*production*); (elec.) series, in series; **fuera de serie** special, unusual; outsize; **Serie Mundial** (baseball) World Series
seriedad *f* seriousness; reliability; sternness, severity; solemnity
serijo or **serillo** *m* small frail
serio -ria *adj* serious; reliable; stern, severe; majestic, solemn; **ir en serio** to become serious; **tomar en serio** to take seriously
Ser.ma or **Serma.** abr. of **Serenísima**
Ser.mo or **Sermo.** abr. of **Serenísimo**
sermón *m* sermon; (fig.) sermon; **sermón de la Montaña** (Bib.) Sermon on the Mount
sermonar *vn* to preach, to preach sermons
sermoneador -dora *adj* sermonizing
sermonear *va* (coll.) to sermonize; *vn* to sermonize
sermoneo *m* (coll.) sermonizing
serna *f* cultivated field
seroja *f* or **serojo** *m* dead leaves; brushwood
serología *f* serology
serón *m* pannier, long narrow frail; **serón caminero** horse pannier
serondo -da *adj* (bot.) serotinous
serosidad *f* (med. & physiol.) serosity
seroso -sa *adj* serous
seroterapia *f* serotherapeutics, serum therapy
serótino -na *adj* var. of **serondo**
serpa *f* (hort.) layer, runner
serpear *vn* var. of **serpentear**
serpentaria *f* (bot.) green dragon; **serpentaria virginiana** (bot.) Virginia snakeroot
serpentario *m* serpentarium; (orn.) secretary bird; (*cap.*) *m* (astr.) Serpent Bearer
serpenteante *adj* winding
serpentear *vn* to wind, meander; to wriggle, to squirm; to gleam, to coruscate
serpenteo *m* winding, meandering; wriggling; coruscation
serpentín *m* coil (*of a still, heater, etc.*); cock of a musket lock; **serpentín enfriador** cooling coil
serpentino -na *adj* serpentine; *f* coiled confetti; (mineral.) serpentine
serpentón *m* large serpent; (mus.) serpent (*wind instrument*)
serpezuela *f* little snake
serpiente *f* serpent; (fig.) snake, serpent (*treacherous person; Satan*); (*cap.*) *f* (astr.) Serpent; **serpiente de cascabel** (zool.) rattlesnake
serpiginoso -sa *adj* serpiginous
serpigo *m* (path.) serpigo
serpol *m* (bot.) wild thyme
serpollar *vn* to sprout, to shoot

serpollo *m* sprout, shoot, sucker
serradizo -za *adj* var. of **aserradizo**
serrado -da *adj* serrate
serrador *m* var. of **aserrador**
serraduras *fpl* sawdust
serrallo *m* seraglio
serranía *f* range of mountains, mountainous country
serraniego -ga *adj* highland, mountain
serranil *m* knife, dagger
serrano -na *adj* highland, mountain; *mf* highlander, mountaineer; *m* (ichth.) sea bass
serrar §18 *va* to saw
serrata *f* (orn.) merganser (*Mergus serrator*)
serrátil *adj* irregular (*pulse*)
serrato *m* (anat.) serratus
serrería *f* sawmill
serreta *f* little saw; cavesson
serretazo *m* jerk on the cavesson; dressing-down, reprimand
serrijón *m* short chain of mountains
serrín *m* sawdust
serriño -ña *adj* mountain; (med.) high and irregular (*pulse*)
serrón *m* large saw; two-handed saw
serruchar *va* (Am.) to saw
serrucho *m* handsaw
serval *m* (zool.) serval; (bot.) service tree
servato *m* (bot.) hog's-fennel
serventesio *m* sirvente (*Provençal moral song*); quatrain with rhyme abab
serventía *f* (Am.) road passing through private property
Servia *f* see **servio**
servible *adj* serviceable, useful
servicial *adj* accommodating, obliging; *m* enema, clyster
serviciar *va* to collect or to pay (*cattle toll, sheepwalk dues, etc.*)
servicio *m* service; enema; chamber pot; (tennis) service, serve; cover (*setting at table for one person*); (Am.) toilet; **de servicio** on duty; **estar en el servicio** (coll.) to serve, to be in the service (*to be a soldier*); **hacer un flaco servicio a** (coll.) to play a dirty trick on; **servicio activo** active service; **servicio de grúa** (aut.) towing service; **servicio de mesa** set of dishes; **servicio de municionamiento** (mil.) ordnance department; **servicio de reparaciones** repair service; **servicio divino** divine service; **servicio informativo** (rad.) news service; **servicio militar** military service; **servicio secreto** secret service; **servicio social** social service
servidero -ra *adj* serviceable, useful; demanding
servidor -dora *mf* servant; humble servant; (tennis) server; **quedo de Vd. atento y seguro servidor** yours respectfully; **servidor de Vd.** your servant, at your service; *m* waiter; suitor; chamber pot; *f* waitress
servidumbre *f* servitude; servants, help; demand; obligation; compulsion; dominance by passion; (law) easement, servitude; **servidumbre de la gleba** serfdom; **servidumbre de luces** (law) right to not have one's windows shut off from light; **servidumbre de paso** (law) right of way; **servidumbre de vía** (rail.) right of way
servil *adj* servile, subservient; *m* (hist.) absolutist
servilismo *m* servility, subservience
servilón -lona *adj* servile; *m* (hist.) absolutist
servilla *f* pump (*low shoe*)
servilleta *f* napkin, serviette; **doblar la servilleta** (coll.) to die
servilletero *m* napkin ring
servio -via *adj* & *mf* Serbian; *m* Serbian (*language*); (*cap.*) *f* Serbia
serviola *f* (naut.) cathead, anchor beam
servir §94 *va* to serve; to help, wait on; to fill (*an order*); to worship; to favor; to court (*a lady*); (tennis) to serve; **ir servido** to get one's deserts; **para servir a Vd.** at your service; **ser servido de** + *inf* to be pleased to + *inf;* **servir de** to serve (*someone*) as ‖ *vn* to serve; to be useful, to be of use; to follow suit (*in cards*); (tennis) to serve; **¿de** or **para qué sirve . . . ?** what is the good of . . . ?; **¿de** or **para qué sirve** + *inf?* what is the good of + *ger?;* **no servir para nada** to be good for nothing, to be of no use; **servir de** to serve as, to act as; to be used as; **servir para** to be used for, to be good for ‖ *vr* to help oneself, to serve oneself (*e.g., at table*); **servirse** + *inf* to have the kindness to + *inf,* to deign to + *inf;* **servirse de** to make use of; **sírvase** + *inf* please + *inf;* **¡sírvase!** please!
serv.° abr. of **servicio**
servocontrol *m* (aer.) servo control
servocroata *adj* & *mf* Serbo-Croatian; *m* Serbo-Croatian (*language*)
servodirección *f* (aut.) power steering
servoembrague *m* automatic clutch
servofreno *m* servo brake
servomecanismo *m* servomechanism
servomotor *m* (mach.) servomotor
serv.°r abr. of **servidor**
sesada *f* brains (*of an animal*); fried brains
sésamo *m* (bot.) sesame; sesame (*magic word*); **¡sésamo ábrete!** open sesame!
sesamoideo -a *adj* sesamoid or sesamoidal
sesear *vn* to pronounce Spanish c and z like s
sesenta *adj* & *m* sixty
sesentavo -va *adj* & *m* sixtieth
sesentón -tona *adj* & *mf* (coll.) sexagenarian
seseo *m* pronunciation of Spanish c and z like s
seseoso -sa *adj* pronouncing Spanish c and z like s
sesera *f* brain; brainpan
sesga *f* see **sesgo**
sesgadamente *adv* slantingly, obliquely, on the bias
sesgado -da *adj* slanting, oblique; beveled
sesgadura *f* slant, obliquity; bevel; skew
sesgar §59 *va* to gore, to cut (*cloth*) on the bias; to slope, bevel, slant; to skew
sesgo -ga *adj* slanting, sloped, oblique; beveled; severe, stern; calm, placid; *m* slope, slant, obliquity; bias, bevel; skew; compromise; turn; **al sesgo** obliquely, on the bias; *f* gore
sésil *adj* (bot.) sessile
sesión *f* session, sitting; meeting, conference; show (*each showing of a movie*); **abrir la sesión** to open the meeting; **levantar la sesión** to adjourn the meeting; **sesión continua** (mov.) continuous showing; **sesión de espiritistas** séance, spiritualistic séance
sesionar *vn* to be in session
seso *m* brain; brains, intelligence; block (*of stone, brick, or iron*) to steady a pot on the fire; **sesos** *mpl* brains (*for food*); **calentarse** or **devanarse los sesos** to rack one's brain; **levantarse la tapa de los sesos** to blow out one's brains; **perder el seso** to go crazy; **tener sorbido el seso a, tener sorbidos los sesos a** (coll.) to dominate, to have unlimited influence on; to be madly in love with; to be deeply immersed in
sesquiáltero -ra *adj* sesquialteral; *f* (mus.) sesquialtera (*interval; organ stop*)
sesquipedal *adj* sesquipedalian (*measuring a foot and a half; very long, containing many syllables*)
sesteadero *m* shady place where cattle rest
sestear *vn* to siesta, to take a siesta; to rest in the shade (*said of cattle*)
sestil *m* var. of **sesteadero**
sestina *f* sextina (*verse form*)
sesudez *f* braininess
sesudo -da *adj* brainy; wise; (Am.) stubborn
seta *f* bristle; toadstool
setáceo -a *adj* setaceous (*bristlelike*)
setal *m* mushroom bed or patch
set.e abr. of **septiembre**
setecientos -tas *adj* & *m* seven hundred; **el Setecientos** the Eighteenth Century
setena *f* seven
setenar *va* to select by lot every seventh of; to punish beyond all measure
setenario -ria *adj* & *m* var. of **septenario**
setenta *adj* & *m* seventy
setentavo -va *adj* & *m* seventieth
setentón -tona *adj* & *mf* (coll.) septuagenarian
setiembre *m* var. of **septiembre**
seto *m* fence; **seto vivo** hedge, quickset
sétter *m* (*pl:* **-ters**) setter (*bird dog*)

setuní *m* (*pl:* **-níes**) var. of **aceituní**
seudohermafroditismo *m* pseudohermaphroditism
seudomorfismo *m* (mineral.) pseudomorphism
seudónimo -ma *adj* pseudonymous; *m* pseudonym, pen name
seudópodo *m* (zool.) pseudopod or pseudopodium
Seúl *f* Seoul
s.e.u.o. abr. of **salvo error u omisión**
severidad *f* severity; sternness, strictness; seriousness
Severna *m* Severn
severo -ra *adj* severe; stern, strict; serious
sevicia *f* ferocity, great cruelty
sevicioso -sa *adj* ferocious, extremely cruel, brutal
Sevilla *f* Seville
sevillano -na *adj* & *mf* Sevillian; **sevillanas** *fpl* sevillanas (*seguidillas of Seville*)
sexagenario -ria *adj* & *mf* sexagenarian or sexagenary
sexagesimal *adj* sexagesimal
sexagésimo -ma *adj* & *m* sixtieth; *f* (eccl.) Sexagesima, Sexigesima Sunday
sexángulo -la *adj* (geom.) sexangular; *m* (geom.) sexangle
sexcentésimo -ma *adj* & *m* six hundredth
sexenal *adj* sexennial, six-year
sexenio *m* sexennium, six years
sexmero *m* township officer
sexmo *m* township
sexo *m* sex; **el bello sexo** the fair sex or the gentle sex; **el sexo barbudo** (Am.) the sterner or the stronger sex; **el sexo débil** the weaker sex; **el sexo feo** or **el sexo fuerte** the sterner sex or the stronger sex
sexología *f* sexology
sexólogo -ga *mf* sexologist
sexta *f* see **sexto**
sextante *m* sextant (*instrument*); (*cap.*) *m* (astr.) Sextant; **sextante de burbuja** bubble sextant
sextavado -da *adj* hexagonal
sextavar *va* to make hexagonal
sexteto *m* (mus.) sextet, sestet
sextil *adj* (astrol.) sextile
sextilla *f* sextain
sextillo *m* (mus.) sextuplet
sextillón *m* British sextillion
sextina *f* sestina (*verse form*); six-line stanza
sexto -ta *adj* sixth; *m* sixth; *f* sequence of six (*in cards*); (mus.) sixth; (eccl.) sext
sextuplicación *f* sextuplication
sextuplicar §86 *va* & *vr* to sextuple
séxtuplo -pla *adj* & *m* sextuple, sixfold
sexual *adj* sexual, sex
sexualidad *f* sexuality
S.G.M. abr. of **Segunda Guerra Mundial**
shogún *m* shogun
shogunado *m* shogunate
si *conj* if; whether; I wonder if; **como si** as if; **por si acaso** just in case; **un si es, no es** a whit, a jot, a soupçon; **si acaso** if by chance; **si no** otherwise; *m* (mus.) si
sí *adv* yes; indeed; (gives emphasis to verb and is often equivalent to English auxiliary verb) **él sí habla español** he does speak Spanish; **él no irá pero yo sí** he will not go but I shall; **por sí o por no** in any case; **sí que** certainly; **sí tal** yes indeed, surely; *m* yes; **dar el sí** to say yes (*especially to a proposal for marriage*); *pron reflex* (used as object of prepositions) himself, herself, itself, themselves; yourself, yourselves; oneself; each other, e.g., **independientes entre sí** independent of each other; **de por sí** separately, by oneself, in itself, by itself; **de sí** separately, in itself; **por sí y ante sí** of his own accord; **sobre sí** cautiously; haughtily
siamés -mesa *adj* & *mf* Siamese; *m* Siamese (*language*); *f* siamoise (*fabric*)
sibarita *adj* & *mf* Sybarite
sibarítico -ca *adj* Sybaritic
sibaritismo *m* sybaritism
Siberia *f* Siberia
siberiano -na *adj* & *mf* Siberian
sibil *m* cave; cellar, vault
sibila *f* sibyl
sibilante *adj* sibilant, hissing, whistling; (phonet.) sibilant
sibilino -na or **sibilítico -ca** *adj* sibylline; (fig.) sibylline
siboney *adj* & *mf* (Am.) Cuban
sicalipsis *f* spiciness, suggestiveness
sicalíptico -ca *adj* spicy, suggestive; ribald
sicamor *m* (bot.) Judas tree
sicano -na *adj* Sicanian
sicario *m* paid assassin
sicastenia *f* var. of **psicastenia**
sicigia *f* (astr.) syzygy
Sicilia *f* Sicily
siciliano -na *adj* & *mf* Sicilian; *m* Sicilian (*dialect*)
siclo *m* shekel
sicoanálisis *m* var. of **psicoanálisis**
sicoanalista *mf* var. of **psicoanalista**
sicoanalítico -ca *adj* var. of **psicoanalítico**
sicoanalizar §76 *va* var. of **psicoanalizar**
sicodinámico -ca *adj* & *f* var. of **psicodinámico**
sicofanta *m* or **sicofante** *m* sycophant (*informer; impostor*)
sicofísica *f* var. of **psicofísica**
sicognostia *f* var. of **psicognostia**
sicología *f* var. of **psicología**
sicológico -ca *adj* var. of **psicológico**
sicólogo -ga *mf* var. of **psicólogo**
sicometría *f* var. of **psicometría**
sicométrico -ca *adj* var. of **psicométrico**
sicómoro *m* (bot.) sycamore
sicón *m* (zool.) sycon
siconeurosis *f* (*pl:* **-sis**) var. of **psiconeurosis**
sicono *m* (bot.) syconium or syconus
sicópata *mf* var. of **psicópata**
sicopatía *f* var. of **psicopatía**
sicopático -ca *adj* var. of **psicopático**
sicopatología *f* var. of **psicopatología**
sicosis *f* (*pl:* **-sis**) (path.) psychosis; (path.) sycosis (*skin affection*)
sicosomático -ca *adj* var. of **psicosomático**
sicote *m* (prov. & Am.) personal uncleanliness, smelliness of feet
sicotecnia *f* var. of **psicotecnia**
sicoterapia *f* var. of **psicoterapia**
sicrómetro *m* var. of **psicrómetro**
sículo -la *adj* & *mf* Sicilian; (hist.) Siculian
sideral or **sidéreo -a** *adj* sidereal
siderita *f* (mineral.) siderite; (bot.) ironwort
siderosa *f* (mineral.) siderite
siderosis *f* (path.) siderosis
siderurgia *f* siderurgy; iron and steel industry
siderúrgico -ca *adj* siderurgical; (pertaining to) iron and steel
sidonio -nia *adj* & *mf* Sidonian
sidra *f* cider
sidrería *f* cider shop
sidrero -ra *adj* (pertaining to) cider
siega *f* reaping; harvest; crop
siembra *f* sowing; seed, seeding; seedtime; sown field
siempre *adv* always; surely; **de siempre** usual; **para siempre** or **por siempre** forever; **por siempre jamás** forever and ever; **siempre que** provided; whenever; **siempre y cuando que** provided
siempreviva *f* (bot.) everlasting flower; **siempreviva mayor** (bot.) houseleek; **siempreviva menor** (bot.) white stonecrop
sien *f* (anat.) temple
siena *m* sienna; **siena tostado** burnt sienna
sienés -nesa *adj* & *mf* Sienese
sienita *f* (mineral.) syenite
sierpe *f* serpent, snake; wild person; ugly-looking person; wriggler; (hort.) tiller
sierra *f* saw; jagged mountain range, sierra; (ichth.) sawfish; (ichth.) sierra; **sierra abrazadera** lumberman's saw; **sierra bracera** two-handed saw; **sierra de mano** handsaw; **sierra caladora** keyhole saw; **sierra circular** buzz saw, circular saw; **sierra continua** band saw; **sierra de armero** hacksaw; **sierra de bastidor** bucksaw; **sierra de cinta** band saw; **sierra de cortar metales** hacksaw; **sierra de hilo** or **hender** ripsaw; **sierra de punta** compass saw; **sierra de tras-**

dós backsaw; **sierra de través** crosscut saw; **sierra de vaivén** jig saw; **sierra sin fin** band saw
siervo -va *mf* slave; humble servant; **siervo de Dios** servant of God; (coll.) poor devil; **siervo de la gleba** serf
sieso *m* (anat.) fundament
siesta *f* siesta; sleep or rest after eating; hottest time of day; afternoon music in church; **dormir** or **echar la siesta** to siesta, to take a nap after lunch; **siesta del carnero** nap before lunch
siete *adj* seven; **las siete** seven o'clock; **las siete colinas** the Seven Hills (*of Rome*); **las siete maravillas del mundo** the Seven Wonders of the World; *m* seven; seventh (*in dates*); V-shaped tear; (carp.) dog clamp; **más que siete** (coll.) too much
sieteenrama *f* (bot.) septfoil
sietemesino -na *adj* born in seven months; (coll.) puny fellow; (coll.) coxcomb
sieteñal *adj* seven-year-old
sífilis *f* (path.) syphilis
sifilítico -ca *adj & mf* syphilitic
sifón *m* siphon; siphon bottle; siphon water; trap (*in a pipe*)
sifonógamo -ma *adj* (bot.) siphonogamic or siphonogamous; *f* (bot.) siphonogam
sifosis *f* var. of **cifosis**
sifué *m* surcingle
sig.[e] abr. of **siguiente**
Sigfrido *m* Siegfried
sigilación *f* sealing, stamping; seal, stamp; concealment
sigilar *va* to seal, to stamp; to conceal, keep silent
sigilo *m* seal; concealment, reserve; **sigilo sacramental** inviolable secrecy of the confessional
sigilografía *f* sigillography
sigiloso -sa *adj* close-lipped, tight-lipped; silent, reserved
sigla *f* initial (*used in an abbreviation*); abbreviation, symbol
siglo *m* century; world (*worldly matters or activities*); age (*long time*); period, epoch, age; times; **en** or **por los siglos de los siglos** world without end, forever and ever; **hasta la consumación de los siglos** until the end of time; **siglo de cobre** (archeol.) Age of Copper; **siglo de hierro** (myth. & fig.) iron age; **siglo de la ilustración** or **de las luces** Age of Enlightenment (*eighteenth century*); **siglo de oro** (myth. & lit.) golden age; **siglo de plata** (myth.) silver age; **siglo dorado** (myth.) golden age; **siglos medios** Middle Ages
sigma *f* sigma
sigmoideo -a *adj* sigmoid
signáculo *m* seal, signet
signar *va* to sign; to put a mark on; to make the sign of the cross over; *vr* to cross oneself
signatario -ria *adj & mf* signatory
signatura *f* library number; signature, sign, stamp, mark; signing; (print.) signature, signature mark; (eccl.) rescript granting indulgence; (mus.) signature, time signature
significación *f* significance; signification
significado -da *adj* known, well-known, important; *m* meaning, signification
significar §86 *va* to signify, to mean; to indicate, to point out, to make known; *vn* to signify, to be important; *vr* to be distinguished
significativo -va *adj* significant; significative
signo *m* sign (*e.g., of rain*); mark; (astr., math., med., mus. & print.) sign; scroll or flourish (*in notary's signature*); mark (*cross made instead of signature*); benediction, sign of the cross; fate, destiny; **signo de admiración** (gram.) exclamation mark; **signo de interrogación** (gram.) question mark; **signo de radicación** (math.) radical sign; **signo diacrítico** (gram.) diacritical mark
siguapa *f* var. of **sijú**
siguiente *adj* following; next
sij *m* (*pl:* **sijs**) Sikh
sijú *m* (*pl:* **-júes**) (orn.) Antillean gnome owl
Sila *m* Sulla (*Roman general*)
sílaba *f* syllable; **última sílaba** (gram.) ultima; **sílaba abierta** (phonet.) open syllable; **sílaba cerrada** (phonet.) closed syllable; **sílaba libre** (phonet.) free syllable; **sílaba trabada** (phonet.) checked syllable
silabar *vn* to syllable
silabario *m* reader with words divided in syllables; syllabary
silabear *va* to syllable, to syllabize, to syllabify; *vn* to syllable
silabeo *m* syllabication, syllabification
silábico -ca *adj* syllabic
sílabo *m* syllabus
silba *f* hiss, hissing
silbador -dora *adj* whistling; hissing; *mf* whistler; hisser
silbante *adj* var. of **sibilante**
silbar *va* to whistle (*a tune*); to blow (*a whistle*); to hiss (*an actor, a play*); *vn* to whistle; to whiz
silbato *m* whistle; whistling or hissing crack (*emitting air or a liquid*)
silbido *m* whistle, whistling, hiss; (rad.) howling, squealing; **silbido de oídos** ringing in the ears
silbo *m* whistle, hiss, whiz
silbón *m* (orn.) widgeon
silboso -sa *adj* whistling, hissing
silenciador *m* silencer (*device for firearms, internal-combustion engines, etc.*); **silenciador de ruidos** (rad.) noise suppressor
silenciar *va* to keep silent about, to avoid mentioning; to silence
silenciero -ra *mf* silencer (*person*)
silencio *m* silence; (mil.) taps (*signal to put out lights*); (mus.) rest; **en silencio** in silence
silencioso -sa *adj* silent, noiseless; still, quiet; *m* (aut.) muffler
Sileno *m* (myth.) Silenus
silente *adj* silent, still, calm, quiet
silepsis *f* (*pl:* **-sis**) (rhet.) syllepsis
silero *m* (agr.) silo
silesiano -na or **silesio -sia** *adj & mf* Silesian
sílex *m* (mineral.) silex
sílfide *f* (myth. & fig.) sylph
silfo *m* (myth.) sylph
silga *f* var. of **sirga**
silgar §59 *va* to tow (*a boat*); *vn* (naut.) to pole
silguero *m* (orn.) linnet
silicato *m* (chem.) silicate
sílice *f* (chem.) silica
silíceo -a *adj* siliceous
silícico -ca *adj* (chem.) silicic
silicio *m* (chem.) silicon
siliciuro *m* (chem.) silicide
silicón *m* (chem.) silicone
silicosis *f* (path.) silicosis
silicua *f* (bot.) silique
silícula *f* (bot.) silicle
silicuoso -sa *adj* (bot.) siliquose or siliquous
silo *m* (agr.) silo; cave, cavern, dark place
Siloé *m* (Bib.) Siloam
silogismo *m* syllogism
silogístico -ca *adj* syllogistic
silogizar §76 *vn* to syllogize
silueta *f* silhouette; **en silueta** in silhouette
siluetear *va* to silhouette
siluriano -na or **silúrico -ca** *adj & m* (geol.) Silurian
siluro *m* (ichth.) sheatfish; self-propelling torpedo
silva *f* miscellany; verse of iambic hendecasyllables intermingled with seven-syllable lines, with some verses rhymed
Silvano *m* Silvan, Sylvanus
silvático -ca *adj* var. of **selvático**
silvestre *adj* wild; uncultivated, rustic; (*cap.*) *m* Silvester or Sylvester
Silvia *f* Sylvia; **silvia blanquinegra** (orn.) black-and-white warbler
silvicultor -tora *mf* forester
silvicultura *f* forestry
silvina *f* (mineral.) sylvite
silvoso -sa *adj* var. of **selvoso**
silla *f* chair; saddle; (eccl.) see; **de silla a silla** tête à tête, two together in private; **silla curul** curule chair; **silla de balanza** (Am.) rocking chair; **silla de cubierta** deck chair; **silla de hamaca** (Am.) rocking chair; **silla de la reina** seat made by two people crossing hands and grasping wrists; **silla de ma-**

nos sedan chair; **silla de montar** saddle, riding saddle; **silla de posta** post chaise; **silla de ruedas** wheel chair; **silla de tijera** folding chair, camp stool; **silla eléctrica** electric chair; **silla giratoria** swivel chair; **Silla peligrosa** Siege Perilous (*at King Arthur's Round Table*); **silla plegadiza** folding chair; **silla poltrona** easy chair, easy armchair; **silla volante** shay (*light carriage*)
sillar *m* ashlar; horseback
sillarejo *m* small ashlar, facing ashlar
sillera *f* see **sillero**
sillería *f* set of chairs; stalls (*in a choir*); ashlar, ashlar masonry; chair factory, chair store; chairmaking, chair business
sillero -ra *mf* chairmaker, chair dealer; *f* (archaic) place for storing sedan chairs
silleta *f* little chair; bedpan; **silletas** *fpl* (prov.) sidesaddle
silletazo *m* blow with a chair
silletero *m* chairman (*one who carries people in a sedan chair or pushes them in a wheel chair*)
silletín *m* little chair; (dial.) stool
sillico *m* chamber pot
sillín *m* light riding saddle; harness saddle; saddle (*e.g., of bicycle*); fancy sidesaddle
sillón *m* armchair, easy chair; sidesaddle; **sillón de hamaca** rocking chair; **sillón de orejas** wing chair; **sillón de ruedas** wheel chair
sima *f* chasm, abyss; (arch.) scotia
simbiosis *f* (biol.) symbiosis
simbiótico -ca *adj* (biol.) symbiotic
simbólico -ca *adj* symbolic or symbolical
simbolismo *m* symbolism
simbolista *adj* symbolistic; *mf* symbolist
simbolización *f* symbolization
simbolizar §76 *va* to symbolize, to symbol
símbolo *m* symbol; adage; mark, device; **Símbolo Atanasiano** Athanasian Creed; **Símbolo de la fe** or **Símbolo de los Apóstoles** Apostles' Creed
Simeón *m* Simeon
simetría *f* symmetry
simétrico -ca *adj* symmetric or symmetrical
simetrizar §76 *va* to symmetrize
simia *f* female ape
símico -ca *adj* simian
simiente *f* seed; germ; semen; **simiente de papagayos** (bot.) bastard saffron
simiesco -ca *adj* apelike, apish
símil *adj* similar; *m* resemblance, similarity; (rhet.) simile
similar *adj* similar
similicuero *m* imitation leather
similiseda *f* imitation silk
similitud *f* similitude
similitudinario -ria *adj* similar
similizar §76 *va* to mercerize
similor *m* similor; **de similor** false, fake, sham
simio *m* (zool.) simian
Simón *m* Simon; (*l.c.*) *m* hack, cab; hackman
simonía *f* simony
simoníaco -ca *adj* simoniacal
simpa *f* (Am.) braid, plait; (Am.) tress
simpar *adj* unequaled, unmatched
simpatectomía *f* var. of **simpaticectomía**
simpatía *f* sympathy; fondness, liking, attachment, affection; friendliness; congeniality; **llevarse la simpatía de** to win the affection of; **tomar simpatía a** to take a liking for
simpática *f* see **simpático**
simpaticectomía *f* (surg.) sympathectomy
simpático -ca *adj* sympathetic; pleasant, agreeable, likable, congenial; (anat., mus., phys. & physiol.) sympathetic; **gran simpático** (anat. & physiol.) sympathetic nervous system; *f* (bot.) phlox
simpatiquísimo -ma *adj super* very or most sympathetic; very or most pleasant, agreeable, or congenial
simpatizador -dora or **simpatizante** *adj* sympathetic; *mf* sympathizer; follower, backer
simpatizar §76 *vn* to be congenial, to get on well together; **simpatizar con** to get on well with, to be friendly toward, to be sympathetic toward
simpétalo -la *adj* (bot.) sympetalous
simple *adj* simple; single; insipid, tasteless; *mf* simple, simpleton; *m* simple (*medicinal plant*); (pharm.) simple
simpleza *f* simpleness, stupidness, dullness; stupidity (*in act or word*)
simplicidad *f* simplicity, simpleness; simpleheartedness
simplicísimo -ma *adj super* very or most simple (*in all senses except that of* unwary, foolish, stupid, *for which* **simplísimo** *is used*)
simplismo *m* simplicity
simplicista *adj* simplistic; *mf* simplist, devotee of simplification
simplificación *f* simplification
simplificar §86 *va* to simplify
simplista *adj* simplistic, oversimplifying; *mf* simplist, person inclined to oversimplify; (med.) simplist, herbalist
simplón -plona *adj* simple-hearted; (coll.) simple, dull; *mf* simple-hearted person
simposio *m* (hist.) symposium
simulación *f* simulation, pretense; malingering
simulacro *m* simulacrum, phantom, vision; image, idol; show, semblance; pretense; sham battle; **simulacro de ataque aéreo** air-raid drill; **simulacro de combate** sham battle; **simulacro de salvamento** lifesaving drill, lifesaving test
simuladamente *adv* feigningly
simulado -da *adj* simulated, pretended, fake; (com.) pro forma
simulador -dora *adj* simulative; *mf* simulator; malingerer
simular *va* to simulate, to feign, to fake; *vn* to malinger; to pretend; **simular** + *inf* to pretend to + *inf*
simultanear *va* to carry out simultaneously; (educ.) to take (*courses of successive years or in different schools*) at the same time
simultaneidad *f* simultaneity
simultáneo -a *adj* simultaneous
simún *m* simoom or simoon
sin *prep* without; without counting; **sin** + *inf* without + *ger*, e.g., **salió sin despedirse** he left without saying good-by; to be + *pp*, e.g., **hay muchas necesidades urgentes sin satisfacer** there are many urgent needs to be satisfied; **sin que** + *subj* without + *ger*, e.g., **entró sin que yo le viese** he came in without my seeing him
sinagoga *f* synagogue
Sinaí, el Sinai (*peninsula*)
sinalagmático -ca *adj* (law) synallagmatic
sinalefa *f* synalepha or synaloepha
sinapismo *m* mustard plaster, sinapism; (coll.) nuisance, bore
sinapsis *f* (*pl:* **-sis**) (biol.) synapsis; (physiol.) synapsis or synapse
sinartrosis *f* (*pl:* **-sis**) (anat.) synarthrosis
sincárpeo -a *adj* (bot.) syncarpous
sincarpo *m* (bot.) syncarp
sincerador -dora *adj* exonerating; *mf* exonerator, defender
sincerar *va* to exonerate, vindicate; *vr* to exonerate oneself, vindicate onself; to speak frankly
sinceridad *f* sincerity
sincero -ra *adj* sincere
sincipucio *m* (anat.) skullcap, sinciput
sinclástico -ca *adj* (math.) synclastic
sinclinal *adj* synclinal; (geol.) synclinal; *m* (geom.) syncline
síncopa *f* (mus. & phonet.) syncopation, syncope
sincopado -da *adj* syncopated
sincopal *adj* syncopal
sincopar *va* (mus. & phonet.) to syncopate; to abridge
síncope *m* (path.) syncope, fainting spell; (phonet.) syncope
sincopizar §76 *va* to make faint, make swoon; *vr* to faint, to swoon
sincrético -ca *adj* syncretic
sincretismo *m* syncretism
sincrisis *f* (rhet.) syncrisis
sincronía *f* synchrony
sincrónico -ca *adj* synchronous; synchronic; (elec.) synchronous

sincronismo *m* synchronism
sincronización *f* synchronization
sincronizador *m* synchronizer
sincronizar §76 *va & vn* to synchronize
síncrono -na *adj* synchronous; (elec.) synchronous
sincronoscopio *m* (elec.) synchronoscope
sincrotrón *m* (phys.) synchrotron
sindéresis *f* discretion, good judgment; (theol.) synteresis
sindicación *f* syndication
sindicado *m* syndicate (*body of syndics*)
sindical *adj* syndical
sindicalismo *m* syndicalism; unionism, trade unionism
sindicalista *adj & mf* syndicalist; unionist, trade unionist
sindicar §86 *va* to accuse, to inform on; to put in trust; to syndicate; *vr* to syndicate
sindicato *m* syndicate; union, labor union, trade union
sindicatura *f* trusteeship; (law) receivership
síndico *m* syndic, trustee; (law) receiver (*in litigation over property or in a bankruptcy*)
sindiós (*pl:* **-diós**) *adj* godless; *mf* godless person, atheist
síndrome *m* (path.) syndrome
sinécdoque *f* (rhet.) synecdoche
sinecura *f* sinecure
sinecurista *mf* sinecurist
sinedrio *m* var. of **sanedrín**
sinéresis *f* (gram.) synaeresis
sinergia *f* synergy
sinestesia *f* (physiol. & psychol.) synesthesia
sinfín *m* endless number, endless amount
sinfinidad *f* (coll.) endless number, infinity
sínfisis *f* (*pl:* **-sis**) (anat. & zool.) symphysis; **sínfisis sacroilíaca** (anat.) sacroiliac joint
sínfito *m* (bot.) comfrey
sinfonía *f* symphony
sinfónico -ca *adj* symphonic
sinfonista *mf* symphonist
Singapur *f* Singapore
singar §59 *vn* (naut.) to pole
singenésico -ca *adj* (bot.) syngenesious
singladura *f* sailing, navigation; boat's speed; (naut.) day (*from noon to noon*); (naut.) day's run
singlar *vn* (naut.) to sail, to travel, to steer
single *adj* (naut.) single
singlón *m* (naut.) yardarm
singular *adj* singular; special; single; (gram.) singular; *m* (gram.) singular; **en singular** in particular
singularidad *f* singularity
singularizar §76 *va* to distinguish, to single out; to put or use in the singular (*a word which is regularly in the plural*); *vr* to distinguish oneself, to stand out; to make oneself conspicuous
singularmente *adv* singularly, strangely; particularly
singulto *m* sob; (path.) hiccup, singultus
sinhueso *f* (coll.) tongue
sinicesis *f* var. of **sinizesis**
sínico -ca *adj* Sinic, Sinitic
siniestra *f* see **siniestro**
siniestrado -da *adj* ill-fated; *m* victim
siniestro -tra *adj* sinister (*on the left; showing ill will; disastrous*); sinistral; (her.) sinister; *m* depravity, perversity; disaster, calamity; *f* left hand, left-hand side
sinistrorso -sa *adj* (bot.) sinistrorse
sinizesis *f* (gram., biol. & path.) synizesis
sinnúmero *m* great amount, great many
sino *conj* but, except; **no . . . sino** only; not . . . but; **no . . . sino que** only; **no sólo . . . sino que** not only . . . but, but also; *m* fate, destiny
sinodal *adj* synodal
sinódico -ca *adj* synodical; (astr.) synodical
sínodo *m* synod; (astr. & astrol.) synod
sinojaponés -nesa *adj* Sino-Japanese
sinología *f* Sinology
sinológico -ca *adj* Sinological
sinólogo -ga *mf* Sinologist
sinonimia *f* synonymy, synonymity; (rhet.) synonymy
sinónimo -ma *adj* synonymous; *m* synonym
sinopsis *f* (*pl:* **-sis**) synopsis
sinóptico -ca *adj* synoptic or synoptical
sinovia *f* (anat.) synovia
sinovial *adj* synovial
sinovitis *f* (path.) synovitis
sinrazón *f* wrong, injustice; unreason, want of reason
sinsabor *m* displeasure, unpleasantness; anxiety, trouble, worry
sinsonte *m* (orn.) mockingbird
sinsubstancia *mf* (coll.) trifler, good-for-nothing
sintáctico -ca *adj* syntactic or syntactical
sintaxis *f* syntax
síntesis *f* (*pl:* **-sis**) synthesis
sintético -ca *adj* synthetic or synthetical
sintetizar §76 *va* to synthesize
sintoísmo *m* Shinto, Shintoism
sintoísta *adj & mf* Shinto, Shintoist
síntoma *m* (med. & fig.) symptom
sintomático -ca *adj* symptomatic
sintonía *f* (elec.) syntony; (rad.) tuning, tune; (rad.) theme song; **sintonía afilada** (rad.) sharp tuning
sintónico -ca *adj* (elec.) syntonic or syntonical
sintonina *f* (biochem.) syntonin
sintonizable *adj* (rad.) tunable
sintonización *f* (rad.) tuning
sintonizador -dora *adj* (rad.) tuning; *m* (rad.) tuner
sintonizar §76 *va* (rad.) to tune; (rad.) to tune in; *vn* to be in tune, to harmonize
sinuosidad *f* sinuosity; hollow
sinuoso -sa *adj* sinuous, winding, wavy; evasive
sinusitis *f* (path.) sinusitis
sinusoidal *adj* sinusoidal
sinusoide *f* (math.) sinusoid
sinvergüencería *f* (coll.) brazenness, shamelessness
sinvergüenza *adj* (coll.) brazen, shameless; *mf* (coll.) scoundrel, rascal, shameless person
Sión *f* Zion
sionista *adj & mf* Zionist
sionismo *m* Zionism
sipedón *m* (zool.) seps
siquiatra *mf* var. of **psiquiatra**
siquiatría *f* var. of **psiquiatría**
siquiátrico -ca *adj* var. of **psiquiátrico**
siquiatro *m* var. of **psiquiatro**
síquico -ca *adj* var. of **psíquico**
siquiera *adv* at least; even; *conj* although, even though; **siquiera . . . siquiera** whether . . . or whether
Siracusa *f* Syracuse
siracusano -na *adj & mf* Syracusan
sirena *f* (aut., phys., myth. & fig.) siren; mermaid; **sirena de la playa** bathing beauty; **sirena de niebla** foghorn
sirenazo *m* blast of a siren or horn
sirenio -nia *adj & m* (zool.) sirenian
sirga *f* (naut.) towrope, towline; line for hauling in seines; **a la sirga** in tow from the shore or bank
sirgar §59 *va* to tow (*a boat*)
sirgo *m* twisted silk; silk fabric
sirguero *m* var. of **jilguero**
Siria *f* see **sirio**
siríaco -ca *adj* Syrian; Syriac; (astr.) Sirian; *mf* Syrian; *m* Syriac (*dialect*)
siringa *f* syrinx (*rustic flute; Panpipe*); (bot.) lilac; (bot.) hevea; (Am.) rubber; (Am.) drunk, spree
siringe *f* syrinx (*vocal organ of birds*)
siringomielia *f* (path.) syringomyelia
siringotomía *f* (surg.) syringotomy
sirio -ria *adj & mf* Syrian; (*cap.*) *m* (astr.) Sirius; (*cap.*) *f* Syria
sirirí *m* (*pl:* **-ríes**) (orn.) Couch's kingbird
sirle *m* sheep manure, goat manure
siro -ra *adj & mf* Syrian
siroco *m* sirocco
sirria *f* var. of **sirle**
sirsaca *f* seersucker
sirte *f* rocky shoal; quicksand, syrtis
sirventés *m* sirvente (*Provençal moral song*)
sirvienta *f* maid, servant girl
sirviente *adj* serving; (law) servient; *m* servant; waiter

sisa *f* snitching, petty theft; sizing (*for gilding*); (sew.) dart; (archaic) excise
sisador -dora *adj* snitching, thieving; *mf* snitcher, petty thief
sisallo *m* (bot.) saltwort
sisar *va* to snitch, filch; to size (*for gilding*); (sew.) to take in; (archaic) to excise
sisarcosis *f* (anat.) syssarcosis
sisear *va* to hiss (*an actor, speaker, scene*); *vn* to hiss; to sizzle
siseo *m* hiss, hissing; sizzle, sizzling
sisero *m* (archaic) excise collector, exciseman
Sísifo *m* (myth.) Sisyphus
sisimbrio *m* (bot.) sisymbrium, hedge mustard
sísmico -ca *adj* seismic
sismo *m* seism, earthquake
sismografía *f* seismography
sismográfico -ca *adj* seismographic or seismographical
sismógrafo *m* seismograph
sismograma *m* seismogram
sismología *f* seismology
sismológico -ca *adj* seismologic or seismological
sismologista *mf* seismologist
sismómetro *m* seismometer
sisón -sona *adj* (coll.) thieving; *mf* (coll.) petty thief; *m* (orn.) little bustard
sistáltico -ca *adj* systaltic
sistema *m* system; **sistema cegesimal** or **sistema centímetro-gramo-segundo** (phys.) centimeter-gram-second system; **sistema de Copérnico** (astr.) Copernican system; **sistema de Tolomeo** (astr.) Ptolemaic system; **sistema mercantil** mercantile system; **sistema métrico** metric system; **sistema nervioso central** (anat. & physiol.) central nervous system; **sistema nervioso simpático** o **del gran simpático** (anat. & physiol.) sympathetic nervous system; **sistema periódico** (chem.) periodic system; **sistema solar** solar system
sistemático -ca *adj* systematic or systematical; (anat. & physiol.) systemic; *f* systematics
sistematización *f* systematization
sistematizar §76 *va* to systematize
sístilo *m* (arch.) systyle
sístole *f* (gram., biol. & physiol.) systole
sistólico -ca *adj* systolic
sistro *m* (mus.) sistrum
sitiador -dora *adj* besieging; *mf* besieger
sitial *m* chair (*seat of honor, dignity, authority, etc.*); seat
sitibundo -da *adj* (poet.) thirsty
sitiar *va* to surround, hem in; to siege, besiege
sitio *m* place, spot, room; location, site; country place; (Am.) cattle ranch; (Am.) taxicab stand; (mil.) siege; **dejar en el sitio** to kill on the spot; **dejar sitio a** to make room for; **levantar el sitio** (mil.) to raise the siege; **poner sitio a** (mil.) to lay siege to; **quedarse en el sitio** to die on the spot
sito -ta *adj* situated, located
sitología *f* sitology
situación *f* situation, position; location; **pedir situación** (aer.) to ask for bearings
situado *m* income, fixed income
situar §33 *va* to situate, locate, place; to invest, to place (*money*); *vr* to take a position; to settle; (aer.) to get one's bearings
sixtino -na *adj* Sistine
Sixto *m* Sixtus (*name of several popes*)
s.l. abr. of **sin lugar**
S.l.n.a. abr. of **sin lugar ni año**
S.M. abr. of **Su majestad**
smoking *m* (*pl:* **-kings**) tuxedo, dinner coat
S.ⁿ abr. of **San**
SO abr. of **sudoeste**
so *prep* under, e.g., **so pena de** under penalty of; *interj* whoa!; (coll.) you . . . !, e.g., **¡so animal!** you beast!
soasar *va* to roast lightly, to roast medium
soba *f* kneading; massage; beating, slapping
sobacal *adj* axillary
sobaco *m* (anat.) armpit, armhole; (arch.) spandrel
sobado -da *adj* rumpled, worn; (cook.) short; (Am.) terrific; *m* kneading
sobadura *f* kneading; massage
sobajadura *f* or **sobajamiento** *m* crushing, rumpling
sobajar *va* to crush, to rumple
sobajeo *m* crushing, rumpling
sobanda *f* lower curve of a cask or barrel
sobaquera *f* armhole (*in clothes*); shield (*for armpit*)
sobaquina *f* sweat under arms
sobar *va* to knead; to massage; to beat, to slap; to cuddle, to pet, to paw, to feel; (coll.) to annoy, be fresh to; (Am.) to tire out (*a horse*)
sobarba *f* noseband
sobarbada *f* sudden check; scolding, dressing-down
sobarbo *m* pallet, pawl; bucket, paddle
sobarcar §86 *va* to carry under the arm; to draw or slide (*clothing*) up to the armpits
sobejos *mpl* leavings
sobeo *m* thong to tie yoke to pole
soberanamente *adv* royally; extremely
soberanear *vn* to domineer, to lord it
soberanía *f* sovereignty; rule, sway; haughtiness
soberano -na *adj* sovereign; superb; *mf* sovereign; *m* sovereign (*coin*)
soberbio -bia *adj* proud, haughty; arrogant, presumptuous; magnificent, superb; fiery; *f* pride, haughtiness; arrogance, presumption; magnificence; frenzy
soberbioso -sa *adj* var. of **soberbio**
sobermejo -ja *adj* dark-red
sobina *f* wooden peg or pin
sobo *m* var. of **soba**
sobón -bona *adj* (coll.) malingering, work-dodging; (coll.) fresh, mushy, spoony
sobordo *m* (naut.) freight list; (naut.) bonus (*paid to crew of freighter in time of war*)
sobornable *adj* corrupt, purchasable
sobornación *f* bribing, bribery
sobornado -da *adj* twisted, out of shape (*said of a loaf of bread*)
sobornador -dora *adj* bribing; *mf* briber
sobornal *m* overload, extra load
sobornar *va* to bribe, to suborn
soborno *m* bribery, subornation; **soborno de testigo** (law) subornation of perjury
sobra *f* extra, excess, surplus; **sobras** *fpl* leavings, offal, leftovers; rubbish, trash; **de sobra** more than enough; superfluous, unnecessary
sobradamente *adv* excessively, too; too well; very well
sobradar *va* to build a garret to
sobradillo *m* penthouse (*sloping roof over window or door*)
sobrado -da *adj* excessive, abundant, more than enough; bold, daring; rich, wealthy; *m* attic, garret; **sobrado** *adv* too
sobrancero -ra *adj* unemployed
sobrante *adj* leftover, remaining, in excess, surplus; *m* leftover, surplus
sobrar *va* to exceed, surpass; *vn* to be more than enough, to be over and above; to be in the way; to be left, to remain
sobrasada *f* high-seasoned Majorcan sausage
sobrasar *va* to add more fire under (*a pot*)
sobre *prep* on, upon, over, above; about; near; after; in addition to; out of, e.g., **en nueve casos sobre diez** in nine out of ten cases; **sobre** + *inf* in addition to + *ger;* *m* envelope; address; **sobre de ventanilla** window envelope; **sobre monedero** coin container or holder (*for mailing coins*); **sobre ventana** window envelope
sobreabundancia *f* superabundance
sobreabundante *adj* superabundant
sobreabundar *vn* to superabound
sobreaguar §23 *vn & vr* to float
sobrealiento *m* hard breathing
sobrealimentación *f* overfeeding; supercharging
sobrealimentar *va* to overfeed; to supercharge; *vn* to overfeed
sobreañadir *va* to superadd
sobreañal *adj* over a year old
sobrearar *va* to plow over again
sobrearco *m* (arch.) relieving arch
sobreasada *f* var. of **sobrasada**
sobreasar *va* to roast again

sobrebarato -ta *adj* very cheap, extra cheap
sobrebarrer *va* to sweep lightly
sobrebeber *vn* to have another drink, to drink too much
sobrecalentamiento *m* overheating; superheating
sobrecalentar §18 *va* to overheat; to superheat
sobrecalza *f* legging
sobrecama *f* bedspread
sobrecaña *f* (vet.) bony tumor on a horse's leg
sobrecarga *f* overload, extra load; supercharge; packing strap; added annoyance; (philately) surcharge
sobrecargar §59 *va* to overload, to overburden; to overlay; to overcharge; (sew.) to fell; (philately) to surcharge: (aer.) to pressurize
sobrecargo *m* (naut.) supercargo; (Am.) purser; *f* (Am.) air hostess, stewardess
sobrecaro -ra *adj* very dear or expensive
sobrecarta *f* envelope (*for a letter*); (law) second notice
sobreceja *f* forehead right above eyebrows
sobrecejo *m* frown; **poner sobrecejo** to frown
sobrecenar *va* to have as a second supper; *vn* to have a second supper
sobreceño *m* frown
sobrecerco *m* (sew.) welt
sobrecerrado -da *adj* well closed, extra tight
sobrecielo *m* canopy, dais
sobrecincha *f* or **sobrecincho** *m* surcingle
sobreclaustra *f* or **sobreclaustro** *m* quarters above a cloister
sobrecoger §49 *va* to surprise, catch; to scare, terrify; *vr* to be surprised; to be scared; **sobrecogerse de** to be seized with
sobrecogimiento *m* surprise, apprehension; seizure
sobrecomida *f* dessert
sobrecomprimir *va* (aer.) to pressurize
sobrecoser *va* (Am.) to fell, to whip
sobrecrecer §34 *vn* to grow too much
sobrecubierta *f* extra cover or wrapping; jacket (*of a book*); (naut.) upper deck
sobrecuello *m* top collar; stock (*kind of cravat*)
sobredicho -cha *adj* above-mentioned
sobrediente *m* snaggletooth
sobredorar *va* to gold-plate (*especially silver*); to palliate, to extenuate
sobreedificar §86 *va* to build on or over
sobreempeine *m* part of leggings covering instep
sobreentender §66 *va & vr* var. of **sobrentender**
sobreestadía *f* (naut.) extra lay day, demurrage
sobreexceder *va* var. of **sobrexceder**
sobreexcitación *f* overexcitement
sobreexcitar *va* to overexcite; *vr* to become overexcited
sobreexpondré *1st sg fut ind of* **sobreexponer**
sobreexponer §69 *va* to overexpose; (phot.) to overexpose
sobreexpongo *1st sg pres ind of* **sobreexponer**
sobreexposición *f* overexposure; (phot.) overexposure
sobreexpuesto -ta *pp of* **sobreexponer**
sobreexpuse *1st sg pret ind of* **sobreexponer**
sobrefalda *f* overskirt
sobrefaz *f* (*pl:* **-faces**) surface, outside
sobrefrenada *f* var. of **sofrenada**
sobrefusión *f* supercooling
sobregirar *va & vn* (com.) to overdraw
sobregiro *m* (com.) overdraft
sobrehaz *f* (*pl:* **-haces**) surface, outside; cover; superficial appearance
sobreherido -da *adj* slightly hurt or wounded
sobrehilado -da *adj* (sew.) overcast; *m* (sew.) overcast, overcasting
sobrehilar *va* (sew.) to overcast
sobrehilo *m* (sew.) overcast, overcasting
sobrehombre *m* superman
sobrehueso *m* work, trouble, annoyance; (vet.) splint (*tumor and bone*); (vet.) splint bone
sobrehumano -na *adj* superhuman
sobreintendencia *f* var. of **superintendencia**

sobrejalma *f* woolen blanket to put over a packsaddle
sobrejuanete *m* (naut.) royal mast, royal sail
sobrejunta *f* splice plate, butt strap
sobrelecho *m* (arch.) underside of stone
sobrellave *f* double lock
sobrellenar *va* to fill to overflowing
sobrelleno -na *adj* filled to overflowing
sobrellevar *va* to bear, carry; to ease (*the burden of another*); to share (*effort or trouble*); to suffer (*annoyances*) with patience; to overlook, be lenient about (*another's shortcomings*)
sobremando *m* (aut.) overdrive
sobremanera *adv* exceedingly, beyond measure
sobremano *f* (vet.) splint on forehoofs
sobremantel *m* center tablecloth
sobremarcha *f* (aut.) overdrive
sobremesa *f* tablecloth, table cover; sitting at table after eating; **de sobremesa** table, for the table; at table after eating; after-dinner
sobremesana *f* (naut.) mizzen topsail
sobremodo *adv* var. of **sobremanera**
sobremodulación *f* (rad.) overmodulation
sobremundano -na *adj* supermundane
sobrenadante *adj* supernatant
sobrenadar *vn* to float
sobrenatural *adj* supernatural
sobrenaturalismo *m* supernaturalism
sobrenaturalizar §76 *va* to make or treat as supernatural, to supernaturalize
sobrenjalma *f* var. of **sobrejalma**
sobrenombrar *va* to surname; to nickname
sobrenombre *m* surname (*epithet*); nickname, agnomen
sobrentender §66 *va* to understand; *vr* to be understood, be implied
sobrentrenar *va & vr* (sport) to overtrain
sobreorgánico -ca *adj* superorganic
sobrepaga *f* increased pay
sobrepaño *m* upper cloth
sobreparto *m* confinement after childbirth; indisposition after childbirth
sobrepasar *va* to excel, surpass, outdo; to overtake; *vr* to outdo each other; to go too far
sobrepaso *m* amble
sobrepeine *adv* (coll.) lightly, superficially, half
sobrepelliz *f* (*pl:* **-llices**) (eccl.) surplice
sobrepeso *m* overweight
sobrepié *m* (vet.) splint on rear hoofs
sobreplán *m* (naut.) rider
sobrepondré *1st sg fut ind of* **sobreponer**
sobreponer §69 *va* to superpose, put on top; to superimpose; *vr* to control oneself; to triumph over adversity; **sobreponerse a** to win over, to overcome
sobrepongo *1st sg pres ind of* **sobreponer**
sobreprecio *m* extra charge, surcharge
sobreproducción *f* overproduction
sobrepuerta *f* cornice over door; door curtain, portière; overdoor, dessus de porte
sobrepuesto -ta *pp of* **sobreponer;** *adj* appliqué; *m* appliqué; honeycomb formed on full hive; basket or earthen jar turned upside down over hive; (Am.) patch, mend
sobrepujamiento *m* excellence, excelling
sobrepujanza *f* great power, might, strength, or vigor
sobrepujar *va* to excel, surpass
sobrepuse *1st sg pret ind of* **sobreponer**
sobrequilla *f* (naut.) keelson
sobrero -ra *adj* extra, spare
sobrerronda *f* var. of **contrarronda**
sobrerropa *f* overcoat
sobresalario *m* extra pay
sobresaldré *1st sg fut ind of* **sobresalir**
sobresalgo *1st sg pres ind of* **sobresalir**
sobresaliente *adj* projecting; outstanding, conspicuous, excellent; distinguished (*in an examination*); *mf* substitute; understudy
sobresalir §81 *vn* to project, jut out; to stand out, excel
sobresaltar *va* to assail, to rush upon, to storm; to frighten, to startle; *vn* to stand out clearly; *vr* to be frightened, be startled; to start; **sobresaltarse de, con** or **por** to be frightened or startled at
sobresalto *m* fright, scare; start, shock; **de sobresalto** unexpectedly, suddenly

sobresanar *vn* to heal on the outside; to try to conceal a defect or shortcoming
sobresano *m* (naut.) tabling; *adv* healing on the outside; with affectation, with concealment
sobresaturación *f* (chem.) supersaturation
sobresaturar *va* to supersaturate
sobrescribir **§17,** 9 *va* to superscribe; to address (*a letter*)
sobrescrito -ta *adj* superscript; *pp* of **sobrescribir;** *m* superscription; address
sobresdrújulo -la *adj* accented on syllable preceding antepenult
sobreseer **§35** *va* (law) to supersede, to stay; *vn* to desist, yield
sobreseguro *adv* without risk
sobreseimiento *m* suspension, discontinuance; (law) stay of proceedings, supersedeas
sobresellar *va* to put a double seal on; to overprint
sobresello *m* double seal; overprint
sobresembrar **§18** *va* to sow over, sow a second time
sobresolar **§77** *va* to resole; to repave, to put a double floor on
sobrestadía *f* var. of **sobreestadía**
sobrestante *m* foreman, boss
sobresuela *f* new sole
sobresueldo *m* extra wages, extra pay
sobresuelo *m* pavement or floor laid over another
sobretarde *f* late afternoon
sobretendón *m* (vet.) tumor on tendon of horse's leg
sobretensión *f* (elec.) surge
sobretiro *m* offprint
sobretodo *m* overcoat, topcoat; *adv* especially
sobreveedor *m* chief overseer
sobrevendré *1st sg fut ind of* **sobrevenir**
sobrevengo *1st sg pres ind of* **sobrevenir**
sobrevenida *f* sudden and unexpected arrival; supervention
sobrevenir **§92** *vn* to happen, take place; to crop up, to set in, to supervene; **sobrevenir a** to come upon, to overtake
sobreverter **§66** *vr* to overflow, to run over
sobrevesta or **sobreveste** *f* overtunic; surcoat (*over armor*)
sobrevestir **§94** *va* to put (*a garment*) over other clothes
sobrevidriera *f* window screen; window grill; storm window
sobrevienta *f* gust of wind; rage, onslaught; start, surprise, consternation; sudden happening; **a sobrevienta** suddenly, unexpectedly
sobreviento *m* gust of wind; **estar** or **ponerse a sobreviento de** (naut.) to have the wind of
sobrevine *1st sg pret ind of* **sobrevenir**
sobreviniendo *ger of* **sobrevenir**
sobrevista *f* beaver (*of helmet*)
sobreviviente *adj* surviving; *mf* survivor
sobrevivir *vn* to survive; **sobrevivir a** to survive, outlive
sobrexceder *va* to exceed, excel, surpass
sobrexcitación *f* overexcitement
sobrexcitar *va* to overexcite; *vr* to become overexcited
sobriedad *f* sobriety, moderation
sobrina *f* niece
sobrinazgo *m* relationship of nephew or niece; nepotism
sobrino *m* nephew
sobrio -bria *adj* sober, moderate, temperate
soca *f* (agr.) ratoon (*of sugar cane*)
socaire *m* (naut.) lee; (naut.) slatch (*slack part of rope*); **al socaire de** (naut.) under the lee of; (coll.) under the shelter of; **estar** or **ponerse al socaire** (coll.) to shirk, to skulk
socairero *adj masc* (naut.) malingering, shirking
socaliña *f* swindle, swindling
socaliñar *va* to swindle (*e.g., money*)
socaliñero -ra *adj* swindling; *mf* swindler
socalzado *m* underpinning
socalzar **§76** *va* to underpin, to shore up
socapa *f* maneuver, subterfuge; **a socapa** clandestinely; cautiously
socapiscol *m* var. of **sochantre**
socarra *f* singe, scorching; craft, cunning
socarrar *va* to singe, scorch
socarrén *m* eaves
socarrena *f* cavity, hollow; space between two rafters
socarrina *f* (coll.) singeing, scorching
socarrón -rrona *adj* sly, cunning, crafty
socarronería *f* slyness, cunning, craftiness
socava *f* undermining; trench around base of plant or tree to hold irrigation water
socavación *f* undermining
socavar *va* to dig under, to undermine; (fig.) to undermine (*e.g., the health*)
socavón *m* cavern; cave-in; (min.) adit, gallery
socaz *m* (*pl:* **-caces**) tailrace
sociabilidad *f* sociability; sociality (*tendency to form social groups*)
sociable *adj* sociable, social; *m* sociable (*carriage*)
social *adj* social; (com.) (pertaining to a) company, e.g., **edificio social** company building
socialismo *m* socialism; **socialismo del estado** state socialism
socialista *adj & mf* socialist
socialización *f* socialization
socializar **§76** *va* to socialize
sociedad *f* society; company, firm; **buena sociedad** society (*fashionable people*); **hallarse en sociedad** to be in society; **sociedad anónima** (com.) stock company; **sociedad comanditaria** or **en comandita** (com.) commandite (*partnership with one or more silent partners*); **sociedad de cartera** investment trust; **sociedad de control** (com.) holding company; **sociedad de inversión** investment trust; **Sociedad de las Naciones** League of Nations; **sociedad financiera** investment trust; **sociedad limitada** (com.) limited company; **sociedad secreta** secret society
societario -ria *adj* labor-union; *mf* member of a labor union
socio -cia *mf* partner; companion; member; *m* fellow; (scornful) fellow, guy; **socio capitalista** financial partner; **socio comanditario** (com.) silent partner, sleeping partner; **socio industrial** working partner
sociología *f* sociology
sociológico -ca *adj* sociological
sociólogo -ga *mf* sociologist
socolar *va* (Am.) to clear of brush and small trees
socolor *m* pretext, subterfuge; **socolor de** under the pretext of
socollada *f* flapping (*of sails*); (naut.) pitching
socoro *m* (eccl.) place under the choir
socorredor -dora *adj* helping, aiding; *mf* helper, aid
socorrer *va* to succor, help, aid; to pay on account
socorrido -da *adj* helping, ready; well stocked; handy, useful; worn, trite, hackneyed
socorrista *mf* first-aider, member of a first-aid association
socorro *m* succor, help, aid; payment on account; (mil.) relief; **acudir en socorro de** to come to the aid of, to come to the help of
socoyote *m* (Am.) baby (*youngest child*)
Sócrates *m* Socrates
socrático -ca *adj* Socratic
socrocio *m* saffron poultice
sochantre *m* (eccl.) subchantor, succentor
soda *f* (chem.) soda; soda, soda water
sódico -ca *adj* (chem.) (pertaining to) sodium
sodio *m* (chem. sodium
Sodoma *f* (Bib.) Sodom
sodomía *f* sodomy
sodomita *mf* Sodomite; sodomite
soez *adj* (*pl:* **-eces**) base, vile, mean, crude
sofá *m* (*pl:* **-fás**) sofa; **sofá cama** (*pl:* **sofás cama**) day bed
sofaldar *va* to tuck up, to truss up; to raise, to uncover
sofaldo *m* tucking up, trussing up; raising
sofí *m* (*pl:* **-fíes**) var. of **sufí**
Sofía *f* Sophia; Sofia (*city*)
sofión *m* snort; harsh refusal; blunderbuss
sofisma *m* sophism
sofismo *m* var. of **sufismo**

sofista *adj* sophistic or sophistical; *m* sophist
sofistería *f* sophistry
sofisticación *f* adulteration; falsification
sofisticar §86 *va* to adulterate; to falsify
sofístico -ca *adj* sophistic or sophistical
sofito *m* (arch.) soffit
soflama *f* glow, flicker; blush; deceit, cheating; hypocritical look; (coll.) speech
soflamar *va* to flimflam; to make blush; *vr* to scorch
soflamero -ra *adj* flimflamming, hypocritical; *mf* flimflammer, hypocrite
sofocación *f* choking, suffocation; (coll.) great annoyance, disappointment; blushing
sofocador -dora or **sofocante** *adj* suffocating, stifling
sofocar §86 *va* to choke, suffocate, stifle, smother; to extinguish, quench; (coll.) to bother, harass; to make blush; *vr* to choke, suffocate; to get out of breath; to flush; **sofocarse por** to get excited over
sofocleo -a *adj* Sophoclean
Sófocles *m* Sophocles
sofoco *m* blush, embarrassment; **pasar un sofoco** (coll.) to get into an embarrassing situation
sofocón *m* (coll.) annoyance, disappointment
Sofonías *m* (Bib.) Zephaniah
sofoquina *f* (coll.) intense annoyance or disappointment
sófora *f* (bot.) Japanese pagoda tree
sofreír §73 & §17, 9 *va* to fry lightly
sofrenada *f* saccade, sudden checking of a horse; self-control; severe reprimand
sofrenar *va* to check (*a horse*) suddenly; to control (*a passion*); to reprimand severely
sofrito -ta *pp of* **sofreír**
soga *f* rope, cord, halter; (mas.) stretcher; (mas.) face (*of brick or stone*); **dar soga a** (coll.) to make fun of; **hacer soga** (coll.) to lag behind; *m* sly fellow
soguería *f* rope-making; rope shop; ropes
soguero *m* ropemaker, rope dealer; street porter
soguilla *f* small rope; small braid; *m* errand boy
sois *2d pl pres ind of* **ser**
soja *f* (bot.) soy, soybean
sojuzgador -dora *adj* subjugating; *mf* conqueror
sojuzgar §59 *va* to subjugate, to subdue
sol *m* sun; sunlight; sunny side (*e.g., of bull ring*); (fig.) day; (chem. & mus.) sol.; (ichth.) sole (*Symphurus plagiusa*); sol (*Peruvian monetary unit*); **soles** *mpl* (poet.) eyes; **al sol naciente** at sunrise; (coll.) fawning on someone about to attain a position of influence; **al sol puesto** at sunset; (coll.) late, inopportunely; **arrimarse al sol que más calienta** to know on which side one's bread is buttered; **de sol a sol** from sunrise to sunset; **hacer sol** to be sunny; **morir sin sol, sin luz y sin moscas** (coll.) to die without a friend in the world; **no dejar a sol ni a sombra** (coll.) to give no rest to, to not leave in peace; **tomar el sol** to bask in the sun; (naut.) to shoot the sun, to take the sun's altitude; **sol de las Indias** (bot.) sunflower; **sol de medianoche** midnight sun; **sol medio** (astr.) mean sun
solacear *va* (archaic) var. of **solazar**
solada *f* dregs, sediment
solado *m* paving, tiling; pavement
solador *m* paver, tiler, tile man
soladura *f* paving, tiling; paving material; tiles
solamente *adv* only, solely; **solamente que** provided that, with the proviso that
solana *f* sunny spot; solarium, sun porch, sunroom
solanáceo -a *adj* (bot.) solanaceous
solanera *f* sunburn; hot sunny spot; hot sunshine
solanina *f* (chem.) solanine
solano *m* easterly wind; (dial.) hot stifling wind; (bot.) nightshade
solapa *f* lapel; pretext, pretense; flap (*of jacket of book*); (vet.) sinus (*of a small wound*); **de solapa** (coll.) sneakily
solapado -da *adj* overlapping; cunning, underhanded, sneaky
solapadura *f* (naut.) clincher work (*in the sides of a ship*)
solapar *va* to put lapels on; to overlap; to conceal, cover up; *vn* to overlap (*said of part of a garment*)
solape *m* lapel
solapo *m* lapel; overlapped part or piece; (coll.) chuck under chin; **a solapo** (coll.) sneakily
solar *adj* solar, (pertaining to the) sun; ancestral; *m* lot, plot, ground; manor house, ancestral mansion; noble lineage; §77 *va* to pave, to floor; to sole (*a shoe*)
solariego -ga *adj* ancestral; manorial
solaz *m* (*pl:* **-laces**) solace, consolation; recreation; **a solaz** with pleasure
solazar §76 *va* to solace, console; to amuse, divert; *vr* to be solaced or consoled; to amuse oneself, enjoy oneself
solazo *m* (coll.) scorching sun or sunshine
solazoso -sa *adj* consoling, comforting
soldada *f* pay, wages
soldadesco -ca *adj* soldier, barrack-room; **a la soldadesca** like a soldier, like soldiers; *f* soldiery; soldiership; undisciplined troops
soldado *m* soldier; **soldado de a caballo** cavalryman; **soldado de a pie** infantryman, foot soldier; **soldado de infantería** infantryman; **soldado de marina** marine; **soldado de primera** private first class; **soldado desconocido** unknown soldier; **soldado raso** buck private
soldador *m* solderer; welder; soldering iron
soldadote *m* gruff old campaigner
soldadura *f* solder; soldering; soldered joint; welding; welded joint; **soldadura al arco** arc welding; **soldadura autógena** welding; **soldadura de forja** blacksmith welding; **soldadura eléctrica** electric welding; **soldadura fuerte** hard solder; **soldadura fundente** welding compound; **soldadura oxiacetilénica** oxyacetylene welding; **soldadura por arco** arc welding; **soldadura tierna** soft solder
soldán *m* var. of **sultán**
soldar §77 *va* to solder; to weld; to patch up (*a mistake*); *vr* to knit (*said of bones*)
soleamiento *m* sunning, basking in the sun
solear *va* to sun; *vr* to sun, to sun oneself
solecismo *m* solecism
soledad *f* solitude, loneliness; longing, grieving, sorrow; lonely place; mournful Andalusian tune, song, and dance
soledoso -sa *adj* solitary, lonely; grieving, sorrowing
solejar *m* sunny place
solemne *adj* solemn; (coll.) terrible, downright (*e.g., mistake*)
solemnidad *f* solemnity; formality
solemnización *f* solemnization
solemnizador -dora *adj* solemnizing; *mf* solemnizer
solemnizar §76 *va* to solemnize
solenoide *m* (elec.) solenoid
soleo *m* gathering of fallen olives
sóleo *m* (anat.) soleus
soler *m* (naut.) underflooring; §63 *vn* (used only in pres & imperf ind and with a following inf) to be accustomed to, e.g., **suele venir los lunes** he is accustomed to come on Monday; **suele llover en este tiempo** it generally rains at this time of the year
solera *f* crossbeam, entablature; lumber, timber; stone base (*for uprights*); floor (*of oven*); bottom (*of channel*); lower millstone: mother liquor (*of wine*), mother of the wine; blend of sherry; old vintage sherry; (Am.) curb; (Am.) brick, tile; **de solera** or **de rancia solera** of the good old school, of the good old times
soleraje *m* vintage wine
solercia *f* skill, zeal, shrewdness
solería *f* paving or flooring material; sole leather
solerte *adj* cunning, crafty, shrewd
soleta *f* patch for sole of stocking; (coll.) brazen woman; **tomar soleta** (coll.) to flee, run away, leave
soletar or **soletear** *va* to patch the sole of (*a stocking*)
soletero -ra *mf* stocking mender

solevación *m* rising; upheaval; revolt
solevamiento *m* rising; upheaval; (geol.) upthrust
solevantado -da *adj* worried, perturbed
solevantamiento *m* var. of **solevamiento**
solevantar *va* to raise up, to upheave; to rouse, stir up, incite; *vr* to rise up, to upheave; to become aroused, to become stirred up
solevar *va* to raise up, to upheave; to excite to rebellion; *vr* to rise up, to upheave; to revolt
solfa *f* (mus.) sol-fa; solmization; musical notation; music, harmony; (coll.) flogging; **poner en solfa** to put in a ridiculous light
solfeador -dora *mf* (mus.) sol-faer
solfear *va* (mus.) to sol-fa; (coll.) to flog, to beat; to criticize severely; *vn* (mus.) to sol-fa
solfeo *m* (mus.) sol-faing, solfeggio; (coll.) flogging, beating
solferino -na *adj* reddish-purple
solfista *mf* (mus.) sol-faist
solicitación *f* solicitation; wooing, courting; (phys.) attraction
solicitador -dora *adj* soliciting; attracting; *m* solicitor, agent
solicitante *mf* petitioner, solicitor; applicant
solicitar *va* to solicit, to ask for; to apply for; to seek after; to woo, to court, to attract (*e.g., attention*); to pull, to drive; to attend to; (phys.) to attract
solícito -ta *adj* solicitous, careful, diligent; obliging; (coll.) fond, affectionate
solicitud *f* solicitude; request, petition; application; **a solicitud** on request; **a solicitud de** at the request of
solidar *va* to harden, to make firm or solid; to establish, to prove
solidariamente *adv* jointly, conjointly
solidaridad *f* solidarity; (law) joint liability
solidario -ria *adj* solidary, jointly liable; jointly binding; involved; **solidario con** or **de** integral with
solidarizar §76 *va* to make jointly liable; *vr* to become jointly liable; to make common cause
solideo *m* (eccl.) calotte, zucchetto
solidez *f* solidity; strength, soundness; firmness, constancy; soundness of judgment; (geom.) volume
solidificación *f* solidification
solidificar §86 *va & vr* to solidify
sólido -da *adj* solid; strong; sound; firm; *m* solid
soliloquiar *vn* (coll.) to talk to oneself; to soliloquize
soliloquio *m* soliloquy
solimán *m* (alchem.) corrosive sublimate; (*cap.*) *m* Solyman
solio *m* throne with canopy, throne
solípedo -da *adj & m* (zool.) soliped
solipsismo *m* (philos.) solipsism
solista *mf* (mus.) soloist; *adj* (mus.) solo (*e.g., instrument*)
solitario -ria *adj* solitary; *mf* solitary, hermit, recluse; *m* solitaire (*game and diamond*); *f* post chaise; tapeworm
sólito -ta *adj* customary, accustomed
soliviadura *f* lifting; getting up partly
soliviantar *va* to rouse, stir up, incite; *vr* to become aroused, to become stirred up
soliviar *va* to lift, lift up; *vr* to rise partly, to get up partly
solivio *m* lifting; upward pressure; getting up partly
solivión *m* hard jerk to throw or pull something off or away
solo -la *adj* only, sole; alone; lonely; straight (*e.g., whiskey*); (mus.) solo; **a solas** alone, by oneself (*unaided*); **a mis solas** alone, by myself (*in solitude*); *m* (mus.) solo
sólo *adv* only, solely; **con sólo que** provided that
solomillo *m* sirloin
solomo *m* sirloin; loin of pork
Solón *m* Solon; (fig.) Solon
solsticial *adj* solstitial
solsticio *m* (astr.) solstice; **solsticio de invierno** or **solsticio hiemal** (astr.) winter solstice; **solsticio de verano** or **solsticio vernal** (astr.) summer solstice
soltadizo -za *adj* slyly let go of, easily loosened, removable, collapsible
soltador -dora *adj* loosening, unfastening; *mf* dropper; **soltador del margen** margin release (*of typewriter*)
soltar §77 *va* to untie, unfasten, loosen; to let loose, to let go, to set free; to let go of; (coll.) to let out, let slip (*a remark*); to give (*a kick or slap*); to turn on (*water*); to solve, explain; **soltar la lengua** to blow off steam; *vr* to get loose or free; to come loose, come off; to burst out; to loosen up; to acquire ease; to cast aside restraint, to thaw out, to let oneself go; **soltarse a** + *inf* to start out to + *inf*
soltera *f* see **soltero**
soltería *f* singleness; bachelorhood; celibacy
soltero -ra *adj* single, unmarried; *m* bachelor; *f* spinster; **de soltera** née
solterón -rona *adj* (coll.) old and unmarried; *m* (coll.) old bachelor; *f* (coll.) old maid, spinster, maiden lady
soltura *f* looseness; ease, agility, freedom; fluency; dissoluteness, licentiousness; release (*of a prisoner*)
solubilidad *f* solubility
soluble *adj* soluble
solución *f* solution; **solución de continuidad** solution of continuity (*break*)
solucionar *va* to solve, resolve
solutivo -va *adj & m* (med.) laxative
soluto *m* (chem.) solute
solvencia *f* settlement; solution; solvency; reliability
solventar *va* to settle, pay up (*what one owes*); to solve (*a difficulty*)
solvente *adj* solvent; reliable; (chem.) solvent; *m* (chem.) solvent
solver §63 & §17, 9 *va* (archaic) to solve, to explain; (obs.) to absolve
sollado *m* (naut.) orlop
sollamar *va* to scorch, to singe
sollastre *m* scullion (*servant; contemptible person*)
sollastría *f* scullery
sollo *m* (ichth.) sturgeon
sollozar §76 *vn* to sob
sollozo *m* sob
soma *f* (biol.) soma; coarse flour
somalí *mf* (*pl:* **-líes**) Somali
Somalía, la Somaliland
somanta *f* (coll.) drubbing, beating
somatén *m* (Sp. hist.) body of armed vigilantes for defense and for maintaining order; (coll.) hubbub, uproar; *interj* war cry of ancient Catalans
somatenista *m* vigilante (*of a somatén*)
somático -ca *adj* somatic
somatología *f* somatology
sombra *f* shade; shadow; shady side (*e.g., of bull ring*); parasol; darkness; ignorance; ghost, spirit, shade; grace, charm, wit; favor, protection; spot, defect; (fig.) shadow (*appearance*); (coll.) luck; (paint.) umber; **a la sombra** in the shade; (coll.) in jail; **a sombra de tejado** (coll.) stealthily, sneakingly; **hacer sombra** to cast a shadow; **hacer sombra a** to stand in the light of, to outshine; to back, to protect; **ni por sombra** by no means; without any notice; **no ser su sombra** to be but a shadow of one's former self; **no tener sombra de** to not have a bit of; **tener buena sombra** (coll.) to be likeable; to be witty; to bring good luck; **tener mala sombra** (coll.) to be disagreeable, be unpopular; to bring bad luck; **sombras chinescas** (theat.) shadow pantomime, shadow play
sombraje *m* sun screen made of branches and twigs
sombrajo *m* sun screen made of branches and twigs; (coll.) shadow (*made by getting in someone's light*); **hacer sombrajos** (coll.) to get in the light, to get in someone's light
sombrar *va* to shade
sombrático -ca or **sombrátil** *adj* shady; obscure, puzzling
sombreado *m* (f.a.) shading, hatching
sombrear *va* to shade; (f.a.) to shade
sombrerada *f* hatful
sombrerazo *m* large hat; blow with a hat; (coll.) hurried doffing of hat
sombrerera *f* see **sombrerero**

sombrerería *f* hat store; millinery shop; hat factory; hat business
sombrerero -ra *mf* hatter, hat maker, milliner; *f* hatter's wife; bandbox, hatbox
sombrerete *m* little hat; hood, bonnet (*of chimney*); spark catcher (*of locomotive*); cap (*of mushroom*); hubcap
sombrerillo *m* little hat; hat (*held out for alms*); cap (*of mushrooms*); (bot.) Venus's-navelwort
sombrero *m* hat; canopy (*of pulpit*); privilege of keeping hat on in presence of king; cap (*of mushrooms*); **pasar el sombrero** to pass the hat; **sombrero apuntado** cocked hat; **sombrero calañés** Andalusian hat with turned-up brim and low cone-shaped crown; **sombrero castoreño** beaver hat; **sombrero cordobés** low, wide-brim felt halt; **sombrero de cabrestante** (naut.) drum of the capstan; **sombrero de candil** cocked hat; **sombrero de copa** or **de copa alta** top hat, high hat; **sombrero de jipijapa** Panama hat; **sombrero del patrón** (naut.) hat money, primage; **sombrero de muelles** opera hat; **sombrero de paja** straw hat; **sombrero de pelo** (Am.) high hat; **sombrero de teja** shovel hat; **sombrero de tres picos** three-cornered hat; **sombrero flexible** soft hat; **sombrero gacho** slouch hat; **sombrero hongo** derby hat; **sombrero jarano** (Am.) sombrero; **sombrero panamá** Panama hat
sombría *f* see **sombrío**
sombrilla *f* parasol, sunshade; **sombrilla de playa** beach umbrella; **sombrilla protectora** (mil.) umbrella
sombrío -a *adj* shady; somber; gloomy; (f.a.) shaded; *f* shady place
sombroso -sa *adj* shady; shadowy, full of shadows
somero -ra *adj* brief, summary; slight; superficial, shallow; on the surface, just above the surface
someter *va* to force to yield, to subdue, to subject; to submit (*e.g., an argument; a problem for consideration or solution*); *vr* to yield, submit, surrender
sometido -da *adj* submissive, docile, humble
sometimiento *m* submission, subjection
somier *m* (*pl:* **-mieres**) bedspring, spring mattress
somnambulismo *m* var. de **sonambulismo**
somnámbulo -la *adj & mf* var. of **sonámbulo**
somnífero -ra *adj* somniferous
somnílocuo -cua *adj* somniloquous, sleep-talking; *mf* somniloquist, sleep talker
somnolento -ta *adj* sleepy, dozy, drowsy, somnolent; lazy
somnolencia *f* drowsiness, somnolence
somontano -na *adj & mf* Upper Aragonese
somonte; de somonte coarse, rough, unpolished
somorgujador *m* diver
somorgujar *va* to duck, to plunge, to submerge; *vn* to dive; *vr* to duck, to plunge, to submerge; to dive
somorgujo *m* (orn.) dabchick, grebe; **a lo somorgujo** or **a somorgujo** under the water; (coll.) secretly, stealthily; **somorgujo castaño** or **menor** (orn.) dabchick (*Podiceps ruficollis*); **somorgujo moñudo** (orn.) crested grebe
somormujar *va* var. of **somorgujar**
somormujo *m* var. of **somorgujo**
somos *1st pl pres ind of* **ser**
sompesar *va* to heft, try the weight of
son *m* sound, sweet sound; news, rumor; pretext, motive; manner, mode; **¿a qué son?** or **¿a son de qué?** (coll.) for what reason?; **a son de** to the sound of; **bailar a cualquier son** (coll.) to be fickle in one's likes and dislikes; **bailar al son que le tocan** (coll.) to adapt oneself to circumstances; **en son de** in the manner of, by way of, on the score of; **sin son** (coll.) without reason; *3d pl pres ind of* **ser**
sonable *adj* loud, noisy; noted, famous
sonada *f* see **sonado**
sonadera *f* blowing the nose
sonadero *m* handkerchief
sonado -da *adj* talked-about, bruited about; noted, famous; **hacer una que sea sonada** (coll.) to cause a scandal, to cause a lot of talk; *f* (mus.) sonata
sonador -dora *adj* noisemaking; *mf* noisemaker; *m* handkerchief
sonaja *f* jingle, metallic disk (*of tambourine*); **sonajas** *fpl* jingle hoop
sonajero *m* child's rattle
sonambulismo *m* sleepwalking, somnambulism
sonámbulo -la *adj* sleepwalking, somnambulistic; *mf* sleepwalker, somnambulist
sonante *adj* sonant, sounding, jingling; *f* (phonet.) sonorant, syllabic consonant
sonar *m* sonar; **§77** *va* to sound, to ring; to play (*a musical instrument*); to blow (*one's nose*); *vn* to sound, to ring; to be sounded (*said of a vowel, consonant, letter, etc.*); to strike (*said of a clock*); to be mentioned; to be reported or bruited about; to seem; (coll.) to sound familiar; (fig.) to ring, to sound (*a certain way*); **ni suena ni truena** (coll.) cuts no figure; **sonar a** to sound like, to have the appearance of; *vr* to blow one's nose; to be rumored
sonata *f* (mus.) sonata
sonatina *f* (mus.) sonatina
sonda *f* sounding; sounder, plummet, lead; drill; (geol.) annular borer; diamond drill; (surg.) catheter; (surg.) probe; **sonda acústica** sonic depth finder
sondable *adj* fathomable
sondaje *m* boring, drilling, sounding
sondaleza *f* (naut.) lead line, sounding line
sondar or **sondear** *va* to sound (*water, subsoil, a person, a person's intentions*); to drill, make borings in; (surg.) to sound, to probe
sondeo *m* sounding, probing
sonecillo *m* little sound, slight noise; joyous sound, merry tune
sonería *f* pealing of bells; set of bells, carillon; striking mechanism (*of clock*)
sonetear *vn* to write sonnets, to sonneteer
sonetico *m* light sonnet; tapping with the fingers
sonetillo *m* short-line sonnet
sonetista *mf* sonneteer
sonetizar §76 *vn* to write sonnets, to sonneteer
soneto *m* sonnet
sónico -ca *adj* sonic
sonido *m* sound; report, rumor; literal meaning
soniquete *m* little sound, unpleasant sound, tapping, rapping
sonlocado -da *adj* mad, wild, reckless, foolish
sonochada *f* evening, early part of night; evening watch
sonochar *vn* to watch in the early part of the night
sonómetro *m* sonometer
sonora *f* see **sonoro**
sonoridad *f* sonority
sonorización *f* recording of sound effects on a film; (phonet.) voicing
sonorizar §76 *va* to record sound effects on (*a film*); (phonet.) to voice; *vr* (phonet.) to voice
sonoro -ra *adj* sonorous; clear, loud, resounding; (phonet.) sonant; *f* (phonet.) sonant
sonoroso -sa *adj* (poet.) sonorous, resounding
sonreír §73 *vn & vr* to smile
sonriente *adj* smiling; *mf* smiling person
sonrisa *f* smile
sonrisueño -ña *adj & mf* var. of **sonriente**
sonrodar §77 *vr* to stick or get stuck in the mud (*said of wheels*)
sonrojar or **sonrojear** *va* to make blush; *vr* to blush
sonrojo *m* blush, blushing; word or remark that causes blushing
sonrosado -da *adj* rosy
sonrosar or **sonrosear** *va* to rose-color; to flush; *vr* to become rose-colored; to flush, to blush
sonroseo *m* flush, blush
sonsaca *f* pilfering; enticement; wresting, eliciting
sonsacador -dora *adj* pilfering; enticing; eliciting; *mf* pilferer; enticer; wheedler; pumper (*of secrets*)
sonsacamiento *m* var. of **sonsaca**

sonsacar §86 *va* to pilfer; to entice away; to elicit, draw out (*e.g., a secret*); **sonsacar un secreto a alguien** to elicit a secret from someone, to draw a secret out of someone
sonsaque *m* var. of **sonsaca**
sonsonete *m* rhythmical tapping; dull rumbling; singsong; smirking tone
sonsoniche *interj* (slang) hush!, silence!
soñación *f* dream; **ni por soñación** (coll.) by no means, far from it
soñador -dora *adj* dreamy; *mf* dreamer; (fig.) dreamer
soñar §77 *va* to dream; **ni soñarlo** (coll.) not even in dreams; *vn* to dream; to daydream; **soñar con** or **en** to dream of; **soñar con** or **en** + *inf* to dream of + *ger;* **soñar despierto** to daydream
soñarrera *f* (coll.) dreaminess; sleepiness; deep sleep
soñera *f* sleepiness
soñolencia *f* drowsiness, somnolence
soñoliento -ta *adj* sleepy, dozy, drowsy, somnolent; lazy; somniferous
sopa *f* sop (*food soaked in milk, etc.*); soup; **sopas** *fpl* slices of bread to put in soup; **a la sopa boba** (coll.) at other people's expense; **andar** or **ir a la sopa** to beg from door to door; **hecho una sopa** (coll.) soaked to the skin, sopping wet, drenched; **sopa de pastas** noodle soup; **sopa juliana** julienne
sopaipa *f* fritter soaked in honey
sopalancar §86 *va* to lift with a lever
sopalanda *f* student's gown
sopanda *f* brace; joist
sopapear *va* (coll.) to chuck under the chin; (coll.) to abuse
sopapina *f* (coll.) beating, drubbing
sopapo *m* chuck under the chin; (coll.) slap, blow; valve
sopar *va* to steep, soak
sopear *va* to steep, soak; to trample on; to abuse
sopeña *f* cavity under a rock
sopero -ra *adj* (pertaining to) soup; *m* soup dish; *f* soup tureen
sopesar *va* to heft, try the weight of
sopetear *va* to dunk; to abuse
sopeteo *m* dunking
sopetón *m* slap, box; toast soaked in olive oil; **de sopetón** suddenly
sopicaldo *m* thin soup
sopista *adj* poverty-stricken; *mf* beggar, object of charity; *m* student making his way on charity
sopladero *m* vent, air hole
soplado -da *adj* (coll.) overnice; (coll.) conceited, stuck up; *m* blowing; (min.) deep fissure
soplador -dora *adj* blowing; *m* blower; ventilator, blowing fan; vent, air hole; (zool.) blower (*whale*); *f* blower
sopladura *f* blowing; blowhole, air hole
soplamocos *m* (*pl:* **-cos**) (coll.) punch in the nose
soplar *va* to blow; to blow away; to blow up, to inflate; to snitch, to swipe; to prompt; to inspire (*a person; verse, poetry*); to whisper (*e.g., an answer to a pupil*); to tip, to tip off; (coll.) to squeal on; (checkers) to huff; *vn* to blow; (zool.) to blow (*said of a whale*); (coll.) to squeal; **¡sopla!** (coll.) gracious me!; *vr* to be puffed up, be conceited; (coll.) to swill, gulp, gobble
soplete *m* blowpipe, torch; **soplete oxiacetilénico** oxyacetylene torch; **soplete oxhídrico** oxyhydrogen torch
soplido *m* blowing, blast
soplillo *m* blowing fan, ventilator; chiffon, silk gauze; light sponge cake
soplo *m* blowing, blast; breath; puff, gust of wind; instant, moment; (coll.) tip (*secret information*); (coll.) squealing; (coll.) squealer; **soplo de vida** breath of life
soplón -plona *adj* (coll.) tattletale; *mf* (coll.) tattletale, squealer
soplonear *va* (coll.) to squeal on
sopón *m* (coll.) beggar
soponcio *m* swoon, faint, fainting
sopor *m* sleepiness, drowsiness; stupor, lethargy
soporífero -ra *adj* soporiferous, soporific; *m* soporific
soporífico -ca *adj* soporific
soporoso -sa *adj* sleepy; soporose
soportable *adj* bearable, endurable, supportable
soportal *m* porch, portico, arcade
soportar *va* to support, bear, hold up; to suffer, endure
soporte *m* support, bearing, rest, standard; base, stand; hanger; bracket
soprano *mf* soprano (*person*); *m* soprano (*voice*)
sopuntar *va* to put dots under (*a letter or word*)
Sor. abr. of **Señor**
sor *f* (used before names of nuns) sister
sorber *va* to sip, to suck; to absorb, to soak up, to swallow up; **sorber los vientos por** (coll.) to be crazy about; *vr* to overcome, get the best of
sorbete *m* sherbet, water ice
sorbetera *f* ice-cream freezer; (Am.) high hat
sorbetón *m* (coll.) gulp, big gulp of liquor
sorbible *adj* to be sipped, that can be sipped; absorbable
sorbo *m* sip; sipping; swallow, gulp; sniff
Sorbona *f* Sorbonne
sorda *f* see **sordo**
sordera *f* deafness
sordez *f* (phonet.) voicelessness
sordidez *f* sordidness
sórdido -da *adj* sordid
sordina *f* (mus.) damper; (mus.) mute; silencer; **a la sordina** silently, on the quiet
sordino *m* (mus.) fiddle
sordo -da *adj* deaf; silent, mute; muffled, dull; dull (*noise; pain*); veiled (*e.g., hostility*); deaf, indifferent; (math. & phonet.) surd; **a la sorda, a lo sordo** or **a sordas** silently, noiselessly; **sordo como una tapia** (coll.) stone-deaf, deaf as a post; *mf* deaf person; **hacerse el sordo** to pretend to be deaf; to turn a deaf ear; *f* (orn.) snipe; (naut.) hawser used for launching; (phonet.) surd
sordomudez *f* deaf-dumbness, deaf-muteness
sordomudo -da *adj* deaf and dumb, deaf-mute; *mf* deaf-mute
sorgo *m* (bot.) sorghum; **sorgo del Sudán** (bot.) Sudan grass
soríasis *f* (path.) psoriasis
sorna *f* slowness; sluggishness; cunning
soro *m* (bot.) sorus
sorochar *vr* (Am.) to become mountain-sick
soroche *m* (Am.) soroche, mountain sickness; (Am.) flush (*caused by heat, shame, etc.*); (Am.) silver-bearing lead sulfide
sóror *f* (eccl.) sister
sorosis *f* (bot.) sorosis
sorprendente *adj* surprising; unusual, extraordinary
sorprender *va* to surprise; to catch; to discover (*a secret*); **sorprender en el hecho** to catch in the act; *vr* to be surprised
sorpresa *f* surprise; surprise package; **coger** or **tomar de sorpresa** to take by surprise
sorpresivamente *adv* unexpectedly, by surprise
sorpresivo -va *adj* unexpected, sudden, surprising
sorra *f* ballast of coarse gravel; half belly of tunny
sorregar §29 *va* to irrigate by overflow from a higher ditch
sorriego *m* irrigation by overflow from a higher ditch; overflow water
sorrostrada *f* insolence, bluntness; **dar sorrostrada a** to insult, upbraid
sorrostrar *va* to insult, upbraid
sorteamiento *m* var. of **sorteo**
sortear *va* to draw or cast lots for; to choose by lot; to dodge, to evade; to duck through (*traffic*); (taur.) to choose by lot (*the bull one is to fight*); (taur.) to make passes at (*a bull*); *vn* to draw or cast lots
sorteo *m* drawing, casting of lots; choosing by lot; dodging, evasion; (taur.) workout, performance
sortero -ra *mf* soothsayer, fortuneteller
sortiaria *f* fortunetelling by cards
sortija *f* ring; curl; hoop; **sortija de sello** signet ring; **sortija solitario** solitaire (*ring*)
sortijilla *f* ringlet; curl
sortijuela *f* ringlet

sortilegio *m* sorcery, witchery, sortilege
sortílego -ga *mf* fortuneteller; *m* sorcerer; *f* sorceress
S O S *m* (rad.) S O S (*signal of distress*)
sosa *f* see **soso**
sosaina *adj* dull, colorless (*person*)
sosal *m* or **sosar** *m* field of glasswort, field of kelp
sosegado -da *adj* calm, quiet, peaceful
sosegador -dora *adj* calming, quieting; *mf* quieter, appeaser
sosegar §29 *va* to calm, to quiet, to allay; *vn* to become calm, to rest; *vr* to calm down, to quiet down; to become calm, to rest
sosera *f* see **sosero**
sosería *f* insipidity, tastelessness; dullness, inanity, nonsense
sosero -ra *adj* (bot.) soda-yielding; *f* insipidity, tastelessness; dullness, inanity, nonsense
sosia *m* double (*counterpart of another person*)
sosiega *f* rest from work; drink when resting; nightcap
sosiego *m* calm, quiet, serenity
soslayar *va* to place obliquely; to duck (*a question*); to evade (*an evil*)
soslayo -ya *adj* oblique, slanting; **al soslayo** or **de soslayo** obliquely, slantingly; at a slant; askance; **mirada de soslayo** side glance; **pegar de soslayo** to glance against, to hit on the slant
soso -sa *adj* insipid, tasteless; dull, inane; *f* (bot.) glasswort; soda ash; (chem.) soda; **sosa cáustica** (chem.) caustic soda
sosobre *m* or **sosobrejuanete** *m* (naut.) skysail, skysail pole
sospecha *f* suspicion
sospechable *adj* suspicious; suspect
sospechar *va* to suspect; *vn* to suspect, be suspicious; **sospechar de** to suspect, distrust
sospechoso -sa *adj* suspicious; suspect; *m* suspect
sospesar *va* to heft, try the weight of
sosquín *m* side blow; sneak blow or punch
sostén *m* support (*person or thing*); brassière; steadiness (*of ship*); *2d sg impv of* **sostener**
sostendré *1st sg fut ind of* **sostener**
sostenedor -dora *adj* supporting, sustaining; *mf* supporter, sustainer
sostener §85 *va* to support, hold up; to sustain; to maintain; to back, uphold; to bear, stand
sostengo *1st sg pres ind of* **sostener**
sostenido -da *adj* & *m* (mus.) sharp; **doble sostenido** (mus.) double sharp
sostenimiento *m* support, sustenance, maintenance
sostuve *1st sg pret ind of* **sostener**
sota *f* jack (*in cards*); jade, hussy; *m* (Am.) boss, foreman
sotabanco *m* attic, garret; (arch.) impost, springer, skewback
sotabarba *f* fringe of whiskers (*around chin from ear to ear*)
sotacola *f* crupper
sotacoro *m* var. of **socoro**
sotalugo *m* second hoop (*of cask or barrel*)
sotaministro *m* var. of **sotoministro**
sotana *f* soutane, cassock; (coll.) beating, drubbing
sotanear *va* (coll.) to beat, to drub, to reprimand harshly
sotaní *m* (*pl:* **-níes**) short skirt without folds
sótano *m* basement, cellar
sotaventar or **sotaventear** *vr* (naut.) to fall to leeward
sotavento *m* (naut.) leeward; **a sotavento** (naut.) alee, to leeward
sotechado *m* shed
soteño -ña *adj* growing in groves
soteriología *f* (theol.) soteriology
soterramiento *m* burial, inhumation
soterraño -ña *adj* underground, subterranean
soterrar §18 to bury, inhume; to hide away
sotileza *f* (prov.) leader (*transparent fiber of fishline*); (archaic) subtlety
soto *m* grove; thicket, brush
sotoministro *m* (eccl.) steward
sotreta *m* (Am.) nag
sotrozo *m* (mach.) key; (arti.) linchpin, axle pin; (naut.) foothook staff
sotuer *m* (her.) saltier
soviet *m* (*pl:* **-viets**) soviet
soviético -ca *adj* soviet, sovietic
sovietismo *m* sovietism
sovietización *f* sovietization
sovietizar §76 *va* to sovietize
sovoz; a sovoz sotto voce, in a low tone
soy *1st sg pres ind of* **ser**
soya *f* var. of **soja**
spre. abr. of **siempre**
S.r or **Sr.** abr. of **Señor**
Sra. abr. of **Señora**
Sría. abr. of **secretaría**
Sr.ta or **Srta.** abr. of **Señorita**
S.S. abr. of **Su Santidad**
S.S.a abr. of **Su Señoría**
SS.mo abr. of **Santísimo**
SS.no abr. of **escribano**
S.S.S. abr. of **su seguro servidor**
ss. ss. abr. of **seguros servidores**
S.S.S. y Capellán (coll.) formula written by priests at the end of a letter
Sta. abr. of **Santa**
stajanovismo *m* Stakhanovism
stajanovista *adj* & *mf* Stakhanovite
Stalingrado *f* Stalingrad
stalinismo *m* Stalinism
stalinista *adj* & *mf* Stalinist
Sto. abr. of **Santo**
stuka *m* Stuka (*German dive bomber*)
su *adj poss* his, her, its, their, your, one's
Suabia *f* Swabia
suabo -ba *adj* & *mf* Swabian
suarda *f* stain, spot; suint (*grease of wool*)
suasorio -ria *adj* suasive, persuasive
suave *adj* suave, smooth; mild, meek; gentle; (phonet.) smooth (*breathing*)
suavidad *f* suavity, smoothness; mildness, meekness
suavizador -dora *adj* smoothing, softening, mollifying; *m* razor strop
suavizar §76 to smooth, to ease, to sweeten, to soften, to mollify; to strop (*a razor*)
subacetato *m* (chem.) subacetate
subácido -da *adj* (chem.) subacid
subacuático -ca *adj* underwater, subaquatic
subácueo -a *adj* subaqueous
subafluente *m* tributary
subagente *m* subagent
subalcaide *m* deputy warden
subalimentación *f* undernourishment
subalquilar *va* var. of **subarrendar**
subalternar *va* to subdue, to subject
subalterno -na *adj* & *mf* subaltern, subordinate
subálveo -a *adj* located under the river bed; *m* place under river bed
subantártico -ca *adj* subantarctic
subarrendador -dora *mf* subletter
subarrendar §18 *va* to sublease; to sublet
subarrendatario -ria *mf* sublessor; sublessee
subarriendo *m* sublease
subártico -ca *adj* subarctic
subasta *f* auction, auction sale; bidding; **sacar a pública subasta** to sell at auction
subastar *va* to auction, sell at auction, auction off; to bid
subatómico -ca *adj* subatomic
subátomo *m* (chem. & phys.) subatom
subcampeón -ona *mf* (sport) runner-up
subcentral *f* (elec.) substation
subclase *f* (biol.) subclass
subclavio -via *adj* (anat.) subclavian
subcolector *m* subcollector, assistant collector
subcomendador *m* deputy commander (*of a military order*)
subcomisión *f* subcommission, subcommittee
subconsciencia *f* subconscious, subconsciousness
subconsciente *adj* subconscious
subcontinente *m* subcontinent
subcontratar *va* & *vn* to subcontract
subcontratista *mf* subcontractor
subcontrato *m* subcontract
subcostal *adj* (anat. & zool.) subcostal
subcrítico -ca *adj* subcritical
subcutáneo -a *adj* subcutaneous
subdecano *m* subdean
subdelirio *m* (path.) subdelirium

subdesarrollado -da *adj* underdeveloped
subdiaconato *m* subdeaconry
subdiácono *m* subdeacon
subdirector -tora *mf* subhead, subdirector
súbdito -ta *adj & mf* subject
subdividir *va & vr* to subdivide
subdivisión *f* subdivision
subdominante *f* (mus.) subdominant
subduplo -pla *adj* (math.) subdouble
subentender §66 *va* to understand; *vr* be understood, be implied
subeo *m* var. of **sobeo**
suberina *f* (biochem.) suberin
suberoso -sa *adj* subereous
subespecie *f* (biol.) subspecies
subestación *f* (elec.) substation
subestimar *va* to underestimate
subestructura *f* substructure; (rail.) roadbed
subexposición *f* (phot.) underexposure
subfamilia *f* subfamily
subfluvial *adj* underriver
subfusil *m* submachine gun; **subfusil ametrallador** submachine gun
subgénero *m* (biol.) subgenus
subgobernador *m* lieutenant governor
subgrupo *m* subgroup
subida *f* see **subido**
subidero -ra *adj* climbing, for climbing; *m* way up, way to go up
subido -da *adj* high, fine, superior; strong, intense; bright (*color*); high, high-priced; **subido de color** off-color; *f* rise; ascent, acclivity; accession (*e.g., to the throne*)
subidor *m* porter; elevator, lift
subilla *f* awl
subimiento *m* rise
subíndice *m* subindex
subinquilino -na *mf* subtenant
subinspección *f* subinspection
subinspector *m* subinspector
subintración *f* underlapping (*of bone*); overlapping (*of fever*)
subintrar *vn* to come in later; to underlap (*said of a fractured bone*); to overlap (*said of onsets of fever*)
subir *va* to raise; to lift, to lift up; to carry up; to go up (*the stairs, a slope*); to swell, increase; (mus.) to raise the pitch of; *vn* to go up, to come up; to rise; to swell, increase; to get worse; to spread; (mus.) to rise (*said of pitch*); **subir a** + *inf* to go or come up to + *inf;* **subir a** to climb (*e.g., a tree*); **subir a** or **en** to climb to; to get in or into, to climb into; to get on, to mount; *vr* to rise; **subírsele a uno a la cabeza** to go to one's head (*said, e.g., of wine*); **subirse a** or **en** to get into
subitáneo -a *adj* sudden, unexpected
súbito -ta *adj* sudden, unexpected; hasty, impetuous; hurried; **súbito** *adv* suddenly; **de súbito** suddenly
subjefe *m* assistant to the chief, subhead
subjetividad *f* subjectivity
subjetivismo *m* (philos.) subjectivism
subjetivo -va *adj* subjective
subjuntivo -va *adj & m* (gram.) subjunctive
sublevación *f* uprising, revolt
sublevado *m* rebel, insurrectionist
sublevamiento *m* var. of **sublevación**
sublevar *va* to incite to rebellion; to stir up the ire of; *vr* to revolt
sublimación *f* sublimation
sublimado -da *adj* sublimated; exalted; *m* (chem.) sublimate
sublimar *va* to sublimate; to sublime, exalt, elevate; *vr* to be sublimated; to be sublimed, be exalted, be elevated
sublime *adj* sublime; **lo sublime** the sublime
sublimidad *f* sublimity
subliminar *adj & f* (psychol.) subliminal
sublingual *adj* (anat.) sublingual
sublunar *adj* sublunar or sublunary
submarginal *adj* submarginal
submarinista *mf* skin diver
submarino -na *adj* submarine; underwater; *m* submarine
submaxilar *adj* submaxillary
submersión *f* var. of **sumersión**
submicroscópico -ca *adj* submicroscopic
submúltiplo -pla *adj & m* (math.) submultiple
subnormal *adj* subnormal; *f* (geom.) subnormal
subnota *f* footnote to a footnote
suboficial *m* sergeant major; noncommissioned officer
suborbital *adj* suborbital
suborden *m* suborder
subordinación *f* subordination
subordinado -da *adj* subordinate; (gram.) subordinate, subordinating; *mf* subordinate
subordinante *adj* (gram.) subordinating, subordinate
subordinar *va* to subordinate; *vr* to be subordinated
subprefecto *m* subprefect
subprefectura *f* subprefecture
subproducto *m* by-product
subrayar *va* to underline; to emphasize
subreino *m* (biol.) subkingdom
subrepción *f* underhandedness, subreption
subrepticio -cia *adj* surreptitious
subrogación *f* substitution; (law) subrogation
subrogar §59 *va* to subrogate; **subrogar con** or **por** to replace with
subsanable *adj* excusable; reparable
subsanación *f* excusal, excusing; reparation
subsanar *va* to excuse, overlook; to correct, repair
subsatélite *m* subsatellite
subscapular *adj* (anat.) subscapular
subscribir §17, 9 *va* to subscribe; to subscribe to, to endorse; to subscribe to or for (*e.g., bonds*); to sign; **subscribir a uno a** to enter or enroll someone for a subscription to; *vr* to subscribe; **subscribirse a** to subscribe to or for (*e.g., a journal*)
subscripción *f* subscription
subscriptor -tora *mf* subscriber
subscrito -ta *pp de* **subscribir**
subscritor -tora *mf* subscriber
subsecretaría *f* undersecretaryship
subsecretario *m* undersecretary
subsecuente *adj* subsequent
subseguir §82 *vn & vr* to follow next; **subseguir de** to follow from
subsidiar *va* to subsidize
subsidiario -ria *adj* subsidiary; (law) ancillary
subsidio *m* subsidy; aid, help; **subsidio de vejez** old-age pension; **subsidio por desempleo** or **subsidios de paro** unemployment compensation
subsiguiente *adj* subsequent, succeeding
subsistencia *f* subsistence, sustenance; (philos.) subsistence
subsistente *adj* subsistent; persistent, lasting
subsistir *vn* to subsist
subsolano *m* east wind
subsónico -ca *adj* subsonic
substancia *f* substance; **en substancia** in substance; **substancia gris** (anat.) gray matter
substanciación *f* abridgment, abstraction; (law) trial
substancial *adj* substantial; important; nourishing
substancialidad *f* substantiality
substanciar *va* to abridge, abstract; (law) to try
substancioso -sa *adj* substantial; nourishing; tasty
substantífico -ca *adj* substantial
substantivar *va* (gram.) substantivize; *vr* (gram.) to become substantivized, to be used as a noun
substantivo -va *adj* substantive; (gram.) substantive; *m* (gram.) substantive
substitución *f* replacement; (alg., chem. & law) substitution
substituíble *adj* replaceable
substituidor -dora *adj* substitute, substitutional; *mf* substitute
substituir §41 *va* to replace, e.g., **substituimos la mantequilla con** or **por la margarina** we replaced butter with margarine; to substitute for, take the place of, e.g., **Juan substituyó a Pedro** John substituted for Peter, John took the place of Peter; **la margarina substituyó a la mantequilla** margarine took the place of butter; *vn* to take someone's or something's place; *vr* to be replaced; to relieve each other

substitutivo -va *adj* substitutive; substitute; *m* substitute (*thing*); **desconfíe de substitutivos** beware of substitutes
substituto -ta *mf* substitute
substracción *f* removal, withdrawal; theft; subtraction
substraendo *m* (math.) subtrahend
substraer §88 *va* to remove, to deduct; to rob, to steal; to subtract; **substraer a** to take away from; to rob from, to steal from; *vr* to withdraw; **substraerse a** to evade, to avoid, to slip away from
substraigo *1st sg pres ind of* **substraer**
substraje *1st sg pret ind of* **substraer**
substrato *m* substratum; (biochem.) substrate
subsuelo *m* subsoil
subsumir *va* to subsume
subsumpción *f* subsumption
subtender §66 *va* (geom. & bot.) to subtend
subtenencia *f* second lieutenancy
subteniente *m* second lieutenant
subtensa *f* (geom.) line subtending, subtense
subterfugio *m* subterfuge
subterráneo -a *adj* subterranean, underground; *m* subterranean (*place*)
subtitular *va* to subtitle
subtítulo *m* subtitle, subhead
subtropical *adj* subtropical
subtrópicos *mpl* subtropics
suburbano -na *adj* outlying, adjacent (*to a city*); suburban; *mf* suburbanite
suburbio *m* suburb; outlying slum
subvención *f* subvention, subsidy
subvencionar *va* to subsidize
subvendré *1st sg fut ind of* **subvenir**
subvengo *1st sg pres ind of* **subvenir**
subvenir §92 *vn* to provide; **subvenir a** to provide for (*e.g., a person's needs*); to meet, defray (*expenses*)
subversión *f* subversion
subversivo -va *adj* subversive
subversor -sora *adj* subversive; *mf* subverter; subversive
subvertir §62 *va* to subvert
subvine *1st sg pret ind of* **subvenir**
subviniendo *ger of* **subvenir**
subyacente *adj* subjacent, underlying
subyugación *f* subjugation
subyugador -dora *adj* subjugating; *mf* subjugator
subyugar §59 *va* to subjugate
succínico -ca *adj* succinic
succino *m* amber
succión *f* sucking; suction
succionador *m* suction cup
succionar *va* to suck, to suck in
sucedáneo -a *adj* & *m* substitute
suceder *va* to succeed, follow, be the successor of; *vn* to happen; **suceder a** to succeed to (*e.g., a throne*); **suceder con** to happen to; *vr* to follow one another, to follow one after the other
sucedido *m* (coll.) happening, event
sucesión *f* succession; issue, offspring; estate
sucesivamente *adv* successively; **y así sucesivamente** and so on
sucesivo -va *adj* successive; **en lo sucesivo** in the future
suceso *m* event, happening; issue, outcome; course, lapse; **sucesos de actualidad** current events
sucesor -sora *adj* succeeding; *mf* successor; heir
suciedad *f* dirt, filth; dirtiness, filthiness, filthy remark
sucintar *vr* to be precise, be brief
sucinto -ta *adj* succinct
sucio -cia *adj* dirty, filthy; low, base; tainted; blurred; (naut.) foul (*because of hidden rocks*); (sport) foul (*blow*); **sucio** *adv* (sport) foully, unfairly
sucísimo -ma *adj super* very or most dirty or filthy
suco *m* (archaic) juice; (Am.) muddy ground
sucoso -sa *adj* (archaic) juicy
sucre *m* sucre (*monetary unit of Ecuador*)
suctorio -ria *adj* suctorial
súcubo *adj masc* succubine; *m* succubus
sucucho *m* corner, nook
súcula *f* windlass, winch
suculencia *f* succulence or succulency
suculento -ta *adj* succulent
sucumbir *vn* to succumb; (law) to lose
sucursal *adj* branch; *f* branch, branch office
sucusión *f* succussation or succussion
sudadero *m* saddlecloth, saddle blanket; sweating room, sudatorium; handkerchief, sweat cloth; moist ground
Sudáfrica *f* South Africa
sudafricano -na *adj* & *mf* South African
Sudamérica *f* South America
sudamericano -na *adj* & *mf* South American
Sudán *m* Sudan; **Sudán Angloegipcio** Anglo-Egyptian Sudan
sudanés -nesa *adj* & *mf* Sudanese
sudante *adj* sweating; *mf* sweater (*person*)
sudar *va* to sweat; (coll.) to cough up; *vn* to sweat; (coll.) to sweat (*to work hard*)
sudario *m* shroud, winding sheet; (archaic) handkerchief, sweat cloth; (archaic) sweating room
sudatorio -ria *adj* sudatory; *m* (hist.) sudatorium
sudcoreano -na *adj* & *mf* South Korean
sudeño -ña *adj* southern
sudestada *f* southeaster
sudestal *adj* southeast; southeasterly
sudeste *m* southeast; southeaster (*wind*); **el Sudeste Asiático** or **de Asia** Southeast Asia; *adj* southeast; southeastern
sudetas *mfpl* Sudeten (*people*)
sudetes *mfpl* Sudeten (*people*); *mpl* Sudeten (*mountains*); **región de los Sudetes** Sudetenland
sudista *m* Southerner (*in U.S. Civil War*)
sudoccidental *adj* southwest
sudoeste *m* southwest; southwest wind
sudor *m* sweat; (fig.) sweat, toil; **sudores** (med.) sweat treatment; **chorrear de sudor** to swelter; **sudor frío** cold sweat
sudoriento -ta *adj* sweaty
sudorífero -ra *adj* sudoriferous
sudorífico -ca *adj* & *m* sudorific
sudoríparo -ra *adj* (anat.) sudoriparous
sudoroso -sa *adj* sweating, sweaty
sudoso -sa *adj* sweaty
sudsudeste *m* south-southeast
sudsudoeste *m* south-southwest
sudueste *m* var. of **sudoeste**
Suecia *f* Sweden; (*l.c.*) *f* suede (*leather*)
sueco -ca *adj* Swedish; *mf* Swede; **hacerse el sueco** (coll.) to pretend to not understand; *m* Swedish (*language*)
suegra *f* mother-in-law; hard crust (*of bread*)
suegro *m* father-in-law
suela *f* sole; sole leather; (ichth.) sole (*Solea vulgaris & Symphurus plagiusa*); leather tip (*of billiard cue*); horizontal beam; **suelas** *fpl* sandals; **de tres, de cuatro** or **de siete suelas** (coll.) downright; **media suela** half sole; **no llegarle a uno a la suela del zapato** (coll.) to not be able to hold a candle to someone
suelda *f* var. of **consuelda**
sueldaconsuelda *m* (bot.) snowberry (*Chiococca alba*)
sueldacostilla *f* (bot.) grape hyacinth
sueldo *m* salary, pay
suelo *m* ground, soil, land; floor, flooring; pavement; bottom; hoof; dregs; end; **arrastrarse por el suelo** (coll.) to crawl, to cringe; **dar consigo en el suelo** to fall down; **echar por los suelos** to ruin; **echarse por los suelos** to be excessively obsequious; **faltarle a uno el suelo** to trip, to fall; **medir el suelo** to stretch out on the ground or on the floor; (coll.) to fall flat on the ground; **no pisar en el suelo** to walk in the clouds, to walk on air; **por el suelo** or **por los suelos** cast off, cast aside; **sin suelo** unlimited; brazenly; **sobre suelo firme** on terra firma; **venir** or **venirse al suelo** to fall to the ground, to collapse, to topple; to fail; **suelo franco** loam; **suelo natal** home country
suelto -ta *adj* loose; free, easy; swift, agile, nimble; fluent, voluble; bold, daring; single (*copy*); blank (*verse*); odd, separate; spare; bulk; **suelto de lengua** loose-tongued; **suelto de manos** ready-fisted; *pp of* **solver;** *m*

small change; news item; *f* release; fetters (*for grazing animals*); relay (*of oxen*); **dar suelta a** to set loose; to give a recess to
sueñecillo *m* nap; **descabezar un sueñecillo** to take a nap
sueño *m* sleep, sleepiness; dream, fancy; (fig.) dream (*something beautiful*); **caerse de sueño** to be overcome with sleep; **conciliar el sueño** to manage to go to sleep; **descabezar el sueño** to doze off; **desperezar el sueño** to shake off sleep by stretching; **echar un sueño** to take a nap; **en sueños** or **entre sueños** dreaming, while dreaming; **espantar el sueño** to scare away or drive away sleep; **ni por sueños** by no means; **no dormir sueño** to not sleep a wink; **tener sueño** to be sleepy; **último sueño** last sleep (*death*); **sueño hecho realidad** dream come true; **sueños dorados** daydreams
suero *m* (biol. & med.) serum; **suero de la leche** serum, whey; **suero terapéutico** serum, antitoxic serum
sueroso -sa *adj* var. of **seroso**
sueroterapia *f* var. of **seroterapia**
suerte *f* luck, fortune, chance; piece of luck; fate, lot; augury; kind, sort; way; trick, feat; grade, quality; (print.) sort; (box.) round; (taur.) play, suerte; (Am.) lottery ticket; **buena suerte** good luck; **de esta suerte** in this way; **de suerte que** so that, with the result that; and so; **echar suertes** to draw lots, to cast lots; **mala suerte** bad luck; **por suerte** by lots; by chance; luckily; **sacar a la suerte** to draw by lots; **tener buena suerte** to be lucky; **tocarle a uno en suerte** to fall to one's lot; **suerte de banderillear** (taur.) planting darts; **suerte de matar** (taur.) death thrust; **suerte de picar** (taur.) lancing the bull
suertero -ra *adj* (Am.) fortunate, lucky; *mf* (Am.) vendor of lottery tickets
sueste *m* southwester or sou'wester (*waterproof hat*)
suéter *m* (*pl:* **-ters**) sweater
Suetonio *m* Suetonius
suévico -ca *adj* Suevian
suevo -va *adj & mf* Suevian
sufí *m* (*pl:* **-fíes**) Sufi
suficiencia *f* sufficiency; fitness, competency; adequacy; **a suficiencia** sufficiently
suficiente *adj* sufficient; fit, competent; adequate
sufijo -ja *adj* (gram.) suffixed; *m* (gram.) suffix
sufismo *m* Sufism
sufra *f* ridgeband
sufragación *f* defrayal or defrayment
sufragáneo -a *adj* suffragan
sufragar §59 *va* to help, support, favor; to defray; *vn* (Am.) to vote
sufragio *m* suffrage; help, succor; (eccl.) suffrage; **en sufragio de** for the benefit of
sufragismo *m* woman suffrage
sufragista *mf* suffragist; woman-suffragist; *f* suffragette
sufrible *adj* sufferable
sufridero -ra *adj* sufferable, endurable; *f* dolly (*in riveting*); iron block or plate for placing under piece to be punched
sufrido -da *adj* long-suffering; serviceable (*color*); complaisant (*husband*); *m* complaisant husband
sufridor -dora *adj* suffering; *mf* sufferer; *m* holder-on (*in riveting gang*)
sufriente *adj* suffering
sufrimiento *m* suffering; sufferance, tolerance
sufrir *va* to suffer; to undergo; to support, hold up; to buck up (*a rivet*); to take (*an examination*); to tolerate; *vn* to suffer
sufusión *f* (path.) suffusion; (path.) cataracts
sugerencia *f* suggestion
sugerente *adj* suggestive
sugerible *adj* suggestible
sugeridor -dora *adj* suggesting
sugerir §62 *va* to suggest; **sugerir** + *inf* to suggest + *ger*
sugestión *f* suggestion; (psychol.) suggestion
sugestionable *adj* suggestible, easily influenced
sugestionador -dora *adj* suggesting, suggestive, influencing
sugestionar *va* to suggest (*by hypnosis*); to influence
sugestivo -va *adj* suggestive, stimulating, striking
suicida *adj* suicidal; *mf* suicide (*person*)
suicidar *va* to force suicide on; *vr* to commit suicide
suicidio *m* suicide (*act*)
suite *f* (mus.) suite
suizo -za *adj & mf* Swiss; *f* fracas, row; (*cap.*) *f* Switzerland
sujeción *f* subjection; surrender; fastening; fastener; (rhet.) rhetorical question
sujetador *m* fastener, clamp, anchor, clip
sujetahilo *m* (elec.) binding post
sujetapapel *m* paper finger (*of typewriter*)
sujetapapeles *m* (*pl:* **-les**) paper clip
sujetar *va* to subject; to subdue; to fasten, hold, tighten; *vr* to subject oneself, to submit; to stick, adhere
sujetatubos *m* (*pl:* **-bos**) pipe clamp
sujeto -ta *adj* subject, liable; fastened; (Am.) able, capable; *m* (gram., med., philos., psychol. & log.) subject; fellow, individual; **buen sujeto** brick, good egg
sulfadiacina *f* (pharm.) sulfadiazine
sulfanilamida *f* (pharm.) sulfanilamide
sulfapiridina *f* (pharm.) sulfapyridine
sulfarsfenamina *f* (pharm.) sulpharsphenamine
sulfas *fpl* (pharm.) sulfas, sulfa drugs
sulfatación *f* sulfation; (elec.) sulfation
sulfatado *m* sulfation
sulfatador *m* (agr.) sprayer (*device*)
sulfatar *va* to sulfate; (elec.) to sulfate; (agr.) to spray (*vines*) with copper sulfate
sulfatiazol *m* (pharm.) sulfathiazole
sulfato *m* (chem.) sulfate; **sulfato de cobre** (chem.) copper sulfate; **sulfato ferroso** (chem.) ferrous sulfate
sulfhídrico -ca *adj* (chem.) sulfhydric or sulphydric
sulfito *m* (chem.) sulfite
sulfonal *m* (pharm.) sulfonal
sulfonamida *f* (chem.) sulfonamide
sulfuración *f* sulfuration
sulfurar *va* to sulfurate; to anger, to annoy; *vr* to get angry, get furious
sulfúreo -a *adj* sulphureous, sulphury
sulfúrico -ca *adj* sulfuric; (chem.) sulfuric
sulfuro *m* (chem.) sulfid or sulfide; **sulfuro de hidrógeno** (chem.) hydrogen sulfide; **sulfuro ferroso** (chem.) ferrous sulfide
sulfuroso -sa *adj* sulfurous; (chem.) sulfurous
sultán *m* sultan; (coll.) sheik (*great lover*)
sultana *f* sultana, sultaness
sultanato *m* sultanate (*government; territory*)
sultanía *f* sultanate (*territory*)
sultánico -ca *adj* sultanic
sulla *f* (bot.) sulla clover, French honeysuckle
suma *f* see **sumo**
sumador -dora *adj* adding; *mf* adder; **sumadora mecánica** adding machine
sumamente *adv* extremely, exceedingly
sumando *m* (math.) addend; added element, contribution
sumar *va* to add, to sum; to sum up; to amount to; *vn* to add; to amount; **sumar y restar** (arith.) to add and subtract; **suma y sigue** add and carry, carried forward; *vr* to add up; **sumarse a** to add up to; to be added to; to adhere to, to become attached to
sumaria *f* see **sumario**
sumariar *va* (law) to indict
sumario -ria *adj* summary; *m* summary, résumé; (law) indictment; *f* (law) indictment (*in military case*)
sumarísimo -ma *adj super* (law) swift, expeditious
sumatrino -na *adj & mf* Sumatran
sumergible *adj* submersible, sinkable; *m* submersible (*boat*)
sumergimiento *m* submersion
sumergir §42 *va & vr* to submerge, submerse
sumerio -ria *adj & mf* Sumerian; *m* Sumerian (*language*)
sumersión *f* submersion
sumidad *f* top, apex, summit
sumidero *m* drain, sewer; sink; sump

sumiller *m* butler (*of royal household*)
sumillería *f* butlership (*in royal household*)
suministración *f* provision, supply
suministrador -dora *adj* providing, supplying; *mf* provider, supplier
suministrar *va* to provide, supply
suministro *m* provision, supply; **suministros** *mpl* (mil.) supplies; **suministro de potencia** (rad.) power supply; **suministros para oficinas** office supplies
sumir *va* to sink; to press down; to overwhelm; (eccl.) to swallow (*the elements of Eucharist*); *vr* to sink; to be sunken (*said, e.g., of cheeks*); (Am.) to shrink, to shrivel; (Am.) to cower; (Am.) to pull down (*e.g., a hat*)
sumisión *f* submission
sumiso -sa *adj* submissive
sumista *adj* compendiary; *mf* summarist; rapid calculator
sumo -ma *adj* high, great, extreme; supreme; **a lo sumo** at most, at the most; **de sumo** completely; **en sumo grado** exceedingly; *f* sum, addition; summary; sum and substance; summa (*of a branch of learning*); **en suma** in short, in a word
súmulas *fpl* compendium of logic
sunción *f* (eccl.) taking of Eucharistic elements (*by priest*)
suncho *m* hoop
suntuario -ria *adj* sumptuary
suntuosidad *f* sumptuousness, sumptuosity
suntuoso -sa *adj* sumptuous
supe *1st sg pret ind of* **saber**
supedáneo *m* pedestal, pedestal of a crucifix
supeditación *f* oppression, subjection
supeditar *va* to hold down, oppress, subject; *vr* to be oppressed, be held in subjection
súper *adj* (coll.) super (*excellent, superfine*)
superable *adj* superable; **difícilmente superable** hard to beat
superabundancia *f* superabundance
superabundante *adj* superabundant
superabundar *vn* to superabound
superación *f* surpassing, excelling; winning, overcoming; superiority
superádito -ta *adj* superadded
superar *va* to surpass, excel; to overcome, conquer
superávit *m* (com.) surplus, superavit
superbomba *f* superbomb
supercapitalización *f* overcapitalization
supercapitalizar §76 *va* to overcapitalize
supercarburante *m* high-test fuel
supercarretera *f* superhighway
superciliar *adj* (anat.) superciliary
superconductividad *f* superconductivity
superconductor *m* (elec.) superconductor
superchería *f* fraud, deceit
superchero -ra *adj* fraudulent, deceitful, tricky; *mf* cheat, trickster
superdominante *f* (mus.) superdominant
supereminente *adj* supereminent
superentender §66 *va* to superintend, to supervise
supererogación *f* supererogation
supererogatorio -ria *adj* supererogatory
superespía *m* superspy
superestado *m* superstate
superestructura *f* superstructure
superfetación *f* superfetation
superficial *adj* superficial; (pertaining to) surface
superficialidad *f* superficiality
superficiario -ria *adj* (law) superficiary
superficie *f* surface; area; outside, exterior; **superficie de caldeo** or **calefacción** heating surface; **superficie de rodadura** (aut.) tread; **superficie de sustentación** or **superficie sustentadora** (aer.) airfoil
superfino -na *adj* superfine
superfluencia *f* great abundance
superfluidad *f* superfluity
superfluo -flua *adj* superfluous
superfortaleza *f* (aer.) superfortress, superfort
superfosfato *m* (chem. & agr.) superphosphate
superheterodino -na *adj* & *m* (rad.) superheterodyne
superhombre *m* superman
superhumeral *m* (eccl.) superhumeral
superintendencia *f* superintendence, superintendency, supervision
superintendente *mf* superintendent, supervisor; **superintendente del patio** (rail.) yardmaster
superior *adj* superior; upper; higher; **superior a** superior to; higher than; more than, greater than, larger than; *m* superior
superiora *f* superioress, mother superior
superiorato *m* superiorship
superioridad *f* superiority; authorities, higher authorities
superlación *f* superlativeness
superlativo -va *adj* superlative; (gram.) superlative; *m* (gram.) superlative
supermercado *m* supermarket
superno -na *adj* supreme, highest, supernal
supernumerario -ria *adj* supernumerary; (mil.) (on the) reserve; *mf* supernumerary
súpero -ra *adj* (bot.) superior, upper
superpista *f* superhighway
superpoblación *f* overpopulation
superpoblar §77 *va* to overpopulate
superpondré *1st sg fut ind of* **superponer**
superponer §69 *va* to superpose
superpongo *1st sg pres ind of* **superponer**
superposición *f* superposition; (geom.) superposition
superpotencia *f* (dipl. & elec.) superpower
superproducción *f* overproduction; superproduction
superpuesto -ta *pp of* **superponer**
superpuse *1st sg pret ind of* **superponer**
superreacción *f* or **superregeneración** *f* (rad.) superregeneration
superregenerativo -va *adj* (rad.) superregenerative
superscripción *f* (pharm.) superscription
supersensible *adj* supersensitive
supersónico -ca *adj* supersonic; *f* supersonics
superstición *f* superstition
supersticioso -sa *adj* superstitious
supérstite *adj* (law) surviving; *mf* (law) survivor
superstructura *f* superstructure
supert.te abr. of **superintendente**
supervención *f* supervention
supervendré *1st sg fut ind of* **supervenir**
supervengo *1st sg pres ind of* **supervenir**
superveniencia *f* var. of **supervención**
supervenir §92 *vn* var. of **sobrevenir**
supervigilancia *f* (Am.) superintendence, supervision
supervigilar *va* (Am.) to superintend, to supervise
supervine *1st sg pret ind of* **supervenir**
superviniendo *ger of* **supervenir**
supervisar *va* to supervise
supervisión *f* supervision
supervisor *m* supervisor
supervivencia *f* survival; (law) survivorship; **supervivencia de los más aptos** (biol.) survival of the fittest
superviviente *adj* & *mf* var. of **sobreviviente**
supervoltaje *m* (phys.) supervoltage
super-yo *m* (psychoanal.) superego
supinación *f* supination; (anat. & physiol.) supination
supinador *m* (anat.) supinator
supino -na *adj* supine; *m* (gram.) supine
súpito -ta *adj* sudden; (coll.) impatient; (dial.) sly, crafty; (Am.) dumfounded
suplantación *f* supplanting (*by treachery*); fraudulent alteration
suplantar *va* to supplant (*by treachery*); to alter fraudulently (*a document*)
supleausencias *mf* (*pl:* **-cias**) substitute
suplefaltas *mf* (*pl:* **-tas**) (coll.) substitute, fill-in
suplemental *adj* supplemental
suplementario -ria *adj* supplementary; (geom.) supplementary
suplemento *m* supplementing; supplement; excess fare; (gram.) complement; (trig.) supplement; **suplemento ilustrado** illustrated supplement (*e.g., of newspaper*)
suplente *adj* & *mf* substitute

supletorio -ria *adj* additional, supplementary
súplica *f* suppliance, supplication; petition; (law) petition; **a súplica** by request, by petition
suplicación *f* supplication; rolled waffle (*for making cones*); cone (*of dough*); (law) petition to a superior court against its sentence; **a suplicación** by petition
suplicacionero -ra *mf* waffle vendor, cone vendor
suplicante *adj & mf* suppliant or supplicant
suplicar §86 *va & vn* to supplicate, entreat, implore; (law) to petition (*a superior court*) against its sentence; **suplicar de la sentencia** (law) to petition against the sentence; **suplicar en revista** (law) to apply for a new trial
suplicatoria *f* (law) communication from a court to a superior court
suplicatorio *m* (law) communication from a court to a superior court; (law) communication from a court to the Senate or Congress requesting permission to initiate legal proceedings against a member of the legislative body
suplicio *m* torture; punishment, execution; place of execution; anguish; **último suplicio** capital punishment
suplidor -dora *adj & mf* substitute
suplir *va* to supplement, make up for; to replace, take the place of; to cover up (*someone's shortcomings*); (gram.) to understand
supl.te abr. of **suplente**
supón *2d sg impv of* **suponer**
supondré *1st sg fut ind of* **suponer**
suponedor -dora *mf* wrong guesser
suponer *m* (coll.) supposition; **§69** *va* to suppose; to assume; to imply, presuppose; to entail; to cause, impose; **suponer + *inf*** to pretend to + *inf;* **suponer que sí** to suppose so; *vn* to have weight, have authority
supongo *1st sg pres ind of* **suponer**
suposición *f* supposition; distinction, high position; imposture, falsehood
supositicio -cia *adj* supposititious
supositivo -va *adj* suppositional
supositorio *m* suppository
supradicho -cha *adj* above-mentioned
supramundano -na *adj* supermundane
supranacional *adj* supranational
supraorbital *adj* (anat.) supraorbital
suprarrenal *adj* (anat.) suprarenal
suprasensible *adj* supersensible
supraspina *f* (anat.) supraspinous fossa
supraspinoso -sa *adj* (anat.) supraspinous
suprema *f* see **supremo**
supremacía *f* supremacy
supremo -ma *adj* supreme; **hora suprema** or **momento supremo** supreme moment (*death*); **sacrificio supremo** supreme sacrifice; *f* Supreme Council of the Inquisition
supresión *f* suppression, elimination, omission
supresivo -va *adj* suppressive
supresor -sora *adj* suppressive; *mf* suppressor
suprimible *adj* suppressible
suprimir *va* to suppress, eliminate, do away with
suprior *m* (eccl.) subprior
sup.te abr. of **suplicante**
supuesto -ta *pp of* **suponer;** *adj* supposed, assumed, hypothetical; **esto supuesto** this being understood; **supuesto que** since, inasmuch as; *m* assumption, hypothesis; **dar por supuesto** to take for granted; **por supuesto** of course, naturally
supuración *f* suppuration
supurante *adj* suppurating, suppurative, runny
supurar *vn* to suppurate
supurativo -va *adj & m* suppurative
supuse *1st sg pret ind of* **suponer**
suputación *f* computation, calculation
suputar *va* to compute, to calculate
sur *m* south; south wind
surá *m* surah (*fabric*)
sural *adj* (anat.) sural
Suramérica *f* South America
surcador -dora *adj* ploughing; *m* plowman; *f* plowwoman
surcar §86 *va* to furrow; to plough, to plough through, to cut through; to streak through
surco *m* furrow; wrinkle, rut, cut; groove (*e.g., of a phonograph record*); **echarse en el surco** (coll.) to lie down on the job
surcoreano -na *adj & mf* South Korean
surculado -da *adj* (bot.) single-stemmed
súrculo *m* (bot.) single stem
surculoso -sa *adj* (bot.) var. of **surculado**
sureño -ña *adj* southern
surgente *adj* spouting, spurting
surgidero *m* (naut.) anchorage, anchoring place
surgimiento *m* spouting, spurting; rise, appearance
surgir §42 *vn* to spout, spurt; to issue, spring up, come forth; to arise, appear; (naut.) to anchor
suripanta *f* (hum.) chorine; (scornful) slut, jade
surnia *f* (orn.) hawk owl
suroriental *adj* southeastern
surrealismo *m* surrealism
surrealista *adj* surrealist, surrealistic; *mf* surrealist
sursuncorda *m* (coll.) anonymous big shot, big so-and-so
surtida *f* see **surtido**
surtidero *m* conduit, outlet; jet, fountain
surtido -da *adj* assorted; *m* spouting, spurting; assortment; line, supply; **de surtido** in common use, stock; *f* side door; sally, sortie; (fort.) sally port; (naut.) slipway
surtidor -dora *adj* supplying, providing; *mf* supplier, provider; *m* jet, spout, fountain; **surtidor de gasolina** gasoline pump
surtimiento *m* provision, supply
surtir *va* to provide, furnish, stock; **surtir efecto** to have the desired effect, to work; *vn* to spout, spurt, shoot up
surto -ta *adj* quiet, still; anchored
sus *interj* take heart!, get going!
Susana *f* Susan
suscepción *f* assumption, reception
susceptibilidad *f* susceptibility; touchiness; (magnetism) susceptibility
susceptible *adj* susceptible; touchy
susceptivo -va *adj* susceptible
suscitación *f* stirring up, provoking
suscitador -dora *mf* originator, promoter
suscitar *va* to stir up, provoke; to raise (*doubts, a question*)
suscribir §17, 9 *va & vr* var. of **subscribir**
suscripción *f* var. of **subscripción**
suscritor -tora *mf* var. of **subscritor**
susidio *m* anxiety, uneasiness, disturbance
susodicho -cha *adj* above-mentioned
suspender *va* to hang; to suspend; to astonish, astound; to postpone; (educ.) to flunk; (educ.) to condition; *vr* to be suspended or stopped; to rear (*said of a horse*)
suspensión *f* suspension; amazement, astonishment; (rhet.) suspension; **suspensión de armas** suspension of arms, suspension of hostilities; **suspensión de fuegos** cease fire
suspensivo -va *adj* suspensive; suspension (*points*)
suspenso -sa *adj* suspended, hanging; baffled, bewildered; (theat.) closed; *m* (educ.) condition; **en suspenso** in suspense, suspended
suspensores *mpl* (Am.) suspenders
suspensorio -ria *adj* suspensory; *m* suspensory, supporter, jockstrap
suspicacia *f* suspicion, distrust; suspiciousness
suspicaz *adj* (*pl:* **-caces**) suspicious, distrustful
suspirado -da *adj* longed for
suspirar *vn* to sigh; **suspirar por** to sigh for, to long for, to covet
suspiro *m* sigh; glass whistle; ladyfinger; (bot.) morning-glory; (mus.) crotchet, quarter rest; **exhalar el último suspiro** to breathe one's last
suspirón -rona *adj* full of sighs
suspiroso -sa *adj* heavy-breathing
sustancia *f* var. of **substancia**
sustanciación *f* var. of **substanciación**
sustancial *adj* var. of **substancial**
sustancialidad *f* var. of **substancialidad**
sustanciar *va* var. of **substanciar**

sustancioso -sa *adj* var. of **substancioso**
sustantífico -ca *adj* var. of **substantífico**
sustantivar *va* var. of **substantivar**
sustantivo -va *adj & m* var. of **substantivo**
sustentable *adj* sustainable, arguable
sustentación *f* sustentation; support, prop; (aer.) lift; (rhet.) suspension
sustentáculo *m* prop, support, stay; holder
sustentador -dora *adj* sustaining; *mf* sustainer, support
sustentamiento *m* sustentation, sustenance
sustentante *adj* sustaining; *m* support; defender (*of a thesis*)
sustentar *va* to sustain, support, feed; to maintain; to defend (*a thesis*)
sustento *m* sustenance, support, food; maintenance
sustitución *f* var. of **substitución**
sustituíble *adj* var. of **substituíble**
sustituir §41 *va & vn* var. of **substituir**
sustitutivo -va *adj & m* var. of **substitutivo**
sustituto -ta *mf* var. of **substituto**
susto *m* scare, fright, dread; **darse un susto** to have a good scare
sustracción *f* var. of **substracción**
sustraendo *m* var. of **substraendo**
sustraer §88 *va & vr* var. of **substraer**
susurración *f* whispering, whispering gossip
susurrador -dora *adj* whispering; *mf* whisperer
susurrar *va* to whisper; *vn* to whisper, murmur, rustle, purl, hum; to be whispered about, be bruited about; *vr* to be whispered about, be bruited about
susurrido *m* murmur, rustle, purling, hum
susurro *m* whisper, murmur, rustle, purling, hum
susurrón -rrona *adj* (coll.) whispering; *mf* (coll.) whisperer
sutás *m* braid
sutil *adj* subtle, subtile; keen, observant
sutileza *f* subtlety, subtility; animal instinct; **sutileza de manos** skill, dexterity, skillful performance; slick pickpocketing
sutilidad *f* subtlety, subtility
sutilizador -dora *adj* hairsplitting; *mf* hairsplitter, quibbler
sutilizar §76 *va* to make thin, to taper; to file, to polish; to discuss with acuity; *vn* to split hairs, to quibble
sutorio -ria *adj* (pertaining to a) shoemaker
sutura *f* (anat., bot., surg. & zool.) suture; **sutura coronal** (anat.) coronal suture
suyo -ya *adj poss* of his, of hers, of yours, of theirs, e.g., **un amigo suyo** a friend of his, of hers, etc.; *pron poss* his, hers, yours, theirs, its, one's; **de suyo** on his (her, etc.) own. on his (her, etc.) own accord: naturally, inherently; **hacer de las suyas** (coll.) to be up to one's old tricks; **los suyos** his (her, your, their) friends; his (her, etc.) men; his (her, etc.) side; **salirse con la suya** to come out ahead, to have one's way; to carry one's point; **ver la suya** (coll.) to have or get one's chance
suzeranía *f* (feud.) suzerainty
suzerano *m* (feud.) suzerain
suzón *m* (bot.) groundsel
svástica *f* swastika

T

T, t *f* twenty-third letter of the Spanish alphabet
t. abr. of **tarde**
ta *interj* careful!, easy!; **¡ta, ta!** rat-a-tat!; tut, tut!
taba *f* anklebone; knucklebone (*of sheep*); knucklebones, dibs (*game*); (Am.) jackstones; (Am.) vent in water pipe; **calentársele a uno las tabas** (Am.) to redouble one's efforts; (Am.) to be anxious to get married; **dar** or **darse vuelta la taba** (Am.) to take a turn (*said of fate*); **darle taba a uno** to have a long-drawn-out conversation with someone; **darle** or **pegarle a uno en la taba** (Am.) to hit someone where it hurts; **menear las tabas** (coll.) to hustle about; **tomar la taba** (coll.) to start talking quickly as soon as another stops
tabacal *m* tobacco field
tabacalero -ra *adj* (pertaining to) tobacco; *mf* tobacco grower; tobacconist; tobacco twister
tabacazo *m* (Am.) tobacco potion (*given as poison*)
tabaco *m* tobacco; cigar; snuff; black rot; **tabaco cimarrón** (bot.) marijuana (*Nicotiana glauca*); **tabaco de humo** smoking tobacco; **tabaco de montaña** arnica; **tabaco de pipa** pipe tobacco; **tabaco de polvo** snuff; **tabaco en rama** leaf tobacco, wrappers; **tabaco indio** (bot.) Indian tobacco; **tabaco torcido** twisted tobacco, cigars; **tomar tabaco** to take snuff; *adj invar* (Am.) bold, determined
tabacoso -sa *adj* (coll.) snuffy (*addicted to use of snuff*); tobacco-stained; attacked by black rot
tabalada *f* (coll.) fall on the behind; (coll.) spanking
tabalario *m* (coll.) behind
tabalear *va* to rock, to shake; *vn* to drum with the fingers; *vr* to rock, to shake
tabaleo *m* rocking; drumming
tabanazo *m* (coll.) spanking; (coll.) slap (*in the face*)
tabanco *m* food stand; stand, stall
tabanera *f* place full of horseflies
tábano *m* (ent.) gadfly, horsefly
tabanque *m* treadle wheel (*of potter's wheel*)
tabaola *f* hubbub, uproar
tabaque *m* wicker basket; large tack
tabaquera *f* see **tabaquero**
tabaquería *f* cigar store, tobacco store; tobacco factory
tabaquero -ra *adj* (pertaining to) tobacco; *mf* tobacconist; cigar maker; *f* snuffbox; bowl (*of a tobacco pipe*)
tabaquismo *m* (path.) tobaccoism
tabaquista *mf* tobacco expert; inveterate user of tobacco
tabardete *m* or **tabardillo** *m* (coll.) sunstroke; (coll.) crazy annoying fellow, harum-scarum
tabardo *m* tabard
tabarra *f* (coll.) tiring speech, boring conversation, bore
tabarrera *f* (coll.) terrible bore
tabasco *f* tabasco (*sauce*); *m* (Am.) banana
tabellar *va* to fold (*cloth*) leaving the selvage visible; to mark with a trademark
taberna *f* tavern, saloon
tabernáculo *m* tabernacle; (*cap.*) *m* (Bib.) Tabernacle
tabernario -ria *adj* vulgar, low; (pertaining to a) saloon
tabernera *f* saloonkeeper's wife; barmaid
tabernería *f* saloon business
tabernero *m* saloonkeeper; bartender
tabes *f* (path.) consumption
tabí *m* (*pl:* **-bíes**) tabby, watered fabric
tabica *f* iron or copper plate; riser (*of stairs*); (arch.) covering board
tabicar §86 *va* to wall up; to close up
tabicón *m* thick partition
tábido -da *adj* rotted; wasted by consumption
tabique *m* thin wall, partition; (Am.) brick; **tabique de panderete** brick-on-edge partition; **tabique sordo** wall with air space
tabiquería *f* partitions
tabiquero *m* partition builder
tabla *f* board; table (*list, contents, synopsis in parallel columns, etc.*); slab (*of stone*); sheet of metal; flat diamond; wide part (*of member of body*); garden patch or bed; strip of land; land between two rows of trees; butcher shop; butcher-shop counter; box pleat; calm stretch of river; broad face of log; panel, painting on a board; (anat.) table; (Am.) cake of chocolate; **tablas** *fpl* boards (*stage*); draw, tie; barrier (*bull ring*); **a raja tabla** (coll.) at any cost, regardless; (Am.) promptly, vigorously; **cantarle a uno la tabla** (Am.) to lay down the law to someone; **en las tablas** (Am.) penniless; **escapar en una tabla** to have a narrow escape; **hacer tablas** to be tied, to be deadlocked; **hacer tabla rasa de** to do without; (Am.) to remove obstacles to; **no dar en tablas** (Am.) not to hit the nail on the head; **no saber por dónde van las tablas** to not know what is going on; **quedar tablas** to be tied, to be deadlocked; **salir a las tablas** to go upon the boards (*the stage*); **salir con las tablas** (Am.) to fail; **salvarse en una tabla** to have a narrow escape; **sobre tabla** (Am.) quickly, extemporaneously; **subir a las tablas** to go upon the boards (*the stage*); **tener tablas** to have stage presence, to be at home on the stage; **tabla de juego** gambling house, gambling stand; **tabla de conversión** conversion table; **tabla de la vaca** noisy group; **tabla de lavar** washboard; **tabla de materias** table of contents; **tabla de multiplicar** multiplication table; **tabla de planchar** ironing board; **tabla de salvación** last recourse, lifesaver; **tabla periódica** (chem.) periodic table; **tabla rasa** unpainted board; untrained mind; clean slate; **Tabla Redonda** (myth.) Round Table (*knights of King Arthur*); **tablas alfonsinas** Alphonsine Tables (*astronomical tables prepared by order of Alfonso X of Castile in 1252*); **tablas de la ley** (Bib.) tables of the law; **tablas reales** backgammon
tablachina *f* wooden shield
tablacho *m* sluice, floodgate
tablado *m* flooring; stage; scaffold; bottom boards of a bedstead
tablaje *m* boarding, planking; shed; gambling house
tablajería *f* gambling; butcher shop
tablajero *m* scaffold builder, stand builder; keeper of a gambling house; butcher
tablar *m* group of garden plots; calm stretch of river; sideboard (*of wagon or cart*)
tablazo *m* blow with a board; shoal
tablazón *f* boarding, planking; (naut.) decking, deck flooring
tableado *m* box pleat
tablear *va* to cut into boards; to divide (*e.g., a garden*) into plots or patches; to level or grade (*ground*) with a board or roller; to hammer into plates; to make box pleats in
tablero *m* board; panel; sheet (*of metal, etc.*); top, table top; timber to be sawed; checkerboard, chessboard; counter; gambling house; cutting table (*of tailor*); (wooden) blackboard; (floor) nail; floor (*of bridge*); (elec.) switchboard; (orn.) petrel; **tableros** *mpl* wooden fence or barrier around inside of bull ring; **estar en el tablero** to be exposed to public

view, to be in the limelight; **poner** or **traer al tablero** to risk; **tablero de ajedrez** chessboard; **tablero de damas** checkerboard; **tablero de instrumentos** (aut.) dashboard, instrument panel
tableta *f* small board; floor board; tablet, writing pad; lozenge; cake of chocolate; **tabletas** *fpl* clappers used in begging for hospitals; **estar en tabletas** to be uncertain, to be dubious (*said of the success of a thing*); **quedarse tocando tabletas** (coll.) to be disappointed, to lose all
tableteado *m* rattling sound
tabletear *vn* to rattle
tableteo *m* rattle, rattling
tablilla *f* small board; slat; shingle; bulletin board; tablet, slab; cushion of billiard table between two pockets; (surg.) splint; showcase; **tablillas de encuadernar** (b.b.) pressing boards; **tablillas de San Lázaro** clappers used in begging for hospitals
tablón *m* plank, heavy board; beam; strake
tabloncillo *m* small plank; seat in the last row (*in bull ring*)
tabloza *f* (painter's) palette
tabú *m* (*pl:* **-búes**) tabu or taboo
tabuco *m* hovel, shack, shanty
tabulación *f* tabulation
tabulador *m* tabulator
tabular *adj* tabular; *va* to tabulate
taburete *m* taboret, stool; small velvet-back chair without arms; **taburetes** *mpl* semicircular rows of benches in the pit (*of old Madrid theaters*); **taburete de piano** piano stool
tac *m* tick (*of clock, heart, etc.*)
taca *f* spot, stain; small closet; crucible plate
tacada *f* stroke (*at billiards*)
tacamaca, tacamacha, or **tacamahaca** *f* (bot.) tacamahac (*tree and resin*)
tacana *f* gray silver ore
tacañear *vn* to be stingy; (archaic) to be cunning
tacañería *f* stinginess; (archaic) cunning
tacaño -ña *adj* stingy, miserly; (archaic) cunning, deceitful
tacar §86 *va* to spot, to mark
tacazo *m* stroke with a cue
taceta *f* copper bowl for pouring olive oil from one vessel to another
tacita *f* little cup; demitasse
tácito -ta *adj* tacit; silent; (*cap.*) *m* Tacitus
taciturnidad *f* taciturnity; melancholy
taciturno -na *adj* taciturn; melancholy
taclobo *m* (zool.) tridacna (*bivalve and shell*)
taco *m* bung, plug; wad, wadding; billiard cue; popgun; rammer; pad; block; almanac pad; package; (coll.) snack, bite to eat; (coll.) drink of wine; (coll.) muddle, mess; (coll.) oath; (Am.) heel (*of shoe*); (Am.) sport; (Am.) rolled maize tortilla; **soltar tacos** (coll.) to swear; **taco de alisar** sanding block; **taco de billetes** pad or block of tickets
tacómetro *m* tachometer
tacón *m* heel (*part of shoe that raises heel of foot*)
taconazo *m* kick with the heel
taconear *va* (Am.) to fill, pack, stuff; *vn* to click the heels; to strut
taconeo *m* clicking of the heels (*in walking or dancing*)
táctico -ca *adj* tactical; *m* tactician; *f* tactics; (mil.) tactics; **gran táctica** (mil.) grand tactics
táctil *adj* tactile, tactual
tactismo *m* (biol.) taxis
tactivo -va *adj* tactual
tacto *m* (sense of) touch; skill; touch (*of piano, pianist, typewriter, or typist*); tact; **al tacto** by touch; **tacto de codos** (mil.) alignment shoulder to shoulder; (fig.) perfect union
tacuaco -ca *adj* (Am.) chubby
tacha *f* fault, defect, flaw; large tack
tachadura *f* erasure
tachar *va* to erase; to strike out; to blame, find fault with; (law) to challenge (*a witness*)
tacho *m* (Am.) boiler with round bottom; (Am.) evaporator, sugar pan; (Am.) tin (*sheet*); (Am.) coffee pot, tea pot; **irse al tacho** (Am.) to fail, to collapse, to die
tachón *m* scratch, erasure; ribbon, trimming; gimp nail, gilt-headed tack, silver-headed tack
tachonar *va* to adorn with ribbon or trimming; to adorn with ornamental tacks; to spangle, to stud
tachonería *f* ornamental work with gimp nails
tachoso -sa *adj* defective, faulty
tachuela *f* large-headed tack, hobnail; bowl; (prov.) crook, rascal; (Am.) metal warming bowl; (Am.) tin cup; (Am.) runt, half pint
Tadeo *m* Thaddeus
tafanario *m* (coll.) buttocks, behind
tafetán *m* taffeta; **tafetanes** *mpl* flags, colors; (coll.) finery; **tafetán adhesivo** adhesive tape; **tafetán de heridas** or **tafetán inglés** court plaster
tafia *f* (Am.) tafia or taffia (*rum*)
tafilete *m* morocco, morocco leather, shagreen; sweatband; **tafilete de Levante** Levant morocco
tafiletear *va* to adorn or finish with morocco leather
tafiletería *f* art of dressing morocco leather; morocco-leather shop
tafón *m* (zool.) striated sea gastropod (*Taphon striatus*)
tafurea *f* flat-bottomed boat for transporting horses
tagalo -la *mf* Tagalog; *m* Tagalog (*language*)
tagarnina *f* (bot.) Spanish oyster plant, golden thistle; (coll.) poor cigar
tagarote *m* (orn.) sparrow hawk; scrivener; (coll.) gawk; (coll.) gentleman sponger
tagarotear *vn* to write in a bold sweeping hand
tagide *adj* (poet.) of the Tagus
tagua *f* (bot.) ivory palm; (Am.) coot, mud hen
taguán *m* (zool.) flying squirrel
taha *f* district, region
tahalí *m* (*pl:* **-líes**) baldric; leather box (*to carry the Koran or Christian relics and prayers*)
taharal *m* var. of **tarayal**
taheño -ña *adj* red (*hair*); red-bearded
tahitiano -na *adj* & *mf* var. of **taitiano**
tahona *f* horse-driven flour mill; bakery
tahonero -ra *mf* miller; baker; *f* miller's wife; baker's wife
tahúr -húra *adj* gambling; cheating; *mf* gambler; cheat
tahurería *f* gaming house, gambling den; gambling; cheating
taicún *m* tycoon (*hereditary lord of Japan*)
taifa *f* faction, party; (coll.) bad lot, gang of bums
tailandés -desa *adj* & *mf* Thai; *m* Thai (*language*)
Tailandia *f* Thailand
taima *f* slyness, slickness, crookedness; (Am.) sullenness, stubbornness
taimado -da *adj* sly, slick, crafty; (Am.) sullen, gruff
taimar *vr* (Am.) to sulk, be stubborn
taimería *f* slyness, slickness, crookedness
taita m (coll.) daddy
taitiano -na *adj* & *mf* Tahitian
taja *f* cut, division; shield; saddle frame
tajada *f* see **tajado**
tajadera *f* curved chopping knife; chopping block; cold chisel
tajadero *m* chopping block
tajadilla *f* small slice; chopped lungs; (prov.) slice of orange or lemon eaten as a relish with brandy
tajado -da *adj* steep, sheer; *f* cut, slice; (coll.) hoarseness; (hum.) drunk; (Am.) slash, gash; **hacer tajadas** (coll.) to slash up, to cut to pieces; **sacar tajada** (coll.) to look out for number one
tajador -dora *adj* cutting, chopping; *mf* cutter, chopper; *m* chopping block
tajadura *f* cutting, slicing, chopping
tajalápiz *m* (*pl:* **-pices**) (Am.) pencil sharpener
tajamar *m* cutwater (*of bridge or ship*); (Am.) dike, dam
tajamiento *m* var. of **tajadura**
tajante *adj* cutting, sharp; incisive; complete, total; *m* butcher
tajaplumas *m* (*pl:* **-mas**) penknife
tajar *va* to cut, slice, chop; to sharpen (*pencil*)
tajea *f* culvert, drainpipe

tajo *m* cut; edge; trench; steep cliff; chopping block; block (*on which a condemned person is beheaded*); line of progress (*of gang of reapers, miners, pavers, etc.*); (*cap.*) *m* Tagus
tajón *m* chopping block
tajuela *f* three-legged rustic stool
tajuelo *m* three-legged rustic stool; (mach.) pillow block
tal *adj indef* such, such a; this; *pron indef* so-and-so; such a thing; someone; *adv* so; in such a way; **como tal** as such; **con tal (de) que** provided (that); **el tal** that; that one; that fellow, e.g., **el tal Juan** that fellow John; **no tal** no, no; **¿qué tal?** how?; hello!, how's everything?; **sí tal** yes, indeed; **un tal** a certain; one such; **tal como** just as; **tal cual** such as; an occasional, one or two, a few; so-so, middling, ordinary; **tal para cual** (coll.) two of a kind
tala *f* felling of trees; destruction, havoc; tipcat (*boys' game*); cat (*used in tipcat*); (mil.) abatis; (bot.) Argentine hackberry
talabarte *m* sword belt
talabartería *f* saddlery, harness shop
talabartero *m* saddler, harness maker
talacha *f*, **talache** *m* or **talacho** *m* (Am.) mattock
taladrador -dora *adj* boring, drilling; piercing; *mf* driller; *f* drill, drilling machine; drill press
taladramiento *m* boring, drilling; piercing
taladrante *adj* boring, drilling; piercing; (fig.) penetrating
taladrar *va* to bore, drill, perforate; to pierce; to punch (*a ticket*); to get to the bottom of (*a problem*)
taladro *m* drill; auger; drill hole; drill press; **taladro de mano** hand drill; **taladro de pecho** breast drill; **taladro de trinquete** ratchet drill; **taladro mecánico** drill press
talamera *f* (hunt.) tree in which a decoy is placed
talamete *m* (naut.) forward deck
talámico -ca *adj* thalamic
tálamo *m* bridal bed; (anat. & bot.) thalamus; **tálamo óptico** (anat.) optic thalamus
talán *m* ding-dong
talanquera *f* breastwork, parapet; cover, place of refuge; (fig.) safety; (Am.) reed fence; **desde talanquera** (coll.) without taking any chances oneself
talante *m* performance; mien, countenance; desire, will, pleasure; **de buen talante** in a good mood; with good grace; **de mal talante** in a bad mood; with bad grace
talar *adj* long (*robe or gown*); **talares** *mpl* (myth.) talaria (*of Mercury*); *va* to fell (*trees*); to destroy, lay waste; (dial. & Am.) to prune
talásico -ca *adj* thalassic
talayote *m* (archeol.) talayot (*Balearic tower-shaped stone structure*)
talco *m* tinsel; (mineral.) talc; **talco en polvo** talcum powder
talcoso -sa *adj* talcose
talcualillo -lla *adj* (coll.) fair, fairly good, so-so; (coll.) somewhat better (*in health*)
taled *m* tallith
talega *f* bag, sack; bagful; hair bag; diaper; **talegas** *fpl* (coll.) money, wealth
talegalo *m* (orn.) brush turkey, mound bird
talego *m* big bag, sack; (coll.) big slob; **tener talego** (coll.) to have money tucked away
taleguilla *f* small bag; bullfighter's breeches; **taleguilla de la sal** (coll.) daily household expenses
talento *m* talent
talentoso -sa or **talentudo -da** *adj* talented
Tales *m* Thales
Talía *f* (myth.) Thalia
talio *m* (chem.) thallium
talión *m* talion
talionar *va* to punish by talion
talismán *m* talisman
talismánico -ca *adj* talismanic
talma *f* talma (*large cape or cloak*)
Talmud *m* Talmud
talmúdico -ca *adj* Talmudic
talmudista *m* Talmudist
talo *m* (bot.) thallus
talocha *f* mason's float
talófita *f* (bot.) thallophyte
talofítico -ca *adj* thallophytic
talón *m* (anat.) heel; heel (*part of shoe or stocking that covers heel of foot*); heelpiece; (arch.) heel (*of a timber*); (arch.) talon (*molding*); (aut.) flange, lug (*on a tire*); (mus.) heel (*of violin bow*); (naut.) heel (*of keel*); (rail.) heel (*of frog*); (com.) check, voucher, coupon (*detached, e.g., from a stub*); stub (*e.g., of check*); monetary standard; **a talón** (coll.) on foot; **apretar** or **levantar los talones** (coll.) to take to one's heels; **pisarle a uno los talones** (coll.) to be at one's heels, to tail after someone; (fig.) to keep up with someone; **talón de Aquiles** Achilles' heel (*vulnerable spot*)
talonada *f* kick with the heels
talonario -ria *adj* (pertaining to a) stub; *m* stub book, checkbook
talonazo *m* kick with the heel
talonear *vn* (coll.) to dash along
talonesco -ca *adj* (coll.) (pertaining to the) heel
talpa or **talparia** *f* mole, wen, talpa
talque *m* tasco (*refractory clay*)
talquita *f* talc schist
talud *m* slope, talus
talvina *f* almond-meal porridge
talla *f* cut; carving; engraving; height, stature; size (*of a person, of a dress*); ransom; reward; height-measuring scale; hand (*at cards*); (naut.) purchase block; (surg.) lithotomy; **poner talla contra** to offer a reward for (*e.g., a criminal*)
tallado -da *adj* shaped, formed; *m* carving; engraving; grinding (*of a lens*)
tallador -dora *mf* carver; cutter; engraver; (Am.) dealer, banker (*at cards*); *f* cutter, cutting machine; **talladora de engranajes** (mach.) gear cutter
talladura *f* carving; engraving; cutting
tallar *adj* ready for cutting into lumber (*said of trees or woodland*); *m* woodland ready for first cutting; young growth of trees; planting of young olive trees; *va* to carve; to engrave; to cut (*a precious stone*); to measure the height of; to appraise; to deal (*cards*); to grind (*a lens*); *vn* (Am.) to chat, converse; (Am.) to make love
tallarín *m* noodle
tallarola *f* knife for cutting velvet pile
talle *m* shape, figure, stature; waist (*of body and of garment*); fit; outline, appearance; (Am.) bodice
tallecer §34 *vn & vr* to shoot, to sprout
taller *m* shop, workshop; mill, factory; atelier, studio; laboratory; casters (*for vinegar and oil*); (educ.) workshop; **taller agremiado** closed shop; **taller de cepillado** planing mill; **taller de reparaciones** repair shop; service station; **talleres gráficos** printing establishment; **taller franco** open shop; **taller mecánico** machine shop; **taller penitenciario** workhouse
tallerista *m* shopworker
tallero -ra *mf* (Am.) vegetable dealer
tallista *mf* wood carver, sculptor
tallo *m* stem, stalk; sprout, shoot; (Am.) cabbage; **tallos** *mpl* (Am.) greens, fresh vegetables
tallón *m* ransom; reward
talludo -da *adj* long-stalked; tall, lanky; inveterate; aging, no longer young
tamal *m* (Am.) tamale; (Am.) intrigue
tamanduá *m* (*pl:* **-duaes**) (zool.) tamandua (*arboreal anteater*)
tamañamente *adv* as greatly
tamañito -ta *adj* so small; very small; disconcerted, confused
tamaño -ña *adj* so big; such a big; very big, very large; **abrir tamaños ojos** to open one's eyes wide; **tamaño como** as big as; *m* size; **tamaño extra** oversize; **tamaño natural** full size
támara *f* (bot.) date palm; growth of date palms; **támaras** *fpl* cluster of dates; brushwood
tamaricáceo -a *adj* (bot.) tamaricaceous
tamarilla *f* (bot.) rockrose (*Cistus clusii*)
tamarindo *m* (bot.) tamarind (*tree and fruit*)

tamarisco *m* (bot.) tamarisk
tamariz *m* (*pl:* **-rices**) (bot.) tamarisk
tamarrizquito -ta or **tamarrusquito -ta** *adj* (coll.) tiny, very small
tambaleante *adj* staggering, tottering, reeling
tambalear *vn & vr* to stagger, totter, reel
tambaleo *m* staggering, tottering, reeling
tambanillo *m* (arch.) tympanum
tambarillo *m* chest with arched lid
tambero -ra *adj* (Am.) (pertaining to an) inn; (Am.) (pertaining to) cattle; *mf* (Am.) innkeeper
también *adv* also, too
tambo *m* (Am.) inn, wayside inn; (Am.) dairy; **tambo de tíos** (Am.) shindy, pandemonium
tambor *m* drum (*cylinder*); (arch. & mus.) drum; (sew.) tambour; sieve, screen; (anat.) eardrum; coffee roaster; (Am.) drum (*container*); **a tambor** or **con tambor batiente** with drums beating; in triumph; **bordar a tambor** to tambour; **tambor mayor** (mil.) drum major
tambora *f* bass drum; (Am.) drum
tamborear *vn* to drum with the fingers
tamboreo *m* drumming with the fingers
tamboreta *f* (orn.) tambourine
tamborete *m* (naut.) cap (*used in joining spars*)
tamboril *m* tabor, timbrel, small drum
tamborilada *f* or **tamborilazo** *m* (coll.) bump, bump on one's bottom; (coll.) slap on the head or shoulders
tamborilear *va* to extol, praise to the skies; (print.) to tap with the planer; *vn* to drum
tamborilero *m* taborer, drummer
tamborilete *m* (mus.) taboret; (print.) planer
tamborín *m* tabor, timbrel
tamborino *m* tabor, timbrel; taborer
tamboritear *vn* to drum
tamboritero *m* taborer, drummer
tamborón *m* big bass drum
tambucho *m* (naut.) hood
Tamerlán *m* Tamerlane
Támesis *m* Thames
tamiz *m* (*pl:* **-mices**) sieve
tamizar §76 *va* to sift, to sieve
tamo *m* fuzz, fluff, dust
tamojo *m* var. of **matojo**
tampa *f* (Am.) tangled hair
tampar *va* (Am.) to tangle, confuse
tampoco *adv* neither, not either, e.g., **tampoco vino** or **no vino tampoco** he did not come either; **ni yo tampoco** nor I either
tampón *m* stamp pad
tamposo -sa *adj* (Am.) tangled, confused
tamtam *m* tom-tom
tamujo *m* (bot.) box-leafed broom
tamul *adj & mf* Tamil; *m* Tamil (*language*)
tan. abr. of **tangente**
tan *adv* so; **tan . . . como** or **cuan** as . . . as; **tan siquiera** at least; *m* boom (*of drum*)
tanaceto *m* (bot.) tansy
tanagra *f* (f.a.) Tanagra (*figurine*)
tanato *m* (chem.) tannate
tanda *f* turn; shift, relay; task; coat; layer; game, match (*especially of billiards*); lot, pack, flock; (Am.) show (*each of a continuous series of performances*); (Am.) habit, bad habit
tándem *m* (*pl:* **tándemes**) tandem
tandeo *m* distribution of irrigating water by turns
tanganillas; en tanganillas shaky, tottery
tanganillo *m* temporary prop or support
tángara *m* (orn.) tanager
tangencia *f* tangency
tangencial *adj* tangential
tangente *adj* tangent; (geom.) tangent; *f* (geom., trig. & mus.) tangent; **escapar, escaparse, irse** or **salir por la tangente** (coll.) to resort to subterfuges, to evade the issue
Tánger *f* Tangier
tangerino -na *adj & mf* Tangerine; *f* tangerine (*orange*)
tangibilidad *f* tangibility
tangible *adj* tangible
tango *m* tango (*dance and music*)
tangón *m* (naut.) outrigger, swinging boom
tanguear *vr* (Am.) to change parties
tánico -ca *adj* (chem.) tannic
tanino *m* (chem.) tannin
tano -na *adj & mf* (Am.) Neapolitan, Italian
tanque *m* tank; bee glue; dipper, drinking cup; (mil.) tank; **tanque del inodoro** toilet tank
tanqueta *f* (mil.) small tank
tantalato *m* (chem.) tantalate
tantálico -ca *adj* (chem.) tantalic
tantalio *m* (chem.) tantalum
tantalita *f* (mineral.) tantalite
tántalo *m* (chem.) tantalum; (orn.) wood ibis; (*cap.*) *m* (myth.) Tantalus
tantán *m* tom-tom; clanging (*e.g., of an anvil*)
tantarantán *m* rub-a-dub; (coll.) hard smack
tanteador -dora *mf* score keeper; *m* score board
tantear *va* to compare; to size up, take the measure of; to test, feel, feel out; to sketch, outline; to keep the score of; (Am.) to estimate; *vn* to keep score; (Am.) to grope, feel one's way; **¡tantee Vd.!** (Am.) fancy that!, just imagine!
tanteo *m* comparison; careful consideration; trial, test; feeler; trial and error; score; **al tanteo** (Am.) by sight, by guess
tanto -ta *adj* so much; such a big; as much; *pron* so much; as much; that; **tantos -tas** *adj & pron pl* so many; as many; **tanto** *adv* so much; so hard; so often; so long; as much; **algún tanto** somewhat, a little; **al tanto** at the same price; **al tanto de** because of; **a tanto** so far, to such a pass, to such an extent; **a tantos de** on a certain day in, on such and such a day in (*e.g., June*); **con tanto que** provided (that); **en tanto** or **entre tanto** in the meantime; **en tanto que** whereas, while; **estar al tanto de** to be or keep informed about, be aware of; **no ser para tanto** to be not so bad, to be not so serious; **otros tantos** as many others; **otro tanto** as much, the same thing; **poner al tanto de** to make aware of, to keep informed of; **por el tanto** at the same price; **por lo tanto** therefore; **por tanto** therefore, wherefore; **un tanto** somewhat, rather; **un tanto por ciento** a certain percentage; **y tantos** odd, or more, e.g., **veinte y tantos** twenty odd, twenty or more; **¡tanto bueno!** or **¡tanto bueno por aquí!** so good to see you!; **tanto como** or **cuanto** as much as; as well as; the same thing as; **tanto . . . como** as much . . . as; both . . . and; **tantos . . . como** as many . . . as; **tantos cual, cuanto** or **que** so many that; **tanto más** (or **menos**) **. . . más** (or **menos**) all the more (or less) . . . (in proportion) as . . . more (or less); **tanto más** (or **menos**) **cuanto que** all the more (or less) because; **tanto mayor (mejor, menos** or **peor)** all the more (better, less or worse); **tanto que** as soon as; *m* copy; counter, chip (*to keep score*); point (*in a score*); (Am.) part, portion; **apuntar** or **señalar los tantos** to keep score; **un tanto por cada día de trabajo** so much for each day's work
tanza *f* casting line
tañedor -dora *mf* player, musician
tañer §84 *va* to play (*a musical instrument*); *vn* to drum with the fingers
tañido *m* sound, tone; twang (*e.g., of guitar*); ring; tang (*ringing sound*)
tañimiento *m* playing an instrument
taño *m* tanbark
taoísmo *m* Taoism
taoísta *adj & mf* Taoist
tapa *f* lid, cover, top, cap; head (*of a cylinder, barrel, etc.*); gate (*of sluice*); shirt front; board cover (*of book*); lift or layer (*of heel*); (aut.) valve cap; **tapas** *fpl* (coll.) appetizer, free lunch; **levantarse** or **saltarse la tapa de los sesos** to blow one's brains out; **tapas de cocina** hot appetizers
tapaagujeros *m* (*pl:* **-ros**) var. of **tapagujeros**
tapabarro *m* (Am.) mudguard
tapaboca *f* slap in the mouth; muffler; (coll.) squelch, squelcher; **tapabocas** *m* (*pl:* **-cas**) muffler; (arti.) tampion
tapacete *m* (naut.) sliding awning
tapacubo or **tapacubos** *m* (*pl:* **-bos**) (aut.) hubcap
tapaculo *m* hip (*of dog rose*)
tapada *f* woman who hides her face with mantle or handkerchief

tapadera *f* lid, cover, cap; blind (*person who shields another*)
tapadero *m* plug, stopper
tapadillo *m* woman's hiding her face with mantle or handkerchief; (mus.) flute-stop of organ; **de tapadillo** secretly, under cover
tapadizo *m* shed
tapador -dora *adj* covering; *mf* coverer; *m* lid, cover, top; plug, stopper; *f* (Am.) bottle capper
tapadura *f* covering; hiding; stopping, obstructing
tapafunda *f* flap of a holster
tapagoteras *m* (*pl:* **-ras**) (Am.) roofer; (Am.) roofing cement, waterproofing material
tapagujeros *m* (*pl:* **-ros**) (coll.) poor plasterer, awkward mason; (coll.) substitute, makeshift (*person*)
tapajuntas *m* (*pl:* **-tas**) strip or molding covering crack between door frame or window frame and wall; bead (*on corner to protect plaster*)
tápalo *m* (Am.) shawl, muffler
tapamiento *m* var. of **tapadura**
tapanga *f* (Am.) housing, trappings
tapapecho *m* (Am.) chuck (*of beef*)
tapaporos *m* (*pl:* **-ros**) primer, filler
tapar *va* to cover; to cover up, to hide; to conceal (*a fugitive*); to plug, stop, stop up; to shut; to obstruct (*the view*); to wrap up; (Am.) to fill (*a tooth*); (Am.) to crumple, crush; **taparlas** (prov.) to inhale (*in smoking*); *vr* to cover oneself; to wrap up, bundle up
tapara *f* (Am.) gourd; **vaciarse como una tapara** (Am.) to spill everything one knows
tápara *f* var. of **alcaparra**
taparo *m* (bot.) gourd tree
taparrabo *m* loincloth; trunks, bathing trunks
tapera *f* (Am.) ruins; (Am.) shack, hovel
taperujar *vr* (coll.) to wrap one's face all up
taperujo *m* (coll.) badly fitting plug; (coll.) awkward way of covering the face
tapetado -da *adj* dark, dark-brown
tapete *m* rug; runner (*of carpet, lace, etc.*); table scarf; **estar sobre el tapete** to be on the carpet (*i.e., under discussion*); **tapete verde** card table, gambling table, green table
tapetito *m* coaster, mat
tapia *f* mud wall, adobe wall
tapiador *m* mud-wall builder
tapial *m* form or mold for making mud walls; (dial. & Am.) mud wall
tapiar *va* to wall up, to wall in, to inclose with a wall; to close up
tapicería *f* tapestries; upholstery; making of tapestry; tapestry shop; upholstery shop
tapicero *m* tapistery maker; carpet maker; carpet layer; upholsterer
tapido -da *adj* closely woven
tapiería *f* mud walls (*of a house, enclosure, etc.*)
tapioca *f* tapioca
tapir *m* (zool.) tapir
tapiz *m* (*pl:* **-pices**) tapestry; **tapiz gobelino** Gobelin tapestry
tapizado *m* upholstery
tapizar **§76** *va* to tapestry; to upholster; to carpet; to cover
tapón *m* stopper, cork; cap; bottle cap; plug, bung; (elec.) fuse; (surg.) tampon; **al primer tapón, zurrapas** (coll.) off to a bad start; **tapón de algodón** (surg.) swab; **tapón de cuba** (coll.) fat, squatty person; **tapón de cubo** (aut.) hubcap; **tapón de desagüe** drain plug; **tapón de llenado** (aut.) gas-tank cap, filler cap; **tapón de radiador** (aut.) radiator cap; **tapón de tráfico** traffic jam; **tapón de vaciado** (aut.) drain plug; **tapón fusible** (elec.) plug fuse
taponado *m* capping, plugging
taponamiento *m* (surg.) tamponage
taponar *va* to plug, stop up; (surg.) to tampon
taponazo *m* pop (*of a cork*)
taponería *f* corks, stoppers; cork factory; cork business; cork store
taponero -ra *adj* (pertaining to) cork; *mf* cork maker; cork dealer
tapsia *f* (bot.) deadly carrot
tapujar *vr* (coll.) to muffle one's face, to cover one's face
tapujo *m* muffler, cover held over the face; (coll.) concealment, subterfuge
taque *m* click (*of a door as it locks or latches*); rap, knock (*at a door*)
taqué *m* (aut.) tappet
taquera *f* rack or stand for billiard cues
taquicardia *f* (path.) tachycardia
taquigrafía *f* tachygraphy; shorthand, stenography; tachygraph
taquigrafiar **§90** *va* to stenograph, take down in shorthand
taquigráfico -ca *adj* tachygraphic or tachygraphical; stenographic, shorthand
taquígrafo -fa *mf* tachygraph or tachygrapher; stenographer
taquilita *f* (mineral.) tachylite
taquilla *f* file (*for letters, papers, etc.*); ticket rack; ticket window; ticket office; box office; take, gate (*money collected for a contest, show, etc.*); (Am.) inn, tavern
taquillero -ra *adj* box-office; *mf* ticket seller, ticket agent
taquimeca *mf* (coll.) shorthand-typist
taquimecanógrafo -fa *mf* shorthand-typist
taquimetría *f* tachymetry
taquimétrico -ca *adj* tachymetric
taquímetro *m* speedometer, tachymeter; (surv.) tachymeter
taquín *m* anklebone
taquisterol *m* (biochem.) tachysterol
taquistoscopio *m* tachistoscope
tara *f* tare (*deduction for weight*); tally (*split stick for recording transactions*); defect; allowance for weight; (Am.) noisemaker (*wooden rattle*); **menos la tara** (coll.) making due allowance for exaggeration
tarabilla *f* millclapper; catch (*to fasten a window*); turnbuckle; (coll.) millclapper, chatterbox; (coll.) jabber, nonsense; **soltar la tarabilla** (coll.) to talk a blue streak
tarabita *f* tongue (*of belt buckle*); (Am.) rope of rope railway
taracea *f* marquetry, inlaid work; inlaid floor
taracear *va* to inlay, to adorn with marquetry
tarado -da *adj* defective
taragallo *m* var. of **trangallo**
taragontía *f* var. of **dragontea**
taraje *m* var. of **taray**
tarambana *adj & mf* (coll.) crackpot
tarando *m* (zool.) reindeer
tarángana *f* cheap blood sausage
tarantela *f* tarantella (*dance and music*)
tarántula *f* (zool.) tarantula; (zool.) gecko, tarente
tarantulado -da *adj* var. of **atarantado**
tarar *va* to tare
tarara *f* or **tarará** *m* sound of trumpet
tararear *va & vn* to hum
tarareo *m* hum, humming
tararira *f* (coll.) noisy goings on; *mf* (coll.) blustery person
tarasca *f* dragon (*in Corpus Christi procession*); gluttony; (coll.) ugly wench, hag
tarascada *f* bite; (coll.) tart reply, rude answer
tarascar **§86** *va* to bite (*said of a dog*)
taray *m* (bot.) salt cedar
tarayal *m* growth of salt cedars
tarazana *f* or **tarazanal** *m* var. of **atarazana**
tarazar **§76** *va* to bite, to tear, or to lacerate with the teeth; to annoy, bother
tarazón *m* slice, chunk
tarbea *f* large hall
tardanza *f* slowness, delay, tardiness
tardar *vn* to be long; to be late; **a más tardar** at the latest; **tardar en** + *inf* to be long in + *ger;* to be late in + *ger;* **tardar . . . en** + *inf* to be . . . in + *ger* or to take . . . to + *inf,* e.g., **tardó dos horas en preparar su lección** he was two hours in preparing his lesson or he took two hours to prepare his lesson; *vr* to be long; to be late
tarde *adv* late; too late; **de tarde en tarde** from time to time; **hacerse tarde** to grow late; **más tarde o más temprano** sooner or later; **para luego es tarde** it's later than you think; (Am.) come on and do it, you'd better hurry up and do it; **tarde o temprano** sooner or later; *f* afternoon, evening; (fig.) evening (*of life*); **buenas tardes** good after-

noon, good evening; **de la tarde a la mañana** overnight; suddenly, in no time; unexpectedly
tardeada *f* (Am.) afternoon party
tardecer **§34** *vn* to grow late, to grow dark
tardecica or **tardecita** *f* nightfall, dusk
tardígrado -da *adj* (zool.) tardigrade
tardío -a *adj* late, delayed, tardy; slow; **tardíos** *mpl* late crops
tardo -da *adj* slow; late; slow, dull, dense
tardón -dona *adj* (coll.) slow, poky; *mf* (coll.) poke, slow poke
tarea *f* task, job; work; care, worry
tarifa *f* tariff; price list; rate; fare; (telp.) toll; **tarifa diferencial** (rail.) differential rate; **tarifa proteccionista** protective tariff; **tarifa recargada** extra fare
tarifar *va* to price; *vn* to quarrel, to fall out
tarificación *f* price fixing
tarima *f* stand; platform; stool; low bench; bunk; board
tarja *f* shield, buckler; tally (*split stick for recording transactions*); (coll.) blow, lash; **beber sobre tarja** (coll.) to drink on tick
tarjador -dora *mf* tally keeper
tarjar *va* to tally
tarjero -ra *mf* tally keeper
tarjeta *f* card; place card; title and imprint (*on a map*); (arch.) tablet; **tarjeta de buen deseo** or **tarjeta de felicitación** greeting card; **tarjeta de felicitación de Año Nuevo** New Year's card; **tarjeta de felicitación de Pascuas** Christmas card; **tarjeta de identidad** identity card; **tarjeta de negocios** business card; **tarjeta de visita** calling card, visiting card; **tarjeta navideña** Christmas card; **tarjeta perforada** punch card, punched card; **tarjeta postal** post card, postal card; **tarjeta registradora** timecard
tarjeteo *m* (coll.) exchange of visiting cards
tarjetero *m* card case; card file, card index
tarlatana *f* tarlatan
taro *m* (bot.) taro
tarpeyo -ya *adj* Tarpeian; (*cap.*) *f* Tarpeia
tarpón *m* (ichth.) tarpon
tarquín *m* mire, slime, mud
tarquinada *f* (coll.) rape
Tarquino *m* Tarquin
tarrago *m* (bot.) meadow sage
tarraja *f* var. of **terraja**
tarraya *f* casting net
tarrico *m* (bot.) saltwort
tarro *m* jar; milk pail; (Am.) horn; (Am.) high hat
tarsiano -na *adj* tarsal
tarso *m* (anat. & zool.) tarsus; (*cap.*) *f* Tarsus
tarta *f* tart; pan
tártago *m* (bot.) caper spurge; (coll.) misfortune; (coll.) poor joke, mean trick; **tártago de Venezuela** (bot.) castor-oil plant
tartaja *adj* (coll.) stuttering; *mf* (coll.) stutterer
tartajear *vn* to stutter
tartajeo *m* stuttering
tartajoso -sa *adj* stuttering; *mf* stutterer
tartalear *vn* (coll.) to stagger, to sway; (coll.) to be dumbfounded, be speechless
tartamudear *vn* to stutter, to stammer
tartamudeo *m* (act of) stuttering, stammering
tartamudez *f* (defect of) stuttering, stammering
tartamudo -da *adj* stuttering, stammering; *mf* stutterer, stammerer
tartán *m* Scotch plaid, tartan
tartana *f* tartana (*two-wheeled round-top carriage of Valencia*); rickety old railroad train; (naut.) tartan
tartanero *m* driver of a tartana
tartáreo -a *adj* Tartarean
Tartaria *f* Tartary
tartárico -ca *adj* var. of **tártrico**
tartarizar **§76** *va* to tartarize
tártaro -ra *adj* & *mf* Tartar; *m* (chem.) tartar; tartar (*on teeth*); **tártaro emético** (chem.) tartar emetic; (*cap.*) *m* (myth.) Tartarus (*underworld*)
tartera *f* pastry pan; lunch basket, dinner pail
tartrato *m* (chem.) tartrate
tártrico -ca *adj* tartaric
tartufo *m* hypocrite
taruga *f* (zool.) guemal (*Hippocamelus antisiensis*)
tarugo *m* wooden plug; wooden paving block; (Am.) cheat; (Am.) dolt
tarumba *adj* (coll.) confused, rattled; **volver tarumba** (coll.) to rattle; **volverse tarumba** (coll.) to get rattled
tas *m* stake (*small anvil*)
tasa *f* appraisal; measure, standard; rate; moderation; ceiling price
tasación *f* appraisal; regulation; **tasación de costas** (law) taxation
tasadamente *adv* with measure; scantily; (coll.) just right
tasador -dora *adj* appraising; *mf* appraiser; **tasador de avería** insurance adjuster
tasajo *m* jerked beef
tasar *va* to appraise; to regulate; to hold down, keep within bounds; to grudge; (law) to tax (*the costs*)
tasca *f* dive, joint
tascador *m* swingle, scutcher
tascar **§86** *va* to swingle, to scutch; to crunch (*grass*); to champ (*the bit*)
tasco *m* stalk of hemp or flax (*after scutching*)
tasconio *m* var. of **talque**
tasmanio -nia *adj* & *mf* Tasmanian; (*cap.*) *f* Tasmania
tasquera *f* (coll.) row, quarrel
tasquil *m* chip, splinter (*of stone*)
tastana *f* hard crust (*of dry earth*); membrane (*dividing the carpels or slices of, e.g., an orange*)
tastaz *m* brass-polishing powder
tasto *m* spoiled taste (*of food*)
tasugo *m* (zool.) badger
tata *m* see **tato**; *f* see **tato**
tatarabuelo -la *mf* great-great-grandparent; *m* great-great-grandfather; *f* great-great-grandmother
tataradeudo -da *mf* remote ancestor
tataranieto -ta *mf* great-great-grandchild; *m* great-great-grandson; *f* great-great-granddaughter
tátaro -ra *adj* & *mf* Tartar, Tatar
tatarrete *m* (coll.) old jar
tate *interj* be careful!, look out!; I get it!, I get you!
tato -ta *adj* stammering, lisping; *m* (dial. & Am.) little brother; (zool.) armadillo; *f* (coll.) nursemaid; (dial. & Am.) little sister; **andar a tatas** (coll.) to toddle; (coll.) to go on all fours; **tata** *m* (dial. & Am.) daddy
tatú *m* (*pl:* **-túes**) (zool.) tatouay
tatuaje *m* tattoo, tattooing
tatuar **§33** *va* & *vr* to tattoo
taujel *m* strip of wood, support of an arch
taujía *f* damascene, damascene work
taumaturgia *f* thaumaturgy
taumatúrgico -ca *adj* thaumaturgic or thaumaturgical
taumaturgo -ga *mf* thaumaturge, wonderworker
taurino -na *adj* taurine, bullfighting; *f* (chem.) taurine
Tauro *m* (astr. & geog.) Taurus
taurófilo -la *mf* bullfight fan
taurómaco -ca *adj* bullfighting, tauromachian; *mf* bullfighter, tauromachian
tauromaquia *f* bullfighting, tauromachy
tauromáquico -ca *adj* bullfighting, tauromachic
taurotraumatólogo *m* medical expert on bullfight wounds
tautoga *f* (ichth.) tautog
tautología *f* tautology
tautológico -ca *adj* tautological
tautomería *f* (chem.) tautomerism
tautómero *m* (chem.) tautomer
taxativamente *adv* rigorously
taxativo -va *adj* rigorous; (law) limitative
taxear *vn* (aer.) to taxi
taxi *m* taxi, taxicab; *f* taxi dancer
taxia *f* (biol.) taxis
taxidermia *f* taxidermy
taxidérmico -ca *adj* taxidermal
taxidermista *mf* taxidermist
taxímetro *m* taximeter
taxis *f* (biol. & surg.) taxis

taxista *mf* taxi driver
taxonomía *f* taxonomy
taxonómico -ca *adj* taxonomic
taxonomista *mf* taxonomist
taylorismo *m* industrial management, efficiency engineering
taz; taz a taz on an even basis; **taz con taz** (Am.) even, tied
taza *f* cup; basin (*of fountain*); bowl (*of toilet*); cup guard (*of sword*)
tazaña *f* dragon (*in Corpus Christi procession*)
tazar §76 *va & vr* to fray
tazón *m* bowl; (prov.) basin
T.B.O. abr. de **tebeo** (*libro cómico*)
te *pron pers & reflex* (used as object of verb) thee, to thee; you, to you; thyself, to thyself; yourself, to yourself; *f* T square; tee (*pipe*)
té *m* (bot.) tea; (bot.) fireweed; tea (*dried leaves; drink; afternoon reception*); **té bailable** tea dance, thé dansant; **té borde** or **de Méjico** (bot.) Mexican tea; **té del Canadá** (bot.) spiceberry; **té del Paraguay** (bot.) Paraguay tea; **té de Pékoë** pekoe; **té de Pensilvania** (bot.) Oswego tea; **té de Suecia** (bot.) twinflower; **té negro** black tea; **té verde** green tea
tea *f* torch, firebrand
teáceo -a *adj* (bot.) theaceous
teantropía *f* theanthropism
teatral *adj* theatrical
teatralidad *f* theatricality
teatrero -ra *mf* (Am.) theater-goer
teatro *m* theater; (fig.) theater (*e.g., of war*); (fig.) scene (*e.g., of an accident*); **dar teatro a** to ballyhoo; **teatro circular** arena theater, theater-in-the-round; **teatro de estreno** first-run house; **teatro de la ópera** opera house; **teatro de repertorio** stock company; repertory theater
teatrólogo -ga *mf* theater critic; actor; *f* actress
tebaico -ca *adj* Thebaic
tebaína *f* (chem.) thebaine
tebano -na *adj & mf* Theban
Tebas *f* Thebes (*of Egypt; of Greece*)
tebeo -a *adj & mf* Theban; *m* comic book
teca *f* (anat. & bot.) theca; (bot.) teak (*tree and wood*); reliquary
tecla *f* key (*of typewriter, piano, etc.*); touchy subject; **dar en la tecla** (coll.) to get the knack of it; (coll.) to fall into a habit; **tocar una tecla** (coll.) to try to start something; (coll.) to feel one's way; **tecla de cambio** shift key; **tecla de escape** margin release; **tecla de espacios** space bar, space key; **tecla del tabulador** tabulator key; **tecla de retroceso** backspacer; **tecla muerta** dead key; **tecla tabulatoria** tabulating key
teclado *m* keyboard (*of typewriter, piano, etc.*); **teclado manual** (mus.) manual (*of organ*); **teclado pedalero** (mus.) pedal keyboard; **teclado universal** standard keyboard (*of typewriter*)
tecle *m* (naut.) single whip
tecleado *m* fingering
teclear *va* (coll.) to feel out (*a matter, deal, etc.*); *vn* to run one's fingers over the keys, to type, to play the piano; to click; (coll.) to wiggle one's fingers; (coll.) to drum, to thrum
tecleo *m* fingering; touch; click (*of typewriter*)
tecnetio *m* (chem.) technetium
técnica *f* see **técnico**
tecnicidad *f* technicality (*technical character*)
tecnicismo *m* technical terminology; technicality (*technical term*)
técnico -ca *adj* technic, technical; *m* technician; expert; *f* technic or technics (*science of an art; skill*); technique (*method; skill*)
tecnicolor *m* technicolor
tecnocracia *f* technocracy
tecnócrata *mf* technocrat
tecnocrático -ca *adj* technocratic
tecnología *f* technology
tecnológico -ca *adj* technologic or technological
tecnólogo -ga *mf* technologist
tecolote *m* (orn.) eagle owl (*of Central America*); **estar tecolote** (Am.) to be tipsy
tectita *f* (geol.) tektite
tectónico -ca *adj* tectonic; *f* tectonics
techado *m* roof; **bajo techado** under cover, indoors
techador *m* roofer
techar *va* to roof, put a roof on
techo *m* ceiling; roof, cover; (aer.) ceiling; (fig.) roof (*house, home*); (slang) lid (*hat*); **subirse al techo** (coll.) to blow one's top; **techo de paja** thatched roof; **techo de servicio** (aer.) service ceiling
techumbre *f* ceiling; roof
tedero *m* cresset, fire basket
tedeum *m* (*pl:* **tedeum**) Te Deum
tediar *va* to loathe, to be sick of
tedio *m* tedium, ennui, boredom
tedioso -sa *adj* tedious, boresome
teelina *f* (biochem.) theelin
tegmen *m* (bot. & zool.) tegmen
tégula *f* (zool.) tegula
tegular *adj* tegular
tegumentario -ria *adj* tegumentary
tegumento *m* (anat., bot. & zool.) tegument
teína *f* (chem.) theine
teinada *f* cattle shed
teísmo *m* theism
teísta *adj* theistic; *mf* theist
teja *f* roofing tile; shovel hat; (bot.) yew; (bot.) linden; **a teja vana** with a plain tile roof; lightly, without concern; **a toca teja** (coll.) for cash; **de tejas abajo** (coll.) in the natural order, without help from above; (coll.) here below; **de tejas arriba** (coll.) in the supernatural order; (coll.) in the other world; **teja canalón** pantile, gutter tile; **teja de cimacio** pantile; **teja de madera** shingle; **teja romana** pantile
tejadillo *m* top, cover
tejado *m* tile roof; roof; **tejado a cuatro aguas** hip roof; **tejado a dos aguas** double-sloping roof; **tejado de media agua** single-sloping roof; **tejado de vidrio** (fig.) glass-house
tejamaní *m* (*pl:* **-níes**) (Am.) shake (*long shingle*)
tejamanil *m* (Am.) var. of **tejamaní**
tejano -na *adj & mf* Texan
tejar *m* tile works; *va* to tile, to roof with tiles
tejaroz *m* eaves
Tejas *m* Texas
tejavana *f* shed; building with plain tile roof; **a tejavana** lightly, without concern
tejedera *f* weaver (*woman*); (ent.) whirligig beetle
tejedor -dora *adj* weaving; (coll.) scheming; *mf* weaver; (coll.) schemer; *m* (ent.) water strider, water skipper; (orn.) weaver, weaver-bird
tejedura *f* weaving; texture
tejeduría *f* (art of) weaving; weaving mill
tejemaneje *m* (coll.) knack, cleverness; (Am.) scheming
tejer *va* to weave; (fig.) to weave (*a story, a plot*); *vn* to weave; **tejer y destejer** to blow hot and cold, to back and fill
tejera *f* see **tejero**
tejería *f* tile business; tile works, tile kiln
tejero -ra *mf* tile maker; *f* tile works
tejido *m* weave, texture; web; fabric, textile; tissue; (biol.) tissue; (fig.) tissue, web; **tejido adhesivo** (elec.) friction tape; **tejido conjuntivo** or **conectivo** (anat.) connective tissue; **tejido criboso** (bot.) sieve tissue; **tejido de encaje** lace fabric; **tejido de malla** netted fabric; **tejido de media** hosiery fabric; **tejido de punto** knitted fabric, jersey
tejo *m* disk, weight (*in shuffleboard*); quoit; bearing, pillow block; metal disk; (bot.) yew, yew tree
tejocote *m* (bot.) hawthorn; haw (*fruit*)
tejoleta *f* broken tile; brickbat; clapper
tejolote *m* (Am.) stone pestle
tejón *m* (zool.) badger; **tejón de Australia** (zool.) wombat; **tejón de Laponia** (zool.) glutton
tejonera *f* burrow of badgers
tejuela *f* broken tile; brickbat; saddletree
tejuelo *m* small tile; (b.b.) label; (b.b.) lettering; (mach.) pillow block
tela *f* cloth, fabric; skin (*e.g., of an onion*); film; web (*of an insect*); subject, something to talk

about; (b.b.) cloth; (paint.) canvas; (hunt.) canvas enclosure; (slang) dough (*money*); **poner en tela de juicio** to question, to doubt; **tela aislante** (elec.) insulating tape, friction tape; **tela de alambre** wire screen; **tela de araña** spider web, cobweb; **tela de crin** horsehair, haircloth; **tela de esmeril** emery cloth; **tela de punto** stockinet; **tela emplástica** court plaster; **tela metálica** chicken wire; **tela polímita** fabric made of many-colored threads

telada *f* gang, outfit, clique

telamón *m* (arch.) telamon

telangiectasia *f* (path.) telangiectasis

telar *m* loom; frame; embroidery frame; (b.b.) sewing press; (theat.) gridiron

telaraña *f* spider web, cobweb; (fig.) cobweb (*something slight or flimsy*); **mirar las telarañas** (coll.) to be stargazing; **tener telarañas en los ojos** (coll.) to look without seeing, to be blind to what is going on

telarañoso -sa *adj* cobwebby, gossamery

telautógrafo or **teleautógrafo** *m* telautograph

teleaudiencia *f* television audience

telecomunicación *f* telecommunication

telecontrol *m* remote control

telediario *m* television newscast

teledifundir *va & vn* to telecast

teledifusión *f* telecasting; telecast; music by wire; wired wireless

teledifusora *f* television transmitter

teleferaje *m* telpherage

teleferar *va* to telpher

teleférico -ca *adj & m* telpher

telefio *m* (bot.) orpin

telefonar *va & vn* (Am.) var. of **telefonear**

telefonazo *m* (slang) telephone call

telefonear *va & vn* to telephone

telefonema *m* telephone message, telephone call

telefonía *f* telephony; **telefonía inalámbrica** or **sin hilos** wireless telephony

telefónico -ca *adj* telephonic

telefonista *mf* operator, telephonist

teléfono *m* telephone; **teléfono automático** dial telephone; **teléfono inalámbrico** or **sin hilos** wireless telephone; **teléfono público** pay station

telefoto *m* (elec.) telephote (*telectric apparatus*); *f* telephoto (*picture*)

telefotografía *f* telephotography; telephotograph

telefotografiar **§90** *va & vn* to telephotograph

telefotográfico -ca *adj* telephoto, telephotographic

telefotógrafo *m* phototelegraph (*apparatus*)

teleg. abr. of **telégrafo** & **telegrama**

telega *f* telega

telegonía *f* (biol.) telegony

telegrafía *f* telegraphy; **telegrafía inalámbrica** or **sin hilos** wireless, wireless telegraphy

telegrafiar **§90** *va & vn* to telegraph

telegráfico -ca *adj* telegraphic

telegrafista *mf* telegrapher; telegraphist

telégrafo *m* telegraph; **hacer telégrafos** (coll.) to talk by signs (*said especially of lovers*); **telégrafo de banderas** (nav.) wigwagging; **telégrafo de máquinas** (naut.) engine-room telegraph; **telégrafo sin hilos** wireless telegraph

telegrama *m* telegram

teleguiado -da *adj* guided by remote control

teleimpresor *m* teletype, teleprinter

teleléctrico -ca *adj* telelectric

Telémaco *m* (myth.) Telemachus

telemando *m* remote control

telemecánico -ca *adj* telemechanic; *m* television repairman; *f* telemechanics

telemedición *f* telemetering

telemetrar *va & vn* to telemeter

telemetría *f* telemetry

telemétrico -ca *adj* telemetric

telémetro *m* telemeter; (mil.) range finder

telemisora *f* television transmitter

telencéfalo *m* (anat.) telencephalon

telendo -da *adj* sprightly, lively, spirited

teleobjetivo *m* telephoto lens

teleología *f* teleology

teleológico -ca *adj* teleological

teleósteo -a *adj & m* (ichth.) teleost

telépata *mf* telepathist

telepatía *f* telepathy

telepático -ca *adj* telepathic

telepatista *mf* telepathist

telequinesia *f* telekinesis

telera *f* plow pin; sheepfold (*enclosed in a board fence*); jaw (*of a vise*); transom (*of gun carriage*); (naut.) rack block

telerán *m* (elec.) teleran

telero *m* stake (*of cart or truck*)

telerreceptor *m* television set, television receiver

telescopaje *m* telescoping (*of one object inside another*)

telescopar *va & vr* to telescope

telescópico -ca *adj* telescopic

telescopio *m* telescope; (*cap.*) *m* (astr.) Telescopium; **telescopio de espejo** reflecting telescope

telesilla *f* chair lift (*for skiers*)

telesillas *m* (*pl:* **-llas**) var. of **telesilla**

telespectador -dora *mf* viewer, televiewer

telesquí *m* ski lift, ski tow

telestereoscopio *m* telestereoscope

telestesia *f* telesthesia

telestudio *m* television broadcasting studio

teleta *f* blotting paper, blotter; sieve in a paper mill

teletermómetro *m* telethermometer

teletipia *f* teletypewriter

teletipiadora *f* teletype

teletipista *mf* teletyper

teletipo *m* teletype

teletransmisora *f* television transmitter

teletubo *m* (telv.) picture tube

televidente *mf* viewer, televiewer

televisar *va* to televise

televisión *f* television; **televisión en circuito cerrado** closed-circuit television; **televisión en colores** color television

televiso -sa *adj* (pertaining to) television

televisor -sora *adj* televising; (pertaining to) television; *m* television set; *f* television transmitter

telilla *f* light camelot; film

telina *f* (zool.) clam

telofase *f* (biol.) telophase

telolecito *adj masc* (embryol.) telolecithal

telón *m* (theat.) drop curtain; **telón contra incendios** (theat.) safety curtain; **telón de acero** (fig.) iron curtain; **telón de boca** (theat.) front curtain; **telón de fondo** or **foro** (theat.) backdrop; **telón de seguridad** (theat.) safety curtain

telonero -ra *mf* first actor in a vaudeville program

telurato *m* (chem.) tellurate

telúrico -ca *adj* telluric; (chem.) telluric

telurio *m* (chem.) tellurium

telurita *f* (mineral.) tellurite

telurito *m* (chem.) tellurite

teluroso -sa *adj* (chem.) tellurous

telururo *m* (chem.) telluride

tellina *f* (zool.) clam

telliz *m* (*pl:* **-llices**) horse blanket, saddle cover

telliza *f* bedspread, quilt

tema *m* theme, subject; exercise; contention; (gram.) stem; (mus.) theme; *f* persistence, insistence; fixed idea, mania; grudge; **a tema** in emulation, in competition; **tener tema** to be stubborn; **tener tema a** to have a grudge against

temario *m* agenda

temático -ca *adj* thematic; persistent, insistent; (gram.) (pertaining to the) stem

tembladal *m* quaking bog

tembladero -ra *adj* shaking, trembling; *mf* trembler; *m* quaking bog; *f* jewel mounted on a spiral spring; bowl of very thin metal or glass; (ichth.) torpedo; (bot.) large quaking grass

temblador -dora *adj* shaking, trembling; *mf* trembler; (rel.) trembler (*Quaker*); *m* (elec.) trembler

temblante *adj* shaking, trembling; *m* bracelet

temblar **§18** *vn* to shake, tremble, quiver; to shiver; **estar temblando** to teeter

tembleque *adj* shaking, trembling; *m* trembler; jewel mounted on a spiral spring
temblequear *vn* (coll.) to shake, to tremble all the time; (coll.) to fake a tremor
temblequeo *m* (coll.) shaking, trembling, constant shaking, constant trembling
tembletear *vn* (coll.) var. of **temblequear**
temblón -blona *adj* (coll.) shaking, tremulous; **hacer la temblona** (coll.) to fake a tremor (*said of a beggar*); *m* (bot.) aspen
temblor *m* tremor, shaking, trembling, quivering; shivering; (path.) tremor; (Am.) earthquake; **temblor de tierra** earthquake
tembloroso -sa or **tembloso -sa** *adj* shaking, tremulous
tembo -ba *adj* (Am.) silly, stupid
temedero -ra *adj* dread, fearful
temedor -dora *adj* fearful, afraid
temer *va* to fear; *vn* to fear; **temer** + *inf* to fear to + *inf*; **temer por** to fear for
temerario -ria *adj* rash, reckless, hasty, foolhardy
temeridad *f* rashness, recklessness, temerity, foolhardiness
temerón -rona *adj* (coll.) blustering; *mf* (coll.) blusterer
temeroso -sa *adj* dread, frightful; timorous, timid; fearful
temescal *m* (Am.) bathhouse
temible *adj* dreadful, terrible, fearful
Temístocles *m* Themistocles
temor *m* fear, dread
temoso -sa *adj* persistent, stubborn
tempanador *m* beekeeper's knife (*used for removing the dome*)
tempanar *va* to put the head on (*a barrel*); to put the cork dome on (*a beehive*)
témpano *m* timbrel, small drum; drumhead, drumskin; head (*of barrel*); flitch (*of bacon*); floe (*of ice*); cork dome (*of beehive*); (arch.) tympan; (mus.) kettledrum; **témpano de hielo** iceberg
temperación *f* tempering
temperadamente *adv* temperately
temperamental *adj* temperamental
temperamento *m* temperament (*peculiar character of a person*); conciliation, compromise; weather, state of the weather; (mus.) temperament
temperancia *f* var. of **templanza**
temperante *adj* temperate (*in indulgence*); conciliatory; (Am.) abstemious; *mf* (Am.) teetotaler
temperar *va* to temper, to soften, to moderate, to calm; (med.) to calm; (mus.) to put in tune (*two or more instruments*); *vn* (Am.) to go to a warmer climate
temperatísimo -ma *adj super* very or most temperate
temperatura *f* temperature; weather; (path.) temperature (*i.e., high temperature, fever*); **temperatura absoluta** (phys.) absolute temperature; **temperatura del cuerpo** body temperature
temperie *f* weather, state of the weather
tempero *m* (agr.) mellowness of soil
tempestad *f* storm, tempest; (orn.) bluebird, western bluebird; **tempestad de arena** sandstorm; **tempestad de lluvia** rainstorm; **tempestades de risas** gales of laughter; **tempestad magnética** (phys.) magnetic storm
tempestear *vn* to storm, be stormy; (coll.) to storm (*to rage, become violent*)
tempestividad *f* opportuneness, timeliness
tempestivo -va *adj* opportune, timely
tempestuoso -sa *adj* stormy, tempestuous; (fig.) stormy, tempestuous
templa *f* (paint.) distemper (*pigment*); (Am.) juice in sugar pan; **templas** *fpl* (anat.) temples
templadera *f* head gate, sluice gate
templado -da *adj* temperate (*in indulgence; in climate*); (lit.) moderate (*style*); lukewarm, medium; (coll.) brave, courageous; (Am.) in love; (Am.) tipsy, drunk; (Am.) austere, severe; **bien templado** good-tempered, well-tempered; (mus.) well-tempered; **mal templado** bad-tempered
templador *m* (mus.) tuning key or hammer; tempering furnace
templadura *f* tempering; moderation; (mus.) tempering
templanza *f* temperance; mildness, temperateness (*of climate*)
templar *va* to temper; to soften; to ease; to dilute; (mus.) to temper; (naut.) to trim (*sails*) to the wind; (paint.) to blend; *vn* to warm up (*said of weather*); *vr* to temper; to be moderate; to moderate (*said of weather*); (Am.) to fall in love; (Am.) to die
Templario *m* Templar, Knight Templar
temple *m* weather, state of the weather; temper (*disposition*); humor; average; dash, boldness; temper (*hardness of steel, glass, etc.*); (mus.) tempering; (paint.) distemper (*art or process*); **al temple** (paint.) in distemper; **estar de buen temple** to be in a good humor; **estar de mal temple** to be in a bad humor
templén *m* temple (*of a loom*)
templete *m* small temple; niche, tabernacle; pavilion; bandstand
templista *mf* (paint.) painter in distemper
templo *m* temple
témpora *f* Ember days; **témporas** *fpl* Ember days
temporada *f* season; period; spell; **de temporada** temporarily; **estar de temporada** to be vacationing
temporal *adj* temporal; temporary; (anat. & gram.) temporal; *m* weather; spell of rainy weather; storm, tempest; (naut.) whole gale; (anat.) temporal bone; **aguantar un temporal** (naut.) to lie to
temporalidad *f* temporality; **temporalidades** *fpl* (eccl.) temporalities
temporalizar §76 *va* to secularize
temporalmente *adv* temporally; temporarily
temporáneo -a or **temporario -ria** *adj* temporary
temporejar *vn* (naut.) to lie to
temporero -ra *adj* substitute, temporary, provisional; *mf* substitute
temporizar §76 *vn* to temporize; to putter around
tempranal *adj* early-yielding (*land, crops, etc.*)
tempranamente *adv* early
tempranero -ra *adj* early
tempranía *f* (coll.) earliness
tempranilla *f* early grape
tempranito *adv* (coll.) pretty early
temprano -na *adj* early; *m* early crop; **temprano** *adv* early; **temprano y con sol** bright and early
temulencia *f* drunkenness, intoxication
temulento -ta *adj* drunk, intoxicated
ten *2d sg impv of* **tener; ten con ten** (coll.) caution
tena *f* cattle shed
tenacear *va* to tear the flesh of (*a person*) with nippers; to torture; *vn* to persist stubbornly
tenacero *m* maker, dealer, or user of pincers, pliers, or tongs
tenacidad *f* tenacity; (phys.) tenacity
tenacillas *fpl* sugar tongs; hair curler; tweezers; snuffers
tenáculo *m* (surg.) tenaculum
tenada *f* cattle shed
tenallón *m* (fort.) tenaillon
tenante *m* (her.) supporter (*of an escutcheon*)
tenar *adj & m* (anat.) thenar
tenaz *adj* (*pl:* **-naces**) tenacious
tenaza *f* tenace (*two high cards of a suit*); (fort.) tenaille; **tenazas** *fpl* pincers, pliers; tongs (*to carry coal, ice, wood, etc.*); pincers (*e.g., of a crab*); (dent.) forceps; **tenazas de chimenea** coal tongs, fire tongs; **tenazas de rizar** curling iron
tenazada *f* hold with pincers, pliers, or tongs; click of pincers or pliers, clink of tongs; hard bite
tenazazo *m* blow with pincers, pliers, or tongs
tenazón; a or **de tenazón** without taking aim; offhand
tenazuelas *fpl* tweezers
tenca *f* (ichth.) tench
tención *f* holding, possession
tendajo *m* var. of **tendejón**

tendal *m* awning; canvas used to catch falling olives; frame for drying clothes; clothes spread out or hung up to dry
tendalera *f* (coll.) litter (*on the floor or ground*)
tendalero *m* drying place, frame for drying clothes
tendear *vn* (Am.) to browse about the stores
tendedera *f* (Am.) clothesline
tendedero *m* var. of **tendalero**
tendedor -dora *mf* spreader, stretcher, tenter, layer, setter; person who hangs or spreads clothes to dry
tendejón *m* little shop; shack; shed
tendel *m* (mas.) chalk line, leveling line; (mas.) layer of mortar
tendencia *f* tendency
tendenciosidad *f* tendentiousness
tendencioso -sa *adj* tendentious
tendente *adj* tending
tender §66 *va* to spread, spread out, stretch out; to extend; to reach out; to offer, to tender; to hang out (*clothes to dry*); to coat (*e.g., with plaster*); to lay (*a cable, a track, etc.*); to throw, to build (*a bridge*); to set (*a trap*); (Am.) to lay out (*a corpse*); *vn* to tend; **tender a** + *inf* to tend to + *inf; vr* to stretch out; to throw one's cards on the table; to run at full gallop; (naut.) to swell; (coll.) to become unconcerned, neglectful
ténder *m* (rail.) tender
tenderete *m* stand, booth; (coll.) litter
tendero -ra *mf* storekeeper, shopkeeper; *m* tent maker
tendezuela *f* little shop
tendido *m* laying (*e.g., of a cable, of a track*); spreading (*e.g., of a curtain of smoke*); hanging, stretching (*of wires*); wires; run of lace; wash (*amount hung up to dry*); batch of bread; coat of plaster; slope of a roof, side of roof; (taur.) uncovered stand, bleachers; (dial.) clear sky; (Am.) bedclothes; **tendido aéreo** overhead wires; **tendido alto** (taur.) upper section (*of seats*); **tendido bajo** (taur.) lower section (*of seats*)
tendinoso -sa *adj* tendinous
tendón *m* (anat.) tendon; **tendón de Aquiles** (anat.) Achilles' tendon
tendré *1st sg fut ind of* **tener**
tenducha *f* or **tenducho** *m* poor little store
tenebrario *m* (eccl.) tenebrae hearse
tenebrosidad *f* darkness, gloom; obscurity
tenebroso -sa *adj* dark, gloomy, tenebrous; dark, shady (*e.g., deal*); obscure (*style, writer*)
tenedero *m* (naut.) place to anchor
tenedor *m* holder; bearer; fork, table fork; (sport) ball boy; **tenedor de acciones** stockholder; **tenedor de bonos** bondholder; **tenedor de libros** bookkeeper; **tenedor de una póliza** (ins.) policyholder
teneduría *f* bookkeeping; **teneduría de libros** bookkeeping
tenencia *f* tenancy, occupancy, tenure; possession; lieutenancy
tener §85 *va* to have; to hold; to keep; to own, possess; to consider; to esteem; to stop; to be the matter with, to ail; **no tenerlas todas consigo** (coll.) to be worried, be scared; **no tener nada que ver con** to have nothing to do with; **no tener sobre qué caerse muerto** (coll.) to not have a cent to one's name; **tener a bien** + *inf* to have the kindness to + *inf;* **tener para sí** to think, to have as one's own opinion; **tener por** to consider as; **tener que** + *inf* to have to + *inf;* **tener que ver con** to have an affair with, to have intercourse with; to have to do with, to deal with; for expressions like **tener hambre** to be hungry, see the noun; *vr* to stop; to catch oneself, to keep from falling; to consider oneself; to fit, to go; **tenerse a** to tend to, attend to; to stick to
tenería *f* tannery
tenesmo *m* (path.) tenesmus
tengo *1st sg pres ind of* **tener**
tenguerengue; en tenguerengue (coll.) teetering
tenia *f* (anat.) taenia; (arch.) taenia, fillet; (zool.) taenia, tapeworm
teniasis *f* (path.) taeniasis
tenicida *adj* taeniacidal; *m* taeniacide
tenida *f* (Am.) meeting, session
tenienta *f* lieutenant; lieutenant's wife
tenientazgo *m* lieutenancy
teniente *adj* holding, having, owning; immature, unripe; mean, miserly; (coll.) hard of hearing; *m* lieutenant; (mil.) lieutenant, first lieutenant; **teniente coronel** (mil.) lieutenant colonel; **teniente general** (mil.) lieutenant general
tenífugo -ga *adj & m* (med.) taeniafuge
tenis *m* (sport) tennis
tenista *mf* tennis player
tenístico -ca *adj* (pertaining to) tennis
tenor *m* tenor, character, import, drift; (mus.) tenor (*person; voice; instrument*): **a este tenor** like this; **a tenor de** in accordance with
tenoriesco -ca *adj* philandering
tenorio *m* lady-killer
tenotomía *f* (surg.) tenotomy
tensar *va* to tighten, to make taut
tensible *adj* tensible
tensión *f* tension; tenseness; (lit.) tenson; (mech.) stress (*molecular resistance to outside forces*): **alta tensión** (elec.) high tension; **baja tensión** (elec.) low tension; **en tensión** (elec.) in series; **tensión arterial** or **sanguínea** (med.) arterial tension; **tensión superficial** (phys.) surface tension
tenso -sa *adj* tense, tight, taut; tense (*person; situation*)
tensón *f* (lit.) tenson
tensor -sora *adj* tensile; *m* tension (*device*); guy; turnbuckle; (anat.) tensor
tentación *f* temptation
tentaculado -da *adj* tentacled
tentacular *adj* tentacular
tentáculo *m* (bot. & zool.) tentacle; **tentáculos** *mpl* (zool.) feelers
tentadero *m* (taur.) testing corral for young bulls
tentador -dora *adj* tempting; *m* tempter; **el tentador** the Tempter (*the Devil*); *f* temptress
tentadura *f* mercury test of silver ore; thrashing, drubbing
tentalear *va* (coll.) to feel for, to examine gropingly
tentar §18 *va* to touch; to feel (*e.g., one's way*); to try, to attempt; to examine; to test, try out (*a person*); to tempt; (surg.) to probe; **tentar a uno a** + *inf* to tempt someone to + *inf*
tentaruja *f* (coll.) mussing, rumpling
tentativo -va *adj* tentative; *f* attempt; preliminary examination; trial, feeler; **tentativa de delito** (law) attempt to commit a crime
ten.te abr. of **teniente**
tente; a tente bonete (coll.) with persistence
tentejuela *f* extreme effort, desperate resistance; **hasta tentejuela** (coll.) to the point of exhaustion
tentemozo *m* prop, support; pole prop; tumbler (*toy*): cheek strap
tentempié *m* (coll.) snack, bite, pick-me-up; tumbler (*toy figure*)
tentenelaire *mf* offspring of mulatto and quadroon; (Am.) half-breed
tentetieso *m* tumbler (*toy*)
tentón *m* (coll.) snatch; **dar un tentón a** (coll.) to snatch at
tenue *adj* tenuous; light, soft; faint, subdued; simple (*style*)
tenuidad *f* tenuity, tenuousness; trifle, triviality
tenzón *f* var. of **tensón**
teñido *m* dyeing; staining
teñidor -dora *mf* dyer; stainer
teñidura *f* dyeing; staining
teñir §74 *va* to color; to dye; to stain; (paint.) to darken
teño -ña *adj* (Am.) light-brown
teobroma *m* (bot.) cacao; chocolate
teobromina *f* (chem.) theobromine
teocali *m* (Am. archeol.) teocalli (*temple*)
teocracia *f* theocracy
teócrata *mf* theocrat
teocrático -ca *adj* theocratic
Teócrito *m* Theocritus
teodicea *f* theodicy
teodolito *m* theodolite
Teodorico *m* Theodoric

Teodoro *m* Theodore
Teodosio *m* Theodosius
Teófilo *m* Theophilus
Teofrasto *m* Theophrastus
teogonía *f* theogony
teogónico -ca *adj* theogonic
teologal *adj* var. of **teológico**
teología *f* theology; **no meterse en teologías** (coll.) to keep out of deep water
teológico -ca *adj* theological
teologizar §76 *vn* to theologize; (coll.) to prate like a theologian
teólogo -ga *adj* theological; *mf* theologian; divinity student, theologue
teorema *m* theorem
teoría *f* theory; **teoría atómica** (chem.) atomic theory; **teoría cuántica** or **teoría de los cuanta** (phys.) quantum theory; **teoría del conocimiento** (philos.) theory of knowledge; **teoría electromagnética** (phys.) electromagnetic theory (*of light*); **teoría electrónica** (phys.) electronic theory (*of light*); **teoría germinal** (biol. & path.) germ theory; **teoría ondulatoria** (phys.) undulatory or wave theory (*of light*); **teoría unitaria** (chem.) unitary theory
teórico -ca *adj* theoretic or theoretical; *mf* theoretician; theorist; *f* theory
teorizante *adj* theorizing; *mf* theorist, theorizer
teorizar §76 *va* to theorize on, to deal theoretically with; *vn* to theorize
teoso -sa *adj* resinous
teosofía *f* theosophy
teosófico -ca *adj* theosophic or theosophical
teósofo -fa *mf* theosophist
tepe *m* sod, turf (*used for making walls*)
tepetate *m* (Am.) whitish yellow rock
tepetomate *m* (bot.) manzanita (*Arctostaphylos tomentosa*)
tequila *m* (Am.) tequila (*distilled liquor*)
terapeuta *mf* therapeutist
terapéutico -ca *adj* therapeutic or therapeutical; *f* therapeutics
terapia *f* therapy; **terapia física** physical therapy
teratología *f* teratology
teratológico -ca *adj* teratological
terbio *m* (chem.) terbium
tercena *f* government warehouse (*especially for tobacco*); (Am.) butcher shop
tercenista *mf* government warehouseman; (Am.) butcher, meat dealer
tercer *adj* apocopated form of **tercero,** used only before masculine singular nouns and adjectives
tercera *f* see **tercero**
tercería *f* mediation; pandering, procuring; temporary occupation (*of castle, fort, etc.*); (law) right of third party
tercerilla *f* tercet in arte menor
tercero -ra *adj* third; *mf* third; mediator; gobetween; *m* procuror, bawd; referee, umpire; (eccl.) tertiary; (geom.) sixtieth of a second (*of a circle*); *f* tierce (*in cards*); procuress; (mus.) third
tercerol *m* (naut.) third (*e.g., oar*)
tercerola *f* short carbine; small barrel, keg, tierce
tercerón -rona *mf* terceron (*offspring of white person and mulatto*)
terceto *m* tercet; (mus.) trio; trio (*group of three*)
tercia *f* see **tercio**
terciado -da *adj* slanting, crosswise; *m* cutlass, broadsword; broad ribbon
tercianario -ria *adj* suffering from tertian fever; infested with tertian fever; *mf* person suffering from tertian fever
tercianela *f* double-thread silk cloth
terciano -na *adj* tertian; *f* (path.) tertian
terciar *va* to place diagonally; to swing (*e.g., a weapon over one's shoulder*); to divide into three parts; to mix; to plow the third time; *vn* to intercede, to mediate; to take part; to fill in; *vr* to suit, be appropriate; to happen, take place, turn out
terciario -ria *adj* tertiary; (geol.) Tertiary; *m* (geol.) Tertiary
terciazón *f* third plowing
tercio -cia *adj* third; *m* third (*one of three equal parts*); pack (*carried by beast of burden*); corps, troop; harbor guild; (archaic) infantry regiment; **tercios** *mpl* tough limbs; **hacer buen tercio a** to do a good turn; **hacer mal tercio a** to do a bad turn; **hacer tercio** to fill in; **mejorado en tercio y quinto** greatly favored; *f* third; tierce (*in cards*); (eccl.) tierce
terciopelado -da *adj* velvety; *m* velours
terciopelero *m* velvet weaver
terciopelo *m* velvet
terco -ca *adj* stubborn; hard, resistant
terebinto *m* (bot.) terebinth
terebrante *adj* boring, piercing (*pain*)
teredo *m* (zool.) teredo
Terencio *m* Terence
Teresa *f* Theresa
tergiversación *f* tergiversation; slanting, twisting, perversion (*of facts, statements, etc.*)
tergiversador -dora *adj* tergiversating; *mf* tergiversator
tergiversar *va* to slant, to twist (*facts, statements, etc.*); *vn* to tergiversate
teriaca *f* var. of **triaca**
teriacal *adj* var. of **triacal**
teriantrópico -ca *adj* therianthropic
teridófita *f* (bot.) pteridophyte
teriomórfico -ca *adj* theriomorphic
terliz *m* ticking
termal *adj* thermal; steam (*power plant*)
termas *fpl* thermae, hot baths
termatizar §76 *va* (phys.) to thermalize or thermatize
termia *f* (phys.) therm
térmico -ca *adj* thermic; (pertaining to) temperature; steam-generated (*power*)
terminabilidad *f* terminability
terminable *adj* terminable
terminación *f* termination; (gram.) termination, ending
terminacho *m* (coll.) vulgar term; (coll.) blunder, barbarism
terminador -dora *adj* finishing; *mf* finisher; *f* finishing machine
terminajo *m* (coll.) var. of **terminacho**
terminal *adj* terminal; *m* (elec.) terminal; **terminales** *mpl* (Am.) bargains at end of season
terminante *adj* final, definitive, peremptory
terminar *va* to terminate, to end; to finish; *vn* to terminate, to end; **terminar por** + *inf* or **terminar** + *ger* to end by + *ger*; *vr* to terminate, to end; to lead, to issue
terminativo -va *adj* terminative
terminista *mf* phrasemaker
término *m* end, limit; boundary; manner, bearing; term; (arch., log. & math.) term; (*cap.*) *m* (myth.) Terminus; **en buenos términos** on good terms; in other words; **estar en buenos términos con** to be on good terms with; **llevar a término** to carry out; **pasar los términos** to go too far; **medio término** subterfuge, evasion; compromise; **poner término a** to put an end to; **por término medio** on an average; **primer término** foreground; (mov.) close-up; **segundo término** middle distance; **último término** background; **término fatal** (law) deadline; **término medio** average; compromise; (log.) middle term; **término municipal** township
terminología *f* terminology
terminológico -ca *adj* terminological
terminote *m* (coll.) big word
termio *m* (phys.) therm
termión *m* (phys.) thermion
termiónico -ca *adj* thermionic; *f* thermionics
termistor *m* (elec.) thermistor
termita *f* (chem.) thermit; (ent. & fig.) termite
termite *m* (ent.) termite
termitero *m* nest of termites
termito *m* (ent.) termite
termo *m* thermos bottle
termobarógrafo *m* thermobarograph
termobarómetro *m* thermobarometer
termocauterio *m* thermocautery
termodinámico -ca *adj* thermodynamic; *f* thermodynamics
termoelectricidad *f* thermoelectricity
termoeléctrico -ca *adj* thermoelectric or thermoelectrical

termoelectromotor -triz (*pl:* **-trices**) *adj* thermoelectromotive
termoelemento *m* (elec.) thermoelement
termoestesia *f* (physiol.) thermesthesia
termofisión *f* (phys.) thermofission
termofusión *f* (phys.) thermofusion
termogénesis *f* (physiol.) thermogenesis
termógeno -na *adj* thermogenetic
termógrafo *m* thermograph
termoiónico -ca *adj* var. of **termiónico**
termolábil *adj* (biochem.) thermolabile
termólisis *f* (chem. & physiol.) thermolysis
termología *f* thermology
termometría *f* thermometry
termométrico -ca *adj* thermometric
termómetro *m* thermometer; **termómetro centígrado** centigrade thermometer; **termómetro clínico** clinical thermometer; **termómetro diferencial** differential thermometer
termomotor -triz (*pl:* **-trices**) *adj* thermomotive; *m* heat engine
termomultiplicador *m* (phys.) thermomultiplier, thermopile
termonuclear *adj* thermonuclear
termopar *m* (elec.) thermocouple
termopila *f* (phys.) thermopile
Termópilas, las Thermopylae
termoplástico -ca *adj* thermoplastic
termoquímico -ca *adj* thermochemical; *f* thermochemistry
termos *m* & *f* (*pl:* **-mos**) thermos bottle; **termos de acumulación** (elec.) off-peak hot-water heater; **termos eléctrico** electric hot-water heater
termoscopio *m* thermoscope
termosifón *m* thermosiphon; boiler, hot-water boiler (*for heating rooms or water*)
termostático -ca *adj* thermostatic
termóstato *m* thermostat
termotropismo *m* (biol.) thermotropism
terna *f* three candidates presented for selection; pair of threes (*at dice*); set of dice
ternado -da *adj* (bot.) ternate
ternario -ria *adj* ternary; *m* three days' devotion
terne *adj* (coll.) strong, husky; (coll.) persistent, stubborn; (coll.) bullying; *m* (coll.) bully; (Am.) gaucho knife
ternejal *adj* (coll.) bullying; *m* (coll.) bully
ternejo -ja *adj* (Am.) peppy, energetic
ternejón -jona *adj* & *mf* (coll.) var. of **ternerón**
ternera *f* calf; veal; **ternera marina** (zool.) sea cow
ternero *m* bull calf
ternerón -rona *adj* (coll.) sentimental, easily moved; *mf* (coll.) sentimental person
terneruela *f* sucking calf
terneza *f* tenderness; fondness, love; **ternezas** *fpl* sweet nothings
ternilla *f* gristle
ternilloso -sa *adj* gristly
ternísimo -ma *adj super* very or most tender
terno *m* suit of clothes; oath, curse; set of three; tern (*in lottery*); (print.) three sheets folded together; (eccl.) group of three priests celebrating high mass; (eccl.) vestments of three priests celebrating high mass; (coll.) piece of luck; **echar ternos** to swear to curse
ternura *f* tenderness; fondness, love
terpeno *m* (chem.) terpene
terpineol *m* (chem.) terpineol
Terpsícore *f* (myth.) Terpsichore
terquear *vn* to be stubborn
terquedad *f* stubbornness, obstinacy, bullheadedness
terracota *f* terra cotta
terrada *f* bitumen
terrado *m* high terrace, flat roof
terraja *f* diestock; modeling board
terraje *m* land rent
terrajero *m* var. of **terrazguero**
terral *adj* land (*breeze*); *m* land breeze
terramicina *f* (pharm.) terramycin
Terranova *f* Newfoundland (*island and province*); *m* Newfoundland (*dog*)
terraplén *m* fill; embankment; terrace, platform; (fort.) earthwork, rampart; (fort.) terreplein
terraplenar *va* to fill, fill in; to embank; to terrace
terráqueo -a *adj* terraqueous (*globe, sphere, planet*)
terrateniente *mf* landholder, landowner
terraza *f* terrace; veranda; flat roof; border, edge (*in garden*); sidewalk café; glazed jar with two handles; (geol.) terrace
terrazgo *m* field for planting; land rent
terrazguero *m* lessee of a field for raising crops
terrazo *m* (paint.) ground, earth (*in a landscape*)
terrear *va* (Am.) to lick (*salt earth*); *vn* to be thinly sown (*said of soil, of a field, of crops*); (Am.) to drag one's feet
terrecer §34 *va* to frighten, terrify
terregoso -sa *adj* cloddy, lumpy
terremoto *m* earthquake
terrenal *adj* earthly, mundane, worldly
terrenidad *f* earthliness
terreno -na *adj* terrestrial; mundane, worldly; *m* land, ground, terrain; plot, lot, piece of land; (geol.) terrane, terrain; (sport) field, course, grounds; (fig.) field, sphere; **ceder terreno** to give ground, to yield ground; **ganar terreno** to gain ground; **medir el terreno** to see how the land lies; **minar el terreno a** to undermine the work of; **perder terreno** to lose ground; **preparar el terreno** to pave the way; **sobre el terreno** on the spot; with data in hand; **terreno de relleno** filled ground, made ground; **terreno echadizo** dump, refuse dump
térreo -a *adj* earthen, earthy
terrero -ra *adj* earthly; of earth; humble; low-flying (*bird*); *m* pile, heap (*of earth, brush, etc.*); mark, target; terrace; public square; alluvium; (min.) dump; **hacer terreros** to make love or to serenade from the street (*in front of lady's house*); *f* steep ground; frail for carrying earth; (orn.) lark
terrestre *adj* terrestrial, land
terrezuela *f* worthless piece of ground
terribilidad *f* terribleness
terribilísimo -ma *adj super* very or most terrible
terrible *adj* terrible; gruff, ill-tempered
terrícola *adj* (bot. & zool.) terricolous; *mf* earth dweller
terrier *m* terrier
terrífico -ca *adj* terrific
terrígeno -na *adj* earthborn
terrino -na *adj* earthy, terrene
territorial *adj* territorial
territorialidad *f* territoriality
territorio *m* territory; **territorio del Labrador** Labrador; **Territorios del Noroeste** Northwest Territories (*of Canada*)
terromontero *m* hill, butte
terrón *m* clod; lump; (coll.) small plot of ground; **terrones** *mpl* farm
terronazo *m* blow with a clod of earth
terror *m* terror; (*cap.*) *m* (hist.) Reign of Terror
terrorífico -ca *adj* terrific, frightful
terrorismo *m* terrorism, frightfulness
terrorista *adj* terrorist, terroristic; *mf* terrorist
terrosidad *f* earthiness; dirtiness
terroso -sa *adj* earthy; dirty
terruño *m* piece of ground; soil; country, native soil
tersar *va* to smooth, to polish, to shine
tersidad *f* var. of **tersura**
Tersites *m* (myth.) Thersites
terso -sa *adj* smooth, glossy, polished; smooth, limpid, flowing (*style*)
tersura *f* smoothness, glossiness, polish; smoothness (*of style*)
tertulia *f* party, social gathering; game room (*in the back of a café*); (Am.) orchestra seat; **estar de tertulia** to go to a party, to sit around and talk; **hacer tertulia** to sit around and talk; to talk (*when one should not, e.g., in class*)
tertuliano -na *adj* party-going; *mf* party-goer, member of a social gathering; (*cap.*) *m* Tertullian
tertuliante *adj* party-going; *mf* party-goer, member of a social gathering

tertuliar *vn* (Am.) to go to a party, to sit around and talk
tertulio -lia *adj & mf* var. of **tertuliante**
tertulión *m* big party, big gathering
terzuelo *m* third; (orn.) tercel, male falcon
Tesalia, la Thessaly
tesaliano -na *adj & mf* Thessalian
tesálico -ca *adj* Thessalian
tesaliense, tesalio -lia or **tésalo -la** *adj & mf* var. of **tesaliano**
tesalonicense *adj & mf* Thessalonian
tesalónico -ca *adj & mf* Thessalonian; (*cap.*) *f* Thessalonica
tesar *va* (naut.) to haul taut; *vn* to back, to pull back (*said of oxen*)
tesauro *m* thesaurus
tesela *f* tessera (*in mosaic work*)
teselado -da *adj* tessellate; *m* tessellated paving, mosaic pavement
Teseo *m* (myth.) Theseus
tésera *f* (hist.) tessera
tesis *f* (*pl:* **-sis**) thesis; (mus.) thesis
tesitura *f* attitude, state of mind; (mus.) tessitura
teso -sa *adj* taut, tight, tense; *m* top of a hill; rough spot (*on smooth surface*)
tesón *m* grit, pluck, tenacity
tesonería *f* obstinacy, stubbornness
tesonero -ra *adj* obstinate, stubborn
tesorería *f* treasury; treasurership
tesorero -ra *mf* treasurer
tesoro *m* treasure; treasury; treasure house; thesaurus
Tespis *m* Thespis
test *m* (educ. & psychol.) test
testa *f* head; front; (bot.) testa; (zool.) test or testa; (coll.) head, brains; **testa coronada** crowned head (*sovereign*); **testa de ferro** (coll.) figurehead, dummy, straw man
testáceo -a *adj & m* (zool.) testacean
testación *f* cancellation, erasure
testado -da *adj* testate; *f* blow with the head
testador -dora *mf* testator; *f* testatrix
testadura *f* var. of **testación**
testaférrea *m* or **testaferro** *m* (coll.) figurehead, dummy, straw man
testamentaría *f* testamentary execution; estate, inheritance; meeting of executors
testamentario -ria *adj* testamentary; *m* executor; *f* executrix
testamentifacción *f* or **testamentificación** *f* (law) power to make a will
testamento *m* testament, will; **Antiguo Testamento** Old Testament; **Nuevo Testamento** New Testament; **Viejo Testamento** Old Testament; **testamento nuncupativo** (law) nuncupative will
testar *va* (law) to seize, to attach; (obs.) to erase; (Am.) to underline; *vn* to make a testament or will
testarada *f* blow with the head; (coll.) stubbornness
testarro *m* piece of junk (*old furniture*); wreck (*sickly, useless person*)
testarrón -rrona *adj* (coll.) var. of **testarudo**
testarronería *f* (coll.) great stubbornness
testarudez *f* stubbornness, pig-headedness
testarudo -da *adj* stubborn, pig-headed
teste *m* (anat.) testis
testera *f* front; forehead (*of animal*); crownpiece (*of harness*); back seat (*of coach*); wall (*of furnace*)
testero *m* front; (min.) overhand stope
testicular *adj* testicular
testículo *m* (anat.) testicle
testificación *f* attestation, testification
testifical *adj* of a witness, of witnesses
testificante *adj* testifying
testificar §86 *va & vn* to testify
testificativo -va *adj* testificatory
testigo *mf* witness; **testigo auricular** auricular witness; **testigo de cargo** witness for the prosecution; **testigo de descargo** witness for the defense; **testigo de oídas** auricular witness; **testigo de vista, testigo ocular** or **testigo presencial** eyewitness; **testigos de Jehová** Jehovah's Witnesses; *m* witness (*evidence*); marker; control (*in an experiment*)
testimonial *adj* testificatory; **testimoniales** *fpl* (eccl.) testimonial
testimoniar *va* to attest, to testify to, to bear witness to
testimoniero -ra *adj* false, perjured; hypocritical
testimonio *m* testimony; false accusation; (Bib.) testimony; **en testimonio de lo cual** in testimony whereof
test.mto abr. of **testamento**
test.o abr. of **testigo**
testolín *m* (ichth.) spotted sea robin
testosterona *f* (biochem.) testosterone
testudinal *adj* (zool.) testudinal
testudíneo -a *adj* testudinous
testudo *m* (hist.) testudo
testuz *m* (*pl:* **-tuces**) nape (*of animal*); forehead (*of animal*)
testuzo *m* var. of **testuz**
tesura *f* var. of **tiesura**
teta *f* teat; breast; hummock, knoll; **dar la teta a** to suckle; **quitar la teta a** to wean; **teta de vaca** conical meringue
tetada *f* feeding, breast feeding
tetania *f* (path.) tetany
tetánico -ca *adj* tetanic
tetanizar §76 *va* to tetanize
tétano or **tétanos** *m* (path.) tetanus
tetar *va* to suckle
tetartoédrico -ca *adj* (cryst.) tetartohedral
tetartoedro *m* (cryst.) tetartohedron
tetera *f* teapot, teakettle
tetero *m* (Am.) nursing bottle
tetigonia *f* (ent.) grouse locust
tetilla *f* nipple (*of male; of nursing bottle*)
Tetis *f* (myth.) Thetis
tetón *m* stub (*of limb of tree*); (naut.) jutting rock
tetraciclina *f* (pharm.) tetracycline
tetracloruro *m* (chem.) tetrachloride
tetracordal *adj* (mus.) tetrachordal
tetracordio *m* (mus.) tetrachord
tetracromía *f* (print.) four-color process
tetradimita *f* (mineral.) tetradymite
tetraédrico -ca *adj* tetrahedral
tetraedro *m* (geom.) tetrahedron
tetraetilo de plomo *m* (chem.) tetraethyl lead
tetragonal *adj* tetragonal
tetrágono *m* (geom.) tetragon
tetralogía *f* (theat.) tetralogy
tetrámetro -tra *adj & m* tetrameter
tetramotor *m* (aer.) four-motor plane
tetrapétalo -la *adj* (bot.) tetrapetalous
tetrarca *m* tetrarch
tetrarquía *f* tetrarchy
tetrasilábico -ca *adj* tetrasyllabic
tetrasílabo -ba *adj* tetrasyllabic; *m* tetrasyllable
tetravalente *adj* (chem.) tetravalent
tétrico -ca *adj* dark, gloomy, sullen
tetril *m* tetryl
tetrodo or **tétrodo** *m* (elec.) tetrode
tetróxido *m* (chem.) tetroxide
tetuaní (*pl:* **-níes**) *adj* (pertaining to) Tetuán; *mf* native or inhabitant of Tetuán
teucali *m* var. of **teocali**
teucro -cra *adj & mf* Teucrian; (*cap.*) *m* (myth.) Teucer
teurgia *f* theurgy
teúrgico -ca *adj* theurgic or theurgical
teurgo *m* theurgist
teutón -tona *adj & mf* Teuton
teutónico -ca *adj* Teutonic; *m* Teutonic (*language*)
textil *adj & m* textile
texto *m* text; textbook; (print.) great primer; **el Sagrado texto** the Bible; **fuera de texto** (b.b.) tipped-in (*e.g., illustration, map*); **grabado fuera de texto** (b.b.) inset, insert
textorio -ria *adj* textile
textual *adj* textual
textualista *m* textualist
textura *f* texture; weaving; (fig.) texture (*structure*)
textural *adj* textural
tez *f* complexion
tezado -da *adj* tan
ti *pron pers* (used as object of preposition) thee; you

tía *f* aunt; old lady; (coll.) coarse woman; (coll.) bawd, prostitute; **no hay tu tía** (coll.) there's no use, there's no chance; **quedar** or **quedarse para tía** (coll.) to be left an old maid; **tía abuela** grandaunt, great-aunt
tialina *f* var. of **ptialina**
tialismo *m* var. of **ptialismo**
tiamina *f* (biochem.) thiamine
tiara *f* tiara
tiazol *m* (chem.) thiazole
Tíber *m* Tiber
tiberio *m* (coll.) noise, hubbub, uproar; (*cap.*) *m* Tiberius
Tibet, el Tibet
tibetano -na *adj & mf* Tibetan; *m* Tibetan (*language*)
tibia *f* see **tibio**
tibial *adj* tibial
tibieza *f* tepidity, lukewarmness; (fig.) tepidity, lukewarmness; (fig.) coolness, coldness
tibio -bia *adj* tepid, lukewarm; (fig.) tepid, lukewarm; *f* (anat.) tibia, shinbone; (mus.) tibia, flute, pipe
tibor *m* large Chinese or Japanese earthen jar; (Am.) chamber pot; (Am.) chocolate cup
tiburón *m* (ichth.) shark
tic *m* (*pl:* **tiques**) (path.) tic; **tic doloroso de la cara** (path.) tic douloureux
Ticiano, El Titian
tictac *m* tick, tick-tock
tiemblo *m* (bot.) aspen, aspen tree
tiempo *m* time; weather; stage; (gram.) tense; (mach.) cycle (*of an internal-combustion engine*); (mus.) tempo; (mus.) movement (*e.g., of a symphony*); **abrir el tiempo** to begin to clear up, to moderate; **al poco tiempo** within a short time; **alzar** or **alzarse el tiempo** to clear up; **a su tiempo** in due time; **a tiempo** in time; **a tiempo que** at the time that; **a tiempo para** + *inf* in time to + *inf;* **a tiempos** at times; **a un tiempo** at the same time; **cargarse el tiempo** to cloud over; **con tiempo** in time; **cuánto tiempo** how long; **darse buen tiempo** to have a good time; **de cuatro tiempos** (mach.) four-cycle; **de dos tiempos** (mach.) two-cycle; **de tiempo en tiempo** from time to time; **de un tiempo a esta parte** for some time, for some time now; **el Tiempo** Father Time; **engañar el tiempo** to kill time; **en los buenos tiempos** in the good old days; **en tiempo** at the right time; **en tiempo de** at the time of; **en tiempo oportuno** in due time; **entretener el tiempo** to kill time, to pass the time away; **fuera de tiempo** untimely, at the wrong time; **ganar tiempo** (coll.) to make time; (coll.) to temporize; **gastar el tiempo** to waste time; **hacer tiempo** to mark time; **hacer buen tiempo** to be clear, to be good weather; **hacer mal tiempo** to be bad weather; **medio tiempo** meantime; **mucho tiempo** a long time; **pasar el tiempo** to fritter away the time; **perder el tiempo** to waste time; **poner a mal tiempo buena cara** to make the best of a bad situation; **tomarse tiempo** to bide one's time; **tiempo de exposición** (phot.) time, exposure time; **tiempo inmemorable** time immemorial, time out of mind; **tiempo inmemorial** (law) time immemorial; **tiempo medio** (astr.) mean time; **tiempo muerto** dull season; **tiempo (solar) verdadero** (astr.) true time
tienda *f* store, shop; tent; tilt (*cloth cover of cart or wagon*); (naut.) awning; **abrir tienda** to set up shop; **alzar** or **levantar tienda** to shut up shop; **ir de tiendas** to go shopping; **tienda de antigüedades** antique shop; **tienda de campaña** army tent; **tienda de descuento** discount house; **tienda de modas** ladies' dress shop; **tienda de objetos de regalo** gift shop; **tienda de oxígeno** (med.) oxygen tent; **tienda de pacotilla** slopshop; **tienda de playa** beach tent; **tienda de raya** company store (*on Mexican ranch*); **tienda de ultramarinos** delicatessen store, grocery store
tienta *f* cleverness, shrewdness· (surg.) probe; sounding rod; (taur.) testing the mettle of a young bull or cow; **andar a tientas** to grope, to grope in the dark; (fig.) to feel one's way
tientaguja *f* sounding rod
tientaparedes *mf* (*pl:* **-des**) groper, groper in the dark
tiento *m* touch; blind man's stick; ropewalker's pole (*for balance*); steady hand; care, caution; (mus.) flourish (*before beginning to play*); (paint.) mahlstick, maulstick; (coll.) blow, hit; (coll.) swig; (zool.) tentacle; **andarse con tiento** to watch one's step; **a tiento** gropingly; with uncertainty; **con tiento** cautiously; **dar tiento a** to test, to try; (coll.) to take a swig from (*a bottle, a jug*); **de tiento en tiento** trying one thing after another; **perder el tiento** to lose one's touch; **por el tiento** gropingly, groping in the dark; **tener a los tientos** (Am.) to keep at hand; (Am.) to keep in sight, to keep an eye on (*a person*); **tener la vida en un tiento** (Am.) to be in great danger; **tomar el tiento a** (coll.) to examine
tierno -na *adj* tender; loving; tearful; soft (*e.g., cushion*)
tierra *f* earth; ground; dirt; land; country; (elec.) ground; **besar la tierra** (coll.) to fall flat on one's face; **caer a tierra** to fall on the ground, to fall on the floor; **dar en tierra con** to upset, overthrow, wreck, ruin; **echar en** or **por tierra** to upset, knock down; to destroy; to overthrow; **echar tierra a** to hush up; **en tierra, mar y aire** on land, on sea, and in the air; **irse a tierra** to topple, to collapse; **la tierra de nadie** (mil.) no man's land; **perder tierra** to lose one's footing; to be swept off one's feet; **poner por tierra** to demolish; **por estas tierras** in these parts; **por tierra** by land, overland; **tomar tierra** to land; to find one's way about; **venir** or **venirse a tierra** to topple, to collapse; **ver tierras** to see the world, to go traveling; **tierra adentro** inland; **tierra de batán** or **de bataneros** fuller's earth; **tierra de Hus** (Bib.) Uz; **tierra de labor** cultivated land; **tierra de ladrillos** brick clay; **tierra de pan llevar** (agr.) wheat land, cereal-growing land; **tierra de pipa** or **pipas** pipe clay; **Tierra de promisión** (Bib.) Land of Promise, Promised Land; **tierra de promisión** (fig.) promised land; **tierra de sombra** umber; **tierra firme** mainland; land, terra firma; **Tierra Firme** Spanish Main; **tierra japónica** (pharm.) terra japonica; **tierra pesada** (mineral.) heavy earth; **Tierra prometida** (Bib.) Promised Land; **tierra prometida** (fig.) promised land; **tierra rara** (chem.) rare earth; **Tierra Santa** Holy Land; **tierras antárticas** Antarctica; **tierra vegetal** vegetable mold
tieso -sa *adj* stiff; tight, taut, tense; strong, well; bold, enterprising; stubborn; stiff, stuck-up; **tenérselas tiesas a** or **con** (coll.) to hold one's ground with, to stand up to; **tenerse tieso** to hold tight; **tieso** *adv* hard
tiesto -ta *adj* stiff; tight, taut, tense; stubborn; **tiesto** *adv* hard; *m* flowerpot; broken piece of earthenware; *f* edge of headings (*of a barrel*)
tiesura *f* stiffness; (fig.) stiffness
tífico -ca *adj* typhous, typhic; typhoid
tifo -fa *adj* (coll.) full, satiated; *m* (path.) typhus; **tifo asiático** (path.) Asiatic cholera; **tifo de América** (path.) yellow fever; **tifo de Oriente** (path.) bubonic plague
tifoideo -a *adj* typhoidal; typhoid
tifón *m* waterspout; typhoon
tifus *m* (path.) typhus; (slang) free seats (*in theater*); **entrar de tifus** (slang) to get in free; **tifus exantemático** (path.) spotted fever, typhus fever; **tifus icteroides** (path.) yellow fever
tigana *f* (orn.) sunbird, sun bittern
tigmotaxia *f* (biol.) thigmotaxis
tigmotropismo *m* (biol.) thigmotropism
tigra *f* female tiger; (Am.) female jaguar
tigre *m* (zool.) tiger; (fig.) tiger (*bloodthirsty person*); (Am.) jaguar; **tigre de Bengala** or **tigre real** Bengal tiger
tigresa *f* tigress
tigrillo *m* (zool.) gray fox
tigrino -na *adj* tigerish, tigrine
tija *f* stem (*of key*)

tijera *f* scissors, shears; sawbuck, sawhorse; day's shearing (*of sheep*); gossip; **tijeras** *fpl* scissors, shears; **buena tijera** (coll.) good cutter; (coll.) good eater, trencherman; (coll.) terrible gossip; **hacer tijera** to twist the mouth (*said of a horse*)
tijerada *f* snip, clip, cut (*with scissors*)
tijereta *f* tendril (*of vine*); (ent.) earwig; (orn.) man-of-war bird; (orn.) fork-tailed flycatcher (*Milvulus tyrannus*); **tijeretas** *fpl* small scissors or shears; **¡tijeretas han de ser!** silly obstinacy!
tijeretada *f* or **tijeretazo** *m* var. of **tijerada**
tijeretear *va* to snip, clip, cut (*with scissors*); (coll.) to deal arbitrarily with (*another person's affairs*); *vn* (Am.) to gossip
tijereteo *m* snipping, clipping, cutting; click, clicking (*of scissors*)
tijerilla or **tijeruela** *f* small scissors; tendril (*of vine*)
til *m* (bot.) til
tila *f* (bot.) linden tree; flower of linden tree; linden-blossom tea; **tomar tila** (coll.) to hold one's tongue
tílburi *m* tilbury
tildar *va* to put a tilde or dash over; to erase, strike out; to brand, stigmatize; **tildar de** to brand as
tilde *m & f* tilde (*on letter n*); accent mark; superior dash; blemish, flaw; censure; (phonet.) til; *f* jot, tittle
tildío *m* (orn.) killdee
tildón *m* scratch, erasure
tiliáceo -a *adj* (bot.) tiliaceous
tiliche *m* (Am.) trinket; (Am.) fragment, piece
tilichero -ra *mf* (Am.) peddler
tilín *m* ting-a-ling; **hacer tilín** (coll.) to be well liked; **tener tilín** (coll.) to be appealing, be winsome
tilio *m* (bot.) wahoo
tilo *m* (bot.) linden tree
tilla *f* (naut.) part deck
tillado *m* board floor
tillar *va* to floor
timador -dora *mf* thief, swindler
tímalo *m* (ichth.) grayling
timar *va* to snitch; to swindle; *vr* (coll.) to make eyes at each other
timba *f* (coll.) game of chance; (coll.) gambling den; (Am.) belly
timbal *m* (mus.) timbal, kettledrum; (cook.) timbale
timbalear *vn* to play the kettledrum
timbalero *m* kettledrummer
timbrado -da *adj* stamped; **bien timbrado** sonorous (*voice*)
timbrar *va* to stamp; (her.) to timbre
timbrazo *m* loud ring (*e.g., of doorbell*)
timbre *m* seal, stamp; tax stamp; stamp duty or tax; bell, electric bell; snare (*of drum*); test pressure (*of boiler*); deed of glory; (her., phonet., & phys.) timbre; (Am.) postage stamp; **timbres** *mpl* (mus.) glockenspiel; **timbre adherido** adhesive stamp; **timbre nasal** twang
timbrófilo -la *adj & mf* philatelist
timeleáceo -a *adj* (bot.) thymelaeaceous
tímico -ca *adj* thymic (*pertaining to thyme*); thymic, thymus
timidez *f* timidity
tímido -da *adj* timid
timo *m* (coll.) theft, swindle; (coll.) lie; (coll.) catch phrase; (anat.) thymus; (ichth.) grayling; **dar un timo a** (coll.) to cheat, swindle, trick
timocracia *f* timocracy
timocrático -ca *adj* timocratic or timocratical
timol *m* (chem.) thymol
timón *m* beam (*of plow*); (naut. & aer.) rudder; (fig.) helm; **timón de dirección** (aer.) vertical rudder; **timón de profundidad** (aer.) elevator, horizontal rudder
timonear *vn* (naut.) to steer
timonel *m* (naut.) helmsman, steersman
timoneo *m* (naut.) steering
timonera *adj fem* (orn.) rectricial; *f* (naut.) pilot house, wheelhouse
timorato -ta *adj* God-fearing; timid, chicken-hearted
Timoteo *m* Timothy
timpa *f* (metal.) tymp; (metal.) hearth, grate
timpánico -ca *adj* (anat. & med.) tympanic
timpanismo *m* (path.) distention of the abdomen
timpanítico -ca *adj* tympanitic
timpanitis *f* (path.) tympanitis (*inflammation of middle ear*); (path.) tympanites (*distention caused by gas*)
timpanizar §76 *vr* (path.) to become distended with gas
tímpano *m* (arch.) tympanum; (anat.) tympanum, eardrum; (mus.) timpano, kettledrum; (print.) tympan
tina *f* large earthen jar; wooden vat or tub; bathtub; juice oozing from heap of olives
tinaco *m* wooden vat
tinada *f* woodpile, fagot; cattle shed
tinado or **tinador** *m* cattle shed
tinaja *f* large earthen jar
tinajero *m* maker or seller of earthen water jars; stand for earthen water jars
tinajón *m* earthen tank (*to catch rain water*)
tinamú *m* (*pl:* **-múes**) (orn.) tinamou
tincal *m* tincal
tincar §86 *va* (Am.) to fillip
tincazo *m* (Am.) fillip
tinción *f* dyeing
tinelo *m* servants' dining room
tinerfeño -ña *adj* (pertaining to) Teneriffe; *mf* native or inhabitant of Teneriffe
tinge *m* big black owl
tingladillo *m* (naut.) clinker work
tinglado *m* shed; temporary board floor; intrigue, trick
tingle *f* glazier's tool for leading window glass
tinieblas *fpl* darkness; (eccl.) Tenebrae
tinillo *m* reservoir of wine press (*for collecting must*)
tino *m* feel (*for things*); good aim; knack; insight, wisdom; stone tank (*in wool factory*); wine press; (bot.) laurustine; **a buen tino** (coll.) by sight, by guess; **a tino** gropingly; **coger el tino** to get the hang of it, to catch on; **sacar de tino** to wallop; to astound, confound; **sin tino** without moderation, without sense
tinta *f* see **tinto**
tintaje *m* inking (*of press or typewriter*)
tintar *va* to color, to tint
tinte *m* dye; dyeing; dyer's shop, dyeing establishment; (fig.) coloring, false appearance
tinterazo *m* blow with an inkwell
tinterillada *f* (Am.) pettifoggery
tinterillo *m* (coll.) clerk, lawyer's clerk; (Am.) pettifogger
tintero *m* inkstand, inkwell; (print.) ink fountain; **dejar en el tintero** (coll.) to forget, to overlook
tintín *m* clink; jingle
tintinar or **tintinear** *vn* to clink; to jingle
tintineo *m* clink, clinking; jingle, jingling
tinto -ta *adj* red; (Am.) dark-red; *m* red table wine; *f* ink; tint, hue; dyeing; paint (*mixed for painting*); (zool.) ink (*e.g., of squid*); **de buena tinta** (coll.) on good authority; **media tinta** (paint. & phot.) half-tone; **medias tintas** (coll.) vague notions; **tinta china** India ink; **tinta de copiar** copying ink; **tinta de imprenta** printer's ink; **tinta simpática** invisible ink, sympathetic ink
tintóreo -a *adj* tinctorial, dyeing
tintorera *f* see **tintorero**
tintorería *f* dyeing; dyeing establishment; dry-cleaning establishment
tintorero -ra *mf* dyer; dry cleaner; *f* (Am.) female shark
tintura *f* dye; dyeing; rouge; (pharm.) tincture; (fig.) tincture, smattering; **tintura compuesta de alcanfor** (pharm.) paregoric; **tintura de tornasol** litmus solution, litmus; **tintura de yodo** (pharm.) iodine
tinturar *va* to tincture; (fig.) to tincture; (fig.) to give a smattering to
tiña *f* (ent.) beehive spider; (path.) tinea; (path.) ringworm; (coll.) stinginess
tiñería *f* (coll.) stinginess
tiñoso -sa *adj* scabby, mangy; (coll.) stingy
tiñuela *f* (bot.) dodder; (zool.) shipworm

tío *m* uncle; (coll.) old man; (coll.) guy, fellow; **tíos** *mpl* uncle and aunt; **tío abuelo** granduncle, great-uncle
tiocianato *m* (chem.) thiocyanate
tiociánico -ca *adj* thiocyanic
tiofeno *m* (chem.) thiophene
tiónico -ca *adj* thionic
tiosinamina *f* (chem.) thiosinamine
tiosulfato *m* (chem.) thiosulfate
tiosulfúrico -ca *adj* thiosulfuric
tiourea *f* (chem.) thiourea
tiovivo *m* merry-go-round, carrousel
tipejo *m* (coll.) ridiculous fellow, sap
tipiadora *f* typewriter (*machine*); typist
tipiar *va & vn* to type, to typewrite
tipicista *adj* regional, local
típico -ca *adj* typical
tipificar §86 *va* to standardize
tipismo *m* characteristic
tipista *mf* typist, typewriter; linotypist
tiple *mf* soprano (*person*); treble-guitar player; *m* soprano (*voice*); treble guitar; (naut.) one-piece mast
tiplisonante *adj* (coll.) treble, soprano
tipo *m* type; (print.) type; rate (*of exchange, discount, interest*); type (*figure on coin or medal*); shape, figure, build; (coll.) fellow, specimen, guy; **tener buen tipo** to have a good figure; **tipo alemán** (print.) German text; **tipo de ensayo** or **de prueba** eye-test chart; **tipo impositivo** tax rate; **tipo menudo** small print
tipocromía *f* color printing
tipografía *f* typography
tipográfico -ca *adj* typographic or typographical
tipógrafo *m* typographer; type-setting machine
tipolitografía *f* typolithography
tipometría *f* typometry
tipómetro *m* type gauge
tipotelégrafo *m* var. of **teletipo**
típula *f* (ent.) crane fly, daddy-longlegs
tiquete *m* (Am.) ticket
tiquismiquis *mpl* (coll.) fussiness; (coll.) obsequiousness
tiquistiquis *m* (bot.) Philippine soapberry
tira *f* strip; **hecho tiras** (Am.) in rags; **sacar las tiras a** (Am.) to beat up, give a beating to; **tira de películas** film strip; **tira emplástica** (Am.) court plaster; **tiras cómicas** comics, funnies (*in the newspaper*)
tirabala *m* popgun
tirabeque *m* string pea; slingshot
tirabotas *m* (*pl:* **-tas**) boot hook
tirabotón *m* buttonhook
tirabraguero *m* truss (*for a rupture*)
tirabuzón *m* corkscrew; curl, hanging curl, corkscrew curl
tiracantos *m* (*pl:* **-tos**) var. of **echacantos**
tiracol *m* or **tiracuello** *m* baldric
tirada *f* see **tirado**
tiradera *f* long horn-tipped Indian arrow
tiradero *m* hunting post, shooting post
tiradilla *f* catgut
tirado -da *adj* plentiful, given away, dirt-cheap; rakish, long and low (*ship*); cursive (*handwriting*); *m* wire drawing; *f* throw; draft; distance, stretch; time, period; printing; edition, issue, run, circulation; tirade; shooting party, hunting party; (mus.) tirade; **de** or **en una tirada** at one stroke; **tirada aparte** reprint
tirador -dora *mf* thrower; drawer; shooter; shot, good shot; fencer; *m* knob; doorknob, pull; pull chain; (elec.) pull cord, pull chain; slingshot; ruling pen, drawing pen; (print.) pressman; **tirador apostado** sniper; **tirador certero** sharpshooter; **tirador de oro** gold wiredrawer; **tirador de plata** silver wiredrawer; **tirador emboscado** sniper
tirafondo *m* wood screw, lag screw; (surg.) bullet-extracting forceps
tiraje *m* draft; printing, edition; (phot.) printing; (phot.) focal length
tirajo *m* (coll.) tatter, shred
tiralíneas *m* (*pl:* **-as**) ruling pen
tiramiento *m* shooting; tension, stretching
tiramira *f* long, narrow range (*of mountains*); string (*of things*); distance, stretch
tiranía *f* tyranny
tiranicida *adj* tyrannicidal; *mf* tyrannicide (*person*)
tiranicidio *m* tyrannicide (*act*)
tiránico -ca *adj* tyrannic or tyrannical
tiranizar §76 *va & vn* to tyrannize
tirano -na *adj* tyrannous; *mf* tyrant; *m* (orn.) kingbird
tirante *adj* tense, taut, tight; (fig.) tense, strained (*relations*); *m* trace (*of harness*); brace, tie rod; tie beam; **tirantes** *mpl* suspenders; **a tirantes largos** with four horses and two coachmen
tirantez *f* tenseness, tautness, tightness; strain; length
tirapié *m* stirrup (*of shoemaker*)
tirapo *m* (Am.) toy pistol
tirar *va* to throw, cast, fling; to throw away, cast off; to shoot, fire (*e.g., a gun*); to draw, pull, stretch (*e.g., wire*); to draw (*a line*); to squander; to give (*e.g., a kick*); to print; to attract; to tear down, to knock down; (phot.) to print; **a más tirar** or **a todo tirar** at the most ‖ *vn* to draw (*said of a chimney*); to pull; to turn (*to the right, to the left*); to last; to appeal, have an appeal; **ir tirando** (coll.) to get along; **tirad** or **tirar** pull (*word on public door*); **tirar a** to shoot at; to handle (*e.g., the sword*); to shade into, e.g., **tirar a verde** to shade into green, to be greenish; **tirar a** + *inf* to tend to + *inf;* to aspire to + *inf;* **tirar de** to pull, to pull on; to draw (*a sword*); to attract; to boast of being; **tirar de largo** or **tirar por largo** (coll.) to spend lavishly; to estimate rather high than low; **tirar por su lado** to go one's own way, to fend for oneself; **tira y afloja** (coll.) give and take; (coll.) hot and cold ‖ *vr* to rush, throw oneself; to give oneself over; to lie down; **tirársela de** (Am.) to boast of
tiratacos *m* (*pl:* **-cos**) popgun
tiratrón *m* (electron.) thyratron
tiravira *f* parbuckle
tirela *f* striped cloth
tirilla *f* neckband (*of shirt*)
tirio -ria *adj & mf* Tyrian
tiritaña *f* thin silk cloth; (coll.) trifle
tiritar *vn* to shiver
tiritón *m* shiver
tiritona *f* (coll.) fake shiver
tiro *m* throw; shot; gun; charge, load (*of gun*); report (*of gun*); range, rifle range; trace (*of harness*); draft (*of chimney; through a window*); team (*of horses*); flight (*of stairs*); reach; length (*e.g., of piece of cloth*); pull cord, pull chain; hoisting rope; hurt, damage; theft; trick; (min.) shaft; depth of shaft; (sport) drive, shot; (fig.) shot (*marksman; remark aimed at someone*); **tiros** *mpl* sword belt; (Am.) suspenders; **a tiro** within range; within reach; **a tiro de ballesta** (coll.) at a glance, from a distance; **a tiro de fusil** within gunshot; **a tiro de piedra** within a stone's throw; **a tiros** with shots; by shooting; **al tiro** (coll.) right away; **de tiros largos** (coll.) all dressed-up; (coll.) spick-and-span; **errar el tiro** to miss the mark; **hacer tiro a** (coll.) to shoot at (*to aspire to, to aim to get*); **matar a tiros** to shoot to death; **ni a tiros** not for love nor money; **poner el tiro muy alto** to aim high, to hitch one's wagon to a star; **salir el tiro por la culata** (coll.) to backfire; **ser un buen tiro** to be a good shot, be a good marksman; **tiro al blanco** target practice; **tiro al platillo** or **al plato** trapshooting; **tiro al vuelo** trapshooting; **tiro de la pesa** (sport) shot-put; **tiro de aspiración** exhaust draft; **tiro de pichón** trapshooting; **tiro de revés** (sport) backhand drive; **tiro par** team of four mules or horses; (*cap.*) *f* Tyre
tirocinio *m* apprenticeship
tiroidectomía *f* (surg.) thyroidectomy
tiroideo -a *adj* thyroid
tiroides *adj* thyroid; *m* (anat.) thyroid (*gland, cartilage*)
tiroidina *f* (pharm.) thyroid, thyroid extract
Tirol, el the Tyrol
tirolés -lesa *adj & mf* Tyrolese; *m* peddler (*of toys and hardware*); *f* Tyrolienne; yodeling

tirón *m* tyro, novice; jerk; tug, pull; (fig.) pull (*attraction*); **de un tirón** all at once, at one stroke; **tres horas de un tirón** three hours at a stretch
tirosina *f* (biochem.) tyrosine
tirosinasa *f* (biochem.) tyrosinase
tirotear *va* to snipe at, to blaze away at; *vr* to fire at each other; to bicker
tiroteo *m* firing, shooting
tirotricina *f* (pharm.) tyrothricin
tiroxina *f* (biochem.) thyroxin
tirreno -na *adj* Tyrrhenian
tirria *f* (coll.) dislike, grudge; **tener tirria a** (coll.) to have a grudge against, to have it in for
tirso *m* (bot. & myth.) thyrsus
tisana *f* tea, infusion
Tisbe *f* (myth.) Thisbe
tísico -ca *adj* phthisical
tisis *f* (path.) phthisis, consumption; **tisis galopante** (path.) galloping consumption
tisú *m* (*pl:* **-súes**) tissue, gold or silver tissue
tisular *adj* (pertaining to) tissue
tít. abr. of **título**
titán *m* titan; titan crane; (*cap.*) *m* (myth.) Titan
titanato *m* (chem.) titanate
Titania *f* Titania
titánico -ca *adj* titanic; (chem.) titanic; (myth.) Titanic
titanio -nia *adj* titanic; *m* (chem.) titanium
titanita *f* (mineral.) titanite
titano *m* (chem.) titanium
titar *vn* (prov.) to gobble (*said of turkey*)
títere *m* marionette, puppet; mania, fixed idea; (coll.) whipper-snapper; (coll.) nincompoop; (fig.) puppet; **títeres** *mpl* puppet show, pantomime; acrobatics; **echar los títeres a rodar** (coll.) to tell them all where to get off at; **hacer títere a** (coll.) to fascinate, enthrall; **no dejar títere con cabeza** or **cara** (coll.) to completely upset the applecart
titerero -ra *mf* var. of **titiritero**
titeretada *f* (coll.) laxity, shabbiness, folly
titerista *mf* var. of **titiritero**
tití *m* (*pl:* **-tíes**) (zool.) marmoset
titilación *f* titillation; quivering; twinkling
titilar *va* to titillate; *vn* to quiver; to twinkle
titileo *m* twinkling
titímalo *m* (bot.) spurge
titirimundi *m* var. of **mundonuevo**
titiritaina *f* (coll.) din of wind instruments; (coll.) noisy merrymaking
titiritar *vn* to shake, to shiver
titiritero -ra *mf* puppeteer; ropewalker, acrobat, juggler
tít.º abr. of **título**
tito *m* (bot.) grass pea; chamber pot; (*cap.*) *m* Titus
titoísmo *m* Titoism
titoísta *adj & mf* Titoist
Titono *m* (myth.) Tithonus
titración *f* (chem.) titration
titrar *va & vn* (chem.) to titrate
titubeante *adj* staggering; tottering; stammering; wavering
titubear *vn* to stagger, totter; to stammer, stutter; to waver, hesitate; **titubear en** + *inf* to waver in + *ger*, to hesitate to + *inf*
titubeo *m* staggering; tottering; stammering; wavering, hesitation
titulación *f* (chem.) titration
titulado -da *adj* titled; so-called; *m* titleholder; titled person; degree holder
titular *adj* titular; official; *m* bearer, holder (*e.g., of a passport*); titleholder; incumbent; headline; *f* (print.) capital letter (*used in a title or headline*); *va* to title, to entitle; (chem.) to titrate; *vn* to receive a title of nobility; (chem.) to titrate; *vr* to receive a title; to be called; to call oneself
titulillo *m* (print.) running head, running title; **andar en titulillos** (coll.) to be a stickler
título *m* title; titled person; regulation; certificate; bond; diploma; degree (*granted by a university*); headline; grade, content (*of ore*); fineness (*of coinage*); strength, concentration (*of alcoholic liquors*); (chem., immun. & physiol.) titer; **títulos** *mpl* qualifications, credentials; **a título de** as a, by way of, on the score of; **a título de información** unofficially; **título de propiedad** (law) title deed
tiza *f* chalk
tizna *f* blackening
tiznadura *f* smudge, stain, spot
tiznajo *m* (coll.) smudge
tiznar *va* to soil with soot; to stain, to spot; to defame; *vr* to become soiled with soot; to get stained or spotted; (Am.) to get drunk
tizne *m & f* soot; *m* half-burned stick, firebrand
tiznón *m* smudge, spot of soot
tizo *m* brand (*partly burned piece of wood*)
tizón *m* brand (*partly burned piece of wood*); bunt, wheat smut; (mas.) header; (fig.) brand (*dishonor*)
tizona *f* (coll.) sword
tizonada *f* or **tizonazo** *m* blow with a firebrand; (coll.) hellfire
tizoncillo *m* bunt, wheat smut
tizonear *vn* to stir up the fire
tizonera *f* charcoal kiln (*made of partly burned wood*)
tlapalería *f* (Am.) paint store, hardware store
tmesis *f* (rhet.) tmesis
tno. abr. of **teléfono**
T.N.T. abr. of **trinitrotolueno**
t.º abr. of **tomo**
toalla *f* towel; pillow sham; **toalla continua** roller towel; **toalla de baño** bath towel; **toalla rusa** Turkish towel; **toalla sin fin** roller towel
toallero *m* towel rack
toalleta *f* small towel; napkin
toar *va* (naut.) to tow
toba *f* (geol.) tufa (*porous limestone*); (geol.) tuff (*volcanic rock*); (dent.) tartar; (bot.) cotton thistle; crust, cover
tobar *m* tufa quarry
tobera *f* (found.) tuyère
Tobías *m* Tobias
tobillera *adj fem* (coll.) flapperish; *f* (coll.) flapper, bobbysoxer; (coll.) subdeb; anklet; (sport) ankle support
tobillo *m* ankle
tobo *m* (Am.) bucket
tobogán *m* toboggan; slide, chute
toboso -sa *adj* tufaceous
toca *f* toque; headdress; veil; cornet (*headdress of Sisters of Charity*)
tocadiscos *m* (*pl:* **-cos**) record player; **tocadiscos automático** record changer
tocado -da *adj* touched (*spoiled; mentally unbalanced*); **tocado de la cabeza** (coll.) touched in the head; *m* hairdo, coiffure; headdress; topknot (*bow of ribbon worn on head*)
tocador -dora *mf* player, performer (*on musical instrument*); *m* boudoir; dressing table; dressing case, toilet case
tocadura *f* hairdo, coiffure; headdress
tocamiento *m* feeling, touching; inspiration
tocante *adj* touching; touching, moving; **tocante a** touching, concerning, with reference to
tocar §86 *va* to feel; to touch; to touch on; to ring; to toll; to strike; to feel, to come to know, to suffer; to do (*the hair*); to touch (*with a touchstone*); (mus.) to play (*an instrument, a composition, a phonograph record*); to beat (*a drum*); (paint.) to touch up ‖ *vn* to touch; **en** or **por lo que toca a** with regard to; **tocar a** to knock at (*a door*); to behoove; to pertain to, to concern; to be related to; to fall to, to fall to the lot of; to be the turn of; to approach (*e.g., the end*); **tocar a** + *inf* to be time to + *inf*; **tocar a uno** + *inf* to be up to someone to + *inf*; **tocar en** to touch at (*a port*); to touch (*land*); to touch on; to approach, border on ‖ *vr* to put one's hat on, cover one's head; to be related (*said of two or more persons*); to touch each other; to become touched (*mentally unbalanced*); to make one's toilet; **tocarse con** to have on, to wear (*on the head*); **tocárselas** (coll.) to beat it, run away
tocasalva *f* var. of **salvilla**
tocata *f* (mus.) toccata; (coll.) drubbing, beating
tocayo -ya *mf* namesake
tocía *f* var. of **atutía**

tocinera *f* see **tocinero**
tocinería *f* bacon and pork shop or stand
tocinero -ra *mf* bacon and pork dealer; *f* pork-salting board or table
tocino *m* bacon; salt pork; (coll.) fast rope skipping; **tocino del cielo** candied yolk of egg
tocio -cia *adj* dwarf (*oak*)
tocoferol *m* (biochem.) tocopherol
tocología *f* tocology, obstetrics
tocólogo -ga *mf* tocologist, obstetrician
tocón *m* stump (*of tree, arm, or leg*)
toconal *m* ground full of stumps; olive grove of new shoots growing from stumps
tocte *m* (bot.) black walnut
tocuyo *m* (Am.) coarse cotton cloth
tochedad *f* roughness, coarseness, crudity
tochimbo *m* (Am.) smelting furnace
tocho -cha *adj* rough, coarse, crude; *m* (found.) bloom, billet
tochura *f* crudity
todabuena or **todasana** *f* (bot.) parkleaves, tutsan
todavía *adv* still, yet; **todavía no** not yet
todo -da *adj* all, whole, every; any; full (*e.g., speed*); *m* whole; everything; **todos** *mpl* all, everybody; **así y todo** even so, anyhow; **ante todo** first of all; **con todo** still, however; **del todo** wholly, entirely; **de todo en todo** through and through, entirely; **jugar el todo por el todo** to stake everything; **por todo** all in all; **ser el todo** (coll.) to be the whole show; **sobre todo** above all, especially; **todo el que** everybody who; **todo lo que** all that; **todos cuantos** all those who
todopoderoso -sa *adj* all-powerful, almighty; **el Todopoderoso** the Almighty (*God*)
tofo *m* (path.) tophus
toga *f* (hist.) toga; gown (*of professor, judge, etc.*)
togado -da *adj* togaed; *m* gownsman
toisón *m* Golden Fleece (*order*); (myth.) Golden Fleece; **toisón de oro** Golden Fleece (*order*); (myth.) Golden Fleece
tojal *m* growth of furze
tojino *m* (naut.) chock; (naut.) round, rundle (*on side of ship*); (naut.) cleat
tojo *m* (bot.) gorse, furze, whin
tolanos *mpl* short hair on back of neck; (vet.) gingivitis
toldadura *f* awning, awnings
toldar *va* to cover with an awning
toldilla *f* (naut.) poop, poop deck
toldo *m* awning; tilt (*cloth covering of cart or wagon*); pride, haughtiness
tole *m* hubbub, uproar; popular clamor (*against something*); **tomar el tole** (coll.) to run away, leave in a hurry; **tole tole** talk, gossip
toledano -na *adj & mf* Toledan
toledo *m* word used by the superstitious instead of thirteen
tolerable *adj* tolerable
tolerancia *f* tolerance; toleration; (mach. & med.) tolerance; tolerance (*in coinage*); **por tolerancia** on suffrance
tolerante *adj* tolerant
tolerantismo *m* toleration; tolerationism
tolerar *va* to tolerate
tolete *m* (naut.) thole, tholepin; (Am.) club, cudgel
tolilo *m* (chem.) tolyl
tolmera *f* place full of tall boulders
tolmo *m* tall boulder
Tolomeo *m* Ptolemy
Tolón *f* Toulon
tolondro -dra *adj* scatterbrained; *mf* scatterbrain; *m* bump, lump; **a topa tolondro** headlong, recklessly
tolondrón -drona *adj* scatterbrained; *m* bump, lump; **a tolondrones** intermittently, piecemeal
Tolosa *f* Toulouse; Tolosa (*town in northern Spain*)
tolteca *adj & mf* Toltec
tolueno *m* (chem.) toluene
toluico -ca *adj* (chem.) toluic
toluidina *f* (chem.) toluidine
toluol *m* (chem.) toluol
tolva *f* hopper; chute
tolvanera *f* dust storm, dust whirl
tolla *f* quagmire, soggy marsh; (Am.) drinking trough
tollina *f* (coll.) beating, drubbing
tollo *m* (hunt.) blind; quagmire; loin of stag; (ichth.) dogfish; (prov.) puddle
tollón *m* narrow pass, narrow road; (bot.) toyon
tom. abr. of **tomo**
toma *f* taking, assumption; seizure, capture; dose; tap; intake, inlet; (elec.) tap, outlet; (elec.) plug; (elec.) terminal; (mov.) take; **toma de antena** (rad.) antenna terminal or connection; **toma de corriente** (elec.) current collecting, current collector; (elec.) tap, outlet; (elec.) plug; **toma de posesión** installation, induction (*into a new office or position*); inauguration (*e.g., of a new president*); **toma de tierra** (aer.) landing; (rad.) ground terminal or connection; **toma directa** (aut.) high gear; **toma media** (elec.) center tap; **toma y daca** *m* give-and-take
toma-corriente *m* or **toma-corrientes** *m* (*pl:* **-tes**) (elec.) current collector; (elec.) tap, outlet; (elec.) plug
tomada *f* seizure, capture
tomadero *m* handle; intake, inlet
tomador -dora *mf* (coll.) thief; (Am.) drinker; *m* (com.) drawee; (naut.) gasket
tomadura *f* taking, assumption; seizure; dose
tomaína *f* (biochem.) ptomaine
tomajón -jona *adj* (coll.) thieving; *mf* (coll.) petty thief
tomar *va* to take; to get; to seize; to take on; to catch (*e.g., cold*); to have (*e.g., breakfast*); **tomar a** to take from; **tomar a bien** to take the right way (*i.e., in the right spirit*); **tomar a mal** to take offense at; **tomarla con** to pick at or on, to fight with; to have a grudge against; **tomarle a uno la risa** to be overcome with laughter; **tomar para sí** to take to oneself; **tomar por** to take for, e.g., **le tomé a Vd. por otra persona** I took you for someone else; **tomar prestado** to borrow; **tomar sobre sí** to take upon oneself; *vn* to take (*to the right, to the left*); **¡toma!** (coll.) why, of course!; (coll.) there you are!; *vr* to take; to have (*e.g., breakfast*); to get rusty; **tomarse con** to pick a quarrel with; **tomarse tiempo** to bide one's time
Tomás *m* Thomas; **Santo Tomás** Saint Thomas; **Santo Tomás de Aquino** Saint Thomas Aquinas; **un Santo Tomás** a doubting Thomas
tomatada *f* fried tomatoes
tomatal *m* tomato patch, tomato field
tomatazo *m* blow with a tomato
tomate *m* (bot.) tomato (*plant and fruit*); (coll.) tear or run (*in stocking*); (Am.) tomatillo; (Am.) cape gooseberry; **tomate de invierno** (bot.) strawberry tomato
tomatero -ra *adj* (pertaining to the) tomato; *mf* tomato raiser or dealer; *f* (bot.) tomato, tomato plant
tomavistas (*pl:* **-tas**) *adj* picture-taking; *m* motion-picture camera; cameraman
toma y daca *m* give-and-take
tombac *m* tombac, Dutch brass
tómbola *f* raffle, charity raffle
tomento *m* coarse tow; (bot.) tomentum
tomentoso -sa *adj* tomentose
tomillar *m* growth of thyme
tomillo *m* (bot.) thyme; **tomillo real** (bot.) savory, winter savory; **tomillo salsero** (bot.) Spanish thyme
tomineja *f* or **tominejo** *m* (orn.) hummingbird
tomismo *m* Thomism
tomista *adj & mf* Thomist
tomiza *f* esparto rope
tomo *m* volume (*one in a set*); bulk; importance, consequence; **de tomo y lomo** of consequence; (coll.) bulky and heavy
tomón -mona *adj & mf* (coll.) var. of **tomajón**
ton. abr. of **tonelada**
ton *m;* **sin ton ni son** without rhyme or reason
tonada *f* air, melody, song
tonadilla *f* light tune; (theat.) musical interlude
tonadillero -ra *mf* composer of musical interludes; popular singer

tonal *adj* tonal
tonalidad *f* (mus. & f.a.) tonality
tonar §77 *vn* (poet.) to thunder, to lighten
tondiz *f* var. of **tundizno**
tonel *m* cask, barrel; (aer.) barrel roll; (coll.) tank (*heavy drinker*)
tonelada *f* ton; tun (*measure equivalent to 252 gallons*); (naut.) ton; **tonelada métrica** metric ton
tonelaje *m* tonnage
tonelería *f* barrelmaking, cooperage; barrel factory; barrels, stock of barrels
tonelero -ra *adj* barrel, barrelmaking; *m* barrelmaker, cooper
tonelete *m* keg; short skirt, kilt; tutu, ballet skirt; (arm.) skirt
tonga *f* coat; layer; (Am.) pile
tongada *f* coat; layer; **en una tongada** (coll.) all at once
tongonear *vr* (Am.) to strut, swagger
tongoneo *m* (Am.) strut, swagger
tonicidad *f* tonicity
tónico -ca *adj* tonic; *m* (med.) tonic; **tónico nervioso** nerve tonic; *f* (mus.) keynote, tonic; (phonet.) tonic
tonificación *f* strengthening, invigoration
tonificador -dora or **tonificante** *adj* strengthening, invigorating
tonificar §86 *va* to strengthen, invigorate
tonillo *m* singsong; accent (*of a region*)
tonina *f* (ichth.) tunny; (zool.) dolphin
tonita *f* tonite
tono *m* tone; tune; (f.a., mus., phonet. & physiol.) tone; (mus.) pitch; (mus.) key; (mus.) slide (*of wind instrument*); **a este tono** like this; **a tono con** in tune with, in harmony with; **bajar el tono** to lower one's tone; **dar el tono** to set the standard; **darse tono** (coll.) to put on airs; **de buen tono** stylish, elegant; **de mal tono** vulgar; **estar a tono** (coll.) to be in style; **mudar de tono** to change one's tone; to change one's tune; **poner a tono** to tune up (*a car engine*); **subir** or **subirse de tono** to become haughty; to live in a grand style; **tono mayor** (mus.) major key; **tono menor** (mus.) minor key
tonómetro *m* tonometer
Tonquín, el Tonkin or Tongking
tonsila *f* (anat.) tonsil
tonsilar *adj* tonsillar
tonsilectomía *f* (surg.) tonsillectomy
tonsilitis *f* (path.) tonsillitis
tonsura *f* shearing, clipping; (eccl.) tonsure
tonsurar *va* to shear, to clip; (eccl.) to tonsure
tontada *f* silliness, nonsense
tontaina *adj* (coll.) foolish; *mf* (coll.) fool
tontear *vn* to talk nonsense, to act foolishly
tontedad *f*, **tontera** or **tontería** *f* foolishness, nonsense; triviality
tontillo *m* farthingale, hoop skirt
tontina *f* tontine
tonto -ta *adj* foolish, stupid; **a tontas y a locas** in disorder, haphazard; *mf* fool, dolt; **como tonto en vísperas** (coll.) in a brown study; **hacerse el tonto** (coll.) to play dumb; **tonto de capirote** (coll.) blockhead
tontuna *f* silliness, nonsense
toña *f* tipcat (*boys' game*); cat (*used in tipcat*)
topacio *m* topaz
topada *f* var. of **topetada**
topadizo -za *adj* bobbing up all the time
topar *va* to butt; to bump; to run into, run across, encounter; *vn* to butt; to take a bet; to come out well, to succeed; (coll.) to guess right; **tope donde tope** (coll.) strike where it may; **topar con** to run into, run across, encounter; **topar en** to run into, run across, encounter; to lie, e.g., **en eso topa la dificultad** there's where the trouble lies
tope *m* butt; bumper, buffer; bump, collision; encounter; top; rub, difficulty; scuffle, fight; (mach.) stop, check; (naut.) masthead; (naut.) topmast head; (naut.) topman; (rail.) bumper; **topes** *mpl* (theat.) stage to left of spectator; **ahí está el tope** there's the rub, that's the trouble; **al tope** or **a tope** end to end; flush; **estar hasta los topes** (naut.) to be loaded to the gunwales; (coll.) to be full, to be satiated; **hasta el tope** to the brim; **tope de puerta** doorstop; **tope máximo** ceiling price; *adj* top (*price*); last (*date*)
topera *f* molehill
topetada *f* butt (*e.g., given by head of a goat*); (coll.) butt (*with the head*); **darse de topetadas** (coll.) to butt each other
topetar *va* to butt; *vn* to butt; **topetar con** (coll.) to bump, bump into; (coll.) to run across
topetazo *m* var. of **topetada**
topetear *va & vn* var. of **topetar**
topetón *m* butt; bump, collision
topetudo -da *adj* butting (*animal*)
topiario -ria *adj & f* topiary
tópico -ca *adj* topical, local; (med.) topical; *m* topic; platitude; (med.) external local application
topinada *f* (coll.) blundering; (coll.) stumbling, awkwardness
topinaria *f* mole, wen, talpa
topinera *f* molehill; **beber como una topinera** to drink like a fish
topo *m* (zool.) mole; (coll.) blunderer; (coll.) stumbler, awkward person; top; **más ciego que un topo** blind as a bat; *adj* (coll.) blundering; (coll.) stumbly, awkward
topografía *f* topography
topográfico -ca *adj* topographic or topographical
topógrafo -fa *mf* topographer
topología *f* (anat. & math.) topology
toponimia *f* toponymy; (anat.) toponymy; toponymics
toponímico -ca *adj* toponymic
topónimo *m* toponym, place name
toponomástica *f* var. of **toponimia**
toque *m* touch; ring; knock; sound; beat (*of drum*); test, check; gist, point; call (*at a port*); (paint.) touch; (coll.) blow; **dar un toque a** (coll.) to put to the test; (coll.) to sound out, to feel out; **toque a muerto** toll, knell; **toque de ánimas** passing bell, burial peal; **toque de corneta** bugle call; **toque de diana** (mil.) reveille; **toque de difuntos** passing bell, burial peal; **toque de queda** curfew; **toque de retreta** (mil.) tattoo; **toque de silbato** whistle
toqueado *m* clapping, stamping, rapping
toquilla *f* triangular kerchief; knitted shawl
tora *f* torah; fireworks in the form of a bull; **la Tora** the Torah
torácico -ca *adj* thoracic
torada *f* drove of bulls
toral *adj* chief, main, principal; *m* unbleached yellow wax; mold for copper bars; copper bar
tórax *m* (*pl:* **-rax**) (anat. & zool.) thorax
torbellino *m* whirlwind; (fig.) whirlwind; (coll.) harum-scarum
torca *f* (geol.) crater, depression
torce *f* loop of necklace or chain
torcecuello *m* (orn.) wryneck
torcedero -ra *adj* crooked; *m* twister (*device*)
torcedor -dora *adj* twisting; *mf* twister; *m* twister, twisting machine; tobacco twister; disappointment, source of disappointment; *f* (ent.) sewer, leaf sewer
torcedura *f* twist, twisting; sprain; dislocation; small wine
torcer §87 *va* to twist; to bend; to turn; to change, turn aside; to twist up, screw up (*one's face*); to turn (*one's ankle*); to twist (*to misconstrue*); to pervert (*the ends of justice*); **andar** or **estar torcido con** (coll.) to be on the outs with; *vn* to turn (*to the right or left*); *vr* to twist; to bend; to sprain, dislocate; to turn; to turn sour; to go crooked, go astray; to turn bad, to fail; **torcérsele a uno la suerte** (Am.) to be out of luck
torcido -da *adj* twisted; crooked; bent; cross (*eyes*); (fig.) crooked (*person or conduct*); (Am.) unlucky; *m* curl (*of hair*); twist (*of cotton, silk, etc.*); twist of candied fruit; look of scorn; *f* wick; curlpaper
torcijón *m* cramps; (vet.) gripes
torcimiento *m* twist, twisting; roundabout way of talking
torculado -da *adj* screw-shaped
tórculo *m* press, screw press
tordella *f* (orn.) missel thrush
tórdiga *f* strip of hide or leather

tordillo -lla *adj* dapple-gray
tordo -da *adj* dapple-gray; *mf* dapple-gray horse; *m* (orn.) thrush; **tordo alirrojo** (orn.) redwing, song thrush; **tordo de agua** (orn.) water ouzel; **tordo de mar** (ichth.) red wrasse; **tordo mayor** (orn.) missel thrush
toreador *m* toreador; (archaic) mounted bullfighter
torear *va* to fight (*bulls*); to banter, tease, string along; *vn* to fight bulls, be a bullfighter
toreo *m* bullfighting
torera *f* see **torero**
torería *f* bullfighters; bullfighters' guild; (Am.) boyish prank
torero -ra *adj* (coll.) (pertaining to) bullfighting; *mf* torero, bullfighter; *f* tight unbuttoned jacket
torés *m* (arch.) torus
torete *m* small bull; (coll.) puzzler, baffling question; (coll.) topic of conversation
tórico -ca *adj* toric; (chem.) thoric
toril *m* (taur.) bull pen
torillo *m* bead, small molding; dowel, pin; (coll.) topic of conversation
torio *m* (chem.) thorium
toriondez *f* rut (*of cattle*)
toriondo -da *adj* ruttish (*cattle*)
torismo *m* Toryism
torita *f* (mineral.) thorite
torloroto *m* shepherd's horn
tormagal *m* or **tormellera** *f* var. of **tolmera**
tormenta *f* storm, tempest; misfortune, adversity; turmoil
tormentila *f* (bot.) bloodroot, tormentil
tormentín *m* (naut.) jib boom
tormento *m* torment; torture; anguish; (hist.) tormentum
tormentoso -sa *adj* stormy; (naut.) storm-ridden (*ship*)
tormera *f* var. of **tolmera**
tormo *m* tall boulder; clod, clump (*of earth*)
torna *f* return; dam; tap; **volver las tornas** to give tit for tat; to turn the tables
tornaboda *f* day after wedding
tornada *f* return; envoy (*stanza ending a poem*); (vet.) gid, water brain
tornadera *f* two-pronged winnowing fork
tornadizo -za *adj* changeable, fickle; renegade; *mf* turncoat, renegade
tornado *m* (meteor.) tornado
tornadura *f* return
tornaguía *f* return receipt
tornalecho *m* bed canopy
tornamiento *m* turn, change
tornapunta *f* prop, brace; strut (*of a gable frame*)
tornar *va* to return, give back; to turn, to make; *vn* to return; to turn; **tornar a** + *inf* verb + again, e.g., **tornó a abrir la puerta** he opened the door again; *vr* to turn, to become
tornasol *m* (bot.) sunflower; (chem.) litmus; iridescence
tornasolado -da *adj* iridescent, changeable (*fabric*)
tornasolar *va* to make iridescent; *vr* to become iridescent
tornátil *adj* turned (*on a lathe*); changeable, fickle
tornatrás *mf* throwback, reversion (*person*); half-breed
tornavía *f* (rail.) turntable
tornaviaje *m* return trip; things brought back from a trip
tornavirón *m* (coll.) slap in the face, smack on the head
tornavoz *m* (*pl:* **-voces**) soundboard, sounding board (*to direct sound to audience*)
torneador *m* turner, lathe operator; tourneyer, jouster
torneaduras *fpl* turnings, chips (*from a lathe*)
tornear *va* to turn, turn up (*on a lathe*); (sport) to curve (*a ball*); *vn* to go around; to tourney; to muse, to meditate
torneo *m* tourney; match, tournament; turning (*on a lathe*); **torneo de tenis** tennis match
tornería *f* turning (*on a lathe*); lathe work; lathe shop, machine shop, turnery
tornero *m* turner, lathe operator
tornillería *f* stock of screws or bolts
tornillero *m* (coll.) deserter (*from army*)
tornillo *m* screw; bolt; vise; clamp; small lathe; (mil.) desertion; **apretar los tornillos a** (coll.) to put the screws on; **faltarle a uno un tornillo** or **tener flojos los tornillos** (coll.) to have a screw loose; **tornillo de Arquímedes** Archimedes' screw; **tornillo de mordazas** jaw vise; **tornillo de ojo** eyebolt; **tornillo de orejas** thumbscrew; **tornillo de presión** setscrew; **tornillo micrométrico** micrometric screw; **tornillo para madera** wood screw; **tornillo para metales** machine screw; **tornillo sin fin** worm gear; **tornillo tensor** turnbuckle
torniquete *m* bell crank; turnstile; turnbuckle (*to fasten a shutter against the wall*); (Am.) fence ratchet (*to stretch wires of fence*); (surg.) tourniquet; **dar torniquete a** to twist the meaning of
torniscón *m* (coll.) slap in the face, smack on the head; (coll.) sharp pinch
torno *m* turn, revolution; lathe; potter's wheel; vise; clamp; winch, windlass; drum; turn (*in a river*); brake (*of carriage*); revolving server (*for passing something through a wall*); **a torno** around; on a lathe; **en torno** around; in exchange; **en torno a** or **de** around; **torno de alfarero** potter's wheel; **torno de hilar** spinning wheel
toro *m* bull; (arch.) molding of convex profile; (anat., bot. & math.) torus; (fig.) bull (*strong, husky fellow*); **toros** *mpl* bullfight; **ciertos son los toros** (coll.) you can depend on that; **correr toros** to fight bulls; **echar** or **soltar el toro a** (coll.) to talk straight off the shoulder to; **toro corrido** (coll.) smart fellow, no easy mark; **toro de lidia** fighting bull; **toro de muerte** (taur.) bull to be fought till killed
torófilo -la *mf* bullfight fan
toroide *m* (geom.) toroid
torón *m* (chem.) thoron; strand (*of cable*)
toronja *f* grapefruit (*fruit*)
toronjil *m* or **toronjina** *f* (bot.) lemon balm, garden balm
toronjo *m* (bot.) grapefruit (*tree*)
toroso -sa *adj* robust, husky
torozón *m* annoyance, worry; (vet.) gripes
torpe *adj* slow, heavy; awkward; dull, stupid; bawdy, lewd; infamous; ugly, crude
torpedeamiento *m* var. of **torpedeo**
torpedear *va* (nav. & fig.) to torpedo
torpedeo *m* torpedoing; (fig.) torpedoing
torpedero *m* (nav.) torpedo boat; (Am.) shortstop
torpedista *m* torpedoist
torpedo *m* (nav., ichth. & rail.) torpedo; (aut.) open car, touring car; **torpedo aéreo** (aer.) aerial torpedo
torpeza *f* torpidity, slowness; awkwardness; dullness, stupidity; bawdiness, lewdness; infamy; ugliness, crudeness
torques *f* (*pl:* **-ques**) torque (*ancient necklace*)
torrar *va* to toast
torre *f* tower; watchtower; castle, rook (*in chess*); (arti. & nav.) turret; (prov.) country house, place in the country, farm; (Am.) chimney of sugar mill; **torre albarrana** watchtower; bartizan; **torre de Babel** Tower of Babel; **torre de burbujeo** bubble tower; **torre de control** (rail.) switch tower; **torre del homenaje** donjon, keep; stronghold; **torre de lanzamiento** launching tower; **torre de mando** (aer.) control tower; (nav.) conning tower; **torre de marfil** (fig.) ivory tower; **torre de señales** signal tower; **torre de viento** castle in the air; **torre de vigía** (naut.) crow's-nest; **torre fraccionadora** fractionating tower; **Torre inclinada** Leaning Tower; **torre maestra** donjon, keep; **torre reloj** clock tower
torrear *va* to fortify with towers or turrets
torrefacción *f* torrefaction; toasting
torrefacto -ta *adj* toasted
torrejón *m* crooked little tower
torrencial *adj* torrential
torrentada *f* flash flood
torrente *m* torrent (*rush of water*); (fig.) torrent
torrentera *f* bed of a torrent; gully

torrentoso -sa *adj* (Am.) torrential
torreón *m* (arch.) turret; fortified tower
torrero *m* lighthouseman
torreta *f* (nav.) turret; (nav.) conning tower (*of submarine*)
torreznada *f* large fry of bacon
torreznero -ra *adj* (coll.) lazy, self-indulgent; *mf* (coll.) loafer, idler
torrezno *m* rasher (*slice of bacon*)
tórrido -da *adj* torrid
torrija *f* slice of bread dipped in milk or wine, fried, and sweetened with sugar or honey
torsión *f* torsion; (mech.) torsion
torsional *adj* torsional
torso *m* torso; (f.a.) torso; (paint.) bust
torta *f* cake; (print.) font; (mas.) roughcast; (coll.) slap; **costar la torta un pan** (coll.) to cost a lot more than expected; **ser tortas y pan pintado** (coll.) to be not so bad; (coll.) to be a cinch; **torta a la plancha** griddlecake, hot cake
tortada *f* meat or chicken pie; layer of mortar; batch of mortar
tortazo *m* (coll.) slap, slap in the face
tortedad *f* twisted state
tortero -ra *mf* cake maker; cake dealer; *m* cake box or basket; *f* flat earthenware baking pan; round cake pan; whorl of spinning wheel
torticero -ra *adj* wrong, unjust
torticolis *m* or **tortícolis** *m* (path.) torticollis, wryneck, stiff neck
tortilla *f* omelet; (Am.) tortilla (*corn-meal cake*); **hacer tortilla a** (coll.) to smash or break to pieces; **volverse la tortilla** (coll.) to turn out contrary to expectations; (coll.) to turn against one, e.g., **se volvió la tortilla** fortune turned against him (her, you, etc.); **tortilla a la española** potato omelet; **tortilla a la francesa** plain omelet
tortillo *m* (her.) bezant
tortillón *m* (f.a.) stump
tórtola *f* (orn.) turtledove; (orn.) ringdove
tórtolo *m* male turtledove; (coll.) turtledove (*affectionate person*)
tortor *m* (naut.) twist; (naut.) heaver
tortuga *f* (zool.) tortoise, turtle; **tortuga gigante** (zool.) giant tortoise; **tortuga lagarto** (zool.) mud turtle, snapping turtle
tortuguilla *f* (ent.) Mexican bean beetle
tortuosidad *f* tortuosity, tortuousness
tortuoso -sa *adj* winding, tortuous; (fig.) tortuous, devious
tortura *f* twisted state; torture
torturador -dora *adj* torturing, torturous
torturar *va* to torture
tórulo *m* (ent.) torulus
torva *f* see **torvo**
torvisca *f* var. of **torvisco**
torviscal *m* field of spurge flax
torvisco *m* (bot.) spurge flax
torvo -va *adj* grim, stern, fierce; *f* rain squall, snow squall
torzal *m* cord, twist
torzaldillo *m* light cord, thin twist
torzón *m* var. of **torozón**
torzonado -da *adj* suffering from gripes
torzuelo *m* (orn.) tercel, male falcon
tos *f* (*pl:* **toses**) cough; coughing; **tos convulsiva** or **ferina** (path.) whooping cough; **tos perruna** barking cough
tosca *f* see **tosco**
toscano -na *adj & mf* Tuscan; *m* Tuscan (*language; dialect*); **la Toscana** Tuscany
tosco -ca *adj* coarse, rough; uncouth; *f* (geol.) tufa; (geol.) tuff
tosegoso -sa *adj* coughing
toser *va* (coll.) to equal, to beat (*especially in valor*); *vn* to cough; **toser fuerte** to boast
tosidura *f* coughing
tosigar §59 *va* to poison
tósigo *m* poison; grief, sorrow
tosigoso -sa *adj* poisoned; coughing
tosiguero *m* (bot.) poison ivy
tosquedad *f* coarseness, roughness; uncouthness
tostada *f* see **tostado**
tostadera *f* toaster; roaster
tostadero *m* (coll.) oven (*hot place*)
tostado -da *adj* tan, sunburned; brown; *m* toasting; roasting; *f* piece of toast; **dar** or **pegar la** or **una tostada a** (coll.) to cheat, to trick, to harm; **no ver la tostada** (coll.) to see no good in it, to not be able to hand it a thing
tostador -dora *adj* toasting; roasting; burning; *mf* toaster; roaster; *m* toaster (*utensil*); roaster (*utensil*)
tostadura *f* toasting; roasting
tostar §77 *va & vr* to toast; to roast; to burn; to tan
tostón *m* roasted chickpea; toast dipped in olive oil; roast pig; scorched piece (*of food*); Mexican silver coin worth 50 centavos
total *adj & m* total; overall; *adv* in a word
totalidad *f* totality; whole; **en su totalidad** in its entirety; **la casi totalidad de** almost all of
totalitario -ria *adj & mf* totalitarian
totalitarismo *m* totalitarianism
totalización *f* totalization
totalizador *m* totalizer; totalizator, pari-mutuel
totalizar §76 *va* to totalize, to add up; to amount to; *vr* to add up; **totalizarse en** to add up to
tótem *m* (*pl:* **-tems**) totem
totémico -ca *adj* totemic
totemismo *m* totemism
totilimundi *m* var. of **mundonuevo**
totipalmo -ma *adj* (zool.) totipalmate
totovía *f* (orn.) crested lark
totuma *f* calabash (*fruit*)
totumo *m* (bot.) calabash tree; calabash (*fruit and vessel made with it*)
tova *f* var. of **totovía**
toxalbúmina *f* var. of **toxialbúmina**
toxemia *f* (path.) toxemia
toxémico -ca *adj* toxemic
toxialbúmina *f* (biochem.) toxalbumin
toxicar §86 *va* to poison
toxicidad *f* toxicity
tóxico -ca *adj & m* toxic
toxicogénico -ca or **toxicógeno -na** *adj* toxicogenic
toxicología *f* toxicology
toxicológico -ca *adj* toxicological
toxicólogo -ga *mf* toxicologist
toxicomanía *f* drug addiction
toxicómano -na *adj* addicted to drugs; *mf* drug addict
toxicosis *f* (*pl:* **-sis**) (path.) toxicosis
toxifobia *f* var. of **toxofobia**
toxina *f* (bact.) toxin
toxofobia *f* (psychopath.) toxiphobia
tozo -za *adj* dwarfish, stumpy; *f* chunk of bark; log with sharp edge
tozolada *f* or **tozolón** *m* blow on the neck
tozudez *f* stubbornness
tozudo -da *adj* stubborn
tozuelo *m* thick neck (*of an animal*)
tpo. abr. of **tiempo**
tr. abr. of **transitivo**
traba *f* tie, bond; clasp, lock; hobble, clog, trammel; obstacle; (law) seizure, attachment; (mas.) bond
trabacuenta *f* mistake (*e.g., in an addition*); dispute, argument
trabadero *m* pastern (*of horse*)
trabado -da *adj* joined, connected; tied, fastened; robust, sinewy; white-footed (*i.e., having white forefeet or a white right forefoot and a white left hind foot*); (phonet.) checked (*syllable*)
trabadura *f* joining, uniting; bond, union
trabajado -da *adj* overworked, worn-out; busy; strained, forced (*e.g., style*)
trabajador -dora *adj* working; industrious, hard-working; *mf* worker, laborer; toiler; *m* workman, workingman; *f* workingwoman
trabajar *va* to work (*e.g., wood*); to till (*the soil*); to bother, disturb; to work, to drive (*a person*); *vn* to work; to strain; to warp; (naut.) to labor (*e.g., in a storm*); **trabajar en** or **por** *+inf* to strive to *+inf; vr* to strive, to exert oneself
trabajera *f* (coll.) bother, nuisance, chore
trabajo *m* work; labor (*as contrasted with capital*); trouble; (phys.) work; **trabajos** *mpl* tribulations, hardships; **trabajo a destajo** piece-

work; **trabajo a domicilio** homework (*work done in home of worker*); **trabajo a jornal** timework; **trabajo a tarea** piecework; **trabajo de campaña** or **de campo** field work; **trabajo de mucho aliento** long undertaking; endless task; **trabajo de taller** shopwork; **trabajo de zapa** underhand work; **trabajo motor** (phys.) work developed by a motor, work done by a force; **trabajo resistente** (phys.) work necessary to overcome a resistance, work done against a force; **trabajos de Hércules** (myth.) labors of Hercules; **trabajos forzados** or **forzosos** hard labor (*penal*); **costar trabajo** to take a lot of effort; **costar trabajo** + *inf* to be hard to + *inf*; **pasar trabajos** to have trouble, to have a hard time; **tomarse el trabajo de** + *inf* to take the trouble to + *inf*
trabajoso -sa *adj* hard, arduous, laborious; pale, sickly; labored; (Am.) unpleasant, demanding; (Am.) bothersome, annoying
trabalenguas *m* (*pl:* **-guas**) tongue twister, jawbreaker
trabamiento *m* joining, uniting
trabanca *f* paperhanger's table
trabanco *m* var. of **trangallo**
trabar *va* to join, unite; to catch, seize; to fasten; to fetter; to lock; to check; to thicken; to set (*a saw; the teeth of a saw*); to begin; to join (*battle*); to strike up (*a conversation, friendship, etc.*); (law) to seize, attach; (mas.) to bond; *vn* to take hold; *vr* to become entangled; to jam; to foul; **trabársele la lengua a uno** to become tongue-tied
trabazón *f* union; bond, connection; thickness, consistency; (mas.) bond
trabe *f* beam
trabécula *f* (anat. & bot.) trabecula
trabilla *f* gaiter strap; end stitch, loose stitch
trabón *m* fetter, hopple
trabuca *f* firecracker
trabucación *f* upset; confusion; mix-up; jumble
trabucaire *adj* bold, arrogant, blustering
trabucar §86 *va* to upset, overturn; to confuse, disturb; to mix up (*words, letters, or syllables*); to jumble; *vr* to upset, overturn; to become confused; to become mixed up; to become jumbled
trabucazo *m* shot with a blunderbuss; (coll.) dismay
trabuco *m* blunderbuss; popgun; catapult; **trabuco naranjero** wide-mouthed blunderbuss
trabujar *va* (carp.) to plane across the grain
trabuquete *m* catapult; seine
trac *m* stage fright
traca *f* string of firecrackers; (naut.) strake
tracalada *f* (Am.) crowd, flock
tracalero -ra *adj* (Am.) cheating, tricky; *mf* (Am.) cheat, trickster
tracamundana *f* (coll.) barter; (coll.) uproar, excitement
tracción *f* traction; (mech.) tension; **de tracción de sangre** animal-drawn; **tracción delantera** (aut.) front drive; **tracción en cuatro ruedas** four-wheel drive
tracería *f* (arch.) tracery
Tracia, la see **tracio**
traciano -na *adj & mf* Thracian
tracio -cia *adj & mf* Thracian; **la Tracia** Thrace
tracista *mf* designer; schemer, trickster
tracoma *m* (path.) trachoma
tracomatoso -sa *adj* trachomatous
tractivo -va *adj* tractive
tracto *m* tract, stretch (*in space or time*)
tractocamión *m* tractor-trailer
tractor *m* tractor; **tractor de oruga** or **tractor oruga** caterpillar tractor
tradición *f* tradition; (law) delivery, transfer
tradicional *adj* traditional
tradicionalismo *m* traditionalism
tradicionista *mf* folklorist
traducción *f* translation; **traducción automática** machine translation
traducianismo *m* (theol.) traducianism
traducible *adj* translatable
traducir §38 *va* to translate; to change; to express
traductor -tora *mf* translator
traduje *1st sg pret ind of* **traducir**
traduzco *1st sg pres ind of* **traducir**
traedizo -za *adj* portable, carried, brought, transported
traedor -dora *mf* porter, carrier, bearer
traer §88 *va* to bring; to bring on; to draw, pull, attract; to adduce; to make, keep; to have, carry; to wear; to lead (*a good or bad life*); to hold out (*one's hands*); **traer a mal traer** (coll.) to abuse, treat roughly; **traer y llevar** (coll.) to peddle (*gossip*); *vn* to carry; **traer y llevar** (coll.) to gossip; *vr* to dress; to comport oneself; to be up to; **traérselas** (coll.) to become more and more of a problem; **traeres** *mpl* finery
trafagador *m* dealer, trader
trafagante *adj* dealing, trading; *mf* dealer, trader
trafagar §59 *va* to travel over or through; *vn* to traffic, to trade; to travel around; to hustle
tráfago *m* traffic, trade; toil, drudgery, treadmill
trafagón -gona *adj* (coll.) hustling, lively; (coll.) slick, tricky; *mf* (coll.) hustler, live wire
trafalgar *m* cotton lining
trafalmeja or **trafalmejas** (*pl:* **-jas**) *adj* (coll.) rattlebrained; *mf* (coll.) rattlebrain
traficación *f* var. of **tráfico**
traficante *adj* dealing, trading; *mf* dealer, trafficker; *m* tradesman
traficar §86 *vn* to traffic, deal, trade; to travel, go about
tráfico *m* traffic (*trade; movement of people and vehicles*); **tráfico de negros** slave trade
tragaaños *mf* (Am.) well-preserved person
tragable *adj* swallowable
tragacanta *f* or **tragacanto** *m* (bot.) tragacanth (*tree and gum*)
tragacete *m* dart, javelin
tragaderas *fpl* throat; (coll.) gullibility; (coll.) tolerance, indulgence, laxity; **tener buenas tragaderas** (coll.) to be gullible
tragadero *m* throat; gulf, abyss; (coll.) gullibility
tragadieces *m* (*pl:* **-ces**) (Am.) juke box
tragador -dora *adj* swallowing; gluttonous; *mf* swallower; **tragador de leguas** (coll.) great walker
tragahombres *m* (*pl:* **-bres**) (coll.) bully
trágala *m*; **cantarle a uno el trágala** (coll.) to force it down one's throat
tragaldabas *mf* (*pl:* **-bas**) (coll.) glutton; (coll.) easy mark
tragaleguas *mf* (*pl:* **-guas**) (coll.) great walker
tragaluz *m* (*pl:* **-luces**) skylight, bull's-eye; cellar window
tragamallas *mf* (*pl:* **-llas**) (coll.) glutton
tragamonedas *m* (*pl:* **-das**) (coll.) slot machine
tragantada *f* swig, big swig
tragante *m* flue (*of reverberatory furnace*); hopper (*of blast furnace*); (dial.) flume
tragantón -tona *adj* (coll.) voracious, gluttonous; *mf* (coll.) big eater; (coll.) glutton; *f* (coll.) big meal, big spread; (coll.) gulp, effort to swallow; (coll.) strained belief, grudging acquiescence
tragaperras *m* (*pl:* **-rras**) (coll.) slot machine
tragar §59 *va* to swallow; to swallow up; to devour, gulp down; (fig.) to swallow (*to believe too easily; to stand for, to tolerate*); to overlook; **no poder tragar** (coll.) to not be able to stomach; *vn* to swallow; *vr* to swallow up; (fig.) to swallow (*to believe too easily; to stand for, to tolerate*); to overlook
tragasable *m* sword swallower
tragasantos *mf* (*pl:* **-tos**) (coll.) churchified person
tragasopas *mf* (*pl:* **-pas**) (coll.) beggar
tragavenado *f* (zool.) anaconda (*arboreal snake of South America which crushes deer and other animals*)
tragavino *m* funnel
tragavirotes *m* (*pl:* **-tes**) (coll.) stuffed shirt
tragazón *f* (coll.) gluttony
tragedia *f* tragedy
trágico -ca *adj* tragic or tragical; *m* tragedian; *f* tragedienne

tragicomedia *f* tragicomedy
tragicómico -ca *adj* tragicomic or tragicomical
trago *m* swallow; swig; (coll.) misfortune, hard time; (anat.) tragus; (Am.) brandy; **a tragos** (coll.) slowly, by degrees; **echar un trago** (coll.) to have or take a drink
tragón -gona *adj* (coll.) gluttonous; *mf* (coll.) glutton
tragonear *va & vn* (coll.) to keep eating all the time
tragonería or **tragonía** *f* (coll.) gluttony
tragontina *f* (bot.) arum lily
traguear *vn* (coll.) to tipple
trágulo *m* (zool.) chevrotain
traición *f* treachery; treason; act of treason; **a traición** or **a la traición** treacherously; **hacer traición a** to betray; **alta traición** high treason
traicionar *va* to betray
traicionero -ra *adj* treacherous; traitorous, treasonous; *mf* traitor
traído -da *adj* threadbare; **traído y llevado** beaten about, knocked about; *f* carrying, bringing; **traída de aguas** water supply
traidor -dora *adj* treasonous, traitorous; treacherous; *mf* betrayer; *m* traitor; villain (*of a novel or play*); *f* traitress
traigo *1st sg pres ind of* **traer**
traílla *f* leash; lash; road scraper
traillar **§75** *va* to scrape, to grade with a scraper
traína *f* deep-sea fish net; net used for fishing sardines
trainera *f* sardine-fishing smack; (sport) long racing rowboat
trainerilla *f* (sport) shell
traíña *f* heavy net used for catching sardines and dragging them to shore
traite *m* napping (*of cloth*)
Trajano *m* Trajan
traje *m* dress, costume; suit; gown; (Am.) mask; **cortar un traje a** (coll.) to gossip about; **vestir su primer traje largo** to come out, to make one's debut; **traje académico** academic costume; **traje a la medida** suit made to order; **traje a presión** pressure suit; **traje de baño** bathing suit; **traje de buzo** diving suit; **traje de calle** street clothes; **traje de ceremonia** or **de etiqueta** dress suit; full dress; evening dress; **traje de faena** working clothes; (mil.) fatigue dress; **traje de luces** bullfighter's costume; **traje de malla** tights; **traje de montar** riding habit; riding clothes; **traje de paisano** civilian clothes; **traje espacial** space suit; **traje hecho** ready-made suit or dress; **traje sastre** lady's tailor-made suit; **traje serio** formal dress; **traje talar** gown, robe (*of a priest*); *1st sg pret ind of* **traer**
trajear *va* to dress, clothe, costume
trajedizo -za *adj* well-dressed
trajín *m* carrying, carting; going and coming; bustle, hustle
trajinante *adj* carrying, carting; *m* carrier, carter, expressman
trajinar *va* to carry, cart, transport; (Am.) to poke into; (Am.) to deceive; *vn* to move around, bustle around; (Am.) to lose patience; *vr* (Am.) to be disappointed
trajinería *f* carrying, carting, cartage
trajinero *m* carrier, carter, expressman
tralla *f* whipcord; lash
trallazo *m* lash; crack (*of a whip*)
trama *f* weft or woof; tram (*twisted silk*); lay (*in ropemaking*); texture; plot, scheme; plot (*of play or novel*); blossoming, blossom (*especially of olive tree*); screen, line screen (*in photoengraving*)
tramador -dora *adj* weaving; plotting, scheming; *mf* weaver; plotter, schemer
tramar *va* to weave; to contrive; to plot, to scheme; to hatch (*a plot*); *vn* to blossom (*said especially of olive trees*)
tramilla *f* twine
tramitación *f* transaction, negotiation; steps, procedure
tramitador -dora *mf* transactor, negotiator
tramitar *va* to transact, negotiate
trámite *m* step, procedure; proceeding
tramo *m* tract, lot; stretch (*of road*); flight (*of stairs*); span (*of bridge*); level (*of canal between locks*); passage (*of writing*)
tramojo *m* band, cord (*used to bind a sheaf*); trouble, sorrow
tramontano -na *adj* tramontane; *f* north; north wind, tramontana; pride, haughtiness, vanity
tramontar *va* to help escape, help get away; *vn* to go over the mountains; to sink behind the mountains (*said of the sun*); *vr* to escape, get away
tramoya *f* stage machinery; scheme, trick, fake
tramoyista *adj* scheming, tricky; *mf* schemer, impostor, humbug; *m* stage machinist; scene shifter, stagehand
trampa *f* trap; trap door; snare, pitfall; flap (*of shop counter*); fly (*of trousers*); trick; bad debt; **armar trampa a** (coll.) to lay a trap for; **caer en la trampa** (coll.) to fall into the trap; **hacer trampas** to cheat; **llevarse la trampa** (coll.) to fall through, to come to naught; **trampa de iones** (telv.) ion trap; **trampa explosiva** (mil.) booby trap
trampal *m* bog, quagmire
trampantojo *m* (coll.) sleight of hand, trick
trampeador -dora *adj & mf* (coll.) var. of **tramposo**
trampear *va* (coll.) to trick, to swindle; *vn* (coll.) to cheat; (coll.) to shift, pull through, manage to get along
trampería *f* trickery, cheating, swindling
trampero *m* trapper
trampilla *f* peephole; door of coalbin; lid (*of a desk*); leaf, hinged leaf (*of table*); fly (*of trousers*)
trampista *adj & mf* var. of **tramposo**
trampolín *m* springboard, diving board; ski jump; (fig.) springboard; **trampolín de acróbata** trampoline
tramposo -sa *adj* tricky, crooked; *mf* trickster, cheat, swindler
tranca *f* beam, pole; bar, crossbar; (Am.) drunk, spree; **a trancas y barrancas** (coll.) through fire and water
trancada *f* big step, long stride; (prov.) blow with a cudgel; **en dos trancadas** (coll.) in a trice
trancahilo *m* stop knot (*on thread or cord*)
trancanil *m* (naut.) waterway
trancar **§86** *va* to bar; *vn* (coll.) to stride along
trancazo *m* blow with a cudgel; (coll.) grippe, influenza
trance *m* critical moment; bad situation; trance; (law) judicial writ (*to enforce settlement of debt*); **a todo trance** at any risk, at any cost; **en trance de** in the act of; at the point of (*death*); **último trance** last stage, end (*of life*); **trance de armas** feat in arms
trancelín *m* (archaic) var. of **trencellín**
tranco *m* big step, long stride; threshold; **a trancos** (coll.) pell-mell; **en dos trancos** (coll.) in a trice
trancha *f* tinsmith's stake
tranchete *m* shoemaker's blade
trangallo *m* stick hung from a dog's collar to keep him from lowering his head to smell the ground
tranquear *vn* (coll.) to stride along
tranquera *f* palisade (*fence*); (Am.) gate (*opening to a field, barnyard, etc.*)
tranquero *m* cut stone (*for parts of doorframe*)
tranquil *m* plumb line
tranquilidad *f* tranquillity
tranquilizador -dora *adj* tranquilizing, calming, quieting; *m* (med.) tranquilizer
tranquilizar **§76** *va, vn & vr* to tranquilize
tranquilo -la *adj* tranquil, calm
tranquilla *f* feeler, leader (*to elicit a reply*); bar, lug, pin
tranquillo *m* knack
tranquillón *m* maslin, mixture of wheat and rye
transacción *f* settlement, compromise; transaction
transaéreo *m* (aer.) air liner
transalpino -na *adj* transalpine
transandino -na *adj* trans-Andean
transar *vn* (Am.) to yield, to compromise

transatlántico -ca *adj* transatlantic; *m* transatlantic ship, transatlantic liner
transbordador -dora *adj* transshipping; transfer; *m* ferry; transporter bridge; transporter car; **transbordador funicular** funicular
transbordar *va* to transship; to transfer; *vn* to change trains, to transfer
transbordo *m* transshipment; transfer
Transcaucasia, la Transcaucasia
transcendencia *f* var. of **trascendencia**
transcendental *adj* var. of **trascendental**
transcendentalismo *m* (philos.) transcendentalism
transcendentalista *mf* transcendentalist
transcendente *adj* var. of **trascendente**
transcender §66 *va & vn* var. of **trascender**
transceptor *m* (rad.) transceiver
transcontinental *adj* transcontinental
transcribir §17, 9 *va* to transcribe; (mus. & rad.) to transcribe
transcripción *f* transcription; (mus. & rad.) transcription
transcripto -ta var. of **transcrito**
transcriptor *m* transcriber
transcrito -ta *pp of* **transcribir**
transcurrir *vn* to pass, to elapse
transcurso *m* course (*of time*)
transductor *m* (phys.) transducer
transepto *m* (arch.) transept
transeúnte *adj* transient; transitory; *mf* transient; passer-by
transferencia *f* transference; (law) transfer
transferible *adj* transferable
transferidor -dora *mf* transferrer
transferir §62 *va* to transfer; to postpone; (law) to transfer
transfiguración *f* transfiguration; (*cap.*) *f* (Bib. & eccl.) Transfiguration
transfigurar *va* to transfigure; *vr* to become transfigured
transfijo -ja *adj* transfixed
transfixión *f* transfixion; (surg.) transfixion
transflor *m* painting on metal (*generally green on gold*)
transflorar *va* to paint on metal; to copy against the light; *vn* to show through
transflorear *va* to paint on metal
transformable *adj* transformable; (aut.) convertible; *m* (aut.) convertible
transformación *f* transformation; transformation (*wig*)
transformador -dora *adj* transforming; *mf* transformer; *m* (elec.) transformer; **transformador de campanilla** (elec.) doorbell transformer; **transformador de corriente** (elec.) current transformer; **transformador de fuerza** (elec.) power transformer; **transformador de entrada** (rad.) input transformer; **transformador de núcleo de aire** (elec.) air-core transformer; **transformador de núcleo de hierro** (elec.) iron-core transformer; **transformador de poder** or **de potencia** (elec.) power transformer; **transformador de salida** (rad.) output transformer; **transformador de tensión** (elec.) voltage transformer; **transformador elevador** (elec.) step-up transformer; **transformador reductor** (elec.) step-down transformer
transformamiento *m* transformation
transformar *va* to transform; (elec., math. & phys.) to transform; *vr* to transform, to become transformed
transformativo -va *adj* transformative
transformismo *m* (biol.) transformism; (theat.) quick-change acting
transformista *adj* (biol.) transformist, transformistic; *mf* (biol.) transformist; (theat.) quick-change artist
transfregar §29 *va* to rub, rumple
transfretano -na *adj* (located) across the strait, across the inlet
transfretar *va* to cross (*the sea*); *vn* to spread out, to extend
tránsfuga *mf* fugitive; turncoat
tránsfugo *m* fugitive; turncoat
transfundición *f* transfusion
transfundir *va* to transfuse; to transmit, to spread
transfusión *f* transfusion; **transfusión de sangre** (med.) transfusion, blood transfusion
transfusionista *mf* (med.) transfusionist
transfusor -sora *adj* transfusing; *mf* transfuser
transgredir §53 *va* to transgress
transgresión *f* transgression
transgresor -sora *adj* transgressing; *mf* transgressor
transiberiano -na *adj* trans-Siberian
transición *f* transition
transido -da *adj* overcome, paralyzed; mean, cheap, stingy
transigencia *f* (act of) compromising; compromise
transigente *adj* compromising
transigir §42 *va* to settle, to compromise; *vn* to settle, to compromise; to agree; **transigir con** to compromise on; **transigir en** + *inf* to agree to + *inf*
Transilvania, la Transylvania
transilvano -na *adj & mf* Transylvanian
transistor *m* (elec.) transistor
transistorizar §76 *va* to transistorize
transitable *adj* passable, practicable
transitar *vn* to go, to walk; to travel, to journey (*sometimes with stopovers*)
transitivo -va *adj* transitive; (gram.) transitive
tránsito *m* transit; traffic; stop; passage; passing (*of a saint*); transfer; **de tránsito** in transit; transient; **hacer tránsito** to make a stop; **tránsito rodado** vehicular traffic
transitoriedad *f* transitoriness, transiency
transitorio -ria *adj* transitory
Transjordán, el or **Transjordania, la** Trans-Jordan or Transjordania
translación *f* var. of **traslación**
transladar *va* var. of **trasladar**
translaticio -cia *adj* var. of **traslaticio**
translativo -va *adj* var. of **traslativo**
translimitación *f* trespass; armed intervention
translimitar *va* to cross without intending to violate (*a border or frontier*); to go beyond (*any limit*)
translinear *vn* (law) to pass an entail from one line of heirs to another
translucidez *f* translucence or translucency
translúcido -da *adj* translucent
translucir §60 *va, vn & vr* var. of **traslucir**
transmarino -na *adj* transmarine, overseas
transmigración *f* transmigration
transmigrar *vn* to transmigrate
transmisibilidad *f* transmissibility
transmisible *adj* transmissible
transmisión *f* transmission; **transmisión de energía** (elec.) power transmission; **transmisión del pensamiento** thought transference
transmisor -sora *adj* transmitting; *mf* transmitter; *m* (rad., telg. & telp.) transmitter; **transmisor de órdenes** (naut.) engine-room telegraph
transmitir *va & vn* to transmit
transmontano -na *adj* tramontane
transmontar *va, vn & vr* var. of **tramontar**
transmudación *f* or **transmudamiento** *m* var. of **transmutación**
transmudar *va* to move, transfer; to transmute; to persuade, convince
transmutable *adj* transmutable
transmutación *f* transmutation; (alchem. & chem.) transmutation
transmutar *va, vn & vr* to transmute
transoceánico -ca *adj* transoceanic
transónico -ca *adj* transonic
transpacífico -ca *adj* transpacific
transpadano -na *adj* transpadane
transparecer §34 *vn* to show through
transparencia *f* transparence or transparency; slide (*for projection in a projector*)
transparentar *vr* to be transparent; to show through; (fig.) to become transparent
transparente *adj* transparent; translucent; (fig.) transparent; *m* transparency (*picture on some translucent substance*); curtain, window curtain; stained-glass window (*at back of*

altar); **transparente de resorte** window blind or shade
transpiración *f* transpiration; sweat, sweating; (bot. & physiol.) transpiration
transpirar *va* to transpire; to sweat; *vn* to transpire; to sweat; (fig.) to transpire (*to become known, leak out*)
transpirenaico -ca *adj* trans-Pyrenean
transpondré *1st sg fut ind of* **transponer**
transponedor -dora *adj* transposing; *mf* transposer
transponer §69 *va* to transpose; to disappear behind, to go around (*e.g., the corner*); to transplant; (alg.) to transpose; *vr* to set (*said of sun, moon, and stars*); to get sleepy
transpongo *1st sg pres ind of* **transponer**
transportable *adj* transportable
transportación *f* transportation, transporting
transportador -dora *adj* transporting; *mf* transporter; *m* conveyor; (surv.) protractor
transportamiento *m* transport; (fig.) transport (*e.g., of joy*)
transportar *va* to transport; to transfer (*a drawing, design, or pattern*); (mus.) to transpose; (elec.) to transmit; (fig.) to transport; *vr* (fig.) to be in transports, to be carried away
transporte *m* transport; transportation; transfer (*of a drawing, design, or pattern*); (aer. & fig.) transport; (naut.) transport, troopship; (mus.) transportation; (elec.) transmission; **transporte ilícito de armas** (law) carrying concealed weapons; **transportes en común** public conveyances
transportista *mf* transport worker
transposición *f* transposition, transposal; (mus.) transposition
transpuesto -ta *pp of* **transponer;** *f* var. of **traspuesta**
transpuse *1st sg pret ind of* **transponer**
transterminar *va* (law) to transfer to another jurisdiction
transtiberino -na *adj & mf* Trasteverine
transubstanciación *f* transubstantiation
transubstancial *adj* transubstantial
transubstanciar *va & vr* to transubstantiate
transuránico -ca *adj* (chem.) transuranic
transuretral *adj* transurethral
transvasar *va* to decant, to transvase, to pour from one vessel into another
transverberación *f* transfixion, transverberation
transversal *adj* transversal; cross (*e.g., street*); collateral
transverso -sa *adj* transverse
transvestido -da *adj & mf* transvestite
transvestismo or **transvestitismo** *m* transvestitism
tranvía *m* streetcar, trolley, trolley car; trolley line; **tranvía de sangre** horsecar
tranviario -ria *adj* trolley; *m* trolley or transit employee
tranviero *m* trolley or transit employee
tranzadera *f* var. of **trenzadera**
tranzar §76 *va* to cut, rip off; to braid, plait
tranzón *m* plot, lot
trapa *f* tramp, tramping (*of feet*); shouting, uproar; (naut.) spilling line; **trapas** *fpl* (naut.) tackle used to fasten a lifeboat on deck
trapacear *vn* to cheat, swindle
trapacería *f* cheat, swindle; fraud, deceit
trapacero -ra *adj* cheating, swindling; *mf* cheat, swindler
trapacete *m* (com.) sales book
trapacista *adj & mf* var. of **trapacero**
trapajería *f* sails of a ship; (prov.) rags, old clothes
trapajo *m* rag, tatter
trapajoso -sa *adj* ragged, tattered, torn; slovenly, untidy
trápala *adj* (coll.) chattering, jabbering; (coll.) cheating, false; *mf* (coll.) chatterbox, jabberer; (coll.) cheat, trickster; *m* (coll.) garrulity, loquacity; *f* noise, uproar, confusion; clatter (*of running horse*); (coll.) cheating, deceit
trapalear *vn* (coll.) to chatter, jabber; (coll.) to lie, cheat, deceive; to clatter along
trapalón -lona *adj* (coll.) cheating, tricky; *mf* (coll.) cheater, trickster
trapatiesta *f* (coll.) brawl, row, roughhouse
trapaza *f* var. of **trapacería**
trapazar §76 *vn* var. of **trapacear**
trapeador *m* (Am.) mop, floor mop
trapear *va* (Am.) to mop; *vn* (dial.) to snow
trapecial *adj* trapezial; (geom.) trapezoidal
trapecio *m* (sport) trapeze; (anat.) trapezium; (anat.) trapezius; (geom.) trapezoid
trapecista *mf* trapeze performer
trapense *adj & mf* Trappist
trapería *f* rags; rag shop
trapero -ra *adj* see **puñalada;** *mf* ragpicker, rag dealer; junk dealer
trapezoedro *m* (cryst.) trapezohedron
trapezoidal *adj* (geom.) trapezial
trapezoide *m* (anat.) trapezoid; (geom.) trapezium
trapiche *m* sugar mill; press, olive press; ore crusher
trapichear *vn* (coll.) to scheme; to deal at retail
trapicheo *m* (coll.) scheming
trapichero *m* sugar-mill worker
trapiento -ta *adj* ragged, raggedy
trapillo *m* (coll.) second-rate gallant; (coll.) soubrette; (coll.) nest egg, small nest egg (*savings*); **de trapillo** (coll.) in house clothes
trapío *m* (coll.) pertness, flipness; (taur.) spirit (*of bull*)
trapisonda *f* (coll.) brawl, uproar; (coll.) intrigue, scheming
trapisondear *vn* (coll.) to intrigue, to scheme
trapisondista *mf* (coll.) intriguer, schemer
trapista *adj & mf* Trappist; *m* (Am.) ragpicker, ragman
trapito *m* small rag; **trapitos de cristianar** (coll.) Sunday best
trapo *m* rag; cleaning rag; (naut.) canvas, sails; (taur.) bullfighter's bright-colored cape; (taur.) cloth (*of muleta*); (theat.) curtain; (Am.) cloth, fabric; **trapos** *mpl* (coll.) rags, duds; **a todo trapo** (naut. & fig.) full sail; **poner como un trapo** (coll.) to rake over the coals; **sacar los trapos a la colada, a relucir** or **al sol** (coll.) to wash one's dirty linen in public; **soltar el trapo** (coll.) to burst out crying, to burst out laughing; **tirar el trapo** (coll.) to withdraw, to give up; **trapos de cristianar** (coll.) Sunday best
traque *m* crack (*of firecracker*); fuse (*of firecracker*); **a traque barraque** (coll.) at any time, for any reason
tráquea *f* (anat., bot. & zool.) trachea
traqueal *adj* tracheal
traquear *va* to shake, agitate; to rattle; (coll.) to tamper with, fool with; *vn* to crackle; to rattle; (mach.) to chatter
traqueida *f* (bot.) tracheid
traqueítis *f* (path.) tracheitis
traqueo *m* crack, crackle; rattle; (mach.) chattering
traqueotomía *f* (surg.) tracheotomy
traquetear *va & vn* var. of **traquear**
traqueteo *m* var. of **traqueo**
traquido *m* crack (*of firecracker; of something breaking*)
traquita *f* (geol.) trachyte
tras *prep* after; behind; **tras** + *inf* after + *ger;* **tras de** behind; in addition to; *m* (coll.) behind; **¡tras, tras!** rat-a-tat!
trasalcoba *f* (arch.) alcove (*adjoining a bedroom*)
trasalpino -na *adj* var. of **transalpino**
trasaltar *m* space behind altar
trasandino -na *adj* var. of **transandino**
trasanteanoche *adv* three nights ago
trasanteayer or **trasantier** *adv* three days ago
trasatlántico -ca *adj* var. of **transatlántico**
trasbarrás *m* thump, thud
trasbordador -dora *adj & m* var. of **transbordador**
trasbordar *va* var. of **transbordar**
trasbordo *m* var. of **transbordo**
trasca *f* leather thong
trascabo *m* trip, tripping
trascantón *m* spur stone; errand boy, street porter; **a trascantón** unexpectedly; **dar trascantón a** (coll.) to shake off
trascantonada *f* spur stone
trascara *f* (hum.) backside, behind

trascendencia *f* penetration, keenness; importance; result, consequence; (philos.) transcendence
trascendental *adj* far-reaching; highly important, very serious; (philos. & math.) transcendental
trascendente *adj* penetrating; important; (philos. & theol.) transcendent
trascender §66 *va* to go into, to dig up; *vn* to smell, be fragrant; to spread; to come to be known, to leak out
trascendido -da *adj* keen, perspicacious
trascocina *f* scullery (*room near kitchen for coarse work*)
trascolar §77 *va* to strain, percolate; to take through, to take to the other side; *vr* to butt in
trasconejar *vr* to squat, to cower (*said of game*); to be mislaid, get lost
trascordado -da *adj* wrong, mistaken, confused
trascordar §77 *vr* to forget, to confuse
trascoro *m* back choir, retrochoir
trascorral *m* back court, back yard; (coll.) backside
trascorvo -va *adj* crookkneed (*horse*)
trascribir §17, 9 *va* var. of **transcribir**
trascripción *f* var. of **transcripción**
trascripto -ta or **trascrito -ta** var. of **transcrito**
trascuarto *m* back room
trascuenta *f* mistake (*e.g., in an addition*)
trascurrir *vn* var. of **transcurrir**
trascurso *m* var. of **transcurso**
trasdobladura *f* trebling
trasdoblar *va* to treble; to fold three times
trasdoblo *m* triple number
trasdós *m* (arch.) extrados
trasdosear *va* (arch.) to strengthen the back of, to strengthen in the back
trasechar *va* to waylay, to ambush
trasegar §29 *va* to upset, turn topsy-turvy; to transfer, to decant
traseñalar *va* to change the mark on, to put a different mark on
trasero -ra *adj* back, rear; *m* buttock, rump; **traseros** *mpl* (coll.) ancestors; *f* back (*of house, door, etc.*)
trasferencia *f* var. of **transferencia**
trasferible *adj* var. of **transferible**
trasferidor -dora *mf* var. of **transferidor**
trasferir §62 *va* var. of **transferir**
trasfiguración *f* var. of **transfiguración**
trasfigurar *va & vr* var. of **transfigurar**
trasfijo -ja *adj* var. of **transfijo**
trasfixión *f* var. of **transfixión**
trasflor *m* var. of **transflor**
trasflorar *va & vn* var. of **transflorar**
trasflorear *va* var. of **transflorear**
trasfollo *m* (vet.) swollen gambrel
trasfondo *m* background
trasformación *f* var. of **transformación**
trasformador -dora *adj & mf* var. of **transformador**
trasformamiento *m* var. of **transformamiento**
trasformar *va & vr* var. of **transformar**
trasformativo -va *adj* var. of **transformativo**
trasfregar §29 *va* var. of **transfregar**
trasfretano -na *adj* var. of **transfretano**
trasfretar *va & vn* var. of **transfretar**
trásfuga *mf* var. of **tránsfuga**
trásfugo *m* var. of **tránsfugo**
trasfundición *f* var. of **transfundición**
trasfundir *va* var. of **transfundir**
trasfusión *f* var. of **transfusión**
trasfusor -sora *adj & mf* var. of **transfusor**
trasgo *m* goblin, hobgoblin; imp (*mischievous youngster*); **dar trasgo a** to spook, to act the spook in order to frighten
trasgredir §53 *va* var. of **transgredir**
trasgresión *f* var. of **transgresión**
trasgresor -sora *adj & mf* var. of **transgresor**
trasguear *vn* to play spook
trasguero -ra *mf* spook (*person who acts the spook*)
trashoguero -ra *adj* stay-at-home, lazy; *m* fireback; big log (*in fireplace*)
trashojar *va* to leaf through (*a book, a batch of papers*)
trashumación *f* or **trashumancia** *f* moving from winter to summer pasture, moving from summer to winter pasture
trashumante *adj* nomadic (*flocks*)
trashumar *vn* to move from winter to summer pasture, to move from summer to winter pasture (*said of sheep and shepherds*)
trasiego *m* upset, disorder; transfer, decantation
trasijado -da *adj* thin-flanked; skinny, lanky
traslación *f* transfer, translation; postponement; copy, transcription; (mech. & telg.) translation
trasladable *adj* movable, traveling
trasladación *f* var. of **traslación**
trasladador -dora *mf* carrier, mover; **trasladadora de vía** (rail.) track shifter
trasladar *va* to transfer, to translate; to postpone; to copy, to transcribe; to transmit; to move; (mech. & telg.) to translate; *vr* to move (*to another place, job, etc.*); to go, to betake oneself
traslado *m* transfer; copy, transcript; moving; (law) notification
traslapado -da *adj* overlapped; double-breasted
traslapar *va & vn* to overlap
traslapo *m* overlap, overlapping
traslaticio -cia *adj* figurative
traslativo -va *adj* transferring, conveying
traslato -ta *adj* var. of **traslaticio**
traslator *m* (telg. & telp.) translator
traslinear *vn* var. of **translinear**
traslúcido -da *adj* var. of **translúcido**
traslucir §60 *va* to infer, to guess; *vn* to become evident, to leak out; *vr* to be translucent; to become evident, to leak out
traslumbramiento *m* dazzlement; sudden disappearance
traslumbrar *va* to dazzle; *vr* to become dazzled; to disappear suddenly, to vanish
trasluz *m* diffused light; glint, gleam; **al trasluz** against the light
trasluzco *1st sg pres ind of* **traslucir**
trasmallo *m* trammel net
trasmano *mf* second hand (*at cards*); **a trasmano** out of reach; out of the way, remote
trasmañana *adv* day after tomorrow
trasmañanar *va* to put off till tomorrow, to put off from day to day, to procrastinate
trasmarino -na *adj* var. of **transmarino**
trasmatar *va* (coll.) to wish (*someone*) dead, to kill off (*in one's mind*)
trasmigración *f* var. of **transmigración**
trasmigrar *vn* var. of **transmigrar**
trasminante *adj* undermining; (Am.) bitter (*cold*)
trasminar *va* to undermine; to permeate, to seep through; *vr* to seep, be penetrating
trasmisibilidad *f* var. of **transmisibilidad**
trasmisible *adj* var. of **transmisible**
trasmisión *f* var. of **transmisión**
trasmisor -sora *adj & mf* var. of **transmisor**
trasmitir *va & vn* var. of **transmitir**
trasmochar *va* to trim (*a tree*) for firewood
trasmontano -na *adj* var. of **transmontano**
trasmontar *va, vn & vr* var. of **tramontar**
trasmóvil *m* (Am.) mobile unit, radio pickup
trasmudación *f* or **trasmudamiento** *m* var. of **transmutación**
trasmudar *va* var. of **transmudar**
trasmundo *m* afterlife, future life
trasmutable *adj* var. of **transmutable**
trasmutación *f* var. of **transmutación**
trasmutar *va, vn & vr* var. of **transmutar**
trasnochado -da *adj* stale, spoiled (*from standing overnight*); haggard, run-down; stale, hackneyed; *f* last night; sleepless night, nightlong wakefulness; (mil.) night attack
trasnochador -dora *mf* nighthawk, night owl
trasnochar *va* to sleep over (*a problem*); *vn* to spend the night; to spend a sleepless night; to keep late hours, to stay up late
trasnoche *m* or **trasnocho** *m* sleepless night
trasnombrar *va* to change the names of
trasnominación *f* (rhet.) metonymy
trasoigo *1st sg pres ind of* **trasoír**
trasoír §64 *va* to hear wrong

trasojado -da *adj* hollow-eyed, having rings under the eyes; careworn, emaciated
trasoñar §77 *va* to imagine wrongly, to have the wrong idea about, to mistake for reality
trasovado -da *adj* (bot.) obovate
traspadano -na *adj* var. of **transpadano**
traspalar or **traspalear** *va* to shovel, to shovel off; to move, to transfer; (prov.) to weed (*vines*) with a hoe
traspaleo *m* shoveling; transfer
traspapelar *va* to mislay (*among one's papers*); *vr* to become mislaid
trasparecer §34 *vn* var. of **transparecer**
trasparencia *f* var. of **transparencia**
trasparentar *vr* var. of **transparentar**
trasparente *adj & m* var. of **transparente**
traspasador -dora *adj* transgressing; *mf* transgressor
traspasamiento *m* var. of **traspaso**
traspasar *va* to cross, cross over; to send; to transfer; to move; to pierce, transfix; to transgress (*a law*); to pain, grieve; to pierce (*the heart with pain or grief*); *vn* (archaic) to set (*said of the sun*); *vr* to go too far
traspaso *m* crossing; transfer; transgression; goods transferred; cost of transfer; pain, grief; (naut.) strait
traspatio *m* (Am.) back yard
traspeinar *va* to touch up with a comb
traspellar *va* to close, shut
traspié *m* slip, stumble; trip; **dar traspiés** to stumble; (coll.) to slip, go wrong
traspillar *va* to close, shut; *vr* to fail, to decline
traspintar *va* to show (*one card*) and play another; *vr* to show through; (coll.) to turn out differently, turn out wrong, be disappointing
traspiración *f* var. of **transpiración**
traspirar *va & vn* var. of **transpirar**
traspirenaico -ca *adj* var. of **transpirenaico**
trasplantable *adj* transplantable
trasplantación *f* transplantation
trasplantador -dora *adj* transplanting; *mf* transplanter; *m* transplanter (*machine*)
trasplantar *va* to transplant; (surg.) to transplant; *vr* to transplant (*to admit of being transplanted*); to emigrate, settle in another country
trasplante *m* transplant; transplantation
traspolar *adj* transpolar
traspondré *1st sg fut ind of* **trasponer**
trasponedor -dora *adj & mf* var. of **transponedor**
trasponer §69 *va & vr* var. of **transponer**
traspongo *1s sg pres ind of* **trasponer**
traspontín *m* small undermattress; (coll.) backside, behind
trasportable *adj* var. of **transportable**
trasportación *f* var. of **transportación**
trasportador -dora *adj & mf* var. of **transportador**
trasportamiento *m* var. of **transportamiento**
trasportar *va & vr* var. of **transportar**
trasporte *m* var. of **transporte**
trasportín *m* small undermattress
trasportista *mf* var. of **transportista**
trasposición *f* var. of **transposición**
traspuesto -ta *pp of* **trasponer;** *f* transposition; rise, elevation; back (*of house*); hiding, disappearance, flight; hiding place
traspunte *m* (theat.) prompter (*in the wings*)
traspuntín *m* small undermattress; folding seat, flap seat
traspuse *1st sg pret ind of* **trasponer**
trasquero *m* dealer in leather thongs
trasquila *f* lopping, cropping; shearing
trasquilador *m* shearer
trasquiladura *f* var. of **trasquila**
trasquilar *va* to lop, crop; to shear (*sheep*); (coll.) to lessen, reduce, curtail
trasquilimocho -cha *adj* (coll.) close-cropped
trasquilón *m* lopping, cropping; shearing; slash (*with scissors*); (coll.) swindle (*amount swindled*)
trasroscado -da *adj* stripped (*screw or nut*)
trasroscar §86 *vr* to be or become stripped, to not fit (*said of a screw or nut*)
trastabillar *vn* var. of **trastrabillar**
trastada *f* (coll.) dirty trick
trastajo *m* piece of junk
trastazo *m* whack, blow
traste *m* (mus.) fret (*of guitar*); **trastes** *mpl* (Am.) dishes; **dar al traste con** to throw away, do away with, ruin, spoil; **ir fuera de trastes** (coll.) to act like a fool, to talk nonsense; **sin trastes** (coll.) without order, without method
trasteado *m* (mus.) set of frets
trastear *va* to fret (*a guitar*); to play (*a guitar*); to wave the muleta at (*the bull*); (coll.) to manage, to steer; *vn* to shove things around; to talk with sparkle
trastejador -dora *adj* tiling; *m* tiler
trastejadura *f* var. of **trastejo**
trastejar *va* to tile; to overhaul
trastejo *m* tiling; overhauling; shuffle
trasteo *m* waving the muleta; (coll.) management, steering
trastera *f* attic, lumber room
trastería *f* pile of junk; (coll.) mean trick
trasterminar *va* var. of **transterminar**
trastesado -da *adj* stiff, taut (*with milk*)
trastesón *m* fullness of milk (*of an udder*)
trastiberino -na *adj & mf* var. of **transtiberino**
trastienda *f* back room (*behind a store*); (coll.) caution, canniness; (coll.) backside, behind
trasto *m* piece of furniture, utensil; piece of junk; (theat.) set piece; (coll.) good-for-nothing (*person*); (coll.) nuisance (*person*); **trastos** *mpl* tools, implements, utensils; arms, weapons; junk; (taur.) muleta and sword; **trastos de pescar** fishing tackle
trastornable *adj* easily upset
trastornador -dora *adj* upsetting; *mf* upsetter; disturber, agitator
trastornar *va* to upset, overturn; to turn upside down; to upset, disturb; to make dizzy; to persuade
trastorno *m* upset; upheaval, disturbance; (path.) upset, disturbance
trastrabado -da *adj* with white right hind foot and left forefoot, with white left hind foot and right forefoot (*said of a horse*)
trastrabar *vr* to become entangled; **trastrabársele la lengua a uno** to become tongue-tied
trastrabillar *vn* to stumble; to stagger, reel, sway; to stammer, stutter
trastrás *m* (coll.) last but one (*in certain children's games*)
trastrocamiento *m* reversal, change
trastrocar §95 *va* to turn around, to reverse, to change the nature of
trastrueco or **trastrueque** *m* var. of **trastrocamiento**
trastulo *m* toy, plaything; fun, amusement
trastumbar *va* to drop, let fall; to upset
trasudación *f* light sweat; sweating (*of an earthen vessel*)
trasudadamente *adv* with toil and sweat
trasudar *va & vn* to sweat lightly
trasudor *m* light sweat
trasueño *m* blurred dream, vague recollection
trasuntar *va* to copy; to abstract, sum up
trasuntivamente *adv* as a copy; compendiously
trasunto *m* copy; record; likeness, faithful image
trasvasar *va* var. of **transvasar**
trasvenar *vr* to spill; to exude through the veins
trasver §93 *va* to see (*something*) on the other side; to see wrong
trasverberación *f* var. of **transverberación**
trasversal *adj* var. of **transversal**
trasverso -sa *adj* var. of **transverso**
trasverter §66 *vn* to run over, to overflow
trasvinar *vr* to leak, ooze out (*said of wine*); (coll.) to become evident, to leak out
trasvisto -ta *pp of* **trasver**
trasvolar §77 *va* to fly over
trata *f* trade, traffic (*in human beings*); slave trade; **trata de blancas** white slavery; **trata de esclavos** or **de negros** slave trade
tratable *adj* friendly, sociable; tractable, manageable
tratadista *mf* writer of a treatise or treatises

tratado *m* treatise (*book*); treaty (*agreement between nations*); agreement; **Tratado de Varsovia** Warsaw Pact
tratador -dora *mf* mediator
tratamiento *m* treatment; title; **apear el tratamiento** to leave off the title; **dar tratamiento a una persona** to give a person his title (*in speaking to him*); **¿Qué tratamiento se da a un gobernador?** How does one address a governor?; **tratamiento expectante** (med.) expectant treatment
tratante *m* dealer, retailer
tratar *va* to handle; to deal with; to treat; **tratar a uno de** to address someone as; to charge someone with being; **tratar con** or **por** (chem.) to treat with ‖ *vn* to deal; to treat; to try; **tratar con** to deal with; to have an affair with; **tratar de** to deal with; to treat of; to come in contact with; **tratar de** + *inf* to try to + *inf;* **tratar en** to deal in ‖ *vr* to deal; to behave, conduct oneself; to live (*well or badly*); **tratarse con** to have to do with; to have an affair with; **tratarse de** to deal with; to be a question of; **tratarse de** + *inf* to be a question of + *ger*
tratero *m* (Am.) pieceworker
trato *m* treatment; manner, way of acting; deal, agreement; business; title; friendly relations; communion with God; **tener buen trato** to be very nice, be very pleasant; **trato colectivo** collective bargaining; **trato de gentes** savoir-vivre; **trato doble** double-dealing; **¡trato hecho!** (coll.) it's a deal!
trauma *m* (path. & psychopath.) trauma
traumaticina *f* (pharm.) traumaticine
traumático -ca *adj* traumatic
traumatismo *m* (path.) traumatism
traversa *f* bolster (*of a wagon*); (fort.) traverse; (naut.) stay
travertino *m* (mineral.) travertine
través *m* bias, bend, turn; crossbeam; reverse, misfortune; (arch. & fort.) traverse; (naut.) beam (*direction at right angles to keel*); **al** or **a través de** through, across; **dar al través con** to do away with, to destroy; **de través** sidewise; **mirar de través** to squint; to look at out of the corner of one's eye; **por el través** (naut.) on the beam
travesaño *m* crosspiece, crosstimber; bolster (*of bed*); rung (*e.g., of a chair*)
travesar §18 *va & vr* var. of **atravesar**
travesear *vn* to jump around, to romp, to carry on; to be witty, to sparkle; to lead a wild life
travesero -ra *adj* cross, transverse; *m* bolster (*of bed*); *f* cross street
travesío -a *adj* wandering, stray (*sheep*); cross, side (*wind*); *m* crossing, crossover; *f* crossroad; cross street; through road; path; crosswise position; crossing, voyage; distance, passage; profit or loss (*in gambling*); sailor's pay per voyage (*in merchant marine*); (fort.) traverse works; (naut.) cross wind, side wind
travestido -da *adj* disguised
travesura *f* prank, antic, mischief; wit, sparkle, keenness; slick trick
travieso -sa *adj* cross, transverse; keen, shrewd; restless, fidgety, naughty, mischievous; dissolute, debauched; *f* crossing, voyage; rafter, crossbeam; transverse wall; side bet; (min.) cross gallery; (rail.) tie, crosstie
trayecto *m* journey, passage, course
trayectoria *f* trajectory; path (*of a storm*)
traza *f* plan, design; scheme, invention; means; appearance, looks; trace, mark; footprint; streak, trait; (geom.) trace; **darse traza** (coll.) to take care of oneself, to manage; **discurrir trazas para** to contrive schemes for; **tener trazas de** to show signs of; to look like
trazable *adj* traceable
trazado -da *adj* traced, outlined; **bien trazado** well-formed, good-looking; **mal trazado** ill-formed, unattractive; *m* plan, design; outline; graph; appearance, looks; route, layout, (*e.g., of a railroad line*)
trazador -dora *adj* planning, designing; plotting; tracing; (chem. & phys.) tracer; *mf* planner, designer; plotter; tracer; *m* (chem. & phys.) tracer
trazante *adj* (chem. & phys.) tracer
trazar §76 *va* to plan, design; to outline; to trace (*a curve; the characteristics of a person or thing*); to draw (*a line*); to lay out, to plot
trazo *m* trace (*line or figure drawn*); outline; line, stroke; (paint.) fold in drapery; **trazo magistral** heavy stroke (*of pen*)
trazumar *vr* to ooze, to seep
trébedes *mpl or fpl* trivet
trebejar *vn* to romp, frolic, gambol
trebejo *m* plaything; chess piece; **trebejos** *mpl* tools, implements, utensils
Trebisonda *f* Trebizond
trébol *m* (bot.) clover, trefoil; (arch.) trefoil; cloverleaf (*intersection*); club (*playing card*); **tréboles** *mpl* clubs (*suit of playing cards*); **trébol acuático** (bot.) buck bean; **trébol amarillo** (bot.) bird's-foot trefoil; **trébol de agua** (bot.) buck bean; **trébol de Holanda** (bot.) Dutch clover; **trébol encarnado** or **del Rosellón** (bot.) crimson clover; **trébol oloroso** or **real** (bot.) sweet clover; **trébol rampante** (bot.) white clover; **trébol rojo** (bot.) red clover; **trébol sueco** (bot.) alsike, Swedish clover
trebolar *m* (Am.) field of clover
trece *adj* thirteen; **las trece** one P.M.; *m* thirteen; thirteenth (*in dates*); **estarse, mantenerse** or **seguir en sus trece** (coll.) to be persistent; (coll.) to stick to one's opinion
treceavo -va *adj & m* var. of **trezavo**
trecemesino -na *adj* thirteen-month
trecenario *m* thirteen days
treceno -na *adj* thirteenth
trecésimo -ma *adj & m* var. of **trigésimo**
trecientos -tas *adj & m* var. of **trescientos**
trecha *f* trick, wile
trechear *va* (min.) to pass along from one man to the next
trechel *m* spring wheat
trecheo *m* (min.) passing along from one man to the next
trecho *m* stretch (*of space or time*); while; **a trechos** at intervals; **de trecho en trecho** from place to place; from time to time; **muy de trecho en trecho** only once in a while, once in a long while
tredécimo -ma *adj* thirteenth
trefe *adj* weak, shaky; false, fake
trefilado *m* wiredrawing
trefilador -dora *mf* wiredrawer; wireworker; *f* drawplate; wiredrawing machine
trefilaje *m* wiredrawing
trefilar *va* to wiredraw
trefilería *f* wiredrawing; wireworks
trefina *f* (surg.) trephine
trefinar *va* (surg.) to trephine
tregua *f* truce; letup, respite, rest; **dar treguas** to ease up; to not be urgent; **sin tregua** without letup, without respite
treinta *adj* thirty; *m* thirty; thirtieth (*in dates*)
treintaidosavo -va *adj* thirty-second; **en treintaidosavo** thirty-twomo
treintaidoseno -na *adj* thirty-second
treintanario *m* thirty days
treintañal *adj* thirty-year-old
treintavo -va *adj & m* thirtieth
treinteno -na *adj* thirtieth; *f* thirty; thirtieth
treja *f* cushion shot
tremadal *m* quaking bog
tremátodo *m* (zool.) trematode
tremebundo -da *adj* frightful, dreadful
tremedal *m* var. of **tremadal**
tremendismo *m* realistic movement in contemporary Spanish fiction and theater which is characterized by emphasis on suffering, horror, and violence
tremendo -da *adj* frightful, terrible, tremendous; awesome; (coll.) tremendous (*very great, enormous*)
trementina *f* turpentine
tremer *vn* to tremble, to shake
tremés or **tremesino -na** *adj* three-month-old
tremielga *f* (ichth.) torpedo, electric ray
tremó *m* (*pl:* **-mós**) pier glass, trumeau
tremol *m* var. of **tremó**
tremolar *va* to wave; to display, make a show of
tremolina *f* rustling; (coll.) bustle, hubbub, uproar

tremolita *f* (mineral.) tremolite
trémolo *m* (mus.) tremolo
tremor *m* tremor, slight tremor
tremulante, tremulento -ta or **trémulo -la** *adj* tremulous, quivering, flickering
tren *m* train (*succession, e.g., of waves*); outfit, equipment; following, retinue; show, pomp; set; way (*e.g., of life*); (mil.) train, convoy; (rail.) train; **llevar el tren** (sport) to set the pace, lead the way; **tren aerodinámico** (rail.) streamliner; **tren ascendente** (rail.) up train; **tren botijo** (rail.) excursion train; **tren carreta** (coll.) accommodation train; **tren correo** (rail.) mail train; **tren de aterrizaje** (aer.) landing gear; **tren de engranajes** (mach.) set of gears; **tren de excursión** or **de recreo** (rail.) excursion train; **tren de juguete** toy train; **tren de laminadores** train of rolls, rolling mill; **tren delantero** (aut.) front assembly; **tren de mercancías** (rail.) freight train; **tren de ondas** (phys.) wave train; **tren de ruedas** running gear; **tren descendente** (rail.) down train; **tren expreso** (rail.) express train; **tren hospital** (mil.) hospital train; **tren mixto** (rail.) mixed train; **tren ómnibus** (rail.) accommodation train; **tren rápido** (rail.) flyer, fast express; **tren trasero** (aut.) rear assembly
trena *f* sash; burnt silver; twist (*roll*); (prov.) jail
trenado -da *adj* reticulated, latticed
trenca *f* crosspiece (*in beehive*); main root
trencellín *m* (archaic) bejeweled gold or silver hatband
trencilla *f* braid
trencillar *va* to braid
trencillo *m* braid; (archaic) bejeweled gold or silver hatband
treno *m* dirge, threnody; jeremiad
Trento *f* Trent
trenza *f* braid, plait; tress; (Am.) string (*e.g., of garlic*)
trenzadera *f* braided cord or ribbon
trenzado *m* braid, plait; tress; caper (*in dancing*); prance (*of horse*); **al trenzado** carelessly
trenzar §76 *va* to braid, to plait; *vn* to caper, cut capers; to prance
treo *m* (naut.) storm lateen sail; (naut.) storm lateen yard
treonina *f* (biochem.) threonine
trepa *f* climb, climbing; drilling, boring; grain (*in polished wood*); twilled braid; (coll.) somersault; (coll.) slyness, deceit; (coll.) flogging, beating
trepación *f* climbing, creeping
trepado -da *adj* strong, husky (*animal*); *m* twilled braid; perforation (*series of holes, e.g., in stamps*)
trepador -dora *adj* climbing; drilling; (bot.) climbing, creeping; *mf* climber; *m* place to climb; climber (*device*); *f* drilling machine; (bot.) climber, creeper; (orn.) climber
trepajuncos *m* (*pl:* **-cos**) (orn.) marsh warbler
trepanación *f* trepanation
trepanar *va* (mach. & surg.) to trepan
trépano *m* (min. & surg.) trepan
trepante *adj* climbing; sly, deceitful
trepar *va* to climb; to drill, bore; to trim with twilled braid; *vn* to climb; (bot.) to climb, creep; **trepar por** to climb up; *vr* to lean back
trepatroncos *m* (*pl:* **-cos**) (orn.) blue titmouse; (orn.) nuthatch
trepe *m* (coll.) scolding, reprimand; **echar un trepe a** (coll.) to give a scolding to
trepidación *f* trepidation, vibration; (path.) trepidation (*clonus*)
trepidar *vn* to shake, vibrate; (Am.) to fear, hesitate, waver
trépido -da *adj* shaking, shivering, flickering
tres *adj* three; **las tres** three o'clock; *m* three; third (*in dates*); **tres en raya** see **juego del tres en raya**
tresalbo -ba *adj* having three white feet (*said of a horse*)
tresañal or **tresañejo -ja** *adj* three-year-old
tresbolillo; a or **al tresbolillo** (hort.) in quincunxes; (mach.) staggered
trescientos -tas *adj & m* three hundred
tresdoblar *va* to treble; to fold three times
tresdoble *adj & m* triple
tresillear *vn* (coll.) to play ombre
tresillista *mf* ombre player, ombre expert
tresillo *m* ombre (*card game*); living-room suit (*of three pieces*); ring set with three stones; (mus.) triplet
tresnal *m* (agr.) shock, stack
trestanto *adv* three times as much; *m* treble
treta *f* trick, scheme; feint (*in fencing*); (Am.) bad habit
Tréveris *f* Treves
trezavo -va *adj & m* thirteenth
tría *f* sorting; tease (*in fabrics*)
triaca *f* (old med.) theriaca; remedy, cure
triacal *adj* theriacal
triache *m* triage (*inferior grade of coffee*)
tríada or **tríade** *f* triad
triadelfo -fa *adj* (bot.) triadelphous
triandro -dra *adj* (bot.) triandrous
triangulación *f* triangulation
triangulado -da *adj* triangulate
triangular *adj* triangular; *va* to triangulate
triángulo -la *adj* triangular; *m* (geom., mus. & fig.) triangle; (*cap.*) *m* (astr.) Triangle
triar §90 *va* to sort; *vn* to swarm in and out a hive; *vr* to show teases (*said of a fabric*); (prov.) to curdle
triásico -ca *adj & m* (geol.) Triassic
triatómico -ca *adj* (chem.) triatomic
triaxial *adj* triaxial
tríbada *f* tribade
tribadismo *m* tribadism
tribal *adj* tribal
tribásico -ca *adj* (chem.) tribasic
trib.l abr. of **tribunal**
tribraquio *m* (pros.) tribrach
tribu *f* tribe
tribual *adj* var. of **tribal**
tribuir §41 *va* var. of **atribuir**
tribulación *f* tribulation
tríbulo *m* (bot.) caltrop (*Tribulus terrestris*)
tribuna *f* tribune, rostrum, platform; (arch.) tribune; stand, grandstand; gallery (*in a church*); parliamentary eloquence; parliament; **tribuna de la prensa** press box; **tribuna del órgano** (mus.) organ loft; **tribuna de los acusados** (law) dock
tribunado *m* tribunate, tribuneship
tribunal *m* tribunal, court; (fig.) tribunal (*of public opinion, of one's own conscience, etc.*); **tribunal de presas marítimas** prize court; **tribunal de primera instancia** court of the first instance; **tribunal de exámenes** (educ.) examining board; **Tribunal internacional** International Court; **Tribunal internacional de La Haya** Hague Court; **Tribunal Permanente de Arbitraje** Permanent Court of Arbitration; **Tribunal Permanente de Justicia Internacional** Permanent Court of International Justice; **Tribunal Supremo** Supreme Court; **tribunal tutelar de menores** juvenile court
tribunicio -cia or **tribúnico -ca** *adj* tribunitian; demagogic
tribuno *m* (hist.) tribune; tribune (*demagogue*)
tributación *f* contribution; tribute; system of taxes, taxation
tributar *va* to pay (*taxes, contributions, etc.*); to pay, to render (*homage, admiration, etc.*)
tributario -ria *adj* tributary; (pertaining to) tax; **ser tributario de** to be indebted to; *mf* tributary; *m* tributary (*stream flowing into larger one or sea*)
tributo *m* tribute; tax; contribution; burden
tricenal *adj* thirty-year
tricentenario *m* tercentenary, tricentennial
tricentésimo -ma *adj & m* three-hundredth
tríceps *m* (anat.) triceps; *adj* (anat.) tricipital
tricésimo -ma *adj & m* var. of **trigésimo**
triciclo *m* tricycle
tricípite *adj* (anat.) tricipital
triclínico -ca *adj* (cryst.) triclinic
triclinio *m* (hist.) triclinium
tricloruro *m* (chem.) trichloride
tricología *f* trichology
tricolor or **tricoloro -ra** *adj* tricolor
tricorne *adj* (poet.) three-horned
tricornio -nia *adj* tricorn, three-horned, three-cornered; *m* tricorn, three-cornered hat

tricot *m* (*pl:* **-cots**) knitted wear; jersey; sweater
tricota *f* (Am.) jersey
tricotomía *f* trichotomy
tricotómico -ca *adj* trichotomic
tricótomo -ma *adj* trichotomous
tricotosa *f* knitting machine
tricroico -ca *adj* trichroic
tricromático -ca *adj* trichromatic
tricromatismo *m* trichromatism
tricromía *f* three-color process; three-color photograph
tricúspide *adj* tricuspid; (anat.) tricuspid; *f* (anat.) tricuspid valve
tridente *adj* trident, tridentate; *m* trident; (hist. & myth.) trident
tridimensional *adj* three-dimensional, tridimensional
triduano -na *adj* three-day
triduo *m* (eccl.) triduum
triedro -dra *adj* trihedral; *m* (geom.) trihedron
trienal *adj* triennial
trienio *m* triennium, triennial
trieñal *adj* var. of **trienal**
trifacial *adj* trifacial
trifásico -ca *adj* (elec.) three-phase
trifenilmetano *m* (chem.) triphenylmethane
trífido -da *adj* trifid
trifilar *adj* (elec.) three-wire
trifloro -ra *adj* three-flowered
trifocal *adj* trifocal
trifoliado -da *adj* (bot.) trifoliate
trifolio *m* (bot.) trifolium
trifoliolado -da *adj* (bot.) trifoliolate
triforio *m* (arch.) triforium
triforme *adj* triform
trifulca *f* (found.) blower mechanism; (coll.) row, squabble
trifurcación *f* trifurcation
trifurcado -da *adj* trifurcate
trifurcar §86 *va & vr* to trifurcate
trigal *m* wheat field
trigémino -na *adj* trigeminal; trigeminous; *m* (anat.) trigeminal nerve
trigésimo -ma *adj & m* thirtieth
trigla *f* (ichth.) red mullet
tríglifo *m* (arch.) triglyph
trigo *m* (bot.) wheat (*plant and grain*); wheat field; (slang) dough, money; **echar por esos trigos** or **por los trigos de Dios** (coll.) to be off the beam; **trigo albarejo** or **albarico** summer wheat; **trigo candeal** bread wheat; **trigo de primavera** spring wheat, summer wheat; **trigo durillo** or **duro** durum; **trigo sarraceno** (bot.) buckwheat
trigon. abr. of **trigonometría**
trigón *m* (mus.) trigon
trigonal *adj* trigonal; (cryst.) trigonal
trígono *m* (astrol. & geom.) trigon
trigonómetra *mf* trigonometer
trigonometría *f* trigonometry; **trigonometría esférica** spherical trigonometry; **trigonometría plana** or **rectilínea** plane trigonometry
trigonométrico -ca *adj* trigonometric or trigonometrical
trigueño -ña *adj* darkish, olive-skinned
triguero -ra *adj* wheat, wheat-growing; *m* wheat dealer, grain merchant; wheat sieve, grain sieve; (orn.) meadow lark; *f* (bot.) wheat grass
trilátero -ra *adj* trilateral
trilingüe *adj* trilingual
trilio *m* (bot.) trillium
trilita *f* (chem.) TNT
trilítero -ra *adj* triliteral
trilito *m* (archeol.) trilithon
trilobado -da *adj* trilobate
trilobites *m* (*pl:* **-tes**) (pal.) trilobite
trilocular *adj* trilocular
trilogía *f* trilogy
trilla *f* (agr.) threshing, threshingtime; (agr.) spike-tooth harrow; (ichth.) red mullet
trilladera *f* (agr.) spike-tooth harrow
trillado -da *adj* beaten (*path*); trite, commonplace
trillador -dora *adj* (agr.) threshing; *mf* (agr.) thresher; *f* (agr.) threshing machine
trilladura *f* (agr.) threshing
trillar *va* (agr.) to thresh; (coll.) to frequent; to abuse, to mistreat
trillizo -za *mf* (coll.) triplet
trillo *m* (agr.) spike-tooth harrow; (agr.) threshing machine
trillón *m* British trillion (*a million million millions*); quintillion (*in U.S.A.*)
trimembre *adj* three-member
trímero -ra *adj* trimerous
trimestral *adj* trimestral or trimestrial, quarterly
trimestre *m* trimester, quarter; *adj* trimestral, quarterly
trímetro *adj masc & m* trimeter
trimielga *f* var. of **tremielga**
trimotor -tora *adj* three-motor; *m* (aer.) three-motor plane
trinado *m* (mus.) trill, warble
trinador -dora *adj* trilling, warbling; *mf* warbler
trinar *vn* to trill, warble, quaver; (coll.) to get angry, to be beside oneself
trinca *f* triad, trinity; (naut.) rope, cable; (naut.) woolding; (coll.) gang
trincadura *f* (naut.) big two-masted barge
trincaesquinas *m* (*pl:* **-nas**) pump drill
trincafía *f* (naut.) marline
trincafiar §90 *va* (naut.) to marl
trincapiñones *m* (*pl:* **-nes**) (coll.) scatterbrain
trincar §86 *va* to tie fast, to lash; to bind, bind the hands or arms of; to break up, crush; (naut.) to woold; (slang) to kill; *vn* (coll.) to drink, take a drink of liquor; (naut.) to lie to
trincha *f* belt, girdle; gouge
trinchador -dora *adj* carving; *mf* carver
trinchante *m* carver; carving table; carving knife
trinchar *va* to carve, to slice; (coll.) to settle, to settle with an air of finality
trinche *m* (Am.) fork
trinchera *f* (mil.) trench; deep cut (*for a road or railway*); trench coat
trinchero *m* trencher (*wooden platter*); carving table, side table
trinchete *m* shoemaker's blade
trineo *m* sleigh, sled
trinervado -da *adj* (bot.) triple-nerved
tringa *f* (orn.) sandpiper
Trinidad *f* (theol.) Trinity; (*l.c.*) *f* (coll.) trinity; (coll.) inseparable three
trinitario -ria *adj & mf* (eccl.) Trinitarian; *f* (bot.) heartsease, wild pansy; **trinitaria de Méjico** (bot.) tigerflower
trinitrocresol *m* (chem.) trinitrocresol
trinitrotolueno *m* (chem.) trinitrotoluene
trinitrotoluol *m* (chem.) trinitrotoluol
trino -na *adj* trinal, threefold; (astr.) trine; *m* (mus.) trill
trinomio *m* (alg.) trinomial
trinquetada *f* (naut.) sailing under foresail
trinquete *m* (mach.) pawl; (mach.) ratchet; (naut.) foremast; (naut.) foresail; (naut.) foreyard; rackets (*game*); **a cada trinquete** (coll.) at every turn
trinquetilla *f* (naut.) foresail, forestaysail; (naut.) small jib
trinquis *m* (*pl:* **-quis**) (coll.) drink, swig
trío *m* sorting; trio; (mus.) trio
triodo *m* (electron.) triode
trióxido *m* (chem.) trioxide
tripa *f* gut, intestine; belly; filler (*of cigar*); **tripas** *fpl* insides; file, dossier; **flotar tripa arriba** to float on one's back; **hacer de tripas corazón** (coll.) to pluck up courage, to put on a bold front; **tener malas tripas** to be cruel, bloodthirsty
tripada *f* (coll.) bellyful
tripaflavina *f* (pharm.) trypaflavine
tripanosoma *m* (zool.) trypanosome
triparsamida *f* (pharm.) tryparsamide
tripartición *f* tripartition
tripartir *va* to divide into three parts
tripartito -ta *adj* tripartite
tripe *m* shag (*fabric*)
tripería *f* tripery, tripeshop
tripero -ra *mf* tripe seller; *m* (coll.) bellyband
tripétalo -la *adj* (bot.) tripetalous
tripicallero -ra *mf* tripe seller, tripemonger
tripicallos *mpl* tripe

tripinado -da *adj* (bot.) tripinnate
triplano *m* (aer.) triplane
triple *adj & m* triple, treble
tripleta *f* three-seated tandem bicycle
triplicación *f* triplication
triplicado -da *adj* triplicate; *m* triplicate; **por triplicado** in triplicate
triplicar §86 *va* to treble, triple, triplicate; to do three times; *vr* to treble, triple
tríplice *adj* triple; (*cap.*) *f* Triple Alliance
triplicidad *f* triplicity
triplo -pla *adj & m* triple, treble
tripo *m* (bot.) mullein, great mullein
trípode *m & f* (hist.) tripod; *m* tripod (*for camera, theodolite, etc.*)
trípol *m* or **trípoli** *m* (mineral.) tripoli, rottenstone
tripolino -na or **tripolitano -na** *adj & mf* Tripolitan
tripolizar §76 *va* to rottenstone
tripón -pona *adj* (coll.) big-bellied, pot-bellied; (Am.) gluttonous
tripsina *f* (biochem.) trypsin
tripso *m* (ent.) thrips
tríptico -ca *adj* (physiol.) tryptic; *m* triptych (*set of three panels; hinged writing tablet*); book or treatise in three parts
triptófano *m* (biochem.) tryptophan
triptongar §59 *va* to pronounce (*three vowels*) as a triphthong
triptongo *m* triphthong
tripudiar *vn* to dance
tripudio *m* dance
tripudo -da *adj* big-bellied, pot-bellied
tripulación *f* crew (*of ship, plane, etc.*)
tripulante *m* crew member
tripular *va* to man (*ship, plane, etc.*); to fit out, equip; to ship on (*a certain vessel*)
trique *m* crack, swish; **a cada trique** (coll.) at every turn
triquíasis *f* (path.) trichiasis
triquina *f* (zool.) trichina
triquinado -da *adj* trichinous, trichinized
triquinosis *f* (path.) trichinosis
triquinoso -sa *adj* trichinous
triquiñuela *f* (coll.) chicanery, evasion, subterfuge
triquita *f* (petrog.) trichite
triquitraque *m* clatter; crack, bang, crash; cracker (*firecracker; paper roll which explodes when pulled at both ends*); **a cada triquitraque** (coll.) at every turn
trirreme *m* (hist.) trireme
tris *m* slight cracking sound; (coll.) trice; (coll.) shave, inch; (coll.) touch; **en un tris** (coll.) almost, within an ace
trisa *f* (ichth.) shad
trisar *va* (Am.) to crack, chip; *vn* to chirp
trisca *f* crushing sound (*made with feet*); noise, rumpus
triscador -dora *adj* noisy, frisky; *m* saw set
triscar §86 *va* to mix, to mingle; to set (*a saw*); *vn* to stamp the feet; to frisk about, romp, caper, prance
trisecar §86 *va* to trisect
trisección *f* trisection
trisemanal *adj* triweekly (*occurring three times a week or every three weeks*)
trisílabo -ba *adj* trisyllabic; *m* trisyllable
trismo *m* (path.) trismus, lockjaw
trispermo -ma *adj* (bot.) trispermous
Tristán *m* (myth.) Tristan or Tristram
triste *adj* sad; dismal, gloomy; mean, low; sorry (*e.g., figure*)
tristeza *f* sadness
tristón -tona *adj* rather sad, wistful
tristura *f* var. of **tristeza**
trisulco -ca *adj* trisulcate
trisulfuro *m* (chem.) trisulfide
tritio *m* (chem.) tritium
tritón *m* merman, expert swimmer; (zool.) eft, newt, triton; (*cap.*) *m* (myth.) Triton
tritono *m* (mus.) tritone
trituración *f* trituration; grinding, pounding
triturador -dora *adj* triturating; *mf* triturator; *f* crusher, crushing machine
triturar *va* to triturate; to abuse, mistreat; to grind, to pound; (fig.) to tear to pieces
triunfada *f* trumping (*at cards*)
triunfador -dora *adj* triumphant; *mf* triumpher, victor, winner
triunfal *adj* triumphal
triunfante *adj* triumphant
triunfar *vn* to triumph; to trump; (coll.) to be lavish, make a great show; **triunfar de** to triumph over; to trump (*opponent's card*)
triunfo *m* triumph; trump; trumping; **costar un triunfo** (coll.) to be a gigantic effort; **en triunfo** in triumph; **sin triunfo** no trump; **triunfo pírrico** Pyrrhic victory
triunviral *adj* triumviral
triunvirato *m* triumvirate
triunviro *m* triumvir
trivalencia *f* (chem.) trivalence or trivalency
trivalente *adj* (chem.) trivalent
trivalvo -va or **trivalvulado -da** *adj* trivalve
trivial *adj* trivial; trite, commonplace; beaten (*path*)
trivialidad *f* triviality; triteness
trivio *m* junction (of three roads); trivium (*three lower subjects of medieval seven liberal arts*)
triza *f* shred, fragment; (naut.) halyard; **hacer trizas** to smash to pieces, to tear to pieces
trizar §76 *va* to break or tear to pieces
trocable *adj* exchangeable
trocada; a la trocada in the opposite way; in exchange
trocadamente *adv* topsy-turvy, in reverse
trocado *m* change; giveaway (*game of checkers*)
trocador -dora *mf* exchanger, barterer
trocaico -ca *adj & m* trochaic
trocamiento *m* exchange; change
trocánter *m* (anat., ent. & zool.) trochanter
trocar *m* (surg.) trocar; §95 *va* to exchange; to barter; to confuse, distort, twist; to vomit; *vr* to change; to change seats
trócar *m* (surg.) trocar
trocatinta *f* (coll.) mistaken exchange
trocatinte *m* changeable color
trocear *va* to divide into pieces, to split up
troceo *m* (naut.) parrel
trociscar §86 *va* to make into troches or lozenges
trocisco *m* (pharm.) troche
trocla *f* pulley
tróclea *f* pulley; (anat.) trochlea
troclear *adj* (anat.) trochlear
trocleario -ria *adj* (bot.) trochlear
troco *m* (ichth.) sunfish
trocoide *f* (geom.) trochoid
trocoideo -a *adj* trochoid
trocha *f* trail, narrow path; (Am.) gauge (*of track*)
trochemoche; a trochemoche (coll.) helter-skelter, pell-mell
trochuela *f* narrow path
trofeo *m* trophy; victory, triumph
trófico -ca *adj* (physiol.) trophic
trofoplasma *m* (biol.) trophoplasm
troglodita *adj* troglodytic; (fig.) troglodytic (*brutal*); (fig.) gluttonous; *m* troglodyte; (fig.) troglodyte (*cruel, brutal person*); (fig.) glutton
troglodítico -ca *adj* troglodytic or troglodytical
troica *f* troika
Troilo *m* (myth.) Troilus
troj *f* or **troje** *f* granary; olive bin
trojero *m* granary keeper or tender
trojezado -da *adj* chopped up, shredded, minced
trola *f* (coll.) deception, lie
trole *m* trolley pole
trolebús *m* trolley bus, trackless trolley
trolero -ra *adj* (coll.) deceptive, false, lying; *mf* (coll.) liar
tromba *f* (meteor.) column, whirl (*of dust, water, etc.*); (fig.) avalanche, rush; **tromba marina** (meteor.) waterspout; **tromba terrestre** (meteor.) tornado
trombina *f* (biochem.) thrombin
trombo *m* (path.) thrombus
trombocito *m* (physiol.) thrombocyte
trombón *m* trombone (*instrument*); trombone, trombonist (*performer*); **trombón de pistones** valve trombone; **trombón de varas** slide trombone
trombosis *f* (path.) thrombosis
trómel *m* (metal.) trommel

trompa *f* (mus.) horn; boy's whistle (*made of onion scape*); humming top; nozzle; trunk (*of elephant*); proboscis (*of certain animals and insects*); vacuum pump; (anat.) tube, duct; (arch.) squinch arch; (found.) trompe; (hum.) proboscis (*person's nose*); (meteor.) whirl, waterspout; (Am.) cowcatcher, pilot (*of locomotive*); **a trompa tañida** at the sound of the trumpet; **a trompa y talega** (coll.) helter-skelter; **trompa de armonía** (mus.) French horn; **trompa de caza** huntinghorn; **trompa de Eustaquio** (anat.) Eustachian tube; **trompa de Falopio** (anat.) Fallopian tube; **trompa de París** or **trompa gallega** jews'-harp; *m* horn player
trompada *f* (coll.) blow or bump with a horn or trumpet; (coll.) bump, collision; (coll.) punch; (naut.) collision, running aground
trompar *vn* to spin a top
trompazo *m* blow with a top; blow or bump with a horn or trumpet; hard bump
trompear *va* (Am.) to bump; *vn* to spin a top
trompero -ra *adj* false, deceptive; *m* top maker, top seller
trompeta *f* trumpet; clarion, bugle; (aut.) axle housing; **trompeta de amor** (bot.) sunflower; *m* trumpet or trumpeter (*player*)
trompetada *f* (coll.) silly remark
trompetazo *m* trumpet blast; (coll.) silly remark
trompetear *va* (coll.) to trumpet; *vn* (coll.) to trumpet, to sound the trumpet
trompeteo *m* trumpeting
trompetería *f* trumpetry, trumpets; trumpets (*of organ*)
trompetero *m* trumpet maker; trumpeter
trompetilla *f* ear trumpet; (bot.) yellow elder, trumpet flower; proboscis (*of mosquito*); conical Philippine cigar; **de trompetilla** buzzing (*mosquito*); **trompetilla acústica** ear trumpet
trompicar §86 *va* to trip, make stumble; (coll.) to promote (*one person*) over another; *vn* to stumble
trompicón *m* or **trompilladura** *f* stumble, stumbling; **a trompicones** by fits and starts
trompillar *va & vn* var. of **trompicar**
trompillo *m* (bot.) trompillo
trompillón *m* (arch.) keystone of a squinch arch
trompis *m* (*pl:* **-pis**) (coll.) punch; **andar a trompis** (coll.) to fight with the fists
trompiza *f* (Am.) fist fight
trompo *m* top (*spinning toy*); man (*at chess*); tub (*clumsy boat*); dolt; (zool.) trochid; **ponerse como un trompo** or **hecho un trompo** (coll.) to eat or drink to excess
trompón *m* big top; bump, collision; (bot.) daffodil; **a** or **de trompón** (coll.) helter-skelter
trompudo -da *adj* (Am.) thick-lipped
trona *f* (mineral.) trona
tronado -da *adj* used, worn; broke, cleaned out; *f* thunderstorm
tronador -dora *adj* thundering; *mf* thunderer; *f* (bot.) yellow elder
tronamenta *f* (Am.) thunderstorm
tronante *adj* thunderous
tronar §77 *va* (Am.) to shoot, to execute; *vn* to thunder; (coll.) to fail, collapse, crash; **por lo que pueda tronar** (coll.) just in case; **tronar con** (coll.) to quarrel with, to break with; **tronar contra** to thunder at; **truena** it is thundering; *vr* (coll.) to fail, collapse, crash; to go to ruin
tronca *f* var. of **truncamiento**
troncal *adj* trunk
troncar §86 *va* to cut off the head of; to cut, slash (*a writing, speech, etc.*)
tronco *m* trunk (*of human or animal body, of tree, of a line or family, of railroad, etc.*); log; team (*of horses*); (anat. & arch.) trunk; (geom.) frustum; (coll.) fathead, sap; **estar hecho un tronco** (coll.) to be knocked out; (coll.) to be sound asleep
troncón *m* trunk (*of human or animal body*); stump
troncha *f* (dial.) cinch, sinecure; (Am.) slice
tronchar *va* to rend, crack, shatter, split
troncho *m* stalk
tronchudo -da *adj* thick-stalked
tronera *f* embrasure, loophole, porthole; louver, small, narrow window; pocket (*of pool table*); *mf* harum-scarum
tronerar *va* var. of **atronerar**
tronero *m* (dial.) thunderhead
trónica *f* gossip
tronido *m* thunderclap; (prov.) show, haughtiness
tronitoso -sa *adj* (coll.) thundering, thunderous
trono *m* throne; (eccl.) shrine; **tronos** *mpl* (eccl.) thrones
tronquista *m* driver, teamster
tronzador *m* two-handed saw; crosscut saw; mechanical saw
tronzar §76 *va* to shatter, break to pieces; to crosscut, to saw transversely; to pleat (*a dress*); to wear out, exhaust
tronzo -za *adj* with one or both ears cropped (*said of a horse*)
troostita *f* (metal.) troostite
tropa *f* troop, flock; (mil.) troops; (mil.) assembly; (Am.) troop, herd, drove; **tropas** *fpl* (mil.) troops; **en tropa** straggling, without formation; **tropa de línea** (mil.) line, regular troops; **tropas de asalto** (mil.) shock troops, storm troops; **tropas francas** (mil.) marauders, guerrillas; **tropas regulares** (mil.) regulars
tropeína *f* (chem.) tropeine
tropel *m* bustle, rush, hurry; hodgepodge, jumble; **de** or **en tropel** in a mad rush
tropelía *f* mad rush; precipitation; outrage; prestidigitation
tropelista *m* prestidigitator
tropeolea *f* (bot.) tropaeolum
tropeolina *f* (chem.) tropaeolin
tropero *m* (Am.) cowboy
tropezadero *m* stumbling place, stumbling block
tropezador -dora *adj* stumbling; *mf* stumbler
tropezadura *f* stumbling
tropezar §31 *va* to hit; to strike; *vn* to stumble; to squabble, wrangle; to slip, to slip into error or wrongdoing; **tropezar con** or **en** to stumble against or over; to trip over; to run into, encounter; to come upon, meet; *vr* to interfere (*said of a horse*)
tropezón -zona *adj* (coll.) stumbly; *m* stumbling; stumbling place; obstacle; **tropezones** *mpl* chopped ham mixed with soup; **a tropezones** (coll.) by fits and starts; falteringly; **dar un tropezón** to stumble, to trip
tropezoso -sa *adj* (coll.) stumbly, faltering
tropical *adj* tropic or tropical
trópico -ca *adj* (rhet.) tropical; *m* (astr. & geog.) tropic; **trópico de Cáncer** tropic of Cancer; **trópico de Capricornio** tropic of Capricorn
tropiezo *m* stumble; stumbling block; slip, error, fault, guilt; cause of guilt; hitch, obstacle; squabble, wrangle
tropina *f* (chem.) tropine
tropismo *m* (biol.) tropism
tropo *m* (mus. & rhet.) trope
tropoesfera *f* var. of **troposfera**
tropología *f* tropology
tropológico -ca *adj* tropologic or tropological
troposfera *f* (meteor.) troposphere
troque *m* knot made in cloth before dyeing to show original color
troquel *m* die (*for stamping coins and medals*)
troquelar *va* to stamp in a die
troquelero *m* diesinker
troqueo *m* trochee
troquilo or **troquillo** *m* trochilus (*scotia*)
trotacalles *mf* (*pl:* **-lles**) (coll.) gadabout, loafer
trotaconventos *f* (*pl:* **-tos**) (coll.) procuress
trotador -dora *adj* trotting
trotamundos *m* (*pl:* **-dos**) globetrotter
trotar *vn* to trot; (coll.) to hustle
trote *m* trot; (coll.) chore; **al** or **a trote** quickly, right away; **para todo trote** (coll.) for everyday wear; **tomar el trote** (coll.) to run away, to dash off; **trote de perro** jog trot
trotil *m* (chem.) trotyl, trinitrotoluene
trotón -tona *adj* trotting; *mf* trotter; *m* horse; *f* chaperone

trotonería *f* constant trotting
trotskismo *m* Trotskyism
trotzkista *adj & mf* Trotskyite
trova *f* verse; parody; lyric; love song; (Am.) fib, lie
trovador -dora *adj* troubadour; *m* troubadour; poet; *f* poetess
trovadoresco -ca *adj* troubadour
trovar *va* to misconstrue; to parody; *vn* to write verse
trovero *m* trouvère
trovo *m* popular love song
Troya *f* Troy; **ahí, allí** or **aquí fué Troya** (coll.) all that's left is ruins; **¡arda Troya!** no matter what happens!
troyano -na *adj & mf* Trojan
troza *f* log (*of wood*); (naut.) truss
trozar §76 *va* to break up, to break to pieces; to cut into logs
trozo *m* piece, bit, fragment; block (*of wood*); excerpt, selection
trucaje *m* (mov.) trick photography
trucar §86 *vn* to pocket a ball (*at pool*)
truco *m* trick, device, contrivance; wrinkle; pocketing of ball; **trucos** *mpl* pool (*game*); **truco de naipes** card trick; **trucos malabares** juggling, acrobatics
truculencia *f* truculency
truculento -ta *adj* truculent
trucha *f* (ichth.) trout; three-legged derrick, crab; **trucha arco iris** (ichth.) rainbow trout; **trucha de mar** (ichth.) hogfish; (ichth.) sea trout; **trucha marina** (ichth.) sea trout; **trucha salmonada** (ichth.) salmon trout
truchero -ra *adj* (pertaining to) trout; *m* trout fisherman; trout seller
truchimán -mana *adj* (coll.) slick, sharp; *mf* (coll.) tricky person
truchuela *f* small dry codfish
trueco *m* var. of **trueque**
trueno *m* thunder, thunderclap; shot, report; (coll.) harum-scarum, wild young fellow; (bot.) wax tree (*Ligustrum lucidum*); **escapar del trueno y dar en el relámpago** to jump from the frying pan into the fire; **trueno gordo** finale (*of fireworks*); (coll.) big scandal
trueque *m* barter; exchange; trade-in; **trueques** *mpl* (Am.) change (*money*); **a trueque de** in exchange for, instead of
trufa *f* (bot.) truffle; lie, story, fib
trufador -dora *adj* lying, fibbing; *mf* liar, fibber
trufar *va* (cook.) to fill or stuff with truffles; *vn* to lie, to fib
trufera *f* truffle bed
truficultura *f* truffle growing
truhán -hana *adj* cheating, crooked, tricky; (coll.) clownish; *mf* cheat, crook, trickster; (coll.) clown, buffoon
truhanada *f* var. of **truhanería**
truhanear *vn* to cheat, swindle; (coll.) to play the buffoon, be clownish
truhanería *f* rascality, crookedness; (coll.) buffoonery; gang of crooks
truhanesco -ca *adj* knavish, crooked, tricky; (coll.) clownish
truísmo *m* truism
truja *f* olive bin
trujal *m* wine press; oil press; oil mill; soda vat (*in soapmaking*)
trujamán -mana *mf* interpreter; *m* adviser, expert
trujamanear *vn* to interpret; to counsel; to deal, to trade
trujamanía *f* interpreting; counseling; dealing, trading
trujimán -mana *mf* var. of **trujamán**
trulla *f* noise, bustle; crowd; trowel
trullo *m* (orn.) teal; vat to catch juice of pressed grapes
truncadamente *adv* with cuts, with omissions
truncado -da *adj* truncate; truncated
truncadura *f* (cryst.) truncation
truncamiento *m* truncation; curtailment
truncar §86 *va* to truncate; to cut off the head of; to cut, slash (*a writing, speech, etc.*); to cut off, leave unfinished
trunco -ca *adj* truncated
trupial *m* (orn.) troupial
truquero *m* keeper of a poolroom
trusas *fpl* trunk hose; (Am.) trunks
tsetsé *f* (ent.) tsetse
T.S.H. abr. of **telefonía sin hilos** & **telegrafía sin hilos**
tu *poss adj* thy; your
tú *pron pers* thou; you; **a tú por tú** (coll.) disrespectfully; **de tú por tú** intimately; **hablar, llamar** or **tratar de tú** to thou, address as thou, be on close or intimate terms with
tuáutem *m* (*pl:* **-temes**) (coll.) indispensable person; (coll.) sine qua non
tuba *f* (mus.) tuba
Tubalcaín *m* (Bib.) Tubal-cain
tubercular *adj* tubercular
tuberculina *f* (bact.) tuberculin
tuberculización *f* tubercularization
tubérculo *m* (anat. & bot.) tuber, tubercle; (path. & zool.) tubercle
tuberculosis *f* (path.) tuberculosis
tuberculoso -sa *adj* tuberculous; tubercular; *mf* tubercular (*person having tuberculosis*)
tubería *f* tubing; piping, pipes; tubeworks
tuberosa *f* see **tuberoso**
tuberosidad *f* tuberosity
tuberoso -sa *adj* tuberous; *f* (bot.) tuberose
tubícola *adj* (zool.) tubicolous
Tubinga *f* Tübingen
tubo *m* tube; pipe; (anat., elec. & rad.) tube; **tubo acústico** speaking tube; **tubo capilar** capillary, capillary tube; **tubo criboso** (bot.) sieve tube; **tubo de burbuja** bubble tube; **tubo de embocadura de flauta** (mus.) flue pipe; **tubo de ensayo** test tube; **tubo de flauta** (mus.) flue pipe; **tubo de Geissler** (elec.) Geissler tube; **tubo de humo** flue; **tubo de imagen** (telv.) picture tube; **tubo de lámpara** lamp chimney; **tubo de lengüeta** (mus.) reed pipe; **tubo de nivel** gauge glass; **tubo de órgano** (mus.) organ pipe; **tubo de radio** radio tube; **tubo de vacío** (rad.) vacuum tube; **tubo digestivo** (anat.) alimentary canal; **tubo fluorescente** fluorescent lamp; **tubo indicador** gauge glass; **tubo lanzatorpedos** (nav.) torpedo tube; **tubo radiógeno** (rad.) broadcasting tube; **tubo sonoro** chime, tubular chime; **tubo tricolor** (telv.) tricolor tube; **tubo Venturi** (hyd.) Venturi tube
tubocurarina *f* (chem.) tubocurarine
tubulación *f* tubulation
tubulado -da *adj* tubulate
tubular *adj* tubular; *m* bicycle tire
tubuloso -sa *adj* (bot.) tubulous
tubulura *f* (chem.) tubulure
tucán *m* (orn.) toucan; (*cap.*) *m* (astr.) Toucan (*constellation of Southern Hemisphere*)
tucía *f* tutty
Tucídides *m* Thucydides
tudel *m* (mus.) crook (*of bassoon*)
tudesco -ca *adj & mf* German
tueca *f* stump
tueco *m* stump; hollow left by wood-boring insect
tuerca *f* (mach.) nut; **tuerca de aletas** or **de mariposa** (mach.) wing nut; **tuerca de orejetas** (mach.) thumb nut
tuerce *m* twist; (Am.) misfortune
tuercecuello *m* (orn.) wryneck
tuero *m* heavy log; stick, sticks; (Am.) hide-and-seek
tuerto -ta *adj* twisted, crooked, bent; one-eyed; **a tuertas** (coll.) backwards, upside down; crosswise; **a tuertas o a derechas** rightly or wrongly; without reflection; **a tuerto** unjustly; **a tuerto o a derecho** rightly or wrongly; without reflection; *mf* one-eyed person; *m* wrong, harm, injustice; **tuertos** *mpl* afterpains
tueste *m* toast, toasting
tuétano *m* (anat.) marrow; (bot.) pith; **hasta los tuétanos** (coll.) through and through, head over heels
tufarada *f* sharp smell or odor
tufillas *mf* (*pl:* **-llas**) (coll.) spitfire
tufo *m* fume, vapor; sidelock; (geol.) tufa; (coll.) foul odor; (coll.) foul breath; **tufos** *mpl* (coll.) airs, conceit

tufoso -sa *adj* fumy, vaporous; foul; conceited, haughty
tugurio *m* shepherd's hut; hovel
tuición *f* protection, custody
tuina *f* long, loose jacket
tuitivo -va *adj* protective, defensive
tul *m* tulle
Tula *f* Gerty
tularemia *f* (path.) tularemia
Tule *f* Thule; **última Tule** ultima Thule; (*l.c.*) *m* (bot.) tule
tulio *m* (chem.) thulium; (*cap.*) *m* Tully
tulipa *f* (bot.) gillyflower; (bot.) small tulip; tulip-shaped glass globe; bell end (*of a pipe*)
tulipán *m* (bot.) tulip (*plant, bulb, and flower*); (bot.) rose of China (*Hibiscus rosa-sinensis*)
tulipanero or **tulipero** *m* (bot.) tulip tree
tullecer §34 *va* to abuse, mistreat; *vn* to become crippled or paralyzed
Tullerías *fpl* Tuileries
tullidez *f* paralysis
tullido -da *adj* crippled, paralyzed; *mf* cripple
tulliduras *fpl* excreta (*of birds of prey*)
tullimiento *m* paralysis; abuse, mistreatment; stiff tendons
tullir §26 *va* to cripple, paralyze; to abuse, mistreat; *vn* to excrete (*said of birds*); *vr* to become crippled or paralyzed
tumba *f* grave, tomb; monument, tombstone; tumble; arched top; (Am.) clearing, felling of timber
tumbacuartillos *mf* (*pl:* **-llos**) (coll.) old toper, rounder
tumbadillo *m* (naut.) roundhouse
tumbado -da *adj* arched, vaulted
tumbador *m* wrecker; feller, woodsman; wrestler; tumbler; (coll.) masher
tumbadora *f* tree-dozer
tumbaga *f* tombac (*alloy*); tombac ring; ring
tumbagón *m* tombac bracelet
tumbaollas *mf* (*pl:* **-llas**) (coll.) glutton
tumbar *va* to knock down, knock over; (coll.) to stun, knock out; to catch, to trick; (Am.) to clear (*land, woods*); *vn* to fall, tumble; (naut.) to capsize; *vr* (coll.) to lie down, go to bed; to ease up, to give up
tumbilla *f* wooden frame (*to hold a bed warmer*)
tumbo *m* fall, tumble, violent shaking; boom, rumble; critical moment; rise and fall of sea; rough surf; archive; **tumbo de dado** imminent danger
tumbón -bona *adj* (coll.) sly, wily; (coll.) lazy; *mf* (coll.) sly person; (coll.) lazy loafer; *m* coach with arched top; coffer or trunk with rounded lid
tumbonear *vn* (coll.) to loaf around
tumefacción *f* swelling, tumefaction
tumefacer §55 (has no compound tenses) *va & vr* to swell, to tumefy
tumefaciente *adj* tumefacient; *m* tumefacient agent
tumefacto -ta *adj* swollen
tumescencia *f* tumescence
tumescente *adj* tumescent
túmido -da *adj* tumid, swollen; (fig.) tumid, pompous, bombastic; bulbous or onion-shaped (*arch or vault*)
tumor *m* (path.) tumor
tumoral *adj* tumorlike
tumoroso -sa *adj* tumorous
tumulario -ria *adj* tumular
túmulo *m* tumulus; catafalque (*with or without corpse*)
tumulto *m* tumult
tumultuar §33 *va* to incite to riot, incite to make a disturbance; *vr* to riot, make a disturbance
tumultuario -ria *adj* tumultuary
tumultuoso -sa *adj* tumultuous
tuna *f* see **tuno**
tunal *m* (bot.) tuna, prickly pear; growth of prickly pears
tunanta *adj fem* crooked, tricky; *f* crook, rascal
tunantada *f* crookedness, trickiness
tunante *adj* bumming, loafing; crooked, tricky; *mf* bum, loafer; crook, rascal
tunantear *vn* to be crooked, be tricky
tunantería *f* crookedness, trickiness
tunar *vn* (coll.) to bum, to loaf
tunda *f* shearing of cloth; (coll.) beating, drubbing
tundear *va* to beat, drub, thrash
tundente *adj* bruising
tundición *f* shearing of cloth
tundidor -dora *adj* cloth-shearing; *mf* cloth shearer; *f* cloth-shearing machine; lawn mower
tundidura *f* shearing of cloth
tundir *va* to shear (*cloth*); to cut, to mow (*grass*); (coll.) to beat, drub, thrash
tundizno *m* short staple wool
tundra *f* tundra
tunear *vn* (coll.) to be crooked, be tricky
tunecí, tunecino -na *adj & mf* Tunisian
túnel *m* tunnel; **túnel aéreo** or **aerodinámico** (aer.) wind tunnel; **túnel a presión** (aer.) pressure tunnel
tunera *f* (bot.) prickly pear
tunes *mpl* (Am.) little steps, first steps
Túnez Tunis (*city*); Tunisia (*state*)
túngaro *m* (zool.) agua toad
tungstato *m* (chem.) tungstate
tungsteno *m* (chem.) tungsten
túngstico -ca *adj* (chem.) tungstic
tungstita *f* (mineral.) tungstite
túnica *f* tunic; (anat., bot. & zool.) tunic
tunicado -da *adj* tunicate; *m* (zool.) tunicate
tunicela *f* tunic; (eccl.) tunicle
tunicina *f* (biochem.) tunicin
túnico *m* robe, gown; (Am.) chemise
tuno -na *adj* crooked, tricky; *mf* crook, rascal; *f* (bot.) tuna, prickly pear (*plant and fruit*); group of students; (coll.) bumming, loafing; **correr la tuna** (coll.) to bum, to loaf
tuntún *m* (zool.) hookworm; **al tuntún** or **al buen tuntún** (coll.) wildly, thoughtlessly, without knowing what one is talking about
tuntunita *f* (Am.) tiresome repetition
tupa *f* stuffing, packing; (coll.) stuffing, overeating
tupé *m* toupee; (coll.) cheek, brass, nerve
tupelo *m* (bot.) tupelo
tupi *m* (Am.) coffee house
tupido -da *adj* thick, dense, heavy, compact; dull, stupid; (Am.) abundant
tupinambo *m* var. of **aguaturma**
tupir *va* to pack tight, make compact; *vr* to stuff, eat too much
turacina *f* (biochem.) turacin
turaco *m* (orn.) touraco
turanio *adj & mf* Turanian
turba *f* crowd, mob; peat, turf
turbación *f* disturbance, confusion
turbadamente *adv* confusedly, excitedly
turbador -dora *adj* disturbing; *mf* disturber
turbal *m* peat bog
turbamiento *m* var. of **turbación**
turbamulta *f* (coll.) mob, rabble
turbante *m* turban
turbar *va* to disturb, upset, trouble; to stir up; *vr* to become disturbed, to get confused or mixed up
turbera *f* peat bog
turbia *f* see **turbio**
turbidimétrico -ca *adj* turbidimetric
turbidímetro *m* turbidimeter
túrbido -da *adj* var. of **turbio**
turbiedad *f* turbidity, muddiness; confusion, obscurity
turbieza *f* (act of) confusing, bewildering
turbina *f* turbine; **turbina a vapor** steam turbine; **turbina axial** axial-flow turbine; **turbina centrífuga** outward-flow turbine; **turbina centrípeta** inward-flow turbine; **turbina de acción** impulse turbine; **turbina de gas** gas turbine; **turbina de impulsión** impulse turbine; **turbina de reacción** reaction turbine; **turbina de vapor** steam turbine; **turbina hidráulica** hydraulic turbine; **turbina límite** limit turbine; **turbina mixta** mixed-flow turbine; **turbina paralela** parallel-flow turbine; **turbina radial** radial-flow turbine
turbinado -da *adj* turbinate (*inversely conical*); (anat.) turbinate
turbino *m* (pharm.) turpeth
turbinto *m* (bot.) pepper tree or shrub

turbio -bia *adj* turbid, muddy, cloudy; troubled, confused; obscure (*language*); **de turbio en turbio** (coll.) drowsy all day (*from having been awake all night*); **turbios** *mpl* dregs, oil dregs; *f* muddiness (*of water*)
turbión *m* squall, heavy shower; thunderstorm; (fig.) rush, sweep; (fig.) hail (*e.g., of bullets*)
turbit *m* (bot.) turpeth
turbobomba *f* turbopump
turbocompresor *m* turbocompressor
turbodínamo *f* turbodynamo
turboeléctrico -ca *adj* turbine-electric
turbogenerador *m* turbogenerator
turbohélice *m* (aer.) turbo-prop
turbomotor *m* turbomotor
turbonada *f* windstorm, thunderstorm
turbopropulsor *m* (aer.) turbo-propeller engine
turborreactor *m* (aer.) turbojet; **turborreactor a postcombustión** (aer.) turbo-ram-jet
turboso -sa *adj* peaty, turfy
turbosoplador *m* turboblower
turbosupercargador *m* turbosupercharger
turboventilador *m* turbofan; turboventilator
turbulencia *f* turbulence or turbulency
turbulento -ta *adj* turbulent
turco -ca *adj* Turkish; (philol.) Turkic; *mf* Turk; *m* Turkish (*language*); (mil.) Turco (*Algerian tirailleur*); **el gran Turco** the Grand Turk (*the Sultan*); **gran turco** (bot.) buckwheat; *f* (coll.) jag, drunk; **coger una turca** (coll.) to go on a jag, to get drunk
turcófilo -la *adj & mf* Turkophile
turcófobo -ba *adj & mf* Turkophobe
turcomano -na *adj* Turkomanic; *mf* Turkoman
turcople *adj & mf* Turko-Greek (*of Turkish father and Greek mother*)
túrdiga *f* strip of hide or leather; sole of a sandal
Turena, la Touraine
turf *m* (*pl:* **turfs**) race track; horse racing; turfmen
turfista *adj* turfy, horsy; *m* turfman
turfístico -ca *adj* racing, horse-racing
turgencia *f* turgidity
turgente *adj* (path. & fig.) turgid; (poet.) raised, elevated, massive
turgescencia *f* turgescence
turgescente *adj* turgescent
túrgido -da *adj* (poet.) raised, elevated, massive
turgita *f* (mineral.) turgite
turibular *va* to incense with the thurible
turibulario *m* (eccl.) thurifer
turíbulo *m* (eccl.) thurible
turiferario *m* (eccl.) thurifer; (coll.) fawner
turificación *f* thurification
turificar §86 *va & vn* to thurify
Turín *f* Turin
Turingia *f* Thuringia
turingiano -na *adj & mf* Thuringian
turión *m* (bot.) turion
turismo *m* touring; tourist business; touring car
turista *mf* tourist
turístico -ca *adj* touring; tourist
Turkmenistán, el the Turkmen Soviet Socialist Republic
turma *f* testicle; **turma de tierra** (bot.) truffle
turmalina *f* (mineral.) tourmaline
turnar *vn* to alternate, to take turns
turneráceo -a *adj* (bot.) turneraceous
turnerita *f* (mineral.) turnerite
turnio -nia *adj* squint, cross (*eyes*); squint-eyed, cross-eyed; (fig.) cross-looking, stern
turno *m* turn, shift; **aguardar turno** to wait one's turn; **a su turno** in his stead; **fuera de turno** out of turn; **por turno** in turn; **por turnos** by turns
turón *m* (zool.) fitch, polecat
turpial *m* var. of **trupial**
turquear *vr* (Am.) to be fagged out
turquesa *f* (mineral.) turquoise; mold; bullet mold
turquesado -da *adj* dark-blue
turquesco -ca *adj* Turkish
Turquestán, el Turkestan; **el Turquestán Chino** Chinese Turkestan; **el Turquestán Ruso** Russian Turkestan
turquí *adj* (*pl:* **-quíes**) deep-blue
Turquía *f* Turkey; **la Turquía de Asia** Turkey in Asia; **la Turquía de Europa** Turkey in Europe; **la Turquía Asiática** Turkey in Asia; **la Turquía Europea** Turkey in Europe
turquino -na *adj* var. of **turquí**
turrar *va* to toast, to roast, to broil
turriculado -da *adj* (zool.) turreted
turrón *m* nougat; (coll.) public office, plum; **romper el turrón** (Am.) to begin to thou each other, to begin to call each other by their first names
turronería *f* nougat shop
turronero -ra *mf* maker or seller of nougats
Turs *f* Tours
turulato -ta *adj* (coll.) stunned, dumbfounded
turumbón *m* (coll.) bump, bump on the head
turuta *f* (coll.) jag, drunk
tus *interj* here, here! (*to call a dog*); **sin decir tus ni mus** (coll.) without saying boo
tusa *f* (Am.) cigar rolled in corn husk; (Am.) corncob; (Am.) corn silk; (Am.) mane (*of horse*); (Am.) pockmark; (Am.) trollop
tusar *vn* (prov. & Am.) to cut, to shear
Túsculo *f* Tusculum
tusícula *f* slight cough
tusilago *m* (bot.) coltsfoot
tusón *m* fleece; unsheared sheepskin; colt under two years old
tusona *f* (prov.) filly under two years old
tusor *m* tussah (*silk*)
tutado -da *adj* (Am.) pock-marked
tutar *vr* (Am.) to become pock-marked
tuteamiento *m* var. of **tuteo**
tutear *va* to thou; to address using the second person singular; to be on close or intimate terms with; *vr* to thou each other; to address each other using the second person singular; to be on close or intimate terms with each other
tutela *f* guardianship, tutelage; protection
tutelar *adj* guardian, tutelar, tutelary; *va* to protect, take under one's wing
tuteo *m* thouing; addressing in the second person singular
tutía *f* var. of **atutía**
tutilimundi *m* var. of **mundonuevo**
tutiplén; a tutiplén (coll.) in abundance, to excess
tutor -tora or **-triz** (*pl:* **-trices**) *mf* guardian, protector; (law) guardian; *m* prop (*for plants*)
tutoría *f* guardianship, tutelage
tutuquear *va* (Am.) to sick (*a dog*)
tuturuto -ta *adj* (Am.) stunned, dumbfounded; *mf* (Am.) go-between
tuturutú *m* (*pl:* **-túes**) bugle call, horn call
tuve *1st sg pret ind of* **tener**
tuyo -ya *adj & pron poss* thine, yours; *f* (bot.) thuja; **tuya articulada** (bot.) sandarac; **tuya de la China** (bot.) China tree
tuza *f* (zool.) gopher, pocket gopher
TV *f* abr. of **televisión**

U

U, u *f* twenty-fourth letter of the Spanish alphabet
U. abr. of **usted**
u *conj* (used for **o** before a word beginning with the vowel sound **o**) or
uapití *m* (*pl:* **-tíes**) (zool.) wapiti
Ubaldo *m* Waldo
ubérrimo -ma *adj super* very or most abundant or fertile
ubicación *f* location, situation, position
ubicar §86 *va* (Am.) to place, locate; *vn & vr* to be located, be situated
ubicuidad *f* ubiquity
ubicuo -cua *adj* ubiquitous
ubiquidad *f* var. of **ubicuidad**
ubiquitario -ria *adj & mf* (eccl.) Ubiquitarian
ubre *f* teat; udder
ubrera *f* (path.) thrush
ucase *m* ukase
-uco -ca *suffix dim & pej* e.g., **ventanucho** ugly little window; **casuca** shack, shanty
ucranio -nia *adj & mf* Ukrainian; *m* Ukrainian (*language*); (*cap.*) *f* Ukraine
-ucho -cha *suffix dim & pej* e.g., **ventanucho** ugly little window; **casucha** shack, shanty
uchuvito -ta *adj* (Am.) drunk
Ud. abr. of **usted**
udómetro *m* udometer
-udo -da *suffix adj* -y, e.g., **carnudo** fleshy; **peludo** hairy; *suffix aug* e.g., **barbudo** long-bearded, heavy-bearded; **cabezudo** big-headed; **zancudo** long-shanked
Uds. abr. of **ustedes**
-uelo -la *suffix dim & pej* indicates smallness with or without concept of ridicule or contempt, e.g., **arroyuelo** rill; **mozuelo** young fellow; **coquetuela** vain coquette; **plazuela** small square
-ueño -ña *suffix adj* -ing, e.g., **halagüeño** charming; **pedigüeño** demanding; **risueño** smiling
uesnorueste *m* var. of **oesnoroeste**
uessudueste *m* var. of **oessudoeste**
ueste *m* var. of **oeste**
uf *interj* pshaw!; humph!; whew!
ufanar *vr* to boast; **ufanarse con** or **de** to boast of, to pride oneself on
ufanía *f* pride, conceit; cheer, satisfaction; smoothness, mastery
ufano -na *adj* proud, conceited, boastful; cheerful, satisfied; easy, smooth, masterly
ufo; a ufo on someone else, at someone else's expense
ujier *m* doorman, usher
ulano *m* (mil.) uhlan
úlcera *f* (path.) sore, ulcer; (bot.) rot; **úlcera de decúbito** bedsore; **úlcera duodenal** (path.) duodenal ulcer; **úlcera gástrica** (path.) gastric ulcer; **úlcera péptica** (path.) peptic ulcer
ulceración *f* ulceration
ulcerar *va & vr* to ulcerate, to fester
ulceroso -sa *adj* ulcerous
ulema *m* ulema
ulero *m* (Am.) rolling pin
ulfilano -na *adj* of Ulfilas (*said of an ancient mode of writing*)
uliginoso -sa *adj* uliginose
Ulises *m* (myth.) Ulysses
ulitis *f* (path.) ulitis
ulmáceo -a *adj* (bot.) ulmaceous
ulmaria *f* (bot.) meadowsweet
ulna *f* (anat.) ulna
ulnar *adj* ulnar
úlster *m* ulster
ulterior *adj* ulterior, later, subsequent
ulteriormente *adv* later, subsequently
ultimación *f* termination, conclusion
últimamente *adv* finally; recently, lately
ultimar *va* to end, finish, terminate, wind up
ultimátum *m* (*pl:* **-mátum** or **-mátumes**) ultimatum; (coll.) definitive decision
ultimidad *f* finality
último -ma *adj* last, latest; excellent, superior; most remote; lowest; final (*said, e.g., of a price*); top (*floor*); late (*hour*); **a última hora** at the eleventh hour; **a últimos de** in the latter part of (*a month*); **a la última** in the latest fashion; **estar a lo último** or **en las últimas** to be up to date, be well-informed; to be near the end, to be on one's last legs; **por último** at last, finally; **última sílaba** (gram.) ultima; **último suplicio** capital punishment
ultra *adv* besides
ultraatmosférico -ca *adj* outer (*space*)
ultrajador -dora *adj* insulting, offensive; *mf* insulter
ultrajar *va* to outrage, insult, offend
ultraje *m* outrage, insult, offense
ultrajoso -sa *adj* outrageous
ultraliberal *adj & mf* ultraliberal
ultramar *m* country overseas; ultramarine (*pigment*); **en ultramar** overseas
ultramarino -na *adj* ultramarine; overseas; *m* ultramarine, ultramarine blue; **ultramarinos** *mpl* delicatessen, overseas foods, groceries
ultramicroscopia *f* ultramicroscopy
ultramicroscópico -ca *adj* ultramicroscopic
ultramicroscopio *m* ultramicroscope
ultramoderno -na *adj* ultramodern
ultramontanismo *m* ultramontanism
ultramontano -na *adj & mf* ultramontane
ultramundano -na *adj* ultramundane, otherworldly
ultramundo *m* other world, future life
ultranza; a ultranza to the death; at any cost, unflinchingly; extreme
ultrarradical *adj* ultraradical
ultrarrápido -da *adj* ultrarapid, extra-fast
ultrarrojo -ja *adj* ultrared, infrared
ultrasónico -ca *adj* supersonic; ultrasonic; *f* ultrasonics
ultratropical *adj* ultratropical
ultratumba *adv* beyond the grave
ultraviolado -da or **ultravioleta** *adj* (phys.) ultraviolet
ultravirus *m* (*pl:* **-rus**) ultravirus
ultrazodiacal *adj* (astr.) ultrazodiacal
úlula *f* (orn.) tawny owl
ululación *f* howl, ululation; hoot (*of owl*); wow (*of phonograph record*)
ululante *adj* ululant
ulular *vn* to ululate; to hoot
ululato *m* howl, ululation; hoot (*of owl*)
-ullo -lla *suffix dim & pej* e.g., **zangandullo** worthless loafer; **ramulla** small wood, dead wood
ulluco *m* (bot.) ulluco (*South American tubercle similar to the potato*)
umbela *f* (bot.) umbel
umbelado -da *adj* umbellate
umbelífero -ra *adj* umbelliferous
umbeliforme *adj* umbellar or umbellate
umbilicado -da *adj* umbilicate
umbilical *adj* umbilical
umbo *m* (anat. & zool.) umbo
umbón *m* umbo (*of shield*)
umbráculo *m* shaded, airy place for plants
umbral *m* threshold; doorsill; (arch.) lintel (*of any opening*); (psychol., physiol. & fig.) threshold; **atravesar los umbrales** to cross the threshold; **estar en los umbrales de** to be on the threshold of; **no atravesar los umbrales** to not darken one's door

umbralada *f*, **umbralado** *m*, or **umbraladura** *f* (Am.) threshold
umbralar *va* (arch.) to put a lintel in
umbrático -ca *adj* umbrageous, shady
umbrela *f* (zool.) umbrella (*of jellyfishes*)
umbrío -a *adj* shady; *f* shade, shady place; shady side; **la Umbría** Umbria
umbro -bra *adj* & *mf* Umbrian; *m* Umbrian (*ancient Italic language*)
umbroso -sa *adj* umbrageous, shady
un, una *art indef* a, an; *adj* one (*numeral*); the form **un** is used before a masculine singular noun or an adjective + a masculine singular noun and before a feminine singular noun beginning with accented **a** or **ha**; see **uno**
unánime *adj* unanimous
unanimidad *f* unanimity
unanimismo *m* unanimism
uncial *adj* & *f* uncial
unciforme *adj* unciform; *m* (anat.) unciform
uncinado -da *adj* uncinate
unción *f* unction; **unciones** *fpl* treatment with mercurial ointment
uncir §50 *va* to yoke; to subjugate
undante *adj* (poet.) wavy, undulating
undecágono *m* undecagon
undécimo -ma *adj* & *m* eleventh
undécuplo -pla *adj* eleven times as large or as much
undísono -na *adj* (poet.) babbling, rippling
undívago -ga *adj* (poet.) wavy
undoso -sa *adj* waving, wavy
undulación *f* undulation; wave; wave motion; **undulación permanente** permanent wave
undulante *adj* undulant; waving
undular *vn* to undulate; to wriggle
undulatorio -ria *adj* undulatory
Unesco *f* Unesco
ungido *m* anointed; **el ungido del Señor** The Lord's Anointed
ungimiento *m* anointment
ungir §42 *va* to anoint; (eccl.) to anoint; (coll.) to dub, to name
ungüentario -ria *adj* unguentary; *mf* maker or dealer in unguents; *m* vessel in which unguents are kept
ungüento *m* unguent, ointment, salve; (fig.) salve, flattery
unguiculado -da *adj* ungual, unguiculate
unguinal *adj* ungual
unguis *m* (*pl:* **-guis**) (anat.) unguis or os unguis
úngula *f* (zool. & geom.) ungula
ungulado -da *adj* & *m* ungulate
ungular *adj* ungular
uniato -ta *adj* & *mf* Uniat
uniaxial, uniáxico -ca or **uniaxil** *adj* uniaxial
únicamente *adv* only, solely; uniquely
unicameral *adj* unicameral
unicelular *adj* unicellular
unicidad *f* unity; uniqueness
único -ca *adj* only, sole; unique; one, e.g., **precio único** one price
unicolor *adj* one-color
unicornio -nia *adj* unicorn; *m* (myth. & Bib.) unicorn
unidad *f* unit; unity; **unidad móvil** (rad.) mobile unit
unidireccional *adj* one-way, unidirectional
unido -da *adj* united; smooth; (fig.) close-knit
unifamiliar *adj* one-family, single-family (*e.g., house*)
unificación *f* unification
unificador -dora *adj* unifying
unificar §86 *va* to unify; *vr* to be or become unified
unifloro -ra *adj* (bot.) uniflorous
unifoliado -da *adj* (bot.) unifoliate
uniformar *va* to uniform; to clothe in uniforms; to make uniform; **uniformar una cosa a** or **con otra** to make one thing uniform with another; *vr* to become uniform
uniforme *adj* & *m* uniform
uniformidad *f* uniformity
unigénito -ta *adj* unigenital, only-begotten
unilateral *adj* unilateral
unión *f* union; double finger ring; (mach.) union; (*cap.*) *f* Union (*U.S.A.*); **unión aduanera** customs union; **Unión de Repúblicas Socialistas Soviéticas** Union of Soviet Socialist Republics; **Unión panamericana** Pan American Union; **Unión Soviética** Soviet Union; **Unión Sudafricana** Union of South Africa
unionismo *m* unionism
unionista *mf* unionist
uníparo -ra *adj* (zool. & bot.) uniparous
unípede *adj* uniped
unipersonal *adj* unipersonal; of one person, one-man (*e.g., government*); (gram.) impersonal
unipolar *adj* (elec.) unipolar, single-pole
unir *va* & *vr* to unite, join
unisexual *adj* unisexual
unisón *m* (mus.) instruments or voices in unison
unisonancia *f* monotony (*of an orator*); (mus.) unison
unisonar *vn* to sound or be in unison
unísono -na *adj* (mus.) unison; unisonous; **al unísono** in unison; unanimously; **al unísono de** in unison with
unitario -ria *adj* unitary; (pertaining to a) unit; Unitarian; *mf* Unitarian
unitarismo *m* (eccl.) Unitarianism
unitivo -va *adj* unitive
univalencia *f* (chem.) univalence
univalente *adj* (chem.) univalent
univalvo -va *adj* (zool.) univalve
universal *adj* universal; *m* (log.) universal (*each one of the five predicables*)
universalidad *f* universality; generality
universalismo *m* universalism; Universalism
universalista *mf* universalist; Universalist
universalizar §76 *va* to universalize
universidad *f* university
universitario -ria *adj* (pertaining to a) university; *mf* (Am.) university student, college student; *m* university professor
universo -sa *adj* universal; *m* universe; **universo aislado** (astr.) island universe
univocación *f* univocity
univocar §86 *vr* to have the same meaning
unívoco -ca *adj* univocal
-uno -na *suffix adj* -ine, e.g., **boyuno** bovine; **cervuno** cervine; **lebruno** leporine; **porcuno** porcine; -ish, e.g., **frailuno** friarish; **hombruno** mannish
uno -na *adj* & *pron indef* one, someone, some one; one and the same; one, they, people, e.g., **uno no sabe qué hacer aquí** one does not know what to do here; **a una** of one accord; **de una** at once; **la una** one o'clock; **somos unos** we are one; **una y no más** once is enough; **uno a otro, unos a otros** each other, one another; **uno que otro** one or more, a few; **unos -nas** some, about; a pair of, e.g., **unas gafas** a pair of glasses; **unos tirantes** a pair of suspenders; **unos cuantos** some, a few; **uno y otro** both; *m* one (*numeral*); see **un**
untador -dora *adj* anointing; greasing; *mf* anointer; greaser
untadura *f* anointing, ointment; greasing, grease
untamiento *m* anointing; greasing
untar *va* to anoint; to smear, grease; (coll.) to bribe; *vr* to get smeared; to grease oneself; (coll.) to take care of oneself, look out for oneself
untaza *f* fat
unto *m* grease; fat; ointment; salve, flattery; **unto de botas, unto de zapatos** (Am.) shoe polish; **unto de Méjico** (coll.) bribe money
untoso -sa *adj* var. of **untuoso**
untuosidad *f* greasiness, stickiness
untuoso -sa *adj* unctuous; greasy, sticky
untura *f* var. of **untadura**
uña *f* nail, fingernail, toenail; nail hole (*in blade of penknife*); claw; hoof, talon; sting (*of scorpion*); thorn; scab; hard tumor on eyelid; short tree stump; plectrum (*e.g., for mandolin*); (mach.) claw, gripper; (mach.) pallet (*of pawl*); fluke, bill (*of anchor*); **a uña de caballo** at full gallop, at full speed; **enseñar** or **mostrar las uñas** to show one's teeth; **ser largo de uñas** to have long fingers; **ser**

uña y carne (coll.) to be in cahoots, to be hand in glove; **tener en la uña** to have on the tip of one's fingers; **uña de caballo** (bot.) coltsfoot
uñada *f* scratch, nail scratch; nip, flip
uñarada *f* nail scratch
uñate *m* (coll.) pinch with the nail; chuckfarthing
uñero *m* ingrowing nail; whitlow; thumb notch
uñeta *f* small fingernail; stonecutter's chisel; chuckfarthing
uñetazo *m* nail scratch
uñir §25 *va* (prov.) to yoke
uñoso -sa *adj* long-nailed, long-clawed
upa *interj* up, up!
upas *m* (bot.) upas (*tree and sap*)
upupa *f* (orn.) hoopoe
ural *adj* Ural; **los Urales** the Urals
urálico -ca *adj* Uralian, Uralic
uralita *f* (mineral.) uralite; asbestos roofing material
uraloaltaico -ca *adj & m* Ural-Altaic
uranálisis *f* (*pl:* **-sis**) urinalysis
Urania *f* see **uranio**
uránico -ca *adj* (chem.) uranic
uranilo *m* (chem.) uranyl
uraninita *f* (mineral.) uraninite
uranio -nia *adj* Uranian; *m* (chem.) uranium; (*cap.*) *f* (myth.) Urania
uranismo *m* uranism
uranita *f* (mineral.) uranite
urano *m* (chem.) uranium; (*cap.*) *m* (astr. & myth.) Uranus
uranocircita *f* (mineral.) uranocircite
uranofano *m* (mineral.) uranophane
uranografía *f* uranography
uranógrafo -fa *mf* uranographer
uranometría *f* uranometry
uranosferita *f* (mineral.) uranosphaerite
uranospatita *f* (mineral.) uranospathite
uranospinita *f* (mineral.) uranospinite
uranotalita *f* (mineral.) uranothallite
uranotila *f* (mineral.) uranotil
uranotorita *f* (mineral.) uranothorite
urao *m* (mineral.) urao, trona
urato *m* (chem.) urate
urbanidad *f* urbanity
urbanismo *m* city planning
urbanista *adj* city-planning; *m* city planner
urbanístico -ca *adj* urbanistic; *f* city planning
urbanización *f* urbanization; city planning
urbanizar §76 *va* to urbanize; *vr* to become urbanized
urbano -na *adj* urban, city; urbane (*courteous, elegant*); (*cap.*) *m* Urban
urbe *f* big city, metropolis
urca *f* (naut.) hooker, dogger; (zool.) killer whale, orca
urce *m* (bot.) heath
urceolado -da *adj* urceolate
urchilla *f* (bot. & chem.) archil
urdemalas *mf* (*pl:* **-las**) (coll.) intriguer, schemer
urdidera *f* warper (*woman*); warping frame
urdidor -dora *adj* warping; scheming; *mf* warper; *f* warping frame
urdidura *f* warping; scheming
urdiembre *f* or **urdimbre** *f* warp; warping chain; scheme, scheming
urdir *va* to beam (*a warp*); to plot, scheme, conspire
urdú *m* Urdu
urea *f* (biochem.) urea
uredospora *f* (bot.) uredospore
ureido *m* (chem.) ureide
uremia *f* (path.) uremia
urémico -ca *adj* uremic
urente *adj* burning, smarting
uréter *m* (anat. & zool.) ureter
uretra *f* (anat.) urethra
uretral *adj* urethral
uretritis *f* (path.) urethritis
uretroscopia *f* urethroscopy
uretroscopio *m* urethroscope
uretrotomía *f* (surg.) urethrotomy
urgencia *f* urgency; emergency; **de urgencia** emergency; special-delivery
urgente *adj* urgent; special-delivery
urgir §42 *vn* to be urgent; **urgir** + *inf* to be urgent to + *inf*
Urías *m* (Bib.) Uriah
úrico -ca *adj* (chem.) uric
urinación *f* urination
urinal *adj* urinary; *m* urinal (*place*)
urinálisis *f* (*pl:* **-sis**) urinalysis
urinario -ria *adj* urinary; *m* urinal (*place*)
urinífero -ra *adj* uriniferous
urna *f* urn; glass case; ballot box; **ir a las urnas** to go to the polls
-uro *suffix m* (chem.) -ide, e.g., **hidruro** hydride; **sulfuro** sulfide; (zool.) -uran, e.g., **braquiuro** brachyuran; **jifosuro** xiphosuran
uro *m* (zool.) aurochs; (zool.) urus
urocisto *m* (anat.) urocyst
urocromo *m* (biochem.) urochrome
urodelo -la *adj & m* (zool.) urodelan
urofeína *f* (biochem.) urophaein or urophein
urogallo *m* (orn.) capercaillie
urogenital *adj* urogenital
urógeno -na *adj* urogenous
urolitiasis *f* (path.) urolithiasis
urolito *m* (path.) urolith
urología *f* urology
urológico -ca *adj* urologic or urological
urólogo -ga *mf* urologist
uromancia or **uromancía** *f* divination by inspection of urine
uropatagio *m* (zool.) uropatagium
uropigal *adj* uropygial
uropigio *m* uropygium
urópodo -da *adj* (zool.) uropodal; *m* (zool.) uropod
uropoiesis *f* or **uropoyesis** *f* uropoiesis
uroscopia *f* uroscopy
urosis *f* (path.) urosis
urotoxia *f* (physiol.) urotoxy
urraca *f* (orn.) magpie
ursiforme *adj* ursiform
ursino -na *adj* ursine
U.R.S.S. abr. of **Unión de Repúblicas Socialistas Soviéticas**
Úrsula *f* Ursula
ursulino -na *adj & f* Ursuline
urticáceo -a *adj* (bot.) urticaceous
urticación *f* (med.) urtication
urticante *adj* urticant
urticaria *f* (path.) hives, urticaria, nettle rash
urubú *m* (*pl:* **-búes**) (orn.) black vulture
Uruguay, el Uruguay
uruguayo -ya *adj & mf* Uruguayan
urunday *m* (Am.) urunday (*timber tree of genus Astronium*)
usadamente *adv* according to custom
usado -da *adj* used (*customarily employed; worn, partly worn-out; accustomed*); skilled; **al usado** at usance; **poco usado** rare (*word*)
usagre *m* (path.) infantile impetigo; (vet.) mange
usanza *f* use; usage, custom
usar *va* to use, make use of; to follow (*a profession*); *vn* to be accustomed; **usar** + *inf* to be accustomed to + *inf*, e.g., **uso salir de paseo por la mañana** I am accustomed to go out for a walk in the morning; **usar de** to use, resort to, indulge in; **usar de la palabra** to speak, make a speech; *vr* to be the custom
usarcé or **usarced** *mf* (obs.) your honor
usencia *mf* (obs.) your reverence
useñoría *mf* your excellence; *m* your lordship; *f* your ladyship
usgo *m* loathing
usía *mf* your excellence; *m* your lordship; *f* your ladyship
usier *m* var. of **ujier**
usina *f* (Am.) plant, factory; (Am.) powerhouse; **usina mareamotriz** (Am.) tide-driven power plant; **usina térmica** (Am.) steam power plant
uso *m* use; custom, usage; habit, practice; wear, wear and tear; **al uso** according to custom; **el uso hace maestro** practice makes perfect; **en buen uso** (coll.) in good condition; **hacer uso de la palabra** to speak, to make a speech; **uso de razón** discretion, discernment
ustaga *f* (naut.) tie
uste *interj* get away!; **sin decir uste ni muste** (coll.) without saying a word

usted *pron pers* (used with third person of verb) you
ustible *adj* combustible
ustión *f* burning, cauterization
ustorio -ria *adj* burning
usual *adj* usual; sociable; usable
usualmente *adv* usually
usuario -ria *adj* (law) having limited use of a thing; *mf* (law) usuary; user
usucapión *f* (law) usucapion
usucapir *va* (law) to usucapt
usufructo *m* (law) usufruct; uses, fruits
usufructuar §33 *va* to usufruct; to enjoy; *vn* to be productive, be fruitful
usura *f* usury; interest; profit; profiteering; **pagar con usura** to pay back (*a favor, an insult, etc.*) a thousandfold
usurar *vn* var. of **usurear**
usurario -ria *adj* usurious
usurear *vn* to practice usury; to profiteer
usurero -ra *mf* usurer; profiteer
usurpación *f* usurpation
usurpador -dora *adj* usurping; *mf* usurper
usurpar *va* usurp
utensilio *m* utensil; **utensilios** *mpl* (mil.) outfit, equipment
uterino -na *adj* uterine
útero *m* (anat.) uterus, womb
uterotomía *f* (surg.) hysterotomy
útil *adj* useful; (law) lawful, legal (*time*); *m* use; tool; **útiles** *mpl* tools, equipment
utilería *f* (Am.) stage equipment, properties; (Am.) scenic effects
utilero -ra *mf* (Am.) person in charge of properties (*in a theater*); *m* (Am.) property man
utilidad *f* utility, usefulness; profit, earning
utilitario -ria *adj* utilitarian
utilitarismo *m* utilitarianism
utilitarista *adj & mf* utilitarian
utilizable *adj* usable, ready for use, ready for service
utilización *f* utilization
utilizar §76 *va* to utilize; *vr* to serve; **utilizarse con, de** or **en** to make use of; **utilizarse para** to be used for, to be good for
utillaje *m* or **utillería** *f* tools, equipment, outfit
utopia or **utopía** *f* utopia or Utopia
utópico -ca *adj* utopian or Utopian
utopismo *m* utopianism
utopista *adj & mf* utopian or Utopian
utrera *f* heifer between two and three years old
utrero *m* bull between two and three years old
utrícula *f* (bot.) utricle
utricularia *f* (bot.) bladderwort
utrículo *m* (anat.) utricle
UU. abr. of **ustedes**
uva *f* grape; berry of barberry; grapevine; wart on eyelid; uvular tumor; **estar hecho una uva** to be soaked, have a load on; **no entrar por uvas** to not risk interceding; **uva canilla** (bot.) white stonecrop; **uva crespa** (bot.) gooseberry; **uva de Corinto** currant; **uva de gato** (bot.) sedum, white stonecrop; **uva de playa** sea-grape berry; **uva de raposa** (bot.) nightshade; **uva espín** or **espina** (bot.) gooseberry; **uva lupina** (bot.) wolfsbane; **uva marina** (bot.) shrubby horsetail; **uva pasa** raisin; **uvas verdes** (fig.) sour grapes (*of Aesop's fable*); **uva tamínea** or **taminia** (bot.) stavesacre; **uva verga** (bot.) wolfsbane
uvada *f* abundance of grapes, rich crop of grapes
uvaduz *f* (bot.) bearberry
uvaguemaestre *m* (mil.) wagon master
uval *adj* grape-like
uvanita *f* (mineral.) uvanite
uvarovita *f* (mineral.) uvarovite
uvate *m* grape preserves
uve *f* letter V
úvea *f* (anat.) uvea
uveral *m* (Am.) growth of sea grapes
uvero -ra *adj* (pertaining to the) grape; *mf* grape seller; *m* (bot.) sea grape
úvula *f* (anat.) uvula
uvular *adj* (anat. & phonet.) uvular
uvulitis *f* (path.) uvulitis
uxoricida *m* uxoricide (*man*)
uxoricidio *m* uxoricide (*act*)
uxorio -ria *adj* uxorial; uxorious (*excessively fond of and doting on one's wife*)
-uza *suffix pej* e.g., **carnuza** coarse cheap meat; **gentuza** rabble
uzarina *f* (chem.) uzarin
uzbeco -ca *adj & mf* Uzbek or Uzbeg; *m* Uzbek or Uzbeg (*language*)
Uzbekistán, el Uzbekistan
-uzco -ca *suffix adj* -ish, e.g., **blancuzco** whitish; **negruzco** blackish

V

V, v *f* twenty-fifth letter of the Spanish alphabet
V. abr. of **usted, véase** & **venerable**
V.A. abr. of **Vuestra Alteza**
va *3d sg pres ind of* **ir**
vaca *f* cow; cowhide; beef; gambling pool; **echar las vacas a** (coll.) to put the blame on; **hacer vacas** (Am.) to play truant; **vaca de la boda** (coll.) clown, laughingstock, goat; friend in need; **vaca de leche** milch cow; **vaca de San Antón** (ent.) ladybird; **vaca gruñidora** (zool.) yak; **vaca lechera** milch cow; **vaca marina** (zool.) sea cow; **vacas lecheras** dairy cattle
vacabuey *m* (bot.) sandpaper tree
vacación *f* vacation; vacancy; **vacaciones** *fpl* vacation; **estar de vacaciones** to be on vacation; **marcharse de vacaciones** to go away on a vacation, to leave for a vacation; **vacaciones retribuídas** vacations with pay
vacacionista *mf* vacationist
vacada *f* drove of cattle
vacancia *f* vacancy
vacante *adj* vacant, unoccupied; *f* vacation; vacancy
vacar §86 *vn* to be vacant, to be unfilled; to be idle, to not work, to be unoccupied; **vacar a** to engage in, to attend to; **vacar de** to lack
vacarí *adj* (*pl* **-ríes**) cowhide, made of cowhide
vaccíneo -a *adj* vaccine, vaccinic
vaccínico -ca *adj* var. of **vaccíneo**
vaciadero *m* drain; drainpipe
vaciadizo -za *adj* cast, molded
vaciado -da *adj* hollow-ground; *m* cast, casting; hollow; plaster cast
vaciador *m* emptier; caster, molder; sharpener
vaciamiento *m* emptying; casting, molding
vaciante *m* ebb tide
vaciar §90 & regular *va* to drain, to empty; to cast, to mold; to hollow out; to sharpen on a grindstone; to transcribe; to expatiate upon; *vn* to flow, to empty; to fall (*as a flood, river, etc.*); *vr* (coll.) to blab, to spill all one knows; **vaciarse de** (coll.) to blab, to spill
vaciedad *f* nonsense, folly
vacilación *f* vacillation; unsteadiness; flickering; hesitation
vacilada *f* (Am.) spree, high time; (Am.) drunk
vacilante *adj* vacillating; unsteady; flickering; hesitant
vacilar *vn* to vacillate, to waver; to shake, be unsteady; to flicker; to hesitate; (Am.) to get drunk; **vacilar en** + *inf* to hesitate to + *inf*
vacío -a *adj* empty; hollow; idle; vain, useless, unsuccessful; lacking; proud, presumptuous; barren (*said of cattle*); *m* emptiness; vacancy; side, flank; hollow; lack; void; (phys.) vacuum; **de vacío** idle, light, unloaded; unsucessfully; **en el vacío** in vacuo; **en vacío** unsteadily; in vain; at nothing, in the air; **hacer el vacío a** to isolate, to keep people away from
vaco -ca *adj* vacant; *m* (coll.) ox
vacuidad *f* emptiness; vacuity
vacuna *f* see **vacuno**
vacunación *f* vaccination
vacunar *va* to vaccinate
vacuno -na *adj* bovine; cowhide, made of cowhide; *f* cowpox; vaccine
vacunoterapia *f* vaccine therapy
vacuo -cua *adj* empty; vacant; stupid, emptyheaded; *m* hollow; vacuum
vacuola *f* (biol.) vacuole
vadeable *adj* fordable; superable
vadeador *m* guide in fording streams
vadeamiento *m* fording
vadear *va* to ford; to overcome; to sound out; *vr* to behave, conduct oneself
vademécum *m* vade mecum; manual; school companion, school portfolio
vadeo *m* var. of **vadeamiento**
vadera *f* wide ford; (prov.) channel made by a freshet or flood
vado *m* ford; resource, expedient; **al vado o a la puente** (coll.) one way or another; **no hallar vado** to have no solution, to see no way out; **tentar el vado** to look into the matter, to feel one's way
vadoso -sa *adj* fordy, shallow, shoaly
vagabundaje *m* vagabondage; vagrancy
vagabundear *vn* to wander, to roam; to idle, to loaf around
vagabundeo *m* vagabondage
vagabundo -da *adj* vagabond; *mf* vagabond, tramp
vagamundear *vn* var. of **vagabundear**
vagamundo -da *adj & mf* var. of **vagabundo**
vagancia *f* vagrancy; idleness
vagante *adj* vagrant; (Am.) untilled
vagar *m* leisure, idleness; slowness; **andar de vagar** to be at leisure, to be idle; **con vagar** slowly; **§59** *vn* to wander, to roam; to lose one's way; to idle, be idle, be at leisure; to lie around (*said of a thing*); to play (*said of a smile on the face of a person*)
vagaroso -sa *adj* errant, wandering; flitting
vagido *m* (med.) vagitus
vagina *f* (bot. & anat.) vagina
vaginado -da *adj* vaginate
vaginal *adj* vaginal
vaginitis *f* (path.) vaginitis
vagínula *f* (bot. & zool.) vaginula
vagneriano -na *adj & mf* Wagnerian
vago -ga *adj* wandering, roaming; vagabond, idle; lazy; lax, loose; hesitating, wavering; vague; blank (*stare*); (paint.) vaporous, indistinct; *m* vagabond; **en vago** unsteadily; in vain; at nothing, in the air; **poner en vago** to tilt (*e.g., a chair*)
vagón *m* railroad car; moving van on flat car; **vagón cama** sleeping car; **vagón cerrado** boxcar; **vagón cisterna** tank car; **vagón cuadra** cattle van; cattle car; **vagón de carga** freight car; **vagón de cola** caboose; **vagón de mercancías** freight car; **vagón de plataforma** flatcar; **vagón de volteo** dump car; **vagón frigorífico** refrigerator car; **vagón grúa** derrick car; **vagón plano** or **raso** flatcar; **vagón salón** chair car; **vagón tanque** (rail.) tank car; **vagón tolva** hopperbottom car; **vagón volquete** dump car
vagonada *f* carload
vagoneta *f* small car; small dump car, tip car; (Am.) delivery truck
vagra *f* (zool.) tapir; (naut.) ribband
vaguada *f* waterway, thalweg
vagueación *f* vagary, flight of fancy
vaguear *vn* to wander, to roam; to be idle, to loaf
vaguedad *f* vagueness; vague remark
vaguemaestre *m* (mil.) wagon master
vaguido -da *adj* dizzy, giddy; *m* dizziness, fainting spell
vagus *m* (anat.) vagus
vahaje *m* gentle breeze
vahar *vn* to emit fumes or vapor; to breathe forth
vaharada *f* exhalation, breathing
vaharera *f* (path.) thrush; (prov.) green melon
vahariento -ta *adj* vaporous
vaharina *f* (coll.) fume, vapor
vahear *vn* to emit fumes or vapor; to breathe forth
vahído *m* dizziness, fainting spell
vaho *m* vapor, fume, steam; breath

vaina *f* sheath, scabbard; knife case; (bot.) pod, shell, husk; (naut.) boltrope tabling, tabling (*e.g., of a flag*); (Am.) casing (*to draw string through*); (Am.) annoyance, nuisance; (Am.) luck, stroke of luck; (Am. slang) intercourse, fornication; **de vaina abierta** quick and ready; **salirse de la vaina** (Am. coll.) to get violent, to lose one's head; **vaina de haba** (Am.) trifle; *mf* (Am.) bore, wretch
vainazas *m* (*pl:* **-zas**) (coll.) sloppy fellow
vainero *m* scabbard-maker
vainica *f* small sheath or scabbard; hemstitch
vainilla *f* small pod; hemstitch; (bot.) vanilla (*plant, bean, and extract*)
vainillar *va* (Am.) to hemstitch
vainillina *f* (chem.) vanillin
vainita *f* (Am.) string bean
vais *2d pl pres ind of* **ir**
vaivén *m* swing, seesaw, backward and forward motion, coming and going, wavering; risk, chance; unsteadiness, inconstancy; (naut.) three-stranded rope or cable
vajilla *f* table service; set of dishes; dishes; **lavar la vajilla** to wash the dishes; **vajilla de oro** gold plate; **vajilla de plata** silverware, silver plate; **vajilla de porcelana** chinaware
val *m* apocopated form of **valle;** *2d sg impv of* **valer**
valaco -ca *adj & mf* Walachian; *m* Walachian (*language*); *f* (Am.) wide hair band
Valaquia *f* Walachia
valar *adj* (pertaining to a) fence, hedge, or stockade
valdense *adj & mf* Waldensian; **valdenses** *mpl* Waldenses
valdepeñero -ra *adj* (pertaining to) Valdepeñas; *mf* native or inhabitant of Valdepeñas
valdgrave *m* waldgrave
valdré *1st sg fut ind of* **valer**
vale *m* bond, promissory note; receipt, voucher; advance note of pardon (*in school*); farewell; (Am.) pal, chum
valedero -ra *adj* valid, binding
valedor -dora *mf* protector, defender; (Am.) friend, companion
valedura *f* (Am.) favor, protection
valencia *f* (chem.) valence, valency
valenciano -na *adj & mf* Valencian; *m* Valencian (*dialect*); f (Am.) cuff (*of trousers*)
valentía *f* valor, bravery; feat, heroic exploit; brag, boast; dash, boldness; bold stroke; **pisar de valentía** to strut
Valentín, San Saint Valentine
valentino -na *adj* Valencian
valentísimo -ma *adj super* very or most valiant; very or most excellent; extremely skilled or finished
valentón -tona *adj* arrogant, boastful; *mf* braggart, boaster; *f* bragging, boasting
valentonada *f* bragging, boasting
valer *m* worth, merit, value ‖ §89 *va* to defend, protect; to favor, patronize; to avail; to bring about, to cause; to amount to; to be worth, be valued at; to be equal to, be equivalent to; to produce, to yield; **no valer un diablo** (coll.) to be not worth a darn; **valer lo que pesa** or **valer tanto como pesa** (coll.) to be worth its (his, her, etc.) weight in gold; **valga lo que valiere** come what may; **¡válgame Dios!** so help me God!, bless my soul ‖ *vn* to have worth; to be worthy; to have force, power, authority; to be valuable; to be valid; to prevail; to hold, to count; to serve as defense; to have influence, to be in favor; **hacer valer** to make felt; to assert (*e.g., one's rights*); to make good (*e.g., a claim*); to turn to account; **más vale** it is better (to); **más vale tarde que nunca** better late than never; **valerle a uno** + *inf* to help someone to + *inf*, to get someone to + *inf*, e.g., **eso le valió ser encarcelado** that got him to be jailed, that got him jailed; **valer para** to be useful for; **valer por** to be equal to, be as good as; **vale tanto como decir** it is as much as to say ‖ *vr* to help oneself, to defend oneself; **no poder valerse** to be helpless; **valerse de** to make use of, to avail oneself of, to take advantage of; **valerse por sí mismo** to help oneself
valeriana *f* (bot.) valerian, setwall; (pharm.) valerian; **valeriana griega** (bot.) Greek valerian
valerosidad *f* bravery, valor; skill
valeroso -sa *adj* brave, valorous; active, effective
valet *m* (*pl:* **-lets**) jack (*in cards*)
valetudinario -ria *adj & mf* valetudinarian
valgo *1st sg pres ind of* **valer**
Valhala, el or **Valhalla, el** (myth.) Valhalla
valí *m* (*pl:* **-líes**) wali
valía *f* value, worth; favor, influence; faction, party; **a las valías** at the highest price; **mayor valía** or **plus valía** increased value, appreciation; unearned increment
validación *f* validation
validar *va* to validate
validez *f* validity; strength, vigor
valido -da *adj* valued, esteemed; influential; *m* prime minister; court favorite
válido -da *adj* valid; strong, robust
valiente *adj* valiant; fine, excellent; terrific; *m* brave fellow; bully
valija *f* valise; mailbag, mailpouch; **valija diplomática** diplomatic pouch
valijero *m* mailbag deliverer
valimiento *m* favor, protection; favoritism, favor at court
valioso -sa *adj* valuable; wealthy; influential
valisoletano -na *adj & mf* var. of **vallisoletano**
valón -lona *adj & mf* Walloon; *m* Walloon (*dialect*); **valones** *mpl* bloomers; *f* Vandyke collar
valor *m* value, worth; meaning, import; efficacy; equivalence; stability, steadiness; resignation; valor, courage; audacity, impudence; (mus.) value; (fig.) asset (*person, thing, or quality worth having*); **valores** *mpl* securities; **valor alimenticio** food value; **valor de rescate** (ins.) surrender value; **valor facial** face value; **valor nominal** (com.) par value, face value
valoración *f* valuation, appraisal
valorar or **valorear** *va* to value, to appraise; to enhance the value of
valorización *f* valorization
valorizar §76 *va* to valorize
valpurgita *f* (mineral.) walpurgite
valquiria *f* (myth.) Valkyrie
vals *m* (*pl:* **valses**) waltz
valsar *vn* to waltz
valuable *adj* ratable, appraisable
valuación *f* valuation, appraisal
valuar §33 *va* to appraise, estimate
valuta *f* (econ.) valuta
valva *f* (biol.) valve
valviforme *adj* valviform, valve-shaped
válvula *f* (anat., mach. & rad.) valve; **sin válvulas** valveless; **válvula corrediza** slide valve; **válvula de admisión** intake valve; **válvula de aguja** needle valve; **válvula de bola** ball valve; **válvula de émbolo** piston valve; **válvula de escape** exhaust valve; **válvula de escape libre** cutout; **válvula de fuerza** (rad.) power tube; **válvula de mariposa** butterfly valve; **válvula de seguridad** safety valve; **válvula en la culata** valve in the head, overhead valve; **válvula mitral** (anat.) mitral valve; **válvula tricúspide** (anat.) tricuspid valve
valvulado -da *adj* valvate
valvular *adj* valvular
valla *f* fence, barricade; obstacle, hindrance; (sport) hurdle; (Am.) cockpit; **valla paranieves** snow fence
valladar *m* fence, barricade; obstacle, hindrance
valladear *va* to fence, to hedge, to fence in
vallado *m* fence, barricade
vallar *adj* (pertaining to a) fence, hedge, or stockade; *va* to fence, to hedge, to fence in
valle *m* valley, vale; river basin; valley dwellings, valley villages; **valle de lágrimas** vale of tears; **valle de Tempe** (hist.) Vale of Tempe
vallico *m* var. of **ballico**
vallisoletano -na *adj* (pertaining to) Valladolid; *mf* native or inhabitant of Valladolid

vamos *1st pl pres ind & impv of* **ir;** *interj* well!; why!; come now!; let's go!; watch out!; stop!
vampiresa *f* vampire (*woman who preys on men*)
vampiro *m* vampire; (zool.) vampire; (fig.) vampire (*extortionist*)
van *3d pl pres ind of* **ir**
vanadio *m* (chem.) vanadium
vanagloria *f* vainglory
vanagloriar §90 & regular *vr* to boast; **vanagloriarse de** or **por** to boast of; **vanagloriarse de** + *inf* to boast of + *ger*
vanaglorioso -sa *adj* vainglorious
vanamente *adv* vainly
vandálico -ca *adj* Vandal; vandal
vandalismo *m* vandalism
vándalo -la *adj & mf* Vandal; vandal
Vandea, la the Vendée (*district in western France*)
vandeano -na *adj & mf* Vendean
vanear *vn* to talk idly, to talk nonsense
vanguardia *f* (mil. & fig.) van, vanguard; **vanguardias** *fpl* abutment (*of bridge*); **a vanguardia** in the vanguard; **estar a** or **en vanguardia** to be in the lead, to be out in front
vanguardismo *m* avant-garde
vanguardista *adj* avant-garde
vanidad *f* vanity; pomp; nonsense, inanity; **ajar la vanidad de** (coll.) to take down a peg; **hacer vanidad de** to boast of
vanidoso -sa *adj* vain, conceited
vanilocuencia *f* empty talk
vanílocuo -cua *adj* chattering, wordy; *mf* empty talker or speaker
vaniloquio *m* empty talk
vanistorio *m* (coll.) vain affectation; (coll.) affected person
vano -na *adj* vain; **en vano** in vain; *m* bay, opening in a wall
vánova *f* (dial.) bedspread
vapor *m* steam, vapor; mist, exhalation; vertigo, faintness; steamer, steamboat; **vapores** *mpl* gas (*belched*); hysterics; attack of blues; **al vapor** by steam; at great speed; **vapor de agua** water vapor; **vapor de paletas** or **ruedas** paddle-wheel steamboat; **vapor volandero** tramp steamer
vapora *f* (coll.) steam launch
vaporable *adj* vaporable
vaporación *f* evaporation
vaporar *va & vr* to evaporate
vaporear *va* to evaporate; *vn* to exhale vapors; *vr* to evaporate
vaporización *f* vaporization; (med.) vaporization
vaporizador *m* vaporizer; sprayer, atomizer
vaporizar §76 *va & vr* to vaporize; to spray, to atomize
vaporoso -sa *adj* vaporous, steamy; light, diaphanous, gauzy
vapulación *f* or **vapulamiento** *m* whipping, flogging
vapular *va* to whip, to flog
vapuleamiento *m* var. of **vapulación**
vapulear *va* var. of **vapular**
vapuleo or **vápulo** *m* var. of **vapulación**
vaquería *f* drove of cattle; dairy
vaquerizo -za *adj* (pertaining to) cattle; *mf* cattle tender; *f* winter stable for cattle
vaquero -ra *adj* (pertaining to) cattle; *mf* cattle tender; *m* cowboy, cow hand
vaqueta *f* leather
vaquillona *f* (Am.) heifer
vara *f* twig, stick; pole, staff, rod; wand; shaft (*of carriage*); (bot.) scape; (taur.) thrust with goad; measure of length: 2.8 ft.; **entrar en vara** to gather together to feed on acorns (*said of hogs*); **tener vara alta** to have the upper hand; **vara alcándara** shaft (*of carriage*); **vara alta** upper hand, sway, authority; **vara buscadora** divining rod (*used professedly to discover water or minerals under ground*); **vara de adivinar** divining rod; **vara de Jesé** (bot.) tuberose; **vara de oro** (bot.) goldenrod; **vara de pescar** fishing rod; **vara de San José** (bot.) goldenrod; **vara mágica** divining rod
vara-alta *m* (coll.) boss
varada *f* beaching (*of a boat*); running aground; (prov.) farm workers; farming season; three-month mine work; quarterly mine earnings
varadera *f* (naut.) skid, skeed
varadero *m* shipyard, repair dock
varadura *f* grounding, running aground
varal *m* perch, long pole; horizontal pole with holes in which to fasten the upright side sticks of a cart; (coll.) tall ungainly person
varano *m* (zool.) monitor
varapalo *m* long pole; blow with stick or rod; (coll.) reverse, setback, disappointment
varar *va* to beach (*a boat*); *vn* to run aground; to come to a standstill (*said of business*)
varaseto *m* treillage, espalier
varazo *m* blow with a stick or pole
varbasco *m* (bot.) great mullein
vardasca *f* green twig
vareaje *m* beating down fruit; measuring or sale by the vara
varear *va* to beat, to strike; to knock (*fruit from a tree*); (taur.) to goad; to measure with a vara; to sell by the vara; *vn* to weaken, to get weak
varec *m* (bot.) wrack
varejón *m* long heavy stick
varenga *f* (naut.) floor timber; (naut.) headrail
vareo *m* beating fruit from trees
vareta *f* small twig or stick; lime twig for catching birds; colored stripe; cutting remark; (coll.) hint; **irse de vareta** (coll.) to have diarrhea
varetazo *m* stroke with a stick; side thrust with the horn (*by bull*)
varetear *va* to make stripes in
varetón *m* young stag having antlers without tines
varga *f* steep part of a slope
varganal *m* stake fence, stockade
várgano *m* stake (*of fence*)
vargueño *m* var. of **bargueño**
variabilidad *f* variability
variable *adj* variable; *f* (math.) variable
variación *f* variation
variado -da *adj* varied; variegated
variamente *adv* variously, diversely, differently
variante *adj & f* variant
variar §90 *va* to vary, to change; *vn* to vary, to change, be different; **variar de** or **en opinión** to change one's mind
varice *f* or **várice** *f* (path.) varix; **varices** *fpl* (path.) varicose veins
varicela *f* (path.) varicella, chicken pox
varicocele *m* (path.) varicocele
varicosidad *f* varicosity (*state of being varicose; varix*)
varicosis *f* (path.) varicosis
varicoso -sa *adj* varicose
variedad *f* variety; **variedades** *fpl* variety, vaudeville; miscellanies
varilarguero *m* (taur.) picador
varilla *f* rod, stem, twig; wand; rib (*of umbrella, fan, etc.*); wire spoke; stay (*of corset*); (coll.) jawbone; (Am.) peddler's wares; **varillas** *fpl* frame of sieve or strainer; **varilla de virtudes, varilla mágica** magician's wand, conjurer's wand; **varilla empujadora** tappet rod; **varilla exploradora** divining rod; **varilla levantaválvula** tappet rod
varillaje *m* ribbing, ribs; type bars, basket of type bars (*of a typewriter*); (mech.) linkage
varillero -ra *mf* (Am.) peddler
vario -ria *adj* various, varied; inconstant; undecided; variegated; **varios -rias** *adj pl* various, several; **varios** *mpl* miscellanea, literary miscellany
varioacoplador *m* (rad.) variocoupler
varioloide *f* (path.) varioloid
varioloso -sa *adj* variolous; pock-marked; *mf* pock-marked person
variómetro *m* (elec., meteor. & rad.) variometer
variórum *adj & m invar* variorum
variz *f* (*pl:* **-rices**) var. of **varice**
varón *m* man, male; adult male; man of standing, man of parts; (naut.) rudder pendant; **santo varón** plain artless fellow; **Varón de Dolores** Man of Sorrows (*Jesus*); *adj* male, e.g., **hijo varón** male child

varona *f* woman, female; mannish woman
varonía *f* male issue, male descent
varonil *adj* manly, virile; courageous, vigorous
varraco *m* var. of **verraco**
varraquear *vn* var. of **verraquear**
varraquera *f* var. of **verraquera**
Varsovia *f* Warsaw
varsoviano -na *adj* (pertaining to) Warsaw; *mf* native or inhabitant of Warsaw; *f* varsoviana, varsovienne (*music and dance*)
vas *2d sg pres ind of* **ir**
vasallaje *m* vassalage; liege money
vasallo -lla *adj & mf* vassal
vasar *m* kitchen shelf, kitchen shelving
vasco -ca *adj & mf* Basque (*of Spain and France*); *m* Basque (*language*)
vascón -cona *adj & mf* Basque (*ancient*)
vascongado -da *adj & mf* Basque (*of Spain*); *m* Basque (*language*); **las Vascongadas** the Basque Provinces
vascónico -ca *adj* Basque (*ancient*)
vascuence *adj & m* Basque (*language*); *m* (coll.) gibberish
vascular *adj* (bot. & zool.) vascular
vasculoso -sa *adj* vasculous, vasculose
vasectomía *f* (surg.) vasectomy
vaselina *f* vaseline
vaselinoso -sa *adj* (coll.) full of schmaltz
vasera *f* kitchen shelf; glass rack, glass basket; case for carrying a glass or tumbler
vasija *f* vessel, receptacle, container; dish; wine casks and jars in wine cellar
vasillo *m* cell (*of honeycomb*); (bot.) navelwort, pennywort
vaso *m* glass, tumbler; glassful; receptacle; vase, flower jar; high urinal; horse's hoof; capacity; (naut.) vessel; (anat.) vas, vessel, duct; (bot.) vessel; (arch.) vase; **vaso de engrase** (mach.) grease cup; **vaso de noche** pot, chamber pot; **vaso de papel** paper cup; **vaso excretorio** chamber pot; **vaso lacrimatorio** lachrymal vase; **vaso sanguíneo** (anat.) blood vessel
vasoligadura *f* (surg.) vasoligation
vasomotor -tora *adj* (physiol.) vasomotor
vástago *m* twig, sapling, shoot; scion, offspring; rod, stem; **vástago de émbolo** piston rod; **vástago de válvula** valve stem
vastedad *f* vastness
vasto -ta *adj* vast
vate *m* poet, bard, seer
váter *m* (coll.) toilet, water closet
vatiaje *m* (elec.) wattage
vaticano -na *adj* (pertaining to the) Vatican; (*cap.*) *m* Vatican
vaticinador -dora *adj* prophesying, predicting; *mf* prophet, predicter
vaticinante *adj* prophesying, predicting
vaticinar *va* to prophesy, to predict, to vaticinate
vaticinio *m* prophecy, prediction
vatídico -ca *adj* prophetical; prophesying; *mf* prophet
vatihorímetro *m* (elec.) watt-hour meter
vatímetro *m* (elec.) wattmeter
vatio *m* (elec.) watt
vatio-hora *m* (*pl:* **vatios-hora**) (elec.) watt-hour
vaya *f* scoff, jest, jeer; *1st sg pres subj of* **ir**
Vd. abr. of **usted**
Vds. abr. of **ustedes**
V.E. abr. of **Vuestra Excelencia**
ve *3d sg pres ind & 2d sg impv of* **ver**
vé *2d sg impv of* **ir**
vecera *f* see **vecero**
vecería *f* drove (*especially of hogs*)
vecero -ra *adj* alternating; yielding in alternate years; *mf* person who takes turns; customer; person who waits his turn; *f* drove (*especially of hogs*)
vecinal *adj* (pertaining to the) neighborhood, local, vicinal
vecinamente *adv* nearby, near at hand
vecindad *f* neighborhood, vicinage, vicinity; **hacer mala vecindad** to be a bad neighbor
vecindario *m* neighborhood, community; population
vecino -na *adj* neighboring, near; similar, like; *mf* neighbor; resident, native, citizen
vectación *f* riding (*in vehicle*)
vector *m* (biol. & math.) vector
vectorial *adj* vector, vectorial
veda *f* prohibition; hindrance; closed season; (*cap.*) *m* Veda
vedado *m* game park, game preserve
vedamiento *m* prohibition; hindrance
vedar *va* to forbid, prohibit; to stop, hinder; to veto; **vedar** + *inf* to forbid to + *inf*
vedegambre *m* (bot.) hellebore
vedeja *f* long lock of hair; lion's mane
védico -ca *adj* Vedaic; *m* Vedaic (*language*)
vedija *f* tuft of wool; mat of hair; matted hair; (anat.) pubes
vedijoso -sa or **vedijudo -da** *adj* having tangled hair; tangly
vedismo *m* Vedism
veedor -dora *adj* curious, prying, spying; *mf* prier, spy, busybody; *m* supervisor, overseer; **veedor del tesoro** controller
veeduría *f* inspectorship; inspector's office
vega *f* fertile plain; (Am.) tobacco plantation; (*cap.*) *f* (astr.) Vega
vegetación *f* vegetation; **vegetaciones adenoideas** adenoids
vegetal *adj* vegetal; *m* vegetable (*plant*)
vegetalismo *m* var. of **vegetarianismo**
vegetalista *adj* var. of **vegetariano**
vegetar *vn* to vegetate; to grow; (fig.) to vegetate
vegetarianismo *m* vegetarianism
vegetariano -na *adj & mf* vegetarian
vegetativo -va *adj* vegetative
vegoso -sa *adj* (Am.) damp, wet (*ground*)
veguero -ra *adj* country; *m* farmer; (Am.) tobacco planter
vehemencia *f* vehemence
vehemente *adj* vehement
vehicular *adj* vehicular
vehículo *m* vehicle; **vehículo espacial** space vehicle; **vehículo motor** motor vehicle
veía *1st sg imperf ind of* **ver**
veintavo -va *adj & m* twentieth
veinte *adj* twenty; **a las veinte** (coll.) inopportunely, very late; **las veinte** eight P.M.; *m* twenty; twentieth (*in dates*)
veintena *f* see **veinteno**
veintenario -ria *adj* twenty-year-old
veinteno -na *adj* twentieth; *f* score, twenty
veintenero *m* (eccl.) succentor
veinteñal *adj* twenty-year
veinticinco *adj* twenty-five; *m* twenty-five; twenty-fifth (*in dates*)
veinticuatreno -na *adj* twenty-fourth
veinticuatría *f* (archaic) prefecture
veinticuatro *adj* twenty-four; **las veinticuatro** twelve midnight; *m* twenty-four; twenty-fourth (*in dates*); (archaic) prefect
veintidós *adj* twenty-two; **las veintidós** ten P.M.; *m* twenty-two; twenty-second (*in dates*)
veintidoseno -na *adj* twenty-second
veintinueve *adj* twenty-nine; *m* twenty-nine; twenty-ninth (*in dates*)
veintiocheno -na *adj* twenty-eighth
veintiocho *adj* twenty-eight; *m* twenty-eight; twenty-eighth (*in dates*)
veintiséis *adj* twenty-six; *m* twenty-six; twenty-sixth (*in dates*)
veintiseiseno -na *adj* twenty-sixth
veintisiete *adj* twenty-seven; *m* twenty-seven; twenty-seventh (*in dates*)
veintitrés *adj* twenty-three; **las veintitrés** eleven P.M.; *m* twenty-three; twenty-third (*in dates*)
veintiún *adj* apocopated form of **veintiuno,** used only before masculine nouns and adjectives
veintiuno -na *adj* twenty-one; **las veintiuna** nine P.M.; *m* twenty-one; twenty-first (*in dates*); *f* twenty-one (*card game*)
vejación *f* vexation, annoyance
vejamen *m* vexation, annoyance; sharp criticism
vejar *va* to vex, annoy; to criticize
vejatorio -ria *adj* vexatious, annoying
vejestorio *m* (coll.) old dodo; (archaic) piece of junk
vejeta *f* (orn.) crested lark
vejete *m* (coll.) little old fellow, silly old fellow
vejez *f* oldness; old age; peevishness of old age; platitude, old story; **a la vejez, viruelas** there's no fool like an old fool

vejiga *f* bladder; blister; pock mark; **vejiga de la bilis** (anat.) gall bladder; **vejiga de perro** (bot.) winter cherry; **vejiga natatoria** air bladder, swimming bladder (*of fish*)
vejigatorio -ria *adj* blistering; *m* blister plaster
vejigazo *m* blow with a bladder full of air
vejigoso -sa *adj* full of blisters
vejiguilla *f* small bladder; pustule; (bot.) winter cherry
vela *f* wakefulness; evening (*devoted to some pursuit*); work (*in the evening*); candle; pilgrimage; (eccl.) vigil (*before Eucharist*); sail; sailboat; awning; **a toda vela** full sail; **a vela** under sail; **a vela llena** under full sail; **dar vela** or **darse a la vela** to set sail; **en vela** awake; **estar entre dos velas** to have a sheet in the wind, to be tipsy; **hacerse a la vela** to set sail; **levantar velas** to hoist sails; to set sail; (coll.) to withdraw, give up; **tender las velas** to take advantage of wind and weather; (fig.) to make the most of an opportunity; **vela al tercio** lugsail; **vela (de) cangreja** fore-and-aft sail; **vela de cruz** square sail; **vela de estay** staysail; **vela de mesana** mizzen (sail); **vela latina** lateen sail; **vela mayor** mainsail; **vela romana** Roman candle
velación *f* watching, vigil, wake; (eccl.) veiling at nuptial mass
velacho *m* (naut.) foretopsail
velado -da *adj* veiled, hidden; (phot.) cloudy; *m* husband; *f* wife; vigil, watch, watching; evening, evening party, soirée
velador -dora *adj* watching; *m* watchman, guard; wooden candlestick; pedestal table; (Am.) night table
veladura *f* (paint.) velatura; (phot.) clouding (*of a film*)
velaje *m* or **velamen** *m* (naut.) canvas, sails
velar *adj & f* (phonet.) velar ‖ *va* to watch, to watch over; to guard; to keep (*guard or watch*); to wake, hold a wake over; to veil; (fig.) to veil, hide, conceal; to veil (*newly married couple*) at nuptial mass; (phot.) to fog ‖ *vn* to stay awake; to work late, to work in the evening or at night; to be solicitous; to stick out of the water (*said of rocks in sea*); to keep up all night (*said of the wind*); (eccl.) to assist by turns before the Holy Sacrament; **velar por** or **sobre** to watch over; **velar por que** to see to it that ‖ *vr* (phot.) to fog, be light-struck
velarización *f* (phonet.) velarization
velarizar §76 *va* (phonet.) to velarize
velarte *m* broadcloth
velatorio *m* wake (*beside corpse*)
veleidad *f* caprice, whim; inconstancy, fickleness, flightiness
veleidoso -sa *adj* capricious, whimsical; inconstant, fickle, flighty
velejar *vn* (naut.) to sail with sails unfurled, to navigate under sail
velería *f* tallow chandler's store; sail loft
velero -ra *adj* (naut.) swift-sailing; fond of vigils; fond of pilgrimages; *mf* tallow chandler; *m* sailmaker; sailboat, sailer; (aer.) sailplane
veleta *f* vane, weathercock, weather vane; rudder, rudder vane (*of windmill*); bob (*of fishing line*); streamer, pennant; **veleta de manga** (aer.) air sleeve, air sock; *mf* weathercock (*fickle person*)
velete *m* small thin veil
velicación *f* (med.) lancing, opening
velicar §86 *va* (med.) to lance, to open
velicomen *m* cup for drinking toasts
velilla *f* small candle
velillo *m* small veil; gauze embroidered with silver thread
velís *m* (Am.) valise
velmez *m* (*pl:* **-meces**) tunic worn under armor
velo *m* veil; white veil thrown over couple at nuptial mass; taking the veil; humeral veil; (biol.) velum; (phot.) fog; (fig.) veil (*mask, disguise*); (fig.) confusion, perplexity; **correr el velo** to pull aside the curtain, to dispel the mystery; **correr** or **echar el velo sobre** to hush up; **tomar el velo** to take the veil; **velo del paladar** (anat.) velum, soft palate; **velo de monja** nun's veiling
velocidad *f* velocity; speed; **en gran velocidad** (rail.) by express; **en pequeña velocidad** (rail.) by freight; **primera velocidad** (aut.) low gear; **segunda velocidad** (aut.) second; **tercera velocidad** (aut.) high gear; **velocidad con respecto al suelo** (aer.) ground speed; **velocidad de escape** escape velocity (*of a satellite*); **velocidad de régimen** working speed, steady speed; **velocidad de sincronismo** (elec.) synchronous speed; **velocidad sobremultiplicada** (aut.) overdrive
velocímetro *m* speedometer; velocimeter (*to measure speed of projectiles*)
velocípedo *m* velocipede
velódromo *m* velodrome
velógrafo *m* hectograph
velómetro *m* speedometer
velón *m* metal olive-oil lamp
velonera *f* lamp stand, lamp bracket
velonero *m* lamp maker, lamp dealer
velorio *m* party, gathering; wake; taking the veil; (coll.) dull party; (Am.) come-on
velorta *f* var. of **vilorta**
velorto *m* var. of **vilorto**
veloz *adj* (*pl:* **-loces**) swift, rapid; agile, quick
veludillo *m* var. of **velludillo**
veludo *m* plush; velvet
vellera *f* (archaic) depilator (*woman*)
vellido -da *adj* var. of **velloso**
vello *m* down (*on fruit and human body*); velvet (*of antlers of deer*); (anat., bot. & zool.) villus
vellocino *m* fleece; unsheared sheepskin
vellón *m* fleece; unsheared sheepskin; lock of wool; copper and silver alloy; copper coin
vellonero *m* gatherer of fleece
vellora *f* knot on wrong side of cloth
vellorí *m* (*pl:* **-ríes**) broadcloth of undyed wool
vellorín *m* var. of **vellorí**
vellorita *f* (bot.) cowslip; (bot.) English daisy
vellosidad *f* downiness, fuzziness, hairiness
vellosilla *f* (bot.) mouse-ear
velloso -sa *adj* downy, fuzzy, hairy, villous
velludillo *m* velveteen
velludo -da *adj* shaggy, hairy, fuzzy; *m* plush; velvet
vellutero *m* silk worker, plush worker
ven *2d sg impv of* **venir**
vena *f* vein; grain (*in stone*); (fig.) streak; (fig.) poetical inspiration; **coger a uno de vena** to find someone receptive; **darle a uno la vena** (coll.) to be bent on folly; **estar en vena** (coll.) to be all set, to be inspired; (coll.) to be sparkling with wit; **reventarse una vena** to burst a blood vessel; **vena ácigos** (anat.) azygous vein; **vena basílica** (anat.) basilic vein; **vena de agua** underground water passage; **vena de loco** fickle disposition; **vena porta** (anat.) portal vein; **vena yugular** (anat.) jugular vein
venable *adj* salable
venablo *m* javelin, dart; **echar venablos** to burst forth in angry words
venación *f* venation (*arrangement of veins*); (archaic) venation, venery (*hunting*)
venadero *m* place frequented by deer
venado *m* deer, stag
venaje *m* fountainheads (*of a river*)
venal *adj* salable; venal, mercenary; venous
venalidad *f* venality
venático -ca *adj* (coll.) fickle, unsteady, inconstant
venatorio -ria *adj* (pertaining to) hunting, venatic
venatriz, la (myth.) the huntress Diana
vencedero -ra *adj* falling due, maturing
vencedor -dora *adj* conquering; *mf* conqueror, victor
vencejo *m* band, string; (orn.) black martin, European swift
vencer §91 *va* to conquer, vanquish; to surpass, outdo, excel; to surmount, overcome; *vn* to conquer, win out; to twist, bend, turn; (com.) to mature, fall due; to expire; to be up (*said of a period of time*); *vr* to control oneself; (Am.) to wear out, to become worthless
vencetósigo *m* (bot.) swallowwort, tame poison
vencible *adj* conquerable, superable, vincible

vencido -da *adj* conquered, overcome; (com.) mature, due, payable; **estar** or **ir de vencida** to be all in; to be all up; to be finished; to be past or over
vencimiento *m* victory; defeat, vanquishment (*state of being conquered*); (com.) maturity, expiration
venda *f* see **vendo**
vendaje *m* bandage, dressing
vendar *va* to bandage; to blindfold; to blind, to hoodwink
vendaval *m* southeasterly wind from the sea; strong wind
vendedera *f* saleslady, saleswoman
vendedor -dora *adj* selling, vending; *m* salesman; *f* saleslady, saleswoman, salesgirl
vendehumos *mf* (*pl:* **-mos**) (coll.) influence peddler, person who trades on his real or supposed influence
vendeja *f* public sale
vender *va* to sell; to sell out, to betray, to give away; **vender de beber** to sell drinks; **vender de comer** to sell food, to serve meals; *vn* to sell; **¡vendo, vendo, vendí!** going, going, gone!; *vr* to sell oneself; to expose oneself to danger; to sell, be for sale; to give oneself away, to show one's hand; **venderse caro** to be sold dear; to be seldom seen, to be a stranger; to be hard to see; **venderse en** to sell for (*e.g., five dollars*); **venderse por** to pretend to be
vendetta *f* vendetta
vendí *m* (*pl:* **-díes**) certificate of sale
vendible *adj* salable, vendible; marketable
vendimia *f* vintage; (fig.) rich profit
vendimiador -dora *mf* vintager
vendimiar *va* to gather (*grapes*); to reap unjustly, to reap with violence; (coll.) to kill, murder
vendo -da *adj* Wendish; *mf* Wend; *m* Wendish (*language*); selvage; *f* bandage; blindfold; regal fillet
vendré *1st sg fut ind of* **venir**
venduta *f* (Am.) vendue, public sale; (Am.) greengrocery
vendutero -ra *mf* (Am.) auctioneer; (Am.) greengrocer
Venecia *f* Venice (*city*); Venetia (*province or district*)
veneciano -na *adj & mf* Venetian; *m* Venetian (*dialect*)
venencia *f* tube for sampling wines
veneno *m* poison, venom; (fig.) bitterness
venenosidad *f* poisonousness
venenoso -sa *adj* poisonous, venomous
venera *f* scallop shell, cockleshell; pilgrim's scallop shell; knight's badge; spring (*of water*); **empeñar la venera** (coll.) to spare no expense, to go all out
venerabilidad *f* venerability
venerabilísimo -ma *adj super* very or most venerable
venerable *adj* venerable
veneración *f* veneration, worship
venerador -dora *adj* venerating, worshiping; *mf* venerator, worshiper
venerando -da *adj* venerable
venerar *va & vn* to venerate, revere; to worship
venéreo -a *adj* venereal; *m* venereal disease
venero *m* spring (*of water*); source, origin; hour mark (*on sundial*); (min.) lode
véneto -ta *adj & mf* Venetian; *m* sea green
venezolanismo *m* Venezuelanism
venezolano -na *adj & mf* Venezuelan
Venezuela *f* Venezuela
vengable *adj* worthy of revenge, capable of being avenged
vengador -dora *adj* avenging; *mf* revenger, avenger
venganza *f* vengeance, revenge
vengar §59 *va* to avenge; *vr* to take revenge; **vengarse de** to take revenge for; **vengarse en** to take revenge on, to avenge oneself on
vengativo -va *adj* vengeful, vindictive
vengo *1st sg pres ind of* **venir**
venia *f* pardon, forgiveness; permission, leave; bow (*with head*); (law) court decree allowing minors to manage own estates; (Am.) (military) salute
venial *adj* venial
venialidad *f* veniality
venida *f* see **venido**
venidero -ra *adj* coming, future; **en lo venidero** in the future; **venideros** *mpl* successors, posterity
venido -da *adj* come, arrived; **bien venido** welcome; *f* coming; return; flood, freshet; impetuosity, rashness
venir §92 *vn* to come, to go; **lo por venir** the future; **que viene** coming, next; **venga lo que viniere** come what may; **venir** + *ger* to be + *ger;* **venir a** + *inf* to come to + *inf;* to end by + *ger,* to amount to + *ger;* to happen to + *inf;* **venir a que** + *subj* to come in order that; **venir a ser** to turn out to be; **venir bien** to become, fit, suit; **venir de** + *inf* to come from + *ger,* e.g., **vengo de pagar unas cuentas** I come from paying some bills, I have just been to pay some bills; *vr* to ferment; **venirse abajo** to collapse
venoso -sa *adj* venous
venta *f* sale, selling; salesmanship; roadside inn; place in the open, unsheltered spot; **de venta** or **en venta** on sale, for sale; **hacer venta** (coll.) to invite in to have something to eat; **ser una venta** (coll.) to be a dear place; to be in the open, to be unprotected; **venta al descubierto** or **a plazo** (com.) short sale
ventada *f* blast, gust of wind
ventaja *f* advantage; extra pay; odds (*in a game*); (tennis) advantage; **llevar la ventaja a** to be ahead of; to have the advantage of
ventajista *mf* sharper, crook
ventajoso -sa *adj* advantageous
ventalla *f* (mach.) valve; (bot.) valve (*of capsule or legume*)
ventalle *m* fan; nosepiece (*of helmet*)
ventana *f* window (*opening in a wall; windowpane*); sash; nostril; (anat.) fenestra; **echar la casa por la ventana** (coll.) to go to a lot of expense (*to entertain or in other ways*); **tirar por la ventana** to ruin, spoil; **ventana a bisagra** or **ventana batiente** casement; **ventana de guillotina** sliding window, sash window; **ventana de la nariz** nostril; **ventana oval** (anat.) fenestra ovalis; **ventana redonda** (anat.) fenestra rotunda; **ventana salediza** bay window
ventanaje *m* (arch.) fenestration, windows (*of a building*)
ventanal *m* large window, church window
ventanazo *m* slamming a window, window slamming
ventanear *vn* (coll.) to be always at the window
ventaneo *m* (coll.) fondness for being at the window
ventanero -ra *adj* fond of being at the window; *mf* person fond of being at the window; *m* windowmaker; window gazer (*man who likes to look in windows where there are women*); *f* woman who spends a lot of time hanging out of the window; woman flirting from a window
ventanico *m* var. of **ventanillo**
ventanilla *f* small window, opening; window (*of railway car; of a bank; of an envelope*); wicket; ticket window; nostril
ventanillo *m* small window; peephole
ventanuco or **ventanucho** *m* ugly little window
ventar §18 *va* to sniff (*said of animals*); *vn* to blow (*said of the wind*)
ventarrón *m* strong wind, windstorm, gale
venteadura *f* wind shake, split in timber caused by wind; (found.) blowhole
ventear *va* to sniff, to scent (*said of animals*); to air, to dry in the wind; to snoop into, to pry into; *vn* to blow (*said of the wind*); to snoop, to pry about; *vr* to split; to blister (*said of baking bricks*); to become spoiled in the air; (coll.) to break wind
venteo *m* sniffing, scenting; airing; snooping; venthole (*in a barrel*)
ventero -ra *adj* scenting (*said of animals*); *mf* innkeeper, keeper of a roadside inn
ventilación *f* ventilation; (fig.) airing
ventilador *m* ventilator; fan; (naut.) funnel; **ventilador aspirador** exhaust fan
ventilar *va* to ventilate; (fig.) to ventilate, to air

ventisca *f* blizzard; drift (*of snow*)
ventiscar §86 *vn* to snow and blow; to drift (*said of snow*)
ventisco *m* var. of **ventisca**
ventiscoso -sa *adj* snowy and stormy; full of snow drifts
ventisquear *vn* var. of **ventiscar**
ventisquero *m* blizzard; snowdrift; snow-capped mountain; glacier
ventola *f* (naut.) strong blast of wind, strong noisy blast of wind
ventolera *f* strong blast of wind; pinwheel; (coll.) vanity, boasting; (coll.) caprice, wild idea
ventolina *f* (naut.) light fresh wind, light air
ventor -tora *adj* scenting, hunting by scent; *m* pointer (*dog*)
ventorrero *m* windy spot
ventorrillo *m* wretched little roadhouse; lunch house in the country
ventorro *m* wretched little roadhouse
ventosa *f* see **ventoso**
ventosear *vn* to break wind
ventosidad *f* windiness; wind (*in intestines or being expelled*)
ventoso -sa *adj* windy; full of wind (*said of intestines*); causing wind (*in intestines*); *f* cupping glass; vacuum cup (*of tire*); (zool.) sucker; vent, air hole; **pegar una ventosa a** (coll.) to swindle
ventral *adj* ventral
ventrecha *f* belly (*of fish*)
ventregada *f* brood, litter; sudden abundance
ventrera *f* bellyband (*of man or beast*)
ventricular *adj* ventricular
ventrículo *m* (anat. & zool.) ventricle
ventril *m* counterpoise (*in olive-oil mill*)
ventrílocuo -cua *adj* ventriloquial; *mf* ventriloquist
ventriloquia *f* or **ventriloquismo** *m* ventriloquism
ventrón *m* large belly; tripe
ventroso -sa or **ventrudo -da** *adj* big-bellied
ventura *f* see **venturo**
venturado -da *adj* lucky, fortunate
venturanza *f* happiness
venturero -ra *adj* adventurous, vagabond; fortunate; *mf* adventurer
venturímetro *m* (hyd.) Venturi meter
venturina *f* (mineral.) aventurin or aventurine
venturo -ra *adj* future, coming; *f* happiness; luck, chance; risk, danger; (orn.) bluebird (*Sialia mexicana*); **a la ventura** at a venture, at random; at a risk; **por ventura** perhaps, perchance; **probar ventura** to try one's luck
venturón *m* stroke of luck
venturoso -sa *adj* lucky, fortunate
Venus *f* (myth.) Venus; Venus (*very beautiful woman*); *m* (astr.) Venus; (*l.c.*) *f* venery
venustez *f* or **venustidad** *f* beauty, gracefulness
venusto -ta *adj* beautiful, graceful
venza *f* goldbeater's skin
veo *1st sg pres ind of* **ver**
ver *m* sight; appearance; opinion; **a mi ver** in my opinion; **tener buen ver** to have a good appearance ‖ §93 *va & vn* to see; to look at; (law) to hear, to try; **a más ver** so long; **a ver** let's see; **estar por ver** to remain to be seen; **hasta más ver** good-bye, so long; **no poder ver** to not be able to bear, to despise; **no tener nada que ver con** to have nothing to do with; **ser de ver** to be worth seeing; **ver** + *inf* to see + *inf*, e.g., **ví pasar el tren** I saw the train go by; to see + *ger*, e.g., **ví llegar al médico** I saw the doctor arriving; to see + *pp*, e.g., **ví ahorcar al criminal** I saw the criminal hanged; **ver de** + *inf* to try to + *inf;* **ver venir** to see what (*someone*) is up to; to wait and see; **ver y creer** seeing is believing ‖ *vr* to be seen; to be obvious; to see oneself; to see each other; to find oneself, to be; to meet; **ya se ve** of course, certainly; **verse con** to see, to have a talk with
vera *f* edge, border; **veras** *fpl* truth, reality; earnestness; **a la vera de** near, beside; **de veras** in truth; in earnest; **jugar de veras** to play in earnest, to play for keeps
veracidad *f* veracity
veracruzano -na *adj* (pertaining to) Vera Cruz; *mf* native or inhabitant of Vera Cruz
veranada *f* summer season (for pasturing)
veranadero *m* summer pasture
veranar *vn* to summer
veranda *f* veranda; bay window, closed porch
veraneante *adj* summering, summer-vacationing; *mf* summer vacationist, summer resident
veranear *vn* to summer
veraneo *m* summering; **ir de veraneo** to summer, to go on a summer vacation
veranero *m* summer grazing land
veraniego -ga *adj* (pertaining to) summer; sickly in the summer; slight, unimportant
veranillo *m* Indian summer; **veranillo de San Martín** Indian summer
verano *m* summer; (Am.) dry season
verascopio *m* stereo camera; stereo viewer
veratrina *f* (chem.) veratrine
veratro *m* (bot.) hellebore
veraz *adj* (*pl:* **-races**) veracious
verba *f* loquacity, eloquence
verbal *adj* verbal; verb; (gram.) verbal; *m* (gram.) verbal
verbalismo *m* verbalism (*predominance of words over concepts*)
verbasco *m* (bot.) great mullein
verbena *f* (bot.) verbena, vervain; night festival on eve of a saint's day; evening party; soirée; fair, village or country fair; **coger la verbena** (coll.) to get up and take a walk early in the morning
verbenáceo -a *adj* (bot.) verbenaceous
verbenear *vn* to move about, to swarm; to abound
verberación *f* beating, striking, pounding
verberar *va* to beat, strike; to beat against (*said of wind and water*)
verbigracia verbi gratia, for example
verbo *m* (gram.) verb; (*cap.*) *m* (theol.) Word (*second person of Trinity*); **verbo auxiliar** (gram.) auxiliary verb
verborragia or **verborrea** *f* (coll.) verbosity, wordiness
verbosidad *f* verbosity, wordiness
verboso -sa *adj* verbose, wordy
verdacho *m* green earth, terre-verte
verdad *f* truth; **¿verdad?** isn't that so?; **a decir verdad** to tell the truth, as a matter of fact; **a la verdad** in truth; as a matter of fact; **decir cuatro verdades (a)** to speak one's mind (to); **en verdad** truly, really; **faltar a la verdad** to lie; **¿no es verdad?** isn't that so? Esta pregunta, que se hace muy a menudo en la conversación después de aseveraciones de todo género, se traduce al inglés de variadísimas maneras. Si la aseveración es negativa, la pregunta que equivale a **¿no es verdad?** será afirmativa, p.ej., **Vd. no trabaja. ¿No es verdad?** You are not working. Are you? Si la aseveración es afirmativa, la pregunta será negativa y se podrán usar las contracciones con 'not', p.ej., **Vd. trabaja. ¿No es verdad?** You are working. Are you not? o Aren't you? Si la aseveración contiene auxiliar, la pregunta contendrá dicho auxiliar menos el infinitivo, el participio pasado o el participio activo del verbo, p.ej., **Llegará mañana por la mañana. ¿No es verdad?** He will arrive tomorrow morning. Won't he?; **Se lo ha dicho. ¿No es verdad?** She has told you. Hasn't she? Si la aseveración no contiene auxiliar ni una forma de la cópula 'to be', la pregunta contendrá el auxiliar 'do' o 'did' menos el infinitivo del verbo, p.ej., **Vd. habla inglés. ¿No es verdad?** You speak English. Don't you?; **Fueron a Madrid. ¿No es verdad?** They went to Madrid. Didn't they? Si el sujeto de la aseveración es un nombre sustantivo, irá representado en la pregunta con un pronombre personal, p.ej., **María no bebería café. ¿No es verdad?** Mary would not drink coffee. Would she?; **ser verdad** to be true; **verdad desnuda** plain truth
verdadero -ra *adj* true; truthful; real
verdal *adj* green (although ripe)
verdasca *f* green twig or branch
verde *adj* green; young, blooming, vigorous; callow (*youth*); sharp (*reprimand*); gay, merry

(*e.g., widow, old man*); shady, off-color; smutty (*person*); **están verdes** (coll.) they're hard to reach or get; **poner verde** (coll.) to abuse, to rake over the coals; *m* green; verdure, foliage; **darse un verde** (coll.) to have a fling, to have a little change; **verde de montaña** or **de tierra** mineral green
verdea *f* greenish wine
verdear *va* to pick for sale (*grapes or olives*); *vn* to look green, to turn green
verdeceledón *m* celadon green
verdecer §34 *vn* to turn green, to grow green
verdecillo *m* (orn.) greenfinch; (orn.) serin
verdegal *m* green field
verdegay *adj & m* light green
verdeguear *vn* to grow green
verdejo -ja *adj* green (although ripe)
verdemar *m* sea green
verdemontaña *m* mineral green (*mineral and color*)
verderol *m* (orn.) greenfinch; (zool.) cockle (*Cardium edule*)
verderón -rona *adj* bright-green; *m* (orn.) greenfinch; (zool.) cockle (*Cardium edule*)
verdete *m* verdigris
verdevejiga *m* bladder green, sap green
verdezuelo *m* (orn.) greenfinch
verdín *m* fresh greenness (*of plants*); mold, pond scum; verdigris; green snuff
verdina *f* see **verdino**
verdinal *m* green spot
verdinegro -gra *adj* dark-green
verdino -na *adj* bright-green; *f* fresh greenness (*of plants*)
verdinoso -sa *adj* moldy, scummy; verdigrisy
verdiseco -ca *adj* half-dried
verdolaga *f* (bot.) purslane
verdón *m* (orn.) greenfinch
verdor *m* verdure; youth
verdoso -sa *adj* greenish
verdoyo *m* fresh greenness
verdugada *f* layer of bricks
verdugado *m* hoop skirt
verdugal *m* thicket, cleared and burned and now covered with growth of young shoots
verdugazo *m* lash with a stick
verdugo *m* twig, shoot, sucker; long slender rapier; scourge, lash; welt; executioner; torment; hoop (*of a ring*); layer of bricks; (orn.) shrike, butcher bird
verdugón *m* large twig; large welt, wale
verduguillo *m* wale on leaves; narrow razor; dueling rapier; earring; half-round strip or fillet; (Am.) stiletto
verdulería *f* greengrocery
verdulero -ra *mf* greengrocer; *f* foul-mouthed woman, fishwife
verdura *f* verdure, verdancy, greenness; smuttiness; (f.a.) verdure (*tapestry*); **verduras** *fpl* vegetables, greens
verdusco -ca *adj* dark-greenish
verecundia *f* var. of **vergüenza**
verecundo -da *adj* var. of **vergonzoso**
vereda *f* path; circular notice sent by messenger; route of traveling preachers; (Am.) sidewalk; **meter por** or **en vereda** to set aright
veredero *m* country messenger over a regular route
veredicto *m* verdict
verga *f* (naut.) yard; penis; steel bow (*of a crossbow*); **verga de abanico** (naut.) sprit; **verga de popa** (naut.) spanker boom; **verga mayor** (naut.) main yard; **vergas en alto** (naut.) ready to sail
vergajo *m* pizzle (*used as a whip*); whip
vergel *m* flower and fruit garden
vergeta *f* var. of **vergueta**
vergeteado -da *adj* (her.) paly
vergonzante *adj* bashful, shamefaced (*beggar*)
vergonzoso -sa *adj* bashful, shy; embarrassing; shameful; private (*parts*); *mf* bashful or shy person; *m* (zool.) armadillo (*species that rolls up in a ball when pursued*)
verguear *va* to whip, to flog
vergüenza *f* shame; bashfulness, shyness; embarrassment; dignity; public punishment; **vergüenzas** *fpl* privates, genitals; **¡qué vergüenza!** for shame!; **tener vergüenza** to be ashamed; **tener vergüenza de** + *inf* to be ashamed to + *inf;* **ser una mala vergüenza** (coll.) to be a shame, to be too bad; **vergüenza torera** (taur.) professional honor or dignity
verguer *m* or **verguero** *m* (prov.) high constable
vergueta *f* rod, stem, twig
vergueteado -da *adj* laid (*paper*)
verguío -a *adj* flexible, leathery (*said of wood*)
vericueto *m* rough uneven ground
verídico -ca *adj* truthful
verificable *adj* verifiable
verificación *f* verification; check; realization; inspection (*of water, gas, and electric meters*); (law) probate (*e.g., of a will*)
verificador -dora *adj* verifying; *m* meter inspector
verificar §86 *va* to verify, to check; to carry out; to inspect (*water, gas, and electric meters*); *vr* to be verified, to prove true; to take place
verificativo -va *adj* corroborative
verija *f* (anat.) pubes
veril *m* (naut.) edge of sandbank or shoal
verilear *vn* (naut.) to sail around a sandbank or shoal
verisímil *adj* likely, probable, versimilar
verisimilitud *f* verisimilitude, probability
verismo *m* verism; truthfulness, spirit of truth
verja *f* grating; iron fence
vermes *mpl* intestinal worms
vermicida *adj* vermicidal; *m* vermicide
vermicular *adj* vermicular
vermiforme *adj* vermiform
vermífugo -ga *adj & m* (med.) vermifuge
verminoso -sa *adj* verminous
vermis *m* (*pl:* **-mis**) (anat.) vermis
vermut *m* (*pl:* **-mutes**) vermouth
vernación *f* (bot.) vernation
vernáculo -la *adj* vernacular
vernal *adj* vernal, spring
vernier *m* (*pl:* **-nieres**) vernier
vero *m* vair (*fur*); **veros** *mpl* (her.) vair
veronal *m* veronal
veronense *adj & mf* Veronese
veronés -nesa *adj & mf* Veronese; **el Veronés** Veronese (*painter*)
verónica *f* (bot.) veronica; veronica (*image of face of Christ impressed on handkerchief of St. Veronica*); (taur.) veronica (*maneuver in which the bullfighter waits for the bull's attack with cape extended in both hands*)
veroniquear *vn* (taur.) to perform veronicas
verosímil *adj* var. of **verisímil**
verraco *m* male hog, boar
verraquear *vn* (coll.) to grunt, to grumble; (coll.) to keep on crying hard
verraquera *f* (coll.) violent crying; (Am.) drunkenness
verriondez *f* rut, heat; withered state; toughness
verriondo -da *adj* rutting, in heat; withered; poorly cooked, tough (*said of vegetables*)
verrón *m* var. of **verraco**
verruga *f* wart; (bot.) wart; (fig.) defect; (coll.) nuisance, bore
verrugo *m* (coll.) miser
verrugoso -sa *adj* warty
versado -da *adj* versed; **versado en** versed in, conversant with
versal *adj & f* capital (*letter*)
versalilla or **versalita** *adj fem & f* small capital (*letter*)
Versalles *f* Versailles
versar *vn* to turn, to go around; to deal; **versar acerca de** or **sobre** to deal with, to treat of; *vr* to become versed
versátil *adj* versatile (*fickle*); (bot. & zool.) versatile
versatilidad *f* versatility (*fickleness*)
versear *vn* (coll.) to versify
versería *f* verses, poems
versicolor *adj* many-colored, variegated
versícula *f* stand for choir books
versiculario *m* chanter of versicles; keeper of choir books
versículo *m* (eccl.) versicle; verse (*in Bible*)
versificación *f* versification
versificador -dora *adj* versifying; *mf* versifier, versemaker

versificar §86 *va & vn* to versify
versión *f* version; translation; (obstet.) version; **versión de los Setenta** (Bib.) Septuagint
versista *mf* versifier; poetaster
verso *m* verse; (print.) verso; **verso alejandrino** Alexandrine; **verso blanco** blank verse; **verso esdrújulo** verse whose last word is accented on antepenult; **verso libre** blank verse; **verso llano** verse whose last word is accented on penult; **versos pareados** couplet, rhymed couplet; **verso suelto** blank verse
versta *f* verst (*Russian measure: 3500 feet*)
vértebra *f* (anat. & zool.) vertebra
vertebración *f* vertebration
vertebrado -da *adj & m* vertebrate
vertebral *adj* vertebral
vertedera *f* moldboard (*of plow*)
vertedero *m* dumping ground, dumping place; weir, spillway
vertedor -dora *adj* emptying, dumping; *m* drain; weir, spillway; pan (*for articles weighed*); (naut.) boat scoop
vertello *m* (naut.) ball (*of parrel*)
verter §66 *va* to pour, to empty; to shed; to dump; to translate; *vn* to flow; *vr* to run, to empty
vertibilidad *f* changeableness
vertible *adj* changeable
vertical *adj* vertical; *m* (astr.) vertical circle; **primer vertical** (astr.) prime vertical; *f* vertical (*line*)
vértice *m* (math. & anat.) vertex
verticilado -da *adj* (bot. & zool.) verticillate
verticilo *m* (bot.) verticil, whorl
vertiente *adj* flowing, pouring; *m & f* slope (*e.g., of a continent or a roof*)
vertiginoso -sa *adj* vertiginous, dizzy, giddy
vértigo *m* vertigo, dizziness; fit of insanity; (vet.) vertigo, staggers
vertimiento *m* emptying; shedding; dumping; flowing
vesania *f* insanity
vesánico -ca *adj* insane; *mf* insane person
vesical *adj* vesical
vesicante *adj & m* vesicant
vesícula *f* (anat., bot., path. & zool.) vesicle; **vesícula biliar** (anat.) gall bladder; **vesícula elemental** or **orgánica** (biol.) cell
vesiculado -da *adj* vesiculate
vesicular *adj* vesicular
vesiculoso -sa *adj* vesiculose
veso *m* (zool.) polecat
Vespasiano *m* Vespasian
vesperal *adj* evening; *m* vesperal (*book*)
Véspero *m* Vesper
vespertilio *m* (zool.) vespertilio (*bat*)
vespertino -na *adj* vespertine, evening; *m* evening sermon; *f* evening discourse at the university; evening sermon
Vesta *f* (myth.) Vesta
vestal *adj* vestal; *f* vestal, vestal virgin
veste *f* (poet.) dress, clothing
Vestfalia *f* Westphalia
vestfaliano -na *adj & mf* Westphalian
vestfálico -ca *adj* Westphalian
vestibular *adj* (anat.) vestibular
vestíbulo *m* vestibule; (anat.) vestibule (*of ear*); (theat.) lobby, foyer
vestido *m* clothing; costume, suit; dress; **vestido de etiqueta** evening clothes, evening dress; **vestido de etiqueta de mujer** or **vestido de noche** evening gown; **vestido de serio** evening clothes, evening dress; **vestido de tarde-noche** cocktail dress; **vestido imperio** Empire gown
vestidura *f* clothing; vestment; **vestiduras** *fpl* vestments, canonicals
vestigial *adj* vestigial
vestigio *m* vestige; track, footprint; (biol.) vestige; (chem.) trace
vestiglo *m* horrible monster
vestimenta *f* clothes; vestment
vestir §94 *va* to clothe, to dress; to adorn, to bedeck; to cover; to disguise; to wear; to put on (*clothing*); to roughcast; **morir vestido** to die a violent death; **vestir el cargo** to look the part ‖ *vn* to dress; to be dressy (*said, e.g., of a material*); **vestir de blanco** to dress in white; **vestir de etiqueta** to dress in evening clothes; **vestir de paisano** to dress in civilian clothes ‖ *vr* to dress, to dress oneself; to be covered; to be up (*from a sick bed*); **vestirse de** to be covered with (*e.g., grass, leaves, clouds*); to assume (*e.g., importance*)
vestuario *m* wardrobe, apparel; dressing room, bathhouse; (mil.) uniform; (theat.) dressing room; checkroom, cloakroom
vestugo *m* sprout of an olive tree
vesubiano -na *adj* Vesuvian
Vesubio, el Vesuvius
veta *f* vein (*in the earth; in wood or stone*); stripe; **descubrir la veta de** (coll.) to be on to
vetado -da veined, striped
vetar *va* to veto
veteado -da *adj* veined, striped; *m* graining
vetear *va* to grain, to stripe
veteranía *f* long service, long experience
veterano -na *adj & mf* veteran
veterinario -ria *adj* veterinary; *mf* veterinary, veterinarian; *f* veterinary medicine, veterinary surgery
vetisesgado -da *adj* diagonal-striped
vetiver *m* (bot.) vetiver
veto *m* veto; prohibition
vetustez *f* great age, antiquity
vetusto -ta *adj* very old, ancient
Veyos *f* Veii
vez *f* (*pl:* **veces**) time; turn; drove; **a la vez** at one time, at the same time; **a la vez que** while, **alguna vez** sometimes; ever, e.g., **¿Ha estado Vd. alguna vez en España?** Have you ever been in Spain?; **a su vez** in turn; on his part; **a veces** at times, sometimes; **cada vez** every time; **cada ves más** more and more; **cada vez que** every time that; **cuántas veces** how often; **de una vez** at one time; once and for all; **de vez en cuando** once in a while; **dos veces más grande que** twice as large as; **en vez de** instead of; **esperar vez** to wait one's turn; **hacer las veces de** to serve as, to take the place of; **las más veces** in most cases, most of the time; **muchas veces** often; **otra vez** again; some other time; **pocas veces** seldom; **rara vez** or **raras veces** seldom, rarely; **repetidas veces** repeatedly, over and over again; **tal cual vez** occasionally; **tal vez** perhaps; **tomar la vez a** (coll.) to get ahead of; **una que otra vez** once in a while; **una vez** once; **una vez que** once; inasmuch as
veza *f* (bot.) vetch, spring vetch
vezar §76 *va* to accustom; *vr* to become accustomed
vg. abr. of **verbigracia** & **virgen**
v.g. & **v.gr.** abr. of **verbigracia**
vía *f* road, route, way; (rail.) track; rail (*of track*); gauge (*of track*); (anat.) passage, tract; (fig.) way; **cuaderna vía** stanza of mester de clerecía (*thirteenth and fourteenth centuries*) consisting of four single-rhymed Alexandrines; **estar en vías de** + *inf* to be + *ger*, to be engaged in + *ger;* **por la vía de** via; **por vía aérea** by air; **por vía bucal** by mouth, orally; **por vía de** by way of; **vía acuática** waterway; **vía aérea** airway; **vía ancha** (rail.) broad gauge; **Vía Apia** Appian Way; **vía de agua** waterway; (naut.) leak; **vía de circunvalación** (rail.) belt line; **vía ejecutiva** (law) seizure, attachment; **vía estrecha** (rail.) narrow gauge; **vía férrea** railway; **Vía Flaminia** Flaminian Way; **vía fluvial** waterway; **vía húmeda** (chem.) wet way; **Vía láctea** (astr.) Milky Way; **vía muerta** (rail.) siding; **vía normal** (rail.) standard gauge; **vía pública** thoroughfare; **vías de hecho** (Am.) violence; (Am.) assault and battery; **vías de comunicación** communications; **vías urinarias** (anat.) urinary tract; *prep* via, e.g., **vía Nueva York** via New York
viabilidad *f* viability; feasibility
viable *adj* viable; feasible
viadera *f* harness shaft (*of loom*)
viador *m* (theol.) traveler (*to the other world*)
viaducto *m* viaduct
viajador -dora *mf* traveler
viajante *adj* traveling; *mf* traveler; *m* traveling salesman, drummer

viajar *va* to sell on the road; to cover (*a certain territory*) as salesman; *vn* to travel, to journey
viajata *f* (coll.) journey
viaje *m* trip, journey, voyage; way, road; travel book; load on each trip; water supply; (arch.) obliquity; **¡buen viaje!** bon voyage!; **viaje de ida y vuelta** or **viaje redondo** round trip; **viajes por el espacio** space travel
viajero -ra *adj* traveling; *mf* traveler; passenger
vial *adj* (pertaining to a) road, highway; *m* avenue (*of trees, shrubs, etc.*)
vialidad *f* road service, highway service, communications
vianda *f* viand, food
viandante *mf* traveler, itinerant, stroller; tramp
viaraza *f* diarrhea
viaticar §86 *va* (eccl.) to administer the viaticum to; *vr* (eccl.) to receive the viaticum
viático *m* viaticum, travel allowance; (eccl.) viaticum
víbora *f* (zool.) viper; (fig.) viper; **víbora cornuda** (zool.) horned viper; **víbora de agua** (zool.) moccasin
viborera *f* (bot.) viper's bugloss, blueweed
viborezno -na *adj* viperous; *m* young viper
vibración *f* vibration
vibrador *m* vibrator
vibrante *adj* vibrant; (phonet.) trilled; (fig.) vibrant (*e.g., style*); *f* (phonet.) trilled consonant (*Spanish sound of r*)
vibrar *va* to vibrate; to brandish; to throw, to hurl; to roll (*the voice; the letter r*); *vn* to vibrate
vibrátil *adj* vibratile
vibratorio -ria *adj* vibrative, vibratory
vibrio *m* (bact.) vibrio
vibrión *m* (bact.) vibrion
vibrisas or **vibrizas** *fpl* whiskers (*e.g., of cat*); hair in the nostrils
viburno *m* (bot.) viburnum
vicaria *f* see **vicario**
vicaría *f* vicarage, vicarship
vicarial *adj* vicarial
vicariato *m* vicarage, vicarship
vicario -ria *adj* vicarious; (physiol.) vicarious; *mf* vicar; **vicario general** vicar-general; **vicarios** *mpl* (bot.) grape hyacinth; *f* assistant mother superior
vicealmirantazgo *m* vice-admiralty
vicealmirante *m* vice-admiral
vicecanciller *m* vice-chancellor
viceconsiliario *m* vice-counsellor
vicecónsul *m* vice-consul
viceconsulado *m* vice-consulate
vicecristo *m* vice-Christ
vicediós *m* vice-God
vicegerencia *f* vicegerency
vicegerente *adj* vicegerent; assistant; *m* vicegerent; assistant manager
vicegobernador *m* vice-governor
vicenal *adj* vicennial
vicenio *m* twenty years
vicense *adj* (pertaining to) Vich; *mf* native or inhabitant of Vich
Vicente *m* Vincent; **San Vicente** Saint Vincent (*island*)
vicepresidencia *f* vice-presidency
vicepresidencial *adj* vice-presidential
vicepresidente -ta *mf* vice-president; *f* wife of vice-president
vicerrector *m* vice-rector
vicesecretaría *f* vice-secretaryship
vicesecretario -ria *mf* vice-secretary
vicésimo -ma *adj & m* twentieth
vicetesorero -ra *mf* vice-treasurer
viceversa *adv* vice versa
vicia *f* (bot.) vetch
viciación *f* vitiation
viciado -da *adj* foul, vitiated
viciar *va* to vitiate, falsify, adulterate; to nullify; (law) to vitiate; *vr* to become vitiated, to give oneself up to vice; to become deeply attached; to warp, become warped
vicio *m* vice; viciousness; defect; overgrowth, luxuriance; **de vicio** from being spoiled; without reason, out of habit; **hablar de vicio** (coll.) to be a chatterbox, to jabber away; **quejarse de vicio** (coll.) to be a chronic complainer; **vicio de dicción** grammatical error, solecism
vicioso -sa *adj* vicious; faulty, defective; strong, robust; licentious; luxuriant, abundant; (coll.) spoiled (*said of a child*)
vicisitud *f* vicissitude
víctima *f* victim; **víctima propiciatoria** scapegoat
victimar *va* to sacrifice; (Am.) to kill, assassinate
victo *m* daily bread
víctor *m & interj* var. of **vítor**
victorear *va* var. of **vitorear**
victoria *f* victory; (bot.) victoria; victoria (*carriage*); **victoria pírrica** Pyrrhic victory
victoriano -na *adj & mf* Victorian
victorioso -sa *adj* victorious
vicuña *f* (zool.) vicuña (*animal, wool, and cloth*)
vid *f* (bot.) grapevine
vida *f* life; living, livelihood; life span; **con vida** alive; **darse buena vida** to enjoy life; to live comfortably; **de por vida** for life; **en mi (tu, su) vida** never; **escapar con vida** to have a narrow escape; **ganar** or **ganarse la vida** to earn one's living; **hacer por la vida** (coll.) to get a bite to eat; **hacer vida** to live together (*as man and wife*); **jugarse la vida** to take one's life in one's hands; **mudar de vida** to mend one's ways; **pasar la vida** to live frugally, to just about get along; **¡por vida!** please!; by Jove!; **quitarse la vida** to take one's life; **tener siete vidas como los gatos** to have nine lives; **vida airada** licentious living; **vida ancha** loose living; **vida canonical** or **de canónigo** (coll.) life of ease; **vida de bohemio** Bohemianism; **vida de familia** or **de hogar** home life; **vida de perros** dog's life; **vida media** (phys.) half life; **vida privada** private life
videncia *f* clear-sightedness; clairvoyance
vidente *adj* seeing; *mf* person with sight; *m* prophet, seer; *f* seeress
vídeo *m* video
videofrecuencia *f* television frequency
videograbación *f* video-tape recording
videoseñal *f* picture signal, video signal
vidorra *f* (prov.) life of ease
vidorria *f* (Am.) dog's life
vidriado -da *adj* brittle; glazed; *m* glazing; glazed earthenware; dishes
vidriar §90 & **regular** *va* to glaze; *vr* to become glazed; to become glassy
vidriera *f* glass window, glass door; (Am.) shopwindow, show window; **vidriera de colores** or **vidriera pintada** stained-glass window
vidriería *f* glasswork; glassworks; glass store
vidriero *m* glassworker, glazier
vidrio *m* glass; piece of glass; glass vessel; window pane; something delicate or brittle; touchy person; **en vidrio** in vitro; **ir al vidrio** to ride backwards (*in a coach*); **pagar los vidrios rotos** (coll.) to be the goat, to take the blame; **vidrio cilindrado** plate glass; **vidrio de aumento** magnifying glass; **vidrio de color** stained glass; **vidrio de cuarzo** quartz glass; **vidrio de plomo** flint glass; **vidrio de seguridad** safety glass; **vidrio deslustrado** ground glass; **vidrio hilado** spun glass; **vidrio pintado** stained glass; **vidrio soluble** water glass; **vidrio tallado** cut glass
vidriosidad *f* glassiness; brittleness; slipperiness
vidrioso -sa *adj* glassy, vitreous; brittle; slippery; (fig.) touchy; (fig.) glassy (*look in eyes*)
vidual *adj* (pertaining to a) widow; widow's; (pertaining to a) widower; widower's
vidueño or **viduño** *m* quality or kind of grapevine
viejo -ja *adj* old, ancient, antique; antiquated, old-fashioned; worn-out; *m* old man; **el viejo de la montaña** (hist.) the Old Man of the Mountain; **viejo verde** old goat, old rake; *f* old woman
viejón -jona *adj* (Am.) oldish
Viena *f* Vienna; Vienne (*French city*)
vienense *adj* Viennese; (pertaining to) Vienne (*France*); *mf* Viennese; native or inhabitant of Vienne

vienés -nesa *adj & mf* Viennese
vientecillo *m* breeze, light wind
viento *m* wind (*air in motion; strong current of air; air filled with animal odor; vanity, conceit*); air; direction, course; guy; (arti.) windage (*space between projectile and bore of gun*); (coll.) wind (*gas in stomach or bowels*); **beber los vientos por** (coll.) to turn everything upside down for; **ceñir el viento** (naut.) to sail close to the wind; **contra viento y marea** come hell and high water, against all odds; **ir viento en popa** to go very well, to get along famously; **moverse a todos vientos** to be as fickle as the wind; (coll.) to be easily led by the nose; **viento bonancible** (*naut.*) moderate breeze; **viento de cola** (aer.) tail wind; **viento de la hélice** (aer.) slip stream; **viento duro** (naut.) fresh gale; **viento flojito** (naut.) light breeze; **viento flojo** (naut.) gentle breeze; **viento frescachón** (naut.) moderate gale; **viento fresco** (naut.) strong breeze; **viento fresquito** (naut.) fresh breeze; **viento muy duro** (naut.) strong gale; **vientos alisios** trade winds; **vientos altanos** winds blowing alternately offshore and off the sea; **vientos antialisios** antitrades; **viento terral** land breeze; **viento trasero** (aer.) tail wind
vientre *m* belly; bowels; womb; **evacuar, exonerar** or **mover el vientre** to defecate, to stool; **vientre flojo** loose bowels
vier. abr. of **viernes**
viera *f* pilgrim's scallop shell; (zool.) scallop
viernes *m* (*pl:* **-nes**) Friday; **comer de viernes** to fast, to abstain from meat; **Viernes santo** Good Friday
viero *m* road worker
vierteaguas *m* (*pl:* **-guas**) flashing
vietnamés -mesa, vietnamiano -na, vietnamiense, or **vietnamita** *adj & mf* Viet-Namese
viga *f* beam, girder, joist, rafter; press; pressing of olives; **estar contando las vigas** (coll.) to gaze blankly at the ceiling
vigencia *f* force, operation; use, vogue; **en vigencia** in force, in effect
vigente *adj* effective, in force
vigesimal *adj* vigesimal
vigésimo -ma *adj* twentieth; vigesimal; *m* twentieth
vigía *f* watch; watchtower; (naut.) rock, reef; *m* lookout, watch; **vigía de incendios** fire-warden
vigiar **§90** *va* to watch for, to lie watching
vigilancia *f* vigilance, watchfulness; **bajo vigilancia médica** under the care of a doctor
vigilante *adj* vigilant, watchful; *mf* vigilante; *m* watchman, guard; **vigilante nocturno** night watchman
vigilar *va* to watch over, to look out for; *vn* to watch, keep guard; **vigilar por** or **sobre** to watch over, to care for
vigilativo -va *adj* causing sleeplessness
vigilia *f* vigil; study, night study; eve; wakefulness; (mil.) watch, guard; (eccl.) vigils; **comer de vigilia** to fast, to abstain from meat; **durante la vigilia** while awake
vigitano -na *adj* (pertaining to) Vich; *mf* native or inhabitant of Vich
vigor *m* vigor; **entrar en vigor** to go into effect; **poner en vigor** to put into effect
vigorizador -dora *adj* invigorating; **vigorizador del cabello** hair tonic
vigorizante *adj* invigorating
vigorizar **§76** *va* to invigorate; to encourage; *vr* to be invigorated; to be encouraged
vigorosidad *f* vigorousness
vigoroso -sa *adj* vigorous
vigota *f* (naut.) deadeye
viguería *f* set of beams
vigués -guesa *adj* (pertaining to) Vigo; *mf* native or inhabitant of Vigo
vigueta *f* small beam, small girder
vil *adj* vile, base; dastardly; *mf* dastard
vilano *m* pappus, burr or down of the thistle
vileza *f* vileness; infamy
vilipendiador -dora *adj* scornful; vilifying; *mf* scorner; vilifier
vilipendiar *va* to scorn; to vilify
vilipendio *m* scorn; vilification
vilipendioso -sa *adj* contemptible
vilo; en vilo in the air; (fig.) up in the air (*uncertain*)
vilordo -da *adj* lazy, dull, slothful
vilorta *f* reed hoop; clasp ring of plow; washer; game like lacrosse
vilorto *m* reed hoop; crosse for playing vilorta; (bot.) clematis, liana
viltrotear *vn* (coll.) to walk the streets, to gad about
viltrotera *f* (coll.) gadabout (*woman*)
villa *f* town; villa, country or suburban house; **la Villa** or **la Villa del Manzanares** Madrid
Villadiego town in the province of Burgos, Spain; **coger** or **tomar las de Villadiego** to beat it, to run away
villaje *m* small town, village
villanada *f* despicable act
villanaje *m* peasantry; (hist.) villeinage
villancejo or **villancete** *m* var. of **villancico**
villancico *m* carol, Christmas carol; **villancico de Nochebuena** or **de Navidad** Christmas carol
villanciquero -ra *mf* caroler (*one who carols*)
villanchón -chona *adj* rustic, crude
villanela *f* villanelle
villanería *f* villainy; (hist.) villeinage
villanesco -ca *adj* rustic, crude, boorish
villanía *f* humble birth; villainy; vile remark
villano -na *adj* coarse, impolite; base, villainous; *mf* peasant; evil person, villain; (hist.) villain, villein
villar *m* village, hamlet
villazgo *m* village charter; village tax
villoría *f* hamlet, farm
villorín *m* var. of **vellorí**
villorrio *m* small country town
vimbre *m* (bot.) osier; wicker
vimbrera *f* (bot.) osier
vinagrada *f* vinegar water (*a drink*)
vinagre *m* vinegar; (coll.) grouch; **vinagre de madera** wood vinegar
vinagrero -ra *mf* vinegarer; *f* vinaigrette; (bot.) sorrel; (Am.) heartburn; **vinagreras** *fpl* cruet stand
vinagreta *f* vinegar sauce
vinagrillo *m* weak vinegar; vinegar lotion (*a cosmetic*)
vinagroso -sa *adj* vinegary (*taste or disposition*)
vinajera *f* (eccl.) burette, cruet; **vinajeras** *fpl* (eccl.) cruets and tray
vinariego *m* vineyardist
vinario -ria *adj* (pertaining to) wine
vinatería *f* wine trade; wine shop
vinatero -ra *adj* (pertaining to) wine; *m* wine dealer, vintner
vinaza *f* poor thin wine
vinazo *m* strong heavy wine
vincapervinca *f* (bot.) cut-finger, large periwinkle
Vincenas *f* Vincennes
vinculable *adj* (law) entailable
vinculación *f* (law) entailment; continuation
vincular *va* to tie, bind, unite; (law) to entail; to continue, perpetuate; to found (*e.g., hopes*)
vínculo *m* bond; vinculum; (law) entail
vindicación *f* vindication; (law) vindication
vindicador -dora *adj* vindicating; *mf* vindicator
vindicar **§86** *va* to avenge; to vindicate; (law) to vindicate
vindicativo -va *adj* vindicative; vindictive
vindicta *f* revenge; **vindicta pública** punishment, justice
vine *1st sg pret ind of* **venir**
vínico -ca *adj* vinic
vinícola *adj* (pertaining to) wine; vinegrowing; *m* vinegrower
vinicultor -tora *mf* vinegrower
vinicultura *f* vinegrowing
viniebla *f* (bot.) hound's-tongue
viniendo *ger of* **venir**
vinífero -ra *adj* wine-producing
vinificación *f* vinification
vinilo *m* (chem.) vinyl
vinillo *m* (coll.) weak wine

vino *m* wine; wine party, sherry reception; **bautizar** or **cristianizar el vino** to water wine; **dormir el vino** to sleep off a drunk; **tener mal vino** to be a quarrelsome drunk; **vino cubierto** dark-red wine; **vino de cuerpo** strong-bodied wine; **vino de Jerez** sherry wine; **vino de lágrima** wine from the juice exuded by ripe grapes; **vino del terruño** wine of the locality; **vino de mesa** table wine; **vino de Oporto** port wine; **vino de orujo** thin, second-run wine; **vino de pasto** table wine; **vino de postre** after-dinner wine; **vino de segunda** second-run wine; **vino de solera** old vintage wine; **vino generoso** generous, rich wine; **vino mulso** mulse; **vino seco** dry wine; **vino tinto** red table wine; *3d sg pret ind of* **venir**
vinolencia *f* excessive use of wine
vinolento -ta *adj* too fond of wine
vinosidad *f* vinousness
vinoso -sa *adj* vinous
vinote *m* residue in boiler after distillation of wine
viña *f* vineyard; **ser una viña** (coll.) to be a mine; **tener una viña** (coll.) to have a sinecure
viñadero *m* guard of vineyard
viñador *m* vinedresser, vineyardist; guard of vineyard
viñatero *m* (Am.) vineyardist, winegrower; (Am.) owner of a vineyard
viñedo *m* vineyard
viñero -ra *mf* owner of a vineyard
viñeta *f* vignette
viola *f* (mus. & bot.) viola; **viola de amor** (mus.) viola d'amore; *mf* viola, viola player
violable *adj* violable
violáceo -a *adj* violaceous
violación *f* violation
violado -da *adj & m* violet (*color*)
violador -dora *adj* violating; *mf* violator
violar *m* bed of violets; *va* violate; to tamper with
violencia *f* violence; **no violencia** nonviolence
violentar *va* to do violence to; to break into; *vr* to force oneself
violento -ta *adj* violent
violero *m* (ent.) mosquito
violeta *f* (bot.) violet; (bot.) damewort; **violeta africana** (bot.) African violet; *m* violet (*color; dye*); **violeta de genciana** gentian violet; **violeta de metilo** methyl violet; *adj invar* violet (*color and scent*)
violetera *f* violet vendor, flower girl
violetero *m* small vase
violeto *m* (bot.) clingstone peach
violín *m* violin (*instrument and performer*); bridge, cue rest (*in billiards*); **segundo violín** second violin; **violín de Ingres** avocation, hobby
violinista *mf* violinist
violón *m* (mus.) bass viol (*instrument and performer*); **estar tocando el violón** (coll.) to talk nonsense
violoncelista *mf* violoncellist, cellist
violoncelo *m* (mus.) violoncello, cello
violonchelista *mf* var. of **violoncelista**
violonchelo *m* var. of **violoncelo**
violle *m* violle (*photometric unit*)
viosterol *m* (pharm.) viosterol
vipéreo -a *adj* viperine
viperino -na *adj* viperine; (fig.) viperish; *f* (bot.) viper's bugloss, blueweed; **viperina de Virginia** (bot.) Virginia snakeroot
vira *f* dart; welt (*of shoe*)
virada *f* turn, change of direction; (naut.) tack, tacking
virado *m* (phot.) toning
virador *m* (naut.) viol; (phot.) toning bath
virago *f* mannish woman
viraje *m* turn, change of direction; (phot.) toning; **viraje en horquilla** hairpin bend, hairpin turn
viral *adj* viral
virar *va* (naut.) to wind, twist, heave; (naut.) to veer, to tack; (phot.) to tone; *vn* to turn; (naut.) to veer, to tack
viratón *m* large dart
virazón *f* sea breeze
vireo *m* (orn.) vireo
víreo *m* (orn.) golden oriole
virescencia *f* (bot.) virescence
virescente *adj* virescent
virgen *f* virgin; upright guide in wine or olive press; (*cap.*) *f* (astr.) Virgin; **la Santísima Virgen** the Blessed Virgin; **las islas Vírgenes** the Virgin Islands; **la Virgen María** the Virgin Mary; *adj* virgin
virgiliano -na *adj* Virgilian
Virgilio *m* Virgil
virginal *adj* virginal, maidenly; *m* (mus.) virginal
virgíneo -a *adj* virginal
Virginia *f* Virginia; (*l.c.*) *m* Virginia tobacco
virginiano -na *adj & mf* Virginian
virginidad *f* virginity
virginio *m* (chem.) virginium
virgo *m* virginity; (*cap.*) *m* (astr.) Virgo
vírgula *f* small rod; light dash; comma; (bact.) bacillus (*Vibrio comma*) causing Asiatic cholera
virgulilla *f* fine stroke, light dash; mark, point, sign, accent (*attached to a letter*)
viril *adj* virile; *m* clear glass bell; (eccl.) small monstrance within larger one
virilidad *f* virility
virio *m* (orn.) golden oriole
viripotente *adj* marriageable; strong, vigorous
virol *m* (her.) virole
virola *f* collar, clasp (*e.g., on a knife, sword, etc.*); check ring on a goad; (mach.) ferrule
virolado -da *adj* provided with a clasp; (her.) viroled
virolento -ta *adj* with smallpox; pock-marked; *mf* person with smallpox; pock-marked person
virología *f* virology
virológico -ca *adj* virological
virólogo -ga *mf* virologist
virotazo *m* hit or wound with an arrow
virote *m* iron-pointed arrow; (coll.) young single man about town; (coll.) stuffed shirt
virotillo *m* short upright brace
virotismo *m* arrogance, haughtiness
virreina *f* vice-queen; wife of a viceroy
virreinal *adj* viceregal
virreinato *m* viceroyalty
virrey *m* viceroy, vice-king
virtual *adj* virtual
virtualidad *f* virtuality
virtud *f* virtue; **en virtud de** by or in virtue of; **virtudes cardinales** cardinal virtues
virtuosidad *f* virtuousness; virtuosity
virtuosismo *m* virtuosity
virtuoso -sa *adj* virtuous; *m* virtuoso
viruela *f* (path.) smallpox, variola; (path.) varioloid; pock mark; **viruelas locas** (path.) chicken pox
virulencia *f* virulence
virulento -ta *adj* virulent
virus *m* (*pl:* **-rus**) virus
viruta *f* shaving (*of wood or metal*)
virutilla *f* thin shaving; **virutillas de acero** steel wool
visa *f* visa, visé
visado *m* visa; **visado de tránsito** transit visa
visaje *m* face, grimace, smirk
visajero -ra *adj* grimacing, making faces
visar *va* to visa, to visé; to endorse, to O.K.; (arti. & surv.) to sight
visayo -ya *adj & mf* Bisayan or Visayan
visceral *adj* visceral
vísceras *fpl* viscera
visco *m* (bot.) mistletoe (*Phoradendron*); birdlime; **visco quercino** (bot.) mistletoe (*Viscum album*)
viscosa *f* see **viscoso**
viscosidad *f* viscosity
viscosilla *f* rayon thread
viscoso -sa *adj* viscous; *f* viscose
visera *f* visor (*of helmet, cap, windshield, etc.*); eye-shade; (Am.) blinder, blinker
visibilidad *f* visibility
visible *adj* visible; evident; conspicuous
visigodo -da *adj* Visigothic; *mf* Visigoth
visigótico -ca *adj* Visigothic
visillo *m* window curtain, window shade
visión *f* vision; view; (coll.) scarecrow, sight (*person*); **ver visiones** (coll.) to be seeing things; **visión negra** blackout (*of aviators*)

visionario -ria *adj & mf* visionary
visiotelefonía *f* video telephony
visir *m* vizier, vizir; **gran visir** grand vizier
visita *f* visit; visitor; **hacer una visita** to make a call; **ir de visitas** to go calling; **pagar una visita** to return a call; **tener visita** to have callers; **visita de aspectos** medical inspection of faces of passengers; **visita de cumplido, de cumplimiento** or **de digestión** formal call; **visita de médico** (coll.) short call
visitable *adj* open to visitors
visitación *f* visitation, visit; (*cap.*) *f* Visitation
visitador -dora *adj* visiting; *mf* visitor, frequent visitor; inspector
visitante *adj* visitant; *mf* visitant; visitor; (sport) visitor
visitar *va* to visit; to inspect; *vr* to visit, to call on each other
visiteo *m* frequent exchange of visits, frequent visiting
visitero -ra *adj* (coll.) visiting; (coll.) fond of visits (*said of a doctor*); *mf* (coll.) visitor
visitón *m* (coll.) long tiresome visit
visivo -va *adj* visual
vislumbrar *va* to glimpse; to suspect, surmise; *vr* to glimmer; to loom, appear indistinctly
vislumbre *f* glimpse, glimmer; inkling, surmise; slight resemblance
Visnú *m* Vishnu
viso *m* sheen, gleam, glint; streak, strain; appearance; thin veneer; colored garment under transparent outer garment; eminence, height; **a dos visos** with a double purpose; **de viso** of importance, prominent
visón *m* (zool.) mink
visor *m* (aer.) bombsight; (phot.) finder; (math.) unit vector
visorio -ria *adj* visual; *m* inspection by an expert
víspera *f* eve, day before; forerunner, cause; imminence; **vísperas** *fpl* (eccl.) vespers; **en vísperas de** on the eve of; **víspera de año nuevo** New Year's Eve; **víspera de Navidad** Christmas Eve; **Vísperas sicilianas** (hist.) Sicilian Vespers
vista *f* see **visto**
vistazo *m* look, glance
vistillas *fpl* eminence, high spot; **irse a las vistillas** (coll.) to try to get a look at the cards of one's opponent
visto -ta *adj* evident, obvious; in view of, e.g., **vista la importancia del asunto** in view of the importance of the matter; **bien visto** looked on with approval; **mal visto** looked on with disapproval; **no visto** or **nunca visto** unheard-of, extraordinary; **por lo visto** evidently, as is clear from the above; **visto bueno** approved, authorized, O.K.; **visto que** whereas, inasmuch as, seeing ‖ *pp of* **ver** ‖ *f* sight, vision; view; vista; glance; appearance, comparison; purpose, design; eye, eyes; (law) trial; (law) hearing; **vistas** *fpl* windows, openings; view, outlook; conference; visible parts, parts that show; collar, cuffs, and bosom of shirt; **a la vista** (com.) at sight; **a primera vista** at first sight; **a simple vista** at a glance; with the naked eye; **a vista de** in view of, within view of, in the sight of; compared with; **con vistas a** + *inf* with a view to + *ger;* **de vista** by sight; **doble vista** second sight; **en vista de** in consideration of; **hacer la vista gorda (a)** to pretend not to see; **hasta la vista** good-bye, au revoir, so long; **medir con la vista** to size up (*a person*); **perder de vista** to lose sight of; **saltar a la vista** to be self-evident; **segunda vista** second sight; **tener a la vista** to have at hand, to have received (*a letter*); to keep one's eyes on; **torcer la vista** to squint; **vista cansada** far-sightedness; **vista corta** near-sightedness; **vista de pájaro** bird's-eye view; **vista doble** double vision; **vista en corte** cross-section view; **vista torcida** cross-eye ‖ **vista** *m* custom-house inspector
vistosidad *f* showiness, loudness, flashiness
vistoso -sa *adj* showy, loud, flashy
Vístula *m* Vistula
visual *adj* visual; *f* line of sight, visual line
visualidad *f* pleasure at sight of showy display
visualización *f* visualization
visualizar §76 *va* to visualize
visuauditivo -va *adj* audio-visual
visura *f* visual examination; inspection by an expert
vitáceo -a *adj* (bot.) vitaceous
vital *adj* vital
vitalicio -cia *adj* lifetime; (lasting for) life; (holding an office, etc. for) life; *m* life-insurance policy; lifetime pension, life annuity
vitalicista *mf* life annuitant
vitalidad *f* vitality
vitalismo *m* vitalism
vitalista *adj* vitalistic; *mf* vitalist
vitalización *f* vitalization
vitalizar §76 *va* to vitalize
vitamina *f* vitamine
vitamínico -ca *adj* vitaminic, vitamine
vitando -da *adj* to be avoided; odious, execrable
vitela *f* vellum
vitelino -na *adj* vitelline; *f* (biochem.) vitellin
vitelo *m* vitellus, yolk of an egg
vitícola *adj* viticultural, grape-growing; *mf* viticulturist, grape grower
viticultor -tora *mf* viticulturist, grape grower
viticultura *f* viticulture, grape growing
vitíligo *m* (path.) vitiligo
vito *m* lively Andalusian dance
vitola *f* calipers for bullets; cigar band; measure of size of cigars; mien, appearance
vítor *m* triumphal pageant; panegryric tablet; *interj* hurray!; long live!
vitorear *va* to cheer, to acclaim, to applaud
vitoriano -na *adj* (pertaining to) Vitoria; *mf* native or inhabitant of Vitoria
vitral *m* stained-glass window
vitre *m* light hempen canvas; light canvas
vítreo -a *adj* vitreous; glassy
vitrificable *adj* vitrifiable
vitrificación *f* vitrification
vitrificar §86 *va & vr* to vitrify
vitrina *f* showcase; display cabinet; glass case; (Am.) shopwindow
vitriolar *va* to vitriolize (*to throw vitriol at, to injure with vitriol*)
vitriólico -ca *adj* (chem.) vitriolic
vitriolizar §76 *va* to vitriolize (*to treat or mix with vitriol*)
vitriolo *m* vitriol; **vitriolo azul** blue vitriol; **vitriolo blanco** white vitriol; **vitriolo de plomo** lead sulphate
vitualla *f* victuals, provisions, food, abundance of food, abundance of vegetables
vituallar *va* to provide with food, to provision
vituperable *adj* vituperable
vituperación *f* vituperation
vituperador -dora *adj* vituperating; *mf* vituperator
vituperar *va* to vituperate
vituperio *m* vituperation
vituperioso -sa or **vituperoso -sa** *adj* vituperative
viuda *f* see **viudo**
viudal *adj* (pertaining to a) widower, widow; widower's, widow's
viudedad *f* widow's pension, dower
viudez *f* widowhood; widowerhood
viudo -da *adj* widowed; *m* widower; *f* widow; (bot.) mourning bride, mourning widow, sweet scabious; (orn.) whidah bird; **viuda de pecho rojo** (orn.) paradise whidah bird, paradise weaver; **viuda de marido vivo** or **viuda de paja** grass widow
viva *m* viva; *interj* viva!, long live!
vivac *m* (*pl:* **vivaques**) var. of **vivaque**
vivacidad *f* vigor; keenness; brightness, brilliancy
vivandero -ra *mf* (mil.) sutler; *f* vivandière
vivaque *m* bivouac; guardhouse; (Am.) police headquarters
vivaquear *vn* to bivouac
vivar *m* warren, burrow; aquarium; **vivar de garzas** heronry; *va* (Am.) to cheer, acclaim, hurrah
vivaracho -cha *adj* (coll.) vivacious, lively, frisky
vivario *m* vivarium

vivaz *adj* (*pl:* **-vaces**) long-lived; active, vigorous; vivacious; keen, perceptive; (bot.) perennial
vivencia *f* (philos.) experience
vivera *f* var. of **vivar**
viveral *m* tree nursery
víveres *mpl* food, victuals, provisions
vivero *m* tree nursery; fishpond; (fig.) hotbed
viveza *f* quickness, agility, briskness; ardor, vehemence; keenness, perception; brightness, brilliancy; witticism; sparkle (*in the eyes*); thoughtlessness (*in word or deed*)
Viviana *f* Vivian
vividero -ra *adj* habitable, livable
vivido -da *adj* based on life or experience (*said of writing*)
vívido -da *adj* lively; vivid
vividor -dora *adj* living; long-lived; thrifty; (coll.) opportunistic; *mf* liver; thrifty person; (coll.) opportunist; (slang) thief, crook; *m* sponger, hanger-on
vivienda *f* dwelling; housing; life, way of living; **vivienda remolque** trailer
viviente *adj* living
vivificación *f* vivification
vivificador -dora *adj* vivifying, life-giving
vivificar §86 *va* to vivify, to enliven
vivífico -ca *adj* full of life; springing from life
vivíparo -ra *adj* viviparous
vivir *m* life; living; *va* to live (*an experience or adventure*); to live out (*e.g., one's life, one's old age*); to live in; *vn* to live; **¿quién vive?** (mil.) who goes there?; **¡viva!** viva!, long live!; **vivir de** to live on (*e.g., bread*); **vivir para ver** to live and learn; **vivir y dejar vivir** to live and let live
vivisección *f* vivisection
viviseccionista *mf* vivisectionist
vivisector *m* vivisector
vivisectorio *m* vivisectorium
vivismo *m* philosophy of Luis Vives
vivo -va *adj* alive, living; live; active, effective, in effect; vivid; intense, bright; sharp; acute, keen, deep; ingenious; expressive; quick; raw (*flesh*); modern, living (*language*); **a lo vivo** or **al vivo** vividly; effectively; **dar en lo vivo** to touch to the quick; **de viva voz** viva voce, by word of mouth; **herir en lo vivo** to cut or hurt to the quick; *mf* living person; (coll.) clever person, shrewd person; **los vivos** the living, the quick; **los vivos y los muertos** the quick and the dead; *m* edging, border; rib, corded seam; (arch.) sharp edge; (vet.) mange
vizcacha *f* (zool.) vizcacha or viscacha (*large South American rodent*)
vizcainada *f* Biscayanism; solecism
vizcaíno -na *adj & mf* Biscayan; *m* Biscayan (*language*)
Vizcaya *f* Biscay (*province of northern Spain*); **llevar hierro a Vizcaya** to carry coals to Newcastle
vizcondado *m* viscountcy, viscountship, or viscounty
vizconde *m* viscount; **vizcondes** *mpl* viscount and viscountess
vizcondesa *f* viscountess
V.M. abr. of **Vuestra Majestad**
V.ºB.º abr. of **visto bueno**
vocablista *mf* punster
vocablo *m* word, term; **jugar del vocablo** to pun
vocabulario *m* vocabulary
vocabulista *mf* vocabulist, lexicographer
vocación *f* vocation; name given to a church, chapel, or altar in dedication to the Virgin or a saint; (theol.) vocation
vocacional *adj* vocational
vocal *adj* vocal; *mf* voter, director; *f* vowel; **vocal abierta** open vowel; **vocal breve** short vowel; **vocal cerrada** close vowel; **vocal débil** weak vowel; **vocal fuerte** strong vowel; **vocal larga** long vowel; **vocal nasal** nasal vowel; **vocal posterior** back vowel
vocálico -ca *adj* vocalic, vowel
vocalismo *m* (phonet.) vocalism
vocalista *mf* vocalist, singer (*e.g., in a night club*)
vocalización *f* (mus. & phonet.) vocalization
vocalizar §76 *va* (phonet.) to vocalize; *vn* (mus.) to vocalize; *vr* (phonet.) to vocalize
vocativo -va *adj & m* vocative
voceador -dora *adj* vociferating; *mf* vociferator; *m* town crier; (Am.) paper boy
vocear *va* to cry, shout, proclaim; to cheer, hail, acclaim; (coll.) to boast publicly about; *vn* to cry out, to shout
vocejón *m* harsh, rough voice
vocería *f* shouting, uproar; spokesmanship
vocerío *m* shouting, uproar
vocero *m* spokesman, mouthpiece
vociferación *f* vociferation
vociferador -dora *adj* vociferous; *mf* vociferator; barker
vociferante *adj & mf* vociferant
vociferar *va* to shout or vociferate (*e.g., insults*); to announce boastfully; *vn* to shout, to vociferate
vocingleo *m* or **vocinglería** *f* shouting, uproar, shrieking
vocinglero -ra *adj* loudmouthed; loquacious, chattering; *mf* loudmouthed person; chatterer
vodca *m* or **vodka** *m* vodka
vodevil *m* light comedy
vodú *m* (*pl:* **-dúes**) voodoo
voduísmo *m* voodooism
voduísta *adj* voodoo, voodooistic; *mf* voodooist
vol. abr. of **volumen** & **voluntad**
volada *f* see **volado**
voladero -ra *adj* flying; fleeting; floating; *m* precipice; *f* float (*of water wheel*)
voladizo -za *adj* projecting; *m* projection
volado -da *adj* (print.) superior (*letter*); **volado de genio** (Am.) quick-tempered; *m* meringue; *f* short flight; (Am.) trick; (Am.) happening
volador -dora *adj* flying; swinging, hanging; running, swift; *m* rocket; flying fish; (ichth.) flying gurnard
voladura *f* flying through the air; explosion, blast
volandas; en volandas in the air, flying in the air; (coll.) swiftly
volandero -ra *adj* ready to fly, starting to fly; hanging, swinging; accidental, unforeseen; incidental; ephemeral; unsettled; wandering; *f* (mach.) washer; grindstone; (print.) galley slice; (coll.) fib, lie
volandillas; en volandillas var. of **en volandas**
volante *adj* flying; volant; unsettled; (her.) volant; *m* shuttlecock; battledore and shuttlecock; flywheel; steering wheel; balance wheel; coining press; lackey, flunkey; outrider; folded sheet of paper, bill, note; slip (*of paper*); (sew.) ruffle; **en el volante** at the wheel (*of an auto*); **un buen volante** a good driver (*of an auto*); **volante compensador** (horol.) compensating balance; **volante de dirección** (aut.) steering wheel; **volante de reloj** (horol.) balance wheel
volantín -tina *adj* unsettled; *m* fish line; (Am.) kite
volantista *m* (coll.) man at the wheel, driver
volantón -tona *adj* ready to fly, starting to fly; *mf* fledgling
volapié *m* (taur.) suerte in which the matador moves in on the standing bull instead of awaiting the bull's charge; **a volapié** half running, half flying; half walking, half swimming
volar §77 *va* to fly (*to transport in an aircraft*); to blow up, to explode; to rouse (*game*); to exasperate; to blow, to fan; (print.) to raise (*a letter, number, etc.*) to the top of the line; *vn* to fly; to flutter; to fly away; to disappear rapidly; to project, to jut out; to spread rapidly (*said, e.g., of news*); to rise in the air (*said, e.g., of a steeple*); (Am.) to bluff (*in poker*); **volar a** + *inf* to fly to + *inf;* **volar sin motor** (aer.) to glide; *vr* to fly, to fly away
volateo *m* shooting at a flying target; **al volateo** on the wing
volatería *f* birdhunting with decoys; birds; random thoughts; shot in the dark; **de volatería** at random, in the dark
volatero -ra *adj* fickle, inconstant
volátil *adj* volatile
volatilidad *f* volatility

volatilización *f* volatilization
volatilizar §76 *va* to volatilize; *vr* to volatilize; (coll.) to fade away, to disappear (*said, e.g., of money*)
volatín *m* ropewalker; feat of ropewalker
volatinero -ra *mf* ropewalker
volatizar §76 *va* var. of **volatilizar**
volcadero *m* tipple
volcán *m* volcano; (fig.) volcano; **estar sobre un volcán** (fig.) to be on the edge of a volcano
volcanera *f* (orn.) wood pigeon (*Columba fasciata*)
volcánico -ca *adj* volcanic
volcanismo *m* volcanism
volcar §95 *va* to upset, to dump; to overturn; to tip, to tilt; to make dizzy or giddy (*said of a strong odor*); to make (*a person*) change his mind; to tease, to irritate; *vn* to upset; *vr* to turn upside down; **volcarse en** to fall all over oneself in (*e.g., praises*)
volea *f* whippletree; (tennis) volley
volear *va* to volley (*a ball*); to sow (*grain*) by throwing it in the air with the hand
voleo *m* (tennis) volley; reeling punch or blow; **al voleo** throwing the grain in the air with the hand; **del primer voleo** or **de un voleo** (coll.) quickly, at one blow
volframio *m* (chem.) wolfram
volframita *f* (mineral.) wolframite, wolfram
volibol *m* volleyball
volición *f* volition
volitar *vn* to flutter
volitivo -va *adj* volitive, volitional
volquear *vr* to tumble, to roll over
volquete *m* dumpcart, tipcart; dump truck; dumping device
volsco -ca *adj & mf* Volscian
voltaico -ca *adj* voltaic
voltaje *m* (elec.) voltage
voltámetro *m* (phys.) voltameter
voltamperímetro *m* (phys.) voltammeter
voltamperio *m* (elec.) volt-ampere
voltariedad *f* fickleness, inconstancy
voltario -ria *adj* fickle, inconstant
volteador -dora *adj* tumbling; *mf* tumbler, acrobat
voltear *va* to upset, to roll over; to turn around; to move, transform; to build (*an arch or vaulting*); *vn* to roll over, to tumble
voltejear *va* to turn around; *vn* (naut.) to tack; (naut.) to maneuver
volteo *m* upset, rolling over; reversal; tumbling; (Am.) passage, journey; (Am.) scolding, dressing-down
voltereta *f* tumble, somersault; turning up card to determine trump
volterianismo *m* Voltairism or Voltairianism
volteriano -na *adj & mf* Voltairian
volteta *f* var. of **voltereta**
voltímetro *m* (elec.) voltmeter
voltio *m* (elec.) volt
voltizo -za *adj* twisted, curled; fickle, inconstant
volubilidad *f* volubility; fickleness, inconstancy
voluble *adj* voluble (*turning easily*); fickle, inconstant; (bot.) voluble, twining
volumen *m* volume (*book; bulk; mass, e.g., of water*); (geom.) volume; **a todo volumen** (rad.) full volume; **volumen sonoro** volume
volumétrico -ca *adj* volumetric
volúmetro *m* volumeter
voluminoso -sa *adj* voluminous; heavy, huge; bulky
voluntad *f* will; love, fondness; **a voluntad** at will; **de buena voluntad** willingly; **de mala voluntad** unwillingly; **ganarse la voluntad de** to win the favor of; **última voluntad** last wish; (law) last will and testament; **voluntad de hierro** iron will; **voluntad de poder** (philos.) will to power
voluntariado *m* (mil.) volunteering
voluntariedad *f* willfulness, self-will
voluntario -ria *adj* voluntary, willful; *mf* volunteer
voluntarioso -sa *adj* willful, self-willed; determined
voluntarismo *m* (philos.) voluntarism
voluptuosidad *f* voluptuousness
voluptuoso -sa *adj* voluptuous; voluptuary; *mf* voluptuary
voluta *f* (arch.) scroll, volute; (fig.) volute; (zool.) volute (*any of Volutidae*)
volva *f* (bot.) volva
volvedor -dora *adj* (Am.) that runs away to get back home (*said of a horse*); *m* screw driver; **volvedor de machos** tap wrench
volver §63 & §17, 9 *va* to turn; to turn over; to turn upside down; to turn inside out; to return, to give back, to send back; to close; to push or pull (*e.g., a door*) to; to change, transform; to make (*a person*) change his mind; to translate; to vomit; to reflect (*sound*); to plow a second time; to give (*change*) ‖ *vn* to turn; to return, come back; **volver a** + *inf* verb + again, e.g., **volvió a leer ese libro** he read that book again; **volver en sí** to come to; **volver por** to defend, to stand up for; **volver sobre** to go back on (*e.g., one's footsteps, a decision*); **volver sobre sí** to recover one's calm; to take stock of oneself or one's conduct; to recover from a loss ‖ *vr* to become; to turn, to turn sour; to return, come back; to change one's mind; **volverse atrás** to back out, to not keep one's word; **volverse contra** to turn on
volvible *adj* turnable, reversible
volvo or **vólvulo** *m* (path.) volvulus
vómer *m* (anat.) vomer, plowshare bone
vomicina *f* (chem.) vomicine
vómico -ca *adj* vomitive
vomitado -da *adj* (coll.) thin, sickly, pale
vomitador -dora *adj* vomiting; *mf* person who vomits
vomitar *va* to vomit, throw up; to belch forth; to utter (*insults, curses, etc.*); to let out (*e.g., a secret*); (coll.) to disgorge, to cough up (*something unjustly held back or stolen*); *vn* to vomit; (coll.) to disgorge
vomitivo -va *adj & m* vomitive
vómito *m* vomit, vomiting; **vómito negro** (path.) black vomit; **vómitos del embarazo** morning sickness
vomitón -tona *adj* vomiting (*said of a suckling child*); *f* (coll.) violent vomiting
voquible *m* (coll.) word
voracidad *f* voracity
vorágine *f* whirlpool, vortex
voraz *adj* (*pl:* **-races**) voracious; fierce, destructive
vormela *f* (zool.) polecat (*Putorius sarmaticus*)
vórtice *m* vortex; center of a cyclone
vorticela *f* (zool.) vorticella
vos *pron pers* (used as subject of verb and as object of preposition in addressing God, the Virgin Mary, a saint, or a person of high position or authority; takes plural form of verb but is singular in meaning; in popular speech in much of Spanish America is used instead of **tú**) you
vosear *va* to use **vos** in speaking to
voseo *m* use of **vos,** use of **vos** for **tú**
Vosgos *mpl* Vosges
vosotros -tras *pron pers* (used as subject of verb and object of preposition in addressing several persons each of whom would be addressed with **tú** and in the formal language of public speech, diplomatic correspondence, etc.) you
votación *f* voting; (total) vote; **por votación** by choice; **por votación oral** by viva-voce vote; **votación de confianza** vote of confidence; **votación por manos levantadas** show of hands
votador -dora *adj* voting; *mf* voter; swearer
votante *adj* voting; *mf* voter
votar *va* to vow; to vote, to vote for, to vote on; **¡voto a tal!** confound it!; goodness!; upon my soul!; *vn* to vow; to vote; to swear; *vr* to vow
votivo -va *adj* votive
voto *m* vow; curse; votive offering; vote; **votos** *mpl* wishes, good wishes; **echar votos** to swear, to curse; **hacer votos** to wish, to hope; **regular los votos** to tally the votes; **ser** or **tener voto** to have a vote; to know what one is talking about; **voto activo** right to vote; **voto de amén** or **de reata** (coll.) vote of a yes man; (coll.) yes man; **voto de calidad**

casting vote (*in case of a tie*); **voto de confianza** vote of confidence; **voto femenino** woman suffrage; **voto informativo** straw vote; **voto pasivo** eligibility; **voto secreto** secret ballot
voy *1st sg pres ind of* **ir**
voz *f* (*pl:* **voces**) voice; word; (gram. & mus.) voice; **voces** *fpl* outcry; **aclarar la voz** to clear one's throat; **alzar la voz** to raise one's voice, to lift up one's voice; **a media voz** in a low tone; with a gentle hint; **a una voz** with one voice; **a voces** shouting; **a voz en cuello** or **a voz en grito** at the top of one's voice; **correr la voz que** to be rumored that; **dar voces** to shout, to cry out; **de viva voz** viva voce, by word of mouth; **en alta voz** aloud; **en voz** verbally; (mus.) in voice; **en voz baja** in a low tone; **estar a la voz** (naut.) to be within hail, to be within hailing distance; **llevar la voz cantante** (coll.) to have the say, to be the boss; **tomar la voz** to take up the discussion; **voz activa** right to vote; (gram.) active voice; **voz de acarreo** (philol.) borrowing, loan word; **voz pasiva** eligibility; (gram.) passive voice
vozarrón *m* (coll.) harsh, loud voice
voznar *vn* to cackle
vro. abr. of **vuestro**
V.S. abr. of **Vueseñoría**
v.to abr. of **vuelto**
vudú *m* (*pl:* **-dúes**) var. of **vodú**
vuduísmo *m* var. of **voduísmo**
vuduísta *adj & mf* var. of **voduísta**
vuecelencia or **vuecencia** contraction of **vuestra excelencia** your Excellency
vuelco *m* upset, overturning; **dar un vuelco** to upset, to turn over; **darle a uno un vuelco el corazón** (coll.) to have a presentiment or misgiving
vuelillo *m* lace cuff trimming
vuelo *m* flight; flying; wing; spread, fullness, flare; projection; lace cuff trimming; woodland; **al vuelo** at once, in a jiffy; on the wing; scattered at random; (chess) en passant; **alzar el vuelo** to take flight; (coll.) to dash off, to leave in a hurry; **cortarle los vuelos a uno** to cut someone's wings; **de un vuelo** in a flash; in a single flight, without letup; **echar a vuelo las campanas** to ring a full peal; **en un vuelo** in a flash; in a single flight, without letup; **levantar el vuelo** to take flight; to become imaginative; to be proud, haughty; **tirar al vuelo** to shoot on the wing; **tocar al vuelo las campanas** to ring a full peal; **tomar vuelo** to progress, to grow; **vuelo a ciegas** or **vuelo ciego** (aer.) blind flying; **vuelo de distancia** (aer.) long-distance flight; **vuelo de ensayo** or **de prueba** (aer.) test flight; **vuelo espacial** space flight; **vuelo planeado** (aer.) volplane; **vuelo por instrumentos** (aer.) instrument flying; **vuelo rasante** (aer.) hedgehopping; **vuelo sin escala** (aer.) nonstop flight; **vuela sin motor** (aer.) glide, gliding; **vuelo sin parar** (aer.) nonstop flight
vuelto -ta *pp of* **volver;** *m* (print.) verso; (Am.) change (*money*); *f* turn, rotation, revolution; change; harshness; return; change (*money*); clock (*in stocking*); reverse, other side; repetition; burden (*of song*); beating, whipping; ploughing; cuff; cuff trimming; (arch.) interior curve; turning up a card; **a la vuelta** on returning; on the other side of the page, please turn page; **a la vuelta de** at the end of, after; at the turn of; around (*e.g., the corner*); **andar a vueltas con** to clash with; **a vuelta de** about; **a vuelta de correo** by return mail; **a vueltas de** in addition to; **dar cien vueltas a** to get far ahead of, to run rings around; **dar la vuelta** to upset; **dar la vuelta de campana** to turn somersault; **darse una vuelta a la redonda** (coll.) to tend to one's own business; **dar una vuelta** to take a stroll or walk; to make a short trip; to go and take a look; to change one's ways; **dar vuelta** to turn sour (*said of wine*); **dar vuelta a** to reverse, to turn around; **dar vueltas** to circle; to look in vain; to travel around; to keep going over the same subject; to swim, to whirl, to be dizzy; **de vuelta** on returning; **estar de vuelta** to be back; **no hay que darle vueltas** there's no use talking about it; **no tener vuelta de hoja** to be undeniable; **ponerle a uno de vuelta y media** to insult a person; **quedarse con la vuelta** to keep the change; **vuelta de braza** (naut.) timber hitch; **vuelta de cabo** (naut.) hitch; **vuelta de campana** somersault; **vuelta del mundo** trip around the world; **vuelta doble** double turn (*of lock*)
vueludo -da *adj* full (*said of a garment*)
vuesarced contraction of **vuestra merced** your Grace, your Honor
vueseñoría contraction of **vuestra señoría** your Lordship, your Ladyship
vuestro -tra (corresponds to **vos** and **vosotros**) *adj poss* your; *pron poss* yours
vulcanio -nia *adj* Vulcanian; vulcanian
vulcanismo *m* vulcanism
vulcanista *mf* vulcanist
vulcanita *f* vulcanite
vulcanización *f* vulcanization
vulcanizador *m* vulcanizer
vulcanizar §76 *va* to vulcanize
Vulcano *m* (myth.) Vulcan
vulcanología *f* volcanology
vulgacho *m* mob, rabble, populace
vulgar *adj* vulgar; vernacular; common, ordinary; popular
vulgaridad *f* vulgarity, commonness; commonplace
vulgarismo *m* vulgarism (*in language*); (philol.) popular word, popular form
vulgarización *f* vulgarization; popularization
vulgarizador -dora *adj* vulgarizing; *mf* vulgarizer; popularizer
vulgarizar §76 *va* to vulgarize; to popularize; to translate into the vernacular; *vr* to become common; to associate with common people, to grow vulgar
Vulgata *f* Vulgate
vulgo *m* common people; laity; *adv* vulgo, commonly
vulnerabilidad *f* vulnerability
vulnerable *adj* vulnerable
vulneración *f* damage to a reputation; breach (*e.g., of law*)
vulnerar *va* to harm, injure, damage (*e.g., a reputation*); to infringe on; to break (*a law*)
vulnerario -ria *adj & m* (med.) vulnerary
vulpécula or **vulpeja** *f* vixen, she-fox
vulpinita *f* (mineral.) vulpinite
vulpino -na *adj* vulpine; *m* (bot.) plume grass
vultuoso -sa *adj* bloated (*said of the face*)
vulturno *m* hot summer breeze
vulva *f* (anat.) vulva
vulvar *adj* vulvar
vulvitis *f* (path.) vulvitis
V.V. or **VV.** abr. of **ustedes**

W, w *f* called **doble v, v doble,** and **u valona** in Spanish, this letter does not belong to the Spanish alphabet
wagneriano -na *adj & mf* var. of **vagneriano**
wagón *m* var. of **vagón**
wapití *m* (*pl:* **-tíes**) var. of **uapití**
wat *m* (*pl:* **wats**) var. of **vatio**
wáter *m* (coll.) var. of **váter**
water-closet *m* (*pl:* **-sets**) toilet, water closet
water-polista *mf* water polo player
water-polo *m* (sport) var. of **polo acuático**
wattman *m* (*pl:* **-men**) motorman
WC *m* abr. of **water-closet**
wesleyano -na *adj & mf* Wesleyan
Westfalia *f* var. of **Vestfalia**
Westfaliano -na *adj & mf* var. of **Vestfaliano**
whisky *m* whiskey or whisky
wolfram *m* var. of **volframio**
wulfenita *f* (mineral.) wulfenite

X, x *f* twenty-sixth letter of the Spanish alphabet
xantalina *f* (chem.) xanthaline
xantato *m* (chem.) xanthate
xanteína *f* (chem.) xanthein
xanteno *m* (chem.) xanthene
xantina *f* (chem.) xanthin; (biochem.) xanthine
Xantipa *f* var. of **Jantipa**
xantocroide *adj & mf* (anthrop.) xanthochroid
xantodermo -ma *mf* (anthrop.) xanthoderm
xantofila *f* (biochem.) xanthophyll
xantógeno *m* (chem.) xanthogen
xantoma *m* (path.) xanthoma
xantopsia *f* (path.) xanthopsia
xantopsina *f* xanthopsin
xantosis *f* (path.) xanthosis
xantoxilina *f* (chem. & pharm.) xanthoxylin
xenia *f* (bot.) xenia
xeno *m* (chem.) xenon
xenofobia *f* xenophobia, dislike of foreigners
xenófobo -ba *mf* xenophobe
xenogénesis *f* (biol.) xenogenesis
xenón *m* var. of **xeno**
xerófito -ta *adj* (bot.) xerophytic; *f* (bot.) xerophyte
xeroftalmía *f* (path.) xerophthalmia
xifisternón *m* (anat.) xiphisternum
xifoides *adj & m* (anat.) xiphoid
xifosuro *m* var. of **jifosuro**
xilán *m* (chem.) xylan
xilema *m* (bot.) xylem
xileno *m* (chem.) xylene
xilidina *f* (chem.) xylidine
xilobálsamo *m* xylobalsamum
xilófago -ga *adj* xylophagous
xilófono *m* (mus.) xylophone
xilografía *f* xylography (*art*); xylograph (*engraving*)
xilográfico -ca *adj* xylographic or xylographical
xilógrafo -fa *mf* xylographer
xilol *m* (chem.) xylol
xilosa *f* (chem.) xylose
xister *m* (surg.) xyster
x.mo abr. of **diezmo**
xpiano abr. of **cristiano**
Xpo abr. of **Cristo**
xptiano abr. of **cristiano**
Xpto abr. of **Cristo**
Xptóbal abr. of **Cristóbal**
xucul *m* (bot.) purslane (*of Mexico*)
xunde *m* (Am.) basket made of reed or palm

Y

Y, y *f* twenty-seventh letter of the Spanish alphabet
y *conj* and
ya *adv* already; now; finally; at once, right away; **no ya** not only; **no . . . ya** no longer; **¡pues ya!** of course!; **ya no** no longer; **ya que** since, inasmuch as; **ya . . . ya** now . . . again, whether . . . or
yaba *f* (bot.) cabbage tree
yac *m* yak (*Tibetan ox*); (naut.) jack (*flag*)
yacedor *m* herdboy who drives horses out for night grazing
yacente *adj* recumbent, jacent; located; *m* (min.) floor of a vein
yacer §96 *vn* to lie; to rest, lie buried; to graze by night; **yacer con** (coll.) to lie with (*to have sexual intercourse with*)
yacija *f* bed, couch; grave, tomb; **ser de mala yacija** to be restless; to sleep poorly; to be a vagrant
yacimiento *m* bed, deposit, field
yago *1st sg pres ind of* **yacer**
yagua *f* (bot.) yagua (*palm tree: Roystonea borinqueana; broad flat stem of its leaf*)
yaguar *m* var. of **jaguar**
yámbico -ca *adj* iambic
yambo *m* iamb, iambus, iambic
yanacona *m* (Am.) serf; (Am.) sharecropper
yanqui *adj & mf* Yankee, American
Yanquilandia *f* Yankeedom
yanquismo *m* Yankeeism
yantar *m* food; *va & vn* (archaic) to eat
yapa *f* (Am.) lagniappe, bonus, extra, allowance; (min.) mercury added to silver ore; **de yapa** (Am.) extra, in the bargain
yarda *f* yard; yardstick
yardaje *m* yardage
yaro *m* (bot.) arum
yatagán *m* yataghan
yate *m* yacht
yazco or **yazgo** *1st sg pres ind of* **yacer**
ye *f* letter Y
yedra *f* var. of **hiedra**
yegua *f* mare; (Am.) cigar butt
yeguada *f* stud (*collection of horses; place for breeding*)
yeguar *adj* (pertaining to a) mare
yegüería *f* var. of **yeguada**
yegüerizo -za *adj* (pertaining to a) mare; *m* keeper of mares
yegüero *m* keeper of mares
yeísmo *m* pronunciation of Spanish **ll** like **y**
yelmo *m* (arm.) helmet
yema *f* yolk (*of egg*); candied yolk; (anat., bot. & zool.) bud; dead (*e.g., of winter*); (fig.) cream; **dar en la yema** (coll.) to hit the nail on the head; **yema del dedo** finger tip; **yema mejida** eggnog
yemenita *adj & mf* Yemenite
yendo *ger of* **ir**
yente *adj* going; **yentes y vinientes** frequenters, habitués
yeral *m* lentil field
yerba *f* var. of **hierba**
yerbajo *m* weed
yermar *va* to strip, lay waste, leave deserted
yermo -ma *adj* deserted, uninhabited, uncultivated; *m* desert, wilderness; waste land
yerno *m* son-in-law
yero *m* (bot.) tare, lentil, bitter vetch (*Ervum ervilia*)
yerro *m* error, mistake; **yerro de imprenta** typographical error
yerto -ta *adj* stiff, rigid
yervo *m* var. of **yero**
yesal *m* or **yesar** *m* gypsum pit or quarry
yesca *f* punk, touchwood, tinder; fuel (*for passion*); **yescas** *fpl* tinderbox
yesería *f* gypsum kiln; plasterer's shop; plastering
yesero -ra *adj* (pertaining to) gypsum; *mf* gypsum maker or dealer; plasterer
yeso *m* gypsum; chalk; plaster; plaster cast; **yeso blanco** finishing plaster; **yeso de París** plaster of Paris; **yeso negro** rough plaster
yesón *m* chunk of plaster
yesoso -sa *adj* gypseous; chalky
yesquero *m* tinder maker or dealer; tinderbox
yeyuno *m* (anat.) jejunum
yezgo *m* (bot.) danewort, dwarf elder
yo *pron pers* I: **soy yo** it is I; *m* ego; (philos.) I, ego
Yocasta *f* (myth.) Jocasta
yod *f* (philol.) yod
yodado -da *adj* iodized; sea-soaked, sea-burned
yodato *m* (chem.) iodate
yodhídrico -ca *adj* (chem.) hydriodic
yódico -ca *adj* (chem.) iodic
yodismo *m* (path.) iodism
yodo *m* (chem.) iodine
yodoformo *m* (chem.) iodoform
yodoso -sa *adj* (chem.) iodous
yoduro *m* (chem.) iodide
yoga *m* yoga
yogui *m* yogi
yogurt *m* yogurt
yola *f* (sport) shell; (sport) sailboat; (naut.) gig
yubarta *f* (zool.) finback
yuca *f* (bot.) yucca; **yuca brava** (bot.) bitter cassava; **yuca dulce** (bot.) sweet cassava
Yucatán, el Yucatan
yucateco -ca *adj* (pertaining to) Yucatan; *mf* native or inhabitant of Yucatan
yugada *f* day's plowing of a yoke of oxen; yoke of oxen; yoke of land
yugo *m* yoke; burden; marriage tie; (naut.) transom; **sacudir el yugo** to throw off the yoke; **sujetarse al yugo de** to bend under the yoke of, to yield to the ascendancy of
Yugoeslavia *f* Yugoslavia
yugoeslavo -va *adj* Yugoslav, Yugoslavic; *mf* Yugoslav
Yugoslavia *f* Yugoslavia
yugoslavo -va *adj & mf* var. of **yugoeslavo**
yuguero *m* plowboy, plowman
yugular *adj & f* (anat.) jugular; *va* to cut off, to throttle (*a disease, an epidemic*)
Yugurta *m* Jugurtha
yunque *m* anvil; (anat.) anvil, incus; long-suffering person; drudge; **estar al yunque** to be long-suffering
yunta *f* see **yunto**
yuntero *m* plowboy, plowman
yunto -ta *adj* close (*said of furrows*); *f* yoke (*of animals*); **yunto** *adv* close; **arar yunto** to plow close
yusera *f* horizontal stone base in olive-oil mill
yusión *f* (law) precept; (law) jussion, command
yusivo -va *adj* (gram.) jussive
yute *m* (bot.) jute (*plant, fiber, and fabric*)
Yuturna *f* (myth.) Juturna
yuxtalineal *adj* in parallel columns (*said of a translation and its original*)
yuxtapondré *1st sg fut ind of* **yuxtaponer**
yuxtaponer §69 *va* to juxtapose; *vr* to become juxtaposed
yuxtapongo *1st sg pres ind of* **yuxtaponer**
yuxtaposición *f* juxtaposition
yuxtapuesto -ta *pp of* **yuxtaponer**
yuxtapuse *1st sg pret ind of* **yuxtaponer**
yuyo *m* (Am.) weed; (Am.) blister between toes; **yuyos** *mpl* (Am.) greens
yuyuba *f* jujube

Z

Z, z *f* twenty-eighth letter of the Spanish alphabet
za *interj* begone!, get out of here! (*said to a dog*)
zabarcera *f* greengrocer, dealer in fresh fruits and vegetables (*woman*)
zabida or **zabila** *f* (bot.) aloe
zaborda *f* or **zabordamiento** *m* (naut.) running aground
zabordar *vn* (naut.) to run aground
zabordo *m* var. of **zaborda**
zaborro *m* fat fellow, fatty
zabucar §86 *va* to stir by shaking
zabullida *f* var. of **zambullida**
zabullidor -dora *adj & mf* var. of **zambullidor**
zabullidura *f* or **zabullimiento** *m* var. of **zambullidura**
zabullir § 26 *va & vr* var. of **zambullir**
zabuqueo *m* stirring, shaking
zaca *f* (min.) leather bag used for bailing
zacapela or **zacapella** *f* shindy, row, rumpus
Zacarías *m* (Bib.) Zechariah; (Bib.) Zachariah
zacate *m* (Am.) hay, fodder; (Am.) grass; **zacate corredor** (bot.) hyssop loosestrife; **zacate de empaque** (Am.) excelsior
zacategordura *f* (bot.) molasses grass
zacatín *m* old-clothes market
zacear *va* to chase away (*e.g., a dog*); *vn* to lisp
zadorija *f* (bot.) large-flowered hypecoum
zafa *f* see **zafo**
zafado -da *adj* (Am.) alert, wide-awake; (Am.) brazen; *f* loosening, untying; freezing; lightening a ship
zafar *va* to adorn, bedeck; to loosen, untie; to free, to clear; to lighten (*a vessel*); *vr* to slip away, hide away; to slip off, come off (*said of a belt*); **zafarse de** to get out of, to dodge
zafariche *m* shelf for water jugs
zafarrancho *m* (naut.) clearing for action; clearing out, forcible evacuation; (coll.) ravage, destruction; (coll.) row, scuffle; **zafarrancho de combate** (naut.) clearing for battle
zafiedad *f* roughness, coarseness, crudeness, uncouthness
zafio -fia *adj* rough, coarse, crude, uncouth
zafir *m* var. of **zafiro**
zafíreo -a *adj* sapphire (*in color*)
zafirino -na *adj* sapphire (*in color*); *f* (mineral.) sapphirine
zafiro *m* sapphire
zafo -fa *adj* intact, unhurt; (naut.) free, clear; *f* basin, bowl
zafones *mpl* var. of **zahones**
zafra *f* drip jar; oil can; ridgeband; sugar crop; sugar making; sugar-making season; (min.) rubbish, muck
zafre *m* (mineral.) zaffer
zafrero *m* (min.) mucker
zaga *f* rear; load carried in the rear; **a la zaga, a zaga** or **en zaga** behind; **no ir en zaga a** (coll.) to keep up with, be as good as
zagal *m* youth; strapping young fellow; shepherd's helper; footboy; skirt
zagala *f* lass, maiden; shepherdess
zagaleja *f* lassie
zagalejo *m* lad; peasant's skirt
zagalón -lona *mf* big youngster
zagual *m* paddle
zaguán *m* vestibule, entry
zaguanete *m* small vestibule; royal guard, royal escort
zaguero -ra *adj* rear, hind; **no quedar zaguero de** to not be behind, to keep up with; *m* backstop; (*football*) back
zahareño -ña *adj* wild, unsociable, intractable; haggard (*falcon*)
zaharrón *m* clown
zaheridor -dora *adj* reproachful, faultfinding; *mf* faultfinder
zaherimiento *m* reproach; calling down
zaherir §62 *va* to reproach, find fault with; to call down; to pique, to provoke
zahína *f* (bot.) sorghum
zahinar *m* sorghum field
zahonado -da *adj* of a different color in the front (*said of the feet of an animal*)
zahondar *va* to dig; *vn* to sink, sink down (*in the ground*)
zahones *mpl* chaps (*cowboy trousers*); hunting breeches
zahora *f* (dial.) party, feast
zahorar *vn* (dial.) to celebrate, to feast
zahorí *m* (*pl:* **-ríes**) diviner, clairvoyant; keen observer
zahorra *f* (naut.) ballast
zahúrda *f* pigpen; (fig.) pigpen
zaida *f* (orn.) demoiselle
zaino -na *adj* treacherous, false; dark-chestnut (*horse*); black (*cattle*); vicious (*horse*); **a lo zaino** or **de zaino** sidewise, askance
zalá *f* (*pl:* **-laes**) Mohammedan prayer; **hacer la zalá a** (coll.) to fawn over, bow down to
zalagarda *f* ambush, ambuscade; skirmish; snare, trap; (coll.) trick; (coll.) surprise disturbance (*caused by a gang of roughnecks*); mock fight
zalama *f*, **zalamelé** *m* or **zalamería** *f* flattery
zalamero -ra *adj* flattering; *mf* flatterer
zalea *f* unsheared sheepskin, pelt
zalear *va* to drag around, to shake; to chase away (*a dog*)
zalema *f* (coll.) salaam
zaleo *m* dragging, shaking; sheepskin left by fox and brought in by shepherd to account for loss of sheep
zaloma *f* (naut.) var. of **saloma**
zalona *f* large unglazed earthen jug
zallar *va* (naut.) to rig out, to run out
zamacuco *m* (coll.) dullard; (coll.) sullen fellow; (coll.) drunkenness
zamanca *f* (coll.) drubbing, beating
zamarra *f* undressed sheepskin; shepherd's undressed sheepskin jacket
zamarrear *va* to shake with the teeth; (coll.) to ill-treat, abuse, knock around; to pin down, pin to the wall
zamarreo *m* shaking with the teeth; (coll.) ill treatment, abuse
zamarrico *m* sheepskin bag
zamarrilla *f* (bot.) poly
zamarro *m* lambskin, sheepskin; shepherd's undressed sheepskin jacket; (coll.) boor, rustic; (coll.) sly fellow; **zamarros** *mpl* (Am.) chaps, riding breeches
zambaigo -ga *adj* half Negro half Indian; (Am.) half Indian half Chinese
zambarco *m* breast strap (*of harness*); strap with buckle
zambear *vn* to be knock-kneed
zámbigo -ga *adj* knock-kneed
zambo -ba *adj* knock-kneed; *mf* (Am.) zambo; *m* (zool.) papion
zamboa *f* citron (*fruit*)
zambomba *f* (mus.) zambomba; *interj* whew!
zambombazo *m* beating, clubbing
zambombo *m* (coll.) boor, lubber, crude fellow
zamborondón -dona, zamborotudo -da or **zamborrotudo -da** *adj* (coll.) awkward, clumsy, ill-shaped; (coll.) bungling; *mf* (coll.) bungler, botcher
zambra *f* Moorish boat; (coll.) din, uproar; (archaic) Moorish celebration, Moorish hullabaloo

zambucar §86 *va* (coll.) to hide away, to slip away
zambuco *m* (coll.) quick hiding or concealment
zambullida *f* dive, plunge; thrust to the breast (*in fencing*)
zambullidor -dora *adj* diving, plunging; *mf* diver, plunger; *m* (orn.) diver; (orn.) dabchick (*Podilymbus podiceps*)
zambullidura *f* or **zambullimiento** *m* diving, plunging
zambullir §26 *va* to duck, give a ducking to; *vr* to dive, plunge, duck under; to hide
zambullo *m* big chamber pot
Zamora *f;* **no se ganó Zamora en una hora** Rome was not built in a day
zampa *f* pile, bearing pile
zampabodigos *mf* (*pl:* **-gos**) (coll.) var. of **zampatortas**
zampabollos *mf* (*pl:* **-llos**) (coll.) var. of **zampatortas**
zampacuartillos *mf* (*pl:* **-llos**) (coll.) soak, toper
zampalimosnas *mf* (*pl:* **-nas**) (coll.) bum, common bum
zampapalo *mf* (coll.) var. of **zampatortas**
zampar *va* to slip away, to hide away; to gobble down; *vr* to slip away, to hide away
zampatortas *mf* (*pl:* **-tas**) (coll.) glutton; (coll.) boor
zampeado *m* (constr.) pilework and rubble, grillage
zampear *va* to strengthen (*soil*) with a grillage
zampón -pona *adj* (coll.) gluttonous; *mf* (coll.) glutton
zampoña *f* rustic flute, shepherd's pipe; boy's flute made of green cane; (coll.) triviality, nonsense
zampuzar §76 *va* to duck, give a ducking to; to slip away, to hide away
zampuzo *m* ducking; hiding
zamuro *m* (orn.) turkey buzzard
zanahoria *f* (bot.) carrot
zanahoriate *m* var. of **azanahoriate**
zanate *m* (Am.) grackle (*Quiscalus macrourus*)
zanca *f* long leg (*of bird*); (coll.) long leg, shank; horse (*of staircase*); **andar en zancas de araña** (coll.) to resort to subterfuge, to shirk; **por zancas o por barrancas** (coll.) by hook or crook
zancada *f* long stride; **en dos zancadas** (coll.) in a jiffy
zancadilla *f* trip, tripping; (coll.) booby trap, trick; **echarle la zancadilla a uno** to stick out one's foot and trip someone
zancajear *vn* to rush around
zancajera *f* footing of running board
zancajiento -ta *adj* var. of **zancajoso**
zancajo *m* heel; heel bone; heel (*of shoe or stocking*); (coll.) ugly little person; **no llegar a los zancajos** or **al zancajo a** (coll.) to not come up to, to not be the equal of; **roer los zancajos a** (coll.) to talk behind the back of
zancajoso -sa *adj* duck-toed; big-heeled; dirty-heeled; with the heels of one's stockings out
zancarrón *m* (coll.) leg bone stripped of flesh; (coll.) skinny, dirty old fellow; (coll.) ignorant teacher, teacher who does not know his subject
zanco *m* stilt; **en zancos** (coll.) in a lofty station
zancón -cona *adj* (coll.) long-shanked, long-legged
zancudo -da *adj* long-shanked, long-legged; (orn.) wading; *m* (Am.) mosquito; *f* (orn.) wader, wading bird
zandía *f* var. of **sandía**
zanfonía *f* hurdy-gurdy
zangala *f* buckram
zangamanga *f* (coll.) trick
zanganada *f* (coll.) impertinence, impropriety
zangandongo -ga, zangandullo -lla or **zangandungo -ga** *mf* (coll.) worthless loafer
zanganear *vn* (coll.) to drone, to loaf, to idle
zángano *m* (ent.) drone; (fig.) drone, idler, sponger
zangarilleja *f* slattern, trollop
zangarrear *vn* (coll.) to thrum a guitar
zangarriana *f* slight recurring indisposition; (vet.) dropsy; (coll.) gloominess, blues
zangarullón *m* (coll.) var. of **zangón**
zangolotear *va* (coll.) to jiggle; *vn* (coll.) to flit around, to fuss around; *vr* (coll.) to jiggle; (coll.) to flop around, to swing, to slam
zangoloteo *m* (coll.) jiggle, jiggling; (coll.) flitting, fuss, bother; (coll.) slam, rattle
zangolotina *f* grown girl who tries to pass as a child
zangolotino *m* grown boy who tries to pass as a child
zangón *m* (coll.) lanky young loafer
zangotear *va* (coll.) to jiggle, jiggle around
zangoteo *m* (coll.) jiggle, jiggling
zanguango -ga *adj* (coll.) slothful; *mf* (coll.) loafer; *f* (coll.) malingering; (coll.) flattery; **hacer la zanguanga** (coll.) to malinger
zanguayo *m* (coll.) sly lanky fellow
zanja *f* ditch, trench; (Am.) gully; **abrir las zanjas** to lay the foundations
zanjar *va* to dig a ditch or ditches in; to settle, clear up, expedite
zanjón *m* deep ditch, deep drain
zanqueador -dora *adj* waddling; *mf* waddler
zanqueamiento *m* waddling
zanquear *vn* to waddle; to rush around
zanquilargo -ga *adj* long-shanked, long-legged
zanquilla *mf* (coll.) short-legged little runt
zanquituerto -ta *adj* bandy-legged
zanquivano -na *adj* (coll.) spindle-shanked, spindle-legged
zapa *f* spade; sap, trenching; sharkskin; shagreen (*rough skin of certain sharks*); sharkskin finish (*on metal*)
zapador *m* (mil.) sapper
zapalote *m* (bot.) plantain
zapapico *m* mattock, pickax
zapar *va & vn* to mine, to excavate
zaparrada *f* blow with claw, clawing
zaparrastrar *vn* (coll.) to trail one's clothes
zaparrastroso -sa *adj* (coll.) ragged, shabby, filthy; *mf* (coll.) ragamuffin, tatterdemalion
zaparrazo *m* (coll.) var. of **zaparrada**
zapata *f* half boot; shoe (*of a brake; of electric car for taking current from third rail*); (naut.) shoe (*of anchor*); (naut.) false keel
zapatazo *m* blow with a shoe; thud, bump, bang; clatter or rattle of horse's hoofs; (naut.) flapping (*of a sail*); **mandar a zapatazos** (coll.) to have an ascendancy over; **tratar a zapatazos** (coll.) to abuse, ill-treat
zapateado *m* clog dance, tap dance
zapateador -dora *adj* clog-dancing; *mf* clog dancer
zapatear *va* to hit with the shoe; to tap with the feet; to touch repeatedly with the button of the foil; (coll.) to abuse, to ill-treat; *vn* to tap-dance; (naut.) to flap (*said of sails*); *vr* to hold out, hold one's own
zapateo *m* tapping with the feet; tap dance, tap dancing
zapatera *f* see **zapatero**
zapateresco -ca *adj* (hum.) shoemaker's, (pertaining to a) shoemaker
zapatería *f* shoemaking; shoe store; shoemaker's shop
zapateril *adj* shoemaker's, (pertaining to a) shoemaker
zapatero -ra *adj* hard, raw, poorly cooked; spoiled (*olive*); *mf* shoemaker; shoe dealer; **quedarse zapatero** (coll.) to not take a trick; **zapatero de viejo** or **zapatero remendón** shoemaker, shoe repairer, cobbler; *m* (ent.) water strider; (ichth.) cutlass fish; *f* shoemaker's wife
zapateta *f* slap on foot or shoe while jumping; *interj* upon my word!
zapatilla *f* slipper; pump (*low shoe*); gasket; leather washer; washer (*e.g., for a spigot*); chamois washer (*for keys of wind instrument*); leather tip or button (*of a foil*); cloven hoof; **zapatilla de baño** bath or bathing slipper; **zapatilla de la reina** (bot.) large-flowered hypecoum; **zapatilla de señorita** (bot.) lady-slipper
zapatillazo *m* blow with a slipper
zapatillero -ra *mf* maker of slippers, dealer in slippers
zapatito *m* little shoe; **zapatito de la reina** (bot.) butterfly pea

zapato *m* shoe, low shoe; **andar con zapatos de fieltro** to gumshoe; **como tres en un zapato** (coll.) like sardines; (coll.) in straits, hard up; **lamer los zapatos a** (coll.) to lick the boots of; **saber (uno) dónde le aprieta el zapato** (coll.) to know one's own mind; **zapato inglés** low shoe; **zapatos papales** overshoes
zapatón -tona *adj* (Am.) tough, leathery; *m* big shoe; (Am.) overshoe; **zapatones** *mpl* spurs (*for fighting cocks*)
zapatudo -da *adj* wearing clodhoppers; big-hoofed; big-clawed; (mach.) provided or equipped with a shoe
zape *interj* scat!
zapear *va* to chase away (*a cat*); (coll.) to scare away
zapote *m* (bot.) sapodilla; **zapote chico** (bot.) marmalade tree; marmalade plum
zapotillo *m* (bot.) marmalade tree
zapuzar §76 *va* to duck
zaque *m* goatskin, wineskin; (coll.) drunk, drunkard
zaquear *va* to rack from one wineskin to another; to carry in wineskins
Zaqueo *m* (Bib.) Zaccheus
zaquizamí *m* (*pl:* **-míes**) garret, attic; hovel, pigpen
zar *m* czar
zarabanda *f* (mus.) saraband; noise, uproar
zarabandista *mf* composer of sarabands; saraband dancer; noisy person, lively person
zarabutear *va* (coll.) var. of **zaragutear**
zarabutero -ra *adj & mf* (coll.) var. of **zaragutero**
zaragalla *f* fine charcoal
zaragata *f* (coll.) row, fight, scuffle
zaragatería *f* rowdyism, hooliganism
zaragatero -ra *adj* (coll.) rowdyish; *mf* (coll.) rowdy, hooligan
zaragatona *f* (bot.) fleawort
Zaragoza *f* Saragossa
zaragozano -na *adj* (pertaining to) Saragossa; *mf* native or inhabitant of Saragossa
zaragüelles *mpl* breeches; (coll.) coarse bloomers; (dial.) drawers; (bot.) reed grass
zaragutear *va* (coll.) to bungle, to botch
zaragutero -ra *adj* (coll.) bungling; *mf* (coll.) bungler
zaramagullón *m* (orn.) dabchick, grebe
zaranda *f* sieve, screen
zarandador -dora *mf* sifter, winnower
zarandajas *fpl* (coll.) trifles, odds and ends
zarandalí *adj* (*pl:* **-líes**) (prov.) black-spotted (*dove*)
zarandar *va* to sift, to screen, to winnow; to slip or slide along; to select, pick out, separate; (coll.) to take the pick of; (coll.) to jiggle; *vr* to slip or slide along; (coll.) to jiggle
zarandear *va* to sift, to screen, to winnow; (coll.) to jiggle; *vr* to toil, to wear oneself out; (coll.) to jiggle
zarandeo *m* sifting, screening, winnowing; toiling, drudgery; (coll.) jiggle, jiggling
zarandero -ra *mf* var. of **zarandador**
zarandillo *m* small sieve, small screen; (coll.) harum-scarum; (coll.) live wire; **traerle a uno como un zarandillo** (coll.) to keep someone on the go
zarapatel *m* salmagundi
zarapico *m* (bot.) candytuft; (orn.) curlew
zarapito *m* (orn.) curlew
zaratán *m* (path.) cancer of the breast
zaraza *f* gingham, chintz, printed cotton; **zarazas** *fpl* animal poison (*made of powdered glass and poisonous substances*)
zarcear *va* to clean out (*pipes, tubes, etc.*) with brambles; *vn* to hunt in the underbrush (*said of a dog*); to rush back and forth
zarceño -ña *adj* brambly
zarceta *f* (orn.) garganey
zarcillitos *mpl* (bot.) quaking grass
zarcillo *m* eardrop; weeding hoe; (bot.) tendril; (dial.) hoop
zarco -ca *adj* light-blue (*eyes*)
zarevitz *m* czarevitch
zargatona *f* var. of **zaragatona**
zariano -na *adj* czarish
zarigüeya *f* (zool.) opossum
zarina *f* czarina
zarismo *m* czarism
zarista *mf* czarist
zarja *f* var. of **azarja**
zarpa *f* paw, claw (*of beast*); (constr.) projection of footing (*of a wall*); mud sticking to lower part of clothing; (naut.) weighing anchor
zarpada *f* blow with claw, clawing
zarpar *va* (naut.) to weigh (*anchor*); *vn* (naut.) to weigh anchor, set sail
zarpazo *m* blow with claw, clawing; thud, bump
zarposo -sa *adj* mud-splashed, mud-bespattered
zarracatería *f* (coll.) insincere flattery
zarracatín *m* (coll.) sharp dealer
zarramplín *m* (coll.) botcher, bungler
zarramplinada *f* (coll.) botch, bungle
zarrapastra *f* (coll.) mud sticking to lower part of clothing
zarrapastrón -trona or **zarrapastroso -sa** *adj & mf* (coll.) var. of **zaparrastroso**
zarria *f* mud sticking to clothes; thong, leather strap; rag, tatter
zarriento -ta or **zarrioso -sa** *adj* mud-splashed, mud-bespattered
zarza *f* (bot.) blackberry, blackberry bush, bramble
zarzagán *m* cold northeast wind
zarzaganillo *m* stormy northeast wind
zarzahán *m* striped colored silk
zarzal *m* blackberry patch; underbrush, brambles
zarzamora *f* blackberry, brambleberry (*fruit*)
zarzaparrilla *f* (bot.) sarsaparilla (*plant, extract, and drink*)
zarzaparrillar *m* sarsaparilla field
zarzaperruna *f* (bot.) dog rose (*plant and fruit*)
zarzarrosa *f* dog rose (*flower*)
zarzo *m* hurdle, wattle
zarzoso -sa *adj* brambly, bushy
zarzuela *f* (theat.) zarzuela (*Spanish musical comedy with alternating music and dialogue*); **zarzuela grande** three-act zarzuela
zarzuelero -ra *adj* (pertaining to the) zarzuela
zarzuelista *mf* composer of zarzuelas
zas *interj* bang!; **¡zas, zas!** bing, bang!
zascandil *m* (coll.) meddler, schemer
zascandilear *vn* to meddle, to scheme
zata or **zatara** *f* raft
zato *m* piece of bread
zazo -za or **zazoso -sa** *adj* stammering, stuttering
Zebedeo *m* (Bib.) Zebedee
zedilla *f* c cedilla; cedilla
zéjel *m* popular Spanish-Arabic verse form consisting of an initial theme and a number of three-line monorhymed stanzas each followed by a line in rhyme with the initial theme
Zelanda, la Zeeland; **Nueva Zelanda** New Zealand
zelandés -desa *adj & mf* var. of **celandés**
Zelandia, la var. of **la Zelanda**
zenit *m* var. of **cenit**
Zenón *m* Zeno
zepelín *m* zeppelin
zeugma or **zeuma** *f* (rhet.) zeugma
Zeus *m* (myth.) Zeus
zigodáctilo -la *adj & f* (orn.) zygodactyl
zigofiláceo -a *adj* var. of **cigofiláceo**
zigoma *f* var. of **cigoma**
zigomático -ca *adj* var. of **cigomático**
zigomorfo -fa *adj* (biol.) zygomorphic or zygomorphous
zigospora *f* (bot.) zygospore
zigoto *m* var. of **cigoto**
zigzag *m* zigzag
zigzaguear *vn* to zigzag
zimasa *f* (biochem.) zymase
zimo *m* var. of **cimo**
zimógeno *m* var. of **cimógeno**
zimótico -ca *adj* var. of **cimótico**
zinc *m* (*pl:* **zinces**) var. of **cinc**
zipizape *m* (coll.) scuffle, row
zircón *m* var. of **circón**
zircona *f* var. of **circona**
zirconio *m* var. of **circonio**
ziriano *m* Zyrian (*a Finno-Ugric language*)

zis, zas *interj* (coll.) bing, bang!
ziszás *m* zigzag; (fort.) zigzag intrenchment
zoantropía *f* (path.) zoanthropy
zoca *f* see **zoco**
zócalo *m* (arch.) socle; (rad.) socket; (Am.) center of public square
zocatear *vr* to become corky or pithy
zocato -ta *adj* corky, pithy (*fruit*); (coll.) left; (coll.) left-handed; *mf* (coll.) left-handed person
zoclo *m* wooden shoe, clog
zoco -ca *adj* (coll.) left; (coll.) left-handed; *mf* (coll.) left-handed person; *m* wooden shoe, clog; Moroccan market or market place; (arch.) socle; **andar de zocos en colodros** to go from bad to worse; *f* public square
zodiacal *adj* zodiacal
zodíaco *m* (astr.) zodiac
zofra *f* Moorish carpet or rug
zoilo *m* envious critic
zolocho -cha *adj* (coll.) simple, silly; *mf* (coll.) simpleton
zollipar *vn* (coll.) to sob
zollipo *m* (coll.) sob
zoma *f* coarse flour, middling
zompo -pa *adj & mf* var. of **zopo**
zona *f* zone; belt, girdle; **zona a batir** target area; **Zona del Canal** Canal Zone; **zona escolar** school zone; **zona glacial** frigid zone; **zona templada** temperate zone; **zona tórrida** torrid zone; **zona tropical** tropics or Tropics; *m* (path.) zona, zoster, shingles
zonado -da *adj* zoned (*striped*)
zonal *adj* zonal
zoncería *f* insipidity; dullness, inanity, nonsense
zonificación *f* zoning
zonote *m* (Am.) var. of **cenote**
zonula *f* zonule
zonzo -za *adj* insipid, tasteless; dull, inane; *mf* boob, simpleton; *m* (orn.) cedarbird
zonzorrión -rriona *adj* (coll.) dull, inane; *mf* (coll.) dullard, dolt
zoo *m* (coll.) zoo (*zoölogical garden*)
zoocecidia *f* (zool.) zoöcecidium
zoófito *m* (zool.) zoöphyte
zoogeografía *f* zoögeography
zooglea *f* (bact.) zoögloea
zoografía *f* zoögraphy
zoología *f* zoölogy
zoológico -ca *adj* zoölogical
zoólogo -ga *mf* zoölogist
zoometría *f* zoömetry
zoométrico -ca *adj* zoömetric
zoomorfismo *m* zoömorphism
zoonosis *f* (path.) zoönosis
zooplancton *m* (zool.) zoöplankton
zooplastia *f* (surg.) zoöplasty
zooquímico -ca *adj* zoöchemical; *f* zoöchemistry
zoospora *f* (bot.) zoöspore
zoosporangio *m* (bot.) zoösporangium
zootecnia *f* zoötechny
zootomía *f* zoötomy
zootropo *m* zoetrope (*optical toy*)
zopas *mf* see **zopo**
zopenco -ca *adj* (coll.) dull, doltish; *mf* (coll.) dullard, dolt
zopetero *m* slope, embankment
zopilote *m* (orn.) carrion crow, black vulture; **zopilote de montaña** (orn.) turkey buzzard
zopisa *f* pitch, tar; pine tar; ointment of pine tar and wax
zopitas *mf* (*pl:* **-tas**) (hum.) lisper
zopo -pa *adj* crippled; *mf* cripple; **zopas** *mf* (*pl:* **-pas**) (coll.) lisper
zoqueta *f* wooden guard to protect the left hand from the sickle
zoquete *m* block, chunk, end (*of wood*); bit of bread; blockhead, chump; (coll.) fat and ugly little runt
zoquetero -ra *mf* bum
zoquetudo -da *adj* coarse, rough
zoroastriano -na *adj & mf* Zoroastrian
zoroástrico -ca *adj* Zoroastrian
zoroastrismo *m* Zoroastrianism
Zoroastro *m* Zoroaster
zorongo *m* Aragonese kerchief (*folded like bandage around head*); flat chignon
zorra *f* (zool.) fox; female fox; (coll.) foxy person; prostitute; drunkenness; truck, dray; (*cap.*) *f* (astr.) Fox, Vulpecula; **pillar una zorra** (coll.) to get drunk; **zorra de mar** (ichth.) fox shark, thresher shark
zorrastrón -trona *adj* (coll.) crafty, tricky; *mf* (coll.) crafty person, tricky person
zorrera *f* see **zorrero**
zorrería *f* foxiness
zorrero -ra *adj* foxy, sly; slow, tardy; fox-hunting (*dog*); large (*shot*); (naut.) heavy-sailing; *m* royal game warden (*whose duty it was to kill foxes, wolves, birds of prey, and other harmful animals*); *f* fox hole; (coll.) confusion, worry; smoke-filled room
zorrillo *m* (zool.) skunk
zorro *m* (zool.) male fox; fox (*fur*); (coll.) fox, foxy fellow; (coll.) person who plays stupid; **zorros** *mpl* duster; **estar hecho un zorro** (coll.) to be overwhelmed with sleep; (coll.) to be dull and sullen; **hacerse el zorro** (coll.) to pretend ignorance, to pretend not to hear; **zorro azul** (zool.) blue fox; **zorro negro** (zool.) raccoon; **zorro plateado** (zool.) silver fox
zorrocloco *m* (coll.) sly boob; (coll.) caress
zorronglón -glona *adj* (coll.) grumbling; *mf* (coll.) grumbler
zorrullo *m* var. of **zurullo**
zorruno -na *adj* foxlike, foxy
zorzal *m* (orn.) fieldfare; sly fellow; (Am.) simpleton, boob; **zorzal marino** (ichth.) black wrasse
zorzaleño -ña *adj* crescent (*olive*)
zoster *f* (path.) zoster, shingles
zote *adj* simple, stupid; *mf* simpleton, dolt
zozobra *f* capsizing, foundering, sinking; worry, anxiety
zozobrar *va* to sink; to wreck (*a business*); *vn* to capsize, founder, sink; to be in jeopardy; to worry, to fret; *vr* to capsize, founder, sink
zozobroso -sa *adj* worried, anxious, restless
zúa *f* var. of **azud**
zuavo *m* (mil.) Zouave
zubia *f* drain, channel
zucarino -na *adj* sugary, sweet
zueco *m* wooden shoe, clog, sabot; wood-soled or cork-soled shoe
zuela *f* var. of **azuela**
-zuelo -la *suffix dim & pej* var. of **-uelo** and attached to polysyllables ending in **d, e, n, r,** an accented vowel, an unaccented diphthong, or an unaccented vowel in a word with a diphthong in its root, e.g., **pobrezuelo** poorish; **ladronzuelo** petty thief; **mujerzuela** woman of no account; **lengüezuela** little tongue; **piedrezuela** little stone; **huevezuelo** little egg. The radical diphthong sometimes disappears when the suffix is added, e.g., **pontezuelo** small bridge; **tendezuela** little shop; **terrezuela** worthless piece of ground
zuingliano -na *adj & mf* Zwinglian
zulacar §86 *va* to waterproof
zulaque *m* waterproof packing; waterproof paving material
zulaquear *va* var. of **zulacar**
zulú (*pl:* **-lús** or **-lúes**) *adj & mf* Zulu
Zululandia *f* Zululand
zulla *f* (bot.) sulla clover, French honeysuckle; (coll.) excrement (*human*)
zullar *vr* (coll.) to have a movement of the bowels; (coll.) to break wind
zullenco -ca *adj* (coll.) windy, flatulent
zullón -llona *adj* (coll.) windy, flatulent; *m* (coll.) wind, flatulence
zumacal *m* planting of sumachs
zumacar *m* planting of sumachs; *va* to dress or tan with sumach
zumacaya *f* var. of **zumaya**
zumaque *m* (bot.) sumach; (coll.) grape wine; **zumaque del Japón** (bot.) tree of heaven; **zumaque venenoso** (bot.) poison sumach, poison ivy
zumaya *f* (orn.) goatsucker; (orn.) tawny owl; (orn.) secretary bird
zumba *f* bell worn by leading mule; whistle (*toy made to spin on end of a string*); fun, joke; **hacer zumba a** to make fun of

zumbador -dora *adj* buzzing; *m* buzzer; (elec.) buzzer; (Am.) hummingbird
zumbar *va* to make fun of; to let have, e.g., **le zumbó una bofetada** he let him have a slap in the face; *vn* to buzz, to hum; to ring (*said of the ears*); **zumbar a** to be close to, e.g., **le zumban los sesenta años** he is close to sixty years of age; *vr* to make fun of each other; **zumbarse de** to make fun of
zumbel *m* string used to spin a top; (coll.) frown
zumbido *m* buzz, hum; (coll.) blow, smack; **zumbido de ocupación** busy signal (*of telephone*); **zumbido de oídos** (path.) ringing in the ears, tinnitus
zumbo *m* buzz, hum; (Am.) gourd
zumbón -bona *adj* funny, playful, waggish; *mf* wag, jester
zumiento -ta *adj* juicy
zumillo *m* (bot.) green dragon; (bot.) deadly carrot
zumo *m* juice; profit, advantage; **zumo de cepas** or **parras** (coll.) fruit of the vine, wine; **zumo de naranja** orange juice; **zumo de uva** grape juice
zumoso -sa *adj* juicy
zuna *f* Sunna or Sunnah; (dial.) treachery; (dial.) viciousness (*of a horse*)
zunchar *va* to band, to hoop, to fasten with a band or hoop
zuncho *m* band, hoop, ring; **zuncho de botalón** (naut.) boom iron
zuño *m* frown
zupia *f* dregs (*of wine*); wine full of dregs; slop; (fig.) scum, trash
zurano -na *adj* wild (*dove or pigeon*)
zurcido *m* darn, darning; **zurcido invisible** invisible mending
zurcidor -dora *adj* darning; *mf* darner
zurcidura *f* darning
zurcir §50 *va* to darn; to strand; to join, unite; (coll.) to hatch, concoct (*a lie*), to weave (*a tissue of lies*)
zurdazo *m* blow with the left (*hand*); (box.) left
zurdear *vn* to be left-handed
zurdería *f* left-handedness
zurdo -da *adj* left; left-handed; (mach.) left-handed (*e.g., screw*); **a zurdas** with the left hand; the wrong way; *mf* left-handed person

zurear *vn* to coo
zureo *m* cooing
zurito -ta *adj* stock (*dove*); *f* (orn.) stock dove
zuro -ra *adj* wild (*dove or pigeon*); *m* stripped corncob
zurra *f* currying, dressing; scuffle, quarrel; grind (*long hard work or study*); drubbing, thrashing
zurrador *m* leather currier or dresser
zurrapa *f* filament, thread; (coll.) trash, rubbish; (coll.) ugly, skinny young fellow; **con zurrapas** (coll.) in an uncleanly way
zurrapelo *m* (coll.) dressing-down, sharp reprimand
zurrapiento -ta or **zurraposo -sa** *adj* dreggy, turbid, roily
zurrar *va* to curry, to dress (*leather*); to get the best of; to dress down; (coll.) to drub, to thrash; *vr* to have an accident, to dirty oneself; (coll.) to be scared to death
zurriaga *f* whip, lash; (dial.) lark (*bird*)
zurriagar §59 *va* to whip, to horsewhip
zurriagazo *m* whipping, lashing; stroke of bad luck; unexpected abuse, unexpected slight
zurriago *m* whip, lash; strap used to spin a top
zurriar §90 *vn* var. of **zurrir**
zurribanda *f* (coll.) rain of blows; (coll.) scuffle, rumpus, row
zurriburri *m* (coll.) cur, contemptible fellow; (coll.) gang of crooks; (coll.) uproar, confusion
zurrido *m* buzzing, grating noise; (coll.) blow with a stick
zurrir *vn* to buzz, to grate
zurrón *m* shepherd's leather bag; husk; placenta; **zurrón de pastor** (bot.) shepherd's-purse
zurrona *f* (coll.) loose, crooked woman
zurronada *f* bagful
zurrusco *m* burnt toast
zurullo *m* (coll.) soft roll (*of anything*); (coll.) turd
zurumbático -ca *adj* stunned, bewildered
zurupeto *m* (coll.) unregistered broker
zutano -na *mf* (coll.) so-and-so
zuzo *interj* var. of **chucho**
zuzón *m* (bot.) groundsel
zuzunga *f* strainer, colander

CENTER SECTION — SECCIÓN CENTRAL

BREVE HISTORIA DE LA LENGUA INGLESA

Los orígenes del inglés. La lengua inglesa pertenece al subgrupo germánico occidental y fué introducida por los invasores anglos y sajones en los siglos quinto y sexto en el territorio que ocupa hoy la Gran Bretaña sobre un substrato celta. En sus orígenes se entremezclan dos corrientes lingüísticas, la germánica y la latina. En su estructura gramatical se parece al alemán, el holandés y las lenguas escandinavas al paso que en su léxico ofrece mucho parecido con el latín, el francés y las otras lenguas neolatinas. Su nombre actual deriva del de la tribu de los anglos de Northumbria que vinieron de la península danesa a mediados del siglo sexto. Con el tiempo adquirió el país asimismo el nombre de *Engla-land* (tierra de los anglos). El inglés como idioma ha tenido existencia independiente por sólo mil quinientos años. Se consideran tres períodos históricos en su evolución: el inglés antiguo (450-1150), que se confunde con el llamado anglosajón, el inglés medio (1150-1500) y el inglés moderno (desde 1500).

El inglés antiguo. El inglés antiguo constituye una lengua homogénea y original. Se caracterizaba por sus numerosas declinaciones de substantivos y adjetivos, muy semejantes a las del alemán moderno. Por otra parte, el verbo era más simple, valiéndose solamente de dos tiempos simples, el presente y el pasado. Había, sin embargo, más de trescientos verbos fuertes (o irregulares), como **speak, spoke, spoken** del inglés moderno, a diferencia de los verbos débiles, más simples y puramente germánicos, como **talk, talked, talked** del inglés moderno. Gran parte de esta estructura gramatical, poco necesaria para la adecuada expresión de las ideas, fué eliminada durante el período del inglés medio.

Durante el período del inglés antiguo la lengua estuvo expuesta a la influencia de varias lenguas extranjeras que le dieron un número considerable de palabras nuevas. Los anglosajones, algún tiempo antes de su llegada al territorio de la Gran Bretaña, habían sostenido prolongadas guerras y más tarde establecido relaciones comerciales con los romanos, aprendiendo de ellos palabras como **caseus** (cheese), **(libras) pondo** (pound), **strata (via)** (street) y **vinum** (wine). Sus relaciones con los celtas trajeron al idioma algunas palabras del celta y otras latinas que los celtas habían aprendido durante la ocupación romana desde el año 43 al 410 de la era cristiana. Al ser convertidos al cristianismo, los ingleses adoptaron, no sólo palabras como **alb, altar, creed** y **priest,** relativas a la Iglesia, sino varios cientos de otras palabras que la elevada cultura del clero les dió a conocer. La influencia extranjera de mayor importancia durante este período fué la de los piratas escandinavos que comenzaron a saquear las costas de Inglaterra en el año 787 y que en el siglo siguiente establecieron colonias de alguna importancia en la isla. Por espacio de más de doscientos años, el inglés y las lenguas escandinavas, especialmente el danés, se hablaron conjuntamente en el nordeste de Inglaterra. Cuán estrecha fué la unión de estos elementos lingüísticos es evidente si se considera que palabras tan comunes como **knife, sister, root, skin, trust** y **window** son todas de origen danés. Aun más significativo es el hecho de que los pronombres **they, their** y **them**, la forma **are** del verbo **be** y la conjunción **though**, palabras que muy raras veces pasan de un idioma a otro, entraron a formar parte del léxico inglés. Así vemos, en el período del inglés antiguo, el comienzo de la costumbre tan marcada en la lengua inglesa, de hacer adopciones frecuentes de otros idiomas, costumbre que constituye una de las características más notables del inglés en sus épocas subsiguientes.

El inglés medio. En el año de 1066, Guillermo, duque de Normandía, cumplió, por medio de la conquista, su pretensión al trono de Inglaterra. La conquista normanda originó una transformación cuyo resultado fué el inglés medio, con diferentes divisiones cronológicas. Así hay el de transición o semisajón (1150-1200), el primitivo (1200-1250), el normal (1250-1400) y el tardío (1400-1500). El léxico se afrancesó con 10.000 palabras relativas a la administración, el ejército, la Iglesia, la arquitectura, el arte, la moda y la vida aristocrática, la mayor parte de las cuales están todavía en uso al paso que la gramática abandonó las leyes flexionales y sintácticas del anglosajón. A raíz de la conquista normanda el substantivo perdió todos sus casos con excepción del posesivo. Los casos se expresan por simples preposiciones; únicamente en las desinencias -'s y -s' se sigue la antigua gramática anglosajona. Las diferentes declinaciones se ordenaron bajo una sola en la cual la s (o es) forma el plural, con excepción de un pequeño número de substantivos como **man** (*pl:* **men**), **tooth** (*pl:* **teeth**) y **child** (*pl:* **children**). El adjetivo y el artículo definido perdieron sus flexiones y son hoy invariables sin consideración del género, número y caso del substantivo que modifican. Y la pérdida de las terminaciones produjo paulatinamente el abandono de los géneros gramaticales. Más de la mitad de los trescientos verbos fuertes del inglés antiguo desaparecieron durante el período del inglés medio y quedan solamente unos setenta en el inglés moderno. Para fines del período, el sistema de flexiones se había reducido poco más o menos a la forma simple actualmente en uso.

El inglés moderno. Durante el Renacimiento, el inglés al latinizarse substituyó al latín como lengua apropiada para materias eruditas. Y en los siglos subsiguientes los sabios continuaron recurriendo a la autoridad de los autores clásicos griegos y romanos para refinar el léxico y fijar la lengua. Los resultados no fueron siempre felices. A principios del siglo dieciocho surgió un movimiento que abogaba por el establecimiento de una academia a imitación de la Academia Francesa, pero el proyecto fracasó. A falta de academia, continúa invocándose el buen uso para resolver los problemas de corrección lingüística.

En los últimos siglos se enriqueció el léxico con muchos neologismos para expresar los nuevos conceptos de la ciencia, la tecnología y la vida modernas. Se regularizó la ortografía, que era en exceso variable y que aún está muy en desacuerdo con la pronunciación.

La formación de palabras. Era característica del sistema de formación de palabras en el inglés antiguo la palabra compuesta que se explica por sí misma. Muchas de estas palabras compuestas fueron reemplazadas por palabras francesas ya completamente formadas, p.ej., **bookhouse** por **library** y **treewright** por **carpenter.** Pero aún hoy se forman palabras compuestas que se explican por sí mismas, como **bridgehead, late-comer** y **nose cone.**

Hay tres maneras en que dos o más palabras pueden ser unidas en nuevas unidades del vocabulario. Primero, algunas palabras van combinadas en una unidad simple, p.ej., **steamboat** buque de vapor. Segundo, algunas van combinadas por medio de un guión, p.ej., **scissors-grinder** afilador de tijeras. Y tercero, algunas van combinadas solamente en la idea, aunque en la forma permanecen separadas, p.ej., **race track** pista de carreras.

El uso del guión. Existe una relación muy estrecha entre muchos nombres del tercer grupo y los adjetivos correspondientes del segundo. Esto consiste en que los nombres del tercer grupo pueden hacerse adjetivos por la simple introducción del guión, p.ej., **air raid** ataque aéreo y **air-raid shelter** refugio contra ataques aéreos. Este empleo del guión para formar adjetivos compuestos se encuentra en particular en combinaciones de adjetivos (o adverbios) y participios activos (o participios pasados), p.ej., **good-looking, high-sounding, well-meaning, high-priced, ill-gotten, well-informed.** También se encuentra en combinaciones de nombres y participios activos (o participios pasados). Tales nombres son objeto directo del participio activo, p.ej., **my beer-drinking friends** mis amigos bebedores de cerveza, pero con el participio pasado tienen la fuerza del agente con la voz pasiva, p.ej., **war-torn Europe** la Europa devastada por la guerra. En combinaciones de nombres y participios activos de verbos intransitivos, el nombre tiene fuerza adverbial, p.ej., **my church-going friends** mis amigos que van a la iglesia (es decir, que frecuentan la iglesia). Las combinaciones de nombres y participios activos pueden usarse también como nombres substantivos, p.ej., **beer-drinking** la costumbre de beber cerveza.

Se emplea asimismo el guión para formar combinaciones adjetivales de un número cardinal y un nombre que denota medida, conservando siempre la forma singular del nombre, p.ej., **a ten-mile walk** una caminata de diez millas, **a two-year course** un curso de dos años. Y tales combinaciones pueden combinarse aun más con un adjetivo que corresponda al nombre que denota medida, p.ej., **a two-mile-long race track** una pista de dos millas de largo, **a three-month-old baby** un rorro de tres meses de edad.

Queremos señalar además que hay muchos compuestos adjetivales que se escriben con guión sólo cuando van delante del nombre substantivo a que califican, p.ej., **this is a worth-while book** éste es un libro de gran mérito, pero **this book is worth while** este libro es de gran mérito.

Variedades del inglés. El inglés moderno ofrece variedades dialectales y regionales. Se admiten, en general, un inglés del norte, que abarca los dialectos escoceses y desciende del antiguo inglés septentrional, un inglés sudoccidental, que desciende del antiguo sajón occidental y un inglés del centro-este, que se puede considerar como el idioma predominante de la isla. Fuera de Inglaterra existen variedades dialectales y coloniales y la lengua se ha enriquecido con voces y giros indígenas. En los Estados Unidos ha adquirido ciertas características distintivas, especialmente en la pronunciación y el léxico. Al mismo tiempo hay fuerzas que tienden a disminuir las dificultades que encuentran para comprenderse los angloparlantes de diversas procedencias. Por ejemplo, la aceptación y vulgarización del cine norteamericano ha familiarizado al público británico con el idioma familiar y popular de los Estados Unidos. En resumen, se puede afirmar la unidad fundamental de la lengua inglesa. Es el lazo de unión entre la gente de origen anglosajón de muchos países y entre diversas nacionalidades y razas de todas las partes del mundo.

RESUMEN DE GRAMÁTICA INGLESA

§1. Símbolos fonéticos. Pueden representarse aproximadamente todos los sonidos del idioma inglés con treinta y cuatro símbolos. En la lista que damos a continuación, cada símbolo va acompañado (1) de una palabra española o francesa que contiene un sonido (impreso en negrilla) más o menos parecido al sonido inglés referido y (2) de palabras inglesas que ejemplifican las varias grafías (también impresas en negrilla) empleadas para representar el sonido en este idioma. El signo ˈ antes de sílaba indica que tal sílaba lleva el acento principal, como en **father** [ˈfɑðər] y el signo ˌ antes de sílaba indica que tal sílaba lleva un acento menos fuerte que el principal, como en **fundamental** [ˌfʌndəˈmɛntəl].

VOCALES

SÍMBOLO	SONIDO	GRAFÍA
1. [æ]	Mucho más cerrado que la **a** de **claro.**	c**a**t [kæt] pl**ai**d [plæd]
2. [ɑ]	Como la **a** de am**a**do.	f**a**ther [ˈfɑðər] p**a**lm [pɑm] w**a**s [wɑz] h**ea**rth [hɑrθ] s**e**rgeant [ˈsɑrdʒənt] h**o**t [hɑt]
3. [e]	Más cerrado que la **e** de habl**é**. Suena a menudo como si fuese seguido de [ɪ], especialmente en final de sílaba acentuada.	f**a**ce [fes] r**ai**n [ren] r**ay** [re] g**ao**l [dʒel] g**au**ge [gedʒ] st**ea**k [stek] v**ei**l [vel] ob**ey** [oˈbe]
4. [ɛ]	Como la **e** de p**e**rro.	s**e**t [sɛt] **e**bb [ɛb] **a**ny [ˈɛnɪ] **ae**sthetic [ɛsˈθɛtɪk] s**ai**d [sɛd] s**ay**s [sɛz] l**ea**ther [ˈlɛðər] h**ei**fer [ˈhɛfər] l**eo**pard [ˈlɛpərd] fr**ie**nd [frɛnd] f**oe**tid [ˈfɛtɪd] b**u**ry [ˈbɛrɪ]
	En la mayor parte de las palabras en que [ɛ] va seguido de **r,** hay tendencia en algunas partes a articularlo más abiertamente y con más duración.	d**a**re [dɛr] **ae**ry [ˈɛrɪ] ch**ai**r [tʃɛr] pr**ay**er [prɛr] w**ea**r [wɛr] th**e**re [ðɛr] th**ei**r [ðɛr]
5. [ə]	Como la **e** del artículo definido francés l**e.**	orph**a**n [ˈɔrfən] mach**i**ne [məˈʃin] mount**ai**n [ˈmaʊntən] syst**e**m [ˈsɪstəm] penc**i**l [ˈpɛnsəl] gall**o**p [ˈgæləp] p**o**tato [pəˈteto] biol**o**gy [baɪˈɔlədʒɪ] aug**u**r [ˈɔgər] porp**oi**se [ˈpɔrpəs] curi**ou**s [ˈkjʊrɪəs]
6. [i]	Como la **i** de m**i**sa.	m**e** [mi] tr**ee** [tri] t**ea**m [tim] dec**ei**ve [dɪˈsiv] k**ey** [ki] p**eo**ple [ˈpipəl] mach**i**ne [məˈʃin] bel**ie**ve [bɪˈliv] **ae**gis [ˈidʒɪs] qu**ay** [ki] amo**e**ba [əˈmibə]

VOCALES

SÍMBOLO	SONIDO	GRAFÍA
7. [ɪ]	Un poco más abierto que la **i** de s**i**lba.	s**i**t [sɪt] s**ie**ve [sɪv] pr**e**tty ['prɪtɪ] b**ee**n [bɪn] b**ee**r [bɪr] w**o**men ['wɪmɪn] b**u**sy ['bɪzɪ] b**ui**ld [bɪld] h**y**mn [hɪm]
	Encuéntrase en sílaba inacentuada.	att**i**c ['ætɪk] fam**i**ne ['fæmɪn] Mond**ay** ['mʌndɪ] cott**a**ge ['kɑtɪdʒ] carr**ia**ge ['kærɪdʒ] sen**a**te ['sɛnɪt] coff**ee** ['kɑfɪ] for**ei**gn ['fɑrɪn] mon**ey** ['mʌnɪ] misch**ie**f ['mɪstʃɪf] cham**o**is ['ʃæmɪ] circ**ui**t ['sʌrkɪt] scarl**e**t ['skɑrlɪt]
8. [o]	Más cerrado que la **o** de b**o**ca. Suena a menudo como si fuese seguido de [ʊ].	n**o**te [not] r**oa**d [rod] c**o**mb [kom] t**oe** [to] br**oo**ch [brotʃ] th**ough** [ðo] kn**ow** [no] **owe** [o] h**au**tboy ['hobɔɪ] b**eau** [bo] s**ew** [so] y**eo**man ['jomən]
	Cuando [o] va seguido de una **r**, se debe sobrentender que se oye [ə] después de [o] en muchas partes de los Estados Unidos, aunque el sonido [ə] no está indicado ni en la ortografía ni en la representación fonética.	fl**oo**r [flor] m**o**re [mor]
9. [ɔ]	Más abierto que la **o** de t**o**rre.	**o**rder ['ɔrdər] wr**o**ng [rɔŋ] g**o**ne [gɔn] br**oa**d [brɔd] c**ou**rt [kɔrt] w**a**rm [wɔrm] s**a**lt [sɔlt] c**au**ght [kɔt] **au**stere [ɔs'tɪr] r**aw** [rɔ]
10. [u]	Como la **u** de d**u**da.	r**u**de [rud] pr**o**ve [pruv] d**o** [du] l**o**se [luz] t**o**mb [tum] can**oe** [kə'nu] f**oo**d [fud] fl**ue** [flu] fr**ui**t [frut] man**eu**ver [mə'nuvər] dr**ew** [dru] tw**o** [tu]
11. [ʊ]	Menos cerrado que la **u** de c**u**lto.	f**u**ll [fʊl] b**u**sh [bʊʃ] w**o**lf [wʊlf] t**ou**r [tʊr] l**oo**k [lʊk] sh**ou**ld [ʃʊd]

DIPTONGOS

SÍMBOLO	SONIDO	GRAFÍA
12. [ʌ]	Algo parecido a **eu** en la palabra francesa s**eu**l.	c**u**p [kʌp] s**u**ch [sʌtʃ] s**o**n [sʌn] c**o**ver ['kʌvər] fr**o**nt [frʌnt] m**o**ther ['mʌðər] m**o**ney ['mʌnɪ] d**oe**s [dʌz] fl**oo**d [flʌd] c**ou**ple ['kʌpəl] t**wo**pence ['tʌpəns]
13. [aɪ]	Como **ai** de habl**ái**s.	n**igh**t [naɪt] t**i**me [taɪm] l**ie** [laɪ] **ai**sle [aɪl] **aye** [aɪ] h**eigh**t [haɪt] **eye** [aɪ] t**ie** [taɪ] b**uy** [baɪ] sk**y** [skaɪ] l**ye** [laɪ]
	Cuando [aɪ] va seguido de una **r**, se debe sobrentender que se oye [ə] después de [aɪ], aunque el sonido [ə] no está indicado ni en la ortografía ni en la representación fonética.	f**i**re [faɪr] t**i**re [taɪr]
14. [aʊ]	Como **au** de p**au**sa.	b**ough** [baʊ] s**ou**nd [saʊnd] h**ow** [haʊ]
15. [ɔɪ]	Como **oy** de d**oy**.	ch**oi**ce [tʃɔɪs] **oi**l [ɔɪl] t**oy** [tɔɪ]
16. [b]	Como la **b** de cam**b**iar.	**b**ell [bɛl] ho**bb**y ['habɪ]
17. [d]	Como la **d** de con**d**e.	**d**ear [dir] la**dd**er ['lædər]
18. [f]	Como la **f** de **f**also.	**f**ace [fes] mu**ff**in ['mʌfɪn] tou**gh** [tʌf]
19. [g]	Como la **g** de **g**olpe.	**g**o [go] **g**ive [gɪv] a**gg**ressive [ə'grɛsɪv] e**x**act [ɛg'zækt]
20. [h]	Sonido más aspirado y más suave que el de la **j** de **j**amás.	**h**ome [hom] alco**h**ol ['ælkəhɔl] **wh**o [hu]
21. [j]	Como la **y** de cu**y**o.	**y**et [jɛt] **u**nit ['junɪt] on**i**on ['ʌnjən] f**eu**d [fjud] f**ew** [fju]
22. [k]	Como la **c** de **c**asa.	**c**ar [kar] a**cc**ount [ə'kaʊnt] **ch**ord [kɔrd] si**ck** [sɪk] **k**eep [kip] bo**x** [baks] a**cq**uaint [ə'kwent]
23. [l]	Como la **l** de **l**ago.	**l**ive [lɪv] a**ll**ow [ə'laʊ]
24. [m]	Como la **m** de **m**anteca.	**m**ore [mor] su**mm**on ['sʌmən]

CONSONANTES

SÍMBOLO	SONIDO	GRAFÍA
25. [n]	Como la **n** de **n**adar.	**n**ot [nɑt] ma**nn**er [ˈmænər]
26. [p]	Como la **p** de ma**p**a.	**p**ay [pe] a**pp**oint [əˈpɔɪnt]
27. [r]	La **r** más común en la mayor parte de los Estados Unidos y en muchas partes de Inglaterra es un sonido semivocal que se articula con la punta de la lengua elevada más hacia el paladar duro que en la **r** fricativa española y aun doblada hacia atrás. Intervocálica y al final de sílaba, es muy débil y casi no se puede oír.	**r**at [ræt] a**r**m [ɑrm] ca**r** [kɑr] ta**rr**y [ˈtærɪ]
	El símbolo [r] precedido de [ʌ] o [ə] representa un solo sonido, el de la llamada vocal de colorido de **r**, producido sin el sonido consonantal. Véase 40 y 41 abajo.	hu**r**t [hʌrt] ea**r**ly [ˈʌrlɪ] fathe**r** [ˈfɑðər] pe**r**ceive [pərˈsiv]
28. [s]	Como la **s** de ca**s**a.	**s**ell [sɛl] **c**ent [sɛnt] fa**ç**ade [fəˈsɑd] bo**x** [bɑks] quart**z** [kwɔrts]
29. [t]	Como la **t** de car**t**a.	**t**ell [tɛl] la**tt**er [ˈlætər] **Th**omas [ˈtɑməs] dripp**ed** [drɪpt]
30. [v]	Como la **v** de la palabra francesa sa**v**oir.	**v**acate [ˈveket] clo**v**er [ˈklovər] o**f** [ɑv]
31. [w]	Como la **u** de h**u**evo.	**w**orse [wʌrs] t**w**ice [twaɪs] pers**u**ade [pərˈswed] q**u**een [kwin] ch**o**ir [kwaɪr]
	Hay dos palabras que no tienen grafía para representar el sonido [w].	one [wʌn] once [wʌns]
32. [z]	Como la **s** de de**s**de.	**z**est [zɛst] snee**z**e [sniz] bu**zz**er [ˈbʌzər] bu**s**y [ˈbɪzɪ] her**s** [hʌrz] matche**s** [ˈmætʃɪz] an**x**iety [æŋˈzaɪətɪ] po**ss**ess [pəˈzɛs]
33. [ð]	Como la **d** de na**d**a.	**th**en [ðɛn] fa**th**er [ˈfɑðər]
34. [θ]	Como la **z** de **z**orro en la pronunciación de Castilla.	**th**in [θɪn] mou**th** [maʊθ] e**th**er [ˈiθər]
35. [ʃ]	Como **ch** de la palabra francesa **ch**emin.	**sh**eet [ʃit] ma**ch**ine [məˈʃin] o**c**ean [ˈoʃən] vi**c**ious [ˈvɪʃəs] man**s**ion [ˈmænʃən] mi**ss**ion [ˈmɪʃən] na**t**ion [ˈneʃən] **s**ugar [ˈʃʊgər] con**sc**ious [ˈkɑnʃəs] an**x**ious [ˈæŋkʃəs]
36. [ʒ]	Como la **j** de la palabra francesa **j**ambe.	a**z**ure [ˈæʒər] gla**z**ier [ˈgleʒər] plea**s**ure [ˈplɛʒər] vi**s**ion [ˈvɪʒən] rou**g**e [ruʒ]
37. [ŋ]	Como la **n** de arra**n**car.	si**ng** [sɪŋ] co**n**quer [ˈkɑŋkər] a**n**xiety [æŋˈzaɪətɪ]

Símbolos Combinados

SÍMBOLOS	SONIDO	GRAFÍA
38. [tʃ]	Como la **ch** de mu**ch**o.	**ch**ief [tʃif] mu**ch** [mʌtʃ] ca**tch** [kætʃ] righ**te**ous ['raɪtʃəs] ques**ti**on ['kwɛstʃən] na**t**ural ['nætʃərəl]
39. [dʒ]	Como la **y** de cón**y**uge y **dj** de la palabra francesa a**dj**acent.	**g**em [dʒɛm] **j**ust [dʒʌst] ver**d**ure ['vʌrdʒər] sol**di**er ['soldʒər] bri**dg**e [brɪdʒ] exa**gg**erate [ɛg'zædʒəret] a**dj**ourn [ə'dʒʌrn]
40. [ʌr]	El símbolo [ʌ] y el símbolo [r] que le sigue, representan en este diccionario un solo sonido, el de la llamada vocal de colorido de **r**, acentuada. Es más largo y más tenso que [ʌ]. Se produce con la lengua en la acostumbrada posición elevada para la **r** pero sin el sonido de **r**. Véase 27 arriba.	h**ur**t [hʌrt] h**er**b [hʌrb] **ear**ly ['ʌrlɪ] b**ir**d [bʌrd] w**or**m [wʌrm] c**olo**nel ['kʌrnəl] c**our**age ['kʌrɪdʒ] m**yr**tle [mʌrtəl]
41. [ər]	El símbolo [ə] y el símbolo [r] que le sigue, representan en este diccionario un solo sonido, el de la llamada vocal de colorido de **r**, inacentuada. Se produce con la lengua en la acostumbrada posición elevada para la **r** pero sin el sonido de **r**. Véase 27 arriba.	fath**er** ['fɑðər] li**ar** ['laɪər] p**er**ceive [pər'siv] mart**yr** ['mɑrtər] cent**re** ['sɛntər]
42. [hw]	Como **ju** en **ju**erga pero con la **j** mucho más suave que en español.	**wh**ile [hwaɪl] **wh**en [hwɛn]
43. [ll]	Mucho más largo que [l] pero de carácter semejante. No tiene nada que ver con la **ll** española.	so**lel**y ['sollɪ] coo**ll**y ['kullɪ] sou**ll**ess ['sollɪs]

Sonidos Extranjeros

SÍMBOLO	SONIDO	GRAFÍA
44. [a]	francés	**a**vant-g**a**rde [avɑ̃'gard]
45. [ɑ̃]	francés	contret**em**ps [kɔ̃trə'tɑ̃]
46. [æ̃]	francés	anc**ien** régime [ɑ̃sjæ̃ re'ʒim]
47. [õ]	francés	b**on** mot [bõ'mo]
48. [ø]	francés	mil**ieu** [mi'ljø]
49. [œ]	alemán	G**ö**ttingen ['gœtɪŋən]
50. [y]	francés	au j**u**s [o'ʒy]
51. [x]	alemán	Ma**ch**e ['mɑxə]

§2. El número. 1. Añaden una **s** [s] para formar el plural los substantivos que terminan en uno de los siguientes sonidos consonantes sordos: [f], [k], [p], [t] y [θ].

SONIDO FINAL	SINGULAR	PLURAL
[f]	**chief** [tʃif] **tariff** [ˈtærɪf] **cough** [kɔf] **fife** [faɪf]	**chiefs** [tʃifs] **tariffs** [ˈtærɪfs] **coughs** [kɔfs] **fifes** [faɪfs]
[k]	**sack** [sæk] **rake** [rek]	**sacks** [sæks] **rakes** [reks]
[p]	**cap** [kæp] **pipe** [paɪp]	**caps** [kæps] **pipes** [paɪps]
[t]	**cat** [kæt] **fate** [fet]	**cats** [kæts] **fates** [fets]
[θ]	**death** [dɛθ]	**deaths** [dɛθs]

(*a*) Sin embargo, la mayor parte de los substantivos que terminan en **f** [f] y **fe** [f] cambian **f** y **fe** en **ves** [vz] para formar el plural.

SINGULAR	PLURAL
calf [kæf]	**calves** [kævz]
half [hæf]	**halves** [hævz]
leaf [lif]	**leaves** [livz]
thief [θif]	**thieves** [θivz]
wolf [wulf]	**wolves** [wulvz]
knife [naɪf]	**knives** [naɪvz]
life [laɪf]	**lives** [laɪvz]
wife [waɪf]	**wives** [waɪvz]

Los siguientes substantivos tienen el plural regular.

SINGULAR	PLURAL
chief [tʃif]	**chiefs** [tʃifs]
dwarf [dwɔrf]	**dwarfs** [dwɔrfs]
handkerchief [ˈhæŋkərtʃɪf]	**handkerchiefs** [ˈhæŋkərtʃɪfs]
proof [pruf]	**proofs** [prufs]
roof [ruf]	**roofs** [rufs]

Los siguientes substantivos tienen el plural regular e irregular.

SINGULAR	PLURAL
scarf [skɑrf]	{ **scarfs** [skɑrfs] { **scarves** [skɑrvz]
wharf [hwɔrf]	{ **wharfs** [hwɔrfs] { **wharves** [hwɔrvz]

(*b*) Añaden **s** [s] para formar el plural la mayor parte de los substantivos que terminan en **th.**

SINGULAR	PLURAL
breath [brɛθ]	**breaths** [brɛθs]
death [dɛθ]	**deaths** [dɛθs]
growth [groθ]	**growths** [groθs]
month [mʌnθ]	**months** [mʌnθs]

Algunos substantivos añaden **s** [z], cambiando el sonido de **th** a [ð].

SINGULAR	PLURAL
mouth [maʊθ]	**mouths** [maʊðz]

Y algunos forman el plural de ambos modos.

SINGULAR	PLURAL
oath [oθ]	**oaths** [oθs] y [oðz]
truth [truθ]	**truths** [truθs] y [truðz]
wreath [riθ]	**wreaths** [riθs] y [riðz]
youth [juθ]	**youths** [juθs] y [juðz]

2. Añaden una **s** [z] para formar el plural los substantivos que terminan en uno de los siguientes sonidos consonantes sonoros: [b], [d], [ð], [g], [l], [m], [n], [ŋ], [r] y [v].

SONIDO FINAL	SINGULAR	PLURAL
[b]	**rib** [rɪb]	**ribs** [rɪbz]
	tube [tjub]	**tubes** [tjubz]
[d]	**lad** [læd]	**lads** [lædz]
	side [saɪd]	**sides** [saɪdz]
[ð]	**lathe** [leð]	**lathes** [leðz]
[g]	**pig** [pɪg]	**pigs** [pɪgz]
	rogue [rog]	**rogues** [rogz]
[l]	**ball** [bɔl]	**balls** [bɔlz]
	tile [taɪl]	**tiles** [taɪlz]
	pebble [ˈpɛbəl]	**pebbles** [ˈpɛbəlz]
[m]	**rim** [rɪm]	**rims** [rɪmz]
	lamb [læm]	**lambs** [læmz]
	hymn [hɪm]	**hymns** [hɪmz]
	name [nem]	**names** [nemz]
[n]	**ton** [tʌn]	**tons** [tʌnz]
	bone [bon]	**bones** [bonz]
[ŋ]	**bung** [bʌŋ]	**bungs** [bʌŋz]
	tongue [tʌŋ]	**tongues** [tʌŋz]
[r]	**bar** [bɑr]	**bars** [bɑrz]
	tire [taɪr]	**tires** [taɪrz]
[v]	**stove** [stov]	**stoves** [stovz]

3. Añaden **s** [ɪz] o **es** [ɪz] para formar el plural los substantivos que terminan en uno de los siguientes sonidos consonantes africados y fricativos: [ʃ], [ʒ], [tʃ], [dʒ], [s] y [z]. Añaden **s** si la grafía termina en **e** muda, **es** si termina en consonante.

SONIDO FINAL	SINGULAR	PLURAL
[ʃ]	**wish** [wɪʃ]	**wishes** [ˈwɪʃɪz]
[ʒ]	**mirage** [mɪˈrɑʒ]	**mirages** [mɪˈrɑʒɪz]
[tʃ]	**latch** [lætʃ]	**latches** [ˈlætʃɪz]
[dʒ]	**edge** [ɛdʒ]	**edges** [ˈɛdʒɪz]
[s]	**class** [klæs]	**classes** [ˈklæsɪz]
	box [bɑks]	**boxes** [ˈbɑksɪz]
	case [kes]	**cases** [ˈkesɪz]
[z]	**buzz** [bʌz]	**buzzes** [ˈbʌzɪz]
	maze [mez]	**mazes** [ˈmezɪz]

El sonido [s] del substantivo **house** cambia en [z] con la adición de la **s** del plural.

SINGULAR	PLURAL
house [haʊs]	**houses** [ˈhaʊzɪz]

4. Añaden **s** [z] para formar el plural los substantivos que terminan en vocal o diptongo.

SINGULAR	PLURAL
sofa [ˈsofə]	**sofas** [ˈsofəz]
sea [si]	**seas** [siz]
eye [aɪ]	**eyes** [aɪz]
toe [to]	**toes** [toz]
shoe [ʃu]	**shoes** [ʃuz]
value [ˈvæljʊ]	**values** [ˈvæljuz]
cow [kaʊ]	**cows** [kaʊz]
boy [bɔɪ]	**boys** [bɔɪz]

(*a*) La mayor parte de los substantivos que terminan en **o** añaden **es** [z] para formar el plural. Hay algunos que añaden **s** [z] y otros que añaden **s** [z] o **es** [z].

SINGULAR	PLURAL
potato [pəˈteto]	**potatoes** [pəˈtetoz]
cameo [ˈkæmɪo]	**cameos** [ˈkæmɪoz]
motto [ˈmɑto]	**mottoes** o **mottos** [ˈmɑtoz]

(*b*) Los substantivos que terminan en **y** cambian la **y** en **ies**, si va precedida de consonante.

SINGULAR	PLURAL
city ['sɪtɪ]	**cities** ['sɪtɪz]
sky [skaɪ]	**skies** [skaɪz]

No cambian la **y** si va precedida de vocal.

SINGULAR	PLURAL
toy [tɔɪ]	**toys** [tɔɪz]
key [ki]	**keys** [kiz]

5. Hay varios substantivos que tienen el plural enteramente irregular.

SINGULAR	PLURAL
man [mæn]	**men** [mɛn]
woman ['wʊmən]	**women** ['wɪmɪn]
child [tʃaɪld]	**children** ['tʃɪldrən]
ox [ɑks]	**oxen** ['ɑksən]
foot [fʊt]	**feet** [fit]
goose [gus]	**geese** [gis]
tooth [tuθ]	**teeth** [tiθ]
louse [laʊs]	**lice** [laɪs]
mouse [maʊs]	**mice** [maɪs]

Los compuestos de estos substantivos forman el plural de la misma manera. Pero los substantivos **German, Mussulman, Roman** y **Ottoman,** que nada tienen que ver con la palabra **man,** añaden **s** para formar el plural: **Germans, Mussulmans, Romans** y **Ottomans.** Y el substantivo **Norman** también añade **s** para formar el plural: **Normans.**

6. Hay muchos substantivos que tienen como plural la misma forma del singular, p.ej., **one sheep, two sheep.** Esto se ve en los nombres de medida y de peces y también en los nombres de nacionalidad que terminan en **ese**, p.ej., **one Japanese, two Japanese.** Los siguientes substantivos de origen latino y francés también tienen como plural la misma forma y la misma pronunciación del singular: **abatis, chamois, forceps, series** y **species.** Y el plural de **corps** tiene la misma forma del singular, aunque la **s,** muda en el singular, va pronunciada en el plural: **corps** [kor] y **corps** [korz].

7. Los substantivos de origen latino que terminan en **us, a** y **um** forman el plural como en la declinación latina. Así es que **us** cambia en **i, a** en **ae,** y **um** en **a.**

SINGULAR	PLURAL
alumnus [ə'lʌmnəs]	**alumni** [ə'lʌmnaɪ]
alumna [ə'lʌmnə]	**alumnae** [ə'lʌmni]
addendum [ə'dɛndəm]	**addenda** [ə'dɛndə]

Algunos de estos substantivos tienen dos plurales, el latino y el regular, p.ej., **vertebra** con **vertebrae** y **vertebras, fungus** con **fungi** y **funguses, stratum** con **strata** y **stratums.**

8. Los substantivos de origen griego que terminan en **is** y **on** forman el plural como en la declinación griega. Así es que **is** cambia en **es** y **on** cambia en **a.**

SINGULAR	PLURAL
crisis ['kraɪsɪs]	**crises** ['kraɪsiz]
automaton [ɔ'tɑmətɑn]	**automata** [ɔ'tɑmətə]

9. Los substantivos de origen latino que terminan en **ex** e **ix** tienen dos plurales, uno como en la declinación latina y uno regular, algunas veces con sentido distinto, p.ej., **vertex** con **vertices** y **vertexes** y **matrix** con **matrices** y **matrixes.**

10. Los substantivos **cherub** y **seraph,** de origen hebreo, tienen dos plurales: **cherubim** y **cherubs, seraphim** y **seraphs.** Y hay otros plurales del tipo hebreo, p.ej., **Sephardim.**

11. Ciertos substantivos se consideran singulares aunque tienen la **s** del plural, p.ej., **gallows, measles, news.** Los substantivos acabados en **ics** pertenecen a este grupo cuando designan artes y ciencias; pero son plurales cuando tienen otro sentido, p.ej., **acoustics** es singular cuando significa acústica (*ciencia de los sonidos*) y plural cuando significa acústica arquitectural (*condiciones de un recinto para la reflexión de los sonidos*).

§3. La comparación de los adjetivos. Añaden **er** (o **r**) [ər] para formar el comparativo y **est** (o **st**) [ɪst] para formar el superlativo (1) los adjetivos monosílabos, (2) los adjetivos bisílabos que terminan en **er, le, ow, y** y **some** inacentuados y (3) algunos adjetivos bisílabos que terminan en sílaba acentuada.

soft	**softer**	**softest**
clever	**cleverer**	**cleverest**
mellow	**mellower**	**mellowest**

(*a*) Si el adjetivo termina en consonante simple precedida de vocal simple acentuada, se dobla la consonante al añadir **er** y **est.**

fat	**fatter**	**fattest**
sad	**sadder**	**saddest**
red	**redder**	**reddest**
dim	**dimmer**	**dimmest**
big	**bigger**	**biggest**
hot	**hotter**	**hottest**

(*b*) Si la vocal no es simple, no se dobla la consonante.

great	**greater**	**greatest**
deep	**deeper**	**deepest**
poor	**poorer**	**poorest**

(*c*) Si el adjetivo termina en **e** muda, se añade simplemente **r** y **st** en la escritura pero [ər] y [ɪst] en la pronunciación.

large [lɑrdʒ]	**larger** [ˈlɑrdʒər]	**largest** [ˈlɑrdʒɪst]
wise [waɪz]	**wiser** [ˈwaɪzər]	**wisest** [ˈwaɪzɪst]
handsome [ˈhænsəm]	**handsomer** [ˈhænsəmər]	**handsomest** [ˈhænsəmɪst]
polite [pəˈlaɪt]	**politer** [pəˈlaɪtər]	**politest** [pəˈlaɪtɪst]
sincere [sɪnˈsɪr]	**sincerer** [sɪnˈsɪrər]	**sincerest** [sɪnˈsɪrɪst]

(*d*) Si el adjetivo termina en **ng** [ŋ], se intercala el sonido [g] al añadir **er** y **est.**

long [lɔŋ]	**longer** [ˈlɔŋgər]	**longest** [ˈlɔŋgɪst]
strong [strɔŋ]	**stronger** [ˈstrɔŋgər]	**strongest** [ˈstrɔŋgɪst]
young [jʌŋ]	**younger** [ˈjʌŋgər]	**youngest** [ˈjʌŋgɪst]

(*e*) Si el adjetivo termina en **y** precedida de consonante, se cambia la **y** en **i** al añadir **er** y **est.**

holy [ˈholɪ]	**holier** [ˈholɪər]	**holiest** [ˈholɪɪst]
happy [ˈhæpɪ]	**happier** [ˈhæpɪər]	**happiest** [ˈhæpɪɪst]

Si la **y** va precedida de vocal, no se cambia en **i.**

coy [kɔɪ]	**coyer** [ˈkɔɪər]	**coyest** [ˈkɔɪɪst]

Anteponen **more** para formar el comparativo y **most** para formar el superlativo los adjetivos de dos sílabas que terminan en **ful, ish** y **ous** y los adjetivos de más de dos sílabas.

helpful	**more helpful**	**most helpful**
selfish	**more selfish**	**most selfish**
vicious	**more vicious**	**most vicious**
excellent	**more excellent**	**most excellent**

Los siguientes adjetivos tienen comparación irregular.

good } **well** }	**better**	**best**
bad } **ill** }	**worse**	**worst**
little	**less, lesser**	**least**
much, many	**more**	**most**
far	**farther**	**farthest**

§4. Presente de indicativo. El presente de indicativo es idéntico al infinitivo con la excepción de la tercera persona del singular, que se forma añadiendo **s** o **es**.

1. Añaden una **s** [s] para formar la tercera persona del singular los verbos que terminan en uno de los siguientes sonidos consonantes sordos: [f], [k], [p], [t] y [θ].

SONIDO FINAL	INFINITIVO	TERCERA PERSONA DEL SINGULAR
[f]	**doff** [dɑf]	**doffs** [dɑfs]
	cough [kɔf]	**coughs** [kɔfs]
	chafe [tʃef]	**chafes** [tʃefs]
[k]	**seek** [sik]	**seeks** [siks]
	bake [bek]	**bakes** [beks]
[p]	**sip** [sɪp]	**sips** [sɪps]
	hope [hop]	**hopes** [hops]
[t]	**sit** [sɪt]	**sits** [sɪts]
	hate [het]	**hates** [hets]
[θ]	**lath** [læθ]	**laths** [læθs]

2. Añaden una **s** [z] para formar la tercera persona del singular los verbos que terminan en uno de los siguientes sonidos consonantes sonoros: [b], [d], [ð], [g], [l], [m], [n], [ŋ], [r] y [v].

SONIDO FINAL	INFINITIVO	TERCERA PERSONA DEL SINGULAR
[b]	**sob** [sɑb]	**sobs** [sɑbz]
	robe [rob]	**robes** [robz]
[d]	**raid** [red]	**raids** [redz]
	hide [haɪd]	**hides** [haɪdz]
[ð]	**smooth** [smuð]	**smooths** [smuðz]
	bathe [beð]	**bathes** [beðz]
[g]	**sag** [sæg]	**sags** [sægz]
[l]	**kill** [kɪl]	**kills** [kɪlz]
	smile [smaɪl]	**smiles** [smaɪlz]
[m]	**seem** [sim]	**seems** [simz]
	name [nem]	**names** [nemz]
[n]	**pin** [pɪn]	**pins** [pɪnz]
	sign [saɪn]	**signs** [saɪnz]
	pine [paɪn]	**pines** [paɪnz]
[ŋ]	**ring** [rɪŋ]	**rings** [rɪŋz]
[r]	**hear** [hɪr]	**hears** [hɪrz]
	care [kɛr]	**cares** [kɛrz]
[v]	**rev** [rɛv]	**revs** [rɛvz]
	give [gɪv]	**gives** [gɪvz]

3. Añaden **s** [ɪz] o **es** [ɪz] para formar la tercera persona del singular los verbos que terminan en uno de los siguientes sonidos consonantes africados y fricativos: [ʃ], [ʒ], [tʃ], [dʒ], [s], y [z]. Añaden **s** si la grafía termina en **e** muda, **es** si termina en consonante.

SONIDO FINAL	INFINITIVO	TERCERA PERSONA DEL SINGULAR
[ʃ]	**wash** [wɑʃ]	**washes** [ˈwɑʃɪz]
	cache [kæʃ]	**caches** [ˈkæʃɪz]
[ʒ]	**massage** [məˈsɑʒ]	**massages** [məˈsɑʒɪz]
[tʃ]	**attach** [əˈtætʃ]	**attaches** [əˈtætʃɪz]
	catch [kætʃ]	**catches** [ˈkætʃɪz]
[dʒ]	**pledge** [plɛdʒ]	**pledges** [ˈplɛdʒɪz]
	urge [ʌrdʒ]	**urges** [ˈʌrdʒɪz]
[s]	**pass** [pæs]	**passes** [ˈpæsɪz]
	race [res]	**races** [ˈresɪz]
[z]	**buzz** [bʌz]	**buzzes** [ˈbʌzɪz]
	praise [prez]	**praises** [ˈprezɪz]

4. Añaden una **s** [z] para formar la tercera persona del singular los verbos que terminan en vocal o diptongo.

SONIDO FINAL	INFINITIVO	TERCERA PERSONA DEL SINGULAR
[ɑ]	**baa** [bɑ]	**baas** [bɑz]
[e]	**play** [ple]	**plays** [plez]
[i]	**see** [si]	**sees** [siz]
[ɔ]	**saw** [sɔ]	**saws** [sɔz]
[o]	**know** [no]	**knows** [noz]
[u]	**woo** [wu]	**woos** [wuz]
[aɪ]	**tie** [taɪ]	**ties** [taɪz]
	sigh [saɪ]	**sighs** [saɪz]
[aʊ]	**plow** [plaʊ]	**plows** [plaʊz]
[ɔɪ]	**toy** [tɔɪ]	**toys** [tɔɪz]

Dos verbos que terminan en vocal añaden **es** [z] para formar la tercera persona del singular: **do** [du], **does** [dʌz] y **go** [go], **goes** [goz].

Los verbos que terminan en **y** cambian la **y** en **ies**, si va precedida de consonante.

INFINITIVO	TERCERA PERSONA DEL SINGULAR
carry [ˈkærɪ]	**carries** [ˈkærɪz]
satisfy [ˈsætɪsfaɪ]	**satisfies** [ˈsætɪsfaɪz]
try [traɪ]	**tries** [traɪz]

No cambian la **y** si va precedida de vocal.

INFINITIVO	TERCERA PERSONA DEL SINGULAR
pray [pre]	**prays** [prez]
buy [baɪ]	**buys** [baɪz]

El presente de indicativo del verbo **be** es muy irregular.

I am [æm]	**we are** [ɑr]
you are [ɑr]	**you are**
he o **she is** [ɪz]	**they are**

Además de **be,** cuatro verbos más tienen la tercera persona del singular irregular en la pronunciación.

INFINITIVO	TERCERA PERSONA DEL SINGULAR
do [du]	**does** [dʌz]
have [hæv]	**has** [hæz]
say [se]	**says** [sɛz]

§5. El gerundio (participio activo). 1. Para formar el gerundio, se añade **ing** al infinitivo, p.ej., **walk** [wɔk], **walking** [ˈwɔkɪŋ]; **eat** [it], **eating** [ˈitɪŋ].

2. Si el infinitivo termina en consonante simple precedida de vocal simple acentuada, se dobla esta consonante al añadir **ing.**

rub [rʌb]	**rubbing** [ˈrʌbɪŋ]
pad [pæd]	**padding** [ˈpædɪŋ]
beg [bɛg]	**begging** [ˈbɛgɪŋ]
dispel [dɪsˈpɛl]	**dispelling** [dɪsˈpɛlɪŋ]
trim [trɪm]	**trimming** [ˈtrɪmɪŋ]
run [rʌn]	**running** [ˈrʌnɪŋ]
sip [sɪp]	**sipping** [ˈsɪpɪŋ]
refer [rɪˈfʌr]	**referring** [rɪˈfʌrɪŋ]
bat [bæt]	**batting** [ˈbætɪŋ]
rev [rɛv]	**revving** [ˈrɛvɪŋ]

Si la vocal no es simple, no se dobla la consonante.

seem [sim]	**seeming** [ˈsimɪŋ]
cook [kʊk]	**cooking** [ˈkʊkɪŋ]
appear [əˈpɪr]	**appearing** [əˈpɪrɪŋ]
soak [sok]	**soaking** [ˈsokɪŋ]

Si la vocal no es acentuada, no se dobla la consonante.

suffer [ˈsʌfər]	**suffering** [ˈsʌfərɪŋ]
labor [ˈlebər]	**laboring** [ˈlebərɪŋ]

Si la consonante es **l** y la vocal no acentuada, se puede dejar la **l** simple o doblarla al añadir **ing.**

travel [ˈtrævəl]	**traveling** [ˈtrævəlɪŋ] o **travelling** [ˈtrævəlɪŋ]

Si el verbo termina en **e** muda, se la omite al añadir **ing.**

make [mek]	**making** [ˈmekɪŋ]
ride [raɪd]	**riding** [ˈraɪdɪŋ]

No se omite la **e** en los gerundios de **dye, singe** y los verbos que terminan en **oe.**

dye [daɪ]	**dyeing** [ˈdaɪɪŋ]
singe [sɪndʒ]	**singeing** [ˈsɪndʒɪŋ]
hoe [ho]	**hoeing** [ˈho·ɪŋ]
tiptoe [ˈtɪpˌto]	**tiptoeing** [ˈtɪpˌto·ɪŋ]

§6. Las clases de los verbos. Los verbos débiles son los que forman el pretérito y el participio pasado sin cambiar la vocal de la raíz y añadiendo **ed, d** o **t,** p.ej., **walk, walked, walked.** Los verbos fuertes son los que forman el pretérito y el participio pasado cambiando la vocal de la raíz y añadiendo **en, n** o **ne,** p.ej., **fly, flew, flown.** Y los verbos mixtos son los que forman el pretérito y el participio pasado cambiando la vocal de la raíz y añadiendo **d** o **t,** p.ej., **tell, told, told.**

Hay verbos débiles que no añaden **d** o **t** porque ya la tienen en el infinitivo, p.ej., **cost, cost, cost** y **spend, spent, spent.** Y hay verbos fuertes que no añaden **en, n** o **ne** en el participio pasado por haberla perdido, p.ej., **awake, awoke, awoke,** o porque ya la tienen en el infinitivo, p.ej., **spin, spun, spun.**

§7. Los verbos débiles. Añaden **ed** [t] o **d** [t] para formar el pretérito y el participio pasado los verbos débiles que terminan en uno de los siguientes sonidos consonantes sordos: [f], [k], [p], [s], [θ], [ʃ] y [tʃ]. La terminación se escribe **ed** si el verbo no termina en **e** muda, **d** si termina en **e** muda.

Verbos que no terminan en **e** muda.

SONIDO FINAL	INFINITIVO	PRETÉRITO Y PARTICIPIO PASADO
[f]	**loaf** [lof]	**loafed** [loft]
	cough [kɔf]	**coughed** [kɔft]
[k]	**mock** [mɑk]	**mocked** [mɑkt]
[p]	**camp** [kæmp]	**camped** [kæmpt]
[s]	**bless** [blɛs]	**blessed** [blɛst]
	mix [mɪks]	**mixed** [mɪkst]
[θ]	**lath** [læθ]	**lathed** [læθt]
[ʃ]	**wash** [wɔʃ]	**washed** [wɔʃt]
[tʃ]	**patch** [pætʃ]	**patched** [pætʃt]

Verbos que terminan en **e** muda.

SONIDO FINAL	INFINITIVO	PRETÉRITO Y PARTICIPIO PASADO
[f]	**knife** [naɪf]	**knifed** [naɪft]
[k]	**bake** [bek]	**baked** [bekt]
[p]	**wipe** [waɪp]	**wiped** [waɪpt]
[ʃ]	**cache** [kæʃ]	**cached** [kæʃt]

Añaden **ed** [d] o **d** [d] para formar el pretérito y el participio pasado los verbos débiles que terminan en uno de los siguientes sonidos consonantes sonoros: [b], [g], [l], [m], [n], [r], [v], [z], [ð], [ʒ], [dʒ] y [ŋ]. La terminación se escribe **ed** si el verbo no termina en **e** muda, **d** si termina en **e** muda.

Verbos que no terminan en **e** muda.

SONIDO FINAL	INFINITIVO	PRETÉRITO Y PARTICIPIO PASADO
[b]	**ebb** [ɛb]	**ebbed** [ɛbd]
[g]	**egg** [ɛg]	**egged** [ɛgd]
[l]	**sail** [sel]	**sailed** [seld]
[m]	**storm** [stɔrm]	**stormed** [stɔrmd]
[n]	**lean** [lin]	**leaned** [lind]
[r]	**smear** [smɪr]	**smeared** [smɪrd]
[z]	**buzz** [bʌz]	**buzzed** [bʌzd]
[ð]	**smooth** [smuð]	**smoothed** [smuðd]
[ŋ]	**bang** [bæŋ]	**banged** [bæŋd]

Verbos que terminan en **e** muda.

SONIDO FINAL	INFINITIVO	PRETÉRITO Y PARTICIPIO PASADO
[b]	**robe** [rob]	**robed** [robd]
[l]	**scale** [skel]	**scaled** [skeld]
[m]	**name** [nem]	**named** [nemd]
[n]	**pine** [paɪn]	**pined** [paɪnd]
[r]	**care** [kɛr]	**cared** [kɛrd]
[v]	**move** [muv]	**moved** [muvd]
[z]	**praise** [prez]	**praised** [prezd]
[ð]	**bathe** [beð]	**bathed** [beðd]
[ʒ]	**massage** [məˈsɑʒ]	**massaged** [məˈsɑʒd]
[dʒ]	**oblige** [əˈblaɪdʒ]	**obliged** [əˈblaɪdʒd]

Añaden **ed** [ɪd] o **d** [ɪd] para formar el pretérito y el participio pasado los verbos que terminan en [d] o [t]. La terminación se escribe **ed** si el verbo no termina en **e** muda, **d** si termina en **e** muda.

Verbos que no terminan en **e** muda.

SONIDO FINAL	INFINITIVO	PRETÉRITO Y PARTICIPIO PASADO
[d]	**end** [ɛnd]	**ended** [ˈɛndɪd]
[t]	**wait** [wet]	**waited** [ˈwetɪd]

Verbos que terminan en **e** muda.

SONIDO FINAL	INFINITIVO	PRETÉRITO Y PARTICIPIO PASADO
[d]	**wade** [wed]	**waded** [ˈwedɪd]
[t]	**invite** [ɪnˈvaɪt]	**invited** [ɪnˈvaɪtɪd]

Añaden **ed** [d] para formar el pretérito y el participio pasado los verbos que terminan en vocal o diptongo.

INFINITIVO	PRETÉRITO Y PARTICIPIO PASADO
baa [bɑ]	**baaed** [bɑd]
pray [pre]	**prayed** [pred]
key [ki]	**keyed** [kid]
mow [mo]	**mowed** [mod]
woo [wu]	**wooed** [wud]
sigh [saɪ]	**sighed** [saɪd]
plow [plaʊ]	**plowed** [plaʊd]
toy [tɔɪ]	**toyed** [tɔɪd]

Los pretéritos y los participios pasados de dos verbos débiles que terminan en **ay** se escriben de modo irregular aunque se pronuncian regularmente.

INFINITIVO	PRETÉRITO Y PARTICIPIO PASADO
lay [le]	**laid** [led]
pay [pe]	**paid** [ped]

Los verbos débiles que terminan en **y** cambian la **y** en **ied** para formar el pretérito y el participio pasado. Si la **y** se pronuncia [aɪ], **ied** se pronuncia [aɪd]. Si la **y** se pronuncia [ɪ], **ied** se pronuncia [ɪd].

INFINITIVO	PRETÉRITO Y PARTICIPIO PASADO
satisfy [ˈsætɪsfaɪ]	**satisfied** [ˈsætɪsfaɪd]
try [traɪ]	**tried** [traɪd]
carry [ˈkærɪ]	**carried** [ˈkærɪd]
pity [ˈpɪtɪ]	**pitied** [ˈpɪtɪd]

Si el verbo termina en consonante simple precedida de vocal simple acentuada, se dobla esta consonante al añadir **ed.**

INFINITIVO	PRETÉRITO Y PARTICIPIO PASADO
rub [rʌb]	**rubbed** [rʌbd]
pad [pæd]	**padded** [ˈpædɪd]
beg [bɛg]	**begged** [bɛgd]
trek [trɛk]	**trekked** [trɛkt]
dispel [dɪsˈpɛl]	**dispelled** [dɪsˈpɛld]
trim [trɪm]	**trimmed** [trɪmd]
tan [tæn]	**tanned** [tænd]
sip [sɪp]	**sipped** [sɪpt]
refer [rɪˈfʌr]	**referred** [rɪˈfʌrd]
bat [bæt]	**batted** [ˈbætɪd]
rev [rɛv]	**revved** [rɛvd]

Si la vocal no es simple, no se dobla la consonante.

INFINITIVO	PRETÉRITO Y PARTICIPIO PASADO
seem [sim]	**seemed** [simd]
cook [kʊk]	**cooked** [kʊkt]
appear [əˈpɪr]	**appeared** [əˈpɪrd]
soak [sok]	**soaked** [sokt]

Si la vocal no va acentuada, no se dobla la consonante.

INFINITIVO	PRETÉRITO Y PARTICIPIO PASADO
suffer [ˈsʌfər]	**suffered** [ˈsʌfərd]
labor [ˈlebər]	**labored** [ˈlebərd]

Si la vocal no va acentuada y la consonante es **l**, se puede dejar la **l** simple o doblarla al añadir **ed.**

INFINITIVO	PRETÉRITO Y PARTICIPIO PASADO
travel [ˈtrævəl]	**traveled** [ˈtrævəld] o **travelled** [ˈtrævəld]

La **e** de **ed** de los participios pasados usados como adjetivos se pronuncia en todos los casos, p.ej., **blessed** [ˈblɛsɪd]; **learned** [ˈlʌrnɪd].

§8. Los verbos débiles irregulares. Algunos verbos débiles que terminan en **n, l** o **ll,** forman el pretérito y el participio pasado con la adición de **ed** [d] en la manera regular o con la adición de **t** y con la simplificación de **ll** en **l.**

INFINITIVO	PRETÉRITO Y PARTICIPIO PASADO
burn [bʌrn]	**burned** [bʌrnd] y **burnt** [bʌrnt]
spoil [spɔɪl]	**spoiled** [spɔɪld] y **spoilt** [spɔɪlt]
smell [smɛl]	**smelled** [smɛld] y **smelt** [smɛlt]

Algunos verbos débiles que terminan en **nd, ld** y **rd** forman el pretérito y el participio pasado cambiando la **d** final en **t.**

INFINITIVO	PRETÉRITO Y PARTICIPIO PASADO
bend [bɛnd]	**bent** [bɛnt]
build [bɪld]	**built** [bɪlt]
gird [gʌrd]	**girt** [gʌrt]

Una veintena de verbos que terminan en **d, t** o **st** no varían en la formación del pretérito y el participio pasado.

INFINITIVO	PRETÉRITO Y PARTICIPIO PASADO
cut [kʌt]	**cut** [kʌt]
hurt [hʌrt]	**hurt** [hʌrt]
rid [rɪd]	**rid** [rɪd]
spread [sprɛd]	**spread** [sprɛd]
cast [kæst]	**cast** [kæst]
cost [kɔst]	**cost** [kɔst]
thrust [θrʌst]	**thrust** [θrʌst]

§9. Los verbos fuertes. Damos abajo una lista de verbos fuertes que ejemplifican todas las variaciones del sonido de la vocal de la raíz en las tres partes principales.

INFINITIVO	PRETÉRITO	PARTICIPIO PASADO
hang [hæŋ]	**hung** [hʌŋ]	**hung** [hʌŋ]
lie [laɪ]	**lay** [le]	**lain** [len]
hide [haɪd]	**hid** [hɪd]	**hidden** ['hɪdən]
write [raɪt]	**wrote** [rot]	**written** ['rɪtən]
abide [ə'baɪd]	**abode** [ə'bod]	**abode** [ə'bod]
strike [straɪk]	**struck** [strʌk]	**struck** [strʌk]
fly [flaɪ]	**flew** [flu]	**flown** [flon]
get [gɛt]	**got** [gɑt]	**gotten** ['gɑtən]
bear [bɛr]	**bore** [bor]	**borne** [born]
break [brek]	**broke** [brok]	**broken** ['brokən]
shake [ʃek]	**shook** [ʃʊk]	**shaken** ['ʃekən]
slay [sle]	**slew** [slu]	**slain** [slen]
bid [bɪd]	**bade** [bæd]	**bidden** ['bɪdən]
sing [sɪŋ]	**sang** [sæŋ]	**sung** [sʌŋ]
give [gɪv]	**gave** [gev]	**given** ['gɪvən]
spin [spɪn]	**spun** [spʌn]	**spun** [spʌn]
eat [it]	**ate** [et]	**eaten** ['itən]
see [si]	**saw** [sɔ]	**seen** [sin]
freeze [friz]	**froze** [froz]	**frozen** ['frozən]
fall [fɔl]	**fell** [fɛl]	**fallen** ['fɔlən]
draw [drɔ]	**drew** [dru]	**drawn** [drɔn]
grow [gro]	**grew** [gru]	**grown** [gron]
run [rʌn]	**ran** [ræn]	**run** [rʌn]
come [kʌm]	**came** [kem]	**come** [kʌm]
choose [tʃuz]	**chose** [tʃoz]	**chosen** ['tʃozən]

§10. Los verbos mixtos. Damos abajo una lista de verbos mixtos que ejemplifican todas las variaciones del sonido de la vocal de la raíz en las tres partes principales.

INFINITIVO	PRETÉRITO	PARTICIPIO PASADO
stand [stænd]	**stood** [stʊd]	**stood** [stʊd]
catch [kætʃ]	**caught** [kɔt]	**caught** [kɔt]
slide [slaɪd]	**slid** [slɪd]	**slid** [slɪd]
fight [faɪt]	**fought** [fɔt]	**fought** [fɔt]
find [faɪnd]	**found** [faʊnd]	**found** [faʊnd]
sell [sɛl]	**sold** [sold]	**sold** [sold]
say [se]	**said** [sɛd]	**said** [sɛd]
sit [sɪt]	**sat** [sæt]	**sat** [sæt]
think [θɪŋk]	**thought** [θɔt]	**thought** [θɔt]
feed [fid]	**fed** [fɛd]	**fed** [fɛd]
teach [titʃ]	**taught** [tɔt]	**taught** [tɔt]
clothe [kloð]	**clad** [klæd]	**clad** [klæd]
hold [hold]	**held** [hɛld]	**held** [hɛld]
shoot [ʃut]	**shot** [ʃɑt]	**shot** [ʃɑt]
lose [luz]	**lost** [lɔst]	**lost** [lɔst]

§11. Los verbos irregulares. Algunos verbos tienen el pretérito y el participio pasado irregulares.

INFINITIVO	PRETÉRITO	PARTICIPIO PASADO
be [bi]	**was** [wɑz] y **were** [wʌr]	**been** [bɪn] o [bin]
do [du]	**did** [dɪd]	**done** [dʌn]
go [go]	**went** [wɛnt]	**gone** [gɔn] o [gɑn]
have [hæv]	**had** [hæd]	**had** [hæd]
make [mek]	**made** [med]	**made** [med]

BRIEF HISTORY OF THE SPANISH LANGUAGE

Vulgar Latin. Latin as a living language was subject to constant change. While the language of the cultivated classes (Classical Latin) became more and more uniform under the conservative influences of culture, learning, and tradition, the language of the people (Vulgar Latin) became more and more altered through contact with other languages, more and more revitalized through innovation and addition, and more and more diversified as it spread with the vast Roman Empire across the continent of Europe. Classical Latin became a dead language while Vulgar Latin developed into what we now call the Neo-Latin or Romance languages.

No great literature has been handed down to us to attest the existence of Vulgar Latin. Our knowledge of it is derived from the following sources: 1) colloquialisms condemned in the works of grammarians, 2) careless mistakes of Classical Latin authors, 3) intentional colloquialisms in Classical Latin comedy, 4) the language of a few works written by poorly educated people, 5) popular forms appearing in the work of stonecutters and early scribes, 6) glosses in popular form in documents written in a more cultivated idiom, and finally, 7) the Romance languages themselves, by a comparative study of which it is possible to reconstruct hypothetically a Latin idiom which is widely different in many respects from Classical Latin.

The Romance Languages. The differentiation of Vulgar Latin from one region to another, which finally resulted in its transformation into the several Romance languages and their dialects, is thought to have been brought about by the following causes: 1) the varying period of Romanization, 2) the relative geographic isolation of one group from another, 3) the variation of cultural and educational conditions, 4) dialectal differences in the language of the Italic colonists, 5) the original languages encountered by the Romans in their penetration of other lands, 6) the languages of later invaders of Romanized areas, and 7) the development of separate political units. The degree of differentiation may be realized by a consideration of the large number of Romance languages and their dialects. The chief Romance languages are Spanish, Portuguese, French, Italian, Provençal-Catalan, Rhaeto-Romanic, and Rumanian.

Castilian. The chief Romance languages of the Iberian Peninsula were Castilian, Leonese, Navarro-Aragonese, Gallaeco-Portuguese, and Catalan. Castilian, by absorbing Leonese and Navarro-Aragonese, became the language of Spain and spread to the New World with Spanish discovery and colonization. It is important as the language of one of the world's great literatures and is spoken by over a hundred and fifty million people in Spain, Central America, South America, Mexico, the West Indies, southwestern United

States, the Philippine Islands, and many other islands of the Atlantic and Pacific.

From Latin to Spanish. The principal changes in the transition from Latin to Spanish were the following:

1. The diphthongization of Latin stressed short **e** to Spanish **ie,** e.g., **tenet** > **tiene, petram** > **piedra** and the diphthongization of Latin stressed short **o** to Spanish **ue,** e.g., **bonum** > **bueno, novem** > **nueve.** These changes account in part for the development of radical-changing verbs for when the vowels are not stressed they do not diphthongize. Accordingly, we have **siento** but **sentamos, duerme** but **dormimos.** And they also account for the difference in the radical vowel of such forms as **ardiente** and **ardentísimo, valiente** and **valentón.**

2. The voicing or fall of certain intervocalic consonants, e.g., **acutum** > **agudo, lupum** > **lobo, profectum** > **provecho, credo** > **creo, legalem** > **leal.**

3. The development of yod and the consequent palatalization of contiguous consonants, e.g., **meliorem** > **mejor, seniorem** > **señor, factum** > **hecho, oculum** > **ojo.**

4. The velarization of **b, p, v,** and **l,** e.g., **capitalem** > **cabdal** > **caudal, captivum** > **cautivo, civitatem** > **ciudad, alterum** > **autro** > **otro.**

5. The change of Latin initial **cl, fl,** and **pl** to Spanish **ll,** e.g., **clavem** > **llave, flammam** > **llama, plorare** > **llorar.**

6. The fall of unaccented vowels, e.g., **delicatum** > **delgado, consuturam** > **costura**; and the consequent development of new consonant groups, e.g., **hominem** > **homne** > **hombre, comitem** > **conde, judicare** > **juzgar.**

7. The partial disappearance of nominal, adjectival, and verbal inflection, e.g., the neuter gender, all cases except the accusative, many tenses, and the passive voice.

8. The emergence of word order as the prime instrument of syntax instead of inflection.

In addition to the words of popular origin, which constitute the chief wealth of the Spanish vocabulary, new Latin words have entered the language from the earliest times. These words came first through the church and the law, later through the work of scholars and men of letters, and still later through science and medicine. They have not undergone all the changes which popular words have undergone, first, because they have often entered the language after certain changes had ceased to take place, and second, because of a conscious effort to preserve their Latin form. The word **matemática** is an example of a learned word. None of its sounds has fallen, none has undergone a fundamental change.

Sometimes a learned or semilearned word already existed as a popular word. The two forms are then called doublets, e.g., **límite** and **linde, minuto** and **menudo, ración** and **razón, examen** and **enjambre.** Borrowings from dialects and other languages may also become doublets, e.g.,**jefe** (from French **chef**) and **cabo,** both from Latin **caput, juerga** (Andalusian) and **huelga,** both from the stem of Latin **follicare.**

Sometimes a popular word was modified or replaced by a Latin word from which it originally came. Such a word is called a regressive word. Thus Old Spanish **aorar** was replaced by **adorar,** Old Spanish **viesso** by **verso.**

Non-Latin Words in Spanish. Many languages have influenced Spanish in the course of its growth and development. But it is generally agreed that with few exceptions this influence did not go beyond vocabulary and did not affect the intrinsic character of the language.

Aside from a large number of place names only a few words, such as **izquierdo, páramo,** and **vega,** were adopted from the language of the original Iberians.

Words of Greek origin entered the language at different periods, frequently through Latin, occasionally through Arabic. The words **bodega, escuela, golpe,** and **huérfano** are popular words of Greek origin, while the words **fisiología, geografía, mecánica,** and **telégrafo** are learned words of Greek origin.

Many words were taken during the Middle Ages from the Germanic and Arabic invaders. The Germanic words were Visigothic, Swabian, and Vandal and were for the most part concerned with the waging of war and violent action, e.g., **guerra, tregua, yelmo,** and **robar.** Of Germanic origin also were many names of persons, e.g., **Elvira, Fernando,** and **Ramiro.**

The Arabic words are fairly numerous and cover practically every aspect of human activity. They give to the Spanish vocabulary an appearance which distinguishes it markedly from that of French and Italian. Here are a few examples of Arabic words: **albacea, albañil, alcalde, algodón, atalaya, noria, quilate,** and **zaguán.**

Since the thirteenth century, that is, after Spanish had passed through its formative stages, the languages from whose vocabularies it has borrowed the largest number of words are French and Italian. The words borrowed from French are, for the most part, words concerned with the church, with chivalry, diplomacy, and literature, e.g., **fraile, galán, homenaje, jardín, jaula, linaje, manjar, mensaje, monje, preste,** and **vergel,** while the words borrowed from Italian are, for the most part, words concerned with literature and the arts, e.g., **esbozo, fachada, gaceta, novela, piano,** and **soneto.**

With the discovery of America many words were adopted from Indian dialects. Some of these have not spread beyond the region of their origin, some have spread throughout Spanish America, and some have spread as far as Spain to become part of the metropolitan language, e.g., **alpaca, cacique, canoa, chocolate, huracán, maíz,** and **tomate.**

Old and Modern Spanish. The first traces of Spanish are found in Latin documents of the eighth century and the first great monument of Spanish literature, the Poem of the Cid, was composed in the twelfth century. As the period of Old Spanish extends to the end of the fifteenth century, the epochal year of 1492 might well be regarded as the turning point to Modern Spanish. In that year the troops of Queen Isabella completed the Reconquest by driving the Moors from Granada, the great humanist, Antonio de Nebrija, published his famous grammar of the Spanish language, and Columbus discovered the New World. Thus, the influence of the Arabs in words, thought, and action, which had been so profound and vigorous for centuries, came to an end; Spanish now began to feel the full impact of the Renaissance, which brought with it, along with new ideas and new ways to express them, the stabilizing influence of grammar, formal literature, and logic; and discovery and colonization, in carrying Spanish to new and unknown lands, introduced new scientific facts and a new view of the universe which required a richer and more flexible language for expression.

Thus the new forces to which Spanish was subjected were just as complex as those of the Middle Ages. If the language of today seems so close to that of the sixteenth century, it is because of the stabilizing influence of grammar, formal literature, and logic mentioned above. This influence was reinforced by the invention of printing, the spread of French Classicism, and the establishment of the Spanish Academy in 1713, whose emblem bears the significant legend: Limpia, fija y da esplendor. At the same time, as a result of the wide geographic spread of the Spanish-speaking regions of the globe, Spanish has grown luxuriantly in keeping pace with the developments of science, art, commerce, and industry in the nineteenth and twentieth centuries.

OUTLINE OF SPANISH GRAMMAR

§12. Spelling and Pronunciation. 1. The letters of the Spanish alphabet are listed below with their names and approximate sounds in terms of equivalent English sounds. Note that **ch, ll, ñ,** and **rr** are considered to be separate single letters in Spanish and that **ch, ll,** and **ñ** (but not **rr**) are treated as separate single letters in the alphabetization of Spanish words. Thus all words beginning in **ch, ll,** and **ñ** are regularly listed after the complete listing of all words beginning in **c, l,** and **n** respectively. And thus, for example, **dúctil** is alphabetized ahead of **ducha, pelo** ahead of **pellejo,** and **vino** ahead of **viña.**

The names of all the letters are feminine and the feminine article is used before **a** and **h** in spite of the fact that they are stressed, viz., **la a** and **la h (la hache).**

LETTER	NAME	APPROXIMATE SOUND
a	a	Like *a* in English *father*, e.g., **taza, fácil.**
b	be	At the beginning of a word and when preceded by **m**, like *b* in English *boat*, e.g., **bola, comba.** Between two vowels and when preceded by a vowel and followed by **l** or **r**, somewhat like *v* in English *voodoo* except that it is formed with both lips (not with the lower lip and the upper teeth), e.g., **caber, tabla, sobre.** It is generally silent and often dropped in spelling before **s**, e.g., **obscuro** or **oscuro, subscribir** or **suscribir.**
c	ce	When followed by **e** or **i**, like *th* in English *think* in Castilian but like *c* in English *cent* in American Spanish, e.g., **nacer, ciento.** When followed by **a, o, u,** or a consonant, like *c* in English *coal*, e.g., **canto, cola, cubo, pacto, creer.** Double **c** is always followed by **e** or **i.** This means that the first **c**, being followed by a consonant, has the sound of *c* in English *coal*, while the second **c**, being followed by **e** or **i**, has in Castilian the sound of *th* in English *think* and in American Spanish the sound of *c* in English *cent*, e.g., **accidente, lección.**
ch	che	Like *ch* in English *such*, e.g., **mucho.**
d	de	Generally, like *d* in English *dance*, e.g., **dar, conde.** Between two vowels, when preceded by a vowel and followed by **r**, and when final, like *th* in English *this*, e.g., **nada, piedra, usted.**
e	e	When ending a syllable, like *e* in English *they* (without the following sound of *y*), e.g., **dedo, menos.** When followed by a consonant in the same syllable, like *e* in English *bet*, e.g., **pérfido, celda.**
f	efe	Like *f* in English *foot*, e.g., **fonda, afectar.**
g	ge	When followed by **e** or **i**, like *h* in English *house*, e.g., **género, gitano.** When followed by **a, o, u,** or a consonant, like *g* in English *goat*, e.g., **gasto, goma, gusano, grande.** The **u** of **ue** and **ui** is silent after **g** unless marked with a diaeresis, when it has the sound of English *w*, e.g., **guerra, guía,** but **agüero, lingüístico.**
h	hache	Always silent, e.g., **hijo, alcohol.**
i	i	Like *i* in English *machine*, e.g., **línea, salido.**
j	jota	Like *h* in English *house*, e.g., **jardín, justo.** Final **j** is generally silent, e.g., **reloj.**
k	ka	Like English *k*, e.g., **kantiano, kilogramo.**
l	ele	Somewhat like *l* in English *lamb*, e.g., **bala, labio.**
ll	elle	Somewhat like *lli* in English *million* in Castilian but like *y* in English *yet* in American Spanish, e.g., **sello, llover.**
m	eme	Like *m* in English *money*, e.g., **tomar, musa.**
n	ene	Generally, like *n* in English *nut*, e.g., **andar, nombre.** But before **v**, like *m* in English *money*, e.g., **invadir, convidar.** And before hard **c** and hard **g**, like *ng* in English *singer*, e.g., **banco, manga.**
ñ	eñe	Somewhat like *ni* in English *onion*, e.g., **empeño, uña.**
o	o	When ending a syllable, like *o* in English *note* (without the following sound of *w* heard in this word), e.g., **solo, poco.** When followed by a consonant in the same syllable, like *o* in English *order*, e.g., **costa, torta.**
p	pe	Like *p* in English *path*, e.g., **puente, complicar.** It is silent in **septiembre** and **séptimo.**
q	cu	Like *c* in English *coal*. This letter is always followed by **ue** or **ui**, in which the **u** is silent, e.g., **quemar, quinta.**
r	ere	At the beginning of a word and when preceded by **l, n,** or **s**, it is strongly trilled, e.g., **ramo, malrotar, conrear, israelita.** Pronounced with a single tap of the tongue in all other positions, e.g., **pero, traigo, hablar.**

LETTER	NAME	APPROXIMATE SOUND
rr	erre	Strongly trilled, e.g., **perro, correr.**
s	ese	Generally, like *s* in English *see,* e.g., **secar, cosa, español.** But before a voiced consonant **(b, d,** hard **g, l, r, m, n),** like *z* in English *zero,* e.g., **esbelto, desde, rasgo, eslavo, mismo, asno.**
t	te	Like *t* in English *top,* e.g., **tejido, pata.**
u	u	Like *u* in English *rule,* e.g., **buzo, mulo.** It is silent in **gue, gui, que,** and **qui,** but not in **güe** and **güi,** e.g., **guerra, guía, quemar, quinta,** but **agüero, lingüístico.**
v	ve *or* uve (*to avoid confusion with* be)	At the beginning of a word and when preceded by **n,** like *b* in English *boat,* e.g., **vengo, invadir.** Between two vowels, somewhat like *v* in English *voodoo* except that it is formed with both lips (not with the lower lip and the upper teeth), e.g., **tuve, severo.**
x	equis	Before a consonant, like *s* in English *see,* e.g., **explicar, sexto.** Between two vowels, with the sound of *gs,* e.g., **examen, máxima**; but in some words, like *s* in English *see,* e.g., **auxilio, exacto.** In **México** (for **Méjico**) like Spanish **j.**
y	ye (*formerly* i griega)	Like *i* in English *machine,* e.g., **y** (conjunction). Before a vowel, like *y* in English *youth,* e.g., **ya, cayó.**
z	zeda *or* zeta	Like *th* in English *think* in Castilian but like *c* in English *cent* in American Spanish, e.g., **zanco, zumbar.**

2. A diphthong is the combination into a single syllable of a vowel sound and the consonant sound of *y* (in English *yet* or English *toy*) or the consonant sound of *w* (in English *woman* or English *now*). The sound of *y* is represented in Spanish by **i** and **y, y** being used in the initial and final positions and between two vowels, the sound of *w* by **u.** Either the vowel sound or the consonant sound may come first.

It is customary to call **a, e,** and **o** strong vowels and **i (y)** and **u** weak vowels. However, in the formation of diphthongs and triphthongs containing **a, e,** and **o, i (y)** and **u** are really consonants.

Diphthongs with Vowel Sound First

DIPHTHONG	APPROXIMATE SOUND
ai	Like *i* in English *night,* e.g., **traigo.**
ay	Like *i* in English *night,* e.g., **estay.**
au	Like *ou* in English *found,* e.g., **causa.**
ei	Like *ey* in English *they,* e.g., **peine.**
ey	Like *ey* in English *they,* e.g., **rey.**
eu	Like *ayw* in English *haywire,* e.g., **deuda.**
oi	Like *oy* in English *toy,* e.g., **oigo.**
oy	Like *oy* in English *toy,* e.g., **doy.**

Diphthongs with Consonant Sound First

DIPHTHONG	APPROXIMATE SOUND
ia	Like *ya* in English *yarn,* e.g., **estudiamos.**
ya	Like *ya* in English *yarn,* e.g., **vayamos.**
ua	Like *wa* in English *wad,* e.g., **cuando.**
ie	Like *ye* in English *yet,* e.g., **tierra.**
ye	Like *ye* in English *yet,* e.g., **yerno.**
ue	Like *wa* in English *wade,* e.g., **bueno.**
io	Like *yo* in English *yoke,* e.g., **naciones.**
yo	Like *yo* in English *yoke,* e.g., **yodo.**
uo	Like *uo* in English *quote,* e.g., **cuota.**
iu	Like *yu* in English *yule,* e.g., **viudo.**
yu	Like *yu* in English *yule,* e.g., **yugo.**
ui	Like *wee* in English *week,* e.g., **cuido.**

3. A triphthong is the combination into a single syllable of the following three elements in the order given: (1) the consonant sound of *y* (represented in Spanish by **i**) or the consonant sound of *w* (represented in Spanish by **u**), (2) a vowel sound, and (3) the consonant sound of *y* (represented in Spanish by **i** or if final, by **y**) or the consonant sound of *w* (represented in Spanish by **u**).

TRIPHTHONG	APPROXIMATE SOUND
iai	Like *yi* in *yipe*, e.g., **estudiáis.**
iau	Like *eow* in *meow*, e.g., **miau.**
iei	Like the English word *yea*, e.g., **estudiéis.**
uai	Like *wi* in *wine*, e.g., **continuáis.**
uay	Like *wi* in *wine*, e.g., **guay.**
uau	Like the English word *wow*, e.g., **guau.**
uei	Like *wei* in *weigh*, e.g., **continuéis.**
uey	Like *wei* in *weigh*, e.g., **buey.**

4. Vowels, diphthongs, and triphthongs are vocalic units and words have as many syllables as they have vocalic units. Spanish words are divided into syllables according to the following principles.

(*a*) When a single consonant (including **ch, ll,** and **rr**) stands between two vocalic units it belongs to the following syllable, e.g., **ca·ja, cau·sa, bue·no, o·cho, se·llo, ca·rro.**

(*b*) When a consonant group consisting of a mute plus a liquid (i.e., of **b, c, d, f, g, p,** or **t** followed by **l** or **r**) stands between two vocalic units, the group belongs to the following syllable, e.g., **ha·blar, bu·cle, so·bre, co·fre, ma·triz.**

(*c*) When a consonant group consisting of any other pair of consonants stands between two vocalic units, the first consonant belongs to the preceding syllable, the second to the following syllable, e.g., **ac·to, en·cen·der, mas·lo, lec·ción.**

(*d*) When a consonant group consisting of more than two consonants stands between two vocalic units, the last two consonants are generally a mute plus a liquid (i.e., **b, c, d, f, g, p,** or **t** followed by **l** or **r**) and they both belong to the following syllable, e.g., **am·blar, pon·dré, ex·pli·car, com·prar.** However, if the second consonant is **s,** it belongs with the first consonant to the preceding syllable, e.g., **cons·tan·te, pers·pi·caz.**

(*e*) When no consonant stands between the two vowels, they belong to separate syllables (unless they combine to form a diphthong), e.g., **sa·e·ta, fe·o, cre·er, to·ar.** In accordance with this principle, when a letter which regularly represents the consonant element of a diphthong or triphthong has the value of a vowel, it belongs to a separate syllable and this is indicated by the written accent, e.g., **ca·í·do, ba·úl, se·rí·a, se·rí·ais.**

(*f*) When the letter **y** stands between two vowels, it forms a diphthong with the following vowel and therefore, belongs to the following syllable, e.g., **va·ya, cu·yo, le·yó.**

(*g*) Prefixes that are felt to be prefixes form separate syllables even if the division is contrary to the above principles, e.g., **ab·ro·gar, sub·le·var, des·a·sir.** But **s** in a three-consonant group is kept with the prefix, e.g., **cons·tan·te, pers·pi·caz.**

5. All Spanish words except compound nouns and adverbs ending in **mente** have but one stress. And the position of this stress is always shown by the spelling in accordance with four simple rules.

(*a*) Words ending in a vowel sound or in **n** or **s** are stressed on the syllable next to the last, e.g., **cosecha, antiguo, serio, comen, casas.**

(*b*) Words ending in a consonant except **n** or **s,** but including **y,** are stressed on the last syllable, e.g., **calor, papel, feliz, Uruguay, estoy.**

(*c*) If the stress does not fall in accordance with one or the other of the above rules, it is indicated by a written accent, e.g., **café, encendí, salís, nación, difícil, lápiz, república.**

(*d*) The stress (and the written accent) falls on the vowel element (strong vowel) of stressed diphthongs and triphthongs, e.g., **traigo, peine, cuando, bueno, habláis, continuáis.** If the letter which regularly represents the consonant element of a diphthong or triphthong has the value of a vowel, it forms a separate stressed syllable and this is indicated by the written accent, e.g., **caído, baúl, sería, seríais.**

Two words spelled alike are often distinguished by the written accent on the stressed vowel of one of them, e.g., **él** *he* and **el** *the,* **éste** *this one* and **este** *this,* **sí** *yes* and **si** *if,* **más** *more* and **mas** *but.* Interrogative and exclamatory pronouns, adjectives, and adverbs are thus distinguished from similarly spelled relative pronouns and subordinating conjunctions, e.g., **quién** and **quien, cuál** and **cual, dónde** and **donde.**

6. Spanish punctuation differs from English chiefly in the use of the inverted question mark before interrogative words and sentences and the inverted exclamation point before exclamatory words and sentences, e.g., **¿Qué hora es?, ¡Qué lástima!**

7. Capitalization is not used as much in Spanish as in English. Nouns and adjectives of nationality, religion, etc., the names of the days of the week, and the names of the months are generally not capitalized, e.g., **un español** *a Spaniard,* **el idioma español** *the Spanish language,* **un metodista** *a Methodist,* **lunes** *Monday,* **marzo** *March.*

§13. Plural of Nouns. Nouns ending in a vowel add **s** to form the plural, e.g., **casa** *house* and **casas** *houses,* **diente** *tooth* and **dientes** *teeth,* **tribu** *tribe* and **tribus** *tribes.* But nouns ending in accented **a, i,** or **u** add **es** to form the plural, e.g., **bajá** *pasha* and **bajaes** *pashas,* **rubí** *ruby* and **rubíes** *rubies,* **iglú** *igloo* and **iglúes** *igloos.* Nouns ending in a consonant (including **y**) add **es** to form the plural, e.g., **balcón** *balcony* and **balcones** *balconies,* **flor** *flower* and **flores** *flowers,* **mes** *month* and **meses** *months,* **rey** *king* and **reyes** *kings.* But nouns ending in **z** change this **z** to **c** and add **es,** e.g., **vez** *time* and **veces** *times,* **lápiz** *pencil* and **lápices** *pencils.* And nouns ending in **s** preceded by an unaccented vowel do not change in the plural, e.g., **crisis** *crisis* and **crisis** *crises,* **lunes** *Monday* and **lunes** *Mondays.*

The syllable stressed in the singular is always stressed in the plural except in a few words such as **carácter** and **régimen,** whose plurals are **caracteres** and **regímenes.** However, the written accent found on the last syllable of the singular of some nouns ending in **n** and **s** is not necessary in the plural and must be accordingly omitted, e.g., **acción** *action* and **acciones** *actions,* **marqués** *marquess* and **marqueses** *marquesses.*

§14. Inflection and Comparison of Adjectives. 1. Adjectives ending in **o** change **o** to **a** to form the feminine, e.g., **alto** and **alta** *high.* Adjectives ending in any other letter have the same form in both genders, e.g., **diferente** *different,* **difícil** *difficult,* and **belga** *Belgian.* However, adjectives of nationality ending in **l, s,** and **z,** adjectives ending in **or** (except comparatives), and adjectives ending in **án** or **ón** add **a** to form the feminine, e.g., **español** and **española** *Spanish,* **francés** and **francesa** *French,* **consolador** and **consoladora** *consoling,* **alazán** and **alazana** *sorrel,* **barrigón** and **barrigona** *big-bellied.* Comparatives ending in **or** do not change to form the feminine, e.g., **mejor** *better* and **inferior** *lower, inferior.*

Adjectives ending in a vowel form their plural by adding **s,** e.g., **alto** and **altos, alta** and **altas** *high,* **diferente** and **diferentes** *different,* **belga** and **belgas** *Belgian.* Adjectives ending in a consonant form their plural by adding **es,** e.g., **fácil** and **fáciles** *easy,* **moral** and **morales** *moral.* But adjectives ending in **z** change this **z** to **c** and add **es,** e.g., **feliz** and **felices** *happy.* When **bueno** *good,* **malo** *bad,* **primero** *first,* and **tercero** *third* are used before a masculine singular noun, they drop their final **o,** e.g., **buen libro** *good book,* **primer capítulo** *first chapter.* When **grande** *large, big, great* is used before a masculine or feminine singular noun, it drops its last syllable **de,** e.g., **gran libro** *large book,* **gran nación** *great nation.* If the noun begins with a vowel or **h,** either **gran** or **grande** may be used, e.g., **gran amigo** or **grande amigo** *great friend.* The masculine **santo** becomes **san** before all names of saints except those beginning with **Do** and **To,** e.g., **San Francisco** *Saint Francis,* but **Santo Domingo** *Saint Dominic,* **Santo Tomás** *Saint Thomas.* Before common nouns it is not shortened, e.g., **el Santo Papa** *the Holy Father.* The indefinite article **un** and the indefinite adjectives **algún** and **ningún** are formed the same way as **buen, mal, primer, tercer,** that is, by dropping the **o** of **uno, alguno,** and **ninguno.**

2. The comparative and superlative of adjectives and adverbs are formed by placing **más** before the adjective or adverb, e.g., **rico** *rich,* **más rico** *richer, richest;* **despacio** *slowly,* **más despacio** *more slowly, most slowly.* The sense generally requires the use of the definite article or a possessive adjective with the superlative in English and Spanish, e.g., **Es el alumno más inteligente de la clase** *He is the most intelligent student in the class.*

Some adjectives and adverbs have irregular comparatives and superlatives.

POSITIVE	SUPERLATIVE
bueno *good, well*	**mejor** *better, best*
grande *large, big*	**mayor** *greater, greatest; older, oldest* **más grande** *larger, largest*
malo *bad, ill*	**peor** *worse, worst*
pequeño *small, little*	**menor** *smaller, smallest; younger, youngest* **más pequeño** *smaller, smallest*
bien *well*	**mejor** *better, best*
mal *badly, poorly*	**peor** *worse, worst*
mucho *much*	**más** *more, most*
muchos *many*	**más** *more, most*
poco *little*	**menos** *less, least*
pocos *few*	**menos** *fewer, fewest*

The expression **más bien** means *rather.*

Comparatives and superlatives ending in **or** do not change in the feminine.

There is also an absolute superlative, which is formed by adding the ending **ísimo** to the stem of the adjective. It does not form comparisons but has intensive force equivalent to **muy** with the positive degree, e.g., **cansadísimo** *most tired, very tired;* **elocuentísimo** *most eloquent, very eloquent.*

Adjectives ending in **co** and **go** change **c** and **g** to **qu** and **gu** respectively, e.g., **rico** *rich,* **riquísimo** *very rich;* **largo** *long,* **larguísimo** *very long.* Adjectives ending in **ble** change this ending to **bilísimo,** e.g., **probable** *probable,* **probabilísimo** *very probable.* And adjectives ending in **io** show a contraction of the **i** of **io** with the **i** of **ísimo,** e.g., **limpio** *clean,* **limpísimo** *very clean.* An important exception is **frío** *cold,* **friísimo** *very cold.* And adjectives containing the accented diphthong **ie** or **ue** change **ie** to **e** and **ue** to **o** when adding **ísimo,** e.g., **ardiente** *ardent,* **ardentísimo** *very ardent;* **nuevo** *new,* **novísimo** *very new.*

§15. Spelling-changing Verbs. Verbs which, though regular to the ear, are irregular in spelling are called spelling-changing verbs. There are two groups, those irregular in the spelling of the stem and those irregular in the spelling of the ending. The first group consists of verbs ending in **car, gar, guar, zar; cer** preceded by a consonant; **cir** preceded by a consonant; **ger, gir, guir,** and **quir.** The second group consists of verbs of the second and third conjugations whose stems end in **ll, ñ,** or a vowel.

FIRST GROUP

MODEL	CHANGE	OCCURRENCE
1. **tocar**	**c** to **qu** before **e,** e.g., **toqué**	In 1st sg. pret. ind. and whole pres. subj.
2. **ligar**	**g** to **gu** before **e,** e.g., **ligué**	
3. **averiguar**	**gu** to **gü** before **e,** e.g., **averigüé**	
4. **rezar**	**z** to **c** before **e,** e.g., **recé**	
5. **vencer**	**c** to **z** before **o** and **a,** e.g., **venzo**	In 1st sg. pres. ind. and whole pres. subj.
6. **esparcir**	**c** to **z** before **o** and **a,** e.g., **esparzo**	
7. **escoger**	**g** to **j** before **o** and **a,** e.g., **escojo**	
8. **dirigir**	**g** to **j** before **o** and **a,** e.g., **dirijo**	
9. **distinguir**	**gu** to **g** before **o** and **a,** e.g., **distingo**	
10. **delinquir**	**qu** to **c** before **o** and **a,** e.g., **delinco**	

SECOND GROUP

MODEL	CHANGE	OCCURRENCE
11. **empeller**	**i** of **ió** and **ie** falls, e.g., **empelló**	In ger., 3d sg. and 3d pl. pret. ind., whole imperf. subj. (**s**-form and **r**-form), and whole fut. subj.
12. **bullir**	**i** of **ió** and **ie** falls, e.g., **bulló**	
13. **tañer**	**i** of **ió** and **ie** falls, e.g., **tañó**	
14. **bruñir**	**i** of **ió** and **ie** falls, e.g., **bruñó**	
15. **creer**	1. **i** of **ió** and **ie** changes to **y,** e.g., **creyó**	In ger., 3d sg. and 3 pl. pret. ind., whole imperf. subj. (**s**-form and **r**-form), and whole fut. subj.
	2. stressed **i** of endings takes accent mark, e.g., **creído**	In 2d sg., 1st pl., and 2d pl. pret. ind. and past participle
16. **oír**	1. **i** of **ió** and **ie** changes to **y,** e.g., **oyó**	In ger., 3d sg. and 3d pl. pret. ind., whole imperf. subj. (**s**-form and **r**-form), and whole fut. subj.
	2. stressed **i** of endings takes accent mark, e.g., **oído**	In 1st pl. pres. ind., 2d sg., 1st pl. and 2d pl. pret. ind., 2d pl. impv., and past participle

§16. Radical-changing Verbs. The irregularity of radical-changing verbs consists in a change in the radical vowel in certain forms. There are four classes of these verbs. The first class consists of verbs of the first and second conjugations with radical **e** and **o**; the second class consists of verbs of the third conjugation with radical **e** and **o**; the third class consists of verbs of the third conjugation with radical **e**; and the fourth class consists of verbs of all three conjugations with radical **ai, au,** and **eu.**

First Class

MODEL	CHANGE	OCCURRENCE
1. **acertar** 2. **perder** 3. **rodar** 4. **morder**	**e** stressed changes to **ie,** e.g., **acierto** **e** stressed changes to **ie,** e.g., **pierdo** **o** stressed changes to **ue,** e.g., **ruedo** **o** stressed changes to **ue,** e.g., **muerdo**	In 1st, 2d, 3d sg. and 3d pl. pres. ind. and subj., and 2d sg. impv.

Second Class

MODEL	CHANGE	OCCURRENCE
5. **mentir**	1. **e** stressed changes to **ie,** e.g., **miento**	In 1st, 2d, 3d sg. and 3d pl. pres. ind. and pres. subj., and 2d sg. impv.
	2. **e** unstressed and followed by an ending containing **a, ió,** or **ie** changes to **i,** e.g., **mintamos**	In ger., 1st and 2d pl. pres. subj., 3d sg. and pl. pret. ind., whole imperf. subj. (**s**-form and **r**-form), and whole future subj.
6. **dormir**	1. **o** stressed changes to **ue,** e.g., **duermo**	In 1st, 2d, 3d sg. and 3d pl. pres. ind. and pres. subj., and 2d sg. impv.
	2. **o** unstressed and followed by an ending containing **a, ió,** or **ie** changes to **u,** e.g., **durmamos**	In ger., 1st and 2d pl. pres. subj., 3d sg. and pl. pret. ind., whole imperf. subj. (**s**-form and **r**-form), and whole future subj.

Third Class

MODEL	CHANGE	OCCURRENCE
7. **vestir**	1. **e** stressed changes to **i,** e.g., **visto**	In 1st, 2d, 3d sg. and 3d pl. pres. ind. and pres. subj., and 2d sg. impv.
	2. **e** unstressed and followed by an ending containing **a, ió,** or **ie** changes to **i,** e.g., **vistamos**	In ger., 1st and 2d pl. pres. subj., 3d sg. and pl. pret. ind., whole imperf. subj. (**s**-form and **r**-form), and whole future subj.

Fourth Class

MODEL	CHANGE	OCCURRENCE
8. **reunir**	**ai, au,** and **eu** stressed change to **aí, aú,** and **eú** repectively, e.g., **reúne**	In 1st, 2d, 3d sg. and 3d pl. pres. ind. and pres. subj., and 2d sg. impv.

9. Some verbs in **iar** and all verbs in **uar** (except those in **cuar** and **guar**) are radical-changing verbs in that the **i** or **u** with which the stem ends becomes the radical vowel in those forms in which the radical vowel is regularly stressed, namely, the whole singular and the third plural of the present indicative and the present subjunctive, and the second singular imperative. This is shown by the written accent on the **i** or **u,** e.g., **varío** from **variar, continúo** from **continuar.**

§17. Irregular Verbs. In addition to the irregularities of spelling-changing verbs and radical-changing verbs, there are other irregularities in certain roots, stems, and endings. These are classified below.

1. The following verbs have irregular stems in the first singular present indicative and the whole present subjunctive.

MODEL	1ST SG. PRES. IND.
argüir	**arguyo**
asir	**asgo**
caber	**quepo**
caer	**caigo**
conocer	**conozco**
crecer	**crezco**
decir	**digo**
deducir	**deduzco**
destruir	**destruyo**
hacer	**hago**
lucir	**luzco**
oír	**oigo**
poner	**pongo**
raer	{ **raigo** / **rayo**
roer	{ **roigo** / **royo**
salir	**salgo**
tener	**tengo**
traer	**traigo**
valer	**valgo**
venir	**vengo**
ver	**veo**
yacer	{ **yazco** / **yazgo** / **yago**

2. The following verbs have irregular endings in the first singular present indicative and the present subjunctive cannot be derived from them.

MODEL	1ST SG. PRES. IND.
dar	**doy**
estar	**estoy**
haber	**he**
ir	**voy**
saber	**sé**
ser	**soy**

3. The following verbs have a **y** inserted between the radical vowel and the vowel of the ending in the second and third singular and the third plural present indicative and the second singular imperative.

MODEL	2D SG. PRES. IND.
argüir	**arguyes**
destruir	**destruyes**
oír	**oyes**

4. The following verbs have irregular imperfect indicatives.

MODEL	1ST SG. IMPERF. IND.
ir	**iba**
ser	**era**
ver	**veía**

5. The following verbs have irregular stems in the future indicative and these stems continue through the whole conditional.

MODEL	1ST SG. FUT. IND.
caber	**cabré**
decir	**diré**
haber	**habré**
hacer	**haré**
poder	**podré**
poner	**pondré**
querer	**querré**
saber	**sabré**
salir	**saldré**
tener	**tendré**
valer	**valdré**
venir	**vendré**

6. The following verbs have irregular radicals (vowel, stem, or both) in the whole preterit indicative, the whole imperfect subjunctive (**s**-form and **r**-form), and the whole future subjunctive. They have the further irregularity in the preterit indicative of having the stress on the radical vowel in the first and third singular forms. If the stem ends in **j**, the third plural preterit indicative, the whole imperfect subjunctive (**s**-form and **r**-form), and the whole future subjunctive have **e** instead of **ie** in the ending. The verb **placer** has these irregularities only in the forms of the third person singular. And one verb, **hacer**, has the orthographic change from **c** to **z** in the third singular preterit indicative.

MODEL	1ST SG. PRET. IND.
andar	**anduve**
caber	**cupe**
decir	**dije** (3d pl.: **dijeron**)
deducir	**deduje** (3d pl.: **dedujeron**)
estar	**estuve**
haber	**hube**
hacer	**hice** (3d sg.: **hizo**)
placer	**plugo**
poder	**pude**
poner	**puse**
querer	**quise**
saber	**supe**
tener	**tuve**
traer	**traje** (3d pl.: **trajeron**)
venir	**vine**

7. The following verbs have irregular preterit indicatives and derived tenses.

MODEL	1ST SG. PRET. IND.
dar	**di**
ir	**fui**
ser	**fui**

8. The following verbs have irregular second singular imperatives.

MODEL	2D SG. IMPV.
decir	**di**
haber	**hé**
hacer	**haz**
ir	**vé**
poner	**pon**
salir	**sal**
ser	**sé**
tener	**ten**
valer	**val**
venir	**ven**
yacer	**yaz**

The compounds of **poner, tener,** and **venir** require a written accent on the second singular imperative, e.g., **supón** (of **suponer**), **retén** (of **retener**), **convén** (of **convenir**). This is true also of the compounds of **ver,** e.g., **entrevé** (of **entrever**). In addition to **benedecir (§24)** and **maldecir** (also **§24**) the compounds of **decir** have second singular imperatives in **-dice,** e.g., **desdice** (of **desdecir**). And **satisfacer** has both a regular and an irregular second singular imperative, viz., **satisface** and **satisfaz.**

9. The following verbs, some regular and some irregular, have irregular past participles. Those in standard type are compounds of those in boldface.

MODEL	PAST PARTICIPLE	MODEL	PAST PARTICIPLE
abrir	**abierto**	prescribir	prescrito
entreabrir	entreabierto	proscribir	proscrito
reabrir	reabierto	reescribir	reescrito
cubrir	**cubierto**	sobrescribir	sobrescrito
descubrir	descubierto	subscribir	subscrito
encubrir	encubierto	transcribir	transcrito
recubrir	recubierto	**freír**	**frito**
redescubrir	redescubierto	refreír	refrito
decir	**dicho**	sofreír	sofrito
antedecir	antedicho	**hacer**	**hecho**
contradecir	contradicho	contrahacer	contrahecho
desdecir	desdicho	deshacer	deshecho
interdecir	interdicho	rehacer	rehecho
predecir	predicho	satisfacer	satisfecho
redecir	redicho	**imprimir**	**impreso**
escribir	**escrito**	reimprimir	reimpreso
adscribir	adscrito	**morir**	**muerto**
circunscribir	circunscrito	entremorir	entremuerto
describir	descrito	premorir	premuerto
inscribir	inscrito	**poner**	**puesto**
manuscribir	manuscrito	anteponer	antepuesto

MODEL	PAST PARTICIPLE	MODEL	PAST PARTICIPLE
componer	compuesto	yuxtaponer	yuxtapuesto
contraponer	contrapuesto	**proveer**	**provisto**
deponer	depuesto	desproveer	desprovisto
descomponer	descompuesto	**pudrir**	**podrido**
desimponer	desimpuesto	repudrir	repodrido
disponer	dispuesto	**romper**	**roto**
exponer	expuesto	**solver**	**suelto**
imponer	impuesto	absolver	absuelto
indisponer	indispuesto	disolver	disuelto
interponer	interpuesto	ensolver	ensuelto
oponer	opuesto	resolver	resuelto
posponer	pospuesto	**ver**	**visto**
predisponer	predispuesto	antever	antevisto
preponer	prepuesto	entrever	entrevisto
presuponer	presupuesto	prever	previsto
proponer	propuesto	rever	revisto
recomponer	recompuesto	trasver	trasvisto
reponer	repuesto	**volver**	**vuelto**
sobreexponer	sobreexpuesto	desenvolver	desenvuelto
sobreponer	sobrepuesto	desvolver	desvuelto
superponer	superpuesto	devolver	devuelto
suponer	supuesto	envolver	envuelto
transponer	transpuesto	revolver	revuelto

INFINITIVE GERUND AND PAST PARTICIPLE	PRESENT INDICATIVE	PRESENT SUBJUNCTIVE	IMPERFECT INDICATIVE	FUTURE INDICATIVE	CONDITIONAL
§18 **acertar** acertando acertado	**acierto** **aciertas** **acierta** acertamos acertáis **aciertan**	**acierte** **aciertes** **acierte** acertemos acertéis **acierten**	acertaba acertabas acertaba acertábamos acertabais acertaban	acertaré acertarás acertará acertaremos acertaréis acertarán	acertaría acertarías acertaría acertaríamos acertaríais acertarían
§19 **agorar** agorando agorado	**agüero** **agüeras** **agüera** agoramos agoráis **agüeran**	**agüere** **agüeres** **agüere** agoremos agoréis **agüeren**	agoraba agorabas agoraba agorábamos agorabais agoraban	agoraré agorarás agorará agoraremos agoraréis agorarán	agoraría agorarías agoraría agoraríamos agoraríais agorarían
§20 **andar** andando andado	ando andas anda andamos andáis andan	ande andes ande andemos andéis anden	andaba andabas andaba andábamos andabais andaban	andaré andarás andará andaremos andaréis andarán	andaría andarías andaría andaríamos andaríais andarían
§21 **argüir** **arguyendo** argüido	**arguyo** **arguyes** **arguye** argüimos argüís **arguyen**	**arguya** **arguyas** **arguya** **arguyamos** **arguyáis** **arguyan**	argüía argüías argüía argüíamos argüíais argüían	argüiré argüirás argüirá argüiremos argüiréis argüirán	argüiría argüirías argüiría argüiríamos argüiríais argüirían
§22 **asir** asiendo asido	**asgo** ases ase asimos asís asen	**asga** **asgas** **asga** **asgamos** **asgáis** **asgan**	asía asías asía asíamos asíais asían	asiré asirás asirá asiremos asiréis asirán	asiría asirías asiría asiríamos asiríais asirían
§23 **averiguar** averiguando averiguado	averiguo averiguas averigua averiguamos averiguáis averiguan	**averigüe** **averigües** **averigüe** **averigüemos** **averigüéis** **averigüen**	averiguaba averiguabas averiguaba averiguábamos averiguabais averiguaban	averiguaré averiguarás averiguará averiguaremos averiguaréis averiguarán	averiguaría averiguarías averiguaría averiguaríamos averiguaríais averiguarían
§24 **bendecir** **bendiciendo** bendecido	**bendigo** **bendices** **bendice** bendecimos bendecís **bendicen**	**bendiga** **bendigas** **bendiga** **bendigamos** **bendigáis** **bendigan**	bendecía bendecías bendecía bendecíamos bendecíais bendecían	bendeciré bendecirás bendecirá bendeciremos bendeciréis bendecirán	bendeciría bendecirías bendeciría bendeciríamos bendeciríais bendecirían
§25 **bruñir** **bruñendo** bruñido	bruño bruñes bruñe bruñimos bruñís bruñen	bruña bruñas bruña bruñamos bruñáis bruñan	bruñía bruñías bruñía bruñíamos bruñíais bruñían	bruñiré bruñirás bruñirá bruñiremos bruñiréis bruñirán	bruñiría bruñirías bruñiría bruñiríamos bruñiríais bruñirían
§26 **bullir** **bullendo** bullido	bullo bulles bulle bullimos bullís bullen	bulla bullas bulla bullamos bulláis bullan	bullía bullías bullía bullíamos bullíais bullían	bulliré bullirás bullirá bulliremos bulliréis bullirán	bulliría bullirías bulliría bulliríamos bulliríais bullirían
§27 **caber** cabiendo cabido	**quepo** cabes cabe cabemos cabéis caben	**quepa** **quepas** **quepa** **quepamos** **quepáis** **quepan**	cabía cabías cabía cabíamos cabíais cabían	**cabré** **cabrás** **cabrá** **cabremos** **cabréis** **cabrán**	**cabría** **cabrías** **cabría** **cabríamos** **cabríais** **cabrían**

PRETERIT INDICATIVE	IMPERF. SUBJ. s-FORM	IMPERF. SUBJ. r-FORM	FUTURE SUBJUNCTIVE	IMPERATIVE	NOTES AND REFERENCES
acerté acertaste acertó acertamos acertasteis acertaron	acertase acertases acertase acertásemos acertaseis acertasen	acertara acertaras acertara acertáramos acertarais acertaran	acertare acertares acertare acertáremos acertareis acertaren	**acierta** acertad	**§16,** 1
agoré agoraste agoró agoramos agorasteis agoraron	agorase agorases agorase agorásemos agoraseis agorasen	agorara agoraras agorara agoráramos agorarais agoraran	agorare agorares agorare agoráremos agorareis agoraren	**agüera** agorad	Like **§77** with diaeresis on **u** of **ue**
anduve **anduviste** **anduvo** **anduvimos** **anduvisteis** **anduvieron**	**anduviese** **anduvieses** **anduviese** **anduviésemos** **anduvieseis** **anduviesen**	**anduviera** **anduvieras** **anduviera** **anduviéramos** **anduvierais** **anduvieran**	**anduviere** **anduvieres** **anduviere** **anduviéremos** **anduviereis** **anduvieren**	anda andad	**§17,** 6
argüí argüiste **arguyó** argüimos argüisteis **arguyeron**	**arguyese** **arguyeses** **arguyese** **arguyésemos** **arguyeseis** **arguyesen**	**arguyera** **arguyeras** **arguyera** **arguyeramos** **arguyerais** **arguyeran**	**arguyere** **arguyeres** **arguyere** **arguyéremos** **arguyereis** **arguyeren**	**arguye** argüid	Like **§41** with diaeresis on **u** before stressed **i**
así asiste asió asimos asisteis asieron	asiese asieses asiese asiésemos asieseis asiesen	asiera asieras asiera asiéramos asierais asieran	asiere asieres asiere asiéremos asiereis asieren	ase asid	**§17,** 1
averigüé averiguaste averiguó averiguamos averiguasteis averiguaron	averiguase averiguases averiguase averiguásemos averiguaseis averiguasen	averiguara averiguaras averiguara averiguáramos averiguarais averiguaran	averiguare averiguares averiguare averiguáremos averiguareis averiguaren	averigua averiguad	**§15,** 3
bendije **bendijiste** **bendijo** **bendijimos** **bendijisteis** **bendijeron**	**bendijese** **bendijeses** **bendijese** **bendijésemos** **bendijeseis** **bendijesen**	**bendijera** **bendijeras** **bendijera** **bendijéramos** **bendijerais** **bendijeran**	**bendijere** **bendijeres** **bendijere** **bendijéremos** **bendijereis** **bendijeren**	**bendice** bendecid	Like **§37** except in fut. ind., cond., impv., and past participle
bruñí bruñiste **bruñó** bruñimos bruñisteis **bruñeron**	**bruñese** **bruñeses** **bruñese** **bruñésemos** **bruñeseis** **bruñesen**	**bruñera** **bruñeras** **bruñera** **bruñéramos** **bruñerais** **bruñeran**	**bruñere** **bruñeres** **bruñere** **bruñéremos** **bruñereis** **bruñeren**	bruñe bruñid	**§15,** 14
bullí bulliste **bulló** bullimos bullisteis **bulleron**	**bullese** **bulleses** **bullese** **bullésemos** **bulleseis** **bullesen**	**bullera** **bulleras** **bullera** **bulléramos** **bullerais** **bulleran**	**bullere** **bulleres** **bullere** **bulléremos** **bullereis** **bulleren**	bulle bullid	**§15,** 12
cupe **cupiste** **cupo** **cupimos** **cupisteis** **cupieron**	**cupiese** **cupieses** **cupiese** **cupiésemos** **cupieseis** **cupiesen**	**cupiera** **cupieras** **cupiera** **cupiéramos** **cupierais** **cupieran**	**cupiere** **cupieres** **cupiere** **cupiéremos** **cupiereis** **cupieren**	cabe cabed	**§17,** 1, 5, & 6

INFINITIVE GERUND AND PAST PARTICIPLE	PRESENT INDICATIVE	PRESENT SUBJUNCTIVE	IMPERFECT INDICATIVE	FUTURE INDICATIVE	CONDITIONAL
§28 **caer** **cayendo** **caído**	**caigo** caes cae caemos caéis caen	**caiga** **caigas** **caiga** **caigamos** **caigáis** **caigan**	caía caías caía caíamos caíais caían	caeré caerás caerá caeremos caeréis caerán	caería caerías caería caeríamos caeríais caerían
§29 **cegar** cegando cegado	**ciego** **ciegas** **ciega** cegamos cegáis **ciegan**	**ciegue** **ciegues** **ciegue** **ceguemos** **ceguéis** **cieguen**	cegaba cegabas cegaba cegábamos cegabais cegaban	cegaré cegarás cegará cegaremos cegaréis cegarán	cegaría cegarías cegaría cegaríamos cegaríais cegarían
§30 **cocer** cociendo cocido	**cuezo** **cueces** **cuece** cocemos cocéis **cuecen**	**cueza** **cuezas** **cueza** **cozamos** **cozáis** **cuezan**	cocía cocías cocía cocíamos cocíais cocían	coceré cocerás cocerá coceremos coceréis cocerán	cocería cocerías cocería coceríamos coceríais cocerían
§31 **comenzar** comenzando comenzado	**comienzo** **comienzas** **comienza** comenzamos comenzáis **comienzan**	**comience** **comiences** **comience** **comencemos** **comencéis** **comiencen**	comenzaba comenzabas comenzaba comenzábamos comenzabais comenzaban	comenzaré comenzarás comenzará comenzaremos comenzaréis comenzarán	comenzaría comenzarías comenzaría comenzaríamos comenzaríais comenzarían
§32 **conocer** conociendo conocido	**conozco** conoces conoce conocemos conocéis conocen	**conozca** **conozcas** **conozca** **conozcamos** **conozcáis** **conozcan**	conocía conocías conocía conocíamos conocíais conocían	conoceré conocerás conocerá conoceremos conoceréis conocerán	conocería conocerías conocería conoceríamos conoceríais conocerían
§33 **continuar** continuando continuado	**continúo** **continúas** **continúa** continuamos continuáis **continúan**	**continúe** **continúes** **continúe** continuemos continuéis **continúen**	continuaba continuabas continuaba continuábamos continuabais continuaban	continuaré continuarás continuará continuaremos continuaréis continuarán	continuaría continuarías continuaría continuaríamos continuaríais continuarían
§34 **crecer** creciendo crecido	**crezco** creces crece crecemos crecéis crecen	**crezca** **crezcas** **crezca** **crezcamos** **crezcáis** **crezcan**	crecía crecías crecía crecíamos crecíais crecían	creceré crecerás crecerá creceremos creceréis crecerán	crecería crecerías crecería creceríamos creceríais crecerían
§35 **creer** **creyendo** **creído**	creo crees cree creemos creéis creen	crea creas crea creamos creáis crean	creía creías creía creíamos creíais creían	creeré creerás creerá creeremos creeréis creerán	creería creerías creería creeríamos creeríais creerían
§36 **dar** dando dado	**doy** das da damos dais dan	**dé** des **dé** demos deis den	daba dabas daba dábamos dabais daban	daré darás dará daremos daréis darán	daría darías daría daríamos daríais darían
§37 **decir** **diciendo** **dicho**	**digo** **dices** **dice** decimos decís **dicen**	**diga** **digas** **diga** **digamos** **digáis** **digan**	decía decías decía decíamos decíais decían	**diré** **dirás** **dirá** **diremos** **diréis** **dirán**	**diría** **dirías** **diría** **diríamos** **diríais** **dirían**

PRETERIT INDICATIVE	IMPERF. SUBJ. s-FORM	IMPERF. SUBJ. r-FORM	FUTURE SUBJUNCTIVE	IMPERATIVE	NOTES AND REFERENCES
caí	**cayese**	**cayera**	**cayere**		**§15,** 15 & **§17,** 1
caíste	**cayeses**	**cayeras**	**cayeres**	cae	
cayó	**cayese**	**cayera**	**cayere**		
caímos	**cayésemos**	**cayéramos**	**cayéremos**		
caísteis	**cayeseis**	**cayerais**	**cayereis**	caed	
cayeron	**cayesen**	**cayeran**	**cayeren**		
cegué	cegase	cegara	cegare		Combination of
cegaste	cegases	cegaras	cegares	**ciega**	**§15,** 2 & **§16,** 1
cegó	cegase	cegara	cegare		
cegamos	cegásemos	cegáramos	cegáremos		
cegasteis	cegaseis	cegarais	cegareis	cegad	
cegaron	cegasen	cegaran	cegaren		
cocí	cociese	cociera	cociere		Like **§87** al-
cociste	cocieses	cocieras	cocieres	**cuece**	though **c** is pre-
coció	cociese	cociera	cociere		ceded by a vowel
cocimos	cociésemos	cociéramos	cociéremos		
cocisteis	cocieseis	cocierais	cociereis	coced	
cocieron	cociesen	cocieran	cocieren		
comencé	comenzase	comenzara	comenzare		Combination of
comenzaste	comenzases	comenzaras	comenzares	**comienza**	**§15,** 4 & **§16,** 1
comenzó	comenzase	comenzara	comenzare		
comenzamos	comenzásemos	comenzáramos	comenzáremos		
comenzasteis	comenzaseis	comenzarais	comenzareis	comenzad	
comenzaron	comenzasen	comenzaran	comenzaren		
conocí	conociese	conociera	conociere		**§17,** 1
conociste	conocieses	conocieras	conocieres	conoce	
conoció	conociese	conociera	conociere		
conocimos	conociésemos	conociéramos	conociéremos		
conocisteis	conocieseis	conocierais	conociereis	conoced	
conocieron	conociesen	conocieran	conocieren		
continué	continuase	continuara	continuare		**§16,** 9
continuaste	continuases	continuaras	continuares	**continúa**	
continuó	continuase	continuara	continuare		
continuamos	continuásemos	continuáramos	continuáremos		
continuasteis	continuaseis	continuarais	continuareis	continuad	
continuaron	continuasen	continuaran	continuaren		
crecí	creciese	creciera	creciere		**§17,** 1
creciste	crecieses	crecieras	crecieres	crece	
creció	creciese	creciera	creciere		
crecimos	creciésemos	creciéramos	creciéremos		
crecisteis	crecieseis	crecierais	creciereis	creced	
crecieron	creciesen	crecieran	crecieren		
creí	**creyese**	**creyera**	**creyere**		**§15,** 15
creíste	**creyeses**	**creyeras**	**creyeres**	cree	
creyó	**creyese**	**creyera**	**creyere**		
creímos	**creyésemos**	**creyéramos**	**creyéremos**		
creísteis	**creyeseis**	**creyerais**	**creyereis**	creed	
creyeron	**creyesen**	**creyeran**	**creyeren**		
di	**diese**	**diera**	**diere**		**§17,** 2 & 7
diste	**dieses**	**dieras**	**dieres**	da	
dio	**diese**	**diera**	**diere**		
dimos	**diésemos**	**diéramos**	**diéremos**		
disteis	**dieseis**	**dierais**	**diereis**	dad	
dieron	**diesen**	**dieran**	**dieren**		
dije	**dijese**	**dijera**	**dijere**		**§16,** 7 & **§17,**
dijiste	**dijeses**	**dijeras**	**dijeres**	**di**	1, 5, 6, 8, & 9
dijo	**dijese**	**dijera**	**dijere**		
dijimos	**dijésemos**	**dijéramos**	**dijéremos**		
dijisteis	**dijeseis**	**dijerais**	**dijereis**	decid	
dijeron	**dijesen**	**dijeran**	**dijeren**		

INFINITIVE GERUND AND PAST PARTICIPLE	PRESENT INDICATIVE	PRESENT SUBJUNCTIVE	IMPERFECT INDICATIVE	FUTURE INDICATIVE	CONDITIONAL
§38 **deducir** deduciendo deducido	**deduzco** deduces deduce deducimos deducís deducen	**deduzca** **deduzcas** **deduzca** **deduscamos** **deduzcáis** **deduzcan**	deducía deducías deducía deducíamos deducíais deducían	deduciré deducirás deducirá deduciremos deduciréis deducirán	deduciría deducirías deduciría deduciríamos deduciríais deducirían
§39 **delinquir** delinquiendo delinquido	**delinco** delinques delinque delinquimos delinquís delinquen	**delinca** **delincas** **delinca** **delincamos** **delincáis** **delincan**	delinquía delinquías delinquía delinquíamos delinquíais delinquían	delinquiré delinquirás delinquirá delinquiremos delinquiréis delinquirán	delinquiría delinquirías delinquiría delinquiríamos delinquiríais delinquirían
§40 **desosar** desosando desosado	**deshueso** **deshuesas** **deshuesa** desosamos desosáis **deshuesan**	**deshuese** **deshueses** **deshuese** desosemos desoséis **deshuesen**	desosaba desosabas desosaba desosábamos desosabais desosaban	desosaré desosarás desosará desosaremos desosaréis desosarán	desosaría desosarías desosaría desosaríamos desosaríais desosarían
§41 **destruir** **destruyendo** destruido	**destruyo** **destruyes** **destruye** destruimos destruís **destruyen**	**destruya** **destruyas** **destruya** **destruyamos** **destruyáis** **destruyan**	destruía destruías destruía destruíamos destruíais destruían	destruiré destruirás destruirá destruiremos destruiréis destruirán	destruiría destruirías destruiría destruiríamos destruiríais destruirían
§42 **dirigir** dirigiendo dirigido	**dirijo** diriges dirige dirigimos dirigís dirigen	**dirija** **dirijas** **dirija** **dirijamos** **dirijáis** **dirijan**	dirigía dirigías dirigía dirigíamos dirigíais dirigían	dirigiré dirigirás dirigirá dirigiremos dirigiréis dirigirán	dirigiría dirigirías dirigiría dirigiríamos dirigiríais dirigirían
§43 **discernir** discerniendo discernido	**discierno** **disciernes** **discierne** discernimos discernís **disciernen**	**discierna** **disciernas** **discierna** discernamos discernáis **disciernan**	discernía discernías discernía discerníamos discerníais discernían	discerniré discernirás discernirá discerniremos discerniréis discernirán	discerniría discernirías discerniría discerniríamos discerniríais discernirían
§44 **distinguir** distinguiendo distinguido	**distingo** distingues distingue distinguimos distinguís distinguen	**distinga** **distingas** **distinga** **distingamos** **distingáis** **distingan**	distinguía distinguías distinguía distinguíamos distinguíais distinguían	distinguiré distinguirás distinguirá distinguiremos distinguiréis distinguirán	distinguiría distinguirías distinguiría distinguiríamos distinguiríais distinguirían
§45 **dormir** **durmiendo** dormido	**duermo** **duermes** **duerme** dormimos dormís **duermen**	**duerma** **duermas** **duerma** **durmamos** **durmáis** **duerman**	dormía dormías dormía dormíamos dormíais dormían	dormiré dormirás dormirá dormiremos dormiréis dormirán	dormiría dormirías dormiría dormiríamos dormiríais dormirían
§46 **empeller** **empellendo** empellido	empello empelles empelle empellemos empelléis empellen	empella empellas empella empellamos empelláis empellan	**empellía** **empellías** **empellía** **empellíamos** **empellíais** **empellían**	**empelleré** **empellerás** **empellerá** **empelleremos** **empelleréis** **empellerán**	**empellería** **empellerías** **empellería** **empelleríamos** **empelleríais** **empellerían**

PRETERIT INDICATIVE	IMPERF. SUBJ. s-FORM	IMPERF. SUBJ. r-FORM	FUTURE SUBJUNCTIVE	IMPERATIVE	NOTES AND REFERENCES
deduje	**dedujese**	**dedujera**	**dedujere**		**§17,** 1 & 6
dedujiste	**dedujeses**	**dedujeras**	**dedujeres**	deduce	
dedujo	**dedujese**	**dedujera**	**dedujere**		
dedujimos	**dedujésemos**	**dedujéramos**	**dedujéremos**		
dedujisteis	**dedujeseis**	**dedujerais**	**dedujereis**	deducid	
dedujeron	**dedujesen**	**dedujeran**	**dedujeren**		
delinquí	delinquiese	delinquiera	delinquiere		**§15,** 10
delinquiste	delinquieses	delinquieras	delinquieres	delinque	
delinquió	delinquiese	delinquiera	delinquiere		
delinquimos	delinquiésemos	delinquiéramos	delinquiéremos		
delinquisteis	delinquieseis	delinquierais	delinquiereis	delinquid	
delinquieron	delinquiesen	delinquieran	delinquieren		
desosé	desosase	desosara	desosare		Like **§77** with **h** before **ue** as in **§65**
desosaste	desosases	desosaras	desosares	**deshuesa**	
desosó	desosase	desosara	desosare		
desosamos	desosásemos	desosáramos	desosáremos		
desosasteis	desosaseis	desosarais	desosareis	desosad	
desosaron	desosasen	desosaran	desosaren		
destruí	**destruyese**	**destruyera**	**destruyere**		**§15,** 15. 1 & **§17,** 1 & 3
destruiste	**destruyeses**	**destruyeras**	**destruyeres**	**destruye**	
destruyó	**destruyese**	**destruyera**	**destruyere**		
destruimos	**destruyésemos**	**destruyéramos**	**destruyéremos**		
destruisteis	**destruyeseis**	**destruyerais**	**destruyereis**	destruid	
destruyeron	**destruyesen**	**destruyeran**	**destruyeren**		
dirigí	dirigiese	dirigiera	dirigiere		**§15,** 8
dirigiste	dirigieses	dirigieras	dirigieres	dirige	
dirigió	dirigiese	dirigiera	dirigiere		
dirigimos	dirigiésemos	dirigiéramos	dirigiéremos		
dirigisteis	dirigieseis	dirigierais	dirigiereis	dirigid	
dirigieron	dirigiesen	dirigieran	dirigieren		
discerní	discerniese	discerniera	discerniere		Third conjugation with irregularities of **§66**
discerniste	discernieses	discernieras	discernieres	**discierne**	
discernió	discerniese	discerniera	discerniere		
discernimos	discerniésemos	discerniéramos	discerniéremos		
discernisteis	discernieseis	discernierais	discerniereis	discernid	
discernieron	discerniesen	discernieran	discernieren		
distinguí	distinguiese	distinguiera	distinguiere		**§15,** 9
distinguiste	distinguieses	distinguieras	distinguieres	distingue	
distinguió	distinguiese	distinguiera	distinguiere		
distinguimos	distinguiésemos	distinguiéramos	distinguiéremos		
distinguisteis	distinguieseis	distinguierais	distinguiereis	distinguid	
distinguieron	distinguiesen	distinguieran	distinguieren		
dormí	**durmiese**	**durmiera**	**durmiere**		**§16,** 6
dormiste	**durmieses**	**durmieras**	**durmieres**	**duerme**	
durmió	**durmiese**	**durmiera**	**durmiere**		
dormimos	**durmiésemos**	**durmiéramos**	**durmiéremos**		
dormisteis	**durmieseis**	**durmierais**	**durmiereis**	dormid	
durmieron	**durmiesen**	**durmieran**	**durmieren**		
empellí	**empellese**	**empellera**	**empellere**		**§15,** 11
empelliste	**empelleses**	**empelleras**	**empelleres**	empelle	
empelló	**empellese**	**empellera**	**empellere**		
empellimos	**empellésemos**	**empelléramos**	**empelléremos**		
empellisteis	**empelleseis**	**empellerais**	**empellereis**	empelled	
empelleron	**empellesen**	**empelleran**	**empelleren**		

INFINITIVE GERUND AND PAST PARTICIPLE	PRESENT INDICATIVE	PRESENT SUBJUNCTIVE	IMPERFECT INDICATIVE	FUTURE INDICATIVE	CONDITIONAL
§47					
erguir	**yergo**	**yerga**	erguía	erguiré	erguiría
	irgo	**irga**			
irguiendo	**yergues**	**yergas**	erguías	erguirás	erguirías
	irgues	**irgas**			
erguido	**yergue**	**yerga**	erguía	erguirá	erguiría
	irgue	**irga**			
	erguimos	**irgamos**	erguíamos	erguiremos	erguiríamos
	erguís	**irgáis**	erguíais	erguiréis	erguiríais
	yerguen	**yergan**	erguían	erguirán	erguirían
	irguen	**irgan**			
§48					
errar	**yerro**	**yerre**	erraba	erraré	erraría
errando	**yerras**	**yerres**	errabas	errarás	errarías
errado	**yerra**	**yerre**	erraba	errará	erraría
	erramos	erremos	errábamos	erraremos	erraríamos
	erráis	erréis	errabais	erraréis	erraríais
	yerran	**yerren**	erraban	errarán	errarían
§49					
escoger	**escojo**	**escoja**	escogía	escogeré	escogería
escogiendo	escoges	**escojas**	escogías	escogerás	escogerías
escogido	escoge	**escoja**	escogía	escogerá	escogería
	escogemos	**escojamos**	escogíamos	escogeremos	escogeríamos
	escogéis	**escojáis**	escogíais	escogeréis	escogeríais
	escogen	**escojan**	escogían	escogerán	escogerían
§50					
esparcir	**esparzo**	**esparza**	esparcía	esparciré	esparciría
esparciendo	esparces	**esparzas**	esparcías	esparcirás	esparcirías
esparcido	esparce	**esparza**	esparcía	esparcirá	esparciría
	esparcimos	**esparzamos**	esparcíamos	esparciremos	esparciríamos
	esparcís	**esparzáis**	esparcíais	esparciréis	esparciríais
	esparcen	**esparzan**	esparcían	esparcirán	esparcirían
§51					
estar	**estoy**	**esté**	estaba	estaré	estaría
estando	**estás**	**estés**	estabas	estarás	estarías
estado	**está**	**esté**	estaba	estará	estaría
	estamos	estemos	estábamos	estaremos	estaríamos
	estáis	estéis	estabais	estaréis	estaríais
	están	**estén**	estaban	estarán	estarían
§52					
forzar	**fuerzo**	**fuerce**	forzaba	forzaré	forzaría
forzando	**fuerzas**	**fuerces**	forzabas	forzarás	forzarías
forzado	**fuerza**	**fuerce**	forzaba	forzará	forzaría
	forzamos	**forcemos**	forzábamos	forzaremos	forzaríamos
	forzáis	**forcéis**	forzabais	forzaréis	forzaríais
	fuerzan	**fuercen**	forzaban	forzarán	forzarían
§53					
garantir			garantía	garantiré	garantiría
garantiendo			garantías	garantirás	garantirías
garantido			garantía	garantirá	garantiría
	garantimos		garantíamos	garantiremos	garantiríamos
	garantís		garantíais	garantiréis	garantiríais
			garantían	garantirán	garantirían
§54					
haber	**he**	**haya**	había	**habré**	**habría**
habiendo	**has**	**hayas**	habías	**habrás**	**habrías**
habido	**ha**	**haya**	había	**habrá**	**habría**
	hemos	**hayamos**	habíamos	**habremos**	**habríamos**
	habéis	**hayáis**	habíais	**habréis**	**habríais**
	han	**hayan**	habían	**habrán**	**habrían**
§55					
hacer	**hago**	**haga**	hacía	**haré**	**haría**
haciendo	haces	**hagas**	hacías	**harás**	**harías**
hecho	hace	**haga**	hacía	**hará**	**haría**
	hacemos	**hagamos**	hacíamos	**haremos**	**haríamos**
	hacéis	**hagáis**	hacíais	**haréis**	**haríais**
	hacen	**hagan**	hacían	**harán**	**harían**

PRETERIT INDICATIVE	IMPERF. SUBJ. S-FORM	IMPERF. SUBJ. R-FORM	FUTURE SUBJUNCTIVE	IMPERATIVE	NOTES AND REFERENCES
erguí erguiste **irguió** erguimos erguisteis **irguieron**	**irguiese** **irguieses** **irguiese** **irguiésemos** **irguieseis** **irguiesen**	**irguiera** **irguieras** **irguiera** **irguiéramos** **irguierais** **irguieran**	**irguiere** **irguieres** **irguiere** **irguiéremos** **irguiereis** **irguieren**	**yergue** **irgue** erguid	**§15,** 9 & **§16,** 5 or 7
erré erraste erró erramos errasteis erraron	errase errases errase errásemos erraseis errasen	errara erraras errara erráramos errarais erraran	errare errares errare erráremos errareis erraren	**yerra** errad	Like **§18** but with initial **ye** for **ie**
escogí escogiste escogió escogimos escogisteis escogieron	escogiese escogieses escogiese escogiésemos escogieseis escogiesen	escogiera escogieras escogiera escogiéramos escogierais escogieran	escogiere escogieres escogiere escogiéremos escogiereis escogieren	escoge escoged	**§15,** 7
esparcí esparciste esparció esparcimos esparcisteis esparcieron	esparciese esparcieses esparciese esparciésemos esparcieseis esparciesen	esparciera esparcieras esparciera esparciéramos esparcierais esparcieran	esparciere esparcieres esparciere esparciéremos esparciereis esparcieren	esparce esparcid	**§15,** 6
estuve **estuviste** **estuvo** **estuvimos** **estuvisteis** **estuvieron**	**estuviese** **estuvieses** **estuviese** **estuviésemos** **estuvieseis** **estuviesen**	**estuviera** **estuvieras** **estuviera** **estuviéramos** **estuvierais** **estuvieran**	**estuviere** **estuvieres** **estuviere** **estuviéremos** **estuviereis** **estuvieren**	**está** estad	**§17,** 2 & 6
forcé forzaste forzó forzamos forzasteis forzaron	forzase forzases forzase forzásemos forzaseis forzasen	forzara forzaras forzara forzáramos forzarais forzaran	forzare forzares forzare forzáremos forzareis forzaren	**fuerza** forzad	Combination of **§15,** 4 & **§16,** 3
garantí garantiste garantió garantimos garantisteis garantieron	garantiese garantieses garantiese garantiésemos garantieseis garantiesen	garantiera garantieras garantiera garantiéramos garantierais garantieran	garantiere garantieres garantiere garantiéremos garantiereis garantieren	garantid	Defective verb used only in forms whose endings begin with **i**
hube **hubiste** **hubo** **hubimos** **hubisteis** **hubieron**	**hubiese** **hubieses** **hubiese** **hubiésemos** **hubieseis** **hubiesen**	**hubiera** **hubieras** **hubiera** **hubiéramos** **hubierais** **hubieran**	**hubiere** **hubieres** **hubiere** **hubiéremos** **hubiereis** **hubieren**	**hé** habed	**§17,** 2, 5, 6, & 8
hice **hiciste** **hizo** **hicimos** **hicisteis** **hicieron**	**hiciese** **hicieses** **hiciese** **hiciésemos** **hicieseis** **hiciesen**	**hiciera** **hicieras** **hiciera** **hiciéramos** **hicierais** **hicieran**	**hiciere** **hicieres** **hiciere** **hiciéremos** **hiciereis** **hicieren**	**haz** haced	**§17,** 1, 5, 6, 8, & 9 *1st & 3d sg pret ind of* **rehacer: rehíce, rehízo**

INFINITIVE GERUND AND PAST PARTICIPLE	PRESENT INDICATIVE	PRESENT SUBJUNCTIVE	IMPERFECT INDICATIVE	FUTURE INDICATIVE	CONDITIONAL
§56 **inquirir** inquiriendo inquirido	**inquiero** **inquieres** **inquiere** inquirimos inquirís **inquieren**	**inquiera** **inquieras** **inquiera** inquiramos inquiráis **inquieran**	inquiría inquirías inquiría inquiríamos inquiríais inquirían	inquiriré inquirirás inquirirá inquiriremos inquiriréis inquirirán	inquiriría inquirirías inquiriría inquiriríamos inquiriríais inquirirían
§57 **ir** **yendo** ido	**voy** **vas** **va** **vamos** **vais** **van**	**vaya** **vayas** **vaya** **vayamos** **vayáis** **vayan**	**iba** **ibas** **iba** **íbamos** **ibais** **iban**	iré irás irá iremos iréis irán	iría irías iría iríamos iríais irían
§58 **jugar** jugando jugado	**juego** **juegas** **juega** jugamos jugáis **juegan**	**juegue** **juegues** **juegue** **juguemos** **juguéis** **jueguen**	jugaba jugabas jugaba jugábamos jugabais jugaban	jugaré jugarás jugará jugaremos jugaréis jugarán	jugaría jugarías jugaría jugaríamos jugaríais jugarían
§59 **ligar** ligando ligado	ligo ligas liga ligamos ligáis ligan	**ligue** **ligues** **ligue** **liguemos** **liguéis** **liguen**	ligaba ligabas ligaba ligábamos ligabais ligaban	ligaré ligarás ligará ligaremos ligaréis ligarán	ligaría ligarías ligaría ligaríamos ligarías ligarían
§60 **lucir** luciendo lucido	**luzco** luces luce lucimos lucís lucen	**luzca** **luzcas** **luzca** **luzcamos** **luzcáis** **luzcan**	lucía lucías lucía lucíamos lucíais lucían	luciré lucirás lucirá luciremos luciréis lucirán	luciría lucirías luciría luciríamos luciríais lucirían
§61 **mecer** meciendo mecido	**mezo** meces mece mecemos mecéis mecen	**meza** **mezas** **meza** **mezamos** **mezáis** **mezan**	mecía mecías mecía mecíamos mecíais mecían	meceré mecerás mecerá meceremos meceréis mecerán	mecería mecerías mecería meceríamos meceríais mecerían
§62 **mentir** **mintiendo** mentido	**miento** **mientes** **miente** mentimos mentís **mienten**	**mienta** **mientas** **mienta** **mintamos** **mintáis** **mientan**	mentía mentías mentía mentíamos mentíais mentían	mentiré mentirás mentirá mentiremos mentiréis mentirán	mentiría mentirías mentiría mentiríamos mentiríais mentirían
§63 **morder** mordiendo mordido	**muerdo** **muerdes** **muerde** mordemos mordéis **muerden**	**muerda** **muerdas** **muerda** mordamos mordáis **muerdan**	mordía mordías mordía mordíamos mordíais mordían	morderé morderás morderá morderemos morderéis morderán	mordería morderías mordería morderíamos morderíais morderían
§64 **oír** **oyendo** **oído**	**oigo** **oyes** **oye** **oímos** oís **oyen**	**oiga** **oigas** **oiga** **oigamos** **oigáis** **oigan**	oía oías oía oíamos oíais oían	oiré oirás oirá oiremos oiréis oirán	oiría oirías oiría oiríamos oiríais oirían
§65 **oler** oliendo olido	**huelo** **hueles** **huele** olemos oléis **huelen**	**huela** **huelas** **huela** olamos oláis **huelan**	olía olías olía olíamos olíais olían	oleré olerás olerá oleremos oleréis olerán	olería olerías olería oleríamos oleríais olerían

PRETERIT INDICATIVE	IMPERF. SUBJ. s-FORM	IMPERF. SUBJ. r-FORM	FUTURE SUBJUNCTIVE	IMPERATIVE	NOTES AND REFERENCES
inquirí	inquiriese	inquiriera	inquiriere		Third conjugation with radical **i** and irregularities of **§66**
inquiriste	inquirieses	inquirieras	inquirieres	**inquiere**	
inquirió	inquiriese	inquiriera	inquiriere		
inquirimos	inquiriésemos	inquiriéramos	inquiriéremos		
inquiristeis	inquirieseis	inquirierais	inquiriereis	inquirid	
inquirieron	inquiriesen	inquirieran	inquirieren		
fui	**fuese**	**fuera**	**fuere**		**§17,** 2, 4, 7, & 8
fuiste	**fueses**	**fueras**	**fueres**	**vé**	
fue	**fuese**	**fuera**	**fuere**		
fuimos	**fuésemos**	**fuéramos**	**fuéremos**	**vamos**	
fuisteis	**fueseis**	**fuerais**	**fuereis**	id	
fueron	**fuesen**	**fueran**	**fueren**		
jugué	jugase	jugara	jugare		Like **§79** but with radical **u**
jugaste	jugases	jugaras	jugares	**juega**	
jugó	jugase	jugara	jugare		
jugamos	jugásemos	jugáramos	jugáremos		
jugasteis	jugaseis	jugarais	jugareis	jugad	
jugaron	jugasen	jugaran	jugaren		
ligué	ligase	ligara	ligare		**§15,** 2
ligaste	ligases	ligaras	ligares	liga	
ligó	ligase	ligara	ligare		
ligamos	ligásemos	ligáramos	ligáremos		
ligasteis	ligaseis	ligarais	ligareis	ligad	
ligaron	ligasen	ligaran	ligaren		
lucí	luciese	luciera	luciere		**§17,** 1
luciste	lucieses	lucieras	lucieres	luce	
lució	luciese	luciera	luciere		
lucimos	luciésemos	luciéramos	luciéremos		
lucisteis	lucieseis	lucierais	luciereis	lucid	
lucieron	luciesen	lucieran	lucieren		
mecí	meciese	meciera	meciere		Like **§91** although **c** is preceded by a vowel
meciste	mecieses	mecieras	mecieres	mece	
meció	meciese	meciera	meciere		
mecimos	meciésemos	meciéramos	meciéremos		
mecisteis	mecieseis	mecierais	meciereis	meced	
mecieron	meciesen	mecieran	mecieren		
mentí	**mintiese**	**mintiera**	**mintiere**		**§16,** 5
mentiste	**mintieses**	**mintieras**	**mintieres**	**miente**	
mintió	**mintiese**	**mintiera**	**mintiere**		
mentimos	**mintiésemos**	**mintiéramos**	**mintiéremos**		
mentisteis	**mintieseis**	**mintierais**	**mintiereis**	mentid	
mintieron	**mintiesen**	**mintieran**	**mintieren**		
mordí	mordiese	mordiera	mordiere		**§16,** 4
mordiste	mordieses	mordieras	mordieres	**muerde**	
mordió	mordiese	mordiera	mordiere		
mordimos	mordiésemos	mordiéramos	mordiéremos		
mordisteis	mordieseis	mordierais	mordiereis	morded	
mordieron	mordiesen	mordieran	mordieren		
oí	**oyese**	**oyera**	**oyere**		**§15,** 16 & **§17,** 1 & 3
oíste	**oyeses**	**oyeras**	**oyeres**	**oye**	
oyó	**oyese**	**oyera**	**oyere**		
oímos	**oyésemos**	**oyéramos**	**oyéremos**		
oísteis	**oyeseis**	**oyerais**	**oyereis**	**oíd**	
oyeron	**oyesen**	**oyeran**	**oyeren**		
olí	oliese	oliera	oliere		Like **§63** but with **h** before **ue**
oliste	olieses	olieras	olieres	**huele**	
olió	oliese	oliera	oliere		
olimos	oliésemos	oliéramos	oliéremos		
olisteis	olieseis	olierais	oliereis	oled	
olieron	oliesen	olieran	olieren		

INFINITIVE GERUND AND PAST PARTICIPLE	PRESENT INDICATIVE	PRESENT SUBJUNCTIVE	IMPERFECT INDICATIVE	FUTURE INDICATIVE	CONDITIONAL
§66 **perder** perdiendo perdido	**pierdo** **pierdes** **pierde** perdemos perdéis **pierden**	**pierda** **pierdas** **pierda** perdamos perdáis **pierdan**	perdía perdías perdía perdíamos perdíais perdían	perderé perderás perderá perderemos perderéis perderán	perdería perderías perdería perderíamos perderíais perderían
§67 **placer** placiendo placido	**plazco** **plazgo** places place placemos placéis placen	**plazca** **plazga** **plazcas** **plazca** **plazcamos** **plazcáis** **plazcan**	placía placías placía placíamos placíais placían	placeré placerás placerá placeremos placeréis placerán	placería placerías placería placeríamos placeríais placerían
§68 **poder** **pudiendo** podido	**puedo** **puedes** **puede** podemos podéis **pueden**	**pueda** **puedas** **pueda** podamos podáis **puedan**	podía podías podía podíamos podíais podían	**podré** **podrás** **podrá** **podremos** **podréis** **podrán**	**podría** **podrías** **podría** **podríamos** **podríais** **podrían**
§69 **poner** poniendo **puesto**	**pongo** pones pone ponemos ponéis ponen	**ponga** **pongas** **ponga** **pongamos** **pongáis** **pongan**	ponía ponías ponía poníamos poníais ponían	**pondré** **pondrás** **pondrá** **pondremos** **pondréis** **pondrán**	**pondría** **pondrías** **pondría** **pondríamos** **pondríais** **pondrían**
§70 **querer** queriendo querido	**quiero** **quieres** **quiere** queremos queréis **quieren**	**quiera** **quieras** **quiera** queramos queráis **quieran**	quería querías quería queríamos queríais querían	**querré** **querrás** **querrá** **querremos** **querréis** **querrán**	**querría** **querrías** **querría** **querríamos** **querríais** **querrían**
§71 **raer** **rayendo** **raído**	**raigo** **rayo** raes rae raemos raéis raen	**raiga** **raya** **raigas** **raiga** **raigamos** **raigáis** **raigan**	raía raías raía raíamos raíais raían	raeré raerás raerá raeremos raeréis raerán	raería raerías raería raeríamos raeríais raerían
§72 **regir** **rigiendo** regido	**rijo** **riges** **rige** regimos regís **rigen**	**rija** **rijas** **rija** **rijamos** **rijáis** **rijan**	regía regías regía regíamos regíais regían	regiré regirás regirá regiremos regiréis regirán	regiría regirías regiría regiríamos regiríais regirían
§73 **reír** **riendo** **reído**	**río** **ríes** **ríe** **reímos** reís **ríen**	**ría** **rías** **ría** **riamos** **riáis** **rían**	reía reías reía reíamos reíais reían	reiré reirás reirá reiremos reiréis reirán	reiría reirías reiría reiríamos reirías reirían
§74 **reñir** **riñendo** reñido	**riño** **riñes** **riñe** reñimos reñís **riñen**	**riña** **riñas** **riña** **riñamos** **riñáis** **riñan**	reñía reñías reñía reñíamos reñíais reñían	reñiré reñirás reñirá reñiremos reñiréis reñirán	reñiría reñirías reñiría reñiríamos reñiríais reñirían

PRETERIT INDICATIVE	IMPERF. SUBJ. s-FORM	IMPERF. SUBJ. r-FORM	FUTURE SUBJUNCTIVE	IMPERATIVE	NOTES AND REFERENCES
perdí perdiste perdió perdimos perdisteis perdieron	perdiese perdieses perdiese perdiésemos perdieseis perdiesen	perdiera perdieras perdiera perdiéramos perdierais perdieran	perdiere perdieres perdiere perdiéremos perdiereis perdieren	**pierde** perded	**§16,** 2
plací placiste plació **plugo** placimos placisteis placieron	placiese placieses placiese **pluguiese** placiésemos placieseis placiesen	placiera placieras placiera **pluguiera** placiéramos placierais placieran	placiere placieres placiere **pluguiere** placiéremos placiereis placiere	place placed	**§17,** 1 & 6
pude **pudiste** **pudo** **pudimos** **pudisteis** **pudieron**	**pudiese** **pudieses** **pudiese** **pudiésemos** **pudieseis** **pudiesen**	**pudiera** **pudieras** **pudiera** **pudiéramos** **pudierais** **pudieran**	**pudiere** **pudieres** **pudiere** **pudiéremos** **pudiereis** **pudieren**		**§16,** 4 & **§17,** 5 and 6; irregular **u** in gerund
puse **pusiste** **puso** **pusimos** **pusisteis** **pusieron**	**pusiese** **pusieses** **pusiese** **pusiésemos** **pusieseis** **pusiesen**	**pusiera** **pusieras** **pusiera** **pusiéramos** **pusierais** **pusieran**	**pusiere** **pusieres** **pusiere** **pusiéremos** **pusiereis** **pusieren**	**pon** poned	**§17,** 1, 5, 6, 8, & 9
quise **quisiste** **quiso** **quisimos** **quisisteis** **quisieron**	**quisiese** **quisieses** **quisiese** **quisiésemos** **quisieseis** **quisiesen**	**quisiera** **quisieras** **quisiera** **quisiéramos** **quisierais** **quisieran**	**quisiere** **quisieres** **quisiere** **quisiéremos** **quisiereis** **quisieren**	**quiere** quered	**§16,** 2 & **§17,** 5 & 6
raí **raíste** **rayó** **raímos** **raísteis** **rayeron**	**rayese** **rayeses** **rayese** **rayésemos** **rayeseis** **rayesen**	**rayera** **rayeras** **rayera** **rayéramos** **rayerais** **rayeran**	**rayere** **rayeres** **rayere** **rayéremos** **rayereis** **rayeren**	rae raed	**§15,** 15 & **§17,** 1
regí registe **rigió** regimos registeis **rigieron**	**rigiese** **rigieses** **rigiese** **rigiésemos** **rigieseis** **rigiesen**	**rigiera** **rigieras** **rigiera** **rigiéramos** **rigierais** **rigieran**	**rigiere** **rigieres** **rigiere** **rigiéremos** **rigiereis** **rigieren**	**rige** regid	Combination of **§15,** 8 & **§16,** 7
reí **reíste** **rió** **reímos** **reísteis** **rieron**	**riese** **rieses** **riese** **riésemos** **rieseis** **riesen**	**riera** **rieras** **riera** **riéramos** **rierais** **rieran**	**riere** **rieres** **riere** **riéremos** **riereis** **rieren**	**ríe** **reíd**	Like **§94** but with contraction of radical **i** and **i** of **ió** and **ie** of endings. Also **§15,** 16. 2
reñí reñiste **riñó** reñimos reñisteis **riñeron**	**riñese** **riñeses** **riñese** **riñésemos** **riñeseis** **riñesen**	**riñera** **riñeras** **riñera** **riñéramos** **riñerais** **riñeran**	**riñere** **riñeres** **riñere** **riñéremos** **riñereis** **riñeren**	**riñe** reñid	Combination of **§15,** 14 & **§16,** 7

INFINITIVE GERUND AND PAST PARTICIPLE	PRESENT INDICATIVE	PRESENT SUBJUNCTIVE	IMPERFECT INDICATIVE	FUTURE INDICATIVE	CONDITIONAL
§75					
reunir	**reúno**	**reúna**	reunía	reuniré	reuniría
reuniendo	**reúnes**	**reúnas**	reunías	reunirás	reunirías
reunido	**reúne**	**reúna**	reunía	reunirá	reuniría
	reunimos	reunamos	reuníamos	reuniremos	reuniríamos
	reunís	reunáis	reuníais	reuniréis	reuniríais
	reúnen	**reúnan**	reunían	reunirán	reunirían
§76					
rezar	rezo	**rece**	rezaba	rezaré	rezaría
rezando	rezas	**reces**	rezabas	rezarás	rezarías
rezado	reza	**rece**	rezaba	rezará	rezaría
	rezamos	**recemos**	rezábamos	rezaremos	rezaríamos
	rezáis	**recéis**	rezabais	rezaréis	rezaríais
	rezan	**recen**	rezaban	rezarán	rezarían
§77					
rodar	**ruedo**	**ruede**	rodaba	rodaré	rodaría
rodando	**ruedas**	**ruedes**	rodabas	rodarás	rodarías
rodado	**rueda**	**ruede**	rodaba	rodará	rodaría
	rodamos	rodemos	rodábamos	rodaremos	rodaríamos
	rodáis	rodéis	rodabais	rodaréis	rodaríais
	ruedan	**rueden**	rodaban	rodarán	rodarían
§78					
roer	roo	roa	roía	roeré	roería
	roigo	**roiga**			
	royo	**roya**			
royendo	roes	roas	roías	roerás	roerías
roído	roe	roa	roía	roerá	roería
	roemos	roamos	roíamos	roeremos	roeríamos
	roéis	roáis	roíais	roeréis	roeríais
	roen	roan	roían	roerán	roerían
§79					
rogar	**ruego**	**ruegue**	rogaba	rogaré	rogaría
rogando	**ruegas**	**ruegues**	rogabas	rogarás	rogarías
rogado	**ruega**	**ruegue**	rogaba	rogará	rogaría
	rogamos	**roguemos**	rogábamos	rogaremos	rogaríamos
	rogáis	**roguéis**	rogabais	rogaréis	rogaríais
	ruegan	**rueguen**	rogaban	rogarán	rogarían
§80					
saber	**sé**	**sepa**	sabía	**sabré**	**sabría**
sabiendo	sabes	**sepas**	sabías	**sabrás**	**sabrías**
sabido	sabe	**sepa**	sabía	**sabrá**	**sabría**
	sabemos	**sepamos**	sabíamos	**sabremos**	**sabríamos**
	sabéis	**sepáis**	sabíais	**sabréis**	**sabríais**
	saben	**sepan**	sabían	**sabrán**	**sabrían**
§81					
salir	**salgo**	**salga**	salía	**saldré**	**saldría**
saliendo	sales	**salgas**	salías	**saldrás**	**saldrías**
salido	sale	**salga**	salía	**saldrá**	**saldría**
	salimos	**salgamos**	salíamos	**saldremos**	**saldríamos**
	salís	**salgáis**	salíais	**saldréis**	**saldríais**
	salen	**salgan**	salían	**saldrán**	**saldrían**
§82					
seguir	**sigo**	**siga**	seguía	seguiré	seguiría
siguiendo	**sigues**	**sigas**	seguías	seguirás	seguirías
seguido	**sigue**	**siga**	seguía	seguirá	seguiría
	seguimos	**sigamos**	seguíamos	seguiremos	seguiríamos
	seguís	**sigáis**	seguíais	seguiréis	seguiríais
	siguen	**sigan**	seguían	seguirán	seguirían
§83					
ser	**soy**	**sea**	**era**	seré	sería
siendo	**eres**	**seas**	**eras**	serás	serías
sido	**es**	**sea**	**era**	será	sería
	somos	**seamos**	**éramos**	seremos	seríamos
	sois	**seáis**	**erais**	seréis	seríais
	son	**sean**	**eran**	serán	serían

PRETERIT INDICATIVE	IMPERF. SUBJ. S-FORM	IMPERF. SUBJ. R-FORM	FUTURE SUBJUNCTIVE	IMPERATIVE	NOTES AND REFERENCES
reuní	reuniese	reuniera	reuniere		
reuniste	reunieses	reunieras	reunieres	**reúne**	**§16,** 8
reunió	reuniese	reuniera	reuniere		
reunimos	reuniésemos	reuniéramos	reuniéremos	reunid	
reunisteis	reunieseis	reunierais	reuniereis		
reunieron	reuniesen	reunieran	reunieren		
recé	rezase	rezara	rezare		**§15,** 4
rezaste	rezases	rezaras	rezares	reza	
rezó	rezase	rezara	rezare		
rezamos	rezásemos	rezáramos	rezáremos		
rezasteis	rezaseis	rezarais	rezareis	rezad	
rezaron	rezasen	rezaran	rezaren		
rodé	rodase	rodara	rodare		**§16,** 3
rodaste	rodases	rodaras	rodares	**rueda**	
rodó	rodase	rodara	rodare		
rodamos	rodásemos	rodáramos	rodáremos		
rodasteis	rodaseis	rodarais	rodareis	rodad	
rodaron	rodasen	rodaran	rodaren		
roí	**royese**	**royera**	**royere**		**§15,** 15 & **§17,** 1
roíste	**royeses**	**royeras**	**royeres**	roe	
royó	**royese**	**royera**	**royere**		
roímos	**royésemos**	**royéramos**	**royéremos**		
roísteis	**royeseis**	**royerais**	**royereis**	roed	
royeron	**royesen**	**royeran**	**royeren**		
rogué	rogase	rogara	rogare		Combination of
rogaste	rogases	rogaras	rogares	**ruega**	**§15,** 2 & **§16,** 3
rogó	rogase	rogara	rogare		
rogamos	rogásemos	rogáramos	rogáremos		
rogasteis	rogaseis	rogarais	rogareis	rogad	
rogaron	rogasen	rogaran	rogaren		
supe	**supiese**	**supiera**	**supiere**		**§17,** 2, 5, & 6
supiste	**supieses**	**supieras**	**supieres**	sabe	
supo	**supiese**	**supiera**	**supiere**		
supimos	**supiésemos**	**supiéramos**	**supiéremos**		
supisteis	**supieseis**	**supierais**	**supiereis**	sabed	
supieron	**supiesen**	**supieran**	**supieren**		
salí	saliese	saliera	saliere		**§17,** 1, 5, & 8
saliste	salieses	salieras	salieres	**sal**	
salió	saliese	saliera	saliere		
salimos	saliésemos	saliéramos	saliéremos		
salisteis	salieseis	salierais	saliereis	salid	
salieron	saliesen	salieran	salieren		
seguí	**siguiese**	**siguiera**	**siguiere**		Combination of
seguiste	**siguieses**	**siguieras**	**siguieres**	**sigue**	**§15,** 9 & **§16,** 7
siguió	**siguiese**	**siguiera**	**siguiere**		
seguimos	**siguiésemos**	**siguiéramos**	**siguiéremos**		
seguisteis	**siguieseis**	**siguierais**	**siguiereis**	seguid	
siguieron	**siguiesen**	**siguieran**	**siguieren**		
fui	**fuese**	**fuera**	**fuere**		**§17,** 2, 4, 7, & 8
fuiste	**fueses**	**fueras**	**fueres**	**sé**	
fue	**fuese**	**fuera**	**fuere**		
fuimos	**fuésemos**	**fuéramos**	**fuéremos**		
fuisteis	**fueseis**	**fuerais**	**fuereis**	sed	
fueron	**fuesen**	**fueran**	**fueren**		

INFINITIVE GERUND AND PAST PARTICIPLE	PRESENT INDICATIVE	PRESENT SUBJUNCTIVE	IMPERFECT INDICATIVE	FUTURE INDICATIVE	CONDITIONAL
§84					
tañer	taño	taña	tañía	tañeré	tañería
tañendo	tañes	tañas	tañías	tañerás	tañerías
tañido	tañe	taña	tañía	tañerá	tañería
	tañemos	tañamos	tañíamos	tañeremos	tañeríamos
	tañéis	tañáis	tañíais	tañeréis	tañeríais
	tañen	tañan	tañían	tañerán	tañerían
§85					
tener	**tengo**	**tenga**	tenía	**tendré**	**tendría**
teniendo	**tienes**	**tengas**	tenías	**tendrás**	**tendrías**
tenido	**tiene**	**tenga**	tenía	**tendrá**	**tendría**
	tenemos	**tengamos**	teníamos	**tendremos**	**tendríamos**
	tenéis	**tengáis**	teníais	**tendréis**	**tendríais**
	tienen	**tengan**	tenían	**tendrán**	**tendrían**
§86					
tocar	toco	**toque**	tocaba	tocaré	tocaría
tocando	tocas	**toques**	tocabas	tocarás	tocarías
tocado	toca	**toque**	tocaba	tocará	tocaría
	tocamos	**toquemos**	tocábamos	tocaremos	tocaríamos
	tocáis	**toquéis**	tocabais	tocaréis	tocaríais
	tocan	**toquen**	tocaban	tocarán	tocarían
§87					
torcer	**tuerzo**	**tuerza**	torcía	torceré	torcería
torciendo	**tuerces**	**tuerzas**	torcías	torcerás	torcerías
torcido	**tuerce**	**tuerza**	torcía	torcerá	torcería
	torcemos	**torzamos**	torcíamos	torceremos	torceríamos
	torcéis	**torzáis**	torcíais	torceréis	torceríais
	tuercen	**tuerzan**	torcían	torcerán	torcerían
§88					
traer	**traigo**	**traiga**	traía	traeré	traería
trayendo	traes	**traigas**	traías	traerás	traerías
traído	trae	**traiga**	traía	traerá	traería
	traemos	**traigamos**	traíamos	traeremos	traeríamos
	traéis	**traigáis**	traíais	traeréis	traeríais
	traen	**traigan**	traían	traerán	traerían
§89					
valer	**valgo**	**valga**	valía	**valdré**	**valdría**
valiendo	vales	**valgas**	valías	**valdrás**	**valdrías**
valido	vale	**valga**	valía	**valdrá**	**valdría**
	valemos	**valgamos**	valíamos	**valdremos**	**valdríamos**
	valéis	**valgáis**	valíais	**valdréis**	**valdríais**
	valen	**valgan**	valían	**valdrán**	**valdrían**
§90					
variar	**varío**	**varíe**	variaba	variaré	variaría
variando	**varías**	**varíes**	variabas	variarás	variarías
variado	**varía**	**varíe**	variaba	variará	variaría
	variamos	variemos	variábamos	variaremos	variaríamos
	variáis	variéis	variabais	variaréis	variaríais
	varían	**varíen**	variaban	variarán	variarían
§91					
vencer	**venzo**	**venza**	vencía	venceré	vencería
venciendo	vences	**venzas**	vencías	vencerás	vencerías
vencido	vence	**venza**	vencía	vencerá	vencería
	vencemos	**venzamos**	vencíamos	venceremos	venceríamos
	vencéis	**venzáis**	vencíais	venceréis	venceríais
	vencen	**venzan**	vencían	vencerán	vencerían
§92					
venir	**vengo**	**venga**	venía	**vendré**	**vendría**
viniendo	**vienes**	**vengas**	venías	**vendrás**	**vendrías**
venido	**viene**	**venga**	venía	**vendrá**	**vendría**
	venimos	**vengamos**	veníamos	**vendremos**	**vendríamos**
	venís	**vengáis**	veníais	**vendréis**	**vendríais**
	vienen	**vengan**	venían	**vendrán**	**vendrían**

PRETERIT INDICATIVE	IMPERF. SUBJ. s-FORM	IMPERF. SUBJ. r-FORM	FUTURE SUBJUNCTIVE	IMPERATIVE	NOTES AND REFERENCES
tañí	**tañese**	**tañera**	**tañere**		**§15,** 13
tañiste	**tañeses**	**tañeras**	**tañeres**	tañe	
tañó	**tañese**	**tañera**	**tañere**		
tañimos	**tañésemos**	**tañéramos**	**tañéremos**		
tañisteis	**tañeseis**	**tañerais**	**tañereis**	tañed	
tañeron	**tañesen**	**tañeran**	**tañeren**		
tuve	**tuviese**	**tuviera**	**tuviere**		**§16,** 2 & **§17,** 1, 5, 6, & 8
tuviste	**tuvieses**	**tuvieras**	**tuvieres**	**ten**	
tuvo	**tuviese**	**tuviera**	**tuviere**		
tuvimos	**tuviésemos**	**tuviéramos**	**tuviéremos**		
tuvisteis	**tuvieseis**	**tuvierais**	**tuviereis**	tened	
tuvieron	**tuviesen**	**tuvieran**	**tuvieren**		
toqué	tocase	tocara	tocare		**§15,** 1
tocaste	tocases	tocaras	tocares	toca	
tocó	tocase	tocara	tocare		
tocamos	tocásemos	tocáramos	tocáremos		
tocasteis	tocaseis	tocarais	tocareis	tocad	
tocaron	tocasen	tocaran	tocaren		
torcí	torciese	torciera	torciere		Combination of **§15,** 5 & **§16,** 4
torciste	torcieses	torcieras	torcieres	**tuerce**	
torció	torciese	torciera	torciere		
torcimos	torciésemos	torciéramos	torciéremos		
torcisteis	torcieseis	torcierais	torciereis	torced	
torcieron	torciesen	torcieran	torcieren		
traje	**trajese**	**trajera**	trajere		**§15,** 15 & **§17,** 1 & 6
trajiste	**trajeses**	**trajeras**	trajeres	trae	
trajo	**trajese**	**trajera**	trajere		
trajimos	**trajésemos**	**trajéramos**	trajéremos		
trajisteis	**trajeseis**	**trajerais**	trajereis	traed	
trajeron	**trajesen**	**trajeran**	trajeron		
valí	valiese	valiera	valiere		**§17,** 1, 5 & 8
valiste	valieses	valieras	valieres	**val** or vale	
valió	valiese	valiera	valiere		
valimos	valiésemos	valiéramos	valiéremos		
valisteis	valieseis	valierais	valiereis	valed	
valieron	valiesen	valieran	valieren		
varié	variase	variara	variare		**§16,** 9
variaste	variases	variaras	variares	**varía**	
varió	variase	variara	variare		
variamos	variásemos	variáramos	variáremos		
variasteis	variaseis	variarais	variareis	variad	
variaron	variasen	variaran	variaren		
vencí	venciese	venciera	venciere		**§15,** 5
venciste	vencieses	vencieras	vencieres	vence	
venció	venciese	venciera	venciere		
vencimos	venciésemos	venciéramos	venciéremos		
vencisteis	vencieseis	vencierais	venciereis	venced	
vencieron	venciesen	vencieran	vencieren		
vine	**viniese**	**viniera**	**viniere**		**§16,** 5 & **§17,** 1, 5, 6, & 8
viniste	**vinieses**	**vinieras**	**vinieres**	**ven**	
vino	**viniese**	**viniera**	**viniere**		
vinimos	**viniésemos**	**viniéramos**	**viniéremos**		
vinisteis	**vinieseis**	**vinierais**	**viniereis**	venid	
vinieron	**viniesen**	**vinieran**	**vinieren**		

INFINITIVE GERUND AND PAST PARTICIPLE	PRESENT INDICATIVE	PRESENT SUBJUNCTIVE	IMPERFECT INDICATIVE	FUTURE INDICATIVE	CONDITIONAL
§93					
ver	**veo**	**vea**	**veía**	veré	vería
viendo	ves	**veas**	**veías**	verás	verías
visto	ve	**vea**	**veía**	verá	vería
	vemos	**veamos**	**veíamos**	veremos	veríamos
	veis	**veáis**	**veíais**	veréis	veríais
	ven	**vean**	**veían**	verán	verían
§94					
vestir	**visto**	**vista**	vestía	vestiré	vestiría
vistiendo	**vistes**	**vistas**	vestías	vestirás	vestirías
vestido	**viste**	**vista**	vestía	vestirá	vestiría
	vestimos	**vistamos**	vestíamos	vestiremos	vestiríamos
	vestís	**vistáis**	vestíais	vestiréis	vestiríais
	visten	**vistan**	vestían	vestirán	vestirían
§95					
volcar	**vuelco**	**vuelque**	volcaba	volcaré	volcaría
volcando	**vuelcas**	**vuelques**	volcabas	volcarás	volcarías
volcado	**vuelca**	**vuelque**	volcaba	volcará	volcaría
	volcamos	**volquemos**	volcábamos	volcaremos	volcaríamos
	volcáis	**volquéis**	volcabais	volcaréis	volcaríais
	vuelcan	**vuelquen**	volcaban	volcarán	volcarían
§96					
yacer	**yazco**	**yazca**	yacía	yaceré	yacería
	yazgo	**yazga**			
	yago	**yaga**			
yaciendo	yaces	**yazcas**	yacías	yacerás	yacerías
yacido	yace	**yazca**	yacía	yacerá	yacería
	yacemos	**yazcamos**	yacíamos	yaceremos	yaceríamos
	yacéis	**yazcáis**	yacíais	yaceréis	yaceríais
	yacen	**yazcan**	yacía	yacerán	yacerían
§97					
arcaizar	**arcaízo**	**arcaíce**	arcaizaba	arcaizaré	arcaizaría
arcaizando	**arcaízas**	**arcaíces**	arcaizabas	arcaizarás	arcaizarías
arcaizado	**arcaíza**	**arcaíce**	arcaizaba	arcaizará	arcaizaría
	arcaizamos	**arcaicemos**	arcaizábamos	arcaizaremos	arcaizaríamos
	arcaizáis	**arcaicéis**	arcaizabais	arcaizaréis	arcaizaríais
	arcaízan	**arcaícen**	arcaizaban	arcaizarán	arcaizarían
§98					
avergonzar	**avergüenzo**	**avergüence**	avergonzaba	avergonzaré	avergonzaría
avergonzando	**avergüenzas**	**avergüences**	avergonzabas	avergonzarás	avergonzarías
avergonzado	**avergüenza**	**avergüence**	avergonzaba	avergonzará	avergonzaría
	avergonzamos	**avergoncemos**	avergonzábamos	avergonzaremos	avergonzaríamos
	avergonzáis	**avergoncéis**	avergonzabais	avergonzaréis	avergonzaríais
	avergüenzan	**avergüencen**	avergonzaban	avergonzarán	avergonzarían
§99					
ahusar	**ahúso**	**ahúse**	ahusaba	ahusaré	ahusaría
ahusando	**ahúsas**	**ahúses**	ahusabas	ahusarás	ahusarías
ahusado	**ahúsa**	**ahúse**	ahusaba	ahusará	ahusaría
	ahusamos	ahusemos	ahusábamos	ahusaremos	ahusaríamos
	ahusáis	ahuséis	ahusabais	ahusaréis	ahusaríais
	ahúsan	**ahúsen**	ahusaban	ahusarán	ahusarían

PRETERIT INDICATIVE	IMPERF. SUBJ. s-FORM	IMPERF. SUBJ. r-FORM	FUTURE SUBJUNCTIVE	IMPERATIVE	NOTES AND REFERENCES
vi viste **vio** vimos visteis vieron	viese vieses viese viésemos vieseis viesen	viera vieras viera viéramos vierais vieran	viere vieres **viere** viéremos viereis vieren	 ve ved	**§17,** 1, 4, & 9
vestí vestiste **vistió** vestimos vestisteis **vistieron**	**vistiese** **vistieses** **vistiese** **vistiésemos** **vistieseis** **vistiesen**	**vistiera** **vistieras** **vistiera** **vistiéramos** **vistierais** **vistieran**	**vistiere** **vistieres** **vistiere** **vistiéremos** **vistiereis** **vistieren**	 **viste** vestid	**§16,** 7
volqué volcaste volcó volcamos volcasteis volcaron	volcase volcases volcase volcásemos volcaseis volcasen	volcara volcaras volcara volcáramos volcarais volcaran	volcare volcares volcare volcáremos volcareis volcaren	 **vuelca** volcad	Combination of **§15,** 1 & **§16,** 3
yací yaciste yació yacimos yacisteis yacieron	yaciese yacieses yaciese yaciésemos yacieseis yaciesen	yaciera yacieras yaciera yaciéramos yacierais yacieran	yaciere yacieres yaciere yaciéremos yaciereis yacieren	 **yaz** yace yaced	**§17,** 1 & 8
arcaicé arcaizaste arcaizó arcaizamos arcaizasteis arcaizaron	arcaizase arcaizases arcaizase arcaizásemos arcaizaseis arcaizasen	arcaizara arcaizaras arcaizara arcaizáramos arcaizarais arcaizaran	arcaizare arcaizares arcaizare arcaizáremos arcaizareis arcaizaren	 **arcaíza** arcaizad	Combination of **§15,** 4 & **§16,** 8
avergoncé avergonzaste avergonzó avergonzamos avergonzasteis avergonzaron	avergonzase avergonzases avergonzase avergonzásemos avergonzaseis avergonzasen	avergonzara avergonzaras avergonzara avergonzáramos avergonzarais avergonzaran	avergonzare avergonzares avergonzare avergonzáremos avergonzareis avergonzaren	 **avergüenza** avergonzad	Combination of **§15,** 4 & **§19**
ahusé ahusaste ahusó ahusamos ahusasteis ahusaron	ahusase ahusases ahusase ahusásemos ahusaseis ahusasen	ahusara ahusaras ahusara ahusáramos ahusarais ahusaran	ahusare ahusares ahusare ahusáremos ahusareis ahusaren	 **ahúsa** ahusad	Applies to verbs with radical **ahí, ahú, ehí, ehú, ohí.** See NUEVAS NORMAS 25

§100. Regular Verbs. All the tenses of model regular verbs of the three conjugations are presented on this and the three following pages. The simple tenses are on the left-hand pages, the compound tenses on the right-hand pages. And each compound tense is placed horizontally in line with the simple tense to which its auxiliary corresponds.

Simple Tenses

The simple tenses are made from three basic stems, which for regular verbs may in turn be derived from the infinitive. These three stems are 1) the infinitive minus the ending **-ar, -er,** or **-ir,** 2) the whole infinitive itself, and 3) the third plural preterit indicative minus the last syllable **-ron.** The first of these stems is used to form the gerund, the past participle, the present indicative, the imperfect indicative, the preterit indicative, the present subjunctive, and the imperative; the second is used to form the future indicative and the conditional; and the third is used to form the imperfect subjunctive (**s**-form and **r**-form) and the future subjunctive.

FIRST CONJUGATION	SECOND CONJUGATION	THIRD CONJUGATION
	INFINITIVE	
habl-ar	**com-er**	**viv-ir**
	GERUND	
habl-ando	com-iendo	viv-iendo
	PAST PARTICIPLE	
habl-ado	com-ido	viv-ido
	PRESENT INDICATIVE	
habl-o habl-as habl-a habl-amos habl-áis habl-an	com-o com-es com-e com-emos com-éis com-en	viv-o viv-es viv-e viv-imos viv-ís viv-en
	IMPERFECT INDICATIVE	
habl-aba habl-abas habl-aba habl-ábamos habl-abais habl-aban	com-ía com-ías com-ía com-íamos com-íais com-ían	viv-ía viv-ías viv-ía viv-íamos viv-íais viv-ían
	PRETERIT INDICATIVE	
habl-é habl-aste habl-ó habl-amos habl-asteis habl-a-ron	com-í com-iste com-ió com-imos com-isteis com-ie-ron	viv-í viv-iste viv-ió viv-imos viv-isteis viv-ie-ron
	FUTURE INDICATIVE	
hablar-é hablar-ás hablar-á hablar-emos hablar-éis hablar-án	comer-é comer-ás comer-á comer-emos comer-éis comer-án	vivir-é vivir-ás vivir-á vivir-emos vivir-éis vivir-án
	CONDITIONAL	
hablar-ía hablar-ías hablar-ía hablar-íamos hablar-íais hablar-ían	comer-ía comer-ías comer-ía comer-íamos comer-íais comer-ían	vivir-ía vivir-ías vivir-ía vivir-íamos vivir-íais vivir-ían

Compound Tenses

The compound tenses are made with the uninflected past participle of the verb preceded by all the simple tenses of the auxiliary **haber** except the imperative and the past participle, for which there are no corresponding compound tenses.

FIRST CONJUGATION	SECOND CONJUGATION	THIRD CONJUGATION
	PERFECT INFINITIVE	
haber hablado	**haber comido**	**haber vivido**
	COMPOUND GERUND	
habiendo hablado	habiendo comido	habiendo vivido
	PERFECT INDICATIVE	
he hablado has hablado ha hablado hemos hablado habéis hablado han hablado	he comido has comido ha comido hemos comido habéis comido han comido	he vivido has vivido ha vivido hemos vivido habéis vivido han vivido
	PLUPERFECT INDICATIVE	
había hablado habías hablado había hablado habíamos hablado habíais hablado habían hablado	había comido habías comido había comido habíamos comido habíais comido habían comido	había vivido habías vivido había vivido habíamos vivido habíais vivido habían vivido
	PRETERIT PERFECT INDICATIVE	
hube hablado hubiste hablado hubo hablado hubimos hablado hubisteis hablado hubieron hablado	hube comido hubiste comido hubo comido hubimos comido hubisteis comido hubieron comido	hube vivido hubiste vivido hubo vivido hubimos vivido hubisteis vivido hubieron vivido
	FUTURE PERFECT INDICATIVE	
habré hablado habrás hablado habrá hablado habremos hablado habréis hablado habrán hablado	habré comido habrás comido habrá comido habremos comido habréis comido habrán comido	habré vivido habrás vivido habrá vivido habremos vivido habréis vivido habrán vivido
	CONDITIONAL PERFECT	
habría hablado habrías hablado habría hablado habríamos hablado habríais hablado habrían hablado	habría comido habrías comido habría comido habríamos comido habríais comido habrían comido	habría vivido habrías vivido habría vivido habríamos vivido habríais vivido habrían vivido

Simple Tenses

FIRST CONJUGATION	SECOND CONJUGATION	THIRD CONJUGATION
	PRESENT SUBJUNCTIVE	
habl-e	com-a	viv-a
habl-es	com-as	viv-as
habl-e	com-a	viv-a
habl-emos	com-amos	viv-amos
habl-éis	com-áis	viv-áis
habl-en	com-an	viv-an
	IMPERF. SUBJ. S-FORM	
habla-se	comie-se	vivie-se
habla-ses	comie-ses	vivie-ses
habla-se	comie-se	vivie-se
hablá-semos	comié-semos	vivié-semos
habla-seis	comie-seis	vivie-seis
habla-sen	comie-sen	vivie-sen
	IMPERF. SUBJ. R-FORM	
habla-ra	comie-ra	vivie-ra
habla-ras	comie-ras	vivie-ras
habla-ra	comie-ra	vivie-ra
hablá-ramos	comié-ramos	vivié-ramos
habla-rais	comie-rais	vivie-rais
habla-ran	comie-ran	vivie-ran
	FUTURE SUBJUNCTIVE	
habla-re	comie-re	vivie-re
habla-res	comie-res	vivie-res
habla-re	comie-re	vivie-re
hablá-remos	comié-remos	vivié-remos
habla-reis	comie-reis	vivie-reis
habla-ren	comie-ren	vivie-ren
	IMPERATIVE	
habl-a	com-e	viv-e
habl-ad	com-ed	viv-id

COMPOUND TENSES

FIRST CONJUGATION	SECOND CONJUGATION	THIRD CONJUGATION
	PERFECT SUBJUNCTIVE	
haya hablado	haya comido	haya vivido
hayas hablado	hayas comido	hayas vivido
haya hablado	haya comido	haya vivido
hayamos hablado	hayamos comido	hayamos vivido
hayáis hablado	hayáis comido	hayáis vivido
hayan hablado	hayan comido	hayan vivido
	PLUPERF. SUBJ. S-FORM	
hubiese hablado	hubiese comido	hubiese vivido
hubieses hablado	hubieses comido	hubieses vivido
hubiese hablado	hubiese comido	hubiese vivido
hubiésemos hablado	hubiésemos comido	hubiésemos vivido
hubieseis hablado	hubieseis comido	hubieseis vivido
hubiesen hablado	hubiesen comido	hubiesen vivido
	PLUPERF. SUBJ. R-FORM	
hubiera hablado	hubiera comido	hubiera vivido
hubieras hablado	hubieras comido	hubieras vivido
hubiera hablado	hubiera comido	hubiera vivido
hubiéramos hablado	hubiéramos comido	hubiéramos vivido
hubierais hablado	hubierais comido	hubierais vivido
hubieran hablado	hubieran comido	hubieran vivido
	FUTURE PERFECT SUBJUNCTIVE	
hubiere hablado	hubiere comido	hubiere vivido
hubieres hablado	hubieres comido	hubieres vivido
hubiere hablado	hubiere comido	hubiere vivido
hubiéremos hablado	hubiéremos comido	hubiéremos vivido
hubiereis hablado	hubiereis comido	hubiereis vivido
hubieren hablado	hubieren comido	hubieren vivido

§101. Spanish and English Cognates. The similarity of many Spanish and English words can be readily detected by noting the following equivalences in spelling, sounds, and endings.

Words of Greek Origin

EQUIVALENCES		EXAMPLES	
SPANISH	ENGLISH	SPANISH	ENGLISH
qu followed by e or **i**	ch [k] followed by e, i, or y	**química** **arquitectura** **monarquía**	chemistry architecture monarchy
c followed by any other letter	ch [k] followed by any other letter	**arcaico** **característico**	archaic characteristic
f	ph	**filosofía** **teléfono**	philosophy telephone
r	rh	**retórica**	rhetoric
rr	rrh	**catarro**	catarrh
t	th	**atleta** **teatro**	athlete theater
i	y	**tipo** **sinfonía**	type symphony
n initial	pn	**neumático**	pneumatic
s initial	ps	**salmo**	psalm
t initial	pt	**tomaína**	ptomaine

Latin Consonant Groups

EQUIVALENCES		EXAMPLES	
SPANISH	ENGLISH	SPANISH	ENGLISH
cc followed by **i** + vowel	ct followed by i + vowel	**sección**	section
ct followed by **a, o, u,** or a consonant	ct followed by a, o, u, or consonant	**actor** **actriz**	actor actress
nt	nct	**instinto**	instinct
cu	qu	**cuarto** **frecuencia**	quarter frequency
es + consonant	s + consonant	**escala** **estudio**	scale study

Latin Double Consonants

EQUIVALENCES		EXAMPLES	
SPANISH	ENGLISH	SPANISH	ENGLISH
b	bb	**abadía**	abbacy
c followed by **a, o,** or **u**	cc followed by a, o, or u	**acompañar** **acusar**	accompany accuse
c followed by **e** + consonant	cc followed by e + consonant	**aceptar**	accept

Latin Double Consonants

EQUIVALENCES		EXAMPLES	
SPANISH	ENGLISH	SPANISH	ENGLISH
cc followed by **e** or **i** + consonant	cc followed by e or i + consonant	**acceso** **accidente**	access accident
d	dd	**adición**	addition
f	ff	**efecto**	effect
g	gg	**agresivo**	aggressive
l	ll	**colegio**	college
m	mm	**recomendar**	recommend
n	nn	**anual**	annual
p	pp	**aplicar**	apply
s	ss	**clásico**	classic
t	tt	**atento**	attentive

Latin double l sometimes corresponds to Spanish **ll,** e.g., **valle** valley and sometimes to English l, e.g., **caballería** cavalry.

If the first m of English mm belongs to the prefix com or the prefix im, the Spanish word will generally have nm, e.g., **conmoción** commotion, **inmediato** immediate.

Double n sometimes corresponds to Spanish **ñ,** e.g., **cañón** cannon.

Double r exists in both Spanish and English, e.g., **corrosión** corrosion, **irregular** irregular. In Spanish it is considered to be a single letter (**§12,** 1).

Endings of Nouns

EQUIVALENCES		EXAMPLES	
SPANISH	ENGLISH	SPANISH	ENGLISH
-acio	-ace	**palacio**	palace
-ada	-ade	**mascarada**	masquerade
-ador	-ator	**orador**	orator
-aje	-age	**personaje**	personage
-al	-al	**canal**	canal
-ancia	{-ance {-ancy	**abundancia** **constancia**	abundance constancy
-ante	-ant	**instante**	instant
-ario	{-arian {-ary	**unitario** **adversario**	unitarian adversary
-ato	-ate	**sulfato**	sulfate
-cia	-cy	**aristocracia**	aristocracy
-ción	-tion	**nación**	nation
-cto	-ct	**conducto**	conduct
-culo	-cle	**círculo**	circle
-dad	-ty	**sociedad**	society
-encia	{-ence {-ency	**violencia** **frecuencia**	violence frequency

Endings of Nouns

EQUIVALENCES		EXAMPLES	
SPANISH	ENGLISH	SPANISH	ENGLISH
-ente	-ent	**accidente**	accident
-gio	-ge	**privilegio**	privilege
-ia	-y	**farmacia**	pharmacy
-ía	-y	**filosofía**	philosophy
-ica	-ic	**música**	music
-icio	-ice	**edificio**	edifice
-ico	-ic	**lógico**	logic
-ina	-ine	**doctrina**	doctrine
-ión	-ion	**religión**	religion
-isco	-isk	**asterisco**	asterisk
-ismo	-ism	**despotismo**	despotism
-ista	-ist	**artista**	artist
-ita	-ite	**fluorita**	fluorite
-ito	-ite	**sulfito**	sulfite
-mento	-ment	**suplemento**	supplement
-miento	-ment	**movimiento**	movement
-monia	-mony	**acrimonia**	acrimony
-o	-us -um	**genio** **museo**	genius museum
-oide	-oid	**alcaloide**	alkaloid
-or	-or	**actor**	actor
-orio	-ory	**promontorio**	promontory
-ota	-ot	**patriota**	patriot
-sis	-sis	**énfasis**	emphasis
-tad	-ty	**libertad**	liberty
-terio	-tery	**misterio**	mystery
-tro	-ter	**centro**	center
-tud	-tude	**multitud**	multitude
-ulo	-ule	**glóbulo**	globule
-ura	-ure	**cultura**	culture
-uro	-ide	**cloruro**	chloride

Endings of Adjectives

EQUIVALENCES		EXAMPLES	
SPANISH	ENGLISH	SPANISH	ENGLISH
-ado	-ate	**duplicado**	duplicate
-al	-al	**natural**	natural
-ano	-an	**pagano**	pagan
-áneo	-aneous	**cutáneo**	cutaneous
-ante	-ant	**constante**	constant

ENDINGS OF ADJECTIVES

EQUIVALENCES		EXAMPLES	
SPANISH	ENGLISH	SPANISH	ENGLISH
-ar	-ar	**circular**	circular
-ario	-arious -ary	**precario** **ordinario**	precarious ordinary
-az	-acious	**tenaz**	tenacious
-ble	-ble	**posible**	possible
-cial	-tial	**substancial**	substantial
-cional	-tional	**nacional**	national
-cto	-ct	**perfecto**	perfect
-ente	-ent	**evidente**	evident
-fero	-ferous	**carbonífero**	carboniferous
-ico	-ic -ical	**público** **crítico**	public critical
-ido	-id	**sólido**	solid
-il	-ile	**dócil**	docile
-ino	-ine	**aquilino**	aquiline
-ito	-ite	**erudito**	erudite
-ivo	-ive	**activo**	active
-no	-nal	**eterno**	eternal
-orio	-ory	**satisfactorio**	satisfactory
-oso	-ose -ous	**verboso** **luminoso**	verbose luminous
-ulento	-ulent	**turbulento**	turbulent
-undo	-und	**moribundo**	moribund
-uro	-ure	**maduro**	mature

ENDINGS OF VERBS

EQUIVALENCES		EXAMPLES	
SPANISH	ENGLISH	SPANISH	ENGLISH
-ar	-ate	**calcular**	calculate
-ducir	-duce	**conducir**	conduce
-ecer	-ish	**establecer**	establish
-ferir	-fer	**diferir**	defer
-iar	-iate -y	**afiliar** **gloriar**	affiliate glory
-ificar	-ify	**modificar**	modify
-iguar	-ify	**apaciguar**	pacify
-izar	-ize	**organizar**	organize
-struir	-struct	**obstruir**	obstruct
-vergir	-verge	**convergir**	converge
-vertir	-vert	**divertir**	divert
-zar	-ce	**comenzar**	commence

NUEVAS NORMAS DE PROSODIA Y ORTOGRAFÍA

NUEVO TEXTO DEFINITIVO

The NUEVAS NORMAS are for the most part emendations of clauses in the Grammar of the Spanish Academy or of entries in its Dictionary. Some are optional, some prescriptive. Some have been observed for years, some have been, still are, and probably will continue to be treated unevenly in the press and other forms of publication. We give them below in slightly condensed form.

1. When the Dictionary (of the Academy) authorizes two forms of accentuation of a word, both will be included in the same entry separated by the conjunction **o,** e.g., **quiromancia** o **quiromancía.**

2. The first form is considered the more common in present-day usage but the second is as fully sanctioned and correct as the first.

3. With regard to the double forms included for the first time in the eighteenth edition of the Dictionary (1956) the order of preference shall be reversed in the following entries, thus: **pentagrama / pentágrama, reuma / reúma.**

4. The first letter of the initial groups **ps, mn, gn** may be dropped, e.g., **sicología** for **psicología.**

5. The contract forms **remplazo, remplazar, rembolso, rembolsar** may be used instead of the forms with double **e.**

6. The accent mark of the first word of a solid compound shall not be used, e.g., **asimismo, piamadre.**

7. Adverbs in **-mente** are an exception to this rule. They shall be pronounced with two accents and written with an accent if the adjective requires it, e.g., **ágilmente, cortésmente.**

8. Compounds of verb form + enclitic + object shall be written without the accent on the verb form, e.g., **sabelotodo.**

9. The stress and the written accent (if one is necessary) of each of the elements of a compound written with a hyphen shall be preserved, e.g., **hispano-belga, anglo-soviético, cántabro-astur.**

10. The infinitive ending **-uir** will continue to be written without an accent.

11. The verb **inmiscuir** may be conjugated regularly or with **y** like verbs ending in **-uir,** e.g., **inmiscuyo.**

12. A combination consisting of an accented strong vowel + an unaccented weak vowel or an unaccented weak vowel + an accented strong vowel forms a diphthong; if a written accent is required on a diphthong it shall be placed on the strong vowel. A combination in which the strong vowel is unaccented and the weak vowel accented does not form a diphthong and the written accent must always be placed on the weak vowel.

13. The diphthong **ui** shall bear the written accent only when it appears in the antepenult or at the end of the word, e.g., **casuístico, benjuí,** but not, e.g., in **casuista.**

14. Words ending in **-ay, -ey, -oy, -uy** shall be written without the accent, e.g., **taray, virrey, convoy.**

15. The monosyllables **fue, fui, dio, vio** shall be written without the accent.

16. All forms of the pronouns **éste, ése, aquél** shall be written without the accent as long as there is no risk of ambiguity.

17. When the word **aun** can be replaced by **todavía** without changing the meaning of the sentence, it shall be written with the accent and pronounced as a dissyllable, e.g., **aún está enfermo, está enfermo aún.** In all other cases, that is, when it has the meaning of **hasta, también, inclusive** (or of **siquiera** in negative sentences), it shall be written without the accent, e.g., **aun los sordos han de oírme; ni hizo nada por él ni aun lo intentó.**

18. The word **solo** used as an adverb may be written with an accent if it is necessary to avoid ambiguity.

19. The written accent shall be omitted in paroxytones ending in **-oo,** e.g., **Feijoo, Campoo.**

20. Foreign proper nouns shall be written without an accent except for accents that may be part of their spelling in the foreign language; they may be marked with an accent in the Spanish manner if their pronunciation and spelling make this feasible. Foreign place names that have become part of the Spanish language shall not be considered foreign and shall be written with the accent in accordance with the general rules.

21. The dieresis shall be required only where it is necessary to show that **u** must be pronounced in the combinations **gue** and **gui,** e.g., **pingüe, pingüino.** It may be used also by poetic license or to show some special pronunciation.

22. Compound names of nationality shall be written solid where there has been geographic or political fusion, e.g., **hispanoamericano, checoslovaco;** where there has been no fusion but rather opposition or contrast, they shall be written with a hyphen, e.g., **franco-prusiano, germano-soviético.**

23. New compounds made of two adjectives shall be written with a hyphen and only the second shall be inflected, e.g., **tratado teórico-práctico, lección teórico-práctica, cuerpos técnico-administrativos.**

24. Compounds do not have to be divided according to their components but may be divided according to the regular rules of syllabification, e.g., **no·sotros** or **nos·otros, de·samparo** or **des·amparo.** Compounds with a medial group consisting of consonant + **h** shall be divided with the **h** attached to the second element, e.g., **al·haraca, in·humación, clor·hidrato, des·hidratar.**

25. Intervocalic **h** does not prevent the vowels from becoming a diphthong, e.g., **de·sahu·cio, sahu·me·rio.** The written accent shall, therefore, be placed on a stressed weak vowel separated by **h** from an unstressed strong vowel, e.g., **vahído, búho, rehúso.**

CONVERSION TABLES

TABLAS DE CONVERSION

Fahrenheit to Celsius (Centigrade)

−50	−45.5	18	−7.7	41	5.0	64	17.7	87	30.5
−40	−40.0	19	−7.2	42	5.5	65	18.3	88	31.0
−30	−34.4	20	−6.6	43	6.1	66	18.8	89	31.5
−20	−28.8	21	−6.1	44	6.6	67	19.4	90	32.1
−10	−23.3	22	−5.5	45	7.2	68	20.0	91	32.6
0	−17.7	23	−5.0	46	7.7	69	20.5	92	33.2
1	−17.2	24	−4.4	47	8.3	70	21.1	93	33.7
2	−16.6	25	−3.8	48	8.8	71	21.6	94	34.3
3	−16.1	26	−3.3	49	9.4	72	22.2	95	34.8
4	−15.5	27	−2.7	50	10.0	73	22.7	96	35.4
5	−15.0	28	−2.2	51	10.5	74	23.3	97	36.0
6	−14.4	29	−1.6	52	11.1	75	23.8	98	36.5
7	−13.8	30	−1.1	53	11.6	76	24.4	99	37.1
8	−13.3	31	−0.5	54	12.2	77	25.0	100	37.6
9	−12.7	32	0	55	12.7	78	25.5	125	51.6
10	−12.2	33	0.5	56	13.3	79	26.1	150	65.5
11	−11.6	34	1.1	57	13.8	80	26.6	175	79.4
12	−11.1	35	1.6	58	14.4	81	27.2	200	93.3
13	−10.5	36	2.2	59	15.0	82	27.7	250	121.1
14	−10.0	37	2.7	60	15.5	83	28.3	300	148.8
15	−9.4	38	3.3	61	16.1	84	28.8	350	176.6
16	−8.8	39	3.8	62	16.6	85	29.4	400	204.6
17	−8.3	40	4.4	63	17.2	86	29.9	450	232.2

Grados centígrados a grados Fahrenheit

−50	−58	1	33,8	26	78,8	51	123,8	76	168,8
−40	−40	2	35,6	27	80,6	52	125,6	77	170,6
−30	−22	3	37,4	28	82,4	53	127,4	78	172,4
−25	−13	4	39,2	29	84,2	54	129,2	79	174,2
−20	−4	5	41,0	30	86,0	55	131,0	80	176,0
−19	−2,2	6	42,8	31	87,8	56	132,8	81	177,8
−18	−0,4	7	44,6	32	89,6	57	134,6	82	179,6
−17,8	0	8	46,4	33	91,4	58	136,4	83	181,4
−16	3,2	9	48,2	34	93,2	59	138,2	84	183,2
−15	5	10	50,0	35	95,0	60	140,0	85	185,0
−14	6,8	11	51,8	36	96,8	61	141,8	86	186,8
−13	8,6	12	53,6	37	98,6	62	143,6	87	188,6
−12	10,4	13	55,4	38	100,4	63	145,4	88	190,4
−11	12,2	14	57,2	39	102,2	64	147,2	89	192,2
−10	14,0	15	59,0	40	104,0	65	149,0	90	194,0
−9	15,8	16	60,8	41	105,8	66	150,8	91	195,8
−8	17,6	17	62,6	42	107,6	67	152,6	92	197,6
−7	19,4	18	64,4	43	109,4	68	154,4	93	199,4
−6	21,2	19	66,2	44	111,2	69	156,2	94	201,2
−5	23,0	20	68,0	45	113,0	70	158,0	95	203,0
−4	24,8	21	69,8	46	114,8	71	159,8	96	204,8
−3	26,6	22	71,6	47	116,6	72	161,6	97	206,6
−2	28,4	23	73,4	48	118,4	73	163,4	98	208,4
−1	30,2	24	75,2	49	120,2	74	165,2	99	210,2
0	32	25	77,0	50	122,0	75	167,0	100	212,0

Feet to Meters

1	0.30	25	7.62	49	14.93	73	22.25	97	29.56
2	0.60	26	7.92	50	15.24	74	22.55	98	29.87
3	0.91	27	8.22	51	15.54	75	22.86	99	30.17
4	1.21	28	8.53	52	15.84	76	23.16	100	30.48
5	1.52	29	8.83	53	16.15	77	23.46	125	38.10
6	1.82	30	9.14	54	16.45	78	23.77	150	45.72
7	2.13	31	9.44	55	16.76	79	24.07	175	53.34
8	2.43	32	9.75	56	17.06	80	24.38	200	60.96
9	2.74	33	10.05	57	17.37	81	24.68	225	68.58
10	3.04	34	10.36	58	17.67	82	24.99	250	76.20
11	3.35	35	10.66	59	17.98	83	25.29	275	83.82
12	3.65	36	10.97	60	18.28	84	25.60	300	91.44
13	3.96	37	11.27	61	18.59	85	25.90	325	99.06
14	4.26	38	11.58	62	18.89	86	26.21	350	106.68
15	4.57	39	11.88	63	19.20	87	26.51	375	114.30
16	4.87	40	12.19	64	19.50	88	26.82	400	121.92
17	5.18	41	12.49	65	19.81	89	27.12	425	129.54
18	5.48	42	12.80	66	20.11	90	27.43	450	137.16
19	5.79	43	13.10	67	20.42	91	27.73	475	144.78
20	6.09	44	13.41	68	20.72	92	28.04	500	152.40
21	6.40	45	13.71	69	21.03	93	28.34	1000	304.80
22	6.70	46	14.02	70	21.33	94	28.65	2000	609.60
23	7.01	47	14.32	71	21.64	95	28.95	3000	914.40
24	7.31	48	14.63	72	21.94	96	29.26	4000	1219.20

Metros a pies

1	3,28	22	72,17	43	141,07	64	209,97	85	278,87
2	6,56	23	75,45	44	144,35	65	213,25	86	282,15
3	9,84	24	78,74	45	147,63	66	216,53	87	285,43
4	13,12	25	82,02	46	150,91	67	219,81	88	288,71
5	16,40	26	85,30	47	154,19	68	223,09	89	291,99
6	19,68	27	88,58	48	157,48	69	226,37	90	295,27
7	22,96	28	91,86	49	160,76	70	229,65	91	298,55
8	26,24	29	95,14	50	164,04	71	232,93	92	301,83
9	29,52	30	98,42	51	167,32	72	236,22	93	305,11
10	32,80	31	101,70	52	170,60	73	239,50	94	308,39
11	36,08	32	104,98	53	173,88	74	242,78	95	311,67
12	39,37	33	108,26	54	177,16	75	246,06	96	314,96
13	42,65	34	111,54	55	180,44	76	249,34	97	318,24
14	45,93	35	114,82	56	183,72	77	252,62	98	321,52
15	49,21	36	118,11	57	187,00	78	255,90	99	324,80
16	52,49	37	121,39	58	190,28	79	259,18	100	328,08
17	55,77	38	126,67	59	193,56	80	262,46	200	656,16
18	59,05	39	127,95	60	196,85	81	265,74	300	984,25
19	62,33	40	131,23	61	200,13	82	269,02	400	1312,33
20	65,61	41	134,51	62	203,41	83	272,30	500	1640,41
21	68,89	42	137,79	63	206,69	84	275,59	1000	3280,82

Pounds to Kilograms

1	.4	32	14.5	63	28.5	94	42.6	125	56.6
2	.9	33	14.9	64	29.0	95	43.0	126	57.1
3	1.3	34	15.4	65	29.4	96	43.5	127	57.6
4	1.8	35	15.8	66	29.9	97	43.9	128	58.0
5	2.2	36	16.3	67	30.3	98	44.4	129	58.5
6	2.7	37	16.7	68	30.8	99	44.9	130	58.9
7	3.1	38	17.2	69	31.2	100	45.3	131	59.4
8	3.6	39	17.6	70	31.7	101	45.8	132	59.8
9	4.0	40	18.1	71	32.2	102	46.2	133	60.3
10	4.5	41	18.5	72	32.6	103	46.7	134	60.7
11	4.9	42	19.0	73	33.1	104	47.1	135	61.2
12	5.4	43	19.5	74	33.5	105	47.6	136	61.6
13	5.8	44	19.9	75	34.0	106	48.0	137	62.1
14	6.3	45	20.4	76	34.4	107	48.5	138	62.5
15	6.8	46	20.8	77	34.9	108	48.9	139	63.0
16	7.2	47	21.3	78	35.3	109	49.4	140	63.5
17	7.7	48	21.7	79	35.8	110	49.8	141	63.9
18	8.1	49	22.2	80	36.2	111	50.3	142	64.4
19	8.6	50	22.6	81	36.7	112	50.8	143	64.8
20	9.0	51	23.1	82	37.1	113	51.2	144	65.3
21	9.5	52	23.5	83	37.6	114	51.7	145	65.7
22	9.9	53	24.0	84	38.1	115	52.1	146	66.2
23	10.4	54	24.4	85	38.5	116	52.5	147	66.6
24	10.8	55	24.9	86	39.0	117	53.0	148	67.1
25	11.3	56	25.4	87	39.4	118	53.5	149	67.5
26	11.7	57	25.8	88	39.9	119	53.9	150	68.0
27	12.2	58	26.3	89	40.3	120	54.4	160	72.5
28	12.7	59	26.7	90	40.8	121	54.8	170	77.1
29	13.1	60	27.2	91	41.2	122	55.3	180	81.6
30	13.6	61	27.6	92	41.7	123	55.7	190	86.1
31	14.0	62	28.1	93	42.1	124	56.2	200	90.7

Kilogramos a libras

1	2,2	21	46,3	41	90,3	61	134,4	81	178,5
2	4,4	22	48,5	42	92,5	62	136,6	82	180,7
3	6,6	23	50,7	43	94,8	63	138,8	83	182,9
4	8,8	24	52,9	44	97,0	64	141,1	84	185,1
5	11,0	25	55,1	45	99,2	65	143,3	85	187,3
6	13,2	26	57,3	46	101,4	66	145,5	86	189,6
7	15,4	27	59,5	47	103,6	67	147,7	87	191,8
8	17,6	28	61,7	48	105,8	68	149,9	88	194,0
9	19,8	29	63,9	49	108,0	69	152,1	89	196,2
10	22,0	30	66,1	50	110,2	70	154,3	90	198,4
11	24,2	31	68,3	51	112,4	71	156,5	91	200,6
12	26,4	32	70,5	52	114,6	72	158,7	92	202,8
13	28,6	33	72,7	53	116,8	73	160,9	93	205,0
14	30,8	34	74,9	54	119,0	74	163,1	94	207,2
15	33,0	35	77,1	55	121,2	75	165,3	95	209,4
16	35,2	36	79,3	56	123,4	76	167,5	96	211,6
17	37,4	37	81,5	57	125,6	77	169,7	97	213,8
18	39,6	38	83,7	58	127,8	78	171,9	98	216,0
19	41,8	39	85,9	59	130,6	79	174,1	99	218,2
20	44,0	40	88,1	60	132,2	80	176,3	100	220,4

Miles to Kilometers

1	1.60	40	64.37
2	3.21	50	80.46
3	4.82	60	96.55
4	6.43	70	112.65
5	8.04	80	128.74
6	9.65	90	144.83
7	11.26	100	160.93
8	12.87	200	321.86
9	14.48	300	482.79
10	16.09	400	643.72
20	32.18	500	804.65
30	48.27	1000	1609.30

Kilómetros a millas

1	0,62	40	24,85
2	1,24	50	31,07
3	1,86	60	37,28
4	2,48	70	43,49
5	3,10	80	49,71
6	3,72	90	55,92
7	4,34	100	62,14
8	4,97	200	124,18
9	5,59	300	186,42
10	6,21	400	248,56
20	12,42	500	310,70
30	18,64	1000	621,40

Gallons to Liters

1	3.7	21	79.4
2	7.5	22	83.2
3	11.3	23	87.0
4	15.1	24	90.8
5	18.9	25	94.6
6	22.7	26	98.4
7	26.4	27	102.2
8	30.2	28	105.9
9	34.0	29	109.7
10	37.8	30	113.5
11	41.6	31	117.3
12	45.4	32	121.1
13	49.2	33	124.9
14	52.9	34	128.7
15	56.7	35	132.4
16	60.5	36	136.2
17	64.3	37	140.0
18	68.1	38	143.8
19	71.9	39	147.6
20	75.7	40	151.4

Litros a galones

1	0,26	21	5,54	41	10,83
2	0,52	22	5,81	42	11,09
3	0,79	23	6,07	43	11,35
4	1,05	24	6,34	44	11,62
5	1,32	25	6,60	45	11,88
6	1,58	26	6,86	46	12,15
7	1,84	27	7,13	47	12,41
8	2,11	28	7,39	48	12,68
9	2,37	29	7,66	49	12,94
10	2,64	30	7,92	50	13,20
11	2,90	31	8,18	51	13,47
12	3,17	32	8,45	52	13,73
13	3,43	33	8,71	53	14,00
14	3,69	34	8,98	54	14,26
15	3,96	35	9,24	55	14,52
16	4,22	36	9,51	56	14,79
17	4,49	37	9,77	57	15,05
18	4,75	38	10,03	58	15,32
19	5,01	39	10,30	59	15,58
20	5,28	40	10,56	60	15,85

TIRE PRESSURE — PRESIÓN DE INFLADO

Pounds per Square Inch	Atmospheres Atmósferas	Kilogramos por centímetro cuadrado
16	1.08	1,12
18	1.22	1,26
20	1.36	1,40
22	1.49	1,54
24	1.63	1,68
26	1.76	1,82
28	1.90	1,96
30	2.04	2,10
32	2.16	2,24
36	2.44	2,52
40	2.72	2,81
50	3.40	3,51
55	3.74	3,85
60	4.08	4,21
70	4.76	4,92

PART II — PARTE SEGUNDA

English-Spanish

Inglés-Español

A, a [e] *s* (*pl:* **A's, a's** [ez]) primera letra del alfabeto inglés
a. abr. de **acre, acres, adjective** y **answer**
A. abr. de **America** y **American**
a [ə] o [e] *art indef* un; por, cada, a; **fifteen cents a pound** quince centavos la libra; se convierte en **an** antes de sonido vocálico, p.ej., **an orange** una naranja, **an hour** una hora
A 1 ['e'wʌn] *adj* de primera clase, excelente
AAA abr. de **Agricultural Adjustment Administration**
A.A.A. abr. de **American Automobile Association**
A.A.A.L. abr. de **American Academy of Arts and Letters**
A.A.A.S. abr. de **American Association for the Advancement of Science**
Aachen ['ɑkən] *s* Aquisgrán
aardvark ['ɑrd,vɑrk] *s* (zool.) cerdo hormiguero
aardwolf ['ɑrd,wʊlf] *s* (zool.) próteles rayado
Aaron ['ɛrən] *s* (Bib.) Aarón
A.B. abr. de **Artium Baccalaureus** (Lat.) **Bachelor of Arts**
abacá [,ɑbɑ'kɑ] *s* (bot.) abacá (*planta y fibra textil*)
aback [ə'bæk] *adv* atrás; (naut.) en facha; **to be taken aback** quedar desconcertado; **to take aback** desconcertar
abacus ['æbəkəs] *s* (*pl:* **-cuses** o **-ci** [saɪ]) ábaco; (arch.) ábaco
abaft [ə'bæft] o [ə'bɑft] *adv* (naut.) a popa, en popa; *prep* (naut.) detrás de
abalone [,æbə'lonɪ] *s* (zool.) abalone, oreja marina
abandon [ə'bændən] *s* abandono; *va* abandonar; **to abandon oneself** abandonarse
abandoned [ə'bændənd] *adj* abandonado
abandonment [ə'bændənmənt] *s* abandono
abase [ə'bes] *va* degradar, humillar, rebajar
abasement [ə'besmənt] *s* degradación, humillación, rebajamiento
abash [ə'bæʃ] *va* azorar, avergonzar
abashment [ə'bæʃmənt] *s* azoramiento, avergonzamiento
abate [ə'bet] *va* disminuir, reducir; suprimir; anular; deducir, substraer; omitir; *vn* disminuir, moderarse
abatement [ə'betmənt] *s* disminución; supresión; anulación; cantidad rebajada; omisión; (law) ocupación, sin derecho, de una finca tras la muerte de su último dueño
abatis ['æbətɪs] *s* (*pl:* **-tis**) (fort.) abatida; barricada de alambre de púas
A battery *s* (rad.) batería para calentar el cátodo
abattoir ['æbətwɑr] *s* matadero
abbacy ['æbəsɪ] *s* (*pl:* **-cies**) abadía
Abbassides [ə'bæsaɪdz] o ['æbəsaɪdz] *spl* abasidas
abbatial [ə'beʃəl] *adj* abacial
abbé ['æbe] *s* abate
abbess ['æbɪs] *s* abadesa
abbey ['æbɪ] *s* abadía
abbot ['æbət] *s* abad
abbr. o **abbrev.** abr. de **abbreviated** y **abbreviation**
abbreviate [ə'brivɪet] *va* abreviar
abbreviation [ə,brivɪ'eʃən] *s* abreviación (*acortamiento*); abreviatura (*forma abreviada*)
abbreviator [ə'brivɪ,etər] *s* abreviador; (eccl.) abreviador
A B C [,e,bi'si] *s* abecé; **A B C's** *spl* abecedario
A.B.C. powers *spl* potencias A B C (*la Argentina, el Brasil, Chile*)
abdicate ['æbdɪket] *va & vn* abdicar
abdication [,æbdɪ'keʃən] *s* abdicación
abdomen ['æbdəmən] o [æb'domən] *s* (anat. & zool.) abdomen
abdominal [æb'dɑmɪnəl] *adj* abdominal
abdominal supporter *s* faja abdominal
abducent [æb'djusənt] o [æb'dusənt] *adj* (physiol.) abductor
abduct [æb'dʌkt] *va* raptar, secuestrar; (physiol.) abducir
abduction [æb'dʌkʃən] *s* rapto, secuestro; (physiol. & log.) abducción
abductor [æb'dʌktər] *s* raptor, secuestrador; (physiol.) abductor
Abe [eb] *s* nombre abreviado de **Abraham**
abeam [ə'bim] *adv* (naut.) de través, por el través
abed [ə'bɛd] *adv* en cama
Abélard ['æbəlɑrd] *s* Abelardo
abele [ə'bil] o ['ebəl] *s* (bot.) álamo blanco
abelmosk ['ebəl,mɑsk] *s* (bot.) abelmosco
aberrant [æb'ɛrənt] *adj* aberrante
aberration [,æbə'reʃən] *s* aberración; (astr. & opt.) aberración
abet [ə'bɛt] (*pret & pp:* **abetted;** *ger:* **abetting**) *va* incitar (*a una persona, especialmente al mal*); fomentar (*p.ej., el crimen*)
abetment [ə'bɛtmənt] *s* incitación (*especialmente al mal*); fomento (*p.ej., del crimen*)
abetter o **abettor** [ə'bɛtər] *s* incitador, instigador
abeyance [ə'beəns] *s* suspensión; **in abeyance** en suspenso
abhor [æb'hɔr] (*pret & pp:* **-horred;** *ger:* **-horring**) *va* aborrecer, detestar
abhorrence [æb'hɑrəns] o [æb'hɔrəns] *s* aborrecimiento, detestación
abhorrent [æb'hɑrənt] o [æb'hɔrənt] *adj* aborrecible, detestable
abide [ə'baɪd] (*pret & pp:* **abode** o **abided**) *va* esperar; soportar, tolerar; *vn* morar, permanecer, continuar; **to abide by** cumplir con; atenerse a
abiding [ə'baɪdɪŋ] *adj* permanente, perdurable
abigail ['æbɪgel] *s* doncella, criada confidente
ability [ə'bɪlɪtɪ] *s* (*pl:* **-ties**) habilidad, capacidad; talento, ingenio
abiogenesis [,æbɪo'dʒɛnɪsɪs] *s* abiogénesis
abiosis [,æbɪ'osɪs] *s* abiosis
abiotic [,ebaɪ'ɑtɪk] *adj* abiótico
abirritant [æb'ɪrɪtənt] *adj* abirritante; *s* remedio abirritante
abirritate [æb'ɪrɪtet] *va* (med.) abirritar
abirritation [æb,ɪrɪ'teʃən] *s* (med.) abirritación
abject ['æbdʒɛkt] o [æb'dʒɛkt] *adj* abyecto
abjection [æb'dʒɛkʃən] *s* abyección
abjuration [,æbdʒʊ'reʃən] *s* abjuración
abjure [æb'dʒʊr] *va* abjurar
abjurement [æb'dʒʊrmənt] *s* abjuración
abl. abr. de **ablative**
ablactate [æb'læktet] *va* ablactar
ablactation [,æblæk'teʃən] *s* ablactación
ablation [æb'leʃən] *s* (surg.) ablación
ablative ['æblətɪv] *adj & s* (gram.) ablativo
ablative absolute *s* (gram.) ablativo absoluto
ablative case *s* (gram.) ablativo
ablaut ['æblaʊt] *s* (phonet.) apofonía
ablaze [ə'blez] *adj* brillante, encendido; ardiente, anhelante; encolerizado; *adv* en llamas
able ['ebəl] *adj* hábil, capaz; talentoso; **to be able to** + *inf* poder + *inf*
able-bodied ['ebəl'bɑdɪd] *adj* sano; fornido, forzudo
able-bodied seaman *s* marinero experto
ablegate ['æblɪget] *s* (eccl.) ablegado
ablepharia [,æblɪ'fɛrɪə] *s* ablefaria
ablepsia [e'blɛpsɪə] *s* ablepsia
abloom [ə'blum] *adj & adv* en flor
ablution [æb'luʃən] *s* ablución
ably ['eblɪ] *adv* hábilmente; talentosamente
abnegate ['æbnɪget] *va* abnegar; *vn* abnegarse

abnegation [ˌæbnɪˈgeʃən] *s* abnegación
abnormal [æbˈnɔrməl] *adj* anormal
abnormality [ˌæbnɔrˈmælɪtɪ] *s* (*pl:* **-ties**) anormalidad
abnormity [æbˈnɔrmɪtɪ] *s* (*pl:* **-ties**) anomalía; monstruosidad
aboard [əˈbord] *adv* (naut.) a bordo; al bordo; **all aboard!** ¡señores viajeros al tren!; **to go aboard** ir a bordo, embarcarse; **to take aboard** embarcar; *prep* en (*p.ej., el tren*); (naut.) al bordo de, al costado de
abode [əˈbod] *s* domicilio, morada; **to take up one's abode** adquirir o fijar domicilio, domiciliarse; *pret & pp de* **abide**
abolish [əˈbɑlɪʃ] *va* suprimir, eliminar
abolition [ˌæbəˈlɪʃən] *s* supresión, eliminación; (hist.) abolición
abolitionism [ˌæbəˈlɪʃənɪzəm] *s* abolicionismo
abolitionist [ˌæbəˈlɪʃənɪst] *s* abolicionista
abomasum [ˌæboˈmesəm] o **abomasus** [ˌæboˈmesəs] *s* (anat.) abomaso
A-bomb [ˈeˌbɑm] *s* bomba atómica
abominable [əˈbɑmɪnəbəl] *adj* abominable
abominate [əˈbɑmɪnet] *va* abominar, abominar de
abomination [əˌbɑmɪˈneʃən] *s* abominación
aboriginal [ˌæbəˈrɪdʒɪnəl] *adj & s* aborigen
aborigines [ˌæbəˈrɪdʒɪniz] *spl* aborígenes
abort [əˈbɔrt] *va & vn* abortar
abortion [əˈbɔrʃən] *s* aborto
abortionist [əˈbɔrʃənɪst] *s* abortista
abortive [əˈbɔrtɪv] *adj* abortivo
abound [əˈbaʊnd] *vn* abundar; **to abound in** o **with** abundar de o en
about [əˈbaʊt] *adv* casi; alrededor; aquí; acá y allá; en la dirección opuesta; uno después del otro; **to be about** estar levantado (*dícese de uno que ha estado enfermo*); **to be about to** + *inf* estar para + *inf; prep* acerca de, alrededor de; con respecto a; por, cerca de; hacia, como, a eso de, p.ej., **about six o'clock** a eso de las seis; **to be about** tratar de
about face *interj* (mil.) ¡media vuelta!
about-face [əˈbaʊtˌfes] *s* media vuelta; cambio de opinión; [əˈbaʊtˈfes] *vn* dar media vuelta; cambiar de opinión
above [əˈbʌv] *adj & s* antedicho, arriba escrito; **from above** desde lo alto; de arriba; del cielo; *adv* arriba, encima; *prep* sobre, encima de, superior a, más arriba de, más alto que; **above all** sobre todo
aboveboard [əˈbʌvˌbord] *adj & adv* franco, francamente, sin rebozo ni disfraz
above-cited [əˈbʌvˌsaɪtɪd] *adj* ya citado
aboveground [əˈbʌvˌgraʊnd] *adj & adv* sobre la superficie de la tierra; vivo, viviente
above-mentioned [əˈbʌvˌmɛnʃənd] *adj* sobredicho, susodicho, dicho antes
Abp. abr. de **Archbishop**
abracadabra [ˌæbrəkəˈdæbrə] *s* abracadabra
abrade [əˈbred] *va* raer, desgastar por fricción
Abraham [ˈebrəhæm] *s* Abrahán
Abraham's bosom *s* seno de Abrahán
abrasion [əˈbreʒən] *s* abrasión, raedura; (med.) abrasión
abrasive [əˈbresɪv] o [əˈbrezɪv] *adj & s* abrasivo
abreast [əˈbrɛst] *adj & adv* de frente; **to be abreast of** o **with** correr parejas con; estar al corriente de; **to keep abreast of the times** ponerse al corriente de las cosas
abridge [əˈbrɪdʒ] *va* abreviar; privar
abridgement o **abridgment** [əˈbrɪdʒmənt] *s* abreviación; privación
abroad [əˈbrɔd] *adv* en el extranjero, al extranjero; en todas partes, a todas partes; fuera de casa
abrogate [ˈæbrəget] *va* abrogar
abrogation [ˌæbrəˈgeʃən] *s* abrogación
abrupt [əˈbrʌpt] *adj* repentino; brusco; áspero; abrupto, escarpado
abruptness [əˈbrʌptnɪs] *s* precipitación; brusquedad; aspereza; desigualdad
Absalom [ˈæbsələm] o [ˈæbsəlɑm] *s* (Bib.) Absalón
abscess [ˈæbsɛs] *s* (path.) absceso
abscessed [ˈæbsɛst] *adj* apostemado
abscissa [æbˈsɪsə] *s* (geom.) abscisa
abscission [æbˈsɪʒən] o [æbˈsɪʃən] *s* abscisión
abscond [æbˈskɑnd] *vn* evadirse, fugarse

absence [ˈæbsəns] *s* ausencia; falta de asistencia (*a la escuela, etc.*); **in the absence of** a falta de; **absence of mind** distracción
absent [ˈæbsənt] *adj* ausente; distraído; [æbˈsɛnt] *va* ausentar; **to absent oneself** ausentarse
absentee [ˌæbsənˈti] *s* absentista; ausente
absentee ballot *s* voto por correspondencia
absenteeism [ˌæbsənˈtiɪzəm] *s* absentismo, ausentismo
absentee landlord *s* absentista
absentee ownership *s* absentismo, ausentismo
absentee voter *s* votante por correspondencia
absently [ˈæbsəntlɪ] *adv* distraídamente
absent-minded [ˈæbsəntˈmaɪndɪd] *adj* distraído
absent-mindedly [ˈæbsəntˈmaɪndɪdlɪ] *adv* distraídamente
absent-mindedness [ˈæbsəntˈmaɪndɪdnɪs] *s* distracción
absinth o **absinthe** [ˈæbsɪnθ] *s* (bot.) absintio, ajenjo; absenta, ajenjo (*bebida*)
absinthin [æbˈsɪnθɪn] *s* (chem.) absintina
absinthism [ˈæbsɪnθɪzəm] o [æbˈsɪnθɪzəm] *s* (path.) absintismo
absolute [ˈæbsəlut] *adj & s* absoluto
absolute alcohol *s* alcohol absoluto
absolutely [ˈæbsəlutlɪ] o [ˌæbsəˈlutlɪ] *adv* absolutamente
absolute monarchy *s* monarquía absoluta
absolute temperature *s* (phys.) temperatura absoluta
absolute zero *s* (phys.) cero absoluto
absolution [ˌæbsəˈluʃən] *s* absolución
absolutism [ˈæbsəlutɪzəm] *s* absolutismo
absolutist [ˈæbsəlutɪst] *s* absolutista
absolve [æbˈsɑlv] o [æbˈzɑlv] *va* absolver
absorb [æbˈsɔrb] o [æbˈzɔrb] *va* absorber
absorbable [æbˈsɔrbəbəl] o [æbˈzɔrbəbəl] *adj* absorbible
absorbed [æbˈsɔrbd] o [æbˈzɔrbd] *adj* absorto, ensimismado
absorbency [æbˈsɔrbənsɪ] o [æbˈzɔrbənsɪ] *s* absorbencia
absorbent [æbˈsɔrbənt] o [æbˈzɔrbənt] *adj & s* absorbente
absorbent cotton *s* algodón hidrófilo
absorbing [æbˈsɔrbɪŋ] o [æbˈzɔrbɪŋ] *adj* absorbente (*interesante*)
absorption [æbˈsɔrpʃən] o [æbˈzɔrpʃən] *s* absorción
abstain [æbˈsten] *vn* abstenerse; **to abstain from** + *ger* abstenerse de + *inf*
abstainer [æbˈstenər] *s* abstinente
abstemious [æbˈstimɪəs] *adj* abstemio, abstinente
abstention [æbˈstɛnʃən] *s* abstención
abstergent [æbˈstʌrdʒənt] *adj & s* abstergente
abstersion [æbˈstʌrʃən] *s* abstersión
abstersive [æbˈstʌrsɪv] *adj* abstersivo
abstinence [ˈæbstɪnəns] *s* abstinencia
abstinent [ˈæbstɪnənt] *adj* abstinente
abstract [ˈæbstrækt] o [æbˈstrækt] *adj* abstracto; [ˈæbstrækt] *s* sumario, resumen; resumen analítico (*de materia científica*); **in the abstract** en abstracto; *va* resumir, compendiar; [æbˈstrækt] *va* abstraer (*una calidad*); quitar
abstracted [æbˈstræktɪd] *adj* abstraído
abstraction [æbˈstrækʃən] *s* abstracción
abstractionism [æbˈstrækʃənɪzəm] *s* (f.a.) abstraccionismo
abstractionist [æbˈstrækʃənɪst] *adj & s* (f.a.) abstraccionista
abstruse [æbˈstrus] *adj* abstruso
absurd [æbˈsʌrd] o [æbˈzʌrd] *adj* absurdo
absurdity [æbˈsʌrdɪtɪ] o [æbˈzʌrdɪtɪ] *s* (*pl:* **-ties**) absurdidad, absurdo
abundance [əˈbʌndəns] *s* abundancia
abundant [əˈbʌndənt] *adj* abundante
abuse [əˈbjus] *s* maltrato; injuria, insulto; abuso (*mal uso; costumbre injusta, injusticia*); [əˈbjuz] *va* maltratar; injuriar, insultar; abusar de (*usar mal de, p.ej., la autoridad*)
abusive [əˈbjusɪv] *adj* injurioso, insultante; abusivo (*que se practica por abuso*)
abut [əˈbʌt] (*pret & pp:* **abutted;** *ger:* **abutting**) *vn* confinar, estar contiguo; **to abut on, upon,** o **against** confinar con, terminar en
abutment [əˈbʌtmənt] *s* (arch.) estribo, contra-

fuerte, botarel; (carp.) empotramiento (*ensamblaje*); confinamiento, contigüidad
Abydos [əˈbaɪdɑs] *s* Abidos
abysm [əˈbɪzəm] *s* var. de **abyss**
abysmal [əˈbɪzməl] *adj* abismal; profundo
abysmally [əˈbɪzməlɪ] *adv* profundamente
abyss [əˈbɪs] *s* abismo
abyssal [əˈbɪsəl] *adj* abisal
Abyssinia [ˌæbɪˈsɪnɪə] *s* Abisinia
Abyssinian [ˌæbɪˈsɪnɪən] *adj & s* abisinio
A.C. o **a.c.** abr. de **alternating current**
acacia [əˈkeʃə] *s* (bot.) acacia; (bot.) acacia falsa (*Robinia pseudoacacia*); goma arábiga
academic [ˌækəˈdɛmɪk] *adj* académico (*escolar; clásico, literario; teórico; amanerado*); *s* estudiante universitario; profesor de la universidad; individuo de una sociedad de eruditos
academical [ˌækəˈdɛmɪkəl] *adj* var. de **academic; academicals** *spl* var. de **academic costume**
academic costume *s* traje de catedrático, traje académico, toga
academic freedom *s* libertad de cátedra
academician [əˌkædəˈmɪʃən] *s* académico
academic subjects *spl* (educ.) materias no profesionales
academic year *s* año escolar, año académico
academize [əˈkædəmaɪz] *va* academizar
Academus [ˌækəˈdiməs] *s* (myth.) Academo
academy [əˈkædəmɪ] *s* (*pl:* **-mies**) academia
academy figure *s* (f.a.) academia
Acadia [əˈkedɪə] *s* Acadia
Acadian [əˈkedɪən] *adj & s* acadiense
acalephan [ˌækəˈlɛfən] *adj & s* (zool.) acalefo
acalycine [eˈkælɪsɪn] o [eˈkælɪsaɪn] *adj* (bot.) acalicino
acanthaceous [ˌækænˈθeʃəs] *adj* (bot.) acantáceo
acanthocephalan [əˌkænθoˈsɛfələn] *adj & s* (zool.) acantocéfalo
acanthopterygian [ˌækænˌθɑptəˈrɪdʒɪən] *adj & s* (ichth.) acantopterigio
acanthus [əˈkænθəs] *s* (*pl:* **-thuses** o **-thi** [θaɪ]) (bot. & arch.) acanto
acarid [ˈækərɪd] *s* (zool.) acárido
acaroid gum o **resin** [ˈækərɔɪd] *s* acaroide, resina acaroide
acarpous [eˈkɑrpəs] *adj* (bot.) acarpo
acarus [ˈækərəs] *s* (*pl:* **-ri** [raɪ]) (zool.) ácaro
acatalectic [eˌkætəˈlɛktɪk] *adj & s* acataléctico
acatalepsia [eˌkætəˈlɛpsɪə] *s* (med.) acatalepsia
acatalepsy [eˈkætəˌlɛpsɪ] *s* (philos.) acatalepsia
acaulescent [ˌækɔˈlɛsənt] *adj* (bot.) acaule
acc. abr. de **accusative**
accede [ækˈsid] *vn* acceder; **to accede to** acceder a, condescender a; ascender o subir a (*p.ej., un trono*)
accelerate [ækˈsɛləret] *va* acelerar; *vn* acelerarse
acceleration [ækˌsɛləˈreʃən] *s* aceleración
accelerator [ækˈsɛləˌretər] *s* (aut.) acelerador
accelerometer [ækˌsɛləˈrɑmɪtər] *s* (aer.) acelerómetro
accent [ˈæksɛnt] *s* acento; [ˈæksɛnt] o [ækˈsɛnt] *va* acentuar
accentual [ækˈsɛntʃuəl] *adj* acentual
accentuate [ækˈsɛntʃuet] *va* acentuar
accentuation [ækˌsɛntʃuˈeʃən] *s* acentuación
accept [ækˈsɛpt] *va* aceptar; (com.) aceptar
acceptability [ækˌsɛptəˈbɪlɪtɪ] *s* aceptabilidad
acceptable [ækˈsɛptəbəl] *adj* aceptable
acceptably [ækˈsɛptəblɪ] *adv* aceptablemente
acceptance [ækˈsɛptəns] *s* aceptación; (com.) aceptación
acceptation [ˌæksɛpˈteʃən] o **acception** [ækˈsɛpʃən] *s* acepción (*sentido*)
acceptor [ækˈsɛptər] *s* aceptador, aceptante; (com.) aceptante
access [ˈæksɛs] *s* acceso; (med.) acceso, ataque; aditamento, aumento
accessary [ækˈsɛsərɪ] *adj* var. de **accessory;** *s* (*pl:* **-ries**) var. de **accessory**
accessibility [ækˌsɛsɪˈbɪlɪtɪ] *s* accesibilidad
accessible [ækˈsɛsɪbəl] *adj* accesible
accession [ækˈsɛʃən] *s* accesión, consentimiento; ascenso (*a una dignidad o empleo*); aditamento, acrecentamiento; adquisición (*p. ej., de libros en una biblioteca*)
accessory [ækˈsɛsərɪ] *adj* accesorio; *s* (*pl:* **-ries**) accesorio; fautor, cómplice
accessory after the fact *s* (law) encubridor en el delito
accessory before the fact *s* (law) instigador de un delito
accidence [ˈæksɪdəns] *s* (gram.) accidentes
accident [ˈæksɪdənt] *s* accidente; (gram. & mus.) accidente; **by accident** por accidente
accidental [ˌæksɪˈdɛntəl] *adj* accidental; *s* (mus.) accidental
accidentally [ˌæksɪˈdɛntəlɪ] *adv* accidentalmente
accident insurance *s* seguro contra accidentes
accident prevention *s* precauciones contra accidentes
accipiter [ækˈsɪpɪtər] *s* (surg.) accípitre
acclaim [əˈklem] *s* aclamación; **to win acclaim** merecer aclamación, merecer aplausos; *va & vn* aclamar
acclamation [ˌækləˈmeʃən] *s* aclamación; **by acclamation** por aclamación
acclimate [əˈklaɪmɪt] o [ˈæklɪmet] *va* aclimatar; **to become acclimated** aclimatarse; *vn* aclimatarse
acclimation [ˌæklɪˈmeʃən] o **acclimatization** [əˌklaɪmətɪˈzeʃən] *s* aclimatación
acclimatize [əˈklaɪmətaɪz] *va & vn* var. de **acclimate**
acclivity [əˈklɪvɪtɪ] *s* (*pl:* **-ties**) cuesta ascendente, subida
accolade [ˌækəˈled] o [ˈækəled] *s* acolada, espaldarazo; elogio, premio; (arch., mus. & paleog.) acolada
accommodate [əˈkɑmədet] *va* acomodar; hospedar, alojar; *vn* conformarse
accommodating [əˈkɑməˌdetɪŋ] acomodadizo, servicial
accommodation [əˌkɑməˈdeʃən] *s* acomodación; hospedaje, alojamiento; (physiol.) acomodación; **accommodations** *spl* facilidades, comodidades; localidad (*p.ej., en un tren*); alojamiento, aposento (*en un hotel*)
accommodation train *s* tren ómnibus
accompaniment [əˈkʌmpənɪmənt] *s* acompañamiento; (mus.) acompañamiento
accompanist [əˈkʌmpənɪst] *s* acompañador, acompañante; (mus.) acompañante
accompany [əˈkʌmpənɪ] *va* (*pret & pp:* **-nied**) *va* acompañar; (mus.) acompañar
accomplice [əˈkɑmplɪs] *s* cómplice
accomplish [əˈkɑmplɪʃ] *va* realizar, llevar a cabo
accomplished [əˈkɑmplɪʃt] *adj* realizado; consumado; culto, elegante
accomplishment [əˈkɑmplɪʃmənt] *s* realización, ejecución, logro; **accomplishments** *spl* prendas, talentos, habilidades
accord [əˈkɔrd] *s* acuerdo; **in accord** de acuerdo; **in accord with** de acuerdo con; **of one's own accord** espontáneamente; **with one accord** de común acuerdo; *va* acordar, componer, conciliar; conceder, otorgar; *vn* concordar, avenirse, ponerse de acuerdo
accordance [əˈkɔrdəns] *s* conformidad; **in accordance with** de acuerdo con, de conformidad con
accordant [əˈkɔrdənt] *adj* acorde, conforme
according [əˈkɔrdɪŋ] *adj* acorde, conforme; **according as** según que; **according to** según, conforme a
accordingly [əˈkɔrdɪŋlɪ] *adv* en conformidad; por consiguiente
accordion [əˈkɔrdɪən] *s* acordeón; *adj* en acordeón, acordeonado
accordionist [əˈkɔrdɪənɪst] *s* acordeonista
accordion pleat *s* (sew.) pliegue acordeonado o en acordeón
accost [əˈkɔst] o [əˈkɑst] *va* abordar, acercarse a
accouchement [əˈkuʃmənt] *s* alumbramiento
account [əˈkaunt] *s* cuenta; relación, informe; importancia, monta; (com.) estado de cuenta; **by all accounts** según el decir general; **of account** de importancia; **of no account** de poca importancia; despreciable; **on account** a cuenta; **on account of** a causa de; por amor de; **on no account** de ninguna manera;

to bring to account pedir cuentas a; **to buy on account** comprar a plazos; **to call to account** pedir cuentas a; **to charge to the account of** cargar en cuenta a; **to give a good account of oneself** dar buena cuenta de sí; **to lose account of** perder la cuenta de; **to pay on account** pagar a buena cuenta; **to settle accounts with** ajustar cuentas con; **to take account of** tomar en cuenta; considerar; **to take account of stock** hacer inventario; **to take into account** tomar en cuenta; **to turn to account** sacar provecho de, hacer valer; *va* considerar, juzgar; *vn* echar la cuenta; **to account for** explicar; responder de, dar razón de
accountability [ə,kaʊntə'bɪlɪtɪ] *s* responsabilidad
accountable [ə'kaʊntəbəl] *adj* responsable; explicable
accountably [ə'kaʊntəblɪ] *adv* explicablemente
accountancy [ə'kaʊntənsɪ] *s* contabilidad
accountant [ə'kaʊntənt] *s* contador, contable
account executive *s* (Brit.) var. de **customers' man**
accounting [ə'kaʊntɪŋ] *s* arreglo de cuentas; estado de cuentas; contabilidad
accounts payable *spl* (com.) cuentas a pagar
accounts receivable *spl* (com.) cuentas a cobrar
accounts rendered *spl* (com.) cuentas pasadas o rendidas
accounts stated *spl* (com.) cuentas convenidas
accouter o **accoutre** [ə'kutər] *va* aviar, equipar
accouterments o **accoutrements** [ə'kutərmənts] *spl* avío, equipo
accredit [ə'krɛdɪt] *va* acreditar; (educ.) acreditar
accreditation [ə,krɛdɪ'teʃən] *s* acreditación; (educ.) acreditación
accretion [ə'kriʃən] *s* acrecentamiento; (mineral. & path.) acreción
accrual [ə'kruəl] *s* acumulación
accrue [ə'kru] *vn* resultar; acumularse
acct. abr. de **account**
accumulate [ə'kjumjələt] *va* acumular; *vn* acumularse
accumulation [ə,kjumjə'leʃən] *s* acumulación
accumulator [ə'kjumjə,letər] *s* acumulador; (Brit.) acumulador (*eléctrico*)
accuracy ['ækjərəsɪ] *s* exactitud, precisión
accurate ['ækjərɪt] *adj* exacto; seguro (*en el cálculo*)
accursed [ə'kʌrsɪd] o [ə'kʌrst] o **accurst** [ə'kʌrst] *adj* maldecido, maldito
accus. abr. de **accusative**
accusable [ə'kjuzəbəl] *adj* acusable
accusation [,ækjə'zeʃən] o [,ækjʊ'zeʃən] *s* acusación
accusative [ə'kjuzətɪv] *adj & s* (gram.) acusativo
accusatory [ə'kjuzə,torɪ] *adj* acusatorio
accuse [ə'kjuz] *va* acusar
accused [ə'kjuzd] *adj & s* acusado
accuser [ə'kjuzər] *s* acusador
accusingly [ə'kjuzɪŋlɪ] *adv* acusando
accustom [ə'kʌstəm] *va* acostumbrar
accustomed [ə'kʌstəmd] *adj* acostumbrado, de costumbre
ace [es] *s* as (*naipes, dados, tenis, aviación*); **to be within an ace of** + *ger* estar a dos dedos de + *inf*
acephalous [e'sɛfələs] *adj* acéfalo
aceraceous [,æsə'reʃəs] *adj* (bot.) aceráceo
acerbate ['æsərbet] *va* agriar; (fig.) exasperar
acerbity [ə'sʌrbɪtɪ] *s* (*pl:* **-ties**) acerbidad
acerose ['æsəros] *adj* (bot.) aceroso
acerous ['æsərəs] *adj* (bot.) aceroso; [e'sɪrəs] *adj* (zool.) acerato (*sin cuernos*)
acetabulum [,æsɪ'tæbjələm] *s* (*pl:* **-la** [lə]) (anat., bot. & zool.) acetábulo
acetanilid [,æsɪ'tænɪlɪd] o **acetanilide** [,æsɪ'tænɪlɪd] o [,æsɪ'tænɪlaɪd] *s* (chem.) acetanilida
acetate ['æsɪtet] *s* (chem.) acetato
acetic [ə'sitɪk] *adj* (chem.) acético
acetic acid *s* (chem.) ácido acético
acetification [ə,sɛtɪfɪ'keʃən] *s* acetificación
acetify [ə'sɛtɪfaɪ] (*pret & pp:* **-fied**) *va* acetificar; *vn* acetificarse
acetimeter [,æsɪ'tɪmɪtər] o **acetometer** [,æsɪ'tɑmɪtər] *s* acetímetro
acetone ['æsɪton] *s* (chem.) acetona
acetonemia [,æsɪto'nimɪə] *s* (path.) acetonemia
acetonuria [,æsɪto'nurɪə] o [,æsɪto'njurɪə] *s* (path.) acetonuria
acetose ['æsɪtos] o **acetous** ['æsɪtəs] o [ə'sitəs] *adj* acetoso
acetyl ['æsɪtɪl] *s* (chem.) acetilo
acetylene [ə'sɛtɪlin] *s* (chem.) acetileno; *adj* acetilénico
acetylene torch *s* soplete oxiacetilénico
Achaea [ə'kiə] *s* Acaya
Achaean [ə'kiən] *adj & s* aqueo
Achaia [ə'keə] o [ə'kaɪə] *s* var. de **Achaea**
Achates [ə'ketiz] *s* (myth.) Acates
ache [ek] *s* dolor continuo, achaque; **to be full of aches and pains** estar lleno de goteras; *vn* doler, p.ej., **my head aches** me duele la cabeza; padecer dolor, estar acongojado; (coll.) suspirar, anhelar
achene [e'kin] *s* (bot.) aquenio
achenial [e'kinɪəl] *adj* aquénico
Acheron ['ækərɑn] *s* (myth.) Aqueronte
achievable [ə'tʃivəbəl] *adj* acabable
achieve [ə'tʃiv] *va* llevar a cabo; alcanzar; ganar; *vn* tener buen éxito
achievement [ə'tʃivmənt] *s* realización, ejecución, logro; hazaña
Achilles [ə'kɪliz] *s* (myth.) Aquiles
Achilles' heel *s* talón de Aquiles (*sitio vulnerable*)
Achilles' tendon *s* (anat.) tendón de Aquiles
achlorhydria [e,klor'haɪdrɪə] *s* (path.) aclorhidria
achromatic [,ækro'mætɪk] *adj* (opt., biol., & mus.) acromático
achromatin [e'kromətɪn] *s* (biol.) acromatina
achromatism [e'kromətɪzəm] *s* acromatismo
achromatize [e'kromətaɪz] *va* acromatizar
achromatosis [e,kromə'tosɪs] *s* (path.) acromatosis
achromatous [e'kromətəs] *adj* acromático
acicular [ə'sɪkjələr] *adj* acicular
aciculate [ə'sɪkjəlɪt] *adj* (bot. & zool.) aciculado
acid ['æsɪd] *adj* ácido; (chem.) ácido; (fig.) agrio, mordaz; *s* (chem.) ácido
acid-forming ['æsɪd,fɔrmɪŋ] *adj* ácido; acidógeno (*dícese de los alimentos*)
acidic [ə'sɪdɪk] *adj* acidificante; (petrog.) ácido
acidiferous [,æsɪ'dɪfərəs] *adj* acidífero
acidification [ə,sɪdɪfɪ'keʃən] *s* acidificación
acidify [ə'sɪdɪfaɪ] (*pret & pp:* **-fied**) *va* acidificar; *vn* acidificarse
acidimeter [,æsɪ'dɪmɪtər] *s* acidímetro
acidity [ə'sɪdɪtɪ] *s* (*pl:* **-ties**) acidez
acidophil ['æsɪdə,fɪl] *adj & s* acidófilo
acidophilus milk [,æsɪ'dɑfɪləs] *s* lactobacilina
acidosis [,æsɪ'dosɪs] *s* (path.) acidosis
acidproof ['æsɪd'pruf] *adj* inatacable por los ácidos
acid test *s* prueba extrema, prueba de fuego
acidulate [ə'sɪdjəlet] *va* acidular
acidulous [ə'sɪdjələs] *adj* acídulo
ack-ack ['æk,æk] *s* (slang) fuego antiaéreo; (slang) artillería antiaérea
acknowledge [æk'nɑlɪdʒ] *va* admitir, confesar, reconocer; acusar (*recibo de una carta, oficios, etc.*); agradecer (*p.ej., un favor*); (law) certificar, testificar
acknowledgment o **acknowledgement** [æk'nɑlɪdʒmənt] *s* admisión, confesión, reconocimiento; acuse (*de recibo*); agradecimiento; (law) certificación, testificación
aclastic [e'klæstɪk] *adj* (opt.) aclástico
acleidian o **aclidian** [e'klaɪdɪən] *adj & s* (anat.) acleido
aclinic [e'klɪnɪk] *adj* (phys.) aclínico
aclinic line *s* (phys.) línea aclínica
acme ['ækmɪ] *s* auge, colmo, pináculo, cima; (med.) acmé
acne ['æknɪ] *s* (path.) acne
acology [ə'kɑlədʒɪ] *s* acología
acolyte ['ækolaɪt] *s* acólito
acolythate [ə'kɑlɪθet] *s* (eccl.) acolitazgo
aconite ['ækənaɪt] *s* (bot.) acónito

aconitine [əˈkɑnɪtin] o [əˈkɑnɪtɪn] *s* (chem.) aconitina
acorn [ˈekɔrn] o [ˈekərn] *s* bellota
acorned [ˈekɔrnd] o [ˈekərnd] *adj* lleno de bellotas, cebado con bellotas; (her.) englandado
acotyledon [eˌkɑtɪˈlidən] *s* (bot.) acotiledón
acotyledonous [eˌkɑtɪˈlidənəs] *adj* (bot.) acotiledón o acotiledóneo
acoustic [əˈkustɪk] o [əˈkaustɪk] *adj* acústico; **acoustics** *ssg* (phys.) acústica; **acoustics** *spl* acústica arquitectural
acoustically [əˈkustɪkəlɪ] o [əˈkaustɪkəlɪ] *adv* acústicamente
acoustical tile *s* azulejo antisonoro
acousticon [əˈkustɪkɑn] o [əˈkaustɪkɑn] *s* (trademark) acusticón
acquaint [əˈkwent] *va* informar, familiarizar, poner al corriente; **to be acquainted** conocerse (*uno a otro*); **to be acquainted with** conocer; estar al corriente de; **to become acquainted** venir a conocerse; **to become acquainted with** venir a conocer; ponerse al corriente de; **to acquaint with** poner al corriente de
acquaintance [əˈkwentəns] *s* conocimiento; conocido (*persona*)
acquaintanceship [əˈkwentənsʃɪp] *s* conocimiento; trato, relaciones
acquiesce [ˌækwɪˈɛs] *vn* consentir, conformarse, condescender
acquiescence [ˌækwɪˈɛsəns] *s* consentimiento, conformidad, condescendencia, aquiescencia
acquiescent [ˌækwɪˈɛsənt] *adj* acomodadizo, conforme, condescendiente, aquiescente
acquire [əˈkwaɪr] *va* adquirir
acquired character *s* (biol.) carácter adquirido
acquirement [əˈkwaɪrmənt] *s* adquisición; **acquirements** *spl* conocimientos
acquisition [ˌækwɪˈzɪʃən] *s* adquisición
acquisitive [əˈkwɪzɪtɪv] *adj* propenso a adquirir, codicioso; (law) adquisitivo
acquisitiveness [əˈkwɪzɪtɪvnɪs] *s* adquisividad
acquisitive prescription *s* (law) prescripción adquisitiva
acquit [əˈkwɪt] (*pret & pp:* **acquitted;** *ger:* **acquitting**) *va* absolver, exculpar; **to acquit oneself** portarse, conducirse
acquittal [əˈkwɪtəl] *s* absolución, exculpación; desempeño
acquittance [əˈkwɪtəns] *s* descargo (*de una deuda*); pago; recibo, finiquito
acre [ˈekər] *s* acre
acreage [ˈekərɪdʒ] *s* acreaje, superficie medida en acres
acrid [ˈækrɪd] *adj* acre, acrimonioso; (fig.) acre, acrimonioso
acridity [əˈkrɪdɪtɪ] *s* acritud, acrimonia; (fig.) acritud, acrimonia
acriflavine [ˌækrɪˈflevɪn] o [ˌækrɪˈflevin] *s* (pharm.) acriflavina
acrimonious [ˌækrɪˈmonɪəs] *adj* acrimonioso
acrimony [ˈækrɪˌmonɪ] *s* (*pl:* **-nies**) acrimonia
acrobat [ˈækrəbæt] *s* acróbata
acrobatic [ˌækrəˈbætɪk] *adj* acrobático; **acrobatics** *spl* acrobacia (*ejercicios*); **acrobatics** *ssg* acrobatismo (*arte o profesión*)
acrogen [ˈækrədʒən] *s* (bot.) acrógena
acromegaly [ˌækroˈmɛgəlɪ] *s* (path.) acromegalia
acronym [ˈækrənɪm] *s* acrónimo
acropolis [əˈkrɑpəlɪs] *s* acrópolis; **the Acropolis** la Acrópolis
acrospore [ˈækrospor] *s* (bot.) acrósporo
across [əˈkrɔs] o [əˈkrɑs] *adv* a través; al otro lado; en cruz, transversalmente; *prep* a través de, al través de; al otro lado de; (elec.) en paralelo con; **to come across** encontrarse con; **to go across** atravesar; **to run across** encontrarse con; **across the way** enfrente
across-the-board [əˈkrɔsðəˈbord] o [əˈkrɑsðəˈbord] *adj* comprensivo, general, para todos sin excepción
acrostic [əˈkrɔstɪk] o [əˈkrɑstɪk] *s* acróstico
acroterium [ˌækroˈtɪrɪəm] *s* (*pl:* **-a** [ə]) (arch.) acrotera; (naut.) acrostolio
acrylic [əˈkrɪlɪk] *adj* (chem.) acrílico
acrylic acid *s* (chem.) ácido acrílico
act [ækt] *s* acto, acción; (law) ley, decreto; (theat.) acto; **an act of treason** una traición; **in the act** en flagrante; *va* representar; desempeñar (*un papel*); desempeñar el papel de; aparentar; **to act the fool** hacer el bufón, hacer de bufón; **to act the part of** hacer el papel de, desempeñar el papel de; *vn* obrar, actuar, funcionar; portarse, conducirse; fingir; (theat.) hacer un papel, actuar; **to act as** actuar de; **to act as if** hacer que, hacer como que; **to act for** representar; **to act on** o **upon** actuar sobre, influir en; seguir, obedecer; **to act up** travesear; **to act up to** portarse en conformidad con; hacer zalamerías a, hacer fiestas a
acting [ˈæktɪŋ] *adj* fingidor, simulador; interino; *s* funcionamiento; simulación; (theat.) actuación, representación, desempeño de un papel
actinic [ækˈtɪnɪk] *adj* actínico
actinism [ˈæktɪnɪzəm] *s* actinismo
actinium [ækˈtɪnɪəm] *s* (chem.) actinio
actinometer [ˌæktɪˈnɑmɪtər] *s* actinómetro
actinomycin [ˌæktɪnoˈmaɪsɪn] *s* (pharm.) actinomicina
actinomycosis [ˌæktɪnomaɪˈkosɪs] *s* (path.) actinomicosis
action [ˈækʃən] *s* acción; (mach.) accionado (*mecanismo*); **actions** *spl* conducta; **in action** en acción, en marcha; **to take action** tomar medidas; (law) poner, entablar un pleito
actionable [ˈækʃənəbəl] *adj* justiciable; procesable
Actium [ˈæktɪəm] o [ˈækʃɪəm] *s* Accio
activate [ˈæktɪvet] *va* activar
activation [ˌæktɪˈveʃən] *s* activación
activator [ˈæktɪˌvetər] *s* activador; (chem.) activador
active [ˈæktɪv] *adj* activo
active service *s* (mil.) servicio activo
active voice *s* (gram.) voz activa
activist [ˈæktɪvɪst] *s* activista
activity [ækˈtɪvɪtɪ] *s* (*pl:* **-ties**) actividad
act of God *s* fuerza mayor
acton [ˈæktən] *s* gambax
actor [ˈæktər] *s* actor, agente; (theat. & law) actor
actress [ˈæktrɪs] *s* (theat.) actriz; (law) actora
Acts of the Apostles *spl* (Bib.) Actas, Actos, o Hechos de los Apóstoles
actual [ˈæktʃuəl] *adj* real, efectivo
actuality [ˌæktʃuˈælɪtɪ] *s* (*pl:* **-ties**) realidad
actualize [ˈæktʃuəlaɪz] *va* realizar
actually [ˈæktʃuəlɪ] *adv* en realidad
actuarial [ˌæktʃuˈɛrɪəl] *adj* actuario, actuarial
actuary [ˈæktʃuˌɛrɪ] *s* (*pl:* **-ies**) actuario, actuario de seguros
actuate [ˈæktʃuet] *va* actuar, poner en acción; estimular, impulsar
acuity [əˈkjuɪtɪ] *s* agudeza, acuidad
acumen [əˈkjumɛn] *s* acumen, cacumen, perspicacia
acuminate [əˈkjumɪnet] *adj* acuminado; (bot. & zool.) acuminado; *va* aguzar; *vn* rematar en punta
acupuncture [ˌækjəˈpʌŋktʃər] *s* (surg.) acupuntura
acute [əˈkjut] *adj* agudo
acute accent *s* acento agudo
acute angle *s* (geom.) ángulo agudo
acute-angled [əˈkjutˈæŋgəld] *adj* acutangulado, acutangular, acutángulo
acuteness [əˈkjutnɪs] *s* agudeza
acyclic [eˈsaɪklɪk] *adj* acíclico
A.D. abr. de **anno Domini** (Lat.) **in the year of our Lord**
ad [æd] *s* (coll.) anuncio
Ada [ˈedə] *s* Ada
adage [ˈædɪdʒ] *s* adagio, refrán
adagio [əˈdɑdʒo] o [əˈdɑdʒɪo] *s* (*pl:* **-gios**) (mus.) adagio
Adam [ˈædəm] *s* Adán; **not to know from Adam** (coll.) no conocer absolutamente; **the old Adam** la inclinación al pecado
adamant [ˈædəmænt] o [ˈædəmənt] *adj* diamantino, duro, inquebrantable; firme, inexorable; *s* adamas
adamantine [ˌædəˈmæntɪn], [ˌædəˈmæntin] o [ˌædəˈmæntaɪn] *adj* adamantino
Adamic [əˈdæmɪk] *adj* adámico
Adam's apple *s* nuez, nuez de la garganta, manzana de Adán

adapt [ə'dæpt] *va* adaptar, adecuar; refundir (*p.ej., un drama*)
adaptability [ə,dæptə'bɪlɪtɪ] *s* adaptabilidad
adaptable [ə'dæptəbəl] *adj* adaptable
adaptation [,ædæp'teʃən] *s* adaptación; refundición (*p.ej., de un drama*)
adapter [ə'dæptər] *s* adaptador; (chem.) alargadera; refundidor
adaptive [ə'dæptɪv] *adj* adaptante, adaptativo
add [æd] *va* añadir, agregar; sumar; *vn* sumar; **to add up to** subir a
added line *s* (mus.) línea suplementaria
addend ['ædɛnd] o [ə'dɛnd] *s* (math.) sumando
addendum [ə'dɛndəm] *s* (*pl:* **-da** [də]) complemento; (mach.) cabeza; (mach.) altura de la cabeza
addendum circle *s* (mach.) círculo de cabeza
adder ['ædər] *s* (zool.) víbora común; serpiente
adder's-tongue ['ædərz,tʌŋ] *s* (bot.) lengua de sierpe (*helecho*); (bot.) eritrono
addible ['ædɪbəl] *adj* añadible
addict ['ædɪkt] *s* enviciado; adicto, partidario; [ə'dɪkt] *va* enviciar; dedicar, entregar; **to addict oneself to** enviciarse en o con; dedicarse a, entregarse a
addicted [ə'dɪktɪd] *adj* enviciado; adicto; **addicted to** enviciado con, apasionado por
addiction [ə'dɪkʃən] *s* enviciamiento; adhesividad
adding machine *s* máquina de sumar, sumadora
Addison's disease ['ædɪsənz] *s* (path.) enfermedad de Addison, cirrosis hipertrófica
addition [ə'dɪʃən] *s* adición; **in addition** además; **in addition to** además de, a más de
additional [ə'dɪʃənəl] *adj* adicional
additionally [ə'dɪʃənəlɪ] *adv* adicionalmente
additive ['ædɪtɪv] *adj & s* aditivo
addle ['ædəl] *adj* huero; (fig.) huero; *va & vn* enhuerar
addlebrained ['ædəl'brend] *adj* atontado, estúpido
address [ə'drɛs] o ['ædrɛs] *s* dirección; (com.) consignación; [ə'drɛs] *s* discurso, alocución; destreza, habilidad; trato, maneras; **addresses** *spl* obsequios amorosos; **to deliver an address** pronunciar un discurso; *va* dirigirse a; dirigir la palabra a; dirigir (*p.ej., una alocución, una carta*); (com.) consignar; (golf) prepararse para golpear (*la pelota*); **How does one address a governor?** ¿Qué tratamiento se da a un gobernador?; **to address oneself to** dirigirse a
addressee [,ædrɛ'si] *s* destinatario; (com.) consignatario
addressing machine *s* máquina para dirigir sobres
addressograph [ə'drɛsəgræf] o [ə'drɛsəgrɑf] *s* (trademark) adresógrafo
adduce [ə'djus] o [ə'dus] *va* aducir
adducent [ə'djusənt] o [ə'dusənt] *adj* (physiol.) aductor
adduct [ə'dʌkt] *va* (physiol.) aducir
adduction [ə'dʌkʃən] *s* aducción; (physiol.) aducción
adductor [ə'dʌktər] *s* (physiol.) aductor, músculo aductor
Adelaide ['ædəled] *s* Adelaida
Adeline ['ædəlaɪn] o ['ædəlin] *s* Adelina
Aden ['ɑdən] o ['edən] *s* Adén
adenia [ə'dinɪə] *s* (path.) adenia
adenitis [,ædɪ'naɪtɪs] *s* (path.) adenitis
adenoid ['ædənɔɪd] *adj* adenoideo; **adenoids** *spl* vegetaciones adenoideas
adenoidal [,ædə'nɔɪdəl] *adj* adenoideo
adenoidectomy [,ædɪnɔɪ'dɛktəmɪ] *s* (*pl:* **-mies**) adenoidectomía
adenoma [,ædɪ'nomə] *s* (*pl:* **-mata** [mətə] o **-mas**) (path.) adenoma
adept [ə'dɛpt] *adj* experto, perito; hábil; adepto; ['ædɛpt] o [ə'dɛpt] *s* experto, perito; adepto (*en alquimia, magia, etc.*)
adequacy ['ædɪkwəsɪ] *s* suficiencia
adequate ['ædɪkwɪt] *adj* suficiente
adhere [æd'hɪr] *vn* adherir, adherirse; conformarse
adherence [æd'hɪrəns] *s* adhesión (*apoyo, fidelidad*)
adherent [æd'hɪrənt] *adj & s* adherente
adhesion [æd'hiʒən] *s* adherencia (*acción de pegarse*); adhesión (*apoyo, fidelidad*); (path.) adherencia; (phys.) adherencia o adhesión
adhesive [æd'hisɪv] o [æd'hizɪv] *adj & s* adhesivo
adhesive tape *s* tafetán adhesivo, cinta adhesiva
ad hoc [æd'hɑk] (Lat.) para aquello de que se trata
adiabatic [,ædɪə'bætɪk] *adj* adiabático
adiaphoresis [,ædɪ,æfo'risɪs] *s* (path.) adiaforesis
adieu [ə'dju] o [ə'du] *s* (*pl:* **adieus** o **adieux** [ə'djuz] o [ə'duz]) adiós; **to bid adieu to** despedirse de; *interj* ¡ adiós!
ad infinitum [æd,ɪnfɪ'naɪtəm] *adv* a lo infinito, hasta lo infinito
adipocere ['ædɪpo,sɪr] *s* adipocira
adipose ['ædɪpos] *adj* adiposo
adiposis [,ædɪ'posɪs] *s* (path.) adiposis
adiposity [,ædɪ'pɑsɪtɪ] *s* adiposidad
adipsia [e'dɪpsɪə] *s* (path.) adipsia
adit ['ædɪt] *s* entrada; acceso; (min.) bocamina, socavón
adjacency [ə'dʒesənsɪ] *s* adyacencia
adjacent [ə'dʒesənt] *adj* adyacente
adjacent angles *spl* (math.) ángulos adyacentes
adjectival [,ædʒɪk'taɪvəl] o ['ædʒɪktɪvəl] *adj* adjetival
adjectivally [,ædʒɪk'taɪvəlɪ] o ['ædʒɪktɪvəlɪ] *adv* adjetivadamente
adjective ['ædʒɪktɪv] *adj & s* adjetivo
adjoin [ə'dʒɔɪn] *va* lindar con; anexar; *vn* colindar
adjoining [ə'dʒɔɪnɪŋ] *adj* colindante
adjourn [ə'dʒʌrn] *va* prorrogar, suspender, aplazar; *vn* prorrogarse, suspenderse; (coll.) trasladarse
adjournment [ə'dʒʌrnmənt] *s* suspensión, aplazamiento; (coll.) translación
Adjt. abr. de **Adjutant**
adjudge [ə'dʒʌdʒ] *va* decretar; sentenciar; condenar; juzgar; adjudicar (*otorgar*)
adjudicate [ə'dʒudɪket] *va* juzgar; *vn* juzgar (*ser juez*)
adjudication [ə,dʒudɪ'keʃən] *s* juicio
adjudicator [ə'dʒudɪ,ketər] *s* juez
adjunct ['ædʒʌŋkt] *adj* adjunto; *s* adjunto, ayudante; (gram.) adjunto
adjuration [,ædʒu'reʃən] *s* orden imperiosa y solemne; conjuro (*ruego encarecido*)
adjure [ə'dʒur] *va* ordenar imperiosa y solemnemente (*en nombre de Dios o mediante juramento*); conjurar (*pedir con instancia*)
adjust [ə'dʒʌst] *va* ajustar, arreglar; (ins.) liquidar; verificar, corregir (*un instrumento*); *vn* ajustarse, acomodarse
adjustable [ə'dʒʌstəbəl] *adj* ajustable, arreglable, componible
adjuster [ə'dʒʌstər] *s* ajustador, arreglador; (ins.) liquidador de la avería, perito en daños
adjustment [ə'dʒʌstmənt] *s* ajuste, arreglo, composición; (ins.) liquidación de la avería, evaluación del daño
adjutancy ['ædʒətənsɪ] *s* (*pl:* **-cies**) (mil.) ayudantía
adjutant ['ædʒətənt] *s* ayudante; (mil.) ayudante; (orn.) argala; *adj* ayudante
adjutant bird *s* (orn.) argala
adjutant general *s* (*pl:* **adjutant generals**) (mil.) ayudante general
adjuvant ['ædʒəvənt] *adj & s* adyuvante
adlib [,æd'lɪb] (*pret & pp:* **adlibbed;** *ger:* **adlibbing**) *va & vn* (coll.) improvisar
Adm. abr. de **Admiral**
Admetus [æd'mitəs] *s* (myth.) Admeto
adminicle [æd'mɪnɪkəl] *s* adminículo; (law) adminículo (*principio que corrobora una prueba*)
administer [æd'mɪnɪstər] *va* administrar; **to administer an oath** tomar juramento; *vn* ejercer el cargo de administrador; **to administer to** ayudar a (*una persona*); contribuir a (*p.ej., necesidades*)
administration [æd,mɪnɪs'treʃən] *s* administración
administrative [æd'mɪnɪs,tretɪv] *adj* administrativo
administrator [æd'mɪnɪs,tretər] *s* administrador; administrador judicial (*de bienes ajenos*)
administratrix [æd,mɪnɪs'tretrɪks] *s* (*pl:*

-trices [trɪsiz]) administradora judicial (*de bienes ajenos*)
admirable ['ædmɪrəbəl] *adj* admirable
admiral ['ædmɪrəl] *s* almirante; buque almirante; (ent.) ninfálido (*especialmente Vanessa atalanta y Basilarchia arthemis*)
Admiral of the Fleet *s* (nav.) capitán general de la armada
admiralty ['ædmɪrəltɪ] *s* (*pl:* **-ties**) almirantazgo
Admiralty Islands *spl* islas Almirantes
admiration [,ædmɪ'reʃən] *s* admiración
admire [æd'maɪr] *va* admirar; *vn* admirarse
admirer [æd'maɪrər] *s* admirador; enamorado
admiring [æd'maɪrɪŋ] *adj* admirativo, admirador
admissibility [æd,mɪsɪ'bɪlɪtɪ] *s* admisibilidad
admissible [æd'mɪsɪbəl] *adj* admisible
admission [æd'mɪʃən] *s* admisión; ingreso (*en una escuela*); precio de entrada; **to gain admission** lograr entrar
admit [æd'mɪt] (*pret & pp:* **-mitted;** *ger:* **-mitting**) *va* admitir; *vn* dar entrada; **to admit of** admitir, permitir
admittance [æd'mɪtəns] *s* admisión; derecho de entrar; (elec.) admitancia; **no admittance** se prohíbe la entrada, acceso prohibido
admittedly [æd'mɪtɪdlɪ] *adv* concedidamente
admix [æd'mɪks] *va* mezclar
admixture [æd'mɪkstʃər] *s* mezcla
admonish [æd'mɑnɪʃ] *va* amonestar
admonishment [æd'mɑnɪʃmənt] *s* amonestamiento, amonestación
admonition [,ædmə'nɪʃən] *s* admonición
admonitory [æd'mɑnɪ,torɪ] *adj* admonitivo
adnate ['ædnet] *adj* (bot. & zool.) adnato
ad nauseam [æd'nɔʃɪæm] o [æd'nɔsɪæm] (Lat.) hasta provocar náuseas
adnexa [æd'nɛksə] *spl* (anat.) anexos
ado [ə'du] *s* bulla, excitación
adobe [ə'dobɪ] *s* adobe; casa de adobe; *adj* adobino, de adobe
adolescence [,ædə'lɛsəns] *s* adolescencia
adolescent [,ædə'lɛsənt] *adj & s* adolescente
Adolph ['ædɑlf] o ['edɑlf] *s* Adolfo
Adonic [ə'dɑnɪk] *adj & s* adónico
Adonis [ə'donɪs] o [ə'dɑnɪs] *s* (myth.) Adonis; (fig.) adonis (*joven de gran belleza*)
adopt [ə'dɑpt] *va* adoptar
adoptable [ə'dɑptəbəl] *adj* adoptable
adopter [ə'dɑptər] *s* adoptante, adoptador
adoption [ə'dɑpʃən] *s* adopción
adoptionism [ə'dɑpʃənɪzəm] *s* adopcionismo
adoptionist [ə'dɑpʃənɪst] *adj & s* adopcionista
adoptive [ə'dɑptɪv] *adj* adoptivo
adorable [ə'dorəbəl] *adj* adorable; (coll.) adorable (*encantador, deleitoso*)
adoration [,ædə'reʃən] *s* adoración
adore [ə'dor] *va* adorar
adorer [ə'dorər] *s* adorador
adorn [ə'dɔrn] *va* adornar
adornment [ə'dɔrnmənt] *s* adorno
adrenal [æd'rinəl] *adj* suprarrenal
adrenal gland *s* (anat.) glándula suprarrenal
adrenalin [æd'rɛnəlɪn] *s* (physiol. & pharm.) adrenalina
Adrian ['edrɪən] *s* Adriano
Adriatic [,edrɪ'ætɪk] o [,ædrɪ'ætɪk] *adj & s* Adriático
adrift [ə'drɪft] *adj & adv* (naut.) al garete, a la deriva; abandonado; divagando
adroit [ə'drɔɪt] *adj* diestro
adroitness [ə'drɔɪtnɪs] *s* destreza
adsorb [æd'sɔrb] o [æd'zɔrb] *va* adsorber
adsorption [æd'sɔrpʃən] o [æd'zɔrpʃən] *s* adsorción
adsorptive [æd'sɔrptɪv] o [æd'zɔrptɪv] *adj* adsorbente
adularia [,ædʒə'lɛrɪə] *s* (mineral.) adularia
adulate ['ædʒəlet] *va* adular
adulation [,ædʒə'leʃən] *s* adulación
adulator ['ædʒə,letər] *s* adulador
adulatory ['ædʒələ,torɪ] *adj* adulatorio
adulatress ['ædʒə,letrɪs] *s* aduladora
adult [ə'dʌlt] o ['ædʌlt] *adj & s* adulto
adult education *s* educación de adultos
adulterant [ə'dʌltərənt] *adj & s* adulterante
adulterate [ə'dʌltəret] *va* adulterar
adulteration [ə,dʌltə'reʃən] *s* adulteración
adulterer [ə'dʌltərər] *s* adúltero
adulteress [ə'dʌltərɪs] *s* adúltera
adulterine [ə'dʌltərɪn] o [ə'dʌltəraɪn] *adj* adulterino
adulterize [ə'dʌltəraɪz] *vn* adulterar
adulterous [ə'dʌltərəs] *adj* adúltero
adultery [ə'dʌltərɪ] *s* (*pl:* **-ies**) adulterio
adulthood [ə'dʌlthud] *s* edad adulta; adultez (Am.)
adumbrate [æd'ʌmbret] o ['ædəmbret] *va* bosquejar; presagiar, anunciar; sombrear
adumbration [,ædəm'breʃən] *s* bosquejo; presagio, anuncio; sombra
adv. abr. de **adverb, adverbial** y **advertisement**
ad. val. abr. de **ad valorem**
ad valorem [ædvə'lorem] (Lat.) según el valor
advance [æd'væns] o [æd'vɑns] *s* adelanto, avance; alza, aumento de precio; (mach.) avance (*del encendido, de la admisión*); **advances** *spl* propuesta, insinuación; requerimiento amoroso; propuesta indecente; **in advance** delante, al frente; por anticipado, de antemano; *adj* adelantado; anticipado; *va* adelantar; *vn* adelantar (*medrar, hacer progresos*); adelantarse (*moverse hacia adelante; irse delante*); subir (*los precios*)
advanced [æd'vænst] o [æd'vɑnst] *adj* avanzado; **advanced in years** avanzado de edad, entrado en años
advanced standing *s* (educ.) traspaso de matrículas, traspaso de crédito académico
advanced studies *spl* altos estudios
advance guard *s* (mil.) avanzada
advancement [æd'vænsmənt] o [æd'vɑnsmənt] *s* adelanto, anticipo; avance, mejora, subida
advance publicity *s* publicidad de lanzamiento
advance sheets *spl* (print.) hojas del autor
advantage [æd'væntɪdʒ] o [æd'vɑntɪdʒ] *s* ventaja; **to have the advantage of** llevar la ventaja a; **to take advantage of** aprovecharse de; abusar de, engañar; **to advantage** ventajosamente; **advantage in** (tennis) ventaja dentro; **advantage out** (tennis) ventaja fuera; *va* aventajar
advantageous [,ædvən'tedʒəs] *adj* ventajoso
advent ['ædvɛnt] *s* advenimiento; (*cap.*) *s* (eccl.) Adviento
Adventism ['ædvɛntɪzəm] *s* adventismo
Adventist ['ædvɛntɪst] *s* adventista
adventitia [,ædvɛn'tɪʃɪə] *s* (anat.) adventicia
adventitious [,ædvɛn'tɪʃəs] *adj* adventicio; (anat., biol., & med.) adventicio
adventive [æd'vɛntɪv] *adj* (bot. & zool.) adventicio
Advent Sunday *s* domingo de Adviento, primera domínica de Adviento
adventure [æd'vɛntʃər] *s* aventura; *va* aventurar; **to adventure an opinion** aventurar una opinión; *vn* aventurarse
adventurer [æd'vɛntʃərər] *s* aventurero
adventuresome [æd'vɛntʃərsəm] *adj* aventurero
adventuress [æd'vɛntʃərɪs] *s* aventurera
adventurous [æd'vɛntʃərəs] *adj* aventurero
adverb ['ædvʌrb] *s* adverbio
adverbial [æd'vʌrbɪəl] *adj* adverbial
adverbialize [æd'vʌrbɪəlaɪz] *va* adverbializar
adverbially [æd'vʌrbɪəlɪ] *adv* adverbialmente
adversaria [,ædvər'sɛrɪə] *spl* adversarios (*notas*)
adversary ['ædvər,sɛrɪ] *s* (*pl:* **-ies**) adversario; **the Adversary** el enemigo malo
adversative [æd'vʌrsətɪv] *adj & s* (gram.) adversativo
adverse [æd'vʌrs] o ['ædvʌrs] *adj* adverso
adversity [æd'vʌrsɪtɪ] *s* (*pl:* **-ties**) adversidad (*infortunio*)
advert [æd'vʌrt] *vn* referirse, aludir
advertent [æd'vʌrtənt] *adj* atento
advertise ['ædvərtaɪz] o [,ædvər'taɪz] *va & vn* anunciar
advertisement [,ædvər'taɪzmənt] o [æd'vʌrtɪzmənt] *s* anuncio
advertiser ['ædvər,taɪzər] o [,ædvər'taɪzər] *s* anunciante
advertising ['ædvər,taɪzɪŋ] o [,ædvər'taɪzɪŋ] *adj* publicitario, anunciador, de anuncios; *s* propaganda, publicidad; anuncios
advertising agency *s* empresa anunciadora
advertising man *s* empresario de publicidad

advertising manager *s* gerente de publicidad
advice [æd'vaɪs] *s* consejo (*parecer, dictamen*); noticia, aviso; **a piece of advice** un consejo
advisability [æd,vaɪzə'bɪlɪtɪ] *s* conveniencia, propiedad
advisable [æd'vaɪzəbəl] *adj* aconsejable
advise [æd'vaɪz] *va* aconsejar, asesorar (*dar consejo a*); avisar, informar; **to advise to** + *inf* aconsejar + *inf; vn* aconsejar; **to advise with** aconsejarse de o con
advised [æd'vaɪzd] *adj* premeditado, deliberado
advisedly [æd'vaɪzɪdlɪ] *adv* premeditadamente, deliberadamente
advisee [,ædvaɪ'zi] *s* aconsejado
advisement [æd'vaɪzmənt] *s* consideración; **to take under advisement** someter a consideración
adviser o **advisor** [æd'vaɪzər] *s* aconsejador, consejero, asesor
advisory [æd'vaɪzərɪ] *adj* consejero, asesor
advocacy ['ædvəkəsɪ] *s* defensa
advocate ['ædvəket] o ['ædvəkɪt] *s* defensor; abogado; ['ædvəket] *va* defender, abogar por
advt. abr. de **advertisement**
adynamia [,ædɪ'nemɪə] *f* (path.) adinamia
adynamic [,ædɪ'næmɪk] *adj* adinámico
adz o **adze** [ædz] *s* azuela
aedile ['idaɪl] *s* edil
Aeëtes [i'itiz] *s* (myth.) Eetes
A.E.F. abr. de **American Expeditionary Force**
Aegean [i'dʒiən] *s* Archipiélago; mar Egeo (*de los antiguos*)
aegis ['idʒɪs] *s* (myth. & fig.) égida
Aegisthus [i'dʒɪsθəs] *s* (myth.) Egisto
Aegospotami [,igəs'pɑtəmɪ] *s* (hist.) Egospótamos
Aegyptus [i'dʒɪptəs] *s* (myth.) Egipto
Aelfric ['ælfrɪk] *s* Aelfrico
Aeneas [i'niəs] *s* (myth.) Eneas
Aeneid [i'niɪd] *s* Eneida
Aeolian [i'olɪən] *adj & s* eolio; (*l.c.*) *adj* (geol.) eoliano
aeolian harp *s* arpa eolia
Aeolic [i'ɑlɪk] *adj & s* eolio (*dialecto*)
Aeolis ['iolɪs] *s* la Eólide
Aeolus ['ioləs] *s* (myth.) Éolo
aeon ['iən] o ['iɑn] *s* eón; (Gnosticism) eón
aerate ['ɛret] o ['eəret] *va* airear
aerated ['ɛretɪd] o ['eər,etɪd] *adj* aireado
aeration [ɛ'reʃən] o [,eə'reʃən] *s* aireación, aeración
aerial ['ɛrɪəl] o [e'ɪrɪəl] *adj* aéreo; ['ɛrɪəl] *s* (rad. & telv.) antena
aerial beacon *s* aerofaro
aerialist ['ɛrɪəlɪst] o [e'ɪrɪəlɪst] *s* volatinero, equilibrista
aerial torpedo *s* (aer.) torpedo aéreo
aerie ['ɛrɪ] o ['ɪrɪ] *s* var. de **eyrie**
aeriferous [ɛ'rɪfərəs] o [,eə'rɪfərəs] *adj* aerífero
aerification [,ɛrɪfɪ'keʃən] o [,eərɪfɪ'keʃən] *s* aerificación
aeriform ['ɛrɪfɔrm] o ['eərɪ,fɔrm] *adj* aeriforme; inmaterial, imaginario
aerify ['ɛrɪfaɪ] o ['eərɪfaɪ] (*pret & pp:* **-fied**) *va* aerificar
aero ['ɛro] o ['eəro] *adj* aeronáutico
aerobatics [,ɛro'bætɪks] o [,eəro'bætɪks] *spl* acrobacia aérea (*ejercicios*); *ssg* acrobacia aérea (*arte*)
aerobe ['ɛrob] o ['eərob] *s* (bact.) aerobio
aerobic [ɛ'robɪk] o [,eə'robɪk] *adj* (bact.) aeróbico
aerodrome ['ɛrədrom] o ['eərə,drom] *s* aeródromo
aerodynamic [,ɛrodaɪ'næmɪk] o [,eərodaɪ'næmɪk] *adj* aerodinámico; **aerodynamics** *ssg* aerodinámica
aeroembolism [,ɛro'ɛmbəlɪzəm] o [,eərə'ɛmbəlɪzəm] *s* (path.) aeroembolismo
aerogram ['ɛrəgræm] o ['eərə,græm] *s* aerograma (*despacho transmitido por vehículo aéreo; radiograma*)
aerolite ['ɛrolaɪt] o ['eəro,laɪt] *s* aerolito
aerologist [ɛ'rɑlədʒɪst] o [,eə'rɑlədʒɪst] *s* aerólogo
aerology [ɛ'rɑlədʒɪ] o [,eə'rɑlədʒɪ] *s* aerología
aeromancer ['ɛro,mænsər] o ['eəro,mænsər] *s* aeromántico
aeromancy ['ɛro,mænsɪ] o ['eəro,mænsɪ] *s* aeromancía
aeromantic [,ɛro'mæntɪk] o [,eəro'mæntɪk] *adj* aeromántico
aeromechanic [,ɛromɪ'kænɪk] o [,eəromɪ'kænɪk] *adj* aeromecánico; *s* mécanico de aviación; **aeromechanics** *ssg* aeromecánica
aeromechanical [,ɛromɪ'kænɪkəl] o [,eəromɪ'kænɪkəl] *adj* aeromecánico
aerometer [ɛ'rɑmɪtər] o [,eə'rɑmɪtər] *s* aerómetro
aeronaut ['ɛrənɔt] o ['eərə,nɔt] *s* aeronauta
aeronautic [,ɛrə'nɔtɪk] o [,eərə'nɔtɪk] *adj* aeronáutico; **aeronautics** *ssg* aeronáutica
aeronautical [,ɛrə'nɔtɪkəl] o [,eərə'nɔtɪkəl] *adj* aeronáutico
aerophagia [,ɛro'fedʒɪə] o [,eəro'fedʒɪə] *s* (path.) aerofagia
aerophobia [,ɛro'fobɪə] o [,eəro'fobɪə] *s* (path.) aerofobia
aerophore ['ɛrofor] o ['eəro,for] *s* (med. & min.) aeróforo
aerophotograph [,ɛrə'fotəgræf], [,eərə'fotəgræf], [,ɛrə'fotəgrɑf] o [,eərə'fotəgrɑf] *s* aerofotografía (*imagen*)
aerophotography [,ɛrəfə'tɑgrəfɪ] o [,eərəfə'tɑgrəfɪ] *s* aerofotografía (*arte*)
aeroplane ['ɛrəplen] o ['eərə,plen] *s* aeroplano, avión
aeroscope ['ɛroskop] o ['eəro,skop] *s* aeroscopio
aerosol ['ɛrosol] o ['eəro,sol] *s* (physical chem.) aerosol
aerospace ['ɛrospes] o ['eəro,spes] *adj* aéroespacial
aerostat ['ɛrostæt] o ['eəro,stæt] *s* aeróstato (*aparato*); aeróstata (*persona*)
aerostatic [,ɛro'stætɪk] o [,eəro'stætɪk] *adj* aerostático; **aerostatics** *ssg* aerostática
aerostatical [,ɛro'stætɪkəl] o [,eəro'stætɪkəl] *adj* aerostático
aerostation [,ɛro'steʃən] o [,eəro'steʃən] *s* aerostación
aerotherapeutics [,ɛro,θɛrə'pjutɪks] o [,eəro,θɛrə'pjutɪks] *ssg* o **aerotherapy** [,ɛro'θɛrəpɪ] o [,eəro'θɛrəpɪ] *s* aeroterapia
aery ['ɛrɪ] o ['ɪrɪ] *s* (*pl:* **-ies**) var. de **eyrie**
Aeschines ['ɛskɪniz] *s* Esquines
Aeschylus ['ɛskɪləs] *s* Esquilo
Aesculapian [,ɛskjə'lepɪən] *s* Esculapio (*cualquier médico*); *adj* de Esculapio; medicinal
Aesculapius [,ɛskjə'lepɪəs] *s* (myth.) Esculapio
Aesop ['isɑp] *s* Esopo
Aesopian [i'sopɪən] *adj* esópico
aesthete ['ɛsθit] *s* esteta
aesthetic [ɛs'θɛtɪk] *adj* estético; **aesthetics** *ssg* estética
aesthetically [ɛs'θɛtɪkəlɪ] *adv* estéticamente
aesthetician [,ɛsθɪ'tɪʃən] *s* estético
aestival ['ɛstɪvəl] o [ɛs'taɪvəl] *adj* estival
aestivate ['ɛstɪvet] *vn* veranear; (zool.) pasar el estío en estado de estivación
aestivation [,ɛstɪ'veʃən] *s* veraneo; (bot. & zool.) estivación
aether ['iθər] *s* éter (*los espacios celestes*); (phys.) éter (*materia hipotética*)
aethereal [ɪ'θɪrɪəl] *adj* etéreo; (phys.) etéreo
aetiology [,itɪ'ɑlədʒɪ] *s* etiología
Aetna, Mount ['ɛtnə] el monte Etna
Aetolia [i'tolɪə] *s* la Etolia
A.F. o **a.f.** abr. de **audio frequency**
afar [ə'fɑr] *adv* lejos; **from afar** de lejos, desde lejos
affability [,æfə'bɪlɪtɪ] *s* afabilidad
affable ['æfəbəl] *adj* afable
affair [ə'fɛr] *s* asunto, negocio; lance, episodio; amorío, aventura; encuentro, combate; **affairs** *spl* negocios
affair of honor *s* lance de honor
affect [ə'fɛkt] *va* influir en; impresionar, enternecer; aficionarse a; afectar (*poner demasiado estudio en; fingir; asumir*)
affectation [,æfɛk'teʃən] *s* afectación
affected [ə'fɛktɪd] *adj* afectado
affecting [ə'fɛktɪŋ] *adj* impresionante, enternecedor
affection [ə'fɛkʃən] *s* afecto, cariño, afección; (med.) afección
affectionate [ə'fɛkʃənɪt] *adj* afectuoso, cariñoso

affective [ə'fɛktɪv] *adj* afectivo
afferent ['æfərənt] *adj* (physiol.) aferente
affiance [ə'faɪəns] *s* palabra de casamiento; confianza; *va* dar palabra de casamiento a
affianced [ə'faɪənst] *adj* prometido
affidavit [,æfɪ'devɪt] *s* declaración jurada, acta notarial, afidávit
affiliate [ə'fɪlɪet] *adj* afiliado; *s* afiliado; (com.) filial; *va* afiliar; **to affiliate oneself with** afiliarse a; *vn* afiliarse; **to affiliate with** afiliarse a
affiliation [ə,fɪlɪ'eʃən] *s* afiliación
affinity [ə'fɪnɪtɪ] *s* (*pl:* **-ties**) afinidad; amante; (biol. & chem.) afinidad
affirm [ə'fʌrm] *va & vn* afirmar
affirmation [,æfər'meʃən] *s* afirmación
affirmative [ə'fʌrmətɪv] *adj* afirmativo; *s* afirmativa
affix ['æfɪks] *s* añadidura; (gram.) afijo; [ə'fɪks] *va* añadir; atribuir (*p.ej., culpa*); poner (*una firma, sello, etc.*)
affixation [,æfɪk'seʃən] *s* (gram.) afijación
afflatus [ə'fletəs] *s* aflato, ciencia infusa
afflict [ə'flɪkt] *va* afligir; **to be afflicted with** sufrir de
affliction [ə'flɪkʃən] *s* aflicción; desgracia, infortunio; achaque, mal
afflictive [ə'flɪktɪv] *adj* aflictivo
affluence ['æfluəns] *s* afluencia, abundancia; opulencia
affluent ['æfluənt] *adj* afluente, abundante; opulento; *s* afluente
afflux ['æflʌks] *s* afluencia (*acción de afluir*); (med.) aflujo
afford [ə'fɔrd] *va* producir, proporcionar; **to be able to afford** tener con que comprar, tener con que pagar, tener los medios para, poder permitirse
afforest [ə'fɑrɪst] o [ə'fɔrɪst] *va* repoblar (*con árboles jóvenes*)
afforestation [ə,fɑrɪs'teʃən] o [ə,fɔrɪs'teʃən] *s* repoblación forestal, aforestalación
affranchise [ə'fræntʃaɪz] *va* var. de **enfranchise**
affray [ə'fre] *s* riña, pendencia
affricate ['æfrɪkɪt] *s* (phonet.) africada
affricative [ə'frɪkətɪv] *adj* (phonet.) africado; *s* (phonet.) africada
affront [ə'frʌnt] *s* afrenta; *va* afrentar; arrostrar
affusion [ə'fjuʒən] *s* (med.) afusión
Afghan ['æfgən] o ['æfgæn] *adj & s* afgano; (*l.c.*) *s* manta de estambre, cubrecama de estambre
Afghanistan [æf'gænɪstæn] *s* el Afganistán
afield [ə'fild] *adv* en el campo, al campo; afuera
afire [ə'faɪr] *adj & adv* ardiendo
aflame [ə'flem] *adj & adv* en llamas
afloat [ə'flot] *adj & adv* a flote; a bordo; sin rumbo; inundado; en circulación
aflutter [ə'flʌtər] *adj & adv* en agitación
afoot [ə'fʊt] *adj & adv* a pie; en movimiento
aforementioned [ə'for'mɛnʃənd] o **aforesaid** [ə'for,sɛd] *adj* ya mencionado
aforethought [ə'for,θɔt] *adj* premeditado; *s* premeditación
aforetime [ə'for,taɪm] *adv* antiguamente
a fortiori [e,fɔrʃɪ'orɪ] (Lat.) con mayor razón
afoul [ə'faʊl] *adj & adv* en colisión; enredado; **to run afoul of** enredarse con
afraid [ə'fred] *adj* asustado, espantado; **to be afraid (of)** tener miedo (a o de); **to be afraid to** + *inf* tener miedo de + *inf*
afresh [ə'frɛʃ] *adv* de nuevo, otra vez
Africa ['æfrɪkə] *s* África
African ['æfrɪkən] *adj & s* africano
Africanist ['æfrɪkənɪst] *s* africanista
African rue *s* (bot.) alárgama
Afrikaans [,æfrɪ'kɑns] *s* afrikaans
Afrikander [,æfrɪ'kændər] *s* africander
Afro-American ['æfroə'mɛrɪkən] *adj & s* afroamericano
Afro-Asian ['æfro'eʒən] o ['æfro'eʃən] *adj* afroasiático
aft [æft] o [ɑft] *adj & adv* (naut.) en popa, a popa
after ['æftər] o ['ɑftər] *adj* siguiente; *adv* después; *prep* después de; según; al cabo de; **to run after** correr tras; **after all** al fin y al cabo; **after you!** ¡Vd. primero!; *conj* después que o después de que
afterbirth ['æftər,bʌrθ] o ['ɑftər,bʌrθ] *s* secundinas
afterburner ['æftər,bʌrnər] o ['ɑftər,bʌrnər] *s* (aer.) posquemador
afterburning ['æftər,bʌrnɪŋ] o ['ɑftər,bʌrnɪŋ] *s* (aer.) poscombustión
aftercare ['æftər,kɛr] o ['ɑftər,kɛr] *s* tratamiento postoperatorio
afterclap ['æftər,klæp] o ['ɑftər,klæp] *s* golpe inesperado
aftercost ['æftər,kɔst] o ['ɑftər,kɔst] *s* gastos adicionales, gastos de mantenimiento
aftercrop ['æftər,krɑp] o ['ɑftər,krɑp] *s* segunda cosecha
afterdamp ['æftər,dæmp] o ['ɑftər,dæmp] *s* (min.) gases de explosión
afterdeck ['æftər,dɛk] o ['ɑftər,dɛk] *s* (naut.) cubierta de popa
after-dinner ['æftər,dɪnər] o ['ɑftər,dɪnər] *adj* de sobremesa
after-dinner speaker *s* orador de sobremesa
after-dinner speech *s* discurso de sobremesa
aftereffect ['æftərɪ,fɛkt] o ['ɑftərɪ,fɛkt] *s* efecto resultante, consecuencia
afterglow ['æftər,glo] o ['ɑftər,glo] *s* brillo prolongado; resplandor crepuscular
after-hours ['æftər'aʊrz] o ['ɑftər'aʊrz] *adv* después del trabajo
afterimage ['æftər,ɪmɪdʒ] o ['ɑftər,ɪmɪdʒ] *s* postimagen
afterlife ['æftər,laɪf] o ['ɑftər,laɪf] *s* trasmundo, vida venidera; resto de la vida
afterlove ['æftər,lʌv] o ['ɑftər,lʌv] *s* segunda pasión, nuevos amores
aftermath ['æftərmæθ] o ['ɑftərmæθ] *s* segunda cosecha; consecuencias, consecuencias desastrosas
aftermost ['æftərmost] o ['ɑftərmost] *adj* último; trasero, posterior
afternoon ['æftər'nun] o ['ɑftər'nun] *s* tarde
afterpains ['æftər,penz] o ['ɑftər,penz] *spl* dolores de sobreparto, entuertos; dolor postoperatorio
after-shaving ['æftər,ʃevɪŋ] o ['ɑftər,ʃevɪŋ] *adj* para después de afeitarse
aftershock ['æftər,ʃɑk] o ['ɑftər,ʃɑk] *s* temblor secundario
aftertaste ['æftər,test] o ['ɑftər,test] *s* resabio, dejo, gustillo
afterthought ['æftər,θɔt] o ['ɑftər,θɔt] *s* idea tardía, expediente tardío, nueva ocurrencia
aftertime ['æftər,taɪm] o ['ɑftər,taɪm] *s* tiempo venidero
afterward ['æftərwərd] o ['ɑftərwərd] o **afterwards** ['æftərwərdz] o ['ɑftərwərdz] *adv* después, luego; **long afterwards** mucho tiempo después
afterwhile ['æftər'hwaɪl] o ['ɑftər'hwaɪl] *adv* dentro de poco
afterworld ['æftər,wʌrld] o ['ɑftər,wʌrld] *s* mundo futuro, vida venidera
again [ə'gɛn] o [ə'gen] *adv* otra vez, de nuevo; además, por otra parte; **as much again** otro tanto más; **now and again** de vez en cuando; **to** + *inf* + **again** volver a + *inf*; **again and again** repetidamente
against [ə'gɛnst] o [ə'genst] *prep* contra; cerca de; en contraste con; por; para; **to be against** oponerse a; **to go against the grain** desagradar, repugnar
agalloch [ə'gælæk] *s* (bot.) agáloco
Agamemnon [,ægə'mɛmnɑn] *s* (myth.) Agamenón
agamic [ə'gæmɪk] *adj* (biol.) ágamo
agamogenesis [,ægəmo'dʒɛnɪsɪs] *s* (biol.) agamogénesis
Aganippe [,ægə'nɪpi] *s* (myth.) Aganipe
agape [ə'gep] *adj & adv* con la boca abierta; abierto de par en par
agar ['ɑgər] o ['ægər] *s* agar-agar; (bot.) agáloco
agar-agar ['ɑgər'ɑgər] o ['ægər'ægər] *s* agar-agar
agaric ['ægərɪk] o [ə'gærɪk] *s* (bot.) agárico; (pharm.) agárico blanco
agate ['ægɪt] *s* (mineral.) ágata; bolilla de cristal ágata; (print.) tipo de 5½ puntos
agateware ['ægɪt,wɛr] *s* porcelana de imita-

ción de ágata; utensilios de hierro, de imitación de ágata
Agatha ['ægəθə] *s* Ágata, Águeda
agave [ə'gevɪ] *s* (bot.) agave
age [edʒ] *s* edad; vejez, ancianidad; generación; siglo (*cien años*); (psychol.) edad mental; (coll.) siglo, eternidad (*largo tiempo*); **ages** *spl* (coll.) siglo, eternidad (*largo tiempo*); **of age** mayor de edad; **to act one's age** actuar (*una persona*) de acuerdo con su edad; **to come of age** alcanzar su mayoría de edad, llegar a mayor edad; **under age** menor de edad; *va* envejecer; *vn* envejecer o envejecerse
aged ['edʒɪd] *adj* viejo, anciano, envejecido; de la vejez; [edʒd] *adj* de la edad de
ageless ['edʒlɪs] *adj* eternamente joven
agelong ['edʒ,lɔŋ] o ['edʒ,lɑŋ] *adj* eterno, secular
agency ['edʒənsɪ] *s* (*pl:* **-cies**) agencia; acción, medio
agenda [ə'dʒɛndə] *spl* cosas que se han de hacer; *ssg* temario, agenda
agennesis [,ædʒə'nisɪs] *s* (physiol.) agenesia
agent ['edʒənt] *s* agente; (gram.) agente; (coll.) agente viajero
agent provocateur [æ'ʒɑ̃ prɔvɔkɑ'tʌr] *s* agente provocador
age of discretion *s* edad de discreción
Age of Enlightenment *s* siglo de las luces (*siglo dieciocho*)
ageratum [,ædʒə'retəm] o [ə'dʒɛrətəm] *s* (bot.) agérato
ageusia [ə'gjusɪə] *s* (path.) ageusia
agglomerant [ə'glɑmərənt] *s* aglomerante
agglomerate [ə'glɑmərɪt] o [ə'glɑməret] *s* aglomeración; (geol.) aglomerado; *adj* aglomerado; [ə'glɑməret] *va* aglomerar; *vn* aglomerarse
agglomeration [ə,glɑmə'reʃən] *s* aglomeración
agglutinate [ə'glutɪnɪt] o [ə'glutɪnet] *adj* aglutinado; [ə'glutɪnet] *va* aglutinar; *vn* aglutinarse
agglutination [ə,glutɪ'neʃən] *s* aglutinación
agglutinative [ə'glutɪ,netɪv] *adj* aglutinante
agglutinative languages *spl* lenguas aglutinantes
agglutinin [ə'glutɪnɪn] *s* (biochem.) aglutinina
aggrandize ['ægrəndaɪz] o [ə'grændaɪz] *va* agrandar, engrandecer; **to aggrandize oneself** agrandarse, engrandecerse
aggrandizement [ə'grændɪzmənt] *s* agrandamiento, engrandecimiento
aggravate ['ægrəvet] *va* agravar; (coll.) irritar, exasperar
aggravating ['ægrə,vetɪŋ] *adj* agravante; (coll.) irritante, exasperante
aggravation [,ægrə'veʃən] *s* agravación, agravamiento; (coll.) irritación
aggregate ['ægrɪgɪt] o ['ægrɪget] *adj & s* agregado; total; ['ægrɪget] *va* agregar, unir, juntar; ascender a
aggregation [,ægrɪ'geʃən] *s* agregación
aggression [ə'grɛʃən] *s* agresión
aggressive [ə'grɛsɪv] *adj* agresivo
aggressor [ə'grɛsər] *s* agresor
aggrieve [ə'griv] *va* afligir, acongojar, oprimir
aghast [ə'gæst] o [ə'gɑst] *adj* horrorizado
agile ['ædʒɪl] o ['ædʒaɪl] *adj* ágil
agility [ə'dʒɪlɪtɪ] *s* agilidad
aging ['edʒɪŋ] *s* envejecimiento; añejamiento (*p.ej., del vino*)
agio ['ædʒɪo] *s* (*pl:* **-os**) agio
agitate ['ædʒɪtet] *va* agitar; *vn* agitar (*promover cuestiones*)
agitation [,ædʒɪ'teʃən] *s* agitación
agitator ['ædʒɪ,tetər] *s* agitador
Aglaia [ə'gleə] *s* (myth.) Aglaya
agleam [ə'glim] *adj & adv* reluciente
aglitter [ə'glɪtər] *adj & adv* rutilante
aglow [ə'glo] *adj & adv* fulgurante
agnate ['ægnet] *adj & s* agnado
agnation [æg'neʃən] *s* agnación; parentesco
Agnes ['ægnɪs] *s* Inés
agnostic [æg'nɑstɪk] *adj & s* agnóstico
agnosticism [æg'nɑstɪsɪzəm] *s* agnosticismo
agnus castus ['ægnəs'kæstəs] *s* (bot.) agnocasto, sauzgatillo
Agnus Dei ['ægnəs'diaɪ] *s* agnusdéi
ago [ə'go] *adj & adv* hace, p.ej., **a long time ago** hace mucho tiempo
agog [ə'gɑg] *adj* ansioso, anhelante; curioso; *adv* con ansiedad; curiosamente; **to set agog** excitar
agonic [e'gɑnɪk] *adj* (geom.) ágono
agonic line *s* (phys.) línea agónica
agonistic [,ægə'nɪstɪk] *adj* agonal, agonístico; **agonistics** *ssg* agonística
agonize ['ægənaɪz] *va* atormentar; *vn* hacer grandes esfuerzos; retorcerse de dolor, sufrir intensamente
agony ['ægənɪ] *s* (*pl:* **-nies**) agonía (*aflicción extremada; lucha postrema contra la muerte*); lucha, esfuerzos; angustia, congoja
agony column *s* (coll.) anuncios en un periódico relativos a parientes o amigos desaparecidos
agora ['ægərə] *s* (*pl:* **-rae** [ri]) *s* ágora
agoraphobia [,ægərə'fobɪə] *s* (psychopath.) agorafobia
agouti [ə'gutɪ] *s* (*pl:* **-tis** o **-ties**) (zool.) acutí
agrarian [ə'grɛrɪən] *adj* agrario; agrariense; *mf* agrariense
agrarianism [ə'grɛrɪənɪzəm] *s* agrarianismo
agree [ə'gri] *vn* concordar, estar de acuerdo, ponerse de acuerdo; sentar bien; (gram.) concordar; **to agree on** convenir en; **to agree with** concordar con, estar de acuerdo con; sentar bien; (gram.) concordar con
agreeable [ə'griəbəl] *adj* agradable; conforme, satisfecho
agreement [ə'grimənt] *s* acuerdo, convenio; concordancia, conformidad; (gram.) concordancia; **in agreement** de acuerdo; **in agreement with** de acuerdo con
agric. abr. de **agriculture**
agricultural [,ægrɪ'kʌltʃərəl] *adj* agrícola
agriculturalist [,ægrɪ'kʌltʃərəlɪst] *s* agricultor
agriculture ['ægrɪ,kʌltʃər] *s* agricultura
agriculturist [,ægrɪ'kʌltʃərɪst] *s* agricultor
agrimony ['ægrɪ,monɪ] *s* (*pl:* **-nies**) (bot.) agrimonia
Agrippa [ə'grɪpə] *s* Agripa
agronomic [,ægrə'nɑmɪk] *adj* agronómico
agronomist [ə'grɑnəmɪst] *s* agrónomo
agronomy [ə'grɑnəmɪ] *s* agronomía
aground [ə'graʊnd] *adj & adv* varado, encallado; **to run aground** varar, encallar
agt. abr. de **agent**
ague ['egju] *s* escalofrío; fiebre intermitente
aguish ['egjuɪʃ] *adj* escalofriado; palúdico
ah [ɑ] *interj* ¡ah!
aha [ɑ'hɑ] *interj* ¡ajá!
ahead [ə'hɛd] *adj & adv* delante, al frente; adelante; **straight ahead** todo seguido; **to get ahead** adelantarse; **to get ahead of** adelantarse a; **to go ahead** seguir adelante; avanzar; continuar; **to send ahead** enviar por delante; **ahead of** antes de; delante de; al frente de
ahem [ə'hɛm] *interj* ¡eh!; ¡ejem!
ahorse [ə'hɔrs] *adj & adv* a caballo
ahoy [ə'hɔɪ] *interj* (naut.) ¡ha!; **ship ahoy!** ¡ah del barco!
aid [ed] *s* ayuda, auxilio; (mil.) ayudante; **to come to the aid of** acudir en socorro a; *va* ayudar; **to aid and abet** auxiliar e incitar, ser cómplice de; *vn* ayudar
aid-de-camp ['eddə'kæmp] *s* (*pl:* **aids-de-camp**) var. de **aide-de-camp**
aide [ed] *s* (mil.) ayudante
aide-de-camp ['eddə'kæmp] *s* (*pl:* **aides-de-camp**) (mil.) ayudante de campo, edecán
aigrette ['egrɛt] o [e'grɛt] *s* airón, penacho; (elec.) airón (*penachos en los ángulos de los cuerpos electrizados*); (orn.) garceta
ail [el] *va* afligir, molestar, inquietar; **what ails you?** ¿qué tiene Vd?; *vn* sufrir, estar enfermo
ailanthus [e'lænθəs] *s* (bot.) ailanto
aileron ['elərɑn] *s* (aer.) alerón
ailing ['elɪŋ] *adj* enfermo, achacoso
ailment ['elmənt] *s* enfermedad, achaque
aim [em] *s* puntería, encaro; intento, blanco, mira; punto de mira; **to miss one's aim** errar el tiro; **to take aim** apuntar; *va* apuntar, encarar; dirigir (*p.ej., una observación*);

vn apuntar; intentar; **to aim to** + *inf* mirar a + *inf*
aimless ['emlɪs] *adj* sin designio, sin objeto
ain't [ent] (dial. & illit.) contracción de **am not** y equivalente a **am not, is not, are not, have not** y **has not**
air [ɛr] *s* aire; (mus.) aire; **by air** por vía aérea, en avión; **in mid air** entre cielo y tierra; **in the open air** al aire libre; **on the air** en antena, en la radio; **to fly through the air** volar por los aires; **to let the air out of** desinflar (*un neumático*); **to put on airs** darse aires; **to put on the air** (rad.) llevar a las antenas; **to walk** o **tread on air** no pisar en el suelo, estar bañado en agua de rosas; *adj* aéreo; aeronáutico; *va* airear, ventilar; radiofundir; (fig.) ventilar
air-atomic ['ɛrə'tɑmɪk] *adj* aéro-atómico
air attack *s* ataque aéreo
air base *s* base aérea
air beacon *s* faro aéreo
air bends *spl* (path.) embolia aérea
air bladder *s* (zool.) vejiga natatoria
air-borne ['ɛr,born] *adj* (mil.) aéreo, aerotransportado; llevado por el aire
air brake *s* freno de aire, freno neumático
air bridge *s* puente aéreo
air brush *s* aerógrafo, pincel aéreo, pulverizador de aire comprimido
air castle *s* castillo en el aire
air chamber *s* cámara de aire
air cock *s* llave de admisión de aire, llave de escape de aire
air-condition ['ɛrkən'dɪʃən] *va* proveer de maquinaria acondicionadora del aire, climatizar
air-conditioned ['ɛrkən'dɪʃənd] *adj* con aire acondicionado
air conditioner *s* acondicionador de aire
air conditioning *s* acondicionamiento del aire, aire acondicionado
air-cool ['ɛr,kul] *va* enfriar por aire
air-cooling ['ɛr,kulɪŋ] *s* enfriamiento por aire
air-core transformer ['ɛr,kor] *s* (elec.) transformador de núcleo de aire
air corps *s* cuerpo de aviación
aircraft ['ɛr,kræft] o ['ɛr,krɑft] *ssg* máquina de volar; *spl* máquinas de volar
aircraft carrier *s* portaaviones
air cushion *s* almohada de aire, colchón de aire
air drill *s* taladro neumático
airdrome ['ɛr,drom] *s* aeródromo
airdrop ['ɛr,drɑp] *s* (aer.) lanzamiento; (*pret & pp:* **-dropped** o **-dropt;** *ger:* **-dropping**) *va* (aer.) lanzar
air field *s* campo de aviación
air fleet *s* flotilla militar aérea
airfoil ['ɛr,fɔɪl] *s* (aer.) superficie de sustentación
air force *s* fuerza aérea, ejército del aire
Air Force Academy *s* (U.S.A.) Academia General del Aire
air frame *s* (aer.) armadura de avión
air gap *s* (phys.) entrehierro
air-ground ['ɛr'graʊnd] *adj* aeroterrestre
air gun *s* escopeta de aire comprimido
air hole *s* respiradero; (aer.) vacío; (found.) sopladura
air hostess *s* azafata, aeromoza
airing ['ɛrɪŋ] *s* ventilación; secamiento al aire; paseo para tomar el aire; (fig.) ventilación; **to take an airing** orearse
air lane *s* ruta aérea
airless ['ɛrlɪs] *adj* sin brisa, tranquilo
airlift ['ɛr,lɪft] *s* puente aéreo; *va* transportar por puente aéreo
air line *s* línea aérea
air liner *s* avión de travesía, transaéreo
air lock *s* cámara intermedia (*entre presiones atmosféricas diferentes*)
air mail *s* correo aéreo, correo por avión
air-mail ['ɛr,mel] *adj* aeropostal
air-mail letter *s* carta por avión, carta aérea
air-mail pilot *s* aviador postal
air-mail stamp *s* sello aéreo
airman ['ɛrmən] o ['ɛr,mæn] *s* (*pl:* **-men**) aviador; (mil.) aviador, soldado del cuerpo de aviación
air map *s* aeromapa
air-minded ['ɛr,maɪndɪd] *adj* adicto a la aviación
Air Ministry *s* (Brit.) Ministerio del Aire
air passage *s* aire aprisionado; fuga o escape de aire
airplane ['ɛr,plen] *s* avión
airplane carrier *s* portaaviones
air plant *s* (bot.) epífita
air pocket *s* (aer.) depresión, bolsa de aire, bache aéreo
airport ['ɛr,port] *s* aeropuerto
air power *s* poder aéreo
air pressure *s* presión atmosférica
air pump *s* bomba de aire, máquina neumática
air raid *s* ataque aéreo
air-raid alarm ['ɛr,red] *s* alarma aérea
air-raid drill *s* ejercicio antiaéreo, simulacro de ataque aéreo
air-raid shelter *s* abrigo antiaéreo, refugio antiaéreo
air-raid warden *s* vigilante contra ataques aéreos
air-raid warning *s* alarma aérea
air rifle *s* escopeta de aire comprimido, escopeta de viento
air sac *s* (orn.) celda para aire
air service *s* servicio aéreo
air shaft *s* respiradero
airship ['ɛr,ʃɪp] *s* aeronave
airsick ['ɛr,sɪk] *adj* mareado en el aire
airsickness ['ɛr,sɪknɪs] *s* mareo del aire, mal de vuelo
air sleeve o **air sock** *s* veleta de manga
airstrip ['ɛr,strɪp] *s* pista de despegue; pista de aterrizaje
air supremacy *s* dominio del aire
airtight ['ɛr'taɪt] *adj* hermético, herméticamente cerrado, estanco al aire
air-traffic control ['ɛr,træfɪk] *s* control de tránsito aéreo
airwaves ['ɛr,wevz] *spl* ondas de radio
airway ['ɛr,we] *s* aerovía, vía aérea; (min.) galería de ventilación
airway lighting *s* (aer.) balizaje
air well *s* respiradero, pozo de ventilación
airwoman ['ɛr,wʊmən] *s* (*pl:* **-women**) aviadora
airworthy ['ɛr,wʌrðɪ] *adj* en condiciones de vuelo
airy ['ɛrɪ] *adj* (*comp:* **-ier;** *super:* **-iest**) airoso; aireado; alegre; impertinente; (coll.) afectado
aisle [aɪl] *s* pasillo (*en el teatro, la iglesia, etc.*); nave (*en una fábrica, tienda, etc.*); alameda, paseo; (arch.) nave lateral
Aix-la-Chapelle [,ekslɑʃɑ'pɛl] *s* Aquisgrán
ajar [ə'dʒɑr] *adj* entreabierto, entornado; en desacuerdo
Ajax ['edʒæks] *s* (myth.) Áyax
Ajax the Less *s* (myth.) Áyax el Pequeño
akene [e'kin] *s* var. de **achene**
akimbo [ə'kɪmbo] *adj & adv* en jarras; **with arms akimbo** en jarras
akin [ə'kɪn] *adj* emparentado; semejante
alabamine [,ælə'bæmin] *s* (chem.) alabamio
alabaster ['ælə,bæstər] o ['ælə,bɑstər] *s* alabastro; *adj* alabastrino
à la carte [ɑlɑ'kɑrt] según lista, a la carta
alacrity [ə'lækrɪtɪ] *s* alacridad, presteza
Aladdin [ə'lædɪn] *s* Aladino
Aladdin's lamp *s* lámpara de Aladino
à la king [ɑlɑ'kɪŋ] con salsa de crema, harina, hongos, pimientos, etc.
à la mode [ɑlɑ'mod] o [,ælə'mod] a la moda; servido con helado encima
Alaric ['ælərɪk] *s* Alarico
alarm [ə'lɑrm] *s* alarma; **to sound the alarm** dar la alarma; *va* alarmar, inquietar
alarm clock *s* despertador, reloj despertador
alarming [ə'lɑrmɪŋ] *adj* alarmante
alarmist [ə'lɑrmɪst] *s* alarmista
alary ['elərɪ] o ['ælərɪ] *adj* alario
Alas. abr. de **Alaska**
alas [ə'læs] o [ə'lɑs] *interj* ¡ay!, ¡ay de mí!
alate ['elet] *adj* alado
alb [ælb] *s* alba (*vestidura de lienzo blanco de sacerdote*)
albacore ['ælbəkor] *s* (ichth.) albacora; (ichth.) germón (*Germo alalunga*)
Albanian [æl'benɪən] *adj & s* albanés o albano

albatross ['ælbətrɔs] o ['ælbətrɑs] *s* (orn.) albatros
albeit [ɔl'biɪt] *conj* aunque
Albert ['ælbərt] *s* Alberto
Albertus Magnus [æl'bʌrtəs 'mægnəs] *s* Alberto Magno
Albigenses [,ælbɪ'dʒɛnsiz] *spl* albigenses
Albigensian [,ælbɪ'dʒɛnsɪən] *adj* albigense
albinic [æl'bɪnɪk] *adj* albino
albinism ['ælbɪnɪzəm] *s* albinismo
albino [æl'baɪno] *s* (*pl:* **-nos**) albino
Albion ['ælbɪən] *s* (poet.) Albión (*Inglaterra*)
albite ['ælbaɪt] *s* (mineral.) albita
albugineous [,ælbjə'dʒɪnɪəs] *adj* albugíneo
albugo [æl'bjugo] *s* (*pl:* **-gines** [dʒɪniz]) (path.) albugo
album ['ælbəm] *s* álbum
albumen [æl'bjumən] *s* (bot.) albumen; (biochem.) albúmina
albumin [æl'bjumɪn] *s* (biochem.) albúmina
albuminimeter [æl,bjumɪ'nɪmɪtər] *s* albuminímetro
albuminoid [æl'bjumɪnɔɪd] *adj* albuminoideo; *s* albuminoide
albuminous [æl'bjumɪnəs] *adj* albuminoso
albuminuria [æl,bjumɪ'njʊrɪə] o [æl,bjumɪ'nʊrɪə] *s* (path.) albuminuria
alburnum [æl'bʌrnəm] *s* alborno, alburno, albura
alcazar ['ælkəzɑr] o [æl'kæzər] *s* alcázar
Alcestis [æl'sɛstɪs] *s* (myth.) Alcestes
alchemic [æl'kɛmɪk] o **alchemical** [æl'kɛmɪkəl] *adj* alquímico
alchemist ['ælkɪmɪst] *s* alquimista
alchemy ['ælkɪmɪ] *s* alquimia
Alcibiades [,ælsɪ'baɪədiz] *s* Alcibíades
Alcmene [ælk'minɪ] *s* (myth.) Alcmena
alcohol ['ælkəhɔl] o ['ælkəhɑl] *s* alcohol
alcoholate ['ælkəhɔlet] o ['ælkəhɑlet] *s* (pharm.) alcoholado, alcoholato
alcoholic [,ælkə'hɔlɪk] o [,ælkə'hɑlɪk] *adj* alcohólico; (path.) alcohólico, alcoholizado; *s* (path.) alcohólico, alcoholizado
alcoholism ['ælkəhɔlɪzəm] o ['ælkəhɑlɪzəm] *s* (path.) alcoholismo
alcoholization [,ælkə,hɔlɪ'zeʃən] o [,ælkə,hɑlɪ'zeʃən] *s* alcoholización
alcoholometer [,ælkəhɔ'lɑmɪtər] o [,ælkəhɑ'lɑmɪtər] *s* alcoholímetro
Alcoran [,ælko'rɑn] o [,ælko'ræn] *s* Alcorán
alcove ['ælkov] *s* (arch.) trasalcoba; gabinete; cenador, glorieta
Alcuin ['ælkwɪn] *s* Alcuino
Alcyone [æl'saɪəni] *s* (astr.) Alción
Ald. abr. de **Alderman**
Aldebaran [æl'dɛbərən] *s* (astr.) Aldebarán
aldehyde ['ældɪhaɪd] *s* (chem.) aldehido
alder ['ɔldər] *s* (bot.) aliso
alder buckthorn *s* (bot.) arraclán, frángula
alderman ['ɔldərmən] *s* (*pl:* **-men**) concejal
aldermanic [,ɔldər'mænɪk] *adj* de un concejal
Alderney ['ɔldərnɪ] *s* vaca de Alderney
Aldine ['ældin] o ['ældɪn] *adj* aldino
Aldm. abr. de **Alderman**
ale [el] *s* ale (*bebida semejante a la cerveza pero más obscura, espesa y amarga*)
aleatory ['elɪə,torɪ] *adj* aleatorio
Aleck ['ælɪk] *s* nombre abreviado de **Alexander**
alee [ə'li] *adv* (naut.) a sotavento
alehouse ['el,haʊs] *s* cervecería
alembic [ə'lɛmbɪk] *s* alambique
Alençon [ə'lɛnsɑn] *s* punto de Alenzón
alepidote [e'lɛpɪdot] *adj* (ichth.) alepídoto
Aleppo [ə'lɛpo] *s* Alepo
Aleppo pine *s* (bot.) pincarrasco
alert [ə'lʌrt] *adj* vigilante; vivo, listo; *s* (mil.) alerta; (aer.) alarma; **to be on the alert** estar alerta, estar sobre aviso; *va* alertar
alertness [ə'lʌrtnɪs] *s* vigilancia; viveza
aleurone [ə'lʊron] *s* (biochem.) aleurona
Aleut ['ælɪut] *s* aleutiano (*natural; idioma*)
Aleutian [ə'luʃən] *adj & s* aleutiano
Aleutian Islands *spl* islas Aleutas, islas Aleutinas
alewife ['el,waɪf] *s* (*pl:* **-wives**) tabernera; (ichth.) cervecera
Alexander [,ælɪg'zændər] *s* Alejandro
Alexander the Great *s* Alejandro Magno
Alexandria [,ælɪg'zændrɪə] *s* Alejandría
Alexandrian [,ælɪg'zændrɪən] *adj* alejandrino
Alexandrine [,ælɪg'zændrɪn] *adj* alejandrino; *s* alejandrino (*natural de Alejandría; verso inglés de doce sílabas y verso castellano de catorce*)
alexia [ə'lɛksɪə] *s* (psychopath.) alexia
alexin [ə'lɛksɪn] *s* (biochem.) alexina
alexipharmic [ə,lɛksɪ'fɑrmɪk] *adj & s* alexifármaco
Alexis [ə'lɛksɪs] *s* Alejo
alfalfa [æl'fælfə] *s* (bot.) alfalfa
Alfred ['ælfrɪd] *s* Alfredo
Alfred the Great *s* Alfredo el Grande
alg. abr. de **algebra**
alga ['ælgə] *s* (*pl:* **algae** ['ældʒi]) (bot.) alga
algal ['ælgəl] *adj* algáceo; *s* (bot.) alga
algebra ['ældʒɪbrə] *s* álgebra
algebraic [,ældʒɪ'breɪk] o **algebraical** [,ældʒɪ'breɪkəl] *adj* algebraico, algébrico
algebraically [,ældʒɪ'breɪkəlɪ] *adv* algebraicamente
algebraist ['ældʒɪ,breɪst] *s* algebrista
Algeria [æl'dʒɪrɪə] *s* Argelia
Algerian [æl'dʒɪrɪən] o **Algerine** [,ældʒə'rin] *adj & s* argelino
algid ['ældʒɪd] *adj* frío, glacial
algidity [æl'dʒɪdɪtɪ] *s* frialdad
Algiers [æl'dʒɪrz] *s* Argel
algology [æl'gɑlədʒɪ] *s* algología
Algonkian [æl'gɑŋkɪən] *adj* (geol.) algonquino; *s* (geol.) algonquina
Algonquian [æl'gɑŋkɪən] o [æl'gɑŋkwɪən] *adj & s* (philol.) algonquino
Algonquin [æl'gɑŋkɪn] o [æl'gɑŋkwɪn] *s* algonquino
algor ['ælgɔr] *s* (path.) algor
algorism ['ælgərɪzəm] *s* (math.) algoritmia, algoritmo
algorithmic [,ælgə'rɪðmɪk] *adj* algorítmico
algous ['ælgəs] *adj* algoso
alias ['elɪəs] *adv* alias; *s* alias, nombre supuesto
alibi ['ælɪbaɪ] *s* (*pl:* **-bis**) coartada; (coll.) excusa, pretexto, comodín; **to prove an alibi** probar la coartada
Alice ['ælɪs] *s* Alicia
Alice in Wonderland *s* Alicia en el país de las maravillas
alidade ['ælɪded] o **alidad** ['ælɪdæd] *s* alidada
alien ['eljən] o ['elɪən] *adj* extranjero; ajeno; *s* extranjero
alienable ['eljənəbəl] o ['elɪənəbəl] *adj* alienable, enajenable
alienate ['eljənet] o ['elɪənet] *va* enajenar, alienar
alienation [,eljən'eʃən] o [,elɪən'eʃən] *s* enajenación, alienación
alienism ['eljənɪzəm] o ['elɪənɪzəm] *s* extranjería; alienismo
alienist ['eljənɪst] o ['elɪənɪst] *s* alienista
alien property custodian *s* administrador de bienes de enemigos
alight [ə'laɪt] *adj* encendido, iluminado; (*pret & pp:* **alighted** o **alit**) *vn* bajar, apearse; **to alight on** posarse sobre; encontrarse con
align [ə'laɪn] *va* alinear; *vn* alinearse
aligner [ə'laɪnər] *s* alineador
alignment [ə'laɪnmənt] *s* alineación; (archeol.) alineamiento; (eng.) alineación; **in alignment** en línea; **out of alignment** fuera de alineación
alike [ə'laɪk] *adj* semejantes, p.ej., **these books are alike** estos libros son semejantes; **to look alike** parecerse; *adv* igualmente, del mismo modo
aliment ['ælɪmənt] *s* alimento
alimentary [,ælɪ'mɛntərɪ] *adj* alimenticio; alimentario (*que suministra la subsistencia*)
alimentary canal *s* (anat.) canal o tubo digestivo, canal alimenticio
alimentation [,ælɪmɛn'teʃən] *s* alimentación
alimony ['ælɪ,monɪ] *s* alimentos, asistencias de divorcio o separación
aline [ə'laɪn] *va & vn* var. de **align**
aliped ['ælɪpɛd] *adj & s* alípedo
aliphatic [,ælɪ'fætɪk] *adj* (chem.) alifático
aliquant ['ælɪkwənt] *adj* (math.) alicuanta
aliquot ['ælɪkwɑt] *adj* (math.) alícuota
alish ['elɪʃ] *adj* acervezado
alit [ə'lɪt] *pret & pp de* **alight**
alive [ə'laɪv] *adj* vivo, viviente, con vida; ac-

tivo, animado; **to look alive** darse prisa, menearse; **alive to** despierto para, sensible a; **alive with** hormigueante en
alizarin [əˈlɪzərɪn] *s* (chem.) alizarina
alkalescence [ˌælkəˈlɛsəns] *s* (chem.) alcalescencia
alkalescent [ˌælkəˈlɛsənt] *adj* (chem.) alcalescente
alkali [ˈælkəlaɪ] *s* (*pl:* **-lis** o **-lies**) (chem.) álcali
alkalimeter [ˌælkəˈlɪmɪtər] *s* alcalímetro
alkaline [ˈælkəlaɪn] o [ˈælkəlɪn] *adj* alcalino
alkaline-earth metals [ˈælkəlaɪnˈʌrθ] o [ˈælkəlɪnˈʌrθ] *spl* (chem.) metales alcalinotérreos
alkaline earths *spl* (chem.) álcalis térreos
alkalinity [ˌælkəˈlɪnɪtɪ] *s* alcalinidad
alkalize [ˈælkəlaɪz] *va* alcalizar
alkaloid [ˈælkəlɔɪd] *s* alcaloide
alkaloidal [ˌælkəˈlɔɪdəl] *adj* alcalóidico
alkalosis [ˌælkəˈlosɪs] *s* (physiol.) alcalosis
alkanet [ˈælkənɛt] *s* (bot.) ancusa; (bot.) ancusa de tintes; (bot.) alcana; (chem.) ancusina
Alkoran [ˌælkoˈrɑn] o [ˌælkoˈræn] *s* Alcorán
all [ɔl] *adj indef* todo, todos; todo el, todos los; *pron indef* todo; todos, todo el mundo; (tennis) iguales; **after all** sin embargo; **at all** del todo; **for all I know** que yo sepa; **for good and all** para siempre; **not at all** nada; no hay de qué; **once and for all** de una vez para siempre; **all in all** en resumen; **all of** todo el, todos los; **all that** todo lo que, todos los que; **all told** en conjunto; *adv* enteramente; **not to be all there** (slang) no estar en su juicio cabal; **to be all up with** no haber remedio para; **all at once** de golpe; **all along** desde el principio; a lo largo de, de un cabo a otro de; **all but** casi; **all in** (slang) agotado, rendido; **all of a sudden** de repente; **all off** (slang) abandonado; **all one** (coll.) igual; **all out** a ultranza; **all over** terminado; por todas partes; exactamente; **all right** está bien, bueno, corriente; **all the better** tanto mejor; **all the worse** tanto peor; **all too** excesivamente, desgraciadamente
Allah [ˈælə] *s* Alá
all-American [ˌɔləˈmɛrɪkən] *adj* que representa todas las partes de los Estados Unidos; exclusivamente estadunidense; (sport) seleccionado como jugador representativo nacional
allantoid [əˈlæntɔɪd] *adj* alantoideo
allantois [əˈlænto·ɪs] *s* (anat.) alantoides
all-around [ˈɔləˌraʊnd] *adj* hábil para muchas cosas
allay [əˈle] *va* aliviar, calmar
all-clear [ˈɔlˈklɪr] *s* cese de alarma, toque o señal de cese de alarma
allegation [ˌælɪˈgeʃən] *s* alegación; (law) alegato
allege [əˈlɛdʒ] *va* alegar
allegedly [əˈlɛdʒɪdlɪ] *adv* según se alega
allegiance [əˈlidʒəns] *s* lealtad, fidelidad; homenaje; **to swear allegiance to** rendir homenaje a; jurar fidelidad a
allegoric [ˌælɪˈgɑrɪk] o [ˌælɪˈgɔrɪk] o **allegorical** [ˌælɪˈgɑrɪkəl] o [ˌælɪˈgɔrɪkəl] *adj* alegórico
allegorize [ˈælɪgəraɪz] *va* alegorizar
allegory [ˈælɪˌgorɪ] *s* (*pl:* **-ries**) alegoría
allegretto [ˌæləˈgrɛto] *s* (*pl:* **-tos**) (mus.) alegreto
allegro [ɑˈlegro] o [əˈlɛgro] *s* (*pl:* **-gros**) (mus.) alegro
alleluia [ˌælɪˈlujə] *s* aleluya; *interj* ¡ aleluya!
allemande [ˌæləˈmænd] *s* alemana o alemanda (*danza*)
allergen [ˈælərdʒɛn] *s* (immun.) alergeno
allergic [əˈlʌrdʒɪk] *adj* alérgico
allergy [ˈælərdʒɪ] *s* (*pl:* **-gies**) (path.) alergia
alleviate [əˈlivɪet] *va* aliviar
alleviation [əˌlivɪˈeʃən] *s* alivio
alleviative [əˈlivɪˌetɪv] *adj* aliviador
alley [ˈælɪ] *s* callejuela, callejón; paseo arbolado, paseo de jardín; pista (*de bolera*); (tennis) espacio lateral
alleyway [ˈælɪˌwe] *s* callejuela, pasadizo
All Fools' Day *s* var. de **April Fools' Day**
all fours *spl* las cuatro patas; **on all fours** a gatas
Allhallows [ˌɔlˈhæloz] *s* día de todos los santos
alliance [əˈlaɪəns] *s* alianza
Alliance for Progress *s* Alianza para el Progreso
alligator [ˈælɪˌgetər] *s* (zool.) caimán; cuero o piel de caimán o cocodrilo
alligator gar *s* (ichth.) pez caimán
alligator pear *s* aguacate
alligator tree *s* (bot.) ocozol
alligator wrench *s* llave de mandíbulas, llave dentada
all-important [ˈɔlɪmˈpɔrtənt] *adj* de toda importancia
all-in [ˈɔlˈɪn] *adj* (Brit.) inclusivo; (Brit.) sin restricción
alliterate [əˈlɪtəret] *va* disponer en forma de aliteración; *vn* usar aliteración
alliteration [əˌlɪtəˈreʃən] *s* aliteración
alliterative [əˈlɪtəˌretɪv] *adj* aliterado
all-knowing [ˈɔlˈno·ɪŋ] *adj* omnisciente
all-metal [ˈɔlˈmɛtəl] *adj* todo de metal, todo metálico
allocate [ˈæloket] *va* asignar, señalar, distribuir
allocation [ˌæloˈkeʃən] *s* asignación, distribución
allocution [ˌæloˈkjuʃən] *s* alocución
allodium [əˈlodɪəm] *s* (*pl:* **-a** [ə]) var. de **alodium**
allogamy [əˈlɑgəmɪ] *s* (bot.) alogamia
allopath [ˈælopæθ] *s* alópata
allopathic [ˌæloˈpæθɪk] *adj* alopático
allopathist [əˈlɑpəθɪst] *s* var. de **allopath**
allopathy [əˈlɑpəθɪ] *s* alopatía
allophone [ˈælofon] *s* miembro del fonema
allot [əˈlɑt] (*pret & pp:* **allotted;** *ger:* **allotting**) *va* asignar, distribuir
allotment [əˈlɑtmənt] *s* asignación, distribución; lote, parte, porción
allotrope [ˈælotrop] *s* alotropo
allotropic [ˌæloˈtrɑpɪk] *adj* alotrópico
allotropism [əˈlɑtrəpɪzəm] *s* alotropismo
allotropy [əˈlɑtrəpɪ] *s* alotropía
all-out [ˈɔlˈaʊt] *adj* total, acérrimo
allover [ˈɔlˌovər] *adj* que tiene un diseño repetido sobre toda la superficie; *s* tela con diseño repetido sobre toda la superficie; diseño repetido sobre toda la superficie
allow [əˈlaʊ] *va* dejar, permitir; admitir; conceder; poner aparte; (coll.) creer; **to allow to** + *inf* dejar + *inf*, permitir + *inf; vn* **to allow for** tener en cuenta; **to allow of** permitir; admitir
allowable [əˈlaʊəbəl] *adj* permisible; admisible
allowance [əˈlaʊəns] *s* permiso; concesión; asignación, pensión; ración, mesada; descuento, rebaja; tolerancia (*en el peso o en las dimensiones*); **to make allowance for** tener en cuenta
alloy [ˈælɔɪ] o [əˈlɔɪ] *s* aleación, liga; impureza, adulteración; [əˈlɔɪ] *va* alear, ligar; adulterar
alloy steel *s* acero de aleación
all-powerful [ˈɔlˈpaʊərfəl] *adj* todopoderoso
all-round [ˈɔlˌraʊnd] *adj* hábil para muchas cosas
All Saints' Day *s* día de todos los santos
all-silk [ˈɔlˌsɪlk] *adj* de pura seda
All Souls' Day *s* día de los difuntos
allspice [ˈɔlˌspaɪs] *s* pimienta inglesa (*fruto seco y molido*)
allspice tree *s* (bot.) pimienta (*Pimenta officinalis*)
all-steel [ˈɔlˈstil] *adj* todo de acero
allude [əˈlud] *vn* aludir
allure [əˈlʊr] *s* tentación, encanto, fascinación; *va* tentar, encantar, fascinar
allurement [əˈlʊrmənt] *s* tentación, encanto, fascinación
alluring [əˈlʊrɪŋ] *adj* tentador, encantador, fascinante
allusion [əˈluʒən] *s* alusión
allusive [əˈlusɪv] *adj* alusivo
alluvial [əˈluvɪəl] *adj* aluvial
alluvion [əˈluvɪən] *s* aluvión; (law) aluvión
alluvium [əˈluvɪəm] *s* (*pl:* **-ums** o **-a** [ə]) aluvión
all-wave [ˈɔlˈwev] *adj* (rad.) de toda onda, de onda universal
all-weather [ˈɔlˈwɛðər] *adj* para todo tiempo, para todas las estaciones
all-wise [ˈɔlˈwaɪz] *adj* infinitamente sabio

ally ['ælaɪ] o [ə'laɪ] *s* (*pl:* **allies**) aliado; [ə'laɪ] (*pret & pp:* **allied**) *va* aliar; **to become allied** aliarse; **to ally oneself** aliarse; *vn* aliarse
allyl ['ælɪl] *s* (chem.) alilo
allylene ['ælɪlin] *s* (chem.) alileno
almagest ['ælmədʒɛst] *s* almagesto
Alma Mater ['ælmə'metər] o ['ɑlmə'mɑtər] *s* (myth.) alma máter; (*l.c.*) *s* alma máter (*universidad donde uno se ha graduado*)
almanac ['ɔlmənæk] *s* almanaque
almighty [ɔl'maɪtɪ] *adj* todopoderoso; (coll.) enorme, grave; **the Almighty** el Todopoderoso (*Dios*)
almond ['ɑmənd] o ['æmənd] *s* (bot.) almendro (*árbol*); almendra (*fruto y semilla del fruto*)
almond brittle *s* crocante
almond cream *s* crema de almendras
almond-eyed ['ɑmənd,aɪd] o ['æmənd,aɪd] *adj* de ojos almendrados
almond-shaped ['ɑmənd,ʃept] o ['æmənd-,ʃept] *adj* almendrado
almoner ['ælmənər] o ['ɑmənər] *s* limosnero
almonry ['ælmənrɪ] o ['ɑmənrɪ] *s* (*pl:* **-ries**) lugar donde se reparten limosnas
almost ['ɔlmost] u [ɔl'most] *adv* casi
alms [ɑmz] *ssg & spl* limosna
almsgiver ['ɑmz,gɪvər] *s* limosnero
almsgiving ['ɑmz,gɪvɪŋ] *adj* limosnero; *s* limosna
almshouse ['ɑmz,haʊs] *s* casa de beneficencia, hospicio
almsman ['ɑmzmən] *s* (*pl:* **-men**) mendigo, pordiosero
almswoman ['ɑmz,wʊmən] *s* (*pl:* **-women**) mendiga, pordiosera
almucantar [,ælmjə'kæntər] *s* (astr.) almicantarada
alnico ['ælnɪko] *s* alnico (*aleación*)
alodial [ə'lodɪəl] *adj* (law) alodial
alodium [ə'lodɪəm] *s* (*pl:* **-a** [ə]) (law) alodio
aloe ['ælo] *s* (bot.) áloe; (bot.) maguey; **aloes** *ssg* (pharm.) áloe; palo áloe, palo de áloe
aloes wood *s* palo áloe, palo de áloe
aloetic [,ælo'ɛtɪk] *adj* aloético
aloft [ə'lɔft] o [ə'lɑft] *adv* arriba, en alto, en los aires; (naut.) en la arboladura; (aer.) en vuelo
aloin ['ælo·ɪn] *s* (chem. & pharm.) aloína
alone [ə'lon] *adj* solo; **let alone** sin mencionar; y mucho menos, p.ej., **he cannot speak his own language, let alone a foreign language** no puede hablar su propio idioma y mucho menos un idioma extranjero; **to leave alone** o **to let alone** no molestar a (*una persona*); no mezclarse en (*una cosa*); *adv* solamente
along [ə'lɔŋ] o [ə'lɑŋ] *prep* a lo largo de; **all along** de un cabo a otro de; *adv* a lo largo; adelante; conmigo, consigo, p.ej., **come along** venga Vd. conmigo; **all along** desde el principio; **to get along** irse; medrar; entenderse; **along with** junto con
alongshore [ə'lɔŋ,ʃor] o [ə'lɑŋ,ʃor] *adv* a la orilla, a lo largo de la costa
alongside [ə'lɔŋ'saɪd] o [ə'lɑŋ'saɪd] *prep* junto a, a lo largo de; (naut.) al costado de; *adv* a lo largo; (naut.) al costado, costado con costado; **to bring alongside** (naut.) acostar; **to come alongside** (naut.) acostarse; **alongside of** junto a
aloof [ə'luf] *adj* apartado; reservado, frío; **to keep aloof from** o **to stand aloof from** mantenerse apartado de; *adv* lejos, a distancia
aloofness [ə'lufnɪs] *s* apartamiento, aislamiento; reserva, frialdad
alopecia [,ælo'piʃɪə] *s* (path.) alopecia
aloud [ə'laʊd] *adv* alto, en voz alta; con voz fuerte
alp [ælp] *s* monte elevado
alpaca [æl'pækə] *s* (zool.) alpaca; alpaca (*lana y tela hecha de esta lana*)
alpenglow ['ælpən,glo] *s* arrebol alpestre
alpenhorn ['ælpən,hɔrn] *s* trompa de los Alpes
alpenstock ['ælpən,stɑk] *s* bastón puntiagudo de los montañeros
alpha ['ælfə] *s* alfa; **alpha and omega** alfa y omega
alphabet ['ælfəbɛt] *s* alfabeto
alphabetic [,ælfə'bɛtɪk] o **alphabetical** [,ælfə'bɛtɪkəl] alfabético
alphabetically [,ælfə'bɛtɪkəlɪ] *adv* alfabéticamente
alphabetization [,ælfə,bɛtɪ'zeʃən] *s* alfabetización
alphabetize ['ælfəbətaɪz] *va* alfabetizar
alpha rays *spl* (phys.) rayos alfa
Alpheus [æl'fiəs] *s* (myth.) Alfeo
Alphonsine [æl'fɑnsɪn] *adj* alfonsino
Alphonsine Tables *spl* tablas alfonsinas
Alphonso [æl'fɑnso] o [æl'fɑnzo] *s* Alfonso
alphorn ['ælp,hɔrn] *s* trompa de los Alpes
alpine ['ælpaɪn] o ['ælpɪn] *adj* alpestre; (*cap.*) *adj* alpino
alpine chough *s* (orn.) chova pinariega, grajo de pico amarillo
Alpinism ['ælpɪnɪzəm] *s* alpinismo
Alpinist ['ælpɪnɪst] *s* alpinista
alpist ['ælpɪst] *s* alpiste (*semilla*)
Alps [ælps] *spl* Alpes
already [ɔl'rɛdɪ] *adv* ya
Alsace ['ælses] o ['ælsæs] *s* Alsacia
Alsace-Lorraine ['ælseslɑ'ren] o ['ælsæslɑ-'ren] *s* Alsacia-Lorena
Alsatian [æl'seʃən] *adj & s* alsaciano
alsike ['ælsaɪk] u ['ɔlsaɪk] *s* (bot.) trébol sueco
also ['ɔlso] *adv* también
alt. abr. de **alternate** y **altitude**
Alta. abr. de **Alberta** (*Canadá*)
Altaic [æl'teɪk] *adj* altaico
altar ['ɔltər] *s* altar; (found.) altar; **to lead to the altar** conducir al altar
altar boy *s* monaguillo, acólito
altar cloth *s* (eccl.) sabanilla, paño de altar, palia
altarpiece ['ɔltər,pis] *s* retablo
altar rail *s* comulgatorio
alter ['ɔltər] *va* alterar; (coll.) arreglar (*castrar*); *vn* alterarse
alterability [,ɔltərə'bɪlɪtɪ] *s* alterabilidad
alterable ['ɔltərəbəl] *adj* alterable
alteration [,ɔltə'reʃən] *s* alteración; reparación, compostura, reforma
alterative ['ɔltə,retɪv] *adj & s* (med.) alterante
altercate ['ɔltərket] o ['æltərket] *vn* altercar
altercation [,ɔltər'keʃən] o [,æltər'keʃən] *s* altercación o altercado
alter ego ['æltər'igo] o ['æltər'ɛgo] (Lat.) álter ego (*otro yo; amigo de confianza*)
alternate ['ɔltərnɪt] o ['æltərnɪt] *s* suplente; *adj* alternante; alterno; (bot. & geom.) alterno; ['ɔltərnet] o ['æltərnet] *va & vn* alternar
alternate angles *spl* (geom.) ángulos alternos
alternate leaves *spl* (bot.) hojas alternas
alternately ['ɔltərnɪtlɪ] o ['æltərnɪtlɪ] *adv* alternadamente, alternativamente
alternating ['ɔltər,netɪŋ] o ['æltər,netɪŋ] *adj* alternante, alternativo
alternating current *s* (elec.) corriente alterna, corriente alternativa
alternation [,ɔltər'neʃən] o [,æltər'neʃən] *s* alternación; (elec.) alternancia
alternation of generations *s* (biol.) alternancia de generaciones
alternative [ɔl'tʌrnətɪv] o [æl'tʌrnətɪv] *adj* alternativo; *s* alternativa
alternative conjunction *s* (gram.) conjunción disyuntiva
alternator ['ɔltər,netər] o ['æltər,netər] *s* (elec.) alternador
althea [æl'θiə] *s* (bot.) altea
althorn ['ælthɔrn] *s* trombón alto
although [ɔl'ðo] *conj* aunque
altimeter [æl'tɪmɪtər] *s* altímetro
altimetrical [,æltɪ'metrɪkəl] *adj* altímetro
altimetry [æl'tɪmɪtrɪ] *s* altimetría
altitude ['æltɪtjud] o ['æltɪtud] *s* altitud, altura
alto ['ælto] *s* (*pl:* **-tos**) (mus.) alto; contralto (*mujer*)
alto-cumulus [,ælto'kjumjələs] *s* (meteor.) altocúmulo
altogether [,ɔltə'gɛðər] *adv* enteramente; en conjunto
alto horn *s* trombón alto
alto-relievo ['æltorɪ'livo] *s* (*pl:* **-vos**) alto relieve
alto-stratus [,ælto'stretəs] *s* (meteor.) altostrato

altruism ['æltruɪzəm] *s* altruísmo
altruist ['æltruɪst] *s* altruísta
altruistic [ˌæltru'ɪstɪk] *adj* altruísta
alula ['æljələ] *s* (*pl:* **-lae** [li]) (orn. & ent.) álula
alum ['æləm] *s* (chem.) alumbre
alumina [ə'lumɪnə] *s* (mineral.) alúmina
aluminate [ə'lumɪnet] *s* (chem.) aluminato
aluminite [ə'lumɪnaɪt] *s* (mineral.) aluminita
aluminium [ˌæljə'mɪnɪəm] *s* var. de **aluminum**
aluminothermy [ə'lumɪnoˌθʌrmɪ] *s* (metal.) aluminotermia
aluminous [ə'lumɪnəs] *adj* alumbroso (*que tiene alumbre*); aluminoso (*que tiene alúmina*); alumínico (*que tiene aluminio*)
aluminum [ə'lumɪnəm] *s* (chem.) aluminio
aluminum bronze *s* bronce de aluminio
aluminum oxide *s* (chem.) óxido de aluminio
aluminum paint *s* pintura de aluminio
alumna [ə'lʌmnə] *s* (*pl:* **-nae** [ni]) graduada
alumni association *s* asociación de graduados
alumnus [ə'lʌmnəs] *s* (*pl:* **-ni** [naɪ]) graduado
alum rock *s* (mineral.) piedra de alumbre
alum schist, shale o **slate** *s* esquisto aluminoso
alum stone *s* var. de **alum rock**
alunite ['æljənaɪt] *s* (mineral.) alunita
alveary ['ælvɪˌɛrɪ] *s* (*pl:* **-ies**) (anat.) alveario
alveolar [æl'viələr] *adj* (anat. & phonet.) alveolar
alveolar process *s* (anat.) apófisis alveolar
alveolus [æl'viələs] *s* (*pl:* **-li** [laɪ]) (anat., phonet., & zool.) alvéolo
alvine ['ælvɪn] o ['ælvaɪn] *adj* (med.) alvino
always ['ɔlwɪz] u ['ɔlwez] *adv* siempre
alyssum [ə'lɪsəm] *s* (bot.) alisón; (bot.) alhelicillo
a.m. o **A.M.** abr. de **ante meridiem** (Lat.) **before noon**
A.M. abr. de **Artium Magister** (Lat.) **Master of Arts**
A.M. o **AM** abr. de **amplitude modulation**
Am. abr. de **America** y **American**
am [æm] *primera persona del sg del pres de ind de* **be**
A.M.A. abr. de **American Medical Association**
amain [ə'men] *adv* con fuerza, con prisa, con vehemencia
Amalekite ['æmələkaɪt] *s* (Bib.) amalecita
amalgam [ə'mælgəm] *s* (chem., mineral. & fig.) amalgama
amalgamate [ə'mælgəmet] *va* (chem. & fig.) amalgamar; *vn* amalgamarse
amalgamation [əˌmælgə'meʃən] *s* amalgamación
amalgamation process *s* (min.) amalgamación
amanita [ˌæmə'naɪtə] *s* (bot.) amanita
amanuensis [əˌmænju'ɛnsɪs] *s* (*pl:* **-ses** [siz]) amanuense
amaranth ['æmərænθ] *s* (bot.) amaranto; (poet.) flor que nunca se marchita; púrpura (*color*)
amaranthaceous [ˌæmərænˈθeʃəs] *adj* (bot.) amarantáceo
amaranthine [ˌæmə'rænθɪn] o [ˌæmə'rænθaɪn] *adj* amarantino; inmarcesible, imperecedero; purpúreo
amaryllis [ˌæmə'rɪlɪs] *s* (bot.) amarilis; (*cap.*) *s* Amarilis (*pastora*)
amass [ə'mæs] *va* acumular, amontonar; amasar (*dinero, una fortuna*)
amateur [ˌæmə'tʌr] o ['æmətʃər] *s* aficionado; chapucero, principiante; *adj* aficionado; de afición; chapucero, principiante
amateurish [ˌæmə'tʌrɪʃ], ['æmətjurɪʃ] o ['æmətʃərɪʃ] *adj* superficial, chapucero
amateurism [ˌæmə'tʌrɪzəm], ['æmətjurɪzəm] o ['æmətʃərɪzəm] *s* estado de aficionado; chapucería
amative ['æmətɪv] *adj* amativo
amatory ['æməˌtorɪ] *adj* amatorio
amaurosis [ˌæmɔ'rosɪs] *s* (path.) amaurosis
amaze [ə'mez] *va* asombrar, pasmar, maravillar; **to be amazed at, by,** o **with** asombrarse de
amazedly [ə'mezɪdlɪ] *adv* con asombro, pasmadamente
amazement [ə'mezmənt] *s* asombro, pasmo, aturdimiento
amazing [ə'mezɪŋ] *adj* asombroso, pasmoso, maravilloso
amazon ['æməzɑn] o ['æməzən] *s* amazona (*mujer varonil*); (*cap.*) *s* Amazonas (*río*); (orn.) amazona (*loro*); (myth.) amazona
Amazonian [ˌæmə'zonɪən] *adj* amazónico
amazonite ['æməzənaɪt] *s* (mineral.) amazonita
ambagious [æm'bedʒəs] *adj* ambagioso
ambassador [æm'bæsədər] *s* embajador
ambassadorial [æmˌbæsə'dorɪəl] *adj* embajatorio
ambassadorship [æm'bæsədərˌʃɪp] *s* embajada (*dignidad, cargo, tiempo que dura el cargo*)
ambassadress [æm'bæsədrɪs] *s* embajadora
amber ['æmbər] *s* ámbar; *adj* ambarino
ambergris ['æmbərgris] *s* ámbar gris
amber jack *s* (ichth.) coronado, medregal; (ichth.) pez limón
ambidexterity [ˌæmbɪdɛks'tɛrɪtɪ] *s* ambidextrismo, ambidexteridad; falsedad, hipocresía
ambidextrous [ˌæmbɪ'dɛkstrəs] *adj* ambidextro; falso, hipócrita
ambient ['æmbɪənt] *adj* ambiente
ambiguity [ˌæmbɪ'gjuɪtɪ] *s* (*pl:* **-ties**) ambigüedad
ambiguous [æm'bɪgjuəs] *adj* ambiguo
ambit ['æmbɪt] *s* ámbito
ambition [æm'bɪʃən] *s* ambición
ambitious [æm'bɪʃəs] *adj* ambicioso
ambivalence [æm'bɪvələns] *s* (psychol.) ambivalencia
ambivalent [æm'bɪvələnt] *adj* ambivalente
amble ['æmbəl] *s* ambladura, paso de ambladura; *vn* amblar
ambler ['æmblər] *s* amblador
amblyopia [ˌæmblɪ'opɪə] *s* (path.) ambliopía
ambo ['æmbo] *s* (*pl:* **-bos**) ambón
Ambrose ['æmbroz] *s* Ambrosio
Ambrose Channel *s* el canal Ambrosio
ambrosia [æm'broʒə] o [æm'broʒɪə] *s* (bot., myth., & fig.) ambrosía
ambrosial [æm'broʒəl] o [æm'broʒɪəl] *adj* ambrosíaco
Ambrosian [æm'broʒən] o [æm'brozɪən] *adj* ambrosiano
Ambrosian chant *s* canto ambrosiano
ambry ['æmbrɪ] *s* (*pl:* **-bries**) armario; despensa
ambulacral [ˌæmbjə'lekrəl] *adj* (zool.) ambulacral
ambulacrum [ˌæmbjə'lekrəm] *s* (*pl:* **-kra** [krə]) (zool.) ambulacro
ambulance ['æmbjələns] *s* ambulancia
ambulance driver *s* ambulanciero
ambulant ['æmbjələnt] *adj* ambulante
ambulate ['æmbjəlet] *vn* ambular, andar, deambular
ambulatory ['æmbjələˌtorɪ] *adj* ambulatorio; *s* (arch.) deambulatorio
ambuscade [ˌæmbəs'ked] *s, va, & vn* var. de **ambush**
ambush ['æmbuʃ] *s* emboscada; **to fall into an ambush** caer en una emboscada; **to lie in ambush** estar emboscado; *va* emboscar, ocultar (*tropas*) para una emboscada; insidiar, poner asechanzas a; *vn* emboscarse
ameba [ə'mibə] *s* (*pl:* **-bas** o **-bae** [bi]) var. de **amoeba**
ameer [ə'mɪr] *s* amir
Amelia [ə'miljə] *s* Amalia
ameliorable [ə'miljərəbəl] *adj* mejorable
ameliorate [ə'miljəret] *va & vn* mejorar
amelioration [əˌmiljə'reʃən] *s* mejoramiento
ameliorative [ə'miljəˌretɪv] *adj* mejorador
amen ['e'mɛn] o ['ɑ'mɛn] *s & interj* amén; **to say amen to** (coll.) decir amén a (*avenirse a*)
amenability [əˌminə'bɪlɪtɪ] o [əˌmɛnə'bɪlɪtɪ] *s* docilidad; responsabilidad
amenable [ə'minəbəl] o [ə'mɛnəbəl] *adj* dócil; responsable
amen corner *s* banco de iglesia en donde se encuentran los fieles más ardientes y chillones (*en las iglesias protestantes*)
amend [ə'mɛnd] *va* enmendar; *vn* enmendarse; **amends** *spl* enmienda; **to make amends for** dar cumplida satisfacción por, enmendar

amendment [ə'mɛndmənt] *s* enmienda; (agr.) enmiendas

amenity [ə'mɛnɪtɪ] o [ə'minɪtɪ] *s* (*pl:* **-ties**) amenidad

amenorrhea [əˌmɛnə'riə] *s* (path.) amenorrea

ament ['æmənt] o ['emənt] *s* (bot.) amento (*inflorescencia*)

amentaceous [ˌæmən'teʃəs] *adj* (bot.) amentáceo

amentia [e'mɛnʃɪə] *s* demencia, locura, imbecilidad

Amer. abr. de **America** y **American**

amerce [ə'mʌrs] *va* multar; castigar

amercement [ə'mʌrsmənt] *s* multa; castigo

America [ə'mɛrɪkə] *s* América

American [ə'mɛrɪkən] *adj* & *s* americano; norteamericano, estadunidense

Americana [əˌmɛrɪ'kenə], [əˌmɛrɪ'kɑnə] o [əˌmɛrɪ'kænə] *spl* escritos americanos, escritos sobre cosas de América

American aloe *s* (bot.) maguey, pita

American Beauty *s* rosa encarnada de gran tamaño

American cheese *s* queso de Cheddar

American eagle *s* águila americana (*escudo de armas de los EE.UU.*)

Americanism [ə'mɛrɪkənɪzəm] *s* americanismo

Americanist [ə'mɛrɪkənɪst] *s* americanista

Americanization [əˌmɛrɪkənɪ'zeʃən] *s* americanización

Americanize [ə'mɛrɪkənaɪz] *va* americanizar; *vn* americanizarse

American ostrich *s* (orn.) avestruz de América, ñandú

American plan *s* cuartos con comidas

americium [ˌæmə'rɪʃɪəm] *s* (chem.) americio

Americomania [əˌmɛrɪko'menɪə] *s* americomanía

Amerind ['æmərɪnd] *s* amerindio

Amerindian [ˌæmə'rɪndɪən] *adj* & *s* amerindio

amethyst ['æmɪθɪst] *s* amatista

ametropia [ˌæmɪ'tropɪə] *s* (path.) ametropía

amiability [ˌemɪə'bɪlɪtɪ] *s* amabilidad

amiable ['emɪəbəl] *adj* amable; bonachón

amicability [ˌæmɪkə'bɪlɪtɪ] *s* amigabilidad

amicable ['æmɪkəbəl] *adj* amigable

amice ['æmɪs] *s* (eccl.) amito

amid [ə'mɪd] *prep* en medio de

amide ['æmɪd] o ['æmaɪd] *s* (chem.) amida

amidine ['æmɪdin] o ['æmɪdɪn] *s* (chem.) amidina

amidogen [ə'midodʒɛn] o [ə'mɪdodʒɛn] *s* (chem.) amidógeno

amidol ['æmɪdɑl] o ['æmɪdol] *s* (chem.) amidol

amidship [ə'mɪdʃɪp] o **amidships** [ə'mɪdʃɪps] *adv* en medio del navío

amidst [ə'mɪdst] *prep* en medio de

amine [ə'min] o ['æmɪn] *s* (chem.) amina

aminic [ə'mɪnɪk] *adj* (chem.) amínico

amino acids ['æmɪno] o [ə'mino] *spl* (chem.) aminoácidos

amir [ə'mɪr] *s* amir

amiss [ə'mɪs] *adj* inoportuno; malo, errado; en mal estado; *adv* inoportunamente; mal, erradamente; en mal estado; **to take amiss** llevar a mal, tomar en mala parte

amitosis [ˌæmɪ'tosɪs] *s* (biol.) amitosis

amity ['æmɪtɪ] *s* (*pl:* **-ties**) amistad, bienquerencia, armonía

ammeter ['æmˌmitər] o ['æmɪtər] *s* (elec.) anmetro, amperímetro

ammonia [ə'monɪə] *s* (chem.) amoníaco; (chem.) agua amoniacal

ammoniac [ə'monɪæk] *adj* amoniacal; *s* amoníaco (*goma resinosa*)

ammoniacal [ˌæmo'naɪəkəl] *adj* amoníaco

ammoniacal liquor *s* líquido amoniacal

ammonia gas *s* (chem.) gas amoníaco

ammonia water *s* (chem.) agua amoniacal

ammonite ['æmənaɪt] *s* (pal.) amonita; (*cap.*) *s* (Bib.) amonita

ammonium [ə'monɪəm] *s* (chem.) amonio; *adj* amónico

ammonium chloride *s* (chem.) cloruro amónico

ammonium hydroxide *s* (chem.) hidrato amónico

ammonium nitrate *s* (chem.) nitrato amónico

ammunition [ˌæmjə'nɪʃən] *s* munición; *va* amunicionar

amnesia [æm'niʒɪə] o [æm'niʒə] *s* (path.) amnesia

amnesic [æm'nisɪk] o [æm'nizɪk] *adj* amnésico

amnesty ['æmnɪstɪ] *s* (*pl:* **-ties**) amnistía; (*pret & pp:* **-tied**) *va* amnistiar

amnion ['æmnɪən] *s* (*pl:* **-ons** o **-a** [ə]) (anat.) amnios

amniote ['æmnɪot] *adj* & *s* (zool.) amniota

amniotic [ˌæmnɪ'ɑtɪk] *adj* (anat.) amniótico

amoeba [ə'mibə] (*pl:* **-bas** o **-bae** [bi]) (zool.) amiba

amoebic [ə'mibɪk] *adj* ami[illegible]o

amoebic dysentery *s* (pat[illegible]) disentería amibiana

amoeboid [ə'mibɔɪd] *adj* amiboideo

amok [ə'mɑk] o [ə'mʌk] *adv* var. de **amuck**

amomum [ə'momam] *s* (bot.) amomo

among [ə'mʌŋ] o **amongst** [ə'mʌŋst] *prep* entre, en medio de, en el número de

amoral [e'mɑrəl] o [e'mɔrəl] *adj* amoral

amorality [ˌemə'rælɪtɪ] *s* amoralidad

amorous ['æmərəs] *adj* amoroso

amorphia [ə'mɔrfɪə] *s* amorfia

amorphism [ə'mɔrfɪzəm] *s* amorfismo

amorphous [ə'mɔrfəs] *adj* amorfo

amortization [ˌæmərtɪ'zeʃən] o [əˌmɔrtɪ'zeʃən] *s* amortización

amortize ['æmərtaɪz] o [ə'mɔrtaɪz] *va* amortizar

amortizement [ə'mɔrtɪzmənt] *s* amortización

Amos ['eməs] *s* Amós

amount [ə'maʊnt] *s* cantidad, importe; *vn* ascender; **to amount to** ascender a, subir a; significar

amour [ə'mʊr] *s* amores, amorío

amour-propre [ɑ'mʊr'prɔprə] *s* amor propio

amp. abr. de **ampere** y **amperage**

ampelite ['æmpəlaɪt] *s* (mineral.) ampelita

ampelography [ˌæmpə'lɑgrəfɪ] *s* ampelografía

amperage [æm'pɪrɪdʒ] o ['æmpɪrɪdʒ] *s* (elec.) amperaje

ampere ['æmpɪr] *s* (elec.) amperio

ampere-hour ['æmpɪr'aʊr] *s* (*pl:* **ampere-hours**) (elec.) amperio hora

ampere turn *s* (elec.) amperio-vuelta

ampersand ['æmpərsænd] *s* la cifra & que significa **and**

amphetamine [æm'fɛtəmin] o [æm'fɛtəmɪn] *s* (pharm.) anfetamina

amphibian [æm'fɪbɪən] *adj* & *s* (aer. & biol.) anfibio

amphibious [æm'fɪbɪəs] *adj* (aer., biol., & fig.) anfibio

amphibole ['æmfɪbol] *s* (mineral.) anfíbol

amphibolite [æm'fɪbolaɪt] *s* (geol.) anfibolita

amphibological [æmˌfɪbo'lɑdʒɪkəl] *adj* anfibológico

amphibology [ˌæmfɪ'bɑlədʒɪ] *s* (*pl:* **-gies**) anfibología

amphiboly [æm'fɪbəlɪ] *s* (*pl:* **-lies**) var. de **amphibology**

amphibrach ['æmfɪbræk] *s* anfíbraco

Amphion [æm'faɪən] *s* (myth.) Anfión

amphipod ['æmfɪpɑd] *adj* & *s* (zool.) anfípodo

amphisbaena [ˌæmfɪs'binə] *s* (zool.) anfisbena

amphiscians [æm'fɪʃɪəns] *spl* anfiscios (*habitantes de la zona tórrida*)

amphitheater ['æmfɪˌθiətər] *s* anfiteatro

Amphitrite [ˌæmfɪ'traɪtɪ] *s* (myth. & zool.) Anfitrite

Amphitryon [æm'fɪtrɪən] *s* (myth.) Anfitrión

amphora ['æmfərə] *s* (*pl:* **-rae** [ri]) ánfora

ample ['æmpəl] *adj* amplio; bastante, suficiente; abundante

amplexicaul [æm'plɛksɪkəl] *adj* (bot.) amplexicaulo

amplification [ˌæmplɪfɪ'keʃən] *s* amplificación; (elec.) amplificación

amplificative ['æmplɪfɪˌketɪv] *adj* amplificativo

amplifier ['æmplɪˌfaɪər] *s* amplificador; (elec.) amplificador

amplify ['æmplɪfaɪ] (*pret & pp:* **-fied**) *va* amplificar; (elec.) amplificar; *vn* espaciarse (*en el discurso*)

amplifying ['æmplɪˌfaɪɪŋ] *adj* amplificador

amplitude ['æmplɪtjud] o ['æmplɪtud] *s* amplitud; (astr., elec., & mech.) amplitud

amplitude modulation *s* (rad.) modulación de altura o de amplitud
amply ['æmplɪ] *adv* ampliamente; bastante, suficientemente; abundantemente
ampoule [æm'pul] *s* (med.) ampolla
ampulla [æm'pʌlə] *s* (anat., bot., eccl., hist. & zool.) ampolla
amputate ['æmpjətet] *va* amputar
amputation [,æmpjə'teʃən] *s* amputación
amputee [,æmpjə'ti] *s* amputado
amt. abr. de **amount**
amuck [ə'mʌk] *adv* frenéticamente; **to run amuck** atacar a c˙ ˙as
amulet ['æmjəlɪt] ˙muleto
amuse [ə'mjuz] *va* ˙vertir, entretener
amusement [ə'mjuzmənt] *s* diversión, entretenimiento; pasatiempo, recreación; atracción (*p.ej., en un circo*)
amusement park *s* parque de atracciones
amusement tax *s* impuesto sobre espectáculos
amusing [ə'mjuzɪŋ] *adj* divertido, gracioso
Amy ['emɪ] *s* Amata
amygdalin [ə'mɪgdəlɪn] *s* (chem.) amigdalina
amygdaloid [ə'mɪgdəlɔɪd] *adj* amigdaloideo; (mineral.) amigdaloide
amyl ['æmɪl] o ['emɪl] *s* (chem.) amilo; *adj* (chem.) amílico
amylaceous [,æmɪ'leʃəs] *adj* amiláceo
amylase ['æmɪles] *s* (biochem.) amilasa
amylene ['æmɪlin] *s* (chem.) amileno
amylic [ə'mɪlɪk] *adj* (chem.) amílico
amyloid ['æmɪlɔɪd] *adj* amiloideo
amyloid degeneration *s* (path.) degeneración amiloidea
amyloidosis [,æmɪlɔɪ'dosɪs] *s* (path.) amiloidosis
amylopsin [,æmɪ'lɑpsɪn] *s* (chem.) amilopsina
an [æn] o [ən] *art indef* (antes de sonido vocal) var. de **a**
Anabaptism [,ænə'bæptɪzəm] *s* anabaptismo
Anabaptist [,ænə'bæptɪst] *adj & s* anabaptista
anabiosis [,ænəbaɪ'osɪs] *s* anabiosis
anabolic [,ænə'bɑlɪk] *adj* anabólico
anabolism [ə'næbəlɪzəm] *s* (biol.) anabolismo
anacardiaceous [,ænə,kɑrdɪ'eʃəs] *adj* (bot.) anacardiáceo
anacardic [,ænə'kɑrdɪk] *adj* (chem.) anacárdico
anachronism [ə'nækrənɪzəm] *s* anacronismo
anachronistic [ə,nækrə'nɪstɪk] o **anachronous** [ə'nækrənəs] *adj* anacrónico
anacoluthon [,ænəko'luθɑn] *s* (*pl:* **-tha** [θə]) (gram.) anacoluto
anaconda [,ænə'kɑndə] *s* (zool.) anaconda
Anacreon [ə'nækrɪɑn] *s* Anacreonte
Anacreontic [ə,nækrɪ'ɑntɪk] *adj* anacreóntico
anadromous [ə'nædroməs] *adj* anadromo
anaemia [ə'nimɪə] *s* (path.) anemia
anaemic [ə'nimɪk] *adj* anémico
anaerobe [æn'ɛrob] o [æn'eərob] *s* anaerobio
anaerobic [,ænɛ'robɪk] o [æn,eə'robɪk] *adj* anaerobio, anaeróbico
anaesthesia [,ænɪs'θiʒə] o [,ænɪs'θiʒɪə] *s* anestesia
anaesthesiologist [,ænɪs,θizɪ'ɑlədʒɪst] *s* anestesiólogo
anaesthesiology [,ænɪs,θizɪ'ɑlədʒɪ] *s* anestesiología
anaesthetic [,ænɪs'θɛtɪk] *adj & s* anestésico
anaesthetist [æ'nɛsθɪtɪst] *s* anestesiador
anaesthetize [æ'nɛsθɪtaɪz] *va* anestesiar
anaglyph ['ænəglɪf] *s* anáglifo
anagnorisis [,ænæg'nɑrɪsɪs] *s* (rhet.) anagnórisis
anagogics [,ænə'gɑdʒɪks] *spl* anagoge o anagogía
anagram ['ænəgræm] *s* anagrama; **anagrams** *spl* anagramas (*juego*)
anagrammatic [,ænəgrə'mætɪk] o **anagrammatical** [,ænəgrə'mætɪkəl] *adj* anagramático
anagrammatism [,ænə'græmətɪzəm] *s* anagramatismo
anal ['enəl] *adj* (anat.) anal
analecta [,ænə'lɛktə] *spl* o **analects** ['ænəlɛkts] *spl* analectas
analeptic [,ænə'lɛptɪk] *adj* analéptico
analgen [æ'nældʒɛn] o **analgene** [æ'nældʒin] *s* (pharm.) analgeno
analgesia [,ænæl'dʒizɪə] *s* (physiol.) analgesia
analgesic [,ænæl'dʒizɪk] *adj & s* analgésico
analog ['ænəlɔg] o ['ænəlɑg] *s* var. de **analogue**
analog computer *s* calculadora analógica
analogical [,ænə'lɑdʒɪkəl] *adj* analógico
analogous [ə'næləgəs] *adj* análogo
analogue ['ænəlɔg] o ['ænəlɑg] *s* análogo; (biol.) análogo
analogy [ə'nælədʒɪ] *s* (*pl:* **-gies**) analogía
analyse ['ænəlaɪz] *va* analizar
analyser ['ænə,laɪzər] *s* analizador
analysis [ə'nælɪsɪs] *s* (*pl:* **-ses** [siz]) análisis
analyst ['ænəlɪst] *s* analista (*analizador; psicoanalista*)
analytic [,ænə'lɪtɪk] *adj* analítico; **analytics** *ssg* geometría analítica; (philos.) analítica
analytical [,ænə'lɪtɪkəl] *adj* analítico
analytic geometry *s* geometría analítica
analyzable ['ænə,laɪzəbəl] *adj* analizable
analyze ['ænəlaɪz] *va* analizar
analyzer ['ænə,laɪzər] *s* analizador; (opt.) analizador
anamniotic [æn,æmnɪ'ɑtɪk] *adj* anamriótico
anamorphosis [,ænə'mɔrfəsɪs] *s* (*pl:* **-ses** [siz]) anamorfosis; (biol. & bot.) anamorfosis
Ananias [,ænə'naɪəs] *s* (Bib.) Ananías
anapaest ['ænəpɛst] *s* anapesto
anapaestic [,ænə'pɛstɪk] *adj* anapéstico
anapest ['ænəpɛst] *s* anapesto
anapestic [,ænə'pɛstɪk] *adj* anapéstico
anaphase ['ænəfez] *s* (biol.) anafase
anaphora [ə'næfərə] *s* (rhet. & astrol.) anáfora
anaphrodisia [æn,æfrə'dɪzɪə] *s* (med.) anafrodisia
anaphrodisiac [æn,æfrə'dɪzɪæk] *adj & s* (med.) anafrodisíaco, antiafrodisíaco
anaphylaxis [,ænəfɪ'læksɪs] *s* (path.) anafilaxis
anaplastic [,ænə'plæstɪk] *adj* anaplástico
anaplasty ['ænə,plæstɪ] *s* (surg.) anaplastia
anaptyxis [,ænæp'tɪksɪs] *s* (phonet.) anaptixis
anarch ['ænɑrk] *s* anarquista
anarchic [æn'ɑrkɪk] o **anarchical** [æn'ɑrkɪkəl] *adj* anárquico
anarchism ['ænərkɪzəm] *s* anarquismo
anarchist ['ænərkɪst] *s* anarquista
anarchistic [,ænər'kɪstɪk] *adj* anarquista
anarchy ['ænərkɪ] *s* anarquía
anasarca [,ænə'sɑrkə] *s* (path.) anasarca
anastatic [,ænəs'tætɪk] *adj* anastático
anastigmatic [æn,æstɪg'mætɪk] *adj* (opt.) anastigmático
anastomose [ə'næstəmoz] *vn* anastomosarse
anastomosis [ə,næstə'mosɪs] *s* (*pl:* **-ses** [siz]) (anat. & biol.) anastomosis
anastomotic [ə,næstə'mɑtɪk] *adj* anastomótico
anastrophe [ə'næstrəfɪ] *s* (gram.) anástrofe
anathema [ə'næθɪmə] *s* anatema; persona anatematizada; persona aborrecida, cosa aborrecida
anathematization [ə,næθɪmətɪ'zeʃən] *s* anatematización
anathematize [ə'næθɪmətaɪz] *va* anatematizar
Anatolian [,ænə'tolɪən] *adj & s* anatolio
anatomic [,ænə'tɑmɪk] o **anatomical** [,ænə'tɑmɪkəl]) *adj* anatómico
anatomist [ə'nætəmɪst] *s* anatomista, anatómico
anatomize [ə'nætəmaɪz] *va* anatomizar
anatomy [ə'nætəmɪ] *s* (*pl:* **-mies**) anatomía
Anaxagoras [,ænæks'ægərəs] *s* Anaxágoras
Anaximander [æ,næksɪ'mændər] *s* Anaximandro
ancestor ['ænsɛstər] *s* antecesor, antepasado
ancestral [æn'sɛstrəl] *adj* ancestral
ancestress ['ænsɛstrɪs] *s* antecesora
ancestry ['ænsɛstrɪ] *s* (*pl:* **-tries**) prosapia, abolengo, alcurnia
Anchises [æn'kaɪsiz] *s* (myth.) Anquises
anchor ['æŋkər] *s* (naut.) ancla o áncora; (horol. & fig.) áncora; (dent.) anclaje; **to cast anchor** echar anclas; **to ride at anchor** estar anclado; **to weigh anchor** levar anclas; *va* (naut.) sujetar con el ancla; asegurar, sujetar, empotrar; *vn* (naut.) anclar, ancorar
anchorage ['æŋkərɪdʒ] *s* anclaje
anchor escapement *s* (horl.) escape de áncora
anchoress ['æŋkərɪs] *s* anacoreta
anchoret ['æŋkərɛt] *s* anacoreta

anchoretic [ˌæŋkəˈrɛtɪk] *adj* anacorético
anchoretism [ˈæŋkərɛtɪzəm] *s* anacoretismo
anchorite [ˈæŋkəraɪt] *s* anacoreta
anchoritic [ˌæŋkəˈrɪtɪk] *adj* anacorético
anchoritism [ˈæŋkəraɪtɪzəm] *s* anacoretismo
anchorless [ˈæŋkərlɪs] *adj* sin ancla; (fig.) inseguro, errante
anchor ring *s* (naut.) arganeo
anchovy [ˈæntʃovɪ] o [ænˈtʃovɪ] *s* (*pl:* **-vies**) (ichth.) alacha, anchoa, anchova, boquerón
ancien régime [ɑ̃sjæ̃·reˈʒim] *s* antiguo régimen
ancient [ˈenʃənt] *adj* antiguo; **the ancients** los antiguos
ancient history *s* la historia antigua; (coll.) cosa vieja
anciently [ˈenʃəntlɪ] *adv* antiguamente
Ancient of Days *s* anciano de los días (*Dios*)
ancillary [ˈænsɪˌlɛrɪ] *adj* ancilar; auxiliar, subordinado
ancon [ˈæŋkɑn] *s* (*pl:* **ancones** [æŋˈkoniz]) (anat. & arch.) ancón
and [ænd], [ənd] o [ən] *conj* y, e; **and so on** o **and so forth** y así sucesivamente
Andalusia [ˌændəˈluʒə] o [ˌændəˈluʃə] *s* Andalucía
Andalusian [ˌændəˈluʒən] o [ˌændəˈluʃən] *adj & s* andaluz
andalusite [ˌændəˈlusaɪt] *s* (mineral.) andalucita
andante [ænˈdæntɪ] o [ɑnˈdɑnte] *s* (mus.) andante
andantino [ˌændænˈtino] o [ˌɑndɑnˈtino] *s* (*pl:* **-nos**) (mus.) andantino
Andean [ænˈdiən] o [ˈændɪən] *adj & s* andino
Andes [ˈændiz] *spl* Andes
andirons [ˈændˌaɪərnz] *spl* morillos
Andorran [ænˈdɔrən] *adj & s* andorrano
Andrew [ˈændru] *s* Andrés
Androcles [ˈændrokliz] *s* Ándrocles
androecium [ænˈdriʃɪəm] *s* (*pl:* **-a** [ə]) (bot.) androceo
androgen [ˈændrədʒən] *s* (biochem.) andrógeno
androgyne [ˈændrodʒɪn] o [ˈændrodʒaɪn] *s* andrógino; (bot.) andrógino
androgynous [ænˈdrɑdʒɪnəs] *adj* andrógino; (bot.) andrógino
android [ˈændrɔɪd] *s* androide (*autómata de forma humana*)
Andromache [ænˈdrɑməkɪ] *s* (myth.) Andrómaca
Andromeda [ænˈdrɑmɪdə] *s* (myth. & astr.) Andrómeda
androphobia [ˌændroˈfobɪə] *s* androfobia
androseme [ænˈdrɑsɪmi] *s* (bot.) androsemo
androsphinx [ˈændrosfɪŋks] *s* (archeol.) androsfinge
androsterone [ænˈdrɑstəron] *s* (biochem.) androsterona
anecdotal [ˈænɪkˌdotəl] *adj* anecdótico
anecdote [ˈænɪkdot] *s* anécdota
anecdotist [ˈænɪkˌdotɪst] *s* anecdotista
anelectric [ˌænɪˈlɛktrɪk] *adj & s* (phys.) aneléctrico
anemia [əˈnimɪə] *s* (path.) anemia
anemic [əˈnimɪk] *adj* anémico
anemometer [ˌænɪˈmɑmɪtər] *s* anemómetro
anemometry [ˌænɪˈmɑmɪtrɪ] *s* anemometría
anemone [əˈnɛmənɪ] *s* (bot.) anemona o anemone
anemoscope [əˈnɛməskop] *s* anemoscopio
anent [əˈnɛnt] *prep* tocante a
anepigraphic [ænˌɛpɪˈgræfɪk] *adj* anepigráfico
aneroid [ˈænərɔɪd] *adj* aneroide
aneroid barometer *s* barómetro aneroide
anesthesia [ˌænɪsˈθiʒə] o [ˌænɪsˈθiʒɪə] *s* anestesia
anesthesiologist [ˌænɪsˌθizɪˈɑlədʒɪst] *s* anestesiólogo
anesthesiology [ˌænɪsˌθizɪˈɑlədʒɪ] *s* anestesiología
anesthetic [ˌænɪsˈθɛtɪk] *adj & s* anestésico
anesthetist [æˈnɛsθɪtɪst] *s* anestesiador
anesthetize [æˈnɛsθɪtaɪz] *va* anestesiar
aneurysm [ˈænjərɪzəm] *s* (path.) aneurisma
aneurysmatic [ˌænjərɪzˈmætɪk] *adj* aneurismático
anew [əˈnju] o [əˈnu] *adv* de nuevo, nuevamente
anfractuosity [ænˌfræktʃʊˈɑsɪtɪ] *s* (*pl:* **-ties**) anfractuosidad
anfractuous [ænˈfræktʃʊəs] *adj* anfractuoso
angaria [æŋˈgɛrɪə] *s* (law) angaria
angel [ˈendʒəl] *s* ángel; (slang) caballo blanco (*persona que provee fondos para una empresa*)
angel cake *s* bizcocho blanco de harina, azúcar y clara de huevo
angelfish [ˈendʒəlˌfɪʃ] *s* (ichth.) angelote, ángel de mar, peje ángel; (ichth.) reina de los ángeles (*Angelichthys ciliaris*)
angelic [ænˈdʒɛlɪk] *adj* angélico o angelical
angelica [ænˈdʒɛlɪkə] *s* (bot.) angélica
angelical [ænˈdʒɛlɪkəl] *adj* var. de **angelic**
Angelic Doctor *s* doctor angélico (*Santo Tomás de Aquino*)
Angelic Salutation *s* salutación angélica
angelin [ˈændʒəlɪn] *s* (bot.) angelín, pangelín
angel sleeve *s* manga de ángel
Angelus [ˈændʒələs] *s* ángelus
anger [ˈæŋgər] *s* ira, cólera; *va* airar, encolerizar
Angevin [ˈændʒɪvɪn] *adj & s* angevino
angina [ænˈdʒaɪnə] o [ˈændʒɪnə] *s* (path.) angina
angina pectoris [ˈpɛktərɪs] *s* (path.) angina de pecho
angiocholitis [ˌændʒɪokoˈlaɪtɪs] *s* (path.) angiocolitis
angiography [ˌændʒɪˈɑgrəfɪ] *s* (anat.) angiografía
angiology [ˌændʒɪˈɑlədʒɪ] *s* angiología
angiosperm [ˈændʒɪoˌspʌrm] *s* (bot.) angiosperma
angiospermous [ˌændʒɪoˈspʌrməs] *adj* (bot.) angiospermo
angle [ˈæŋgəl] *s* ángulo; codo, ángulo de hierro, hierro en ángulo; (fig.) punto de vista; **Angles** *spl* anglos; **at an angle** en ángulo; *vn* pescar con caña; (fig.) intrigar; **to angle for** intrigar por conseguir
angle iron *s* hierro angular, ángulo de hierro
angle of attack *s* (aer.) ángulo de ataque
angle of incidence *s* (phys.) ángulo de incidencia
angler [ˈæŋglər] *s* pescador de caña; (ichth.) pejesapo; (fig.) intrigante
anglesite [ˈæŋgləsaɪt] *s* (mineral.) anglesita
angleworm [ˈæŋgəlˌwʌrm] *s* lombriz de tierra
Anglia [ˈæŋglɪə] *s* Anglia
Anglian [ˈæŋglɪən] *adj & s* anglo
Anglican [ˈæŋglɪkən] *adj & s* anglicano; inglés
Anglicanism [ˈæŋglɪkənɪzəm] *s* anglicanismo
Anglicism [ˈæŋglɪsɪzəm] *s* anglicismo, inglesismo
Anglicization [ˌæŋglɪsɪˈzeʃən] *s* anglicización
Anglicize [ˈæŋglɪsaɪz] *va* inglesar
angling [ˈæŋglɪŋ] *s* pesca con caña
Anglo-American [ˌæŋgloəˈmɛrɪkən] *adj & s* angloamericano, anglonorteamericano
Anglo-Catholic [ˌæŋgloˈkæθəlɪk] *adj & s* anglocatólico
Anglo-Catholicism [ˌæŋglokəˈθɑlɪsɪzəm] *s* anglocatolicismo
Anglo-Egyptian Sudan [ˌæŋglo·ɪˈdʒɪpʃən] *s* Sudán Angloegipcio
Anglo-Indian [ˌæŋgloˈɪndɪən] *adj & s* angloindio
Anglo-Iranian [ˌæŋgloaɪˈrenɪən] *adj & s* angloiranio
Anglomania [ˌæŋgloˈmenɪə] *s* anglomanía
Anglomaniac [ˌæŋgloˈmenɪæk] *s* anglómano
Anglo-Norman [ˌæŋgloˈnɔrmən] *adj & s* anglonormando
Anglophile [ˈæŋglofaɪl] *adj & s* anglófilo
Anglophobe [ˈæŋglofob] *adj & s* anglófobo
Anglophobia [ˌæŋgloˈfobɪə] *s* anglofobia
Anglo-Saxon [ˌæŋgloˈsæksən] *adj & s* anglosajón
Angora [æŋˈgorə] *s* angora (*gato o cabra*)
Angora cat *s* gato de Angora
Angora goat *s* cabra de Angora
angostura [ˌæŋgəsˈtjurə] o [ˌæŋgəsˈturə] *s* angostura (*corteza medicinal*); (pharm.) angosturina (*tónico*)
angostura bark *s* corteza de angostura
angostura bitters *spl* (trademark) (amargo de) angostura
Angoulême [ˌɑ̃ˌguˈlɛm] *s* Angulema
angrily [ˈæŋgrɪlɪ] *adv* airadamente

angry ['æŋgrɪ] *adj* (*comp:* **-grier;** *super:* **-griest**) enojado, airado, encolerizado; tormentoso; (path.) irritado, inflamado; **to become angry at** enojarse de (*una cosa*); **to become angry with** enojarse con o contra (*una persona*)
angstrom ['æŋgstrəm] *s* (phys.) angstrom
anguish ['æŋgwɪʃ] *s* angustia, congoja; *va* angustiar, acongojar
angular ['æŋgjələr] *adj* angular; anguloso (*dícese, p.ej., de las facciones*)
angularity [ˌæŋgjə'lærɪtɪ] *s* (*pl:* **-ties**) angularidad; angulosidad
angular momentum *s* (mech.) momento angular
anhydrid [æn'haɪdrɪd] o **anhydride** [æn'haɪdraɪd] o [æn'haɪdrɪd] *s* (chem.) anhídrido
anhydrite [æn'haɪdraɪt] *s* (mineral.) anhidrita
anhydrous [æn'haɪdrəs] *adj* (chem.) anhidro
anil ['ænɪl] *s* (bot.) añil (*planta, color y tintura*)
anilin ['ænɪlɪn] *s* (chem.) anilina
aniline ['ænɪlɪn] o ['ænɪlaɪn] *s* var. de **anilin**
aniline dyes *spl* colores de anilina
anility [ə'nɪlɪtɪ] *s* (*pl:* **-ties**) ancianidad femenil, senilidad en la mujer
animadversion [ˌænɪmæd'vʌrʒən] o [ˌænɪmæd'vʌrʃən] *s* animadversión
animadvert [ˌænɪmæd'vʌrt] *va* reparar, observar, advertir; *vn* reparar, observar, advertir; **to animadvert on** *ó* **upon** censurar, reprochar
animal ['ænɪməl] *adj & s* animal
animalcule [ˌænɪ'mælkjʊl] *s* animálculo
animal husbandry *s* ganadería
animalism ['ænɪməlɪzəm] *s* animalismo
animalist ['ænɪməlɪst] *s* animalista
animalistic [ˌænɪmə'lɪstɪk] *adj* animalista
animality [ˌænɪ'mælɪtɪ] *s* animalidad
animalization [ˌænɪməlɪ'zeʃən] *s* animalización
animalize ['ænɪməlaɪz] *va* animalizar
animal kingdom *s* reino animal
animal magnetism *s* magnetismo animal
animal spirits *spl* ardor, vigor, vivacidad
animate ['ænɪmɪt] *adj* animado; ['ænɪmet] *va* animar
animated ['ænɪˌmetɪd] *adj* animado, vivo, alegre
animated cartoon *s* película de dibujos, dibujo animado
animation [ˌænɪ'meʃən] *s* animación
animator ['ænɪˌmetər] *s* animador; (mov.) animador
animism ['ænɪmɪzəm] *s* animismo
animist ['ænɪmɪst] *s* animista
animistic [ˌænɪ'mɪstɪk] *adj* animista
animosity [ˌænɪ'mɑsɪtɪ] *s* (*pl:* **-ties**) animosidad
animus ['ænɪməs] *s* ánimo; mala voluntad, odio
anion ['ænˌaɪən] *s* (elec.) anión
anise ['ænɪs] *s* (bot.) anís (*planta y semilla*)
aniseed ['ænɪsid] *s* grano de anís
anisette [ˌænɪ'zɛt] *s* anisete
anisomerous [ˌænaɪ'sɑmərəs] *adj* (bot.) anisómero
anisometric [ænˌaɪso'mɛtrɪk] *adj* (mineral.) anisométrico
anisophyllous [ænˌaɪso'fɪləs] *adj* (bot.) anisofilo
ankle ['æŋkəl] *s* tobillo
anklebone ['æŋkəlˌbon] *s* hueso del tobillo
ankle support *s* (sport) tobillera
anklet ['æŋklɪt] *s* brazalete para el tobillo, ajorca; tobillera (*calcetín corto; abrazadera o vendaje para el tobillo*)
ankylose ['æŋkɪlos] *va* anquilosar; *vn* anquilosarse
ankylosis [ˌæŋkɪ'losɪs] *s* (path.) anquilosis
Ann [æn] o **Anna** ['ænə] *s* Ana
annalist ['ænəlɪst] *s* analista
annals ['ænəlz] *spl* anales
Annamese [ˌænə'miz] *adj* anamita; *s* (*pl:* **-mese**) anamita
annatto [ɑ'nɑto] *s* (bot.) bija (*árbol y colorante*)
annatto tree *s* (bot.) achiote, bija
Anne [æn] *s* Ana
anneal [ə'nil] *va* recocer; (fig.) fortalecer
annealing [ə'nilɪŋ] *s* recocido
annelid ['ænəlɪd] *adj & s* (zool.) anélido
annex ['ænɛks] *s* anexo; pabellón (*edificio*); [ə'nɛks] *va* anexar
annexation [ˌænɛks'eʃən] *s* anexión
annexationism [ˌænɛks'eʃənɪzəm] *s* anexionismo
annexationist [ˌænɛks'eʃənɪst] *adj & s* anexionista
annihilate [ə'naɪɪlet] *va* aniquilar
annihilation [əˌnaɪɪ'leʃən] *s* aniquilación
anniversary [ˌænɪ'vʌrsərɪ] *adj* aniversario; *s* (*pl:* **-ries**) aniversario
anno Domini ['æno'dɑmɪnaɪ] (Lat.) año de Cristo
annonaceous [ˌæno'neʃəs] *adj* anonáceo
annotate ['ænotet] *va* anotar
annotation [ˌæno'teʃən] *s* anotación
annotator ['ænoˌtetər] *s* anotador
announce [ə'naʊns] *va* anunciar
announcement [ə'naʊnsmənt] *s* anuncio, aviso
announcer [ə'naʊnsər] *s* anunciador; (rad.) locutor
annoy [ə'nɔɪ] *va* molestar, fastidiar
annoyance [ə'nɔɪəns] *s* molestia, fastidio
annoying [ə'nɔɪɪŋ] *adj* molesto, fastidioso
annual ['ænjʊəl] *adj* anual; *s* publicación anual; (bot.) planta anual
annually ['ænjʊəlɪ] *adv* anualmente
annual ring *s* (bot.) capa anual
annuitant [ə'njuɪtənt] o [ə'nuɪtənt] *s* censualista, rentista
annuity [ə'njuɪtɪ] o [ə'nuɪtɪ] *s* (*pl:* **-ties**) anualidad; renta vitalicia
annul [ə'nʌl] (*pret & pp:* **-nulled;** *ger:* **-nulling**) *va* anular, invalidar; revocar; destruir
annular ['ænjələr] *adj* anular
annulet ['ænjəlɪt] *s* anillejo, anillete; (her. & zool.) anillo
annulment [ə'nʌlmənt] *s* anulación; revocación; abolición; descasamiento
annulus ['ænjələs] *s* (*pl:* **-li** [laɪ] o **-luses**) (anat., arch., & bot.) anillo
annum ['ænəm] *s* (Lat.) año; **per annum** por año, al año
annunciate [ə'nʌnʃɪet] o [ə'nʌnsɪet] *va* anunciar
annunciation [əˌnʌnsɪ'eʃən] *s* anunciación; (*cap.*) *s* Anunciación
annunciator [ə'nʌnʃɪˌetər] o [ə'nʌnsɪˌetər] *s* anunciador; (elec.) cuadro indicador
annunciator wire *s* alambre para timbres eléctricos
anode ['ænod] *s* (elec.) ánodo
anodic [æn'ɑdɪk] *adj* anódico
anodize ['ænodaɪz] *va* (metal.) anodizar
anodyne ['ænədaɪn] *adj & s* anodino
anodynia [ˌænə'dɪnɪə] *s* anodinia
anoint [ə'nɔɪnt] *va* ungir, untar; (eccl.) ungir
anointed [ə'nɔɪntɪd] *s* ungido
anointment [ə'nɔɪntmənt] *s* ungimiento, untamiento
anomalistic [əˌnɑmə'lɪstɪk] *adj* anomalístico
anomalistic month *s* (astr.) mes anomalístico
anomalistic year *s* (astr.) año anomalístico
anomalous [ə'nɑmələs] *adj* anómalo
anomaly [ə'nɑməlɪ] *s* (*pl:* **-lies**) anomalía
anomuran [ˌæno'mjʊrən] *adj & s* (zool.) anomuro
anon. abr. de **anonymous**
anon [ə'nɑn] *adv* en breve; otra vez
anonym ['ænənɪm] *s* anónimo
anonymity [ˌænə'nɪmɪtɪ] *s* anonimato, anónimo; **to preserve one's anonymity** guardar o conservar el anónimo
anonymous [ə'nɑnɪməs] *adj* anónimo
anopheles [ə'nɑfəliz] *s* (*pl:* **-les**) (ent.) anofeles
anorexia [ˌæno'rɛksɪə] *s* (path.) anorexia
anosmia [æ'nɑzmɪə] *s* (path.) anosmia
another [ə'nʌðər] *adj & pron indef* otro; uno más; **one another** uno a otro, unos a otros
anoxemia [ˌænɑks'imɪə] *s* (path.) anoxemia
ans. abr. de **answer**
Anselm, Saint ['ænsɛlm] San Anselmo
anserine ['ænsəraɪn] o ['ænsərɪn] *adj* ansarino; tonto, necio, mentecato
answer ['ænsər] o ['ɑnsər] *s* respuesta, contestación; explicación; solución (*a un problema o un enigma*); (law) contestación a la demanda; *va* responder a, contestar; resolver (*un problema o un enigma*); **to answer a purpose**

convenir a un designio; **to answer the bell, the door, the telephone** contestar el timbre, la puerta, el teléfono; *vn* responder, contestar; bastar; **to answer back** ser respondón; **to answer for** responder de (*una cosa*); responder por (*una persona*); **to answer to the name of** responder al nombre de; atender (*p.ej., un perro*) por
answerable ['ænsərəbəl] o ['ɑnsərəbəl] *adj* responsable; contestable; soluble
ant [ænt] *s* (ent.) hormiga
antacid [ænt'æsɪd] *adj & s* antiácido
Antaeus [æn'tiəs] *s* (myth.) Anteo
antagonism [æn'tægənɪzəm] *s* antagonismo
antagonist [æn'tægənɪst] *s* antagonista
antagonistic [æn,tægə'nɪstɪk] *adj* antagónico
antagonize [æn'tægənaɪz] *va* oponerse a; enemistar, enajenar
antarctic [ænt'ɑrktɪk] *adj* antártico; *s* tierras antárticas
Antarctica [ænt'ɑrktɪkə] *s* la Antártica o Antártida
antarctic circle *s* círculo polar antártico
Antarctic Continent *s* continente antártico
Antarctic Ocean *s* océano Antártico
Antarctic zone *s* zona antártica
Antares [æn'tɛriz] *s* (astr.) Antarés
ant bear *s* (zool.) oso hormiguero
ante ['æntɪ] *s* puesta, tanto (*en juegos de naipes*); *va* apostar; pagar; *vn* poner su apuesta; pagar su apuesta; pagar su cuota
anteater ['ænt,itər] *s* (zool.) oso hormiguero; (zool.) cerdo hormiguero; mamífero o pájaro que come hormigas
ante-bellum ['æntɪ'bɛləm] *adj* anterior a la guerra, de antes de la guerra
antecedence [,æntɪ'sidəns] *s* antecedencia o antecedente
antecedent [,æntɪ'sidənt] *adj* antecedente; *s* antecedente; (gram., log., & math.) antecedente; **antecedents** *spl* antepasados; antecedentes
antechamber ['æntɪ,tʃembər] *s* antecámara
antechapel ['æntɪ,tʃæpəl] *s* (eccl.) antecapilla
antechoir ['æntɪ,kwaɪr] *s* (arch.) antecoro
antedate ['æntɪ,det] *s* antedata; *va* antedatar; retrotraer; preceder
antediluvian [,æntɪdɪ'luvɪən] *adj* antediluviano
antefix ['æntɪfɪks] *s* (arch.) antefija
antelope ['æntɪlop] *s* (zool.) antílope
antemeridian [,æntɪmə'rɪdɪən] *adj* antemeridiano
antenatal [,æntɪ'netəl] *adj* antenatal
antenna [æn'tɛnə] *s* (*pl:* **-nae** [ni]) (ent.) antena; (*pl:* **-nas**) (rad.) antena
antenna connection *s* (rad.) toma de antena
antenuptial [,æntɪ'nʌpʃəl] *adj* antenupcial
antependium [,æntɪ'pɛndɪəm] *s* (*pl:* **-a** [ə]) (eccl.) antipendio
antepenult [,æntɪ'pinʌlt] *s* antepenúltima
antepenultimate [,æntɪpɪ'nʌltɪmɪt] *adj* antepenúltimo
anterior [æn'tɪrɪər] *adj* anterior
anteriority [,æntɪrɪ'ɔrɪtɪ] *s* anterioridad
anteroom ['æntɪ,rum] o ['æntɪ,rʊm] *s* antecámara
anteversion [,æntɪ'vʌrʒən] o [,æntɪ'vʌrʃən] *s* (path.) anteversión
anthelion [ænt'hilɪən] o [æn'θilɪən] *s* (meteor.) antelio
anthem ['ænθəm] *s* himno; (eccl.) antífona
anthemion [æn'θimɪən] *s* (*pl:* **-a** [ə]) (f.a.) antemio o antemión
anther ['ænθər] *s* (bot.) antera
antheridium [,ænθə'rɪdɪəm] *s* (*pl:* **-a** [ə]) (bot.) anteridio
antherozoid [,ænθərə'zo·ɪd] o ['ænθərəzɔɪd] *s* (bot.) anterozoide
anthesis [æn'θisɪs] *s* (bot.) antesis
anthill ['ænt,hɪl] *s* hormiguero
anthocyan [,ænθo'saɪən] o **anthocyanin** [,ænθo'saɪənɪn] *s* (biochem.) antocianina
anthodium [æn'θodɪəm] *s* (*pl:* **-a** [ə]) (bot.) antodio
anthologist [æn'θɑlədʒɪst] *s* antólogo
anthology [æn'θɑlədʒɪ] *s* (*pl:* **-gies**) antología
Anthony ['ænθənɪ] *s* Antonio
anthophyte ['ænθofaɪt] *s* (bot.) antofita
anthozoans [,ænθo'zoənz] *spl* (zool.) antozoos
anthracene ['ænθrəsin] *s* (chem.) antraceno
anthracite ['ænθrəsaɪt] *s* antracita; *adj* antracitoso
anthracnose [æn'θræknos] *s* (bot.) antracnosis
anthrax ['ænθræks] *s* (path.) ántrax
anthropoid ['ænθropɔɪd] *adj* antropoide; *s* (zool.) antropoideo (*mono antropoideo*)
anthropoidal [,ænθro'pɔɪdəl] *adj* antropoideo
anthropological [,ænθropə'lɑdʒɪkəl] *adj* antropológico
anthropologist [,ænθro'pɑlədʒɪst] *s* antropólogo
anthropology [,ænθro'pɑlədʒɪ] *s* antropología
anthropometric [,ænθropə'mɛtrɪk] o **anthropometrical** [,ænθropə'mɛtrɪkəl] *adj* antropométrico
anthropometry [,ænθro'pɑmɪtrɪ] *s* antropometría
anthropomorphic [,ænθropə'mɔrfɪk] *adj* antropomórfico
anthropomorphism [,ænθropə'mɔrfɪzəm] *s* antropomorfismo
anthropomorphous [,ænθropə'mɔrfəs] *adj* antropomorfo
anthropophagi [,ænθro'pɑfədʒaɪ] *spl* antropófagos
anthropophagy [,ænθro'pɑfədʒɪ] *s* antropofagía
Anthropopithecus [,ænθropopɪ'θikəs] *s* (pal.) antropopiteco
anti ['æntaɪ] o ['æntɪ] *s* (*pl:* **-tis**) (coll.) adversario, contrario
anti-aircraft [,æntɪ'ɛr,kræft] o [,æntɪ'ɛr,krɑft] *adj* antiaéreo
anti-aircraft gun *s* cañón antiaéreo, ametralladora antiaérea
antialcoholism [,æntɪ'ælkəhɔlɪzəm] o [,æntɪ'ælkəhɑlɪzəm] *s* antialcoholismo
antiar ['æntɪɑr] *s* antiar (*goma muy tóxica*)
antiarin ['æntɪərɪn] *s* (chem.) antiarina
antibacterial [,æntɪbæk'tɪrɪəl] *adj* antibactérico
antibiosis [,æntɪbaɪ'osɪs] *s* (biol.) antibiosis
antibiotic [,æntɪbaɪ'ɑtɪk] *adj & s* antibiótico
antibody ['æntɪ,bɑdɪ] *s* (*pl:* **-ies**) (bact.) anticuerpo
anticatarrhal [,æntɪkə'tɑrəl] *adj & s* anticatarral
anticathode [,æntɪ'kæθod] *s* anticátodo
anti-Catholic [,æntɪ'kæθəlɪk] *adj & s* anticatólico
antichlor ['æntɪklor] *s* (chem.) anticloro
antichresis [,æntɪ'krisɪs] *s* (*pl:* **-ses** [siz]) (law) anticresis
antichretic [,æntɪ'kritɪk] *adj* anticrético
Antichrist ['æntɪ,kraɪst] *s* Anticristo
anti-Christian [,æntɪ'krɪstʃən] *adj & s* anticristiano
anticipate [æn'tɪsɪpet] *va* esperar, prever; cumplir, llevar a cabo antes; anticipar, acelerar; anticiparse a; prevenir, impedir; prometerse (*p.ej., un placer*); temerse (*algo desagradable*)
anticipation [æn,tɪsɪ'peʃən] *s* anticipación; esperanza, previsión
anticlerical [,æntɪ'klɛrɪkəl] *adj* anticlerical
anticlericalism [,æntɪ'klɛrɪkəlɪzəm] *s* anticlericalismo
anticlimax [,æntɪ'klaɪmæks] *s* (rhet.) anticlímax; acontecimiento desengañador
anticlinal [,æntɪ'klaɪnəl] *adj* anticlinal
anticline ['æntɪklaɪn] *s* (geol.) anticlinal
anticlinorium [,æntɪklaɪ'norɪəm] *s* (*pl:* **-a** [ə]) (geol.) anticlinorio
anticommunist [,æntɪ'kɑmjʊnɪst] *adj & s* anticomunista
antics ['æntɪks] *spl* cabriolas, gracias, travesuras
anticyclone ['æntɪ,saɪklon] *s* (meteor.) anticiclón
anticyclonic [,æntɪsaɪ'klɑnɪk] *adj* anticiclonal
antidemocratic [,æntɪ,dɛmə'krætɪk] *adj* antidemocrático
antidote ['æntɪdot] *s* antídoto; (fig.) antídoto
antiemetic [,æntɪɪ'mɛtɪk] *adj & s* antiemético
antifederal [,æntɪ'fɛdərəl] *adj* antifederalista
antifederalist [,æntɪ'fɛdərəlɪst] *s* antifederalista
antifreeze [,æntɪ'friz] *s* anticongelante
antifriction [,æntɪ'frɪkʃən] *s* antifricción

antifriction metal *s* metal antifricción
antigen ['æntɪdʒən] *s* (bact.) antígeno
antigenic [ˌæntɪ'dʒɛnɪk] *adj* antigénico
antiglare [ˌæntɪ'glɛr] *adj* antideslumbrante
Antigone [æn'tɪgəni] *s* (myth.) Antígone
antigrippe [ˌæntɪ'grɪp] *adj* antigripal
antihistamine [ˌæntɪ'hɪstəmin] o [ˌæntɪ'hɪstəmɪn] *adj & s* (pharm.) antihistamínico
anti-inflationary [ˌæntɪɪn'fleʃəˌnɛrɪ] *adj* antiinflacionista
anti-Jewish [ˌæntɪ'dʒuɪʃ] *adj* antijudío
antiknock [ˌæntɪ'nɑk] *adj & s* antidetonante
antilabor [ˌæntɪ'lebər] *adj* antiobrero
Antillean [ˌæntɪ'liən] o [æn'tɪlɪən] *adj & s* antillano
Antilles [æn'tɪliz] *spl* Antillas
antilogarithm [ˌæntɪ'lɔgərɪðəm] o [ˌæntɪ'lɑgərɪðəm] *s* (math.) antilogaritmo
antimacassar [ˌæntɪmə'kæsər] *s* antimacasar o paño de adorno
antimatter ['æntɪˌmætər] *s* (phys.) antimateria
antimilitarism [ˌæntɪ'mɪlɪtərɪzəm] *s* antimilitarismo
antimilitarist [ˌæntɪ'mɪlɪtərɪst] *adj & s* antimilitarista
antimissile missile [ˌæntɪ'mɪsɪl] *s* proyectil antiproyectil, proyectil destructor de proyectiles
antimonarchical [ˌæntɪmə'nɑrkɪkəl] *adj* antimonárquico
antimonial [ˌæntɪ'monɪəl] *adj* (chem.) antimonial
antimonite ['æntɪˌmonaɪt] *s* (chem. & mineral.) antimonita
antimony ['æntɪˌmonɪ] *s* (chem.) antimonio
antinode ['æntɪˌnod] *s* (phys.) antinodo
antinomic [ˌæntɪ'nɑmɪk] *adj* antinómico
antinomy [æn'tɪnəmɪ] *s* (*pl:* **-mies**) antinomia
Antioch ['æntɪɑk] *s* Antioquía
Antiochian [ˌæntɪ'okɪən] *adj & s* antioqueno
Antiochus [æn'taɪəkəs] *s* Antíoco
antiparty [ˌæntɪ'pɑrtɪ] *adj & s* antipartido
antipasto [ˌɑntɪ'pɑsto] *s* (*pl:* **-tos**) aperitivo, entremés
antipathetic [ˌæntɪpə'θɛtɪk] o **antipathetical** [ˌæntɪpə'θɛtɪkəl] *adj* antipático; antagónico
antipathy [æn'tɪpəθɪ] *s* (*pl:* **-thies**) antipatía; cosa aborrecida, aversión
antipersonnel [ˌæntɪˌpʌrsə'nɛl] *adj* (mil.) contra personal, contra las personas
antiphlogistic [ˌæntɪflo'dʒɪstɪk] *adj* antiflogístico
antiphon ['æntɪfɑn] *s* (eccl.) antífona
antiphonal [æn'tɪfənəl] *adj & s* antifonal
antiphrasis [æn'tɪfrəsɪs] *s* (rhet.) antífrasis
antipodal [æn'tɪpədəl] *adj* antípoda
antipode ['æntɪpod] *s* antípoda (*el contrario*); **antipodes** [æn'tɪpədiz] *spl* antípodas (*lugares y habitantes*); **Antipodes** [æn'tɪpədiz] *spl* Antípodas (*islas*)
antipodean [ænˌtɪpə'diən] *adj* var. de **antipodal**
antipolio [ˌæntɪ'polɪo] *adj* antipoliomielítico
antipope ['æntɪˌpop] *s* antipapa
antiproton [ˌæntɪ'protɑn] *s* (chem. & phys.) antiprotón
antipyretic [ˌæntɪpaɪ'rɛtɪk] *adj & s* antipirético
antipyrine [ˌæntɪ'paɪrɪn] o [ˌæntɪ'paɪrin] *s* antipirina
antiquarian [ˌæntɪ'kwɛrɪən] *adj & s* anticuario
antiquary ['æntɪˌkwɛrɪ] *s* (*pl:* **-ies**) anticuario
antiquate ['æntɪkwet] *va* anticuar
antiquated ['æntɪˌkwetɪd] *adj* anticuado
antique [æn'tik] *adj* antiguo; anticuado; antiguo por imitación; *s* antigualla
antique dealer *s* anticuario
antique store *s* tienda de antigüedades
antiquity [æn'tɪkwɪtɪ] *s* (*pl:* **-ties**) antigüedad; **antiquities** *spl* antigüedades
antirabic [ˌæntɪ'ræbɪk] *adj* antirrábico
antirachitic [ˌæntɪrə'kɪtɪk] *adj & s* antirraquítico
antireligious [ˌæntɪrɪ'lɪdʒəs] *adj* antirreligioso
antisaloon [ˌæntɪsə'lun] *adj* enemigo de las tabernas, antialcohólico
antiscians [æn'tɪʃənz] *spl* antecos, antiscios
antiscorbutic [ˌæntɪskər'bjutɪk] *adj & s* antiescorbútico
anti-Semite [ˌæntɪ'sɛmaɪt] o [ˌæntɪ'simaɪt] *s* antisemita
anti-Semitic [ˌæntɪsɪ'mɪtɪk] *adj* antisemítico
anti-Semitism [ˌæntɪ'sɛmɪtɪzəm] *s* antisemitismo
antisepsis [ˌæntɪ'sɛpsɪs] *s* antisepsia o antisepsis; antiséptico
antiseptic [ˌæntɪ'sɛptɪk] *adj & s* antiséptico
antiseptically [ˌæntɪ'sɛptɪkəlɪ] *adv* antisépticamente
antislavery [ˌæntɪ'slevərɪ] *adj* antiesclavista
antisocial [ˌæntɪ'soʃəl] *adj* antisocial
anti-Soviet [ˌæntɪ'sovɪɛt] *adj* antisoviético
anti-Spanish [ˌæntɪ'spænɪʃ] *adj* antiespañol
antispasmodic [ˌæntɪspæz'mɑdɪk] *adj* antiespasmódico
Antisthenes [æn'tɪsθəniz] *s* Antístenes
antistrophe [æn'tɪstrəfɪ] *s* antistrofa
antisubmarine [ˌæntɪ'sʌbməˌrin] *adj* antisubmarino
antitank [ˌæntɪ'tæŋk] *adj* antitanque
antithesis [æn'tɪθɪsɪs] *s* (*pl:* **-ses** [siz]) antítesis
antithetic [ˌæntɪ'θɛtɪk] o **antithetical** [ˌæntɪ'θɛtɪkəl] *adj* antitético
antitoxic [ˌæntɪ'tɑksɪk] *adj* antitóxico
antitoxin [ˌæntɪ'tɑksɪn] *s* (bact.) antitoxina
antitrades ['æntɪˌtredz] *spl* vientos antialisios
antitragus [æn'tɪtrəgəs] *s* (*pl:* **-gi** [dʒaɪ]) (anat.) antitrago
antitrust [ˌæntɪ'trʌst] *adj* anticartel
antitwilight [ˌæntɪ'twaɪˌlaɪt] *s* anticrepúsculo
antivenin [ˌæntɪ'vɛnɪn] *s* antiveneno
antiviral [ˌæntɪ'vaɪrəl] *adj* antiviral, antivirulento
antivivisectionist [ˌæntɪˌvɪvɪ'sɛkʃənɪst] *adj & s* antiviviseccionista
antler ['æntlər] *s* cuerna, cornamenta
antlered ['æntlərd] *adj* cornudo
ant lion *s* (ent.) hormiga león
Antoinette [ˌæntwɑ'nɛt] *s* Antonieta
Antoninus [ˌæntə'naɪnəs] *s* Antonino
Antonius [æn'tonɪəs] *s* Antonio
antonomasia [ˌæntəno'meʒə] *s* (rhet.) antonomasia
antonym ['æntənɪm] *s* antónimo
antrum ['æntrəm] *s* (*pl:* **-tra** [trə]) antro; (anat.) antro
antrum of Highmore ['haɪmor] *s* (anat.) antro de Highmoro
Antwerp ['æntwərp] *s* Amberes
anus ['enəs] *s* (anat.) ano
anvil ['ænvɪl] *s* yunque; (anat.) yunque
anxiety [æŋ'zaɪətɪ] *s* (*pl:* **-ties**) ansiedad, inquietud; anhelo
anxiety neurosis *s* (psychoanal.) neurosis de ansiedad
anxious ['æŋkʃəs] *adj* ansioso, inquieto; anhelante; **to be anxious to** + *inf* tener vivos deseos de + *inf*
anxious seat *s* ansiedad, inquietud
any ['ɛnɪ] *adj indef* algún, cualquier; todo; **any place** dondequiera, en cualquier parte; **any time** cuando quiera; alguna vez; *pron indef* alguno, cualquiera; *adv* algo; **not . . . any longer** ya no; **not . . . any more** no . . . más; ya no
anybody ['ɛnɪˌbɑdɪ] *pron indef* alguno, alguien, cualquiera, quienquiera; todo el mundo; **not anybody** ninguno, nadie; *s* (*pl:* **-ies**) cualquiera (*persona de poca importancia*); personaje (*persona de importancia*)
anyhow ['ɛnɪhaʊ] *adv* de cualquier modo; de todos modos; sin embargo
anyone or **any one** ['ɛnɪwʌn] *pron indef* alguno, alguien, cualquiera
anything ['ɛnɪθɪŋ] *pron indef* algo, alguna cosa; todo cuanto; cualquier cosa; **like anything** (coll.) hasta más no poder; **not anything** nada; **anything at all** cualquier cosa que sea; **anything else** cualquier otra cosa; **anything else?** ¿algo más?
anyway ['ɛnɪwe] *adv* de cualquier modo; de todos modos; por lo menos, sin embargo; sin esmero, sin orden ni concierto

anywhere ['ɛnɪhwɛr] *adv* dondequiera, en cualquier parte; adondequiera, a cualquier parte; **not anywhere** en ninguna parte; a ninguna parte
anywise ['ɛnɪwaɪz] *adv* de cualquier modo; del todo
Aonian [e'onɪən] *adj* aonio
aorist ['eərɪst] *s* (gram.) aoristo
aorta [e'ɔrtə] *s* (*pl:* **-tas** o **-tae** [ti]) (anat.) aorta
aortic [e'ɔrtɪk] *adj* aórtico
Ap. abr. de **April**
A.P. o **AP** abr. de **Associated Press**
apace [ə'pes] *adv* aprisa
apache [ə'pɑʃ] o [ə'pæʃ] *s* (*pl:* **apache** o **apaches**) apache (*bandido, salteador*); (*cap.*) [ə'pætʃɪ] *s* apache (*piel roja*)
apanage ['æpənɪdʒ] *s* var. de **appanage**
apart [ə'pɑrt] *adv* aparte; en partes, en pedazos; **to come apart** desunirse; desprenderse; **to fall apart** caerse a pedazos; desunirse; (fig.) ir al desastre; **to live apart** vivir aislado; vivir separados; **to pull apart** separar por tracción; romper en dos; **to set apart** reservar, poner a un lado; **to stand apart** mantenerse apartado; **to take apart** descomponer, desarmar, desmontar; **to tear apart** romper en dos; **to tell apart** distinguir; **apart from** aparte; aparte de, a parte de; *adj* aparte, separado
apartheid [ə'pɑrt·haɪt] *s* política de segregación racial contra los negros en la Unión Sudafricana
apartment [ə'pɑrtmənt] *s* apartamento, departamento, piso
apartment house *s* casa de pisos, casa de departamentos
apathetic [,æpə'θɛtɪk] *adj* apático
apathetically [,æpə'θɛtɪkəlɪ] *adv* apáticamente
apathy ['æpəθɪ] *s* (*pl:* **-thies**) apatía
apatite ['æpətaɪt] *s* (mineral.) apatita
ape [ep] *s* (zool.) mono; (fig.) mona (*persona que imita a las demás*); *va* imitar, remedar
apeak [ə'pik] *adv* (naut.) a pique (*en posición vertical*)
Apelles [ə'pɛliz] *s* Apeles
Apennines ['æpənaɪnz] *spl* Apeninos
apepsia [e'pɛpsɪə] *s* (path.) apepsia
aperient [ə'pɪrɪənt] *adj & s* laxante
aperiodic [e,pɪrɪ'ɑdɪk] *adj* aperiódico
apéritif [ɑperi'tif] *s* aperitivo
aperitive [ə'pɛrətɪv] *adj & s* (med.) aperitivo
aperture ['æpərtʃər] *s* abertura, orificio
apetalous [e'pɛtələs] *adj* (bot.) apétalo
apex ['epɛks] *s* (*pl:* **apexes** o **apices** ['æpɪsiz] o ['epɪsiz]) ápex o ápice; (gram. & hist.) ápex; (math.) ápice
aphaeresis [ə'fɛrəsɪs] *s* (gram.) aféresis
aphanipterous [,æfə'nɪptərəs] *adj* (zool.) afaníptero
aphasia [ə'feʒə] o [ə'feʒɪə] *s* (path.) afasia
aphelion [æ'filɪən] *s* (*pl:* **-ons** o **-a** [ə]) (astr.) afelio
apheresis [ə'fɛrəsɪs] *s* var. de **aphaeresis**
aphid ['efɪd] o ['æfɪd] *s* (ent.) áfido
aphis ['efɪs] *s* (*pl:* **aphides** ['æfɪdiz]) var. de **aphid**
aphlogistic [,eflo'dʒɪstɪk] *adj* aflogístico
aphonia [e'fonɪə] *s* (path.) afonía
aphonic [e'fɑnɪk] *adj* (path. & phonet.) afónico
aphonous ['æfonəs] *adj* áfono
aphorism ['æfərɪzəm] *s* aforismo
aphoristic [,æfə'rɪstɪk] *adj* aforístico
aphoristically [,æfə'rɪstɪkəlɪ] *adv* aforísticamente
aphrodisia [,æfrə'dɪzɪə] *s* (path.) afrodisia
aphrodisiac [,æfrə'dɪzɪæk] *adj & s* afrodisíaco
Aphrodite [,æfrə'daɪtɪ] *s* (myth.) Afrodita; (zool.) Afrodita (*anélido marino*)
aphtha ['æfθə] *s* (*pl:* **-thae** [θi]) (path.) afta
aphthous ['æfθəs] *adj* aftoso
aphthous fever *s* (vet.) fiebre aftosa
aphyllose [e'fɪlos] o **aphyllous** [e'fɪləs] *adj* áfilo
apiary ['epɪ,ɛrɪ] *s* (*pl:* **-ies**) abejar, colmenar
apical ['æpɪkəl] o ['epɪkəl] *adj* apical; (phonet.) apical
apiculture ['epɪ,kʌltʃər] *s* apicultura
apiculturist [,epɪ'kʌltʃərɪst] *s* apicultor
apiculus [ə'pɪkjələs] *s* (*pl:* **-li** [laɪ]) apículo
apiece [ə'pis] *adv* cada uno; por persona
apish ['epɪʃ] *adj* simiesco, monesco; necio, tonto
aplanatic [,æplə'nætɪk] *adj* (opt.) aplanético
aplenty [ə'plɛntɪ] *adv* en abundancia
aplomb [ə'plɑm] *s* aplomo, sangre fría
apocalypse [ə'pɑkəlɪps] *s* revelación; (*cap.*) *s* (Bib.) Apocalipsis
apocalyptic [ə,pɑkə'lɪptɪk] o **apocalyptical** [ə,pɑkə'lɪptɪkəl] *adj* apocalíptico; (fig.) apocalíptico
apocarpous [,æpə'kɑrpəs] *adj* (bot.) apocárpico
apocopate [ə'pɑkəpet] *va* (gram.) apocopar
apocope [ə'pɑkəpɪ] *s* (gram.) apócope
apocrypha [ə'pɑkrɪfə] *spl* libros apócrifos; (*cap.*) *spl* Libros Apócrifos (*de la Biblia*)
apocryphal [ə'pɑkrɪfəl] *adj* apócrifo; (*cap.*) *adj* apócrifo
apocynaceous [ə,pɑsɪ'neʃəs] *adj* (bot.) apocináceo
apodal ['æpədəl] *adj* ápodo
apodictic [,æpə'dɪktɪk] o **apodictical** [,æpə'dɪktɪkəl] *adj* (log.) apodíctico
apodosis [ə'pɑdəsɪs] *s* (*pl:* **-ses** [siz]) (gram.) apódosis
apogee ['æpədʒi] *s* (astr. & fig.) apogeo
apograph ['æpəgræf] o ['æpəgrɑf] *s* apógrafo
Apollinaris water [ə,pɑlɪ'nɛrɪs] *s* agua de Apollinaris
Apollo [ə'pɑlo] *s* (myth.) Apolo
Apollyon [ə'pɑljən] *s* (Bib.) Apollión
apologetic [ə,pɑlə'dʒɛtɪk] *adj* apologético; lleno de excusas; **apologetics** *ssg* apologética
apologetically [ə,pɑlə'dʒɛtɪkəlɪ] *adv* excusándose, pidiendo perdón, con muchas excusas
apologia [,æpə'lodʒɪə] *s* apología
apologist [ə'pɑlədʒɪst] *s* apologista
apologize [ə'pɑlədʒaɪz] *vn* excusarse, disculparse; apologizar; **to apologize for** disculparse de; **to apologize to** disculparse con
apologue ['æpəlɔg] o ['æpəlɑg] *s* apólogo
apology [ə'pɑlədʒɪ] *s* (*pl:* **-gies**) apología; excusa, justificación; expediente
apomorphine [,æpə'mɔrfin] *s* (pharm.) apomorfina
aponeurosis [,æpənju'rosɪs] o [,æpənu'rosɪs] *s* (*pl:* **-ses** [siz]) (anat.) aponeurosis
aponeurotic [,æpənju'rɑtɪk] o [,æpənu'rɑtɪk] *adj* aponeurótico
aponeurotome [,æpə'njurətom] o [,æpə'nurətom] *s* (surg.) aponeurótomo
apophthegm ['æpəθɛm] *s* var. de **apothegm**
apophyge [ə'pɑfɪdʒɪ] *s* (arch.) apófige
apophysis [ə'pɑfɪsɪs] *s* (*pl:* **-ses** [siz]) (anat., geol., & zool.) apófisis
apoplectic [,æpə'plɛktɪk] *adj & s* apoplético
apoplexy ['æpə,plɛksɪ] *s* (path.) apoplejía
aport [ə'port] *adv* (naut.) a babor
apostasy [ə'pɑstəsɪ] *s* (*pl:* **-sies**) apostasía
apostate [ə'pɑstet] o [ə'pɑstɪt] *s* apóstata
apostatize [ə'pɑstətaɪz] *vn* apostatar
apostematous [,æpə'stɛmətəs] *adj* apostematoso
apostle [ə'pɑsəl] *s* apóstol
Apostle of the Gentiles *s* (Bib.) apóstol de los gentiles o las gentes
Apostles' Creed *s* Símbolo de los Apóstoles
apostolate [ə'pɑstəlet] o [ə'pɑstəlɪt] *s* apostolado
apostolic [,æpəs'tɑlɪk] o **apostolical** [,æpəs'tɑlɪkəl] *adj* apostólico
Apostolic Fathers *spl* Padres apostólicos
Apostolic See *s* Sede apostólica
apostrophe [ə'pɑstrəfɪ] *s* (rhet.) apóstrofe; (gram.) apóstrofo
apostrophize [ə'pɑstrəfaɪz] *va* apostrofar
apothecaries' measure *s* sistema de medidas para líquidos usado en los Estados Unidos por los boticarios
apothecaries' weight *s* sistema de pesos usado en los Estados Unidos y la Gran Bretaña por los boticarios
apothecary [ə'pɑθɪ,kɛrɪ] *s* (*pl:* **-ies**) boticario, droguero
apothecary's jar *s* bote de porcelana
apothegm ['æpəθɛm] *s* apotegma (*sentencia breve e instructiva*)
apothem ['æpəθɛm] *s* (geom.) apotema

apotheosis [ə,pɑθɪ'osɪs] o [,æpə'θiəsɪs] *s* (*pl:* **-ses** [siz]) apoteosis
apotheosize [ə'pɑθɪosaɪz] o [,æpə'θiəsaɪz] *va* deificar, endiosar
apozem ['æpəzɛm] *s* (pharm.) apócema
appal [ə'pɔl] (*pret & pp:* **-palled;** *ger:* **-palling**) *va* var. de **appall**
Appalachian [,æpə'letʃən] o [,æpə'lætʃən] *adj* apalache; **Appalachians** *spl* Apalaches (*montes*)
Appalachian Mountains *spl* montes Apalaches
appall [ə'pɔl] *va* espantar, aterrar; desmayar, desanimar
appalling [ə'pɔlɪŋ] *adj* espantoso, aterrador; desanimador
appanage ['æpənɪdʒ] *s* pertenencia, cosa accesoria; dependencia; infantado
apparatus [,æpə'retəs] o [,æpə'rætəs] *s* (*pl:* **-tus** o **-tuses**) aparato; (anat.) aparato
apparatus criticus ['krɪtɪkəs] *s* aparato crítico
apparel [ə'pærəl] *s* ropa, vestido; (naut.) aparejo; (*pret & pp:* **-eled** o **-elled;** *ger:* **-eling** o **-elling**) *va* vestir, ataviar, adornar
apparent [ə'pærənt] o [ə'pɛrənt] *adj* aparente; manifiesto, evidente
apparently [ə'pærəntlɪ] o [ə'pɛrəntlɪ] *adv* aparentemente; evidentemente, por lo visto
apparition [,æpə'rɪʃən] *s* aparición
appeal [ə'pil] *s* súplica, instancia; recurso; solicitud; atracción, interés; (law) apelación; *vn* ser atrayente; **to appeal for** solicitar; **to appeal from** (law) apelar de; **to appeal to** suplicar a (*una persona*); atraer a, interesar a (*una persona*); recurrir a; (law) apelar a
appear [ə'pɪr] *vn* aparecer; parecer; semejar; (law) comparecer
appearance [ə'pɪrəns] *s* aparición, aparecimiento; apariencia, aspecto; (law) comparecencia; **for appearances** por el bien parecer; **to judge by appearances** juzgar por las apariencias; **to keep up appearances** salvar las apariencias
appease [ə'piz] *va* apaciguar
appeasement [ə'pizmənt] *s* apaciguamiento
appeaser [ə'pizər] *s* apaciguador
appellant [ə'pɛlənt] *s* (law) apelante
appellate court [ə'pɛlɪt] o [ə'pɛlet] *s* (law) tribunal de apelación
appellation [,æpə'leʃən] *s* apellidamiento; nombre, título
appellative [æ'pɛlətɪv] *adj & s* (gram.) apelativo
appellee [,æpə'li] *s* (law) apelado
append [ə'pɛnd] *va* añadir, anexar; atar
appendage [ə'pɛndɪdʒ] *s* apéndice; (biol.) apéndice
appendant [ə'pɛndənt] *adj* anexo, adjunto; accesorio; *s* apéndice; accesorio
appendectomy [,æpən'dɛktəmɪ] *s* (*pl:* **-mies**) (surg.) apendectomía o apendicectomía
appendicitis [ə,pɛndɪ'saɪtɪs] *s* (path.) apendicitis
appendicular [,æpən'dɪkjələr] *adj* apendicular
appendix [ə'pɛndɪks] *s* (*pl·* **-dixes** o **-dices** [dɪsiz]) apéndice; (aer.) apéndice; (anat.) apéndice vermiforme
apperception [,æpər'sɛpʃən] *s* (philos.) apercepción
apperceptive [,æpər'sɛptɪv] *adj* (philos.) aperceptivo
appertain [,æpər'ten] *vn* relacionarse; **to appertain to** relacionarse con
appetite ['æpɪtaɪt] *s* apetito; **to whet the appetite** abrir el apetito
appetizer ['æpɪ,taɪzər] *s* apetite, aperitivo
appetizing ['æpɪ,taɪzɪŋ] *adj* apetitoso
Appian Way ['æpɪən] *s* Vía Apia
applaud [ə'plɔd] *va & vn* aplaudir
applause [ə'plɔz] *s* aplauso, aplausos
apple ['æpəl] *s* (bot.) manzano (*árbol*); manzana (*fruto*); *adj* manzanil
apple butter *s* mermelada de manzana espesa y condimentada con especias
applecart ['æpəl,kɑrt] *s* carretilla para ir vendiendo manzanas por las calles; **to upset the applecart** (coll.) revolver la feria
applejack ['æpəl,dʒæk] *s* aguardiente de manzana
apple mint *s* (bot.) madrastra
apple of discord *s* manzana de la discordia
apple of the eye *s* niña del ojo
apple orchard *s* manzanar
apple pie *s* pastel de manzanas
apple-pie order ['æpəl,paɪ] *s* condición perfecta
apple polisher *s* (slang) lameculos, quitamotas
applesauce ['æpəl,sɔs] *s* mermelada de manzana; (slang) halagos insinceros; (slang) música celestial
apple tree *s* manzano
apple worm *s* gusano de la manzana
appliance [ə'plaɪəns] *s* artificio, dispositivo, aparato; aplicación
applicability [,æplɪkə'bɪlɪtɪ] *s* aplicabilidad
applicable ['æplɪkəbəl] *adj* aplicable
applicant ['æplɪkənt] *s* aspirante, pretendiente, candidato, solicitante
application [,æplɪ'keʃən] *s* aplicación; pretensión, candidatura, solicitud
applied [ə'plaɪd] *adj* aplicado
appliqué [,æplɪ'ke] *adj* aplicado; *s* aplicación (*ornamentación sobrepuesta*); *va* aplicar sobrepuesto
appliqué lace *s* encaje de aplicación
apply [ə'plaɪ] (*pret & pp:* **-plied**) *va* aplicar; **to apply oneself** aplicarse; *vn* aplicarse (*ser pertinente*); dirigirse, recurrir; **to apply for** pedir, solicitar
appoggiatura [ə,pɑdʒə'turə] *s* (mus.) apoyatura
appoint [ə'pɔɪnt] *va* nombrar, designar; establecer, sentar; amueblar
appointee [ə,pɔɪn'ti] *s* electo
appointive [ə'pɔɪntɪv] *adj* electivo
appointment [ə'pɔɪntmənt] *s* nombramiento, designación; empleo, puesto; cita
apportion [ə'porʃən] *va* prorratear
apportionment [ə'porʃənmənt] *s* prorrateo
appose [æ'poz] *va* aplicar; yuxtaponer
apposite ['æpəzɪt] *adj* oportuno, conveniente, apropiado
apposition [,æpə'zɪʃən] *s* yuxtaposición; (gram.) aposición
appositive [ə'pɑzɪtɪv] *adj & s* (gram.) apositivo
appraisal [ə'prezəl] *s* tasación, valuación, apreciación
appraise [ə'prez] *va* tasar, valuar, apreciar
appraisement [ə'prezmənt] *s* var. de **appraisal**
appraiser [ə'prezər] *s* tasador, apreciador
appreciable [ə'priʃɪəbəl] *adj* apreciable; sensible
appreciably [ə'priʃɪəblɪ] *adv* apreciablemente; sensiblemente
appreciate [ə'priʃɪet] *va* apreciar; aprobar; comprender; estar agradecido por; aumentar el valor de; *vn* subir en valor
appreciation [ə,priʃɪ'eʃən] *s* aprecio, apreciación; agradecimiento, reconocimiento; plusvalía, aumento en valor
appreciative [ə'priʃɪ,etɪv] *adj* apreciador; agradecido
apprehend [,æprɪ'hɛnd] *va* aprehender, prender; temer; comprender
apprehension [,æprɪ'hɛnʃən] *s* aprehensión; comprensión; aprensión (*miedo, inquietud*)
apprehensive [,æprɪ'hɛnsɪv] *adj* aprensivo o aprehensivo (*receloso, miedoso*); penetrante, perspicaz
apprentice [ə'prɛntɪs] *s* aprendiz; *va* poner de aprendiz
apprenticeship [ə'prɛntɪsʃɪp] *s* aprendizaje; **to serve one's apprenticeship** hacer su aprendizaje
apprise o **apprize** [ə'praɪz] *va* informar, enterar; apreciar, valuar, tasar
approach [ə'protʃ] *s* acercamiento; vía de acceso, vía de entrada; proposición; enfoque (*de un problema*); **approaches** *spl* (mil.) aproches; *va* acercar (*poner más cerca*); abordar; acercarse a; parecerse a; *vn* acercarse, aproximarse
approachability [ə,protʃə'bɪlɪtɪ] *s* accesibilidad
approachable [ə'protʃəbəl] *adj* abordable, accesible
approbation [,æprə'beʃən] *s* aprobación

appropriable [ə'proprɪəbəl] *adj* apropiable
appropriate [ə'proprɪɪt] *adj* apropiado, a propósito; [ə'proprɪet] *va* apropiarse; asignar, destinar
appropriation [ə,proprɪ'eʃən] *s* apropiación; asignación
approval [ə'pruvəl] *s* aprobación; **on approval** a prueba
approve [ə'pruv] *va* aprobar; probar; *vn* aprobar; **to approve of** aprobar
approvingly [ə'pruvɪŋlɪ] *adv* con aprobación
approximate [ə'prɑksɪmɪt] *adj* aproximado, aproximativo; [ə'prɑksɪmet] *va* aproximar; *vn* aproximarse
approximately [ə'prɑksɪmɪtlɪ] *adv* aproximadamente
approximation [ə,prɑksɪ'meʃən] *s* aproximación
appurtenance [ə'pʌrtɪnəns] *s* pertenencia, accesorio
appurtenant [ə'pʌrtɪnənt] *adj* perteneciente, accesorio; *s* pertenencia, accesorio
Apr. abr. de **April**
apraxia [e'præksɪə] *s* (path.) apraxia
apricot ['eprɪkɑt] o ['æprɪkɑt] *s* (bot.) albaricoquero (*árbol*); albaricoque (*fruto*)
April ['eprɪl] *s* abril; *adj* abrileño
April fool *s* el que es burlado el primero de abril; **to make an April fool of** coger por inocente
April Fools' Day *s* primer día de abril, que corresponde al día de engañabobos o día de los santos inocentes—28 de diciembre—en que se coge por inocente a la gente
apriorism [,eprɪ'orɪzəm] *s* (philos.) apriorismo
aprioristic [,eprɪə'rɪstɪk] *adj* apriorístico
apriority [,eprɪ'ɑrɪtɪ] *s* (philos.) aprioridad
apron ['eprən] *s* delantal; mandil (*de obrero; de francmasón*); batiente (*de un dique*); (naut.) albitana; (aer.) rampa (*pavimento frente a un hangar*); **tied to the apron strings of** cosido o pegado a las faldas de
apropos [,æprə'po] *adj* oportuno; *adv* a propósito; **apropos of** a propósito de, acerca de
apse [æps] *s* (arch.) ábside
apsidiole [æp'sɪdɪol] *s* (arch.) absidiolo
apsis ['æpsɪs] *s* (*pl:* **apsides** ['æpsɪdiz] o [æp'saɪdiz]) (astr.) ápside
apsychia [æp'sɪkɪə] o [æp'saɪkɪə] *s* (med.) apsiquia
apt [æpt] *adj* apto; a propósito; dispuesto, propenso, tendente; **he is apt to come this morning** es fácil que venga esta mañana
apterous ['æptərəs] *adj* áptero
aptitude ['æptɪtjud] o ['æptɪtud] *s* aptitud
aptitude test *s* prueba de aptitud
aptness ['æptnɪs] *s* aptitud
Apuleius [,æpjə'liəs] *s* Apuleyo
apyretic [,epaɪ'rɛtɪk] o [,æpaɪ'rɛtɪk] *adj* apirético
apyrexia [,epaɪ'rɛksɪə] o [,æpaɪ'rɛksɪə] *s* (path.) apirexia
aqua ['ækwə] o ['ekwə] *s* (*pl:* **aquas** o **aquae** ['ækwi] o ['ekwi]) (pharm.) agua
aquacade ['ækwə,ked] *s* espectáculo acuático
aqua fortis ['fɔrtɪs] *s* agua fuerte (*ácido nítrico; estampa*)
aquafortist [,ækwə'fɔrtɪst] o [,ekwə'fɔrtɪst] *s* aguafuertista
aqualung ['ækwə,lʌŋ] *s* aparato de buceo autónomo
aquamarine [,ækwəmə'rin] *s* aguamarina (*mineral y color*); *adj* de color aguamarina
aquamarine chrysolite *s* (mineral.) aguamarincrisolita
aquaplane ['ækwə,plen] *s* acuaplano; *vn* correr en acuaplano
aqua regia ['ridʒɪə] *s* (chem.) agua regia
aquarium [ə'kwɛrɪəm] *s* (*pl:* **-ums** o **-a** [ə]) acuario
Aquarius [ə'kwɛrɪəs] *s* (astr.) Acuario
aquatic [ə'kwætɪk] o [ə'kwatɪk] *adj.* acuático; *s* animal acuático; planta acuática; **aquatics** *spl* (sports) deportes acuáticos
aquatint ['ækwə,tɪnt] *s* acuatinta
aqua vitae ['vaɪti] *s* licor alcohólico, aguardiente
aqueduct ['ækwɪdʌkt] *s* acueducto; (anat.) acueducto
aqueous ['ekwɪəs] o ['ækwɪəs] *adj* ácueo, acuoso
aqueous humor *s* (anat.) humor acuoso
aquiline ['ækwɪlaɪn] o ['ækwɪlɪn] *adj* aguileño
aquiline nose *s* nariz aguileña
Aquinas, Saint Thomas [ə'kwaɪnəs] Santo Tomás de Aquino
Aquitaine ['ækwɪten] *s* Aquitania
Aquitanian [,ækwɪ'tenɪən] *adj & s* aquitano
Arab ['ærəb] *adj* árabe; *s* árabe; caballo árabe
arabesque [,ærə'bɛsk] *adj* (f.a.) arabesco; caprichoso; *s* (f.a.) arabesco
Arabia [ə'rebɪə] *s* la Arabia
Arabian [ə'rebɪən] *adj & s* árabe
Arabian Desert *s* Desierto Arábigo
Arabian jasmine *s* (bot.) jazmín de Arabia, sampaguita
Arabian Nights *spl* Mil y una noches
Arabian Sea *s* mar Arábigo
Arabic ['ærəbɪk] *adj* arábigo; *s* árabe o arábigo (*idioma*)
arabic acid *s* (chem.) ácido arábico
Arabic figure *s* cifra arábiga
Arabic numeral *s* número arábigo
Arabism ['ærəbɪzəm] *s* arabismo
Arabist ['ærəbɪst] *s* arabista
Arabize ['ærəbaɪz] *va* arabizar
arable ['ærəbəl] *adj* arable
Araby ['ærəbɪ] *s* (poet.) Arabia
araceous [ə'reʃəs] *adj* (bot.) aráceo
Arachne [ə'ræknɪ] *s* (myth.) Aracne
arachnid [ə'ræknɪd] *s* (zool.) arácnido
arachnidan [ə'ræknɪdən] *adj & s* (zool.) arácnido
arachnoid [ə'ræknɔɪd] *s* (anat.) aracnoides
Aragon ['ærəgɑn] *s* Aragón
Aragonese [,ærəgə'niz] *adj* aragonés; *s* (*pl:* **-nese**) aragonés
aragonite [ə'rægənaɪt] o ['ærəgənaɪt] *s* (mineral.) aragonita, aragonito
aralia [ə'relɪə] *s* (bot. & pharm.) aralia
araliaceous [ə,relɪ'eʃəs] *adj* (bot.) araliáceo
Aral Sea ['ærəl] *s* mar Aral
Aramaean [,ærə'miən] *adj & s* arameo
Aramaic [,ærə'meɪk] *adj & s* aramaico
Araucan [ə'rɔkən] *s* araucano
Araucanian [,ærɔ'kenɪən] *adj & s* araucano
araucaria [,ærɔ'kɛrɪə] *s* (bot.) araucaria
arbalest o **arbalist** ['ɑrbəlɪst] *s* ballesta; (math.) arbalestrilla
arbiter ['ɑrbɪtər] *s* árbitro
arbitrable ['ɑrbɪtrəbəl] *adj* arbitrable
arbitrage ['ɑrbɪtrɪdʒ] *s* arbitraje
arbitrage of exchange *s* arbitraje de cambio
arbitral ['ɑrbɪtrəl] *adj* arbitral
arbitrament [ɑr'bɪtrəmənt] *s* arbitramento
arbitrary ['ɑrbɪ,trɛrɪ] *adj* arbitrario
arbitrate ['ɑrbɪtret] *va & vn* arbitrar
arbitration [,ɑrbɪ'treʃən] *s* arbitraje
arbitrator ['ɑrbɪ,tretər] *s* árbitro, arbitrador
arbitress ['ɑrbɪtrɪs] *s* árbitra
arbor ['ɑrbər] *s* cenador, glorieta, emparrado; (mach.) árbol
Arbor Day *s* (U.S.A.) fiesta del árbol
arboreal [ɑr'borɪəl] *adj* arbóreo
arborescence [,ɑrbə'rɛsəns] *s* arborescencia
arborescent [,ɑrbə'rɛsənt] *adj* arborescente
arboretum [,ɑrbə'ritəm] *s* (*pl:* **-tums** o **-ta** [tə]) jardín botánico de árboles
arboriculture ['ɑrbərɪ,kʌltʃər] *s* arboricultura
arboriculturist ['ɑrbərɪ,kʌltʃərɪst] *s* arboricultor
arboriform ['ɑrbərɪfɔrm] *adj* arboriforme
arborist ['ɑrbərɪst] *s* arbolista
arborization [,ɑrbərɪ'zeʃən] *s* (anat. & mineral.) arborización
arbor vitae ['ɑrbər'vaɪti] *s* (Bib.) árbol de la vida; (bot.) tuya, árbol de la vida; (anat.) árbol de la vida
arbutus [ɑr'bjutəs] *s* (bot.) madroño; (bot.) epigea rastrera
arc [ɑrk] *s* (geom. & elec.) arco; (*pret & pp:* **arced** [ɑrkt] o **arcked;** *ger:* **arcing** ['ɑrkɪŋ] o **arcking**) *vn* (elec.) formar arco
arcade [ɑr'ked] *s* (arch.) arcada
Arcadia [ɑr'kedɪə] *s* la Arcadia
Arcadian [ɑr'kedɪən] *adj* árcade, arcadio; (fig.) arcádico (*simple, campestre*); *s* árcade, arcadio

Arcady [ˈɑrkədɪ] *s* (poet.) la Arcadia
arcane [ɑrˈken] *adj* arcano
arcanum [ɑrˈkenəm] *s* (*pl:* **-nums** o **-na** [nə]) arcano
arch. abr. de **archaic, archaism, archipelago, architect, architectural** y **architecture**
arch [ɑrtʃ] *adj* astuto; travieso, picaresco; principal, insigne; *s* (arch. & anat.) arco; *va* arquear, enarcar; atravesar
archaeological [ˌɑrkɪəˈlɑdʒɪkəl] *adj* arqueológico
archaeologist [ˌɑrkɪˈɑlədʒɪst] *s* arqueólogo
archaeology [ˌɑrkɪˈɑlədʒɪ] *s* arqueología
archaic [ɑrˈkeɪk] *adj* arcaico
archaism [ˈɑrkeɪzəm] *s* arcaísmo
archaist [ˈɑrkeɪst] *s* arcaísta
archaize [ˈɑrkeaɪz] *va & vn* arcaizar
archangel [ˈɑrkˌendʒəl] *s* arcángel
archangelic [ˌɑrkænˈdʒɛlɪk] o **archangelical** [ˌɑrkænˈdʒɛlɪkəl] *adj* arcangélico
archbishop [ˈɑrtʃˈbɪʃəp] *s* arzobispo
archbishopric [ˌɑrtʃˈbɪʃəprɪk] *s* arzobispado
archdeacon [ˈɑrtʃˈdikən] *s* arcediano, archidiácono
archdeaconry [ˌɑrtʃˈdikənrɪ] *s* (*pl:* **-ries**) arcedianato
archdiocese [ˈɑrtʃˈdaɪəsis] o [ˈɑrtʃˈdaɪəsɪs] *s* arquidiócesis
archducal [ˌɑrtʃˈdjukəl] o [ˌɑrtʃˈdukəl] *adj* archiducal
archduchess [ˈɑrtʃˈdʌtʃɪs] *s* archiduquesa
archduchy [ˈɑrtʃˈdʌtʃɪ] *s* (*pl:* **-ies**) archiducado
archduke [ˈɑrtʃˈdjuk] o [ˈɑrtʃˈduk] *s* archiduque
arched [ɑrtʃt] *adj* arqueado, enarcado, combado
archegonium [ˌɑrkɪˈgonɪəm] *s* (*pl:* **-a** [ə]) (bot.) arquegonio
archenemy [ˈɑrtʃˌɛnɪmɪ] *s* (*pl:* **-mies**) archienemigo (*enemigo principal*); Satanás, el enemigo malo
archeological [ˌɑrkɪəˈlɑdʒɪkəl] *adj* arqueológico
archeologist [ˌɑrkɪˈɑlədʒɪst] *s* arqueólogo
archeology [ˌɑrkɪˈɑlədʒɪ] *s* arqueología
Archeozoic [ˌɑrkɪəˈzo·ɪk] *adj* (geol.) arqueozoico; *s* (geol.) era arqueozoica, era arcaica
archer [ˈɑrtʃər] *s* arquero, flechero
archery [ˈɑrtʃərɪ] *s* tiro de flechas, tiro de arco
archetype [ˈɑrkɪtaɪp] *s* arquetipo
archfiend [ˈɑrtʃˈfind] *s* demonio principal; Satanás, el enemigo malo
archiepiscopal [ˌɑrkɪɪˈpɪskəpəl] *adj* arquiepiscopal o arzobispal
archil [ˈɑrkɪl] *s* (bot. & chem.) orchilla
Archimedean [ˌɑrkɪˈmidɪən] o [ˌɑrkɪmɪˈdiən] *adj* arquimédico
Archimedean screw *s* rosca de Arquímedes, tornillo de Arquímedes
Archimedes [ˌɑrkɪˈmidiz] *s* Arquímedes
Archimedes' screw *s* rosca de Arquímedes, tornillo de Arquímedes
archipelago. [ˌɑrkɪˈpɛləgo] *s* (*pl:* **-gos** o **-goes**) archipiélago
architect [ˈɑrkɪtɛkt] *s* arquitecto
architectonic [ˌɑrkɪtɛkˈtɑnɪk] *adj* arquitectónico
architectural [ˌɑrkɪˈtɛktʃərəl] *adj* arquitectural
architecture [ˈɑrkɪˌtɛktʃər] *s* arquitectura
architrave [ˈɑrkɪtrev] *s* (arch.) arquitrabe
archives [ˈɑrkaɪvz] *spl* archivo
archivist [ˈɑrkɪvɪst] *s* archivero, archivista
archivolt [ˈɑrkɪvolt] *s* (arch.) archivolta
archpriest [ˈɑrtʃˈprist] *s* arcipreste
archpriesthood [ˌɑrtʃˈpristhʊd] *s* arciprestazgo
archway [ˈɑrtʃˌwe] *s* arcada
arc lamp *s* lámpara de arco
arc light *s* lámpara de arco; alumbrado de arco
arctic [ˈɑrktɪk] *adj* ártico; **arctics** *spl* chanclos impermeables; (*cap.*) *s* Ártico
arctic circle *s* círculo polar ártico
Arctic Ocean *s* océano Ártico
Arctic Zone *s* zona ártica
Arcturus [ɑrkˈtjʊrəs] o [ɑrkˈtʊrəs] *s* (astr.) Arturo
arc welding *s* soldadura de o por arco
ardency [ˈɑrdənsɪ] *s* ardor
ardent [ˈɑrdənt] *adj* ardiente
ardent spirits *spl* licores espirituosos
ardor [ˈɑrdər] *s* ardor
ardour [ˈɑrdər] *s* (Brit.) var. de **ardor**
arduous [ˈɑrdʒʊəs] o [ˈɑrdjʊəs] *adj* arduo, difícil; enérgico; escabroso, escarpado; riguroso
are [ɛr] o [ɑr] *s* área (*medida agraria*); [ɑr] *segunda persona del sg y primera, segunda y tercera personas del pl del pres de ind de* **be**
area [ˈɛrɪə] *s* área, superficie; extensión; región, comarca; zona; patio; entrada baja de un sótano
areaway [ˈɛrɪəˌwe] *s* entrada baja de un sótano; pasaje angosto entre edificios
areca [ˈærəkə] o [əˈrikə] *s* (bot.) areca (*palma y nuez*)
arena [əˈrinə] *s* arena o arenas
arenaceous [ˌærɪˈneʃəs] *adj* arenáceo
arena theater *s* teatro circular
arenation [ˌærɪˈneʃən] *s* (med.) arenación
aren't [ɑrnt] contracción de **are not**
areola [əˈriələ] *s* (*pl:* **-lae** [li] o **-las**) (anat., bot., path., & zool.) aréola
areolar [əˈriələr] *adj* areolar
areometer [ˌærɪˈɑmɪtər] *s* areómetro
Areopagus [ˌærɪˈɑpəgəs] *s* Areópago
areostyle [əˈriəstaɪl] *s* (arch.) areóstilo
Ares [ˈɛriz] *s* (myth.) Ares
Arethusa [ˌærɪˈθuzə] o [ˌærɪˈθusə] *s* (myth.) Aretusa
argali [ˈɑrgəlɪ] *s* (*pl:* **-li** o **-lis**) (zool.) argalí
argan [ˈɑrgən] *s* argán (*fruto*)
argan tree *s* (bot.) argán, erguen
argent [ˈɑrdʒənt] *adj* argénteo; *s* (her.) argén; (poet.) argento
argentiferous [ˌɑrdʒənˈtɪfərəs] *adj* argentífero
Argentina [ˌɑrdʒənˈtinə] *s* la Argentina
Argentine [ˈɑrdʒəntin] o [ˈɑrdʒəntaɪn] *adj & s* argentino; **the Argentine** la Argentina; (*l.c.*) *adj* argentino (*de plata*)
Argentinean [ˌɑrdʒənˈtɪnɪən] *s* argentino
argil [ˈɑrdʒɪl] *s* arcilla figulina
Argive [ˈɑrdʒaɪv] *adj & s* argivo
Argo [ˈɑrgo] *s* (myth.) Argos (*nave*); (astr.) Argos
Argolic [ɑrˈgɑlɪk] *adj* argólico
Argolis [ˈɑrgəlɪs] *s* la Argólide
argon [ˈɑrgɑn] *s* (chem.) argo o argón
Argonaut [ˈɑrgənɔt] *s* (myth.) argonauta; (*l.c.*) *s* (zool.) argonauta
Argonautic [ˌɑrgəˈnɔtɪk] *adj* (myth.) argonáutico
Argo Navis [ˈnevɪs] *s* (astr.) Navío Argo
Argos [ˈɑrgɑs] *s* Argos (*ciudad de la antigua Grecia*)
argosy [ˈɑrgəsɪ] *s* (*pl:* **-sies**) buque con cargamento valioso; buques valiosos
argot [ˈɑrgo] o [ˈɑrgət] *s* jerga
argue [ˈɑrgju] *va* debatir (*un proyecto*); persuadir con razones; sostener; argüir (*indicar, probar; acusar*); **to argue into** + *ger* persuadir (*a una persona*) a + *inf;* **to argue out of** + *ger* disuadir (*a una persona*) de + *inf; vn* argüir, disputar; **to argue against** argüir contra
arguer [ˈɑrgjʊər] *s* argumentador, argumentista
argument [ˈɑrgjəmənt] *s* argumento; discusión, disputa
argumentation [ˌɑrgjəmɛnˈteʃən] *s* argumentación
argumentative [ˌɑrgjəˈmɛntətɪv] *adj* argumentador; argumentativo
Argus [ˈɑrgəs] *s* (myth.) Argos (*monstruo*); argos (*persona muy vigilante*)
Argus-eyed [ˈɑrgəsˌaɪd] *adj* hecho un argos
argyrol [ˈɑrdʒɪrɔl] *s* (trademark) argirol
aria [ˈɑrɪə] o [ˈɛrɪə] *s* (mus.) aria
Ariadne [ˌærɪˈædnɪ] *s* (myth.) Ariadna
Arian [ˈɛrɪən] *adj & s* arriano
Arianism [ˈɛrɪənɪzəm] *s* arrianismo
arid [ˈærɪd] *adj* árido
aridity [əˈrɪdɪtɪ] *s* aridez
Aries [ˈɛrɪiz] *m* (astr.) Aries
aright [əˈraɪt] *adv* acertadamente; **to set aright** rectificar
aril [ˈærɪl] *s* (bot.) arilo
arillate [ˈærɪlet] *adj* (bot.) arilado
arise [əˈraɪz] (*pret:* **arose;** *pp:* **arisen**) *vn*

levantarse; subir; aparecer, presentarse; **to arise from** provenir de, proceder de
arisen [əˈrɪzən] *pp de* **arise**
Aristides [ˌærɪsˈtaɪdiz] *s* Arístides
aristocracy [ˌærɪsˈtɑkrəsɪ] *s* (*pl:* **-cies**) aristocracia
aristocrat [əˈrɪstəkræt] o [ˈærɪstəkræt] *s* aristócrata
aristocratic [əˌrɪstəˈkrætɪk] o [ˌærɪstəˈkrætɪk] *adj* aristocrático
aristocratically [əˌrɪstəˈkrætɪkəlɪ] o [ˌærɪstəˈkrætɪkəlɪ] *adv* aristocráticamente
Aristophanes [ˌærɪsˈtɑfəniz] *s* Aristófanes
Aristophanic [ˌærɪstəˈfænɪk] *adj* aristofánico; *s* (rhet.) aristofánico
Aristotelian [ˌærɪstəˈtilɪən] *adj & s* aristotélico
Aristotelianism [ˌærɪstəˈtilɪənɪzəm] *s* aristotelismo
Aristotle [ˈærɪsˌtɑtəl] *s* Aristóteles
Aristotle's lantern *s* (zool.) linterna de Aristóteles
arith. abr. de **arithmetic**
arithmetic [əˈrɪθmətɪk] *s* aritmética
arithmetical [ˌærɪθˈmɛtɪkəl] *adj* aritmético
arithmetically [ˌærɪθˈmɛtɪkəlɪ] *adv* aritméticamente
arithmetical progression *s* progresión aritmética
arithmetician [əˌrɪθməˈtɪʃən] o [ˌærɪθməˈtɪʃən] *s* aritmético
arithmomania [əˌrɪθməˈmenɪə] *s* aritmomanía
arithmometer [ˌærɪθˈmɑmɪtər] *s* aritmómetro
Arius [əˈraɪəs] o [ˈɛrɪəs] *s* Arrio
Ariz. abr. de **Arizona**
Ark. abr. de **Arkansas**
ark [ɑrk] *s* (Bib.) arca de Noé; lanchón; arca, caja
ark of the covenant *s* (Bib.) arca de la alianza
arkose [ɑrˈkos] *s* arcosa
arm [ɑrm] *s* brazo (*del cuerpo, de una silla, del mar, de la ley, etc.*); arma; ejército (*cada una de las tres ramas de las fuerzas militares*); **in arms** de pecho, de teta (*dícese de un niño*); **to arms!** ¡a las armas!; **to bear arms** llevar las armas; **to be the right arm of** ser el brazo derecho de; **to be up in arms** alzarse en armas, estar en armas; **to carry arms** tener armas consigo; **to keep at arm's length** mantener a distancia; mantenerse a distancia; **to lay down one's arms** rendir las armas; **to present arms** presentar armas; **to rise up in arms** alzarse en armas; **to take up arms** tomar (las) armas; **under arms** sobre las armas; **with arms folded** de brazos cruzados; **with open arms** con los brazos abiertos; **arm in arm** de bracero, asidos del brazo; **arm's reach** alcance del brazo; *va* armar; acorazar; *vn* armarse
armada [ɑrˈmɑdə] o [ɑrˈmedə] *s* armada; **the Armada** la Armada Invencible
armadillo [ˌɑrməˈdɪlo] *s* (*pl:* **-los**) (zool.) armadillo
Armageddon [ˌɑrməˈgɛdən] *s* (Bib.) Armagedón (*lugar de grande y terrible conflicto*); (fig.) lucha suprema
armament [ˈɑrməmənt] *s* armamento; *adj* armamentista
armament race *s* carrera de los armamentos, carrera armamentista
armature [ˈɑrmətʃər] *s* armadura; (zool.) coraza; (elec.) armadura (*de imán, condensador, motor, etc.*); (elec.) inducido (*órgano giratorio de dínamo o motor*); (elec.) coraza alambrada
armature winding *s* (elec.) arrollamiento del inducido
arm band *s* brazal
armchair [ˈɑrmˌtʃɛr] *s* sillón, silla de brazos
armed [ɑrmd] *adj* armado; (her.) armado; **armed attack** ataque a mano armada
armed forces *spl* fuerzas armadas
Armenia [ɑrˈminɪə] *s* Armenia
Armenian [ɑrˈminɪən] *adj & s* armenio
armet [ˈɑrmɛt] *s* almete
armful [ˈɑrmfʊl] *s* brazado
armhole [ˈɑrmˌhol] *s* sobaquera; (anat.) sobaco, hueco de la axila
armillary [ˈɑrmɪˌlɛrɪ] o [ɑrˈmɪlərɪ] *adj* armilar
armillary sphere *s* esfera armilar
Arminian [ɑrˈmɪnɪən] *adj & s* arminiano
Arminianism [ɑrˈmɪnɪənɪzəm] *s* arminianismo
Arminius [ɑrˈmɪnɪəs] *s* Arminio
armistice [ˈɑrmɪstɪs] *s* armisticio
armless [ˈɑrmlɪs] *adj* inerme; sin brazos
armlet [ˈɑrmlɪt] *s* brazalete; brazal o avambrazo (*de la armadura*); pequeño brazo del mar
armload [ˈɑrmˌlod] *s* brazado
armor [ˈɑrmər] *s* armadura; coraza, blindaje; *va* acorazar, blindar
armor-bearer [ˈɑrmərˌbɛrər] *s* armígero
armored car *s* (mil.) carro blindado
armorer [ˈɑrmərər] *s* armero
armorial [ɑrˈmorɪəl] *adj* heráldico; *s* armorial
armorial bearings *spl* escudo de armas
armor-piercing [ˈɑrmərˌpɪrsɪŋ] *adj* perforante
armor plate *s* plancha de blindaje
armor-plate [ˈɑrmərˌplet] *va* acorazar, blindar
armory [ˈɑrmərɪ] *s* (*pl:* **-ies**) armería (*fábrica de armas; arte del armero*); arsenal; cuartel; (her.) armería
armour [ˈɑrmər] *s & va* (Brit.) var. de **armor**
armpit [ˈɑrmˌpɪt] *s* (anat.) sobaco, hueco de la axila
armrack [ˈɑrmˌræk] *s* armero (*aparato para tener las armas*)
armrest [ˈɑrmˌrɛst] *s* apoyabrazos
arm signal *s* (naut.) señal de brazos
army [ˈɑrmɪ] *s* (*pl:* **-mies**) ejército; (fig.) ejército; *adj* castrense
army chaplain *s* capellán de ejército, capellán castrense
army corps *s* (mil.) cuerpo de ejército
arnica [ˈɑrnɪkə] *s* (bot. & pharm.) árnica
Arnold [ˈɑrnəld] *s* Arnaldo
aroma [əˈromə] *s* aroma, fragancia
aromacity [ˌærəˈmæsɪtɪ] *s* aromaticidad
aromatic [ˌærəˈmætɪk] *adj* aromático; *s* (bot.) aromática; (chem. & med.) aromático
aromatization [əˌromətɪˈzeʃən] *s* aromatización
aromatize [əˈromətaɪz] *va* aromatizar
arose [əˈroz] *pret de* **arise**
around [əˈraʊnd] *adv* alrededor, a la redonda, en torno; a la vuelta; en la dirección opuesta; por todos lados; *prep* alrededor de, en torno de; cerca de; por todos lados de; a la vuelta de (*la esquina*)
arouse [əˈraʊz] *va* mover, excitar, incitar; despertar
arpeggio [ɑrˈpɛdʒo] *s* (*pl:* **-gios**) (mus.) arpegio
arrack [ˈærək] *s* raque (*aguardiente*)
arraign (əˈren] *va* acusar, denunciar; (law) presentar al tribunal
arraignment [əˈrenmənt] *s* acusación, denuncia; (law) presentación al tribunal
arrange [əˈrendʒ] *va* disponer, arreglar; (mus.) adaptar, refundir
arrangement [əˈrendʒmənt] *s* disposición, arreglo; (mus.) adaptación, refundición
arrant [ˈærənt] *adj* redomado, consumado; descarado, infame
arras [ˈærəs] *s* tapicería de Arrás
array [əˈre] *s* orden; orden de batalla; adorno, atavío; *va* poner en orden; poner en orden de batalla; adornar, ataviar
arrearage [əˈrɪrɪdʒ] *s* demora, tardanza; deudas; reserva
arrears [əˈrɪrz] *spl* atrasos; trabajo no acabado; **in arrears** atrasado en pagos
arrest [əˈrɛst] *s* arresto, prisión; parada, detención; **under arrest** bajo arresto; *va* arrestar; parar, detener; atraer (*la atención*)
arrester [əˈrɛstər] *s* detenedor; (elec.) pararrayos; (elec.) apagachispas; (mach.) detenedor
arresting [əˈrɛstɪŋ] *adj* impresionante
arrhizal [əˈraɪzəl] *adj* (bot.) arrizo
arrhythmia [əˈrɪθmɪə] *s* (path.) arritmia
arrhythmic [əˈrɪðmɪk] o [əˈrɪθmɪk] *adj* arrítmico
arris [ˈærɪs] *s* (arch.) arista
arrival [əˈraɪvəl] *s* llegada; llegado (*persona que llega*)
arrive [əˈraɪv] *vn* llegar; tener éxito; **to arrive at** llegar a

arrogance ['ærəgəns] *s* arrogancia
arrogant ['ærəgənt] *adj* arrogante
arrogate ['æroget] *va* arrogarse; atribuir; **to arrogate to oneself** arrogarse
arrogation [,æro'geʃən] *s* arrogación; atribución
arrow ['æro] *s* flecha
arrowhead ['æro,hɛd] *s* punta de flecha; (bot.) sagitaria, saetilla
arrowroot ['æro,rut] o ['æro,rʊt] *s* (bot.) maranta; fécula de maranta, arrurruz
arrowweed ['æro,wid] *s* (bot.) cachanilla
arrowwood ['æro,wʊd] *s* (bot.) viburno; (bot.) cachanilla; (bot.) arraclán, frángula
arrowy ['æro·ɪ] o ['ærəwɪ] *adj* aflechado; (fig.) veloz, cortante, penetrante
arsenal ['ɑrsɪnəl] *s* arsenal
arsenate ['ɑrsɪnet] o ['ɑrsɪnɪt] *s* (chem.) arseniato
arsenic ['ɑrsɪnɪk] *s* (chem. & mineral.) arsénico; [ɑr'sɛnɪk] *adj* (chem.) arsénico
arsenic acid *s* (chem.) ácido arsénico
arsenical [ɑr'sɛnɪkəl] *adj* arsenical
arsenide ['ɑrsɪnaɪd] o ['ɑrsɪnɪd] *s* (chem.) arseniuro
arsenious [ɑr'siniəs] *adj* (chem.) arsenioso
arsenite ['ɑrsɪnaɪt] *s* (chem.) arsenito
arson ['ɑrsən] *s* incendio premeditado, delito de incendio
arsphenamine [,ɑrsfɛnə'min] o [,ɑrsfɛ'næmɪn] *s* (pharm.) arsfenamina
art. abr. de **article**
art [ɑrt] *s* arte; *segunda persona del sg del pres de ind de* **be**
Artaxerxes [,ɑrtə'zɛrksiz] *s* Artajerjes
Artemis ['ɑrtɪmɪs] *s* (myth.) Artemis o Artemisa
arterial [ɑr'tɪrɪəl] *adj* arterial
arterialization [ɑr,tɪrɪəlɪ'zeʃən] *s* arterialización
arterialize [ɑr'tɪrɪəlaɪz] *va* arterializar
arterial tension *s* (med.) tensión arterial o sanguínea
arteriole [ɑr'tɪrɪol] *s* arteriola
arteriosclerosis [ɑr,tɪrɪosklɪ'rosɪs] *s* (path.) arteriosclerosis
arterious [ɑr'tɪrɪəs] *adj* arterioso
arteritis [,ɑrtə'raɪtɪs] *s* (path.) arteritis
artery ['ɑrtərɪ] *s* (*pl:* **-ies**) (anat.) arteria; (fig.) arteria (*gran vía*)
artesian well [ɑr'tiʒən] *s* pozo artesiano
artful ['ɑrtfəl] *adj* mañoso, astuto, artificioso; artificial; artístico; diestro, ingenioso
arthritic [ɑr'θrɪtɪk] *adj & s* artrítico
arthritis [ɑr'θraɪtɪs] *s* (path.) artritis
arthromere ['ɑrθromɪr] *s* (zool.) artrómera
arthropod ['ɑrθrəpɑd] *adj & s* (zool.) artrópodo
Arthur ['ɑrθər] *s* Arturo; **King Arthur** el rey Arturo, el rey Artús
Arthurian [ɑr'θʊrɪən] *adj* arturiano o artúrico
Arthurian Cycle *s* (lit.) ciclo de Artús
artichoke ['ɑrtɪtʃok] *s* (bot.) alcachofa (*planta y su piña*)
article ['ɑrtɪkəl] *s* artículo; **an article of clothing** una prenda; **an article of food** un alimento; **an article of furniture** un mueble; **an article of luggage** un bulto de equipaje; *va & vn* articular
articular [ɑr'tɪkjələr] *adj* articular
articulate [ɑr'tɪkjəlɪt] *adj* articulado; claro, distinto; capaz de hablar; *s* (zool.) articulado; [ɑr'tɪkjəlet] *va* articular; *vn* articularse
articulation [ɑr,tɪkjə'leʃən] *s* articulación; (anat., bot., zool., & phonet.) articulación
artifact ['ɑrtɪfækt] *s* artefacto; (biol.) artefacto
artifice ['ɑrtɪfɪs] *s* artificio
artificer [ɑr'tɪfɪsər] *s* artífice; (mil.) artificiero
artificial [,ɑrtɪ'fɪʃəl] *adj* artificial
artificial insemination *s* inseminación artificial
artificiality [,ɑrtɪ,fɪʃɪ'ælɪtɪ] *s* (*pl:* **-ties**) falta de naturalidad, afectación; cosa artificial
artillerist [ɑr'tɪlərɪst] *s* artillero
artillery [ɑr'tɪlərɪ] *s* artillería
artilleryman [ɑr'tɪlərɪmən] *s* (*pl:* **-men**) artillero
artiodactyl o **artiodactyle** [,ɑrtɪo'dæktɪl] *adj & s* (zool.) artiodáctilo
artisan ['ɑrtɪzən] *s* artesano
artist ['ɑrtɪst] *s* artista
artistic [ɑr'tɪstɪk] *adj* artístico
artistically [ɑr'tɪstɪkəlɪ] *adv* artísticamente
artistry ['ɑrtɪstrɪ] *s* arte, habilidad artística; obra del artista
artless ['ɑrtlɪs] *adj* sencillo, natural, sin arte; chabacano; imperito
art paper *s* papel cuché
arts and crafts *spl* artes y oficios
arty ['ɑrtɪ] *adj* (*comp:* **-ier;** *super:* **-iest**) (coll.) ostentosamente artístico
arum ['ɛrəm] *s* (bot.) aro; (bot.) aro de Etiopía
arum lily *s* (bot.) aro de Etiopía
Aryan ['ɛrɪən] o ['ɑrjən] *adj & s* ario
as [æz] o [əz] *pron rel* que; **the same as** el mismo que; **such as** tal cual; *adv* tan; **so as to** + *inf* para + *inf;* **as . . . as** tan . . . como; **as far as** hasta, hasta donde; **as far as he is concerned** por lo que le toca a él; **as far as I know** que yo sepa; **as for** en cuanto a; **as if** como si; **as if to** + *inf* como para + *inf;* **as long as** mientras que; ya que; **as many as** tantos como; **as much as** tanto como; **as of** en el día de; **as per** según; **as regards** en cuanto a; **as soon as** tan pronto como; **as soon as possible** cuanto antes, lo más pronto posible; **as though** como si; **as to** en cuanto a; **as well** también; **as well as** así como; **as yet** hasta ahora; *conj* como; que, ya que; a medida que; **all the more** (o **less**) **. . . (in proportion) as . . . more** (o **less**) tanto más (o menos) . . . cuanto más (o menos); **as it seems** por lo visto, según parece; **as it were** por decirlo así; *prep* por, como; **as a rule** por regla general
asafetida o **asafoetida** [,æsə'fɛtɪdə] *s* asafétida o asa fétida
asarabacca [,æsərə'bækə] *s* (bot.) asarabácara o ásaro
asbestos o **asbestus** [æs'bɛstəs] *s* asbesto; *adj* asbestino
ascarid ['æskərɪd] *s* (zool.) ascáride
ascend [ə'sɛnd] *va* subir (*p.ej., una cuesta*); **to ascend the throne** empuñar el cetro; *vn* ascender
ascendance [ə'sɛndəns] o **ascendancy** [ə'sɛndənsɪ] *s* ascendiente (*poder, influjo*); dominio, ventaja
ascendant [ə'sɛndənt] *adj* ascendente; predominante; *s* ascendiente (*poder, influjo*); (astrol.) ascendiente; **in the ascendant** predominante, con influencia cada vez mayor, ganando poder
ascendence [ə'sɛndəns] o **ascendency** [ə'sɛndənsɪ] *s* var. de **ascendance**
ascendent [ə'sɛndənt] *adj & s* var. de **ascendant**
ascension [ə'sɛnʃən] *s* ascensión; (*cap.*) *s* Ascensión (*subida de Cristo; fiesta; isla en el Atlántico*)
ascensional [ə'sɛnʃənəl] *adj* ascensional
Ascension Day *s* la Ascensión, fiesta de la Ascensión
ascent [ə'sɛnt] *s* ascensión, subida; ascenso, promoción
ascertain [,æsər'ten] *va* averiguar
ascertainable [,æsər'tenəbəl] *adj* averiguable
ascertainment [,æsər'tenmənt] *s* averiguación
ascetic [ə'sɛtɪk] *adj* ascético; *s* asceta
asceticism [ə'sɛtɪsɪzəm] *s* ascetismo
ascians ['æʃɪənz] o ['æʃənz] *spl* ascios
ascidian [ə'sɪdɪən] *s* (zool.) ascidia
ascites [ə'saɪtiz] *s* (path.) ascitis
Asclepius [æs'klipɪəs] *s* (myth.) Asclepio
ascomycete [,æskomaɪ'sit] *s* (bot.) ascomiceto
ascon ['æskɑn] *s* (zool.) ascón
ascorbic acid [ə'skɔrbɪk] *s* (biochem.) ácido ascórbico
ascospore ['æskospor] *s* (bot.) ascospora
ascot ['æskət] *s* corbata a la inglesa
ascribable [ə'skraɪbəbəl] *adj* atribuíble
ascribe [ə'skraɪb] *va* atribuir
ascription [ə'skrɪpʃən] *s* atribución
ascus ['æskəs] *s* (*pl:* **asci** ['æsaɪ]) (bot.) asca
asepsis [ə'sɛpsɪs] o [e'sɛpsɪs] *s* (med.) asepsia
aseptic [ə'sɛptɪk] o [e'sɛptɪk] *adj* aséptico
asexual [e'sɛkʃʊəl] *adj* asexual
ash [æʃ] *s* ceniza; (bot.) fresno; **ashes** *spl* ceniza, cenizas; (fig.) cenizas (*restos mortales*)

ashamed [ə'ʃemd] *adj* avergonzado; **to be ashamed** tener vergüenza; **to be ashamed to** + *inf* tener vergüenza de + *inf*
ash can *s* recipiente de hojalata para ceniza
ashen ['æʃən] *adj* ceniciento; fresnal
ash fire *s* borrajo, rescoldo
ashlar o **ashler** ['æʃlər] *s* sillar; sillería
ashman ['æʃ,mæn] *s* (*pl:* **-men**) basurero
ashore [ə'ʃor] *adv* en tierra, a tierra; **to come ashore** o **to go ashore** desembarcar; **to run ashore** encallar, varar
ashpan ['æʃ,pæn] *s* cenicero, guardacenizas
ashpit ['æʃ,pɪt] *s* cenizal, foso para cenizas
ash tray *s* cenicero
Ash Wednesday *s* miércoles de ceniza
ashy ['æʃɪ] *adj* cenizoso
Asia ['eʒə] o ['eʃə] *s* Asia
Asia Minor *s* el Asia Menor
Asian ['eʒən] o ['eʃən] o **Asiatic** [,eʒɪ'ætɪk] o [,eʃɪ'ætɪk] *adj* & *s* asiático
Asiatic cholera *s* (path.) cólera asiático
Asiaticism [,eʒɪ'ætɪsɪzəm] o [,eʃɪ'ætɪsɪzəm] *s* asiaticismo
aside [ə'saɪd] *adv* aparte, a un lado; **to step aside** hacerse a un lado, quitarse de en medio; **aside from** además de; *s* aparte (*observación*)
asinine ['æsɪnaɪn] *adj* tonto, necio
asininity [,æsɪ'nɪnɪtɪ] *s* (*pl:* **-ties**) asnería
ask [æsk] o [ɑsk] *va* pedir (*suplicar, exigir*); preguntar (*hacer preguntas a*); hacer (*una pregunta*); invitar; **to ask someone for something** pedir algo a alguien; **to ask someone something** preguntar algo a alguien; **to ask someone to** + *inf* pedir a alguien que + *subj;* invitar a alguien a + *inf; vn* pedir; preguntar; **to ask about, after** o **for** preguntar por; **to ask for** pedir; **to ask for it** (coll.) buscársela
askance [ə'skæns] o **askant** [ə'skænt] *adv* al sesgo, de soslayo; sospechosamente, con desdén
askew [ə'skju] *adj* sesgado, oblicuo; *adv* al sesgo, oblicuamente; con desdén
asking ['æskɪŋ] o ['ɑskɪŋ] *s* ruego, petición; **for the asking** sin más que pedirlo
aslant [ə'slænt] o [ə'slɑnt] *adv* oblicuamente; *prep* a través de
asleep [ə'slip] *adj* dormido; muerto, entumecido; **to fall asleep** dormirse
aslope [ə'slop] *adv* en declive
Asmodeus [,æzmə'diəs] o [,æsmə'diəs] *s* Asmodeo
asp [æsp] *s* (zool.) áspid; (poet.) tiemblo (*árbol*)
asparagus [ə'spærəgəs] *s* (bot.) espárrago (*planta y tallos*); espárragos (*tallos que se comen*)
asparkle [ə'spɑrkəl] *adj* centelleante
aspect ['æspɛkt] *s* aspecto; (astr., astrol. & gram.) aspecto
aspen ['æspən] *s* (bot.) álamo temblón, tiemblo; *adj* tremulante
aspergillum [,æspər'dʒɪləm] *s* (*pl:* **-la** [lə] o **-lums**) (eccl.) hisopo
asperity [æs'pɛrɪtɪ] *s* (*pl:* **-ties**) aspereza
asperse [ə'spʌrs] *va* difamar, calumniar; asperjar
aspersion [ə'spʌrʒən] o [ə'spʌrʃən] *s* difamación, calumnia; aspersión (*rociamiento*); **to cast aspersions on** insinuar calumnias contra
asphalt ['æsfɔlt] o ['æsfælt] *s* asfalto; (mineral.) asfalto; *adj* asfaltado; *va* asfaltar
asphaltic [æs'fɔltɪk] o [æs'fæltɪk] *adj* asfáltico
asphaltum [æs'fæltəm] *s* (mineral.) asfalto
asphodel ['æsfədɛl] *s* (bot.) asfódelo
asphyxia [æs'fɪksɪə] *s* (path.) asfixia
asphyxiate [æs'fɪksɪet] *va* asfixiar
asphyxiation [æs,fɪksɪ'eʃən] *s* asfixia
aspic ['æspɪk] *s* (zool.) áspid; manjar de gelatina, carne picada, jugo de tomate, etc.
aspidistra [,æspɪ'dɪstrə] *s* (bot.) aspidistra
aspirant [ə'spaɪrənt] o ['æspɪrənt] *s* pretendiente, candidato
aspirate ['æspɪrɪt] *adj* (phonet.) aspirado; *s* (phonet.) aspirada (*letra*); ['æspɪret] *va* (phonet.) aspirar
aspiration [,æspɪ'reʃən] *s* aspiración
aspirator ['æspɪ,retər] *s* aspirador
aspire [ə'spaɪr] *vn* aspirar; elevarse; **to aspire after** o **to** aspirar a; **to aspire to** + *inf* aspirar a + *inf*
aspirin ['æspɪrɪn] *s* (pharm.) aspirina
asquint [ə'skwɪnt] *adv* de soslayo
ass [æs] *s* asno; (fig.) asno
assafetida o **assafoetida** [,æsə'fɛtɪdə] *s* var. de **asafetida**
assagai ['æsəgaɪ] *s* azagaya
assail [ə'sel] *va* asaltar, acometer
assailable [ə'seləbəl] *adj* atacable
assailant [ə'selənt] *s* asaltador, asaltante
assassin [ə'sæsɪn] *s* asesino
assassinate [ə'sæsɪnet] *va* asesinar
assassination [ə,sæsɪ'neʃən] *s* asesinato
assassin bug *s* (ent.) reduvio
assault [ə'sɔlt] *s* asalto; *va* asaltar
assault and battery *spl* (law) vías de hecho, violencias
assay [ə'se] o ['æse] *s* ensaye; muestra de ensaye; [ə'se] *va* ensayar (*mineral, aleación, etc.*); apreciar
assayer [ə'seər] *s* ensayador, contraste, quilatador
assemblage [ə'sɛmblɪdʒ] *s* asamblea; reunión (*de personas o cosas*); (mach.) montaje
assemble [ə'sɛmbəl] *va* reunir; (mach.) armar, montar; *vn* reunirse
assembly [ə'sɛmblɪ] *s* (*pl:* **-blies**) asamblea; reunión (*de personas o cosas*); (mach.) montaje, armadura; (mil.) asamblea
assembly hall *s* aula magna, salón de sesiones, paraninfo
assembly line *s* línea de montaje
assemblyman [ə'sɛmblɪmən] *s* (*pl:* **-men**) asambleísta
assembly plant *s* fábrica de montaje
assembly room *s* sala de reunión; (mach.) taller de montaje
assent [ə'sɛnt] *s* asenso; *vn* asentir
assert [ə'sʌrt] *va* afirmar, aseverar, declarar; **to assert oneself** hacer valer sus derechos
assertion [ə'sʌrʃən] *s* aserción
assertive [ə'sʌrtɪv] *adj* asertivo; agresivo
assess [ə'sɛs] *va* gravar (*una propiedad inmueble*); fijar (*daños y perjuicios*); amillarar, prorratear; apreciar, estimar
assessable [ə'sɛsəbəl] *adj* gravable
assessment [ə'sɛsmənt] *s* gravamen; fijación; amillaramiento, prorrateo; apreciación, estimación
assessor [ə'sɛsər] *s* tasador
asset ['æsɛt] *s* posesión, ventaja; (fig.) valor (*persona, cosa o cualidad dignas de ser poseídas*); (com.) partida del activo; **assets** *spl* (com.) activo
asseverate [ə'sɛvəret] *va* aseverar
asseveration [ə,sɛvə'reʃən] *s* aseveración
assibilate [ə'sɪbɪlet] *va* (phonet.) asibilar; *vn* (phonet.) asibilarse
assibilation [ə,sɪbɪ'leʃən] *s* (phonet.) asibilación
assiduity [,æsɪ'djuɪtɪ] o [,æsɪ'duɪtɪ] *s* asiduidad
assiduous [ə'sɪdʒuəs] o [ə'sɪdjuəs] *adj* asiduo
assign [ə'saɪn] *s* (law) cesionario; *va* asignar
assignable [ə'saɪnəbəl] *adj* asignable
assignat ['æsɪgnæt] *s* asignado (*papel moneda en Francia durante la Revolución*)
assignation [,æsɪg'neʃən] *s* asignación; cita con una muchacha
assignee [,æsɪ'ni] *s* (law) cesionario
assignment [ə'saɪnmənt] *s* asignación, cometido; lección; (law) escritura de cesión
assignor [,æsɪ'nɔr] *s* (law) cesionista
assimilable [ə'sɪmɪləbəl] *adj* asimilable
assimilate [ə'sɪmɪlet] *va* asimilarse (*p.ej., los alimentos, el conocimiento*); asimilar; *vn* asimilar
assimilation [ə,sɪmɪ'leʃən] *s* asimilación
assimilative [ə'sɪmɪ,letɪv] *adj* asimilativo
Assisi [ə'sizɪ] *s* Asís
assist [ə'sɪst] *va* asistir, ayudar, socorrer, auxiliar
assistance [ə'sɪstəns] *s* asistencia, ayuda, socorro
assistant [ə'sɪstənt] *adj* & *s* ayudante
assistant manager *s* subdirector
assistant professor *s* ayudante de profesor, profesor agregado
assizes [ə'saɪzɪz] *spl* sesión del tribunal de justicia
assn. o **Assn.** abr. de **association**

assoc. abr. de **associate** y **association**
associate [ə'soʃɪɪt] o [ə'soʃɪet] *adj* asociado; *s* asociado, socio; [ə'soʃɪet] *va* asociar; *vn* asociarse
associate professor *s* profesor adjunto
association [əˌsosɪ'eʃən] o [əˌsoʃɪ'eʃən] *s* asociación
association football *s* (sport) asociación o fútbol asociación
associationism [əˌsosɪ'eʃənɪzəm] o [əˌsoʃɪ'eʃənɪzəm] *s* (psychol.) asociacionismo
associative [ə'soʃɪˌetɪv] *adj* asociativo
assonance ['æsənəns] *s* asonancia; asonante (*sonido, sílaba o letra*)
assonanced ['æsənənst] *adj* asonantado
assonant ['æsənənt] *adj & s* asonante
assonate ['æsənet] *vn* asonantar, asonar
assort [ə'sɔrt] *va* ordenar, clasificar; *vn* convenir, asociarse
assorted [ə'sɔrtɪd] *adj* surtido, variado; clasificado; apareado
assortment [ə'sɔrtmənt] *s* surtido; clasificación; clase, grupo
asst. o **Asst.** abr. de **assistant**
assuage [ə'swedʒ] *va* mitigar, aliviar
assuagement [ə'swedʒmənt] *s* mitigación, alivio
assume [ə'sum] o [ə'sjum] *va* asumir (*p.ej., el mando, responsabilidades, grandes proporciones*); adoptar; arrogarse; suponer, dar por sentado; *vn* presumir
assumed [ə'sumd] o [ə'sjumd] *adj* supuesto; fingido, pretendido, falso
assuming [ə'sumɪŋ] o [ə'sjumɪŋ] *adj* presuntuoso, presumido
assumption [ə'sʌmpʃən] *s* asunción; adopción; arrogación; suposición; presunción; (*cap.*) *s* (eccl.) Asunción
Assumptionist [ə'sʌmpʃənɪst] *s* asuncionista
assumptive [ə'sʌmptɪv] *adj* supuesto; arrogante, presuntuoso
assurance [ə'ʃurəns] *s* aseguramiento; seguridad, confianza; descaro; (com.) seguro
assure [ə'ʃur] *va* asegurar; (com.) asegurar
assured [ə'ʃurd] *adj* seguro, confiado; descarado; (com.) asegurado
Assyria [ə'sɪrɪə] *s* Asiria
Assyrian [ə'sɪrɪən] *adj & s* asirio
Assyriologist [əˌsɪrɪ'alədʒɪst] *s* asiriólogo
Assyriology [əˌsɪrɪ'alədʒɪ] *s* asiriología
astatic [e'stætɪk] *adj* astático
astatine ['æstətin] o ['æstətɪn] *s* (chem.) astatino o ástato
aster ['æstər] *s* (bot. & biol.) aster; (bot.) reina Margarita (*Callistephus chinensis*)
asterisk ['æstərɪsk] *s* asterisco
asterism ['æstərɪzəm] *s* (astr. & phys.) asterismo
astern [ə'stʌrn] *adv* (naut.) por la popa, a popa
asteroid ['æstərɔɪd] *adj* asteroide (*de figura de estrella*); *s* (astr.) asteroide; (bot.) asteroidea; (zool.) asteroideo, estrella de mar
asteroidean [ˌæstə'rɔɪdɪən] *adj & s* (zool.) asteroideo
asthenia [æs'θinɪə] *s* (path.) astenia
asthenic [æs'θenɪk] *adj & s* asténico
asthma ['æzmə] o ['æsmə] *s* (path.) asma
asthmatic [æz'mætɪk] o [æs'mætɪk] *adj & s* asmático
astigmatic [ˌæstɪg'mætɪk] *adj* astigmático
astigmatism [ə'stɪgmətɪzəm] *s* (med.) astigmatismo
astigmometer [ˌæstɪg'mamɪtər] *s* astigmómetro
astir [ə'stʌr] *adv* en movimiento, en actividad; levantado de la cama
astonish [ə'stanɪʃ] *va* asombrar
astonishing [ə'stanɪʃɪŋ] *adj* asombroso
astonishment [ə'stanɪʃmənt] *s* asombro
astound [ə'staund] *va* pasmar, aturdir
astounding [ə'staundɪŋ] *adj* pasmoso
astrachan ['æstrəkən] *s* astracán
astraddle [ə'strædəl] *adv* a horcajadas
astragal ['æstrəgəl] *s* (anat., arch. & arti.) astrágalo; (carp.) contrapilastra
astrakhan ['æstrəkən] *s* var. de **astrachan**
astral ['æstrəl] *adj* astral
astral body *s* (theosophy) cuerpo astral
astral lamp *s* lámpara astral
astray [ə'stre] *adv* por mal camino; **to go astray** extraviarse; **to lead astray** extraviar
astriction [ə'strɪkʃən] *s* astricción
astrictive [ə'strɪktɪv] *adj* astrictivo
astride [ə'straɪd] *adv* a horcajadas; *prep* a horcajadas en
astringency [ə'strɪndʒənsɪ] *s* astringencia; (fig.) austeridad
astringent [əs'trɪndʒənt] *adj* astringente; (fig.) austero; *s* astringente
astrodome ['æstrədom] *s* (aer.) astródomo
astrolabe ['æstrəleb] *s* (astr.) astrolabio
astrologer [ə'stralədʒər] *s* astrólogo
astrological [ˌæstrə'ladʒɪkəl] *adj* astrológico
astrologize [ə'stralədʒaɪz] *va & vn* astrologar
astrology [ə'stralədʒɪ] *s* astrología
astronaut ['æstrənɔt] *s* astronauta
astronautic [ˌæstrə'nɔtɪk] *adj* astronáutico; **astronautics** *ssg* astronáutica
astronautical [ˌæstrə'nɔtɪkəl] *adj* astronáutico
astronavigation [ˌæstroˌnævɪ'geʃən] *s* astronavegación
astronomer [ə'stranəmər] *s* astrónomo
astronomic [ˌæstrə'namɪk] o **astronomical** [ˌæstrə'namɪkəl] *adj* astronómico; (fig.) astronómico (*extraordinariamente grande*)
astronomical year *s* año astronómico
astronomy [ə'stranəmɪ] *s* astronomía
astrophotography [ˌæstrəfə'tagrəfɪ] *s* astrofotografía
astrophotometry [ˌæstrəfo'tamɪtrɪ] *s* astrofotometría
astrophysical [ˌæstro'fɪzɪkəl] *adj* astrofísico
astrophysics [ˌæstro'fɪzɪks] *ssg* astrofísica
Asturian [æs'turɪən] *adj & s* asturiano
astute [æs'tjut] o [æs'tut] *adj* astuto, sagaz
astuteness [æs'tjutnɪs] o [æs'tutnɪs] *s* astucia
Astyanax [æs'taɪənæks] *s* (myth.) Astianacte
asunder [ə'sʌndər] *adv* a pedazos, en dos; **to tear asunder** romper en dos
asylum [ə'saɪləm] *s* asilo
asymmetric [ˌesɪ'metrɪk] o [ˌæsɪ'metrɪk] o **asymmetrical** [ˌesɪ'metrɪkəl] o [ˌæsɪ'metrɪkəl] *adj* asimétrico
asymmetry [e'sɪmɪtrɪ] *s* asimetría
asymptote ['æsɪmtot] *s* (math.) asíntota
asynchronism [e'sɪŋkrənɪzəm] o [e'sɪnkrənɪzəm] *s* asincronismo
asynchronous [e'sɪŋkrənəs] o [e'sɪnkrənəs] *adj* asincrónico
asyndeton [ə'sɪndətən] o [ə'sɪndɪtan] *s* (rhet.) asíndeton
asystole [e'sɪstəli] *s* (path.) asistolia
asystolic [ˌesɪs'talɪk] *adj* asistólico
at [æt] o [ət] *prep* en, p.ej., **he was at the theater last night** estuvo en el teatro anoche; **at that time** en aquel entonces; a, p.ej., **he was waiting for me at the door** me esperaba a la puerta; **at eight o'clock** a las ocho; por, p.ej., **go in at the front door** entre Vd. por la puerta principal; **at my order** por mi orden; de, p.ej., **to be surprised at** estar sorprendido de; **to laugh at** reírse de; en casa de p.ej., **at Mary's** en casa de María; en la oficina de; en la tienda de; en el taller de; en el restaurante de
atacamite [ə'tækəmaɪt] *s* (mineral.) atacamita
ataractic [ˌætə'ræktɪk] *adj* ataráxico
ataraxia [ˌætə'ræksɪə] *s* ataraxia
atavism ['ætəvɪzəm] *s* (biol.) atavismo
atavistic [ˌætə'vɪstɪk] *adj* atávico
ataxia [ə'tæksɪə] *s* ataxia; (path.) ataxia
ataxic [ə'tæksɪk] *adj & s* atáxico
ataxy [ə'tæksɪ] *s* var. de **ataxia**
ate [et] *pret de* **eat**; (*cap.*) ['etɪ] *s* (myth.) Até
atelier ['ætəlje] *s* taller (*de artista*)
athanasia [ˌæθə'neʒə] *s* atanasia (*inmortalidad*)
Athanasian [ˌæθə'neʒən] *adj* atanasiano
Athanasian Creed *s* Símbolo Atanasiano
Athanasius, Saint [ˌæθə'neʃəs] San Atanasio
athanor ['æθənɔr] *s* atanor, hornillo de atenor
atheism ['eθiɪzəm] *s* ateísmo
atheist ['eθiɪst] *adj & s* ateo
atheistic [ˌeθi'ɪstɪk] o **atheistical** [ˌeθi'ɪstɪkəl] *adj* ateo
Athena [ə'θinə] *s* (myth.) Atena o Atenea
athenaeum o **atheneum** [ˌæθɪ'niəm] *s* ateneo
Athene [ə'θinɪ] *s* var. de **Athena**

Athenian [ə'θinɪən] *adj & s* ateniense
Athens ['æθɪnz] *s* Atenas
atherine ['æθərɪn] o ['æθəraɪn] *s* (ichth.) pejerrey, pez de rey
athermancy [e'θʌrmənsɪ] *s* (phys.) atermancia
athermanous [e'θʌrmənəs] *adj* atérmano
atherosclerosis [,æθəroskl ɪ'rosɪs] *s* (path.) aterosclerosis
athirst [ə'θʌrst] *adj* sediento
athlete ['æθlit] *s* atleta
athlete's foot *s* (path.) pie de atleta
athlete's heart *s* (path.) corazón atlético
athletic [æθ'lɛtɪk] *adj* atlético; **athletics** *ssg* atletismo (*doctrina acerca de los ejercicios atléticos*); atlética (*arte o habilidad*); *spl* atletismo (*ejercicios atléticos*)
athletic field *s* campo de deportes
at-home [æt'hom] *s* recepción, recibimiento
athwart [ə'θwɔrt] *adv* de través; *prep* por el través de; contra
atilt [ə'tɪlt] *adv* en posición inclinada; dando una lanzada
atingle [ə'tɪŋgəl] *adj* estremeciéndose
atinkle [ə'tɪŋkəl] *adj* tintineando
Atlantean [,ætlæn'tiən] *adj* atlántico (*perteneciente al gigante Atlas o Atlante*)
atlantes [æt'læntiz] *spl* (arch.) atlantes
Atlantic [æt'læntɪk] *adj & s* Atlántico
Atlantic Charter *s* carta del Atlántico
Atlantic Coast *s* Costa del Atlántico
Atlantic Ocean *s* océano Atlántico
Atlantides [æt'læntɪdiz] *spl* (astr. & myth.) Atlántidas
Atlantis [æt'læntɪs] *s* Atlántida
atlas ['ætləs] *s* atlas (*libro de mapas geográficos*); (anat.) atlas; (*cap.*) *s* (myth.) Atlas o Atlante
atlas folio *s* folio atlántico
Atlas Mountains, the el Atlas
atmosphere ['ætməsfɪr] *s* atmósfera; (fig.) atmósfera
atmospheric [,ætməs'fɛrɪk] *adj* atmosférico; **atmospherics** *spl* (rad.) parásitos atmosféricos
atmospheric pressure *s* presión atmosférica
atoll ['ætɑl] o [ə'tɑl] *s* atolón
atom ['ætəm] *s* átomo; (chem.) átomo
atom bomb *s* bomba atómica
atomic [ə'tɑmɪk] *adj* atómico
atomic age *s* era atómica
atomic air power *s* poder aéreo atómico
atomic bomb *s* bomba atómica
atomic energy *s* (phys.) energía atómica
atomicity [,ætə'mɪsɪtɪ] *s* (chem.) atomicidad
atomic number *s* (chem.) número atómico
atomic pile *s* (phys.) pila atómica
atomic reactor *s* (phys.) reactor atómico
atomic theory *s* (chem.) teoría atómica
atomic war *s* guerra atómica
atomic weapon *s* arma atómica
atomic weight *s* (chem.) peso atómico
atomism ['ætəmɪzəm] *s* atomismo
atomist ['ætəmɪst] *s* atomista
atomistic [,ætə'mɪstɪk] *adj* atomístico; **atomistics** *ssg* atomística
atomize ['ætəmaɪz] *va* atomizar
atomizer ['ætə,maɪzər] *s* atomizador, pulverizador
atom smasher *s* (phys.) rompeátomos
atomy ['ætəmɪ] *s* (*pl:* **-mies**) átomo; pigmeo
atonal [e'tonəl] *adj* (mus.) atonal
atonalism [e'tonəlɪzəm] *s* (mus.) atonalismo
atonality [,etə'nælɪtɪ] *s* (mus.) atonalidad
atone [ə'ton] *vn* dar reparación; **to atone for** dar reparación por; expiar
atonement [ə'tonmənt] *s* reparación; expiación; (theol.) redención
atonic [ə'tɑnɪk] *adj* (gram. & med.) átono, atónico
atonicity [,ætə'nɪsɪtɪ] o [,etə'nɪsɪtɪ] *s* (med.) atonicidad
atony ['ætənɪ] *s* (path. & phonet.) atonía
atop [ə'tɑp] *adv* encima; *prep* encima de
atrabilious [,ætrə'bɪljəs] *adj* atrabiliario
atresia [ə'triʒɪə] *s* (med.) atresia
Atreus ['etrus] o ['etrɪəs] *s* (myth.) Atreo
atrium ['etrɪəm] *s* (*pl:* **-a** [ə]) atrio; (anat.) atrio
atrocious [ə'troʃəs] *adj* atroz; (coll.) muy malo, abominable
atrocity [ə'trɑsɪtɪ] *s* (*pl:* **-ties**) atrocidad
atrophy ['ætrəfɪ] *s* atrofia; (*pret & pp:* **-phied**) *va* atrofiar; *vn* atrofiarse
atropine ['ætrəpin] o ['ætrəpɪn] *s* (chem. & pharm.) atropina
Atropos ['ætropɑs] *s* (myth.) Átropos
attach [ə'tætʃ] *va* atar, pegar, ligar, juntar; atribuir (*p.ej., importancia*); (law) embargar, incautarse, secuestrar (*propiedad*); *vn* pertenecer
attaché [,ætə'ʃe] o [ə'tæʃe] *s* agregado
attached [ə'tætʃt] *adj* adherido; **attached to** encariñado con, aficionado a
attachment [ə'tætʃmənt] *s* atadura, unión, enlace; atribución; apego, cariño; aditamento, accesorio; (law) embargo, secuestro, ejecución
attack [ə'tæk] *s* ataque; **an attack of pneumonia** una pulmonía, un ataque de pulmonía; *va* atacar; (chem.) atacar
attain [ə'ten] *va* lograr, alcanzar, conseguir; *vn* alcanzar; **to attain to** alcanzar a
attainable [ə'tenəbəl] *adj* alcanzable, realizable
attainder [ə'tendər] *s* muerte civil; (obs.) deshonra
attainment [ə'tenmənt] *s* logro, consecución; **attainments** *spl* dotes, prendas
attaint [ə'tent] *s* mancha, baldón; (vet.) alcanzadura; *va* condenar a muerte civil
attar ['ætər] *s* aceite esencial fragante
attar of roses *s* aceite esencial de rosas
attempt [ə'tɛmpt] *s* tentativa (*intento, prueba*); atentado; conato; *va* procurar, intentar; atentar a o contra
attend [ə'tɛnd] *va* atender, asistir; asistir a (*la iglesia, la escuela, etc.*); auxiliar (*a un moribundo*); *vn* atender; **to attend to** atender a
attendance [ə'tɛndəns] *s* asistencia, concurrencia; **to dance attendance** hacer antesala; **to dance attendance on** servir obsequiosa y constantemente
attendant [ə'tɛndənt] *adj & s* asistente; concomitante
attention [ə'tɛnʃən] *s* atención; **attentions** *spl* atenciones (*agasajo, obsequio*); **to attract attention** llamar la atención; **to call attention to** hacer presente; **to come to the attention of someone** hacérsele presente a uno; **to pay attention** hacer caso; **to stand at attention** cuadrarse (*los soldados*); *interj* ¡atención!, ¡firmes!
attentive [ə'tɛntɪv] *adj* atento
attenuate [ə'tɛnjʊet] *va* atenuar; *vn* atenuarse
attenuation [ə,tɛnjʊ'eʃən] *s* atenuación
attest [ə'tɛst] *va* atestar, atestiguar; juramentar; *vn* dar fe; **to attest to** dar fe de
attestation [,ætɛs'teʃən] *s* atestación, atestiguación
Attic ['ætɪk] *adj & s* ático; (*l.c.*) *s* (anat. & arch.) ático; buharda
Attica ['ætɪkə] *s* el Ática
Atticism ['ætɪsɪzəm] *s* aticismo
Atticist ['ætɪsɪst] *s* aticista
Attic salt *s* sal ática
Attila ['ætɪlə] *s* Atila
attire [ə'taɪr] *s* atavío, traje; *va* ataviar, vestir
attitude ['ætɪtjud] o ['ætɪtud] *s* actitud, ademán, postura; (paint. & sculp.) ademán; (aer.) posición; (fig.) actitud (*disposición de la mente*)
attorney [ə'tʌrnɪ] *s* procurador; abogado
attorney at law *s* procurador judicial
attorney general *s* (*pl:* **attorneys general** o **attorney generals**) procurador de síndico, procurador general; (*caps.*) *s* (U.S.A.) ministro de Justicia
attract [ə'trækt] *va* atraer; llamar (*la atención*)
attractable [ə'træktəbəl] *adj* atraíble
attraction [ə'trækʃən] *s* atracción; atractivo (*gracia personal*)
attractive [ə'træktɪv] *adj* atractivo; atrayente (*agradable, interesante*)
attractiveness [ə'træktɪvnɪs] *s* atractivo
attributable [ə'trɪbjətəbəl] *adj* atribuíble
attribute ['ætrɪbjʊt] *s* atributo; (gram.) atributo; [ə'trɪbjʊt] *va* atribuir
attribution [,ætrɪ'bjuʃən] *s* atribución

attributive [ə'trɪbjətɪv] *adj* atributivo; (gram.) atributivo
attrition [ə'trɪʃən] *s* (phys. & theol.) atrición; (fig.) agotamiento, consunción
attune [ə'tjun] o [ə'tun] *va* acordar, afinar
atty. abr. de **attorney**
at. wt. abr. de **atomic weight**
atypical [e'tɪpɪkəl] *adj* atípico
auburn ['ɔbərn] *adj & s* castaño rojizo
Aubusson [oby'sõ] *s* tapiz de Aubusson
auction ['ɔkʃən] *s* almoneda, remate, subasta; **to put up at auction** poner en pública subasta; *va* rematar, subastar
auction bridge *s* bridge-remate
auctioneer [,ɔkʃən'ɪr] *s* pregonero, subastador; *va* rematar, subastar
auction room *s* sala de subastas
audacious [ɔ'deʃəs] *adj* audaz
audacity [ɔ'dæsɪtɪ] *s* (*pl:* **-ties**) audacia
audibility [,ɔdɪ'bɪlɪtɪ] *s* audibilidad
audible ['ɔdɪbəl] *adj* audible
audience ['ɔdɪəns] *s* audiencia; público, auditorio
audience room *s* audiencia (*lugar destinado para dar audiencias*)
audio frequency ['ɔdɪo] *s* (rad.) audiofrecuencia
audio-frequency [,ɔdɪo'frikwənsɪ] *adj* (rad.) de audiofrecuencia
audiology [,ɔdɪ'ɑlədʒɪ] *s* audiología
audiometer [,ɔdɪ'ɑmɪtər] *s* audímetro, audiómetro
audion ['ɔdɪɑn] *s* (rad.) audión
audiophile ['ɔdiofaɪl] *s* aficionado a la música de alta fidelidad
audio-visual ['ɔdɪo'vɪʒuəl] *adj* audio-visual
audiphone ['ɔdɪfon] *s* audífono
audit ['ɔdɪt] *s* (com.) intervención; *va* intervenir (*una cuenta*)
audition [ɔ'dɪʃən] *s* audición; *va* dar audición a
auditor ['ɔdɪtər] *s* oyente (*en la escuela*); (com.) interventor
auditorium [,ɔdɪ'torɪəm] *s* (*pl:* **-ums** o **-a** [ə]) auditorio, anfiteatro, paraninfo
auditory ['ɔdɪ,torɪ] *adj* auditivo; *s* (*pl:* **-ries**) auditorio, anfiteatro
auditory canal *s* (anat.) conducto auditivo
auditory nerve *s* (anat.) nervio auditivo
Aug. abr. de **August**
Augean Stables [ɔ'dʒiən] *spl* (myth.) establos de Augías
auger ['ɔgər] *s* barrena
aught [ɔt] *s* alguna cosa; cifra; nada; *adv* absolutamente; en cualquier respecto
augite ['ɔdʒaɪt] *s* (mineral.) augita
augment [ɔg'mɛnt] *va* aumentar; *vn* aumentar o aumentarse
augmentation [,ɔgmɛn'teʃən] *s* aumento; (her.) aumentación
augmentative [ɔg'mɛntətɪv] *adj & s* (gram.) aumentativo
augmented [ɔg'mɛntɪd] *adj* (mus.) aumentado
au gratin [o'grɑtən] *adv* (cook.) al gratín
Augsburg Confession ['ɔgzbʌrg] *s* confesión de Augsburgo
augur ['ɔgər] *s* augur; *va & vn* augurar; **to augur ill** ser de mal agüero; **to augur well** ser de buen agüero
augural ['ɔgjərəl] *adj* augural
augurate ['ɔgjərɪt] *s* augurado
augury ['ɔgjərɪ] *s* (*pl:* **-ries**) augurio
august [ɔ'gʌst] *adj* augusto; (*cap.*) ['ɔgəst] *s* agosto; *adj* agostero
Augustan [ɔ'gʌstən] *adj* augustal
Augustan age *s* siglo de Augusto (*de la literatura romana*); siglo de la reina Ana (*de la literatura inglesa*); siglo de Luis Catorce (*de la literatura francesa*)
Augustine ['ɔgəstin] u [ɔ'gʌstɪn] *s* Agustín; **Saint Augustine** San Agustín
Augustinian [,ɔgəs'tɪnɪən] *adj & s* agustino o agustiniano
Augustinianism [,ɔgəs'tɪnɪənɪzəm] *s* agustinianismo
Augustinian Order *s* (eccl.) orden de San Agustín
Augustus [ɔ'gʌstəs] *s* Augusto
au jus [o'ʒy] *adv* (cook.) en su jugo
auk [ɔk] *s* (orn.) alca
au naturel [onaty'rɛl] *adv* al natural
aunt [ænt] o [ɑnt] *s* tía
aura ['ɔrə] *s* (*pl:* **-ras** o **-rae** [ri]) efluvio, emanación; (med.) aura
aural ['ɔrəl] *adj* aural
aureate ['ɔrɪet] u ['ɔrɪɪt] *adj* áureo
Aurelian [ɔ'rilɪən] *s* Aureliano
Aurelius, Marcus [ɔ'rilɪəs] Marco Aurelio
aureole ['ɔrɪol] *s* (meteor., theol., f.a., & fig.) aureola; *va* aureolar
aureomycin [,ɔrɪo'maɪsɪn] *s* (pharm.) aureomicina
au revoir [orə'vwɑr] *interj* ¡ hasta la vista!
auricle ['ɔrɪkəl] *s* (anat.) aurícula
auricula [ɔ'rɪkjələ] *s* (*pl:* **-lae** [li] o **-las**) (bot.) aurícula
auricular [ɔ'rɪkjələr] *adj* auricular; (anat.) auricular
auricular witness *s* testigo de vista o testigo auricular
auriculate [ɔ'rɪkjəlɪt] *adj* (bot. & zool.) auriculado
auriferous [ɔ'rɪfərəs] *adj* aurífero
Auriga [ɔ'raɪgə] *s* (astr.) Auriga
aurist ['ɔrɪst] *s* aurista
aurochs ['ɔrɑks] *s* (zool.) uro
aurora [ɔ'rorə] *s* aurora; (meteor.) aurora polar; (*cap.*) *s* (myth.) Aurora
aurora australis [ɔs'trelɪs] *s* (meteor.) aurora austral
aurora borealis [,borɪ'elɪs] o [,borɪ'ælɪs] *s* (meteor.) aurora boreal
auroral [ɔ'rorəl] *adj* auroral
auscultate ['ɔskəltet] *va & vn* auscultar
auscultation [,ɔskəl'teʃən] *s* auscultación
auspice ['ɔspɪs] *s* auspicio; **under the auspices of** bajo los auspicios de
auspicious [ɔs'pɪʃəs] *adj* propicio, auspicioso
austere [ɔs'tɪr] *adj* austero
austerity [ɔs'tɛrɪtɪ] *s* (*pl:* **-ties**) austeridad
Austin ['ɔstɪn] *s* Agustín
austral ['ɔstrəl] *adj* austral
Australasia [,ɔstrəl'eʒə] u [,ɔstrəl'eʃə] *s* la Australasia
Australasian [,ɔstrəl'eʒən] u [,ɔstrəl'eʃən] *adj* australasiático
Australia [ɔs'treljə] *s* Australia
Australian [ɔs'treljən] *adj & s* australiano
Australian crawl *s* (swimming) brazada australiana
Australian pea *s* (bot.) caracolillo
Austria ['ɔstrɪə] *s* Austria
Austria-Hungary ['ɔstrɪə'hʌŋgərɪ] *s* Austria-Hungría
Austrian ['ɔstrɪən] *adj & s* austríaco
Austro-Hungarian [,ɔstrohʌŋ'gɛrɪən] *adj & s* austrohúngaro
autarchic [ɔ'tɑrkɪk] o **autarchical** [ɔ'tɑrkɪkəl] *adj* autárquico
autarchy ['ɔtɑrkɪ] *s* (*pl:* **-chies**) autarquía
autarkic [ɔ'tɑrkɪk] o **autarkical** [ɔ'tɑrkɪkəl] *adj* autárcico o autárquico
autarky ['ɔtɑrkɪ] *s* (*pl:* **-kies**) autarcía o autarquía (*independencia económica*)
authentic [ɔ'θɛntɪk] *adj* auténtico
authentically [ɔ'θɛntɪkəlɪ] *adv* auténticamente
authenticate [ɔ'θɛntɪket] *va* autenticar
authentication [ɔ,θɛntɪ'keʃən] *s* autenticación
authenticity [,ɔθɛn'tɪsɪtɪ] *s* autenticidad
author ['ɔθər] *s* autor
authoress ['ɔθərɪs] *s* autora
authoritarian [ɔ,θɑrɪ'tɛrɪən] u [ɔ,θɔrɪ'tɛrɪən] *adj & s* autoritario
authoritarianism [ɔ,θɑrɪ'tɛrɪənɪzəm] u [ɔ,θɔrɪ'tɛrɪənɪzəm] *s* autoritarismo
authoritative [ɔ'θɑrɪ,tetɪv] u [ɔ'θɔrɪ,tetɪv] *adj* autorizado; autoritario (*imperioso*)
authority [ɔ'θɑrɪtɪ] u [ɔ'θɔrɪtɪ] *s* (*pl:* **-ties**) autoridad; **on good authority** de buena tinta
authorization [,ɔθərɪ'zeʃən] *s* autorización
authorize ['ɔθəraɪz] *va* autorizar; **to authorize to** + *inf* autorizar a o para + *inf*
Authorized Version *s* versión autorizada (*de la Biblia*)
authorship ['ɔθərʃɪp] *s* profesión de autor; paternidad literaria
auto ['ɔto] *s* (*pl:* **-tos**) (coll.) auto
autobiographer [,ɔtobaɪ'ɑgrəfər] u [,ɔtobɪ'ɑgrəfər] *s* autobiógrafo
autobiographic [,ɔto,baɪə'græfɪk] o **autobio-**

graphical [ˌɔtoˌbaɪə'græfɪkəl] *adj* autobiográfico
autobiography [ˌɔtobaɪ'ɑgrəfɪ] u [ˌɔtobɪ'ɑgrəfɪ] *s* autobiografía
autoblast ['ɔtoblæst] *s* (biol.) autoblasto
autobus ['ɔtoˌbʌs] *s* autobús
autocade ['ɔtoˌked] *s* caravana de automóviles
autochthon [ɔ'tɑkθən] *s* autóctono
autochthonous [ɔ'tɑkθənəs] *adj* autóctono
autochthony [ɔ'tɑkθənɪ] *s* autoctonía
autoclave ['ɔtoklev] *s* autoclave
autocracy [ɔ'tɑkrəsɪ] *s* (*pl:* **-cies**) autocracia
autocrat ['ɔtəkræt] *s* autócrata
autocratic [ˌɔtə'krætɪk] o **autocratical** [ˌɔtə'krætɪkəl] *adj* autocrático
auto-da-fé ['ɔtodə'fe] o ['autodə'fe] *s* (*pl:* **autos-da-fé**) auto de fe
auto driver training school *s* var. de **driving school**
autofrettage [ˌɔto'frɛtɪdʒ] *s* autofretage
autogenesis [ˌɔto'dʒɛnɪsɪs] *s* autogénesis
autogenous [ɔ'tɑdʒɪnəs] *adj* autógeno
autogiro [ˌɔto'dʒaɪro] *s* (*pl:* **-ros**) autogiro
autograph ['ɔtəgræf] u ['ɔtəgrɑf] *adj* autógrafo (*escrito de mano de su mismo autor*); *s* autógrafo; *va* autografiar
autographic [ˌɔtə'græfɪk] o **autographical** [ˌɔtə'græfɪkəl] *adj* autográfico
autograph seeker *s* cazador de autógrafos
autography [ɔ'tɑgrəfɪ] *s* autografía
autogyro [ˌɔto'dʒaɪro] *s* (*pl:* **-ros**) var. de **autogiro**
autohypnosis [ˌɔtohɪp'nosɪs] *s* autohipnosis
autoinfection [ˌɔto·ɪn'fɛkʃən] *s* (path.) autoinfección
autointoxication [ˌɔto·ɪnˌtɑksɪ'keʃən] *s* (path.) autointoxicación
autoist ['ɔto·ɪst] *s* (coll.) automovilista
automat ['ɔtəmæt] *s* restaurante automático, bar automático
automate ['ɔtəmet] *va* automatizar
automatic [ˌɔtə'mætɪk] *adj* automático
automatically [ˌɔtə'mætɪkəlɪ] *adv* automáticamente
automatic rifle *s* fusil ametrallador
automation [ˌɔtə'meʃən] *s* automatización
automatism [ɔ'tɑmətɪzəm] *s* automacia, automatismo
automaton [ɔ'tɑmətɑn] *s* (*pl:* **-tons** o **-ta** [tə]) autómata; (fig.) autómata (*persona*)
automobile [ˌɔtə'mobɪl] *adj* automóvil; automovilista; [ˌɔtəmo'bil] u [ˌɔtə'mobil] *s* automóvil
automobile show *s* salón del automóvil
automobilist [ˌɔtəmo'bilɪst] u [ˌɔtə'mobɪlɪst] *s* automovilista
automotive [ˌɔtə'motɪv] *adj* automotor
automotive engineer *s* autotécnico
automotive engineering *s* autotécnica
autonomic [ˌɔtə'nɑmɪk] *adj* autonómico
autonomist [ɔ'tɑnəmɪst] *s* autonomista
autonomous [ɔ'tɑnəməs] *adj* autónomo
autonomy [ɔ'tɑnəmɪ] *s* autonomía
autoplastic [ˌɔto'plæstɪk] *adj* autoplástico
autoplasty ['ɔtoˌplæstɪ] *s* (surg.) autoplastia
autopsy ['ɔtɑpsɪ] *s* (*pl:* **-sies**) autopsia; (*pret & pp:* **-sied**) *va* autopsiar
auto radio *s* autorradio
autosuggestion [ˌɔtosəg'dʒɛstʃən] *s* autosugestión
autotrophic [ˌɔto'trɑfɪk] *adj* autótrofo
autotropism [ɔ'tɑtrəpɪzəm] *s* (bot.) autotropismo
autotruck ['ɔtoˌtrʌk] *s* autocamión
autumn ['ɔtəm] *s* otoño
autumnal [ɔ'tʌmnəl] *adj* otoñal, autumnal
autumnal equinox *s* (astr.) equinoccio otoñal o de otoño
autumn crocus *s* (bot.) cólquico
autunite ['ɔtənaɪt] *s* (mineral.) autunita
Auvergne [o'vʌrn], [o'vɛrn] u [o'vɛrnjə] *s* Auvernia
aux. abr. de **auxiliary**
auxiliary [ɔg'zɪljərɪ] *adj* auxiliar; (gram.) auxiliar; *s* (*pl:* **-ries**) auxiliar; (gram.) auxiliar (*verbo*); **auxiliaries** *spl* tropas auxiliares
auxiliary verb *s* (gram.) verbo auxiliar
auxochrome ['ɔksəkrom] *s* (chem.) auxocromo
av. abr. de **avenue, average,** y **avoirdupois**
A.V. abr. de **Authorized Version**
avail [ə'vel] *s* provecho, utilidad; *va* beneficiar; **to avail oneself of** aprovecharse de, valerse de; *vn* aprovechar
availability [əˌvelə'bɪlɪtɪ] *s* disponibilidad
available [ə'veləbəl] *adj* disponible, aprovechable; **to make available to** poner a la disposición de
available assets *spl* disponibilidades
avalanche ['ævəlæntʃ] o ['ævəlɑntʃ] *s* alud, avalancha; (fig.) alud, avalancha, torrente
avant-garde [avɑ̃'gard] *adj* vanguardista; *s* vanguardismo
avant-gardist [avɑ̃'gardɪst] *s* vanguardista
avarice ['ævərɪs] *s* avaricia
avaricious [ˌævə'rɪʃəs] *adj* avaricioso, avariento
avast [ə'væst] o [ə'vɑst] *interj* (naut.) ¡forte!
avatar [ˌævə'tɑr] *s* avatar
avaunt [ə'vɔnt] o [ə'vɑnt] *interj* (archaic) ¡fuera!, ¡largo de aquí!
Ave. abr. de **Avenue**
Ave Maria ['ɑvemə'riə] o ['evɪmə'raɪə] *s* avemaría
avenge [ə'vɛndʒ] *va* vengar; **to avenge oneself on** vengarse en
avenger [ə'vɛndʒər] *s* vengador
avens ['ævɪnz] *s* (bot.) cariofilata, hierba de San Benito
aventurine [ə'vɛntʃərɪn] *s* (mineral.) venturina
avenue ['ævɪnju] o ['ævɪnu] *s* avenida
aver [ə'vʌr] (*pret & pp:* **averred;** *ger:* **averring**) *va* afirmar, declarar
average ['ævərɪdʒ] *s* promedio, término medio; (naut.) avería; **on an average** por término medio; *adj* medio, de término medio; mediano, común, ordinario; *va* calcular el término medio de; prorratear; hacer un promedio de; ser de un promedio de, ser por término medio
averment [ə'vʌrmənt] *s* afirmación, declaración
Avernus [ə'vʌrnəs] *s* (myth.) Averno
Averroism [ˌævə'ro·ɪzəm] *s* averroísmo
Averroist [ˌævə'ro·ɪst] *s* averroísta
averse [ə'vʌrs] *adj* renuente, contrario
aversion [ə'vʌrʒən] o [ə'vʌrʃən] *s* desviación; aversión, antipatía; cosa aborrecida
avert [ə'vʌrt] *va* apartar, desviar, separar; impedir
aviary ['evɪˌɛrɪ] *s* (*pl:* **-ies**) avería, pajarera
aviation [ˌevɪ'eʃən] *s* aviación; *adj* aviatorio
aviation medicine *s* aeromedicina
aviator ['evɪˌetər] *s* aviador
aviatrix [ˌevɪ'etrɪks] *s* aviadora, aviatriz
aviculture ['evɪˌkʌltʃər] *s* avicultura
avid ['ævɪd] *adj* ávido
avidity [ə'vɪdɪtɪ] *s* avidez
Avignon [avi'njõ] *s* Aviñón
avitaminosis [eˌvaɪtəmɪ'nosɪs] *s* (path.) avitaminosis
avocado [ˌævo'kɑdo] *s* (*pl:* **-dos**) (bot.) aguacate (*árbol y fruto*)
avocation [ˌævə'keʃən] *s* diversión, distracción, ocupación accesoria
avocet ['ævosɛt] *s* (orn.) avoceta
avoid [ə'vɔɪd] *va* evitar; (law) anular; **to avoid** + *ger* evitar + *inf*
avoidable [ə'vɔɪdəbəl] *adj* evitable
avoidance [ə'vɔɪdəns] *s* evitación; (law) anulación
avoirdupois [ˌævərdə'pɔɪz] o ['ævərdəˌpɔɪz] *s* sistema de pesos británico y estadounidense; (coll.) peso, gordura
avoirdupois weight *s* peso avoirdupois (*cuya unidad es la libra de dieciséis onzas, que equivale a 453,50 gramos*)
avoset ['ævosɛt] *s* var. de **avocet**
avouch [ə'vautʃ] *va* afirmar; garantizar; reconocer
avow [ə'vau] *va* admitir, confesar
avowal [ə'vauəl] *s* admisión, confesión
avowedly [ə'vauɪdlɪ] *adv* concedidamente
avulsion [ə'vʌlʃən] *s* (law) avulsión
avuncular [ə'vʌŋkjələr] *adj* avuncular
await [ə'wet] *va* aguardar, esperar
awake [ə'wek] *adj* despierto; (*pret & pp:* **awoke** o **awaked**) *va & vn* despertar
awaken [ə'wekən] *va & vn* despertar
awakening [ə'wekənɪŋ] *adj* despertador; *s* despertamiento

award [ə'wɔrd] *s* concesión; recompensa, premio; condecoración; adjudicación; *va* conceder; adjudicar
aware [ə'wɛr] *adj* enterado; **to become aware of** enterarse de, ponerse al corriente de, darse cuenta de
awareness [ə'wɛrnɪs] *s* conocimiento, conciencia
awash [ə'wɑʃ] o [ə'wɔʃ] *adv* a flor de agua
away [ə'we] *adj* ausente; distante; *adv* lejos; a lo lejos; alejándose; con ahinco; sin cesar; (sport) en campo ajeno; **to do away with** deshacerse de; matar; **to get away** escapar; **to go away** irse; **to lead away** llevar consigo; **to make away with** robar, hurtar; **to make away with oneself** darse la muerte; **to run away** fugarse; **to send away** enviar; despedir; **to take away** llevarse; quitar; **away from** lejos de; **away with you!** ¡márchese Vd.!; ¡lárguese Vd.!
awe [ɔ] *s* temor, temor reverencial; *va* infundir temor reverencial a
aweary [ə'wɪrɪ] *adj* (poet.) cansado, aburrido
aweigh [ə'we] *adj* (naut.) levado; **with anchor aweigh** con ancla levada, levada el ancla
awesome ['ɔsəm] *adj* imponente, pasmoso
awestricken ['ɔ,strɪkən] o **awestruck** ['ɔ,strʌk] *adj* pasmado, espantado
awful ['ɔfəl] *adj* atroz, horrible, tremendo; impresionante, majestuoso; (coll.) muy malo, muy feo, enorme
awfully ['ɔfəlɪ] *adv* atrozmente, horriblemente; majestuosamente; (coll.) muy, excesivamente
awhile [ə'whaɪl] *adv* un rato, algún tiempo
awkward ['ɔkwərd] *adj* desmañado, torpe, lerdo; embarazoso, delicado
awkwardness ['ɔkwərdnɪs] *s* desmaña, torpeza; embarazo, delicadeza
awkward squad *s* (mil.) pelotón de los torpes
awl [ɔl] *s* alesna, lezna
awn [ɔn] *s* (bot.) arista
awned [ɔnd] *adj* (bot.) aristado
awning ['ɔnɪŋ] *s* toldo
awoke [ə'wok] *pret & pp de* **awake**
A.W.O.L. (mil.) ausente sin licencia
awry [ə'raɪ] *adv* de través; equivocadamente, erradamente
ax o **axe** [æks] *s* hacha; **to have an ax to grind** tener algún fin interesado, tener ocultas intenciones
axeman ['æksmən] *s* (*pl:* **-men**) leñador, hachero; (mil.) hachero, gastador
axhammer ['æks,hæmər] *s* martillo de dos filos para desbastar piedra
axial ['æksɪəl] *adj* axil, axial
axial-flow turbine ['æksɪəl'flo] *s* turbina axial
axil ['æksɪl] *s* (bot.) axila
axile ['æksɪl] o ['æksaɪl] *adj* (bot.) axilar
axilla [æk'sɪlə] *s* (*pl:* **-lae** [li]) (anat., bot., & zool.) axila
axillar ['æksɪlər] *adj* axilar; *s* (ent.) axilar
axillary ['æksɪ,lɛrɪ] o [æk'sɪlərɪ] *adj* (anat., bot., & zool.) axilar
axinite ['æksɪnaɪt] *s* (mineral.) axinita
axiology [,æksɪ'ɑlədʒɪ] *s* axiología
axiom ['æksɪəm] *s* axioma
axiomatic [,æksɪə'mætɪk] *adj* axiomático
axion ['æksɪɑn] *s* (anat.) axión
axis ['æksɪs] *s* (*pl:* **axes** ['æksiz]) *s* eje; (math.) eje; (anat.) axis; (*cap.*) *s* Eje (*Alemania e Italia*)
axis cylinder *s* (anat. & physiol.) cilindroeje
Axis nations *spl* naciones del Eje
axle ['æksəl] *s* eje, árbol
axletree ['æksəl,tri] *s* eje, eje de carretón
axman ['æksmən] *s* (*pl:* **-men**) leñador, hachero; (mil.) hachero, gastador
axoid ['æksɔɪd] o **axoidean** [æk'sɔɪdɪən] *adj* (anat.) axoideo
axolotl ['æksəlɑtəl] *s* (zool.) ajolote
axon ['æksɑn] *s* (anat.) axón
axone ['ækson] *s* (anat. & physiol.) axón
axunge ['æksʌndʒ] *s* enjundia
ay [aɪ] *adv & s* sí; [e] *adv* siempre; **for ay** por siempre; [e] *interj* ¡ay!; **ay me!** ¡ay de mí!
aye [aɪ] *adv & s* sí; [e] *adv* siempre; **for aye** por siempre
aye-aye ['aɪ,aɪ] *s* (zool.) ayeaye
azalea [ə'zeljə] *s* (bot.) azalea
azarole ['æzərol] *s* (bot.) acerolo (*arbusto*); acerola (*fruto*)
azedarach [ə'zɛdəræk] *s* (bot.) acederaque
Azerbaijan [,ɑzərbaɪ'dʒɑn] *s* el Azerbeiyán
azimuth ['æzɪməθ] *s* acimut
azimuthal ['æzɪ,mʌθəl] *adj* acimutal
azoic [ə'zo·ɪk] *adj* (chem. & geol.) azoico
Azores [ə'zorz] o ['ezorz] *spl* Azores
azote ['æzot] o [ə'zot] *s* (chem.) ázoe
Aztec ['æztɛk] *adj & s* azteca
azure ['æʒər] o ['eʒər] *adj* azul; *s* azul; (her.) azur, blao
azurite ['æʒəraɪt] *s* (mineral.) azurita
azygos ['æzɪgɑs] *s* (anat.) ácigos
azygous vein ['æzɪgəs] *s* (anat.) vena ácigos
azymous ['æzɪməs] *adj* ázimo

B

B, b [bi] *s* (*pl:* **B's, b's** [biz]) segunda letra del alfabeto inglés
b. abr. de **base, bass, basso, bay, book, born, breadth** y **brother**
B. abr. de **bay, Bible, British** y **Brotherhood**
B.A. abr. de **Baccalaureus Artium** (Lat.) **Bachelor of Arts**
baa [bɑ] *s* be (*balido*); *vn* balar
babbitt [ˈbæbɪt] *s* metal de babbitt; *va* revestir o forrar de metal de babbitt
Babbitt metal *s* metal de babbitt
babbittry [ˈbæbɪtrɪ] *s* (U.S.A.) concepto de la moral y las costumbres de la clase media
babble [ˈbæbəl] *s* barboteo; charla, parloteo; murmullo (*de un arroyo*); *va* barbotar; decir indiscretamente; *vn* barbotar; charlar, parlotear; murmurar (*un arroyo*)
babbler [ˈbæblər] *s* charlatán
babbling [ˈbæblɪŋ] *adj* charlatán; murmurante; *s* charlatanería
Babcock test [ˈbæbkɑk] *s* prueba de Babcock
babe [beb] *s* nene, rorro; niño (*persona inocente e inexperta*)
babel o **Babel** [ˈbebəl] *s* babel
babies'-breath [ˈbebɪzˌbrɛθ] *s* (bot.) gipsófila
babirusa, babiroussa o **babirussa** [ˌbæbɪˈrusə] *s* (zool.) babirusa
baboon [bæˈbun] *s* (zool.) babuíno, mandril
baby [ˈbebɪ] *s* (*pl:* **-bies**) nene, rorro, criatura, bebé; pequeño (*de un animal*); benjamín (*el menor de una familia o un grupo*); *adj* aniñado, infantil, pequeño; (*pret & pp:* **-bied**) *va* mimar
baby beef *s* ternerillo para el matadero
baby carriage *s* cochecillo para niños, coche cuna
baby face *s* cara aniñada
baby grand *s* piano de media cola
babyhood [ˈbebɪhud] *s* infancia
babyish [ˈbebɪɪʃ] *adj* aniñado, infantil
Babylon [ˈbæbɪlən] o [ˈbæbɪlɑn] *s* Babilonia (*antigua ciudad; cualquier gran ciudad rica y desmoralizada*)
Babylonia [ˌbæbɪˈlonɪə] *s* Babilonia (*antiguo imperio*)
Babylonian [ˌbæbɪˈlonɪən] *adj* babilónico, babilonio; (fig.) babilónico (*fastuoso*); *s* babilonio
Babylonian willow *s* (bot.) sauce de Babilonia
baby sitter *s* (coll.) niñera por horas
baby talk *s* habla aniñada
baby teeth *s* dientes de leche
baccalaureate [ˌbækəˈlɔrɪɪt] *s* bachillerato; (U.S.A.) sermón que se predica a los graduandos del bachillerato
baccara o **baccarat** [ˈbækərɑ] *s* bacará
Bacchae [ˈbæki] *spl* bacantes
bacchanal [ˈbækənəl] *adj* bacanal; *s* bacanal (*orgía*); **bacchanals** *spl* bacanales
bacchanalia [ˌbækəˈnelɪə] *spl* bacanal (*orgía tumultuosa*); (*cap.*) *spl* bacanales
bacchanalian [ˌbækəˈnelɪən] *adj* bacanal; *s* borracho, juerguista
bacchant [ˈbækənt] *s* sacerdote o devoto de Baco; juerguista
bacchante [bəˈkæntɪ] o [bəˈkænt] *s* bacante
Bacchic [ˈbækɪk] *adj* báquico; (*l.c.*) *adj* báquico (*borracho, desenfrenado*)
Bacchus [ˈbækəs] *s* (myth.) Baco
bacciferous [bækˈsɪfərəs] *adj* (bot.) bacífero
bachelor [ˈbætʃələr] *s* soltero (*hombre no casado*); bachiller (*persona que ha recibido el primer grado académico*); doncel (*joven noble*)
bachelor-at-arms [ˈbætʃələrətˈɑrmz] *s* doncel
bachelorhood [ˈbætʃələrˌhud] *s* soltería
bachelor's-button [ˈbætʃələrzˈbʌtən] *s* (bot.) azulejo, aciano (*Centaurea cyanus*); (bot.) margarita de los prados (*Bellis perennis*)
bachelor's degree *s* bachillerato
bacillary [ˈbæsɪˌlɛrɪ] *adj* bacilar
bacillus [bəˈsɪləs] *s* (*pl:* **-li** [laɪ]) bacilo
back [bæk] *adj* trasero; posterior; pasado; atrasado; del interior; posterior (*diente*); (phonet.) posterior ‖ *adv* atrás, detrás; otra vez; de vuelta; hace, p.ej., **some weeks back** hace algunas semanas; **as far back as** ya en (*cierta época*); **to be back** estar de vuelta; **to come back** volver; **to go back** volver; **to go back and forth** ir y venir; **to go back on** volver sobre (*sus pasos*); (coll.) volver sobre (*p.ej., una decisión*); (coll.) faltar a (*p.ej., una promesa*); (coll.) abandonar, traicionar; **to go back to** remontarse a; **to send back** mandar para atrás, hacer volver (*a una persona*); devolver (*una cosa*); **back and forth** de una parte a otra; **back in** allá por (*cierta época*); **back of** detrás de; apoyando ‖ *s* espalda, dorso; respaldo, espaldar (*de una silla*); reverso (*de una moneda*); lomo (*de un animal, un libro o un cuchillo*); dorso (*de la mano; de un grabado, un programa, etc.*); fondo (*p.ej., de una sala*); final (*del libro*), p.ej., **you will find the passage in the back of the book** Vd. hallará el pasaje al final o hacia el final del libro; (football) defensa, zaguero; **behind one's back** a espaldas de uno; **on one's back** postrado, en cama; a cuestas; **to break the back of** deslomar, derrengar; **to get one's back up** enojarle a uno; enojarse; **to turn one's back on** volver las espaldas a; **with one's back to the wall** entre la espada y la pared; **back to back** espalda con espalda, dándose las espaldas ‖ *va* mover hacia atrás; dar marcha atrás a; respaldar (*apoyar, defender*); (naut.) engalgar (*una áncora*); (print.) retirar; **to back up** mover hacia atrás; respaldar (*apoyar, defender*); **to back water** (naut. & fig.) ciar ‖ *vn* moverse hacia atrás; dar marcha atrás; **to back and fill** zigzaguear; seguir mudando de opinión; **to back down** u **out** volverse atrás; (fig.) volverse atrás, ceder, echarse atrás
backache [ˈbækˌek] *s* dolor de espalda
backbite [ˈbækˌbaɪt] (*pret:* **-bit;** *pp:* **-bit** o **-bitten**) *va* cortar un traje a, calumniar solapadamente; *vn* murmurar (*en perjuicio de un ausente*)
backbone [ˈbækˌbon] *s* espinazo; nervura (*de un libro*); firmeza, decisión
backbreaking [ˈbækˌbrekɪŋ] *adj* deslomador
back comb *s* peineta
back country *s* afueras del poblado; zona fronteriza
backcross [ˈbækˌkrɔs] o [ˈbækˌkrɑs] *s* cruzamiento retrógrado
backdoor [ˈbækˌdor] *adj* secreto, clandestino
back door *s* puerta excusada, falsa o trasera
backdown [ˈbækˌdaʊn] *s* (coll.) palinodia
backdrop [ˈbækˌdrɑp] *s* telón de foro
back electromotive force *s* (elec.) fuerza contraelectromotriz
backer [ˈbækər] *s* sostenedor, defensor; impulsor (*de un proyecto comercial*)
backfield [ˈbækˌfild] *s* (football) terreno detrás de la línea delantera; (football) defensas, zagueros, jugadores detrás de la línea delantera
backfire [ˈbækˌfaɪr] *s* (aut.) petardeo; quema que se hace para evitar que se extienda un incendio; *vn* (aut.) petardear; hacer una quema para evitar que se extienda un incendio; (fig.) salir el tiro por la culata
back formation *s* (philol.) derivación regresiva; (philol.) derivado regresivo

backgammon ['bæk,gæmən] o [,bæk'gæmən] *s* chaquete
background ['bæk,graʊnd] *s* fondo, último término; antecedentes, educación; olvido, obscuridad; **in the background** al fondo, en el fondo; en la obscuridad
background music *s* música de fondo
background noise *s* ruidos de fondo
backhand ['bæk,hænd] *s* revés; escritura inclinada a la izquierda; *adj* dado con la mano vuelta; inclinado a la izquierda
backhanded ['bæk,hændɪd] *adj* dado con la mano vuelta; inclinado a la izquierda; desmañado; falto de sinceridad
backhouse ['bæk,haʊs] *s* trascuarto; común o retrete (*detrás de la casa*)
backing ['bækɪŋ] apoyo, sostén; garantía
backlash ['bæk,læʃ] *s* movimiento trepidante de piezas mal articuladas; juego; contragolpe, pérdida de carrera, culateo
backlining ['bæk,laɪnɪŋ] *s* (b.b.) forro del lomo del libro
backlog ['bæk,lɔg] o ['bæk,lɑg] *s* leño trasero en un hogar; (com.) reserva, reserva de pedidos pendientes
back number *s* número atrasado, viejo número (*de un periódico o revista*); (coll.) persona atrasada
back pay *s* sueldo retrasado
back porch *s* galería
back pressure *s* contrapresión
backsaw ['bæk,sɔ] *s* sierra de trasdós
back seat *s* asiento de atrás; (fig.) puesto secundario; **to take a back seat** (fig.) ceder su puesto, perder influencia
backset ['bæk,sɛt] *s* revés, contrariedad; remolino
backsheesh o **backshish** ['bækʃiʃ] *s* propina entre los árabes y turcos
backside ['bæk,saɪd] *s* espalda; trasero, nalgas
backslide ['bæk,slaɪd] (*pret:* **-slid**; *pp:* **-slidden** o **-slid**) *vn* reincidir
backslider ['bæk,slaɪdər] *s* reincidente
backspacer ['bæk,spesər] *s* tecla de retroceso
backspin ['bæk,spɪn] *s* giro hacia atrás (*de una pelota o de una bola de billar*)
backstage ['bæk'stedʒ] *adv* (theat.) detrás del telón; (theat.) al o en el camarín de un actor o una actriz
backstairs ['bæk,stɛrz] *adj* indirecto, intrigante, secreto
back stairs *spl* escalera de servicio, escalera trasera; medios indirectos
backstay ['bæk,ste] *s* refuerzo de espaldar; (naut.) brandal, traversa
backstitch ['bæk,stɪtʃ] *s* pespunte; *va & vn* pespuntar
backstop ['bæk,stɑp] *s* reja o red para detener la pelota; meta, jugador que detiene la pelota
back street *s* callejón
backstroke ['bæk,strok] *s* arrastre de espalda, brazada que se emplea al nadar de espaldas; revés
backswept wing ['bæk,swɛpt] *s* (aer.) ala en flecha
back swimmer *s* (ent.) barquillero de los estanques
back talk *s* respuesta insolente, mala contestación
backtrack ['bæk,træk] *vn* volver pies atrás, retirarse
backup ['bæk,ʌp] *s* apoyo, sostén; retroceso, retiro; represa, estancación; acumulación; reserva; (print.) retiración; *adj* de reserva
back vowel *s* (phonet.) vocal posterior
backward ['bækwərd] *adj* vuelto hacia atrás; atrasado, tardío; tímido, retraído; *adv* atrás; de espaldas; al revés; hacia atrás; cada vez peor; **to go backward** andar de espaldas; ir hacia atrás; **to go backward and forward** ir y venir; **to read backward** leer para atrás
backward and forward motion *s* vaivén
backwardness ['bækwərdnɪs] *s* atraso, retraso, tardanza; torpeza; timidez
backwards ['bækwərdz] *adv* var. de **backward**
backwash ['bæk,wɑʃ] o ['bæk,wɔʃ] *s* agua de rechazo; (fig.) contracorriente, consecuencias
backwater ['bæk,wɔtər] o ['bæk,wɑtər] *s* remanso, rebalsa; contracorriente, remolino; (fig.) atraso, incultura
backwoods ['bæk,wʊdz] *spl* monte, región apartada de los centros de población
backwoodsman ['bæk,wʊdzmən] *s* (*pl:* **-men**) hombre que habita el monte
back yard *s* corral trasero, patio trasero
bacon ['bekən] *s* tocino; **to bring home the bacon** (coll.) sacarse el gordo, tener éxito
Baconian [be'konɪən] *adj* baconiano; *s* baconista
Baconian theory *s* teoría de que la obra dramática de Shakespeare fué escrita por Francisco Bacon
bacteria [bæk'tɪrɪə] *pl de* **bacterium**
bacterial [bæk'tɪrɪəl] *adj* bacteriano
bactericidal [bæk,tɪrɪ'saɪdəl] *adj* bactericida
bactericide [bæk'tɪrɪsaɪd] *s* bactericida
bacteriological [bæk,tɪrɪə'lɑdʒɪkəl] *adj* bacteriológico
bacteriologist [bæk,tɪrɪ'ɑlədʒɪst] *s* bacteriólogo
bacteriology [bæk,tɪrɪ'ɑlədʒɪ] *s* bacteriología
bacteriolysis [bæk,tɪrɪ'ɑlɪsɪs] *s* bacteriólisis
bacteriophage [bæk'tɪrɪəfedʒ] *s* (bact.) bacteriófago
bacteriostasis [bæk,tɪrɪə'stesɪs] *s* (bact.) bacteriostasis
bacteriostatic [bæk,tɪrɪə'stætɪk] *adj* bacteriostático
bacterium [bæk'tɪrɪəm] *s* (*pl:* **-a** [ə]) bacteria
Bactrian ['bæktrɪən] *adj & s* bactriano
Bactrian camel *s* (zool.) camello bactriano
bad [bæd] *adj* (*comp:* **worse;** *super:* **worst**) malo; incobrable (*deuda*); falso (*aplícase a la moneda*); **a bad one** un mal sujeto; **from bad to worse** de mal en peor; **not bad, not half bad** o **not so bad** bastante bueno; **to be too bad** ser lástima; **to go to the bad** caer en el mal, arruinarse; **to look bad** tener mala cara; **to the bad** en el debe (*de uno*)
bad blood *s* mala sangre, mala voluntad
bad breath *s* mal aliento
bade [bæd] *pret de* **bid**
bad egg *s* (slang) mal sujeto, calavera, buena alhaja
bad form *s* conducta reprobable (*por propasarse de lo que admite la buena sociedad*)
badge [bædʒ] *s* divisa, insignia; placa (*de metal*); (fig.) señal, símbolo
badger ['bædʒər] (zool.) tejón; *va* molestar, atormentar
badinage [,bædɪ'nɑʒ] o ['bædɪnɪdʒ] *s* broma, chanza
Bad Lands *spl* Tierras malas (*comarcas yermas en los estados de Nebraska y Dakota del Sur, EE.UU.*)
badly ['bædlɪ] *adv* mal, malamente; muy, con urgencia; gravemente
badly off *adj* malparado, maltrecho; muy enfermo
badminton ['bædmɪntən] *s* juego del volante
badness ['bædnɪs] *s* maldad; imperfección
bad order *s* desarreglo
bad-tempered ['bæd'tɛmpərd] *adj* de mal genio
Baedeker ['bedəkər] *s* Baedeker (*guía del turismo*)
baffle ['bæfəl] *s* (mach.) deflector; (rad.) pantalla acústica; *va* deslumbrar, confundir; *vn* luchar en vano
bafflement ['bæfəlmənt] *s* deslumbramiento, confusión
baffle plate *s* chicana, placa deflectora
baffling ['bæflɪŋ] *adj* deslumbrador, perplejo
B.Ag. abr. de **Bachelor of Agriculture**
bag [bæg] *s* saco, bolso; saquito de mano; bolsa (*de un vestido o tela*); rodillera (*del pantalón en las rodillas*); caza (*animales después de cazados*); (anat.) bolsita, vejiguilla; (zool.) bolsa (*del marsupial*); (baseball) almohadilla; **to be in the bag** (slang) ser cosa segura; **to be left holding the bag** (coll.) quedarse con la carga en las costillas; (*pret & pp:* **bagged;** *ger:* **bagging**) *va* ensacar; coger, cazar; (slang) robar; *vn* hacer bolsa o pliegue (*un vestido o tela*)
bag and baggage *adv* con todas sus pertenencias, enteramente
bagasse [bə'gæs] *s* bagazo
bagatelle [,bægə'tɛl] *s* bagatela

baggage ['bægɪdʒ] *s* equipaje; (mil.) bagaje
baggage car *s* (rail.) coche de equipajes, furgón
baggage check *s* talón, contraseña de equipajes
baggage master *s* jefe de equipajes
baggage rack *s* red de equipaje
baggage room *s* sala de equipajes
bagging ['bægɪŋ] *s* harpillera
baggy ['bægɪ] *adj* (*comp:* **-gier;** *super:* **-giest**) flojo, holgado, que hace bolsa
bagman ['bægmən] *s* (*pl:* **-men**) (Brit.) agente viajero
bagnio ['bænjo] o ['bɑnjo] *s* (*pl:* **bagnios**) baño (*cárcel mora o turca*); mancebía, casa de prostitutas
bagpipe ['bæg,paɪp] *s* gaita, cornamusa
bagpiper ['bæg,paɪpər] *s* gaitero
B.Agr. abr. de **Bachelor of Agriculture**
baguet o **baguette** [bæ'gɛt] *s* joya rectangular; (arch.) astrágalo pequeño
bah [bɑ] *interj* ¡bah!
Bahama Islands [bə'hemə] o [bə'hɑmə] *spl* islas Bahamas, islas Lucayas
Bahamas *spl* Bahama, archipiélago de Bahama
bail [bel] *s* fianza, caución; achicador; aro, zuncho; **to go bail for** salir fiador por; **to jump bail** (slang) fugarse estando bajo fianza; *va* afianzar; achicar (*la embarcación; el agua de la embarcación*); zunchar (*fijar con un zuncho*); **to bail out** salir fiador por; achicar; *vn* achicar; **to bail out** (aer.) lanzarse en paracaídas
bailable ['beləbəl] *adj* afianzable
bail bond *s* escritura de fianza
bailiff ['belɪf] *s* alguacil, corchete
bailiwick ['belɪwɪk] *s* alguacilazgo; bailía; competencia, pertenencia; **to be in the bailiwick of** ser de la pertenencia de
bailment ['belmənt] *s* afianzamiento; depósito
bailsman ['belzmən] *s* (*pl:* **-men**) fianza, fiador
bain-marie [,bæ̃,mɑ'ri] *s* (*pl:* **bains-marie**) baño maría
Baird's sandpiper [bɛrdz] *s* (orn.) chorlito unicolor, pollito de mar
bairn [bɛrn] *s* (Scottish) niño
bait [bet] *s* carnada, cebo; añagaza, señuelo; **to swallow the bait** (fig.) tragar el anzuelo; *va* cebar; azuzar, hostigar
baize [bez] *s* bayeta
bake [bek] *s* cocción al horno; cosa cocida al horno; *va* cocer al horno; **to bake on** aplicar en caliente; *vn* hornear
baked meat *s* carne asada al horno
bakelite ['bekəlaɪt] *s* (trademark) baquelita
baker ['bekər] *s* panadero; (orn.) hornero
baker's dozen *s* docena del fraile (*trece*)
bakery ['bekərɪ] *s* (*pl:* **-ies**) panadería
baking ['bekɪŋ] *s* cochura, hornada
baking powder *s* polvo para hornear, levadura química
baking soda *s* bicarbonato de sosa
baksheesh o **bakshish** ['bækʃiʃ] *s* propina entre los árabes y turcos
Baku [bɑ'ku] *s* Bakú
bal. abr. de **balance**
Balaam ['beləm] *s* (Bib.) Balaán
balaclava helmet [,bælə'klɑvə] *s* pasamontaña
balalaika [,bælə'laɪkə] *s* (mus.) balalaika
balance ['bæləns] *s* balanza (*instrumento para pesar*); (com.) balance; equilibrio; resto (*lo que queda*); (com.) saldo (*a favor o en contra de uno*); volante de reloj; **in the balance** en balanza; **to lose one's balance** perder el equilibrio; **to strike a balance** hacer o pasar balance; *va* balancear (*en la balanza*); equilibrar; equilibrar, nivelar (*el presupuesto*); *vn* equilibrarse; balancear (*vacilar*)
balance beam *s* balancín
balanced diet *s* régimen alimenticio bien equilibrado
balance of payments *s* balanza de pagos
balance of power *s* (dipl.) equilibrio político, equilibrio europeo
balance of trade *s* balanza de comercio
balancer ['bælənsər] *s* balanceador; balancín (*de insecto*)
balance sheet *s* (com.) balance, avanzo
balance wheel *s* volante de reloj
balas ['bæləs] *s* balaje (*rubí espinela*)
balbriggan [bæl'brɪgən] *s* tejido de algodón o de lana para medias y ropa interior
balcony ['bælkənɪ] *s* (*pl:* **-nies**) balcón; (theat.) galería, paraíso
bald [bɔld] *adj* calvo; franco, directo, sencillo, sin adornos
baldachin ['bældəkɪn] o ['bɔldəkɪn] *s* baldaquín, palio; (arch.) baldaquín
bald eagle *s* (orn.) águila de cabeza blanca
balderdash ['bɔldərdæʃ] *s* disparate, música celestial
baldheaded ['bɔld'hɛdɪd] *adj* calvo
baldness ['bɔldnɪs] *s* calvicie
baldpate ['bɔld,pet] *s* persona calva; (orn.) lavanco, mareca
baldric ['bɔldrɪk] *s* tahalí
bald spot *s* calva
Baldwin ['bɔldwɪn] *s* Balduíno
baldy ['bɔldɪ] *adj* (coll.) calvito; *s* (*pl:* **-ies**) (coll.) calvito
bale [bel] *s* bala (*de papel, algodón, etc.*); *va* embalar
Balearic [,bælɪ'ærɪk] *adj* balear
Balearic Islands *spl* islas Baleares
baleen [bə'lin] *s* ballena (*lámina córnea en la mandíbula superior de la ballena*)
balefire ['bel,faɪr] *s* hoguera; señal luminosa; pira funeraria
baleful ['belfəl] *adj* funesto, nocivo
Balinese [,bɑlɪ'niz] *adj* baliaga, balinés; *s* (*pl:* **-nese**) baliaga, balinés
balk [bɔk] *s* lomo entre surcos; viga; contratiempo, obstáculo; desliz, descuido; (billiards) cabaña; (billiards) cuadro; *va* evitar; burlar, frustrar; malograr, perder; *vn* detenerse bruscamente; emperrarse, resistirse; repropiarse (*un caballo*)
Balkan ['bɔlkən] *adj* balcánico; **the Balkans** los Balcanes
Balkanize ['bɔlkənaɪz] *va* balcanizar
Balkan Mountains *spl* montes Balcanes
Balkan Peninsula *s* Península Balcánica, Península de los Balcanes
Balkan States *spl* estados de los Balcanes
balk line *s* (sport) línea de salida; (billiards) línea o raya a la cabecera de la mesa; (billiards) línea paralela a la banda
balky ['bɔkɪ] *adj* (*comp:* **-ier;** *super:* **-iest**) rebelón, repropio
ball [bɔl] *s* bola, pelota; balón (*pelota grande*); globo, esfera; ovillo (*de hilo, lana, etc.*); yema (*del dedo*); (hort.) cepellón (*tierra pegada a las raíces*); bala (*proyectil*); baile (*festejo en que se baila*); **to carry the ball** (coll.) tener toda la responsabilidad; **to have something on the ball** (slang) tener gran capacidad o talento; **to play ball** emprender la jugada; (coll.) seguir la corriente, obrar en armonía; *va* convertir en bola; **to ball up** (slang) enredar, confundir; *vn* convertirse en bola
ballad ['bæləd] *s* balada; romance
ballade [bə'lɑd] *s* (mus.) balada
ball and chain *s* bola de hierro atada con una cadena; (fig.) restricción, freno
ball-and-socket joint ['bɔlənd'sɑkɪt] *s* (mach.) articulación esférica
ballast ['bæləst] *s* (naut. & aer.) lastre; (rail.) balasto; (fig.) lastre (*juicio*); *va* (naut. & aer.) lastrar; (rail.) balastar
ball bearing *s* juego de bolas, cojinete de bolas
ball cock *s* (mach.) llave de bola o flotador
ballerina [,bælə'rinə] *s* bailarina
ballet ['bæle] o [bæ'le] *s* ballet, baile
ball float *s* flotador esférico
ball governor *s* (mach.) regulador de bolas, regulador de fuerza centrífuga
ballista [bə'lɪstə] *s* (*pl:* **-tae** [ti]) balista
ballistic [bə'lɪstɪk] *adj* balístico; **ballistics** *ssg* balística
ballistocardiogram [bə,lɪsto'kɑrdɪo,græm] *s* balistocardiograma
ballistocardiograph [bə,lɪsto'kɑrdɪo,græf] o [bə,lɪsto'kɑrdɪo,grɑf] *s* balistocardiógrafo
ballistocardiography [bə,lɪsto,kɑrdɪ'ɑgrəfɪ] *s* balistocardiografía
ball of fire *s* (slang) pólvora (*persona viva, pronta y eficaz*)
ballonet [,bælə'nɛt] *s* globo interior (*de un dirigible*)

balloon [bə'lun] *s* globo; *vn* subir o viajar en un globo; hincharse como un globo
balloon barrage *s* barrera de globos
balloonist [bə'lunɪst] *s* ascensionista
balloon tire *s* (aut.) llanta balón
balloon vine *s* (bot.) farolillo
ballot ['bælət] *s* papeleta, balota, cédula para votar; sufragio; *vn* balotar, votar
ballot box *s* urna electoral; **to stuff the ballot box** echar votos fraudulentos en la urna electoral
ball park *s* estadio de béisbol
ballplayer ['bɔl,pleər] *s* pelotero, jugador de pelota; beisbolero
ball point pen *s* bolígrafo o polígrafo, pluma esferográfica
ballroom ['bɔl,rum] o ['bɔl,rʊm] *s* salón de baile, sala de fiestas
ball valve *s* (mach.) válvula de bola
ballyhoo ['bælɪhu] *s* alharaca, bombo, propaganda sensacional; ['bælihu] o [,bælɪ'hu] *va* dar teatro a, dar bombo a; *vn* hacer propaganda sensacional
balm [bɑm] *s* bálsamo; (bot.) toronjil; (fig.) bálsamo (*consuelo, alivio*)
balm of Gilead *s* (bot.) balsamea; bálsamo de Judea o de la Meca (*resina y ungüento*)
balmy ['bɑmɪ] *adj* (*comp:* **-ier;** *super:* **-iest**) balsámico; bonancible, suave (*tiempo*); (slang) loco
baloney [bə'lonɪ] *s* (slang) tonterías, música celestial
balsa ['bɔlsə] o ['bælsə] *s* balsa; (bot.) balsa
balsam ['bɔlsəm] *s* bálsamo; (fig.) bálsamo (*consuelo, alivio*); (bot.) balsamina; (bot.) abeto de la parte oriental de Norteamérica (*Abies balsamea*); (bot.) madama (*Impatiens balsamina*)
balsam apple *s* (bot.) balsamina
balsam fir *s* (bot.) abeto de la parte oriental de Norteamérica (*Abies balsamea*)
Balt [bɔlt] *s* balto
Balthasar [bæl'θezər] *s* Baltasar
Baltic ['bɔltɪk] *adj* báltico; *s* Báltico
Baltic Provinces *spl* provincias bálticas
Baltic Sea *s* mar Báltico
Baltic States *spl* países bálticos, estados bálticos
Baltimore oriole ['bɔltɪmor] *s* (orn.) cacique veranero
Baluchistan [bə,lutʃɪ'stæn] *s* el Beluchistán
baluster ['bæləstər] *s* balaustre
balustrade [,bæləs'tred] *s* balaustrada
bambino [bæm'bino] *s* (*pl:* **-ni** [ni]) niño pequeño; niño Jesús (*imagen*)
bamboo [bæm'bu] *s* (bot.) bambú (*planta y caña*)
bamboo curtain *s* (fig.) cortina de bambú
bamboozle [bæm'buzəl] *va & vn* (coll.) embaucar, engañar, confundir
bamboozler [bæm'buzlər] *s* (coll.) engañabobos, embaucador, engañador
ban [bæn] *s* prohibición; maldición; bando de destierro; **bans** *spl* amonestaciones; (*pret & pp:* **banned;** *ger:* **banning**) *va* prohibir; maldecir; excomulgar
banal ['benəl], [bə'næl] o ['bænəl] *adj* trivial, trillado
banality [bə'nælɪtɪ] *s* (*pl:* **-ties**) trivialidad
banana [bə'nænə] *s* (bot.) banano, bananero, plátano (*árbol*); banana, plátano (*fruto*); *adj* bananero, platanero
banana oil *s* acetato de amilo, esencia de pera
Banat, the [bɑ'nɑt] el Banato
band [bænd] *s* banda; cenefa; raya, filete (*línea fina*); cuadrilla (*de personas*); cintillo (*de sombrero*); anillo (*de cigarro*); liga de goma; música, banda; (min.) veta, vena; (rad.) banda; cadena, grillete; correa; *va* orlar; zunchar; rayar; reunir, abanderizar; *vn* reunirse, abanderizarse
bandage ['bændɪdʒ] *s* venda; *va* vendar
bandana o **bandanna** [bæn'dænə] *s* pañuelo de hierbas
bandbox ['bænd,bɑks] *s* sombrerera
band brake *s* freno de cinta
bandeau [bæn'do] o ['bændo] *s* (*pl:* **-deaux** [doz]) prendedero
banderole o **banderol** ['bændərol] *s* banderola, banderita
band filter *s* (elec.) filtro de bandas
bandicoot ['bændɪkut] *s* (zool.) bandicut
bandit ['bændɪt] *s* (*pl:* **-dits** o **-ditti** ['dɪtɪ]) bandido
banditry ['bændɪtrɪ] *s* banditismo, bandidaje
bandmaster ['bænd,mæstər] o ['bænd,mɑstər] *s* director de banda, músico mayor
bandog ['bæn,dɔg] o ['bæn,dɑg] *s* mastín, sabueso; perro de guarda atado
bandoleer o **bandolier** [,bændə'lɪr] *s* bandolera; cartuchera colgada de una bandolera
band-pass filter ['bænd,pæs] o ['bænd,pɑs] *s* (elec.) filtro de bandas
band saw *s* sierra continua, sierra de cinta, sierra sin fin
band shell *s* quiosco de música con cubierta en forma de concha
bandsman ['bændzmən] *s* (*pl:* **-men**) músico de banda
band spread *s* (rad.) esparcimiento de banda, ensanche de banda
bandstand ['bænd,stænd] *s* plataforma de banda, templete, quiosco
bandwagon ['bænd,wægən] *s* carro de banda de música; (coll.) partido que gana; **to climb aboard the bandwagon** (coll.) adherirse al partido que gana
bandy ['bændɪ] *adj* arqueado, estevado; (*pret & pp.* **-died**) *va* tirar de una parte a otra; trocar (*palabras*); *vn* contender
bandy-legged ['bændɪ,lɛgɪd] o ['bændɪ,lɛgd] *adj* patiestevado
bane [ben] *s* azote; calamidad, ruina, muerte
baneberry ['ben,bɛrɪ] *s* (*pl:* **-ries**) (bot.) hierba de San Cristóbal
baneful ['benfəl] *adj* nocivo, venenoso; funesto, mortal
banewort ['ben,wʌrt] *s* (bot.) belladona; (bot.) flámula
bang [bæŋ] *s* golpazo, ruido de un golpe; portazo; **bangs** *spl* flequillo; *adv* de repente, de golpe; con estrépito; *interj* ¡pum!; *va* golpear con ruido, golpear con violencia; cortar (*el cabello*) en flequillo; *vn* hacer estrépito; **to bang against** dar con ruido contra
bangle ['bæŋgəl] *s* ajorca
bang-up ['bæŋ,ʌp] *adj* (slang) excelente, de primera clase
banian ['bænjən] *s* baniano; (bot.) baniano
banish ['bænɪʃ] *va* desterrar; despedir; (fig.) despedir (*p.ej., sospechas*)
banishment ['bænɪʃmənt] *s* destierro; despedida
banister ['bænɪstər] *s* balaustre; **banisters** *spl* balaustrada
banjo ['bændʒo] *s* (*pl:* **-jos** o **-joes**) banjo
banjoist ['bændʒo·ɪst] *s* banjoísta
banjo signal *s* (rail.) señal de guitarra, señal de disco
bank [bæŋk] *s* banco; banca (*en ciertos juegos*); alcancía (*vasija con una hendidura estrecha, donde se echan monedas*); ribera, margen, orilla (*de un río*); montón (*de tierra, nieve, nubes, etc.*); banda (*de la mesa de billar*); hilera; hilera de remos; teclado; (elec.) batería (*de lámparas*); (elec.) fila (*de transformadores*); (aer.) inclinación lateral (*en un viraje*); **to break the bank** hacer saltar la banca (*en el juego*); *va* amontonar; represar; cubrir (*un fuego*) con cenizas o con carbón; depositar (*dinero*); guardar (*dinero*) en un banco; poner en filas; (aer.) ladear; *vn* depositar dinero; ser banquero; (aer.) ladearse; **to bank on** (coll.) contar con
bank acceptance *s* giro contra un banco aceptado por éste
bank account *s* cuenta de banco, cuenta corriente
bank bill *s* cédula de banco; billete de banco
bankbook ['bæŋk,bʊk] *s* libreta de banco
bank discount *s* descuento corriente
banker ['bæŋkər] *s* banquero
bank holiday *s* día feriado para los bancos
banking ['bæŋkɪŋ] *adj* bancario; *s* banca
banking house *s* casa de banca
banking indicator *s* (aer.) inclinómetro
bank note *s* billete de banco
bank of issue *s* banco de emisión
bank roll *s* lío de papel moneda
bankrupt ['bæŋkrʌpt] *adj & s* bancarrotero; **to**

go bankrupt hacer bancarrota; *va* hacer quebrar; arruinar
bankruptcy ['bæŋkrʌptsɪ] o ['bæŋkrəpsɪ] *s* bancarrota, quiebra; (fig.) bancarrota (*fracaso*)
bank vault *s* caja fuerte
banner ['bænər] *s* bandera, estandarte; encabezamiento; *adj* primero, dominante
banner cry *s* grito de combate
banneret o **bannerette** [,bænə'rɛt] *s* banderета, banderín
banns [bænz] *spl* amonestaciones; banas (Am.)
banquet ['bæŋkwɪt] *s* banquete; *va & vn* banquetear
banquette [bæŋ'kɛt] *s* (eng. & fort.) banqueta; acera, banqueta
banshee o **banshie** ['bænʃi] o [bæn'ʃi] *s* (Irish & Scottish) hada o genio cuyos lamentos bajo la ventana anuncian una muerte en la familia
bantam ['bæntəm] *adj* pequeño, ligero; *s* persona de pequeña talla y amiga de pelear; gallo Bantam
bantamweight ['bæntəm,wet] *s* (box.) peso gallo
banter ['bæntər] *s* burla, chanza; *va* burlarse de, chancearse con; *vn* burlar, chancear
banteringly ['bæntərɪŋlɪ] *adv* chanceando
bantling ['bæntlɪŋ] *s* chicuelo
Bantu ['bæntu] *adj* bantu o bantú; *s* (*pl:* **-tu** o **-tus**) bantu o bantú
banyan ['bænjən] *s* (bot.) baniano
baobab ['beobæb] *s* (bot.) baobab
Bap. o **Bapt.** abr. de **Baptist**
baptism ['bæptɪzəm] *s* bautizo o bautismo; (eccl.) bautismo
baptismal [bæp'tɪzməl] *adj* bautismal
baptismal name *s* nombre de pila
baptism of fire *s* bautismo de fuego
Baptist ['bæptɪst] *adj & s* bautista, baptista
baptistery ['bæptɪstərɪ] *s* (*pl:* **-ies**) baptisterio o bautisterio
baptistry ['bæptɪstrɪ] *s* (*pl:* **-tries**) var. de **baptistery**
baptize [bæp'taɪz] o ['bæptaɪz] *va* bautizar; limpiar, purificar
baptizer [bæp'taɪzər] *s* bautista
bar. abr. de **barometer, barometric, barrel** y **barrister**
Bar. abr. de **Baruch**
B.Ar. abr. de **Bachelor of Architecture**
bar [bɑr] *s* barra (*de metal, etc.; banco de arena; insignia militar; mostrador en un bar*); tranca (*detrás de una puerta o ventana*); reja (*de una ventana, especialmente de una cárcel*); bar (*establecimiento donde se venden licores alcohólicos para beber en el mostrador*); barrera, impedimento; raya, lista; (her.) barra; (mus.) compás; (mus.) barra, divisoria; abogacía; curia (*conjunto de abogados*); tribunal; **behind bars** entre rejas; **to be admitted to the bar** recibirse de abogado; **to tend bar** ser barman, despachar bebidas en la barra de un bar; *prep* excepto; **bar none** sin excepción; (*pret & pp:* **barred;** *ger:* **barring**) *va* barrar, barretear, atrancar; impedir, estorbar; prohibir; excluir
Barabbas [bə'ræbəs] *s* (Bib.) Barrabás
barb [bɑrb] *s* púa; lengüeta (*de un anzuelo o dardo*); barbilla (*de una pluma*); caballo de Berbería; *va* armar con púas; armar con lengüetas
Barbados [bɑr'bedoz] *s* la Barbada
barbarian [bɑr'bɛrɪən] *adj & s* bárbaro
barbaric [bɑr'bærɪk] *adj* bárbaro, barbárico
barbarism ['bɑrbərɪzəm] *s* barbaridad; (gram.) barbarismo
barbarity [bɑr'bærɪtɪ] *s* (*pl:* **-ties**) barbarie
barbarous ['bɑrbərəs] *adj* bárbaro
Barbary ['bɑrbərɪ] *s* Berbería
Barbary ape *s* (zool.) mono de Gibraltar, mona
Barbary States *spl* Estados Berberiscos
barbecue ['bɑrbəkju] *s* barbacoa, churrasco; *va* churrasquear
barbed [bɑrbd] *adj* armado de púas; mordaz, punzante
barbed wire *s* alambre de púas, espino artificial; (mil.) alambrada
barbel ['bɑrbəl] *s* barbilla (*alrededor de la boca de algunos peces*); (ichth.) barbo
bar bell *s* barra de balas
barber ['bɑrbər] *s* barbero, peluquero; *adj* barberil; *va* hacer la barba a
barber pole *s* percha (*de barbero*)
barberry ['bɑr,bɛrɪ] *s* (*pl:* **-ries**) (bot.) bérbero, agracejo (*arbusto*); bérbero, agracejina (*fruto*)
barbershop ['bɑrbər,ʃɑp] *s* barbería, peluquería
barber's itch *s* sarna de los barberos
barbette [bɑr'bɛt] *s* (fort.) barbeta; **in barbette** a barbeta
barbican ['bɑrbɪkən] *s* (fort.) barbacana
barbiturate [bɑr'bɪtʃəret] o [,bɑrbɪ'tjuret] *s* (chem.) barbiturato
barbituric acid [,bɑrbɪ'tjurɪk] o [,bɑrbɪ'turɪk] *s* (chem.) ácido barbitúrico
barcarole o **barcarolle** ['bɑrkərol] *s* (mus.) barcarola
bard [bɑrd] *s* bardo; barda (*armadura del caballo*)
Bard of Avon ['evən] o ['ævən] *s* Cisne del Avon (*Shakespeare*)
bare [bɛr] *adj* desnudo; descubierto (*sin sombrero*); raído (*gastado por el uso*); desamueblado; mero, sencillo; sin aislar (*dícese del alambre*); **to lay bare** poner a descubierto; *va* desnudar; descubrir, manifestar
bareback ['bɛr,bæk] *adj* montado en pelo; *adv* en pelo, sin silla
barefaced ['bɛr,fest] *adj* desembozado; descarado, desvergonzado
barefoot ['bɛr,fut] *adj* descalzo; *adv* con los pies desnudos
barefooted ['bɛr,futɪd] *adj* descalzo
barège [,bɑ'rɛʒ] *s* barés
barehanded ['bɛr,hændɪd] *adj* con las manos desnudas; desprovisto
bareheaded ['bɛr,hɛdɪd] *adj* descubierto; *adv* con la cabeza descubierta
barelegged ['bɛr,lɛgɪd] o ['bɛr,lɛgd] *adj* en pernetas
barely ['bɛrlɪ] *adv* solamente; apenas
bareness ['bɛrnɪs] *s* desnudez
barfly ['bɑr,flaɪ] *s* (*pl:* **-flies**) frecuentador habitual de bares o tabernas
bargain ['bɑrgɪn] *s* negocio, trato de compra y venta; negocio ventajoso para el comprador; ganga (*cosa comprada barato*); **at a bargain** baratísimo; **into the bargain** de añadidura; **to strike a bargain** cerrar un trato; *va* estipular; **to bargain away** vender regalado; *vn* negociar; (coll.) regatear; **to bargain for** estar dispuesto para, contar con
bargain counter *s* baratillo, puesto para la venta de saldos
bargain sale *s* venta con rebajas, liquidación
barge [bɑrdʒ] *s* barcaza, gabarra; *vn* moverse pesadamente; **to barge in** entrar sin pedir permiso; **to barge in on** entrar a ver sin llamar a la puerta; **to barge into** entremeterse en (*una conversación*); irrumpir en (*un cuarto*)
bargeboard ['bɑrdʒ,bord] *s* (arch.) guardamalleta
bargee [bɑr'dʒi] *s* var. de **bargeman**
bargeman ['bɑrdʒmən] *s* (*pl:* **-men**) gabarrero
bar hole *s* (naut.) bocabarra (*del cabrestante*)
barilla [bə'rɪlə] *s* (bot. & chem.) barrilla
bar iron *s* hierro en barras
barite ['bɛraɪt] *s* (mineral.) baritina
baritone ['bærɪton] *s* (mus.) barítono
barium ['bɛrɪəm] *s* (chem.) bario
barium enema *s* (med.) enema opaca, enema de bario
bark [bɑrk] *s* corteza (*del árbol*); ladrido (*del perro*); estampido (*del cañón*); tos; (naut.) barca, bricbarca; (poet.) barca; *va* descortezar; cubrir con una capa de corteza; curtir (*las pieles*); pelar, raspar; ladrar (*p.ej., injurias*); *vn* ladrar; (fig.) ladrar
barkeeper ['bɑr,kipər] *s* tabernero, cantinero, mozo que despacha bebidas alcohólicas
barkentine ['bɑrkəntin] *s* (naut.) barca-goleta
barker ['bɑrkər] *s* ladrador; descortezador; vociferador, pregonero
barley ['bɑrlɪ] *s* (bot.) cebada
barleycorn ['bɑrlɪ,kɔrn] *s* grano de cebada;

John Barleycorn personificación humorística de las bebidas alcohólicas
barley sugar *s* azúcar cande o candi
barley water *s* hordiate
barm [bɑrm] *s* jiste
bar magnet *s* barra imantada
barmaid ['bɑr,med] *s* moza de taberna
barman ['bɑrmən] *s* (*pl:* **-men**) (Brit.) tabernero, cantinero, barman
Barmecide feast ['bɑrmɪsaɪd] *s* comida fingida, sin manjares; abundancia ilusoria
barmy ['bɑrmɪ] *adj* (*comp:* **-ier;** *super:* **-iest**) espumoso, lleno de jiste; (coll.) alocado, cambiadizo
barn [bɑrn] *s* granero, pajar, troje; cuadra, establo, caballeriza; cochera
Barnaby ['bɑrnəbɪ] *s* Bernabé
barnacle ['bɑrnəkəl] *s* (zool.) cirrópodo; (zool.) anatifa (*Lepas*); (zool.) bálano (*Balanus*); (zool.) percebe (*Pollicipes*); (orn.) bernicla, ganso monjita; pegote (*persona que se pega a otra*); **barnacles** *spl* (her. & vet.) acial; (coll.) anteojos
barnacle goose *s* (orn.) bernicla, ganso monjita
Barney ['bɑrnɪ] *s* Bernardo
barn owl *s* (orn.) lechuza, oliva
barnstorm ['bɑrn,stɔrm] *vn* (coll.) dar funciones de teatro o pronunciar discursos en las aldeas o en el campo
barnstormer ['bɑrn,stɔrmər] *s* (coll.) cómico de la legua
barn swallow *s* (orn.) golondrina; (orn.) golondrina cola tijera (*Hirundo erythrogastra*)
barnyard ['bɑrn,jɑrd] *s* corral, patio de granja
barnyard fowl *spl* aves de corral
barogram ['bærəgræm] *s* barograma
barograph ['bærəgræf] o ['bærəgrɑf] *s* barógrafo
barometer [bə'rɑmɪtər] *s* barómetro; (fig.) barómetro
barometric [,bærə'mɛtrɪk] o **barometrical** [,bærə'mɛtrɪkəl] *adj* barométrico
baron ['bærən] *s* barón; (coll.) potentado
baronage ['bærənɪdʒ] *s* baronía; nobleza; **the baronage** todos los barones
baroness ['bærənɪs] *s* baronesa
baronet ['bærənɪt] *s* baronet
baronetage ['bærənɪtɪdʒ] *s* dignidad de baronet; **the baronetage** todos los baronets
baronetcy ['bærənɪtsɪ] *s* (*pl:* **-cies**) dignidad de baronet; documento que confiere la dignidad de baronet
baronial [bə'ronɪəl] *adj* baronial
barony ['bærənɪ] *s* (*pl:* **-nies**) baronía
baroque [bə'rok] o [bə'rɑk] *adj & s* barroco
baroque pearl *s* barrueco
baroscope ['bærəskop] *s* baroscopio
barouche [bə'ruʃ] *s* barrocho
bar pin *s* alfiler en forma de barra
barque [bɑrk] *s* (poet.) barca; (naut.) barca o corbeta
barracan ['bærəkæn] *s* barragán
barracks ['bærəks] *spl* barracón; (mil.) cuartel
barracuda [,bærə'kudə] *s* (ichth.) barracuda, picuda
barrage [bə'rɑʒ] *s* presa; (mil.) barrera
barrage balloon *s* globo de barrera
barratry ['bærətrɪ] *s* (law) baratería; (naut. law) baratería de capitán o de patrón
barrel ['bærəl] *s* barril, tonel; cañón (*de escopeta, pluma, etc.*); tambor de cabrestante; cilindro (*p.ej., del émbolo*); (*pret & pp:* **-reled** o **-relled;** *ger:* **-reling** o **-relling**) *va* embarrilar, entonelar; *vn* (slang) avanzar con gran velocidad
barrel organ *s* (mus.) órgano de cilindro; (mus.) órgano de manubrio, organillo
barrel roll *s* (aer.) tonel
barrel vault *s* (arch.) bóveda en cañón
barren ['bærən] *adj* estéril, árido; **barrens** *spl* tierra yerma
barrenness ['bærənnɪs] *s* esterilidad, aridez
barrette [bə'rɛt] *s* broche para el cabello
barricade [,bærɪ'ked] *s* barricada; *va* barrear
barricado [,bærɪ'kedo] *s* (*pl:* **-does**) var. de **barricade;** *va* var. de **barricade**
barrier ['bærɪər] *s* barrera
barrier reef *s* barrera de arrecifes
barring ['bɑrɪŋ] *prep* salvo, excepto, sin
barrister ['bærɪstər] *s* (Brit.) abogado que tiene el derecho de alegar ante cualquier tribunal; (coll.) abogado
barroom ['bɑr,rum] o ['bɑr,rʊm] *s* bar, cantina
barrow ['bæro] *s* angarillas; carretón de mano; carretilla; túmulo (*encima de una sepultura antigua*); cerdo castrado
bar shot *s* (nav.) palanqueta
bar solder *s* soldadura en barras
barstool ['bɑr,stul] *s* taburete de la barra de un bar
Bart. abr. de **baronet**
bartender ['bɑr,tɛndər] *s* tabernero, cantinero, barman
barter ['bɑrtər] *s* trueque (*de un objeto por otro*); *va* trocar; **to barter away** trocar en desventajas; vender (*su honor*); *vn* trocar
Bartholomew [bɑr'θɑləmju] *s* Bartolomé
bartizan ['bɑrtɪzən] o [,bɑrti'zæn] *s* torre albarrana (*en una muralla*)
Baruch ['bɛrək] *s* (Bib.) Baruc
barysphere ['bærɪsfɪr] *s* (geol.) barisfera
baryta [bə'raɪtə] *s* (chem.) barita
barytone ['bærɪton] *s* var. de **baritone**
basal ['besəl] *adj* basal
basal metabolism *s* metabolismo basal
basalt [bə'sɔlt] o ['bæsɔlt] *s* basalto
basaltic [bə'sɔltɪk] *adj* basáltico
basanite ['bæzənaɪt] *s* (petrog.) basanita
bascule ['bæskjul] *s* juego de contrapesos iguales y contrarios
bascule bridge *s* puente basculante
base [bes] *s* base; culote (*de proyectil*); (arch.) basa; (elec.) culote (*de válvula de radio o de lámpara eléctrica*); (mus.) bajo; *adj* bajo, humilde; infame, vil; tosco; bajo de ley (*dícese de los metales*); *va* basar
baseball ['bes,bɔl] *s* béisbol; pelota de béisbol
baseboard ['bes,bord] *s* rodapié
baseborn ['bes'bɔrn] *adj* de humilde cuna; bastardo
baseburner ['bes'bʌrnər] *s* horno de alimentación automática
base hit *s* (baseball) golpe con que el batter gana la primera base
Basel ['bɑzəl] *s* Basilea
baseless ['beslɪs] *adj* infundado
base line *s* línea de base; (tennis) línea de fondo
basely ['beslɪ] *adv* bajamente, vilmente
baseman ['besmən] *s* (*pl:* **-men**) (baseball) jugador de cuadro
basement ['besmənt] *s* sótano
baseness ['besnɪs] *s* bajeza, vileza
base salary *s* salario base
bash [bæʃ] *s* (coll.) golpe que quiebra; *va* (coll.) quebrar a golpes
bashaw [bə'ʃɔ] o ['bæʃɔ] *s* bajá; persona de campanillas
bashful ['bæʃfəl] *adj* tímido, vergonzoso, encogido
bashfulness ['bæʃfəlnɪs] *s* timidez, vergüenza, encogimiento
basic ['besɪk] *adj* básico; (chem.) básico
basically ['besɪkəlɪ] *adv* fundamentalmente
Basic English *s* el inglés básico
basicity [be'sɪsɪtɪ] *s* basicidad
basidiomycete [bə,sɪdɪomaɪ'sit] *s* (bot.) basidiomiceto
basidium [bə'sɪdɪəm] *s* (*pl:* **-a** [ə]) (bot.) basidio
basil ['bæzɪl] *s* (bot.) albahaca
basilar ['bæsɪlər] *adj* basilar
Basilian [bə'sɪlɪən] *adj & s* basilio
basilica [bə'sɪlɪkə] *s* basílica
basilic vein [bə'sɪlɪk] *s* (anat.) vena basílica
basilisk ['bæsɪlɪsk] *s* (zool. & myth.) basilisco
basin ['besən] *s* palangana, jofaina; tazón (*de una fuente*); cuenca (*de un río*); dársena
basinet ['bæsɪnɛt] *s* bacinete
basis ['besɪs] *s* (*pl:* **-ses** [siz]) base; **on the basis of** a base de o en base a
bask [bæsk] o [bɑsk] *va* asolear, calentar; *vn* asolearse, calentarse, confortarse al sol o junto al fuego
basket ['bæskɪt] o ['bɑskɪt] *s* cesta; cesto (*cesta grande*); canasta (*cesto con dos asas*); excusabaraja (*cesta con tapadera*); (aer.) cesto, barquilla; (sport) cesto, red

basketball ['bæskɪt,bɔl] o ['bɑskɪt,bɔl] *s* baloncesto, basquetbol; *adj* baloncestístico
basketball player *s* baloncestista
basket-handle arch ['bæskɪt,hændəl] o ['bɑskɪt,hændəl] *s* arco carpanel
basket hilt *s* cazoleta
basketry ['bæskɪtrɪ] o ['bɑskɪtrɪ] *s* cestería
basket weave *s* tejido que se parece al de una cesta
basketwork ['bæskɪt,wʌrk] o ['bɑskɪt,wʌrk] *s* cestería
basking shark *s* (ichth.) cetorrino
Basle [bɑl] *s* Basilea
basque [bæsk] *s* jubón; (*cap.*) *adj* & *s* vasco (*de España y Francia*); vascongado (*de España*); vascón (*de la España antigua*); vasco, vascongado, vascuence (*idioma*)
Basque Country, the el País Vasco
Basque Provinces, the las Provincias Vascongadas o las Vascongadas
bas-relief [,bɑrɪ'lif] o [,bæsrɪ'lif] *s* bajo relieve
bass [bes] *adj* (mus.) bajo; *s* (mus.) bajo; [bæs] *s* (ichth.) róbalo; (ichth.) perca; (ichth.) pomosio; (bot.) tilo; (bot.) líber
bass clef [bes] *s* (mus.) clave de fa
bass drum [bes] *s* (mus.) bombo
basset ['bæsɪt] *s* perro basset
bass horn [bes] *s* (mus.) tuba
bassinet [,bæsɪ'nɛt] o ['bæsɪnɛt] *s* cuna o cochecillo en forma de cesto
basso ['bæso] o ['bɑso] *adj* (mus.) bajo; *s* (*pl:* **-sos** o **-si** [sɪ]) (mus.) bajo
bassoon [bə'sun] *s* (mus.) bajón
bassoonist [bə'sunɪst] *s* bajonista
basso profundo ['bɑso pro'fʌndo] *s* (mus.) bajo profundo
bass viol [bes] *s* (mus.) violón, contrabajo
basswood ['bæs,wud] *s* (bot.) tilo, tilo americano
bast [bæst] *s* (bot.) líber
bastard ['bæstərd] *adj* & *s* bastardo
bastardly ['bæstərdlɪ] *adj* bastardo; bastardeado
bastard title *s* (print.) anteportada
bastardy ['bæstərdɪ] *s* bastardía
baste [best] *va* azotar, apalear; (sew.) hilvanar; (cook.) pringar, enlardar
bastille o **bastile** [bæs'til] *s* bastida (*máquina militar antigua*); bastilla (*fuerte pequeño*); prisión
bastinado [,bæstɪ'nedo] *s* (*pl:* **-does**) bastonada o bastonazo; bastón, porra; *va* bastonear
bastion ['bæstʃən] o ['bæstɪən] *s* bastión
bastioned ['bæstʃənd] o ['bæstɪənd] *adj* (fort.) bastionado
bat. abr. de **battalion** y **battery**
bat [bæt] *s* palo; (coll.) golpe; (slang) parranda, borrachera; (zool.) murciélago; **blind as a bat** más ciego que un topo; **right off the bat** (slang) de repente, sin deliberación; **to go on a bat** (slang) andar de parranda; (*pret & pp:* **batted;** *ger:* **batting**) *va* golpear; **without batting an eye** sin pestañear, sin inmutarse; *vn* golpear
Bataan [bə'tæn] *s* el Bataán
Batavian [bə'tevɪən] *adj* & *s* bátavo
batch [bætʃ] *s* cochura, hornada; colección; grupo; lío (*de papeles*); (coll.) soltero
bate [bet] *va* disminuir, suspender; **with bated breath** con aliento entrecortado; *vn* disminuirse
bath [bæθ] o [bɑθ] *s* baño; **to take a bath** tomar un baño
bathe [beð] *va* bañar; *vn* bañarse; **to go bathing** ir a bañarse
bather [beðər] *s* bañista
bathhouse ['bæθ,haus] o ['bɑθ,haus] *s* casa de baños; caseta o casilla de baños
bathing beach *s* playa de baños
bathing beauty *s* sirena de la playa
bathing cap *s* gorro de baño
bathing resort *s* estación balnearia
bathing slipper *s* zapatilla de baño
bathing soap *s* jabón de baño
bathing suit *s* traje de baño, bañador
bathing trunks *spl* taparrabo
bath mat *s* alfombra de baño
batholith ['bæθəlɪθ] *s* (geol.) batolito
bathometer [bə'θɑmɪtər] *s* batómetro
bathos ['beθɑs] *s* paso ridículo de lo sublime a lo trivial o vulgar; trivialidad; sensiblería
bath powder *s* polvos de baño
bathrobe ['bæθ,rob] o ['bɑθ,rob] *s* bata de baño, albornoz; bata, peinador
bathroom ['bæθ,rum] o ['bɑθ,rum] *s* baño, cuarto de baño
bathroom fixtures *spl* aparatos sanitarios, juego de baño
bath salts *spl* sales para el baño
Bathsheba [bæθ'ʃibə] o ['bæθʃɪbə] *s* (Bib.) Betsabé
bath slipper *s* zapatilla de baño
bath soap *s* jabón de baño
bath sponge *s* esponja de baño
bath towel *s* toalla de baño
bathtub ['bæθ,tʌb] o ['bɑθ,tʌb] *s* bañera, bañadera, baño
bathybius [bə'θɪbɪəs] *s* (zool.) batibio
bathyscaphe ['bæθɪskef] *s* batiscafo
bathysphere ['bæθɪsfɪr] *s* batisfera
batik [bə'tik] o ['bætɪk] *s* batik
batiste [bə'tist] *s* batista de Escocia; cámbric (*tejido elástico de algodón con que se hacen vendas*)
batman ['bætmən] *s* (*pl:* **-men**) (Brit.) ordenanza
baton [bæ'tɑn] o ['bætən] *s* bastón; (mus.) batuta
batrachian [bə'trekɪən] *adj* & *s* (zool.) batracio
batsman ['bætsmən] *s* (*pl:* **-men**) (sport) batter
batt. abr. de **battalion** y **battery**
batt [bæt] *s* hoja de algodón; algodón en hojas
battalion [bə'tæljən] *s* (mil. & fig.) batallón; **battalions** *spl* (mil.) fuerzas, tropas
batten ['bætən] *s* listón; tabla para pisos; *va* engordar; enlistonar; **to batten down the hatches** (naut.) asegurar las escotillas con listones de madera; **to batten up** cerrar con listones; *vn* engordar; medrar
batter ['bætər] *s* batido, pasta; talud; (baseball) bateador; *va* golpear; magullar, mellar, estropear; (baseball) batear; ataludar (*dar talud a*)
battering ram *s* ariete
battery ['bætərɪ] *s* (*pl:* **-ies**) batería; (elec.) pila; (elec.) acumulador; (elec.) batería (*dos o más pilas o acumuladores unidos entre sí*); (baseball) batería; (law) violencia
battery charger *s* (elec.) cargador de acumulador
battery eliminator *s* (rad.) eliminador de baterías
battery tester *s* (elec.) probador de acumuladores
batting ['bætɪŋ] *s* algodón en hojas; (baseball) bateo
battle ['bætəl] *s* batalla; **to do battle** librar batalla; *va* batallar con; *vn* batallar
battle array *s* orden de batalla; **in battle array** en batalla
battleax o **battleaxe** ['bætəl,æks] *s* hacha de armas, hacha de combate
battle cruiser *s* (nav.) crucero de combate
battle cry *s* grito de batalla, grito de combate
battledore ['bætəldor] *s* raqueta; **battledore and shuttlecock** volante, raqueta y volante
battlefield ['bætəl,fild] *s* campo de batalla
battle front *s* frente de combate
battleground ['bætəl,graund] *s* campo de batalla
battlement ['bætəlmənt] *s* almenaje, crestería
battle piece *s* (paint.) batalla
battleplane ['bætəl,plen] *s* avión de combate
battle royal *s* riña promiscua; lucha hasta el último trance
battle-scarred ['bætəl,skɑrd] *adj* lisiado en batalla
battleship ['bætəl,ʃɪp] *s* acorazado
battle stations *spl* puestos de combate
battology [bə'tɑlədʒɪ] *s* batología
battue [bæ'tu] o [bæ'tju] *s* batida; matanza general
batty ['bætɪ] *adj* (*comp:* **-tier;** *super:* **-tiest**) (slang) extravagante, necio, loco
bauble ['bɔbəl] *s* chuchería; cetro de bufón
Baucis ['bɔsɪs] *s* (myth.) Baucis

baulk [bɔk] *s, va & vn* var. de **balk**
bauxite ['bɔksaɪt] o ['bozaɪt] *s* (mineral.) bauxita
Bavaria [bə'verɪə] *s* Baviera
Bavarian [bə'verɪən] *adj & s* bávaro
bawd [bɔd] *s* alcahuete o alcahueta, tercero o tercera
bawdry ['bɔdrɪ] *s* indecencia, obscenidad
bawdy ['bɔdɪ] *adj* (*comp:* **-ier;** *super:* **-iest**) indecente, obsceno
bawdyhouse ['bɔdɪ,haʊs] *s* mancebía, lupanar
bawl [bɔl] *s* voces, gritos; *va* vocear; **to bawl out** (slang) dar una calada a; *vn* vocear, gritar, chillar
bay [be] *s* bahía; (arch.) ventana salediza; (arch.) intercolumnio; ladrido, aullido; granero, pajar; apuro, trance; bayo; caballo bayo; (bot.) laurel; **bays** *spl* corona de laurel; lauro, fama; **at bay** acosado, acorralado, a raya; *adj* bayo; *vn* ladrar, aullar; **to bay at the moon** ladrar a la luna
bayadere [,bɑjə'dɪr] *s* bayadera (*bailarina y cantadora india*)
Bayard, Seigneur de ['beərd] señor de Bayardo
bayberry ['be,berɪ] *s* (*pl:* **-ries**) (bot.) arrayán brabántico; baya del arrayán brabántico; (bot.) malagueta (*Pimenta acris*)
Bay of Bengal *s* golfo de Bengala
Bay of Biscay *s* mar Cantábrico, golfo de Vizcaya, golfo de Gascuña
bayonet ['beənɪt] *s* bayoneta; *va* herir con bayoneta; forzar a la bayoneta; bayonetear (Am.)
bayonet socket *s* (elec.) portalámparas de bayoneta
Bayonne [,bæ'jɔn] *s* Bayona
bay rum *s* ron de laurel, ron de malagueta
bay tree *s* (bot.) laurel
bay window *s* galería, mirador, ventana salediza; (slang) barriga, panza
baywood ['be,wʊd] *s* (bot.) caoba del golfo de Campeche (*Swietenia macrophylla*)
bazaar o **bazar** [bə'zɑr] *s* bazar; quermese, venta para reunir fondos para obras caritativas
bazooka [bə'zukə] *s* (mil.) bazuca (*cañón cohete portátil*)
B.B.A. abr. de **Bachelor of Business Administration**
B battery *s* (rad.) batería del circuito de la placa
bbl. abr. de **barrel** o **barrels**
bbls. abr. de **barrels**
B.C. abr. de **before Christ** y **British Columbia**
B.C.E. abr. de **Bachelor of Chemical Engineering** y **Bachelor of Civil Engineering**
B complex *s* (biochem.) complejo B
bd. abr. de **board**
B.D. abr. de **Bachelor of Divinity**
bdellium ['delɪəm] *s* bedelio
bdl. abr. de **bundle**
be [bi] (*pres:* **am, is, are;** *pret:* **was, were;** *pp:* **been**) *v aux* estar, p.ej., **he is eating** está comiendo; ser, p.ej., **she is loved by everybody** es amada por todo el mundo; haber, p.ej., **he is gone** ha ido; deber, p.ej., **what are we to do?** ¿qué debemos hacer?; *v impers* ser, p.ej., **it is easy to learn Spanish** es fácil aprender el español; **so be it** o **be it so** así sea; **be that as it may** sea lo que fuere, sea como fuere; haber, p.ej., **it is foggy** hay neblina; **it is muddy** hay lodo; **it is sunny** hay sol; **there is** o **there are** hay; **what is the matter?** ¿qué hay?; **what is wrong?** ¿qué hay?; hacer, p.ej., **how is the weather?** ¿qué tiempo hace?; **it is cold** hace frío; **it is fine weather** hace buen tiempo; **it is hot** o **it is warm** hace calor; *vn* estar, p.ej., **I am tired** estoy cansado; **he is in Madrid** está en Madrid; ser, p.ej., **she is very old** es muy vieja; **I am a doctor** soy médico; tener, p.ej., **to be ashamed** tener vergüenza; **to be cold** tener frío; **to be hot** tener calor; **to be hungry** tener hambre; **to be in a hurry** tener prisa; **to be the matter with** tener p.ej., **what is the matter with you?** ¿qué tiene Vd.?; **to be right** tener razón; **to be thirsty** tener sed; **to be warm** tener calor; **to be wrong** no tener razón; **to be . . . years old** tener . . . años; **to be** futuro, p.ej., **my wife to be** mi futura esposa; **to be in** estar en casa, en la tienda, en la oficina, etc.; **to be in with** (coll.) ser muy amigo de, gozar del favor de; **to be off** irse; estar equivocado; **to be out** estar fuera de casa, estar en la calle; **to be out of** (coll.) no tener más; **to be up to** estar a la altura de, ser competente para; estar haciendo, estar urdiendo; andar en (*p.ej., travesuras*); tocar a, depender de
beach [bitʃ] *s* playa; *va* varar; *vn* varar, encallar
beachcomb ['bitʃ,kom] *vn* raquear; **to go beachcombing** andar al raque
beachcomber ['bitʃ,komər] *s* ola encrestada; raquero, vagabundo de las playas
beach flea *s* (zool.) pulga de mar
beachhead ['bitʃ,hed] *s* (mil.) cabeza de playa
beach robe *s* albornoz
beach robin *s* (U.S.A.) revuelvepiedras; (Brit.) canut (*Calidris canutus*)
beach shoe *s* playera
beach umbrella *s* parasol de playa, sombrilla de colores
beach wagon *s* rubia, coche rural
beachy ['bitʃɪ] *adj* (*comp:* **-ier;** *super:* **-iest**) guijoso, cascajoso
beacon ['bikən] *s* almenara, señal luminosa; faro; hacho (*sitio elevado cerca de la costa*); (rad.) radiofaro; (fig.) guía; *va* señalar con almenara; iluminar, guiar; *vn* brillar
bead [bid] *s* cuenta, abalorio; cuenta (*de rosario*); cuentecilla, mostacilla; perla; gota, burbuja; botón (*de fundente*); reborde (*borde saliente*); talón (*de neumático*); mira globular; (arch.) astrágalo; guardavivos (*moldura para proteger las esquinas*); listón separador; **beads** *spl* sarta de cuentas; rosario; **to count one's beads** rezar el rosario; **to draw a bead on** (coll.) apuntar; **to say** o **to tell one's beads** rezar el rosario; *va* adornar con abalorios; rebordear; *vn* formar reborde; burbujear
beading ['bidɪŋ] *s* abalorio; (arch.) astrágalo; (arch.) contero
beadle ['bidəl] *s* bedel; (eccl.) pertiguero
beadsman ['bidzmən] *s* (*pl:* **-men**) hombre que reza por otro; pobre, mendigo
bead tree *s* (bot.) acederaque
beadwork ['bid,wʌrk] *s* abalorio; (arch.) astrágalo; (arch.) contero
beady ['bidɪ] *adj* (*comp:* **-ier;** *super:* **-iest**) adornado con abalorios; que tiene apariencia de gotas brillantes; burbujeante
beagle ['bigəl] *s* sabueso
beak [bik] *s* pico; boquilla (*de un instrumento de viento*); (slang) nariz, nariz corva; mechero de gas; rostro (*del barco antiguo*); cabo, promontorio
beaked [bikt] *adj* picudo
beaker ['bikər] *s* tazón; (chem.) vaso con pequeño pico
beakhead ['bik,hed] *s* (naut.) beque
beam [bim] *s* viga; viga maestra; timón (*del arado*); (naut.) bao; (naut.) bao mayor; (naut.) manga (*anchura mayor*); (naut.) través (*dirección perpendicular a la de la quilla*); rayo (*de luz, de calor, de radio*); astil (*de la balanza*); balanza de cruz; (mach.) balancín; (fig.) rayo (*p.ej., de esperanza*); **on the beam** siguiendo el haz (*del radiofaro*); (naut.) por el través; (slang) siguiendo el buen camino; *va* emitir (*luz, ondas, etc.*); *vn* destellar, brillar; sonreír alegremente
beamed [bimd] *adj* envigado
beaming ['bimɪŋ] *adj* brillante, radiante; alegre, risueño
beam sea *s* (naut.) mar de costado
beamy ['bimɪ] *adj* (*comp:* **-ier;** *super:* **-iest**) brillante, radiante; alegre, risueño; macizo, grueso
bean [bin] *s* (bot.) haba (*Vicia faba*); (bot.) alubia, frijol, habichuela, judía (*Phaseolus vulgaris*), vaina del haba; haba (*simiente del café y el cacao*); (slang) cabeza; *va* (slang) golpear en la cabeza con una pelota

beanbag ['bin,bæg] *s* saquito de habas (*que usan los niños en ciertos juegos*)
bean ball *s* (slang) lanzamiento a la cabeza del bateador (*en el béisbol*)
beanpole ['bin,pol] *s* estaca para habas o frijoles; (fig.) poste de telégrafo (*persona muy alta y delgada*)
beanstalk ['bin,stɔk] *s* tallo de haba, tallo de frijol
bear [bɛr] *s* oso; bajista (*en la Bolsa*); hombre ceñudo ‖ (*pret:* **bore;** *pp:* **borne**) *va* cargar; traer; llevar (*p.ej., armas, una inscripción*); apoyar, sostener; aguantar, sufrir; sentir, experimentar; dejar, permitir; producir, rendir (*p.ej., frutos, interés*); parir; referir, relatar; tener (*odio o amor*); **to bear a grudge against** guardar rencor a, tener inquina a; **to bear date** llevar fecha; **to bear in mind** tener presente, tener en cuenta; **to bear interest** devengar interés; **to bear out** apoyar, sostener; confirmar; **to bear the charges** pagar los gastos; **to bear the market** jugar a la baja; **to bear witness** dar testimonio ‖ *vn* dirigirse, seguir, volver; **to bear down** ejercer presión hacia abajo; hacer bajar por fuerza (*dícese de la mujer que está de parto*); **to bear down on** o **upon** apretar hacia abajo; contener, reprimir; correr sobre, arrojarse impetuosamente sobre; **to bear on** o **upon** referirse a; **to bear up** cobrar ánimo, no perder la esperanza; **to bear up against** resistir; arrostrar; **to bear with** ser indulgente para con, ser paciente con
bearable ['bɛrəbəl] *adj* soportable, sufrible
bearbaiting ['bɛr,betɪŋ] *s* deporte que consiste en echar perros a pelear con un oso encadenado
bearberry ['bɛr,bɛrɪ] *s* (*pl:* **-ries**) (bot.) gayuba, aguavilla
beard [bɪrd] *s* barba; (bot.) arista; *va* mesar; retar, desafiar; poner barba a
bearded ['bɪrdɪd] *adj* barbado, barbudo; (bot.) aristado
bearded eagle o **vulture** *s* (orn.) águila barbuda
bearer ['bɛrər] *s* portador; (com.) portador; árbol fructífero; posesor (*de un cargo u oficio*); portaféretro
bear garden *s* patio de los osos; corral donde los perros pelean con un oso encadenado; merienda de negros
bearing ['bɛrɪŋ] *s* apoyo; porte, presencia, maneras; aguante, paciencia; referencia, relación; fuerza (*p.ej., de una observación*); (her.) blasón; (mach.) cojinete; **bearings** *spl* orientación; **to ask for bearings** (aer.) pedir situación; **to lose one's bearings** desorientarse
bearish ['bɛrɪʃ] *adj* osuno; ceñudo; que juega a la baja; que tiende a bajar
bear's-ear ['bɛrz,ɪr] *s* (bot.) oreja de oso
bearskin ['bɛr,skɪn] *s* piel de oso; morrión (*gorro militar*); bayetón (*tela de lana peluda*)
beast [bist] *s* bestia; persona abrutada; (coll.) cosa muy mala, p.ej., **a beast of a day** un día muy malo
beastly ['bistlɪ] *adj* (*comp:* **-lier;** *super:* **-liest**) bestial; (coll.) muy malo, detestable; *adv* (coll.) muy, detestablemente
beast of burden *s* bestia de carga
beast of prey *s* animal de rapiña
beat [bit] *s* golpe; latido (*del corazón*); compás (*del ritmo*); marca del compás (*con la mano o el pie*); (mus.) tiempo; (phys.) batimiento; (rad.) batido; ronda (*p.ej., de un policía*); (coll.) ganador, vencedor; (slang) gorrón, embestidor; anticipación de una noticia (*por un periódico*); **off one's beat** fuera del camino trillado; **outside the beat of** fuera de la competencia de; *adj* (coll.) deslomado, derrengado; (rad.) de batido ‖ (*pret:* **beat;** *pp;* **beaten** o **beat**) *va* batir; sacudir (*una alfombra*); aventajar, ganar; (mus.) llevar (*el compás*); tocar (*un tambor*); azotar, pegar; (coll.) confundir; (coll.) engañar, estafar; **to beat a retreat** emprender la retirada; **to beat back** rechazar; **to beat down** abatir, derribar; (coll.) rebajar (*un precio*) regateando; **to beat it** (slang) largarse; **to beat off** rechazar; **to beat to death** matar a golpes; **to beat up** batir (*p.ej., huevos*); (slang) acometer, aporrear ‖ *vn* batir; latir (*el corazón*); (coll.) ganar; (naut.) barloventear; **to beat about** ir buscando; **to beat about the bush** (coll.) andarse por las ramas; **to beat against** azotar, estrellarse contra; **to beat down on** batir (*dar fuertemente en*)
beaten ['bɪtən] *adj* batido, martillado, trillado; vencido, derrotado; deslomado, derrengado; *pp de* **beat**
beater ['bitər] *s* batidor (*persona o instrumento*)
beatific [,biə'tɪfɪk] *adj* beatífico
beatification [bɪ,ætɪfɪ'keʃən] *s* beatificación
beatify [bɪ'ætɪfaɪ] (*pret & pp:* **-fied**) beatificar
beating ['bitɪŋ] *s* golpeo; pulsación; paliza, zurra; aleteo; derrota; **to take a beating** recibir una paliza; salir derrotado; (com.) salir con pérdidas
beatitude [bɪ'ætɪtjud] o [bɪ'ætɪtud] *s* beatitud; (*cap.*) *s* beatitud (*Sumo Pontífice*); **the Beatitudes** (theol.) las bienaventuranzas
beatnik ['bitnɪk] *s* bohemio que rechaza los valores convencionales de la sociedad
beat reception *s* (rad.) recepción por batido
Beatrice ['biətrɪs] *s* Beatriz
beau [bo] *s* (*pl:* **beaus** o **beaux** [boz]) pretendiente, cortejo; novio; petimetre, currutaco
Beau Brummell ['brʌməl] *s* el hermoso Brummell, el Petronio, el rey de la moda; petimetre, currutaco
beau geste [ʒɛst] *s* (*pl:* **beaux gestes** [bo'ʒɛst]) (Fr.) acción generosa; (Fr.) generosidad fingida
beau ideal [aɪ'diəl] *s* bello ideal
beau monde [mɑnd] *s* (Fr.) gente de moda
beauteous ['bjutɪəs] *adj* bello, hermoso
beautification [,bjutɪfɪ'keʃən] *s* embellecimiento
beautiful ['bjutɪfəl] *adj* bello, hermoso
beautify ['bjutɪfaɪ] (*pret & pp:* **-fied**) *va* embellecer, hermosear; *vn* embellecerse, hermosearse
beauty ['bjutɪ] *s* (*pl:* **-ties**) beldad, belleza (*hermosura, mujer muy hermosa*)
beauty contest *s* concurso de belleza
beauty parlor *s* salón de belleza
beauty queen *s* reina de belleza
beauty sleep *s* primer sueño (*antes de medianoche*)
beauty spot *s* lunar postizo, grano de belleza; sitio pintoresco
beaver ['bivər] *s* (zool.) castor; piel de castor; castor (*tejido de lana*); sombrero castoreño; sombrero de copa; sobrevista (*del morrión*); (arm.) babera, baberol; (arm.) visera
bebeerine [bə'bɪrin] o [bə'bɪrɪn] *s* (pharm.) bebirina
becalm [bɪ'kɑm] *va* serenar, calmar; **to be becalmed** (naut.) encalmarse
became [bɪ'kem] *pret de* **become**
because [bɪ'kɔz] *conj* porque; **because of** por, por causa de, a causa de, con motivo de; **because of** + *ger* por + *inf*
beccafico [,bɛkə'fiko] *s* (*pl:* **-cos**) (orn.) becafigo
béchamel [beʃɑ'mɛl] *s* bechamela
bechance [bɪ'tʃæns] o [bɪ'tʃɑns] *vn* acontecer, suceder
Bechuanaland [,bɛtʃu'ɑnə,lænd] o [,bɛkju'ɑnə,lænd] *s* la Bechuanalandia
beck [bɛk] *s* seña (*con la cabeza o la mano*); **at the beck and call of** a disposición de; completamente entregado a
beckon ['bɛkən] *s* seña (*con la cabeza o la mano*); *va* llamar con señas; atraer, tentar; *vn* hacer seña (*con la cabeza o la mano*)
becloud [bɪ'klaud] *va* anublar, obscurecer
become [bɪ'kʌm] (*pret:* **-came;** *pp:* **-come**) *va* convenir; sentar bien; *vn* hacerse, p.ej., **my brother became a doctor** mi hermano se hizo médico; **he will become rich but not happy** se hará rico pero no feliz; llegar a ser, p.ej., **he will become a general** llegará a ser general; meterse, p.ej., **he became a soldier** se metió soldado; ponerse, p.ej., **she became very ill** se puso muy enferma; volverse, p.ej., **the clouds became black** se volvieron negras las nubes; convertirse en,

p.ej., **the water became wine** se convirtió el agua en vino; (philos.) devenir; **to become of** ser de, p.ej., **what will become of me?** ¿qué será de mí?; hacerse de, p.ej., **what became of my hat?** ¿qué se ha hecho de mi sombrero?; este verbo, seguido de un adjetivo, se traduce a veces por un verbo neutro o reflexivo que corresponda al adjetivo, p.ej., **to become crazy** enloquecer; **to become useless** inutilizarse
becoming [bɪˈkʌmɪŋ] *adj* conveniente; que sienta bien; *s* (philos.) (el) devenir
bed [bɛd] *s* cama, lecho; (mas.) lecho; lecho (*del río, de la vía; asiento; capa, estrato*); (min.) yacimiento; macizo (*de jardín*); **to get up on the wrong side of the bed** levantarse por los pies de la cama; **to go to bed** acostarse; **to make the bed** hacer la cama; **to stay in bed** guardar cama; **to take to one's bed** encamarse; (*pret & pp:* **bedded;** *ger:* **bedding**) *va* acostar; dar cama a; sembrar o plantar en un macizo; poner en capas sobrepuestas; *vn* acostarse; formar una masa compacta; cohabitar, hacer vida marital
bedabble [bɪˈdæbəl] *va* salpicar
bed and board *s* techo y sustento
bedaub [bɪˈdɔb] *va* embadurnar; adornar vistosamente; vilipendiar; alabar con exceso
bedaze [bɪˈdez] *va* aturdir, atolondrar
bedazzle [bɪˈdæzəl] *va* deslumbrar
bedbug [ˈbɛd,bʌg] *s* (ent.) chinche
bedchamber [ˈbɛd,tʃembər] *s* alcoba, cuarto de dormir
bedclothes [ˈbɛd,kloz] *spl* ropa de cama
bedcover [ˈbɛd,kʌvər] *s* cubierta de cama
bedding [ˈbɛdɪŋ] *s* ropa de cama; paja para jergón; lecho (*asiento; capa inferior*); (geol.) estratificación
Bede [bid] *s* Beda; **the Venerable Bede** el venerable Beda
bedeck [bɪˈdɛk] *va* acicalar, adornar, engalanar
bedevil [bɪˈdɛvəl] (*pret & pp:* **-iled** o **-illed;** *ger:* **-iling** o **-illing**) *va* atormentar; confundir; endemoniar, hechizar
bedevilment [bɪˈdɛvəlmənt] *s* tormento; confusión; hechizo
bedew [bɪˈdju] o [bɪˈdu] *va* rociar
bedfast [ˈbɛd,fæst] o [ˈbɛd,fast] *adj* postrado en cama
bedfellow [ˈbɛd,fɛlo] *s* compañero o compañera de cama; compañero, compañera
Bedford cord [ˈbɛdfərd] *s* paño Bedford
bedgown [ˈbɛd,gaʊn] *s* camisa de dormir; chaqueta (*de las mujeres del norte de Inglaterra*)
bedight [bɪˈdaɪt] (*pret & pp:* **-dight** o **-dighted**) *va* (archaic) adornar, guarnecer
bedim [bɪˈdɪm] (*pret & pp:* **-dimmed;** *ger:* **-dimming**) *va* obscurecer
bedizen [bɪˈdaɪzən] o [bɪˈdɪzən] *va* emperejilar
bedlam [ˈbɛdləm] *s* confusión, bullicio; casa de orates, manicomio
bedlamite [ˈbɛdləmaɪt] *s* loco, orate
bed linen *s* ropa de cama
bed of roses *s* canonjía, sinecura
Bedouin [ˈbɛduɪn] *adj* beduíno; *s* beduíno; nómada
bedpan [ˈbɛd,pæn] *s* calentador de cama; silleta
bedpost [ˈbɛd,post] *s* pilar de cama
bedraggle [bɪˈdrægəl] *va* ensuciar o manchar arrastrando por el suelo
bedrail [ˈbɛd,rel] *s* baranda o barandilla de la cama
bedrid [ˈbɛd,rɪd] o **bedridden** [ˈbɛd,rɪdən] *adj* postrado en cama
bedrock [ˈbɛd,rɑk] *s* lecho de roca, roca sólida; fondo; base, fundamento
bedroom [ˈbɛd,rum] o [ˈbɛd,rʊm] *s* alcoba, cuarto de dormir
bedroom suit *s* juego de alcoba
bedside [ˈbɛd,saɪd] *s* lado de cama; cabecera; espacio entre la cama y la pared; *adj* del lado de cama; con los enfermos; práctico en cuidar a los enfermos
bedside table *s* velador, mesa de noche
bedsore [ˈbɛd,sor] *s* úlcera de decúbito; **to have** or **to get bedsores** decentarse
bedspread [ˈbɛd,sprɛd] *s* sobrecama
bedspring [ˈbɛd,sprɪŋ] *s* colchón de muelles
bedstead [ˈbɛd,stɛd] *s* cuja
bedstraw [ˈbɛd,strɔ] *s* paja para jergón; (bot.) amor de hortelano, cuajaleche; (bot.) pegapega (*Desmodium uncinatum*)
bedtick [ˈbɛd,tɪk] *s* cutí
bedtime [ˈbɛd,taɪm] *s* hora de acostarse
bedtime story *s* cuento que se dice a los niños al acostarse
bed warmer *s* calientacamas
bee [bi] *s* (ent.) abeja; reunión, tertulia; capricho extravagante; **to be busy as a bee** estar muy metido en el trabajo; **to have a bee in one's bonnet** u **one's head** tener una idea fija en la mente; ser ligero de cascos; (*cap.*) *s* nombre abreviado de **Beatrice**
beebread [ˈbi,brɛd] *s* ámago
beech [bitʃ] *s* (bot.) haya
beechen [ˈbitʃən] *adj* de haya, hecho de haya
beechnut [ˈbitʃ,nʌt] *s* hayuco
beechwood [ˈbitʃ,wʊd] *s* madera de haya
bee eater *s* (orn.) abejaruco
beef [bif] *s* (*pl:* **beeves** o **beefs**) carne de vaca o toro; ganado vacuno de engorde; (coll.) fuerza muscular; (coll.) peso; (*pl:* **beefs**) (slang) queja; *va* **to beef up** (coll.) reforzar; *vn* (slang) quejarse
beef cattle *s* ganado vacuno de engorde
beefeater [ˈbif,itər] *s* persona muy gorda; (Brit.) alabardero de palacio; (Brit.) alabardero de la Torre de Londres; (orn.) espulgabueyes, picabueyes
bee fly *s* (ent.) mosca abeja
beefsteak [ˈbif,stek] *s* biftec o bistec
beef tea *s* caldo concentrado de carne
beefy [ˈbifɪ] *adj* (*comp:* **-ier;** *super:* **-iest**) fornido, musculoso, pesado
bee glue *s* tanque, propóleos
beehive [ˈbi,haɪv] *s* colmena
beekeeper [ˈbi,kipər] *s* colmenero
beeline [ˈbi,laɪn] *s* línea recta; **to make a beeline for** ir en línea recta hacia
Beelzebub [bɪˈɛlzɪbʌb] *s* (Bib.) Belcebú
been [bɪn] *pp de* **be**
beer [bɪr] *s* cerveza; bebida gaseosa hecha de raíces; **dark beer** cerveza parda o negra; **light beer** cerveza clara
beer and skittles *spl* diversión, placer
beer garden *s* cervecería al aire libre
beer saloon *s* cervecería
beery [ˈbɪrɪ] *adj* (*comp:* **-ier;** *super:* **-iest**) cervecero, de cerveza, de la cerveza
beestings [ˈbistɪŋz] *spl* calostro
beeswax [ˈbiz,wæks] *s* cera de abejas; *va* encerar
beeswing [ˈbiz,wɪŋ] *s* películas del oporto; viejo oporto
beet [bit] *s* (bot.) remolacha (*planta y raíz*)
beetle [ˈbitəl] *s* (ent.) escarabajo; martillo de madera; pisón; *adj* saliente; *va* martillar con martillo de madera; pisar con pisón; *vn* destacar, sobresalir
beetle-browed [ˈbitəl,braʊd] *adj* cejudo; (fig.) ceñudo
beetling [ˈbitlɪŋ] *adj* saliente, sobresaliente
beet root *s* raíz de remolacha
beet sugar *s* azúcar de remolacha
befall [bɪˈfɔl] (*pret:* **-fell;** *pp:* **-fallen**) *va* acontecer a; *vn* acontecer
befell [bɪˈfɛl] *pret de* **befall**
befit [bɪˈfɪt] (*pret & pp:* **-fitted;** *ger:* **-fitting**) *va* convenir, venir bien, cuadrar
befitting [bɪˈfɪtɪŋ] *adj* conveniente
befog [bɪˈfɑg] o [bɪˈfɔg] (*pret & pp:* **-fogged;** *ger:* **-fogging**) *va* envolver en niebla; obscurecer, confundir
befool [bɪˈful] *va* engañar, embaucar
before [bɪˈfor] *adv* delante, enfrente; antes; ya, más arriba; *prep* delante de, enfrente de; antes de; ante (*en presencia de*); *conj* antes (de) que
beforehand [bɪˈfor,hænd] *adv* de antemano, con anticipación; *adj* hecho de antemano
beforetime [bɪˈfor,taɪm] *adv* (archaic) en tiempos pasados
befoul [bɪˈfaʊl] *va* ensuciar, emporcar; enredarse en
befriend [bɪˈfrɛnd] *va* amparar, favorecer, ofrecer amistad a
befuddle [bɪˈfʌdəl] *va* aturdir, confundir

beg [bɛg] (*pret & pp:* **begged;** *ger:* **begging**) *va* rogar, pedir, solicitar; mendigar; **to beg someone for something** pedir algo a alguien; **to beg the question** dar por sentado lo mismo que se trata de probar; **to beg someone to** + *inf* pedir a alguien que + *subj; vn* mendigar; **to go begging** andar mendigando; no hallar comprador, no tener demanda; **to beg for** solicitar; **to beg off** excusarse; **to beg to** + *inf* permitirse + *inf*
began [bɪˈgæn] *pret de* **begin**
beget [bɪˈgɛt] (*pret:* **-got;** *pp:* **-gotten** o **-got;** *ger:* **-getting**) *va* engendrar
beggar [ˈbɛgər] *s* mendigo; pobre de solemnidad; pícaro, bribón; tipo, sujeto, individuo; *va* empobrecer, arruinar; excederse de
beggardom [ˈbɛgərdəm] *s* pobretería
beggar-lice [ˈbɛgərˌlaɪs] *ssg & spl* var. de **beggar's-lice**
beggarly [ˈbɛgərlɪ] *adj* pobre, miserable, mezquino, despreciable
beggar's-lice [ˈbɛgərzˌlaɪs] *ssg & spl* (bot.) bardana, cadillo, pegarropa (*planta y frutos espinosos que se adhieren al vestido*)
beggar's-tick [ˈbɛgərzˌtɪk] *s* aquenio del bidente; **beggar's-ticks** *spl* (bot.) bidente; (bot.) bardana, cadillo, pegarropa
beggary [ˈbɛgərɪ] *s* (*pl:* **-ies**) mendicidad; pobretería
begin [bɪˈgɪn] (*pret:* **-gan;** *pp:* **-gun;** *ger:* **-ginning**) *va* comenzar, empezar; *vn* comenzar, empezar; tomar principio; **to not begin to** ni por asomo, ni con mucho; **to begin by** + *ger* comenzar por + *inf;* **to begin to** + *inf* comenzar o empezar a + *inf;* **to begin** + *ger* comenzar + *ger*; **beginning with** a partir de
beginner [bɪˈgɪnər] *s* principiante, novicio; iniciador, originador
beginning [bɪˈgɪnɪŋ] *s* comienzo, principio; origen; punto de partida
begirt [bɪˈgʌrt] *adj* ceñido, cercado, rodeado
begone [bɪˈgɔn] o [bɪˈgɑn] *interj* ¡fuera!, ¡vete de aquí!
begonia [bɪˈgonɪə] *s* (bot.) begonia
begoniaceous [bɪˌgonɪˈeʃəs] *adj* (bot.) begoniáceo
begot [bɪˈgɑt] *pret & pp de* **beget**
begotten [bɪˈgɑtən] *pp de* **beget**
begrime [bɪˈgraɪm] *va* embarrar, tiznar
begrudge [bɪˈgrʌdʒ] *va* dar de mala gana; envidiar
begrudgingly [bɪˈgrʌdʒɪŋlɪ] *adv* de mala gana
beguile [bɪˈgaɪl] *va* engañar, seducir; divertir, entretener; defraudar; **to beguile the time** engañar el tiempo
begun [bɪˈgʌn] *pp de* **begin**
behalf [bɪˈhæf] o [bɪˈhɑf] *s* favor, patrocinio, interés; **in behalf of** a favor de; **on behalf of** en nombre de; a favor de
behave [bɪˈhev] *vn* actuar, funcionar; portarse, conducirse; portarse bien
behavior [bɪˈhevjər] *s* conducta, comportamiento; porte, modales; funcionamiento
behaviorism [bɪˈhevjərɪzəm] *s* (psychol.) comportamentismo, behaviorismo
behaviorist [bɪˈhevjərɪst] *s* comportamentista, behaviorista
behavioristic [bɪˌhevjəˈrɪstɪk] *adj* comportamentista, behaviorístico
behead [bɪˈhɛd] *va* descabezar
beheld [bɪˈhɛld] *pret & pp de* **behold**
behemoth [bɪˈhiməθ] o [ˈbiɪmɑθ] *s* (coll.) gigante, bestia colosal
behind [bɪˈhaɪnd] *s* (slang) culo, trasero; *adv* detrás; hacia atrás; más allá; con retraso; **from behind** por detrás; **to stay behind** quedarse atrás; *prep* detrás de; **to be behind the times** no estar al corriente de las cosas; **behind the back of** a espaldas de; **behind time** tarde
behindhand [bɪˈhaɪndˌhænd] *adv* con atraso; *adj* atrasado; tardío; atrasado en pagos
behold [bɪˈhold] (*pret & pp:* **-held**) *va* mirar, contemplar; *interj* ¡he aquí!
beholden [bɪˈholdən] *adj* obligado
behoof [bɪˈhuf] *s* provecho, utilidad, ventaja
behoove [bɪˈhuv] o **behove** [bɪˈhuv] o [bɪˈhov] *va* convenir, corresponder, tocar
beige [beʒ] *adj & s* beige (*amarillento*)

being [ˈbiɪŋ] *s* ser, ente; *adj* existente; **for the time being** por ahora, por el momento; *ger de* **be**
bejewel [bɪˈdʒuəl] (*pret & pp:* **-eled** o **-elled;** *ger:* **-eling** o **-elling**) *va* alhajar, enjoyar
bejeweled [bɪˈdʒuəld] *adj* enjoyelado, enjoyado
bel [bɛl] *s* (phys.) belio
belabor [bɪˈlebər] *va* apalear; ridiculizar
belated [bɪˈletɪd] *adj* atrasado; sorprendido por la noche
belay [bɪˈle] *va* (naut.) amarrar (*una cuerda*) dando vueltas en una cabilla; (coll.) detener
belaying pin *s* (naut.) cabilla de maniobra
belch [bɛltʃ] *s* eructo, regüeldo; *va* vomitar (*p.ej., llamas, humo, injurias*); *vn* eructar, regoldar; salir con fuerza (*llamas, humo, etc.*)
beldam o **beldame** [ˈbɛldəm] *s* tarasca, bruja
beleaguer [bɪˈligər] *va* sitiar, bloquear, cercar
belemnite [ˈbɛləmnaɪt] *s* (pal.) belemnita
belfry [ˈbɛlfrɪ] *s* (*pl:* **-fries**) campanario
Belg. abr. de **Belgian** y **Belgium**
Belgian [ˈbɛldʒən] *adj* belga, bélgico; *s* belga
Belgian Congo *s* el Congo Belga
Belgium [ˈbɛldʒəm] *s* Bélgica
Belgrade [bɛlˈgred] o [ˈbɛlgred] *s* Belgrado
belie [bɪˈlaɪ] (*pret & pp:* **-lied;** *ger:* **-lying**) *va* desmentir; calumniar, difamar; representar falsamente
belief [bɪˈlif] *s* creencia
believable [bɪˈlivəbəl] *adj* creíble
believe [bɪˈliv] *va* creer; *vn* creer; **to believe in** creer en (*p.ej., Dios*); aprobar; contar con
believer [bɪˈlivər] *s* creyente; fiel (*cristiano*)
belike [bɪˈlaɪk] *adv* (archaic & dial.) tal vez, probablemente
Belisarius [ˌbɛlɪˈsɛrɪəs] *s* Belisario
belittle [bɪˈlɪtəl] *va* desalabar, despreciar; empequeñecer
Belize [bɛˈliz] *s* Bélice
bell [bɛl] *s* campana; timbre (*campanilla eléctrica*); cencerro (*que se ata al pescuezo de las reses*); cascabel (*bolita hueca que contiene un pedacito de hierro*); campanada (*toque de campana*); (arch.) campana; (mus.) pabellón (*de instrumento de viento*); galardón, premio; **to bear the bell** ganar el premio, ser el primero; **to ring a bell** (coll.) sonar, p.ej., **this name rings a bell for me** este nombre me suena; *va* poner campana a; acampanar; **to bell the cat** ponerle el cascabel al gato; *vn* acampanarse; crecer (*p.ej., una flor*) en figura de campana; bramar, berrear
Bella [ˈbɛlə] *s* nombre abreviado de **Arabella** e **Isabella**
belladonna [ˌbɛləˈdɑnə] *s* (bot. & pharm.) belladona
belladonna lily *s* (bot.) amarilis
bellbird [ˈbɛlˌbʌrd] *s* (orn.) campanero
bellboy [ˈbɛlˌbɔɪ] *s* botones
bell buoy *s* (naut.) boya de campana
belle [bɛl] *s* beldad o belleza (*mujer muy hermosa*); buena moza
Bellerophon [bəˈlɛrəfɑn] *s* (myth.) Belerofonte
belles-lettres [ˌbɛlˈlɛtrə] *spl* bellas letras
bellflower [ˈbɛlˌflaʊər] *s* (bot.) campánula
bell gable *s* espadaña
bell glass *s* campana de cristal; fanal (*para resguardar una péndola, luz, etc.*)
bellhop [ˈbɛlˌhɑp] *s* (slang) botones
bellicose [ˈbɛlɪkos] *adj* belicoso
bellicosity [ˌbɛlɪˈkɑsɪtɪ] *s* belicosidad
belligerence [bəˈlɪdʒərəns] o **belligerency** [bəˈlɪdʒərənsɪ] *s* beligerancia
belligerent [bəˈlɪdʒərənt] *adj & s* beligerante
bell jar *s* var. de **bell glass**
bellman [ˈbɛlmən] *s* (*pl:* **-men**) pregonero de campana
bell metal *s* metal campanil, metal de campana, bronce de campanas
bell-mouthed [ˈbɛlˌmaʊðd] o [ˈbɛlˌmaʊθt] *adj* acampanado, abocinado, abocardado
bellow [ˈbɛlo] *s* bramido; **bellows** [ˈbɛloz] o [ˈbɛləs] *ssg o spl* fuelle; barquín (*fuelle usado en las herrerías*); (phot.) fuelle (*de la máquina fotográfica*); **bellow** [ˈbɛlo] *va* gritar, vociferar; *vn* bramar
bellows blower *s* entonador
bell ringer *s* campanero
bell-shaped [ˈbɛlˌʃept] *adj* acampanado

bell tent *s* pabellón
bell transformer *s* (elec.) transformador para timbres
bellwether [ˈbɛlˌwɛðər] *s* manso
bell wire *s* (elec.) alambre para timbres
belly [ˈbɛlɪ] *s* (*pl:* **-lies**) vientre, barriga; estómago; (*pret & pp:* **-lied**) *vn* hacer barriga; hacer bolso (*las velas*); pandearse
bellyache [ˈbɛlɪˌek] *s* (slang) dolor de barriga· *vn* (slang) quejarse
bellyband [ˈbɛlɪˌbænd] *s* ventrera; barriguera (*de las caballerías*); cincha (*para asegurar la silla a las caballerías*)
belly dancer *s* (coll.) bailarina ombliguista
bellyful [ˈbɛlɪful] *s* (slang) panzada
belong [bɪˈlɔŋ] o [bɪˈlɑŋ] *vn* pertenecer; deber estar, p.ej., **the chair belongs in this room** la silla debe estar en este cuarto; **to belong to** pertenecer a
belongings [bɪˈlɔŋɪŋz] o [bɪˈlɑŋɪŋz] *spl* pertenencias; (coll.) familia; **to gather one's belongings** liar los bártulos
beloved [bɪˈlʌvid] o [bɪˈlʌvd] *adj* dilecto, querido, amado; *s* querido, amado
below [bɪˈlo] *adv* abajo; más abajo; en el infierno; bajo cero, p.ej., **ten below** diez grados bajo cero; *prep* debajo de; inferior a
Belshazzar [bɛlˈʃæzər] *s* (Bib.) Baltasar
belt [bɛlt] *s* cinto, cinturón; (aer.) correa; (mach.) correa; (geog.) faja, zona; (slang) correazo; **below the belt** (sport) de cintura abajo, sucio, suciamente; **to tighten one's belt** ceñirse; *va* ceñir; poner correa a (*una máquina*); unir con correa; (slang) golpear con correa
belt conveyor *s* correa transportadora, cinta de transporte
belt course *s* (arch.) cordón
belt drive *s* transmisión por correa
belting [ˈbɛltɪŋ] *s* correa (*material*); correaje
belt line *s* (rail.) línea o vía de circunvalación
beluga [bəˈlugə] *s* (zool.) beluga; (ichth.) esturión blanco
belvedere [ˌbɛlvəˈdɪr] *s* belvedere; glorieta
bemaul [bɪˈmɔl] *va* aporrear, maltratar a golpes
bemazed [bɪˈmezd] *adj* aturdido, confundido
bemedaled o **bemedalled** [bɪˈmɛdəld] *adj* condecorado con muchas medallas
bemire [bɪˈmaɪr] *va* enlodar, embarrar
bemoan [bɪˈmon] *va* deplorar, lamentar
bemock [bɪˈmɑk] *va* mofarse de, reírse de
bemuse [bɪˈmjuz] *va* atolondrar, aturdir, confundir. pasmar
Ben [bɛn] *s* nombre abreviado de **Benjamin**
bench [bɛntʃ] *s* banco; (law) tribunal; (law) judicatura; meseta; plataforma (*de una exposición canina*); **to be on the bench** (law) ser juez, ejercer sus funciones (*un juez*); *va* proveer de bancos; sentar en un banco; exhibir (*un perro*); poner en un tribunal; (baseball) enviar a las duchas
bench dog *s* perro exhibido (*en una exposición canina*)
bencher [ˈbɛntʃər] *s* el que trabaja en un banco; remador; frecuentador de tabernas; (Brit.) decano de un colegio de abogados
bench mark *s* (top.) cota, punto topográfico de referencia
bench root *s* (agr.) raíces trabadas
bench show *s* exposición canina
bench warmer *s* (slang) arrimón
bench warrant *s* (law) auto de prisión expedido por un juez o un tribunal
bend [bɛnd] *s* curva; recodo (*de un camino, río, etc.*); inclinación; gaza (*lazo en el extremo de un cabo*); (her.) banda; **bends** *spl* (naut.) cinta; (coll) enfermedad de los cajones de aire comprimido; (*pret & pp:* **bent**) *va* encorvar, combar; doblar; torcer; inclinar; dirigir; someter; (naut.) envergar (*una vela*); (naut.) entalingar (*el chicote del cable*); **to bend one's efforts** dirigir sus esfuerzos; **to bend the head** inclinar la cabeza; **to bend the head to one side** ladear la cabeza; **to bend the knee** doblar la rodilla; hincar la rodilla (*en el suelo*); *vn* encorvarse; doblarse; inclinarse; volver; someterse; **to bend down** u **over** inclinarse
bended [ˈbɛndɪd] (archaic) *pret & pp de* **bend; on bended knee** o **knees** arrodillado
bender [ˈbɛndər] *s* torcedor; (mach.) doblador (*de un tubo, carril, etc.*); (slang) juerga, jolgorio
beneath [bɪˈniθ] *adv* abajo, debajo; *prep* debajo de; inferior a
benedicite [ˌbɛnɪˈdɪsɪtɪ] *s* benedícite (*invocación*); (*cap.*) *s* (eccl.) benedícite
benedict [ˈbɛnɪdɪkt] *s* casado, recién casado, solterón acabado de casar; (*cap.*) *s* Benito; Benedicto (*papa*)
Benedictine [ˌbɛnɪˈdɪktin] o [ˌbɛnɪˈdɪktaɪn] *adj & s* benedictino; (*l.c.*) [ˌbɛnɪˈdɪktin] *s* benedictino (*licor*)
Benedictine rule *s* regla de San Benito
benediction *s* [ˌbɛnɪˈdɪkʃən] *s* bendición
Benedictus [ˌbɛnɪˈdɪktəs] *s* (eccl.) benedictus
benefaction [ˌbɛnɪˈfækʃən] *s* beneficencia; beneficio
benefactor [ˈbɛnɪˌfæktər] o [ˌbɛnɪˈfæktər] *s* bienhechor
benefactress [ˈbɛnɪˌfæktrɪs] o [ˌbɛnɪˈfæktrɪs] *s* bienhechora
benefice [ˈbɛnɪfɪs] *s* (eccl.) beneficio
beneficence [bɪˈnɛfɪsəns] *s* beneficencia; beneficio
beneficent [bɪˈnɛfɪsənt] *adj* benéfico, bienhechor
beneficial [ˌbɛnɪˈfɪʃəl] *adj* beneficioso
beneficiary [ˌbɛnɪˈfɪʃɪˌɛrɪ] o [ˌbɛnɪˈfɪʃərɪ] *s* (*pl:* **-ies**) beneficiario; (eccl.) beneficiado
benefit [ˈbɛnɪfɪt] *s* beneficio; (theat.) beneficio, **for the benefit of** a beneficio de; *va* beneficiar; *vn* beneficiar; **to benefit from** beneficiar de, aprovechar
benevolence [bɪˈnɛvələns] *s* benevolencia
benevolent [bɪˈnɛvələnt] *adj* benévolo; benéfico (*dícese, p.ej., de una institución*)
Bengal [bɛŋˈgɔl] *s* Bengala
Bengalese [ˌbɛŋgəˈliz] *adj* bengalí; *s* (*pl:* **-lese**) bengalí
Bengali [bɛŋˈgɔlɪ] *adj* bengalí; *s* bengalí (*habitante e idioma*); (orn.) bengalí
bengaline [ˈbɛŋgəlin] o [ˌbɛŋgəˈlin] *s* bengalina
Bengal light *s* luz de Bengala
Bengal tiger *s* tigre de Bengala o tigre real
benighted [bɪˈnaɪtɪd] *adj* sorprendido por la noche; ignorante, depravado
benign [bɪˈnaɪn] *adj* benigno; (path.) benigno
benignancy [bɪˈnɪgnənsɪ] *s* benignidad
benignant [bɪˈnɪgnənt] *adj* benigno; (path.) benigno
benignity [bɪˈnɪgnɪtɪ] *s* (*pl:* **-ties**) benignidad; bondad
benison [ˈbɛnɪzən] o [ˈbɛnɪsən] *s* bendición
Benjamin [ˈbɛndʒəmɪn] *s* Benjamín; (*l.c.*) *s* benjuí (*resina aromática*)
benne [ˈbɛnɪ] *s* (bot.) sésamo de la India u oriental
bent [bɛnt] *s* encorvadura; inclinación, propensión; (bot.) hierba amófila; (dial.) páramo, matorral; *adj* encorvado; doblado; torcido; **bent on** resuelto a, empeñado en; **bent over** cargado de espaldas; *pret & pp de* **bend**
benthos [ˈbɛnθɑs] *s* (biol.) bentos
benumb [bɪˈnʌm] *va* entorpecer
benzedrine [ˈbɛnzədrin] o [ˈbɛnzədrɪn] *s* (trademark) bencedrina
benzene [ˈbɛnzin] o [bɛnˈzin] *s* (chem.) benceno
benzene ring *s* (chem.) núcleo bencénico
benzidine [ˈbɛnzɪdin] o [ˈbɛnzɪdɪn] *s* (chem.) bencidina
benzine [ˈbɛnzin] o [bɛnˈzin] *s* bencina
benzoate [ˈbɛnzoet] *s* (chem.) benzoato
benzoic [bɛnˈzo·ɪk] *adj* (chem.) benzoico
benzoic acid *s* (chem.) ácido benzoico
benzoin [ˈbɛnzo·ɪn] o [ˈbɛnzɔɪn] *s* benjuí (*resina aromática*); (bot.) benzoin; (chem.) benzoína
benzol [ˈbɛnzɑl] *s* (chem.) benzol
bepearl [bɪˈpʌrl] *va* aljofarar
bepraise [bɪˈprez] *va* alabar con exceso, lisonjear con exageración
bequeath [bɪˈkwið] o [bɪˈkwiθ] *va* (law & fig.) legar
bequeathal [bɪˈkwiðəl] *s* manda, donación
bequest [bɪˈkwɛst] *s* manda; legado

berate [bɪ'ret] *va* zaherir, reñir, regañar
Berber ['bʌrbər] *adj & s* bereber
bereave [bɪ'riv] (*pret & pp:* **-reaved** o **-reft**) *va* despojar, privar; desconsolar, desolar
bereavement [bɪ'rivmənt] *s* despojo, privación; aflicción, desconsuelo, duelo
bereft [bɪ'rɛft] *pret & pp de* **bereave**
beret [bɛ'rɛ] o ['bɛrɛ] *s* boina, boina francesa
berg [bʌrg] *s* banquisa, iceberg
bergamot ['bʌrgəmɑt] *s* (bot.) bergamoto (*limero; peral*); (bot.) sándalo de agua, té de Pensilvania; bergamota (*lima; pera; aceite esencial; tabaco en polvo*); (*cap.*) *s* bérgama (*tapicería*)
beribboned [bɪ'rɪbənd] *adj* encintado
beriberi ['bɛrɪ'bɛrɪ] *s* (path.) beriberi
beringed [bɪ'rɪŋd] *adj* que lleva muchas sortijas
berkelium [bər'kilɪəm] *s* (chem.) berkelio
berlin [bʌr'lɪn] o ['bʌrlɪn] *s* berlina; estambre; (*cap.*) [bʌr'lɪn] *s* Berlín
Berliner [bʌr'lɪnər] *s* berlinés
berm [bʌrm] *s* (fort.) berma
Bermuda [bər'mjudə] *s* las Bermudas
Bermuda onion *s* cebolla común de las Bermudas, Tejas y California
Bermudian [bər'mjudɪən] *adj & s* bermudeño
Bern [bʌrn] o [bɛrn] *s* Berna
Bernard ['bʌrnərd] o [bər'nɑrd] *s* Bernardo
Bernese [bʌr'niz] *adj* bernés; *s* (*pl:* **-nese**) bernés
berry ['bɛrɪ] *s* (*pl:* **-ries**) baya; grano, haba (*simiente, p.ej., del cafeto*); polidrupa (*de la fresa, la frambuesa, etc.*); (*pret & pp:* **-ried**) *vn* coger fresas, frambuesas, grosellas, etc.; producir (*una planta*) fresas, frambuesas, grosellas, etc.
berserk ['bʌrsʌrk] *adj* frenético; *adv* con frenesí; **to go berserk** embestir frenéticamente a diestro y siniestro
Bert [bʌrt] *s* nombre abreviado de **Albert, Bertram** y **Herbert**
berth [bʌrθ] *s* litera (*cama fija en los buques y el ferrocarril*); (naut.) camarote (*dormitorio*); (naut.) amarradero; (naut.) dársena; puesto, empleo; **to give a wide berth to** apartarse de, evitar el encuentro de; *va & vn* (naut.) atracar
bertha ['bʌrθə] *s* berta (*cuello*); (*cap.*) *s* Berta; (slang) Berta (*cañón alemán*)
Bertillon system ['bʌrtɪlɑn] *s* bertillonaje
Bertram ['bʌrtrəm] *s* Beltrán
beruffled [bɪ'rʌfəld] *adj* adornado con volantes, fruncido
beryl ['bɛrɪl] *s* (mineral.) berilo
beryllium [bə'rɪlɪəm] *s* (chem.) berilio
beseech [bɪ'sitʃ] (*pret & pp:* **-sought** o **-seeched**) *va* suplicar
beseem [bɪ'sim] *va & vn* convenir
beset [bɪ'sɛt] (*pret & pp:* **-set;** *ger:* **-setting**) *va* acometer, acosar; cercar, sitiar; engastar
besetting [bɪ'sɛtɪŋ] *adj* constante, dominante
beshrew [bɪ'ʃru] *va* (archaic) echar maldiciones a
beside [bɪ'saɪd] *adv* además, también, por otra parte; *prep* cerca de, junto a; en comparación de; excepto, fuera de; **beside oneself** fuera de sí, **beside the point** que no viene al caso
besides [bɪ'saɪdz] *adv* además, también, por otra parte; *prep* además de; excepto, fuera de
besiege [bɪ'sidʒ] *va* asediar, sitiar; apretar, apiñar; (fig.) asediar
besmear [bɪ'smɪr] *va* embadurnar
besmirch [bɪ'smʌrtʃ] *va* ensuciar, manchar
besom ['bizəm] *s* escoba
besot [bɪ'sɑt] (*pret & pp:* **-sotted;** *ger:* **-sotting**) *va* entontecer, embrutecer; emborrachar
besought [bɪ'sɔt] *pret & pp de* **beseech**
bespangle [bɪ'spæŋgəl] *va* adornar con lentejuelas
bespatter [bɪ'spætər] *va* salpicar
bespeak [bɪ'spik] (*pret:* **-spoke;** *pp:* **-spoken** o **-spoke**) *va* apalabrar, reservar; indicar, demostrar; pedir, solicitar; (poet. & archaic) dirigir la palabra a
bespectacled [bɪ'spɛktəkəld] *adj* con gafas, con anteojos
bespoke [bɪ'spok] *pret & pp de* **bespeak**
bespoken [bɪ'spokən] *pp de* **bespeak**
bespread [bɪ'sprɛd] (*pret & pp:* **-spread**) *va* derramar, recubrir
besprinkle [bɪ'sprɪŋkəl] *va* rociar, salpicar; espolvorear
Bess [bɛs] *s* nombre abreviado de **Elizabeth**
Bessarabia [,bɛsə'rebɪə] *s* la Besarabia
Bessemer converter ['bɛsəmər] *s* convertidor Bessemer
Bessemer process *s* procedimiento Bessemer
Bessemer steel *s* acero Bessemer
best [bɛst] *adj super* mejor; mayor; *adv super* mejor; **had best** debería; *s* lo mejor; lo más; **all for the best** conducente al bien a la larga; **at best** a lo más; **to do one's best** hacer todo lo posible; **to get** o **to have the best of** aventajar, sobresalir; **to make the best of** salir lo mejor posible de
bestead [bɪ'stɛd] *adj* situado; **bestead with dangers** rodeado de peligros; *va* ayudar
best girl *s* (coll.) novia, amiga preferida
bestial ['bɛstjəl] o ['bɛstʃəl] *adj* bestial
bestiality [,bɛstɪ'ælɪtɪ] o [,bɛstʃɪ'ælɪtɪ] *s* bestialidad
bestiary ['bɛstɪ,ɛrɪ] *s* (*pl:* **-ies**) bestiario
bestir [bɪ'stʌr] (*pret & pp:* **-stirred;** *ger:* **-stirring**) *va* incitar, excitar; **to bestir oneself** esforzarse, menearse
best man *s* padrino de boda
bestow [bɪ'sto] *va* otorgar, conferir; emplear, dedicar
bestowal [bɪ'stoəl] *s* otorgamiento, donación; empleo, dedicación
bestraddle [bɪ'strædəl] *va* montar a horcajadas
bestrew [bɪ'stru] (*pret:* **-strewed;** *pp:* **-strewed** o **-strewn**) *va* desparramar, esparcir; sembrar, salpicar; estar esparcido en o por
bestrid [bɪ'strɪd] *pret & pp de* **bestride**
bestridden [bɪ'strɪdən] *pp de* **bestride**
bestride [bɪ'straɪd] (*pret:* **-strode** o **-strid;** *pp:* **-stridden** o **-strid**) *va* montar a horcajadas; cruzar de un tranco
bestrode [bɪ'strod] *pret de* **bestride**
best seller *s* éxito de venta; éxito de librería, libro de mayor venta; autor que más se vende
bestud [bɪ'stʌd] (*pret & pp:* **-studded;** *ger:* **-studding**) *va* tachonar
bet. abr. de **between**
bet [bɛt] *s* apuesta; postura (*cantidad que se apuesta*); (*pret & pp:* **bet** o **betted;** *ger:* **betting**) *va & vn* apostar; **to bet on** apostar por (*p.ej., un caballo*); **I bet** a que, apuesto a que; **you bet** (slang) ya lo creo
beta ['betə] o ['bitə] *s* beta
betake [bɪ'tek] (*pret:* **-took;** *pp:* **-taken**) *va* **to betake oneself** dirigirse; darse, aplicarse (*p.ej., al estudio*)
betaken [bɪ'tekən] *pp de* **betake**
beta rays *spl* (phys.) rayos beta
betatron ['betətrɑn] o ['bitətrɑn] *s* (phys.) betatrón
betel ['bitəl] *s* (bot.) betel
Betelgeuse ['bitəldʒuz] o ['bɛtəldʒʌz] *s* (astr.) Betelgeuze
betel nut *s* nuez de betel
betel palm *s* (bot.) palmera de betel
bête noire ['bet'nwɑr] *s* (Fr.) aversión, persona o cosa que inspira gran aversión
Bethany ['bɛθənɪ] *s* (Bib.) Betania
bethel ['bɛθəl] *s* casa de Dios, lugar santificado; iglesia o capilla para marineros; (Brit.) capilla de los disidentes
bethink [bɪ'θɪŋk] (*pret & pp:* **-thought**) *va* recapacitar; **to bethink oneself of** considerar, acordarse de
Bethlehem ['bɛθlɪəm] o ['bɛθlɪhɛm] *s* Belén
Bethlehemite ['bɛθlɪəmaɪt] o ['bɛθlɪhɛmaɪt] *s* betlemita
bethought [bɪ'θɔt] *pret & pp de* **bethink**
Bethsaida [bɛθ'sedə] *s* (Bib.) Betsaida
betide [bɪ'taɪd] *va* acontecer a; presagiar; *vn* acontecer
betimes [bɪ'taɪmz] *adv* temprano, pronto, con tiempo
betoken [bɪ'tokən] *va* indicar, anunciar, presagiar
betony ['bɛtənɪ] *s* (*pl:* **-nies**) (bot.) betónica
betook [bɪ'tʊk] *pret de* **betake**

betray [bɪ'tre] *va* traicionar; extraviar, violar; revelar, descubrir, mostrar
betrayal [bɪ'treəl] *s* traición; violación; revelación, descubrimiento
betrayer [bɪ'treər] *s* traicionero
betroth [bɪ'troð] o [bɪ'trɔθ] *va* prometer en matrimonio; **to be** o **to become betrothed** desposarse
betrothal [bɪ'troðəl] o [bɪ'trɔθəl] *s* desposorios, esponsales
betrothed [bɪ'troðd] o [bɪ'trɔθt] *s* novio, prometido
better ['bɛtər] *adj comp* mejor; **it is better to** + *inf* más vale + *inf;* **to grow better** mejorarse; **to make better** mejorar; *adv comp* mejor; más, p.ej., **better than a hundred** más de una centena; **had better** debería; más vale que; **to like better** preferir; **to think better of** mudar de opiníon acerca de; **you ought to know better** deberías tener vergüenza; *s* superior; ventaja; apostador; **It is changing and not for the better** Esto cambia pero no para mejorar; **This is for the better** Así es mejor, **our betters** nuestros superiores; **to get** o **to have the better of** llevar la ventaja a; *va* mejorar; aventajar; **to better oneself** mejorar su posición
better half *s* (hum.) cara mitad (*esposa*)
betterment ['bɛtərmənt] *s* mejoramiento; mejoría (*en una enfermedad*)
better off *adj* más acomodado, en mejores circunstancias
bettor ['bɛtər] *s* apostador
Betty ['bɛtɪ] *s* nombre abreviado de **Elizabeth**
betulaceous [,betʃu'leʃəs] *adj* (bot.) betuláceo
between [bɪ'twin] *adv* en medio, entremedias; **in between** en medio, entremedias; *prep* entre; **between you and me** entre Vd. y yo
between-decks [bɪ'twin,dɛks] *s* (naut.) entrecubiertas, entrepuentes; *adv* (naut.) entre cubiertas
between decks *adv* (naut.) entre cubiertas
betwixt [bɪ'twɪkst] *adv* (archaic & poet.) en medio; **betwixt and between** entre lo uno y lo otro; *prep* (archaic & poet.) entre
bevel ['bɛvəl] *adj* biselado; *s* cartabón, falsa escuadra; (*pret & pp:* **-eled** o **-elled;** *ger:* **-eling** o **-elling**) *va* biselar
bevel cut *s* corte en bisel
bevel edge *s* bisel
bevel gauge *s* falsa escuadra
bevel gear *s* engranaje cónico, engranaje en bisel
bevel protractor *s* transportador-saltarregla
bevel square *s* falsa escuadra, saltarregla, baivel
bevel wheel *s* rueda cónica
beverage ['bɛvərɪdʒ] *s* bebida
bevy ['bɛvɪ] *s* (*pl:* **-ies**) bandada (*de aves*); grupo (*de muchachas*)
bewail [bɪ'wel] *va & vn* lamentar
beware [bɪ'wɛr] *va* guardarse de, precaverse de; *vn* tener cuidado; **to beware of** guardarse de, precaverse de; **beware!** ¡ojo!; **beware of . . .!** ¡ojo con . . .!, ¡cuidado con . . .!
bewigged [bɪ'wɪgd] *adj* pelucón
bewilder [bɪ'wɪldər] *va* aturdir, dejar perplejo
bewilderment [bɪ'wɪldərmənt] *s* aturdimiento, perplejidad
bewitch [bɪ'wɪtʃ] *va* embrujar, hechizar, encantar
bewitching [bɪ'wɪtʃɪŋ] *adj* hechicero, encantador
beyond [bɪ'jand] *adv* más allá, más lejos; *prep* más allá de; además de, fuera de; no capaz de, no susceptible de; **beyond the reach of** fuera del alcance de; **beyond the seas** allende los mares; *s* **the beyond** o **the great beyond** el más allá, el otro mundo
bezant ['bɛzənt] o [bə'zænt] *s* bezante (*moneda*); (f.a. & her.) bezante
bezel ['bɛzəl] *s* bisel; faceta (*de piedra preciosa tallada*); engaste (*de una joya o una sortija*)
bezique [bə'zik] *s* besigue (*juego de naipes*)
bezoar ['bizor] *s* bezoar
b.f. o **bf** abr. de **bold-faced type**
B.F.A. abr. de **Bachelor of Fine Arts**
bg. abr. de **bag**

bhang [bæŋ] *s* (bot.) cáñamo de la India; hachich
biangular [baɪ'æŋgjələr] *adj* biangular
biannual [baɪ'ænjuəl] *adj* semestral
bias ['baɪəs] *s* sesgo, diagonal; predisposición; prejuicio; (rad.) polarización negativa (*de la rejilla*); **to cut on the bias** cortar al sesgo; *adj* sesgo, diagonal; *adv* al sesgo; (*pret & pp:* **biased** o **biassed;** *ger:* **biasing** o **biassing**) *va* predisponer, prevenir
biatomic [,baɪə'tamɪk] *adj* (chem.) biatómico
biaxial [baɪ'æksɪəl] *adj* biaxil
Bib. abr. de **Bible** y **Biblical**
bib [bɪb] *s* babador, babero; pechera (*del delantal*)
bib and tucker *s* (coll.) ropa, vestido
bibcock ['bɪb,kak] *s* grifo
bibelot [bi'blo] o ['bɪblo] *s* objeto pequeño de lujo
Bibl. abr. de **Biblical** y **bibliographical**
Bible ['baɪbəl] *s* Biblia
Bible Belt *s* (U.S.A.) zona de la ortodoxia protestante
Bible paper *s* papel biblia
Biblical o **biblical** ['bɪblɪkəl] *adj* bíblico
Biblicist ['bɪblɪsɪst] *s* biblicista
bibliographer [,bɪblɪ'agrəfər] *s* bibliógrafo
bibliographic [,bɪblɪo'græfɪk] o **bibliographical** [,bɪblɪo'græfɪkəl] *adj* bibliográfico
bibliography [,bɪblɪ'agrəfɪ] *s* (*pl:* **-phies**) bibliografía
bibliomania [,bɪblɪo'menɪə] *s* bibliomanía
bibliomaniac [,bɪblɪo'menɪæk] *adj & s* bibliómano
bibliophil ['bɪblɪofɪl] o **bibliophile** ['bɪblɪofaɪl] o ['bɪblɪofɪl] *s* bibliófilo
bibulous ['bɪbjələs] *adj* bíbulo (*absorbente*); bebedor, borrachín
bicameral [baɪ'kæmərəl] *adj* bicameral
bicarbonate [baɪ'karbənɪt] o [baɪ'karbənet] *s* (chem.) bicarbonato
bicarbonate of soda *s* (chem.) bicarbonato sódico o de sosa
bice [baɪs] *s* verde mar, azul de montaña
bicentenary [baɪ'sɛntɪ,nɛrɪ] o [,baɪsɛn'tinərɪ] *s* (*pl:* **-ies**) bicentenario; *adj* bicentenario
bicentennial [,baɪsɛn'tɛnɪəl] *adj & s* bicentenario
bicephalous [baɪ'sɛfələs] *adj* bicéfalo
biceps ['baɪsɛps] *s* (anat.) bíceps
bichlorid [baɪ'klorɪd] o **bichloride** [baɪ'kloraɪd] o [baɪ'klorɪd] *s* (chem.) dicloruro; (chem.) cloruro mercúrico
bichromate [baɪ'kromet] *s* (chem.) bicromato
bichromate cell *s* (elec.) pila de bicromato
bicipital [baɪ'sɪpɪtəl] *adj* bicípite
bicker ['bɪkər] *s* quisquilla; charla; *vn* pararse en quisquillas; charlar; destellar
bicolor ['baɪ,kʌlər] o **bicolored** ['baɪ,kʌlərd] *adj* bicolor
biconcave [baɪ'kankev] o [,baɪkan'kev] *adj* bicóncavo
biconvex [baɪ'kanvɛks] o [,baɪkan'vɛks] *adj* biconvexo
bicuspid [baɪ'kʌspɪd] *adj* bicúspide; (anat.) bicúspide; *s* (anat.) bicúspide
bicuspidate [baɪ'kʌspɪdet] *adj* bicuspidado
bicycle ['baɪsɪkəl] *s* bicicleta
bicyclist ['baɪsɪklɪst] *s* biciclista, ciclista
bid [bɪd] *s* oferta, postura; (bridge) envite, declaración; (*pret:* **bade** o **bid;** *pp:* **bidden;** *ger:* **bidding**) *va* mandar, ordenar; proclamar; dar (*la bienvenida*); decir (*adiós*); (*pret & pp:* **bid;** *ger:* **bidding**) *va* ofrecer; pujar, licitar; (bridge) envidar, declarar; **to bid defiance to** desafiar; **to bid up** pujar; *vn* ofrecer un precio; (bridge) envidar, declarar; **to bid fair to** + *inf* prometer + *inf*, dar indicios de + *inf*
biddable ['bɪdəbəl] *adj* dócil, obediente; (bridge) declarable
bidden ['bɪdən] *pp de* **bid**
bidder ['bɪdər] *s* postor; (bridge) declarante; **the highest bidder** el mejor postor
bidding ['bɪdɪŋ] *s* mandato; invitación; remate: (bridge) remate; **to close the bidding** (bridge) cerrar el remate; **to do the bidding of** cumplir el mandato de; **to open the bidding** (bridge) abrir el remate, abrir las declaraciones

biddy [ˈbɪdɪ] *s* (*pl:* **-dies**) pollo, gallina; (coll.) criada irlandesa
bide [baɪd] *va* hacer cara a; **to bide one's time** esperar la hora propicia, tomarse el tiempo; *vn* quedarse; morar
bidentate [baɪˈdɛntet] *adj* bidente
biennial [baɪˈɛnɪəl] *adj* bienal; *s* acontecimiento bienal; planta bienal
biennially [baɪˈɛnɪəlɪ] *adv* bienalmente
biennium [baɪˈɛnɪəm] *s* (*pl:* **-a** [ə]) bienio
bier [bɪr] *s* féretro, andas
biferous [ˈbɪfərəs] *adj* (bot.) bífero
biff [bɪf] *s* (slang) bofetada, puñetazo; *va* (slang) dar una bofetada a, dar un puñetazo a
bifid [ˈbaɪfɪd] *adj* bífido
biflorous [baɪˈflorəs] *adj* bifloro
bifocal [baɪˈfokəl] *adj* bifocal; *s* lente bifocal; **bifocals** *spl* anteojos bifocales
biform [ˈbaɪˌfɔrm] *adj* biforme
bifurcate [ˈbaɪfərket] o [baɪˈfʌrket] *adj* bifurcado; *va* dividir en dos ramales o brazos; *vn* bifurcarse
bifurcation [ˌbaɪfərˈkeʃən] *s* bifurcación
big [bɪg] *adj* (*comp:* **bigger;** *super:* **biggest**) grande; abultado; adulto; importante; engreído; preñado; **big with child** preñada; *adv* (coll.) con jactancia; **to go big** (slang) tener gran éxito; **to talk big** (slang) echar bravatas
bigamist [ˈbɪgəmɪst] *s* bígamo o bígama
bigamous [ˈbɪgəməs] *adj* bígamo
bigamy [ˈbɪgəmɪ] *s* bigamia
big-bellied [ˈbɪgˌbɛlɪd] *adj* panzudo
Big Ben *s* campana en el reloj del Parlamento de Londres; el reloj del Parlamento
big board *s* (coll.) mercado de valores de Nueva York
big-boned [ˈbɪgˌbond] *adj* huesudo
big brother *s* hermano mayor; hombre que sirve de hermano o otro; jefe de un gobierno o movimiento autoritarios
big business *s* (coll.) comercio acaparador
Big Dipper *s* (astr.) Carro mayor
big-eared [ˈbɪgˌɪrd] *adj* orejudo
big end *s* (mach.) cabeza de la biela
big game *s* caza mayor; (fig.) caza mayor
biggish [ˈbɪgɪʃ] *adj* grandote
big gun *s* (coll.) magnate, señorón
big head *s* (coll.) orgullo, envanecimiento
big-headed [ˈbɪgˌhɛdɪd] *adj* cabezudo; (coll.) orgulloso, soberbio
big-hearted [ˈbɪgˌhɑrtɪd] *adj* cordial, generoso
bighorn [ˈbɪgˌhɔrn] *s* (zool.) carnero cimarrón de las Montañas Rocosas
big house *s* (slang) presidio
bight [baɪt] *s* codo, recodo; ensenada; gaza
bigmouthed [ˈbɪgˌmaʊðd] o [ˈbɪgˌmaʊθt] *adj* bocudo; ruidoso, hablador
bigness [ˈbɪgnɪs] *s* grandeza
bignonia [bɪgˈnonɪə] *s* (bot.) bignonia
big-nosed [ˈbɪgˌnozd] *adj* narigudo
bigot [ˈbɪgət] *s* intolerante, fanático
bigoted [ˈbɪgətɪd] *adj* intolerante, fanático
bigotry [ˈbɪgətrɪ] *s* (pl: **-ries**) intolerancia, fanatismo
big shot *s* (slang) personaje, señorón, persona de campanillas, señor de horca y cuchillo
big stick *s* palo en alto (*poder de coacción*)
big time *s* (slang) teatro de variedades de primera clase en las grandes ciudades; (slang) gran éxito; (slang) parranda, jaleo; **to be in the big time** (slang) asociarse con gente de influencia, tener gran éxito
big-time [ˈbɪgˈtaɪm] *adj* (slang) influyente, de campanillas
big toe *s* dedo gordo o grande del pie
big top *s* (coll.) techado de una tienda de circo; (coll.) circo
big tree *s* (bot.) secoya
bigwig [ˈbɪgˌwɪg] *s* (coll.) pájaro de cuenta
bijou [ˈbiʒu] *s* (*pl:* **-joux** [ʒuz]) joya; alhaja
bijouterie [biˈʒutəri] *s* joyería
bijugate [ˈbaɪdʒuget] o **bijugous** [ˈbaɪdʒugəs] *adj* (bot.) biyugado
bike [baɪk] *s* (coll.) bici; *vn* (coll.) ir o montar en bicicleta
bilabial [baɪˈlebɪəl] *adj* & *s* (phonet.) bilabial
bilabiate [baɪˈlebɪet] *adj* (bot.) bilabiado
bilateral [baɪˈlætərəl] *adj* bilateral
bilberry [ˈbɪlˌbɛrɪ] *s* (*pl:* **-ries**) (bot.) arándano
bilbo [ˈbɪlbo] *s* (*pl:* **-boes**) (hist.) espada, estoque; **bilboes** *spl* cepo con grillos
bile [baɪl] *s* (physiol. & fig.) bilis
bile duct *s* (anat.) conducto biliar
bilge [bɪldʒ] *s* (naut.) pantoque; agua de pantoque; barriga de barril; disparate, tontería; *va* combar; (naut.) desfondar; *vn* combarse; (naut.) hacer agua; (naut.) desfondarse
bilge pump *s* (naut.) bomba de sentina
bilge water *s* (naut.) agua de pantoque
bilge ways *spl* (naut.) anguilas
biliary [ˈbɪlɪˌɛrɪ] *adj* biliario
bilingual [baɪˈlɪŋgwəl] *adj* bilingüe
bilingualism [baɪˈlɪŋgwəlɪzəm] *s* bilingüismo
bilious [ˈbɪljəs] *adj* bilioso; (fig.) bilioso
bilirubin [ˌbɪlɪˈrubɪn] *s* (biochem.) bilirrubina
biliteral [baɪˈlɪtərəl] *adj* bilítero
biliverdin [ˌbɪlɪˈvʌrdɪn] *s* (biochem.) biliverdina
bilk [bɪlk] *s* estafa, trampería; estafador, tramposo; *va* estafar, trampear
bill [bɪl] *s* cuenta, factura; billete (*que reemplaza monedas*); aviso, cartel; cartel de teatro; función de teatro; hoja suelta; cédula, escrito; proyecto de ley; (com.) giro, letra de cambio; (law) pedimento; pico (*de ave*); pica, alabarda; podadera; (naut.) uña (*de ancla*); (*cap.*) *s* nombre abreviado de **William; to fill the bill** (coll.) llenar los requisitos; **to foot the bill** (coll.) pagar la cuenta; (coll.) sufragar los gastos; *va* facturar; cargar en cuenta a; anunciar por carteles; fijar carteles en; *vn* darse el pico (*las palomas*); acariciarse (*los enamorados*); **to bill and coo** acariciarse y arrullarse (*como las palomas*)
billboard [ˈbɪlˌbord] *s* cartelera
billet [ˈbɪlɪt] *s* (mil.) orden escrita de alojamiento; (mil.) lugar de alojamiento; (mil.) boleta; empleo, oficio; zoquete (*de madera*); palanquilla (*hierro de sección cuadrada*); tocho (*de hierro o acero*); *va* (mil.) alojar (*tropas*)
billet-doux [ˈbɪleˈdu] *s* (*pl:* **billets-doux** [ˈbɪleˈduz]) esquela amorosa
billfold [ˈbɪlˌfold] *s* billetero, cartera de bolsillo
billhead [ˈbɪlˌhɛd] *s* encabezamiento de factura
billhook [ˈbɪlˌhʊk] *s* podadera
billiard [ˈbɪljərd] *s* (coll.) carambola (*lance*); **billiards** *ssg* billar (*juego*); **to play billiards** jugar al billar
billiard ball *s* bola de billar
billiard cloth *s* paño de billar
billiard player *s* jugador de billar, billarista
billiard pocket *s* tronera de billar
billiard table *s* mesa de billar
billingsgate [ˈbɪlɪŋzˌget] *s* lenguaje bajo y obsceno
billion [ˈbɪljən] *s* (U.S.A.) mil millones; (Brit.) billón (*un millón de millones*)
billionaire [ˌbɪljənˈɛr] *adj* & *s* billonario
billionth [ˈbɪljənθ] *adj* & *s* billonésimo
bill of attainder *s* (law) ley que condena a muerte civil
bill of exchange *s* (com.) letra de cambio
bill of fare *s* lista de comidas, menú
bill of goods *s* (com.) consignación de mercancías; **to sell a bill of goods** (coll.) dar gato por liebre
bill of health *s* patente de sanidad
bill of lading *s* (com.) conocimiento de embarque
bill of particulars *s* (law) declaración de hechos (*del demandante o del demandado*)
bill of rights *s* declaración de derechos
bill of sale *s* escritura de venta
billow [ˈbɪlo] *s* ondulación, oleada; *vn* ondular, hincharse
billowy [ˈbɪlo·ɪ] o [ˈbɪləwɪ] *adj* ondulante, hinchado
billposter [ˈbɪlˌpostər] *s* cartelero, fijacarteles; cartel
billy [ˈbɪlɪ] *s* (*pl:* **-lies**) cachiporra; (*cap.*) *s* nombre abreviado de **William**
billy goat *s* (coll.) cabrón, bode, macho cabrío
bilocation [ˌbaɪloˈkeʃən] *s* bilocación

bilocular [baɪ'lakjələr] *adj* bilocular
bimetallic [,baɪmɪ'tælɪk] *adj* bimetálico; bimetalista
bimetallism [baɪ'mɛtəlɪzəm] *s* bimetalismo
bimetallist [baɪ'mɛtəlɪst] *adj & s* bimetalista
bimonthly [baɪ'mʌnθlɪ] *adj* bimestral o bimestre (*que se repite cada dos meses*); bimensual (*que se repite dos veces al mes*); *adv* bimestralmente; bimensualmente; *s* (*pl:* **-lies**) revista o publicación bimestre; revista o publicación bimensual
bimotored (baɪ'motərd] *adj* (aer.) bimotor
bin [bɪn] *s* arcón, hucha; (*pret & pp:* **binned;** *ger:* **binning**) *va* guardar en arcón o hucha
binary ['baɪnərɪ] *adj* binario
binary star *s* (astr.) estrella doble
binate ['baɪnet] *adj* binado
bination [baɪ'neʃən] *s* (eccl.) binación
binaural [bɪn'ɔrəl] *adj* binaural o binauricular
bind [baɪnd] *s* lazo, enlace; (mus.) ligadura; (*pret & pp:* **bound**) *va* atar, ligar; unir, juntar; ceñir; enguirnaldar; ribetear; fajar; vendar (*una herida*); agavillar (*p.ej., las mieses*); encuadernar (*libros*); estreñir; contener, refrenar; obligar, precisar; escriturar; poner en aprendizaje, poner a servir; **to bind in boards** encartonar; **to bind over** (law) obligar moral o legalmente (*p.ej., a comparecer ante un juez, a mantener la paz*); *vn* atiesarse, endurecerse; agarrotarse; ser obligatorio
binder ['baɪndər] *s* atador; (agr.) atadora, agavilladora; encuadernador; substancia aglomerante, substancia aglutinante; (mas.) perpiaño; sobretripa (*de cigarro*); (ins.) documento provisional de protección
bindery ['baɪndərɪ] *s* (*pl:* **-ies**) encuadernación (*taller*)
binding ['baɪndɪŋ] *adj* atador; que estriñe; obligatorio; *s* atadura; encuadernación; ribete
binding post *s* (elec.) borne, sujetahilo
bindweed ['baɪnd,wid] *s* (bot.) enredadera
bine [baɪn] *s* sarmiento (*de la vid*); vástago de enredadera; vástago del lúpulo; lúpulo
Binet test [bɪ'ne] *s* examen de inteligencia de Binet
binge [bɪndʒ] *s* (slang) jarana, borrachera; **to go on a binge** (slang) andar de jarana, tomar una borrachera
binnacle ['bɪnəkəl] *s* (naut.) bitácora
binocle ['bɪnəkəl] *s* binóculo, gemelos
binocular [bɪ'nakjələr] o [baɪ'nakjələr] *adj* binocular; **binoculars** *spl* prismáticos, gemelos
binomial [baɪ'nomɪəl] *adj* binomial, binomio; *s* (alg. & biol.) binomio
binomial theorem *s* (alg.) teorema binomial, binomio de Newton
biochemical [,baɪo'kɛmɪkəl] *adj* bioquímico
biochemist [,baɪo'kɛmɪst] *s* bioquímico
biochemistry [,baɪo'kɛmɪstrɪ] *s* bioquímica
biodynamics [,baɪodaɪ'næmɪks] o [,baɪodɪ'næmɪks] *ssg* biodinámica
biog. abr. de **biographical** y **biography**
biogenesis [,baɪo'dʒɛnɪsɪs] *s* (biol.) biogénesis
biographee [baɪ,agrə'fi] o [bɪ,agrə'fi] *s* biografiado
biographer [baɪ'agrəfər] o [bɪ'agrəfər] *s* biógrafo
biographic [,baɪə'græfɪk] o **biographical** [,baɪə'græfɪkəl] *adj* biográfico
biography [baɪ'agrəfɪ] o [bɪ'agrəfɪ] *s* (*pl:* **-phies**) biografía
biol. abr. de **biological** y **biology**
biologic [,baɪə'ladʒɪk] o **biological** [,baɪə'ladʒɪkəl] *adj* biológico
biological warfare *s* guerra biológica
biologist [baɪ'alədʒɪst] *s* biólogo
biology [baɪ'alədʒɪ] *s* biología
biomedical [,baɪo'mɛdɪkəl] *adj* biomédico
biometric [,baɪo'mɛtrɪk] o **biometrical** [,baɪo'mɛtrɪkəl] *adj* biométrico
biometry [baɪ'amɪtrɪ] *s* biometría
biophysical [,baɪo'fɪzɪkəl] *adj* biofísico
biophysics [,baɪo'fɪzɪks] *ssg* biofísica
biopsy ['baɪapsɪ] *s* (med.) biopsia
biostatic [,baɪo'stætɪk] *adj* biostático; **biostatics** *ssg* biostática
biostatical [,baɪo'stætɪkəl] *adj* biostático
biota [baɪ'otə] *s* biota
biotic [baɪ'atɪk] o **biotical** [baɪ'atɪkəl] *adj* biótico
biotite ['baɪotaɪt] *s* (mineral.) biotita
biotype ['baɪotaɪp] *s* (biol.) biotipo
biparous ['bɪpərəs] *adj* (bot. & zool.) bíparo
bipartisan [baɪ'partɪzən] *adj* de (los) dos partidos políticos
bipartite [baɪ'partaɪt] *adj* bipartido o bipartito
biped ['baɪpɛd] *adj & s* bípedo
bipetalous [baɪ'pɛtələs] *adj* (bot.) bipétalo
bipinnate [baɪ'pɪnet] *adj* (bot.) bipinado
biplane ['baɪ,plen] *s* (aer.) biplano
bipolar [baɪ'polər] *adj* bipolar
birch [bʌrtʃ] *s* (bot.) abedul; férula, palmatoria; *va* varear
birchen ['bʌrtʃən] *adj* de abedul, hecho de abedul
bird [bʌrd] *s* ave o pájaro; (slang) sujeto, tío, tipo; **the bird has flown** voló el golondrino; **to kill two birds with one stone** matar dos pájaros de una pedrada; **bird in the hand** pájaro en mano; **bird of ill omen** pájaro de mal agüero; **birds of a feather** pájaros de una misma pluma, gente de una calaña; *vn* andar a caza de pájaros
bird bath *s* baño para pájaros
bird cage *s* jaula
bird call *s* reclamo
bird dog *s* perro de ajeo, perro cobrador de aves
birdie ['bʌrdɪ] *s* avecilla, pajarillo
birdlime ['bʌrd,laɪm] *s* liga, ajonje
birdman ['bʌrd,mæn] o ['bʌrdmən] *s* (*pl:* **-men**) (coll.) aviador
bird of paradise *s* ave del paraíso
bird of passage *s* ave de paso; (fig.) ave de paso
bird of peace *s* paloma (*que simboliza la paz*)
bird of prey *s* ave de rapiña
birdseed ['bʌrd,sid] *s* alpiste, cañamones
bird's-eye view ['bʌrdz,aɪ] *s* vista de pájaro, vista a ojo de pájaro
bird shot *s* perdigones
birdwoman ['bʌrd,wʊmən] *s* (*pl:* **-women**) (coll.) aviadora o aviatriz
birectangular [,baɪrɛk'tæŋgjələr] *adj* birrectángulo
birefringence [,baɪrɪ'frɪndʒəns] *s* birrefringencia
bireme ['baɪrim] *adj & s* birreme
biretta [bɪ'rɛtə] *s* birreta
birth [bʌrθ] *s* nacimiento; parto; camada, lechigada; linaje, alcurnia; **by birth** de nacimiento; **to give birth to** parir, dar el ser a, dar a luz
birth certificate *s* partida de nacimiento
birth control *s* control de los nacimientos, esterilidad voluntaria
birthday ['bʌrθ,de] *s* natal; cumpleaños, aniversario del nacimiento; aniversario (*de cualquier suceso*)
birthday present *s* cuelga, regalo de cumpleaños
birthmark ['bʌrθ,mark] *s* marca de nacimiento
birthplace ['bʌrθ,ples] *s* patria, suelo nativo, lugar de nacimiento, casa natal
birth rate *s* natalidad
birthright ['bʌrθ,raɪt] *s* derechos de nacimiento; primogenitura
birthstone ['bʌrθ,ston] *s* piedra preciosa que simboliza las influencias del mes en que uno ha nacido
birthwort ['bʌrθ,wʌrt] *s* (bot.) aristoloquia
bis [bɪs] *adv* (mus.) bis
Bisayan [bɪ'sajən] *adj & s* bisayo o visayo
Bisayas [bɪ'sajas] *spl* islas Bisayas o Visayas
Biscay ['bɪske] o ['bɪskɪ] *s* Vizcaya
Biscayan [bɪs'keən] o ['bɪskeən] *adj & s* vizcaíno
biscuit ['bɪskɪt] *s* bizcocho (*pan y loza*)
bisect ['baɪsɛkt] *s* (philately) sello cortado por la mitad; [baɪ'sɛkt] *va* dividir en dos partes; (geom.) bisecar; (philately) cortar por la mitad; *vn* empalmar (*p.ej., dos caminos*)
bisection [baɪ'sɛkʃən] *s* división en dos partes; (geom.) bisección
bisector [baɪ'sɛktər] *s* (geom.) bisectriz
bisexual [baɪ'sɛkʃʊəl] *adj & s* bisexual

bishop ['bɪʃəp] *s* (eccl.) obispo; alfil (*en el juego de ajedrez*)
bishopric ['bɪʃəprɪk] *s* obispado
bishop's-weed ['bɪʃəps,wid] *s* (bot.) ameos, biznaga
bismuth ['bɪzməθ] *s* (chem.) bismuto
bismutite ['bɪzmətaɪt] *s* (mineral.) bismutita
bison ['baɪsən] o ['baɪzən] *s* (zool.) bisonte
bisque [bɪsk] *s* sopa de cangrejos; sopa hecha con espárragos, tomates, etc., pasados por un tamiz; helado hecho con almendrados y nueces molidas; bizcocho (*loza sin barniz*)
bissextile [bɪ'sɛkstɪl] *adj & s* bisiesto
bister ['bɪstər] *s* (paint.) bistre
bistort ['bɪstɔrt] *s* (bot.) bistorta
bistoury ['bɪsturɪ] *s* (*pl:* **-ries**) (surg.) bisturí
bisulfate [baɪ'sʌlfet] *s* (chem.) bisulfato
bisulfid [baɪ'sʌlfɪd] o **bisulfide** [baɪ'sʌlfaɪd] o [baɪ'sʌlfɪd] *s* (chem.) bisulfuro
bisulfite [baɪ'sʌlfaɪt] *s* (chem.) bisulfito
bisyllabic [,baɪsɪ'læbɪk] *adj* bisílabo
bit [bɪt] *s* pedacito, pizca, poquito; bocado (*de comida*); ratito; bocado, freno; hoja de corte; barrena; paletón (*de llave*); soldador (*punta del instrumento*); **a good bit** una buena cantidad; **not a bit** ni pizca; **to blow to bits** hacer pedazos; **to take the bit in the teeth** desbocarse; rebelarse; **two bits** (coll.) veinte y cinco centavos; **bit by bit** poco a poco; *pret de* **bite**; (*pret & pp:* **bitted**; *ger:* **bitting**) *va* enfrenar; contener, refrenar
bitch [bɪtʃ] *s* perra, zorra, loba; (vulg.) mujer, mujer de mal genio, ramera; (slang) queja; *va* (slang) chapucear, echar a perder; *vn* (slang) quejarse
bite [baɪt] *s* mordedura; picadura (*de ave o insecto*); resquemo (*sensación picante en la lengua*); bocado; tentempié, refrigerio; (print.) lardón (*blanco en la impresión*); **to take a bite** morder; comer algo; (*pret:* **bit**; *pp:* **bit** o **bitten**) *va* morder; picar (*los peces, los insectos, etc.*); resquemar (*un alimento*); comerse (*las uñas*); **to bite off** quitar mordiendo; *vn* morder; picar; resquemar; (slang) picar (*tragar el anzuelo, caer en el lazo*); **to bite at** querer morder
biting ['baɪtɪŋ] *adj* penetrante; mordaz, picante, acre
bit part *s* (theat.) papel de ínfima importancia
bit player *s* (theat.) parte de por medio
bitstock ['bɪt,stɑk] *s* berbiquí, manubrio de taladro
bitt [bɪt] *s* (naut.) bita; *va* (naut.) abitar
bitten ['bɪtən] *pp de* **bite**
bitter ['bɪtər] *adj* amargo; encarnizado, p.ej., **a bitter struggle** una lucha encarnizada; **to taste bitter** ser de gusto amargo; **to the bitter end** hasta el extremo; hasta la muerte; *adv* (dial.) picantemente; **bitter cold** (dial.) frío cortante; *s* amargo, amargura; **bitters** *spl* bítter
bitter almond *s* (bot.) almendro amargo; almendra amarga (*semilla*)
bitter-end ['bɪtər'ɛnd] *adj* (coll.) intransigente, irreconciliable
bitter-ender ['bɪtər'ɛndər] *s* (coll.) persona intransigente, persona irreconciliable
bitterish ['bɪtərɪʃ] *adj* algo amargo
bitterling ['bɪtərlɪŋ] *s* (ichth.) bermejuela
bittern ['bɪtərn] *s* (orn.) avetoro, ave toro; agua madre de la cristalización de la sal; composición amarga de cuasia, tabaco, cocculus indicus para adulterar la cerveza
bitterness ['bɪtərnɪs] *s* amargor, amargura; encarnizamiento (*p.ej., de una lucha*)
bitter pill *s* lance humillante
bittersweet ['bɪtər,swit] *s* mezcla de lo dulce y lo amargo; (bot.) dulcamara; (bot.) evónimo norteamericano. *adj* dulce y amargo a la vez, agridulce; semidulce (*chocolate*)
bitter vetch *s* (bot.) yero, alcareña
bitterwood ['bɪtər,wud] *s* (bot. & pharm.) cuasia de Jamaica; (bot.) cuasia amarga; (pharm.) cuasia
bitterwort ['bɪtər,wʌrt] *s* (bot.) genciana amarilla, gencianilla; (bot.) diente de león
bitumen [bɪ'tjumən] o [bɪ'tumən] *s* betún
bituminize [bɪ'tjumɪnaɪz] o [bɪ'tumɪnaɪz] *va* embetunar, convertir en betún
bituminous [bɪ'tjumɪnəs] o [bɪ'tumɪnəs] *adj* bituminoso
bituminous coal *s* carbón bituminoso
bivalence [baɪ'veləns] o ['bɪvələns] *s* (chem.) bivalencia
bivalent [baɪ'velənt] o ['bɪvələnt] *adj* (chem.) bivalente
bivalve ['baɪ,vælv] *adj* bivalvo; *s* (zool.) molusco bivalvo
bivouac ['bɪvuæk] o ['bɪvwæk] *s* vivaque; (*pret & pp:* **-acked**; *ger:* **-acking**) *vn* vivaquear
biweekly [baɪ'wiklɪ] *adj* quincenal; bisemanal; *adv* quincenalmente; bisemanalmente; *s* (*pl:* **-lies**) revista o publicación quincenal o bisemanal
bixaceous [bɪk'seʃəs] *adj* (bot.) bixáceo
biyearly [baɪ'jɪrlɪ] *adj* semestral; *adv* semestralmente
bizarre [bɪ'zɑr] *adj* raro, extravagante
bk. abr. de **bank, block** y **book**
bkg. abr. de **banking**
bkt. abr. de **basket**
bl. abr. de **bale** y **barrel**
b.l. abr. de **bill of lading**
B.L. abr. de **Bachelor of Laws**
blab [blæb] *s* chisme, hablilla; chismoso; (*pret & pp:* **blabbed**; *ger:* **blabbing**) *va* chismear, soltar indiscretamente; *vn* chismear, vaciarse
black [blæk] *adj* negro; ceñudo; *adv* con ceño, p.ej., **to look black at** mirar con ceño; *s* negro; luto; *va* ennegrecer; embetunar, limpiar (*los zapatos*); **to black out** apagar (*las luces*); obscurecer (*una estancia*) contra el bombardeo aéreo; *vn* ennegrecer; **to black out** apagar las luces; desmayarse, perder el sentido; **to black up** pintarse de negro
black amber *s* ámbar negro
blackamoor ['blækəmur] *s* (offensive) negro
black-and-blue ['blækənd'blu] *adj* amoratado, lívido, acardenalado
black-and-blue mark *s* cardenal
black and white *s* dibujo en blanco y negro; **in black and white** en blanco y negro (*por escrito*)
black-and-white ['blækənd'hwaɪt] *adj* en blanco y negro
black-and-white creeper o **warbler** *s* (orn.) reinita trepadora, silvia blanquinegra
black art *s* magia negra, nigromancia
blackball ['blæk,bɔl] *s* bola negra; *va* bolear, dar bola negra a
black bass [bæs] *s* (ichth.) micróptero
black bear *s* (zool.) baribal; (zool.) oso del Tibet
black-bellied plover ['blæk,bɛlɪd] *s* (orn.) chorlito gris, chorlito playero
black belt *s* región muy fértil de los estados de Alabama y Misisipí, EE.UU.; (U.S.A.) región donde hay más negros que blancos
blackberry ['blæk,bɛrɪ] *s* (*pl:* **-ries**) (bot.) zarza; zarzamora (*fruto*)
blackbird ['blæk,bʌrd] *s* (orn.) mirlo
blackboard ['blæk,bord] *s* pizarra, encerado
black book *s* lista negra
black bread *s* pan negro
blackcap ['blæk,kæp] *s* ave de cabeza negra; (orn.) curruca de cabeza negra; (bot.) frambuesa negra; (bot.) espadaña
blackdamp ['blæk,dæmp] *s* (min.) mofeta
Black Death *s* peste negra (*del siglo XIV*)
black diamond *s* diamante negro (*carbonado*); **black diamonds** *spl* carbón de piedra
black drum *s* (ichth.) corvina negra
blacken ['blækən] *va* ennegrecer; denigrar, desacreditar; *vn* ennegrecer
black eye *s* ojo amoratado por un golpe; (coll.) mala fama, descrédito
black-eyed ['blæk,aɪd] *adj* ojinegro
black-eyed bean *s* (bot.) caragilate, garrubia, judía de carete, frijol de ojos negros
black-eyed Susan *s* (bot.) rudbequia; (bot.) ojo de poeta, ojo de Venus (*Thunbergia alata*)
blackface ['blæk,fes] *adj* carinegro; *s* actor que se pinta de negro; pintura que se emplea para hacer el papel de negro; (print.) letra negrilla
blackfish ['blæk,fɪʃ] *s* (ichth.) tautoga; (zool.) cabeza de olla
black flag *s* bandera negra (*de los piratas*)

black fly *s* (ent.) jején (*del género Simulium*)
Black Forest *s* Selva Negra (*en Alemania*)
Black Friar *s* fraile negro (*dominico*)
Black Friday *s* viernes aciago; viernes santo
black grouse *s* (orn.) gallo de bosque
blackguard ['blægɑrd] *s* bribón, pillo, tunante; *va* injuriar, vilipendiar
blackguardly ['blægɑrdlɪ] *adj* bribón, pillo, tunante
black-haired ['blæk,hɛrd] *adj* pelinegro
Black Hand *s* mano negra
blackhead ['blæk,hɛd] *s* (path.) espinilla, comedón; (orn.) coquinero; (vet.) enterohepatitis infecciosa
black-hearted ['blæk,hɑrtɪd] *adj* malvado, perverso
blacking ['blækɪŋ] *s* ennegrecimiento; betún (*para dar lustre a los zapatos*)
blackish ['blækɪʃ] *adj* negruzco
blackjack ['blæk,dʒæk] *s* cachiporra con puño flexible; escudilla de metal charolado; veintiuna (*juego de naipes*); bandera negra (*de los piratas*); (bot.) roble norteamericano (*Quercus marilandica*); *va* aporrear
black lead [lɛd] *s* grafito, plombagina
blackleg ['blæk,lɛg] *s* petardista, fullero; (Brit.) esquirol; (vet.) morriña negra
black letter *s* (print.) letra gótica; (print.) letra negrilla
black-letter ['blæk,lɛtər] *adj* (print.) gótico; (print.) impreso en negrilla; aciago, infausto
black list *s* lista negra
black-list ['blæk,lɪst] *va* poner en la lista negra
black magic *s* magia negra, nigromancia
blackmail ['blæk,mel] *s* chantaje; dinero obtenido por chantaje; *va* amenazar con chantaje; arrancar dinero por chantaje a (*una persona*)
blackmailer ['blæk,melər] *s* chantajista
Black Maria [mə'raɪə] *s* (coll.) coche celular
black mark *s* marca negra (*de censura*); mala nota (*de los estudiantes*)
black market *s* estraperlo, mercado negro
black marketeer *s* estraperlista
black martin *s* (orn.) vencejo
black measles *s* (path.) sarampión hemorrágico, sarampión negro
Black Monk *s* monje negro (*benedictino*)
blackness ['blæknɪs] *s* negrura
black nightshade *s* (bot.) hierba mora
black oak *s* (bot.) cuercitrón
blackout ['blæk,aʊt] *s* apagón (*para la defensa antiaérea*); (theat.) apagamiento de luces; visión negra (*ceguera repentina y pasajera de los aviadores*); pérdida de la memoria
black pepper *s* (bot.) pimentero; pimienta negra (*fruto*)
blackpoll ['blæk,pol] *s* (orn.) reinita cabeza negra
black pope *s* papa negro
black poplar *s* (bot.) álamo negro
black powder *s* pólvora negra
Black Prince *s* Príncipe negro
black pudding *s* morcilla
black race *s* raza negra
black sanicle *s* (bot.) astrancia mayor
black scoter *s* (orn.) negreta
Black Sea *s* mar Negro
black sheep *s* oveja negra, (el) malo entre los buenos
black shirt *s* camisa negra (*fascista*)
blacksmith ['blæk,smɪθ] *s* herrero; herrador (*de caballos*)
blacksmith welding *s* soldadura de forja
blacksnake ['blæk,snek] *s* (zool.) culebra de color prieto (*Zamenis constrictor*); látigo de cuero retorcido
black spruce *s* (bot.) variedad de pícea (*Picea mariana*)
blacktail ['blæk,tel] *s* (zool.) ciervo mulo, bura
black tea *s* té negro
blackthorn ['blæk,θɔrn] *s* (bot.) espino negro, acacia bastarda, endrino; porra o bastón hecho de la rama del endrino
black tie *s* corbata de smoking, media etiqueta
black top *s* superficie bituminosa
black vomit *s* (path.) vómito negro
black walnut *s* (bot.) nogal negro
black whale *s* (zool.) calderón, cabeza de olla
black widow *s* (ent.) araña hembra (*Latrodectus mactans*)
bladder ['blædər] *s* (anat.) vejiga; vejiga (*saco de goma o de piel*)
bladder green *s* verdevejiga
bladder senna *s* (bot.) espantalobos
bladderwort ['blædər,wʌrt] *s* (bot.) utricularia
blade [bled] *s* hoja (*de un arma o instrumento*); espada (*arma o persona*); hojita de hierba, tallo de hierba; (bot.) lámina, limbo (*de una hoja*); aleta (*de hélice*); pala (*de remo, de la azada, etc.*); (elec.) cuchilla (*de un interruptor*); gallardo joven, buen mozo
bladed ['bledɪd] *adj* que tiene hoja u hojas
bladesmith ['bled,smɪθ] *s* espadero
blah [blɑ] *s* (slang) pamplina, nonada; *interj* (slang) ¡bah!
blain [blen] *s* ampolla, úlcera
blamable ['bleməbəl] *adj* culpable
blame [blem] *s* culpa; **to put the blame on someone for something** echar la culpa a uno de una cosa; *va* culpar; **to be to blame for** tener la culpa de
blameless ['blemlɪs] *adj* inculpable, intachable
blameworthy ['blem,wʌrðɪ] *adj* culpable
blanch [blæntʃ] o [blɑntʃ] *va* blanquear; blanquecer (*p.ej., la plata*); (cook. & hort.) blanquear; hacer pálido; *vn* blanquear; palidecer
Blanch o **Blanche** [blæntʃ] o [blɑntʃ] *s* Blanca
blancmange [blə'mɑnʒ] *s* manjar blanco
bland [blænd] *adj* blando
blandish ['blændɪʃ] *va* engatusar, lisonjear
blandishment ['blændɪʃmənt] *s* engatusamiento, lisonja
blank [blæŋk] *adj* en blanco (*no escrito o impreso*); blanco (*vacío, hueco*); ciego (*obstruído, cerrado*), p.ej., **blank key** llave ciega; confuso, turbado; insípido, sin interés; entero, cabal; vago, p.ej., **blank stare** mirada vaga; *s* blanco; papel blanco; formulario; cospel (*disco para hacer moneda*); tejo (*para ser estampado*); *va* esconder; borrar, cancelar; obstruir; estampar (*una chapa de metal*); (sport) impedir (*a uno*) que gane ni un solo tanto
blank cartridge *s* cartucho en blanco, cartucho sin bala
blank check *s* cheque en blanco; (fig.) carta blanca
blanket ['blæŋkɪt] *s* manta; capa (*p.ej., de niebla*); (fig.) manto; *adj* combinado, general, comprensivo; *va* cubrir con manta; cubrir, obscurecer; mantear; (mil. & nav.) atajar (*el fuego enemigo*) interponiendo un buque o tropas amigas; (naut.) quitar el viento a (*un buque*); (rad.) neutralizar, paralizar (*un radiorreceptor*) por medio de ondas perturbadoras
blank signature *s* firma en blanco
blank verse *s* verso blanco, libre o suelto
blare [blɛr] *s* fragor; son de trompetas; resplandor, color muy brillante; *va* tocar o sonar con mucho ruido; vociferar; *vn* hacer estruendo, resonar
blarney ['blɑrnɪ] *s* zalamerías; *va* hacer zalamerías a; *vn* hacer zalamerías
blasé [blɑ'ze] o ['blɑze] *adj* hastiado, indiferente
blaspheme [blæs'fim] *va* blasfemar contra; *vn* blasfemar; **to blaspheme against** blasfemar contra
blasphemous ['blæsfɪməs] *adj* blasfemo
blasphemy ['blæsfɪmɪ] *s* (*pl:* **-mies**) blasfemia
blast [blæst] o [blɑst] *s* ráfaga (*de aire o viento*); chorro (*de aire, agua, arena, etc.*); soplo (*de un fuelle*); toque o sonido (*de bocina, trompeta, pito, etc.*); carga de pólvora, carga de barreno; explosión, voladura; arruinamiento; tizón, añublo (*honguillo parásito*); **at** o **in full blast** en plena marcha; *va* volar (*p.ej., con dinamita*); arruinar; atizonar, añublar; maldecir, infamar; **to blast open** abrir con explosivos; **to blast out** arrojar (*al enemigo*) con explosivos; *vn* atizonar, añublarse
blasted ['blæstɪd] o ['blɑstɪd] *adj* arruinado; marchito; maldito
blastema [blæs'timə] *s* (*pl:* **-mata** [mətə]) (embryol.) blastema
blast furnace *s* alto horno

blasting ['blæstɪŋ] o ['blɑstɪŋ] *s* voladura; arruinamiento; atizonamiento (*de los cereales*)
blasting cap *s* (min.) detonador, casquete explosivo
blasting machine *s* explosor
blastocoele ['blæstəsil] *s* (embryol.) blastocele
blastocyst ['blæstəsɪst] *s* (embryol.) blastocisto
blastoderm ['blæstədʌrm] *s* (embryol.) blastodermo
blastoff ['blæst,ɔf] o ['blɑst,ɔf] *s* lanzamiento de cohete
blastula ['blæstʃulə] *s* (*pl:* **-lae** [li]) (embryol.) blástula
blast wave *s* onda de choque (*de una explosión nuclear*)
blat [blæt] (*pret & pp:* **blatted;** *ger:* **blatting**) *va* decir o soltar sin consideración y con mucho ruido; *vn* balar; hablar sin consideración y con mucho ruido
blatancy ['bletənsɪ] *s* vocinglería; molestia
blatant ['betənt] *adj* vocinglero; molesto, intruso
blather ['blæðər] *s* charla, disparate; *vn* charlar
blatherskite ['blæðərskaɪt] *s* (coll.) hablador, charlatán
blaze [blez] *s* llamarada, llama muy brillante; hoguera; incendio; luz brillante; resplandor; explosión (*de cólera*); estrella (*en la frente del caballo o la vaca*); señal hecha en los árboles para servir de guía; **in a blaze** en llamas, resplandeciente; *va* encender, inflamar; marcar (*los árboles*) con cortes y señales para que sirvan de guía; publicar, proclamar; **to blaze a trail** abrir o marcar una senda; *vn* encenderse, arder con llama; resplandecer; **to blaze away** (coll.) comenzar o continuar a tirar; (coll.) seguir criticando, regañando, etc.
blazer ['blezər] *s* (sport) chaqueta ligera de franela o seda
blazon ['blezən] *s* blasón; ostentación, boato; *va* blasonar; adornar, decorar; publicar, proclamar; exhibir, mostrar
blazonry ['blezənrɪ] *s* blasón; decoración brillante
bldg. abr. de **building**
bleach [blitʃ] *s* blanqueo; blanquimento; *va* blanquear, blanquear al sol o con la acción química; *vn* blanquear; palidecer
bleacher ['blitʃər] *s* blanqueador; blanquimiento; **bleachers** *spl* (sport) gradas al aire libre
bleachery ['blitʃərɪ] *s* (*pl:* **-ies**) blanquería
bleaching powder *s* polvos de blanqueo, polvos de gas
bleak [blik] *adj* desierto, solitario; sombrío, triste, frío, helado
blear [blɪr] *adj* turbio, legañoso; *va* enturbiar; engañar
bleareye ['blɪr,aɪ] *s* (path.) legaña
blear-eyed ['blɪr,aɪd] *adj* enturbiado, legañoso; torpe de entendimiento
bleary ['blɪrɪ] *adj* (*comp:* **-ier;** *super:* **-iest**) turbio, legañoso
bleat [blit] *s* balido; *vn* balar
bleb [blɛb] *s* ampolla; burbuja
bled [blɛd] *pret & pp de* **bleed**
bleed [blid] (*pret & pp:* **bled**) *va* sangrar; sacar dinero a; **to bleed white** desangrar; arrancar hasta el último céntimo a; *vn* sangrar; verter su sangre, sufrir, morir; exudar (*las plantas*); llorar (*la vid*); penar, afligirse; **to bleed to death** morir de desangramiento
bleeder ['blidər] *s* sangrador; hemofílico; (mach.) dispositivo de sangrar
bleeding heart *s* (bot.) dicentra
blemish ['blɛmɪʃ] *s* mancha, tacha; lunar; *va* manchar
blench [blɛntʃ] *va* blanquear; *vn* acobardarse, recular; palidecer
blend [blɛnd] *s* mezcla, combinación; armonía; (*pret & pp:* **blended** o **blent**) *va* mezclar, combinar; armonizar; fusionar; *vn* mezclarse, combinarse; armonizar; fusionarse
blende [blɛnd] *s* (mineral.) blenda (*sulfuro de cinc*); (mineral.) sulfuro de brillo metaloideo
blending ['blɛndɪŋ] *s* mezcla, combinación; armonía; (philol.) cruce de palabras, fusión de voces
blennorrhea [,blɛnə'riə] *s* (path.) blenorrea
blenny ['blɛnɪ] *s* (*pl:* **-nies**) (ichth.) blenia
blent [blɛnt] *pret & pp de* **blend**
blepharitis [,blɛfə'raɪtɪs] *s* (path.) blefaritis
bless [blɛs] (*pret & pp:* **blessed** o **blest**) *va* bendecir; amparar, proteger; **bless my soul!** ¡válgame Dios!
blessed ['blɛsɪd] *adj* bendito, bienaventurado, santo, feliz; (for emphasis) santo, p.ej., **the whole blessed day** todo el santo día; maldito, p.ej., **to not know a blessed thing about the matter** no saber maldita la cosa del asunto; [blɛst] *pret & pp de* **bless**
blessedness ['blɛsɪdnɪs] *s* bienaventuranza, santidad, felicidad
Blessed Virgin *s* Santísima Virgen
blessing ['blɛsɪŋ] *s* bendición
blest [blɛst] *pret & pp de* **bless**
blether ['blɛðər] *s & vn* var. de **blather**
blew [blu] *pret de* **blow**
blight [blaɪt] *s* roya; (fig.) plaga, infortunio, daño grave; *va* atizonar, añublar; arruinar; frustrar (*las esperanzas*); *vn* atizonar
blimp [blɪmp] *s* pequeño dirigible no rígido
blind [blaɪnd] *adj* ciego; oculto, secreto; obscuro; (arch.) ciego (*dícese, p.ej., de una ventana o puerta*); (fig.) ciego, p.ej., **blind with anger** ciego de ira; **blind with jealousy** ciego con celos; **blind as a bat** más ciego que un topo; **blind of** o **in one eye** que no ve con un ojo, tuerto; *s* velo; venda (*para los ojos*); anteojera (*para los ojos del caballo*); disfraz, subterfugio, pretexto; estor, transparente de resorte; persiana; pantalla (*persona que encubre a otra*); (fort.) blinda; escondrijo del cazador; **to be a blind for someone** (slang) ser pantalla o tapadera de alguien; *va* cegar; deslumbrar
blindage ['blaɪndɪdʒ] *s* (fort.) blindaje
blind alley *s* callejón sin salida; (fig.) atolladero
blind date *s* (slang) cita a ciegas (*cita entre un muchacho y una muchacha que no se conocen*)
blinder ['blaɪndər] *s* anteojera
blind flying *s* (aer.) vuelo a ciegas
blindfold ['blaɪnd,fold] *adj* vendado (*de ojos*); deslumbrado; descuidado, atolondrado; *s* venda en los ojos; *va* vendar los ojos a
blind landing *s* (aer.) aterrizaje a ciegas
blind man *s* ciego
blindman's buff ['blaɪndmænz] *s* gallina ciega (*juego*)
blindness ['blaɪndnɪs] *s* ceguedad
blind spot *s* (anat.) punto ciego; (rad.) lugar ciego; (fig.) punto acerca de que uno, sin darse cuenta de ello, tiene pocos informes o mucho prejuicio
blind stitch *s* puntada invisible
blindstitch ['blaɪnd,stɪtʃ] *va* coser a puntadas invisibles
blind-tool ['blaɪnd'tul] *va* (b.b.) estampar en seco
blind tooling *s* (b.b.) estampación en seco
blindworm ['blaɪnd,wʌrm] *s* (zool.) lución
blink [blɪŋk] *s* mirada, vista; guiñada, parpadeo; **on the blink** (slang) incapacitado; (slang) desconcertado; *va* guiñar (*el ojo*); desconocer; señalar por luz intermitente; *vn* guiñar, parpadear; mirar con los ojos entreabiertos; oscilar (*la luz*)
blinker ['blɪŋkər] *s* anteojera; proyector de destellos; (naut.) señales por luz intermitente (*con el alfabeto Morse*); (slang) ojo
blip [blɪp] *s* (radar) bache (*indicación visual*)
bliss [blɪs] *s* bienaventuranza, felicidad
blissful ['blɪsfəl] *adj* bienaventurado, muy feliz
blister ['blɪstər] *s* ampolla, vejiga; *va* ampollar, avejigar; censurar acerbamente; *vn* ampollarse, avejigarse
blister beetle *s* (ent.) cantárida, abadejo
blister gas *s* gas vesicante
blister pearl *s* perla de ampolla
blister plaster *s* vejigatorio
blithe [blaɪð] o [blaɪθ] o **blithesome** ['blaɪðsəm] o ['blaɪθsəm] *adj* alegre, gozoso, animado
blitz [blɪts] *s & va* (coll.) var. de **blitzkrieg**
blitzkrieg ['blɪts,krig] *s* guerra relámpago; *va* atacar con guerra relámpago, arrasar por bombardeo aéreo

blizzard ['blɪzərd] *s* ventisca
bloat [blot] *va* hinchar; ahumar, curar al humo (*el arenque*); *vn* hincharse, abotagarse
bloater ['blotər] *s* arenque ahumado
blob [blɑb] *s* gota, burbuja; burujo
bloc [blɑk] *s* (pol.) bloque
block [blɑk] *s* bloque, zoquete, canto; tajo (*para partir la carne; sobre el cual se cortaba la cabeza a los reos*); plataforma en que se hace venta pública; plataforma en que se vendían los esclavos en subasta; (mach.) bloque (*de cilindros*); horma, cáliz (*pieza de madera torneada que usan los sombrereros*); polea, garrucha; (naut.) motón; (print.) bloque; (rail.) tramo; bloque (*tableta para apuntes*); cepo (*de yunque*); cuadrado; manzana (*de una ciudad*); cuadrito (*de sellos de correo*); estorbo, obstáculo; grupo, conjunto; (pol.) bloque; **blocks** *spl* piezas de madera de construcciones infantiles; **to go to the block** ir a ser decapitado; venderse en pública subasta; *va* cegar, cerrar, obstruir; bloquear; conformar (*un sombrero*); calzar (*una rueda*); parar (*una pelota, una jugada*); **to block in** o **to block out** delinear, esbozar; **to block up** cegar, tapar, taponar; apoyar mediante trozos de madera o piedra
blockade [blɑ'ked] *s* (mil. & naut.) bloqueo; obstrucción; **to run the blockade** (naut.) burlar, forzar o violar el bloqueo; *va* (mil. & naut.) bloquear; obstruir
blockade runner *s* (naut.) forzador de bloqueo
block and tackle *s* aparejo de poleas, polea con aparejo
block anesthesia *s* anestesia de bloque, anestesia regional
blockbuster ['blɑk,bʌstər] *s* (coll.) bomba rompemanzanas
blockhead ['blɑk,hɛd] *s* zoquete, zopenco, tonto
blockhouse ['blɑk,haʊs] *s* (fort.) blocao
blockish ['blɑkɪʃ] *adj* tonto, estúpido
block plane *s* cepillo de contrafibra
block printing *s* impresión de plancha de madera
block signal *s* (rail.) señal de tramo
block system *s* (rail.) sistema de tramos
blocky ['blɑkɪ] *adj* rechoncho; dividido en cuadrados alternados de luz y sombra
blond [blɑnd] *adj* rubio, blondo; *s* rubio (*hombre rubio*)
blonde [blɑnd] *adj* rubio, blondo; *s* rubia (*mujer rubia*)
blond lace *s* blonda
blood [blʌd] *s* sangre; jugo o zumo; efusión de sangre, matanza; ira, cólera; temperamento; vida; hombre animoso; libertino; caballo de pura raza; **in cold blood** a sangre fría; **to draw blood** hacer correr sangre; **to have one's blood run cold** helársele a uno la sangre
blood bank *s* banco de sangre
blood brother *s* hermano carnal; hermano por mezcla de sangre
blood count *s* (med.) recuento sanguíneo
bloodcurdling ['blʌd,kʌrdlɪŋ] *adj* horripilante, espeluznante
blood donor *s* donador de sangre, donante de sangre
blood group *s* grupo sanguíneo
bloodguilty ['blʌd,gɪltɪ] *adj* culpable del derramamiento de sangre, culpable de homicidio
blood heat *s* calor de la sangre
bloodhound ['blʌd,haʊnd] *s* sabueso; (slang) sabueso (*detective*)
bloodless ['blʌdlɪs] *adj* exangüe, desangrado, desanimado; insensible; sin efusión de sangre
bloodletting ['blʌd,lɛtɪŋ] *s* sangría, flebotomía
blood money *s* dinero que se paga por el derramamiento de sangre; dinero que se paga como indemnización por el derramamiento de sangre
blood orange *s* naranja sanguínea o roja
blood plasma *s* plasma sanguíneo
blood poisoning *s* (path.) envenenamiento de la sangre (*septicemia, toxemia, piohemia*)
blood pressure *s* presión sanguínea, tensión arterial
blood pudding *s* morcilla
blood red *s* color rojo sangre
blood relation *s* pariente consanguíneo
blood relationship *s* consanguinidad
blood relative *s* var. de **blood relation**
bloodroot ['blʌd,rut] o ['blʌd,rʊt] *s* (bot.) sanguinaria del Canadá; (bot.) tormentila
blood royal *s* sangre real
bloodshed ['blʌd,ʃɛd] *s* efusión de sangre, matanza
bloodshot ['blʌd,ʃɑt] *adj* ensangrentado, inyectado de sangre
bloodstained ['blʌd,stend] *adj* manchado de sangre, homicida
bloodstone ['blʌd,ston] *s* (mineral.) restañasangre; (mineral.) hematites
blood stream *s* corriente sanguínea
bloodsucker ['blʌd,sʌkər] *s* (zool.) sanguijuela; (fig.) sanguijuela; (fig.) sablista, gorrista
blood test *s* análisis de sangre
bloodthirsty ['blʌd,θʌrstɪ] *adj* sanguinario
blood transfusion *s* transfusión sanguínea o transfusión de sangre
blood vessel *s* (anat.) vaso sanguíneo; **to burst a blood vessel** reventarse una vena
bloody ['blʌdɪ] *adj* (*comp:* **-ier;** *super:* **-iest**) sangriento; sanguíneo; (Brit. slang) maldito; *adv* (Brit. slang) muy; (*pret & pp:* **-ied**) *va* ensangrentar; herir
Bloody Mary *s* La Sanguinaria (*María I, reina de Inglaterra*)
bloom [blum] *s* florescencia, florecimiento; flor; lozanía; (found.) changote; (found.) tocho (*barra*); masa de vidrio candente; *vn* florecer; lozanear
bloomer ['blumər] *s* (slang) gazapatón (*en el hablar*); **bloomers** *spl* calzones cortos y holgados de mujer
blooming ['blumɪŋ] *adj* floreciente, lozano
blooming mill *s* (found.) laminadero desbastador de tochos
bloomy ['blumɪ] *adj* (*comp:* **-ier;** *super:* **-iest**) floreciente, lozano; lleno de polvillo
bloop [blup] *s* (mov.) ruido de empalme
blossom ['blɑsəm] *s* flor; brote, pimpollo; florescencia; **in blossom** en cierne; *vn* florecer; brotar
blossomy ['blɑsəmɪ] *adj* lleno de flores, lleno de botones
blot [blɑt] *s* borrón (*mancha de tinta*); (fig.) borrón, mancha; (*pret & pp:* **blotted;** *ger:* **blotting**) *va* borrar, emborronar; manchar; secar con papel secante; **to blot out** borrar; *vn* borrarse, emborronarse; echar borrones (*una pluma*)
blotch [blɑtʃ] *s* manchón; erupción (*en la piel*); *va* emborronar, cubrir con manchones; cubrir con erupciones
blotchy ['blɑtʃɪ] *adj* (*comp:* **-ier;** *super:* **-iest**) lleno de manchones; lleno de erupciones
blot on the escutcheon *s* borrón en el escudo, mancha en el honor de uno
blotter ['blɑtər] *s* teleta; borrador, libro borrador
blotting paper *s* papel secante
blotto ['blɑto] *adj* (slang) borracho perdido
blouse [blaʊs] o [blaʊz] *s* blusa
blow [blo] *s* golpe; soplo, soplido; ventarrón; toque, trompetazo; estocada (*cosa que ocasiona dolor*); (bot.) florescencia; (metal.) hornada; larva de mosca depositada en carne; (slang) fanfarrón; **at one blow** de un solo golpe; **to come to blows** venir a las manos; **without striking a blow** sin dar un golpe, sin esfuerzo ninguno; se traduce a menudo al español por medio del sufijo **-azo**, p.ej., **blow of a horn** bocinazo; **blow with the fist** puñetazo ‖ (*pret:* **blew;** *pp:* **blown**) *va* soplar; limpiar o vaciar a soplos; sonar o tocar (*un instrumento de viento o un silbato*); silbar (*un silbato*); volar, hacer saltar; sonarse (*las narices*); desalentar; depositar larvas en (*carne*); quemar (*un fusible*); echar (*flores*); divulgar; (slang) malgastar (*dinero*); (slang) convidar; **to blow down** derribar; **to blow in** (metal.) dar fuego a, poner a funcionar; (slang) malgastar (*dinero*); **to blow open** abrir; abrir con explosivos; **to blow out** hacer salir soplando; apagar soplando; quemar (*un fusible*); **to blow up** volar, hacer saltar; soplar, inflar; (phot.) ampliar ‖ *vn* soplar; sonar; jadear, resoplar; (zool.)

soplar (*echar agua la ballena*); quemarse (*un fusible*); abrirse (*las flores*); (slang) fanfarronear; (slang) irse, marcharse; **to blow hot and cold** estar entre sí y no; **to blow in** (slang) llegar inesperadamente; **to blow off** escaparse (*el vapor*); descargarse (*una caldera*); (slang) fanfarronear; **to blow on** (slang) delatar, traicionar; **to blow open** abrirse (*por causa del viento*); **to blow out** apagarse (*por causa del viento*); quemarse (*un fusible*); reventar (*un neumático*); **to blow over** pasar; ser olvidado; **to blow shut** cerrarse (*por causa del viento*); **to blow up** volarse, reventarse; fracasar; (slang) estallar o reventar (*de ira*)
blower [ˈbloər] *s* soplador (*persona y máquina; cetáceo*)
blowfly [ˈbloˌflaɪ] *s* (*pl:* **-flies**) (ent.) moscarda
blowgun [ˈbloˌgʌn] *s* cerbatana, bodoquera
blowhole [ˈbloˌhol] *s* respiradero; (found.) sopladura, venteadura, escarabajo; (zool.) espiráculo; agujero en el hielo adonde vienen las ballenas, focas, etc. para respirar
blown [blon] *adj* agotado, desalentado; corrompido por las moscas; *pp de* **blow**
blown glass *s* vidrio soplado
blowoff [ˈbloˌɔf] o [ˈbloˌɑf] *s* escape (*p.ej., de vapor*); (slang) fanfarrón
blowout [ˈbloˌaʊt] *s* reventón, estalladura; (elec.) quemadura (*de fusible*); (slang) banquete, tertulia concurrida
blowout patch *s* (aut.) parche para neumático
blowpipe [ˈbloˌpaɪp] *s* soplete; cerbatana, bodoquera
blowtorch [ˈbloˌtɔrtʃ] *s* lámpara de soldar, antorcha a soplete
blowup [ˈbloˌʌp] *s* explosión; (fig.) explosión (*de ira o cólera*); (phot.) ampliación
blowy [ˈblo·ɪ] *adj* (*comp:* **-ier;** *super:* **-iest**) ventoso; ligero
blowzy [ˈblaʊzɪ] *adj* (*comp:* **-ier;** *super:* **-iest**) desaliñado, desmelenado; coloradote
bls. abr. de **barrels**
blubber [ˈblʌbər] *s* grasa de ballena; grasa (*de una persona o animal*); lloro ruidoso; *va* decir llorando ruidosamente; *vn* llorar con mucho ruido, llorar hasta hincharse los carrillos
blubber lip *s* bezo
blucher [ˈblukər] o [ˈblutʃər] *s* zapato de orejas sueltas
bludgeon [ˈblʌdʒən] *s* cachiporra; *va* aporrear; amedrentar, intimidar
blue [blu] *adj* (*comp:* **bluer;** *super:* **bluest**) azul; amoratado, lívido; abatido, triste; **to turn blue** azular; azularse; *s* azul, color azul; **the blue** el cielo; el mar; **the blues** la morriña; (*pret & pp:* **blued;** *ger:* **bluing** o **blueing**) *va* azular; añilar, dar azulete a (*la ropa blanca*); pavonar (*el hierro o el acero*); *vn* azularse
blue baby *s* niño azul
Bluebeard [ˈbluˌbɪrd] *s* Barba Azul
bluebell [ˈbluˌbɛl] *s* (bot.) campánula
blueberry [ˈbluˌbɛrɪ] *s* (*pl:* **-ries**) (bot.) vaccinio
bluebird [ˈbluˌbʌrd] *s* (orn.) pájaro azul (*Sialia sialis*); (orn.) tempestad, ventura (*Sialia mexicana*)
blue-black [ˈbluˈblæk] *adj* negro azulado, azul obscuro
blue blood *s* sangre azul (*sangre noble*); (coll.) aristócrata
blue-blooded [ˈbluˌblʌdɪd] *adj* de sangre azul
bluebonnet [ˈbluˌbɑnɪt] *s* bonete azul; (bot.) azulejo, aciano
blue book *s* (coll.) anuario de la alta sociedad; (U.S.A.) registro de empleados del gobierno; (U.S.A.) librito de exámenes; (Brit.) libro azul (*que contiene documentos diplomáticos*)
bluebottle [ˈbluˌbɑtəl] *s* (bot.) aciano, azulejo; (ent.) moscarda, mosca de color azul metálico
blue cheese *s* queso de vaca, semejante al queso de Roquefort y de fabricación norteamericana
bluecoat [ˈbluˌkot] *s* policía (*que lleva uniforme azul*)
blue devils *spl* abatimiento, melancolía; delirio debido al abuso del alcohol
bluefish [ˈbluˌfɪʃ] *s* (ichth.) pomátomo saltador, anchoa de banco
blue flag *s* (bot.) lirio azul
bluegrass [ˈbluˌgræs] o [ˈbluˌgrɑs] *s* (bot.) gramínea norteamericana de tallo verde azulado (*del género Poa*)
blue grosbeak *s* (orn.) alondra azul
blue gum *s* (bot.) eucalipto
blueing [ˈbluɪŋ] *s & ger* var. de **bluing**
bluejacket [ˈbluˌdʒækɪt] *s* marinero de buque de guerra
bluejay [ˈbluˌdʒe] *s* (orn.) gayo
blue laws *spl* (U.S.A.) leyes puritánicas severas
blue lead [lɛd] *s* (mineral.) galena; plomo azul (*pigmento*)
Blue Monday *s* lunes que precede a la Cuaresma; lunes, día triste por la necesidad de volver al trabajo
Blue Nile *s* Nilo Azul
blue-pencil [ˈbluˈpɛnsəl] (*pret & pp:* **-ciled** o **-cilled;** *ger:* **-ciling** o **-cilling**) *va* marcar, corregir o borrar con lápiz azul
bluepoint [ˈbluˌpɔɪnt] *s* ostra pequeña (*que se come cruda*)
blueprint [ˈbluˌprɪnt] *s* cianotipia; cianotipo; (fig.) plan detallado; *va* copiar a la cianotipia
blue racer *s* (zool.) culebra de color azulado (*Coluber constrictor flaviventris*)
blue ribbon *s* cinta azul concedida al que gana el primer premio; divisa azul de una sociedad contra el uso del alcohol; (naut.) gallardete azul (*trofeo*); (Brit.) cinta de terciopelo azul (*de la Orden de la Jarretera*)
blue-ribbon [ˈbluˈrɪbən] *adj* muy perito, muy inteligente; de capacidad especial
blue-sky law [ˈbluˈskaɪ] *s* (coll.) ley para impedir la venta de acciones u obligaciones sin valor
bluestocking [ˈbluˌstɑkɪŋ] *s* (coll.) marisabidilla
bluestone [ˈbluˌston] *s* arenisca azulada; (chem.) piedra azul
blue streak *s* (coll.) rayo; **to talk a blue streak** (coll.) soltar la tarabilla
bluet [ˈbluɪt] *s* (bot.) azulejo, aciano; (bot.) houstonia cerúlea
blue titmouse *s* (orn.) herrerillo, trepatroncos
blue vitriol *s* (chem.) vitriolo azul
blueweed [ˈbluˌwid] *s* (bot.) viborera
blue wildebeest *s* (zool.) ñu
blue-winged teal [ˈbluˌwɪŋd] *s* (orn.) pato chiquito, pato zarcel
bluff [blʌf] *adj* escarpado; brusco, francote; *s* peñasco escarpado, risco; falsas apariencias; amenaza que no se puede realizar; fanfarrón; **to call someone's bluff** cogerle la palabra a uno; *va* tratar de engañar con falsas apariencias, tratar de intimidar con amenazas que no se pueden realizar; *vn* blufar, fanfarronear, baladronear
bluffer [ˈblʌfər] *s* fanfarrón
bluffing [ˈblʌfɪŋ] *s* fanfarronada, baladronada, faramalla
bluing [ˈbluɪŋ] *s* añil, azulete, pasta para lavandera; pavonado; *ger de* **blue**
bluish [ˈbluɪʃ] *adj* azulado, azulino
blunder [ˈblʌndər] *s* disparate, desatino, patochada; *va* chapucear, chafallar; descolgarse con, decir desatinadamente; *vn* disparatar, desatinar; **to blunder into, on** o **upon** tropezar con, hallar por accidente
blunderbuss [ˈblʌndərbʌs] *s* trabuco; desatinado (*el que habla o procede sin juicio*)
blunderer [ˈblʌndərər] *s* desatinado
blunt [blʌnt] *adj* embotado, despuntado; obtuso, lerdo; franco, brusco, directo; *va* embotar, despuntar; *vn* embotarse, despuntarse
bluntness [ˈblʌntnɪs] *s* embotadura; franqueza, brusquedad
blur [blʌr] *s* obscuridad; forma confusa; mancha, borrón; (*pret & pp:* **blurred;** *ger:* **blurring**) *va* empañar, velar; manchar; *vn* empañarse, velarse
blurb [blʌrb] *s* anuncio efusivo
blurry [ˈblʌrɪ] *adj* manchado, confuso, borroso; grasiento
blurt [blʌrt] *va* descolgarse con, soltar a tontas y a locas; **to blurt out** descolgarse con, soltar a tontas y a locas

blush [blʌʃ] *s* rubor, sonrojo; color de rosa; **at first blush** a primera vista; *vn* ruborizarse, sonrojarse, ponerse colorado
blushing ['blʌʃɪŋ] *adj* ruboroso; *s* rubor, sonrojo
bluster ['blʌstər] *s* borrasca ruidosa; ruido tempestuoso; tempestad de gritos; jactancia, fanfarronada; *va* hacer con gritos y violencia, decir con gritos y violencia; forzar, intimidar; conseguir por gritos y violencia; *vn* bramar, soplar con furia (*el viento*); fanfarronear, pavonearse, bravear
blustery ['blʌstərɪ] *adj* tempestuoso, ruidoso; fanfarrón
blvd. abr. de **boulevard**
boa ['boə] *s* (zool.) boa; boa (*prenda de pieles o plumas*)
boa constrictor *s* (zool.) boa, boa constrictor
Boadicea [ˌboədɪ'siə] *s* Boadicea
boar [bor] *s* (zool.) verraco; (zool.) jabalí (*Sus scrofa*)
board [bord] *s* tabla, plancha; tablero; tablilla (*para anuncios*); (elec.) cuadro; cartón; mesa; junta, consejo; pensión; canto, borde; (naut.) bordo; (naut.) bordada (*camino entre dos viradas*); **bound in boards** en cartoné, encartonado; **on board** (naut.) a bordo; en el tren; **the boards** las tablas (*la escena del teatro*); **to go by the boards** (naut.) caer por el costado del buque; fracasar; ser echado a un lado, ser abandonado; **to tread the boards** ser actor o actriz, representar un papel; *va* entablar, enmaderar; dar de comer u hospedar regularmente bajo pago; subir a (*un tren*); (naut.) embarcarse en; (naut.) abordar; *vn* hacer las comidas, hospedarse regularmente bajo pago; (naut.) dar de bordadas; (naut.) navegar de bolina
board and lodging *s* cuarto y comida, pensión completa
boarder ['bordər] *s* huésped; interno (*en una escuela*); (naut.) abordador
board foot *s* pie de tabla (*unidad que equivale a una tabla de un pie cuadrado y de un espesor de una pulgada*)
boarding ['bordɪŋ] *s* tablazón; entablado; tabique de tablas; (naut.) abordaje
boarding house *s* casa de huéspedes
boarding school *s* internado
board measure *s* medida de tabla (*cuya unidad es el pie de tabla*)
Board of Admiralty *s* (Brit.) ministerio de Marina
board of directors *s* directorio, junta directiva
board of health *s* junta de sanidad
board of trade *s* junta de comercio; (*caps.*) *s* (Brit.) ministerio de Comercio
board of trustees *s* junta de síndicos, consejo de administración
board room *s* sala de junta; sala del tablero indicador de las cotizaciones de bolsa
boardwalk ['bordˌwɔk] *s* paseo entablado a la orilla del mar
boarhound ['borˌhaʊnd] *s* perro jabalinero
boarish ['borɪʃ] *adj* cochino, puerco; lascivo; cruel
boast [bost] *s* jactancia, baladronada; *va* jactarse de; ostentar; *vn* jactarse; **it is nothing to boast of** no es cosa para jactarse
boastful ['bostfəl] *adj* jactancioso
boat [bot] *s* barco, embarcación, nave; buque, navío; bote; barca, lancha; salsera (*vasija para la salsa*); **in the same boat** en una misma situación, corriendo los mismos peligros; **to burn one's boats** quemar las naves; *va* poner a bordo, llevar a bordo; **to boat oars** desarmar los remos; *vn* ir o pasear en bote
boat bridge *s* puente de barcas
boat hook *s* bichero
boathouse ['botˌhaʊs] *s* casilla de botes
boating ['botɪŋ] *s* paseo en barco
boatload ['botˌlod] *s* barcada
boatman ['botmən] *s* (*pl:* **-men**) barquero; botero (*patrón*)
boat race *s* regata
boatswain ['bosən] o ['botˌswen] *s* (naut.) contramaestre
boatswain's chair *s* asiento colgante; (naut.) guindola
boatswain's mate *s* (naut.) segundo contramaestre
bob [bɑb] *s* sacudida, meneo brusco; cola cortada de un caballo; pelo cortado corto; lenteja (*de la péndola del reloj*); plomo (*peso de una plomada*); corcho (*de una caña de pescar*); (Brit. slang) chelín; (*cap.*) *s* nombre abreviado de **Robert;** (*pret & pp:* **bobbed;** *ger:* **bobbing**) *va* cortar corto; menear bruscamente, *vn* menearse, agitarse; **to bob at** o **for an apple** tratar de coger con la boca una manzana colgada de un hilo o que flota en el agua; **to bob up** dejarse ver repentina e inesperadamente; **to bob up and down** fluctuar, subir y bajar con sacudidas cortas
bobbin ['bɑbɪn] *s* carrete; canilla, broca (*de la máquina de coser*)
bobbinet [ˌbɑbɪ'nɛt] o ['bɑbɪnɛt] *s* bobiné
bobbin lace *s* encaje de bolillos
bobby ['bɑbɪ] *s* (*pl:* **-bies**) (Brit. slang) policía
bobby pin *s* horquilla de puntas apretadas para el cabello
bobbysocks ['bɑbɪˌsɑks] *spl* (coll.) tobilleras (*de jovencita*)
bobbysoxer ['bɑbɪˌsɑksər] *s* (coll.) tobillera
bobcat ['bɑbˌkæt] *s* (zool.) lince
bobolink ['bɑbəlɪŋk] *s* (orn.) chambergo
bobsled ['bɑbˌslɛd] *s* bob-sleigh; (*pret & pp:* **-sledded;** *ger:* **-sledding**) *vn* descender en bob-sleigh
bobsleigh ['bɑbˌsle] *s & vn* var. de **bobsled**
bobstay ['bɑbˌste] *s* (naut.) barbiquejo
bobtail ['bɑbˌtel] *adj* rabón; escaso, incompleto; *s* cola corta; cola cortada; animal rabón; *va* cortar muy corta la cola a
bobwhite ['bɑb'hwaɪt] *s* (orn.) colín de Virginia
Boche o **boche** [bɑʃ] o [boʃ] *s* (slang) boche (*alemán*)
bock [bɑk] o **bock beer** *s* cerveza de marzo (*cerveza muy fuerte de color obscuro*)
bode [bod] *va & vn* presagiar, prefigurar, indicar por señales; **to bode ill** ser un mal presagio; **to bode well** ser un buen presagio; *pret de* **bide**
bodice ['bɑdɪs] *s* almilla, jubón, corpiño; cinturón ancho
bodiless ['bɑdɪlɪs] *adj* incorporal, incorpóreo; sin tronco
bodily ['bɑdɪlɪ] *adj* corporal, corpóreo; *adv* en persona; en conjunto, todos juntos
bodkin ['bɑdkɪn] *s* espadilla (*para sujetar el pelo de las mujeres*); aguja de jareta; punzón (*para abrir ojales*); (obs.) daga, puñal
Bodleian [bɑd'liən] o ['bɑdlɪən] *s* biblioteca bodleyana (*de Oxford*)
body ['bɑdɪ] *s* (*pl:* **-ies**) cuerpo; tronco (*de un árbol*); nave (*de una iglesia*); caja; carrocería (*de un coche o carro*); extensión (*de agua*); masa (*de aire*); (coll.) persona; **to keep body and soul together** seguir viviendo; (*pret & pp:* **-ied**) *va* informar, dar cuerpo a; espesar (*un líquido*); **to body forth** dar forma a, representar; presagiar
body and fender repairman *s* (aut.) chapista carrocero, mecánico chapista
bodyguard ['bɑdɪˌgɑrd] *s* guardia de corps; guardaespaldas; salvaguardia
body politic *s* entidad política
body snatcher *s* ladrón de cadáveres
body temperature *s* temperatura del cuerpo
Boeotia [bi'oʃə] *s* Beocia
Boeotian [bi'oʃən] *adj* beocio; (fig.) beocio (*torpe, estúpido*); *s* beocio
Boer [bor] o [bʊr] *adj & s* bóer
Boer War *s* guerra del Transvaal
bog [bɑg] *s* pantano; (*pret & pp:* **bogged;** *ger:* **bogging**) *vn* atascarse, hundirse; **to bog down** atascarse, hundirse
bog asphodel *s* (bot.) abama
bogey ['bogɪ] *s* duende, demonio; coco; aversión, persona que inspira gran aversión; (golf) norma de perfección
bogeyman ['bogɪˌmæn] *s* (*pl:* **-men**) duende; coco
boggle ['bɑgəl] *s* chapucería; desatino, disparate; *vn* asustarse, vacilar; retroceder; chapucear

boggy ['bɑgɪ] *adj* (*comp:* **-gier;** *super:* **-giest**) pantanoso
bogie ['bogɪ] *s* duende, demonio; coco; aversión, persona que inspira gran aversión; (golf) norma de perfección; (Brit. rail.) bogie
bogle ['bogəl] o ['bɑgəl] *s* duende, demonio; coco; aversión
bogus ['bogəs] *adj* (U.S.A.) falso, fingido, espurio
bogy ['bogɪ] *s* (*pl:* **-gies**) duende, demonio; coco; aversión, persona que inspira gran aversión
Bohemia [bo'himɪə] *s* Bohemia
Bohemian [bo'himɪən] *adj & s* bohemio; (fig.) bohemio
Bohemianism [bo'himɪənɪzəm] *s* bohemia, vida de bohemio
boil [bɔɪl] *s* ebullición, hervor; cocción; (path.) divieso; **to bring to a boil** calentar (*el agua*) hasta que hierva; **to come to a boil** comenzar a hervir; *va* herventar; hacer hervir (*el agua*); **to boil down** reducir hirviendo; reducir a su más simple expresión; *vn* hervir, bullir, cocer; (fig.) hervir (*una persona*); **to boil away** consumirse (*un líquido*) a fuerza de cocer; **to boil down** reducirse hirviendo; reducirse; **to boil over** rebosar con la ebulición; **to boil up** borbollar
boiler ['bɔɪlər] *s* caldera; hervidor; termosifón (*para calentar agua y para calentar por medio de agua caliente*)
boilermaker ['bɔɪlər,mekər] *s* calderero
boiler plate *s* plancha de caldera
boiler room *s* sala de calderas
boiler shell *s* casco o cuerpo de caldera
boiler tube *s* tubería de caldera
boiling ['bɔɪlɪŋ] *adj* hirviente; *s* ebullición, hervor
boiling point *s* punto de ebullición; **at the boiling point** muy encolerizado
boisterous ['bɔɪstərəs] *adj* alborotado, ruidoso, turbulento, bullicioso
Bokhara [bo'kɑrə] *s* Bujara (*ciudad*); la Bujara (*estado*)
Bol. abr de **Bolivia**
bold [bold] *adj* audaz, osado, atrevido, arrojado; impudente, descarado; temerario; vigoroso; acantilado, escarpado; **to make bold to** + *inf* osar + *inf*, tomar la libertad de + *inf*
boldface ['bold,fes] *s* individuo descarado; (print.) negrilla
boldine ['bɑldin] o ['bɑldɪn] *s* (pharm.) boldina
boldness ['boldnɪs] *s* audacia, osadía, arrojo; impudencia, descaro; temeridad; vigor
bole [bol] *s* tronco de árbol
bolero [bo'lɛro] *s* (*pl:* **-ros**) bolero (*baile y música, chaquetilla de señora*)
boletus [bo'litəs] *s* (bot.) boleto
Boleyn, Anne ['bulɪn] Ana Bolena
bolide ['bolaɪd] o ['bolɪd] *s* (astr.) bólido
Bolivia [bo'lɪvɪə] *s* Bolivia
Bolivian [bo'lɪvɪən] *adj & s* boliviano
boll [bol] *s* (bot.) cápsula de algodón o lino
Bollandist ['bɑləndɪst] *s* bolandista
bollard ['bɑlərd] *s* (naut.) bolardo
boll weevil *s* (ent.) picudo, gorgojo del algodón
bollworm ['bol,wʌrm] *s* (zool.) larva de una mariposa que causa grandes estragos al maíz y el algodón (*Heliothis armigera*)
Bologna [bə'lonjə] *s* Bolonia
boloney [bə'lonɪ] *s* var. de **baloney**
Bolshevik ['bɑlʃəvɪk] o ['bolʃəvɪk] *adj* bolchevique; *s* (*pl:* **-viki** ['vikɪ] o **-viks**) bolchevique
Bolshevism ['bɑlʃəvɪzəm] o ['bolʃəvɪzəm] *s* bolchevismo o bolcheviquismo
Bolshevist ['bɑlʃəvɪst] o ['bolʃəvɪst] *adj & s* bolchevista, bolcheviquista
Bolshevistic o **bolshevistic** [,bɑlʃə'vɪstɪk] o [,bolʃə'vɪstɪk] *adj* bolchevista, bolcheviquista
Bolshevization o **bolshevization** [,bɑlʃəvɪ'zeʃən] o [,bolʃəvɪ'zeʃən] *s* bolchevización
Bolshevize o **bolshevize** ['bɑlʃəvaɪz] o ['bolʃəvaɪz] *va* bolchevizar
bolster ['bolstər] *s* almohadón; travesaño (*para la cabecera de la cama*); refuerzo, sostén, soporte; *va* apoyar con almohadón; apoyar, sostener; **to bolster up** apoyar, sostener; animar, alentar
bolt [bolt] *s* perno; cerrojo, pestillo, pasador; grillete; cuadrillo (*saeta*); chorro cilíndrico (*de agua*); rayo; fuga, salto repentino; rollo (*de tela o papel*); bolo alimenticio; ataque, argumento; disidencia (*de un partido político*); **to shoot one's bolt** hacer (*uno*) todo cuanto en él cabe; *adv* repentinamente; directamente; **bolt upright** enhiesto, derecho y rígido; *va* acerrojar; empernar; amarrar con grillos; deglutir de una vez; descolgarse con; cerner, cribar, tamizar; arrojar; disidir de (*un partido político*); separar, examinar, escudriñar; *vn* lanzarse, salir de repente; desbocarse (*un caballo*); disidir; **to bolt in** entrar de repente; **to bolt off** u **out** salir de repente
bolter ['boltər] *s* caballo desbocado; disidente (*en asuntos políticos*); criba, tamiz
bolt from the blue *s* rayo en cielo sin nubes; (fig.) acontecimiento inesperado
boltrope ['bolt,rop] *s* (naut.) relinga
bolus ['boləs] *s* bolo (*píldora gruesa u otra masa esférica*)
bomb [bɑm] *s* bomba; (fig.) acontecimiento inesperado, sorpresa inquietante; *va* bombear
bombard [bɑm'bɑrd] *va* bombardear; (phys.) bombardear; (fig.) asediar (*p.ej., de preguntas*)
bombardier [,bɑmbər'dɪr] *s* bombardero
bombardment [bɑm'bɑrdmənt] *s* bombardeo
bombasine [,bɑmbə'zin] o ['bɑmbəzin] *s* alepín
bombast ['bɑmbæst] *s* ampulosidad
bombastic [bɑm'bæstɪk] *adj* ampuloso
bombastically [bɑm'bæstɪkəlɪ] *adv* ampulosamente
bombazine [,bɑmbə'zin] o ['bɑmbəzin] *s* alepín
bomb bay *s* (aer.) compartimiento de las bombas
bomb crater *s* (mil.) embudo de bomba
bomber ['bɑmər] *s* bombardero (*tripulante y avión*)
bombing ['bɑmɪŋ] *s* bombeo, bombardeo
bombproof ['bɑm,pruf] *adj* a prueba de bombas
bomb release *s* (aer.) lanzabombas, disparador de bombas
bombshell ['bɑm,ʃɛl] *s* bomba; sorpresa asoladora; **to fall like a bombshell** caer como una bomba
bomb shelter *s* refugio antiaéreo
bombsight ['bɑm,saɪt] *s* (aer.) mira de bombardero, visor
bona fide ['bonə 'faɪdɪ] *adj & adv* de buena fe
bonanza [bo'nænzə] *s* (min.) bonanza; (fig.) bonanza (*prosperidad*)
Bonapartist ['bonə,pɑrtɪst] *s* bonapartista
bonbon ['bɑn,bɑn] *s* bombón
bond [bɑnd] *s* enlace, lazo, unión, vínculo; contrato; bono, obligación; caución, fianza; fiador; depósito de mercancías hasta el pago de los impuestos; (mas.) aparejo, trabazón; conexión eléctrica de dos carriles; **bonds** *spl* cadenas, grillos; cautiverio; **in bond** en depósito bajo fianza; *va* hipotecar; obligar por fianza; depositar (*mercancías*) hasta pago de los impuestos; enlazar, unir
bondage ['bɑndɪdʒ] *s* cautiverio, esclavitud, servidumbre
bonded ['bɑndɪd] *adj* consolidado, afianzado con bonos; depositado bajo fianza
bonded warehouse *s* depósito comercial
bonderize ['bɑndəraɪz] *va* (trademark) bonderizar
bondholder ['bɑnd,holdər] *s* obligacionista, tenedor de bonos
bondmaid ['bɑnd,med] *s* esclava
bondman ['bɑndmən] *s* (*pl:* **-men**) esclavo
bond servant *s* esclavo
bondsman ['bɑndzmən] *s* (*pl:* **-men**) fiador
bondstone ['bɑnd,ston] *s* (mas.) perpiaño
bondwoman ['bɑnd,wumən] *s* (*pl:* **-women**) esclava
bone [bon] *s* hueso; espina (*de los peces*); barba de ballena; armazón (*p.ej., de un buque*); **bones** *spl* esqueleto; huesos (*restos mortales*); castañuelas; (coll.) dados; **to feel in one's bones** estar seguro de (*una cosa*) sin saber por qué;

to have a bone to pick with tener que habérselas con; **to make no bones about** (coll.) no andarse con rodeos en; *va* desosar; quitar las espinas a; emballenar (*un corsé*); abonar con huesos molidos; *vn* (slang) estudiar con ahinco; **to bone up on** (slang) estudiar (*una cosa*) con ahinco, empollar sobre
boneblack ['bon,blæk] *s* negro animal, carbón animal
bone-dry ['bon'draɪ] *adj* enteramente seco; (coll.) absolutamente abstemio; (coll.) sin venta de licor
bonehead ['bon,hɛd] *s* (slang) mentecato, zopenco
bone lace *s* encaje de bolillos
boneless ['bonlɪs] *adj* mollar; desosado; sin espinas
bone meal *s* huesos molidos, harina de huesos
bone of contention *s* materia de discordia, manzana de la discordia
boner ['bonər] *s* (slang) patochada, plancha, error
boneset ['bon,sɛt] *s* (bot.) eupatorio; (bot.) consuelda
bonfire ['bɑn,faɪr] *s* hoguera, fogata
bonhomie [,bɑno'mi] *s* bonhomía, buen natural
Boniface ['bɑnɪfes] *s* Bonifacio; (*l.c.*) *s* hostelero, dueño de una posada
bonito [bo'nito] *s* (*pl:* **-tos** o **-toes**) (ichth.) bonito
bon mot [bõ'mo] *s* (*pl:* **bons mots** [bõ'mo]) donaire, agudeza
bonne [bɑn] o [bʌn] *s* niñera; criada
bonnet ['bɑnɪt] *s* papalina; gorra escocesa; penacho de plumas (*de los pieles rojas norteamericanos*); (naut.) boneta; (anat. & fort.) bonete; sombrerete (*de chimenea*); (aut.) cubierta, capó; *va* cubrir (*la cabeza*)
bonnie o **bonny** ['bɑnɪ] *adj* (*comp:* **-nier;** *super:* **-niest**) (Scottish) bonito, lindo, excelente, lozano
bonnyclabber ['bɑnɪ,klæbər] *s* leche cuajada
bonus ['bonəs] *s* prima, extra, plus; (bridge) bonificación
bon voyage [bõvwɑ'jɑʒ] *interj* ¡buen viaje!
bony ['bonɪ] *adj* (*comp:* **-ier;** *super:* **-iest**) osudo, huesudo; óseo, huesoso; descarnado; espinoso (*pez*)
bonze [bɑnz] *s* bonzo (*sacerdote del culto de Buda*)
boo [bu] *s* abucheo; bu; **to not say boo** no decir ni chus ni mus; *interj* ¡bu!; *va* abuchear (*p.ej., a un cantante*); hacer el bu a; *vn* abuchear; hacer el bu
boo-boo ['bu,bu] *s* (slang) patochada, plancha
booby ['bubɪ] *s* (*pl:* **-bies**) zopenco, bobalicón; el peor jugador de todos; (orn.) pato bobo
booby hatch *s* (naut.) tambucho; (coll.) manicomio; (slang) cárcel
booby prize *s* último premio, premio de consolación
booby trap *s* (mil.) trampa explosiva; (fig.) zancadilla (*engaño*)
boodle ['budəl] *s* (slang) cuadrilla; (slang) dinero; (slang) soborno
boogie-woogie ['bugɪ'wugɪ] *s* bugui-bugui (*manera de tocar el piano y baile norteamericanos*)
boohoo [,bu'hu] *s* lloro ruidoso y sollozante; *vn* llorar ruidosamente y con sollozos
book [bʊk] *s* libro; libreta (*p.ej., de la caja de ahorros*); librillo (*de papel de fumar, de panes de oro, de sellos, etc.*); libro en que se apuntan las apuestas (*en las carreras de caballos*); (bridge) conjunto de las seis primeras bazas; (com.) libro-registro; **by the book** con exactitud, según las reglas; **the Book** la Biblia; **to bring someone to book** llamar o traer a uno a capítulo; regañarle a uno; **to close the books** (com.) cerrar el borrador; **to keep books** (com.) llevar libros; **to know like a book** saber de todo en todo; conocer a fondo; *va* asentar en un libro; notar en un registro; inscribir; anotar (*un pedido, mercancías*) para despacho; reservar (*un pasaje en una embarcación*); escriturar (*a un actor para una función*)
bookbinder ['bʊk,baɪndər] *s* encuadernador
bookbindery ['bʊk,baɪndərɪ] *s* (*pl:* **-ies**) encuadernación (*taller*)
bookbinding ['bʊk,baɪndɪŋ] *s* encuadernación (*acción; arte*)
bookcase ['bʊk,kes] *s* armario o estante para libros
book end *s* sujetalibros, apoyalibros
bookie ['bʊkɪ] *s* (coll.) corredor de apuestas (*en las carreras de caballos*)
booking ['bʊkɪŋ] *s* reservación (*de un pasaje*); escritura (*de un actor*)
booking clerk *s* vendedor de billetes de pasaje o teatro
booking office *s* despacho de pasajes
bookish ['bʊkɪʃ] *adj* libresco
bookkeeper ['bʊk,kipər] *s* tenedor de libros
bookkeeping ['bʊk,kipɪŋ] *s* teneduría de libros
book learning *s* ciencia libresca
booklet ['bʊklɪt] *s* librete, libretín
booklore ['bʊk,lor] *s* ciencia libresca
booklover ['bʊk,lʌvər] *s* aficionado a los libros
bookmaker ['bʊk,mekər] *s* recopilador; (print.) impresor encargado de la imposición; corredor de apuestas (*en las carreras de caballos*)
bookmark ['bʊk,mark] *s* registro
bookmobile ['bʊkmo'bil] *s* biblioteca rodante
Book of Common Prayer *s* devocionario de la Iglesia anglicana
Book of Mormon *s* libro del Mormón, libro sagrado del mormonismo
bookplate ['bʊk,plet] *s* ex libris
bookrack ['bʊk,ræk] *s* atril; estante
book review *s* reseña
bookseller ['bʊk,sɛlər] *s* librero
bookshelf ['bʊk,ʃɛlf] *s* (*pl:* **-shelves**) estante para libros
bookstall ['bʊk,stɔl] *s* puesto para la venta de libros
bookstand ['bʊk,stænd] *s* atril; mostrador para libros; puesto para la venta de libros
bookstore ['bʊk,stor] *s* librería
book value *s* (com.) valor de las acciones de una sociedad en el libro de cuenta de la sociedad
bookworm ['bʊk,wʌrm] *s* polilla que roe los libros; (fig.) ratón de biblioteca
boom [bum] *s* trueno, estampido; auge, alza rápida, prosperidad repentina, fomento enérgico; aguilón (*de una grúa*); (naut.) botalón; (naut.) botavara (*de una vela*); (naut.) cadena de troncos, barrera de un puerto; *adj* que aumenta, crece o medra repentinamente; *va* fomentar enérgicamente; expresar con estruendo; dar (*el reloj, p.ej., las tres*) con estruendo; *vn* tronar, hacer estampido; estar en auge, medrar, estar en bonanza
boomerang ['bumərænŋ] *s* bumerang; (fig.) cosa que redunda en perjuicio del que la originó; *vn* redundar (*una cosa*) en perjuicio del que la originó
boom iron *s* (naut.) zuncho de botalón
boom town *s* pueblo que está en bonanza
boon [bun] *s* dicha, bendición; (archaic) favor, gracia; *adj* alegre, festivo; (archaic) bondadoso, generoso
boon companion *s* buen compañero
boondocks ['bun,dɑks] *spl* (slang) monte, monte bajo; (slang) afueras del poblado
boondoggle ['bun,dɑgəl] *s* (slang) trabajo sin provecho; *vn* (slang) trabajar sin provecho
boor [bʊr] *s* patán
boorish ['bʊrɪʃ] *adj* grosero, chabacano
boost [bust] *s* empujón hacia arriba; alza (*de precios*); alabanza; ayuda; *va* empujar hacia arriba; alzar (*los precios*); alabar; ayudar
booster ['bustər] *s* aumentador de presión; detonador auxiliar; cohete de lanzamiento; (coll.) bombista, fomentador; (elec.) elevador de tensión; (med.) inyección secundaria; (rail.) propulsor
booster battery *s* (elec.) batería elevadora
booster pump *s* bomba reforzadora
booster rocket *s* cohete de lanzamiento
boot [but] *s* bota; calceta (*usada como tormento*); pesebrón (*del coche*); toldo para el cochero; **boots** *ssg* (Brit.) limpiabotas; **the boot is on the other leg** los papeles están trastrocados; **to be in the boots of** estar en el pellejo de; **to bet your boots** estar absolutamente se-

guro; **to boot** de añadidura; **to die with one's boots on** morir con las botas puestas, morir al pie del cañón; **to get the boot** (coll.) ser echado a la calle; **to lick the boots of** lamer los zapatos a (*adular con exceso*); **to wipe one's boots on** insultar, maltratar; *va* calzar, poner las botas a; dar un puntapié a; (slang) poner en la calle; **to boot it** ir a pie; *vn* calzarse las botas; ir a pie

bootblack ['but,blæk] *s* limpiabotas

booted ['butɪd] *adj* calzado con botas

bootee [bu'ti] *s* calzado de punto para niños; bota corta de mujer

Boötes [bo'otiz] *s* (astr.) Bootes

booth [buθ] o [buð] *s* (*pl:* **booths** [buðz]) casilla o quiosco (*de información*); cabina (*telefónica; de votación; para oír discos de fonógrafo*); puesto de feria o mercado

boot hook *s* tirabotas

bootjack ['but,dʒæk] *s* sacabotas

bootleg ['but,lɛg] *s* caña de bota; (slang) contrabando de licores; *adj* (slang) contrabandista; (*pret & pp:* **-legged;** *ger:* **-legging**) *va* (slang) pasar, llevar o vender (*licores*) de contrabando; *vn* (slang) contrabandear en licores

bootlegger ['but,lɛgər] *s* (slang) contrabandista, destilador clandestino

bootlegging ['but,lɛgɪŋ] *s* contrabando de licores

bootless ['butlɪs] *adj* inútil, sin provecho

bootlicker ['but,lɪkər] *s* (slang) lameculos, quitamotas

boots and saddles *spl* (mil.) botasilla

bootstrap ['but,stræp] *s* elástico o tirante de la bota

boot tree *s* horma de bota

booty ['butɪ] *s* (*pl:* **-ties**) botín, presa; ganancia, premio

booze [buz] *s* (coll.) licor; (coll.) borrachera, ataque de borrachera; *vn* (coll.) borrachear

boozer ['buzər] *s* (coll.) borracho

boozy ['buzɪ] *adj* (coll.) chispo; (coll.) borracho

bop [bɑp] (*pret & pp:* **bopped;** *ger:* **bopping**) *va* (slang) golpear, pegar

bopeep [bo'pip] *s* juego de niños que consiste en descubrirse los ojos rápidamente después de tenerlos tapados con las manos; **Little Bopeep** pastorcita, en un cuento de niños, que ha perdido sus ovejas

bor. abr. de **borough**

boracic [bo'ræsɪk] *adj* (chem.) bórico

boracite ['borəsaɪt] *s* (mineral.) boracita

borage ['bʌrɪdʒ], ['bɑrɪdʒ] o ['bɔrɪdʒ] *s* (bot.) borraja

borate ['boret] *s* (chem.) borato

borated ['boretɪd] *adj* boratado

borax ['boræks] *s* (chem.) bórax

Bordeaux [bɔr'do] *s* Burdeos; burdeos (*vino*)

Bordeaux mixture *s* (hort.) caldo de Burdeos, caldo bordelés

Bordeaux red *s* rojo de Burdeos

border ['bɔrdər] *s* borde, margen; frontera, confín; ribete, orla; repulgo, dobladillo; arriate (*de jardín*); **borders** *spl* (theat.) bambalina; *adj* frontero; *va* limitar, deslindar, ribetear, orlar; repulgar, dobladillar; *vn* confinar; **to border on** o **upon** confinar con, rayar en; (fig.) bordear

border clash *s* encuentro fronterizo, choque en la frontera

borderer ['bɔrdərər] *s* habitante fronterizo

borderland ['bɔrdər,lænd] *s* zona fronteriza; región intermedia, espacio indefinido

borderline ['bɔrder,laɪn] *s* frontera; *adj* fronterizo; límite, intermedio; indefinido, incierto

bordure ['bɔrdʒər] *s* (her.) bordura, bordadura

bore [bor] *s* barreno (*agujero*); calibre; ánima, alma (*del cañón del arma de fuego*); alesaje (*del cilindro de un motor*); machaca (*persona*); fastidio, molienda; maremoto (*grande ola al subir la marea*); *va* agujerear; barrenar; fastidiar; *vn* agujerear; adelantarse; **to bore from within** atacar por traición desde adentro; *pret de* **bear**

boreal ['borɪəl] *adj* boreal

Boreas ['borɪəs] *s* (myth.) Bóreas; bóreas (*viento del norte*)

boredom ['bordəm] *s* aburrimiento, fastidio, tedio

borer ['borər] *s* barrena, taladro; (ent.) barrenillo

boresome ['borsəm] *adj* aburrido, fastidioso, tedioso

boric ['borɪk] *adj* (chem.) bórico

boric acid *s* (chem.) ácido bórico

boring ['borɪŋ] *adj* aburrido, fastidioso

born [bɔrn] *adj* nacido; nato, innato, p.ej., **born criminal** criminal nato; **born liar** mentiroso innato; **in all my born days** (coll.) en mi vida; **to be born** nacer; **to be born again** renacer, volver a nacer

borne [born] *pp de* **bear**

boron ['borɑn] *s* (chem.) boro

borough ['bʌro] *s* villa; distrito administrativo de municipio

borrow ['bɑro] o ['bɔro] *va* pedir prestado, tomar prestado, tomar a préstamo; apropiarse, tomar para sí; **to borrow from** pedir prestado a; **to borrow trouble** darse molestia sin ningún motivo

borrower ['bɑroər] o ['bɔroər] *s* prestatario

borrowing ['bɑro·ɪŋ] o ['bɔro·ɪŋ] *s* préstamo; préstamo lingüístico

borrow pit *s* préstamo

borzoi ['bɔrzɔɪ] *s* barzoi (*galgo ruso*)

boscage ['bɑskɪdʒ] *s* boscaje

bosh [bɑʃ] *s* etalaje (*de alto horno*); (coll.) tontería, música celestial

bosk [bɑsk] *s* bosquecillo, maleza

bosky ['bɑskɪ] *adj* nemoroso, boscoso; frondoso, umbroso

bo's'n ['bosən] *s* var. de **boatswain**

Bosnian ['bɑznɪən] *adj & s* bosníaco o bosnio

bosom ['buzəm] *s* seno; pechera (*de camisa*); amor, cariño; *adj* íntimo, de la mayor confianza; *va* guardar en el seno, encerrar en el pecho

Bosporus ['bɑspərəs] *s* Bósforo

boss [bɔs] o [bɑs] *s* (coll.) jefe, mandamás; (coll.) amo, gallo, capataz, gerente; (coll.) cacique (*en asuntos políticos*); protuberancia, figura de relieve; (arch.) crucería (*en las bóvedas góticas*); *va* (coll.) regentar, dominar; trabajar en relieve, adornar en relieve

bossism ['bɔsɪzəm] o ['bɑsɪzəm] *s* caciquismo, gamonalismo

bossy ['bɔsɪ] o ['bɑsɪ] *adj* (*comp:* **-ier;** *super:* **-iest**) mandón; adornado en relieve

boston ['bɔstən] o ['bɑstən] *s* bostón (*juego de naipes; vals*)

Bostonian [bɔs'tonɪən] o [bɑs'tonɪən] *adj & s* bostoniano

Boston Tea Party *s* (hist.) motín del té

bostryx ['bɑstrɪks] *s* (bot.) bóstrice

bosun ['bosən] *s* var. de **boatswain**

bot [bɑt] *s* (ent.) rezno

botanic [bə'tænɪk] o **botanical** [bə'tænɪkəl] *adj* botánico

botanist ['bɑtənɪst] *s* botanista, botánico

botanize ['bɑtənaɪz] *va* explorar la flora de; *vn* botanizar

botany ['bɑtənɪ] *s* botánica

botch [bɑtʃ] *s* chapucería, remiendo chapucero; *va* chapucear, remendar chapuceramente

botchy ['bɑtʃɪ] *adj* (*comp:* **-ier;** *super:* **-iest**) chapucero, mal hecho

botfly ['bɑt,flaɪ] *s* (*pl:* **-flies**) (ent.) estro, moscardón

both [boθ] *adj* ambos; *pron* ambos, los dos, uno y otro; **both of** ambos; **both of them** ellos dos, los dos; **both of us** nosotros dos; *conj* a la vez; **both . . . and** tanto . . . como, así . . . como, al par . . . y; *adv* igualmente

bother ['bɑðər] *s* incomodidad, molestia; persona o cosa molesta; *va* incomodar, molestar; *vn* molestarse; **to bother about** o **with** molestarse con; **to bother to** + *inf* molestarse en + *inf*

botheration [,bɑðə'reʃən] *s* (coll.) incomodidad, molestia; *interj* ¡caramba! (*para expresar enfado*)

bothersome ['bɑðərsəm] *adj* incómodo, molesto

bott [bɑt] *s* var. de **bot**

bottle ['bɑtəl] *s* botella; biberón (*para la lactancia artificial*); **the bottle** las bebidas alcohólicas; *va* embotellar; **to bottle up** embotellar

bottle brush *s* escobilla para limpiar botellas; (bot.) cola de rata, equiseto menor
bottle gourd *s* (bot.) cogorda
bottle green *s* verde botella
bottle imp *s* (phys.) diablillo de Descartes
bottleneck ['bɑtəl,nɛk] *s* gollete, cuello de botella; embotellamiento, congestión del tráfico; embotellado, obstáculo
bottle nose *s* nariz hinchada por el mucho beber
bottlenose ['bɑtəl,noz] *s* (zool.) delfín de hocico de botella
bottle opener *s* abrebotellas, descapsulador; destapacorona (Am.)
bottler ['bɑtlər] *s* embotellador
bottle rack *s* botellero
bottle tit *s* (orn.) alionín, chamarón
bottom ['bɑtəm] *s* fondo; fundamento, cimiento; fundación; asiento (*de una silla*); final (*de una página*); (coll.) trasero; (naut.) fondo; (naut.) casco, nave, buque; (fig.) fondo (*lo principal*); **bottoms** *spl* hondonada; **at bottom** en el fondo, en la realidad; **to be at the bottom of** ser la causa de; ser el último de (*p.ej., la clase*); **to begin at the bottom** (fig.) empezar el oficio por abajo; **to get to the bottom of** entrar en el fondo de; **to go the bottom** irse a pique; *adj* fundamental, del fondo; (coll.) más bajo, p.ej., **the bottom price** el precio más bajo; (coll.) último, p.ej., **his bottom dollar** su último dólar; *va* fundar; profundizar; poner asiento a (*una silla*)
bottom land *s* hondonada
bottomless ['bɑtəmlɪs] *adj* sin fondo; sin asiento; infundado; profundo; abismal; insondable; ilimitado, inagotable
bottomless pit, the el abismo, el infierno
bottomry ['bɑtəmrɪ] *s* (naut.) contrato a la gruesa
botulism ['bɑtʃəlɪzəm] *s* (path.) botulismo
bouclé [bu'kle] *s* bouclé; *adj* de bouclé
boudoir [bu'dwɑr] *s* tocador, gabinete; saloncito
bougainvillea [,bugən'vɪlɪə] *s* (bot.) buganvilla
bough [baʊ] *s* rama
bought [bɔt] *pp de* **buy**
boughten ['bɔtən] *adj* (dial.) no casero, comprado
bougie ['budʒɪ], ['buʒɪ] o [bu'ʒi] *s* bujía (*vela de cera*); (surg.) bujía, candelilla
bouillabaisse [,buljə'bes] *s* bullabesa
bouillon ['buljɑn] o [bul'jɑn] *s* caldo
bouillon cube *s* cubito de caldo concentrado
boulder ['boldər] *s* guijarro grande, canto rodado
boulevard ['buləvɑrd] o ['buləvɑrd] *s* bulevar
boulter ['boltər] *s* palangre
bounce [baʊns] *s* bote; jactancia; (slang) despedida; *va* hacer botar; (slang) despedir; *vn* botar; dar saltos al andar; saltar repentinamente; precipitarse ruidosamente y sin ceremonia
bouncer ['baʊnsər] *s* cosa de gran tamaño; (coll.) fanfarrón; (slang) apagabroncas, guardián fornido que echa a la calle a los alborotadores de un café, bar, etc.
bouncing ['baʊnsɪŋ] *adj* fuerte, frescachón
bouncing Bess o **Bet** *s* (bot.) jabonera
bound [baʊnd] *s* salto; bote (*de una pelota*); límite, margen, raya; **bounds** *spl* zona fronteriza, región, comarca; **out of bounds** fuera de los límites, más allá de los límites; **within bounds** a raya; *adj* obligado; encuadernado; estreñido; puesto en aprendizaje; (coll.) determinado, resuelto; **bound for** con destino a; **bound up in** o **with** relacionado estrechamente con; muy adicto a; absorto en; *va* limitar; deslindar; *vn* saltar; botar; confinar, rayar; *pret & pp de* **bind**
boundary ['baʊndərɪ] *s* (*pl:* **-ries**) límite, margen, frontera
boundary stone *s* mojón
bounden ['baʊndən] *adj* obligatorio; obligado
bounder ['baʊndər] *s* advenedizo vulgar y malcriado
boundless ['baʊndlɪs] *adj* ilimitado, infinito; vasto, inmenso
bounteous ['baʊntɪəs] o **bountiful** ['baʊntɪfəl] *adj* generoso, liberal; abundante, copioso
bounty ['baʊntɪ] *s* (*pl:* **-ties**) generosidad, liberalidad; dádiva, regalo; premio, galardón; prima (*premio del gobierno*); (mil.) premio de enganche
bouquet [bu'ke] o [bo'ke] *s* ramo, ramillete; nariz (*perfume del vino*)
Bourbon ['burbən] *s* Borbón; conservador; (*l.c.*) ['burbən] o ['bʌrbən] *s* aguardiente de maíz
Bourbonism ['burbənɪzəm] *s* borbonismo; conservatismo excesivo
bourgeois [bur'ʒwɑ] o ['burʒwɑ] *adj* burgués; *s* (*pl:* **-geois** [ʒwɑ]) burgués; [bʌr'dʒɔɪs] *s* (print.) tipo de nueve puntos
bourgeoisie [,burʒwɑ'zi] *s* burguesía
bourn o **bourne** [born] *s* arroyo, riachuelo; [born] o [burn] *s* meta; margen; límite; región, dominio
bourse [burs] *s* bolsa
boustrophedon [,bustrə'fidən] o [,baʊstrə'fidən] *s* bustrófedon
bout [baʊt] *s* encuentro; rato; ataque (*de una enfermedad*)
boutonnière o **boutonniere** [,butə'njɛr] *s* flor que se lleva en el ojal
bovine ['bovaɪn] o ['bovɪn] *adj* bovino; lerdo, estúpido; impasible; *s* bovino
bow [baʊ] *s* inclinación, reverencia; (naut.) proa; **to make a bow** hacer una reverencia; **to make one's bow** presentarse; *va* inclinar (*la cabeza*); inclinarse en señal de (*p.ej., agradecimiento*); **to bow one's way in** entrar haciendo reverencias; **to bow one's way out** salir haciendo reverencias; *vn* inclinarse; ceder, someterse; **to bow and scrape** hacer reverencias profundas, mostrarse muy obsequioso; **to bow to** saludar, inclinarse delante; [bo] *s* arco; lazo, nudo; ojo (*de la llave*); (mus.) arco; *adj* arqueado; *va* (mus.) tocar con arco; *vn* arquearse; alabearse
bow compass [bo] *s* bigotera
bowdlerize ['baʊdlərаɪz] *va* expurgar
bowel ['baʊəl] *s* parte del intestino; **bowels** *spl* (anat.) intestinos; (fig.) entrañas (*lo más oculto*); (archaic) entrañas (*compasión, ternura*); **to keep the bowels open** tener el vientre libre
bowel movement *s* evacuación del vientre
bower ['boər] *s* músico de arco; ['baʊər] *s* emparrado, enramada; cenador, glorieta; (naut.) ancla de proa, ancla de servidumbre; **right bower** sota del triunfo; **left bower** sota del mismo color del triunfo; *va* emparrar
bowerbird ['baʊər,bʌrd] *s* (orn.) tilonorrinco
bowery ['baʊərɪ] *adj* frondoso, emparrado, sombreado; *s* (*pl:* **-ies**) (hist.) finca, granja; (*cap.*) *s* calle y barrio de Nueva York con tabernas y hoteles de mala calidad
bowfin ['bo,fɪn] *s* (ichth.) amia
bowie knife ['bo·ɪ] o ['bu·ɪ] *s* cuchillo puñal
bowknot ['bo,nɑt] *s* nudo corredizo
bowl [bol] *s* escudilla; jofaina, palangana (*para lavarse las manos*); tazón (*de fuente*); taza (*de inodoro*); paleta (*de la cuchara*); hornillo (*de la pipa*); copa (*vaso con pie para beber*); cuenco, concavidad; anfiteatro al aire libre en forma de cuenco; bola (*en el juego de bolos*); turno (*en el juego de bolos*); **bowls** *spl* bolos (*juego*); *va* arrojar (*la bola en la vilorta*); **to bowl down** derribar; **to bowl over** tumbar; (coll.) confundir, desconcertar; *vn* jugar a los bolos; rodar; **to bowl along** rodar
bowlder ['boldər] *s* var. de **boulder**
bowleg ['bo,lɛg] *s* pierna arqueada; arqueo de las piernas
bowlegged ['bo,lɛgɪd] o ['bo,lɛgd] *adj* estevado, patiestevado
bowler ['bolər] *s* jugador de bolos; (Brit.) sombrero hongo
bowline ['bolɪn] o ['bolaɪn] *s* (naut.) bolina; as de guía; **on a bowline** (naut.) de bolina
bowline knot *s* as de guía
bowling ['bolɪŋ] *s* juego de bolos; *adj* bolístico
bowling alley *s* bolera
bowling green *s* bolera encespada
bowman ['bomən] *s* (*pl:* **-men**) arquero, flechero
bow oar [baʊ] *s* (naut.) remo de proa; (naut.) proel (*marinero*)
bowshot ['bo,ʃɑt] *s* tiro de flecha, alcance de la flecha

bowsprit ['bauspr ɪt] o ['bosprɪt] *s* (naut.) bauprés
bowstring ['bo,strɪŋ] *s* cuerda de arco; cuerda para estrangular; (*pret & pp:* **-stringed** o **-strung**) *va* estrangular con cuerda
bowstring beam *s* viga de cuerda y arco
bow tie [bo] *s* corbata de mariposa, corbata de lazo, pajarita
bow window [bo] *s* ventana salediza en forma de arco
bowwow ['bau,wau] *s* guau guau (*ladrido del perro*); perro; *interj* ¡guau!; *vn* ladrar; gruñir, regañar
bowwow theory *s* (philol.) teoría de la onomatopeya
box [bɑks] *s* caja; casilla de establo; pescante (*asiento de cochero*); garita; bofetada; (theat.) palco; (mach.) cárter; (elec.) caja (*para llaves, tomas de corriente, etc.*); (bot.) boj; (baseball) puesto del lanzador; (baseball) puesto del cogedor; recuadro (*p.ej., en un periódico*); *va* encajonar, embalar; abofetear; **to box up** encerrar, encerrar en una caja; *vn* (sport) boxear
boxcar ['bɑks,kɑr] *s* (rail.) vagón cerrado, vagón cubierto, vagón encajonado
box couch *s* diván arca
box coupling *s* (mach.) manguito, collar de acoplamiento
box elder *s* (bot.) negondo o negundo
boxer ['bɑksər] *s* embalador; (sport) boxeador; bóxer (*perro*); (*cap.*) *s* bóxer (*en China*)
boxing ['bɑksɪŋ] *s* embalaje; encajonamiento; madera para encajonar; marco de puerta o de ventana; (sport) boxeo; *adj* boxístico
Boxing Day *s* (Brit.) día festivo que se celebra, con regalos a los empleados, el primer día de trabajo después de Navidad
boxing gloves *spl* guantes de boxeo
box kite *s* cometa celular *f*
box office *s* despacho de localidades, contaduría, taquilla; **good box office** (slang) éxito de taquilla
box-office ['bɑks,ɔfɪs] o ['bɑks,ɑfɪs] *adj* de taquilla, taquillero
box-office record *s* marca de taquilla
box pleat o **plait** *s* (sew.) pliegue de tabla
box seat *s* (theat.) asiento de palco
boxwood ['bɑks,wud] *s* (bot.) boj
box wrench *s* llave de cubo
boy [bɔɪ] *s* muchacho; mozo (*criado*); (coll.) hombre, compadre
boyar [bo'jɑr] o ['bɔɪər] o **boyard** [bo'jɑrd] o ['bɔɪərd] *s* boyardo
boycott ['bɔɪkɑt] *s* boicot; boicoteo; *va* boicotear
boyhood ['bɔɪhud] *s* muchachez; muchachería, muchachos; juventud masculina
boyish ['bɔɪɪʃ] *adj* amuchachado, muchachil
boy scout *s* explorador, niño explorador
Bp. abr. de **bishop**
b.p. o **B/P** abr. de **bills payable** y **boiling point**
B.P.E. abr. de **Bachelor of Physical Education**
B.Ph. abr. de **Bachelor of Philosophy**
br. abr. de **brand, brig** y **brother**
Br. abr. de **Britain** y **British**
b.r. o **B/R** abr. de **bills receivable**
bra [brɑ] *s* (coll.) portasenos, sostén
Brabant [brə'bænt] o ['brɑbənt] *s* Brabante
brace [bres] *s* riostra, tirante; apoyo; (print.) corchete; (carp.) berbiquí; (naut.) braza (*cabo para sujetar las vergas*); par; **braces** *spl* (Brit.) tirantes (*del pantalón*); *va* arriostrar; apoyar; asegurar, vigorizar; **to brace oneself** (coll.) cobrar ánimo; *vn* **to brace up** (coll.) cobrar ánimo
brace and bit *s* berbiquí y barrena
bracelet ['breslɪt] *s* brazalete, pulsera; (hum.) esposa, grillete
bracer ['bresər] *s* persona o cosa que fortifica; (coll.) trago fortificante; brazal de arquero
brachial ['brekɪəl] o ['brækɪəl] *adj* braquial
brachiopod ['brekɪə,pɑd] o ['brækɪə,pɑd] *s* (zool.) braquiópodo
brachycephalic [,brækɪsɪ'fælɪk] *adj* (anthrop.) braquicéfalo
brachyuran [,brækɪ'jurən] *adj & s* (zool.) braquiuro
bracing ['bresɪŋ] *adj* fortificante, tónico; *s* arriostramiento, refuerzo
bracken ['brækən] *s* (bot.) helecho común; helechal
bracket ['brækɪt] *s* puntal, soporte; escuadra; anaquel asegurado con ménsulas; brazo de lámpara asegurado en la pared; (arch.) ménsula, repisa; corchete o paréntesis cuadrado; clase, categoría; *va* asegurar con ménsulas; acorchetar, poner entre corchetes cuadrados; agrupar
brackish ['brækɪʃ] *adj* salobre
bract [brækt] *s* bráctea
bractlet ['bræktlɪt] *s* (bot.) bractéola
brad [bræd] *s* puntilla, clavito, clavito de ala de mosca
bradawl ['bræd,ɔl] *s* lezna para puntillas o clavitos
bradycardia [,brædɪ'kɑrdɪə] *s* (path.) bradicardia
bradypepsia [,brædɪ'pɛpsɪə] *s* (path.) bradipepsia
brae [bre] *s* (Scottish) cuesta, pendiente
brag [bræg] *s* jactancia; (*pret & pp:* **bragged;** *ger:* **bragging**) *va* jactarse de; *vn* jactarse
braggadocio [,brægə'doʃɪo] *s* (*pl:* **-os**) fanfarronada; fanfarrón
braggart ['brægərt] *adj & s* fanfarrón
brahma ['brɑmə] o ['bremə] *s* gallina brahma; (*cap.*) ['brɑmə] *s* (rel.) Brahma
Brahman ['brɑmən] *s* (*pl:* **-mans**) brahmán
Brahmanism ['brɑmənɪzəm] *s* brahmanismo
Brahmin ['brɑmɪn] *s* brahmán; aristócrata culto
braid [bred] *s* trenza, galón, pasamano, sutás; *va* trenzar, galonear, encintar
brail [brel] *s* (naut.) candeliza; *va* (naut.) halar por medio de candelizas
Braille o **braille** [brel] *s* sistema Braille; letras Braille
brain [bren] *s* (anat. & zool.) cerebro; **brains** *spl* cerebro, inteligencia; sesos (*que se comen*); **to beat one's brains** esforzarse por recordar algo; **to blow one's brains out** saltarse la tapa de los sesos; **to have on the brain** (coll.) tener la manía de, estar dominado por la idea de; **to rack one's brains** devanarse los sesos, romperse la cabeza; *va* descerebrar
brain cell *s* (anat.) neurona cerebral
brain child *s* parto del ingenio, obra del cerebro de uno
brainfag ['bren,fæg] *s* fatiga cerebral
brain fever *s* (path.) fiebre cerebral
braininess ['brenɪnɪs] *s* sesudez, inteligencia
brainless ['brenlɪs] *adj* tonto, insensato, sin sesos
brainpan ['bren,pæn] *s* (anat.) cráneo
brain sand *s* (anat.) acérvula
brainsick ['bren,sɪk] *adj* loco
brain storm *s* agitación repentina y transitoria; (coll.) buena idea, inspiración, hallazgo
brain trust *s* grupo de consejeros intelectuales
brain washing *s* (coll.) lavado cerebral o de cerebro
brain wave *s* (coll.) buena idea, inspiración, hallazgo; **brain waves** *spl* (med.) ondas encefálicas
brain work *s* trabajo intelectual
brainy ['brenɪ] *adj* (*comp:* **-ier;** *super:* **-iest**) (coll.) sesudo, inteligente
braise [brez] *va* (cook.) dorar (*la carne*) rápidamente y cocerla a fuego lento en una vasija bien tapada y con muy poca agua
brake [brek] *s* freno; agramadera; amasadera; break (*carruaje*); (bot.) helecho común; matorral; *va* frenar; agramar (*el lino o el cáñamo*); amasar (*la harina o la tierra*); *vn* trabajar como guardafrenos
brake band *s* (aut.) banda de freno, cinta de freno
brake drum *s* (aut.) tambor o campana de freno
brake light *s* (aut.) luz de frenado
brake lining *s* (aut.) forro de freno, guarnición de freno, cinta de freno
brakeman ['brekmən] *s* (*pl:* **-men**) (rail.) guardafrenos
brake pedal *s* (aut.) pedal de freno
brake shoe *s* zapata de freno
brake wheel *s* (aut.) tambor de freno

Bramantesque [ˌbrɑmən'tɛsk] *adj* (arch.) bramantesco
bramble ['bræmbəl] *s* (bot.) frambueso, zarza
brambly ['bræmblɪ] *adj* (*comp:* **-blier;** *super:* **-bliest**) zarzoso
bran [bræn] *s* afrecho, salvado
branch [bræntʃ] o [brɑntʃ] *s* rama (*del árbol, de un linaje; parte accesoria*); ramo (*rama de segundo orden; rama cortada del árbol; parte de una ciencia, arte, etc.*); sarmiento (*de la vid*); ramal (*de un camino, vía férrea, etc.*); brazo (*de un río, candelabro, etc.*); sucursal (*de un establecimiento, tienda, etc.*); pierna (*del compás*); *adj* dependiente; sucursal; *vn* ramificarse; **to branch off** ramificarse; bifurcarse; **to branch out** ramificarse; extenderse (*en los negocios*)
branchia ['bræŋkɪə] *s* (*pl:* **-chiae** [kɪi]) (ichth.) branquia
branchial ['bræŋkɪəl] *adj* branquial
branchiferous [bræŋ'kɪfərəs] *adj* branquífero
branch line *s* (rail.) ramal, línea de empalme
branch office *s* sucursal
brand [brænd] *s* marca (*de cualquier producto*); marca de fábrica; clase, género, especie; hierro (*que se pone a las reses*); hierro de marcar; tea; tizón (*palo a medio quemar*); (fig.) tizón (*deshonra*); (poet.) relámpago; (archaic & poet.) espada; *va* poner marca de fábrica en; imprimir de modo indeleble; herrar (*con hierro candente*); tiznar (*la reputación de una persona*); **to brand as** motejar de, tildar de
Brandenburg ['brændənbʌrg] *s* Brandeburgo (*ciudad, provincia y adorno militar*)
brandied ['brændɪd] *adj* macerado en aguardiente
branding iron *s* hierro de marcar
brandish ['brændɪʃ] *s* molinete, floreo; *va* blandear; *vn* blandear o blandearse
brand-new ['brænd'nju] o ['brænd'nu] *adj* flamante, nuevo flamante, nuevecito
brandy ['brændɪ] *s* (*pl:* **-dies**) aguardiente
bran-new ['bræn'nju] o ['bræn'nu] *adj* var. de **brand-new**
brant [brænt] *s* (orn.) branta, ganso marino; (orn.) ganso monjita atlántico; (orn.) ganso de las nieves
brash [bræʃ] *adj* temerario, impetuoso; insolente, respondón; (dial.) quebradizo; *s* (dial.) enfermedad repentina, sarpullido
brasier ['breʒər] *s* var. de **brazier**
brasiletto [ˌbrɑsɪ'lɛto] *s* (bot.) brasilete
brasilin ['bræzɪlɪn] *s* var. de **brazilin**
brasque [bræsk] o [brɑsk] *s* (found.) brasca; *va* (found.) brascar
brass [bræs] o [brɑs] *s* latón; (mach.) bronce; (mus.) cobre; (Brit. slang) dinero; (U.S. slang) los jefazos, los mandamases (*especialmente en el ejército y la marina*); color de latón; (coll.) descaro, desvergüenza; **brasses** *spl* cobre (*utensilios de cocina de cobre*); (mus.) cobres; *adj* hecho de latón; **to get down to brass tacks** (coll.) entrar en materia, ir al grano
brassard ['bræsɑrd] o [bræ'sɑrd] o **brassart** ['bræsərt] *s* brazal
brass band *s* (mus.) charanga
brass hat *s* (slang) espadón (*oficial de estado mayor*)
brassie ['bræsɪ] o ['brɑsɪ] *s* (golf) maza de madera con cabo plano de metal
brassière [brə'zɪr] o [ˌbræsɪ'ɛr] *s* portasenos, sostén
brass knuckles *spl* bóxer
brassware ['bræsˌwɛr] o ['brɑsˌwɛr] *s* latonería, obra de latón
brass-wind ['bræsˌwɪnd] o ['brɑsˌwɪnd] *adj* (mus.) de los cobres, de boquilla
brass winds *spl* (mus.) cobres, instrumentos de boquilla
brasswork ['bræsˌwʌrk] o ['brɑsˌwʌrk] *s* latonería (*arte*); **brassworks** *spl* latonería (*taller*)
brassy ['bræsɪ] o ['brɑsɪ] *adj* (*comp:* **-ier;** *super:* **-iest**) de latón, hecho de latón; áspero, metálico; (coll.) descarado, desvergonzado; *s* (*pl:* **-ies**) (golf) maza de madera con cabo plano de metal
brat [bræt] *s* (scornful) braguillas (*niño mal dispuesto*)
brattice ['brætɪs] *s* tabique de ventilación; *va* poner tabique de ventilación en
bravado [brə'vɑdo] *s* (*pl:* **-does** o **-dos**) bravata
brave [brev] *adj* bravo, valiente; airoso, garboso; *s* valiente; guerrero indio norteamericano; *va* arrostrar, hacer frente a; desafiar, retar
bravery ['brevərɪ] *s* bravura (*ánimo, valor; buen aire, apostura*); gala, atavío
bravo ['brɑvo] o ['brevo] *s* (*pl:* **-voes** o **-vos**) bravo (*asesino*); ['brɑvo] *s* (*pl:* **-vos**) bravo (*grito de aplauso*); *interj* ¡bravo!
bravura [brə'vjʊrə] o [brə'vʊrə] *s* arrojo, brío, pujanza; (mus.) bravura
brawl [brɔl] *s* pendencia, reyerta; alboroto, vocerío; ruido (*de un arroyo*); *vn* armar pendencia; alborotar; correr ruidosamente (*un arroyo*)
brawler ['brɔlər] *s* pendenciero, alborotador
brawn [brɔn] *s* músculo; carne adobada de verraco
brawny ['brɔnɪ] *adj* (*comp:* **-ier;** *super:* **-iest**) musculoso, fornido
bray [bre] *s* rebuzno; *va* triturar, pulverizar; *vn* rebuznar
Braz. abr. de **Brazil** y **Brazilian**
braze [brez] *s* soldadura de latón, soldadura fuerte; *va* soldar con latón, soldar en fuerte; cubrir de latón; broncear; adornar con latón
brazen ['brezən] *adj* hecho de latón; bronceado; bronco, áspero; descarado, desvergonzado; *va* arrostrar descaradamente; envalentonar; **to brazen out** o **through** llevar a cabo descaradamente
brazier ['breʒər] *s* brasero (*vasija*); latonero
Brazil [brə'zɪl] *s* el Brasil
Brazilian [brə'zɪljən] *adj* & *s* brasileño
brazilin ['bræzɪlɪn] *s* (chem.) brasilina
Brazil nut *s* castaña de Pará, castaña del Marañón
Brazil-nut tree [brə'zɪl ˌnʌt] *s* (bot.) juvia, almendrón
brazilwood [brə'zɪlˌwʊd] *s* palo brasil, palo del Brasil
breach [britʃ] *s* abertura, hendidura, grieta; brecha (*en una pared o muralla*); violación; abuso (*de confianza*); *va* practicar una abertura en; abrir una brecha en
breach of faith *s* falta de fidelidad
breach of peace *s* perturbación del orden público
breach of promise *s* incumplimiento de promesa matrimonial
breach of trust *s* abuso de confianza
bread [brɛd] *s* pan; **on bread and water** a pan y agua; **to break bread with** sentarse a la mesa con; **to cast one's bread upon the waters** hacer el bien sin mirar a quién; **to know which side one's bread is buttered on** arrimarse al sol que más calienta; *va* (cook.) empanar (*envolver en ralladuras de pan*)
bread and butter *s* pan con mantequilla; (coll.) pan de cada día
bread-and-butter ['brɛdən'bʌtər] *adj* juvenil; práctico; prosaico; de consumo o uso general
bread-and-butter letter *s* carta de agradecimiento enviada después de una visita
breadboard ['brɛdˌbord] *s* tablero para amasar o cortar pan
bread crumbs *spl* pan rallado
breaded ['brɛdɪd] *adj* empanado
breadfruit ['brɛdˌfrut] *s* fruto del pan; (bot.) árbol del pan
breadfruit tree *s* (bot.) árbol del pan
bread line *s* cola del pan
bread mold *s* moho del pan
breadstuff ['brɛdˌstʌf] *s* cereales, granos, harina (*que sirven para hacer el pan*); pan
breadth [brɛdθ] *s* anchura; paño (*ancho de una tela*); extensión, espaciosidad; tolerancia
breadthways ['brɛdθˌwez] o **breadthwise** ['brɛdθˌwaɪz] *adv* a lo ancho
breadwinner ['brɛdˌwɪnər] *s* persona que gana el pan de la familia, sostén de la familia
break [brek] *s* rompimiento; interrupción; intervalo, pausa; cambio repentino; fragmento; grieta, hendidura, raja; blanco (*en los escritos*); claro (*en las nubes*); huída, evasión (*p.ej., de la cárcel*); gallo (*nota falsa en el canto*); ruptura

(*entre amigos*); (slang) disparate; (slang) suerte (*buena o mala*); (pros.) cesura; (elec.) corte, interrupción; (com.) baja (*de los precios*); **to give someone a break** abrirle a uno la puerta; **to make a break** escaparse; romper relaciones; (slang) cometer un disparate ‖ (*pret:* **broke;** *pp:* **broken**) *va* romper; domar; cambiar (*un billete*); comunicar (*p.ej., una mala noticia*); amortiguar (*p.ej., un golpe*); moderar (*la velocidad*); suspender (*relaciones*); faltar a (*la palabra, un juramento*); (mil.) degradar; (sport) batir (*un record*); (elec.) cortar (*un circuito*); (phonet.) diptongar; quebrantar (*un hábito; un testamento; la prisión o la cárcel*); romper (*una ley*); descompletar (*un juego de piezas iguales*); **to break asunder** separar en dos partes; despedazar; **to break down** analizar; **to break in** forzar (*p.ej., una puerta*); **to break oneself of a habit** deshacerse de un hábito; **to break open** abrir rompiendo; abrir con violencia, abrir por la fuerza; **to break up** desmenuzar; disolver (*p.ej., una reunión*); esparcir (*p.ej., una muchedumbre*); (coll.) desconcertar; **to break wind** ventosear ‖ *vn* romperse; romper (*las olas, el día*); quebrarse, interrumpirse; dispersarse (*la multitud*); emitirse (*un grito*); reventar; (box.) separarse; aclarar (*el tiempo*); bajar (*los precios*); (phonet.) diptongarse; romperse (*el corazón*), p.ej., **his heart is breaking** se le rompe el corazón; quebrantarse (*la salud*), p. ej., **his health is breaking** se le quebranta la salud; estallar (*la ira; una persona con ira; una noticia*); mudar (*la voz de un muchacho*); cascarse (*perder la calidad musical una voz*); cesar (*la sequía*); salir (*bien o mal*); **to break asunder** separarse; desmenuzarse; **to break away** escaparse; irse súbitamente; cambiar súbitamente; salir antes de la señal de partida; **to break down** descomponerse, desbaratarse; perder la salud; prorrumpir en llanto; **to break even** salir en paz, salir sin ganar ni perder; **to break forth** romper, salir repentinamente; brotar; exclamar; **to break in** entrar por fuerza; irrumpir, entrar de repente; irrumpir en; **to break into** forzar (*p.ej., una puerta*); allanar (*una casa*); soltarse en (*p.ej., lágrimas*); **to break into a run** empezar a correr, salir corriendo; **to break loose** desprenderse; escaparse; desencadenarse (*p.ej., la tempestad*); desbocarse (*un caballo; una persona en injurias*); **to break off** desprenderse; pararse repentinamente; **to break out** estallar (*una guerra, una tempestad*); declararse (*un incendio, una epidemia*); brotar granos (*en la piel*); romper (*en risa, en llanto*); **to break through** abrir paso por entre; abrirse paso; **to break up** desmenuzarse; disolverse, levantarse (*una reunión*); dispersarse (*la multitud*); **to break with** romper con, enemistarse con

breakable [ˈbrekəbəl] *adj* rompible, quebradizo

breakage [ˈbrekɪdʒ] *s* fractura, rotura; estropicio; indemnización por objetos quebrados

breakax o **breakaxe** [ˈbrekˌæks] *s* (bot.) quiebrahacha

breakdown [ˈbrekˌdaʊn] *s* parada imprevista, avería repentina; pana (*de automóvil*); fracaso, mal éxito; ruptura (*p.ej., de negociaciones*); análisis; (chem.) descomposición; (med.) colapso; (U.S.A.) baile ruidoso

breaker [ˈbrekər] *s* cachón (*ola*); triturador; barril pequeño; (elec.) disyuntor

breaker points *spl* (aut.) contactos de distribuidor

breakfast [ˈbrɛkfəst] *s* desayuno; *vn* desayunar o desayunarse; **to breakfast on** desayunarse con

breakfast food *s* cereal para el desayuno

breakneck [ˈbrekˌnɛk] *adj* vertiginoso, precipitado; **at breakneck speed** a mata caballo

break of day *s* amanecer

breakthrough [ˈbrekˌθru] *s* (mil.) ruptura, brecha; (min.) rompimiento; (fig.) adelanto repentino e inesperado

breakup [ˈbrekˌʌp] *s* separación; disolución, dispersión; parada, terminación; desplome; (med.) postración

breakwater [ˈbrekˌwɔtər] o [ˈbrekˌwɑtər] *s* rompeolas

bream [brim] *s* (ichth.) brema; *va* (naut.) dar fuego a (*fondos*)

breast [brɛst] *s* pecho, seno; pechuga (*del ave*); pechera (*de una prenda de vestir*); testera, frente, fachada; (min.) cara, frente; **to beat one's breast** darse golpes de pecho; **to make a clean breast of** reconocer con franqueza; **to make a clean breast of it** confesarlo todo; **to nurse at the breast** criar a los pechos; *va* arrostrar, acometer, embestir

breastband [ˈbrɛstˌbænd] *s* petral

breastbone [ˈbrɛstˌbon] *s* (anat.) esternón

breast collar *s* petral

breast drill *s* taladro o berbiquí de pecho

breasthook [ˈbrɛstˌhʊk] *s* (naut.) buzarda

breastpin [ˈbrɛstˌpɪn] *s* alfiler de pecho

breastplate [ˈbrɛstˌplet] *s* (arm.) peto; pectoral (*del sumo sacerdote hebreo*)

breastrail [ˈbrɛstˌrel] *s* (arch. & naut.) cairel

breast stroke *s* brazada de pecho

breastsummer [ˈbrɛstˌsʌmər] o [ˈbrɛsˌsʌmər] *s* (arch.) dintel

breast wheel *s* (hyd.) rueda de costado, rueda de pecho

breastwork [ˈbrɛstˌwʌrk] *s* (fort.) parapeto; (naut.) propao

breath [brɛθ] *s* respiración, aliento; hálito, soplo, perfume; respiro (*descanso, alivio*); vida, espíritu; susurro, murmullo; (phonet.) explosión; (phonet.) aspiración; **at every breath** a cada instante; **below one's breath** por lo bajo, en voz baja; **in the same breath** al mismo tiempo; **to catch one's breath** suspender un ratito la respiración, tomar aliento; **to gasp for breath** respirar anhelosamente; **to hold one's breath** contener el aliento; **to save one's breath** guardar silencio; **out of breath** sin aliento; **short of breath** corto de resuello; **under one's breath** por lo bajo, en voz baja

breathe [brið] *va* respirar; inspirar, infundir; desalentar; exhalar; (phonet.) aspirar; (fig.) respirar (*p.ej., amor, bondad*); **not to breathe a word** no respirar; **to breathe life into** alentar; **to breathe one's last** dar el último suspiro; *vn* respirar; soplar suavemente; **to breathe freely** respirar, cobrar aliento; **to breathe in** aspirar; **to breathe out** espirar

breather [ˈbriðər] *s* respiradero; respiro, rato de descanso; ejercicio físico que hace perder la respiración

breathing [ˈbriðɪŋ] *s* respiración; brisa suave, soplo de viento; (phonet.) aspiración (*de la h*); (gram.) espíritu (*en el griego*)

breathing space *s* lugar de descanso; rato de descanso

breathing spell *s* respiro, rato de descanso

breathless [ˈbrɛθlɪs] *adj* falto de aliento, jadeante; intenso, vivo; muerto; sin aire, tranquilo; **to leave breathless** dejar sin aliento

breath of life *s* soplo de vida

breathtaking [ˈbrɛθˌtekɪŋ] *adj* emocionante, imponente, conmovedor

breccia [ˈbrɛtʃɪə] o [ˈbrɛʃɪə] *s* (geol.) brecha

bred [brɛd] *pret & pp de* **breed**

breech [britʃ] *s* trasero (*del animal*); trasera (*de una cosa*); culata, recámara (*del cañón de un arma de fuego*); **breeches** [ˈbrɪtʃɪz] *spl* calzones; (coll.) pantalones; **to wear the breeches** llevar los calzones, ponerse los pantalones (*una mujer*); [britʃ] o [brɪtʃ] *va* poner los calzones a

breechblock [ˈbritʃˌblɑk] *s* cierre de cañón

breechcloth [ˈbritʃˌklɔθ] o [ˈbritʃˌklɑθ] o **breechclout** [ˈbritʃˌklaʊt] *s* taparrabo

breeches buoy [ˈbritʃɪz] *s* (naut.) boya pantalón, pantalón de salvamento

breeching [ˈbrɪtʃɪŋ] o [ˈbritʃɪŋ] *s* retranca

breechloader [ˈbritʃˌlodər] *s* arma de retrocarga

breechloading [ˈbritʃˌlodɪŋ] *adj* de retrocarga

breed [brid] *s* raza, casta (*de animales*); clase, especie; (*pret & pp:* **bred**) *va* criar; *vn* criarse

breeder [ˈbridər] *s* criador (*de animales*); reproductor (*animal*); criadero (*animal fecundo*); paridera (*hembra fecunda*); fuente, origen

breeder reactor *s* (phys.) reactor de cría, reactor-generador

breeding [ˈbridɪŋ] *s* cría; cría y reproducción;

crianza, modales; **bad breeding** mala crianza; **good breeding** buena crianza
breeding ground *s* criadero de animales
breeding pond *s* vivar, vivero de peces
breeze [briz] *s* brisa, airecillo; (coll.) agitación, alboroto
breezy ['brizɪ] *adj* (*comp:* **-ier;** *super:* **-iest**) airoso; animado, vivo, alegre; (coll.) ligero, vivaracho
Brenner ['brɛnər] *s* Brenero
br'er [brʌr] *s* (dial.) hermano
brethren ['brɛðrɪn] *spl* hermanos (*p.ej., de una hermandad*)
Breton ['brɛtən] *adj & s* bretón
breve [briv] *s* (mus.) breve; (gram.) marca curva que se pone sobre las vocales para indicar su brevedad
brevet [brə'vɛt] o ['brɛvɪt] *s* (mil.) comisión honoraria; *adj* (mil.) honorario; (*pret & pp:* **-veted** o **-vetted;** *ger:* **-veting** o **-vetting**) *va* (mil.) conceder una comisión honoraria a
breviary ['brivɪ,ɛrɪ] o ['brɛvɪ,ɛrɪ] *s* (*pl:* **-ies**) breviario; (eccl.) breviario
brevier [brə'vɪr] *s* (print.) breviario
brevipennate [,brɛvɪ'pɛnet] *adj* (orn.) brevipenne
brevity ['brɛvɪtɪ] *s* (*pl:* **-ties**) brevedad
brew [bru] *s* calderada de cerveza; mezcla; *va* bracear (*cerveza*); cocer (*tisana*); fraguar; tramar, urdir; *vn* fabricar cerveza; formarse, prepararse; amenazar (*p.ej., una tormenta*)
brewer ['bruər] *s* bracero, cervecero
brewer's yeast *s* levadura de cerveza
brewery ['bruərɪ] *s* (*pl:* **-ies**) cervecería, fábrica de cerveza
briar ['braɪər] *s* var. de **brier**
Briareus [braɪ'ɛrɪəs] *s* (myth.) Briareo
briarwood ['braɪər,wʊd] *s* var. de **brierwood**
briary ['braɪərɪ] *adj* var. de **briery**
bribe [braɪb] *s* soborno; *va* sobornar
bribery ['braɪbərɪ] *s* (*pl:* **-ies**) soborno
bric-à-brac o **bric-a-brac** ['brɪkə,bræk] *s* curiosidades
brick [brɪk] *s* ladrillo; ladrillos; (coll.) buen sujeto; *adj* de ladrillo; *va* enladrillar; **to brick up** enladrillar, tapar con ladrillos
brickbat ['brɪk,bæt] *s* pedazo de ladrillo; (coll.) palabra hiriente
brick ice cream *s* queso helado, helado al corte
brickkiln ['brɪk,kɪl] o ['brɪk,kɪln] *s* horno de ladrillos
bricklayer ['brɪk,leər] *s* ladrillador
bricklaying ['brɪk,leɪŋ] *s* enladrillado
brick-red ['brɪk,rɛd] *adj* ladrilloso, rojo ladrillo
brickwork ['brɪk,wʌrk] *s* enladrillado
brickyard ['brɪk,jɑrd] *s* ladrillal
bridal ['braɪdəl] *adj* nupcial; de novia, de la novia; *s* boda
bridal wreath *s* corona nupcial; (bot.) espirea
bride [braɪd] *s* novia; **the bride and groom** los novios, los recién casados
bridegroom ['braɪd,grum] o ['braɪd,grʊm] *s* novio
bridesmaid ['braɪdz,med] *s* madrina de boda
bridewell ['braɪdwɛl] *s* (Brit.) casa de corrección; (coll.) cárcel
bridge [brɪdʒ] *s* puente; (naut.) puente; (mus.) puente (*del violín*); puente dental; caballete (*de la nariz*); (billiards) violín; bridge (*juego de naipes*); **in bridge** (elec.) en paralelo; *va* tender un puente sobre; salvar (*un obstáculo*); ayudar a salir de (*una dificultad*)
bridgeboard ['brɪdʒ,bord] *s* (carp.) gualdera, larguero de escalera
bridgehead ['brɪdʒ,hɛd] *s* entrada de puente; (mil.) cabeza de puente
Bridge of Sighs *s* puente de los suspiros
Bridget ['brɪdʒɪt] *s* Brígida
bridgework ['brɪdʒ,wʌrk] *s* construcción de puentes; puente dental
bridle ['braɪdəl] *s* brida, freno; (naut.) frenillo; (fig.) freno; *va* embridar; (naut.) frenillar; (fig.) embridar; *vn* engallarse, levantar la cabeza (*en son de orgullo, desdén, resentimiento, etc.*)
bridle path *s* camino de herradura
bridoon [brɪ'dun] *s* bridón
Brie [bri] *s* brie (*queso*)

brief [brif] *adj* breve; *s* resumen; (law) escrito; (eccl.) breve; **in brief** en resumen, en pocas palabras; **to hold a brief for** abogar por; *va* resumir; dar instrucciones o consejos anticipados a; (law) alegar
brief case *s* portapapeles, cartera
briefing ['brifɪŋ] *s* instrucciones breves dadas a la tripulación de un avión de combate poco antes de emprender el vuelo
briefless ['briflɪs] *adj* sin pleitos, sin clientes
briefness ['brifnɪs] *s* brevedad
brier ['braɪər] *s* (bot.) zarza; (bot.) brezo blanco; (bot.) rosal silvestre; zarzal; pipa hecha de madera de brezo blanco
brierwood ['braɪər,wʊd] *s* madera de las raíces del brezo blanco; pipa hecha de madera de brezo blanco
briery ['braɪərɪ] *adj* zarzoso, espinoso
Brig. abr. de **Brigadier**
brig [brɪg] *s* (naut.) bergantín; (naut.) calabozo en buques de guerra
brigade [brɪ'ged] *s* brigada; (mil.) brigada
brigadier [,brɪgə'dɪr] *s* (mil.) general de brigada
brigadier general *s* (*pl:* **brigadier generals**) (mil.) general de brigada
brigand ['brɪgənd] *s* bandolero
brigandage ['brɪgəndɪdʒ] *s* bandolerismo
brigandine ['brɪgəndin] o ['brɪgəndaɪn] *s* (arm.) brigantina
brigantine ['brɪgəntin] o ['brɪgəntaɪn] *s* (naut.) bergantín goleta
bright [braɪt] *adj* brillante; claro, transparente; subido (*color*); listo, inteligente; vivo, alegre; preclaro, eximio; luminoso (*pensamiento, idea*)
bright and early *adv* temprano y con sol
brighten ['braɪtən] *va* abrillantar; avivar; alegrar; *vn* avivarse; avivar, cobrar vida; alegrarse; despejarse (*el cielo*)
bright lights *spl* luces brillantes del barrio de los teatros y cabarets; (aut.) faros, lámparas o luces de carretera
brightness ['braɪtnɪs] *s* brillantez; claridad, transparencia; inteligencia; viveza, alegría
Bright's disease *s* (path.) brightismo, mal de Bright
brill [brɪl] *s* (ichth.) rodaballo; (ichth.) rodaballo menor (*Rhombus laevis*)
brilliance ['brɪljəns] o **brilliancy** ['brɪljənsɪ] *s* brillantez. brillo; (fig.) brillantez, brillo
brilliant ['brɪljənt] *adj* brillante; (fig.) brillante; *s* brillante (*piedra brillante*); (print.) tipo de tres puntos y medio
brilliantine [,brɪljən'tin] o ['brɪljəntin] *s* brillantina (*aceite para los cabellos; tela lustrosa*)
brim [brɪm] *s* borde; labio (*de un vaso*); ala (*de sombrero*); (*pret & pp:* **brimmed;** *ger:* **brimming**) *va* llenar hasta el borde; *vn* estar de bote en bote
brimful ['brɪm,fʊl] *adj* lleno hasta el borde
brimmer ['brɪmər] *s* copa o vaso lleno
brimstone ['brɪm,ston] *s* azufre; mujer regañona
brindle ['brɪndəl] *adj* leonado mosqueado o rayado; *s* animal de color leonado mosqueado o rayado; color leonado mosqueado o rayado
brindled ['brɪndəld] *adj* leonado mosqueado o rayado
brindled gnu *s* (zool.) ñu
brine [braɪn] *s* salmuera; agua salobre; mar; (poet.) lágrimas; *va* remojar en salmuera
bring [brɪŋ] (*pret & pp:* **brought**) *va* traer; llevar (*traer consigo en la mano, el bolsillo, etc.; producir; persuadir*); hacer venir; contribuir; armar (*un pleito*); **to bring about** efectuar; **to bring around** sacar de un desmayo; persuadir; **to bring away** llevarse; **to bring back** devolver; **to bring down** bajar; abatir; (fig.) abatir, humillar; **to bring down the house** hacer venirse abajo el teatro (*con aplausos*); **to bring forth** parir; producir; poner de manifiesto; sacar, dar a luz; **to bring forward** poner de manifiesto; presentar (*un argumento*); (com.) llevar (*una suma*) a otra cuenta; **to bring home** traer a casa; conducir a casa; hacer sentir claramente, demostrar de modo concluyente; **to bring in** sacar o traer a colación (*hacer mención de*); introducir

(*p.ej., una moda*); presentar (*una cuenta*); servir (*una comida*); dar (*un fallo*); entrar (*a una persona en una sala*); **to bring into play** poner en juego; **to bring off** rescatar; exculpar· llevar a cabo; **to bring on** causar, producir; **to bring oneself to** + *inf* resignarse a + *inf;* **to bring out** sacar; demostrar; presentar al público; **to bring round** sacar de un desmayo; reanimar, curar; persuadir; ganar, convertir; **to bring suit** poner pleito; **to bring to** sacar de un desmayo; parar, detener; **to bring to bear** traer (*influencia*); asestar, apuntar, dirigir; **to bring to book** llamar o traer a capítulo, pedir cuenta a; **to bring together** reunir; confrontar; reconciliar; **to bring to pass** efectuar, realizar; **to bring up** subir; acercar, arrimar (*p.ej., una silla*); educar; sacar a colación; parar de repente; **to bring upon oneself** atraerse (*p.ej., un infortunio*)

bringing-up [ˈbrɪŋɪŋˈʌp] *s* educación

brink [brɪŋk] *s* borde, margen; **on the brink of** al borde de; **on the brink of** + *ger* a punto de + *inf*

brinkmanship [ˈbrɪŋkmənʃɪp] *s* (coll.) práctica de llevar las cosas muy cerca de la línea fronteriza del peligro ineludible

briny [ˈbraɪnɪ] *adj* (*comp:* **-ier;** *super:* **-iest**) salado, salobre; **the briny** (coll.) el mar

briquet o **briquette** [brɪˈkɛt] *s* briqueta (*de carbón*); comprimido, pan

Briseis [braɪˈsiɪs] *s* (myth.) Briseida

brisk [brɪsk] *adj* animado, vivo; fuerte; rápido

brisket [ˈbrɪskɪt] *s* pecho de animal; carne cortada del pecho de un animal

briskness [ˈbrɪsknɪs] *s* animación, viveza; fuerza, vigor; rapidez

bristle [ˈbrɪsəl] *s* cerda; pelusa (*que se desprende de las telas*); *va* poner cerda a; erizar (*el cabello*); *vn* erizarse; erizar las cerdas (*un animal*); encresparse, montar en cólera; cubrirse, llenarse; **to bristle with** estar erizado de (*p.ej., dificultades*)

bristletail [ˈbrɪsəlˌtel] *s* (ent.) lepisma

bristly [ˈbrɪslɪ] *adj* (*comp:* **-tlier;** *super:* **-tliest**) cerdoso, erizado. sedeño

Bristol board [ˈbrɪstəl] *s* brístol

Brit. abr. de **Britain** y **British**

Britain [ˈbrɪtən] *s* Bretaña; la Gran Bretaña

Britannia [brɪˈtænɪə] *s* Bretaña; la Gran Bretaña; el Imperio Británico; (*l.c.*) *s* metal inglés, metal britannia

britannia metal *s* metal britannia, metal británico, metal inglés

Britannic [brɪˈtænɪk] *adj* británico

Briticism [ˈbrɪtɪsɪzəm] *s* modismo o vocablo del inglés hablado en Inglaterra

British [ˈbrɪtɪʃ] *adj* británico; **the British** los britanos

British Columbia *s* la Colombia Británica

British Commonwealth of Nations *s* Comunidad Británica de Naciones

British East Africa *s* el África Oriental Inglesa

British Empire *s* Imperio Británico

Britisher [ˈbrɪtɪʃər] *s* britano

British Guiana *s* la Guayana Inglesa

British Honduras *s* la Honduras Británica

British India *s* la India Inglesa

British Isles *spl* islas Británicas

British Malaya *s* la Malaya Británica

British Museum *s* Museo Británico

British Somaliland *s* la Somalía Británica

British thermal unit *s* unidad térmica británica

British West Africa *s* el África Occidental Inglesa

British West Indies *spl* Indias Occidentales Británicas

Briton [ˈbrɪtən] *s* britano

Brittany [ˈbrɪtənɪ] *s* Bretaña; bretaña (*tela*)

brittle [ˈbrɪtəl] *adj* quebradizo, vidrioso

bro. abr. de **brother**

broach [brotʃ] *s* asador, espetón; espita; broche, prendedero; (mach.) escariador, mandril; *va* sacar a colación; espetar; decantar, trasegar (*un líquido*); (mach.) brochar; *vn* emerger (*p.ej., una ballena, un submarino*); **to broach to** (naut.) tomar por avante

broad [brɔd] *adj* ancho; liberal, tolerante; general, comprensivo; lato (*sentido de una palabra*); claro, franco, sencillo; grosero, tosco; verde, libre; pleno (*día, mediodía, etc.*); (phonet.) abierto; dialectal; **as broad as it is long** que igual da que sea o que se haga de uno o de otro modo; **broad hint** insinuación clara, indirecta del padre Cobos; **broad in one's outlook** de amplias miras e ideas

broadax o **broadaxe** [ˈbrɔdˌæks] *s* hacha de carpintero; doladera (*de tonelero*); hacha de armas

broadbrim [ˈbrɔdˌbrɪm] *s* sombrero de alas anchas; (*cap.*) *s* (coll.) cuáquero

broadcast [ˈbrɔdˌkæst] o [ˈbrɔdˌkɑst] *s* difusión, esparcimiento; radiodifusión; audición (*programa radiotelefónico*); *adj* difundido, esparcido; radiodifundido; *adv* por todas partes; (*pret & pp:* **-cast**) *va* difundir, esparcir; (*pret & pp:* **-cast** o **-casted**) *va* radiodifundir, emitir, radiar

broadcasting [ˈbrɔdˌkæstɪŋ] o [ˈbrɔdˌkɑstɪŋ] *adj* emisor, radiodifusor; *s* emisión, radiodifusión

broadcasting station *s* estación de radiodifusión, emisora, radiodifusora

broadcloth [ˈbrɔdˌklɔθ] o [ˈbrɔdˌklɑθ] *s* velarte

broaden [ˈbrɔdən] *va* ensanchar; *vn* ensancharse

broad-gauge [ˈbrɔdˌgedʒ] o **broad-gauged** [ˈbrɔdˌgedʒd] *adj* de vía ancha (*de 56 y ½ pulgadas inglesas*); tolerante, de amplias miras

broad jump *s* (sport) salto de longitud

broadloom [ˈbrɔdˌlum] *adj* tejido en telar ancho y en color sólido

broad-minded [ˈbrɔdˈmaɪndɪd] *adj* tolerante, de amplias miras

broadness [ˈbrɔdnɪs] *s* anchura; tolerancia; abertura (*de una vocal*)

broad-shouldered [ˈbrɔdˈʃoldərd] *adj* ancho de espaldas

broadside [ˈbrɔdˌsaɪd] *s* (naut.) costado; batería del costado; (naut.) andanada; lado o superficie uniforme y ancha; cara de un pliego de papel; hoja suelta impresa en un solo lado; (coll.) torrente de injurias; *adv* por lo ancho; con el costado vuelto de través

broadsword [ˈbrɔdˌsord] *s* espada ancha, chafarote

Brobdingnagian [ˈbrɑbdɪŋˈnægɪən] *adj* gigantesco, colosal, enorme; *s* gigante

brocade [broˈked] *s* brocado; *va* tejer o decorar con brocado

brocaded [broˈkedɪd] *adj* brocado

brocatel [ˌbrɑkəˈtɛl] *s* brocatel (*tejido y mármol*)

broccoli [ˈbrɑkəlɪ] *s* (bot.) brécol, brécoles o bróculi

brochette [broˈʃɛt] *s* broqueta

brochure [broˈʃʊr] *s* folleto

brogan [ˈbrogən] *s* zapato fuerte y basto

brogue [brog] *s* zapato fuerte y basto; zapato basto de orejas sueltas; acento irlandés; idioma corrompido

broil [brɔɪl] *s* carne asada a la parrilla; camorra, pendencia; *va* asar a la parrilla; calentar con exceso; *vn* asarse (*padecer calor*)

broiled meat *s* carne asada a la parrilla

broiler [ˈbrɔɪler] *s* parrilla; polla para asar en parrillas

broke [brok] *adj* (slang) sin blanca; *pret de* **break**

broken [ˈbrokən] *adj* quebrado, fragoso; interrumpido. desigual, disparejo; suelto, separado; agotado, debilitado; amansado, sumiso; chapurrado; *pp de* **break**

broken-down [ˈbrokənˈdaʊn] *adj* abatido, arruinado; deshecho, descompuesto

broken-hearted [ˈbrokənˈhɑrtɪd] *adj* acongojado, traspasado de dolor

broken-winded [ˈbrokənˈwɪndɪd] *adj* corto de aliento; (vet.) atacado de huélfago

broker [ˈbrokər] *s* corredor

brokerage [ˈbrokərɪdʒ] *s* corretaje

bromate [ˈbromet] *s* (chem.) bromato

brome grass [brom] *s* (bot.) bromo

bromeliaceous [broˌmilɪˈeʃəs] *adj* (bot.) bromeliáceo

bromic [ˈbromɪk] *adj* (chem.) brómico

bromid [ˈbromɪd] o **bromide** [ˈbromaɪd] o

['bromɪd] *s* (chem.) bromuro; (pharm.) bromuro de potasio; (slang) trivialidad
bromidic [bro'mɪdɪk] *adj* (coll.) común, trivial
bromin ['bromɪn] o **bromine** ['bromin] o ['bromɪn] *s* (chem.) bromo
bronchia ['braŋkɪə] *spl* (anat.) bronquíolos
bronchial ['braŋkɪəl] *adj* bronquial
bronchial tubes *spl* (anat.) bronquios, bronquíolos
bronchiole ['braŋkɪol] *s* (anat.) bronquíolo
bronchitic [braŋ'kɪtɪk] *adj* bronquítico
bronchitis [braŋ'kaɪtɪs] *s* (path.) bronquitis
broncho ['braŋko] *s* (*pl:* **-chos**) var. de **bronco**
bronchopneumonia [,braŋkonju'monjə] o [,braŋkonu'monjə] *s* (path.) bronconeumonía
bronchorrea [,braŋkə'riə] *s* (path.) broncorrea
bronchoscope ['braŋkəskop] *s* broncoscopio
bronchoscopy [braŋ'kaskəpɪ] *s* broncoscopia
bronchus ['braŋkəs] *s* (*pl:* **-chi** [kaɪ]) (anat.) bronquio; (anat.) bronquíolo
bronco ['braŋko] *s* (*pl:* **-cos**) (U.S.A.) potro cerril, potro sin domar
broncobuster ['braŋko,bʌstər] *s* chalán, picador, domador de potros
brontosaurus [,brantə'sɔrəs] *s* (pal.) brontosauro
bronze [branz] *s* bronce (*aleación; objeto de arte; polvo*); *adj* de bronce, hecho de bronce; bronceado; *va* broncear; *vn* broncearse
bronze age *s* (myth.) edad de bronce; (*caps.*) *s* (archeol.) edad del bronce
bronzesmith ['branz,smɪθ] *s* broncista
brooch [brotʃ] o [brutʃ] *s* alfiler de pecho, prendedero
brood [brud] *s* camada, cría; nidada; familia; raza, casta; *va* empollar; cobijar, albergar; *vn* enclocar, encobar; **to brood on** u **over** meditar con tristeza
brooder ['brudər] *s* incubadora; clueca (*gallina*); rumión
broody ['brudɪ] *adj* (*comp:* **-ier**; *super:* **-iest**) clueco; (fig.) triste, melancólico
brook [brʊk] *s* arroyo; *va* tolerar, permitir
brooklet ['brʊklɪt] *s* arroyuelo
brooklime ['brʊk,laɪm] *s* (bot.) berro de caballo; (bot.) becabunga
brook trout *s* (ichth.) trucha norteamericana (*Salvelinus fontinalis*)
brookweed ['brʊk,wid] *s* (bot.) pamplina de agua
broom [brum] o [brʊm] *s* escoba; (bot.) hiniesta, retama
broomcorn ['brum,kɔrn] o ['brʊm,kɔrn] *s* (bot.) sorgo común
broomcorn millet *s* (bot.) millo de escoba
broom goosefoot *s* (bot.) ceñiglo de jardín
broomstick ['brum,stɪk] o ['brʊm,stɪk] *s* palo de escoba
bros. abr. de **brothers**
broth [brɔθ] o [brɑθ] *s* caldo; (bact.) caldo de cultivo
brothel ['brɑθəl] o ['brɑðəl] *s* burdel
brother ['brʌðər] *s* hermano
brotherhood ['brʌðərhʊd] *s* hermandad
brother-in-law ['brʌðərɪn,lɔ] *s* (*pl:* **brothers-in-law**) cuñado, hermano político; concuñado
Brother Jonathan *s* el hermano Jonatás (*los EE.UU. o el pueblo de los EE.UU.*)
brotherly ['brʌðərlɪ] *adj* fraternal; amistoso, bondadoso; *adv* fraternalmente, como hermano, como hermanos
brougham [brum], ['bruəm] o ['broəm] *s* brougham (*carruaje; automóvil*)
brought [brɔt] *pret & pp de* **bring**
brow [braʊ] *s* frente *f*; ceja; (fig.) ceja (*de monte*); borde (*de despeñadero*); **to knit one's brow** fruncir las cejas
browbeat ['braʊ,bit] (*pret:* **-beat**; *pp:* **-beaten**) *va* intimidar mirando con ceño; intimidar con amenazas
brown [braʊn] *adj* pardo, moreno, castaño; tostado del sol; *s* pardo, color pardo; *va* poner pardo o moreno; broncear; tostar, quemar; (cook.) dorar; *vn* ponerse pardo o moreno; broncearse; tostarse, quemarse; (cook.) dorarse
brown bear *s* (zool.) oso pardo
brown betty *s* pudín de manzana y pan
brown bread *s* pan bazo, pan moreno
brown coal *s* lignito
brown hyena *s* (zool.) hiena parda
Brownian movement ['braʊnɪən] *s* (phys.) movimiento browniano
brownie ['braʊnɪ] *s* duende moreno y benévolo; tortita de chocolate y nueces
brownish ['braʊnɪʃ] *adj* pardusco
brown race *s* raza cobriza
brown rat *s* (zool.) rata de alcantarilla
brown rice *s* arroz no pulimentado
brown shirt *s* camisa parda (*nazi*)
brownstone ['braʊn,ston] *s* arenisca de color pardo rojizo
brown study *s* absorción, suspensión, pensamiento profundo
brown sugar *s* azúcar terciado, azúcar moreno
brown thrasher *s* (orn.) túrdido norteamericano (*Toxostoma rufum*)
browse [braʊz] *s* ramón; *va* comer (*las ramitas y las hojas de los árboles*); pacer (*la hierba*); *vn* ramonear; pacer; hojear un libro ociosamente; **to browse about** o **around** examinar ociosamente libros u obras de arte; recorrer las tiendas, más por curiosidad que por ánimo de comprar
brucellosis [,brusə'losɪs] *s* (path. & vet.) brucelosis
brucine ['brusin] o ['brusɪn] *s* (pharm.) brucina
brucite ['brusaɪt] *s* (mineral.) brucita
Bruges ['brudʒɪz] o [bruʒ] *s* Brujas
bruin ['bruɪn] *s* oso
bruise [bruz] *s* contusión, magulladura; *va* contundir, magullar; majar; *vn* contundirse, magullarse
bruiser ['bruzər] *s* púgil; matón
bruit [brut] *va* esparcir, divulgar; **to bruit about** esparcir, divulgar
brunet [bru'nɛt] *adj* moreno; *s* moreno (*hombre moreno*)
brunette [bru'nɛt] *adj* moreno; *s* morena (*mujer morena*)
Brunhild ['brunhɪld] *s* Brunilda
brunt [brʌnt] *s* fuerza, empuje; **the brunt** lo más difícil; **to bear the brunt of the battle** llevar el peso de la batalla
brush [brʌʃ] *s* cepillo, escobilla; brocha; pincel; cola peluda (*de un perro*); cepilladura; brochada; roce; escaramuza, encuentro; ramojo; broza (*despojo de las plantas; maleza*); (elec.) escobilla; *va* cepillar; quitar frotando; rozar; **to brush aside** echar bruscamente a un lado; **to brush up** retocar (*un cuadro*); repasar, refrescar (*la pintura de una casa*); *vn* moverse apresuradamente; **to brush by** pasar cerca de (*una persona*) sin hacer caso de ella; **to brush up on** renovar el conocimiento de (*un asunto*)
brush discharge *s* (elec.) efluvio
brush holder *s* (elec.) portaescobillas
brush-off ['brʌʃ,ɔf] o ['brʌʃ,ɑf] *s* (slang) despedida, desaire; **to give the brush-off to** (slang) despedir noramala, rehusar, desairar
brush shift *s* (elec.) decalaje de escobillas
brushwood ['brʌʃ,wʊd] *s* broza (*despojo de las plantas; maleza*)
brushy ['brʌʃɪ] *adj* (*comp:* **-ier**; *super:* **-iest**) cerdoso, peludo; zarzoso
brusque [brʌsk] *adj* brusco
brusqueness ['brʌsknɪs] *s* brusquedad
Brussels ['brʌsəlz] *s* Bruselas
Brussels carpet *s* alfombra de Bruselas
Brussels lace *s* encaje de Bruselas
Brussels sprouts *spl* (bot.) bretones, col de Bruselas
brutal ['brutəl] *adj* brutal
brutality [bru'tælɪtɪ] *s* (*pl:* **-ties**) brutalidad
brutalize ['brutəlaɪz] *va* brutalizar
brute [brut] *adj & s* bruto
brutish ['brutɪʃ] *adj* bruto
Brutus ['brutəs] *s* Bruto
bryology [braɪ'ɑlədʒɪ] *s* briología
bryony ['braɪənɪ] *s* (*pl:* **-nies**) (bot.) brionia, nueza
bryophyte ['braɪəfaɪt] *s* (bot.) briofita
b.s. abr. de **balance sheet** y **bill of sale**
B.S. abr. de **Baccalaureus Scientiae** (Lat.) **Bachelor of Science**

B.S.A. abr. de **Bachelor of Scientific Agriculture** y **Boy Scouts of America**
B.Sc. abr. de **Baccalaureus Scientiae** (Lat.) **Bachelor of Science**
Bt. abr. de **baronet**
B.T. o **B.Th.** abr. de **Baccalaureus Theologiae** (Lat.) **Bachelor of Theology**
B.T.U. abr. de **British thermal unit**
bu. abr. de **bushel**
bubal ['bjubəl] *s* (zool.) búbalo
bubble ['bʌbəl] *s* burbuja, borbollón; ampolla; quimera, ilusión, sueño descabellado y efímero; *vn* burbujear, borbotar; **to bubble over** desbordar, rebosar; **to bubble over with joy** desbordar o rebosar de gozo
bubble dance *s* baile de los globos
bubble gum *s* chicle de globo, chicle de burbuja, chicle hinchable
bubble sextant *s* sextante de burbuja
bubble tower *s* torre de burbujeo
bubble tube *s* tubo de burbuja
bubbling ['bʌblɪŋ] *adj* burbujeante; (fig.) efusivo; *s* burbujeo, borbollón
bubbly ['bʌblɪ] *adj* espumoso, efervescente
bubo ['bjubo] *s* (*pl:* **-boes**) (path.) buba, bubón
buboed ['bjubod] *adj* buboso
bubonic [bju'bɑnɪk] *adj* bubónico
bubonic plague *s* (path.) peste bubónica
buccal ['bʌkəl] *adj* bucal
buccaneer [,bʌkə'nɪr] *s* bucanero
buccinator ['bʌksɪ,netər] *s* (anat.) bucinador
Bucephalus [bju'sɛfələs] *s* Bucéfalo
Bucharest [,bjukə'rɛst] o [,bukə'rɛst] *s* Bucarest
buchu ['bjukju] o ['buku] *s* (pharm.) buchú
buck [bʌk] *s* (zool.) cabrón; (zool.) gamo, ciervo, conejo (*macho*); caballete, cabrilla; petimetre, pisaverde; encorvada, corveta (*de un caballo*); colada (*lejía*); (coll.) indio o negro varón; (slang) dólar; **to pass the buck** (coll.) echar la carga a otro; *va* (coll.) hacer frente a, resistir; (coll.) tirar (*al jinete*) encorvándose; (coll.) embestir, arrojarse sobre; (coll.) acornear; (mil.) castigar atando los codos, muñecas y rodillas; colar (*la ropa*); *vn* encorvarse, (elec.) ser contrario; **to buck against** embestir contra; **to buck up** (coll.) animarse, cobrar ánimo
buckaroo ['bʌkəru] o [,bʌkə'ru] *s* (*pl:* **-roos**) vaquero
buck bean *s* (bot.) trébol acuático o de agua
buckboard ['bʌk,bord] *s* carretón de cuatro ruedas sin muelles
bucket ['bʌkɪt] *s* balde, cubo; pozal (*de un pozo*); paleta (*de turbina u otra rueda*); cangilón (*de la noria*); cucharón o pala (*de excavadora*); **to kick the bucket** (slang) liar el petate, estirar la pata
bucketful ['bʌkɪtful] *s* balde, cubo (*contenido*)
bucket seat *s* (aut.) baquet
bucket shop *s* agencia que compra y vende acciones para otros maladministrando los intereses de éstos
bucket wheel *s* rueda de cangilones
buckeye ['bʌk,aɪ] *s* (bot.) castaño de Indias
Buckingham Palace ['bʌkɪŋəm] *s* palacio Buckingham
buckle ['bʌkəl] *s* hebilla; pandeo; *va* abrochar con hebilla; *vn* pandear; **to buckle down to** dedicarse con empeño a; **to buckle with** luchar con
buckler ['bʌklər] *s* escudo, broquel
buckling ['bʌklɪŋ] *s* pandeo
buck private *s* (slang) soldado raso
buckram ['bʌkrəm] *s* percalina, bocací; tiesura, ceremonia excesiva
bucksaw ['bʌk,sɔ] *s* sierra de bastidor
buckshot ['bʌk,ʃɑt] *s* perdigón zorrero
buckskin ['bʌk,skɪn] *s* ante; badana; **buckskins** *spl* calzones de ante
buckthorn ['bʌk,θɔrn] *s* (bot.) espino cerval
bucktooth ['bʌk,tuθ] *s* (*pl:* **-teeth**) diente saliente
buckwheat ['bʌk,hwit] *s* (bot.) alforfón, trigo sarraceno
buckwheat cake *s* panqué hecho de harina de trigo sarraceno
bucolic [bju'kɑlɪk] *adj* bucólico; *s* bucólica (*composición poética*); (hum.) pastor, campesino
bucranium [bjʊ'krenɪəm] *s* (*pl:* **-a** [ə]) (arch.) bucráneo
bud [bʌd] *s* botón; brote; joven; niña que se pone de largo; (anat., bot. & zool.) yema; **to nip in the bud** cortar de raíz, atajar desde los principios; (*pret & pp:* **budded**; *ger:* **budding**) *va* injertar (*una yema en otra planta*); *vn* abotonar; brotar
Buddha ['budə] *s* Buda
Buddhic ['budɪk] *adj* búdico
Buddhism ['budɪzəm] *s* budismo
Buddhist ['budɪst] *adj* & *s* budista
buddy ['bʌdɪ] *s* (*pl:* **-dies**) (coll.) compañero; (coll.) muchachito
budge [bʌdʒ] *va* bullir, mover un poco; *vn* bullir, bullirse, p.ej., **he did not dare to budge** no osaba bullirse
budgerigar [,bʌdʒərɪ'gɑr] *s* (orn.) periquito de Australia
budget ['bʌdʒɪt] *s* presupuesto; acumulación, colección; *va & vn* presuponer
budgetary ['bʌdʒɪ,tɛrɪ] *adj* presupuestario
budgie ['bʌdʒɪ] *s* (coll.) var. de **budgerigar**
Buenos Aires ['bonəs'ɛriz] *s* Buenos Aires
buff [bʌf] *s* ante; color de ante; chaqueta de soldado hecha de ante; rueda pulidora; (coll.) piel desnuda; *adj* hecho de ante; de color de ante; *va* pulimentar con ante; pulimentar; amortiguar el choque de
buffalo ['bʌfəlo] *s* (*pl:* **-loes, -los** o **-lo**) (zool.) búfalo; (zool.) bisonte; piel de bisonte con pelo; *vn* (slang) confundir; (slang) impresionar
buffalo bird *s* (orn.) garrapatero
buffalo grass *s* (bot.) hierba de la pradera (*Buchloë dactyloides y Bouteloua*)
buffalo robe *s* piel de bisonte con pelo
buffer ['bʌfər] *s* tope; (rail.) tope, paragolpes; amortiguador de choques; pulidor (*persona o instrumento*)
buffer state *s* estado tapón, país situado entre dos naciones rivales
buffet [bu'fe] *s* aparador; chinero; ambigú; fonda de ferrocarril; caja (*de órgano*); ['bʌfɪt] *s* puñada; bofetada; golpe; *va* dar de puñadas; abofetear; golpear; *vn* luchar, pelear
buffet car [bu'fe] *s* (rail.) coche donde se sirven refrescos
buffet lunch [bu'fe] *s* servicio de buffet
buffet supper [bu'fe] *s* ambigú
buffing wheel *s* rueda pulidora
buffoon [bə'fun] *s* bufón
buffoonery [bə'funərɪ] *s* (*pl:* **-ies**) bufonada
bug [bʌg] *s* bicho, sabandija, insecto; (Brit.) chinche; microbio; (coll.) estorbo, traba; (slang) loco; (slang) manía; (slang) entusiasta
bugaboo ['bʌgəbu] *s* (*pl:* **-boos**) espantajo
bugbear ['bʌg,bɛr] *s* espantajo; aversión; coco
bug-eyed ['bʌg,aɪd] *adj* (slang) de ojos saltones
buggy ['bʌgɪ] *s* (*pl:* **-gies**) calesa de cuatro ruedas; *adj* (*comp:* **-gier**; *super:* **-giest**) lleno de bichos, sabandijas, chinches, etc.; (slang) loco
bughouse ['bʌg,haʊs] *s* (slang) casa de locos, manicomio; *adj* (slang) loco
bugle ['bjugəl] *s* (mus.) corneta, corneta de llaves; cañutillo (*tubido de vidrio usado en pasamanería*); (bot.) consuelda media; *va* llamar con toque de corneta; *vn* tocar la corneta
bugle call *s* toque de corneta
bugle horn *s* corneta, corneta de llaves
bugler ['bjuglər] *s* corneta
bugleweed ['bjugəl,wid] *s* marrubio acuático; (bot.) consuelda media
bugloss ['bjuglɑs] o ['bjuglɔs] *s* (bot.) buglosa
buhl [bul] *s* taracea de Boulle; mueble de Boulle
buhl saw *s* sierra de calar, serrezuela
build [bɪld] *s* estructura; talle (*del cuerpo humano*); (*pret & pp:* **built**) *va* edificar, construir, fabricar; fundar, establecer; componer; desarrollar; **to build up** componer; desarrollar; tapar, rellenar; armar; construir muchas casas en; crearse (*p.ej., una clientela*); *vn* edificar, construir; **to build on** o **upon** edificar sobre; contar con

builder [ˈbɪldər] *s* constructor; maestro de obras
building [ˈbɪldɪŋ] *s* edificio; construcción; pabellón (*p.ej., de una exposición*); *adj* de construcción, para construcciones
building and loan association *s* sociedad de crédito de construcción, sociedad de préstamos para edificación
building line *s* línea municipal, línea de edificación, alineamiento
building lot *s* solar
building permit *s* permiso de edificación
build-up [ˈbɪld,ʌp] *s* composición; (coll.) propaganda anticipada a favor de una persona o cosa
built [bɪlt] *pret & pp de* **build**
built-in [ˈbɪlt,ɪn] *adj* inamovible, integrante, empotrado, incorporado o montado en la construcción
built-in antennas (rad.) antena interior incorporada
built-up [ˈbɪltˈʌp] *adj* compuesto, armado; aglomerado
Bukhara [bʊˈkɑrə] *s* var. de **Bokhara**
bulb [bʌlb] *s* (anat. & bot.) bulbo; (bot.) planta bulbosa; ampolleta, bombilla (*de luz eléctrica*); ampolleta, bola, cubeta (*del termómetro y el barómetro*); ampolla, pera (*de jeringa*); ensanche, protuberancia
bulbil [ˈbʌlbɪl] *s* (bot.) bulbillo
bulbous [ˈbʌlbəs] *adj* bulboso; ampollar
bulbul [ˈbʊlbʊl] *s* (orn.) picnonoto; (orn.) ave canora persa (*tal vez Luscinia golzii*)
Bulgar [ˈbʌlgɑr] o [ˈbʊlgɑr] *adj & s* búlgaro
Bulgaria [bʌlˈgɛrɪə] o [bʊlˈgɛrɪə] *s* Bulgaria
Bulgarian [bʌlˈgɛrɪən] o [bʊlˈgɛrɪən] *adj & s* búlgaro
bulge [bʌldʒ] *s* bombeo, pandeo; protuberancia; *vn* bombearse, pandearse; saltar, sobresalir
bulging [ˈbʌldʒɪŋ] *s* bombeo, pandeo; *adj* pando; protuberante
bulgy [ˈbʌldʒɪ] *adj* (*comp:* **-ier;** *super:* **-iest**) pando; protuberante
bulk [bʌlk] *s* bulto, volumen; grueso; **in bulk** a granel (*sin envase*); en pilas, en fardos; *adj* suelto; *va* amontonar; abultar; calcular el bulto de; *vn* abultar; hincharse; tener importancia
bulkhead [ˈbʌlk,hɛd] *s* (naut.) mamparo; escotillón; muro ribereño de contención; tabique hermético
bulky [ˈbʌlkɪ] *adj* (*comp:* **-ier;** *super:* **-iest**) abultado, grueso
bull [bʊl] *s* toro; elefante macho; macho de la ballena, la foca; (fig.) toro (*hombre muy robusto y fuerte*); alcista (*en la Bolsa*); (slang) agente de policía, detective; bula (*sello; documento pontificio*); disparate, dicho absurdo; (slang) música celestial; **to take the bull by the horns** irse a la cabeza del toro; *adj* robusto, fuerte; bramante; alcista; *va* cubrir (*el toro a la vaca*); (slang) chapucear; **to bull the market** jugar al alza; *vn* (slang) chapucear; (slang) tratar de encubrir sus desperfectos
bulla [ˈbʊlə] o [ˈbʌlə] *s* (*pl:* **-lae** [li]) bula; (path.) flictena
bull bat *s* (orn.) chotacabras norteamericano
bull briar *s* (bot.) bejuco de corona
bulldog [ˈbʊl,dɔg] o [ˈbʊl,dɑg] *s* dogo; *adj* porfiado, terco; valiente
bulldoze [ˈbʊl,doz] *va* (coll.) intimidar con amenazas o usando la violencia
bulldozer [ˈbʊl,dozər] *s* (coll.) valentón; (mach.) topadora, empujadora niveladora; (mach.) dobladora de ángulos
bullet [ˈbʊlɪt] *s* bala; plomada (*de pescador*)
bullet-head [ˈbʊlɪt,hɛd] *s* cabeza redonda; persona de cabeza redonda; (coll.) persona obstinada
bullet-headed [ˈbʊlɪt,hɛdɪd] *adj* de cabeza redonda; (coll.) obstinado
bulletin [ˈbʊlətɪn] *s* boletín; anuncio; anuario (*p.ej., de la universidad*)
bulletin board *s* tablilla o tablón de anuncios
bulletproof [ˈbʊlɪt,pruf] *adj* a prueba de bala
bullfight [ˈbʊl,faɪt] *s* toros, corrida de toros
bullfighter [ˈbʊl,faɪtər] *s* torero
bullfighting [ˈbʊl,faɪtɪŋ] *s* toreo; *adj* torero
bullfinch [ˈbʊl,fɪntʃ] *s* (orn.) pinzón real
bullfrog [ˈbʊl,frɑg] o [ˈbʊl,frɔg] *s* (zool.) rana toro
bullhead [ˈbʊl,hɛd] *s* persona obstinada y poco inteligente; (ichth.) amiuro; (ichth.) siluro; (orn.) chorlito
bullheaded [ˈbʊl,hɛdɪd] *adj* obstinado, terco; obstinado y poco inteligente
bullion [ˈbʊljən] *s* entorchado (*bordado del uniforme*); oro o plata en barras, lingotes de oro o plata
bullish [ˈbʊlɪʃ] *adj* parecido al toro; obstinado, estúpido; optimista; en alza; alcista
bullnecked [ˈbʊl,nɛkt] *adj* de cuello grueso
bullock [ˈbʊlək] *s* buey
bull pen *s* toril; (coll.) prevención de policía
bull ring *s* plaza de toros; (mach.) anillo de presión
bull's-eye [ˈbʊlz,aɪ] *s* centro del blanco; tiro que da en el centro del blanco; lente ojo de buey; lente con vidrio abombado; linterna sorda; (arch.) ojo de buey; (naut.) cristal de patente; (*cap.*) *s* (astr.) Ojo del Toro; **to hit the bull's-eye** o **to score a bull's-eye** hacer diana
bull terrier *s* bull-terrier
bully [ˈbʊlɪ] *s* (*pl:* **-lies**) matón, valentón; *adj* (coll.) excelente, magnífico; *interj* (coll.) ¡bravo!; (*pret & pp:* **-lied**) *va* intimidar con amenazas y gritería; **to bully someone into doing something** forzar a uno con amenazas y gritería a que haga una cosa; *vn* gallear
bully beef *s* carne de vaca encurtida o conservada en latas
bullyrag [ˈbʊlɪ,ræg] (*pret & pp:* **-ragged;** *ger:* **-ragging**) *va* atormentar, maltratar, molestar, intimidar con amenazas
bully tree *s* (bot.) balata
bulrush [ˈbʊl,rʌʃ] *s* (bot.) junco; (bot.) junco de laguna; (bot.) papiro; (bot.) anea
bulwark [ˈbʊlwərk] *s* (fort. & fig.) baluarte; (naut.) macarrón; *va* fortificar con baluarte; amparar, defender
bum [bʌm] *s* (slang) holgazán, holgazán borracho; (slang) vagabundo; (slang) sablista, mendigo; (slang) jarana, juerga, parranda; *adj* (*comp:* **bummer;** *super:* **bummest**) (slang) inferior, chapucero; (slang) inservible; **to feel bum** (slang) sentirse muy malo; (*pret & pp:* **bummed;** *ger:* **bumming**) *va* (slang) mendigar (*dinero, comidas, etc.*); *vn* (slang) holgazanear; (slang) vagabundear; (slang) beber a pote; (slang) sablear, mendigar
bumble [ˈbʌmbəl] *va* (dial.) chapucear; *vn* (dial.) zumbar (*como un abejorro*); (dial.) menearse; (dial.) chapucear
bumblebee [ˈbʌmbəl,bi] *s* (ent.) abejorro
bumboat [ˈbʌm,bot] *s* bote vivandero
bump [bʌmp] *s* topetón (*choque*); batacazo (*golpe al caer*); aspereza (*del terreno*); sacudida; rebote (*del avión en el aire agitado*); bollo, hinchazón; chichón (*en la cabeza*); joroba, protuberancia; *va* topar, dar contra; empujar violentamente; abollar; **to bump off** (slang) matar; *vn* chocar; dar sacudidas (*p.ej., un coche*); **to bump against** chocar contra; **to bump off** (slang) morirse
bumper [ˈbʌmpər] *s* tope; (rail.) parachoques o paratopes (*de final de línea*); (aut.) parachoques o amortiguador; copa o vaso lleno; (coll.) cosa muy grande; *adj* (coll.) muy grande, abundante
bumping post *s* (rail.) parachoques o paratopes
bumpkin [ˈbʌmpkɪn] *s* patán; (naut.) pescante
bumptious [ˈbʌmpʃəs] *adj* presuntuoso
bumpy [ˈbʌmpɪ] *adj* (*comp:* **-ier;** *super:* **-iest**) abollado; áspero (*terreno*); agitado (*aire*)
bun [bʌn] *s* bollo
buna [ˈbunə] o [ˈbjunə] *s* (chem.) buna
bunch [bʌntʃ] *s* manojo; ristra (*de tallos de ajos, cebollas, etc.*); racimo (*de uvas*); ramillete (*de flores*); manada (*de animales*); grupo (*de personas*); montón; *va* agrupar, juntar; amontonar, *vn* arracimarse
bunchberry [ˈbʌntʃ,bɛrɪ] *s* (*pl:* **-ries**) (bot.) cornejo canadiense
bunch grass *s* (bot.) poa
bunchy [ˈbʌntʃɪ] *adj* (*comp:* **-ier;** *super:* **-iest**) racimoso, amanojado

bunco [ˈbʌŋko] *s* (*pl:* **-cos**) (slang) estafa; banca (*juego de naipes*); *va* (slang) estafar
buncombe [ˈbʌŋkəm] *s* (coll.) discurso o lenguaje altisonante e insincero
bundle [ˈbʌndəl] *s* lío, bulto; paquete; fardo; legajo (*de papeles*); haz (*de leña, hierba, etc.*); *va* liar, atar, empaquetar, envolver; **to bundle off** u **out** despachar precipitadamente; **to bundle up** arropar; *vn* escaparse precipitadamente; meterse en cama juntos sin desnudarse (*dos amantes*); **to bundle up** arroparse
bung [bʌŋ] *s* bitoque; piquera (*boca para sacar el vino*); *va* atarugar; tapar con bitoque; tapar, cerrar, obstruir; (slang) abollar, magullar, machucar
bungalow [ˈbʌŋgəlo] *s* bungalow, casa de campo, de un solo piso
bunghole [ˈbuŋˌhol] *s* piquera, boca de tonel
bungle [ˈbʌŋgəl] *s* chapucería; *va & vn* chapucear
bungler [ˈbʌŋglər] *s* chapucero
bungling [ˈbʌŋglɪŋ] *s* chapucería; *adj* chapucero
bunion [ˈbʌnjən] *s* (path.) juanete
bunk [bʌŋk] *s* tarima (*entablado para dormir*); (slang) habla altisonante e insincera; (slang) música celestial; *vn* (coll.) dormir en tarima, dormir, hospedarse
bunker [ˈbʌŋkər] *s* carbonera; (naut.) pañol del carbón; (golf) hoya de arena; (fort.) fortín
bunko [ˈbʌŋko] *s* (*pl:* **-kos**) var. de **bunco**; *va* var. de **bunco**
bunkum [ˈbʌŋkəm] *s* var. de **buncombe**
bunny [ˈbʌnɪ] *s* (*pl:* **-nies**) conejito; pequeña ardilla
Bunsen burner [ˈbʌnsən] *s* mechero Bunsen
bunt [bʌnt] *s* empellón, empujón; topetada (*con la cabeza*); (naut.) centro de una vela redonda; (baseball) golpe dado sin fuerza de modo que la pelota dé en el suelo y no vaya lejos; *va* empellar, empujar; topetar; (baseball) golpear (*la pelota*) sin fuerza de modo que dé en el suelo y no vaya lejos
bunting [ˈbʌntɪŋ] *s* lanilla para banderas; empavesado (*de un barco*); banderas colgadas como adorno; (orn.) gorrión triguero; (orn.) plectrófanes
buntline [ˈbʌntlɪn] o [ˈbʌntlaɪn] *s* (naut.) briol
buoy [bɔɪ] o [ˈbu·ɪ] *s* (naut.) boya; (naut.) guindola, boya salvavidas; *va* aboyar, señalar con boyas; mantener a flote; animar, alentar; **to buoy up** mantener a flote; animar, alentar
buoyancy [ˈbɔɪənsɪ] o [ˈbujənsɪ] *s* flotación (*facultad de flotar*); fuerza ascensional; alegría, viveza
buoyant [ˈbɔɪənt] o [ˈbujənt] *adj* boyante; ascensional; alegre, vivaz
buprestid [bjuˈprɛstɪd] *s* (ent.) bupresto
bur [bʌr] *s* erizo (*p.ej., de la castaña*); planta que tiene erizos; persona o cosa muy pegadiza; (*pret & pp:* **burred**; *ger:* **burring**) *va* quitar los erizos a
burble [ˈbʌrbəl] *s* burbujeo; charla; *vn* burbujear; charlar
burbot [ˈbʌrbət] *s* (ichth.) lota
burden [ˈbʌrdən] *s* carga; (fig.) carga; (naut.) arqueo (*capacidad de una embarcación*); (naut.) peso de la carga; tema (*de un discurso, ensayo, etc.*); estribillo (*verso*); *va* cargar; (fig.) cargar, gravar, agobiar
burden of proof *s* peso de la prueba
burdensome [ˈbʌrdənsəm] *adj* oneroso, gravoso, pesado
burdock [ˈbʌrˌdɑk] *s* (bot.) bardana
bureau [ˈbjuro] *s* (*pl:* **-reaus** o **-reaux** [roz]) cómoda; (Brit.) escritorio, buró; oficina, dirección; negociado (*sección administrativa*); departamento del gobierno
bureaucracy [bjuˈrɑkrəsɪ] o [bjuˈrokrəsɪ] *s* (*pl:* **-cies**) burocracia
bureaucrat [ˈbjurokræt] *s* burócrata
bureaucratic [ˌbjuroˈkrætɪk] *adj* burocrático
burette [bjuˈrɛt] *s* (chem.) bureta
burg [bʌrg] *s* (coll.) pueblo, ciudad
burgeon [ˈbʌrdʒən] *s* (bot.) retoño; (bot.) yema; *vn* (bot.) retoñar
burgess [ˈbʌrdʒɪs] *s* vecino de una villa, pueblo, etc.; alcalde; miembro de la cámara baja de la legislatura colonial de los estados de Virginia y Maryland, EE.UU.
burgh [bʌrg] o [ˈbʌro] *s* (Scottish) villa
burgher [ˈbʌrgər] *s* vecino de una villa, pueblo, etc.; ciudadano
burglar [ˈbʌrglər] *s* escalador
burglar alarm *s* alarma de ladrones
burglar insurance *s* seguro contra robos
burglarious [bərˈglɛrɪəs] *adj* escalador
burglarize [ˈbʌrgləraɪz] *va* (coll.) escalar para robar
burglarproof [ˈbʌrglərˌpruf] *adj* a prueba de escaladores
burglary [ˈbʌrglərɪ] *s* (*pl:* **-ies**) robo con escalo
burgle [ˈbʌrgəl] *va & vn* (coll.) escalar para robar
burgomaster [ˈbʌrgoˌmæstər] o [ˈbʌrgoˌmɑstər] *s* burgomaestre
burgonet [ˈbʌrgonɛt] *s* (arm.) borgoñota, celada borgoñota
burgrave [ˈbʌrgrev] *s* burgrave
burgraviate [bʌrˈgrevɪɪt] *s* burgraviato
Burgundian [bərˈgʌndɪən] *adj & s* borgoñés o borgoñón
Burgundy [ˈbʌrgəndɪ] *s* la Borgoña; borgoña (*vino*)
burial [ˈbɛrɪəl] *s* entierro
burial ground *s* cementerio
burial service *s* oficio de sepultura
burin [ˈbjurɪn] *s* buril; cincel; (fig.) buril (*estilo o modo del grabador*)
burl [bʌrl] *s* nudo (*en la madera*); mota (*en el paño*); *va* desmotar, despinzar
burlap [ˈbʌrlæp] *s* harpillera
burlesque [bərˈlɛsk] *adj* extravagante; de music-hall; (lit.) festivo; *s* parodia; (theat.) music-hall; *va* parodiar
burley o **Burley** [ˈbʌrlɪ] *s* tabaco de hojas delgadas cultivado en el estado de Kentucky, EE.UU.
burly [ˈbʌrlɪ] *adj* (*comp:* **-lier**; *super:* **-liest**) membrudo, fornido
Burma [ˈbʌrmə] *s* Birmania
Burma Road *s* ruta de Birmania
Burmese [bʌrˈmiz] *adj* birmano; *s* (*pl:* **-mese**) birmano
burn [bʌrn] *s* quemadura; (Scottish) arroyo, riachuelo; (*pret & pp:* **burned** o **burnt**) *va* quemar; incendiar; inflamar (*encender; irritar*); cocer (*ladrillos*); calcinar (*minerales calcáreos*); vidriar (*la loza*); soldar o fundir (*el plomo*); (chem.) oxidar; (surg.) cauterizar; quemar (*el carbón del motor de combustión interna; el combustible para producir calor*); practicar quemando; funcionar con, p.ej., **this motor burns gasoline** este motor funciona con gasolina; **to burn out** quemar (*un cojinete, fusible, motor, transformador*); fundir (*una bombilla eléctrica*); **to burn together** reunir por fusión; **to burn up** consumir; (slang) llenar de indignación; *vn* quemarse; arder (*el fuego, el combustible*); asarse (*sentir mucho calor*); inflamarse (*encenderse; irritarse*); arder de o en deseos; (coll.) quemarse (*estar uno muy cerca de hallar lo que busca*); estar encendido, p.ej., **the light is burning in my room** la luz está encendida en mi cuarto; **to burn out** quemarse (*un fusible*); fundirse (*una bombilla eléctrica*); apagarse (*el fuego, la luz*); **to burn to death** morir quemado; **to burn to** + *inf* arder por + *inf*; **to burn with** arder de o en (*deseos, celos, etc.*); **to burn within** requemarse
burner [ˈbʌrnər] *s* quemador (*persona o aparato*); mechero
burnet [ˈbʌrnɪt] *s* (bot.) sanguisorba
Burnett salmon [ˈbʌrnɪt] *s* (ichth.) barramunda
burning [ˈbʌrnɪŋ] *s* quemadura; cocción; soldadura (*de plomo*); *adj* quemador; ardiente; (fig.) ardiente; **to be burning hot** (coll.) estar que quema; (coll.) hacer mucho calor
burning glass *s* espejo ustorio
burning question *s* cuestión batallona, cuestión palpitante
burning shame *s* vergüenza enorme
burnish [ˈbʌrnɪʃ] *s* bruñido; *va* bruñir; *vn* bruñirse
burnisher [ˈbʌrnɪʃər] *s* bruñidor

burnoose o **burnous** [bʌrˈnus] o [ˈbʌrnus] *s* albornoz
burnsides [ˈbʌrnˌsaɪdz] *spl* patillas
burnt [bʌrnt] *pret & pp de* **burn**
burnt almond *s* almendra dulce tostada
burnt offering *s* holocausto
burnt sienna *s* siena tostado
burnt umber *s* tierra de sombra quemada
bur oak [bʌr] *s* (bot.) roble macrocarpo
burr [bʌr] *s* erizo (*p.ej., de la castaña*); planta que tiene erizos; persona o cosa muy pegadiza; rebaba (*en el borde de un corte*); fresa (*de dentista*); sonido bronco de la erre; pronunciación bronca y gutural; zumbido; *va* quitar los erizos a; quitar las rebabas a; *vn* sonar la erre con sonido bronco; hablar con pronunciación bronca y gutural; zumbar
burrow [ˈbʌro] *s* madriguera; conejera; refugio subterráneo; *va* socavar; hacer madrigueras en; *vn* amadrigarse; esconderse; buscar, hacer pesquisas
bursa [ˈbʌrsə] *s* (*pl:* **-sas** o **-sae** [si]) (anat.) bolsa
bursar [ˈbʌrsər] *s* tesorero universitario
bursary [ˈbʌrsərɪ] *s* (*pl:* **-ries**) tesorería universitaria
bursitis [bərˈsaɪtɪs] *s* (path.) bursitis
burst [bʌrst] *s* reventón; explosión; ráfaga (*de metralla*); salida brusca, arranque, llamarada; (*pret & pp:* **burst**) *va* reventar; quebrar; *vn* reventar, reventarse; entrar o salir repentina o violentamente; arrojarse, precipitarse; partirse (*el corazón*); **to burst into** irrumpir en (*p.ej., una habitación*); desatarse en (*amenazas, improperios, etc.*); prorrumpir en, deshacerse en (*lágrimas*); **to burst out crying** romper a llorar; **to burst out laughing** echarse a reír; **to burst with laughter** reventar de risa
bursted [ˈbʌrstɪd] *adj* (dial.) reventado
bursted bubble *s* burbuja deshecha, proyecto desbaratado
burstwort [ˈbʌrstˌwʌrt] *s* (bot.) milgranos, quebrantapiedras
burthen [ˈbʌrðən] *s* (archaic) var. de **burden**
bury [ˈbɛrɪ] (*pret & pp:* **-ied**) *va* enterrar; (fig.) enterrar (*esconder; relegar al olvido; sobrevivir*); **to be buried in thought** estar absorto en meditación; **to bury the hatchet** envainar la espada, hacer la paz, echar pelillos a la mar
burying beetle *s* (ent.) enterrador, escarabajo sepulturero
burying ground *s* cementerio
bus. abr. de **business** y **bushel**
bus [bʌs] *s* (*pl:* **busses** o **buses**) ómnibus, autobús; autocar (*para servicio de carreteras*)
bus bar *s* (elec.) barra colectora
bus boy *s* ayudante de camarero
busby [ˈbʌzbɪ] *s* (*pl:* **-bies**) gorra de húsar
bush. abr. de **bushel**
bush [bʊʃ] *s* arbusto; matorral, monte; (mach.) buje, tejuelo, forro de metal; **to beat around the bush** andarse en chiquitas, andar con rodeos; *va* poblar de arbustos; igualar (*el terreno*) arrastrando matas; proteger con matas; poner buje o tejuelo a; *vn* crecer espeso
bushel [ˈbʊʃəl] *s* medida de capacidad para áridos, que equivale a 35,23 litros en los EE.UU. y 36,35 litros en Inglaterra; (*pret & pp:* **-eled** o **-elled; ger:** **-eling** o **-elling**) *va* reparar o modificar (*los vestidos*)
bushhammer [ˈbʊʃˌhæmər] *s* escoda
bushing [ˈbʊʃɪŋ] *s* (mach.) buje, tejuelo, forro de metal; (elec.) atravesador, pasatapas (*de un transformador*)
bushman [ˈbʊʃmən] *s* (*pl:* **-men**) montaraz, campesino; colonizador de la floresta australiana; (*cap.*) *s* bosquimán o bosquimano (*salvaje nómada sudafricano*)
bushmaster [ˈbʊʃˌmæstər] o [ˈbʊʃˌmɑstər] *s* (zool.) mapanare
bushranger [ˈbʊʃˌrendʒər] *s* montaraz; bandido australiano
bushwhacker [ˈbʊʃˌhwækər] *s* montaraz; guerrillero; guadaña para segar el arbusto, la zarza, etc.
bushy [ˈbʊʃɪ] *adj* (*comp:* **-ier;** *super:* **-iest**) espeso; peludo, lanudo; matoso; lleno de arbustos
busily [ˈbɪzɪlɪ] *adv* atareadamente, diligentemente
business [ˈbɪznɪs] *s* negocio, negocios, comercio; ocupación, empleo; cuestión, asunto; empresa; (theat.) acción; **going out of business** saldos por cambio de negocio (o por traslado); **on business** por negocios; de negocios; **to be in business** estar establecido; **to have no business** + *ger* no tener derecho a + *inf;* **to make it one's business to** + *inf* proponerse + *inf;* **to mean business** (coll.) actuar en serio, hablar en serio; **to mind one's own business** ocuparse en lo que le toca a uno, no meterse donde no le llaman a uno; **to send about one's business** echar, enviar o mandar a paseo; *adj* de negocios, comercial
business college *s* escuela de comercio
business connections *spl* relaciones comerciales
business cycle *s* ciclo comercial
business deal *s* trato comercial
business district *s* barrio comercial
business expert *s* perito mercantil
business house *s* casa de comercio, establecimiento mercantil
businesslike [ˈbɪznɪsˌlaɪk] *adj* metódico, práctico, serio, eficaz
businessman [ˈbɪznɪsˌmæn] *s* (*pl:* **-men**) hombre de negocios, comerciante
business reply card [ˈbɪznɪsrɪˈplaɪ] *s* tarjeta de respuesta comercial
business suit *s* traje civil, traje de calle
business trip *s* viaje de negocios
businesswoman [ˈbɪznɪsˌwʊmən] *s* (*pl:* **-women**) mujer de negocios
busk [bʌsk] *s* ballena (*de metal u otro material*); (dial.) corsé
buskin [ˈbʌskɪn] *s* borceguí; coturno; (fig.) drama trágico
buskined [ˈbʌskɪnd] *adj* coturnado; trágico
busman [ˈbʌsmən] *s* (*pl:* **-men**) conductor de autobús
busman's holiday *s* día de fiesta, pasado trabajando en trabajo igual al de todos los días
buss [bʌs] *s* (coll.) beso, beso sonado; *va* (coll.) besar, besar con resonancia; *vn* (coll.) dar besos; (coll.) darse besos
bust [bʌst] *s* busto; pecho de mujer; (slang) reventón; (slang) fracaso; (slang) borrachera, parranda; *va* (slang) hacer quebrar, arruinar; (slang) pegar, golpear; *vn* (slang) reventar; (slang) fracasar
bustard [ˈbʌstərd] *s* (orn.) avutarda (*Otis tarda*); (orn.) sisón (*Otis tetrax*)
buster [ˈbʌstər] *s* (slang) cosa muy grande, cosa extraordinaria; (coll.) muchachito
bustle [ˈbʌsəl] *s* alboroto, bullicio; polisón (*para abultar la falda por detrás*); *va* apresurar, impeler al trabajo; *vn* apresurarse ruidosamente
bustle pipe *s* portaviento
bustler [ˈbʌslər] *s* bullebulle
busy [ˈbɪzɪ] *adj* (*comp:* **-ier;** *super:* **-iest**) ocupado; de mucha actividad; bullicioso; entremetido, intruso; (*pret & pp:* **-ied**) *va* ocupar; **to busy oneself with** atarearse con o en
busybody [ˈbɪzɪˌbɑdɪ] *s* (*pl:* **-ies**) buscavidas, entremetido, metemuertos
busy signal *s* (telp.) zumbido de ocupación, señal de ocupado
but [bʌt] *s* pero, objeción; *adv* sólo, solamente; *prep* excepto, menos; *conj* pero, mas; sino, p.ej., **nobody knows it but John** nadie lo sabe sino Juan; sino que, p.ej., **he does not speak Spanish but he reads it very well** no habla español sino que lo lee muy bien; que no, p.ej., **she is not so tired but she can keep on talking** no está tan cansada que no pueda seguir hablando; **all but** casi; **cannot but** + *inf* no poder menos de + *inf*, no poder dejar de + *inf;* **nothing . . . but** no . . . más que; **the last but one** el penúltimo; **but for** a no ser por; **but little** muy poco
butadiene [ˌbjutəˈdaɪin] o [ˌbjutədaɪˈin] *s* (chem.) butadieno
butane [ˈbjuten] o [bjuˈten] *s* (chem.) butano
butcher [ˈbʊtʃər] *s* carnicero; (fig.) carnicero (*hombre cruel y sanguinario*); *va* matar (*reses para el consumo*); dar muerte a; chapucear; *vn* ser carnicero, matar el ganado; hacer una carnicería

butcher bird *s* (orn.) alcaudón, verdugo, pájaro verdugo, desollador
butcher knife *s* cuchilla de carnicero
butcher's-broom ['butʃərz'brum] o ['butʃərz'brʊm] *s* (bot.) brusco
butcher shop *s* carnicería (*tienda*)
butchery ['butʃərɪ] *s* (*pl:* **-ies**) carnicería; oficio de carnicero; matadero; (fig.) carnicería
butene ['bjutin] *s* (chem.) buteno
butler ['bʌtlər] *s* despensero, mayordomo
butler's pantry *s* despensa (*entre la cocina y el comedor*)
butomaceous [,bjuto'meʃəs] *adj* (bot.) butomáceo
butt [bʌt] *s* culata (*de un arma de fuego*); mocho (*de un instrumento*); tocón (*de un árbol cortado*); punta o colilla (*de cigarro*); cabezada (*golpe*); bisagra; (mach.) cabeza de biela; blanco; hazmerreír; pipa (*tonel; medida de capacidad para vinos*); **the butts** sitio para tirar al blanco; *va* topar; dar cabezadas a; acornear; apoyar; (mach.) juntar a tope; *vn* dar cabezadas; **to butt against** terminar en, confinar con; **to butt in** (slang) entremeterse; **to butt on** o **upon** terminar en, confinar con
butte [bjut] *s* terromontero
butter ['bʌtər] *s* mantequilla; **smooth as butter** como manteca; *va* untar con mantequilla, pringar con mantequilla; (coll.) adular, lisonjear
buttercup ['bʌtər,kʌp] *s* (bot.) ranúnculo; (bot.) botón de oro, hierba belida; (bot.) hierba velluda
butter dish *s* mantequera, mantequillera
butterfat ['bʌtər,fæt] *s* materia grasa de la leche
butterfingers ['bʌtər,fɪŋgərz] *s* (coll.) persona con dedos de mantequilla; (coll.) descuidado, desmañado
butterfish ['bʌtər,fɪʃ] *s* (ichth.) cagavino; (ichth.) blenio
butterfly ['bʌtər,flaɪ] *s* (*pl:* **-flies**) (ent. & fig.) mariposa
butterfly damper *s* mariposa reguladora de tiro
butterfly fish *s* (ichth.) baboso, budión; (ichth.) mariposa
butterfly valve *s* válvula de mariposa
butterfly weed *s* (bot.) seda vegetal, pelo de gato, plumerillo
butterine ['bʌtərin] o ['bʌtərɪn] *s* mantequilla artificial
butteris ['bʌtərɪs] *s* pujavante
butter knife *s* cuchillo mantequillero
buttermilk ['bʌtər,mɪlk] *s* leche de manteca
butternut ['bʌtər,nʌt] *s* (bot.) nogal ceniciento, nogal de Cuba; nuez de Cuba
butter sauce *s* mantequilla fundida
butterscotch ['bʌtər,skɑtʃ] *s* dulce de azúcar terciado con mantequilla
butter spreader *s* var. de **butter knife**
buttery ['bʌtərɪ] *adj* mantecoso; ['bʌtərɪ] o ['bʌtrɪ] *s* (*pl:* **-ies**) despensa
butt joint *s* junta de tope, junta de cubrejunta
buttocks ['bʌtəks] *spl* nalgas
button ['bʌtən] *s* botón; **buttons** *ssg* (coll.) botones (*mozo de hotel*); *va* abotonar; *vn* abotonarse
buttonhole ['bʌtən,hol] *s* ojal; *va* abrir ojales en; coser a puntadas de ojal; obligar a escuchar, detener con conversación
buttonhole stitch *s* puntada de ojal
buttonhook ['bʌtən,huk] *s* abotonador, abrochador
buttonmold ['bʌtən,mold] *s* hormilla
buttonwood ['bʌtən,wʊd] *s* (bot.) plátano de occidente; (bot.) botoncillo (*Conocarpus*)
buttress ['bʌtrɪs] *s* (arch.) contrafuerte; apoyo, refuerzo, sostén; *va* reforzar con contrafuerte, poner contrafuerte a; apoyar, reforzar, sostener
butt weld *s* soldadura a tope
butyl ['bjutɪl] *s* (chem.) butilo
butylene ['bjutɪlin] *s* (chem.) butileno
butyric [bju'tɪrɪk] *adj* (chem.) butírico
butyric acid *s* (chem.) ácido butírico
butyrin ['bjutɪrɪn] *s* (chem.) butirina
butyrometer [,bjutɪ'rɑmɪtər] *s* butirómetro
butyrous ['bjutɪrəs] *adj* butiroso
buxaceous [bʌks'eʃəs] *adj* (bot.) buxáceo
buxom ['bʌksəm] *adj* rollizo, frescachón
buy [baɪ] *s* (coll.) compra; (*pret & pp:* **bought**) *va* comprar; **to buy back** recomprar; **to buy off** comprar (*sobornar*); libertar pagando; **to buy out** comprar la parte de (*un socio*); **to buy up** acaparar
buyer ['baɪər] *s* comprador
buyer's market *s* mercado del comprador
buzz [bʌz] *s* zumbido; *va* expresar zumbando; (coll.) llamar por teléfono; (aer.) saludar (*a una persona*) volando muy bajo; *vn* zumbar; **to buzz about** cazcalear, andar muy ocupado; **to buzz off** cortar una conversación telefónica
buzzard ['bʌzərd] *s* (orn.) alfaneque, busardo, águila ratonera; (orn.) zopilote de montaña
buzz bomb *s* (mil.) bomba volante
buzzer ['bʌzər] *s* zumbador; (elec.) zumbador
buzz saw *s* sierra circular
B.V. abr. de **Beata Virgo** (Lat.) **Blessed Virgin**
B.W.I. abr. de **British West Indies**
bx. abr. de **box** o **boxes**
bxs. abr. de **boxes**
by [baɪ] *adv* cerca; a solas; más allá; aparte, a un lado; **by and by** luego, pronto, de aquí a poco; **by and large** en todo respecto, de un modo general; *prep* por; por o de (*para denotar el agente con la voz pasiva*); de (*día, noche*); (math.) por (*para indicar multiplicación*); para, p.ej., **by two o'clock** para las dos; cerca de, junto a, al lado de; **by far** con mucho; **by the by** a propósito; **by the way** de paso; a propósito
by-and-by ['baɪənd'baɪ] *s* porvenir
bye [baɪ] *s* (sport) jugador sin contrario en los juegos en que los jugadores han sido escogidos por parejas; (cricket) carrera hecha sin haber golpeado la pelota; (golf) hoyo u hoyos que se quedan sin ser jugados al fin de la partida; **by the bye** a propósito
bye-bye ['baɪ'baɪ] *interj* (coll.) ¡adiosito!; ¡ro ro! (*para arrullar a los niños*)
by-election ['baɪɪ,lɛkʃən] *s* (Brit.) elección especial para cubrir una vacante
Byelorussian [,bɛlə'rʌʃən] *adj & s* bielorruso
bygone ['baɪ,gɔn] o ['baɪ,gɑn] *adj* pasado; *s* pasado; **let bygones be bygones** olvidemos lo pasado
bylaw ['baɪ,lɔ] *s* estatuto; reglamento, ley o regla secundaria
by-line ['baɪ,laɪn] *s* (U.S.A.) línea al comienzo de un artículo de periódico o revista dando el nombre del autor
by-name ['baɪ,nem] *s* sobrenombre; apodo
by-pass ['baɪ,pæs] o ['baɪ,pɑs] *s* desviación; (mach.) tubo de paso; (elec.) derivación; *va* desviar
by-pass condenser *s* (elec.) condensador de paso o derivación
by-path ['baɪ,pæθ] o ['baɪ,pɑθ] *s* trocha, senda
by-play ['baɪ,ple] *s* (theat.) acción aparte
by-product ['baɪ,prɑdəkt] *s* subproducto, derivado
byre [baɪr] *s* establo de vacas
by-road ['baɪ,rod] *s* camino apartado
Byronic [baɪ'rɑnɪk] *adj* byroniano
byssus ['bɪsəs] *s* (*pl:* **-suses** o **-si** [saɪ]) (hist. & zool.) biso
bystander ['baɪ,stændər] *s* circunstante, espectador
by-street ['baɪ,strit] *s* callejuela
byway ['baɪ,we] *s* camino apartado, camino poco frecuentado
byword ['baɪ,wʌrd] *s* oprobio, objeto de oprobio; refrán, proverbio; apodo
Byzantine ['bɪzəntin] o [bɪ'zæntin] *adj & s* bizantino
Byzantine Empire *s* Imperio Bizantino
Byzantium [bɪ'zænʃɪəm] o [bɪ'zæntɪəm] *s* Bizancio

C

C, c [si] *s* (*pl:* **C's, c's** [siz]) tercera letra del alfabeto inglés

c. abr. de **cent** o **cents**

C. abr. de **centigrade**

C.A. abr. de **Central America**

cab [kæb] *s* taxi; cabriolé, coche de plaza; berlina; casilla (*de locomotora o camión*)

cabal [kə'bæl] *s* cábala; (*pret & pp:* **-balled;** *ger:* **-balling**) *va & vn* tramar, maquinar

cabala ['kæbələ] o [kə'bɑlə] *s* cábala

cabalistic [,kæbə'lɪstɪk] *adj* cabalístico

cabaret [,kæbə're] o ['kæbəre] *s* cabaret

cabbage ['kæbɪdʒ] *s* (bot.) col; coles (*cabeza y hojas que se comen*); *va* sisar; *vn* sisar; repollar

cabbage palm *s* (bot.) palma real, col palma; (bot.) palmito de tierra firme

cabby ['kæbɪ] *s* (*pl:* **-bies**) (coll.) var. de **cabman**

cab driver *s* var. de **cabman**

cabin ['kæbɪn] *s* cabaña, choza; (naut.) camarote; (aer.) cabina; *va* apretar, encerrar; *vn* vivir en cabaña o choza

cabin boy *s* (naut.) mozo de cámara

cabin class *s* (naut.) clase de cámara

cabinet ['kæbɪnɪt] *s* escaparate, vitrina; armario; caja, estuche; caja o mueble (*p.ej., de un aparato de radio*); gabinete (*de un gobierno; colección de objetos; pieza retirada*); *adj* ministerial; digno de figurar en gabinete; secreto, reservado

cabinetmaker ['kæbɪnɪt,mekər] *s* ebanista

cabinetwork ['kæbɪnɪt,wʌrk] *s* ebanistería

cable ['kebəl] *s* cable; cable eléctrico; cableado eléctrico (*de un coche, radio, televisor, etc.*); cablegrama; *adj* cablegráfico; *va* cablegrafiar; atar o amarrar con cable; *vn* cablegrafiar

cable address *s* dirección cablegráfica

cable car *s* carro arrastrado por cable; tranvía de cable

cable chain *s* cadena de cable

cablegram ['kebəlgræm] *s* cablegrama

cable-laid ['kebəl,led] *adj* (naut.) acalabrotado

cable railroad *s* andarivel

cable ship *s* buque cablero

cable's length *s* cable (*medida*)

cable vault *s* (elec.) caja de empalme de cables

cableway ['kebəl,we] *s* cable transportador, cablecarril

cabman ['kæbmən] *s* (*pl:* **-men**) cochero; taxista; conductor de automóvil de alquiler

caboodle [kə'budəl] *s* (slang) conjunto, grupo, lío

caboose [kə'bus] *s* (rail.) carro o furgón de cola; (naut.) cocina (*en el puente del buque*)

cabriolet [,kæbrɪo'le] *s* cabriolé (*carruaje y automóvil*)

cab signal *s* (rail.) señal en la cabina del maquinista que repite la indicación de la señal fija externa

cabstand ['kæb,stænd] *s* punto de coches

cacao [kə'kɑo] o [kə'keo] *s* (*pl:* **-os**) (bot.) cacao (*árbol y semilla*)

cacao butter *s* manteca de cacao

cachalot ['kæʃəlɑt] o ['kæʃəlo] *s* (zool.) cachalote

cache [kæʃ] *s* escondite, escondrijo; víveres escondidos; *va* depositar en un escondrijo; encubrir, ocultar

cachectic [kə'kɛktɪk] o **cachectical** [kə'kɛktɪkəl] *adj* caquéctico

cachepot ['kæʃpɑt] o [kɑʃ'po] *s* vasija de adorno (*para ocultar una maceta tosca*)

cache-sexe [kɑʃ'sɛks] *s* cubresexo

cachet [kæ'ʃe] o ['kæʃe] *s* sello particular; marca de distinción; carácter, originalidad; sello medicinal

cachexia [kə'kɛksɪə] *s* (path.) caquexia

cachinnate ['kækɪnet] *vn* reír a carcajadas

cachinnation [,kækɪ'neʃən] *s* carcajada, risotada

cackle ['kækəl] *s* cacareo; risa aguda y sacudida; cháchara, charla; *vn* cacarear; reírse ásperamente; chacharear, charlar

cacochymia [,kæko'kɪmɪə] *s* (path.) cacoquimia

cacodylate ['kækodɪlet] *s* (chem.) cacodilato

cacodylic [,kæko'dɪlɪk] *adj* (chem.) cacodílico

cacomistle ['kækə,mɪsəl] *s* (zool.) basáride

cacophonous [kə'kɑfənəs] *adj* cacofónico

cacophony [kə'kɑfənɪ] *s* (*pl:* **-nies**) cacofonía

cactaceous [kæk'teʃəs] *adj* (bot.) cactáceo

cactus ['kæktəs] *s* (*pl:* **-tuses** o **-ti** [taɪ]) (bot.) cacto

cad [kæd] *s* canalla, sinvergüenza, persona malcriada

cadastral [kə'dæstrəl] *adj* catastral

cadastre [kə'dæstər] *s* catastro

cadaver [kə'dævər] *s* cadáver

cadaverous [kə'dævərəs] *adj* cadavérico

caddie ['kædɪ] *s* (golf) muchacho que lleva los instrumentos de juego; (*pret & pp:* **-died;** *ger:* **-dying**) *vn* servir de muchacho de golf

caddis ['kædɪs] *s* jerguilla de lana; cinta de seda y estambre; (ent.) gusano de la paja

caddis fly *s* (ent.) frígano

caddish ['kædɪʃ] *adj* malcriado

caddis worm *s* (ent.) gusano de la paja

caddy ['kædɪ] *s* (*pl:* **-dies**) cajita, botecito o lata para té; (golf) muchacho que lleva los instrumentos de juego; (*pret & pp:* **-died;** *ger:* **-dying**) *vn* servir de muchacho de golf

cade [ked] *adj* manso; mimado; *s* cordero manso; animal mimado; (bot.) enebro de la miera

cadence ['kedəns] *s* cadencia; (mus.) cadencia; (mil.) cadencia del paso

cadenza [kə'dɛnzə] o [kə'dɛntsə] *s* (mus.) cadencia

cadet [kə'dɛt] *s* cadete; hijo menor, hermano menor; (slang) alcahuete

cadetship [kə'dɛtʃɪp] *s* grado o puesto de cadete

cadge [kædʒ] *va* (coll.) obtener mendigando; *vn* (coll.) mendigar, gorronear, vivir de gorra; (dial.) ir vendiendo de casa en casa

cadi ['kɑdɪ] o ['kedɪ] *s* (*pl:* **-dis**) cadí

Cadmean [kæd'miən] *adj* cadmeo

cadmium ['kædmɪəm] *s* (chem.) cadmio

cadmium cell *s* (elec.) elemento de cadmio

Cadmus ['kædməs] *s* (myth.) Cadmo

cadre ['kɑdər] *s* armazón; ['kædrɪ] *s* (mil.) cuadro

caduceus [kə'djusɪəs] o [kə'dusɪəs] *s* (*pl:* **-cei** [sɪaɪ]) caduceo

caducity [kə'djusɪtɪ] o [kə'dusɪtɪ] *s* caducidad; (law) caducidad

caducous [kə'djukəs] o [kə'dukəs] *adj* caduco; (bot. & law) caduco

caecal ['sikəl] *adj* cecal

caecum ['sikəm] *s* (*pl:* **-ca** [kə]) (anat.) intestino ciego

Caedmon ['kædmən] *s* Cedmón

Caesar ['sizər] *s* César

Caesarea [,sɛsə'riə] o [,sɛzə'riə] *s* Cesarea

Caesarean [sɪ'zɛrɪən] *adj* cesáreo (*imperial*); cesariano (*perteneciente a César*); (surg.) cesáreo; *s* (surg.) operación cesárea

Caesarean operation *s* (surg.) operación cesárea

Caesarean section *s* (surg.) sección cesárea

Caesarian [sɪ'zɛrɪən] *adj & s* var. de **Caesarean**

caesarism ['sizərɪzəm] *s* cesarismo

caesium ['sizɪəm] *s* var. de **cesium**

caesura [sɪ'ʒurə] o [sɪ'zjurə] *s* (*pl:* **-ras** o **-rae** [ri]) (pros.) cesura

café [kæ'fe] *s* café, restaurante; bar; cabaret

café au lait [kæ'fe o 'le] *s* (Fr.) café con leche; color de café con leche
café society *s* gente alegre que frecuenta los cabarets de moda
cafeteria [,kæfə'tɪrɪə] *s* cafetería, restaurante en que uno mismo se sirve
caffein o **caffeine** ['kæfin] o ['kæfɪɪn] *s* (pharm.) cafeína
caftan ['kæftən] *s* cafetán o caftán
cage [kedʒ] *s* jaula; (elec., mach. & min.) jaula; cárcel; *va* enjaular
cageling ['kedʒlɪŋ] *s* pájaro enjaulado
cagey ['kedʒɪ] *adj* (*comp:* **cagier**; *super:* **cagiest**) (coll.) zorro, astuto
cahoots [kə'huts] *s* (slang) acuerdo, consorcio; **in cahoots** (slang) de acuerdo, asociados; **to go cahoots** (slang) entrar por partes iguales
Caiaphas ['keəfəs] o ['kaɪəfəs] *s* (Bib.) Caifás
caiman ['kemən] *s* (*pl:* **-mans**) (zool.) caimán
Cain [ken] *s* (Bib.) Caín; **to raise Cain** (slang) armar bochinche
caïque [kɑ'ik] *s* (naut.) caique
cairn [kɛrn] *s* montón de piedras que sirve de mojón, lápida, etc.
Cairo ['kaɪro] *s* El Cairo
caisson ['kesən] o ['kesɑn] *s* (mil.) cajón; (eng.) cajón hidráulico, cajón de aire comprimido; (naut.) cajón de suspensión; (arch.) artesón, casetón
caisson disease *s* (path.) enfermedad de los cajones de aire comprimido, enfermedad de los buzos
caitiff ['ketɪf] *adj & s* belitre, pícaro, cobarde
cajole [kə'dʒol] *va* halagar, camelar; **to cajole a person into something** conseguir por medio de halagos que una persona haga una cosa; **to cajole a person out of something** conseguir una cosa de una persona por medio de halagos
cajolery [kə'dʒolərɪ] *s* (*pl:* **-ies**) halago, lisonja, camelo
cake [kek] *s* bollo, tortita, pastelillo; bizcocho; fritada (*p.ej., de pescado*); pan o pastilla (*de jabón, cera, etc.*); **to take the cake** (slang) ganar el premio; (slang) llevarse la mapa, ser el colmo; *vn* apelmazarse, aterronarse
cakewalk ['kek,wɔk] *s* cake-walk; *vn* bailar el cake-walk
Cal. abr. de **California**
calaba ['kæləbə] *s* (bot.) calambuco, árbol de María
calabash ['kæləbæʃ] *s* (bot.) calabacera; calabaza (*fruto; botella o escudilla*); (mus.) calabazo
calabash tree *s* (bot.) calabacero, árbol de las calabazas, güira
calaboose ['kæləbus] *s* (coll.) calabozo
Calabrian [kə'lebrɪən] *adj & s* calabrés
calabur tree ['kæləbʌr] *s* (bot.) memiso, capulín
caladium [kə'ledɪəm] *s* (bot.) caladio, papagayo
calamanco [,kælə'mæŋko] *s* calamaco
calambac ['kæləmbæk] *s* calambac (*madera*)
calamine ['kæləmaɪn] o ['kæləmɪn] *s* (mineral.) calamina
calamint ['kæləmɪnt] *s* (bot.) calamento, calaminta
calamistrum [,kælə'mɪstrəm] *s* (*pl:* **-tra** [trə]) (zool.) calamistro
calamitous [kə'læmɪtəs] *adj* calamitoso
calamity [kə'læmɪtɪ] *s* (*pl:* **-ties**) calamidad
calamus ['kæləməs] *s* (*pl:* **-mi** [maɪ]) (bot.) ácoro, cálamo; (pharm.) cálamo aromático
calander [kə'lændər] *s* (orn.) calandria
calash [kə'læʃ] *s* carretela (*carruaje*); capota plegable; capota de señora (*de los siglos diez y ocho y diez y nueve*)
calcareous [kæl'kɛrɪəs] *adj* calcáreo; cálcico
calceolaria [,kælsɪə'lɛrɪə] *s* (bot.) calceolaria
Calchas ['kælkəs] *s* (myth.) Calcas
calcic ['kælsɪk] *adj* (chem.) cálcico
calciferous [kæl'sɪfərəs] *adj* calcífero
calcification [,kælsɪfɪ'keʃən] *s* calcificación
calcify ['kælsɪfaɪ] (*pret & pp:* **-fied**) *va* calcificar; *vn* calcificarse
calcimeter [kæl'sɪmɪtər] *s* calcímetro
calcimine ['kælsɪmaɪn] o ['kælsɪmɪn] *s* lechada; *va* lechar
calcination [,kælsɪ'neʃən] *s* calcinación
calcine ['kælsaɪn] *va* calcinar; *vn* calcinarse
calcite ['kælsaɪt] *s* (mineral.) calcita
calcium ['kælsɪəm] *s* (chem.) calcio
calcium carbide *s* (chem.) carburo de calcio
calcium carbonate *s* (chem.) carbonato de calcio
calcium chloride *s* (chem.) cloruro de calcio
calcium cyanamide *s* (chem.) cianamida de calcio
calcium hydroxide *s* (chem.) hidróxido de calcio
calcium light *s* luz de calcio
calcium phosphate *s* (chem.) fosfato cálcico
calcium sulfate *s* (chem.) sulfato de calcio
calcspar ['kælk,spɑr] *s* (mineral.) espato calizo
calculable ['kælkjələbəl] *adj* calculable
calculate ['kælkjəlet] *va* calcular; **calculated to** + *inf* (coll.) aprestado para + *inf*; *vn* calcular; **to calculate on** contar con
calculating ['kælkjə,letɪŋ] *adj* calculador; de calcular; astuto; intrigante
calculating machine *s* máquina de calcular, calculadora
calculation [,kælkjə'leʃən] *s* cálculo
calculative ['kælkjə,letɪv] *adj* calculatorio
calculator ['kælkjə,letər] *s* calculador; calculadora (*máquina*)
calculous ['kælkjələs] *adj* (path.) calculoso
calculus ['kælkjələs] *s* (*pl:* **-li** [laɪ] o **-luses**) (math. & path.) cálculo
Calcutta [kæl'kʌtə] *s* Calcuta
caldron ['kɔldrən] *s* calderón
Caledonian [,kælɪ'donɪən] *adj & s* caledonio
calendar ['kæləndər] *s* calendario; calendario escolar; programa; orden *m* del día; (law) lista de pleitos; *va* poner o entrar en el calendario; poner en la lista, reducir a lista
calendar day *s* día civil
calendar month *s* mes del año
calendar year *s* año civil
calender ['kæləndər] *s* calandria (*para dar lustre al papel*); *vn* calandrar (*el papel*)
calends ['kælɪndz] *spl* calendas (*primer día de cada mes*)
calendula [kə'lɛndjələ] o [kə'lɛndjʊlə] *s* (bot.) caléndula
calenture ['kæləntʃər] *s* (path.) calentura
calf [kæf] o [kɑf] *s* (*pl:* **calves**) ternero o ternera; cría del rinoceronete y otros animales; piel de ternero; cuero hecho de piel de ternero; pantorrilla (*de la pierna*); (coll.) bobo, mentecato; **to kill the fatted calf** preparar una fiesta para dar la bienvenida
calf love *s* (coll.) var. de **puppy love**
calfskin ['kæf,skɪn] o ['kɑf,skɪn] *s* piel de ternero; cuero hecho de piel de ternero
caliber ['kælɪbər] *s* calibre; (fig.) calaña (*de una persona*); (fig.) calibre (*de una cosa*)
calibrate ['kælɪbret] *va* calibrar
calibration [,kælɪ'breʃən] *s* calibración
calicle ['kælɪkəl] *s* (anat. & zool.) calículo
calico ['kælɪko] *s* (*pl:* **-coes** o **-cos**) calicó, indiana; *adj* hecho de calicó; que tiene manchas de otro color
calicoback ['kælɪko,bæk] *s* (ent.) chinche de jardín
Calif. abr. de **California**
calif ['kelɪf] o ['kælɪf] *s* var. de **caliph**
California condor [,kælɪ'fɔrnɪə] *s* (orn.) cóndor de California
Californian [,kælɪ'fɔrnɪən] *adj & s* californiano
California poppy *s* (bot.) amapola de California, copa de oro
californium [,kælɪ'fɔrnɪəm] *s* (chem.) californio
caliper compass ['kælɪpər] *s* compás de calibres
caliper gauge *s* calibrador fijo
calipers ['kælɪpərz] *spl* calibrador
caliper square *s* pie de rey
caliph ['kelɪf] o ['kælɪf] *s* califa
caliphate ['kælɪfet] *s* califato
calisaya bark [,kælɪ'sejə] *s* (pharm.) calisaya
calisthenic [,kælɪs'θɛnɪk] *adj* calisténico; **calisthenics** *spl* calistenia
calk [kɔk] *s* ramplón (*para las herraduras del caballo*); crampón (*para los zapatos del hombre*); callo (*de herradura*); *va* poner ramplones en; poner crampones en; calafatear

calker [ˈkɔkər] *s* calafate o calafateador
calking [ˈkɔkɪŋ] *s* calafateo
call [kɔl] *s* llamada; grito; invitación; visita, parada; escala (*de buque o avión*); citación (*ante un juez*); reclamo (*del ave*); balitadera (*del gamo*); (hunt.) chilla; (mil.) llamada; derecho; obligación; (coll.) demanda (*p.ej., de fondos*); **on call** disponible; (com.) a solicitud, al pedir; **within call** al alcance de la voz ‖ *va* llamar; señalar; invitar; despertar; citar; mandar; considerar, juzgar; apreciar, estimar; llamar por teléfono; convocar (*una sesión, huelga, etc.*); (sport) dar por terminada (*la partida*); (poker) exigir (*a un jugador*) la exposición de su mano; **to call aside** llamar aparte; **to call back** hacer volver; volver a llamar por teléfono; **to call down** pedir al cielo (*p.ej., favores divinos*); (slang) regañar; **to call forth** sacar (*p.ej., una respuesta*); **to call in** hacer entrar; recoger, retirar; **to call off** aplazar, dar por terminado; disuadir; **to call out** llamar (*a uno*) a que salga; desafiar; **to call together** convocar, reunir; **to call up** llamar por teléfono; recordar ‖ *vn* llamar, gritar; hacer una visita, pararse un rato; (naut.) hacer escala; **to call at** pasar por la casa o la oficina de; **to call for** ir o venir por; exigir; rezar, p.ej., **the newspaper calls for rain** el periódico reza agua; **to call on** o **upon** acudir a (*en busca de auxilio*); visitar; **to call out** llamar a gritos, gritar; **to go calling** ir de visitas
calla [ˈkælə] *s* (bot.) cala (*Zantedeschia aethiopica y Calla palustris*)
calla lily *s* (bot.) cala (*Zantedeschia aethiopica*)
call bell *s* timbre de llamada
callboy [ˈkɔlˌbɔɪ] *s* botones, mozo de hotel, paje de cámara; (theat.) avisador
call button *s* botón para llamar
caller [ˈkɔlər] *s* llamador; visita
call girl *s* (coll.) chica de cita
calligraphic [ˌkælɪˈgræfɪk] *adj* caligráfico
calligraphy [kəˈlɪgrəfɪ] *s* caligrafía
calling [ˈkɔlɪŋ] *s* invitación, convite; mandamiento; citación (*ante un juez*); vocación, profesión
calling card *s* tarjeta de visita
calliope [kəˈlaɪəpɪ] o [ˈkælɪop] *s* (mus.) órgano de vapor; (*cap.*) [kəˈlaɪəpɪ] *s* (myth.) Calíope
calliopsis [ˌkælɪˈɑpsɪs] *s* (bot.) coreópsida
callipers [ˈkælɪpərz] *spl* var. de **calipers**
callisthenic [ˌkælɪsˈθenɪk] *adj* calisténico; **callisthenics** *spl* calistenia
Callisto [kəˈlɪsto] *s* (myth.) Calisto
call letters *spl* (telg.) indicativo de llamada, letras de identificación
call loan *s* préstamo que debe pagarse a demanda
call money *s* dinero prestado que debe pagarse a demanda
call number *s* número de teléfono; número de clasificación (*de un libro*)
call of the wild *s* ansia de vagar, atracción de la vida silvestre
callose [ˈkælos] *s* (bot. & biochem.) callosa
callosity [kəˈlɑsɪtɪ] *s* (*pl:* **-ties**) callosidad; insensibilidad
callous [ˈkæləs] *adj* calloso; duro, insensible
callow [ˈkælo] *adj* joven e inexperto; desplumado (*sin plumas adecuades para volar*)
call sign *s* var. de **call letters**
call slip *s* papeleta de biblioteca
call to arms *s* (mil.) llamada; **to sound the call to arms** (mil.) tocar o batir llamada
call to the colors *s* (mil.) llamada a filas
callus [ˈkæləs] *s* callo
calm [kɑm] *s* calma; quietud, serenidad; (naut.) calma; **dead calm** calma chicha o muerta; *adj* tranquilo, bonancible; quieto, sereno; *va* calmar; *vn* calmarse; calmar, abonanzar, pacificarse (*el tiempo*)
calmness [ˈkɑmnɪs] *s* calma, tranquilidad
calomel [ˈkæləmɛl] *s* (pharm.) calomel
calomel electrode *s* (physical chem.) electrodo de calomel
caloric [kəˈlɑrɪk] o [kəˈlɔrɪk] *adj* calórico; *s* (old chem.) calórico
caloricity [ˌkæləˈrɪsɪtɪ] *s* (physiol.) caloricidad
calorie [ˈkælərɪ] *s* (phys. & physiol.) caloría; **gram calorie** o **small calorie** caloría gramo o caloría pequeña; **kilogram calorie** o **large calorie** caloría kilogramo o caloría grande
calorific [ˌkæləˈrɪfɪk] *adj* calorífico
calorification [kəˌlɑrɪfɪˈkeʃən] *s* calorificación
calorimeter [ˌkæləˈrɪmɪtər] *s* calorímetro
calorimetric [ˌkælərɪˈmɛtrɪk] o **calorimetrical** [ˌkælərɪˈmɛtrɪkəl] *adj* calorimétrico
calorimetry [ˌkæləˈrɪmɪtrɪ] *s* calorimetría
calory [ˈkælərɪ] *s* (*pl:* **-ries**) var. de **calorie**
calotte [kəˈlɑt] *s* casquete; (eccl.) solideo; (arch.) casquete
caltrop [ˈkæltrəp] *s* (bot. & mil.) abrojo
calumba [kəˈlʌmbə] *s* (pharm.) colombo
calumet [ˈkæljumɛt] *s* pipa larga que fuman los indios norteamericanos en las ceremonias solemnes y sobre todo en los acuerdos de paz
calumniate [kəˈlʌmnɪet] *va* calumniar
calumniator [kəˈlʌmnɪˌetər] *s* calumniador
calumnious [kəˈlʌmnɪəs] *adj* calumnioso
calumny [ˈkæləmnɪ] *s* (*pl:* **-nies**) calumnia
Calvary [ˈkælvərɪ] *s* (Bib.) Calvario; (*l.c.*) *s* (*pl:* **-ries**) calvario (*representación*); humilladero (*en la entrada de un pueblo*)
calve [kæv] o [kɑv] *va & vn* parir (*dícese de la vaca*)
Calvin [ˈkælvɪn] *s* Calvino
Calvinism [ˈkælvɪnɪzəm] *s* calvinismo
Calvinist [ˈkælvɪnɪst] *adj & s* calvinista
Calvinistic [ˌkælvɪˈnɪstɪk] *adj* calvinista
calx [kælks] *s* (*pl:* **calxes** o **calces** [ˈkælsiz]) residuo cenizoso de un metal o mineral calcinado; cal
calycle [ˈkælɪkəl] *s* (bot. & zool.) calículo
calycular [kəˈlɪkjələr] *adj* (bot.) calicular
calyculus [kəˈlɪkjələs] *s* (*pl:* **-li** [laɪ]) (anat. & zool.) calículo
calypso [kəˈlɪpso] *s* (*pl:* **-sos**) calipso (*canto improvisado*); (bot.) calipso; (*cap.*) *s* (myth.) Calipso
calyx [ˈkelɪks] o [ˈkælɪks] *s* (*pl:* **calyxes** o **calyces** [ˈkælɪsiz] o [ˈkelɪsiz]) (anat. & bot.) cáliz
cam [kæm] *s* (mach.) leva
camaraderie [ˌkɑməˈrɑdərɪ] *s* camaradería
camarilla [ˌkæməˈrɪlə] *s* camarilla
camass [ˈkæmæs] *s* (bot.) camasia
camber [ˈkæmbər] *s* comba, combadura; (aut.) inclinación (*de las ruedas*); convexidad (*del camino*); *va* combar, arquear; *vn* combarse, arquearse
cambium [ˈkæmbɪəm] *s* (bot.) cámbium o cambio
Cambodia [kæmˈbodɪə] *s* Camboya
Cambodian [kæmˈbodɪən] *adj & s* camboyano
Cambrian [ˈkæmbrɪən] *adj & s* cambriano o cámbrico; (geol.) cambriano o cámbrico
cambric [ˈkembrɪk] *s* batista
cambric tea *s* bebida hecha de agua caliente, leche y azúcar, y a veces un poquito de té
Cambyses [kæmˈbaɪsiz] *s* Cambises
came [kem] *pret de* **come**
camel [ˈkæməl] *s* (zool.) camello; (naut.) camello (*mecanismo para suspender un buque*)
camel grass *s* (bot.) esquenanto
camellia [kəˈmiljə] *s* (bot.) camelia
camelopard [kəˈmɛləpɑrd] o [ˈkæmələˌpɑrd] *s* (zool.) camello pardal
camel's hair *s* pelo de camello
camel's-hair [ˈkæməlzˌhɛr] *adj* de pelo de camello
camel's-hair brush *s* pincel de pelo de camello
Camembert [ˈkæməmbɛr] *s* camembert (*queso*)
cameo [ˈkæmɪo] *s* (*pl:* **-os**) camafeo
camera [ˈkæmərə] *s* cámara fotográfica; cámara apostólica; (law) sala particular del juez; **in camera** (law) en la sala particular del juez; en secreto
camera lucida [ˈlusɪdə] *s* (opt.) cámara clara o lúcida
cameraman [ˈkæmərəˌmæn] *s* (*pl:* **-men**) (mov.) cámara *m*, camarógrafo
camera obscura [ɑbˈskjurə] *s* (opt.) cámara oscura
camera stand *s* sostén de cámara
Cameroons [ˌkæməˈrunz] *s* Camerón
Cameroun [kɑmˈrun] *s* el Camerón francés
camion [ˈkæmɪən] *s* camión
camisole [ˈkæmɪsol] *s* camiseta de mujer; camisola (*de hombre*); cubrecorsé; camisa de fuerza

camlet ['kæmlɪt] *s* camelote
camomile ['kæməmaɪl] *s* (bot. & pharm.) camomila, manzanilla
Camorra [kə'mɑrə] o [kə'mɔrə] *s* Camorra
camouflage ['kæməflɑʒ] *s* camuflaje; *va* camuflar
camp [kæmp] *s* campamento, campo; **in the same camp** de acuerdo, del mismo partido; **to break camp** (mil.) levantar el campo; *vn* acampar; (coll.) alojarse transitoriamente
campaign [kæm'pen] *s* (mil. & fig.) campaña; *vn* hacer campaña
campaigner [kæm'penər] *s* persona que hace campaña o ha hecho campaña; veterano
campanile [ˌkæmpə'nilɪ] *s* campanario
campanula [kæm'pænjʊlə] *s* (bot.) campánula
campanulaceous [kæmˌpænjʊ'leʃəs] *adj* (bot.) campanuláceo
camp chair *s* silla plegadiza
camper ['kæmpər] *s* acampador
campfire ['kæmpˌfaɪr] *s* hoguera de campamento; reunión de tropas, de niños exploradores, etc., alrededor de una hoguera
camp follower *s* vivandero u otro no combatiente que sigue al ejército
campground ['kæmpˌgraʊnd] *s* campamento
camphor ['kæmfər] *s* alcanfor
camphorate ['kæmfəret] *va* alcanforar
camphorated oil *s* (pharm.) aceite alcanforado
camphor ball *s* bola de alcanfor
camphor tree *s* (bot.) alcanforero, árbol del alcanfor
camp hospital *s* hospital de campaña
campion ['kæmpɪən] *s* (bot.) colleja, cruz de Malta
camp kitchen *s* cocina de campaña
camp meeting *s* campamento de devotos
campstool ['kæmpˌstul] *s* silla ligera de tijera, catrecillo
campus ['kæmpəs] *s* campo, terreno, recinto (*de la universidad*)
camshaft ['kæmˌʃæft] o ['kæmˌʃɑft] *s* (mach.) árbol de levas, eje de levas
Can. abr. de **Canada** y **Canadian**
can [kæn] *s* lata, bote, envase; vasito para beber; (*pret & pp:* **canned**; *ger:* **canning**) *va* enlatar, envasar; (slang) despedir, echar a la calle; (*pret & cond:* **could**) *v aux* poder; saber, p.ej., **he can swim** sabe nadar
Canaan ['kenən] *s* (Bib.) Tierra de Canaán; (fig.) tierra de promisión
Canaanite ['kenənaɪt] *adj & s* (Bib.) cananeo
Canada ['kænədə] *s* el Canadá
Canada balsam *s* (bot.) bálsamo canadiense
Canada goose *s* (orn.) ganso de corbata
Canada thistle *s* (bot.) cardo negro
Canadian [kə'nedɪən] *adj & s* canadiense
canaille [kə'nel] o [kə'naɪ] *s* canalla, gentuza
canal [kə'næl] *s* canal *m*
canal boat *s* bote de canal
canalization [kəˌnælɪ'zeʃən] o [ˌkænəlɪ'zeʃən] *s* canalización
canalize [kə'nælaɪz] o ['kænəlaɪz] *va* canalizar
canal rays *spl* (phys.) rayos canales
Canal Zone *s* Zona del Canal (*Panamá*)
canapé [ˌkænə'pe] o ['kænəpe] *s* canapé (*para excitar el apetito*)
canard [kə'nɑrd] o [kə'nɑr] *s* bola, embuste, noticia falsa
Canarian [kə'nɛrɪən] *adj & s* canario
canary [kə'nɛrɪ] *s* (*pl:* **-ies**) (orn.) canario; color de canario; vino de las islas Canarias; **Canaries** *spl* Canarias
canary bird *s* (orn.) canario
canary grass *s* (bot.) alpiste
Canary Islands *spl* islas Canarias
canary yellow *adj & s* amarillo canario
canasta [kə'næstə] *s* canasta (*juego de naipes*)
can buoy *s* (naut.) boya de tambor
cancan ['kænkæn] *s* cancán
cancel ['kænsəl] *s* supresión, eliminación, canceladura; (*pret & pp:* **-celed** o **-celled**; *ger:* **-celing** o **-celling**) *va* suprimir, eliminar, cancelar; matasellar, obliterar (*sellos de correo*)
canceler ['kænsələr] *s* matasellos
cancellation [ˌkænsə'leʃən] *s* supresión, eliminación, cancelación; obliteración (*inutilización de los sellos de correo; raya o marca de inutilización*)
cancer ['kænsər] *s* (path.) cáncer; (*cap.*) *s* (astr.) Cáncer
cancerous ['kænsərəs] *adj* canceroso
cancroid ['kæŋkrɔɪd] *adj* cancroideo
candelabrum [ˌkændə'lɑbrəm] o [ˌkændə'lebrəm] *s* (*pl:* **-bra** [brə] o **-brums**) *s* candelabro
candescence [kæn'dɛsəns] *s* candencia, incandescencia
candescent [kæn'dɛsənt] *adj* candente, incandescente
candid ['kændɪd] *adj* cándido; justo, imparcial
candidacy ['kændɪdəsɪ] *s* candidatura
candidate ['kændɪdet] o ['kændɪdɪt] *s* candidato; graduando
candidature ['kændɪˌdetʃər] *s* candidatura
candid camera *s* máquina fotográfica de reducidas dimensiones, para poder tomar instantáneas de escenas de la vida diaria, sin llamar la atención, cámara indiscreta
candied ['kændɪd] *adj* convertido en azúcar; almibarado, azucarado; **candied words** palabras melosas
candle ['kændəl] *s* candela, bujía, vela; (eccl.) cirio; **to burn the candle at both ends** gastar locamente fuerzas y dinero, consumir la vida; **to not be able to hold a candle to** (coll.) no llegar a la suela del zapato a, no poder compararse con; *va* examinar (*huevos*) al trasluz
candleholder ['kændəlˌholdər] *s* candelero
candlelight ['kændəlˌlaɪt] *s* luz de vela; crepúsculo
candlelighter ['kændəlˌlaɪtər] *s* encendedor de velas; acólito
Candlemas ['kændəlməs] *s* candelaria
candle power *s* bujía
candlestick ['kændəlˌstɪk] *s* palmatoria
candlewick ['kændəlˌwɪk] *s* pabilo, mecha de la vela
candlewood ['kændəlˌwʊd] *s* cuelmo, tea
candor ['kændər] *s* candor; justicia, imparcialidad
candour ['kændər] *s* (Brit.) var. de **candor**
candy ['kændɪ] *s* (*pl:* **-dies**) bombón, confite, dulce; dulces; (*pret & pp:* **-died**) *va* confitar; almibarar, azucarar; *vn* cristalizarse
candy box *s* bombonera
candytuft ['kændɪˌtʌft] *s* (bot.) carraspique, zarapico
cane [ken] *s* bastón; caña (*tallo de varias plantas*); *va* bastonear; fabricar de caña; poner asiento de rejilla o de mimbre a (*una silla*)
canebrake ['kenˌbrek] *s* cañaveral
cane seat *s* asiento de rejilla
cane sugar *s* azúcar de caña
cangue [kæŋ] *s* canga
can hooks *spl* gafas
canicular [kə'nɪkjələr] *adj* canicular
canine ['kenaɪn] o ['kænaɪn] *adj* canino; *s* (anat.) canino (*colmillo*); can, perro
canine tooth *s* (anat.) diente canino
Canis Major ['kenɪs 'medʒər] *s* (astr.) Can Mayor
Canis Minor ['kenɪs 'maɪnər] *s* (astr.) Can Menor
canistel [ˌkænɪs'tɛl] *s* canisté o canistel (*fruto*)
canister ['kænɪstər] *s* bote, frasco, lata (*para té, café, tabaco, etc.*)
canker ['kæŋkər] *s* (path.) llaga o úlcera gangrenosa; úlcera en la boca; (bot.) cancro; (ent.) oruga; *va* ulcerar; corromper; *vn* ulcerarse; corromperse
cankerous ['kæŋkərəs] *adj* ulceroso, gangrenoso; ulcerativo
canker rash *s* (path.) escarlatina
cankerworm ['kæŋkərˌwʌrm] *s* (ent.) oruga (*Alsophila pometaria y Paleacrita vernata*)
canna ['kænə] *s* (bot.) cañacoro
cannabinaceous [ˌkænəbɪ'neʃəs] *adj* (bot.) canabíneo
cannaceous [kə'neʃəs] *adj* (bot.) canáceo
canned goods *spl* conservas alimenticias
canned music *s* (slang) música impresa (*en discos, cintas, etc.*)
cannel ['kænəl] o **cannel coal** *s* carbón mate, carbón de bujía
canner ['kænər] *s* envasador (*persona que envasa víveres en latas*)

cannery ['kænərɪ] *s* (*pl:* **-ies**) fábrica de conservas alimenticias, conservera
cannibal ['kænɪbəl] *adj & s* caníbal
cannibalism ['kænɪbəlɪzəm] *s* canibalismo
cannibalistic [ˌkænɪbə'lɪstɪk] *adj* caníbal, canibalino, del canibalismo
cannikin ['kænɪkɪn] *s* lata o vaso pequeño de metal
canning ['kænɪŋ] *s* envase (*en latas*); *adj* conservero
cannon ['kænən] *s* cañón; cañonería, artillería (*conjunto de cañones*); (zool.) metatarso
cannonade [ˌkænə'ned] *s* cañoneo; *va* acañonear
cannon ball *s* bala de cañón
cannon bone *s* (zool.) metatarso
cannon cracker *s* triquitraque grande
cannoneer [ˌkænə'nɪr] *s* cañonero, artillero
cannon fodder *s* carne de cañón
cannon metal *s* metal o bronce para cañones
cannonry ['kænənrɪ] *s* (*pl:* **-ries**) cañoneo; cañonería
cannon shot *s* balas de cañón; cañonazo, tiro de cañón; alcance de un cañón
cannot ['kænɑt] contracción de **can not**
cannula ['kænjələ] *s* (*pl:* **-lae** [li]) (surg.) cánula
cannular ['kænjələr] *adj* canular
canny ['kænɪ] *adj* (*comp:* **-nier;** *super:* **-niest**) astuto, sagaz; cauteloso; parco, económico; lindo; cómodo
canoe [kə'nu] *s* canoa; (*pret & pp:* **-noed;** *ger:* **-noeing**) *va* llevar en canoa; *vn* pasear en canoa
canoeist [kə'nuɪst] *s* canoero
canon ['kænən] *s* canon; (Bib., eccl. & mus.) canon; canónigo (*sacerdote*); (print.) gran canon; (*cap.*) *s* (eccl.) canon (*parte de la misa que empieza Te igitur*)
cañon ['kænjən] *s* var. de **canyon**
canoness ['kænənɪs] *s* canonesa
canonical [kə'nɑnɪkəl] *adj* (Bib. & eccl.) canónico; aceptado, auténtico; **canonicals** *spl* vestiduras
canonical hours *spl* horas canónicas
canonization [ˌkænənɪ'zeʃən] *s* canonización
canonize ['kænənaɪz] *va* canonizar
canon law *s* cánones, derecho canónico
canonry ['kænənrɪ] *s* (*pl:* **-ries**) canonjía
can opener *s* abrelatas, abridor de latas
canopy ['kænəpɪ] *s* (*pl:* **-pies**) dosel, pabellón; sombrero (*del púlpito*); cielo (*de la cama*); conopeo (*baldaquino en forma de tienda portátil*); (arch.) doselete (*sobre las estatuas, sepulcros, etc.*); (elec.) campana; casquete (*del paracaídas*); (fig.) cielo; (*pret & pp:* **-pied**) *va* endoselar
canopy of heaven *s* bóveda celeste, capa del cielo
cant [kænt] *s* lenguaje insincero, hipocresía, gazmoñería; germanía (*de ladrones*); jerga (*de una profesión*); inclinación, sesgo; bisel, chaflán; tumbo; *adj* insincero, hipócrita, gazmoño; de una jerga; inclinado, sesgado; *va* inclinar, sesgar; arrojar, lanzar; tumbar, derribar; *vn* hablar en jerga; hablar con gazmoñería
can't [kænt] o [kɑnt] contracción de **can not**
Cantab. abr. de **Cantabrigiensis** (Lat.) **of Cambridge**
Cantabrigian [ˌkæntə'brɪdʒɪən] *adj* perteneciente a Cambridge; *s* natural o habitante de Cambridge
cantaloup o **cantaloupe** ['kæntəlop] *s* cantalupo
cantankerous [kæn'tæŋkərəs] *adj* pendenciero, quimerista, avieso
cantata [kən'tɑtə] *s* (mus.) cantata
canteen [kæn'tin] *s* cantina; cantimplora
canter ['kæntər] *s* medio galope; *vn* andar (*el caballo*) a medio galope
Canterburian [ˌkæntər'bjʊrɪən] *adj & s* cantuariense
Canterbury ['kæntərˌbɛrɪ] *s* Cantórbery
Canterbury bell *s* (bot.) farolillo, campánula
cantharides [kæn'θærɪdiz] *spl* (pharm.) polvo de cantárida
cantharis ['kænθərɪs] *s* (*pl:* **cantharides** [kæn'θærɪdiz]) (ent.) cantárida
cant hook *s* palanca de gancho (*para dar vuelta a los troncos*)
canticle ['kæntɪkəl] *s* cántico; **Canticles** *spl* (Bib.) Cantar de los Cantares
Canticle of Canticles *s* (Bib.) Cantar de los Cantares
cantilever ['kæntɪˌlɛvər] o ['kæntɪˌlivər] *s* viga voladiza; ménsula
cantilever bridge *s* puente cantilever, puente voladizo
cantilever spring *s* (aut.) muelle voladizo
cantilever wing *s* (aer.) ala voladiza, ala en cantilever
cantle ['kæntəl] *s* arzón trasero
canto ['kænto] *s* (*pl:* **-tos**) canto
canton ['kæntən] o [kæn'tɑn] *s* cantón; (her.) cantón; [kæn'tɑn] o [kæn'ton] *va* acantonar
cantonal ['kæntənəl] *adj* cantonal
Canton crepe ['kæntən] *s* burato
Cantonese [ˌkæntə'niz] *adj* cantonés; *s* (*pl:* **-ese**) cantonés
Canton flannel *s* moletón
cantonment [kæn'tɑnmənt] o ['kæntənmənt] *s* acantonamiento
cantor ['kæntər] o ['kæntɔr] *s* chantre; cantor principal (*de una sinagoga*)
Canuck [kə'nʌk] *adj & s* (slang) canadiense, francocanadiense
canvas ['kænvəs] *s* cañamazo, lona; (naut.) vela, lona; (naut.) velamen; (paint.) lienzo; **under canvas** (mil.) en tiendas; (naut.) con las velas izadas
canvasback ['kænvəsˌbæk] *s* (orn.) pato pelucón
canvass ['kænvəs] *s* escrutinio, pesquisa, inspección; solicitación (*de votos*); *va* escudriñar; solicitar (*votos*); discutir; *vn* solicitar votos, pedidos comerciales, fondos, opiniones, etc.
canvasser ['kænvəsər] *s* inspector, examinador; solicitador (*de votos, pedidos comerciales, etc.*)
canyon ['kænjən] *s* cañón (*paso estrecho entre montañas*)
canzonet [ˌkænzə'nɛt] *s* cancioneta
caoutchouc ['kaʊtʃʊk] o ['kutʃʊk] *s* caucho
cap. abr. de **capital, capitalize** y **capital letter**
cap [kæp] *s* gorra, gorrilla de visera; tapa, tapón, tapita; cima, cumbre; gorra, bonete (*del traje de catedrático*); caballete (*de la chimenea*); cápsula (*de una botella o un arma de percusión*); (naut.) tamborete (*que sujeta dos palos sobrepuestos*); (bot.) sombrero o sombrerete (*de seta u hongo*); **to put on one's thinking cap** reflexionar con madurez; **to set one's cap for** (coll.) proponerse conquistar para novio; (*pret & pp:* **capped;** *ger:* **capping**) *va* cubrir con gorra; capsular (*una botella*); poner tapa a; poner cima a; poner remate a, acabar; exceder, sobrepujar; saludar descubriéndose la cabeza; **to cap the climax** ser el colmo; *vn* descubrirse en señal de reverencia
capability [ˌkepə'bɪlɪtɪ] *s* (*pl:* **-ties**) capacidad, habilidad
capable ['kepəbəl] *adj* capaz, hábil; **capable of** capaz de; sujeto a
capacious [kə'peʃəs] *adj* capaz, espacioso
capacitance [kə'pæsɪtəns] *s* (elec.) capacitancia
capacitor [kə'pæsɪtər] *s* (elec.) capacitor
capacity [kə'pæsɪtɪ] *s* (*pl:* **-ties**) capacidad; (elec. & phys.) capacidad
cap and bells *spl* gorro con campanillas (*del bufón*)
cap and gown *spl* toga y bonete
cap-a-pie o **cap-à-pie** [ˌkæpə'pi] *adv* de pies a cabeza
caparison [kə'pærɪsən] *s* caparazón; equipo, traje o vestido rico; *va* engualdrapar; vestir soberbiamente
cape [kep] *s* capa, esclavina; cabo, promontorio
Cape Breton Island ['brɪtən] o ['brɛtən] *s* la Isla del cabo Bretón
Cape buffalo *s* (zool.) búfalo cafre, búfalo de Cafrería
Cape Colony *s* la Colonia del Cabo
Cape Horn *s* el Cabo de Hornos
Cape hunting dog *s* (zool.) perro hiena
Cape jasmine *s* (bot.) jazmín del Cabo
capelin ['kæpəlɪn] *s* (ichth.) capelán
capeline ['kæpəlɪn] *s* (arm. & surg.) capellina

Cape of Good Hope *s* cabo de Buena Esperanza
caper ['kepər] *s* cabriola; travesura; (bot.) alcaparra; **capers** *spl* alcaparrones (*botones de la flor de la alcaparra*); **to cut capers** dar cabriolas; hacer travesuras; *vn* cabriolar
capercaillie [ˌkæpər'keljɪ] *s* (orn.) urogallo, grigallo
Capernaum [kə'pʌrnɪəm] *s* Cafarnaúm
Capetian [kə'piʃən] *adj & s* capetiano, capetino
Capetown ['kepˌtaun] o **Cape Town** *s* El Cabo, la Ciudad del Cabo
Cape Verde [vʌrd] *s* Cabo Verde
Cape Verde Islands *spl* islas de Cabo Verde
capias ['kepɪɑs] o ['kæpɪɑs] *s* (law) orden de arresto
capillarity [ˌkæpɪ'lærɪtɪ] *s* capilaridad
capillary ['kæpɪˌlɛrɪ] *adj* capilar; *s* (*pl:* **-ies**) tubo capilar; (anat.) capilar, vaso capilar
capillary attraction *s* (phys.) atracción capilar
capillary tube *s* tubo capilar
capita ['kæpɪtə] *pl de* **caput**
capital ['kæpɪtəl] *adj* capital; excelente, magnífico; *s* capital *m* (*dinero*); capital *f* (*ciudad*); (fort.) capital *f*; (arch.) capitel; (tech.) capitel (*del alambique*); **to make capital out of** sacar partido de
capital expenditure *s* inversión de capital para ampliar o mejorar el negocio
capital gains *spl* ganancias capitales
capital goods *spl* bienes capitales (*elementos de producción*)
capitalism ['kæpɪtəlɪzəm] *s* capitalismo
capitalist ['kæpɪtəlɪst] *adj & s* capitalista
capitalistic [ˌkæpɪtə'lɪstɪk] *adj* capitalista
capitalization [ˌkæpɪtəlɪ'zeʃən] *s* capitalización; aprovechamiento; total del capital; escritura o impresión en mayúscula
capitalize ['kæpɪtəlaɪz] *va* capitalizar; aprovechar; escribir o imprimir con mayúscula; *vn* capitalizar; **to capitalize on** aprovecharse de
capital letter *s* letra capital, letra mayúscula
capitally ['kæpɪtəlɪ] *adv* excelentemente, admirablemente
capital punishment *s* pena capital, pena de muerte
capital ship *s* (nav.) acorazado grande
capital sin *s* pecado capital, pecado mortal
capital stock *s* capital social
capitate ['kæpɪtet] *adj* (bot.) capitado
capitation [ˌkæpɪ'teʃən] *s* capitación
capitol ['kæpɪtəl] *s* capitolio; (*cap.*) *s* Capitolio
Capitoline ['kæpɪtəlaɪn] o [kə'pɪtəlaɪn] *adj* capitolino; *s* monte Capitolino
capitular [kə'pɪtʃələr] *adj* capitular
capitulary [kə'pɪtʃəˌlɛrɪ] *s* (*pl:* **-ies**) capitular; **capitularies** *spl* (hist.) capitulares
capitulate [kə'pɪtʃəlet] *vn* capitular
capitulation [kəˌpɪtʃə'leʃən] *s* capitulación; resumen, recapitulación
Cap'n ['kæpən] *s* capitán
capnomancy ['kæpnoˌmænsɪ] *s* capnomancia
capon ['kepən] o ['kepɑn] *s* capón (*pollo castrado*); capón cebado
capote [kə'pot] *s* capote (*capa*); capota (*cubierta de coche; sombrero sujeto con cintas*)
Cappadocian [ˌkæpə'doʃən] *adj & s* capadocio
capparidaceous [ˌkæpærɪ'deʃəs] *adj* (bot.) caparidáceo
capriccio [kə'prɪtʃɪo] o [kə'pritʃo] *s* (*pl:* **-cios**) travesura; capricho; (mus.) capricho
caprice [kə'pris] *s* capricho; veleidad, inconstancia; (mus.) capricho
capricious [kə'prɪʃəs] *adj* caprichoso, caprichudo
Capricorn ['kæprɪkɔrn] *s* (astr.) Capricornio
caprificate ['kæprɪfɪket] o [kə'prɪfɪket] *va* cabrahigar
caprification [ˌkæprɪfɪ'keʃən] *s* cabrahigadura
caprifig ['kæprɪˌfɪg] *s* (bot.) cabrahigo
caprifoliaceous [ˌkæprɪˌfolɪ'eʃəs] *adj* (bot.) caprifoliáceo
capriole ['kæprɪol] *s* cabriola; *vn* cabriolar
caps. abr. de **capital letters**
capsaicin [kæp'seɪsɪn] *s* (chem.) capsaicina
cap screw *s* tornillo de cabeza cuadrada o hexagonal
capsicum ['kæpsɪkəm] *s* (bot.) pimiento (*planta y fruto*)
capsize ['kæpsaɪz] *va* volcar; *vn* volcar; tumbar (*un barco*)
capstan ['kæpstən] *s* cabrestante, argüe; **to rig the capstan** guarnir el cabrestante
capstan bar *s* (naut.) manuella, barra del cabrestante
capstan lathe *s* torno revólver
capstone ['kæpˌston] *s* (arch.) albardilla, coronamiento; (fig.) coronamiento
capsular ['kæpsələr] o ['kæpsjulər] *adj* capsular
capsule ['kæpsəl] o ['kæpsjul] *s* (anat., bot., pharm. & zool.) cápsula; cápsula (*de un cohete espacial*)
Capt. abr. de **Captain**
captain ['kæptɪn] *s* capitán (*p.ej., de un equipo de fútbol*); (mil., naut. & nav.) capitán; *va* capitanear
captaincy ['kæptɪnsɪ] *s* (*pl:* **-cies**) capitanía
captain general *s* (*pl:* **captains general**) (mil. & Sp. hist.) capitán general
captainship ['kæptɪnʃɪp] *s* capitanía
caption ['kæpʃən] *s* título; (mov.) subtítulo; *va* intitular, poner título a
captious ['kæpʃəs] *adj* criticón, reparón; insidioso
captivate ['kæptɪvet] *va* fascinar, cautivar
captivation [ˌkæptɪ'veʃən] *s* fascinación
captive ['kæptɪv] *adj & s* cautivo
captive balloon *s* globo cautivo
captivity [kæp'tɪvɪtɪ] *s* (*pl:* **-ties**) cautiverio, cautividad
captor ['kæptər] *s* captor, apresador
capture ['kæptʃər] *s* apresamiento, captura; toma (*de una plaza*); prisionero; presa, botín; *va* apresar, capturar; tomar (*una plaza*); captar (*la confianza de uno*)
capture cross section *s* (phys.) sección de captura
capuchin ['kæpjutʃɪn] o ['kæpjuʃɪn] *s* (zool.) capuchino (*mono*); (orn.) paloma capuchina; capucho (*pieza del vestido*); (*cap.*) *s* capuchino (*monje*)
Capuchin nun *s* capuchina
caput ['kepət] o ['kæpət] *s* (*pl:* **capita** ['kæpɪtə]) (Lat.) cabeza; **per capita** por cabeza, por persona
capybara [ˌkæpɪ'bɑrə] *s* (zool.) capibara, carpincho
car [kɑr] *s* coche (*carro de ferrocarril; automóvil*); caja o carro (*de ascensor*); barquilla (*de un globo aerostático*)
carabao [ˌkɑrə'bɑo] *s* (*pl:* **-os**) (zool.) carabao
carabineer o **carabinier** [ˌkærəbɪ'nɪr] *s* carabinero
caracal ['kærəkæl] *s* (zool.) caracal, lince de las estepas
caracole ['kærəkol] *s* caracol (*del caballo*); *vn* caracolear (*el caballo*)
caracul ['kærəkəl] *s* caracul (*piel rizada*); cordero de astracán, oveja caracul
carafe [kə'ræf] o [kə'rɑf] *s* garrafa
caramel ['kærəməl] o ['kɑrməl] *s* caramelo, azúcar quemado; confite plástico que sabe a caramelo; *va* acaramelar; *vn* acaramelarse
caramelize ['kærəməlaɪz] *va* acaramelizar; *vn* acaramelizarse
carapace ['kærəpes] *s* carapacho
carat ['kærət] *s* quilate
caravan ['kærəvæn] *s* caravana; carricoche; (Brit.) coche-habitación
caravansary [ˌkærə'vænsərɪ] *s* (*pl:* **-ries**) caravanera o caravansera; posada grande
caravanserai [ˌkærə'vænsəraɪ] o [ˌkærə'vænsəre] *s* var. de **caravansary**
caravan site *s* (Brit.) var. de **trailer camp**
caravel ['kærəvɛl] *s* (naut.) carabela
caraway ['kærəwe] *s* (bot.) alcaravea (*planta y simiente*)
caraway seeds *spl* alcaravea, carvi
carbarn ['kɑrˌbɑrn] *s* cochera de tranvías, cobertizo para tranvías
carbide ['kɑrbaɪd] o ['kɑrbɪd] *s* (chem.) carburo (*especialmente el de calcio*)
carbine ['kɑrbaɪn] *s* carabina
carbineer [ˌkɑrbɪ'nɪr] *s* var. de **carabineer**
carbinol ['kɑrbɪnol] o ['kɑrbɪnɑl] *s* (chem.) carbinol

carbodynamite [ˌkɑrbo'daɪnəmaɪt] *s* carbodinamita
carbohydrate [ˌkɑrbo'haɪdret] *s* (chem.) carbohidrato, hidrato de carbono
carbolated ['kɑrbəˌletɪd] *adj* mezclado con ácido carbólico
carbolic [kɑr'bɑlɪk] *adj* carbólico
carbolic acid *s* (chem.) ácido carbólico
carbolineum [ˌkɑrbo'lɪnɪəm] *s* (trademark) carbolíneo
carbolize ['kɑrbəlaɪz] *va* mezclar o tratar con ácido carbólico
carbon ['kɑrbən] *s* (chem.) carbono; (elec.) carbón (*de una pila o una lámpara de arco*); papel carbón; copia en papel carbón; (aut.) carbonilla o carboncillo (*en los cilindros*)
carbonaceous [ˌkɑrbə'neʃəs] *adj* carbonoso
carbonado [ˌkɑrbə'nedo] *s* (*pl:* **-does** o **-dos**) carne asada a la parrilla; carbonado (*diamante negro*); *va* asar a la parrilla; acuchillar
carbonate ['kɑrbənet] o ['kɑrbənɪt] *s* (chem.) carbonato; ['kɑrbənet] *va* carbonatar
carbon copy *s* copia en papel carbón, copia al carbón
carbon diamond *s* carbonado, diamante negro
carbon dioxide *s* (chem.) dióxido de carbono, anhídrido carbónico
carbon dioxide snow *s* (chem.) nieve carbónica
carbonic [kɑr'bɑnɪk] *adj* carbónico
carbonic-acid gas [kɑr'bɑnɪk'æsɪd] *s* (chem.) gas carbónico, dióxido de carbono
carboniferous [ˌkɑrbə'nɪfərəs] *adj* carbonífero; (*cap.*) *adj* (geol.) carbonífero; *s* (geol.) período carbonífero; (geol.) carbonífero, formación carbonífera
carbonization [ˌkɑrbənɪ'zeʃən] *s* carbonización
carbonize ['kɑrbənaɪz] *va* carbonizar; *vn* carbonizarse
carbon monoxide *s* (chem.) óxido de carbono, monóxido de carbono
carbon paper *s* papel carbón
carbon tetrachloride [ˌtɛtrə'kloraɪd] *s* (chem.) tetracloruro de carbono
carbonyl ['kɑrbənɪl] *s* (chem.) carbonilo
carborundum [ˌkɑrbə'rʌndəm] *s* (trademark) carborundo
carborundum detector *s* (rad.) detector de cristales de carborundo
carboxyl group [kɑr'bɑksɪl] *s* (chem.) grupo carboxilo
carboy ['kɑrbɔɪ] *s* bombona, garrafón
carbuncle ['kɑrbʌŋkəl] *s* carbunclo o carbúnculo (*rubí o granate*); (path. & vet.) carbunco o carbunclo; grano (*tumorcillo pequeño*)
carburet ['kɑrbəret] o ['kɑrbjəret] (*pret & pp:* **-reted** o **-retted;** *ger:* **-reting** o **-retting**) *va* carburar
carburetion [ˌkɑrbə'reʃən] o [ˌkɑrbjə'reʃən] *s* carburación
carburetor o **carburettor** ['kɑrbəˌretər] o ['kɑrbjəˌretər] *s* carburador
carcanet ['kɑrkənɛt] *s* (archaic) gargantilla o collar de piedras preciosas u oro
carcase o **carcass** ['kɑrkəs] *s* cadáver (*especialmente de animal*); res muerta; esqueleto o armazón (*de una casa, un navío, etc.*); (mil.) carcasa
Carcassonne [ˌkɑrˌkɑ'sɔn] *s* Carcasona
carcinogen [kɑr'sɪnədʒən] *s* (path.) carcinógeno
carcinoma [ˌkɑrsɪ'nomə] *s* (*pl:* **-mata** [mətə] o **-mas**) (path.) carcinoma
card [kɑrd] *s* tarjeta; carta, naipe; ficha; rosa náutica; (coll.) tipo, sujeto; carda, cardencha (*para cardar lana*); **cards** *spl* naipes (*juego*); **in** u **on the cards** probable; **to cut the cards** cortar el naipe; **to deal the cards** dar las cartas; **to have a card up one's sleeve** tener otro recurso, tener ayuda en reserva; **to play cards** jugar a los naipes; **to put one's cards on the table** poner las cartas boca arriba, jugar a cartas vistas; **to shuffle the cards** barajar las cartas; *va* dar un naipe a; poner en una tarjeta o ficha; cardar (*p.ej., la lana*)
cardamom o **cardamum** ['kɑrdəməm] o **cardamon** ['kɑrdəmən] *s* (bot.) cardamomo
cardboard ['kɑrdˌbord] *s* cartón
cardboard binding *s* encuadernación en pasta
cardboard box *s* cartón, caja de cartón
card-carrying communist ['kɑrd'kærɪɪŋ] *s* comunista que lleva consigo la tarjeta de afiliación al partido
card case *s* tarjetero
card catalogue *s* catálogo de fichas
carder ['kɑrdər] *s* cardador
card game *s* juego de cartas; partida de cartas
cardia ['kɑrdɪə] *s* (anat.) cardias
cardiac ['kɑrdɪæk] *adj* cardíaco; *s* remedio cardíaco; (coll.) cardíaco (*persona que padece del corazón*)
cardigan ['kɑrdɪgən] *s* rebeca, chaqueta de lana tejida, albornoz
cardinal ['kɑrdɪnəl] *adj* cardinal; *s* purpurado; (eccl. & orn.) cardenal; número cardinal
cardinalate ['kɑrdɪnəlet] *s* cardenalato
cardinal bird *s* (orn.) cardenal
cardinal flower *s* (bot.) lobelia escarlata
cardinal grosbeak *s* (orn.) cardenal
cardinal number *s* número cardinal
cardinal points *spl* puntos cardinales
cardinal virtues *spl* virtudes cardinales
card index *s* fichero, tarjetero
carding ['kɑrdɪŋ] *s* cardadura (*acción*); cardada (*porción de lana cardada*)
cardiogram ['kɑrdɪoˌgræm] *s* cardiograma
cardiograph ['kɑrdɪoˌgræf] o ['kɑrdɪoˌgrɑf] *s* cardiógrafo
cardiography [ˌkɑrdɪ'ɑgrəfɪ] *s* cardiografía
cardiology [ˌkɑrdɪ'ɑlədʒɪ] *s* cardiología
cardiovascular [ˌkɑrdɪo'væskjələr] *adj* cardiovascular
carditis [kɑr'daɪtɪs] *s* (path.) carditis
cardoon [kɑr'dun] *s* (bot.) cardo de comer
card party *s* tertulia de baraja
cardsharp ['kɑrdˌʃɑrp] *s* fullero, tahur
card table *s* mesa de baraja
card trick *s* truco de naipes
care [kɛr] *s* cuidado, inquietud, solicitud; esmero; cargo, custodia; **to have a care** o **to take care** tener cuidado; **to take care of** cuidar, cuidar de; (coll.) tratar con, tratar de; **to take care not to** + *inf* guardarse de + *inf;* **to take care of oneself** cuidarse (*mirar por su salud; darse buena vida*); **to write in care of** escribir a manos de; **care of** suplicada en casa de; *vn* tener cuidado; interesarse; **to care about** preocuparse de o por, cuidarse de (*p.ej., el qué dirán*); **to care for** querer, amar; desear; interesarse en; cuidar de; **to care to** + *inf* tener ganas de + *inf*, cuidar de + *inf*
careen [kə'rin] *s* (naut.) carena; inclinación, vuelco; *va* (naut.) inclinar o volcar (*un buque*); (naut.) carenar, despalmar (*reparar o componer*); inclinar o volcar; *vn* (naut.) carenar; inclinarse o volcarse; mecerse precipitadamente
careenage [kə'rinɪdʒ] *s* (naut.) despalmador (*sitio*); despalmadura (*reparo o compostura*)
career [kə'rɪr] *s* carrera; *adj* de carrera; *vn* correr a carrera tendida
career diplomat *s* diplomático de carrera
careerist [kə'rɪrɪst] *s* profesional de carrera
career woman *s* (coll.) mujer que se consagra a una profesión
carefree ['kɛrˌfri] *adj* desenfadado, despreocupado, alegre
careful ['kɛrfəl] *adj* cuidadoso; esmerado (*hecho con esmero*)
carefulness ['kɛrfəlnɪs] *s* cuidado; esmero
careless ['kɛrlɪs] *adj* descuidado; inconsiderado; indiferente; alegre, sin cuidado
carelessness ['kɛrlɪsnɪs] *s* descuido; inconsideración; indiferencia; alegría
caress [kə'rɛs] *s* caricia; *va* acariciar; *vn* acariciarse
caret ['kærət] *s* signo de intercalación
caretaker ['kɛrˌtekər] *s* curador, custodio, guardián; portero; casero (*que cuida de una casa y vive en ella*)
caretaker government *s* gobierno provisional
careworn ['kɛrˌworn] *adj* agobiado de inquietud
carfare ['kɑrˌfɛr] *s* pasaje (*en tren, tranvía, autobús*); pequeña cantidad de dinero
cargo ['kɑrgo] *s* (*pl:* **-goes** o **-gos**) (naut.) carga, cargamento
cargo boat *s* barco de carga

carhop [ˈkɑrˌhɑp] *s* (slang) moza de restaurante que sirve a los automovilistas en sus coches
Carib [ˈkærɪb] *s* caribe
Caribbean [ˌkærɪˈbiən] o [kəˈrɪbɪən] *adj* caribe; *s* mar Caribe
Caribbean Sea *s* mar Caribe, mar de las Antillas
caribou [ˈkærɪbu] *s* (zool.) caribú
caricature [ˈkærɪkətʃər] *s* caricatura; *va* caricaturizar
caricaturist [ˈkærɪkətʃərɪst] *s* caricaturista
caries [ˈkɛrɪz] o [ˈkɛrɪiz] *s* (path.) caries
carillon [ˈkærɪlɑn] o [kəˈrɪljən] *s* (mus.) carillón, órgano de campanas; (*pret & pp:* **-lonned;** *ger:* **-lonning**) *vn* tocar el carillón
carillonneur [ˌkærɪləˈnʌr] *s* (mus.) campanero
cariole [ˈkærɪol] *s* carriola; carro pequeño
carious [ˈkɛrɪəs] *adj* cariado
carking [ˈkɑrkɪŋ] *adj* molesto; inquieto
carl o **carle** [kɑrl] *s* (archaic) campesino; (Scottish) patán, palurdo
carline thistle [ˈkɑrlɪn] *s* (bot.) ajonjera, angélica carlina
Carlism [ˈkɑrlɪzəm] *s* carlismo
Carlist [ˈkɑrlɪst] *adj & s* carlista
carload [ˈkɑrˌlod] *s* vagonada, furgonada, carga de carro
carloadings [ˈkɑrˌlodɪŋz] *spl* (com.) vagones cargados (*p.ej., en una semana*)
carload lot *s* (rail.) carro completo o entero
Carlovingian [ˌkɑrloˈvɪndʒɪən] *adj & s* carlovingio
carmagnole [ˌkɑrməˈnjol] *s* carmañola (*chaqueta, canción y danza*)
carman [ˈkɑrmən] *s* (*pl:* **-men**) carretero; conductor (*de un tranvía*)
Carmel, Mount [ˈkɑrməl] *s* el monte Carmelo
Carmelite [ˈkɑrməlaɪt] *adj* carmelita, carmelitano; *s* carmelita
carminative [kɑrˈmɪnətɪv] o [ˈkɑrmɪˌnetɪv] *adj & s* (med.) carminativo
carmine [ˈkɑrmɪn] o [ˈkɑrmaɪn] *adj* carmíneo; *s* carmín (*materia colorante y color*); *va* carminar
carminite [ˈkɑrmɪnaɪt] *s* (mineral.) carminita
carnage [ˈkɑrnɪdʒ] *s* carnicería, mortandad
carnal [ˈkɑrnəl] *adj* carnal
carnality [kɑrˈnælɪtɪ] *s* (*pl:* **-ties**) carnalidad
carnallite [ˈkɑrnəlaɪt] *s* (mineral.) carnalita
carnation [kɑrˈneʃən] *s* (bot.) clavel, clavel reventón; encarnado; *adj* encarnado
carnelian [kɑrˈniljən] *s* (mineral.) cornalina, cornerina
carnification [ˌkɑrnɪfɪˈkeʃən] *s* (path.) carnificación
carnival [ˈkɑrnɪvəl] *s* carnaval; feria, espectáculo de atracciones; *adj* carnavalesco
carnivore [ˈkɑrnɪvor] *s* (zool. & bot.) carnívoro
carnivorous [kɑrˈnɪvərəs] *adj* carnívoro, carnicero
carnosine [ˈkɑrnosin] *s* (chem.) carnosina
Carnot cycle [kɑrˈno] *s* (phys.) ciclo de Carnot
carnotite [ˈkɑrnətaɪt] *s* (mineral.) carnotita
carob [ˈkærəb] *s* (bot.) algarrobo
carol [ˈkærəl] *s* canción alegre; villancico; (*pret & pp:* **-oled** u **-olled;** *ger:* **-oling** u **-olling**) *va & vn* cantar con alegría; celebrar con villancicos
Carolina poplar [ˌkærəˈlaɪnə] *s* (bot.) chopo de la Carolina
Caroline [ˈkærəlaɪn] o [ˈkærəlɪn] *s* Carolina; *adj* carolino
Caroline Islands *spl* islas Carolinas
Carolingian [ˌkærəˈlɪndʒɪən] *adj & s* carolingio
carom [ˈkærəm] *s* carambola; rebote; *vn* carambolear; rebotar
carotene [ˈkærətin] *s* (chem.) caroteno
carotid [kəˈrɑtɪd] *adj* carotídeo; *s* (anat.) carótida, arteria carótida
carotid gland *s* (anat.) glándula carótida
carotin [ˈkærətɪn] *s* var. de **carotene**
carousal [kəˈraʊzəl] *s* jarana, gresca, borrachera
carouse [kəˈraʊz] *s* jarana, gresca, borrachera; *vn* jaranear, emborracharse
carousel [ˌkærəˈzɛl] *s* var. de **carrousel**
carp [kɑrp] *s* (ichth.) carpa; *vn* regañar, quejarse
carpal [ˈkɑrpəl] *adj* (anat.) carpiano; *s* (anat.) hueso del carpo
car park *s* (Brit.) var. de **parking lot**
Carpathian Mountains [kɑrˈpeθɪən] o **Carpathians** *spl* Cárpatos
carpel [ˈkɑrpəl] *s* (bot.) carpelo
carpenter [ˈkɑrpəntər] *s* carpintero; *vn* carpintear
carpenter ant *s* (ent.) hormiga carpintera
carpenter bee *s* (ent.) abeja carpintera
carpentry [ˈkɑrpəntrɪ] *s* carpintería
carpet [ˈkɑrpɪt] *s* alfombra; **to be on the carpet** estar sobre el tapete (*ser examinado, ser discutido*); (coll.) ser reprobado; *va* alfombrar, tapizar; (fig.) felpar (*p.ej., de hierba*)
carpetbag [ˈkɑrpɪtˌbæg] *s* saco de viaje hecho de tejido de alfombra
carpetbagger [ˈkɑrpɪtˌbægər] *s* aventurero, explotador; (scornful) politicastro del Norte de los EE.UU. que iba al Sur, después de la guerra entre Norte y Sur, a aprovecharse de la situación política
carpetbeater [ˈkɑrpɪtˌbitər] *s* sacudidor de alfombras (*instrumento*)
carpet beetle *s* (ent.) polilla de los tapices
carpet dealer *s* alfombrista
carpeting [ˈkɑrpɪtɪŋ] *s* alfombrado; tela para alfombras
carpet knight *s* soldado de gabinete
carpet maker *s* alfombrero
carpet moth *s* (ent.) polilla de los paños
carpet slipper *s* zapatilla de fieltro
carpet sweeper *s* barredera de alfombras
carping [ˈkɑrpɪŋ] *adj* criticón, reparón
carpology [kɑrˈpɑlədʒɪ] *s* carpología
carport [ˈkɑrˌport] *s* alpende para automóvil
carpus [ˈkɑrpəs] *s* (*pl:* **-pi** [paɪ]) (anat.) carpo; (anat.) muñeca
carrack [ˈkærək] *s* (naut.) carraca (*galeón*)
car radio *s* radio para auto
carrageen [ˈkærəˌgin] *s* (bot.) carragaen, musgo de Irlanda
carrel o **carrell** [ˈkærəl] *s* gabinete de estudio (*anejo a los depósitos de libros de una biblioteca*)
car-rental service [ˈkɑrˈrɛntəl] *s* alquiler de coches
carriage [ˈkærɪdʒ] *s* carruaje; (arti.) cureña; (mach.) carro (*p.ej., de la máquina de escribir*); porte, continente; porte, transporte
carriage-free [ˈkærɪdʒˈfri] *adj* franco de porte
carriage horse *s* caballo de coche
carriage trade *s* clientela de personas ricas
Carrie [ˈkærɪ] *s* nombre abreviado de **Caroline**
carrier [ˈkærɪər] *s* porteador, portador; (path.) portador de gérmenes; empresa de transportes; cartero; (nav.) portaaviones; (rad.) onda portadora
carrier-based plane [ˈkærɪərˌbest] *s* avión con base en portaaviones
carrier pigeon *s* paloma de raza carrier; paloma mensajera
carrier wave *s* (rad.) onda portadora, onda portante
carriole [ˈkærɪol] *s* var. de **cariole**
carrion [ˈkærɪən] *s* carroña; podredumbre; inmundicia; *adj* carroño; que se alimenta de carroña; inmundo
carrion crow *s* (orn.) corneja; (orn.) zopilote (*Catharista atrata*)
carronade [ˌkærəˈned] *s* carronada
carrot [ˈkærət] *s* (bot.) zanahoria
carroty [ˈkærətɪ] *adj* amarillo rojizo; pelirrojo
carrousel [ˌkærəˈzɛl] *s* caballitos, tiovivo
carry [ˈkærɪ] *s* (*pl:* **-ries**) alcance (*de un arma*); transporte en los hombros; trecho no navegable (*de un río*) ‖ (*pret & pp:* **-ried**) *va* llevar, traer, portar; acarrear, transportar; sostener (*una carga*); contener, comprender, incluir; ganar, lograr (*p.ej., elecciones, un premio*); ganar las elecciones en; hacer aceptar (*una proposición*); extender, llevar más lejos; influir en; llevar consigo; tener en existencia (*mercancías*); (arith.) llevar; **to carry about** llevar de un lado para otro; **to carry along** llevar consigo; **to carry away** llevarse; encantar, entusiasmar; llevar con violencia; **to carry back** devolver, restituir; **to carry**

down bajar; **to carry forward** llevar adelante; (com.) llevar o pasar (*en las cuentas*); **to carry into effect** llevar a cabo, poner en ejecución; **to carry off** llevarse; **to carry on** conducir, dirigir; promover; continuar; **to carry oneself** comportarse; **to carry one's point** salirse con la suya; **to carry out** realizar, llevar a cabo; **to carry over** aplazar; guardar para más tarde; pasar a otra página, cuenta, etc.; **to carry the day** quedar victorioso, ganar la palma; **to carry through** realizar, llevar a cabo; ayudar o sostener hasta el fin; **to carry up** subir; **to carry weight** ser de peso, ser de influencia; **carried forward** suma y sigue ‖ *vn* alcanzar; **to carry on** continuar; (coll.) travesear (*portarse de manera ridícula*); **to carry over** sobrar
carryall [ˈkærɪˌɔl] *s* coche ligero y cubierto, de un solo caballo
carrying charges *spl* gastos de mantenimiento; gastos adicionales en la compra a plazos (*p.ej., intereses, seguros*)
carry-over [ˈkærɪˌovər] *s* sobrante, exceso; (com.) suma anterior, suma que pasa de una página o cuenta a otra
car-sick [ˈkɑrˌsɪk] *adj* mareado (*en un automóvil o tren*)
cart [kɑrt] *s* carreta; **to put the cart before the horse** empezar la casa por el tejado; *va* carretear, acarrear
cartage [ˈkɑrtɪdʒ] *s* carretaje, acarreo
carte [kɑrt] *s* lista de comidas; **à la carte** según lista, a la carta
carte blanche [ˈkɑrt ˈblɑnʃ] *s* carta blanca
cartel [kɑrˈtɛl] o [ˈkɑrtəl] *s* cartel (*escrito de desafío*); (econ., dipl. & pol.) cartel
carter [ˈkɑrtər] *s* carretero
Cartesian [kɑrˈtiʒən] *adj & s* cartesiano
Cartesian coördinates *spl* (math.) coordenadas cartesianas
Cartesian devil, diver o **imp** *s* (phys.) diablillo de Descartes
Cartesianism [kɑrˈtiʒənɪzəm] *s* cartesianismo
Carthage [ˈkɑrθɪdʒ] *s* Cartago
Carthaginian [ˌkɑrθəˈdʒɪnɪən] *adj & s* cartaginés
cart horse *s* caballo de tiro
Carthusian [kɑrˈθuʒən] *adj & s* cartujo
cartilage [ˈkɑrtɪlɪdʒ] *s* (anat.) cartílago
cartilaginous [ˌkɑrtɪˈlædʒɪnəs] *adj* cartilaginoso; (ichth.) cartilaginoso, cartilagíneo
cartload [ˈkɑrtˌlod] *s* carretada
cartographer [kɑrˈtɑgrəfər] *s* cartógrafo
cartographic [ˌkɑrtoˈgræfɪk] *adj* cartográfico
cartography [kɑrˈtɑgrəfɪ] *s* cartografía
carton [ˈkɑrtən] *s* cartón, caja de cartón
cartoon [kɑrˈtun] *s* caricatura; tira cómica; cartón (*modelo de frescos, tapices, etc.*); (mov.) dibujo animado; *va* caricaturizar
cartoonist [kɑrˈtunɪst] *s* caricaturista
cartouche [kɑrˈtuʃ] *s* (arch.) cartucho, cartela
cartridge [ˈkɑrtrɪdʒ] *s* cartucho; cabeza (*del fonocaptor*); (phot.) rollo de películas
cartridge belt *s* canana, cartuchera
cartridge box *s* cartuchera
cartridge case *s* casco de cartucho
cartridge clip *s* peine de balas
cartridge fuse *s* (elec.) fusible de cartucho
cart wheel *s* rueda de carro; salto mortal de lado; (slang) dólar
caruncle [ˈkærʌŋkəl] o [kəˈrʌŋkəl] *s* (anat., bot. & zool.) carúncula
caruncular [kəˈrʌŋkjələr] *adj* caruncular
caruncolate [kəˈrʌŋkjəlet] *adj* carunculado
carve [kɑrv] *va* trinchar (*carne*); esculpir, tallar; cincelar, grabar; **to carve out** crearse, labrarse (*p.ej., un porvenir, una fortuna*)
carvel [ˈkɑrvəl] *s* var. de **caravel**
carvel-built [ˈkɑrvəlˌbɪlt] *adj* (naut.) con juntas a tope, construído a tope
carvel joint *s* (naut.) junta a tope
carver [ˈkɑrvər] *s* trinchador; trinchante (*cuchillo*); tallista (*de madera*); escultor; grabador
carving [ˈkɑrvɪŋ] *s* acción de trinchar; arte de trinchar; escultura; talladura; tallado, obra de talla
carving knife *s* trinchante
car washer *s* lavacoches
caryatid [ˌkærɪˈætɪd] *s* (*pl:* **-ids** o **-ides** [ɪdiz]) (arch.) cariátide
caryophyllaceous [ˌkærɪofɪˈleʃəs] *adj* (bot.) cariofiláceo
caryopsis [ˌkærɪˈɑpsɪs] *s* (*pl:* **-ses** [siz] o **-sides** [sɪdiz]) (bot.) cariópside
casaba [kəˈsɑbə] *s* melón de Indias
Casbah [ˈkɑzbɑ] *s* casba (*alcazaba y barrio musulmano de Argel y otras ciudades norteafricanas*)
cascade [kæsˈked] *s* cascada
cascade amplification *s* (elec.) amplificación en cascada
cascade connection *s* (elec.) conexión en cascada
cascade control *s* (elec.) control a cascada
cascara [kæsˈkɛrə] *s* (bot. & pharm.) cáscara sagrada
cascara sagrada [səˈgredə] *s* (pharm.) cáscara sagrada
case [kes] *s* caso; (gram. & med.) caso; (law) causa, pleito; argumento convincente; estuche; caja; funda, vaina; bastidor, marco (*p.ej., de una ventana*); (print.) caja; (slang) persona extravagante, persona divertida; **in case** caso que, en caso que; **in case of** en caso de; **in any case** en todo caso, de todos modos; **in no case** de ninguna manera; **in such a case** en tal caso; *adj* (gram.) casual; *va* encajonar; enfundar
casease [ˈkesɪes] *s* (biochem.) caseasa
caseation [ˌkesɪˈeʃən] *s* (path.) caseificación
casebook [ˈkesˌbuk] *s* libro de texto conteniendo casos selectos clasificados
case ending *s* (gram.) desinencia casual
caseharden [ˈkesˌhɑrdən] *va* endurecer la superficie de (*p.ej., la madera*); (metal.) cementar; (fig.) volver insensible
caseic [ˈkesɪɪk] o [kəˈsiɪk] *adj* caseico
casein [ˈkesɪɪn] *s* (biochem.) caseína
caseinogen [ˌkesɪˈɪnədʒɛn] *s* (biochem.) caseinógeno
case knife *s* cuchillo provisto de una vaina; cuchillo de mesa
casemate [ˈkesmet] *s* (fort. & naut.) casamata
casemated [ˈkesmetɪd] *adj* acasamatado
casement [ˈkesmənt] *s* ventana a bisagra, ventana batiente; bastidor, marco (*de una ventana*); caja, funda; (poet.) ventana
caseous [ˈkesɪəs] *adj* caseoso
caserns o **casernes** [kəˈzʌrnz] *spl* (mil.) cuartel
case work *s* trabajo con casos
cash [kæʃ] *s* dinero contante; pago al contado; **for cash** al contado; por pago al contado; **to convert into cash** convertir en dinero efectivo; **to pay cash** pagar al contado; **cash on delivery** contra reembolso; *va* pagar al contado por; cobrar, hacer efectivo (*un cheque*); *vn* cobrar; **to cash in** (coll.) morir; **to cash in on** (coll.) sacar provecho de; (coll.) emplear útilmente
cash and carry *s* pago al contado con transporte por parte del comprador
cashbook [ˈkæʃˌbuk] *s* libro de caja
cashbox [ˈkæʃˌbɑks] *s* caja
cashew [ˈkæʃu] o [kəˈʃu] *s* (bot.) anacardo (*planta y nuez*)
cashew bird *s* (orn.) paují
cashew nut *s* anacardo, nuez de acajú
cashier [kæˈʃɪr] *s* cajero; *va* destituir; degradar
cashier's check *s* cheque de caja
cashier's desk *s* caja
cashmere [ˈkæʃmɪr] *s* casimir o cachemir; lana muy fina de cabras; chal de lana fina de cabras; (*cap.*) *s* Cachemira
cash on delivery *s* entrega contra pago, pago contra reembolso
cash on hand *s* efectivo en caja
cash payment *s* pago al contado
cash prize *s* premio en metálico
cash register *s* caja registradora
casing [ˈkesɪŋ] *s* cubierta, caja, envoltura; tubería de revestimiento; cerco o marco (*de puerta o ventana*); (aut.) cubierta (*de neumático*); (sew.) jareta
casino [kəˈsino] *s* (*pl:* **-nos**) casino
cask [kæsk] o [kɑsk] *s* tonel, casco, pipa
casket [ˈkæskɪt] o [ˈkɑskɪt] *s* cajita, cofrecito; caja, ataúd
Caspian [ˈkæspɪən] *adj & s* caspio

Caspian Sea *s* mar Caspio
casque [kæsk] *s* capacete, casco, casquete
cassaba [kəˈsɑbə] *s* var. de **casaba**
Cassandra [kəˈsændrə] *s* (myth. & fig.) Casandra
cassation [kæˈseʃən] *s* (law) casación
cassava [kəˈsɑvə] *s* (bot.) mandioca (*planta y harina fina de su raíz*)
casserole [ˈkæsərol] *s* cacerola; timbal (*pastel relleno*); (chem.) cacerola
cassia [ˈkæʃə] o [ˈkæsɪə] *s* (bot.) casia; (pharm.) canela de la China
cassimere [ˈkæsɪmɪr] *s* casimir o cachemir
cassino [kəˈsino] *s* (*pl:* **-nos**) casino (*juego de naipes*)
Cassiopeia [ˌkæsɪoˈpiə] *s* (myth. & astr.) Casiopea
cassis [kɑˈsis] *s* (bot.) casis (*planta y licor*)
cassiterite [kəˈsɪtəraɪt] *s* (chem.) casiterita
Cassius [ˈkæʃəs] *s* Casio
cassock [ˈkæsək] *s* sotana, balandrán; **to doff the cassock** colgar los hábitos
cassowary [ˈkæsəˌwerɪ] *s* (*pl:* **-ies**) (orn.) casuario
cast [kæst] o [kɑst] *s* echada; forma, molde; pieza fundida; (theat.) reparto; aire, apariencia, semblante; clase; tinte, matiz; mirada bizca; (*pret & pp:* **cast**) *va* echar, lanzar; echar fuera, desechar; echar, volver (*los ojos*); proyectar (*una sombra*); fundir, vaciar; adicionar, calcular; (theat.) repartir (*los papeles*); echar (*balotas*); **to cast about** arrojar por todos lados; **to cast aside** desechar; **to cast away** desechar, abandonar; **to cast down** derribar; desanimar; **to cast forth** despedir, exhalar; **to cast loose** soltar; **to cast off** abandonar, echar de sí; (sew.) hacer (*la última hilera de puntadas*); **to cast on** echarse (*un vestido*) rápidamente; (sew.) empezar con (*la primera hilera de puntadas*); **to cast out** arrojar, echar fuera; despedir, desterrar; *vn* echar dados; arrojar el sedal de pescar; adicionar; **to cast about** buscar, hacer planes, revolver proyectos; **to cast off** (naut.) desamarrar
Castalides [kæsˈtælɪdiz] *spl* (myth.) Castálidas
castanet [ˌkæstəˈnɛt] *s* castañuela o castañeta
castaway [ˈkæstəˌwe] o [ˈkɑstəˌwe] *adj & s* náufrago; proscrito, réprobo
caste [kæst] o [kɑst] *s* casta; régimen de castas; **to lose caste** perder el prestigio
castellan [ˈkæstələn] *s* castellán o castellano
castellated [ˈkæstəˌletɪd] *adj* encastillado
caster [ˈkæstər] o [ˈkɑstər] *s* echador; fundidor, vaciador; ruedecilla de mueble; frasco para aceite, vinagre, sal, etc.; angarillas, vinagreras
castigate [ˈkæstɪget] *va* castigar
castigation [ˌkæstɪˈgeʃən] *s* castigo
castigator [ˈkæstɪˌgetər] *s* castigador
Castile [kæsˈtil] *s* Castilla
Castile soap *s* jabón de Castilla
Castilian [kæsˈtɪljən] *adj & s* castellano
casting [ˈkæstɪŋ] o [ˈkɑstɪŋ] *s* fundición, vaciado; pieza fundida; pesca de lanzamiento; (falc.) curalle; (theat.) reparto (*de los papeles*)
casting line *s* tanza, sedal
casting net *s* esparavel
casting vote *s* voto de calidad, voto decisivo (*en caso de empate*)
cast iron *s* hierro colado, hierro fundido
cast-iron [ˈkæstˈaɪərn] o [ˈkɑstˈaɪərn] *adj* hecho de hierro fundido; fuerte, endurecido; duro, inflexible
cast-iron stomach *s* (coll.) estómago de avestruz
castle [ˈkæsəl] o [ˈkɑsəl] *s* castillo; palacio (*edificio suntuoso*); (chess) roque, torre; *va & vn* (chess) enrocar
castle in Spain o **castle in the air** *s* castillo en el aire
castling [ˈkæslɪŋ] o [kɑslɪŋ] *s* (chess) enroque
castoff [ˈkæstˌɔf] o [ˈkɑstˌɔf] *adj* abandonado, desechado; *s* persona o cosa abandonada o desechada, plato de segunda mesa; (print.) cálculo de espacio
castor [ˈkæstər] o [ˈkɑstər] *s* ruedecilla de mueble; frasco para aceite, vinagre, sal, etc.; angarillas, vinagreras; sombrero de castor; castóreo (*substancia aceitosa*); (*cap.*) *s* (myth., astr. & naut.) Cástor
Castor and Pollux *spl* (myth., astr. & naut.) Cástor y Pólux
castor bean *s* (pharm.) semilla de ricino; (bot.) ricino
castor oil *s* aceite de ricino
castor-oil plant [ˈkæstərˈɔɪl] o [ˈkɑstərˈɔɪl] *s* (bot.) ricino
castrametation [ˌkæstrəməˈteʃən] *s* (mil.) castrametación
castrate [ˈkæstret] *va* castrar, capar; expurgar (*un libro*)
castration [kæsˈtreʃən] *s* castración, capadura; expurgación (*de un libro*)
cast steel *s* acero colado, acero fundido
cast stone *s* sillar de concreto, piedra artificial
casual [ˈkæʒuəl] *adj* casual; impensado, descuidado, indiferente; *s* obrero casual; persona que recibe caridad de vez en cuando; (mil.) soldado en espera de asignación
casualty [ˈkæʒuəltɪ] *s* (*pl:* **-ties**) accidente, desgracia; víctima; muerte; baja (*en la guerra*)
casualty list *s* (mil.) lista de bajas
casuist [ˈkæʒuɪst] *s* casuísta; sofista
casuistic [ˌkæʒuˈɪstɪk] o **casuistical** [ˌkæʒuˈɪstɪkəl] *adj* casuístico; sofístico
casuistry [ˈkæʒuɪstrɪ] *s* (*pl:* **-ries**) casuística; razonamiento hábil y falso
casus belli [ˈkesəs ˈbɛlaɪ] *s* casus belli, motivo de guerra
cat. abr. de **catalogue** y **catechism**
cat [kæt] *s* gato; mujer rencorosa; (ichth.) siluro, bagre, amicuro; (naut.) aparejo de gato; gato de nueve colas, azote con nueve ramales; **to bell the cat** ponerle cascabel al gato; **to let the cat out of the bag** revelar el secreto; (*pret & pp:* **catted;** *ger:* **catting**) *va* (naut.) levantar y trincar (*el ancla*)
catabolism [kəˈtæbəlɪzəm] *s* (biol.) catabolismo
catachresis [ˌkætəˈkrisɪs] *s* (*pl:* **-ses** [siz]) (rhet.) catacresis
cataclysm [ˈkætəklɪzəm] *s* cataclismo
cataclysmal [ˌkætəˈklɪzməl] o **catclysmic** [ˌkætəˈklɪzmɪk] *adj* cataclísmico
catacomb [ˈkætəkom] *s* catacumba
catadioptric [ˌkætədaɪˈɑptrɪk] *adj* (phys.) catadióptrico
catafalque [ˈkætəfælk] *s* catafalco
Catalan [ˈkætəlæn] *adj & s* catalán
Catalan forge o **furnace** *s* forja a la catalana
catalase [ˈkætəles] *s* (chem.) catalasa
catalectic [ˌkætəˈlɛktɪk] *adj* cataléctico
catalepsis [ˌkætəˈlɛpsɪs] o **catalepsy** [ˈkætəˌlɛpsɪ] *s* (path.) catalepsia
cataleptic [ˌkætəˈlɛptɪk] *adj & s* cataléptico
catalog o **catalogue** [ˈkætəlɔg] o [ˈkætəlɑg] *s* catálogo; anuario (*p.ej., de la universidad*); *va* catalogar
catalogue card *s* ficha catalográfica (*de una biblioteca*)
Catalonia [ˌkætəˈlonɪə] *s* Cataluña
Catalonian [ˌkætəˈlonɪən] *adj* catalán
catalpa [kəˈtælpə] *s* (bot.) catalpa
catalysis [kəˈtælɪsɪs] *s* (*pl:* **-ses** [siz]) (chem.) catálisis
catalyst [ˈkætəlɪst] *s* (chem.) catalizador
catalytic [ˌkætəˈlɪtɪk] *adj* catalítico
catalyzer [ˈkætəˌlaɪzər] *s* (chem.) catalizador
catamaran [ˌkætəməˈræn] *s* (naut.) catamarán; armadía, balsa; (coll.) persona pendenciera, mujer pendenciera
catamount [ˈkætəmaʊnt] *s* (zool.) puma; (zool.) lince, gato montés
cataphoresis [ˌkætəfəˈrisɪs] *s* (med. & chem.) cataforesis
catapult [ˈkætəpʌlt] *s* catapulta; honda; (aer.) catapulta; *va* catapultar
cataract [ˈkætərækt] *s* catarata; aguacero, inundación; (path.) catarata
catarrh [kəˈtɑr] *s* (path.) catarro
catarrhal [kəˈtɑrəl] *adj* catarral
catastrophe [kəˈtæstrəfɪ] *s* catástrofe; (theat. & geol.) catástrofe
catastrophic [ˌkætəˈstrɑfɪk] *adj* catastrófico
catbird [ˈkætˌbʌrd] *s* (orn.) pájaro gato
catboat [ˈkætˌbot] *s* (naut.) laúd
catcall [ˈkætˌkɔl] *s* rechifla; *va & vn* rechiflar
catch [kætʃ] *s* cogida (*de la pelota*); pestillo, cerradera; broche; presa, botín; pesca (*lo que se ha pescado*); trampa; buen partido; rondó; **catch in the voice** voz entrecortada ‖ *adj*

atractivo, llamativo; engañoso, tramposo ‖ (*pret & pp:* **caught**) *va* asir, coger, atrapar; sorprender; comprender; (sport) coger, parar; tomar (*frío*), coger (*un resfriado*); **to catch alive** cazar vivo; **to catch fire** encenderse, inflamarse; **to catch hold of** prenderse en; apoderarse de; **to catch it** (coll.) merecerse castigo, merecerse un regaño; **to catch oneself** contenerse; recobrar el equilibrio; **to catch out** (baseball) sacar fuera a (*un jugador*) cogiendo la pelota antes de que caiga ésta al suelo; **to catch up** asir, coger súbitamente; coger al vuelo; coger la palabra a; cazar (*sorprender en error o un descuido*) ‖ *vn* pegarse, transmitirse fácilmente (*una enfermedad*); enredarse, engancharse; encenderse; **to catch at** tratar de asir o coger; asir fuertemente o con anhelo; **to catch on** prender en (*p.ej., un gancho*); comprender; coger el tino; **to catch on to** ponerse al tanto de; **to catch up** emparejar, salir del atraso; ponerse al día (*en las deudas*); **to catch up with** emparejar con

catchall ['kætʃ,ɔl] *s* armario, cesto o cajón destinado a contener toda clase de objetos; vaso de seguridad

catch basin *s* cisterna de desagüe

catch crop *s* (agr.) siembra intermedia entre otras dos siembras o entre las hileras de una siembra

catch drain *s* cuneta

catcher ['kætʃər] *s* agarrador, cogedor; (baseball) receptor, parador, catcher

catchfly ['kætʃ,flaɪ] *s* (*pl:* **-flies**) (bot.) pegamoscas

catching ['kætʃɪŋ] *adj* contagioso; atrayente, fascinador

catchment ['kætʃmənt] *s* captación; depósito de abastecimiento

catchment area o **basin** *s* cuenca de captación

catchpenny ['kætʃ,pɛnɪ] *adj* barato, de pacotilla; *s* (*pl:* **-nies**) engañifa, baratija

catchpole o **catchpoll** ['kætʃ,pol] *s* alguacil, corchete

catch question *s* pega

catch stitch *s* (b.b.) punto alto y bajo; (sew.) punto espigado

catch title *s* título corto y expresivo

catchup ['kætʃəp] o ['kɛtʃəp] *s* var. de **catsup**

catchword ['kætʃ,wʌrd] *s* reclamo, lema, palabra de efecto; (print.) reclamo; (theat.) pie

catchy ['kætʃɪ] *adj* (*comp:* **-ier**; *super:* **-iest**) pegajoso, insidioso; animado, vivo

cate [ket] *s* (archaic) golosina

catechetical [,kætɪ'kɛtɪkəl] *adj* catequístico

catechise o **catechize** ['kætɪkaɪz] *va* catequizar; interrogar minuciosamente

catechism ['kætɪkɪzəm] *s* catecismo; serie de preguntas

catechist ['kætɪkɪst] *s* catequista

catechizer ['kætɪ,kaɪzər] *s* catequizador

catechu ['kætətʃu] *s* catecú

catechumen [,kætɪ'kjumən] *s* (eccl. & fig.) catecúmeno

catechumenate [,kætɪ'kjumənet] *s* catecumenado

categorical [,kætɪ'gɑrɪkəl] o [,kætɪ'gɔrɪkəl] *adj* categórico

categorical imperative *s* (philos.) imperativo categórico

category ['kætɪ,gorɪ] *s* (*pl:* **-ries**) categoría

catenary ['kætɪ,nɛrɪ] *adj* catenario; *s* (*pl:* **-ies**) (math.) catenaria

catenate ['kætɪnet] *va* encadenar, enlazar

catenulate [kə'tɛnjəlet] *adj* catenular

cater ['ketər] *va & vn* abastecer, proveer; **to cater for** abastecer, proveer; **to cater to** proveer a (*p.ej., el gusto popular*)

cater-cornered ['kætər,kɔrnərd] *adj* diagonal; *adv* diagonalmente

caterer ['ketərər] *s* proveedor de alimentos y bebidas a domicilio, especialmente para fiestas y reuniones

cateress ['ketərɪs] *s* abastecedora, proveedora

caterpillar ['kætər,pɪlər] *s* (ent.) oruga; (mach.) oruga (*mecanismo de arrastre*); (trademark) tractor de oruga

caterpillar chain *s* cadena de oruga

caterpillar tractor *s* (trademark) tractor de oruga

caterpillar tread *s* rodado tipo oruga

caterwaul ['kætərwɔl] *s* marramao; chillido; *vn* marramizar (*el gato*); chillar

catfish ['kæt,fɪʃ] *s* (ichth.) siluro, bagre, amiuro

catgut ['kæt,gʌt] *s* (mus.) cuerda de tripa; (surg.) catgut

Cath. abr. de **Catholic**

catharsis [kə'θɑrsɪs] *s* (aesthetics, med. & psychoanal.) catarsis

cathartic [kə'θɑrtɪk] *adj* catártico, purgante; *s* purgante

Cathay [kæ'θe] *s* Catay

cathead ['kæt,hɛd] *s* (naut.) serviola

cathedra [kə'θidrə] o ['kæθɪdrə] *s* cátedra

cathedral [kə'θidrəl] *s* catedral; *adj* catedral, catedralicio; episcopal

Catherine ['kæθərɪn] *s* Catalina

catheter ['kæθɪtər] *s* (surg.) catéter

catheterization [,kæθɪtərɪ'zeʃən] *s* (surg.) cateterismo o cateterización

catheterize ['kæθɪtəraɪz] *va* (surg.) cateterizar

cathetometer [,kæθɪ'tɑmɪtər] *s* (phys.) catetómetro

cathode ['kæθod] *s* (elec.) cátodo

cathode-ray ['kæθod're] *adj* (phys.) de rayos catódicos

cathode rays *spl* (phys.) rayos catódicos

cathode-ray tube *s* (phys.) tubo o válvula de rayos catódicos

cathodic [kə'θɑdɪk] *adj* catódico

catholic ['kæθəlɪk] *adj* católico (*universal*); liberal, de amplias miras; (*cap.*) *adj & s* católico

catholicism [kə'θɑlɪsɪzəm] *s* catolicidad (*universalidad*); (*cap.*) *s* catolicismo

catholicity [,kæθə'lɪsɪtɪ] *s* catolicidad (*universalidad*); (*cap.*) *s* catolicidad

catholicize [kə'θɑlɪsaɪz] *va* catolizar; *vn* catolizarse

cation ['kæt,aɪən] *s* (elec.) catión

catkin ['kætkɪn] *s* (bot.) amento (*inflorescencia*)

catmint ['kæt,mɪnt] *s* (bot.) hierba gatera

cat nap *s* siesta corta

catnip ['kætnɪp] *s* (bot.) hierba gatera

Cato ['keto] *s* Catón

Catonian [ke'tonɪən] *adj* catoniano

cat-o'-nine-tails [,kætə'naɪn,telz] *s* gato de nueve colas, azote con nueve ramales

catoptric [kə'tɑptrɪk] *adj* catóptrico; **catoptrics** *ssg* (opt.) catóptrica

cat-rigged ['kæt,rɪgd] *adj* (naut.) aparejado como un laúd

cat's cradle *s* cunas, juego de la cuna

cat's-eye ['kæts,aɪ] *s* (mineral.) ojo de gato

cat's-paw o **catspaw** ['kæts,pɔ] *s* instrumento, hombre de paja, mano de gato; (naut.) soplo ligero

cat's-tail ['kæts,tel] *s* (bot.) cola de rata (*Equisetum arvense*); (bot.) viborera; (bot.) espadaña; (bot.) fleo; (meteor.) cola de gato (*cirro*)

catsup ['kætsəp] o ['kɛtʃəp] *s* salsa de tomate con cebollas, sal, azúcar y especias

cat tackle *s* (naut.) aparejo de gata

cattail ['kæt,tel] *s* (bot.) espadaña, anea (*Typha latifolia*); (bot.) anea (*Typha angustifolia*); (bot.) amento (*inflorescencia*)

cat thyme *s* (bot.) hierba del papa

cattiness ['kætɪnɪs] *s* gatada; chismería

cattish ['kætɪʃ] *adj* gatuno; engañoso, trampista; rencoroso, malicioso; chismoso

cattle ['kætəl] *s* ganado, ganado vacuno; gente despreciable

cattle car *s* vagón cuadra, vagón jaula

cattle crossing *s* paso de ganado

cattleman ['kætəlmən] *s* (*pl:* **-men**) ganadero

cattle pump *s* bomba automática para el ganado

cattle raising *s* ganadería

cattle ranch *s* hacienda de ganado

cattle show *s* exposición de ganado

cattle thief *s* ladrón de ganado

cattle tick *s* (ent.) garrapata

catty ['kætɪ] *adj* (*comp:* **-tier**; *super:* **-tiest**) gatesco; arisco; rencoroso, malicioso; chismoso

Catullus [kə'tʌləs] *s* Catulo

catwalk ['kæt,wɔk] *s* pasadizo, pasarela

cat whisker *s* (rad.) bigote de gato

Caucasian [kɔ'keʒən] o [kɔ'keʃən] *adj & s*

caucásico (*blanco*); caucáseo o caucasiano (*del Cáucaso*)
Caucasus ['kɔkəsəs] *s* Cáucaso
caucus ['kɔkəs] *s* camarilla política; *vn* reunirse en camarilla política
caudal ['kɔdəl] *adj* (zool.) caudal
caudate ['kɔdet] *adj* caudato
Caudine Forks ['kɔdaɪn] *spl* Horcas Caudinas
caudle ['kɔdəl] *s* bebida caliente compuesta de azúcar, huevos, especias y vino o cerveza (*para los enfermos*)
caught [kɔt] *pret & pp de* **catch**
caul [kɔl] *s* redaño
cauldron ['kɔldrən] *s* var. de **caldron**
caulescent [kɔ'lɛsənt] *adj* (bot.) caulescente
caulicle ['kɔlɪkəl] *s* (bot.) caulícula
cauliculus [kɔ'lɪkjələs] *s* (*pl:* **-li** [laɪ]) (arch.) caulículo
cauliflower ['kɔlɪ,flauər] *s* (bot.) coliflor
cauliflower excrescence *s* (path.) coliflor
caulk [kɔk] *va* calafatear
caulker ['kɔkər] *s* calafate o calafateador
causal ['kɔzəl] *adj* causal
causality [kɔ'zælɪtɪ] *s* (*pl:* **-ties**) causalidad
causation [kɔ'zeʃən] *s* causa; causalidad (*relación de causa a efecto*)
causative ['kɔzətɪv] *adj* causativo (*que es causa de alguna cosa*)
cause [kɔz] *s* causa; causante; (law) causa; **to make common cause with** hacer causa común con; *va* causar
causeless ['kɔzlɪs] *adj* sin causa; infundado
causerie [,kozə'ri] *s* charla, plática; artículo corto
causeway ['kɔz,we] *s* calzada, arrecife; calzada elevada, terraplén
caustic ['kɔstɪk] *adj* (chem., math., opt. & fig.) cáustico; *s* (chem.) cáustico; (math. & opt.) cáustica
caustically ['kɔstɪkəlɪ] *adv* cáusticamente
causticity [kɔs'tɪsɪtɪ] *s* causticidad; (fig.) causticidad
caustic potash *s* (chem.) potasa cáustica
caustic soda *s* (chem.) sosa cáustica
cauterization [,kɔtərɪ'zeʃən] *s* cauterización
cauterize ['kɔtəraɪz] *va* cauterizar
cautery ['kɔtərɪ] *s* (*pl:* **-ies**) cauterio
caution ['kɔʃən] *s* cautela; advertencia, amonestación; (coll.) persona o cosa extraordinaria; *va* advertir, amonestar
cautionary ['kɔʃə,nɛrɪ] *adj* amonestador
cautious ['kɔʃəs] *adj* cauto, cauteloso
Cav. abr. de **Cavalry**
cavalcade [,kævəl'ked] o ['kævəlked] *s* cabalgata
cavalier [,kævə'lɪr] *s* caballero; galán (*que sirve de escolta a una dama*); *adj* altivo, desdeñoso; brusco, inceremonioso; desenvuelto, despreocupado
cavalry ['kævəlrɪ] *s* (*pl:* **-ries**) (mil.) caballería
cavalry charge *s* carga de caballería
cavalryman ['kævəlrɪmən] *s* (*pl:* **-men**) (mil.) soldado de caballería
cavatina [,kævə'tinə] *s* (mus.) cavatina
cave [kev] *s* cueva; *va* ahuecar, excavar; **to cave in** quebrar; *vn* **to cave in** derrumbarse; (coll.) ceder, rendirse
caveat ['kevɪæt] *s* advertencia; (law) información a un juez u otro funcionario para que suspenda algún procedimiento hasta más tarde
cave dweller *s* cavernícola
cave-in ['kev,ɪn] *s* (coll.) socavón, hundimiento, derrumbe
cave man *s* cavernícola, hombre de caverna; hombre grosero
cavern ['kævərn] *s* caverna
cavernous ['kævərnəs] *adj* cavernoso
cavesson ['kævəsən] *s* cabezón
cavetto [kə'vɛto] *s* (*pl:* **-ti** [tɪ] o **-tos**) (arch.) caveto, esgucio
caviar o **caviare** ['kævɪɑr] o ['kɑvɪɑr] *s* caviar; **caviar to the general** cosa demasiado buena para ser estimada por la gente ordinaria
cavicorn ['kævɪkɔrn] *adj* (zool.) cavicornio
cavil ['kævɪl] *s* cavilación; (*pret & pp:* **-iled** o **-illed**; *ger:* **-iling** o **-illing**) *va & vn* cavilar
cavitation [,kævɪ'teʃən] *s* (mach. & path.) cavitación
cavity ['kævɪtɪ] *s* (*pl:* **-ties**) cavidad
cavort [kə'vɔrt] *vn* (coll.) cabriolar
cavy ['kevɪ] *s* (*pl:* **-vies**) (zool.) cavia, conejillo de Indias
caw [kɔ] *s* graznido; *vn* graznar
cay [ke] o [ki] *s* cayo
cayenne [kaɪ'ɛn] o [ke'ɛn] *s* pimentón (*polvo*); (*cap.*) *s* Cayena
cayenne pepper *s* pimentón (*polvo*)
cayman ['kemən] *s* (*pl:* **-mans**) (zool.) caimán
cayuse [kaɪ'jus] *s* (U.S.A.) jaca india
C battery *s* (rad.) batería de rejilla
cc. o **c.c.** abr. de **cubic centimeter** o **cubic centimeters**
cd. abr. de **cord** o **cords**
cd. ft. abr. de **cord foot**
cearin ['siərɪn] *s* (pharm.) cearina
cease [sis] *s* cesación; **without cease** sin cesar; *va* parar, suspender; *vn* cesar; **to cease** + *ger* cesar de + *inf*
cease fire *s* cese de fuego, alto el fuego
cease-fire ['sis'faɪr] *vn* suspender hostilidades
ceaseless ['sislɪs] *adj* incesante, continuo
Cecil ['sisɪl] o ['sɛsɪl] *s* Cecilio
Cecilia [sɪ'sɪljə] *s* Cecilia
Cecropia moth [sɪ'kropɪə] *s* (ent.) mariposa del gusano de seda (*Samia cecropia*)
cedar ['sidər] *s* (bot.) cedro; *adj* cedrino
cedarbird ['sidər,bʌrd] o **cedar waxwing** *s* (orn.) filomeno, zonzo
cedar chest *s* cofre o arca de cedro
cedar of Lebanon *s* (bot.) cedro del Líbano
cede [sid] *va* ceder, traspasar
cedilla [sɪ'dɪlə] *s* cedilla
cedrium ['sidrɪəm] *s* cedria
ceil [sil] *va* forrar, revestir (*la pared o el techo interior*)
ceiling ['silɪŋ] *s* techo, cielo raso; (aer.) techo, cielo máximo
ceiling price *s* precio tope
celadon green ['sɛlədɑn] *s* verdeceledón
celandine ['sɛləndaɪn] *s* (bot.) celidonia, hierba de las golondrinas
celebrant ['sɛlɪbrənt] *s* celebrante (*sacerdote*)
celebrate ['sɛlɪbret] *va* celebrar; proclamar; festejar (*p.ej., un día de fiesta*); *vn* celebrar (*decir misa*); divertirse, festejarse, parrandear
celebrated ['sɛlɪ,bretɪd] *adj* célebre
celebration [,sɛlɪ'breʃən] *s* celebración; tertulia, diversión
celebrator ['sɛlɪ,bretər] *s* celebrante; contertulio; parrandista
celebrity [sɪ'lɛbrɪtɪ] *s* (*pl:* **-ties**) celebridad (*calidad y persona*)
celeriac [sɪ'lɛrɪæk] *s* (bot.) apio-nabo
celerity [sɪ'lɛrɪtɪ] *s* celeridad
celery ['sɛlərɪ] *s* (bot.) apio
celesta [sɪ'lɛstə] *s* (mus.) celesta; (mus.) celeste (*registro del órgano*)
celestial [sɪ'lɛstʃəl] *adj* celestial (*perteneciente al paraíso; perteneciente al firmamento*); celeste (*perteneciente al firmamento y a la astronomía*); (fig.) celestial (*perfecto, delicioso*); (*cap.*) *adj & s* celeste (*chino*)
celestial body *s* cuerpo celeste
Celestial Empire *s* celeste imperio, imperio celeste (*China*)
celestial globe *s* (astr.) globo celeste
celestial mechanics *s* (astr.) mecánica celeste
celestial sphere *s* (astr.) esfera celeste
celibacy ['sɛlɪbəsɪ] *s* (*pl:* **-cies**) celibato
celibate ['sɛlɪbɪt] o ['sɛlɪbet] *adj & s* célibe
cell [sɛl] *s* celda (*aposento en un convento, cárcel, etc.*); celdilla (*de los panales de las abejas*); (biol., elec. & pol.) célula; (elec.) elemento (*de una pila o acumulador*); (aer.) celda, globo (*de dirigible*); (aer.) célula (*de avión*); (bot.) celdilla (*lóculo*)
cellar ['sɛlər] *s* sótano, bodega
cellarage ['sɛlərɪdʒ] *s* sótanos, bodegas; almacenaje en una bodega
cellarer ['sɛlərər] *s* bodeguero
cellaret [,sɛlə'rɛt] *s* licorera
celled [sɛld] *adj* celulado
cellist o **'cellist** ['tʃɛlɪst] *s* violoncelista
cello o **'cello** ['tʃɛlo] *s* (*pl:* **-los**) (mus.) violoncelo
celloidin [sə'lɔɪdɪn] *s* (chem.) celoidina
cellophane ['sɛləfen] *s* (trademark) celofán
cellular ['sɛljələr] *adj* celular

cellule ['sɛljul] *s* celulilla; (aer.) célula (*de avión*)
cellulitis [,sɛljə'laɪtɪs] *s* (path.) celulitis
celluloid ['sɛljəlɔɪd] *s* (trademark) celuloide; (fig.) celuloide (*película cinematográfica*)
cellulose ['sɛljəlos] *s* (chem.) celulosa
cellulous ['sɛljələs] *adj* celuloso
celom ['siləm] *s* var. de **coelom**
Celt [sɛlt] o [kɛlt] *s* celta
Celtiberia [,sɛltɪ'bɪrɪə] *s* Celtiberia
Celtiberian [,sɛltɪ'bɪrɪən] *adj & s* celtibérico
Celtic ['sɛltɪk] o ['kɛltɪk] *adj* céltico; *s* celta (*idioma*)
Celticism ['sɛltɪsɪzəm] o ['kɛltɪsɪzəm] *s* celtismo
Celticist ['sɛltɪsɪst] o ['kɛltɪsɪst] *s* celtista
cement [sɪ'mɛnt] *s* cemento; (anat., dent. & geol.) cemento; *va* revestir de cemento; unir con cemento; (metal.) cementar; unir, pegar; consolidar (*p.ej., la amistad, la alianza*); *vn* unirse, pegarse
cementation [,simən'teʃən] *s* (metal.) cementación
cement block *s* bloque de hormigón
cement mill *s* fábrica de cemento
cement mixer *s* var. de **concrete mixer**
cemetery ['sɛmɪ,tɛrɪ] *s* (*pl:* **-ies**) cementerio
cen. abr. de **central**
Cenacle ['sɛnəkəl] *s* Cenáculo (*sala de la última cena*)
Cenis, Mont [mõ sə'ni] el monte Cenís, Moncenisio
cenobite ['sinobaɪt] o ['sɛnobaɪt] *s* cenobita
cenobitism ['sinobaɪtɪzəm] o ['sɛnobaɪtɪzəm] *s* cenobitismo
cenotaph ['sɛnətæf] o ['sɛnətɑf] *s* cenotafio
Cenozoic [,sino'zo·ɪk] o [,sɛno'zo·ɪk] *adj* (geol.) cenozoico; *s* (geol.) era cenozoica, formaciones cenozoicas
censer ['sɛnsər] *s* incensario
censor ['sɛnsər] *s* censor; *va* censurar
censorial [sɛn'sorɪəl] *adj* censorio
censorious [sɛn'sorɪəs] *adj* censurista, criticón
censorship ['sɛnsərʃɪp] *s* censura
censurable ['sɛnʃərəbəl] *adj* censurable
censure ['sɛnʃər] *s* censura; *va* censurar
census ['sɛnsəs] *s* censo; **to take the census** levantar el censo; *adj* censal
census taker *s* enumerador censal
census taking *s* levantamiento del censo o de los censos
cent. abr. de **centigrade, central** y **century**
cent [sɛnt] *s* centavo
centaur ['sɛntɔr] *s* (myth.) centauro
centaury ['sɛntɔrɪ] *s* (*pl:* **-ries**) (bot.) centaura
centenarian [,sɛntɪ'nɛrɪən] *adj & s* centenario
centenary ['sɛntɪ,nɛrɪ] o [sɛn'tinərɪ] *adj* centenario; *s* (*pl:* **-ies**) centenario
centennial [sɛn'tɛnɪəl] *adj & s* centenario
centennially [sɛn'tɛnɪəlɪ] *adv* cada cien años
center ['sɛntər] *s* centro; *adj* centrista; *va* centrar; concentrar; (mil.) centrar (*fuego, ataque, etc.*); *vn* estar en el centro; concentrarse; concurrir
centerboard ['sɛntər,bord] *s* (naut.) orza de deriva
center drill *s* broca de centrar
center field *s* (baseball) jardín central
centering ['sɛntərɪŋ] *s* centraje; (arch.) cimbra
center of attraction *s* (astr.) centro de atracción; (fig.) centro de interés
center of gravity *s* (mech.) centro de gravedad
centerpiece ['sɛntər,pis] *s* centro de mesa
center punch *s* granete, punzón de marcar
center service line *s* (tennis) línea de mitad, línea de media red
center tap *s* (elec.) toma media, derivación central
centesimal [sɛn'tɛsɪməl] *adj* centesimal; *s* centésimo
centiare ['sɛntɪ,ɛr] *s* centiárea
centigrade ['sɛntɪgred] *adj* centígrado
centigrade thermometer *s* termómetro centígrado
centigram o **centigramme** ['sɛntɪgræm] *s* centigramo
centiliter ['sɛntɪ,litər] *s* centilitro
centime ['sɑntim] *s* céntimo
centimeter ['sɛntɪ,mitər] *s* centímetro
centimeter-gram-second system ['sɛntɪ,mitər'græm'sɛkənd] *s* (phys.) sistema cegesimal, sistema centímetro-gramo-segundo
centipede ['sɛntɪpid] *s* (zool.) ciempiés o cientopiés
central ['sɛntrəl] *adj* central; *s* (telp.) central; (telp.) telefonista
Central America *s* Centro América, la América Central
Central American *adj & s* centroamericano
central heating *s* (Brit.) calefacción central; (U.S.A.) calefacción central de un grupo de edificios
centralism ['sɛntrəlɪzəm] *s* centralismo
centralist ['sɛntrəlɪst] *adj & s* centralista
centralization [,sɛntrəlɪ'zeʃən] *s* centralización
centralize ['sɛntrəlaɪz] *va* centralizar; *vn* centralizarse
centrally ['sɛntrəlɪ] *adv* en el centro, hacia el centro
central nervous system *s* (anat. & physiol.) sistema nervioso central
Central Powers *spl* Potencias centrales
Central time *s* (U.S.A.) hora legal correspondiente al meridiano 90°
centre ['sɛntər] *s, adj, va, & vn* var. de **center**
centric ['sɛntrɪk] *adj* céntrico
centrifugal [sɛn'trɪfjʊgəl] *adj* centrífugo
centrifugal force *s* fuerza centrífuga
centrifugal machine *s* centrifugadora
centrifugal pump *s* bomba centrífuga
centrifuge ['sɛntrɪfjudʒ] *s* centrífuga; *va* centrifugar
centripetal [sɛn'trɪpɪtəl] *adj* centrípeto
centripetal force *s* fuerza centrípeta
centrist ['sɛntrɪst] *s* centrista
centrobaric [,sɛntro'bærɪk] *adj* centrobárico
centrosome ['sɛntrəsom] *s* (biol.) centrosoma
centrosphere ['sɛntrə,sfɪr] *s* (biol.) centroesfera
centuple ['sɛntjʊpəl] o ['sɛntʊpəl] *adj* céntuplo; *va* centuplicar
centurion [sɛn'tjʊrɪən] o [sɛn'tʊrɪən] *s* centurión
century ['sɛntʃərɪ] *s* (*pl:* **-ries**) siglo, centuria; (hist.) centuria; grupo de cien personas o cosas
century plant *s* (bot.) pita
cephalic [sɪ'fælɪk] *adj* cefálico
cephalochordate [,sɛfəlo'kɔrdet] *adj* (zool.) cefalocordado
cephalopod ['sɛfəlo,pɑd] *adj & s* (zool.) cefalópodo
cephalothorax [,sɛfəlo'θoræks] *s* (zool.) cefalotórax
Cepheid ['sɛfɪɪd] *adj* (astr.) cefeido; *s* (astr.) cefeida; **Cepheid variable** (astr.) cefeida variable
Cepheus ['sifjus] o ['sifɪəs] *s* (myth. & astr.) Cefeo
ceramic [sɪ'ræmɪk] *adj* cerámico; **ceramics** *ssg* cerámica (*arte*); *spl* cerámica (*objetos*)
ceramist ['sɛrəmɪst] *s* ceramista
cerargyrite [sɪ'rɑrdʒɪraɪt] *s* (mineral.) querargirita
cerastes [sɪ'ræstiz] *s* (zool.) cerasta
cerate ['sɪret] *s* (pharm.) cerato
Cerberus ['sʌrbərəs] *s* (myth. & fig.) Cancerbero
cere [sɪr] *s* (orn.) cera
cereal ['sɪrɪəl] *adj & s* cereal
cerebellum [,sɛrɪ'bɛləm] *s* (*pl:* **-lums** o **-la** [lə]) (anat.) cerebelo
cerebral ['sɛrɪbrəl] *adj* cerebral
cerebral palsy *s* (path.) parálisis cerebral infantil, diplejía espástica
cerebrate ['sɛribret] *vn* pensar, reflexionar
cerebration [,sɛrɪ'breʃən] *s* cerebración; pensamiento
cerebrospinal [,sɛrɪbro'spaɪnəl] *adj* (anat.) cerebroespinal
cerebrospinal meningitis *s* (path.) meningitis cerebroespinal
cerebrum ['sɛrɪbrəm] *s* (*pl:* **-brums** o **-bra** [brə]) (anat.) cerebro (*encéfalo; parte anterior del encéfalo*)

cerecloth ['sɪr,klɔθ] o ['sɪr,klɑθ] *s* encerado; mortaja encerada
cerement ['sɪrmənt] *s* mortaja encerada
ceremonial [,serɪ'monɪəl] *adj* ceremonial; *s* ceremonial; (eccl.) ceremonial (*libro*)
ceremonious [,serɪ'monɪəs] *adj* ceremonioso
ceremony ['serɪ,monɪ] *s* (*pl:* **-nies**) ceremonia; **to stand on ceremony** hacer ceremonias
Ceres ['sɪriz] *s* (myth.) Ceres
cereus ['sɪrɪəs] *s* (bot.) pitahaya, acacana
cerise [sə'riz] o [sə'ris] *s* cereza, color de cereza; *adj* de color de cereza
cerium ['sɪrɪəm] *s* (chem.) cerio
cerium metals *spl* (chem.) céridos
cero ['sɪro] *s* (*pl:* **-ros**) (ichth.) pintada, sierra
ceroplastics [,sɪro'plæstɪks] o [,sero'plæstɪks] *ssg* ceroplástica
cerotic [sɪ'rɑtɪk] *adj* (chem.) cerótico
cerotic acid *s* (chem.) ácido cerótico
certain ['sʌrtən] *adj* cierto; **a certain** cierto; **for certain** por cierto; **to be certain to** + *inf* no poder dejar de + *inf*
certainly ['sʌrtənlɪ] *adv* ciertamente, con certeza; con mucho gusto
certainty ['sʌrtəntɪ] *s* (*pl:* **-ties**) certeza o certidumbre; cosa cierta; **with certainty** a ciencia cierta
certes ['sʌrtiz] *adv* (archaic) seguramente, en verdad
certifiable ['sʌrtɪ,faɪəbəl] *adj* certificable
certificate [sər'tɪfɪkɪt] *s* certificado, certificación; título (*documento que representa valor comercial*); [ser'tɪfɪket] *va* certificar
certificate of baptism *s* partida de bautismo
certificate of death *s* partida de defunción
certificate of marriage *s* certificado de matrimonio, partida de casamiento
certificate of origin *s* (com.) certificado de origen
certification [,sʌrtɪfɪ'keʃən] *s* certificación
certificatory [sər'tɪfɪkə,torɪ] *adj* certificatorio
certified check *s* (com.) cheque certificado
certified public accountant *s* censor jurado de cuentas, contador público titulado
certify ['sʌrtɪfaɪ] (*pret & pp:* **-fied**) *va* certificar; garantizar la calidad de
certiorari [,sʌrʃɪo'rerɪ] *s* (law) auto de avocación
certitude ['sʌrtɪtjud] o ['sʌrtɪtud] *s* certidumbre
cerulean [sɪ'rulɪən] *adj* cerúleo
cerumen [sɪ'rumen] *s* (physiol.) cerumen
ceruse ['sɪrus] o [sɪ'rus] *s* (chem.) cerusa
cerussite ['sɪrəsaɪt] *s* (mineral.) cerusita
Cervantist [sər'væntɪst] *s* cervantista
cervical ['sʌrvɪkəl] *adj* cervical
cervical rib *s* (anat.) costilla cervical
cervicitis [,sʌrvɪ'saɪtɪs] *s* (path.) cervicitis
cervine ['sʌrvaɪn] o ['sʌrvɪn] *adj* cervino
cervix ['sʌrvɪks] *s* (*pl:* **cervices** [sər'vaɪsiz] o ['sʌrvɪsiz] o **cervixes**) (anat.) cerviz
Cesarean o **Cesarian** [sɪ'zerɪən] *adj & s* var. de **Caesarean**
cesium ['sizɪəm] *s* (chem.) cesio
cespitose ['sespɪtos] *adj* cespitoso
cessation [se'seʃən] *s* cesación
cessation of hostilities *s* suspensión de hostilidades
cession ['seʃən] *s* cesión
cesspool ['ses,pul] *s* pozo negro; sitio inmundo
cestode ['sestod] *s* (zool.) cestodo
cestus ['sestəs] *s* (hist.) cesto (*armadura de la mano*); (myth.) cinturón de Venus
cesura [sɪ'ʒurə] o [sɪ'zjurə] *s* (*pl:* **-ras** o **-rae** [ri]) var. de **caesura**
cetacean [sɪ'teʃən] *adj & s* (zool.) cetáceo
cetaceous [sɪ'teʃəs] *adj* (zool.) cetáceo
cetane ['siten] *s* (chem.) cetano
cetane number *s* (chem.) número de cetano
cetin ['sitən] *s* (chem.) cetina
cetrarin [sɪ'trerɪn] o ['setrərɪn] *s* (chem.) cetrarina
Cetus ['sitəs] *s* (astr.) Ballena
cetyl ['setɪl] o ['sitɪl] *s* (chem.) cetilo
Ceylon [sɪ'lɑn] *s* Ceilán
Ceylonese [,silə'niz] *adj* ceilanés; *s* (*pl:* **-nese**) ceilanés
cf. abr. de **confer** (Lat.) **compare**

c.f.i. o **C.F.I.** abr. de **cost, freight, and insurance**
cg. abr. de **centigram** o **centigrams**
c.g.s. o **cgs** abr. de **centimeter-gram-second (system)**
ch. abr. de **chapter** y **church**
chaconne [ʃɑ'kɔn] *s* (mus.) chacona
Chaeronea [,kerə'niə] *s* Queronea
chafe [tʃef] *s* frotamiento; desgaste; irritación; *va* frotar; escocer; desgastar, raer; irritar; *vn* desgastarse, raerse; irritarse, escocerse
chafer ['tʃefər] *s* (ent.) abejorro
chaff [tʃæf] o [tʃɑf] *s* barcia, aechaduras; paja menuda; broza, desperdicio; zumba, vaya, chanza ligera; *va* zumbarse de
chaffer ['tʃæfər] *s* regateo; *va* regatear; trocar (*palabras*); **to chaffer away** gastar; *vn* regatear
chaffinch ['tʃæfɪntʃ] *s* (orn.) pinzón
chaffy ['tʃæfɪ] o ['tʃɑfɪ] *adj* (*comp:* **-ier**; *super:* **-iest**) lleno de barcia; brozoso, inútil; chancero
chafing dish ['tʃefɪŋ] *s* cocinilla, infernillo
chagrin [ʃə'grɪn] *s* pesadumbre, desazón, disgusto; *va* apesadumbrar, desazonar, disgustar
chain [tʃen] *s* cadena; (chem. & rad.) cadena; *va* encadenar
chain cable *s* (naut.) cadena de ancla
chain drive *s* transmisión de cadena
chain gang *s* collera, cadena de presidiarios, cuerda de presos
chain gear *s* rueda de cadena
chain lightning *s* relámpagos en zigzag
chain-link fencing ['tʃen'lɪŋk] *s* cercado eslabonado
chain mail *s* cota de malla
chainman ['tʃenmən] *s* (*pl:* **-men**) cadenero
chain of mountains *s* cordillera, cadena de montañas
chain-pull socket ['tʃen,pul] *s* (elec.) portalámparas de cadena
chain pump *s* bomba de cadena
chain reaction *s* (phys.) reacción en cadena, acción eslabonada
chain saw *s* sierra de cadena
chain shot *s* (mil.) balas enramadas
chain smoker *s* cigarrista, fumador de un pitillo tras otro
chain stitch *s* punto de cadeneta
chain-stitch ['tʃen,stɪtʃ] *va* coser empleando el punto de cadeneta
chain store *s* empresa con cadena de tiendas; tienda de una cadena
chain tongs *spl* llave de cadena
chain wheel *s* rueda dentada para cadena
chair [tʃer] *s* silla; cátedra (*de profesor*); silla de manos; sillón del presidente; presidente (*de una reunión*); (rail.) cojinete; **to take the chair** abrir la sesión; presidir la reunión; *va* asentar; llevar en una silla; presidir (*una reunión*)
chair car *s* (rail.) vagón salón
chair lift *s* telesilla (*para los esquiadores*)
chairman ['tʃermən] *s* (*pl:* **-men**) presidente; silletero (*el que lleva una silla de manos o empuja una silla de ruedas*)
chairmanship ['tʃermənʃɪp] *s* presidencia
Chair of Saint Peter *s* cátedra de San Pedro (*dignidad del Sumo Pontífice; silla situada en la Basílica del Vaticano*)
chair rail *s* guardasilla
chairwoman ['tʃer,wumən] *s* (*pl:* **-women**) presidenta
chaise [ʃez] *s* calesa, calesín, silla volante
chaise longue [lɔŋg] *s* meridiana, chaise longue
chalaza [kə'lezə] *s* (*pl:* **-zas** o **-zae** [zi]) (bot. & embryol.) chalaza
Chalcedon ['kælsɪdɑn] o [kæl'sidən] *s* Calcedonia
chalcedony [kæl'sedənɪ] o ['kælsɪ,donɪ] *s* (*pl:* **-nies**) (mineral.) calcedonia
chalcid ['kælsɪd] *s* (ent.) calcídido
chalcopyrite [,kælkə'paɪraɪt] o [,kælkə'pɪraɪt] *s* (mineral.) calcopirita
Chaldaic [kæl'deɪk] *adj* caldaico, caldeo; *s* caldeo
Chaldea [kæl'diə] *s* Caldea
Chaldean [kæl'diən] *adj & s* caldeo; (fig.) caldeo (*astrólogo; mágico*)

Chaldee [kæl'di] o ['kældi] *adj & s* caldeo
chalet [ʃæ'le] o ['ʃæle] *s* chalet
chalice ['tʃælɪs] *s* (bot., eccl. & poet.) cáliz
chalk [tʃɔk] *s* creta; tiza (*con que se escribe en las pizarras*); *va* marcar, escribir o dibujar con tiza; mezclar o frotar con creta; enyesar; **to chalk up** apuntar; (sport) apuntar; (sport) ganar (*un tanto*); obtener (*un triunfo*)
chalk talk *s* conferencia esclarecida con ejemplos o dibujos hechos con tiza en una pizarra
chalky ['tʃɔkɪ] *adj* (*comp:* **-ier;** *super:* **-iest**) cretoso; pálido
challenge ['tʃælɪndʒ] *s* desafío; demanda; (mil.) quién vive; (law) recusación; *va* desafiar, retar; demandar, exigir; disputar; dudar; (mil.) dar el quién vive a; (law) recusar; **to challenge to** + *inf* desafiar a + *inf*
challenger ['tʃælɪndʒər] *s* desafiador, retador
challenging ['tʃælɪndʒɪŋ] *adj* desafiador, retador; provocador
challie o **challis** ['ʃælɪ] *s* chalí
chalybeate [kə'lɪbɪet] o [kə'lɪbɪɪt] *adj* calibeado, ferruginoso; *s* medicamento ferruginoso, agua ferruginosa
chamber ['tʃembər] *s* cámara; recámara (*de un arma de fuego*); (anat.) cámara; aposento, dormitorio; **chambers** *spl* oficina de abogado o juez; (Brit.) serie de cámaras que sirven de habitaciones u oficinas
chambered ['tʃembərd] *adj* que tiene cámara o cámaras; dividido en compartimientos
chamberlain ['tʃembərlɪn] *s* chambelán; tesorero
chambermaid ['tʃembər,med] *s* camarera
chamber music *s* música de cámara
chamber of commerce *s* cámara de comercio
chamber orchestra *s* orquesta de cámara
chamber pot *s* orinal, vaso de noche
chambray ['ʃæmbre] *s* cambray
chameleon [kə'milɪən] *s* (zool. & fig.) camaleón
chamfer ['tʃæmfər] *s* chaflán; *va* chaflanar; acanalar, estirar
chamois ['ʃæmɪ] *s* (*pl:* **-ois** [ɪ]) (zool.) gamuza; gamuza (*piel*)
champ [tʃæmp] *s* (slang) campeón; mordisco; *va & vn* mordiscar; **to champ the bit** morder o tascar el freno
champagne [ʃæm'pen] *s* champaña *m* (*vino*); (*cap.*) *s* la Champaña
champaign [ʃæm'pen] *adj* llano y abierto; *s* campiña
champion ['tʃæmpɪən] *s* campeón; (fig.) campeón; paladín; *adj* campeón, p.ej., **champion cyclist** campeón ciclista; *va* defender (*a veces contra el dictamen ajeno*)
championess ['tʃæmpɪənɪs] *s* campeona
championship ['tʃæmpɪən,ʃɪp] *s* campeonato
champlevé [,ʃæmplə've] *s* esmalte campeado o vaciado
Champs Elysées [ʃɑ̃zeli'ze] *spl* Campos Elíseos (*paseo de París*)
chance [tʃæns] o [tʃɑns] *s* ocasión, oportunidad; posibilidad, probabilidad; casualidad; suerte, fortuna; riesgo, peligro; acontecimiento, suceso; **by chance** por acaso, por casualidad; **on the chance that** por si acaso; **the chances are even that . . .** las probabilidades corren parejas que . . .; **the chances are that . . .** (coll.) es probable que . . .; **to let the chance slip** perder la ocasión; **to look out for the main chance** estar a caza de su provecho; **to not stand a chance** no tener probabilidad; **to take a chance** probar fortuna, probar suerte; comprar un billete (*p.ej., de lotería*); **to take one's chances** aventurarse, probar fortuna; *adj* casual, imprevisto; *va* (coll.) arriesgar; *vn* acontecer, suceder; **to chance on** o **upon** tropezar con
chancel ['tʃænsəl] o ['tʃɑnsəl] *s* (eccl.) entrecoro
chancellery ['tʃænsələrɪ] o ['tʃɑnsələrɪ] *s* (*pl:* **-ies**) cancillería
chancellor ['tʃænsələr] o ['tʃɑnsələr] *s* canciller
Chancellor of the Exchequer *s* (Brit.) Canciller del echiquier, ministro de hacienda
chancellorship ['tʃænsələr,ʃɪp] o ['tʃɑnsələr,ʃɪp] *s* cancillería
chancery ['tʃænsərɪ] o ['tʃɑnsərɪ] *s* (*pl:* **-ies**) chancillería (*tribunal de justicia*); cancillería; justicia; archivo (*de documentos públicos*); (wrestling) presa a la cabeza; **in chancery** en litigio en un tribunal de justicia; en situación muy difícil; (wrestling) debajo del brazo del contrario (*dícese de la cabeza*)
chancre ['ʃæŋkər] *s* (path.) chancro
chancrous ['ʃæŋkrəs] *adj* chancroso
chancy ['tʃænsɪ] o ['tʃɑnsɪ] *adj* (*comp:* **-ier;** *super:* **-iest**) (coll.) arriesgado
chandelier [,ʃændə'lɪr] *s* araña de luces
chandler ['tʃændlər] *s* cerero, velero; abacero, tendero
chandlery ['tʃændlərɪ] *s* (*pl:* **-ies**) cerería, velería; cirios, velas, candelas, etc.
change [tʃendʒ] *s* cambio, mudanza; variedad; dinero menudo, moneda suelta; vuelta (*dinero devuelto*); muda (*de ropa*); **for a change** por cambiar, por variedad; **to keep the change** quedarse con la vuelta; **to ring the changes** tocar las campanas de todas las maneras; obrar de varias maneras; **to ring the changes on** hacer (*una cosa*) de varias maneras; decir (*una cosa*) de varias maneras; *va* cambiar, mudar; reemplazar; **to change clothes** cambiar de ropa; **to change color** demudarse; **to change gears** cambiar de velocidades; **to change hands** cambiar de dueño; **to change money** cambiar moneda; **to change one's mind** cambiar de opinión; **to change one's tune** cambiar de actitud; **to change trains** cambiar de tren, transbordar; *vn* cambiar, mudar; corregirse
'change [tʃendʒ] *s* bolsa, lonja
changeability [,tʃendʒə'bɪlɪtɪ] *s* alterabilidad, mutabilidad
changeable ['tʃendʒəbəl] *adj* cambiable, mudable; variable; cambiadizo, inconstante
changeful ['tʃendʒfəl] *adj* cambiante; variable, inconstante
changeless ['tʃendʒlɪs] *adj* inmutable, constante
changeling ['tʃendʒlɪŋ] *s* niño cambiado en secreto por otro; (archaic) niño bobo, tonto o malparecido
change of clothing *s* muda de ropa
change of heart *s* conversión, cambio de sentimiento, arrepentimiento
change of life *s* (physiol.) menopausia
change of time *s* cambio de hora
change of venue *s* (law) cambio de tribunal (*en un proceso*)
change of voice *s* muda (*de los muchachos*)
change-over ['tʃendʒ,ovər] *s* cambio, conmutación
channel ['tʃænəl] *s* canal *m & f;* álveo, cauce (*de un río*); vía (*p.ej., de comunicaciones*); ranura, surco; conducto; (mil.) conducto regular; (naut.) mesa o meseta de guarnición; (rad. & telv.) canal *m;* **the Channel** el canal de la Mancha; (*pret & pp:* **-neled** o **-nelled;** *ger:* **-neling** o **-nelling**) *va* acanalar; canalizar (*p.ej., dinero, esfuerzos*)
channel iron *s* hierro de canal
Channel Islands *spl* islas Anglonormandas, islas del Canal, islas Normandas
chant [tʃænt] o [tʃɑnt] *s* canción; canto; salmo; *va* cantar; *vn* cantar; cantar la misma cantinela
chanter ['tʃæntər] o ['tʃɑntər] *s* cantor; chantre; (mus.) puntero (*de gaita*)
chantey ['ʃæntɪ] o ['tʃæntɪ] *s* (naut.) saloma
chanteyman ['ʃæntɪmən] o ['tʃæntɪmən] *s* (*pl:* **-men**) (naut.) salomador
chanticleer ['tʃæntɪklɪr] *s* gallo
chantry ['tʃæntrɪ] o ['tʃɑntrɪ] *s* (*pl:* **-tries**) capilla; dotación para decirse misas especiales en una capilla
chanty ['ʃæntɪ] o ['tʃæntɪ] *s* (*pl:* **-ties**) var. de **chantey**
chaos ['keɑs] *s* caos
chaotic [ke'ɑtɪk] *adj* caótico
chaotically [ke'ɑtɪkəlɪ] *adv* caóticamente
chap. abr. de **chaplain** y **chapter**
chap [tʃæp] o [tʃɑp] *s* mandíbula; mejilla; [tʃæp] *s* grieta, hendedura; (coll.) muchacho, chico; **chaps** *spl* zahones, chaparreras (*calzones de cuero*); (*pret & pp:* **chapped;** *ger:* **chapping**) *va* agrietar, hender, rajar; *vn* agrietarse, henderse, rajarse
chaparral [,tʃæpə'ræl] *s* chaparral

chapbook ['tʃæp,bʊk] *s* librete de cuentos, coplas, etc., que se vendía en las calles
chapel ['tʃæpəl] *s* capilla; oficio celebrado en una capilla; (Brit.) capilla destinada al culto de los que no pertenecen a la Iglesia establecida; imprenta; personal de la imprenta
chapel of ease *s* ayuda de parroquia
chaperon o **chaperone** ['ʃæpəron] *s* acompañanta de señoritas, señora de compañía; *va* acompañar (*una señora a una o más señoritas*)
chaperonage ['ʃæpə,ronɪdʒ] *s* deberes de acompañanta de señoritas
chapfallen ['tʃɑp,fɔlən] o ['tʃæp,fɔlən] *adj* alicaído, desanimado
chaplain ['tʃæplɪn] *s* capellán
chaplaincy ['tʃæplɪnsɪ] *s* (*pl:* **-cies**) capellanía
chaplainship ['tʃæplɪnʃɪp] *s* capellanía
chaplet ['tʃæplɪt] *s* guirnalda; gargantilla, collar; rosario; (arch.) moldura de cuentas
chapleted ['tʃæplɪtɪd] *adj* enguirnaldado
chapman ['tʃæpmən] *s* (*pl:* **-men**) (Brit.) buhonero
chaptalization [,ʃæptəlɪ'zeʃən] *s* (wine mfg.) captalización
chaptalize ['tʃæptəlaɪz] *va* captalizar
chapter ['tʃæptər] *s* capítulo; capítula (*pasaje de la Sagrada Escritura*)
chapter and verse *adv* con todos sus pelos y señales
chapter house *s* casa capitular; casa de una confraternidad universitaria
char [tʃɑr] *s* tarea de ocasión, trabajo a jornal; (*pret & pp:* **charred;** *ger:* **charring**) *va* carbonizar; socarrar (*quemar ligeramente*); *vn* hacer tareas de ocasión, trabajar a jornal; carbonizarse
char-à-banc ['ʃærə,bæŋ] *s* (*pl:* **-bancs** [,bæŋz]) charabán, autobús grande para excursiones
character ['kærɪktər] *s* carácter; personaje; (theat.) papel; (theat.) personaje; (coll.) tipo, sujeto; (bot., zool., print. & theol.) carácter; **in character** con verdad, conforme al tipo; **out of character** impropio, contrario al tipo
character actor *s* (theat.) actor de carácter
character assassination *s* calumnia hecha con propósito de destruir la confianza del público en una persona
characteristic [,kærɪktə'rɪstɪk] *adj* característico; *s* característica; (math. & rad.) característica
characteristically [,kærɪktə'rɪstɪkəlɪ] *adv* característicamente
characterization [,kærɪktərɪ'zeʃən] *s* caracterización
characterize ['kærɪktəraɪz] *va* caracterizar
character loan *s* préstamo sin garantía colateral
character piece *s* pieza breve para piano, que expresa un estado de alma o impresión simple
character sketch *s* semblanza; (theat.) representación de un personaje de carácter bien definido
character study *s* retrato literario
character witness *s* testigo que da testimonio de la buena reputación y la moralidad de una persona
charactery ['kærɪktərɪ] *s* simbolismo; símbolos, caracteres
charade [ʃə'red] o [ʃə'rɑd] *s* charada
charcoal ['tʃɑr,kol] *s* carbón de leña; carboncillo (*para dibujar*); dibujo al carbón
charcoal burner *s* carbonero; horno para hacer carbón de leña
chard [tʃɑrd] *s* (bot.) acelga
chare [tʃɛr] *s* tarea de ocasión, trabajo a jornal; *vn* hacer tareas de ocasión, trabajar a jornal
charge [tʃɑrdʒ] *s* carga (*de un arma de fuego, un horno, etc.*); cargo (*responsabilidad; acusación; cuidado, custodio; gravamen, impuesto*); encargo, orden, mando; coste, precio; (mil. & elec.) carga; (her.) blasón; **in charge** encargado; **in charge of** a cargo de (*una persona*); encargado de (*una cosa*); **to reverse the charges** (telp.) cobrar al número llamado; **to take charge of** hacerse cargo de; *va* cargar; cobrar (*cierto precio*); encargar, ordenar, mandar; embestir; (mil. & elec.) cargar; **to charge off** poner (*algo*) en cuenta restándolo como pérdida; anotar en el libro de cuentas; **to charge to the account of someone** (com.) cargarle a uno en cuenta; **to charge with** cargar de, acusar de; *vn* embestir
chargeable ['tʃɑrdʒəbəl] *adj* acusable; cobradero
charge account *s* (com.) cuenta corriente
chargé d'affaires [ʃɑr'ʒedæ'fɛr] *s* (*pl:* **chargés d'affaires**) encargado de negocios
charger ['tʃɑrdʒər] *s* cargador; caballo de guerra; (elec.) cargador (*de acumuladores*); (archaic) fuente o plato grande
charging ['tʃɑrdʒɪŋ] *adj* (her.) furioso
charging rate *s* (elec.) corriente de carga (*de un acumulador*)
chariot ['tʃærɪət] *s* carro romano, carro de guerra; carroza
charioteer [,tʃærɪə'tɪr] *s* auriga, carretero
charism ['kærɪzəm] *s* (theol.) carisma
charitable ['tʃærɪtəbəl] *adj* caritativo, benéfico
charity ['tʃærɪtɪ] *s* (*pl:* **-ties**) caridad
charivari [,ʃɑrɪ'vɑrɪ], [ʃə,rɪvə'ri] o ['ʃɪvəri] *s* cencerrada (*en particular, la dada al viudo que se vuelve a casar, la noche de bodas*); cantaleta
charlatan ['ʃɑrlətən] *s* charlatán (*embaidor; curandero*)
charlatanism ['ʃɑrlətənɪzəm] o **charlatanry** ['ʃɑrlətənrɪ] *s* charlatanismo
Charlemagne ['ʃɑrləmen] *s* Carlomagno
Charles [tʃɑrlz] *s* Carlos
Charles's Wain ['tʃɑrlzɪz'wen] *s* (astr.) la Osa Mayor
Charley o **Charlie** ['tʃɑrlɪ] *s* forma familiar de **Charles;** Carlitos (*se aplica a niños*)
charley horse *s* (coll.) calambre
charlock ['tʃɑrlɑk] *s* (bot.) mostaza silvestre
Charlotte ['ʃɑrlət] *s* Carlota; (*l.c.*) *s* carlota (*torta*)
charlotte russe ['ʃɑrlət 'rus] *s* carlota rusa (*pastel de nata*)
charm [tʃɑrm] *s* encanto, hechizo; dije, amuleto; **charms** *spl* hechizos (*de una mujer*); *va* encantar, hechizar
charmer ['tʃɑrmər] *s* encantador
charmeuse [ʃɑr'mʌz] *s* charmeuse (*tejido*)
charming ['tʃɑrmɪŋ] *adj* encantador
charnel ['tʃɑrnəl] *adj* sepulcral, cadavérico, horrible; *s* carnero, osario
charnel house *s* carnero
Charon ['kɛrɑn] *s* (myth.) Carón o Caronte
chart [tʃɑrt] *s* mapa geográfico; (naut.) carta de marear; lista, tabla; cuadro, diagrama; *va* poner en una carta de marear; **to chart a course** trazar o planear un derrotero
charter ['tʃɑrtər] *s* carta; *va* estatuir; (naut.) fletar (*un barco*); alquilar (*un autobús*)
chartered accountant *s* (Brit.) perito mercantil, contador perito
charterhouse ['tʃɑrtər,haʊs] *s* cartuja
charter member *s* socio fundador
charter party *s* (naut.) carta partida, carta de fletamento
chartometer [kɑr'tɑmɪtər] *s* cartómetro
chartreuse [ʃɑr'trʌz] *s* chartreuse
charwoman ['tʃɑr,wʊmən] *s* (*pl:* **-women**) criada por horas, alquilona, asistenta
chary ['tʃɛrɪ] *adj* (*comp:* **-ier;** *super:* **-iest**) cuidadoso; esquivo, asustado; parco; **to be chary of** ser avaro de (*p.ej., elogios*); tener miedo de (*p.ej., los extranjeros*); **to be chary of** + *ger* vacilar en + *inf*
Charybdis [kə'rɪbdɪs] *s* (geog. & myth.) Caribdis
Chas. abr. de **Charles**
chase [tʃes] *s* caza; persecución; ranura, muesca; (print.) rama; **to give chase** dar caza; *va* cazar; perseguir; filetear, grabar; **to chase away** ahuyentar; *vn* (coll.) precipitarse
chaser ['tʃesər] *s* cazador; perseguidor; avión de caza; cazasubmarinos; grabador; buril, cincel; (coll.) bebida que se toma después de un licor fuerte
chasm ['kæzəm] *s* grieta; abismo, desfiladero; laguna, vacío; (fig.) abismo (*entre dos personas o cosas*)
chasseur [ʃɑ'sʌr] *s* cazador (*soldado*); criado vestido de uniforme
chassis ['ʃæsɪ] o ['tʃæsɪ] *s* (*pl:* **-sis** [sɪz]) (aut. & rad.) chasis; (aer.) armazón

chaste [tʃest] *adj* casto; castizo, simple, sin adorno
chasten [ˈtʃesən] *va* castigar
chaste tree *s* (bot.) agnocasto, sauzgatillo
chastise [tʃæsˈtaɪz] *va* castigar
chastisement [ˈtʃæstɪzmənt] o [tʃæsˈtaɪzmənt] *s* castigo
chastity [ˈtʃæstɪtɪ] *s* castidad; casticidad, simpleza, falta de adorno
chastity belt *s* cinturón de castidad
chasuble [ˈtʃæzjubəl] *s* casulla
chat [tʃæt] *s* charla, plática; (orn.) cagaestacas; (*pret & pp:* **chatted;** *ger:* **chatting**) *vn* charlar, platicar
chatelaine [ˈʃætəlen] *s* castellana (*señora de un castillo*); muelle, cadena con dijes o llavero que llevan las mujeres en la cintura
chattel [ˈtʃætəl] *s* bienes muebles
chatter [ˈtʃætər] *s* charla, cháchara; chirrido, rechinido; castañeteo (*de los dientes*); *vn* charlar, chacharear; chirriar, rechinar; castañetear (*los dientes*); (mach.) traquear, traquetear
chatterbox [ˈtʃætər,bɑks] *s* charlador, tarabilla
chatty [ˈtʃætɪ] *adj* (*comp:* **-tier;** *super:* **-tiest**) gárrulo, locuaz
chauffeur [ˈʃofər] o [ʃoˈfʌr] *s* chófer
chautauqua o **Chautauqua** [ʃəˈtɔkwə] *s* (U.S.A.) reunión cultural (*que consta de conferencias, conciertos, etc., que se ofrecen durante varios días*)
chauvinism [ˈʃovɪnɪzəm] *s* chauvinismo
chauvinist [ˈʃovɪnɪst] *s* chauvinista
chauvinistic [,ʃovɪˈnɪstɪk] *adj* chauvinista
Ch.E. abr. de **Chemical Engineer**
cheap [tʃip] *adj* barato; barateado; baratero (*que vende barato*); mal pagado (*dícese del trabajo*); cursi, de mal gusto; **to feel cheap** sentirse inferior, sentir vergüenza; *adv* barato
cheapen [ˈtʃipən] *va* abaratar; *vn* abaratar, abaratarse
cheapness [ˈtʃipnɪs] *s* baratura
cheat [tʃit] *s* trampa, timo, fraude; trampista, timador, defraudador; *va* trampear, timar, defraudar; **to cheat someone out of something** defraudar algo a alguien
cheater [ˈtʃitər] *s* trampista, timador, defraudador
check [tʃɛk] *s* parada súbita; rechazo, repulsa; freno, restricción; (mach.) tope; amortiguador (*de puerta*); cheque (*de banco*); talón, contraseña (*de equipajes*); billete de reclamo; cuenta (*en un restaurante*); billete de salida, contraseña de salida (*en el teatro o cine*); comprobación, verificación; inspección; marca, señal; tela tejida a cuadros; cuadro (*de una tela tejida a cuadros*); grieta; jaque (*lance en el juego de ajedrez*); **in check** en jaque (*en el juego de ajedrez*); **to hold in check** contener, refrenar, reprimir ‖ *interj* ¡jaque! (*en el juego de ajedrez*) ‖ *va* parar súbitamente; rechazar, repulsar; refrenar, restringir; trabar; amortiguar; facturar, depositar (*equipajes*); controlar, comprobar, verificar; inspeccionar; marcar, señalar; marcar con cuadros; agrietar; jaquear, dar jaque a (*en ajedrez*); **to check off** marcar para indicar una comprobación; **to check up** comprobar, verificar ‖ *vn* pararse súbitamente; **to check in** llegar a un hotel e inscribir su nombre en el registro; (slang) morir; **to check out** despedirse en un hotel despúes de pagar la cuenta; (slang) morir
checkbook [ˈtʃɛk,bʊk] *s* libreta de cheques, libro talonario
checked [tʃɛkt] *adj* ajedrezado; (phonet.) trabado
checked syllable *s* (phonet.) sílaba trabada
checker [ˈtʃɛkər] *s* tela tejida a cuadros; cuadro (*de una tela tejida a cuadros*); ficha, pieza (*del juego de damas*); **checkers** *spl* damas, juego de damas; *va* cuadricular, dividir en cuadros, marcar con cuadros; diversificar, variar; *vn* diversificarse, variarse
checkerberry [ˈtʃɛkər,bɛrɪ] *s* (*pl:* **-ries**) (bot.) gaulteria; baya de la gaulteria; aceite de gaulteria
checkerboard [ˈtʃɛkər,bord] *s* damero
checkered [ˈtʃɛkərd] *adj* ajedrezado, escaqueado; diversificado, irregular
check girl *s* guardarropa (*joven encargada de custodiar vestidos, sombreros, etc.*)
checking account *s* cuenta corriente
check list *s* lista para la comprobación de nombres, etc.
check mark *s* marca, señal
checkmate [ˈtʃɛk,met] *s* mate o jaque mate; (fig.) derrota completa; *va* dar mate a, dar jaque mate a; (fig.) derrotar completamente
checkpoint [ˈtʃɛk,pɔɪnt] *s* punto de comprobación, punto de inspección
checkrein [ˈtʃɛk,ren] *s* engallador
checkroom [ˈtʃɛk,rum] o [ˈtʃɛk,rʊm] *s* guardarropa (*sitio*); (rail.) consigna
checkup [ˈtʃɛk,ʌp] *s* verificación rigurosa; reconocimiento general (*del estado de la salud de uno*); revisión (*p.ej., de un automóvil*)
check valve *s* válvula de retención
checky [ˈtʃɛkɪ] *adj* (her.) escacado, jaquelado
Cheddar [ˈtʃɛdər] *s* queso de Cheddar
Che.E. abr. de **Chemical Engineer**
cheek [tʃik] *s* mejilla, carrillo; (coll.) frescura, descaro, insolencia; (mach.) quijada; **to have one's tongue in one's cheek** decir una cosa queriendo decir otra
cheekbone [ˈtʃik,bon] *s* (anat.) pómulo, hueso de la mejilla
cheek by jowl *adv* cara a cara, lado a lado; en la mayor intimidad
cheek pouch *s* abazón (*de los monos*)
cheek strap *s* quijera (*de la cabezada del caballo*)
cheeky [ˈtʃikɪ] *adj* (*comp:* **-ier;** *super:* **-iest**) (coll.) fresco, cara dura
cheep [tʃip] *s* chillido (*del ave pequeña*); pío (*del pollo*); *vn* chillar; piar
cheer [tʃɪr] *s* alegría, ánimo, alivio; viva, aplauso; alimento; humor, estado de ánimo; **what cheer?** ¿qué tal?; *va* alegrar, animar, aliviar; vitorear, aplaudir; instar o animar con vivas o aplausos; saludar o dar la bienvenida a (*una persona*) con vivas o aplausos; *vn* alegrarse, animarse, aliviarse; **cheer up!** ¡ánimo!, ¡cobre ánimo!
cheerful [ˈtʃɪrfəl] *adj* alegre (*persona, noticia, ambiente, etc.*); pronto, complaciente
cheerfully [ˈtʃɪrfəlɪ] *adv* alegremente; de buena gana
cheerfulness [ˈtʃɪrfəlnɪs] *s* alegría; complacencia
cheerio [ˈtʃɪrɪo] *interj* (coll.) ¡qué tal!, ¡hola!; ¡adiós!, ¡hasta la vista!; ¡viva!
cheerless [ˈtʃɪrlɪs] *adj* triste, sombrío
cheery [ˈtʃɪrɪ] *adj* (*comp:* **-ier;** *super:* **-iest**) alegre (*persona, noticia, ambiente, etc.*)
cheese [tʃiz] *s* queso; *va* (slang) dejarse de; **cheese it!** (slang) ¡déjese de eso!; (slang) ¡cállese la boca!; (slang) ¡lárguese!
cheesecake [ˈtʃiz,kek] *s* quesadilla; (slang) fotografías de los hechizos de una mujer
cheesecloth [ˈtʃiz,klɔθ] o [ˈtʃiz,klɑθ] *s* estopilla
cheeseflower [ˈtʃiz,flaʊər] *s* (bot.) malva común
cheese fly *s* (ent.) mosca del queso
cheese mite *s* (ent.) ácaro del queso
cheesemonger [ˈtʃiz,mʌŋgər] *s* quesero
cheeseparing [ˈtʃiz,pɛrɪŋ] *adj* tacaño, mezquino; *s* cosa sin valor; tacañería, mezquindad
cheese rennet *s* (bot.) cuajaleche
cheese skipper *s* gusano del queso
cheesy [ˈtʃizɪ] *adj* (*comp:* **-ier;** *super:* **-iest**) caseoso; (slang) tosco, de mala calidad, sin valor
cheetah [ˈtʃitə] *s* (zool.) leopardo cazador
chef [ʃɛf] *s* primer cocinero, jefe de cocina
Chefoo [ˈtʃiˈfu] *s* Chefú
Cheka [ˈtʃɛkɑ] *s* Checa (*policía secreta soviética*)
chela [ˈkilə] *s* (*pl:* **-lae** [li]) (zool.) quela
chelicera [kɪˈlɪsərə] *s* (*pl:* **-ae** [i]) (ent.) quelícero
chelonian [kɪˈlonɪən] *adj & s* (zool.) quelonio
chem. abr. de **chemical, chemist** y **chemistry**
chemic [ˈkɛmɪk] *adj* (archaic) químico, alquímico
chemical [ˈkɛmɪkəl] *adj* químico; *s* substancia química, producto químico
chemical engineer *s* ingeniero químico

chemical engineering *s* ingeniería química
chemically ['kɛmɪkəlɪ] *adv* químicamente
chemical warfare *s* guerra química
chemise [ʃə'miz] *s* camisa de mujer
chemism ['kɛmɪzəm] *s* quimismo
chemist ['kɛmɪst] *s* químico; (Brit.) boticario, farmacéutico
chemistry ['kɛmɪstrɪ] *s* química
chemosphere ['kɛməsfɪr] *s* quimiosfera
chemosurgery [,kɛmo'sʌrdʒərɪ] *s* quimiocirugía
chemosynthesis [,kɛmo'sɪnθɪsɪs] *s* quimiosíntesis
chemotaxis [,kɛmo'tæksɪs] *s* (biol.) quimiotaxis
chemotherapy [,kɛmo'θɛrəpɪ] *s* quimioterapia
chemurgy ['kɛmʌrdʒɪ] *s* química agrícola industrial
chenille [ʃə'nil] *s* felpilla
chenopod ['kinəpɑd] o ['kɛnəpɑd] *s* (bot.) quenopodio
chenopodiaceous [,kinə,podɪ'eʃəs] o [,kɛnə,podɪ'eʃəs] *adj* (bot.) quenopodiáceo
cheque ['tʃɛk] *s* (Brit.) cheque
chequer ['tʃɛkər] *s, va & vn* var. de **checker; chequers** *spl* var. de **checkers**
Cherbourg ['ʃɛrbʊrg] *s* Cherburgo
cherish ['tʃɛrɪʃ] *va* acariciar (*tratar con ternura; abrigar, p.ej., esperanzas*)
cheroot [ʃə'rut] *s* cigarro puro truncado por los dos extremos
cherry ['tʃɛrɪ] *s* (*pl:* **-ries**) (bot.) cerezo; cereza (*fruto; color*)
cherry brandy *s* aguardiente de cerezas
cherry laurel *s* (bot.) lauroceraso
cherry orchard *s* cerezal
cherry red *s* rojo cereza
cherry stone *s* hueso de cereza; (zool.) almeja redonda (*Venus mercenaria*)
chersonese ['kʌrsəniz] o ['kʌrsənis] *s* quersoneso; **the Chersonese** el quersoneso de Tracia (*la península de Gallipoli*)
cherub ['tʃɛrəb] *s* (*pl:* **-ubim** [əbɪm]) (Bib., f.a. & theol.) querubín; (*pl:* **-ubs**) niño angelical; persona de rostro regordete e inocente
cherubic [tʃə'rubɪk] *adj* querúbico
chervil ['tʃʌrvɪl] *s* (bot.) cerafolio, perifollo
chess [tʃɛs] *s* ajedrez
chessboard ['tʃɛs,bord] *s* tablero de ajedrez
chessman ['tʃɛs,mæn] *s* (*pl:* **-men**) pieza de ajedrez, trebejo
chess player *s* ajedrecista
chess set *s* ajedrez (*conjunto de las piezas*)
chest [tʃɛst] *s* (anat.) pecho; arca, cajón, cofre; cómoda, guardarropa; caja (*para dinero*); (mach.) caja
chestnut ['tʃɛsnʌt] *s* (bot.) castaño (*árbol y madera*); castaña (*fruto*); castaño (*color*); caballo de color castaño; (vet.) espejuelo; (coll.) broma gastada, chiste sabido por todo el mundo; **to pull someone's chestnuts out of the fire** (coll.) sacarle a uno las castañas del fuego; *adj* castaño, marrón
chest of drawers *s* cómoda
chesty ['tʃɛstɪ] *adj* (*comp:* **-ier**; *super:* **-iest**) (slang) engreído, soberbio, orgulloso
chetah ['tʃitə] *s* var. de **cheetah**
cheval-de-frise [ʃə'vældə'friz] *s* (*pl:* **chevaux-de-frise** [ʃə'vodə'friz]) erizo (*que corona lo alto de una muralla*); (mil.) caballo de frisa
cheval glass [ʃə'væl] *s* psique (*espejo*)
chevalier [,ʃɛvə'lɪr] *s* caballero
cheviot ['ʃɛvɪət] *s* cheviot
chevron ['ʃɛvrən] *s* (her.) cheurón; (mil.) insignia, galón
chevron molding *s* (arch.) cheurón
chevrony ['ʃɛvrənɪ] *adj* (her.) cheuronado
chevrotain ['ʃɛvrəten] o ['ʃɛvrətɪn] *s* (zool.) trágulo
chevy ['tʃɛvɪ] o ['tʃɪvɪ] *s* (*pl:* **-ies**) (Brit.) caza, grito de caza; (*pret & pp:* **-ied**) *va* (Brit.) cazar, perseguir; (Brit.) acosar, atormentar; *vn* (Brit.) correr, precipitarse
chew [tʃu] *s* mascadura; *va* mascar, masticar; **to chew the cud** rumiar; (fig.) rumiar (*meditar*); **to chew the rag** (slang) dar la lengua; *vn* mascar, masticar; (coll.) mascar tabaco
chewing gum *s* goma de mascar
chewink [tʃɪ'wɪŋk] *s* (orn.) pájaro fringílido norteamericano (*Pipilo erythrophthalmus*)
chg. abr. de **charge**
chgd. abr. de **charged**
Chian ['kaɪən] *adj & s* quío
Chianti [kɪ'ɑntɪ] o [kɪ'æntɪ] *s* quianti o chianti (*vino*)
chiaroscuro [kɪ,ɑrə'skjuro] *s* (*pl:* **-ros**) (paint.) claroscuro
chiasma [kaɪ'æzmə] *s* (*pl:* **-mata** [mətə]) (anat. & biol.) quiasma
chiasmus [kaɪ'æzməs] *s* (*pl:* **-mi** [maɪ]) (rhet.) quiasma
chibouk o **chibouque** [tʃɪ'buk] o [tʃɪ'bʊk] *s* chibuquí
chic [ʃik] o [ʃɪk] *adj* elegante, gracioso; *s* chic
chicane [ʃɪ'ken] *s* triquiñuela, embuste; *va* defraudar; cavilar; *vn* andar con triquiñuelas
chicanery [ʃɪ'kenərɪ] *s* (*pl:* **-ies**) triquiñuela, embuste
chick [tʃɪk] *s* pollito, polluelo
chickadee ['tʃɪkədi] *s* (orn.) paro, paro de cabeza negra
chickaree ['tʃɪkəri] *s* (zool.) chicari (*ardilla norteamericana de pelaje rojizo*)
chicken ['tʃɪkən] *s* pollo; gallina o gallo; (fig.) pollo (*persona joven*); (fig.) polla (*mocita*); **she is no chicken** (coll.) ella ya no es muy joven; **to go to bed with the chickens** acostarse con las gallinas; *adj* joven, pequeño
chicken cholera *s* (vet.) cólera de las gallinas
chicken coop *s* gallinero
chicken feed *s* (slang) pequeña cantidad de dinero; (slang) calderilla, dinero menudo
chicken-hearted ['tʃɪkən,hɑrtɪd] *adj* gallina (*cobarde, tímido*)
chicken pox *s* (path.) viruelas locas, varicela
chicken wire *s* alambrada, tela metálica
chickpea ['tʃɪk,pi] *s* (bot.) garbanzo (*planta y semilla*)
chickweed ['tʃɪk,wid] *s* (bot.) álsine, pamplina de canarios, hierba pajarera
chicle ['tʃɪkəl] *s* chicle (*gomorresina*)
chicory ['tʃɪkərɪ] *s* (*pl:* **-ries**) (bot.) achicoria
chid [tʃɪd] *pret & pp de* **chide**
chidden ['tʃɪdən] *pp de* **chide**
chide [tʃaɪd] (*pret:* **chided** o **chid;** *pp:* **chided, chid** o **chidden**) *va & vn* reprobar, reprender, regañar
chief [tʃif] *s* jefe; cacique (*de pieles rojas*); (her.) jefe; **in chief** en jefe; *adj* principal
chief burgess *s* alcalde
chief clerk *s* oficial mayor
chief executive *s* jefe del estado; primer mandatario (Am.)
chief justice *s* presidente de sala; presidente de la corte suprema
chiefly ['tʃiflɪ] *adv* principalmente, mayormente; ante todo, sobre todo
chief of staff *s* (mil.) jefe de estado mayor
chieftaincy ['tʃiftənsɪ] o **chieftainship** ['tʃiftənʃɪp] *s* jefatura
chiffon [ʃɪ'fɑn] o ['ʃɪfɑn] *s* gasa, soplillo; **chiffons** *spl* encajes, cintas, atavíos
chiffonier [,ʃɪfə'nɪr] *s* cómoda alta
chigger ['tʃɪgər] *s* (ent.) ácaro; (ent.) garrapata; (ent.) nigua
chignon ['ʃinjɑn] *s* castaña, moño de pelo
chigoe ['tʃɪgo] *s* (ent.) nigua
chilblain ['tʃɪl,blen] *s* sabañón
child [tʃaɪld] *s* (*pl:* **children** ['tʃɪldrən]) niño; hijo; descendiente; **to be with child** estar encinta
childbearing ['tʃaɪld,bɛrɪŋ] *s* parto
childbed ['tʃaɪld,bɛd] *s* parturición
childbirth ['tʃaɪld,bʌrθ] *s* parto, alumbramiento
child care *s* puericultura
Childermas ['tʃɪldərməs] *s* (obs.) día de los inocentes
childhood ['tʃaɪldhʊd] *s* niñez, infancia
childish ['tʃaɪldɪʃ] *adj* aniñado, pueril
childishness ['tʃaɪldɪʃnɪs] *s* puerilidad
child labor *s* trabajo de menores
childless ['tʃaɪldlɪs] *adj* sin hijos
childlike ['tʃaɪld,laɪk] *adj* aniñado, infantil, pueril
child prodigy *s* niño prodigio
child psychology *s* psicología infantil
children ['tʃɪldrən] *pl de* **child**

children of Israel *spl* israelitas, hijos de Israel
Children's Crusade *s* cruzada de los Niños
child's play *s* juego de niños (*cosa muy fácil*)
child welfare *s* bienestar del niño
chile ['tʃɪlɪ] *s* var. de **chili;** (*cap.*) *s* Chile
Chilean ['tʃɪlɪən] *adj & s* ehileno
chile con carne *s* var. de **chili con carne**
Chile saltpeter *s* nitro de Chile
chili ['tʃɪlɪ] *s* (*pl:* **-ies**) (bot.) chile (*planta y fruto*)
chili con carne [kɑn'kɑrnɪ] *s* chile con carne
chili sauce *s* ajiaco, salsa de ají
chill [tʃɪl] *s* frío desapacible; frialdad; calofrío, escalofrío; estremecimiento (*p.ej., que recorre una multitud*); abatimiento, desaliento; (fig.) frialdad (*falta de cordialidad*); *adj* desapaciblemente frío; (fig.) frío; (fig.) depresivo; *va* enfriar; abatir, desalentar; (metal.) enfriar; *vn* calofriarse, enfriarse
chilli ['tʃɪlɪ] *s* (*pl:* **-lies**) var. de **chili**
chilly ['tʃɪlɪ] *adj* (*comp:* **-ier;** *super:* **-iest**) frío; escalofriado, friolento; (fig.) frío
chime [tʃaɪm] *s* carillón, juego de campanas; tubo sonoro; repique, campaneo; armonía; conformidad; *va* repicar (*una campana o un juego de campanas*); decir en cadencia; *vn* repicar; sonar con armonía; hablar en cadencia, hablar monótonamente; estar en armonía; **to chime in** hacer coro, unisonar; (coll.) unirse, asociarse; (coll.) entremeterse; **to chime in with** armonizar con
chime clock *s* péndola de carillón, reloj de carillón
chimera o **chimaera** [kɪ'mɪrə] o [kaɪ'mɪrə] *s* (myth., f.a. & fig.) quimera
chimeric [kɪ'mɪrɪk] o [kaɪ'mɪrɪk] o **chimerical** [kɪ'mɪrɪkəl] o [kaɪ'mɪrɪkəl] *adj* quimérico
chimney ['tʃɪmnɪ] *s* chimenea; tubo de vidrio de lámpara; **to smoke like a chimney** echar más humo que una chimenea
chimney cap *s* caperuza, mitra de chimenea
chimney corner *s* rincón de chimenea
chimney jack *s* mitra giratoria de chimenea; reparador de altas chimeneas
chimney piece *s* delantera de chimenea; adorno de chimenea
chimney pot *s* mitra de chimenea, guardavientos
chimney sweep *s* limpiachimeneas, limpiador de chimenea, deshollinador
chimney swift *s* (orn.) vencejo americano (*Chaetura pelagica*)
chimpanzee [tʃɪm'pænzɪ] o [,tʃɪmpæn'zi] *s* (zool.) chimpancé
Chin. abr. de **Chinese**
chin [tʃɪn] *s* barba, mentón; **to keep one's chin up** (coll.) no desanimarse; (*pret & pp:* **chinned;** *ger:* **chinning**) *va* **to chin oneself** colgarse de una barra alzándose con las manos hasta tocarla con la barba; *vn* (coll.) charlar, parlotear
china ['tʃaɪnə] *s* china, porcelana; (*cap.*) *s* China, la China
China aster *s* (bot.) reina Margarita, extraña
chinaberry ['tʃaɪnə,bɛrɪ] *s* (*pl:* **-ries**) (bot.) jabonero de las Antillas; (bot.) acederaque
china closet *s* chinero
Chinaman ['tʃaɪnəmən] *s* (*pl:* **-men**) chino
China pink *s* (bot.) clavel de China
China rose *s* (bot.) rosa de China, tulipán (*Hibiscus rosa-sinensis*)
China Sea *s* mar de la China
China silk *s* china
Chinatown ['tʃaɪnə,taʊn] *s* (U.S.A.) barrio chino
China tree *s* (bot.) acederaque, cinamomo, agriaz, tuya de la China
chinaware ['tʃaɪnə,wɛr] *s* porcelana, vajilla de porcelana
chincapin ['tʃɪŋkəpɪn] *s* var. de **chinquapin**
chinch [tʃɪntʃ] *s* (ent.) chinche; (ent.) chinche de los cereales
chinch bug *s* (ent.) chinche de los cereales
chinchilla [tʃɪn'tʃɪlə] *s* (zool.) chinchilla (*animal y piel*); tela de lana muy espesa (*se usa para sobretodos*)
chine [tʃaɪn] *s* espinazo; lomo (*carne del lomo del animal*); cresta, cima (*de las montañas*)
Chinese [tʃaɪ'niz] *adj* chino; *s* (*pl:* **-nese**) chino
Chinese anise *s* (bot.) badián
Chinese gong *s* (mus.) batintín
Chinese lantern *s* linterna china
Chinese puzzle *s* problema muy complicado
Chinese Turkestan *s* el Turquestán Chino
Chinese Wall *s* Gran muralla de la China
chink [tʃɪŋk] *s* grieta, hendedura, rajadura; sonido metálico; *va* agrietar, hender, rajar; rellenar (*junturas entre ladrillos*); *vn* agrietarse, henderse, rajarse; sonar metálicamente
chinkapin ['tʃɪŋkəpɪn] *s* (bot.) chincapino
chinook [tʃɪ'nuk] o [tʃɪ'nʊk] *s* chinuco (*viento que aparece por la parte oriental de las Montañas Rocosas*); (*cap.*) *s* chinuco (*indio norteamericano; idioma*)
chinquapin ['tʃɪŋkəpɪn] *s* (bot.) chincapino
chin strap *s* barbuquejo, carrillera
chintz [tʃɪnts] *s* quimón, zaraza
chiolite ['kaɪolaɪt] *s* (mineral.) chiolita
Chios ['kaɪɑs] *s* Quío
chip [tʃɪp] *s* astilla, brizna; saltadura (*defecto en la superficie de la piedra*); raspadura (*de la corteza del pan*); pedacito (*de alimento, dulce, etc.*); ficha (*en el póker*); viruta (*de madera*); (naut.) barquilla; **chip off the old block** hijo de su padre, hijo de su madre; **chip on one's shoulder** (coll.) propensión a pendencias; (*pret & pp:* **chipped;** *ger:* **chipping**) *va* astillar, descascarillar, desconchar; picar, tajar con cincel o hacha; **to chip in** (coll.) dar, contribuir; (coll.) contribuir con su cuota; *vn* saltar, astillarse, descascarillarse, desconcharse; **to chip in** (coll.) contribuir; (coll.) pagar en la apuesta
chip ax *s* azuela
chipmunk ['tʃɪpmʌŋk] *s* (zool.) ardilla listada
chipper ['tʃɪpər] *adj* (coll.) alegre, jovial, vivo
chipping sparrow *s* (orn.) gorrión norteamericano (*Spizella passerina*)
chippy ['tʃɪpɪ] *s* (*pl:* **-pies**) (zool.) ardilla listada; (orn.) gorrión norteamericano (*Spizella passerina*); (slang) chica; (slang) ramera
chirk [tʃʌrk] *adj* (coll.) alegre, vivo; *va* (coll.) alegrar, avivar; *vn* (coll.) alegrarse, avivarse
chirographer [kaɪ'rɑgrəfər] *s* quirógrafo
chirographic [,kaɪro'græfɪk] *adj* quirográfico
chirography [kaɪ'rɑgrəfɪ] *s* quirografía
chiromancer ['kaɪro,mænsər] *s* quiromántico
chiromancy ['kaɪro,mænsɪ] *s* quiromancía
chiromantic [,kaɪro'mæntɪk] o **chiromantical** [,kaɪro'mæntɪkəl] *adj* quiromántico
Chiron ['kaɪrɑn] *s* (myth.) Quirón
chiropodist [kaɪ'rɑpədɪst] o [kɪ'rɑpədɪst] *s* quiropodista
chiropody [kaɪ'rɑpədɪ] o [kɪ'rɑpədɪ] *s* quiropodia
chiropractic [,kaɪro'præktɪk] *adj* quiropráctico; *s* quiropráctica (*método de tratamiento*); quiropráctico (*persona*)
chiropractor ['kaɪro,præktər] *s* quiropráctico
chiropteran [kaɪ'rɑptərən] *adj & s* (zool.) quiróptero
chirp [tʃʌrp] *s* gorjeo; chirrido (*del grillo*); *va* decir de manera chirriante; *vn* gorjear; chirriar (*el grillo*); hablar alegremente
chirr [tʃʌr] *s* trino agudo (*p.ej., del saltón*); *vn* trinar agudamente
chirrup ['tʃɪrəp] o ['tʃʌrəp] *s* gorjeo repetido; chirrido repetido; chasquido (*de la lengua*); *va* decir de manera chirriante; *vn* gorjear repetidas veces; chirriar continuamente; chascar la lengua
chisel ['tʃɪzəl] *s* escoplo, formón; cincel (*para labrar piedras o metales*); (*pret & pp:* **-eled** o **-elled;** *ger:* **-eling** o **-elling**) *va & vn* escoplear; cincelar (*piedras o metales*); (slang) estafar, timar
chiseler o **chiseller** ['tʃɪzələr] *s* escopleador; (slang) estafador, timador
chit [tʃɪt] *s* chiquillo; chiquilla descarada; (Brit.) carta breve, esquela
chit-chat ['tʃɪt,tʃæt] *s* charla, palique; chisme, hablilla
chitin ['kaɪtɪn] *s* (chem.) quitina
chitinous ['kaɪtɪnəs] *adj* quitinoso
chiton ['kaɪtɑn] *s* (hist. & zool.) quitón
chitterlings ['tʃɪtərlɪŋz] *spl* menudos comestibles del puerco
chivalric ['ʃɪvəlrɪk] o [ʃɪ'vælrɪk] *adj* caba-

lleresco (*perteneciente a la caballería*); caballeroso (*propio del caballero*)
chivalrous ['ʃɪvəlrəs] *adj* caballeroso (*propio del caballero*); caballeresco (*perteneciente a la caballería*)
chivalry ['ʃɪvəlrɪ] *s* caballería (*especialmente de la Edad Media; conjunto de caballeros*); caballerosidad (*calidad del caballero ideal; proceders del caballero*); caballeros, personas de consideración
chive [tʃaɪv] *s* (bot.) cebollino, ajo moruno
Ch.J. abr. de **Chief Justice**
chlamys ['klemɪs] o ['klæmɪs] *s* (*pl:* **-myses** o **-mydes** [mɪdiz]) clámide
Chloe [klo·ɪ] *s* Cloe
chloral ['klorəl] *s* (chem.) cloral; (chem.) hidrato de cloral
chloral hydrate *s* (chem.) hidrato de cloral
chlorate ['kloret] o ['klorɪt] *s* (chem.) clorato
chloric ['klorɪk] *adj* (chem.) clórico
chloric acid *s* (chem.) ácido clórico
chlorid ['klorɪd] o **chloride** ['kloraɪd] o ['klorɪd] *s* (chem.) cloruro; (chem.) sal del ácido clorhídrico
chloride of lime *s* (chem.) cloruro de cal
chlorin ['klorɪn] *s* var. de **chlorine**
chlorinate ['klorɪnet] *va* clorinar; desinfectar con cloro
chlorination [,klorɪ'neʃən] *s* clorinación; desinfección con cloro
chlorine ['klorin] o ['klorɪn] *s* (chem.) cloro
Chloris ['klorɪs] *s* (myth.) Cloris
chlorite ['kloraɪt] *s* (chem.) clorito; (mineral.) clorita
chloritic [klo'rɪtɪk] *adj* clorítico
chloroform ['klorəfɔrm] *s* (chem.) cloroformo; *va* (med.) cloroformizar; matar aplicando cloroformo
chloromycetin [,klorəmaɪ'sitɪn] *s* (pharm.) cloromicetina
chlorophyl o **chlorophyll** ['klorəfɪl] *s* (bot. & biochem.) clorofila
chlorophyllin [,klorə'fɪlɪn] *s* (biochem.) clorofilina
chlorophyllous [,klorə'fɪləs] *adj* clorofílico
chloropicrin [,klorə'pɪkrɪn] o [,klorə'paɪkrɪn] *s* (chem.) cloropicrina
chloroplast ['klorəplæst] *s* (bot.) cloroplasto
chloroprene ['klorəprin] *s* (chem.) cloropreno
chlorosis [klo'rosɪs] *s* (bot. & path.) clorosis
chlorotic [klo'rɑtɪk] *adj* clorótico
chlorous ['klorəs] *adj* (chem.) cloroso
chlortetracycline [klor,tɛtrə'saɪklin] o [klor,tɛtrə'saɪklɪn] *s* (pharm.) clortetraciclina
chm. abr. de **chairman**
choana ['koənə] *s* (anat.) coana
chock [tʃɑk] *s* cuña, calzo; (naut.) choque; *adv* lo más cerca posible, lo más estrechamente posible; enteramente, completamente; *va* acuñar, calzar; afianzar o apretar con calzos; (naut.) calzar
chock-a-block ['tʃɑkə'blɑk] *adj* (naut.) a besar; apretado
chock-full ['tʃɑk'fʊl] *adj* colmado, de bote en bote
chocolate ['tʃɔkəlɪt] o ['tʃɑkəlɪt] *s* chocolate; *adj* hecho de chocolate; achocolatado, de color de chocolate
chocolate candy *s* confite o dulce de chocolate
choice [tʃɔɪs] *s* elección, selección, escogimiento; opción; lo selecto, lo más escogido; **to have no choice** no tener alternativa; *adj* selecto, escogido, excelente, superior
choir [kwaɪr] *s* coro; (mus., arch. & theol.) coro; *va & vn* corear
choirboy ['kwaɪr,bɔɪ] *s* infante de coro, niño de coro
choir desk *s* facistol
choir loft *s* coro
choirmaster ['kwaɪr,mæstər] o ['kwaɪr,mɑstər] *s* jefe de coro, maestro de capilla
choir practice *s* ensayo de coro
choir stall *s* asiento del coro; **choir stalls** *spl* sillería
choke [tʃok] *s* estrangulación; (aut.) cierre u obturador (*del carburador*); (elec.) choque; *va* sofocar, ahogar, estrangular; reprimir, suprimir; tapar, obstruir; (aut.) obturar; **to choke back** contener, retener; **to choke down** oprimir, sujetar; atragantar; **to choke off** parar, detener; poner fin a; deshacerse de; **to choke up** tapar, obstruir; *vn* sofocarse; no poder respirar; atragantarse; **to choke on** atragantarse con; **to choke up** atragantarse; taparse, obstruirse
chokeberry ['tʃok,bɛrɪ] *s* (*pl:* **-ries**) (bot.) amelanquier
chokebore ['tʃok,bor] *s* (arti.) calibre estrangulado; arma de fuego de calibre estrangulado
chokecherry ['tʃok,tʃɛrɪ] *s* (*pl:* **-ries**) (bot.) cerezo silvestre norteamericano (*Prunus virginiana*); cereza silvestre
choke coil *s* (elec.) bobina de choque
chokedamp ['tʃok,dæmp] *s* (min.) mofeta
choker ['tʃokər] *s* ahogador, sofocador, estrangulador; (mach.) obturador; (elec.) bobina de reacción; (coll.) ahogador, cuello alto; (coll.) pena (*joya que se anudaba al cuello*)
cholagogue ['kɑləgɑg] *adj & s* (med.) colagogo
cholecystectomy [,kɑləsɪs'tɛktəmɪ] *s* (*pl:* **-mies**) (surg.) colecistectomía
cholecystostomy [,kɑləsɪs'tɑstəmɪ] *s* (*pl:* **-mies**) (surg.) colecistostomía
choler ['kɑlər] *s* cólera, ira
cholera ['kɑlərə] *s* (path.) cólera
cholera infantum [ɪn'fæntəm] *s* (path.) cólera infantil
cholera morbus ['mɔrbəs] *s* (path.) cólera morbo
cholera nostras ['nɑstræs] *s* (path.) cólera nostras
choleric ['kɑlərɪk] *adj* colérico (*irascible*)
cholerine ['kɑlərɪn] o ['kɑləraɪn] *s* (path.) colerina
cholesterin [kə'lɛstərɪn] *s* (biochem.) colesterina
cholesterol [kə'lɛstərol] o [kə'lɛstərɑl] *s* (biochem.) colesterol
choline ['kolin] o ['kɑlin] *s* (biochem.) colina
cholla ['tʃoljɑ] *s* (bot.) cholla
chondriome ['kɑndrɪom] *s* (biol.) condrioma
chondriosome ['kɑndrɪo,som] *s* (biol.) condriosoma
chondrology [kɑn'drɑlədʒɪ] *s* condrología
choose [tʃuz] (*pret:* **chose;** *pp:* **chosen**) *va* elegir, escoger; optar por; *vn* optar; **to choose between** optar entre (*p.ej., dos candidatos*); **to choose to** + *inf* optar por + *inf*
choosy ['tʃuzɪ] *adj* (slang) melindroso, quisquilloso
chop [tʃɑp] *s* golpe cortante; tajada; chuleta (*costilla con carne*); mandíbula; mejilla; marca, sello; licencia, permiso; (box.) martillazo; (coll.) grado, calidad; **chops** *spl* quijada; boca, labios; (*pret & pp:* **chopped;** *ger:* **chopping**) *va* cortar, tajar; desmenuzar; picar (*la carne*); abrirse (*paso*) cortando; arrojar, mover a tirones; **to chop off** tronchar; *vn* moverse a tirones; cambiar, variar súbito; virar (*el viento*); **to chop at** querer cortar; tratar de atrapar con la boca
chophouse ['tʃɑp,haus] *s* restaurán donde se sirven principalmente chuletas, bifteks, etc.
chopine [tʃo'pin] o ['tʃɑpɪn] *s* chapín (*chanclo de corcho de mujer*)
chopper ['tʃɑpər] *s* hachero, tajador; hacha, hachuela; cortante (*cuchilla grande del carnicero*)
chopping block *s* tajo
choppy ['tʃɑpɪ] *adj* (*comp:* **-pier;** *super:* **-piest**) agitado (*mar*); variable (*viento*); cortado (*estilo*)
chopsticks ['tʃɑp,stɪks] *spl* palillos (*de que se sirven los chinos para comer*)
chop suey [,tʃɑp'suɪ] *s* chopsuey (*olla china*)
choral ['korəl] *adj* (mus.) coral; [ko'rɑl] o ['korəl] *s* (mus.) coral
chorale [ko'rɑl] o ['korəl] *s* (mus.) coral
choral music *s* música coreada
choral society *s* orfeón
chord [kɔrd] *s* (mus.) acorde; (aer., anat., eng. & geom.) cuerda; (fig.) cuerda sensible
chordate ['kɔrdet] *adj & s* (zool.) cordado
chore [tʃor] *s* faena, tarea, quehacer
chorea [ko'riə] *s* (path.) corea
choreographer [,korɪ'ɑgrəfər] *s* coreógrafo
choreographic [,korɪə'græfɪk] *adj* coreográfico
choreography [,korɪ'ɑgrəfɪ] *s* coreografía
choriamb ['korɪæmb] o ['kɑrɪæmb] *s* coriambo

choriambic [ˌkorɪˈæmbɪk] o [ˌkɑrɪˈæmbɪk] *adj & s* coriámbico
choric [ˈkorɪk] *adj* coral
chorine [ˈkorin] o [koˈrin] *s* (slang) corista
chorion [ˈkorɪɑn] *s* (embryol. & zool.) corión
chorister [ˈkɑrɪstər] o [ˈkɔrɪstər] *s* corista; infante o niño de coro; jefe de coro
chorographer [koˈrɑgrəfər] *s* corógrafo
chorographic [ˌkorəˈgræfɪk] o **chorographical** [ˌkorəˈgræfɪkəl] *adj* corográfico
chorography [koˈrɑgrəfɪ] *s* corografía
choroid [ˈkorɔɪd] *adj* coroideo, coroides; *s* (anat.) coroides, membrana coroides
chortle [ˈtʃɔrtəl] *s* resoplido alegre; *vn* resoplar alegremente
chorus [ˈkorəs] *s* (theat. & mus.) coro; concierto; estribillo; **in chorus** en coro; *vn* hablar o cantar en coro; contestar a una voz
chorus girl *s* (theat.) corista
chorus man *s* (theat.) corista
chose [tʃoz] *pret de* **choose**
chosen [ˈtʃozən] *adj* selecto, escogido; *pp de* **choose**
chough [tʃʌf] *s* (orn.) chova; (orn.) chova piñariega, grajo de pico amarillo
chow [tʃaʊ] *s* chao (*perro chino*); (slang) comida, alimento
chow-chow [ˈtʃaʊˌtʃaʊ] *s* conserva china; encurtidos con mostaza, divididos y mezclados
chowder [ˈtʃaʊdər] *s* sancocho de almejas o pescado, con patatas, cebollas, etc.
chow mein [ˌtʃaʊˈmen] *s* fideos fritos servidos con un guisado de carne, cebollas, apio, etc.
Chr. abr. de **Christian**
chrestomathy [krɛsˈtɑməθɪ] *s* (*pl:* **-thies**) crestomatía
Chris [krɪs] *s* nombre abreviado de **Christopher**
chrism [ˈkrɪzəm] *s* (eccl.) crisma
chrismal [ˈkrɪzməl] *adj & s* (eccl.) crismal
chrismatory [ˈkrɪzməˌtorɪ] *s* (*pl:* **-ries**) crismera
chrismon [ˈkrɪzmɑn] *s* (*pl:* **-ma** [mə]) crismón
Christ [kraɪst] *s* Cristo
christcross [ˈkrɪsˌkrɔs] o [ˈkrɪsˌkrɑs] *s* cristus
christen [ˈkrɪsən] *va* bautizar (*a una persona; un buque; dar nombre a*); (coll.) estrenar (*usar por primera vez*)
Christendom [ˈkrɪsəndəm] *s* cristiandad
christening [ˈkrɪsənɪŋ] *s* bautismo, bautizo
Christian [ˈkrɪstʃən] *adj* cristiano; (coll.) honesto, decente; *s* cristiano; (coll.) persona honesta, persona decente; Cristián (*nombre de varón*)
Christian Brothers *spl* hermanos de la doctrina (cristiana)
Christian Era *s* era cristiana, era de Cristo
Christianity [ˌkrɪstʃɪˈænɪtɪ] *s* cristianismo
Christianization [ˌkrɪstʃənɪˈzeʃən] *s* cristianización
Christianize [ˈkrɪstʃənaɪz] *va* cristianizar
Christianly [ˈkrɪstʃənlɪ] *adj* cristiano; *adv* cristianamente
Christian name *s* nombre de pila o de bautismo
Christian Science *s* ciencia cristiana
Christian Scientist *s* adepto de la ciencia cristiana
Christine [krɪsˈtin] *s* Cristina
Christlike [ˈkraɪstˌlaɪk] o **Christly** [ˈkraɪstlɪ] *adj* propio de Jesucristo, evangélico
Christmas [ˈkrɪsməs] *s* Navidad; *adj* navideño
Christmas card *s* tarjeta navideña, aleluya navideña, christmas
Christmas carol *s* villancico, villancico de Nochebuena o de Navidad
Christmas Day *s* Navidad, día de Navidad
Christmas Eve *s* víspera de Navidad, nochebuena
Christmas gift *s* aguinaldo, regalo de Navidad
Christmas holidays *spl* fiestas navideñas
Christmas rose *s* (bot.) eléboro negro
Christmastide [ˈkrɪsməsˌtaɪd] *s* tiempo de Navidad
Christmas tree *s* árbol de Navidad
Christopher [ˈkrɪstəfər] *s* Cristóbal
Christ's-thorn [ˈkraɪstsˌθɔrn] *s* (bot.) espina santa
chromate [ˈkromet] *s* (chem.) cromato
chromatic [kroˈmætɪk] *adj* cromático; (mus.) cromático; **chromatics** *ssg* cromática
chromatic aberration *s* (opt.) aberración cromática
chromatically [kroˈmætɪkəlɪ] *adv* cromáticamente
chromatic scale *s* (mus.) escala cromática
chromatin [ˈkromətɪn] *s* (biol.) cromatina
chromatism [ˈkromətɪzəm] *s* cromatismo; (bot.) cromismo
chromatophore [ˈkromətəˌfor] *s* (biol.) cromatóforo
chrome [krom] *s* (chem.) cromo; *adj* cromado; *va* cromar
chrome green *s* verde de cromo
chrome red *s* rojo de cromo
chrome steel *s* acerocromo
chrome yellow *s* amarillo de cromo
chromic [ˈkromɪk] *adj* (chem.) crómico
chrominance [ˈkromɪnəns] *s* (phys.) crominancia
chromite [ˈkromaɪt] *s* (chem.) cromito; (mineral.) cromita
chromium [ˈkromɪəm] *s* (chem.) cromo
chromium plating *s* cromado
chromium steel *s* acerocromo
chromo [ˈkromo] *s* (*pl:* **-mos**) cromo (*estampa*); (slang) trasto
chromogen [ˈkromədʒən] *s* (chem.) cromógeno
chromogenic [ˌkroməˈdʒɛnɪk] *adj* cromógeno
chromolithograph [ˌkromoˈlɪθəgræf] o [ˌkromoˈlɪθəgrɑf] *s* cromolitografía (*estampa*); *va* cromolitografiar
chromolithographer [ˌkromolɪˈθɑgrəfər] *s* cromolitógrafo
chromolithographic [ˌkromoˌlɪθəˈgræfɪk] *adj* cromolitográfico
chromolithography [ˌkromolɪˈθɑgrəfɪ] *s* cromolitografía
chromophore [ˈkroməfor] *s* (chem.) cromóforo
chromoplasm [ˈkroməplæzəm] *s* (biol.) cromoplasma
chromoplast [ˈkroməplæst] *s* (bot.) cromoplasto
chromoscope [ˈkroməskop] *s* (telv.) cromoscopio
chromosome [ˈkroməsom] *s* (biol.) cromosoma
chromosphere [ˈkroməsfɪr] *s* (astr.) cromosfera
chromotypography [ˌkromotaɪˈpɑgrəfɪ] *s* cromotipografía
chromous [ˈkroməs] *adj* (chem.) cromoso
chron. abr. de **chronological** y **chronology**
Chron. abr. de **Chronicles**
chronic [ˈkrɑnɪk] *adj* crónico
chronically [ˈkrɑnɪkəlɪ] *adv* crónicamente
chronicle [ˈkrɑnɪkəl] *s* crónica; **Chronicles** *spl* (Bib.) Crónicas (*nombre que dan los protestantes a los Paralipómenos*); *va* historiar, anotar o poner en una crónica; contar, narrar
chronicler [ˈkrɑnɪklər] *s* cronista
chronograph [ˈkrɑnəgræf] o [ˈkrɑnəgrɑf] *s* cronógrafo
chronologic [ˌkrɑnəˈlɑdʒɪk] o **chronological** [ˌkrɑnəˈlɑdʒɪkəl] *adj* cronológico
chronologist [krəˈnɑlədʒɪst] *s* cronologista o cronólogo
chronology [krəˈnɑlədʒɪ] *s* (*pl:* **-gies**) cronología
chronometer [krəˈnɑmɪtər] *s* cronómetro
chronometry [krəˈnɑmɪtrɪ] *s* cronometría
chronoscope [ˈkrɑnəskop] *s* cronoscopio
chrysalid [ˈkrɪsəlɪd] *s* var. de **chrysalis**
chrysalis [ˈkrɪsəlɪs] *s* (*pl:* **chrysalises** o **chrysalides** [krɪˈsælɪdiz]) *s* (ent.) crisálida
chrysanthemum [krɪˈsænθɪməm] *s* (bot.) crisantemo
Chryseis [kraɪˈsiɪs] *s* (myth.) Criseida
chrysoberyl [ˈkrɪsoˌbɛrɪl] *s* (mineral.) crisoberilo
chrysolite [ˈkrɪsolaɪt] *s* (mineral.) crisólito
chrysoprase [ˈkrɪsoprez] *s* (mineral.) crisoprasa
Chrysostom, Saint John [ˈkrɪsəstəm] o [krɪsˈɑstəm] San Juan Crisóstomo
chrysotile [ˈkrɪsətɪl] *s* (mineral.) crisotilo
chub [tʃʌb] *s* (ichth.) cacho
chubby [ˈtʃʌbɪ] *adj* (*comp:* **-bier**; *super:* **-biest**) rechoncho, gordiflón
chuck [tʃʌk] *s* mamola (*bajo la barbilla de una*

persona); echada, tirada; (mach.) mandril, portaherramienta; lomo (*tajada de carne de vaca*); *va* hacer la mamola a; arrojar
chuck-full [ˈtʃʌkˈfʊl] *adj* colmado, de bote en bote
chuckhole [ˈtʃʌkˌhol] *s* badén
chuckle [ˈtʃʌkəl] *s* risa ahogada; *vn* reírse ahogadamente
chucklehead [ˈtʃʌkəlˌhɛd] *s* (coll.) tonto, estúpido
chug [tʃʌg] *s* ruido explosivo corto; (*pret & pp:* **chugged;** *ger:* **chugging**) *vn* (coll.) hacer ruidos explosivos repetidos; (coll.) moverse con ruidos explosivos repetidos
chukkar o **chukker** [ˈtʃʌkər] *s* (sport) período en el juego de polo
chum [tʃʌm] *s* (coll.) compinche; (coll.) compañero de cuarto; (*pret & pp:* **chummed;** *ger:* **chumming**) *vn* (coll.) ser compinche, ser compinches; (coll.) compartir un cuarto, vivir en un mismo cuarto
chummy [ˈtʃʌmɪ] *adj* (*comp:* **-mier;** *super:* **-miest**) (coll.) íntimo, muy amigable
chump [tʃʌmp] *s* tarugo, zoquete, leño grueso; extremidad gruesa; (coll.) tonto, estúpido; (slang) cabeza
chunk [tʃʌŋk] *s* pedazo grueso (*p.ej., de madera*); (coll.) persona rechoncha
chunky [ˈtʃʌŋkɪ] *adj* (*comp:* **-ier;** *super:* **-iest**) (coll.) corto y grueso; (coll.) rechoncho
church [tʃʌrtʃ] *s* iglesia; **to go into the church** entrar en la iglesia (*el estado eclesiástico*); **to go to church** ir a la iglesia
churchgoer [ˈtʃʌrtʃˌgoər] *s* devoto, fiel; iglesiero (Am.)
churchly [ˈtʃʌrtʃlɪ] *adj* eclesiástico
churchman [ˈtʃʌrtʃmən] *s* (*pl:* **-men**) sacerdote, eclesiástico; miembro de una iglesia, feligrés
church member *s* miembro de una iglesia, feligrés
church militant *s* iglesia militante
church music *s* música de iglesia, música sagrada
Church of Christ, Scientist *s* Iglesia de la ciencia cristiana
Church of England *s* Iglesia de Inglaterra, Iglesia anglicana
Church of Jesus Christ of Latter-day Saints *s* Iglesia de Jesucristo de los santos del día final (*iglesia de los mormones*)
Church Slavic o **Slavonic** *s* eslavoeclesiástico (*idioma*)
church supplies *spl* artículos del culto
church triumphant *s* iglesia triunfante
churchwarden [ˈtʃʌrtʃˌwɔrdən] *s* capiller; (coll.) pipa de fumar larga, hecha de arcilla
churchwoman [ˈtʃʌrtʃˌwʊmən] *s* (*pl:* **-women**) mujer miembro de una iglesia, feligresa
churchyard [ˈtʃʌrtʃˌjɑrd] *s* patio de iglesia; cementerio
churl [tʃʌrl] *s* patán, palurdo
churlish [ˈtʃʌrlɪʃ] *adj* palurdo, grosero, insolente
churn [tʃʌrn] *s* agitación; batido; mantequera; *va* mazar (*leche*), batir en una mantequera, hacer (*mantequilla*) en una mantequera; agitar, revolver
churr [tʃʌr] *s & vn* var. de **chirr**
chute [ʃut] *s* canal o conducto inclinado; tolva; cascada, salto de agua; recial
chutney [ˈtʃʌtnɪ] *s* salsa picante compuesta de frutas, hierbas, pimienta, etc.
chyle [kaɪl] *s* (physiol.) quilo
chyliferous [kaɪˈlɪfərəs] *adj* quilífero
chylification [ˌkaɪlɪfɪˈkeʃən] *s* (physiol.) quilificación
chylify [ˈkaɪlɪfaɪ] (*pret & pp:* **-fied**) *va* (physiol.) quilificar; *vn* (physiol.) quilificarse
chylous [ˈkaɪləs] *adj* quiloso
chyme [kaɪm] *s* (physiol.) quimo
chymification [ˌkaɪmɪfɪˈkeʃən] o [ˌkɪmɪfɪˈkeʃən] *s* (physiol.) quimificación
chymify [ˈkaɪmɪfaɪ] (*pret & pp:* **-fied**) (physiol.) *va* quimificar
chymous [ˈkaɪməs] *adj* quimoso
ciborium [sɪˈborɪəm] *s* (*pl:* **-a** [ə]) (arch.) ciborio, baldaquín; (eccl.) copón
cicada [sɪˈkedə] o [sɪˈkɑdə] *s* (*pl:* **-das** o **-dae** [di]) (ent.) cigarra
cicatrice [ˈsɪkətrɪs] *s* var. de **cicatrix**
cicatricle [ˈsɪkəˌtrɪkəl] *s* (bot. & embryol.) cicatrícula
cicatrix [ˈsɪkətrɪks] o [sɪˈketrɪks] *s* (*pl:* **cicatrices** [ˌsɪkəˈtraɪsiz]) cicatriz; (bot.) cicatriz
cicatrize [ˈsɪkətraɪz] *va* cicatrizar; *vn* cicatrizarse
cicely [ˈsɪsəlɪ] *s* (*pl:* **-lies**) (bot.) perifollo oloroso
Cicero [ˈsɪsəro] *s* Cicerón
cicerone [ˌtʃitʃəˈrone] o [ˌsɪsəˈronɪ] *s* (*pl:* **-ni** [nɪ] o **-nes**) cicerone
Ciceronian [ˌsɪsəˈronɪən] *adj* ciceroniano
cider [ˈsaɪdər] *s* sidra
cider press *s* lagar para sacar el zumo de las manzanas
c.i.f. o **C.I.F.** abr. de **cost, insurance, and freight**
cigar [sɪˈgɑr] *s* cigarro, cigarro puro
cigar band *s* anillo (de cigarro)
cigar case *s* cigarrera
cigar cutter *s* cortacigarros, cortapuros
cigaret o **cigarette** [ˌsɪgəˈrɛt] *s* cigarrillo, pitillo
cigarette case *s* pitillera
cigarette holder *s* boquilla
cigarette lighter *s* encendedor de cigarrillos
cigarette paper *s* papel de fumar
cigar holder *s* boquilla
cigar lighter *s* encendedor de cigarros
cigar store *s* estanco, tabaquería
cilia [ˈsɪlɪə] *spl* cilios, pestañas; (bot. & zool.) cilios
ciliary [ˈsɪlɪˌɛrɪ] *adj* (anat.) ciliar
ciliate [ˈsɪlɪet] o [ˈsɪlɪɪt] *adj* ciliado; *s* (zool.) ciliado
ciliated [ˈsɪlɪˌetɪd] *adj* ciliado
Cimmerian [sɪˈmɪrɪən] *adj* cimerio; obscuro, sombrío; *s* cimerio
cinch [sɪntʃ] *s* cincha (*de una silla o albarda*); (coll.) agarro firme; (slang) breva (*cosa fácil*); *va* cinchar; (slang) agarrar
cinchona [sɪnˈkonə] *s* (bot.) quino, cascarillo; (pharm.) quina, cascarilla
cinchona bark *s* (pharm.) quina, corteza del cascarillo
cinchonism [ˈsɪnkənɪzəm] *s* (path.) quinismo
cincture [ˈsɪŋktʃər] *s* cinturón, cincho; cerco; *va* cercar
cinder [ˈsɪndər] *s* carbonilla, ceniza; *va* reducir a cenizas
cinder block *s* bloque de concreto de cenizas
Cinderella [ˌsɪndəˈrɛlə] *s* la Cenicienta
cinder path *s* sendero de cenizas
cinder track *s* pista de cenizas para carreras a pie
cinema [ˈsɪnɪmə] *s* cine
cinematograph [ˌsɪnɪˈmætəgræf] o [ˌsɪnɪˈmætəgrɑf] *s* cinematógrafo; *va & vn* cinematografiar
cineraria [ˌsɪnəˈrɛrɪə] *s* (bot.) cineraria
cinerarium [ˌsɪnəˈrɛrɪəm] *s* (*pl:* **-a** [ə]) lugar cinerario
cinerary [ˈsɪnəˌrɛrɪ] *adj* cinerario
cingulum [ˈsɪŋgjələm] *s* (*pl:* **-la** [lə]) cíngulo (*del alba de un sacerdote*); (anat., bot. & zool.) cíngulo
cinnabar [ˈsɪnəbɑr] *s* cinabrio (*mineral y color*)
cinnamic [sɪˈnæmɪk] o [ˈsɪnəmɪk] *adj* (chem.) cinámico
cinnamon [ˈsɪnəmən] *s* (bot.) canelo; canela (*corteza y especia*); *adj* acanelado
cinquefoil [ˈsɪŋkˌfɔɪl] *s* (bot.) cincoenrama, quinquefolio; (arch.) rosetón de cinco lóbulos
cion [ˈsaɪən] *s* (hort. & fig.) vástago
cipher [ˈsaɪfər] *s* cifra; cero; clave (*de una cifra*); monograma, cifra; (fig.) cero, cero a la izquierda; *adj* cifrado; de ningún valor, de ninguna importancia; *va* cifrar (*escribir en cifra*); numerar, calcular; *vn* numerar, calcular
cipher device *s* cifrador
cipher message *s* mensaje cifrado
circa [ˈsʌrkə] *prep* a eso de, cerca de, hacia
Circassian [sərˈkæʃən] *adj & s* circasiano
Circe [ˈsʌrsɪ] *s* (myth.) Circe
circinate [ˈsʌrsɪnet] *adj* (bot.) circinado
circle [ˈsʌrkəl] *s* círculo; circo; **to square the circle** cuadrar el círculo; *va* circuir, circun-

dar; dar la vuelta a; girar alrededor de; *vn* dar vueltas
circlet [ˈsʌrklɪt] *s* anillo; círculo pequeño; adorno en forma de círculo
circuit [ˈsʌrkɪt] *s* circuito; (elec.) circuito; *va* circular por; contornear; *vn* circular; hacer un circuito
circuit breaker *s* (elec.) disyuntor, interruptor automático
circuit court *s* (law) tribunal cuyos jueces administran justicia a intervalos regulares en varios lugares de un distrito
circuitous [sərˈkjuɪtəs] *adj* tortuoso, indirecto
circuit rider *s* clérigo metodista que andaba de sitio en sitio para pronunciar sermones
circuitry [ˈsʌrkɪtrɪ] *s* (*pl:* **-ries**) (elec.) trazado de circuito; conjunto de los elementos de un circuito; sistema de circuitos
circular [ˈsʌrkjələr] *adj* circular; tortuoso, indirecto; *s* circular, carta circular
circularity [ˌsʌrkjəˈlærɪtɪ] *s* circularidad
circularize [ˈsʌrkjələraɪz] *va* dirigir circulares a; dar forma circular a
circular measure *s* medición del círculo en grados sexagesimales
circular saw *s* sierra circular
circulate [ˈsʌrkjəlet] *va & vn* circular
circulating capital *s* (econ.) capital circulante
circulating library *s* biblioteca circulante
circulation [ˌsʌrkjəˈleʃən] *s* circulación
circulatory [ˈsʌrkjələˌtorɪ] *adj* circulatorio
circumambient [ˌsʌrkəmˈæmbɪənt] *adj* circumambiente
circumcise [ˈsʌrkəmsaɪz] *va* circuncidar
circumcision [ˌsʌrkəmˈsɪʒən] *s* circuncisión
circumference [sərˈkʌmfərəns] *s* circunferencia
circumferential [sərˌkʌmfəˈrɛnʃəl] *adj* circunferencial
circumflex [ˈsʌrkəmflɛks] *adj* (anat. & gram.) circunflejo; *s* (gram.) circunflejo
circumflex accent *s* acento circunflejo
circumfluent [sərˈkʌmflʊənt] *adj* circunfluente
circumfuse [ˌsʌrkəmˈfjuz] *va* difundir en derredor
circumjacent [ˌsʌrkəmˈdʒesənt] *adj* circunyacente
circumlocution [ˌsʌrkəmloˈkjuʃən] *s* circunlocución, circunloquio
circumnavigate [ˌsʌrkəmˈnævɪget] *va* circunnavegar
circumnavigation [ˌsʌrkəmˌnævɪˈgeʃən] *s* circunnavegación
circumnavigator [ˌsʌrkəmˈnævɪˌgetər] *s* circunnavegador
circumpolar [ˌsʌrkəmˈpolər] *adj* circumpolar
circumscribe [ˌsʌrkəmˈskraɪb] *va* circunscribir; (geom.) circunscribir
circumscript [ˈsʌrkəmskrɪpt] *adj* circunscrito
circumscription [ˌsʌrkəmˈskrɪpʃən] *s* circunscripción
circumspect [ˈsʌrkəmspɛkt] *adj* circunspecto
circumspection [ˌsʌrkəmˈspɛkʃən] *s* circunspección
circumstance [ˈsʌrkəmstæns] *s* circunstancia; ostentación, ceremonia; **to be in easy circumstances** estar acomodado; **under no circumstances** de ninguna manera, no importa cuáles sean las circunstancias; **under the circumstances** en las circunstancias
circumstantial [ˌsʌrkəmˈstænʃəl] *adj* circunstancial; circunstanciado (*detallado*)
circumstantial evidence *s* (law) indicios vehementes, evidencia circunstancial
circumstantiate [ˌsʌrkəmˈstænʃɪet] *va* relatar con todas las circunstancias, probar o sostener detalladamente
circumvallate [ˌsʌrkəmˈvælet] *va* circunvalar
circumvallation [ˌsʌrkəmvəˈleʃən] *s* circunvalación
circumvent [ˌsʌrkəmˈvɛnt] *va* embaucar, engañar; entrampar; evitar, desviarse de
circumvention [ˌsʌrkəmˈvɛnʃən] *s* embaucamiento, engaño; evitación
circumvolution [ˌsʌrkəmvəˈluʃən] *s* circunvolución
circus [ˈsʌrkəs] *s* circo; (coll.) persona o cosa muy divertida; *adj* circense
Circus Maximus [ˈmæksɪməs] *s* circo máximo
cirque [sʌrk] *s* circo; (geol.) circo; (poet.) anillo, círculo pequeño
cirrhosis [sɪˈrosɪs] *s* (path.) cirrosis
cirrhotic [sɪˈrɑtɪk] *adj* cirrótico
cirriped [ˈsɪrɪpɛd] *adj & s* (zool.) cirrípedo o cirrópodo
cirro-cumulus [ˌsɪroˈkjumjələs] *s* (meteor.) cirrocúmulo
cirro-stratus [ˌsɪroˈstretəs] *s* (meteor.) cirrostrato
cirrus [ˈsɪrəs] *s* (*pl:* **-ri** [raɪ]) (bot., zool. & meteor.) cirro
cisalpine [sɪsˈælpaɪn] o [sɪsˈælpɪn] *adj* cisalpino
cisandine [sɪsˈændaɪn] o [sɪsˈændɪn] *adj* cisandino
cisatlantic [ˌsɪsætˈlæntɪk] *adj* cisatlántico
cisco [ˈsɪsko] *s* (*pl:* **-coes** o **-cos**) (ichth.) arenque de lago (*Leucichthys*)
cissoid [ˈsɪsɔɪd] *s* (geom.) cisoide
cistaceous [sɪsˈteʃəs] *adj* (bot.) cistáceo
Cistercian [sɪsˈtʌrʃən] *adj & s* cisterciense
Cistercian Order *s* orden *f* del Cister
cistern [ˈsɪstərn] *s* cisterna; (anat.) cisterna
citadel [ˈsɪtədəl] *s* (fort.) ciudadela
citation [saɪˈteʃən] o [sɪˈteʃən] *s* citación; (law) citación; (mil.) mención
cite [saɪt] *va* citar; (law) citar; (mil.) mencionar; mover, incitar
cithara [ˈsɪθərə] *s* (mus.) cítara (*lira griega*)
cither [ˈsɪθər] *s* (mus.) cítara (*lira griega; instrumento músico parecido a la guitarra*)
cithern [ˈsɪθərn] *s* (mus.) cítara (*instrumento músico parecido a la guitarra*)
citified [ˈsɪtɪfaɪd] *adj* urbanizado
citizen [ˈsɪtɪzən] *s* ciudadano; paisano (*el que no es militar*); *adj* ciudadano
citizeness [ˈsɪtɪzənɪs] *s* ciudadana
citizen of the world *s* ciudadano del mundo
citizenry [ˈsɪtɪzənrɪ] *s* ciudadanos, conjunto de ciudadanos
citizenship [ˈsɪtɪzənˌʃɪp] *s* ciudadanía
citrate [ˈsɪtret] o [ˈsaɪtret] *s* (chem.) citrato
citrate of magnesia *s* (med.) citrato de magnesia
citric [ˈsɪtrɪk] *adj* (chem.) cítrico
citric acid *s* (chem.) ácido cítrico
citrin [ˈsɪtrɪn] *s* (biochem.) citrina
citron [ˈsɪtrən] *s* (bot.) cidro (*Citrus medica*); cidra (*fruto*); cidrada (*corteza confitada*)
citronella [ˌsɪtrəˈnɛlə] *s* (bot.) limoncillo; esencia de limoncillo
citron melon *s* (bot.) sandía de carne blanca
citrous [ˈsɪtrəs] *adj* auranciáceo
citrus [ˈsɪtrəs] *adj* auranciáceo; *s* (bot.) cidro (*cualquier planta del género Citrus*); cidra (*fruto*)
citrus fruit *s* agrios (*fruto de cualquier planta del género Citrus*)
cittern [ˈsɪtərn] *s* var. de **cithern**
city [ˈsɪtɪ] *s* (*pl:* **-ies**) ciudad; **the City** el centro comercial, bancario y bursátil de Londres; **City** Interior o Ciudad (*palabra que se pone al sobrescrito de una carta que va al interior de la ciudad*); *adj* ciudadano; urbano
city clerk *s* archivero de municipio
city council *s* ayuntamiento
city editor *s* (U.S.A.) redactor de periódico encargado de las noticias locales; (Brit.) redactor de periódico encargado de las noticias comerciales y bancarias
city fathers *spl* concejales
city hall *s* ayuntamiento, casa consistorial, palacio municipal
city limits *spl* casco urbano
city manager *s* administrador municipal escogido por el ayuntamiento o por alguna comisión
City of Brotherly Love *s* ciudad del amor fraternal (*Filadelfia*)
City of David *s* ciudad de David (*Jerusalén; Belén*)
City of God *s* ciudad de Dios (*el paraíso*)
City of Masts *s* ciudad de los mástiles (*Londres*)
City of the Seven Hills *s* ciudad de las siete colinas (*Roma*)
city plan *s* plano de la ciudad
city planner *s* urbanista
city planning *s* urbanismo, urbanización

city room *s* redacción de un periódico (*lugar donde se redacta; conjunto de los redactores*)
city-state ['sɪtɪ'stet] *s* ciudad-estado
civet ['sɪvɪt] *s* algalia, civeto
civet bean (bot.) frijol iztagapa
civet cat *s* (zool.) algalia, civeta, gato de algalia
civic ['sɪvɪk] *adj* cívico; **civics** *ssg* estudio de los deberes, derechos y privilegios de los ciudadanos
civies ['sɪvɪz] *spl* (coll.) traje de paisano, ropas civiles; **in civies** (coll.) de paisano
civil ['sɪvɪl] *adj* civil
civil defense *s* defensa civil, protección civil
civil disobedience *s* desobediencia civil
civil engineer *s* ingeniero civil
civil engineering *s* ingeniería civil
civilian [sɪ'vɪljən] *adj* civil; *s* hombre civil, paisano
civilian clothes *spl* traje de paisano
civility [sɪ'vɪlɪtɪ] *s* (*pl:* **-ties**) civilidad
civilization [ˌsɪvɪlɪ'zeʃən] *s* civilización
civilize ['sɪvɪlaɪz] *va* civilizar; *vn* civilizarse
civilized ['sɪvɪlaɪzd] *adj* civilizado
civil law *s* derecho civil
civil liberty *s* libertad civil
civilly ['sɪvɪlɪ] *adv* civilmente
civil marriage *s* matrimonio civil
civil rights *s* derechos civiles
civil servant *s* empleado de servicio civil oficial
civil service *s* servicio civil oficial
civil war *s* guerra civil; **Civil War** *s* (U.S.A.) Guerra civil, Guerra entre Norte y Sur
civil year *s* año civil
civism ['sɪvɪzəm] *s* civismo
civvies ['sɪvɪz] *spl* (coll.) var. de **civies**
clabber ['klæbər] *s* cuajada de leche agria; *vn* cuajarse agriándose
clack [klæk] *s* ruido corto y agudo; charla; *vn* producir ruidos cortos y agudos; charlar
clack valve *s* (hyd.) chapaleta
clad [klæd] *pret & pp de* **clothe**
cladoceran [klə'dɑsərən] *adj & s* (zool.) cladócero
cladode ['klædod] *s* (bot.) cladodio
claim [klem] *s* demanda; reclamación; afirmación, declaración; (min.) pertenencia; **to jump a claim** usurpar el terreno o la mina que una persona ha denunciado; **to lay claim to** reclamar, reivindicar; *va* demandar; reclamar; afirmar, declarar; (min.) denunciar; **to claim to be** pretender ser
claim agent *s* agente de reclamación
claimant ['klemənt] *s* demandante; reclamante; (min.) denunciante; pretendiente (*al trono*)
claim check *s* comprobante
clairvoyance [klɛr'vɔɪəns] *s* clarividencia (*penetración, perspicacia; doble vista*)
clairvoyant [klɛr'vɔɪənt] *adj* clarividente (*perspicaz; que pretende poseer la doble vista*); *s* clarividente (*persona que pretende poseer la doble vista*)
clam [klæm] *s* (zool.) almeja; (coll.) chiticalla (*persona muy callada*); (*pret & pp:* **clammed;** *ger:* **clamming**) *vn* pescar almejas
clambake ['klæmˌbek] *s* jira campestre en que se asan almejas
clamber ['klæmbər] *s* trepa desmañada o difícil; *vn* trepar, subir gateando
clammy ['klæmɪ] *adj* (*comp:* **-mier;** *super:* **-miest**) frío y húmedo
clamor ['klæmər] *s* clamor, clamoreo; *va & vn* clamorear
clamorous ['klæmərəs] *adj* clamoroso
clamp [klæmp] *s* abrazadera; tornillo de banco; (naut.) contradurmiente; *va* afianzar o sujetar con abrazadera; asegurar en el tornillo de banco; *vn* pisar recio; **to clamp down on** (coll.) coaccionar, apretar los tornillos a
clamshell ['klæmˌʃɛl] *s* concha de almeja; cucharón de almeja o de quijadas, pala de doble concha
clamshell bucket *s* cucharón de almeja o de quijadas, pala de doble concha
clan [klæn] *s* clan
clandestine [klæn'dɛstɪn] *adj* clandestino
clang [klæŋ] *s* fuerte sonido metálico como de campana; tantán (*de un yunque*); *va* hacer sonar fuertemente; *vn* sonar fuertemente
clangor ['klæŋgər] o ['klæŋər] *s* sonido metálico desapacible, estruendo
clangorous ['klæŋgərəs] o ['klæŋərəs] *adj* estrepitoso, retumbante
clank [klæŋk] *s* sonido metálico seco; *va* hacer sonar secamente; *vn* sonar secamente
clannish ['klænɪʃ] *adj* tribal; exclusivista
clansman ['klænzmən] *s* (*pl:* **-men**) miembro de un clan
clap [klæp] *s* golpe seco, estampido; trueno; palmoteo; (slang) gonorrea; (*pret & pp:* **clapped;** *ger:* **clapping**) *va* batir (*palmas*); aplaudir; poner o colocar de prisa; **to clap eyes on** (coll.) clavar la vista en; **to clap shut** cerrar de golpe; **to clap up** poner en la cárcel; *vn* estallar; palmear, palmotear
clapboard ['klæbərd] o ['klæpˌbord] *s* chilla, tabla de chilla; *va* cubrir con tablas de chilla
clap of thunder *s* estampido de trueno
clapper ['klæpər] *s* golpeador; palmoteador; badajo (*de campana*); tarabilla, cítola; castañuelas; (coll.) lengua
claptrap ['klæpˌtræp] *s* faramalla, engañabobos; latiguillo (*de actor*); *adj* faramallón
claque [klæk] *s* claque
Clare [klɛr] *s* Clara; clarisa (*religiosa*)
clarence ['klærəns] *s* clarens (*coche*)
claret ['klærɪt] *s* clarete; rojo purpurado; (slang) sangre
clarification [ˌklærɪfɪ'keʃən] *s* clarificación
clarifier ['klærɪˌfaɪər] *s* clarificador; clarificadora (*vasija en que se clarifica el guarapo del azúcar*)
clarify ['klærɪfaɪ] (*pret & pp:* **-fied**) *va* clarificar
clarinet [ˌklærɪ'nɛt] *s* (mus.) clarinete
clarinetist o **clarinettist** [ˌklærɪ'nɛtɪst] *s* clarinete o clarinetista (*músico que toca el clarinete*)
clarion ['klærɪən] *s* (mus.) clarín (*instrumento músico; registro del órgano*); (poet.) sonido del clarín; (poet.) sonido de clarín; *adj* claro y agudo
clarionet [ˌklærɪə'nɛt] *s* var. de **clarinet**
clarity ['klærɪtɪ] *s* claridad
clary ['klɛrɪ] *s* (*pl:* **-ies**) (bot.) amaro, esclarea
clash [klæʃ] *s* choque, encontrón; estruendo; *va* batir, golpear ruidosamente; *vn* chocar
clasp [klæsp] o [klɑsp] *s* broche, corchete; cierre; hebilla; abrazadera; abrazo; agarro; *va* abrochar, encorchetar; abrazar; agarrar, apretar (*la mano*); apretarse (*la mano*)
clasp knife *s* navaja (*cuya hoja puede doblarse y quedar guardada dentro del mango*)
class. abr. de **classical**
class [klæs] o [klɑs] *s* clase; (slang) excelencia; (slang) elegancia, buen tono; **the classes** las clases más altas de la sociedad; *va* clasificar; *vn* clasificarse
classbook ['klæsˌbʊk] o ['klɑsˌbʊk] *s* libro de clase; libro publicado por una clase de la escuela (*sobre todo la que está para graduarse*)
class-conscious ['klæs'kɑnʃəs] o ['klɑs'kɑnʃəs] *adj* consciente de su clase social
class consciousness *s* conciencia o conocimiento de la clase social a que uno pertenece
class day *s* (U.S.A.) día en que los miembros de una clase que va a graduarse celebran su graduación
class hour *s* (educ.) hora de clase
classic ['klæsɪk] *adj & s* clásico; **the classics** las obras clásicas (*de la literatura romana y griega*)
classical ['klæsɪkəl] *adj* clásico
classically ['klæsɪkəlɪ] *adv* clásicamente
classical scholar *s* erudito en las lenguas clásicas
classicism ['klæsɪsɪzəm] *s* clasicismo
classicist ['klæsɪsɪst] *s* clasicista
classification [ˌklæsɪfɪ'keʃən] *s* clasificación
classification yard *s* (rail.) patio de clasificación
classified ['klæsɪfaɪd] *adj* clasificado; clasificado como secreto
classified ads *spl* anuncios clasificados (en secciones)
classifier ['klæsɪˌfaɪər] *s* (min.) clasificador
classify ['klæsɪfaɪ] (*pret & pp:* **-fied**) *va* clasificar
class legislation *s* legislación clasista
classmate ['klæsˌmet] o ['klɑsˌmet] *s* compañero de clase, condiscípulo

classroom ['klæsˌrum] o ['klɑsˌrum] *s* sala de clase
class struggle *s* lucha de clases
classy ['klæsɪ] *adj* (*comp:* **-ier;** *super:* **-iest**) (slang) elegante, de categoría
clatter ['klætər] *s* martilleo, estruendo confuso; algazara, gresca; trápala (*del trote de un caballo*); *va* hacer chocar ruidosamente; *vn* chocar ruidosamente; moverse o caer con estruendo confuso; hablar rápida y ruidosamente; **to clatter down the steps** bajar la escalera ruidosamente
Claud o **Claude** [klɔd] o **Claudius** ['klɔdɪəs] *s* Claudio
clause [klɔz] *s* cláusula (*disposición de un contrato u otro documento*); (gram.) oración dependiente
claustral ['klɔstrəl] *adj* var. de **cloistral**
claustrophobia [ˌklɔstrə'fobɪə] *s* (path.) claustrofobia
claustrum ['klɔstrəm] *s* (*pl:* **-tra** [trə]) (anat.) claustro
clava ['klevə] *s* (*pl:* **-vae** [vi]) (anat.) clava
clavate ['klevet] *adj* (bot. & zool.) claviforme
clavichord ['klævɪkɔrd] *s* (mus.) clavicordio
clavicle ['klævɪkəl] *s* (anat.) clavícula
clavicular [klə'vɪkjələr] *adj* clavicular
claviculate [klə'vɪkjəlet] *adj* (zool.) claviculado
clavier ['klævɪər] o [klə'vɪr] *s* (mus.) teclado; (mus.) teclado sin sonido para practicar; [klə'vɪr] *s* (mus.) clave, clavicordio, piano u otro instrumento musical con teclado
claw [klɔ] *s* (zool.) garra; (zool.) uña; (zool.) pinza (*de langosta, cangrejo, etc.*); oreja (*de martillo, llave de tuerca, etc.*); arañazo; mano, dedos; *va* agarrar; desgarrar; arañar; *vn* arañar, arañar ligeramente
claw bar *s* sacaclavos de horquilla
claw clutch *s* (mach.) embrague de garra
claw hammer *s* martillo de orejas, martillo sacaclavos; (coll.) frac
clay [kle] *s* arcilla; *va* arcillar; (agr.) arcillar
clayey ['kleɪ] *adj* (*comp:* **clayier;** *super:* **clayiest**) arcilloso
claymore ['klemor] *s* claymore (*espada escocesa*)
clay pigeon *s* pichón de barro (*disco de arcilla lanzado al aire en el tiro al blanco*)
clay pipe *s* pipa de fumar hecha de arcilla, pipa de tierra
clay pit *s* gredal, mina de arcilla
clay soil *s* terreno arcilloso
clay stone *s* piedra arcillosa; piedra formada a base de arcilla
claytonia [kle'tonɪə] *s* (bot.) claitonia
clean [klin] *adj* limpio; neto, distinto; completo, perfecto; liso, parejo; diestro, hábil; bien hecho, bien proporcionado; *adv* completamente, totalmente; limpio, limpiamente; **to come clean** (slang) confesarlo todo; *va* limpiar, asear; **to be cleaned out** (slang) quedar limpio (*sin dinero*); **to clean out** limpiar vaciando; limpiar (*p.ej., las ramas pequeñas de un árbol*); agotar, consumir; (slang) limpiar (*hurtando o en el juego*); **to clean up** limpiar completamente; arreglar; (mach.) alinear; (coll.) acabar, completar; (slang) sacar de ganancia; *vn* limpiarse, asearse; **to clean up** limpiarse, asearse; (coll.) llevárselo todo; (coll.) hacer mesa limpia (*en el juego*); (slang) ganar mucho dinero; **to clean up after someone** limpiar lo que alguno ha ensuciado
clean bill of health *s* patente limpia de sanidad; certificado de aptitud
clean-cut ['klinˌkʌt] *adj* bien definido; bien tallado; claro, definido; de buen parecer
cleaner ['klinər] *s* limpiador; tintorero; quitamanchas (*persona y substancia*); **to send to the cleaners** (slang) dejar limpio, limpiarle a (*uno*) todo el dinero
cleanhanded ['klin'hændɪd] *adj* con las manos limpias, sin culpa
cleaning ['klinɪŋ] *s* limpiadura, aseo; **cleanings** *spl* limpiaduras (*desperdicios*)
cleaning fluid *s* quitamanchas
cleaning rag *s* trapo para limpiar, paño de limpiar
cleaning rod *s* (arti.) baqueta de limpieza
cleaning woman *s* criada que limpia la casa
clean-limbed ['klin'lɪmbd] *adj* de piernas bien proporcionadas
cleanliness ['klɛnlɪnɪs] *s* limpieza habitual; esmero (*en la compostura de la persona*)
cleanly ['klɛnlɪ] *adj* (*comp:* **-lier;** *super:* **-liest**) limpio (*que tiene el hábito de la limpieza*); ['klinlɪ] *adv* limpiamente
cleanness ['klinnɪs] *s* limpieza, aseo
cleanse [klɛnz] *va* limpiar, depurar, purificar
clean-shaven ['klin'ʃevən] *adj* lisamente afeitado
cleanup ['klinˌʌp] *s* limpieza general; (slang) gran ganancia; **to make a cleanup** (slang) hacer su pacotilla
clear [klɪr] *adj* claro; despejado (*sin nubes*); libre (*de culpa, deudas, estorbos, etc.*); seguro, cierto; neto, líquido; entero, completo; **clear of** libre de (*p.ej., deudas*); a distancia de; **in the clear** por dentro ‖ *adv* claro, claramente; enteramente, completamente; sin tocar, sin alcanzar; **clear through** de lado a lado ‖ *va* aclarar; clarificar; desembarazar; desmontar, rebajar (*un terreno*); salvar, saltar por encima de; pasar por un lado de, sin tocar; abonar, acreditar; absolver, probar la inocencia de; sacar (*una ganancia neta*); desocupar (*un cuarto*); (naut.) despachar en la aduana; (com.) pasar (*un cheque*) por un banco de liquidación; (com.) liquidar (*una cuenta*); **to clear a ship for action** (nav.) alistar un buque para el combate; **to clear an equation of fractions** (math.) quitar los denominadores de una ecuación; **to clear away** u **off** quitar (*estorbos u obstáculos*); desocupar; desmontar, rebajar; quitar (*la mesa*); **to clear out** limpiar, desembarazar desechando o vaciando; **to clear the way** abrir camino; **to clear up** aclarar, clarificar; arreglar, ordenar; desembarazar ‖ *vn* aclararse; clarificarse; desembarazarse; justificarse; (naut.) despacharse después de pagados los derechos de aduana; **to clear away** u **off** irse, desaparecer; **to clear out** (coll.) irse, salirse, escabullirse; **to clear up** abonanzar (*el tiempo o una situación embarazosa*); despejarse (*el cielo, el tiempo*)
clearance ['klɪrəns] *s* aclaración; abono, acreditación; espacio libre (*entre dos cosas que pasan la una al lado de la otra sin tocarse*); (mach.) espacio muerto (*en un cilindro*); (mach.) intersticio (*p.ej., de una turbina hidráulica*); (elec.) distancia radial (*entre el polo y el inducido*); (com.) compensación
clearance sale *s* venta de liquidación
clear-cut ['klɪrˌkʌt] *adj* claro, definido; bien delineado
clear-headed ['klɪr'hɛdɪd] *adj* inteligente, perspicaz
clearing ['klɪrɪŋ] *s* claro (*en un bosque*); (com.) compensación
clearing house *s* (com.) cámara de compensación
clearness ['klɪrnɪs] *s* claridad
clear-sighted ['klɪr'saɪtɪd] *adj* perspicaz; (fig.) perspicaz
clearstarch ['klɪrˌstɑrtʃ] *va* almidonar con una mezcla ligera de almidón y agua
clearstory ['klɪrˌstorɪ] *s* (*pl:* **-ries**) var. de **clerestory**
cleat [klit] *s* abrazadera, listón, fiador; (naut.) tojino; (naut.) cornamusa (*para amarrar cabos*); *va* enlistonar; (naut.) asegurar con o en tojino, cornamusa, etc.
cleavage ['klivɪdʒ] *s* hendedura, división; (biol.) segmentación del óvulo; (fig.) desunión
cleave [kliv] (*pret:* **cleaved, cleft** o **clove;** *pp:* **cleaved, cleft** o **cloven**) *va* hender, rajar, dividir; penetrar; abrir (*trocha en la selva*); cortar (*la cabeza*); partir (*el corazón*); hender (*las aguas un buque, los aires una flecha, las nubes un avión, etc.*); *vn* henderse, rajarse; (*pret & pp:* **cleaved**) *vn* adherirse, pegarse; ser fiel, ser leal
cleaver ['klivər] *s* rajadera, cortante, cuchilla de carnicero; **cleavers** *s* (*pl:* **-ers**) (bot.) presera, galio
cleek [klik] *s* (golf) maza de hierro para lanzamientos a distancia
clef [klɛf] *s* (mus.) clave
cleft [klɛft] *s* raja, grieta, hendedura; *adj* rajado, hendido; *pret & pp de* **cleave**

cleft palate *s* palatosquisis, fisura del paladar
cleistogamous [klaɪs'tɑgəməs] *adj* (bot.) cleistógamo
clematis ['klɛmətɪs] *s* (bot.) clemátide
clemency ['klɛmənsɪ] *s* (*pl:* **-cies**) clemencia; benignidad, suavidad
clement ['klɛmənt] *adj* clemente; benigno, suave; (*cap.*) *s* Clemente
clench [klɛntʃ] *s* agarro; *va* agarrar; cerrar o apretar (*el puño, los dientes*); remachar (*la punta de un clavo ya clavado*)
Cleon ['kliɑn] *s* Cleón
clepsydra ['klɛpsɪdrə] *s* (*pl:* **-dras** o **-drae** [dri]) reloj de agua, clepsidra
clerestory ['klɪr,storɪ] *s* (*pl:* **-ries**) (arch.) claraboya
clergy ['klʌrdʒɪ] *s* (*pl:* **-gies**) clero, clerecía
clergyman ['klʌrdʒɪmən] *s* (*pl:* **-men**) clérigo, sacerdote, eclesiástico, pastor
cleric ['klɛrɪk] *adj* clerical; *s* clérigo
clerical ['klɛrɪkəl] *adj* clerical; oficinesco; *s* clérigo; clerical (*partidario del clero*); **clericals** *spl* (coll.) hábitos clericales
clerical error *s* error de pluma
clericalism ['klɛrɪkəlɪzəm] *s* clericalismo
clericalist ['klɛrɪkəlɪst] *s* clerical
clerical work *s* trabajo de oficina
clerk [klʌrk] *s* dependiente de tienda, vendedor; oficinista, escribiente; archivero (*de municipio*); (law) escribano; lego, seglar (*en una iglesia*); (hist.) clérigo (*hombre de estudios*); *vn* trabajar como dependiente, oficinista, etc.
clerkly ['klʌrklɪ] *adj* (*comp:* **-lier;** *super:* **-liest**) de dependiente; clerical
clerkship ['klʌrkʃɪp] *s* empleo de dependiente, empleo de oficinista; (law) escribanía; secretaría
cleveite ['klivaɪt] *s* (mineral.) cleveíta
clever ['klɛvər] *adj* inteligente; hábil, diestro, mañoso
cleverness ['klɛvərnɪs] *s* inteligencia; habilidad, destreza, maña; gracia
clevis ['klɛvɪs] *s* horquilla, abrazadera
clew [klu] *s* indicio, pista, guía; ovillo; (naut.) puño; (naut.) anillo de hierro fijado al puño; *va* (naut.) levantar (*la vela*) sirviéndose del anillo fijado al puño
cliché [kli'ʃe] *s* (print.) clisé; (fig.) cliché (*frase hecha, idea gastada*)
click [klɪk] *s* golpecito; tecleo (*de la máquina de escribir*); piñoneo (*del arma de fuego*); taconeo; chasquido (*de la lengua*); *va* chascar (*la lengua*); **to click the heels** taconear; cuadrarse (*militarmente*); *vn* sonar con un golpecito seco; piñonear (*un arma de fuego*)
client ['klaɪənt] *s* cliente; cliente de abogado
clientele [,klaɪən'tɛl] *s* clientela
cliff [klɪf] *s* risco, escarpa, precipicio
cliff dweller *s* hombre de las rocas
cliff dwelling *s* casa o cueva construída en las rocas
cliff swallow *s* (orn.) golondrina de las rocas
climacteric [klaɪ'mæktərɪk] o [,klaɪmæk'tɛrɪk] *adj* climatérico; *s* climatérico o climaterio
climactic [klaɪ'mæktɪk] *adj* climáxico, culminante
climate ['klaɪmɪt] *s* clima
climatic [klaɪ'mætɪk] *adj* climático
climatically [klaɪ'mætɪkəlɪ] *adv* climáticamente
climatology [,klaɪmə'tɑlədʒɪ] *s* climatología
climax ['klaɪmæks] *s* (rhet.) clímax; colmo; **to cap the climax** ser el colmo; *va & vn* terminar
climb [klaɪm] *s* trepa; subida; subidero; *va* trepar, escalar, subir; *vn* trepar, escalar, subir; **to climb down** bajar a gatas; descender; (coll.) cejar, rendirse; **to climb up** trepar por
climber ['klaɪmər] *s* trepador; subidor; ambicioso de figurar; garfio, trepador (*clavo puntiagudo fijado en el zapato para facilitar la subida*); (bot.) trepadora, enredadera; (orn.) trepadora; **climber of hills** (aut.) subidor de cuestas
climb indicator *s* (aer.) ascensómetro, indicador de ascensión
climbing belt *s* cinturón de seguridad
climbing fish *s* (ichth.) anabas
climbing irons *spl* garfios, trepadores, crampones
clime [klaɪm] *s* (poet.) clima, país, región, plaga
clinch [klɪntʃ] *s* agarro; abrazo; remache, roblón; (box.) clincha; (naut.) entalingadura; **to be in a clinch** estar agarrados, estar abrazados; *va* agarrar; abrazar; afianzar, sujetar o fijar con firmeza; apretar (*el puño, los dientes*); remachar, roblar (*un clavo ya clavado*); afirmar, resolver decisivamente; (naut.) entalingar; *vn* abrazarse fuertemente; luchar cuerpo a cuerpo
clincher ['klɪntʃər] *s* remachador; clavo de remachar; (coll.) argumento decisivo; neumático de talón
clincher tire *s* neumático de talón
cling [klɪŋ] (*pret & pp:* **clung**) *vn* adherirse, pegarse
clingstone ['klɪŋ,ston] *s* pavía, albérchiga, peladillo; *adj* de hueso adherente, de carne pegada al hueso (*dícese del melocotón o pérsico*)
clingy ['klɪŋɪ] *adj* pegajoso
clinic ['klɪnɪk] *s* clínica
clinical ['klɪnɪkəl] *adj* clínico
clinical chart *s* hoja clínica
clinically ['klɪnɪkəlɪ] *adv* clínicamente
clinical thermometer *s* termómetro clínico
clinician [klɪ'nɪʃən] *s* clínico
clink [klɪŋk] *s* tintín (*sonido metálico ligero*); (coll.) cárcel; *va* hacer tintinar; *vn* tintinar
clinker ['klɪŋkər] *s* escoria de hulla; escoria de cemento; ladrillo muy duro; masa de ladrillos derretidos; *vn* formar escorias
clinker-built ['klɪŋkər,bɪlt] *adj* de tingladillo
clinker work *s* tingladillo
clinometer [klaɪ'nɑmɪtər] *s* clinómetro
Clio ['klaɪo] *s* (myth.) Clío
clip [klɪp] *s* tijereteo, cercenadura, esquileo; movimiento rápido; grapa, pinza; sujetapapeles, presilla de alambre; (coll.) golpe seco y súbito; **clips** *spl* tijeras; **at a good clip** a paso rápido; (*pret & pp:* **clipped;** *ger:* **clipping**) *va* tijeretear, cercenar, esquilar; cercenar (*el borde de las monedas*) dañandolas; agarrar, afianzar; recortar (*p.ej., un cupón*), acortar; (phonet.) apocopar; (coll.) golpear súbito con golpe seco; **to clip the wings of** cortar las alas a, cortar los vuelos a; *vn* moverse con rapidez
clipped word *s* palabra apocopada (*como* **prof** [prɑf] *por* **professor**)
clipper ['klɪpər] *s* cercenador; recortador; tijera, cizalla; (naut. & aer.) clíper; **clippers** *spl* maquinilla para cortar el pelo; guadañadora, tijeras podadoras
clipper-built ['klɪpər,bɪlt] *adj* (naut.) construído y aparejado para gran rapidez
clipping ['klɪpɪŋ] *s* recorte; tijereteo; esquileo; *adj* (coll.) rápido; (slang) excelente, de primera clase
clique [klik] *s* pandilla, compadraje, corrillo
cliquish ['klikɪʃ] *adj* exclusivista
clitellum [klɪ'tɛləm] o [klaɪ'tɛləm] *s* (*pl:* **-la** [lə]) (zool.) clitelo
clitoris ['klaɪtərɪs] o ['klɪtərɪs] *s* (anat.) clítoris
clk. abr. de **clerk** y **clock**
cloaca [klo'ekə] *s* (*pl:* **-cae** [si]) cloaca; (zool.) cloaca
cloak [klok] *s* capa, capote; disimulo, excusa; *va* encapotar; disimular, encubrir
cloak-and-dagger ['klokən'dægər] *adj* de capa y espada
cloak-and-sword ['klokənd'sord] *adj* de capa y espada
cloak hanger *s* cuelgacapas
cloakroom ['klok,rum] o ['klok,rʊm] *s* guardarropa (*sitio*); (Brit.) excusado, retrete
clobber ['klɑbər] *va* (slang) apalear, tundir; (slang) derrotar completamente
cloche [kloʃ] *s* campana de cristal; sombrero de mujer de ajuste estrecho
clock [klɑk] *s* reloj; cuadrado (*en las medias*); **round the clock** noche y día, todas las horas del día; **to turn the clock back** retrasar el reloj; quitarse años, fingir menos edad; remontarse al pasado; *va* registrar; (sport) cronometrar; bordar con cuadrado; *vn* **to clock in** marcar (*el obrero o el empleado*) la hora de

entrada en el reloj registrador; **to clock out** marcar (*el obrero o el empleado*) la hora de salida en el reloj registrador
clockmaker ['klɑk,mekər] *s* relojero
clock meter *s* (elec.) limitador de corriente
clock tower *s* torre reloj
clockwise ['klɑk,waɪz] *adj & adv* en el sentido de las agujas del reloj
clockwork ['klɑk,wʌrk] *s* aparato de relojería; **like clockwork** como un reloj
clod [klɑd] *s* tierra; terrón; palurdo, zoquete
clodhopper ['klɑd,hɑpər] *s* destripaterrones, patán; **clodhoppers** *spl* zapatos grandes y fuertes
clog [klɑg] *s* estorbo, obstáculo; traba (*para atar los pies del caballo*); chanclo, galocha; zueco (*usado en bailes*); zapateado; (*pret & pp:* **clogged;** *ger:* **clogging**) *va* atascar; estorbar; *vn* atascarse; bailar el zapateado
clog dance *s* zapateado
clog dancer *s* zapateador
cloisonné [,klɔɪzə'ne] *s* esmalte alveolado o tabicado
cloister ['klɔɪstər] *s* claustro; *va* enclaustrar
cloistral ['klɔɪstrəl] *adj* claustral
clonic ['klɑnɪk] *adj* clónico
clonus ['klonəs] *s* (path.) clono
close [klos] *adj* cercano, próximo; estrecho; casi igual, casi a la par, con corta distancia; cerrado, apretado; compacto (*p.ej., tejido*); exacto, estricto, riguroso; pesado, sofocante; mal ventilado; encerrado; limitado; avaro, mezquino; escaso; minucioso; reñido (*combate, carrera, etc.*); (phonet.) cerrado; **at close range** de cerca, a corta distancia ‖ *s* cercado, recinto; atrio (*de una catedral o abadía*) ‖ [kloz] *s* fin, terminación; cierre (*p.ej., de la Bolsa*); **at the close of day** a la caída de la tarde ‖ [kloz] *va* cerrar; tapar; concluir; cerrar (*un trato, un contrato*); saldar (*una cuenta*); (elec.) cerrar (*un circuito*); **to close down** cerrar completamente; **to close in** cerrar, encerrar; **to close out** vender en liquidación; saldar (*una cuenta*); **to close ranks** estrechar las distancias; (mil.) cerrar las filas; **to close up** poner más cerca; cerrar por completo; **close quote** fin de la cita ‖ *vn* cerrarse; reunirse; concordarse; (sport) luchar cuerpo a cuerpo; **to close down** cerrarse por completo; **to close in** acercarse rodeando; **to close in on** cercar, rodear; **to close up** ponerse más cerca; cerrarse por completo; cicatrizarse; **to close with** cerrar con (*p.ej., el enemigo*)
close call *s* (coll.) escape difícil o milagroso, escape por un pelo
close column *s* (mil.) columna cerrada
close confinement *s* prisión estrecha, estado de incomunicado
close connection *s* intimidad, relación estrecha; combinación de trenes sin mucho margen entre la llegada de un tren y la salida del siguiente
close corporation *s* (com.) sociedad anónima cuyos dignatarios son dueños de las acciones
closed car *s* automóvil o coche cerrado, conducción interior
closed chapter *s* asunto concluído
closed circuit *s* (elec.) circuito cerrado
closed-circuit battery ['klozd'sʌrkɪt] *s* (elec.) pila de circuito cerrado
closed-circuit television *s* televisión en circuito cerrado
closed season *s* veda
closed shop *s* taller agremiado
closed syllable *s* (phonet.) sílaba cerrada
close election *s* elección muy reñida
close fertilization *s* (bot.) autofecundación
closefisted ['klos'fɪstɪd] *adj* manicorto, cicatero, tacaño
close-fitting ['klos'fɪtɪŋ] *adj* ajustado, ceñido al cuerpo
close-grained ['klos'grend] *adj* de grano fino o cerrado
close-hauled ['klos'hɔld] *adj* (naut.) de bolina
close-lipped ['klos'lɪpt] *adj* callado, reservado
closely ['kloslɪ] *adv* de cerca; estrechamente; estrictamente; fielmente; sólidamente; con avaricia; **closely printed** de impresión compacta
close-mouthed ['klos'maʊðd] o ['klos'maʊθt] *adj* callado, reservado
closeness ['klosnɪs] *s* cercanía, proximidad; estrechez, intimidad; avaricia, tacañería; reserva, discreción; pesantez (*de la atmósfera*); falta de aire, mala ventilación; fidelidad (*de una traducción*)
close order *s* (mil.) formación cerrada
close quarters *spl* lucha casi cuerpo a cuerpo; posición muy cerrada, lugar muy estrecho
close shave *s* afeitado a ras; (coll.) escape difícil o milagroso, escape por un pelo
closet ['klɑzɪt] *s* armario, alacena; gabinete, retrete; gabinete privado; aposento, gabinete (*muchas veces situado debajo de la escalera*); guardarropa *m*; *va* encerrar en un gabinete para una entrevista secreta
close to the wind *adj* (naut.) de bolina
close translation *s* traducción fiel
close-up ['klos,ʌp] *s* vista de cerca; fotografía de cerca
close-woven ['klos'wovən] *adj* estrechamente tejido
closing ['klozɪŋ] *s* cerradura; (phonet.) cerrazón
closure ['kloʒər] *s* cierre; encierro; fin, término, conclusión; (phonet.) oclusión; clausura (*de un debate*)
clot [klɑt] *s* grumo, coágulo, cuajarón; (*pret & pp:* **clotted;** *ger:* **clotting**) *vn* engrumecerse, coagularse, cuajarse
cloth [klɔθ] o [klɑθ] *s* (*pl:* **cloths** [klɔðz], [klɑðz], [klɔθs] o [klɑθs]) *s* tela, paño; trapo; vestidura clerical; clerecía; (b.b.) tela; (naut.) vela, lona
clothe [kloð] (*pret & pp:* **clothed** o **clad**) *va* vestir; trajear; cubrir, revestir; investir (*p.ej., de autoridad*); **clothes** [kloz] o [kloðz] *spl* ropa, vestidos; ropa de cama; **to change clothes** cambiar de ropa
clothesbasket ['kloz,bæskɪt] *s* cesto grande para ropa, cesto de la colada
clothesbrush ['kloz,brʌʃ] *s* cepillo de ropa
clothes dryer *s* secadora de ropa
clothes hanger *s* colgador de ropa
clotheshorse ['kloz,hɔrs] *s* enjugador, secarropa de travesaños
clothesline ['kloz,laɪn] *s* cordel para tender la ropa
clothespin ['kloz,pɪn] s alfiler de madera, pinza (*para tender la ropa*)
clothes pole *s* berlinga
clothes press *s* guardarropa, armario para guardar ropa
clothes rack *s* colgadero, perchero
clothes tree *s* percha
clothes wringer *s* exprimidor de ropa
clothier ['kloðjər] *s* fabricante de ropa; ropero; pañero
clothing ['kloðɪŋ] *s* ropa, vestidos; ropaje
Clotho ['kloθo] *s* (myth.) Cloto
cloth of gold *s* tela de oro
cloth prover *s* cuentahilos
cloth yard *s* yarda (*medida que equivale a 91 centímetros*)
cloture ['klotʃər] *s* clausura (*de un debate*)
cloud [klaʊd] *s* nube (*masa de vapores suspendida en el aire; multitud; mancha o sombra que se nota en piedras preciosas; cualquier cosa que altera la serenidad*); nubarrón (*nube grande y negra*); **in the clouds** entre las nubes, altísimo; ilusorio, quimérico; teórico: distraído, lleno de ensueños; **under a cloud** desacreditado, bajo sospecha; en aprietos; sombrío, melancólico; *va* anublar; entristecer; *vn* anublarse
cloud bank *s* mar de nubes
cloudberry ['klaʊd,bɛrɪ] *s* (*pl:* **-ries**) (bot.) camemoro; baya del camemoro
cloudburst ['klaʊd,bʌrst] *s* chaparrón, turbión
cloud-capped ['klaʊd,kæpt] *adj* coronado de nubes, altísimo
cloud chamber *s* (phys.) cámara anublada, cámara de niebla
cloudiness ['klaʊdɪnɪs] *s* nubosidad, nebulosidad
cloudless ['klaʊdlɪs] *adj* sin nubes
cloudlet ['klaʊdlɪt] *s* nube pequeña
cloud of dust *s* polvareda, nube de polvo
cloud rack *s* masa de nubes altas y algo separadas

cloud seeding *s* siembra de una substancia en las nubes para producir lluvia artificial
cloudy ['klaʊdɪ] *adj* (*comp:* **-ier;** *super:* **-iest**) nublado; vaporoso; turbio; obscuro, confuso; sombrío, melancólico; ceñudo; (phot.) velado; **it is cloudy** está nublado
clough [klʌf] o [klaʊ] *s* vallecico, cañada
clout [klaʊt] *s* paño blanco al cual se le tira con el arco; flechazo; (coll.) bofetada, golpe seco de mano; (archaic) trapo, paño; *va* (coll.) abofetear, dar golpe seco de mano a
clove [klov] *s* (bot.) clavero; clavo de especia (*flor*); (cook.) clavo; diente de ajo; *pret de* **cleave**
clove hitch *s* (naut.) ballestrinque
cloven ['klovən] *adj* rajado, dividido; *pp de* **cleave**
cloven foot *s* pie hendido
cloven-footed ['klovən'fʊtɪd] *adj* patihendido, bisulco; diabólico
cloven hoof *s* pie hendido, pata hendida; **to show the cloven hoof** descubrir la oreja, sacar la pata
cloven-hoofed ['klovən'huft] o ['klovən'hʊft] *adj* patihendido, bisulco; diabólico
clover ['klovər] *s* (bot.) trébol; **to be in clover** vivir lujosamente, gozar de una vida de abundancia
clover dodder *s* (bot.) epítimo, barba de capuchino
cloverleaf ['klovər,lif] *s* (*pl:* **-leaves**) cruce en trébol (*para la circulación de automóviles*)
Clovis ['klovɪs] *s* Clodoveo
clown [klaʊn] *s* payaso, bufón, clown; patán; *vn* bufonear, hacer el payaso; conducirse de manera ridícula
clownery ['klaʊnərɪ] *s* (*pl:* **-ies**) payasada, bufonada
clownish ['klaʊnɪʃ] *adj* bufonesco; rústico; grosero
cloy [klɔɪ] *va & vn* hastiar, empalagar
club [klʌb] *s* clava, porra, cachiporra; (sport) bate; club, casino, círculo; trébol (*naipe que corresponde al basto*); **clubs** *spl* tréboles (*palo que corresponde al de bastos*); (*pret & pp:* **clubbed;** *ger:* **clubbing**) *va* aporrear; *vn* unirse para un mismo fin; pagar todos su escote
club car *s* (rail.) coche club, coche bar
clubfoot ['klʌb,fʊt] *s* (*pl:* **-feet**) (path.) pie calcáneo, pie talo
clubhouse ['klʌb,haʊs] *s* casino
clubman ['klʌbmən] *s* (*pl:* **-men**) clubista (*hombre*)
club moss *s* (bot.) azufre vegetal, musgo terrestre
clubwoman ['klʌb,wʊmən] *s* (*pl:* **-women**) clubista (*mujer*)
cluck [klʌk] *s* cloqueo, clo clo; *vn* cloquear (*la gallina*)
clue [klu] *s & va* var. de **clew**
clumber ['klʌmbər] *s* clumber (*perro de aguas de pies cortos y cuerpo pesado*)
clump [klʌmp] *s* grupo (*de árboles, arbustos, etc.*); terrón; trozo sin forma; pisada fuerte; (bact.) acúmulo; *va* formar un grupo de (*árboles, arbustos, etc.*); colocar en grupos; plantar en grupos; *vn* andar pesadamente; **to clump along** andar torpemente con pisadas fuertes
clumpy ['klʌmpɪ] *adj* lleno de grupos o montones; fuerte y torpe
clumsy ['klʌmzɪ] *adj* (*comp:* **-sier;** *super:* **-siest**) torpe, desmañado; chapucero, mal hecho; difícil, embarazoso
clung [klʌŋ] *pret & pp de* **cling**
Cluniac ['klunɪæk] *adj & s* cluniacense
Cluny lace ['klunɪ] *s* encaje de Cluny
cluster ['klʌstər] *s* racimo; grupo; manada; *va* agrupar, apiñar, juntar; *vn* arracimarse; agruparse, apiñarse, juntarse; **to cluster around** reunirse en torno de
clutch [klʌtʃ] *s* agarro, apretón fuerte; garra, uña, mano agarradora; gobierno, mando, poder; (aut.) embrague; (aut.) pedal de embrague; nidada; cría de pollos; **to fall into the clutches of** caer en las garras de; **to throw the clutch in** embragar; **to throw the clutch out** desembragar; *va* agarrar, empuñar; arrebatar
clutch band *s* (aut.) cinta de embrague
clutch housing *s* (aut.) caja de embrague
clutch lever *s* (aut.) palanca del embrague
clutch pedal *s* (aut.) pedal de embrague
clutter ['klʌtər] *s* confusión, desorden; alboroto, baraúnda; *va* poner en confusión o desorden; cubrir o llenar desordenadamente; *vn* reunirse en desorden; alborotar
clypeus ['klɪpɪəs] *s* (*pl:* **-i** [aɪ]) (archeol., bot. & zool.) clípeo
clyster ['klɪstər] *s* (med.) clistel o clister; *va* clisterizar
Clytemnestra [,klaɪtəm'nɛstrə] *s* (myth.) Clitemnestra
cm. abr. de **centimeter** o **centimeters**
cml. abr. de **commercial**
Cnossus ['nɑsəs] *s* var. de **Knossos**
c.o. o **c/o** abr. de **in care of** y **carried over**
co. o **Co.** abr. de **Company** y **County**
C.O. abr. de **Commanding Officer**
coach [kotʃ] *s* coche, diligencia; (rail.) coche de viajeros, coche ordinario; (aut.) coche cerrado; maestro particular, preceptor; (sport) entrenador; *va* llevar en coche; aleccionar, instruir; (sport) entrenar; *vn* pasear en coche; estudiar con un preceptor; **to coach with** ser aleccionado por
coach-and-four [,kotʃənd'for] *s* coche o carroza de cuatro caballos
coach box *s* pescante
coach dog *s* perro dalmático
coach horse *s* caballo de coche
coach house *s* cochera
coaching ['kotʃɪŋ] *s* lecciones particulares; (sport) entrenamiento
coachman ['kotʃmən] *s* (*pl:* **-men**) cochero
coach stand *s* parada o estación de coches
coadjutor [ko'ædʒətər] o [,koə'dʒutər] *s* coadjutor
coagulant [ko'ægjələnt] *s* coagulante
coagulate [ko'ægjəlet] *va* coagular; *vn* coagularse
coagulation [ko,ægjə'leʃən] *s* coagulación
coagulative [ko'ægjə,letɪv] *adj* coagulador, coagulante
coagulin [ko'ægjəlɪn] *s* (biochem.) coagulina
coagulum [ko'ægjələm] *s* (physiol.) coágulo
coal [kol] *s* carbón; carbón de piedra, carbón mineral; carbón de leña; pedazo de carbón; ascua, brasa; **to haul, drag** o **rake over the coals** dar una calada a, poner como un trapo; **to heap coals of fire on one's head** avergonzarle a uno, devolviendo bien por mal; *va* proveer de carbón, cargar de carbón; *vn* proveerse de carbón, tomar carbón
coal basin *s* cuenca hullera
coalbin ['kol,bɪn] *s* carbonera
coal bunker *s* carbonera
coal car *s* vagón carbonero
coaldealer ['kol,dilər] *s* carbonero
coaler ['kolər] *s* carbonero (*obrero o comerciante*); barco carbonero, ferrocarril carbonero
coalesce [,koə'lɛs] *vn* unirse, incorporarse
coalescence [,koə'lɛsəns] *s* unión, combinación
coal field *s* yacimiento de carbón
coal gas *s* gas de hulla
coal heaver *s* cargador de carbón
coaling ['kolɪŋ] *adj* carbonero; *s* toma de carbón
coaling station *s* estación carbonera
coalition [,koə'lɪʃən] *s* unión, combinación; coalición
coalitionist [,koə'lɪʃənɪst] *s* coalicionista
coal measures *spl* (geol.) estratos de carbón, yacimientos de carbón
coal mine *s* mina de carbón, mina hullera
coal miner *s* minero de carbón
coal oil *s* aceite mineral, keroseno
coal pipe *s* veta delgada e irregular de hulla
coalpit ['kol,pɪt] *s* mina de carbón
coal scuttle *s* cubo para carbón
coal ship *s* barco carbonero
coal tar *s* alquitrán de carbón, alquitrán de hulla
coal titmouse *s* (orn.) azabache
coal tongs *spl* tenazas de chimenea
coalyard ['kol,jɑrd] *s* carbonería
coaming ['komɪŋ] *s* (naut.) brazola
coaptation [,koæp'teʃən] *s* coaptación
coarse [kors] *adj* burdo, basto; grueso (*dícese,*

por ejemplo, de la arena); común, inferior, ordinario; grosero, rudo, vulgar
coarse-grained ['kors'grend] *adj* de grano grueso; tosco, grosero, rudo
coarsen ['korsen] *va* volver burdo, grueso o grosero; *vn* hacerse burdo, grueso o grosero
coarseness ['korsnɪs] *s* basteza; grosura; grosería, vulgaridad
coast [kost] *s* (naut.) costa; **the coast is clear** ha pasado el peligro, no hay moros en la costa; *va* costear; *vn* pasar; costear; navegar en cabotaje; deslizarse cuesta abajo (*en trineo, bicicleta u otro vehículo*); **to coast along** avanzar sin esfuerzo; **to coast to a stop** avanzar por gravedad o por impulso propio hasta pararse
coastal ['kostəl] *adj* costero
coastal plain *s* llanura costera
coast artillery *s* artillería de costa
coaster ['kostər] *s* práctico de costa; barco de cabotaje, buque costero; deslizador; trineo; montaña rusa; salvamanteles (*pieza de cristal para debajo de los vasos*)
coaster brake *s* freno de contrapedal (*de bicicleta*)
coast guard *s* (los) guardacostas, cuerpo o servicio de guardacostas; guardia (*individuo*) de los guardacostas; tercios de frontera y costas (*en España*)
coast guard cutter *s* guardacostas, escampavía de los guardacostas
coasting ['kostɪŋ] *s* (naut.) navegación costera; marcha por gravedad o por impulso propio
coasting trade *s* (naut.) cabotaje
coastland ['kost,lænd] *s* litoral
coastline ['kost,laɪn] *s* línea de la costa
coastward ['kostwərd] *adj* dirigido hacia la costa; *adv* hacia la costa
coastwards ['kostwərdz] *adv* hacia la costa
coastways ['kost,wez] *adv* a lo largo de la costa
coastwise ['kost,waɪz] *adj* costanero; *adv* a lo largo de la costa
coat [kot] *s* saco, americana, levita; abrigo, sobretodo; capa, mano (*de pintura*); lana, pelo (*de un animal*); **to turn one's coat** cambiarse la camisa, pasarse al partido opuesto; *va* proveer de saco, americana, etc.; cubrir, revestir; dar una capa o una mano de pintura a
coated ['kotɪd] *adj* revestido; bañado; saburroso (*dícese de la lengua*)
coatee [ko'ti] *s* saquete, casaquilla; vestidura exterior corta
coat hanger *s* colgador
coati [ko'ɑtɪ] *s* (*pl:* **-tis**) (zool.) coatí
coating ['kotɪŋ] *s* capa; revestimiento; enlucido, blanqueo; tela para casacas, abrigos, etc.
coat of arms *s* escudo de armas
coat of mail *s* cota de malla
coat of tan *s* solanera, atezamiento (*de la piel al sol*)
coatroom ['kot,rum] o ['kot,rʊm] *s* guardarropa
coattail ['kot,tel] *s* faldón
coauthor [ko'ɔθər] *s* coautor
coax [coks] *va* engatusar; obtener mediante caricias, halagos, etc.
coaxial [ko'æksɪəl] *adj* coaxial
coaxial cable *s* cable coaxial
cob [kɑb] *s* zuro (*de la mazorca del maíz*); jaca fuerte; cisne macho; **to eat corn on the cob** comer maíz en o de la mazorca
cobalt ['kobɔlt] *s* (chem.) cobalto
cobalt bloom *s* flores de cobalto, eritrita
cobalt blue *s* azul de cobalto
cobaltic [ko'bɔltɪk] *adj* (chem.) cobáltico
cobaltite [ko'bɔltaɪt] o ['kobɔltaɪt] *s* (mineral.) cobaltina
cobble ['kɑbəl] *s* guijarro; *va* empedrar con guijarros; apedazar, remendar; chalfallar; *vn* remendar zapatos
cobbler ['kɑblər] *s* remendón, zapatero de viejo; chapucero; pastel de frutas; bebida helada (*que contiene vino, frutas y jugo de frutas*)
cobblestone ['kɑbəl,ston] *s* guijarro
cobelligerent [,kobɪ'lɪdʒərənt] *s* cobeligerante
Coblenz ['koblɛnts] *s* Coblenza
cobra ['kobrə] *s* (zool.) cobra, culebra de anteojos
Coburg ['kobʌrg] *s* Coburgo
cobweb ['kɑb,wɛb] *s* telaraña; hilo de telaraña; (fig.) red, ardid; (fig.) telaraña (*cosa sutil de poca entidad*)
cobwebby ['kɑb,wɛbɪ] *adj* entelarañado, telarañoso
coca ['kokə] *s* (bot. & pharm.) coca
cocain o **cocaine** [ko'ken] o ['koken] *s* cocaína
cocainism [ko'kenɪzəm] *s* (path.) cocainismo
cocainization [ko,kenɪ'zeʃən] *s* cocainización
cocainize [ko'kenaɪz] *va* cocainizar
coccobacillus [,kɑkobə'sɪləs] *s* (bact.) cocobacilo
coccus ['kɑkəs] *s* (*pl:* **cocci** ['kɑksaɪ]) (bact.) coco; (bot.) carpelo; cochinilla (*materia colorante*)
coccyx ['kɑksɪks] *s* (*pl:* **coccyges** [kɑk'saɪdʒiz]) (anat.) cóccix
Cochin o **cochin** ['kotʃɪn] o ['kɑtʃɪn] *s* cochinchina (*gallina*)
Cochin Bantam *s* cochinchina enana (*gallina*)
Cochin China *s* la Cochinchina
cochineal [,kɑtʃɪ'nil] o ['kɑtʃɪnil] *s* cochinilla (*materia colorante*)
cochineal insect *s* (ent.) cochinilla
cochlea ['kɑklɪə] *s* (*pl:* **-ae** [i]) (anat.) cóclea, caracol
cochlear ['kɑklɪər] *adj* coclear
cock [kɑk] *s* gallo; macho de ave; espita, grifo; martillo (*de un arma de fuego*); giraldilla, veleta; jefe, caudillo; vuelta airosa hacia arriba (*de los ojos, de la nariz*); vuelta (*del ala de un sombrero*); montón (*de paja o heno*); *va* amartillar (*un arma de fuego*); enderezar, volver hacia arriba (*el ala del sombrero*); ladear (*la cabeza*); amontonar (*paja o heno*); *vn* volverse airosamente hacia arriba (*los ojos, la nariz*); contonearse, engreírse
cockade [kɑ'ked] *s* escarapela, cucarda
cock-a-doodle-doo ['kɑkə,dudəl'du] *s* quiquiriquí
Cockaigne [kɑ'ken] *s* tierra imaginaria de deleite y pereza
cock-and-bull story ['kɑkənd'bʊl] *s* cuento absurdo, exagerado o increíble
cockatoo [,kɑkə'tu] o ['kɑkətu] *s* (*pl:* **-toos**) (orn.) cacatúa
cockatrice ['kɑkətrɪs] *s* (myth.) basilisco
cockchafer ['kɑk,tʃefər] *s* (ent.) abejorro (*Melolontha vulgaris*)
cockcrow ['kɑk,kro] *s* aurora, tiempo del canto del gallo
cocked hat *s* sombrero de ala vuelta hacia arriba; sombrero de candil o de tres picos; **to knock into a cocked hat** (slang) arruinar, demoler o destruir completamente
cocker ['kɑkər] *s* cocker
cockerel ['kɑkərəl] *s* gallipollo
cocker spaniel *s* cocker
cockeyed ['kɑk,aɪd] *adj* bisojo, bizco; (slang) ladeado, encorvado, torcido; (slang) disparatado, extravagante
cockfight ['kɑk,faɪt] o **cockfighting** ['kɑk,faɪtɪŋ] *s* combate o pelea de gallos
cockhorse ['kɑk'hɔrs] *s* caballo mecedor
cockle ['kɑkəl] *s* (zool.) cardio, berberecho; (bot.) cizaña, joyo; (bot.) ballico perenne; barquichuelo; arruga, pliegue; **the cockles of the heart** las profundidades del corazón, lo íntimo del corazón; *va* arrugar, fruncir; *vn* arrugarse, fruncirse
cockleboat ['kɑkəl,bot] *s* barquichuelo
cocklebur ['kɑkəl,bʌr] *s* (bot.) cachurrera menor, bardana menor; (bot.) bardana
cockle hat *s* sombrero con venera (*especialmente del peregrino que va a Santiago de Compostela*)
cockleshell ['kɑkəl,ʃɛl] *s* concha de cardio; venera; barquichuelo; cascarón de nuez (*embarcación pequeña*)
cockloft ['kɑk,lɔft] o ['kɑk,lɑft] *s* desván gatero
cockney ['kɑknɪ] *s* habitante del barrio pobre de Londres que habla un dialecto particular; dialecto del barrio pobre de Londres
cock of the rock *s* (orn.) gallo de roca, rupícola anaranjado
cock of the walk *s* gallito del lugar
cockpit ['kɑk,pɪt] *s* gallera, valla (*para las*

riñas de gallos); (aer.) carlinga; (naut.) recámaras situadas debajo del puente (*en los buques de guerra antiguos*); sitio de muchos combates
cockroach ['kak,rotʃ] *s* (ent.) cucaracha
cock robin *s* (orn.) petirrojo (*macho*)
cockscomb ['kaks,kom] *s* cresta de gallo; gorro de bufón; (bot.) cresta de gallo, moco de pavo; mequetrefe; baladrón, fanfarrón
cocksure ['kak'ʃur] *adj* completamente seguro; demasiado seguro
cockswain ['kaksən] o ['kakswen] *s* var. de **coxswain**
cocktail ['kak,tel] *s* coctel; aperitivo (*de frutas, almejas, ostras, etc.*); (meteor.) rabos de gallo (*cirro o nube cirrosa*)
cocktail dress *s* vestido de tarde-noche
cocktail party *s* coctel (*reunión donde se ofrecen cocteles*)
cocktail shaker *s* coctelera
cocky ['kakɪ] *adj* (*comp:* **-ier**; *super:* **-iest**) (coll.) arrogante, hinchado, fanfarrón
coco ['koko] *s* (*pl:* **-cos**) (bot.) coco, cocotero
cocoa ['koko] *s* cacao en polvo; chocolate (*bebida*); (bot.) coco, cocotero
cocoa bean *s* semilla del cacao
cocoa butter *s* manteca de cacao
cocoanut o **coconut** ['koko,nʌt] *s* coco (*fruto*)
coconut butter *s* manteca de coco
coconut fiber *s* bonote, coir
coconut milk *s* leche de coco
coconut oil *s* aceite de coco
coconut palm *s* (bot.) cocotero, coco, palma indiana
coconut tree *s* (bot.) cocotero, coco
cocoon [kə'kun] *s* capullo
coco plum *s* (bot.) hicaco o icaco (*árbol y fruto*)
Cocytus [ko'saɪtəs] *s* (myth.) Cocito
c.o.d. o **C.O.D.** abr. de **collect on delivery** (U.S.A.) y **cash on delivery** (Brit.)
cod [kad] *s* (ichth.) abadejo, bacalao
coda ['kodə] *s* (mus.) coda
coddle ['kadəl] *va* mimar, consentir; cocer (*huevos*) en agua caliente sin hervir
code [kod] *s* código; clave o cifra (*escritura secreta*); (com.) cifrario; **in code** en cifra; *va* cifrar (*escribir en cifra*); cambiar o traducir en código o clave; escribir o transmitir en código o clave
code flag *s* (naut.) señal del código
codein ['kodɪɪn] o **codeine** ['kodɪɪn] o ['kodin] *s* (chem.) codeína
code of honor *s* código de honor
code pennant *s* (naut.) señal del código
code word *s* (telg.) clave telegráfica
codex ['kodɛks] *s* (*pl:* **codices** ['kodɪsiz] o ['kadɪsiz]) códice
codfish ['kad,fɪʃ] *s* (ichth.) abadejo, bacalao; (com.) pez palo
codfish cake *s* albóndiga de bacalao
codger ['kadʒər] *s* (coll.) tipo
codicil ['kadɪsɪl] *s* (law) codicilo; apéndice
codicillary [,kadɪ'sɪlərɪ] *adj* codicilar
codification [,kadɪfɪ'keʃən] o [,kodɪfɪ'keʃən] *s* codificación
codify ['kadɪfaɪ] o ['kodɪfaɪ] (*pret & pp:* **-fied**) *va* codificar
codling ['kadlɪŋ] *s* manzana no madura; manzana pequeña y de calidad inferior; manzana de forma larga y algo cónica; (ichth.) pescadilla; (ichth.) brótola (*Urophycis*)
codling moth *s* (ent.) tiña (*Carpocapsa pomonella*)
cod liver *s* hígado de bacalao
cod-liver oil ['kad,lɪvər] *s* aceite de hígado de bacalao
coed o **co-ed** ['ko,ɛd] *s* (coll.) alumna de una escuela coeducacional
coeducation [,ko,ɛdʒə'keʃən] o [,ko,ɛdʒu'keʃən] *s* coeducación
coeducational [,ko,ɛdʒə'keʃənəl] o [,ko,ɛdʒu'keʃənəl] *adj* coeducacional
coefficient [,ko·ɪ'fɪʃənt] *s* (math. & phys.) coeficiente; *adj* coeficiente
coefficient of expansion *s* (phys.) coeficiente de dilatación
coelenterate [si'lɛntəret] *adj & s* (zool.) celenterado
coeliac ['silɪæk] *adj* (anat.) celíaco
coelom ['siləm] *s* (anat. & zool.) celoma
coelomate [si'lomet] *adj & s* (zool.) celomado
coenesthesis [,sinɛs'θisɪs] *s* (psychol.) cenestesia
coenobite ['sinobaɪt] o ['sɛnobaɪt] *s* cenobita
coenobium [sɪ'nobɪəm] *s* (*pl:* **-a** [ə]) (biol. & bot.) cenobio
coequal [ko'ikwəl] *adj & s* coigual
coerce [ko'ʌrs] *va* coactar, forzar; coercer, restringir
coercion [ko'ʌrʃən] *s* coacción, compulsión; gobierno por fuerza; coerción, restricción
coercive [ko'ʌrsɪv] *adj* coactivo; coercitivo
coercive force *s* (phys.) fuerza coercitiva
coeternal [,ko·ɪ'tʌrnəl] *adj* coeterno
coeval [ko'ivəl] *adj & s* coetáneo, contemporáneo
coexist [,koɛg'zɪst] *vn* coexistir
coexistence [,koɛg'zɪstəns] *s* coexistencia
coexistent [,koɛg'zɪstənt] *adj* coexistente
coextend [,koɛks'tɛnd] *va* extender igualmente; *vn* coextenderse
coextension [,koɛks'tɛnʃən] *s* coextensión
coextensive [,koɛks'tɛnsɪv] *adj* coextensivo
coffee ['kɔfɪ] o ['kafɪ] *s* café; (bot.) cafeto; **black coffee** café solo
coffee bean *s* grano de café
coffee break *s* rato de descanso para tomar el café
coffee cake *s* pastelillo o bollo que se come con el café
coffee grinder *s* molinillo de café
coffee grounds *spl* heces del café
coffee house *s* café
coffee mill *s* molinillo de café
coffee plant *s* (bot.) cafeto
coffee plantation *s* cafetal, finca cafetera
coffee pot *s* cafetera
coffee shop *s* café
coffee table *s* mesa de té
coffee tree *s* (bot.) cafeto
coffer ['kɔfər] o ['kafər] *s* cofre, arca; (arch.) artesón, casetón; (hyd.) ataguía; (fort.) cofre; **coffers** *spl* tesoro, fondos
cofferdam ['kɔfər,dæm] o ['kafər,dæm] *s* ataguía, caja-dique
coffin ['kɔfɪn] o ['kafɪn] *s* ataúd; *va* poner en un ataúd; encerrar estrechamente
coffin bone *s* (zool.) bolillo
C. of S. abr. de **Chief of Staff**
cog [kag] *s* diente (*de rueda dentada*); rueda dentada; (carp.) espiga; **to slip a cog** equivocarse; (*pret & pp:* **cogged;** *ger:* **cogging**) *va* poner dientes a; (carp.) ensamblar con espigas; cargar (*un dado*)
cogency ['kodʒənsɪ] *s* fuerza (*de un argumento*)
cogent ['kodʒənt] *adj* fuerte, convincente
cogged [kagd] *adj* dentado, engranado
cogitate ['kadʒɪtet] *va & vn* meditar, reflexionar
cogitation [,kadʒɪ'teʃən] *s* meditación, reflexión
cogitative ['kadʒɪ,tetɪv] *adj* cogitativo (*que tiene facultad de pensar*); meditabundo, reflexivo
cognac ['konjæk] o ['kanjæk] *s* coñac
cognate ['kagnet] *adj & s* cognado
cognition [kag'nɪʃən] *s* cognición (*proceso mental*)
cognitive ['kagnɪtɪv] *adj* cognoscitivo
cognizable ['kagnɪzəbəl] o ['kanɪzəbəl] *adj* cognocible; (law) justiciable
cognizance ['kagnɪzəns] o ['kanɪzəns] *s* conocimiento; (law) competencia; **to have** o **take cognizance of** venir en conocimiento de
cognizant ['kagnɪzənt] o ['kanɪzənt] *adj* sabedor; (law) competente
cognomen [kag'nomɛn] *s* (*pl:* **-mens** o **-mina** [mɪnə]) apellido; sobrenombre; apodo
cogon grass [ko'gon] *s* (bot.) cisca, cogón
cograil ['kag,rel] *s* cremallera
cogwheel ['kag,hwil] *s* rueda dentada
cohabit [ko'hæbɪt] *vn* cohabitar
cohabitation [ko,hæbɪ'teʃən] *s* cohabitación
coheir [ko'ɛr] *s* coheredero
coheiress [ko'ɛrɪs] *s* coheredera
cohere [ko'hɪr] *vn* adherirse, pegarse; enlazarse, corresponder
coherence [ko'hɪrəns] o **coherency** [ko'hɪrənsɪ] *s* coherencia

coherent [koˈhɪrənt] *adj* coherente; (bot.) coherente
coherer [koˈhɪrər] *s* (rad.) cohesor
cohesion [koˈhiʒən] *s* cohesión; (phys.) cohesión
cohesive [koˈhisɪv] *adj* cohesivo; coherente
cohobate [ˈkohobet] *va* (chem.) cohobar
cohort [ˈkohɔrt] *s* cohorte; compañero
coif [kɔɪf] *s* cofia; (arm.) cofia; *va* cubrir con cofia
coiffeur [kwɑˈfʌr] *s* peluquero
coiffure [kwɑˈfjʊr] *s* peinado; tocado
coign [kɔɪn] *s* esquina saliente
coign of vantage *s* posición ventajosa
coil [kɔɪl] *s* rollo; vuelta (*de un rollo*); serpentín (*p.ej., de un alambique*); rizo (*de cabellos*); (elec.) carrete; (naut.) adujada; (naut.) aduja (*vuelta de una adujada*); (archaic) desorden; *va* arrollar, enrollar; (naut.) adujar; *vn* arrollarse, enrollarse; serpentear; andar en círculos
coil spring *s* resorte espiral
coin [kɔɪn] *s* moneda; cuña; **to pay back in his own coin** pagar en la misma moneda; *va* acuñar, troquelar; amonedar; forjar (*palabras o frases*); **to coin money** (coll.) ganar mucho dinero, enriquecerse
coinage [ˈkɔɪnɪdʒ] *s* acuñación; amonedación; monedas; sistema monetario; invención
coincide [ˌko·ɪnˈsaɪd] *vn* coincidir; ponerse de acuerdo
coincidence [koˈɪnsɪdəns] *s* coincidencia
coincident [koˈɪnsɪdənt] o **coincidental** [koˌɪnsɪˈdɛntəl] *adj* coincidente
coiner [ˈkɔɪnər] *s* monedero; monedero falso; inventor
coinsurance [ˌko·ɪnˈʃʊrəns] *s* coaseguro
coir [kɔɪr] *s* coir, bonote, roya
coition [koˈɪʃən] o **coitus** [ˈko·ɪtəs] *s* coito
coke [kok] *s* coque; *va & vn* coquizar
coke oven *s* horno de coque
col. abr. de **colored, colony** y **column**
Col. abr. de **Colonel, Colorado** y **Colossians**
colander [ˈkʌləndər] o [ˈkɑləndər] *s* escurridor, colador
colchicine [ˈkɑlkɪsin] o [ˈkɑlkɪsɪn] *s* (chem.) colquicina
colchicum [ˈkɑlkɪkəm] *s* (bot. & pharm.) cólquico
Colchis [ˈkɑlkɪs] *s* la Cólquida
colcothar [ˈkɑlkəθər] *s* (chem.) colcótar
cold [kold] *adj* frío; (fig.) frío, indiferente; (coll.) frío (*lejos de lo que se busca*); **to be cold** hacer frío (*dícese del tiempo*); tener frío (*p.ej., una persona*); *s* frío; resfriado; **to catch** o **to take cold** tomar frío, resfriarse; **to leave out in the cold** dejar colgado, menospreciar con premeditación
cold blood *s* sangre fría; **in cold blood** a sangre fría
cold-blooded [ˈkoldˈblʌdɪd] *adj* insensible; cruel, despiadado; friolento (*muy sensible al frío*); (zool.) de sangre fría
cold chisel *s* cortafrío
cold cream *s* colcrén, crema
cold cuts *spl* fiambres
cold feet *s* (coll.) miedo, desánimo
cold frame *s* (hort.) cajonera
cold front *s* (meteor.) frente frío
cold-hearted [ˈkoldˈhɑrtɪd] *adj* duro, insensible
cold light *s* luz fría
cold meat *s* carne fiambre
coldness [ˈkoldnɪs] *s* frialdad
cold pack *s* (med.) compresa fría
cold-pack [ˈkoldˈpæk] *va* aplicar una compresa fría a
cold-rolled [ˈkoldˈrold] *adj* laminado en frío
cold shoulder *s* (coll.) frialdad; **to turn a cold shoulder on** (coll.) tratar con frialdad, despedir con desaire
cold-shoulder [ˈkoldˈʃoldər] *va* (coll.) tratar con frialdad, despedir con desaire
cold snap *s* corto rato de frío agudo
cold sore *s* (path.) fuegos en la boca o los labios
cold steel *s* arma de acero, arma blanca
cold storage *s* conservación en cámara frigorífica
cold-storage [ˈkoldˈstorɪdʒ] *adj* frigorífico; *va* conservar en cámara frigorífica
cold sweat *s* sudor frío
cold war *s* guerra fría
cold wave *s* ola de frío; permanente en frío
cole [kol] *s* (bot.) naba
colectomy [kəˈlɛktəmɪ] *s* (*pl:* **-mies**) (surg.) colectomía
coleopterous [ˌkolɪˈɑptərəs] o [ˌkɑlɪˈɑptərəs] *adj* (ent.) coleóptero
coleorhiza [ˌkolɪəˈraɪzə] o [ˌkɑlɪəˈraɪzə] *s* (bot.) coleorriza
coleslaw [ˈkolˌslɔ] *s* ensalada de col
coleus [ˈkolɪəs] *s* (bot.) coleo
colewort [ˈkolˌwʌrt] *s* (bot.) col rizada, berza verde
coli [ˈkolaɪ] *s* (bact.) colibacilo
colibacillosis [ˌkolɪˌbæsɪˈlosɪs] *s* (path.) colibacilosis
colic [ˈkɑlɪk] *adj* (anat. & path.) cólico; *s* (path.) cólico
colicky [ˈkɑlɪkɪ] *adj* cólico
coliseum [ˌkɑlɪˈsiəm] *s* coliseo; (*cap.*) *s* Coliseo
colitis [koˈlaɪtɪs] *s* (path.) colitis
coll. abr. de **colleague, collection, collector, college** y **colloquial**
collaborate [kəˈlæbəret] *vn* colaborar
collaboration [kəˌlæbəˈreʃən] *s* colaboración
collaborationist [kəˌlæbəˈreʃənɪst] *s* colaboracionista
collaborator [kəˈlæbəˌretər] *s* colaborador
collagen [ˈkɑlədʒɛn] *s* (biochem.) colágeno
collapse [kəˈlæps] *s* hundimiento, desplome; aplastamiento; fracaso; (path. & fig.) colapso; *va* aplastar; *vn* hundirse, desplomarse; aplastarse; fracasar; postrarse, sufrir colapso
collapse therapy *s* colapsoterapia
collapsible [kəˈlæpsɪbəl] *adj* colapsible, plegable, abatible
collapsible boat *s* bote plegable
collapsible target *s* blanco abatible
collar [ˈkɑlər] *s* cuello; collar (*de perro, caballo, buey; raya de color que rodea el pescuezo de un animal*); (mach.) collar; **to slip the collar** escaparse, desenredarse; *va* ceñir con cuello, collar, etc.; poner cuello o collar a; agarrar por el cabezón; (coll.) coger, prender (*p.ej., a un reo*)
collarband [ˈkɑlərˌbænd] *s* cabezón
collar beam *s* (arch.) entrecinta
collarbone [ˈkɑlərˌbon] *s* (anat.) clavícula
collate [kɑˈlet] o [ˈkɑlet] *va* colacionar, cotejar, compulsar
collateral [kəˈlætərəl] *adj* colateral; *s* colateral (*pariente*); (com.) colateral, resguardo
collation [kɑˈleʃən] *s* colación (*cotejo; comida ligera*)
collator [kɑˈletər] o [ˈkɑletər] *s* colacionador
colleague [ˈkɑlig] *s* colega
collect [ˈkɑlɛkt] *s* (eccl.) colecta; [kəˈlɛkt] *va* acumular, reunir; coleccionar (*p.ej., sellos de correo*); colectar (*p.ej., impuestos*); cobrar (*p.ej., pasajes*); recoger (*p.ej., billetes*); suponer; **to collect oneself** recobrarse, reponerse; *vn* acumularse, reunirse; **collect on delivery** contra reembolso
collectable [kəˈlɛktəbəl] *adj* cobrable
collected [kəˈlɛktɪd] *adj* sosegado, a sangre fría
collectible [kəˈlɛktɪbəl] *adj* var. de **collectable**
collection [kəˈlɛkʃən] *s* colección; recaudación (*p.ej., de impuestos*); recogida (*p.ej., del correo*); (eccl.) colecta; montón
collective [kəˈlɛktɪv] *adj* colectivo; (gram.) colectivo; *s* (gram.) nombre colectivo
collective bargaining *s* trato colectivo entre gremios y patronos respecto a sueldos, horas y condiciones de trabajo
collectively [kəˈlɛktɪvlɪ] *adv* colectivamente
collective noun *s* (gram.) nombre colectivo
collective security *s* seguridad colectiva
collectivism [kəˈlɛktɪvɪzəm] *s* colectivismo
collectivist [kəˈlɛktɪvɪst] *s* colectivista
collectivistic [kəˌlɛktɪˈvɪstɪk] *adj* colectivista
collectivity [ˌkɑlɛkˈtɪvɪtɪ] *s* colectividad
collectivization [kəˌlɛktɪvɪˈzeʃən] *s* colectivización
collectivize [kəˈlɛktɪvaɪz] *va* colectivizar
collector [kəˈlɛktər] *s* coleccionador (*p.ej., de mapas, medallas*); recaudador (*p.ej., de impuestos*); (elec.) colector

collectorship [kəˈlɛktərʃɪp] *s* colecturía; distrito donde actúa el recaudador o colector
colleen [ˈkɑlin] o [kɑˈlin] *s* (Irish) muchacha
college [ˈkɑlɪdʒ] *s* colegio; colegio universitario
College of Cardinals *s* Colegio de cardenales
collegian [kəˈlidʒɪən] *s* colegial
collegiate [kəˈlidʒɪɪt] *adj* colegial, colegiado; universitario
collegiate church *s* colegiata, iglesia colegial
collide [kəˈlaɪd] *vn* chocar; **to collide with** chocar con
collie [ˈkɑlɪ] *s* collie, perro de pastor escocés
collier [ˈkɑljər] *s* barco carbonero; minero de carbón
colliery [ˈkɑljərɪ] *s* (*pl:* **-ies**) mina de carbón, hullera
collimate [ˈkɑlɪmet] *va* alinear; enfocar las líneas de mira de (*p.ej., un telescopio*)
collimation [ˌkɑlɪˈmeʃən] *s* (astr. & opt.) colimación
collimator [ˈkɑlɪˌmetər] *s* (opt.) colimador
collision [kəˈlɪʒən] *s* colisión
collocate [ˈkɑloket] *va* colocar, disponer, arreglar
collocation [ˌkɑloˈkeʃən] *s* colocación, disposición, arreglo
collodion [kəˈlodɪən] *s* (chem.) colodión
colloid [ˈkɑlɔɪd] *adj & s* (chem.) coloide
colloidal [kəˈlɔɪdəl] *adj* coloidal
collop [ˈkɑləp] *s* trocito, pedacito; tajada de carne; pliegue, doblez (*de piel en el cuerpo*)
colloquial [kəˈlokwɪəl] *adj* familiar, coloquial
colloquialism [kəˈlokwɪəlɪzəm] *s* locución familiar, palabra familiar; estilo familiar
colloquy [ˈkɑləkwɪ] *s* (*pl:* **-quies**) coloquio
collude [kəˈlud] *vn* confabularse, coludir
collusion [kəˈluʒən] *s* confabulación, colusión; **to be in collusion with** estar en inteligencia con
collusive [kəˈlusɪv] *adj* colusorio
collyrium [kəˈlɪrɪəm] *s* (*pl:* **-a** [ə] o **-ums**) colirio
Colo. abr. de **Colorado**
colocynth [ˈkɑləsɪnθ] *s* (bot.) coloquíntida
cologne [kəˈlon] *s* colonia, agua de Colonia; (*cap.*) *s* Colonia
Colombia [kəˈlʌmbɪə] *s* Colombia
Colombian [kəˈlʌmbɪən] *adj & s* colombiano
colon [ˈkolən] *s* (anat.) colon; (gram.) dos puntos
colonel [ˈkʌrnəl] *s* coronel
colonelcy [ˈkʌrnəlsɪ] *s* (*pl:* **-cies**) coronelía
colonial [kəˈlonɪəl] *adj* colonial; colonialista (*país*); *s* colono
colonialism [kəˈlonɪəlɪzəm] *s* colonialismo
colonic [kəˈlɑnɪk] *adj* colónico
colonist [ˈkɑlənɪst] *s* colonizador; colono
colonization [ˌkɑlənɪˈzeʃən] *s* colonización
colonize [ˈkɑlənaɪz] *va & vn* colonizar
colonnade [ˌkɑləˈned] *s* columnata
colonnaded [ˌkɑləˈnedɪd] *adj* (arch.) con columnatas
colony [ˈkɑlənɪ] *s* (*pl:* **-nies**) colonia
colophon [ˈkɑləfɑn] *s* colofón
colophony [ˈkɑləˌfonɪ] o [kəˈlɑfənɪ] *s* colofonia
color [ˈkʌlər] *s* color; **off color** descolorido; indispuesto; (slang) colorado, libre, verde; **the colors** los colores (*la bandera*); ceremonia de enarbolar la bandera por la mañana y bajarla por la noche; el ejército y la marina, el servicio militar; **to call to the colors** llamar al servicio militar; **to change color** mudar de color (*palidecer; sonrojarse*); **to give** o **to lend color to** dar impresión de probabilidad o verdad a, hacer parecer probable o verdadero; **to hoist the colors** enarbolar la bandera; **to lose color** palidecer; **to show one's colors** dejarse ver en su carácter verdadero, declarar sus opiniones o proyectos; **under color of** so color de, so pretexto de; **with flying colors** (mil.) con banderas desplegadas; con lucimiento; *va* colorar, colorear; (fig.) colorear; dar calidad distinta a; *vn* sonrojarse, encenderse
colorable [ˈkʌlərəbəl] *adj* plausible, admisible; especioso
coloration [ˌkʌləˈreʃən] *s* coloración
coloratura [ˌkʌlərəˈtjurə] o [ˌkʌlərəˈturə] *s* (mus.) coloratura
colorbearer [ˈkʌlərˌbɛrər] *s* abanderado, portaestandarte
color-blind [ˈkʌlərˌblaɪnd] *adj* acromatópsico, daltoniano, ciego para los colores
color blindness *s* (path.) acromatopsia, daltonismo, ceguera para los colores
color chart *s* carta de colores, guía colorimétrica
color company *s* (mil.) compañía abanderada
colored [ˈkʌlərd] *adj* de color (*que no es blanco ni negro; que no pertenece a la raza blanca*); colorado, especioso; persuadido engañosamente
color film *s* película en colores
color filter *s* filtro cromofotográfico
colorful [ˈkʌlərfəl] *adj* colorido; pintoresco
color guard *s* (mil.) guardia de la bandera
colorimeter [ˌkʌləˈrɪmɪtər] *s* colorímetro
colorimetry [ˌkʌləˈrɪmɪtrɪ] *s* colorimetría
coloring [ˈkʌlərɪŋ] *s* colorido; colorante (*substancia*); (fig.) colorido
colorist [ˈkʌlərɪst] *s* colorista
colorless [ˈkʌlərlɪs] *adj* incoloro
color line *s* diferencia social, económica y política entre la raza blanca y las de color
color photography *s* fotografía en colores
color salute *s* (mil.) saludo con la bandera
color sargent *s* (mil.) sargento abanderado
color screen *s* (phot.) pantalla de color
color sentinel *s* (mil.) centinela de la bandera
color television *s* televisión en colores, televisión a color
colossal [kəˈlɑsəl] *adj* colosal
Colosseum [ˌkɑləˈsiəm] *s* Coliseo
Colossian [kəˈlɑʃən] *adj & s* colosense; **Colossians** *spl* (Bib.) Epístola a los colosenses
colossus [kəˈlɑsəs] *s* (*pl:* **-si** [saɪ] o **-suses**) coloso
Colossus of Rhodes *s* coloso de Rodas
colostomy [kəˈlɑstəmɪ] *s* (*pl:* **-mies**) (surg.) colostomía
colostrum [kəˈlɑstrəm] *s* calostro
colour [ˈkʌlər] *s, va & vn* (Brit.) var. de **color**
colporteur [ˈkɑlˌportər] *s* repartidor ambulante de escritos religiosos
colt [kolt] *s* potro; mozuelo sin juicio; persona joven e inexperta; (*cap.*) *s* (trademark) revólver Colt
colter [ˈkoltər] *s* reja del arado
coltish [ˈkoltɪʃ] *adj* jugetón, retozón
coltsfoot [ˈkoltsˌfut] *s* (*pl:* **-foots**) (bot.) uña de caballo
columbarium [ˌkɑləmˈbɛrɪəm] *s* (*pl:* **-a** [ə]) columbario
Columbia [kəˈlʌmbɪə] *s* Colombia (*nombre dado a los EE.UU. de la América del Norte*)
Columbian [kəˈlʌmbɪən] *adj* colombino (*perteneciente a Cristóbal Colón*); americano
columbine [ˈkɑləmbaɪn] *adj* columbino; *s* (bot.) aguileña; (*cap.*) *s* Colombina
columbium [kəˈlʌmbɪəm] *s* (chem.) colombio
Columbus [kəˈlʌmbəs] *s* Colón
Columbus Day *s* día de la raza, fiesta de la hispanidad
columella [ˌkɑljəˈmɛlə] *s* (*pl:* **-lae** [li]) (arch., anat., bot. & zool.) columela
column [ˈkɑləm] *s* columna
columnar [kəˈlʌmnər] *adj* columnario
columned [ˈkɑləmd] *adj* con columnas
columniation [kəˌlʌmnɪˈeʃən] *s* (arch.) columnata
columnist [ˈkɑləmnɪst] o [ˈkɑləmɪst] *s* columnista
colure [ˈkoljʊr] *s* (astr.) coluro
colza [ˈkɑlzə] *s* (bot.) colza; semilla de colza
colza oil *s* aceite de colza
com. abr. de **comedy, commerce, common** y **commonly**
Com. abr. de **Commander, Commissioner, Committee** y **Commodore**
coma [ˈkomə] *s* (*pl:* **-mas**) (path.) coma; (*pl:* **-mae** [mi]) *s* (astr.) cabellera; (bot.) copete, manojo; (bot.) manojito (*de hebras sedosas en la extremidad de una semilla*)
comatose [ˈkɑmətos] o [ˈkomətos] *adj* comatoso
coma vigil *s* (path.) coma vigil
comb [kom] *s* peine; almohaza (*para limpiar el pelo del caballo*); cresta (*del gallo y otras aves*); panal (*de cera que forman las abejas*); cresta de ola, cima de ola; *va* peinar; cardar (*la lana*); explorar con minuciosidad, examinar por to-

das partes; rastrillar (*el lino*); *vn* encresparse y romper (*las olas*)
combat ['kɑmbæt] *s* combate; ['kɑmbæt] o [kəm'bæt] (*pret & pp:* **-bated** o **-batted;** *ger:* **-bating** o **-batting**) *va* combatir; *vn* combatir, combatirse
combatant ['kɑmbətənt] *adj* combatiente; combativo; *s* combatiente
combat car *s* (mil.) carro de combate
combat duty *s* (mil.) servicio de frente
combative ['kɑmbətɪv] o [kəm'bætɪv] *adj* combativo
combe o **comb** [kum] o [kom] *s* valle estrecho; hoyo profundo cercado de alturas por tres lados
comber ['komər] *s* peinador; cardador (*de lana*); ola encrestada, ola rompiente
combination [,kɑmbɪ'neʃən] *s* combinación; combinación (*ropa interior*)
combination faucet *s* mezclador automático
combination fuse *s* espoleta de doble efecto
combination lock *s* cerradura de combinación
combine ['kɑmbaɪn] o [kəm'baɪn] *s* (coll.) combinación (*de personas reunidas para un mismo fin*); monopolio; (agr.) segadora trilladora; [kəm'baɪn] *va* combinar; (chem.) combinar; *vn* combinarse; (chem.) combinarse
combings ['komɪŋz] *spl* cabellos quitados por el peine, peinadura
combining form *s* (gram.) elemento de compuestos
comb perforation *s* (philately) dentado de peine
combustibility [kəm,bʌstɪ'bɪlɪtɪ] *s* combustibilidad
combustible [kəm'bʌstɪbəl] *adj* combustible; ardiente, impetuoso; *s* combustible
combustion [kəm'bʌstʃən] *s* combustión
combustion chamber *s* (mach.) cámara de combustión
combustion engine *s* motor de combustión
Comdr. abr. de **Commander**
Comdt. abr. de **Commandant**
come [kʌm] (*pret:* **came;** *pp:* **come**) *vn* venir; ir, p.ej., **I'm coming** ya voy; ascender, subir; **come!** ¡venga!, ¡mire!, ¡deténgase!; ¡estése Vd. quieto!; **come along!** ¡vamos!; **come on!** ¡vamos!; ¡adelante!; **to come about** girar, cambiar de dirección; suceder; (naut.) cambiar de amura; **to come across** atravesar; encontrarse con; (slang) entregar lo que se tiene en manos; **to come after** venir detrás de, venir después de; venir por o en busca de; **to come again** volver, venir otra vez; **to come apart** desunirse; desprenderse; caerse a pedazos; **to come around** o **round** restablecerse (*de una enfermedad*); cobrar nuevo vigor; volver en sí; ceder, rendirse; ponerse de acuerdo; girar, cambiar de dirección; **to come at** alcanzar, conseguir; arrojarse sobre; **to come away** apartarse, retirarse; **to come back** volver; retroceder; (coll.) recobrarse, rehabilitarse; **to come before** anteponerse; llegar antes; **to come between** interponerse; dividir, separar, desunir; **to come by** conseguir, obtener; **to come down** bajar; desplomarse; descender (*respecto a la posición social, el estado financiero, etc.*); ser transmitido (*de una persona a otra*); **to come down on** caer sobre, acometer de prisa; (coll.) regañar; **to come downstairs** bajar (*de un piso a otro*); **to come down with** enfermar de; **to come for** venir por, venir a buscar; **to come forth** salir; aparecer; **to come forward** avanzar; presentarse; ofrecerse a hacer algún trabajo; **to come from** venir de; provenir de; **to come in** entrar; empezar; ponerse en uso; **to come in for** obtener, recibir; **to come into** entrar; obtener, recibir; heredar; **to come into one's own** ser reconocido, hacer reconocer sus derechos; **to come off** separarse, desprenderse; acontecer; hacerse, llegar a ser; salir; conducirse; librarse; **to come on** adelantar, mejorar; encontrarse con; principiar, p.ej., **the fever came on him this morning** la fiebre le principió esta mañana; **to come out** salir; salir a luz; estrenarse, debutar; ponerse de largo; declararse; resultar; **to come out for** anunciar su apoyo de; **to come out of** dejar (*alguna actividad*); salir de (*un cuidado, negocio, etc.*); **to come out with** decir, mostrar, revelar, publicar; **to come over** asir, coger; dejarse persuadir; pasar, p.ej., **what has come over him?** ¿qué le pasó?; **to come over to** pasarse a; **to come through** salir bien, tener éxito; ganar; (slang) entregar lo que se tiene en manos; **to come to** volver en sí; (naut.) anclar; (naut.) orzar; **to come together** juntarse, reunirse; **to come to oneself** volver en sí; **to come true** resultar verdadero; hacerse realidad; realizarse; **to come up** subir; surgir; presentarse; **to come upon** encontrarse con; **to come upstairs** subir (*de un piso a otro*); **to come up to** acercarse a; subir a; estar a la altura de; **to come up with** llegar a reunirse con; proponer; **come true** hecho realidad, p.ej., **a dream come true** un sueño hecho realidad
come-at-able [kʌm'ætəbəl] *adj* (coll.) alcanzable, asequible
comeback ['kʌm,bæk] *s* (coll.) rehabilitación; (slang) respuesta hábil, respuesta aguda; (slang) motivo para quejarse
comedian [kə'midɪən] *s* cómico; autor de comedias
comedienne [kə,midɪ'en] *s* cómica
comedown ['kʌm,daʊn] *s* desazón, revés, pérdida de fortuna, dignidad, etc.; humillación
comedy ['kɑmədɪ] *s* (*pl:* **-dies**) comedia, comedia cómica; comicidad (*calidad de cómico*); (fig.) comedia; **cut the comedy!** (slang) ¡basta de risas!; (slang) ¡estáte quieto!
comedy of character *s* comedia de carácter
comedy of intrigue *s* comedia de enredo
comedy of manners *s* comedia de costumbres
comeliness ['kʌmlɪnɪs] *s* gracia, donaire; propiedad, conveniencia
comely ['kʌmlɪ] *adj* (*comp:* **-lier;** *super:* **-liest**) gracioso, donairoso; propio, conveniente
come-on ['kʌm,ɑn] *s* (slang) añagaza (*artificio para atraer con engaño*); (slang) desafío; (slang) bobo, crédulo
comer ['kʌmər] *s* llegado, recién llegado; (coll.) persona que promete; **the first comer** el primero que se presente
comestible [kə'mɛstɪbəl] *adj & s* comestible
comet ['kɑmɪt] *s* (astr.) cometa
come-uppance [,kʌm'ʌpəns] *s* (coll.) reprensión, castigo merecido
comfit ['kʌmfɪt] o ['kɑmfɪt] *s* confite, dulce
comfort ['kʌmfərt] *s* confort, comodidad; confortación; confortador; colcha, cobertor; (law) ayuda, sostén; *va* acomodar, dar comodidad a; confortar; (law) ayudar, sostener
comfortable ['kʌmfərtəbəl] *adj* cómodo (*aplícase a las personas o las cosas*); desahogado (*dícese de una posición, fortuna, etc.*); holgado (*que, sin ser rico, vive con bienestar*); *s* colcha, cobertor
comforter ['kʌmfərtər] *s* confortador; colcha, cobertor; bufanda de lana; **the Comforter** el Consolador (*el Espíritu Santo*)
comforting ['kʌmfərtɪŋ] *adj* confortador, confortante
comfortless ['kʌmfərtlɪs] *adj* desconsolado, inconsolable; incómodo
comfort station *s* lavatorio con excusado, quiosco de necesidad
comfrey ['kʌmfrɪ] *s* (bot.) consuelda, sínfito
comic ['kɑmɪk] *adj* cómico; *s* cómico (*actor; lo que es propio para hacer reír*); (coll.) periódico cómico; **comics** *spl* (coll.) tiras cómicas (*de los periódicos*)
comical ['kɑmɪkəl] *adj* cómico
comic book *s* tebeo
comic opera *s* (mus.) ópera cómica, ópera bufa
comic relief *s* alivio de la tensión dramática, alivio cómico (*en lo dramático*)
comic strip *s* tira cómica, historieta gráfica
Cominform [,kɑmɪn'fɔrm] *s* Cominform
coming ['kʌmɪŋ] *adj* que viene, venidero; (coll.) en camino hacia la importancia o la celebridad; *s* venida, llegada; advenimiento (*de Cristo*)
coming out *s* (com.) emisión (*de títulos*); entrada en sociedad, puesta de largo
coming-out party ['kʌmɪŋ'aʊt] *s* recepción de una muchacha que se pone de largo
Comintern [,kɑmɪn'tʌrn] *s* Cominterno
comitia [kə'mɪʃɪə] *spl* comicios

comity ['kamɪtɪ] *s* (*pl:* **-ties**) cortesía
comma ['kamə] *s* (gram.) coma
comma bacillus *s* (bact.) comabacilo
command [kə'mænd] o [kə'mand] *s* mandato, orden; mando, dominio, imperio; (mil.) comando; comandancia (*dignidad o cargo; territorio; cuerpo de soldados, flota de buques, etc. bajo un comandante*); dominio (*p.ej., de un idioma extranjero*); alcance de vista; **to be at the command of** estar a la disposición de; **to be in command** estar al mando; **to have command of** u **over oneself** saber dominarse, tener dominio de sí mismo; **to take command** tomar el mando; *va* mandar, ordenar; (mil.) comandar; imponer; dominar; merecer (*p.ej., respeto*); *vn* mandar
commandant [,kamən'dænt] o [,kamən'dant] *s* comandante (*de un fuerte, arsenal, etc.*)
commandeer [,kamən'dɪr] *va* reclutar forzosamente; expropiar; (coll.) apoderarse de
commander [kə'mændər] o [kə'mandər] *s* (mil.) comandante; (nav.) capitán de fragata; comendador (*de una orden militar*)
commander in chief *s* jefe supremo, comandante en jefe
commanding [kə'mændɪŋ] o [kə'mandɪŋ] *adj* poderoso; autorizado; imponente; dominante
commanding officer *s* (mil.) jefe, comandante en jefe
commandment [kə'mændmənt] o [kə'mandmənt] *s* mandato, orden; (Bib.) mandamiento
commando [kə'mændo] o [kə'mando] *s* (*pl:* **-dos** o **-does**) (mil.) comando (*tropa o soldado*)
command of the air *s* (mil.) dominio del aire
command performance *s* función mandada (*por orden real, presidencial, etc.*)
commemorable [kə'mɛmərəbəl] *adj* conmemorable
commemorate [kə'mɛməret] *va* conmemorar
commemoration [kə,mɛmə'reʃən] *s* conmemoración; **in commemoration of** en conmemoración de
commemorative [kə'mɛmə,retɪv] *adj* conmemorativo
commemoratory [kə'mɛmərə,torɪ] *adj* conmemoratorio
commence [kə'mɛns] *va & vn* comenzar, empezar
commencement [kə'mɛnsmənt] *s* comienzo, principio; día de graduación; ceremonias de graduación
commend [kə'mɛnd] *va* alabar, ensalzar; recomendar; encargar, encomendar
commendable [kə'mɛndəbəl] *adj* loable, recomendable, meritorio
commendam [kə'mɛndəm] *s* (eccl.) encomienda; **in commendam** (eccl.) en encomienda
commendation [,kamən'deʃən] *s* alabanza, encomio; recomendación; encargo, encomienda
commendatory [kə'mɛndə,torɪ] *adj* recomendatorio, laudatorio; (eccl.) comendaticio
commensal [kə'mɛnsəl] *s* comensal; (biol.) comensal
commensurability [kə,mɛnʃərə'bɪlɪtɪ] *s* conmensurabilidad
commensurable [kə'mɛnʃərəbəl] *adj* conmensurable
commensurate [kə'mɛnʃərɪt] *adj* proporcionado; conmensurable; igual
commensuration [kə,mɛnʃə'reʃən] *s* conmensuración
comment ['kamɛnt] *s* comento; comentario; observación; *vn* comentar; **to comment on** comentar
commentary ['kamən,tɛrɪ] *s* (*pl:* **-ies**) comentario
commentator ['kamən,tetər] *s* comentador, comentarista; (rad.) locutor
commerce ['kamərs] *s* comercio
commercial [kə'mʌrʃəl] *adj* comercial; *s* (rad.) anuncio comercial, programa comercial; (Brit.) agente viajero
commercialism [kə'mʌrʃəlɪzəm] *s* mercantilismo; costumbre de comercio; locución mercantil
commercialization [kə,mʌrʃəlɪ'zeʃən] *s* comercialización
commercialize [kə'mʌrʃəlaɪz] *va* comercializar
commercial traveler *s* agente viajero
commination [,kamɪ'neʃən] *s* conminación
commingle [kə'mɪŋgəl] *va* mezclar; *vn* mezclarse
comminute ['kamɪnjut] o ['kamɪnut] *va* moler, triturar, pulverizar
comminuted fracture *s* (surg.) fractura conminuta
comminution [,kamɪ'njuʃən] o [,kamɪ'nuʃən] *s* molienda, trituración, pulveración; (surg.) fractura conminuta
commiserate [kə'mɪzəret] *va* compadecer; *vn* condolerse; **to commiserate with** condolerse de
commiseration [kə,mɪzə'reʃən] *s* conmiseración
commissar [,kamɪ'sar] *s* comisario (*en una república soviética*)
commissariat [,kamɪ'sɛrɪæt] *s* comisaría o comisariato
commissary ['kamɪ,sɛrɪ] *s* (*pl:* **-ies**) economato (*tienda*); comisario; (mil.) comisario
commission [kə'mɪʃən] *s* comisión; (mil.) nombramiento; patente; **to put in commission** poner en uso, hacer funcionar; poner (*un buque*) en servicio activo; **to put out of commission** descomponer, inutilizar; retirar (*un buque*) del servicio activo; *va* comisionar; (mil.) nombrar; poner en uso; poner (*un buque*) en servicio activo
commissioned officer *s* (mil. & nav.) oficial
commissioner [kə'mɪʃənər] *s* comisionado; comisario
commissionership [kə'mɪʃənər,ʃɪp] *s* cargo de comisionado
commission government *s* gobierno municipal dirigido por una comisión electiva
commission merchant *s* comisionista
commissure ['kamɪʃur] *s* (anat., bot. & zool.) comisura
commit [kə'mɪt] (*pret & pp:* **-mitted;** *ger:* **-mitting**) *va* confiar, entregar; cometer (*p.ej., un negocio a uno; un crimen, una falta*); someter (*a una comisión para su consideración*); comprometer; dar (*la palabra*); internar (*a un demente*); encomendar (*a la memoria*); **to commit oneself** declararse; comprometerse; **to commit to paper** o **to writing** poner por escrito
commitment [kə'mɪtmənt] *s* comisión; internación; auto de prisión; compromiso, promesa, cometido
committal [kə'mɪtəl] *s* comisión; entierro; compromiso, promesa
committee [kə'mɪtɪ] *s* comité
committeeman [kə'mɪtɪmən] *s* (*pl:* **-men**) comisionado
committee of the whole *s* comité compuesto de la totalidad de los miembros de una asamblea, un club, etc.
commix [ka'mɪks] *va* mezclar; *vn* mezclarse
commixture [ka'mɪkstʃər] *s* conmistión
commode [kə'mod] *s* cómoda; lavabo; servicio, sillico
commodious [kə'modɪəs] *adj* cómodo, espacioso, holgado
commodity [kə'madɪtɪ] *s* (*pl:* **-ties**) mercancía; comodidad, cosa útil
commodore ['kamədor] *s* comodoro; navío del comodoro
common ['kamən] *adj* común; *s* campo común, ejido; **commons** *spl* estado llano; refectorio (*de un colegio*); víveres; **in common** en común; **the Commons** (Brit.) los Comunes, la Cámara de los Comunes
commonage ['kamənɪdʒ] *s* derecho de pastar en común; propiedad de terrenos en común; campo común; estado llano, gente común
commonalty ['kamənəltɪ] *s* (*pl:* **-ties**) generalidad de personas, común de las gentes; estado llano; miembros de una corporación o sociedad
common bile duct *s* (anat.) conducto biliar común, colédoco
common carrier *s* empresa de transporte público
common cold *s* catarro común, resfriado común
common council *s* ayuntamiento
common councilman *s* concejal

common denominator *s* (math. & fig.) denominador común
common divisor *s* (math.) común divisor
commoner ['kamənər] *s* plebeyo; (Brit.) miembro de la Cámara de los Comunes; (Brit.) estudiante que no tiene beca ni plaza
common era *s* era común, cristiana o vulgar
common fraction *s* (math.) fracción común, quebrado
common gender *s* (gram.) género común
common law *s* derecho consuetudinario, derecho no legislado
common-law marriage ['kamən'lɔ] *s* matrimonio consensual, unión matrimonial contraída sin intervención de la iglesia ni la autoridad civil
commonly ['kamənlɪ] *adv* comúnmente
common noun *s* (gram.) nombre apelativo o común
commonplace ['kamən,ples] *adj* común, trivial, ordinario; *s* cosa común u ordinaria; lugar común, trivialidad, observación evidente
common pleas *spl* (law) pleitos civiles; (law) tribunal civil
common prayer *s* liturgia de la Iglesia anglicana
common room *s* casino, sala de reunión
common salt *s* sal común
common school *s* escuela elemental
common sense *s* sentido común
common-sense ['kamən,sɛns] *adj* cuerdo, razonable
common stock *s* (com.) acción ordinaria, acciones ordinarias
commonweal ['kamən,wil] *s* bienestar general, bien público
commonwealth ['kamən,wɛlθ] *s* nación; república; estado (*de los Estados Unidos de América*); mancomunidad; estado libre asociado
Commonwealth of Australia *s* Federación Australiana
commotion [kə'moʃən] *s* conmoción
communal ['kamjʊnəl] o [kə'mjunəl] *adj* comunal
communalism ['kamjʊnəlɪzəm] o [kə'mjunəlɪzəm] *s* sistema de confederación de comunas
commune ['kamjun] *s* comunión (*trato familiar*); (eccl.) comunión; comuna; (*cap.*) *s* Comuna; [kə'mjun] *vn* conversar, comunicarse; (eccl.) comulgar
communicable [kə'mjunɪkəbəl] *adj* comunicable
communicant [kə'mjunɪkənt] *adj* comunicante; *s* comunicante; (eccl.) comulgante
communicate [kə'mjunɪket] *va* comunicar; (eccl.) comulgar; *vn* comunicar; comunicarse; (eccl.) comulgar
communicating [kə'mjunɪ,ketɪŋ] *adj* comunicador; **to be communicating** mandarse (*dos piezas de un edificio*)
communication [kə,mjunɪ'keʃən] *s* comunicación; **communications** *spl* comunicaciones (*teléfonos, correos, etc.*); vías de comunicación
communicative [kə'mjunɪ,ketɪv] *adj* comunicativo
communion [kə'mjunjən] *s* comunión; (*cap.*) *s* (eccl.) comunión
communion of saints *s* (eccl.) comunión de los santos
communion rail *s* comulgatorio
Communion service *s* oficio del sacramento de la Eucaristía
communiqué [kə,mjunɪ'ke] o [kə'mjunɪke] *s* comunicado, parte
communism ['kamjʊnɪzəm] *s* comunismo
communist ['kamjʊnɪst] *adj & s* comunista
communistic [,kamjʊ'nɪstɪk] *adj* comunista
Communist International *s* Internacional Comunista
community [kə'mjunɪtɪ] *s* (*pl:* **-ties**) comunidad, colectividad; vecindario
community center *s* centro social, centro comunal
community chest *s* caja de beneficencia, fondos de beneficencia
community house *s* centro social
communize ['kamjʊnaɪz] *va* comunizar
commutable [kə'mjutəbəl] *adj* conmutable
commutate ['kamjʊtet] *va* (elec.) conmutar
commutation [,kamjʊ'teʃən] *s* conmutación; (coll.) uso de un billete de abono; (elec. & law) conmutación
commutation ticket *s* billete de abono
commutative [kə'mjutətɪv] o ['kamjʊ,tetɪv] *adj* conmutativo
commutator ['kamjʊ,tetər] *s* (elec.) conmutador; (elec.) colector (*de dínamo*)
commutator bar *s* (elec.) delga
commute [kə'mjut] *va* conmutar; (law) conmutar; *vn* ser abonado al ferrocarril, viajar con billete de abono
commuter [kə'mjutər] *s* abonado al ferrocarril
comp. abr. de **compare, comparative, composer, composition, compositor** y **compound**
compact [kəm'pækt] *adj* compacto; breve, conciso; compuesto; **compact of** compuesto de; ['kampækt] *s* estuche de afeites; [kəm'pækt] *va* hacer compacto, consolidar, condensar, comprimir; componer
companion [kəm'pænjən] *s* compañero (*persona o cosa*); acompañador; caballero de la orden más baja; (naut.) chupeta de escala; (naut.) escalera de cámara; *va* acompañar, estar o ir en compañía de
companionable [kəm'pænjənəbəl] *adj* sociable, simpático
companion-at-arms [kəm'pænjənət'armz] *s* (*pl:* **companions-at-arms**) compañonero de armas, conmilitón
companionate [kəm'pænjənɪt] *adj* de compañeros, de compañerismo
companionate marriage *s* matrimonio de compañerismo
companionship [kəm'pænjənʃɪp] *s* compañerismo
companionway [kəm'pænjən,we] *s* (naut.) escalera de cámara
company ['kʌmpənɪ] *s* (*pl:* **-nies**) compañía; (com.) compañía, empresa; (mil. & theat.) compañía; compañero o compañeros; compañerismo; (coll.) huésped o huéspedes; (coll.) visita o visitas; (naut.) tripulación; **to bear company** acompañar; **to join company** incorporarse; **to be good company** ser compañero simpático, ser compañero alegre; **to keep bad company** asociarse con gente mala; **to keep company** ir juntos (*un hombre y una mujer*); **to keep company with** cortejar (*a una mujer*); recibir galanteos de (*un hombre*); **to keep good company** asociarse con gente buena; **to keep someone company** hacerle compañía a una persona; **to part company** tomar rumbos distintos; separarse; enemistarse; **to part company with** separarse de; enemistarse con; *adj* social, p.ej., **company building** edificio social
company union *s* gremio interno, gremio controlado por los patronos
compar. abr. de **comparative**
comparable ['kampərəbəl] *adj* comparable
comparative [kəm'pærətɪv] *adj* comparativo; comparado (*dícese, p.ej., de la anatomía*); (gram.) comparativo; *s* (gram.) comparativo
comparatively [kəm'pærətɪvlɪ] *adv* comparativamente
comparator ['kampə,retər] *s* (phys.) comparador
compare [kəm'pɛr] *s* comparación; **beyond compare** sin comparación, incomparable; *va* comparar; **not to be compared with** no ser comparable con, no poder compararse con
comparison [kəm'pærɪsən] *s* comparación; (gram.) comparación; **in comparison with** en comparación con, comparado con
compartment [kəm'partmənt] *s* compartimiento; (rail.) compartimiento, departamento
compass ['kʌmpəs] *s* brújula o compás; raya, confín; círculo, circunferencia; circuito, recinto, ámbito; alcance, extensión; compás (*extensión de la voz, etc.*); **compass** *s* o **compasses** *spl* compás (*para trazar curvas, etc.*); **to box the compass** (naut.) cuartear la aguja; (fig.) volver a su punto de partida; *va* contornear, rodear; circundar; maquinar, urdir; entender, comprender
compass card *s* (naut.) rosa náutica, rosa de los vientos
compassion [kəm'pæʃən] *s* compasión; **to move to compassion** mover a compasión

compassionate [kəm'pæʃənɪt] *adj* compasivo
compass needle *s* aguja de brújula
compass plant *s* (bot.) planta magnética
compass saw *s* serrucho de calar, sierra de punta
compaternity [ˌkampə'tʌrnɪtɪ] *s* compadrazgo, compaternidad
compatibility [kəmˌpætɪ'bɪlɪtɪ] *s* compatibilidad
compatible [kəm'pætɪbəl] *adj* compatible
compatriot [kəm'petrɪət] o [kəm'pætrɪət] *s* compatriota
compeer [kam'pɪr] o ['kampɪr] *s* par, igual; compañero, camarada
compel [kəm'pɛl] (*pret & pp:* **-pelled;** *ger:* **-pelling**) *va* compeler; imponer (*p.ej., respeto*); **to compel to** + *inf* compeler a + *inf*
compend ['kampɛnd] *s* var. de **compendium**
compendious [kəm'pɛndɪəs] *adj* compendioso
compendium [kəm'pɛndɪəm] *s* (*pl:* **-ums** o **-a** [ə]) compendio
compensate ['kampənset] *va & vn* compensar; **to compensate for** compensar
compensating balance *s* (horol.) volante compensador, balanza de compensación
compensating pendulum *s* compensador
compensation [ˌkampən'seʃən] *s* compensación; retribución (*pago*); indemnización
compensation balance *s* (horol.) volante compensador
compensation pendulum *s* péndulo de compensación
compensative ['kampənˌsetɪv] o [kəm'pɛnsətɪv] *adj* compensativo
compensator ['kampənˌsetər] *s* compensador
compensatory [kəm'pɛnsəˌtorɪ] *adj* compensatorio
compete [kəm'pit] *vn* competir
competence ['kampɪtəns] o **competency** ['kampɪtənsɪ] *s* competencia; (un) buen pasar; (law) competencia
competent ['kampɪtənt] *adj* competente; (law) competente
competition [ˌkampɪ'tɪʃən] *s* competencia; oposición (*para la obtención de un premio, cátedra, etc. por medio de un examen*); **in competition with** en competencia de
competitive [kəm'pɛtɪtɪv] *adj* de concurso, de oposición
competitor [kəm'pɛtɪtər] *s* competidor
compilation [ˌkampɪ'leʃən] *s* compilación, recopilación
compile [kəm'paɪl] *va* compilar, recopilar
complacence [kəm'plesəns] o **complacency** [kəm'plesənsɪ] *s* satisfacción de sí mismo; complacencia
complacent [kəm'plesənt] *adj* complacido, satisfecho de sí mismo; complaciente
complain [kəm'plen] *vn* quejarse; **to complain about** u **of** quejarse de; **to complain of** + *ger* quejarse de + *inf*
complainant [kəm'plenənt] *s* querellante; (law) demandante
complaint [kəm'plent] *s* queja; agravio; mal, enfermedad; (law) querella, demanda; **to lodge a complaint** hacer una reclamación
complaisance [kəm'plezəns] o [ˌkample'zæns] *adj* complacencia, amabilidad, condescendencia
complaisant [kəm'plezənt] o [ˌkample'zænt] *adj* complaciente, amable, condescendiente
complement ['kamplɪmənt] *s* complemento; (gram., math. & mus.) complemento; (naut.) dotación; ['kamplɪmɛnt] *va* complementar
complemental [ˌkamplɪ'mɛntəl] *adj* completivo, complementario
complementary [ˌkamplɪ'mɛntərɪ] *adj* complementario
complementary angle *s* (geom.) ángulo complementario
complementary colors *spl* colores complementarios
complement fixation *s* (bact.) fijación del complemento
complete [kəm'plit] *adj* completo; *va* completar
completeness [kəm'plitnɪs] *s* entereza, perfección
completion [kəm'pliʃən] *s* completamiento; cumplimiento, terminación
completory [kəm'plitərɪ] *s* (*pl:* **-ries**) (eccl.) completas
complex [kəm'plɛks] o ['kamplɛks] *adj* complejo; ['kamplɛks] *s* complejo; (psychol.) complejo; (coll.) idea fija, prejuicio irracional
complex fraction *s* (math.) fracción compleja
complexion [kəm'plɛkʃən] *s* complexión, tez; aspecto general, carácter
complexity [kəm'plɛksɪtɪ] *s* (*pl:* **-ties**) complejidad
complex sentence *s* (gram.) frase compleja
compliance [kəm'plaɪəns] *s* condescendencia, sumisión; complacencia, rendimiento; **in compliance with** accediendo a; de acuerdo con
compliancy [kəm'plaɪənsɪ] *s* var. de **compliance**
compliant [kəm'plaɪənt] *adj* condescendiente, sumiso; complaciente, servicial
complicate ['kamplɪket] *va* complicar; entrelazar, torcer juntos
complicated ['kamplɪˌketɪd] *adj* complicado
complication [ˌkamplɪ'keʃən] *s* complicación
complicity [kəm'plɪsɪtɪ] *s* (*pl:* **-ties**) complicidad
compliment ['kamplɪmənt] *s* alabanza, halago; cumplimiento; **to send compliments** enviar saludos; ['kamplɪmɛnt] *va* cumplimentar
complimentary [ˌkamplɪ'mɛntərɪ] *adj* lisonjero; gratuito, de regalo, de cortesía
complimentary copy *s* ejemplar de cortesía
complimentary ticket *s* billete de regalo, pase de cortesía
complin ['kamplɪn] o **compline** ['kamplaɪn] o ['kamplɪn] *s* (eccl.) completas
complot ['kamplat] *s* complot; [kəm'plat] (*pret & pp:* **-plotted;** *ger:* **-plotting**) *vn* complotar
comply [kəm'plaɪ] (*pret & pp:* **-plied**) *vn* conformarse, condescender; **to comply with** conformarse con, obrar de acuerdo con
componé [kam'pone] *adj* (her.) componado
component [kəm'ponənt] *adj* componente; *s* componente *m;* (mech.) componente *f*
comport [kəm'port] *va* acarrear; **to comport oneself** comportarse; *vn* convenir, concordar
comportment [kəm'portmənt] *s* comportamiento
compose [kəm'poz] *va* componer; (mus., lit. & print.) componer; **to be composed of** constar de, estar compuesto de; *vn* componer; componerse, combinarse
composed [kəm'pozd] *adj* tranquilo, sosegado
composer [kəm'pozər] *s* componedor; (mus.) compositor; autor, escritor
composing stick *s* (print.) componedor
composite [kəm'pazɪt] *adj* compuesto; (*cap.*) *adj* (arch.) compuesto; (*l.c.*) *s* compuesto; (bot.) compuesta
composite photograph *s* fotografía compuesta, fotografía de superposición
composition [ˌkampə'zɪʃən] *s* composición
composition of forces *s* (mech.) composición de fuerzas
compositor [kəm'pazɪtər] *s* (print.) componedor, cajista
compost ['kampost] *s* compuesto; (agr.) abono compuesto; *va* (agr.) abonar, estercolar
composure [kəm'poʒər] *s* compostura, serenidad, calma
compote ['kampot] *s* compota; compotera (*vasija*)
compound ['kampaʊnd] o [kam'paʊnd] *adj* compuesto; (elec. & mach.) compound; ['kampaʊnd] *s* compuesto; (chem.) compuesto; (gram.) vocablo compuesto, palabra compuesta; recinto; [kam'paʊnd] *va* componer, combinar; **to compound a felony** (law) aceptar dinero para no procesar; *vn* componerse; **to compound with** capitular con
compound fraction *s* (math.) fracción compuesta, quebrado compuesto
compound fracture *s* (surg.) fractura complicada
compound interest *s* interés compuesto
compound number *s* (math.) número compuesto
compound sentence *s* (gram.) oración compuesta
comprehend [ˌkamprɪ'hɛnd] *va* comprender

comprehensibility [,kamprɪ,hɛnsɪ'bɪlɪtɪ] *s* comprensibilidad

comprehensible [,kamprɪ'hɛnsɪbəl] *adj* comprensible

comprehension [,kamprɪ'hɛnʃən] *s* comprensión

comprehensive [,kamprɪ'hɛnsɪv] *adj* comprensivo (*que tiene la facultad de entender; que incluye o contiene*); completo, que lo abarca todo

compress ['kamprɛs] *s* (med.) compresa; compresor (*para comprimir el algodón en balas*); [kəm'prɛs] *va* comprimir

compressed [kəm'prɛst] *adj* comprimido

compressed air *s* aire comprimido

compressed-air drill [kəm'prɛst'ɛr] *s* perforadora de aire comprimido

compressibility [kəm,prɛsɪ'bɪlɪtɪ] *s* compresibilidad

compressible [kəm'prɛsɪbəl] *adj* compresible

compression [kəm'prɛʃən] *s* compresión

compression ratio *s* (mach.) índice de compresión

compression stroke *s* (mach.) carrera de compresión

compressive [kəm'prɛsɪv] *adj* compresivo

compressor [kəm'prɛsər] *s* compresor; (anat., mach. & surg.) compresor

comprise o **comprize** [kəm'praɪz] *va* abarcar, comprender, constar de

compromise ['kamprəmaɪz] *s* componenda, compromiso; (coll.) término medio; (canon law) compromiso; *va* arreglar, componer (*por medio de concesiones mutuas*); comprometer, exponer; *vn* transigir

comprovincial [,kamprə'vɪnʃəl] *adj* (eccl.) comprovincial; *s* (eccl.) comprovincial; comprovinciano (*persona de la misma provincia*)

comptometer [kamp'tamɪtər] *s* (trademark) contómetro

comptroller [kən'trolər] *s* contralor, interventor

comptrollership [kən'trolərʃɪp] *s* contraloría, intervención

compulsion [kəm'pʌlʃən] *s* compulsión

compulsive [kəm'pʌlsɪv] *adj* compulsivo

compulsory [kəm'pʌlsərɪ] *adj* obligatorio; compulsivo

compunction [kəm'pʌŋkʃən] *s* compunción

computation [,kampjʊ'teʃən] *s* computación

compute [kəm'pjut] *va & vn* computar, calcular

computer [kəm'pjutər] *s* calculador; ordenador (*aparato*)

comrade ['kamræd] o ['kamrɪd] *s* camarada

comrade in arms *s* compañero de armas

comradeship ['kamrædʃɪp] o ['kamrɪdʃɪp] *s* camaradería

con. abr. de **conclusion, consolidated** y **contra** (Lat.) **against**

con [kan] contra; *s* contra (*concepto opuesto*); (*pret & pp:* **conned;** *ger:* **conning**) *va* estudiar, aprender de memoria

conation [ko'neʃən] *s* (psychol.) conación

concatenate [kan'kætɪnet] *adj* concatenado; *va* concatenar

concatenation [kan,kætɪ'neʃən] *s* concatenación

concave ['kankev] o [kan'kev] *adj* cóncavo; ['kankev] *s* cóncavo

concavity [kan'kævɪtɪ] *s* (*pl:* **-ties**) concavidad

concavo-convex [kan'kevokan'vɛks] *adj* cóncavoconvexo

conceal [kən'sil] *va* encubrir, ocultar, disimular

concealment [kən'silmənt] *s* encubrimiento, disimulación; escondite

concede [kən'sid] *va* conceder

conceit [kən'sit] *s* orgullo, engreimiento; concepto, dicho ingenioso, capricho

conceited [kən'sitɪd] *adj* orgulloso, engreído

conceivable [kən'sivəbəl] *adj* concebible

conceive [kən'siv] *va* concebir; *vn* concebir; **to conceive of** formar concepto de

concentrate ['kansəntret] *s* substancia concentrada; (min.) gandinga; *va* concentrar; *vn* concentrarse; **to concentrate on** concentrar la atención en

concentration [,kansən'treʃən] *s* concentración

concentration camp *s* campo de concentración

concentric [kan'sɛntrɪk] o **concentrical** [kan'sɛntrɪkəl] *adj* concéntrico

concept ['kansɛpt] *s* concepto

conception [kən'sɛpʃən] *s* concepción

conceptual [kən'sɛptʃuəl] *adj* conceptual

conceptualism [kən'sɛptʃuəlɪzəm] *s* (philos.) conceptualismo

conceptualist [kən'sɛptʃuəlɪst] *s* (philos.) conceptualista

conceptualistic [kən,sɛptʃuə'lɪstɪk] *adj* (philos.) conceptualista

concern [kən'sʌrn] *s* interés; inquietud; negocio, asunto importante; empresa, casa comercial, compañía; concernencia; **of concern** de interés, de importancia; *va* atañer, concernir, importar; interesar; **as concerns** respecto de; **as far as he is concerned** en cuanto le toca a él; **to concern oneself** interesarse, ocuparse; inquietarse; **to whom it may concern** a quien pueda interesar

concerned [kən'sʌrnd] *adj* interesado; ocupado; inquietado

concerning [kən'sʌrnɪŋ] *prep* concerniente a, respecto de

concernment [kən'sʌrnmənt] *s* interés, importancia; inquietud; asunto

concert ['kansərt] *s* concierto; (mus.) concierto (*sesión musical*); **in concert** de concierto; *adj* (mus.) para conciertos; [kən'sʌrt] *va & vn* concertar

concerted [kən'sʌrtɪd] *adj* concertado; (mus.) concertante

concert grand *s* (mus.) gran piano para conciertos

concertina [,kansər'tinə] *s* (mus.) concertina

concertmaster ['kansərt,mæstər] o ['kansərt,mastər] o **concertmeister** [kən'tsɛrt,maɪstər] *s* (mus.) concertino

concerto [kan'tʃɛrto] *s* (*pl:* **-tos** o **-ti** [ti]) (mus.) concierto, concerto (*composición*)

concession [kən'sɛʃən] *s* concesión

concessionaire [kən,sɛʃə'nɛr] *s* concesionario

concessive [kən'sɛsɪv] *adj* concesivo; (gram.) concesivo

conch [kaŋk] o [kantʃ] *s* (*pl:* **conchs** [kaŋks] o **conches** ['kantʃɪz]) *s* caracola; (arch.) concha

concha ['kaŋkə] *s* (*pl:* **-chae** [ki]) *s* (anat. & arch.) concha

conchiferous [kaŋ'kɪfərəs] *adj* conquífero

conchoid ['kaŋkɔɪd] *s* (geom.) concoide

conchoidal [kaŋ'kɔɪdəl] *adj* concoideo; (mineral.) concoideo

conchologist [kaŋ'kalədʒɪst] *s* conquiliólogo

conchology [kaŋ'kalədʒɪ] *s* conquiliología

concierge [,kansɪ'ʌrʒ] *s* conserje

conciliate [kən'sɪlɪet] *va* conciliar

conciliation [kən,sɪlɪ'eʃən] *s* conciliación

conciliative [kən'sɪlɪ,etɪv] *adj* conciliativo

conciliator [kən'sɪlɪ,etər] *s* conciliador

conciliatory [kən'sɪlɪə,torɪ] *adj* conciliador, conciliatorio

concise [kən'saɪs] *adj* conciso

concision [kən'sɪʒən] *s* concisión

conclave ['kanklev] *s* conclave; (eccl.) conclave

conclavist ['kanklevɪst] *s* conclavista

conclude [kən'klud] *va* concluir; *vn* concluir o concluirse

conclusion [kən'kluʒən] *s* conclusión; despedida (*de una carta*); **in conclusion** en conclusión; **to try conclusions with** participar en una contienda con

conclusive [kən'klusɪv] *adj* concluyente

concoct [kan'kakt] *va* confeccionar; tramar, maquinar; forjar (*mentiras*)

concoction [kan'kakʃən] *s* confección; trama, maquinación; forja (*p.ej., de mentiras*)

concolorous [kan'kʌlərəs] *adj* concoloro

concomitance [kan'kamɪtəns] *s* concomitancia

concomitant [kan'kamɪtənt] *adj & s* concomitante

concord ['kaŋkərd] *s* concordia; (gram. & mus.) concordancia

concordance [kan'kɔrdəns] *s* concordancia, acuerdo; concordancias (*lista de palabras con citas*)

concordant [kan'kɔrdənt] *adj* concordante

concordat [kɑnˈkɔrdæt] *s* concordato; (eccl.) concordato
Concord grape *s* uva Concord
concourse [ˈkɑŋkors] *s* confluencia (*p.ej., de dos ríos*); concurso (*de gente*); (rail.) gran salón; bulevar, gran vía
concrescence [kɑnˈkrɛsəns] *s* concrescencia; (biol.) concrescencia
concrete [ˈkɑnkrit] o [kɑnˈkrit] *adj* concreto; de hormigón, de concreto, para concreto; cuajado, duro, sólido; *s* hormigón, concreto; *va* concretar; [kɑnˈkrit] *va* solidificar, endurecer; *vn* solidificarse, endurecerse
concrete block *s* bloque de hormigón
concrete mixer *s* mezcladora de hormigón, hormigonera
concrete number *s* (arith.) número concreto
concretion [kɑnˈkriʃən] *s* concreción; (geol. & path.) concreción
concubinage [kɑnˈkjubɪnɪdʒ] *s* concubinato
concubine [ˈkɑŋkjʊbaɪn] *s* concubina; casada de condición y derechos inferiores
concupiscence [kɑnˈkjupɪsəns] *s* concupiscencia
concupiscent [kɑnˈkjupɪsənt] *adj* concupiscente
concupiscible [kɑnˈkjupɪsɪbəl] *adj* concupiscible
concur [kənˈkʌr] (*pret & pp:* **-curred;** *ger:* **-curring**) *vn* concurrir
concurrence [kənˈkʌrəns] *s* concurrencia; acuerdo
concurrent [kənˈkʌrənt] *adj* concurrente; *s* acontecimiento concurrente
concussion [kənˈkʌʃən] *s* concusión; (path.) concusión
condemn [kənˈdɛm] *va* condenar; expropiar; **to condemn to be burned** condenar a la hoguera; **to condemn to** + *inf* condenar a + *inf*
condemnation [ˌkɑndɛmˈneʃən] *s* condenación; expropiación
condemnatory [kənˈdɛmnəˌtorɪ] *adj* condenatorio
condensation [ˌkɑndɛnˈseʃən] *s* condensación
condense [kənˈdɛns] *va* condensar; *vn* condensarse
condensed milk *s* leche condensada
condenser [kənˈdɛnsər] *s* condensador
condescend [ˌkɑndɪˈsɛnd] *vn* dignarse; **to condescend to** + *inf* dignarse + *inf*
condescending [ˌkɑndɪˈsɛndɪŋ] *adj* que trata con aire protector a inferiores, que tiene aire de superioridad
condescension [ˌkɑndɪˈsɛnʃən] *s* dignación, aire protector
condign [kənˈdaɪn] *adj* condigno, merecido (*castigo*)
condiment [ˈkɑndɪmənt] *s* condimento
condisciple [ˌkɑndɪˈsaɪpəl] *s* condiscípulo
condition [kənˈdɪʃən] *s* condición; **on condition that** a condición (de) que; *va* acondicionar; (educ.) suspender; (textiles) condicionar
conditional [kənˈdɪʃənəl] *adj* condicional; (gram.) condicional
conditioned [kənˈdɪʃənd] *adj* condicionado
conditioned reflex o **response** *s* (psychol.) reflejo condicionado
condole [kənˈdol] *vn* condolerse
condolence [kənˈdoləns] *s* condolencia
condominium [ˌkɑndəˈmɪnɪəm] *s* condominio
condonation [ˌkɑndoˈneʃən] *s* condonación
condone [kənˈdon] *va* condonar
condor [ˈkɑndər] *s* (orn.) cóndor
condottiere [ˌkondotˈtjɛre] *s* (*pl:* **-ri** [ri]) condotiero
conduce [kənˈdjus] o [kənˈdus] *vn* conducir
conducive [kənˈdjusɪv] o [kənˈdusɪv] *adj* conducente, contribuyente
conduct [ˈkɑndʌkt] *s* conducta; **to be on one's good conduct** conducirse bien; [kənˈdʌkt] *va & vn* conducir; **to conduct oneself** conducirse, comportarse
conductance [kənˈdʌktəns] *s* (elec.) conductancia
conductibility [kənˌdʌktɪˈbɪlɪtɪ] *s* conductibilidad
conductible [kənˈdʌktɪbəl] *adj* conductible; conductivo
conduction [kənˈdʌkʃən] *s* conducción; (phys. & physiol.) conducción
conduction anesthesia *s* anestesia de conducción, anestesia regional
conductive [kənˈdʌktɪv] *adj* conductivo; (phys.) conductor
conductivity [ˌkɑndʌkˈtɪvɪtɪ] *s* conductividad
conductor [kənˈdʌktər] *s* conductor, guía; (mus.) director; (phys.) conductor; (rail.) conductor, revisor; cobrador (*de billetes en un tranvía*)
conduit [ˈkɑndɪt] o [ˈkɑndʊɪt] *s* conducto; (elec.) conducto, canal, canal para alambres
conduplicate [kɑnˈdjuplɪkɪt] o [kɑnˈduplɪkɪt] *adj* (bot.) conduplicado
condyle [ˈkɑndɪl] *s* (anat.) cóndilo
cone [kon] *s* (geom. & bot.) cono; barquillo (*hoja de pasta de harina arrollada en forma de cono o cucurucho*)
cone bearing *s* cojinete de cono
cone brake *s* freno de cono
cone clutch *s* embrague de cono
cone gear *s* engranaje cónico
cone pulley *s* cono de poleas
Conestoga wagon [ˌkɑnɪsˈtogə] *s* carromato que empleaban los norteamericanos para atravesar las llanuras del oeste antes del ferrocarril transcontinental
coney [ˈkonɪ] *s* var. de **cony**
confab [ˈkɑnfæb] *s* (coll.) confabulación; (*pret & pp:* **-fabbed;** *ger:* **-fabbing**) *vn* (coll.) confabular
confabulate [kənˈfæbjəlet] *vn* confabular
confabulation [kənˌfæbjəˈleʃən] *s* confabulación
confection [kənˈfɛkʃən] *s* confección, hechura; confite, confitura; confección caprichosa, sombrero caprichoso
confectioner [kənˈfɛkʃənər] *s* confitero
confectionery [kənˈfɛkʃəˌnɛrɪ] *s* (*pl:* **-ies**) confitería; confituras
confederacy [kənˈfɛdərəsɪ] *s* (*pl:* **-cies**) confederación; cábala; (*cap.*) *s* (U.S.A.) Estados confederados
confederate [kənˈfɛdərɪt] *adj* confederado; *s* confederado; cómplice; [kənˈfɛdəret] *va* confederar; *vn* confederarse
Confederate States of America *s* (U.S.A.) Estados confederados
confederation [kenˌfɛdəˈreʃən] *s* confederación
confederative [kənˈfɛdəˌretɪv] *adj* confederativo
confer [kənˈfʌr] (*pret & pp:* **-ferred;** *ger:* **-ferring**) *va* conferir; *vn* conferir, conferenciar
conferee [ˌkɑnfəˈri] *s* conferenciante; conferido
conference [ˈkɑnfərəns] *s* conferencia
conferment [kənˈfʌrmənt] *s* otorgamiento, donación
confess [kənˈfɛs] *va* confesar; (eccl.) confesar (*sus pecados; a un penitente*); *vn* confesar o confesarse; (eccl.) confesar o confesarse; **to confess to** confesar o confesarse a (*Dios*); confesarse con (*un sacerdote*)
confessedly [kənˈfɛsɪdlɪ] *adv* reconocidamente
confession [kənˈfɛʃən] *s* confesión
confessional [kənˈfɛʃənəl] *adj* confesional; *s* confesonario; confesión, costumbre de confesar los pecados al sacerdote
confession of faith *s* confesión, profesión de fe
confessor [kənˈfɛsər] *s* confesor (*creyente; sacerdote*); confesante (*persona que confiesa delitos o pecados*)
confetti [kənˈfɛtɪ] *spl* confeti; serpentina (*en tiras o cintas*)
confidant [ˌkɑnfɪˈdænt] o [ˈkɑnfɪdænt] *s* confidente
confidante [ˌkɑnfɪˈdænt] o [ˈkɑnfɪdænt] *s* confidenta
confide [kənˈfaɪd] *va* confiar (*p.ej., algún negocio*); fiar, decir en confianza (*secretos*); *vn* confiar o confiarse; **to confide in** decir confidencias a
confidence [ˈkɑnfɪdəns] *s* confianza; confidencia, secreto; **in strictest confidence** bajo la mayor reserva; **to place one's confidence in** depositar su confianza en

confidence game *s* fraude en que el timador se gana la confianza de su víctima
confidence man *s* timador que se gana la confianza de su víctima
confident ['kanfɪdənt] *adj* confiado; seguro; *s* confidente, confidenta
confidential [,kanfɪ'denʃəl] *adj* confidencial
confiding [kən'faɪdɪŋ] *adj* confiado
configuration [kən,fɪgjə'reʃən] *s* configuración
confine ['kanfaɪn] *s* confín; **the confines** los confines; [kən'faɪn] *va* limitar; confinar, encerrar; **to be confined** estar de parto; **to be confined to bed** tener que guardar cama, estar enfermo en cama; *vn* lindar, estar contiguos (*p.ej., dos países*)
confinement [kən'faɪnmənt] *s* limitación; confinamiento, encierro; parto, sobreparto
confirm [kən'fʌrm] *va* confirmar
confirmation [,kanfər'meʃən] *s* confirmación
confirmative [kən'fʌrmətɪv] *adj* confirmativo
confirmatory [kən'fʌrmə,torɪ] *adj* confirmatorio
confirmed [kən'fʌrmd] *adj* confirmado; inveterado
confiscate ['kanfɪsket] *va* confiscar
confiscation [,kanfɪs'keʃən] *s* confiscación
confiscator ['kanfɪs,ketər] *s* confiscador
confiscatory [kən'fɪskə,torɪ] *adj* confiscador
confiture ['kanfɪtʃur] *s* confitura
conflagration [,kanflə'greʃən] *s* conflagración
conflict ['kanflɪkt] *s* conflicto; incompatibilidad (*p.ej., de intereses, de horas de clase*); [kən'flɪkt] *vn* combatir; chocar, desavenirse
conflicting [kən'flɪktɪŋ] *adj* contradictorio; incompatible
confluence ['kanfluəns] *s* confluencia
confluent ['kanfluənt] *adj* confluente
conflux ['kanflʌks] *s* confluencia
conform [kən'fɔrm] *va* conformar; *vn* conformar, conformarse
conformable [kən'fɔrməbəl] *adj* conforme
conformance [kən'fɔrməns] *s* conformidad
conformation [,kanfɔr'meʃən] *s* conformación
conformist [kən'fɔrmɪst] *s* conformista
conformity [kən'fɔrmɪtɪ] *s* (*pl:* **-ties**) conformidad
confound [kan'faund] *va* confundir; [kan'faund] o ['kan'faund] *va* condenar, maldecir; **confound it!** ¡demontre!; **confound you!** ¡vete al demonio!
confounded [kan'faundɪd] o ['kan'faundɪd] *adj* maldito; (coll.) aborrecible, odioso
confraternal [,kanfrə'tʌrnəl] *adj* confraternal
confraternity [,kanfrə'tʌrnɪtɪ] *s* (*pl:* **-ties**) confraternidad
confrere ['kanfrer] *s* colega, compañero
confront [kən'frʌnt] *va* encontrar cara a cara; confrontarse con, enfrentarse con, hacer frente a (*un acontecimiento, un enemigo, la necesidad*); confrontar (*poner en presencia; cotejar*)
Confucian [kən'fjuʃən] *adj & s* confuciano
Confucianism [kən'fjuʃənɪzəm] *s* confucianismo
Confucianist [kən'fjuʃənɪst] *adj & s* confucianista
Confucius [kən'fjuʃəs] *s* Confucio
confuse [kən'fjuz] *va* confundir
confused [kən'fjuzd] *adj* confuso
confusedly [kən'fjuzɪdlɪ] o [kən'fjuzdlɪ] *adv* confusamente
confusion [kən'fjuʒən] *s* confusión
confusion of tongues *s* (Bib.) confusión de lenguas
confutation [,kanfju'teʃən] *s* confutación
confute [kən'fjut] *va* confutar; anular, invalidar
confuter [kən'fjutər] *s* confutador
Cong. abr. de **Congregation, Congregational, Congregationalist** y **Congressional**
congeal [kən'dʒil] *va* congelar; *vn* congelarse
congener ['kandʒɪnər] *s* congénere
congenial [kən'dʒinjəl] *adj* congenial, simpático; compatible; agradable
congeniality [kən,dʒinɪ'ælɪtɪ] *s* simpatía; compatibilidad; agrado
congenital [kən'dʒenɪtəl] *adj* congénito
conger ['kaŋgər] o **conger eel** *s* (ichth.) congrio
congeries [kan'dʒɪriz] o [kan'dʒɪrɪiz] *ssg & spl* congerie
congest [kən'dʒest] *va* apiñar, congestionar; (path.) congestionar; *vn* apiñarse, congestionarse
congestion [kən'dʒestʃən] *s* congestión; (path.) congestión
congestive [kən'dʒestɪv] *adj* congestivo
conglomerate [kən'glamərɪt] *adj & s* conglomerado; [kən'glaməret] *va* conglomerar; *vn* conglomerarse
conglomeration [kən,glamə'reʃən] *s* conglomeración
conglutinate [kən'glutɪnet] *va* conglutinar; *vn* conglutinarse
conglutination [kən,glutɪ'neʃən] *s* conglutinación
conglutinative [kən'glutɪ,netɪv] *adj* conglutinativo
Congo ['kaŋgo] *s* Congo
Congoese [,kaŋgo'iz] *adj* congoleño o congolés; *s* (*pl:* **-ese**) congoleño o congolés
Congo Free State *s* Estado libre del Congo
Congolese [,kaŋgo'liz] *adj* var. de **Congoese**; *s* (*pl:* **-lese**) var. de **Congoese**
congo monkey *s* (zool.) congo
congo snake *s* (zool.) anfiumo
congratulate [kən'grætʃəlet] *va* congratular, felicitar; **to congratulate on** congratular de o por
congratulation [kən,grætʃə'leʃən] *s* congratulación, felicitación, enhorabuena
congratulatory [kən'grætʃələ,torɪ] *adj* congratulatorio
congregate ['kaŋgrɪget] *va* congregar; *vn* congregarse
congregation [,kaŋgrɪ'geʃən] *s* congregación; reunión; concurso, auditorio; fieles (*de una iglesia*)
congregational [,kaŋgrɪ'geʃənəl] *adj* congregacionalista; (*cap.*) *adj* congregacionalista
congregationalism [,kaŋgrɪ'geʃənəlɪzəm] *s* congregacionalismo; (*cap.*) *s* congregacionalismo
Congregationalist [,kaŋgrɪ'geʃənəlɪst] *adj & s* congregacionalista
congress ['kaŋgrɪs] *s* congreso; diputación; (*cap.*) *s* Congreso de los EE.UU.; Congreso de los Diputados (*de las Cortes*)
congress boot *s* botín que tiene un trozo de materia elástica en los lados
congressional [kən'greʃənəl] *adj* congresional, de congreso; (*cap.*) *adj* congresional, del Congreso
Congressional Record *s* (U.S.A.) Diario de Sesiones del Congreso
congressman ['kaŋgrɪsmən] *s* (*pl:* **-men**) congresista; diputado
congresswoman ['kaŋgrɪs,wumən] *s* (*pl:* **-women**) congresista; diputada
congruence ['kaŋgruəns] o **congruency** ['kaŋgruənsɪ] *s* congruencia; (math.) congruencia
congruent ['kaŋgruənt] *adj* congruente; (geom.) congruente
congruity [kən'gruɪtɪ] *s* (*pl:* **-ties**) congruencia; (geom.) congruencia
congruous ['kaŋgruəs] *adj* congruo; (geom.) congruente
conic ['kanɪk] *adj* cónico; **conics** *ssg* curvas cónicas, secciones cónicas
conical ['kanɪkəl] *adj* cónico
conic projection *s* proyección cónica
conic section *s* (math.) sección cónica; **conic sections** *spl* secciones cónicas (*parte de la geometría*)
conidiophore [ko'nɪdɪə,for] *s* (bot.) conidióforo
conidium [ko'nɪdɪəm] *s* (*pl:* **-a** [ə]) (bot.) conidio
conifer ['konɪfər] o ['kanɪfər] *s* (bot.) conífera
coniferous [ko'nɪfərəs] *adj* (bot.) conífero
conirostral [,konɪ'rastrəl] *adj* (orn.) conirrostro
conj. abr. de **conjugation** y **conjunction**
conjectural [kən'dʒektʃərəl] *adj* conjetural
conjecture [kən'dʒektʃər] *s* conjetura; *va & vn* conjeturar
conjoin [kən'dʒɔɪn] *va* juntar, unir, asociar; *vn*

juntarse, unirse, asociarse; (astr.) estar en conjunción
conjoint [kən'dʒɔɪnt] o ['kandʒɔɪnt] *adj* conjunto
conjointly [kən'dʒɔɪntlɪ] o ['kandʒɔɪntlɪ] *adv* conjuntamente, de mancomún
conjugal ['kandʒugəl] *adj* conyugal
conjugate ['kandʒuget] o ['kandʒugɪt] *adj* conjunto; (gram.) congénere; (bot. & math.) conjugado; *s* (gram.) palabra congénere; (bot.) conjugada; ['kandʒəget] *va* conjugar; (gram. & biol.) conjugar; *vn* (gram. & biol.) conjugarse
conjugation [,kandʒə'geʃən] *s* conjugación; (biol. & gram.) conjugación
conjunct [kən'dʒʌŋkt] o ['kandʒʌŋkt] *adj* conjunto
conjunction [kən'dʒʌŋkʃən] *s* conjunción; (astr. & gram.) conjunción
conjunctiva [,kandʒʌŋk'taɪvə] *s* (anat.) conjuntiva
conjunctival [,kandʒʌŋk'taɪvəl] *adj* conjuntival
conjunctive [kən'dʒʌŋktɪv] *adj* conjuntivo; conjunto; (gram.) conjuntivo; (gram.) afijo (*pronombre*); *s* (gram.) conjunción
conjunctivitis [kən,dʒʌŋktɪ'vaɪtɪs] *s* (path.) conjuntivitis
conjuncture [kən'dʒʌŋktʃər] *s* coyuntura
conjuration [,kandʒu'reʃən] *s* conjuro (*invocación supersticiosa*); magia, hechizo; (archaic) conjuro (*ruego, súplica*); (archaic) adjuración (*hecha en nombre de Dios o una cosa santa*)
conjure [kən'dʒur] *va* adjurar, conjurar (*pedir con instancia*); ['kʌndʒər] o ['kandʒər] *va* conjurar (*exorcizar; alejar, p.ej., un peligro*); evocar (*por medio de invocaciones mágicas*); hacer o efectuar por arte mágica; **to conjure away** conjurar (*exorcizar; alejar, p.ej., un peligro*); **to conjure up** evocar (*hacer aparecer por medio de invocaciones mágicas; traer a la memoria; traer a la memoria de alguien*); crear, suscitar (*p.ej., dificultades*); *vn* hacer aparecer a un demonio; practicar las artes mágicas; hacer juegos de manos
conjurer o **conjuror** ['kʌndʒərər] o ['kandʒərər] *s* mágico; prestidigitador; [kən'dʒurər] *s* conjurante (*persona que suplica*)
Conn. abr. de **Connecticut**
connatural [kə'nætʃərəl] *adj* connatural
connect [kə'nɛkt] *va* conectar, enlazar; conexionar, asociar, relacionar; *vn* enlazarse; conexionarse, asociarse, relacionarse; enlazar o empalmar (*p.ej., dos trenes*)
connected [kə'nɛktɪd] *adj* conexo; conectado; **to be connected with** estar asociado con; estar empleado por
connecter [kə'nɛktər] *s* var. de **connector**
connecting rod *s* (mach.) biela
connection [kə'nɛkʃən] *s* conexión; pariente; relación; comunicación; combinación, enlace, empalme (*de trenes, etc.*); (mach.) acoplamiento; **in connection with** con respecto a; juntamente con
connective [kə'nɛktɪv] *adj* conectivo; *s* conectador; (gram.) palabra conjuntiva
connective tissue *s* (anat.) tejido conjuntivo
connector [kə'nɛktər] *s* conectador; (elec.) conectador, enchufe
connexion [kə'nɛkʃən] *s* (Brit.) var. de **connection**
conning tower ['kanɪŋ] *s* (nav.) torre de mando; (nav.) torreta (*de un submarino*)
conniption [kə'nɪpʃən] *s* (coll.) rabieta
connivance [kə'naɪvəns] *s* connivencia, confabulación
connive [kə'naɪv] *vn* hacer la vista gorda, fingir ceguedad o ignorancia; cooperar secretamente; **to connive at** hacer la vista gorda respecto de; **to connive with** confabularse con
connivent [kə'naɪvənt] *adj* (anat. & bot.) connivente
connoisseur [,kanɪ'sʌr] *s* conocedor (*especialmente en materia de arte*)
connotation [,kano'teʃən] *s* connotación
connotative [kə'notətɪv] o ['kano,tetɪv] *adj* connotativo
connote [kə'not] *va* connotar
connubial [kə'njubɪəl] o [kə'nubɪəl] *adj* conyugal, connubial
conoid ['konɔɪd] *adj* conoide; *s* (geom.) conoide
conoidal [ko'nɔɪdəl] *adj* conoidal
conquer ['kaŋkər] *va* vencer; conquistar (*a fuerza de armas*); *vn* vencer
conquerable ['kaŋkərəbəl] *adj* vencible; conquistable
conqueror ['kaŋkərər] *s* vencedor; conquistador; **the Conqueror** el Conquistador (*Guillermo I de Inglaterra, Jaime I de Aragón, Alfonso I de Portugal*)
conquest ['kaŋkwɛst] *s* conquista (*acción; persona o cosa*); **the Conquest** la conquista de Inglaterra por los normandos
conquistador [kan'kwɪstədɔr] *s* conquistador (*español en las Américas en el siglo XVI*)
Conrad ['kanræd] *s* Conrado
consanguineous [,kansæŋ'gwɪnɪəs] *adj* consanguíneo
consanguinity [,kansæŋ'gwɪnɪtɪ] *s* consanguinidad
conscience ['kanʃəns] *s* conciencia; **in all conscience** en conciencia; razonablemente; seguramente
conscience clause *s* cláusula de conciencia
conscience money *s* dinero que se paga para descargar la conciencia
conscience-stricken ['kanʃəns,strɪkən] *adj* arrepentido, contrito, lleno de remordimientos
conscientious [,kanʃɪ'ɛnʃəs] *adj* concienzudo
conscientious objector *s* objetante de conciencia (*el que por escrúpulos de conciencia se niega a prestar servicios militares*)
conscionable ['kanʃənəbəl] *adj* justo, razonable
conscious ['kanʃəs] *adj* consciente; tímido, encogido; intencional, p.ej., **conscious lie** mentira intencional; **to be conscious** tener conocimiento; **to be conscious of** tener conciencia de; **to become conscious** volver en sí; **conscious of** consciente de (*p.ej., sus derechos*); confiado en (*p.ej., sus fuerzas*)
consciousness ['kanʃəsnɪs] *s* conciencia, conocimiento; **to lose consciousness** perder el conocimiento; **to regain consciousness** recobrar el conocimiento
conscript ['kanskrɪpt] *s* conscripto; [kən'skrɪpt] *va* reclutar; tomar para el uso del Estado
conscript fathers *spl* padres conscriptos
conscription [kən'skrɪpʃən] *s* conscripción; imposición de contribuciones, trabajos, etc., para el uso del Estado
consecrate ['kansɪkret] *adj* consagrado; *va* consagrar
consecration [,kansɪ'kreʃən] *s* consagración
consecrator ['kansɪ,kretər] *s* consagrante
consecutive [kən'sɛkjətɪv] *adj* consecutivo; consecuente; (gram.) consecutivo
consensual [kən'sɛnʃuəl] *adj* (law) consensual
consensus [kən'sɛnsəs] *s* consenso
consent [kən'sɛnt] *s* consentimiento; **by common consent** según la opinión unánime; *vn* consentir; **to consent to** consentir en; **to consent to** + *inf* consentir en + *inf*
consequence ['kansɪkwɛns] *s* consecuencia; **in consequence** por consiguiente; **in consequence of** de resultas de; **to take the consequences** aceptar las consecuencias
consequent ['kansɪkwɛnt] *adj* consiguiente; *s* consecuencia; (log. & math.) consecuente
consequential [,kansɪ'kwɛnʃəl] *adj* consiguiente; altivo, arrogante; de consecuencia
consequently ['kansɪkwɛntlɪ] *adv* por consiguiente, por lo tanto
conservation [,kansər'veʃən] *s* conservación; conservación de los bosques, ríos, etc.; bosque bajo cuidado oficial
conservationist [,kansər'veʃənɪst] *s* persona que aboga por la conservación de los bosques, ríos, etc.
conservation of energy *s* (phys.) conservación de la energía
conservation of mass *s* (phys.) conservación de la masa
conservation of matter *s* (phys.) conservación de la materia
conservatism [kən'sʌrvətɪzəm] *s* conservadurismo

conservative [kən'sʌrvətɪv] *adj* conservativo (*que conserva*); cauteloso, moderado; (pol.) conservador; *s* preservativo; (pol.) conservador
Conservative Party *s* (Brit.) conservadurismo, partido conservador
conservatoire [kən,sʌrvə'twɑr] *s* conservatorio
conservator ['kɑnsər,vetər] o [kən'sʌrvətər] *s* conservador
conservatory [kən'sʌrvə,torɪ] *adj* conservatorio; *s* (*pl:* **-ries**) conservatorio (*establecimiento dedicado a la enseñanza de la música y las artes*); invernadero
conserve [kən'sʌrv] o ['kɑnsʌrv] *s* conserva, compota; [kən'sʌrv] *va* conservar
consider [kən'sɪdər] *va* considerar
considerable [kən'sɪdərəbəl] *adj* considerable
considerably [kən'sɪdərəblɪ] *adv* considerablemente
considerate [kən'sɪdərɪt] *adj* considerado, cortés, respetuoso
consideration [kən,sɪdə'reʃən] *s* consideración; **in consideration of** en consideración a; en cambio de; **on no consideration** bajo ningún concepto, de ninguna manera; **to take into consideration** tomar en consideración; **under consideration** en consideración; **without due consideration** sin reflexión, inconsideradamente
considered [kən'sɪdərd] *adj* considerado
considering [kən'sɪdərɪŋ] *adv* teniendo en cuenta las circunstancias; **considering that** en vista de que; *prep* en consideración a, en vista de
consign [kən'saɪn] *va* consignar; confiar, encomendar; (com.) consignar
consignee [,kɑnsaɪ'ni] *s* (com.) consignatario
consigner [kən'saɪnər] *s* var. de **consignor**
consignment [kən'saɪnmənt] *s* consignación; (com.) consignación; **on consignment** (com.) a consignación
consignor [kən'saɪnər] *s* (com.) consignador
consist [kən'sɪst] *vn* consistir; **to consist in** consistir en (*residir en, estar incluído en*); **to consist of** consistir en, constar de (*estar compuesto de*); **to consist with** concordar con
consistence [kən'sɪstəns] *s* var. de **consistency**
consistency [kən'sɪstənsɪ] *s* (*pl:* **-cies**) consistencia; consecuencia
consistent [kən'sɪstənt] *adj* consistente; consecuente
consistorial [,kɑnsɪs'torɪəl] *adj* consistorial
consistory [kən'sɪstərɪ] *s* (*pl:* **-ries**) consistorio
consolation [,kɑnsə'leʃən] *s* consolación, consuelo
consolation match *s* (sport) partido o match de consolación
consolation prize *s* premio de consuelo
consolation race *s* (sport) carrera de consolación
consolatory [kən'sɑlə,torɪ] *adj* consolatorio
console ['kɑnsol] *s* consola, mesa de consola; (arch., mus. & rad.) consola; [kən'sol] *va* consolar
console table ['kɑnsol] *s* consola, mesa de consola
consolidate [kən'sɑlɪdet] *va* consolidar; *vn* consolidarse
consolidation [kən,sɑlɪ'deʃən] *s* consolidación
consoling [kən'solɪŋ] *adj* consolador
consols ['kɑnsɑlz] o [kən'sɑlz] *spl* consolidados (*de la deuda británica*)
consommé [,kɑnsə'me] *s* consumado, consomé
consonance ['kɑnsənəns] o **consonancy** ['kɑnsənənsɪ] *s* consonancia
consonant ['kɑnsənənt] *adj & s* consonante
consonantal [,kɑnsə'næntəl] *adj* consonántico
consort ['kɑnsɔrt] *s* consorte (*esposo o esposa*); (naut.) buque que acompaña a otro; [kən'sɔrt] *va* asociar; *vn* asociarse; concordar
consortium [kən'sɔrʃɪəm] *s* (*pl:* **-tia** [ʃɪə]) consorcio
conspectus [kən'spɛktəs] *s* vista general; sumario, resumen
conspicuous [kən'spɪkjuəs] *adj* manifiesto, ostensible; conspicuo (*ilustre, insigne*); llamativo, vistoso; notable
conspiracy [kən'spɪrəsɪ] *s* (*pl:* **-cies**) conspiración
conspirator [kən'spɪrətər] *s* conspirador
conspiratorial [kən,spɪrə'torɪəl] *adj* conspiratorio
conspire [kən'spaɪr] *va* maquinar; *vn* conspirar; **to conspire to** + *inf* conspirar a o para + *inf*
constable ['kɑnstəbəl] o ['kʌnstəbəl] *s* policía, guardia de seguridad; condestable (*antiguo oficial superior de milicia*); guardián de un fuerte o castillo
constabulary [kən'stæbjə,lɛrɪ] *s* (*pl:* **-ies**) policía (*de un distrito*); guardia civil
Constance ['kɑnstənz] *s* Constanza (*nombre propio de mujer*)
constancy ['kɑnstənsɪ] *s* constancia; fidelidad, lealtad
constant ['kɑnstənt] *adj* constante; incesante, continuo; fiel, leal; *s* (math. & phys.) constante
Constantine ['kɑnstəntaɪn] o ['kɑnstəntin] *s* Constantino
Constantinople [,kɑnstæntɪ'nopəl] *s* Constantinopla
constantly ['kɑnstəntlɪ] *adv* constantemente; incesantemente, continuamente; fielmente, lealmente
constellation [,kɑnstə'leʃən] *s* (astr. & astrol.) constelación; cielo constelado; reunión brillante
consternation [,kɑnstər'neʃən] *s* consternación
constipate ['kɑnstɪpet] *va* estreñir
constipated ['kɑnstɪ,petɪd] *adj* estreñido
constipation [,kɑnstɪ'peʃən] *s* estreñimiento
constituency [kən'stɪtʃuənsɪ] *s* (*pl:* **-cies**) grupo de votantes; distrito electoral; grupo de comitentes
constituent [kən'stɪtʃuənt] *adj* constitutivo; (pol.) constituyente; *s* constitutivo; (pol.) elector; (law) poderdante, comitente
constituent assembly *s* (pol.) cortes constituyentes
constitute ['kɑnstɪtjut] o ['kɑnstɪtut] *va* constituir
constitution [,kɑnstɪ'tjuʃən] o [,kɑnstɪ'tuʃən] *s* constitución
constitutional [,kɑnstɪ'tjuʃənəl] o [,kɑnstɪ'tuʃənəl] *adj* constitucional
constitutionality [,kɑnstɪ,tjuʃən'ælɪtɪ] o [,kɑnstɪ,tuʃən'ælɪtɪ] *s* constitucionalidad
constitutionally [,kɑnstɪ'tjuʃənəlɪ] o [,kɑnstɪ'tuʃənəlɪ] *adv* constitucionalmente
constitutional monarchy *s* monarquía constitucional
constitutive ['kɑnstɪ,tjutɪv] o ['kɑnstɪ,tutɪv] *adj* constitutivo; constituidor
constrain [kən'stren] *va* constreñir, obligar; restringir, reprimir; encerrar, detener
constrained [kən'strend] *adj* constreñido; forzado, p.ej., **constrained smile** risa forzada
constraint [kən'strent] *s* constreñimiento; sujeción; encierro; embarazo, encogimiento
constrict [kən'strɪkt] *va* apretar, estrechar, encoger
constriction [kən'strɪkʃən] *s* constricción; (med.) constricción
constrictive [kən'strɪktɪv] *adj* constrictivo
constrictor [kən'strɪktər] *s* (zool.) culebra constrictora; (anat.) constrictor
constringent [kən'strɪndʒənt] *adj* constringente
construct [kən'strʌkt] *va* construir; (geom. & gram.) construir
construction [kən'strʌkʃən] *s* construcción; interpretación, explicación, sentido; (gram.) construcción; **under construction** en construcción
constructional [kən'strʌkʃənəl] *adj* estructural
constructionist [kən'strʌkʃənɪst] *s* interpretador
constructive [kən'strʌktɪv] *adj* constructor; constructivo; creador; (law) implícito
constructor [kən'strʌktər] *s* constructor
construe [kən'stru] o ['kɑnstru] *va* interpretar, explicar; deducir, inferir; traducir; (gram.) construir, analizar
consubstantial [,kɑnsəb'stænʃəl] *adj* consubstancial

consubstantiality [ˌkɑnsəbˌstænʃɪˈælɪtɪ] *s* consubstancialidad
consubstantiation [ˌkɑnsəbˌstænʃɪˈeʃən] *s* (theol.) consubstanciación
consuetude [ˈkɑnswɪtjud] o [ˈkɑnswɪtud] *s* costumbre
consuetudinary [ˌkɑnswɪˈtjudɪˌnɛrɪ] o [ˌkɑnswɪˈtudɪˌnɛrɪ] *adj* consuetudinario
consul [ˈkɑnsəl] *s* cónsul
consular [ˈkɑnsələr] o [ˈkɑnsjələr] *adj* consular
consular agent *s* agente consular
consular invoice *s* factura consular
consulate [ˈkɑnsəlɪt] o [ˈkɑnsjəlɪt] *s* consulado
consulate general *s* (*pl:* **consulates general**) consulado general
consul general *s* (*pl:* **consuls general**) cónsul general
consulship [ˈkɑnsəlʃɪp] *s* consulado
consult [kənˈsʌlt] *va & vn* consultar
consultant [kənˈsʌltənt] *s* consultor
consultation [ˌkɑnsəlˈteʃən] *s* consulta, consultación
consultative [kənˈsʌltətɪv] *adj* consultivo
consumable [kənˈsuməbəl] o [kənˈsjuməbəl] *adj* consumible
consume [kənˈsum] o [kənˈsjum] *va* consumir; **consumed with** preocupado con; *vn* consumirse
consumedly [kənˈsumɪdlɪ] o [kənˈsjumɪdlɪ] *adv* muchísimo, demasiado
consumer [kənˈsumər] o [kənˈsjumər] *s* consumidor
consumer credit *s* crédito para comprar a plazos, crédito dado al consumidor
consumer resistence *s* resistencia del consumidor a la venta
consumers' goods *spl* bienes de consumo
consumer spending *s* gastos de consumo
consummate [kənˈsʌmɪt] *adj* consumado; [ˈkɑnsəmet] *va* consumar
consummation [ˌkɑnsəˈmeʃən] *s* consumación
consumption [kənˈsʌmpʃən] *s* consunción, destrucción, extinción; consumo (*p.ej., de comestibles*); (path.) consunción
consumptive [kənˈsʌmptɪv] *adj* consuntivo, consumidor; (path.) tísico; *s* (path.) tísico
cont. abr. de **containing, contents, continent, continental, continue** y **continued**
Cont. abr. de **Continental**
contact [ˈkɑntækt] *s* contacto; (elec.) contacto; (elec.) toma de corriente; **to put in contact with** poner en contacto con; *va* (coll.) ponerse en contacto con; *vn* contactar
contact breaker *s* (elec.) ruptor
contact firing *s* (arti.) fuego de contacto
contact goniometer *s* goniómetro de aplicación
contact lens *s* lente de contacto, lente invisible
contactor [ˈkɑntæktər] *s* (elec.) contactor
contact plane *s* (mil.) aeroplano de contacto
contact rail *s* (elec.) carril conductor
contagion [kənˈtedʒən] *s* contagio
contagious [kənˈtedʒəs] *adj* contagioso
contain [kənˈten] *va* contener; (math.) ser exactamente divisible por; **to contain oneself** contenerse, refrenarse
container [kənˈtenər] *s* continente; envase, vasija, caja
containment [kənˈtenmənt] *s* refrenamiento, contención
contaminate [kənˈtæmɪnet] *va* contaminar
contamination [kənˌtæmɪˈneʃən] *s* contaminación; (philol.) cruce de palabras, contaminación
contd. abr. de **continued**
contemn [kənˈtɛm] *va* desacatar, despreciar
contemplate [ˈkɑntəmplet] *va & vn* contemplar; **to contemplate** + *ger* pensar + *inf*
contemplation [ˌkɑntəmˈpleʃən] *s* contemplación; proyecto, intención
contemplative [ˈkɑntəmˌpletɪv] o [kənˈtɛmplətɪv] *adj* contemplativo
contemporaneous [kənˌtɛmpəˈrenɪəs] *adj* contemporáneo
contemporaneously [kənˌtɛmpəˈrenɪəslɪ] *adv* contemporáneamente
contemporary [kənˈtɛmpəˌrɛrɪ] *adj* contemporáneo, coetáneo; *s* (*pl:* **-ies**) contemporáneo, coetáneo
contempt [kənˈtɛmpt] *s* desacato, desprecio; (law) contumacia
contemptible [kənˈtɛmptɪbəl] *adj* despreciable
contempt of court *s* menosprecio a la justicia, desacato a la autoridad del tribunal
contemptuous [kənˈtɛmptʃuəs] *adj* desdeñoso, despreciativo
contend [kənˈtɛnd] *va* sostener, mantener, defender; *vn* contender
contender [kənˈtɛnder] *s* contendiente, concurrente
content [kənˈtɛnt] *adj* contento; *s* contento; **to one's heart's content** a gusto; [ˈkɑntɛnt] *s* contenido; sustancia; cabida; volumen; **contents** [ˈkɑntɛnts] *spl* contenido; [kənˈtɛnt] *va* contentar
contented [kənˈtɛntɪd] *adj* contento, satisfecho
contentedness [kənˈtɛntɪdnɪs] *s* contentamiento, satisfacción
contention [kənˈtɛnʃən] *s* contención; argumento
contentious [kənˈtɛnʃəs] *adj* contencioso; (law) contencioso
contentment [kənˈtɛntmənt] *s* contento, contentamiento
conterminous [kɑnˈtʌrmɪnəs] *adj* contérmino; coextensivo
contest [ˈkɑntɛst] *s* competencia, concurso; contienda; [kənˈtɛst] *va* disputar, impugnar; tratar de conseguir; *vn* contender
contestant [kənˈtɛstənt] *s* contendiente
context [ˈkɑntɛkst] *s* contexto
contextual [kənˈtɛkstʃuəl] *adj* del contexto
contexture [kənˈtɛkstʃər] *s* contextura
contiguity [ˌkɑntɪˈgjuɪtɪ] *s* (*pl:* **-ties**) contigüidad; continuo
contiguous [kənˈtɪgjuəs] *adj* contiguo
continence [ˈkɑntɪnəns] *s* continencia
continent [ˈkɑntɪnənt] *adj* continente; *s* continente; **the Continent** la Europa continental
continental [ˌkɑntɪˈnɛntəl] *adj* continental; *s* papel moneda puesto en circulación durante la Revolución norteamericana; **not worth a continental** sin valor; (*cap.*) *s* habitante del continente europeo; soldado del ejército continental norteamericano durante la Revolución
continental divide *s* divisoria continental, parteaguas continental
contingency [kənˈtɪndʒənsɪ] *s* (*pl:* **-cies**) contingencia
contingent [kənˈtɪndʒənt] *adj* contingente; *s* contingente; (mil.) contingente
continual [kənˈtɪnjuəl] *adj* continuo
continually [kənˈtɪnjuəlɪ] *adv* continuamente, continuadamente
continuance [kənˈtɪnjuəns] *s* continuación; (law) aplazamiento
continuation [kənˌtɪnjuˈeʃən] *s* continuación
continuative [kənˈtɪnjuˌetɪv] *adj* (gram.) continuativo; *s* (gram.) continuativa
continuator [kənˈtɪnjuˌetər] *s* continuador
continue [kənˈtɪnju] *va* continuar; mantener, conservar; aplazar; **to be continued** continuará; **to continue** + *ger* o **to continue to** + *inf* continuar + *ger; vn* continuar; continuarse (*extenderse*)
continued fever *s* (path.) fiebre continua
continued fraction *s* (math.) fracción continua
continuer [kənˈtɪnjuər] *s* continuador
continuity [ˌkɑntɪˈnjuɪtɪ] o [ˌkɑntɪˈnuɪtɪ] *s* (*pl:* **-ties**) continuidad; (mov.) escenario; (rad.) comentarios o anuncios que se dan entre las partes de un programa
continuous [kənˈtɪnjuəs] *adj* continuo
continuous current *s* var. de **direct current**
continuous showing *s* (mov.) sesión continua
continuous waves *spl* (rad.) ondas continuas, ondas entretenidas
continuum [kənˈtɪnjuəm] *s* (*pl:* **-a** [ə]) continuo
contort [kənˈtɔrt] *va* retorcer, deformar
contortion [kənˈtɔrʃən] *s* contorsión
contortionist [kənˈtɔrʃənɪst] *s* contorsionista
contour [ˈkɑntur] *s* contorno
contour chair *s* silla de contorno
contour line *s* curva de nivel
contour map *s* plano acotado
contourné [kɑnˈturne] *adj* (her.) contornado

contr. abr. de **contract, contracted** y **contraction**
contraband [ˈkɑntrəbænd] *s* contrabando; *adj* de contrabando, contrabandista
contrabandist [ˈkɑntrəˌbændɪst] *s* contrabandista
contraband of war *s* contrabando de guerra
contrabass [ˈkɑntrəˌbes] *s* (mus.) contrabajo; *adj* (mus.) de contrabajo
contraception [ˌkɑntrəˈsɛpʃən] *s* contracepción
contraceptive [ˌkɑntrəˈsɛptɪv] *adj & s* contraceptivo
contract [ˈkɑntrækt] *s* contrato; contrato de matrimonio; bridge contrato; [kənˈtrækt] *adj* (gram.) contracto; *va* contraer; (gram.) contraer; *vn* contraerse; [ˈkɑntrækt] o [kənˈtrækt] *va* contraer (*p.ej., matrimonio*); *vn* comprometerse por contrato; **to contract for** contratar; **to contract to** + *inf* comprometerse por contrato a + *inf*
contract bridge [ˈkɑntrækt] *s* bridge contrato, bridge contratado
contracted [kənˈtræktɪd] *adj* contraído; prometido; escaso, retardado, torpe; pobre de ánimo; nada liberal
contractible [kənˈtræktɪbəl] *adj* contractable, contráctil
contractile [kənˈtræktɪl] *adj* contráctil; contractivo
contractility [ˌkɑntrækˈtɪlɪtɪ] *s* contractilidad
contraction [kənˈtrækʃən] *s* contracción
contractive [kənˈtræktɪv] *adj* contractivo; contráctil
contractor [ˈkɑntræktər] o [kənˈtræktər] *s* contratista, contratante; empresario
contractual [kənˈtræktʃʊəl] *adj* contractual
contracture [kənˈtræktʃər] *s* (arch. & path.) contractura
contradance [ˈkɑntrəˌdæns] o [ˈkɑntrəˌdɑns] *s* contradanza
contradict [ˌkɑntrəˈdɪkt] *va* contradecir
contradiction [ˌkɑntrəˈdɪkʃən] *s* contradicción
contradictory [ˌkɑntrəˈdɪktərɪ] *adj* contradictorio; contradictor; *s* (*pl:* **-ries**) (log.) contradictoria
contradistinction [ˌkɑntrədɪsˈtɪŋkʃən] *s* distinción por oposición o contraste; **in contradistinction to** a diferencia de, en contraste con
contrail [ˈkɑnˌtrel] *s* (aer.) estela de vapor, rastro de condensación
contraindicant [ˌkɑntrəˈɪndɪkənt] *s* (med.) contraindicante
contraindicate [ˌkɑntrəˈɪndɪket] *va* (med.) contraindicar
contraindication [ˌkɑntrəˌɪndɪˈkeʃən] *s* (med.) contraindicación
contralateral [ˌkɑntrəˈlætərəl] *adj* contralateral
contralto [kənˈtrælto] *s* (*pl:* **-tos**) (mus.) contralto (*voz y persona*); *adj* (mus.) de contralto, para contralto
contraposition [ˌkɑntrəpəˈzɪʃən] *s* contraposición
contraption [kənˈtræpʃən] *s* (coll.) artificio, invención, dispositivo
contrapuntal [ˌkɑntrəˈpʌntəl] *adj* (mus.) contrapuntístico
contrapuntist [ˌkɑntrəˈpʌntɪst] *s* contrapuntista
contrariety [ˌkɑntrəˈraɪətɪ] *s* (*pl:* **-ties**) contrariedad
contrariwise [ˈkɑntrɛrɪˌwaɪz] *adv* en contrario; al contrario; [ˈkɑntrɛrɪˌwaɪz] o [kənˈtrɛrɪˌwaɪz] *adv* obstinadamente, tercamente
contrary [ˈkɑntrɛrɪ] *adj* contrario; [ˈkɑntrɛrɪ] o [kənˈtrɛrɪ] *adj* obstinado, terco; [ˈkɑntrɛrɪ] *adv* contrariamente, en contrario; *s* (*pl:* **-ries**) contraria (*cosa opuesta a otra*); contrario (*contradicción*); **on the contrary** al contrario; **to the contrary** en contrario
contrary to fact sentence *s* (gram.) oración condicional de negación implícita
contrast [ˈkɑntræst] *s* contraste; [kənˈtræst] *va* hacer contrastar, poner en contraste; *vn* contrastar
contravallation [ˌkɑntrəvəˈleʃən] *s* (fort.) contravalación
contravene [ˌkɑntrəˈvin] *va* contravenir a (*p.ej., una ley*); contradecir, oponerse a
contravention [ˌkɑntrəˈvɛnʃən] *s* contravención; contradicción, oposición
contrayerva [ˌkɑntrəˈjʌrvə] *s* (bot.) contrahierba
contredanse [kõtrəˈdɑ̃s] *s* var. de **contradance**
contretemps [kõtrəˈtɑ̃] *s* contratiempo; (mus.) contratiempo
contribute [kənˈtrɪbjʊt] *va & vn* contribuir; **to contribute to** + *ger* contribuir a + *inf*
contribution [ˌkɑntrɪˈbjuʃən] *s* contribución; colaboración (*a una revista, coloquio, etc.*)
contributive [kənˈtrɪbjʊtɪv] *adj* contribuidor
contributor [kənˈtrɪbjʊtər] *s* contribuidor, contribuyente
contributory [kənˈtrɪbjʊˌtorɪ] *adj* contribuidor
contrite [ˈkɑntraɪt] *adj* contrito
contrition [kənˈtrɪʃən] *s* contrición
contrivance [kənˈtraɪvəns] *s* invención; artefacto; inventiva; plan, designio
contrive [kənˈtraɪv] *va* inventar; gestionar, procurar; efectuar; maquinar; *vn* maquinar; **to contrive to** + *inf* ingeniarse a + *inf*
control [kənˈtrol] *s* gobierno, mando, dominio; dirección; derecho para intervenir; control, contrarregistro, norma de comprobación; testigo (*en un experimento de laboratorio*); (mach.) regulador; (spiritualism) comunicante; **controls** *spl* mandos; **to get under control** conseguir dominar (*p.ej., un incendio*); (*pret & pp:* **-trolled;** *ger:* **-trolling**) *va* gobernar, mandar, dominar; regular; controlar, comprobar; **to control oneself** dominarse, poseerse
control car *s* (aer.) barquilla de gobierno (*de un dirigible*)
control center *s* centro de control
control experiment *s* control
controllable [kənˈtroləbəl] *adj* gobernable, manejable, controlable
controller [kənˈtrolər] *s* interventor, contralor; director; (elec.) combinador; (mach.) regulador
controllership [kənˈtrolərʃɪp] *s* oficio de interventor; dirección
controlling interest *s* (com.) interés predominante, mayoría
control panel *s* (aer.) tablero de instrumentos
control room *s* (rad. & telv.) sala de control, sala de mando
control stick *s* (aer.) mango de escoba, palanca de mando
control tower *s* (aer.) torre de mando
controversial [ˌkɑntrəˈvʌrʃəl] *adj* controvertible, disputable; contencioso
controversialist [ˌkɑntrəˈvʌrʃəlɪst] *s* controversista
controversy [ˈkɑntrəˌvʌrsɪ] *s* (*pl:* **-sies**) controversia
controvert [ˈkɑntrəvʌrt] o [ˌkɑntrəˈvʌrt] *va* controvertir; contradecir; *vn* controvertir
controvertible [ˌkɑntrəˈvʌrtɪbəl] *adj* controvertible
contumacious [ˌkɑntjʊˈmeʃəs] o [ˌkɑntʊˈmeʃəs] *adj* contumaz
contumacy [ˈkɑntjʊməsɪ] o [ˈkɑntʊməsɪ] *s* (*pl:* **-cies**) contumacia
contumelious [ˌkɑntjʊˈmilɪəs] o [ˌkɑntʊˈmilɪəs] *adj* contumelioso
contumely [ˈkɑntjʊmɪlɪ] o [ˈkɑntʊmɪlɪ] *s* (*pl:* **-lies**) contumelia
contuse [kənˈtjuz] o [kənˈtuz] *va* contundir, contusionar
contusion [kənˈtjuʒən] o [kənˈtuʒən] *s* contusión
conundrum [kəˈnʌndrəm] *s* acertijo, adivinanza; problema complicado
convalesce [ˌkɑnvəˈlɛs] *vn* convalecer
convalescence [ˌkɑnvəˈlɛsəns] *s* convalecencia
convalescent [ˌkɑnvəˈlɛsənt] *adj* convaleciente; de convalecencia; *s* convaleciente
convalescent home *s* clínica de reposo
convection [kənˈvɛkʃən] *s* transporte; (phys.) convección
convection current *s* (elec.) corriente de convección

convene [kən'vin] *va* convocar; *vn* convenir, juntarse, reunirse
convenience [kən'vinjəns] *s* comodidad; proximidad; **at one's convenience** cuando le sea cómodo a uno; **at your earliest convenience** a su más pronta conveniencia
conveniency [kən'vinjənsɪ] *s* (*pl:* **-cies**) var. de **convenience**
convenient [kən'vinjənt] *adj* cómodo; alcanzadizo; **convenient to** (coll.) vecino a
convent ['kanvent] *s* convento (*de religiosas*)
conventicle [kən'ventɪkəl] *s* conventículo
convention [kən'venʃən] *s* convención; asamblea, congreso
conventional [kən'venʃənəl] *adj* convencional, de convención; formalista
conventionalism [kən'venʃənəlɪzəm] *s* convencionalismo; formalismo
conventionality [kən,venʃə'nælɪtɪ] *s* convencionalidad; formalismo
conventionalize [kən'venʃənəlaɪz] *va* estilizar
conventual [kən'ventʃuəl] *adj* conventual; *s* conventual (*religioso*); religiosa que vive en convento
converge [kən'vʌrdʒ] *va* hacer convergir; *vn* convergir
convergence [kən'vʌrdʒəns] o **convergency** [kən'vʌrdʒənsɪ] *s* convergencia
convergent [kən'vʌrdʒənt] *adj* convergente
conversable [kən'vʌrsəbəl] *adj* conversable; propio a la conversación
conversant ['kanvərsənt] o [kən'vʌrsənt] *adj* versado; **conversant with** versado en, al corriente de
conversation [,kanvər'seʃən] *s* conversación
conversational [,kanvər'seʃənəl] *adj* conversacional; amigo de la conversación
conversationalist [,kanvər'seʃənəlɪst] *s* conversador
conversationally [,kanvər'seʃənəlɪ] *adv* de manera propia a la conversación; en conversación
conversation piece *s* (paint.) cuadro de un grupo de personas de la alta sociedad; mueble de interés especial
converse ['kanvʌrs] *adj* contrario; inverso; *s* contraria; (log.) inversa; conversación; [kən'vʌrs] *vn* conversar
conversely ['kanvʌrslɪ] o [kən'vʌrslɪ] *adv* a la inversa, contrariamente
conversion [kən'vʌrʒən] o [kən'vʌrʃən] *s* conversión; apropiación ilícita para uso propio; (mil.) conversión (*mutación de frente*)
conversion table *s* tabla de conversión
conversive [kən'vʌrsɪv] *adj* conversivo
convert ['kanvʌrt] *s* converso, convertido; [kən'vʌrt] *va* convertir; apropiar ilícitamente para uso propio; *vn* convertirse
converted [kən'vʌrtɪd] *adj* converso
converter [kən'vʌrtər] *s* (elec.) convertidor, conmutatriz; (metal.) convertidor; (rad.) conversor; (com.) comerciante que termina la preparación de telas para la venta
convertibility [kən,vʌrtɪ'bɪlɪtɪ] *s* convertibilidad
convertible [kən'vʌrtɪbəl] *adj* convertible; (aut.) descapotable, transformable; *s* (aut.) descapotable, transformable
convertiplane [kən'vʌrtɪplen] *s* avión convertible, convertiplano
convex ['kanveks] o [kan'veks] *adj* convexo
convexity [kan'veksɪtɪ] *s* (*pl:* **-ties**) convexidad
convey [kən've] *va* conducir, transportar; transmitir (*p.ej., una corriente eléctrica*); expresar; participar; transferir, traspasar (*p.ej., bienes de una persona a otra*)
conveyance [kən'veəns] *s* conducción, transporte; transmisión; participación, comunicación; vehículo; traspaso de dominio; escritura de traspaso
conveyancer [kən'veənsər] *s* escribano que prepara escrituras de traspaso
conveyancing [kən'veənsɪŋ] *s* preparación de escrituras de traspaso
conveyer o **conveyor** [kən'veər] *s* conductor, portador; transportador
conveyor belt *s* correa transportadora
conveyor chain *s* cadena para transportador
convict ['kanvɪkt] *s* convicto; presidiario; [kən'vɪkt] *va* probar la culpabilidad de; declarar convicto a (*un acusado*); convencer de alguna culpa
conviction [kən'vɪkʃən] *s* convicción; (law) condena judicial
convince [kən'vɪns] *va* convencer
convincible [kən'vɪnsɪbəl] *adj* convencible
convincing [kən'vɪnsɪŋ] *adj* convencedor; convincente (*razón, argumento*)
convivial [kən'vɪvɪəl] *adj* jovial, festivo
conviviality [kən,vɪvɪ'ælɪtɪ] *s* (*pl:* **-ties**) jovialidad
convocation [,kanvo'keʃən] *s* convocación; asamblea
convoke [kan'vok] *va* convocar
convolute ['kanvəlut] *adj* enrollado; (bot.) convolutado
convolution [,kanvə'luʃən] *s* circunvolución, convolución; (anat.) circunvolución
convolution of Broca ['brokə] *s* (anat.) circunvolución de Broca
convolvulaceous [kən,valvjə'leʃəs] *adj* (bot.) convolvuláceo
convolvulus [kən'valvjələs] *s* (*pl:* **-luses** o **-li** [laɪ]) (bot.) convólvulo
convoy ['kanvɔɪ] *s* convoy; [kan'vɔɪ] *va* convoyar
convulse [kən'vʌls] *va* agitar; crispar, convulsionar; mover a risas convulsivas; *vn* agitarse; crisparse
convulsion [kən'vʌlʃən] *s* convulsión; ataque o paroxismo de risa; (path.) convulsión
convulsive [kən'vʌlsɪv] *adj* convulsivo; convulso
cony ['konɪ] *s* (*pl:* **-nies**) conejuna, pelo de conejo; (zool.) damán; (zool.) ochotona; (archaic) conejo
coo [ku] *s* arrullo; *va & vn* arrullar
cooee o **cooey** ['kuɪ] *s* grito largo y agudo
cook [kuk] *s* cocinero; *va* cocer, cocinar; (coll.) ajar; (slang) arruinar, echar a perder; **to cook up** preparar; (coll.) falsear, falsificar; (coll.) tramar, maquinar; *vn* cocer; cocinar (*ocuparse en cosas de cocina*)
cookbook ['kuk,buk] *s* libro de cocina
cooker ['kukər] *s* hervidor; (Brit.) cocina económica
cookery ['kukərɪ] *s* (*pl:* **-ies**) cocina (*arte o empleo; lugar*)
cookhouse ['kuk,haus] *s* cocina; cocina móvil de campaña; (naut.) fogón
cookie ['kukɪ] *s* var. de **cooky**
cooking ['kukɪŋ] *s* cocina, arte culinaria
cooking soda *s* (coll.) bicarbonato sódico
cookshop ['kuk,ʃap] *s* casa de comidas, pequeño restaurante
cookstove ['kuk,stov] *s* cocina, cocina económica
cooky ['kukɪ] *s* (*pl:* **-ies**) pastelito dulce, pasta seca
cool [kul] *adj* fresco; sereno, tranquilo; indiferente; de color azul, gris o verde; (coll.) sin calificación, sin exageración; *va* refrescar; atemplar, moderar; **to cool one's heels** (coll.) hacer antesala, estar esperando mucho tiempo; *vn* refrescarse; atemplarse, moderarse; **to cool off** refrescarse; serenarse, tranquilizarse
coolant ['kulənt] *s* líquido refrigerador
cooler ['kulər] *s* refrigerador; heladera; refrigerante; (slang) cárcel
cool-headed ['kul'hedɪd] *adj* sereno, tranquilo; juicioso, sensato
coolie ['kulɪ] *s* culí
cooling ['kulɪŋ] *s* enfriamiento; *adj* refrescante; refrigerante
cooling coil *s* serpentín enfriador
cooling jacket *s* camisa refrigerante
cooling time *s* (law) tiempo durante el cual se apaciguan las pasiones de los litigantes
coolish ['kulɪʃ] *adj* fresquito, algo fresco
coolly ['kulɪ] o ['kullɪ] *adv* frescamente; serenamente, tranquilamente; indiferentemente; con descaro
coolness ['kulnɪs] *s* frescura; tranquilidad; indiferencia
cooly ['kulɪ] *s* (*pl:* **-lies**) var. de **coolie**
coomb [kum] o [kom] *s* var. de **combe**
coon [kun] *s* (zool.) mapache, oso lavador; piel de mapache; (U.S.A.) miembro del partido re-

publicano en la época de la Revolución; (coll.) marrullero; (offensive) negro
coon's age *s* (coll.) mucho tiempo
coop [kup] *s* gallinero; jaula o redil para conejos u otros animales pequeños; (slang) caponera (*cárcel*); *va* encerrar en un gallinero; enjaular, emparedar
coöp. abr. de **coöperative**
coöp [ko'ɑp] o ['koɑp] *s* tienda cooperativa
cooper ['kupər] o ['kʊpər] *s* barrilero, tonelero; *va* fabricar o concertar (*barriles, toneles, etc.*); **to cooper out** o **up** acabar, elaborar; *vn* ser barrilero, ser tonelero
cooperage ['kupərɪdʒ] o ['kʊpərɪdʒ] *s* barrilería, tonelería; precio pagado por la fabricación de barriles, toneles, etc.
coöperate [ko'ɑpəret] *vn* cooperar; **to coöperate in** + *ger* cooperar a + *inf*
coöperation [koˌɑpə'reʃən] *s* cooperación
coöperative [ko'ɑpəˌretɪv] *adj* cooperativo; *s* cooperativa, sociedad cooperativa
coöperative store *s* tienda cooperativa
coöperator [ko'ɑpəˌretər] *s* cooperador, cooperario; socio de una cooperativa
cooper's adz *s* doladera de tonelero
coöpt [ko'ɑpt] *va* cooptar
coöptation [ˌkoɑp'teʃən] *s* cooptación
coördinate [ko'ɔrdɪnɪt] *adj* coordinado; de igual importancia; (math.) coordenado; (gram.) coordinante; *s* igual, semejante; (math.) coordenado; [ko'ɔrdɪnet] *va & vn* coordinar
coördinate geometry *s* geometría analítica
coördinating conjunction *s* (gram.) conjunción coordinante
coördination [koˌɔrdɪ'neʃən] *s* coordinación
coördinative [ko'ɔrdɪˌnetɪv] *adj* coordinativo
coördinator [ko'ɔrdɪˌnetər] *s* coordinador
coot [kut] *s* (orn.) fúlica; (orn.) fúlica negra, foja; (orn.) negreta; (coll.) bobalicón
cootie ['kutɪ] *s* (slang) piojo
cop [kɑp] *s* rollo de hilos ahusado; tubo de enrollar hilos de seda u otros; (slang) polizonte; (*pret & pp:* **copped;** *ger:* **copping**) *va* (slang) coger, prender; (slang) hurtar, robar
copaiba [ko'pebə] o [ko'paɪbə] *s* (pharm.) copaiba
copaiba balsam *s* (pharm.) bálsamo de copaiba
copal ['kopəl] *s* copal
copartner [ko'pɑrtnər] *s* consocio, copartícipe
copartnership [ko'pɑrtnərʃɪp] *s* asociación, coparticipación
cope [kop] *s* (eccl.) capa pluvial; (mas.) albardilla; *va* vestir con capa pluvial; poner albardilla a, rematar con albardilla; *vn* hacer frente; **to cope with** hacer frente a, enfrentarse con
copeck ['kopɛk] *s* var. de **kopeck**
Copenhagen [ˌkopən'hegən] *s* Copenhague
copepod ['kopɪpɑd] *adj & s* (zool.) copépodo
Copernican [ko'pʌrnɪkən] *adj & s* copernicano
Copernican system *s* (astr.) sistema de Copérnico
Copernicus [ko'pʌrnɪkəs] *s* Copérnico
copestone ['kopˌston] *s* piedra de albardilla; (fig.) coronamiento
copier ['kɑpɪər] *s* copiador, imitador; copiante, copista
copilot ['koˌpaɪlət] *s* (aer.) copiloto
coping ['kopɪŋ] *s* (mas.) albardilla
coping saw *s* serrucho de calar, sierra caladora
copious ['kopɪəs] *adj* copioso
copper ['kɑpər] *s* cobre; calderilla, vellón (*moneda de cobre*); caldero (*vasija*); (slang) polizonte; *adj* cobreño; cobrizo (*en el color*); *va* cubrir o revestir con cobre
copperas ['kɑpərəs] *s* (chem.) caparrosa verde
copper glance *s* (mineral.) calcosina
copperhead ['kɑpərˌhɛd] *s* (zool.) víbora de cabeza de cobre; (*cap.*) *s* (U.S.A.) habitante de los Estados del Norte que simpatizaba con los Estados confederados del Sur
copperplate ['kɑpərˌplet] *s* plancha de cobre (*que sirve para grabar*); grabado en lámina de cobre; grabadura en cobre; *va* grabar en cobre
copper pyrites *s* (mineral.) pirita de cobre
coppersmith ['kɑpərˌsmɪθ] *s* cobrero
copper sulfate *s* (chem.) sulfato de cobre
coppery ['kɑpərɪ] *adj* encobrado, cobreño; cobrizo (*en el color*)
coppice ['kɑpɪs] *s* var. de **copse**
copra ['kɑprə] *s* copra
coproduction [ˌkopro'dʌkʃən] *s* coproducción
coprolite ['kɑprəlaɪt] *s* (pal.) coprolito
copse [kɑps] *s* soto, matorral, monte bajo
Copt [kɑpt] *s* copto
Coptic ['kɑptɪk] *adj* copto, cóptico; *s* copto (*idioma*)
Coptic Church *s* Iglesia copta
copula ['kɑpjələ] *s* cópula; (anat., gram., law, log. & med.) cópula
copulate ['kɑpjəlet] *vn* copularse
copulation [ˌkɑpjə'leʃən] *s* copulación
copulative ['kɑpjəˌletɪv] *adj* copulativo; *s* (gram.) palabra copulativa
copy ['kɑpɪ] *s* (*pl:* **-ies**) copia; modelo; ejemplar (*p.ej., de un libro*); número (*p.ej., de un periódico*); (print.) original, manuscrito, material; (*pret & pp:* **-ied**) *va* copiar; *vn* copiar; **to copy after** contrahacer
copybook ['kɑpɪˌbʊk] *s* cuaderno de escritura; (com.) libro copiador; *adj* común, ordinario
copyhold ['kɑpɪˌhold] *s* (English law) posesión en virtud de una copia del rollo del tribunal señorial; tierras poseídas en virtud de una copia del rollo señorial
copyholder ['kɑpɪˌholdər] *s* lector de pruebas (*el que lee en alta voz al corrector*); atendedor (*el que sigue la lectura que hace el corrector*); portacopia, sujetacuartillas (*dispositivo en que se coloca el manuscrito que se va a copiar*); (English law) poseedor en virtud de una copia del rollo señorial
copying ink *s* tinta de copiar
copyist ['kɑpɪɪst] *s* copiante, copista; copiador, imitador
copyreader ['kɑpɪˌridər] *s* revisor de manuscritos
copyright ['kɑpɪˌraɪt] *s* (derecho de) propiedad literaria; *va* proteger solicitando la propiedad literaria; inscribir en el registro de la propiedad literaria
copy writer *s* escritor de anuncios
copy writing *s* preparación de material publicitario
coquet [ko'kɛt] (*pret & pp:* **-quetted;** *ger:* **-quetting**) *vn* coquetear; bromear, burlarse
coquetry ['kokətrɪ] o [ko'kɛtrɪ] *s* (*pl:* **-ries**) coquetería; broma, burla
coquette [ko'kɛt] *s* coqueta
coquettish [ko'kɛtɪʃ] *adj* coqueta; coquetón
coquina [ko'kinə] *s* coquina
cor. abr. de **corner, coroner, corrected, correction** y **corresponding**
Cor. abr. de **Corinthians** y **Coroner**
coracle ['kɑrəkəl] o ['kɔrəkəl] *s* (Brit.) barquilla casi redonda y en forma de canasta
coracoid ['kɑrəkɔɪd] o ['kɔrəkɔɪd] *adj & s* (anat.) coracoides
coracoid process *s* (anat.) apófisis coracoides
coral ['kɑrəl] o ['kɔrəl] *adj* coralino; *s* (zool.) coral (*pólipo, secreción calcárea, color, etc.*)
coralline ['kɑrəlɪn] o ['kɑrəlaɪn] *adj* coralino; *s* (bot. & zool.) coralina
coral reef *s* arrecife de coral
Coral Sea *s* mar del Coral
coral snake *s* (zool.) coral, coralillo
corbel ['kɔrbəl] *s* (arch.) ménsula, repisa; sostén; (*pret & pp:* **-beled** o **-belled;** *ger:* **-beling** o **-belling**) *va* proveer de ménsula o repisa; sostener por medio de una ménsula o repisa
corbie ['kɔrbɪ] *s* (Scotch) cuervo
corbie gable *s* (arch.) aguilón escalonado
corbiestep ['kɔrbɪˌstɛp] *s* (arch.) escalón de aguilón escalonado
cord [kɔrd] *s* cuerda; (anat. & elec.) cordón; corduroy; **cords** *spl* pantalones de corduroy; *va* acordonar; poner (*leña*) en cuerdas
cordage ['kɔrdɪdʒ] *s* cordaje, cordería; leña medida por cuerdas
cordate ['kɔrdet] *adj* cordiforme, cordato
corded ['kɔrdɪd] *adj* con cordoncillos; encordelado; hecho de cuerdas, provisto de cuerdas; puesto en cuerdas (*aplícase a la leña*)
cordial ['kɔrdʒəl] o ['kɔrdjəl] *adj* cordial; *s* cordial (*bebida confortante*); licor, licor tónico
cordiality [kɔr'dʒælɪtɪ] o [ˌkɔrdɪ'ælɪtɪ] *s* (*pl:* **-ties**) cordialidad
Cordilleran [ˌkɔrdɪl'jɛrən] o [kɔr'dɪlərən] *adj* cordillerano

cordite ['kɔrdaɪt] *s* cordita
cordon ['kɔrdən] *s* cordón (*cinta o cuerda ornamental*); (arch., fort., her., hort. & mil.) cordón
Cordova ['kɔrdovə] o [kɔr'dovə] *s* Córdoba
Cordovan ['kɔrdovən] o [kɔr'dovən] *adj & s* cordobés; (*l.c.*) *adj* de cordobán; *s* cordobán (*piel*)
cord tire *s* (aut.) neumático de cordones o de cuerdas
corduroy ['kɔrdərɔɪ] *s* pana, corduroy; **corduroys** *spl* pantalones de pana; traje o vestido de pana; *adj* de pana, de corduroy
corduroy road *s* camino de troncos
cordwainer ['kɔrdwenər] *s* (archaic) cordobanero; (obs.) zapatero
cordwood ['kɔrd,wʊd] *s* leña apilada en cuerdas; leña que se vende en cuerdas; leña cortada en trozos de a 4 pies
core [kor] *s* corazón (*p.ej., de ciertas frutas*); quid (*de un problema*); alma, devanador (*del ovillo*); foco (*de un absceso*); (elec.) alma (*de un cable conductor*); (elec.) núcleo (*de un electroimán*); (found.) ánima (*de un molde*); *va* quitar el corazón de (*p.ej., una manzana*)
Corea [ko'riə] *s* Corea
Corean [ko'riən] *adj & s* coreano
coreligionist [,korɪ'lɪdʒənɪst] *s* correligionario
coreopsis [,korɪ'ɑpsɪs] *s* (bot.) coreópsida
corespondent [,korɪs'pɑndənt] *s* (law) acusado como cómplice del demandado en un pleito de divorcio
coriaceous [,korɪ'eʃəs] *adj* coriáceo
coriander [,korɪ'ændər] *s* (bot.) cilantro o culantro
Corinth ['kɑrɪnθ] o ['kɔrɪnθ] *s* Corinto
Corinthian [kə'rɪnθɪən] *adj* corintio; *s* corintio; **Corinthians** *spl* (Bib.) Epístola de San Pablo a los corintios
Coriolanus [,kɑrɪə'lenəs] o [,kɔrɪə'lenəs] *s* Coriolano
corium ['korɪəm] *s* (*pl:* **-a** [ə]) (anat. & zool.) corión
cork [kɔrk] *s* corcho; corcho, tapón de corcho; tapón (*de cualquier materia*); (angling) corcho (*flotador*); *adj* corchoso (*parecido al corcho*); corchero (*perteneciente al corcho*); corchotaponero (*perteneciente a la fabricación de los tapones de corcho*); *va* tapar con corcho; encerrar; restringir; pintar con corcho quemado
corking ['kɔrkɪŋ] *adj* (slang) excelente, extraordinario
cork jacket *s* salvavidas de corcho
cork oak *s* (bot.) alcornoque
corkscrew ['kɔrk,skru] *s* sacacorchos, tirabuzón, descorchador; *adj* espiral, en forma de sacacorchos; *vn* zigzaguear; (aer.) volar en espiral
corkscrew flower *s* (bot.) caracol real
cork tree *s* var. de **cork oak**
corkwood ['kɔrk,wʊd] *s* (bot.) balsa o balso; (bot.) anona; (bot.) majagua (*Pariti tiliaceum*); madera de estos árboles
corky ['kɔrkɪ] *adj* (*comp:* **-ier;** *super:* **-iest**) corchoso; (coll.) alegre, vivaz; que sabe a corcho (*dícese del vino*)
corm [kɔrm] *s* (bot.) cormo
cormophyte ['kɔrməfaɪt] *s* (bot.) cormofita
cormorant ['kɔrmərənt] *s* (orn.) cormorán, corvejón, cuervo marino, mergo; (fig.) avaro, avariento; *adj* avaro, avariento
corn [kɔrn] *s* (U.S.A.) maíz; (England) trigo; (Scotland) avena; grano (*de maíz, trigo, etc.*); callo, clavo (*dureza de la piel*); (coll.) aguardiente de maíz; (slang) trivialidad; (slang) broma cansada o gastada; *va* acecinar, curar, salar
cornaceous [kɔr'neʃəs] *adj* (bot.) cornáceo
Corn Belt *s* (U.S.A.) zona del maíz
corn borer *s* (ent.) mariposa del maíz
corn bread *s* pan de maíz
corncake ['kɔrn,kek] *s* tortilla de maíz
corncob ['kɔrn,kɑb] *s* mazorca de maíz, carozo; pipa de fumar hecha de una mazorca de maíz
corn cockle *s* (bot.) neguilla, neguillón
corn crake *s* (orn.) guión de las codornices, rey de codornices
corncrib ['kɔrn,krɪb] *s* granero para maíz
corn cure *s* callicida
corn cutter *s* (U.S.A.) máquina para cortar el maíz
corncutter ['kɔrn,kʌtər] *s* callista, cortacallos
cornea ['kɔrnɪə] *s* (anat.) córnea
corneal ['kɔrnɪəl] *adj* corneal
corned [kɔrnd] *adj* acecinado
cornel ['kɔrnel] *s* (bot.) cornejo; (bot.) sanguiñuelo o sanapudio blanco
Cornelia [kɔr'niljə] *s* Cornelia
cornelian [kɔr'niljən] *s* (mineral.) cornalina
cornelian cherry *s* (bot.) cornejo macho
Cornelius [kɔr'niljəs] *s* Cornelio
corneous ['kɔrnɪəs] *adj* córneo
corner ['kɔrnər] *s* ángulo; esquina (*especialmente donde se encuentran dos calles*); rincón (*ángulo interior formado por dos o tres superficies que se encuentran; lugar retirado; parte, región*); comisura (*de los labios, los párpados, etc.*); apuro, aprieto, situación difícil; (com.) acaparamiento, monopolio; **around the corner** a la vuelta de la esquina; **out of the corner of one's eye** con el rabillo del ojo; **to cut corners** atajar; economizar acortando gastos, esfuerzos, tiempo, etc.; **to get someone in a corner** arrinconarle a uno; poner a uno en situación difícil; **to turn the corner** pasar el punto más peligroso; *adj* de esquina, p.ej., **corner room** habitación de esquina; *va* arrinconar; (com.) acaparar, monopolizar
corner bead *s* guardavivo
corner block *s* (carp.) coda
corner chair *s* silla de rincón
corner cupboard *s* rinconera (*armario*)
cornerstone ['kɔrnər,ston] *s* piedra angular; primera piedra (*de un nuevo edificio*); (fig.) piedra angular; **to lay the cornerstone** poner la primera piedra
cornerways ['kɔrnər,wez] o **cornerwise** ['kɔrnər,waɪz] *adv* diagonalmente
cornet [kɔr'nɛt] *s* (mus.) corneta, cornetín; ['kɔrnɛt] o [kɔr'nɛt] *s* cucurucho (*papel arrollado en forma de cono*); toca (*de las hermanas de la caridad*); (Brit.) corneta (*oficial de caballería que llevaba el estandarte*); (Brit.) helado de barquillo, cucurucho
cornetist o **cornettist** [kɔr'nɛtɪst] *s* (mus.) corneta, cornetín
corn exchange *s* bolsa de granos
cornfield ['kɔrn,fild] *s* (U.S.A.) maizal; (England) trigal; (Scotland) avenal
corn flour *s* harina de maíz
cornflower ['kɔrn,flaʊər] *s* (bot.) cabezuela, aciano; (bot.) neguillón; (Brit.) almidón de maíz
corn gromwell *s* (bot.) mijo de sol agreste
cornhusk ['kɔrn,hʌsk] *s* perfolla
cornice ['kɔrnɪs] *s* sobrepuerta; cornisa (*crestería de nieve*); (arch.) cornisa
Cornish ['kɔrnɪʃ] *adj* córnico; *s* córnico (*idioma*)
Cornishman ['kɔrnɪʃmən] *s* (*pl:* **-men**) habitante de Cornualles
Corn Laws *spl* (Brit.) leyes que prohibían o limitaban la importación del trigo
corn liquor *s* chicha
corn meal *s* harina de maíz
corn on the cob *s* maíz en la mazorca
corn pith *s* meollo del tallo del maíz
corn plaster *s* emplasto para los callos
corn pone *s* pan de maíz
corn popper *s* tostador de maíz
corn poppy *s* (bot.) amapola
corn rose *s* (bot.) amapola; (bot.) neguillón
corn salad *s* (bot.) valerianilla
corn shock *s* hacina de tallos de maíz
corn silk *s* cabellos, barbas del maíz
cornstalk ['kɔrn,stɔk] *s* tallo de maíz
cornstarch ['kɔrn,stɑrtʃ] *s* almidón de maíz
corn sugar *s* azúcar hecho de almidón de maíz
corn syrup *s* jarabe hecho de maíz
cornu ['kɔrnjʊ] *s* (*pl:* **-nua** [njʊə]) (anat.) cuerno
cornu ammonis [ə'monɪs] *s* (anat. & pal.) cuerno de Amón
cornucopia [,kɔrnə'kopɪə] *s* cornucopia
Cornwall ['kɔrnwɔl] o ['kɔrnwəl] *s* Cornualles
corn worm *s* (ent.) gusano del maíz
corny ['kɔrnɪ] *adj* (*comp:* **-ier;** *super:* **-iest**)

de maíz; de trigo; calloso; (dial.) que sabe a malta; (coll.) falto de espontaneidad, muy sentimental (*dícese de la música*); (slang) muy malo, muy pesado; (slang) gastado, trillado, trivial
corolla [kəˈrɑlə] *s* (bot.) corola
corollary [ˈkɑrəˌlɛrɪ] o [ˈkɔrəˌlɛrɪ] *s* (*pl:* **-ies**) corolario; deducción; consecuencia natural
corona [kəˈronə] *s* (*pl:* **-nas** o **-nae** [ni]) corona; (astr., elec. & meteor.) corona
Corona Australis [ɔˈstrelɪs] *s* (astr.) Corona austral
Corona Borealis [ˌborɪˈælɪs] o [ˌborɪˈelɪs] *s* (astr.) Corona boreal
coronach [ˈkɔrənəx] *s* (Scotch) endecha, canto fúnebre
coronal [ˈkɑrənəl] o [ˈkɔrənəl] *adj* coronal; *s* corona
coronal suture *s* (anat.) sutura coronal
coronary [ˈkɑrəˌnɛrɪ] o [ˈkɔrəˌnɛrɪ] *adj* coronario
coronary thrombosis *s* (path.) trombosis coronaria, trombosis de las coronarias
coronation [ˌkɑrəˈneʃən] o [ˌkɔrəˈneʃən] *s* coronación
coroner [ˈkɑrənər] o [ˈkɔrənər] *s* juez de guardia, córoner
coroner's inquest *s* pesquisa dirigida por el juez de guardia
coroner's jury *s* jurado del juez de guardia
coronet [ˈkɑrənɛt] o [ˈkɔrənɛt] *s* corona (*que corresponde a un título nobiliario*); diadema (*que sirve de ornamento para la cabeza*); (vet.) corona (*de la cuartilla de un caballo*)
coronium [kəˈronɪəm] *s* (chem.) coronio
corp. o **Corp.** abr. de **Corporal** y **Corporation**
corporal [ˈkɔrpərəl] *adj* corporal; *s* (mil.) cabo; (eccl.) corporal (*lienzo*)
corporally [ˈkɔrpərəlɪ] *adv* corporalmente
corporal punishment *s* (law) castigo corporal
corporate [ˈkɔrpərɪt] *adj* corporativo; colectivo
corporately [ˈkɔrpərɪtlɪ] *adv* corporativamente; corporalmente
corporation [ˌkɔrpəˈreʃən] *s* corporación; sociedad anónima; (coll.) vientre abultado
corporeal [kɔrˈporɪəl] *adj* corpóreo; material, tangible
corposant [ˈkɔrpəzænt] *s* fuego de Santelmo
corps [kor] *s* (*pl:* **corps** [korz]) cuerpo (*conjunto de personas que obran juntamente*); (mil.) cuerpo, cuerpo de ejército
corps area *s* (U.S.A.) distrito militar
corps de ballet [kɔr də bæˈlɛ] *s* cuerpo de baile, cuerpo coreográfico
corpse [kɔrps] *s* cadáver (humano)
corpulence [ˈkɔrpjələns] o **corpulency** [ˈkɔrpjələnsɪ] *s* corpulencia
corpulent [ˈkɔrpjələnt] *adj* corpulento
corpus [ˈkɔrpəs] *s* (*pl:* **corpora** [ˈkɔrpərə]) cadáver; cuerpo (*colección de escritos, leyes, etc.*); (anat.) cuerpo
corpus callosum [kəˈlosəm] *s* (*pl:* **corpora callosa**) (anat.) cuerpo calloso
Corpus Christi [ˈkrɪstɪ] o [ˈkrɪstaɪ] *s* (eccl.) Corpus, día del Cuerpo de Cristo
corpuscle [ˈkɔrpʌsəl] *s* (bot., chem. & phys.) corpúsculo; (physiol.) glóbulo
corpuscular [kɔrˈpʌskjələr] *adj* corpuscular
corpus delicti [dɪˈlɪktaɪ] *s* (law) cuerpo del delito
corpus juris [ˈdʒurɪs] *s* cuerpo de leyes
corpus luteum [ˈlutɪəm] *s* (*pl:* **corpora lutea**) (embryol.) cuerpo lúteo
corr. abr. de **correspondence, correspondent** y **corresponding**
corral [kəˈræl] *s* corral; (*pret & pp:* **-ralled;** *ger:* **-ralling**) *va* acorralar
correct [kəˈrɛkt] *adj* correcto; cumplido (*en muestras de urbanidad*); *va* corregir
correction [kəˈrɛkʃən] *s* corrección
correctional [kəˈrɛkʃənəl] *adj & s* correccional
corrective [kəˈrɛktɪv] *adj & s* correctivo
correctness [kəˈrɛktnɪs] *s* corrección
correlate [ˈkɑrəlet] o [ˈkɔrəlet] *va* correlacionar; *vn* correlacionarse
correlation [ˌkɑrəˈleʃən] o [ˌkɔrəˈleʃən] *s* correlación
correlative [kəˈrɛlətɪv] *adj & s* correlativo

correspond [ˌkɑrɪˈspɑnd] o [ˌkɔrɪˈspɑnd] *vn* corresponder; corresponderse (*escribirse*)
correspondence [ˌkɑrɪˈspɑndəns] o [ˌkɔrɪˈspɑndəns] *s* correspondencia
correspondence course *s* curso por correspondencia
correspondence school *s* escuela por correspondencia
correspondent [ˌkɑrɪˈspɑndənt] o [ˌkɔrɪˈspɑndənt] *adj* correspondiente; *s* correspondiente, corresponsal
corresponding [ˌkɑrɪˈspɑndɪŋ] o [ˌkɔrɪˈspɑndɪŋ] *adj* correspondiente
correspondingly [ˌkɑrɪˈspɑndɪŋlɪ] o [ˌkɔrɪˈspɑndɪŋlɪ] *adv* correspondientemente
corresponding secretary *s* secretario que atiende la correspondencia
corridor [ˈkɑrɪdər] o [ˈkɔrɪdər] *s* corredor, pasillo; (pol.) corredor
corrigendum [ˌkɑrɪˈdʒɛndəm] o [ˌkɔrɪˈdʒɛndəm] *s* (*pl:* **-da** [də]) error por corregir (*en un manuscrito, libro, etc.*)
corrigible [ˈkɑrɪdʒɪbəl] o [ˈkɔrɪdʒɪbəl] *adj* corregible
corroborant [kəˈrɑbərənt] *adj & s* corroborante
corroborate [kəˈrɑbəret] *va* corroborar
corroboration [kəˌrɑbəˈreʃən] *s* corroboración
corroborative [kəˈrɑbəˌretɪv] o **corroboratory** [kəˈrɑbərəˌtorɪ] *adj* corroborativo
corrode [kəˈrod] *va* corroer; (fig.) corroer (*agobiar, consumir*); *vn* corroerse
corrodible [kəˈrodɪbəl] *adj* corrosible
corrosion [kəˈroʒən] *s* corrosión
corrosive [kəˈrosɪv] *adj & s* corrosivo
corrosive sublimate *s* (chem.) argento vivo sublimado, sublimado corrosivo
corrugate [ˈkɑrəget] o [ˈkɔrəget] *va* acanalar, ondular; corrugar (*el cartón*); arrugar
corrugated iron [ˈkɑrəˌgetɪd] o [ˈkɔrəˌgetɪd] *s* hierro acanalado, hierro ondulado
corrugated paper *s* papel corrugado
corrugation [ˌkɑrəˈgeʃən] o [ˌkɔrəˈgeʃən] *s* acanaladura, ondulación; corrugación; arruga
corrupt [kəˈrʌpt] *adj* corrompido; *va* corromper; *vn* corromperse
corruptibility [kəˌrʌptɪˈbɪlɪtɪ] *s* corruptibilidad
corruptible [kəˈrʌptɪbəl] *adj* corruptible
corruption [kəˈrʌpʃən] *s* corrupción
corruptive [kəˈrʌptɪv] *adj* corruptivo
corsage [kɔrˈsɑʒ] *s* corpiño, jubón; ramillete que llevan las mujeres a la cintura, el hombro, etc.
corsair [ˈkɔrsɛr] *s* (naut.) corsario (*pirata; barco de piratas; embarcación armada en corso*)
corselet [ˈkɔrslɪt] *s* coselete (*armadura*); (zool.) coselete (*tórax de los insectos*); [ˌkɔrsəˈlɛt] *s* cuerpecillo, ajustador, corsé ligero
corset [ˈkɔrsɪt] *s* corsé
corset cover *s* cubrecorsé
Corsica [ˈkɔrsɪkə] *s* Córcega
Corsican [ˈkɔrsɪkən] *adj & s* corso; **the Corsican** el Corso (*Napoleón*)
Corsican pine *s* (bot.) pino salgareño, pino negral
corslet [ˈkɔrslɪt] *s* coselete (*armadura*); (zool.) coselete (*tórax de los insectos*)
cortege o **cortège** [kɔrˈtɛʒ] *s* procesión; cortejo, comitiva, séquito
cortex [ˈkɔrtɛks] *s* (*pl:* **-tices** [tɪsiz]) (anat. & bot.) corteza
cortical [ˈkɔrtɪkəl] *adj* cortical
corticate [ˈkɔrtɪket] o **corticated** [ˈkɔrtɪˌketɪd] *adj* cortezudo, corticado
corticotropin [ˌkɔrtɪkoˈtropɪn] *s* (physiol. & pharm.) corticotropina
cortisone [ˈkɔrtɪzon] *s* (physiol. & pharm.) cortisono
corundum [kəˈrʌndəm] *s* (mineral.) corindón
Corunna [koˈrʌnə] *s* La Coruña
coruscate [ˈkɑrəsket] o [ˈkɔrəsket] *vn* brillar, fulgurar, relampaguear
coruscation [ˌkɑrəsˈkeʃən] o [ˌkɔrəsˈkeʃən] *s* brillo, fulgor, relampagueo
corvée [kɔrˈve] *s* prestación vecinal; trabajo impuesto por la ley
corvet o **corvette** [kɔrˈvɛt] *s* (naut.) corbeta
corvine [ˈkɔrvaɪn] o [ˈkɔrvɪn] *adj* corvino
Corybant [ˈkɑrɪbænt] o [ˈkɔrɪbænt] *s* (*pl:*

-bantes ['bæntiz]) coribante (*sacerdote de Cibeles*)
Corybantic [,karɪ'bæntɪk] o [,kɔrɪ'bæntɪk] *adj* de coribantes, de los coribantes
Corycian Cave [kə'rɪʃən] *s* gruta Coriciana
corylaceous [,karɪ'leʃəs] *adj* (bot.) coriláceo
corymb ['karɪmb] o ['kɔrɪmb] *s* (bot.) corimbo
corymbose [ko'rɪmbos] *adj* corimboso
coryphaeus [,karɪ'fiəs] *s* (*pl:* **-phaei** ['fiaɪ]) corifeo
coryphee [,korɪ'fe] *s* bailarina; primera bailarina
coryza [ko'raɪzə] *s* (path.) coriza
cos abr. de **cosine**
cos [kas] o [kɔs] *s* (bot.) lechuga Cos
cosec abr. de **cosecant**
cosecant [ko'sikənt] *s* (trig.) cosecante
cosignatory [ko'sɪgnə,torɪ] *adj* cosignatario; *s* (*pl:* **-ries**) cosignatario
cosine ['kosaɪn] *s* (trig.) coseno
cos lettuce *s* var. de **cos**
cosmetic [kaz'mɛtɪk] *adj & s* cosmético
cosmic ['kazmɪk] *adj* cósmico
cosmically ['kazmɪkəlɪ] *adv* según las leyes cósmicas; vastamente, con gran extensión
cosmic rays *spl* (phys.) rayos cósmicos
cosmogonic [,kazmə'ganɪk] o **cosmogonical** [,kazmə'ganɪkəl] *adj* cosmogónico
cosmogony [kaz'magənɪ] *s* (*pl:* **-nies**) cosmogonía
cosmographer [kaz'magrəfər] *s* cosmógrafo
cosmographic [,kazmə'græfɪk] o **cosmographical** [,kazmə'græfɪkəl] *adj* cosmográfico
cosmography [kaz'magrəfɪ] *s* cosmografía
cosmologist [kaz'malədʒɪst] *s* cosmólogo
cosmology [kaz'malədʒɪ] *s* cosmología
cosmonaut ['kazmənɔt] *s* cosmonauta
cosmopolitan [,kazmə'palɪtən] *adj & s* cosmopolita
cosmopolitanism [,kazmə'palɪtənɪzəm] *s* cosmopolitismo
cosmopolite [kaz'mapəlaɪt] *s* cosmopolita
cosmorama [,kazmə'ræmə] o [,kazmə'ramə] *s* cosmorama
cosmos ['kazməs] o ['kazmas] *s* cosmos (*universo*); (bot.) cosmos
Cossack ['kasæk] *adj & s* cosaco
cosset ['kasɪt] *s* cordero domesticado y mimado; animal domesticado y mimado; *va* mimar, acariciar
cost [kɔst] o [kast] *s* costa, coste, costo; **costs** *spl* (law) costas; **at cost** a precio de coste, a coste y costas; **at all costs** o **at any cost** a toda costa; (*pret & pp:* **cost**) *va & vn* costar; **cost what it may** cueste lo que cueste
cost accounting *s* (com.) escandallo
costal ['kastəl] o ['kɔstəl] *adj* (anat.) costal
costard ['kastərd] o ['kɔstərd] *s* variedad de manzana inglesa; (hum.) cabeza
Costa Rican ['kastə 'rikən] o ['kɔstə 'rikən] *adj & s* costarriqueño
coster ['kastər] o ['kɔstər] o **costermonger** ['kastər,mʌŋgər] o ['kɔstər,mʌŋgər] *s* (Brit.) vendedor ambulante de frutas, legumbres, pescado, etc.
cost, insurance, and freight *s* (com.) costo, seguro y flete
costive ['kastɪv] o ['kɔstɪv] *adj* estreñido
costliness ['kɔstlɪnɪs] o ['kastlɪnɪs] *s* carestía; suntuosidad
costly ['kɔstlɪ] o ['kastlɪ] *adj* (*comp:* **-lier**; *super:* **-liest**) costoso, dispendioso; suntuoso
costmary ['kast,mɛrɪ] o ['kɔst,mɛrɪ] *s* (bot.) hierba de Santa María, costo hortense; (bot.) hierba lombriguera
cost of living *s* costo de la vida
cost-price squeeze ['kɔst'praɪs] o ['kast'praɪs] *s* (coll.) disminución de beneficios debida a la relación estrecha entre el costo de producción y el precio resultante de la competencia
costume ['kastjum] o ['kastum] *s* traje; disfraz; manera de vestirse; [kas'tjum] o [kas'tum] *va* trajear, vestir
costume ball *s* baile de trajes
costume jewelry *s* joyas de fantasía, bisutería
costumer [kas'tjumər] o [kas'tumər] o **costumier** [kas'tjumɪər] o [kas'tumɪər] *s* sastre de máscaras, sastre de teatro, mascarero; percha
cosy ['kozɪ] *adj* (*comp:* **-sier**; *super:* **-siest**) var. de **cozy**; *s* (*pl:* **-sies**) var. de **cozy**
cot abr. de **cotangent**
cot [kat] *s* catre (*cama ligera*); catre de tijera; cabaña, choza; envoltura; (naut.) coy
cotangent [ko'tændʒənt] *s* (trig.) cotangente
cote [kot] *s* abrigo para aves o animales pequeños
Côte-d'Or [,kot'dɔr] *s* Costa de Oro (*en Francia*)
cotenant [ko'tɛnənt] *s* coinquilino
coterie ['kotərɪ] *s* grupo, círculo, cofradía; corrillo
coterminous [ko'tʌrmɪnəs] *adj* var. de **conterminous**
cotillion [kə'tɪljən] *s* cotillón
cottage ['katɪdʒ] *s* cabaña; casita de campo, casita en un lugar de veraneo
cottage cheese *s* naterón, názula, requesón
cottage pudding *s* pudín con salsa dulce
cottager ['katɪdʒər] *s* veraneante que vive en una casita de campo
cottar o **cotter** ['katər] *s* campesino escocés que trabaja por cuenta de algún hacendado y que recibe como parte de su remuneración una cabaña y una porción de terreno
cotter ['katər] o **cotter pin** *s* (mach.) chaveta
cotton ['katən] *s* algodón; (bot.) algodonero; cotón (*tela*); *vn* (coll.) convenir, estar de acuerdo; (coll.) aficionarse
cotton bagging *s* tela de algodón para sacos, sacos de tela de algodón
cotton batting *s* algodón en hojas
cotton field *s* algodonal
cotton flannel *s* franela de algodón
cotton gin *s* desmotadera de algodón
cotton moth *s* (ent.) mariposa del gusano del algodón
cottonmouth ['katən,mauθ] *s* (zool.) mocasín, víbora de agua
cotton picker *s* recogedor de algodón; máquina para recolectar el algodón
cotton plant *s* (bot.) algodonero
cotton plantation *s* plantación de algodón
cotton rose *s* (bot.) amor al uso, flor de la vida
cottonseed ['katən,sid] *s* semilla de algodón
cottonseed meal *s* harina de las semillas del algodón
cottonseed oil *s* aceite de algodón
cottontail ['katən,tel] *s* (zool.) liebre de cola blanca
cotton thistle *s* (bot.) acantio, cardo borriqueño, toba
cotton waste *s* hilacha de algodón, desperdicios de algodón
cottonwood ['katən,wud] *s* (bot.) chopo de la Carolina; (bot.) chopo de Virginia
cotton wool *s* algodón en rama
cotton worm *s* gusano del algodón
cottony ['katənɪ] *adj* algodonoso
cotton yarn *s* hilaza de algodón
cotyledon [,katɪ'lidən] *s* (bot. & embryol.) cotiledón
cotyledonous [,katɪ'lidənəs] *adj* (bot.) cotiledóneo
cotyloid ['katɪlɔɪd] *adj* (anat.) cotiloideo
couch [kautʃ] *s* canapé, sofá, yacija; cama, lecho; *va* poner en canapé, sofá o yacija; expresar; bajar o inclinar en posición de ataque; enristrar (*p.ej., una lanza*); *vn* acostarse en canapé, sofá o yacija; agacharse o esconderse para atacar
couch grass *s* (bot.) hierba rastrera; (bot.) grama del norte
Couch's kingbird *s* (orn.) burlisto grande, sirirí
cougar ['kugər] *s* (zool.) puma
cough [kɔf] o [kaf] *s* tos; *va* **to cough down** hacer callar tosiendo; **to cough up** arrojar del pecho tosiendo; (slang) dar, conceder, entregar, sudar; *vn* toser
cough drop *s* pastilla para la tos
cough syrup *s* jarabe para la tos
could [kud] *v aux* pude, p.ej., **I could not come yesterday** no pude venir ayer; podría, p.ej., **I could see you tomorrow** podría ver a Vd. mañana
couldn't ['kudənt] contracción de **could not**

coulee [ˈkulɪ] o **coulée** [kuˈle] *s* cañada, quebrada; raudal de lava
coulomb [kuˈlɑm] *s* (elec.) culombio
coulter [ˈkolter] *s* var. de **colter**
council [ˈkaʊnsəl] *s* consejo (*cuerpo consultivo y administrativo*); ayuntamiento, concejo (*de un municipio*); (eccl.) concilio
councilman [ˈkaʊnsəlmən] *s* (*pl:* **-men**) concejal
council of state *s* consejo de estado
Council of Trent *s* concilio de Trento
council of war *s* consejo de guerra
councilor o **councillor** [ˈkaʊnsələr] *s* conciliar; concejal
counsel [ˈkaʊnsəl] *s* consejo; deliberación; consultor, consejero; grupo de consultores o consejeros; abogado consultor; **to keep one's own counsel** ser muy reservado, no revelar su propio pensamiento; **to take counsel** tomar consejo; (*pret & pp:* **-seled** o **-selled;** *ger:* **-seling** o **-selling**) *va* aconsejar; *vn* aconsejarse
counselor o **counsellor** [ˈkaʊnsələr] *s* consejero; abogado
count [kaʊnt] *s* cuenta; recuento; suma, total; conde; (law) cargo (*cada falta de que se acusa a uno*); (sport) cuento de 10 segundos antes de declarar vencido a un pugilista; **to take the count** (box.) dejarse contar diez; *va* contar; **to count noses** contar personas o cabezas; **to count off** separar contando; **to count out** no incluir, no tener en cuenta; (coll.) vencer en una elección contando incorrectamente los votos; (sport) declarar vencido (*a un pugilista que no puede levantarse después de contarle los 10 segundos*); *vn* contar; tenerse en cuenta; ponerse en cuenta; valer; **to count for** valer; **to count on** contar con; **to count on** + *ger* contar + *inf;* **to count on one's fingers** contar con o por los dedos
countable [ˈkaʊntəbəl] *adj* contable
count-down [ˈkaʊnt,daʊn] *s* recuento descendente hasta cero
countenance [ˈkaʊntɪnəns] *s* semblante; apoyo, patrocinio; serenidad, compostura; **to be out of countenance** estar desconcertado, estar conturbado; **to keep one's countenance** contenerse, estar tranquilo; abstenerse de sonreír o reír; **to lose countenance** agitarse, conturbarse; **to put out of countenance** confundir, avergonzar; *va* dar su aprobación a
counter [ˈkaʊntər] *s* contador (*persona o cosa*); mostrador; ficha; pecho del caballo; (box.) contragolpe; (fencing) contra; (naut.) bovedilla; *adj* contrario, de sentido opuesto; *adv* en el sentido opuesto, al revés; **to run counter to** oponerse a; *va* oponerse a; contradecir; devolver (*p.ej., un golpe*); **to counter with** contestar (*una pregunta, proyecto*) con (*otra pregunta, proyecto, etc.*); *vn* (box.) dar un contragolpe
counteract [,kaʊntərˈækt] *va* contrariar, contrarrestar, neutralizar
counteraction [,kaʊntərˈækʃən] *s* acción contraria, contrarresto, neutralización
counteractive [,kaʊntərˈæktɪv] *adj & s* contrario
counterambush [,kaʊntərˈæmbʊʃ] *s* contraemboscada
counterapproach [ˈkaʊntərə,protʃ] *s* (fort.) contraaproches
counterattack [ˈkaʊntərə,tæk] *s* contraataque; [,kaʊntərəˈtæk] *va & vn* contraatacar
counterattraction [,kaʊntərəˈtrækʃən] *s* atracción contraria
counterbalance [ˈkaʊntər,bæləns] *s* contrapeso, contrabalanza; (rail.) contrapeso (*de la rueda motriz de la locomotora*); [,kaʊntərˈbæləns] *va* contrapesar, contrabalanzar
counterbattery [ˈkaʊntər,bætərɪ] *s* (mil.) contrabatería
counterbrace [ˈkaʊntər,bres] *s* barra de contratensión; *va* contrabracear
countercheck [ˈkaʊntər,tʃɛk] *s* oposición, obstáculo; segunda comprobación; *va* resistir, contrarrestar, estorbar; comprobar por segunda vez
counterclaim [ˈkaʊntər,klem] *s* contrarreclamación; *vn* contrarreclamar
counterclockwise [,kaʊntərˈklɑk,waɪz] *adj* contrario a las agujas de reloj; *adv* en sentido contrario al de las agujas de reloj
countercurrent [ˈkaʊntər,kʌrənt] *s* contracorriente
counterdike [ˈkaʊntər,daɪk] *s* contradique
counter electromotive force *s* (elec.) fuerza contraelectromotriz
counterespionage [ˈkaʊntər,ɛspɪənɪdʒ] o [ˈkaʊntər,ɛspiəˈnɑʒ] *s* contraespionaje
counterfeit [ˈkaʊntərfɪt] *adj* contrahecho, falsificado, fingido; *s* contrahechura, falsificación; moneda falsa; *va* contrahacer; *vn* contrahacer; contrahacerse
counterfeiter [ˈkaʊntər,fɪtər] *s* contrahacedor, falsificador; falsificador de moneda, monedero falso
counterfeit money *s* moneda falsa
counterfessed [,kaʊntərˈfɛst] *adj* (her.) contrafajado
counterflory [,kaʊntərˈflorɪ] *adj* (her.) contraflorado
counterfoil [ˈkaʊntər,fɔɪl] *s* talón (*p.ej., de un cheque*)
counterfort [ˈkaʊntər,fort] *s* (arch.) contrafuerte
counterfugue [ˈkaʊntər,fjug] *s* (mus.) contrafuga
counterguard [ˈkaʊntər,gɑrd] *s* (fort.) contraguardia
counterintelligence [ˈkaʊntərɪnˈtɛlɪdʒəns] *s* contrainteligencia
counterirritant [,kaʊntərˈɪrɪtənt] *adj & s* (med.) contrairritante
counterirritation [ˈkaʊntər,ɪrɪˈteʃən] *s* (med.) contrairritación
counterjumper [ˈkaʊntər,dʒʌmpər] *s* (slang) vendedor o dependiente de tienda
countermand [ˈkaʊntərmænd] o [ˈkaʊntərmɑnd] *s* contramandato, contraorden; [,kaʊntərˈmænd], [,kaʊntərˈmɑnd], [ˈkaʊntərmænd] o [ˈkaʊntərmɑnd] *va* contramandar; revocar, hacer volver
countermarch [ˈkaʊntər,mɑrtʃ] *s* contramarcha; *vn* contramarchar
countermark [ˈkaʊntər,mɑrk] *s* contramarca; [,kaʊntərˈmɑrk] *va* contramarcar
countermeasure [ˈkaʊntər,mɛʒər] *s* paso contrario, contramedida
countermine [ˈkaʊntər,maɪn] *s* (mil.) contramina; *va* (mil. & fig.) contraminar
counteroffensive [,kaʊntərəˈfɛnsɪv] *s* (mil.) contraofensiva
counteropening [ˈkaʊntər,opənɪŋ] *s* (surg.) contraabertura
counterpaly [ˈkaʊntər,pelɪ] *adj* (her.) contrapalado
counterpane [ˈkaʊntər,pen] *s* cubrecama
counterpart [ˈkaʊntər,pɑrt] *s* copia; duplicado; contrafigura; contraparte; (theat.) contrafigura
counterplot [ˈkaʊntər,plɑt] *s* contratreta; (*pret & pp:* **-plotted;** *ger:* **-plotting**) *va* complotar contra; contraminar
counterpoint [ˈkaʊntər,pɔɪnt] *s* (mus.) contrapunto
counterpoise [ˈkaʊntər,pɔɪz] *s* contrapeso; (rad.) contraantena; *va* contrapesar
counterpoison [ˈkaʊntər,pɔɪzən] *s* contraveneno
counterproposal [,kaʊntərprəˈpozəl] *s* contrapropuesta
counterquartered [,kaʊntərˈkwɔrtərd] *adj* (her.) contracuartelado
counterreconnaissance [,kaʊntərrɪˈkɑnɪsəns] *s* (mil.) contrarreconocimiento
counterreformation [ˈkaʊntər,rɛfərˈmeʃən] *s* contrarreforma
Counter Reformation *s* Contrarreforma
counterrevolution [ˈkaʊntər,rɛvəˈluʃən] *s* contrarrevolución
counterround [ˈkaʊntər,raʊnd] *s* (mil.) contrarronda
counterscarp [ˈkaʊntər,skɑrp] *s* (fort.) contraescarpa
countershaft [ˈkaʊntər,ʃæft] o [ˈkaʊntər,ʃɑft] *s* (mach.) contraárbol, contraeje
countersign [ˈkaʊntər,saɪn] *s* contraseña; refrendata (*firma*); (mil.) contraseña; *va* refrendar

countersignature [ˌkauntər'sɪgnətʃər] *s* refrendata
countersink ['kauntərˌsɪŋk] *s* agujero avellanado; avellanador, broca de avellanar; (*pret & pp:* **-sunk**) *va* avellanar; meter (*un tornillo*) en agujero avellanado
countersinking bit *s* broca de avellanar
counterspy ['kauntərˌspaɪ] *s* contraespía
counterstimulant [ˌkauntər'stɪmjələnt] *s* (med.) contraestimulante
counterstroke ['kauntərˌstrok] *s* contragolpe
countersunk ['kauntərˌsʌŋk] *adj* avellanado, perdido; *pret & pp de* **countersink**
countervail ['kauntərˌvel] *va* contrarrestar; contrapesar, compensar; *vn* ser de fuerza igual
counterweight ['kauntərˌwet] *s* contrapeso
countess ['kauntɪs] *s* condesa
counting house *s* despacho, escritorio, oficina
counting room *s* oficina de contabilidad
countless ['kauntlɪs] *adj* incontable, sin cuento
countrified ['kʌntrɪfaɪd] *adj* campesino, rústico; rural
country ['kʌntrɪ] *s* (*pl:* **-tries**) país; campo (*en oposición a la ciudad*); patria (*país a que uno pertenece como ciudadano*); *adj* campestre, rural
country club *s* club campestre
country cousin *s* pariente rústico
country-dance ['kʌntrɪˌdæns] o ['kʌntrɪˌdɑns] *s* baile campestre; contradanza
country estate *s* hacienda de campo, heredad
countryfolk ['kʌntrɪˌfok] *s* gente del campo, campesinos
country gentleman *s* caballero de provincia, dueño acomodado de finca rural
country house *s* quinta, casa de campo
country jake *s* (coll.) patán
country life *s* vida campestre
countryman ['kʌntrɪmən] *s* (*pl:* **-men**) compatriota; campesino, hombre de o del campo
country people *spl* gente del campo
country road *s* camino rural
countryseat ['kʌntrɪˌsit] *s* finca, hacienda, casa de campo algo pretenciosa
countryside ['kʌntrɪˌsaɪd] *s* campiña, campo
country-wide ['kʌntrɪˌwaɪd] *adj* nacional
countrywoman ['kʌntrɪˌwumən] *s* (*pl:* **-women**) compatriota; campesina
countship ['kauntʃɪp] *s* condado
county ['kauntɪ] *s* (*pl:* **-ties**) partido (*distrito*); (hist.) condado
county farm *s* (U.S.A.) hospicio mantenido por el partido
county seat *s* cabeza de partido
coup [ku] *s* golpe, golpe maestro
coup de grâce [ˌkudə'grɑs] *s* golpe de gracia, puñalada de misericordia
coup d'état [ˌkude'tɑ] *s* golpe de estado
coupé [ku'pe] o [kup] *s* cupé (*automóvil*); [ku'pe] *s* cupé (*coche*)
couple ['kʌpəl] *s* par (*conjunto de dos cosas de la misma especie; macho y hembra*); matrimonio (*marido y mujer*); pareja (*dos personas unidas, p.ej., para un baile*); (mech.) par de fuerzas; (elec.) par voltaico; (coll.) dos más o menos; *va* juntar, unir; aparear; (coll.) casar, unir en matrimonio; *vn* juntarse, unirse; aparease; copularse
coupler ['kʌplər] *s* (mach. & rad.) acoplador; (rail.) enganche
couplet ['kʌplɪt] *s* pareado (*dos versos rimados entre sí*); par
coupling ['kʌplɪŋ] *s* junta, unión; acoplamiento; (elec.) acoplador; (rail.) enganche
coupling box *s* (mach.) manguito, collar de acoplamiento; (elec.) caja de empalme
coupling pin *s* (rail.) pasador de enganche
coupling rod *s* (mach.) biela de acoplamiento
coupon ['kupɑn] o ['kjupɑn] *s* cupón
courage ['kʌrɪdʒ] *s* valor, ánimo; firmeza, resolución; **to have the courage of one's convictions** ajustarse abiertamente con su conciencia; **to pluck up courage** hacer de tripas corazón
courageous [kə'redʒəs] *adj* valiente, animoso
courbaril ['kurbərɪl] *s* (bot.) curbaril
courbaril copal *s* anime (*resina*)
courier ['kʌrɪər] o ['kurɪər] *s* estafeta (*mensajero*); guía
Courland ['kurlənd] *s* Curlandia
course [kors] *s* curso; asignatura; decurso; (arti.) trayectoria; (naut.) rumbo, derrota; (naut.) papahigo; (mas.) hilada; plato (*de una comida*); proceder; campo de golf; **in due course** oportunamente, a su debido tiempo; **in the course of** en el decurso de, durante; **of course** por supuesto, naturalmente; **to give course to** dar curso a (*p.ej. las lágrimas*); *va* cazar con perros; correr por; (mas.) poner en hiladas; *vn* correr; corretear; tomar parte en una carrera
courser ['korsər] *s* (poet.) corcel
court [kort] *s* corte (*de un rey*); (law) corte, tribunal; patio, atrio; callejuela; pista (*p.ej., de tennis*); **in open court** en pleno tribunal; **out of court** sin merecer consideración; **to pay court to** hacer la corte a (*un magnate, una mujer, etc.*); *va* cortejar; hacer la corte a; solicitar, buscar
court card *s* carta de figura
court day *s* (law) día hábil
courteous ['kʌrtɪəs] *adj* cortés
courtesan ['kʌrtɪzən] o ['kortɪzən] *s* cortesana
courtesy ['kʌrtɪsɪ] *s* (*pl:* **-sies**) cortesía; **by courtesy** por cortesía
courtezan ['kʌrtɪzən] o ['kortɪzən] *s* var. de **courtesan**
court hand *s* letra de curia
courthouse ['kortˌhaus] *s* casa de tribunales, palacio de justicia
courtier ['kortɪər] *s* cortesano (*palaciego*); cortejador (*el que corteja*)
court jester *s* bufón
courtly ['kortlɪ] *adj* (*comp:* **-lier**; *super:* **-liest**) cortesano, cortés; cortejador, obsequioso
courtly love *s* amor cortés
court-martial ['kort'mɑrʃəl] *s* (*pl:* **courts-martial**) consejo de guerra; juicio por el consejo de guerra; (*pret & pp:* **-tialed** o **-tialled**; *ger:* **-tialing** o **-tialling**) *va* someter a consejo de guerra
court of record *s* tribunal de actas perpetuas
Court of St. James *s* Corte de San Jaime (*corte del soberano británico*)
court of the first instance *s* (law) tribunal de primera instancia
court plaster *s* esparadrapo, tafetán inglés
courtroom ['kortˌrum] o ['kortˌrum] *s* tribunal, sala de justicia
courtship ['kortʃɪp] *s* cortejo (*acción de cortejar a una mujer*); noviazgo
courtyard ['kortˌjɑrd] *s* patio, atrio
cousin ['kʌzən] *s* primo o prima
cousin-german ['kʌzən'dʒʌrmən] *s* (*pl:* **cousins-german**) primo hermano o prima hermana
cousinly ['kʌzənlɪ] *adj* de primo; *adv* como primo
cousinship ['kʌzənʃɪp] *s* primazgo
cove [kov] *s* (naut.) ensenada; escondrijo, rincón protegido; (arch.) bovedilla; (slang) mozo u hombre, tipo raro; *va* (arch.) abovedar
covenant ['kʌvənənt] *s* pacto, convenio; contrato; (Bib.) alianza; *va & vn* pactar, convenir; (*cap.*) *s* pacto firmado entre los presbiterianos escoceses y el parlamento inglés
covenanter ['kʌvənəntər] *s* contratante; (*cap.*) ['kʌvənəntər] o [ˌkʌvə'næntər] *s* Covenantario (*partidario de la liga en defensa de la religión presbiteriana*)
Covenant of the League of Nations *s* Pacto de la Sociedad de las Naciones
covenant of warranty *s* (law) cláusula de evicción de saneamiento
Coventry ['kʌvəntrɪ] o ['kɑvəntrɪ] *s* ciudad del condado de Warwick, Inglaterra; **to send to Coventry** evitar relaciones con
cover ['kʌvər] *s* cubierta; cubierto (*servicio de mesa para una persona*); portada (*de una revista*); **to break cover** salir al aire libre, salir a campo raso; dejarse ver; salir de la espesura; **to take cover** ocultarse; **under cover** bajo cubierto, bajo techado; secreto, oculto; disfrazado; en secreto, cubiertamente; **under cover of** a cubierto de (*p.ej., la noche*); so pretexto de, bajo la apariencia de; **under separate cover** bajo cubierta separada, por separado;

va cubrir; revestir; recorrer (*cierta distancia*); cubrirse (*la cabeza*); empollar; incluir; apuntar con un arma de fuego; cubrir (*el caballo a la yegua*); (mil.) cubrir (*p.ej., la retirada*); **to cover up** cubrir completamente; *vn* cubrirse; (coll.) cubrirse (*satisfacer una deuda o alcance*)

coverage [ˈkʌvərɪdʒ] *s* alcance, envergadura (*cantidad o espacio cubierto*); (ins.) agregado de los riesgos contra los cuales se contrata un seguro; reportaje

coveralls [ˈkʌvərˌɔlz] *spl* mono (*traje de faena*)

cover charge *s* precio del cubierto (*en los restaurantes*)

cover crop *s* (agr.) siembra de cubierta

covered bridge *s* puente cubierto

covered wagon *s* carro entalamado

covered way *s* (fort.) camino cubierto, estrada encubierta

covered wire *s* (elec.) alambre forrado

cover girl *s* (coll.) muchacha hermosa en la portada de una revista

cover glass *s* cubreobjeto, cubierta de vidrio (*para muestras microscópicas*)

covering [ˈkʌvərɪŋ] *s* cubierta, envoltura

covering letter *s* carta adjunta

coverlet [ˈkʌvərlɪt] o **coverlid** [ˈkʌvərlɪd] *s* cubierta, envoltura; cubrecama, sobrecama

coversed sine [ˈkovʌrst] *s* (trig.) coseno verso

cover slip *s* var. de **cover glass**

covert [ˈkʌvərt] *adj* cubierto; secreto, disimulado, furtivo; (law) bajo la protección del marido; *s* abrigo; guarida, escondrijo

covert cloth *s* tela cruzada de lana, generalmente de color pardo

coverture [ˈkʌvərtʃər] *s* cubierta; abrigo, escondrijo

covet [ˈkʌvɪt] *va & vn* codiciar

covetous [ˈkʌvɪtəs] *adj* codicioso

covetousness [ˈkʌvɪtəsnɪs] *s* codicia

covey [ˈkʌvɪ] *s* nidada, pollada; bandada; grupo (*p.ej., de muchachas*)

cow [kaʊ] *s* vaca; elefanta; *va* acobardar, intimidar

coward [ˈkaʊərd] *adj & s* cobarde

cowardice [ˈkaʊərdɪs] *s* cobardía

cowardly [ˈkaʊərdlɪ] *adj* cobarde; *adv* cobardemente

cowbane [ˈkaʊˌben] *s* (bot.) cicuta acuática; (bot.) cicuta mayor

cowbell [ˈkaʊˌbɛl] *s* cencerro

cowbird [ˈkaʊˌbʌrd] *s* (orn.) enmantecado, garrapatero

cowboy [ˈkaʊˌbɔɪ] *s* vaquero, gaucho, caballista

cowboy hat *s* sombrero de vaquero norteamericano

cowcatcher [ˈkaʊˌkætʃər] *s* (rail.) rastrillo delantero; (rail.) trompa (Am.)

cower [ˈkaʊər] *vn* agacharse

cowfish [ˈkaʊˌfɪʃ] *s* (ichth.) pez cofre

cow hand *s* vaquero

cowherd [ˈkaʊˌhʌrd] *s* pastor de vacas, pastor de ganado

cowhide [ˈkaʊˌhaɪd] *s* cuero; zurriago; *va* zurriagar

cowl [kaʊl] *s* cogulla; capucha (*parte superior de la cogulla*); (aut.) bóveda, cubretablero; (aer.) cubierta del motor; (mach.) caperuza; sombrerete de chimenea; *va* poner cogulla a, encapuchar; cubrir con tapa, tapar

cowled [kaʊld] *adj* encapuchado; cuculiforme

cowlick [ˈkaʊˌlɪk] *s* remolino, mechón (*que se levanta sobre la frente*)

cowling [ˈkaʊlɪŋ] *s* (aer.) cubierta del motor

co-worker [koˈwʌrkər] *s* coadjutor; colaborador

cowpea [ˈkaʊˌpi] *s* (bot.) caupí, frijol de maíz, frijol de vaca

cowpox [ˈkaʊˌpɑks] *s* vacuna

cowpuncher [ˈkaʊˌpʌntʃər] *s* (coll.) vaquero, gaucho

cowrie o **cowry** [ˈkaʊrɪ] *s* (*pl:* **-ries**) cauri (*concha que se usa como moneda en muchos pueblos de África*)

cowskin [ˈkaʊˌskɪn] *s* cuero

cowslip [ˈkaʊslɪp] *s* (bot.) primavera; (bot.) hierba centella

cow tree *s* (bot.) árbol de la leche, árbol de vaca

cowwheat [ˈkaʊˌhwit] *s* (bot.) melámpiro

coxa [ˈkɑksə] *s* (*pl:* **-ae** [i]) (anat.) coxal; (ent.) coxa

coxal [ˈkɑksəl] *adj* coxal

coxalgia [kɑkˈsældʒɪə] *s* (path.) coxalgia

coxalgic [kɑkˈsældʒɪk] *adj* coxálgico

coxcomb [ˈkɑksˌkom] *s* mequetrefe; baladrón, fanfarrón; cresta de gallo; gorro de bufón; (bot.) cresta de gallo

coxcombry [ˈkɑksˌkomrɪ] *s* (*pl:* **-ries**) fanfarronería; fanfarronada

coxofemoral [ˌkɑksəˈfɛmərəl] *adj* coxofemoral

coxswain [ˈkɑksən] o [ˈkɑkswen] *s* (naut.) timonel

coy [kɔɪ] *adj* recatado, reservado; retrechero

coyote [kaɪˈotɪ] o [ˈkaɪot] *s* (zool.) coyote

coypu [ˈkɔɪpu] *s* (zool.) coipo

coz [kʌz] *s* (coll.) primo o prima

cozen [ˈkʌzən] *va* trampear, defraudar, engañar, entretener

cozenage [ˈkʌzənɪdʒ] *s* trampa, fraude, engaño, entretenimiento

cozy [ˈkozɪ] *adj* (*comp:* **-zier**; *super:* **-ziest**) cómodo; contento; (Brit.) sociable, charlador; *s* (*pl:* **-zies**) cubretetera

cp. abr. de **compare**

c.p. abr. de **chemically pure** y **candle power**

C.P. abr. de **Chemically Pure, Common Pleas, Common Prayer** y **Court of Probate**

C.P.A. abr. de **certified public accountant**

cpd. abr. de **compound**

cr. abr. de **credit** y **creditor**

crab [kræb] *s* (zool.) cangrejo; (mach.) cabria; (coll.) malhumorado, persona de mal genio; (*cap.*) *s* (astr.) Cáncer; **to catch a crab** (rowing) sacar cangrejos; (*pret & pp:* **crabbed;** *ger:* **crabbing**) *va* (coll.) criticar, censurar; (coll.) echar a perder; *vn* coger cangrejos; (coll.) regañar

crab apple *s* manzana silvestre (*muy estimada para hacer conservas*); (bot.) manzano silvestre

crabbed [ˈkræbɪd] *adj* avinagrado, ceñudo; enredoso, embrollado; escabroso, desigual

crab grass *s* (bot.) hierba rastrera; (bot.) garranchuelo (*Digitaria sanguinalis*)

crab louse *s* (ent.) piojo pegadizo, ladilla

crab tree *s* (bot.) manzano silvestre

crack [kræk] *s* grieta; crujido, estallido; (coll.) golpe estruendoso; (coll.) instante, momento; (slang) prueba; (slang) esfuerzo; (slang) chiste; **at the crack of dawn** al romper el alba ‖ *adj* (coll.) excelente, de primera clase; (coll.) certero (*tirador*) ‖ *va* agrietar; romper haciendo crujir; chasquear (*un látigo*); (coll.) golpear, produciendo un ruido súbito y agudo; (slang) descubrir (*un secreto*); (slang) romper, desbaratar (*una fuerza enemiga*); (slang) decir con gracejo; enloquecer; fraccionar (*petróleo*); abrir (*una caja fuerte*) por la fuerza; **to crack a book** (slang) abrir un libro para estudiarlo; **to crack a bottle** (slang) abrir una botella y beber lo que contiene; **to crack a code** llegar a descifrar un código; **to crack a joke** (slang) decir algo gracioso, decir un chiste; **to crack a smile** (slang) sonreír; **to crack up** (coll.) alabar, elogiar ‖ *vn* agrietarse; crujir; cascarse (*la voz de una persona*); enloquecerse; ceder, someterse; (slang) desbaratarse; fraccionarse (*el petróleo*); **to crack down on** (coll.) reprender severamente, castigar violentamente; **to crack up** fracasar; perder el ánimo, perder la salud; estrellarse (*un avión*)

crackbrain [ˈkrækˌbren] *s* loco, mentecato

crack-brained [ˈkrækˌbrend] *adj* loco, mentecato

crackdown [ˈkrækˌdaʊn] *s* (coll.) reprensión severa

cracked [krækt] *adj* agrietado; picado (*hielo*); chillón; perjudicado; (coll.) loco, mentecato

cracker [ˈkrækər] *s* galleta, galletita; triquitraque (*cohete; rollo de papel que contiene dulces y que produce una pequeña detonación cuando se arrancan las dos extremidades*); (U.S.A.) blanco de baja clase que habita una región apartada de los centros de población en los estados de Georgia y la Florida

cracker-barrel [ˈkrækərˌbærəl] *adj* (coll.) sencillo, íntimo, familiar, sin concierto ni propósito fijo (*dícese de la charla de los aldeanos*)

crackerjack ['krækər,dʒæk] *adj* (slang) excelente, de órdago, muy hábil, muy capaz; *s* (slang) cosa excelente, individuo de gran habilidad
crack filler *s* relleno para hendeduras
cracking ['krækɪŋ] *s* fraccionamiento (*del petróleo*)
crackle ['krækəl] *s* crujido, crepitación; (f.a.) acabado escarchado, pintura jaspeada; (f.a.) grietado (*superficie finamente estriada*); *vn* crujir, crepitar
crackleware ['krækəl,wɛr] *s* (f.a.) grietado
crackling ['kræklɪŋ] *s* crujido, crepitación; chicharrón; chicharrón de pellejo
cracknel ['kræknəl] *s* coscarana, bizcocho duro y quebradizo; **cracknels** *spl* chicharrones; chicharrones de manteca
crack of doom *s* señal del juicio final, señal del fin del mundo
crackpot ['kræk,pɑt] *adj & s* (slang) excéntrico, loco, tarambana
cracksman ['kræksmən] *s* (*pl:* **-men**) (slang) escalador (*ladrón*)
crack-up ['kræk,ʌp] *s* fracaso; colisión; derrota; (coll.) colapso; (aer.) aterrizaje violento
Cracow ['kreko] o ['krækaʊ] *s* Cracovia
cradle ['kredəl] *s* cuna; (min.) artesa oscilante (*para lavar el oro*); (naut.) cuna; armazón (*de la guadaña armada*); (constr.) cuna, plataforma colgante; (surg.) tablilla (*para entablillar huesos rotos*); (telp.) horquilla (*del microteléfono*); (aut.) cojeclavos; (fig.) cuna (*lugar de nacimiento u origen*); **to rob the cradle** escoger un compañero o casarse con una persona mucho más joven; *va* meter o acostar en la cuna; acunar, mecer; (fig.) acunar (*proteger durante la infancia*); (min.) lavar (*el oro*) con artesa oscilante; (naut.) sostener por medio de una cuna; segar con guadaña armada
cradle scythe *s* guadaña armada
cradlesong ['kredəl,sɔŋ] o ['kredəl,sɑŋ] *s* arrullo, canción de cuna
craft [kræft] o [krɑft] *s* arte, arte manual; astucia, maña; oficio, empleo; gremio; embarcación, barco; máquina de volar; *spl* embarcaciones, barcos; máquinas de volar
craftiness ['kræftɪnɪs] o ['krɑftɪnɪs] *s* astucia, maña
craftsman ['kræftsmən] o ['krɑftsmən] *s* (*pl:* **-men**) artesano (*el que ejerce un arte mecánico*); artífice (*artista*)
craftsmanship ['kræftsmənʃɪp] o ['krɑftsmənʃɪp] *s* artesanía
crafty ['kræftɪ] o ['krɑftɪ] *adj* (*comp:* **-ier;** *super:* **-iest**) astuto, mañoso
crag [kræg] *s* despeñadero, peñasco, cima del despeñadero
cragged ['krægɪd] o **craggy** ['krægɪ] *adj* peñascoso, escarpado
crake [krek] *s* (orn.) guión de las codornices; (orn.) rascón de agua
cram [kræm] (*pret & pp:* **crammed;** *ger:* **cramming**) *va* embutir, atracar; (coll.) cargar (*la cabeza a alguien*) con datos o conocimientos; (coll.) aprender apresuradamente; *vn* atracarse; (coll.) sobrecargar la memoria con datos o conocimientos; (coll.) aprender apresuradamente (*especialmente antes de un examen*)
crambo ['kræmbo] *s* juego de hallar rimas o consonantes
cramp [kræmp] *s* grapa, laña; abrazadera, torno; aprieto; calambre (*contracción de los músculos*); *adj* apretado, restringido; nudoso, dificultoso; *va* engrapar, lañar; apretar, restringir; dar o causar calambre a; **to cramp one's style** (slang) cortarle las alas a uno, impedirle a uno manifestar su habilidad
crampfish ['kræmp,fɪʃ] *s* (ichth.) tremielga, torpedo
crampon ['kræmpən] *s* tenazas de garfios (*dispositivo de garfios y cadenas para izar cajas o sillares*); crampón (*para andar por el hielo*); (bot.) raicilla aérea trepadora
cranberry ['kræn,bɛrɪ] *s* (*pl:* **-ries**) (bot.) arándano agrio
cranberry bog *s* arandanedo
cranberry bush *s* (bot.) arándano agrio (*arbusto*); (bot.) mundillo, sauquillo
cranberry tree *s* (bot.) mundillo, sauquillo
crane [kren] *s* (mach.) grúa; aguilón, cigüeña o pescante de chimenea; (naut.) abanico; (orn.) grulla; (orn.) garza; *va* mover o levantar con grúa; estirar (*el cuello como hace la grulla*); *vn* estirar el cuello
crane fly *s* (ent.) típula
crane's-bill o **cranes-bill** ['krenz,bɪl] *s* (bot.) geranio, pico de grulla
cranial ['krenɪəl] *adj* craneal
craniology [,krenɪ'ɑlədʒɪ] *s* craneología
craniometry [,krenɪ'ɑmɪtrɪ] *s* craneometría
craniotomy [,krenɪ'ɑtəmɪ] *s* (*pl:* **-mies**) (surg.) craneotomía
cranium ['krenɪəm] *s* (*pl:* **-niums** o **-nia** [nɪə]) (anat.) cráneo
crank [kræŋk] *s* manivela, manubrio; idea, concepto; capricho; (coll.) maniático; (coll.) malhumorado; *adj* inestable, inseguro; *va* (aut.) hacer girar o hacer arrancar (*el motor*) con la manivela; encorvar para dar forma de manivela
crankcase ['kræŋk,kes] *s* (mach.) cárter del cigüeñal, cárter del motor
crankcase service *s* (aut.) limpieza del cárter
crank handle *s* mango de la manivela; (aut.) manivela de arranque
crankshaft ['kræŋk,ʃæft] o ['kræŋk,ʃɑft] *s* (mach.) cigüeñal, eje motor
cranky ['kræŋkɪ] *adj* (*comp:* **-ier;** *super:* **-iest**) caprichoso, maniático; malhumorado, irritable; inestable, inseguro; encorvado, sinuoso
crannied ['krænɪd] *adj* grietoso
cranny ['krænɪ] *s* (*pl:* **-nies**) grieta, rendija, hendedura
crape [krep] *s* crespón; crespón fúnebre, crespón negro, paño de tumba, gasa
crapehanger ['krep,hæŋər] *s* (slang) aguafiestas
crappie ['kræpɪ] *s* (ichth.) pomosio
craps [kræps] *s* juego de dados; **to shoot craps** jugar o tirar a los dados
crapshooter ['kræp,ʃutər] *s* jugador de dados
crash [kræʃ] *s* desplome; colisión; estallido, crac; fracaso; quiebra, crac financiero; lienzo grueso, cotí burdo; (aer.) aterrizaje violento; *va* romper estrepitosamente; estrellar; hacer mover o ir con fuerza y estrépito; **to crash a party** (slang) asistir a una tertulia sin invitación; **to crash the gate** (slang) colarse, colarse de gorra; *vn* desplomarse; caer, encontrar, chocar o romperse con violencia y estrépito; estallar; quebrar (*en el comercio*); aterrizar violentamente, estrellarse (*un avión*); **to crash against** o **into** estrellarse contra
crash dive *s* (nav.) sumersión instantánea (*de un submarino*)
crash helmet *s* (aer.) casco protector
crash landing *s* aterrizaje violento
crash program *s* programa intensivo
crasis ['kresɪs] *s* (*pl:* **-ses** [siz]) crasia, crasis; (gram.) crasis
crass [kræs] *adj* tosco, espeso; craso (*error*)
crassulaceous [,kræsjə'leʃəs] *adj* (bot.) crasuláceo
Crassus ['kræsəs] *s* Craso
crate [kret] *s* banasta, cesto, cuévano; jaula (*embalaje de tablas colocadas a cierta distancia unas de otras*); *va* embalar en jaula, embalar con tablas
crater ['kretər] *s* cráter; (elec. & mil.) cráter; crátera (*vasija*); (*cap.*) *s* (astr.) Cráter
crating ['kretɪŋ] *s* embalaje en jaulas
cravat [krə'væt] *s* corbata
crave [krev] *va* ansiar, anhelar; pedir (*indulgencia*); *vn* suplicar; **to crave after** ansiar, anhelar; **to crave for** ansiar, anhelar; pedir, pedir con insistencia
craven ['krevən] *adj & s* cobarde; **to cry craven** rendirse
cravenette [,krævə'nɛt] o [,krevə'nɛt] *s* (trademark) tela impermeable; impermeable (*sobretodo*)
craving ['krevɪŋ] *s* ansia, anhelo, sed
craw [krɔ] *s* buche
crawfish ['krɔ,fɪʃ] *s* (zool.) cámbaro, cangrejo de río; (zool.) langosta; *vn* (coll.) desdecirse, retroceder, ceder
crawl [krɔl] *s* reptación; marcha lenta; gateo; (swimming) arrastre; corral (*jaula en el agua*

para encerrar peces, tortugas, etc.); *vn* reptar, arrastrarse; andar o marchar paso a paso; gatear; andar furtivamente; hormiguear (*experimentar cierta sensación en la piel*); **to crawl along** andar o marchar paso a paso; **to crawl forth** u **out** avanzar o salir arrastrándose; **to crawl under** meterse debajo de; **to crawl up** trepar
crawly ['krɔlɪ] *adj* (coll.) hormigueante
crayfish ['kre,fɪʃ] *s* (zool.) cámbaro, cangrejo de río; (zool.) langosta
crayon ['kreən] o ['kreɑn] *s* creyón; dibujo al creyón; *va* dibujar con creyón
craze [krez] *s* moda, boga; manía, locura; estrías finas en la superficie de ciertas especies de vajilla; *va* enloquecer; estriar finamente (*la superficie de la vajilla*)
crazy ['krezɪ] *adj* (*comp:* **-zier;** *super:* **-ziest**) loco, demente; desvencijado; achacoso, débil; loco (*que procede como loco*); **to be crazy about** (coll.) estar loco por; **to drive crazy** volver loco; **crazy as a bedbug** o **as a loon** (slang) loco de atar, loco rematado
crazy bone *s* hueso de la alegría
crazy quilt *s* centón
crazyweed ['krezɪ,wid] *s* (bot.) loco, cascabelito
creak [krik] *s* chirrido, rechinamiento; *va* hacer chirriar o rechinar; *vn* chirriar, rechinar, chillar
creaky ['krikɪ] *adj* (*comp:* **-ier;** *super:* **-iest**) chirriadero, chirriador, rechinador
cream [krim] *s* crema; nata y flor, crema (*p.ej., de la sociedad*); *va* proveer de crema; poner crema en; cocinar con crema o salsa de crema; desnatar (*la leche*); *vn* criar o producir nata; espumar
cream cheese *s* queso crema
creamer ['krimər] *s* cremera
creamery ['krimərɪ] *s* (*pl:* **-ies**) mantequería, quesería, lechería, granja
cream of tartar *s* crémor tártaro
creamometer [kri'mɑmɪtər] *s* cremómetro
cream puff *s* bollo de crema
cream sauce *s* salsa de crema
cream separator *s* desnatadora, descremadora
creamy ['krimɪ] *adj* (*comp:* **-ier;** *super:* **-iest**) cremoso; de color de crema
crease [kris] *s* arruga, pliegue; raya (*de los pantalones*); cris (*daga*); *va* arrugar, plegar; *vn* arrugarse, plegarse
create [kri'et] *va* crear
creation [kri'eʃən] *s* creación; **the Creation** la Creación
creationism [kri'eʃənɪzəm] *s* (philos. & theol.) creacionismo
creative [kri'etɪv] *adj* creador, creativo
creator [kri'etər] *s* creador; **the Creator** el Creador
creature ['kritʃər] *s* criatura; (U.S.A.) animalejo, bicho; criatura (*hechura de otra persona*)
creature comforts *spl* cosas (*alimentos, vestidos*) que confortan el cuerpo
crèche [kreʃ] o [krɛʃ] *s* belén, nacimiento; casa de expósitos; guardería infantil
credence ['kridəns] *s* creencia, fe; credencia, aparador; (eccl.) credencia; **to give credence to** dar fe a, dar crédito a
credential [krɪ'dɛnʃəl] *adj & s* credencial; **credentials** *spl* credenciales; (dipl.) carta credencial
credibility [,krɛdɪ'bɪlɪtɪ] *s* credibilidad
credible ['krɛdɪbəl] *adj* creíble
credit ['krɛdɪt] *s* crédito; (com. & educ.) crédito; **on credit** (com.) a crédito; **to do credit to** acreditar, dar crédito a; **to give a person credit for** concederle a una persona el mérito de; **to give credit to** creer, dar crédito a; (com.) abrir crédito a; **to take credit for** atribuirse el mérito de; *va* creer; (com. & educ.) acreditar; **to credit a person with** atribuirle a una persona el mérito de
creditable ['krɛdɪtəbəl] *adj* honorable, estimable
credit balance *s* saldo acreedor
credit card *s* (com.) tarjeta de crédito
credit line *s* referencia que da el nombre del autor de un escrito que se ha reproducido
credit man *s* investigador de ventas al fiado
creditor ['krɛdɪtər] *s* acreedor
credit union *s* asociación o banco cooperativo
credo ['krido] o ['kredo] *s* (*pl:* **-dos**) credo; (mus.) credo
credulity [krɪ'djulɪtɪ] o [krɪ'dulɪtɪ] *s* credulidad
credulous ['krɛdʒələs] *adj* crédulo
creed [krid] *s* credo
creek [krik] o [krɪk] *s* arroyo; (naut.) ensenada
creel [kril] *s* cesta para pescados; jaula de mimbres (*para coger langostas, etc.*)
creep [krip] *s* arrastramiento; marcha lenta; **the creeps** (coll.) hormigueo (*en la piel*); (*pret & pp:* **crept**) *vn* arrastrarse; andar o mover cautelosa o furtivamente; gatear; trepar; desviarse; hormiguear, sentir hormigueo; **to creep forward** andar avanzando despacio; acercarse insensible o cautelosamente; **to creep in** o **into** insinuarse en; entrar cautelosa o furtivamente en; **to creep out** salir arrastrándose; salir cautelosa o furtivamente; **to creep up on** acercarse a, insensible o cautelosamente
creepage ['kripɪdʒ] *s* (elec.) fluencia, corrimiento, escurrimiento; (elec.) ascenso capilar
creeper ['kripər] *s* rastrero; (bot.) planta rastrera, planta trepadora; (orn.) trepador; **creepers** *spl* crampón, ramplón; prenda de vestir para niños (*comprende la blusa y el pantalón*)
creeping ['kripɪŋ] *s* arrastramiento; marcha lenta; desviación, deslizamiento; *adj* lento; progresivo; (bot.) rastrero
creeping barrage *s* (mil.) barrera de fuego móvil
creeping paralysis *s* (path.) parálisis progresiva
creeping sickness *s* (path.) ergotismo
creepy ['kripɪ] *adj* (*comp:* **-ier;** *super:* **-iest**) (coll.) hormigueante; lento; **to feel creepy** (coll.) hormiguear; (coll.) tener carne de gallina
creese [kris] *s* cris (*daga*)
cremate ['krimet] o [krɪ'met] *va* incinerar
cremation [krɪ'meʃən] *s* cremación, incineración de cadáveres
cremator ['krimetər] o [krɪ'metər] *s* persona que incinera cadáveres; horno crematorio
crematory ['krimə,torɪ] o ['krɛmə,torɪ] *adj* crematorio; *s* (*pl:* **-ries**) crematorio; horno crematorio
crème [krɛm] *s* crema (*nata; licor espeso y dulce*)
crème de menthe [krɛmdə'mɑ̃t] *s* crema de menta
Cremona [krɪ'monə] *s* violín de Cremona
crenate ['krinet] *adj* (bot.) crenato
crenation [krɪ'neʃən] *s* (bot.) crena, muesca; (anat.) crena
crenelate o **crenellate** ['krɛnəlet] *va* (fort.) almenar
Creole ['kriol] *adj & s* criollo; (*l.c.*) *s* criollo, negro criollo
creosol ['kriəsol] *s* (chem.) creosol
creosote ['kriəsot] *s* creosota; *va* creosotar
creosote oil *s* aceite de creosota
crepe o **crêpe** [krep] *s* crespón
crepe de Chine [,krepdə'ʃin] *s* crespón de la China
crepitant ['krɛpɪtənt] *adj* crepitante
crepitate ['krɛpɪtet] *vn* crepitar
crepitation [,krɛpɪ'teʃən] *s* crepitación; (med.) crepitación
crept [krɛpt] *pret & pp de* **creep**
crepuscular [krɪ'pʌskjələr] *adj* crepuscular
crescendo [krə'ʃɛndo] *s* (*pl:* **-dos**) (mus.) crescendo
crescent ['krɛsənt] *adj* creciente; *s* media luna (*figura de cuarto de luna creciente o menguante; mahometismo; imperio turco*); panecillo (*de figura de media luna*); (astr.) creciente, creciente de la luna; (her.) creciente
cresol ['krisɑl] *s* (chem.) cresol
cress [krɛs] *s* (bot.) mastuerzo
cresset ['krɛsɪt] *s* hachón, almenar, tedero
Cressida ['krɛsɪdə] *s* (myth.) Criseida
crest [krɛst] *s* cresta (*copete, penacho de las aves; cima de una ola; cima, copete de una montaña; cimera sobre el morrión*); (anat., arch., bot., mach. & zool.) cresta; (her.) cimera, crista

crested [ˈkrɛstɪd] *adj* crestado
crested grebe *s* (orn.) somorgujo moñudo
crested lark *s* (orn.) cochevís, cogujada, vejeta
crestfallen [ˈkrɛstˌfɔlən] *adj* cabizbajo, con las orejas caídas
cretaceous [krɪˈteʃəs] *adj* cretáceo; (*cap.*) *adj & s* (geol.) cretáceo
Cretan [ˈkritən] *adj & s* cretense
Crete [krit] *s* Creta
cretin [ˈkritɪn] *s* cretino
cretinism [ˈkritɪnɪzəm] *s* (path.) cretinismo
cretonne [krɪˈtɑn] o [ˈkritɑn] *s* cretona
crevasse [krəˈvæs] *s* grieta en un alud; (U.S.A.) brecha en un dique o malecón
crevice [ˈkrɛvɪs] *s* grieta
crew [kru] *s* equipo; personal; tripulación o dotación (*de un buque o máquina de volar*); cuadrilla, banda; (sport) remo (*deporte de los remeros para carreras*); (sport) dotación (*de remeros*); *pret de* **crow**
crew cut *s* corte de pelo a cepillo
crewel [ˈkruəl] *s* estambre (*para bordar*)
crew member *s* tripulante, miembro de la tripulación
crib [krɪb] *s* camilla de niño; pesebre; granero; chiribitil (*cuarto muy pequeño*); (constr.) armazón de sustentación; (hyd.) cofre, cajón; (min.) brocal de entibación; (slang) chuleta (*notas que se usan a hurtadillas en un examen*); (coll.) plagio; (*pret & pp:* **cribbed**; *ger:* **cribbing**) *va* enjaular o encerrar dentro de un espacio muy pequeño; (coll.) plagiar; *vn* (slang) usar a hurtadillas claves o notas (*en un examen*)
cribbage [ˈkrɪbɪdʒ] *s* juego de naipes en que se cuentan los tantos con clavijas que encajan en una tableta
crick [krɪk] *s* calambre; *va* hacer padecer un calambre
cricket [ˈkrɪkɪt] *s* (ent.) grillo; (sport) cricquet; escabel, taburete; (coll.) juego limpio; *vn* (sport) jugar al cricquet
cricketer [ˈkrɪkɪtər] *s* (sport) cricquetero
cricoid [ˈkraɪkɔɪd] *adj & s* (anat.) cricoides
crier [ˈkraɪər] *s* pregonero; baladrero; lamentador
crime [kraɪm] *s* crimen, delito
Crimea [kraɪˈmiə] o [krɪˈmiə] *s* Crimea
Crimean [kraɪˈmiən] o [krɪˈmiən] *adj* de Crimea
Crimean War *s* guerra de Crimea
criminal [ˈkrɪmɪnəl] *adj & s* criminal
criminal code *s* (law) código penal
criminal conversation *s* (law) adulterio
criminality [ˌkrɪmɪˈnælɪtɪ] *s* (*pl:* **-ties**) criminalidad
criminal law *s* derecho penal, jurisprudencia criminal
criminally [ˈkrɪmɪnəlɪ] *adv* criminalmente
criminal negligence *s* imprudencia temeraria
criminate [ˈkrɪmɪnet] *va* criminar
crimination [ˌkrɪmɪˈneʃən] *s* criminación
criminatory [ˈkrɪmɪnəˌtorɪ] *adj* acriminador
criminological [ˌkrɪmɪnəˈlɑdʒɪkəl] *adj* criminológico
criminologist [ˌkrɪmɪˈnɑlədʒɪst] *s* criminólogo
criminology [ˌkrɪmɪˈnɑlədʒɪ] *s* criminología
crimp [krɪmp] *s* encrespadura, rizado; arruga; rizo (*de pelo*); persona que recluta con fuerza o engaño; **to put a crimp in** (slang) estorbar, impedir; *va* encrespar, rizar; arrugar; reclutar con fuerza o engaño
crimping iron *s* encrespador, rizador
crimple [ˈkrɪmpəl] *va* encrespar, rizar, arrugar; *vn* encresparse, rizarse, arrugarse
crimpy [ˈkrɪmpɪ] *adj* (*comp:* **-ier**; *super:* **-iest**) encrespado, rizado, arrugado
crimson [ˈkrɪmzən] *adj & s* carmesí; *va* teñir de carmesí; enrojecer; *vn* enrojecerse
crimson clover *s* (bot.) trébol encarnado, trébol del Rosellón
cringe [krɪndʒ] *s* adulación, bajeza; *vn* arrastrarse, reptar, encogerse
cringle [ˈkrɪŋgəl] *s* (naut.) garrucho
crinière [ˌkriˈnjɛr] *s* (arm.) capizana
crinkle [ˈkrɪŋkəl] *s* arruga, pliegue; rizo u onda (*en el agua*); susurro, crujido; *va* arrugar, plegar; *vn* arrugarse; serpentear; susurrar, crujir
crinkly [ˈkrɪŋklɪ] *adj* (*comp:* **-klier**; *super:* **-kliest**) arrugado; ondulado; susurrante, crujidero
crinoid [ˈkraɪnɔɪd] o [ˈkrɪnɔɪd] *adj & s* (zool.) crinoideo
crinoline [ˈkrɪnəlɪn] o [ˈkrɪnəlin] *s* crinolina
cripple [ˈkrɪpəl] *adj & s* lisiado, baldado, estropeado; *va* lisiar, baldar, estropear; dañar, perjudicar; (naut.) desarbolar, desmantelar
crisis [ˈkraɪsɪs] *s* (*pl:* **-ses** [siz]) crisis
crisp [krɪsp] *adj* frágil, quebradizo; crespo, rizado; agudo; decisivo; refrescante; *va* hacer frágil o quebradizo; encrespar, rizar; ondular; *vn* encresparse, rizarse; ondularse
crispy [ˈkrɪspɪ] *adj* (*comp:* **-ier**; *super:* **-iest**) var. de **crisp**
crisscross [ˈkrɪsˌkrɔs] o [ˈkrɪsˌkrɑs] *s* cruz (*figura; firma*); líneas cruzadas; cristus; juego del tres en raya; *adj* cruzado; *adv* en cruz, en forma de cruz; *va* marcar o cubrir con líneas cruzadas; *vn* entrecruzarse
criterion [kraɪˈtɪrɪən] *s* (*pl:* **-a** [ə] u **-ons**) criterio
critic [ˈkrɪtɪk] *s* crítico; criticón (*persona que todo lo critica*)
critical [ˈkrɪtɪkəl] *adj* crítico; criticón
critical angle *s* (aer. & opt.) ángulo crítico
critical edition *s* edición crítica
critical mass *s* (phys.) masa crítica
critical pressure *s* (phys.) presión crítica
critical temperature *s* (phys.) temperatura crítica
criticise [ˈkrɪtɪsaɪz] *va & vn* var. de **criticize**
criticism [ˈkrɪtɪsɪzəm] *s* crítica; (philos.) criticismo
criticize [ˈkrɪtɪsaɪz] *va & vn* criticar
critique [krɪˈtik] *s* crítica; ensayo crítico
croak [krok] *s* graznido (*p.ej., del cuervo*); canto de las ranas; *va* (slang) matar; *vn* graznar (*el cuervo, el grajo, etc.*); croar (*la rana*); gruñir; presagiar el mal; (slang) reventar (*morir*)
croaker [ˈkrokər] *s* gruñidor, refunfuñador; graznador; (ichth.) roncador, corvina blanca
Croat [ˈkroæt] *s* croata (*natural o habitante; idioma*)
Croatia [kroˈeʃə] *s* Croacia
Croatian [kroˈeʃən] *adj & s* croata
crocein [ˈkrosɪɪn] *s* (chem.) croceína
crochet [kroˈʃe] *s* croché; (*pret & pp:* **-cheted** [ˈʃed]; *ger:* **-cheting** [ˈʃeɪŋ]) *va* trabajar con aguja de croché; *vn* hacer croché
crochet needle *s* aguja de croché, aguja de gancho
crocin [ˈkrosɪn] *s* (chem.) crocina
crock [krɑk] *s* vasija de barro cocido, vasija de loza, cacharro
crockery [ˈkrɑkərɪ] *s* loza
crocket [ˈkrɑkɪt] *s* (arch.) follaje
crocodile [ˈkrɑkədaɪl] *s* (zool.) cocodrilo
crocodile tears *spl* lágrimas de cocodrilo
crocodilian [ˌkrɑkəˈdɪlɪən] *adj & s* (zool.) cocodriliano
crocus [ˈkrokəs] *s* (bot.) azafrán
Croesus [ˈkrisəs] *s* (biog. & fig.) Creso
croft [krɔft] o [krɑft] *s* (Brit.) campo pequeño encerrado; (Brit.) granja muy pequeña
crofter [ˈkrɔftər] o [ˈkrɑftər] *s* (Brit.) persona que cultiva una granja muy pequeña
Cro-Magnon [kroˈmægnɑn] *adj* (anthrop.) cromañonense; *s* (anthrop.) cromañón
cromlech [ˈkrɑmlɛk] *s* crómlech o crónlech
crone [kron] *s* vieja acartonada
Cronos [ˈkronɑs] o **Cronus** [ˈkronəs] *s* (myth.) Cronos
crony [ˈkronɪ] *s* (*pl:* **-nies**) camarada, compinche
crook [krʊk] *s* gancho, garfio; curva, curvatura; cayado (*que usan los pastores*); (mus.) tudel (*del bajón*); (coll.) fullero, ladrón; *va* encorvar; (slang) empinar (*el codo*); *vn* encorvarse
crooked [ˈkrʊkɪd] *adj* curvo, encorvado, torcido; (fig.) torcido (*dícese de una persona o su conducta*); **to go crooked** (coll.) torcerse (*desviarse del camino recto de la virtud*)
Crookes space [krʊks] *s* (phys.) espacio de Crookes
Crookes tube *s* (phys.) tubo de Crookes

crookneck ['krʊk,nɛk] *s* (bot.) calabaza de cuello torcido
crooknecked ['krʊk,nɛkt] *adj* de cuello torcido
croon [krun] *s* canturreo; *va & vn* cantar con voz suave, cantar con melancolía exagerada
crooner ['krunər] *s* cantor de voz suave, cantor melancólico
crop [krɑp] *s* cosecha; (fig.) cosecha (*p.ej., de mentiras*); cabellera; cabello corto; señal producida recortando las orejas a los animales; buche (*del ave*); látigo mocho, remate de látigo; (fig.) hornada (*de citas, héroes, etc.*); (*pret & pp:* **cropped;** *ger:* **cropping**) *va* sembrar y cosechar; cortar; desorejar; desmochar; esquilar, trasquilar; pacer (*la hierba*); *vn* cosechar; **to crop out** o **up** (min.) aflorar; asomar, dejarse ver, manifestarse inesperadamente
crop dusting *s* aerofumigación, fumigación aérea, pulverización agrícola
cropper ['krɑpər] *s* cultivador; (coll.) caída pesada; (coll.) fracaso; **to come a cropper** (coll.) caer pesadamente; (coll.) fracasar
croquet [kro'ke] *s* argolla, croquet (*juego*)
croquette [kro'kɛt] *s* croqueta
crosier ['kroʒər] *s* cayado, báculo pastoral; (bot.) fronda circinada (*de los helechos*)
cross [krɔs] o [krɑs] *s* cruz; cruce (*de dos caminos; de razas*); (elec.) cruzamiento; (fig.) cruz, calvario (*sufrimiento moral*); **the Cross** la Cruz, la Santa Cruz; **to make the sign of the cross** hacerse la señal de la cruz; **to take the cross** cruzarse (*alistarse en una cruzada*) ‖ *adj* transversal; travieso; cruzado (*de raza mixta*); malhumorado ‖ *va* cruzar; contrariar; frustrar; **to cross a person's path** cruzar el camino de una persona; **to cross a road** atravesar o cruzar un camino; **to cross off** u **out** borrar; **to cross oneself** hacerse la señal de la cruz; **to cross one's fingers** cruzar los dedos (*por superstición*); **to cross one's heart** hacerse la señal de la cruz sobre el corazón (*como juramento de integridad*); **to cross one's legs** cruzar las piernas; **to cross one's mind** ocurrírsele a uno; **to cross swords** cruzar las espadas (*batirse*); **to cross the Atlantic** cruzar el Atlántico; **to cross the street** atravesar o cruzar la calle; **to cross up** servir de obstáculo a ‖ *vn* cruzar; cruzarse; **to cross over** atravesar de un lado a otro
crossbar ['krɔs,bɑr] o ['krɑs,bɑr] *s* travesaño; raya o lista al través o transversal
crossbeam ['krɔs,bim] o ['krɑs,bim] *s* viga transversal
crossbill ['krɔs,bɪl] o ['krɑs,bɪl] *s* (orn.) piquituerto
cross bond *s* (elec.) conexión entre riel y alimentador; (mas.) aparejo cruzado
crossbones ['krɔs,bonz] o ['krɑs,bonz] *spl* huesos cruzados (*símbolo de la muerte*)
crossbow ['krɔs,bo] o ['krɑs,bo] *s* ballesta
crossbowman ['krɔs,bomən] o ['krɑs,bomən] *s* (*pl:* **-men**) ballestero
cross bracing *s* arriostramiento transversal
crossbred ['krɔs,brɛd] o ['krɑs,brɛd] *adj* cruzado (*de raza*)
crossbreed ['krɔs,brid] o ['krɑs,brid] *s* híbrido; (*pret & pp:* **-bred**) *va* cruzar (*animales o plantas*)
cross-breeding ['krɔs,bridɪŋ] o ['krɑs,bridɪŋ] *s* cruzamiento
cross bun *s* bollo marcado con la figura de una cruz (*que se come el viernes santo*)
cross-country ['krɔs,kʌntrɪ] o ['krɑs,kʌntrɪ] *adj* a campo traviesa; a través del país, transcontinental; *s* (sport) carrera a pie y a campo traviesa
cross-country flight *s* (aer.) vuelo a través del país
crosscurrent ['krɔs,kʌrənt] o ['krɑs,kʌrənt] *s* contracorriente; (fig.) tendencia contraria
crosscut ['krɔs,kʌt] o ['krɑs,kʌt] *adj* para cortar transversalmente; cortado transversalmente; *s* sierra de través; corte transversal; atajo (*senda*); (min.) galería transversal; (*pret & pp:* **-cut;** *ger:* **-cutting**) *va* cortar o aserrar transversalmente
crosscut file *s* lima de doble picadura
crosscut saw *s* sierra de través, tronzador
crosse [krɔs] o [krɑs] *s* (sport) raquetón (*que sirve para jugar a la crosse*)
crossed anesthesia *s* anestesia cruzada
cross-examination ['krɔsɛg,zæmɪ'neʃən] o ['krɑsɛg,zæmɪ'neʃən] *s* (law) repregunta; interrogatorio riguroso
cross-examine ['krɔsɛg'zæmɪn] o ['krɑsɛg'zæmɪn] *va* (law) repreguntar; interrogar rigurosamente
cross-eye ['krɔs,aɪ] o ['krɑs,aɪ] *s* (path.) estrabismo convergente, vista torcida
cross-eyed ['krɔs,aɪd] o ['krɑs,aɪd] *adj* bisojo, bizco, ojituerto
cross-fertilization ['krɔs,fʌrtɪlɪ'zeʃən] o ['krɑs,fʌrtɪlɪ'zeʃən] *s* (bot. & biol.) fertilización cruzada
cross-fertilize ['krɔs'fʌrtɪlaɪz] o ['krɑs'fʌrtɪlaɪz] *va* fecundar por fertilización cruzada; *vn* fecundarse por fertilización cruzada
cross fire *s* (mil.) fuego cruzado
cross-grained ['krɔs'grend] o ['krɑs'grend] *adj* de contrafibra, de contrahilo; intratable, terco
cross hair *s* (opt.) hilo cruzado
crosshatch ['krɔs,hætʃ] o ['krɑs,hætʃ] *va* marcar con rayitas cruzadas; *vn* marcarse con rayitas cruzadas
crosshead ['krɔs,hɛd] o ['krɑs,hɛd] *s* (mach.) cruceta
crossing ['krɔsɪŋ] o ['krɑsɪŋ] *s* cruce (*de líneas, calles, etc.*); travesía (*del mar*); vado (*de un río*); crucero, paso a nivel (*de ferrocarril*); (arch.) crucero (*sitio en que se cruzan las naves transversal y principal de una iglesia*)
crossing gate *s* (rail.) barrera, barrera de paso a nivel
crossing point *s* punto de cruce
crossjack ['krɔs,dʒæk] o ['krɑs,dʒæk] *s* (naut.) vela de mesana
cross-legged ['krɔs'lɛgɪd], ['krɑs'lɛgɪd], ['krɔs,lɛgd] o ['krɑs,lɛgd] *adj* con los pies cruzados; con las piernas cruzadas
crosslet ['krɔslɪt] o ['krɑslɪt] *s* crucecita
cross-over ['krɔs,ovər] o ['krɑs,ovər] *s* crucero, traspaso; (biol.) recombinación, cruzamiento intercromosómico; (elec.) cruce de conductores
crosspatch ['krɔs,pætʃ] o ['krɑs,pætʃ] *s* (coll.) malhumorado, gruñón
crosspiece ['krɔs,pis] o ['krɑs,pis] *s* travesaño; cruceta (*de un enrejado*)
cross-pollinate ['krɔs'pɑlɪnet] o ['krɑs'pɑlɪnet] *va* fecundar por polinización cruzada; *vn* fecundarse por polinización cruzada
cross-pollination ['krɔs,pɑlɪ'neʃən] o ['krɑs,pɑlɪ'neʃən] *s* (bot.) polinización cruzada
cross-purpose ['krɔs'pʌrpəs] o ['krɑs'pʌrpəs] *s* disposición contraria, propósito contrario; **cross-purposes** *spl* juego de preguntas y respuestas en el cual se usan palabras de diferentes significados; **at cross-purposes** sin comprenderse uno a otro; oponiéndose uno a otro involuntariamente
cross-question ['krɔs'kwɛstʃən] o ['krɑs'kwɛstʃən] *s* (law) repregunta; *va* (law) repreguntar
crossrail ['krɔs,rel] o ['krɑs,rel] *s* travesaño
cross-refer [,krɔsrɪ'fʌr] o [,krɑsrɪ'fʌr] (*pret & pp:* **-ferred;** *ger:* **-ferring**) *va & vn* contrarreferir
cross reference *s* contrarreferencia, remisión
crossroad ['krɔs,rod] o ['krɑs,rod] *s* vía o camino transversal; vía conectadora; **crossroads** *spl* cruce, encrucijada; **at the crossroads** en el momento crítico
crossruff ['krɔs,rʌf] o ['krɑs,rʌf] *s* (cards) jugada en la cual cada compañero juega un naipe que se puede matar con el triunfo del otro
cross sea *s* (naut.) mar alborotada en que las olas corren en sentidos opuestos
cross section *s* sección transversal, corte transversal; (fig.) sección representativa (*de un grupo de personas, cosas, etc.*)
cross spider *s* (ent.) araña epeira
cross-staff ['krɔs,stæf] o ['krɑs,stɑf] *s* escuadra de agrimensor; (naut.) ballestilla
cross-stitch ['krɔs,stɪtʃ] o ['krɑs,stɪtʃ] *s* puntada cruzada; bordado hecho con puntadas cruzadas; *va* bordar o coser con puntadas cruzadas
cross street *s* calle de travesía, calle traviesa
crosstie ['krɔs,taɪ] o ['krɑs,taɪ] *s* (rail.) traviesa, durmiente

crosstree ['krɔs,tri] o ['krɑs,tri] *s* (naut.) cruceta
cross vault *s* (arch.) bóveda por arista
crossway ['krɔs,we] o ['krɑs,we] *s* var. de **crossroad**
crossways ['krɔs,wez] o ['krɑs,wez] o **crosswise** ['krɔs,waɪz] o ['krɑs,waɪz] *adv* al través; en cruz; mal, equivocadamente
cross wire *s* (opt.) hilo cruzado
crossworder ['krɔs,wʌrdər] o ['krɑs,wʌrdər] *s* crucigramista
crossword puzzle ['krɔs,wʌrd] o ['krɑs,wʌrd] *s* crucigrama
crosswort ['krɔs,wʌrt] o ['krɑs,wʌrt] *s* (bot.) cruciata
crossyard ['krɔs,jɑrd] o ['krɑs,jɑrd] *s* (naut.) palo o verga en cruz
crotch [krɑtʃ] *s* bifurcación; bragadura, horcajadura, entrepiernas; (naut.) pique
crotched [krɑtʃt] *adj* bifurcado
crotchet ['krɑtʃɪt] *s* capricho, rareza; ganchito; (mus.) suspiro (*pausa*); (mus.) negra
crotchety ['krɑtʃɪtɪ] *adj* caprichoso, excéntrico
croton ['krotən] *s* (bot.) crotón; (bot.) buenavista
Croton bug *s* (ent.) cucaracha
croton oil *s* aceite de crotón
crouch [krautʃ] *s* encogimiento; posición agachada; *va* doblar o inclinar muy bajo; *vn* encogerse, agacharse; doblar las rodillas inclinándose muy bajo
croup [krup] *s* (path.) crup, garrotillo; anca, grupa (*del caballo*)
croupier ['krupɪər] *s* crupié, coime
croupous ['krupəs] *adj* crupal
croupy ['krupɪ] *adj* cruposo; crupal
crouton ['krutɑn] *s* cuscurro, cortezón
crow [kro] *s* (orn.) corneja; (orn.) grajo; (orn.) chova; barra, palanca; quiquiriquí (*del gallo*); arrullo (*de los niños pequeños*); **as the crow flies** en línea recta, por el camino más corto; **to eat crow** (coll.) cantar la palinodia; **to have a crow to pick with** (coll.) tener que habérselas con; (*pret:* **crowed** o **crew;** *pp:* **crowed**) *vn* cantar (*el gallo*); (*pret & pp:* **crowed**) *vn* bravear, jactarse; **to crow over** jactarse de
crowbar ['kro,bɑr] *s* palanca, pie de cabra, alzaprima
crowd [kraud] *s* gentío, afluencia, multitud; vulgo, populacho; caterva, tropel; (coll.) grupo, clase; **to follow the crowd** irse al hilo o tras el hilo de la gente (*hacer lo que hacen los otros*); *va* apretar, apiñar, atestar; empujar; **to crowd on sail** (naut.) hacer fuerza de vela; *vn* apretarse, atestarse; arremolinarse; impelerse con fuerza
crowded ['kraudɪd] *adj* apretado, apiñado, atestado; lleno, tupido
crowfoot ['kro,fut] *s* (*pl:* **-foots**) (bot.) ranúnculo; (*pl:* **-feet**) araña (*para sostener toldos*); (elec.) electrodo de cinc (*de una pila de gravedad*); (mil.) abrojo
crown [kraun] *s* corona; (dent.) corona; corona (*moneda*); (naut.) cruz (*del ancla*); copa (*de sombrero*); *adj* coronario; *va* coronar; abombar, abovedar; poner corona artificial a (*un diente*); (checkers) coronar; (slang) golpear en la cabeza
crown colony *s* colonia de la Corona (*colonia del imperio británico que no tiene autonomía*)
crowned head *s* testa coronada (*soberano*)
crown glass *s* crown-glass (*cristal muy puro*); vidrio en hojas circulares para ventanas
crown lens *s* lente convexa de crown-glass
crown prince *s* príncipe heredero
crown princess *s* consorte del príncipe heredero; princesa heredera
crown saw *s* sierra de corona cilíndrica
crown sheet *s* cielo del hogar (*de las cajas de fuego*)
crown wheel *s* (mach.) rueda de dientes laterales
crownwork ['kraun,wʌrk] *s* (dent.) corona artificial; (fort.) corona, obra de corona
crow's-foot ['kroz,fut] *s* (*pl:* **-feet**) pata de gallo (*arruga en el rabo del ojo*); puntada de tres puntas (*que se usa en los bordados*); (mil.) abrojo
crow's-nest ['kroz,nɛst] *s* (naut.) torre de vigía
croze [kroz] *s* gárgol, jable (*ranura*); argallera, jabladera (*serrucho*); *va* ruñar
crozier ['kroʒər] *s* var. de **crosier**
crucial ['kruʃəl] *adj* crucial, decisivo; penoso, severo; (surg.) crucial
crucible ['krusɪbəl] *s* crisol; (fig.) crisol
crucible furnace *s* horno de crisol
crucible steel *s* acero de crisol
crucifer ['krusɪfər] *s* (eccl.) crucero, crucíferario; (bot.) crucífera
crucified ['krusɪfaɪd] *adj* crucificado; **the Crucified** el Crucificado (*Jesucristo*)
crucifix ['krusɪfɪks] *s* crucifijo; cruz
crucifixion [,krusɪ'fɪkʃən] *s* crucifixión; (*cap.*) *s* Crucifixión
cruciform ['krusɪfɔrm] *adj* cruciforme
crucify ['krusɪfaɪ] (*pret & pp:* **-fied**) *va* crucificar; (fig.) crucificar
crude [krud] *adj* grosero, tosco; crudo (*no refinado; no preparado*); sin labrar
crudity ['krudɪtɪ] *s* (*pl:* **-ties**) grosería, tosquedad; crudeza
cruel ['kruəl] *adj* cruel
cruelty ['kruəltɪ] *s* (*pl:* **-ties**) crueldad
cruet ['kruɪt] *s* ampolleta, vinagrera
cruet stand *s* angarillas, vinagreras
cruise [kruz] *s* travesía, viaje por mar; excursión; (naut. & aer.) crucero; *va* (naut.) cruzar; *vn* (naut.) cruzar; (aer.) volar en crucero; (coll.) andar de un punto a otro
cruiser ['kruzər] *s* (nav.) crucero; aeroplano, taxi o embarcación que hace viajes de ida y vuelta
cruising ['kruzɪŋ] *s* (naut.) crucero; *adj* de crucero, p.ej., **cruising speed** velocidad de crucero
cruising radius *s* autonomía (*de un buque, avión, etc.*)
cruller ['krʌlər] *s* buñuelo
crumb [krʌm] *s* migaja (*partícula del pan; porción pequeña de cualquier cosa*); miga (*parte más blanda del pan*); *va* desmenuzar; desmigar (*el pan*); (cook.) cubrir con migajas; (coll.) limpiar (*la mesa*) de migajas; *vn* desmigarse
crumb brush *s* recogemigas
crumble ['krʌmbəl] *va* desmenuzar; *vn* desmenuzarse; desmoronarse
crumbly ['krʌmblɪ] *adj* (*comp:* **-blier;** *super:* **-bliest**) desmenuzable; desmoronadizo
crumb tray *s* bandeja en que se recogen las migajas
crumby ['krʌmɪ] *adj* (*comp:* **-ier;** *super:* **-iest**) lleno de migajas; blando, tierno
crummy ['krʌmɪ] *adj* (*comp:* **-mier;** *super:* **-miest**) (slang) desaseado, sucio; (slang) gastado, p.ej., **a crummy joke** una broma gastada
crump [krʌmp] *s, va & vn* var. de **crunch**
crumpet ['krʌmpɪt] *s* bollo blando tostado
crumple ['krʌmpəl] *s* arruga o pliegue que se hace aplastando una cosa; *va* arrugar, plegar, hacer contraerse en arrugas; *vn* arrugarse, plegarse, contraerse en arrugas
crunch [krʌntʃ] *s* roznido, mascadura; crujido; *va* ronzar, mascar ruidosamente; *vn* contraerse con ruido, crujir
crunk [krʌŋk] o [kruŋk] *vn* (dial.) gruir (*la grulla*)
cruor ['kruɔr] *s* (physiol.) crúor
crupper ['krʌpər] *s* baticola; anca, grupa (*del caballo*); (hum.) nalgas
crural ['krurəl] *adj* (anat.) crural
crusade [kru'sed] *s* cruzada; *vn* hacerse cruzado, abrazar una cruzada; **to crusade for** hacer campaña por
crusader [kru'sedər] *s* cruzado
cruse [kruz] o [krus] *s* ampolleta, cazuela, olla
crush [krʌʃ] *s* presión violenta; aplastamiento; bullaje (*de gente*); **to have a crush on** (slang) estar perdido por, perder la chaveta por (*una persona*); *va* aplastar, magullar; moler; bocartear (*el mineral*); abrumar, p.ej., **I was crushed by the news** me quedé abrumado con la noticia
crush hat *s* sombrero flexible; clac
crust [krʌst] *s* corteza; corteza de pan; corteza de papel; mendrugo; costra, escara; *va* encostrar; *vn* encostrarse

crustacean [krʌs'teʃən] *adj & s* crustáceo
crustaceous [krʌs'teʃəs] *adj* crustáceo; (zool.) crustáceo
crusty ['krʌstɪ] *adj* (*comp:* **-ier;** *super:* **-iest**) costroso; rudo, grosero, áspero
crutch [krʌtʃ] *s* muleta; (fig.) muleta
crux [krʌks] *s* (*pl:* **cruxes** o **cruces** ['krusiz]) punto capital; enigma, cuestión perpleja
cry [kraɪ] *s* (*pl:* **cries**) grito; lloro; gritería; pregón; grito de guerra; aullido (*del lobo*); bramido (*del toro*); **in full cry** en persecución inmediata; **to have a good cry** prorrumpir en lágrimas abundantes ‖ (*pret & pp:* **cried**) *va* decir a gritos; pregonar; **to cry down** gritar (*p.ej., una comedia*); despreciar, menospreciar; **to cry off** renunciar, romper (*p.ej., un acuerdo*); **to cry one's eyes** o **heart out** llorar amargamente; **to cry out** decir a gritos; pregonar o publicar en alta voz; **to cry up** alabar, elogiar; dar por importante ‖ *vn* gritar; llorar; aullar (*el lobo*); bramar (*el toro*); **to cry aloud** gritar fuertemente; llorar a gritos; **to cry for** clamar por; **to cry for joy** llorar de alegría; **to cry out** clamar; **to cry out against** clamar contra; **to cry out for** clamar, clamar por; **to cry out to** clamar a; **to cry to heaven** clamar al cielo
crybaby ['kraɪ,bebɪ] *s* (*pl:* **-bies**) llorón o llorona, lloraduelos
crying ['kraɪɪŋ] *adj* llorón; enorme, atroz
cryogen ['kraɪədʒən] *s* criógeno, substancia criógena
cryogenic [,kraɪo'dʒɛnɪk] *adj* criogénico
cryohydrate [,kraɪo'haɪdret] *s* (chem.) criohidrato
cryolite ['kraɪəlaɪt] *s* (mineral.) criolita
cryology [kraɪ'ɑlədʒɪ] *s* criología
cryometer [kraɪ'ɑmɪtər] *s* criómetro
cryoscope ['kraɪəskop] *s* crioscopio
cryoscopy [kraɪ'ɑskəpɪ] *s* crioscopia
cryostat ['kraɪostæt] *s* crióstato
cryotherapy [,kraɪo'θɛrəpɪ] *s* (med.) crioterapia
crypt [krɪpt] *s* cripta; (anat.) cripta
cryptic ['krɪptɪk] o **cryptical** ['krɪptɪkəl] *adj* secreto, misterioso
cryptogam ['krɪptogæm] *s* (bot.) criptógama
cryptogamic [,krɪpto'gæmɪk] *adj* criptogámico
cryptogamous [krɪp'tɑgəməs] *adj* criptógamo
cryptogram ['krɪptogræm] *s* criptograma
cryptograph ['krɪptogræf] o ['krɪptogrɑf] *s* criptógrafo (*aparato*); criptograma
cryptographer [krɪp'tɑgrəfər] *s* criptógrafo (*persona*)
cryptographic [,krɪpto'græfɪk] *adj* criptográfico
cryptography [krɪp'tɑgrəfɪ] *s* criptografía
crystal ['krɪstəl] *s* cristal (*vidrio*); abalorio, cristal; (chem., mineral. & rad.) cristal; (fig.) cristal (*agua*); cristal de reloj; cristal de roca; **as clear as crystal** tan claro como el agua; *adj* cristalino
crystal ball *s* bola de cristal (*que sirve para adivinar lo porvenir*)
crystal cartridge *s* (elec.) cápsula de cristal
crystal detector *s* (rad.) detector de cristal
crystal gazing *s* sortilegio que se hace mirando fijamente en un cristal
crystalline ['krɪstəlɪn] o ['krɪstəlaɪn] *adj* cristalino
crystalline lens *s* (anat.) cristalino
crystallite ['krɪstəlaɪt] *s* (mineral.) cristalito
crystallization [,krɪstəlɪ'zeʃən] *s* cristalización
crystallize ['krɪstəlaɪz] *va* cristalizar; *vn* cristalizarse
crystallographic [,krɪstələ'græfɪk] o **crystallographical** [,krɪstələ'græfɪkəl] *adj* cristalográfico
crystallography [,krɪstə'lɑgrəfɪ] *s* cristalografía
crystalloid ['krɪstəlɔɪd] *adj* cristaloideo; *s* cristaloide
crystal set *s* (rad.) receptor con detector de cristal
crystal violet *s* var. de **gentian violet**
C.S. abr. de **Christian Science** y **Civil Service**
C.S.A. abr. de **Confederate States Army** y **Confederate States of America**
CSC abr. de **Civil Service Commission**
C.S.T. abr. de **Central Standard Time**
ct. abr. de **cent**
Ct. abr. de **Connecticut**
cts. abr. de **cents**
cu. abr. de **cubic**
cub [kʌb] *s* cachorro (*de león, oso, lobo, etc.*); muchacho desmañado
Cuban ['kjubən] *adj & s* cubano
Cuban lily *s* (bot.) jacinto estrellado
cubbyhole ['kʌbɪ,hol] *s* chiribitil
cube [kjub] *s* cubo; (math.) cubo; *va* dar forma de cubo a; (math.) cubicar
cubeb ['kjubɛb] *s* (bot. & pharm.) cubeba; cigarrillo de cubeba
cube root *s* (math.) raíz cúbica
cubic ['kjubɪk] *adj* cúbico; (cryst. & math.) cúbico
cubical ['kjubɪkəl] *adj* cúbico
cubicle ['kjubɪkəl] *s* cubículo
cubic measure *s* cubicación
cubism ['kjubɪzəm] *s* (f.a.) cubismo
cubist ['kjubɪst] *adj & s* (f.a.) cubista
cubit ['kjubɪt] *s* codo (*medida antigua*)
cubital ['kjubɪtəl] *adj* cubital
cubitus ['kjubɪtəs] *s* (*pl:* **-ti** [taɪ]) (anat.) cúbito
cuboid ['kjubɔɪd] *adj* cuboideo; (anat.) cuboides; *s* cubo; (anat.) cuboides
cub reporter *s* (coll.) reportero novato, aprendiz de reportero
cuckold ['kʌkəld] *adj & s* cornudo; *va* encornudar, hacer cornudo a (*un marido*)
cuckoo ['kuku] *s* (orn.) cuclillo; (orn.) cuclillo de las lluvias; cucú (*canto del cuclillo*); *adj* (slang) mentecato, loco
cuckoo clock *s* reloj de cuclillo
cuckoopint ['kuku,pɪnt] *s* (bot.) aro
cu. cm. abr. de **cubic centimeter** o **cubic centimeters**
cucullate ['kjukəlet] o [kju'kʌlet] *adj* cuculiforme, cuculado
cucumber ['kjukʌmbər] *s* (bot.) cohombro, pepino (*planta y fruto*); **cool as a cucumber** muy fresco; sereno, tranquilo
cucurbitaceous [kju,kʌrbɪ'teʃəs] *adj* (bot.) cucurbitáceo
cud [kʌd] *s* bolo alimenticio; **to chew the cud** rumiar; (fig.) rumiar (*meditar*)
cuddle ['kʌdəl] *s* abrazo cariñoso; *va* abrazar con cariño; *vn* estar abrazados; arrimarse afectuosa o cómodamente
cuddy ['kʌdɪ] *s* (*pl:* **-dies**) pequeño cuarto; aparador; (naut.) camarote; (naut.) despensa
cudgel ['kʌdʒəl] *s* garrote, porra; **to take up the cudgels for** defender con vehemencia, entrar en la lucha en defensa de; (*pret & pp:* **-eled** o **-elled;** *ger:* **-eling** o **-elling**) *va* apalear, aporrear; **to cudgel one's brains** devanarse los sesos
cue [kju] *s* señal, indicación; papel; humor, disposición; coleta (*de cabellos*); cola (*de personas que esperan*); taco (*de billar*); (theat.) apunte; *va* trenzar
cue rest *s* (billiards & pool) diablo
cuff [kʌf] *s* puño; doblez (*del pantalón*); manilla; bofetada; *va* abofetear, dar de bofetadas
cuff button *s* botón del puño de la camisa
cuff links *spl* gemelos (*para los puños de la camisa*)
cu. ft. abr. de **cubic foot** o **cubic feet**
cu. in. abr. de **cubic inch** o **cubic inches**
cuirass [kwɪ'ræs] *s* (arm. & zool.) coraza; (arm.) peto (*de la coraza*); *va* armar o cubrir de coraza
cuirassier [,kwɪrə'sɪr] *s* coracero
cuish [kwɪʃ] *s* var. de **cuisse**
cuisine [kwɪ'zin] *s* cocina
cuisse [kwɪs] *s* (arm.) quijote
cul-de-sac ['kʊldə'sæk] o ['kʌldə'sæk] *s* callejón sin salida
culex ['kjulɛks] *s* (*pl:* **-lices** [lɪsiz]) (ent.) mosquito común
culinary ['kjulɪ,nɛrɪ] *adj* culinario
cull [kʌl] *s* entresaca de lo inferior y sin valor; *va* entresacar, escoger, extraer
cullet ['kʌlɪt] *s* vidrio de desecho
cullis ['kʌlɪs] *s* canal de tejado

culm [kʌlm] *s* cisco; antracita de mala calidad; (bot.) caña, tallo (*de las gramíneas*)
culminate ['kʌlmɪnet] *vn* culminar; (astr.) culminar; **to culminate in** conducir a, terminar en
culmination [,kʌlmɪ'neʃən] *s* culminación; (astr.) culminación
culpability [,kʌlpə'bɪlɪtɪ] *s* culpabilidad
culpable ['kʌlpəbəl] *adj* culpable
culprit ['kʌlprɪt] *s* culpado; reo
cult [kʌlt] *s* culto; secta, conjunto de personas que siguen la misma doctrina
cultism ['kʌltɪzəm] *s* devoción a un culto; culteranismo, cultismo
cultist ['kʌltɪst] *s* adicto a un culto; culterano
cultivable ['kʌltɪvəbəl] *adj* cultivable
cultivate ['kʌltɪvet] *va* cultivar
cultivated ['kʌltɪ,vetɪd] *adj* culto
cultivation [,kʌltɪ'veʃən] *s* cultivo (*de la tierra, las artes, la memoria, etc.*); cultura
cultivator ['kʌltɪ,vetər] *s* cultivador; cultivadora, extirpador (*máquina agrícola*)
cultural ['kʌltʃərəl] *adj* cultural
culture ['kʌltʃər] *s* cultura; (bact.) cultivo; *va* culturar; (bact.) cultivar
cultured ['kʌltʃərd] *adj* culto
cultus ['kʌltəs] *s* culto, culto religioso
culverin ['kʌlvərɪn] *s* culebrina
culvert ['kʌlvərt] *s* alcantarilla
Cumae ['kjumi] *s* Cumas
cumber ['kʌmbər] *s* estorbo, impedimento; *va* estorbar, impedir; incomodar, molestar
cumbersome ['kʌmbərsəm] o **cumbrous** ['kʌmbrəs] *adj* pesado, incómodo, molesto
cumin o **cummin** ['kʌmɪn] *s* (bot.) comino
cuminseed ['kʌmɪn,sid] *s* comino
cum laude [kʌm 'lɔdi] o [kʊm 'laʊde] (Lat.) con honor
cummerbund ['kʌmər,bʌnd] *s* faja que se lleva con traje de etiqueta en vez de chaleco
cumquat ['kʌmkwɑt] *s* var. de **kumquat**
cumulate ['kjumjəlet] *va* acumular
cumulation [,kjumjə'leʃən] *s* acumulación
cumulative ['kjumjə,letɪv] *adj* acumulativo
cumulo-cirrus [,kjumjəlo'sɪrəs] *s* (meteor.) cumulocirro
cumulo-nimbus [,kjumjəlo'nɪmbəs] *s* (meteor.) cúmulonimbo
cumulo-stratus [,kjumjəlo'stretəs] *s* (meteor.) cumulostrato
cumulous ['kjumjələs] *adj* en forma de cúmulo; compuesto de cúmulos
cumulus ['kjumjələs] *s* (*pl:* **-li** [laɪ]) cúmulo; (meteor.) cúmulo
cuneate ['kjunɪet] o ['kjunɪɪt) *adj* cuneiforme; (bot.) cuneiforme, cuneado
cuneiform [kjʊ'niɪfɔrm] o ['kjunɪɪ,fɔrm] *adj* cuneiforme; (anat.) cuneiforme; *s* caracteres cuneiformes; (anat.) cuneiforme
cunner ['kʌnər] *s* (ichth.) tenolabro
cunning ['kʌnɪŋ] *adj* astuto; hábil; gracioso, mono; *s* astucia
cup [kʌp] *s* taza, jícara; copa; bebida; (eccl.) cáliz; (eccl.) vino sagrado (*que se sirve en la misa*); (mach.) vaso de engrase; cubeta (*del barómetro*); (sport) copa; (fig.) copa (*del dolor, la desgracia, etc.*); (fig.) fortuna, suerte; (*cap.*) *s* (astr.) Copa; **in one's cups** ebrio, borracho; (*pret & pp:* **cupped**; *ger:* **cupping**) *va* ahuecar en forma de copa o taza; tomar o poner en copa, taza, etc.; aplicar ventosa a
cupbearer ['kʌp,bɛrər] *s* copero
cupboard ['kʌbərd] *s* alacena, aparador
cupcake [['kʌp,kek] *s* torta hecha en una vasija de forma de copa o taza
cupel ['kjupɛl] o [kju'pɛl] *s* copela; (*pret & pp:* **-peled** o **-pelled**; *ger:* **-peling** o **-pelling**) *va* copelar
cupellation [,kjupə'leʃən] *s* copelación
cupful ['kʌpful] *s* taza (*lo que contiene una taza*)
cup grease *s* grasa lubricante
cupid ['kjupɪd] *s* cupido (*niño alado, símbolo del amor*); (*cap.*) *s* (myth.) Cupido
cupidity [kjʊ'pɪdɪtɪ] *s* codicia
cupola ['kjupələ] *s* (arch., anat. & nav.) cúpula; (arch.) cupulino (*remate, linterna*); (found.) cubilote
cupping ['kʌpɪŋ] *s* aplicación de ventosa
cupping glass *s* ventosa
cupreous ['kjuprɪəs] *adj* cobreño; cobrizo
cupressineous [,kjuprɛ'sɪnɪəs] *adj* (bot.) cupresíneo
cupric ['kjuprɪk] *adj* (chem.) cúprico
cupriferous [kju'prɪfərəs] *adj* cuprífero
cuprite ['kjupraɪt] *s* (mineral.) cuprita
cupronickel [,kjupro'nɪkəl] *s* cuproníquel
cuprous ['kjuprəs] *adj* (chem.) cuproso
cup shake *s* acebolladura
cupule ['kjupjul] *s* (bot. & zool.) cúpula
cupuliferous [,kjupjə'lɪfərəs] *adj* (bot.) cupulífero
cur [kʌr] *s* perro mestizo, perro de mala raza; drope (*hombre despreciable*)
curability [,kjʊrə'bɪlɪtɪ] *s* curabilidad
curable ['kjʊrəbəl] *adj* curable
curaçao [,kjʊrə'so] *s* curasao (*licor*); (*cap.*) *s* Curazao
curacy ['kjʊrəsɪ] *s* (*pl:* **-cies**) curato
curare [kjʊ'rɑrɪ] *s* curare
curarize ['kjʊrəraɪz] o [kjʊ'rɑraɪz] *va* curarizar
curate ['kjʊrɪt] *s* cura
curative ['kjʊrətɪv] *adj* curativo; *s* curativa
curator [kjʊ'retər] *s* conservador
curb [kʌrb] *s* barbada (*del freno*); encintado (*borde de la acera*); brocal de pozo; restricción; (com.) bolsín; (vet.) corva; *va* proveer de encintado; proveer de brocal; contener, refrenar
curb bit *s* freno con barbada
curbing ['kʌrbɪŋ] *s* materia para construir el encintado; encintado; refrenamiento
curb market *s* bolsín
curbstone ['kʌrb,ston] *s* piedra de encintado; encintado; brocal de pozo
curculio [kʌr'kjulɪo] *s* (*pl:* **-os**) (ent.) rincóforo
curcuma paper ['kʌrkjəmə] *s* (chem.) papel de cúrcuma
curd [kʌrd] *s* cuajada; *va* cuajar; *vn* cuajarse
curdle ['kʌrdəl] *va* cuajar; **to curdle the blood** causar horror u horripilación; *vn* cuajarse
curdy ['kʌrdɪ] *adj* cuajado
cure [kjʊr] *s* cura, curación; curato; *va* curar (*una enfermedad, un mal; carnes, pieles, etc.; restituir a la salud*); *vn* curar; curarse
curé [kjʊ're] *s* cura, párroco
cure-all ['kjʊr,ɔl] *s* sánalotodo, panacea
curettage [kjʊ'rɛtɪdʒ] o [,kjʊrə'tɑʒ] *s* (surg.) curetaje
curette [kjʊ'rɛt] *s* (surg.) cureta
curfew ['kʌrfju] *s* queda, cubrefuego
curia ['kjʊrɪə] *s* (hist.) curia
curie ['kjʊri] o [kjʊ'ri] *s* (phys.) curie
curio ['kjʊrɪo] *s* (*pl:* **-os**) curiosidad (*objeto curioso*)
curiosity [,kjʊrɪ'ɑsɪtɪ] *s* (*pl:* **-ties**) curiosidad
curiosity shop *s* tienda de curiosidades
curious ['kjʊrɪəs] *adj* curioso
curium ['kjʊrɪəm] *s* (chem.) curio
curl [kʌrl] *s* bucle, rizo; tirabuzón (*rizo pendiente en espiral*); ondulación, sinuosidad; rizado; espiral (*de humo*); *va* encrespar, ensortijar, rizar; arrollar; torcer; fruncir (*los labios*); **to curl up** arrollar; *vn* encresparse, ensortijarse, rizarse; arrollarse; torcerse; **to curl up** arrollarse; tirar las piernas hacia arriba (*al acostarse*); (coll.) abatirse, desbaratarse
curlew ['kʌrlu] o ['kʌrlju] *s* (orn.) zarapito
curlicue ['kʌrlɪkju] *s* plumada, rasgo, ringorrango
curling ['kʌrlɪŋ] *s* (sport) curling (*juego sobre campo de hielo*)
curling iron *s* rizador, encrespador, maquinilla de rizar
curlpaper ['kʌrl,pepər] *s* torcida, papelito para rizar el pelo
curly ['kʌrlɪ] *adj* (*comp:* **-ier**; *super:* **-iest**) encrespado, ensortijado, rizado; ondulado
curly n *s* ñ (*n con tilde*)
curmudgeon [kʌr'mʌdʒən] *s* cicatero, erizo
currant ['kʌrənt] *s* pasa de Corinto; grosella; (bot.) grosellero
currency ['kʌrənsɪ] *s* (*pl:* **-cies**) moneda corriente; uso corriente; valor corriente
current ['kʌrənt] *adj* corriente; *s* corriente; (elec.) corriente
current account *s* (com.) cuenta corriente
current collector *s* (elec.) toma de corriente

current density *s* (elec.) densidad de corriente
current events *spl* actualidades, sucesos de actualidad
current limiter *s* (elec.) limitador de corriente, limitacorrientes
currently ['kʌrəntlɪ] *adv* actualmente; por lo general
curricle ['kʌrɪkəl] *s* carrocín
curricular [kə'rɪkjələr] *adj* del plan de estudios
curriculum [kə'rɪkjələm] *s* (*pl:* **-lums** o **-la** [lə]) *s* programa o plan de estudios
currier ['kʌrɪər] *s* curtidor; almohazador
currish ['kʌrɪʃ] *adj* perruno; gruñón, arisco, descortés
curry ['kʌrɪ] *s* (*pl:* **-ries**) cari (*polvo, salsa y guisado*); (*pret & pp:* **-ried**) *va* curtir (*las pieles*); almohazar (*el caballo*); preparar o sazonar con cari; **to curry favor** procurar complacer
currycomb ['kʌrɪˌkom] *s* almohaza; *va* almohazar
curry powder *s* polvo de cari
curse [kʌrs] *s* maldición; maleficio; calamidad; (*pret & pp:* **cursed** o **curst**) *va* maldecir; **to be cursed with** sufrir, padecer; *vn* blasfemar
cursed ['kʌrsɪd] o [kʌrst] *adj* maldito; aborrecible, abominable
cursive ['kʌrsɪv] *adj* cursivo; *s* cursiva
cursorial [kʌr'sorɪəl] *adj* propio para correr; que tiene piernas propias para correr
cursory ['kʌrsərɪ] *adj* apresurado, rápido, precipitado; superficial, de paso, por encima
curst [kʌrst] *adj* var. de **cursed;** *pret & pp de* **curse**
curt [kʌrt] *adj* corto, conciso; brusco, áspero
curtail [kʌr'tel] *va* acortar, abreviar, reducir; privar
curtailment [kʌr'telmənt] *s* acortamiento, abreviación, reducción; privación
curtain ['kʌrtən] *s* cortina; (theat.) telón; **to draw the curtain** correr la cortina; **to drop the curtain** (theat.) bajar el telón; *va* proveer de cortina; separar con cortina; cubrir, ocultar; **to curtain off** separar con cortina
curtain call *s* (theat.) aplauso de llamamiento
curtain lecture *s* regaño privado, reprimenda conyugal
curtain of fire *s* (mil.) cortina de fuego
curtain raiser *s* (theat.) pieza preliminar
curtain ring *s* anilla
curtain rod *s* barra de cortina, riel para cortinas
curtation [kʌr'teʃən] *s* (astr.) acortamiento, curtación
curtesy ['kʌrtəsɪ] *s* (*pl:* **-sies**) (law) título del derecho del marido a los bienes raíces de su mujer muerta
curtsey ['kʌrtsɪ] *s* cortesía, reverencia
curtsy ['kʌrtsɪ] *s* (*pl:* **-sies**) cortesía, reverencia; (*pret & pp:* **-sied**) *vn* hacer una cortesía, hacer una reverencia
curule ['kjurul] *adj* curul
curule chair *s* silla curul
curvaceous [kʌr'veʃəs] *adj* (coll.) curvilíneo (*dícese de una mujer*)
curvature ['kʌrvətʃər] *s* curvatura
curve [kʌrv] *s* curva; (baseball) curva; *adj* curvo; *va* encorvar; *vn* encorvarse; voltear en curva
curvet ['kʌrvɛt] *s* corveta; [kʌr'vɛt] o ['kʌrvɛt] (*pret & pp:* **-vetted** o **-veted;** *ger:* **-vetting** o **-veting**) *vn* corvetear
curvilineal [ˌkʌrvɪ'lɪnɪəl] o **curvilinear** [ˌkʌrvɪ'lɪnɪər] *adj* curvilíneo
curvometer [kʌr'vɑmɪtər] *s* curvímetro
cushion ['kuʃən] *s* cojín, almohadón; banda o baranda (*de la mesa de billar*); (mach.) amortiguador; *va* asentar o poner sobre cojín; sostener con cojines; proteger por medio de cojines; amortiguar, someter a acción amortiguadora; acojinar (*un pistón*)
cusk [kʌsk] *s* (ichth.) pez marino comestible (*Brosmius brosme*); (ichth.) lota
cusp [kʌsp] *s* cúspide; punta (*del creciente*); (anat.) cúspide (*de un diente*)
cuspid ['kʌspɪd] *s* (anat.) cúspide (*diente*)
cuspidal ['kʌspɪdəl] *adj* de cúspide; puntiagudo
cuspidate ['kʌspɪdet] *adj* cuspídeo
cuspidor ['kʌspɪdɔr] *s* escupidera
cuss [kʌs] *s* (coll.) maldición; (coll.) tipo insignificante o impertinente; *va & vn* (coll.) maldecir
cussed ['kʌsɪd] *adj* (coll.) maldito; (coll.) terco
custard ['kʌstərd] *s* flan, natillas
custard apple *s* (bot.) anona; (bot.) anona blanca (*Annona squamosa*); (bot.) anona colorada, corazón, mamón, riñón (*Annona reticulata*); (bot.) papayo; papaya (*fruto*); (bot.) asimina
custodial [kʌs'todɪəl] *adj* del custodio, de la custodia
custodian [kʌs'todɪən] *s* custodio
custodianship [kʌs'todɪənˌʃɪp] *s* custodia
custody ['kʌstədɪ] *s* (*pl:* **-dies**) custodia; **in custody** en prisión; **to take into custody** arrestar, prender
custom ['kʌstəm] *s* costumbre; parroquia, clientela (*de una tienda*); **customs** *spl* aduana; derechos de aduana; *adj* hecho según pedido; hecho a la medida
customary ['kʌstəmˌɛrɪ] *adj* acostumbrado
custom-built ['kʌstəmˌbɪlt] *adj* hecho o construído según pedido
customer ['kʌstəmər] *s* parroquiano, cliente; (coll.) individuo, tipo
customers' man *s* (coll.) empleado del corredor de bolsa que solicita y aconseja a los clientes
customhouse ['kʌstəmˌhaus] *s* aduana; *adj* aduanero
custom-made ['kʌstəmˌmed] *adj* hecho a la medida
customs barrier *s* barrera aduanera
customs clearance *s* despacho de aduana
customs declaration *s* declaración de aduana
customs officer *s* aduanero
customs union *s* unión aduanera
custom tailor *s* sastre que hace vestidos a la medida
custom work *s* trabajo hecho según pedido
cut [kʌt] *s* corte; tajada (*porción cortada*); cuchillada (*herida*); desmonte, excavación; atajo (*camino más corto*); reducción (*de precios, sueldos, etc.*); golpe cortante; hechura (*de un traje*); (tennis) golpe cortante; parte (*de las ganancias que corresponde a cada uno de los asociados en alguna empresa*); (cards) corte; (print.) estampa, grabado; (print.) clisé; (coll.) falta de asistencia (*a la clase*); (coll.) desaire; (coll.) palabra hiriente; **a cut above** (coll.) un dedo más arriba de; **cut of one's jib** (coll.) aspecto exterior de uno; *adj* cortado; tallado, labrado ‖ (*pret & pp:* **cut;** *ger:* **cutting**) *va* cortar; practicar (*p.ej., un agujero*); capar, castrar; pegar con golpe cortante; disolver; (coll.) hacer, formar, ejecutar; (coll.) faltar a, ausentarse de (*la clase*); (coll.) desairar; (coll.) herir (*con palabra hiriente*); **to cut across** cortar al través; **to cut asunder (away)** separar (quitar) cortando; **to cut back** acortar (*cortando el extremo de una cosa*); **to cut down** cortar; derribar cortando; aminorar, castigar (*gastos*); **to cut in** (elec.) intercalar, introducir (*un circuito*); **to cut off** cortar; desheredar; amputar (*p.ej., una pierna*); (elec.) cortar (*la corriente*); (aut.) cortar (*la ignición*); (aut.) cerrar (*el carburador*); **to cut open** abrir cortando; **to cut out** cortar; quitar o sacar cortando; tallar, labrar; omitir, suprimir; desbancar; soplar (*la dama a un rival*); (slang) dejarse de (*p.ej., disparates*); **to cut short** terminar de repente; chafar (*en la conversación*); **to cut teeth** endentecer; **to cut up** desmenuzar, despedazar; criticar severamente; (coll.) acongojar, afligir; **cut it out!** ¡déjese de eso!, ¡no hable más de eso! ‖ *vn* cortar; cortarse, poderse cortar; pasar rápidamente, apartarse rápidamente; salir (*los dientes*); (coll.) fumarse la clase; **to cut across** atravesar, ir a través de; **to cut back** volver de repente; **to cut in** entrar de repente; interrumpir; cortar o separar la pareja (*en el baile*); **to cut under** vender a menor precio que; **to cut up** (slang) travesear; (slang) jaranear
cut and dried *adj* ya dispuesto para el uso; monótono, poco interesante
cutaneous [kju'tenɪəs] *adj* cutáneo
cutaway ['kʌtəˌwe] o **cutaway coat** *s* chaqué
cute [kjut] *adj* (coll.) mono, monono; (coll.) astuto

cut gear *s* engranaje de dientes tallados a máquina
cut glass *s* cristal tallado
cuticle ['kjutɪkəl] *s* (anat. & bot.) cutícula
cuticular [kju'tɪkjələr] *adj* cuticular
cutin ['kjutɪn] *s* (biochem.) cutina
cutireaction [,kjutɪrɪ'ækʃən] *s* (med. & vet.) cutirreacción
cutis ['kjutɪs] *s* (anat.) dermis
cutlass ['kʌtləs] *s* alfanje
cutler ['kʌtlər] *s* cuchillero
cutlery ['kʌtlərɪ] *s* cuchillería; cubiertos (*cucharas, tenedores y cuchillos*); cuchillos, tijeras y otros instrumentos cortantes
cutlet ['kʌtlɪt] *s* chuleta; fritada de carne picada, fritada de pescado picado
cutoff ['kʌt,ɔf] o ['kʌt,ɑf] *s* atajo; (mach.) cierre de vapor; (mach.) cortavapor (*aparato*); (elec.) frecuencia de corte
cutoff valve *s* (mach.) corredera auxiliar de expansión
cutout ['kʌt,aut] *s* recortado, diseño o figura para recortar; (mach.) válvula de escape libre; (elec.) portafusible
cutover ['kʌt,ovər] *adj* desmontado (*terreno*)
cutpurse ['kʌrt,pʌrs] *s* cortabolsas, carterista
cut-rate ['kʌt'ret] *adj* (U.S.A.) de precio reducido
cutter ['kʌtər] *s* cortador (*persona*); cortadora (*máquina*); freso (*de una fresadora*); (anat.) cortador (*diente incisivo*); (naut.) cúter (*embarcación de un solo palo*); (naut.) escampavía
cutthroat ['kʌt,θrot] *s* asesino; *adj* asesino; cruel, sanguinario; implacable
cutting ['kʌtɪŋ] *adj* cortante; mordaz, hiriente; *s* corte, cortadura; recorte (*de un periódico*); (hort.) esqueje, rampollo
cuttle ['kʌtəl] *s* var. de **cuttlefish**
cuttlebone ['kʌtəl,bon] *s* jibión
cuttlefish ['kʌtəl,fɪʃ] *s* (zool.) jibia
cutup ['kʌt,ʌp] *s* (slang) bromista; **cutups** *spl* diseños o figuras para recortar
cutwater ['kʌt,wɔtər] o ['kʌt,wɑtər] *s* espolón, tajamar (*de barco o puente*)
cutworm ['kʌt,wʌrm] *s* (ent.) larva de agrótida
cuvette [kju'vɛt] *s* (phot.) cubeta
CW abr. de **continuous wave**
cwt. abr. de **hundredweight**
cyanamide [saɪ'ænəmaɪd] o [,saɪə'næmaɪd] *s* (chem.) cianamida; (com.) cianamida de calcio
cyanate ['saɪənet] *s* (chem.) cianato
cyanic [saɪ'ænɪk] *adj* (chem.) ciánico; cianótico (*azulado*)
cyanic acid *s* (chem.) ácido ciánico
cyanid ['saɪənɪd] o **cyanide** ['saɪənaɪd] o ['saɪənɪd] *s* (chem.) cianuro
cyanide of potassium *s* (chem.) cianuro de potasio
cyanite ['saɪənaɪt] *s* (mineral.) cianita
cyanogen [saɪ'ænədʒən] *s* (chem.) cianógeno
cyanophycean [,saɪəno'fɪʃən] *adj* (bot.) cianofíceo; *s* (bot.) cianofícea
cyanosis [,saɪə'nosɪs] *s* (path.) cianosis
cyanotic [,saɪə'nɑtɪk] *adj* (path.) cianótico
Cybele ['sɪbəli] *s* (myth.) Cibeles
cybernetics [,saɪbər'nɛtɪks] *ssg* cibernética
cycad ['saɪkæd] *s* (bot.) cicadácea
Cyclades ['sɪklədiz] *spl* Cícladas
cyclamen ['sɪkləmɛn] *s* (bot.) ciclamen, pamporcino
cyclamin ['sɪkləmɪn] *s* (chem.) ciclamina
cyclas ['sɪklæs] o ['saɪklæs] *s* (*pl:* **cyclades** ['sɪklədiz]) cíclada (*de las romanas*); ciclatón (*tela de la Edad Media*)
cycle ['saɪkəl] *s* ciclo; bicicleta, velocípedo; (phys.) período; (mach.) tiempo (*de un motor de combustión interna*); *vn* hacer o completar un ciclo; ocurrir repetidamente en el mismo orden; andar o montar en bicicleta
cyclic ['saɪklɪk] o ['sɪklɪk] o **cyclical** ['saɪklɪkəl] o ['sɪklɪkəl] *adj* cíclico
cycling ['saɪklɪŋ] *s* ciclismo
cyclist ['saɪklɪst] *s* ciclista
cycloid ['saɪklɔɪd] *adj* cicloidal; *s* (geom.) cicloide
cyclometer [saɪ'klɑmɪtər] *s* ciclómetro
cyclonal [saɪ'klonəl] *adj* ciclonal
cyclone ['saɪklon] *s* ciclón
cyclonic [saɪ'klɑnɪk] o **cyclonical** [saɪ'klɑnɪkəl] *adj* ciclónico
cyclopaedia [,saɪklo'pidɪə] *s* var. de **cyclopedia**
cyclopean [,saɪklo'piən] *adj* ciclópeo; (*cap.*) *adj* (myth.) ciclópeo
cyclopedia [,saɪklo'pidɪə] *s* enciclopedia
cyclopedic [,saɪklo'pidɪk] *adj* enciclopédico
cyclopentane [,saɪklo'pɛnten] o [,sɪklo'pɛnten] *s* (chem.) ciclopentano
Cyclopic [saɪ'klɑpɪk] *adj* ciclópico
cycloplegia [,saɪklo'plidʒɪə] o [,sɪklo'plidʒɪə] *s* (path.) cicloplejía
cyclopropane [,saɪklo'propen] o [,sɪklo'propen] *s* (chem.) ciclopropano
Cyclops ['saɪklɑps] *s* (*pl:* **Cyclopes** [saɪ'klopiz]) (myth.) Cíclope
cyclorama [,saɪklo'ræmə] o [,saɪklo'rɑmə] *s* ciclorama
cyclostome ['saɪklostom] o ['sɪklostom] *s* (ichth.) ciclóstoma
cyclotron ['saɪklotrɑn] o ['sɪklotrɑn] *s* (phys.) ciclotrón
Cydnus ['sɪdnəs] *s* Cidno
cygnet ['sɪgnɪt] *s* (orn.) pollo de cisne
Cygnus ['sɪgnəs] *s* (astr.) Cisne
cyl. abr. de **cylinder** y **cylindrical**
cylinder ['sɪlɪndər] *s* cilindro; *va* proveer de cilindro o cilindros; cilindrar
cylinder block *s* (mach.) bloque de cilindros
cylinder bore *s* alesaje
cylinder capacity *s* cilindrada
cylinder head *s* tapa del cilindro (*de una máquina de vapor*); culata del cilindro (*de un motor de gasolina*)
cylinder lock *s* cerradura de cilindro
cylindric [sɪ'lɪndrɪk] o **cylindrical** [sɪ'lɪndrɪkəl] *adj* cilíndrico
cylindroid ['sɪlɪndrɔɪd] *adj* cilindroide; *s* (geom. & med.) cilindroide
cymbal ['sɪmbəl] *s* (mus.) címbalo, platillo
cymbalist ['sɪmbəlɪst] *s* (mus.) cimbalero, cimbalista
cyme [saɪm] *s* (bot.) cima
cymene ['saɪmin] *s* (chem.) cimeno
cymophane ['saɪmofen] *s* (mineral.) cimofana
cymose ['saɪmos] o [saɪ'mos] *adj* (bot.) cimoso
Cymric ['kɪmrɪk] o ['sɪmrɪk] *adj & s* címrico
Cymry ['kɪmrɪ] *spl* cimris
cynic ['sɪnɪk] *adj & s* cínico (*burlón, volteriano*); (*cap.*) *adj & s* cínico
cynical ['sɪnɪkəl] *adj* cínico (*burlón, volteriano*)
cynicism ['sɪnɪsɪzəm] *s* cinismo (*burlonería, volterianismo*); (*cap.*) *s* cinismo
cynic spasm *s* (path.) espasmo cínico
cynosure ['saɪnəʃʊr] o ['sɪnəʃʊr] *s* miradero (*objeto de la atención*); guía, norte; (*cap.*) *s* (astr.) Cinosura
Cynthia ['sɪnθɪə] *s* (myth.) Cintia
cyperaceous [,saɪpə'reʃəs] *adj* (bot.) ciperáceo
cypher ['saɪfər] *s, adj, va & vn* var. de **cipher**
cypress ['saɪprəs] *s* (bot.) ciprés; *adj* cipresino
Cyprian ['sɪprɪən] *adj & s* chipriota; (fig.) lujurioso
Cypriot ['sɪprɪət] o **Cypriote** ['sɪprɪot] *adj & s* chipriota
cypripedium [,sɪprɪ'pidɪəm] *s* (*pl:* **-a** [ə]) (bot.) cipripedio
Cyprus ['saɪprəs] *s* Chipre
Cyrenaic [,saɪrɪ'neɪk] o [,sɪrɪ'neɪk] *adj & s* cirenaico
Cyrenaica [,saɪrɪ'neɪkə] o [,sɪrɪ'neɪkə] *s* la Cirenaica
Cyrene [saɪ'rinɪ] *s* Cirene (*ciudad*)
Cyril ['sɪrɪl] *s* Cirilo
Cyrillic [sɪ'rɪlɪk] *adj* cirílico
Cyrus ['saɪrəs] *s* Ciro
cyst [sɪst] *s* (bot., path. & zool.) quiste
cystic ['sɪstɪk] *adj* (anat.) cístico; (path.) quístico
cystic duct *s* (anat.) cístico, conducto cístico
cysticercosis [,sɪstɪsər'kosɪs] *s* (path.) cisticercosis
cysticercus [,sɪstɪ'sʌrkəs] *s* (*pl:* **-ci** [saɪ]) (zool.) cisticerco
cystitis [sɪs'taɪtɪs] *s* (path.) cistitis
cystoscope ['sɪstoskop] *s* cistoscopio
cystotomy [sɪs'tɑtəmɪ] *s* (*pl:* **-mies**) (surg.) cistotomía
cytase ['saɪtes] *s* (biochem.) citasa

Cytherea [ˌsɪθəˈriə] *s* (myth.) Citerea
Cytherean [ˌsɪθəˈriən] *adj* citereo
cytisine [ˈsɪtɪsin] o [ˈsɪtɪsɪn] *s* (pharm.) citisina
cytisus [ˈsɪtɪsəs] *s* (*pl:* **-si** [saɪ]) (bot.) cítiso
cytochemistry [ˌsaɪtoˈkemɪstrɪ] *s* citoquímica
cytologist [saɪˈtɑlədʒɪst] *s* citólogo
cytology [saɪˈtɑlədʒɪ] *s* citología
cytoplasm [ˈsaɪtoplæzəm] *s* (biol.) citoplasma
cytoplasmic [ˌsaɪtoˈplæzmɪk] *adj* (biol.) citoplásmico
C.Z. abr. de **Canal Zone**
czar [zɑr] *s* zar; (fig.) autócrata
czardas [ˈtʃɑrdɑʃ] o [ˈzɑrdæs] *s* (mus.) csardas
czarevitch [ˈzɑrɪvɪtʃ] *s* zarevitz
czarevna [zɑˈrevnə] *s* czarevna
czarina [zɑˈrinə] *s* zarina
czarism [ˈzɑrɪzəm] *s* zarismo
czarist [ˈzɑrɪst] *s* zarista
Czech [tʃek] *adj & s* checo
Czechish [ˈtʃekɪʃ] *adj* checo
Czecho-Slovak o **Czechoslovak** [ˈtʃekoˈslovæk] *adj & s* checoeslovaco o checoslovaco
Czecho-Slovakia o **Czechoslovakia** [ˌtʃekosloˈvɑkɪə] o [ˌtʃekosloˈvækɪə] *s* Checoeslovaquia o Checoslovaquia
Czecho-Slovakian o **Czechoslovakian** [ˌtʃekosloˈvɑkɪən] o [ˌtʃekosloˈvækɪən] *adj & s* var. de **Czecho-Slovak**

D

D, d [di] *s* (*pl:* **D's, d's** (diz]) cuarta letra del alfabeto inglés
d. abr. de **date, day, daughter, dead, degree, delete, diameter, died, dime, dollar** y **denarius (English penny, pence)**
D. abr. de **December, Democrat, Democratic, Duchess, Duke** y **Dutch**
D.A. abr. de **District Attorney**
dab [dæb] *s* golpecito, toque ligero; masa pastosa; brochazo (*hecho con pintura*); pizca; (ichth.) platija, lenguado, barbada; (*pret & pp:* **dabbed;** *ger:* **dabbing**) *va* golpear ligeramente, tocar ligeramente, frotar suavemente; embadurnar; aplicar (*pintura*) con brochazos ligeros
dabble ['dæbəl] *va* salpicar, rociar; *vn* chapotear; trabajar superficialmente; **to dabble in** mangonear en, meterse en; jugar a (*la bolsa*); especular en (*p.ej., granos*)
dabbler ['dæblər] *s* aficionado, diletante
dabchick ['dæb,tʃɪk] *s* (orn.) zambullidor (*Podilymbus podiceps*); (orn.) somorgujo castaño o menor (*Podiceps ruficollis*)
dabster ['dæbstər] *s* (coll.) chapucero, principiante; (dial.) perito
dace [des] *s* (ichth.) albur, leucisco, dardo
dachshund ['dɑks,hunt] o ['dæks,hund] *s* perro de casta alemana corto de patas y de cuerpo largo
Dacia ['deʃə] *s* la Dacia
Dacian ['deʃən] *adj & s* dacio
dactyl ['dæktɪl] *s* dáctilo
dactylic [dæk'tɪlɪk] *adj* dactílico
dactyliography [dæk,tɪlɪ'ɑgrəfɪ] *s* dactiliografía
dactyliology [dæk,tɪlɪ'ɑlədʒɪ] *s* dactiliología
dactylogram ['dæktɪlə,græm] o [dæk'tɪləgræm] *s* dactilograma
dactyloscopic [,dæktɪlə'skɑpɪk] *adj* dactiloscópico
dactyloscopy [,dæktɪ'lɑskəpɪ] *s* dactiloscopia
dad [dæd] *s* (coll.) papá
Dadaism ['dɑdəɪzəm] *s* dadaísmo
daddy ['dædɪ] *s* (*pl:* **-dies**) (coll.) var. de **dad**
daddy-longlegs [,dædɪ'lɔŋ,lɛgz] o [,dædɪ'lɑŋ,lɛgz] *s* (*pl:* **-legs**) (ent.) típula; (ent.) segador; (orn.) candelero, comalteca; (*cap.*) *s* Papaíto piernas largas
dado ['dedo] *s* (*pl:* **-does**) friso; (arch.) dado
Daedalus ['dɛdələs] o ['didələs] *s* (myth.) Dédalo
daemon ['dimən] *s* var. de **demon**
daffodil ['dæfədɪl] *s* (bot.) narciso trompón
daffy ['dæfɪ] *adj* (*comp:* **-ier;** *super:* **-iest**) (coll.) chiflado
daft [dæft] *adj* chiflado; necio
dagger ['dægər] *s* daga, puñal; (print.) cruz, obelisco; **to look daggers (at)** apuñalar con la mirada
daguerreotype [də'gɛrətaɪp] *s* daguerrotipo; *va* daguerrotipar
dahlia ['dæljə], ['deljə] o ['dɑljə] *s* (bot.) dalia
daily ['delɪ] *adj* diario, cotidiano; *adv* diariamente; *s* (*pl:* **-lies**) diario
daily double *s* apuesta doble (*en las carreras de caballos*)
daily dozen *spl* rato diario de gimnasia; quehaceres rutinarios
dainty ['dentɪ] *adj* (*comp:* **-tier;** *super:* **-tiest**) delicado; *s* (*pl:* **-ties**) golosina
dairy ['dɛrɪ] *s* (*pl:* **-ies**) lechería, quesería, vaquería
dairy cattle *s* vacas lecheras
dairymaid ['dɛrɪ,med] *s* lechera
dairyman ['dɛrɪmən] *s* (*pl:* **-men**) lechero
dais ['de·ɪs] *s* estrado
daisy ['dezɪ] *s* (*pl:* **-sies**) (bot.) margarita; (bot.) margarita mayor; (slang) primor
dale [del] *s* vallecico
dalliance ['dælɪəns] *s* coquetería, frivolidad
dally ['dælɪ] (*pret & pp:* **-lied**) *vn* juguetear, retozar; tardar, holgar, perder el tiempo
Dalmatia [dæl'meʃə] *s* Dalmacia
Dalmatian [dæl'meʃən] *adj* dálmata, dalmático; *s* dálmata; perro dalmático
dalmatic [dæl'mætɪk] *s* dalmática (*vestidura*)
Daltonism ['dɔltənɪzəm] *s* (path.) daltonismo
dam [dæm] *s* presa, dique; madre (*de cuadrúpedos*); (dent.) dique; (found.) dama; (*pret & pp:* **dammed;** *ger:* **damming**) *va* represar, estancar; contener con diques; cerrar, tapar, obstruir
damage ['dæmɪdʒ] *s* daño, perjuicio, deterioro; desdoro (*en la reputación*); pérdida; (com.) avería; (slang) costo; **damages** *spl* daños y perjuicios; *va* dañar, perjudicar; averiar; *vn* dañarse; averiarse
damaging ['dæmɪdʒɪŋ] *adj* perjudicial; desdoroso (*p.ej., en la reputación*)
damascene ['dæməsin] o [,dæmə'sin] *adj* ataujiado; damasquino, damasquinado; *s* ataujía (*obra de metal adornada con embutidos de oro, plata y esmaltes*); damasquinado (*hierro o acero con líneas ondeantes; obra de metal adornada con embutidos de oro, plata y esmaltes*); *va* ataujiar; damasquinar; (*cap.*) *adj & s* damasceno
damascene work *s* ataujía; damasquinado
Damascus [də'mæskəs] *s* Damasco
Damascus steel *s* acero damasquino, acero adamascado
damask ['dæməsk] *s* damasco (*tejido*); ataujía; damasquinado; acero damasquino; *adj* adamascado; damasceno (*de Damasco*); damasquino (*dícese, p.ej., del acero*); *va* adamascar
damask rose *s* (bot.) rosa de Damasco
damask steel *s* acero damasquino, acero adamascado
dame [dem] *s* dama, señora; (slang) tía, mujer
damewort ['dem,wʌrt] *s* (bot.) juliana
damn [dæm] *s* terno; **I don't give a damn** (slang) maldito lo que me importa; **that's not worth a damn** (slang) eso no vale un pito; *va* condenar (a pena eterna); condenar; maldecir; **to damn with faint praise** condenar por medio de alabanzas poco entusiastas; *vn* maldecir, echar ternos
damnable ['dæmnəbəl] *adj* condenable; detestable, infame, abominable
damnation [dæm'neʃən] *s* damnación; (theol.) condenación
damned [dæmd] *adj* condenado (a pena eterna), maldito; condenado; detestable, abominable; **the damned** los condenados (a pena eterna), los malditos
Damocles ['dæməkliz] *s* (myth.) Damocles o Dámocles
Damon ['demən] *s* (myth.) Damón
damp [dæmp] *adj* húmedo, mojado; *s* humedad; grisú; abatimiento, desaliento; *va* humedecer, mojar; amortecer, amortiguar; abatir, desalentar; (elec.) amortiguar (*ondas electromagnéticas*)
damped wave *s* (elec.) onda amortiguada
dampen ['dæmpən] humedecer; apagar, amortecer, amortiguar; abatir, desalentar; (elec.) amortiguar (*ondas electromagnéticas*); *vn* humedecerse; amortecerse
dampener ['dæmpənər] *s* (mach.) amortiguador
damper ['dæmpər] *s* registro, regulador de tiro de chimenea; llave de estufa; apagador, sordina (*del piano*); desalentador
dampish ['dæmpɪʃ] *adj* algo húmedo

dampness ['dæmpnɪs] *s* humedad
damsel ['dæmzəl] *s* damisela, señorita, muchacha
damson ['dæmzən] *s* (bot.) ciruelo damasceno; ciruela damascena (*fruto*)
Danae ['dænɪi] *s* (myth.) Dánae
Danaides o **Danaïdes** [də'neɪdiz] *spl* (myth.) Danaides
Danaus o **Danaüs** ['dæneəs] *s* (myth.) Danao
dance [dæns] o [dɑns] *s* baile, danza; **formal dance** baile de etiqueta; *adj* de baile, para bailar, bailable; *va* bailar, danzar (*p.ej., una polca*); *vn* bailar, danzar; (fig.) bailar, danzar; **to dance to the music** bailar al son que se toca
danceable ['dænsəbəl] o ['dɑnsəbəl] *adj* bailable
dance band *s* orquesta de jazz
dance hall *s* salón de baile
dance floor *s* pista de baile
dance music *s* música de baile, música bailable
dance of death *s* danza de la muerte
dancer ['dænsər] o ['dɑnsər] *s* bailador, danzador; bailarín (*profesional*)
dancing partner *s* pareja (de baile)
dandelion ['dændɪ,laɪən] *s* (bot.) amargón o diente de león
dander ['dændər] *s* (coll.) ira, cólera, mal genio; caspa (*escamilla a raíz de los cabellos*); **to get one's dander up** (coll.) enojarse, perder la paciencia
dandle ['dændəl] *va* mecer, hacer saltar sobre las rodillas; acariciar, mimar
dandler ['dændlər] *s* niñero
dandruff ['dændrəf] *s* caspa
dandy ['dændɪ] *s* (*pl:* **-dies**) currutaco; (slang) cosa excelente; *adj* (*comp:* **-dier;** *super:* **-diest**) currutaco; (slang) excelente, magnífico
dandyism ['dændɪɪzəm] *s* dandismo
Dane [den] *s* danés o dinamarqués
danewort ['den,wʌrt] *s* (bot.) actea, yezgo
danger ['dendʒər] *s* peligro; **out of danger** fuera de peligro
dangerous ['dendʒərəs] *adj* peligroso
dangle ['dæŋgəl] *va & vn* colgar en el aire, colgar flojamente; **to dangle after** seguir, ir tras de
dangling ['dæŋglɪŋ] *adj* colgante en el aire, colgante flojamente
dangling participle *s* (gram.) participio inconexo
Daniel ['dænjəl] *s* Daniel
Danish ['denɪʃ] *adj* danés o dinamarqués; *s* danés o dinamarqués (*idioma*); **the Danish** los daneses, los dinamarqueses
dank [dæŋk] *adj* liento, húmedo
danse macabre [dɑ̃s mɑ'kɑbrə] *s* danza macabra
danseuse [dɑ̃'søz] *s* bailarina
Dantesque [dæn'tɛsk] *adj* dantesco
Danube ['dænjʊb] o ['dænjub] *s* Danubio
Danubian [dæn'jubɪən] *adj* danubiano
daphne ['dæfnɪ] *s* (bot.) laurel; (bot.) adelfilla; (*cap.*) *s* (myth.) Dafne
dapper ['dæpər] *adj* aseado, apuesto, gallardo; vivaracho
dapple ['dæpəl] *s* apariencia moteada; animal rodado, caballo rodado; *adj* rodado, habado; *va* motear
dappled ['dæpəld] *adj* rodado, habado
dapple gray *s* caballo rucio rodado
dapple-gray ['dæpəl,gre] *adj* rucio rodado
Dardan ['dɑrdən] o **Dardanian** [dɑr'denɪən] *adj* dardanio o dárdano; *s* dárdano
Dardanelles [,dɑrdə'nɛlz] *spl* Dardanelos
Dardanus ['dɑrdənəs] *s* (myth.) Dárdano
dare [dɛr] *s* reto, provocación; *va* retar, provocar; arrostrar, resistir; *vn* atreverse; **I dare say** acaso, quizá; **to dare (to)** + *inf* atreverse a + *inf*, osar + *inf*
daredevil ['dɛr,dɛvəl] *adj & s* temerario
daring ['dɛrɪŋ] *adj* osado, atrevido; *s* osadía, atrevimiento
Darius [də'raɪəs] *s* Darío
dark [dɑrk] *adj* obscuro; trigueño, moreno; secreto, oculto; ignorante; triste, tétrico; malvado, perverso; atroz; pardo (*dícese de la cerveza*); **to become dark** o **get dark** obscurecerse; hacerse de noche, anochecer; **to keep dark** callar, tener reservado; *s* obscuridad, tinieblas; anochecer, noche; color obscuro; (paint.) sombra obscura; **in the dark** a obscuras; (fig.) a obscuras
dark ages o **Dark Ages** *spl* edad media; primera mitad de la edad media
dark-complexioned ['dɑrkkəm'plɛkʃənd] *adj* moreno
Dark Continent *s* Continente Negro
darken ['dɑrkən] *va* obscurecer; manchar; desconcertar, confundir; entristecer; *vn* obscurecerse
darkey ['dɑrkɪ] *s* (offensive) negro
dark horse *s* caballo desconocido; ganador desconocido; (pol.) candidato nombrado inesperadamente
darkish ['dɑrkɪʃ] *adj* algo obscuro
dark lantern *s* linterna sorda
darkle ['dɑrkəl] *va* obscurecer, volver obscuro; *vn* obscurecerse, parecer obscuro
darkling ['dɑrklɪŋ] *adj* obscurecido; *adv* a obscuras
darkly ['dɑrklɪ] *adv* obscuramente; secretamente; misteriosamente
dark meat *s* carne del ave fuera de la pechuga
darkness ['dɑrknɪs] *s* obscuridad; secreto; ignorancia; tristeza; maldad, perversidad
darkroom ['dɑrk,rum] o ['dɑrk,rʊm] *s* (phot.) cuarto obscuro
darksome ['dɑrksəm] *adj* (poet.) obscuro, sombrío
darky ['dɑrkɪ] *s* (*pl:* **-ies**) (offensive) negro
darling ['dɑrlɪŋ] *adj & s* querido; predilecto
darn [dɑrn] *s* zurcido; (coll.) maldición; *va & vn* zurcir; (coll.) maldecir
darnel ['dɑrnəl] *s* (bot.) cizaña; (bot.) ballico perenne
darner ['dɑrnər] *s* zurcidor; aguja de zurcir
darning ['dɑrnɪŋ] *s* zurcidura; cosas zurcidas; cosas por zurcir; *adj* zurcidor; de zurcir
darning needle *s* aguja de zurcir; (ent.) caballito del diablo
dart [dɑrt] *s* dardo, saeta; movimiento rápido; rehilete (*que se lanza por diversión*); aguijón (*de los insectos*); (sew.) sisa; (arch.) saetilla, dardo (*puntas de flechas que alternan con las ovas*); *vn* lanzarse, precipitarse; volar como dardo
darter ['dɑrtər] *s* flechador; (ichth.) eteostoma; (orn.) pájaro culebra
dartle ['dɑrtəl] *va* lanzar repetidamente; *vn* lanzarse repetidamente
Darwinian [dɑr'wɪnɪən] *adj* darviniano; *s* darvinista
Darwinism ['dɑrwɪnɪzəm] *s* darvinismo
Darwinist ['dɑrwɪnɪst] *adj* darviniano; *s* darvinista
dash [dæʃ] *s* rociada; arremetida, arranque; choque, colisión; revés repentino; poquito, pequeña cantidad; carrera corta; brío, espíritu; jactancia; guardafango, guardalodos; (aut.) tablero de instrumentos; raya (*en la imprenta, la escritura y la telegrafía*); **at one dash** de un golpe; **to cut a dash** hacer gran papel; *va* lanzar, tirar; quebrar, romper, estrellar; desanimar; frustrar; rociar, salpicar; mezclar; **to dash against** estampar contra; **to dash away** desechar, arrojar de sí; **to dash off** escribir de prisa; **to dash to pieces** hacer añicos, hacer mil pedazos; *vn* chocar, estrellarse (*p.ej., las olas del mar*); lanzarse; **to dash by** pasar corriendo; **to dash in** entrar como un rayo, entrar de estampía; **to dash out** salir como un rayo, salir de estampía
dashboard ['dæʃ,bord] *s* guardafango, guardalodos; (aut.) tablero de instrumentos
dasher ['dæʃər] *s* persona briosa; agitador (*de mantequera o sorbetera*)
dashing ['dæʃɪŋ] *adj* brioso; vistoso, ostentoso; *s* embate (*p.ej., de las olas*)
dastard ['dæstərd] *adj & s* vil, miserable, cobarde
dastardly ['dæstərdlɪ] *adj* vil, miserable, cobarde
dat. abr. de **dative**
data processing *s* tramitación automática de datos
datary ['detərɪ] *s* (*pl:* **-ries**) dataría (*cargo*); datario (*cardenal*)
date [det] *s* fecha, data; (coll.) cita; (bot.) datilera; dátil (*fruto*); **out of date** fuera de mo-

da, anticuado; **to bring up to date** poner al día; **to date** hasta la fecha; **under date of** con fecha de; **up to date** hasta la fecha; **what is the date?** ¿cuál es la fecha de hoy?; *va* fechar, datar; (coll.) tener cita o citas con; *vn* datar; llevar fecha; **to date from** datar de
dated ['detɪd] *adj* fechado; anticuado, fuera de moda
dateless ['detlɪs] *adj* sin fecha; sin fin; inmemorial
date line *s* línea (efectiva) de cambio de fecha
date palm *s* (bot.) palmera datilera
date shell *s* (zool.) dátil
dative ['detɪv] *adj & s* (gram.) dativo
datum (['detəm] o ['dætəm] *s* (*pl:* **data** ['detə] o ['dætə]) dato
datum level *s* (surv.) nivel de referencia
datum plane *s* (surv.) plano de referencia
datura [də'tjʊrə] *s* (bot.) datura
dau. abr. de **daughter**
daub [dɔb] *s* embadurnamiento; pintarrajo (*pintura mal hecha*); *va* embadurnar; pintarrajear; *vn* embadurnarse; pintarrajear
dauber ['dɔbər] *s* embadurnador; mal pintor
daughter ['dɔtər] *s* hija
daughter-in-law ['dɔtərɪn,lɔ] *s* (*pl:* **daughters-in-law**) nuera
daughterly ['dɔtərlɪ] *adj* filial, como una hija
daughter of Eve *s* hija de Eva
daunt [dɔnt] o [dɑnt] *va* espantar, asustar; desanimar, acobardar
dauntless ['dɔntlɪs] o ['dɑntlɪs] *adj* impávido, intrépido, atrevido
dauphin ['dɔfɪn] *s* delfín
dauphiness ['dɔfɪnɪs] *s* delfina
davenport ['dævənport] *s* pequeño escritorio; sofá cama tapizado
David ['devɪd] *s* David
davit ['dævɪt] o ['devɪt] *s* (naut.) pescante, grúa de bote
Davy Jones's locker ['devɪ 'dʒonzɪz] *s* el fondo del mar
Davy lamp *s* lámpara de Davy, lámpara de seguridad para los mineros
daw [dɔ] *s* (orn.) corneja
dawdle ['dɔdəl] *va* malgastar (*tiempo*); *vn* malgastar el tiempo, haronear
dawdler ['dɔdlər] *s* holgazán, haragán
dawn [dɔn] *s* amanecer, alba, aurora; (fig.) aurora, principio, comienzo; *vn* amanecer; despuntar (*el día, la mañana, etc.*); empezar a mostrarse; **to dawn on** o **upon one** venírsele a uno a las mientes; empezar uno a comprender, p.ej., **the truth dawned on him** empezó a comprender la verdad
day [de] *s* día; jornada (*p.ej., de trabajo, de inquietud*); victoria, triunfo; **any day** de un día a otro, de un día para otro; **by day** de día; **by the day** a jornal; **from day to day** de día en día, de un día para otro; **the day after** el día siguiente; **the day after tomorrow** pasado mañana; **the day before** la víspera, la víspera de; **the day before yesterday** anteayer; **to call it a day** (coll.) dejar de trabajar; **to have one's day** tener sus días; **to this day** hasta el día de hoy; **to win the day** ganar la palma, ganar la victoria; **day after day** día tras día; **day by day** día por día; **day in, day out** día tras día, sin cesar; *adj* diurno
day bed *s* sofá cama, diván cama, canapé cama
day book *s* diario; (com.) libro diario; (naut.) cuaderno de bitácora
daybreak ['de,brek] *s* amanecer, aurora; **at daybreak** al amanecer
day coach *s* (rail.) coche de viajeros
daydream ['de,drim] *s* ensueño, sueño de vigilia; *vn* soñar despierto
day laborer *s* jornalero
day letter *s* telegrama diurno
daylight ['de,laɪt] *s* día, luz del día; amanecer; luz, publicidad; (slang) abertura, espacio, intervalo; **in broad daylight** en pleno día; **to scare the daylights out of** (slang) pasmar de terror; **to see daylight** comprender; (coll.) ver el fin de una tarea difícil
daylight saving *s* aprovechamiento de la luz
daylight-saving time ['de,laɪt'sevɪŋ] *s* hora de verano
day lily *s* (bot.) azucena amarilla
daylong ['de,lɔŋ] o ['de,lɑŋ] *adj* de todo el día; *adv* todo el día
day nursery *s* guardería infantil
Day of Atonement *s* día de la expiación
day off *s* día de holgar o de huelga, día de vacación, asueto
Day of Judgment *s* día del juicio
day of reckoning *s* día de ajustar cuentas, día de la justicia
day school *s* escuela diurna; escuela de semana; externado, escuela de externos
day shift *s* turno diurno
days of grace *spl* (com.) días de gracia
dayspring ['de,sprɪŋ] *s* aurora, albor
daystar ['de,stɑr] *s* lucero del alba; (poet.) sol
daytime ['de,taɪm] *s* día; **in the daytime** de día
daze [dez] *s* aturdimiento; deslumbramiento; **in a daze** aturdido; *va* aturdir; deslumbrar
dazzle ['dæzəl] *s* deslumbramiento, ofuscamiento; *va* deslumbrar, ofuscar
dazzling ['dæzlɪŋ] *adj* deslumbrante
d.c. abr. de **direct current**
D.C. abr. de **direct current** y **District of Columbia**
DDT ['di'di'ti] *s* símbolo de **dichlorodiphenyl-trichloroethane**
deacon ['dikən] *s* diácono
deaconess ['dikənɪs] *s* diaconisa
deaconry ['dikənrɪ] *s* (*pl:* **-ries**) diaconato
dead [dɛd] *adj* muerto; anticuado, fuera de uso; (coll.) cansado; (sport) muerto; *adv* absolutamente, completamente; directamente; *s* época o tiempo lóbrego; **deads** *spl* (min.) escombros; **the dead** los muertos; **the dead of night** el profundo silencio de la noche; **the dead of winter** lo más frío del invierno
dead air *s* (rad.) interrupción del programa (*por avería*)
dead beat *s* (slang) gorrón; (slang) holgazán
dead-beat ['dɛd'bit] *adj* (coll.) muerto de cansancio
deadbeat ['dɛd,bit] *adj* (phys.) sin oscilación
dead bolt *s* cerrojo dormido
dead center *s* (mach.) punto muerto; (mach.) punta fija (*p.ej., en un torno*)
dead-drunk ['dɛd'drʌŋk] *adj* difunto de taberna
dead duck *s* (slang) persona acabada, persona sin porvenir, cosa arruinada
deaden ['dɛdən] *va* amortiguar, amortecer; insonorizar
dead end *s* extremo cerrado, callejón sin salida; (rad.) punto muerto; (fig.) atolladero
dead-end ['dɛd,ɛnd] *adj* sin salida; (rad.) muerto
deadeye ['dɛd,aɪ] *s* (naut.) vigota
dead freight *s* (naut.) falso flete
deadhead ['dɛd,hɛd] *s* persona exenta de pagar (*en el teatro, el ferrocarril, etc.*); (found.) mazarota; (naut.) boya de madera; (naut.) poste de amarra
dead heat *s* carrera indecisa
dead key *s* tecla muerta (*de una máquina de escribir*)
dead language *s* lengua muerta
deadlatch ['dɛd,lætʃ] *s* aldaba dormida
dead letter *s* carta no reclamada; (fig.) letra muerta (*práctica caída en desuso, ley que ya no se cumple*)
dead-letter office ['dɛd'lɛtər] *s* oficina de cartas no reclamadas
deadline ['dɛd,laɪn] *s* línea vedada; fin del plazo
deadlock ['dɛd,lɑk] *s* cerradura dormida; estancación, callejón sin salida; *va* estancar; *vn* estancarse
deadly ['dɛdlɪ] *adj* (*comp:* **-lier;** *super:* **-liest**) mortal; fatigoso, abrumador; *adv* mortalmente; excesivamente, sumamente
deadly carrot *s* (bot.) tapsia
deadly nightshade *s* (bot.) belladona; (bot.) hierba mora
deadly sins *spl* siete pecados capitales
dead march *s* (mus.) marcha fúnebre
dead pan *s* (slang) semblante sin expresión
dead point *s* punto muerto
dead reckoning *s* (naut.) estima
dead ringer *s* segunda edición (*persona o cosa que se parece mucho a otra*)
dead rise *s* (naut.) delgado

Dead Sea *s* mar Muerto
dead set *adj* (coll.) muy resuelto, muy determinado
dead-smooth file ['dɛd,smuð] *s* lima sorda
dead soldier *s* (slang) botella vacía
dead-stick landing ['dɛd,stɪk] *s* (aer.) aterrizaje con motor muerto
dead stop *s* parada completa, parada en seco
dead weight *s* peso muerto, peso propio; carga onerosa
deadwood ['dɛd,wʊd] *s* leña seca; gente inútil, material inútil
deaf [dɛf] *adj* sordo; **as deaf as a post** sordo como una tapia; **to turn a deaf ear** hacerse sordo
deaf and dumb *adj* sordomudo
deaf-and-dumb alphabet ['dɛfənd'dʌm] *s* alfabeto para sordomudos, alfabeto dactilológico
deaf-dumbness ['dɛf'dʌmnɪs] *s* sordomudez
deafen ['dɛfən] *va* asordar, ensordecer; insonorizar (*p.ej., una pared*); apagar (*un sonido*); aturdir
deafening ['dɛfənɪŋ] *adj* ensordecedor; aturdidor
deaf-mute ['dɛf,mjut] *adj & s* sordomudo
deafness ['dɛfnɪs] *s* sordera
deal [dil] *s* negocio, negociación; (coll.) trato; reparto, repartición; mano (*p.ej., de naipes*); turno de dar (*los naipes*); parte, porción; tabla de pino, tabla de abeto; (coll.) convenio secreto; **a good deal (of)** o **a great deal (of)** mucho, p.ej., **he has a good deal of money** tiene mucho dinero; **a good deal faster** mucho más rápidamente; **it's a deal** (coll.) trato hecho; **to make a great deal of** estimar mucho; hacer fiestas a; (*pret & pp:* **dealt**) *va* asestar, dar (*un golpe*); repartir, dar (*la baraja*); *vn* negociar, comerciar; mediar, intervenir; portarse, conducirse; ser mano (*en juegos de naipes*); **to deal with** ocuparse en, entender en; tratar con, entenderse con; tratar de
dealer ['dilər] *s* comerciante, negociante; concesionario; repartidor (*de naipes*)
dealing ['dilɪŋ] *s* negocio, negociación; conducta; repartición; **dealings** *spl* negocios; relaciones de amistad
dealt [dɛlt] *pret & pp de* **deal**
dean [din] *s* decano (*de una escuela*); (eccl.) deán; (fig.) decano
deanery ['dinərɪ] *s* (*pl:* **-ies**) decanato
deanship ['dinʃɪp] *s* decanato; (eccl.) deanato o deanazgo
dear [dɪr] *adj* querido; caro, costoso; carero (*que vende caro*); **dear me!** ¡Dios mío!; ¡válgame Dios!; *adv* afectuosamente; caro; *s* querido
dearie ['dɪrɪ] *s* (coll.) queridito
dearness ['dɪrnɪs] *s* cariño; carestía, precio alto
dearth [dʌrθ] *s* carestía, escasez
deary ['dɪrɪ] *s* (*pl:* **-ies**) (coll.) queridito
death [dɛθ] *s* muerte; (*cap.*) *s* muerte (*esqueleto con una guadaña*); **to be at death's door** estar a la muerte; **to beat to death** matar a golpes; **to be bored to death** morirse de aburrimiento; **to be death on** (slang) estar loco por, amar locamente; (slang) odiar locamente; **to bleed to death** morir desangrado; **to bore to death** matar de aburrimiento; **to burn to death** morir quemado; **to choke to death** estrangular; morir atragantado; **to death** a muerte; excesivamente; **to die a violent death** morir vestido; **to do to death** dar la muerte a; **to freeze to death** morir helado; **to put to death** dar la muerte a; **to shock to death** electrocutar; **to shoot to death** matar a tiros; **to starve to death** matar de hambre; morir de hambre; **to stone to death** matar a pedradas; **to the death** a muerte; excesivamente; **to whip to death** matar a latigazos
deathbed ['dɛθ,bɛd] *s* lecho de muerte
deathblow ['dɛθ,blo] *s* golpe mortal
death certificate *s* fe de óbito, partida de defunción
death cup *s* (bot.) canaleja
deathful ['dɛθfəl] *adj* mortal, de muerte
death house *s* capilla (*de los reos de muerte*)
deathless ['dɛθlɪs] *adj* inmortal, eterno
deathlike ['dɛθ,laɪk] *adj* mortal; cadavérico
deathly ['dɛθlɪ] *adj* mortal, de muerte; *adv* mortalmente; excesivamente, sumamente
death mask *s* mascarilla (*sacada sobre el rostro de un cadáver*)
death penalty *s* pena de muerte
death rate *s* mortalidad
death rattle *s* estertor agónico
death's-head ['dɛθs,hɛd] *s* calavera
death toll *s* doble, toque de difuntos; número de muertos
deathtrap ['dɛθ,træp] *s* lugar inseguro y peligroso; situación peligrosa
Death Valley *s* valle de la Muerte (*en el estado de California, EE.UU.*)
death warrant *s* sentencia de muerte; fin de toda esperanza
deathwatch ['dɛθ,wɑtʃ] *s* velación de un moribundo, velación de un cadáver; guardia de un reo de muerte; (ent.) reloj de la muerte
debacle [de'bɑkəl] o [dɪ'bækəl] *s* desastre, catástrofe, ruina; derrota; deshielo (*de un río*); inundación violenta
debar [dɪ'bɑr] (*pret & pp:* **-barred;** *ger:* **-barring**) *va* excluir; prohibir
debark [dɪ'bɑrk] *va & vn* desembarcar
debarkation [,dibɑr'keʃən] *s* desembarco (*de pasajeros*); desembarque (*de mercancías*)
debarment [dɪ'bɑrmənt] *s* exclusión; prohibición
debase [dɪ'bes] *va* rebajar, degradar, envilecer; alterar, falsificar
debasement [dɪ'besmənt] *s* rebajamiento, degradación, envilecimiento; depreciación; alteración, falsificación
debatable [dɪ'betəbəl] *adj* disputable, discutible
debate [dɪ'bet] *s* debate, discusión; *va* debatir; *vn* debatir; deliberar
debater [dɪ'betər] *s* polemista, controversista
debauch [dɪ'bɔtʃ] *s* libertinaje; lujuria; *va* corromper, seducir; *vn* entregarse a la lujuria
debauchee [,dɛbɔ'ʃi] o [,dɛbɔ'tʃi] *s* libertino, disoluto
debaucher [dɪ'bɔtʃər] *s* corruptor, seductor
debauchery [dɪ'bɔtʃərɪ] *s* (*pl:* **-ies**) libertinaje; lujuria; corrupción
debauchment [dɪ'bɔtʃmənt] *s* corrupción, seducción
debenture [dɪ'bɛntʃər] *s* (com.) vale, orden de pago; (com.) obligación
debilitate [dɪ'bɪlɪtet] *va* debilitar
debilitation [dɪ,bɪlɪ'teʃən] *s* debilitación
debility [dɪ'bɪlɪtɪ] *s* (*pl:* **-ties**) debilidad
debit ['dɛbɪt] *s* (com.) debe; (com.) cargo (*entrada en el debe*); *va* (com.) debitar, adeudar, cargar
debit balance *s* saldo deudor
debonair o **debonaire** [,dɛbə'nɛr] *adj* alegre, de buen humor; cortés, urbano
Deborah ['dɛbərə] *s* Débora
debouch [dɪ'buʃ] *vn* desembocar
debouchment [dɪ'buʃmənt] *s* desembocadura
débride [de'brid] *va* (surg.) desbridar
débridement [de'bridmənt] *s* (surg.) desbridamiento
debrief [di'brif] *va* interrogar (*p.ej., a un piloto de avión*) para conseguir datos informativos
debris o **débris** [de'bri] o ['debri] *s* ruinas, escombros; desecho; (geol.) despojos
debt [dɛt] *s* deuda; (Bib.) deuda (*pecado*); **to be deeply in debt** estar lleno de deudas o trampas; **to run into debt** endeudarse
debt of honor *s* deuda de honor, deuda de juego
debtor ['dɛtər] *s* deudor
debunk [di'bʌŋk] *va* (slang) desenmascarar, desbaratar
debut o **début** [de'bju] o ['debju] *s* estreno, debut; **to make one's debut** estrenarse, debutar; presentarse en sociedad, ponerse de largo
debutante o **débutante** [,dɛbjʊ'tɑnt] o ['dɛbjətænt] *s* principiante, debutante; muchacha que se pone de largo
dec. abr. de **deceased** y **decimeter**
Dec. abr. de **December**
decade ['dɛked] *s* década, decenio
decadence [dɪ'kedəns] o ['dɛkədəns] o **deca-**

dency [dɪˈkedənsɪ] o [ˈdɛkədənsɪ] *s* decadencia; (lit.) decadentismo
decadent [dɪˈkedənt] o [ˈdɛkədənt] *adj* decadente; (lit.) decadentista; *s* (lit.) decadentista
decagon [ˈdɛkəgɑn] *adj & s* (geom.) decágono
decagram o **decagramme** [ˈdɛkəgræm] *s* decagramo
decahedron [ˌdɛkəˈhidrən] *s* (*pl:* **-drons** o **-dra** [drə]) (geom.) decaedro
decalcomania [dɪˌkælkəˈmenɪə] *s* calcomanía o decalcomanía
decalescence [ˌdikəˈlɛsəns] *s* (metal.) decalescencia
decaliter o **decalitre** [ˈdɛkəˌlitər] *s* decalitro
decalog o **decalogue** [ˈdɛkəlɔg] o [ˈdɛkəlɑg] *s* decálogo
decalvant [dɪˈkælvənt] *adj* (med.) decalvante
decameter o **decametre** [ˈdɛkəˌmitər] *s* decámetro
decamp [dɪˈkæmp] *vn* decampar; fugarse, escapar
decampment [dɪˈkæmpmənt] *s* levantamiento del campamento; fuga, escape
decanal [ˈdɛkənəl] o [dɪˈkenəl] *adj* de decano, del decanato
decant [dɪˈkænt] *va* decantar
decantation [ˌdikænˈteʃən] *s* decantación
decanter [dɪˈkæntər] *s* garrafa
decapitate [dɪˈkæpɪtet] *va* decapitar, descabezar
decapitation [dɪˌkæpɪˈteʃən] *s* decapitación, descabezamiento
decapod [ˈdɛkəpɑd] *adj & s* (zool.) decápodo
decarbonate [diˈkɑrbənet] *va* descarbonatar
decarbonization [diˌkɑrbənɪˈzeʃən] *s* descarburación
decarbonize [diˈkɑrbənaɪz] *va* descarburar
decare [ˈdɛkɛr] o [dɛˈkɛr] *s* decárea
decastere [ˈdɛkəstɪr] *s* decastéreo
decasyllabic [ˌdɛkəsɪˈlæbɪk] *adj* decasílabo
decasyllable [ˈdɛkəˌsɪləbəl] *adj & s* decasílabo
decathlon [dɪˈkæθlɑn] *s* (sport) decatlo
decay [dɪˈke] *s* podredumbre; decaimiento, descaecimiento; caries (*p.ej., de los dientes*); *va* pudrir; *vn* pudrirse; cariarse (*los dientes*); decaer
decease [dɪˈsis] *s* fallecimiento; *vn* fallecer
deceased [dɪˈsist] *adj & s* difunto, muerto
decedent [dɪˈsidənt] *s* difunto, muerto
deceit [dɪˈsit] *s* engaño; mentira, fraude; falsedad, duplicidad
deceitful [dɪˈsitfəl] *adj* mentiroso, engañoso
deceivable [dɪˈsivəbəl] *adj* engañadizo
deceive [dɪˈsiv] *va* engañar; *vn* mentir
deceiver [dɪˈsivər] *s* engañador, impostor
decelerate [diˈsɛləret] *va* retardar, desacelerar; *vn* retardarse, desacelerarse
deceleration [diˌsɛləˈreʃən] *s* retardación, desaceleración
December [dɪˈsɛmbər] *s* diciembre; *adj* decembrino
decemvir [dɪˈsɛmvər] *s* decenviro
decemviral [dɪˈsɛmvərəl] *adj* decenviral
decemvirate [dɪˈsɛmvərɪt] o [dɪˈsɛmvəret] *s* decenvirato; cuerpo de diez personas
decency [ˈdisənsɪ] *s* (*pl:* **-cies**) decencia, honestidad; **decencies** *spl* buenas costumbres; comodidades
decennial [dɪˈsɛnɪəl] *adj* decenal; *s* décimo aniversario; fiestas celebradas cada diez años
decent [ˈdisənt] *adj* decente, honesto
decentralization [diˌsɛntrəlɪˈzeʃən] *s* descentralización
decentralize [diˈsɛntrəlaɪz] *va* descentralizar
deception [dɪˈsɛpʃən] *s* decepción, engaño
deceptive [dɪˈsɛptɪv] *adj* engañoso
deciare [ˈdɛsɪɛr] *s* deciárea
decibel [ˈdɛsɪbɛl] *s* (phys.) decibel o decibelio
decide [dɪˈsaɪd] *va* decidir; *vn* decidir, decidirse; **to decide on** decidir (*p.ej., cierta gestion*); **to decide to** + *inf* decidir + *inf*, decidirse a + *inf*
decided [dɪˈsaɪdɪd] *adj* decidido
decidedly [dɪˈsaɪdɪdlɪ] *adv* decididamente
deciduous [dɪˈsɪdʒʊəs] o [dɪˈsɪdjʊəs] *adj* (bot. & zool.) deciduo
decigram o **decigramme** [ˈdɛsɪgræm] *s* decigramo
deciliter o **decilitre** [ˈdɛsɪˌlitər] *s* decilitro
decillion [dɪˈsɪljən] *s* (Brit.) decillón
decimal [ˈdɛsɪməl] *adj & s* decimal
decimal fraction *s* fracción decimal
decimalize [ˈdɛsɪməlaɪz] *va* decimalizar
decimally [ˈdɛsɪməlɪ] *adv* decimalmente
decimal point *s* punto decimal; coma (*usada más comúnmente en español*)
decimate [ˈdɛsɪmet] *va* diezmar
decimation [ˌdɛsɪˈmeʃən] *s* decimación
decimeter o **decimetre** [ˈdɛsɪˌmitər] *s* decímetro
decipher [dɪˈsaɪfər] *va* descifrar
decipherable [dɪˈsaɪfərəbəl] *adj* descifrable
decipherer [dɪˈsaɪfərər] *s* descifrador
decipherment [dɪˈsaɪfərmənt] *s* descifre
decision [dɪˈsɪʒən] *s* decisión
decisive [dɪˈsaɪsɪv] *adj* decisivo; resuelto, determinado
decistere [ˈdɛsɪstɪr] *s* deciestéreo
deck [dɛk] *s* (naut.) cubierta; baraja (*de naipes*); **on deck** (coll.) visible, listo, disponible; **to hit the deck** (slang) levantarse pronto; (slang) extenderse boca abajo; (slang) prepararse para obrar; *va* cubrir, ocultar; adornar, ataviar, engalanar, vestir
deck chair *s* (naut.) silla de cubierta
deck hand *s* (naut.) grumete, marinero de cubierta
deck-land [ˈdɛkˌlænd] *vn* (aer.) apontizar
deck-landing [ˈdɛkˌlændɪŋ] *s* (aer.) apontizaje
deckle [ˈdɛkəl] *s* cubierta (*bastidor*); barba (*desigualdad en los bordes del papel*)
deckle edge *s* barba
deckle-edged [ˈdɛkəlˌɛdʒd] *adj* barbado
declaim [dɪˈklem] *va & vn* declamar
declaimer [dɪˈklemər] *s* declamador
declamation [ˌdɛkləˈmeʃən] *s* declamación
declamatory [dɪˈklæməˌtorɪ] *adj* declamatorio
declarable [dɪˈklɛrəbəl] *adj* declarable
declarant [dɪˈklɛrənt] *s* declarante
declaration [ˌdɛkləˈreʃən] *s* declaración
Declaration of Independence *s* Declaración de la independencia
declarative [dɪˈklærətɪv] *adj* declarativo; (gram.) aseverativo, enunciativo
declaratory [dɪˈklærəˌtorɪ] *adj* declaratorio
declare [dɪˈklɛr] *va & vn* declarar
declension [dɪˈklɛnʃən] *s* declinación; (gram.) declinación
declinable [dɪˈklaɪnəbəl] *adj* declinable
declination [ˌdɛklɪˈneʃən] *s* declinación; (astr. & magnetism) declinación
declinatory compass [dɪˈklaɪnəˌtorɪ] *s* declinatorio
declinatory plea *s* (law) declinatoria
decline [dɪˈklaɪn] *s* declinación, bajada; baja (*de los precios*); bajón (*en la salud, el caudal, etc.*); ocaso (*del sol*); (coll.) consunción, tisis; **to be on the decline** (coll.) ir cabeza abajo (*decaer*); *va* rehusar, declinar; inclinar hacia abajo; (gram.) declinar; *vn* declinar; (gram.) declinar; **to decline to** + *inf* excusarse de + *inf*
declivity [dɪˈklɪvɪtɪ] *s* (*pl:* **-ties**) declividad
decoct [dɪˈkɑkt] *va* extraer por decocción
decoction [dɪˈkɑkʃən] *s* decocción; (pharm.) decocción
decode [diˈkod] *va* descifrar
decoder [diˈkodər] *s* descifrador
decoding [diˈkodɪŋ] *s* descifre
decoherer [ˌdikoˈhɪrər] *s* (rad.) descohesor
décolletage [ˌdekɑlˈtɑʒ] *s* escote o escotadura
décolleté [ˌdekɑlˈte] *adj* escotado (*dícese del vestido o la persona*)
decolorization [diˌkʌlərɪˈzeʃən] *s* decoloración
decolorize [diˈkʌləraɪz] *va* decolorar
decompose [ˌdikəmˈpoz] *va* descomponer; *vn* descomponerse
decomposition [ˌdikɑmpəˈzɪʃən] *s* descomposición
decompression [ˌdikəmˈprɛʃən] *s* descompresión
decompression chamber *s* cámara de descompresión
decontaminate [ˌdikənˈtæmɪnet] *va* descontaminar
decontamination [ˌdikənˌtæmɪˈneʃən] *s* descontaminación
decontamination squad *s* cuadrilla de descontaminación
decontrol [ˌdikənˈtrol] *s* supresión o termina-

ción del control; *va* suprimir o terminar el control de
décor [de'kɔr] *s* decoración; (theat.) decorado
decorate ['dɛkəret] *va* decorar; empapelar (*una pared*); pintar (*p.ej., una pared*); condecorar (*con una insignia de honor*)
decoration [,dɛkə'reʃən] *s* decoracion; condecoración (*insignia de honor*)
Decoration Day *s* (U.S.A.) día señalado para decorar las tumbas de los soldados muertos en batalla (*el 30 de mayo*)
decorative ['dɛkə,retɪv] *adj* decorativo
decorator ['dɛkə,retər] *s* decorador
decorous ['dɛkərəs] o [dɪ'korəs] *adj* decoroso
decorum [dɪ'korəm] *s* decoro
decoy [dɪ'kɔɪ] o ['dikɔɪ] *s* señuelo, añagaza; reclamo (*ave amaestrada*); trampa; entruchón (*persona*); [dɪ'kɔɪ] *va* atraer con señuelo; entruchar
decrease ['dikris] o [dɪ'kris] *s* disminución, decrecimiento; [dɪ'kris] *va* disminuir; *vn* disminuir, disminuirse, decrecer
decree [dɪ'kri] *s* decreto; *va* decretar
decree law *s* decreto-ley
decrement ['dɛkrɪmənt] *s* decremento, disminución; (rad.) decremento
decremeter [dɪ'krɛmɪtər] *s* (rad.) decrémetro
decrepit [dɪ'krɛpɪt] *adj* decrépito
decrepitude [dɪ'krɛpɪtjud] o [dɪ'krɛpɪtud] *s* decrepitud
decrescendo [,dekrə'ʃɛndo] *m* (*pl:* **-dos**) (mus.) decrescendo
decretal [dɪ'kritəl] *adj* decretal; *s* decretal; **decretals** *spl* decretales
decretalist [dɪ'kritəlɪst] *s* (theol.) decretalista
decretist [dɪ'kritɪst] *s* decretista
decrial [dɪ'kraɪəl] *s* vituperio; rebaja
decry [dɪ'kraɪ] (*pret & pp:* **-cried**) *va* vituperar; rebajar, desacreditar
decubitus [dɪ'kjubɪtəs] *s* (med.) decúbito; (path.) decúbito (*úlcera*)
decumbent [dɪ'kʌmbənt] *adj* decumbente; (bot.) decumbente
decuple ['dɛkjupəl] *adj & s* décuplo; *va* decuplar o decuplicar
decurrent [dɪ'kʌrənt] *adj* (bot.) decurrente
decury ['dɛkjərɪ] *s* (*pl:* **-ries**) decuria
decussate [dɪ'kʌsɪt] o [dɪ'kʌset] *adj* decuso o decusado; (bot.) decuso o decusado
dedicate ['dɛdɪket] *va* dedicar
dedication [,dɛdɪ'keʃən] *s* dedicación; dedicatoria (*p.ej., de un libro*)
dedicative ['dɛdɪ,ketɪv] *adj* dedicativo
dedicator ['dɛdɪ,ketər] *s* dedicante
dedicatory ['dɛdɪkə,torɪ] *adj* dedicatorio
dedolation [,dɛdə'leʃən] *s* (surg.) dedolación
deduce [dɪ'djus] o [dɪ'dus] *va* deducir; derivar
deducible [dɪ'djusɪbəl] o [dɪ'dusɪbəl] *adj* deducible
deduct [dɪ'dʌkt] *va* deducir
deductible [dɪ'dʌktɪbəl] *adj* deducible
deduction [dɪ'dʌkʃən] *s* deducción
deductive [dɪ'dʌktɪv] *adj* deductivo
deed [did] *s* acto, hecho; hazaña, proeza; (law) escritura; **in deed** en verdad; de obra, de hecho; *va* (law) traspasar por escritura
deed of gift *s* escritura de donación
deem [dim] *va & vn* pensar, creer, juzgar, conceptuar
deemphasize [di'ɛmfəsaɪz] *va* quitar importancia a
deep [dip] *adj* profundo; grave (*sonido*); subido (*color*); astuto; sagaz; de hondo, p.ej., **ten inches deep** diez pulgadas de hondo; **to go off the deep end** (coll.) adoptar una resolución temeraria; **deep in debt** cargado de deudas; **deep in politics** muy metido en política; **deep in thought** absorto en la meditación; **the deep** lo profundo; lo más intenso; la mar; el infierno; *adv* hondo; **deep into the night** hasta muy tarde la noche
deep-chested ['dip,tʃɛstɪd] *adj* ancho de pecho
deepen ['dipən] *va* profundizar; *vn* profundizarse
deep-felt ['dip,fɛlt] *adj* sentido, hondamente sentido
deep-freeze ['dip'friz] *s* (trademark) congeladora; (*pret:* **-froze;** *pp:* **-frozen**) *va* congelar; almacenar en congeladora
deep-laid ['dip,led] *adj* dispuesto con astucia
deep mourning *s* luto riguroso
deep-rooted ['dip,rutɪd] o ['dip,rʊtɪd] *adj* arraigado profundamente; afirmado, asegurado
deep-sea ['dip,si] *adj* de las profundidades del mar
deep-sea fishing *s* pesca de gran altura
deep-sea lead [lɛd] *s* (naut.) plomada para el sondeo profundo
deep-seated ['dip,sitɪd] *adj* arraigado profundamente; hundido; fijo sólidamente
deep-set ['dip,sɛt] *adj* puesto profundamente; fijo sólidamente
Deep South *s* (U.S.A.) el extremo meridional de los estados de Alabama, Georgia, Luisiana y Misisipí (*considerado como representante de la cultura y las tradiciones del Sur de los EE.UU.*)
deepwater ['dip,wɔtər] o ['dip,wɑtər] *adj* de gran altura
deer [dɪr] *s* (zool.) ciervo, venado
deerhound ['dɪr,haʊnd] *s* galgo escocés de pelo lanoso
deerskin ['dɪr,skɪn] *s* gamuza, piel de ciervo
deerstalking ['dɪr,stɔkɪŋ] *s* caza del venado al acecho
def. abr. de **defendant, deferred, defined, definite** y **definition**
deface [dɪ'fes] *va* desfigurar
defacement [dɪ'fesmənt] *s* desfiguración
de facto [di'fækto] *adv* de hecho; (law) de hecho
defalcate [dɪ'fælket] o ['difælket] *vn* desfalcar
defalcation [,difæl'keʃən] o [,dɛfəl'keʃən] *s* desfalco
defamation [,dɛfə'meʃən] o [,difə'meʃən] *s* difamación
defamatory [dɪ'fæmə,torɪ] *adj* difamatorio
defame [dɪ'fem] *va* difamar
defamer [dɪ'femər] *s* difamador
default [dɪ'fɔlt] *s* omisión, descuido; falta, incumplimiento; (law) rebeldía; **by default** (sport) por no presentarse; **in default of** por falta de; *va* dejar de cumplir; no pagar; (law) condenar en rebeldía; (sport) perder por no presentarse; *vn* faltar; (law) caer en rebeldía; (sport) perder por no presentarse
defaulter [dɪ'fɔltər] *s* delincuente; desfalcador; (law) rebelde
defeat [dɪ'fit] *s* vencimiento, derrota; *va* vencer, derrotar
defeatism [dɪ'fitɪzəm] *s* derrotismo
defeatist [dɪ'fitɪst] *adj & s* derrotista
defecate ['dɛfɪket] *va* defecar, clarificar; *vn* defecar
defecation [,dɛfɪ'keʃən] *s* defecación
defect [dɪ'fɛkt] o ['difɛkt] *s* defecto; [dɪ'fɛkt] *vn* desertar
defection [dɪ'fɛkʃən] *s* defección; fracaso, mal éxito
defective [dɪ'fɛktɪv] *adj* defectivo, defectuoso, deficiente; (gram.) defectivo
defence [dɪ'fɛns] *s* (Brit.) var. de **defense**
defend [dɪ'fɛnd] *va* defender; (law) defender
defendant [dɪ'fɛndənt] *s* (law) demandado; (law) acusado, reo
defender [dɪ'fɛndər] *s* defensor
defense [dɪ'fɛns] *s* defensa; (law & sport) defensa
defense in depth *s* (mil.) defensa en profundidad
defenseless [dɪ'fɛnslɪs] *adj* indefenso
defense mechanism *s* (physiol. & psychoanal.) defensa
defensible [dɪ'fɛnsɪbəl] *adj* defendible
defensive [dɪ'fɛnsɪv] *adj* defensivo; *s* defensiva; **to be on the defensive** estar a la defensiva
defer [dɪ'fʌr] (*pret & pp:* **-ferred;** *ger:* **-ferring**) *va* diferir, aplazar, dilatar; *vn* deferir; **to defer to** deferir a (*p.ej., el parecer de otro*)
deference ['dɛfərəns] *s* deferencia
deferent ['dɛfərənt] *adj* deferente; (anat.) deferente
deferential [,dɛfə'rɛnʃəl] *adj* deferente
deferment [dɪ'fʌrmənt] *s* aplazamiento, dilación
defiance [dɪ'faɪəns] *s* desafío; oposición obsti-

nada; **in defiance of** a despecho de; **to bid defiance to** o **to set at defiance** desafiar
defiant [dɪ'faɪənt] *adj* desafiador; provocante
deficiency [dɪ'fɪʃənsɪ] *s* (*pl:* **-cies**) deficiencia, carencia; (com.) descubierto
deficiency disease *s* (med.) enfermedad por carencia, enfermedad carencial
deficient [dɪ'fɪʃənt] *adj* deficiente
deficit ['dɛfɪsɪt] *s* déficit; *adj* deficitario
deficit spending *s* gasto que produce déficit
defier [dɪ'faɪər] *s* desafiador; provocador
defilade [,dɛfɪ'led] *s* (mil.) desenfilada; *va* (fort. & mil.) desenfilar; *vn* (fort. & mil.) desenfilarse
defile [dɪ'faɪl] o ['difaɪl] *s* desfiladero; [dɪ'faɪl] *va* manchar, corromper, violar, deshonrar; *vn* desfilar
defilement [dɪ'faɪlmənt] *s* corrupción, violación, deshonra
defiler [dɪ'faɪlər] *s* corruptor, violador, deshonrador
definable [dɪ'faɪnəbəl] *adj* definible
define [dɪ'faɪn] *va* definir
definite ['dɛfɪnɪt] *adj* definido; (gram.) definido, determinado
definite article *s* (gram.) artículo definido, artículo determinado
definition [,dɛfɪ'nɪʃən] *s* definición; (opt.) definición
definitive [dɪ'fɪnɪtɪv] *adj* definitivo; *s* sentencia definitiva; (gram.) palabra limitativa
deflagrate ['dɛfləgret] *va* (chem.) hacer deflagrar; *vn* (chem.) deflagrar
deflagration [,dɛflə'greʃən] *s* (chem.) deflagración
deflate [dɪ'flet] *va* desinflar; (fig.) desinflar (*a una persona*)
deflation [dɪ'fleʃən] *s* desinflación; (econ.) deflación
deflationary [dɪ'fleʃən,ɛrɪ] *adj* deflacionista
deflect [dɪ'flɛkt] *va* desviar; *vn* desviarse
deflection [dɪ'flɛkʃən] *s* desviación, deflexión
deflective [dɪ'flɛktɪv] *adj* desviador
deflector [dɪ'flɛktər] *s* deflector; (naut.) deflector
defloration [,dɛflə'reʃən] *s* desfloración
deflower [di'flaʊər] *va* desflorar
defoliate [dɪ'folɪet] *va* deshojar; *vn* deshojarse
defoliation [dɪ,folɪ'eʃən] *s* defoliación
deforce [di'fors] *va* (law) detentar
deforcement [dɪ'forsmənt] *s* (law) detentación
deforciant [dɪ'forʃənt] *s* (law) detentador
deforest [di'fɑrɪst] o [di'fɔrɪst] *va* desforestar
deforestation [di,fɑrɪs'teʃən] o [di,fɔrɪs'teʃən] *s* desforestación
deform [dɪ'fɔrm] *va* deformar
deformation [,difɔr'meʃən] o [,dɛfər'meʃən] *s* deformación
deformed [dɪ'fɔrmd] *adj* deforme
deformity [dɪ'fɔrmɪtɪ] *s* (*pl:* **-ties**) deformidad
defraud [dɪ'frɔd] *va* defraudar
defrauder [dɪ'frɔdər] *s* defraudador
defray [dɪ'fre] *va* sufragar, subvenir a
defrayal [dɪ'freəl] o **defrayment** [dɪ'fremənt] *s* pago, sufragación
defrost [di'frɔst] o [di'frɑst] *va* deshelar, descongelar
defroster [di'frɔstər] o [di'frɑstər] *s* desescarchador, descongelador
defrosting [di'frɔstɪŋ] o [di'frɑstɪŋ] *s* descongelación, deshielo
deft [dɛft] *adj* diestro, hábil; ligero
deftness ['dɛftnɪs] *s* destreza, habilidad; ligereza
defunct [dɪ'fʌŋkt] *adj* difunto
defy [dɪ'faɪ] o ['difaɪ] *s* (*pl:* **-fies**) (slang) desafío; [dɪ'faɪ] (*pret & pp:* **-fied**) *va* desafiar; oponerse obstinadamente a; resistir
deg. abr. de **degree** o **degrees**
degas [di'gæs] (*pret & pp:* **-gassed;** *ger:* **-gassing**) *va* desgasificar
degasify [di'gæsɪfaɪ] (*pret & pp:* **-fied**) *va* var. de **degas**
de Gaullist [də'golɪst] *adj & s* degaullista
degauss [dɪ'gaʊs] o [dɪ'gɔs] *va* desgausar
degeneracy [dɪ'dʒɛnərəsɪ] *s* degeneración
degenerate [dɪ'dʒɛnərɪt] *adj & s* degenerado; [dɪ'dʒɛnəret] *vn* degenerar
degeneration [dɪ,dʒɛnə'reʃən] *s* degeneración
degenerative [dɪ'dʒɛnə,retɪv] *adj* degenerativo
deglutition [,diglu'tɪʃən] o [,dɛglu'tɪʃən] *s* deglución
degradation [,dɛgrə'deʃən] *s* degradación; (geol.) degradación
degrade [dɪ'gred] *va* degradar; (geol.) degradar
degrading [dɪ'gredɪŋ] *adj* degradante
degree [dɪ'gri] *s* grado; (educ.) grado (*p.ej., de bachiller*); (gram., math. & mus.) grado; **by degrees** de grado en grado; **to a degree** algo, un poco; en sumo grado; **to take a degree** recibir un grado o título
dehisce [di'hɪs] *vn* abrirse, hendirse
dehiscence [di'hɪsəns] *s* (biol. & bot.) dehiscencia
dehiscent [di'hɪsənt] *adj* dehiscente
dehorn [di'hɔrn] *va* descornar
dehumanization [di,hjumənɪ'zeʃən] *s* deshumanización
dehumanize [di'hjumənaɪz] *va* deshumanizar
dehumidifier [,dihju'mɪdɪ,faɪər] *s* deshumedecedor, reductor de humedad
dehumidify [,dihju'mɪdɪfaɪ] (*pret & pp:* **-fied**) *va* deshumedecer, deshumidificar
dehydrate [di'haɪdret] *va* deshidratar; *vn* deshidratarse
dehydration [,dihaɪ'dreʃən] *s* deshidratación
dehypnotize [di'hɪpnətaɪz] *va* deshipnotizar
deice [di'aɪs] *va* (aer.) deshelar
deicer [di'aɪsər] *s* (aer.) deshelador
deicidal [,diɪ'saɪdəl] *adj* deicida
deicide ['diɪsaɪd] *s* deicida (*persona*); deicidio (*acción*)
deific [di'ɪfɪk] *adj* deífico
deification [,diɪfɪ'keʃən] *s* deificación
deify ['diɪfaɪ] (*pret & pp:* **-fied**) *va* deificar
deign [den] *va* dignarse dar o conceder; *vn* dignarse; **to deign to** + *inf* dignarse + *inf*
deism ['diɪzəm] *s* deísmo
deist ['diɪst] *s* deísta
deistic [di'ɪstɪk] o **deistical** [di'ɪstɪkəl] *adj* deísta
deity ['diɪtɪ] *s* (*pl:* **-ties**) deidad; **the Deity** Dios
deject [dɪ'dʒɛkt] *va* abatir, desanimar
dejected [dɪ'dʒɛktɪd] *adj* abatido, desanimado
dejection [dɪ'dʒɛkʃən] *s* abatimiento, desánimo; (physiol.) deyección
dekaliter ['dɛkə,litər] *s* var. de **decaliter**
dekameter ['dɛkə,mitər] *s* var. de **decameter**
del. abr. de **delegate** y **delete**
Del. abr. de **Delaware**
delay [dɪ'le] *s* dilación, retraso, tardanza; *va* dilatar, retrasar; *vn* tardar, demorarse
delayed-action fuse [dɪ'led'ækʃən] *s* (mil.) espoleta de explosión retardada
delayed-time switch [dɪ'led'taɪm] *s* (elec.) llave de tiempo atrasado
dele ['dilɪ] *s* (print.) dele; *va* (print.) suprimir
delectable [dɪ'lɛktəbəl] *adj* deleitable
delectation [,dilɛk'teʃən] *s* delectación
delegacy ['dɛlɪgəsɪ] *s* (*pl:* **-cies**) delegación
delegate ['dɛlɪget] o ['dɛlɪgɪt] *s* delegado; congresista; ['dɛlɪget] *va* delegar
delegation [,dɛlɪ'geʃən] *s* delegación
delete [dɪ'lit] *va* suprimir
deleterious [,dɛlɪ'tɪrɪəs] *adj* deletéreo
deletion [dɪ'liʃən] *s* supresión
delft [dɛlft] o **delftware** ['dɛlft,wɛr] *s* porcelana de Delft
Delian ['dilɪən] *adj & s* delio
deliberate [dɪ'lɪbərɪt] *adj* reflexionado, pensado; circunspecto, cauto; espacioso, lento, tardo; [dɪ'lɪbəret] *va & vn* deliberar
deliberation [dɪ,lɪbə'reʃən] *s* deliberación
deliberative [dɪ'lɪbə,retɪv] *adj* deliberativo; deliberante
delicacy ['dɛlɪkəsɪ] *s* (*pl:* **-cies**) delicadeza; golosina (*manjar delicado*)
delicate ['dɛlɪkɪt] *adj* delicado
delicatessen [,dɛlɪkə'tɛsən] *s* ultramarinos; tienda de ultramarinos, tienda de fiambres, ensaladas, queso, pescado ahumado, etc.
delicious [dɪ'lɪʃəs] *adj* delicioso, sabroso
delight [dɪ'laɪt] *s* deleite, delicia; **to take delight in** deleitarse con o en; **to take delight in** + *ger* deleitarse en + *inf;* *va* deleitar; **to be**

delighted to + *inf* deleitarse en + *inf; vn* deleitarse; **to delight in** deleitarse con o en; **to delight in** + *ger* deleitarse en + *inf*
delightful [dɪˈlaɪtfəl] *adj* deleitoso, delicioso
Delilah [dɪˈlaɪlə] *s* (Bib.) Dalila
delimit [dɪˈlɪmɪt] *va* delimitar
delimitation [dɪˌlɪmɪˈteʃən] *s* delimitación
delineate [dɪˈlɪnɪet] *va* delinear
delineation [dɪˌlɪnɪˈeʃən] *s* delineación
delineator [dɪˈlɪnɪˌetər] *s* delineador, delineante
delinquency [dɪˈlɪŋkwənsɪ] *s* (*pl:* **-cies**) culpa, delincuencia; morosidad (*en el pago*)
delinquent [dɪˈlɪŋkwənt] *adj* culpado, delincuente; moroso (*en el pago, etc.*); debido y no pagado; *s* culpado; deudor moroso
deliquesce [ˌdelɪˈkwes] *vn* liquidarse lentamente, atrayendo la humedad del aire; derretirse
deliquescence [ˌdelɪˈkwesəns] *s* delicuescencia
deliquescent [ˌdelɪˈkwesənt] *adj* delicuescente
delirious [dɪˈlɪrɪəs] *adj* delirante; **to be delirious** delirar
delirium [dɪˈlɪrɪəm] *s* (*pl:* **-ums** o **-a** [ə]) delirio
delirium tremens [ˈtrimənz] *s* (path.) delírium tremens
deliver [dɪˈlɪvər] *va* librar, libertar; entregar; distribuir (*el correo*); dar, asestar, descargar (*un golpe*); lanzar (*p.ej., una pelota*); recitar, pronunciar (*un discurso*); rendir, transmitir (*energía*); partear (*a la mujer que está de parto*); **to be delivered** parir; **to deliver oneself of** aliviarse de; comunicar
deliverance [dɪˈlɪvərəns] *s* libramiento, liberación; rescate; profesión, dictamen; alumbramiento
deliverer [dɪˈlɪvərər] *s* librador, salvador; entregador; relator; distribuidor
delivery [dɪˈlɪvərɪ] *s* (*pl:* **-ies**) liberación; rescate; entrega; distribución (*del correo*); parto, alumbramiento; discurso, modo de expresarse
deliveryman [dɪˈlɪvərɪmən] *s* (*pl:* **-men**) entregador, recadero, mozo de reparto
delivery room *s* sala de alumbramiento (*de un hospital*)
delivery table *s* (print.) sacador
delivery truck *s* furgoneta, sedán de reparto
dell [del] *s* vallecito, vallejuelo
Delos [ˈdilɑs] *s* Delos
delouse [diˈlaʊs] o [diˈlaʊz] *va* despiojar, espulgar
Delphi [ˈdelfaɪ] *s* Delfos
Delphian [ˈdelfɪən] *adj* délfico; ambiguo
Delphic [ˈdelfɪk] *adj* délfico; ambiguo
Delphic oracle *s* oráculo délfico o de Delfos
delphinium [delˈfɪnɪəm] *s* (bot.) espuela de caballero (*Delphinium ajacis*); (bot.) consólida real (*Delphinium consolida*)
delta [ˈdeltə] *s* delta
delta connection *s* (elec.) conexión en delta
delta wing *s* (aer.) ala en delta
deltoid [ˈdeltɔɪd] *adj* deltoides (*triangular*); (anat.) deltoides; *s* (anat.) deltoides
deltoid muscle *s* (anat.) deltoides
delude [dɪˈlud] *va* deludir, engañar
deluder [dɪˈludər] *s* delusor, engañador
deluge [ˈdeljudʒ] *s* diluvio; (fig.) diluvio; **the Deluge** el Diluvio; *va* inundar; **to deluge with** inundar de
delusion [dɪˈluʒən] *s* engaño, decepción
delusive [dɪˈlusɪv] o **delusory** [dɪˈlusərɪ] *adj* delusorio; ilusivo
de luxe [dɪˈlʊks] o [dɪˈlʌks] *adj & adv* de lujo
delve [delv] *va* cavar; *vn* cavar; insudar (*afanarse*); buscar (*explorar*); **to delve into** sondear, profundizar
Dem. abr. de **Democrat** y **Democratic**
demagnetization [diˌmægnɪtɪˈzeʃən] *s* desimanación, desimantación
demagnetize [diˈmægnɪtaɪz] *va* desimanar, desimantar
demagog [ˈdeməgɑg] *s* demagogo
demagogic [ˌdeməˈgɑdʒɪk] o [ˌdeməˈgɑgɪk] *adj* demagógico
demagogue [ˈdeməgɑg] *s* var. de **demagog**
demagoguery [ˈdeməˌgɑgərɪ] o **demagogy** [ˈdeməˌgɑdʒɪ] o [ˈdeməˌgɑgɪ] *s* demagogia
demand [dɪˈmænd] o [dɪˈmɑnd] *s* demanda; (com.) demanda; (law) demanda (*reclamación*); **on demand** a la presentación; **to be in demand** tener demanda; *va* demandar; pedir perentoriamente
demanding [dɪˈmændɪŋ] o [dɪˈmɑndɪŋ] *adj* exigente
demarcate [ˈdimɑrket] o [dɪˈmɑrket] *va* demarcar
demarcation [ˌdimɑrˈkeʃən] *s* demarcación
démarche [deˈmɑrʃ] *s* gestión, paso; (dipl.) diligencia, gestión
demean [dɪˈmin] *va* degradar; **to demean oneself** degradarse; portarse, conducirse; *vn* portarse, conducirse
demeanor [dɪˈminər] *s* porte, conducta, comportamiento
demeanour [dɪˈminər] *s* (Brit.) var. de **demeanor**
demented [dɪˈmentɪd] *adj* demente
dementia [dɪˈmenʃə] *s* demencia
dementia praecox [ˈprikɑks] *s* (path.) demencia precoz
demerit [diˈmerɪt] *s* demérito; nota de desaprobación
demesne [dɪˈmen] o [dɪˈmin] *s* tierra solariega; heredad; dominio; región
Demeter [dɪˈmitər] *s* (myth.) Deméter o Demetria
demigod [ˈdemɪˌgɑd] *s* semidiós
demigoddess [ˈdemɪˌgɑdɪs] *s* semidiosa
demigorge [ˈdemɪˌgɔrdʒ] *s* (fort.) semigola
demijohn [ˈdemɪdʒɑn] *s* damajuana
demilitarization [diˌmɪlɪtərɪˈzeʃən] *s* desmilitarización
demilitarize [diˈmɪlɪtəraɪz] *va* desmilitarizar
demimondaine [ˌdemɪmɑnˈden] *s* mujer mundana
demimonde [ˈdemɪmɑnd] *s* mujeres mundanas, mujeres de reputación equívoca
demineralization [diˌmɪnərəlɪˈzeʃən] *s* (med.) desmineralización
demise [dɪˈmaɪz] *s* fallecimiento; transmisión de la corona; (law) traslación de dominio; *va* (law) transferir, transferir por testamento o por arriendo
demisemiquaver [ˈdemɪˈsemɪˌkwevər] *s* (mus.) fusa
demission [dɪˈmɪʃən] *s* dimisión
demit [dɪˈmɪt] (*pret & pp:* **-mitted;** *ger:* **-mitting**) *va & vn* dimitir
demitasse [ˈdemɪˌtæs] o [ˈdemɪˌtɑs] *s* taza pequeña, tacita de café
Demiurge [ˈdemɪʌrdʒ] *s* (philos.) demiurgo
demobilization [diˌmobɪlɪˈzeʃən] *s* desmovilización
demobilize [diˈmobɪlaɪz] *va* desmovilizar
democracy [dɪˈmɑkrəsɪ] *s* (*pl:* **-cies**) democracia
democrat [ˈdeməkræt] *s* demócrata
democratic [ˌdeməˈkrætɪk] *adj* demócrata; democrático
democratically [ˌdeməˈkrætɪkəlɪ] *adv* democráticamente
democratization [dɪˌmɑkrətɪˈzeʃən] *s* democratización
democratize [dɪˈmɑkrətaɪz] *va* democratizar; *vn* democratizarse
Democritus [dɪˈmɑkrɪtəs] *s* Demócrito
demodulate [diˈmɑdʒəlet] *va* (rad.) desmodular
Demogorgon [ˌdimoˈgɔrgən] o [ˌdemoˈgɔrgən] *s* (myth.) Demogorgón
demographic [ˌdiməˈgræfɪk] o **demographical** [ˌdiməˈgræfɪkəl] *adj* demográfico
demography [dɪˈmɑgrəfɪ] *s* demografía
demoiselle [ˌdemwɑˈzel] *s* damisela; (orn.) antropoide, grulla de Numidia; (ent.) caballito del diablo
demolish [dɪˈmɑlɪʃ] *va* demoler
demolisher [dɪˈmɑlɪʃər] *s* demoledor
demolishment [dɪˈmɑlɪʃmənt] *s* demolición
demolition [ˌdeməˈlɪʃən] o [ˌdiməˈlɪʃən] *s* demolición
demolition bomb *s* bomba de demolición
demolition squad *s* cuadrilla de demolición
demon [ˈdimən] *s* demonio
demonetization [diˌmɑnɪtɪˈzeʃən] o [diˌmʌnɪtɪˈzeʃən] *s* desmonetización
demonetize [diˈmɑnɪtaɪz] o [diˈmʌnɪtaɪz] *va* desmonetizar
demoniac [dɪˈmonɪæk] *adj & s* demoníaco

demoniacal [ˌdiməˈnaɪəkəl] *adj* demoníaco
demonic [diˈmɑnɪk] *adj* demoníaco
demonism [ˈdimənɪzəm] *s* demonismo
demonolatry [ˌdimənˈɑlətrɪ] *s* demonolatría
demonology [ˌdimənˈɑlədʒɪ] *s* demonología
demonomancy [ˌdimənˈɑmənsɪ] *s* demonomancia
demonstrability [dɪˌmɑnstrəˈbɪlɪtɪ] o [ˌdɛmənstrəˈbɪlɪtɪ] *s* demostrabilidad
demonstrable [dɪˈmɑnstrəbəl] o [ˈdɛmənstrəbəl] *adj* demostrable
demonstrably [dɪˈmɑnstrəblɪ] o [ˈdɛmənstrəblɪ] *adv* demostrablemente
demonstrate [ˈdɛmənstret] *va* demostrar; *vn* manifestar
demonstration [ˌdɛmənˈstreʃən] *s* demostración; manifestación (*reunión pública para dar a conocer un sentimiento u opinión*)
demonstrative [dɪˈmɑnstrətɪv] *adj* demostrativo; (gram.) demostrativo; *s* (gram.) demostrativo
demonstrator [ˈdɛmənˌstretər] *s* demostrador; vehículo de demostraciones; alborotador, manifestante
demoralization [dɪˌmɑrəlɪˈzeʃən] o [dɪˌmɔrəlɪˈzeʃən] *s* desmoralización
demoralize [dɪˈmɑrəlaɪz] o [dɪˈmɔrəlaɪz] *va* desmoralizar
demoralizing [dɪˈmɑrəlaɪzɪŋ] o [dɪˈmɔrəlaɪzɪŋ] *adj* desmoralizador
Demosthenes [dɪˈmɑsθəniz] *s* Demóstenes
demote [dɪˈmot] *va* degradar
demotic [dɪˈmɑtɪk] *adj* demótico
demotion [dɪˈmoʃən] *s* degradación
demount [diˈmaʊnt] *va* desmontar
demountable [diˈmaʊntəbəl] *adj* desmontable
demulcent [dɪˈmʌlsənt] *adj* & *s* demulcente
demulsibility [dɪˌmʌlsɪˈbɪlɪtɪ] *s* (chem.) demulsibilidad
demulsify [dɪˈmʌlsɪfaɪ] (*pret* & *pp:* **-fied**) *va* (chem.) demulsionar
demur [dɪˈmʌr] *s* objeción; vacilación, irresolución; (*pret* & *pp:* **-murred;** *ger:* **-murring**) *vn* objetar; vacilar
demure [dɪˈmjʊr] *adj* recatado, modesto; gazmoño; serio, sobrio, grave
demurrage [dɪˈmʌrɪdʒ] *s* (com.) estadía
demurrer [dɪˈmʌrər] *s* objeción; persona que objeta; (law) excepción
demy [dɪˈmaɪ] *s* (*pl:* **-mies**) papel marquilla; becario de Magdalen College, Oxford
Den. abr. de **Denmark**
den [dɛn] *s* madriguera (*de animales o ladrones*); cuchitril (*habitación pequeña y sucia*); antro, nido (*de gente de mala conducta*); cuarto de estudio; (Bib.) fosa (*de los leones*)
denarius [dɪˈnɛrɪəs] *s* (*pl:* **-i** [aɪ]) denario
denationalization [diˌnæʃənəlɪˈzeʃən] *s* desnacionalización
denationalize [diˈnæʃənəlaɪz] *va* desnacionalizar
denaturalization [diˌnætʃərəlɪˈzeʃən] *s* desnaturalización
denaturalize [diˈnætʃərəlaɪz] *va* desnaturalizar
denaturation [diˌnetʃəˈreʃən] *s* (chem.) desnaturalización
denature [diˈnetʃər] *va* (chem.) desnaturalizar
denatured alcohol *s* alcohol desnaturalizado
denazification [diˌnɑtsɪfɪˈkeʃən] o [diˌnætsɪfɪˈkeʃən] *s* desnazificación
denazify [diˈnɑtsɪfaɪ] o [diˈnætsɪfaɪ] (*pret* & *pp:* **-fied**) *va* desnazificar
dendriform [ˈdɛndrɪfɔrm] *adj* dendriforme
dendrite [ˈdɛndraɪt] *s* (anat., physiol. & mineral.) dendrita
dendritic [dɛnˈdrɪtɪk] o **dendritical** [dɛnˈdrɪtɪkəl] *adj* dendrítico
dendrography [dɛnˈdrɑgrəfɪ] *s* dendrografía
dendroid [ˈdɛndrɔɪd] *adj* dendroide
dendrometer [dɛnˈdrɑmɪtər] *s* dendrómetro
dengue [ˈdɛŋge] o [ˈdɛŋgɪ] *s* (path.) dengue
deniable [dɪˈnaɪəbəl] *adj* negable
denial [dɪˈnaɪəl] *s* negación; abnegación
denier [dɪˈnaɪər] *s* negador
denim [ˈdɛnɪm] *s* dril de algodón
Denis [ˈdɛnɪs] *s* Dionisio; **Saint Denis** San Dionisio
denitrification [diˌnaɪtrɪfɪˈkeʃən] *s* desnitrificación
denitrify [diˈnaɪtrɪfaɪ] (*pret* & *pp:* **-fied**) *va* desnitrificar
denizen [ˈdɛnɪzən] *s* habitante; extranjero naturalizado; animal naturalizado, planta naturalizada, voz naturalizada
Denmark [ˈdɛnmɑrk] *s* Dinamarca
den of vice *s* nido de vicios
denominate [dɪˈnɑmɪnɪt] o [dɪˈnɑmɪnet] *adj* denominado; [dɪˈnɑmɪnet] *va* denominar
denomination [dɪˌnɑmɪˈneʃən] *s* denominación; categoría, clase; valor; (eccl.) secta, confesión
denominational [dɪˌnɑmɪˈneʃənəl] *adj* sectario
denominationalism [dɪˌnɑmɪˈneʃənəlɪzəm] *s* sectarismo
denominative [dɪˈnɑmɪˌnetɪv] *adj* denominativo; (gram.) denominativo; *s* (gram.) denominativo
denominator [dɪˈnɑmɪˌnetər] *s* denominador; (math.) denominador
denotation [ˌdinoˈteʃən] *s* denotación
denotative [dɪˈnotətɪv] *adj* denotativo
denote [dɪˈnot] *va* denotar
denouement o **dénouement** [deˈnumɑ̃] *s* desenlace
denounce [dɪˈnaʊns] *va* denunciar; censurar; (dipl. & min.) denunciar
denouncement [dɪˈnaʊnsmənt] *s* denuncia, denunciación; censura; (min.) denuncio
denouncer [dɪˈnaʊnsər] *s* denunciador; censurador
de novo [diˈnovo] (Lat.) de nuevo
dense [dɛns] *adj* denso; estúpido
densimeter [dɛnˈsɪmɪtər] *s* densímetro
densimetry [dɛnˈsɪmɪtrɪ] *s* densimetría
density [ˈdɛnsɪtɪ] *s* (*pl:* **-ties**) densidad
dent [dɛnt] *s* abolladura; *va* abollar; *vn* abollarse
dental [ˈdɛntəl] *adj* dental; (phonet.) dental; *s* (phonet.) dental
dental floss *s* hilo dental, seda encerada
dentalization [ˌdɛntəlɪˈzeʃən] *s* (phonet.) dentalización
dentalize [ˈdɛntəlaɪz] *va* (phonet.) dentalizar
dental pulp *s* (anat.) pulpa
dental surgeon *s* cirujano-dentista
dentate [ˈdɛntet] *adj* dentado
dentex [ˈdɛntɛks] *s* (ichth.) dentón
denticulate [dɛnˈtɪkjəlet] *adj* dentellado, denticulado
denticulation [dɛnˌtɪkjəˈleʃən] *s* denticulación
dentifrice [ˈdɛntɪfrɪs] *s* dentífrico
dentil [ˈdɛntɪl] *s* (arch.) dentellón, dentículo
dentilabial [ˌdɛntɪˈlebɪəl] *adj* & *s* (phonet.) dentilabial
dentilingual [ˌdɛntɪˈlɪŋgwəl] *adj* & *s* (phonet.) dentilingual
dentin [ˈdɛntɪn] o **dentine** [ˈdɛntin] o [ˈdɛntɪn] *s* (anat.) dentina
dentiroster [ˌdɛntɪˈrɑstər] *s* (orn.) dentirrostro
dentirostral [ˌdɛntɪˈrɑstrəl] *adj* dentirrostro
dentist [ˈdɛntɪst] *s* dentista
dentistry [ˈdɛntɪstrɪ] *s* dentistería, odontología
dentition [dɛnˈtɪʃən] *s* dentición
denture [ˈdɛntʃər] *s* dentadura; dentadura artificial
denudate [ˈdɛnjudet] o [dɪˈnjudɪt] *adj* denudado; [ˈdɛnjudet] o [dɪˈnjudet] *va* desnudar
denudation [ˌdɛnjuˈdeʃən] *s* denudación; desposeimiento
denude [dɪˈnjud] o [dɪˈnud] *va* desnudar; desposeer; *vn* desposeer
denunciate [dɪˈnʌnsɪet] o [dɪˈnʌnʃɪet] *va* denunciar
denunciation [dɪˌnʌnsɪˈeʃən] o [dɪˌnʌnʃɪˈeʃən] *s* denunciación, denuncia; censura; (dipl. & min.) denuncia
denunciator [dɪˈnʌnsɪˌetər] o [dɪˈnʌnʃɪˌetər] *s* denunciador
denunciatory [dɪˈnʌnsɪəˌtorɪ] o [dɪˈnʌnʃɪəˌtorɪ] *adj* denunciatorio
deny [dɪˈnaɪ] (*pret* & *pp:* **-nied**) *va* negar; **to deny having** + *pp* negar haber + *pp;* **to deny oneself** negarse a sí mismo; **to deny oneself to callers** negarse; *vn* negar
Denys, Saint [ˈdɛnɪs] var. de **Denis, Saint**

deobstruent [di'abstruənt] *adj & s* (med.) desobstruyente
deodar ['diodar] *s* (bot.) cedro deodara, cedro de la India
deodorant [di'odərənt] *adj & s* desodorante
deodorization [di,odərɪ'zeʃən] *s* desodorización
deodorize [di'odəraɪz] *va* desodorizar
deodorizer [di'odə,raɪzər] *s* desodorante, inodoro
deontology [,dian'taləd͡ʒɪ] *s* deontología
deoxidation [di,aksɪ'deʃən] *s* desoxidación
deoxidizable [di'aksɪ,daɪzəbəl] *adj* desoxidable
deoxidize [di'aksɪdaɪz] *va* desoxidar
deoxidizer [di'aksɪ,daɪzər] *s* desoxidante, desoxigenante
deoxygenate [di'aksɪd͡ʒənet] *va* desoxigenar
deoxygenation [di,aksɪd͡ʒə'neʃən] *s* desoxigenación
deozonize [di'ozonaɪz] *va* desozonizar
dep. abr. de **department, departs, deponent** y **deputy**
depart [dɪ'part] *va* **to depart this life** partir de esta vida; *vn* partir; fallecer, morir; apartarse, desistir
departed [dɪ'partɪd] *adj* difunto; pasado; *s* difunto; *spl* difuntos
department [dɪ'partmənt] *s* departamento; ministerio
departmental [,dipart'mɛntəl] *adj* departamental
Department of Defense *s* (U.S.A.) ministerio de Defensa Nacional
Department of Justice *s* (U.S.A.) ministerio de Justicia
Department of State *s* (U.S.A.) ministerio de Asuntos Exteriores
Department of the Air Force *s* (U.S.A.) ministerio del Aire
Department of the Army *s* (U.S.A.) ministerio del Ejército
Department of the Interior *s* (U.S.A.) ministerio de la Gobernación
Department of the Lord Chancellor *s* (Brit.) ministerio de Justicia
Department of the Navy *s* (U.S.A.) ministerio de Marina
department store *s* grandes almacenes
departure [dɪ'partʃər] *s* salida, partida; desviación; nuevo curso
depend [dɪ'pɛnd] *vn* depender; pender, colgar; **that depends** según y conforme; **to depend on** o **upon** depender de
dependability [dɪ,pɛndə'bɪlɪtɪ] *s* confiabilidad
dependable [dɪ'pɛndəbəl] *adj* confiable, seguro, fidedigno
dependant [dɪ'pɛndənt] *adj & s* var. de **dependent**
dependence [dɪ'pɛndəns] *s* dependencia
dependency [dɪ'pɛndənsɪ] *s* (*pl:* **-cies**) dependencia; posesión (*territorio, país*)
dependent [dɪ'pɛndənt] *adj* dependiente; pendiente, colgante; *s* dependiente, carga de familia, familiar dependiente
dephase [di'fez] *va* (elec.) defasar
dephlegmate [di'flɛgmet] *va* deflegmar
depict [dɪ'pɪkt] *va* pintar; dibujar, representar, describir
depiction [dɪ'pɪkʃən] *s* pintura; representación, descripción
depilate ['dɛpɪlet] *va* depilar
depilation [,dɛpɪ'leʃən] *s* depilación
depilatory [dɪ'pɪlə,torɪ] *adj & s* depilatorio
deplete [dɪ'plit] *va* agotar; depauperar
depletion [dɪ'pliʃən] *s* agotamiento; depauperación
deplorable [dɪ'plorəbəl] *adj* deplorable
deplore [dɪ'plor] *va* deplorar
deploy [dɪ'plɔɪ] *va* (mil.) desplegar; *vn* (mil.) desplegarse
deployment [dɪ'plɔɪmənt] *s* (mil.) despliegue
depolarization [di,polərɪ'zeʃən] *s* (chem. & phys.) despolarización
depolarize [di'poləraɪz] *va* (chem. & phys.) despolarizar
depolarizer [di'polə,raɪzər] *s* (chem. & phys.) despolarizador
depone [dɪ'pon] *va & vn* (law) deponer
deponent [dɪ'ponənt] *adj* (gram.) deponente; *s* (law) deponente; (gram.) verbo deponente
depopulate [di'papjəlet] *va* despoblar
depopulation [di,papjə'leʃən] *s* despoblación
deport [dɪ'port] *va* deportar; **to deport oneself** portarse, conducirse
deportation [,dipor'teʃən] *s* deportación
deportee [,dipor'ti] *s* deportado
deportment [dɪ'portmənt] *s* porte, conducta, comportamiento
deposal [dɪ'pozəl] *s* deposición
depose [dɪ'poz] *va* deponer; (law) deponer; *vn* (law) deponer
deposit [dɪ'pazɪt] *s* depósito; señal (*dinero que se da como anticipo*); (min.) yacimiento; **on deposit** en depósito; en el banco; *va* depositar; dar para señal; *vn* depositarse
deposit account *s* cuenta corriente
depositary [dɪ'pazɪ,tɛrɪ] *s* (*pl:* **-ies**) depositario (*persona*); depósito, almacén
deposition [,dɛpə'zɪʃən] o [,dipə'zɪʃən] *s* deposición; depósito; (law) deposición
depositor [dɪ'pazɪtər] *s* depositador, cuentacorrentista, imponente
depository [dɪ'pazɪ,torɪ] *adj* depositario; *s* (*pl:* **-ries**) depósito, almacén; depositario (*persona*); depositaría
depot ['dipo] o ['dɛpo] *s* depósito, almacén; (rail.) estación; (mil.) depósito
depravation [,dɛprə'veʃən] *s* depravación
deprave [dɪ'prev] *va* depravar
depraved [dɪ'prevd] *adj* depravado
depravity [dɪ'prævɪtɪ] *s* (*pl:* **-ties**) depravación
deprecate ['dɛprɪket] *va* desaprobar
deprecation [,dɛprɪ'keʃən] *s* desaprobación
deprecative ['dɛprɪ,ketɪv] *adj* deprecativo
deprecatory ['dɛprɪkə,torɪ] *adj* de desaprobación; deprecatorio
depreciate [dɪ'priʃɪet] *va* depreciar (*rebajar el valor o el precio de*); despreciar, desestimar; *vn* depreciarse
depreciation [dɪ,priʃɪ'eʃən] *s* depreciación (*disminución del valor*); desaprecio, desestimación
depreciative [dɪ'priʃɪ,etɪv] o **depreciatory** [dɪ'priʃɪə,torɪ] *adj* despreciativo
depredate ['dɛprɪdet] *va* depredar
depredation [,dɛprɪ'deʃən] *s* depredación; (law) depredación
depress [dɪ'prɛs] *va* deprimir; desalentar, desanimar, entristecer; bajar (*p.ej., los precios*)
depressant [dɪ'prɛsənt] *adj & s* (med.) deprimente
depressed [dɪ'prɛst] *adj* deprimido; desalentado, desanimado, entristecido; necesitado
depression [dɪ'prɛʃən] *s* depresión; desaliento, desanimación, entristecimiento; crisis (*económica*); (path. & meteor.) depresión
depressive [dɪ'prɛsɪv] *adj* depresivo; deprimente
depressor [dɪ'prɛsər] *s* (anat., physiol., & surg.) depresor
deprivation [,dɛprɪ'veʃən] *s* privación
deprive [dɪ'praɪv] *va* privar
dept. abr. de **department**
depth [dɛpθ] *s* profundidad; fondo (*extensión interior de un edificio*); (naut.) braceaje (*del mar*); **in the depth of** en pleno, p.ej., **in the depth of winter** en pleno invierno; **to go beyond one's depth** meterse en agua demasiado profunda; (fig.) meterse en honduras
depth bomb *s* bomba de profundidad
depth charge *s* carga de profundidad
depurative ['dɛpjə,retɪv] *adj & s* (med.) depurativo
deputation [,dɛpjə'teʃən] *s* diputación
depute [dɪ'pjut] *va* diputar
deputize ['dɛpjətaɪz] *va* diputar, delegar
deputy ['dɛpjətɪ] *s* (*pl:* **-ties**) diputado; *adj* teniente
derail [di'rel] *va* hacer descarrilar; *vn* descarrilar
derailment [di'relmənt] *s* descarriladura o descarrilamiento
derange [dɪ'rend͡ʒ] *va* desarreglar, descomponer; volver loco
derangement [dɪ'rend͡ʒmənt] *s* desarreglo, descompostura; locura

derat [di'ræt] (*pret & pp:* **-ratted;** *ger:* **-ratting**) *va* desratizar
derby ['dʌrbɪ] *s* (*pl:* **-bies**) sombrero hongo; (*cap.*) ['dʌrbɪ] o ['dɑrbɪ] *s* (*pl:* **-bies**) derby (*carrera de caballos que se celebra anualmente*)
derelict ['dɛrɪlɪkt] *adj* abandonado; negligente; *s* (naut.) derrelicto (*buque*); pelafustán
dereliction [,dɛrɪ'lɪkʃən] *s* derrelicción, abandono; negligencia; colapso (*de las fuerzas vitales*)
deride [dɪ'raɪd] *va* mofarse de, ridiculizar
de rigueur [dərɪ'gʌr] *adj & adv* de rigor
derision [dɪ'rɪʒən] *s* irrisión, burla
derisive [dɪ'raɪsɪv] *adj* mofador
derisory [dɪ'raɪsərɪ] *adj* mofador, burlador; ridículo, irrisorio
derivation [,dɛrɪ'veʃən] *s* derivación; (gram., math., & med.) derivación
derivative [dɪ'rɪvətɪv] *adj* derivativo; (gram.) derivativo, derivado; (med.) derivativo; *s* derivativo; (gram.) derivativo, derivado; (med.) derivativo; (math.) derivada
derive [dɪ'raɪv] *va* derivar; *vn* derivar o derivarse
derma ['dʌrmə] *s* (anat.) dermis; piel, cutis
dermal ['dʌrməl] *adj* dérmico
dermatitis [,dʌrmə'taɪtɪs] *s* (path.) dermatitis
dermatographia [,dʌrmətə'græfɪə] *s* (path.) dermatografía
dermatography [,dʌrmə'tɑgrəfɪ] *s* dermatografía (*descripción de la piel*)
dermatological [,dʌrmətə'lɑdʒɪkəl] *adj* dermatológico
dermatologist [,dʌrmə'tɑlədʒɪst] *s* dermatólogo
dermatology [,dʌrmə'tɑlədʒɪ] *s* dermatología
dermatosis [,dʌrmə'tosɪs] *s* (path.) dermatosis
dermic ['dʌrmɪk] *adj* dérmico
dermis ['dʌrmɪs] *s* (anat.) dermis
dermographia [,dʌrmə'græfɪə] o **dermographism** [dər'mɑgrəfɪzəm] *s* (path.) dermografía o dermografismo
derogate ['dɛrəget] *vn* desmerecer, empeorar, degenerar; **to derogate from** quitar mérito a
derogation [,dɛrə'geʃən] *s* menosprecio, desprecio; disminución, deterioración, derogación
derogative [dɪ'rɑgətɪv] *adj* despreciativo
derogatory [dɪ'rɑgə,torɪ] *adj* despreciativo, menospreciativo
derout [dɪ'raʊt] *s* derrota; *va* derrotar
derrick ['dɛrɪk] *s* grúa; torre de perforar (*sobre un pozo de petróleo*)
derring-do ['dɛrɪŋ'du] *s* proeza
dervish ['dʌrvɪʃ] *s* derviche
desalt [di'sɔlt] *va* desalar
descant ['dɛskænt] *s* discante; (mus.) discante; [dɛs'kænt] *va* (mus.) discantar; *vn* discantar; (mus.) discantar
descend [dɪ'sɛnd] *va* descender, bajar (*la escalera*); *vn* descender; (mus.) descender; **to descend from** descender de; **to descend on** o **upon** invadir, caer sobre; **to descend to** descender a, rebajarse a
descendant [dɪ'sɛndənt] *adj* descendente; *s* descendiente; **in the descendant** menguante, con influencia cada vez menor
descendent [dɪ'sɛndənt] *adj* descendente
descent [dɪ'sɛnt] *s* descenso (*acción de descender o bajar; caída de una situación o estado a otro inferior*); descendimiento (*acción de bajar a una persona o cosa*); descendencia (*casta, estirpe; hijos, prole*); cuesta, bajada; herencia; invasión
describable [dɪ'skraɪbəbəl] *adj* descriptible
describe [dɪ'skraɪb] *va* describir
describer [dɪ'skraɪbər] *s* descriptor
description [dɪ'skrɪpʃən] *s* descripción; género, clase, calidad
descriptive [dɪ'skrɪptɪv] *adj* descriptivo
descry [dɪ'skraɪ] (*pret & pp:* **-scried**) *va* avistar, divisar; descubrir, percibir
desecrate ['dɛsɪkret] *va* profanar
desecration [,dɛsɪ'kreʃən] *s* profanación
desecrator ['dɛsɪ,kretər] *s* profanador
desegregate [di'sɛgrɪget] *va* desegregar
desegregation [di,sɛgrɪ'geʃən] *s* desegregación
desensitize [di'sɛnsɪtaɪz] *va* desensibilizar, insensibilizar; (phot.) hacer insensible a la luz
desert ['dɛzərt] *s* desierto; yermo; *adj* desierto; [dɪ'zʌrt] *s* merecimiento, mérito, merecido, p.ej., **he received his just deserts** llevó su merecido; *va* desertar, desertar de; *vn* desertar
deserter [dɪ'zɛrtər] *s* (mil. & fig.) desertor
desertion [dɪ'zʌrʃən] *s* deserción; abandono de cónyuge
deserve [dɪ'zʌrv] *va & vn* merecer; **to deserve to** + *inf* merecer + *inf*
deservedly [dɪ'zʌrvɪdlɪ] *adj* merecidamente
deserving [dɪ'zʌrvɪŋ] *adj* merecedor
deshabille [,dɛzə'bil] *s* ropa suelta, desabillé
desiccant ['dɛsɪkənt] *adj & s* desecante
desiccate ['dɛsɪket] *va* desecar; *vn* desecarse
desiccation [,dɛsɪ'keʃən] *s* desecación
desiccative ['dɛsɪ,ketɪv] *adj* desecativo
desiccator ['dɛsɪ,ketər] *s* desecador
desideratum [dɪ,sɪdə'retəm] *s* (*pl:* **-ta** [tə]) desiderátum
design [dɪ'zaɪn] *s* diseño, trazado (*esbozo, bosquejo*); dibujo (*delineación; disposición de detalles; arte del dibujo; objeto trabajado con arte*); designio (*plan, proyecto*); modelo; intención, mala intención; **by design** intencionalmente; **to have designs on** poner la mira en; *va* diseñar, trazar, dibujar; estudiar; idear, proyectar, proponerse; destinar (*a una persona para algún fin*); *vn* dibujar
designate ['dɛzɪgnet] *adj* designado; *va* señalar (*indicar por señal*); denominar (*nombrar con un título particular*); designar (*destinar para determinado fin*)
designation [,dɛzɪg'neʃən] *s* señalamiento (*indicación definida*); denominación (*nombre o título*); designación (*destinación para algún fin*)
designedly [dɪ'zaɪnɪdlɪ] *adv* adrede, de propósito
designer [dɪ'zaɪnər] *s* dibujante; proyectista; maquinador, intrigante
designing [dɪ'zaɪnɪŋ] *adj* maquinador, intrigante; previsor; *s* dibujo
desirability [dɪ,zaɪrə'bɪlɪtɪ] *s* deseabilidad
desirable [dɪ'zaɪrəbəl] *adj* deseable
desire [dɪ'zaɪr] *s* deseo; *va* desear; **to desire to** + *inf* desear + *inf*
desirous [dɪ'zaɪrəs] *adj* deseoso
desist [dɪ'zɪst] *vn* desistir
desistance [dɪ'zɪstəns] *s* desistimiento
desk [dɛsk] *s* pupitre, escritorio; atril; caja (*donde se pagan las cuentas en los hoteles*)
desk clerk *s* cajero (*en los hoteles*)
desk set *s* juego de escritorio
desk work *s* trabajo de escritorio; trabajo oficinesco; trabajo literario
desolate ['dɛsəlɪt] *adj* desolado, arruinado; desierto; solitario; infeliz, triste; lúgubre; ['dɛsəlet] *va* desolar, arruinar, arrasar; despoblar; entristecer, desconsolar
desolation [,dɛsə'leʃən] *s* desolación; soledad (*estado y lugar*)
desolator ['dɛsə,letər] *s* desolador
despair [dɪ'spɛr] *s* desesperación; *vn* desesperar, desesperarse; **to despair of** desesperar de
despairing [dɪ'spɛrɪŋ] *adj* desesperado
despatch [dɪ'spætʃ] *s & va* var. de **dispatch**
despatcher [dɪ'spætʃər] *s* var. de **dispatcher**
desperado [,dɛspə'redo] o [,dɛspə'rɑdo] *s* (*pl:* **-does** o **-dos**) criminal desesperado
desperate ['dɛspərɪt] *adj* desesperado; encarnizado; heroico (*p.ej., remedio*)
desperation [,dɛspə'reʃən] *s* desesperación
despicable ['dɛspɪkəbəl] o [dɛs'pɪkəbəl] *adj* desdeñable, despreciable
despise [dɪ'spaɪz] *va* despreciar, desdeñar
despite [dɪ'spaɪt] *s* insulto, afrenta, odio, desafío; **in despite of** a despecho de; *prep* a despecho de, a pesar de
despiteful [dɪ'spaɪtfəl] *adj* malicioso, vengativo
despoil [dɪ'spɔɪl] *va* despojar
despoilment [dɪ'spɔɪlmənt] o **despoliation** [dɪ,spolɪ'eʃən] *s* despojo
despond [dɪ'spɑnd] *s* abatimiento; *vn* desanimarse
despondence [dɪ'spɑndəns] *s* desaliento, desánimo, abatimiento
despondency [dɪ'spɑndənsɪ] *s* (*pl:* **-cies**) var. de **despondence**

despondent [dɪ'spɑndənt] o **desponding** [dɪ'spɑndɪŋ] *adj* desalentado, desanimado, abatido
despot ['dɛspɑt] o ['dɛspət] *s* déspota
despotic [dɛs'pɑtɪk] *adj* despótico
despotically [dɛs'pɑtɪkəlɪ] *adj* despóticamente
despotism ['dɛspətɪzəm] *s* despotismo
desquamate ['dɛskwəmet] *vn* descamarse
desquamation [ˌdɛskwə'meʃən] *s* descamación
dessert [dɪ'zʌrt] *s* postre
dessertspoon [dɪ'zʌrtˌspun] *s* cuchara de postre
destalinization [diˌstɑlɪnɪ'zeʃən] *s* destalinización o desestalinización
destalinize [di'stɑlɪnaɪz] *va* destalinizar o desestalinizar
destination [ˌdɛstɪ'neʃən] *s* destinación (*acción de destinar; fin, objeto*); destino (*consignación para determinado fin; lugar a donde va una persona o cosa*)
destine ['dɛstɪn] *va* destinar; **to destine for** destinar para; **to destine to** + *inf* destinar (*p.ej., dinero*) a + *inf*
destiny ['dɛstɪnɪ] *s* (*pl:* **-nies**) destino; (*cap.*) *s* (myth.) Destino
destitute ['dɛstɪtjut] o ['dɛstɪtut] *adj* indigente; **destitute of** desprovisto de
destitution [ˌdɛstɪ'tjuʃən] o [ˌdɛstɪ'tuʃən] *s* indigencia
destroy [dɪ'strɔɪ] *va* destruir; matar; invalidar
destroyer [dɪ'strɔɪər] *s* destruidor o destructor; (nav.) destructor
destroyer escort *s* (nav.) destructor de escolta
destructibility [dɪˌstrʌktɪ'bɪlɪtɪ] *s* destructibilidad
destructible [dɪ'strʌktɪbəl] *adj* destruíble o destructible
destruction [dɪ'strʌkʃən] *s* destrucción
destructive [dɪ'strʌktɪv] *adj* destructivo
desuetude ['dɛswɪtjud] o ['dɛswɪtud] *s* desuetud, desuso
desulfurization [diˌsʌlfjərɪ'zeʃən] *s* desulfuración
desulfurize [di'sʌlfjəraɪz] *va* desulfurar
desulphurize [di'sʌlfjəraɪz] *va* var. de **desulfurize**
desultory ['dɛsəlˌtorɪ] *adj* descosido, deshilvanado
detach [dɪ'tætʃ] *va* separar, desprender; (mil.) destacar
detachable [dɪ'tætʃəbəl] *adj* separable, desmontable
detached [dɪ'tætʃt] *adj* separado, suelto; imparcial, desinteresado
detachment [dɪ'tætʃmənt] *s* separación, desprendimiento; aislamiento; imparcialidad, desinterés; (mil.) destacamento
detail [dɪ'tel] o ['ditel] *s* detalle, pormenor; (f.a.) detalle; (mil.) destacamento; **in detail** en detalle, detalladamente; **to go into detail** menudear; [dɪ'tel] *va* detallar; (mil.) destacar
detain [dɪ'ten] *va* detener
detainer [dɪ'tenər] *s* detenedor; (law) detentación; (law) detención ilegal; (law) auto de detención
detainment [dɪ'tenmənt] *s* detención
detect [dɪ'tɛkt] *va* detectar; (elec. & rad.) detectar
detectable [dɪ'tɛktəbəl] o **detectible** [dɪ'tɛktɪbəl] *adj* perceptible
detection [dɪ'tɛkʃən] *s* detección; (elec. & rad.) detección
detective [dɪ'tɛktɪv] *s* detective; *adj* detectivesco
detective story *s* novela policíaca, novela policial
detector [dɪ'tɛktər] *s* detector; (elec. & rad.) detector
detention [dɪ'tɛnʃən] *s* detención
deter [dɪ'tʌr] (*pret & pp:* **-terred;** *ger:* **-terring**) *va* refrenar, impedir, detener
deterge [dɪ'tʌrdʒ] *va* deterger
detergent [dɪ'tʌrdʒənt] *adj & s* detergente
deteriorate [dɪ'tɪrɪəret] *va* deteriorar; *vn* deteriorarse
deterioration [dɪˌtɪrɪə'reʃən] *s* deterioro o deterioración
determinability [dɪˌtʌrmɪnə'bɪlɪtɪ] *s* determinabilidad
determinable [dɪ'tʌrmɪnəbəl] *adj* determinable
determinant [dɪ'tʌrmɪnənt] *adj* determinante; *s* determinante; (biol., log., & math.) determinante
determinate [dɪ'tʌrmɪnɪt] *adj* determinado
determination [dɪˌtʌrmɪ'neʃən] *s* determinación
determinative [dɪ'tʌrmɪˌnetɪv] *adj* determinativo; (gram.) determinativo
determine [dɪ'tʌrmɪn] *va* determinar; *vn* determinarse
determined [dɪ'tʌrmɪnd] *adj* determinado, resuelto
determinism [dɪ'tʌrmɪnɪzəm] *s* (philos.) determinismo
determinist [dɪ'tʌrmɪnɪst] *adj & s* (philos.) determinista
deterrent [dɪ'tɛrənt] o [dɪ'tʌrənt] *adj* impeditivo, disuasivo; *s* refrenamiento, impedimento, detención; **to act as a deterrent** servir como un freno
detersion [dɪ'tʌrʃən] *s* detersión
detersive [dɪ'tʌrsɪv] *adj & s* detersivo
detest [dɪ'tɛst] *va* detestar
detestable [dɪ'tɛstəbəl] *adj* detestable
detestation [ˌditɛs'teʃən] *s* detestación; persona detestada, cosa detestada
dethrone [dɪ'θron] *va* destronar
dethronement [dɪ'θronmənt] *s* destronamiento
detin [di'tɪn] (*pret & pp:* **-tinned;** *ger:* **-tinning**) *va* desestañar; *vn* desestañarse; recuperar estaño
detonate ['dɛtonet] o ['ditonet] *va* hacer detonar; *vn* detonar
detonation [ˌdɛto'neʃən] o [ˌdito'neʃən] *s* detonación
detonator ['dɛtoˌnetər] o ['ditoˌnetər] *s* detonador
detour ['ditʊr] o [dɪ'tʊr] *s* desvío, rodeo, vuelta; manera indirecta; *va* desviar (*p.ej., el tránsito*); *vn* desviarse
detract [dɪ'trækt] *va* detraer, apartar; *vn* detraer; **to detract from** disminuir, rebajar; quitar atractivo, belleza, crédito, reputación, mérito, etc. a
detraction [dɪ'trækʃən] *s* detracción
detractive [dɪ'træktɪv] *adj* detractor
detractor [dɪ'træktər] *s* detractor
detrain [di'tren] *va* hacer salir del tren; *vn* salir del tren
detrainment [di'trenmənt] *s* salida del tren
detriment ['dɛtrɪmənt] *s* perjuicio, detrimento; **to the detriment of** en perjuicio de
detrimental [ˌdɛtrɪ'mɛntəl] *adj* perjudicial, dañoso, nocivo
detrital [dɪ'traɪtəl] *adj* (geol.) detrítico
detrition [dɪ'trɪʃən] *s* detricción
detritus [dɪ'traɪtəs] *s* (geol.) detrito; (fig.) restos
Deucalion [dju'kelɪən] o [du'kelɪən] *s* (myth.) Deucalión
deuce [djus] o [dus] *s* dos (*en los juegos de naipes y dados*); a dos (*en el tenis*); **the deuce!** ¡demonio!
deuced ['djusɪd], ['dusɪd], [djust] o [dust] *adj* diabólico, excesivo; *adv* diabólicamente, excesivamente
deucedly ['djusɪdlɪ] o ['dusɪdlɪ] *adv* diabólicamente, excesivamente
Deut. abr. de **Deuteronomy**
deuterium [dju'tɪrɪəm] o [du'tɪrɪəm] *s* (chem.) deuterio
deuteron ['djutərɑn] o ['dutərɑn] *s* (chem.) deuterión
Deuteronomy [ˌdjutə'rɑnəmɪ] o [ˌdutə'rɑnəmɪ] *s* (Bib.) Deuteronomio
deuton ['djutɑn] o ['dutɑn] *s* (chem.) deutón (*es decir, deuterión*)
deutoplasm ['djutoplæzəm] o ['dutoplæzəm] *s* (biol.) deutoplasma
devaluate [di'væljuet] *va* desvalorizar, desvalorar
devaluation [diˌvælju'eʃən] *s* devaluación, desvalorización
devalue [di'vælju] *va* desvalorizar, desvalorar
devastate ['dɛvəstet] *va* devastar
devastating ['dɛvəsˌtetɪŋ] *adj* devastador; (slang) abrumador, arrollador

devastation [ˌdɛvəsˈteʃən] *s* devastación
devastator [ˈdɛvəsˌtetər] *s* devastador
develop [dɪˈvɛləp] *va* desarrollar, desenvolver; (math.) desarrollar; (phot.) desarrollar, revelar; explotar (*p.ej., una mina*); *vn* desarrollarse, desenvolverse; evolucionar; crecer
developable [dɪˈvɛləpəbəl] *adj* desarrollable
developer [dɪˈvɛləpər] *s* (phot.) revelador
development [dɪˈvɛləpmənt] *s* desarrollo, desenvolvimiento; explotación (*p.ej., de una mina*); nuevo cambio, acontecimiento nuevo; construcción de casas, caserío nuevo; (phot.) revelado
developmental [dɪˌvɛləpˈmɛntəl] *adj* evolucionista; del desarrollo; experimental
deviate [ˈdiviet] *va* desviar; *vn* desviarse
deviation [ˌdiviˈeʃən] *s* desviación
deviationism [ˌdiviˈeʃənɪzəm] *s* desviacionismo
deviationist [ˌdiviˈeʃənɪst] *s* desviacionista (*comunista que no sigue la línea del partido*)
device [dɪˈvaɪs] *s* dispositivo, artefacto, artificio, aparato; treta, ardid; patrón, dibujo; divisa heráldica; lema, divisa; **to leave someone to his own devices** dejar a uno que haga lo que se le antoje
devil [ˈdɛvəl] *s* diablo; (mach.) diablo; **between the devil and the deep blue sea** entre la espada y la pared; **like the devil** (coll.) como el diablo; **poor devil** pobre diablo; **talk of the Devil and he will appear** en nombrando al ruin de Roma, luego asoma; **the Devil** el Diablo, Satán; **the devil!** ¡diablos!; **the devil take the hindmost** quien se quede en zaga, con el diablo se las haya; **there will be the devil to pay** ahí será el diablo; **to give the devil his due** ser justo hasta con un diablo; **to raise the devil** (slang) armarla, armar un alboroto; (*pret & pp:* **-iled** o **-illed;** *ger:* **-iling** o **-illing**) *va* condimentar con picantes; (coll.) molestar, incomodar
deviled [ˈdɛvəld] *adj* condimentado con picantes
deviled eggs *spl* huevos duros rellenos con su propia yema y condimentados con picantes
devilfish [ˈdɛvəlˌfɪʃ] *s* (ichth.) raya, manta; (zool.) pulpo
devil incarnate *s* diablo encarnado
devilish [ˈdɛvəlɪʃ] o [ˈdɛvlɪʃ] *adj* diabólico; (coll.) diabólico (*excesivamente malo*); (coll.) excesivo; *adv* (coll.) excesivamente
devilled [ˈdɛvəld] *adj* var. de **deviled**
devil-may-care [ˈdɛvəlmeˈkɛr] *adj* atolondrado, irresponsable
devilment [ˈdɛvəlmənt] *s* maldad, perversidad; diablura (*travesura grande; acción temeraria*)
devilry [ˈdɛvəlrɪ] *s* (*pl:* **-ries**) var. de **deviltry**
devil's advocate *s* (eccl. & fig.) abogado del diablo
devil's-darning-needle [ˈdɛvəlzˈdɑrnɪŋˌnidəl] *s* (ent.) caballito del diablo; (bot.) peine de Venus
Devil's Island *s* Isla del Diablo
deviltry [ˈdɛvəltrɪ] *s* (*pl:* **-tries**) maldad, perversidad, crueldad; diablura (*travesura grande; acción temeraria*)
devious [ˈdivɪəs] *adj* apartado, desviado; tortuoso (*dícese de un camino, una persona, etc.*)
devise [dɪˈvaɪz] *s* (law) legado; (law) testamento; (law) propiedad legada; *va* idear, inventar, proyectar; (law) legar; *vn* formar proyectos
devisee [ˌdɛvɪˈze] o [dɪˌvaɪˈzi] *s* (law) legatario
deviser [dɪˈvaɪzər] *s* autor, inventor
devisor [dɪˈvaɪzər] o [dɪˈvaɪzɔr] *s* (law) testador
devitalization [diˌvaɪtəlɪˈzeʃən] *s* desvitalización
devitalize [diˈvaɪtəlaɪz] *va* desvitalizar
devitrify [diˈvɪtrɪfaɪ] (*pret & pp:* **-fied**) *va* desvitrificar
devoid [dɪˈvɔɪd] *adj* desprovisto; vacío
devoir [dəˈvwɑr] o [ˈdɛvwɑr] *s* cumplido, homenaje; deber, obligación
devolution [ˌdɛvəˈluʃən] *s* traspaso, transmisión de una persona a otra; (biol.) degeneración; (eccl.) devolución
devolve [dɪˈvɑlv] *va* transmitir, transferir; *vn* pasar, transferirse; **to devolve on, to,** o **upon** pasar a, incumbir a

Devonian [dɪˈvonɪən] *adj & s* devoniano; (geol.) devoniano
Devonic [dɪˈvɑnɪk] *adj* (geol.) devónico, devoniano
devote [dɪˈvot] *va* dedicar; **to devote oneself to** dedicarse a; **to devote oneself to** + *inf* dedicarse a + *inf*
devoted [dɪˈvotɪd] *adj* devoto (*afecto, aficionado*); dedicado
devotee [ˌdɛvəˈti] *s* devoto
devotion [dɪˈvoʃən] *s* devoción; dedicación (*p.ej., al estudio, al trabajo*); **devotions** *spl* preces, oraciones
devotional [dɪˈvoʃənəl] *adj* devoto
devour [dɪˈvaʊr] *va* devorar; (fig.) devorar
devourer [dɪˈvaʊrər] *s* devorador
devouring [dɪˈvaʊrɪŋ] *adj* devorador, devorante
devout [dɪˈvaʊt] *adj* devoto; cordial, sincero
dew [dju] o [du] *s* rocío; *va* rociar
Dewar vessel [ˈdjuər] o [ˈduər] *s* vasija de Dewar
dewberry [ˈdjuˌbɛrɪ] o [ˈduˌbɛrɪ] *s* (*pl:* **-ries**) (bot.) zarza; (bot.) zarza de los rastrojos (*Rubus caesius*)
dewclaw [ˈdjuˌklɔ] o [ˈduˌklɔ] *s* espolón, pesuño falso
dewdrop [ˈdjuˌdrɑp] o [ˈduˌdrɑp] *s* gota de rocío
dewlap [ˈdjuˌlæp] o [ˈduˌlæp] *s* papada
dew point *s* (physical chem.) punto de rocío
dewy [ˈdjuɪ] o [ˈduɪ] *adj* (*comp:* **-ier;** *super:* **-iest**) rociado; (fig.) rutilante, suave, efímero (*como el rocío*)
dexter [ˈdɛkstər] *adj* diestro; (her.) diestro
dexterity [dɛksˈtɛrɪtɪ] *s* destreza
dexterous [ˈdɛkstərəs] *adj* diestro
dextral [ˈdɛkstrəl] *adj* diestro; derecho
dextrin o **dextrine** [ˈdɛkstrɪn] *s* (chem.) dextrina
dextrocardia [ˌdɛkstroˈkɑrdɪə] *s* (anat.) dextrocardia
dextrogyrous [ˌdɛkstroˈdʒaɪrəs] *adj* (phys.) dextrógiro
dextrorotatory [ˌdɛkstroˈrotəˌtorɪ] *adj* (phys.) dextrorrotatorio
dextrorse [ˈdɛkstrɔrs] o [dɛksˈtrɔrs] *adj* (bot.) dextrorso
dextrose [ˈdɛkstros] *s* (biochem.) dextrosa
dextrous [ˈdɛkstrəs] *adj* var. de **dexterous**
D.F. abr. de **Defender of the Faith**
dg. abr. de **decigram** o **decigrams**
diabase [ˈdaɪəbes] *s* (mineral.) diabasa
diabetes [ˌdaɪəˈbitɪs] o [ˌdaɪəˈbitiz] *s* (path.) diabetes
diabetic [ˌdaɪəˈbɛtɪk] o [ˌdaɪəˈbitɪk] *adj & s* diabético
diabetometer [ˌdaɪəbɪˈtɑmɪtər] *s* diabetómetro
diablerie [dɪˈɑblərɪ] *s* hechicería; diablura (*travesura grande; acción temeraria*); dominio de diablos
diabolic [ˌdaɪəˈbɑlɪk] o **diabolical** [ˌdaɪəˈbɑlɪkəl] *adj* diabólico
diabolism [daɪˈæbəlɪzəm] *s* diabolismo (*doctrina*); hechicería; maldad, perversidad; posesión demoníaca
diachronic [ˌdaɪəˈkrɑnɪk] *adj* diacrónico
diachrony [daɪˈækrənɪ] *s* diacronía
diachylon [daɪˈækɪlɑn] *s* diaquilón
diacodion [ˌdaɪəˈkodɪən] *s* (pharm.) diacodión
diaconal [daɪˈækənəl] *adj* diaconal
diaconate [daɪˈækənɪt] o [daɪˈækənet] *s* diaconado
diacritic [ˌdaɪəˈkrɪtɪk] *adj* (gram. & med.) diacrítico; *s* (gram.) signo diacrítico
diacritical [ˌdaɪəˈkrɪtɪkəl] *adj* (gram. & med.) diacrítico
diacritical mark *s* (gram.) signo diacrítico
diadelphous [ˌdaɪəˈdɛlfəs] *adj* (bot.) diadelfo
diadem [ˈdaɪədɛm] *s* diadema
diaeresis [daɪˈɛrɪsɪs] *s* (*pl:* **-ses** [siz]) diéresis
diagnose [ˌdaɪəgˈnos] o [ˌdaɪəgˈnoz] *va* diagnosticar
diagnosis [ˌdaɪəgˈnosɪs] *s* (*pl:* **-ses** [siz]) (bot., zool. & med.) diagnosis
diagnostic [ˌdaɪəgˈnɑstɪk] *adj & s* diagnóstico
diagnostician [ˌdaɪəgnɑsˈtɪʃən] *s* médico experto en hacer el diagnóstico

diagonal [daɪˈægənəl] *adj & s* diagonal
diagonal cloth *s* diagonal
diagonally [daɪˈægənəlɪ] *adv* diagonalmente
diagram [ˈdaɪəgræm] *s* diagrama, esquema; (*pret & pp:* **-gramed** o **-grammed;** *ger:* **-graming** o **-gramming**) *va* esquematizar, dibujar en forma de diagrama
diagrammatic [ˌdaɪəgrəˈmætɪk] o **diagrammatical** [ˌdaɪəgrəˈmætɪkəl] *adj* diagramático
diagrammatically [ˌdaɪəgrəˈmætɪkəlɪ] *adv* diagramáticamente
diagraph [ˈdaɪəgræf] o [ˈdaɪəgrɑf] *s* diágrafo
dial. abr. de **dialect** y **dialectal**
dial [ˈdaɪəl] *s* esfera, cuadrante, muestra; (rad.) cuadrante; disco selector (*del teléfono*); (*pret & pp:* **dialed** o **dialled;** *ger:* **dialing** o **dialling**) *va* sintonizar (*el radiorreceptor o el radiotransmisor*); marcar (*el número teléfonico*); llamar (*a una persona*) por teléfono automático; *vn* (telp.) marcar
dialect [ˈdaɪəlɛkt] *s* dialecto
dialectal [ˌdaɪəˈlɛktəl] *adj* dialectal
dialectic [ˌdaɪəˈlɛktɪk] *adj* dialéctico; dialectal; *s* dialéctica; **dialectics** *ssg* dialéctica
dialectical [ˌdaɪəˈlɛktɪkəl] *adj* dialéctico; dialectal
dialectician [ˌdaɪəlɛkˈtɪʃən] *s* dialéctico
dialecticism [ˌdaɪəˈlɛktɪsɪzəm] *s* dialectalismo
dialectology [ˌdaɪəlɛkˈtɑlədʒɪ] *s* dialectología
dialing o **dialling** [ˈdaɪəlɪŋ] *s* (telp.) marcaje
diallage [ˈdaɪəlɪdʒ] *s* (mineral.) diálaga
dialogic [ˌdaɪəˈlɑdʒɪk] *adj* dialogal
dialogism [daɪˈælədʒɪzəm] *s* (rhet.) dialogismo
dialogist [daɪˈælədʒɪst] *s* dialoguista (*escritor*)
dialogue [ˈdaɪəlɔg] o [ˈdaɪəlɑg] *s* diálogo; *va & vn* dialogar
dial telephone *s* teléfono automático
dial tone *s* (telp.) señal para marcar
dialycarpous [ˌdaɪəlɪˈkɑrpəs] *adj* (bot.) dialicarpelar
dialysis [daɪˈælɪsɪs] *s* (*pl:* **-ses** [siz]) diálisis
dialytic [ˌdaɪəˈlɪtɪk] *adj* dialítico
dialyze [ˈdaɪəlaɪz] *va* dializar
dialyzer [ˈdaɪəˌlaɪzər] *s* (physical chem.) dializador
diam. abr. de **diameter**
diamagnetic [ˌdaɪəmægˈnɛtɪk] *adj & s* diamagnético
diamagnetism [ˌdaɪəˈmægnɪtɪzəm] *s* diamagnetismo
diamantiferous [ˌdaɪəmənˈtɪfərəs] *adj* diamantífero
diamat [ˈdaɪəmæt] *s* materialismo dialéctico (*teoría de Carlos Marx y Federico Engels, basada en el método de Hegel*)
diameter [daɪˈæmɪtər] *s* diámetro
diametric [ˌdaɪəˈmɛtrɪk] o **diametrical** [ˌdaɪəˈmɛtrɪkəl] *adj* diametral
diamond [ˈdaɪəmənd] o [ˈdaɪmənd] *s* diamante; losange (*figura de rombo*); (baseball) losange; carró, rombo o diamante (*naipe que corresponde al oro*); **diamonds** *spl* carrós, rombos o diamantes (*palo que corresponde al de oros*); **diamond in the rough** diamante en bruto; (fig.) diamante en bruto; *adj* diamantino
diamond cutter *s* diamantista
diamond edition *s* (print.) edición diamante
diamond wedding *s* bodas de diamante
Dian [ˈdaɪæn] *s* (poet.) Diana
Diana [daɪˈænə] *s* (myth.) Diana
diandrous [daɪˈændrəs] *adj* diandro
diapalma [ˌdaɪəˈpælmə] *s* (pharm.) diapalma
diapason [ˌdaɪəˈpezən] o [ˌdaɪəˈpesən] *s* (mus.) diapasón
diapason normal *s* (mus.) diapasón normal
diapedesis [ˌdaɪəpɪˈdisɪs] *s* (physiol.) diapédesis
diaper [ˈdaɪəpər] *s* pañal (*de niño*); labor con motivos uniformemente repetidos; *va* labrar con motivos uniformemente repetidos; proveer con pañal, renovar el pañal de
diaphanous [daɪˈæfənəs] *adj* diáfano
diaphoresis [ˌdaɪəfoˈrisɪs] *s* (med.) diaforesis
diaphoretic [ˌdaɪəfoˈrɛtɪk] *adj & s* diaforético
diaphoretical [ˌdaɪəfoˈrɛtɪkəl] *adj* diaforético
diaphragm [ˈdaɪəfræm] *s* diafragma; (telp. & rad.) membrana fónica o diafragma
diaphragmatic [ˌdaɪəfrægˈmætɪk] *adj* diafragmático
diaphysis [daɪˈæfɪsɪs] *s* (*pl:* **-ses** [siz]) (anat. & bot.) diáfisis
diapositive [ˌdaɪəˈpɑzɪtɪv] *s* (phot.) diapositiva
diarist [ˈdaɪərɪst] *s* diarista
diarrhea o **diarrhoea** [ˌdaɪəˈriə] *s* (path.) diarrea
diarthrosis [ˌdaɪɑrˈθrosɪs] *s* (anat.) diartrosis
diary [ˈdaɪərɪ] *s* (*pl:* **-ries**) diario
diascordium [ˌdaɪəˈskɔrdɪəm] *s* (pharm.) diascordio
Diaspora [daɪˈæspərə] *s* (Bib. & fig.) Diáspora
diaspore [ˈdaɪəspor] *s* (mineral.) diásporo
diastase [ˈdaɪəstes] *s* (biochem.) diastasa
diastasic [ˌdaɪəˈstesɪk] *adj* (biochem. & surg.) diastásico
diastasis [daɪˈæstəsɪs] *s* (surg.) diastasis
diastole [daɪˈæstəli] *s* (physiol. & gram.) diástole
diastolic [ˌdaɪəˈstɑlɪk] *adj* diastólico
diastrophism [daɪˈæstrəfɪzəm] *s* (geol.) diastrofismo
diastyle [ˈdaɪəstaɪl] *s* (arch.) diástilo
diatessaron [ˌdaɪəˈtɛsərɑn] *s* (ancient mus., ancient pharm., & rel.) diatesarón
diathermanous [ˌdaɪəˈθʌrmənəs] *adj* (phys.) diatérmano
diathermic [ˌdaɪəˈθʌrmɪk] *adj* (med. & phys.) diatérmico
diathermy [ˈdaɪəˌθʌrmɪ] *s* (med.) diatermia
diathesis [daɪˈæθɪsɪs] *s* (med.) diátesis
diathetic [ˌdaɪəˈθɛtɪk] *adj* diatésico
diatom [ˈdaɪətɑm] *s* (bot.) diatomea
diatomaceous [ˌdaɪətoˈmeʃəs] *adj* diatomáceo
diatonic [ˌdaɪəˈtɑnɪk] *adj* (mus.) diatónico
diatonic scale *s* (mus.) escala diatónica
diatribe [ˈdaɪətraɪb] *s* diatriba
dibasic [daɪˈbesɪk] *adj* (chem.) dibásico
dibble [ˈdɪbəl] *s* plantador; *va* plantar con plantador
dice [daɪs] *spl* dados; cubitos (*p.ej., de zanahorias*); **to load the dice** cargar los dados; *va* perder (*dinero*) jugando a los dados; cortar (*p.ej., zanahorias*) en cubitos; *vn* jugar a los dados
dicebox [ˈdaɪsˌbɑks] *s* cubilete; cuchumbo (Am.)
dicer [ˈdaɪsər] *s* jugador de dados
dichasium [daɪˈkeʒɪəm] *s* (*pl:* **-a** [ə]) (bot.) dicasio
dichloride [daɪˈkloraɪd] o [daɪˈklorɪd] *s* (chem.) dicloruro
dichlorodiphenyl-trichloroethane [daɪˌklorodaɪˌfɛnɪltraɪˌkloroˈɛθen] *s* (chem.) diclorodifeniltricloroetano
dichotomic [ˌdaɪkəˈtɑmɪk] *adj* dicotómico
dichotomize [daɪˈkɑtəmaɪz] *va* dividir en dos
dichotomous [daɪˈkɑtəməs] *adj* dicótomo
dichotomy [daɪˈkɑtəmɪ] *s* (*pl:* **-mies**) dicotomía; (astr., biol., bot. & log.) dicotomía
dichroic [daɪˈkro·ɪk] *adj* dicroico
dichroism [daɪˈkro·ɪzəm] *s* dicroísmo
dichromate [daɪˈkromet] *s* (chem.) dicromato
dichromatic [ˌdaɪkroˈmætɪk] *adj* dicromático
dichromatism [daɪˈkromətɪzəm] *s* (path.) dicromatismo
Dick [dɪk] *s* nombre abreviado de **Richard**
dickens [ˈdɪkənz] *s* (coll.) diantre, dianche; **the dickens!** ¡diantre!, ¡dianche!
dicker [ˈdɪkər] *s* regateo, cambalache; *va & vn* regatear, cambalachear
dickey [ˈdɪkɪ] *s* camisolín, pechera postiza; cuello separado; babero de niño; (aut.) asiento del conductor; asiento descubierto detrás de un coche; (coll.) pajarito, pájaro pequeño; asno
dicky [ˈdɪkɪ] *s* (*pl:* **-ies**) var. de **dickey**
diclinous [ˈdaɪklɪnəs] o [daɪˈklaɪnəs] *adj* (bot.) diclino
dicotyledon [daɪˌkɑtɪˈlidən] *s* (bot.) dicotiledón
dicotyledonous [daɪˌkɑtɪˈlidənəs] *adj* (bot.) dicotiledóneo
dict. abr. de **dictionary**
dictaphone [ˈdɪktəfon] *s* (trademark) dictadora, dictáfono
dictate [ˈdɪktet] *s* mandato; **dictates** *spl* dictados; [ˈdɪktet] o [dɪkˈtet] *va & vn* dictar; mandar, disponer
dictation [dɪkˈteʃən] *s* dictado; mandato; **to take dictation** escribir al dictado
dictator [ˈdɪktetər] o [dɪkˈtetər] *s* dictador; persona que dicta cartas
dictatorial [ˌdɪktəˈtorɪəl] *adj* dictatorio (*per-*

teneciente al dictador); dictatorial (*perteneciente al dictador; imperioso, soberbio*)
dictatorship [ˈdɪktetər,ʃɪp] o [dɪkˈtetər,ʃɪp] *s* dictadura
diction [ˈdɪkʃən] *s* dicción
dictionary [ˈdɪkʃən,ɛrɪ] *s* (*pl:* **-ies**) diccionario
dictograph [ˈdɪktəgræf] o [ˈdɪktəgrɑf] *s* (trademark) dictógrafo
dictum [ˈdɪktəm] *s* (*pl:* **-ta** [tə]) dictamen; sentencia, aforismo; (law) fallo u opinión judicial sobre un punto no esencial al juicio principal
did [dɪd] *pret de* **do**
didactic [daɪˈdæktɪk] o [dɪˈdæktɪk] *adj* didáctico; **didactics** *ssg* didáctica
didactical [daɪˈdæktɪkəl] o [dɪˈdæktɪkəl] *adj* didáctico
didacticism [daɪˈdæktɪsɪzəm] o [dɪˈdæktɪsɪzəm] *s* método didáctico
didactylous [daɪˈdæktɪləs] *adj* didáctilo
diddle [ˈdɪdəl] *va* (coll.) estafar; (coll.) arruinar, quebrar; (coll.) perder (*el tiempo*); *vn* (coll.) zarandearse
didelphian [daɪˈdɛlfɪən] *adj & s* (zool.) didelfo
didn't [ˈdɪdənt] contracción de **did not**
dido [ˈdaɪdo] *s* (*pl:* **-dos** o **-does**) (coll.) travesura; **to cut didos** (coll.) hacer travesuras; (*cap.*) *s* (myth.) Dido
didymium [daɪˈdɪmɪəm] o [dɪˈdɪmɪəm] *s* (chem.) didimio
didymous [ˈdɪdɪməs] *adj* (bot. & zool.) dídimo
die [daɪ] *s* (*pl:* **dice** [daɪs]) dado; cubito (*p.ej., de zanahorias*); **the die is cast** la suerte está echada, el dado está tirado ‖ *s* (*pl:* **dies** [daɪz]) (arch.) dado; (mach.) troquel (*para acuñar monedas o estampar metales*); (mach.) hembra de terraja, cojinete de roscar ‖ (*pret & pp:* **died;** *ger:* **dieing**) *va* cortar con troquel; roscar ‖ (*pret & pp:* **died;** *ger:* **dying**) *va* morir (*p.ej., una muerte dolorosa*) ‖ *vn* morir; **to be dying to** + *inf* (coll.) morirse por + *inf;* **to die away, down** u **out** acabarse gradualmente, desaparecer gradualmente; enflaquecerse gradualmente; **to die hard** resistir hasta la muerte, rendirse de mala gana; **to die laughing** morir de risa
die-cast [ˈdaɪ,kæst] o [ˈdaɪ,kɑst] (*pret & pp:* **-cast**) *va* fundir a troquel
die casting *s* pieza fundida a troquel
diecious [daɪˈiʃəs] *adj* (biol. & bot.) dioico
die-hard [ˈdaɪ,hɑrd] *adj & s* intransigente
dielectric [,daɪɪˈlɛktrɪk] *adj & s* dieléctrico
dieresis [daɪˈɛrɪsɪs] *s* (*pl:* **-ses** [siz]) diéresis
Diesel-electric [ˈdizəlɪˈlɛktrɪk] *adj* dieseleléctrico
Diesel engine [ˈdizəl] s motor Diesel
Dieselization [,dizəlɪˈzeʃən] *s* dieselización
Diesel motor *s* motor Diesel
diesinker [ˈdaɪ,sɪŋkər] *s* grabador en hueco, troquelero
diesis [ˈdaɪɪsɪs] *s* (*pl:* **-ses** [siz]) (mus.) diesis; (print.) obelisco doble
diestock [ˈdaɪ,stɑk] *s* terraja, portacojinete
diet [ˈdaɪət] *s* dieta, régimen alimenticio; dieta (*asamblea*); **to be on a diet** estar a dieta; **to put on a diet** poner a dieta; *va* adietar; *vn* estar a dieta
dietary [ˈdaɪə,tɛrɪ] *adj* dietético; *s* (*pl:* **-ies**) dieta, sistema dietético; tratado sobre dietas
dietetic [,daɪəˈtɛtɪk] *adj* dietético; **dietetics** *ssg* dietética
dietician o **dietitian** [,daɪəˈtɪʃən] *s* dietista, especialista en dietética
diff. abr. de **difference** y **different**
differ [ˈdɪfər] *vn* diferenciar, discordar; diferenciarse, diferir
difference [ˈdɪfərəns] *s* diferencia; **it makes no difference** lo mismo da, no importa; **to not know the difference** no darse cuenta de ello; **to split the difference** partir la diferencia; **what difference does it make?** ¿qué más da?
difference of potential *s* (phys.) diferencia de potencial
different [ˈdɪfərənt] *adj* diferente
differentia [,dɪfəˈrɛnʃɪə] *s* (*pl:* **-ae** [i]) (log.) diferencia
differential [,dɪfəˈrɛnʃəl] *adj* diferencial; *s* (mach.) diferencial *m;* (math.) diferencial *f*
differential calculus *s* (math.) cálculo diferencial
differential coefficient *s* (math.) coeficiente diferencial
differential equation *s* (math.) ecuación diferencial
differential gear *s* (mach.) engranaje diferencial
differential housing *s* (aut.) caja del diferencial
differential rate *s* (rail.) tarifa diferencial
differential thermometer *s* termómetro diferencial
differentiate [,dɪfəˈrɛnʃɪet] *va* diferenciar; (math.) diferenciar; *vn* diferenciarse; (bot.) diferenciarse
differentiation [,dɪfə,rɛnʃɪˈeʃən] *s* diferenciación
difficult [ˈdɪfɪkʌlt] *adj* difícil
difficulty [ˈdɪfɪkʌltɪ] *s* (*pl:* **-ties**) dificultad; **difficulties** *spl* aprietos, apuros
diffidation [,dɪfɪˈdeʃən] *s* difidación, declaración de guerra
diffidence [ˈdɪfɪdəns] *s* timidez, apocamiento
diffident [ˈdɪfɪdənt] *adj* tímido, apocado
diffluence [ˈdɪfluəns] *s* difluencia
diffluent [ˈdɪfluənt] *adj* difluente
diffract [dɪˈfrækt] *va* difractar
diffraction [dɪˈfrækʃən] *s* difracción
diffraction grating *s* (opt.) red de difracción
diffractive [dɪˈfræktɪv] *adj* difractivo, difrangente
diffuse [dɪˈfjus] *adj* difuso; [dɪˈfjuz] *va* difundir; *vn* difundirse
diffuser [dɪˈfjuzər] *s* difusor
diffusibility [dɪ,fjuzɪˈbɪlɪtɪ] *s* difusibilidad
diffusible [dɪˈfjuzɪbəl] *adj* difusible
diffusion [dɪˈfjuʒən] *s* difusión; (anthrop., chem. & phys.) difusión
diffusionist theory [dɪˈfjuʒənɪst] *s* (anthrop.) difusionismo
diffusive [dɪˈfjusɪv] *adj* difusivo; difuso (*superabundante en palabras*)
dig [dɪg] *s* empuje, codazo; (coll.) pulla, puyazo, palabra hiriente; (*pret & pp:* **dug** o **digged;** *ger:* **digging**) *va* cavar, excavar; ahondar, escudriñar; **to dig up** desenterrar; (fig.) desenterrar; *vn* cavar, excavar; trabajar con azada, etc.; abrirse paso cavando; (coll.) trabajar mucho; **to dig in** (mil.) atrincherarse, afosarse; poner manos a la obra; **to dig into** (coll.) ocuparse mucho en; **to dig under** socavar
digest [ˈdaɪdʒɛst] *s* resumen, compendio; (law) digesto; [dɪˈdʒɛst] o [daɪˈdʒɛst] *va* (physiol. & chem.) digerir; (fig.) digerir (*meditar con cuidado, tratar de entender; sufrir con paciencia*); (fig.) resumir, compendiar; *vn* digerir, digerirse
digester [dɪˈdʒɛstər] o [daɪˈdʒɛstər] *s* compendiador; (med.) digestivo; digestor (*vasija cerrada a tornillo*)
digestibility [dɪ,dʒɛstɪˈbɪlɪtɪ] o [daɪ,dʒɛstɪˈbɪlɪtɪ] *s* digestibilidad
digestible [dɪˈdʒɛstɪbəl] o [daɪˈdʒɛstɪbəl] *adj* digerible, digestible
digestion [dɪˈdʒɛstʃən] o [daɪˈdʒɛstʃən] *s* digestión
digestive [dɪˈdʒɛstɪv] o [daɪˈdʒɛstɪv] *adj & s* digestivo
digger [ˈdɪgər] *s* cavador; azadón
digger wasp *s* (ent.) avispa cavadora
diggings [ˈdɪgɪŋz] *spl* excavaciones; (coll.) alojamiento
digit [ˈdɪdʒɪt] *s* (arith. & astr.) dígito; (hum.) dedo
digital [ˈdɪdʒɪtəl] *adj* digital; *s* (hum.) dedo; tecla
digital computer *s* calculadora numérica
digitalin [,dɪdʒɪˈtelɪn] o [ˈdɪdʒɪtəlɪn] *s* (chem. & pharm.) digitalina
digitalis [,dɪgɪˈtælɪs] o [,dɪdʒɪˈtelɪs] *s* (bot. & pharm.) digital
digitate [ˈdɪdʒɪtet] *adj* digitado; (bot.) digitado
digitigrade [ˈdɪdʒɪtɪ,gred] *adj & s* (zool.) digitígrado
dignification [,dɪgnɪfɪˈkeʃən] *s* dignificación
dignified [ˈdɪgnɪfaɪd] *adj* digno, grave, decoroso

dignify ['dɪgnɪfaɪ] (*pret & pp:* **-fied**) *va* dignificar; dar un título altisonante a
dignitary ['dɪgnɪ,tɛrɪ] *s* (*pl:* **-ies**) dignatario
dignity ['dɪgnɪtɪ] *s* (*pl:* **-ties**) dignidad; **to be beneath one's dignity** no estar de acuerdo con la dignidad de uno, ser impropio de la dignidad de uno; **to stand upon one's dignity** ponerse tan alto
digram ['daɪgræm] *s* digrama
digraph ['daɪgræf] o ['daɪgrɑf] *s* digrafía, dígrafo
digress [dɪ'grɛs] o [daɪ'grɛs] *vn* divagar
digression [dɪ'grɛʃən] o [daɪ'grɛʃən] *s* digresión; (astr.) digresión
digressive [dɪ'grɛsɪv] o [daɪ'grɛsɪv] *adj* digresivo
dihedral [daɪ'hidrəl] *adj* (geom.) diedro
diiamb [,daɪaɪ'æmb] *s* diyambo
dike [daɪk] *s* dique; zanja, arrecife; (geol.) dique; *va* contener por medio de un dique; desaguar con zanjas
dilacerate [dɪ'læsəret] *va* dilacerar
dilaceration [dɪ,læsə'reʃən] *s* dilaceración
dilapidate [dɪ'læpɪdet] *va* dilapidar (*malgastar*); desmantelar; *vn* desmantelarse (*abandonarse o arruinarse, p.ej., una casa*)
dilapidated [dɪ'læpɪ,detɪd] *adj* desmantelado
dilapidation [dɪ,læpɪ'deʃən] *s* dilapidación (*derroche*); desmantelamiento
dilatability [daɪ,letə'bɪlɪtɪ] *s* dilatabilidad
dilatable [daɪ'letəbəl] *adj* dilatable
dilatation [,dɪlə'teʃən] o [,daɪlə'teʃən] *s* dilatación
dilate [daɪ'let] o [dɪ'let] *va* dilatar; *vn* dilatarse
dilation [daɪ'leʃən] o [dɪ'leʃən] *s* dilatación
dilative [daɪ'letɪv] o [dɪ'letɪv] *adj* dilatativo
dilatometer [,daɪlə'tɑmɪtər] o [,dɪlə'tɑmɪtər] *s* (phys.) dilatómetro
dilator [daɪ'letər] o [dɪ'letər] *s* (anat. & surg.) dilatador
dilatory ['dɪlə,torɪ] *adj* tardío (*aplícase a acciones y personas*); (law) dilatorio
dilemma [dɪ'lɛmə] *s* dilema, disyuntiva; aprieto, conflicto; (log.) dilema
dilettante [,dɪlə'tæntɪ] *adj* diletante; *s* (*pl:* **-tes** o **-ti** [tɪ]) diletante
dilettanteism [,dɪlə'tæntɪɪzəm] or **dilettantism** [,dɪlə'tæntɪzəm] *s* diletantismo
diligence ['dɪlɪdʒəns] *s* diligencia
diligent ['dɪlɪdʒənt] *adj* diligente
dill [dɪl] *s* (bot.) eneldo
dill pickle *s* pepinillo encurtido sazonado con eneldo
dillydally ['dɪlɪ,dælɪ] (*pret & pp:* **-lied**) *vn* holgazanear, perder el tiempo
diluent ['dɪljʊənt] *s* (med.) diluente
dilute [dɪ'lut] *adj* diluído; *va* diluir; *vn* diluirse
dilution [dɪ'luʃən] *s* dilución
diluvial [dɪ'luvɪəl] o **diluvian** [dɪ'luvɪən] *adj* diluviano
dim. abr. de **diminuendo** y **diminutive**
dim [dɪm] *adj* (*comp:* **dimmer;** *super:* **dimmest**) débil, mortecino; poco claro, obscuro, confuso, indistinto; lerdo, torpe; **to take a dim view of** mirar escépticamente, no entusiasmarse por; (*pret & pp:* **dimmed;** *ger:* **dimming**) *va* amortiguar, velar (*la luz*); poner a media luz (*p.ej., un faro*); obscurecer; *vn* obscurecerse
dime [daɪm] *s* (U.S.A.) moneda de diez centavos
dime novel *s* novela sensacional de ningún mérito literario
dimension [dɪ'mɛnʃən] *s* dimensión
dimensional [dɪ'mɛnʃənəl] *adj* dimensional
dimeter ['dɪmɪtər] *s* (pros.) dímetro
dimetria [daɪ'mitrɪə] *s* (med.) dimetría
dimin. abr. de **diminuendo** y **diminutive**
diminish [dɪ'mɪnɪʃ] *va* disminuir; *vn* disminuir, disminuirse
diminished [dɪ'mɪnɪʃt] *adj* (mus.) diminuto
diminuendo [dɪ,mɪnjʊ'ɛndo] *s* (*pl:* **-dos**) (mus.) diminuendo
diminution [,dɪmɪ'njuʃən] o [,dɪmɪ'nuʃən] *s* diminución, disminución
diminutive [dɪ'mɪnjətɪv] *adj* diminuto; (gram.) diminutivo; *s* persona diminuta, cosa diminuta; (gram.) diminutivo
dimissory letters ['dɪmɪ,sorɪ] *spl* (eccl.) dimisorias
dimity ['dɪmɪtɪ] *s* (*pl:* **-ties**) cotonía
dimmer ['dɪmər] *s* amortiguador de luz; (aut.) faro, lámpara o luz de cruce
dimorphism [daɪ'mɔrfɪzəm] *s* dimorfismo
dimorphous [daɪ'mɔrfəs] *adj* dimorfo
dimple ['dɪmpəl] *s* hoyuelo; *va* formar hoyuelos en; *vn* formarse hoyuelos
dimply ['dɪmplɪ] *adj* que tiene hoyuelos
din [dɪn] *s* ruido ensordecedor y continuado; (*pret & pp:* **dinned;** *ger:* **dinning**) *va* atolondrar con ruido ensordecedor y continuado; repetir insistentemente; *vn* hacer un ruido ensordecedor y continuado
Dinah ['daɪnə] *s* Dina
Dinaric Alps [dɪ'nærɪk] *spl* Alpes dináricos
dine [daɪn] *va* dar de comer a; *vn* comer; **to dine out** comer fuera de casa
diner ['daɪnər] *s* convidado (a una comida); (rail.) coche-comedor; restaurante que se parece a un coche-comedor
dinette [daɪ'nɛt] *s* comedorcito, comedor pequeño junto a la cocina
ding [dɪŋ] *s* sonido, repique (*de campanas*); *va* repicar (*las campanas*); (coll.) repetir insistentemente; *vn* resonar
Ding an sich [dɪŋɑn'zɪx] *s* (philos.) cosa en sí
ding-dong ['dɪŋ,dɔŋ] o ['dɪŋ,dɑŋ] *s* dindán, tintín; *va* importunar regañando; *vn* retiñir
ding-dong theory *s* (philol.) teoría de la invención
dingey ['dɪŋgɪ] *s* dinga
dinghy ['dɪŋgɪ] *s* (*pl:* **-ghies**) dinga
dinginess ['dɪndʒɪnɪs] *s* deslustre
dingle ['dɪŋgəl] *s* cañada pequeña
dingo ['dɪŋgo] *s* (*pl:* **-goes**) dingo (*perro salvaje*)
dingus ['dɪŋəs] *s* (slang) chisme, adminículo
dingy ['dɪndʒɪ] *adj* (*comp.* **-gier;** *super:* **-giest**) empañado, deslustrado, sucio, manchado; ['dɪŋgɪ] *s* (*pl:* **-gies**) dinga
dining car *s* (rail.) coche-comedor
dining room *s* comedor
dining-room suit ['daɪnɪŋ,rum] o ['daɪnɪŋ,rʊm] *s* juego de comedor
dinkey ['dɪŋkɪ] *s* (coll.) locomotora pequeña de maniobras
dinky ['dɪŋkɪ] *adj* (*comp:* **-ier;** *super:* **-iest**) (slang) diminuto, insignificante
dinner ['dɪnər] *s* comida; banquete
dinner coat o **dinner jacket** *s* smoking
dinner pail *s* fiambrera, portaviandas
dinner set *s* vajilla
dinner time *s* hora de la comida
dinornis [daɪ'nɔrnɪs] *s* (pal.) dinornis
dinosaur ['daɪnəsɔr] o **dinosaurian** [,daɪnə'sɔrɪən] *s* (pal.) dinosaurio
dinothere ['daɪnəθɪr] *s* (pal.) dinoterio
dint [dɪnt] *s* golpe; abolladura; fuerza; **by dint of** a fuerza de; *va* abollar
diocesan [daɪ'ɑsɪsən] *adj & s* diocesano
diocese ['daɪəsis] o ['daɪəsɪs] *s* diócesi o diócesis
Diocletian [,daɪə'kliʃən] *s* Diocleciano
diode ['daɪod] *s* (electron.) diodo
dioecious [daɪ'iʃəs] *adj* (biol. & bot.) dioico
Diogenes [daɪ'ɑdʒɪniz] *s* Diógenes
Diomede ['daɪəmid] o **Diomedes** [,daɪə'midiz] *s* (myth.) Diomedes
Dionysia [,daɪə'nɪʃɪə] o [,daɪə'nɪsɪə] *spl* Dionisias, Dionisíacas (*fiestas*)
Dionysiac [,daɪə'nɪsɪæk] *adj* dionisíaco
Dionysius [,daɪə'nɪʃɪəs] *s* Dionisio
Dionysos o **Dionysus** [,daɪə'naɪsəs] *s* (myth.) Dionisios o Dionisos
diopter [daɪ'ɑptər] *s* dioptra, alidada; (opt.) dioptria (*unidad*)
dioptric [daɪ'ɑptrɪk] *adj* dióptrico; **dioptrics** *ssg* dióptrica
dioptrical [daɪ'ɑptrɪkəl] *adj* dióptrico
diorama [,daɪə'ræmə] o [,daɪə'rɑmə] *s* diorama
dioramic [,daɪə'ræmɪk] *adj* diorámico
diorite ['daɪəraɪt] *s* (mineral.) diorita
dioscoreaceous [,daɪɑs,korɪ'eʃəs] *adj* (bot.) dioscoreáceo
Dioscuri [,daɪɑs'kjuraɪ] *spl* (myth.) Dioscuros
dioxide [daɪ'ɑksaɪd] o [daɪ'ɑksɪd] *s* (chem.) dióxido
dip [dɪp] *s* inmersión, zambullida; baño corto; depresión (*p.ej., en un camino*); inclinación;

grado de inclinación; vela de sebo chorreada; (mach.) cuchara de lubricación; (geol.) buzamiento; (*pret & pp:* **dipped;** *ger:* **dipping**) *va* sumergir; sumergir para lavar o limpiar; sumergir en un tinte; sacar, levantar con cuchara, pala, etc.; bajar y alzar prontamente (*p.ej., una bandera*); *vn* sumergirse; bajar súbitamente, desaparecer súbitamente; inclinarse hacia abajo; (geol.) buzar; **to dip into** hojear, repasar (*p.ej., un libro*); empeñarse en, meterse en (*p.ej., un comercio*)
dipetalous [daɪˈpɛtələs] *adj* dipétalo
diphase [ˈdaɪˌfez] *adj* (elec.) difásico
diphtheria [dɪfˈθɪrɪə] *s* (path.) difteria
diphtherial [dɪfˈθɪrɪəl] o **diphtheritic** [ˌdɪfθəˈrɪtɪk] *adj* diftérico
diphtheritis [ˌdɪfθəˈraɪtɪs] *s* (path.) difteritis
diphtheroid [ˈdɪfθərɔɪd] *adj* difteroide
diphthong [ˈdɪfθɔŋ] o [ˈdɪfθɑŋ] *s* diptongo
diphthongal [dɪfˈθɔŋgəl] o [dɪfˈθɑŋgəl] *adj* de diptongo, del diptongo
diphthongization [ˌdɪfθɔŋgɪˈzeʃən] o [ˌdɪfθɑŋgɪˈzeʃən] *s* diptongación
diphthongize [ˈdɪfθɔŋgaɪz] o [ˈdɪfθɑŋgaɪz] *va* diptongar; *vn* diptongarse
diphyllous [daɪˈfɪləs] *adj* (bot.) dífilo
diplegia [daɪˈplidʒɪə] *s* (path.) diplejía
diplochlamydeous [ˌdɪpləkləˈmɪdɪəs] *adj* (bot.) diploclamídeo
diplococcus [ˌdɪpləˈkɑkəs] *s* (*pl:* **-cocci** [ˈkɑksaɪ]) (bact.) diplococo
diplodocus [dɪˈplɑdəkəs] *s* (pal.) diplodoco
diploma [dɪˈplomə] *s* diploma
diplomacy [dɪˈploməsɪ] *s* (*pl:* **-cies**) diplomacia
diplomat [ˈdɪpləmæt] *s* diplomático
diplomate [ˈdɪpləmɪt] o [ˈdɪpləmet] *s* diplomado
diplomatic [ˌdɪpləˈmætɪk] *adj* diplomático; **diplomatics** *ssg* diplomática (*arte de conocer los diplomas; diplomacia*)
diplomatically [ˌdɪpləˈmætɪkəlɪ] *adv* diplomáticamente
diplomatic corps *s* cuerpo diplomático
diplomatic edition *s* edición diplomática
diplomatic pouch *s* valija diplomática
diplomatist [dɪˈplomətɪst] *s* diplomático
diplopia [dɪˈplopɪə] *s* (med.) diplopía
dipolar [daɪˈpolər] *adj* dipolar
dipole [ˈdaɪˌpol] *s* (chem. & phys.) dipolo
dipole antenna *s* (rad.) antena dipolo
dipper [ˈdɪpər] *s* cazo, cucharón; cuchara (*de pala mecánica*); (orn.) zambullidor, mirlo de agua; **the Dipper** (astr.) el Carro
dipsomania [ˌdɪpsoˈmenɪə] *s* (path.) dipsomanía
dipsomaniac [ˌdɪpsoˈmenɪæk] *s* dipsomaníaco
dipsomaniacal [ˌdɪpsoməˈnaɪəkəl] *adj* dipsomaníaco
dipstick [ˈdɪpˌstɪk] *s* varilla de nivel
dipteral [ˈdɪptərəl] *adj* (zool. & arch.) díptero
dipteran [ˈdɪptərən] *adj & s* (zool.) díptero
dipteros [ˈdɪptərɑs] *s* (arch.) díptero (*edificio*)
dipterous [ˈdɪptərəs] *adj* (zool.) díptero
diptych [ˈdɪptɪk] *s* díptica (*tablas*); díptico (*cuadro*)
Dircaen [dʌrˈsiən] *adj* dirceo
Dircaen Swan *s* cisne dirceo (*Píndaro*)
Dirce [ˈdʌrsi] *s* (myth.) Dirce
dire [daɪr] *adj* horrendo, terrible, deplorable
direct [dɪˈrɛkt] o [daɪˈrɛkt] *adj* directo; sincero, franco, abierto; exacto, preciso; (gram.) directo; *va* dirigir; ordenar, mandar
direct action *s* acción directa
direct current *s* (elec.) corriente continua
direct discourse *s* (gram.) estilo directo
direct distance dialing *s* (telp.) marcaje directo a distancia
direct hit *s* blanco directo, impacto directo; **to score a direct hit** conseguir un impacto directo
direction [dɪˈrɛkʃən] o [daɪˈrɛkʃən] *s* dirección; instrucción; **in the direction of** en la dirección de, con rumbo a
directional [dɪˈrɛkʃənəl] o [daɪˈrɛkʃənəl] *adj* direccional
directional antenna *s* (rad.) antena direccional
direction finder *s* (rad.) radiogoniómetro
directive [dɪˈrɛktɪv] o [daɪˈrɛktɪv] *adj* directivo; *s* directorio, directriz
directly [dɪˈrɛktlɪ] o [daɪˈrɛktlɪ] *adj* directamente; inmediatamente, en seguida; exactamente, absolutamente
directness [dɪˈrɛktnɪs] o [daɪˈrɛktnɪs] *s* derechura
direct object *s* (gram.) complemento directo
Directoire [ˌdɪrɛkˈtwɑr] *s* Directorio
director [dɪˈrɛktər] o [daɪˈrɛktər] *s* director; vocal (*de un directorio*)
directorate [dɪˈrɛktərɪt] o [daɪˈrɛktərɪt] *s* dirección, directorio
director-general [dɪˈrɛktərˈdʒɛnərəl] o [daɪˈrɛktərˈdʒɛnərəl] *s* (*pl:* **director-generals**) director general
directorial [dɪˌrɛkˈtorɪəl] o [ˌdaɪrɛkˈtorɪəl] *adj* directoral (*del director*); directorio, directorial
directorship [dɪˈrɛktərʃɪp] o [daɪˈrɛktərʃɪp] *s* dirección, directorio
directory [dɪˈrɛktərɪ] o [daɪˈrɛktərɪ] *adj* directorio; *s* (*pl:* **-ries**) directorio (*junta directiva; libro de nombres y señas*); guía telefónica
direct ratio *s* (math.) razón directa
directress [dɪˈrɛktrɪs] o [daɪˈrɛktrɪs] *s* directora
directrix [dɪˈrɛktrɪks] o [daɪˈrɛktrɪks] *s* (geom.) directriz
direct tax *s* contribución directa
direful [ˈdaɪrfəl] *adj* terrible, calamitoso, espantoso
dirge [dʌrdʒ] *s* endecha, canto fúnebre; (eccl.) oficio de difuntos; (eccl.) misa de réquiem
dirigible [ˈdɪrɪdʒɪbəl] *adj & s* dirigible
dirk [dʌrk] *s* daga, puñal
dirt [dʌrt] *s* lodo, barro; polvo; tierra, suelo; bajeza, vileza; suciedad, porquería; obscenidad
dirt-cheap [ˈdʌrtˈtʃip] *adj* tirado, sumamente barato
dirt farmer *s* (coll.) agricultor practicón
dirty [ˈdʌrtɪ] *adj* (*comp:* **-ier;** *super:* **-iest**) enlodado, barroso; polvoriento; bajo, vil; sucio, puerco; obsceno; (*pret & pp:* **-tied**) *va* ensuciar
dirty linen *s* ropa sucia, ropa para lavar; **to air one's dirty linen** sacar los trapos sucios a relucir
dirty trick *s* (slang) perrada, perrería (*vileza*)
disability [ˌdɪsəˈbɪlɪtɪ] *s* (*pl:* **-ties**) inhabilidad, incapacidad; impedimento
disable [dɪsˈebəl] *va* inhabilitar; (law) descalificar
disablement [dɪsˈebəlmənt] *s* inhabilitación
disabuse [ˌdɪsəˈbjuz] *va* desengañar
disaccord [ˌdɪsəˈkɔrd] *s* desacuerdo; *vn* discordar
disadvantage [ˌdɪsədˈvæntɪdʒ] o [ˌdɪsədˈvɑntɪdʒ] *s* desventaja; *va* dañar, perjudicar
disadvantageous [dɪsˌædvənˈtedʒəs] *adj* desventajoso
disaffect [ˌdɪsəˈfɛkt] *va* indisponer, enemistar
disaffected [ˌdɪsəˈfɛktɪd] *adj* desafecto
disaffection [ˌdɪsəˈfɛkʃən] *s* desafección, desafecto
disagree [ˌdɪsəˈgri] *vn* desconvenir, desconvenirse, desavenirse; altercar, contender; **to disagree with** no estar de acuerdo con; no sentar bien a
disagreeable [ˌdɪsəˈgriəbəl] *adj* desagradable
disagreeably [ˌdɪsəˈgriəblɪ] *adv* desagradablemente
disagreement [ˌdɪsəˈgrimənt] *s* desacuerdo; altercado; desemejanza
disallow [ˌdɪsəˈlaʊ] *va* desaprobar, rechazar
disallowance [ˌdɪsəˈlaʊəns] *s* desaprobación, rechazamiento
disappear [ˌdɪsəˈpɪr] *vn* desaparecer, desaparecerse
disappearance [ˌdɪsəˈpɪrəns] *s* desaparecimiento, desaparición
disappoint [ˌdɪsəˈpɔɪnt] *va* decepcionar, desilusionar, frustrar; **to be disappointed** llevarse chasco
disappointment [ˌdɪsəˈpɔɪntmənt] *s* decepción, desilusión, frustración, chasco
disapprobation [ˌdɪsæprəˈbeʃən] o **disapproval** [ˌdɪsəˈpruvəl] *s* desaprobación
disapprove [ˌdɪsəˈpruv] *va & vn* desaprobar
disapprovingly [ˌdɪsəˈpruvɪŋlɪ] *adv* con desaprobación
disarm [dɪsˈɑrm] *va & vn* desarmar

disarmament [dɪsˈɑrməmənt] *s* desarme o desarmamiento
disarmed [dɪsˈɑrmd] *adj* desarmado; (her.) moznado
disarrange [ˌdɪsəˈrendʒ] *va* desarreglar, descomponer
disarrangement [ˌdɪsəˈrendʒmənt] *s* desarreglo, descomposición
disarray [ˌdɪsəˈre] *s* desarreglo, desorden; desatavío; *va* desarreglar, desordenar; desataviar
disarticulate [ˌdɪsɑrˈtɪkjəlet] *va* desarticular; (surg.) desarticular; *vn* desarticularse
disarticulation [ˌdɪsɑrˌtɪkjəˈleʃən] *s* desarticulación; (surg.) desarticulación
disassemble [ˌdɪsəˈsɛmbəl] *va* desarmar, desmontar
disassimilate [ˌdɪsəˈsɪmɪlet] *va* (physiol.) desasimilar
disassimilation [ˌdɪsəˌsɪmɪˈleʃən] *s* (physiol.) desasimilación
disassociate [ˌdɪsəˈsoʃɪet] *va* disociar
disassociation [ˌdɪsəˌsosɪˈeʃən] o [ˌdɪsəˌsoʃɪˈeʃən] *s* disociación
disaster [dɪzˈæstər] o [dɪzˈɑstər] *s* desastre
disastrous [dɪzˈæstrəs] o [dɪzˈɑstrəs] *adj* desastroso, funesto
disavow [ˌdɪsəˈvaʊ] *va* negar, desconocer
disavowal [ˌdɪsəˈvaʊəl] *s* negación, desconocimiento
disband [dɪsˈbænd] *va* disolver; licenciar (*tropas*); *vn* desbandarse
disbandment [dɪsˈbændmənt] *s* disolución; licenciamiento
disbar [dɪsˈbɑr] (*pret & pp:* **-barred**; *ger:* **-barring**) *va* (law) excluir del foro
disbarment [dɪsˈbɑrmənt] *s* (law) exclusión del foro
disbelief [ˌdɪsbɪˈlif] *s* incredulidad, descreimiento
disbelieve [ˌdɪsbɪˈliv] *va & vn* descreer
disburden [dɪsˈbʌrdən] *va* descargar; *vn* descargarse
disburse [dɪsˈbʌrs] *va* desembolsar
disbursement [dɪsˈbʌrsmənt] *s* desembolso
disbursement office *s* pagaduría
disburser [dɪsˈbʌrsər] *s* pagador
disc. abr. de **discount, discovered** y **discoverer**
disc [dɪsk] *s* var. de **disk**
discalced [dɪsˈkælst] *adj* descalzo (*fraile*)
discard [ˈdɪskɑrd] *s* descarte; **to put** o **to throw in the discard** (coll.) echar a un lado; [dɪsˈkɑrd] *va* descartar; *vn* descartarse
discern [dɪˈzʌrn] o [dɪˈsʌrn] *va & vn* discernir, percibir
discerner [dɪˈzʌrnər] o [dɪˈsʌrnər] *s* discernidor
discernible [dɪˈzʌrnɪbəl] o [dɪˈsʌrnɪbəl] *adj* discernible
discerning [dɪˈzʌrnɪŋ] o [dɪˈsʌrnɪŋ] *adj* discerniente, discernidor, perspicaz
discernment [dɪˈzʌrnmənt] o [dɪˈsʌrnmənt] *s* discernimiento, percepción, perspicacia
discharge [dɪsˈtʃɑrdʒ] *s* descarga; descargo (*pago de una deuda; disculpa*); cumplimiento, desempeño (*de un deber*); liberación (*de un preso*); despedida, remoción; descarga unitaria; (elec.) descarga; (med.) derrame; (mil.) certificado de licencia; *va* descargar; desempeñar (*p.ej., un deber*); libertar, soltar (*a un preso*); despedir, despachar, remover; dar de alta (*a un enfermo*); (elec.) descargar; (mil.) licenciar; *vn* descargar (*dícese de un tubo, conducto, río, etc.*); descargarse (*un arma de fuego*); correrse (*un tinte*)
disciple [dɪˈsaɪpəl] *s* discípulo
discipleship [dɪˈsaɪpəlʃɪp] *s* discipulado
disciplinable [ˈdɪsɪplɪnəbəl] *adj* disciplinable; castigable, punible
disciplinal [ˌdɪsɪˈplaɪnəl] *adj* disciplinal
disciplinarian [ˌdɪsɪplɪˈnɛrɪən] *adj* disciplinario; *s* ordenancista
disciplinary [ˈdɪsɪplɪˌnɛrɪ] *adj* disciplinario
discipline [ˈdɪsɪplɪn] *s* disciplina; castigo; *va* disciplinar; castigar
discipular [dɪˈsɪpjələr] *adj* discipular
disclaim [dɪsˈklem] *va* negar, desconocer; (law) renunciar
disclaimer [dɪsˈklemər] *s* negación, desconocimiento; (law) renuncia
disclose [dɪsˈkloz] *va* descubrir; revelar, divulgar, publicar
disclosure [dɪsˈkloʒər] *s* descubrimiento; revelación, divulgación, publicación
discoidal [dɪsˈkɔɪdəl] *adj* discoidal
discolor [dɪsˈkʌlər] *adj* (bot.) discoloro; *va* descolorar, manchar; *vn* descolorarse, mancharse
discoloration [dɪsˌkʌləˈreʃən] *s* descoloración, descoloramiento
discomfit [dɪsˈkʌmfɪt] *va* derrotar; burlar, frustrar; desconcertar
discomfiture [dɪsˈkʌmfɪtʃər] *s* derrota; burla, frustración; desconcierto
discomfort [dɪsˈkʌmfərt] *s* incomodidad; *va* incomodar
discompose [ˌdɪskəmˈpoz] *va* agitar, inquietar, descomponer, desconcertar
discomposure [ˌdɪskəmˈpoʒər] *s* agitación, inquietud, descomposición, desconcierto
disconcert [ˌdɪskənˈsʌrt] *va* desconcertar, agitar, confundir
disconcerting [ˌdɪskənˈsʌrtɪŋ] *adj* desconcertante
disconformity [ˌdɪskənˈfɔrmɪtɪ] *s* disconformidad
disconnect [ˌdɪskəˈnɛkt] *va* desunir, desacoplar; (elec. & mach.) desconectar
disconnected [ˌdɪskəˈnɛktɪd] *adj* inconexo, incoherente; (elec. & mach.) desconectado
disconnection [ˌdɪskəˈnɛkʃən] *s* desunión; desconexión
disconsolate [dɪsˈkɑnsəlɪt] *adj* desconsolado
disconsolation [dɪsˌkɑnsəˈleʃən] *s* desconsuelo
discontent [ˌdɪskənˈtɛnt] *adj & s* descontento; *va* descontentar
discontented [ˌdɪskənˈtɛntɪd] *adj* descontento
discontentment [ˌdɪskənˈtɛntmənt] *s* descontentamiento, descontento
discontinuance [ˌdɪskənˈtɪnjʊəns] o **discontinuation** [ˌdɪskənˌtɪnjʊˈeʃən] *s* descontinuación o discontinuación
discontinue [ˌdɪskənˈtɪnjʊ] *va* descontinuar o discontinuar
discontinuity [ˌdɪskɑntɪˈnjuɪtɪ] o [ˌdɪskɑntɪˈnuɪtɪ] *s* discontinuidad
discontinuous [ˌdɪskənˈtɪnjʊəs] *adj* descontinuo o discontinuo
discophile [ˈdɪskofaɪl] *s* discófilo
discord [ˈdɪskɔrd] *s* discordia, desacuerdo; disonancia; [dɪsˈkɔrd] *vn* discordar
discordance [dɪsˈkɔrdəns] o **discordancy** [dɪsˈkɔrdənsɪ] *s* discordancia; (geol.) discordancia
discordant [dɪsˈkɔrdənt] *adj* discordante; (geol.) discordante
discount [ˈdɪskaʊnt] *s* descuento; **at a discount** al descuento; mal acogido; [ˈdɪskaʊnt] o [dɪsˈkaʊnt] *va* descontar; considerar exagerado
discountable [dɪsˈkaʊntəbəl] *adj* descontable
discountenance [dɪsˈkaʊntɪnəns] *va* desaprobar; avergonzar
discount house *s* tienda de descuento
discount rate *s* tipo de descuento; tipo de redescuento
discourage [dɪsˈkʌrɪdʒ] *va* desalentar, desanimar; desaprobar; disuadir; **to discourage from** + *ger* disuadir de + *inf*
discouragement [dɪsˈkʌrɪdʒmənt] *s* desaliento, desánimo; desaprobación; disuasión
discourse [ˈdɪskors] o [dɪsˈkors] *s* discurso; [dɪsˈkors] *vn* discurrir
discourteous [dɪsˈkʌrtɪəs] *adj* descortés
discourtesy [dɪsˈkʌrtɪsɪ] *s* (*pl:* **-sies**) descortesía
discover [dɪsˈkʌvər] *va* descubrir
discoverer [dɪsˈkʌvərər] *s* descubridor
discovery [dɪsˈkʌvərɪ] *s* (*pl:* **-ies**) descubrimiento
Discovery Day *s* día de la raza, fiesta de la hispanidad
discredit [dɪsˈkrɛdɪt] *s* descrédito; *va* desacreditar; descreer
discreditable [dɪsˈkrɛdɪtəbəl] *adj* ignominioso, deshonroso, vergonzoso
discreditably [dɪsˈkrɛdɪtəblɪ] *adv* ignominiosamente, deshonrosamente, vergonzosamente
discreet [dɪsˈkrit] *adj* discreto (*moderado en*

sus acciones o palabras; que incluye discreción)
discrepancy [dɪsˈkrɛpənsɪ] *s* (*pl:* **-cies**) discrepancia
discrepant [dɪsˈkrɛpənt] *adj* discrepante
discrete [dɪsˈkrit] *adj* discreto (*discontinuo; que se compone de partes separadas*); (math. & med.) discreto
discretion [dɪsˈkrɛʃən] *s* discreción; **at discretion** a discreción
discretional [dɪsˈkrɛʃənəl] o **discretionary** [dɪsˈkrɛʃəˌnɛrɪ] *adj* discrecional
discriminant [dɪsˈkrɪmɪnənt] *adj* discriminante; *s* (math.) discriminante
discriminate [dɪsˈkrɪmɪnet] *va* discriminar; *vn* discriminar; hacer distinciones injustas; **to be discriminated against** ser tratado desfavorablemente; **to discriminate against** hacer distinción en perjuicio de; **to discriminate between** distinguir entre
discriminating [dɪsˈkrɪmɪˌnetɪŋ] *adj* distintivo, discerniente, discriminante; diferencial (*dícese de los derechos de aduana*); injusto, parcial
discrimination [dɪsˌkrɪmɪˈneʃən] *s* distinción, discernimiento, discriminación (*especialmente contra una persona o varias personas*)
discriminative [dɪsˈkrɪmɪˌnetɪv] o **discriminatory** [dɪsˈkrɪmɪnəˌtorɪ] *adj* distintivo, discerniente, discriminativo; injusto, parcial
discrown [dɪsˈkraʊn] *va* quitar la corona a, destronar
discursive [dɪsˈkʌrsɪv] *adj* digresivo, divagador
discus [ˈdɪskəs] *s* (sport) disco
discuss [dɪsˈkʌs] *va* discutir; hablar de, tratar de; (hum.) catar, probar (*un manjar, una bebida*); *vn* discutir
discussion [dɪsˈkʌʃən] *s* discusión
discus thrower *s* discóbolo
disdain [dɪsˈden] *s* desdén; *va* desdeñar
disdainful [dɪsˈdenfəl] *adj* desdeñoso
disease [dɪˈziz] *s* enfermedad; *adj* patógeno; *va* enfermar
diseased [dɪˈzizd] *adj* enfermo; morboso
disembark [ˌdɪsɛmˈbɑrk] *va & vn* desembarcar
disembarkation [dɪsˌɛmbɑrˈkeʃən] *s* desembarco (*de pasajeros*); desembarque (*de mercancías*)
disembarrass [ˌdɪsɛmˈbærəs] *va* desembarazar; librar de turbación
disembodiment [ˌdɪsɛmˈbɑdɪmənt] *s* separación del alma y el cuerpo
disembody [ˌdɪsɛmˈbɑdɪ] (*pret & pp:* **-ied**) *va* desencarnar; **disembodied spirit** espíritu desencarnado
disembowel [ˌdɪsɛmˈbaʊəl] (*pret & pp:* **-eled;** o **-elled;** *ger:* **-eling** o **-elling**) *va* desentrañar
disembowelment [ˌdɪsɛmˈbaʊəlmənt] *s* desentrañamiento
disenchant [ˌdɪsɛnˈtʃænt] o [ˌdɪsɛnˈtʃɑnt] *va* desencantar
disenchantment [ˌdɪsɛnˈtʃæntmənt] o [ˌdɪsɛnˈtʃɑntmənt] *s* desencantamiento o desencanto
disencumber [ˌdɪsɛnˈkʌmbər] *va* descombrar
disencumbrance [ˌdɪsɛnˈkʌmbrəns] *s* descombro
disendow [ˌdɪsɛnˈdaʊ] *va* privar de dotación, privar de subvención
disendowment [ˌdɪsɛnˈdaʊmənt] *s* privación de dotación, privación de subvención
disenfranchise [ˌdɪsɛnˈfræntʃaɪz] *va* var. de **disfranchise**
disengage [ˌdɪsɛnˈgedʒ] *va* desembarazar; desasir, desunir, desenganchar, soltar; desempeñar
disengaged [ˌdɪsɛnˈgedʒd] *adj* desembarazado; separado; desocupado
disengagement [ˌdɪsɛnˈgedʒmənt] *s* desembarazo; desasimiento; desempeño
disentangle [ˌdɪsɛnˈtæŋgəl] *va* desenredar
desentanglement [ˌdɪsɛnˈtæŋgəlmənt] *s* desenredo
disenthrone [ˌdɪsɛnˈθron] *va* var. de **dethrone**
disentwine [ˌdɪsɛnˈtwaɪn] *va* desenredar, desenmarañar
disepalous [daɪˈsɛpələs] *adj* (bot.) disépalo
disestablish [ˌdɪsɛsˈtæblɪʃ] *va* separar (*la Iglesia*) del Estado
disestablishment [ˌdɪsɛsˈtæblɪʃmənt] *s* separación de la Iglesia del Estado
disesteem [ˌdɪsɛsˈtim] *s* desestima o desestimación; *va* desestimar
diseuse [diˈzøz] *s* recitadora
disfavor [dɪsˈfevər] *s* disfavor, desgracia; *va* desfavorecer
disfigure [dɪsˈfɪgjər] *va* desfigurar
disfigurement [dɪsˈfɪgjərmənt] *s* desfiguración o desfiguramiento
disfranchise [dɪsˈfræntʃaɪz] *va* privar de derechos de ciudadanía
disfranchisement [dɪsˈfræntʃɪzmənt] *s* privación de derechos de ciudadanía
disgorge [dɪsˈgɔrdʒ] *va* vomitar; desembuchar (*dícese de las aves*); (fig.) vomitar (*arrojar de sí; entregar de mala gana*); *vn* vomitar; (fig.) vomitar
disgrace [dɪsˈgres] *s* deshonra, ignominia; desgracia, disfavor; **in disgrace** desacreditado; sin favor, en la desgracia; *va* deshonrar, desacreditar; despedir con ignominia
disgraceful [dɪsˈgresfəl] *adj* deshonroso, ignominioso, vergonzoso
disgruntle [dɪsˈgrʌntəl] *va* descontentar, disgustar, enfadar
disgruntlement [dɪsˈgrʌntəlmənt] *s* descontento, disgusto, enfado
disguise [dɪsˈgaɪz] *s* disfraz; *va* disfrazar
disgust [dɪsˈgʌst] *s* repugnancia, asco; *va* repugnar, dar asco a
disgusting [dɪsˈgʌstɪŋ] *adj* repugnante, asqueroso
dish [dɪʃ] *s* plato; vasija; **dishes** *spl* vajilla, vajilla de mesa; **to wash the dishes** lavar la vajilla, lavar los platos; *va* servir en un plato; formar una concavidad en; (slang) vencer, arruinar
dishabille [ˌdɪsəˈbil] *s* var. de **deshabille**
disharmony [dɪsˈhɑrmənɪ] *s* (*pl:* **-nies**) discordia, disonancia
dishcloth [ˈdɪʃˌklɔθ] o [ˈdɪʃˌklɑθ] *s* albero, paño de cocina
dishearten [dɪsˈhɑrtən] *va* abatir, desalentar, desanimar, descorazonar
disheartening [dɪsˈhɑrtənɪŋ] *adj* desalentador
dishevel [dɪˈʃɛvəl] (*pret & pp:* **-eled** o **-elled;** *ger:* **-eling** o **-elling**) *va* desgreñar, desmelenar
dishonest [dɪsˈɑnɪst] *adj* ímprobo, no honrado, fraudulento
dishonesty [dɪsˈɑnɪstɪ] *s* (*pl:* **-ties**) improbidad, falta de honradez, fraude
dishonor [dɪsˈɑnər] *s* deshonra, deshonor; *va* deshonrar, deshonorar; (com.) no aceptar (*un giro*); no pagar (*un cheque*)
dishonorable [dɪsˈɑnərəbəl] *adj* deshonroso
dishpan [ˈdɪʃˌpæn] *s* paila de lavar platos
dish rack *s* escurreplatos
dishrag [ˈdɪʃˌræg] *s* albero
dishtowel [ˈdɪʃˌtaʊəl] *s* paño para secar platos
dishwasher [ˈdɪʃˌwɑʃər] o [ˈdɪʃˌwɔʃər] *s* fregona; lavadora de platos o de vajilla, máquina de lavar platos, lavaplatos
dishwater [ˈdɪʃˌwɔtər] o [ˈdɪʃˌwɑtər] *s* agua de lavar platos
disillusion [ˌdɪsɪˈluʒən] *s* desilusión; *va* desilusionar
disillusionment [ˌdɪsɪˈluʒənmənt] *s* desilusión
disinclination [dɪsˌɪnklɪˈneʃən] *s* aversión, mala gana, repugnancia
disincline [ˌdɪsɪnˈklaɪn] *va* desinclinar; *vn* desinclinarse
disinclined [ˌdɪsɪnˈklaɪnd] *adj* desinclinado
disincrust [ˌdɪsɪnˈkrʌst] *va* desincrustar
disincrustant [ˌdɪsɪnˈkrʌstənt] *s* desincrustante
disinfect [ˌdɪsɪnˈfɛkt] *va* desinfectar, desinficionar
disinfectant [ˌdɪsɪnˈfɛktənt] *adj & s* desinfectante
disinfection [ˌdɪsɪnˈfɛkʃən] *s* desinfección
disinfest [ˌdɪsɪnˈfɛst] *va* desinfestar
disingenuous [ˌdɪsɪnˈdʒɛnjʊəs] *adj* doble, falso, disimulado
disinherit [ˌdɪsɪnˈhɛrɪt] *va* desheredar
disinheritance [ˌdɪsɪnˈhɛrɪtəns] *s* desheredación

disintegrate [dɪs'ɪntɪgret] *va* desagregar, desintegrar, disgregar; *vn* desagregarse, desintegrarse, disgregarse
disintegration [dɪs,ɪntɪ'greʃən] *s* desagregación, desintegración, disgregación; (geol.) desagregación
disintegrator [dɪs'ɪntɪ,gretər] *s* disgregador
disinter [,dɪsɪn'tʌr] (*pret & pp:* **-terred;** *ger:* **-terring**) *va* desenterrar; (fig.) desenterrar, descubrir
disinterested [dɪs'ɪntərɛstɪd] o [dɪs'ɪntrɪstɪd] *adj* desinteresado, imparcial
disinterestedness [dɪs'ɪntərɛstɪdnɪs] o [dɪs'ɪntrɪstɪdnɪs] *s* desinterés
disinterment [,dɪsɪn'tʌrmənt] *s* desenterramiento
disjoin [dɪs'dʒɔɪn] *va* desunir, separar
disjoint [dɪs'dʒɔɪnt] *va* desarticular, dislocar, descoyuntar, desarreglar; *vn* desarticularse, dislocarse, descoyuntarse, desarreglarse
disjointed [dɪs'dʒɔɪntɪd] *adj* desarticulado, dislocado, descoyuntado; desunido; inconexo, incoherente
disjunction [dɪs'dʒʌŋkʃən] *s* disyunción; (log.) disyunción
disjunctive [dɪs'dʒʌŋktɪv] *adj* disyuntivo; *s* (gram.) conjunción disyuntiva; (log.) proposición disyuntiva
disk [dɪsk] *s* disco; (astr., bot., & zool.) disco
disk harrow *s* (agr.) grada de discos
disk jockey *s* (rad.) locutor de un programa de discos
dislike [dɪs'laɪk] *s* aversión, antipatía; **to take a dislike for** cobrar aversión a; *va* tener aversión a, desamar
dislocate ['dɪsloket] *va* dislocar, dislocarse (*p.ej., un hueso*)
dislocation [,dɪslo'keʃən] *s* dislocación; (geol.) dislocación
dislodge [dɪs'lɑdʒ] *va* desalojar
dislodgment [dɪs'lɑdʒmənt] *s* desalojamiento
disloyal [dɪs'lɔɪəl] *adj* desleal
disloyalty [dɪs'lɔɪəltɪ] *s* (*pl:* **-ties**) deslealtad
dismal ['dɪzməl] *adj* obscuro, tenebroso, lúgubre; miserable, desgraciado
Dismal Swamp *s* Pantano maldito (*en los estados de Virginia y la Carolina del Norte, EE.UU.*)
dismantle [dɪs'mæntəl] *va* desarmar, desmontar, desmantelar; desguarnecer; desamueblar; (naut.) desaparejar
dismast [dɪs'mæst] o [dɪs'mɑst] *va* (naut.) desarbolar
dismay [dɪs'me] *s* consternación; *va* consternar
dismember [dɪs'mɛmbər] *va* desmembrar
dismemberment [dɪs'mɛmbərmənt] *s* desmembración
dismiss [dɪs'mɪs] *va* despedir, destituir; dar permiso a (*una persona*) para irse; echar en olvido; (law) rechazar (*p.ej., una demanda*); (mil.) licenciar
dismissal [dɪs'mɪsəl] *s* despedida, destitución; permiso para irse; (law) rechazamiento; (mil.) licenciamiento
dismission [dɪs'mɪʃən] *s* var. de **dismissal**
dismount [dɪs'maʊnt] *va* desmontar; *vn* desmontar, desmontarse
disobedience [,dɪsə'bidɪəns] *s* desobediencia
disobedient [,dɪsə'bidɪənt] *adj* desobediente
disobey [,dɪsə'be] *va & vn* desobedecer
disoblige [,dɪsə'blaɪdʒ] *va* desobligar
disobliging [,dɪsə'blaɪdʒɪŋ] *adj* poco servicial
disorder [dɪs'ɔrdər] *s* desorden; *va* desordenar
disorderly [dɪs'ɔrdərlɪ] *adj* desordenado; alborotador; *adv* desordenadamente; turbulentamente
disorderly conduct *s* conducta escandalosa, perturbación del orden público
disorderly house *s* burdel (*casa de niñas, casa de prostitución; casa en que se falta al decoro con ruido y confusión*); casa de juego
disorganization [dɪs,ɔrgənɪ'zeʃən] *s* desorganización
disorganize [dɪs'ɔrgənaɪz] *va* desorganizar
disorganizer [dɪs'ɔrgə,naɪzər] *s* desorganizador
disorientation [dɪs,orɪɛn'teʃən] *s* (psycopath.) desorientación
disown [dɪs'on] *va* desconocer, repudiar
disparage [dɪ'spærɪdʒ] *va* desdorar; desacreditar
disparagement [dɪ'spærɪdʒmənt] *s* desdoro; descrédito
disparagingly [dɪ'spærɪdʒɪŋlɪ] *adv* con desdoro; desacreditando
disparate ['dɪspəret] o ['dɪspərɪt] *adj* dispar, disparejo
disparity [dɪ'spærɪtɪ] *s* (*pl:* **-ties**) disparidad
dispart [dɪs'pɑrt] *va* despartir; *vn* despartirse, partirse
dispassion [dɪs'pæʃən] *s* desinterés, imparcialidad
dispassionate [dɪs'pæʃənɪt] *adj* desapasionado
dispatch [dɪ'spætʃ] *s* despacho; *va* despachar; (coll.) despabilar (*alimento, una comida*)
dispatcher [dɪ'spætʃər] *s* despachador
dispel [dɪ'spɛl] (*pret & pp:* **-pelled;** *ger:* **-pelling**) *va* desvanecer, dispersar
dispensable [dɪ'spɛnsəbəl] *adj* dispensable; poco importante
dispensary [dɪ'spɛnsərɪ] *s* (*pl:* **-ries**) dispensario
dispensation [,dɪspɛn'seʃən] *s* dispensación; designio divino, acto providencial
dispensatory [dɪ'spɛnsə,torɪ] *s* (*pl:* **-ries**) dispensatorio (*farmacopea; dispensario*)
dispense [dɪ'spɛns] *va* dispensar, otorgar, distribuir; eximir; administrar (*p.ej., justicia*); preparar (*medicamentos compuestos*); *vn* conceder dispensa; **to dispense with** pasar sin; deshacerse de
dispenser [dɪ'spɛnsər] *s* dispensador, surtidor, expedidor
dispeople [dɪs'pipəl] *va* despoblar
dispersal [dɪ'spʌrsəl] *s* dispersión
disperse [dɪ'spʌrs] *va* dispersar; *vn* dispersarse
dispersion [dɪ'spʌrʒən] o [dɪ'spʌrʃən] *s* dispersión; (phys.) dispersión
dispersive [dɪ'spʌrsɪv] *adj* dispersivo
dispireme [daɪ'spaɪrim] *s* (biol.) dispirema
dispirit [dɪ'spɪrɪt] *va* desalentar, desanimar
displace [dɪs'ples] *va* dislocar; tomar el lugar de; destituir; desplazar (*un volumen de agua*); (chem.) reemplazar
displaced person *s* persona desplazada
displacement [dɪs'plesmənt] *s* dislocación; cambio de situación; destitución; desplazamiento (*de un volumen de agua*); (chem.) reemplazo; (geol.) falla, quiebra; cilindrada (*de un pistón o émbolo*)
display [dɪ'sple] *s* despliegue; exhibición; ostentación; **on display** en exhibición; *va* desplegar; exhibir; ostentar
display cabinet *s* escaparate, vitrina
display window *s* escaparate de tienda
displease [dɪs'pliz] *va* desplacer, desagradar, disgustar
displeasing [dɪs'plizɪŋ] *adj* desagradable
displeasure [dɪs'plɛʒər] *s* desplacer, desagrado, disgusto
disport [dɪ'sport] *s* diversión; *va* divertir; **to disport oneself** divertirse; *vn* divertirse; retozar, juguetear
disposable [dɪ'spozəbəl] *adj* disponible
disposal [dɪ'spozəl] *s* disposición; arreglo, ajuste; distribución; venta, liquidación; colocación; evacuación; eliminación, destrucción; **at the disposal of** a la disposición de; **to have at one's disposal** disponer de
dispose [dɪ'spoz] *va* disponer, arreglar, componer; mover, inducir, decidir; exponer; *vn* disponer; **to dispose of** disponer de; deshacerse de; dar; vender; comer, beber; arreglar, componer
disposition [,dɪspə'zɪʃən] *s* disposición; índole, genio, natural; arreglo, ajuste; distribución; venta
dispossess [,dɪspə'zɛs] *va* desposeer; desahuciar (*expulsar*)
dispossession [,dɪspə'zɛʃən] *s* desposeimiento; desahucio (*expulsión*)
dispraise [dɪs'prez] *s* censura, desaprobación; *va* censurar, desaprobar
disproof [dɪs'pruf] *s* confutación, refutación
disproportion [,dɪsprə'porʃən] *s* desproporción; *va* desproporcionar
disproportional [,dɪsprə'porʃənəl] *adj* desproporcionado

disproportionally [ˌdɪsprəˈporʃənəlɪ] *adv* desproporcionadamente
disproportionate [ˌdɪsprəˈporʃənɪt] *adj* desproporcionado
disproportionately [ˌdɪsprəˈporʃənɪtlɪ] *adv* desproporcionadamente
disprove [dɪsˈpruv] *va* confutar, refutar
disputable [dɪˈspjutəbəl] *adj* disputable
disputant [ˈdɪspjutənt] *adj & s* disputador
disputation [ˌdɪspjuˈteʃən] *s* disputa
disputatious [ˌdɪspjuˈteʃəs] o **disputative** [dɪˈspjutətɪv] *adj* disputador
dispute [dɪˈspjut] *s* disputa; **beyond dispute** sin disputa; **in dispute** disputado, cuestionado; *va & vn* disputar
disqualification [ˌdɪsˌkwɑlɪfɪˈkeʃən] *s* inhabilitación; descalificación; (sport) desclasificación, descalificación
disqualify [dɪsˈkwɑlɪfaɪ] (*pret & pp:* **-fied**) *va* inhabilitar, incapacitar; descalificar (*privar de un derecho, etc.*); (sport) desclasificar, descalificar
disquiet [dɪsˈkwaɪət] *s* inquietud, desasosiego; *va* inquietar, desasosegar
disquietude [dɪsˈkwaɪətjud] o [dɪsˈkwaɪətud] *s* inquietud
disquisition [ˌdɪskwɪˈzɪʃən] *s* disertación, disquisición
disregard [ˌdɪsrɪˈgɑrd] *s* desatención, desaire; *va* desatender, desairar; pasar por alto
disregardful [ˌdɪsrɪˈgɑrdfəl] *adj* desatento, negligente
disrelish [dɪsˈrɛlɪʃ] *s* aversión, repugnancia; *va* sentir aversión a, sentir repugnancia a
disremember [ˌdɪsrɪˈmɛmbər] *va* (coll.) olvidar
disrepair [ˌdɪsrɪˈpɛr] *s* mal estado, desconcierto
disreputable [dɪsˈrɛpjətəbəl] *adj* desacreditado, de mala fama; deshonroso, desdoroso, ignominioso
disrepute [ˌdɪsrɪˈpjut] *s* descrédito, mala fama; **in disrepute** desacreditado; **to bring into disrepute** desacreditar
disrespect [ˌdɪsrɪˈspɛkt] *s* desacato; *va* desacatar
disrespectful [ˌdɪsrɪˈspɛktfəl] *adj* irrespetuoso, desacatador
disrobe [dɪsˈrob] *va* desnudar; *vn* desnudarse
disrupt [dɪsˈrʌpt] *va* romper; desbaratar, desorganizar
disruption [dɪsˈrʌpʃən] *s* rompimiento; desbarate, desorganización
disruptive [dɪsˈrʌptɪv] *adj* rompedor; desorganizador; (elec.) disruptivo
dissatisfaction [ˌdɪssætɪsˈfækʃən] *s* descontento, desagrado
dissatisfactory [ˌdɪssætɪsˈfæktərɪ] *adj* poco satisfactorio, nada satisfactorio
dissatisfied [dɪsˈsætɪsfaɪd] *adj* descontento, malcontento
dissatisfy [dɪsˈsætɪsfaɪ] (*pret & pp:* **-fied**) *va* descontentar, desagradar
dissect [dɪˈsɛkt] *va* disecar; (fig.) disecar
dissected [dɪˈsɛktɪd] *adj* dividido; cortado en pedazos; (bot.) disecado (*dícese especialmente de algunas hojas*)
dissection [dɪˈsɛkʃən] *s* disección; objecto disecado; (fig.) disección (*análisis minuciosa*)
dissector [dɪˈsɛktər] *s* disector; instrumento para disecar
disseize [dɪsˈsiz] *va* (law) desposeer injustamente
disseizin [dɪsˈsizɪn] *s* (law) desposeimiento injusto
dissemble [dɪˈsɛmbəl] *va* disimular; *vn* ser hipócrita
disseminate [dɪˈsɛmɪnet] *va* diseminar, difundir
dissemination [dɪˌsɛmɪˈneʃən] *s* diseminación, difusión
disseminator [dɪˈsɛmɪˌnetər] *s* diseminador
dissension [dɪˈsɛnʃən] *s* disensión
dissent [dɪˈsɛnt] *s* disensión, disenso; (eccl.) disidencia; *vn* disentir; (eccl.) disidir
dissenter [dɪˈsɛntər] *s* disidente
dissentient [dɪˈsɛnʃənt] *adj & s* disidente
dissertation [ˌdɪsərˈteʃən] *s* disertación
disserve [dɪsˈsʌrv] *va* deservir
disservice [dɪsˈsʌrvɪs] *s* deservicio
dissever [dɪˈsɛvər] *va* separar, desunir
dissidence [ˈdɪsɪdəns] *s* disidencia
dissident [ˈdɪsɪdənt] *adj & s* disidente
dissimilar [dɪˈsɪmɪlər] *adj* disímil, disimilar, desemejante
dissimilarity [dɪˌsɪmɪˈlærɪtɪ] *s* (*pl:* **-ties**) disimilitud, desemejanza
dissimilate [dɪˈsɪmɪlet] *va* disimilar; *vn* disimilarse
dissimilation [dɪˌsɪmɪˈleʃən] *s* disimilación
dissimilitude [ˌdɪsɪˈmɪlɪtjud] o [ˌdɪsɪˈmɪlɪtud] *s* disimilitud
dissimulate [dɪˈsɪmjəlet] *va & vn* disimular
dissimulation [dɪˌsɪmjəˈleʃən] *s* disimulación
dissipate [ˈdɪsɪpet] *va* disipar; *vn* disiparse; entregarse a los placeres o los vicios
dissipated [ˈdɪsɪˌpetɪd] *adj* disipado, disoluto
dissipation [ˌdɪsɪˈpeʃən] *s* disipación; (fig.) disipación (*conducta de una persona que se entrega a los placeres o los vicios*); (fig.) diversión, recreo
dissociate [dɪˈsoʃɪet] *va* disociar; *vn* disociarse
dissociation [dɪˌsosɪˈeʃən] o [dɪˌsoʃɪˈeʃən] *s* disociación
dissociative [dɪˈsoʃɪˌetɪv] *adj* disociador
dissolubility [dɪˌsɑljəˈbɪlɪtɪ] *s* disolubilidad
dissoluble [dɪˈsɑljəbəl] *adj* disoluble
dissolute [ˈdɪsəlut] *adj* disoluto
dissolution [ˌdɪsəˈluʃən] *s* disolución (*de una familia, aparcería, gobierno, tratado, contrato, etc.*); muerte, deceso
dissolutive [ˈdɪsəˌlutɪv] *adj* disolutivo
dissolve [dɪˈzɑlv] *va* disolver; (law) disolver; *vn* disolver; disolverse
dissolvent [dɪˈzɑlvənt] *adj & s* disolvente
dissonance [ˈdɪsənəns] *s* disonancia
dissonant [ˈdɪsənənt] *adj* disonante
dissuade [dɪˈswed] *va* disuadir; **to dissuade from** + *ger* disuadir de + *inf*
dissuasion [dɪˈsweʒən] *s* disuasión
dissuasive [dɪˈswesɪv] *adj* disuasivo
dissyllabic [ˌdɪssɪˈlæbɪk] *adj* disílabo o disilábico
dissyllable [dɪˈsɪləbəl] *s* disílabo
dissymmetric [ˌdɪssɪˈmɛtrɪk] o **dissymetrical** [ˌdɪssɪˈmɛtrɪkəl] *adj* disimétrico
dissymmetry [dɪsˈsɪmɪtrɪ] *s* (*pl:* **-tries**) disimetría
dist. abr. de **distance, distinguish** y **district**
distaff [ˈdɪstæf] o [ˈdɪstɑf] *s* rueca; quehaceres de mujer; (fig.) rueca, mujeres
distaff side *s* lado de la madre, hembras de la familia
distal [ˈdɪstəl] *adj* (anat.) distal
distance [ˈdɪstəns] *s* distancia; (fig.) distancia (*falta de amistad, frialdad*); **at a distance** a distancia; **in the distance** a lo lejos, en lontananza; **to keep at a distance** mantener a distancia; no tratar con familiaridad; **to keep one's distance** mantenerse a distancia; *va* distanciar; dejar atrás, tomar la delantera a
distant [ˈdɪstənt] *adj* distante; indiferente, frío; lejano (*pariente*)
distaste [dɪsˈtest] *s* aversión, antipatía, disgusto
distasteful [dɪsˈtestfəl] *adj* desabrido, desagradable
distemper [dɪsˈtɛmpər] *s* enfermedad; (vet.) moquillo; tumulto, alboroto; (paint.) temple (*procedimiento*); (paint.) templa (*mezcla para desleír los colores*); (paint.) pintura al temple; *va* destemplar, desconcertar; (paint.) pintar al temple
distend [dɪˈstɛnd] *va* ensanchar, hinchar, distender; *vn* ensancharse, hincharse, distenderse
distensible [dɪsˈtɛnsɪbəl] *adj* dilatable, distensible
distension o **distention** [dɪsˈtɛnʃən] *s* ensanche, hinchazón, distensión
distich [ˈdɪstɪk] *s* dístico
distichous [ˈdɪstɪkəs] *adj* (bot.) dístico
distil o **distill** [dɪˈstɪl] (*pret & pp:* **-tilled;** *ger:* **-tilling**) *va & vn* destilar
distillable [dɪˈstɪləbəl] *adj* destilable
distillate [ˈdɪstɪlet] o [dɪˈstɪlet] *s* destilado
distillation [ˌdɪstɪˈleʃən] *s* destilación
distiller [dɪˈstɪlər] *s* destilador
distillery [dɪˈstɪlərɪ] *s* (*pl:* **-ies**) destilería o destilatorio

distinct [dɪˈstɪŋkt] *adj* distinto; inequívoco, cierto, indudable
distinction [dɪˈstɪŋkʃən] *s* distinción; distintivo; **in distinction from** o **to** a distinción de
distinctive [dɪˈstɪŋktɪv] *adj* distintivo
distinctly [dɪˈstɪŋktlɪ] *adv* distintamente; inequívocamente
distinctness [dɪˈstɪŋktnɪs] *s* distinción
distingué [ˌdɪstæŋˈge] o [dɪˈstæŋge] *adj* distinguido
distinguish [dɪˈstɪŋgwɪʃ] *va* distinguir
distinguishable [dɪˈstɪŋgwɪʃəbəl] *adj* distinguible
distinguished [dɪˈstɪŋgwɪʃt] *adj* distinguido
distomatous [daɪˈstɑmətəs] o [daɪˈstomətəs] *adj* (zool.) dístomo
distort [dɪsˈtɔrt] *va* torcer, deformar; (fig.) torcer, falsear (*p.ej., la verdad*)
distortion [dɪsˈtɔrʃən] *s* torcimiento, deformación; (fig.) torcimiento, falseamiento, distorción; (rad.) distorsión, deformación
distract [dɪˈstrækt] *va* distraer (*p.ej., la atención*); aturdir, confundir; enloquecer
distraction [dɪˈstrækʃən] *s* distracción; aturdimiento, confusión; locura
distrain [dɪˈstren] *va & vn* (law) embargar, secuestrar, ejecutar
distraint [dɪˈstrent] *s* (law) embargo, secuestro, ejecución
distrait [dɪˈstre] *adj* distraído
distraught [dɪˈstrɔt] *adj* distraído; aturdido, confundido; loco
distress [dɪˈstrɛs] *s* pena, dolor, angustia, aflicción; apuro, revés, infortunio, peligro; (law) embargo, secuestro; *va* apenar, angustiar, afligir; poner en aprieto; (law) embargar, secuestrar
distressful [dɪˈstrɛsfəl] *adj* penoso, congojoso; afligido
distressing [dɪˈstrɛsɪŋ] *adj* penoso, congojoso
distress signal *s* señal de socorro
distribute [dɪsˈtrɪbjʊt] *va* distribuir, repartir; (print.) desempastelar (*pastel*)
distributed capacity *s* (rad.) capacidad distribuída
distributer [dɪˈstrɪbjətər] *s* distribuidor
distribution [ˌdɪstrɪˈbjuʃən] *s* distribución, repartimiento
distributive [dɪˈstrɪbjətɪv] *adj* distributivo; *s* (gram.) distributivo (*substantivo*); (gram.) conjunción distributiva
distributively [dɪˈstrɪbjətɪvlɪ] *adv* distributivamente
distributor [dɪˈstrɪbjətər] *s* distribuidor; (aut.) distribuidor
distributor points *spl* (aut.) plaquitas del distribuidor
district [ˈdɪstrɪkt] *s* comarca, región; barrio (*de una ciudad*); distrito (*división administrativa*); *va* dividir en distritos
district attorney s fiscal, fiscal de distrito, acusador público
district court *s* tribunal de distrito; tribunal federal de primera instancia
District of Columbia *s* Distrito de Columbia
distrust [dɪsˈtrʌst] *s* desconfianza; *va* desconfiar de
distrustful [dɪsˈtrʌstfəl] *adj* desconfiado
disturb [dɪˈstʌrb] *va* disturbar, alborotar; inquietar; desordenar, revolver, descasar; perturbar (*el orden público*)
disturbance [dɪˈstʌrbəns] *s* disturbio, alboroto; inquietud; desorden; trastorno
disturber [dɪˈstʌrbər] *s* alborotador; **disturber of the peace** alborotador, perturbador del orden público
disulfide o **disulphide** [daɪˈsʌlfaɪd] o [daɪˈsʌlfɪd] *s* (chem.) disulfuro
disunion [dɪsˈjunjən] *s* desunión
disunite [ˌdɪsjʊˈnaɪt] *va* desunir; *vn* desunirse
disuse [dɪsˈjus] *s* desuso; [dɪsˈjuz] *va* desusar
ditch [dɪtʃ] *s* zanja; (fort.) foso; **to the last ditch** hasta quemar el último cartucho; *va* zanjar; echar en una zanja; (slang) zafarse de, desembarazarse de; *vn* (aer.) amarar forzosamente
ditch reed *s* (bot.) carrizo
ditheism [ˈdaɪθiɪzəm] *s* diteísmo
ditheist [ˈdaɪθiɪst] *s* diteísta
ditheistic [ˌdaɪθiˈɪstɪk] *adj* diteísta
dither [ˈdɪðər] *s* (dial.) estremecimiento; **in a dither** estremecido, muy excitado; *va* (dial.) estremecer; *vn* (dial.) estremecerse
dithyramb [ˈdɪθɪræm] *s* ditirambo
dithyrambic [ˌdɪθɪˈræmbɪk] *adj* ditirámbico
ditone [ˈdaɪˌton] *s* (mus.) dítono
dittany [ˈdɪtənɪ] *s* (*pl:* **-nies**) (bot.) díctamo
ditto [ˈdɪto] *s* (*pl:* **-tos**) ídem; principio de comillas (*que se emplea en lugar de "ídem"*); copia, duplicado; *va* copiar, duplicar
ditto mark *s* principio de comillas (*que se emplea en lugar de "ídem"*)
ditty [ˈdɪtɪ] *s* (*pl:* **-ties**) cancioneta
ditty bag *s* saco de costura de marinero
ditty box *s* caja de costura de marinero
diuresis [ˌdaɪjʊˈrisɪs] *s* (path.) diuresis
diuretic [ˌdaɪjʊˈrɛtɪk] *adj & s* (med.) diurético
diurnal [daɪˈʌrnəl] *adj* diurno; diario; *s* (eccl.) diurno
diurnally [daɪˈʌrnəlɪ] *adv* de día; diariamente
diuturnal [ˌdaɪjʊˈtʌrnəl] *adj* diuturno
diuturnity [ˌdaɪjʊˈtʌrnɪtɪ] *s* diuturnidad
div. abr. de **dividend, divided** y **division**
diva [ˈdivə] *s* (mus.) diva
divagate [ˈdaɪvəget] *vn* divagar
divagation [ˌdaɪvəˈgeʃən] *s* divagación
divan [dɪˈvæn] *s* diván (*consejo turco y sala donde se reúne; colección de poesías*); [ˈdaɪvæn] o [dɪˈvæn] *s* diván (*canapé*); fumadero
divaricate [daɪˈværɪket] o [dɪˈværɪket] *adj* divergente; (bot.) divaricado; *va* dividir en dos ramales; desplegar; *vn* bifurcarse
divarication [daɪˌværɪˈkeʃən] o [dɪˌværɪˈkeʃən] *s* divaricación; divergencia (*de opiniones*)
dive [daɪv] *s* salto, zambullida; salto ornamental; sumersión (*de un submarino*); (aer.) picado; (coll.) tasca, casa de juego de mala fama; (*pret & pp:* **dived** o **dove**) *vn* zambullirse (*meterse debajo del agua con ímpetu; ocultarse, esconderse*); bucear (*trabajar como buzo*); sumergirse (*un submarino*); meter de repente la mano (*p.ej., en el bolsillo*); enfrascarse (*p.ej., en el trabajo, los negocios*); (aer.) picar
dive-bomb [ˈdaɪvˌbɑm] *va & vn* bombardear en picado
dive bomber *s* (aer.) bombardero en picado, avión de bombardeo en picado
dive bombing *s* (aer.) bombardeo en picado
diver [ˈdaɪvər] *s* zambullidor; buzo (*provisto o no de una escafandra*); (orn.) somorgujo
diverge [dɪˈvʌrdʒ] o [daɪˈvʌrdʒ] *vn* divergir
divergence [dɪˈvʌrdʒəns] o [daɪˈvʌrdʒəns] *s* divergencia
divergency [dɪˈvʌrdʒənsɪ] o [daɪˈvʌrdʒənsɪ] *s* (*pl:* **-cies**) var. de **divergence**
divergent [dɪˈvʌrdʒənt] o [daɪˈvʌrdʒənt] *adj* divergente
divers [ˈdaɪvərz] *adj* diversos, varios
diverse [dɪˈvʌrs], [daɪˈvʌrs] o [ˈdaɪvʌrs] *adj* diverso; variado
diversely [dɪˈvʌrslɪ], [daɪˈvʌrslɪ] o [ˈdaɪvʌrslɪ] *adv* diversamente; variamente
diver's helmet *s* casco de escafandra
diversification [dɪˌvʌrsɪfɪˈkeʃən] o [daɪˌvʌrsɪfɪˈkeʃən] *s* diversificación
diversiform [dɪˈvʌrsɪfɔrm] o [daɪˈvʌrsɪfɔrm] *adj* diversiforme
diversify [dɪˈvʌrsɪfaɪ] o [daɪˈvʌrsɪfaɪ] (*pret & pp:* **-fied**) *va* diversificar; *vn* diversificarse
diversion [dɪˈvʌrʒən] o [daɪˈvʌrʒən] *s* diversión; (mil.) diversión
diversity [dɪˈvʌrsɪtɪ] o [daɪˈvʌrsɪtɪ] *s* (*pl:* **-ties**) diversidad
divert [dɪˈvʌrt] o [daɪˈvʌrt] *va* apartar, desviar; divertir, entretener; (mil.) divertir
diverticular [ˌdaɪvərˈtɪkjələr] *adj* diverticular
diverticulitis [ˌdaɪvərˌtɪkjəˈlaɪtɪs] *s* (path.) diverticulitis
diverticulum [ˌdaɪvərˈtɪkjələm] *s* (*pl:* **-la** [lə]) (anat. & path.) divertículo
diverting [dɪˈvʌrtɪŋ] o [daɪˈvʌrtɪŋ] *adj* divertido
divertissement [divɛrtisˈmɑ̃] *s* divertimiento; (mus.) divertimiento
divertive [dɪˈvʌrtɪv] o [daɪˈvʌrtɪv] *adj* divertido
divest [dɪˈvɛst] o [daɪˈvɛst] *va* desnudar; desposeer, despojar

divide [dɪˈvaɪd] *s* (geog.) divisoria; *va* dividir; *vn* dividirse
dividend [ˈdɪvɪdɛnd] *s* (math. & com.) dividendo
divider [dɪˈvaɪdər] *s* divisor; **dividers** *spl* compás de división
divination [ˌdɪvɪˈneʃən] *s* adivinación
divinatory [dɪˈvɪnəˌtorɪ] *adj* adivinatorio
divine [dɪˈvaɪn] *s* sacerdote, predicador, clérigo; *adj* divino; (fig.) divino; *va & vn* adivinar
divine grace *s* (theol.) influencia, divina gracia
divinely [dɪˈvaɪnlɪ] *adv* divinamente
diviner [dɪˈvaɪnər] *s* adivinador
divine right of kings *s* derecho divino de los reyes
divine service *s* servicio divino
diving [ˈdaɪvɪŋ] *s* zambullida, buceo
diving attack *s* (aer.) ataque en picado
diving bell *s* campana de bucear, campana de buzo
diving board *s* trampolín
diving suit *s* escafandra o escafandro
divining [dɪˈvaɪnɪŋ] *adj* adivinatorio
divining rod *s* vara de adivinar, vara mágica; vara buscadora, varilla exploradora (*que se emplea para determinar la presencia de agua, metal o mineral subterráneos*)
divinity [dɪˈvɪnɪtɪ] *s* (*pl:* **-ties**) divinidad; teología; **the Divinity** Dios
divinize [ˈdɪvɪnaɪz] *va* divinizar
divisibility [dɪˌvɪzɪˈbɪlɪtɪ] *s* divisibilidad
divisible [dɪˈvɪzɪbəl] *adj* divisible
division [dɪˈvɪʒən] *s* división; (math. & mil.) división
divisional [dɪˈvɪʒənəl] *adj* divisional
divisive [dɪˈvaɪsɪv] *adj* divisivo
divisor [dɪˈvaɪzər] *s* (math.) divisor
divorce [dɪˈvors] *s* divorcio; **to get a divorce from** divorciarse de; *va* divorciar (*los cónyuges*); divorciarse de (*la mujer o el marido*); (fig.) divorciar; *vn* divorciarse
divorcé [dɪvorˈse] *s* hombre divorciado
divorcee [dɪvorˈsi] *s* persona divorciada
divorcée [dɪvorˈse] *s* mujer divorciada
divorcement [dɪˈvorsmənt] *s* divorcio
divot [ˈdɪvət] *s* terrón arrancado con el palo de golf
divulge [dɪˈvʌldʒ] *va* divulgar, publicar, revelar
Dixie [ˈdɪksɪ] *s* el Sur de los Estados Unidos
dizen [ˈdaɪzən] o [ˈdɪzən] *va* emperejilar
dizziness [ˈdɪzɪnɪs] *s* vértigo, desvanecimiento; aturdimiento, confusión, perplejidad
dizzy [ˈdɪzɪ] *adj* (*comp:* **-zier;** *super:* **-ziest**) vertiginoso; aturdido, confuso, perplejo; tonto, mentecato
dl. abr. de **deciliter** o **deciliters**
D.Lit. o **D.Litt.** abr. de **Doctor of Literature**
dm. abr. de **decimeter** o **decimeters**
do. abr. de **ditto**
do [du] (*pret:* **did;** *pp:* **done;** *ger:* **doing**) *va* hacer; terminar; rendir, tributar (*homenaje*); ser suficiente para; trabajar en, ocuparse de o en; resolver (*un problema*); andar, recorrer (*una distancia*); cocinar suficientemente; cumplir con (*un deber*); aprender (*una lección*); arreglar, componer (*el cuarto, la cama*); tocar (*el cabello*); pasar (*cierto tiempo*) en la cárcel; (coll.) ver, visitar (*un país extranjero*); (coll.) engañar, estafar; traducir; hacer de; **to be well done** estar bien asado; **to be done for** (coll.) estar cansado; (coll.) estar arruinado, estar destruído; (coll.) estar muerto; **to have nothing to do with** no tener nada que ver con; **to do in** (slang) apalear, azotar; (slang) rendir, vencer; (slang) despachar, matar; **to do one a world of good** sentarle a uno a las mil maravillas; **to do one's best** hacer todo lo posible; **to do over** volver a hacer; renovar; repetir; **to do over with** cubrir con, revestir con; **to do right by** tratar bien, portarse bien para con; **to do someone out of something** (coll.) defraudar algo a alguien; **to do to death** despachar, matar; **to do up** liar, empaquetar; arreglar, poner en orden; almidonar y planchar (*p.ej., una camisa*); conservar (*fruto*); (coll.) cansar, deslomar ‖ *vn* estar, hallarse, ir; conducirse, proceder; actuar, obrar; servir, ser suficiente; **how do you do?** ¿cómo está Vd.?, ¿cómo se halla Vd.?; **that will do** basta ya, eso es bastante; eso sirve; calla, no digas más; **that won't do** eso no sirve, eso no vale; **to have done** haber terminado; **to have done with** haber terminado; no tener más que ver con; **to have to do with** tratar de; **to do away with** suprimir; matar; **to do for** bastar para, servir para; **to do well in an examination** salir bien de un examen; **to do with** servirse de; **to do without** pasar sin ‖ *v aux* empléase (1) para dar énfasis a la oración, p.ej., **I do eat spinach** yo sí como espinacas; (2) para hacer una pregunta, p.ej., **Do you see me?** ¿Me ve Vd?; (3) para señalar la negación, p.ej., **He did not come** No vino; (4) para reemplazar otro verbo que va omitido, p.ej., **Do you speak Spanish? Yes, I do** ¿Habla Vd. español? Sí, lo hablo; (5) en el orden invertido después de un adverbio, p.ej., **seldom does she complain** ella rara vez se queja
doable [ˈduəbəl] *adj* factible
do-all [ˈduˌɔl] *s* factótum
doat [dot] *vn* var. de **dote**
dobbin [ˈdɑbɪn] *s* caballo lento y manso
Docetism [doˈsitɪzəm] *s* docetismo
docile [ˈdɑsɪl] *adj* dócil
docility [doˈsɪlɪtɪ] *s* docilidad
docimastic [ˌdɑsɪˈmæstɪk] *adj* docimástico
docimasy [ˈdɑsɪməsɪ] *s* (*pl:* **-sies**) docimasia
dock [dɑk] *s* muñón de cola; (naut.) dique; (naut.) muelle; (law) tribuna de los acusados; (bot.) romaza; *va* derrabar, descolar, cercenar; (naut.) poner en dique; reducir, suprimir (*el salario*); *vn* (naut.) entrar en muelle
dockage [ˈdɑkɪdʒ] *s* entrada en un dique; muellaje; reducción, rebaja
docket [ˈdɑkɪt] *s* rótulo, marbete; minuta, sumario, extracto; (law) lista de causas pendientes; (law) orden del día; **on the docket** (coll.) pendiente, entre manos, en consideración; *va* rotular; hacer la minuta de, extractar; (law) poner en la lista de causas pendientes; (law) poner en el orden del día
dock hand o **dock worker** *s* portuario
dockyard [ˈdɑkˌjɑrd] *s* (naut.) arsenal
doctor [ˈdɑktər] *s* médico; doctor (*en ciencias, letras, derecho, etc.*); *va* (coll.) medicinar; (coll.) alterar y adulterar; (coll.) reparar, componer, concertar; *vn* (coll.) practicar la medicina; (coll.) tomar medicinas
doctoral [ˈdɑktərəl] *adj* doctoral
doctorate [ˈdɑktərɪt] *s* doctorado
doctrinaire [ˌdɑktrɪˈnɛr] *adj & s* doctrinario
doctrinairism [ˌdɑktrɪˈnɛrɪzəm] *s* doctrinarismo
doctrinal [ˈdɑktrɪnəl] *adj* doctrinal
doctrine [ˈdɑktrɪn] *s* doctrina
document [ˈdɑkjəmənt] *s* documento; [ˈdɑkjəmɛnt] *va* documentar
documental [ˌdɑkjəˈmɛntəl] *adj* documental
documentary [ˌdɑkjəˈmɛntərɪ] *adj* documental; *s* (*pl:* **-ries**) (mov.) documental (*película*)
documentation [ˌdɑkjəmɛnˈteʃən] *s* documentación
dodder [ˈdɑdər] *s* (bot.) cúscuta; *vn* temblar, tambalear
doddering [ˈdɑdərɪŋ] *adj* sandio, chocho
dodecagon [doˈdɛkəgɑn] *s* (geom.) dodecágono
dodecagonal [ˌdodɛˈkægənəl] *adj* (geom.) dodecágono
dodecahedron [ˌdodɛkəˈhidrən] *s* (*pl:* **-drons** o **-dra** [drə]) (geom.) dodecaedro
dodecahedral [ˌdodɛkəˈhidrəl] *adj* (geom.) dodecaédrico
Dodecanese Islands [doˌdɛkəˈnis] *spl* Dodecaneso, islas del Dodecaneso
dodecasyllabic [ˌdodɛkəsɪˈlæbɪk] *adj* dodecasílabo
dodge [dɑdʒ] *s* regate; (fig.) regate; *va* evadir (*p.ej., un golpe*) moviéndose rápidamente a un lado; (coll.) evitar mañosamente; *vn* regatear, hurtar el cuerpo; **to dodge around the corner** voltear la esquina
dodger [ˈdɑdʒər] *s* persona que hace regates; trampista; anuncio pequeño; pan de maíz
dodo [ˈdodo] *s* (*pl:* **-dos** o **-does**) (orn.) dodo o dodó; (coll.) inocente de ideas atrasadas
doe [do] *s* cierva, gama; hembra del conejo, el antílope, la liebre, el canguro

doer [ˈduər] *s* hacedor
does [dʌz] *tercera persona del sg del pres de ind de* **do**
doeskin [ˈdoˌskɪn] *s* ante, piel de ante; tejido fino de lana
doesn't [ˈdʌzənt] contracción de **does not**
doff [dɑf] o [dɔf] *va* quitarse (*p.ej., el sombrero o chaqueta*); quitarse de encima, deshacerse de
dog [dɔg] o [dɑg] *s* perro; zorro, lobo (*macho*); tunante; (coll.) hombre, sujeto, individuo; fiador, asidor; morillo; (coll.) ínfulas; **to go to the dogs** darse al abandono, arruinarse; **to put on the dog** (coll.) darse ínfulas; **to teach an old dog new tricks** conseguir que un viejo cambie de ideas o hábitos; (*pret & pp:* **dogged;** *ger:* **dogging**) *va* seguir los pasos de, seguir las pisadas de, perseguir
dogbane [ˈdɔgˌben] o [ˈdɑgˌben] *s* (bot.) apocino
dogberry [ˈdɔgˌbɛrɪ] o [ˈdɑgˌbɛrɪ] *s* (*pl:* **-ries**) (bot.) cornejo hembra, sanguiñuelo, sanapudio blanco
dogcart [ˈdɔgˌkɑrt] o [ˈdɑgˌkɑrt] *s* carro pequeño tirado por perros; dócar (*carruaje de dos ruedas, con dos asientos colocados espalda contra espalda*)
dogcatcher [ˈdɔgˌkætʃər] o [ˈdɑgˌkætʃər] *s* lacero, perrero (*persona*); cazaperros (*animal*)
dog clutch *s* (mach.) embrague de mordaza
dog days *spl* canícula, caniculares
doge [dodʒ] *s* dux
dog-ear [ˈdɔgˌɪr] o [ˈdɑgˌɪr] *s & va* var. de **dog's-ear**
dogfight [ˈdɔgˌfaɪt] o [ˈdɑgˌfaɪt] *s* lucha de perros; refriega; (aer.) combate violento entre aviones pequeños y rápidos
dogfish [ˈdɔgˌfɪʃ] o [ˈdɑgˌfɪʃ] *s* (ichth.) tiburón; (ichth.) cazón
dogged [ˈdɔgɪd] o [ˈdɑgɪd] *adj* tenaz, terco, obstinado
dogger [ˈdɔgər] o [ˈdɑgər] *s* dogre (*embarcación de pesca*)
doggerel [ˈdɔgərəl] o [ˈdɑgərəl] *s* coplas de ciego; *adj* malo, poco artístico
doggie [ˈdɔgɪ] o [ˈdɑgɪ] *s* perrito
doggy [ˈdɔgɪ] o [ˈdɑgɪ] *s* (*pl:* **-gies**) perrito; *adj* (*comp:* **-gier;** *super:* **-giest**) emperejilado, aparatoso
doghouse [ˈdɔgˌhaʊs] o [ˈdɑgˌhaʊs] *s* perrera; **to be in the doghouse** (slang) estar en desgracia
dogie [ˈdogɪ] *s* ternero sin madre
dog in the manger *s* (coll.) el perro del hortelano
dog Latin *s* latinajo, latín de cocina
dogma [ˈdɔgmə] o [ˈdɑgmə] *s* (*pl:* **-mas** o **-mata** [mətə]) dogma
dogmatic [dɔgˈmætɪk] o [dɑgˈmætɪk] o **dogmatical** [dɔgˈmætɪkəl] o [dɑgˈmætɪkəl] *adj* dogmático
dogmatism [ˈdɔgmətɪzəm] o [ˈdɑgmətɪzəm] *s* dogmatismo
dogmatist [ˈdɔgmətɪst] o [ˈdɑgmətɪst] *s* dogmatizador
dogmatize [ˈdɔgmətaɪz] o [ˈdɑgmətaɪz] *va & vn* dogmatizar
do-gooder [ˈduˌgʊdər] *s* (scornful) reformador visionario y algo tonto
dog racing *s* carrera de galgos
dog rose *s* (bot.) escaramujo (*planta y fruto*); (bot.) agavanzo (*planta*); agavanza (*fruto*); zarzarrosa (*flor*)
dog's-ear [ˈdɔgzˌɪr] o [ˈdɑgzˌɪr] *s* orejón (*de la hoja de un libro*); *va* doblar o plegar la punta de (*la hoja de un libro*)
dog show *s* exposición canina
dog sledge *s* rastra tirada por perros
dog's letter *s* letra canina (*la rr*)
dog's life *s* vida de perros, vida miserable
Dog Star *s* (astr.) Canícula; (astr.) Proción
dog's-tooth violet [ˈdɔgzˌtuθ] o [ˈdɑgzˌtuθ] *s* var. de **dogtooth violet**
dog-tired [ˈdɔgˌtaɪrd] o [ˈdɑgˌtaɪrd] *adj* cansadísimo
dogtooth [ˈdɔgˌtuθ] o [ˈdɑgˌtuθ] *s* (*pl:* **-teeth** [ˌtiθ]) (anat.) colmillo; (arch.) diente de perro
dogtooth violet *s* (bot.) diente de perro
dogtrot [ˈdɔgˌtrɑt] o [ˈdɑgˌtrɑt] *s* trote de perro
dogwatch [ˈdɔgˌwɑtʃ] o [ˈdɑgˌwɑtʃ] *s* (naut.) guardia de cuartillo
dogwood [ˈdɔgˌwʊd] o [ˈdɑgˌwʊd] *s* (bot.) cornejo
dogy [ˈdogɪ] *s* (*pl:* **-gies**) var. de **dogie**
doily [ˈdɔɪlɪ] *s* (*pl:* **-lies**) paño pequeño de adorno, pañito de adorno
doings [ˈduɪŋz] *spl* actos, hechos; conducta, proceder; (slang) actividad, tremolina
do-it-yourself [ˈduɪtjʊrˈsɛlf] *adj* (slang) ideado para el que quiere hacer sus propios trabajos manuales del hogar
doldrums [ˈdɑldrəmz] *spl* (naut.) zona de calmas ecuatoriales; abatimiento, desanimación
dole [dol] *s* limosna; distribución en pequeñas porciones; socorro del gobierno a los desocupados; *va* dar limosna a; distribuir en pequeñas porciones; **to dole out** distribuir en pequeñas porciones
doleful [ˈdolfəl] *adj* triste, lúgubre
dolichocephalic [ˌdɑlɪkəsɪˈfælɪk] *adj* (anthrop.) dolicocéfalo
doll [dɑl] *s* muñeca; (fig.) muñeca (*mujer pequeñita; mozuela linda y necia*); *va* (slang) engalanar, emperejilar; *vn* (slang) engalanarse, emperejilarse; **to doll up** (slang) engalanarse, emperejilarse
dollar [ˈdɑlər] *s* dólar
dollar diplomacy *s* diplomacia del dólar
dollar mark *s* signo del dólar
dolly [ˈdɑlɪ] *s* (*pl:* **-ies**) muñequita; plataforma con rodillo, gato rodante; (mach.) sufridera
dolman [ˈdɑlmən] *s* (*pl:* **-mans**) dormán (*de los turcos, húsares, etc.*); capa de mujer de mangas perdidas
dolmen [ˈdɑlmɛn] *s* dolmen
dolmenic [dɑlˈmɛnɪk] *adj* dolménico
dolomite [ˈdɑləmaɪt] *s* (mineral.) dolomía o dolomita
dolomitic [ˌdɑləˈmɪtɪk] *adj* dolomítico
dolor [ˈdolər] *s* (poet.) dolor
dolorous [ˈdɑlərəs] o [ˈdolərəs] *adj* doloroso
dolphin [ˈdɑlfɪn] *s* (zool.) delfín; (ichth.) dorado de altura; (naut.) poste de amarra; (naut.) boya de anclaje; (*cap.*) *s* (astr.) Delfín
dolphin striker *s* (naut.) moco del bauprés
dolt [dolt] *s* bobalicón, mastuerzo
doltish [ˈdoltɪʃ] *adj* bobalicón, tonto
dom. abr. de **domestic** y **dominion**
domain [doˈmen] *s* dominio, imperio; heredad, propiedad; campo (*p.ej., de la erudición*)
dome [dom] *s* (arch.) domo, cúpula, cimborrio; (aut.) techo abovedado; cimborrio (*de un carro tanque, carro de riego, etc.*); *va* cubrir con un domo o cúpula; dar forma de domo o cúpula a; *vn* elevarse como un domo o cúpula
dome light *s* (aut.) lámpara de techo
Domesday Book [ˈdumzˌde] o [ˈdomzˌde] *s* Libro del día del Juicio final (*libro que registra los nombres, extensión, valor y otros datos de todas las propiedades de Inglaterra, que Guillermo el Conquistador hizo compilar en 1086*)
domestic [dəˈmɛstɪk] *adj* doméstico; *s* doméstico (*criado que sirve en una casa*)
domesticable [dəˈmɛstɪkəbəl] *adj* domesticable
domestically [dəˈmɛstɪkəlɪ] *adv* domésticamente
domesticate [dəˈmɛstɪket] *va* domesticar; *vn* domesticarse
domestication [dəˌmɛstɪˈkeʃən] *s* domesticación
domesticity [ˌdomɛsˈtɪsɪtɪ] *s* (*pl:* **-ties**) domesticidad; **domesticities** *spl* asuntos domésticos
domicile [ˈdɑmɪsɪl] o [ˈdɑmɪsaɪl] *s* domicilio; *va* domiciliar; *vn* domiciliarse
domiciliary [ˌdɑmɪˈsɪlɪˌɛrɪ] *adj* domiciliario
domiciliate [ˌdɑmɪˈsɪlɪet] *va* domiciliar; *vn* domiciliarse
dominance [ˈdɑmɪnəns] o **dominancy** [ˈdɑmɪnənsɪ] *s* dominación; (biol.) dominancia
dominant [ˈdɑmɪnənt] *adj* dominante; (astrol., biol., & mus.) dominante; *s* (mus.) dominante
dominate [ˈdɑmɪnet] *va & vn* dominar
domination [ˌdɑmɪˈneʃən] *s* dominación; **dominations** *spl* dominaciones (*cuarto coro de ángeles*)
domineer [ˌdɑmɪˈnɪr] *va & vn* dominar

domineering [ˌdɑmɪˈnɪrɪŋ] *adj* dominante, dominador
Dominic, Saint [ˈdɑmɪnɪk] Santo Domingo
Dominica [ˌdɑmɪˈnikə] o [doˈmɪnɪkə] *s* la Dominica (*isla de las Antillas*)
Dominican [doˈmɪnɪkən] *adj* dominicano (*perteneciente a la orden de Santo Domingo; perteneciente a la República Dominicana*); dominico (*perteneciente a la orden de Santo Domingo*); *s* dominicano; dominico
Dominican Republic *s* República Dominicana
dominie [ˈdɑmɪnɪ] *s* dómine; [ˈdomɪnɪ] *s* cura, clérigo
dominion [dəˈmɪnjən] *s* dominio
domino [ˈdɑmɪno] *s* (*pl:* **-noes** o **-nos**) dominó (*traje que se usa en los bailes de máscara*); careta o antifaz usado con el dominó; persona que usa el dominó; ficha (*del juego de dominó*); **dominoes** *spl* dominó (*juego*)
Domitian [doˈmɪʃən] *s* Domiciano
don [dɑn] *s* caballero, señor; personaje de alta categoría; (coll.) rector, preceptor, socio (*de un colegio de las universidades de Oxford y Cambridge, Inglaterra*); (*cap.*) *s* don (*tratamiento español de cortesía que se da a los hombres y se antepone a los nombres de pila*); (*pret & pp:* **donned;** *ger:* **donning**) *va* ponerse, vestirse
Donald [ˈdɑnəld] *s* Donaldo
Donald Duck *s* el pato Donaldo
donate [ˈdonet] *va* dar, donar
donation [doˈneʃən] *s* donación, donativo
Donatism [ˈdɑnətɪzəm] *s* donatismo
Donatist [ˈdɑnətɪst] *adj & s* donatista
done [dʌn] *adj* hecho, acabado, terminado; (coll.) cansado, rendido; bien asado; *pp de* **do**
donee [ˌdoˈni] *s* donatario
done for *adj* (coll.) cansado; (coll.) agotado; (coll.) fuera de combate; (coll.) arruinado; (coll.) muerto
donjon [ˈdʌndʒən] o [ˈdɑndʒən] *s* torre del homenaje, torre maestra
Don Juan [dɑnˈdʒuən] *s* Don Juan (*personaje legendario que simboliza al hombre libertino; hombre libertino*)
Don Juanism [dɑnˈdʒuənɪzəm] *s* donjuanismo
donkey [ˈdɑŋkɪ] *s* burro, asno; (fig.) asno
donkey engine *s* pequeña máquina de vapor, máquina auxiliar
donnish [ˈdɑnɪʃ] *adj* profesoral; pedantesco
Donnybrook [ˈdɑnɪbrʊk] *s* (coll.) alboroto, riña general; (coll.) disputa acalorada y bulliciosa entre grupos contrarios
donor [ˈdonər] *s* donador, donante, dador
do-nothing [ˈduˌnʌθɪŋ] *adj* dejado, inactivo, indiferente; *s* haragán, ocioso
don't [dont] contracción de **do not**
doodad [ˈduˌdæd] *s* (coll.) chisme, adminículo; (coll.) chuchería
doodle [ˈdudəl] *va & vn* borrajear
doodlebug [ˈdudəlˌbʌg] *s* (ent.) larva de hormiga león; vara buscadora, dispositivo para determinar la presencia de minerales subterráneos; (Brit.) bomba volante
doodlesack [ˈdudəlˌsæk] *s* gaita escocesa
doohickey [ˈduˌhɪkɪ] *s* (coll.) chisme, adminículo
doom [dum] *s* destino, hado, suerte; ruina, perdición, muerte; condena, juicio, sentencia; juicio final; *va* predestinar a la ruina, a la muerte; condenar; sentenciar a muerte
doom palm *s* (bot.) duma
doomsday [ˈdumzˌde] *s* día del Juicio final; día del juicio
Doomsday Book *s* var. de **Domesday Book**
door [dor] *s* puerta; portezuela (*de un coche o automóvil*); hoja, batiente (*de una puerta en dos partes*); **behind closed doors** a puertas cerradas; **from door to door** de puerta en puerta; **to lay at one's door** echarle a uno la culpa de; **to show a person to the door** despedir a una persona en la puerta; pedir a una persona que salga
doorbell [ˈdorˌbɛl] *s* campanilla de puerta, timbre de llamada
doorbell transformer *s* (elec.) transformador de campanilla
door check *s* amortiguador, freno de puerta
doorframe [ˈdorˌfrem] *s* alfajía, marco de puerta, bastidor de puerta
doorhead [ˈdorˌhɛd] *s* dintel
doorjamb [ˈdorˌdʒæm] *s* jamba de puerta
doorkeeper [ˈdorˌkipər] *s* portero
doorknob [ˈdorˌnɑb] *s* pomo de puerta, tirador de puerta
door latch *s* pestillo
doorman [ˈdormən] o [ˈdorˌmæn] *s* (*pl:* **-men**) portero; abrecoches
door mat *s* alfombrilla
doornail [ˈdorˌnel] *s* clavo grande para puertas; **dead as a doornail** (coll.) absolutamente muerto
doorplate [ˈdorˌplet] *s* rótulo, letrero de la puerta
doorpost [ˈdorˌpost] *s* quicial de puerta, jamba de puerta
door scraper *s* limpiabarros
doorsill [ˈdorˌsɪl] *s* umbral
doorstep [ˈdorˌstɛp] *s* escalón o escalones exteriores de puerta
doorstop [ˈdorˌstɑp] *s* tope de puerta
doorway [ˈdorˌwe] *s* puerta, vano de puerta, portal
dooryard [ˈdorˌjɑrd] *s* patio cerca de la puerta, jardín interior
dope [dop] *s* grasa lubricante; material absorbente; (aer.) nobabia, barniz; (slang) narcótico, opio; (slang) informes; (slang) persona muy estúpida; *vn* (slang) aletargar o atontar con un narcótico; (slang) pronosticar
dope fiend *s* (slang) toxicómano
dope sheet *s* (slang) hoja informativa sobre los caballos que van a correr
Doppler effect [ˈdɑplər] *s* (phys.) efecto de Doppler
dor [dɔr] *s* (ent.) escarabajo estercolero
Dorcas [ˈdɔrkəs] *s* (Bib.) Dorcas
Dordogne [dɔrˈdɔnjə] *s* Dordoña
Dorian [ˈdorɪən] *adj & s* dorio
Doric [ˈdɑrɪk] o [ˈdɔrɪk] *adj* dórico; *s* dórico (*dialecto*)
Doris [ˈdorɪs] *s* la Dóride; (myth.) Doris
dormancy [ˈdɔrmənsɪ] *s* letargo, inactividad; latencia
dormant [ˈdɔrmənt] *adj* durmiente, inactivo; latente
dormer [ˈdɔrmər] *s* buharda o buhardilla (*ventana y su caballete*)
dormered [ˈdɔrmərd] *adj* (arch.) abuhardillado
dormer window *s* buharda o buhardilla, lumbrera
dormitory [ˈdɔrmɪˌtorɪ] *s* (*pl:* **-ries**) dormitorio
dormouse [ˈdɔrˌmaʊs] *s* (*pl:* **-mice**) (zool.) lirón; (zool.) moscardino
Dorothy [ˈdɔrəθɪ] o [ˈdɑrəθɪ] *s* Dorotea
dorsal [ˈdɔrsəl] *adj* dorsal
dory [ˈdorɪ] *s* (*pl:* **-ries**) bote de remos; (ichth.) gallo, ceo, pez de San Pedro
dosage [ˈdosɪdʒ] *s* dosificación, dosis
dose [dos] *s* dosis; (fig.) píldora, mal trago; **dose of patience** dosis de paciencia; *va* administrar una dosis a; mezclar; dosificar (*medicamento*); medicinar; *vn* medicinarse
dosimeter [doˈsɪmɪtər] *s* dosímetro
dosimetric [ˌdosɪˈmɛtrɪk] *adj* dosimétrico
dosimetry [doˈsɪmɪtrɪ] *s* dosimetría
dossier [ˈdɑsɪe] *s* expediente
dot [dɑt] *s* punto; dote; **on the dot** (coll.) en punto, a la hora exacta; (*pret & pp:* **dotted;** *ger:* **dotting**) *va* poner punto a; puntear, motear; salpicar; **to dot one's i's** poner los puntos sobre las íes (*perfeccionar una cosa minuciosamente*); **to dot the i's and cross the t's** fijar la atención en lo más insignificante
dotage [ˈdotɪdʒ] *s* chochera, chochez
dotal [ˈdotəl] *adj* dotal
dotard [ˈdotərd] *s* persona chocha, viejo chocho
dote [dot] *vn* chochear; **to dote on** o **upon** estar locamente enamorado de, idolatrar
doting [ˈdotɪŋ] *adj* chocho (*locamente cariñoso, locamente enamorado; que chochea de viejo*)
dots and dashes *spl* (telg.) puntos y rayas
dotted line [ˈdɑtɪd] *s* línea de puntos, línea punteada; **to sign on the dotted line** echar una firma, firmar ciegamente
dotterel [ˈdɑtərəl] *s* (orn.) chorlito real; (orn.) caradrida; (dial.) tonto, necio
dotty [ˈdɑtɪ] *adj* moteado, punteado; (coll.) trémulo, débil, vacilante; (coll.) bobo, imbécil
double [ˈdʌbəl] *adj* doble; *adv* doble; dos veces;

dos juntos; *s* doble; (theat. & mov.) doble; (bridge) doblo; **doubles** *spl* (tennis) juego de dobles; *va* doblar; ser el doble de; (bridge) doblar; *vn* doblarse; (theat. & mov.) doblar; (bridge) doblar; **to double back** volver atrás; **to double up** doblarse, doblarse en dos; vivir en una misma habitación, dormir en una misma cama (*dos personas*)
double-acting ['dʌbəl'æktɪŋ] *adj* (mach.) de doble efecto
double-barreled ['dʌbəl'bærəld] *adj* de dos cañones; (fig.) de dos propósitos, para dos fines
double bass [bes] *s* (mus.) contrabajo
double bassoon *s* (mus.) contrabajón
double bed *s* cama de matrimonio
double boiler *s* marmita doble, baño maría
double bottom *s* (naut.) doble fondo
double-breasted ['dʌbəl'brɛstɪd] *adj* traslapado, cruzado, de dos hileras de botones, de dos pechos
double chin *s* papada
double consciousness *s* (psychopath.) conciencia doble
double cross *s* (slang) traición hecha a un cómplice
double-cross ['dʌbəl'krɔs] o ['dʌbəl'krɑs] *va* (slang) traicionar (*a un socio o cómplice*)
double-crosser ['dʌbəl'krɔsər] o ['dʌbəl'krɑsər] *s* (slang) traidor de un cómplice
double-cut file ['dʌbəl,kʌt} *s* lima de doble picadura
double dagger *s* (print.) cruz doble, obelisco doble
double date *s* cita de dos parejas
double-dealer ['dʌbəl'dilər] *s* hombre doble, persona doble
double-dealing ['dʌbəl'dilɪŋ] *adj* doble; *s* trato doble, doblez, duplicidad
double-decker ['dʌbəl'dɛkər] *s* navío de dos cubiertas; ómnibus de dos pisos, ómnibus con imperial; cama-litera; (slang) emparedado de tres pedazos de pan
double eagle *s* doble águila (*antigua moneda de oro de los EE.UU.*)
double-edged ['dʌbəl'ɛdʒd] *adj* de dos filos, de doble filo
double entry *s* (com.) partida doble
double-faced ['dʌbəl'fest] *adj* de dos caras; doble, hipócrita
double feature *s* (mov.) programa doble
double-feature ['dʌbəl'fitʃər] *adj* (mov.) de dos películas de largo metraje
double flat *s* (mus.) doble bemol
double-header ['dʌbəl'hɛdər] *s* tren arrastrado por dos locomotoras; (baseball) dos partidos seguidos, doble juego
double house *s* casa con corredor central; casa doble
double-jointed ['dʌbəl'dʒɔɪntɪd] *adj* con articulaciones dobles
double-lock ['dʌbəl'lɑk] *va* cerrar con dos vueltas de llave; cerrar con dos cerrojos
double-park ['dʌbəl'pɑrk] *va & vn* (aut.) aparcar en doble hilera
double play *s* (baseball) maniobra que pone fuera a dos jugadores
double pneumonia *s* (path.) neumonía doble
double-pole switch ['dʌbəl'pol] *s* (elec.) interruptor de dos polos
double-quick ['dʌbəl'kwɪk] *adj & adv* (mil.) a paso ligero; *s* (mil.) paso ligero; *vn* (mil.) marchar a paso ligero
double room *s* habitación doble
double sharp *s* (mus.) doble sostenido
double-sloping roof ['dʌbəl'slopɪŋ] *s* tejado a dos aguas
double-spaced ['dʌbəl'spest] *adj* a dos espacios
double standard *s* norma de conducta restrictiva para la mujer, especialmente en materia sexual
double star *s* (astr.) estrella doble
doublet ['dʌblɪt] *s* jubón; doblete (*piedra falsa*); (philol.) doblete
double tackle *s* polea de dos ruedas acanaladas
double talk *s* habla ambigua para engañar; galimatías, guirigay
double-throw switch ['dʌbəl'θro] *s* (elec.) conmutador de doble caída
double time *s* pago doble por sobretiempo; (mil.) paso ligero
doubleton ['dʌbəltən] *s* (bridge) doblete
double track *s* (rail.) doble vía
double-track ['dʌbəl'træk] *adj* (rail.) de doble vía
doubletree ['dʌbəl,tri] *s* volea
double turn *s* segunda, vuelta doble (*de una cerradura*)
double vision *s* vista doble
doubloon [dʌb'lun] *s* doblón
doubly ['dʌblɪ] *adv* doblemente; dos a la vez
doubt [daʊt] *s* duda; **beyond doubt** sin duda; **in doubt** incierto; **no doubt** sin duda; **to call in doubt** poner en duda; **without doubt** sin duda; *va & vn* dudar; **to doubt having** + *pp* dudar haber + *pp*
doubtable ['daʊtəbəl] *adj* dudable
doubter ['daʊtər] *s* incrédulo
doubtful ['daʊtfəl] *adj* dudoso
doubting Thomas, a un Santo Tomás (*persona que lo duda todo*)
doubtless ['daʊtlɪs] *adj* indudable, indubitable
douche [duʃ] *s* ducha; jeringa; *va* duchar; *vn* ducharse
dough [do] *s* masa, pasta; (slang) pasta (*dinero*)
doughboy ['do,bɔɪ] *s* (coll.) soldado de infantería norteamericano
doughnut ['do,nʌt] *s* buñuelo, rosquilla
doughty ['daʊtɪ] *adj* (*comp:* **-tier;** *super:* **-tiest**) (hum.) bravo, valiente, esforzado
doughy ['do·ɪ] (*comp:* **-ier;** *super:* **-iest**) pastoso
Douglas fir ['dʌgləs] *s* (bot.) seudotsuga
doum [dum] o **doum palm** *s* (bot.) duma
dour [dur], [dʊr] o [daʊr] *adj* abatido, triste, melancólico; (Scottish) austero, severo, duro; (Scottish) terco, obstinado
douse [daʊs] *va* zambullir; empapar; (coll.) apagar (*la luz*); (coll.) quitarse (*una prenda de vestir*); arriar; (naut.) cerrar (*una porta*); *vn* zambullirse; empaparse
dove [dʌv] *s* (orn.) paloma; (fig.) paloma; [dov] *pret & pp* (coll.) *de* **dive**
dovecot ['dʌv,kɑt] o **dovecote** ['dʌv,kot] o ['dʌv,kɑt] *s* palomar
dovetail ['dʌv,tel] *s* (carp.) cola de milano, cola de pato, ensambladura de cola de milano, ensambladura de cola de pato; *va* machihembrar, ensamblar a cola de milano, ensamblar a cola de pato; encajar; *vn* encajar; concordar, conformar
dowager ['daʊədʒər] *s* viuda que goza el título o los bienes del marido, p.ej., condesa viuda, duquesa viuda, princesa viuda; (coll.) señora anciana acaudalada, matrona con pretensiones
dowdy ['daʊdɪ] *adj* (*comp:* **-dier;** *super:* **-diest**) basto, desaliñado; *s* (*pl:* **-dies**) mujer basta, mujer desaliñada
dowel ['daʊəl] *s* clavija; *va* (*pret & pp:* **-eled** o **-elled;** *ger:* **-eling** o **-elling**) enclavijar
dower ['daʊər] *s* viudedad; dote; prenda; *va* señalar viudedad a; dotar
down [daʊn] *adv* abajo; hacia abajo, para abajo; en tierra; al sur; a precio reducido; en un papel, por escrito; de pronto, al contado; **to be down on** (coll.) tener inquina a; **to get down to work** aplicarse resueltamente al trabajo; **to go down** bajar; **to lie down** acostarse; **to sit down** sentarse; **down and out** arruinado; fuera de combate; **down below** allá abajo; **down from** desde; **down in the mouth** cariacontecido; **down on one's knees** de rodillas; **down to** hasta; **down to date** hasta la fecha; hasta nuestros días; **down under** entre los antípodas; **down with . . . !** ¡abajo . . . !; *prep* bajando; abajo de; **down the river** río abajo; **down the street** calle abajo; *adj* descendente; de abajo; malo, enfermo; triste, abatido; echado, acostado; agotado (*p.ej., acumulador*); anticipado (*pago, dinero*); *s* vello (*en las frutas y el cuerpo humano*); plumón (*pluma muy fina de las aves*); baja, caída; revés de fortuna; descenso; terreno undulado y cubierto de hierba; duna; *va* (coll.) tragar; derribar, echar por tierra; *vn* acostarse
downcast ['daʊn,kæst] o ['daʊn,kɑst] *adj* inclinado; abatido, desanimado

downcomer [ˈdaʊnˌkʌmər] *s* conducto de tubo descendente
downfall [ˈdaʊnˌfɔl] *s* caída, ruina; chaparrón; nevazo
downfallen [ˈdaʊnˌfɔlən] *adj* caído, arruinado
downgrade [ˈdaʊnˌgred] *adj* (coll.) pendiente, en declive; *adv* (coll.) cuesta abajo; *s* bajada; **to be on the downgrade** ir cabeza abajo (*decaer, declinar*); *va* disminuir la categoría, el sueldo, etc. de
downhearted [ˈdaʊnˌhartɪd] *adj* abatido, desanimado
downhill [ˈdaʊnˈhɪl] *adj* pendiente, en declive; peor; *adv* cuesta abajo
down payment *s* pago inicial, cuota de entrada
downpour [ˈdaʊnˌpor] *s* chaparrón, aguacero
downright [ˈdaʊnˌraɪt] *adj* absoluto, categórico, completo; claro, patente; *adv* absolutamente, completamente
downstairs [ˈdaʊnˈstɛrz] *adj* de abajo; *adv* abajo; *s* piso inferior; piso bajo
downstream [ˈdaʊnˈstrim] *adv* aguas abajo, río abajo
downstroke [ˈdaʊnˌstrok] *s* (mach.) carrera descendente
downtown [ˈdaʊnˈtaʊn] *adj* céntrico; *adv* al centro de la ciudad, en el centro de la ciudad
down town *s* barrios céntricos, calles céntricas
downtrend [ˈdaʊnˌtrɛnd] *s* tendencia a la baja
downtrodden [ˈdaʊnˌtradən] *adj* pisoteado; oprimido, tiranizado
downward [ˈdaʊnwərd] *adj* descendente; *adv* hacia abajo; hacia una época posterior
downwards [ˈdaʊnwərdz] *adv* hacia abajo; hacia una época posterior
downwind [ˈdaʊnˈwɪnd] *adv* en la dirección en que sopla el viento, en sitio hacia donde sopla el viento
downwind landing *s* (aer.) aterrizaje con viento de cola
downy [ˈdaʊnɪ] *adj* (*comp:* **-ier;** *super:* **-iest**) velloso (*blando como vello*); plumoso (*cubierto de plumón*)
dowry [ˈdaʊrɪ] *s* (*pl:* **-ries**) dote
dowse [daʊs] *va & vn* var. de **douse;** [daʊz] *vn* practicar la radiestesia
doxology [daksˈalədʒɪ] *s* (*pl:* **-gies**) *s* doxología; **greater doxology** gran doxología; **lesser doxology** pequeña doxología
doz. abr. de **dozen** o **dozens**
doze [doz] *s* sueño ligero; *vn* dormitar; **to doze off** quedarse medio dormido
dozen [ˈdʌzən] *s* docena
dozenth [ˈdʌzənθ] *adj* doceno
dozy [ˈdozɪ] *adj* soñoliento
D.P. abr. de **displaced person**
dpt. abr. de **department** y **deponent**
dr. abr. de **debtor, drawer, dram** o **drams**
Dr. abr. de **debtor** y **Doctor**
drab [dræb] *adj* (*comp:* **drabber;** *super:* **drabbest**) gris parduzco, gris amarillento; monótono; *s* gris parduzco, gris amarillento; ramera, puta; mujer desaliñada
drachm [dræm] *s* dracma; (pharm.) dracma
drachma [ˈdrækmə] *s* (*pl:* **-mas** o **-mae** [mi]) dracma
Draco [ˈdreko] *s* Dracón
Draconian [drəˈkonɪən] *adj* draconiano; (fig.) draconiano; (*l.c.*) *adj* draconiano
draff [dræf] *s* heces, poso
draffish [ˈdræfɪʃ] o **draffy** [ˈdræfɪ] *adj* inútil, sin valor, despreciable
draft [dræft] o [draft] *s* corriente de aire; tiro (*de chimenea; acción de tirar una carga*); borrador (*escrito de primera intención*); bosquejo (*primer apunte, plan, proyecto*); trago, bebida; inspiración; aire, humo inspirado; (com.) giro, letra de cambio, libranza; (naut.) calado; (mil.) quinta, conscripción; **drafts** *spl* damas, juego de damas; **on draft** a presión, servido al grifo, directo del barril; **to be exempted from the draft** redimirse de las quintas; *va* dibujar; bosquejar; hacer un borrador de; redactar (*un documento*); (mil.) quintar; **to be drafted** ir a quintas
draft age *s* edad de quintas
draft beer *s* var. de **draught beer**
draft board *s* junta de reclutamiento
draft call *s* llamada a quintas
draft dodger *s* (coll.) emboscado
draftee [ˌdræfˈti] o [ˌdrafˈti] *s* (mil.) quinto, conscripto
draft horse *s* caballo de tiro
drafting board *s* tabla para dibujar
draftsman [ˈdræftsmən] o [ˈdraftsmən] *s* (*pl:* **-men**) dibujante; redactor; peón (*del juego de damas*)
draftsmanship [ˈdræftsmənʃɪp] o [ˈdraftsmənʃɪp] *s* arte del dibujante, labor de dibujante; redacción (*p.ej., de un proyecto de ley*)
draft treaty *s* proyecto de convenio
drafty [ˈdræftɪ] o [ˈdraftɪ] *adj* (*comp:* **-ier;** *super:* **-iest**) airoso, lleno de corrientes de aire
drag [dræg] *s* rastra; (naut.) rastra; rastreamiento; (naut.) rastreo; narria (*para llevar arrastrando cosas de gran peso*); (aer.) resistencia al avance; (fig.) estorbo, impedimento, obstáculo; (slang) enchufe (*influencia*); (*pret & pp:* **dragged;** *ger:* **dragging**) *va* arrastrar; (naut.) rastrear; **to drag on** u **out** hacer demasiado largo, hacer demasiado lento; *vn* arrastrarse por el suelo; avanzar demasiado lentamente; decaer (*el interés*); **to drag on** u **out** avanzar demasiado lentamente, ser interminable, hilar largo
draggle [ˈdrægəl] *va* ensuciar arrastrando; *vn* ensuciarse arrastrando; rezagarse, quedarse atrás
drag link *s* contramanivela; contrabrazo (*del mecanismo de dirección*)
dragnet [ˈdrægˌnɛt] *s* red barredera; (fig.) red barredera
dragoman [ˈdrægomən] *s* (*pl:* **-mans** o **-men**) dragomán
dragon [ˈdrægən] *s* dragón (*animal fabuloso*); (mil.) dragoncillo (*escopeta*); (vet.) dragón (*en el ojo de un caballo*); (fig.) fiera (*persona*); mujer muy severa; *adj* dragontino
dragoness [ˈdrægənɪs] *s* dragona
dragonfly [ˈdrægənˌflaɪ] *s* (*pl:* **-flies**) (ent.) libélula, caballito del diablo
dragonnade [ˌdrægəˈned] *s* dragonada
dragonné [ˈdrægəne] *adj* (her.) dragonado
dragon's-mouth [ˈdrægənzˌmaʊθ] *s* (bot.) boca de dragón
dragon's tail *s* (astr.) cola del dragón
dragon tree *s* (bot.) drago
dragoon [drəˈgun] *s* (mil.) dragón; *va* tiranizar; **to dragoon one into working** precisar a uno a trabajar, constreñir a uno que trabaje
dragrope [ˈdrægˌrop] *s* cable de arrastre; (aer.) cuerda freno
drain [dren] *s* dren, desaguadero (*conducto de desagüe*); consumo; (surg.) dren; desagüe; desangramiento (*desagüe completo*); (fig.) desaguadero (*ocasión de continuo gasto*); *va* drenar, desaguar; avenar (*terrenos húmedos*); desangrar; escurrir (*una vasija; un líquido*); **to drain off** u **out** desangrar; *vn* desaguar; escurrirse
drainage [ˈdrenɪdʒ] *s* drenaje, desagüe, avenamiento
drainage basin *s* cuenca de un río
drainboard [ˈdrenˌbord] *s* escurridero (*mesa inclinada que sirve para escurrir platos*)
drain cock *s* llave de purga
drainer [ˈdrenər] *s* persona que avena las tierras; colador
drainpipe [ˈdrenˌpaɪp] *s* tubo de desagüe
drain plug *s* tapón de desagüe, tapón de purga; (aut.) tapón de vaciado
drake [drek] *s* (orn.) pato
dram [dræm] *s* (pharm.) dracma; trago de aguardiente; porción pequeña
drama [ˈdramə] o [ˈdræmə] *s* drama (*pieza de teatro; género; suceso de la vida real*)
dramamine [ˈdræməmin] *s* (trademark) dramamina
dramatic [drəˈmætɪk] *adj* dramático; **dramatics** *ssg* (theat.) representación de aficionados; *spl* dramas presentados por aficionados
dramatically [drəˈmætɪkəlɪ] *adv* dramáticamente
dramatis personae [ˈdræmətɪs pərˈsoni] *spl* personajes dramáticos
dramatist [ˈdræmətɪst] *s* dramático (*autor*)
dramatization [ˌdræmətɪˈzeʃən] *s* dramatización
dramatize [ˈdræmətaɪz] *va* dramatizar
dramaturgic [ˌdræməˈtʌrdʒɪk] *adj* dramático

dramaturgist [ˈdræmə,tʌrdʒɪst] *s* dramaturgo
dramaturgy [ˈdræmə,tʌrdʒɪ] *s* dramaturgia
dramshop [ˈdræm,ʃɑp] *s* bar, taberna
Drang nach Osten [drɑŋ nɑx ˈɔstən] *s* marcha hacia el este
drank [dræŋk] *pret de* **drink**
drape [drep] *s* colgadura, ropaje; *va* cubrir con colgaduras, adornar con telas colgantes; arreglar los pliegues de (*una prenda de vestir*)
draper [ˈdrepər] *s* tapicero; (Brit.) pañero
drapery [ˈdrepərɪ] *s* (*pl:* **-ies**) colgaduras, ropaje; (Brit.) paño, paños; (Brit.) pañería
drastic [ˈdræstɪk] *adj* drástico; (med.) drástico
drastically [ˈdræstɪkəlɪ] *adv* drásticamente, rápida y violentamente, extensamente
draught [dræft] o [drɑft] *s & va* var. de **draft**
draught beer *s* cerveza a presión
draughtboard [ˈdræft,bord] o [ˈdrɑft,bord] *s* tablero de damas
draughtsman [ˈdræftsmən] o [ˈdrɑftsmən] *s* (*pl:* **-men**) var. de **draftsman**
draughty [ˈdræftɪ] o [ˈdrɑftɪ] *adj* (*comp:* **-ier;** *super:* **-iest**) var. de **drafty**
Dravidian [drəˈvɪdɪən] *adj & s* dravidiano
draw [drɔ] *s* tiro (*p.ej., de una chimenea*); (coll.) función que atrae mucha gente; empate (*en un juego o contienda*); tablas (*en damas y ajedrez*); robo (*naipe o naipes que se toman de la baceta*); sorteo (*p.ej., de una lotería*); jugada, suerte (*en un juego, lotería, etc.*); barranco; piso o compuerta (*de un puente levadizo*) ‖ (*pret:* **drew;** *pp:* **drawn**) *va* tirar (*alambre, una línea; atraer*); tirar de (*arrastrar, traer hacia sí*); sacar (*p.ej., un clavo, una espada, agua, una conclusión*); aspirar, inspirar (*el aire*); atraer (*a la gente*); llamar (*la atención*); atraerse (*aplausos*); contraer, encoger; dar (*un suspiro*); correr, descorrer (*una cortina*); tender (*un arco*); cobrar (*un salario*); sacarse (*un premio*); levantar (*un puente levadizo*); preparar por infusión; empatar (*una partida*); robar (*naipes, fichas*); (com.) girar, librar; hacer (*una comparación*); (naut. & weaving) calar; (elec.) consumir (*amperios*); dibujar; redactar; **to draw a bead on** (coll.) apuntar; **to draw aside** apartar; **to draw along** arrastrar; **to draw back** hacer retroceder; **to draw forth** hacer salir; **to draw interest** devengar interés; **to draw off** sacar, extraer; trasegar (*un líquido*); retirar; **to draw on** ocasionar, producir; provocar; ponerse (*p.ej., guantes*); (com.) girar a cargo de; **to draw oneself up** enderezarse con dignidad; **to draw out** sacar; sonsacar, tirar de la lengua a; **to draw together** juntar, unir; **to draw up** extender, redactar (*un documento*); (mil.) ordenar para el combate ‖ *vn* tirar, tirar bien (*una chimenea*); contraerse, encogerse; empatar; (naut.) calar; dibujar; echar suertes; atraer mucha gente, atraer concurrencia; (com.) girar; **to draw aside** apartarse; **to draw back** retroceder, retirarse; **to draw near** acercarse; acercarse a; **to draw to a close** estar para terminar; **to draw together** juntarse, unirse; **to draw up** pararse, detenerse; **to draw up at the curb** arrimarse a la acera
drawback [ˈdrɔ,bæk] *s* desventaja, inconveniente; (com.) drawback (*reembolso, p.ej., de derechos de aduana*)
drawbridge [ˈdrɔ,brɪdʒ] *s* puente levadizo, puente giratorio
drawee [,drɔˈi] *s* (com.) girado, librado
drawer [drɔr] *s* cajón, gaveta; [ˈdrɔər] *s* dibujante; (com.) girador, librador; **drawers** [drɔrz] *spl* calzoncillos
drawing [ˈdrɔ·ɪŋ] *s* dibujo; sorteo (*en una lotería*)
drawing account *s* cuenta corriente
drawing board *s* tablero de dibujo
drawing card *s* atracción (*actor, orador, función, etc., que atraen a mucha gente*)
drawing knife *s* var. de **drawknife**
drawing room *s* sala; recepción; (rail.) departamento reservado
drawing table *s* mesa para dibujante
drawknife [ˈdrɔ,naɪf] *s pl:* **-knives**) plana curvada, cuchilla de dos mangos
drawl [drɔl] *s* habla lenta y pesada; *va* pronunciar lenta y pesadamente; *vn* hablar lenta y pesadamente
drawn [drɔn] *pp de* **draw**
drawn butter *s* mantequilla derretida
drawn work *s* (sew.) calado
drawplate [ˈdrɔ,plet] *s* (mach.) hilera
drawshave [ˈdrɔ,ʃev] *s* var. de **drawknife**
drawsheet [ˈdrɔ,ʃit] *s* alezo
drawtube [ˈdrɔ,tjub] o [ˈdrɔ,tub] *s* tubo telescópico (*del microscopio*)
draw well *s* pozo de noria
dray [dre] *s* carro; narria; *va* acarrear
drayage [ˈdreɪdʒ] *s* acarreo
dray horse *s* caballo de tiro
drayman [ˈdremən] *s* (*pl:* **-men**) acarreador, carretonero
dread [drɛd] *s* pavor, temor; *adj* terrible, espantoso; *va & vn* temer; **to dread to** + *inf* temer + *inf*
dreadful [ˈdrɛdfəl] *adj* terrible, espantoso; (coll.) desagradable
dreadfully [ˈdrɛdfəlɪ] *adv* terriblemente; (coll.) sumamente, excesivamente
dreadnought [ˈdrɛd,nɔt] *s* (nav.) gran buque acorazado, dreadnought
dream [drim] *s* ensueño, sueño; (fig.) sueño (*cosa de gran belleza*); **dream come true** sueño hecho realidad; (*pret & pp:* **dreamed** o **dreamt**) *va* soñar; pasar (*p.ej., el día*) soñando; **to dream up** (coll.) ingeniar, imaginar; *vn* soñar; **to dream of** soñar con o en; **to dream of** + *ger* soñar con + *inf*
dreamer [ˈdrimər] *s* soñador; (fig.) soñador
dreamland [ˈdrim,lænd] *s* reino del ensueño; utopia; tierra de las hadas; sueño
dreamt [drɛmt] *pret & pp de* **dream**
dreamy [ˈdrimɪ] *adj* (*comp:* **-ier;** *super:* **-iest**) soñador; lleno de sueños; vago, ligero
dreary [ˈdrɪrɪ] *adj* (*comp:* **-ier;** *super:* **-iest**) triste; monótono, pesado
dredge [drɛdʒ] *s* draga; rastra; *va* dragar; rastrear; espolvorear
dredger [ˈdrɛdʒər] *s* persona que draga; draga (*máquina o buque*); polvorera
dredging [ˈdrɛdʒɪŋ] *s* dragado
dregs [drɛgz] *spl* heces; (fig.) heces
drench [drɛntʃ] *s* mojada; solución para empapar, solución para remojar; bebida; bebida purgante; *va* mojar, empapar; purgar con violencia
drenching [ˈdrɛntʃɪŋ] *adj* mojador; torrencial (*lluvia*)
Dresden [ˈdrɛzdən] *s* Dresde
dress [drɛs] *s* indumentaria; vestido; vestido exterior de mujer o niña; falda; traje de etiqueta, vestido de gala; (*pret & pp:* **dressed** o **drest**) *va* vestir; trajear; vestir de etiqueta; adornar, ataviar; preparar; peinar (*el pelo*); curar (*una herida*); adobar y curtir (*pieles*); podar (*plantas*); (naut.) empavesar; (mil.) alinear; **to dress down** (coll.) azotar, pegar; (coll.) calentar las orejas a; **to get dressed** vestirse; *vn* vestir (*ir vestido*); vestirse (*ponerse el vestido*); (mil.) alinearse; **to dress up** vestirse de etiqueta; prenderse de veinticinco alfileres
dress ball *s* baile de etiqueta
dress coat *s* frac
dresser [ˈdrɛsər] *s* cómoda con espejo; aparador; **to be a good dresser** vestir con elegancia, vestir con buen gusto
dress form *s* maniquí
dress goods *spl* géneros para vestidos
dressing [ˈdrɛsɪŋ] *s* aderezamiento, adorno; (cook.) aliño, salsa; (cook.) relleno; (agr.) abono; (surg.) vendaje; (coll.) regaño
dressing-down [ˈdrɛsɪŋˈdaʊn] *s* (coll.) azotamiento; (coll.) regaño, repasata
dressing gown *s* bata, peinador
dressing room *s* cuarto de vestir; (theat.) camarín
dressing station *s* (mil.) puesto de socorro
dressing table *s* tocador
dressmaker [ˈdrɛs,mekər] *s* costurera, modista
dressmaking [ˈdrɛs,mekɪŋ] *s* costura, modistería
dress parade *s* (mil.) parada
dress rehearsal *s* (theat.) ensayo general
dress shirt *s* camisa de pechera dura
dress shop *s* casa de modas

dress suit *s* traje de etiqueta
dress tie *s* corbata de smoking, corbata de frac
dressy [ˈdrɛsɪ] *adj* (*comp:* **-ier;** *super:* **-iest**) (coll.) acicalado, aficionado a ataviarse; (coll.) elegante, vistoso
drest [drɛst] *pret & pp de* **dress**
drew [dru] *pret de* **draw**
dribble [ˈdrɪbəl] *s* goteo, caída en gotas; derrame ligero; (coll.) llovizna; (sport) dribbling; *va* hacer caer gota a gota; (sport) driblar; *vn* gotear; babear; (sport) driblar
dribbler [ˈdrɪblər] *s* persona que babea; (sport) jugador que dribla
driblet [ˈdrɪblɪt] *s* gotita; adarme
dried beef [draɪd] *s* cecina
dried fig *s* higo paso
drier [ˈdraɪər] *s* enjugador (*persona o utensilio*); desecante; secador (*para el cabello*); secadora (*máquina para secar la ropa*)
drift [drɪft] *s* cosa llevada por la corriente; corriente de agua, corriente de aire; montón (*de nieve, arena, etc.*); ventisca; impulsión, impulso; dirección, rumbo; tenor, sentido, significación; (geol.) terrenos de acarreo; (aer. & naut.) deriva; (min.) socavón; (rad. & telv.) desviación; *va* llevar; amontonar; (mach.) mandrilar; *vn* ser llevado por la corriente, ir arrastrado por la corriente; amontonarse; ventiscar; (aer. & naut.) derivar, ir a la deriva; (fig.) vivir sin rumbo
driftage [ˈdrɪftɪdʒ] *s* cosa llevada por la corriente; (aer. & naut.) deriva
drift angle *s* (aer. & naut.) ángulo de deriva
drifter [ˈdrɪftər] *s* vago, vagabundo
drift ice *s* hielo flotante, hielo acarreado por el agua
drift meter *s* (aer. & naut.) derivómetro
driftpin [ˈdrɪftˌpɪn] *s* (mach.) mandril de ensanchar
driftwood [ˈdrɪftˌwʊd] *s* madera flotante, madera acarreada por el agua, madera arrojada a la playa por el agua
drill [drɪl] *s* taladro; (agr.) sembradora mecánica; hilera de semillas sembradas en un surco; disciplina, instrucción; (mil.) ejercicio; dril (*tejido*); (zool.) dril (*mandril*); *va* taladrar; disciplinar, instruir; plantar en hileras, plantar en un surco; (mil.) enseñar el ejercicio a; *vn* (mil.) hacer el ejercicio
drilling [ˈdrɪlɪŋ] *s* perforación; (mil.) ejercicio; dril (*tejido*)
drillmaster [ˈdrɪlˌmæstər] o [ˈdrɪlˌmɑstər] *s* maestro de ejercicios
drill press *s* prensa taladradora, taladro mecánico
drily [ˈdraɪlɪ] *adv* secamente
drink [drɪŋk] *s* bebida; beber, exceso en la bebida; **the drinks are on the house!** ¡convida la casa!; **to take a drink** echar un trago; (*pret:* **drank;** *pp:* **drunk**) *va* beber; beberse (*p.ej., su sueldo*); **to drink down** beber de una vez; **to drink in** beberse (*p.ej., un libro*); beber (*las palabras de una persona*); aspirar (*aire*); *vn* beber; **to drink out of** beber de o en (*p.ej., una fuente*); **to drink to** beber a o por, brindar a o por
drinkable [ˈdrɪŋkəbəl] *adj* bebible, potable
drinker [ˈdrɪŋkər] *s* bebedor
drinking [ˈdrɪŋkɪŋ] *s* (el) beber; *adj* de beber, para beber; bebedor
drinking bout *s* juerga de borrachera
drinking cup *s* tanque, taza para beber
drinking fountain *s* fuente de agua corriente para beber, fuente de beber
drinking glass *s* vaso para beber
drinking horn *s* aliara, cuerna, vaso de cuerno
drinking song *s* canción para beber, canción de taberna, canción báquica
drinking trough *s* abrevadero
drinking water *s* agua para beber, agua potable
drip [drɪp] *s* goteo; gotas; gotera (*p.ej., del techo*); tubo gotero; (arch.) alero; (*pret & pp:* **dripped** o **dript;** *ger:* **dripping**) *va* verter gota a gota, hacer gotear; *vn* caer gota a gota, gotear
drip coffee *s* café de maquinilla
drip-dry [ˈdrɪpˌdraɪ] *adj* de lava y pon, p.ej., **drip-dry shirt** camisa de lava y pon
drip feed *s* engrase por goteo
drip pan *s* cubeta de goteo; (aut.) colector de aceite, recogegotas
dripping [ˈdrɪpɪŋ] *s* goteo; **drippings** *spl* líquidos que gotean; pringue (*grasa que suelta la carne con el calor*)
dripping pan *s* grasera, pringuera
dripstone [ˈdrɪpˌston] *s* (arch.) alero de piedra; carbonato cálcico de las estalactitas y estalagmitas
dript [drɪpt] *pret & pp de* **drip**
drive [draɪv] *s* calzada para coches, calzada para automóviles; paseo en coche, paseo en automóvil; energía, vigor, fuerza; urgencia, presión; campaña vigorosa; venta a bajo precio; golpe fuerte; medio de impulsión; mecanismo de dirección; mecanismo de transmisión; mecanismo de funcionamiento; **an hour's drive** una hora de coche ‖ (*pret:* **drove;** *pp:* **driven**) *va* impeler, empujar; estimular, aguijonear; compeler, forzar; clavar, hincar; actuar, mover; llevar, conducir (*p.ej., ganado*); arrear (*a las bestias*); guiar, conducir (*p.ej., un automóvil*); llevar en coche; efectuar, ejecutar; hacer excavando, hacer ahondando; obligar a trabajar mucho; (sport) golpear con gran fuerza; **to drive a good bargain** hacer un buen trato; **to drive away** ahuyentar; **to drive back** rechazar, obligar a retroceder; **to drive in** hacer entrar por fuerza; **to drive mad** volver loco; **to drive off** ahuyentar; **to drive out** echar fuera, hacer salir, expulsar ‖ *vn* ir en coche, ir en automóvil; trabajar mucho; **to drive at** tener puesta la mira en; querer decir; **to drive away** trabajar mucho; **to drive in** entrar en coche, entrar en (*un sitio*) en coche; **to drive on the right** (u **on the left**) circular por la derecha (o por la izquierda); **to drive out** salir en coche
drive-in motion-picture theater [ˈdraɪvˌɪn] *s* auto-teatro (*cine al aire libre en que los espectadores motorizados ven la cinta desde los coches*)
drive-in restaurant *s* restaurante en que sirven a los automovilistas sin que salgan de los coches
drivel [ˈdrɪvəl] *s* baba; bobería; (*pret & pp:* **-eled** o **-elled;** *ger:* **-eling** o **-elling**) *va* hacer babear; gastar (*tiempo*) tontamente; *vn* babear; bobear
driveler o **driveller** [ˈdrɪvələr] *s* baboso; bobo
driven [ˈdrɪvən] *pp de* **drive**
driven well *s* pozo abisinio
driver [ˈdraɪvər] *s* conductor; cochero; maquinista (*de una locomotora*); rueda motriz (*de locomotora*); (golf) conductor; (mach.) pieza impulsora; persona despótica que fuerza a trabajar
driver's license *s* (aut.) permiso de conducir, carnet de conducir
driver training school *s* var. de **driving school**
drive shaft *s* (mach.) árbol de mando, árbol o eje motor
driveway [ˈdraɪvˌwe] *s* calzada para coches; entrada para coches, calzada de acceso
drivewell [ˈdraɪvˌwɛl] *s* var. de **driven well**
drive wheel *s* (mach.) rueda motriz
drive-yourself service [ˈdraɪvjʊrˈsɛlf] *s* alquiler sin chófer
driving school *s* auto-escuela
drizzle [ˈdrɪzəl] *s* llovizna; *vn* lloviznar
drogue [drog] *s* (aer.) paracaídas estabilizador, paracaídas desacelerador; (aer.) embudo de reaprovisionamiento en vuelo; (meteor.) cono de viento; (naut.) ancla flotante
drogue gun *s* (aer.) cañón eyector de paracaídas
droll [drol] *adj* chusco, gracioso
drollery [ˈdrolərɪ] *s* (*pl:* **-ies**) chuscada, bufonería
dromedary [ˈdrɑməˌdɛrɪ] *s* (*pl:* **-ies**) dromedario
drone [dron] *s* (ent.) zángano; (fig.) zángano; zumbido; bordón o roncón (*de la gaita*); avión radiodirigido; *va* decir monótonamente; *vn* zanganear; zumbar; hablar monótonamente
drool [drul] *s* baba; (slang) bobería; *vn* babear; (slang) bobear
droop [drup] *s* inclinación; *va* inclinar; dejar caer; *vn* inclinarse; estar pendiente, colgar;

decaer, descaecer; consumirse, marchitarse; encamarse (*las mieses*); abatirse, entristecerse
drooping ['drupɪŋ] *adj* caído (*dícese de los párpados, los hombros, etc.*)
drop [drɑp] *s* gota; pendiente (*cuesta o declive; arete*); baja, caída repentina; descenso (*de temperatura*); lanzamiento (*p.ej., de víveres desde un aeroplano*); traguito; pastilla; escotillón; horca; **drops** *spl* gotas (*medicamento*); **at the drop of a hat** al dar la señal; de buena gana, con gusto; **a drop in the bucket** cosa insignificante; **to get** o **to have the drop on** coger la delantera a, llevar la ventaja a; **drop by drop** gota a gota ‖ (*pret & pp:* **dropped** o **dropt;** *ger:* **dropping**) *va* dejar caer; hacer caer; derribar; matar; poner en tierra; bajar (*una cortina*); echar al buzón; soltar (*una palabra*) casualmente; escribir (*una esquela, unos renglones*); omitir, suprimir; abandonar, dejar; despedir; borrar de la lista (*a un alumno*); lanzar (*bombas, suministros, etc. de un avión*); escalfar (*huevos*); **to drop a hint** soltar una indirecta; **to drop anchor** echar el ancla; **to drop a line** poner unos renglones, escribir unas palabras; **to drop a subject** cambiar de asunto ‖ *vn* caer, caer de repente; dejarse caer; caer agotado, caer herido, caer muerto; bajar; cesar, terminar, parar; **to drop asleep** quedarse dormido; **to drop behind** quedarse atrás; **to drop dead** caer muerto; **to drop in, to drop over** entrar al pasar, visitar de paso; **to drop off** desaparecer; quedarse dormido; morir de repente; **to drop out** desaparecer; retirarse; darse de baja (*dejar de pertenecer voluntariamente a una sociedad, etc.*)
drop box *s* buzón
drop curtain *s* (theat.) telón
drop-forge ['drɑp'fordʒ] *va* forjar a martinete
drop hammer *s* martinete, martillo pilón
drop kick *s* (football) puntapié que se da a la pelota en el momento en que rebota
drop-kick ['drɑp,kɪk] *va* (football) dar un puntapié a (*la pelota*) en el momento en que rebota
drop-leaf table ['drɑp,lif] *s* mesa de hoja plegadiza
droplet ['drɑplɪt] *s* gotita
droplight ['drɑp,laɪt] *s* lámpara de extensión, lámpara colgante
dropper ['drɑpər] *s* cuentagotas
dropping ['drɑpɪŋ] *s* goteo; líquido que gotea; **droppings** *spl* excrementos de animales
drop shutter *s* (phot.) obturador de guillotina
dropsical ['drɑpsɪkəl] *adj* hidrópico
dropsy ['drɑpsɪ] *s* (path.) hidropesía
dropt [drɑpt] *pret & pp de* **drop**
drop table *s* mesa perezosa
dropwort ['drɑp,wʌrt] *s* (bot.) filipéndula
drosera ['drɑsərə] *s* (pharm.) drosera
droseraceous [,drɑsə'reʃəs] *adj* (bot.) droseráceo
drosometer [drə'sɑmɪtər] *s* drosómetro
drosophila [dro'sɑfɪlə] *s* (*pl:* **-lae** [li]) (ent.) drosófila
dross [drɔs] o [drɑs] *s* escoria (*de metales*); basura, desecho
drought [draʊt] *s* sequía (*temporada seca*); sequedad
drought-stricken ['draʊt,strɪkən] *adj* asolado por la sequía
droughty ['draʊtɪ] *adj* árido, seco
drouth [draʊθ] *s* var. de **drought**
drove [drov] *s* manada; gentío, multitud; *pret de* **drive**
drover ['drovər] *s* ganadero
drown [draʊn] *va* anegar, ahogar; apagar (*un sonido*); ahogar (*p.ej., pesares*); **to drown out** ahuyentar inundando; apagar (*un sonido, una voz*); apagar la voz de; *vn* anegarse, ahogarse, perecer ahogado
drowse [draʊz] *s* somnolencia, modorra; *va* adormecer; pasar (*el tiempo*) adormeciéndose; *vn* adormecerse, estar amodorrado
drowsiness ['draʊzɪnɪs] *s* somnolencia, modorra
drowsy ['draʊzɪ] *adj* (*comp:* **-sier;** *super:* **-siest**) soñoliento
drub [drʌb] (*pret & pp:* **drubbed;** *ger:* **drubbing**) *va* apalear, tundir; (sport) derrotar completamente
drubbing ['drʌbɪŋ] *s* paliza, zurra; (sport) derrota aplastante
drudge [drʌdʒ] *s* ganapán; yunque, esclavo del trabajo; *vn* afanarse
drudgery ['drʌdʒərɪ] *s* (*pl:* **-ies**) afán, trabajo penoso
drug [drʌg] *s* droga; narcótico; macana, artículo de comercio que queda sin fácil salida; **to be a drug on the market** ser invendible; (*pret & pp:* **drugged;** *ger:* **drugging**) *va* narcotizar; poner narcótico en; aletargar o atontar con un narcótico
drug addict *s* adicto a las drogas narcóticas
drug addiction *s* adicción a las drogas narcóticas
drugget ['drʌgɪt] *s* droguete
druggist ['drʌgɪst] *s* farmacéutico, boticario; droguero, droguista
drug habit *s* vicio de los narcóticos
drug store *s* farmacia, botica; droguería
drug traffic *s* contrabando de narcóticos
druid o **Druid** ['druɪd] *s* druida
druidess ['druɪdɪs] *s* druidesa
druidic [dru'ɪdɪk] o **druidical** [dru'ɪdɪkəl] *adj* druídico
druidism ['druɪdɪzəm] *s* druidismo
drum [drʌm] *s* tambor (*cilindro*); bidón (*p.ej., para aceite, gasolina*); (anat., arch. & mus.) tambor; (*pret & pp:* **drummed;** *ger:* **drumming**) *va* reunir a toque de tambor; **to drum a lesson into someone** meterle a uno la lección en la cabeza; **to drum out** (mil.) expulsar a toque de tambor; **to drum up** reunir a toque de tambor; reunir; **to drum up trade** fomentar ventas; *vn* tocar el tambor; teclear
drum armature *s* (elec.) inducido de tambor
drumbeat ['drʌm,bit] *s* toque de tambor
drum corps *s* banda de tambores
drumfire ['drʌm,faɪr] *s* fuego graneado
drumfish ['drʌm,fɪʃ] *s* (ichth.) corvina negra
drumhead ['drʌm,hed] *s* piel de tambor; (anat.) tambor
drumhead court-martial *s* (mil.) consejo de guerra en marcha o en el campo de batalla
drumlin ['drʌmlɪn] *s* (geol.) colina oval alargada, constituída por materiales detríticos de origen glacial
drum major *s* (mil.) tambor mayor
drummer ['drʌmər] *s* tambor (*persona*); (coll.) viajante
drumstick ['drʌm,stɪk] *s* baqueta, palillo; (coll.) muslo (*de ave cocida*)
drunk [drʌŋk] *adj* borracho; **to get drunk** emborracharse; *s* (slang) borracho; (slang) borrachera; *pp de* **drink**
drunkard ['drʌŋkərd] *s* borrachín
drunken ['drʌŋkən] *adj* borracho, emborrachado, embriagado
drunken driver *s* conductor embriagado
drunken driving *s* acto de conducir en estado de embriaguez; **he was arrested for drunken driving** fué arrestado por conducir en estado de embriaguez
drunkenness ['drʌŋkənnɪs] *s* embriaguez
drupaceous [dru'peʃəs] *adj* (bot.) drupáceo
drupe [drup] *s* (bot.) drupa
drupelet ['druplɪt] *s* (bot.) drupa pequeña
druse [druz] *s* (bot. & mineral.) drusa; (*cap.*) *s* druso
Drusean ['druzɪən] *adj* druso
dry [draɪ] *s* (coll.) prohibicionista; *adj* (*comp:* **drier;** *super:* **driest**) seco, árido; sediento; árido (*aburrido, falto de interés*); sin mantequilla (*dícese del pan*); (coll.) seco (*prohibicionista*); (*pret & pp:* **dried**) *va* secar; enjugar; **to dry up** secar rápidamente, secar completamente; *vn* secarse; **to dry up** secarse rápidamente, secarse completamente; (slang) dejar de hablar, callarse
dryad ['draɪæd] *s* (myth.) dríada
dry battery *s* (elec.) batería seca; (elec.) pila seca
dry cell *s* (elec.) pila seca
dry-clean ['draɪ,klin] *va* limpiar en seco
dry cleaner *s* tintorero
dry cleaning *s* lavado a seco, limpieza en seco
dry-cleaning establishment *s* tintorería
dry dock *s* (naut.) dique, dique de carena
dry-dock ['draɪ,dɑk] *va* (naut.) poner en dique de carena

dryer ['draɪər] *s* var. de **drier**
dry-eyed ['draɪ,aɪd] *adj* ojienjuto, sin lágrimas
dry-farm ['draɪ,fɑrm] *va* cultivar (*terrenos de secano*)
dry farmer *s* cultivador de terrenos de secano
dry farming *s* cultivo de secano
dry goods *spl* mercancías generales, géneros, lencería, pañería
dry ice *s* hielo carbónico, hielo seco o nieve carbónica
dry law *s* (U.S.A.) ley seca
dryly ['draɪlɪ] *adv* secamente
dry measure *s* medida para áridos
dryness ['draɪnɪs] *s* sequedad
dry nurse *s* ama seca
dry-nurse ['draɪ,nʌrs] *va* ser ama seca de
dry point *s* (f.a.) punta seca; grabado a punta seca
dry rot *s* (bot.) pudrición seca; (bot.) podredumbre causada por honguillos; (fig.) corrupción interna, deterioro
dry sand *s* (found.) arena de estufa, arena seca
dry season *s* estación de la seca
dry-shod ['draɪ,ʃɑd] *adj* a pie enjuto
dry-stone ['draɪ,ston] *adj* de piedra seca, de piedra en seco
dry wash *s* lavado secado pero no planchado
d.s. abr. de **days after sight** y **daylight saving**
D.S. abr. de **Dental Surgeon** y **Doctor of Science**
D.Sc. abr. de **Doctor of Science**
D.S.C. abr. de **Distinguished Service Cross**
D.S.M. abr. de **Distinguished Service Medal**
D.S.T. abr. de **Daylight Saving Time**
d.t.'s ['di'tiz] *spl* (coll.) delírium tremens; (coll.) diablos azules (Am.)
dual ['djuəl] o ['duəl] *adj* binario, dual; (gram.) dual; *s* (gram.) dual
dual drive *s* (aut.) mando doble
dualism ['djuəlɪzəm] o ['duəlɪzəm] *s* dualismo
dualist ['djuəlɪst] o ['duəlɪst] *s* dualista
dualistic [,djuə'lɪstɪk] o [,duə'lɪstɪk] *adj* dualista
duality [dju'ælɪtɪ] o [du'ælɪtɪ] *s* (*pl:* **-ties**) dualidad
dub [dʌb] *s* (slang) jugador desmañado; (*pret & pp:* **dubbed;** *ger:* **dubbing**) *va* apellidar, titular; armar caballero a; alisar; (mov.) doblar (*una película, generalmente en otro idioma*)
dubiety [dju'baɪətɪ] o [du'baɪətɪ] *s* (*pl:* **-ties**) incertidumbre; cosa dudosa
dubious ['djubɪəs] o ['dubɪəs] *adj* dudoso
dubitative ['djubɪ,tetɪv] o ['dubɪ,tetɪv] *adj* dubitativo
dubitative conjunction *s* (gram.) conjunción dubitativa
ducal ['djukəl] o ['dukəl] *adj* ducal
ducat ['dʌkət] *s* ducado
duce ['dutʃe] *s* caudillo
duchess ['dʌtʃɪs] *s* duquesa
duchy ['dʌtʃɪ] *s* (*pl:* **-ies**) ducado
duck [dʌk] *s* (orn.) pato; (orn.) pata; dril; terliz (*tejido*); agachada rápida (*para evitar un golpe*); zambullida (*en el agua*); (coll.) querida; **ducks** *spl* (coll.) pantalones de dril; **like water off a duck's back** sin tener ningún efecto; **to make ducks and drakes of** o **to play ducks and drakes with** malgastar, derrochar; *va* agachar rápidamente (*p.ej., la cabeza*); (coll.) evitar (*un golpe*) agachándose rápidamente; chapuzar, zambullir; *vn* agacharse; chapuzar, zambullirse; **to duck out** (slang) escaparse
duckbill ['dʌk,bɪl] *s* (zool.) ornitorrinco
duck hawk *s* (orn.) halcón peregrino patero
ducking ['dʌkɪŋ] *s* caza de patos silvestres; zambullida, chapuz
ducking stool *s* silla de chapuzar
duckling ['dʌklɪŋ] *s* anadeja, patito
duckpins ['dʌk,pɪnz] *spl* juego de bolos
duck soup *s* (slang) breva, ganga, cosa apreciable lograda con poco esfuerzo
duck-toed ['dʌk,tod] *adj* zancajoso
duckweed ['dʌk,wid] *s* (bot.) lenteja acuática o lenteja de agua
duct [dʌkt] *s* conducto, tubo, canal; (anat.) conducto
ductile ['dʌktɪl] *adj* dúctil; (fig.) dúctil
ductility [dʌk'tɪlɪtɪ] *s* (*pl:* **-ties**) ductilidad
ductless gland ['dʌktlɪs] *s* (anat.) glándula cerrada, glándula de secreción interna
dud [dʌd] *s* (coll.) prenda de vestir; (slang) bomba que no estalla, granada que no estalla; (slang) fracaso; **duds** *spl* (coll.) prendas de vestir, trapos; (coll.) pertenencias
dude [djud] o [dud] *s* petimetre, caballerete
dude ranch *s* (U.S.A.) rancho para turistas
dudgeon ['dʌdʒən] *s* inquina, ojeriza; **in high dudgeon** resentido, airado
dudish ['djudɪʃ] o ['dudɪʃ] *adj* peripuesto, lechuguino
due [dju] o [du] *adj* debido; pagadero; aguardado, esperado; **in due time** a su debido tiempo; **to become due** o **to fall due** vencer; **when is the train due?** ¿cuándo llega el tren?, ¿a qué hora debe llegar el tren?; **due to** debido a, ocasionado por; *adv* derecho, directamente, exactamente; *s* deuda; **dues** *spl* derechos; cuota (*de un miembro*); **to get one's due** llevar su merecido; **to give the devil his due** ser justo hasta con el diablo
duel ['djuəl] o ['duəl] *s* duelo; (*pret & pp:* **dueled** o **duelled;** *ger:* **dueling** o **duelling**) *va* combatir en duelo, matar en duelo; *vn* batirse en duelo
duelist o **duellist** ['djuəlɪst] o ['duəlɪst] *s* duelista
duenna [dju'ɛnə] o [du'ɛnə] *s* dueña; señora de compañía
dues-paying ['djuz,peɪŋ] o ['duz,peɪŋ] *adj* cotizante
duet [dju'ɛt] o [du'ɛt] *s* (mus.) dúo
duettist [dju'ɛtɪst] o [du'ɛtɪst] *s* (mus.) duetista
duff [dʌf] *s* pudín de harina cocido en un saco
duffel ['dʌfəl] *s* paño de lana basta; (coll.) pertrechos, pertrechos para acampar
duffel bag *s* (mil.) talego para efectos de uso personal
duffer ['dʌfər] *s* (coll.) estúpido, persona muy torpe, chapucero
dug [dʌg] *s* teta, ubre; *pret & pp de* **dig**
dugong ['dugɑŋ] *s* (zool.) dugón
dugout ['dʌg,aut] *s* (mil.) cueva de refugio, cueva de protección, defensa subterránea; piragua; (baseball) cobertizo bajo para los jugadores
duke [djuk] o [duk] *s* duque; **dukes** *spl* (slang) puños
dukedom ['djukdəm] o ['dukdəm] *s* ducado
dulcet ['dʌlsɪt] *adj* dulce, suave, melodioso
dulcimer ['dʌlsɪmər] *s* (mus.) dulcémele
dull [dʌl] *adj* embotado, romo, obtuso; apagado (*color*); sordo (*sonido; dolor*); insípido, insulso; aburrido, tedioso; insensible; deslustrado, deslucido; lerdo, torpe, tardo de comprensión; desanimado, inactivo, muerto (*negocios*); *va* embotar, enromar; entorpecer; deslustrar, deslucir; enfriar (*p.ej., el entusiasmo*); *vn* embotarse, enromarse; entorpecerse; deslustrarse, deslucirse
dullard ['dʌlərd] *s* estúpido
dullish ['dʌlɪʃ] *adj* algo embotado, algo obtuso; algo lerdo; algo inactivo
dullness ['dʌlnɪs] *s* falta de punta, embotadura; estupidez, torpeza; deslustre; pereza, pesadez; desanimación, inactividad
dully ['dʌllɪ] *adv* de modo obtuso; lentamente; sin brillo, sin lustre; estúpidamente
dulness ['dʌlnɪs] *s* var. de **dullness**
dulse [dʌls] *s* (bot.) rodimenia
duly ['djulɪ] o ['dulɪ] *adv* debidamente
duma ['dumɑ] *s* duma
dumb [dʌm] *adj* mudo; (coll.) torpe, estúpido
dumbbell ['dʌm,bɛl] *s* halterio (*de gimnasia*); (slang) estúpido
dumbfound [,dʌm'faund] *va* var. de **dumfound**
dumb show *s* pantomima
dumbwaiter ['dʌm,wetər] *s* montaplatos; estante giratorio
dumdum bullet ['dʌmdʌm] *s* bala dumdum
dumfound [,dʌm'faund] *va* confundir, pasmar, dejar sin habla
dummy ['dʌmɪ] *s* (*pl:* **-mies**) maniquí (*para exhibir prendas de vestir*); cabeza para pelucas; testaferro (*persona que presta su nombre en un asunto ajeno*); muerto (*en los naipes*); cartas del muerto; muñeco (*figura de hombre*);

(print.) maqueta (*libro en blanco*); (rail.) locomotora de máquina condensadora; imitación, copia; (slang) estúpido; **to be dummy** hacer de muerto (*en los naipes*); *adj* falso, fingido, simulado, de imitación; de testaferro
dump [dʌmp] *s* montón de basuras; basurero (*sitio en donde se amontona la basura*); terreno echadizo; (min.) terrero; (mil.) depósito de municiones; **dumps** *spl* murria; **to be down in the dumps** tener murria, estar abatido; *va* descargar, verter; (coll.) inundar el mercado con; vaciar de golpe; *vn* arrojar la basura
dump body *s* caja de volquete (*de un camión*)
dump car *s* vagón de volteo, vagón volquete
dumpcart [ˈdʌmpˌkɑrt] *s* volquete
dumping [ˈdʌmpɪŋ] *s* descarga; inundación del mercado con mercancías a bajo precio
dumpish [ˈdʌmpɪʃ] *adj* lerdo, torpe; abatido, murrio
dumpling [ˈdʌmplɪŋ] *s* bola de pasta rellena de fruta o carne; bolita de pasta cocida con vapor
dump truck *s* camión volquete
dumpy [ˈdʌmpɪ] *adj* (*comp:* **-ier;** *super:* **-iest**) regordete; abatido, mohino, hosco
dun [dʌn] *s* acreedor importuno; apremio; color bruno; *adj* bruno, pardo; sombrío; (*pret & pp:* **dunned;** *ger:* **dunning**) *va* importunar, requerir para el pago
dunce [dʌns] *s* zopenco, estúpido
dunce cap o **dunce's cap** *s* gorro de forma de cono que se le pone al niño torpe
dunderhead [ˈdʌndərˌhɛd] *s* bodoque
dune [djun] o [dun] *s* duna
dung [dʌŋ] *s* estiércol; *va & vn* estercolar
dungaree [ˌdʌŋgəˈri] *s* tela basta de algodón; **dungarees** *spl* pantalones de tela basta de algodón
dungeon [ˈdʌndʒən] *s* calabozo, mazmorra; torre del homenaje, torre maestra; *va* encalabozar
dunghill [ˈdʌŋˌhɪl] *s* estercolar, estercolero; lugar emporcado; persona vil
dungy [ˈdʌŋɪ] *adj* estercolizo
dunk [dʌŋk] *va & vn* sopetear, ensopar, remojar
Dunkirk [ˈdʌnkʌrk] o [dʌnˈkʌrk] *s* Dunquerque
dunlin [ˈdʌnlɪn] *s* (orn.) tringa alpina
dunnage [ˈdʌnɪdʒ] *s* equipaje; (naut.) abarrote, maderos de estibar
duo [ˈdjuo] o [ˈduo] *s* (*pl:* **duos** o **dui** [ˈdjui] o [ˈdui]) var. de **duet**
duodecimal [ˌdjuoˈdɛsɪməl] o [ˌduoˈdɛsɪməl] *adj & s* duodecimal; **duodecimals** *spl* sistema duodecimal
duodecimo [ˌdjuoˈdɛsɪmo] o [ˌduoˈdɛsɪmo] *adj* en dozavo; *s* (*pl:* **-mos**) libro en dozavo
duodecuple [ˌdjuoˈdɛkjəpəl] o [ˌduoˈdɛkjəpəl] *adj* duodécuplo
duodenal [ˌdjuoˈdinəl] o [ˌduoˈdinəl] *adj* duodenal
duodenal ulcer *s* (path.) úlcera duodenal
duodenum [ˌdjuoˈdinəm] o [ˌduoˈdinəm] *s* (*pl:* **-na** [nə]) (anat.) duodeno
dupe [djup] o [dup] *s* primo, víctima, inocentón; *va* embaucar, engañar
duple [ˈdjupəl] o [ˈdupel] *adj* duplo, doble
duplex [ˈdjuplɛks] o [ˈduplɛks] *adj* doble, duplo, dúplice
duplex apartment *s* apartamiento cuyas piezas están en dos pisos
duplex house *s* casa para dos familias
duplex lock *s* cerradura de dos cilindros
duplex process *s* (metal.) dúplex
duplex telegraphy *s* dúplex
duplicate [ˈdjuplɪkɪt] o [ˈduplɪkɪt] *adj & s* duplicado; **in duplicate** por duplicado; en doble ejemplar; [ˈdjuplɪket] o [ˈduplɪket] *va* duplicar
duplication [ˌdjuplɪˈkeʃən] o [ˌduplɪˈkeʃən] *s* duplicación; duplicado
duplicator [ˈdjuplɪˌketər] o [ˈduplɪˌketər] *s* duplicador, multicopista
duplicity [djuˈplɪsɪtɪ] o [duˈplɪsɪtɪ] *s* (*pl:* **-ties**) duplicidad
durability [ˌdjurəˈbɪlɪtɪ] o [ˌdurəˈbɪlɪtɪ] *s* (*pl:* **-ties**) durabilidad
durable [ˈdjurəbəl] o [ˈdurəbəl] *adj* durable, duradero
durable goods *spl* artículos duraderos
duralumin [djuˈræljəmɪn] o [duˈræljəmɪn] *s* (trademark) duraluminio
dura mater [ˈdjurəˈmetər] o [ˈdurəˈmetər] *s* (anat.) duramadre o duramáter
duramen [djuˈremɛn] o [duˈremɛn] *s* (bot.) duramen
durance [ˈdjurəns] o [ˈdurəns] *s* prisión, cautividad; sempiterna (*tela*)
duration [djuˈreʃən] o [duˈreʃən] *s* duración; **for the duration (of the war)** para el término o la duración del conflicto
durative [ˈdjurətɪv] o [ˈdurətɪv] *adj* durativo; (gram.) durativo
durbar [ˈdʌrbɑr] *s* durbar
duress [ˈdjurɛs], [ˈdurɛs], [djuˈrɛs] o [duˈrɛs] *s* coacción, compulsión; prisión, cautividad
during [ˈdjurɪŋ] o [ˈdurɪŋ] *prep* durante
durmast [ˈdʌrmæst] o [ˈdʌrmɑst] *s* (bot.) melojo, roble borne (*Quercus pubescens*); (bot.) roble albero (*Quercus sessiliflora*)
durra [ˈdurə] *s* (bot.) durra, maíz de Guinea
durum [ˈdjurəm] o [ˈdurəm] *s* (bot.) trigo durillo, trigo duro
dusk [dʌsk] *s* crepúsculo vespertino, caída de la noche; *adj* obscuro; *va* obscurecer; *vn* anochecer
dusky [ˈdʌskɪ] *adj* (*comp:* **-ier;** *super:* **-iest**) obscuro, negruzco; abatido, lúgubre, triste
dust [dʌst] *s* polvo; cenizas (*restos mortales*); cosa inútil; condición vil; (slang) dinero; **to bite the dust** morder el polvo; **to kick up a dust** armar un alboroto; **to lick the dust** morder el polvo; **to raise a dust** armar un alboroto; **to shake the dust off one's feet** irse enojado; **to throw dust in one's eyes** engañarle a uno; *va* desempolvar (*quitar el polvo a*); polvorear (*esparcir polvo sobre*); **to dust off** desempolvar; **to dust one's jacket** (slang) sacudirle el polvo a uno
dustbin [ˈdʌstˌbɪn] *s* receptáculo para polvo, cenizas, etc.
dust bowl *s* cuenca de polvo
dustcloth [ˈdʌstˌklɔθ] o [ˈdʌstˌklɑθ] *s* trapo de polvo
dust cloud *s* polvareda, nube de polvo
duster [ˈdʌstər] *s* plumero, sacudidor (*mazo de plumas para quitar el polvo*); guardapolvo (*sobretodo*)
dust jacket *s* sobrecubierta (*de un libro encuadernado*)
dustless [ˈdʌstlɪs] *adj* sin polvo
dustpan [ˈdʌstˌpæn] *s* pala de recoger la basura
dust rag *s* trapo del polvo
dust storm *s* vendaval de polvo, tolvanera
dusty [ˈdʌstɪ] *adj* (*comp:* **-ier;** *super:* **-iest**) polvoriento, empolvado; grisáceo
Dutch [dʌtʃ] *adj* holandés; (slang) alemán; *spl* holandeses; (slang) alemanes; *ssg* holandés (*idioma*); (slang) alemán (*idioma*); **in Dutch** (slang) en la desgracia; (slang) en un apuro; **to beat the Dutch** (coll.) ser sorprendente, ser extraordinario; **to go Dutch** (coll.) pagar cada uno su escote
Dutch bond *s* (mas.) aparejo flamenco u holandés
Dutch Borneo [ˈbɔrnɪo] o [ˈbornɪo] *s* el Borneo Holandés
Dutch brass *s* tombac
Dutch cheese *s* queso de Holanda; naterón
Dutch clover *s* (bot.) trébol de Holanda
Dutch East Indies *spl* Indias Orientales Holandesas
Dutch Guiana *s* la Guayana Holandesa
Dutchman [ˈdʌtʃmən] *s* (*pl:* **-men**) holandés; buque holandés; (slang) alemán
Dutchman's-breeches [ˈdʌtʃmənzˈbrɪtʃɪz] *ssg & spl* (bot.) dicentra
Dutch New Guinea *s* la Nueva Guinea Holandesa
Dutch oven *s* cacerola con tapa bien cerrada; horno portátil
Dutch tile *s* azulejo
Dutch treat *s* (coll.) convite a escote
Dutch uncle *s* (coll.) mentor muy duro
Dutch West Indies *spl* Indias Occidentales Holandesas
duteous [ˈdjutɪəs] o [ˈdutɪəs] *adj* obediente, obsequioso

dutiable ['djutɪəbəl] o ['dutɪəbəl] *adj* sujeto a derechos de aduana
dutiful ['djutɪfəl] o ['dutɪfəl] *adj* obediente, sumiso, respetuoso; concienzudo
duty ['djutɪ] o ['dutɪ] *s* (*pl:* **-ties**) deber, obligación; obediencia, sumisión; quehacer, tarea, faena; derechos de aduana; **off duty** libre; **on duty** de servicio; de guardia; **to do duty for** servir en lugar de; **to take up one's duties** entrar en funciones
duty-free ['djutɪ'fri] o ['dutɪ'fri] *adj* libre de derechos
duumvir [dju'ʌmvər] o [du'ʌmvər] *s* (*pl:* **-virs** o **-viri** [vɪraɪ]) duunviro
duumviral [dju'ʌmvərəl] o [du'ʌmvərəl] *adj* duunviral
duumvirate [dju'ʌmvərɪt] o [du'ʌmvərɪt] *s* duunvirato
duvetyn ['duvətin] *s* tejido de lana que tiene una lanilla aterciopelada
D.V. abr. de **Deo volente** (Lat.) **God willing**
dwarf [dwɔrf] *adj & s* enano; *va* impedir el desarrollo de, impedir el crecimiento de; achicar, empequeñecer; *vn* achicarse, empequeñecerse
dwarf elder *s* (bot.) actea, yezgo
dwarf fan palm *s* (bot.) palmito, palmera enana o de abanico
dwarfish ['dwɔrfɪʃ] *adj* enano, diminuto
dwarf mallow *s* (bot.) malva de hoja redonda
dwarf star *s* (astr.) estrella enana
dwell [dwɛl] (*pret & pp:* **dwelled** o **dwelt**) *vn* vivir, morar; **to dwell on** o **upon** explayarse en; hacer hincapié en
dweller ['dwɛlər] *s* habitante, morador
dwelling ['dwɛlɪŋ] *s* vivienda, morada
dwelling house *s* casa, domicilio
dwelling place *s* habitación, morada
dwelt [dwɛlt] *pret & pp de* **dwell**
dwindle ['dwɪndəl] *va* disminuir; abatir, rebajar; *vn* disminuirse; consumirse
dwt. abr. de **pennyweight** o **pennyweights**
DX o **D.X.** (rad.) abr. de **distance**
dye [daɪ] *s* tinte; color, matiz; **of blackest dye** u **of deepest dye** de la clase más vil; (*pret & pp:* **dyed**; *ger:* **dyeing**) *va* teñir, tinturar
dyed-in-the-wool ['daɪdɪnðə,wʊl] *adj* teñido en rama; (fig.) intransigente, acérrimo
dyeing ['daɪɪŋ] *s* tintorería; tinte, tintura; *ger de* **dye**
dyer ['daɪər] *s* tintorero
dyer's-weed ['daɪərz,wid] *s* (bot.) retama de tintes o de tintoreros (*Genista tinctoria*); (bot.) gualda (*Reseda luteola*); (bot.) hierba pastel (*Isatis tinctoria*)
dyestuff ['daɪ,stʌf] *s* materia de tinte, materia colorante
dyeweed ['daɪ,wid] *s* (bot.) retama de tintes o de tintoreros
dyewood ['daɪ,wʊd] *s* madera de tinte
dying ['daɪɪŋ] *adj* moribundo, agonizante; mortal; *ger de* **die**
dyke [daɪk] *s & va* var. de **dike**
dynamic [daɪ'næmɪk] o [dɪ'næmɪk] *adj* dinámico; (fig.) dinámico; **dynamics** *ssg* dinámica
dynamical [daɪ'næmɪkəl] o [dɪ'næmɪkəl] *adj* dinámico
dynamic speaker *s* (rad.) altoparlante dinámico
dynamism ['daɪnəmɪzəm] o ['dɪnəmɪzəm] *s* (philos.) dinamismo
dynamist ['daɪnəmɪst] o ['dɪnəmɪst] *s* dinamista
dynamistic [,daɪnə'mɪstɪk] o [,dɪnə'mɪstɪk] *adj* dinamista
dynamite ['daɪnəmaɪt] *s* dinamita; *va* dinamitar
dynamiter ['daɪnə,maɪtər] *s* dinamitero
dynamo ['daɪnəmo] *s* (*pl:* **-mos**) dínamo
dynamoelectric [,daɪnəmo·ɪ'lɛktrɪk] *adj* dinamoeléctrico
dynamometer [,daɪnə'mɑmɪtər] *s* dinamómetro
dynamometric [,daɪnəmo'mɛtrɪk] *adj* dinamométrico
dynamometry [,daɪnə'mɑmɪtrɪ] *s* (mech.) dinamometría
dynamotor ['daɪnə,motər] *s* (elec.) dinamotor
dynast ['daɪnæst] o ['daɪnəst] *s* dinasta
dynastic [daɪ'næstɪk] o [dɪ'næstɪk] *adj* dinástico
dynasty ['daɪnəstɪ] *s* (*pl:* **-ties**) dinastía
dynatron ['daɪnətrɑn] *s* (phys. & rad.) dinatrón
dyne [daɪn] *s* (phys.) dina
dyschroa ['dɪskroə] *s* (path.) discromía
dyschromatopsia [,dɪskromə'tɑpsɪə] *s* (path.) discromatopsia
dyscrasia [dɪs'kreʒɪə] *s* (path.) discrasia
dysenteric [,dɪsən'tɛrɪk] *adj* disentérico
dysentery ['dɪsən,tɛrɪ] *s* (path.) disentería
dysesthesia [,dɪsɛs'θiʒɪə] *s* (path.) disestesia
dysfunction [dɪs'fʌŋkʃən] *s* (med.) disfunción
dyslalia [dɪs'lelɪə] *s* (med.) dislalia
dysmenorrhea o **dysmenorrhoea** [,dɪsmɛnə'riə] *s* (path.) dismenorrea
dyspepsia [dɪs'pɛpsɪə] o [dɪs'pɛpʃə] *s* (path.) dispepsia
dyspeptic [dɪs'pɛptɪk] *adj* dispéptico; triste, melancólico; *s* dispéptico
dyspeptically [dɪs'pɛptɪkəlɪ] *adv* con la dispepsia; como un dispéptico; tristemente, melancólicamente
dysphagia [dɪs'fedʒɪə] *s* (med.) disfagía
dysphasia [dɪs'feʒɪə] *s* (med.) disfasia
dyspnea [dɪsp'niə] *s* (path.) disnea
dysprosium [dɪs'prosɪəm] o [dɪs'proʃɪəm] *s* (chem.) disprosio
dystrophy ['dɪstrəfɪ] *s* (path.) distrofia
dysuria [dɪs'jʊrɪə] *s* (path.) disuria
dz. abr. de **dozen** o **dozens**

E

E, e [i] *s* (*pl:* **E's, e's** [iz]) quinta letra del alfabeto inglés
E. abr. de **east, eastern** y **engineer**
E abr. de **east, eastern** y **Excellent**
ea. abr. de **each**
each [itʃ] *adj indef* cada; *pron indef* cada uno, cada cual; **of each other** el uno del otro, los unos de los otros, p.ej., **they took leave of each other** se despidieron los unos de los otros; **each other** nos, os, se; uno a otro, unos a otros, p.ej., **they looked at each other** se miraron uno a otro; *adv* para o por cada uno; por persona
eager [ˈigər] *adj* anhelante, ansioso; ardiente, fogoso; encarnizado (*combate*); **to be eager for** anhelar o anhelar por; **to be eager to** + *inf* anhelar + *inf*, ansiar + *inf*
eager beaver *s* (coll.) entusiasta diligente
eagerness [ˈigərnɪs] *s* anhelo, ansia; ardor, fogosidad; encarnizamiento
eagle [ˈigəl] *s* (orn.) águila; (fig.) águila (*emblema; moneda de oro de los EE.UU.*); (*cap.*) *s* (astr.) Águila
eagle eye *s* ojo avizor
eagle-eyed [ˈigəlˌaɪd] *adj* de vista de águila; **to be eagle-eyed** tener vista de águila
eagle owl *s* (orn.) búho
eagle ray *s* (ichth.) águila
eaglestone [ˈigəlˌston] *s* (mineral.) etites
eaglet [ˈiglɪt] *s* (orn.) aguilucho
eaglewood [ˈigəlˌwʊd] *s* (bot.) agáloco
ear [ɪr] *s* oreja; oído (*sentido*); asa, asidero; mazorca (*de maíz*); (bot.) espiga; **by ear** de oído; **to be all ears** (coll.) abrir tanto oído o tanto el oído, ser todo oídos; **to fall on deaf ears** no recibir atención; **to give ear to** prestar oído a; **to go in one ear and out the other** entrar por un oído y salir por el otro; **to have a good ear** tener oído, tener buen oído; **to have** o **to keep an ear to the ground** (coll.) prestar atención para estar al corriente; **to have an ear for music** tener oído para la música; **to have the ear of** gozar de la confianza de, tener influencia con; **to lend an ear** abrir los oídos, prestar el oído o los oídos; **to prick up one's ears** aguzar los oídos, aguzar las orejas; **to set by the ears** enemistar, malquistar; **to turn a deaf ear** hacerse sordo, hacer oídos de mercader; **to turn a deaf ear to** no dar oídos a; **up to one's ears** (coll.) hasta los ojos (*p.ej., en amor, en trabajo*); *vn* espigar
earache [ˈɪrˌek] *s* dolor de oído
eardrop [ˈɪrˌdrɑp] *s* arete
eardrum [ˈɪrˌdrʌm] *s* (anat.) tímpano (*del oído*)
earflap [ˈɪrˌflæp] *s* orejera
earing [ˈɪrɪŋ] *s* (naut.) empuñidura
earl [ʌrl] *s* conde
earlap [ˈɪrˌlæp] *s* punta de la oreja; pabellón de la oreja; orejera (*de la gorra*)
earldom [ˈʌrldəm] *s* condado
early [ˈʌrlɪ] *adj* (*comp:* **-lier;** *super:* **-liest**) temprano; primero, antiguo; pronto, próximo, cercano; **at an early date** en fecha próxima; **the early part of** el principio de; **earlier** anterior; **early mass** misa de prima; **early times** tiempos remotos; *adv* (*comp:* **-lier;** *super:* **-liest**) temprano; al principio; en los primeros tiempos; **as early as** ya a (*cierta hora*); ya en (*cierta temporada, cierta época*); **as early as possible** lo más pronto posible; **early in** a principios de (*p.ej., el mes de febrero*); **early in the morning** muy de mañana; **one hour early** con una hora de anticipación; **to rise early** madrugar
early bird *s* madrugador
earmark [ˈɪrˌmɑrk] *s* marca en la oreja; señal, distintivo; *va* distinguir, designar, poner aparte (*para cierto uso*)
earmuff [ˈɪrˌmʌf] *s* orejera
earn [ʌrn] *va* ganar, ganarse; merecerse; obtener, conseguir, conquistar
earnest [ˈʌrnɪst] *adj* serio; celoso, diligente; **in earnest** en serio; de veras; *s* arras, prenda
earnest money *s* arras
earnestness [ˈʌrnɪstnɪs] *s* seriedad; celo, diligencia
earning [ˈʌrnɪŋ] *s* ganancia, rédito; salario
earphone [ˈɪrˌfon] *s* casquete o teléfono de cabeza, auricular
earpick [ˈɪrˌpɪk] *s* escarbaorejas
earring [ˈɪrˌrɪŋ] *s* arete
earshot [ˈɪrˌʃɑt] *s* alcance del oído; **within earshot** al alcance del oído
ear-splitting [ˈɪrˌsplɪtɪŋ] *adj* ensordecedor
earth [ʌrθ] *s* tierra; mundo; madriguera; (rad.) tierra; (chem.) tierra rara; **down to earth** práctico, prosaico; **to come back to earth** bajar de las nubes; **to run to earth** cazar hasta alcanzar, buscar hasta hallar
earthboard [ˈʌrθˌbord] *s* orejera del arado
earthborn [ˈʌrθˌbɔrn] *adj* terrígeno; mortal, humano; de nacimiento humilde
earthbound [ˈʌrθˌbaʊnd] *adj* ligado por los intereses terrenales
earthbred [ˈʌrθˌbrɛd] *adj* humilde, bajo, vil
earthen [ˈʌrθən] *adj* de tierra; de barro
earthenware [ˈʌrθənˌwɛr] *s* loza de barro; trastos, cacharros
earth inductor compass *s* (aer.) brújula de inducción terrestre
earthling [ˈʌrθlɪŋ] *s* habitante de la tierra; persona mundana
earthly [ˈʌrθlɪ] *adj* (*comp:* **-lier;** *super:* **-liest**) terrenal, mundano; concebible, posible; **to be of no earthly use** no servir para nada
earthnut [ˈʌrθˌnʌt] *s* (bot.) fruto subterráneo
earthquake [ˈʌrθˌkwek] *s* terremoto, temblor de tierra
earth-return circuit [ˈʌrθrɪˌtʌrn] *s* (elec.) circuito de retorno por tierra
earthward [ˈʌrθwərd] *adj & adv* hacia la tierra
earthwards [ˈʌrθwərdz] *adv* hacia la tierra
earthwork [ˈʌrθˌwʌrk] *s* (fort.) terraplén
earthworm [ˈʌrθˌwʌrm] *s* (zool.) gusano o lombriz de tierra
earthy [ˈʌrθɪ] *adj* (*comp:* **-ier;** *super:* **-iest**) terroso; basto, grosero; mundanal
ear trumpet *s* trompetilla acústica
earwax [ˈɪrˌwæks] *s* cera de los oídos, cerumen
earwig [ˈɪrˌwɪg] *s* (ent.) punzaorejas, tijereta
ease [iz] *s* facilidad; comodidad, soltura, desenvoltura, bienestar; **at ease** tranquilo, cómodo; (mil.) a discreción descanso; **to take one's ease** descansar, holgar; **with ease** con facilidad, sin esfuerzos; *va* facilitar; aliviar, mitigar; aligerar (*el peso*); aflojar, soltar; (naut.) arriar, lascar; **to ease someone of** u **out of something** (coll.) robar algo a alguien; **to ease someone out of a job** o **position** (coll.) facilitar la salida o la dimisión de una persona de un empleo o cargo; *vn* aliviarse, disminuir, aflojar; moverse lenta y suavemente
easel [ˈizəl] *s* caballete
easement [ˈizmənt] *s* alivio, comodidad; (law) servidumbre
easily [ˈizɪlɪ] *adv* fácilmente; sin duda; sobradamente, con mucho; probablemente
easiness [ˈizɪnɪs] *s* facilidad; soltura, desenvoltura; descuido, indiferencia
east [ist] *s* este, oriente; **down East** en o hacia la Nueva Inglaterra, EE.UU.; *adj* del este, oriental; *adv* al este
East Berlin *s* el Berlín-Este

East China Sea *s* mar Oriental, mar de la China Oriental
Easter ['istər] *s* pascua de flores, pascua florida, pascua de resurrección
Easter egg *s* huevo duro decorado que sirve de regalo en el día de Pascuas
Easter Island *s* Isla de Pascua
easterly ['istərlɪ] *adj* oriental; que viene desde el este; que va hacia el este; *adv* desde el este; hacia el este
Easter Monday *s* lunes de Pascua (*de resurrección*)
eastern ['istərn] *adj* oriental
eastern cardinal *s* (orn.) cardenal de Virginia
Eastern Church *s* Iglesia de Oriente
easterner ['istərnər] *s* habitante del este
Eastern Hemisphere *s* hemisferio oriental
easternmost ['istərnmost] *adj* (el) más oriental
Eastern Roman Empire *s* Imperio de Oriente
Eastern standard time *s* (U.S.A.) hora legal correspondiente al meridiano 75°
Easter Sunday *s* domingo de resurrección
Eastertide ['istər,taɪd] *s* aleluya
East Germany *s* la Alemania Oriental
East India *s* o **East Indies** *spl* Indias Orientales
East Indian *adj* & *s* indiano
east-northeast ['ist,nɔrθ'ist] *s* esnordeste o lesnordeste
East Prussia *s* la Prusia Oriental
east-southeast ['ist,saʊθ'ist] *s* essudeste, essueste o lesueste
eastward ['istwərd] *adj* que va hacia el este; *s* este; *adv* hacia el este
eastwardly ['istwərdlɪ] *adj* que va hacia el este; *adv* hacia el este
eastwards ['istwərdz] *adv* hacia el este
easy ['izɪ] *adj* (*comp:* **-ier**; *super:* **-iest**) fácil; cómodo, holgado; holgazán; lento, pausado, moderado; (coll.) fácil de engañar; (com.) abundante (*dinero*); **on easy street** (coll.) con el bolsillo lastrado; *adv* (coll.) fácilmente; (coll.) despacio; **to take it easy** (coll.) descansar, holgar; (coll.) no afanarse; (coll.) ir despacio; (coll.) proceder con cuidado; **easy there!** (coll.) ¡despacio!
easy chair *s* poltrona
easy-going ['izɪ'go·ɪŋ] *adj* despacioso, holgazán, dejado y flojo, flojo y condescendiente
easy mark *s* inocentón
easy money *s* dinero ganado sin pena
easy payments *spl* facilidades de pago
eat [it] (*pret:* **ate**; *pp:* **eaten**) *va* comer; comerse (*producir comiendo*); **to eat away** corroer; **to eat crow** (coll.) cantar la palinodia; **to eat humble pie** humillarse cediendo; **to eat one's heart out** sufrir en silencio; **to eat one's words** retractarse, retirar sus palabras; **to eat up** devorar; destruir; *vn* comer
eatable ['itəbəl] *adj* comestible, comible; **eatables** *spl* comestibles, alimentos
eaten ['itən] *pp de* **eat**
eater ['itər] *s* comedor; comilón
Eau de Cologne [,o də kə'lon] *s* agua de Colonia
eau de vie [,o də 'vi] *s* aguardiente
eaves [ivz] *spl* alero, tejaroz, socarrén
eaves board *s* contrapar
eavesdrop ['ivz,drɑp] (*pret & pp:* **-dropped**; *ger:* **-dropping**) *vn* escuchar a las puertas, estar de escucha
eavesdropper ['ivz,drɑpər] *s* escuchador a las puertas, escuchador escondido
ebb [ɛb] *s* (naut.) menguante, reflujo; decadencia; **at low ebb** decaído; *vn* bajar (*la marea*); decaer
ebb and flow *s* flujo y reflujo
ebb tide *s* marea menguante
ebenaceous [,ɛbɪ'neʃəs] *adj* (bot.) ebenáceo
ebonite ['ɛbənaɪt] *s* ebonita
ebony ['ɛbənɪ] *s* (*pl:* **-ies**) (bot.) ébano (*árbol y madera*); *adj* de ébano, hecho de ébano; negro
ebullience [ɪ'bʌljəns] *s* ebullición; exaltación, entusiasmo
ebullient [ɪ'bʌljənt] *adj* hirviente; exaltado, entusiasta
ebulliometer [ɪ,bʌlɪ'ɑmɪtər] *s* ebullómetro
ebullioscope [ɪ'bʌlɪə,skop] *s* ebulloscopio
ebullition [,ɛbə'lɪʃən] *s* ebullición; arranque, viva emoción
eburnation [,ibər'neʃən] *s* (path.) eburnación
écarté [,ekɑr'te] *s* ecarté
ecce homo ['ɛksɪ'homo] *s* eccehomo (*imagen*)
eccentric [ɛk'sɛntrɪk] *adj* excéntrico; *s* excéntrico; (mach.) excéntrica
eccentrically [ɛk'sɛntrɪkəlɪ] *adv* excéntricamente
eccentricity [,ɛksɛn'trɪsɪtɪ] *s* (*pl:* **-ties**) excentricidad
ecchymosis [,ɛkɪ'mosɪs] *s* (*pl:* **-ses** [siz]) (path.) equimosis
Eccl. o **Eccles.** abr. de **Ecclesiastes**
Ecclesiastes [ɪ,klizɪ'æstiz] *s* (Bib.) el Eclesiastés
ecclesiastic [ɪ,klizɪ'æstɪk] *adj* & *s* eclesiástico
ecclesiastical [ɪ,klizɪ'æstɪkəl] *adj* eclesiástico
Ecclesiasticus [ɪ,klizɪ'æstɪkəs] *s* (Bib.) el Eclesiástico
echelon ['ɛʃəlɑn] *s* escalón (*grado a que se asciende en autoridad*); (mil.) escalón; *va* (mil.) escalonar
echidna [ɪ'kɪdnə] *s* (zool.) equidna
echinococcus [ɪ,kaɪnə'kɑkəs] *s* (*pl:* **-cocci** ['kɑksaɪ]) (zool.) equinococo
echinoderm [ɪ'kaɪnədʌrm] *s* (zool.) equinodermo
echinus [ɪ'kaɪnəs] *s* (*pl:* **-ni** [naɪ]) (arch. & zool.) equino
echo ['ɛko] *s* (*pl:* **-oes**) eco; (*cap.*) *s* (myth.) Eco; (*l.c.*) *va* repetir (*un sonido*); imitar; *vn* hacer eco, resonar
echoic [ɛ'ko·ɪk] *adj* ecoico
echolalia [,ɛko'lelɪə] *s* (psychol.) ecolalia
éclair [e'klɛr] *s* pastelillo o bollo de crema
eclampsia [ɛk'læmpsɪə] *s* (path.) eclampsia
éclat [e'klɑ] *s* brillo, resplandor; éxito brillante; renombre; aclamación
eclectic [ɛk'lɛktɪk] *adj* & *s* ecléctico
eclecticism [ɛk'lɛktɪsɪzəm] *s* eclecticismo
eclipse [ɪ'klɪps] *s* (astr. & fig.) eclipse; *va* (astr. & fig.) eclipsar
ecliptic [ɪ'klɪptɪk] *adj* eclíptico; *s* eclíptica
ecliptical [ɪ'klɪptɪkəl] *adj* eclíptico
eclogue ['ɛklɔg] o ['ɛklɑg] *s* égloga
ecologist [i'kɑlədʒɪst] *s* ecólogo
ecology [i'kɑlədʒɪ] *s* ecología
economic [,ikə'nɑmɪk] o [,ɛkə'nɑmɪk] *adj* económico; **economics** *ssg* economía política
economical [,ikə'nɑmɪkəl] o [,ɛkə'nɑmɪkəl] *adj* económico
economically [,ikə'nɑmɪkəlɪ] o [,ɛkə'nɑmɪkəlɪ] *adv* económicamente
economist [ɪ'kɑnəmɪst] *s* economista
economize [ɪ'kɑnəmaɪz] *va* & *vn* economizar
economizer [ɪ'kɑnə,maɪzər] *s* (mach.) economizador
economy [ɪ'kɑnəmɪ] *s* (*pl:* **-mies**) economía
ecru o **écru** ['ɛkru] o ['ekru] *adj* crudo, sin blanquear; *s* tejido sin blanquear
ecstasy ['ɛkstəsɪ] *s* (*pl:* **-sies**) éxtasis
ecstatic [ɛk'stætɪk] *adj* extático
ecstatically [ɛk'stætɪkəlɪ] *adv* extáticamente
ectasia [ɛk'teʒɪə] *s* (path.) ectasia
ectasis ['ɛktəsɪs] *s* (pros.) ectasis
ectoblast ['ɛktoblæst] *s* (embryol.) ectoblasto
ectoderm ['ɛktodʌrm] *s* (embryol.) ectodermo
ectoparasite [,ɛkto'pærəsaɪt] *s* (zool.) ectoparásito
ectopia [ɛk'topɪə] *s* (path.) ectopia
ectoplasm ['ɛktoplæzəm] *s* (biol. & spiritualism) ectoplasma
ectropion [ɛk'tropɪən] *s* (path.) ectropión
Ecuador ['ɛkwədɔr] *s* el Ecuador
Ecuadoran [,ɛkwə'dorən] o **Ecuadorian** [,ɛkwə'dorɪən] *adj* & *s* ecuatoriano
Ecuadorianism [,ɛkwə'dorɪənɪzəm] *s* ecuatorianismo
ecumenic [,ɛkjʊ'mɛnɪk] o **ecumenical** [,ɛkjʊ'mɛnɪkəl] *adj* ecuménico
eczema ['ɛksɪmə] o [ɛg'zimə] *s* (path.) eczema
eczematous [ɛk'zɛmətəs] *adj* eczematoso
ed. abr. de **edited, edition** y **editor**
Ed [ɛd] *s* nombre abreviado de **Edward, Edwin, Edgar** y **Edmund**
Edam cheese ['idæm] o ['idəm] *s* queso de Edam, queso de Holanda
edaphology [,ɛdə'fɑlədʒɪ] *s* edafología
Edda ['ɛdə] *s* (lit.) edda

eddy [ˈɛdɪ] *s* (*pl:* **-dies**) remolino; (*pret & pp:* **-died**) *va & vn* remolinear
eddy current *s* (elec.) corriente parásita, corriente de Foucault
edelweiss [ˈedəlvaɪs] *s* (bot.) edelweiss, estrella de los Alpes, pie de león
edema [iˈdimə] *s* (*pl:* **-mata** [mətə]) (path.) edema
edematous [iˈdɛmətəs] *adj* edematoso
Eden [ˈidən] *s* (Bib. & fig.) edén
Edenic [iˈdɛnɪk] *adj* edénico
edentate [iˈdɛntet] *adj* desdentado; *s* (zool.) desdentado
edge [ɛdʒ] *s* filo (*de un instrumento cortante*); margen, borde, orilla; ángulo, esquina, punta; canto (*p.ej., de una mesa*); corte (*de cuchillo, espada o libro*); (sew.) ribete; (fig.) punta, acrimonia; (slang) ventaja; **on edge** de canto; (fig.) nervioso; **to have the edge on** (slang) llevar ventaja a; **to set on edge** poner nervioso; **to set the teeth on edge** dar dentera; **to take the edge off** embotar; (fig.) embotar ‖ *va* afilar, aguzar; bordear; (sew.) ribetear; aguijonear, incitar; abrirse (*paso*) marchando de lado; mover poco a poco de canto; **to edge out** hacer salir empujando poco a poco ‖ *vn* avanzar de lado; **to edge in** abrirse paso, lograr entrar; **to edge up** subir un poco
edgeways [ˈɛdʒˌwez] *adv* de filo, de canto, de lado; **to get a word in edgeways** lograr decir una palabra; **to not let a person get a word in edgeways** no dejarle a uno meter baza
edgewise [ˈɛdʒˌwaɪz] *adv* var. de **edgeways**
edging [ˈɛdʒɪŋ] *s* orla, ribete; pestaña (*encaje*)
edgy [ˈɛdʒɪ] *adj* angular; nervioso, irritable
edibility [ˌɛdɪˈbɪlɪtɪ] *s* (lo) comestible
edible [ˈɛdɪbəl] *adj & s* comestible
edict [ˈidɪkt] *s* edicto
edification [ˌɛdɪfɪˈkeʃən] *s* edificación (*enseñanza, beneficios espirituales*)
edifice [ˈɛdɪfɪs] *s* edificio
edify [ˈɛdɪfaɪ] (*pret & pp:* **-fied**) *va* edificar (*instruir o inspirar en materia de moral, fe, etc.*)
edifying [ˈɛdɪˌfaɪɪŋ] *adj* edificante
edile [ˈidaɪl] *s* edil
Edinburgh [ˈɛdɪnbərə] o [ˈɛdɪnˌbʌro] *s* Edimburgo
edit. abr. de **edited, edition** y **editor**
edit [ˈɛdɪt] *va* preparar para la imprenta; corregir para la imprenta; dirigir, redactar (*un periódico*)
Edith [ˈidɪθ] *s* Edita
edition [ɪˈdɪʃən] *s* edición
editor [ˈɛdɪtər] *s* director, redactor (*de un periódico o revista*); revisor (*de un manuscrito*); editor (*de artículos de fondo*)
editorial [ˌɛdɪˈtorɪəl] *adj* editorial; de redacción; *s* editorial, artículo de fondo
editorialize [ˌɛdɪˈtorɪəlaɪz] *vn* editorializar, expresar opiniones en un artículo de fondo
editorially [ˌɛdɪˈtorɪəlɪ] *adv* en un editorial; como en un editorial
editorial staff *s* redacción, cuerpo de redacción, consejo de redacción
editor in chief *s* jefe de redacción
editorship [ˈɛdɪtərˌʃɪp] *s* redacción; dirección (*de un periódico o revista*)
Edmund [ˈɛdmənd] *s* Edmundo
educable [ˈɛdʒəkəbəl] o [ˈɛdʒʊkəbəl] *adj* educable
educate [ˈɛdʒəket] o [ˈɛdʒʊket] *va* educar
education [ˌɛdʒəˈkeʃən] o [ˌɛdʒʊˈkeʃən] *s* educación, instrucción; instrucción pública
educational [ˌɛdʒəˈkeʃənəl] o [ˌɛdʒʊˈkeʃənəl] *adj* educacional
educational institution *s* centro docente
educative [ˈɛdʒəˌketɪv] o [ˈɛdʒʊˌketɪv] *adj* educativo
educator [ˈɛdʒəˌketər] o [ˈɛdʒʊˌketər] *s* educador
educe [ɪˈdjus] o [ɪˈdus] *va* educir
Edward [ˈɛdwərd] *s* Eduardo
Edwardian [ɛdˈwərdɪən] *adj* eduardiano
Edwin [ˈɛdwɪn] *s* Eduíno
eel [il] *s* (ichth.) anguila; (ichth.) lamprea; **to be as slippery as an eel** escurrirse como una anguila
eelgrass [ˈilˌgræs] o [ˈilˌgrɑs] *s* (bot.) zostera marina
eelpot [ˈilˌpɑt] *s* nasa para anguilas
eelpout [ˈilˌpaʊt] *s* (ichth.) zoarce
eelworm [ˈilˌwʌrm] *s* (zool.) anguílula
e'en [in] *adv* (poet.) var. de **even**
e'er [ɛr] *adv* (poet.) var. de **ever**
eerie o **eery** [ˈɪrɪ] o [ˈirɪ] *adj* (*comp:* **-rier**; *super:* **-riest**) misterioso, espectral; miedoso, tímido
effect [ɪˈfɛkt] *s* efecto; **effects** *spl* efectos; **for effect** sólo por impresionar; **in effect** en efecto, en realidad; vigente, en operación; **of no effect** sin resultado; **to feel the effect of** resentirse de; **to give effect to** activar, poner en efecto; **to go into effect** o **to take effect** hacerse vigente, ponerse en operación; **to put into effect** poner en vigor; **to the effect that** en el sentido de que; *va* efectuar
effective [ɪˈfɛktɪv] *adj* eficaz; vigente; impresionante; **effectives** *spl* (mil.) efectivos
effectual [ɪˈfɛktʃʊəl] *adj* eficaz
effectually [ɪˈfɛktʃʊəlɪ] *adv* eficazmente
effectuate [ɪˈfɛktʃʊet] *va* efectuar
effeminacy [ɪˈfɛmɪnəsɪ] *s* afeminación, afeminamiento
effeminate [ɪˈfɛmɪnɪt] *adj* afeminado; [ɪˈfɛmɪnet] *va* afeminar; *vn* afeminarse
effemination [ɪˌfɛmɪˈneʃən] *s* afeminación
effendi [ɪˈfɛndɪ] *s* (*pl:* **-dis**) efendi
efferent [ˈɛfərənt] *adj* (physiol.) eferente
effervesce [ˌɛfərˈvɛs] *vn* estar en efervescencia
effervescence [ˌɛfərˈvɛsəns] *s* efervescencia
effervescent [ˌɛfərˈvɛsənt] *adj* efervescente
effete [ɪˈfit] *adj* usado, gastado; estéril, infructuoso; decadente
efficacious [ˌɛfɪˈkeʃəs] *adj* eficaz
efficacy [ˈɛfɪkəsɪ] *s* (*pl:* **-cies**) eficacia
efficiency [ɪˈfɪʃənsɪ] *s* (*pl:* **-cies**) eficiencia; (mech.) rendimiento, efecto útil, eficiencia
efficiency engineering *s* taylorismo, organización científica
efficient [ɪˈfɪʃənt] *adj* eficiente; (mech.) de buen rendimiento
effigy [ˈɛfɪdʒɪ] *s* (*pl:* **-gies**) efigie; **to burn in effigy** quemar en efigie; **to hang in effigy** ahorcar en efigie
effloresce [ˌɛfloˈrɛs] *vn* florecer, echar flores; (chem.) eflorecerse
efflorescence [ˌɛfloˈrɛsəns] *s* (bot. & chem.) eflorescencia
efflorescent [ˌɛfloˈrɛsənt] *adj* (bot. & chem.) eflorescente
effluence [ˈɛflʊəns] *s* efluencia, emanación
effluent [ˈɛflʊənt] *adj* efluente; *s* corriente efluente
effluvium [ɪˈfluvɪəm] *s* (*pl:* **-via** [vɪə] o **-viums**) efluvio
effort [ˈɛfərt] *s* esfuerzo; obra; **to make every effort to** + *inf* hacer lo posible por + *inf*
effrontery [ɪˈfrʌntərɪ] *s* (*pl:* **-ies**) desfachatez, impudencia
effulgence [ɪˈfʌldʒəns] *s* refulgencia
effulgent [ɪˈfʌldʒənt] *adj* refulgente
effuse [ɪˈfjuz] *va* verter, derramar; *vn* emanar
effusion [ɪˈfjuʒən] *s* efusión; (fig.) efusión
effusive [ɪˈfjusɪv] *adj* efusivo; (geol. & fig.) efusivo
eft [ɛft] *s* (zool.) tritón; (zool.) lagartija
e.g. abr. de **exempli gratia** (Lat.) **for example**
Eg. abr. de **Egypt** y **Egyptian**
egg [ɛg] *s* huevo; (arch.) ova (*que alterna con el dardo*); (slang) sujeto, buen sujeto; **to have** o **to put all one's eggs in one basket** jugarlo todo a una carta; *va* mezclar o cubrir con huevos; (coll.) arrojar huevos a; **to egg on** incitar
egg beater *s* batidor de huevos
egg cell *s* (biol.) óvulo
eggcup [ˈɛgˌkʌp] *s* huevera
egg glass *s* reloj de arena de unos tres minutos para hervir huevos
egghead [ˈɛgˌhɛd] *s* (slang) intelectual
eggnog [ˈɛgˌnɑg] *s* yema mejida, caldo de la reina, ponche de huevo
eggplant [ˈɛgˌplænt] o [ˈɛgˌplɑnt] *s* (bot.) berenjena
egg-shaped [ˈɛgˌʃept] *adj* oviforme

eggshell ['ɛg,ʃɛl] *s* cáscara de huevo, cascarón
egg whisk *s* (Brit.) var. de **egg beater**
egis ['idʒɪs] *s* var. de **aegis**
eglantine ['ɛgləntaɪn] *s* (bot.) eglantina (*Rosa eglanteria y R. canina*); (bot.) rosa fétida; (bot.) madreselva
ego ['igo] o ['ɛgo] *s* (*pl:* **-gos**) yo; (coll.) egotismo
egocentric [,igo'sɛntrɪk] o [,ɛgo'sɛntrɪk] *adj & s* egocéntrico
egoism ['igo·ɪzəm] o ['ɛgo·ɪzəm] *s* egoísmo; egotismo
egoist ['igo·ɪst] o ['ɛgo·ɪst] *s* egoísta; egotista
egoistic [,igo'ɪstɪk] o [,ɛgo'ɪstɪk] *adj* egoísta; egotista
egotism ['igotɪzəm] o ['ɛgotɪzəm] *s* egotismo; egoísmo
egotist ['igotɪst] o ['ɛgotɪst] *s* egotista; egoísta
egotistic [,igo'tɪstɪk] o [,ɛgo'tɪstɪk] o **egotistical** [,igo'tɪstɪkəl] o [,ɛgo'tɪstɪkəl] *adj* egotista; egoísta
egregious [ɪ'gridʒəs] *adj* (obs.) egregio; atroz, enorme
egress ['igrɛs] *s* salida
egret ['igrɛt] *s* var. de **aigrette**
Egypt ['idʒɪpt] *s* Egipto
Egyptian [ɪ'dʒɪpʃən] *adj & s* egipcio; gitano
Egyptian vulture *s* (orn.) alimoche
Egyptological [ɪ,dʒɪptə'lɑdʒɪkəl] *adj* egiptológico
Egyptologist [,idʒɪp'tɑlədʒɪst] *s* egiptólogo
Egyptology [,idʒɪp'tɑlədʒɪ] *s* egiptología
eh [e] *interj* ¡eh!
E.I. abr. de **East Indian**
eider ['aɪdər] *s* (orn.) eíder, pato de flojel
eider down *s* edredón
eider duck *s* (orn.) eíder, pato de flojel
eight [et] *adj* ocho; *s* ocho; **eight o'clock** las ocho
eight ball *s* bola negra del juego de trucos, señalada con el número ocho; **behind the eight ball** (slang) en situación peligrosa, en situación dificultosa
eight-cylinder ['et,sɪlɪndər] *adj* (mach.) de ocho cilindros; **an eight-cylinder V motor** un ocho cilindros en V
eight-day clock ['et'de] *s* reloj de ocho días cuerda
eighteen ['e'tin] *adj & s* dieciocho o diez y ocho
eighteenth ['e'tinθ] *adj* décimoctavo; dieciochavo; *s* décimoctavo; dieciochavo; dieciocho (*en las fechas*)
eighteenth-century ['e'tinθ'sɛntʃərɪ] *adj* dieciochesco, dieciochista
eightfold ['et,fold] *adj & s* óctuple, óctuplo; *adv* ocho veces
eighth [etθ] *adj* octavo; *s* octavo; ocho (*en las fechas*); (mus.) octava
eight hundred *adj & s* ochocientos
eightieth ['etɪɪθ] *adj & s* octogésimo; ochentavo
eighty ['etɪ] *adj* ochenta; *s* (*pl:* **-ties**) ochenta
eikon ['aɪkɑn] *s* var. de **icon**
einsteinium [aɪn'staɪnɪəm] *s* (chem.) einsteinio
Eire ['ɛrə] *s* Eire
either ['iðər] o ['aɪðər] *adj* uno u otro, cualquier . . . de los dos; cada (*de los dos*); *pron* uno u otro, cualquiera de los dos; *adv* tampoco; *conj* o sea; **either . . . or** o . . . o
ejaculate [ɪ'dʒækjəlet] o [i'dʒækjʊlet] *va & vn* proferir de repente; (physiol.) eyacular
ejaculation [ɪ,dʒækjə'leʃən] o [i,dʒækjʊ'leʃən] *s* exclamación; jaculatoria (*oración breve y ferviente*); (physiol.) eyaculación
ejaculatory [ɪ'dʒækjələ,torɪ] o [i'dʒækjʊlə,torɪ] *adj* exclamatorio; jaculatorio (*breve y ferviente*); (physiol.) eyaculador
ejaculatory duct *s* (anat.) conducto eyaculador
eject [ɪ'dʒɛkt] *va* echar, arrojar, expulsar
ejection [ɪ'dʒɛkʃən] *s* expulsión; deyección (*p.ej., de un volcán*)
ejection seat *s* (aer.) asiento lanzable
ejectment [ɪ'dʒɛktmənt] *s* expulsión, exclusión
ejector [ɪ'dʒɛktər] *s* expulsador; (mach.) eyector; expulsor (*de arma de fuego*)
eke [ik] *va* aumentar con dificultad; **to eke out** ganar a duras penas
el [ɛl] *s* ana (*medida*); pabellón (*edificio contiguo*); (coll.) ferrocarril aéreo, ferrocarril elevado
elaborate [ɪ'læbərɪt] *adj* elaborado; complicado; [ɪ'læbəret] *va* elaborar; (physiol.) elaborar; *vn* explicarse con muchos detalles
elaboration [ɪ,læbə'reʃən] *s* elaboración
elaeagnaceous [,ɛlɪæg'neʃəs] *adj* (bot.) eleagnáceo
Elaine [ɪ'len] *s* Elena
élan [e'lɑ̃] *s* entusiasmo, vivacidad
eland ['ilənd] *s* (zool.) oreas
élan vital [vi'tɑl] *s* fuerza vital
elapse [ɪ'læps] *vn* pasar, transcurrir, mediar
elasmobranch [ɪ'læsməbræŋk] o [ɪ'læzməbræŋk] *s* (ichth.) elasmobranquio
elastic [ɪ'læstɪk] *adj & s* elástico
elastically [ɪ'læstɪkəlɪ] *adv* elásticamente
elasticity [ɪ,læs'tɪsɪtɪ] o [,ilæs'tɪsɪtɪ] *s* elasticidad
elastin [ɪ'læstɪn] *s* (biochem.) elastina
elate [ɪ'let] *va* regocijar, exaltar
elated [ɪ'letɪd] *adj* regocijado, exaltado
elaterin [ɪ'lætərɪn] *s* (chem.) elaterina
elation [ɪ'leʃən] *s* regocijo, exaltación, viva alegría
elbow ['ɛlbo] *s* codo (*del brazo o la manga*); (mach.) codo; recodo (*p.ej., de un río*); brazo (*de sillón*); **at one's elbow** a la mano, muy cerca; **out at the elbow** andrajoso; **to crook the elbow** (slang) empinar el codo; **to rub elbows with** rozarse mucho con; **up to the elbows** hasta los codos; *va* empujar codeando; **to elbow one's way through** abrirse paso codeando, abrirse paso a codazos; *vn* codear; formar recodos
elbow bender *s* (slang) aficionado a empinar el codo
elbow grease *s* (coll.) trabajo manual, duro esfuerzo, jugo de muñeca, betún de saliva, manteca de codo
elbow patch *s* codera
elbow rest *s* ménsula
elbowroom ['ɛlbo,rum] o ['ɛlbo,rʊm] *s* amplio espacio, espacio suficiente; libertad de acción
elder ['ɛldər] *adj* mayor; *s* mayor; anciano; señor mayor; (eccl.) anciano; (bot.) saúco
elderberry ['ɛldər,bɛrɪ] *s* (*pl:* **-ries**) (bot.) saúco; baya del saúco
elderly ['ɛldərlɪ] *adj* viejo, anciano, mayor
eldership ['ɛldərʃɪp] *s* señorío
eldest ['ɛldɪst] *adj super* (el) más viejo, (el) mayor
El Dorado [ɛldə'rɑdo] *s* (*pl:* **-dos**) Eldorado
Eleanor ['ɛlənər] *s* Leonor
Eleatic [,ɛlɪ'ætɪk] *adj & s* eleático
elec. abr. de **electrical** y **electricity**
elecampane [,ɛlɪkəm'pen] *s* (bot.) énula campana, helenio
elect [ɪ'lɛkt] *adj* elegido, electo; *s* electo; **the elect** los elegidos o los escogidos (*por Dios*); los privilegiados; *va* elegir
election [ɪ'lɛkʃən] *s* elección; (theol.) elección, predestinación
electioneer [ɪ,lɛkʃə'nɪr] *vn* solicitar votos, hacer campaña electoral
elective [ɪ'lɛktɪv] *adj* electivo; *s* curso o asignatura electiva
elector [ɪ'lɛktər] *s* elector
electoral [ɪ'lɛktərəl] *adj* electoral
electoral college *s* colegio electoral
electorate [ɪ'lɛktərɪt] *s* electorado
Electra [ɪ'lɛktrə] *s* (myth.) Electra
Electra complex *s* (psychoanal.) complejo de Electra
electress [ɪ'lɛktrɪs] *s* electriz (*mujer o viuda de un príncipe elector*); electora (*mujer que tiene derecho para elegir*)
electric [ɪ'lɛktrɪk] *adj* eléctrico; *s* (coll.) tranvía eléctrico, ferrocarril eléctrico
electrical [ɪ'lɛktrɪkəl] *adj* eléctrico
electrical engineer *s* ingeniero electricista
electrical engineering *s* electrotecnia, ingeniería electricista, ingeniería eléctrica
electrically [ɪ'lɛktrɪkəlɪ] *adv* eléctricamente
electrical transcription *s* transcripción eléctrica
electric blanket *s* cobija eléctrica
electric chair *s* silla eléctrica
electric clock *s* reloj eléctrico
electric column *s* pila voltaica

electric eel *s* (ichth.) anguila eléctrica
electric eye *s* ojo eléctrico
electric fan *s* ventilador eléctrico
electric heating pad *s* almohadilla caliente eléctrica
electric hot-water heater *s* termos eléctrico
electrician [ɪ,lɛk'trɪʃən] o [,ɛlɛk'trɪʃən] *s* electricista
electricity [ɪ,lɛk'trɪsɪtɪ] o [,ɛlɛk'trɪsɪtɪ] *s* electricidad
electric percolator *s* cafetera eléctrica
electric-powered [ɪ'lɛktrɪk'paʊərd] *adj* accionado eléctricamente
electric ray *s* (ichth.) pez eléctrico, tremielga, torpedo
electric razor *s* máquina de afeitar eléctrica
electric refrigerator *s* nevera eléctrica
electric shaver *s* electroafeitadora
electric steel *s* acero de horno eléctrico
electric tape *s* cinta aislante
electric varnish *s* barniz aislador
electrification [ɪ,lɛktrɪfɪ'keʃən] *s* electrificación
electrify [ɪ'lɛktrɪfaɪ] (*pret & pp:* **-fied**) *va* electrificar, electrizar; (fig.) electrizar
electrocardiogram [ɪ,lɛktro'kardɪo,græm] *s* electrocardiograma
electrocardiograph [ɪ,lɛktro'kardɪo,græf] o [ɪ,lɛktro'kardɪo,graf] *s* electrocardiógrafo
electrochemical [ɪ,lɛktro'kɛmɪkəl] *adj* electroquímico
electrochemistry [ɪ,lɛktro'kɛmɪstrɪ] *s* electroquímica
electro-convulsive treatment [ɪ,lɛktrokən'vʌlsɪv] *s* electroshockterapia
electrocute [ɪ'lɛktrəkjut] *va* electrocutar
electrocution [ɪ,lɛktrə'kjuʃən] *s* electrocución
electrode [ɪ'lɛktrod] *s* electrodo
electrodynamic [ɪ,lɛktrodaɪ'næmɪk] *adj* electrodinámico; **electrodynamics** *ssg* electrodinámica
electrolier [ɪ,lɛktro'lɪr] *s* araña de lámparas eléctricas
electrolysis [ɪ,lɛk'tralɪsɪs] o [,ɛlɛk'tralɪsɪs] *s* (chem. & surg.) electrólisis; depilación con aguja electrificada
electrolyte [ɪ'lɛktrolaɪt] *s* electrólito
electrolytic [ɪ,lɛktro'lɪtɪk] *adj* electrolítico
electrolytically [ɪ,lɛktro'lɪtɪkəlɪ] *adv* electrolíticamente
electrolytic condenser *s* (rad.) condensador electrolítico
electrolyzation [ɪ,lɛktrəlɪ'zeʃən] *s* electrolización
electrolyze [ɪ'lɛktrolaɪz] *va* electrolizar
electromagnet [ɪ,lɛktro'mægnɪt] *s* electroimán, electro
electromagnetic [ɪ,lɛktromæg'nɛtɪk] *adj* electromagnético
electromagnetic induction *s* (elec.) inducción electromagnética
electromagnetic speaker *s* (rad.) altavoz o altoparlante electromagnético
electromagnetism [ɪ,lɛktro'mægnɪtɪzəm] *s* electromagnetismo
electrometallurgy [ɪ,lɛktro'mɛtəlʌrdʒɪ] *s* electrometalurgia
electrometer [ɪ,lɛk'tramɪtər] o [,ɛlɛk'tramɪtər] *s* electrómetro
electrometric [ɪ,lɛktro'mɛtrɪk] *adj* electrométrico
electrometry [ɪ,lɛk'tramɪtrɪ] o [,ɛlɛk'tramɪtrɪ] *s* electrometría
electromotive [ɪ,lɛktro'motɪv] *adj* electromotor
electromotive force *s* fuerza electromotriz
electromotor [ɪ,lɛktro'motər] *s* electromotor, motor eléctrico; aparato electrógeno
electron [ɪ'lɛktran] *s* (phys. & chem.) electrón
electronegative [ɪ,lɛktro'nɛgətɪv] *adj* electronegativo
electronic [ɪ,lɛk'tranɪk] o [,ɛlɛk'tranɪk] *adj* electrónico; **electronics** *ssg* electrónica
electronic brain *s* cerebro electrónico
electron microscope *s* microscopio electrónico
electron spin *s* (phys.) giro electrónico
electron volt *s* (phys.) electrón voltio
electrophonic [ɪ,lɛktro'fanɪk] *adj* electrofónico
electrophorus [ɪ,lɛk'trafərəs] o [,ɛlɛk'trafərəs] *s* (*pl:* **-ri** [raɪ]) (phys.) electróforo
electroplate [ɪ'lɛktro,plet] *s* artículo galvanizado; *va* galvanizar
electroplating [ɪ'lɛktro,pletɪŋ] *s* galvanoplastia
electropneumatic [ɪ,lɛktronju'mætɪk] o [ɪ,lɛktronu'mætɪk] *adj* (mus.) electroneumático (*órgano*)
electropositive [ɪ,lɛktro'pazɪtɪv] *adj* electropositivo
electroscope [ɪ'lɛktrəskop] *s* (phys.) electroscopio
electroshock [ɪ'lɛktro,ʃak] *s* electrochoque
electrostatic [ɪ,lɛktro'stætɪk] *adj* electrostático; **electrostatics** *ssg* electrostática
electrosurgery [ɪ,lɛktro'sʌrdʒərɪ] *s* electrocirugía
electrotechnical [ɪ,lɛktro'tɛknɪkəl] *adj* electrotécnico
electrotherapy [ɪ,lɛktro'θɛrəpɪ] *s* electroterapia
electrotype [ɪ'lɛktrotaɪp] *s* electrotipo; *va* electrotipar
electrotypy [ɪ'lɛktro,taɪpɪ] *s* electrotipia
electrum [ɪ'lɛktrəm] *s* electro (*aleación*); plata alemana
electuary [ɪ'lɛktʃʊ,ɛrɪ] *s* (*pl:* **-ies**) electuario
eleemosynary [,ɛlɪ'masɪ,nɛrɪ] *adj* limosnero; mendicante
elegance ['ɛlɪgəns] *s* elegancia
elegancy ['ɛlɪgənsɪ] *s* (*pl:* **-cies**) var. de **elegance**
elegant ['ɛlɪgənt] *adj* elegante
elegiac [,ɛlɪ'dʒaɪæk] o [ɛ'lidʒɪæk] *adj* elegíaco
elegy ['ɛlɪdʒɪ] *s* (*pl:* **-gies**) elegía
element ['ɛlɪmənt] *s* elemento; (anat., biol. & elec.) elemento; (chem.) elemento, cuerpo simple; **the four elements** los cuatro elementos (*fuego, agua, aire y tierra*); **the elements** los elementos (*primeros principios; las fuerzas naturales*); **to be in one's element** estar en su elemento
elemental [,ɛlɪ'mɛntəl] *adj* elemental
elementary [,ɛlɪ'mɛntərɪ] *adj* elemental
elemi ['ɛlɪmɪ] *s* (*pl:* **-mis**) elemí
elephant ['ɛlɪfənt] *s* elefante
elephant fish *s* (ichth.) pez elefante
elephant grass *s* (bot.) hierba elefante (*Pennisetum purpureum*)
elephantiac [,ɛlɪ'fæntɪæk] *adj & s* elefancíaco
elephantiasis [,ɛlɪfæn'taɪəsɪs] *s* (path.) elefantiasis
elephantine [,ɛlɪ'fæntɪn] o [,ɛlɪ'fæntaɪn] *adj* elefantino
elephant seal *s* (zool.) foca de trompa, elefante marino
elephant's-ear ['ɛlɪfənts,ɪr] *s* (bot.) begonia; (bot.) taro
Eleusinian [,ɛlju'sɪnɪən] *adj & s* eleusino
Eleusinian mysteries *spl* misterios de Eleusis
elevate ['ɛlɪvet] *va* elevar; regocijar
elevated ['ɛlɪ,vetɪd] *adj* elevado; alegre; *s* (coll.) ferrocarril aéreo, ferrocarril elevado
elevated railroad *s* ferrocarril aéreo, ferrocarril elevado
elevation [,ɛlɪ'veʃən] *s* elevación; (arch. & astr). elevación; (*cap.*) *s* (eccl.) elevación
elevator ['ɛlɪ,vetər] *s* ascensor, elevador; montacargas; elevador de granos; depósito de cereales; (aer.) timón de profundidad
elevator shaft *s* caja o pozo de ascensor
eleven [ɪ'lɛvən] *adj* once; *s* once; (football) once (*equipo de jugadores*); **eleven o'clock** las once
elevenfold [ɪ'lɛvən,fold] *adj & s* undécuplo; *adv* once veces
eleventh [ɪ'lɛvənθ] *adj* undécimo, onceno; onzavo; *s* undécimo, onceno; onzavo; once (*en las fechas*)
eleventh hour *s* último minuto
elf [ɛlf] *s* (*pl:* **elves**) elfo, duende; enano; niño travieso
elfin ['ɛlfɪn] *adj* elfino, travieso; *s* elfo
elfish ['ɛlfɪʃ] *adj* elfino, travieso
elflock ['ɛlf,lak] *s* greña de pelo
Eli ['ilaɪ] *s* (Bib.) Elí
elicit [ɪ'lɪsɪt] *va* sacar, sonsacar
elicitation [ɪ,lɪsɪ'teʃən] *s* sacamiento, sonsacamiento
elide [ɪ'laɪd] *va* elidir

eligibility [ˌɛlɪdʒɪ'bɪlɪtɪ] *s* (*pl:* **-ties**) elegibilidad
eligible ['ɛlɪdʒɪbəl] *adj* elegible; admisible, aceptable
Elijah [ɪ'laɪdʒə] *s* (Bib.) Elías
eliminate [ɪ'lɪmɪnet] *va* eliminar; (math. & physiol.) eliminar
elimination [ɪˌlɪmɪ'neʃən] *s* eliminación; (physiol.) eliminación
elimination match o **race** *s* (sport) eliminatoria
Eliot ['ɛlɪət] *s* Elías
Elisha [ɪ'laɪʃə] *s* (Bib.) Elíseo
elision [ɪ'lɪʒən] *s* elisión
élite o **elite** [e'lit] *s* lo escogido, lo selecto; **the élite of society** la élite de la sociedad
elixir [ɪ'lɪksər] *s* elixir o elíxir
Elizabeth [ɪ'lɪzəbəθ] *s* Isabel
Elizabethan [ɪˌlɪzə'biθən] o [ɪˌlɪzə'bɛθən] *adj & s* isabelino
elk [ɛlk] *s* (zool.) alce
ell [ɛl] *s* ana (*medida*); pabellón (*edificio contiguo*)
Elliott ['ɛlɪət] *s* Elías
ellipse [ɪ'lɪps] *s* (geom.) elipse
ellipsis [ɪ'lɪpsɪs] *s* (*pl:* **-ses** [siz]) (gram.) elipsis
ellipsograph [ɪ'lɪpsəgræf] o [ɪ'lɪpsəgrɑf] *s* elipsógrafo
ellipsoid [ɪ'lɪpsɔɪd] *s* (geom.) elipsoide
elliptic [ɪ'lɪptɪk] o **elliptical** [ɪ'lɪptɪkəl] *adj* (geom. & gram.) elíptico
elliptically [ɪ'lɪptɪkəlɪ] *adv* elípticamente
Ellis ['ɛlɪs] *s* Elías
elm [ɛlm] *s* (bot.) olmo
elocution [ˌɛlə'kjuʃən] *s* elocución
elocutionary [ˌɛlə'kjuʃənˌɛrɪ] *adj* declamatorio
elocutionist [ˌɛlə'kjuʃənɪst] *s* declamador, recitador
Eloise [ˌɛlo'iz] *s* Eloísa
elongate [ɪ'lɔŋget] o [ɪ'lɑŋget] *adj* alargado; *va* alargar, extender; *vn* alargarse, extenderse
elongation [ˌilɔŋ'geʃən] o [ˌilɑŋ'geʃən] *s* alargamiento, extensión; (astr.) elongación
elope [ɪ'lop] *vn* fugarse con un amante; huir, evadirse, escaparse
elopement [ɪ'lopmənt] *s* fuga con un amante; fuga, escapada
eloquence ['ɛləkwəns] *s* elocuencia
eloquent ['ɛləkwənt] *adj* elocuente
El Salvador [ɛl'sælvədɔr] *s* El Salvador
else [ɛls] *adj* otro, diferente; más; *adv* de otro modo, de otra manera; si no; **or else** o bien
elsewhere ['ɛlshwɛr] *adv* en otra parte, a otra parte
elsewhither ['ɛlsˌhwɪðər] *adv* a otra parte
elucidate [ɪ'lusɪdet] *va* elucidar
elucidation [ɪˌlusɪ'deʃən] *s* elucidación
elude [ɪ'lud] *va* eludir
elusion [ɪ'luʒən] *s* evasiva, efugio
elusive [ɪ'lusɪv] o **elusory** [ɪ'lusərɪ] *adj* deslumbrador, difícil de comprender; evasivo
elver ['ɛlvər] *s* (ichth.) anguila joven
elvish ['ɛlvɪʃ] *adj* var. de **elfish**
Elysian [ɪ'lɪʒən] *adj* elíseo o elisio
Elysian Fields *spl* (myth.) campos elíseos o elisios
Elysium [ɪ'lɪʒəm] o [ɪ'lɪzɪəm] *s* (myth. & fig.) Elíseo o Elisio
elytrum ['ɛlɪtrəm] *s* (*pl:* **-tra** [trə]) (ent.) élitro
Elzevir ['ɛlzəvər] o ['ɛlzəvɪr] *adj* elzeviriano; *s* (bibliog. & print.) elzevir o elzevirio
em [ɛm] *s* (print.) eme
em o **'em** [əm] *pron pers pl* (coll.) var. de **them**
emaciate [ɪ'meʃɪet] *va* enflaquecer; *vn* enflaquecerse
emaciation [ɪˌmeʃɪ'eʃən] *s* enflaquecimiento, emaciación
emanate ['ɛmənet] *vn* emanar
emanation [ˌɛmə'neʃən] *s* emanación
emancipate [ɪ'mænsɪpet] *va* emancipar
emancipation [ɪˌmænsɪ'peʃən] *s* emancipación
emancipator [ɪ'mænsɪˌpetər] *s* emancipador, libertador
emasculate [ɪ'mæskjəlɪt] *adj* debilitado, afeminado; [ɪ'mæskjəlet] *va* emascular; (fig.) debilitar, mutilar
emasculation [ɪˌmæskjə'leʃən] *s* emasculación; (fig.) debilitación, mutilación
embalm [ɛm'bɑm] *va* embalsamar (*un cadáver; el aire*); conservar, conservar en la memoria
embalmer [ɛm'bɑmər] *s* embalsamador
embalmment [ɛm'bɑmmənt] *s* embalsamamiento
embank [ɛm'bæŋk] *va* terraplenar
embankment [ɛm'bæŋkmənt] *s* terraplén
embargo [ɛm'bɑrgo] *s* (*pl:* **-goes**) embargo; *va* embargar
embark [ɛm'bɑrk] *va* embarcar; (fig.) embarcar, lanzar (*en una empresa*); (fig.) invertir (*dinero*) en una empresa; *vn* embarcarse
embarkation [ˌɛmbɑr'keʃən] o **embarkment** [ɛm'bɑrkmənt] *s* embarco (*de personas*); embarque (*de mercancías*)
embarrass [ɛm'bærəs] *va* avergonzar, desconcertar; embarazar, estorbar; poner en aprieto
embarrassing [ɛm'bærəsɪŋ] *adj* vergonzoso, desconcertador; embarazoso
embarrassment [ɛm'bærəsmənt] *s* vergüenza, desconcierto; embarazo, estorbo; apuros, dificultades
embassador [ɛm'bæsədər] *s* var. de **ambassador**
embassy ['ɛmbəsɪ] *s* (*pl:* **-sies**) embajada
embattle [ɛm'bætəl] *va* preparar para la batalla; (fort.) almenar
embay [ɛm'be] *va* abrigar o cerrar en una bahía; encerrar
embed [ɛm'bɛd] (*pret & pp:* **-bedded;** *ger:* **-bedding**) *va* hincar, encajar, empotrar, plantar
embellish [ɛm'bɛlɪʃ] *va* embellecer
embellishment [ɛm'bɛlɪʃmənt] *s* embellecimiento
ember ['ɛmbər] *s* ascua, pavesa; **embers** *spl* rescoldo
Ember days *spl* témpora, témporas
embezzle [ɛm'bɛzəl] *va* malversar, desfalcar
embezzlement [ɛm'bɛzəlmənt] *s* malversación, desfalco
embezzler [ɛm'bɛzlər] *s* malversador
embitter [ɛm'bɪtər] *va* amargar
emblazon [ɛm'blezən] *va* blasonar; engalanar o esmaltar con colores brillantes; (fig.) blasonar, ensalzar
emblazonment [ɛm'blezənmənt] *s* var. de **emblazonry**
emblazonry [ɛm'blezənrɪ] *s* (*pl:* **-ries**) blasón; adorno brillante
emblem ['ɛmbləm] *s* emblema
emblematic [ˌɛmblə'mætɪk] o **emblematical** [ˌɛmblə'mætɪkəl] *adj* emblemático
embodiment [ɛm'bɑdɪmənt] *s* incorporación; encarnación, personificación
embody [ɛm'bɑdɪ] (*pret & pp:* **-ied**) *va* incorporar; encarnar, personificar
embolden [ɛm'boldən] *va* envalentonar
embolectomy [ˌɛmbə'lɛktəmɪ] *s* (*pl:* **-mies**) (surg.) embolectomía
embolism ['ɛmbəlɪzəm] *s* embolismo (*para igualar el calendario*); (path.) embolia
embolismic [ˌɛmbə'lɪzmɪk] *adj* embolismal o embolísmico
embolus ['ɛmbələs] *s* (*pl:* **-li** [laɪ]) (path.) émbolo
embonpoint [ɑ̃bɔ̃'pwæ̃] *s* redondez de cuerpo
embosom [ɛm'bʊzəm] *va* ensenar, guardar en el seno, encerrar en el pecho; envolver, abrigar, proteger cariñosamente
emboss [ɛm'bɔs] o [ɛm'bɑs] *va* abollonar; realzar, labrar de o al realce
embossment [ɛm'bɔsmənt] o [ɛm'bɑsmənt] *s* abollonadura; realce, relieve
embouchure [ˌɑmbu'ʃʊr] *s* desembocadura (*de un río*); embocadura (*de un instrumento músico*)
embower [ɛm'baʊər] *va* emparrar
embrace [ɛm'bres] *s* abrazo; *va* abrazar; *vn* abrazarse (*dos personas*)
embrasure [ɛm'breʒər] *s* (arch.) alféizar; (fort.) aspillera, tronera; *va* aspillerar
embrocate ['ɛmbroket] *va* (med.) bañar y frotar con una embrocación
embrocation [ˌɛmbro'keʃən] *s* (med.) embrocación
embroider [ɛm'brɔɪdər] *va* bordar, recamar; (fig.) bordar, embellecer
embroidery [ɛm'brɔɪdərɪ] *s* (*pl:* **-ies**) bordado, recamado

embroidery frame *s* bastidor para bordar
embroil [ɛm'brɔɪl] *va* embrollar; envolver (*p.ej., en una contienda*)
embroilment [ɛm'brɔɪlmənt] *s* embrollo; envolvimiento
embrown [ɛm'braʊn] *va* embazar, poner pardo
embryo ['ɛmbrɪo] *s* (*pl:* **-os**) (biol., bot. & fig.) embrión; **in embryo** en embrión; *adj* embrionario
embryogenic [,ɛmbrɪo'dʒɛnɪk] *adj* embriogénico
embryogeny [,ɛmbrɪ'ɑdʒənɪ] *s* (biol.) embriogenia
embryologic [,ɛmbrɪo'lɑdʒɪk] o **embryological** [,ɛmbrɪo'lɑdʒɪkəl] *adj* embriológico
embryologist [,ɛmbrɪ'ɑlədʒɪst] *s* embriólogo
embryology [,ɛmbrɪ'ɑlədʒɪ] *s* embriología
embryonal ['ɛmbrɪənəl] *adj* embrional
embryonic [,ɛmbrɪ'ɑnɪk] *adj* embrionario
emeer [ə'mɪr] *s* emir
emend [ɪ'mɛnd] *va* enmendar
emendation [,imɛn'deʃən] o [,ɛmɛn'deʃən] *s* enmienda
emerald ['ɛmərəld] *s* esmeralda; *adj* esmeraldino
emerge [ɪ'mʌrdʒ] *vn* emerger
emergence [ɪ'mʌrdʒəns] *s* emergencia; (bot.) emergencia
emergency [ɪ'mʌrdʒənsɪ] *s* (*pl:* **-cies**) emergencia; urgencia; caso urgente; *adj* de auxilio, de emergencia, de socorro, de fortuna, de prevención
emergency brake *s* freno de auxilio, freno de emergencia
emergency exit *s* salida de auxilio
emergency landing *s* (aer.) aterrizaje forzoso, aterrizaje de emergencia
emergency landing field *s* (aer.) campo de emergencia, aeródromo de urgencia
emergent [ɪ'mʌrdʒənt] *adj* emergente; urgente
emeritus [ɪ'mɛrɪtəs] *adj* emérito, honorario
emeritus professor *s* profesor honorario
emersion [ɪ'mʌrʒən] o [ɪ'mʌrʃən] *s* emersión; (astr.) emersión
emery ['ɛmərɪ] *s* esmeril
emery cloth *s* tela de esmeril
emery grinder *s* muela de esmeril
emery paper *s* papel de esmeril
emery stone *s* piedra de esmeril
emery wheel *s* rueda de esmeril
emetic [ɪ'mɛtɪk] *adj & s* emético
E.M.F. o **e.m.f.** abr. de **electromotive force**
emigrant ['ɛmɪgrənt] *adj & s* emigrante
emigrate ['ɛmɪgret] *vn* emigrar
emigration [,ɛmɪ'greʃən] *s* emigración
émigré [emi'gre] o ['ɛmɪgre] *s* emigrado
Emily ['ɛmɪlɪ] *s* Emilia
eminence ['ɛmɪnəns] *s* eminencia; (*cap.*) *s* (eccl.) eminencia
éminence grise [eminɑ̃s griz] *s* eminencia gris (*persona que tiene influencia insospechada*)
eminency ['ɛmɪnənsɪ] *s* (pl: **-cies**) eminencia (*dignidad, distinción*)
eminent ['ɛmɪnənt] *adj* eminente
eminent domain *s* (law) dominio eminente
eminently ['ɛmɪnəntlɪ] *adv* eminentemente
emir [ə'mɪr] *s* emir
emissary ['ɛmɪ,sɛrɪ] *s* (*pl:* **-ies**) emisario
emission [ɪ'mɪʃən] *s* emisión
emissive [ɪ'mɪsɪv] *adj* emisivo
emit [ɪ'mɪt] (*pret & pp:* **-mitted;** *ger:* **-mitting**) *va* emitir
Emma ['ɛmə] *s* Ema
Emmanuel [ɪ'mænjʊəl] *s* (Bib.) Emanuel
emmenagogue [ə'mɛnəgɑg] o [ə'minəgɑg] *adj & s* (med.) emenagogo
emmer ['ɛmər] *s* (bot.) escandia
emmetrope ['ɛmɪtrop] *s* emétrope
emmetropia [,ɛmɪ'tropɪə] *s* emetropía
emollient [ɪ'mɑljənt] *adj & s* emoliente
emolument [ɪ'mɑljəmənt] *s* emolumento
emotion [ɪ'moʃən] *s* emoción
emotional [ɪ'moʃənəl] *adj* emocional
emotionalism [ɪ'moʃənəlɪzəm] *s* emocionalismo
emotive [ɪ'motɪv] *adj* emotivo
empanel [ɛm'pænəl] (*pret & pp:* **-eled** o **-elled;** *ger:* **-eling** o **-elling**) *va* var. de **impanel**
empathy ['ɛmpəθɪ] *s* (psychol.) empatía
Empedocles [ɛm'pɛdəkliz] *s* Empédocles
empennage [,ɑ̃pɛ'nɑʒ] *s* (aer.) empenaje
emperor ['ɛmpərər] *s* emperador
emphasis ['ɛmfəsɪs] *s* (*pl:* **-ses** [siz]) énfasis
emphasize ['ɛmfəsaɪz] *va* dar énfasis a, acentuar; (fig.) acentuar
emphatic [ɛm'fætɪk] *adj* enfático
emphatically [ɛm'fætɪkəlɪ] *adv* enfáticamente
emphysema [,ɛmfɪ'simə] *s* (path.) enfisema
emphyteusis [,ɛmfɪ'tjusɪs] o [,ɛmfɪ'tusɪs] *s* (law) enfiteusis
emphyteuta [,ɛmfɪ'tjutə] o [,ɛmfɪ'tutə] *s* (*pl:* **-tae** [ti]) enfiteuta
emphyteutic [,ɛmfɪ'tjutɪk] o [,ɛmfɪ'tutɪk] *adj* enfitéutico
empire ['ɛmpaɪr] *s* imperio; (*cap.*) *adj* (f.a.) imperio, de estilo imperio
Empire gown *s* vestido imperio
Empire of the Rising Sun *s* Imperio del sol naciente (*el Japón*)
Empire State *s* estado de Nueva York, EE.UU.
empiric [ɛm'pɪrɪk] *adj* empírico; *s* empírico; curandero, charlatán
empirical [ɛm'pɪrɪkəl] *adj* empírico
empiricism [ɛm'pɪrɪsɪzəm] *s* empirismo
empiricist [ɛm'pɪrɪsɪst] *s* empírico, empirista; curandero, charlatán
emplacement [ɛm'plesmənt] *s* sitio, colocación, emplazamiento
employ [ɛm'plɔɪ] *s* empleo; *va* emplear
employe, employé o **employee** [ɛm'plɔɪi] o [,ɛmplɔɪ'i] *s* empleado
employer [ɛm'plɔɪər] *s* patrón
employment [ɛm'plɔɪmənt] *s* empleo, ocupación
employment agency *s* agencia de colocaciones o empleos
emporium [ɛm'porɪəm] *s* (*pl:* **-riums** o **-ria** [rɪə]) emporio
empower [ɛm'paʊər] *va* facultar, habilitar; autorizar
empress ['ɛmprɪs] *s* emperatriz
emptiness ['ɛmptɪnɪs] *s* vacío, vacuidad
empty ['ɛmptɪ] *adj* (*comp:* **-tier;** *super:* **-tiest**) vacío; vano, inútil; (coll.) hambriento; (*pret & pp:* **-tied**) *va & vn* vaciar
empty-handed ['ɛmptɪ'hændɪd] *adj* manivacío
empty-headed ['ɛmptɪ'hɛdɪd] *adj* tonto, estúpido
empurple [ɛm'pʌrpəl] *va* empurpurar; *vn* empurpurarse
empyema [,ɛmpɪ'imə] *s* (*pl:* **-mata** [mətə]) (path.) empiema
empyreal [ɛm'pɪrɪəl] o [,ɛmpɪ'riəl] *adj* empíreo
empyrean [,ɛmpɪ'riən] *adj & s* empireo
empyreuma [,ɛmpɪ'rumə] *s* (*pl:* **-mata** [mətə]) (chem.) empireuma
emu ['imju] *s* (orn.) emú
emulate ['ɛmjəlet] *va & vn* emular
emulation [,ɛmjə'leʃən] *s* emulación
emulative ['ɛmjə,letɪv] *adj* emulador
emulator ['ɛmjə,letər] *s* emulador
emulgent [ɪ'mʌldʒənt] *adj* emulgente
emulous ['ɛmjələs] *adj* émulo
emulsification [ɪ,mʌlsɪfɪ'keʃən] *s* emulsionamiento; (phot.) albuminaje, emulsionamiento
emulsify [ɪ'mʌlsɪfaɪ] (*pret & pp:* **-fied**) *va* emulsionar; (phot.) albuminar, emulsionar
emulsion [ɪ'mʌlʃən] *s* emulsión
emulsive [ɪ'mʌlsɪv] *adj* emulsivo
emunctory [ɪ'mʌŋktərɪ] *adj* emuntorio; *s* (*pl:* **-ries**) emuntorio
en [ɛn] *s* (print.) mitad de una eme
enable [ɛn'ebəl] *va* habilitar, permitir
enact [ɛn'ækt] *va* decretar; dar o promulgar (*una ley*); desempeñar el papel de; *vn* actuar, desempeñar un papel
enactment [ɛn'æktmənt] *s* ley, estatuto; promulgación (*de una ley*); representación
enallage [ɛn'ælədʒɪ] *s* (gram.) enálage
enamel [ɛn'æməl] *s* esmalte; (anat.) esmalte; (*pret & pp:* **-eled** o **-elled;** *ger:* **-eling** o **-elling**) *va* esmaltar
enamelware [ɛn'æməl,wɛr] *s* utensilios de cocina hechos de hierro esmaltado; enlozado (Am.)
enamor [ɛn'æmər] *va* enamorar
enarthrosis [,ɛnɑr'θrosɪs] *s* (anat.) enartrosis

en bloc [ɛn'blɑk] en bloque, en una pieza, juntos
encamp [ɛn'kæmp] *va* acampar; *vn* acampar o acamparse
encampment [ɛn'kæmpmənt] *s* campamento
encase [ɛn'kes] *va* encajonar, encerrar
encaustic [ɛn'kɔstɪk] *adj* (f.a.) encáustico; *s* (f.a.) encausto
encaustic painting *s* (f.a.) pintura al encausto
encaustic tile *s* azulejo
enceinte [ɛn'sent] *adj* encinta, preñada; *s* (fort.) recinto
encephalic [,ɛnsɪ'fælɪk] *adj* encefálico
encephalitis [ɛn,sɛfə'laɪtɪs] *s* (path.) encefalitis
encephalomyelitis [ɛn,sɛfəlo,maɪə'laɪtɪs] *s* (path.) encefalomielitis
encephalon [ɛn'sɛfəlɑn] *s* (*pl:* **-la** [lə]) (anat.) encéfalo
encephalopathy [ɛn,sɛfə'lɑpəθɪ] *s* (path.) encefalopatía
enchain [ɛn'tʃen] *va* encadenar
enchant [ɛn'tʃænt] o [ɛn'tʃɑnt] *va* encantar
enchanting [ɛn'tʃæntɪŋ] o [ɛn'tʃɑntɪŋ] *adj* encantador
enchantment [ɛn'tʃæntmənt] o [ɛn'tʃɑntmənt] *s* encantamiento, encanto
enchantress [ɛn'tʃæntrɪs] o [ɛn'tʃɑntrɪs] *s* encantadora
enchase [ɛn'tʃes] *va* engastar
encircle [ɛn'sʌrkəl] *va* circuir, rodear, encerrar, circunvalar; (mil.) envolver
encirclement [ɛn'sʌrkəlmənt] *s* rodeo, circuición, encerramiento, circunvalación; (mil.) envolvimiento
encircling [ɛn'sʌrklɪŋ] *adj* (mil.) envolvente
enclave ['ɛnklev] *s* (geog.) enclave; [ɛn'klev] *va* enclavar
enclavement [ɛn'klevmənt] *s* (med.) enclavamiento
enclitic [ɛn'klɪtɪk] *adj* (gram. & obstet.) enclítico; *s* (gram.) enclítico, partícula enclítica
enclose [ɛn'kloz] *va* cercar, encerrar, incluir; **to enclose herewith** remitir adjunto (*con una carta*)
enclosure [ɛn'kloʒər] *s* cercamiento, encerramiento, inclusión; cerca, encierro, recinto; cosa inclusa, carta inclusa, copia inclusa
encomiast [ɛn'komɪæst] *s* encomiasta
encomiastic [ɛn,komɪ'æstɪk] *adj* encomiástico
encomium [ɛn'komɪəm] *s* (*pl:* **-ums** o **-a** [ə]) encomio
encompass [ɛn'kʌmpəs] *va* abarcar, encuadrar
encompassment [ɛn'kʌmpəsmənt] *s* abarcamiento, encuadramiento
encore ['ɑŋkor] *s* (theat.) bis, repetición; *interj* (theat.) ¡bis!, ¡que se repita!; *va* (theat.) pedir la repetición a o de
encounter [ɛn'kaʊntər] *s* encuentro; (mil.) encuentro; *va* encontrar, encontrarse con; *vn* encontrarse; batirse
encourage [ɛn'kʌrɪdʒ] *va* animar, alentar; fomentar; **to encourage to** + *inf* animar a, alentar a + *inf*
encouragement [ɛn'kʌrɪdʒmənt] *s* animación, ánimo; fomento; **to give encouragement to** dar ánimo o ánimos a
encouraging [ɛn'kʌrɪdʒɪŋ] *adj* animador, alentador
encroach [ɛn'krotʃ] *vn* pasar los límites; **to encroach on** o **upon** pasar los límites de, invadir; abusar de
encroachment [ɛn'krotʃmənt] *s* invasión; abuso
encrust [ɛn'krʌst] *va* incrustar; *vn* incrustarse
encumber [ɛn'kʌmbər] *va* embarazar, estorbar; impedir; gravar
encumbrance [ɛn'kʌmbrəns] *s* embarazo, estorbo; impedimento; gravamen; hijo menor de edad
ency. o **encyc.** abr. de **encyclopedia**
encyclical [ɛn'sɪklɪkəl] o [ɛn'saɪklɪkəl] *adj* circular, general; *s* encíclica
encyclopedia o **encyclopaedia** [ɛn,saɪklo'pidɪə] *s* enciclopedia
encyclopedic o **encyclopaedic** [ɛn,saɪklo'pidɪk] *adj* enciclopédico
encyclopedism o **encyclopaedism** [ɛn,saɪklo'pidɪzəm] *s* enciclopedismo
encyclopedist o **encyclopaedist** [ɛn,saɪklo'pidɪst] *s* enciclopedista
encyst [ɛn'sɪst] *va* enquistar; *vn* enquistarse
encystment [ɛn'sɪstmənt] *s* enquistamiento
end [ɛnd] *s* fin, límite; fines (*p.ej., del mes*); extremidad, extremo, cabo, remate; fin, objeto, mira, intento; pieza, fragmento; (football) extremo, ala; **at loose ends** en desorden; desarreglado; **at the end of** a fines de; **from one end to the other** de un extremo a otro, de cabo a cabo; **in the end** al fin; **no end of** (coll.) un sin fin de; **on end** de canto, derecho; uno después de otro; **to come out on the small end of a deal** llevarse lo peor, salir perdiendo; **to come to an end** acabarse, terminarse; **to keep one's end up** no aflojar, hacer lo que a uno le corresponde; **to make an end of** acabar con; **to make both ends meet** proveer a sus necesidades con trabajo o dificultad, pasar con lo que se tiene; **to no end** sin efecto; **to put an end to** poner fin a; **to the end that** a fin de que; **end to end** punta a punta, cabeza contra cabeza ‖ *adj* final, terminal ‖ *va* acabar, terminar ‖ *vn* acabar, terminar; desembocar (*p.ej., una calle*); **to end up** acabar, morir; **to end up as** parar en (*p.ej., ladrón*); **to end up in** ir a parar en
end-all ['ɛnd,ɔl] *s* punto final; golpe de gracia
endanger [ɛn'dendʒər] *va* poner en peligro
endear [ɛn'dɪr] *va* hacer querer; **to endear oneself** hacerse querer
endearment [ɛn'dɪrmənt] *s* encariñamiento; caricia, palabra cariñosa
endeavor [ɛn'dɛvər] *s* esfuerzo, empeño, conato; *vn* esforzarse, empeñarse; **to endeavor to** + *inf* esforzarse por + *inf*
endemic [ɛn'dɛmɪk] *adj* endémico; *s* endemia
en déshabillé [ɑ̃ dezabi'je] a medio vestir, desaliñado, de trapillo
ending ['ɛndɪŋ] *s* fin, terminación; (gram.) desinencia, terminación
endive ['ɛndaɪv] o ['ɑndiv] *s* (bot.) escarola, endibia
endless ['ɛndlɪs] *adj* interminable; (mach.) continuo, sin fin
endless chain *s* cadena sin fin
endless screw *s* tornillo sin fin
end man *s* último hombre de una fila de hombres; (theat.) el actor a cada extremo de una fila de cómicos disfrazados de negro
endmost ['ɛndmost] *adj* último, extremo
endocarditis [,ɛndokɑr'daɪtɪs] *s* (path.) endocarditis
endocardium [,ɛndo'kɑrdɪəm] *s* (anat.) endocardio
endocarp ['ɛndokɑrp] *s* (bot.) endocarpio
endocrine ['ɛndokraɪn] o ['ɛndokrɪn] *adj* (physiol.) endocrino; *s* (physiol.) endocrina
endocrine gland *s* (anat.) glándula endocrina
endocrinology [,ɛndokraɪ'nɑlədʒɪ] o [,ɛndokrɪ'nɑlədʒɪ] *s* endocrinología
endodermis [,ɛndo'dʌrmɪs] *s* (bot.) endodermo
endogamy [ɛn'dɑgəmɪ] *s* endogamia; (biol.) endogamia
endogenesis [,ɛndo'dʒɛnɪsɪs] *s* var. de **endogeny**
endogenous [ɛn'dɑdʒɪnəs] *adj* endógeno
endogeny [ɛn'dɑdʒɪnɪ] *s* (biol.) endogénesis
endolymph ['ɛndolɪmf] *s* (anat.) endolinfa
endomysium [,ɛndo'mɪsɪəm] o [,ɛndo'mɪzɪəm] *s* (anat.) endomisio
endoparasite [,ɛndo'pærəsaɪt] *s* (zool.) endoparásito
endoplasm ['ɛndoplæzəm] *s* (biol.) endoplasma
endorse [ɛn'dɔrs] *va* endosar; apoyar, aprobar
endorsee [,ɛndɔr'si] *s* endosatario
endorsement [ɛn'dɔrsmənt] *s* endoso; apoyo, aprobación
endorser [ɛn'dɔrsər] *s* endosante
endoscope ['ɛndoskop] *s* (med.) endoscopio
endoskeleton [,ɛndo'skɛlɪtən] *s* (zool.) endoesqueleto
endosmosis [,ɛndɑs'mosɪs] *s* (physical chem. & physiol.) endósmosis
endosperm ['ɛndospʌrm] *s* (bot.) endospermo
endospore ['ɛndospor] *s* (bot. & bact.) endospora
endothecium [,ɛndo'θiʃɪəm] o [,ɛndo'θisɪəm] *s* (*pl:* **-cia** [ʃɪə] o [sɪə]) (bot.) endotecio
endothelium [,ɛndo'θilɪəm] *s* (*pl:* **-lia** [lɪə]) (anat.) endotelio

endothermic [ˌɛndoˈθʌrmɪk] *adj* (chem.) endotérmico
endow [ɛnˈdaʊ] *va* dotar
endowment [ɛnˈdaʊmənt] *s* dotación; dote, prenda, gracia
endowment insurance *s* seguro dotal
endowment policy *s* póliza dotal
end paper *s* (b.b.) hoja de encuadernador
end play *s* (mach.) juego longitudinal
end product *s* producto final
endue [ɛnˈdju] o [ɛnˈdu] *va* dotar, investir; poner, vestir
endurance [ɛnˈdjurəns] o [ɛnˈdurəns] *s* aguante, paciencia, tolerancia; resistencia, duración; continuación; (sport) endurancia, resistencia, fortaleza
endurance race *s* (sport) carrera de resistencia
endurance record *s* marca de duración
endure [ɛnˈdjur] o [ɛnˈdur] *va* aguantar, tolerar, endurar; *vn* durar, perdurar; continuar; sufrir con paciencia, sufrir sin rendirse
enduring [ɛnˈdjurɪŋ] o [ɛnˈdurɪŋ] *adj* durable, permanente, resistente; sufrido, paciente
end view *s* vista de la extremidad
endways [ˈɛndˌwez] o **endwise** [ˈɛndˌwaɪz] *adv* de punta, de pie; derecho, erguido; longitudinalmente; topando
Endymion [ɛnˈdɪmɪən] *s* (myth.) Endimión
enema [ˈɛnɪmə] *s* (med.) enema, ayuda; lavativa, mangueta (*para echar ayudas*)
enemy [ˈɛnɪmɪ] *s* (*pl:* **-mies**) enemigo; *adj* enemigo
enemy alien *s* extranjero enemigo
enemy number one, the el enemigo número uno
energetic [ˌɛnərˈdʒɛtɪk] *adj* enérgico; **energetics** *ssg* energética
energetically [ˌɛnərˈdʒɛtɪkəlɪ] *adv* enérgicamente
energize [ˈɛnərdʒaɪz] *va* activar, excitar; *vn* obrar con energía
energumen [ˌɛnərˈgjumɛn] *s* energúmeno
energy [ˈɛnərdʒɪ] *s* (*pl:* **-gies**) energía
enervate [ˈɛnərvet] *adj* enervado; *va* enervar
enervation [ˌɛnərˈveʃən] *s* enervación
en famille [ɑ̃ faˈmi] en familia
enfeeble [ɛnˈfibəl] *va* debilitar
enfeeblement [ɛnˈfibəlmənt] *s* debilitación, debilidad
enfeoff [ɛnˈfɛf] o [ɛnˈfif] *va* (law) enfeudar (*dar en feudo*); (law) dar feudo a
enfeoffment [ɛnˈfɛfmənt] o [ɛnˈfifmənt] *s* (law) enfeudación
enfilade [ˌɛnfɪˈled] *s* enfilamiento; (mil.) enfilada; *va* enfilar; (mil.) enfilar
enfiled [ɛnˈfaɪld] *adj* (her.) enfilado
enfleurage [ɑ̃flʌˈrɑʒ] *s* enfloración
enfold [ɛnˈfold] *va* envolver, arrollar, abrazar, estrechar
enforce [ɛnˈfors] *va* hacer cumplir, poner en vigor; obtener por fuerza; imponer a la fuerza
enforcement [ɛnˈforsmənt] *s* ejecución (*de una ley*); compulsión, coacción
enfranchise [ɛnˈfræntʃaɪz] *va* franquear, manumitir, enfranquecer; conceder el derecho de sufragio a
enfranchisement [ɛnˈfræntʃɪzmənt] *s* franqueo, manumisión; concesión del sufragio
eng. abr. de **engineer, engineering** y **engraving**
Eng. abr. de **England** y **English**
engage [ɛnˈgedʒ] *va* apalabrar; ocupar, emplear; reservar, alquilar; atraer (*p.ej., la atención*); empotrar en; engranar con; trabar batalla con; **to be engaged (to be married)** estar prometido, estar comprometido para casarse; *vn* ocuparse; empeñarse, comprometerse; **to engage in** ocuparse en; empotrar en; engranar con
engaged [ɛnˈgedʒd] *adj* prometido
engaged column *s* (arch.) columna embebida, columna entregada
engagement [ɛnˈgedʒmənt] *s* ajuste, contrato, empeño; palabra de casamiento, esponsales; noviazgo; obligación; cita; (theat.) ajuste, contrato; (mil.) acción, batalla
engagement ring *s* anillo de compromiso, anillo de pedida
engaging [ɛnˈgedʒɪŋ] *adj* agraciado, insinuante, simpático
engender [ɛnˈdʒɛndər] *va* engendrar
engine [ˈɛndʒən] *s* máquina, aparato, instrumento; motor (*p.ej., de un automóvil*); (rail.) máquina, locomotora
engine block *s* bloque del motor
engine driver *s* maquinista, conductor de locomotora
engineer [ˌɛndʒəˈnɪr] *s* ingeniero; maquinista (*p.ej., de locomotora*); *va* construir o dirigir como ingeniero; dirigir o llevar a cabo con acierto
engineering [ˌɛndʒəˈnɪrɪŋ] *s* ingeniería; *adj* de ingeniería, ingenieril
engine failure *s* avería del motor
engine house *s* cuartel de bomberos; casa de máquinas
engine lathe *s* torno de engranaje para roscar
engineman [ˈɛndʒənmən] *s* (*pl:* **-men**) maquinista, conductor de locomotora
engine room *s* sala de máquinas; (naut.) cámara de las máquinas
engine-room telegraph [ˈɛndʒənˌrum] *s* (naut.) transmisor de órdenes, telégrafo de máquinas
engine runner *s* var. de **engine driver**
enginery [ˈɛndʒənrɪ] *s* maquinaria; ingenios de guerra; maña, ardid
England [ˈɪŋglənd] *s* Inglaterra
Englander [ˈɪŋgləndər] *s* natural inglés
English [ˈɪŋglɪʃ] *adj* inglés; *spl* ingleses; *ssg* inglés (*idioma*); (print.) tipo de 14 puntos; (billiards) efecto; *va* traducir al inglés
English bond *s* (mas.) aparejo inglés
English Channel *s* canal de la Mancha
English daisy *s* (bot.) maya, vellorita, margarita de los prados
English horn *s* (mus.) corno o cuerno inglés
Englishman [ˈɪŋglɪʃmən] *s* (*pl:* **-men**) inglés
English setter *s* perdiguero
English sonnet *s* soneto inglés (*rimado abab, cdcd, efef, gg*)
English sparrow *s* (orn.) gorrión
English-speaking [ˈɪŋglɪʃˈspikɪŋ] *adj* de habla inglesa
English walnut *s* (bot.) nogal; nuez (*fruto*)
Englishwoman [ˈɪŋglɪʃˌwumən] *s* (*pl:* **-women**) inglesa
engorge [ɛnˈgɔrdʒ] *va* atracar; *vn* atracarse
engouled [ɛnˈguld] *adj* (her.) engolado
engraft [ɛnˈgræft] o [ɛnˈgrɑft] *va* (hort. & surg.) injertar; (fig.) implantar
engrailed [ɛnˈgreld] *adj* (her.) angrelado
engrave [ɛnˈgrev] *va* grabar; burilar; imprimir con grabado; (fig.) grabar (*p.ej., en la memoria*)
engraver *s* [ɛnˈgrevər] *s* grabador
engraving [ɛnˈgrevɪŋ] *s* grabado (*acción, arte, lámina y estampa*)
engross [ɛnˈgros] *va* absorber; copiar o transcribir caligráficamente; poner en limpio, redactar en forma legal
engrossing [ɛnˈgrosɪŋ] *adj* absorbente, acaparador
engrossment [ɛnˈgrosmənt] *s* absorción, ensimismamiento; copia o transcripción caligráfica
engulf [ɛnˈgʌlf] *va* hundir, inundar
enhance [ɛnˈhæns] o [ɛnˈhɑns] *va* realzar, engrandecer
enhancement [ɛnˈhænsmənt] o [ɛnˈhɑnsmənt] *s* realce, engrandecimiento
enharmonic [ˌɛnhɑrˈmɑnɪk] *adj* (mus.) enarmónico
enigma [ɪˈnɪgmə] *s* enigma
enigmatic [ˌɪnɪgˈmætɪk] o **enigmatical** [ˌɪnɪgˈmætɪkəl] *adj* enigmático
enjambment o **enjambement** [ɛnˈdʒæmmənt] o [ɛnˈdʒæmbmənt] *s* (pros.) encabalgamiento
enjoin [ɛnˈdʒɔɪn] *va* mandar, encargar, ordenar; **to enjoin from** prohibir, vedar
enjoy [ɛnˈdʒɔɪ] *va* gozar (*p.ej., buena salud; la conversación*); **to enjoy** + *ger* gozarse en + *inf;* **to enjoy oneself** divertirse
enjoyable [ɛnˈdʒɔɪəbəl] *adj* deleitable, agradable
enjoyment [ɛnˈdʒɔɪmənt] *s* goce, placer
enkindle [ɛnˈkɪndəl] *va* encender
enlace [ɛnˈles] *va* enlazar, entrelazar; encerrar, rodear
enlarge [ɛnˈlɑrdʒ] *va* agrandar, abultar, am-

pliar, ensanchar; (phot.) ampliar; *vn* agrandarse, abultarse, ampliarse, ensancharse; explayarse; exagerar; **to enlarge on** o **upon** tratar con más extensión; exagerar

enlargement [ɛnˈlɑrdʒmənt] *s* agrandamiento, abultamiento, ampliación, ensanchamiento; (phot.) ampliación

enlarger [ɛnˈlɑrdʒər] *s* ampliador; (phot.) ampliadora

enlighten [ɛnˈlaɪtən] *va* iluminar, ilustrar

enlightened despotism *s* despotismo ilustrado

enlightenment [ɛnˈlaɪtənmənt] *s* iluminación, ilustración; **the Enlightenment** el siglo de las luces (*el siglo dieciocho*)

enlist [ɛnˈlɪst] *va* conseguir el apoyo de, emplear; alistar; *vn* poner empeño; alistarse

enlisted man *s* soldado raso

enlistment [ɛnˈlɪstmənt] *s* consecución, empleo; alistamiento, enganche

enliven [ɛnˈlaɪvən] *va* avivar, vivificar

en masse [ɛn ˈmæs] en masa

enmesh [ɛnˈmɛʃ] *va* enredar, entrampar

enmity [ˈɛnmɪtɪ] *s* (*pl:* **-ties**) enemistad

ennoble [ɛnˈnobəl] *va* ennoblecer

ennoblement [ɛnˈnobəlmənt] *s* ennoblecimiento

ennui [ˈɑnwi] *s* tedio, fastidio, aburrimiento

enormity [ɪˈnɔrmɪtɪ] *s* (*pl:* **-ties**) enormidad

enormous [ɪˈnɔrməs] *adj* enorme

enormously [ɪˈnɔrməslɪ] *adv* enormemente

enough [ɪˈnʌf] *adj, adv & s* bastante; *interj* ¡basta!, ¡no más!

enounce [ɪˈnaʊns] *va* enunciar; pronunciar

enow [ɪˈnaʊ] o [ɪˈno] *adj, adv & s* (archaic) var. de **enough**

en passant [ɑ̃ pɑˈsɑ̃] de paso; (chess) al vuelo, al paso

enplane [ɛnˈplen] *vn* embarcarse en un avión, salir en avión

enquire [ɛnˈkwaɪr] *va & vn* var. de **inquire**

enquiry [ɛnˈkwaɪrɪ] *s* (*pl:* **-ies**) var. de **inquiry**

enrage [ɛnˈredʒ] *va* enrabiar

en rapport [ɑ̃ rɑˈpɔr] de acuerdo

enrapt [ɛnˈræpt] *adj* embelesado, transportado

enrapture [ɛnˈræptʃər] *va* embelesar, transportar

enrich [ɛnˈrɪtʃ] *va* enriquecer

enrichment [ɛnˈrɪtʃmənt] *s* enriquecimiento

enroll o **enrol** [ɛnˈrol] (*pret & pp:* **-rolled;** *ger:* **-rolling**) *va* alistar, inscribir; redactar en forma legal; poner en limpio; enrollar, envolver; *vn* alistarse, inscribirse

enrollment o **enrolment** [ɛnˈrolmənt] *s* alistamiento, inscripción

en route [ɑ̃ ˈrut] o [ɑn ˈrut] en camino; **en route to** camino de, con rumbo a

ensanguine [ɛnˈsæŋgwɪn] *va* ensangrentar

ensconce [ɛnˈskɑns] *va* esconder, poner en seguro; acomodar, situar

ensemble [ɑnˈsɑmbəl] *s* conjunto; (mus.) grupo de músicos que tocan o cantan juntos; (mus.) ejecución por un grupo de músicos; (mus.) conjunto (*relación conveniente entre todas las partes*); traje de mujer armonioso

enshrine [ɛnˈʃraɪn] *va* encerrar o guardar en un relicario; abrigar, guardar con cariño y respeto

enshrinement [ɛnˈʃraɪnmənt] *s* encierro en un relicario; abrigo

ensiform [ˈɛnsɪfɔrm] *adj* (anat., bot. & zool.) ensiforme

ensign [ˈɛnsaɪn] *s* bandera, enseña; divisa, insignia; [ˈɛnsən] o [ˈɛnsaɪn] *s* (nav.) alférez de fragata

ensigncy [ˈɛnsənsɪ] o [ˈɛnsaɪnsɪ] o **ensignship** [ˈɛnsənʃɪp] o [ˈɛnsaɪnʃɪp] *s* alferazgo

ensilage [ˈɛnsɪlɪdʒ] *s* ensilaje; *va* ensilar

enslave [ɛnˈslev] *va* esclavizar

enslavement [ɛnˈslevmənt] *s* esclavización

ensnare [ɛnˈsnɛr] *va* entrampar

ensue [ɛnˈsu] o [ɛnˈsju] *vn* seguirse

ensuing [ɛnˈsuɪŋ] o [ɛnˈsjuɪŋ] *adj* siguiente; resultante

ensure [ɛnˈʃʊr] *va* asegurar

entablature [ɛnˈtæblətʃər] *s* (arch.) cornisamento

entail [ɛnˈtel] *s* (law) vínculo; *va* ocasionar, imponer; (law) vincular

entailment [ɛnˈtelmənt] *s* (law) vinculación

entangle [ɛnˈtæŋgəl] *va* enmarañar, enredar; *vn* enmarañarse, enredarse

entanglement [ɛnˈtæŋgəlmənt] *s* enmarañamiento, enredo

entasia [ɛnˈteʒɪə] *s* (path.) entasia

entasis [ˈɛntəsɪs] *s* (arch.) éntasis

entelechy [ɛnˈtɛləkɪ] *s* (*pl:* **-chies**) (philos.) entelequia

entellus [ɛnˈtɛləs] *s* (zool.) entelo

entente [ɑnˈtɑnt] *s* (dipl.) entente, trato secreto

enter [ˈɛntər] *va* entrar en; asentar, registrar; aduanar; matricular (*a un alumno*); ingresar (*p.ej., a un menor en un asilo*); ingresar en, matricularse en; hacer miembro a; hacerse miembro de; emprender; **to enter an order** asentar un pedido; **to enter one's head** metérsele a uno en la cabeza; *vn* entrar; (theat.) entrar en escena, salir; **to enter into** entrar en; participar en; celebrar (*p.ej., un contrato*); **to enter on** o **upon** emprender; tomar posesión de

enteralgia [ˌɛntəˈrældʒɪə] *s* (path.) enteralgia

enterectomy [ˌɛntəˈrɛktəmɪ] *s* (*pl:* **-mies**) (surg.) enterectomía

enteric [ɛnˈtɛrɪk] *adj* entérico

enteric fever *s* (path.) fiebre entérica

enteritis [ˌɛntəˈraɪtɪs] *s* (path.) enteritis

enterohepatitis [ˌɛntəroˌhɛpəˈtaɪtɪs] *s* (path.) enterohepatitis

enterology [ˌɛntəˈrɑlədʒɪ] *s* enterología

enterostomy [ˌɛntəˈrɑstəmɪ] *s* (*pl:* **-mies**) (surg.) enterostomía

enterotomy [ˌɛntəˈrɑtəmɪ] *s* (*pl:* **-mies**) (surg.) enterotomía

enterprise [ˈɛntərpraɪz] *s* empresa; espíritu emprendedor

enterprising [ˈɛntərˌpraɪzɪŋ] *adj* emprendedor

entertain [ˌɛntərˈten] *va* entretener, divertir; recibir; festejar; abrigar (*ideas, esperanzas, etc.*); considerar; *vn* recibir; dar tertulias

entertainer [ˌɛntərˈtenər] *s* actor, vocalista, músico, etc. (*p.ej., en un café cantante*); anfitrión; festejador

entertaining [ˌɛntərˈtenɪŋ] *adj* entretenido

entertainment [ˌɛntərˈtenmənt] *s* entretenimiento, diversión; recepción; festejo; espectáculo; abrigo (*de una idea, esperanza, etc.*)

enthrall o **enthral** [ɛnˈθrɔl] (*pret & pp:* **-thralled;** *ger:* **-thralling**) *va* encantar, dominar; esclavizar, sojuzgar

enthrallment o **enthralment** [ɛnˈθrɔlmənt] *s* encantamiento, dominación; subyugación

enthrone [ɛnˈθron] *va* entronizar

enthronement [ɛnˈθronmənt] *s* entronización

enthuse [ɛnˈθuz] o [ɛnˈθjuz] *va* (coll.) entusiasmar; *vn* (coll.) entusiasmarse

enthusiasm [ɛnˈθuzɪæzəm] o [ɛnˈθjuzɪæzəm] *s* entusiasmo

enthusiast [ɛnˈθuzɪæst] o [ɛnˈθjuzɪæst] *s* entusiasta

enthusiastic [ɛnˌθuzɪˈæstɪk] o [ɛnˌθjuzɪˈæstɪk] *adj* entusiástico

enthusiastically [ɛnˌθuzɪˈæstɪkəlɪ] o [ɛnˌθjuzɪˈæstɪkəlɪ] *adv* entusiásticamente

enthymeme [ˈɛnθɪmim] *s* (log.) entimema

entice [ɛnˈtaɪs] *va* atraer con halagos; tentar, inducir al mal; **to entice someone into** + *ger* tentar a uno a que + *subj*

enticement [ɛnˈtaɪsmənt] *s* atracción halagüeña; tentación

entire [ɛnˈtaɪr] *adj* entero; (bot.) entero, enterísimo

entirely [ɛnˈtaɪrlɪ] *adv* enteramente; solamente

entirety [ɛnˈtaɪrtɪ] *s* (*pl:* **-ties**) entereza; todo, cosa entera; **in its entirety** en su totalidad

entitle [ɛnˈtaɪtəl] *va* intitular; dar derecho a

entity [ˈɛntɪtɪ] *s* (*pl:* **-ties**) entidad

entomb [ɛnˈtum] *va* sepultar

entombment [ɛnˈtummənt] *s* sepultura

entomologic [ˌɛntəməˈlɑdʒɪk] o **entomological** [ˌɛntəməˈlɑdʒɪkəl] *adj* entomológico

entomologist [ˌɛntəˈmɑlədʒɪst] *s* entomólogo

entomology [ˌɛntəˈmɑlədʒɪ] *s* entomología

entourage [ˌɑntuˈrɑʒ] *s* séquito, cortejo

entozoan [ˌɛntəˈzoən] *s* (zool.) entozoario

entrails [ˈɛntrelz] o [ˈɛntrəlz] *spl* entrañas; (fig.) entrañas (*p.ej., de la tierra*)

entrain [ɛnˈtren] *va* despachar (*p.ej., tropas*); *vn* embarcar, salir en tren

entrance ['ɛntrəns] *s* entrada; ingreso; (theat.) entrada en escena; [ɛn'træns] o [ɛn'trɑns] *va* encantar, embelesar, arrebatar
entrance examination *s* examen de ingreso; **to take entrance examinations** examinarse de ingreso
entrancement [ɛn'trænsmənt] o [ɛn'trɑnsmənt] *s* encanto, embeleso
entranceway ['ɛntrəns,we] *s* entrada; portal, zaguán
entrancing [ɛn'trænsɪŋ] o [ɛn'trɑnsɪŋ] *adj* encantador, embelesador
entrant ['ɛntrənt] *s* entrante; principiante; (sport) concurrente
entrap [ɛn'træp] (*pret & pp:* **-trapped;** *ger:* **-trapping**) *va* entrampar
entreat [ɛn'trit] *va* rogar, suplicar
entreaty [ɛn'tritɪ] *s* (*pl:* **-ies**) ruego, súplica
entree o **entrée** ['ɑntre] *s* entrada, ingreso; (cook.) entrada, principio
entrench [ɛn'trɛntʃ] *va* atrincherar; establecer firmemente; *vn* atrincherarse; **to entrench on** o **upon** infringir, violar
entrenchment [ɛn'trɛntʃmənt] *s* atrincheramiento
entrepôt ['ɑntrəpo] *s* almacén; emporio, centro comercial
entrepreneur [,ɑntrəprə'nʌr] *s* empresario
entresol ['ɛntərsɑl] o ['ɑntrəsɑl] *s* entresuelo
entropy ['ɛntrəpɪ] *s* (*pl:* **-pies**) (thermodynamics) entropía
entrust [ɛn'trʌst] *va* confiar; **to entrust to** confiar a; **to entrust someone with something** confiar algo a alguien
entry ['ɛntrɪ] *s* (*pl:* **-tries**) entrada; (com.) entrada, partida; entrada, vestíbulo, zaguán; artículo (*cada palabra alfabetizada en un diccionario, etc.*); entrada en la aduana; rival (*en una carrera, concurso, etc.*)
entwine [ɛn'twaɪn] *va* entretejer, entrelazar
entwist [ɛn'twɪst] *va* retorcer
enucleate [ɪ'njuklɪet] o [ɪ'nuklɪet] *va* enuclear
enucleation [ɪ,njuklɪ'eʃən] o [ɪ,nuklɪ'eʃən] *s* (surg.) enucleación
enumerate [ɪ'njuməret] o [ɪ'numəret] *va* enumerar
enumeration [ɪ,njumə'reʃən] o [ɪ,numə'reʃən] *s* enumeración
enumerative [ɪ'njumə,retɪv] o [ɪ'numə,retɪv] *adj* enumerativo
enumerator [ɪ'njumə,retər] o [ɪ'numə,retər] *s* enumerador
enunciate [ɪ'nʌnsɪet] o [ɪ'nʌnʃɪet] *va* enunciar; pronunciar
enunciation [ɪ,nʌnsɪ'eʃən] o [ɪ,nʌnʃɪ'eʃən] *s* enunciación; pronunciación
enuresis [,ɛnjə'risɪs] *s* (path.) enuresis
envelop [ɛn'vɛləp] *s* sobre, cubierta; envoltura; (aer.) envoltura; (bot.) túnica, envoltura; *va* envolver
envelope ['ɛnvəlop] o ['ɑnvəlop] *s* sobre, cubierta; envoltura; (aer.) envoltura; (bot.) túnica, envoltura
envelopment [ɛn'vɛləpmənt] *s* envolvimiento; cubierta, envoltura
envenom [ɛn'vɛnəm] *va* envenenar
enviable ['ɛnvɪəbəl] *adj* envidiable
envious ['ɛnvɪəs] *adj* envidioso
environ [ɛn'vaɪrən] *va* encerrar, rodear, ceñir; **environs** [ɛn'vaɪrənz] o ['ɛnvɪrənz] *spl* alrededores, cercanías, inmediaciones
environment [ɛn'vaɪrənmənt] *s* encierro; medio ambiente; alrededores, cercanías, inmediaciones
environmental [ɛn,vaɪrən'mɛntəl] *adj* circunvecino, ambiente, ambiental
envisage [ɛn'vɪzɪdʒ] *va* encarar, encararse con; representarse, considerar
envoi ['ɛnvɔɪ] *s* tornada, despedida (*en una composición poética*)
envoy ['ɛnvɔɪ] *s* enviado; tornada, despedida (*en una composición poética*)
envy ['ɛnvɪ] *s* (*pl:* **-vies**) envidia; (*pret & pp:* **-vied**) *va* envidiar
enwomb [ɛn'wum] *va* sepultar, entrañar
enwrap [ɛn'ræp] (*pret & pp:* **-wrapped;** *ger:* **-wrapping**) *va* arropar, envolver
enwreathe [ɛn'rið] *va* enguirnaldar
enzoötic [,ɛnzo'ɑtɪk] *s* (vet.) enzootia
enzymatic [,ɛnzaɪ'mætɪk] o [,ɛnzɪ'mætɪk] *adj* enzímico
enzyme ['ɛnzaɪm] o ['ɛnzɪm] *s* (biochem.) enzima
Eocene ['iosin] *adj & s* (geol.) eoceno
Eolian [i'olɪən] *adj & s* var. de **Aeolian**
eolithic [,io'lɪθɪk] *adj* (archeol.) eolítico
eon ['iən] o ['iɑn] *s* var. de **aeon**
Eos ['iɑs] *s* (myth.) Eos
eosin ['iosɪn] *s* (chem.) eosina
epact ['ipækt] *s* epacta
epaulet o **epaulette** ['ɛpəlɛt] *s* hombrera, charretera
ependyma [ɛ'pɛndɪmə] *s* (anat.) epéndimo
epenthesis [ɛ'pɛnθɪsɪs] *s* (*pl:* **-ses** [siz]) (gram.) epéntesis
epenthetic [,ɛpɛn'θɛtɪk] *adj* epentético
epergne [ɪ'pʌrn] o [e'pɛrn] *s* centro de mesa, ramillete
Eph. abr. de **Ephesians**
ephedrine [ɪ'fɛdrɪn] o ['ɛfɪdrin] *s* (pharm.) efedrina
ephemeral [ɪ'fɛmərəl] *adj* efímero
ephemerid [ɪ'fɛmərɪd] *s* (ent.) efemérido
ephemeris [ɪ'fɛmərɪs] *s* (*pl:* **ephemerides** [,ɛfɪ'mɛrɪdiz]) efemérides; efemérides astronómicas
Ephesian [ɪ'fiʒən] *adj & s* efesino o efesio; **Ephesians** *spl* (Bib.) Epístola de San Pablo a los Efesios
Ephesus ['ɛfɪsəs] *s* Éfeso
Ephraim ['ifrɪəm] *s* (Bib.) Efraín
epic ['ɛpɪk] *adj* épico; *s* epopeya; (fig.) epopeya
epical ['ɛpɪkəl] *adj* épico
epicalyx [,ɛpɪ'kelɪks] o [,ɛpɪ'kælɪks] *s* (bot.) epicáliz, calículo
epicarp ['ɛpɪkɑrp] *s* (bot.) epicarpio
epicedium [,ɛpɪ'sidɪəm] *s* (*pl:* **-a** [ə]) epicedio
epicene ['ɛpɪsin] *adj* (gram.) epiceno
epicenter ['ɛpɪ,sɛntər] *s* epicentro
epicotyl [,ɛpɪ'kɑtɪl] *s* (bot.) epicotilo
Epictetus [,ɛpɪk'titəs] *s* Epicteto
epicure ['ɛpɪkjʊr] *s* epicúreo
Epicurean [,ɛpɪkjʊ'riən] *adj & s* epicúreo; (*l.c.*) *adj & s* epicúreo
Epicureanism [,ɛpɪkjʊ'riənɪzəm] *s* epicureísmo
Epicurus [,ɛpɪ'kjʊrəs] *s* Epicuro
epicycle ['ɛpɪ,saɪkəl] *s* (astr. & geom.) epiciclo
epicyclic [,ɛpɪ'saɪklɪk] o [,ɛpɪ'sɪklɪk] *adj* epicíclico
epicycloid [,ɛpɪ'saɪklɔɪd] *s* (geom.) epicicloide
epidemic [,ɛpɪ'dɛmɪk] *adj* epidémico; *s* epidemia
epidemical [,ɛpɪ'dɛmɪkəl] *adj* epidémico
epidemicity [,ɛpɪdɪ'mɪsɪtɪ] *s* epidemicidad
epidemiologist [,ɛpɪ,dimɪ'ɑlədʒɪst] *s* epidemiólogo
epidemiology [,ɛpɪ,dimɪ'ɑlədʒɪ] *s* epidemiología
epidermal [,ɛpɪ'dʌrməl] *adj* epidérmico
epidermis [,ɛpɪ'dʌrmɪs] *s* (anat.) epidermis
epidote ['ɛpɪdot] *s* (mineral.) epidota
epigastric [,ɛpɪ'gæstrɪk] *adj* epigástrico
epigastrium [,ɛpɪ'gæstrɪəm] *s* (anat. & zool.) epigastrio
epigene ['ɛpɪdʒin] *adj* (geol.) epigénico
epiglottis [,ɛpɪ'glɑtɪs] *s* (anat.) epiglotis
epigram ['ɛpɪgræm] *s* epigrama
epigrammatic [,ɛpɪgrə'mætɪk] *adj* epigramático
epigrammatically [,ɛpɪgrə'mætɪkəlɪ] *adv* epigramáticamente
epigraph ['ɛpɪgræf] o ['ɛpɪgrɑf] *s* epígrafe
epigrapher [ɪ'pɪgrəfər] *s* epigrafista
epigraphic [,ɛpɪ'græfɪk] *adj* epigráfico
epigraphy [ɪ'pɪgrəfɪ] *s* epigrafía
epilepsy ['ɛpɪ,lɛpsɪ] *s* (path.) epilepsia
epileptic [,ɛpɪ'lɛptɪk] *adj & s* epiléptico
epilog o **epilogue** ['ɛpɪlɔg] o ['ɛpɪlɑg] *s* epílogo
Epiphany [ɪ'pɪfənɪ] *s* (eccl.) Epifanía; (*l.c.*) *s* epifanía (*aparición*)
epiphonema [,ɛpɪfo'nimə] *s* (rhet.) epifonema
epiphora [ɪ'pɪfərə] *s* (path.) epífora
epiphysis [ɪ'pɪfɪsɪs] *s* (*pl:* **-ses** [siz]) (anat.) epífisis
epiphyte ['ɛpɪfaɪt] *s* (bot.) epífita
epiphytic [,ɛpɪ'fɪtɪk] *adj* epífito, epifítico
Epirus [ɪ'paɪrəs] *s* el Epiro

Epis. abr. de **Episcopal, Episcopalians** y **Epistle**
Episc. abr. de **Episcopal**
episcopacy [ɪˈpɪskəpəsɪ] *s* (*pl:* **-cies**) episcopado
episcopal [ɪˈpɪskəpəl] *adj* episcopal; (*cap.*) *adj* episcopal
Episcopalian [ɪˌpɪskəˈpeljən] *adj* & *s* episcopalista
Episcopalianism [ɪˌpɪskəˈpeljənɪzəm] *s* episcopalismo
episcopalism [ɪˈpɪskəpəlɪzəm] *s* (eccl.) episcopalismo
episcopate [ɪˈpɪskəpet] o [ɪˈpɪskəpɪt] *s* episcopado
episode [ˈɛpɪsod] *s* episodio
episodic [ˌɛpɪˈsɑdɪk] o **episodical** [ˌɛpɪˈsɑdɪkəl] *adj* episódico
epispastic [ˌɛpɪˈspæstɪk] *adj* & *s* (med.) epispástico
epistaxis [ˌɛpɪˈstæksɪs] *s* (path.) epistaxis
epistemological [ɪˌpɪstɪməˈlɑdʒɪkəl] *adj* epistemológico
epistemology [ɪˌpɪstɪˈmɑlədʒɪ] *s* epistemología
epistle [ɪˈpɪsəl] *s* epístola; (*cap.*) *s* (eccl.) epístola
Epistle side *s* (eccl.) lado de la epístola
epistolary [ɪˈpɪstəˌlɛrɪ] *adj* epistolar; *s* (eccl.) epistolario
epistyle [ˈɛpɪstaɪl] *s* (arch.) epistilo
epitaph [ˈɛpɪtæf] o [ˈɛpɪtɑf] *s* epitafio
epithalamium [ˌɛpɪθəˈlemɪəm] *s* (*pl:* **-miums** o **-mia** [mɪə]) epitalamio
epithelial [ˌɛpɪˈθilɪəl] *adj* epitelial
epithelioma [ˌɛpɪˌθilɪˈomə] *s* (*pl:* **-mata** [mətə] o **-mas**) (path.) epitelioma
epithelium [ˌɛpɪˈθilɪəm] *s* (*pl:* **-lia** [lɪə] o **-liums**) (anat.) epitelio
epithem [ˈɛpɪθɛm] *s* (med.) epítema
epithet [ˈɛpɪθɛt] *s* epíteto
epitome [ɪˈpɪtəmɪ] *s* epítome
epitomize [ɪˈpɪtəmaɪz] *va* epitomar
epizoötic [ˌɛpɪzoˈɑtɪk] *adj* epizoótico; *s* epizootia
epoch [ˈɛpək] o [ˈipɑk] *s* época; (astr. & geol.) época
epochal [ˈɛpəkəl] *adj* trascendental, memorable
epoch-making [ˈɛpəkˌmekɪŋ] o [ˈipɑkˌmekɪŋ] *adj* que hace época; trascendental, memorable
epode [ˈɛpod] *s* epoda o epodo
eponymous [ɛˈpɑnɪməs] *adj* epónimo
epsilon [ˈɛpsɪlɑn] *s* épsilon
epsomite [ˈɛpsəmaɪt] *s* (mineral.) epsomita
Epsom salts [ˈɛpsəm] *spl* sal de Epsom, sal de la Higuera
eq. abr. de **equal** y **equivalent**
equability [ˌɛkwəˈbɪlɪtɪ] o [ˌikwəˈbɪlɪtɪ] *s* igualdad, uniformidad; constancia, tranquilidad
equable [ˈɛkwəbəl] o [ˈikwəbəl] *adj* igual, uniforme; constante, tranquilo
equal [ˈikwəl] *adj* igual; **equal to** suficiente para, bastante para; a la altura de, al nivel de, con fuerzas para; *s* igual; (*pret & pp:* **equaled** o **equalled;** *ger:* **equaling** *o* **equalling**) *va* igualar (*poner igual*); igualarse a o con (*ser igual a; ponerse al nivel de*)
equalitarian [ɪˌkwɑlɪˈtɛrɪən] *adj* & *s* igualitario
equality [ɪˈkwɑlɪtɪ] *s* (*pl:* **-ties**) igualdad
equalization [ˌikwəlɪˈzeʃən] *s* igualamiento, igualación
equalize [ˈikwəlaɪz] *va* igualar
equally [ˈikwəlɪ] *adv* igualmente
equanimity [ˌikwəˈnɪmɪtɪ] o [ˌɛkwəˈnɪmɪtɪ] *s* ecuanimidad
equate [iˈkwet] *va* igualar; (math.) igualar
equation [iˈkweʒən] o [iˈkweʃən] *s* (math., astr. & chem.) ecuación
equator [iˈkwetər] *s* ecuador
equatorial [ˌikwəˈtorɪəl] *adj* ecuatorial; *s* (astr.) ecuatorial (*instrumento*)
equerry [ˈɛkwərɪ] o [ɪˈkwɛrɪ] *s* (*pl:* **-ries**) caballerizo; (Brit.) caballerizo del rey
equestrian [ɪˈkwɛstrɪən] *adj* ecuestre; *s* jinete
equestrienne [ɪˌkwɛstrɪˈɛn] *s* amazona
equiangular [ˌikwɪˈæŋgjələr] *adj* (geom.) equiángulo
equid [ˈɛkwɪd] *s* (zool.) équido
equidistance [ˌikwɪˈdɪstəns] *s* equidistancia
equidistant [ˌikwɪˈdɪstənt] *adj* equidistante
equilateral [ˌikwɪˈlætərəl] *adj* equilátero
equilibrant [ɪˈkwɪlɪbrənt] *s* (phys.) fuerza equilibrante
equilibrate [ˌikwɪˈlaɪbret] o [ɪˈkwɪlɪbret] *va* equilibrar
equilibration [ˌikwɪlaɪˈbreʃən] o [ɪˌkwɪlɪˈbreʃən] *s* equilibración
equilibrist [ɪˈkwɪlɪbrɪst] *s* equilibrista
equilibrium [ˌikwɪˈlɪbrɪəm] *s* equilibrio
equine [ˈikwaɪn] *adj* & *s* equino
equinoctial [ˌikwɪˈnɑkʃəl] *adj* equinoccial; *s* equinoccial, línea equinoccial; tempestad equinoccial
equinoctial line *s* línea equinoccial
equinoctial point *s* punto equinoccial
equinox [ˈikwɪnɑks] *s* (astr.) equinoccio
equip [ɪˈkwɪp] (*pret & pp:* **equipped;** *ger:* **equipping**) *va* equipar
equipage [ˈɛkwɪpɪdʒ] *s* equipaje, equipo; carruaje
equipment [ɪˈkwɪpmənt] *s* equipo; material, maquinaria, avíos; aptitud, habilitación
equipment bond *s* (rail.) bono respaldado por material rodante
equipment trust *s* (rail.) escritura fiduciaria sobre material rodante
equipoise [ˈikwɪpɔɪz] o [ˈɛkwɪpɔɪz] *s* equilibrio; contrapeso; *va* equilibrar; contrapesar
equipotential [ˌikwɪpəˈtɛnʃəl] *adj* (phys.) equipotencial
equisetaceous [ˌɛkwɪsɪˈteʃəs] *adj* (bot.) equisetáceo
equisetum [ˌɛkwɪˈsitəm] *s* (*pl:* **-tums** o **-ta** [tə]) (bot.) equiseto
equitable [ˈɛkwɪtəbəl] *adj* equitativo
equitation [ˌɛkwɪˈteʃən] *s* equitación
equity [ˈɛkwɪtɪ] *s* (*pl:* **-ties**) equidad; (law) equidad; (coll.) diferencia entre el valor de una propiedad y la hipoteca que la grava
equity of redemption *s* (law) derecho de rescate
equivalence [ɪˈkwɪvələns] *s* equivalencia
equivalent [ɪˈkwɪvələnt] *adj* & *s* equivalente
equivocal [ɪˈkwɪvəkəl] *adj* equívoco
equivocate [ɪˈkwɪvəket] *vn* mentir, usar palabras o frases equívocas para engañar
equivocation [ɪˌkwɪvəˈkeʃən] *s* equívoco
equivocator [ɪˈkwɪvəˌketər] *s* equivoquista
era [ˈɪrə] o [ˈirə] *s* era; (geol.) era
eradicable [ɪˈrædɪkəbəl] *adj* erradicable
eradicate [ɪˈrædɪket] *va* erradicar
eradication [ɪˌrædɪˈkeʃən] *s* erradicación
eradicator [ɪˈrædɪˌketər] *s* arrancarraíces; líquido para quitar grasa, aceite, tinta, etc.; líquido borratintas
erase [ɪˈres] *va* borrar
erase head *s* cabeza de borrado (*del magnetófono*)
eraser [ɪˈresər] *s* borrador, goma de borrar
Erasmian [ɪˈræzmɪən] *adj* & *s* erasmiano
Erasmus [ɪˈræzməs] *s* Erasmo
erasure [ɪˈreʃər] o [ɪˈreʒər] *s* borradura
Erato [ˈɛrəto] *s* (myth.) Erato
erbium [ˈʌrbɪəm] *s* (chem.) erbio
ere [ɛr] *prep* antes de; *conj* antes que; más bien que
Erebus [ˈɛrɪbəs] *s* (myth.) Erebo (*infierno*)
erect [ɪˈrɛkt] *adj* erguido, derecho; erizado; *va* erigir; armar, montar, instalar
erectile [ɪˈrɛktɪl] *adj* eréctil
erectility [ɪˌrɛkˈtɪlɪtɪ] o [ˌirɛkˈtɪlɪtɪ] *s* erectilidad
erection [ɪˈrɛkʃən] *s* erección; (physiol.) erección
erector [ɪˈrɛktər] *s* erector
Erector set *s* (trademark) mecano
erelong [ˌɛrˈlɔŋ] o [ˌɛrˈlɑŋ] *adv* en breve, dentro de poco
eremite [ˈɛrɪmaɪt] *s* eremita, ermitaño
erepsin [ɪˈrɛpsɪn] *s* (biochem.) erepsina
erethism [ˈɛrɪθɪzəm] *s* (physiol.) eretismo
erg [ʌrg] *s* (phys.) ergio
ergo [ˈʌrgo] *adv* & *conj* (Lat.) pues, por tanto, por consiguiente
ergosterol [ʌrˈgɑstərol] *s* (pharm.) ergosterol
ergot [ˈʌrgət] o [ˈʌrgɑt] *s* (bot. & pharm.) cornezuelo; (plant path.) ergotismo
ergotin [ˈʌrgətɪn] *s* (pharm.) ergotina

ergotism ['ʌrgətɪzəm] *s* ergotismo (*sofistería*); (path.) ergotismo
Eric ['ɛrɪk] *s* Erico
ericaceous [ˌɛrɪ'keʃəs] *adj* (bot.) ericáceo
Erin ['ɛrɪn] o ['ɪrɪn] *s* (poet.) la Verde Erín
Erinys [ɪ'rɪnɪs] o [ɪ'raɪnɪs] *s* (*pl:* **Erinyes** [ɪ'rɪnɪiz]) (myth.) Erinia
eristic [ɛ'rɪstɪk] *adj* erístico; *s* erística (*arte de disputar*)
Eritrea [ˌɛrɪ'triə] *s* Eritrea
Eritrean [ˌɛrɪ'triən] *adj & s* eritreo
erlking ['ʌrlˌkɪŋ] *s* (myth.) rey de los duendes
ermine ['ʌrmɪn] *s* (zool. & her.) armiño; (fig.) toga, judicatura; **ermines** *s* (her.) contraarmiños; *adj* armiñado
ermined ['ʌrmɪnd] *adj* armiñado
erne [ʌrn] *s* (orn.) águila marina
Ernest ['ʌrnɪst] *s* Ernesto
erode [ɪ'rod] *va* erosionar; *vn* erosionarse
Eros ['ɪrɑs], ['irɑs] o ['ɛrɑs] *s* (myth.) Eros
erosion [ɪ'roʒən] *s* erosión; (geol.) erosión
erosive [ɪ'rosɪv] *adj* erosivo
erotic [ɪ'rɑtɪk] *adj* erótico; erotómano; *s* persona erótica, erotómano; poema erótico
erotism ['ɛrətɪzəm] *s* erotismo
erotomania [ɪˌrotə'menɪə] o [ɪˌrɑtə'menɪə] *s* (path.) erotomanía
err [ʌr] *vn* marrar
errand ['ɛrənd] *s* recado, mandado, comisión; **to run an errand** hacer un mandado; **to send on an errand** enviar a un recado
errand boy *s* mandadero, recadero
errant ['ɛrənt] *adj* errante, andante; erróneo, equivocado
errantry ['ɛrəntrɪ] *s* (*pl:* **-ries**) caballería andante
erratic [ɪ'rætɪk] *adj* irregular, inconstante; excéntrico; (geol.) errático
erratically [ɪ'rætɪkəlɪ] *adv* irregularmente, inconstantemente; excéntricamente
erratum [ɪ'retəm] o [ɪ'rɑtəm] *s* (*pl:* **-ta** [tə]) errata
erroneous [ɪ'ronɪəs] *adj* erróneo
error ['ɛrər] *s* error
ersatz [ɛr'zɑts] *adj & s* sucedáneo
Erse [ʌrs] *adj & s* erso
erstwhile ['ʌrstˌhwaɪl] *adj* antiguo, de otro tiempo; *adv* (archaic) antiguamente
eruct [ɪ'rʌkt] o **eructate** [ɪ'rʌktet] *va* arrojar, echar de sí, vomitar; *vn* eructar
eructation [ɪˌrʌk'teʃən] o [ˌɛrək'teʃən] *s* eructo; vómito
erudite ['ɛrudaɪt] o ['ɛrjudaɪt] *adj* erudito
erudition [ˌɛru'dɪʃən] o [ˌɛrju'dɪʃən] *s* erudición
erupt [ɪ'rʌpt] *va* arrojar (*llamas, lava, etc.*); *vn* hacer erupción (*p.ej., la piel, los dientes de un niño*); erumpir (*un volcán*)
eruption [ɪ'rʌpʃən] *s* erupción; (path. & dent.) erupción
eruptive [ɪ'rʌptɪv] *adj* eruptivo
Erymanthian boar [ˌɛrɪ'mænθɪən] *s* (myth.) jabalí de Erimanto
erysipelas [ˌɛrɪ'sɪpələs] o [ˌɪrɪ'sɪpələs] *s* (path.) erisipela
erysipeloid [ˌɛrɪ'sɪpəlɔɪd] o [ˌɪrɪ'sɪpəlɔɪd] *s* (path.) erisipeloide
erythema [ˌɛrɪ'θimə] *s* (path.) eritema
erythrin [ɪ'rɪθrɪn] *s* (chem.) eritrina
erythrite [ɪ'rɪθraɪt] *s* (mineral.) eritrita
erythroblast [ɪ'rɪθroblæst] *s* (anat.) eritroblasto
erythrocyte [ɪ'rɪθrosaɪt] *s* (anat.) eritrocito
erythroxylaceous [ˌɛrɪˌθrɑksɪ'leʃəs] *adj* (bot.) eritroxiláceo
Esau ['isɔ] *s* (Bib.) Esaú
escadrille [ˌɛskə'drɪl] *s* (nav.& aer.) escuadrilla
escalade [ˌɛskə'led] *s* escalada; *va* escalar
escalate ['ɛskəlet] *va* escalarse
escalator ['ɛskəˌletər] *s* (trademark) escalera mecánica, escalera móvil, escalera rodante
escalator clause *s* cláusula contractual de revisión de jornales por variación del costo de la vida
escallop [ɛs'kɑləp] o [ɛs'kæləp] *s* (zool.) concha de peregrino; venera (*de los peregrinos*); (sew.) festón; *va* hornear a la crema y con migajas de pan; cocer (*p.ej., ostras*) en su concha
escapade [ˌɛskə'ped] o ['ɛskəped] *s* escapada; travesura, calaverada, aventura atolondrada
escape [ɛs'kep] *s* escape, escapatoria; (fig.) escapatoria (*de atenciones, deberes, etc.*); *va* evitar, eludir; escapársele a uno, p.ej., **nothing escapes him** no se le escapa nada; olvidársele a uno, p.ej., **his name escapes me** se me olvida su nombre; salírsele a uno, p.ej., **a cry escaped his lips** se le salió un grito; escapar a (*p.ej., la muerte*); *vn* escapar o escaparse; **to escape from** escaparse a (*una persona*); escaparse de (*p.ej., la cárcel*)
escape artist *s* ilusionista que sabe desprenderse de toda suerte de ataduras y trabas
escapee [ˌɛskə'pi] *s* evadido
escape hatch *s* escotillón de escape
escape literature *s* literatura de escape
escapement [ɛs'kepmənt] *s* escape
escapement wheel *s* (horol.) rueda de escape
escape velocity *s* velocidad de escape (*de un satélite*)
escape wheel *s* var. de **escapement wheel**
escapism [ɛs'kepɪzəm] *s* escapismo
escapist [ɛs'kepɪst] *adj & s* escapista
escarole ['ɛskərol] *s* (bot.) escarola
escarp [ɛs'kɑrp] *s* escarpa; (fort.) escarpa; *va* (fort.) escarpar
escarpment [ɛs'kɑrpmənt] *s* escarpa, escarpadura; (fort.) escarpa
escharotic [ˌɛskə'rɑtɪk] *adj & s* (med.) escarótico
eschatological [ˌɛskətə'lɑdʒɪkəl] *adj* escatológico
eschatology [ˌɛskə'tɑlədʒɪ] *s* (theol.) escatología
escheat [ɛs'tʃit] *s* (law) reversión al estado o al señor de bienes del que muere sin testar; (law) bienes del que muere sin testar que revierten al estado o al señor; *va* (law) transferir al estado o al señor; *vn* (law) revertir al estado o al señor (*los bienes del que muere sin testar*)
eschew [ɛs'tʃu] *va* evitar
escort ['ɛskɔrt] *s* escolta; (aer. & nav.) escolta; [ɛs'kɔrt] *va* escoltar
escort carrier *s* (nav.) portaaviones de escolta
escort fighter *s* (aer.) caza de escolta
escritoire [ˌɛskrɪ'twɑr] *s* escritorio
escrow [ɛs'kro] o ['ɛskro] *s* (law) plica, documento que se pone en manos de una tercera persona para entregarlo al donatario y que no tiene valor ni efecto hasta cumplidas ciertas condiciones; **in escrow** en custodia de una tercera persona
esculent ['ɛskjələnt] *adj & s* comestible
escutcheon [ɛs'kʌtʃən] *s* escudo de armas; escudo, escudete (*planchuela de metal delante de la cerradura*)
Esd. abr. de **Esdras**
Esdras ['ɛzdrəs] *s* (Bib.) Esdras; (Bib.) libro de Esdras
Eskimo ['ɛskɪmo] *s* (*pl:* **-mos** o **-mo**) esquimal
Eskimoan [ˌɛskɪ'moən] *adj* esquimal
Eskimo dog *s* perro de los esquimales
esophagus [i'sɑfəgəs] *s* (*pl:* **-gi** [dʒaɪ]) (anat.) esófago
esoteric [ˌɛso'tɛrɪk] *adj* esotérico
esotropia [ˌɛso'tropɪə] *s* (path.) esotropia
esp. abr. de **especially**
espagnolette [ˌɛsˌpɑnjo'lɛt] *s* falleba
espalier [ɛs'pæljər] *s* espaldar, espalera; planta extendida sobre el espaldar; *va* extender sobre el espaldar; proveer de espaldar
esparto [ɛs'pɑrto] o **esparto grass** *s* (bot.) esparto
espec. abr. de **especially**
especial [ɛs'pɛʃəl] *adj* especial
especially [ɛs'pɛʃəlɪ] *adv* especialmente
Esperantist [ˌɛspə'rɑntɪst] o [ˌɛspə'ræntɪst] *adj & s* esperantista
Esperanto [ˌɛspə'rɑnto] o [ˌɛspə'rænto] *s* esperanto
espial [ɛs'paɪəl] *s* espionaje (*acción de espiar*); observación
espionage ['ɛspɪənɪdʒ] o [ˌɛspɪə'nɑʒ] *s* espionaje
esplanade [ˌɛsplə'ned] o [ˌɛsplə'nɑd] *s* explanada; (fort.) explanada
espousal [ɛs'pauzəl] *s* desposorios; adhesión (*p.ej., a un dictamen*); **espousals** *spl* desposorios
espouse [ɛs'pauz] *va* casarse con; abogar por, adherirse a (*p.ej., un dictamen*)

esprit de corps [ɛs'pri də 'kɔr] *s* espíritu de cuerpo, compañerismo
espy [ɛs'paɪ] (*pret & pp:* **-pied**) *va* divisar
Esq. abr. de **Esquire**
Esquimau ['ɛskɪmo] *s* (*pl:* **-maux** [mo] o [moz]) var. de **Eskimo**
esquire [ɛs'kwaɪr] *s* escudero (*paje que llevaba el escudo del caballero*); (Brit.) terrateniente de antigua heredad; (Brit.) hombre de la clase inferior a la de los caballeros; acompañante (*de una señora*); (*cap.*) *s* título de honor que se escribe después del apellido y que corresponde a Mr.
-ess *suffix s* -esa, p.ej., **abbess** abadesa; **countess** condesa; -isa, p.ej., **poetess** poetisa; **priestess** sacerdotisa
essay ['ɛse] *s* (lit.) ensayo; ['ɛse] o [ɛ'se] *s* conato, esfuerzo, ensayo; [ɛ'se] *va* ensayar (*especialmente metales, minerales*); intentar; *vn* esforzarse
essayist ['ɛseɪst] *s* ensayista
essence ['ɛsəns] *s* esencia; (chem.) esencia; **in essence** en esencia
essential [ɛ'sɛnʃəl] *adj & s* esencial
essentially [ɛ'sɛnʃəlɪ] *adv* esencialmente
essential oil *s* (chem.) aceite esencial
est. abr. de **established, estate, estimated** y **estuary**
E.S.T. abr. de **Eastern Standard Time**
estab. abr. de **established**
establish [ɛs'tæblɪʃ] *va* establecer
established church *s* iglesia oficial
establishment [ɛs'tæblɪʃmənt] *s* establecimiento
estate [ɛs'tet] *s* heredad, finca, hacienda; bienes, propiedad; bienes relictos, herencia; estado, condición; **the fourth estate** el cuarto poder (*la prensa, el periodismo*); **the three estates** los tres estados (*la nobleza, el clero y el estado llano*)
Estates-General [ɛs'tets'dʒɛnərəl] *spl* var. de **States-General**
esteem [ɛs'tim] *s* estima; *va* estimar
ester ['ɛstər] *s* (chem.) éster
Esth. abr. de **Esther**
Esther ['ɛstər] *s* Ester
esthete ['ɛsθit] *s* var. de **aesthete**
esthetic [ɛs'θɛtɪk] *adj* var. de **aesthetic; esthetics** *ssg* var. de **aesthetics**
esthetically [ɛs'θɛtɪkəlɪ] *adv* var. de **aesthetically**
esthetician [,ɛsθɪ'tɪʃən] *s* var. de **aesthetician**
Esthonia [ɛs'θonɪə] *s* var. de **Estonia**
estimable ['ɛstɪməbəl] *adj* estimable
estimate ['ɛstɪmɪt] o ['ɛstɪmet] *s* estimación; presupuesto (*p.ej., del coste de una obra*); proyecto de presupuesto; ['ɛstɪmet] *va* estimar; presuponer
estimation [,ɛstɪ'meʃən] *s* estimación
estival ['ɛstɪvəl] o [ɛs'taɪvəl] *adj* var. de **aestival**
estivate ['ɛstɪvet] *vn* var. de **aestivate**
estivation [,ɛstɪ'veʃən] *s* var. de **aestivation**
Estonia [ɛs'tonɪə] *s* Estonia
Estonian [ɛs'tonɪən] *adj & s* estonio
estop [ɛs'tɑp] (*pret & pp:* **-topped;** *ger:* **-topping**) *va* obstruir; impedir; (law) impedir (*a uno*) que declare en una acción lo que sea contrario a actas o manifestaciones
estoppel [ɛs'tɑpəl] *s* impedimento; (law) imposibilidad en que se coloca uno de declarar lo que sea contrario a actas o manifestaciones anteriores
estrange [ɛs'trendʒ] *va* apartar; enajenar, enemistar
estrangement [ɛs'trendʒmənt] *s* enajenamiento, extrañeza (*p.ej., entre amigos*)
estray [ɛs'tre] *s* (law) animal doméstico descarriado
estrogen ['ɛstrədʒən] *s* (biochem.) estrógeno
estrone ['ɛstron] *s* (biochem.) estrona
estuary ['ɛstʃʊ,ɛrɪ] *s* (*pl:* **-ies**) estuario; ría (*valle bajo que inunda el mar*)
et al. abr. de **et alii** (Lat.) **and others** y de **et alibi** (Lat.) **and elsewhere**
etc. abr. de **et cetera** (Lat.) **and others** y **and so forth**
etceteras [ɛt'sɛtərəz] *spl* adiciones, apéndices
etch [ɛtʃ] *va & vn* grabar al agua fuerte
etcher ['ɛtʃər] *s* aguafortista
etching ['ɛtʃɪŋ] *s* aguafuerte
eternal [ɪ'tʌrnəl] *adj* eterno, eternal
Eternal City *s* Ciudad Eterna (*Roma*)
eternal feminine, the (lit.) el eterno femenino
eternal recurrence *s* (philos.) retorno eterno
eternity [ɪ'tʌrnɪtɪ] *s* (*pl:* **-ties**) eternidad
eternize [ɪ'tʌrnaɪz] *va* eternizar
etesian [ɪ'tiʒən] o [ɪ'tizɪən] *adj & s* etesio
ethane ['ɛθen] *s* (chem.) etano
Ethelred ['ɛθəlrɛd] *s* Etelredo
ether ['iθər] *s* éter (*los espacios celestes*); (phys.) éter (*materia hipotética*); (chem.) éter (R_2O)
ethereal [ɪ'θɪrɪəl] *adj* etéreo; (phys. & chem.) etéreo
etherealize [ɪ'θɪrɪəlaɪz] *va* espiritualizar
etherification [ɪ,θɛrɪfɪ'keʃən] *s* (chem.) eterificación
etherify [ɪ'θɛrɪfaɪ] (*pret & pp:* **-fied**) *va* (chem.) eterificar
etherization [,iθərɪ'zeʃən] *s* (med.) eterización
etherize ['iθəraɪz] *va* (med.) eterizar; eterificar
ethic ['ɛθɪk] *adj* ético; **ethics** *ssg* ética
ethical ['ɛθɪkəl] *adj* ético
ethically ['ɛθɪkəlɪ] *adv* éticamente
Ethiop ['iθɪɑp] *adj & s* etíope
Ethiopia [,iθɪ'opɪə] *s* Etiopía
Ethiopian [,iθɪ'opɪən] *adj & s* etíope; (coll.) etíope (*de la raza negra*)
Ethiopic [,iθɪ'ɑpɪk] o [,iθɪ'opɪk] *adj* etiópico; *s* lengua etiópica
ethmoid ['ɛθmɔɪd] *adj & s* (anat.) etmoides
ethnic ['ɛθnɪk] o **ethnical** ['ɛθnɪkəl] *adj* étnico
ethnographer [ɛθ'nɑgrəfər] *s* etnógrafo
ethnographic [,ɛθnə'græfɪk] o **ethnographical** [,ɛθnə'græfɪkəl] *adj* etnográfico
ethnography [ɛθ'nɑgrəfɪ] *s* etnografía
ethnologic [,ɛθnə'lɑdʒɪk] o **ethnological** [,ɛθnə'lɑdʒɪkəl] *adj* etnológico
ethnologist [ɛθ'nɑlədʒɪst] *s* etnólogo
ethnology [ɛθ'nɑlədʒɪ] *s* etnología
ethopoeia [,iθo'pijə] *s* (rhet.) etopeya
ethyl ['ɛθɪl] *s* (chem.) etilo; plomo tetraetilo; (trademark) gasolina etílica
ethyl alcohol *s* (chem.) alcohol etílico
ethyl chloride *s* (chem.) cloruro de etilo
ethylene ['ɛθɪlin] *s* (chem.) etileno
Ethyl gas *s* (trademark) etilgasolina
ethylic [ɪ'θɪlɪk] *adj* etílico
etiology [,itɪ'ɑlədʒɪ] *s* var. de **aetiology**
etiquette ['ɛtɪkɛt] *s* etiqueta
Etna, Mount ['ɛtnə] el monte Etna
Etnean [ɛt'niən] *adj* étneo
Eton jacket ['itən] *s* chaqueta corta de los escolares del colegio de Eton (*Inglaterra*); chaqueta corta de mujer
Etrurian [ɪ'trʊrɪən] *adj & s* etrurio
Etruscan [ɪ'trʌskən] *adj & s* etrusco
et seq. abr. de **et sequens, et sequentes** y **et sequentia** (Lat.) **and the following**
étude [e'tjud] *s* (mus.) estudio
etymological [,ɛtɪmə'lɑdʒɪkəl] *adj* etimológico
etymologically [,ɛtɪmə'lɑdʒɪkəlɪ] *adv* etimológicamente
etymologist [,ɛtɪ'mɑlədʒɪst] *s* etimologista
etymology [,ɛtɪ'mɑlədʒɪ] *s* (*pl:* **-gies**) etimología
etymon ['ɛtɪmɑn] *s* (*pl:* **-mons** o **-ma** [mə]) (philol.) étimo o étimon
Euboea [ju'biə] *s* Eubea
eucaine [ju'ken] *s* (pharm.) eucaína
eucalyptol [,jukə'lɪptol] o [,jukə'lɪptɑl] *s* eucaliptol
eucalyptus [,jukə'lɪptəs] *s* (*pl:* **-tuses** o **-ti** [taɪ]) (bot.) eucalipto
Eucharist ['jukərɪst] *s* (eccl.) Eucaristía
Eucharistic [,jukə'rɪstɪk] *adj* eucarístico
euchre ['jukər] *s* juego de naipes en el que el valet del triunfo es la carta más alta; *va* vencer en el juego de euchre; (slang) ser más listo que
Euclid ['juklɪd] *s* Euclides
Euclidean [ju'klɪdɪən] *adj* euclidiano
Euclidean space *s* (geom.) espacio euclidiano
eucrasia [ju'kreʒɪə] *s* (med.) eucrasia
eudaemonism [ju'dimənɪzəm] *s* eudemonismo
eudiometer [,judɪ'ɑmɪtər] *s* eudiómetro
Eugene [jʊ'dʒin] *s* Eugenio
Eugenia [jʊ'dʒinɪə] *s* Eugenia

eugenic [jʊ'dʒɛnɪk] *adj* eugenésico; **eugenics** *ssg o spl* eugenesia
eugenically [jʊ'dʒɛnɪkəlɪ] *adv* de manera eugenésica
eulogist ['julədʒɪst] *s* elogiador
eulogistic [,julə'dʒɪstɪk] *adj* elogiador, elogioso
eulogistically [,julə'dʒɪstɪkəlɪ] *adv* laudatoriamente
eulogium [jʊ'lodʒɪəm] *s* (*pl:* **-giums** o **-gia** [dʒɪə]) elogio
eulogize ['julədʒaɪz] *va* elogiar
eulogy ['julədʒɪ] *s* (*pl:* **-gies**) elogio
Eumenides [ju'mɛnɪdiz] *spl* (myth.) Euménides
eunuch ['junək] *s* eunuco
eupatorium [,jupə'torɪəm] *s* (bot.) eupatorio
eupepsia [ju'pɛpsɪə] o [ju'pɛpʃə] *s* (med.) eupepsia
eupeptic [ju'pɛptɪk] *adj* eupéptico
euphemism ['jufɪmɪzəm] *s* eufemismo
euphemist ['jufɪmɪst] *s* persona que emplea el eufemismo
euphemistic [,jufɪ'mɪstɪk] *adj* eufemístico
euphemistically [,jufɪ'mɪstɪkəlɪ] *adv* eufemísticamente
euphemize ['jufɪmaɪz] *va* expresar con eufemismo; *vn* hacer uso del eufemismo
euphonic [ju'fɑnɪk] *adj* eufónico
euphonious [ju'fonɪəs] *adj* eufono
euphonium [ju'fonɪəm] *s* (mus.) eufonio (*instrumento que tiene tubos de vidrio y barras de acero*); (mus.) eufonia (*tuba*)
euphony ['jufənɪ] *s* (*pl:* **-nies**) eufonía
euphorbia [ju'fɔrbɪə] *s* (bot. & pharm.) euforbio
euphorbiaceous [ju,fɔrbɪ'eʃəs] *adj* (bot.) euforbiáceo
euphoria [ju'forɪə] *s* (psychol.) euforia
euphoric [ju'fɑrɪk] *adj* eufórico
euphrasy ['jufrəsɪ] *s* (bot.) eufrasia
Euphrates [ju'fretiz] *s* Éufrates
Euphrosyne [ju'frɑsɪni] *s* (myth.) Eufrosina
euphuism ['jufjʊɪzəm] *s* eufuísmo
euphuist ['jufjʊɪst] *s* eufuísta
euphuistic [,jufjʊ'ɪstɪk] *adj* eufuístico
Eur. abr. de **Europe** y **European**
Eurasia [jʊ'reʒə] o [jʊ'reʃə] *s* Eurasia
Eurasian [jʊ'reʒən] o [jʊ'reʃən] *adj & s* eurasiano
eureka [jʊ'rikə] *interj* ¡eureka!
eurhythmic [jʊ'rɪðmɪk] *adj* (f.a.) eurítmico
eurhythmy [jʊ'rɪðmɪ] *s* (f.a.) euritmia
Euripides [jʊ'rɪpɪdiz] *s* Eurípides
Europa [jʊ'ropə] *s* (myth.) Europa
Europa Point *s* punta de Europa
Europe ['jʊrəp] *s* Europa
European [,jʊrə'piən] *adj & s* europeo
European Common Market *s* Mercado Común Europeo
Europeanism [,jʊrə'piənɪzəm] *s* europeísmo
Europeanize [,jʊrə'piənaɪz] *va* europeizar
European plan *s* cuarto sin comidas
European swift *s* (orn.) vencejo
europium [jʊ'ropɪəm] *s* (chem.) europio
Eurydice [jʊ'rɪdɪsi] *s* (myth.) Eurídice
eurythmic [jʊ'rɪðmɪk] *adj* var. de **eurhythmic**
eurythmy [jʊ'rɪðmɪ] *s* var. de **eurhythmy**
Eustace ['justɪs] *s* Eustaquio
Eustachian tube [jʊ'stekɪən] o [jʊ'steʃən] *s* (anat.) trompa de Eustaquio
eustyle ['ju,staɪl] *s* (arch.) éustilo
Euterpe [ju'tʌrpɪ] *s* (myth.) Euterpe
euthanasia [,juθə'neʒə] *s* eutanasia
euthenics [ju'θɛnɪks] *ssg* euténica
Eutychian [ju'tɪkɪən] *adj & s* eutiquiano
Euxine Sea ['juksɪn] o ['juksaɪn] *s* Ponto Euxino (*antiguo nombre del mar Negro*)
evacuant [ɪ'vækjʊənt] *adj & s* (med.) evacuante
evacuate [ɪ'vækjʊet] *va* evacuar; (mil.) evacuar; *vn* (mil.) evacuar
evacuation [ɪ,vækjʊ'eʃən] *s* evacuación
evacuee [ɪ,vækjʊ'i] *s* evacuado
evade [ɪ'ved] *va* evadir; *vn* evadirse
evaluate [ɪ'væljʊet] *va* evaluar
evaluation [ɪ,væljʊ'eʃən] *s* evaluación
evanesce [,ɛvə'nɛs] *vn* desvanecerse
evanescence [,ɛvə'nɛsəns] *s* desvanecimiento
evanescent [,ɛvə'nɛsənt] *adj* evanescente; (bot.) evanescente
evangel [ɪ'vændʒəl] *s* buena nueva; evangelio (*doctrina de Jesucristo*); evangelizador; (*cap.*) *s* Evangelio (*cada uno de los cuatro primeros libros del Nuevo Testamento*)
evangelic [,ivæn'dʒɛlɪk] o [,ɛvən'dʒɛlɪk] o **evangelical** [,ivæn'dʒɛlɪkəl] o [,ɛvən'dʒəlɪkəl] *adj* evangélico
evangelicalism [,ivæn'dʒɛlɪkəlɪzəm] o [,ɛvən'dʒɛlɪkəlɪzəm] *s* doctrina de la iglesia evangélica
evangelism [ɪ'vændʒəlɪzəm] *s* evangelismo
evangelist [ɪ'vændʒəlɪst] *s* evangelizador; (*cap.*) *s* Evangelista
evangelistic [ɪ,vændʒə'lɪstɪk] *adj* evangélico
evangelization [ɪ,vændʒəlɪ'zeʃən] *s* evangelización
evangelize [ɪ'vændʒəlaɪz] *va & vn* evangelizar
evaporable [ɪ'væpərəbəl] *adj* evaporable
evaporate [ɪ'væpəret] *va* evaporar, vaporar; *vn* evaporarse (*convertirse en vapor; desaparecer, desvanecerse*)
evaporated milk [ɪ'væpə,retɪd] *s* leche evaporada
evaporation [ɪ,væpə'reʃən] *s* evaporación
evaporator [ɪ'væpə,retər] *s* evaporador
evasion [ɪ'veʒən] *s* evasiva, evasión
evasive [ɪ'vesɪv] *adj* evasivo
eve [iv] *s* víspera; (poet.) tardecita; (*cap.*) *s* Eva; **on the eve of** en vísperas de
evection [ɪ'vɛkʃən] *s* (astr.) evección
even ['ivən] *adj* igual, llano, liso, parejo; uniforme, semejante; constante, invariable; apacible, sereno; justo, imparcial; exacto; a nivel; sin deudas; (math.) par; **to be even** estar en paz; no deber nada a nadie; **to get even with** desquitarse con; *adv* aun, hasta; también; sin embargo; igualmente; exactamente; **not even** ni . . . siquiera; **to break even** (coll.) salir sin ganar ni perder; (coll.) salir en paz (*en juego*); **even as** así como; **even if** aunque, aun cuando; **even so** así; así y todo; **even though** aunque, aun cuando; **even when** aun cuando; *s* (poet.) tardecita; *va* igualar, allanar; desquitar
even-handed ['ivən'hændɪd] *adj* justo, imparcial
evening ['ivnɪŋ] *s* tarde; (fig.) tarde (*de la vida*); *adj* vespertino
evening clothes *spl* o **evening dress** *s* traje de etiqueta
evening gown *s* vestido de etiqueta de mujer, vestido de noche
evening primrose *s* (bot.) hierba del asno
evening star *s* estrella vespertina
evening wear *s* vestido de etiqueta
evenness ['ivənnɪs] *s* igualdad; uniformidad; constancia; serenidad; imparcialidad; exactitud
even number *s* número par
evensong ['ivən,sɔŋ] o ['ivən,sɑŋ] *s* (eccl.) vísperas; canción de la tarde; (archaic) tarde, anochecher
event [ɪ'vɛnt] *s* acontecimiento, suceso; resultado, consecuencia; acto (*hecho público*); (sport) lucha, corrida; **at all events** o **in any event** en todo caso; **in the event of** en caso de; **in the event that** en caso que
even-tempered ['ivən'tɛmpərd] *adj* tranquilo, sereno
eventful [ɪ'vɛntfəl] *adj* lleno de acontecimientos; memorable
eventide ['ivən,taɪd] *s* (poet.) caída de la tarde
eventual [ɪ'vɛntʃʊəl] *adj* final; eventual (*posible, contingente*)
eventuality [ɪ,vɛntʃʊ'ælɪtɪ] *s* (*pl:* **-ties**) eventualidad; **for any eventuality** a todo evento
eventually [ɪ'vɛntʃʊəlɪ] *adv* finalmente, con el tiempo
eventuate [ɪ'vɛntʃʊet] *vn* concluir, resultar, terminarse
ever ['ɛvər] *adv* siempre; por casualidad; jamás, p.ej., **Who has ever seen such a thing?** ¿Quién ha visto jamás semejante cosa?; nunca, p.ej., **the best book ever written** el mejor libro que se haya escrito nunca; **he is happier than ever** es más feliz que nunca; alguna vez, p.ej., **Have you ever been in Spain?** ¿Ha estado Vd. alguna vez en España?; **as ever** como siempre; tanto como; **be it**

ever so + *adj* por + *adj* + que sea; **did you ever!** ¡qué cosa!; **for ever and ever** por siempre jamás; **hardly ever** casi nunca; **not . . . ever** no . . . nunca; **scarcely ever** casi nunca; **ever and anon** de vez en cuando, una y otra vez; **ever since** desde entonces; después de que; **ever so** muy; **ever so much** muchísimo
everglade ['ɛvərgled] *s* tierra baja pantanosa cubierta de altas hierbas; **Everglades** *spl* pantanos en el sur de la Florida (*E.U.A.*)
evergreen ['ɛvər,grin] *adj* siempre verde; *s* planta siempre verde; **evergreens** *spl* ramas que se emplean para adorno
everlasting [,ɛvər'læstɪŋ] o [,ɛvər'lɑstɪŋ] *adj* sempiterno, perpetuo; duradero; aburrido, cansado; *s* eternidad; sempiterna (*tela*); (bot.) siempreviva; **the Everlasting** el Eterno (*Dios*)
evermore [,ɛvər'mor] o ['ɛvərmor] *adv* eternamente; **for evermore** para siempre jamás
eversion [ɪ'vʌrʃən] o [ɪ'vʌrʒən] *s* (med.) eversión
evert [ɪ'vʌrt] *va* volver (*p.ej., los bordes de una herida*) hacia fuera
every ['ɛvrɪ] *adj* todos los, p.ej., **every day** todos los días; todo, p.ej., **every loyal American** todo fiel americano; cada, p.ej., **every time** cada vez; **every bit** (coll.) todo, p.ej., **every bit a man** todo un hombre; **every now and then** de vez en cuando; **every once in a while** una que otra vez; **every one of them** todos ellos; **every other day** cada dos días, un día sí y otro no, cada tercer día; **every which way** (coll.) por todas partes; (coll.) en desarreglo
everybody ['ɛvrɪ,bɑdɪ] *pron indef* todos, todo el mundo
everyday ['ɛvrɪ,de] *adj* diario, cotidiano; acostumbrado, común, ordinario; de los días de trabajo
every man Jack *s* cada hijo de vecino
everyone o **every one** ['ɛvrɪ,wʌn] *pron indef* todos, todo el mundo, cada uno
everything ['ɛvrɪ,θɪŋ] *pron indef & s* todo
everywhere ['ɛvrɪ,hwɛr] *adv* en o por todas partes; a todas partes
evict [ɪ'vɪkt] *va* desahuciar
eviction [ɪ'vɪkʃən] *s* desahucio; (law) evicción
evidence ['ɛvɪdəns] *s* evidencia; (law) prueba; **direct evidence** (law) prueba directa; **indirect evidence** (law) prueba indirecta; **in evidence** visible, manifiesto, notorio; *va* evidenciar
evident ['ɛvɪdənt] *adj* evidente
evidential [,ɛvɪ'dɛnʃəl] *adj* indicador, probatorio
evidently ['ɛvɪdəntlɪ] o [,ɛvɪ'dɛntlɪ] *adv* evidentemente, por lo visto
evil ['ivəl] *adj* malo; *s* mal
evildoer ['ivəl,duər] *s* malhechor
evildoing ['ivəl,duɪŋ] *s* malhecho
evil eye *s* aojo, aojadura, mal de ojo
evil-minded ['ivəl'maɪndɪd] *adj* malicioso, mal pensado
Evil One, the el Malo (*el demonio*)
evince [ɪ'vɪns] *va* mostrar, revelar, indicar
eviscerate [ɪ'vɪsəret] *va* desentrañar, destripar
evisceration [ɪ,vɪsə'reʃən] *s* desentrañamiento, destripamiento; (surg.) evisceración
evocation [,ɛvo'keʃən] *s* evocación
evocative [ɪ'vɑkətɪv] *adj* evocador
evoke [ɪ'vok] *va* evocar
evolution [,ɛvə'luʃən] *s* evolución; (biol., philos., mil. & nav.) evolución; (biol.) evolucionismo (*teoría*); desprendimiento (*p.ej., de calor, gases*); (math.) extracción de raíces, radicación
evolutional [,ɛvə'luʃənəl] o **evolutionary** [,ɛvə'luʃən,ɛrɪ] *adj* evolucionista, evolutivo
evolutionist [,ɛvə'luʃənɪst] *s & adj* evolucionista
evolve [ɪ'vɑlv] *va* desarrollar; desprender (*p.ej., calor, gases*); *vn* evolucionar
evolvement [ɪ'vɑlvmənt] *s* desarrollo; desprendimiento (*p.ej., de calor, gases*); evolución
ewe [ju] *s* oveja
ewe lamb *s* cordera
ewer ['juər] *s* aguamanil
ex. abr. de **examination, examined, example, except, exchange, excursion, executed** y **executive**
Ex. abr. de **Exodus**
ex [ɛks] *prep* (com.) sin participación en; (com.) sin incluir
exacerbate [ɛg'zæsərbet] o [ɛks'æsərbet] *va* exacerbar
exacerbation [ɛg,zæsər'beʃən] o [ɛks,æsər'beʃən] *s* exacerbación
exact [ɛg'zækt] *adj* exacto; *va* exigir
exacting [ɛg'zæktɪŋ] *adj* exigente
exaction [ɛg'zækʃən] *s* exacción
exactitude [ɛg'zæktɪtjud] o [ɛg'zæktɪtud] *s* exactitud
exactly [ɛg'zæktlɪ] *adv* exactamente; en punto, p.ej., **it is exactly two o'clock** son las dos en punto
exactness [ɛg'zæktnɪs] *s* var. de **exactitude**
exact science *s* ciencia exacta
exaggerate [ɛg'zædʒəret] *va* exagerar
exaggeration [ɛg,zædʒə'reʃən] *s* exageración
exaggerator [ɛg'zædʒə,retər] *s* exagerador
exalt [ɛg'zɔlt] *va* exaltar
exaltation [,ɛgzɔl'teʃən] *s* exaltación
exam [ɛg'zæm] *s* (coll.) examen
examination [ɛg,zæmɪ'neʃən] *s* examen; reconocimiento (*médico*); **to take an examination** sufrir un examen, examinarse; **to take an examination in** examinarse de
examine [ɛg'zæmɪn] *va & vn* examinar; **to examine into** examinar, indagar, averiguar
examinee [ɛg,zæmɪ'ni] *s* examinando
examiner [ɛg'zæmɪnər] *s* examinador
example [ɛg'zæmpəl] o [ɛg'zɑmpəl] *s* ejemplo; ejemplar (*caso que sirve de escarmiento*); problema (*p.ej., de matemáticas*); **for example** por ejemplo; **to follow the example of** seguir el ejemplo de; **to set an example** dar ejemplo
exanimation [ɛg,zænɪ'meʃən] *s* exanimación
exanthema [ɛk,sæn'θimə] *s* (*pl:* **-mata** [mətə]) (path.) exantema
exanthematic [ɛk,sænθɪ'mætɪk] *adj* exantemático
exasperate [ɛg'zæspəret] *va* exasperar
exasperation [ɛg,zæspə'reʃən] *s* exasperación
ex cathedra [ɛks kə'θidrə] o [ɛks 'kæθɪdrə] (Lat.) ex cáthedra (*en tono doctoral y decisivo; con autoridad*)
excavate ['ɛkskəvet] *va* excavar
excavation [,ɛkskə'veʃən] *s* excavación
excavator ['ɛkskə,vetər] *s* excavador (*persona*); (dent. & surg.) excavador; excavadora (*máquina*)
exceed [ɛk'sid] *va* exceder; exceder de; sobrepasar (*p.ej., el límite de velocidad*); *vn* excederse
exceeding [ɛk'sidɪŋ] *adj* extraordinario, extremo; *adv* (archaic) sumamente, sobremanera
exceedingly [ɛk'sidɪŋlɪ] *adv* sumamente, sobremanera
excel [ɛk'sɛl] (*pret & pp:* **-celled;** *ger:* **-celling**) *va* aventajar, exceder; *vn* sobresalir
excellence ['ɛksələns] *s* excelencia
excellency ['ɛksələnsɪ] *s* (*pl:* **-cies**) excelencia; (*cap.*) *s* Excelencia (*tratamiento*)
excellent ['ɛksələnt] *adj* excelente
excelsior [ɛk'sɛlsɪər] *s* virutas de madera, pajilla de madera; [ɛk'sɛlsɪɔr] *adj* siempre más alto; lema del estado de Nueva York; *interj* ¡excelsior! (*¡más arriba!*)
Excelsior State *s* estado de Nueva York
except [ɛk'sɛpt] *prep* excepto; **except for** sin; **except that** sin que, a menos que; *va* exceptuar; *vn* objetar, desaprobar
exception [ɛk'sɛpʃən] *s* excepción; **to take exception** objetar, desaprobar; ofenderse; **with the exception of** a excepción de
exceptionable [ɛk'sɛpʃənəbəl] *adj* recusable, tachable
exceptional [ɛk'sɛpʃənəl] *adj* excepcional
excerpt ['ɛksʌrpt] o [ɛk'sʌrpt] *s* excerta, selección, cita; [ɛk'sʌrpt] *va* escoger, citar; *vn* hacer selecciones
excess [ɛk'sɛs] *s* exceso; (fig.) exceso (*abuso; demasía en comer y beber*); **in excess of** más que, superior a; **to excess** en exceso o por exceso; ['ɛksɛs] o [ɛk'sɛs] *adj* excedente, sobrante
excess baggage *s* exceso de equipaje
excess fare *s* suplemento

excessive [ɛk'sɛsɪv] *adj* excesivo
excessively [ɛk'sɛsɪvlɪ] *adv* excesivamente
excess-profits tax ['ɛksɛs'prɑfɪts] *s* impuesto sobre ganancias superiores al promedio durante cierto período de condiciones normales, impuesto a los beneficios extraordinarios
excess weight *s* exceso de peso
exchange [ɛks'tʃendʒ] *s* cambio; canje (*p.ej., de prisioneros, mercancías, periódicos, credenciales*); periódico o revista de canje; (com.) cambio; (com.) bolsa, lonja; estación telefónica, central de teléfonos; **in exchange for** en cambio de; *va* cambiar; canjear; darse, hacerse (*p.ej., cortesías*); **to exchange greetings** cambiar el saludo (*dos personas*); **to exchange shots** cambiar disparos
exchangeable [ɛks'tʃendʒəbəl] *adj* cambiable, canjeable
exchange professor *s* profesor de intercambio
exchequer [ɛks'tʃɛkər] o ['ɛkstʃɛkər] *s* tesorería; fondos; (*cap.*) *s* (Brit.) echiquier, tribunal de hacienda; (Brit.) despacho del tribunal de hacienda; (Brit.) fondos del gobierno inglés
excipient [ɛk'sɪpɪənt] *s* (pharm.) excipiente
excise [ɛk'saɪz] o ['ɛksaɪz] *s* impuesto sobre ciertas mercancías de comercio interior; (Brit.) recaudación de impuestos interiores; [ɛk'saɪz] *va* sacar o quitar cortando; borrar; ahuecar; someter a impuesto
exciseman [ɛk'saɪzmən] *s* (*pl:* **-men**) (Brit.) recaudador de impuestos interiores
excise tax *s* impuesto sobre ciertas mercancías de comercio interior
excision [ɛk'sɪʒən] *s* excisión; corte (*en una composición literaria*)
excitability [ɛk,saɪtə'bɪlɪtɪ] *s* excitabilidad
excitable [ɛk'saɪtəbəl] *adj* excitable
excitant [ɛk'saɪtənt] o ['ɛksɪtənt] *s* (physiol.) excitante
excitation [,ɛksaɪ'teʃən] o [,ɛksɪ'teʃən] *s* excitación; (phys. & physiol.) excitación
excitative [ɛk'saɪtətɪv] *adj* excitativo
excite [ɛk'saɪt] *va* excitar; (elec. & physiol.) excitar
excitement [ɛk'saɪtmənt] *s* excitación
exciter [ɛk'saɪtər] *s* excitador; (elec.) excitador (*para sacar chispas*); (elec.) excitatriz (*para producir un campo magnético*)
exciting [ɛk'saɪtɪŋ] *adj* excitante, estimulante; emocionante, conmovedor
exclaim [ɛks'klem] *va* decir con vehemencia; *vn* exclamar; **to exclaim against** o **at** clamar contra (*p.ej., la injusticia*)
exclamation [,ɛksklə'meʃən] *s* exclamación
exclamation mark o **point** *s* punto de admiración
exclamatory [ɛks'klæmə,torɪ] *adj* exclamatorio
exclude [ɛks'klud] *va* excluir
exclusion [ɛks'kluʒən] *s* exclusión; **to the exclusion of** con exclusión de
exclusive [ɛks'klusɪv] *adj* exclusivo; exclusivista; **exclusive of** fuera de, sin contar
exclusively [ɛks'klusɪvlɪ] *adv* exclusivamente
excogitate [ɛks'kɑdʒɪtet] *va* excogitar
excommunicate [,ɛkskə'mjunɪket] *va* excomulgar
excommunication [,ɛkskə,mjunɪ'keʃən] *s* excomunión
excoriate [ɛks'korɪet] *va* excoriar, desollar; (fig.) vituperar
excoriation [ɛks,korɪ'eʃən] *s* excoriación, desolladura; (fig.) vituperio
excrement ['ɛskrɪmənt] *s* excremento
excremental [,ɛkskrɪ'mɛntəl] *adj* excremental o excrementicio
excrescence [ɛks'krɛsəns] *s* excrecencia
excrescent [ɛks'krɛsənt] *adj* excrecente
excreta [ɛks'kritə] *spl* (physiol.) excreta
excrete [ɛks'krit] *va* (physiol.) excretar
excretion [ɛks'kriʃən] *s* (physiol.) excreción
excretive [ɛks'kritɪv] *adj* (physiol.) excrementicio
excretory ['ɛkskrɪ,torɪ] o [ɛks'kritərɪ] *adj* (physiol.) excretorio
excruciating [ɛks'kruʃɪ,etɪŋ] *adj* atroz, agudísimo (*dolor*)
exculpate ['ɛkskʌlpet] o [ɛks'kʌlpet] *va* exculpar
exculpation [,ɛkskʌl'peʃən] *s* exculpación
excursion [ɛks'kʌrʒən] o [ɛks'kʌrʃən] *s* excursión
excursionist [ɛks'kʌrʒənɪst] o [ɛks'kʌrʃənɪst] *s* excursionista
excursion train *s* tren de excursión, tren botijo, tren de recreo
excursive [ɛks'kʌrsɪv] *adj* divagador
excusable [ɛks'kjuzəbəl] *adj* excusable
excuse [ɛks'kjus] *s* excusa; **to look for an excuse** buscar excusa; [ɛks'kjuz] *va* excusar, dispensar; **to excuse for** + *ger* dispensar que + *subj*, p.ej., **excuse me for keeping you** dispénseme que le detenga; **to excuse from** + *ger* dispensar de + *inf;* **to excuse someone for something** excusarle a uno de algo
execrable ['ɛksɪkrəbəl] *adj* execrable
execrate ['ɛksɪkret] *va* execrar
execration [,ɛksɪ'kreʃən] *s* execración; persona o cosa aborrecidas
executant [ɛg'zɛkjʊtənt] *s* ejecutante
execute ['ɛksɪkjut] *va* ejecutar
execution [,ɛksɪ'kjuʃən] *s* ejecución
executioner [,ɛksɪ'kjuʃənər] *s* ejecutor de la justicia, verdugo
executive [ɛg'zɛkjʊtɪv] *adj* ejecutivo; ejecutor; *s* ejecutor; poder ejecutivo, jefe del estado; dirigente (*p.ej., de una empresa, un centro docente*); ejecutivo (Am.)
Executive Mansion *s* (U.S.A.) palacio del jefe del estado; (U.S.A.) casa oficial del gobernador
executor ['ɛksɪ,kjutər] *s* ejecutor; [ɛg'zɛkjʊtər] *s* albacea, ejecutor testamentario
executrix [ɛg'zɛkjʊtrɪks] *s* (*pl:* **executrices** [ɛg,zɛkjʊ'traɪsiz] o **executrixes**) albacea, ejecutora testamentaria
exedra ['ɛksɪdrə] o [ɛk'sidrə] *s* (arch.) exedra
exegesis [,ɛksɪ'dʒisɪs] *s* (*pl:* **-ses** [siz]) exégesis
exegetic [,ɛksɪ'dʒɛtɪk] o **exegetical** [,ɛksɪ'dʒɛtɪkəl] *adj* exegético
exemplar [ɛg'zɛmplər] o [ɛg'zɛmplɑr] *s* ejemplar
exemplary [ɛg'zɛmplərɪ] o ['ɛgzəm,plɛrɪ] *adj* ejemplar
exemplification [ɛg,zɛmplɪfɪ'keʃən] *s* ejemplificación; ejemplo; (law) copia notarial
exemplify [ɛg'zɛmplɪfaɪ] (*pret & pp:* **-fied**) *va* ejemplificar
exempt [ɛg'zɛmpt] *adj* exento; *va* exentar, eximir; **to exempt from** + *ger* eximir de + *inf*
exemption [ɛg'zɛmpʃən] *s* exención
exequatur [,ɛksɪ'kwetər] *s* exequátur
exequies ['ɛksɪkwɪz] *spl* exequias
exercise ['ɛksərsaɪz] *s* ejercicio; uso constante; ceremonia; **to take exercise** hacer ejercicio; *va* ejercer (*una profesión, influencia, etc.*); ejercitar (*adiestrar con el ejercicio*); inquietar, preocupar; poner (*cuidado*); *vn* ejercitarse; hacer ejercicio
exergue [ɛg'zʌrg] o ['ɛksʌrg] *s* exergo
exert [ɛg'zʌrt] *va* ejercer (*p.ej., una fuerza*); **to exert oneself** esforzarse
exertion [ɛg'zʌrʃən] *s* ejercicio, uso constante; esfuerzo
exeunt ['ɛksɪənt] (Lat.) éxeunt (*ellos salen*)
exfoliate [ɛks'folɪet] *va* exfoliar; *vn* exfoliarse
exfoliation [ɛks,folɪ'eʃən] *s* exfoliación
exhalation [,ɛkshə'leʃən] o [,ɛgzə'leʃən] *s* exhalación; espiración (*del aire aspirado*); evaporación
exhale [ɛks'hel] o [ɛg'zel] *va* exhalar (*gases, olores*); espirar; evaporar; *vn* exhalarse; espirar (*expeler el aire aspirado*); evaporarse
exhaust [ɛg'zɔst] *s* escape; tubo de escape; *adj* de escape; aspirador; *va* agotar; hacer el vacío en, extraer el aire de; apurar (*todos los medios*); *vn* escapar, salir (*el gas, el vapor*)
exhaust cam *s* leva de escape
exhaust draft *s* tiro de aspiración
exhaust fan *s* ventilador aspirador
exhaustible [ɛg'zɔstɪbəl] *adj* agotable
exhaustion [ɛg'zɔstʃən] *s* agotamiento
exhaustive [ɛg'zɔstɪv] *adj* exhaustivo, comprensivo, detallado
exhaustless [ɛg'zɔstlɪs] *adj* inagotable
exhaust manifold *s* múltiple de escape, colector de escape
exhaust port *s* lumbrera de escape

exhaust stroke *s* carrera de escape

exhaust valve *s* válvula de escape

exhibit [ɛg'zɪbɪt] *s* exhibición; (law) documento de prueba; *va* exhibir; (law) exhibir (*un documento*); (med.) administrar (*un remedio*)

exhibition [,ɛksɪ'bɪʃən] *s* exhibición

exhibitionism [,ɛksɪ'bɪʃənɪzəm] *s* (psychol.) exhibicionismo

exhibitionist [,ɛksɪ'bɪʃənɪst] *s* exhibicionista

exhibitor o **exhibiter** [ɛg'zɪbɪtər] *s* expositor

exhilarate [ɛg'zɪləret] *va* excitar, alegrar, regocijar

exhilaration [ɛg,zɪlə'reʃən] *s* excitación, alegría, regocijo

exhort [ɛg'zɔrt] *va* exhortar; **to exhort to** + *inf* exhortar a + *inf*

exhortation [,ɛgzɔr'teʃən] o [,ɛksɔr'teʃən] *s* exhortación

exhortative [ɛg'zɔrtətɪv] *adj* exhortativo

exhortatory [ɛg'zɔrtə,torɪ] *adj* exhortatorio

exhorter [ɛg'zɔrtər] *s* exhortador

exhumation [,ɛkshju'meʃən] *s* exhumación

exhume [ɛks'hjum] o [ɛg'zjum] *va* exhumar

exigence ['ɛksɪdʒəns] *s* exigencia

exigency ['ɛksɪdʒənsɪ] *s* (*pl:* **-cies**) var. de **exigence**

exigent ['ɛksɪdʒənt] *adj* exigente

exiguity [,ɛksɪ'gjuɪtɪ] *s* exigüidad

exiguous [ɛg'zɪgjuəs] o [ɛk'sɪgjuəs] *adj* exiguo

exile ['ɛgzaɪl] o ['ɛksaɪl] *s* destierro; desterrado (*persona*); *va* desterrar, extrañar

exist [ɛg'zɪst] *vn* existir

existence [ɛg'zɪstəns] *s* existencia

existent [ɛg'zɪstənt] *adj* existente

existentialism [,ɛgzɪs'tɛnʃəlɪzəm] *s* (philos.) existencialismo

existentialist [,ɛgzɪs'tɛnʃəlɪst] *adj & s* existencialista

existing [ɛg'zɪstɪŋ] *adj* existente

exit ['ɛgzɪt] o ['ɛksɪt] (Lat.) éxit (*él o ella sale*); *s* salida; salida de la escena; **to make one's exit** salir, marcharse, desaparecer

ex libris [ɛks 'laɪbrɪs] o [ɛks 'librɪs] (Lat.) de entre los libros de; *s* (*pl:* **-bris**) ex libris

exobiology [,ɛksobaɪ'ɑlədʒɪ] *s* exobiología

Exod. abr. de **Exodus**

exodontia [,ɛkso'dɑnʃə] o [,ɛkso'dɑnʃɪə] *s* exodoncia

exodus ['ɛksədəs] *s* éxodo; (*cap.*) *s* (Bib.) Éxodo

ex officio [ɛks ə'fɪʃɪo] (Lat.) en virtud de autoridad o cargo

exogamy [ɛks'ɑgəmɪ] *s* exogamia; (biol.) exogamia

exogenous [ɛks'ɑdʒənəs] *adj* exógeno

exonerate [ɛg'zɑnəret] *va* exculpar; exonerar (*p.ej., de una obligación*)

exoneration [ɛg,zɑnə'reʃən] *s* exculpación; exoneración (*de una obligación*)

exophthalmic [,ɛksɑf'θælmɪk] *adj* exoftálmico

exophthalmos [,ɛksɑf'θælmɑs] *s* (path.) exoftalmía o exoftalmos

exorable ['ɛksərəbəl] *adj* exorable

exorbitance [ɛg'zɔrbɪtəns] o **exorbitancy** [ɛg'zɔrbɪtənsɪ] *s* exorbitancia

exorbitant [ɛg'zɔrbɪtənt] *adj* exorbitante

exorbitantly [ɛg'zɔrbɪtəntlɪ] *adv* exorbitantemente

exorcise ['ɛksɔrsaɪz] *va* exorcizar

exorcism ['ɛksɔrsɪzəm] *s* exorcismo

exorcist ['ɛksɔrsɪst] *s* exorcista

exorcize ['ɛksɔrsaɪz] *va* var. de **exorcise**

exordium [ɛg'zɔrdɪəm] o [ɛk'sɔrdɪəm] *s* (*pl:* **-diums** o **-dia** [dɪə]) exordio

exoskeleton [,ɛkso'skɛlɪtən] *s* (zool.) exosqueleto, dermatoesqueleto

exosmosis [,ɛksɑs'mosɪs] *s* (physical chem. & physiol.) exósmosis

exosphere ['ɛksəsfɪr] *s* exosfera

exospore ['ɛksospor] *s* (bot.) exospora

exoteric [,ɛkso'tɛrɪk] *adj* exotérico

exothermic [,ɛksə'θʌrmɪk] *adj* (chem.) exotérmico

exotic [ɛg'zɑtɪk] o [ɛks'ɑtɪk] *adj* exótico

exoticism [ɛg'zɑtɪsɪzəm] o [ɛks'ɑtɪsɪzəm] *s* exotismo

exp. abr. de **expenses, expired, export, exportation, exported, exporter** y **express**

expand [ɛks'pænd] *va* extender; dilatar; ampliar, ensanchar; (math.) desarrollar (*p.ej., una ecuación*); *vn* extenderse; dilatarse; ampliarse, ensancharse

expanded metal *s* metal desplegado

expanse [ɛks'pæns] *s* extención

expansibility [ɛks,pænsɪ'bɪlɪtɪ] *s* expansibilidad

expansible [ɛks'pænsɪbəl] *adj* expansible

expansile [ɛks'pænsɪl] *adj* expansible

expansion [ɛks'pænʃən] *s* expansión; (math.) desarrollo

expansion bolt *s* perno de expansión

expansionism [ɛks'pænʃənɪzəm] *s* expansionismo

expansionist [ɛks'pænʃənɪst] *adj & s* expansionista

expansion stroke *s* carrera de expansión

expansive [ɛks'pænsɪv] *adj* expansivo; (fig.) expansivo

expatiate [ɛks'peʃɪet] *vn* espaciarse

expatiation [ɛks,peʃɪ'eʃən] *s* espaciamiento

expatriate [ɛks'petrɪɪt] *adj & s* expatriado; [ɛks'petrɪet] *va* expatriar, extrañar; *vn* expatriarse

expatriation [ɛks,petrɪ'eʃən] *s* expatriación

expect [ɛks'pɛkt] *va* esperar, prometerse; (coll.) suponer

expectance [ɛks'pɛktəns] *s* var. de **expectancy**

expectancy [ɛks'pɛktənsɪ] *s* (*pl:* **-cies**) expectación, expectativa

expectant [ɛks'pɛktənt] *adj* expectante

expectant mother *s* mujer encinta, futura madre

expectant treatment *s* (med.) tratamiento expectante

expectation [,ɛkspɛk'teʃən] *s* expectación, expectativa; (med.) expectación

expectation of life *s* expectativa de vida

expectorant [ɛks'pɛktərənt] *adj & s* expectorante

expectorate [ɛks'pɛktəret] *va & vn* expectorar

expectoration [ɛks,pɛktə'reʃən] *s* expectoración

expedience [ɛks'pidɪəns] *s* conveniencia, utilidad, oportunidad; ventaja personal

expediency [ɛks'pidɪənsɪ] *s* (*pl:* **-cies**) var. de **expedience**

expedient [ɛks'pidɪənt] *adj* conveniente, útil, oportuno; ventajoso; egoísta; *s* expediente

expedite ['ɛkspɪdaɪt] *va* apresurar, facilitar, despachar

expedition [,ɛkspɪ'dɪʃən] *s* expedición; (fig.) expedición

expeditionary [,ɛkspɪ'dɪʃən,ɛrɪ] *adj* expedicionario

expeditious [,ɛkspɪ'dɪʃəs] *adj* expeditivo

expel [ɛks'pɛl] (*pret & pp:* **-pelled**; *ger:* **-pelling**) *va* expeler, expulsar; despedir

expend [ɛks'pɛnd] *va* expender, gastar; consumir

expendable [ɛks'pɛndəbəl] *adj* gastable

expenditure [ɛks'pɛndɪtʃər] *s* gasto; consumo

expense [ɛks'pɛns] *s* gasto; **expenses** *spl* gastos, expensas; **at any expense** a toda costa; **at the expense of** a expensas de; **to cover expenses** cubrir gastos; **to go to the expense of** meterse en gastos con; **to meet the expenses** hacer frente a los gastos

expense account *s* cuenta de gastos

expensive [ɛks'pɛnsɪv] *adj* caro, dispendioso; carero (*que vende caro*)

expensively [ɛks'pɛnsɪvlɪ] *adv* costosamente

experience [ɛks'pɪrɪəns] *s* experiencia (*enseñanza que se adquiere con la práctica o sólo con el vivir; cosa que uno ha experimentado, suceso en que uno ha participado*); **by experience** con su propia experiencia; *va* experimentar

experienced [ɛks'pɪrɪənst] *adj* experimentado

experiential [ɛks,pɪrɪ'ɛnʃəl] *adj* experimental

experiment [ɛks'pɛrɪmənt] *s* experimento o experiencia; [ɛks'pɛrɪmɛnt] *vn* experimentar

experimental [ɛks,pɛrɪ'mɛntəl] *adj* experimental

experimentally [ɛks,pɛrɪ'mɛntəlɪ] *adv* experimentalmente

experimental psychology *s* psicología experimental

experimentation [ɛks,pɛrɪmɛn'teʃən] *s* experimentación
experimenter [ɛks'pɛrɪmɛntər] *s* experimentador
expert ['ɛkspʌrt] o [ɛks'pʌrt] *adj* experto; ['ɛkspʌrt] *s* experto
expertise [,ɛks,pɛr'tiz] *s* pericia
expiable ['ɛkspɪəbəl] *adj* expiable
expiate ['ɛkspɪet] *va* expiar
expiation [,ɛkspɪ'eʃən] *s* expiación
expiatory ['ɛkspɪə,torɪ] *adj* expiatorio
expiration [,ɛkspɪ'reʃən] *s* espiración (*del aire*); expiración
expiratory [ɛk'spaɪrə,torɪ] *adj* (physiol.) espirador
expire [ɛks'paɪr] *va* expeler (*especialmente el aire*); *vn* expirar (*expeler el aire aspirado; morir; acabarse, p.ej., el plazo*)
expiry [ɛk'spaɪrɪ] o ['ɛkspɪrɪ] *s* (*pl:* **-ries**) expiración (*p.ej., de un contrato*)
explain [ɛks'plen] *va* explicar; **to explain away** apartar, descartar con explicaciones; **to explain oneself** explicarse; *vn* explicar; explicarse
explainable [ɛks'plenəbəl] *adj* explicable
explanation [,ɛksplə'neʃən] *s* explicación; **to demand an explanation** pedir explicaciones
explanatory [ɛks'plænə,torɪ] *adj* explicatorio, explicativo
expletive ['ɛksplɪtɪv] *adj* expletivo; *s* partícula expletiva; reniego, interjección
explicable ['ɛksplɪkəbəl] *adj* explicable
explicate ['ɛksplɪket] *va* explicar, exponer
explicatory ['ɛksplɪkə,torɪ] *adj* explicatorio
explicit [ɛks'plɪsɪt] *adj* explícito
explode [ɛks'plod] *va* volar, hacer saltar; desautorizar, refutar (*una teoría*); (phonet.) pronunciar con explosión; *vn* estallar, explotar, reventar; **to explode with laughter** echarse a reír
exploit ['ɛksplɔɪt] o [ɛks'plɔɪt] *s* hazaña, proeza; [ɛks'plɔɪt] *va* explotar
exploitation [,ɛksplɔɪ'teʃən] *s* explotación
exploration [,ɛksplə'reʃən] *s* exploración
explorative [ɛks'plorətɪv] *adj* explorativo
exploratory [ɛks'plorə,torɪ] *adj* exploratorio, explorador
explore [ɛks'plor] *va & vn* explorar
explorer [ɛks'plorər] *s* explorador; (med.) explorador (*instrumento*)
explosimeter [,ɛksplo'zɪmɪtər] *s* explosímetro
explosion [ɛks'ploʒən] *s* explosión; (phonet.) explosión; (fig.) refutación (*de una teoría*)
explosive [ɛks'plosɪv] *adj* explosivo; (phonet.) explosivo; *s* explosivo; (phonet.) explosiva
exponent [ɛks'ponənt] *s* exponente, expositor; representante, ejemplar, símbolo; (alg.) exponente
exponential [,ɛkspo'nɛnʃəl] *adj* (math.) exponencial
export ['ɛksport] *s* exportación (*acción o artículo*); **exports** *spl* exportación (*mercaderías que se exportan*); *adj* de exportación; [ɛks'port] o ['ɛksport] *va & vn* exportar
exportation [,ɛkspor'teʃən] *s* exportación
exporter [ɛks'portər] o ['ɛksportər] *s* exportador
expose [ɛks'poz] *va* exponer; desenmascarar; (phot.) exponer; (eccl.) exponer o manifestar (*el Santísimo Sacramento*)
exposé [,ɛkspo'ze] *s* desenmascaramiento, revelación (*p.ej., de un crimen*)
exposition [,ɛkspə'zɪʃən] *s* exposición; (rhet.) exposición
expositive [ɛks'pɑzɪtɪv] *adj* expositivo
expositor [ɛks'pɑzɪtər] *s* expositor
expository [ɛks'pɑzɪ,torɪ] *adj* expositivo, expositor
ex post facto [,ɛks post 'fækto] (Lat.) retroactivo
expostulate [ɛks'pɑstʃəlet] *vn* protestar; **to expostulate with someone about, for, on** o **upon something** reconvenirle a uno con, de, por o sobre algo
expostulation [ɛks,pɑstʃə'leʃən] *s* protesta, reconvención
expostulator [ɛks'pɑstʃə,letər] *s* amonestador
expostulatory [ɛks'pɑstʃələ,torɪ] *adj* amonestador
exposure [ɛks'poʒər] *s* exposición (*acción de exponer; situación con relación a los puntos cardinales*); desenmascaramiento; (phot.) exposición; toma (*de una fotografía*)
exposure meter *s* (phot.) exposímetro
expound [ɛks'paʊnd] *va* exponer
expounder [ɛks'paʊndər] *s* expositor
ex-president ['ɛks'prɛzɪdənt] *s* ex presidente
express [ɛks'prɛs] *adj* expreso (*claro, especificado; con particular intento*); expreso (*tren, carro, ascensor, etc.*); *s* expreso; **by express** (rail.) en gran velocidad; *adv* expresamente; por expreso; *va* expresar; enviar por expreso; exprimir (*extraer apretando*); **to express oneself** expresarse
expressage [ɛks'prɛsɪdʒ] *s* servicio del expreso; costo del expreso
express company *s* compañía de expreso
expressible [ɛks'prɛsɪbəl] *adj* decible, expresable; exprimible
expression [ɛks'prɛʃən] *s* expresión; (math.) expresión
expressive [ɛk'sprɛsɪv] *adj* expresivo
expressly [ɛks'prɛslɪ] *adv* expresamente
expressman [ɛks'prɛsmən] *s* (*pl:* **-men**) (U.S.A.) empleado del expreso
express train *s* tren expreso
expressway [ɛks'prɛs,we] *s* supercarretera
expropriate [ɛks'proprɪet] *va* expropiar
expropriation [ɛks,proprɪ'eʃən] *s* expropiación
expugnable [ɛks'pʌgnəbəl] *adj* expugnable
expulsion [ɛks'pʌlʃən] *s* expulsión
expulsive [ɛks'pʌlsɪv] *adj* expulsivo
expunge [ɛks'pʌndʒ] *va* borrar, cancelar, destruir
expurgate ['ɛkspərget] *va* expurgar
expurgation [,ɛkspər'geʃən] *s* expurgación
expurgatory [ɛks'pʌrgə,torɪ] *adj* expurgatorio
exquisite ['ɛkskwɪzɪt] o [ɛks'kwɪzɪt] *adj* exquisito; agudo, sensible
ex-service [,ɛks'sʌrvɪs] *adj* ex militar
ex-serviceman [,ɛks'sʌrvɪs,mæn] *s* (*pl:* **-men**) ex militar, ex combatiente
extant ['ɛkstənt] o [ɛks'tænt] *adj* existente
extemporaneous [ɛks,tɛmpə'renɪəs] o **extemporary** [ɛks'tɛmpə,rɛrɪ] *adj* improvisado; sin previa preparación; provisional
extempore [ɛks'tɛmpərɪ] *adj* improvisado; *adv* de improviso, improvisadamente
extemporization [ɛks,tɛmpərɪ'zeʃən] *s* improvisación
extemporize [ɛks'tɛmpəraɪz] *va & vn* improvisar
extend [ɛks'tɛnd] *va* extender; prorrogar (*p.ej., un plazo*); dar, conceder, ofrecer; *vn* extenderse
extended [ɛks'tɛndɪd] *adj* extendido; extenso; prolongado
extensible [ɛks'tənsɪbəl] *adj* extensible
extensile [ɛks'tɛnsɪl] *adj* extensible; extensor
extension [ɛks'tɛnʃən] *s* extensión; (telp.) extensión (*línea accesoria*); prolongación; (com.) prórroga; (mach.) alargadera; *adj* de extensión
extension bit *s* barrena de extensión
extension cord *s* (elec.) cordón de extensión
extension ladder *s* escalera extensible, escalera de largueros corredizos
extension table *s* mesa de extensión
extensity [ɛks'tɛnsɪtɪ] *s* extensión; (psychol.) extensión
extensive [ɛks'tɛnsɪv] *adj* extensivo; extenso, vasto, dilatado; (agr.) extensivo
extensor [ɛks'tɛnsər] *s* (anat.) extensor, músculo extensor
extent [ɛks'tɛnt] *s* extensión; alcance, grado; **to a certain extent** hasta cierto punto; **to a great extent** en sumo grado; **to a lesser extent** en menor grado; **to such an extent** hasta tal punto; **to that extent** hasta ese grado, hasta ahí; **to the extent that** en la medida que; hasta el punto que; **to the full extent** en toda su extensión
extenuate [ɛks'tɛnjuet] *va* extenuar (*debilitar; enflaquecer*); atenuar (*aminorar, p.ej., la gravedad de un delito*)
extenuating circumstances *spl* circunstancias atenuantes
extenuation [ɛks,tɛnjʊ'eʃən] *s* extenuación (*debilitación; enflaquecimiento*); atenuación (*p.ej., de la gravedad de un delito*)

exterior [ɛksˈtɪrɪər] *adj & s* exterior
exterminable [ɛksˈtʌrmɪnəbəl] *adj* exterminable
exterminate [ɛksˈtʌrmɪnet] *va* exterminar
extermination [ɛksˌtʌrmɪˈneʃən] *s* exterminio
exterminator [ɛksˈtʌrmɪˌnetər] *s* exterminador (*persona o aparato*)
external [ɛksˈtʌrnəl] *adj* externo; (anat.) externo; **externals** *spl* exterioridad (*apariencia de las cosas*)
externality [ˌɛkstərˈnælɪtɪ] *s* (*pl:* **-ties**) exterioridad (*calidad de externo; cosa externa*)
externally [ɛksˈtʌrnəlɪ] *adv* externamente, exteriormente
extinct [ɛksˈtɪŋkt] *adj* extinto
extinction [ɛksˈtɪŋkʃən] *s* extinción
extinctive [ɛksˈtɪŋktɪv] *adj* extintivo; (law) extintivo
extine [ˈɛkstɪn] o [ˈɛkstaɪn] *s* (bot.) exina o extina (*del polen*)
extinguish [ɛksˈtɪŋgwɪʃ] *va* extinguir
extinguishable [ɛksˈtɪŋgwɪʃəbəl] *adj* extinguible
extinguisher [ɛksˈtɪŋgwɪʃər] *s* apagador (*persona o aparato; cono para apagar las luces*)
extirpate [ˈɛkstərpet] o [ɛksˈtʌrpet] *va* extirpar
extirpation [ˌɛkstərˈpeʃən] *s* extirpación
extol o **extoll** [ɛksˈtol] o [ɛksˈtɑl] (*pret & pp:* **-tolled;** *ger:* **-tolling**) *va* ensalzar
extort [ɛksˈtɔrt] *va* obtener por fuerza o engaño
extortion [ɛksˈtɔrʃən] *s* extorción; exacción (*de una promesa*)
extortionate [ɛksˈtɔrʃənɪt] *adj* injusto, gravoso, opresivo; excesivo
extortioner [ɛksˈtɔrʃənər] o **extortionist** [ɛksˈtɔrʃənɪst] *s* concusionario, desollador
extra [ˈɛkstrə] *adj* extra; de repuesto; *adv* extraordinariamente; *s* extra (*de un periódico; adehala, gaje, plus*); (theat.) extra; repuesto, pieza de repuesto
extract [ˈɛkstrækt] *s* selección, cita; (pharm.) extracto; [ɛksˈtrækt] *va* seleccionar, citar (*pasajes de un libro*); extraer; (math.) extraer (*una raíz*)
extractable [ɛksˈtræktəbəl] o **extractible** [ɛksˈtræktɪbəl] *adj* extractivo
extraction [ɛksˈtrækʃən] *s* extracción
extractive [ɛksˈtræktɪv] *adj* extractivo
extractor [ɛksˈtræktər] *s* extractor (*persona o aparato*)
extra current *s* (elec.) extracorriente
extracurricular [ˌɛkstrəkəˈrɪkjələr] *adj* extracurricular
extraditable [ˈɛkstrəˌdaɪtəbəl] *adj* extraditable
extradite [ˈɛkstrədaɪt] *va* entregar por extradición; obtener la extradición de
extradition [ˌɛkstrəˈdɪʃən] *s* extradición
extrados [ɛksˈtredɑs] *s* (arch.) extradós
extra fare *s* tarifa recargada, recargo de tarifa
extrajudicial [ˌɛkstrədʒuˈdɪʃəl] *adj* extrajudicial
extralegal [ˌɛkstrəˈligəl] *adj* extralegal
extramural [ˌɛkstrəˈmjʊrəl] *adj* extramural
extraneous [ɛksˈtrenɪəs] *adj* ajeno, extraño
extraordinarily [ɛksˈtrɔrdɪˌnɛrɪlɪ] o [ˌɛkstrəˈɔrdɪˌnɛrɪlɪ] *adv* extraordinariamente
extraordinary [ɛksˈtrɔrdɪˌnɛrɪ] o [ˌɛkstrəˈɔrdɪˌnɛrɪ] *adj* extraordinario
extrapolate [ɛksˈtræpəlet] *va & vn* (math.) extrapolar
extrapolation [ˌɛkstrəpoˈleʃən] o [ɛksˌtræpəˈleʃən] *s* (math.) extrapolación
extrasensory [ˌɛkstrəˈsɛnsərɪ] *adj* extrasensorial
extrasystole [ˌɛkstrəˈsɪstəlɪ] *s* (path.) extrasístole
extraterritorial [ˈɛkstrəˌtɛrɪˈtorɪəl] *adj* extraterritorial
extraterritoriality [ˈɛkstrəˌtɛrɪˌtorɪˈælɪtɪ] *s* extraterritorialidad
extravagance [ɛksˈtrævəgəns] *s* derroche, despilfarro, gasto excesivo; lujo excesivo; exorbitancia (*de los precios*); extravagancia
extravagant [ɛksˈtrævəgənt] *adj* despilfarrado, gastador; exorbitante; excesivo; extravagante
extravaganza [ɛksˌtrævəˈgænzə] *s* obra musical o composición literaria extravagante y fantástica
extravasate [ɛksˈtrævəset] *va* extravasar; *vn* (physiol.) extravasarse
extravasation [ɛksˌtrævəˈseʃən] *s* extravasación
extraversion [ˌɛkstrəˈvʌrʃən] *s* (psychol.) extraversión
extreme [ɛksˈtrim] *adj* extremo; *s* extremo; **in the extreme** en sumo grado; **to go from one extreme to the other** pasar de un extremo a otro; **to go to extremes** excederse, propasarse
extremely [ɛksˈtrimlɪ] *adv* extremamente, extremadamente
extreme unction *s* (eccl.) extremaunción
extremism [ɛksˈtrimɪzəm] *s* extremismo
extremist [ɛksˈtrimɪst] *s* extremista
extremity [ɛksˈtrɛmɪtɪ] *s* (*pl:* **-ties**) extremidad; medida extrema; extrema (*escasez grande*); **extremities** *spl* extremidades (*pies y manos*)
extricate [ˈɛkstrɪket] *va* librar
extrication [ˌɛkstrɪˈkeʃən] *s* libramiento
extrinsic [ɛksˈtrɪnsɪk] *adj* extrínseco
extrinsically [ɛksˈtrɪnsɪkəlɪ] *adv* extrínsecamente
extrorse [ɛksˈtrɔrs] *adj* (bot.) extrorso
extroversion [ˌɛkstroˈvʌrʒən] o [ˌɛkstroˈvʌrʃən] *s* (path.) extroversión; (psychol.) extraversión
extrovert [ˈɛkstrovʌrt] *s* extrovertido
extrude [ɛksˈtrud] *va* forzar o empujar hacia fuera; (metal.) estrujar; *vn* resaltar, sobresalir
extrusion [ɛksˈtruʒən] *s* expulsión; resalto; (metal.) estrujamiento, extrusión
extrusive [ɛksˈtrusɪv] *adj* expulsivo; resaltante; (geol.) efusivo
exuberance [ɛgˈzubərəns] o [ɛgˈzjubərəns] *s* exuberancia
exuberancy [ɛgˈzubərənsɪ] o [ɛgˈzjubərənsɪ] *s* (*pl:* **-cies**) var. de **exuberance**
exuberant [ɛgˈzubərənt] o [ɛgˈzjubərənt] *adj* exuberante
exudate [ˈɛksjʊdet] *s* exudado
exudation [ˌɛksjʊˈdeʃən] *s* exudación
exude [ɛgˈzud], [ɛgˈzjud] o [ɛksˈjud] *va & vn* exudar
exult [ɛgˈzʌlt] *vn* exultar
exultant [ɛgˈzʌltənt] *adj* regocijado, alborozado, ufano
exultation [ˌɛgzʌlˈteʃən] o [ˌɛksʌlˈteʃən] *s* exultación
ex-voto [ɛksˈvoto] *s* (*pl:* **-tos**) exvoto
-ey *suffix adj* var. de **-y,** que se usa cuando la palabra termina en **y,** p.ej., **clayey** arcilloso; **eyey** ojoso; *suffix dim* var. de **-y** en algunos nombres propios, p.ej., **Charley** Carlitos
eyas [ˈaɪəs] *s* halcón niego; pájaro que no ha dejado el nido
eye [aɪ] *s* (anat.) ojo; (fig.) ojo (*p.ej., de aguja, del queso, de una herramienta; yema o botón de las plantas; abertura redonda; mirada, vista; atención; aptitud para apreciar las cosas*); (sew.) corcheta; **an eye for an eye** ojo por ojo; **before one's eyes** delante de los ojos de uno; **in the eyes of** a los ojos de; **to catch one's eye** llamar la atención a uno; **to feast one's eyes on** deleitar la vista en; **to have an eye to** prestar atención a; vigilar; **to have an eye to the main chance** abrir los ojos; **to have one's eye on** (coll.) tener los ojos en; (coll.) echar el ojo a (*mirar con deseo*); **to keep an eye on** tener los ojos en; **to keep one's eyes open** abrir el ojo; **to lay eyes on** alcanzar a ver; **to make eyes at** hacer guiños a; **to not take one's eyes off** no quitar los ojos de; **to open one's eyes** abrir los ojos (*salir del error*); **to open someone's eyes** abrirle los ojos a uno (*desengañarle a uno*); **to roll one's eyes** poner los ojos en blanco; **to see eye to eye** estar completamente de acuerdo; **to set eyes on** (coll.) alcanzar a ver; **to shut one's eyes to** hacer la vista gorda ante; **with an eye to** con la intención de, con vistas a; **without batting an eye** sin pestañear, sin inmutarse; **with the naked eye** a simple vista; (*pret & pp:* **eyed;**

ger: **eying** o **eyeing**) *va* ojear; **to eye up and down** mirar de hito en hito
eyeball ['aɪ,bɔl] *s* globo del ojo
eyebolt ['aɪ,bolt] *s* perno de argolla, cáncamo de ojo
eyebright ['aɪ,braɪt] *s* (bot.) eufrasia
eyebrow ['aɪ,braʊ] *s* ceja
eye-catching ['aɪ,kætʃɪŋ] *adj* atrayente, llamativo, sugestivo
eyecup ['aɪ,kʌp] *s* ojera, lavaojos
eyeful ['aɪfʊl] *s* (coll.) buena ojeada
eyeglass ['aɪ,glæs] o ['aɪ,glɑs] *s* ocular (*del anteojo, microscopio, etc.*); ojera, lavaojos (*copita para bañar el ojo*); **eyeglasses** *spl* gafas, anteojos
eyehole ['aɪ,hol] *s* ojete; cuenca del ojo; atisbadero, mirilla
eyelash ['aɪ,læʃ] *s* pestaña
eyeless ['aɪlɪs] *adj* sin ojos, sin vista
eyelet ['aɪlɪt] *s* ojete, ojal; mirilla, atisbadero; *va* ojetear
eyeleteer [,aɪlɪ'tɪr] *s* punzón para abrir ojetes
eyelet punch *s* ojeteadora
eyelid ['aɪ,lɪd] *s* párpado
eye of day, eye of the morning, eye of heaven *s* sol
eye opener *s* acontecimiento asombroso, noticia inesperada e increíble; (slang) trago de licor que se toma por la mañana
eyepiece ['aɪ,pis] *s* ocular
eye-shade ['aɪ,ʃed] *s* visera
eyeshot ['aɪ,ʃɑt] *s* alcance de la vista
eyesight ['aɪ,saɪt] *s* vista; alcance de la vista
eye socket *s* (anat.) cuenca del ojo
eyesore ['aɪ,sor] *s* mácula, cosa que ofende la vista
eyespot ['aɪ,spɑt] *s* (zool.) mancha ocular
eyestrain ['aɪ,stren] *s* cansancio o irritación de los ojos
eye-test chart ['aɪ,tɛst] *s* gráfico para prueba oftalmométrica, tabla de graduación, tipo de ensayo o prueba
eyetooth ['aɪ,tuθ] *s* (*pl:* **-teeth** [,tiθ]) colmillo, diente canino; **to cut one's eyeteeth** (coll.) tener el colmillo retorcido; **to give one's eyeteeth for** (coll.) dar los ojos de la cara por
eyewash ['aɪ,wɑʃ] o ['aɪ,wɔʃ] *s* colirio; (slang) alabanza para engañar
eyewinker ['aɪ,wɪŋkər] *s* pestaña
eyewitness ['aɪ,wɪtnɪs] *s* testigo de vista o testigo ocular
eyey ['aɪ·ɪ] *adj* ojoso
eyrie o **eyry** ['ɛrɪ] *s* (*pl:* **-ries**) aguilera, nido de águilas; nido de ave de rapiña; nidada de aguiluchos; (fig.) morada elevada, altura
Ezek. abr. de **Ezekiel**
Ezekiel [ɪ'zikjəl] *s* (Bib.) Ecequiel o Ezequiel (*profeta y libro*)

F, f [ɛf] *s* (*pl:* **F's, f's** [ɛfs]) sexta letra del alfabeto inglés
f. abr. de **farthing, female, feminine, folio, forte** y **franc**
F. abr. de **Fahrenheit, French** y **Friday**
Fabian [ˈfebɪən] *adj* fabiano; *s* fabiano; Fabián (*nombre propio de varón*)
fable [ˈfebəl] *s* fábula; *va* inventar (*fábulas*); *vn* inventar fábulas, contar fábulas; fingir, mentir
fabled [ˈfebəld] *adj* contado en fábulas, legendario; ficticio, fingido
fabric [ˈfæbrɪk] *s* género, tejido, tela de uso o adorno; textura; fábrica
fabricate [ˈfæbrɪket] *va* fabricar
fabrication [ˌfæbrɪˈkeʃən] *s* fabricación; mentira
fabricator [ˈfæbrɪˌketər] *s* fabricante; fabricador (*p.ej., de mentiras*)
fabrikoid [ˈfæbrɪkɔɪd] *s* (trademark) fabricoide
fabulist [ˈfæbjəlɪst] *s* fabulista
fabulous [ˈfæbjələs] *adj* fabuloso
façade [fəˈsɑd] *s* fachada
face [fes] *s* cara; haz (*de las telas, las hojas de las plantas, etc.*); faz (*p.ej., de la tierra*); cara, dibujo (*de un naipe*); aspecto, semblante; mueca (*visaje ridículo*); esfera, muestra (*del reloj*); ancho (*de una polea*); cotillo (*del martillo*); paramento (*de un muro*); pundonor; (coll.) descaro; (com.) valor neto; (cryst. & geom.) cara; (mach.) cabeza (*de diente de rueda*); (mach.) superficie de contacto o de trabajo (*de la válvula de corredera*); (min.) cara de trabajo, fondo, frente (*p.ej., de la galería*); (print.) ojo (*relieve de las letras que produce la impresión*); (print.) carácter (*forma de las letras*); **in the face of** ante, en presencia de; a pesar de, luchando contra; **on the face of it** según las apariencias; **to keep a straight face** contener la risa; **to lose face** desprestigiarse, sufrir pérdida de prestigio; **to make a wry face** torcer el rostro (*mostrando desagrado*); **to make faces** hacer muecas; **to one's face** en la cara de uno, en la presencia de uno; **to pull a long face** poner la cara larga; **to save face** salvar las apariencias; **to set one's face against** mostrarse contrario a; **to show one's face** dejarse ver; **face to face** cara a cara, faz a faz ‖ *va* mirar hacia, volver la cara hacia; estar enfrente de; encararse con, arrostrar; forrar (*un vestido*); revestir (*un muro*); bruñir (*un metal*); acabar, alisar, labrar; **to face it out** no cejar, mantenerse firme; **to face out** sostener audazmente, insistir descaradamente en; **to face with** carear (*a uno*) con ‖ *vn* carear; volver la mirada; **to face about** volver la mirada; dar media vuelta; cambiar de opinión; **to face on** dar a, dar sobre; **to face up to** encararse con
face card *s* figura, naipe de figura
face lathe *s* torno de plato
face lifting *s* cirugía cosmética, decorativa o estética
faceplate [ˈfesˌplet] *s* (mach.) plato de mandril; (mach.) placa de recubrimiento
face powder *s* polvos blancos faciales
facer [ˈfesər] *s* puñetazo dado en la cara; revés violento e inesperado
facet [ˈfæsɪt] *s* faceta; (arch., zool. & fig.) faceta; *va* labrar facetas en, labrar en facetas
facetious [fəˈsiʃəs] *adj* chistoso, gracioso, salado
face value *s* valor facial; valor aparente o nominal; significado literal
face wheel *s* (mach.) rueda de dientes laterales
facial [ˈfeʃəl] *adj* facial; *s* (coll.) masaje facial
facial angle *s* ángulo facial
facile [ˈfæsɪl] *adj* fácil; vivo, listo
facilitate [fəˈsɪlɪtet] *va* facilitar
facilitation [fəˌsɪlɪˈteʃən] *s* facilitación
facility [fəˈsɪlɪtɪ] *s* (*pl:* **-ties**) facilidad; **facilities** *spl* facilidades (*comodidades*)
facing [ˈfesɪŋ] *s* encaramiento; paramento, revestimiento; (sew.) guarnición; **facings** *spl* vueltas
facsim. abr. de **facsimile**
facsimile [fækˈsɪmɪlɪ] *s* facsímile; **in facsimile** a facsímile; *adj* facsimilar; *va* facsimilar, hacer facsímile de
fact [fækt] *s* hecho; **in fact** de hecho, en realidad; **the fact is that** ello es que
faction [ˈfækʃən] *s* facción; discordia, disensión
factional [ˈfækʃənəl] *adj* faccionario
factionalism [ˈfækʃənəlɪzəm] *s* parcialidad, partidismo
factionalist [ˈfækʃənəlɪst] *s* faccionario
factious [ˈfækʃəs] *adj* faccioso
factitious [fækˈtɪʃəs] *adj* facticio
factor [ˈfæktər] *s* factor (*elemento que contribuye a producir un resultado*); (biochem., biol., law, math. & physiol.) factor; *va* (math.) dividir o descomponer en factores
factorage [ˈfæktərɪdʒ] *s* factoraje (*empleo de factor*); comisión pagada a un factor
factorial [fækˈtorɪəl] *s* (math.) factorial
factory [ˈfæktərɪ] *s* (*pl:* **-ries**) fábrica; factoría (*establecimiento comercial en país extranjero*)
factotum [fækˈtotəm] *s* factótum
factual [ˈfæktʃuəl] *adj* objetivo, basado en hechos, real, verdadero
facula [ˈfækjələ] *s* (*pl:* **-lae** [li]) (astr.) fácula
facultative [ˈfækəlˌtetɪv] *adj* facultativo; (biol.) facultativo
faculty [ˈfækəltɪ] *s* (*pl:* **-ties**) facultad
fad [fæd] *s* chifladura, tema, manía; diversión favorita, novedad
faddish [ˈfædɪʃ] *adj* caprichoso, maniático; aficionado a novedades
faddist [ˈfædɪst] *s* caprichoso, maniático; aficionado a novedades
fade [fed] *va* marchitar; desteñir; cubrir la apuesta de (*en el juego de dados*); *vn* marchitarse; desteñirse; apagarse (*un sonido*); desvanecerse; (rad.) desvanecerse; **to fade away** desvanecerse; **to fade in** aparecer gradualmente; **to fade out** desaparecerse gradualmente
fadeless [ˈfedlɪs] *adj* inmarcesible
fadeout [ˈfedˌaut] *s* desaparición gradual (*de sonido o imagen*); (mov.) imagen que desaparece lentamente
fading [ˈfedɪŋ] *s* (rad.) fáding, desvanecimiento (*de la señal*)
faecal [ˈfikəl] *adj* var. de **fecal**
faeces [ˈfisiz] *spl* var. de **feces**
faerie [ˈfɛrɪ] *s* (archaic) hada; (archaic) tierra de las hadas; *adj* (archaic) de hada, de hadas
faery [ˈfɛrɪ] *s* (*pl:* **-ies**) (archaic) var. de **faerie**; *adj* (archaic) var. de **faerie**
fag [fæg] *s* yunque, esclavo del trabajo; afán, trabajo penoso; (coll.) cigarrillo, pitillo; (Brit.) alumno que sirve a los alumnos mayores; (*pret & pp:* **fagged**; *ger:* **fagging**) *va* cansar, fatigar; hacer trotar; exigir faenas groseras a; *vn* trabajar duramente, hacer faenas rudas, desfallecer de cansancio
fagaceous [fəˈgeʃəs] *adj* (bot.) fagáceo
fag end *s* cabo, final; resto, retal; sobra, desperdicio; cadillos, pezolada; flecos, hilachas; (naut.) cordón
faggot [ˈfægət] *s & va* var. de **fagot**
faggoting [ˈfægətɪŋ] *s* var. de **fagoting**
fagot [ˈfægət] *s* haz de leña; fajina (*haz de leña*

ligera); haz de barras de hierro o acero; *va* atar o liar en haces; (sew.) adornar con vainicas

fagoting ['fægətɪŋ] *s* (sew.) vainicas

Fahr. abr. de **Fahrenheit**

Fahrenheit thermometer ['færənhaɪt] o ['farənhaɪt] *s* termómetro de Fahrenheit

faïence [faɪ'ans] o [fe'ans] *s* faenza

fail [fel] *s* falta; **without fail** sin falta; *va* faltar a, faltar a sus obligaciones a; (coll.) reprobar, suspender (*a un alumno*); (coll.) salir mal en (*un examen*); *vn* faltar; fracasar, malograrse; (coll.) salir suspendido, salir mal (*un alumno*); (com.) quebrar, hacer bancarrota; fallar (*p.ej., un motor*); **to fail to** + *inf* no poder + *inf;* no acertar a + *inf,* no llegar a + *inf;* dejar de + *inf,* p.ej., **don't fail to come** no deje Vd. de venir

failing ['felɪŋ] *s* falta; flaqueza; fracaso, malogro; *adj* decadente; *prep* sin, a falta de

faille [fel] *s* faya (*tejido de seda*); (archaic) falla (*cobertura de la cabeza que usaban las mujeres*)

failure ['feljər] *s* falta; fracaso, malogro; quiebra, bancarrota; fracasado; quebrado; perdigón (*alumno que pierde el curso*); **the failure to** + *inf* el dejar de + *inf*

fain [fen] *adj* (archaic & poet.) obligado, resignado; (archaic & poet.) dispuesto, deseoso; *adv* (archaic & poet.) gustosamente, de buena gana

faint [fent] *s* desmayo, desfallecimiento; **faints** *spl* productos impuros y débiles de la destilación; **to fall into a faint** desmayarse; *adj* débil; desmayado; **to be faint with** desmayarse a consecuencia de, morirse de; **to feel faint** sentirse mareado o débil; *vn* desmayarse, desfallecer; (archaic) desfallecer de ánimo

faintheart ['fent,hart] *s* cobarde

faint-hearted ['fent'hartɪd] *adj* cobarde, medroso

faintness ['fentnɪs] *s* debilidad; desmayo, desfallecimiento

fair [fɛr] *adj* justo; imparcial; honrado; legal; cortés; corriente, ordinario, regular; favorable, propicio; bien formado, hermoso; distinto, legible; rubio (*de pelo*); blanco (*de tez*); despejado, sereno (*cielo*); bueno, bonancible (*tiempo*); limpio; admisible; bueno, p.ej., **to be in a fair way to succeed** estar en buen camino de prosperar; **fair and square** (coll.) honrado a carta cabal; *adv* directamente; favorablemente; **to bid fair to** + *inf* prometer + *inf,* dar indicios de + *inf;* **to play fair** jugar limpio; **to speak one fair** hablarle a uno cortésmente; *s* feria; quermese, verbena; (archaic) mujer; (archaic) amada, querida

fair ball *s* (baseball) buen batazo, golpe bueno

fair copy *s* copia en limpio

fair game *s* caza legal; blanco u objeto legítimo

fairground ['fɛr,graund] *s* real (*campo donde se celebra una feria*)

fair-haired ['fɛr'hɛrd] *adj* pelirrubio; favorito, predilecto

fairish ['fɛrɪʃ] *adj* bastante bueno, bastante grande, bastante bien

fairly ['fɛrlɪ] *adv* justamente; imparcialmente; efectivamente; regularmente; distintamente; bastante, medianamente

fair-minded ['fɛr'maɪndɪd] *adj* imparcial, justo

fairness ['fɛrnɪs] *s* justicia; imparcialidad; honradez; legalidad; cortesía; hermosura; serenidad (*del cielo*); blancura (*de tez*); limpieza

fair play *s* juego limpio, proceder leal

fair sex *s* bello sexo

fair-spoken ['fɛr'spokən] *adj* cortés, bien hablado

fair to middling *adj* (coll.) mediano, bastante bueno

fair-trade agreement ['fɛr'tred] *s* convenio entre el fabricante y el comerciante en que se fija el precio mínimo de las manufacturas

fairway ['fɛr,we] *s* (naut.) canalizo; (golf) terreno entre tees donde no hay obstáculos

fair-weather ['fɛr,wɛðər] *adj* del buen tiempo; de los días prósperos; **fair-weather friend** amigo del buen viento

fairy ['fɛrɪ] *s* (*pl:* **-ies**) hada; *adj* de hada, de hadas, feérico

fairy godmother *s* hada madrina

fairyland [fɛrɪ,lænd] *s* tierra de las hadas; lugar hermoso y encantador

fairy ring *s* corro de bruja o de brujas (*círculo hecho en la hierba por ciertos hongos*)

fairy tale *s* cuento de hadas; (fig.) cuento de hadas, bella poesía

fait accompli [fɛtakõ'pli] *s* (Fr.) hecho consumado, hecho cumplido

faith [feθ] *s* fe; **in bad faith** de mala fe; **in good faith** de buena fe; **in faith** en verdad; **to break faith with** faltar a la palabra dada a; **to have faith in** tener fe en; **to keep faith with** cumplir la palabra dada a; **to pin one's faith on** tener puesta su esperanza en; **upon my faith!** ¡a fe mía!, ¡por mi fe!; *interj* ¡en verdad!

faith cure *s* curación por fe

faithful ['feθfəl] *adj* fiel, leal; **the faithful** los fieles, los creyentes

faithfulness ['feθfəlnɪs] *s* fidelidad

faithless ['feθlɪs] *adj* sin fe, infiel, desleal, falso

fake [fek] *s* (coll.) falsificación; (coll.) impostura, patraña; (coll.) farsante, impostor, patrañero; (naut.) aduja; *adj* (coll.) falso, falsificado, fingido; farsante; *va* (coll.) falsificar, fingir; (naut.) adujar; *vn* (coll.) falsificar, fingir

faker ['fekər] *s* (coll.) falsificador; (coll.) impostor, patrañero; (coll.) embustero; (coll.) buhonero

fakir [fə'kɪr] o ['fekər] *s* faquir

Falange ['felændʒ] *s* (pol.) Falange

Falangist [fə'lændʒɪst] *adj & s* falangista

falcate ['fælket] *adj* falcado

falchion ['fɔltʃən] *s* faca; (poet.) espada

falciform ['fælsɪfɔrm] *adj* falciforme

falcon ['fɔkən] o ['fɔlkən] *s* (orn.) halcón; (arti.) falcón

falconer ['fɔkənər] o ['fɔlkənər] *s* cetrero, halconero

falconry ['fɔkənrɪ] o ['fɔlkənrɪ] *s* cetrería, halconería

falderal ['fældə,ræl] o **falderol** ['fældə,ral] *s* chuchería, menudencia, retazo; disparate, tontería; estribillo de una canción que no significa nada

faldstool ['fɔld,stul] *s* faldistorio; facistol (*atril*)

Falkland Islands [,fɔklənd] *spl* islas Malvinas

fall [fɔl] *s* caída; catarata, salto de agua; baja (*de precios*); desembocadura (*de un río*); otoño; (naut.) tira de aparejo; (sport) partido de lucha grecorromana; **falls** *spl* cataratas, salto de agua; (naut.) aparejo de bajar o izar los botes; **the Fall** la Caída (*pecado del primer hombre*); **to ride for a fall** ir por mal camino, ir a acabar mal; *adj* otoñal; (*pret:* **fell;** *pp:* **fallen**) *vn* caer o caerse; ponerse triste (*la expresión del rostro*); **to fall aboard** (naut.) chocar con; **to fall across** dar con, encontrarse con; **to fall apart** caerse a pedazos; (fig.) ir al desastre; **to fall away** apostatar; reincidir; enflaquecer; **to fall back** (mil.) replegarse; faltar a su palabra; **to fall back on** o **upon** (mil.) replegarse hacia; echar mano de, recurrir a; **to fall backward** caer de espaldas; **to fall behind** quedarse atrás, perder terreno; **to fall down** caerse; postrarse; (slang) fracasar; **to fall due** caer o vencer (*p.ej., una letra*); **to fall flat** caer tendido, caer largo; no surtir efecto, no tener éxito; **to fall for** (slang) ser engañado por; (slang) enamorarse de; **to fall in** desplomarse (*p.ej., un techo*); caducar, terminar; ponerse de acuerdo; (mil.) ponerse en su lugar; **to fall into** abrazar, adoptar; adquirir (*p.ej., un hábito*); acceder a obrar de acuerdo con; tomar su lugar en; **to fall in upon** encontrarse con, tropezar con; visitar de repente o inesperadamente; **to fall in with** encontrarse con; trabar amistades con; conformarse con; ponerse de acuerdo con; juntarse con; **to fall off** caerse; caer de o desde; apostatar; decaer; disminuir; enemistarse; dirigirse, inclinarse; (naut.) abatir; **to fall on** asaltar, echarse sobre; encontrarse con; empezar; echar mano de, recurrir a; caer o bajar rápidamente sobre; recaer sobre; (phonet.) cargar en (*dícese del acento de una palabra*); **to fall out** caerse; desavenirse; acontecer; ve-

nir a ser, resultar; **to fall out of** caerse de (*p.ej., un árbol*); **to fall out with** reñirse con; esquinarse con; **to fall over** caerse; volcarse, venirse abajo; desertar; (slang) adular, halagar; **to fall through** fracasar, malograrse; **to fall to** venir a las manos; cerrarse por sí mismo; recaer (*la herencia, la elección, etc.*) en; tocar, corresponder a; (mil.) caer en poder de; (coll.) empezar a comer; **to fall to** + *ger* empezar a + *inf;* **to fall under** estar sujeto o subordinado a; estar entre, estar comprendido en; **to fall upon** asaltar, echarse sobre; encontrarse con; echar mano de, recurrir a; recaer sobre; **to fall within** estar dentro de; estar entre, estar comprendido en
fallacious [fəˈleʃəs] *adj* erróneo; delusorio; falaz (*que halaga con falsas apariencias*)
fallacy [ˈfæləsɪ] *s* (*pl:* **-cies**) error, falsedad; carácter erróneo; (log.) falacia
fallal [ˌfæˈlæl] *s* faralá, adorno excesivo; modo afectado
fallen [ˈfɔlən] *adj* caído; **the fallen** los caídos (*en la lucha*); *pp de* **fall**
fallen angel *s* ángel caído
fall guy *s* (slang) pato, cabeza de turco
fallibility [ˌfælɪˈbɪlɪtɪ] *s* falibilidad
fallible [ˈfælɪbəl] *adj* falible
falling [ˈfɔlɪŋ] *adj* cayente; (phonet.) decreciente (*diptongo*)
falling sickness *s* (path.) mal caduco
falling star *s* estrella fugaz
fall line *s* borde de una meseta formado por una línea de cataratas; (U.S.A.) línea que va de norte a sur, al este de los Apalaches, donde terminan los estratos duros y comienzan los terrenos blandos de la costa del este
Fallopian tube [fəˈlopɪən] *s* (anat.) trompa de Falopio
fallout [ˈfɔlˌaut] *s* caída radiactiva, precipitación radiactiva
fallout shelter *s* refugio antiatómico
fallow [ˈfælo] *adj* barbechado; flavo; **to let lie fallow** dejar en barbecho; **to lie fallow** estar en barbecho; *s* barbecho; *va* barbechar
fallow deer *s* (zool.) gamo, paleto
fall wheat *s* trigo sembrado en el otoño
false [fɔls] *adj* falso; postizo; *adv* falsamente; **to play false** traicionar
false acacia *s* (bot.) acacia falsa
false alarm *s* falsa alarma
false bottom *s* fondo falso
false colors *spl* bandera falsa; pretextos falsos
false face *s* careta, mascarilla; carantamaula (*careta fea*)
false hair *s* pelo postizo o falso
false-hearted [ˈfɔlsˈhɑrtɪd] *adj* pérfido, traidor
falsehood [ˈfɔlshud] *s* falsedad
false imprisonment *s* detención o prisión ilegal
false keel *s* (naut.) falsa quilla
false key *s* llave falsa
falseness [ˈfɔlsnɪs] *s* falsedad
false pretenses *spl* (law) estafa, dolo
false pride *s* falso orgullo
false relation *s* (mus.) falsa relación
false return *s* declaración falsa
false ribs *spl* (anat.) costillas falsas
false step *s* tropiezo; (fig.) paso en falso
false teeth *spl* dientes postizos o falsos
falsetto [fɔlˈsɛto] *s* (*pl:* **-tos**) falsete (*voz*); falsetista (*persona*); **in a falsetto** de falsete; *adj* del falsete; que canta de falsete; (fig.) artificial, poco natural; *adv* de falsete
falsification [ˌfɔlsɪfɪˈkeʃən] *s* falsificación; mentira; refutación
falsify [ˈfɔlsɪfaɪ] (*pret & pp:* **-fied**) *va* falsificar; refutar; *vn* falsificar; mentir
falsity [ˈfɔlsɪtɪ] *s* (*pl:* **-ties**) falsedad
falter [ˈfɔltər] *s* vacilación; balbuceo; *va* decir titubeando; *vn* vacilar; balbucear
falx [fælks] *s* (*pl:* **falces** [ˈfælsiz]) (anat.) falce, hoz
falx cerebelli [ˌsɛrɪˈbɛlaɪ] *s* (anat.) hoz del cerebelo
falx cerebri [ˈsɛrɪbraɪ] *s* (anat.) hoz del cerebro
fame [fem] *s* fama; *va* afamar
famed [femd] *adj* afamado
familiar [fəˈmɪljər] *adj* familiar; **to be familiar to** ser familiar a; **to be familiar with** estar familiarizado con (*una persona o cosa*); tener muy sabido; *s* familiar; (eccl.) familiar
familiarity [fəˌmɪlɪˈærɪtɪ] *s* (*pl:* **-ties**) familiaridad; conocimiento, p.ej., **familiarity with algebra** conocimiento del álgebra
familiarization [fəˌmɪljərɪˈzeʃən] *s* familiarización
familiarize [fəˈmɪljəraɪz] *va* familiarizar; **to familiarize oneself with** familiarizarse con
family [ˈfæmɪlɪ] *s* (*pl:* **-lies**) familia; *adj* familiar, p.ej., **family ties** lazos familiares; **in a family way** sin ceremonia; **in the family way** (coll.) embarazada, encinta
family circle *s* círculo de la familia; (theat.) gallinero, paraíso
family man *s* padre de familia; hombre casero
family name *s* apellido, nombre de familia
family physician *s* médico de cabecera
family skeleton *s* cosa vergonzosa en una familia que se intenta guardar en secreto
family tree *s* árbol genealógico
famine [ˈfæmɪn] *s* hambre; carestía
famish [ˈfæmɪʃ] *va & vn* hambrear
famished [ˈfæmɪʃt] *adj* famélico
famous [ˈfeməs] *adj* famoso; (coll.) famoso (*excelente*)
famulus [ˈfæmjələs] *s* (*pl:* **-li** [laɪ]) fámulo
fan [fæn] *s* abanico; ventilador; aventador (*para aventar el fuego*); aventadora (*para aventar los granos*); (slang) aficionado (*a deportes, películas, etc.*); (*pret & pp:* **fanned;** *ger:* **fanning**) *va* abanicar; aventar; ahuyentar con abanico; activar o avivar (*el fuego*); excitar (*las pasiones*); azotar (*el viento, p.ej., el rostro*); abrir o extender en abanico; (slang) pegar, zurrar; (baseball) hacer golpear mal la pelota tres veces; **to fan oneself** abanicarse; *vn* abanicarse; moverse impulsado por la brisa; soplar (*el viento*); abrirse o extenderse en abanico; salir (*un camino*) en todas direcciones; (baseball) golpear mal la pelota tres veces
fanatic [fəˈnætɪk] *adj & s* fanático
fanatical [fəˈnætɪkəl] *adj* fanático
fanaticism [fəˈnætɪsɪzəm] *s* fanatismo
fan belt *s* correa de ventilador
fan blade *s* paleta de ventilador
fancied [ˈfænsɪd] *adj* imaginado, imaginario
fancier [ˈfænsɪər] *s* aficionado; criador aficionado (*de aves, animales, etc.*); soñador, visionario
fanciful [ˈfænsɪfəl] *adj* fantástico; imaginativo
fancy [ˈfænsɪ] *s* (*pl:* **-cies**) fantasía; antojo, capricho; afición, gusto, cariño; (mus.) fantasía; **to strike one's fancy** antojársele a uno; **to take a fancy to** prendarse de, coger cariño a; *adj* (*comp:* **-cier;** *super:* **-ciest**) fantástico; extravagante (*idea*); de fantasía, de imitación; de lujo, fino; ornamental, de adorno; primoroso; vendedor de géneros de fantasía; vendedor de géneros de lujo; criado o cultivado por afición; (*pret & pp:* **-cied**) *va* imaginar; aficionarse a; prendarse de; criar (*aves, animales, etc.*) por afición; *vn* fantasear; prendarse de amor
fancy ball *s* baile de trajes
fancy dive *s* salto ornamental
fancy diving *s* buceo acrobático, saltos ornamentales
fancy dress *s* traje de fantasía, traje de capricho
fancy-dress ball [ˈfænsɪˌdrɛs] *s* baile de trajes
fancy foods *spl* comestibles de lujo
fancy-free [ˈfænsɪˈfri] *adj* libre del poder del amor, no enamorado
fancy goods *spl* géneros de fantasía
fancy jewelry *s* joyas de fantasía, joyas de imitación
fancy skater *s* patinador de fantasía
fancy skating *s* patinaje de fantasía
fancy woods *spl* maderas preciosas
fancywork [ˈfænsɪˌwʌrk] *s* (sew.) labor
fane [fen] *s* (archaic & poet.) templo
fanfare [ˈfænfɛr] *s* fanfarria (*pompa excesiva; tocata de caza*); (mus.) fanfarria
fanfaronade [ˌfænfərəˈned] *s* fanfarronada
fang [fæŋ] *s* colmillo (*del lobo, las fieras, etc.*); diente (*del reptil; del tenedor, la horquilla, etc.*); raíz (*de diente*)

fanion ['fænjən] *s* banderola; (surv.) banderola
fanlight ['fæn,laɪt] *s* (arch.) abanico
fan mail *s* (sport) correo de hinchas; (taur.) correo de aficionados; (theat.) correo de admiradores
Fannie o **Fanny** ['fænɪ] *s* Paquita
fanning mill *s* (agr.) máquina aventadora
fanon ['fænən] *s* (eccl.) fanón
fan palm *s* (bot.) miraguano, palmera de abanico
fan-shaped ['fæn,ʃept] *adj* en forma de abanico
fantail ['fæn,tel] *s* (orn.) paloma colipava; (carp.) cola de abanico; (arch.) bovedilla; mechero de mariposa
fan-tan ['fæn,tæn] *s* juego chino por dinero; juego de naipes en el cual gana quien pierde sus naipes primero
fantasia [fæn'tɑzɪə] o [,fæntə'ziə] *s* (mus.) fantasía
fantastic [fæn'tæstɪk] o **fantastical** [fæn'tæstɪkəl] *adj* fantástico
fantasy ['fæntəzɪ] o ['fæntəsɪ] *s* (*pl:* **-sies**) fantasía; (mus.) fantasía
fan tracery *s* (arch.) red decorativa de bóveda de abanico
fan vaulting *s* (arch.) bóveda de abanico
fan window *s* (arch.) abanico
fanwise ['fæn,waɪz] *adv* en abanico
far [fɑr] *adj* (*comp:* **farther;** *super:* **farthest**) lejano; más lejano; largo (*viaje*); posterior; **on the far side of** del otro lado de; *adv* (*comp:* **farther;** *super:* **farthest**) lejos; más lejos; muy, p.ej., **far different** muy diferente; mucho, p.ej., **far better** mucho mejor; **as far as** hasta, hasta donde; tan lejos como; en cuanto, según que; **as far as I am concerned** por lo que a mí me toca; **as far as I know** que yo sepa, según parece; **by far** con mucho; **how far** cuán lejos, hasta dónde, hasta qué punto; **how far is it?** ¿cuánto hay de aquí?; **in so far as** en cuanto, en tanto que; **so far** hasta ahora, hasta entonces; hasta aquí, hasta ahí; **so far as** hasta, hasta donde; en cuanto, según que; **so far so good** mientras siga así, todo va bien; **that is going too far** eso es demasiado fuerte; **thus far** hasta ahora; **thus far this year** en lo que va del año; **to be far from** + *ger* estar lejos de + *inf;* **to go far** ir lejos; alcanzar para mucho; durar mucho; **to go far to** o **toward** contribuir mucho a; **far and near** o **far and wide** por todas partes; **far away** muy lejos; **far be it from me** no permita Dios; **far from** lejos de (*p.ej., la ciudad, el ánimo de uno*); **far from it** ni con mucho, muy al contrario; **far into** hasta muy adentro de; hasta muy tarde de, hasta las altas horas de (*la noche*); hasta muy avanzado (*p.ej., el verano*); **far more** mucho más; **far off** a lo lejos, a gran distancia
farad ['færæd] *s* (elec.) faradio
faradic [fə'rædɪk] *adj* farádico
faradism ['færədɪzəm] *s* faradismo; (med.) faradismo
faradization [,færədɪ'zeʃən] *s* (med.) faradización
faradize ['færədaɪz] *va* (med.) faradizar
faradmeter ['færæd,mitər] *s* (elec.) faradímetro
farandole ['færəndol] *s* farándola o farándula (*baile*)
faraway ['fɑrə,we] *adj* lejano; abstraído, preocupado
farce [fɑrs] *s* (theat.) farsa; (fig.) farsa, cosa de reír; *va* embutir (*un escrito*) de pasajes o citas chistosas
farceur [fɑr'sʌr] *s* bromista, chancero; farsante (*cómico*)
farcical ['fɑrsɪkəl] *adj* absurdo, ridículo, improbable; (vet.) muermoso
far cry *s* gran distancia, gran diferencia
farcy ['fɑrsɪ] *s* (vet.) muermo
fardel ['fɑrdəl] *s* (archaic) carga, lío, paquete
fare [fɛr] *s* pasaje; pasajero; alimento, comida; **to collect fares** cobrar el pasaje; *vn* acontecer, suceder; pasarlo; irle a uno (*bien o mal*), p.ej., **how did you fare?** ¿cómo le ha ido a Vd.?; vivir (*bien o mal*); comer; (archaic) ir, viajar; **to fare forth** ponerse en camino
Far East *s* Extremo Oriente, Lejano Oriente
farewell ['fɛr'wɛl] *s* despedida, adiós; salida; **to bid farewell to** o **to take farewell of** despedirse de; *adj* de despedida, p.ej., **farewell song** canción de despedida; *interj* ¡adiós!
far-fetched ['fɑr'fɛtʃt] *adj* forzado, traído por los pelos
far-flung ['fɑr'flʌŋ] *adj* extenso, vasto, de gran alcance
farina [fə'rinə] *s* harina; almidón; fécula; (zool.) polvo harinoso
farinaceous [,færɪ'neʃəs] *adj* (bot.) farináceo
farkleberry ['fɑrkəl,bɛrɪ] *s* (*pl:* **-ries**) (bot.) batodendrón
farm [fɑrm] *s* granja; terreno agrícola; plantación; *adj* agrícola; agropecuario; *va* cultivar o labrar (*la tierra*); arrendar; hacer contrato por el cuidado de (*p.ej., los indigentes*); **to farm out** ceder (*un trabajo*) por contrato; *vn* cultivar la tierra y criar animales
farmer ['fɑrmər] *s* granjero; agricultor, labrador
farmerette [,fɑrmə'rɛt] *s* (coll.) agricultora, labradora
farmerish ['fɑrmərɪʃ] *adj* apatanado
Farmer-Labor Party ['fɑrmər'lebər] *s* (U.S.A.) partido obrero-campesino
farm hand *s* peón, mozo de granja
farmhouse ['fɑrm,haʊs] *s* cortijo, alquería
farming ['fɑrmɪŋ] *s* agricultura, labranza
farm produce *s* productos del suelo
farm school *s* granja escuela
farmstead ['fɑrmstɛd] *s* granja
farmyard ['fɑrm,jɑrd] *s* corral de granja
faro ['fɛro] *s* faraón (*juego de cartas*)
far-off ['fɑr,ɔf] o ['fɑr,ɑf] *adj* lejano, distante
farrago [fə'rego] *s* (*pl:* **-goes**) fárrago
far-reaching ['fɑr'ritʃɪŋ] *adj* de mucho alcance
farrier ['færɪər] *s* herrador; albéitar
farriery ['færɪərɪ] *s* (*pl:* **-ies**) herrería; albeitería
farrow ['færo] *s* lechigada de puercos; parto de la marrana; *adj* horra (*vaca*); *va & vn* parir (*la marrana*)
far-seeing ['fɑr'siɪŋ] *adj* longividente; previsor, precavido
far-sighted ['fɑr'saɪtɪd] *adj* longividente; previsor, precavido; présbita
far-sightedness ['fɑr'saɪtɪdnɪs] *s* buena visión, penetración; previsión; presbicia
farther ['fɑrðər] *adj comp* más lejano; más, adicional; *adv comp* más lejos, más allá; además, también; **how much farther** cuánto más; **farther on** más adelante
farthermost ['fɑrðərmost] *adj super* más lejano (*de todos*)
farthest ['fɑrðɪst] *adj super* más lejano (*de todos*); último; *adv super* más lejos, a más distancia; más
farthing ['fɑrðɪŋ] *s* (Brit.) cuarto de penique
farthingale ['fɑrðɪŋgel] *s* verdugado, miriñaque
Far West *s* lejano oeste (*de los EE.UU.*)
fasces ['fæsiz] *spl* fasces
fascia ['fæʃɪə] *s* (*pl:* **-ae** [i]) (anat.) fascia; (arch.) faja; (surg.) faja o fascia
fascial ['fæʃɪəl] *adj* fascial
fascicle ['fæsɪkəl] *s* fascículo (*de un libro*); manojo, racimo; (anat. & bot.) fascículo
fascicled ['fæsɪkəld] *adj* fasciculado
fasciculus [fə'sɪkjələs] *s* (*pl:* **-li** [laɪ]) fascículo (*de un libro*); (anat.) fascículo
fascinate ['fæsɪnet] *va* fascinar; (archaic) fascinar (*aojar; hechizar*)
fascinating ['fæsɪ,netɪŋ] *adj* fascinador o fascinante
fascination [,fæsɪ'neʃən] *s* fascinación; (archaic) fascinación (*aojo*)
fascinator ['fæsɪ,netər] *s* fascinador; mantilla ligera de ganchillo
fascine [fæ'sin] *s* haz de leña, fajina; (fort.) fajina
fascism ['fæʃɪzəm] *s* fascismo
fascist ['fæʃɪst] *adj & s* fascista
fashion ['fæʃən] *s* moda, boga; estilo, manera; elegancia, buen tono; alta sociedad, gente de buen tono; **after** o **in a fashion** hasta cierto punto, en cierto modo, así así; **in fashion** de

moda; **out of fashion** fuera de moda, pasado de moda; **to go out of fashion** pasar de moda; *va* labrar, forjar
fashionable ['fæʃənəbəl] *adj* elegante, de moda, de buen tono
fashion designing *s* alta costura
fashion piece *s* (naut.) aleta
fashion plate *s* figurín (*dibujo*); (coll.) figurín, elegante (*persona*)
fashion shop *s* casa de modas
fast [fæst] o [fɑst] *s* ayuno; día de ayuno; asegurador; (naut.) cable de amarra; **to break one's fast** desayunarse; romper el ayuno; *adj* rápido, veloz; adelantado (*reloj*); disipado, disoluto; fijo; estable; fiel (*amigo*); **to pull a fast one** (slang) jugar una mala pasada; *adv* rápidamente, velozmente; firmemente; completamente; profundamente; (archaic) cerca; **fast by** cerca de; **to hold fast** mantenerse firme; **to hold fast to** agarrarse bien de; afirmarse en; **to play fast and loose** proceder de manera poco sincera; **to live fast** entregarse a los placeres o los vicios; *vn* ayunar
fast and loose pulleys *spl* (mach.) contramarcha (*juego de dos poleas, una fija y la otra libre o loca, que sirven para embragar o desembragar un árbol*)
fast day *s* día de ayuno
fasten ['fæsən] o ['fɑsən] *va* fijar; cerrar, cerrar con llave; atar; abrochar; ajustarse (*p.ej., el cinturón*); aplicar (*la culpa*); imprimir; *vn* fijarse; cuajarse; **to fasten on** o **upon** agarrarse o asirse a o de
fastener ['fæsənər] o ['fɑsənər] *s* asilla, asegurador, cierre
fastening ['fæsənɪŋ] o ['fɑsənɪŋ] *s* aseguramiento; asegurador (*instrumento*); cerradura; cerrojo; botón; broche; corchete
fastidious [fæs'tɪdɪəs] *adj* quisquilloso; arrogante, desdeñoso
fastigium [fæs'tɪdʒɪəm] *s* (*pl:* **-a** [ə]) (anat. & arch.) fastigio
fasting ['fæstɪŋ] o ['fɑstɪŋ] *s* ayuno
fastness ['fæstnɪs] o ['fɑstnɪs] *s* rapidez; adelanto (*del reloj*); disipación; estrechez (*de la amistad*); fijeza, firmeza; estabilidad o solidez (*de materias colorantes*); plaza fuerte
fat [fæt] *adj* (*comp:* **fatter;** *super:* **fattest**) gordo; lerdo, pesado, torpe; fuerte, poderoso; opulento; pingüe, provechoso; fértil; (aut.) caliente (*chispa*); **to get fat** engordar; *s* gordo, grasa; (chem.) grasa; **the fat of the land** lo mejor y más rico de la tierra; (*pret & pp:* **fatted;** *ger:* **fatting**) *va & vn* engordar
fatal ['fetəl] *adj* fatal
fatalism ['fetəlɪzəm] *s* fatalismo
fatalist ['fetəlɪst] *s* fatalista
fatalistic [,fetə'lɪstɪk] *adj* fatalista
fatality [fe'tælɪtɪ] o [fə'tælɪtɪ] *s* (*pl:* **-ties**) fatalidad; muerte
fatally ['fetəlɪ] *adv* fatalmente
Fata Morgana ['fɑtə mɔr'gɑnə] *s* (meteor.) Fata Morgana; (myth.) Morgana
fate [fet] *s* hado; **Fates** *spl* (myth.) Parcas
fated ['fetɪd] *adj* fatal; predestinado a la ruina, la muerte, etc.
fateful ['fetfəl] *adj* fatal; fatídico
fathead ['fæt,hed] *s* (coll.) tronco, estúpido
father ['fɑðər] *s* padre; (eccl.) padre; tío (*tratamiento que se da a los hombres ancianos*); *va* engendrar; prohijar; servir de padre a, tratar como hijo; inventar, originar, producir; atribuir
father confessor *s* (eccl.) padre espiritual; confidente
fatherhood ['fɑðərhʊd] *s* paternidad
father-in-law ['fɑðərɪn,lɔ] *s* (*pl:* **fathers-in-law**) suegro
fatherland ['fɑðər,lænd] *s* patria
fatherless ['fɑðərlɪs] *adj* huérfano de padre; abandonado, sin amparo de padre
fatherly ['fɑðərlɪ] *adj* paternal; *adv* paternalmente
Father of his Country *s* padre de la patria (*título de honor concedido a los emperadores romanos y después a otros monarcas y príncipes y en EE.UU. a Jorge Wáshington*)
Father of Waters *s* padre de las aguas (*el río Misisipí*)
fathers of the church *spl* padres de la iglesia, santos padres
Father Time *s* el Tiempo (*representación del tiempo en figura de un anciano con una guadaña en una mano y un reloj de arena en la otra*)
fathom ['fæðəm] *s* (naut.) braza; *va* sondear; desenmarañar, profundizar
fathomable ['fæðəməbəl] *adj* sondable; comprensible
fathomless ['fæðəmlɪs] *adj* insondable; (fig.) insondable, incomprensible
fatidic [fe'tɪdɪk] o [fə'tɪdɪk] *adj* fatídico
fatigue [fə'tig] *s* fatiga; (mech. & physiol.) fatiga; (mil.) faena, trabajo distinto del manejo de las armas; *va* fatigar, cansar
fatigue clothes *spl* (mil.) traje de faena
fatigue duty *s* (mil.) faena, trabajo distinto del manejo de las armas
fatigue party *s* (mil.) pelotón de castigo
fatiguing [fə'tigɪŋ] *adj* fatigoso
fatling ['fætlɪŋ] *s* ceboncillo
fatness ['fætnɪs] *s* gordura; graseza; fertilidad
fatten ['fætən] *va & vn* engordar
fatty ['fætɪ] *adj* (*comp:* **-tier;** *super:* **-tiest**) graso; gordiflón; (chem.) graso; (path.) grasoso; *s* (*pl:* **-ties**) (slang) gordiflón
fatty acid *s* (chem.) ácido graso
fatty degeneration *s* (path.) degeneración grasosa
fatty heart *s* (path.) corazón grasoso
fatuity [fə'tjuɪtɪ] o [fə'tuɪtɪ] *s* (*pl:* **-ties**) fatuidad; irrealidad, ilusión
fatuous ['fætʃʊəs] *adj* fatuo; irreal, ilusivo
faucal ['fɔkəl] *adj* faucal
fauces ['fɔsiz] *spl* (anat.) fauces
faucet ['fɔsɪt] *s* grifo
faugh [fɔ] *interj* ¡puf!, ¡bah!
fault [fɔlt] *s* falta, culpa; (geol. & min.) falla; (sport) falta; (elec.) fuga de corriente, avería del circuito; **at fault** culpable; perplejo; **in fault** culpable; **it's your fault** Vd. tiene la culpa; **to a fault** excesivamente; **to find fault with** criticar, culpar; hallar defecto en; *va* culpar; (geol.) producir falla en
faultfinder ['fɔlt,faɪndər] *s* criticón, reparón
faultfinding ['fɔlt,faɪndɪŋ] *adj* criticón, reparón; *s* crítica, manía de criticar
faultless ['fɔltlɪs] *adj* intachable; perfecto
faulty ['fɔltɪ] *adj* (*comp:* **-ier;** *super:* **-iest**) defectuoso, imperfecto; culpable
faun [fɔn] *s* (myth.) fauno
fauna ['fɔnə] *s* fauna; (*cap.*) *s* (myth.) Fauna
faunal ['fɔnəl] *adj* fáunico
Faust [faʊst] *s* Fausto
Faustian ['faʊstɪən] o ['fɔstɪən] *adj* fáustico
faux pas [fo 'pɑ] *s* (*pl:* **faux pas** [fo 'pɑ] o [fo 'pɑz]) (Fr.) paso en falso
favor ['fevər] *s* favor; grata o atenta (*la carta de que se acusa recibo*); (fig.) favor (*regalo, señal, cinta*); **favors** *spl* favores (*de una mujer*); (fig.) regalos de fiesta (*tales como serpentinas, matracas, sombreros, panderetas*); **by your favor** con permiso de Vd.; **do me the favor of** + *ger* hágame Vd. el favor de + *inf;* **to be in favor** estar en favor (*tener buena aceptación*); **to be in favor of** estar por, ser partidario de; **to be in favor with** disfrutar del favor de, tener el apoyo de; **to be out of favor** no estar en favor; *va* favorecer; abstenerse de usar, usar con precaución; (coll.) parecerse a
favorable ['fevərəbəl] *adj* favorable
favored ['fevərd] *adj* favorecido; encarado, p.ej., **ill-favored** mal encarado; dotado, p.ej., **favored by nature** dotado por la naturaleza; **favored with beauty** dotado de hermosura
favorite ['fevərɪt] *adj* favorito, predilecto; *s* favorito
favorite son *s* (pol.) candidato favorito de un estado (*para la presidencia de los EE.UU.*)
favoritism ['fevərɪtɪzəm] *s* favoritismo
favose ['fevos] o [fe'vos] *adj* favoso
favour ['fevər] *s & va* (Brit.) var. de **favor**
favus ['fevəs] *s* (path.) favo
fawn [fɔn] *s* (zool.) cervato; corzo, gamito (*de menos de un año*); color de cervato; *vn* parir (*la cierva*); arrastrarse, reptar; hacer fiestas (*p.ej., el perro*); **to fawn on** o **upon** adular servilmente; hacer fiestas a

fay [fe] *s* hada; (archaic) fe; *va* empalmar, juntar; *vn* empalmarse, juntarse
faze [fez] *va* (coll.) inquietar, molestar, turbar, desanimar
FBI abr. de **Federal Bureau of Investigation**
fealty ['fiəltɪ] *s* (*pl:* **-ties**) homenaje; fidelidad, lealtad
fear [fɪr] *s* temor, miedo; **for fear of** por temor de, por miedo de; **for fear that** por miedo (de) que; **no fear** no hay peligro; **to be in fear of** tener miedo de; *va & vn* temer; **to fear for** temer por; **to fear to** + *inf* temer + *inf*
fearful ['fɪrfəl] *adj* medroso; (coll.) enorme, numeroso, excesivo, muy malo
fearless ['fɪrlɪs] *adj* intrépido, sin temor, arrojado
fearsome ['fɪrsəm] *adj* medroso
feasibility [,fizɪ'bɪlɪtɪ] *s* viabilidad
feasible ['fizɪbəl] *adj* viable, factible
feast [fist] *s* fiesta (*día; solemnidad; regocijo*); festín, banquete; *va* banquetear; *vn* banquetear; festejarse; **to feast on** regalarse con (*p.ej., golosinas*)
feat [fit] *s* hazaña, proeza, juego de destreza
feather ['fɛðər] *s* pluma; penacho (*adorno de plumas; vanidad*); condición, estado; vestido; clase, género; humor; mechón (*de pelo*); nada, p.ej., **to laugh at a feather** reírse de nada; (carp.) espiga, lengüeta; (mach.) chaveta, pestaña, soporte de refuerzo; (mach.) cuña, llave; (naut.) estela del periscopio (*del submarino*); **feathers** *spl* (poet.) alas; **in feather** plumado; **in fine, good** o **high feather** de buen humor; en buena salud; **to show the white feather** acobardarse, volver las espaldas; **feather in one's cap** timbre de honor, triunfo personal; *adj* de pluma, de plumas; leve, suave; *va* emplumar; poner pluma a (*una flecha*); cortar (*el aire*) volando; adelgazar, sutilizar; volver (*la pala del remo*) al sacarla del agua, poniéndola casi horizontal; (carp.) machihembrar; *vn* emplumecer; crecer, extenderse o moverse como pluma; volver la pala del remo al sacarla del agua, poniéndola casi horizontal
feather bed *s* colchón de plumas; (fig.) lecho de plumas
featherbed ['fɛðər,bɛd] (*pret & pp:* **-bedded;** *ger:* **-bedding**) *vn* exigir el empleo de más trabajadores de lo necesario
featherbrain ['fɛðər,bren] *s* cascabelero
featherbrained ['fɛðər,brend] *adj* cascabelero
feather duster *s* plumero
feathered ['fɛðərd] *adj* plumado; alado; ligero, veloz
featheredge ['fɛðər,ɛdʒ] *s* filván; bisel, canto vivo; (b.b.) barba; *adj* con filván; barbado (*papel*); *va* dejar filván en; biselar
featheredged ['fɛðər,ɛdʒd] *adj* con filván
feathered hyacinth *s* (bot.) jacinto de penacho
feather grass *s* (bot.) espolín
featherless ['fɛðərlɪs] *adj* implume
featherstitch ['fɛðər,stɪtʃ] *s* punto de espina, punto ruso; *va* adornar con punto de espina; *vn* hacer punto de espina
featherweight ['fɛðər,wet] *s* persona o cosa de muy poco peso; (box.) peso pluma; persona o cosa de poca importancia; imbécil, tonto; *adj* muy ligero; poco importante; (box.) de peso pluma
featherwork ['fɛðər,wʌrk] *s* arte plumaria
feathery ['fɛðərɪ] *adj* plumoso
feature ['fitʃər] *s* facción; característica, rasgo distintivo; atracción principal, película principal, artículo principal, tira cómica principal; especialidad; **features** *spl* facciones (*cara, rostro*); *va* delinear, representar; ofrecer (*como cosa principal*); (coll.) destacar, hacer resaltar; (coll.) parecerse a
featured ['fitʃərd] *adj* encarado, p.ej., **well-featured** bien encarado; (coll.) anunciado de modo destacado
featureless ['fitʃərlɪs] *adj* sin rasgos distintivos, poco interesante
Feb. abr. de **February**
febrifuge ['fɛbrɪfjudʒ] *adj & s* febrífugo
febrile ['fibrɪl] o ['fɛbrɪl] *adj* febril
February ['fɛbru,ɛrɪ] *s* febrero
fecal ['fikəl] *adj* fecal
fecalith ['fikəlɪθ] *s* (path.) fecalito
feces ['fisiz] *spl* heces (*excremento; poso, sedimento*)
feckless ['fɛklɪs] *adj* abatido, débil, sin valor
fecula ['fɛkjulə] *s* (*pl:* **-lae** [li]) fécula
feculent ['fɛkjulənt] *adj* feculento (*que tiene heces*)
fecund ['fikənd] o ['fɛkənd] *adj* fecundo
fecundate ['fikəndet] o ['fɛkəndet] *va* fecundar; (biol.) fecundar
fecundation [,fikən'deʃən] o [,fɛkən'deʃən] *s* fecundación; (biol.) fecundación
fecundative [fɪ'kʌndətɪv] *adj* fecundativo
fecundity [fɪ'kʌndɪtɪ] *s* fecundidad
fed [fɛd] *pret & pp de* **feed**
federal ['fɛdərəl] *adj & s* federal; (*cap.*) *s* (U.S.A.) soldado o partidario del gobierno central durante la guerra entre Norte y Sur
federalism ['fɛdərəlɪzəm] *s* federalismo
federalist ['fɛdərəlɪst] *adj & s* federalista
federalize ['fɛdərəlaɪz] *va* federar
Federal Reserve Bank *s* (U.S.A.) cada uno de los doce bancos de los distritos del sistema de Reserva Federal, establecidos para regularizar y ayudar a los bancos miembros de ese sistema
Federal Reserve Board *s* (U.S.A.) grupo de nueve personas elegidas por el presidente de los EE.UU. para controlar el sistema de la Reserva Federal
Federal Reserve System *s* (U.S.A.) sistema de la Reserva Federal
federate ['fɛdərɪt] o ['fɛdəret] *adj* federado; ['fɛdəret] *va* federar
Federated Malay States *spl* Estados Malayos Federados
federation [,fɛdə'reʃən] *s* federación
federative ['fɛdə,retɪv] *adj* federativo
fedora [fɪ'dorə] *s* sombrero de fieltro suave con ala vuelta
fed up *adj* harto; (fig.) harto; **fed up with** harto de
fee [fi] *s* honorarios; derechos; propina; (law) hacienda de patrimonio, herencia; (feud.) dominio; **to hold in fee** poseer, ser dueño de; *va* pagar, premiar; dar propina a
feeble ['fibəl] *adj* débil
feeble-minded ['fibəl'maɪndɪd] *adj* imbécil; irresoluto, vacilante
feebleness ['fibəlnɪs] *s* debilidad
feebly ['fiblɪ] *adv* débilmente
feed [fid] *s* alimento; alimentación; (coll.) comida, comida abundante; (mach.) dispositivo de alimentación, movimiento de alimentación; (*pret & pp:* **fed**) *va* alimentar; *vn* comer, alimentarse; **to feed on** o **upon** alimentarse de
feedback ['fid,bæk] *s* (elec.) regeneración, realimentación
feed-back circuit ['fid,bæk] *s* (elec.) circuito de regeneración
feed-back coil *s* (elec.) bobina de regeneración
feed bag *s* cebadera, morral
feeder ['fidər] *s* alimentador; fuente; afluente (*de un río*); (elec.) conductor de alimentación; (min.) filón ramal; (rail.) ramal tributario
feedhead ['fid,hɛd] *s* depósito de alimentación; (found.) canal de mazarota
feed line *s* (elec.) conductor de alimentación
feed pump *s* bomba alimenticia o bomba de alimentación
feed trough *s* artesa, comedero; (rail.) atarjea de alimentación
feed wire *s* (elec.) conductor de alimentación
feel [fil] *s* sensación; tacto; tino; (*pret & pp:* **felt**) *va* palpar, tentar; sentir; tomar (*el pulso*); resentirse de; tantear (*el camino*); **to feel out** dar un toque a, tantear; *vn* palpar; sentirse (*enfermo, obligado, etc.*); ser (*áspero, suave, etc.*) al tacto; estar (*caliente*); tener (*calor, frío, hambre, sed*); **to feel bad** sentirse mal; condolerse; **to feel cheap** avergonzarse, sentirse inferior; **to feel comfortable** sentirse a gusto; **to feel for** buscar tentando; condolerse de; **to feel like** (coll.) tener ganas de; **to feel like** + *ger* (coll.) tener ganas de + *inf;* **to feel (like) oneself** tener la salud, vigor, ánimo, etc. acostumbrados; **to feel safe** sentirse a salvo; **to feel sorry** sentir; arrepentirse; **to feel sorry for** compadecer

feeler ['filər] *s* persona o cosa que palpa; tentativa, tanteo (*que se hace para descubrir los sentimientos ajenos*); (mach.) calibrador de espesor, tira calibradora; **feelers** *spl* palpos, anténulas (*del insecto*); tentáculos (*del molusco y el zoófito*)
feeling ['filɪŋ] *s* sensación; tacto; sentimiento; parecer, opinión; presentimiento; **feelings** *spl* sensibilidad, sentimientos delicados
feelingly ['filɪŋlɪ] *adv* con emoción
fee simple *s* (law) herencia libre de condición
feet [fit] *pl de* **foot**
fee tail *s* (law) herencia cuyo derecho de sucesión está restringido a los herederos directos
feign [fen] *va* aparentar, fingir; *vn* fingir; **to feign to** + *inf* fingir + *inf;* **to feign to be** fingirse
feint [fent] *s* fingimiento; finta (*amago*); *vn* hacer una finta
feldspar ['fɛld,spɑr] *s* (mineral.) feldespato
feldspathic [fɛld'spæθɪk] o **feldspathose** ['fɛldspæθos] *adj* feldespático
felicitate [fɪ'lɪsɪtet] *va* felicitar
felicitation [fɪ,lɪsɪ'teʃən] *s* felicitación
felicitous [fɪ'lɪsɪtəs] *adj* feliz (*dicho, idea, etc.*); elocuente
felicity [fɪ'lɪsɪtɪ] *s* (*pl:* **-ties**) felicidad; aptitud o gracia de expresión; idea feliz, expresión feliz
felid ['filɪd] *s* (zool.) félido
feline ['filaɪn] *adj* (zool. & fig.) felino; *s* (zool.) felino
fell [fɛl] *s* tala (*de árboles*); todos los árboles cortados en una estación; (sew.) sobrecarga; pellejo; (Scotch) colina, montaña; (Scotch) páramo o brezal elevado; *adj* cruel, feroz; destructivo, mortal; *va* derribar; talar (*árboles*); (sew.) sobrecargar; *pret de* **fall**
fellah ['fɛlə] *s* (*pl:* **fellaheen** o **fellahin** [,fɛlə'hin] o **fellahs**) felá
felloe ['fɛlo] *s* aro de la rueda; pina (*pieza del aro de la rueda*)
fellow ['fɛlo] *s* (coll.) hombre, mozo, tipo, sujeto; (coll.) pretendiente; pícaro, pillo; compañero; igual; pareja; congénere, prójimo; miembro (*de un colegio, sociedad, etc.*); pensionista (*estudiante que disfruta una pensión o beca*)
fellow being *s* prójimo
fellow citizen *s* conciudadano
fellow countryman *s* compatriota
fellow creature *s* prójimo
fellow feeling *s* afinidad, compañerismo, simpatía
fellow man *s* prójimo
fellow member *s* consocio
fellow passenger *s* compañero de viaje
fellow prisoner *s* compañero de prisión
fellowship ['fɛloʃɪp] *s* compañerismo; coparticipación; hermandad; pensión (*para ampliar estudios*)
fellow student *s* condiscípulo
fellow traveler *s* simpatizante; compañero de viaje, comunistizante
fellow worker *s* compañero de trabajo
felly ['fɛlɪ] *s* (*pl:* **-lies**) var. de **felloe**
felon ['fɛlən] *adj* felón, traidor; brutal, cruel; *s* (law) delincuente de mayor cuantía; (path.) panadizo
felonious [fɪ'lonɪəs] *adj* felón, traidor; perverso; (law) delincuente
felony ['fɛlənɪ] *s* (*pl:* **-nies**) (law) delito de mayor cuantía; (feud.) felonía; **to compound a felony** (law) aceptar dinero para no procesar
felsite ['fɛlsaɪt] *s* (mineral.) felsita
felspar ['fɛl,spɑr] *s* var. de **feldspar**
felt [fɛlt] *s* fieltro; *adj* de fieltro; *va* fieltrar; *pret & pp de* **feel**
felucca [fɪ'lʌkə] *s* (naut.) falucho
fem. abr. de **feminine**
female ['fimel] *adj* femenino; hembra, p.ej., **a female fish** un pez hembra; (bot.) femenino; (bot. & mach.) hembra; *s* hembra; (bot.) hembra; (mach.) hembrilla
feminine ['fɛmɪnɪn] *adj* femenino; afeminado; (gram.) femenino; *s* (gram.) femenino (*género*); (gram.) palabra femenina
feminine rhyme *s* (pros.) rima femenina
femininity [,fɛmɪ'nɪnɪtɪ] *s* feminidad; bello sexo
feminism ['fɛmɪnɪzəm] *s* feminismo
feminist ['fɛmɪnɪst] *adj & s* feminista
feministic [,fɛmɪ'nɪstɪk] *adj* feminista
femoral ['fɛmərəl] *adj* femoral
femur ['fimər] *s* (*pl:* **femurs** o **femora** ['fɛmərə]) (anat. & ent.) fémur
fen [fɛn] *s* pantano
fence [fɛns] *s* cerca; esgrima; destreza, habilidad para el debate; alcahuete (*encubridor y vendedor de cosas robadas*); guía (*de la sierra*); **on the fence** (coll.) indeciso, irresoluto; (coll.) no comprometido; *va* cercar; defender, proteger; **to fence in** encerrar con cerca; **to fence off** separar con cerca, obstruir con cerca; **to fence out** excluir con cerca; *vn* esgrimir; defenderse con fintas o evasivas, eludir preguntas con palabras ambiguas; saltar una cerca (*el caballo*); **to fence with** eludir una contestación directa a
fence post *s* poste para cercas
fencer ['fɛnsər] *s* esgrimidor; caballo adiestrado a saltar cercas
fencing ['fɛnsɪŋ] *s* esgrimadura (*acción*); esgrima (*arte*); materiales para construir cercas; cercas
fencing academy *s* escuela de esgrima
fencing master *s* maestro de esgrima
fend [fɛnd] *va* parar, apartar; **to fend off** resguardarse de; *vn* defenderse, resistir; **to fend for oneself** (coll.) tirar por su lado, arreglárselas
fender ['fɛndər] *s* defensa, protección; (aut.) guardafango, guardabarros; (naut.) defensa; (rail.) trompa, quitapiedras; salvavidas (*del tranvía*); guardafuego (*de la chimenea*)
fenestra [fɪ'nɛstrə] *s* (*pl:* **-trae** [tri]) (anat.) ventana
fenestra ovalis [o'velɪs] *s* (anat.) ventana oval
fenestra rotunda [ro'tʌndə] *s* (anat.) ventana rotunda
fenestration [,fɛnɪs'treʃən] *s* (arch.) ventanaje
Fenian ['finɪən] *adj & s* feniano
Fenianism ['finɪənɪzəm] *s* fenianismo
fennel ['fɛnəl] *s* (bot.) hinojo (*Foeniculum vulgare*); (bot.) cáñamo
fennelflower ['fɛnəl,flaʊər] *s* (bot.) neguilla (*cualquier planta del género Nigella*); (bot.) toda especia (*Nigella sativa*)
fennel giant *s* (bot.) var. de **giant fennel**
fenny ['fɛnɪ] *adj* pantanoso
fenugreek ['fɛnjʊgrik] *s* (bot.) alholva, fenogreco
feoff [fɛf] o [fif] *s* var. de **fief**
feracious [fə'reʃəs] *adj* feraz
feracity [fə'ræsɪtɪ] *s* feracidad
feral ['fɪrəl] *adj* salvaje; feral, cruel
fer-de-lance [,fɛrdə'lɑ̃s] *s* (zool.) mapanare
Ferdinand ['fʌrdɪnænd] *s* Fernando
ferment ['fʌrmɛnt] *s* fermento; fermentación; (fig.) fermentación; [fər'mɛnt] *va & vn* fermentar; (fig.) fermentar
fermentable [fər'mɛntəbəl] *adj* fermentable
fermentation [,fʌrmɛn'teʃən] *s* fermentación; (fig.) fermentación
fermentative [fər'mɛntətɪv] *adj* fermentativo
fermium ['fʌrmɪəm] *s* (chem.) fermio
fern [fʌrn] *s* (bot.) helecho
fernery ['fʌrnərɪ] *s* (*pl:* **-ies**) helechal, lugar donde se crían los helechos
ferny ['fʌrnɪ] *adj* de helechos; abundante en helechos
ferocious [fɪ'roʃəs] *adj* feroz
ferocity [fɪ'rɑsɪtɪ] *s* (*pl:* **-ties**) ferocidad
ferrate ['fɛret] *s* (chem.) ferrato
ferreous ['fɛrɪəs] *adj* férreo
ferret ['fɛrɪt] *s* (zool.) hurón; *va* huronear; **to ferret out** huronear; *vn* huronear
ferric ['fɛrɪk] *adj* (chem.) férrico
ferric acid *s* (chem.) ácido férrico
Ferris wheel ['fɛrɪs] *s* noria, rueda de feria, gran rueda (*rueda grande y giratoria que tiene sillas en la pina, empleada en parques de recreo, ferias, etc.*)
ferroaluminum [,fɛroə'lumɪnəm] *s* ferroaluminio
ferrocerium [,fɛro'sɪrɪəm] *s* ferrocerio
ferrochrome ['fɛrokrom] o **ferrochromium** [,fɛro'kromɪəm] *s* ferrocromo

ferroconcrete [ˌfɛroˈkankrit] o [ˌfɛrokanˈkrit] *s* ferroconcreto, ferrohormigón

ferrocyanide [ˌfɛroˈsaɪənaɪd] o [ˌfɛroˈsaɪənɪd] *s* (chem.) ferrocianuro

ferromagnetic [ˌfɛromægˈnɛtɪk] *adj* (phys.) ferromagnético

ferromanganese [ˌfɛroˈmæŋgənis] o [ˌfɛroˈmæŋgəniz] *s* ferromanganeso

ferronickel [ˌfɛroˈnɪkəl] *s* ferroníquel

ferroprussiate [ˌfɛroˈprʌʃɪet] o [ˌfɛroˈprʌsɪet] *s* (chem.) ferroprusiato

ferrotungsten [ˌfɛroˈtʌŋstən] *s* ferrotungsteno

ferrotype [ˈfɛrotaɪp] *s* (phot.) ferrotipo; (phot.) ferrotipia (*procedimiento*)

ferrous [ˈfɛrəs] *adj* ferroso; (chem.) ferroso

ferrous sulfate *s* (chem.) sulfato ferroso

ferrous sulfide *s* (chem.) sulfuro ferroso

ferruginous [fəˈrudʒɪnəs] *adj* ferruginoso; rojizo, herrumbroso

ferrule [ˈfɛrul] o [ˈfɛrəl] *s* regatón; (elec.) tapa de contacto; (mach.) virola

ferry [ˈfɛrɪ] *s* (*pl:* **-ries**) balsa o barco de pasar el río; balsa o barco portatrén; balsadero, embarcadero; transbordador; (*pret & pp:* **-ried**) *va* balsear (*un río*); pasar (*viajeros, mercancías o trenes de ferrocarril*) a través del río; *vn* cruzar el río en barco

ferryboat [ˈfɛrɪˌbot] *s* balsa o barco de pasar el río; balsa o barco portatrén

ferryman [ˈfɛrɪmən] *s* (*pl:* **-men**) balsero, dueño, encargado o empleado de un paso de río

fertile [ˈfʌrtɪl] *adj* fértil; (biol.) fecundo; (fig.) fértil

fertility [fərˈtɪlɪtɪ] *s* fertilidad; fecundidad

fertilization [ˌfʌrtɪlɪˈzeʃən] *s* fertilización; fecundación

fertilize [ˈfʌrtɪlaɪz] *va* fertilizar, abonar; fecundar

fertilizer [ˈfʌrtɪˌlaɪzər] *s* fertilizante (*persona o cosa que fertiliza; abono*)

ferulaceous [ˌfɛrjuˈleʃəs] o [ˌfɛruˈleʃəs] *adj* (bot.) feruláceo

ferule [ˈfɛrul] o [ˈfɛrəl] *s* férula; var. de **ferrule;** *va* castigar con férula

fervency [ˈfʌrvənsɪ] *s* fervor

fervent [ˈfʌrvənt] *adj* fervoroso, ferviente

fervid [ˈfʌrvɪd] *adj* fervoroso

fervor [ˈfʌrvər] *s* fervor

fervour [ˈfʌrvər] *s* (Brit.) var. de **fervor**

fescue [ˈfɛskju] *s* (bot.) cañuela; puntero

fess o **fesse** [fɛs] *s* (her.) faja

festa [ˈfɛstə] *s* fiesta

festal [ˈfɛstəl] *adj* festivo

fester [ˈfɛstər] *s* úlcera; *va* enconar, ulcerar; *vn* enconarse, ulcerarse, pudrir; (fig.) enconarse

festival [ˈfɛstɪvəl] *s* fiesta; festival (*especialmente musical*); *adj* festivo

festive [ˈfɛstɪv] *adj* festivo (*alegre, regocijado*)

festivity [fɛsˈtɪvɪtɪ] *s* (*pl:* **-ties**) festividad

festoon [fɛsˈtun] *s* festón; *va* festonear

festooned [fɛsˈtund] *adj* afestonado

fetal [ˈfitəl] *adj* fetal

fetch [fɛtʃ] *s* acción de ir a buscar, acción de traer; ardid, estratagema, treta; alcance, espacio, extensión; doble; aparecido, espectro; *va* ir por, traer, hacer venir; venderse a o por; proferir (*un gemido, suspiro*); cebar (*una bomba*); tomar (*aliento*); (coll.) encantar, atraer; (coll.) golpear; (dial.) alcanzar; **to fetch down** abatir; bajar; **to fetch up** elevar, levantar; descubrir, recordar; recobrar (*el tiempo perdido*); *vn* ir, moverse; **to fetch and carry** servir rastreramente; andar chismeando; realizar múltiples quehaceres de poca monta; **to fetch up** pararse; aparecer, dejarse ver

fetching [ˈfɛtʃɪŋ] *adj* (coll.) encantador, atractivo

fete o **fête** [fet] *s* fiesta; *va* festejar

fetich [ˈfitɪʃ] o [ˈfɛtɪʃ] *s* var. de **fetish**

feticidal [ˌfitɪˈsaɪdəl] *adj* feticida

feticide [ˈfitɪsaɪd] *s* feticidio (*acción*)

fetid [ˈfɛtɪd] o [ˈfitɪd] *adj* fétido

fetidity [fɛˈtɪdɪtɪ] o [fiˈtɪdɪtɪ] *s* fetidez

fetish [ˈfitɪʃ] o [ˈfɛtɪʃ] *s* fetiche

fetishism [ˈfitɪʃɪzəm] o [ˈfɛtɪʃɪzəm] *s* fetichismo

fetishist [ˈfitɪʃɪst] o [ˈfɛtɪʃɪst] *s* fetichista

fetishistic [ˌfitɪˈʃɪstɪk] o [ˌfɛtɪˈʃɪstɪk] *adj* fetichista

fetlock [ˈfɛtlak] *s* espolón (*prominencia*); cernejas (*pelo*)

fetor [ˈfitər] *s* hedor

fetter [ˈfɛtər] *s* grillo, grillete; *va* engrillar, encadenar; impedir, limitar

fettle [ˈfɛtəl] *s* condición, estado; **in fine fettle** en buena condición, bien preparado; *va* (found.) brascar

fetus [ˈfitəs] *s* (embryol.) feto

feud [fjud] *s* enemistad heredada entre familias o tribus; enemistad entre dos personas o grupos; (law) feudo

feudal [ˈfjudəl] *adj* feudal

feudalism [ˈfjudəlɪzəm] *s* feudalismo

feudalistic [ˌfjudəˈlɪstɪk] *adj* feudal

feudality [fjuˈdælɪtɪ] *s* (*pl:* **-ties**) feudalidad; feudo

feudal system *s* sistema feudal

feudatory [ˈfjudəˌtorɪ] *adj* feudatario; feudado; *s* (*pl:* **-ries**) feudatario; feudo

feudist [ˈfjudɪst] *s* camorrista; (law) feudista (*autor*)

fever [ˈfivər] *s* (path. & fig.) fiebre

fever blister *s* (path.) fuegos en los labios, escupidura, pupa

fevered [ˈfivərd] *adj* febril

feverfew [ˈfivərfju] *s* (bot.) matricaria

feverish [ˈfivərɪʃ] *adj* febril; calenturiento; febrígeno

feverless [ˈfivərlɪs] *adj* sin fiebre

feverous [ˈfivərəs] *adj* var. de **feverish**

feverroot [ˈfivərˌrut] o [ˈfivərˌrʊt] *s* (bot.) triosteo

fever sore *s* var. de **fever blister**

few [fju] *adj & pron indef* unos cuantos, pocos; **a few** unos cuantos; **not a few** no pocos; **quite a few** muchos; **few and far between** poquísimos

fewness [ˈfjunɪs] *s* corto número

fez [fɛz] *s* (*pl:* **fezzes**) fez

ff. abr. de **and the following** o **and what follows, folios** y **fortissimo**

fiancé [ˌfiɑnˈse] *s* novio, prometido

fiancée [ˌfiɑnˈse] *s* novia, prometida

fiasco [fɪˈæsko] *s* (*pl:* **-cos** o **-coes**) fiasco

fiat [ˈfaɪət] o [ˈfaɪæt] *s* fíat, autorización, mandato

fiat money *s* billetes sin respaldo ni garantía, emitidos por el gobierno

fib [fɪb] *s* mentirilla; (*pret & pp:* **fibbed;** *ger:* **fibbing**) *vn* decir mentirillas

fibber [ˈfɪbər] *s* mentiroso

fiber [ˈfaɪbər] *s* fibra; carácter, índole

fiberboard [ˈfaɪbərˌbord] *s* plancha o tabla de fibra

fiberglas [ˈfaɪbərˌglæs] o [ˈfaɪbərˌglas] *s* (trademark) fibravidrio, vidrio fibroso

fibre [ˈfaɪbər] *s* var. de **fiber**

fibril [ˈfaɪbrɪl] *s* (anat. & bot.) fibrilla

fibrillation [ˌfaɪbrɪˈleʃən] *s* (path.) fibrilación

fibrin [ˈfaɪbrɪn] *s* (bot.) fibrina, glutenfibrina; (physiol.) fibrina

fibrinogen [faɪˈbrɪnədʒən] *s* (physiol.) fibrinógeno

fibrinous [ˈfaɪbrɪnəs] *adj* fibrinoso

fibrocartilage [ˌfaɪbroˈkartɪlɪdʒ] *s* (anat.) fibrocartílago

fibroid [ˈfaɪbrɔɪd] *adj* fibroideo; *s* (path.) fibroma, fibroide

fibroin [ˈfaɪbro·ɪn] *s* (biochem.) fibroína

fibroma [faɪˈbromə] *s* (*pl:* **-mata** [mətə] o **-mas**) (path.) fibroma

fibrous [ˈfaɪbrəs] *adj* fibroso

fibula [ˈfɪbjələ] *s* (*pl:* **-lae** [li] o **-las**) (anat.) fíbula, peroné; (archeol.) fíbula

fibular [ˈfɪbjələr] *adj* peroneo, fibular

fichu [ˈfɪʃu] *s* pañoleta

fickle [ˈfɪkəl] *adj* inconstante, veleidoso

fickleness [ˈfɪkəlnɪs] *s* inconstancia, veleidad

fiction [ˈfɪkʃən] *s* ficción; (law) ficción; (lit.) novelística, género novelístico; **pure fiction!** ¡puro cuento!

fictional [ˈfɪkʃənəl] *adj* ficcionario; (lit.) novelesco (*propio de las novelas*); (lit.) novelístico (*perteneciente a la novela*)

fictionalize [ˈfɪkʃənəlaɪz] *va* novelizar

fictitious [fɪkˈtɪʃəs] *adj* ficticio

fid [fɪd] *s* barra de sostén; tarugo grande de ma-

dera; burel (*para abrir cordones de los cables*); (naut.) cuña de mastelero
fiddle ['fɪdəl] *s* (coll.) violín; **fit as a fiddle** en buena salud; **to play second fiddle** desempeñar el papel de segundón; **to play second fiddle to** estar subordinado a; *va* (coll.) tocar (*un aire*) al violín; **to fiddle away** desperdiciar, malgastar (*dinero, tiempo, etc.*); *vn* (coll.) tocar el violín; mover los dedos o las manos rápidamente; ocuparse en fruslerías; **to fiddle with** ocuparse sin provecho en; manosear
fiddle block *s* (naut.) motón de dos ejes con poleas diferenciales
fiddle bow [bo] *s* arco de violín
fiddle-de-dee [ˌfɪdəldɪ'di] *s* disparate; *interj* ¡disparate!
fiddle-faddle ['fɪdəlˌfædəl] *s* (coll.) disparate; *interj* (coll.) ¡disparate!; *vn* (coll.) ocuparse en fruslerías
fiddler ['fɪdlər] *s* (coll.) violinista
fiddler crab *s* (zool.) barrilete
fiddlestick ['fɪdəlˌstɪk] *s* arco de violín; bagatela; **fiddlesticks** *interj* ¡disparate!
fiddlestring ['fɪdəlˌstrɪŋ] *s* cuerda de violín; bagatela
fiddling ['fɪdlɪŋ] *adj* (coll.) insignificante, trivial
fideicommissary [ˌfaɪdɪaɪ'kɑmɪˌsɛrɪ] *adj* (law) fideicomisario; *s* (*pl:* **-ies**) (law) fideicomisario
fideicommissioner [ˌfaɪdɪaɪkə'mɪʃənər] *s* fideicomitente
fideicommissum [ˌfaɪdɪaɪkə'mɪsəm] *s* (*pl:* **-sa** [sə]) (law) fideicomiso
fidelity [faɪ'dɛlɪtɪ] o [fɪ'dɛlɪtɪ] *s* (*pl:* **-ties**) fidelidad
fidget ['fɪdʒɪt] *s* persona agitada, persona inquieta; *va* agitar, inquietar; *vn* agitarse, inquietarse; **to fidget with** manosear
fidgety ['fɪdʒɪtɪ] *adj* azogado, agitado, inquieto, revoltoso
fid hole *s* (naut.) ojo de la cuña de mastelero
fiduciary [fɪ'djuʃɪˌɛrɪ] o [fɪ'duʃɪˌɛrɪ] *adj* fiduciario; *s* (*pl:* **-ies**) fiduciario
fie [faɪ] *interj* ¡qué vergüenza!
fief [fif] *s* feudo
field [fild] *s* campo; sembrado (*tierra sembrada*); (her., phys. & sport) campo; (elec.) inductor; (elec.) campo magnético; (fig.) campo (*de varias actividades*); (baseball) jardín (*campo fuera del cuadro*); (baseball) (los) jardineros; (sport) los que participan en una carrera, partida, etc.; (sport) todos los que entran en una carrera, excepto el favorito; *va* (baseball) parar y devolver (*la pelota*)
field artillery *s* artillería de campaña
field battery *s* (mil.) batería de campaña
field day *s* día de ejercicios atléticos; día de ejercicios militares; día de actividad extraordinaria; día de excursión científica
fielder ['fildər] *s* (baseball) jardinero, jugador situado en el terreno fuera del cuadro para interceptar la pelota
fieldfare ['fildˌfɛr] *s* (orn.) zorzal
field judge *s* (football) juez de línea
field glass *s* anteojos de campaña, gemelos de campo
field gun *s* cañón de campaña
field hockey *s* (sport) hockey sobre hierba
field hospital *s* (mil.) hospital de campaña o de sangre
field kitchen *s* (mil.) cocina de campaña
field lark *s* (orn.) chirlota, triguero (*Sturnella magna*); (orn.) enchilado (*Sturnella neglecta*)
field magnet *s* (elec.) imán inductor
field marshal *s* (mil.) mariscal de campo; (Brit.) capitán general de ejército
field mouse *s* (zool.) ratón de campo
field officer *s* (mil.) jefe (*coronel, teniente coronel o comandante*)
field of honor *s* campo del honor, terreno de honor
fieldpiece ['fildˌpis] *s* cañón de campaña
field trip *s* excursión científicoescolar
field winding *s* (elec.) arrollamiento inductor
fieldwork [fildˌwʌrk] *s* (fort.) obras de campo
field work *s* trabajo científico de campo o en el terreno
fiend [find] *s* diablo; fiera (*persona muy cruel*); (coll.) monomaníaco; **the Fiend** el diablo; **to be a fiend for** ser una fiera para (*p.ej., el trabajo*)
fiendish ['findɪʃ] *adj* diabólico
fierce [fɪrs] *adj* fiero, feroz; furioso (*p.ej., viento*); ardiente, vehemente; (slang) desagradable, muy malo
fierceness ['fɪrsnɪs] *s* fiereza, ferocidad; furia, violencia; ardor, vehemencia
fiery ['faɪrɪ] o ['faɪərɪ] *adj* (*comp:* **-ier**; *super:* **-iest**) ardiente, caliente
fiery cross *s* cruz ardiente
fiesta [fɪ'ɛstə] *s* fiesta
fife [faɪf] *s* (mus.) pífano; *vn* tocar el pífano
fifteen ['fɪf'tin] *adj* & *s* quince; **fifteen all** (tennis) quince iguales
fifteenth ['fɪf'tinθ] *adj* décimoquinto; quinzavo; *s* décimoquinto; quinzavo; quince (*en las fechas*)
fifth [fɪfθ] *adj* quinto; *s* quinto; cinco (*en las fechas*); quinto de galón (*p.ej., de whisky*); (mus.) quinta
fifth column *s* quinta columna
fifth columnist *s* quintacolumnista
fifthly ['fɪfθlɪ] *adv* en quinto lugar
fifth wheel *s* rodete (*de un coche*); quinta rueda (*persona o cosa superfluas*)
fiftieth ['fɪftɪɪθ] *adj* & *s* quincuagésimo; cincuentavo
fifty ['fɪftɪ] *adj* cincuenta; *s* (*pl:* **-ties**) cincuenta
fifty-fifty ['fɪftɪ'fɪftɪ] *adj* & *adv* (coll.) mitad y mitad, a medias; **to go fifty-fifty** ir a medias
fig. abr. de **figure, figurative** y **figuratively**
fig [fɪg] *s* (bot.) higuera; higo (*fruto*); breva (*higo de color purpúreo*); bledo; (coll.) traje, adorno, gala; (coll.) condición; **in fine fig** (coll.) en buena condición, entrenado; **in full fig** (coll.) de veinticuatro alfileres; **to not give a fig for** no dársele a uno un bledo de, p.ej., **I don't give a fig for that** no se me da un bledo de ello
figeater ['fɪgˌitər] *s* (ent.) escarabajo norteamericano (*Cotinis nitida*)
fight [faɪt] *s* lucha, pelea; ánimo de reñir, combatividad; ánimo, brío, pujanza; **to pick a fight with** meterse con, buscar la lengua a; **to show fight** enseñar los dientes; (*pret & pp:* **fought**) *va* combatir, luchar con; alcanzar peleando; dar (*batalla*); hacer reñir (*p.ej., a los gallos*); lidiar (*al toro*); **to fight another's battles** tomar la defensa de otro; **to fight it out** decidirlo luchando; **to fight one's way** luchar por abrirse paso; *vn* luchar, pelear, lidiar; **to fight against odds** luchar con desventaja; **to fight for** luchar o pelear por; **to fight shy of** evitar, tratar de evitar
fighter ['faɪtər] *s* luchador, peleador; combatiente; porfiador (*persona que porfía mucho*); (aer.) avión de combate
fighter bomber *s* (aer.) cazabombardero
fighter pilot *s* (aer.) piloto de caza
fighting ['faɪtɪŋ] *adj* luchador, pugnante; batallador, combatiente; de pelea; de lidia; *s* lucha, pelea; riña; combate
fighting chance *s* (coll.) posibilidad de éxito después de larga lucha, posibilidad de recobrar la salud
fighting cock *s* gallo de pelea; (coll.) persona pendenciera
fig leaf *s* hoja de higuera; hoja de parra (*en las estatuas*); cobertura ligera
figment ['fɪgmənt] *s* ficción, invención
figpecker ['fɪgˌpɛkər] *s* (orn.) papafigo
figuline ['fɪgjəlɪn] *adj* figulino; *s* figurilla figulina, estatua figulina
figurant ['fɪgjurænt] *s* (theat.) figurante
figurante [ˌfɪgju'rɑnt] *s* (theat.) figuranta
figuration [ˌfɪgjə'reʃən] *s* figuración; forma, figura; (mus.) figuración
figurative ['fɪgjərətɪv] *adj* figurativo; figurado (*lenguaje, estilo, etc.*)
figure ['fɪgjər] *s* figura; (arith., geom., log. & rhet.) figura; talle (*disposición del cuerpo humano*); precio; figura, dibujo (*p.ej., en la tela*); **to be good at figures** ser listo en aritmética; **to cut a figure** hacer figura, hacer papel; **to have a good figure** tener buen tipo; **to keep one's figure** conservar la línea; *va* figurar; adornar con figuras, adornar con dibujos; ima-

ginar, suponer; calcular, computar; **to figure out** descifrar, resolver; explicarse; **to figure up** calcular, computar; *vn* figurar (*formar parte; tener autoridad o representación*); figurarse, imaginarse; **to figure on** contar con; incluir
figured [ˈfɪgjərd] *adj* adornado; labrado; estampado, floreado; figurado (*lenguaje*)
figurehead [ˈfɪgjərˌhɛd] *s* (naut.) figurón de proa, mascarón de proa; (fig.) testaferro
figure of speech *s* (rhet.) tropo; exageración
figure skater *s* patinador de figura
figure skating *s* patinaje de figura, patinaje artístico
figurine [ˌfɪgjəˈrin] *s* figurina, figurilla
figwort [ˈfɪgˌwʌrt] *s* (bot.) escrofularia; (bot.) celidonia menor
Fiji [ˈfidʒɪ] *s* Fijí (*archipiélago*); fijiano (*natural*)
Fijian [ˈfidʒɪən] o [fɪˈdʒiən] *adj & s* fijiano
filament [ˈfɪləmənt] *s* filamento; (bot. & elec.) filamento
filament circuit *s* (rad.) circuito de filamento
filament current *s* (rad.) corriente de filamento
filamentous [ˌfɪləˈmɛntəs] *adj* filamentoso
filander [fɪˈlændər] *s* (zool.) filandria
filaria [fɪˈlɛrɪə] *s* (*pl:* **-ae** [i]) (zool.) filaria
filariasis [ˌfɪləˈraɪəsɪs] *s* (path.) filariosis
filbert [ˈfɪlbərt] *s* (bot.) avellano; avellana (*fruto*)
filch [fɪltʃ] *va* ratear, hurtar, birlar
file [faɪl] *s* lima (*instrumento*); fila, hilera; archivo (*de documentos*); fichero; archivador (*carpeta*); **on file** archivado; *va* limar; poner en fila; archivar, clasificar; anotar, asentar, registrar; **to file away** archivar; *vn* desfilar; **to file by** desfilar; **to file in** entrar en fila; **to file out** salir en fila
file brush o **card** *s* carda para limas, cardo
file case *s* fichero
file clerk *s* fichador
file cutter *s* (mach.) picador de limas
filefish [ˈfaɪlˌfɪʃ] *s* (ichth.) alútero
filet [fɪˈle] o [ˈfɪle] *s* filete (*lonja de carne o de pescado*); encaje o red de malla cuadrada; *va* cortar (*carne o pescado*) en filetes
filial [ˈfɪlɪəl] o [ˈfɪljəl] *adj* filial
filiation [ˌfɪlɪˈeʃən] *s* filiación
filibuster [ˈfɪlɪˌbʌstər] *s* obstruccionista (*miembro de un cuerpo legislativo que impide la aprobación de una ley por discursos largos u otros medios*); obstrucción (*de la aprobación de una ley*); filibustero (*el que lucha contra otro país sin la autorización de su propio gobierno*); *va* obstruir (*la aprobación de una ley*); *vn* obstruir la aprobación de una ley; ser filibustero, filibustear
filicidal [ˌfɪlɪˈsaɪdəl] *adj* filicida
filicide [ˈfɪlɪsaɪd] *s* filicidio (*acción*); filicida (*persona*)
filiform [ˈfɪlɪfɔrm] o [ˈfaɪlɪfɔrm] *adj* filiforme
filigree [ˈfɪlɪgri] *s* filigrana; *adj* afiligranado; *va* afiligranar
filigreed [ˈfɪlɪgrid] *adj* afiligranado
filing [ˈfaɪlɪŋ] *s* clasificación (*de documentos*); limadura; **filings** *spl* limaduras, limalla
filing cabinet *s* archivador, carpetero, clasificador
filing card *s* ficha
Filipine [ˈfɪlɪpin] *adj* filipino
Filipino [ˌfɪlɪˈpino] *adj* filipino; *s* (*pl:* **-nos**) filipino
fill [fɪl] *s* hartazgo; terraplén; **to have** o **get one's fill of** darse un hartazgo de (*uvas, leer, etc.*). ‖ *va* llenar; rellenar; despachar, servir (*un pedido*); tapar (*un agujero*); empastar (*un diente*); inflar (*un neumático*); llenar, ocupar (*un puesto*); ocupar completamente (*un espacio*); **to be filled to overflowing** llenarse a rebosar; **to fill in** rellenar; añadir para completar, completar llenando; colmar (*lagunas*); poner al corriente; terraplenar; **to fill in on** poner al corriente de; **to fill out** ampliar, ensanchar, redondear; completar, llevar a cabo; llenar (*un formulario*); **to fill up** rellenar; (coll.) imprimir falsedades en la mente de ‖ *vn* llenarse; rellenarse; ampliarse, ensancharse, redondearse; bañarse (*los ojos*) de lágrimas; ahogarse de emoción; **to fill in** prestar sus servicios provisionalmente; terciar, hacer tercio; **to fill out** ampliarse, ensancharse, redondearse; **to fill up** atascarse, atorarse; ahogarse de emoción
filler [ˈfɪlər] *s* llenador; relleno; tripa (*del cigarro*); (journ.) relleno; (paint.) aparejo, imprimación
filler cap *s* (aut.) tapón de llenado
filler neck o **spout** *s* cuello de relleno
fillet [ˈfɪlɪt] *s* prendedero (*para asegurar el pelo*); cinta, tira, lista; (arch. & b.b.) filete; *va* filetear (*adornar con filetes*); [ˈfɪle] o [ˈfɪlɪt] *s* filete (*lonja de carne o de pescado*); encaje o red de malla cuadrada; *va* cortar (*carne o pescado*) en filetes
filling [ˈfɪlɪŋ] *s* relleno; tripa (*del cigarro*); trama (*del tejido*); (cook.) relleno; (dent.) empastadura (*acción*); (dent.) empaste, pasta
filling station *s* estación gasolinera, estación de servicio de gasolina
fillip [ˈfɪlɪp] *s* capirotazo; estímulo, aguijón; *va* dar un capirotazo a; tirar o impeler con un capirotazo; estimular, incitar; *vn* dar un capirotazo
filly [ˈfɪlɪ] *s* (*pl:* **-lies**) potra; (slang) muchacha vivaz
film [fɪlm] *s* película; (phot.) película; (mov.) film, película; **to shoot a film** (coll.) rodar una película; *adj* (mov.) fílmico; *va* cubrir con película; filmar, hacer una película de; *vn* cubrirse de una película; filmarse; **to film with tears** humedecerse (*los ojos*) de lágrimas
filming [ˈfɪlmɪŋ] *s* filmación
film library *s* filmoteca
film pack *s* (phot.) película en paquetes
film star *s* estrella del cine, estrella de la pantalla
film strip *s* tira de película
filmy [ˈfɪlmɪ] *adj* (*comp:* **-ier;** *super:* **-iest**) pelicular; delgadísimo, diáfano, sutil
filose [ˈfaɪlos] *adj* filiforme
filter [ˈfɪltər] *s* filtro; (elec. & opt.) filtro; *va* filtrar; *vn* filtrarse
filterable [ˈfɪltərəbəl] *adj* filtrable
filter cigaret *s* cigarrillo con filtro
filtering [ˈfɪltərɪŋ] *s* filtraje
filter paper *s* papel de filtro
filter press *s* filtro-prensa
filter tip *s* boquilla filtrónica, embocadura de filtro (*de un cigarrillo*)
filth [fɪlθ] *s* suciedad, inmundicia, mugre
filthiness [ˈfɪlθɪnɪs] *s* suciedad, inmundicia, porquería
filthy [ˈfɪlθɪ] *adj* (*comp:* **-ier;** *super:* **-iest**) sucio, inmundo, mugriento
filthy lucre *s* dinero mal ganado; (coll.) el vil metal (*dinero*)
filtrable [ˈfɪltrəbəl] *adj* var. de **filterable**
filtrate [ˈfɪltret] *s* filtrado; *va* filtrar; *vn* filtrarse
filtration [fɪlˈtreʃən] *s* filtración
fin. abr. de **financial**
Fin. abr. de **Finland** y **Finnish**
fin [fɪn] *s* aleta (*de pez, avión, etc.*); rebaba; los peces; (slang) aleta (*mano, brazo*); (*pret & pp:* **finned;** *ger:* **finning**) *va* cortar las aletas de (*un pescado*); *vn* aletear
finagle [fɪˈnegəl] *va* timar, trampear; conseguir por artimañas; *vn* timar, trampear
final [ˈfaɪnəl] *adj* final; último; decisivo, terminante; *s* cosa final; examen final; sonido final; letra final; **finals** *spl* final, p.ej., **I did not get to the finals** no llegué a la final
finale [fɪˈnɑlɪ] *s* final; (mus.) final, concertante
finalism [ˈfaɪnəlɪzəm] *s* (philos.) finalismo
finalist [ˈfaɪnəlɪst] *s* (philos. & sport) finalista
finality [faɪˈnælɪtɪ] *s* (*pl:* **-ties**) decisión, determinación; cosa final
finalize [ˈfaɪnəlaɪz] *va* (coll.) finalizar; (coll.) aprobar; *vn* (coll.) finalizar
finally [ˈfaɪnəlɪ] *adv* finalmente
finance [fɪˈnæns] o [ˈfaɪnæns] *s* finanzas; **finances** *spl* finanzas; *va* financiar; manejar los fondos de
financial [fɪˈnænʃəl] o [faɪˈnænʃəl] *adj* financiero
financially [fɪˈnænʃəlɪ] o [faɪˈnænʃəlɪ] *adv* financieramente
financier [ˌfɪnənˈsɪr] o [ˌfaɪnænˈsɪr] *s* financiero

financing [fɪˈnænsɪŋ] o [ˈfaɪnænsɪŋ] *s* financiación
finback [ˈfɪn,bæk] *s* (zool.) rorcual
finch [fɪntʃ] *s* (orn.) pinzón
find [faɪnd] *s* hallazgo; (*pret & pp:* **found**) *va* hallar, encontrar; declarar, decidir; proveer; **to find oneself** encontrarse a sí mismo, descubrir sus aptitudes; **to find out** averiguar, darse cuenta de; llegar a saber cuál es el verdadero carácter de; *vn* (law) pronunciar fallo o sentencia; **to find out** informarse; **to find out about** informarse de
finder [ˈfaɪndər] *s* hallador; (astr.) buscador; (phot.) visor; portaobjeto cuadriculado (*del microscopio*)
fin-de-siècle [fædəˈsjɛkəl] *adj* finisecular
finding [ˈfaɪndɪŋ] *s* descubrimiento; (law) resultando; **findings** *spl* herramientas y avíos de un artesano; mercería (*alfileres, cintas, etc.*); constataciones, conclusiones
fine [faɪn] *adj* fino; bueno, p.ej., **fine weather** buen tiempo; magnífico; divertido (*rato*); (iron.) bueno, lindo; *adv* (coll.) muy bien; **to feel fine** (coll.) sentirse muy bien de salud; *s* multa; *va* multar
fine arts *spl* bellas artes
fine-drawn [ˈfaɪn,drɔn] *adj* estirado en un hilo finísimo; fino, sutil
fine-grained [ˈfaɪn,grend] *adj* de grano fino
fineness [ˈfaɪnnɪs] *s* fineza (*de grano, de la arena*); finura, excelencia; ley (*de las ligas de metales preciosos*)
fineness ratio *s* (aer.) finura
fine print *s* tipo menor, letra menuda
finery [ˈfaɪnərɪ] *s* (*pl:* **-ies**) adorno, galas, vestido de gala, atavíos
fines herbes [fin ˈzɛrb] *spl* hierbas finas (*aderezo de hongos, chalotes, perejil, etc. picados*)
fine-spun [ˈfaɪn,spʌn] *adj* estirado en hilo finísimo, hilado en hoja finísima; alambicado
finesse [fɪˈnɛs] *s* tino, sutileza, artificio; (bridge) impás, fineza, jugada por bajo; *va* atraer o cambiar empleando artificios; (bridge) hacer el impás con, tomar la fineza con (*cierto naipe*); *vn* valerse de artificios; (bridge) hacer un impás, hacer o tirar una fineza
fine-tooth [ˈfaɪn,tuθ] o **fine-toothed** [ˈfaɪn,tuθt] o [ˈfaɪn,tuðd] *adj* de dientes finos
fine-tooth o **fine-toothed comb** *s* peine de dientes finos; **to go over with a fine-tooth comb** o **fine-toothed comb** escudriñar minuciosamente
finger [ˈfɪŋgər] *s* dedo; **to burn one's fingers** cogerse los dedos; **to have a finger in the pie** tomar parte en un asunto; **to have long fingers** ser largo de uñas; **to put one's finger in the pie** meter su cucharada; **to put one's finger on** acertar; **to put one's finger on the sore spot** poner el dedo en la llaga; **to slip between the fingers** irse de entre los dedos; **to twist around one's little finger** conquistar fácilmente, manejar completamente; *va* tocar con los dedos; manosear; ejecutar con los dedos; hurtar, robar; (slang) designar, identificar; (slang) acechar, espiar, traicionar; (mus.) señalar la digitación en; (mus.) pulsar; *vn* teclear
finger board *s* (mus.) batidor, diapasón (*p.ej., de la guitarra*); (mus.) teclado (*del piano*)
finger bowl *s* lavadedos, lavafrutas
fingerbreadth [ˈfɪŋgər,brɛdθ] *s* dedo, anchura de un dedo
finger dexterity *s* (mus.) dedeo
fingered [ˈfɪŋgərd] *adj* con dedos; (bot. & mus.) digitado
fingering [ˈfɪŋgərɪŋ] *s* manoseo; obra ejecutada primorosamente con los dedos; (mus.) digitación
fingerling [ˈfɪŋgərlɪŋ] *s* pececillo (*del tamaño del dedo de un hombre*); cosa muy pequeña
fingernail [ˈfɪŋgər,nel] *s* uña
fingernail polish *s* esmalte para las uñas
finger plate *s* chapa de guarda
finger post *s* poste indicador (*con una mano que indica el camino*)
fingerprint [ˈfɪŋgər,prɪnt] *s* huella digital, dactilograma; *va* tomar las huellas digitales de
fingerstall [ˈfɪŋgər,stɔl] *s* dedil
finger tip *s* punta del dedo; **to have at one's finger tips** tener en la punta de los dedos, saber al dedillo; **to one's finger tips** al dedillo, perfectamente
finger-tip control [ˈfɪŋgər,tɪp] *s* mando a punta de dedo
finger wave *s* ondulado o peinado al agua
finial [ˈfɪnɪəl] *s* (arch. & f.a.) florón
finical [ˈfɪnɪkəl], **finicking** [ˈfɪnɪkɪŋ] o **finicky** [ˈfɪnɪkɪ] *adj* delicado, melindroso
finish [ˈfɪnɪʃ] *s* final; acabado; finura de ejecución; pulimento; finura, primor; (sport) llegada a la meta; (sport) línea de llegada; (sport) carrera final; **to be in at the finish** estar presente en la conclusión; **to have a rough finish** estar sin pulir, estar al natural; *va* acabar; afinar; (coll.) vencer completamente; (coll.) acabar (*matar*); (coll.) acabar con (*destruir*); **to finish off** acabar (*completar; matar*); **to finish up** acabar (*completar; consumir*); *vn* acabar; seguir el curso de una escuela de educación social para señoritas; **to finish** + *ger* acabar de + *inf*, concluir de + *inf;* **to finish by** + *ger* acabar por + *inf;* **to finish with** acabar; enemistarse con
finished [ˈfɪnɪʃt] *adj* acabado; pulimentado; fabricado, elaborado
finisher [ˈfɪnɪʃər] *s* acabador; máquina acabadora
finishing nail *s* alfilerillo, puntilla francesa
finishing school *s* escuela particular de educación social para señoritas
finishing touch *s* retoque, última mano
finite [ˈfaɪnaɪt] *adj* finito; (gram.) que expresa número, persona y tiempo determinados; **the finite** lo finito
finite verb *s* forma verbal flexional
Finland [ˈfɪnlənd] *s* Finlandia
Finlander [ˈfɪnləndər] *s* finlandés
Finn [fɪn] *s* finlandés (*natural de Finlandia*); finés (*individuo de cualquier pueblo de habla finesa*)
finnan haddie [ˈfɪnən ˈhædɪ] *s* eglefino ahumado
Finnic [ˈfɪnɪk] *adj* finés
Finnish [ˈfɪnɪʃ] *adj* finlandés; *s* finlandés (*idioma*)
Finno-Ugric [,fɪnoˈugrɪk] *adj* finoúgrio
finny [ˈfɪnɪ] *adj* aletado; abundante en peces
fiord [fjord] *s* fiord o fiordo
fir [fʌr] *s* (bot.) abeto
fire [faɪr] *s* fuego; incendio; martirio, suplicio; (fig.) fuego, fogosidad; **between two fires** entre dos fuegos; **to be on fire** estar ardiendo; **to be under enemy fire** estar expuesto al fuego del enemigo; **to catch fire** encenderse; **to catch on fire** incendiarse; **to go through fire and water** pasar las de Dios es Cristo; **to hang fire** demorarse, tardar, estar en suspenso; **to lay a fire** preparar un fuego; **to miss fire** fallar (*la escopeta; los cilindros*); fracasar; **to open fire** abrir fuego, romper el fuego; **to play with fire** jugar con fuego; **to set on fire, to set fire to** pegar fuego a; **to take fire** encenderse; **under fire** bajo el fuego del enemigo; acusado, inculpado ‖ *interj* (mil.) ¡fuego! ‖ *va* encender; incendiar (*lo que no era destinado a arder*); calentar (*el horno*); cargar (*el hogar*); encender (*la caldera*); cocer (*ladrillos*); calentar, secar al horno (*pintura, esmalte*); disparar (*un arma de fuego*); pegar (*un tiro*); lanzar (*un torpedo, una bomba*); hacer explotar (*una mina*); enrojecer; hacer (*una salva de cañonazos; un saludo nacional*); excitar (*la imaginación*); (coll.) despedir (*a un empleado*) ‖ *vn* encenderse; hacer fuego, tirar; dar explosiones (*un motor*); enrojecerse; **to fire away** (coll.) comenzar, empezar; (coll.) ponerse en marcha; **to fire on** hacer fuego sobre, hacer un disparo sobre; **to fire up** calentar el horno; cargar el hogar; encender la caldera; enfurecerse
fire alarm *s* alarma de incendios; avisador o timbre de incendios; **to sound the fire alarm** tocar a fuego
firearm [ˈfaɪr,ɑrm] *s* arma de fuego
fireball [ˈfaɪr,bɔl] *s* bola de fuego; bólido; rayo en bola; globo lleno de pólvora
fire basket *s* var. de **cresset**
fire beetle *s* (ent.) cucuyo
firebird [ˈfaɪr,bʌrd] *s* pajarillo de color ana-

ranjado subido como el cacique veranero, la piranga y el rubí
fireboat ['faɪr,bot] *s* buque con mangueras para incendios
firebox ['faɪr,bɑks] *s* caja de fuego, fogón
firebrand ['faɪr,brænd] *s* tizón; (fig.) botafuego
firebreak ['faɪr,brek] *s* raya (*para impedir la comunicación del incendio en los campos*)
firebrick ['faɪr,brɪk] *s* ladrillo refractario
fire brigade *s* cuerpo de bomberos
firebug ['faɪr,bʌg] *s* (coll.) incendiario
fire clay *s* arcilla refractaria
fire company *s* cuerpo de bomberos; compañía de seguros
fire control *s* (nav.) dirección de tiro; (mil.) conducción del fuego
firecracker ['faɪr,krækər] *s* triquitraque
firecrest ['faɪr,krɛst] *s* (orn.) abadejo
firedamp ['faɪr,dæmp] *s* (min.) grisú, mofeta
fire department *s* servicio de bomberos, servicio de incendios
firedog ['faɪr,dɔg] o ['faɪr,dɑg] *s* morillo
fire door *s* puerta incombustible, puerta contrafuego; boca de carga, puerta del hogar
fire drill *s* ejercicio o disciplina para caso de incendio
fire-eater ['faɪr,itər] *s* titiritero que finge tragarse brasas; (fig.) matamoros; (coll.) bombero muy intrépido
fire engine *s* bomba de incendios, coche bomba
fire escape *s* escalera de escape, escalera de salvamento
fire extinguisher *s* apagafuego, extintor
fire fighter *s* el que combate los incendios
firefly ['faɪr,flaɪ] *s* (*pl:* **-flies**) (ent.) bicho de luz, luciérnaga
fire grenade *s* extintor de granada
fireguard ['faɪr,gɑrd] *s* guardafuego; (forestry) cortafuego
fire hose *s* manguera contra encendios
firehouse ['faɪr,haʊs] *s* cuartel de bomberos, estación de incendios
fire hydrant *s* boca de incendio
fire insurance *s* seguro de incendios, seguros contra incendios
fire irons *spl* badil y tenazas
fire ladder *s* escalera de salvamento
fireless ['faɪrlɪs] *adj* sin fuego
fireless cooker *s* cocinilla sin fuego
firelight ['faɪr,laɪt] *s* luz de un fuego
firelock ['faɪr,lɑk] *s* pedreñal, trabuco de pedernal
fireman ['faɪrmən] *s* (*pl:* **-men**) bombero (*que apaga los incendios*); fogonero (*que cuida del fogón en las máquinas de vapor*)
fireplace ['faɪr,ples] *s* chimenea o chimenea francesa
fire plug *s* boca de agua
fire pot *s* hornillo
fire power *s* (mil.) potencia de fuego
fireproof ['faɪr,pruf] *adj* incombustible; *va* hacer incombustible
fireproofing ['faɪr,prufɪŋ] *s* incombustibilización; materiales refractarios
fire sale *s* venta de mercancías averiadas en un incendio
fire screen *s* pantalla de chimenea
fire ship *s* brulote
fire shovel *s* badil
fireside ['faɪr,saɪd] *s* hogar
fireside chat *s* (coll.) charla de chimenea
fire station *s* parque de incendios
fire tongs *spl* tenazas para coger las brasas, tenazas de chimenea
fire tower *s* torre con atalaya para la observación de incendios; caja de escalera de escape
firetrap ['faɪr,træp] *s* edificio que se puede encender fácilmente; edificio sin medios adecuados de escape en caso de incendio
fire-tube boiler ['faɪr,tjub] o ['faɪr,tub] *s* caldera tubular de humo
fire wall *s* cortafuego
firewarden ['faɪr,wɔrdən] *s* vigía de incendios
firewater ['faɪr,wɔtər] o ['faɪr,wɑtər] *s* aguardiente
fireweed ['faɪr,wid] *s* (bot.) té (*Erechtites hieracifolia*); (bot.) pascueta, hierba del burro (*Lactuca canadensis*); (bot.) hierba hedionda (*Datura stramonium*)
firewood ['faɪr,wʊd] *s* leña
fireworks ['faɪr,wʌrks] *spl* fuegos artificiales; (coll.) muestra de temperamento
fire worshiper *s* adorador del fuego, ignícola
firing ['faɪrɪŋ] *s* encendimiento; alimentación de fuego; carga de hogar; combustible, carbón, leña; cocción (*p.ej., de ladrillos*); disparo (*de un arma de fuego*); tiroteo; encendido (*de un motor de combustión interna*); (coll.) despedida (*de un empleado*)
firing chart *s* (arti.) cuadro de tiro
firing line *s* (mil.) línea de fuego, frente de batalla; **on the firing line** en vanguardia, en medio del ataque
firing order *s* (aut.) orden *m* del encendido
firing pin *s* percutor, aguja de percusión
firing squad *s* piquete de salvas; pelotón de fusilamiento, piquete de ejecución
firkin ['fʌrkɪn] *s* cuñete; medida de capacidad de 40,914 litros en Inglaterra y de 34,068 litros en EE.UU.
firm [fʌrm] *adj* firme; *s* razón social, firma; *va* poner firme; *vn* ponerse firme
firmament ['fʌrməmənt] *s* firmamento
firman ['fʌrmən] o [fər'mɑn] *s* (*pl:* **-mans**) firmán
firmness ['fʌrmnɪs] *s* firmeza
first [fʌrst] *adj* primero; (mus.) principal; *adv* primero (*primeramente; antes; más bien*); **first and last** bajo todos los conceptos; **first of all** ante todo; *s* primero; (aut.) primera velocidad; (mus.) voz cantante, voz principal; **firsts** *spl* (com.) artículos de primera calidad; **at first** en primer lugar; al principio; **from the first** desde el principio; **the first to** + *inf* el primero en + *inf*
first aid *s* primeros auxilios, cura de urgencia
first-aid ['fʌrst'ed] *adj* de primeros auxilios
first-aider [,fʌrst'edər] *s* socorrista
first-aid kit *s* botiquín, equipo de urgencia
first-aid station *s* casa de socorro
first base *s* (baseball) primera base *f* (*puesto*); (baseball) primera base *m* (*jugador*); **to not get to first base** (slang) no poder dar el primer paso (*en una empresa*)
first baseman *s* (baseball) primera base *m* (*jugador*)
first-born ['fʌrst,bɔrn] *adj & s* primogénito
first class *s* primera clase
first-class ['fʌrst,klæs] o ['fʌrst,klɑs] *adj* de primera clase; *adv* en primera clase
First Day *s* domingo (*en el lenguaje de los cuáqueros*)
first-day cover ['fʌrst,de] *s* (philately) sobre de primer día
first draft *s* borrador
first edition *s* edición príncipe, primera edición
first finger *s* dedo índice o mostrador
first-flight cover ['fʌrst,flaɪt] *s* (philately) sobre de primer vuelo
first floor *s* (U.S.A.) piso bajo; (Brit.) piso principal
first fruits *spl* primicia; (fig.) primicias (*primeros resultados*)
first-hand ['fʌrst,hænd] *adj & adv* de primera mano
first lady of the land *s* (U.S.A.) primera dama de la nación (*esposa del Presidente*)
first lieutenant *s* (mil.) teniente
firstling ['fʌrstlɪŋ] *s* primero (*en su clase*); primogénito; primer resultado
firstly ['fʌrstlɪ] *adv* primeramente, en primer lugar
first mate *s* (naut.) piloto
first name *s* nombre de pila
first night *s* (theat.) noche de estreno
first-nighter [,fʌrst'naɪtər] *s* (theat.) estrenista
first officer *s* (naut.) piloto
first papers *spl* (coll.) aplicación preliminar para la carta de naturaleza
first person *s* (gram.) primera persona
first quarter *s* cuarto creciente (*de la luna*)
first-rate ['fʌrst,ret] *adj* de primer orden, de mayor cuantía; (coll.) excelente; *adv* (coll.) muy bien
first-run house ['fʌrst,rʌn] *s* teatro de estreno
first-string ['fʌrst,strɪŋ] *adj* regular; de mayor cuantía, del primer rango
first water *s* primera calidad, primer rango

firth [fʌrθ] *s* estuario
fisc [fɪsk] *s* fisco
fiscal ['fɪskəl] *adj* económico, monetario; fiscal; *s* fiscal (*el que representa el ministerio en los tribunales*)
fiscal year *s* ejercicio, año económico
fish [fɪʃ] *s* pez; pescado (*pez que se saca del agua para comer; carne de pescado*); (carp.) cubrejunta; (rail.) eclisa; (naut.) jimelga; (rel.) pez (*símbolo*); (coll.) individuo, tipo; **to be like a fish out of water** estar como gallina en corral ajeno; **to be neither fish nor fowl** no ser carne ni pescado; **to drink like a fish** beber como una esponja; **to have other fish to fry** tener otras cosas que hacer; *va* pescar; pescar en (*cierto lugar*); juntar con cubrejunta; (rail.) eclisar; (naut.) enjimelgar; (elec.) pescar; **to fish out** pescar (*sacar del agua*); agotar el pescado en (*p.ej., un lago*); *vn* pescar **to fish for** buscar, tratar de conseguir con maña; **to fish for compliments** buscar alabanzas; **to go fishing** ir de pesca; **to take fishing** llevar de pesca
fishbone ['fɪʃ,bon] *s* espina, espina de pez
fish bowl *s* pecera
fish day *s* día de pescado
fisher ['fɪʃər] *s* pescador; animal pescador; embarcación de pesca; (zool.) marta del Canadá
fisherman ['fɪʃərmən] *s* (*pl:* **-men**) pescador; embarcación de pesca, barco pesquero
fishery ['fɪʃərɪ] *s* (*pl:* **-ies**) pesca (*ejercicio de los pescadores*); pesquería (*trato de los pescadores*); pesquería, pesquera (*lugar*)
fishgig ['fɪʃ,gɪg] *s* fisga (*arpón para pescar*)
fish globe *s* pecera
fish glue *s* cola de pescado
fish hawk *s* (orn.) halieto, águila pescadora
fishhook ['fɪʃ,hʊk] *s* anzuelo
fishing ['fɪʃɪŋ] *adj* pesquero; *s* pesca
fishing ground *s* pesquería, pesquera
fishing reel *s* carrete de pescar
fishing rod *s* caña o vara de pescar
fishing smack *s* barco pesquero, queche
fishing tackle *s* aparejo de pescar, avíos o trastos de pescar
fish joint *s* (rail.) junta de eclisa
fish line *s* sedal
fish market *s* pescadería
fishmonger ['fɪʃ,mʌŋgər] *s* pescadero
fish oil *s* aceite de pescado
fishplate ['fɪʃ,plet] *s* (rail.) eclisa
fish pole *s* vara de pescar
fishpool ['fɪʃ,pul] *s* piscina
fish spear *s* fisga
fish story *s* (coll.) burlería, patraña; **to tell fish stories** (coll.) mentir por la barba
fishtail ['fɪʃ,tel] *adj* de cola de pescado; *s* (aer.) coleadura; *vn* (aer.) colear
fishtail bit *s* barrena de cola de pescado
fish tape *s* (elec.) cinta pescadora
fishwife ['fɪʃ,waɪf] *s* (*pl:* **-wives**) pescadera; verdulera (*mujer malhablada*)
fish wire *s* (elec.) cinta pescadora
fishworm ['fɪʃ,wʌrm] *s* lombriz de tierra (*que sirve de cebo para pescar*)
fishy ['fɪʃɪ] *adj* (*comp:* **-ier**; *super:* **-iest**) que huele o sabe a pescado; abundante en peces; sin brillo (*dícese de los ojos*); sin visos (*dícese de las joyas*); (coll.) dudoso, inverosímil
fissile ['fɪsɪl] *adj* físil
fission ['fɪʃən] *s* escisión; (biol.) escisión; (phys.) fisión
fissionable ['fɪʃənəbəl] *adj* fisionable
fissionable material *s* (phys.) material fisionable
fissiparous [fɪ'sɪpərəs] *adj* fisíparo
fissiped ['fɪsɪpɛd] *adj* & *s* (zool.) fisípedo
fissirostral [,fɪsɪ'rɑstrəl] *adj* (orn.) fisirrostral
fissure ['fɪʃər] *s* grieta, hendedura; (anat., path. & min.) fisura; *va* hender; *vn* henderse
fist [fɪst] *s* puño; (print.) manecilla; (coll.) mano; (coll.) escritura; (coll.) esfuerzo; **to shake one's fist at** amenazar con el puño; *va* apuñear, dar de puñadas a; apuñar, empuñar
fist fight *s* pelea con los puños
fistic ['fɪstɪk] *adj* pugilístico
fisticuff ['fɪstɪ,kʌf] *s* puñetazo; **fisticuffs** *spl* pelea a puñetazos; *va* dar puñetazos a; *vn* pelear a puñetazos
fistula ['fɪstʃulə] *s* (*pl:* **-las** o **-lae** [li]) fístula; (path.) fístula
fistular ['fɪstʃulər] *adj* fistular
fistulous ['fɪstʃuləs] *adj* fistuloso
fit [fɪt] *s* ajuste, talle; encaje (*de una pieza en otra*); ataque; acceso (*p.ej., de tos*); arranque (*de amor, cólera, etc.*); rato; **by fits and starts** a empujones; *adj* (*comp:* **fitter;** *super:* **fittest**) apto, a propósito; apropiado, conveniente; listo, preparado; adiestrado; sano, de buena salud; bueno, p.ej., **fit to eat** bueno de comer; **to be fit for** poder hacer; **to see** o **to think fit** juzgar conveniente; **to see** o **to think fit to** + *inf* tener a bien + *inf;* **fit to be tied** (coll.) impaciente; (coll.) encolerizado; (*pret* & *pp:* **fitted;** *ger:* **fitting**) *va* ajustar, entallar; encajar; sentar, cuadrar; cuadrar con, p.ej., **he does not fit the description** no cuadra con las señas; equipar, preparar; estar de acuerdo con (*p.ej., los hechos*); servir para; **to fit out** o **up** pertrechar, proveer de todo lo necesario; *vn* ajustar, entallar; encajar; sentar; **to fit in** caber en; encajar en; **to fit in with** concordar con; llevarse bien con
fitch [fɪtʃ], **fitchet** ['fɪtʃɪt] o **fitchew** ['fɪtʃu] *s* (zool.) turón, veso
fitful ['fɪtfəl] *adj* espasmódico, caprichoso
fitly ['fɪtlɪ] *adv* aptamente; acertadamente; convenientemente
fitness ['fɪtnɪs] *s* aptitud; conveniencia; buena salud
fitter ['fɪtər] *s* ajustador; montador; proveedor; (sew.) probador
fitting ['fɪtɪŋ] *adj* propio, apropiado, conveniente, a propósito; *s* prueba (*de una prenda de vestir*); pieza de unión (*en las tuberías*); **fittings** *spl* accesorios, avíos; herrajes; muebles
fittingly ['fɪtɪŋlɪ] *adv* convenientemente, a propósito
five [faɪv] *adj* cinco; *s* cinco; equipo de baloncesto (*compuesto de cinco jugadores*); **fives** *spl* juego de pelota (*estilo inglés*); **five o'clock** las cinco
five-and-ten ['faɪvənd'tɛn] o ['faɪvən'tɛn] *s* (coll.) tienda de cinco y diez centavos
five-day week ['faɪv,de] *s* semana laboral de cinco días
fivefold ['faɪv,fold] *adj* & *s* quíntuplo
five hundred *adj* & *s* quinientos
five-year ['faɪv,jɪr] *adj* quinquenal
five-year plan *s* plan quinquenal
fix [fɪks] *s* (coll.) aprieto; **in a tight fix** (coll.) en calzas prietas; **to be in a fix** (coll.) hallarse en un aprieto; (*pret* & *pp:* **fixed** o **fixt**) *va* fijar; arreglar, componer, reparar; calar o montar (*la bayoneta*); (phot.) fijar; (coll.) apretar las clavijas a; (coll.) castigar, pagar en la misma moneda; **to fix up** (coll.) arreglar, componer, reparar; (coll.) muñir; *vn* fijarse; **to fix on** o **upon** elegir, escoger
fixation [fɪks'eʃən] *s* fijación; (chem., phot., psychoanal. & psychol.) fijación
fixation abscess *s* (med.) absceso de fijación
fixative ['fɪksətɪv] *adj* & *s* fijativo
fixed [fɪkst] *adj* fijo
fixed condenser *s* (elec.) condensador fijo
fixed idea *s* idea fija
fixed income *s* renta fija
fixedly ['fɪksɪdlɪ] *adv* fijamente
fixed star *s* (astr.) estrella fija
fixer ['fɪksər] *s* reparador; (slang) perito en daños, liquidador de la avería; (slang) mediador entre criminales y la policía; (phot.) fijador
fixing ['fɪksɪŋ] *s* fijación; (phot.) fijado, fijación; **fixings** *spl* (coll.) accesorios, guarniciones
fixing bath *s* (phot.) fijador
fixity ['fɪksɪtɪ] *s* (*pl:* **-ties**) fijeza; cosa fija
fixt [fɪkst] *adj* var. de **fixed;** *pret* & *pp de* **fix**
fixture ['fɪkstʃər] *s* accesorio, artefacto; órgano de montaje; instalación fija; mueble fijo; brazo o sostén (*de lámpara, lavabo, etc.*); soporte de herramienta; persona que se queda mucho tiempo en un sitio, empleo, etc.; **fixtures** *spl* habilitaciones (*p.ej., de una tienda o almacén*); guarniciones de alumbrado eléctrico; aparatos sanitarios
fixture wire *s* (elec.) alambre para artefactos
fiz [fɪz] *s* ruido sibilante; gaseosa, bebida ga-

seosa; champaña; agitación, bulla; (*pret & pp:* **fizzed;** *ger:* **fizzing**) *vn* hacer un ruido sibilante
fizgig [ˈfɪzˌgɪg] *s* moza casquivana y coqueta; carretilla, buscapiés; fisga (*arpón para pescar*)
fizz [fɪz] *s & vn* var. de **fiz**
fizzle [ˈfɪzəl] *s* chisporroteo; bocazo (*explosión que no produce efecto*); (coll.) fracaso; *vn* chisporrotear débilmente; (coll.) salir calabaza, fracasar; **to fizzle out** (coll.) chisporrotear al apagarse; (coll.) fracasar
fizzy [ˈfɪzɪ] *adj* (*comp:* **-ier;** *super:* **-iest**) que chisporrotea; efervescente
fjord [fjord] *s* var. de **fiord**
fl. abr. de **florin, flourished** y **fluid**
Fla. abr. de **Florida**
flabbergast [ˈflæbərgæst] *va* (coll.) pasmar, dejar sin habla
flabby [ˈflæbɪ] *adj* (*comp:* **-bier;** *super:* **-biest**) flojo, lacio
flabellate [fləˈbɛlɪt] o [fləˈbɛlet] *adj* flabelado
flabelliform [fləˈbɛlɪfɔrm] *adj* flabeliforme
flabellum [fləˈbɛləm] *s* (*pl:* **-la** [lə]) (eccl., bot. & zool.) flabelo
flaccid [ˈflæksɪd] *adj* fláccido
flaccidity [flækˈsɪdɪtɪ] *s* flaccidez
flacon [flɑˈkõ] *s* pomo, frasco para perfume
flag [flæg] *s* bandera; cola de venado; pluma larga de la pata (*de las aves*); pluma secundaria del ala (*de las aves*); piedra laminada, roca laminada; losa; (bot.) lirio; (bot.) ácoro; (*pret & pp:* **flagged;** *ger:* **flagging**) *va* hacer señales con una bandera a; hacer (*señales*) con una bandera; hacer señal de parada a (*un tren*); cazar con banderín; adornar con bandera o banderas; pavimentar o solar con losas; *vn* aflojar, falsear, flaquear, disminuir
flag captain *s* (nav.) capitán de bandera
Flag Day *s* (U.S.A.) fiesta de la bandera (*el catorce de junio*)
flagellant [ˈflædʒələnt] o [fləˈdʒɛlənt] *adj & s* flagelante; (*cap.*) *s* flagelante
flagellate [ˈflædʒəlet] *adj* (bot. & biol.) flagelado; *s* (bot.) flagelado; *va* flagelar
flagellation [ˌflædʒəˈleʃən] *s* flagelación
flagellator [ˈflædʒəˌletər] *s* flagelador
flagellum [fləˈdʒɛləm] *s* (*pl:* **-la** [lə] o **-lums**) flagelo; (biol.) flagelo; (bot.) brote rastrero
flageolet [ˌflædʒoˈlɛt] *s* (mus.) chirimía, caramillo, dulzaina
flagging [ˈflægɪŋ] *adj* flojo, lánguido; *s* enlosado; losas
flaggy [ˈflægɪ] *adj* (*comp:* **-gier;** *super:* **-giest**) flojo, lánguido; lleno de lirios; laminado
flagman [ˈflægmən] *s* (*pl:* **-men**) abanderado; (rail.) guardavía; (rail.) guardafrenos
flag of convenience *s* (naut.) pabellón de conveniencia
flag officer *s* (nav.) jefe de escuadra
flag of truce *s* bandera de parlamento o de paz
flagon [ˈflægən] *s* jarro; botella que contiene unos dos litros; (bot.) ácoro bastardo, espadaña fina
flagpole [ˈflægˌpol] *s* asta de bandera; mástil para una bandera; (surv.) jalón
flagrancy [ˈflegrənsɪ] *s* enormidad, escándalo
flagrant [ˈflegrənt] *adj* enorme, escandaloso
flagship [ˈflægˌʃɪp] *s* (nav.) capitana
flagstaff [ˈflægˌstæf] o [ˈflægˌstɑf] *s* (*pl:* **-staffs** o **-staves** [ˌstevz]) asta de bandera; mástil para una bandera
flag station *s* (rail.) estación de bandera, apeadero
flagstone [ˈflægˌston] *s* piedra laminada, roca laminada; losa
flail [flel] *s* mayal; (mil.) mangual; *va* golpear con mayal; golpear, azotar
flair [flɛr] *s* instinto, penetración; disposiciones (*p.ej., para el teatro*); (hunt.) olfateo; *va* olfatear
flak [flæk] *s* fuego antiaéreo
flake [flek] *s* hojuela, escama; copo (*de nieve*); chispa; (hort.) clavel rayado; *va* formar o separar en hojuelas o escamas; cubrir con hojuelas o escamas; rayar en láminas; *vn* desprenderse en hojuelas o escamas; caer en copos pequeños
flake white *s* albayalde, cerusa o blanco de plomo
flaky [ˈflekɪ] *adj* (*comp:* **-ier;** *super:* **-iest**) escamoso, laminoso; desmenuzable
flambeau [ˈflæmbo] *s* (*pl:* **-beaux** [boz] o **-beaus**) antorcha; candelabro
flamboyance [flæmˈbɔɪəns] *s* (lo) flameante; rimbombancia
flamboyant [flæmˈbɔɪənt] *adj* flameante; (arch.) flameante, flamígero; rimbombante
flame [flem] *s* llama; color de llama; (slang) enamorado o enamorada; *va* iluminar con llama; hacer saber señalando con llama; tratar con la llama; flamear (*esterilizar con la llama*); *vn* llamear; inflamarse; **to flame forth, out** o **up** inflamarse; **to flame out** apagársele repentinamente la llama a (*un motor a chorro*)
flamen [ˈflemen] *s* (*pl:* **flamens** o **flamines** [ˈflæmɪniz]) (hist.) flamen
flameout [ˈflemˌaʊt] *s* (aer.) extinción repentina de la llama de un motor a chorro
flame thrower *s* (mil.) lanzallamas
flaming [ˈflemɪŋ] *adj* llameante; flamante, resplandeciente; ardiente, apasionado, vehemente
flamingo [fləˈmɪŋgo] *s* (*pl:* **-gos** o **-goes**) (orn.) flamenco
Flaminian Way [fləˈmɪnɪən] *s* Vía Flaminia
flammable [ˈflæməbəl] *adj* inflamable
Flanders [ˈflændərz] *s* Flandes
flange [flændʒ] *s* pestaña; (found.) herramienta para formar pestañas; *va* hacer pestaña a; ensanchar en forma de pestaña; *vn* ensancharse en forma de pestaña
flange coupling *s* acoplamiento de bridas
flange joint *s* junta de pestañas remachadas
flange rail *s* riel con pestaña; riel en T
flangeway [ˈflændʒˌwe] *s* canal, ranura o vía de pestaña
flank [flæŋk] *s* flanco; (fort., mach., mil. & nav.) flanco; *va* flanquear
flannel [ˈflænəl] *s* franela; moletón; **flannels** *spl* ropa hecha de franela; ropa interior de lana; *adj* hecho de franela
flannelet o **flannelette** [ˌflænəˈlɛt] *s* moletón
flap [flæp] *s* falda (*parte que cae suelta de una prenda*); oreja (*del zapato*); cartera (*del bolsillo*); ala (*del sombrero*); hoja plegadiza (*de una mesa*); solapa (*de la cubierta de un libro*); faldón (*de la silla de montar*); trampa (*del mostrador de una tienda*); corbata (*de un neumático*); bofetada, cachete, golpe, palmada; lonja, rebanada; aletazo, aleteo; (phonet.) golpe de lengua (*como en la pronunciación de la r*); (*pret & pp:* **flapped;** *ger:* **flapping**) *va* golpear con ruido seco; batir o sacudir (*las alas*); *vn* aletear; flamear ruidosamente
flapdoodle [ˈflæpˌdudəl] *s* (coll.) disparate, tontería
flapjack [ˈflæpˌdʒæk] *s* hojuela, torta de masa frita en una plancha metálica
flapper [ˈflæpər] *s* batidor; falda; pajarito que apenas sabe volar; (coll.) tobillera; (slang) chica descarada; (slang) mano
flare [flɛr] *s* llamarada, destello; bengala, señal luminosa; cohete de señales; abocinamiento; vuelo (*de una falda*); *va* señalar por medio de luces o cohetes de señales; abocinar; ensanchar; *vn* arder con gran llamarada, destellar; abocinarse; **to flare out** o **up** inflamarse; recrudecer (*una enfermedad*)
flareback [ˈflɛrˌbæk] *s* retroceso de la llama; (gun.) salida de gases de la culata; (fig.) réplica brusca y reprensiva; (fig.) retorno súbito y violento (*p.ej., del invierno*)
flare-up [ˈflɛrˌʌp] *s* llamarada; retroceso (*de una enfermedad*); (coll.) llamarada, arrebato de cólera
flash [flæʃ] *s* relámpago; instante, momento; rayo (*p.ej., de esperanza*); sentimiento o manifestación súbita y breve; acceso (*de alegría*); rasgo (*de ingenio*); ostentación; mensaje urgente enviado por radio, telégrafo, etc.; esclusa, represa; rebaba; preparación para teñir los líquidos; sonrisa; (mov.) proyección momentánea explicativa; (slang) ojeada; *va* inflamar; quemar (*pólvora*); despedir (*luz, destellos, etc.*); echar (*llamas*); (coll.) hacer ostentación de; enviar (*un mensaje*) como un rayo; despachar por radio, telégrafo, etc.; proteger (*la techumbre o parte de ella*) contra la lluvia con hoja de plomo o cinc; cubrir (*cristal*) con película de otro color; vaporizar (*el agua*) ins-

tantáneamente; *vn* relampaguear (*p.ej., los ojos*); pasar como un rayo; (coll.) alardear, fachendear
flashback ['flæʃ,bæk] *s* (mov.) episodio intercalado (*para aclarar la historia*)
flash bulb *s* (phot.) luz de magnesio, bombilla de destello, bombilla relámpago, relámpago fotogénico
flash flood *s* avenida repentina, torrentada
flashing ['flæʃɪŋ] *s* vierteaguas, despidiente de agua
flash in the pan *s* fogonazo sin descarga; esfuerzo o tentativa repentina y ostentosa que no tiene éxito
flashlight ['flæʃ,laɪt] *s* fanal de destellos, luz intermitente (*de faro*); linterna eléctrica, lámpara eléctrica de bolsillo; (phot.) magnesio (*luz de magnesio; fotografía al magnesio*), relámpago fotogénico
flashlight battery *s* pila de linterna
flashlight bulb *s* bombilla de linterna, bombilla de lámpara eléctrica de bolsillo
flashlight photography *s* fotografía instantánea de relámpago
flash point *s* punto de inflamación
flash sign *s* anuncio intermitente
flash welding *s* soldadura por arco con presión
flashy ['flæʃɪ] *adj* (*comp:* **-ier;** *super:* **-iest**) relampagueante; chillón, llamativo, de relumbrón
flask [flæsk] o [flɑsk] *s* frasco; frasco de bolsillo; matraz, redoma; caja de moldear
flat [flæt] *adj* (*comp:* **flatter;** *super:* **flattest**) plano; chato (*dícese, p.ej., de la nariz, de una embarcación*); mate, deslustrado; insípido; muerto (*dícese, p.ej., de la cerveza*); desafinado, desentonado; obscuro (*sonido*); desinflado (*neumático*); redondo (*precio*); terminante; (mus.) bemol; *adv* completamente; exactamente; desafinadamente; **to fall flat** caer de plano; no surtir efecto, no tener éxito; *s* plano; barca chata; carro de plataforma; pala de remo; alma de botón; banco, bajío; pantano; piso (*de una casa de vecinos*); (mus.) bemol; (coll.) neumático desinflado; (*pret & pp:* **flatted;** *ger:* **flatting**) *va* allanar, aplanar; aplastar; achatar; deslustrar; cubrir con capa mate; quitar el lustre a (*la pintura*); bajar de tono; *vn* allanarse, aplanarse; aplastarse; achatarse; deslustrarse; aflojar, flaquear; desafinar por lo bajo
flatboat ['flæt,bot] *s* chalana
flat-bottomed ['flæt,bɑtəmd] *adj* de fondo plano (*dícese de una vasija, buque, etc.*); planudo (*buque*)
flatcar ['flæt,kɑr] *s* (rail.) vagón de plataforma, vagón plano, vagón raso, batea
flatfish ['flæt,fɪʃ] *s* (ichth.) pez pleuronecto (*p.ej., lenguado, rodaballo, platija*)
flatfoot ['flæt,fʊt] *s* (*pl:* **-feet**) pie achatado; (path.) pie plano; (slang) agente de policía
flat-footed ['flæt,fʊtɪd] *adj* de pies achatados; (coll.) inflexible
flathead ['flæt,hɛd] *s* cabeza chata (*p.ej., de un perno*); clavo de cabeza chata, tornillo de cabeza chata, perno de cabeza chata; (coll.) bobo, mentecato
flat-headed ['flæt,hɛdɪd] *adj* de cabeza chata
flatiron ['flæt,aɪərn] *s* plancha
flat-lock seaming ['flæt,lɑk] *s* (mach.) engatillado
flatness ['flætnɪs] *s* planicidad; chatedad; insipidez; deslustre; desafinación; decisión, determinación
flatten ['flætən] *va* allanar, aplanar; aplastar, chafar; arrasar; achatar; desazonar; quitar el lustre a (*la pintura*); abatir, desalentar; **to flatten out** poner horizontal; (aer.) enderezar; *vn* allanarse, aplanarse; aplastarse; achatarse; desazonarse; desalentarse; **to flatten out** ponerse horizontal; (aer.) enderezarse
flatter ['flætər] *va* lisonjear; favorecer, p.ej., **that hat flatters you** ese sombrero le favorece; **to flatter oneself** lisonjearse; *vn* lisonjear
flatterer ['flætərər] *s* lisonjero
flattering ['flætərɪŋ] *adj* lisonjero; *s* lisonja
flattery ['flætərɪ] *s* (*pl:* **-ies**) lisonja
flattish ['flætɪʃ] *adj* algo plano; algo insípido
flattop ['flæt,tɑp] *s* (nav.) portaaviones
flatulence ['flætʃələns] *s* flatulencia; hinchazón, vanidad
flatulent ['flætʃələnt] *adj* flatulento; hinchado, vanidoso
flatus ['fletəs] *s* (*pl:* **-tuses** o **-tus**) flato; golpe de viento; hinchazón (*efecto de hincharse*)
flatware ['flæt,wɛr] *s* vajilla de plata; vajilla de porcelana
flatways ['flæt,wez] o **flatwise** ['flæt,waɪz] *adv* horizontalmente; con el lado plano hacia arriba, hacia adelante o en contacto
flatwork ['flæt,wʌrk] *s* ropa blanca que puede ser aprestada por medio de una mangle
flatworm ['flæt,wʌrm] *s* (zool.) gusano plano, platelminto
flaunt [flɔnt] o [flɑnt] *s* ostentación; *va* ostentar, hacer gala de; *vn* hacer ostentación; ondear ostentosamente
flautist ['flɔtɪst] *s* flautista
flavor ['flevər] *s* sabor; condimento; perfume; clase (*de helada*); (fig.) sabor; *va* saborear; condimentar, sazonar; aromatizar, perfumar; *vn* **to flavor of** saber a
flavoring ['flevərɪŋ] *s* condimento; perfume
flavour ['flevər] *s, va & vn* (Brit.) var. de **flavor**
flaw [flɔ] *s* defecto, imperfección, tacha; grieta (*algunas veces inadvertida*); ráfaga; *va* ajar; violar; agrietar; *vn* ajarse; agrietarse
flawless ['flɔlɪs] *adj* entero, perfecto, sin tacha
flawy ['flɔ·ɪ] *adj* (*comp:* **-ier;** *super:* **-iest**) defectuoso, imperfecto; agrietado; con ráfagas
flax [flæks] *s* (bot.) lino (*planta y fibra textil*)
flaxen ['flæksən] *adj* de lino; palizo; rubio
flaxseed ['flæks,sid] *s* linaza
flay [fle] *va* desollar; desollar vivo, flagelar; hurtar, robar
flea [fli] *s* (ent.) pulga; **flea in one's ear** reprensión; desaire, desprecio; insinuación inesperada
fleabane ['fli,ben] *s* (bot.) erígeron; (bot.) hierba pulguera
fleabite ['fli,baɪt] *s* picadura de pulga; molestia insignificante
flea-bitten ['fli,bɪtən] *adj* picado por pulgas; blanco mosqueado en colorado (*dícese, p.ej., del caballo*)
fleam [flim] *s* (surg.) lanceta, sangradera
fleawort ['fli,wʌrt] *s* (bot.) pulguera, zaragatona, coniza
flèche [fleʃ] *s* aguja (*de campanario*); (fort.) flecha
fleck [flɛk] *s* punto de color o luz; vedija; copo; *va* puntear, vetear
flection ['flɛkʃən] *s* flexión; (gram.) flexión
flectional ['flɛkʃənəl] *adj* (gram.) flexional
fled [flɛd] *pret & pp de* **flee**
fledge [flɛdʒ] *va* emplumar (*p.ej., una saeta*); criar (*un pajarito*) hasta que sepa volar; *vn* emplumar, emplumecer (*echar plumas las aves*)
fledgling o **fledgeling** ['flɛdʒlɪŋ] *s* pajarito, volantón, cría; pollo, novato
flee [fli] (*pret & pp:* **fled**) *va & vn* huir
fleece [flis] *s* lana; vellón, vellocino; capa o cobertura (*p.ej., de nieve*); *va* esquilar; pelar, dejar sin blanca
fleecy ['flisɪ] *adj* (*comp:* **-ier;** *super:* **-iest**) lanudo; blanco y blando, aborregado (*como un vellón*)
fleer [flɪr] *s* risa falsa, mueca, pulla; *va* mirar con un gesto de desprecio; *vn* reírse o sonreírse groseramente o con desprecio
fleet [flit] *s* armada, marina de guerra; (naut., nav. & aer.) flota; (fig.) flota (*p.ej., de automóviles, camiones*); *adj* veloz; *vn* pasar o moverse rápidamente
fleeting ['flitɪŋ] *adj* efímero, fugaz; transitorio
fleetness ['flitnɪs] *s* velocidad
Fleming ['flɛmɪŋ] *s* flamenco
Flemish ['flɛmɪʃ] *adj* flamenco; *spl* flamencos; *ssg* flamenco (*idioma*)
Flemish bond *s* (mas.) aparejo flamenco u holandés
flesh [flɛʃ] *s* carne; gordura; género humano; familia, deudos; **in the flesh** vivo; en persona; **to lose flesh** perder carnes; **to put on flesh** cobrar carnes, echar carnes; *va* meter (*un arma blanca*) en la carne; apelambrar (*cueros*); incitar o inflamar las pasiones a; cebar (*halcones,*

perros, etc.) con carne; engordar; **to flesh out** suplir, completar, detallar; *vn* engordar
flesh and blood *s* carne y sangre; el cuerpo
flesh-colored ['flɛʃ,kʌlərd] *adj* encarnado, de color de carne
flesh fly *s* (ent.) mosca de la carne, moscarda
fleshings ['flɛʃɪŋz] *spl* calzas ajustadas de color de carne; raeduras de carne (*que se quitan a los pellejos antes de curtirlos*)
fleshless ['flɛʃlɪs] *adj* descarnado
fleshly ['flɛʃlɪ] *adj* (*comp:* **-lier;** *super:* **-liest**) corpóreo; carnal, sensual
fleshpot ['flɛʃ,pɑt] *s* olla; **fleshpots** *spl* vida regalona
flesh wound *s* herida superficial, herida a flor de carne
fleshy ['flɛʃɪ] *adj* (*comp:* **-ier;** *super:* **-iest**) carnoso; gordo
Fletcherism ['flɛtʃərɪzəm] *s* fletcherismo
fleur-de-lis [,flʌrdə'li] o [,flʌrdə'lis] *s* (*pl:* **fleurs-de-lis** [,flʌrdə'liz]) flor de lis (*escudo de armas de Françia*); (her.) flor de lis; (bot.) lirio de Florencia; (f.a.) flor de lis florenzada
fleury ['flʊrɪ] *adj* (her.) flordelisado; (her.) floronado (*dícese de una cruz*)
flew [flu] *pret de* **fly**
flex [flɛks] *va* doblar; *vn* doblarse
flexibility [,flɛksɪ'bɪlɪtɪ] *s* flexibilidad
flexible ['flɛksɪbəl] o **flexile** ['flɛksɪl] *adj* flexible
flexible cord *s* (elec.) flexible
flexion ['flɛkʃən] *s* var. de **flection**
flexor ['flɛksər] *s* (anat.) flexor, músculo flexor
flexuous ['flɛkʃʊəs] *adj* flexuoso
flexure ['flɛkʃər] *s* flexión; corvadura
flibbertigibbet ['flɪbərtɪ,dʒɪbɪt] *s* persona casquivana; charlador, bachiller
flick [flɪk] *s* golpe rápido y ligero; ruido seco; mancha pequeña, raya, salpicadura; *va* golpear rápida y ligeramente; chasquear (*un látigo*); *vn* moverse rápida y ligeramente, revolotear
flicker ['flɪkər] *s* luz mortecina, llama trémula; chispa; parpadeo; temblor momentáneo (*de emoción*); (orn.) picamaderos norteamericano (*Colaptes auratus*); *va* hacer brillar con luz mortecina; hacer temblar; *vn* brillar con luz mortecina, flamear con llama trémula; fluctuar, lengüetear, oscilar
flier ['flaɪər] *s* persona o cosa que vuela; aviador; autobús, tren o vapor rápido; (slang) empresa arriesgada, negocio arriesgado; (U.S.A.) hoja volante
flight [flaɪt] *s* fuga, huída; vuelo; bandada (*de pájaros*); escuadrilla (*de aviones*); trayecto (*de un avión*); tramo (*de escalera*); ímpetu, arranque (*p.ej., de la fantasía*); **to put to flight** poner en fuga; **to take flight** alzar el vuelo; **to take to flight** ponerse en fuga
flight deck *s* (nav.) cubierta de aterrizaje, cubierta de vuelo
flight feather *s* (orn.) remera
flightiness ['flaɪtɪnɪs] *s* frivolidad, veleidad
flightless ['flaɪtlɪs] *adj* incapaz de volar
flight officer *s* oficial de aviación
flight path *s* (aer.) línea de vuelo
flight recorder *s* (aer.) registrador de vuelo
flighty ['flaɪtɪ] *adj* (*comp:* **-ier;** *super:* **-iest**) frívolo, veleidoso; alocado, casquivano
flimflam ['flɪm,flæm] *s* (coll.) tontería; (coll.) trampa, engaño; (*pret & pp:* **-flammed;** *ger:* **-flamming**) *va* (coll.) trampear
flimflammer ['flɪm,flæmər] *s* (coll.) trampeador
flimsy ['flɪmzɪ] *adj* (*comp:* **-sier;** *super:* **-siest**) débil, endeble; baladí, fútil; *s* papel muy delgado que usan los repórters; informe escrito en papel delgado; (slang) billete de banco
flinch [flɪntʃ] *s* titubeo, vacilación; juego en que se usan naipes especiales numerados de 1 a 14; *vn* acobardarse, encogerse de miedo, desistir de miedo
flinder ['flɪndər] *s* astilla, fragmento
fling [flɪŋ] *s* echamiento violento; baile escocés de compás rápido; **to go on a fling** echar una cana al aire; **to have a fling at** ensayar (*una cosa*); escarnecer (*a una persona*); **to have one's fling** darse a los placeres mientras se puede; (*pret & pp:* **flung**) *va* arrojar, tirar; echar (*p.ej., a la cárcel, al suelo*); mandar precipitadamente (*p.ej., nuevas tropas al frente*); **to fling about** esparcir; **to fling open** abrir de golpe; **to fling out** arrojar con fuerza; hacer ondear (*una bandera*); **to fling shut** cerrar de golpe; *vn* arrojarse, lanzarse, precipitarse; cocear, corcovear
flint [flɪnt] *s* pedernal (*variedad de cuarzo; piedra de chispa*); cosa sumamente dura
flint glass *s* vidrio de plomo
flint-hearted ['flɪnt,hɑrtɪd] *adj* pedernalino, apedernalado
flintlock ['flɪnt,lɑk] *s* llave de chispa; pedreñal, trabuco de chispa
flint paper *s* papel de lija de pedernal
flinty ['flɪntɪ] *adj* (*comp:* **-ier;** *super:* **-iest**) pedernalino, de pedernal; (fig.) apedernalado, empedernido
flip [flɪp] *adj* (*comp:* **flipper;** *super:* **flippest**) (coll.) petulante, impertinente; *s* capirotazo, tirón; bebida de vino o cerveza caliente con azúcar y especias; (*pret & pp:* **flipped;** *ger:* **flipping**) *va* echar de un capirotazo (*p.ej., una moneda sobre el mostrador*); mover rápidamente, mover de un tirón; quitar de golpe; lanzar al aire; **to flip shut** cerrar de golpe (*p.ej., un abanico*); *vn* dar un capirotazo; moverse de un tirón; **to flip up** echar a cara o cruz
flippancy ['flɪpənsɪ] *s* petulancia, impertinencia, ligereza
flippant ['flɪpənt] *adj* petulante, impertinente, ligero
flipper ['flɪpər] *s* aleta (*de foca*); (slang) aleta (*mano*)
flirt [flʌrt] *s* coqueta; galanteador; golpe rápido, meneo rápido, tirón; *va* agitar (*p.ej., un abanico*); mover rápidamente, mover de un tirón; *vn* flirtear; coquetear (*una mujer*); galantear (*un hombre*); **to flirt with** flirtear con; acariciar (*una idea*) con poca seriedad; jugar con (*la muerte*)
flirtation [flʌr'teʃən] *s* flirtación, coqueteo, galanteo; amorío
flirtatious [flʌr'teʃəs] *adj* coqueta; de coqueteo; galanteador; de galanteo
flirting ['flʌrtɪŋ] *s* flirteo; coqueteo; galanteo
flit [flɪt] *s* movimiento rápido y ligero; (*pret & pp:* **flitted;** *ger:* **flitting**) *vn* revolotear, volar; pasar rápidamente (*p.ej., por la imaginación*)
flitch [flɪtʃ] *s* hoja o lonja de tocino
flitter ['flɪtər] *s* pedacitos de metal que sirven de adorno; (coll.) andrajo, harapo; *vn* (archaic & dial.) revolotear, lengüetear
flittermouse ['flɪtər,maʊs] *s* (*pl:* **-mice**) (zool.) murciélago
flitting ['flɪtɪŋ] *adj* fugaz
flivver ['flɪvər] *s* (slang) automóvil o avión pequeño y barato
float [flot] *s* flotador (*especialmente, el corcho de la caña de pescar*); boya (*corcho en las redes*); balsa; palo (*de remo*); paleta (*de rueda*); carroza alegórica, carro alegórico (*de procesiones, fiestas, etc.*); (bot. & mach.) flotador; (mas.) llana; *va* poner a flote; cubrir con agua, inundar, regar; allanar con llana; (com.) lanzar (*una empresa*); (com.) emitir; *vn* flotar
floatability [,flotə'bɪlɪtɪ] *s* flotabilidad
floatable ['flotəbəl] *adj* flotable
float chamber *s* cuba del flotador (*del carburador*)
float-cut file ['flot,kʌt] *s* lima de picadura
floater ['flotər] *s* flotador; (coll.) persona que siempre se está mudando de domicilio o de lugar de empleo; (U.S.A.) persona que en las elecciones echa su voto en varios sitios, ilegalmente
floating ['flotɪŋ] *adj* flotante; no anclado; trashumante
floating axle *s* (mach.) eje flotante, puente flotante
floating battery *s* (elec.) acumulador flotante
floating bridge *s* pontón flotante
floating debt *s* deuda flotante
floating dock *s* dique flotante
floating dry dock *s* dique de carena flotante
floating island *s* isla flotante, isla artificial; (cook.) natillas con merengue
floating kidney *s* (path.) riñón flotante
floating ribs *spl* (anat.) costillas flotantes
floatstone ['flot,ston] *s* (mineral.) cuarzo esponjoso

flocculent ['flɑkjələnt] *adj* lanudo, velludo; (chem.) floculento
flock [flɑk] *s* bandada (*de aves*); rebaño (*de ganado lanar*); gentío, muchedumbre; copo (*p.ej., de lana*); borra, tamo; hatajo (*p.ej., de disparates*); sinnúmero; (fig.) rebaño (*de los fieles*); *vn* congregarse, reunirse; llegar en tropel, agolparse
floe [flo] *s* témpano, banquisa
flog [flɑg] (*pret & pp:* **flogged;** *ger:* **flogging**) *va* azotar
flogging ['flɑgɪŋ] *s* azotamiento
flood [flʌd] *s* inundación, diluvio; avenida, crecida; pleamar; (fig.) inundación, diluvio, torrente (*de luz, palabras, etc.*); (poet.) mar, lago, río; **the Flood** (Bib.) el Diluvio, el Diluvio universal; *va* inundar; abrumar; *vn* desbordar; entrar a raudales, salir a raudales
flood control *s* obras de defensa contra las inundaciones
floodgate ['flʌd,get] *s* compuerta (*de una presa*); esclusa (*de un canal*)
floodlight ['flʌd,laɪt] *s* faro de inundación; *va* iluminar con faro de inundación
flood plain *s* llanura aluvial
flood tide *s* (naut.) pleamar, creciente del mar, marea creciente
floor [flor] *s* piso, suelo; piso (*alto de escalera*); fondo (*de una piscina, del mar, etc.*); hemiciclo (*de una asamblea*); lugar donde se verifican las operaciones de compra y venta (*en las bolsas*); (naut.) varenga; **to ask for the floor** pedir la palabra; **to have the floor** tener la palabra; **to take the floor** tomar la palabra; *va* solar; entarimar; enladrillar, enlosar; derribar, echar al suelo; (coll.) abrumar, vencer; (coll.) dejar turulato, revolcar (*al adversario en controversia*)
floorage ['florɪdʒ] *s* superficie del piso o de los pisos
floor board *s* (aut.) tabla de piso
floorcovering ['flor,kʌvərɪŋ] *s* alfombrado: revestimiento del piso
flooring ['florɪŋ] *s* piso, suelo; pisos, suelos; material para pisos
floor lamp *s* lámpara de pie
floor leader *s* (U.S.A.) jefe de partido (*en la Cámara de Representantes o el Senado*)
floor mop *s* aljofifa, trapeador
floor plan *s* planta
floor show *s* espectáculo de cabaret
floor slab *s* losa de piso
floor space *s* área del piso o los pisos
floor timber *s* (naut.) varenga
floorwalker ['flor,wɔkər] *s* superintendente de división (*en los grandes almacenes*)
floor wax *s* cera de o para pisos
flop [flɑp] *s* agitación (*como de pez recién sacado del agua*); (coll.) fracaso; (coll.) caída (*de una pieza teatral*); **to take a flop** (coll.) caerse; (*pret & pp:* **flopped;** *ger:* **flopping**) *vn* agitarse (*como pez recién sacado del agua*); caerse; dejarse caer o arrojarse pesada y desmañadamente; venirse abajo; mudarse repentinamente; (coll.) salir calabaza, salir huero, fracasar; **to flop over** volcarse, dar un vuelco; cambiar de partido
flophouse ['flɑp,haʊs] *s* posada de baja categoría
floppy ['flɑpɪ] *adj* (*comp:* **-pier;** *super:* **-piest**) (coll.) dado a agitarse; colgante de modo desgarbado (*como las orejas del podenco*); flojo, holgado, flexible
flora ['florə] *s* flora; (*cap.*) *s* (myth.) Flora
floral ['florəl] *adj* floral; de flores
floral emblem *s* flor o planta emblemática (*de un país, una ciudad, etc.*)
Florence ['flɑrəns] o ['flɔrəns] *s* Florencia (*ciudad de Italia; nombre de mujer*)
Florentine ['flɑrəntin] o ['flɔrəntin] *adj & s* florentino
Florentine iris *s* (bot.) lirio de Florencia
florescence [flo'rɛsəns] *s* (bot.) florescencia
florescent [flo'rɛsənt] *adj* floreciente
floret ['florɪt] *s* florecilla, florecita; (bot.) flósculo
floriculture ['florɪ,kʌltʃər] *s* floricultura
floriculturist [,florɪ'kʌltʃərɪst] *s* floricultor
florid ['flɑrɪd] o ['flɔrɪd] *adj* encarnado (*dícese de la tez*); florido, elegante; (lit.) florido
Florida ['flɑrɪdə] o ['flɔrɪdə] *s* la Florida
Florida Keys *spl* Cayos de la Florida
Florida moss *s* (bot.) cabello del rey, barbas de viejo, barba española
Floridan ['flɑrɪdən] o ['flɔrɪdən] o **Floridian** [flo'rɪdɪən] *adj & s* floridano
Florida Strait *s* canal o estrecho de la Florida
floriferous [flo'rɪfərəs] *adj* florífero
florin ['flɑrɪn] o ['flɔrɪn] *s* florín (*moneda*)
floripondio [,florɪ'pɑndɪo] *s* (bot.) floripondio
florist ['florɪst] *s* florero, florista; floricultor
floscule ['flɑskjʊl] *s* (bot.) flósculo
flosculous ['flɑskjʊləs] *adj* flosculoso
floss [flɔs] o [flɑs] *s* cadarzo (*seda basta de la camisa del capullo*); seda floja (*sin torcer*); seda vegetal; (bot.) barbas, cabellos (*del maíz*)
floss silk *s* cadarzo; seda floja
flossy ['flɔsɪ] o ['flɑsɪ] *adj* (*comp:* **-ier;** *super:* **-iest**) len; ligero, velloso; (slang) aparatoso, vistoso, cursi
flotation [flo'teʃən] *s* flotación; lanzamiento (*de un buque*); (com.) lanzamiento (*de una empresa, de una emisión de valores, etc.*); (metal.) flotación
flotilla [flo'tɪlə] *s* flotilla
flotsam ['flɑtsəm] *s* (naut.) pecio, pecios; objetos flotantes
flotsam and jetsam *spl* pecios, despojos que arroja el mar a la orilla; baratijas; gente desocupada y trashumante; gente perdida
flounce [flaʊns] *s* sacudida rápida del cuerpo (*efecto del enojo*); vuelta rápida, torsión, tirón; (sew.) volante; *va* (sew.) adornar con volantes; *vn* andar exagerando los movimientos del cuerpo (*para mostrar enojo*); moverse violentamente, torciendo el cuerpo; **to flounce out** salir airadamente
flounder ['flaʊndər] *s* (ichth.) pleuronecto (*especialmente Platichthys flesus*); lenguado (*Paralichthys brasiliensis*); (ichth.) platija (*Pleuronectes platessa*); forcejeo; *vn* forcejear, andar sin poder avanzar mucho, proceder torpemente; **to flounder through** llegar tropezando al fin de
flour [flaʊr] *s* harina; *adj* harinero; *va* enharinar
flour bolt *s* cedazo, tamiz
flourish ['flʌrɪʃ] *s* molinete (*hecho con el bastón o espada*); plumada, rasgo; rúbrica (*hecha como parte de la firma*); alarde, ostentación; (mus.) floreo; *va* hacer molinetes con (*un bastón, una espada*); hacer alarde de; *vn* florecer; hacer molinetes; hacer rúbricas
flourishing ['flʌrɪʃɪŋ] *adj* floreciente
flour mill *s* molino de harina, molino harinero
floury ['flaʊrɪ] *adj* harinoso; enharinado
flout [flaʊt] *s* mofa, escarnio; insulto; *va* mofarse de, escarnecer; insultar; *vn* mofarse
flow [flo] *s* flujo; (naut.) flujo; *va* derramar; inundar; esparcir (*p.ej., pintura*) en una capa espesa; *vn* fluir; subir (*la marea*); caer o colgar (*los cabellos*); moverse o deslizarse suavemente; ondear; abundar; **to flow away** deslizarse; **to flow into** desaguar en; **to flow over** rebosar; **to flow with** abundar en, nadar en
flower ['flaʊər] *s* flor; (fig.) flor (*lo más escogido*); **flowers** *spl* (chem.) flor; **in flower** en flor; *va* florear, adornar con flores; *vn* florecer
flower bed *s* macizo, parterre
flower beetle *s* (ent.) cetoína
flowered ['flaʊərd] *adj* floreado; espolinado
floweret ['flaʊərɛt] *s* florecilla, florecita
flower garden *s* jardín de flores
flower girl *s* florera; damita de honor
flowering ['flaʊərɪŋ] *adj* floreciente; *s* florecimiento
flowering dogwood *s* (bot.) cornejo florido
flowering fern *s* (bot.) helecho florido
flowering maple *s* (bot.) abutilón
flowering rush *s* (bot.) junco florido
flowerless ['flaʊərlɪs] *adj* sin flores; (bot.) criptogámico
flower of an hour *s* (bot.) aurora común, flor de una hora
flower piece *s* ramillete; (f.a.) florero
flowerpot ['flaʊər,pɑt] *s* tiesto, maceta
flowers of antimony *spl* (chem.) flor de antimonio
flowers of sulphur *spl* (chem.) flor de azufre
flower stand *s* florero (*mueble*)

flowery ['flaʊərɪ] *adj* (*comp:* **-ier;** *super:* **-iest**) florido; (lit.) florido
flowing ['flo·ɪŋ] *adj* corriente; flotante, ondeante; fácil, flúido
flown [flon] *pp de* **fly**
flow sheet *s* gráfico de las fases de un proceso industrial
flu [flu] *s* (coll.) gripe
flubdub ['flʌb,dʌb] *s* (coll.) ínfulas
fluctuant ['flʌktʃuənt] *adj* fluctuante
fluctuate ['flʌktʃuet] *vn* fluctuar
fluctuation [,flʌktʃu'eʃən] *s* fluctuación; (biol. & med.) fluctuación
flue [flu] *s* cañón de chimenea, humero; tubo de humo, tubo de caldera; (mus.) tubo de embocadura de flauta (*del órgano*)
fluency ['fluənsɪ] *s* fluencia; afluencia, facundia; fluidez (*del lenguaje, estilo*)
fluent ['fluənt] *adj* fluente (*que fluye*); afluente, facundo; flúido (*lenguaje, estilo*)
fluently ['fluəntlɪ] *adv* corrientemente
flue pipe *s* (mus.) tubo de flauta, tubo de embocadura de flauta
fluff [flʌf] *s* pelusa, plumón, tamo; lanilla; copo (*de lana*); masa esponjosa (*p.ej., de crema batida*); (coll.) gazapo de actor; *va* mullir, esponjar; *vn* esponjarse
fluffy ['flʌfɪ] *adj* (*comp:* **-ier;** *super:* **-iest**) fofo, esponjoso; velloso, velludo
fluid ['fluɪd] *adj* flúido; cambiante; *s* flúido
fluid diet *s* régimen de alimentos líquidos
fluid dram *s* dracma líquida (*octava parte de la onza líquida*)
fluidity [flu'ɪdɪtɪ] *s* fluidez
fluid mechanics *ssg* mecánica de los flúidos
fluid ounce *s* onza líquida (*29,6 centímetros cúbicos en EE.UU. y 28,4 en Gran Bretaña*)
fluke [fluk] *s* uña (*de ancla, de arpón*); aleta (*de la cola de la ballena*); (ichth.) pleuronecto; (zool.) trematodo, duela del hígado; chiripa (*en el billar, suerte que se gana por casualidad; casualidad favorable*); **to win by a fluke** ganar por chiripa; *va* chiripear; *vn* chiripear; fracasar
flume [flum] *s* garganta profunda por cuyo fondo pasa un río o arroyo; caz, saetín; acueducto, canal de madera
flummery ['flʌmərɪ] *s* (*pl:* **-ies**) manjar blanco; pasta de harina cocida; alabanza insincera; disparates, tonterías
flung [flʌŋ] *pret & pp de* **fling**
flunk [flʌŋk] *s* (coll.) reprobación (*en un examen o asignatura*); (coll.) nota de suspenso; *va* (coll.) colgar, reprobar, dar calabazas a; perder (*un examen o asignatura*); **to flunk out** (coll.) reprobar definitivamente; *vn* (coll.) salir mal, fracasar; **to flunk out** (coll.) tener que abandonar los estudios por haber sido reprobado
flunkey ['flʌŋkɪ] *s* var. de **flunky**
flunky ['flʌŋkɪ] *s* (*pl:* **-ies**) lacayo; adulador
flunkyism ['flʌŋkɪɪzəm] *s* servilismo
fluor ['fluər] *s* (mineral.) fluorita
fluoresce [,fluə'rɛs] *vn* despedir rayos de luz fluorescente
fluorescein [,fluə'rɛsɪɪn] *s* (chem.) fluoresceína
fluorescence [,fluə'rɛsəns] *s* fluorescencia
fluorescent [,fluə'rɛsənt] *adj* fluorescente
fluorescent lamp *s* tubo fluorescente
fluorescent lighting *s* alumbrado fluorescente
fluorescent screen *s* (phys.) pantalla fluorescente
fluoric [flu'ɑrɪk] o [flu'ɔrɪk] *adj* fluórico
fluorid ['fluərɪd] o **fluoride** ['fluəraɪd] o ['fluərɪd] *s* (chem.) fluoruro
fluoridate ['fluərɪdet] *va* fluorizar
fluoridation [,fluərɪ'deʃən] *s* fluorización (*del agua potable*); (geol.) fluorización
fluorin ['fluərɪn] o **fluorine** ['fluərin] o ['fluərɪn] *s* (chem.) flúor
fluorite ['fluəraɪt] *s* (mineral.) fluorita
fluoroscope ['fluərəskop] *s* fluoroscopio
fluoroscopic [,fluərə'skɑpɪk] *adj* fluoroscópico
fluoroscopy [,fluə'rɑskəpɪ] *s* fluoroscopia
fluor spar *s* (mineral.) espato flúor
flurry ['flʌrɪ] *s* (*pl:* **-ries**) ráfaga; chaparrón; nevisca; agitación, aturdimiento; (*pret & pp:* **-ried**) *va* agitar, aturdir
flush [flʌʃ] *s* flujo repentino; rubor, bochorno, llamarada, sonrojo; acceso (*p.ej., de alegría*); floración repentina (*p.ej., en la primavera*); vigor (*de la juventud*); chorro del inodoro; flux (*en el póker*); *adj* rasante, nivelado; enrasado, parejo; embutido; abundante, copioso; robusto, vigoroso; pródigo, próspero; rubicundo; rebosante; bien provisto; (print.) justificado; **flush with** a ras de, al mismo nivel que; *adv* ras con ras, al mismo nivel; directamente, sin errar el golpe; *va* abochornar; exaltar, regocijar; engreír; limpiar con un chorro de agua, lavar con agua a presión; hacer saltar (*una liebre*); hacer volar (*una perdiz*); *vn* abochornarse; estar encendido (*p.ej., el rostro*); fluir repentinamente; brotar; saltar o volar de repente
flush deck *s* (naut.) cubierta corrida
Flushing ['flʌʃɪŋ] *s* Flesinga
flush-mounted switch ['flʌʃ'maʊntɪd] *s* (elec.) llave para embutir, llave embutida
flush outlet *s* (elec.) caja de enchufe embutida
flush switch *s* (elec.) llave para embutir, llave embutida
flush tank *s* depósito de limpia, tanque de inundación
flush toilet *s* inodoro con chorro de agua
fluster ['flʌstər] *s* confusión, aturdimiento; *va* confundir, aturdir
flute [flut] *s* (mus.) flauta; (mus.) flautado (*registro del órgano*); estría (*de una columna*); *va* acanalar, estriar; *vn* flautear, tocar la flauta; cantar o silbar remedando el sonido de la flauta
fluted ['flutɪd] *adj* acanalado, estriado; flauteado
fluting ['flutɪŋ] *s* acanaladura, estriadura
flutist ['flutɪst] *s* flautista
flutter ['flʌtər] *s* aleteo, revoloteo; aturdimiento, confusión, turbación; **in a flutter** aturdido; **to make a flutter** causar alboroto; *va* agitar; aturdir, confundir, turbar; *vn* aletear, revolotear; agitarse; flamear, ondear; alterarse (*el pulso*); palpitar (*el corazón*)
fluvial ['fluvɪəl] *adj* fluvial
flux [flʌks] *s* flujo; fusión (*estado líquido producido por el calor*); continua mudanza; (chem. & metal.) flujo o fundente; (phys. & path.) flujo; *va* fundir; unir por medio de la fusión; mezclar con un fundente; *vn* fundirse
flux density *s* (phys.) densidad de flujo
fluxion ['flʌkʃən] *s* flujo; (math. & path.) fluxión
fluxmeter ['flʌks,mitər] *s* (phys.) flujómetro
fly [flaɪ] *s* (*pl:* **flies**) (ent.) mosca; mosca artificial (*con anzuelo de pescar escondido*); pliegue (*para cubrir botones*); bragueta (*abertura de los pantalones*); toldo que se extiende por encima de una tienda de campaña; lona que tapa la puerta de una tienda de campaña; calesín; (mach.) hélice; **on the fly** al vuelo, en el aire; **to die like flies** morir como chinches; **to hit a fly** (baseball) pegar una planchita, elevar una palomita; **flies** *spl* (theat.) bambalina ‖ (*pret:* **flew;** *pp:* **flown**) *va* hacer volar (*una cometa, un halcón*); dirigir (*un avión*); volar (*llevar en un aparato de aviación*); atravesar en avión; desplegar, llevar (*una bandera*); huir ‖ *vn* volar; huir; ondear (*una bandera*); **to fly at** lanzarse sobre; **to fly away** irse volando; escaparse; **to fly off** salir volando; desprenderse; **to fly open** abrirse de repente; **to fly over** trasvolar; **to fly shut** cerrarse de repente; **to fly to** + *inf* volar a + *inf* ‖ (*pret & pp:* **flied**) *vn* (baseball) pegar una planchita, elevar una palomita
flyaway ['flaɪə,we] *adj* flameante, ondeante; casquivano, frívolo
fly ball *s* (baseball) planchita, palomita
flyblow ['flaɪ,blo] *s* cresa; *va* llenar (*la carne*) de cresas; contaminar
flyblown ['flaɪ,blon] *adj* lleno de cresas; (fig.) contaminado, manchado, infamado
flyboat ['flaɪ,bot] *s* (naut.) filibote; buque muy rápido
fly book *s* cartera (*para moscas artificiales*)
fly-by-night ['flaɪbaɪ,naɪt] *adj* indigno de confianza, poco confiable; *s* noctámbulo; (slang) persona que se escapa por la noche para evitar acreedores
fly-casting ['flaɪ,kæstɪŋ] o ['flaɪ,kɑstɪŋ] *s* lanzamiento de mosca (*manera de pescar*)
flycatcher ['flaɪ,kætʃər] *s* (orn.) papamoscas, cazamoscas, doral, moscareta
flyer ['flaɪər] *s* var. de **flier**

fly-fisher [ˈflaɪˌfɪʃər] *s* pescador que pesca con moscas artificiales
fly-fishing [ˈflaɪˌfɪʃɪŋ] *s* pesca con moscas artificiales
flying [ˈflaɪɪŋ] *adj* volante, volador; flameante, ondeante; apresurado, rápido, veloz; breve; *s* vuelo; aviación
flying boat *s* (aer.) hidroavión
flying bomb *s* bomba volante
flying buttress *s* (arch.) arbotante
flying circus *s* escuadrilla de aviones de caza; acrobacia aeronáutica
flying colors *spl* gran éxito, triunfo
flying column *s* (mil.) columna volante
flying dragon *s* (zool.) dragón, dragón volador
Flying Dutchman, the el Holandés errante; el Barco fantasma
flying field *s* campo de aviación
flying fish *s* (ichth.) volador, pez volador
flying fortress *s* (aer.) fortaleza volante
flying fox *s* (zool.) bermejizo
flying frog *s* (zool.) rana voladora
flying gurnard *s* (ichth.) pez volador
flying jib *s* (naut.) petifoque
flying jib boom *s* (naut.) botalón de petifoque
flying machine *s* máquina de volar
flying saucer *s* platillo volador o volante
flying sickness *s* mal de altura
flying squadron *s* (nav.) escuadra ligera
flying squirrel *s* (zool.) ardilla voladora
fly in the ointment *s* mosca muerta que malea el perfume (*cosa insignificante que estropea una cosa valiosa*)
flyleaf [ˈflaɪˌlif] *s* (*pl:* **-leaves**) (b.b.) guarda, hoja de guarda
fly net *s* mosquitero (*colgadura de cama*); espantamoscas (*para poner a los caballos*)
flypaper [ˈflaɪˌpepər] *s* matamoscas, papel pegajoso (*que se usa para coger moscas*)
flyspeck [ˈflaɪˌspɛk] *s* mancha de mosca; *va* manchar con manchas de mosca
fly swatter *s* matamoscas, paño de aporrear moscas
flytrap [ˈflaɪˌtræp] *s* espantamoscas (*para coger moscas*); (bot.) atrapamoscas, dionea; (bot.) apocino; (bot.) nepente
flyweight [ˈflaɪˌwet] *s* (box.) peso mosca
flywheel [ˈflaɪˌhwil] *s* volante
fm. abr. de **fathom**
F.M. o **FM** abr. de **frequency modulation**
foal [fol] *s* potro (*caballo*); pollino (*asno*); *va & vn* parir (*dícese de la yegua o asna*)
foam [fom] *s* espuma; *va* hacer espumar; *vn* espumar; espumajear
foam extinguisher *s* lanzaespumas, extintor de espuma
foam rubber *s* caucho esponjoso, espuma de caucho
foamy [ˈfomɪ] *adj* (*comp:* **-ier;** *super:* **-iest**) espumoso, espumajoso
f.o.b. o **F.O.B.** abr. de **free on board**
fob [fɑb] *s* faltriquera de reloj; leopoldina (*cadena del reloj de bolsillo*); dije (*de la leopoldina*); (*pret & pp:* **fobbed;** *ger:* **fobbing**) *va* embolsar; engañar; **to fob off** evadir con fraude
focal [ˈfokəl] *adj* focal
focal distance *s* (opt.) distancia focal
focal infection *s* (path.) infección focal
focalization [ˌfokəlɪˈzeʃən] *s* focalización
focalize [ˈfokəlaɪz] *va* enfocar
focal length *s* var. de **focal distance**
focal plane *s* (opt.) plano focal
focal point *s* (math.) punto focal
focus [ˈfokəs] *s* (*pl:* **-cuses** o **-ci** [saɪ]) enfoque (*acción de enfocar*); (math., med., phys., opt., seismol. & fig.) foco; **in focus** enfocado; **out of focus** fuera de foco, desenfocado; (*pret & pp:* **-cused** o **-cussed;** *ger:* **-cusing** o **-cussing**) *va* enfocar; fijar (*la atención*); *vn* enfocarse
fodder [ˈfɑdər] *s* forraje; *va* dar forraje a
foe [fo] *s* enemigo
foeman [ˈfomən] *s* (*pl:* **-men**) enemigo
foetal [ˈfitəl] *adj* var. de **fetal**
foetus [ˈfitəs] *s* var. de **fetus**
fog [fɑg] o [fɔg] *s* niebla; (phot.) velo; (fig.) niebla, confusión; (*pret & pp:* **fogged;** *ger:* **fogging**) *va* envolver en niebla, obscurecer; empañar; (phot.) velar; *vn* ponerse brumoso; empañarse; (phot.) velarse
fog bank *s* banco de nieblas
fog bell *s* campana de nieblas
fogbound [ˈfɑgˌbaʊnd] o [ˈfɔgˌbaʊnd] *adj* inmovilizado por la niebla
fogey [ˈfogɪ] *s* var. de **old fogey**
foggy [ˈfɑgɪ] o [ˈfɔgɪ] *adj* (*comp:* **-gier;** *super:* **-giest**) neblinoso, brumoso; borroso; confuso; (phot.) velado; **it is foggy** hay niebla
foghorn [ˈfɑgˌhɔrn] o [ˈfɔgˌhɔrn] *s* bocina de bruma, sirena de niebla; voz gritona y destemplada
fog signal *s* señal de nieblas
fog whistle *s* silbato de niebla
fogy [ˈfogɪ] *s* (*pl:* **-gies**) var. de **old fogey**
foible [ˈfɔɪbəl] *s* flaqueza, flaco, lado flaco
foil [fɔɪl] *s* hojuela (*de metal*); capa metálica, azogado, plateado (*de un espejo*); pan de oro o plata que se coloca bajo una piedra preciosa para que brille más; contraste, realce; florete (*espadín*); rastro, huella (*de un animal*); malogro; (arch.) lóbulo; **foils** *spl* esgrima; *va* frustrar; azogar o platear (*un espejo*); realzar; (arch.) adornar con lóbulos
foist [fɔɪst] *va* vender con engaño; insertar clandestinamente; **to foist something on someone** venderle a uno una cosa con engaño; lograr mediante un engaño que alguien acepte una cosa
fol. abr. de **folio, followed** y **following**
fold [fold] *s* pliegue, doblez; arruga; aprisco; rebaño, redil; iglesia; feligresía; rebaño (*de los fieles*); (geol.) pliegue, plegamiento; *va* plegar, doblar; recoger (*p.ej., un pájaro sus alas*); envolver, abrazar con ternura; apriscar; cruzar (*los brazos*); **to fold up** doblar (*p.ej., un mapa*); *vn* plegarse, doblarse; **to fold up** reducirse en tamaño doblándose; fracasar; quebrar (*en el comercio*)
folder [ˈfoldər] *s* plegador, doblador; plegadora mecánica, máquina de plegar; carpeta; cuadernillo, folleto, pliego
folderol [ˈfɑldəˌrɑl] *s* fruslería, tontería; bagatela, trivialidad
folding [ˈfoldɪŋ] *adj* plegable, plegadizo; plegador
folding box o **carton** *s* caja de cartón plegable
folding camera *s* cámara plegadiza, aparato fotográfico plegadizo, cámara de fuelle
folding chair *s* silla de tijera, silla plegadiza
folding cot *s* catre de tijera
folding door *s* puerta plegadiza; puerta corrediza; hoja o batiente de puerta
folding machine *s* plegadora mecánica
folding rule *s* metro plegadizo
folding seat *s* catrecillo
foliaceous [ˌfolɪˈeʃəs] *adj* foliáceo
foliage [ˈfolɪɪdʒ] *s* follaje; (arch.) follaje
foliar [ˈfolɪər] *adj* foliar
foliate [ˈfolɪɪt] o [ˈfolɪet] *adj* (bot.) foliado; [ˈfolɪet] *va* follar (*formar en hojas*); adornar con follaje; foliar (*los folios de un libro*); laminar; azogar (*un espejo*); *vn* echar hojas
foliated [ˈfolɪˌetɪd] *adj* follado; laminado; (arch.) lobulado
foliation [ˌfolɪˈeʃən] *s* foliación (*de los folios de un libro*); (bot. & geol.) foliación; (arch. & f.a.) follajería
foliature [ˈfolɪətʃər] *s* foliatura
folic acid [ˈfolɪk] *s* (biochem.) ácido fólico
folio [ˈfolɪo] *s* ((*pl:* **-os**) folio (*hoja de un libro*); infolio, libro en folio; (bookkeeping) folio; **in folio** en folio; *adj* en folio; *va* foliar (*los folios de un libro*)
foliole [ˈfolɪol] *s* (bot.) folíolo
folk [fok] *s* (*pl:* **folk** o **folks**) gente; (*pl:* **folks**) (archaic) gente, nación, tribu; **folks** *spl* (coll.) gente (*familia*); *adj* popular, del pueblo
folk dance *s* baile popular
folk etymology *s* etimología popular
folklore [ˈfokˌlor] *s* folklore
folklorist [ˈfokˌlorɪst] *s* folklorista
folk music *s* música del pueblo, música tradicional
folk song *s* canción popular, canción típica
folksy [ˈfoksɪ] *adj* (*comp:* **-sier;** *super:* **-siest**) (coll.) plebeyo; (coll.) tratable, sociable
folk tale *s* cuento popular

folkway [ˈfok,we] *s* costumbre tradicional de un pueblo
follicle [ˈfɑlɪkəl] *s* (anat. & bot.) folículo
follicular [fəˈlɪkjələr] *adj* folicular
folliculin [fəˈlɪkjəlɪn] *s* (trademark) foliculina
follow [ˈfɑlo] *va* seguir; seguir el hilo de (*un argumento*); interesarse en, estar al corriente de (*las noticias del día*); **to follow out** llevar hasta el fin, llevar a cabo; **to follow through** llevar hasta el fin (*una jugada o golpe*) sin flaquear ni desviarse; **to follow up** perseguir con ahinco; llevar hasta el fin; reforzar con nuevos esfuerzos o nuevas gestiones; *vn* seguir; seguirse, resultar; **as follows** como sigue(n); **it follows** síguese; **is as follows** es lo siguiente; **to follow on** seguir por el mismo camino, continuar en la misma forma
follower [ˈfɑloər] *s* seguidor; secuaz, partidario; imitador; criado
following [ˈfɑlo·ɪŋ] *adj* siguiente; *s* séquito; secuaces, partidarios; **the following** el siguiente, los siguientes
follow-up [ˈfɑlo,ʌp] *adj* consecutivo; recordativo; *s* carta recordativa, circular recordativa
folly [ˈfɑlɪ] *s* (*pl:* **-lies**) desatino, tontería, locura; empresa temeraria
foment [foˈmɛnt] *va* fomentar (*p.ej., el encono*); (med.) fomentar
fomentation [,fomɛnˈteʃən] *s* fomento; (med.) fomento, fomentación
fomenter [foˈmɛntər] *s* fomentador
fond [fɑnd] *adj* cariñoso, afectuoso; **fond of** encariñado con (*una persona*); aficionado a; amigo de
fondant [ˈfɑndənt] *s* pasta de azúcar (*que se usa en la confitería*)
fondle [ˈfɑndəl] *va* acariciar, mimar
fondness [ˈfɑndnɪs] *s* cariño, afición
fondue [fɑnˈdu] o [ˈfɑndu] *s* flan de queso
font [fɑnt] *s* pila (*de bautismo o de agua bendita*); fuente (*de bautismo; manantial de agua; origen*); (print.) fundición
fontal [ˈfɑntəl] *adj* fontal, fontanal
fontanel [,fɑntəˈnɛl] *s* (anat.) fontanela
food [fud] *s* alimento, comida; (fig.) alimento, pábulo, materia; **food for thought** materia en que pensar; *adj* alimenticio
food drop *s* (aer.) lanzamiento de víveres
foodstuff [ˈfud,stʌf] *s* producto alimenticio, comestible
food supplement *s* aditivo alimenticio
food value *s* valor alimenticio
foofaraw [ˈfufərɔ] *s* (coll.) oropel, relumbrón; (coll.) tontería
fool [ful] *s* tonto, necio; bufón; víctima (*de un engaño*); **to make a fool of** poner en ridículo; **to make a fool of oneself** ponerse en ridículo; **to play the fool** hacer el tonto; *va* engañar, embaucar; **to fool away** malgastar (*tiempo, dinero*); *vn* chancear, tontear; **to fool around** (coll.) bromear, malgastar el tiempo neciamente; **to fool with** (coll.) meterse neciamente en; (coll.) ajar, manosear
foolery [ˈfulərɪ] *s* (*pl:* **-ies**) tontería, bufonada
foolhardy [ˈful,hɑrdɪ] *adj* (*comp:* **-dier;** *super:* **-diest**) arriesgado, temerario
fooling [ˈfulɪŋ] *s* chacota, broma; engaño; **no fooling** (coll.) sin broma, hablando en serio
foolish [ˈfulɪʃ] *adj* tonto, necio, disparatado; ridículo
foolishness [ˈfulɪʃnɪs] *s* tontería, necedad; ridiculez
foolproof [ˈful,pruf] *adj* (coll.) a prueba de impericia, a prueba de mal trato; (coll.) cierto, infalible
foolscap [ˈfulz,kæp] *s* papel de oficio; gorro de bufón; gorro de forma de cono que se le pone al niño torpe
fool's cap *s* gorro de bufón; gorro de forma de cono que se le pone al niño torpe
fool's errand *s* caza de grillos
fool's gold *s* pirita amarilla
fool's paradise *s* felicidad que tiene por fundamento esperanzas o creencias falsas
fool's-parsley [ˈfulz,pɑrslɪ] *s* (bot.) cicuta menor, etusa, perejil de perro
fool's scepter *s* cetro de locura
foot [fʊt] *s* (*pl:* **feet**) pie (*de animal, media, bota, verso, etc.; medida lineal*); (mil.) infantería; (naut.) pujamen (*de una vela*); **on foot** a pie; de pie; avanzando, haciendo progresos; **to carry off one's feet** arrebatar, cautivar; **to drag one's feet** (coll.) tardar en obrar, ir a paso de caracol (*intencionadamente*); **to have one foot in the grave** estar con un pie en la sepultura; **to put one's best foot forward** andar lo más aprisa posible; hacer grandes esfuerzos; (coll.) hacer méritos, tratar de impresionar, tratar de ganarse la buena voluntad; **to put one's foot down** (coll.) proceder con gran energía; (coll.) vedarle a otro su deseo; **to put one's foot in it** (coll.) meter la pata; (coll.) tirarse una plancha; **to trample under foot** pisotear; **to tread under foot** hollar (*pisar; despreciar; destruir*); **under foot** estorbando el paso; en el poder de uno; *va* poner el pie (o los pies) a; sumar (*una columna de guarismos*); pagar (*la cuenta*); **to foot it** andar a pie; bailar; *vn* andar a pie; bailar
footage [ˈfʊtɪdʒ] *s* largura o distancia en pies; paga por pie de trabajo; (mov.) longitud de película en pies (*in Spanish* metraje, *i.e., length of film in meters, is used*)
foot-and-mouth disease [ˈfʊtənˈmaʊθ] *s* (vet.) glosopeda, fiebre aftosa
football [ˈfʊt,bɔl] *s* balompié, fútbol (*juego*); balón (*pelota*); (fig.) juguete; *adj* balompédico, futbolístico
football player *s* futbolista
foot bath *s* pediluvio, baño de pies
footboard [ˈfʊt,bord] *s* estribo; pie (*de cama*); pedal
foot brake *s* freno de pedal, freno de pie
footbridge [ˈfʊt,brɪdʒ] *s* puente para peatones, pasarela
foot-candle [ˈfʊtˈkændəl] *s* bujía-pie o piebujía
footcloth [ˈfʊt,klɔθ] o [ˈfʊt,klɑθ] *s* gualdrapa; alfombra
footfall [ˈfʊt,fɔl] *s* paso (*movimiento y ruido*)
foot fault *s* (tennis) falta de pie
footgear [ˈfʊt,gɪr] *s* calzado
foothill [ˈfʊt,hɪl] *s* falda, colina al pie de un monte o sierra
foothold [ˈfʊt,hold] *s* espacio en que se afirma el pie; pie, arraigo, posición establecida; **to gain a foothold** ganar pie (*p.ej., en costa enemiga*)
footing [ˈfʊtɪŋ] *s* pie, p.ej., **he lost his footing and fell** perdió el pie y se cayó; arraigo, posición establecida; condición, estado; suma de guarismos; suma, total; (el) caminar; (el) bailar; **on a friendly footing** en relaciones amistosas; **on an equal footing** en un mismo pie de igualdad; **on a war footing** en pie de guerra
footless [ˈfʊtlɪs] *adj* sin pies; sin fundamento; (coll.) desmañado, torpe
footlights [ˈfʊt,laɪts] *spl* candilejas, batería; (fig.) tablas, profesión de actor
foot-loose [ˈfʊt,lus] *adj* libre (*para hacer lo que a uno se le antoje*)
footman [ˈfʊtmən] *s* (*pl:* **-men**) lacayo; soldado de a pie
footmark [ˈfʊt,mɑrk] *s* huella
footnote [ˈfʊt,not] *s* nota al pie de una página
footpace [ˈfʊt,pes] *s* paso lento, paso del que camina normalmente; descanso (*de escalera*)
footpad [ˈfʊt,pæd] *s* salteador que camina a pie
footpath [ˈfʊt,pæθ] o [ˈfʊt,pɑθ] *s* senda para peatones
foot-pound [ˈfʊt,paʊnd] *s* (mech.) librapié
foot-poundal [ˈfʊt,paʊndəl] *s* (mech.) piepoundal
foot-pound-second system [ˈfʊt,paʊndˈsɛkənd] *s* (phys.) sistema pie-libra-segundo
footprint [ˈfʊt,prɪnt] *s* huella
foot race *s* carrera a pie
foot racing *s* pedestrismo
footrest [ˈfʊt,rɛst] *s* apoyapié, descansapié
footrope [ˈfʊt,rop] *s* (naut.) marchapié
foot rule *s* regla de un pie
foot soldier *s* (mil.) infante, soldado de a pie
footsore [ˈfʊt,sor] *adj* despeado
footsoreness [ˈfʊt,sornɪs] *s* despeadura
footstalk [ˈfʊt,stɔk] *s* (bot. & zool.) pedúnculo
footstep [ˈfʊt,stɛp] *s* paso; **to follow** o **tread**

in the footsteps of seguir las huellas o los pasos de
footstone [ˈfʊtˌston] *s* lápida que se coloca al pie de una sepultura
footstool [ˈfʊtˌstul] *s* escabel, escañuelo
foot warmer *s* calientapiés
footway [ˈfʊtˌwe] *s* senda para peatones; (Brit.) acera
footwear [ˈfʊtˌwɛr] *s* calzado
footwork [ˈfʊtˌwʌrk] *s* juego de piernas (*en los deportes o el bailar*)
footworn [ˈfʊtˌwɔrn] *adj* asendereado, trillado (*camino*); despeado
foozle [ˈfuzel] *s* chambonada; (coll.) vejestorio; *va* chafallar; errar (*un golpe*) de manera chambona; *vn* chambonear
foozler [ˈfuzlər] *s* chambón
fop [fɑp] *s* currutaco, majadero presumido
foppery [ˈfɑpərɪ] *s* (*pl:* **-ies**) presunción de currutaco; perifollos
foppish [ˈfɑpɪʃ] *adj* alechuguinado, currutaco
for. abr. de **foreign** y **forestry**
for [fɔr] *prep* para; por; como, p.ej., **I use coal for fuel** uso carbón como combustible; en honor de; a pesar de, p.ej., **for all her intelligence** a pesar de su inteligencia; de, p.ej., **time for dinner** hora de comer; desde hace, p.ej., **I have been here for three months** estoy aquí desde hace tres meses; **O! for . . . !** ¡quién tuviera . . . !; *conj* pues, porque
forage [ˈfɑrɪdʒ] o [ˈfɔrɪdʒ] *s* forraje; *adj* forrajero; *va* dar forraje a; forrajear; *vn* forrajear
forage cap *s* (Brit.) gorra militar
forager [ˈfɑrɪdʒər] o [ˈfɔrɪdʒər] *s* forrajeador
foramen [foˈremən] *s* (*pl:* **-ramina** [ˈræmɪnə] o **-ramens**) foramen; (anat. & bot.) foramen
foraminifera [foˌræmɪˈnɪfərə] *spl* (zool.) foraminíferos
forasmuch as [ˌfɔrəzˈmʌtʃæz] *conj* porque, puesto que, visto que
foray [ˈfɑre] o [ˈfɔre] *s* correría, saqueo; *va* saquear, despojar
forbade o **forbad** [fɔrˈbæd] *pret de* **forbid**
forbear [ˈfɔrbɛr] *s* antepasado; [fɔrˈbɛr] (*pret:* **-bore;** *pp:* **-borne**) *va* abstenerse de; *vn* contenerse, tener paciencia
forbearance [fɔrˈbɛrəns] *s* abstención; dominio sobre sí mismo, paciencia
forbid [fɔrˈbɪd] (*pret:* **-bade** o **-bad;** *pp:* **-bidden;** *ger:* **-bidding**) *va* prohibir; **God forbid!** ¡no lo permita Dios!; **to forbid to** + *inf* prohibir + *inf*
forbidden [fɔrˈbɪdən] *pp de* **forbid**
Forbidden City *s* ciudad prohibida (*Lhassa, capital del Tibet; parte amurallada de Pequín*)
forbidden fruit *s* fruta prohibida
forbidding [fɔrˈbɪdɪŋ] *adj* repugnante; formidable
forbore [fɔrˈbor] *pret de* **forbear**
forborne [fɔrˈborn] *pp de* **forbear**
force [fors] *s* fuerza; personal; cuerpo (*de tropas, de policía, etc.*); (phys.) fuerza; **forces** *spl* (mil. & nav.) fuerzas; **by force** a la fuerza, por fuerza; **by force of** a fuerza de; **by force of habit** por la fuerza de la costumbre; **by main force** con todas sus fuerzas; **in force** en vigor, vigente; en gran número; **to join forces** coligarse, juntar diestra con diestra; **to meet force with force** oponer la fuerza a la fuerza, enfrentar la fuerza con la fuerza; *va* forzar; (agr.) forzar; **to force away** obligar a marcharse; **to force back** impeler hacia atrás, hacer retroceder; **to force down** obligar a bajar, obligar a bajarse; hacer tragar por fuerza; **to force from** echar o sacar fuera por fuerza, arrancar violentamente; **to force in** clavar o introducir por fuerza; **to force oneself** hacer esfuerzos violentos; **to force out** echar o sacar fuera por fuerza; **to force through** hacer penetrar por fuerza; llevar a cabo por fuerza; **to force to** + *inf* forzar a + *inf* o forzar a que + *subj;* **to force up** hacer subir por fuerza
forced [forst] *adj* forzado; (fig.) forzado (*dícese, p.ej., de una sonrisa*)
forced air *s* aire a presión
forced draft *s* tiro forzado
forced landing *s* (aer.) aterrizaje forzado o forzoso
forced march *s* (mil.) marcha forzada
forced ventilation *s* ventilación por presión
force feed *s* (mach.) alimentación forzada, lubricación a presión
force-feeding [ˈforsˌfidɪŋ] *s* (med.) alimentación forzada
forceful [ˈforsfəl] *adj* eficaz, poderoso, vigoroso
force majeure [fɔrs mɑˈʒœr] *s* (law) fuerza mayor
forcemeat [ˈforsˌmit] *s* carne picada y condimentada que sirve de relleno
forceps [ˈfɔrsəps] *s* (*pl:* **-ceps** o **-cipes** [sɪpiz]) (obstet. & zool.) fórceps; (dent. & surg.) pinzas
force pump *s* bomba impelente o impulsora
forcible [ˈforsɪbəl] *adj* forzado, violentado; eficaz, poderoso, vigoroso, convincente
forcipressure [ˌfɔrsɪˈprɛʃər] *s* (surg.) forcipresión
ford [ford] *s* vado; *va* vadear
fordable [ˈfordəbəl] *adj* vadeable
fore [for] *adj* anterior, delantero; (naut.) de proa; *adv* anteriormente, antes; delante, en la delantera; (naut.) avante; *interj* (golf) ¡ojo!, ¡cuidado!; *s* cabeza, delantera, frente; **to the fore** en la delantera; destacado; dispuesto; a mano; a la vista; vivo
fore and aft *adv* (naut.) a proa y a popa, en proa y en popa; (naut.) de popa a proa
fore-and-aft [ˈforəndˌæft] o [ˈforəndˌɑft] *adj* (naut.) de popa a proa
fore-and-aft sail *s* (naut.) vela cangreja
forearm [ˈforˌɑrm] *s* antebrazo; [forˈɑrm] *va* armar de antemano; prevenir de antemano
forebear [ˈforbɛr] *s* antepasado
forebode [forˈbod] *va* presentir, prever con recelo; presagiar
foreboding [forˈbodɪŋ] *s* presentimiento; presagio; *adj* presagioso, ominoso
forebrain [ˈforˌbren] *s* (anat.) cerebro (*parte anterior del encéfalo*)
forecast [ˈforˌkæst] o [ˈforˌkɑst] *s* pronóstico; previsión; proyecto, plan; (*pret & pp:* **-cast** o **-casted**) *va* pronosticar; prever; proyectar
forecastle [ˈfoksəl], [ˈforˌkæsəl] o [ˈforˌkɑsəl] *s* (naut.) castillo, castillo de proa; (naut.) camarote o camarotes en el castillo de proa (*en que se aloja la tripulación*)
forecastle deck *s* (naut.) castillo
foreclose [forˈkloz] *va* excluir; impedir; (law) extinguir el derecho de redimir (*una hipoteca*); (law) privar del derecho de redimir una hipoteca
foreclosure [forˈkloʒər] *s* (law) extinción del derecho de redimir una hipoteca
foredoom [forˈdum] *va* predestinar a la condenación, predestinar al fracaso
fore edge *s* canal *f* (*de un libro*)
forefather [ˈforˌfɑðər] *s* antepasado
forefend [forˈfɛnd] *va* var. de **forfend**
forefinger [ˈforˌfɪŋgər] *s* dedo índice, dedo mostrador
forefoot [ˈforˌfʊt] *s* (*pl:* **-feet**) pata delantera
forefront [ˈforˌfrʌnt] *s* puesto delantero; sitio de mayor importancia, sitio de actividad más intensa; **in the forefront** a vanguardia
foregather [forˈgæðər] *vn* var. de **forgather**
forego [forˈgo] (*pret:* **-went;** *pp:* **-gone**) *va* renunciar, privarse de; preceder; *vn* preceder
foregoing [ˈforˌgo·ɪŋ] o [forˈgo·ɪŋ] *adj* anterior, precedente
foregone [ˈforgɔn] o [ˈforgɑn] *adj* pasado, previo; [forˈgɔn] o [forˈgɑn] *pp de* **forego**
foregone conclusion *s* conclusión inevitable; decisión adoptada de antemano
foreground [ˈforˌgraʊnd] *s* frente, delantera; primer término, primer plano; **in the foreground** al frente; en primer término
forehand [ˈforˌhænd] *s* posición delantera; posición superior; ventaja; golpe derecho; *adj* dado con la palma de la mano hacia delante
forehanded [ˈforˌhændɪd] *adj* ahorrado, frugal; hecho de antemano, oportuno
forehead [ˈfɑrɪd] o [ˈfɔrɪd] *s* frente *f* (*de la cara*); parte delantera
foreign [ˈfɑrɪn] o [ˈfɔrɪn] *adj* extranjero, exterior; extraño; ajeno
foreign affairs *spl* asuntos exteriores
foreign-born [ˈfɑrɪnˌbɔrn] o [ˈfɔrɪnˌbɔrn]

adj nacido en el extranjero, extranjero de nacimiento
foreign commerce *s* comercio exterior
foreigner ['farɪnər] o ['fɔrɪnər] *s* extranjero
foreign exchange *s* cambio exterior o extranjero; divisa
foreignism ['farɪnɪzəm] o ['fɔrɪnɪzəm] *s* extranjerismo
foreign legion *s* (mil.) legión extranjera
foreign minister *s* ministro de asuntos exteriores
foreign missions *spl* (eccl.) misiones
foreign office *s* ministerio de asuntos exteriores; (*caps.*) *s* (Brit.) ministerio de Asuntos Exteriores
foreign trade *s* comercio exterior
forejudge [for'dʒʌdʒ] *va* prejuzgar
foreknew [for'nju] o [for'nu] *pret de* **foreknow**
foreknow [for'no] (*pret:* **-knew;** *pp:* **-known**) *va* saber con anticipación
foreknowledge ['for,nalɪdʒ] o [for'nalɪdʒ] *s* presciencia; (theol.) presciencia divina
foreknown [for'non] *pp de* **foreknow**
foreland ['for,lænd] o ['forlənd] *s* cabo, promontorio
foreleg ['for,lɛg] *s* brazo, pata delantera (*del cuadrúpedo*)
forelock ['for,lak] *s* mechón de pelo que cae sobre la frente; copete (*del caballo*); (mach.) chaveta; **to take time by the forelock** asir, coger o tomar la ocasión por el copete, por la melena o por los cabellos
foreman ['formən] *s* (*pl:* **-men**) capataz, sobrestante, mayoral; contramaestre (*en un taller mecánico*); director, regente; (law) presidente de jurado
foremast ['formәst], ['for,mæst] o ['for,mast] *s* (naut.) palo de trinquete
foremost ['formost] *adj* delantero; primero; principal, más eminente (*de todos*); *adv* primero
forename ['for,nem] *s* nombre de pila
forenamed ['for,nemd] *adj* susodicho
forenoon ['for,nun] *s* mañana; *adj* matinal
forensic [fə'rɛnsɪk] *adj* forense
foreordain [,forər'den] *va* preordinar
foreordination [,forɔrdɪ'neʃən] *s* preordinación
forepart ['for,part] *s* parte delantera; principio, primera parte
forepaw ['for,pɔ] *s* pata delantera, zarpa delantera
forepeak ['for,pik] *s* (naut.) bodega de proa
forequarter ['for,kwɔrtər] *s* cuarto delantero (*de la res*)
foreran [for'ræn] *pret de* **forerun**
forereach [for'ritʃ] *va* (naut.) alcanzar (*otra embarcación*); (naut.) dejar atrás (*otra embarcación*); (fig.) aventajarse a; *vn* (naut.) ganar terreno
forerun [for'rʌn] (*pret:* **-ran;** *pp:* **-run**) *va* preceder; prevenir; dejar atrás
forerunner ['for,rʌnər] o [for'rʌnər] *s* precursor; presagio; antepasado; predecesor; **the Forerunner** el precursor de Cristo (*San Juan*)
foresail ['forsəl] o ['for,sel] *s* (naut.) trinquete; (naut.) trinquetilla
foresaw [for'sɔ] *pret de* **foresee**
foresee [for'si] (*pret:* **-saw;** *pp:* **-seen**) *va* prever
foreseeable [for'siəbəl] *adj* previsible
foreshadow [for'ʃædo] *va* presagiar, prefigurar
foresheet ['for,ʃit] *s* (naut.) escota del trinquete; **foresheets** *spl* (naut.) parte delantera de un buque abierto
foreshore ['for,ʃor] *s* playa comprendida entre los límites de pleamar y bajamar
foreshorten [for'ʃɔrtən] *va* (f.a.) escorzar
foreshortening [for'ʃɔrtənɪŋ] *s* (f.a.) escorzo
foreshow [for'ʃo] (*pret:* **-showed;** *pp:* **-shown**) *va* presagiar, prefigurar
foresight ['for,saɪt] *s* previsión, presciencia; prudencia
foresighted ['for,saɪtɪd] o [,for'saɪtɪd] *adj* previsor, presciente; prudente
foreskin ['for,skɪn] *s* (anat.) prepucio
forest ['farɪst] o ['fɔrɪst] *s* bosque; *adj* forestal; *va* plantar (*un terreno*) de árboles, convertir (*un terreno*) en bosque
forestall [for'stɔl] *va* impedir, prevenir; (com.) acaparar
forestation [,farɪs'teʃən] o [,fɔrɪs'teʃən] *s* silvicultura
forestay ['for,ste] *s* (naut.) estay del trinquete
forestaysail [,for'stesəl] o [,for'ste,sel] *s* (naut.) trinquetilla
forester ['farɪstər] o ['fɔrɪstər] *s* silvicultor; guardabosques; (zool.) canguro gigante
forest ranger *s* guarda forestal
forest reserve *s* (U.S.A.) bosque nacional
forestry ['farɪstrɪ] o ['fɔrɪstrɪ] *s* silvicultura, dasonomía, ciencia forestal
foretackle ['for,tækəl] *s* (naut.) aparejo del gancho del trinquete
foretaste ['for,test] *s* anticipación, goce anticipado; [for'test] *va* anticipar, catar o conocer con anticipación
foretell [for'tɛl] (*pret & pp:* **-told**) *va* predecir
foretellable [for'tɛləbəl] *adj* pronosticable
forethought ['for,θɔt] *s* premeditación, providencia, prudencia
foretoken ['for,tokən] *s* presagio; [for'tokən] *va* presagiar
foretold [for'told] *pret & pp de* **foretell**
foretop ['fortəp] o ['for,tap] *s* (naut.) cofa de trinquete; ['for,tap] copete (*del caballo*)
foretopgallant mast [,fortə'gælənt] o [,fortap'gælənt] *s* (naut.) mastelerillo de juanete de proa
foretopmast [for'tapməst] *s* (naut.) mastelero de velacho, mastelero de proa
foretopmast staysail *s* (naut.) contrafoque
foretopsail [,for'tapsəl] o [,for'tap,sel] *s* (naut.) velacho
forever [fɔr'ɛvər] *adv* siempre; para siempre o por siempre
forever and a day o **forever and ever** *adv* por siempre jamás
forevermore [fɔr,ɛvər'mor] *adv* por siempre, por siempre jamás
forewarn [for'wɔrn] *va* prevenir con anticipación
forewent [for'wɛnt] *pret de* **forego**
foreword ['for,wʌrd] *s* advertencia, prefacio
forfeit ['fɔrfɪt] *s* multa, pena; prenda perdida; **forfeits** *spl* prendas (*juego*); *adj* perdido; *va* perder, perder el derecho a
forfeiture ['fɔrfɪtʃər] *s* multa, pena; prenda perdida
forfend [fɔr'fɛnd] *va* defender, proteger; (archaic) impedir, evitar
forgather [fɔr'gæðər] *vn* reunirse; encontrarse (*por casualidad*); **to forgather with** asociarse con, fraternizar con
forgave [fɔr'gev] *pret de* **forgive**
forge [fordʒ] *s* fragua (*fogón*); herrería (*taller del herrero*); fundición (*fábrica*); *va* fraguar, forjar; falsificar (*la firma de otra persona*); (fig.) fraguar, forjar (*p.ej., mentiras*); *vn* fraguar, forjar; falsificar; **to forge ahead** avanzar despacio y con esfuerzo; **to forge ahead of** alcanzar y dejar atrás haciendo esfuerzos
forger ['fordʒər] *s* fraguador, forjador; falsificador
forgery ['fordʒərɪ] *s* (*pl:* **-ies**) falsificación; (philately) falso (*sello falsificado*)
forget [fɔr'gɛt] (*pret:* **-got;** *pp:* **-gotten** o **-got;** *ger:* **-getting**) *va* olvidar, olvidarse de; olvidársele a uno, p.ej., **I forgot my passport** se me olvidó mi pasaporte; **forget it!** (coll.) ¡dejémoslo!; **to forget oneself** interesarse por los demás sin pensar en sí mismo; ser distraído; propasarse; **to forget to** + *inf* olvidar + *inf*, olvidarse de + *inf*, olvidársele a uno + *inf*, p.ej., **I forgot to close the window** se me olvidó cerrar la ventana
forgetful [fɔr'gɛtfəl] *adj* olvidado, olvidadizo; descuidado
forgetfulness [fɔr'gɛtfəlnɪs] *s* olvido, falta de memoria; descuido
forget-me-not [fɔr'gɛtmi,nat] *s* (bot.) nomeolvides
forgettable [fɔr'gɛtəbəl] *adj* olvidable
forging ['fordʒɪŋ] *s* forjadura; pieza forjada
forgivable [fɔr'gɪvəbəl] *adj* perdonable
forgive [fɔr'gɪv] (*pret:* **-gave;** *pp:* **-given**) *va* perdonar
forgiven [fɔr'gɪvən] *pp de* **forgive**

forgiveness [fɔr'gɪvnɪs] *s* perdón
forgiving [fɔr'gɪvɪŋ] *adj* perdonador, clemente
forgo [fɔr'go] (*pret:* **-went;** *pp:* **-gone**) *va* renunciar, privarse de
forgone [fɔr'gɔn] o [fɔr'gɑn] *pp de* **forgo**
forgot [fɔr'gɑt] *pret & pp de* **forget**
forgotten [fɔr'gɑtən] *pp de* **forget**
fork [fɔrk] *s* horca; horquilla (*de jardinero; de la bicicleta*); horqueta u horcadura (*de un árbol*); horcajo (*de dos ríos*); bieldo (*para aventar*); tenedor (*utensilio de mesa*); bifurcación; púa (*de horca*); ramal (*de ferrocarril*); afluente (*de un río*); *va* ahorquillar; cargar o hacinar con horquilla; cavar con horquilla; beldar; (chess) atacar o amenazar (*dos piezas*) a la vez; **to fork out** u **over** (slang) entregar; *vn* bifurcarse
forked [fɔrkt] *adj* ahorquillado, bifurcado
forked lightning *s* relámpago en zigzag
fork lift truck *s* carretilla de horquilla, montacarga de horquilla
forlorn [fɔr'lɔrn] *adj* abandonado, desamparado; triste; desesperado; **forlorn of** privado de
forlorn hope *s* (mil.) centinela perdida; (fig.) empresa desesperada
form [fɔrm] *s* forma; estado; formulario; banco (*para sentarse*); grado (*en las escuelas*); encofrado (*para el hormigón*); (print.) molde; **in due form** en debida forma; **in form** en forma; (sport) en forma; *va* formar; (elec.) formar (*las placas de un acumulador*); *vn* formarse
formal ['fɔrməl] *adj* formal; de etiqueta; ceremonioso; en forma
formal attire *s* vestido de etiqueta
formal call *s* visita de cumplido
formaldehyde [fɔr'mældɪhaɪd] *s* (chem.) formaldehido
formal garden *s* jardín de estilo francés, jardín a la francesa
formalin ['fɔrməlɪn] *s* (chem.) formalina
formalism ['fɔrməlɪzəm] *s* formalismo
formalist ['fɔrməlɪst] *s* formalista
formalistic [,fɔrmə'lɪstɪk] *adj* formalista
formality [fɔr'mælɪtɪ] *s* (*pl:* **-ties**) formalidad; etiqueta, ceremonia
formalize ['fɔrməlaɪz] *va* formalizar
formal party *s* recepción de gala, reunión de etiqueta
formal speech *s* discurso de aparato
format ['fɔrmæt] *s* formato
formate ['fɔrmet] *s* (chem.) formiato
formation [fɔr'meʃən] *s* formación; (elec., geol. & mil.) formación
formative ['fɔrmətɪv] *adj* formativo
former ['fɔrmər] *adj* anterior; antiguo, pasado; primero (*de dos*); **the former** aquél; *s* formador; plantilla
formerly ['fɔrmərlɪ] *adv* antes, en otro tiempo
form-fitting ['fɔrm'fɪtɪŋ] *adj* ajustado, ceñido al cuerpo; que se adapta bien al cuerpo
formic ['fɔrmɪk] *adj* fórmico
formic acid *s* (chem.) ácido fórmico
formidable ['fɔrmɪdəbəl] *adj* formidable
formless ['fɔrmlɪs] *adj* informe, sin forma
form letter *s* carta general
formol ['fɔrmol] o ['fɔrmɑl] *s* (chem.) formol
formula ['fɔrmjələ] *s* (*pl:* **-las** o **-lae** [li]) fórmula
formulary ['fɔrmjə,lɛrɪ] *adj* formulario; *s* (*pl:* **-ies**) formulario; (pharm.) formulario
formulate ['fɔrmjəlet] *va* formular
formulation [,fɔrmjə'leʃən] *s* formulación
formulator ['fɔrmjə,letər] *s* formulador
fornicate ['fɔrnɪket] *vn* fornicar
fornication [,fɔrnɪ'keʃən] *s* fornicación
fornicator ['fɔrnɪ,ketər] *s* fornicador
forsake [fɔr'sek] (*pret:* **-sook;** *pp:* **-saken**) *va* abandonar, desamparar; dejar, desechar
forsaken [fɔr'sekən] *adj* abandonado, desamparado; *pp de* **forsake**
forsook [fɔr'suk] *pret de* **forsake**
forsooth [fɔr'suθ] *adv* en verdad, por cierto
forspent [fɔr'spɛnt] *adj* agotado de fuerzas
forswear [fɔr'swɛr] (*pret:* **-swore;** *pp:* **-sworn**) *va* abjurar; negar con juramento; **to forswear oneself** perjurarse; *vn* perjurar
forswore [fɔr'swor] *pret de* **forswear**
forsworn [fɔr'sworn] *adj* perjuro; *pp de* **forswear**
forsythia [fɔr'sɪθɪə] o [fɔr'saɪθɪə] *s* (bot.) forsitia
fort [fort] *s* fortín, fuerte; **to hold the fort** defenderse contra ataque
forte [fort] *s* fuerte (*afición o talento de uno*)
forth [forθ] *adv* adelante, delante, hacia adelante; fuera; afuera; a la vista; **and so forth** y así sucesivamente; **from this day forth** de hoy en adelante; **to go forth** salir
forthcoming ['forθ,kʌmɪŋ] o [,forθ'kʌmɪŋ] *adj* próximo, venidero; disponible; *s* salida, venida
forthright ['forθ,raɪt] o [,forθ'raɪt] *adj* derecho, sincero, extremoso, sin ambages; *adv* derecho, siempre adelante; francamente; luego, en seguida
forthwith [,forθ'wɪð] o [,forθ'wɪθ] *adv* inmediatamente, sin dilación
fortieth ['fɔrtɪɪθ] *adj & s* cuadragésimo; cuarentavo
fortification [,fɔrtɪfɪ'keʃən] *s* fortificación
fortify ['fɔrtɪfaɪ] (*pret & pp:* **-fied**) *va* fortificar; encabezar (*vinos*); *vn* fortificarse
fortitude ['fɔrtɪtjud] o ['fɔrtɪtud] *s* fortaleza, firmeza, valor
fortnight ['fɔrtnaɪt] o ['fɔrtnɪt] *s* quincena, quince días
fortnightly ['fɔrtnaɪtlɪ] *adj* quincenal; *adv* quincenalmente; *s* (*pl:* **-lies**) periódico quincenal
fortress ['fɔrtrɪs] *s* fortaleza, plaza fuerte
fortuitous [fɔr'tjuɪtəs] o [fɔr'tuɪtəs] *adj* fortuito, casual
fortuity [fɔr'tjuɪtɪ] o [fɔr'tuɪtɪ] *s* (*pl:* **-ties**) fortuitez, casualidad; accidente; caso imprevisto
fortunate ['fɔrtʃənɪt] *adj* afortunado
Fortunate Islands *spl* (myth.) islas Afortunadas
fortune ['fɔrtʃən] *s* fortuna; **to tell one's fortune** decirle a uno la buenaventura
fortune hunter *s* el que quiere emparentar con una familia rica, cazador de fortunas
fortuneteller ['fɔrtʃən,tɛlər] *s* adivino, agorero, sortílego
forty ['fɔrtɪ] *adj* cuarenta; *s* (*pl:* **-ties**) cuarenta
forty hours' devotion *s* (eccl.) las cuarenta horas
Forty-Niners [,fɔrtɪ'naɪnərz] *spl* gente que fué a California en busca del oro en 1849
forty winks *spl* una siestecita
forum ['forəm] *s* (*pl:* **-rums** o **-ra** [rə]) (hist. & law) foro; asamblea (*en que se tratan asuntos públicos*); (fig.) tribunal (*p.ej., de la opinión pública*)
forward ['fɔrwərd] *adj* delantero; adelantado, precoz; ansioso, listo; atrevido, impertinente; de avance, p.ej., **forward step** paso de avance; *adv* adelante; hacia adelante; en la delantera; **to bring forward** aducir; **to carry forward** (coll.) pasar a cuenta nueva; **to come** o **to go forward** adelantarse; **to look forward to** esperar con placer anticipado; *va* reexpedir, hacer seguir; fomentar, patrocinar; **please forward** hágase seguir, reexpídase, dele curso; *s* (sport) delantero
forward delivery *s* (coll.) entrega en fecha futura
forwarder ['fɔrwərdər] *s* agente expedidor, comisionista expedidor
forwardness ['fɔrwərdnɪs] *s* adelantamiento; precocidad; ansia, ahinco; impertinencia, descaro
forward pass *s* (football) lanzamiento del balón en dirección de la meta del equipo contrario
forwards ['fɔrwərdz] *adv* adelante; hacia adelante; en la delantera
forwent [fɔr'wɛnt] *pret de* **forgo**
fossa ['fɑsə] *s* (*pl:* **-sae** [si]) (anat.) fosa
fosse [fɑs] *s* foso; (fort.) foso
fossil ['fɑsɪl] *adj & s* fósil; (fig.) fósil
fossiliferous [,fɑsɪ'lɪfərəs] *adj* fosilífero
fossilization [,fɑsɪlɪ'zeʃən] *s* fosilización
fossilize ['fɑsɪlaɪz] *va* convertir en fósil; *vn* fosilizarse
foster ['fɑstər] o ['fɔstər] *adj* adoptivo, alle-

gado (*por la crianza y no por la sangre*); *va* fomentar; criar; cuidar con ternura
foster brother *s* hermano de leche, hermano de crianza
foster child *s* alumno, niño criado como si fuera hijo
foster daughter *s* hija de leche, hija adoptiva
foster father *s* padre adoptivo
foster home *s* hogar de adopción, hogar en que se asigna a un menor por orden judicial
foster land *s* país adoptivo
foster mother *s* madre adoptiva; ama de leche
foster parent *s* padre o madre adoptiva
foster sister *s* hermana de leche, hermana de crianza
foster son *s* hijo de leche, hijo adoptivo
Foucault current [fu'ko] *s* (elec.) corriente de Foucault
fought [fɔt] *pret & pp de* **fight**
foul [faʊl] *adj* asqueroso, puerco; fétido; viciado (*aire*); obsceno; pérfido; nefando; contrario (*viento*); malo (*dícese, p.ej., del tiempo*); atascado, obstruído; (baseball) fuera del cuadro; (naut.) enredado; (naut.) sin carenar; (print.) lleno de errores y correcciones; (sport) sucio, innoble; **to go, fall** o **run foul of** chocar contra; enredarse en; (fig.) enredarse con; *va* ensuciar; engrasar; atascar, obstruir; (naut.) chocar contra; (naut.) enredarse en; (naut.) cubrir (*las lapas el casco de un barco*); (baseball) volear (*la pelota*) fuera del cuadro; (sport) hacer una jugada prohibida contra; *vn* ensuciarse; engrasarse (*un motor*); (baseball) volear la pelota fuera del cuadro; (sport) hacer una jugada prohibida
foulard [fu'lɑrd] *s* fular
foul ball *s* (baseball) mal batazo, pelota que cae fuera del cuadro
foul-mouthed ['faʊl'maʊðd] o ['faʊl'maʊθt] *adj* deslenguado, malhablado
foulness ['faʊlnɪs] *s* asquerosidad, porquería; fetidez; obscenidad; perfidia; maldad
foul play *s* traición, violencia; (sport) juego sucio, jugada prohibida
foul-spoken ['faʊl'spokən] *adj* malhablado
found [faʊnd] *va* fundar; fundir (*un metal; una estatua*); **to found on** o **upon** fundar en o sobre; *pret & pp de* **find**
foundation [faʊn'deʃən] *s* fundación (*acción o efecto de fundar; donación; institución benéfica*); fundamento (*base, fondo*); (arch.) cimiento; **to dig the foundations** abrir los cimientos
foundation stone *s* piedra fundamental
founder ['faʊndər] *s* fundador; fundidor (*de metales*); (vet.) infosura, hormiguillo; *va* maltratar (*un caballo*); hundir, echar a pique; *vn* desplomarse; tropezar, despearse (*un caballo*); fracasar; hundirse, irse a fondo, irse a pique
foundling ['faʊndlɪŋ] *s* expósito, niño expósito
foundling hospital *s* casa de expósitos
foundry ['faʊndrɪ] *s* (*pl:* **-ries**) fundición (*acción; fábrica*)
foundryman ['faʊndrɪmən] *s* (*pl:* **-men**) fundidor
fount [faʊnt] *s* fuente
fountain ['faʊntən] *s* fuente
fountainhead ['faʊntən,hɛd] *s* nacimiento (*de un río*); (fig.) nacimiento (*origen primitivo*)
Fountain of Youth *s* Fuente de la juventud
fountain pen *s* pluma fuente, pluma estilográfica
fountain syringe *s* mangueta
four [for] *adj* cuatro; *s* cuatro; **on all fours** a cuatro pies, a gatas; igual, parejo, al mismo nivel; **four o'clock** las cuatro; **four of a kind** quínola
four-cornered ['for'kɔrnərd] *adj* cuadrangular
four-cycle ['for,saɪkəl] *adj* (mach.) de cuatro tiempos; *s* (mach.) ciclo de cuatro tiempos
four-cylinder ['for,sɪlɪndər] *adj* (mach.) de cuatro cilindros; **a four-cylinder motor** un cuatro cilindros
four-dimensional ['fordɪ'mɛnʃənəl] *adj* de cuatro dimensiones
four flush *s* (poker) cuatro naipes del mismo palo; bluff, finta
four-flush ['for,flʌʃ] *vn* (slang) bravear, fanfarronear, papelonear
fourflusher ['for,flʌʃər] *s* (slang) bravucón, fanfarrón, impostor, embustero
fourfold ['for,fold] *adj* cuádruple
four-footed ['for'fʊtɪd] *adj* cuadrúpedo
four-handed ['for'hændɪd] *adj* que tiene cuatro manos; cuadrúmano; para cuatro jugadores; (mus.) a cuatro manos
four hundred *adj* cuatrocientos; *s* cuatrocientos; **the four hundred** la alta sociedad
Fourierism ['fʊrɪərɪzəm] *s* furierismo
four-in-hand ['forɪn,hænd] *adj* tirado por cuatro caballos (*coche*); de nudo corredizo (*corbata*); *s* coche tirado por cuatro caballos; tiro de cuatro caballos; corbata de nudo corredizo
four-in-hand tie *s* corbata de nudo corredizo, corbata de pañuelo
four-lane ['for'len] *adj* cuadriviario
four-leaf ['for,lif] o **four-leaved** ['for,livd] *adj* cuadrifoliado
four-legged ['for'lɛgɪd] o ['for'lɛgd] *adj* de cuatro piernas; cuadrúpedo
four-letter word ['for'lɛtər] *s* palabra impúdica de cuatro letras (*o muy corta*)
four-motor ['for'motər] *adj* cuadrimotor
four-motor plane *s* (aer.) cuadrimotor
four-o'clock ['forə,klɑk] *s* (bot.) arrebolera, dondiego
fourpence ['forpəns] *s* cuatro peniques; moneda de cuatro peniques
fourpenny ['for,pɛnɪ] o ['forpənɪ] *s* (*pl:* **-nies**) cuatro peniques; moneda de cuatro peniques; *adj* de cuatro peniques
four-poster ['for'postər] *s* cama imperial
fourscore ['for'skor] *s* cuatro veintenas; *adj* ochenta
four seas *spl* los mares que circundan las Islas Británicas
four-seater ['for'sitər] *s* coche de cuatro plazas; (aer.) cuadriplaza
foursome ['forsəm] *s* cuatrinca; (sport) partida en la que cada uno de los dos bandos se compone de dos personas; (sport) conjunto de cuatro jugadores
foursquare ['for'skwɛr] *adj* cuadrado; franco, sincero; firme, constante; ['for,skwɛr] *s* cuadrado
four-stroke cycle ['for,strok] *s* (mach.) ciclo de cuatro tiempos
fourteen ['for'tin] *adj & s* catorce
Fourteen Points, The los catorce puntos (*del presidente Wilson*)
fourteenth ['for'tinθ] *adj* décimocuarto; catorzavo; *s* décimocuarto; catorzavo; catorce (*en las fechas*)
fourth [forθ] *adj* cuarto; *s* cuarto; cuatro (*en las fechas*); (mus.) cuarta
fourth dimension *s* (math.) cuarta dimensión
fourth estate *s* cuarto poder (*la prensa, el periodismo*)
fourthly ['forθlɪ] *adv* en cuarto lugar
Fourth of July *s* cuatro de julio (*fiesta nacional de los EE.UU.*)
four-way ['for,we] *adj* de cuatro direcciones, de cuatro pasos
four-way switch *s* (elec.) conmutador de cuatro terminales
four-wheel ['for'hwil] *adj* de cuatro ruedas; en las cuatro ruedas
four-wheel brakes *spl* (aut.) frenos en las cuatro ruedas
four-wheel drive *s* propulsión o tracción en cuatro ruedas
fovea ['fovɪə] *s* (*pl:* **-ae** [i]) fóvea; (bot.) fóvea
fovea centralis [sɛn'trelɪs] *s* (anat.) fóvea central
fowl [faʊl] *s* ave; gallo, gallina, pollo; carne de ave; *vn* cazar aves de caza
fowler ['faʊlər] *s* cazador de aves
fowling piece *s* escopeta
fox [fɑks] *s* (zool.) zorra; zorro (*piel*); (fig.) zorro (*persona muy taimada*); *va* engañar con astucia; descolorar, manchar
foxglove ['fɑks,glʌv] *s* (bot.) dedalera
foxhole ['fɑks,hol] *s* (mil.) pozo de lobo
foxhound ['fɑks,haʊnd] *s* perro raposero
fox hunt *s* caza de zorras
foxiness ['fɑksɪnɪs] *s* zorrería
fox squirrel *s* (zool.) ardilla negra
foxtail ['fɑks,tel] *s* rabo de zorra; (bot.) rabo de zorra

foxtail grass *s* (bot.) alopecuro
foxtail millet *s* (bot.) panizo
fox terrier *s* fox-térrier
fox trot *s* trote corto (*de caballo*); fox-trot (*danza y música*)
fox-trot ['faks,trat] (*pret & pp:* **-trotted;** *ger:* **-trotting**) *vn* ir al trote corto; bailar el fox-trot
foxy ['faksɪ] *adj* (*comp:* **-ier;** *super:* **-iest**) astuto, taimado; descolorado, manchado
foyer ['fɔɪər] o [fwa'je] *s* salón de entrada; (theat.) salón de descanso, foyer
F.P.S. abr. de **foot-pound-second**
fr. abr. de **fragment, franc** y **from**
Fr. abr. de **Father, France, French** y **Friday**
Fra [fra] *s* fray
fracas ['frekəs] *s* altercado, gresca, riña
fraction ['frækʃən] *s* fracción; pequeña porción; (math.) fracción, quebrado
fractional ['frækʃənəl] *adj* fraccionario; fraccionado; fraccionario (*dinero, moneda*); insignificante
fractional distillation *s* (chem.) destilación fraccionada
fractionate ['frækʃənet] *va* (chem.) fraccionar
fractionating tower ['frækʃə,netɪŋ] *s* torre fraccionadora
fractionation [,frækʃə'neʃən] *s* (chem.) fraccionamiento
fractionize ['frækʃənaɪz] *va* fraccionar
fractious ['frækʃəs] *adj* reacio, rebelón; displicente, regañón
fracture ['fræktʃər] *s* fractura; (geol. & surg.) fractura; *va* fracturar; *vn* fracturarse
fraenum ['frinəm] *s* (*pl:* **-na** [nə]) var. de **frenum**
fragile ['frædʒɪl] *adj* frágil
fragility [frə'dʒɪlɪtɪ] *s* fragilidad
fragment ['frægmənt] *s* fragmento
fragmental [fræg'mentəl] o **fragmentary** ['frægmən,terɪ] *adj* fragmentario
fragmentation [,frægmən'teʃən] *s* fragmentación; (biol.) fragmentación
fragrance ['fregrəns] *s* fragancia
fragrant ['fregrənt] *adj* fragante
frail [frel] *adj* frágil, débil
frailty ['freltɪ] *s* (*pl:* **-ties**) fragilidad, debilidad
fraise [frez] *s* fresa (*gorguera*); (fort.) frisa; *va* (mach.) fresar
frambesia [fræm'biʒə] *s* (path.) frambesia
frame [frem] *s* armazón, esqueleto, estructura; marco (*de un cuadro, espejo, etc.*); armadura, montura (*de unas gafas*); complexión, constitución; bastidor (*para bordar*); sistema (*p.ej., de gobierno*); (mov. & telv.) encuadre; (naut.) cuaderna; *va* formar, forjar; idear; ajustar, construir; enmarcar; formular, redactar; (slang) incriminar (*a un inocente*) por medio de una estratagema; (slang) prefijar (*un resultado deseado*) por medios fraudulentos
frame house *s* casa de madera
frame of mind *s* estado de ánimo, manera de pensar
frame of reference *s* (math.) sistema de coordenadas o de ejes de coordenadas; puntos de referencia
framer ['fremər] *s* constructor; carpintero de obra de afuera; fabricante de marcos
frame-up ['frem,ʌp] *s* (slang) treta, estratagema para incriminar a un inocente
framework ['frem,wʌrk] *s* armazón, esqueleto, estructura, marco
franc [fræŋk] *s* franco
France [fræns] o [frans] *s* Francia
Frances ['frænsɪs] o ['fransɪs] *s* Francisca
Franche-Comté [frɑ̃ʃkõ'te] *s* el Franco Condado
franchise ['fræntʃaɪz] *s* franquicia, privilegio; sufragio
Francis ['frænsɪs] o ['fransɪs] *s* Francisco
Franciscan [fræn'sɪskən] *adj & s* franciscano
francium ['frænsɪəm] *s* (chem.) francio
Franco-German ['fræŋko'dʒʌrmən] *adj* francoalemán
Francophile ['fræŋkofaɪl] *adj & s* francófilo
Francophobe ['fræŋkofob] *adj & s* francófobo
Franco-Prussian War ['fræŋko'prʌʃən] *s* guerra Francoprusiana
franc-tireur [frɑ̃ti'rœr] *s* (*pl:* **francs-tireurs** [frɑ̃ti'rœr]) francotirador
frangible ['frændʒɪbəl] *adj* frangible
frank [fræŋk] *adj* franco; *s* carta franca, envío franco; franquicia de correos; sello indicador de franquicia; *va* franquear; (*cap.*) *s* Franco; Paco, Francho (*nombre abreviado de Francisco*)
Frankenstein ['fræŋkənstaɪn] *s* personaje fabuloso que crea un monstruo que no puede gobernar; cosa que llega a ser causa de la ruina de su inventor
Frankfurt am Main ['fraŋkfurt am 'maɪn] *s* Francfort del Main
Frankfurt an der Oder [an dər 'odər] *s* Francfurt del Oder
frankfurter ['fræŋkfərtər] *s* salchicha (*de carne de vaca y de cerdo*)
frankincense ['fræŋkɪnsɛns] *s* olíbano
Frankish ['fræŋkɪʃ] *adj* franco; *s* franco (*idioma*)
franklin ['fræŋklɪn] *s* (Brit.) poseedor de feudo franco (*de los siglos XIV y XV*)
frankness ['fræŋknɪs] *s* franqueza (*candor, sinceridad, abertura*)
frantic ['fræntɪk] *adj* frenético
frantically ['fræntɪkəlɪ] *adv* frenéticamente
Franz Josef Land ['frants 'jozɛf ,lænd] *s* archipiélago de Francisco José
frappé [fræ'pe] *adj* helado; *s* helado (*de jugo de fruta azucarado*)
frat [fræt] *s* (slang) club de estudiantes (*en las universidades norteamericanas*)
fraternal [frə'tʌrnəl] *adj* fraternal
fraternal twins *spl* gemelos fraternos o heterólogos
fraternity [frə'tʌrnɪtɪ] *s* (*pl:* **-ties**) fraternidad; cofradía; asociación secreta; (U.S.A.) club de estudiantes
fraternization [,frætərnɪ'zeʃən] *s* fraternización
fraternize ['frætərnaɪz] *vn* fraternizar
fratricidal [,frætrɪ'saɪdəl] o [,fretrɪ'saɪdəl] *adj* fratricida
fratricide ['frætrɪsaɪd] o ['fretrɪsaɪd] *s* fratricidio (*acción*); fratricida (*persona*)
fraud [frɔd] *s* fraude; (coll.) impostor
fraudulence ['frɔdʒələns] o **fraudulency** ['frɔdʒələnsɪ] *s* fraudulencia
fraudulent ['frɔdʒələnt] *adj* fraudulento
fraught [frɔt] *adj* cargado, lleno; **fraught with** cargado de, lleno de
Fraunhofer lines ['fraun,hofər] *spl* (phys.) rayas de Fraunhofer
fraxinella [,fræksɪ'nɛlə] *s* (bot.) fresnillo, díctamo blanco
fray [fre] *s* batalla, combate, riña; *va* desgastar, ludir; raer; *vn* raerse, deshilacharse
frazzle ['fræzəl] *s* condición de deshilachado; jirón; gran cansancio; **in a frazzle** deshilachado; rendido de cansancio; *va* desgastar, raer; hacer jirones; rendir de cansancio
freak [frik] *s* curiosidad, monstruosidad, rareza; fenómeno (*persona*); capricho, extravagancia; *adj* muy raro e inesperado
freakish ['frikɪʃ] *adj* muy raro; antojadizo, caprichoso
freckle ['frɛkəl] *s* peca; *va* motear; *vn* ponerse pecoso
freckle-faced ['frɛkəl,fest] *adj* pecoso
freckly ['frɛklɪ] *adj* pecoso
Fred [frɛd] o **Freddy** ['frɛdɪ] *s* Federiquito
Frederica [,frɛdə'rikə] *s* Federica
Frederick ['frɛdərɪk] *s* Federico
free [fri] *adj* (*comp:* **freer** ['friər]; *super:* **freest** ['friɪst]) libre; franco, gratis; liberal, generoso; **to be free with** dar abundantemente; usar de, abundantemente; **to make free with** disponer de (*una cosa*) como si fuera cosa propia; **to set free** libertar; *adv* libremente; en libertad; gratis, de balde; *va* libertar, poner en libertad; manumitir; soltar, desembarazar; exentar, eximir
free alongside ship *adj* libre al costado del vapor
free and easy *adj* despreocupado, sin ceremonia
freeboard ['fri,bord] *s* (naut.) francobordo, obra muerta
freebooter ['fri,butər] *s* pirata, forbante
freebooting ['fri,butɪŋ] *s* piratería

freeborn ['fri,bɔrn] *adj* nacido libre; propio o digno de un pueblo libre
free city *s* ciudad libre
free delivery *s* (U.S.A.) distribución gratuita del correo
freedman ['fridmən] *s* (*pl:* **-men**) liberto, manumiso
freedom ['fridəm] *s* libertad; **to receive the freedom of the city** ser recibido como ciudadano de honor
freedom of assembly *s* libertad de reunión
freedom of speech *s* libertad de palabra
freedom of the press *s* libertad de imprenta o de prensa
freedom of the seas *s* libertad de los mares
freedom of worship *s* libertad de cultos
freedwoman ['frid,wʊmən] *s* (*pl:* **-women**) liberta, manumisa
free energy *s* (phys.) energía libre
free enterprise *s* libertad de empresa
free fight *s* sarracina, riña tumultuaria
free-for-all ['frifər,ɔl] *adj* para todos; *s* concurso, carrera, pugna, etc. abiertas a todo el mundo; sarracina, riña tumultuaria
free hand *s* carta blanca, plena libertad
freehand ['fri,hænd] *adj* a pulso (*dícese del dibujo*)
freehanded ['fri,hændɪd] *adj* dadivoso, liberal
freehold ['fri,hold] *s* (law) feudo franco; (law) posesión de un feudo franco
freeholder ['fri,holdər] *s* poseedor de feudo franco
free lance *s* soldado mercenario; hombre despreocupado e independiente; periodista, artista u otra persona que trabaja independientemente
free-lance ['fri'læns] o ['fri'lɑns] *adj* mercenario; independiente; *vn* ser independiente
free list *s* (com.) lista de artículos exentos de derechos de aduana
freeloader ['fri,lodər] *s* (slang) esponja, gorrón
free lunch *s* tapas, tapitas
freeman ['frimən] *s* (*pl:* **-men**) hombre libre; ciudadano
Freemason ['fri,mesən] *s* francmasón
Freemasonic [,frimə'sɑnɪk] *adj* francmasónico
Freemasonry ['fri,mesənrɪ] *s* francmasonería; (*l.c.*) *s* comprensión mutua, compañerismo, simpatía natural
free of charge *adj* gratis, de balde
free on board *adj* franco a bordo
free port *s* puerto franco
freesia ['friʒə] *s* (bot.) fresia
free silver *s* acuñación libre de la plata
freesilverite [,fri'sɪlvəraɪt] *s* argentista
free-spoken ['fri'spokən] *adj* franco, sin reserva
freestone ['fri,ston] *adj* abridero, de hueso libre; *s* piedra franca; abridero, fruta abridera
free syllable *s* (phonet.) sílaba libre
freethinker ['fri'θɪŋkər] *s* librepensador
freethinking ['fri'θɪŋkɪŋ] *adj* librepensador; *s* librepensamiento
free thought *s* librepensamiento
free trade *s* libre cambio, librecambio
freetrader ['fri'tredər] *s* librecambista
free-trading ['fri'tredɪŋ] *adj* librecambista
free verse *s* poesía libre de toda traba
freeway ['fri,we] *s* autopista
freewheel ['fri'hwil] *s* (mach.) rueda libre
freewheeling ['fri'hwilɪŋ] *s* (mach.) marcha a rueda libre
free will *s* libre albedrío; propia voluntad
freewill ['fri'wɪl] *adj* voluntario; del libre albedrío
freeze [friz] *s* helada; (*pret:* **froze;** *pp:* **frozen**) *va* helar; congelar (*p.ej., los créditos*); **to freeze out** (coll.) deshacerse de (*p.ej., un rival*) quitándole la clientela; *vn* helarse; congelarse; helársele a uno la sangre (*p.ej., de miedo*); **to freeze on to** (coll.) quedar fuertemente agarrado a; **to freeze to death** morir helado, morir de frío
freezer ['frizər] *s* congelador; heladora, sorbetera
freezing mixture *s* mezcla refrigerante
freezing point *s* punto de congelación
freight [fret] *s* carga; mercancías, tren de mercancías; (naut.) flete; **by freight** por carga, como carga; (rail.) en pequeña velocidad; *va* cargar, enviar por carga
freightage ['fretɪdʒ] *s* carga; transporte
freight agent *s* (rail.) agente de carga
freight car *s* (rail.) vagón de carga, vagón de mercancías
freight engine *s* (rail.) locomotora de mercancías
freighter ['fretər] *s* (naut.) buque de carga, buque carguero
freight platform *s* (rail.) muelle
freight station *s* (rail.) estación de carga
freight train *s* mercancías, tren de mercancías
freight yard *s* (rail.) patio de carga
French [frɛntʃ] *adj* francés; *spl* franceses; *ssg* francés (*idioma*)
French and Indian War *s* guerra entre Francia e Inglaterra en tierras americanas
French Canadian *s* francocanadiense
French-Canadian ['frɛntʃkə'nedɪən] *adj* francocanadiense
French chalk *s* jaboncillo de sastre
French Congo *s* el Congo Francés
French doors *spl* puertas vidrieras dobles
French drain *s* desagüe de piedra en una zanja
French dressing *s* aliño francés, salsa francesa (*para ensaladas*)
French Equatorial Africa *s* el África Ecuatorial Francesa
French fried potatoes *spl* patatas fritas en trocitos
French Guiana *s* la Guayana Francesa
French Guinea *s* la Guinea Francesa
French honeysuckle *s* (bot.) zulla
French horn *s* (mus.) trompa de armonía
French horsepower *s* (mech.) caballo de fuerza, caballo de vapor (*736 vatios*)
Frenchify ['frɛntʃɪfaɪ] (*pret & pp:* **-fied**) *va* afrancesar
French Indochina *s* la Indochina Francesa
French leave *s* despedida a la francesa; **to take French leave** despedirse, irse o marcharse a la francesa
Frenchman ['frɛntʃmən] *s* (*pl:* **-men**) francés
French marigold *s* (bot.) damasquina, clavel de las Indias
French Morocco *s* el Marruecos Francés
French telephone *s* var. de **handset**
French toast *s* pan frito después de ser empapado en una mezcla de leche y huevos batidos
French West Africa *s* el África Occidental Francesa
French West Indies *spl* Antillas Francesas
French window *s* ventana de dos hojas de cristal
Frenchwoman ['frɛntʃ,wʊmən] *s* (*pl:* **-women**) francesa
Frenchy ['frɛntʃɪ] *s* (*pl:* **-chies**) (coll.) franchote
frenum ['frinəm] *s* (*pl:* **-na** [nə]) (anat.) frenillo
frenzied ['frɛnzɪd] *adj* frenético
frenzy ['frɛnzɪ] *s* (*pl:* **-zies**) frenesí
freon ['friɑn] *s* freón
frequency ['frikwənsɪ] *s* (*pl:* **-cies**) frecuencia
frequency changer *s* (elec.) cambiador de frecuencia
frequency control *s* (rad.) control de la frecuencia
frequency converter *s* (elec.) convertidor de frecuencia
frequency curve *s* (statistics) curva de frecuencias
frequency distribution *s* (statistics) distribución de frecuencias
frequency list *s* lista de frecuencia (*de palabras*)
frequency meter *s* (elec.) frecuencímetro
frequency modulation *s* (rad.) modulación de frecuencia, frecuencia modulada
frequent ['frikwənt] *adj* frecuente; [frɪ'kwɛnt] *va* frecuentar
frequentation [,frikwən'teʃən] *s* frecuentación
frequentative [frɪ'kwɛntətɪv] *adj & s* (gram.) frecuentativo
frequenter [frɪ'kwɛntər] *s* frecuentador

frequently ['frikwəntlɪ] *adv* frecuentemente, con frequencia
fresco ['frɛsko] *s* (*pl:* **-coes** o **-cos**) fresco (*arte; cuadro*); **in fresco** al fresco; *va* pintar al fresco
frescoer ['frɛskoər] *s* fresquista
fresh [frɛʃ] *adj* fresco; puro (*dícese del aire, agua, etc.*); dulce (*agua*); inexperto, novicio; (naut.) fresquito (*viento*); (slang) atrevido (*para con las mujeres*); (slang) fresco, desvergonzado; **fresh paint!** ¡recién pintado!, ¡ojo, mancha!; *adv* frescamente, recientemente; **I am fresh out of coffee** (coll.) el café está recién agotado
fresh breeze *s* (naut.) viento fresquito
freshen ['frɛʃən] *va* refrescar; hacer menos salado; *vn* refrescarse; refrescar (*el viento*)
freshet ['frɛʃɪt] *s* crecida, avenida; corriente impetuosa de agua dulce que penetra en el mar
fresh gale *s* (naut.) viento duro
freshman ['frɛʃmən] *s* (*pl:* **-men**) novato; estudiante de primer año
freshness ['frɛʃnɪs] *s* frescura; pureza (*del aire, agua, etc.*); (slang) frescura, descaro
fresh-water ['frɛʃ,wɔtər] o ['frɛʃ,wɑtər] *adj* de agua dulce; no acostumbrado a navegar; bisoño, inexperto; provinciano
fret [frɛt] *s* calado; (mus.) ceja o traste (*de la guitarra*); queja, displicencia; (*pret & pp:* **fretted;** *ger:* **fretting**) *va* adornar con calados; irritar; raer, gastar estregando; corroer; agitar (*el agua*); *vn* irritarse, quejarse; agitarse (*el agua*); raerse
fretful ['frɛtfəl] *adj* irritable, displicente, descontentadizo
fret saw *s* sierra de calados
fretted ['frɛtɪd] *adj* calado; (her.) freteado
fretwork ['frɛt,wʌrk] *s* calado
Freudian ['frɔɪdɪən] *adj & s* freudiano
Freudianism ['frɔɪdɪənɪzəm] *s* freudismo
Fri. abr. de **Friday**
friability [,fraɪə'bɪlɪtɪ] *s* friabilidad
friable ['fraɪəbəl] *adj* friable
friar ['fraɪər] *s* fraile; (print.) fraile
friary ['fraɪərɪ] *s* (*pl:* **-ies**) convento de frailes; orden de frailes
fricassee [,frɪkə'si] *s* fricasé; *va* guisar a la fricasé
fricative ['frɪkətɪv] *adj* (phonet.) fricativo; *s* (phonet.) fricativa
friction ['frɪkʃən] *s* fricción, rozamiento; (mech.) fricción, rozamiento; (fig.) fricción, desavenencia, rozamiento
frictional ['frɪkʃənəl] *adj* friccional, de fricción, de rozamiento
friction tape *s* (elec.) cinta aislante, tela aisladora
Friday ['fraɪdɪ] *s* viernes; servidor fiel y muy adicto
fried [fraɪd] *adj* frito
friedcake ['fraɪd,kek] *s* buñuelo
fried egg *s* huevo a la plancha
fried potatoes *spl* patatas fritas
friend [frɛnd] *s* amigo; gente de paz (*expresión con que se contesta al que pregunta ¿quién?*); (*cap.*) *s* cuáquero; **to be close friends** ser muy amigos; **to be friends with** ser amigo de; **to make friends** trabar amistades; ganarse amigos; **to make friends with** hacerse amigo de
friend at court *s* amigo en alto lugar; **to have a friend at court** tener el padre alcalde
friendliness ['frɛndlɪnɪs] *s* amigabilidad, cordialidad
friendly ['frɛndlɪ] *adj* (*comp:* **-lier;** *super:* **-liest**) amigable, amistoso, cordial
Friendly Islands *spl* islas de los Amigos
friendship ['frɛndʃɪp] *s* amistad
Friesland ['frizlənd] *s* Frisia
frieze [friz] *s* frisa (*tela de lana*); (arch.) friso; *va* frisar (*el paño*)
frigate ['frɪgɪt] *s* (naut.) fragata
frigate bird *s* (orn.) fragata, rabihorcado
fright [fraɪt] *s* susto, terror; (coll.) espantajo, mamarracho; **to take fright at** asustarse de; *va* (poet.) asustar
frighten ['fraɪtən] *va* asustar; espantar; **to frighten away** espantar, ahuyentar; *vn* asustar; asustarse
frightful ['fraɪtfəl] *adj* espantoso, horroroso; (coll.) muy feo, repugnante; (coll.) muy grande, tremendo
frightfulness ['fraɪtfəlnɪs] *s* espanto, horror; terrorismo
frigid ['frɪdʒɪd] *adj* frío; (fig.) frío (*indiferente; sin gracia*)
frigidity [frɪ'dʒɪdɪtɪ] *s* frialdad; (fig.) frialdad (*indiferencia, desafecto*); (path.) frialdad, frigidez (*falta de deseos sexuales*)
frigid zone *s* zona glacial
frill [frɪl] *s* lechuga, escarola; collarín (*de aves, animales*); (coll.) adorno inútil, ringorrango; (coll.) afectación (*en el vestir, el hablar, etc.*); *va* alechugar, escarolar; *vn* alechugarse
fringe [frɪndʒ] *s* franja, orla; borde, margen; *va* franjar, orlar; (fig.) orlar (*los árboles un camino*)
fringe benefits *spl* beneficios accesorios
fringillid [frɪn'dʒɪlɪd] *s* (orn.) fringílido
frippery ['frɪpərɪ] *s* (*pl:* **-ies**) cursilería; perifollos, perejiles
Frisco ['frɪsko] *s* (coll.) nombre abreviado de **San Francisco** (*California*)
Frisian ['frɪʒən] *adj & s* frisón
frisk [frɪsk] *va* (slang) cachear; (slang) robar con ratería; *vn* cabriolar, juguetear, retozar
frisket ['frɪskɪt] *s* (print.) frasqueta
frisky ['frɪskɪ] *adj* (*comp:* **-ier;** *super:* **-iest**) juguetón, retozón, vivaracho; fogoso (*caballo*)
frit [frɪt] *s* frita; (*pret & pp:* **fritted;** *ger:* **fritting**) *va* fritar (*las materias con que se fabrica el vidrio*)
frith [frɪθ] *s* estuario, brazo de mar
fritillary ['frɪtɪ,lɛrɪ] *s* (*pl:* **-ies**) (bot. & ent.) fritilaria
fritter ['frɪtər] *s* fruta de sartén, frisuelo; parte pequeña, fragmento; *va* desmenuzar; **to fritter away** desperdiciar o malgastar a poquitos
frivolity [frɪ'vɑlɪtɪ] *s* (*pl:* **-ties**) frivolidad
frivolous ['frɪvələs] *adj* frívolo
friz o **frizz** [frɪz] *s* (*pl:* **frizzes**) bucle, rizo, pelo rizado muy apretadamente; (*pret & pp:* **frizzed;** *ger:* **frizzing**) *va* rizar, rizar muy apretadamente
frizzle ['frɪzəl] *s* rizo pequeño y apretado; chirrido, siseo; *va* rizar apretadamente; asar o freír en parrillas; *vn* chirriar, sisear
frizzly ['frɪzlɪ] o **frizzy** ['frɪzɪ] *adj* muy ensortijado
fro [fro] *adv* atrás, hacia atrás; **to and fro** de una parte a otra, de aquí para allá
frock [frɑk] *s* vestido; bata, blusa; vestido talar (*de los sacerdotes*); levita; *va* vestir con vestido, bata, vestido talar, etc.
frock coat *s* levita
frog [frɑg] o [frɔg] *s* (zool. & rail.) rana; ranilla (*del casco de las caballerías*); alamar (*presilla y botón*); ronquera; (elec.) renacuajo
frog in the throat *s* ronquera, gallo en la garganta
frogman ['frɑg,mæn] o ['frɔg,mæn] *s* (*pl:* **-men**) hombre rana
frolic ['frɑlɪk] *s* juego alegre; travesura; jaleo, holgorio, fiesta; (*pret & pp:* **-icked;** *ger:* **-icking**) *vn* juguetear, retozar, travesear, jaranear
frolicsome ['frɑlɪksəm] *adj* juguetón, retozón, travieso
from [frɑm] o [frəm] *prep* de; desde; de parte de; según; a, p.ej., **to take something away from someone** quitar algo a alguien
frond [frɑnd] *s* (bot.) fronda
frondage ['frɑndɪdʒ] *s* frondas, frondosidad
frondescence [frɑn'dɛsəns] *s* (bot.) frondescencia
frondescent [frɑn'dɛsənt] *adj* frondescente
front [frʌnt] *s* frente *m & f;* frontalera (*de la brida del caballo*); pechera (*de la camisa*); principio (*de un libro*), p.ej., **you will find the passage in the front of the book** Vd. hallará el pasaje al principio o hacia el principio del libro; porción de terreno colindante con un río, calle, etc.; apariencia falsa (*de riqueza, grandeza, etc.*); ademán estudiado; (fort., mil. & pol.) frente *m;* **in front** delante, al frente, en frente; **in front of** delante de, en frente de, frente a; **to put on a front** (coll.) gastar mucho oropel; **to put up a bold front** hacer de tripas corazón (*poner buena cara a cosa desagradable*); *interj* ¡botones!;

adj delantero; primero; anterior (*diente*); (phonet.) anterior; *va* dar a; afrontar, arrostar; estar al frente de; poner frente o fachada a; *vn* adelantarse; **to front on** dar a; **to front towards** mirar hacia
frontage ['frʌntɪdʒ] *s* fachada, frontera; extensión frontera; terreno frontero
frontal ['frʌntəl] *adj* frontal; *s* frontal; (anat., arch. & eccl.) frontal
front door *s* puerta de entrada, puerta principal
front drive *s* (aut.) tracción delantera
frontier [frʌn'tɪr] o ['frɑntɪr] *s* frontera; *adj* fronterizo
frontiersman [frʌn'tɪrzmən] *s* (*pl:* **-men**) habitante de la frontera, colonizador, explorador
frontispiece ['frʌntɪspis] *s* portada, frontispicio (*de un libro*); (arch.) frontispicio
frontlet ['frʌntlɪt] *s* frente de un animal; venda o adorno para la frente
front line *s* (mil.) línea del frente
front matter *s* preliminares (*de un libro*)
front page *s* primera plana
front-page ['frʌnt,pedʒ] *adj* de la primera plana (*de un periódico*); muy importante
front porch *s* soportal
front room *s* cuarto que da a la calle
front row *s* delantera, primera fila
front seat *s* asiento delantero
front steps *spl* quicio, pretorio (*escalones en la puerta exterior de la casa*)
front view *s* vista de frente
front vowel *s* (phonet.) vocal anterior
frost [frɔst] o [frɑst] *s* helada (*congelación*); escarcha (*rocío helado*); (coll.) frialdad (*en el trato*); (slang) fracaso; *va* cubrir de escarcha; escarchar (*p.ej., confituras*); quemar (*el hielo las plantas*); deslustrar (*el vidrio*)
frostbite ['frɔst,baɪt] o [frɑst,baɪt] *s* daño sufrido por causa de la helada; (*pret:* **-bit;** *pp:* **-bitten**) *va* helar; quemar (*el hielo las plantas*)
frosted foods *spl* var. de **frozen foods**
frosted glass *s* vidrio deslustrado, vidrio amolado
frosting ['frɔstɪŋ] o ['frɑstɪŋ] *s* (cook.) capa de clara de huevo y azúcar; imitación de la escarcha (*en el acabado de los metales*)
frosty ['frɔstɪ] o ['frɑstɪ] *adj* (*comp:* **-ier;** *super:* **-iest**) cubierto de escarcha; helado; escarchado; frío, poco amistoso; canoso, gris
froth [frɔθ] o [frɑθ] *s* espuma; frivolidad, bachillerías; *va* hacer espumar; cubrir de espuma; emitir como espuma; batir (*un líquido*) hasta que espume; *vn* espumar, echar espuma; **to froth at the mouth** espumajear, echar espumarajos por la boca
frothy ['frɔθɪ] o ['frɑθɪ] *adj* (*comp:* **-ier;** *super:* **-iest**) espumoso; frívolo
frou-frou ['fru,fru] *s* frufrú
froward ['froward] *adj* indócil, díscolo
frown [fraʊn] *s* ceño, entrecejo; *va* mirar con ceño; expresar (*enojo*) frunciendo el entrecejo; *vn* fruncir el entrecejo, estar de mal semblante; **to frown at** mirar con ceño; desaprobar; **to frown on** desaprobar
frowsy o **frowzy** ['fraʊzɪ] *adj* (*comp:* **-ier;** *super:* **-iest**) desaliñado, desaseado; mal peinado; maloliente
froze [froz] *pret de* **freeze**
frozen ['frozən] *pp de* **freeze**
frozen foods *spl* viandas heladas, alimentos o comestibles congelados
F.R.S. abr. de **Fellow of the Royal Society**
frt. abr. de **freight**
fructiferous [frʌk'tɪfərəs] *adj* fructífero
fructification [,frʌktɪfɪ'keʃən] *s* fructificación
fructify ['frʌktɪfaɪ] (*pret & pp:* **-fied**) *va* fecundar, fertilizar; *vn* fructificar
fructose ['frʌktos] *s* (chem.) fructosa
fructuous ['frʌktʃʊəs] *adj* fructuoso
frugal ['frugəl] *adj* parco, comedido; escaso
frugality [fru'gælɪtɪ] *s* parquedad; escasez
frugivorous [fru'dʒɪvərəs] *adj* frugívoro
fruit [frut] *s* fruta (*p.ej., fresa, manzana, pera*); frutas, p.ej., **I like fruit** me gustan las frutas; (bot.) fruto (*parte que contiene la semilla*); (fig.) fruto (*resultado; producción*), p.ej., **the fruit of much effort** el fruto de mucho trabajo; **the fruits of the earth** los frutos de la tierra; *adj* frutal (*árbol*); frutero (*buque, plato, etc.*); *vn* frutar, dar fruto
fruitage ['frutɪdʒ] *s* fructificación
fruit cake *s* torta de frutas
fruit cup *s* compotera de frutas picadas (*sin cocer*)
fruit dish *s* plato frutero
fruiter ['frutər] *s* buque frutero; árbol frutal; cultivador de frutas
fruiterer ['frutərər] *s* frutero; buque frutero
fruit fly *s* (ent.) mosca del vinagre; (ent.) mosca de las frutas, mosca mediterránea
fruitful ['frutfəl] *adj* fructuoso, fructífero
fruitfulness ['frutfəlnɪs] *s* fructuosidad
fruition [fru'ɪʃən] *s* cumplimiento, buen resultado; complacencia, goce, fruición; fructificación; **to come to fruition** lograrse cumplidamente
fruit jar *s* tarro para frutas
fruit juice *s* jugo de frutas
fruitless ['frutlɪs] *adj* infructuoso
fruit ranch *s* finca dedicada a la fruticultura
fruit salad *s* ensalada de frutas, macedonia de frutas
fruit stand *s* puesto de frutas
fruit store *s* frutería
fruit sugar *s* (chem.) azúcar de fruta
fruit tree *s* árbol frutal
fruitwoman ['frut,wʊmən] *s* (*pl:* **-women**) frutera
fruity ['frutɪ] *adj* (*comp:* **-ier;** *super:* **-iest**) que huele o sabe a fruta, de olor o sabor de fruta
frumenty ['frumәntɪ] *s* frangollo cocido con leche y condimentado con azúcar y canela
frump [frʌmp] *s* mujer descuidada en el vestir
frumpish ['frʌmpɪʃ] *adj* desaliñado; malhumorado
frumpy ['frʌmpɪ] *adj* (*comp:* **-ier;** *super:* **-iest**) var. de **frumpish**
frustrate ['frʌstret] *va* frustrar
frustration [frʌs'treʃən] *s* frustración; desazón, desengaño
frustule ['frʌstʃʊl] *s* (bot.) frústula
frustum ['frʌstəm] *s* (*pl:* **-tums** o **-ta** [tə]) (geom.) tronco
frutescent [fru'tɛsənt] *adj* frutescente
fruticose ['frutɪkos] *adj* fruticoso
fry [fraɪ] *s* (*pl:* **fries**) fritada; *spl* pececillos; cardumen de peces pequeños; prole, hijos; (*pret & pp:* **fried**) *va* freír
frying pan *s* sartén; **to jump from the frying pan into the fire** saltar de la sartén y dar en las brasas, huir de las cenizas y caer en las brasas
ft. abr. de **foot** o **feet**
fucaceous [fju'keʃəs] *adj* (bot.) fucáceo
fuchsia ['fjuʃə] *s* (bot.) fucsia
fuchsin ['fʊksɪn] o **fuchsine** ['fuksɪn] o ['fuksin] *s* (chem.) fucsina
fuddle ['fʌdəl] *va* emborrachar; confundir
fuddy-duddy ['fʌdɪ,dʌdɪ] *adj* (coll.) atrasado, anticuado; (coll.) alharaquiento, quisquilloso; *s* (*pl:* **-dies**) (coll.) persona de ideas o costumbres atrasadas o anticuadas; (coll.) persona alharaquienta, persona quisquillosa; (coll.) tragavirotes
fudge [fʌdʒ] *s* dulce de chocolate (*de la consistencia de la raspadura*); *interj* ¡ tonterías!; *va* hacer de modo chapucero, hacer de modo superficial y mecánico, hacer con mala fe
Fuegian [fju'idʒɪən] *adj & s* fueguino
fuel ['fjuəl] *s* combustible; (fig.) aliciente, pábulo; (*pret & pp:* **fueled** o **fuelled;** *ger:* **fueling** o **fuelling**) *va* aprovisionar de combustible; *vn* aprovisionarse de combustible
fuel gauge *s* indicador de nivel del combustible
fuel oil *s* aceite combustible
fuel tank *s* depósito de combustible
fugacious [fju'geʃəs] *adj* fugaz; (bot.) fugaz
fugitive ['fjudʒɪtɪv] *adj* fugitivo; de interés pasajero; errante, vagabundo; *s* fugitivo
fugleman ['fjugəlmən] *s* (*pl:* **-men**) (mil.) jefe de fila; (fig.) modelo (*persona digna de ser imitada*)
fugue [fjug] *s* (mus.) fuga
fulcrum ['fʌlkrəm] *s* (*pl:* **-crums** o **-cra** [krə]) (bot., ent., ichth. & mach.) fulcro
-ful *suffix adj* -oso p.ej., **frightful** espantoso;

painful doloroso; *suffix s* -ado, p.ej., **armful** brazado; **handful** puñado; -ada p.ej., **spoonful** cucharada; **shovelful** palada
fulfil o **fulfill** [fʊlˈfɪl] (*pret & pp:* **-filled;** *ger:* **-filling**) *va* cumplir (*un deseo, un plazo, una orden*); cumplir con (*una obligación*); llenar (*una condición, un requisito*); realizar
fulfilment o **fulfillment** [fʊlˈfɪlmənt] *s* cumplimiento, ejecución, realización
fulgent [ˈfʌldʒənt] *adj* fulgente
fulgide [ˈfʌldʒaɪd] o [ˈfʌldʒɪd] *s* (chem.) fúlgido
fulgurate [ˈfʌlgjəret] *vn* fulgurar
fulgurite [ˈfʌlgjəraɪt] *s* fulgurita
fulgurous [ˈfʌlgjərəs] *adj* fulguroso
fuliginous [fjuˈlɪdʒɪnəs] *adj* fuliginoso
full [fʊl] *adj* lleno; pleno; amplio, holgado (*vestido*); de etiqueta (*traje*); fuerte, sonoro (*dícese de la voz*); **full of fun** muy divertido, muy chistoso; **full of play** muy juguetón, muy retozón; **full to overflowing** lleno a rebosar; *adv* de lleno; **full many (a)** muchísimos; **full well** muy bien, perfectamente; *s* colmo, máximum; plentitud; **in full** por completo, totalmente; sin abreviar; **to the full** completamente, enteramente; *va* dar amplitud a; abatanar (*el paño*); *vn* llegar (*la Luna*) al plenilunio
fullback [ˈfʊl,bæk] *s* (football) defensa, jugador trasero
full blast *s* pleno tiro; pleno ejercicio; toda velocidad; **at** o **in full blast** a pleno tiro; en pleno ejercicio; a toda velocidad
full-blooded [ˈfʊlˈblʌdɪd] *adj* vigoroso; pletórico; de raza
full-blown [ˈfʊlˈblon] *adj* abierto (*dícese de las flores*); maduro, desarrollado
full-bodied [ˈfʊlˈbɑdɪd] *adj* consistente, fuerte, espeso; aromático
full dress *s* traje de etiqueta; (mil.) uniforme de gala
full-dress coat [ˈfʊl,drɛs] *s* frac
fuller [ˈfʊlər] *s* batanero
fuller's earth *s* tierra de batán, tierra de bataneros
full-faced [ˈfʊlˈfest] *adj* carilleno; de cuadrado (*mirado frente a frente*); de rostro entero (*dícese de un retrato*)
full-fashioned [ˈfʊlˈfæʃənd] *adj* de costura francesa (*dícese de las medias*)
full-fledged [ˈfʊlˈflɛdʒd] *adj* acabado, completo; hecho y derecho, nada menos que
full-grown [ˈfʊlˈgron] *adj* crecido, completamente desarrollado, maduro
full house *s* lleno, entrada llena; (poker) fulján
full-length mirror [ˈfʊlˈlɛŋθ] *s* espejo de cuerpo entero, espejo de vestir
full-length motion picture *s* cinta de largo metraje
full load *s* plena carga; (aer.) peso total
full moon *s* luna llena, plenilunio
full name *s* nombre y apellidos
fullness [ˈfʊlnɪs] *s* (lo) lleno; plenitud, llenura
fullness of time *s* plenitud de los tiempos
full of the moon *s* lleno de la luna
full-page [ˈfʊl,pedʒ] *adj* a página entera
full powers *spl* amplias facultades, plenos poderes
full-rigged [ˈfʊlˈrɪgd] *adj* pertrechado completamente; (naut.) aparejado completamente
full sail *adv* (naut.) a toda vela, a todo trapo; (fig.) a todo trapo
full-sized [ˈfʊlˈsaɪzd] *adj* de tamaño natural
full stop *s* parada completa; (gram.) punto final
full swing *s* plena operación, actividad máxima; **in full swing** en plena actividad
full tilt *adv* a toda velocidad
full time *s* las horas de costumbre, jornada ordinaria
full-time [ˈfʊl,taɪm] *adj* a tiempo completo
full-view [ˈfʊlˈvju] *adj* de vista completa
full volume *s & adv* (rad.) todo volumen
full-wave [ˈfʊl,wev] *adj* (elec.) de onda completa
fully [ˈfʊlɪ] o [ˈfʊllɪ] *adv* completamente; llenamente, abundantemente; cabalmente, exactamente
fulminate [ˈfʌlmɪnet] *s* (chem.) fulminato; *va* hacer saltar, volar; fulminar (*censuras, amenazas, etc.*); *vn* fulminar; **to fulminate against** tronar contra
fulminating powder *s* (chem.) pólvora fulminante
fulmination [,fʌlmɪˈneʃən] *s* fulminación
fulminic [fʌlˈmɪnɪk] *adj* fulmínico
fulminic acid *s* (chem.) ácido fulmínico
fulminous [ˈfʌlmɪnəs] *adj* fulmíneo o fulminoso
fulness [ˈfʊlnɪs] *s* var. de **fullness**
fulsome [ˈfʊlsəm] o [ˈfʌlsəm] *adj* craso, de mal gusto; repugnante
fumarole [ˈfjumərol] *s* fumarola
fumble [ˈfʌmbəl] *s* (football) falta que consiste en dejar caer el balón; *va* manosear desmañadamente; dejar caer (*el balón o la pelota*) desmañadamente; *vn* buscar con las manos (*p.ej., en los bolsillos*); revolver papeles; andar a tientas; titubear (*en la elección o pronunciación de las palabras*)
fume [fjum] *s* emanación, gas, humo, vapor; mal humor, arranque de cólera; *va* ahumar; avahar; *vn* ahumar; avaharse; humear, exhalar vapores; echar pestes; **to fume at** echar pestes contra
fumed oak *s* roble ahumado
fumigate [ˈfjumɪget] *va* fumigar
fumigation [,fjumɪˈgeʃən] *s* fumigación
fumigator [ˈfjumɪ,getər] *s* fumigador (*persona o aparato*)
fumitory [ˈfjumɪ,torɪ] *s* (*pl:* **-ries**) (bot.) fumaria
fun [fʌn] *s* diversión, chacota, broma; **for fun** o **in fun** por gusto, por divertirse; **to be fun** ser divertido; **to have fun** divertirse; **to make fun of** o **to poke fun at** burlarse de, reírse de; **to play for fun** jugar de burlas
function [ˈfʌŋkʃən] *s* función; *vn* funcionar
functional [ˈfʌŋkʃənəl] *adj* funcional
functionalism [ˈfʌŋkʃənəlɪzəm] *s* funcionalismo
functionary [ˈfʌŋkʃə,nɛrɪ] *s* (*pl:* **-ies**) funcionario
fund [fʌnd] *s* fondo; (fig.) fondo (*p.ej., de sabiduría*); **funds** *spl* fondos (*caudales, dinero*); *va* colocar en un fondo; consolidar (*una deuda*)
fundable [ˈfʌndəbəl] *adj* consolidable
fundamental [,fʌndəˈmɛntəl] *adj* fundamental; *s* fundamento; (mus.) nota fundamental
fundamentalism [,fʌndəˈmɛntəlɪzəm] *s* (rel.) fundamentalismo
fundamentalist [,fʌndəˈmɛntəlɪst] *s* (rel.) fundamentalista
fundus [ˈfʌndəs] *s* (anat.) fondo
funeral [ˈfjunərəl] *adj* funeral; *s* funeral, funerales, pompa fúnebre (*de corpore insepulto*); (slang) desgracia, mala suerte; **it's not my funeral** (slang) no corre a mi cuidado
funeral director *s* director de funeraria
funeral march *s* (mus.) marcha fúnebre
funeral parlor *s* funeraria
funeral service *s* misa de cuerpo presente
funerary [ˈfjunə,rɛrɪ] *adj* funerario
funereal [fjuˈnɪrɪəl] *adj* funeral; fúnebre
fungicidal [,fʌndʒɪˈsaɪdəl] *adj* fungicida
fungicide [ˈfʌndʒɪsaɪd] *s* fungicida
fungoid [ˈfʌŋgɔɪd] *adj* fungoideo
fungology [fʌŋˈgɑlədʒɪ] *s* fungología
fungosity [fʌŋˈgɑsɪtɪ] *s* (*pl:* **-ties**) fungosidad; (path.) fungosidad
fungous [ˈfʌŋgəs] *adj* fungoso; que aparece de repente y dura poco
fungus [ˈfʌŋgəs] *adj* fungoso; que aparece de repente y dura poco; *s* (*pl:* **-guses** o **fungi** [ˈfʌndʒaɪ]) (bot.) hongo; (path.) hongo, fungo
funicle [ˈfjunɪkəl] *s* var. de **funiculus**
funicular [fjuˈnɪkjələr] *adj & s* funicular
funicular railway *s* ferrocarril funicular
funiculate [fjuˈnɪkjəlɪt] o [fjuˈnɪkjəlet] (bot.) *adj* funiculado
funiculus [fjuˈnɪkjələs] *s* (*pl:* **-li** [laɪ]) (anat., bot. & zool.) funículo
funk [fʌŋk] *s* (coll.) temor, temor pánico; (coll.) cobarde; **in a funk** (coll.) atemorizado; *va* (coll.) encogerse de miedo por, retraerse con temor de; (coll.) atemorizar; *vn* (coll.) encogerse de miedo, retraerse con temor
funnel [ˈfʌnəl] *s* embudo; (naut.) chimenea (*de un vapor*); (naut.) manguera, ventilador; (*pret & pp:* **-neled** o **-nelled;** *ger:* **-neling** o

-nelling) *va* verter por medio de un embudo; (fig.) concentrar
funny ['fʌnɪ] *adj* (*comp:* **-nier;** *super:* **-niest**) cómico, ridículo; divertido, chistoso; (coll.) extraño, raro; **to strike someone as funny** hacerle a uno gracia; *s* (*pl:* **-nies**) (Brit.) pequeño bote de remos de tingladillo; **funnies** *spl* (slang) tiras cómicas, páginas cómicas (*del periódico*)
funny bone *s* var. de **crazy bone**
funny paper *s* páginas cómicas (*del periódico*)
fur. abr. de **furlong** y **furnished**
fur [fʌr] *s* piel, piel con su lana o pelo; abrigo o adorno de pieles; sarro (*p.ej., en la lengua*); caza de pelo; (her.) forro; **to make the fur fly** (coll.) armar camorra, ser origen de pelotera; **to stroke a person's fur the wrong way** irritarle a una persona; *adj* de piel, de pieles; (*pret & pp:* **furred;** *ger:* **furring**) *va* guarnecer o forrar con pieles; depositar sarro en; aplicar tiras de madera a, clavar tiras de madera en; *vn* formarse incrustaciones
furbelow ['fʌrbəlo] *s* faralá, ringorrango; *va* adornar con volantes, lazos, etc.
furbish ['fʌrbɪʃ] *va* acicalar, limpiar, pulir; **to furbish up** renovar, restaurar
furcate ['fʌrket] *adj* horcado
fur coat *s* abrigo de pieles
furfur ['fʌrfər] *s* (*pl:* **furfures** ['fʌrfjuriz]) (path.) fúrfura
furfuraceous [,fʌrfjə'reʃəs] *adj* furfuráceo; (bot.) furfuráceo
furious ['fjʊrɪəs] *adj* furioso
furl [fʌrl] *va* arrollar; (naut.) aferrar
fur-lined ['fʌr,laɪnd] *adj* forrado con pieles
furlong ['fʌrlɔŋ] o ['fʌrlɑŋ] *s* estadio
furlough ['fʌrlo] *s* (mil.) licencia; *va* (mil.) dar licencia a
furnace ['fʌrnɪs] *s* horno; calorífero (*para calentar una casa*); lugar de calor intenso; prueba penosa
furnaceman ['fʌrnɪsmən] *s* (*pl:* **-men**) hornero; hombre encargado del calorífero
furnish ['fʌrnɪʃ] *va* amueblar; proporcionar, suministrar; aducir (*pruebas*); **to furnish with** proveer de
furnished room *s* cuarto amueblado
furnishings ['fʌrnɪʃɪŋz] *spl* muebles, mueblaje; accesorios; artículos (*p.ej., para caballeros*)
furniture ['fʌrnɪtʃər] *s* muebles, mueblaje; arreos, avíos; (naut.) aparejo; **a piece of furniture** un mueble; **a suit of furniture** un moblaje, un mobiliario, un juego de muebles
furniture polish *s* pulimento para muebles
furor ['fjʊrɔr] *s* furor
furrier ['fʌrɪər] *s* peletero
furriery ['fʌrɪərɪ] *s* (*pl:* **-ies**) peletería
furring ['fʌrɪŋ] *s* adorno o forro de pieles; sarro; tiras de madera
furrow ['fʌro] *s* surco; *va* surcar
furry ['fʌrɪ] *adj* (*comp:* **-rier;** *super:* **-riest**) adornado con pieles; hecho de pieles; peludo; sarroso
fur seal *s* (zool.) oso marino (*Callorhinus alascanus*)
further ['fʌrðər] *adj comp* adicional, nuevo; más lejano; más; *adv comp* además; más lejos; *va* adelantar, promover, apoyar, fomentar
furtherance ['fʌrðərəns] *s* adelantamiento, promoción, apoyo, fomento
furtherer ['fʌrðərər] *s* promotor, patrón, fomentador
furthermore ['fʌrðərmor] *adv* además
furthermost ['fʌrðərmost] *adj super* más lejano (*de todos*)
furthest ['fʌrðɪst] *adj super* más lejano (*de todos*); más; *adv super* más lejos; más
furtive ['fʌrtɪv] *adj* furtivo
furuncle ['fjʊrʌŋkəl] *s* (path.) furúnculo
fury ['fjʊrɪ] *s* (*pl:* **-ries**) furia (*ira; violencia; prisa; persona irritada*): (*cap.*) *s* Furia; **to be in a fury** estar furioso, estar dado a los demonios; **like fury** a toda furia
furze [fʌrz] *s* (bot.) aliaga, aulaga, tojo; (bot.) retama de escoba
furzy ['fʌrzɪ] *adj* retamero
fuse [fjuz] *s* mecha; (elec.) fusible, cortacircuitos; (elec.) tapón fusible; (mil.) espoleta; **to burn** o **burn out a fuse** (elec.) quemar un fusible; *va* fundir; poner la espoleta a; (fig.) fusionar; *vn* fundirse; (fig.) fusionarse
fuse box *s* (elec.) caja de fusibles
fusee [fju'zi] *s* fósforo grande que no apaga el viento; (horol.) caracol, fusé; (rail.) luz de bengala que sirve de señal
fuselage ['fjuzəlɪdʒ] o [,fjuzə'lɑʒ] *s* (aer.) fuselaje
fuse link *s* (elec.) elemento fusible
fusel oil ['fjuzəl] *s* (chem.) aceite de fusel
fusibility [,fjuzɪ'bɪlɪtɪ] *s* fusibilidad
fusible ['fjuzɪbəl] *adj* fusible o fundible
fusiform ['fjuzɪfɔrm] *adj* fusiforme
fusileer o **fusilier** [,fjuzɪ'lɪr] *s* fusilero
fusillade [,fjuzɪ'led] *s* fusilería; (fig.) andanada (*p.ej., de preguntas*); *va* atacar con una descarga de fusilería, fusilar
fusion ['fjuʒən] *s* fusión; (fig.) fusión
fusionism ['fjuʒənɪzəm] *s* (pol.) fusionismo
fusionist ['fjuʒənɪst] *adj & s* fusionista
fuss [fʌs] *s* alharaca, bulla innecesaria; hazañería, desvelos innecesarios; (slang) disputa por ligero motivo; **to make a fuss** hacer alharacas; **to make a fuss over** hacer fiestas a; disputar sobre; *va* molestar, inquietar, atolondrar; dejar hecho un mico; *vn* hacer alharacas, inquietarse por pequeñeces; **to fuss with** manosear
fuss and feathers *s* (coll.) fanfarria, magnificencia, pompa
fussbudget ['fʌs,bʌdʒɪt] *s* (coll.) persona alharaquienta, persona quisquillosa
fussy ['fʌsɪ] *adj* (*comp:* **-ier;** *super:* **-iest**) alharaquiento; descontentadizo, exigente; melindroso; peliagudo; muy adornado; con muchos ringorrangos (*vestido*)
fustian ['fʌstʃən] *s* fustán (*tela gruesa*); pana; cultedad, follaje; *adj* de fustán; de pana; culterano, altisonante
fustic ['fʌstɪk] *s* (bot.) fustete, palo de Cuba; tintura de fustete
fusty ['fʌstɪ] *adj* (*comp:* **-ier;** *super:* **-iest**) mohoso, rancio, que huele a cosa pasada, que huele a cerrado; del tiempo de Maricastaña, pasado de moda
fut. abr. de **future**
futile ['fjutɪl] *adj* estéril (*inútil, vano*); fútil (*de poca importancia*)
futility [fju'tɪlɪtɪ] *s* (*pl:* **-ties**) esterilidad; futilidad
futtock ['fʌtək] *s* (naut.) genol
future ['fjutʃər] *adj* futuro; *s* futuro, porvenir; (gram.) futuro; **futures** *spl* (com.) futuros; **in the future** en lo sucesivo, en el futuro; **in the near future** en fecha próxima
future life *s* vida futura
futurism ['fjutʃərɪzəm] *s* futurismo
futurist ['fjutʃərɪst] *adj & s* futurista
futuristic [,fjutʃə'rɪstɪk] *adj* futurista
futurity [fju'tjʊrɪtɪ] o [fju'tʊrɪtɪ] *s* (*pl:* **-ties**) futuro, porvenir; estado futuro; acontecimiento futuro
fuze [fjuz] *s* mecha; (elec.) fusible; (mil.) espoleta; *va* poner la espoleta a
fuzee [fju'zi] *s* var. de **fusee**
fuzz [fʌz] *s* borra, tamo (*en los bolsillos, rincones, etc.*); pelusa, plumón, vello
fuzzy ['fʌzɪ] *adj* (*comp:* **-ier;** *super:* **-iest**) borroso; cubierto de pelusa o plumón, velloso
fyke [faɪk] *s* nasa para pescar
fylfot ['fɪlfɑt] *s* cruz gamada

G

G, g [dʒi] *s* (*pl:* **G's, g's** [dʒiz]) séptima letra del alfabeto inglés
g. abr. de **gauge, gender, genitive, gram** y **guinea**
G. abr. de **German** y **Gulf**
Ga. abr. de **Georgia**
G.A. abr. de **General Agent** y **General Assembly**
gab [gæb] *s* (coll.) parleta, cotorreo; (*pret & pp:* **gabbed;** *ger:* **gabbing**) *vn* (coll.) picotear, parlotear
gabardine ['gæbərdin] *s* gabardina
gabble ['gæbəl] *s* cotorreo, parloteo; *vn* cotorrear, parlotear
gabbler ['gæblər] *s* picotero
gaberdine ['gæbərdin] *s* var. de **gabardine**
gabion ['gebɪən] *s* (fort. & hyd.) gavión
gable ['gebəl] *s* aguilón (*del tejado*); gablete, frontón (*encima de puertas o ventanas*)
gable end *s* hastial
gable roof *s* tejado de caballete, tejado de dos aguas
gable wall *s* pared de caballete
Gabriel ['gebrɪəl] *s* Gabriel
gaby ['gebɪ] *s* (*pl:* **-bies**) (coll.) tonto, necio
gad [gæd] *s* aguijada, aguijón; *interj* (archaic) ¡pardiez!; (*pret & pp:* **gadded;** *ger:* **gadding**) *vn* callejear, andar de aquí para allá
gadabout ['gædə,baʊt] *adj* callejero; *s* cirigallo; hombre placero
gadfly ['gæd,flaɪ] *s* (*pl:* **-flies**) (ent.) tábano
gadget ['gædʒɪt] *s* (coll.) adminículo, chisme, dispositivo ingenioso
gadid ['gædɪd] *s* (ichth.) gádido
gadolinium [,gædə'lɪnɪəm] *s* (chem.) gadolinio
Gaea ['dʒiə] *s* (myth.) Gea
Gael [gel] *s* gaélico (*natural o habitante celta*)
Gaelic ['gelɪk] *adj* gaélico; *s* gaélico (*idioma*)
gaff [gæf] *s* arpón, garfio; espolón de acero con que se calza a los gallos de pelea; (naut.) cangrejo; **to blow the gaff** (slang) revelar el secreto; **to stand the gaff** (slang) tener mucha resistencia; *va* arponear
gaffer ['gæfər] *s* vejestorio
gafftopsail [,gæf'tɑpsəl] o [,gæf'tɑp,sel] *s* (naut.) escandalosa
gag [gæg] *s* mordaza; mordaza dental; (fig.) mordaza; (slang) morcilla (*añadidura que mete un actor en su papel*); (slang) chiste, payasada; (*pret & pp:* **gagged;** *ger:* **gagging**) *va* amordazar; dar bascas a; (fig.) amordazar; *vn* sentir bascas, arquear
gage [gedʒ] *s* gaje (*de desafío*); desafío; prenda; *va* (archaic) apostar, dar en prenda; *s & va* var. de **gauge**
gaiety ['geɪtɪ] *s* (*pl:* **-ties**) alegría, regocijo; diversión alegre; galas
Gaillard Cut ['gelɑrd] o [gɪl'jɑrd] *s* corte de Gaillard
gaily ['gelɪ] *adv* alegremente; vistosamente
gain [gen] *s* ganancia; aumento; (carp.) gárgol, ranura; (elec.) ganancia; **gains** *spl* ganancias; *va* ganar; conquistar; alcanzar; adelantarse (*p.ej., cinco minutos un reloj*); **to gain over** conquistar; *vn* ir en progreso; ganar terreno; mejorar (*un enfermo*); **to gain on** ir alcanzando
gainer ['genər] *s* ganancioso; zambullida para cuya ejecución hay que colocarse de espaldas al agua y dar un salto mortal en el aire
gainful ['genfəl] *adj* ganancioso
gainsaid [,gen'sɛd] *pret & pp de* **gainsay**
gainsay [,gen'se] (*pret & pp:* **-said** o **-sayed**) *va* contradecir, negar
gainst o **'gainst** [gɛnst] o [genst] *prep* (poet.) var. de **against**
gait [get] *s* paso, manera de andar; **at a good gait** a buen paso
gaiter ['getər] *s* polaina corta; botina con elásticos por los lados
gal. abr. de **gallon** o **gallons**
Gal. abr. de **Galatians**
gala ['gelə] o ['gælə] *s* fiesta; *adj* de gala, de fiesta
galactagogue [gə'læktəgɑg] *adj & s* (med. & vet.) galactagogo
galactic [gə'læktɪk] *adj* lácteo; (astr.) galáctico
galactite [gə'læktaɪt] *s* (mineral.) galactita
galactometer [,gælæk'tɑmɪtər] *s* galactómetro
galactose [gə'læktos] *s* (chem.) galactosa
Galahad ['gæləhæd] *s* Galaad; (fig.) hombre de costumbres muy puras
galantine ['gæləntin] *s* (cook.) galantina
Galápagos Islands [gə'lɑpəgos] *s* islas de (los) Galápagos
Galatea [,gælə'tiə] *s* (myth.) Galatea
Galatia [gə'leʃə] *s* Galacia
Galatian [gə'leʃən] *adj & s* gálata; **Galatians** *spl* (Bib.) Epístola de San Pablo a los Gálatas
galaxy ['gæləksɪ] *s* (*pl:* **-ies**) (astr.) galaxia; grupo o reunión brillante (*de artistas, cortesanos, etc.*)
galbanum ['gælbənəm] *s* gálbano
galbulus ['gælbjələs] *s* (*pl:* **-li** [laɪ]) (bot.) gálbula
gale [gel] *s* ventarrón, viento muy fuerte; (coll.) explosión (*de risas*); (poet.) brisa; (bot.) mirto de Brabante; **to weather the gale** correr el temporal; (fig.) ir tirando
Galen ['gelən] *s* Galeno; (fig.) Galeno (*médico*)
galena [gə'linə] o **galenite** [gə'linaɪt] *s* (mineral.) galena
Galenic [ge'lɛnɪk] o [ge'linɪk] *adj* galénico
Galenism ['gelɪnɪzəm] *s* galenismo
Galicia [gə'lɪʃə] *s* Galicia (*de Polonia y de España*)
Galician [gə'lɪʃən] *adj & s* gallego (*de España*); galiciano (*de Polonia y de España*)
Galilean [,gælɪ'liən] *adj* galileo; (phys.) de Galileo; *s* galileo; **the Galilean** el Galileo (*Jesucristo*)
Galilee ['gælɪli] *s* Galilea; (*l.c.*) *s* galilea (*pórtico*)
galiot ['gælɪət] *s* (naut.) galeota
galipot ['gælɪpɑt] *s* galipodio (*oleorresina*)
gall [gɔl] *s* bilis, hiel; (anat.) vejiga de la bilis, vesícula biliar; (bot.) agalla; hiel (*cosa muy amarga*); rencor, odio; rozadura, matadura; (slang) descaro; *va* lastimar rozando, hacer un desollón o desollones en; irritar, molestar grandemente; *vn* raerse
gallant ['gælənt] o [gə'lænt] *adj* galante (*atento con las damas*); amoroso; ['gælənt] *adj* gallardo, valiente, noble; hazañoso; imponente; festivo, vistoso; *s* hombre valiente; galán; galanteador
gallantry ['gæləntrɪ] *s* (*pl:* **-ries**) gallardía, valor, nobleza; galantería (*para con las damas*); galanteo; (archaic) lujo, ostentación
gall bladder *s* (anat.) vejiga de la bilis, vesícula biliar
galleass ['gælɪæs] *s* (naut.) galeaza
galleon ['gælɪən] *s* (naut.) galeón
gallery ['gælərɪ] *s* (*pl:* **-ies**) galería; tribuna (*en las iglesias, etc.*); galería fotográfica; galería de tiro; conjunto de espectadores; (fort. min., naut. & theat.) galería; **to play to the gallery** (coll.) hablar para la galería
galley ['gælɪ] *s* (naut. & print.) galera; (naut.) fogón
galley proof *s* (print.) galerada, pruebas de segundas
galley slave *s* galeote; (fig.) esclavo del trabajo
gallfly ['gɔl,flaɪ] *s* (*pl:* **-flies**) (ent.) cinípido
galliard ['gæljərd] *s* gallarda (*danza*)

Gallic ['gælɪk] *adj* gálico, galo; (*l.c.*) *adj* (chem.) gálico
gallic acid *s* (chem.) ácido gálico
Gallican ['gælɪkən] *adj* (eccl.) galicano
Gallicanism ['gælɪkənɪzəm] *s* galicanismo
Gallicism ['gælɪsɪzəm] *s* galicismo
Gallicize ['gælɪsaɪz] *va* afrancesar; *vn* afrancesarse
galligaskins [,gælɪ'gæskɪnz] *spl* calzacalzón; polainas
gallinaceous [,gælɪ'neʃəs] *adj* (orn.) gallináceo
galling ['gɔlɪŋ] *adj* irritante, ofensivo
gallinule ['gælɪnjul] o ['gælɪnul] *s* (orn.) polla
gallipot ['gælɪpɑt] *s* galipodio (*oleorresina*); orza (*vasija*); (coll.) boticario
gallium ['gælɪəm] *s* (chem.) galio
gallivant ['gælɪvænt] *vn* andar a placer de aquí para allá
gallnut ['gɔl,nʌt] *s* (bot.) agalla
gall oak *s* (bot.) cajiga o quejigo
Gallomania [,gælo'menɪə] *s* galomanía
gallon ['gælən] *s* galón (*medida*)
galloon [gə'lun] *s* galón (*cinta estrecha*)
gallop ['gæləp] *s* galope; paseo a galope; *va* hacer ir a galope; *vn* galopar; **to gallop through** hacer muy aprisa
galloping ['gæləpɪŋ] *adj* galopante
galloping consumption *s* (path.) tisis galopante
Gallo-Roman [,gælo'romən] *adj* galorromano
gallows ['gæloz] *s* (*pl:* **-lowses** o **-lows**) horca; pena de muerte en la horca; (min.) castillete de mina
gallows bird *s* (coll.) carne de horca
gallstone ['gɔl,ston] *s* cálculo biliario
gall wasp *s* var. de **gallfly**
galop ['gæləp] *s* galopa (*baile*); *vn* galopar (*bailar la galopa*)
galore [gə'lor] *adv* en abundancia
galosh [gə'lɑʃ] *s* chanclo alto de goma o de tela engomada
gals. abr. de **gallons**
galvanic [gæl'vænɪk] *adj* galvánico; sorprendente
galvanism ['gælvənɪzəm] *s* galvanismo
galvanization [,gælvənɪ'zeʃən] *s* galvanización
galvanize ['gælvənaɪz] *va* galvanizar; (fig.) galvanizar
galvanized iron *s* hierro galvanizado
galvanocautery [,gælvəno'kɔtərɪ] o [gæl,væno'kɔtərɪ] *s* (*pl:* **-ies**) (med.) galvanocauterio
galvanometer [,gælvə'nɑmɪtər] *s* galvanómetro
galvanometric [,gælvənə'mɛtrɪk] o [gæl,vænə'mɛtrɪk] *adj* galvanométrico
galvanometry [,gælvə'nɑmɪtrɪ] *s* galvanometría
galvanoplastic [,gælvəno'plæstɪk] o [gæl,væno'plæstɪk] *adj* galvanoplástico; **galvanoplastics** *ssg* galvanoplástica
galvanoplasty [,gælvəno'plæstɪ] o [gæl,væno'plæstɪ] *s* galvanoplastia
galvanoscope ['gælvəno,skop] o [gæl'vænəskop] *s* galvanoscopio
galvanotropism [,gælvə'nɑtrəpɪzəm] *s* (biol.) galvanotropismo
gama grass ['gɑmə] *s* (bot.) maicillo
gambier ['gæmbɪr] *s* (pharm.) gambir
gambit ['gæmbɪt] *s* gambito
gamble ['gæmbəl] *s* (coll.) juego, empresa arriesgada, cosa incierta; *va* jugar, aventurar en el juego; **to gamble away** perder en el juego; *vn* jugar; especular, aventurarse mucho (*p.ej., en las operaciones de bolsa*)
gambler ['gæmblər] *s* jugador; tahúr, garitero
gambling ['gæmblɪŋ] *s* juego (*por dinero*)
gambling house *s* casa de juego
gambling machine *s* máquina de apostar, sacaperras
gambling table *s* mesa de juego
gamboge [gæm'buʒ] o [gæm'bodʒ] *s* gomaguta, resina de Camboya
gambol ['gæmbəl] *s* cabriola, retozo; (*pret & pp:* **-boled** o **-bolled;** *ger:* **-boling** o **-bolling**) *vn* cabriolar, retozar
gambrel ['gæmbrəl] *s* corvejón (*de caballo*); caballete de suspensión (*de los mataderos*); (arch.) techo a la holandesa
gambrel roof *s* (arch.) techo a la holandesa
game [gem] *s* juego; partida (*de juego*); tantos (*de una partida en cualquier momento*); deporte; caza; (bridge) manga; (sport) juego (*cierto número de tantos ganados*); (fig.) juego (*p.ej., de la diplomacia*); (fig.) jugada (*estratagema, treta*); (fig.) asunto, actividad; **the game is up** hemos perdido el juego, estamos frescos; **to be out of the game** estar inútil para el juego; **to make game of** burlarse de; **to play a good game** jugar muy bien, ser muy diestro; **to play the game** jugar limpio, proceder lealmente; *adj* de caza; animoso, bravo, peleón; (coll.) cojo (*dícese de la pierna*); *va* perder en el juego; *vn* jugar por dinero
game bag *s* morral
game bird *s* ave de caza
gamecock ['gem,kɑk] *s* gallo de combate, de pelea o de riña
game fish *s* pez animoso y muy estimado de los pescadores deportivos
game fowl *s* gallo o gallina de la raza de los gallos de riña
gamekeeper ['gem,kipər] *s* guardabosque
game law *s* ley que regula la caza y la pesca
game of chance *s* juego de azar, juego de suerte
game preserve *s* vedado, vedado de caza, coto
gamesome ['gemsəm] *adj* juguetón, retozón
gamester ['gemstər] *s* jugador; tahúr, garitero
gametangium [,gæmɪ'tændʒɪəm] *s* (*pl:* **-a** [ə]) (bot.) gametangio
gamete ['gæmit] o [gə'mit] *s* (biol.) gameto
gametogenesis [,gæmɪto'dʒɛnɪsɪs] *s* (biol.) gametogénesis
gametophyte [gə'mitəfaɪt] *s* (bot.) gametofita
game warden *s* guardabosque
gaming ['gemɪŋ] *s* juego (*por dinero*)
gaming house *s* casa de juego
gaming table *s* mesa de juego
gamma ['gæmə] *s* gama
gammadion [gə'medɪɑn] *s* (*pl:* **-a** [ə]) cruz gamada
gamma globulin *s* (physiol.) globulina gama
gamma rays *spl* (phys.) rayos gama
gammer ['gæmər] *s* abuelita, vieja
gammon ['gæmən] *s* extremo inferior de una lonja de tocino; jamón; (coll.) tejido de falsedades
gamogenesis [,gæmo'dʒɛnɪsɪs] *s* (biol.) gamogénesis
gamopetalous [,gæmo'pɛtələs] *adj* (bot.) gamopétalo
gamophyllous [,gæmo'fɪləs] *adj* (bot.) gamofilo
gamosepalous [,gæmo'sɛpələs] *adj* (bot.) gamosépalo
gamp [gæmp] *s* gran paraguas
gamut ['gæmət] *s* (mus. & fig.) gama
gamy ['gemɪ] *adj* (*comp:* **-ier;** *super:* **-iest**) salvajino; animoso, bravo, peleón
gan o **'gan** [gæn] *pret de* **gin** [gɪn]
gander ['gændər] *s* ganso
gang [gæŋ] *s* pandilla (*de pistoleros*); cuadrilla, brigada (*de braceros*); juego (*de herramientas o máquinas*); *adj* múltiple; *vn* apandillar; acuadrillarse, agavillarse; (Scotch) ir, caminar; **to gang up against** conspirar contra; atacar en cuadrilla
gang condenser *s* (rad.) condensador múltiple
gangling ['gæŋglɪŋ] *adj* larguirucho, larguirucho y desgarbado
ganglion ['gæŋglɪən] *s* (*pl:* **-a** [ə] o **-ons**) (anat. & path.) ganglio; (fig.) centro de actividad
ganglionic [,gæŋglɪ'ɑnɪk] *adj* ganglionar
gangly ['gæŋglɪ] *adj* (coll.) var. de **gangling**
gangplank ['gæŋ,plæŋk] *s* plancha, pasarela
gang plow *s* arado de reja múltiple
gangrene ['gæŋgrin] *s* (path.) gangrena; *va* gangrenar; *vn* gangrenarse
gangrenous ['gæŋgrɪnəs] *adj* gangrenoso
gangster ['gæŋstər] *s* (coll.) pandillero, pistolero
gangsterism ['gæŋstərɪzəm] *s* (coll.) bandolerismo, pistolerismo, gangsterismo
gangue [gæŋ] *s* (min.) ganga
gang warfare *s* lucha entre pandillas
gangway ['gæŋ,we] *s* (naut.) portalón (*abertura en el costado del buque*); plancha, pa-

sarela; *interj* ¡afuera!, ¡abran paso!, ¡paso libre!
gannet [ˈgænɪt] *s* (orn.) alcatraz, planga
ganoid [ˈgænɔɪd] *adj & s* (ichth.) ganoideo
gantlet [ˈgɑntlɪt] *s* (rail.) vía traslapada, vía de garganta; var. de **gauntlet**
gantry [ˈgæntrɪ] *s* (*pl:* **-tries**) caballete, poíno; puente transversal de grúa corrediza; (rail.) puente transversal de señales
gantry crane *s* grúa de caballete
Ganymede [ˈgænɪmid] *s* (myth.) Ganimedes
gaol [dʒel] *s* (Brit.) var. de **jail**
gaoler [ˈdʒelər] *s* (Brit.) var. de **jailer**
gap [gæp] *s* boquete (*p.ej., en una pared*); laguna (*claro, interrupción*); garganta, quebrada; (aer.) entreplanos; (fig.) sima (*entre dos puntos de vista*); (*pret & pp:* **gapped;** *ger:* **gapping**) *va* hacer brecha en; hacer muesca en
gape [gep] o [gæp] *s* abertura, brecha; bostezo; mirada de asombro (*con la boca abierta*); **the gapes** necesidad imperiosa de estar bostezando; enfermedad de las gallinas causada por el gusano rojo; *vn* abrirse mucho; bostezar; embobarse; **to gape at** embobarse de, con o en; **to stand gaping** embobarse
gapeworm [ˈgep,wʌrm] o [ˈgæp,wʌrm] *s* (zool.) gusano rojo
G.A.R. abr. de **Grand Army of the Republic**
gar [gɑr] *s* var. de **garfish**
garage [gəˈrɑʒ] *s* garage; *va* dejar en garage
garb [gɑrb] *s* traje, vestidura; apariencia, aspecto; *va* vestir
garbage [ˈgɑrbɪdʒ] *s* bazofia, basuras, desperdicios
garbage can *s* cubo para basuras, bote de basura
garbage collector *s* basurero, recogedor de bazofia, colector de basuras
garbage disposal *s* evacuación de basuras, remoción de basuras
garbage truck *s* camión basurero
garble [ˈgɑrbəl] *va* mutilar engañosamente (*un texto, discurso, etc.*); entresacar engañosamente (*hechos, cifras de la estadística, etc.*)
garboard [ˈgɑr,bord] *s* (naut.) aparadura
garden [ˈgɑrdən] *s* huerto (*de hortalizas*); jardín (*de flores y plantas ornamentales*); sitio de recreo; sitio deleitoso; región fértil y cultivada; *adj* de huerto; de jardín; común, ordinario; *va* cultivar (*un terreno*) para producir hortalizas o flores; *vn* cultivar huertos o jardines
garden balm *s* (bot.) melisa, toronjil
garden balsam *s* (bot.) balsamina de jardín; (bot.) trébol oloroso
garden city *s* ciudad jardín
gardener [ˈgɑrdnər] *s* hortelano; jardinero
gardenia [gɑrˈdinɪə] *s* (bot.) gardenia
gardening [ˈgɑrdnɪŋ] *s* horticultura; jardinería
Garden of Eden *s* (Bib.) jardín del Edén
garden party *s* fiesta que se da en un jardín o parque
garden pink *s* (bot.) clavel coronado o clavellina de pluma
garden rocket *s* (bot.) juliana; (bot.) roqueta, ruca
garden warbler *s* (orn.) andahuertas
garfish [ˈgɑr,fɪʃ] *s* (ichth.) aguja de mar, pez aguja; (ichth.) pez caimán
garganey [ˈgɑrgənɪ] *s* (orn.) cerceta
Gargantuan [gɑrˈgæntʃuən] *adj* enorme, gigantesco
garget [ˈgɑrgɪt] *s* (vet.) inflamación de la cabeza o la garganta del ganado; (vet.) inflamación de la ubre de las vacas; (bot.) hierba carmín
gargle [ˈgɑrgəl] *s* gargarismo (*líquido*); *va* enjuagarse (*la boca o la garganta*); *vn* gargarizar
gargling [ˈgɑrglɪŋ] *s* gárgara, gargarismo
gargoyle [ˈgɑrgɔɪl] *s* (arch.) gárgola
garish [ˈgɛrɪʃ] *adj* charro, chillón, deslumbrante
garland [ˈgɑrlənd] *s* guirnalda; (naut.) roñada; *va* enguirnaldar
garlic [ˈgɑrlɪk] *s* (bot.) ajo; ajos (*que se usan como condimento*)
garlicky [ˈgɑrlɪkɪ] *adj* cepáceo, aliáceo
garlic mustard *s* (bot.) aliaria
garment [ˈgɑrmənt] *s* prenda, prenda de vestir; *va* vestir
garner [ˈgɑrnər] *s* troj, granero; acopio, provisión; *va* entrojar; acopiar
garnet [ˈgɑrnɪt] *s* granate (*piedra y color*); *adj* granate
garnish [ˈgɑrnɪʃ] *s* adorno; (cook.) condimento de adorno; *va* adornar; (cook.) adornar (*p.ej., con perejil*); (law) notificar; (law) embargar
garnishee [,gɑrnɪˈʃi] *s* (law) persona que ha sido notificada de un entredicho; *va* (law) notificar de un entredicho; (law) embargar
garnishment [ˈgɑrnɪʃmənt] *s* adorno; (law) entredicho; (law) embargo de crédito; (law) emplazamiento
garniture [ˈgɑrnɪtʃər] *s* adorno, embellecimiento, guarnición
Garonne [gɑˈrɑn] *s* Garona
garotte [gəˈrɑt] *s & va* var. de **garrote**
garret [ˈgærɪt] *s* desván, buhardilla
garrison [ˈgærɪsən] *s* (mil.) guarnición; plaza fuerte; *va* guarnecer, guarnicionar; poner (*la tropa*) en guarnición
garrot [ˈgærət] *s* (orn.) clángula
garrote [gəˈrɑt] o [gəˈrot] o **garrotte** [gəˈrɑt] *s* estrangulación (*con robo*); garrote (*forma de ejecución de la pena de muerte; aro de hierro que sirve para tal ejecución*); *va* estrangular; estrangular para robar; agarrotar, dar garrote a
garrulity [gəˈrulɪtɪ] *s* garrulidad
garrulous [ˈgærələs] o [ˈgærjələs] *adj* gárrulo
garter [ˈgɑrtər] *s* liga; (*cap.*) *s* Jarretera (*orden; insignia de la orden*); *va* atar con liga
garter snake *s* (zool.) culebrita no venenosa (*Thamnophis*); (zool.) serpiente de coral
garter stitch *s* punto de media
garth [gɑrθ] *s* patio de claustro
gas [gæs] *s* gas; (coll.) gasolina; (slang) parloteo; **to cut off the gas** (aut.) cerrar el carburador; (*pret & pp:* **gassed;** *ger:* **gassing**) *va* abastecer o proveer de gas; gasear (*atacar, envenenar o asfixiar con gas*); (chem.) gasear; (coll.) abastecer o proveer de gasolina; *vn* despedir gas; (slang) parlotear
gas attack *s* ataque con gases
gasbag [ˈgæs,bæg] *s* (aer.) cámara de gas; (slang) charlatán
gas burner *s* mechero de gas
gas chamber *s* cámara de gases
Gascon [ˈgæskən] *adj & s* gascón; (*l.c.*) *s* fanfarrón
gasconade [,gæskəˈned] *s* gasconada; *vn* fanfarronear
Gasconism [ˈgæskənɪzəm] *s* gasconismo
Gascony [ˈgæskənɪ] *s* Gascuña
gas engine *s* motor de gas
gaseous [ˈgæsɪəs] *adj* gaseoso
gas fitter *s* gasista
gas fittings *spl* cañerías, mecheros y accesorios de gas
gas fixtures *spl* guarniciones de gas
gas generator *s* gasógeno
gash [gæʃ] *s* cuchillada, chirlo; *va* acuchillar, herir con arma blanca
gas heat *s* calefacción por gas
gasholder [ˈgæs,holdər] *s* gasómetro
gasification [,gæsɪfɪˈkeʃən] *s* gasificación
gasiform [ˈgæsɪfɔrm] *adj* gasiforme
gasify [ˈgæsɪfaɪ] (*pret & pp:* **-fied**) *va* gasificar; *vn* gasificarse
gas jet *s* mechero de gas; llama de mechero de gas
gasket [ˈgæskɪt] *s* junta, empaquetadura; (naut.) tomador
gaslight [ˈgæs,laɪt] *s* mechero de gas; luz de gas
gas main *s* cañería de gas, cañería maestra de gas
gas mantle *s* manguito de incandescencia, camiseta
gas mask *s* mascarilla contra gases asfixiantes, máscara contra gases, careta antigás
gas meter *s* contador de gas
gasolene o **gasoline** [ˈgæsəlin] o [,gæsəˈlin] *s* gasoleno o gasolina
gasoline pump *s* surtidor de gasolina, poste distribuidor de gasolina
gasometer [gæsˈɑmɪtər] *s* gasómetro
gasp [gæsp] o [gɑsp] *s* anhelo; grito sofocado; **at the last gasp** a punto de echar el último suspiro; *va* pronunciar con sonidos sofocados;

vn anhelar, sofocarse, boquear, abrir la boca de asombro
gas pipe *s* tubo de conducción de gas, tubería de gas
gas producer *s* gasógeno
gas range *s* cocina a gas
gas shell *s* (mil.) granada de gas
gas station *s* estación gasolinera
gas stove *s* cocina a gas
gassy ['gæsɪ] *adj* (*comp:* **-sier;** *super:* **-siest**) gaseoso; (coll.) hinchado
gas tank *s* gasómetro (municipal); (aut.) depósito de gasolina
gas-tank cap ['gæs,tæŋk] *s* (aut.) tapón de llenado
gastight ['gæs,taɪt] *adj* hermético, a prueba de gas
gastralgia [gæs'trældʒɪə] *s* (path.) gastralgia
gastrectomy [gæs'trɛktəmɪ] *s* (*pl:* **-mies**) (surg.) gastrectomía
gastric ['gæstrɪk] *adj* gástrico
gastric juice *s* (physiol.) jugo gástrico
gastric ulcer *s* (path.) úlcera gástrica
gastritis [gæs'traɪtɪs] *s* (path.) gastritis
gastroenteritis [,gæstro,ɛntə'raɪtɪs] *s* (path.) gastroenteritis
gastroenterology [,gæstro,ɛntə'rɑlədʒɪ] *s* gastroenterología
gastrointestinal [,gæstro·ɪn'tɛstɪnəl] *adj* gastrointestinal
gastronome ['gæstrənom] o **gastronomer** [gæs'trɑnəmər] *s* gastrónomo
gastronomic [,gæstrə'nɑmɪk] o **gastronomical** [,gæstrə'nɑmɪkəl] *adj* gastronómico
gastronomy [gæs'trɑnəmɪ] *s* gastronomía
gastropod ['gæstrəpɑd] *adj & s* (zool.) gastrópodo
gastrovascular [,gæstro'væskjələr] *adj* gastrovascular
gastrula ['gæstrʊlə] *s* (*pl:* **-lae** [li]) (embryol.) gástrula
gas turbine *s* turbina de gas
gasworker ['gæs,wʌrkər] *s* gasista
gasworks ['gæs,wʌrks] *ssg o spl* fábrica de gas
gat [gæt] *s* (slang) arma de fuego, revólver
gate [get] *s* puerta (*de cercado*); portillo; (hyd.) compuerta; (rail.) barrera; entrada, taquilla, entrada de taquilla (*número de personas que asisten a un espectáculo y cantidad de dinero que pagan*); (fig.) entrada, camino, vía; **to crash the gate** (slang) colarse de gorra
gatecrasher ['get,kræʃər] *s* (slang) intruso (*persona que se cuela en alguna parte sin pagar la entrada o sin ser invitado*)
gatekeeper ['get,kipər] *s* portero; (rail.) guardabarrera
gate-leg table ['get,lɛg] o **gate-legged table** ['get,lɛgd] *s* mesa de hojas y patas plegadizas
gate money *s* entrada, taquilla (*dinero cobrado por las entradas a un espectáculo*)
gatepost ['get,post] *s* poste de una puerta de cercado
gateway ['get,we] *s* entrada, paso; (fig.) entrada, camino, vía
gather ['gæðər] *s* (sew.) frunce; *va* recoger, reunir; acumular; cosechar, recolectar; coger (*leña, flores, etc.*); calcular, deducir; cobrar (*fuerzas*); cubrirse de, llenarse de (*polvo*); recoger (*una persona sus pensamientos*); (sew.) fruncir; (b.b.) alzar; **to be gathered to one's fathers** morir y ser enterrado; **to gather speed** ir cada vez más rápidamente; **to gather up** recoger; *vn* reunirse; acumularse; condensarse; formar pus; amontonarse (*p.ej., nubes*); saltar (*p.ej., lágrimas*); **to gather oneself together** componerse, tranquilizarse y cobrar fuerzas
gathering ['gæðərɪŋ] *s* reunión; acumulación; recolección; hacinamiento; (path.) divieso, grano; (b.b.) alzado; (sew.) frunce
Gatun Lake [gɑ'tun] *s* lago de Gatún
gauche [goʃ] *adj* torpe; falto de tino
gaucherie [,goʃə'ri] *s* torpeza; falta de tino
Gaucho ['gaʊtʃo] *adj* gaucho, gauchesco; *s* (*pl:* **-chos**) gaucho
gaud [gɔd] *s* dije, adorno cursi
gaudy ['gɔdɪ] *adj* (*comp:* **-ier;** *super:* **-iest**) chillón, llamativo, vistoso, cursi
gauge [gedʒ] *s* norma de medida; calibre, calibrador; indicador, manómetro, nivel; plantilla; gramil (*de carpintero*); tamaño; capacidad; medidor (*p.ej., de gasolina*); (constr.) porción de tejas, tablas de ripia, etc., que queda expuesta al aire; (rail.) ancho de vía, entrevía; *va* medir; calibrar; graduar; comprobar; aforar, apreciar; (hyd.) aforar, (naut.) arquear
gauge cock *s* grifo del indicador, llave de prueba
gauge glass *s* tubo indicador, vidrio de nivel
Gaul [gɔl] *s* la Galia; galo (*natural*)
Gaulish ['gɔlɪʃ] *s* galo (*idioma*)
gaultheria [gɔl'θɪrɪə] *s* (bot.) gaulteria
gaunt [gɔnt] o [gɑnt] *adj* desvaído, demacrado; triste, sombrío
gauntlet ['gɔntlɪt] o ['gɑntlɪt] *s* guantelete; guante con puño abocinado; puño abocinado; (surg.) guantelete; (mil. & fig.) carrera de baquetas; **to run the gauntlet** (mil. & fig.) correr baquetas o pasar por baquetas; **to take up the gauntlet** recoger el guante; **to throw down the gauntlet** arrojar el guante
gauntleted ['gɔntlɪtɪd] o ['gɑntlɪtɪd] *adj* enguantado con guantelete o con guante
gauss [gaʊs] *s* (phys.) gausio
gauze [gɔz] *s* gasa, cendal
gauzy ['gɔzɪ] *adj* (*comp:* **-ier;** *super:* **-iest**) diáfano, sutilísimo
gavage [gə'vɑʒ] *s* gavaje
gave [gev] *pret de* **give**
gavel ['gævəl] *s* mazo o martillo (*de los presidentes de asambleas, etc.*)
gavial ['gevɪəl] *s* (zool.) gavial
gavotte [gə'vɑt] *s* gavota (*danza y música*)
Gawain ['gɑwɪn] o ['gɔwɪn] *s* Galván (*de la Mesa Redonda y el Amadís de Gaula*)
gawk [gɔk] *s* (coll.) palurdo, papanatas; *vn* (coll.) mirar de modo impertinente; (coll.) papar moscas
gawky ['gɔkɪ] *adj* (*comp:* **-ier;** *super:* **-iest**) torpe, desgarbado, bobo
gay [ge] *adj* alegre, festivo; amigo de los placeres, ligero de cascos; vistoso
gayety ['geɪtɪ] *s* (*pl:* **-ties**) var. de **gaiety**
gay science *s* gaya ciencia (*poesía amatoria*)
gaz. abr. de **gazette** y **gazetteer**
gazabo [gə'zebo] *s* (*pl:* **-bos** o **-boes**) mirador (*balcón con cristales*); miranda; (slang) adefesio, mamarracho
gaze [gez] *s* mirada fija; *vn* mirar con fijeza
gazebo [gə'zibo] *s* (*pl:* **-bos** o **-boes**) var. de **gazabo**
gazehound ['gez,haʊnd] *s* perro que sigue la caza con la vista
gazelle [gə'zɛl] *s* (zool.) gacela
gazette [gə'zɛt] *s* gaceta; *va* anunciar o publicar en gaceta
gazetteer [,gæzə'tɪr] *s* gacetero; director de una gaceta oficial; diccionario geográfico
G.B. abr. de **Great Britain**
g.c.d. o **G.C.D.** abr. de **greatest common divisor**
g.c.m. o **G.C.M.** abr. de **greatest common measure**
gear [gɪr] *s* arneses, pertrechos, utensilios; aparato, mecanismo (*de transmisión, de gobierno, etc.*); engranaje, rueda dentada; **out of gear** desengranado; descompuesto; **to put in gear** o **to throw into gear** engranar; **to throw out of gear** desengranar; (fig.) trastornar; *va* pertrechar; engranar; *vn* engranar; funcionar (*los engranajes*); **to gear into** engranar con
gearbox ['gɪr,bɑks] *s* (mach.) caja de engranajes, cárter de engranajes; (aut.) caja de velocidades
gear case *s* (mach.) caja de engranajes, cárter de engranajes
gear cutter *s* talladora de engranajes
gearing ['gɪrɪŋ] *s* (mach.) engranaje, tren de engranajes
gear ratio *s* relación o razón de engranajes
gearshift ['gɪr,ʃɪft] *s* (aut.) cambio de marchas, cambio de velocidades, aparato de cambios
gearshift lever *s* (aut.) palanca de cambio
gearwheel ['gɪr,hwil] *s* (mach.) rueda dentada
gecko ['gɛko] *s* (*pl:* **-os** u **-oes**) (zool.) geco, salamanquesa
gee [dʒi] *interj* ¡caramba!; ¡a la derecha!; *va* arrear hacia la derecha; *vn* torcer o volver hacia la derecha

geese [gis] *pl de* **goose**
Gehenna [gɪˈhɛnə] *s* (Bib.) gehena
Geiger counter [ˈgaɪgər] *s* (phys.) contador de Geiger
geisha [ˈgeʃə] *s* (*pl:* **-sha** o **-shas**) geisha
Geissler tube [ˈgaɪslər] *s* (elec.) tubo de Geissler
gel [dʒɛl] *s* (chem. & phys.) gel; (*pret & pp:* **gelled**; *ger:* **gelling**) *vn* cuajarse en forma de gel
gelatin o **gelatine** [ˈdʒɛlətɪn] *s* gelatina
gelatinous [dʒɪˈlætɪnəs] *adj* gelatinoso
gelation [dʒɪˈleʃən] *s* gelación
geld [gɛld] (*pret & pp:* **gelded** o **gelt**) *va* castrar
Gelderland [ˈgɛldərlænd] *s* Güeldres
gelding [ˈgɛldɪŋ] *s* animal castrado
gelid [ˈdʒɛlɪd] *adj* gélido, helado, muy frío
gelidity [dʒəˈlɪdɪtɪ] *s* frío extremo
gelsemium [dʒɛlˈsimɪəm] *s* (pharm.) gelsemio
gelt [gɛlt] *pret & pp de* **geld**
gem [dʒɛm] *s* gema, piedra preciosa; (fig.) joya, preciosidad; (*pret & pp:* **gemmed**; *ger:* **gemming**) *va* adornar con piedras preciosas; tachonar (*p.ej., el cielo las estrellas*)
gemellus [dʒɪˈmɛləs] *s* (anat.) gemelo
geminate [ˈdʒɛmɪnet] *adj* geminado; *va* geminar; *vn* geminarse
gemination [ˌdʒɛmɪˈneʃən] *s* geminación; (phonet. & rhet.) geminación
Gemini [ˈdʒɛmɪnaɪ] *ssg* (astr.) Géminis o Gemelos (*constelación*); (astr.) Géminis (*signo del zodíaco*); *spl* (myth.) Cástor y Pólux
gemma [ˈdʒɛmə] *s* (*pl:* **-mae** [mi]) (bot. & zool.) yema
gemmate [ˈdʒɛmet] *adj* (bot.) gemífero; *vn* (bot.) gemificar
gemmation [dʒɛˈmeʃən] *s* (bot. & zool.) gemación
gemmiferous [dʒɛˈmɪfərəs] *adj* gemífero; (bot. & zool.) gemífero
gemmiparous [dʒɛˈmɪpərəs] *adj* (biol.) gemíparo
gemmule [ˈdʒɛmjul] *s* (bot., zool. & biol.) gémula
gemsbok [ˈgɛmzˌbɑk] *s* (zool.) antílope sudafricano (*Oryx gazella*)
gen. abr. de **gender, general, generic, genitive** y **genus**
Gen. abr. de **General** y **Genesis**
gendarme [ˈʒɑndɑrm] *s* gendarme
gendarmerie [ˌʒɑndɑrmˈri] *s* gendarmería
gender [ˈdʒɛndər] *s* (gram.) género; (coll.) sexo
gene [dʒin] *s* (biol.) gen; (*cap.*) *s* nombre abreviado de **Eugene**
genealogical [ˌdʒɛnɪəˈlɑdʒɪkəl] o [ˌdʒinɪəˈlɑdʒɪkəl] *adj* genealógico
genealogical tree *s* árbol genealógico
genealogist [ˌdʒɛnɪˈælədʒɪst] o [ˌdʒinɪˈælədʒɪst] *s* genealogista
genealogy [ˌdʒɛnɪˈælədʒɪ] o [ˌdʒinɪˈælədʒɪ] *s* (*pl:* **-gies**) genealogía
general [ˈdʒɛnərəl] *adj* general; *s* (mil.) general, oficial general; (mil.) capitán general (*grado supremo del generalato*); **in general** en general o por lo general; (*pret & pp:* **-aled** o **-alled**; *ger:* **-aling** o **-alling**) *va* mandar en calidad de general
general anesthesia *f* anestesia general
General Assembly *s* asamblea legislativa de ciertos estados de los EE.UU.; Asamblea General (*de las Naciones Unidas*)
general average *s* (naut.) avería gruesa
General Court *s* asamblea legislativa de los estados de Massachusetts y de Nuevo Hampshire, EE.UU.
general delivery *s* lista de correos
general in chief *s* (mil.) general en jefe
generalissimo [ˌdʒɛnərəˈlɪsɪmo] *s* (*pl:* **-mos**) generalísimo
generality [ˌdʒɛnəˈrælɪtɪ] *s* (*pl:* **-ties**) generalidad
generalization [ˌdʒɛnərəlɪˈzeʃən] *s* generalización
generalize [ˈdʒɛnərəlaɪz] *va & vn* generalizar
generally [ˈdʒɛnərəlɪ] *adv* generalmente
general officer *s* (mil.) oficial general
General of the Army *s* (mil.) capitán general de ejército
general practitioner *s* médico general
general-purpose [ˈdʒɛnərəlˈpʌrpəs] *adj* para toda clase de objetivos
generalship [ˈdʒɛnərəlˌʃɪp] *s* generalato; don de mando
general staff *s* (mil.) estado mayor general
general store *s* tienda de variedades
generate [ˈdʒɛnəret] *va* engendrar, generar; (geom.) engendrar; (elec.) generar
generating station *s* (elec.) central generadora, central de fuerza
generating unit *s* var. de **generator unit**
generation [ˌdʒɛnəˈreʃən] *s* generación
generative [ˈdʒɛnəˌretɪv] *adj* generativo
generator [ˈdʒɛnəˌretər] *s* generador; (elec.) generador (*dínamo*); (mach.) generador (*caldera de vapor*)
generator unit *s* (elec.) grupo electrógeno
generatrix [ˌdʒɛnəˈretrɪks] *s* (*pl:* **generatrices** [ˌdʒɛnərəˈtraɪsiz]) (elec. & geom.) generatriz
generic [dʒɪˈnɛrɪk] *adj* genérico
generically [dʒɪˈnɛrɪkəlɪ] *adv* genéricamente
generosity [ˌdʒɛnəˈrɑsɪtɪ] *s* (*pl:* **-ties**) generosidad
generous [ˈdʒɛnərəs] *adj* generoso; abundante, grande
genesic [dʒɪˈnɛsɪk] *adj* genésico
genesis [ˈdʒɛnɪsɪs] *s* (*pl:* **-ses** [siz]) génesis; (*cap.*) *s* (Bib.) el Génesis
genet [ˈdʒɛnɪt] *s* (zool.) jineta; jaca chica española
genetic [dʒɪˈnɛtɪk] *adj* genético; **genetics** *ssg* genética
genetically [dʒɪˈnɛtɪkəlɪ] *adv* genéticamente
geneticist [dʒɪˈnɛtɪsɪst] *s* genetista
Geneva [dʒɪˈnivə] *s* Ginebra
Genevan [dʒɪˈnivən] *adj & s* var. de **Genevese**
Genevese [ˌdʒɛnɪˈviz] *adj* ginebrés o ginebrino; calvinista; *s* (*pl:* **-vese**) ginebrés o ginebrino; calvinista
Genevieve [ˈdʒɛnəviv] *s* Genoveva
genial [ˈdʒinjəl] *adj* afable, complaciente; confortante, suave; (anat. & zool.) geniano
geniality [ˌdʒinɪˈælɪtɪ] *s* afabilidad, complacencia
geniculate [dʒɪˈnɪkjəlɪt] o [dʒɪˈnɪkjəlet] *adj* geniculado
geniculation [dʒɪˌnɪkjəˈleʃən] *s* geniculación
genie [ˈdʒinɪ] *s* var. de **jinn**
genii [ˈdʒinɪaɪ] *pl de* **genius**
genipap [ˈdʒɛnɪpæp] *s* (bot.) genipa
genital [ˈdʒɛnɪtəl] *adj* genital; **genitals** *spl* (anat.) genitales, órganos genitales
genitive [ˈdʒɛnɪtɪv] *adj & s* (gram.) genitivo
genitourinary [ˌdʒɛnɪtoˈjurɪˌnɛrɪ] *adj* génitourinario
genius [ˈdʒinjəs] o [ˈdʒinɪəs] *s* (*pl:* **geniuses**) genio (*fuerza creadora, don altísimo de invención; persona que lo posee*); (*pl:* **genii** [ˈdʒinɪaɪ]) genio (*espíritu tutelar; deidad pagana*)
Genoa [ˈdʒɛnoə] *s* Génova
genocidal [ˌdʒɛnəˈsaɪdəl] *adj* genocida
genocide [ˈdʒɛnəsaɪd] *s* genocidio (*acción*); genocida (*persona*)
Genoese [ˌdʒɛnoˈiz] *adj* genovés; *s* (*pl:* **-ese**) genovés
genom [ˈdʒɛnɑm] o **genome** [ˈdʒɛnom] *s* (biol.) genoma
genotype [ˈdʒɛnotaɪp] *s* (biol.) genotipo
genre [ˈʒɑnrə] *s* (f.a. & lit.) género; *adj* (f.a.) de género, p.ej., **genre painter** pintor de género
gent. o **Gent.** abr. de **gentleman** o **gentlemen**
genteel [dʒɛnˈtil] *adj* gentil, elegante; cortés, urbano; afectado, exquisito
gentian [ˈdʒɛnʃən] *s* (bot. & pharm.) genciana (*planta y raíz*)
gentianaceous [ˌdʒɛnʃɪəˈneʃəs] *adj* (bot.) gencianáceo
gentian violet *s* violeta de genciana
gentile o **Gentile** [ˈdʒɛntaɪl] *adj & s* no judío; cristiano; gentil (*pagano*); **gentile** [ˈdʒɛntɪl] o [ˈdʒɛntaɪl] *adj & s* (gram.) gentilicio
gentility [dʒɛnˈtɪlɪtɪ] *s* (*pl:* **-ties**) gentileza, cortesía; nobleza; **gentilities** *spl* exquisiteces
gentle [ˈdʒɛntəl] *adj* apacible, benévolo; suave, dulce, manso; noble, bien nacido; bueno, honrado; cortés, fino; ligero (*golpecito*); moderado, poco abrupto
gentle breeze *s* (naut.) viento flojo
gentlefolk [ˈdʒɛntəlˌfok] *s* gente bien nacida

gentleman ['dʒɛntəlmən] *s* (*pl:* **-men**) caballero, señor
gentleman in waiting *s* gentilhombre de cámara
gentlemanly ['dʒɛntəlmənlɪ] *adj* caballeroso
gentleman of fortune *s* caballero de industria
gentleman of leisure *s* señor que se da vida de marqués
gentleman of the road *s* salteador de caminos
gentleman's agreement *s* acuerdo verbal, pacto de caballeros
gentleness ['dʒɛntəlnɪs] *s* apacibilidad; suavidad, dulzura, mansedumbre; nobleza; cortesía; ligereza
gentle sex *s* bello sexo, sexo débil
gentlewoman ['dʒɛntəl,wʊmən] *s* (*pl:* **-women**) señora, dama; dama de honor
gently ['dʒɛntlɪ] *adv* suavemente, dulcemente, mansamente; poco a poco, despacio
gentry ['dʒɛntrɪ] *s* gente bien nacida; (Brit.) alta burguesía; (hum.) gente
genuflect ['dʒɛnjʊflɛkt] *vn* doblar las rodillas en señal de reverencia
genuflection o **genuflexion** [,dʒɛnjʊ'flɛkʃən] *s* genuflexión
genuine ['dʒɛnjʊɪn] *adj* genuino, legítimo; franco, sincero
genuineness ['dʒɛnjʊɪnnɪs] *s* autenticidad; sinceridad
genus ['dʒinəs] *s* (*pl:* **genera** ['dʒɛnərə] o **genuses**) (biol. & log.) género
Geo. abr. de **George**
geocentric [,dʒio'sɛntrɪk] o **geocentrical** [,dʒio'sɛntrɪkəl] *adj* geocéntrico
geochemistry [,dʒio'kɛmɪstrɪ] *s* geoquímica
geode ['dʒiod] *s* (geol.) geoda
geodesic [,dʒio'dɛsɪk] *adj* geodésico
geodesic line *s* (math.) línea geodésica
geodesist [dʒɪ'ɑdɪsɪst] *s* geodesta
geodesy [dʒɪ'ɑdɪsɪ] *s* geodesia
geodetic [,dʒio'dɛtɪk] *adj* geodésico
Geoffrey ['dʒɛfrɪ] *s* Geofredo
geog. abr. de **geographer, geographical** y **geography**
geognosy [dʒɪ'ɑgnəsɪ] *s* geognosia
geographer [dʒɪ'ɑgrəfər] *s* geógrafo
geographic [,dʒiə'græfɪk] o **geographical** [,dʒiə'græfɪkəl] *adj* geográfico
geographically [,dʒiə'græfɪkəlɪ] *adv* geográficamente
geographical mile *s* (naut.) milla marina, milla geográfica
geography [dʒɪ'ɑgrəfɪ] *s* (*pl:* **-phies**) geografía
geoid ['dʒiɔɪd] *s* geoide
geol. abr. de **geological, geologist** y **geology**
geologic [,dʒiə'lɑdʒɪk] o **geological** [,dʒiə'lɑdʒɪkəl] *adj* geológico
geologically [,dʒiə'lɑdʒɪkəlɪ] *adv* geológicamente
geologist [dʒɪ'ɑlədʒɪst] *s* geólogo
geology [dʒɪ'ɑlədʒɪ] *s* (*pl:* **-gies**) geología
geom. abr. de **geometrical** y **geometry**
geomagnetic [,dʒiomæg'nɛtɪk] *adj* geomagnético
geomancer ['dʒiə,mænsər] *s* geomántico
geomancy ['dʒiə,mænsɪ] *s* geomancía
geomantic [,dʒiə'mæntɪk] *adj* geomántico
geometer [dʒɪ'ɑmɪtər] *s* geómetra; (zool.) geómetra
geometric [,dʒiə'mɛtrɪk] o **geometrical** [,dʒiə'mɛtrɪkəl] *adj* geométrico
geometrician [dʒɪ,ɑmɪ'trɪʃən] *s* geómetra
geometric progression *s* progresión geométrica
geometric ratio *s* razón geométrica
geometrid [dʒɪ'ɑmɪtrɪd] *s* (ent.) geométrido
geometrize [dʒɪ'ɑmɪtraɪz] *va & vn* geometrizar
geometry [dʒɪ'ɑmɪtrɪ] *s* (*pl:* **-tries**) geometría
geomorphology [,dʒiəmər'fɑlədʒɪ] *s* geomorfología
geophagy [dʒɪ'ɑfədʒɪ] *s* geofagía
geophysical [,dʒio'fɪzɪkəl] *adj* geofísico
geophysicist [,dʒio'fɪzɪsɪst] *s* geofísico
geophysics [,dʒio'fɪzɪks] *ssg* geofísica
geophyte ['dʒiəfaɪt] *s* (bot.) geófita
geopolitical [,dʒiəpə'lɪtɪkəl] *adj* geopolítico
geopolitics [,dʒiə'pɑlɪtɪks] *ssg* geopolítica
geoponic [,dʒiə'pɑnɪk] *adj* geopónico; **geoponics** *ssg* geopónica o geoponía
georama [,dʒio'ræmə] o [,dʒio'rɑmə] *s* georama
George [dʒɔrdʒ] *s* Jorge
georgette [dʒɔr'dʒɛt] o **georgette crepe** *s* crespón de seda muy diáfano
Georgia ['dʒɔrdʒə] *s* Jorja (*nombre de mujer*)
Georgian ['dʒɔrdʒən] *adj & s* georgiano
Georgiana [,dʒɔrdʒɪ'ænə] o [,dʒɔrdʒɪ'ɑnə] *s* Georgina (*nombre de mujer*)
georgic ['dʒɔrdʒɪk] *s* geórgica (*poema*)
Georgina [dʒɔr'dʒinə] *s* var. de **Georgiana**
geosynclinal [,dʒiosɪn'klaɪnəl] *adj & s* (geol.) geosinclinal
geotaxis [,dʒio'tæksɪs] *s* geotaxia o geotactismo
geotectonic [,dʒiotɛk'tɑnɪk] *adj* geotectónico; **geotectonics** *ssg* geotectónica
geothermal [,dʒio'θʌrməl] *adj* geotérmico
geotropic [,dʒio'trɑpɪk] *adj* geotrópico
geotropism [dʒɪ'ɑtrəpɪzəm] *s* (biol.) geotropismo
ger. abr. de **gerund**
Ger. abr. de **German, Germanic** y **Germany**
Gerald ['dʒɛrəld] *s* Gerardo
geraniaceous [dʒɪ,renɪ'eʃəs] *adj* (bot.) geraniáceo
geranium [dʒɪ'renɪəm] *s* (bot.) geranio
Gerard [dʒɪ'rɑrd] o ['dʒɛrɑrd] *s* var. de **Gerald**
gerent ['dʒɪrənt] *s* gerente
gerfalcon ['dʒʌr,fɔkən] o ['dʒʌr,fɔlkən] *s* (orn.) gerifalte
geriatrical [,dʒɛrɪ'ætrɪkəl] *adj* geriátrico
geriatrician [,dʒɛrɪə'trɪʃən] *s* geriatra
geriatrics [,dʒɛrɪ'ætrɪks] *ssg* geriatría
germ [dʒʌrm] *s* (bact., biol., embryol. & fig.) germen; *adj* germinal
german ['dʒʌrmən] *adj* carnal (*dícese del hermano o el primo*); *s* cotillón; fiesta en que se baila el cotillón; (*cap.*) *adj* alemán; *s* (*pl:* **-mans**) alemán
germander [dʒər'mændər] *s* (bot.) germandrina, camedrio
germane [dʒər'men] *adj* relacionado, pertinente
Germania [dʒər'menɪə] *s* (hist. & fig.) Germania
Germanic [dʒər'mænɪk] *adj* germánico; *s* germánico (*grupo de lenguas*)
Germanism ['dʒʌrmənɪzəm] *s* germanismo
Germanist ['dʒʌrmənɪst] *s* germanista
germanium [dʒər'menɪəm] *s* (chem.) germanio
Germanization [,dʒʌrmənɪ'zeʃən] *s* germanización
Germanize ['dʒʌrmənaɪz] *va* germanizar; *vn* germanizarse
German measles *s* (path.) rubéola, sarampión alemán
Germanophile [dʒər'mænofaɪl] *adj & s* germanófilo
Germanophobe [dʒər'mænofob] *adj & s* germanófobo
German script *s* letra alemana
German shepherd dog *s* perro pastor alemán
German silver *s* melchor, plata alemana
German text *s* (print.) tipo alemán
Germany ['dʒʌrmənɪ] *s* Alemania
germ cell *s* (biol.) célula germen
germicidal [,dʒʌrmɪ'saɪdəl] *adj* germicida
germicide ['dʒʌrmɪsaɪd] *s* germicida
germinal ['dʒʌrmɪnəl] *adj* germinal
germinant ['dʒʌrmɪnənt] *adj* germinante
germinate ['dʒʌrmɪnet] *va* hacer germinar; *vn* germinar
germination [,dʒʌrmɪ'neʃən] *s* germinación
germinative ['dʒʌrmɪ,netɪv] *adj* germinativo
germinator ['dʒʌrmɪ,netər] *s* germinador
germ plasm *s* germen plasma
germ theory *s* (biol. & path.) teoría germinal
germ war o **warfare** *s* guerra bacteriana o guerra bacteriológica
gerontology [,dʒɛrən'tɑlədʒɪ] *s* gerontología
gerrymander ['gɛrɪ,mændər] o ['dʒɛrɪ,mændər] *s* demarcación arbitraria e injusta de los distritos electorales; [,gɛrɪ'mændər] o [,dʒɛrɪ'mændər] *va* dividir arbitrariamente (*un estado*) en distritos electorales (*para sacar ventaja de ello*); manejar injustamente (*los resortes políticos*)

Gertrude ['gʌrtrud] *s* Gertrudis
Gerty ['gʌrtɪ] *s* Tula
gerund ['dʒɛrənd] *s* gerundio
gerundial [dʒɪ'rʌndɪəl] *adj* del gerundio
gerundive [dʒɪ'rʌndɪv] *s* gerundino (*en gramática latina*); gerundio adjetivado
gest [dʒɛst] *s* (archaic) gesta
Gestalt psychology [gə'ʃtɑlt] *s* psicología de la forma, gestaltismo
Gestapo [gə'stɑpo] *s* gestapo (*policía secreta del gobierno nazi*)
gestation [dʒɛs'teʃən] *s* gestación; (fig.) gestación
gesticulate [dʒɛs'tɪkjəlet] *vn* accionar, manotear
gesticulation [dʒɛs,tɪkjə'leʃən] *s* manoteo, ademán
gesticulative [dʒɛs'tɪkjə,letɪv] *adj* manoteador
gesticulator [dʒɛs'tɪkjə,letər] *s* manoteador
gesture ['dʒɛstʃər] *s* ademán, gesto; muestra, demostración, gesto; *vn* hacer ademanes, hacer gestos
get [gɛt] (*pret:* **got;** *pp:* **got** o **gotten;** *ger:* **getting**) *va* obtener, recibir; conseguir; buscar, ir por; traer; tomar (*p.ej., un billete*); llevar, hacer llegar; alcanzar; proporcionar; hallar, localizar; preparar, hacer (*p.ej., la comida*); adquirir (*p.ej., destreza*); aprender de memoria; resolver (*un problema*); (coll.) comprender; (coll.) captar, conseguir sintonizar (*una estación emisora*); (slang) irritar; **let's get this over!** ¡pecho al agua!; **to have got** tener, p.ej., **I've got enough money** tengo bastante dinero; **to have got to** + *inf* tener que + *inf*, p.ej., **I've got to walk** tengo que ir a pie; **to get across** (coll.) hacer aceptar, hacer comprender; **to get back** recobrar; **to get by** conseguir que se deje pasar (*una cosa*); **to get down** descolgar; tragar; **to get going** poner en marcha; **to get in** conseguir meter (*una cosa*) en (*otra*); **to get off** quitar (*p.ej., una mancha*); quitarse (*los zapatos*); ayudar a partir o a escaparse; despachar; **to get on** ponerse (*los zapatos*); **to get out** publicar (*p.ej., un libro*); ayudar a partir o a escaparse; **to get out of** hacer confesar, lograr sacar de; **to get out of the way** quitar de en medio; **to get over** (slang) hacer aceptar, hacer comprender; conseguir pasar (*una cosa*) por encima de o más allá de (*otra*); **to get something away from someone** quitar algo a alguien; **to get through** lograr pasar (*una cosa*) por (*otra*); **to get to** + *inf* conseguir, lograr que + *subj*, p.ej., **I got him to leave** conseguí que saliese; **to get** + *pp* hacer + *inf*, p.ej., **he got his hair cut** se hizo cortar el pelo; hacer que + *subj*, p.ej., **I got him appointed** hice que le nombraran ‖ *vn* hacerse, ponerse, volverse; meterse; llegar (coll.) largarse; **to get about** mostrarse activo; estar levantado (*un convaleciente*); **to get abroad** divulgarse; **to get across** tener éxito; **to get along** marcharse; seguir andando; ir tirando; tener éxito; llevarse bien; pasarlo, p.ej., **how are you getting along?** ¿cómo lo pasa Vd.?; **to get along in years** ponerse viejo; **to get along with** congeniar con; **to get around** salir mucho, ir a todas partes; difundirse, divulgarse; eludir, pasar por alto; manejar (*a una persona*); mandarse, estar levantado (*un convaleciente*); **to get at** alcanzar, llegar hasta; averiguar, descubrir; (coll.) intimidar; (coll.) sobornar; **to get away** alejarse; conseguir marcharse; ponerse en marcha; evadirse; **to get away with** llevarse, escaparse con; (coll.) hacer impunemente; **to get away with it** (coll.) arreglárselas, quedar sin castigo; **to get back** regresar, volver; **to get back at** (slang) desquitarse con; **to get behind** quedarse atrás; apoyar; penetrar (*p.ej., la máscara de una persona*); **to get by** lograr pasar; burlar, burlar la vigilancia de; (coll.) arreglárselas; **to get going** ponerse en marcha; **to get gone** salir, irse; **to get in** conseguir entrar en; llegar (*p.ej., un tren*); volver a casa (*por la noche*); **to get into** conseguir entrar en; meterse en (*p.ej., dificultades*); **to get in with** llegar a ser amigo de, llegar a tener influencia con; **to get left** (slang) llevarse un chasco; **to get off** apearse, bajar; bajar de (*p.ej., un tranvía*); descolgarse; marcharse; escaparse; **to get off with** salir con (*p.ej., una pena leve*); **to get on** subir; subir a (*p.ej., un tranvía*); ponerse encima de; ir tirando, tener éxito; llevarse bien; **to get on with** congeniar con; tener éxito con o en; **to get out** salir; marcharse; escaparse; divulgarse; dejar un negocio, asociación, etc.; **to get out of** bajar de (*p.ej., un coche*); librarse de; evadir, escaparse de; **to get out of the way** quitarse de en medio; **to get over** atravesar, pasar por encima de, pasar más allá de; olvidar (*un disgusto*); vencer (*un obstáculo*); recobrarse de; curarse de; **to get through** pasar por entre; terminar; **to get through with** concluir de hacer; **to get to be** llegar a ser; **to get under** meterse o ponerse debajo de; **to get under way** ponerse en camino; (naut.) hacerse a la vela; **to get up** levantarse; **to get up on** subir a lo alto de; **to not get over it** (coll.) no volver de su asombro; **when I get through with you!** ¡cuando yo te deje!; **get out!** ¡aprieta! (*para expresar incredulidad*); **get up!** ¡arre! (*para arrear a las bestias*); este verbo, seguido de un adjetivo, se traduce a veces por un verbo neutro o reflexivo que corresponda al adjetivo, p.ej., **to get old** envejecer; **to get angry** enfadarse; seguido de un participio pasivo, se traduce a veces por un verbo reflexivo o por la voz pasiva, p.ej., **to get married** casarse; **to get run over** ser atropellado
getaway ['gɛtə,we] *s* escapatoria; (sport) comienzo de una carrera; (aut.) arranque, facilidad y rapidez del arranque
Gethsemane [gɛθ'sɛmənɪ] *s* (Bib.) Getsemaní
get-together ['gɛttu,gɛðər] *s* (coll.) reunión, tertulia
get-up ['gɛt,ʌp] *s* (coll.) presentación; (coll.) atavío, traje
gewgaw ['gjugɔ] *s* fruslería; adorno charro; *adj* charro, chillón
geyser ['gaɪzər] *s* géiser
ghastly ['gæstlɪ] o ['gɑstlɪ] *adj* (*comp:* **-lier;** *super:* **-liest**) horrible; cadavérico, espectral; *adv* horriblemente, extremadamente
Ghent [gɛnt] *s* Gante
gherkin ['gʌrkɪn] *s* (bot.) pepinillo (*Cucumis Anguria y fruto; pepino pequeño encurtido*)
ghetto ['gɛto] *s* (*pl:* **-tos**) ghetto, judería
Ghibelline ['gɪbəlin] *adj & s* gibelino
ghost [gost] *s* espectro, fantasma; alma (*de persona muerta*); alma en pena; asomo apenas perceptible; (opt.) imagen falsa; (telv.) fantasma; (coll.) escritor cuyos escritos aparecen bajo la firma de otra persona; **not a ghost of a** ni la más remota idea de, ni la más remota posibilidad de, ni sombra de; **to give up the ghost** dar, entregar o rendir el alma; *va* (coll.) componer escritos por
ghost image *s* (telv.) imagen fantasma, imagen falsa
ghostly ['gostlɪ] *adj* (*comp:* **-lier;** *super:* **-liest**) espectral; espiritual
ghost story *s* cuento de fantasmas
ghostwrite ['gost,raɪt] *va & vn* escribir bajo la firma de otra persona
ghost writer *s* escritor cuyos escritos aparecen bajo la firma de otra persona, colaborador anónimo
ghoul [gul] *s* demonio que se alimenta con la carne de los cadáveres; profanador de cadáveres, robador de cementerios; persona que se deleita con cosas brutales y horribles
ghoulish ['gulɪʃ] *adj* brutal, horrible, espantoso
G.H.Q. abr. de **General Headquarters**
G.I. ['dʒi'aɪ] *adj* de munición, del ejército norteamericano; (coll.) de reglamento; (coll.) soldadesco; *s* (coll.) soldado raso (*del ejército norteamericano*)
giant ['dʒaɪənt] *adj* gigante; gigantesco; *s* gigante
giant cactus *s* (bot.) saguaro
giantess ['dʒaɪəntɪs] *s* giganta
giant fennel *s* (bot.) cañaheja
giantism ['dʒaɪəntɪzəm] *s* gigantez; (path.) gigantismo
giant panda *s* (zool.) panda gigante

giant powder *s* pólvora gigante
giant salamander *s* (zool.) salamandra gigante
Giant's Causeway *s* Calzada de los Gigantes (*en Irlanda*)
giant's stride *s* (sport) pasos de gigante
giant tortoise *s* (zool.) tortuga gigante
gibber ['dʒɪbər] o ['gɪbər] *s* guirigay; *vn* farfullar, parlotear
gibberish ['dʒɪbərɪʃ] o ['gɪbərɪʃ] *s* guirigay
gibbet ['dʒɪbɪt] *s* picota; horca; *va* empicotar; ahorcar; poner en picota, poner a la vergüenza
gibbon ['gɪbən] *s* (zool.) gibón
gibbosity [gɪ'bɑsɪtɪ] *s* (*pl:* **-ties**) gibosidad
gibbous ['gɪbəs] *adj* giboso
gibe [dʒaɪb] *s* remoque, pulla; *vn* mofarse; **to gibe at** mofarse de
giblets ['dʒɪblɪts] *spl* menudillos
Gibraltar [dʒɪ'brɔltər] *s* Gibraltar
gid [gɪd] *s* (vet.) modorra, tornada
giddiness ['gɪdɪnɪs] *s* vértigo, desvanecimiento; atolondramiento, falta de juicio
giddy ['gɪdɪ] *adj* (*comp:* **-dier;** *super:* **-diest**) vertiginoso; casquivano, ligero de cascos; (vet.) modorro
Gideon ['gɪdɪən] *s* (Bib.) Gedeón
gift [gɪft] *s* regalo; don, dote, prenda; *va* obsequiar; dotar
gifted ['gɪftɪd] *adj* de talento, talentoso
gift horse *s* caballo regalado, p.ej., **never look a gift horse in the mouth** a caballo regalado no se le mira el diente
gift of gab *s* (coll.) facundia, labia
gift package *s* paquete regalo
gift shop *s* tienda de objetos de regalo, comercio de artículos de regalo
gift tax *s* impuesto sobre donaciones, impuesto sobre transferencias a título gratuito
gift-wrap ['gɪft,ræp] (*pret & pp:* **-wrapped;** *ger:* **-wrapping**) *va* envolver en paquete regalo
gig [gɪg] *s* calesa (*de dos ruedas*); fisga, arpón; (naut.) falúa; (*pret & pp:* **gigged;** *ger:* **gigging**) *va & vn* pescar con fisga o arpón
gigantean [,dʒaɪgæn'tiən] *adj* giganteo
gigantesque [,dʒaɪgæn'tɛsk] *adj* gigantesco
gigantic [dʒaɪ'gæntɪk] *adj* gigantesco
gigantism ['dʒaɪgæntɪzəm] o [dʒaɪ'gæntɪzəm] *s* var. de **giantism**
giggle ['gɪgəl] *s* retozo de la risa; *vn* reírse nerviosamente, reír con una risilla tonta
giggly ['gɪglɪ] *adj* de risa fácil e inoportuna
gigolo ['dʒɪgəlo] *s* (*pl:* **-los**) acompañante profesional de mujeres; hombre que vive a expensas de una mujer
gigot ['dʒɪgət] *s* manga hueca y subida; pernil de carnero, de ternera, etc.
Gila monster ['hilə] *s* (zool.) monstruo de Gila
gilbert ['gɪlbərt] *s* (phys.) gilbertio; (*cap.*) *s* Gilberto
gild [gɪld] *s* gremio; asociación de carácter benéfico; (*pret & pp:* **gilded** o **gilt**) *va* dorar; dar brillo o lustre a; dar un brillo falso a
gilder ['gɪldər] *s* dorador
gilding ['gɪldɪŋ] *s* doradura; dorado
Gilead ['gɪlɪəd] *s* (Bib.) Galaad
Giles [dʒaɪlz] *s* Gil
gill [gɪl] *s* papada, papadilla; agalla (*de pez*); barba (*del gallo*); (bot.) hojuela o laminilla (*debajo del sombrerillo del hongo*); [dʒɪl] *s* medida para líquidos, equivalente a la cuarta parte de una pinta
gillie ['gɪlɪ] *s* (Scotch) ayudante o paje de un cazador o pescador; (Scotch) criado, secuaz
gilly ['gɪlɪ] *s* (*pl:* **-lies**) var. de **gillie**
gillyflower ['dʒɪlɪ,flaʊər] *s* (bot.) alhelí, alhelí amarillo, alhelí encarnado
gilt [gɪlt] *adj & s* dorado; *pret & pp de* **gild**
gilt-edged ['gɪlt,ɛdʒd] *adj* con cantos dorados; de toda confianza, de lo mejor que hay
gimbals ['dʒɪmbəlz] o ['gɪmbəlz] *spl* balancines de brújula
gimcrack ['dʒɪm,kræk] *s* chuchería; *adj* brillante y de poco valor, de oropel
gimlet ['gɪmlɪt] *s* barrena de mano
gimlet-eyed ['gɪmlɪt,aɪd] *adj* de ojos taladradores
gimmick ['gɪmɪk] *s* (slang) adminículo, dispositivo ingenioso; (slang) adminículo mágico
gimp [gɪmp] *s* bocadillo; (coll.) energía, vigor
gimp nail *s* tachón o tachuela para tapicería
gin o **'gin** [gɪn] (*pret:* **gan** o **'gan;** *pp:* **gun** o **'gun;** *ger:* **ginning** o **'ginning**) *va & vn* (archaic & poet.) comenzar
gin [dʒɪn] *s* ginebra; desmotadora de algodón; garlito, trampa; poste grúa, torno de izar; (*pret & pp:* **ginned;** *ger:* **ginning**) *va* desmotar (*algodón*); coger con garlito
gin fiz o **fizz** *s* ginebra con gaseosa
ginger ['dʒɪndʒər] *s* (bot.) jengibre (*planta, rizoma y especia*); color de jengibre; (coll.) energía, viveza; *adj* de color de jengibre
ginger ale o **beer** *s* cerveza de jengibre gaseosa
gingerbread ['dʒɪndʒər,brɛd] *s* pan de jengibre; adorno charro; *adj* recargado de adornos charros
gingerly ['dʒɪndʒərlɪ] *adj* cuidadoso, cauteloso; *adv* cuidadosamente, cautelosamente
gingersnap ['dʒɪndʒər,snæp] *s* galletita de jengibre
gingery ['dʒɪndʒərɪ] *adj* que sabe a jengibre; picante; de color de jengibre
gingham ['gɪŋəm] *s* guinga, zaraza; *adj* de guinga, de zaraza
gingival [dʒɪn'dʒaɪvəl] *adj* gingival
gingivitis [,dʒɪndʒɪ'vaɪtɪs] *s* (path.) gingivitis
gingko ['gɪŋko] o ['dʒɪŋko] *s* (*pl:* **-koes**) (bot.) gingo
ginglymus ['dʒɪŋglɪməs] o ['gɪŋglɪməs] *s* (*pl:* **-mi** [maɪ]) (anat.) gínglimo
ginkgo ['gɪŋko] o ['dʒɪŋko] *s* (*pl:* **-goes**) var. de **gingko**
ginseng ['dʒɪnsɛŋ] *s* (bot.) ginsén (*planta y raíz*)
gipsy ['dʒɪpsɪ] *adj* var. de **gypsy;** *s* (*pl:* **-sies**) var. de **gypsy;** (*cap.*) *s* var. de **Gypsy**
giraffe [dʒɪ'ræf] o [dʒɪ'rɑf] *s* (zool.) jirafa
girandole ['dʒɪrəndol] *s* girándula
gird [gʌrd] *s* (archaic) remoque; (*pret & pp:* **girded**) *va* mofarse de; *vn* mofar; (*pret & pp:* **girt** o **girded**) *va* ceñir; aprestar; dotar
girder ['gʌrdər] *s* viga, trabe
girdle ['gʌrdəl] *s* faja, ceñidor; corsé de poca anchura; *va* ceñir; circundar; ir alrededor de; quitar a (*un árbol*) una tira circular de corteza
girl [gʌrl] *s* niña; muchacha; criada; (coll.) novia; (coll.) mujer
girl friend *s* (coll.) amiguita
girlhood ['gʌrlhʊd] *s* muchachez; muchachas; juventud femenina
girlie ['gɪrlɪ] *s* (coll.) niña, chica
girlish ['gʌrlɪʃ] *adj* de niña, de muchacha, juvenil
girl scout *s* niña exploradora
Girondist [dʒɪ'rɑndɪst] *adj & s* (hist.) girondino
girt [gʌrt] *va* ceñir; asediar; *pret & pp de* **gird**
girth [gʌrθ] *s* cincha; pretina; circunferencia; *va* cinchar; ceñir
gist [dʒɪst] *s* enjundia, substancia, esencia
gittern ['gɪtərn] *s* var. de **cithern**
give [gɪv] *s* elasticidad ‖ (*pret:* **gave;** *pp:* **given**) *va* dar; ofrecer; causar, ocasionar (*p.ej., molestia, trabajo*); representar (*una obra dramática*); pronunciar (*un discurso*); dedicar (*sus energías o el tiempo disponible*); **to give and take** cambiar (*unas cosas por otras*) libremente; **to give away** regalar, dar de balde; revelar, divulgar; malvender; llevar (*a la novia*); (coll.) traicionar; **to give back** devolver; **to give forth** producir; divulgar; despedir, echar (*p.ej., olores*); **to give in** ceder, entregar; **to give it to** (coll.) dar una paliza a; (coll.) regañar; **to give off** despedir, echar (*p.ej., olores*); **to give oneself up** entregarse (*a las autoridades*); **to give oneself up to** entregarse a, dedicarse a; abandonarse a; **to give out** distribuir, repartir; divulgar; proclamar; despedir, echar (*p.ej., olores*); **to give over** entregar; desistir de; **to give up** entregar; abandonar, dejar (*un empleo*); renunciar; privarse de; desahuciar; **to give up** + *ger* dejar de + *inf;* privarse de + *inf;* **to give up . . . to** dedicar (*p.ej., el día entero*) a ‖ *vn* hacer regalos; prestar, dar de sí; romperse (*una cuerda*); **to give in** ceder, rendirse; consentir; **to give out** agotarse; no poder más; descomponerse; **to give up** abandonarse, darse

por vencido; **to give upon** dar a (*p.ej., un jardín*)
give-and-take [ˈgɪvəndˈtek] *s* toma y daca, concesiones mutuas; conversación sazonada de burlas
giveaway [ˈgɪvəˌwe] *s* (coll.) revelación involuntaria; (coll.) traición, revelación intencional; (coll.) ganapierde (*modo de jugar a las damas*); **to play giveaway** jugar al o a la ganapierde
given [ˈgɪvən] *adj* dado; (math.) conocido; **given that** suponiendo que; **given to** dado a (*propenso a*); *pp de* **give**
given name *s* nombre de pila
giver [ˈgɪvər] *s* dador, donador
gizzard [ˈgɪzərd] *s* molleja (*de ave*); proventrículo (*de insecto*); (hum.) vientre
Gk. abr. de **Greek**
glabrous [ˈglebrəs] *adj* (bot. & zool.) glabro
glacé [glæˈse] *adj* glaseado; helado; *va* glasear (*las frutas, la piel, etc.*)
glacial [ˈgleʃəl] *adj* glacial; (chem.) glacial
glacial epoch *s* (geol.) época glacial
glacial period *s* (geol.) período glacial
glaciate [ˈgleʃɪet] *va* cubrir con heleros o con hielo glacial; congelar; someter a la acción glaciaria
glaciation [ˌgleʃɪˈeʃən] o [ˌglesɪˈeʃən] *s* glaciación
glacier [ˈgleʃər] *s* glaciar, helero
glacis [ˈglesɪs] o [ˈglæsɪs] *s* glacis; (fort.) glacis
glad [glæd] *adj* (*comp:* **gladder;** *super:* **gladdest**) alegre; gozoso, festivo; vistoso; **to be glad** alegrarse; **to be glad to** + *inf* alegrarse de + *inf*, tener mucho gusto en + *inf*
gladden [ˈglædən] *va* alegrar; *vn* alegrarse
gladdon [ˈglædən] *s* (bot.) íride; (bot.) espadaña, gladíolo
glade [gled] *s* claro, claro herboso (*en un bosque*)
glad hand *s* (slang) acogida efusiva
gladiator [ˈglædɪˌetər] *s* gladiador
gladiatorial [ˌglædɪəˈtorɪəl] *adj* gladiatorio
gladiola [ˌglædɪˈolə] o [gləˈdaɪələ] *s* (bot.) estoque
gladiolus [ˌglædɪˈoləs] o [gləˈdaɪələs] *s* (*pl:* **-luses** o **-li** [laɪ]) (bot.) estoque; [gləˈdaɪələs] *s* (*pl:* **-luses** o **-li** [laɪ]) (anat.) gladíolo (*mesosternón*)
gladius [ˈgledɪəs] *s* (*pl:* **-i** [aɪ]) (zool.) gladio
gladly [ˈglædlɪ] *adv* alegremente; con placer, con mucho gusto
gladness [ˈglædnɪs] *s* alegría, regocijo
glad rags *spl* (slang) trapos elegantes
gladsome [ˈglædsəm] *adj* alegre; festivo; agradable, delicioso
Gladstone bag [ˈglædstən] o [ˈglædston] *s* maleta que al abrirse se desdobla en dos mitades
glair [glɛr] *s* clara de huevo; aderezo o engomado hecho de clara de huevo
glaive [glev] *s* (hist.) alabarda; (archaic) chafarote
glamor [ˈglæmər] *s* var. de **glamour**
glamorous [ˈglæmərəs] *adj* encantador, hechicero, fascinador
glamour [ˈglæmər] *s* encanto, hechizo, fascinación
glamour girl *s* (slang) belleza exótica
glamourous [ˈglæmərəs] *adj* var. de **glamorous**
glance [glæns] o [glɑns] *s* golpe de vista, ojeada, vistazo; destello; desviación oblicua; alusión breve; **at first glance** a primera vista; **at a glance** de un vistazo; *vn* lanzar una mirada; destellar; desviarse de soslayo; **to glance at** lanzar una mirada a; mirar por encima, examinar de paso; aludir a; **to glance off** desviarse de soslayo; desviarse al chocar con; **to glance over** examinar de paso
glancing [ˈglænsɪŋ] o [ˈglɑnsɪŋ] *adj* de soslayo (*dícese de un golpe*)
gland [glænd] *s* (anat. & bot.) glándula; (mach.) casquillo del prensaestopas
glanderous [ˈglændərəs] *adj* muermoso
glanders [ˈglændərz] *s* (vet.) muermo
glandular [ˈglændʒələr] *adj* glandular
glandulous [ˈglændʒələs] *adj* glanduloso
glare [glɛr] *s* fulgor deslumbrante, relumbrón; luz intensa; mirada feroz y penetrante; mirada de indignación; aspecto deslumbrante; superficie lisa y brillante (*p.ej., de hielo*); *adj* liso y brillante; *va* expresar (*p.ej., indignación*) con miradas feroces; *vn* relumbrar; lanzar miradas feroces o de indignación; ser de aspecto deslumbrante
glaring [ˈglɛrɪŋ] *adj* deslumbrante, brillante; relumbrante; de miradas feroces; evidente, notorio
glary [ˈglɛrɪ] *adj* deslumbrante, brillante; alisado, resbaloso
glass [glæs] o [glɑs] *s* vidrio; cristal; vaso; vajilla de cristal; espejo; **glasses** *spl* anteojos, gafas; *adj* de vidrio, de cristal; *va* encerrar entre vidrios; poner vidrios a (*una ventana*); reflejar
glass blower *s* vidriero, soplador de vidrio
glass blowing *s* elaboración del vidrio mediante el soplete
glass case *s* vitrina
glass cutter *s* cortavidrios
glass door *s* puerta vidriera
glassful [ˈglæsfʊl] o [ˈglɑsfʊl] *s* vaso (*cantidad que cabe en un vaso*)
glasshouse [ˈglæsˌhaʊs] o [ˈglɑsˌhaʊs] *s* vidriería; invernadero; galería fotográfica; (fig.) tejado de vidrio
glassiness [ˈglæsɪnɪs] o [ˈglɑsɪnɪs] *s* vidriosidad
glass snake *s* (zool.) lución norteamericano
glassware [ˈglæsˌwɛr] o [ˈglɑsˌwɛr] *s* cristalería; vajilla de cristal
glass wool *s* cristal hilado, lana de vidrio, tela de vidrio
glasswork [ˈglæsˌwʌrk] o [ˈglɑsˌwʌrk] *s* vidriería, cristalería; **glassworks** *ssg o spl* vidriería, cristalería (*fábrica o taller*)
glassworker [ˈglæsˌwʌrkər] o [ˈglɑsˌwʌrkər] *s* vidriero
glasswort [ˈglæsˌwʌrt] o [ˈglɑsˌwʌrt] *s* (bot.) almajo, almajo salado, alacranera
glassy [ˈglæsɪ] o [ˈglɑsɪ] *adj* (*comp:* **-ier;** *super:* **-iest**) vidrioso; (fig.) de mirada fija y estúpida (*dícese de los ojos*); (fig.) vidrioso (*dícese de los ojos o la mirada*)
Glaswegian [glæsˈwidʒən] o [glɑsˈwidʒən] *adj* perteneciente a Glasgow; *s* natural o habitante de Glasgow
glauberite [ˈglaʊbəraɪt] o [ˈglɔbəraɪt] *s* (chem.) glauberita
Glauber's salt [ˈglaʊbərz] o [ˈglɔbərz] *s* (pharm.) sal de Glauber
glaucoma [glɔˈkomə] *s* (path.) glaucoma
glaucomatous [glɔˈkomətəs] o [glɔˈkɑmətəs] *adj* glaucomatoso
glaucous [ˈglɔkəs] *adj* glauco; (bot.) glauco
glaze [glez] *s* barniz vítreo, esmalte; superficie lisa; capa lisa y resbaladiza (*p.ej., la que produce la lluvia al congelarse*); *va* vidriar, esmaltar; lustrar (*un tejido*); poner vidrio o vidrios a (*una ventana o un marco*); cubrir con vidrio; garapiñar; *vn* vidriarse
glazier [ˈgleʒər] *s* vidriero
glazier's point *s* punta de vidriar
glazing [ˈglezɪŋ] *s* oficio de vidriero; trabajo de vidriero; vidrios (*puestos o que han de ponerse*); barniz vítreo, esmalte
gleam [glim] *s* destello, rayo de luz; luz tenue o momentánea; rayo (*de esperanza*); manifestación momentánea (*p.ej., de inteligencia*); *vn* destellar, fulgurar; brillar con luz tenue o momentánea; aparecer de repente, dejarse ver momentáneamente
glean [glin] *va* espigar; (fig.) espigar
gleaner [ˈglinər] *s* espigador
gleaning [ˈglinɪŋ] *s* espigadura, espigueo
glebe [glib] *s* (poet.) tierra, césped; (archaic) campo sembrado o labrado; (eccl.) terreno anejo a un beneficio o curato
glee [gli] *s* alegría, regocijo; (mus.) canción para tres o más solistas a capella
glee club *s* orfeón
gleeful [ˈglifəl] *adj* alegre, regocijado
gleeman [ˈglimən] *s* (*pl:* **-men**) (archaic) cantor, trovador
gleesome [ˈglisəm] *adj* var. de **gleeful**
glen [glɛn] *s* vallecico, valle angosto
glengarry [glɛnˈgærɪ] *s* (*pl:* **-ries**) gorra escocesa
glenoid [ˈglinɔɪd] *adj* glenoideo

glib [glɪb] *adj* (*comp:* **glibber;** *super:* **glibbest**) locuaz, de mucha labia; fácil e insincero
glide [glaɪd] *s* deslizamiento suave, movimiento suave y silencioso; (aer.) vuelo sin motor, planeo; (mus.) ligadura; (phonet.) semivocal; *vn* deslizarse; (aer.) volar sin motor, planear; **to glide along** correr o pasar suavemente; **to glide by** pasarse (*p.ej., los años*) sin sentir
glider ['glaɪdər] *s* persona o cosa que se desliza; (aer.) deslizador, planeador
gliding angle *s* (aer.) ángulo de planeo
gliding boat *s* (aer.) hidrodeslizador
gliding machine *s* (aer.) deslizador, planeador
glim [glɪm] *s* luz (*de candil o de vela*); candil, vela; (slang) ojo
glimmer ['glɪmər] *s* luz tenue y vacilante; vislumbre; *vn* brillar con luz tenue y vacilante; vislumbrarse
glimmering ['glɪmərɪŋ] *adj* trémulo, tenue y vacilante; *s* luz tenue y vacilante; vislumbre
glimpse [glɪmps] *s* vislumbre, vista momentánea; manifestación momentánea; **to catch a glimpse of** vislumbrar; *va* vislumbrar, ver momentáneamente, alcanzar a ver; *vn* brillar con luz tenue y vacilante; lanzar una mirada
glint [glɪnt] *s* destello, rayo, relumbrón
glioma [glaɪ'omə] *s* (*pl:* **-mata** [mətə] o **-mas**) (path.) glioma
glisten ['glɪsən] *s* centelleo; *vn* centellear
glitter ['glɪtər] *s* brillo, resplandor; *vn* brillar, resplendecer
glittering ['glɪtərɪŋ] o **glittery** ['glɪtərɪ] *adj* brillante, resplandeciente
gloaming ['glomɪŋ] *s* crepúsculo vespertino, media luz del anochecer
gloat [glot] *vn* gozarse, relamerse; **to gloat over** gozarse en la contemplación de
global ['globəl] *adj* globoso, esférico; mundial, global
globate ['globet] *adj* globoso, esférico
globe [glob] *s* globo; globo terráqueo o terrestre (*Tierra; mapa de la Tierra en forma de bola*); (astr.) globo celeste; *va* dar forma de globo a; *vn* tomar forma de globo
globe amaranth *s* (bot.) sempiterna, perpetua, amarantina
globefish ['glob,fɪʃ] *s* (ichth.) orbe
globeflower ['glob,flaʊər] *s* (bot.) calderones
globe sight *s* mira esférica
globetrotter ['glob,trɑtər] *s* trotamundos
globose ['globos] o **globous** ['globəs] *adj* globoso
globular ['glɑbjələr] *adj* globular
globule ['glɑbjʊl] *s* glóbulo; (bot.) glóbulo
globulin ['glɑbjəlɪn] *s* (biochem.) globulina
globulose ['glɑbjəlos] *adj* globuloso
glockenspiel ['glɑkən,spil] *s* (mus.) órgano de campanas, timbres, juego de timbres
glomerate ['glɑmərɪt] *adj* aglomerado
glomerule ['glɑmərʊl] *s* (bot.) glomérula
glomerulus [glo'mɛrjʊləs] o [glo'mɛrʊləs] *s* (*pl:* **-li** [laɪ]) (anat.) glomérulo
gloom [glum] *s* lobreguez, tinieblas; abatimiento, tristeza; aspecto abatido, aspecto triste; *vn* obscurecerse; entristecerse, ponerse fúnebre; parecer triste
gloomy ['glumɪ] *adj* (*comp:* **-ier;** *super:* **-iest**) lóbrego (*obscuro; triste*)
gloria ['glorɪə] *s* gloria (*tejido; aureola*); canto en loor de Dios; (*cap.*) *s* (eccl.) Gloria
glorifiable ['glorɪ,faɪəbəl] *adj* glorificable
glorification [,glorɪfɪ'keʃən] *s* glorificación; realce; (coll.) celebración, fiesta
glorify ['glorɪfaɪ] (*pret & pp:* **-fied**) *va* glorificar; realzar
glorious ['glorɪəs] *adj* glorioso; espléndido, excelente
glory ['glorɪ] *s* (*pl:* **-ries**) gloria; **to be in one's glory** estar en sus glorias; **to go to glory** ganar la gloria (*morirse*); (slang) fracasar, sufrir colapso; (*pret & pp:* **-ried**) *va* gloriar, glorificar; *vn* gloriarse; **to glory in** gloriarse de (*p.ej., sus hazañas*); gloriarse en (*p.ej., el Señor*)
gloss [glɔs] o [glɑs] *s* brillo, lustre; apariencia engañosa; glosa; glosario; glosa (*composición poética*); *va* abrillantar, lustrar; satinar, glasear; disculpar, paliar; glosar; *vn* glosar; **to gloss over** disculpar, paliar
glossa ['glɑsə] *s* (*pl:* **-sae** [si]) (zool.) glosis
glossarial [glɑ'sɛrɪəl] *adj* de glosario; a modo de glosario
glossary ['glɑsərɪ] *s* (*pl:* **-ries**) glosario
glossator [glɑ'setər] *s* glosador
glossectomy [glɑ'sɛktəmɪ] *s* (*pl:* **-mies**) (surg.) glosectomía
glossitis [glɑ'saɪtɪs] *s* (path.) glositis
glossy ['glɔsɪ] o ['glɑsɪ] *adj* (*comp:* **-ier;** *super:* **-iest**) brillante, lustroso; satinado, glaseado
glottal ['glɑtəl] *adj* glótico
glottal stop *s* (phonet.) choque glótico
glottis ['glɑtɪs] *s* (anat.) glotis
glove [glʌv] *s* guante; **to handle with gloves** manejar o tratar con sumo cuidado; **to handle without gloves** manejar o tratar sin miramientos; **to take up the glove** recoger el guante; **to throw down the glove** arrojar o echar el guante
glove compartment *s* (aut.) portaguantes, guantera o guantero
glover ['glʌvər] *s* guantero
glove stretcher *s* ensanchador, juanas
glow [glo] *s* resplandor (*de una cosa que arde sin llama*); brillo, esplendor (*p.ej., de los arreboles de la puesta del sol*); sensación agradable de calor corporal; color en las mejillas, color en todo el cuerpo; manifestación o señales de interés muy vivo; *vn* brillar intensamente y sin llama; manifestar calor corporal (*por el color en las mejillas o en todo el cuerpo*); tener las mejillas encendidas; estar muy animado, estar vehemente; estar anhelante (*p.ej., de interés*); arder (*p.ej., la zona tórrida*); (fig.) brillar
glower ['glaʊər] *s* ceño, mirada hosca; *vn* tener la mirada hosca; **to glower at** mirar hoscamente
glowing ['glo·ɪŋ] *adj* ardiente, encendido; radiante; entusiasta
glowworm ['glo,wʌrm] *s* (ent.) gusano de luz
gloxinia [glɑk'sɪnɪə] *s* (bot.) gloxínea
gloze [gloz] *va* disculpar, paliar; abrillantar; *vn* glosar; brillar
glucina [glu'saɪnə] *s* (chem.) glucina
glucinium [glu'sɪnɪəm] o **glucinum** [glu'saɪnəm] *s* (chem.) glucinio
glucoprotein [,gluko'protiɪn] o [,gluko'protin] *s* var. de **glycoprotein**
glucose ['glukos] *s* (biochem.) glucosa
glucoside ['glukosaɪd] o ['glukosɪd] *s* (chem.) glucósido
glucosuria [,gluko'sʊrɪə] *s* var. de **glycosuria**
glue [glu] *s* cola; *va* encolar; pegar fuertemente, unir fuertemente
glue pot *s* cacerola para cola, pote de la cola
gluey ['gluɪ] *adj* (*comp:* **gluier;** *super:* **gluiest**) pegajoso; encolado
glug [glʌg] *s* gluglú (*sonido del agua*); (*pret & pp:* **glugged;** *ger:* **glugging**) *vn* hacer gluglú (*el agua*)
glum [glʌm] *adj* (*comp:* **glummer;** *super:* **glummest**) hosco, sombrío, tétrico
glume [glum] *s* (bot.) gluma
glut [glʌt] *s* abundancia, gran acopio; exceso, plétora; (*pret & pp:* **glutted;** *ger:* **glutting**) *va* hartar, saciar; inundar (*el mercado*); obstruir; *vn* hartarse, saciarse
gluteal [glu'tiəl] o ['glutɪəl] *adj* (anat.) glúteo
gluten ['glutən] *s* gluten
gluten bread *s* pan de gluten
gluten flour *s* harina de gluten
glutenous ['glutɪnəs] *adj* glutenoso
glutinous ['glutɪnəs] *adj* glutinoso
glutton ['glʌtən] *s* glotón; (zool.) glotón (*Gulo gulo*); (zool.) carcayú (*Gulo luscus*)
gluttonous ['glʌtənəs] *adj* glotón
gluttony ['glʌtənɪ] *s* (*pl:* **-ies**) glotonería
glyceric [glɪ'sɛrɪk] o ['glɪsərɪk] *adj* glicérico
glyceric acid *s* (chem.) ácido glicérico
glyceride ['glɪsəraɪd] o ['glɪsərɪd] *s* (chem.) glicérido
glycerin o **glycerine** ['glɪsərɪn] *s* glicerina
glycerol ['glɪsərol] o ['glɪsərɑl] *s* (chem.) glicerol
glyceryl ['glɪsərɪl] *s* (chem.) glicerilo
glycine ['glaɪsin] o [glaɪ'sin] *s* (chem.) glicina
glycogen ['glaɪkədʒən] *s* (biochem.) glicógeno
glycogenic [,glaɪkə'dʒɛnɪk] *adj* glicogénico

glycol ['glaɪkol] o ['glaɪkɑl] *s* (chem.) glicol
glycoprotein [,glaɪko'protiɪn] o [,glaɪko'protin] *s* (biochem.) glucoproteína
glycosuria [,glaɪko'surɪə] *s* (path.) glucosuria
glyph [glɪf] *s* (arch.) glifo
glyptography [glɪp'tɑgrəfɪ] *s* gliptografía
gm. abr. de **gram** o **grams**
G.M. abr. de **general manager, Grand Marshal** y **Grand Master**
G-man ['dʒi,mæn] *s* (*pl:* **-men**) (U.S.A.) agente secreto federal
G.M.T. abr. de **Greenwich mean time**
gnar [nɑr] (*pret & pp:* **gnarred;** *ger:* **gnarring**) *vn* gruñir, refunfuñar
gnarl [nɑrl] *s* nudo (*en un árbol, una tabla, etc.*); *va* torcer; *vn* gruñir, refunfuñar
gnarled [nɑrld] *adj* nudoso, retorcido; de contrafibra; pendenciero, terco
gnarly ['nɑrlɪ] *adj* (*comp:* **-ier;** *super:* **-iest**) var. de **gnarled**
gnash [næʃ] *va* rechinar (*los dientes*); morder haciendo crujir los dientes; *vn* rechinar
gnat [næt] *s* (ent.) jején; (ent.) mosquito; **to strain at a gnat** afanarse o molestarse por pequeñeces
gnathion ['neθɪɑn] o ['næθɪɑn] *s* (anat.) gnatión
gnaw [nɔ] (*pret:* **gnawed;** *pp:* **gnawed** o **gnawn**) *va* roer; practicar (*un agujero*) royendo; *vn* morder; **to gnaw at** roer
gneiss [naɪs] *s* (geol.) gneis
gneissic ['naɪsɪk] *adj* gnéisico
gnome [nom] *s* gnomo; (myth.) gnomo
gnomic ['nomɪk] *adj* gnómico
gnomon ['nomɑn] *s* gnomon
Gnostic ['nɑstɪk] *adj & s* gnóstico
Gnosticism ['nɑstɪsɪzəm] *s* gnosticismo
gnu [nu] o [nju] *s* (zool.) gnu o ñu
go [go] *s* (*pl:* **goes**) ida, ir; (coll.) ánimo, energía, ímpetu; (coll.) estado, situación; (coll.) boga, furor; (coll.) ensayo; éxito; paso libre (*de la circulación de los automóviles*); **it's a go** es un trato hecho; es un gran éxito; **it's all the go** está muy en boga, hace furor; **it's no go** es inútil, es imposible; es un fracaso; **on the go** en continuo movimiento; de viaje; **this is a pretty go** estamos frescos; **to have a go at** ensayar, tentar; **to have plenty of go** estar muy animado; **to make a go of** lograr éxito en ‖ (*pret:* **went;** *pp:* **gone**) *va* ir por, llevar (*un camino*); (coll.) soportar, tolerar; (coll.) llegar hasta, aventurarse hasta; (coll.) apostar; **to go better** apostar más que; llevar la ventaja a; vencer; **to go it** (coll.) ir con gran rapidez; **to go it alone** obrar sin ayuda ‖ *vn* ir; irse, marcharse; funcionar, marchar; caminar; andar (*p.ej., desnudo, con hambre*); avanzar, seguir; correr, pasar; cundir; ponerse, volverse (*p.ej., loco*); desaparecer; estar bien; alcanzar, extenderse; venderse, tener venta; conducir, tender; surtir efecto, tener éxito; colocarse, guardarse; sonar; decirse; hacer, p.ej., **when you swim, go like this** cuando Vd. nada, haga así; **so it goes** así va el mundo; **to be going to** + *inf* o **to go to** + *inf* ir a + *inf;* **to be gone** haberse agotado; haberse gastado; haberse roto; haberse muerto; haber dejado de ser; haberse vuelto inservible; **to go** + *ger* ir de + *noun,* p.ej., **to go fishing** ir de pesca; **to go hunting** ir de caza; **to go about** andar de un sitio para otro; dar vuelta; andar (*p.ej., desnudo*); emprender (*una tarea*); ocuparse en (*los negocios de uno*); (naut.) cambiar de amura; **to go against** ir en contra de, oponerse a, chocar con; **to go ahead** seguir adelante; **to go around** andar de un sitio para otro; dar vuelta; dar vueltas; andar (*p.ej., desnudo*); alcanzar para todos; circundar; dar vueltas a, ir alrededor de; **to go at** emprender; acometer; **to go away** irse, marcharse; pasar (*p.ej., un dolor de cabeza*); **to go by** pasar, pasar por; guiarse por (*p.ej., una serie de señales*); atenerse a, regirse por; conocerse por (*un nombre, un apodo*); usar (*un nombre falso*); **to go down** bajar; hundirse (*un buque, el sol*); **to go down fighting** hundirse peleando; **to go for** ir por; favorecer; ser tenido por; pasar (*p.ej., días enteros*); (coll.) acometer; **to go get** ir por, ir a buscar; **to go in** entrar; entrar en; encajar en; caber en; **to go in for** (coll.) interesarse por, dedicarse a; **to go into** entrar en; encajar en; caber en; discutir; investigar; (aut.) poner (*p.ej., primera*); **to go in with** juntarse con, asociarse con; **to go off** irse, marcharse; estallar; dispararse; tener lugar; llevarse a cabo; **to go off very well** ser un gran éxito; **to go on** seguir adelante; ir tirando; enfurecerse; **to go on** + *ger* continuar, seguir + *ger;* **to go on with** continuar, proseguir; **to go out** salir; pasar de moda; apagarse; declararse en huelga; salir (*a tertulias, teatros, etc.*); **to go over** pasar por encima de; examinar, repasar, revisar; releer; tener éxito; **to go over to** pasarse a las filas de; **to go through** pasar por; hacer completamente, llegar al fin de; hallarse en (*una situación desagradable*); ser aprobado; disipar rápidamente, agotar (*una fortuna*); **to go through with** llevar a su término; **to go with** ir con, acompañar; salir con (*una muchacha*); hacer juego con, armonizar con; **to go without** pasarse sin, andarse sin
goa ['goə] *s* (zool.) antílope tibetano
goad [god] *s* aguijada, aguijón; *va* aguijonear
go-ahead ['goə,hɛd] *adj* (coll.) emprendedor; *s* (coll.) señal para seguir adelante
goal [gol] *s* (sport & fig.) meta; (football) gol
goalkeeper ['gol,kipər] *s* (sport) portero, guardameta
goal line *s* (sport) raya de la meta
goal post *s* (sport) poste de la meta
goat [got] *s* (zool.) cabra, macho cabrío; (slang) víctima inocente; **to be the goat** (slang) pagar el pato; **to get one's goat** (slang) enojar, tomar el pelo a; **to ride the goat** (coll.) recibir la iniciación en una sociedad secreta
goatee [go'ti] *s* perilla, pera
goat grass *s* (bot.) rompesacos
goatherd ['got,hʌrd] *s* cabrero
goatish ['gotɪʃ] *adj* cabrerizo, cabrío; lascivo, lujurioso
goatsbeard ['gots,bɪrd] *s* (bot.) barba cabruna; (bot.) clavaria
goatskin ['got,skɪn] *s* piel de cabra
goat's-rue ['gots,ru] *s* (bot.) galega, ruda cabruna; (bot.) tefrosia
goatsucker ['got,sʌkər] *s* (orn.) chotacabras
goat willow *s* (bot.) sauce cabruno
gob [gɑb] *s* (coll.) masa informe y pequeña; (slang) marinero de guerra
gobang [go'bæŋ] *s* juego japonés algo parecido a las damas
gobbet ['gɑbɪt] *s* pedazo; masa pequeña, terrón
gobble ['gɑbəl] *s* gluglú (*voz del pavo*); *va* engullir; **to gobble up** engullirse ávidamente; (coll.) posesionarse ávidamente de; *vn* gluglutear, gorgonear, titar (*el pavo*); engullir
gobbledygook ['gɑbəldɪ,guk] *s* (coll.) galimatías, lenguaje obscuro e incomprensible
gobbler ['gɑblər] *s* (orn.) pavo, gallipavo
Gobelin tapestry ['gɑbəlɪn] *s* tapiz gobelino
go-between ['gobɪ,twin] *s* medianero; alcahuete; conector
goblet ['gɑblɪt] *s* copa (*con pie*)
goblin ['gɑblɪn] *s* duende, gobelino
goby ['gobɪ] *s* (*pl:* **-bies**) (ichth.) gobio
go-by ['go,baɪ] *s* (coll.) desaire; **to give the go-by to** (coll.) desairar, negarse al trato de
gocart ['go,kɑrt] *s* cochecito para niños; andaderas; carruaje ligero
god [gɑd] *s* dios; (*cap.*) *s* Dios; **God forbid** no lo quiera Dios; **God grant** permita Dios; **God willing** Dios mediante
godchild ['gɑd,tʃaɪld] *s* (*pl:* **-children**) ahijado, ahijada
goddaughter ['gɑd,dɔtər] *s* ahijada
goddess ['gɑdɪs] *s* diosa; (fig.) diosa (*mujer sumamente bella*)
godfather ['gɑd,fɑðər] *s* padrino
God-fearing ['gɑd,fɪrɪŋ] *adj* timorato; devoto, pío
Godforsaken ['gɑdfər,sekən] *adj* dejado de la mano de Dios; (coll.) descuidado, desierto, desolado
Godfrey ['gɑdfrɪ] *s* Godofredo
God-given ['gɑd,gɪvən] *adj* que ha dado Dios; que viene como anillo al dedo
godhead ['gɑdhɛd] *s* divinidad; (*cap.*) *s* Dios
godhood ['gɑdhud] *s* divinidad

godless ['gɑdlɪs] *adj* descreído, sin religión; malvado, desalmado
godlike ['gɑd,laɪk] *adj* deiforme; propio para Dios, propio para un dios
godliness ['gɑdlɪnɪs] *s* devoción, piedad, santidad
godly ['gɑdlɪ] *adj* (*comp:* **-lier;** *super:* **-liest**) devoto, pío, piadoso; (archaic) divino
godmother ['gɑd,mʌðər] *s* madrina
godparent ['gɑd,pɛrənt] *s* padrino o madrina
God's acre *s* campo santo
godsend ['gɑd,sɛnd] *s* cosa llovida del cielo
godship ['gɑdʃɪp] *s* divinidad
God's house *s* casa de Dios (*iglesia*)
godson ['gɑd,sʌn] *s* ahijado
Godspeed ['gɑd,spid] *s* bienandanza; *interj* ¡ buena suerte!, ¡ feliz viaje!
Godward ['gɑdwərd] o **Godwards** ['gɑdwərdz] *adv* hacia Dios
godwit ['gɑdwɪt] *s* (orn.) agujeta
goes [goz] *tercera persona del sg del pres de ind de* **go**
go-getter ['go'gɛtər] *s* (slang) buscavidas, trafagón, persona emprendedora que se las sabe arreglar para todo
goggle ['gɑgəl] *adj* saltón (*dícese de los ojos*); **goggles** *spl* anteojos de camino; *vn* volver los ojos; abrir los ojos desmesuradamente; abrirse desmesuradamente (*los ojos*)
goggle-eyed ['gɑgəl,aɪd] *adj* de ojos saltones
going ['go·ɪŋ] *s* ida, partida; estado del camino; marcha; *adj* en marcha, funcionando; (naut.) que marcha viento en popa; **going on** casi, p.ej., **it is going on two o'clock** son casi las dos; *ger de* **go**
going concern *s* empresa que marcha
goings on *spl* actividades; bulla, jarana
goiter ['gɔɪtər] *s* (path.) bocio
gold [gold] *s* oro; *adj* áureo, de oro; dorado
goldbeater ['gold,bitər] *s* batidor de oro, batihoja
goldbeater's skin *s* venza, película de tripa de buey
gold brick *s* (coll.) estafa, embuste; **to sell a gold brick** (coll.) vender gato por liebre
Gold Coast *s* Costa de Oro (*en África*)
goldcrest ['gold,krɛst] *s* (orn.) reyezuelo moñudo
gold digger *s* (slang) extractora de oro, buscadora de oro
gold dust *s* oro en polvo
golden ['goldən] *adj* áureo, de oro; dorado; brillante; excelente; muy valioso; muy importante; muy favorable; próspero, floreciente; rubio
golden age *s* (myth.) edad de oro, siglo de oro; siglo de oro (*de la literatura castellana*)
Golden Book *s* libro de oro (*de la nobleza veneciana*)
golden calf *s* (Bib. & fig.) becerro de oro
golden chain *s* (bot.) lluvia de oro
golden eagle *s* (orn.) águila caudal, águila real
goldeneye ['goldən,aɪ] *s* (orn.) clángula
Golden Fleece *s* toisón, toisón de oro (*orden*); (myth.) toisón de oro, vellocino de oro
Golden Gate *s* Puerta de Oro (*entrada de la bahía de San Francisco*)
golden glow *s* (bot.) rudbequia
Golden Horn *s* Cuerno de Oro
golden mean *s* justo medio
golden oriole *s* (orn.) oropéndola, virio
golden pheasant *s* (orn.) faisán dorado
golden plover *s* (orn.) chorlito
goldenrod ['goldən,rɑd] *s* (bot.) vara de oro, vara de San José, plumeros amarillos
golden rule *s* regla de la caridad cristiana (*Todas las cosas que quisierais que los hombres hiciesen con vosotros, así también haced vosotros con ellos*); (arith.) regla áurea, regla de oro
golden thistle *s* (bot.) cardillo, tagarnina
golden wedding *s* bodas de oro
gold-filled ['gold,fɪld] *adj* revestido de oro, enchapado en oro
goldfinch ['gold,fɪntʃ] *s* (orn.) jilguero, pintacilgo
goldfish ['gold,fɪʃ] *s* pez de color, cola de cometa, carpa dorada
gold foil *s* pan de oro, oro batido
goldilocks ['goldɪ,lɑks] *s* (coll.) rubiales (*persona rubia*); (bot.) ranúnculo turbante dorado; (bot.) calderones
gold leaf *s* pan de oro finísimo
gold mine *s* mina de oro; (coll.) mina, filón, Potosí; **to strike a gold mine** (fig.) encontrar una mina
gold number *s* (chem.) índice de oro
gold-of-pleasure ['goldəv'plɛʒər] *s* (bot.) camelina
gold plate *s* vajilla de oro
gold-plate ['gold'plet] *va* dorar (*cubrir con un baño de oro*)
gold rush *s* gran agolpamiento de exploradores en busca de veneros de oro
goldsmith ['gold,smɪθ] *s* orfebre
gold standard *s* patrón de oro, patrón oro
golf [gɑlf] *s* (sport) golf; *vn* jugar al golf
golf club *s* palo de golf; asociación de jugadores de golf
golfer ['gɑlfər] *s* (sport) golfista
golf links *spl* (sport) campo de golf
Golgotha ['gɑlgəθə] *s* (Bib.) el Gólgota
Goliath [go'laɪəθ] *s* (Bib.) Goliat
golliwog o **golliwogg** ['gɑlɪwɑg] *s* muñeca negra ridícula; persona ridícula
golosh [gə'lɑʃ] *s* var. de **galosh**
Gomorrah o **Gomorrha** [gə'mɑrə] o [gə'mɔrə] *s* (Bib.) Gomorra; (fig.) lugar o centro de depravación
gonad ['gɑnæd] o ['gonæd] *s* (anat.) gónada
gondola ['gɑndələ] *s* góndola; (aer.) barquilla, cabina; (rail.) vagón de carga abierto, góndola
gondolier [,gɑndə'lɪr] *s* gondolero
gone [gɔn] o [gɑn] *adj* agotado; arruinado; pasado; desaparecido; muerto; débil, desfallecido; **far gone** muy adelantado; muy comprometido; **gone on** (coll.) enamorado de; *pp de* **go**
goneness ['gɔnnɪs] o ['gɑnnɪs] *s* desfallecimiento, debilidad
goner ['gɔnər] o ['gɑnər] *s* (coll.) persona desahuciada, persona muerta, animal muerto, animal que se está muriendo, cosa echada a perder
gonfalon ['gɑnfələn] *s* confalón
gonfalonier [,gɑnfələ'nɪr] *s* confaloniero
gong [gɔŋ] o [gɑŋ] *s* gongo; campana en forma de tazón
Gongorism ['gɑŋgərɪzəm] *s* gongorismo
Gongorist ['gɑŋgərɪst] *s* gongorino
Gongoristic [,gɑŋgə'rɪstɪk] *adj* gongorino
gonidium [gə'nɪdɪəm] *s* (*pl:* **-a** [ə]) (bot.) gonidio
goniometer [,gonɪ'ɑmɪtər] *s* goniómetro
goniometry [,gonɪ'ɑmɪtrɪ] *s* goniometría
gonium ['gonɪəm] *s* (*pl:* **-a** [ə]) (biol.) gonia
gonococcus [,gɑnə'kɑkəs] *s* (*pl:* **-cocci** ['kɑksaɪ]) (bact.) gonococo
gonophore ['gɑnəfor] *s* (bot. & zool.) gonóforo
gonorrhea o **gonorrhoea** [,gɑnə'riə] *s* (path.) gonorrea
gonorrheal [,gɑnə'riəl] *adj* gonorreico
goo [gu] *s* (slang) substancia muy pegajosa
goober ['gubər] *s* (bot.) cacahuete (*planta y fruto*)
good [gʊd] *adj* (*comp:* **better;** *super:* **best**) bueno; **a good one** (iron.) buen chiste, buena noticia, buena jugada; **as good as** casi; **to be good at** tener talento para; **to be no good** (coll.) no servir para nada; (coll.) ser un perdido; **to hold good** seguir vigente, ser valedero; **to make good** tener éxito; probar (*un aserto*); cumplir (*sus promesas*); responder de (*los daños*); pagar o satisfacer (*una deuda*); llevar a cabo (*una evasión*); **good and** (coll.) bien, p.ej., **good and late** bien tarde; **good for** bueno para; capaz de hacer; capaz de pagar; capaz de durar o de vivir (*cierto tiempo*); *s* bien, provecho, utilidad, ventaja; **goods** *spl* efectos; géneros, mercancías; (Brit.) carga; **for good** para siempre; **for good and all** de una vez para siempre; **the good** lo bueno; los buenos; **to be up to no good** llevar mala intención; **to catch with the goods** (slang) coger con el hurto en las manos, coger en flagrante; **to deliver the goods** (slang) cumplir lo esperado, cumplir lo prometido; **to do good** hacer el bien; aprovechar; dar salud o fuerzas a; **to have** o **get the goods on** (slang) tener

la prueba de la culpa de; **to the good** de sobra, en el haber; **what is the good of . . . ?** ¿de o para qué sirve . . . ?; **what is the good of** + *ger?* ¿de o para qué sirve + *inf?*
good afternoon *s* buenas tardes
Good Book *s* Biblia
good-by [ˌgʊd'baɪ] *s* (*pl:* **-bys**) adiós; *interj* ¡adiós!
good-bye [ˌgʊd'baɪ] *s* (*pl:* **-byes**) var. de **good-by**; *interj* var. de **good-by**
good cheer *s* alegría; buenas viandas; ánimo, valor
good day *s* buenos días
good evening *s* buenas tardes, buenas noches
good fellow *s* (coll.) buen chico, buen sujeto; (coll.) jaranero
good fellowship *s* compañerismo, camaradería
good form *s* buenas formas, conducta ajustada a los cánones sociales
good-for-nothing ['gʊdfər,nʌθɪŋ] *adj* inútil, sin valor; *s* pelafustán, perdido, haragán
Good Friday *s* Viernes santo
good graces *spl* favor, amistad, estimación
good-hearted ['gʊd'hɑrtɪd] *adj* de buen corazón
good humor *s* buen humor
good-humored ['gʊd'hjumərd] o ['gʊd'jumərd] *adj* de buen humor; afable, jovial
goodish ['gʊdɪʃ] *adj* bastante bueno; considerable
goodliness ['gʊdlɪnɪs] *s* excelencia; hermosura, gracia
good liver *s* (coll.) gastrónomo
good-looking ['gʊd'lʊkɪŋ] *adj* guapo, bien parecido, buen mozo
good looks *spl* buen aspecto, hermosura
goodly ['gʊdlɪ] *adj* (*comp:* **-lier**; *super:* **-liest**) agradable, excelente; bien parecido, hermoso; considerable
goodman ['gʊdmən] o ['gʊd,mæn] *s* (*pl:* **-men**) (archaic) marido, amo de casa; (archaic) tío (*título*)
good morning *s* buenos días
good nature *s* natural alegre, buen natural
good-natured ['gʊd'netʃərd] *adj* afable, bonachón
Good Neighbor Policy *s* política de la buena vecindad
goodness ['gʊdnɪs] *s* bondad; *interj* ¡válgame Dios!; **for goodness' sake!** ¡por Dios!; **thank goodness!** ¡gracias a Dios!; **goodness gracious!** ¡santo Dios!; **goodness knows!** ¡quién sabe!
good night *s* buenas noches
good offices *spl* (dipl.) buenos oficios
Good Samaritan *s* (Bib.) buen samaritano; persona que socorre generosamente al prójimo
good sense *s* sensatez
Good Shepherd *s* (Bib.) Buen Pastor
good-sized ['gʊd'saɪzd] *adj* de buen tamaño, bastante grande
good speed *s* adiós y buena suerte
goods train *s* (Brit.) mercancías, tren de mercancías
good-tempered ['gʊd'tɛmpərd] *adj* afable, alegre, de natural apacible
good time *s* rato agradable; **to have a good time** pasar un buen rato, divertirse; **to make good time** llegar en poco tiempo
good turn *s* favor
goodwife ['gʊd,waɪf] *s* (*pl:* **-wives**) (archaic) ama de casa; (archaic) señá
good will *s* buena voluntad, buena gana; buen nombre (*de un negocio*)
good works *spl* buena obra, obras de misericordia
goody ['gʊdɪ] *adj* (coll.) beatuco, santurrón; *interj* (coll.) ¡qué alegría!; *s* (*pl:* **-ies**) (coll.) golosina
goody-goody ['gʊdɪ'gʊdɪ] *adj* (coll.) beatuco, santurrón; *s* (*pl:* **-ies**) beatuco, santurrón
gooey ['guɪ] *adj* (*comp:* **gooier**; *super:* **gooiest**) (slang) muy pegajoso, fangoso
goof [guf] *s* (slang) mentecato; *va & vn* (slang) chapucear
goofy ['gufɪ] *adj* (*comp:* **-ier**; *super:* **-iest**) (slang) mentecato
goon [gun] *s* (slang) terrorista de alquiler; (slang) estúpido; (slang) canalla, gamberro
goop [gup] *s* (slang) palurdo
goosander [gu'sændər] *s* (orn.) pato sierra
goose [gus] *s* (*pl:* **geese**) (orn.) ánsar, ganso, oca; bobo; **the goose hangs high** todo va a pedir de boca; **to cook one's goose** malbaratarle a uno los planes, perderle a uno; **to shoe the goose** holgar; emborracharse; *s* (*pl:* **gooses**) plancha de sastre
goose barnacle *s* (zool.) anatifa
gooseberry ['guz,bɛrɪ] o ['gus,bɛrɪ] *s* (*pl:* **-ries**) (bot.) uva crespa, uva espina, grosellero silvestre; grosella silvestre
goose egg *s* huevo de oca; (slang) cero
goose flesh *s* carne de gallina
goosefoot ['gus,fʊt] *s* (*pl:* **-foots**) quenopodio, hierba del zorrillo
goosegirl ['gus,gʌrl] *s* ansarera
gooseherd ['gus,hʌrd] *s* ansarero
gooseneck ['gus,nɛk] *s* cuello de cisne; flexo (*de una lámpara*); (naut.) gancho de botalones
goose pimples *spl* carne de gallina
goose step *s* (mil.) paso de ganso
goose-step ['gus,stɛp] (*pret & pp:* **-stepped**; *ger:* **-stepping**) *vn* (mil.) marchar con paso de ganso
G.O.P. abr. de **Grand Old Party**
gopher ['gofər] *s* (zool.) ardillón, ardilla de tierra (*Spermophilus*); (zool.) tuza (*Geomys*)
gopherwood ['gofər,wʊd] *s* (bot.) árbol tintóreo norteamericano (*Cladrastis lutea*); madera amarilla (*de Cladrastis lutea*); (Bib.) madera de gopher
Gordian ['gɔrdɪən] *adj* gordiano
Gordian knot *s* (myth.) nudo gordiano; **to cut the Gordian knot** (myth. & fig.) cortar el nudo gordiano
gore [gor] *s* sangre derramada; sangre cuajada; (sew.) nesga; *va* acornar, herir con los cuernos; (sew.) nesgar
gorge [gɔrdʒ] *s* garganta, desfiladero; (anat.) gorja, garganta; (arch.) garganta; atasco (*p.ej., de hielo en un río*); contenido del estómago; hartazgo, panzada; asco; indignación; (fort.) gola; *va* engullir; atiborrar; *vn* atiborrarse
gorgeous ['gɔrdʒəs] *adj* brillante, de mucho esplendor, magnífico
gorgerin ['gɔrdʒərɪn] *s* (arch.) gorguera, collarín
gorget ['gɔrdʒɪt] *s* cuello, collar; griñón, impla; (arm.) gorguera, gorjal; (mil.) gola (*insignia militar*); (surg.) gorjerete (*para fístulas*); (zool.) mancha (*en el cuello*)
Gorgon ['gɔrgən] *adj* gorgóneo; *s* (myth.) Gorgona; (*l.c.*) *s* mujer muy fea y feroz
Gorgonian [gɔr'gonɪən] *adj* gorgóneo
Gorgonzola [,gɔrgən'zolə] *s* gorgonzola (*queso*)
gorilla [gə'rɪlə] *s* (zool.) gorila
gormand ['gɔrmənd] *s* var. de **gourmand**
gormandize ['gɔrməndaɪz] *va* comer glotonamente; *vn* glotonear
gorse [gɔrs] *s* (bot.) aulaga, tojo
gory ['gorɪ] *adj* (*comp:* **-ier**; *super:* **-iest**) ensangrentado; sangriento
gosh [gɑʃ] *interj* ¡caramba!
goshawk ['gɑs,hɔk] *s* (orn.) azor, accípitre
gosling ['gɑzlɪŋ] *s* ansarino
gospel ['gɑspəl] *s* Evangelio (*doctrina y vida de Jesucristo*); evangelio (*religión cristiana; verdad indiscutible*); *adj* evangélico; (*cap.*) *s* Evangelio (*cada uno de los cuatro primeros libros del Nuevo Testamento*)
gospeler o **gospeller** ['gɑspələr] *s* (eccl.) evangelistero; fanático, sectario; (scornful) protestante, puritano
Gospel side *s* (eccl.) lado del evangelio
gospel truth *s* evangelio (*verdad indiscutible*)
gossamer ['gɑsəmər] *s* telaraña, hilo de telaraña; gasa sutilísima; tela impermeable muy delgada; impermeable de tela muy delgada; *adj* sutil, diáfano, finísimo, delgadísimo
gossamery ['gɑsəmərɪ] *adj* telarañoso
gossip ['gɑsɪp] *s* chismes, chismería; chismoso; **piece of gossip** chisme; *vn* chismear
gossip columnist *s* periodista chismoso
gossipy ['gɑsɪpɪ] *adj* chismoso
gossoon [gɑ'sun] *s* muchacho; mozo, criado
got [gɑt] *pret & pp de* **get**
Goth [gɑθ] *s* godo; (fig.) bárbaro
Gothic ['gɑθɪk] *adj* gótico; (f.a.) gótico; bár-

baro; *s* gótico (*idioma*); (f.a.) gótico; (print.) gótica, letra gótica; (*l.c.*) *s* (print.) futura, letra futura
Gothicism ['gɑθɪsɪzəm] *s* goticismo; (*l.c.*) *s* barbarie
gotten ['gɑtən] *pp de* **get**
Göttingen ['gœtɪŋən] *s* Gotinga
gouache [gwɑʃ] *s* (paint.) aguazo (*pintura*); aguada (*procedimiento; pintura*)
gouge [gaʊdʒ] *s* (carp.) gubia; acanaladura, estría (*hecha con gubia*); muesca, mella (*producida por un instrumento afilado o un objeto esquinado*); (coll.) estafa; *va* excavar con gubia; acanalar, estriar; mellar (*como con gubia*); sacar el ojo a; cavar (*un canal el torrente*); (coll.) estafar; **to gouge out one's eyes** sacarle a uno los ojos (*p.ej., con el pulgar*)
goulash ['gulɑʃ] *s* puchero húngaro, estofado húngaro (*muy condimentado*)
gourd [gord] o [gʊrd] *s* calabaza (*fruto; calabacino*); (bot.) calabacera; frasco
gourmand ['gʊrmənd] *s* goloso
gourmet ['gʊrme] *s* gastrónomo, buen paladar
gout [gaʊt] *s* (path.) gota; (archaic) gota, salpicadura (*especialmente de sangre*)
gouty ['gaʊtɪ] *adj* (*comp:* **-ier**; *super:* **-iest**) gotoso
gov. abr. de **governor** y **government**
Gov. abr. de **Governor**
govern ['gʌvərn] *va* gobernar; (gram.) regir, pedir; *vn* gobernar
governable ['gʌvərnəbəl] *adj* gobernable
governance ['gʌvərnəns] *s* gobierno
governess ['gʌvərnɪs] *s* aya, institutriz
government ['gʌvərnmənt] *s* gobierno; (gram.) régimen; **to form a government** formar ministerio; *adj* del estado
governmental [,gʌvərn'mɛntəl] *adj* gubernamental, gubernativo
government in exile *s* gobierno exilado
governor ['gʌvərnər] *s* gobernador; alcaide (*de cárcel, castillo, etc.*); (mach.) regulador; (coll.) padre, papá
governor general *s* (*pl:* **governors general**) gobernador general
governorship ['gʌvərnər,ʃɪp] *s* gobierno (*cargo y tiempo que dura*)
govt. o **Govt.** abr. de **government**
gowan ['gaʊən] *s* (Scotch) margarita (*flor*)
gown [gaʊn] *s* vestido (*de mujer*); toga (*de profesor, juez, etc.*); traje talar (*del sacerdote*); bata, peinador; camisa de dormir; conjunto de estudiantes, profesores y demás personas de la universidad; *va* poner vestido de mujer a; vestir con toga
gownsman ['gaʊnzmən] *s* (*pl:* **-men**) togado; paisano (*no militar*)
G.P.O. abr. de **General Post Office** *y* **Government Printing Office**
gr. abr. de **gram** o **grams, grain** o **grains** y **gross**
Gr. abr. de **Grecian, Greece** y **Greek**
grab [græb] *s* arrebatiña; presa; (coll.) robo; (mach.) gancho, gancho agarrador, arrancasondas; (mach.) pala de doble concha; (*pret & pp:* **grabbed;** *ger:* **grabbing**) *va* arrebatar; asir, agarrar; *vn* arrebatar; **to grab at** tratar de arrebatar
grab bucket *s* pala de doble concha
Gracchus ['grækəs] *s* (*pl:* **-chi** [kaɪ]) Graco
grace [gres] *s* gracia (*donaire; favor; perdón*); bendición de la mesa; demora; excelencia, mérito; (mus.) nota o notas de adorno; (theol.) gracia; (*cap.*) *s* Engracia (*nombre de mujer*); **the Graces** (myth.) las Gracias; **to be in the bad graces of** haber caído de la gracia de; **to be in the good graces of** estar en gracia cerca de, gozar del favor de; **to fall from grace** reincidir; **to get in the bad graces of** caer de la gracia de; **to get in the good graces of** congraciarse con; **to have the grace to** + *inf* tener la discreción de + *inf;* **to say grace** bendecir la mesa; **with bad grace** de mal talante; **with good grace** de buen talante; **Your Grace** Su Señoría, Su Señoría Ilustrísima, Su Alteza; *va* adornar, engalanar; agraciar, favorecer; (mus.) poner notas de adorno a
graceful ['gresfəl] *adj* gracioso, agraciado
gracefulness ['gresfəlnɪs] *s* graciosidad, gracia, donaire
graceless ['greslɪs] *adj* desgraciado (*falto de gracia o atractivo*); depravado
grace note *s* (mus.) apoyatura, nota de adorno
gracile ['græsɪl] *adj* grácil
gracious ['greʃəs] *adj* gracioso, graciable; benigno; misericordioso; *interj* ¡ válgame Dios!
grackle ['grækəl] *s* (orn.) estornino de los pastores; (orn.) quiscal
grad. abr. de **graduate** y **graduated**
gradation [gre'deʃən] *s* gradación; grado, paso, matiz; graduación
grade [gred] *s* grado (*estado, valor relativo; sección escolar según la edad de los alumnos*); clase, calidad; calificación, nota (*que reciben los alumnos*); pendiente; grado de pendiente; **at grade** a nivel; **down grade** cuesta abajo; (fig.) cuesta abajo; **the grades** la escuela pública elemental; **to make the grade** lograr subir la cuesta; vencer los obstáculos; **up grade** cuesta arriba; (fig.) cada vez mejor; *va* graduar, calificar, clasificar; dar nota a (*un alumno*); leer y poner nota a (*un tema*); nivelar, explanar; **to grade as** graduar de o por (*bueno, malo, etc.*); *vn* cambiarse (*pasando por una serie de gradaciones*); **to grade into** convertirse gradualmente en
grade crossing *s* (rail.) paso a nivel, cruce a nivel
grade line *s* rasante
grader ['gredər] *s* graduador; nivelador; niveladora (*máquina*); alumno de cierto grado, p.ej., **first grader** alumno del primer grado
grade school *s* escuela elemental
gradient ['gredɪənt] *adj* ambulante; pendiente; *s* pendiente, declive; inclinación; (math. & meteor.) gradiente
gradin ['gredɪn] *s* grada; (eccl.) gradilla
gradine [grə'din] *s* gradina
grading ['gredɪŋ] *s* graduación; clasificación; nivelación, explanación
gradual ['grædʒʊəl] *adj* gradual; *s* (eccl.) gradual
gradually ['grædʒʊəlɪ] *adv* paulatinamente, poco a poco
graduate ['grædʒʊɪt] *adj* graduado; de graduados o para graduados; *s* graduado; frasco graduado, vasija graduada; ['grædʒʊet] *va* graduar; *vn* cambiarse gradualmente; graduarse
graduate school *s* escuela de graduados, escuela superior
graduate student *s* estudiante graduado
graduate work *s* altos estudios, estudios avanzados para graduados de bachiller
graduation [,grædʒʊ'eʃən] *s* graduación; ceremonias de graduación
graduator ['grædʒʊ,etər] *s* (elec.) graduador, derivador
graffito [grə'fito] *s* (pl: **-ti** [ti]) (archeol.) grafito
graft [græft] o [grɑft] *s* (hort. & surg.) injerto; (coll.) malversación, soborno político, ganancia ilegal; *va & vn* (hort. & surg.) injertar; (coll.) malversar
graftage ['græftɪdʒ] o ['grɑftɪdʒ] *s* (hort.) injertación
grafter ['græftər] o ['grɑftər] *s* injertador; (coll.) malversador
grafting ['græftɪŋ] o ['grɑftɪŋ] *s* (hort. & surg.) injertación
grafting knife *s* navaja de injertar, abridor
graham bread ['greəm] *s* pan hecho de harina de trigo sin cerner
graham flour *s* harina de trigo sin cerner
Grail [grel] *s* Graal o Grial
grain [gren] *s* grano; granos; fibra (*de la madera*); vena (*de la piedra*); grano (*de una piel; de una superficie más o menos rugosa; peso*); veteado; carácter, índole; partícula; pizca, p.ej., **not a grain of truth** ni pizca de verdad; **across the grain** transversalmente a la fibra; **against the grain** contra la dirección de la fibra; **to go against the grain** hacérsele a uno cuesta arriba, p.ej., **it goes against the grain** se me hace cuesta arriba; **in the grain** en rama; **with a grain of salt** con un grano de sal; *va* granear (*la masa de pólvora; una piedra litográfica*); vetear, crispir (*la ma-*

dera); granular (*una piel*); teñir en rama; alimentar con cereales
grain alcohol *s* alcohol de grano
grained lac *s* laca en grano
grain elevator *s* elevador de granos; depósito de cereales
grainfield ['gren,fild] *s* sembrado de trigo (*avena, etc.*)
graining ['greniŋ] *s* veteado
gram [græm] *s* gramo
gram atom *s* (chem.) átomo-gramo
gramercy [grə'mʌrsɪ] *interj* (archaic) ¡muchas gracias!; (archaic) ¡válgame Dios!
gramineous [grə'mɪnɪəs] *adj* gramíneo
graminivorous [,græmɪ'nɪvərəs] *adj* graminívoro
gram ion *s* (chem.) gramión
grammar ['græmər] *s* gramática; *adj* de gramática
grammarian [grə'mɛrɪən] *s* gramático
grammar school *s* (U.S.A.) escuela pública elemental; (Brit.) escuela de humanidades
grammatical [grə'mætɪkəl] *adj* gramático, gramatical
grammatically [grə'mætɪkəlɪ] *adv* gramaticalmente
gramme [græm] *s* var. de **gram**
gram-molecular [,græmmə'lɛkjələr] *adj* molecular-gramo
gram molecule *s* (chem.) molécula-gramo
gramophone ['græməfon] *s* (trademark) gramófono
Grampian Hills ['græmpɪən] *spl* montes Grampianos
Grampians, the los Grampianos
grampus ['græmpəs] *s* (zool.) grampo; (zool.) orca
granary ['grænərɪ] o ['grenərɪ] *s* (*pl:* **-ries**) granero; (fig.) granero (*país*)
grand [grænd] *adj* grande y magnífico; grandioso, espléndido; importante, principal; excelente
grandam ['grændæm] o **grandame** ['grændem] *s* abuela; anciana, vieja
Grand Army of the Republic *s* (U.S.A.) asociación de veteranos de la guerra entre Norte y Sur
grandaunt ['grænd,ænt] o ['grænd,ɑnt] *s* tía abuela
Grand Bank *s* Gran Banco (*a lo largo de la costa de Terranova*)
Grand Canal *s* Gran Canal (*de la China*); Canal Grande (*de Venecia*)
Grand Canyon *s* Gran Cañón
grandchild ['grænd,tʃaɪld] *s* (*pl:* **-children**) nieto o nieta
granddaughter ['grænd,dɔtər] *s* nieta
grand duchess *s* gran duquesa
grand duchy *s* gran ducado
grand duke *s* gran duque
grandee [græn'di] *s* grande de España; grande, persona de campanillas
grandeur ['grændʒər] o ['grændʒʊr] *s* grandeza, magnificencia, esplendor
grandfather ['grænd,fɑðər] *s* abuelo; antepasado
grandfatherly ['grænd,fɑðərlɪ] *adj* de abuelo, p.ej., **grandfatherly advice** consejos de abuelo
grandfather's clock *s* reloj de caja
grand guard *s* granguardia
grandiloquence [græn'dɪləkwəns] *s* grandilocuencia
grandiloquent [græn'dɪləkwənt] *adj* grandilocuente
grandiose ['grændɪos] *adj* grandioso; ampuloso, hinchado
grand jury *s* (law) jurado de acusación
grand larceny *s* (law) robo de cantidad importante
grand lodge *s* gran oriente, gran logia (*logia masónica central*)
grandma ['grænd,mɑ], ['græm,mɑ] o ['græmə] *s* (coll.) abuela, abuelita
grandmamma ['grændmə,mɑ] *s* abuela
grand march *s* marcha de sarao (*que consiste en el desfile de todos los convidados*)
grand master *s* gran maestre; gran o grande maestro (*en la orden masónica*)
grandmother ['grænd,mʌðər] *s* abuela; antepasada
grandmotherly ['grænd,mʌðərlɪ] *adj* de abuela, p.ej., **grandmotherly advice** consejos de abuela
grandnephew ['grænd,nɛfju] o ['grænd,nɛvju] *s* resobrino
grandniece ['grænd,nis] *s* resobrina
Grand Old Party *s* (U.S.A.) partido republicano
grand opera *s* (mus.) ópera seria
grandpa ['grænd,pɑ], ['græm,pɑ] o ['græmpə] *s* (coll.) abuelo, abuelito
grandpapa ['grændpə,pɑ] *s* abuelo
grandparent ['grænd,pɛrənt] *s* abuelo o abuela
grand piano *s* gran piano, piano de cola
grandsire ['grænd,saɪr] *s* (archaic) abuelo; (archaic) antepasado; (archaic) viejo
grand slam *s* (bridge) bola, grande eslam
grandson ['grænd,sʌn] *s* nieto
grandstand ['grænd,stænd] *s* gradería cubierta, tribuna
grandstand play *s* (sport) jugada espectacular que hace un jugador, no para ganar sino para impresionar al público; (coll.) cosa hecha para impresionar o para granjearse aplausos
grand strategy *s* (mil.) alta estrategia
grand tactics *ssg* (mil.) gran táctica
grand total *s* gran total, suma de totales
Grand Turk *s* gran señor, gran Turco
granduncle ['grænd,ʌŋkəl] *s* tío abuelo
grand vizier *s* gran visir
grange [grendʒ] *s* granja; cámara agrícola
granger ['grendʒər] *s* granjero
granite ['grænɪt] *s* granito; *adj* agranitado; granítico
graniteware ['grænɪt,wɛr] *s* platos, tazas, utensilios, etc. de hierro con esmalte de porcelana color de granito
granitic [græ'nɪtɪk] *adj* granítico
granivorous [græ'nɪvərəs] *adj* granívoro
grannie o **granny** ['grænɪ] *s* (*pl:* **-nies**) (coll.) abuela, abuelita; (coll.) anciana, vieja; (coll.) malhumorado, melindroso
granny knot *s* gorupo
grant [grænt] o [grɑnt] *s* concesión; subvención; donación; transferencia de propiedad; *va* conceder, otorgar; dar (*permiso, perdón, etc.*); transferir (*el título a bienes inmuebles*); **to take for granted** dar por supuesto, dar por sentado, dar por descontado; tratar con indiferencia, no hacer caso de
grantee [græn'ti] o [grɑn'ti] *s* cesionario, donatario
grant-in-aid ['græntɪn'ed] o ['grɑntɪn'ed] *s* (*pl:* **grants-in-aid**) pensión (*auxilio pecuniario concedido para estimular conocimientos literarios, científicos, etc.*)
grantor [græn'tɔr] o [grɑn'tɔr] *s* cesionista, donador
granular ['grænjələr] *adj* granular; (path.) granuloso
granulate ['grænjəlet] *va* granular; granelar; *vn* granularse; (path.) granularse
granulation [,grænjə'leʃən] *s* granulación
granule ['grænjʊl] *s* gránulo; (bot. & pharm.) gránulo
granulite ['grænjəlaɪt] *s* (geol.) granulita
granulose ['grænjəlos] *s* (chem.) granulosa
grape [grep] *s* (bot.) vid; uva (*fruto*)
grape arbor *s* parral, emparrado de la vid
grapefruit ['grep,frut] *s* (bot.) toronjo, pamplemusa, pomelo; toronja, pamplemusa, pomelo (*fruto*)
grape hyacinth *s* (bot.) sueldacostilla, jacinto racimoso silvestre
grape juice *s* zumo de uva
grapeshot ['grep,ʃɑt] *s* metralla
grape sugar *s* azúcar de uva
grapevine ['grep,vaɪn] *s* (bot.) vid, parra; **by the grapevine** o **by grapevine telegraph** por vías misteriosas (*dícese de los rumores que se propalan sin que se sepa cómo*)
graph [græf] o [grɑf] *s* gráfica; (gram.) grafía; *va* representar mediante una gráfica, construir la gráfica de
graphic ['græfɪk] o **graphical** ['græfɪkəl] *adj* gráfico
graphic arts *spl* artes gráficas
graphite ['græfaɪt] *s* grafito

graphology [græ'fɑlədʒɪ] *s* grafología

graphomania [ˌgræfə'menɪə] *s* grafomanía

graphometer [græ'fɑmɪtər] *s* grafómetro

graph paper *s* papel cuadriculado

grapnel ['græpnəl] *s* garabato; rezón (*ancla pequeña*)

grapple ['græpəl] *s* asimiento; (sport) presa; rezón; garabato, arpeo; *va* asir, agarrar; apretar; luchar a brazo partido con; *vn* agarrarse; luchar a brazo partido; **to grapple for** tratar de pescar; **to grapple with** luchar a brazo partido con; tratar de resolver, tratar de vencer

grappling hook o **iron** *s* arpeo, garfio

grapy ['grepɪ] *adj* de uvas, hecho de uvas

grasp [græsp] o [grɑsp] *s* asimiento; alcance, mano, poder; apretón (*de la mano*); comprensión; **to have a good grasp of** saber a fondo; **within the grasp of** al alcance de; *va* asir, empuñar; apoderarse de; comprender; **grasp all, lose all** quien mucho abarca poco aprieta; *vn* extender la mano (*queriendo asir una cosa*); **to grasp at** tratar de asir o coger; aceptar con avidez

grasping ['græspɪŋ] o ['grɑspɪŋ] *adj* avaro, codicioso

grass [græs] o [grɑs] *s* hierba; césped; **to go to grass** ir al pasto; disfrutar de una temporada de descanso; acabarse, arruinarse; morirse; **to not let the grass grow under one's feet** no dormirse en las pajas; *va* apacentar; cubrir de hierba; *vn* pastar; cubrirse de hierba

grasshopper ['græsˌhɑpər] o ['grɑsˌhɑpər] *s* (ent.) saltamontes

grassland ['græsˌlænd] o ['grɑsˌlænd] *s* campo de pastoreo

grass pea *s* (bot.) almorta

grass pink *s* (bot.) clavel coronado o clavellina de pluma

grass-roots ['græsˌruts] o ['grɑsˌruts] *adj* (coll.) del pueblo, de la gente común

grass seed *s* semilla de césped

grass snake *s* (zool.) culebrita inofensiva que vive entre la hierba (*Natrix natrix, Liopeltis vernalis y Thamnophis sirtalis*)

grass widow *s* viuda de paja, viuda de marido vivo

grass widower *s* hombre divorciado; hombre que vive separado de su mujer

grassy ['græsɪ] o ['grɑsɪ] *adj* (*comp:* **-ier;** *super:* **-iest**) herboso; herbáceo

grate [gret] *s* reja; parrilla; *va* enrejar; hacer rechinar; rallar (*p.ej., queso*); *vn* rechinar, crujir; **to grate on** (fig.) rallar

grateful ['gretfəl] *adj* agradecido, reconocido; agradable, grato; confortante, refrescante

grater ['gretər] *s* ralladera, rallador

gratification [ˌgrætɪfɪ'keʃən] *s* gratificación, recompensa; complacencia, placer, satisfacción

gratify ['grætɪfaɪ] (*pret & pp:* **-fied**) *va* gratificar, complacer, satisfacer; (archaic) gratificar (*recompensar*)

gratifying ['grætɪˌfaɪɪŋ] *adj* grato, satisfactorio

grating ['gretɪŋ] *adj* áspero, chirriante; irritante, fastidioso; *s* enrejado; (opt.) red

gratis ['gretɪs] o ['grætɪs] *adj* gracioso, gratuito; *adv* gratis, de balde

gratitude ['grætɪtjud] o ['grætɪtud] *s* gratitud

gratuitous [grə'tjuɪtəs] o [grə'tuɪtəs] *adj* gratuito

gratuity [grə'tjuɪtɪ] o [grə'tuɪtɪ] *s* (*pl:* **-ties**) dádiva; propina, gratificación

gratulation [ˌgrætʃə'leʃən] *s* gratulación

gratulatory ['grætʃələˌtorɪ] *adj* gratulatorio

gravamen [grə'vemən] *s* (*pl:* **-vamens** o **-vamina** ['væmɪnə]) agravio, motivo para quejarse; (law) materia de un cargo

grave [grev] *adj* grave, serio, solemne; grave, bajo (*sonido*); (gram.) grave (*acento*); *s* sepulcro, sepultura; **to have one foot in the grave** estar con un pie en la sepultura; (*pret:* **graved;** *pp:* **graven** o **graved**) *va* grabar; (naut.) despalmar; (fig.) grabar (*p.ej., en la memoria*)

grave accent *s* acento grave

graveclothes ['grevˌkloz] *spl* mortaja

gravedigger ['grevˌdɪgər] *s* sepulturero, enterrador

gravel ['grævəl] *s* grava, guijo, recebo; (path.) gravela; (*pret & pp:* **-eled** o **-elled;** *ger:* **-eling** o **-elling**) *va* cubrir de grava o guijo, recebar; desconcertar, dejar perplejo

gravelly ['grævəlɪ] *adj* guijoso, cascajoso

gravel pit *s* cascajal

gravel walk *s* vereda de grava

graveness ['grevnɪs] *s* gravedad, seriedad

graven image ['grevən] *s* ídolo, imagen

graver ['grevər] *s* buril, punzón

gravestone ['grevˌston] *s* lápida sepulcral

graveyard ['grevˌjɑrd] *s* cementerio, camposanto

gravid ['grævɪd] *adj* grávido

gravidity [grə'vɪdɪtɪ] *s* gravidez

gravimetric [ˌgrævɪ'mɛtrɪk] o **gravimetrical** [ˌgrævɪ'mɛtrɪkəl] *adj* gravimétrico

gravimetry [grə'vɪmɪtrɪ] *s* gravimetría

graving dock *s* (naut.) dique de carena

gravitate ['grævɪtet] *vn* gravitar; **to gravitate to** o **toward** sentir la atracción de, tender hacia

gravitation [ˌgrævɪ'teʃən] *s* (phys.) gravitación; atracción, tendencia

gravitational [ˌgrævɪ'teʃənəl] *adj* de gravitación, gravitacional

gravity ['grævɪtɪ] *s* (*pl:* **-ties**) gravedad; (phys. & mus.) gravedad

gravity cell *s* (elec.) pila de gravedad

gravity feed *s* (mach.) alimentación por gravedad

gravure [grə'vjʊr] o ['grevjʊr] *s* fotograbado

gravy ['grevɪ] *s* (*pl:* **-vies**) jugo, grasa; salsa; (slang) ganga, breva

gravy dish o **boat** *s* salsera

gravy train *s* (slang) pingüe destino, enchufe

gray [gre] *adj* gris; cano, encanecido; viejo; lúgubre, obscuro; *s* gris; traje gris, vestido gris; tela gris; caballo tordo; media luz (*del crepúsculo*); *va* poner gris; *vn* ponerse gris; encanecer

graybeard ['greˌbɪrd] *s* anciano, viejo

Gray Friar *s* franciscano

gray-headed ['greˌhɛdɪd] *adj* canoso

grayhound ['greˌhaʊnd] *s* galgo; (fig.) galgo (*vapor transoceánico*)

gray iron *s* fundición gris

grayish ['greɪʃ] *adj* grisáceo; entrecano

graylag ['greˌlæg] *s* (orn.) ganso silvestre (*Anser anser*)

grayling ['grelɪŋ] *s* (ichth.) tímalo

gray matter *s* (anat.) substancia gris; (coll.) materia gris cerebral (*inteligencia*)

gray mullet *s* (ichth.) mújol

gray partridge *s* (orn.) perdiz pardilla, estarna

gray squirrel *s* (zool.) ardilla gris

graywacke ['greˌwæk] o ['greˌwækə] *s* (geol.) grauvaca

gray wolf *s* (zool.) lobo gris (*Canis occidentalis*)

graze [grez] *s* roce; arañazo, rasguño; *va* rozar; arañar, rasguñar; pacer (*la hierba*); apacentar (*el ganado*); pastar (*conducir al pasto*); *vn* pacer, pastar

grazier ['greʒər] *s* ganadero

grazing ['grezɪŋ] *s* pasto; campo de pastoreo

Gr. Br. o **Gr. Brit.** abr. de **Great Britain**

grease [gris] *s* grasa; lana en bruto y sin limpiar; (slang) lisonja, soborno; [gris] o [griz] *va* engrasar; (slang) untar, sobornar

grease cup [gris] *s* (mach.) vaso de engrase, caja de sebo, engrasador

grease gun *s* jeringa de engrase, engrasador de pistón, pistola engrasadora, bomba de engrase

grease lift *s* (aut.) puente de engrase

grease pit *s* (aut.) fosa de engrase

greaser ['grisər] o ['grizər] *s* engrasador; (offensive) mejicano, hispanoamericano

grease rack *s* var. de **grease lift**

grease spot *s* lámpara (*mancha de aceite o grasa*)

greasewood ['grisˌwʊd] *s* (bot.) arbusto quenopodiáceo (*Sarcobatus vermiculatus*)

greasy ['grisɪ] o ['grizɪ] *adj* (*comp:* **-ier;** *super:* **-iest**) grasiento; liso, resbaladizo

great [gret] *adj* grande; muy usado, muy popular; (coll.) excelente; magno, grande, p.ej., **Alexander the Great** Alejandro Magno; **Peter the Great** Pedro el Grande; **the great** los grandes

great-aunt ['gret,ænt] o ['gret,ɑnt] *s* tía abuela
Great Barrier Reef *s* Gran Barrera
Great Basin *s* Cuenca Grande
Great Bear *s* (astr.) Osa mayor
Great Britain *s* la Gran Bretaña
great bustard *s* (orn.) avutarda
great circle *s* (astr. & geom.) círculo máximo
greatcoat ['gret,kot] *s* gabán de mucho abrigo
Great Dane *s* mastín danés
Great Divide *s* divisoria continental
Great Dog *s* (astr.) Can mayor
Greater Antilles *spl* Antillas Mayores
Greater London *s* el Gran Londres
Greater New York *s* el Gran Nueva York
greater weever *s* (ichth.) araña, dragón, dragón marino
greater yellowlegs *s* (orn.) chorlo grande de patas amarillas, chorlo real
greatest common divisor *s* (math.) máximo común divisor
great-grandchild [,gret'grænd,tʃaɪld] *s* (*pl:* **-children** [,tʃɪldrən]) bisnieto, bisnieta
great-granddaughter [,gret'grænd,dɔtər] *s* bisnieta
great-grandfather [,gret'grænd,fɑðər] *s* bisabuelo
great-grandmother [,gret'grænd,mʌðər] *s* bisabuela
great-grandparent [,gret'grænd,pɛrənt] *s* bisabuelo o bisabuela
great-grandson [,gret'grænd,sʌn] *s* bisnieto
great-hearted ['gret,hɑrtɪd] *adj* generoso, noble; valiente
great horned owl *s* (orn.) buho americano (*Bubo virginianus*)
Great Lakes *spl* Grandes Lagos
greatly ['gretlɪ] *adv* grandemente; grandiosamente
great mogul *s* autócrata, magnate; **Great Mogul** *s* gran Mogol
great mullein *s* (bot.) gordolobo, verbasco
great-nephew ['gret,nɛfju] o ['gret,nɛvju] *s* resobrino
greatness ['gretnɪs] *s* grandeza
great-niece ['gret,nis] *s* resobrina
Great Plains *s* Pradera (*inmensas pampas de la cuenca del Misisipí y sus afluentes*)
great primer ['prɪmər] *s* (print.) texto
Great Pyramid *s* gran Pirámide
Great Russian *s* gran ruso
Great Salt Lake *s* Gran Lago Salado
great Scott *interj* ¡ válgame Dios!
great seal *s* gran sello
Great Spirit *s* Gran Espíritu (*dios de varias tribus de indios norteamericanos*)
great titmouse *s* (orn.) herrerillo
great-uncle ['gret,ʌŋkəl] *s* tío abuelo
Great Wall of China *s* Gran Muralla de la China
Great War *s* Gran Guerra
Great White Way *s* Gran Vía Blanca (*Broadway*)
greave [griv] *s* greba; **greaves** *spl* chicharrón
grebe [grib] *s* (orn.) castañero, colimbo; plumas de la pechuga del colimbo (*para adornar sombreros*)
Grecian ['griʃən] *adj* griego; *s* griego; helenista
Grecian nose *s* nariz helénica
Grecism ['grisɪzəm] *s* grecismo
Grecize ['grisaɪz] *va & vn* grecizar
Greco-Latin [,griko'lætɪn] o [,griko'lætən] *adj* grecolatino
Greco-Roman [,griko'romən] *adj* grecorromano
Greece [gris] *s* Grecia
greed [grid] *s* codicia, avaricia, glotonería
greediness ['gridɪnɪs] *s* codicia, avaricia, glotonería
greedy ['gridɪ] *adj* (*comp:* **-ier;** *super:* **-iest**) codicioso, avaro, glotón
Greek [grik] *adj* griego; *s* griego; **it's Greek to me** me es chino; (*l.c.*) *s* griego (*fullero*)
Greek calends *spl* calendas griegas (*tiempo que no ha de llegar*)
Greek cross *s* cruz griega
Greek fire *s* fuego griego
Greek Orthodox Church *s* Iglesia griega ortodoxa
Greek rite *s* rito griego
Greek valerian *s* (bot.) valeriana griega
green [grin] *adj* verde; inexperto, novato; candoroso, bobo; demudado (*por el miedo, la envidia, etc.*); *s* verde; césped, prado, terreno verdoso; (golf) terreno cubierto de césped muy fino que circunda cada agujero; **greens** *spl* verduras; ramos verdes colocados para servir de adorno
greenback ['grin,bæk] *s* (U.S.A.) billete de banco (*de dorso verde*)
greenbrier ['grin,braɪər] *s* (bot.) cocolmeca
green corn *s* maíz tierno
green crab *s* (zool.) cámbaro, cangrejo de mar
green dragon (bot.) dragón verde, dragontea
green earth *s* verdacho
greenery ['grinərɪ] *s* (*pl:* **-ies**) verdura; invernáculo
green-eyed ['grin,aɪd] *adj* de ojos verdes; celoso
greengage ['grin,gedʒ] *s* reina claudia, ciruela verdal
green grasshopper *s* (ent.) langostón
greengrocer ['grin,grosər] *s* verdulero
greengrocery ['grin,grosərɪ] *s* (*pl:* **-ies**) verdulería
greenhorn ['grin,hɔrn] *s* pipiolo, novato; bobo, palurdo
greenhouse ['grin,haus] *s* invernáculo
greening ['grinɪŋ] *s* variedad de manzana de color verdoso
greenish ['grinɪʃ] *adj* verdoso
Greenland ['grinlənd] *s* Groenlandia
Greenlander ['grinləndər] *s* groenlandés
Greenlandic [grin'lændɪk] *adj* groenlandés
green manure *s* estiércol reciente; abono vegetal
greenness ['grinnɪs] *s* verdura, verdor; falta de experiencia
greenroom ['grin,rum] o ['grin,rʊm] *s* saloncillo (*de descanso de los actores*); chismería de teatro; local para almacenar loza cruda, tela acabada de hacer, etc.
greensand ['grɪn,sænd] *s* arenisca verde
green sand *s* (found.) arena verde
greensward ['grin,swɔrd] *s* césped
green table *s* tapete verde
green tea *s* té verde
green thumb *s* don de criar plantas
green turtle *s* (zool.) tortuga marina de color verde (*Chelonia mydas*)
green vegetables *spl* verduras
greenwing ['grin,wɪŋ] *s* (orn.) cerceta de verano
greenwood ['grin,wʊd] *s* floresta, bosque frondoso
green woodpecker *s* (orn.) picamaderos, pájaro carpintero
greet [grit] *va* saludar; recibir (*p.ej., con palabras de bienvenida, con palabras airadas, con imprecaciones, etc.*); presentarse a (*los ojos de una persona*)
greeting ['gritɪŋ] *s* saludo, salutación; buena acogida, bienvenida; **greetings!** ¡ salud!
greeting card *s* tarjeta de felicitación
gregarious [grɪ'gɛrɪəs] *adj* gregario; sociable
Gregorian [grɪ'gorɪən] *adj* gregoriano
Gregorian calendar *s* calendario gregoriano
Gregorian chant *s* canto gregoriano
Gregory ['grɛgərɪ] *s* Gregorio
gremial ['grimɪəl] *s* (eccl.) gremial
gremlin ['grɛmlɪn] *s* hado, duende de los aviones
grenade [grɪ'ned] *s* granada; granada extintora
grenadier [,grɛnə'dɪr] *s* granadero
grenadine [,grɛnə'din] o ['grɛnədin] *s* granadina (*tejido; zumo*)
grew [gru] *pret de* **grow**
grewsome ['grusəm] *adj* var. de **gruesome**
grey [gre] *adj, s, va & vn* var. de **gray**
greyhound ['gre,haund] *s* galgo; (fig.) galgo (*vapor transoceánico*)
greyhound race *s* carrera de galgos
grid [grɪd] *s* rejilla, parrilla; (elec. & rad.) rejilla; (Brit.) red nacional de distribución eléctrica
grid bias *s* (rad.) polarización de rejilla
grid circuit *s* (rad.) circuito de rejilla
grid condenser *s* (rad.) condensador de rejilla

grid current *s* (rad.) corriente de rejilla
griddle ['grɪdəl] *s* tortera, plancha; *va* cocer (*tortillas*) en una plancha
griddlecake ['grɪdəl,kek] *s* torta o tortita a la plancha
gride [graɪd] *s* rechinamiento; *va* hacer rechinar; *vn* rechinar
gridiron ['grɪd,aɪərn] *s* parrilla; rejilla (*parecida a una parrilla*); (U.S.A.) campo de fútbol (*marcado a manera de parrilla*); (theat.) telar
grid leak *s* (rad.) resistencia de rejilla, escape de rejilla
grief [grif] *s* aflicción, pena, pesar, quebranto; (coll.) disgusto, disgustos; **good grief!** ¡voto al chápiro!; **to come to grief** tener muchos quebrantos; fracasar, arruinarse
grievance ['grivəns] *s* agravio, injusticia; motivo para quejarse
grieve [griv] *va* afligir, apenar; *vn* afligirse, apenarse; **to grieve over** añorar
grievous ['grivəs] *adj* doloroso, penoso; atroz, cruel, horrible; lastimoso
griffin ['grɪfɪn] o **griffon** ['grɪfən] *s* (myth.) grifo
grig [grɪg] *s* angula (*cría de la anguila*); (ent.) grillo, saltamontes; persona vivaracha
grill [grɪl] *s* parrilla; ración de carne asada, ración de pescado asado; parrilla (*restaurante o comedor de hotel cuya especialidad es la carne asada o el pescado asado*); *va* emparrillar; dar tormento de fuego a; interrogar de modo muy apremiante (*a un acusado*)
grillage ['grɪlɪdʒ] *s* (constr.) zampeado
grille [grɪl] *s* reja, verja; parrilla, rejilla (*p.ej., de automóvil*)
grillroom ['grɪl,rum] o ['grɪl,rʊm] *s* parrilla (*restaurante o comedor de hotel cuya especialidad es la carne asada o el pescado asado*)
grilse [grɪls] *s* cría del salmón que habiendo pasado el invierno en el mar vuelve al agua dulce de un río
grim [grɪm] *adj* (*comp:* **grimmer;** *super:* **grimmest**) austero, severo; ceñudo; fiero, cruel; horrible
grimace [grɪ'mes] *s* mueca, sonrisa falsa o mala; *vn* hacer muecas, fruncir el hocico
grimalkin [grɪ'mælkɪn] o [grɪ'mɔlkɪn] *s* gato; gata vieja; vieja malévola
grime [graɪm] *s* mugre, tiznado; *va* ensuciar, tiznar
grimness ['grɪmnɪs] *s* austeridad, severidad; fiereza, crueldad; horror
grimy ['graɪmɪ] *adj* (*comp:* **-ier;** *super:* **-iest**) sucio, mugriento, tiznado
grin [grɪn] *s* sonrisa bonachona; esguince, regaño, mueca de dolor o de cólera (*mostrando los dientes*); (*pret & pp:* **grinned;** *ger:* **grinning**) *va* expresar (*p.ej., aprobación*) sonriendo bonachonamente; *vn* sonreírse bonachonamente; hacer una mueca de dolor, de cólera o de desdén (*enseñando los dientes*)
grind [graɪnd] *s* molienda; rechinamiento; (coll.) zurra (*trabajo o estudio continuado*); (coll.) empollón, estudiantón; (*pret & pp:* **ground**) *va* moler; afilar, amolar; tallar (*lentes*); picar (*carne*); pulverizar; hacer rechinar; dar vueltas a (*un manubrio*); **to grind out** producir (*música*) dando vueltas a un manubrio; *vn* hacer molienda; molerse; pulverizarse; rozar; rechinar; (coll.) echar los bofes
grinder ['graɪndər] *s* molendero; amolador; esmerilador; amoladora; esmeriladora; molino o molinillo (*para moler café, pimienta, etc.*); muela (*piedra para afilar*); (anat.) muela; **grinders** *spl* (slang) herramienta (*dientes*)
grindstone ['graɪnd,ston] *s* muela, piedra de amolar; **to have, keep** o **put one's nose to the grindstone** trabajar con ahinco, echar los bofes
gringo ['grɪŋgo] *s* (*pl:* **-gos**) (scornful) gringo (*inglés o norteamericano*)
grip [grɪp] *s* asimiento; agarradero; apretón (*de la mano*); modo de darse la mano (*en las asociaciones secretas*); saco de mano; dolor punzante; comprensión; (mach.) mordaza; (path.) gripe; **to come to grips (with)** luchar a brazo partido (con); arrostrarse (con), enfrentarse (con); (*pret & pp:* **gripped** o **gript;** *ger:* **gripping**) *va* asir, agarrar; apretar; tener asido, agarrarse a; absorber la atención a; *vn* agarrarse; absorber la atención
gripe [graɪp] *s* asimiento; sujeción; **gripes** *spl* (naut.) obenques; (path.) retortijón de tripas; *va* asir, apretar; fastidiar, molestar; dar retortijones a; (slang) molestar sobremanera; *vn* sufrir retortijones; (slang) refunfuñar, quejarse mucho
grippe [grɪp] *s* (path.) gripe
gripping ['grɪpɪŋ] *adj* conmovedor, impresionante
gripsack ['grɪp,sæk] *s* saco de mano, maleta
gript [grɪpt] *pret & pp de* **grip**
grisaille [grɪ'zel] *s* (f.a.) grisalla
grisette [grɪ'zɛt] *s* griseta (*muchacha obrera de París*)
grisly ['grɪzlɪ] *adj* (*comp:* **-lier;** *super:* **-liest**) espantoso, horrible, espeluznante
grist [grɪst] *s* harina; molienda (*cantidad que se muele de una vez*); malta molido; (coll.) acervo, acopio; **to be grist to one's mill** (coll.) serle a uno de mucho provecho
gristle ['grɪsəl] *s* cartílago, ternilla
gristly ['grɪslɪ] *adj* (*comp:* **-tlier;** *super:* **-tliest**) cartilaginoso, ternilloso
gristmill ['grɪst,mɪl] *s* molino harinero
grit [grɪt] *s* arena, guijo muy fino; asperón, arenisca silícea; tesón, ánimo, valor; **grits** *spl* farro, sémola, maíz o avena a medio moler; (*pret & pp:* **gritted;** *ger:* **gritting**) *va* cerrar fuertemente (*los dientes*); hacer rechinar (*los dientes*)
gritrock ['grɪt,rɑk] o **gritstone** ['grɪt,ston] *s* asperón, arenisca silícea
gritty ['grɪtɪ] *adj* (*comp:* **-tier;** *super:* **-tiest**) arenoso; valiente, resuelto
grizzled ['grɪzəld] *adj* gris; grisáceo; canoso
grizzly ['grɪzlɪ] *adj* (*comp:* **-zlier;** *super:* **-zliest**) gris; grisáceo; canoso; *s* (*pl:* **-zlies**) (zool.) oso gris; (min.) cribón, parrilla
grizzly bear *s* (zool.) oso gris
groan [gron] *s* gemido, quejido; *va* expresar con voz quejumbrosa; *vn* gemir, quejarse; crujir (*por exceso de peso*); estar muy cargado, p.ej., **the table groaned with good food** estaba la mesa muy cargada de platos deliciosos; estar agobiado, p.ej., **he groaned beneath his burden** estaba agobiado por la carga
groat [grot] *s* blanca, ardite; **groats** *spl* farro, sémola, maíz o avena a medio moler
grocer ['grosər] tendero de ultramarinos; abarrotero (Am.)
grocery ['grosərɪ] *s* (*pl:* **-ies**) tienda de ultramarinos, tienda de comestibles; abarrotería (Am.); **groceries** *spl* comestibles, víveres; abarrotes (Am.)
grocery store *s* tienda de ultramarinos, tienda de comestibles; abarrotería (Am.)
grog [grɑg] *s* grog (*ron diluído en agua; bebida espirituosa*)
groggery ['grɑgərɪ] *s* (*pl:* **-ies**) taberna
groggy ['grɑgɪ] *adj* (*comp:* **-gier;** *super:* **-giest**) (coll.) vacilante, inseguro; (coll.) atontado (*p.ej., de un golpe*); (coll.) borracho
grogram ['grɑgrəm] *s* cordellate, gorgorán
grogshop ['grɑg,ʃɑp] *s* taberna
groin [grɔɪn] *s* (anat.) ingle; (arch.) arista de encuentro; *va* (arch.) construir con aristas de encuentro
grommet ['grɑmɪt] *s* ojal; (naut.) roñada
gromwell ['grɑmwəl] *s* (bot.) granos de amor, mijo gris
groom [grum] o [grʊm] *s* novio; mozo de caballos; (Brit.) camarero, caballerizo o ayuda de cámara de la casa real; (archaic) criado; *va* asear, acicalar, poner en orden; preparar y enseñar (*a un político*) en el modo de presentarse candidato en las elecciones
groomsman ['grumzmən] o ['grʊmzmən] *s* (*pl:* **-men**) padrino de boda
groove [gruv] *s* ranura, acanaladura; garganta (*de polea*); surco (*p.ej., de un disco*); rodada (*señal que deja la rueda*); (coll.) rutina, hábito arraigado; **groove and tongue** a ranura y lengüeta; *va* ranurar, acanalar
groove-and-tongue joint ['gruvənd'tʌŋ] *s* (carp.) ensambladura de ranura y lengüeta
grooving machine *s* ranuradora
grooving plane *s* cepillo de ranurar

grooving saw *s* sierra ranuradora
grope [grop] *va* tentar (*p.ej., el camino en la obscuridad*); *vn* andar a tientas, palpar; pujar (*por expresarse*); **to grope for** buscar a tientas, buscar sin hallar; **to grope through** palpar (*p.ej., las tinieblas*)
gropingly ['gropɪŋly] *adv* a tientas; (fig.) a tientas
grosbeak ['gros,bik] *s* (orn.) pico duro (*Pinicola enucleator*); (orn.) degollado; (orn.) cardenal de Virginia; (orn.) cascapiñones, pico gordo (*Coccothraustes coccothraustes*)
grosgrain ['gro,gren] *s* gro
gross [gros] *adj* total; craso (*error*); grosero; grueso; denso, espeso; bruto; *s* (*pl:* **gross**) gruesa (*doce docenas*); *s* (*pl:* **grosses**) conjunto, totalidad; **in gross** o **in the gross** en grueso
gross anatomy *s* anatomía macroscópica
grossly ['groslɪ] *adv* excesivamente; groseramente; aproximadamente
gross national product *s* renta nacional, producto total de la economía nacional
grossness ['grosnɪs] *s* grosería; densidad, espesor
gross ton *s* tonelada gruesa (*2.240 libras o 1.016,06 kg.*)
grossulariaceous [,grɑsjə,lerɪ'eʃəs] *adj* (bot.) grosulariáceo
grot [grɑt] *s* (poet.) gruta
grotesque [gro'tɛsk] *adj* grotesco (*ridículo*); (f.a.) grutesco o grotesco; *s* (f.a.) grutesco o grotesco
Grotius ['groʃɪəs] *s* Grocio
grotto ['grɑto] *s* (*pl:* **-toes** o **-tos**) gruta
grouch [graʊtʃ] *s* (coll.) mal humor; (coll.) cascarrabias, vinagre (*persona*); *vn* (coll.) estar de mal humor, refunfuñar
grouchy ['graʊtʃɪ] *adj* (*comp:* **-ier;** *super:* **-iest**) (coll.) malhumorado, refunfuñador
ground [graʊnd] *s* tierra; terreno; causa, fundamento; campo (*de batalla*); (elec.) tierra; (elec.) borne de conexión con tierra; (elec.) masa (*p.ej., de un automóvil*); (paint.) campo, fondo; **grounds** *spl* terreno; jardines; causa, fundamento; poso, heces; **above ground** vivo; **from the ground up** de abajo arriba; completamente; **on the ground of** con motivo de; **to be on one's own ground** estar en su elemento; **to break ground** empezar la excavación; abrir los cimientos; **to cover the ground** hacer completamente lo que hay que hacer; atravesar la distancia debida; correr mucho; **to cut the ground from under one's feet** anticiparle a uno las razones en una polémica; **to fall to the ground** fracasar, abandonarse (*un proyecto*); **to gain ground** ganar terreno; **to give ground** ceder terreno; **to hold one's ground** mantenerse firme; **to lose ground** perder terreno; **to run into the ground** (slang) abusar de (*p.ej., un recurso*); **to shift one's ground** cambiar de posición; cambiar de táctica; **to stand one's ground** mantenerse firme; **to yield ground** ceder terreno; **ground for complaint** motivo de queja ‖ *adj* a ras de tierra, terrestre; fundamental ‖ *va* poner en tierra; descansar (*armas*); cimentar, establecer, fundar; (elec.) poner a tierra; (paint.) dar campo o fondo a; **to be grounded** estar sin volar (*un avión*); **to be well grounded** ser muy versado; estar bien fundado (*un juicio*) ‖ *vn* (naut.) encallar, varar ‖ *pret & pp de* **grind**
ground connection *s* (rad.) toma de tierra
ground-controlled approach ['graʊndkən'trold] *s* (aer.) acceso dirigido desde tierra, aproximación controlada desde tierra
ground crew *s* (aer.) personal de tierra
grounder ['graʊndər] *s* (baseball) pelota rodada
ground floor *s* piso bajo
ground game *s* caza de pelo
ground glass *s* vidrio deslustrado
ground hog *s* (zool.) marmota de América
ground ivy *s* (bot.) hiedra terrestre
ground lead [lid] *s* (elec.) conductor a tierra
groundless ['graʊndlɪs] *adj* infundado
ground line *s* línea de tierra
groundling ['graʊndlɪŋ] *s* animal o planta terrestres; pez que habita en el fondo del mar; lector poco culto y sin gusto
groundnut ['graʊnd,nʌt] *s* (bot.) chufa; (bot.) cacahuete
ground pine *s* (bot.) pinillo, pinillo oloroso; (bot.) licopodio
ground plan *s* planta (*de un edificio*); primer proyecto, proyecto fundamental
ground return *s* (elec.) retorno por tierra, retorno por masa
groundsel ['graʊndsəl] *s* (bot.) hierba cana, zuzón
groundsill ['graʊndsɪl] *s* (constr.) carrera inferior, solera de base
ground speed *s* (aer.) velocidad con respecto al suelo
ground squirrel *s* (zool.) tuza; (zool.) ardilla listada
ground support *s* (aer.) apoyo terrestre
ground swell *s* marejada de fondo, mar de fondo
ground troops *spl* (mil.) tropas terrestres
ground water *s* agua de pozo, agua subterránea
ground wire *s* (rad.) alambre de tierra, hilo de tierra; (aut.) hilo de masa
groundwork ['graʊnd,wʌrk] *s* cimiento, fundamento
group [grup] *s* grupo; *adj* colectivo; *va* agrupar; *vn* agruparse
grouper ['grupər] *s* (ichth.) cabrilla, cherna, mero
group insurance *s* seguro a grupos
grouse [graʊs] *s* (orn.) gallo de bosque; (orn.) bonasa americana; (orn.) lagópedo de Escocia; (slang) refunfuño; *vn* (slang) refunfuñar
grout [graʊt] *s* lechada; *va* enlechar
grove [grov] *s* arboleda, bosquecillo
grovel ['grʌvəl] o ['grɑvəl] (*pret & pp:* **-eled** o **-elled;** *ger:* **-eling** o **-elling**) *vn* arrastrarse (*a los pies de un poderoso*); envilecerse, deleitarse en vilezas
groveling o **grovelling** ['grʌvəlɪŋ] o ['grɑvəlɪŋ] *adj* servil, rastrero
grow [gro] (*pret:* **grew;** *pp:* **grown**) *va* cultivar; criar; producir; dejarse (*la barba, el bigote*); *vn* crecer; desarrollarse; cultivarse; criarse; producirse; brotar, nacer; irse aumentando; hacerse, ponerse, volverse; **to grow into** hacerse, llegar a ser; **to grow on** influir cada vez más en; interesar cada vez más; **to grow out of** tener su origen en; perder (*p.ej., la costumbre*); **to grow to** adherirse a, pegarse a; llegar a, llegar a ser; **to grow together** adherirse el uno al otro; **to grow up** hacerse un adolescente, salir de la niñez; este verbo, seguido de un adjetivo, se traduce a veces por un verbo neutro o reflexivo que corresponda al adjetivo, p.ej., **to grow old** envejecer; **to grow angry** enfadarse
grower ['groər] *s* agricultor, cultivador; criador; planta que crece de cierto modo, p.ej., **quick grower** planta que crece rápidamente
growing ['gro·ɪŋ] *adj* creciente; de creces, p.ej., **growing child** muchacho de creces; *s* crecimiento; cultivo; cría
growing pains *spl* dolores causados (*según comúnmente se cree*) por el desarrollo rápido del cuerpo; dificultades iniciales (*p.ej., de una nueva empresa*)
growl [graʊl] *s* gruñido (*del perro*); refunfuño; *va* manifestar (*p.ej., desaprobación*) refunfuñando; *vn* gruñir (*el perro*); refunfuñar
growler ['graʊlər] *s* gruñidor; perro gruñidor; (slang) jarro en el que se trae cerveza desde la cervecería
grown [gron] *adj* crecido; llegado a su mayor desarrollo; adulto; cubierto de hierbas, maleza, etc.; *pp de* **grow**
grown-up ['gron,ʌp] *adj* adulto; serio, juicioso; *s* (*pl:* **grown-ups**) adulto
growth [groθ] *s* crecimiento; desarrollo; aumento; cobertura (*p.ej., forestal, herbosa*); (path.) tumor
growth stock *s* (com.) acción crecedera
grub [grʌb] *s* esclavo del trabajo; (ent.) gorgojo; (slang) condumio (*alimento, comida*); (*pret & pp:* **grubbed;** *ger:* **grubbing**) *va* arrancar (*tocones*); desmalezar (*un terreno*); *vn* cavar;

hozar (*el puerco*); emplearse en menesteres humildes
grubby ['grʌbɪ] *adj* (*comp:* **-bier;** *super:* **-biest**) gorgojoso; sucio, roñoso
grubstake ['grʌb,stek] *s* (coll.) anticipo de dinero que se da al explorador para comprar pertrechos y provisiones, pensando cobrar después de hallado el filón de mineral que se busca; *va* (coll.) subvencionar (*a un explorador*)
Grub Street *s* (hist.) calle de Londres habitada por escritores famélicos; escritores necesitados
grudge [grʌdʒ] *s* inquina, rencor; **to bear** o **to have a grudge against** tener inquina a, guardar rencor a; *va* dar de mala gana; envidiar
grudgingly ['grʌdʒɪŋlɪ] *adv* de mala gana
gruel ['gruəl] *s* avenate; (*pret & pp:* **-eled** o **-elled;** *ger:* **-eling** o **-elling**) *va* desbaratar, agotar, incapacitar
grueling o **gruelling** ['gruəlɪŋ] *adj* muy molesto y agotador; *s* lance muy molesto y agotador
gruesome ['grusəm] *adj* horrible, horripilante
gruff [grʌf] *adj* áspero, rudo, brusco, poco amistoso; ronco
grum [grʌm] *adj* (*comp:* **grummer;** *super:* **grummest**) áspero, hosco, malhumorado
grumble ['grʌmbəl] *s* gruñido, refunfuño; ruido sordo; *va* manifestar gruñendo o refunfuñando; *vn* gruñir, refunfuñar; producir un ruido sordo
grume [grum] *s* grumo
grumpy ['grʌmpɪ] *adj* (*comp:* **-ier;** *super:* **-iest**) gruñón, rezongón, malhumorado
Grundy, Mrs. ['grʌndɪ] *s* el qué dirán; **what will Mrs. Grundy say?** ¿qué dirá la gente?
grunt [grʌnt] *s* gruñido (*del cerdo; de una persona*); (ichth.) ronco; *va* decir entre gruñidos; *vn* gruñir
gruyère [grɪ'jɛr] *s* gruyère
gryphon ['grɪfən] o ['graɪfən] *s* var. de **griffin**
G string *s* cubresexo
gt. abr. de **great** y **gutta** (Lat.) **drop**
Gt. Br. o **Gt. Brit.** abr. de **Great Britain**
g.t.c. abr. de **good till canceled** y **good till countermanded**
g.u. abr. de **genitourinary**
Guadeloupe [,gwadə'lup] *s* Guadalupe
guaiacol ['gwaɪəkol] o ['gwaɪəkal] *s* (chem.) guayacol
guaiacum ['gwaɪəkəm] *s* (bot.) guayacán
guanaco [gwa'nako] *s* (*pl:* **-cos**) (zool.) guanaco
guanidine ['gwænɪdin] o ['gwanɪdin] *s* (chem.) guanidina
guanine ['gwanin] o ['guənin] *s* (chem.) guanina
guano ['gwano] *s* (*pl:* **-nos**) guano
Guarani [,gwara'ni] *adj* guaraní; *s* (*pl:* **-nis**) guaraní
guarantee [,gærən'ti] *s* garantía; garante; persona asegurada por una garantía; *va* garantizar
guaranteed annual wage *s* salario anual garantizado
guarantor ['gærəntər] *s* garante
guaranty ['gærəntɪ] *s* (*pl:* **-ties**) garantía; (*pret & pp:* **-tied**) *va* garantizar
guard [gard] *s* guarda (*acción de guardar; guarnición de la espada; persona que guarda una cosa*); guardia (*cuerpo de hombres armados; individuo de tal cuerpo; manera de defenderse en la esgrima*); salvavidas (*delante de los tranvías*); (sport) coraza; (football) guarda, defensor; **off guard** desprevenido; **on guard** prevenido, en guardia; de centinela; (fencing) en guardia; **to mount guard** montar la guardia; **under guard** a buen recado; *va* guardar; *vn* estar de centinela, hacer centinela; **to guard against** guardarse de, precaverse de; **to guard against** + *ger* guardarse de + *inf*
guarded ['gardɪd] *adj* guardado, protegido; cauteloso, circunspecto
guardhouse ['gard,haus] *s* cuartel de la guardia; cárcel militar
guardian ['gardɪən] *s* guardián; (law) tutor, curador; (eccl.) guardián; *adj* tutelar
guardian angel *s* ángel custodio, ángel de la guarda
guardianship ['gardɪən,ʃɪp] *s* protección; (law) tutela, curaduría; (eccl.) guardianía (*en la orden franciscana*)
guardrail ['gard,rel] *s* baranda; (rail.) contracarril; (naut.) barandilla
guardroom ['gard,rum] o ['gard,rʊm] *s* cuarto de guardia; calabozo militar
guard ship *s* (naut.) navío de guardia
guardsman ['gardzmən] *s* (*pl:* **-men**) guarda; guardia, soldado de guardia; centinela
guard wire *s* (elec.) alambre de guardia
Guatemala [,gwatɪ'malə] *s* Guatemala
Guatemalan [,gwatɪ'malən] *adj & s* guatemalteco
guava ['gwavə] *s* (bot.) guayabo (*árbol*); guayaba (*fruto*); (bot.) ingá, guamo
guayule [gwa'julɛ] *s* (bot.) guayule (*arbusto y caucho*)
gubernatorial [,gjubərnə'torɪəl] *adj* de gobernador, del gobernador
gudgeon ['gʌdʒən] *s* (ichth.) gobio; (mach.) gorrón; (naut.) muñonera, hembra de gorrón; bobo, mentecato; chiripa, ganga; *va* estafar
gudgeon pin *s* (aut.) perno de émbolo
guelder-rose ['gɛldər,roz] *s* (bot.) rosa de güeldres, mundillo, sauquillo
Guelf o **Guelph** [gwɛlf] *s* güelfo
Guelfic o **Guelphic** ['gwɛlfɪk] *adj* güelfo
guerdon ['gʌrdən] *s* (poet.) galardón
guerilla [gə'rɪlə] *s & adj* var. de **guerrilla**
guernsey ['gʌrnzɪ] *s* camiseta de punto (*de los marineros*)
guerrilla [gə'rɪlə] *s* guerrillero; *adj* de guerrilla, de guerrillero
guerrilla warfare *s* guerra de guerrillas
guess [gɛs] *s* conjetura, suposición; *va & vn* conjeturar, suponer; acertar, adivinar; (coll.) creer, suponer; **I guess so** (coll.) creo que sí, me parece que sí
guessable ['gɛsəbəl] *adj* adivinable
guessing game *s* juego de adivinanzas; partido de adivinanzas
guesswork ['gɛs,wʌrk] *s* conjetura; **by guesswork** por conjeturas
guest [gɛst] *s* huésped; convidado; visita; pensionista, inquilino; cliente (*de un hotel*)
guest conductor *s* (mus.) conductor visitante, conductor huésped
guest of honor *s* invitado de honor, huésped de honor
guest room *s* alcoba de respeto, cuarto del huésped
guest rope *s* (naut.) falsa amarra
guffaw [gʌ'fɔ] *s* risotada; *vn* risotear
Guiana [gɪ'anə] o [gɪ'ænə] *s* Guayana
Guianan [gɪ'anən] o [gɪ'ænən] *adj & s* var. de **Guianese**
Guianese [,gia'niz] o [,giæ'niz] *adj* guayanés; *s* (*pl:* **-nese**) guayanés
guidance ['gaɪdəns] *s* guía, gobierno, dirección; **for your guidance** para su gobierno
guide [gaɪd] *s* guía (*persona; libro o tratado*); dirección, indicación; (mil.) guía; poste indicador; (mach.) guía, guiadera; *va* guiar
guideboard ['gaɪd,bord] *s* señal de carretera
guidebook ['gaɪd,bʊk] *s* guía, guía del viajero
guided missile *s* (mil.) proyectil dirigido, proyectil teleguiado
guideline ['gaɪd,laɪn] *s* cuerda de guía; línea trazada de un cambio tipográfico a un signo en el margen; pauta, norma (*p.ej., de conducta*)
guidepost ['gaɪd,post] *s* poste indicador
guide rope *s* arrastradera (*de globo aerostático*); cuerda de guía
guidon ['gaɪdən] *s* (mil.) guión; (mil.) portaguión
guild [gɪld] *s* gremio; asociación de carácter benéfico
guildhall ['gɪld,hɔl] *s* casa de un gremio; casa consistorial, casa de ayuntamiento
guildsman ['gɪldzmən] *s* (*pl:* **-men**) gremial
guile [gaɪl] *s* dolo, astucia, maña
guileful ['gaɪlfəl] *adj* doloso, astuto, mañoso
guileless ['gaɪllɪs] *adj* cándido, sencillo, sincero

guillemot ['gɪlɪmɑt] *s* (orn.) uría
guilloche [gɪ'loʃ] *s* (f.a.) güilogis
guillotine ['gɪlətin] *s* guillotina; (surg. & law) guillotina; [ˌgɪlə'tin] *va* guillotinar
guillotine shears *spl* cizalla de guillotina
guilt [gɪlt] *s* culpa
guiltiness ['gɪltɪnɪs] *s* culpabilidad
guiltless ['gɪltlɪs] *adj* libre de culpa, inocente
guilty ['gɪltɪ] *adj* (*comp:* **-ier;** *super:* **-iest**) culpable; culpado
guimpe [gɪmp] o [gæmp] *s* canesú
guinea ['gɪnɪ] *s* guinea (*moneda*); gallina de Guinea; (*cap.*) *s* Guinea; *adj* guineo
Guinea corn *s* (bot.) maíz de Guinea
guinea fowl *s* pintada, gallina de Guinea
guinea grass *s* (bot.) gramalote, hierba de Guinea
guinea hen *s* var. de **guinea fowl**
guinea pig *s* (zool. & fig.) conejillo de Indias
Guinever ['gwɪnəvər] o **Guinevere** ['gwɪnəvɪr] *s* (myth.) Ginebra
guipure [gɪ'pjʊr] *s* guipur; guarnición de cuerdas entretejidas, con refuerzo de alambre
guise [gaɪz] *s* traje; semejanza, aspecto; capa, pretexto; **in the guise of** disfrazado de; **under the guise of** so capa de
guitar [gɪ'tɑr] *s* (mus.) guitarra
guitarist [gɪ'tɑrɪst] *s* guitarrista
gulch [gʌltʃ] *s* barranco, quebrada
gules [gjulz] *s* (her.) gules; *adj* (her.) de gules
gulf [gʌlf] *s* golfo; vorágine, torbellino
Gulf of Aden *s* golfo de Adén
Gulf of Bothnia ['bɑθnɪə] *s* golfo de Botnia
Gulf of Corinth *s* golfo de Corinto
Gulf of Mexico *s* golfo de Méjico
Gulf of Oman [o'mɑn] *s* mar de Omán
Gulf of Panama *s* golfo de Panamá
Gulf of St. Lawrence *s* golfo de San Lorenzo
Gulf of Venice *s* golfo de Venecia
Gulf States *spl* estados de EE.UU. que confinan con el golfo de Méjico
Gulf Stream *s* Corriente del Golfo
gulfweed ['gʌlfˌwid] *s* (bot.) sargazo
gull [gʌl] *s* (orn.) gaviota; bobo; *va* engañar, estafar
gullet ['gʌlɪt] *s* garguero, gaznate; esófago
gullibility [ˌgʌlɪ'bɪlɪtɪ] *s* credulidad
gullible ['gʌlɪbəl] *adj* crédulo; **to be too gullible** tener buenas tragaderas
gully ['gʌlɪ] *s* (*pl:* **-lies**) arroyada, hondonada; badén (*zanja que forman las aguas llovedizas*)
gulp [gʌlp] *s* gorgorotada, trago; *va* engullir; **to gulp down** engullir; reprimir (*p.ej., sollozos*); *vn* estrangularse momentáneamente; no poder hablar (*por pena, susto o vergüenza*)
gum [gʌm] *s* goma; (bot.) gomero, árbol gomífero; (anat.) encía; chanclo de goma; (*pret & pp:* **gummed;** *ger:* **gumming**) *va* engomar; volver pegajoso; atascar, entorpecer; *vn* manar goma; volverse pegajoso
gum ammoniac *s* goma amoníaco
gum arabic *s* goma arábiga
gumbo ['gʌmbo] *s* (*pl:* **-bos**) (bot.) quingombó; sopa de quingombó; lodo muy pegajoso; dialecto criollo de la Luisiana
gumboil ['gʌmˌbɔɪl] *s* (path.) párulis, flemón
gum boot *s* bota de goma, bota de agua
gumdrop ['gʌmˌdrɑp] *s* pastilla de goma
gum elastic *s* goma elástica
gum guttae ['gʌti] *s* var. de **gamboge**
gumma ['gʌmə] *s* (*pl:* **-mata** [mətə]) (path.) goma
gummiferous [gʌm'ɪfərəs] *adj* gomífero
gummosis [gʌ'mosɪs] *s* (plant path.) gomosis
gummy ['gʌmɪ] *adj* (*comp:* **-mier;** *super:* **-miest**) gomoso
gumption ['gʌmpʃən] *s* (coll.) energía, iniciativa; (coll.) juicio, seso
gum resin *s* gomorresina
gumshoe ['gʌmˌʃu] *s* chanclo de goma; (slang) detective; **gumshoes** *spl* zapatos silenciosos (*con suela de goma y lo demás de lona*); (*pret & pp:* **-shoed;** *ger:* **-shoeing**) *vn* (slang) andar con zapatos de fieltro, andar espiando
gum succory *s* (bot.) condrila
gum tree *s* (bot.) gomero, árbol gomífero
gum water *s* aguagoma
gumwood ['gʌmˌwʊd] *s* madera de árbol gomífero
gun [gʌn] *s* escopeta, fusil; cañón; jeringa (*para inyectar materias blandas*); cañón (*de cemento*); cañonazo (*cada uno de los que componen una salva*); (coll.) revólver, pistola; **to spike one's guns** clavarle a uno los cañones, reducirle a uno a la impotencia; **to stick to one's guns** mantenerse en sus trece, mantenerse con la suya; (*pret & pp:* **gunned;** *ger:* **gunning**) *va* hacer fuego sobre, hacer un disparo sobre; (slang) acelerar rápidamente (*un avión, un motor*); *vn* andar a caza; hacer fuego, disparar; **to gun for** ir en busca de, tratar de conseguir; buscar para matar
gun o **'gun** [gʌn] *pp de* **gin** [gɪn]
gun barrel *s* cañón de fusil
gunboat ['gʌnˌbot] *s* cañonero, lancha cañonera
gun carriage *s* cureña
guncotton ['gʌnˌkɑtən] *s* pólvora de algodón, algodón pólvora, fulmicotón
gunfire ['gʌnˌfaɪr] *s* fuego (*de armas de fuego*); cañoneo, tiroteo; uso de armas de fuego
gunlock ['gʌnˌlɑk] *s* llave de fusil
gunman ['gʌnmən] *s* (*pl:* **-men**) pistolero, bandido armado
gun metal *s* bronce de cañón; bronce empavonado, metal pavonado
gun-metal ['gʌnˌmɛtəl] *adj* empavonado, pavonado
gunnel ['gʌnəl] *s* (ichth.) blenia; (naut.) borda, regala
gunner ['gʌnər] *s* artillero; cazador; (nav.) condestable
gunnery ['gʌnərɪ] *s* artillería
gunning ['gʌnɪŋ] *s* tiro; caza
gunny ['gʌnɪ] *s* (*pl:* **-nies**) yute; saco de yute
gunny sack *s* saco de yute
gunpowder ['gʌnˌpaʊdər] *s* pólvora
gunrunner ['gʌnˌrʌnər] *s* contrabandista de armas de fuego
gunrunning ['gʌnˌrʌnɪŋ] *s* contrabando de armas de fuego
gunshot ['gʌnˌʃɑt] *s* balazo, escopetazo, tiro de fusil; alcance de un fusil; **within gunshot** a tiro de fusil
gunshot wound *s* balazo, escopetazo
gunsmith ['gʌnˌsmɪθ] *s* armero
gunstock ['gʌnˌstɑk] *s* caja de fusil
Gunter's chain ['gʌntərz] *s* cadena de agrimensor o de Gúnter
gunwale ['gʌnəl] *s* (naut.) borda, regala
guppy ['gʌpɪ] *s* (*pl:* **-pies**) (ichth.) lebistes
gurgle ['gʌrgəl] *s* gluglú (*del agua*); gorjeo (*del niño*); *va* expresar con gorjeos, decir entre gorjeos; *vn* hacer gluglú (*el agua*); gorjearse (*el niño*)
gurnard ['gʌrnərd] o **gurnet** ['gʌrnɪt] *s* (ichth.) trilla; (ichth.) rubio volador
gush [gʌʃ] *s* borbollón, chorro; (coll.) efusión, extremos (*de cariño o entusiasmo*); *va* derramar (*p.ej., sangre*) a borbollones; *vn* surgir, salir a borbollones; (coll.) hacer extremos
gusher ['gʌʃər] *s* pozo surgente; (coll.) persona extremosa
gushing ['gʌʃɪŋ] *adj* surgente; extremoso; *s* borbollón, chorro; (coll.) efusión, extremos
gushy ['gʌʃɪ] *adj* (*comp:* **-ier;** *super:* **-iest**) efusivo, extremoso
gusset ['gʌsɪt] *s* (sew.) escudete; (constr.) esquinal, escuadra; (naut.) curvatón
gusset plate *s* cartabón
gust [gʌst] *s* ráfaga (*de viento*); bocanada (*de humo*); aguacero; explosión (*de ruido*); arrebato (*de cólera, entusiasmo, etc.*)
gustative ['gʌstətɪv] *adj* gustativo
gustatory ['gʌstəˌtorɪ] *adj* gustatorio
Gustavus [gʌs'tevəs] *s* Gustavo
Gustavus Adolphus [ə'dɑlfəs] *s* Gustavo Adolfo
gusto ['gʌsto] *s* (*pl:* **-tos**) gusto; sumo placer, deleite, entusiasmo, satisfacción evidente; **with gusto** con sumo placer
gusty ['gʌstɪ] *adj* (*comp:* **-ier;** *super:* **-iest**) tempestuoso, impetuoso, explosivo
gut [gʌt] *s* tripa; cuerda de tripa; estrecho, desfiladero; **guts** *spl* tripas; (slang) agallas; (*pret & pp:* **gutted;** *ger:* **gutting**) *va* destripar; pillar lo interior de; destruir lo interior de
gutta-percha ['gʌtə'pʌrtʃə] *s* gutapercha

gutter ['gʌtər] *s* cuneta (*al lado del camino*); arroyo (*en la calle*); canal (*en los tejados*); badén (*zanja que forman las aguas llovedizas*); acanaladura, estría; barrio bajo; *va* acanalar, estriar; *vn* acanalarse; correr, manar; gotear (*las velas*); **to gutter out** apagarse
guttersnipe ['gʌtər,snaɪp] *s* (coll.) pilluelo, hijo de la miseria
guttiferous [gʌ'tɪfərəs] *adj* (bot.) gutífero
guttural ['gʌtərəl] *adj* gutural; (phonet.) gutural; *s* (phonet.) sonido gutural
guy [gaɪ] *s* viento, cable de retén; (coll.) tipo, sujeto, tío; (coll.) adefesio, mamarracho; (*cap.*) *s* Guido; (*l.c.*) *va* sujetar con vientos; (coll.) dar vaya a, burlarse de
guy wire *s* viento de alambre
guzzle ['gʌzəl] *va* beber con avidez y de modo grosero; *vn* ser muy bebedor
guzzler ['gʌzlər] *s* pellejo, borrachín
gym [dʒɪm] *s* (coll.) gimnasio
gymnasium [dʒɪm'nezɪəm] *s* (*pl:* **-ums** o **-a** [ə]) gimnasio
gymnast ['dʒɪmnæst] *s* gimnasta
gymnastic [dʒɪm'næstɪk] *adj* gimnástico; **gymnastics** *spl* gimnástica o gimnasia
gymnosperm ['dʒɪmnəspʌrm] *s* (bot.) gimnosperma
gymnospermous [,dʒɪmnə'spʌrməs] *adj* gimnospermo
gynaeceum [,dʒɪnɪ'siəm] o [,dʒaɪnɪ'siəm] *s* (*pl:* **-a** [ə]) (hist.) gineceo (*departamento de las mujeres*); (bot.) gineceo
gynaecology [,gaɪnə'kɑlədʒɪ], [,dʒaɪnə'kɑlədʒɪ] o [,dʒɪnə'kɑlədʒɪ] *s* var. de **gynecology**
gynandrous [dʒaɪ'nændrəs] o [dʒɪ'nændrəs] *adj* (bot.) ginandro
gynecological [,gaɪnəkə'lɑdʒɪkəl], [,dʒaɪnəkə'lɑdʒɪkəl] o [,dʒɪnəkə'lɑdʒɪkəl] *adj* ginecológico
gynecologist [,gaɪnə'kɑlədʒɪst], [,dʒaɪnə'kɑlədʒɪst] o [,dʒɪnə'kɑlədʒɪst] *s* ginecólogo
gynecology [,gaɪnə'kɑlədʒɪ], [,dʒaɪnə'kɑlədʒɪ] o [,dʒɪnə'kɑlədʒɪ] *s* ginecología
gyniatrics [,dʒaɪnɪ'ætrɪks] o [,dʒɪnɪ'ætrɪks] *ssg* giniatría
gynoecium [dʒaɪ'nisɪəm] o [dʒɪ'nisɪəm] *s* (*pl:* **-a** [ə]) (bot.) gineceo
gynophore ['dʒaɪnəfor] o ['dʒɪnəfor] *s* (bot.) ginóforo
gyp [dʒɪp] *s* (slang) estafa, timo; (slang) estafador, timador; (*pret & pp:* **gypped;** *ger:* **gypping**) *va* (slang) estafar, timar
gypsophila [dʒɪp'sɑfɪlə] *s* (bot.) gipsófila
gypsum ['dʒɪpsəm] *s* yeso
gypsy ['dʒɪpsɪ] *adj* gitano; *s* (*pl:* **-sies**) gitano; (*cap.*) *s* gitano (*idioma*)
gypsyish ['dʒɪpsɪɪʃ] *adj* gitanesco
gypsyism ['dʒɪpsɪɪzəm] *s* gitanismo
gypsy moth *s* (ent.) lagarta
gyrate ['dʒaɪret] o [dʒaɪ'ret] *vn* girar
gyration [dʒaɪ'reʃən] *s* giro, vuelta
gyratory ['dʒaɪrə,torɪ] *adj* giratorio
gyrfalcon ['dʒʌr,fɔkən] o ['dʒʌr,fɔlkən] *s* var. de **gerfalcon**
gyro ['dʒaɪro] *s* (*pl:* **-ros**) autogiro; girocompás; giroscopio
gyrocompass ['dʒaɪro,kʌmpəs] *s* girocompás
gyrofin ['dʒaɪrəfɪn] *s* (naut.) giroaleta
gyrometer [dʒaɪ'rɑmɪtər] *s* girómetro
gyron ['dʒaɪrən] *s* (her.) jirón
gyropilot ['dʒaɪro,paɪlət] *s* (aer.) giropiloto
gyroplane ['dʒaɪro,plen] *s* (aer.) giroplano, giravión
gyroscope ['dʒaɪrəskop] *s* giroscopio
gyroscopic [,dʒaɪrə'skɑpɪk] *adj* giroscópico
gyrostabilizer [,dʒaɪro'stebɪ,laɪzər] *s* (aer. & naut.) giroestabilizador
gyrostat ['dʒaɪrəstæt] *s* giróstato
gyrostatic [,dʒaɪrə'stætɪk] *adj* girostático; **gyrostatics** *ssg* girostática
gyve [dʒaɪv] *s* grillo; *va* encadenar con grillos

H, h [etʃ] *s* (*pl:* **H's, h's** ['etʃɪz]) octava letra del alfabeto inglés
h. abr. de **harbor, hard, height, high, hour** y **husband**
H. abr. de **harbor, hard, high** y **hour**
ha [hɑ] *interj* ¡ha!; ¡ja!
Hab. abr. de **Habakkuk**
Habakkuk [hə'bækək] o ['hæbəkʌk] *s* (Bib.) Habacuc
habeas corpus ['hebɪəs 'kɔrpəs] *s* (law) hábeas corpus
haberdasher ['hæbər,dæʃər] *s* camisero; mercero
haberdashery ['hæbər,dæʃərɪ] *s* (*pl:* **-ies**) camisería; mercería
habergeon ['hæbərdʒən] *s* cota de malla sin mangas; camisote
habiliment [hə'bɪlɪmənt] *s* ropa, vestido; **habiliments** *spl* prendas de vestir
habit ['hæbɪt] *s* hábito (*costumbre; inclinación adquirida por la repetición; vestido*); manera de crecer; amazona (*traje de mujer que sirve para montar a caballo*); **to be in the habit of** + *ger* acostumbrar + *inf; va* vestir
habitable ['hæbɪtəbəl] *adj* habitable
habitant ['hæbɪtənt] *s* habitante
habitat ['hæbɪtæt] *s* habitación (*morada, residencia*); ámbito natural; (biol.) habitación o habitat
habitation [,hæbɪ'teʃən] *s* habitación
habit-forming ['hæbɪt,fɔrmɪŋ] *adj* enviciador
habitual [hə'bɪtʃuəl] *adj* habitual
habituate [hə'bɪtʃuet] *va* habituar
habituation [hə,bɪtʃu'eʃən] *s* habituación
habitué [hə,bɪtʃu'e] o [hə,bɪtju'e] *s* habituado (*parroquiano; aficionado*)
hachure [hə'ʃur] o ['hæʃur] *s* plumeado; [hə'ʃur] *va* plumear
hack [hæk] *s* corte, cuchillada, hachazo, mella, machetazo; herramienta de cuchilla; tos seca; coche de punto, coche de alquiler; caballo de alquiler; rocín; caballo de silla; escritor mercenario; *adj* alquiladizo; trillado, gastado; mercenario; *va* cortar, acuchillar, picar, mellar; **to hack apart** partir a hachazos; *vn* dar cuchilladas; toser con tos seca; ir a caballo
hackamore ['hækəmor] *s* cabezada, jáquima
hackberry ['hæk,berɪ] *s* (*pl:* **-ries**) (bot.) almez, ramón; almeza (*fruto*)
hackle ['hækəl] *s* rastrillo; pluma del pescuezo (*de ciertas aves*); mosca artificial para pescar; **hackles** *spl* cerdas eréctiles del pescuezo y lomo del perro; *va* rastrillar; cortar toscamente, machetear, estropear a cuchilladas o a hachazos
hackman ['hækmən] *s* (*pl:* **-men**) cochero de punto
hackmatack ['hækmə,tæk] *s* (bot.) alerce americano (*Larix laricina*)
hackney ['hæknɪ] *s* caballo de silla; coche de alquiler; *adj* alquilado, de alquiler; *va* gastar, usar con exceso
hackneyed ['hæknɪd] *adj* gastado, muy usado, trillado
hacksaw ['hæk,sɔ] *s* sierra de armero, sierra de cortar metales
had [hæd] *pret & pp de* **have**
haddock ['hædək] *s* ((ichth.) eglefino (*pez parecido a la merluza*)
Hades ['hediz] *s* (myth. & Bib.) Hades; (*l.c.*) *s* (coll.) infierno
hadn't ['hædənt] contracción de **had not**
Hadrian ['hedrɪən] *s* Adriano
haematic [hi'mætɪk] *adj* var. de **hematic**
haematin ['hemətɪn] o ['himətɪn] *s* var. de **hematin**
haematite ['hemətaɪt] o ['himətaɪt] *s* var. de **hematite**
haematocele ['hemәto,sil] o ['himәto,sil] *s* var. de **hematocele**
haematoma [,himə'tomə] o [,hemə'tomə] *s* var. de **hematoma**
haematopoiesis [,hemətopɔɪ'isɪs] o [,himətopɔɪ'isɪs] *s* var. de **hematopoiesis**
haematosis [,himə'tosɪs] o [,hemə'tosɪs] *s* var. de **hematosis**
haematoxylin [,himə'tɑksɪlɪn] o [,hemə'tɑksɪlɪn] *s* var de **hematoxylin**
haemin ['himɪn] *s* var. de **hemin**
haemocyanin [,himo'saɪənɪn] o [,hemo'saɪənɪn] *s* var. de **hemocyanin**
haemoglobin [,himo'globɪn] o [,hemo'globɪn] *s* var. de **hemoglobin**
haemoleucocyte [,himə'lukəsaɪt] o [,hemə'lukəsaɪt] *s* var. de **hemoleucocyte**
haemolysin [,himə'laɪsɪn], [,hemə'laɪsɪn] o [hɪ'mɑlɪsɪn] *s* var. de **hemolysin**
haemolysis [hɪ'mɑlɪsɪs] *s* var. de **hemolysis**
haemophilia [,himə'fɪlɪə] o [,hemə'fɪlɪə] *s* var. de **hemophilia**
haemophiliac [,himə'fɪlɪæk] o [,hemə'fɪlɪæk] *s* var. de **hemophiliac**
haemophilic [,himə'fɪlɪk] o [,hemə'fɪlɪk] *adj* var. de **hemophilic**
haemorrhage ['hemərɪdʒ] *s* var. de **hemorrhage**
haemorrhoids ['hemərɔɪdz] *spl* var. de **hemorrhoids**
haemostat ['himəstæt] o ['heməstæt] *s* var. de **hemostat**
haemostatic [,himə'stætɪk] o [,hemə'stætɪk] *adj & s* var. de **hemostatic**
hafnium ['hæfnɪəm] *s* (chem.) hafnio
haft [hæft] o [hɑft] *s* mango, puño; *va* poner mango o puño a
Hag. abr. de **Haggai**
hag [hæg] *s* tarasca (*mujer fea y desenvuelta*); bruja
hagfish ['hæg,fɪʃ] *s* (ichth.) lamprea glutinosa
Haggai ['hægeaɪ] *s* (Bib.) Ageo
haggard ['hægərd] *adj* macilento, ojeroso, agobiado de inquietud; zahareño (*halcón*)
haggis ['hægɪs] *s* manjar escocés hecho con el estómago de carnero relleno del menudo de este animal mezclado con harina de avena
haggle ['hægəl] *s* regateo; *va* tajar toscamente, machetear; *vn* regatear; altercar, cavilar
hagiographer [,hægɪ'ɑgrəfər] o [,hedʒɪ'ɑgrəfər] *s* hagiógrafo
hagiographic [,hægɪə'græfɪk] o [,hedʒɪə'græfɪk] o **hagiographical** [,hægɪə'græfɪkəl] o [,hedʒɪə'græfɪkəl] *adj* hagiográfico
hagiography [,hægɪ'ɑgrəfɪ] o [,hedʒɪ'ɑgrəfɪ] *s* (*pl:* **-phies**) hagiografía
hagiology [,hægɪ'ɑlədʒɪ] o [,hedʒɪ'ɑlədʒɪ] *s* (*pl:* **-gies**) hagiología; santoral (*lista de los santos*)
hagridden ['hæg,rɪdən] *adj* atormentado, vejado
Hague, The [heg] La Haya
Hague Court *s* Tribunal internacional de La Haya
hah [hɑ] *interj* var. de **ha**
hail [hel] *s* saludo; viva, aplauso; llamada; granizo; **within hail** al alcance del oído; (naut.) al habla; *interj* ¡salud!, ¡salve!; **hail to . . . !** ¡viva . . . !; *va* saludar; dar vivas a, acoger con vivas; aclamar; llamar; granizar (*p.ej., golpes*); (naut.) ponerse al habla con; *vn* granizar; **to hail from** venir de, ser oriundo de
hail fellow well met *adj* muy afable y simpático; *s* hombre muy afable y simpático
Hail Mary *s* avemaría
hailstone ['hel,ston] *s* piedra de granizo
hailstorm ['hel,stɔrm] *s* granizada; (fig.) granizada

hair [hɛr] *s* pelo; cabello; vello (*pelo corto y suave*); cerda (*pelo grueso y duro*); filamento; **to a hair** con la mayor exactitud; **to make one's hair stand on end** ponerle a uno los pelos de punta; **to not turn a hair** no inmutarse, quedarse tan fresco; **to split hairs** andar en quisquillas, pararse en pelillos; *adj* de pelo; para el cabello
hairbreadth [ˈhɛr,brɛdθ] *s* ancho de un pelo, casi nada; **to escape by a hairbreadth** librarse por un pelo, librarse milagrosamente
hairbrush [ˈhɛr,brʌʃ] *s* cepillo de cabeza
haircloth [ˈhɛr,klɔθ] o [ˈhɛr,klɑθ] *s* cilicio, tela de crin
hair curler *s* rizador, tenacillas, tenazas de rizar
haircut [ˈhɛr,kʌt] *s* corte de cabello, corte de pelo; **to get a haircut** cortarse el cabello o el pelo
hairdo [ˈhɛr,du] *s* (*pl:* **-dos**) peinado, tocado
hairdresser [ˈhɛr,drɛsər] *s* peinador, peluquero
hair dye *s* tinte para el pelo
hairless [ˈhɛrlɪs] *adj* pelón, calvo, sin pelo
hairline [ˈhɛr,laɪn] *s* rayita; estría filiforme
hair net *s* redecilla
hairpin [ˈhɛr,pɪn] *s* horquilla
hairpin bend *s* curva de retorno, viraje cerrado, curva de horquilla
hair-raising [ˈhɛr,rezɪŋ] *adj* (coll.) espeluznante, horripilante
hair restorer *s* crecepelo
hair ribbon *s* cinta para el cabello
hair's-breadth o **hairsbreadth** [ˈhɛrz,brɛdθ] *s* var. de **hairbreadth**
hair set *s* fijapeinados
hair shirt *s* cilicio
hair space *s* (print.) espacio de pelo
hairsplitter [ˈhɛr,splɪtər] *s* sutilizador, persona quisquillosa
hairsplitting [ˈhɛr,splɪtɪŋ] *adj* quisquilloso; *s* quisquillas
hairspring [ˈhɛr,sprɪŋ] *s* (horol.) espiral, pelo
hair tonic *s* vigorizador del cabello, tónico para el cabello
hair trigger *s* pelo (*de un arma de fuego*)
hairy [ˈhɛrɪ] *adj* (*comp:* **-ier;** *super:* **-iest**) peloso, peludo, cabelludo; velloso, hirsuto
Haiti [ˈhetɪ] *s* Haití
Haitian [ˈhetɪən] o [ˈheʃən] *adj & s* haitiano
hake [hek] *s* (ichth.) merluza; (ichth.) fice
halazone [ˈhæləzon] *s* (pharm.) halazona
halberd [ˈhælbərd] *s* alabarda
halberdier [,hælbərˈdɪr] *s* alabardero
halbert [ˈhælbərt] *s* var. de **halberd**
halcyon [ˈhælsɪən] *s* (myth. & orn.) alción; *adj* apacible, tranquilo
halcyon days *spl* (meteor. & myth.) alciόneos; (fig.) días tranquilos, época de paz
hale [hel] *adj* sano, fuerte, robusto; **hale and hearty** sano y fuerte; *va* arrastrar, llevar a la fuerza
half [hæf] o [hɑf] *adj* medio; a medias, p.ej., **half owner** dueño a medias; **a half** medio, p.ej., **a half pound** media libra; **half a** medio, p.ej., **half an apple** media manzana; **half the** la mitad de, p.ej., **half the money** la mitad del dinero; *adv* medio, p.ej., **half asleep** medio dormido; a medio, p.ej., **half finished** a medio acabar; a medias, p.ej., **only half done** hecho solamente a medias; **not half as good as** ni la mitad de bueno que; **not half as much money as** ni la mitad del dinero que; **not half bad** bastante bueno; **half after** o **half past** y media, p.ej., **half after two** o **half past two** las dos y media; **half . . . half** medio . . . medio; *s* (*pl:* **halves**) mitad; (arith.) medio; **by half** con mucho; **by halves** a medias; **in half** por la mitad; **to go halves (with)** ir a medias (con)
half-and-half [ˈhæfəndˈhæf] o [ˈhɑfəndˈhɑf] *adj* mitad y mitad; indeterminado; *adv* a medias, p.ej., **money acquired half-and-half by two persons** dinero adquirido a medias por dos personas; *s* mezcla de leche y crema; mezcla de dos cervezas inglesas
halfback [ˈhæf,bæk] o [ˈhɑf,bæk] *s* (football) medio
half-baked [ˈhæf,bekt] o [ˈhɑf,bekt] *adj* a medio cocer; incompleto, a medio formular; inexperto, poco juicioso
half binding *s* (b.b.) media pasta, encuadernación a la holandesa
half blood *s* parentesco entre hermanos de padre o de madre
half-blood [ˈhæf,blʌd] o [ˈhɑf,blʌd] *s* mestizo; medio hermano o media hermana
half-blooded [ˈhæf,blʌdɪd] o [ˈhɑf,blʌdɪd] *adj* que tiene solamente el mismo padre o la misma madre; mestizo
half boot *s* bota de media caña
half-bound [ˈhæf,baʊnd] o [ˈhɑf,baʊnd] *adj* (b.b.) a la holandesa
half-breed [ˈhæf,brid] o [ˈhɑf,brid] *s* mestizo
half brother *s* medio hermano
half-caste [ˈhæf,kæst] o [ˈhɑf,kɑst] *s* mestizo; mestizo de sangre europea y asiática
half cock *s* posición de medio amartillado; **to go off at half cock** (coll.) hablar u obrar precipitadamente
half-cocked [ˈhæfˈkɑkt] o [ˈhɑfˈkɑkt] *adj* medio amartillado; *adv* (coll.) precipitadamente, sin preparación
half crown *s* (Brit.) moneda de plata de dos chelines y medio
half dollar *s* medio dólar
half door *s* compuerta, media puerta
half dozen *s* media docena
half eagle *s* (U.S.A.) moneda de oro de cinco dólares
half fare *s* medio billete
half-full [ˈhæfˈfʊl] o [ˈhɑfˈfʊl] *adj* mediado
half-hearted [ˈhæf,hɑrtɪd] o [ˈhɑf,hɑrtɪd] *adj* frío, indiferente, sin ánimo; débil
half hitch *s* media llave
half holiday *s* mañana o tarde de asueto
half hose *spl* calcetines
half-hour [ˈhæfˈaʊr] o [ˈhɑfˈaʊr] *s* media hora; **on the half-hour** a la media en punto, cada media hora; *adj* de media hora
half leather *s* var. de **half binding**
half-length [ˈhæfˈlɛŋθ] o [ˈhɑfˈlɛŋθ] *adj* de medio cuerpo
half life *s* (phys.) vida media, período medio (*de una substancia radiactiva*)
half light *s* media luz
half-mast [ˈhæfˈmæst] o [ˈhɑfˈmɑst] *s* media asta; **at half-mast** a media asta
half moon *s* media luna
half mourning *s* medio luto
half nelson [ˈnɛlsən] *s* (sport) presa empleada en la lucha a brazo partido, que consiste en pasar el brazo por debajo del sobaco del contrario, elevando después la mano para agarrarle por el cogote
half note *s* (mus.) nota blanca
half pay *s* media paga; medio sueldo
halfpence [ˈhepəns] *spl* medios peniques
halfpenny [ˈhepənɪ] o [ˈhepnɪ] *s* (*pl:* **-pence** o **-pennies**) medio penique; *adj* de medio penique; insignificante, de muy poco valor
half pint *s* media pinta (*medida*); (slang) gorgojo, mirmidón
half round *s* medio bocel
half-round [ˈhæfˈraʊnd] o [ˈhɑfˈraʊnd] *adj* semicircular, de forma semicircular
half-round file *s* mediacaña, lima de mediacaña
half-seas over [ˈhæf,siz] o [ˈhɑf,siz] *adj* (slang) entre dos velas, medio borracho
half shell *s* concha (*cada una de las dos partes del caparazón de los moluscos bivalvos*); **on the half shell** en su concha (*dícese de las ostras*); en una concha (*dícese de otros alimentos servidos así*)
half-silk [ˈhæf,sɪlk] o [ˈhɑf,sɪlk] *adj* de media seda
half sister *s* media hermana
half sole *s* media suela
half-sole [ˈhæf,sol] o [ˈhɑf,sol] *va* poner media suela a
half sovereign *s* (Brit.) moneda de oro de diez chelines
half-staff [ˈhæfˈstæf] o [ˈhɑfˈstɑf] *s* media asta; **at half-staff** a media asta
half step *s* (mus.) semitono
half tide *s* (naut.) media marea
half-timbered [ˈhæf,tɪmbərd] o [ˈhɑf,tɪmbərd] *adj* entramado, de pared entramada
half title *s* (print.) portadilla, anteportada, falsa portada

half tone *s* (mus.) semitono
half-tone ['hæf,ton] o ['hɑf,ton] *s* fotograbado; (paint. & phot.) media tinta
half-tone screen *s* retícula, trama
half-track ['hæf,træk] o ['hɑf,træk] *s* semitractor, media oruga
half-truth ['hæf,truθ] o ['hɑf,truθ] *s* (*pl:* **-truths** [,truðz] o [,truθs]) reticencia, verdad a medias
half-wave ['hæf,wev] o ['hɑf,wev] *adj* (elec.) de media onda
halfway ['hæf,we] o ['hɑf,we] *adj* a medio camino, situado a mitad del camino; hecho a medias, incompleto, insuficiente; **halfway between** a medio camino entre, a mitad de la distancia entre, equidistante de; *adv* a medio camino; **to meet halfway** partir el camino con; partir la diferencia con; hacer concesiones a; hacer concesiones mutuas; **halfway through** a la mitad de
half-wit ['hæf,wɪt] o ['hɑf,wɪt] *s* imbécil; necio, tonto
half-witted ['hæf,wɪtɪd] o ['hɑf,wɪtɪd] *adj* imbécil; necio, tonto
half-yearly [,hæf'jɪrlɪ] o [,hɑf'jɪrlɪ] *adj* semestral; *adv* semestralmente
halibut ['hælɪbət] *s* (ichth.) halibut, hipogloso
Halicarnassus [,hælɪkɑr'næsəs] *s* Halicarnaso
halide ['hælaɪd] o ['helaɪd] *adj* haloideo; *s* (chem.) haluro
halidom ['hælɪdəm] o **halidome** ['hælɪdom] *s* (archaic) lugar santo, santuario; (archaic) reliquia
Haligonian [,hælɪ'gonɪən] *adj* perteneciente a Halifax; *s* natural o habitante de Halifax
halite ['hælaɪt] o ['helaɪt] *s* (mineral.) halita (*sal gema*)
halitosis [,hælɪ'tosɪs] *s* halitosis
halitus ['hælɪtəs] *s* hálito
hall [hɔl] *s* pasillo, corredor; vestíbulo, zaguán; sala o salón (*p.ej., de conferencias*); paraninfo (*de una universidad*); edificio (*de una universidad*); (Brit.) casa señorial
halleluiah o **hallelujah** [,hælɪ'lujə] *s* aleluya; *interj* ¡ aleluya!
halliard ['hæljərd] *s* var. de **halyard**
hallmark ['hɔl,mɑrk] *s* marca del contraste; (fig.) sello (*distintivo*)
hallo [hə'lo] *s* (*pl:* **-los**) grito, llamada, grito de sorpresa; *interj* ¡ hola!; *vn* gritar
halloa [hə'lo] *s, interj & vn* var. de **hallo**
Hall of Fame *s* galería de la Fama (*galería en Nueva York que encierra bustos y placas conmemorativas de personajes célebres en la historia y la vida norteamericanas*)
halloo [hə'lu] *s* (*pl:* **-loos**) grita; llamada; *interj* ¡ hola!; (hunt.) ¡ sus!, ¡ busca!; *vn* gritar
hallow [hə'lo] *s* grita; llamada; *interj* ¡ hola!; (hunt.) ¡ sus!, ¡ busca!; *vn* gritar; ['hælo] *va* santificar (*hacer santo; honrar como santo*)
hallowed ['hælod] *adj* sagrado, santo; ['hæləwɪd] *adj* santificado
Halloween o **Hallowe'en** [,hælo'in] *s* víspera de Todos los Santos
Hallowmas ['hæloməs] *s* (archaic) día de Todos los Santos
hallucinate [hə'lusɪnet] *va* alucinar
hallucination [hə,lusɪ'neʃən] *s* alucinación
hallway ['hɔl,we] *s* pasillo, corredor; vestíbulo, zaguán
halo ['helo] *s* (*pl:* **-los** o **-loes**) (meteor.) halo; (f.a. & fig.) halo, aureola; *va* aureolar
halogen ['hælodʒən] *s* (chem.) halógeno
halogenation [,hælədʒɪ'neʃən] *s* halogenación
haloid ['hælɔɪd] o ['helɔɪd] *adj & s* (chem.) haloideo
halophilous [hə'lɑfɪləs] *adj* (bot.) halófilo
halophyte ['hæləfaɪt] s (bot.) halófita
halophytic [,hælə'fɪtɪk] *adj* (bot.) halófito
halt [hɔlt] *adj* (archaic) cojo, renco; *s* alto, parada; (archaic) cojera; **to call a halt** mandar hacer alto; **to call a halt to** atajar; **to come to a halt** pararse, interrumpirse; *va* detener, parar; *vn* hacer alto, parar; vacilar; tartamudear; (archaic) cojear, renquear
halter ['hɔltər] *s* cabestro, ronzal; dogal, cuerda de ahorcar; muerte en la horca; (*pl:* **halteres** [hæl'tɪriz]) balancín o halterio (*de insecto*); *va* cabestrar
halting ['hɔltɪŋ] *adj* cojo, renco; vacilante; imperfecto
halve [hæv] o [hɑv] *va* partir por la mitad, partir en dos; reducir por la mitad
halyard ['hæljərd] *s* (naut.) driza
ham [hæm] *s* pernil del cerdo; jamón (*pernil del cerdo curado*); (anat.) corva; (slang) comicastro; (slang) aficionado (*p.ej., a la radio*); **hams** *spl* nalgas
hamadryad [,hæmə'draɪæd] *s* (myth.) hamadríada
hamamelidaceous [,hæmə,milɪ'deʃəs] *adj* (bot.) hamamelidáceo
Haman ['hemən] *s* (Bib.) Amán
ham and eggs *spl* huevos con jamón
Hamburg ['hæmbʌrg] *s* Hamburgo
hamburger ['hæmbʌrgər] *s* albondigón, carne de vaca picada y frita; hamburguesa (*bocadillo o emparedado de carne de vaca picada y frita*)
Hamburg steak *s* albondigón, carne de vaca picada y frita en forma de tortilla
hames [hemz] *spl* horcate (*arreo*)
Hamilcar [hə'mɪlkɑr] *s* Amílcar
Hamite ['hæmaɪt] *s* camita, hamita
Hamitic [hæ'mɪtɪk] *adj* camítico
hamlet ['hæmlɪt] *s* aldehuela, caserío
hammer ['hæmər] *s* martillo; (anat.) martillo; macillo o martinete (*del piano*); **to come** o **to go under the hammer** venderse en subasta; *va* martillar; clavar (*con martillo*); hacer penetrar a martillazos; (coll.) apalear, regañar; **to hammer out** sacar a martillazos; forjar, formar a martillazos; elaborar trabajosamente; sacar en limpio a fuerza de mucho pensar o hablar; *vn* martillar; **to hammer at** trabajar asiduamente en, dedicarse con ahinco a; **to hammer away** trabajar asiduamente; **to hammer away on the same old subject** estar siempre con la misma canción
hammer and sickle, the la hoz y el martillo
hammer and tongs *adv* con violencia, con todas sus fuerzas
hammerhead ['hæmər,hɛd] *s* (ichth.) cornudilla, pez martillo
hammerless ['hæmərlɪs] *adj* sin martillo; de gatillo interior
hammer lock *s* (sport) presa empleada en la lucha a brazo partido, que consiste en torcer el brazo del contrario y doblarlo detrás de su espalda
hammer mill *s* machacadora de martillos
hammock ['hæmək] *s* hamaca; (naut.) coy
hamper ['hæmpər] *s* cesto grande (*generalmente con tapa*); *va* estorbar, embarazar, impedir
hamster ['hæmstər] *s* (zool.) hámster, marmota de Alemania, rata del trigo
hamstring ['hæm,strɪŋ] *s* (anat.) tendón de la corva; (*pret & pp:* **-strung**) *va* desjarretar; (fig.) estropear, incapacitar
hand [hænd] *s* mano; obrero, peón; carácter de letra, escritura, puño y letra; firma; perito; salva de aplausos; palmo menor; mano o manecilla (*de reloj*); mano (*lance entero en un juego*); juego (*conjunto de naipes en la mano*); jugador; fuente (*de una noticia*); manojo (*de tabaco*); **all hands** (naut.) toda la tripulación; (coll.) todos; **at first hand** de primera mano; de buena tinta, directamente; **at hand** a la mano (*cerca*); disponible; **by hand** a mano; **by the hand** de la mano; **in hand** en sujeción, dominado; entre manos; de contado; marchando bien; **in his own hand** de su propio puño; **in one's hands** en manos de uno; **off one's hands** desechado, despachado; **on hand** a la mano, entre manos (*cerca*); disponible; en existencia; listo; **on one's hands** en mano de uno, entre manos; **on the one hand** por una parte; **on the other hand** por otra parte; **out of hand** en seguida, luego; desbocado, desmandado; terminado; **to be at hand** obrar en mi (nuestro) poder (*una carta*); **to bear a hand** dar la mano, prestar ayuda; **to change hands** mudar de manos; **to clap hands** batir palmas; **to eat out of one's hand** aceptar dócilmente la autoridad de uno, entregarse a la voluntad de uno; **to fall into the hands of** caer en manos de; **to force one's hand** obligar a uno a hacer

lo que no quiere hacer, obligar a uno a poner de manifiesto sus intenciones; **to get one's hands on** lograr echar la garra a; **to hand** a mano; en poder de uno; **to have a hand in** tomar parte en, jugar en; **to have one's hands full** estar ocupadísimo; **to hold hands** tomarse de las manos; **to hold up one's hands** alzar las manos (*p.ej., en señal de rendición*); **to hold up the hands of** apoyar, sostener; **to join hands** darse las manos; casarse; **to keep one's hands in** seguir teniendo práctica; mantener su interés en; **to keep one's hands off** no tocar, no meterse en; **to lay hands on** tomar, coger; prender; conseguir; tener al alcance de la mano; (eccl.) imponer las manos; **to lend a hand** dar la mano, prestar ayuda; **to live from hand to mouth** vivir al día, vivir de la mano a la boca; **to not do a hand's turn** ser incapaz de mover un brazo; **to not lift a hand** no levantar paja del suelo; **to play into the hands of** hacer el caldo gordo a; **to shake hands** estrecharse la mano; **to show one's hand** descubrir su juego (*p.ej., en los naipes*); (fig.) descubrir su juego; **to take in hand** hacerse cargo de; dominar; tratar, estudiar (*una cuestión*); ensayar; **to take off one's hands** quitarle a uno de encima (*p.ej., un problema*); **to try one's hand** probar la mano; **to turn one's hand to** dedicarse a, ocuparse en; **to wash one's hands of** lavarse las manos de; **under my hand** de mi puño y letra, con mi firma, bajo mi firma; **under the hand and seal of** firmado y sellado por; **hand and glove** o **hand in glove** uña y carne; **hand in hand** de las manos, asidos de la mano; juntos; **hands up!** ¡arriba las manos!; **hand to hand** cuerpo a cuerpo ‖ *adj* de mano; manual ‖ *va* dar, pasar, entregar; poner en manos de; conducir por la mano; **to hand down** pasar de arriba abajo; transmitir; **to hand in** entregar; **to hand on** pasar a otro, transmitir; **to hand out** dar, repartir; **to hand over** entregar; **to hand up** pasar de abajo arriba

handbag ['hænd,bæg] *s* bolso de mano, faltriquera; maletilla

hand baggage *s* equipaje de mano

handball ['hænd,bɔl] *s* pelota; juego de pelota (*estilo norteamericano*)

handbarrow ['hænd,bæro] *s* parihuelas; carretilla de mano

handbill ['hænd,bɪl] *s* hoja volante (*que se entrega en manos de los transeúntes*)

handbook ['hænd,bʊk] *s* manual; guía (*de turistas*); registro para apuestas; sitio donde se hacen las apuestas

hand brake *s* freno de mano

handbreadth ['hænd,brɛdθ] *s* ancho de la mano

handcar ['hænd,kɑr] *s* (rail.) carrito de mano

handcart ['hænd,kɑrt] *s* carretilla de mano

hand control *s* mando a mano

handcuff ['hænd,kʌf] *s* manilla; **handcuffs** *spl* esposas; *va* poner manilla a, poner esposas a

handful ['hændfʊl] *s* puñado; (fig.) puñado (*corta cantidad*); (coll.) persona o cosa difícil de dominar

hand glass *s* espejo de mano; lente para leer; campana de vidrio (*que sirve de protección a una planta*)

hand grenade *s* granada de mano; granada extintora de mano

handhold ['hænd,hold] *s* asidero

handicap ['hændɪkæp] *s* desventaja, impedimento, obstáculo; (sport) carrera con caballos de peso igualado; (sport) carrera, lucha o torneo en que se dan ciertas ventajas a los menos aventajados; (sport) ventaja que se da o impedimento que se impone; (*pret & pp:* **-capped;** *ger:* **-capping**) *va* estorbar, poner trabas a; (sport) imponer impedimento a

handicraft ['hændɪkræft] o ['hændɪkrɑft] *s* destreza manual; arte mecánica

handicraftsman ['hændɪ,kræftsmən] o ['hændɪ,krɑftsmən] *s* (*pl:* **-men**) artesano

handily ['hændɪlɪ] *adv* diestramente; fácilmente

handiwork ['hændɪ,wʌrk] *s* obra manual; obra de las manos de uno; trabajo, producción

handkerchief ['hæŋkərtʃɪf] *s* pañuelo

handle ['hændəl] *s* asa (*de cesta, vasija, etc.*); mango (*de azadón, pala, etc.*); puño (*de bastón, paraguas, espada, etc.*); tirador (*de cajón, puerta, etc.*); manubrio (*p.ej., de organillo*); guimbalete (*de bomba de agua*); (fig.) asidero (*ocasión, pretexto*); **handles** *spl* (coll.) perejiles (*títulos o signos de dignidad*); **to fly off the handle** (slang) salirse de sus casillas, perder los estribos; *va* tocar, manosear; manejar, manipular; dirigir, gobernar, mandar; tratar; comerciar en; *vn* manejarse (*bien o mal*)

handle bar *s* manillar, guía (*de bicicleta*)

handler ['hændlər] *s* tratante; (box.) entrenador

handless ['hændlɪs] *adj* manco, sin mano

handmade ['hænd,med] *adj* hecho a mano

handmaid ['hænd,med] o **handmaiden** ['hænd,medən] *s* criada; asistenta

hand-me-down ['hændmi,daʊn] *adj* (slang) hecho de antemano; (slang) de segunda mano, barato; (slang) poco elegante, de poco gusto; *s* (slang) prenda de vestir de segunda mano

hand organ *s* organillo

handout ['hænd,aʊt] *s* (slang) comida que se da a un mendigo

hand-picked ['hænd,pɪkt] *adj* escogido a mano; escogido escrupulosamente; escogido con motivos ocultos

handrail ['hænd,rel] *s* barandilla, pasamano

handsaw ['hænd,sɔ] *s* serrucho, sierra de mano

hand's-breadth ['hændz,brɛdθ] *s* var. de **handbreadth**

handsel ['hændsəl] o ['hænsəl] *s* estrena; aguinaldo; primera paga (*de dinero*); cantidad de dinero cobrado por un tendero por la mañana; dinero cobrado por un tendero al poner una tienda nueva; indicio anticipado, goce anticipado; (*pret & pp:* **-seled** o **-selled;** *ger:* **-seling** o **-selling**) *va* dar estrena a; estrenar, inaugurar; probar (*una cosa*) antes que otro, ser el primero en probar o en tener conocimiento de

handset ['hænd,sɛt] *s* (telp.) microteléfono (*aparato con el micrófono y el auricular dispuestos a cada extremo de un mango de ebonita*)

handshake ['hænd,ʃek] *s* apretón de manos

handsome ['hænsəm] *adj* hermoso, guapo, buen mozo; liberal, considerable; donairoso, elegante

handspike ['hænd,spaɪk] *s* palanca, barra (*p.ej., del cabrestante*)

handspring ['hænd,sprɪŋ] *s* voltereta sobre las manos

hand-to-hand ['hændtʊ,hænd] *adj* cuerpo a cuerpo; de mano en mano

hand-to-mouth ['hændtʊ,maʊθ] *adj* precario, inseguro; impróvido

hand-tooled ['hænd'tuld] *adj* labrado a mano

handwork ['hænd,wʌrk] *s* obra hecha a mano, trabajo a mano

hand-wrestle ['hænd,rɛsəl] *vn* pulsear

handwriting ['hænd,raɪtɪŋ] *s* escritura; letra (*forma de letra que cada uno tiene*)

handy ['hændɪ] *adj* (*comp:* **-ier;** *super:* **-iest**) a la mano, próximo; diestro, hábil; útil; **to come in handy** venir a pelo

handy man *s* factótum, dije

hang [hæŋ] *s* caída (*p.ej., de un vestido, una cortina*); pausa; declive; tino (*destreza, acierto*); significado (*de un argumento*); **I don't care a hang** no me importa un ardite; **to get the hang of it** coger el tino ‖ (*pret & pp:* **hung**) *va* colgar; fijar (*p.ej., un letrero*); tender (*la ropa mojada para que se seque*); pegar (*el papel en una pared*); bajar, inclinar (*la cabeza, por vergüenza*); (law) hacer imposible el fallo de (*un jurado*) singularizándose en opinión contraria; **to hang out** colgar fuera; desplegar (*p.ej., una bandera por una ventana*); tender (*la ropa mojada para que se seque*); **to hang up** colgar (*p.ej., el sombrero*); estorbar, impedir los progresos de; **hang it!** ¡caramba! ‖ *vn* colgar, pender; estar fijado; inclinarse; agarrarse, estar agarrado; vacilar, estar indeciso; **to hang around** andar haraganeando, esperar sin hacer nada; rondar, no alejarse de; **to hang back** resistirse a pasar adelante; vacilar, estar indeciso; **to hang down** colgar, estar pendiente; **to hang from** colgar de (*p.ej., un clavo*); **to hang on** colgar de (*p.ej., un clavo*); depender de; estar pendiente de (*las palabras de una persona*); agarrarse; insistir, persistir, estar en sus trece; estar sin acabar de morir; **to hang on to** agarrarse a, estar agarrado a; no querer soltar, no querer deshacerse de; **to hang out** asomarse demasiado; asomarse a (*una ventana*) echando fuera el busto; (slang) alojarse, vivir; **to hang over** cernerse sobre (*amenazar*); (coll.) persistir (*como efecto de un estado anterior*); **to hang together** permanecer unidos, mantenerse unidos; tener cohesión; **to hang up** (telp.) colgar ‖ (*pret & pp:* **hanged** o **hung**) *va* ahorcar; *vn* ahorcarse

hangar ['hæŋər] o ['hæŋgɑr] *s* cobertizo; (aer.) hangar

hangbird ['hæŋ,bʌrd] *s* (orn.) pájaro de nido colgante; (orn.) cacique veranero

hangdog ['hæŋ,dɔg] o ['hæŋ,dɑg] *adj* avergonzado; rastrero, vil

hanger ['hæŋər] *s* colgador, suspensión, brazo o hierro suspensor; colgadero; anillo de suspensión; (aut.) soporte colgante

hanger-on ['hæŋər'ɑn] o ['hæŋər'ɔn] *s* (*pl:* **hangers-on**) secuaz, protegido; pegote; habituado, concurrente

hanging ['hæŋɪŋ] *adj* colgante, pendiente, suspendido; de suspensión; digno de la horca; *s* ahorcadura, muerte en la horca; **hangings** *spl* colgaduras

hanging scaffold *s* andamio volante, puente volante, puente suspendido

hangman ['hæŋmən] *s* (*pl:* **-men**) verdugo

hangnail ['hæŋ,nel] *s* respigón, padrastro (*de las uñas*)

hangout ['hæŋ,aut] *s* (slang) guarida, nidal, querencia

hangover ['hæŋ,ovər] *s* efecto persistente de circunstancias anteriores; (slang) resaca (*malestar que se siente al acabar de dormir la mona*)

hank [hæŋk] *s* madeja (*de hilo, de pelo*); (naut.) anillo

hanker ['hæŋkər] *vn* sentir anhelo; **to hanker after** o **for** sentir anhelo por

hankering ['hæŋkərɪŋ] *s* anhelo; **to have a hankering for** sentir anhelo por

hanky-panky ['hæŋkɪ'pæŋkɪ] *s* (coll.) supercherla; (coll.) prestidigitación

Hannibal ['hænɪbəl] *s* Aníbal

Hanoverian [,hæno'vɪrɪən] *adj & s* hanoveriano

hanse [hæns] *s* ansa (*gremio mercantil medieval*)

Hanseatic [,hænsɪ'ætɪk] *adj* anseático

Hanseatic League *s* Liga anseática

hansel ['hænsəl] *s* var. de **handsel;** (*pret & pp:* **-seled** o **-selled;** *ger:* **-seling** o **-selling**) *va* var. de **handsel**

hansom ['hænsəm] *s* cab (*cabriolé de dos ruedas con pescante elevado por detrás*)

hap [hæp] *s* (archaic) destino, suerte; (archaic) acaso, lance; (*pret & pp:* **happed;** *ger:* **happing**) *vn* (archaic) acontecer

haphazard [,hæp'hæzərd] *adj* casual, descuidado, impensado; *adv* al acaso, al azar, a la ventura; ['hæp,hæzərd] *s* casualidad, accidente

hapless ['hæplɪs] *adj* desgraciado, desventurado

haploid ['hæplɔɪd] *adj & s* (biol.) haploide

haplology [hæp'lɑlədʒɪ] *s* (philol.) haplología

haply ['hæplɪ] *adv* por casualidad

happen ['hæpən] *vn* acontecer, suceder, ocurrir; resultar, p.ej., **it happened as we planned it** resultó tal como lo habíamos proyectado; pasar, p.ej., **what happened?** ¿qué pasó?; **don't let anything happen to you** que no le pase nada; dar la casualidad, p.ej., **it happens that I do not like that fellow** da la casualidad de que a mí no me gusta ese tipo; **no matter what happens** suceda lo que suceda; **to happen to** hacerse de, p.ej., **what happened to my hat?** ¿qué se ha hecho de mi sombrero?; a diferencia de los verbos acontecer, suceder, ocurrir, etc., el verbo **happen** se puede emplear en las primeras y segundas personas; **to happen in** entrar por casualidad; **to happen on** o **upon** acertar con, encontrarse con; **to happen to** + *inf* por casualidad, p.ej., **I happened to be there** me encontraba allí por casualidad; **I happened to see your name in the paper** ví por casualidad su nombre en el periódico; suceder que + *ind*, p.ej., **you happened to fall asleep** sucedió que Vd. se quedó dormido; resultar que + *ind*, p.ej., **I happen to know it** resulta que lo sé; el caso es que + *ind*, p.ej., **I don't happen to agree with you** el caso es que no estoy de acuerdo con Vd.

happening ['hæpənɪŋ] *s* acontecimiento, suceso

happily ['hæpɪlɪ] *adv* felizmente

happiness ['hæpɪnɪs] *s* felicidad

happy ['hæpɪ] *adj* (*comp:* **-pier;** *super:* **-piest**) feliz; contento; **to be happy to** + *inf* alegrarse de + *inf*, tener gusto en + *inf*

happy event *s* venturoso acontecimiento (*nacimiento de un niño*)

happy-go-lucky ['hæpɪgo'lʌkɪ] *adj* impróvido, irresponsable, imperturbable; *adv* a la buena ventura

happy hunting grounds *spl* tierra de caza abundante (*paraíso de los pieles rojas norteamericanos*)

happy medium *s* justo medio

happy motoring *interj* ¡feliz viaje!

Happy New Year *interj* ¡Feliz Año Nuevo!, ¡Próspero Año Nuevo!

hara-kari ['hɑrɑ'kɑrɪ] o **hara-kiri** ['hɑrɑ'kɪrɪ] *s* var. de **hari-kari**

harangue [hə'ræŋ] *s* arenga; *va & vn* arengar

harass ['hærəs] o [hə'ræs] *va* acosar, hostigar

harassment ['hærəsmənt] o [hə'ræsmənt] *s* acosamiento, hostigamiento

harbinger ['hɑrbɪndʒər] *s* precursor; anuncio, presagio; *va* anunciar, presagiar

harbor ['hɑrbər] *s* puerto; (fig.) puerto (*asilo, amparo*); *adj* portuario; *va* albergar; conservar o guardar (*p.ej., sentimientos de odio*); alcahuetear, encubrir (*delincuentes u objetos robados*); *vn* ir a ampararse

harborage ['hɑrbərɪdʒ] *s* puerto; (fig.) puerto, albergue, refugio

harborer ['hɑrbərər] *s* amparador; encubridor (*de delincuentes u objetos robados*)

harbor master *s* capitán de puerto

harbor pilot *s* piloto de puerto, práctico de puerto

harbour ['hɑrbər] *s, adj, va & vn* (Brit.) var. de **harbor**

hard [hɑrd] *adj* duro; difícil; asiduo (*trabajador*); crudo o duro (*dícese del agua*); fuerte (*dícese de la soldadura*); espiritoso, fuertemente alcohólico; (phonet.) gutural, velar; (phonet.) sordo; (phys.) duro (*rayo; tubo al vacío*); **to be hard on** gastar (*p.ej., zapatos*); echar a perder (*p.ej., un libro*); estar muy duro con; **to find it hard to** + *inf* hacérsele a uno cuesta arriba + *inf;* **to make it hard for** causar estorbo o trabajo a; **hard to** + *inf* malo de + *inf*, p.ej., **this lesson is hard to understand** esta lección es mala de entender; *adv* duro; mucho; fuerte; de firme, p.ej., **to drink, to rain, to work hard** beber, trabajar, llover de firme; con dificultad; con violencia; enteramente, hasta el límite; **to go hard with one** costarle a uno caro, serle a uno penoso; verse uno tratado con gran rigor (*por una culpa cometida*); **hard upon** a raíz de

hard and fast *adj* inflexible, riguroso; *adv* firmemente

hard-bitten ['hɑrd'bɪtən] *adj* duro, inflexible, terco

hard-boiled ['hɑrd'bɔɪld] *adj* duro, muy cocido (*huevo*); (coll.) endurecido, inflexible

hard by *adv* cerca; *prep* cerca de

hard candy *s* caramelos

hard cash *s* metálico, dinero contante y sonante

hard cider *s* sidra muy fermentada

hard coal *s* hulla magra, hulla seca

hard-drawn ['hɑrd,drɔn] *adj* (metal.) estirado en frío

hard drinker *s* bebedor empedernido

hard-earned ['hɑrd'ʌrnd] *adj* ganado a pulso

harden ['hɑrdən] *va* endurecer; solidificar; *vn* endurecerse; solidificarse

hardened ['hardənd] *adj* endurecido; empedernido
hardening ['hardənıŋ] *s* endurecimiento; **hardening of the arteries** (path.) endurecimiento arterial
hard facts *spl* realidades
hard-featured ['hard'fitʃərd] *adj* de facciones duras, de semblante hosco
hard-fisted ['hard'fıstıd] *adj* de puños rudos; tacaño
hard-fought ['hard'fɔt] *adj* arduo, reñido
hardhack ['hard,hæk] *s* (bot.) espirea tomentosa
hard-handed ['hard'hændıd] *adj* de manos callosas; duro, cruel, inhumano
hard-headed ['hard'hɛdıd] *adj* astuto, de mucha trastienda; terco, tozudo
hard-hearted ['hard'hartıd] *adj* duro de corazón
hardihood ['hardıhʊd] *s* audacia, atrevimiento, descaro, entereza de carácter
hardiness ['hardınıs] *s* fuerza, robustez, resistencia física; audacia, atrevimiento, descaro
hard labor *s* trabajos forzados
hard lines o **hard luck** *s* mala suerte; *interj* ¡qué mala suerte!
hard-luck story ['hard'lʌk] *s* (coll.) cuento de penas; **to tell a hard-luck story** (coll.) contar lástimas
hardly ['hardlı] *adv* apenas; a duras penas; casi no; difícilmente; duramente, severamente
hardness ['hardnıs] *s* dureza; crudeza (*del agua*)
hard of hearing *adj* corto de oído, medio sordo
hard palate *s* (anat.) paladar duro
hardpan ['hard,pæn] *s* capa arcillosa y dura debajo de terreno blando; (fig.) base sólida; (fig.) fondo de realidad (*algo desagradable o poco lisonjero*)
hard pressed *adj* acosado; apurado, falto de caudal
hard put to it *adj* en apuros, en un aprieto
hard rubber *s* caucho duro o endurecido
hard sauce *s* mantequilla azucarada
hard sell *s* (coll.) método enérgico e insistente de anunciar o vender mercancías
hard-set ['hard'sɛt] *adj* en calzas prietas; resuelto; terco, inflexible
hard-shell ['hard,ʃɛl] *adj* de cáscara o caparazón duros; intransigente
hard-shelled clam ['hard,ʃɛld] *s* (zool.) almeja redonda (*Venus mercenaria*)
hard-shelled crab *s* cangrejo antes de la muda
hardship ['hardʃıp] *s* apuro, fatiga, penalidad
hard sledding *s* apuros, dificultades, condiciones desfavorables
hard soap *s* jabón duro, jabón de piedra
hard steel *s* acero duro
hardtack ['hard,tæk] *s* galleta, sequete
hard times *spl* período duro, período de miseria
hard to please *adj* difícil de contentar
hard up *adj* (coll.) alcanzado, apurado
hardware ['hard,wɛr] *s* quincalla, objetos de metal, ferretería; herraje (*piezas metálicas para guarnecer algo*)
hardwareman ['hard,wɛrmən] *s* (*pl:* **-men**) quincallero, ferretero
hardware store *s* quincallería, ferretería
hard water *s* agua dura, agua cruda
hard-won ['hard,wʌn] *adj* ganado a pulso, conseguido con dificultad
hardwood ['hard,wʊd] *s* madera dura, madera preciosa; árbol de hojas caducas
hardwood floor *s* entarimado
hardy ['hardı] *adj* (*comp:* **-dier;** *super:* **-diest**) fuerte, robusto; atrevido, audaz; temerario; (bot.) resistente
hare [hɛr] *s* (zool.) liebre
harebell ['hɛr,bɛl] *s* (bot.) campánula
harebrained ['hɛr,brend] *adj* atolondrado, ligero de cascos
harelip ['hɛr,lıp] *s* labio leporino
harelipped ['hɛr,lıpt] *adj* labihendido
harem ['hɛrəm] *s* harem o harén
hare's-ear ['hɛrz,ır] *s* (bot.) perfoliada o perfoliata
hari-kari ['harı'karı] *s* harakiri
hark [hark] *interj* ¡oíd!; *vn* escuchar; **to hark back** (hunt.) volver sobre la pista (*dícese de la jauría*); (fig.) volver al asunto
harken ['harkən] *vn* escuchar, atender
harlequin ['harləkwın] *s* arlequín; *adj* arlequinesco; abigarrado; (*cap.*) *s* Arlequín
harlequinade [,harləkwı'ned] *s* arlequinada
harlequin beetle *s* (ent.) arlequín de Cayena
harlequinesque [,harləkwı'nɛsk] *adj* arlequinesco
harlequin ice cream *s* arlequín (*helado*)
harlot ['harlət] *s* ramera
harlotry ['harlətrı] *s* prostitución
harm [harm] *s* daño, perjuicio; *va* dañar, hacer daño a, perjudicar
harmful ['harmfəl] *adj* dañoso, perjudicial, nocivo
harmless ['harmlıs] *adj* inofensivo, inocuo, inocente
harmonic [har'manık] *adj & s* (mus. & phys.) armónico; **harmonics** *ssg* (mus.) teoría musical
harmonica [har'manıkə] *s* armónica
harmonious [har'monıəs] *adj* armonioso
harmonist ['harmənıst] *s* músico, compositor
harmonium [har'monıəm] *s* (mus.) armonio
harmonization [,harmənı'zeʃən] *s* armonización
harmonize ['harmənaız] *va & vn* armonizar
harmony ['harmənı] *s* (*pl:* **-nies**) armonía
harness ['harnıs] *s* guarniciones, arreos, arneses, montura; (archaic) arnés (*armadura*); **in harness** en funciones, trabajando; **to get back in the harness** volver a trabajar, volver a la rutina; **to die in the harness** morir al pie del cañón; *va* enjaezar, poner guarniciones a (*una caballería*); captar, represar (*las aguas de un río*); (archaic) armar con arnés
harness maker *s* guarnicionero
harness race *s* carrera con sulky
Harold ['hærəld] *s* Haroldo
harp [harp] *s* (mus.) arpa; *vn* tañer el arpa; **to harp on** porfiar importunamente sobre, dar en la gracia de decir
harpist ['harpıst] *s* arpista
harpoon [har'pun] *s* arpón; *va* arponar o arponear
harpooner [har'punər] *s* arponero
harpoon gun *s* cañón lanzaarpones
harpsichord ['harpsıkɔrd] *s* (mus.) clave
harpy ['harpı] *s* (*pl:* **-pies**) arpía (*persona muy codiciosa*); (*cap.*) *s* (myth.) arpía
harpy bat *s* (zool.) harpía
harpy eagle *s* (orn.) águila moneva
harquebus ['harkwıbəs] *s* arcabuz
harquebusier [,harkwıbəs'ır] *s* arcabucero
harridan ['hærıdən] *s* bruja (*vieja viciosa y regañona*)
harrier ['hærıər] *s* acosador, asolador; corredor por el campo; perro lebrel; (orn.) busardo
Harriet ['hærıət] *s* Enriqueta
harrow ['hæro] *s* (agr.) grada; *va* (agr.) gradar; lacerar; atormentar, martirizar
harrowing ['hæro·ıŋ] *adj* horripilante, espeluznante; *s* (agr.) gradeo
harry ['hærı] (*pret & pp:* **-ried**) *va* acosar, hostilizar, asolar; inquietar, atormentar; (*cap.*) *s* Enriquito
harsh [harʃ] *adj* áspero (*al tacto, al gusto, al oído; estilo*); cruel, duro
harshness ['harʃnıs] *s* aspereza; crueldad, dureza
hart [hart] *s* (zool.) ciervo
hartebeest ['hartı,bist] o ['hart,bist] *s* (zool.) caama, ciervo del Cabo
hartshorn ['harts,hɔrn] *s* cuerno de ciervo; (pharm.) cuerno de ciervo
hart's-tongue ['harts,tʌŋ] *s* (bot.) lengua de ciervo, lengua cerval
harum-scarum ['hɛrəm'skɛrəm] *adj* tarambana; *adv* atolondradamente; *s* tarambana, torbellino
haruspex [hə'rʌspɛks] o ['hærəspɛks] *s* (*pl:* **haruspices** [hə'rʌspısiz]) arúspice
harvest ['harvıst] *s* cosecha; (fig.) cosecha (*fruto, p.ej., de buena o mala conducta*); *va* cosechar; (fig.) recoger (*el fruto de una acción*); *vn* cosechar
harvester ['harvıstər] *s* cosechero; jornalero por el agosto; segadora, máquina segadora
harvester-thresher ['harvıstər'θrɛʃər] *s* segadora trilladora

harvest home *s* final de la cosecha; fiesta de segadores; canción de segadores
harvestman ['hɑrvɪstmən] *s* (*pl:* **-men**) cosechero; jornalero por el agosto; (ent.) segador
harvest moon *s* plenilunio en la época de la cosecha
harvest mouse *s* (zool.) ratón silvestre
has [hæz] *tercera persona del sg del pres de ind de* **have**
has-been ['hæz,bɪn] *s* (coll.) persona que ya no sirve, cosa que ya no sirve
Hasdrubal ['hæzdrubəl] *s* Asdrúbal
hash [hæʃ] *s* picadillo; mezcla confusa, embrollo, lío; **to settle one's hash** (coll.) meterle a uno en cintura, acabar con uno; *va* picar, desmenuzar; embrollar; **to hash up everything** enredarlo todo
hasheesh o **hashish** ['hæʃiʃ] *s* hachich o hachís o haxix
haslet ['hæslɪt] o ['hezlɪt] *s* asadura de puerco
hasn't ['hæzənt] contracción de **has not**
hasp [hæsp] o [hɑsp] *s* portacandado; broche, manecilla (*para cerrar un libro*)
hassle ['hæsəl] *s* (coll.) disputa, controversia, pendencia
hassock ['hæsək] *s* cojín (*para los pies, para rezar arrodillado, etc.*); montecillo de hierbas crecientes (*en un terreno pantanoso*)
hastate ['hæstet] *adj* (bot.) alabardado
haste [hest] *s* prisa; precipitación; **in haste** de prisa; **to make haste** darse prisa
hasten ['hesən] *va* apresurar; apretar (*el paso*); *vn* apresurarse, darse prisa; **to hasten to** + *inf* apresurarse a + *inf*
hasty ['hestɪ] *adj* (*comp:* **-ier;** *super:* **-iest**) apresurado; hecho de prisa; inconsiderado; colérico
hasty pudding *s* gachas de harina de maíz; gachas de harina o avena
hat [hæt] *s* sombrero; capelo (*de cardenal*); cardenalato; sombrerillo (*para recoger las limosnas*); **to keep under one's hat** (slang) callar, no divulgar; **to pass the hat** pasar el sombrero (o la gorra); pasar el cepillo; **to take one's hat off to** (coll.) reconocer la superioridad de; **to throw one's hat in the ring** (coll.) decidirse a bajar a la arena; (*pret & pp:* **hatted;** *ger:* **hatting**) *va* dar sombrero a; cubrir con sombrero
hatband ['hæt,bænd] *s* cintillo (*de sombrero*)
hat block *s* hormillón, peana
hatbox ['hæt,bɑks] *s* sombrerera
hatch [hætʃ] *s* cría, nidada; salida del cascarón; trampa, escotillón; compuerta, media puerta; (f.a.) línea de sombreado; (naut.) escotilla; (naut.) cuartel (*armazón de tablas para cerrar la escotilla*); *va* sacar (*pollos*) del cascarón; empollar (*huevos*); (f.a.) sombrear, plumear; idear, maquinar, tramar; *vn* salir del huevo; empollarse
hat-check girl ['hæt,tʃɛk] *s* guardarropa (*joven encargada de custodiar los sombreros, etc.*)
hatchel ['hætʃəl] *s* rastrillo (*para limpiar el lino o el cáñamo*); (*pret & pp:* **-eled** o **-elled;** *ger:* **-eling** o **-elling**) *va* rastrillar (*lino o cáñamo*); atormentar, molestar
hatchery ['hætʃərɪ] *s* (*pl:* **-ies**) criadero (*p.ej., de peces*)
hatchet ['hætʃɪt] *s* destral; hacha de guerra (*de los pieles rojas*); **to bury the hatchet** envainar la espada, hacer la paz, echar pelillos a la mar; **to dig up the hatchet** hacer la guerra
hatchet face *s* cara de cuchillo
hatchet vetch *s* (bot.) encorvada, hierba de la segur
hatching ['hætʃɪŋ] *s* (f.a.) sombreado, plumeado
hatchment ['hætʃmənt] *s* placa cuadrada, colocada diagonalmente, en que está grabado el escudo de armas de un caballero o dama muertos
hatchway ['hætʃ,we] *s* escotillón (*puerta en el suelo*); (naut.) escotilla
hate [het] *s* odio, aborrecimiento; *va & vn* odiar, aborrecer; **to hate to** + *inf* detestar + *inf*, p.ej., **I hate to go out in the rain** detesto salir con la lluvia
hateful ['hetfəl] *adj* odiable, odioso; maligno, malévolo
hatefulness ['hetfəlnɪs] *s* odiosidad; malignidad
hatemonger ['het,mʌŋgər] *s* (coll.) alborotador, cizañador
hatpin ['hæt,pɪn] *s* pasador o aguja de sombrero
hatrack ['hæt,ræk] *s* percha (*para colgar sombreros*)
hatred ['hetrɪd] *s* odio, aborrecimiento
hatter ['hætər] *s* sombrerero
Hattie o **Hatty** ['hætɪ] *s* nombre abreviado de **Harriet**
haubergeon ['hɔbərdʒən] *s* var. de **habergeon**
hauberk ['hɔbərk] *s* camisote
haughtiness ['hɔtɪnɪs] *s* altanería, altivez
haughty ['hɔtɪ] *adj* (*comp:* **-tier;** *super:* **-tiest**) altanero, altivo
haul [hɔl] *s* tirón; recorrido, trayecto; redada; (fig.) redada (*p.ej., de ladrones*); *va* acarrear, transportar, arrastrar; (naut.) virar (*una nave*); **to haul up** (coll.) pedir cuentas a; (naut.) virar (*una nave*); *vn* tirar; cambiar de rumbo; **to haul off** levantar el puño (*para asestar un golpe*); retirarse; (naut.) virar (*para apartar la nave de un objeto cualquiera*); **to haul on the wind, to haul to the wind** o **to haul up** (naut.) virar para navegar ciñendo
haulage ['hɔlɪdʒ] *s* acarreo, transporte, arrastre; coste o gastos de acarreo
haunch [hɔntʃ] o [hɑntʃ] *s* cadera (*parte donde se unen el muslo y el tronco*); anca (*cada una de las dos partes posteriores de los animales*); pierna (*de carnero, venado, etc.*)
haunt [hɔnt] o [hɑnt] *s* guarida, nidal, querencia; refugio; (dial.) fantasma, aparecido; *va* frecuentar; andar por, vagar por; perseguir (*una idea a una persona*); estar siempre en la memoria de
haunted house *s* casa de fantasmas
haunting ['hɔntɪŋ] o ['hɑntɪŋ] *adj* persistente, inolvidable, obsesionante
hautboy ['hobɔɪ] u ['obɔɪ] *s* var. de **oboe**
hauteur [ho'tʌr] u [o'tʌr] *s* arrogancia, altivez
Havana [hə'vænə] *s* La Habana; habano (*cigarro o tabaco de Cuba*)
Havanese [,hævə'niz] *adj* habanero; *s* (*pl:* **-nese**) habanero
have [hæv] (*pret & pp:* **had**) *va* tener; tomar, p.ej., **have a cigar** tome Vd. un puro; manifestar (*p.ej., respeto*); sentir (*p.ej., dolor*); conservar (*en la memoria*); tomar (*p.ej., lecciones*); decir, p.ej., **they will have it so** dicen que es así; saber, p.ej., **he has no Latin** no sabe latín; (coll.) llevar ventaja a; (slang) estafar; **there are few to be had** se consiguen difícilmente; **to have and to hold** (úsase sólo en el infinitivo) en propiedad, para ser poseído en propiedad; **to have it in for** (coll.) tener tirria a, tenérsela jurada a; **to have it out** discutir o pelear hasta poner fin al asunto; **to have it out with** emprenderla con, habérselas con; **to have on** llevar puesto; **to have to do with** tener que ver con; **to have** + *inf* hacer o mandar + *inf*, p.ej., **I had him sit down** le hice sentar; **to have** + *pp* hacer o mandar + *inf*, p.ej., **he had his watch repaired** hizo componer su reloj; **I had a suit made** mandé hacer un traje ‖ *vn* **to have at** atacar, embestir; **to have to** tener que; **to have to do with** tratar de; tener relaciones con ‖ *v aux* haber, p.ej., **I have spoken** he hablado; **I had spoken** había hablado
havelock ['hævlɑk] *s* cogotera
haven ['hevən] *s* puerto; buen puerto, abrigo, asilo; *va* abrigar, dar abrigo a
have-not ['hæv,nɑt] *s* (coll.) persona o nación desposeídas; **the haves and the have-nots** (coll.) los ricos y los desposeídos
haven't ['hævənt] contracción de **have not**
haversack ['hævərsæk] *s* barjuleta; (mil.) mochila
havoc ['hævək] *s* estrago, estragos; **to play havoc with** hacer grandes estragos en, destruir
haw [hɔ] *s* baya o simiente del espino; tosecilla, tos nerviosa (*al hablar*); *interj* ¡ apartа!; *va* hacer volver a la izquierda; *vn* destoserse; hablar tartaleando; doblar a la izquierda
Hawaiian [hə'waɪjən] *adj & s* hawaiano

Hawaiian Islands *spl* islas Hawai
hawfinch ['hɔ,fɪntʃ] *s* (orn.) cascapiñones
haw-haw ['hɔ,hɔ] o [hɔ'hɔ] *s* carcajada; *vn* reír a carcajadas
hawk [hɔk] *s* (orn.) halcón, cernícalo, gavilán, gerifalte, azor; (fig.) ave de presa (*persona*); carraspeo; esparavel; *va* pregonar (*mercancías; una noticia; un secreto*); **to hawk up** arrojar tosiendo; *vn* cazar aves con halcones; carraspear
hawker ['hɔkər] *s* halconero, cetrero; buhonero
hawk-eyed ['hɔk,aɪd] *adj* de ojos linces, de ojo avizor
hawking ['hɔkɪŋ] *s* halconería, cetrería
hawklike ['hɔk,laɪk] *adj* halconado
hawk moth *s* (ent.) esfinge
hawk-nosed ['hɔk,nozd] *adj* de nariz aguileña
hawk owl *s* (orn.) surnia
hawk's-bill o **hawksbill** ['hɔks,bɪl] o **hawksbill turtle** *s* (zool.) carey
hawkweed ['hɔk,wid] *s* (bot.) oreja de ratón, pelosilla
hawse [hɔz] *s* (naut.) escobén (*agujero*); (naut.) frente de los escobenes; (naut.) distancia entre un buque anclado y sus anclas
hawsehole ['hɔz,hol] *s* (naut.) escobén
hawser ['hɔzər] *s* (naut.) guindaleza, estacha
hawthorn ['hɔθɔrn] *s* (bot.) espino, oxiacanto
hay [he] *s* heno; **to hit the hay** (slang) acostarse; **to make hay while the sun shines** aprovechar la ocasión; *va* henear; echar heno a (*la caballería o el ganado*)
haycock ['he,kɑk] *s* pequeña niara de heno
hay fever *s* (path.) fiebre del heno
hayfield ['he,fild] *s* henar
hayfork ['he,fɔrk] *s* horca (*para levantar el heno*); elevador de heno
hayloft ['he,lɔft] o ['he,lɑft] *s* henil
haymaker ['he,mekər] *s* heneador; (slang) golpe que pone fuera de combate (*en el boxeo*)
haymow ['he,maʊ] *s* henil; acopio de heno (*en el henil*)
hayrack ['he,ræk] *s* pesebre; armazón que se monta en un carro para transportar el heno
hayrick ['he,rɪk] *s* almiar
hay ride *s* paseo de placer en un carro de heno
hayseed ['he,sid] *s* simiente de heno, simiente de hierbas; (coll.) patán, rústico, campesino
haystack ['he,stæk] *s* almiar
haywire ['he,waɪr] *s* alambre que se usa para el embalaje del heno; *adj* (slang) desarreglado, descompuesto; (slang) barrenado, loco
hazard ['hæzərd] *s* peligro, riesgo; acaso, azar; (golf) obstáculo; **at all hazards** por grande que sea el riesgo; *va* arriesgar; aventurar (*p.ej., una opinión*)
hazardous ['hæzərdəs] *adj* peligroso, arriesgado, aventurado
haze [hez] *s* calina; confusión, vaguedad, falta de claridad; *va* dar novatada a
hazel ['hezəl] *s* (bot.) avellano; *adj* avellanado (*de color de avellana*)
hazelnut ['hezəl,nʌt] *s* avellana
hazing ['hezɪŋ] *s* novatada
hazy ['hezɪ] *adj* (*comp:* **-zier;** *super:* **-ziest**) calinoso; confuso, vago, poco claro
H-bomb ['etʃ,bɑm] *s* bomba de hidrógeno
H.C. abr. de **House of Commons**
H.C.F. o **h.c.f.** abr. de **highest common factor**
hd. abr. de **head**
hdkf. abr. de **handkerchief**
hdqrs. abr. de **headquarters**
H.E. abr. de **His Eminence** y **His Excellency**
he [hi] *pron pers* (*pl:* **they**) él; *s* (*pl:* **hes**) macho, varón; *interj* ¡ji!
head [hɛd] *s* cabeza (*parte superior del cuerpo del hombre y el animal; razón, inteligencia; juicio, talento; parte superior de una página, de un clavo o alfiler, de un martillo; cumbre de una montaña; fuente, origen, manantial; frente de una procesión, ejército, etc.; sitio honorífico en la mesa; jefe, director; dirección; persona; res; punta de un dardo; repollo de col o de lechuga; parte grabadora o reproductora del magnetófono*); cabecera (*de cama*); encabezamiento, título; división o sección (*de un escrito*); centro (*de un divieso*); espuma (*en un vaso de cerveza*); parche (*de un tambor*); puño (*de bastón*); fondo o tapa (*de un cilindro, barril, etc.*); montera (*de la caldera de un alambique*); crisis, punto decisivo; avance, progreso; (bot.) cabezuela (*inflorescencia*); (hyd.) altura de caída; (mach.) culata (*de cilindro*); **heads** *spl* cara (*de una moneda*); **from head to foot** de pies a cabeza; **on** o **upon one's head** a responsabilidad de uno, sobre la cabeza de uno; **off** u **out of one's head** (coll.) delirante, fuera de sí, destornillado; **out of one's own head** de su cosecha, por su cabeza; **over one's head** fuera del alcance de uno; por encima de uno (*dirigiéndose a una autoridad superior*); **to be out of one's head** delirar; **to be the head** hacer cabeza (*en un negocio*); **to bother one's head about** quebrarse la cabeza con; **to come into one's head** pasarle a uno por la cabeza; **to come to a head** madurar; llegar a un punto decisivo; supurar (*un absceso*); **to eat one's head off** ser muy comilón; consumir más de lo que uno vale; **to gather head** ir en progreso; **to get something in one's head** metérsele a uno en la cabeza una cosa; **to give one his head** darle a uno rienda suelta; **to go to one's head** marearle a uno; volverle a uno el juicio; subírsele a uno a la cabeza; **to hang** o **hide one's head** caérsele a uno la cara de vergüenza; **to keep one's head** no perder la cabeza, tenerse en los estribos, mantener su sangre fría; **to keep one's head above water** mantenerse a flote; no dejarse vencer (*por las desgracias, la miseria, etc.*); **to lay** o **put heads together** consultarse (*dos o más personas*) entre sí; conspirar, confabularse, **to lose one's head** perder los estribos; **to not make head or tail of** no ver pies ni cabeza a; **to take it into one's head to** + *inf* metérsele a uno en la cabeza + *inf;* **to turn the head of** trastornar; apasionar; subirse a la cabeza, p.ej., **praise turns his head** los elogios se le suben a la cabeza; **head on** de cabeza; **head over heels** en un salto mortal; absolutamente, completamente, hasta los tuétanos; precipitadamente; **heads or tails** cara o cruz ‖ *adj* delantero, primero; más alto, superior; principal; (naut.) de proa ‖ *va* acaudillar, dirigir, mandar; aventajar, sobrepujar; estar a la cabeza de (*p.ej., la clase*); venir primero en (*p.ej., una lista*); poner cabeza a; descabezar; desmochar (*un árbol*); conducir (*un coche, un avión, etc., en cierta dirección*); **to head off** alcanzar e interceptar (*a uno que huye*); atajar (*un mal*) ‖ *vn* dirigirse; supurar (*un absceso*); repollar (*p.ej., la lechuga*); **to head towards** dirigirse hacia
headache ['hɛd,ek] *s* (path.) dolor de cabeza
headband ['hɛd,bænd] *s* venda, faja, cinta (*para la cabeza*); (b.b.) cabezada
headboard ['hɛd,bord] *s* cabecera de cama
headcheese ['hɛd,tʃiz] *s* queso de cerdo
headdress ['hɛd,drɛs] *s* tocado
headed ['hɛdɪd] *adj* que tiene cabeza; encabezado, titulado; repolludo; **headed for** con rumbo a
header ['hɛdər] *s* desmochador; cámara de circulación; cabeza, jefe; (carp.) brochal, embrochalado; (mas.) hilada, tizón; (coll.) caída de cabeza; **to take a header** (coll.) irse de cabeza
header course *s* (mas.) hilada atizonada o de cabezal
headfirst ['hɛd'fʌrst] o **headforemost** ['hɛd'formost] *adj* de cabeza; precipitadamente, temerariamente
headframe ['hɛd,frem] *s* (min.) castillete de mina
head gate *s* (hyd.) compuerta, paradera; (hyd.) compuerta de cabecera o de toma
headgear ['hɛd,gɪr] *s* sombrero (*de cualquier forma*); tocado (*de mujer*); cabezada (*de guarnición para caballo*); (football) casco de cuero
head-hunter ['hɛd,hʌntər] *s* cazador de cabezas
heading ['hɛdɪŋ] *s* encabezamiento, título; membrete; rumbo; (min.) galería de avance
headland ['hɛdlənd] *s* promontorio
headledge ['hɛd,lɛdʒ] *s* (naut.) contrabrazola
headless ['hɛdlɪs] *adj* acéfalo; descabezado; sin jefe o director; estúpido, tonto

headlight [ˈhɛd,laɪt] *s* (aut.) faro; (rail.) farol; (naut.) farol de tope
headline [ˈhɛd,laɪn] *s* cabecera (*de una plana de periódico*); título de página, titulillo; *va* poner cabecera a, poner título a; (slang) dar cartel a, destacar, hacer resaltar (*a un actor*)
headliner [ˈhɛd,laɪnər] *s* (slang) atracción principal (*en los anuncios de cine o teatro*)
headlong [ˈhɛd,lɔŋ] o [ˈhɛd,lɑŋ] *adj* de cabeza; precipitado; *adv* de cabeza; precipitadamente
headman [ˈhɛd,mæn] o [ˈhɛdmən] *s* (*pl:* **-men**) jefe, caudillo, cacique
headmaster [ˈhɛdˈmæstər] o [ˈhɛdˈmɑstər] *s* director (*de un colegio*)
headmastership [ˈhɛdˈmæstərʃɪp] o [ˈhɛdˈmɑstərʃɪp] *s* cargo de director (*de un colegio*)
headmost [ˈhɛdmost] *adj* delantero, primero
head office *s* casa matriz, oficina central
head of hair *s* cabellera
head-on [,hɛdˈɑn] o [,hɛdˈɔn] *adj* de frente, p.ej., **head-on collision** colisión de frente
headphone [ˈhɛd,fon] *s* auricular de casco, receptor de cabeza
headpiece [ˈhɛd,pis] *s* sombrero; tocado; casco, morrión, yelmo; cabeza, juicio, inteligencia; auricular de casco; cabecera de cama; (print.) cabecera, viñeta
head pin *s* bolo delantero (*en el juego de bolos*)
headquarters [ˈhɛd,kwɔrtərz] *ssg o spl* sede; jefatura, centro de dirección; (mil.) cuartel general
headrace [ˈhɛd,res] *s* caz de traída
headrail [ˈhɛd,rel] *s* peinazo superior de puerta; (naut.) varenga, brazal
headrest [ˈhɛd,rɛst] *s* apoyo para la cabeza
headset [ˈhɛd,sɛt] *s* auricular de casco, receptor de cabeza
headship [ˈhɛdʃɪp] *s* jefatura, dirección, mando
headstall [ˈhɛd,stɔl] *s* cabezada (*de freno*)
headstock [ˈhɛd,stɑk] *s* (mach.) cabezal (*de un torno*)
headstone [ˈhɛd,ston] *s* piedra angular; lápida sepulcral
headstream [ˈhɛd,strim] *s* afluente principal (*de un río*)
headstrong [ˈhɛd,strɔŋ] o [ˈhɛd,strɑŋ] *adj* cabezudo, terco, testarudo
head tone *s* (mus.) voz de cabeza
headwaiter [ˈhɛdˈwetər] *s* encargado de comedor, jefe de camareros
headwaters [ˈhɛd,wɔtərz] o [ˈhɛd,wɑtərz] *spl* cabecera (*de un río*)
headway [ˈhɛd,we] *s* avance, progreso; espacio libre (*entre la cabeza y un dintel, entre un vehículo y un arco de puente, etc.*); (rail.) intervalo entre dos trenes en una misma vía; **to make headway** avanzar, adelantar, progresar
head wind *s* (naut.) viento de frente, viento por la proa
headwork [ˈhɛd,wʌrk] *s* trabajo intelectual
heady [ˈhɛdɪ] *adj* (*comp:* **-ier;** *super:* **-iest**) precipitado, impetuoso; cabezudo (*vino*)
heal [hil] *va* curar, sanar; cicatrizar; remediar (*un daño*); *vn* curar, sanar; cicatrizarse; remediarse; **to heal up** cicatrizarse
healer [ˈhilər] *s* sanador, curador
healing [ˈhilɪŋ] *adj* curativo; *s* curación
health [hɛlθ] *s* salud; **to be in bad health** estar mal de salud; **to be in good health** estar bien de salud; **to drink to the health of** beber a la salud de; **to enjoy wonderful health** gastar salud; **to your health!** ¡a su salud!
health examination *s* reconocimiento sanitario
healthful [ˈhɛlθfəl] *adj* sano, saludable
health insurance *s* seguro de enfermedad
healthy [ˈhɛlθɪ] *adj* (*comp:* **-ier;** *super:* **-iest**) sano (*de buena salud; saludable*)
heap [hip] *s* montón; (coll.) montón (*número considerable*); *va* amontonar, apilar; colmar, llenar, henchir (*p.ej., de favores, insultos*); dar generosamente; *vn* amontonarse, apilarse
hear [hɪr] (*pret & pp:* **heard**) *va* oír; dar audiencia a; tomar la lección a; otorgar; (law) ver; **to hear** + *ger* oír + *inf*, p.ej., **I heard the girl singing** oí cantar a la muchacha; **to hear** + *inf* oír + *inf*, p.ej., **I heard my brother come in** oí entrar a mi hermano; **to hear** + *pp* oír + *inf*, p.ej., **I heard the bell rung** oí tocar la campana; **to hear it said** oírlo decir; **to hear someone out** oír a uno hasta que concluya de hablar; *vn* oír; **he will not hear of it** no quiere ni pensar en ello, no lo permitirá de ningún modo; **to hear about** oír hablar de; **to hear from** saber de, recibir o tener noticias de; **to hear of** oír hablar de; enterarse de; **to hear tell of** oír hablar de; **to hear that** oír decir que; **hear! hear!** ¡bravo!
heard [hʌrd] *pret & pp de* **hear**
hearer [hɪrər] *s* oyente
hearing [ˈhɪrɪŋ] *s* oída (*acción*); oído (*sentido*); audiencia; (law) examen de testigos; **in the hearing of** en la presencia de; **within hearing** al alcance del oído
hearing aid *s* acústico, audífono, aparato auditivo
hearken [ˈhɑrkən] *vn* var. de **harken**
hearsay [ˈhɪr,se] *s* rumor, voz común; **by hearsay** de o por oídas
hearsay evidence *s* (law) testimonio de oídas, prueba de oídas
hearse [hʌrs] *s* coche fúnebre, carroza fúnebre; (eccl.) tenebrario; *va* colocar en un coche fúnebre; enterrar, sepultar
hearsecloth [ˈhʌrs,klɔθ] o [ˈhʌrs,klɑθ] *s* paño mortuorio
heart [hɑrt] *s* corazón; cogollo (*p.ej., de una lechuga*); corazón (*naipe que corresponde a la copa*); **hearts** *spl* corazones (*palo que corresponde al de copas*); **after one's heart** enteramente del gusto de uno; **at heart** verdaderamente, en el fondo; **by heart** de memoria; **dear heart** vida mía; **from one's heart** de todo corazón; **in one's heart of hearts** en lo más recóndito del corazón de uno; **near one's heart** que a uno le toca en lo más sensible, que a uno le interesa grandemente; **to break the heart of** quebrar o partir el corazón de; **to die of a broken heart** morir de pena, morir de desengaño; **to do one's heart good** alegrarle a uno el corazón; **to eat one's heart out** afligirse sobremanera, dejarse morir de tristeza; **to get to the heart of** profundizar, llegar al fondo de; **to have one's heart in one's boots** o **mouth** estar con el alma en la boca, estar muerto de miedo; **to have one's heart in one's work** esmerarse en su trabajo, trabajar con entusiasmo; **to have one's heart in the right place** tener buenas intenciones; **to lay to heart** tener presente; pensar (*una cosa*) seriamente; **to lose heart** descorazonarse; **to not have the heart to** + *inf* no tener corazón para + *inf;* **to open one's heart** descubrir el pecho; **to open one's heart to** abrirse con, descubrirse con; **to take heart** cobrar aliento; **to take the heart out of** desalentar, desanimar; **to take to heart** tomar a pecho; **to wear one's heart on one's sleeve** llevar el corazón en la mano; **with all one's heart** con toda el alma de uno; **with one's heart in one's mouth** con el credo en la boca; **heart and soul** de todo corazón, con toda el alma de uno
heartache [ˈhɑrt,ek] *s* angustia, congoja, pesar
heart attack *s* ataque cardíaco, ataque de corazón
heartbeat [ˈhɑrt,bit] *s* latido del corazón
heartbreak [ˈhɑrt,brek] *s* angustia, dolor abrumador
heartbreaker [ˈhɑrt,brekər] *s* ladrón de corazones; (hum.) tirabuzón (*rizo de cabello*)
heartbreaking [ˈhɑrt,brekɪŋ] *adj* angustioso
heartbroken [ˈhɑrt,brokən] *adj* acongojado, transido de dolor
heartburn [ˈhɑrt,bʌrn] *s* (path.) rescoldera; envidia, celos
heartburning [ˈhɑrt,bʌrnɪŋ] *s* envidia, celos
heart disease *s* enfermedad del corazón
hearten [ˈhɑrtən] *va* animar, alentar
heart failure *s* paro del corazón; desmayo, desfallecimiento
heartfelt [ˈhɑrt,fɛlt] *adj* cordial, sincero
heart-free [ˈhɑrt,fri] *adj* libre de amor

hearth [hɑrθ] *s* hogar; (metal. & fig.) hogar; (metal.) obra (*del alto horno*)
hearth money *s* fogaje (*tributo antiguo*)
hearthside ['hɑrθ,saɪd] *s* hogar
hearthstone ['hɑrθ,ston] *s* solera del hogar; hogar (*domicilio*)
heartily ['hɑrtɪlɪ] *adv* cordialmente, sinceramente; de buena gana, con entusiasmo; con buen apetito; bien, mucho, completamente
heartiness ['hɑrtɪnɪs] *s* cordialidad, sinceridad; buena salud, vigor; espontaneidad; entusiasmo
heartless ['hɑrtlɪs] *adj* cruel, empedernido; apocado, pusilánime
heart-lung machine ['hɑrt'lʌŋ] *s* (surg.) corazón-pulmón, aparato corazón-pulmón
heart-rending ['hɑrt,rɛndɪŋ] *adj* que parte el corazón, que causa mucha angustia
heartsease o **heart's-ease** ['hɑrts,iz] *s* serenidad de ánimo; (bot.) pensamiento, trinitaria
heartseed ['hɑrt,sid] *s* (bot.) farolillo
heartsick ['hɑrt,sɪk] *adj* desconsolado, muy abatido
heartsore ['hɑrt,sor] *adj* acongojado, dolorido
heart-stricken ['hɑrt,strɪkən] *adj* transido de dolor, angustiado
heartstrings ['hɑrt,strɪŋz] *spl* fibras del corazón, entretelas (*entrañas, misericordia*)
heartthrob ['hɑrt,θrɑb] *s* emoción vehemente
heart-to-heart ['hɑrttʊ,hɑrt] *adj* franco, sincero
heart trouble *s* enfermedad del corazón; **to have heart trouble** enfermar del corazón
heart-whole ['hɑrt,hol] *adj* libre de amor; cordial, sincero
heartwood ['hɑrt,wʊd] *s* madera de corazón
hearty ['hɑrtɪ] *adj* (*comp:* **-ier;** *super:* **-iest**) cordial, sincero; sano, robusto; espontáneo; nutritivo, substancioso; grande, abundante; comilón, voraz; *s* (*pl:* **-ies**) (naut.) compañero
heat [hit] *s* calor; calefacción; ardor, ímpetu; celo (*de las bestias*); (sport) carrera (*en las carreras de caballos*); (metal.) hornada, turno de fundición; **in heat** en celo; **to turn on the heat** (slang) aumentar la intensidad, apretar los tornillos; *adj* térmico; *va* calentar; calefaccionar; acalorar, excitar; *vn* calentarse; acalorarse, excitarse
heat barrier *s* var. de **thermal barrier**
heated ['hitɪd] *adj* acalorado
heatedly ['hitɪdlɪ] *adv* acaloradamente
heat engine *s* motor térmico
heater ['hitər] *s* calentador; (rad.) calefactor
heat exchanger [ɛks'tʃendʒər] *s* (phys.) cambiador de calor, cambiador térmico
heath [hiθ] *s* (bot.) brezo; brezal; **native heath** patria chica
heathbird ['hiθ,bʌrd] *s* (orn.) gallo de bosque
heathen ['hiðən] *adj* gentil, pagano; sin religión; inculto; *s* (*pl:* **-thens** o **-then**) gentil, pagano
heathendom ['hiðəndəm] *s* gentilidad
heathenish ['hiðənɪʃ] *adj* gentílico
heathenism ['hiðənɪzəm] *s* gentilidad; irreligión, incultura
heathenize ['hiðənaɪz] *va* gentilizar
heather ['hɛðər] *s* (bot.) brezo
heathery ['hɛðərɪ] *adj* brezoso; cubierto o poblado de brezos
heathy ['hiθɪ] *adj* brezoso
heating ['hitɪŋ] *adj* calentador; *s* calefacción
heating coil *s* (elec.) bobina térmica
heating element *s* (elec.) elemento calentador; (rad.) elemento de caldeo
heating pad *s* almohadilla caliente
heating surface *s* superficie de caldeo o calefacción
heat lightning *s* fucilazo, relámpago de calor
heatproof ['hit'pruf] *adj* antitérmico
heat shield *s* escudo térmico, blindaje térmico (*de una cápsula espacial*)
heatstroke ['hit,strok] *s* (path.) golpe de calor
heat unit *s* (phys.) unidad térmica
heat wave *s* (phys.) onda calorífica; (coll.) ola de calor
heave [hiv] *s* esfuerzo para levantar una cosa pesada, esfuerzo para levantarse; echada, tirada; henchidura (*de las olas*); jadeo; **heaves** *ssg* (vet.) huélfago; (*pret & pp:* **heaved** o **hove**) *va* levantar y lanzar (*una cosa pesada*); levantar con algún esfuerzo; exhalar (*un suspiro*); **to heave to** (naut.) poner al pairo o en facha; *vn* lanzar con esfuerzo; levantarse y bajarse alternativamente (*las olas*); palpitar (*el pecho*); combarse, elevarse; jadear; arquear, hacer esfuerzos por vomitar; **heave ho!** (naut.) ¡iza!
heaven ['hɛvən] *s* cielo; (*cap.*) *s* cielo (*mansión de los bienaventurados; Dios*); **heavens** *spl* cielo (*firmamento*); **for heaven's sake!** o **good heavens!** ¡válgame Dios!; **to move heaven and earth** mover cielo y tierra
heavenly ['hɛvənlɪ] *adj* celeste (*cuerpo*); celestial (*p.ej., mansión*); (fig.) celestial
heavenly body *s* astro, cuerpo celeste
heavenly home *s* mansión celestial, patria celestial
heavenward ['hɛvənwərd] *adj & adv* hacia el cielo
heavenwards ['hɛvənwərdz] *adv* hacia el cielo
heaver ['hivər] *s* (naut.) cargador; (naut.) tortor
heavier-than-air [,hɛvɪər ðən'ɛr] *adj* (aer.) más pesado que el aire
heaviness ['hɛvɪnɪs] *s* pesadez; espesura; densidad; grosor (*p.ej., de una línea*); abundancia; fuerza (*p.ej., de la lluvia*); ímpetu (*de las olas*); languidez, modorra; cargazón (*en el estómago, la cabeza, etc.; en el estilo literario*); abatimiento; opresión; (com.) postración (*del mercado*)
Heaviside layer ['hɛvɪsaɪd] *s* (rad.) capa de Heaviside
heavy ['hɛvɪ] *adj* (*comp:* **-ier;** *super:* **-iest**) pesado; espeso o denso (*líquido*); denso (*tráfico*); grueso (*dícese de la tela, el papel, la mar, una línea, etc.*); tupido (*dícese de la tela, el monte, etc.*); copioso, abundante (*dícese, p.ej., de las cosechas*); recio, fuerte (*dícese de la lluvia*); fuerte (*dícese de los gastos, pérdidas, pagos, rebajas, etc.*); agravado (*dícese de los ojos*); basto (*dícese de las facciones*); fragoroso (*cañoneo*); malo, pésimo (*camino*); empinado (*dícese de una cuesta*); grande (*bebedor*); cargado (*estilo, dibujo*); abatido, cansado; triste, oprimido (*corazón*); grave, serio; sombrío; importante, considerable (*dícese de las deudas, las reparaciones*); encinta; (com.) pesado (*dícese de los géneros*); (com.) postrado (*mercado*); *adv* pesadamente; fuerte; **to hang heavy** pasar con extremada lentitud (*dícese del tiempo o las horas*); *s* (*pl:* **-ies**) (theat.) personaje perverso; **heavies** *spl* (coll.) ropa interior gruesa
heavy-armed ['hɛvɪ'ɑrmd] *adj* armado de armas pesadas, armado de armadura pesada
heavy-duty ['hɛvɪ'djutɪ] o ['hɛvɪ'dutɪ] *adj* de servicio pesado, extrafuerte; de altos derechos de aduana
heavy earth *s* (mineral.) tierra pesada
heavy-eyed ['hɛvɪ,aɪd] *adj* de ojos dormidos
heavy-footed ['hɛvɪ'fʊtɪd] *adj* de andar torpe o desmañado; despeado
heavy-handed ['hɛvɪ'hændɪd] *adj* opresor, agobiador; desmañado, torpe
heavy-hearted ['hɛvɪ'hɑrtɪd] *adj* acongojado, afligido, triste
heavy hydrogen *s* (chem.) hidrógeno pesado
heavy industry *s* industria pesada
heavy-laden ['hɛvɪ'ledən] *adj* recargado; agobiado, oprimido
heavy-set ['hɛvɪ'sɛt] *adj* espaldudo, costilludo
heavy spar *s* (mineral.) espato pesado
heavy water *s* (chem.) agua pesada
heavyweight ['hɛvɪ,wet] *s* persona que pesa mucho; persona de mucho pesquis, persona de campanillas; (box.) peso pesado, peso fuerte
Heb. abr. de **Hebrews**
hebdomadal [hɛb'dɑmədəl] *adj* hebdomadario
Hebe ['hibɪ] *s* (myth.) Hebe
hebetude ['hɛbɪtjud] o ['hɛbɪtud] *s* torpeza, estupidez
Hebraic [hɪ'breɪk] *adj* hebraico
Hebraism ['hibreɪzəm] *s* hebraísmo
Hebraist ['hibreɪst] *s* hebraísta; hebraizante
Hebraistic [,hibre'ɪstɪk] *adj* hebreo
Hebraize ['hibreaɪz] *va* hacer hebreo; *vn* hebraizar
Hebrew ['hibru] *adj & s* hebreo; **Hebrews** *spl* (Bib.) Epístola de San Pablo a los Hebreos

Hebrew calendar *s* calendario hebreo
Hebrides, the ['hɛbrɪdiz] las Hébridas
Hecate ['hɛkətɪ] *s* (myth.) Hécate
hecatomb ['hɛkətom] o ['hɛkətum] *s* hecatombe
heckle ['hɛkəl] *va* interrumpir (*a un orador*) con preguntas impertinentes o molestas
hectare ['hɛktɛr] *s* hectárea
hectic ['hɛktɪk] *adj* hético; (coll.) turbulento, agitado; *s* fiebre hética; rubor hético; hético (*enfermo*)
hectocotylus [,hɛktə'katɪləs] *s* (*pl:* **-li** [laɪ]) (zool.) hectocótilo
hectogram o **hectogramme** ['hɛktəgræm] *s* hectogramo
hectograph ['hɛktəgræf] o ['hɛktəgrɑf] *s* hectógrafo; *va* copiar en el hectógrafo
hectoliter ['hɛktə,litər] *s* hectólitro
hectometer ['hɛktə,mitər] *s* hectómetro
Hector ['hɛktər] *s* (myth.) Héctor; (*l.c.*) *s* matón, valentón; *va & vn* atormentar o intimidar con bravatas
Hecuba ['hɛkjubə] *s* (myth.) Hécuba
he'd [hid] contracción de **he had** y de **he would**
hedge [hɛdʒ] *s* seto vivo, cerca viva; cercado, vallado; apuesta compensatoria; operación de bolsa compensatoria; *va* cercar con seto vivo; cercar con vallado; **to hedge in** encerrar, rodear; poner trabas a; *vn* eludir la respuesta, no querer comprometerse; hacer apuestas compensatorias; hacer operaciones de bolsa compensatorias (*para no perder dinero*)
hedgehog ['hɛdʒ,hag] o ['hɛdʒ,hɔg] *s* (zool.) erizo; (zool.) puerco espín
hedgehop ['hɛdʒ,hap] (*pret & pp:* **-hopped;** *ger:* **-hopping**) *vn* (aer.) volar rasando el suelo
hedge mustard *s* (bot.) sisimbrio; (bot.) erisimo; (bot.) epazote
hedge nettle *s* (bot.) ortiga hedionda
hedgerow ['hɛdʒ,ro] *s* cercado de arbustos o árboles pequeños
hedge sparrow *s* (orn.) acentor de bosque
hedonism ['hidənɪzəm] *s* hedonismo
hedonist ['hidənɪst] *s* hedonista
heed [hid] *s* atención, cuidado; **to take heed** poner atención; *va* atender a, hacer caso de; *vn* atender, hacer caso
heedful ['hidfəl] *adj* atento, cuidadoso
heedless ['hidlɪs] *adj* desatento, descuidado; aturdido, incauto
heedlessness ['hidlɪsnɪs] *s* desatención, descuido; aturdimiento, imprudencia
heehaw ['hi,hɔ] *s* rebuzno (*del asno*); risotada; *vn* rebuznar; risotear, reír groseramente
heel [hil] *s* (anat.) calcañar o talón; talón (*parte de la media o el zapato que cubre el calcañar*); tacón (*pieza semicircular del zapato debajo del calcañar*); parte inferior o trasera (*de ciertas cosas*); fin, conclusión; pedazo que queda de un pan o queso casi consumidos; (arch.) talón; (mus.) talón (*del arco del violín*); (naut.) talón (*de la quilla*); (naut.) coz o pie de palo; (rail.) talón (*de la aguja*); (slang) sinvergüenza; **at heel** a los talones; **down at the heel** con el talón muy gastado; desaliñado, mal vestido; desvalido; **out at the heels** destalonado; desaliñado, mal vestido; desvalido; **to cool one's heels** (coll.) hacer antesala, estar esperando mucho tiempo; **to heel** a los talones; **to be at one's heels** pisarle a uno los talones; **to kick one's heels** hacer antesala; esperar impacientemente; **to kick up one's heels** (slang) mostrarse alegre y retozón; (slang) morir; **to lay by the heels** echar a la cárcel, echar al cepo; **to show a clean pair of heels** o **to take to one's heels** poner pies en polvorosa, apretar los talones, batir los talones; **heels over head** patas arriba; *va* seguir de cerca; poner talón a; poner tacón a; poner espolones a (*un gallo de pelea*); *vn* seguir de cerca al amo (*dícese de los perros*); taconear (*al bailar*); (naut.) escorar
heeler ['hilər] *s* taconero; (slang) muñidor (*de cacique político*)
heel lift *s* tapa (*del tacón del zapato*)
heelpiece ['hil,pis] *s* talón
heeltap ['hil,tæp] *s* tapa (*del tacón del zapato*); vino, aguardiente, etc. que se deja en el vaso después de beber
heft [hɛft] *s* (coll.) influencia; **the heft of** (coll.) la mayor parte de, lo más de; *va* levantar; (coll.) sopesar (*tantear el peso de*)
hefty ['hɛftɪ] *adj* (*comp:* **-ier;** *super:* **-iest**) pesado; (coll.) fornido, recio
Hegelian [he'gelɪən] o [hi'dʒilɪən] *adj & s* hegeliano
Hegelianism [he'gelɪənɪzəm] o [hi'dʒilɪənɪzəm] *s* hegelianismo
hegemony [hɪ'dʒɛmənɪ] o ['hɛdʒɪ,monɪ] *s* (*pl:* **-nies**) hegemonía
hegira [hɪ'dʒaɪrə] o ['hɛdʒɪrə] *s* fuga, huída; fuga de Mahoma desde la Meca a Medina; héjira (*era de los mahometanos*)
heifer ['hɛfər] *s* novilla, vaquilla
heigh [haɪ] o [he] *interj* ¡ea! (*para animar*); ¡eh! (*para llamar*); ¡ah! (*para expresar sorpresa*)
heigh-ho ['haɪ'ho] o ['he'ho] *interj* ¡ay!
height [haɪt] *s* altura; cima (*lo más alto*); colmo (*p.ej., de la locura*); crisis (*de la fiebre*)
heighten ['haɪtən] *va* elevar; aumentar; realzar; intensificar; *vn* elevarse; aumentarse; realzarse; intensificarse
heinous ['henəs] *adj* atroz, infame, nefando
heir [ɛr] *s* heredero
heir apparent *s* (*pl:* **heirs apparent**) (law) heredero forzoso
heirdom ['ɛrdəm] *s* herencia
heiress ['ɛrɪs] *s* heredera
heirloom ['ɛr,lum] *s* joya de familia, reliquia de familia
heir presumptive *s* (*pl:* **heirs presumptive**) (law) heredero presuntivo
heirship ['ɛrʃɪp] *s* herencia
hejira [hɪ'dʒaɪrə] o ['hɛdʒɪrə] *s* var. de **hegira**
hektare ['hɛktɛr] *s* var. de **hectare**
hektogram ['hɛktəgræm] *s* var. de **hectogram**
held [hɛld] *pret & pp de* **hold**
Helen ['hɛlən] *s* Elena; (myth.) Helena (*de Troya*)
heliacal [hɪ'laɪəkəl] *adj* (astr.) helíaco
helianthemum [,hilɪ'ænθɪməm] *s* (bot.) heliantemo
helianthin [,hilɪ'ænθɪn] o **helianthine** [,hilɪ'ænθɪn] o [,hilɪ'ænθin] *s* heliantina
helianthus [,hilɪ'ænθəs] *s* (bot.) helianto
helical ['hɛlɪkəl] *adj* hélico
helicoid ['hɛlɪkɔɪd] *adj* helicoide; (bot. & zool.) helicideo; *s* (geom.) helicoide
helicoidal [,hɛlɪ'kɔɪdəl] *adj* helicoidal
helicoid cyme *s* (bot.) cima helicoidea
Helicon ['hɛlɪkan] *s* (hist., myth. & fig.) Helicón; (*l.c.*) *s* (mus.) helicón
Heliconian [,hɛlɪ'konɪən] *adj* heliconio
helicopter [,hɛlɪ'kaptər] *s* (aer.) helicóptero
heliocentric [,hilɪo'sɛntrɪk] *adj* heliocéntrico
helioengraving ['hilɪoɛn,grevɪŋ] *s* heliograbado
heliograph ['hilɪo,græf] o ['hilɪo,grɑf] *s* heliógrafo; *va & vn* comunicar por medio del heliógrafo
heliography [,hilɪ'agrəfɪ] *s* heliografía
Helios ['hilɪas] *s* (myth.) Helios
helioscope ['hilɪo,skop] *s* helioscopio
heliostat ['hilɪo,stæt] *s* helióstato
heliotherapy ['hilɪo,θɛrəpɪ] *s* helioterapia
heliotrope ['hilɪətrop] *s* (bot. & mineral.) heliotropo
heliotropism [,hilɪ'atrəpɪzəm] *s* (biol.) heliotropismo
heliotype ['hilɪo,taɪp] *s* heliotipia; heliotipo
heliport ['hɛlɪ,port] *s* helipuerto
helium ['hilɪəm] *s* (chem.) helio
helix ['hilɪks] *s* (*pl:* **helixes** o **helices** ['hɛlɪsiz]) hélice (*espiral*); (anat., elec. & geom.) hélice; (arch.) voluta
he'll [hil] contracción de **he shall** y de **he will**
hell [hɛl] *s* infierno; madriguera (*de gente maleante*); garito; cajón de sastre; (print.) caja de letras inservibles
Hellas ['hɛləs] *s* Hélade (*Grecia*)
hellbender ['hɛl,bɛndər] *s* (zool.) salamandra gigante norteamericana; (slang) borrachera descabellada
hell-bent ['hɛl'bɛnt] *adj* (slang) muy resuelto,

muy determinado; **hell-bent on** (slang) empeñado en, dirigiéndose con mucho empeño a
hellbroth ['hɛl,brɔθ] o ['hɛl,brɑθ] *s* caldo alterado, caldo infernal
hellcat ['hɛl,kæt] *s* bruja; arpía, mujer perversa
helldiver ['hɛl,daɪvər] *s* (orn.) zambullidor, acintle
helleboraster [,hɛlɪbə'ræstər] *s* (bot.) eleborastro
hellebore ['hɛlɪbor] *s* (bot. & pharm.) eléboro
Hellene ['hɛlin] *s* heleno
Hellenic [hɛ'lɛnɪk] o [hɛ'linɪk] *adj* helénico
Hellenism ['hɛlənɪzəm] *s* helenismo
Hellenist ['hɛlənɪst] *s* helenista
Hellenistic [,hɛlə'nɪstɪk] *adj* helenístico
Hellenization [,hɛlənɪ'zeʃən] *s* helenización
Hellenize ['hɛlənaɪz] *va* helenizar; *vn* helenizarse
Hellespont ['hɛlɪspɑnt] *s* Helesponto
hellfire ['hɛl,faɪr] *s* fuego del infierno
hellgrammite ['hɛlgrəmaɪt] *s* (ent.) larva de insecto neuróptero (*Corydalis cornuta*)
hellhound ['hɛl,haʊnd] *s* perro de los infiernos; demonio; fiera (*persona cruel*)
hellion ['hɛljən] *s* (coll.) pícaro, bribón
hellish ['hɛlɪʃ] *adj* infernal, diabólico
hello [hɛ'lo] *s* (*pl:* **-los**) grito, saludo; *interj* ¡hola!, ¡qué tal!; ¡aló!, ¡diga! (*en el teléfono*); *vn* gritar, saludar
hello girl *s* (coll.) chica telefonista
helm [hɛlm] *s* (naut.) barra o caña del timón, rueda del timón; (fig.) timón; (archaic) yelmo; **to luff the helm** (naut.) tirar del timón para orzar; *va* dirigir, gobernar; (archaic) dar yelmo a, cubrir con yelmo
helmet ['hɛlmɪt] *s* casco (*de la armadura; de soldado, bombero, buzo, etc.*)
helmeted ['hɛlmɪtɪd] *adj* que lleva casco
helminth ['hɛlmɪnθ] *s* ((zool.) helminto
helminthiasis [,hɛlmɪn'θaɪəsɪs] *s* (path.) helmintiasis
helminthology [,hɛlmɪn'θɑlədʒɪ] *s* helmintología
helmsman ['hɛlmzmən] *s* (*pl:* **-men**) (naut.) timonel
Héloïse [elo'iz] *s* Eloísa
helot ['hɛlət] o ['hilət] *s* ilota; (*cap.*) *s* ilota
helotism ['hɛlətɪzəm] o ['hilətɪzəm] *s* ilotismo
helotry ['hɛlətrɪ] o ['hilətrɪ] *s* ilotismo; los ilotas
help [hɛlp] *s* ayuda, socorro; colaboración; ración (*de alimento*); remedio, p.ej., **there is no help for it** no hay remedio para ello; ayudante; criado, criados; empleado, empleados; obreros; **by the help of** con la ayuda de; **to be a great help to** prestar servicios importantes a, ser el brazo derecho de; **to be good help** ser buen ayudante; **to come to the help of** acudir en socorro de ‖ *interj* ¡socorro! ‖ *va* ayudar, socorrer; servir; aliviar, mitigar; remediar, evitar; **it can't be helped** no hay (más) remedio; **so help me God!** ¡así Dios me salve!; **to help along** ayudar (*a uno*) para que siga su camino o para que vaya tirando; **to help down** ayudar a bajar; **to help one with his coat** ayudarle a uno a ponerse el abrigo; **to help oneself** valerse por sí mismo; servirse; **to help one to** servirle a uno (*carne, pan, etc.*); **to help out** ayudar; ayudar a salir; **to help out of** ayudar a salir de; **to help to** + *inf* o **to help** + *inf* ayudar a + *inf;* **to help up** ayudar a subir; ayudar a levantarse; **to not be able to help** + *ger* no poder menos de + *inf,* p.ej., **I couldn't help laughing** no pude menos de reír; **to not be able to help but** + *inf* (coll.) no poder menos de + *inf,* p.ej., **he cannot help but come** no puede menos de venir ‖ *vn* ayudar; servir; **to help out** ayudar
helper ['hɛlpər] *s* ayudante; apoyo; mancebo (*p.ej., en una farmacia o barbería*)
helpful ['hɛlpfəl] *adj* útil, servicial; provechoso
helping ['hɛlpɪŋ] *s* ración, porción (*de alimento*)
helpless ['hɛlplɪs] *adj* débil, impotente; desvalido; incapaz, imposibilitado
helplessness ['hɛlplɪsnɪs] *s* debilidad, impotencia; desamparo; incapacidad
helpmate ['hɛlp,met] o **helpmeet** ['hɛlp,mit] *s* compañero; compañera (*esposa*)
helter-skelter ['hɛltər'skɛltər] *adj, adv & s* cochite hervite
helve [hɛlv] *s* astil, mango
Helvetia [hɛl'viʃə] *s* la Helvecia
Helvetian [hɛl'viʃən] *adj & s* helvecio
Helvetic [hɛl'vɛtɪk] *adj* helvético; *s* protestante suizo
hem [hɛm] *s* tos fingida; (sew.) bastilla, dobladillo, repulgo; *interj* ¡ejem!; (*pret & pp:* **hemmed;** *ger:* **hemming**) *va* (sew.) bastillar, dobladillar, repulgar; **to hem about, around** o **in** encerrar estrechamente; poner trabas a; **to hem out** impedir (*a uno*) que entre; *vn* destoserse; tartalear; **to hem and haw** toser y retoser; tartalear; vacilar
hematic [hi'mætɪk] *adj* hemático
hematin ['hɛmətɪn] o ['himətɪn] *s* (physiol.) hematina
hematite ['hɛmətaɪt] o ['himətaɪt] *s* (mineral.) hematites
hematocele ['hɛməto,sil] o ['himəto,sil] *s* (path.) hematocele
hematocrit ['hɛməto,krɪt] *s* hematócrito
hematoma [,himə'tomə] o [,hɛmə'tomə] *s* (*pl:* **-mata** [mətə] o **-mas**) (path.) hematoma
hematopoiesis [,hɛmətopɔɪ'isɪs] o [,himətopɔɪ'isɪs] *s* (physiol.) hematopoyesis
hematosis [,himə'tosɪs] o [,hɛmə'tosɪs] *s* (physiol.) hematosis
hematoxylin [,himə'tɑksɪlɪn] o [,hɛmə'tɑksɪlɪn] *s* (chem.) hematoxilina
hemelytral [hɛ'mɛlɪtrəl] *adj* hemélitro
hemelytron [hɛ'mɛlɪtrɑn] o **hemelytrum** [hɛ'mɛlɪtrəm] *s* (*pl:* **-tra** [trə]) (ent.) hemélitro
hemeralopia [,hɛmərə'lopɪə] *s* (path.) hemeralopía
hemicellulose [,hɛmɪ'sɛljəlos] *s* (chem.) hemicelulosa
hemicrania [,hɛmɪ'krenɪə] *s* (path.) hemicránea
hemicycle ['hɛmɪ,saɪkəl] *s* hemiciclo
hemihedral [,hɛmɪ'hidrəl] *adj* (cryst.) hemiédrico o hemiedro
hemin ['himɪn] *s* (biochem.) hemina
hemina [hɪ'maɪnə] *s* (*pl:* **-nae** [ni]) (hist.) hemina
hemionus [hɪ'maɪənəs] *s* (zool.) hemíono
hemiplegia [,hɛmɪ'plidʒɪə] *s* (path.) hemiplejía
hemipterous [hɪ'mɪptərəs] *adj* (ent.) hemíptero
hemisphere ['hɛmɪsfɪr] *s* hemisferio
hemispherical [,hɛmɪ'sfɛrɪkəl] *adj* hemisférico
hemispheroid [,hɛmɪ'sfɪrɔɪd] *s* (geom.) hemisferoide
hemistich ['hɛmɪstɪk] *s* hemistiquio
hemiterpene [,hɛmɪ'tʌrpin] *s* (chem.) hemiterpeno
hemline ['hɛm,laɪn] *s* bastilla de la falda, ruedo de la falda, bajo de la falda; **in the coming season the hemline will be higher** en la próxima temporada la falda se llevará más corta
hemlock ['hɛmlɑk] *s* (bot.) cicuta; (bot.) cicuta mayor (*Conium maculatum*); (bot.) abeto del Canadá (*Tsuga canadensis*); cicuta (*veneno*)
hemmer ['hɛmər] *s* repulgador (*persona y máquina*)
hemocyanin [,himo'saɪənɪn] o [,hɛmo'saɪənɪn] *s* (biochem.) hemocianina
hemoglobin [,himo'globɪn] o [,hɛmo'globɪn] *s* (biochem.) hemoglobina
hemoleucocyte [,himə'lukəsaɪt] o [,hɛmə'lukəsaɪt] *s* (anat.) hemoleucocito
hemolysin [,himə'laɪsɪn], [,hɛmə'laɪsɪn] o [hɪ'mɑlɪsɪn] *s* (immun.) hemolisina
hemolysis [hɪ'mɑlɪsɪs] *s* (immun.) hemólisis
hemophilia [,himə'fɪlɪə] o [,hɛmə'fɪlɪə] *s* (path.) hemofilia
hemophiliac [,himə'fɪlɪæk] o [,hɛmə'fɪlɪæk] *s* hemofílico
hemophilic [,himə'fɪlɪk] o [,hɛmə'fɪlɪk] *adj* hemofílico
hemoptysis [hɪ'mɑptɪsɪs] *s* (path.) hemoptisis
hemorrhage ['hɛmərɪdʒ] *s* (path.) hemorragia
hemorrhagic [,hɛmə'rædʒɪk] *adj* hemorrágico

hemorrhagic septicemia *s* (vet.) septicemia hemorrágica
hemorrhoidal [,hɛmə'rɔɪdəl] *adj* hemorroidal
hemorrhoidectomy [,hɛmərɔɪ'dɛktəmɪ] *s* (*pl:* **-mies**) (surg.) hemorroidectomía
hemorrhoids ['hɛmərɔɪdz] *spl* (path.) hemorroides
hemostat ['himəstæt] o ['hɛməstæt] *s* hemostato, pinza hemostática
hemostatic [,himə'stætɪk] o [,hɛmə'stætɪk] *adj & s* (med.) hemostático
hemp [hɛmp] *s* (bot.) cáñamo (*planta y fibra*); hachich
hempen ['hɛmpən] *adj* cañameño
hempseed ['hɛmp,sid] *s* cañamón; (slang) carne de horca
hemstitch ['hɛm,stɪtʃ] *s* (sew.) vainica; *va* (sew.) hacer una vainica en; *vn* (sew.) hacer vainica
hen [hɛn] *s* gallina
henbane ['hɛn,ben] *s* (bot.) beleño
hence [hɛns] *adv* de aquí; fuera de aquí; desde ahora; por lo tanto, por consiguiente; de aquí a, p.ej., **three months hence** de aquí a tres meses; **years hence** cuando hayan pasado muchos años; *interj* ¡fuera de aquí!; **hence with . . . !** ¡quítenme de delante . . . !
henceforth [,hɛns'forθ] o **henceforward** [,hɛns'fɔrwərd] *adv* de aquí en adelante
henchman ['hɛntʃmən] *s* (*pl:* **-men**) secuaz, servidor; muñidor
hencoop ['hɛn,kup] o ['hɛn,kʊp] *s* gallinero
hendecagon [hɛn'dɛkəgɑn] *s* (geom.) endecágono
hendecasyllabic [,hɛndɛkəsɪ'læbɪk] *adj* endecasílabo
hendecasyllable [,hɛndɛkə'sɪləbəl] *s* endecasílabo
hendiadys [hɛn'daɪədɪs] *s* (rhet.) endíadis
henequen o **henequin** ['hɛnɪkɪn] *s* (bot.) henequén (*planta y su filamento*)
henhouse ['hɛn,haʊs] *s* gallinero
henna ['hɛnə] *s* (bot.) alheña, alcana (*Lawsonia inermis*); henna (*materia colorante*); color de alheña; *va* alheñarse (*el pelo*)
hennery ['hɛnərɪ] *s* (*pl:* **-ies**) gallinero
henotheism [,hɛnə'θiɪzəm] *s* henoteísmo
henpeck ['hɛn,pɛk] *va* importunar, tener subordinado (*al marido*)
henpecked husband *s* marido dominado e importunado por su mujer, marido que se deja mandar por su mujer
Henrietta [,hɛnrɪ'ɛtə] *s* Enriqueta
Henry ['hɛnrɪ] *s* Enrique; (*l.c.*) *s* (*pl:* **-ries** o **-rys**) (elec.) henrio
hep [hɛp] *adj* (slang) enterado; **to be hep to** (slang) estar al corriente de; **to put someone hep to** (slang) poner a uno al corriente de
heparin ['hɛpərɪn] *s* (pharm.) heparina
hepatic [hɪ'pætɪk] *adj* hepático; de color del hígado
hepatica [hɪ'pætɪkə] *s* (bot.) hepática
hepatitis [,hɛpə'taɪtɪs] *s* (path.) hepatitis
hepatization [,hɛpətɪ'zeʃən] *s* (path.) hepatización
hepcat ['hɛp,kæt] *s* (slang) experto en jazz, aficionado al jazz
Hephaestus [hɪ'fɛstəs] *s* (myth.) Hefestos
heptagon ['hɛptəgɑn] *s* (geom.) heptágono
heptagonal [hɛp'tægənəl] *adj* heptagonal
heptahedron [,hɛptə'hidrən] *s* (*pl:* **-drons** o **-dra** [drə]) (geom.) heptaedro
heptameter [hɛp'tæmɪtər] *s* heptámetro
heptane ['hɛpten] *s* (chem.) heptano
heptangular [hɛp'tæŋgjələr] *adj* heptangular
heptarchy ['hɛptɑrkɪ] *s* (*pl:* **-chies**) heptarquía; **the Heptarchy** la Heptarquía anglosajona
heptasyllabic [,hɛptəsɪ'læbɪk] *adj* heptasílabo
heptasyllable [,hɛptə'sɪləbəl] *s* heptasílabo
Heptateuch ['hɛptətjuk] o ['hɛptətuk] *s* (Bib.) Heptateuco
her [hʌr] *adj poss* su; el (o su) . . . de ella; *pron pers* la; ella; **to her** le; a ella
Hera ['hirə] o ['hɪrə] *s* (myth.) Hera
Heracles ['hɛrəkliz] *s* (myth.) Heracles
Heraclitus [,hɛrə'klaɪtəs] *s* Heráclito
Herakles ['hɛrəkliz] *s* var. de **Heracles**
herald ['hɛrəld] *s* heraldo; anunciador, precursor; *va* anunciar, ser precursor de
heraldic [hɛ'rældɪk] *adj* heráldico
heraldry ['hɛrəldrɪ] *s* (*pl:* **-ries**) heráldica; blasón, escudo de armas; heraldía (*cargo u oficio de heraldo*); pompa heráldica, ceremonias heráldicas
herb [ʌrb] o [hʌrb] *s* hierba (*planta cuyo tallo nace todos los años*); hierba medicinal, hierba aromática
herbaceous [hʌr'beʃəs] *adj* herbáceo
herbage ['ʌrbɪdʒ] o ['hʌrbɪdʒ] *s* herbaje
herbal ['hʌrbəl] o ['ʌrbəl] *adj* herbario; *s* herbario (*libro*)
herbalist ['hʌrbəlɪst] o ['ʌrbəlɪst] *s* herbolario, simplista
herbarium [hʌr'bɛrɪəm] *s* (*pl:* **-ums** o **-a** [ə]) herbario (*colección; local*)
herb bennet ['bɛnɪt] *s* (bot.) hierba de San Benito
herb doctor *s* herbolario
herbiferous [hʌr'bɪfərəs] *adj* herbífero
herbivorous [hʌr'bɪvərəs] *adj* herbívoro
herbman ['ʌrbmən] o ['hʌrbmən] *s* (*pl:* **-men**) herbolario
herb mercury *s* (bot.) mercurial
herby ['ʌrbɪ] o ['hʌrbɪ] *adj* herboso
Herculaneum [,hʌrkjə'lenɪəm] *s* Herculano
Herculean [hʌr'kjulɪən] o [,hʌrkjə'liən] *adj* hercúleo (*perteneciente a Hércules*); (*l.c.*) *adj* hercúleo (*forzudo, fornido*); laborioso, penoso
Hercules ['hʌrkjəliz] *s* (astr. & myth.) Hércules
herd [hʌrd] *s* manada, hato, rebaño; multitud; chusma; manadero, vaquero; *va* reunir en manada; juntar; *vn* reunirse en manada, ir en manada; ir juntos
herd instinct *s* instinto de rebaño
herdsman ['hʌrdzmən] *s* (*pl:* **-men**) manadero, vaquero
here [hɪr] *adv* aquí; acá; **that's neither here nor there** eso no viene al caso; **the here and the hereafter** esta vida y la futura; **here and there** acá y allá; **here below** acá abajo (*acá en la tierra*); **here is** o **are** aquí tiene Vd.; **here's to you!** ¡a la salud de Vd.!; *adj* presente; *interj* ¡presente!; (*cap.*) ['hiri] *s* (myth.) Hera
hereabout ['hɪrə,baʊt] o **hereabouts** ['hɪrə,baʊts] *adv* por aquí, cerca de aquí
hereafter [hɪr'æftər] o [hɪr'ɑftər] *adv* de aquí en adelante; en lo futuro; en la vida futura; *s* estado futuro; **the hereafter** lo futuro; la vida futura
hereat [hɪr'æt] *adv* en esto; por esto
hereby [hɪr'baɪ] *adv* por este medio; por éstas, por la presente
hereditable [hɪ'rɛdɪtəbəl] *adj* heredable
hereditary [hɪ'rɛdɪ,tɛrɪ] *adj* hereditario
heredity [hɪ'rɛdɪtɪ] *s* (*pl:* **-ties**) (biol.) herencia
herein [hɪr'ɪn] *adv* adjunto, aquí dentro; en esto, en este asunto
hereinafter [,hɪrɪn'æftər] o [,hɪrɪn'ɑftər] *adv* más abajo, más adelante
hereinbefore [hɪr,ɪnbɪ'for] *adv* en lo precedente; **as hereinbefore stated** como queda dicho en los párrafos precedentes
hereinto [hɪr'ɪntu] *adv* en esto
hereof [hɪr'ɑv] *adv* de esto
hereon [hɪr'ɑn] o [hɪr'ɔn] *adv* en esto, sobre esto
here's [hɪrz] contracción de **here is**
heresiarch [hɪ'risɪɑrk] *s* heresiarca
heresy ['hɛrəsɪ] *s* (*pl:* **-sies**) herejía
heretic ['hɛrətɪk] *s* hereje; *adj* herético
heretical [hɪ'rɛtɪkəl] *adj* herético
hereto [hɪr'tu] *adv* a esto, para esto
heretofore [,hɪrtʊ'for] *adv* antes, hasta ahora
hereunder [hɪr'ʌndər] *adv* abajo; en virtud de esto
hereunto [,hɪrʌn'tu] *adv* a esto, para esto
hereupon [,hɪrə'pɑn] *adv* en esto, sobre esto; en seguida
herewith [hɪr'wɪð] o [hɪr'wɪθ] *adv* con esto; adjunto, con la presente; por este medio, de este modo
heritable ['hɛrɪtəbəl] *adj* heredable; heredero
heritage ['hɛrɪtɪdʒ] *s* herencia

herma [ˈhʌrmə] *s* (*pl:* **-mae** [mi] o **-mai** [maɪ]) (hist.) herma
hermaphrodite [hʌrˈmæfrədaɪt] *adj & s* hermafrodita
hermaphrodite brig *s* (naut.) bergantín goleta
hermaphroditic [hʌr,mæfrəˈdɪtɪk] o **hermaphroditical** [hʌr,mæfrəˈdɪtɪkəl] *adj* hermafrodita
hermaphroditism [hʌrˈmæfrədaɪtɪzəm] *s* (biol.) hermafroditismo
hermeneutic [,hʌrməˈnjutɪk] o [,hʌrməˈnutɪk] *adj* hermenéutico; **hermeneutics** *ssg* hermenéutica
Hermes [ˈhʌrmiz] *s* (myth.) Hermes
hermetic [hʌrˈmɛtɪk] o **hermetical** [hʌrˈmɛtɪkəl] *adj* hermético
Hermione [hʌrˈmaɪənɪ] *s* (myth.) Hermíone
hermit [ˈhʌrmɪt] *s* ermitaño
hermitage [ˈhʌrmɪtɪdʒ] *s* ermita
hermit crab *s* (zool.) ermitaño
hermit thrush *s* (orn.) tordo norteamericano (*Hylocichla guttata*)
hernia [ˈhʌrnɪə] *s* (*pl:* **-as** o **-ae** [i]) (path.) hernia
hernial [ˈhʌrnɪəl] *adj* herniario
hero [ˈhɪro] *s* (*pl:* **-roes**) héroe; (*cap.*) *s* (myth.) Hero
Herod [ˈhɛrəd] *s* (Bib.) Herodes
Herodian [hɪˈrodɪən] *adj* herodiano
Herodias [hɪˈrodɪəs] *s* (Bib.) Herodías
Herodotus [hɪˈrɑdətəs] *s* Heródoto
heroic [hɪˈro·ɪk] *adj* heroico; (med.) heroico; *s* poema heroico; **heroics** *spl* lenguaje rimbombante; acto extravagante; verso heroico
heroic age *s* edad heroica, tiempos heroicos
heroical [hɪˈro·ɪkəl] *adj* heroico
heroic couplet *s* estrofa de dos versos heroicos pareados, de cinco yambos cada uno
heroicomic [hɪ,ro·ɪˈkɑmɪk] *adj* heroicocómico
heroic verse *s* verso heroico (*verso que en cada idioma se tiene por más a propósito para la poesía heroica: el pentámetro yámbico en inglés y el endecasílabo yámbico en español*)
heroin [ˈhɛro·ɪn] *s* (pharm.) heroína
heroine [ˈhɛro·ɪn] *s* heroína
heroism [ˈhɛro·ɪzəm] *s* heroísmo
heron [ˈhɛrən] *s* (orn.) garza; (orn.) garza real, airón (*Ardea cinerea*)
heronry [ˈhɛrənrɪ] *s* (*pl:* **-ries**) vivar de garzas
heron's-bill [ˈhɛrənz,bɪl] *s* (bot.) pico de cigüeña
hero worship *s* culto de los héroes
herpes [ˈhʌrpiz] *s* (path.) herpe
herpetic [hərˈpɛtɪk] *adj* herpético
herpetology [,hʌrpɪˈtɑlədʒɪ] *s* herpetología
herring [ˈhɛrɪŋ] *s* (ichth.) arenque
herringbone [ˈhɛrɪŋ,bon] *s* espina de pescado (*en los tejidos*); punto de Hungría, espinapez (*en los entarimados*); *adj* de espina de pescado; a punto de Hungría
herring gull *s* (orn.) gaviota
hers [hʌrz] *pron poss* el suyo, el de ella; **a friend of hers** un amigo suyo
herself [hərˈsɛlf] *pron pers* ella misma; se; sí, sí misma; **with herself** consigo
Hertzian [ˈhɛrtsɪən] *adj* (elec.) herciano o hertziano
Hertzian wave *s* (elec.) onda herciana o hertziana
he's [hiz] contracción de **he is** y de **he has**
Hesiod [ˈhisɪəd] *s* Hesíodo
hesitance [ˈhɛzɪtəns] *s* var. de **hesitancy**
hesitancy [ˈhɛzɪtənsɪ] *s* (*pl:* **-cies**) vacilación
hesitant [ˈhɛzɪtənt] *adj* vacilante
hesitate [ˈhɛzɪtet] *vn* vacilar; **don't hesitate to** + *inf* no tema + *inf*, no tenga miedo de + *inf;* **to hesitate to** + *inf* vacilar en + *inf*
hesitatingly [ˈhɛzɪ,tetɪŋlɪ] *adv* de modo vacilante
Hesper [ˈhɛspər] *s* var. de **Hesperus**
Hesperia [hɛsˈpɪrɪə] *s* Hesperia (*España o Italia*)
Hesperian [hɛsˈpɪrɪən] *adj* hespérido (*occidental*); hesperio (*perteneciente a España o Italia*)
Hesperides [hɛsˈpɛrɪdiz] *spl* (myth.) Hespérides (*cuatro ninfas*); (myth.) jardín de las Hespérides (*cuyos árboles producían manzanas de oro*)
hesperidin [hɛsˈpɛrɪdɪn] *s* (chem.) hesperidina
hesperidium [,hɛspəˈrɪdɪəm] *s* (*pl:* **-a** [ə]) (bot.) hesperidio
Hesperus [ˈhɛspərəs] *s* Héspero (*el planeta Venus*)
Hessian [ˈhɛʃən] *adj* hesiense; *s* hesiense; soldado mercenario hesiense
Hessian boots *spl* botas adornadas con borlas, muy usadas en Inglaterra en el siglo XIX
Hessian crucible *s* crisol de arcilla muy refractaria
Hessian fly *s* (ent.) cecidomio
hetaera [hɪˈtɪrə] *s* (*pl:* **-rae** [ri]) (hist.) hetera
hetaira [hɪˈtaɪrə] *s* (*pl:* **-rai** [raɪ]) var. de **hetaera**
heterocercal [,hɛtərəˈsʌrkəl] *adj* (ichth.) heterocerco
heterochlamydeous [,hɛtərəkləˈmɪdɪəs] *adj* (bot.) heteroclamídeo
heteroclite [ˈhɛtərə,klaɪt] *adj* heteróclito; *s* persona o cosa heteróclitas; (gram.) palabra heteróclita
heterocyclic [,hɛtərəˈsaɪklɪk] o [,hɛtərəˈsɪklɪk] *adj* (chem.) heterocíclico
heterodox [ˈhɛtərədɑks] *adj* heterodoxo
heterodoxy [ˈhɛtərə,dɑksɪ] *s* (*pl:* **-ies**) heterodoxia
heterodyne [ˈhɛtərə,daɪn] *adj* (rad.) heterodino; *s* (rad.) heterodina (*oscilador*); *va & vn* (rad.) heterodinar
heterodyne reception *s* (rad.) recepción heterodina
heteroecism [,hɛtəˈrisɪzəm] *s* (biol.) heteroecia
heterogamous [,hɛtəˈrɑgəməs] *adj* (bot.) heterógamo
heterogamy [,hɛtəˈrɑgəmɪ] *s* heterogamia
heterogeneity [,hɛtərədʒɪˈniɪtɪ] *s* (*pl:* **-ties**) heterogeneidad
heterogeneous [,hɛtərəˈdʒinɪəs] *adj* heterogéneo
heteronym [ˈhɛtərə,nɪm] *s* heterónimo
heteronymous [,hɛtəˈrɑnɪməs] *adj* heterónimo
heterophyllous [,hɛtərəˈfɪləs] *adj* (bot.) heterofilo
heterophylly [ˈhɛtərə,fɪlɪ] *s* (bot.) heterofilia
heteroplasty [ˈhɛtərə,plæstɪ] *s* (surg.) heteroplastia
heterotrophic [,hɛtərəˈtrɑfɪk] *adj* (biol.) heterótrofo
hetman [ˈhɛtmən] *s* (*pl:* **-mans**) hetmán (*caudillo de cosacos*)
heuristic [hjuˈrɪstɪk] *adj* heurístico
hew [hju] (*pret:* **hewed**; *pp:* **hewed** o **hewn**) *va* cortar, tajar; hachear; desbastar; picar (*piedra*); labrar (*madera, piedra*); **to hew down** cortar, destroncar, derribar o tumbar a hachazos; **to hew one's way through** abrirse paso a fuerza de hachazos por entre; *vn* dar hachazos; **to hew close to the line** (coll.) hilar delgado
hewn [hjun] *pp de* **hew**
hex [hɛks] *s* (coll.) bruja, hechicera; *va* (coll.) embrujar
hexachord [ˈhɛksəkɔrd] *s* (mus.) hexacordo
hexafluoride [,hɛksəˈfluəraɪd] o [,hɛksəˈfluərɪd] *s* (chem.) hexafluoruro
hexagon [ˈhɛksəgɑn] *s* (geom.) hexágono
hexagonal [hɛksˈægənəl] *adj* hexagonal
hexagram [ˈhɛksəgræm] *s* hexagrama
hexahedral [,hɛksəˈhidrəl] *adj* hexaédrico
hexahedron [,hɛksəˈhidrən] *s* (*pl:* **-drons** o **-dra** [drə]) (geom.) hexaedro
hexameter [hɛksˈæmɪtər] *adj & s* hexámetro
hexamethylenetetramine [,hɛksə,mɛθɪlin,tɛtrəˈmin] *s* (chem.) hexametilenotetramina
hexane [ˈhɛksen] *s* (chem.) hexano
hexangular [hɛksˈæŋgjələr] *adj* hexángulo
hexapetalous [,hɛksəˈpɛtələs] *adj* (bot.) hexapétalo
hexapod [ˈhɛksəpɑd] *adj* hexápodo; *s* (ent.) hexápodo
Hexateuch [ˈhɛksətjuk] o [ˈhɛksətuk] *s* (Bib.) Hexateuco
hexose [ˈhɛksos] *s* (chem.) hexosa
hey [he] *interj* ¡eh!, ¡oiga!, ¡oye!

heyday ['he,de] *s* época de esplendor, época de mayor prosperidad, vigor, etc.
Hezekiah [,hezɪ'kaɪə] *s* (Bib.) Ezequías
hf. abr. de **half**
hg. abr. de **hectogram**
H.H. abr. de **Her Highness, His Highness** y **His Holiness**
hhd. abr. de **hogshead**
H.I. abr. de **Hawaiian Islands**
hiatus [haɪ'etəs] *s* (*pl:* **-tuses** o **-tus**) abertura, laguna; hiato (*en un manuscrito o texto impreso*); (anat., gram. & pros.) hiato
hibernal [haɪ'bʌrnəl] *adj* hibernal, invernal
hibernate ['haɪbərnet] *vn* invernar; (biol.) hibernar
hibernation [,haɪbər'neʃən] *s* invernación; (biol.) invernación, hibernación
Hibernian [haɪ'bʌrnɪən] *adj & s* hibernés o hiberniano
hibiscus [hɪ'bɪskəs] o [haɪ'bɪskəs] *s* (bot.) hibisco
hiccough o **hiccup** ['hɪkʌp] *s* hipo; *va* decir con hipos; *vn* hipar
hick [hɪk] *adj & s* (slang) campesino; (slang) palurdo
hickey ['hɪkɪ] *s* adminículo, chisme; (elec.) casquillo conectador, manguito sujetador; (elec.) doblador de tubos
hickory ['hɪkərɪ] *s* (*pl:* **-ries**) (bot.) nuez dura
hickory nut *s* nuez dura
hid [hɪd] *pret & pp de* **hide**
hidden ['hɪdən] *pp de* **hide;** *adj* escondido, oculto; recóndito, obscuro; secreto
hide [haɪd] *s* cuero, piel; **hides** *spl* corambre, curtidos; **neither hide nor hair** ni un vestigio; **to tan someone's hide** (coll.) zurrarle a uno la badana; (*pret & pp:* **hided**) *va* aporrear, medir las costillas a; (*pret:* **hid;** *pp:* **hidden** o **hid**) *va* esconder, ocultar; encubrir; disimular; *vn* esconderse, ocultarse; **to hide out** (coll.) recatarse (*en lugar apartado*)
hide-and-seek ['haɪdənd'sik] *s* escondite; **to play hide-and-seek** jugar al escondite
hidebound ['haɪd,baʊnd] *adj* que tiene la piel pegada a los huesos; dogmático, obstinado, fanático
hideous ['hɪdɪəs] *adj* feote; horrible, espantoso
hideousness ['hɪdɪəsnɪs] *s* fealdad; horribilidad
hide-out ['haɪd,aʊt] *s* (coll.) guarida, escondrijo, refugio
hiding ['haɪdɪŋ] *s* ocultación; escondite; (coll.) tunda, zurra; **in hiding** escondido, oculto; emboscado
hidrosis [hɪ'drosɪs] *s* (path.) hidrosis
hie [haɪ] (*pret & pp:* **hied;** *ger:* **hieing** o **hying**) *va* apresurar; incitar; **hie thee** date prisa; **hie thee home** apresúrate a volver a casa; *vn* correr, volar, ir volando
hierarch ['haɪərɑrk] *s* jerarca
hierarchic [,haɪə'rɑrkɪk] o **hierarchical** [,haɪə'rɑrkɪkəl] *adj* jerárquico
hierarchize ['haɪərɑrkaɪz] *va* jerarquizar
hierarchy ['haɪə,rɑrkɪ] *s* (*pl:* **-chies**) jerarquía
hieratic [,haɪə'rætɪk] o **hieratical** [,haɪə'rætɪkəl] *adj* hierático
hieroglyph ['haɪərə,glɪf] *s* jeroglífico
hieroglyphic [,haɪərə'glɪfɪk] *adj & s* jeroglífico
hieroglyphical [,haɪərə'glɪfɪkəl] *adj* jeroglífico
Hieronymite [,haɪə'rɑnɪmaɪt] *adj & s* jerónimo
hierophant ['haɪərəfænt] o [haɪ'ɛrəfænt] *s* hierofanta o hierofante
hi-fi ['haɪ'faɪ] *adj* (coll.) de alta fidelidad; *s* (coll.) alta fidelidad
hi-fi fan *s* (coll.) aficionado a la alta fidelidad
higgle ['hɪgəl] *vn* regatear, discutir (*sobre precios*)
higgledy-piggledy ['hɪgəldɪ'pɪgəldɪ] *adj* confuso, revuelto; *adv* confusamente, a río revuelto, sin orden ni concierto; *s* confusión
high [haɪ] *adj* alto; de alto, de altura; sumo (*pontífice*); crecido (*río*); agudo (*sonido*); fuerte (*viento*); bueno (*ánimo, humor*); altanero (*modo de proceder*); (coll.) borracho; (cook.) manido; **high and dry** en seco; plantado, abandonado, desamparado; **high and mighty** (coll.) muy arrogante; *adv* altamente, sumamente; en sumo grado; a gran precio; **to aim high** poner el tiro muy alto; **to come high** venderse caro; **to fly high** ser muy optimista; ser muy ambicioso, confiar mucho en su buena estrella; **high and low** por todas partes; **higher than** más alto que; más arriba de (*sobre*); *s* colmo; (aut.) toma directa, marcha directa; (com.) (el) precio más alto; **on high** en las alturas, en el cielo
high altar *s* altar mayor
highball ['haɪ,bɔl] *s* highball (*whisky con hielo y agua gaseosa*); *vn* (slang) avanzar o pasar con rapidez
high-blooded ['haɪ'blʌdɪd] *adj* de noble alcurnia
high blood pressure *s* (path.) hipertensión arterial
highborn ['haɪ,bɔrn] *adj* de ilustre cuna, linajudo
highboy ['haɪ,bɔɪ] *s* cómoda alta sostenida por patas altas
highbred ['haɪ,brɛd] *adj* de familia ilustre; cortés, fino
highbrow ['haɪ,braʊ] *adj* (slang) erudito, docto; (slang) de o para gente erudita; *s* (slang) erudito, docto
high chair *s* silla alta
High Church *s* alta iglesia (*rama conservadora de la Iglesia anglicana*)
High-Church ['haɪ,tʃʌrtʃ] *adj* ritualista
high-colored ['haɪ,kʌlərd] *adj* de color subido; encarnado
high comedy *s* alta comedia
high command *s* (mil.) alto mando, alto comando
high commissioner *s* alto comisario
high-compression ['haɪkəm'prɛʃən] *adj* de alta compresión
high cost of living *s* carestía de la vida
high day *s* día de fiesta
higher criticism *s* alta crítica (*especialmente de la Biblia*)
higher education *s* enseñanza superior
higher-up [,haɪər'ʌp] *s* (coll.) superior jerárquico
high explosive *s* explosivo rompedor
highfalutin o **highfaluting** [,haɪfə'lutən] *adj* (coll.) pomposo; (coll.) soberbio, presuntuoso
high fashion *s* alta costura
high fidelity *s* (rad.) alta fidelidad
high-fidelity ['haɪfaɪ'dɛlɪtɪ] o ['haɪfɪ'dɛlɪtɪ] *adj* (rad.) de alta fidelidad
highflier ['haɪ,flaɪər] *s* persona, cosa, pájaro de alto vuelo; extravagante; despilfarrador
high-flown ['haɪ,flon] *adj* ampuloso, pomposo; extravagante; soberbio, presuntuoso
highflyer ['haɪ,flaɪər] *s* var. de **highflier**
high frequency *s* (elec.) alta frecuencia
high-frequency ['haɪ'frikwənsɪ] *adj* (elec.) de alta frecuencia
high-gain ['haɪ'gen] *adj* (rad.) de alta ganancia
high gear *s* (aut.) toma directa, marcha directa
High German *s* altoalemán
High-German ['haɪ'dʒʌrmən] *adj* altoalemán
high-grade ['haɪ'gred] *adj* de calidad superior
high hand *s* arbitrariedad, despotismo, altanería
high-handed ['haɪ'hændɪd] *adj* arbitrario, despótico, altanero
high hat *s* sombrero de copa
high-hat ['haɪ'hæt] *adj* (slang) esnob; (slang) elegante, que es el colmo de la elegancia; **to be high-hat** (slang) tener mucho copete; [,haɪ'hæt] (*pret & pp:* **-hatted;** *ger:* **-hatting**) *va* (slang) desairar, tratar con desprecio estudiado
high-heeled shoe ['haɪ,hild] *s* zapato de tacón alto
high horse *s* presunción, ademán arrogante; **on a high horse** muy arrogante
highjack ['haɪ,dʒæk] *va* (coll.) var. de **hijack**
highjacker ['haɪ,dʒækər] *s* (coll.) var. de **hijacker**
high jinks [dʒɪŋks] *s* (coll.) jarana, jaleo, payasada
high jump *s* (sport) salto de altura

highland ['haɪlənd] *adj* de (las) tierras altas; *s* meseta, región montañosa; **highlands** *spl* tierras altas, montañas; **Highlands** *spl* región montañosa de Escocia
highlander ['haɪləndər] *s* montañés; (*cap.*) *s* montañés de Escocia; soldado de un regimiento de montañeses de Escocia
Highland fling *s* baile muy vivo de las tierras altas de Escocia
high life *s* alta sociedad, gran mundo
high light *s* (lo) más notable o interesante (*de un viaje, fiesta, etc.*); toque de luz (*de una pintura, fotografía, etc.*)
highlight ['haɪ,laɪt] *va* inundar de luz; (fig.) destacar
highly ['haɪlɪ] *adv* altamente, sumamente; en sumo grado; con aplauso general; a gran precio; **to speak highly of** decir mil bienes de
High Mass *s* (eccl.) misa cantada o mayor
high-minded ['haɪ'maɪndɪd] *adj* noble, magnánimo; arrogante, orgulloso
highness ['haɪnɪs] *s* altura; (*cap.*) *s* Alteza (*título*)
high noon *s* pleno mediodía; **at high noon** en pleno mediodía
high-octane gasoline [,haɪ'ɑkten] *s* gasolina de alto octanaje
high-pass filter ['haɪ,pæs] o ['haɪ,pɑs] *s* (elec.) filtro paso superior, filtro de paso alto
high-pitched ['haɪ'pɪtʃt] *adj* agudo, aflautado, chillón; escarpado; tenso, impresionable
high-powered ['haɪ'pauərd] *adj* de gran potencia, de alta potencia
high-pressure ['haɪ'prɛʃər] *adj* de alta presión; (fig.) emprendedor, enérgico; *va* (coll.) apremiar, instar; **to high-pressure someone to do something** (coll.) instarle a uno a que haga una cosa
high-priced ['haɪ'praɪst] *adj* de alto costo, de precio elevado
high priest *s* sumo sacerdote
high relief *s* alto relieve
highroad ['haɪ,rod] *s* carretera, camino real; (fig.) camino real
high school *s* instituto, instituto de segunda enseñanza
high sea *s* mar gruesa; **high seas** *spl* alta mar
high society *s* alta sociedad, gran mundo
high-sounding ['haɪ,saundɪŋ] *adj* altisonante
high-speed ['haɪ'spid] *adj* rápido, de alta velocidad
high-speed drill *s* broca de alta velocidad
high-speed steel *s* acero rápido, acero de corte rápido
high-spirited ['haɪ'spɪrɪtɪd] *adj* orgulloso; animoso, valiente; fogoso (*caballo*)
high spirits *spl* alegría, buen humor; **in high spirits** alegre, animoso
high-strung ['haɪ'strʌŋ] *adj* tenso, impresionable, excitable
high style *s* alta costura
hight [haɪt] *adj* (archaic) llamado
high tension *s* (elec.) alta tensión
high-tension ['haɪ'tɛnʃən] *adj* (elec.) de alta tensión
high terms *s* palabras lisonjeras
high-test ['haɪ'tɛst] *adj* que pasa pruebas rigurosas; de alta volatilidad
high-test fuel *s* supercarburante
high tide *s* (naut.) marea alta, pleamar; (fig.) apogeo
high time *s* hora, p.ej., **it is high time for you to leave** ya es hora de que se marche Vd.; (slang) jarana, parranda, francachela
high-toned ['haɪ'tond] *adj* agudo, aflautado, chillón; noble, caballeroso; (coll.) elegante, de buen tono
high treason *s* alta traición
high-up ['haɪ'ʌp] *adj* de alto copete
high-voltage ['haɪ'voltɪdʒ] *adj* (elec.) de alto voltaje, de alta tensión
high water *s* aguas altas; marea alta, pleamar
high-water mark ['haɪ'wɔtər] o ['haɪ'wɑtər] *s* línea de aguas altas; línea de la marea alta; (fig.) apogeo, colmo
highway ['haɪ,we] *s* carretera, camino real; (fig.) camino real
highway department *s* servicio de tránsito de caminos
highwayman ['haɪ,wemən] *s* (*pl:* **-men**) bandolero, salteador de caminos
highway robber *s* salteador de caminos
highway robbery *s* salteamiento
highway signals *spl* señales de ruta
high words *spl* palabras airadas, palabras ofensivas
H.I.H. abr. de **His** o **(Her) Imperial Highness**
hijack ['haɪ,dʒæk] *va* (coll.) asaltar a un contrabandista quitándole (*el licor u otro contrabando en camino*); (coll.) asaltar (*a un contrabandista*); (coll.) robar; (coll.) apoderarse violentamente de (*un avión en vuelo*)
hijacker ['haɪ,dʒækər] *s* (coll.) salteador o atracador (*cuyas víctimas son otros bandidos o contrabandistas*); (coll.) robador
hike [haɪk] *s* (coll.) caminata; (coll.) aumento; *va* elevar de un tirón, sacar violentamente; (coll.) aumentar; *vn* (coll.) dar una caminata o caminatas, caminar por lugares agrestes
hiker ['haɪkər] *s* (coll.) caminante, aficionado a las caminatas
hilarious [hɪ'lɛrɪəs] o [haɪ'lɛrɪəs] *adj* regocijado, jubiloso
hilarity [hɪ'lærɪtɪ] o [haɪ'lærɪtɪ] *s* hilaridad, regocijo bullicioso
Hilary ['hɪlərɪ] *s* Hilario
hill [hɪl] *s* colina, collado, cerro; montoncillo; *va* amontonar; (agr.) acobijar, aporcar, recalzar; *vn* amontonarse
hillbilly ['hɪl,bɪlɪ] *s* (*pl:* **-lies**) (coll.) rústico montañés (*del sur de los EE.UU.*)
hilling ['hɪlɪŋ] *s* amontonamiento; (agr.) acobijo, aporcado
hillock ['hɪlək] *s* altozano, cerrejón
hillside ['hɪl,saɪd] *s* ladera
hilly ['hɪlɪ] *adj* (*comp:* **-ier;** *super:* **-iest**) colinoso, montuoso; empinado
hilt [hɪlt] *s* empuñadura, puño; **up to the hilt** completamente
hilum ['haɪləm] *s* (*pl:* **-la** [lə]) (anat.) hilio; (bot.) hilo
H.I.M. abr. de **His** o **(Her) Imperial Majesty**
him [hɪm] *pron pers* le, lo; él; **to him** le; a él
Himalaya, The [hɪ'mɑljə] o [,hɪmə'leə] el Himalaya; **The Himalayas** el Himalaya, los montes Himalaya
Himalaya Mountains *spl* montes Himalaya
Himalayan [hɪ'mɑljən] o [,hɪmə'leən] *adj* himalayo
himself [hɪm'sɛlf] *pron pers* él mismo; se; sí, sí mismo; **with himself** consigo
Hind. abr. de **Hindu, Hindustan** y **Hindustani**
hind [haɪnd] *adj* trasero, posterior; *s* (*pl:* **hinds** o **hind**) cierva; (*pl:* **hinds**) labriego, gañán, campesino
hindbrain ['haɪnd,bren] *s* (anat.) rombencéfalo; (anat.) metencéfalo
hinder ['haɪndər] *adj* trasero, posterior; ['hɪndər] *va* estorbar, impedir, dificultar; **to hinder from** + *ger* impedir + *inf* o impedir que + *subj*
hindermost ['haɪndərmost] *adj* var. de **hindmost**
hind-foremost ['haɪnd'formost] *adv* (dial.) con lo de atrás delante
Hindi ['hɪndi] *s* hindí
hindmost ['haɪndmost] *adj* postrero, último
Hindoo ['hɪndu] *adj* & *s* var. de **Hindu**
hindquarter ['haɪnd,kwɔrtər] *s* cuarto trasero
hindrance ['hɪndrəns] *s* estorbo, impedimento, obstáculo
hindsight ['haɪnd,saɪt] *s* percepción a posteriori, percepción tardía; mira posterior (*de un arma de fuego*)
Hindu ['hɪndu] *adj* & *s* hindú
Hinduism ['hɪnduɪzəm] *s* hinduísmo
Hindustan [,hɪndu'stɑn] *s* el Indostán
Hindustani [,hɪndu'stɑnɪ] *adj* indostánico; *s* indostaní o hindustaní (*lengua*)
hinge [hɪndʒ] *s* charnela, bisagra, gozne; (b.b.) cartivana; (mach.) charnela; (zool.) charnela (*de las dos valvas de los moluscos*); (fig.) punto capital, (lo) más esencial; *va* engoznar; *vn* girar sobre un gozne; **to hinge on** o **upon** depender de

hinged [hɪndʒd] *adj* articulado, de bisagra
hinge joint *s* (anat.) gínglimo
hinny [ˈhɪnɪ] *s* (*pl:* **-nies**) burdégano
hint [hɪnt] *s* indirecta, puntada, insinuación; consejo; **to take the hint** darse por aludido; *va* insinuar; indicar; *vn* echar una indirecta; echar indirectas; **to hint at** insinuar; dar a entender que se desea (*una cosa*)
hinterland [ˈhɪntər,lænd] *s* interior (*de un territorio colonial*); región lejana de los centros urbanos
hip [hɪp] *s* (anat.) cadera; escaramujo (*fruto*); lima, caballete (*arista formada por el encuentro de dos vertientes*); (arch.) lima tesa (*ángulo*); **to have someone on** o **upon the hip** tenerle a uno acorralado, tenerle a uno entre la espada y la pared; **hip and thigh** duramente, sin piedad
hipbone [ˈhɪp,bon] *s* (anat.) cía, hueso de la cadera
Hipparchus [hɪˈpɑrkəs] *s* Hiparco
hipped [hɪpt] *adj* renco; a cuatro aguas (*tejado*); (coll.) triste, melancólico; (coll.) enojado, ofendido; (coll.) obsesionado; **hipped on** (coll.) obsesionado por
hippety-hoppety [ˈhɪpɪtɪˈhɑpɪtɪ] *adv* (coll.) a coxcojita
hippo [ˈhɪpo] *s* (*pl:* **-pos**) (coll.) hipopótamo
hippocampus [,hɪpəˈkæmpəs] *s* (*pl:* **-pi** [paɪ]) (anat., ichth. & myth.) hipocampo
hippocras [ˈhɪpəkræs] *s* hipocrás
Hippocrates [hɪˈpɑkrətiz] *s* Hipócrates
Hippocratic [,hɪpoˈkrætɪk] *adj* hipocrático
Hippocratic oath *s* juramento de Hipócrates
Hippocrene [ˈhɪpokrin] o [,hɪpoˈkrinɪ] *s* (myth.) Hipocrene
hippodrome [ˈhɪpədrom] *s* hipódromo
hippogriff [ˈhɪpəgrɪf] *s* (myth.) hipogrifo
Hippolytus [hɪˈpɑlɪtəs] *s* (myth.) Hipólito
hippopotamus [,hɪpəˈpɑtəməs] *s* (*pl:* **-muses** o **-mi** [maɪ]) (zool.) hipopótamo
hip rafter *s* lima
hip roof *s* tejado a cuatro aguas
hipshot [ˈhɪp,ʃɑt] *adj* renco
hircine [ˈhʌrsaɪn] o [ˈhʌrsɪn] *adj* hircino
hircocervus [,hʌrkəˈsʌrvəs] *s* (myth.) hircocervo
hire [haɪr] *s* alquiler; salario; **for hire** u **on hire** de alquiler; **to work for hire** trabajar por salario; *va* alquilar (*p.ej., un coche*); ajustar (*p.ej., a un criado*); *vn* **to hire out** (coll.) alquilarse, ajustarse
hired girl *s* criada
hired man *s* (coll.) mozo de campo
hireling [ˈhaɪrlɪŋ] *adj* alquiladizo; mercenario; *s* alquiladizo
hire purchase *s* (Brit.) arriendo con opción de compra
hirsute [ˈhʌrsut] o [ˈhʌrsjut] *adj* hirsuto
his [hɪz] *adj poss* su; el (o su) . . . de él; *pron poss* el suyo, el de él; **a friend of his** un amigo suyo
Hispania [hɪsˈpenɪə] *s* Hispania
Hispanic [hɪsˈpænɪk] *adj* hispánico
Hispanicism [hɪsˈpænɪsɪzəm] *s* hispanismo
Hispanicize [hɪsˈpænɪsaɪz] *va* hispanizar
Hispaniola [,hɪspənˈjolə] *s* Santo Domingo (*isla dividida en dos partes: Haití y la República Dominicana*)
hispanist [ˈhɪspənɪst] o [hɪsˈpænɪst] *s* hispanista
Hispano-Moresque [hɪsˈpenomoˈrɛsk] *adj* hispanoárabe
Hispanophile [hɪsˈpænofaɪl] *adj & s* hispanófilo
Hispanophobe [hɪsˈpænofob] *adj & s* hispanófobo
hispid [ˈhɪspɪd] *adj* híspido
hiss [hɪs] *s* silbido, siseo; *va* silbar, sisear (*una escena, a un actor por malo*); expresar o manifestar (*desagrado*) con siseos; *vn* silbar, sisear
hist. abr. de **historian** y **history**
hist [hɪst] *interj* ¡chitón!; ¡ce!
histamine [ˈhɪstəmin] o [ˈhɪstəmɪn] *s* (chem.) histamina
histidine [ˈhɪstɪdin] o [ˈhɪstɪdɪn] *s* (chem.) histidina
histologist [hɪsˈtɑlədʒɪst] *s* histólogo
histology [hɪsˈtɑlədʒɪ] *s* histología
histolysis [hɪsˈtɑlɪsɪs] *s* (biol.) histólisis
histone [ˈhɪston] *s* (biochem.) histona
historian [hɪsˈtorɪən] *s* historiador
historiated [hɪsˈtorɪ,etɪd] *adj* (arch.) historiado
historic [hɪsˈtɑrɪk] o [hɪsˈtɔrɪk] o **historical** [hɪsˈtɑrɪkəl] o [hɪsˈtɔrɪkəl] *adj* histórico
historically [hɪsˈtɑrɪkəlɪ] o [hɪsˈtɔrɪkəlɪ] *adv* históricamente
historicity [,hɪstəˈrɪsɪtɪ] *s* historicidad
historiographer [hɪs,torɪˈɑgrəfər] *s* historiógrafo
historiography [hɪs,torɪˈɑgrəfɪ] *s* historiografía
history [ˈhɪstərɪ] *s* (*pl:* **-ries**) historia
histrionic [,hɪstrɪˈɑnɪk] *adj* histriónico; teatral, insincero; **histrionics** *spl* histrionismo; actitud teatral, modales teatrales o insinceros
hit [hɪt] *s* golpe; tiro certero, golpe bien dado; censura acerba; (coll.) éxito; (baseball) batazo; **to make a hit** (coll.) dar golpe; **to make a hit with** (coll.) caer en la gracia a; (*pret & pp:* **hit;** *ger:* **hitting**) *va* golpear, pegar; chocar con, dar con, dar contra; dar en (*p.ej., el blanco*); tropezar con (*una dificultad, un problema, etc.*); afectar mucho (*una cosa a una persona*); censurar acerbamente; ser del gusto de; **to hit it off** avenirse bien, llevarse bien; **to hit off** remedar; describir o representar con gran acierto; *vn* chocar; acertar; **to hit against** dar contra; **to hit on** o **upon** dar con (*lo que se busca*); llegar a; ocurrirse, p.ej., **how did you hit on that?** ¿cómo se le ocurrió eso?; **hit or miss** a la buena de Dios, salga pez o salga rana
hit-and-run [ˈhɪtənˈrʌn] *adj* que atropella y se da a la huída, que abandona a la víctima
hitch [hɪtʃ] *s* tirón; cojera; broche, traba; fiador, pasador, postillo; dificultad, impedimento; obstáculo; (naut.) vuelta de cabo; **without a hitch** sin tropiezo, a pedir de boca; *va* mover a tirones, adelantar a poquitos; atar, sujetar; enganchar (*un caballo*); uncir (*bueyes*); (slang) casar; **to hitch up** enganchar (*un caballo*); uncir (*bueyes*); alzar (*p.ej., los pantalones*) de un tirón; (slang) casar; *vn* cojear; enredarse; (coll.) armonizar; **to hitch up** (slang) casarse
hitchhike [ˈhɪtʃ,haɪk] *vn* (coll.) hacer auto-stop, ir por auto-stop
hitching post *s* poste para atar a las cabalgaduras
hither [ˈhɪðər] *adv* acá, hacia acá; **hither and thither** acá y allá; *adj* citerior, de la parte de acá
hithermost [ˈhɪðərmost] *adj* (el) más cercano
hitherto [,hɪðərˈtu] o [ˈhɪðər,tu] *adv* hasta ahora, hasta aquí
hitherward [ˈhɪðərwərd] o **hitherwards** [ˈhɪðərwərdz] *adv* hacia acá
Hitlerism [ˈhɪtlərɪzəm] *s* hitlerismo
Hitlerite [ˈhɪtləraɪt] *s* hitleriano
hit-or-miss [ˈhɪtərˈmɪs] *adj* descuidado, casual, fortuito
hit parade *s* (rad.) los números musicales que gozan de más popularidad en la actualidad
hit record *s* (coll.) disco de mucho éxito
hit-run [ˈhɪtˈrʌn] *adj* var. de **hit-and-run**
hit song *s* canción de mucho éxito
hitter [ˈhɪtər] *s* golpeador
Hittite [ˈhɪtaɪt] *adj & s* heteo o hitita
hive [haɪv] *s* colmena; (fig.) enjambre; **hives** *spl* (path.) urticaria; *va* encorchar (*abejas*); acopiar (*miel*) en colmena; (fig.) hacer acopio de; *vn* entrar (*el enjambre*) en la colmena; vivir aglomerados
H.J. abr. de **hic jacet** (Lat.) **here lies**
hl. abr. de **hectoliter**
hm. abr. de **hectometer**
H.M. abr. de **Her Majesty** y **His Majesty**
H.M.S. abr. de **Her** o **(His) Majesty's Service** y **Her** o **(His) Majesty's Ship**
ho [ho] *interj* ¡ah!; ¡oiga!
hoar [hor] *adj* (archaic) var. de **hoary**
hoard [hord] *s* cúmulo; tesoro escondido; *va* atesorar; acaparar, acumular secretamente; *vn* guardar víveres, atesorar dinero
hoarding [ˈhordɪŋ] *s* atesoramiento; acaparamiento, acumulación secreta; (Brit.) valla de tablas provisional que encierra un edificio que se está construyendo o reparando; (Brit.) cartelera

hoarfrost ['hor,frɔst] o ['hor,frɑst] *s* helada blanca, escarcha
hoarhound ['hor,haʊnd] *s* var. de **horehound**
hoarse [hors] *adj* ronco
hoarseness ['horsnɪs] *s* ronquedad; ronquera (*afección de la laringe*)
hoary ['horɪ] *adj* (*comp:* **-ier;** *super:* **-iest**) cano; vetusto
hoary-headed ['horɪ'hɛdɪd] *adj* encanecido
hoatzin [ho'ætsɪn] *s* (orn.) hoazín
hoax [hoks] *s* mistificación, pajarota; *va* mistificar
hob [hɑb] *s* repisa interior de la chimenea; hito (*en el juego de tejos*); duende; (mach.) fresa; **to play** o **to raise hob** (coll.) causar trastornos; **to play hob with** (coll.) trastornar
hobble ['hɑbəl] *s* cojera; traba, manea; (fig.) dificultad, atolladero; *va* dejar cojo; trabar, manear; dificultar, poner trabas a; *vn* cojear; tambalear
hobbledehoy ['hɑbəldɪ,hɔɪ] *s* mozalbete; muchacho grandullón
hobble skirt *s* falda de medio paso
hobby ['hɑbɪ] *s* (*pl:* **-bies**) comidilla (*tema, manía*); trabajo preferido (*fuera del habitual*); **to ride a hobby** entregarse demasiado al tema favorito, distraerse mucho con la ocupación favorita
hobbyhorse ['hɑbɪ,hɔrs] *s* caballito (*palo en que los niños montan a caballo*); caballo mecedor
hobgoblin ['hɑb,gɑblɪn] *s* duende, trasgo; bu, coco
hobnail ['hɑb,nel] *s* tachuela; *va* clavetear con tachuelas; (fig.) atropellar
hobnob ['hɑb,nɑb] (*pret & pp:* **-nobbed;** *ger:* **-nobbing**) *vn* rozarse, codearse; beber juntos; **to hobnob with** codearse con
hobo ['hobo] *s* (*pl:* **-bos** o **-boes**) vagabundo
Hobson's choice ['hɑbsənz] *s* alternativa entre la cosa ofrecida o ninguna
hock [hɑk] *s* corvejón (*del caballo; de varias aves gallináceas*); vino del Rin; (slang) empeño; *va* desjarretar; (slang) empeñar
hockey ['hɑkɪ] *s* (sport) hockey, chueca
hockey stick *s* hockey, palo de hockey
hocus ['hokəs] (*pret & pp:* **-cused** o **-cussed;** *ger:* **-cusing** o **-cussing**) *va* burlar, engañar; narcotizar, atontar con drogas; echar una droga estupefaciente a (*una copa de licor*)
hocus-pocus ['hokəs'pokəs] *s* abracadabra; burla, engaño; juego de manos; (*pret & pp:* **-cused** o **-cussed;** *ger:* **-cusing** o **-cussing**) *va* (coll.) estafar; *vn* (coll.) estafar; (coll.) hacer juegos de manos
hod [hɑd] *s* capacho, cuezo (*para llevar argamasa, ladrillos, etc.*); cubo para carbón
hod carrier *s* peón de albañil, peón de mano
hodden ['hɑdən] *s* (Scotch) tejido basto de lana sin teñir
hodgepodge ['hɑdʒ,pɑdʒ] *s* baturrillo, ensaladilla, salpicón
hodman ['hɑdmən] *s* (*pl:* **-men**) peón de albañil, peón de mano; escritor mercenario
hoe [ho] *s* azada, azadón; (*pret & pp:* **hoed;** *ger:* **hoeing**) *va & vn* azadonar
hoecake ['ho,kek] *s* torta o pan de maíz
hog [hɑg] o [hɔg] *s* (zool.) cerdo, puerco; (coll.) cerdo, puerco; **to go the whole hog** (slang) entregarse sin reservas, llegar hasta el último límite; (*pret & pp:* **hogged;** *ger:* **hogging**) *va* (slang) tragarse lo mejor de
hogback ['hɑg,bæk] o ['hɔg,bæk] *s* cuchilla (*cerro escarpado*)
hog cholera *s* (vet.) cólera de los cerdos
hoggish ['hɑgɪʃ] o ['hɔgɪʃ] *adj* puerco; comilón, glotón; egoísta
hog Latin *s* latín de cocina
hogmanay ['hɑgmə'ne] *s* (Scotch) la noche vieja
hognose snake ['hɑg,noz] o ['hɔg,noz] *s* (zool.) heterodón (*reptil*)
hog plum *s* (bot.) jobo
hog's-fennel ['hɑgz,fɛnəl] o ['hɔgz,fɛnəl] *s* (bot.) servato
hogshead ['hɑgz,hɛd] o ['hɔgz,hɛd] *s* pipa que contiene de 63 a 140 galones norteamericanos; medida de capacidad que equivale a 63 galones norteamericanos, o sea 238,5 litros
hogtie ['hɑg,taɪ] o ['hɔg,taɪ] (*pret & pp:* **-tied;** *ger:* **-tying**) *va* atar las patas de, atar las manos y los pies de; (coll.) inmovilizar, paralizar
hogwash ['hɑg,wɑʃ] o ['hɔg,wɔʃ] *s* bazofia
hoiden ['hɔɪdən] *s* var. de **hoyden**
hoi polloi, the [,hɔɪ pə'lɔɪ] la gente común, las masas
hoist [hɔɪst] *s* (coll.) alzamiento, empujón hacia arriba; torno izador, montacargas; grúa; *va* alzar, levantar; enarbolar; izar
hoity-toity ['hɔɪtɪ'tɔɪtɪ] *adj* arrogante, altanero; frívolo, veleidoso; **to be hoity-toity** ponerse tan alto; *s* arrogancia, altanería; frivolidad, veleidad; *interj* ¡ caramba!
hokey-pokey ['hokɪ'pokɪ] *s* (coll.) abracadabra; (coll.) burla, engaño; (coll.) juego de manos; (coll.) helado barato que se vende en las calles
hokum ['hokəm] *s* (slang) payasadas, chistes de baja ley (*en el teatro*); (slang) sensiblerías; (slang) tonterías, música celestial
hold [hold] *s* agarro; asa, mango; autoridad, influencia, dominio; (mus.) calderón; (naut.) bodega; (aer.) cabina de carga; (sport) presa (*en la lucha*); **to get, lay** o **take hold of** agarrar, coger; apoderarse de; **to loosen one's hold** desasirse; **to take hold** morder (*un tornillo*) ‖ (*pret & pp:* **held**) *va* tener, guardar, retener; apoyar, sostener; agarrar, coger; sujetar (*p.ej., con un alfiler*); contener, tener cabida para; ocupar (*un cargo, puesto, etc.*); celebrar (*una reunión*); sostener (*una opinión*); juzgar, hacer (*responsable*); (mus.) sostener (*una nota*); **to hold back** detener; retener; contener, refrenar; **to hold down** tener sujeto; oprimir; (slang) mantenerse en (*un cargo, puesto, etc.*); **to hold in** refrenar; **to hold off** mantener alejado; refrenar; **to hold one's own** mantenerse firme, no perder terreno; **to hold out** extender, ofrecer; excluir; retener; **to hold over** aplazar, diferir; **to hold together** impedir que (*una cosa*) se despegue o se descomponga o se deshaga; mantener juntos; **to hold up** apoyar, sostener; detener; alzar, tener suspendido; (coll.) atracar, robar ‖ *vn* mantenerse firme o fiel; seguir vigente, ser valedero; seguir, continuar; asirse; pegarse; opinar; **to hold back** detenerse; contenerse, refrenarse; **to hold forth** arengar, declamar, perorar; **to hold in** contenerse; **to hold off** esperar; mantenerse a distancia, mostrarse frío; **to hold on** agarrarse bien, tenerse bien agarrado; aguantar; **to hold on to** agarrarse bien de, asirse de; afirmarse en; **to hold out** no cejar; ir tirando; durar; (slang) retener algo prometido o debido; **to hold out for** insistir en; **to hold over** continuar desempeñando un cargo (*cuando lo natural sería dejarlo*); **to hold to** agarrarse bien de; afirmarse en; **to hold together** no despegarse, no descomponerse, no deshacerse; mantenerse juntos; **to hold up** continuar, durar; **to hold with** convenir con, estar de acuerdo con; **hold on!** ¡ un momento!; **hold on there!** ¡ paso a paso!, ¡ ténganse todos!
holdall ['hold,ɔl] *s* funda
holdback ['hold,bæk] *s* estorbo, restricción; cejadero (*en los carruajes*); calapuerta
holder ['holdər] *s* posesor, tenedor; arrendatario; agarrador, cojinillo (*para coger, p.ej., un plato caliente*); boquilla (*para poner el cigarro o cigarrillo*); poseedor (*p.ej., de un récord*); titular (*p.ej., de un pasaporte*); sostén, sostenedor (*persona y cosa*); mango, puño, asa, sustentáculo; (com.) portador (*de una letra*); porta- (*en palabras compuestas españolas*), p.ej., **electrode holder** portaelectrodo
holder-on ['holdər'ɑn] o ['holdər'ɔn] *s* sufridor (*obrero*); sufridera
holdfast ['hold,fæst] o ['hold,fɑst] *s* aldabilla; agarradero; (bot.) disco adhesivo
holding ['holdɪŋ] *s* posesión, tenencia; terreno; **holdings** *spl* valores habidos
holding company *s* sociedad de control, compañía tenedora (*de valores de otras empresas*)
holding pattern *s* (aer.) circuito cerrado en que un avión da vueltas a una altura fija hasta recibir la orden de aterrizar
holdover ['hold,ovər] *s* (coll.) continuación, resto; (coll.) consecuencias; (com.) suma que

pasa de una página o cuenta a otra; (slang) malestar que se siente al acabar de dormir la mona
holdup [ˈhold,ʌp] *s* detención; (slang) atraco, asalto
holdup man *s* (slang) atracador
hole [hol] *s* agujero; cavidad, hueco, hoyo; ojo (*en el queso, pan, etc.*); guarida (*de animales; de gente maleante*); cochitril (*habitación estrecha y desaseada*); calabozo; charco, remanso (*en un río*); ancón, ensenada; (sport) agujero; (coll.) atascadero, bache (*en un camino*); (coll.) apuro, aprieto; (coll.) defecto; **in a hole** (slang) en un aprieto; **in the hole** (coll.) adeudado, perdidoso; **to burn a hole in one's pocket** írsele a uno (*el dinero*) de entre las manos; **to make a hole in** agotar gran cantidad de; **to make a hole in one** (golf) conseguir de un solo golpe desde el tee que la pelota entre en el agujero; **to pick holes in** (coll.) hallar defectos en, poner reparos a ‖ *va* agujerear; (golf) meter en el agujero ‖ *vn* encovarse; **to hole out** (golf) conseguir que la pelota entre en el agujero; **to hole up** encovarse; buscar un escondrijo, buscar un rincón cómodo; hibernar (*un animal*)
holey [ˈholɪ] *adj* agujereado, hoyoso
holiday [ˈhɑlɪde] *s* día de fiesta; vacación; *adj* de fiesta, festivo
holiday attire *s* trapos de cristianar
holidays with pay *spl* (Brit.) vacaciones retribuídas
holiness [ˈholɪnɪs] *s* santidad; **his Holiness** su Santidad
holla [həˈlɑ] o [ˈhɑlə] *s, interj, va & vn* var. de **hollo**
Holland [ˈhɑlənd] *s* Holanda; (*l.c.*) *s* tela de lino o de lino y algodón (*que se usa para fabricar transparentes, para cubrir muebles, etc.*); **Hollands** *s* ginebra holandesa
hollandaise sauce [ˈhɑlən,dez] *s* salsa holandesa
Hollander [ˈhɑləndər] *s* holandés
Holland gin *s* ginebra holandesa
hollo [həˈlo] o [ˈhɑlo] *s* (*pl:* **-los**) grito; saludo; grito de triunfo; *interj* ¡ah!; ¡hola!; ¡vítor!; *va* decir a gritos; *vn* gritar
holloa [həˈlo] o [ˈhɑlo] *s, interj, va & vn* var. de **hollo**
hollow [ˈhɑlo] *adj* hueco, ahuecado; ahuecado, sepulcral (*dícese de la voz*); hundido (*dícese de los ojos o las mejillas*); hambriento; falso, engañoso, insincero, sin substancia; *adv* **to beat all hollow** (coll.) vencer completamente; *s* cavidad, hueco; depresión; vallecito; hueco (*de la mano*); *va* ahuecar, excavar; **to hollow out** ahuecar, excavar
hollow-eyed [ˈhɑlo,aɪd] *adj* con los ojos hundidos, trasojado
hollow-ground [ˈhɑloˈgraʊnd] *adj* afilado con cara cóncava, vaciado
holly [ˈhɑlɪ] *s* (*pl:* **-lies**) (bot.) acebo
hollyhock [ˈhɑlɪhɑk] *s* (bot.) malva arbórea, loca, real o rósea
holm [hom] *s* vega; isleta de río; (bot.) encina
holmium [ˈholmɪəm] *s* (chem.) holmio
holm oak *s* (bot.) encina
holocaine [ˈhɑləken] *s* (pharm.) holocaína
holocaust [ˈhɑləkɔst] *s* holocausto (*sacrificio; destrucción total causado por un incendio; estrago general*)
Holocene [ˈhɑləsin] *adj* (geol.) holoceno
Holofernes [,hɑləˈfʌrniz] *s* (Bib.) Holofernes
holograph [ˈhɑləgræf] o [ˈhɑləgrɑf] *adj & s* ológrafo
holohedral [,hɑləˈhidrəl] *adj* (cryst.) holoédrico
holothurian [,hɑləˈθʊrɪən] *s* (zool.) holoturia
holster [ˈholstər] *s* pistolera
holy [ˈholɪ] *adj* (*comp:* **-lier;** *super:* **-liest**) santo; sagrado
Holy Alliance *s* Santa Alianza
Holy Bible *s* Santa Biblia
Holy City *s* Ciudad Santa (*Jerusalén, Roma, la Meca, etc.*); cielo, mansión de Dios
Holy Communion *s* sagrada comunión
holyday [ˈholɪ,de] o **holy day** *s* (eccl.) fiesta, día de guardar, día de precepto
holyday of obligation *s* (eccl.) día de guardar, día de precepto
Holy Father *s* Padre Santo
Holy Ghost *s* Espíritu Santo
Holy Grail *s* Santo Grial
Holy Land *s* Tierra santa (*lugares de Palestina*)
Holy Office *s* Santo Oficio
holy of holies *s* sanctasanctórum
holy oil *s* santo óleo
holy orders *spl* (eccl.) órdenes sagradas o sagradas órdenes; **to take holy orders** ordenarse, recibir las órdenes sagradas
Holy Roman Empire *s* Sacro Imperio Romano-Germánico
holy rood *s* crucifijo; (*caps.*) *s* Santa Cruz
Holy Sacrament *s* santísimo sacramento
Holy Saturday *s* sábado de gloria, sábado santo
Holy Scripture *s* Sagrada Escritura
Holy See *s* Santa Sede
Holy Sepulcher *s* santo sepulcro
Holy Spirit *s* Espíritu Santo
holystone [ˈholɪ,ston] *s* (naut.) piedra de cubierta; *va* (naut.) limpiar con piedra y arena
Holy Synod *s* santo sínodo (*de la Iglesia rusa*)
Holy Thursday *s* Jueves Santo; (Anglican Church) fiesta de la Ascensión
holy water *s* agua bendita
Holy Week *s* semana santa
Holy Writ *s* Sagrada Escritura
homage [ˈhɑmɪdʒ] o [ˈɑmɪdʒ] *s* homenaje (*respeto*); (feud.) homenaje, pleito homenaje
home [hom] *s* casa, domicilio, hogar; patria chica; asilo (*para enfermos, pobres, etc.*); patria (*p.ej., de las artes*); (biol.) habitación; (sport) meta, límite, término; **at home** en casa; en su propio país; a gusto; de recibo; al corriente; (sport) en campo propio; **away from home** fuera de casa; **make yourself at home** está Vd. en su casa, haga como si estuviera en su casa, siéntase Vd. en su casa; *adj* casero, doméstico; nativo; regional; nacional; certero, eficaz; *adv* en casa; a casa; a o en su suelo nativo; **to bring** o **to drive home** exponer de modo muy convincente; **to see home** acompañar a casa, llevar a casa; **to strike home** dar en lo vivo; *va* mandar a casa; dar domicilio a; *vn* volver a casa; habitar; buscar la querencia
home appliances *spl* utensilios domésticos
homebody [ˈhom,bɑdɪ] *s* (*pl:* **-ies**) hogareño; acaserado (Am.)
homebred [ˈhom,brɛd] *adj* casero; sencillo, inculto, tosco
home-brew [ˈhomˈbru] *s* vino o aguardiente caseros
home-coming [ˈhom,kʌmɪŋ] *s* regreso al hogar
home country *s* suelo natal
home delivery *s* distribución a domicilio
home economics *s* economía doméstica
home fleet *s* escuadra que defiende la metrópoli inglesa
home freezer *s* heladora casera
home front *s* frente doméstico
home-grown [ˈhomˈgron] *adj* casero (*dícese de las verduras y frutas*)
homeland [ˈhom,lænd] *s* patria, tierra natal; (*cap.*) *s* (Brit.) metrópoli (*a distinción de las colonias*)
homeless [ˈhomlɪs] *adj* sin casa ni hogar; inhabitable, inhospedable
home life *s* vida de familia, vida de hogar
homelike [ˈhom,laɪk] *adj* como de casa; cómodo
home-loving [ˈhom,lʌvɪŋ] *adj* casero, hogareño; acaserado (Am.)
homely [ˈhomlɪ] *adj* (*comp:* **-lier;** *super:* **-liest**) feo; sencillo, simple, llano; casero, doméstico
homemade [ˈhomˈmed] *adj* casero
homemaker [ˈhom,mekər] *s* ama de casa
home office *s* casa central, oficina o establecimiento central o principal; (*caps.*) *s* (Brit.) ministerio de la Gobernación
homeopath [ˈhomɪəpæθ] o [ˈhɑmɪəpæθ] *s* homeópata
homeopathic [,homɪəˈpæθɪk] o [,hɑmɪəˈpæθɪk] *adj* homeopático
homeopathist [,homɪˈɑpəθɪst] o [,hɑmɪˈɑpəθɪst] *s* var. de **homeopath**

homeopathy [ˌhomɪ'ɑpəθɪ] o [ˌhɑmɪ'ɑpəθɪ] *s* homeopatía
home plate *s* (baseball) puesto meta
home port *s* puerto de origen
Homer ['homər] *s* Homero; (*l.c.*) *s* (coll.) paloma mensajera; (baseball) jonrón
Homeric [ho'mɛrɪk] *adj* homérico
Homeric laughter *s* risa homérica
home rule *s* autonomía, gobierno autónomo
home run *s* (baseball) cuadrangular, jonrón
Home Secretary *s* (Brit.) ministro de Gobernación
homesick ['homˌsɪk] *adj* nostálgico; **to be homesick (for)** sentir nostalgia (de)
homesickness ['homˌsɪknɪs] *s* nostalgia, morriña de la tierra
homespun ['homˌspʌn] *adj* casero, hilado en casa; sencillo, llano; *s* cachera, tela de fabricación casera; tela que remeda la de fabricación casera
homestead ['homstɛd] *s* heredad, casa y sus terrenos; finca rural inalienable
homesteader ['homstɛdər] *s* dueño de una heredad; (U.S.A.) colono que ha recibido sus tierras del gobierno nacional
home stretch *s* último trecho, esfuerzo final (*de una carrera*)
home town *s* ciudad natal
homeward ['homwərd] *adj* de regreso; *adv* hacia casa; hacia su país
homewards ['homwərdz] *adv* hacia casa; hacia su país
homework ['homˌwʌrk] *s* trabajo en casa, trabajo a domicilio; trabajo escolar, deber
homey ['homɪ] *adj* (*comp:* **homier;** *super:* **homiest**) (coll.) agradable, cómodo, sosegado, íntimo
homicidal [ˌhɑmɪ'saɪdəl] *adj* homicida
homicide ['hɑmɪsaɪd] *s* homicidio (*acción*); homicida (*persona*)
homiletic [ˌhɑmɪ'lɛtɪk] *adj* de la homilía o las homilías; exhortatorio; **homiletics** *ssg* homilética
homiliarium [ˌhɑmɪlɪ'ɛrɪəm] *s* homiliario
homilist ['hɑmɪlɪst] *s* homilista
homily ['hɑmɪlɪ] *s* (*pl:* **-lies**) homilía
homing ['homɪŋ] *adj* querencioso; (mil.) buscador del blanco, seguidor
homing pigeon *s* paloma mensajera
hominy ['hɑmɪnɪ] *s* maíz molido
homocercal [ˌhomə'sʌrkəl] *adj* (ichth.) homocerco
homochlamydeous [ˌhomәklə'mɪdɪəs] *adj* (bot.) homoclamídeo
homogeneity [ˌhomodʒɪ'niɪtɪ] o [ˌhɑmodʒɪ'niɪtɪ] *s* (*pl:* **-ties**) homogeneidad
homogeneous [ˌhomo'dʒinɪəs] o [ˌhɑmo'dʒinɪəs] *adj* homogéneo
homogenization [hoˌmɑdʒɪnɪ'zeʃən] o [ˌhoməˌdʒinɪ'zeʃən] *s* homogenización, homogeneización
homogenize [ho'mɑdʒɪnaɪz] o ['homədʒənaɪz] *va* homogenizar, homogeneizar
homogenized milk leche homogeneizada
homograph ['hɑməgræf] o ['hɑməgrɑf] *s* homógrafo
homographic [ˌhɑmə'græfɪk] *adj* homógrafo
homologous [ho'mɑləgəs] *adj* homólogo
homologue ['hɑmələg] o ['hɑmәlɑg] *s* cosa homóloga; (biol.) parte u órgano homólogos
homology [ho'mɑlədʒɪ] *s* (*pl:* **-gies**) homología
homonym ['hɑmənɪm] *s* homónimo
homonymous [ho'mɑnɪməs] *adj* homónimo
homonymy [ho'mɑnɪmɪ] *s* homonimia
homophone ['hɑməfon] *s* palabra homófona; letra homófona
homophonic [ˌhɑmə'fɑnɪk] *adj* (mus.) homófono
homophonous [ho'mɑfənəs] *adj* (phonet.) homófono
homophony [ho'mɑfənɪ] o ['hɑməˌfonɪ] *s* (phonet. & mus.) homofonía
homopterous [ho'mɑptərəs] *adj* (ent.) homóptero
homosexual [ˌhomə'sɛkʃuəl] *adj* & *s* homosexual
homosexuality [ˌhoməˌsɛkʃu'ælɪtɪ] *s* homosexualidad
homunculus [ho'mʌŋkjələs] *s* (*pl:* **-li** [laɪ]) homúnculo, hombrecillo; figurín
hon. abr. de **honorably** y **honorary**
Hon. abr. de **Honorable**
Honduran [hɑn'durən] *adj* & *s* hondureño
Honduras [hɑn'durəs] *s* Honduras
hone [hon] *s* piedra de afilar; *va* afilar con piedra
honest ['ɑnɪst] *adj* honrado, recto, probo; honesto (*recatado, decente*); genuino; bien habido o bien adquirido (*dinero*)
honesty ['ɑnɪstɪ] *s* honradez, rectitud, probidad; honestidad; (bot.) hierba de la plata
honey ['hʌnɪ] *s* miel; dulzura; (coll.) vida mía, querido, querida; **it's a honey** (slang) es una preciosidad; *adj* meloso, dulce; (coll.) querido; (*pret & pp:* **-eyed** o **-ied**) *va* enmelar, untar con miel, endulzar con miel; adular, lisonjear; *vn* hablar con cariño, portarse blanda y suavemente
honeybee ['hʌnɪˌbi] *s* (ent.) abeja de miel, abeja doméstica
honeycomb ['hʌnɪˌkom] *s* panal; *adj* apanalado; *va* disponer a manera de panal; acribillar; llenar, penetrar
honeycomb coil *s* (rad.) bobina de panal, bobina nido de abeja
honeycomb radiator *s* (aut.) radiador de colmena, radiador de panal
honeycomb stomach *s* (zool.) redecilla
honey creeper *s* (orn.) azucarero
honeydew ['hʌnɪˌdju] o ['hʌnɪˌdu] *s* liga dulce (*de ciertas plantas e insectos*); melón muy dulce, blanco y terso
honeyed ['hʌnɪd] *adj* enmelado; meloso, dulce
honey locust *s* (bot.) acacia de tres espinas
honeymoon ['hʌnɪˌmun] *s* luna de miel; viaje de bodas, viaje de novios; *vn* pasar la luna de miel
honey of rose *s* (pharm.) miel rosada, rodomiel
honeysuckle ['hʌnɪˌsʌkəl] *s* (bot.) madreselva
honeywort ['hʌnɪˌwʌrt] *s* (bot.) ceriflor; (bot.) cruciata
honied ['hʌnɪd] *adj* var. de **honeyed**
honk [hɑŋk] o [hɔŋk] *s* graznido (*del ganso silvestre*); pitazo, bocinazo (*del automóvil*); *va* tocar (*la bocina*); *vn* graznar; tocar la bocina, pitar
honkytonk ['hɑŋkɪtɑŋk] o ['hɔŋkɪtɔŋk] *s* (slang) tasca, taberna de mala muerte
honor ['ɑnər] *s* honor; (*cap.*) *s* señoría (*título*); **honors** *spl* honores; (bridge) honores; **in honor of** en honor de; **to deem it an honor to** + *inf* honrarse de + *inf;* **to do** o **to show honor to** hacer honor a; **to do the honors** hacer los honores; *va* honrar; hacer honor a (*su firma*); aceptar, pagar
honorable ['ɑnərəbəl] *adj* honrado (*comerciante, negocio, etc.*); honroso (*comportamiento, puesto, etc.*); honorable (*digno de ser honrado*); (*cap.*) *adj* Honorable (*título*)
honorable mention *s* mención honorífica, mención honrosa
honorarium [ˌɑnə'rɛrɪəm] *s* (*pl:* **-ums** o **-a** [ə]) honorario
honorary ['ɑnəˌrɛrɪ] *adj* honorario
honorary doctor's degree *s* título de doctor honorario
honorary member *s* miembro de honor
honorific [ˌɑnə'rɪfɪk] *adj* honorífico; *s* antenombre
honors of war *spl* honores de la guerra
honor system *s* acatamiento voluntario del reglamento
honour ['ɑnər] *s* & *va* (Brit.) var. de **honor**
hooch [hutʃ] *s* (slang) licor, bebida alcohólica; (slang) licor de contrabando
-hood *suffix s* -dad, p.ej., **brotherhood** hermandad; **falsehood** falsedad; **likelihood** probabilidad; -ez, p.ej., **childhood** niñez; **widowhood** viudez
hood [hud] *s* capilla; capirote (*que cubre el rostro*); capillo o capirote (*de las aves de cetrería*); muceta o capirote (*de los doctores en los actos universitarios*); sombrerete (*de chimenea*); (aut.) capó, cubierta; (naut.) tambucho; (slang) gamberro; *va* encapirotar; ocultar; encapillar (*a un halcón*)

hooded ['hʊdɪd] *adj* capilludo; encapirotado; encapillado (*halcón*)
hoodlum ['hudləm] *s* (coll.) gamberro, maleante, matón
hoodman-blind ['hʊdmən,blaɪnd] *s* (archaic) gallina ciega (*juego*)
hoodoo ['hudu] *s* vodú o vudú; (coll.) aojo, mala suerte; (coll.) cenizo o gafe; *va* aojar, traer mala suerte a
hoodwink ['hʊdwɪŋk] *va* vendar los ojos a; burlar, engañar, emprimar
hooey ['huɪ] *s* (slang) música celestial; *interj* (slang) ¡música celestial!
hoof [huf] o [hʊf] *s* casco, pezuña; pata (*de caballo, toro, etc.*); (hum.) pata (*del hombre*); animal ungulado; **on the hoof** en pie (*viviente; dícese del ganado*); *va & vn* (coll.) caminar; **to hoof it** (coll.) caminar, ir a pie; (slang) bailar
hoofbeat ['huf,bit] o ['hʊf,bit] *s* pisada (*de animal ungulado, aludiendo al ruido*)
hoofed [huft] o [hʊft] *adj* ungulado
hook [hʊk] *s* gancho; aldabilla (*gancho para cerrar una puerta, ventana, etc.*); anzuelo (*para pescar*); enganche (*para unir*); ángulo, recodo; hoz; (baseball & golf) vuelo torcido (*de la pelota*); (box.) crochet, golpe de gancho; (mus.) rabo (*de una corchea*); (fig.) anzuelo (*trampa*); **by hook or by crook** por fas o por nefas, a todo trance; **on one's own hook** (coll.) por cuenta propia; **to get the hook** (coll.) ser silbado (*un actor*); (coll.) ser echado de patitas a la calle; **to swallow the hook** (coll.) picar en el anzuelo, tragar el anzuelo ‖ *va* enganchar; encorvar, doblar; dar forma de anzuelo a; pescar, coger (*un pez*); acornar, herir con los cuernos; (baseball) lanzar (*la pelota*) imponiéndole vuelo torcido; (box.) dar un golpe de gancho a; (coll.) birlar, robar; **to hook in** echar el gancho a; **to hook it** (slang) irse, huir; **to hook on** acoplar con; **to hook up** enganchar; sujetar con corchetes; (elec.) montar ‖ *vn* engancharse; encorvarse, doblarse; tener forma de anzuelo; **to hook on** acoplarse con
hooka o **hookah** ['hʊkə] o ['hukə] *s* narguile
hook and eye *s* corchete (*broche compuesto de macho y hembra*)
hook and ladder *s* carro de escaleras de incendio
hooked [hʊkt] *adj* ganchudo, encorvado
hooked rug *s* tapete de crochet (*generalmente de fabricación casera*)
hooker ['hʊkər] *s* (naut.) balandro; (naut.) barcarrón
hook ladder *s* escalera de ganchos
hookup ['hʊk,ʌp] *s* montaje; (rad.) montaje; (rad.) esquema de montaje; (coll.) alianza, pacto
hookworm ['hʊk,wʌrm] *s* (zool.) anquilostoma; (path.) anquilostomiasis, anemia de los túneles, clorosis de Egipto
hookworm disease *s* (path.) anquilostomiasis, anemia de los túneles, clorosis de Egipto
hooky ['hʊkɪ] *adj* ganchudo, encorvado; *s* **to play hooky** hacer novillos
hooligan ['hulɪgən] *s* gamberro
hooliganism ['hulɪgənɪzəm] *s* gamberrismo
hoop [hup] o [hʊp] *s* aro; (croquet) aro; *va* enarcar, enzunchar
hooper ['hupər] o ['hʊpər] *s* tonelero
hoopoe ['hupu] *s* (orn.) abubilla, upupa
hoop skirt *s* miriñaque
hooray [hʊ're] *s, interj, va & vn* var. de **hurrah**
Hoosier ['huʒər] *s* natural o habitante del estado de Indiana, EE.UU.
hoot [hut] *s* ululato, resoplido; sofión; grito; *va* dar grita a; silbar, reprobar a gritos; manifestar a gritos; echar a gritos (*p.ej., a un cómico*); *vn* ulular, resoplar
hoot owl *s* (orn.) autillo, cárabo
hop [hɑp] *s* brinquito, saltito; (coll.) vuelo en avión; (coll.) sarao; (coll.) baile; (bot.) lúpulo u hombrecillo; **hops** *spl* lúpulo (*flores disecadas*); (*pret & pp:* **hopped**; *ger:* **hopping**) *va* (coll.) cruzar o saltar de un salto; (coll.) atravesar (*p.ej., el mar*) en avión; (coll.) subir a (*un tren, taxi, etc.*); mezclar el lúpulo en (*la cerveza*); *vn* brincar, saltar; avanzar a saltitos; saltar a la pata coja (*saltar en un pie*); recoger lúpulo; **to hop off** (coll.) partir en avión; (coll.) bajar de (*un tren, taxi, etc.*); **to hop on** (coll.) subir a (*un tren, taxi, etc.*)
hope [hop] *s* esperanza; **to hope against hope** esperar desesperando; *va & vn* esperar; **to hope for** esperar; **to hope to** + *inf* esperar + *inf*
hope chest *s* arca que encierra la ropa, etc., que una joven guarda para cuando se case
hopeful ['hopfəl] *adj* esperanzado (*que tiene esperanza*); esperanzador (*que da esperanzas*); **young hopeful** muchacho prometedor, muchacha prometedora
hopeless ['hoplɪs] *adj* desesperanzado, desahuciado; desesperado (*p.ej., caso*)
hoplite ['hɑplaɪt] *s* hoplita
hop-o'-my-thumb ['hɑpəmaɪ'θʌm] *s* enano, gorgojo
hopper ['hɑpər] *s* persona o cosa que avanza a saltitos; persona o cosa que salta a la pata coja; (ent.) saltamontes; tolva; tragante (*de un alto horno*)
hopper-bottom car ['hɑpər,bɑtəm] *s* (rail.) vagón tolva
hopscotch ['hɑp,skɑtʃ] *s* infernáculo
hop tree *s* (bot.) cola de zorrillo
Horace ['hɑrɪs] o ['hɔrɪs] *s* Horacio
Horatian [ho'reʃən] *adj* horaciano
horde [hord] *s* horda
horehound ['hor,haʊnd] *s* (bot.) marrubio; extracto de marrubio; dulce de marrubio
horizon [hə'raɪzən] *s* horizonte; (fig.) horizonte
horizontal [,hɑrɪ'zɑntəl] o [,hɔrɪ'zɑntəl] *adj & s* horizontal
horizontal bars *spl* (sport) barras horizontales
horizontal hold *s* (telv.) bloqueo horizontal
horizontal rudder *s* (aer.) timón de profundidad
horizontal stabilizer *s* (aer.) plano de profundidad
hormonal [hɔr'monəl] *adj* hormonal
hormone ['hɔrmon] *s* (physiol.) hormón u hormona
horn [hɔrn] *s* cuerno (*prolongación ósea; materia*); asta o cuerno (*del toro*); (ent.) cuerno (*antena*); (fig.) cuerno (*de la luna, del yunque, etc.*); (mus. & naut.) cuerno; (mus.) trompa de armonía; bocina (*del automóvil o el fonógrafo*); promontorio; **to blow the horn** tocar la bocina; **to blow** o **toot one's own horn** cantar sus propias alabanzas; **to draw in** o **to pull in one's horns** contenerse, volverse atrás; *adj* de cuerno; *va* acornar, dar cornadas a; proveer de cuernos; *vn* tocar un cuerno; **to horn in** (slang) entremeterse (en)
hornbeam ['hɔrn,bim] *s* (bot.) carpe; (bot.) lechillo, palo de barranco (*Carpinus caroliniana*)
hornbill ['hɔrn,bɪl] *s* (orn.) cálao
hornblende ['hɔrn,blɛnd] *s* (mineral.) hornablenda
hornbook ['hɔrn,bʊk] *s* cartel (*para enseñar a leer*); cartilla (*para aprender a leer*)
horned [hɔrnd] *adj* cornudo, enastado
horned toad *s* (zool.) lagarto cornudo
horned viper *s* (zool.) víbora cornuda
hornet ['hɔrnɪt] *s* (ent.) avispón, crabrón
hornet's nest *s* panal del avispón; **to stir up a hornet's nest** (coll.) armar cisco, revolver el ajo
hornfels ['hɔrn,fɛls] *s* (geol.) corneana
horn lightning arrester *s* pararrayos de cuernos
horn of a dilemma *s* miembro de un dilema
horn of plenty *s* cuerno de la abundancia
hornpipe ['hɔrn,paɪp] *s* (mus.) chirimía; antigua danza inglesa que ejecuta una sola persona
hornpout ['hɔrn,paʊt] *s* (ichth.) amiuro nebuloso
horn-rimmed spectacles ['hɔrn,rɪmd] *spl* anteojos de concha
horn ring *s* (aut.) arco de la bocina
horn silver *s* (mineral.) plata córnea
hornswoggle ['hɔrn,swɑgəl] *va* (slang) estafar, embaucar, mistificar

hornwork ['hɔrn,wʌrk] *s* obra de cuerno; objetos de cuerno; (fort.) hornabeque
horny ['hɔrnɪ] *adj* (*comp:* **-ier;** *super:* **-iest**) córneo; cornudo; calloso
horny-handed ['hɔrnɪ'hændɪd] *adj* con manos callosas
horologe ['hɑrəlodʒ] o ['hɔrəlodʒ] *s* reloj (*solar, de agua, de arena, etc.*); (eccl.) horologio
horologer [ho'rɑlədʒər] *s* persona entendida en horología
horology [ho'rɑlədʒɪ] *s* horología
horopter [ho'rɑptər] *s* (opt.) horópter
horopteric [,hɑrɑp'terɪk] *adj* horoptérico
horoscope ['hɑrəskop] o ['hɔrəskop] *s* (astrol.) horóscopo; **to cast a horoscope** (astrol.) sacar un horóscopo
horoscopy [ho'rɑskəpɪ] *s* horoscopia
horrendous [hɑ'rɛndəs] *adj* horrendo
horrible ['hɑrɪbəl] o ['hɔrɪbəl] *adj* horrible; (coll.) muy desagradable, asombroso
horrid ['hɑrɪd] o ['hɔrɪd] *adj* horrible, horroroso; (coll.) muy desagradable
horrify ['hɑrɪfaɪ] o ['hɔrɪfaɪ] (*pret & pp:* **-fied**) *va* horrorizar
horripilation [hɑ,rɪpɪ'leʃən] *s* (path.) horripilación
horror ['hɑrər] o ['hɔrər] *s* horror; (coll.) horror (*atrocidad*); **horrors!** ¡qué horror!; **the horrors** melancolía, morriña; (coll.) espasmo de horror; **to have a horror of** tener horror a
hors de combat ['ɔrdə'kɑmbɑ] *adv* fuera de combate
hors d'oeuvre [ɔr'dʌvrə] *s* (*pl:* **-vres** [vrə]) entremés
horse [hɔrs] *s* caballo; caballete (*de carpintero*); gualdera o zanca (*de escalera*); potro (*de gimnasio*); (mil.) caballería (*cuerpo de soldados*); **hold your horses** pare Vd. el carro (*conténgase Vd.*); **to back the wrong horse** (coll.) jugar a la carta mala; **to horse!** ¡a caballo!; **horse of another color** harina de otro costal; *adj* caballar, hípico; montado; *va* proveer de un caballo o de caballos; cargar con, llevar a cuestas; azotar; cubrir (*el caballo a la yegua*); (naut.) calafatear; (slang) acosar, fatigar; (slang) ridiculizar; *vn* andar a caballo; estar (*la yegua*) salida; **to horse around** (slang) hacer payasadas, usar de chanzas pesadas
horseback ['hɔrs,bæk] *s* lomo de caballo; **on horseback** a caballo; *adv* a caballo; **to ride horseback** montar a caballo
horse bean *s* (bot.) haba caballuna o panosa
horse blanket *s* manta para caballos
horse block *s* montadero
horse box *s* (Brit.) vagón de transportar caballos
horsebreaker ['hɔrs,brekər] *s* caballista, domador de caballos
horsecar ['hɔrs,kɑr] *s* tranvía de sangre; vagón o carro de transportar caballos
horse chestnut *s* (bot.) castaño de Indias; castaña de Indias (*fruto*)
horse collar *s* collera
horse dealer *s* chalán
horse doctor *s* veterinario
horseflesh ['hɔrs,flɛʃ] *s* carne de caballo; caballos
horsefly ['hɔrs,flaɪ] *s* (*pl:* **-flies**) (ent.) tábano; (ent.) mosca borriquera
Horse Guards *spl* (Brit.) brigada de guardias montadas; cuartel general del ejército de la Gran Bretaña
horsehair ['hɔrs,hɛr] *s* pelo de caballo; cerda de caballo; tela de crin; *adj* hecho de cerda de caballo; rellenado de cerda de caballo; cubierto con tela de crin
horsehide ['hɔrs,haɪd] *s* cuero de caballo (*curtido o sin curtir*)
horse latitudes *spl* latitudes de calma (*cerca del grado 30 de latitud norte o sur*)
horse laugh *s* risotada
horseleech ['hɔrs,litʃ] *s* (ent.) sanguijuela borriquera
horseless ['hɔrslɪs] *adj* sin caballo; automóvil
horse mackerel *s* (ichth.) atún; (ichth.) bonito
horseman ['hɔrsmən] *s* (*pl:* **-men**) jinete; caballista
horsemanship ['hɔrsmənʃɪp] *s* equitación, manejo
horse marine *s* individuo de un cuerpo legendario de soldados de marina metidos a soldados de caballería; persona fuera de su elemento natural
horse meat *s* carne de caballo
horse mint *s* (bot.) mastranzo
horse nail *s* clavo de herrar
horse opera *s* (slang) cine espeluznante que se desarrolla en el oeste de los EE.UU.
horse pistol *s* pistola de arzón
horseplay ['hɔrs,ple] *s* payasada, chanza pesada
horsepower ['hɔrs,paʊər] *s* (mech.) caballo de vapor inglés (*746 vatios*)
horsepower-hour ['hɔrs,paʊər'aʊr] *s* (mech.) caballo de fuerza hora, caballo hora
horse race *s* carrera de caballos
horse racing *s* carreras, hipismo
horseradish ['hɔrs,rædɪʃ] *s* (bot.) rábano picante o rusticano; raíz de rábano picante o rusticano; mostaza de los alemanes
horse sense *s* (coll.) sentido común
horseshoe ['hɔrs,ʃu] *s* herradura; **horseshoes** *spl* juego parecido al de tejos en el que se tira a un hito con herraduras
horseshoe arch *s* (arch.) arco de herradura
horseshoe crab *s* (zool.) cangrejo bayoneta
horseshoe magnet *s* imán de herradura
horseshoe nail *s* clavo de herradura, clavo de herrar
horseshoer ['hɔrs,ʃuər] *s* herrador; encasquillador (Am.)
horse show *s* concurso hípico
horsetail ['hɔrs,tel] *s* cola de caballo; (bot.) cola de caballo, equiseto
horse thief *s* cuatrero
horse tick *s* (ent.) mosca borriquera, hipobosco
horse-trade ['hɔrs,tred] *vn* (fig.) chalanear
horse trading *s* (fig.) chalaneo
horse-trading ['hɔrs,tredɪŋ] *adj* (fig.) chalanesco
horsewhip ['hɔrs,hwɪp] *s* látigo; (*pret & pp:* **-whipped;** *ger:* **-whipping**) *va* dar latigazos a
horsewoman ['hɔrs,wʊmən] *s* (*pl:* **-women**) amazona, caballista
horsy ['hɔrsɪ] *adj* (*comp:* **-ier;** *super:* **-iest**) caballar, hípico; turfista, carrerista; (slang) desmañado
hortative ['hɔrtətɪv] o **hortatory** ['hɔrtə,torɪ] *adj* hortatorio
Hortense [hɔr'tɛns] *s* Hortensia
horticultural [,hɔrtɪ'kʌltʃərəl] *adj* hortícola
horticulture ['hɔrtɪ,kʌltʃər] *s* horticultura
horticulturist [,hɔrtɪ'kʌltʃərɪst] *s* horticultor
Hos. abr. de **Hosea**
hosanna [ho'zænə] *s & interj* hosanna
Hosanna Sunday *s* domingo de ramos
hose [hoz] *spl* calzas; *s* (*pl:* **hose**) media; calcetín; (*pl:* **hose** o **hoses**) manguera; *va* regar o limpiar con un chorro de agua (*que sale de una manguera*)
Hosea [ho'ziə] o [ho'zeə] *s* (Bib.) Oseas
hoseman ['hozmən] *s* (*pl:* **-men**) manguero
hosier ['hoʒər] *s* mediero, calcetero
hosiery ['hoʒərɪ] *s* medias, calcetas o calcetines; géneros de punto; calcetería
hosiery shop *s* calcetería
hospice ['hɑspɪs] *s* hospicio
hospitable ['hɑspɪtəbəl] o [hɑs'pɪtəbəl] *adj* hospitalario
hospital ['hɑspɪtəl] *s* hospital
hospitaler ['hɑspɪtələr] *s* (Brit.) hospitalero; (hist.) hospitalario; (*cap.*) *s* (hist.) hospitalario
hospitality [,hɑspɪ'tælɪtɪ] *s* (*pl:* **-ties**) hospitalidad
hospitalization [,hɑspɪtəlɪ'zeʃən] *s* hospitalización
hospitalize ['hɑspɪtəlaɪz] *va* hospitalizar
hospital ship *s* (mil.) buque hospital
hospital train *s* (mil.) tren hospital
host [host] *s* anfitrión; huésped (*persona que hospeda a otra*); mesonero, posadero; hueste (*ejército*); multitud, sinnúmero; (bot. & zool.) huésped; (*cap.*) *s* (eccl.) hostia; **to reckon without one's host** echar la cuenta sin la huéspeda o no contar con la huéspeda
hostage ['hɑstɪdʒ] *s* rehén; **to be held a hostage** quedar en rehenes; **to carry off as a hostage** llevarse en rehenes; **to give hos-**

tages to fortune tener prendas que perder; **to hold as a hostage** retener como rehén
hostel ['hɑstəl] *s* parador; casa de huéspedes (*para caminantes, biciclistas, etc.*); (Brit.) residencia de estudiantes
hostelry ['hɑstəlrɪ] *s* (*pl:* **-ries**) parador
hostess ['hostɪs] *s* huéspeda; dueña, patrona; maestra de ceremonias (*en un cabaret*); (aer.) azafata
hostile ['hɑstɪl] *adj* hostil
hostility [hɑs'tɪlɪtɪ] *s* (*pl:* **-ties**) hostilidad; **hostilities** *spl* hostilidades (*guerra*); **to cease hostilities** cesar en las hostilidades; **to start hostilities** romper las hostilidades
hostler ['hɑslər] o ['ɑslər] *s* establero, mozo de cuadra, mozo de paja y cebada; (rail.) encargado de la locomotora al fin del recorrido
hot [hɑt] *adj* (*comp:* **hotter;** *super:* **hottest**) caliente (*agua, café, aire, etc.*); cálido (*clima, país, etc.; sabor*); en caliente (*remachado*); acre, picante; caluroso, apasionado; violento (*genio*); fresco, reciente (*rastro de un animal*); caliente (*en celo*); enérgico (*p.ej., perseguimiento*); muy activo; (coll.) intolerable; (coll.) caliente (*cerca de lo que se busca*); (coll.) cargado (*de electricidad*); (coll.) muy radiactivo; (slang) recién robado, recién pasado de contrabando; (slang) chic, de la última moda; **to be hot** hacer calor (*dícese del tiempo*); tener calor (*p.ej., una persona*); **to blow hot and cold** ser veleta, mudar a todos los vientos; **to make it hot for** (coll.) hostilizar; *adv* con calor; ardientemente, apasionadamente; sin piedad; **to run hot** recalentarse (*un motor, un cojinete*); **hot and heavy** airadamente; con violencia, sin piedad
hot air *s* (slang) palabrería, música celestial
hot-air engine ['hɑt'ɛr] *s* máquina de aire caliente
hot-air furnace *s* calorífero de aire
hot-air heating *s* calefacción por aire caliente
hot and cold running water *s* circulación de agua fría y caliente
hot atom *s* (phys.) átomo cálido
hot baths *spl* caldas, termas, baños termales
hotbed ['hɑt,bɛd] *s* (hort.) almajara (*abrigada artificialmente*); (fig.) sementera, semillero
hot-blast stove ['hɑt,blæst] o ['hɑt,blɑst] *s* (metal.) recuperador de Cowper
hot-blooded ['hɑt'blʌdɪd] *adj* de malas pulgas; apasionado, de sangre ardiente; temerario, irreflexivo
hotbox ['hɑt,bɑks] *s* (rail.) cojinete recalentado
hot bulb *s* (mach.) bola caliente
hot cake *s* torta o tortita a la plancha; **to sell like hot cakes** (coll.) venderse como pan bendito
hotchpotch ['hɑtʃ,pɑtʃ] *s* var. de **hodgepodge**
hot cross bun *s* bollo marcado con la figura de una cruz (*que se come el viernes santo*)
hot dog *s* (slang) perro caliente
hotel [ho'tɛl] *s* hotel; *adj* hotelero
hotelkeeper [ho'tɛl,kipər] *s* hotelero
hotfoot ['hɑt,fʊt] *adv* (coll.) más que de prisa; *va* (coll.) seguir o perseguir a toda prisa; **to hotfoot it** (coll.) ir más que de prisa; *vn* (coll.) ir más que de prisa
hot-galvanize ['hɑt'gælvənaɪz] *va* galvanizar en caliente, cincar al fuego
hothead ['hɑt,hɛd] *s* persona irritable, persona de mal genio; persona temeraria o impetuosa; agitador, alborotador
hot-headed ['hɑt'hɛdɪd] *adj* caliente de cascos; temerario, irreflexivo, impetuoso; agitador, alborotador
hothouse ['hɑt,haʊs] *s* invernáculo, estufa
hot pad *s* almohadilla caliente eléctrica
hot plate *s* calientaplatos, hornillo (*portátil*)
hot-press ['hɑt,prɛs] *s* prensa térmica; prensa de satinar papel en caliente; *va* prensar en caliente
hot rod *s* (slang) bólido (*automóvil desguarnecido y con motor reforzado*)
hot seat *s* (coll.) situación dificultosa; (coll.) situación de gran responsabilidad; (aer.) asiento lanzable; (slang) silla eléctrica
hotshot ['hɑt,ʃɑt] *adj* (slang) rápido, diestro, próspero, ostentoso, importante; *s* tren rápido de mercancías perecederas; vehículo muy rápido, avión muy rápido; obrero muy perito; deportista muy diestro (*especialmente en golpeando una pelota*); (slang) persona de muchas campanillas
hot spot *s* punto caliente; (coll.) cabaret
hot springs *spl* fuentes termales
hotspur ['hɑt,spʌr] *s* persona temeraria o impetuosa
hot stuff *s* (slang) persona extraordinaria, cosa formidable
hot-tempered ['hɑt'tɛmpərd] *adj* irascible, de genio vivo y colérico
Hottentot ['hɑtəntɑt] *adj* & *s* hotentote
hot water *s* (coll.) lío, aprieto, dificultades
hot-water bag ['hɑt'wɔtər] o ['hɑt'wɑtər] *s* bolsa de agua caliente
hot-water boiler *s* termosifón (*para calentar agua o un edificio*)
hot-water bottle *s* bolsa de agua caliente
hot-water heater *s* calentador de agua, calentador de acumulación; calefón (Am.)
hot-water heating *s* calefacción por agua caliente
hot-water tank *s* depósito de agua caliente
hot-wire ['hɑt,waɪr] *adj* (elec.) de hilo caliente
hot-wire ammeter *s* (elec.) amperímetro de hilo caliente, amperímetro térmico
houdah ['haʊdə] *s* var. de **howdah**
hough [hɑk] *s* corvejón (*del caballo; de varias aves gallináceas*)
hound [haʊnd] *s* podenco; perro; canalla; **to follow the hounds** o **to ride to hounds** cazar con jauría; *va* rondar, acosar
hound's-tongue ['haʊndz,tʌŋ] *s* (bot.) cinoglosa, viniebla
houppelande ['huplænd] *s* hopalanda
hour [aʊr] *s* hora; hora actual, momento; **Hours** *spl* (myth.) Horas; **after hours** fuera de horas; **at all hours** a todas horas; muy tarde; **by the hour** por horas; **in an evil hour** en hora mala; **to keep late hours** trasnochar, acostarse tarde; **on the hour** a la hora en punto, cada hora; **to work long hours** trabajar muchas horas cada día; **hours on end** horas enteras
hour circle *s* (astr.) círculo horario
hourglass ['aʊr,glæs] o ['aʊr,glɑs] *s* reloj de arena
hour hand *s* horario
houri ['hʊrɪ] o ['haʊrɪ] *s* (*pl:* **-ris**) hurí (*del paraíso de Mahoma*)
hourly ['aʊrlɪ] *adj* de cada hora, repetido cada hora; repetido, frecuente; *adv* cada hora; muy a menudo
house [haʊs] *s* (*pl:* **houses** ['haʊzɪz]) casa; cámara (*legislativa*); edificio; teatro (*edificio y público*); entrada (*número de personas que asisten a un espectáculo*), p.ej., **a good house** mucha entrada; **on the house** a expensas del dueño; **to bring down the house** (coll.) hacer venirse abajo el teatro (*con aplausos*); **to clean house** hacer la limpieza de la casa; poner fin al desbarajuste (*municipal, del estado, de una casa de comercio, etc.*); **to keep house** tener casa propia; gobernar su casa; ser ama de su casa; hacer los quehaceres domésticos; **to put** o **to set one's house in order** arreglar sus asuntos; *adj* domiciliario; doméstico; de la casa; casero; [haʊz] *va* alojar, hospedar; domiciliar; (agr.) entrojar; (carp. & mach.) encajar; **to house in** cubrir, encerrar; *vn* morar, albergarse
house arrest *s* arresto domiciliario
houseboat ['haʊs,bot] *s* barco-habitación, casa flotante, embarcación en forma de casa flotante que sirve de habitación
housebreaker ['haʊs,brekər] *s* escalador
housebreaking ['haʊs,brekɪŋ] *s* escalo, allanamiento de morada
housebroken ['haʊs,brokən] *adj* (*perro o gato*) hecho a la casa, enseñado (*a hábitos de limpieza*)
house cleaning *s* limpieza de la casa; (fig.) limpieza
house coat *s* bata
house current *s* (elec.) red o sector de distribución, canalización de consumo; corriente de red
house dog *s* perro de casa; perro de guardia
housefly ['haʊs,flaɪ] *s* (*pl:* **-flies**) (ent.) mosca doméstica
houseful ['haʊsfʊl] *s* casa llena, p.ej., **a**

houseful of guests una casa llena de convidados
housefurnishings ['haus,fʌrnɪʃɪŋz] *spl* ajuar, menaje, enseres domésticos
household ['haushold] *s* casa, familia; *adj* casero, doméstico
household bread *s* pan casero, pan bazo
householder ['haus,holdər] *s* amo o dueño de casa; jefe de familia
household goods *spl* enseres domésticos
household linen *s* var. de **flatwork**
household word *s* frase hecha, palabra de uso corriente
house hunting *s* busca de casa; **to go house hunting** ir a buscar casa
housekeeper ['haus,kipər] *s* mujer de casa, ama de casa; casera, ama de llaves; mujer de gobierno
housekeeping ['haus,kipɪŋ] *s* quehaceres domésticos; manejo doméstico, gobierno doméstico; **to set up housekeeping** poner casa
housekeeping apartment *s* cuarto o piso con cocina
houseleek ['haus,lik] *s* (bot.) hierba puntera, barba de Júpiter, siempreviva mayor
houseline ['haus,laɪn] *s* (naut.) piola
housemaid ['haus,med] *s* criada de casa
housemaid's knee *s* (path.) sinovitis de la rodilla, rodilla de fregona
house meter *s* contador de abonado
housemother ['haus,mʌðər] *s* mujer encargada de una residencia de alumnos
house mouse *s* (zool.) ratón casero
house of assignation *s* casa de citas
house of cards *s* castillo de naipes
House of Commons *s* (Brit.) Cámara de los Comunes
house of correction *s* casa de corrección
house of God *s* casa de Dios (*iglesia*)
house of ill fame o **ill repute** *s* burdel, lupanar
House of Lords *s* (Brit.) Cámara de los Lores
house of prayer *s* casa de oración
House of Representatives *s* (U.S.A.) Cámara de Representantes
house of worship *s* edificio destinado al culto
house painter *s* pintor de brocha gorda
house party *s* convite o tertulia de varios días (*especialmente en la casa de campo del anfitrión*); (los) convidados
house physician *s* médico residente (*de un hospital*); médico de asiento (*en un hotel*)
house plant *s* planta de invernadero, planta de maceta
houseroom ['haus,rum] o ['haus,rʊm] *s* alojamiento, cabida (*en una casa*)
housetop ['haus,tɑp] *s* tejado (*parte superior y exterior de la casa*); **to shout from the housetops** pregonar a los cuatro vientos
housewares ['haus,wɛrz] *spl* ajuar, menaje
housewarming ['haus,wɔrmɪŋ] *s* tertulia para celebrar el estreno de una casa; **to have a housewarming** estrenar la casa
housewife ['haus,waɪf] *s* (*pl:* **-wives** [,waɪvz]) ama o dueña de casa; madre de familia; ['hʌzɪf] *s* (*pl:* **-wives** [ɪvz]) estuche de costura
housewifely ['haus,waɪflɪ] *adj* de ama de casa, propio de un ama de casa; hacendosa
housewifery ['haus,waɪfərɪ] o ['haus,waɪfrɪ] *s* quehaceres domésticos, gobierno doméstico (*del ama de casa*)
housework ['haus,wʌrk] *s* quehaceres domésticos
housing ['hauzɪŋ] *s* alojamiento; abrigo, albergue; edificación (*de casas*); casas; gualdrapa (*del caballo*); (aut.) cárter; (carp.) encaje, muesca; (mach.) caja, bastidor; (naut.) piola; **housings** *spl* arreos, jaeces
housing development *s* colonia, viviendas nuevas
housing shortage *s* crisis de vivienda
hove [hov] *pret & pp de* **heave**
hovel ['hʌvəl] o ['hɑvəl] *s* casucha, choza, pocilga; cobertizo
hover ['hʌvər] o ['hɑvər] *va* mover (*las alas*) sin avanzar; cubrir con las alas; *vn* cernerse (*un ave*); revolotear; andar cerca; dudar, vacilar; asomar (*p.ej., una sonrisa en los labios de una persona*); estar algún tiempo (*p.ej., entre la vida y la muerte*)
how [hau] *adv* cómo; a cómo p.ej., **how do you sell the apples?** ¿a cómo vende Vd. las manzanas?; **how early** cuándo, a qué hora; **how else** de qué otra manera; **how far** qué distancia; a qué distancia; hasta dónde; cuánto, p.ej., **how far is it to the station?** ¿cuánto hay de aquí a la estación?; **how late** cuándo, a qué hora; **how long** cuánto, cuánto tiempo; hasta cuándo; **how many** cuántos; **how much** cuánto; lo mucho que, p.ej., **you don't know how much I have traveled in Spain** no sabe Vd. lo mucho que he viajado por España; **how now?** ¿pues qué?; **how often** cuántas veces; **how old are you?** ¿cuántos años tiene Vd.?; **how so?** ¿cómo así?; **how soon** cuándo, a qué hora; **how** + *adj* qué + *adj*, p.ej., **how beautiful she is!** ¡qué hermosa es!; cuán + *adj* o *adv.*, p.ej., **you do not know how rich he is** Vd. no sabe cuán rico es; lo + *adj*, p.ej., **do you realize how hard it is?** ¿se da Vd. cuenta de lo difícil que es?
howbeit [hau'biɪt] *adv* no obstante, sin embargo
howdah ['haudə] *s* castillo (*montura sobre un elefante*)
how-do-you-do ['haudəjə'du] *s* (coll.) situación enojosa; **that's a fine** (o **pretty** o **nice**) **how-do-you-do!** (coll.) ¡buena es ésa (o ésta)!
howe'er [hau'ɛr] *adv* var. de **however**
however [hau'ɛvər] *adv* sin embargo, a pesar de eso; por muy . . . que, p.ej., **however hard it is** por muy difícil que sea; por mucho . . . que, p.ej., **however cold it is** por mucho frío que haga; como quiera que, p.ej., **however you do it, do it well** como quiera que lo haga, hágalo bien; (coll.) cómo, p.ej., **however did you manage to get it?** ¿cómo se ingenió Vd. para conseguirlo?; **however much** por mucho que
howitzer ['hauɪtsər] *s* obús, cañón obús
howl [haul] *s* aullido, alarido; chillido; risa muy aguda; bramido (*del viento*); *va* decir a gritos; echar a gritos; **to howl down** imponerse a gritos a (*una persona*); *vn* aullar, dar alaridos; chillar; bramar (*el viento*); reír a más no poder
howler ['haulər] *s* aullador; (zool.) aullador, mono aullador; (coll.) plancha, desacierto
howling ['haulɪŋ] *adj* aullador; (slang) clamoroso, ruidoso (*éxito*); *s* (rad.) aullido
howling monkey *s* (zool.) mono aullador, mono chillón
howsoever [,hauso'ɛvər] *adv* como quiera que; por muy . . . que
hoyden ['hɔɪdən] *s* muchacha traviesa, tunantuela
hoydenish ['hɔɪdənɪʃ] *adj* traviesa, tunantuela
HP, H.P., hp. o **h.p.** abr. de **horsepower**
hr. abr. de **hour** o **hours**
H.R. abr. de **House of Representatives**
H.R.H. abr. de **Her Royal Highness** y **His Royal Highness**
hrs. abr. de **hours**
ht. abr. de **height**
H.T. abr. de **Hawaiian Territory**
hub [hʌb] *s* cubo (*de rueda*); (fig.) eje, centro
hubble ['hʌbəl] *s* elevación, prominencia, aspereza
hubble-bubble ['hʌbəl,bʌbəl] *s* narguile; gluglú (*de un líquido*); vocerío confuso
hubbly ['hʌblɪ] *adj* fragoso, quebrado, áspero
hubbub ['hʌbʌb] *s* alboroto, tumulto; gritería
hubcap ['hʌb,kæp] *s* (aut.) sombrerete, tapón de cubo, tapacubo
huck [hʌk] o **huckaback** ['hʌkəbæk] *s* tejido granito
huckleberry ['hʌkəl,bɛrɪ] *s* (*pl:* **-ries**) (bot.) planta ericácea y su baya (*Gaylussacia baccata*)
huckster ['hʌkstər] *s* buhonero; vendedor ambulante (*especialmente de hortalizas*); traficante despreciable; sujeto ruin; (slang) empresario de publicidad; *vn* vender por las calles; regatear
huddle ['hʌdəl] *s* pelotón, tropel; confusión, precipitación; (football) círculo que forman los jugadores para recibir señas; (coll.) reunión secreta; **to go into a huddle** (slang) conferenciar en secreto; *va* hacer o terminar

aprisa y mal; ponerse (*la ropa*) aprisa y mal; amontonar desordenadamente; **to huddle oneself up** arrimarse cómodamente; *vn* amontonarse; acurrucarse, arrimarse; (football) formar círculo para recibir señas

Hudson seal ['hʌdsən] *s* piel de almizclera teñida (*que remeda la piel de foca*)

hue [hju] *s* tinte, matiz, color; grita, gritería; **hue and cry** vocería de alarma o de indignación

huff [hʌf] *s* arrebato de cólera, enojo súbito; **in a huff** encolerizado, ofendido; *va* encolerizar, ofender; (checkers) soplar

huffy ['hʌfɪ] *adj* (*comp:* **-ier;** *super:* **-iest**) enojadizo, resentido

hug [hʌg] *s* abrazo (*de cariño, de oso, de luchador, etc.*); (*pret & pp:* **hugged;** *ger:* **hugging**) *va* abrazar, apretar con los brazos; ahogar entre los brazos (*dícese de un oso*); afirmarse en (*una opinión*); navegar muy cerca de (*la costa u orilla*); ceñirse a (*p.ej., un muro*); *vn* abrazarse; arrimarse

huge [hjudʒ] *adj* enorme, inmenso, descomunal

hugger-mugger ['hʌgər'mʌgər] *s* confusión, desorden, embrollo; *adj* confuso, embrollado, sin pies ni cabeza; *adv* desordenadamente

Hugh [hju] *s* Hugo

Huguenot ['hjugənɑt] *s* hugonote

huh [hʌ] *interj* ¡eh!

hula-hula ['hulə'hulə] *s* baile típico de Hawai

hulk [hʌlk] *s* casco (*de un barco más o menos inservible*); carcamán, carraca (*buque malo y pesado*); pontón (*que sirve de cárcel*); armatoste (*máquina o mueble tosco; persona corpulenta e inútil*)

hulking ['hʌlkɪŋ] *adj* pesado, grueso

hull [hʌl] *s* casco (*de un barco o hidroavión*); armazón (*de un dirigible rígido*); vaina, hollejo (*de ciertas legumbres*); cáliz (*p.ej., de la fresa*); **hull down** (naut.) que se ven sólo las jarcias (*dícese de un barco en el horizonte*); *va* dar en el casco de (*un barco*); desvainar, deshollejar; mondar, pelar

hullabaloo ['hʌləbə,lu] o [,hʌləbə'lu] *s* alboroto, baraúnda, gritería, tumulto

hullo [hə'lo] *s* (*pl:* **-los**) var. de **hello** y **hollo;** *interj & vn* var. de **hello** y **hollo**

hum [hʌm] *s* tarareo, canturreo; zumbido (*de una abeja, máquina, etc.*); *interj* ¡ejem!; (*pret & pp:* **hummed;** *ger:* **humming**) *va* tararear, canturrear; **to hum to sleep** arrullar; *vn* tararear, canturrear; zumbar; (coll.) estar muy activo; **to keep things humming** o **to make things hum** (coll.) ejecutar las cosas de una manera viva y fogosa

human ['hjumən] *adj & s* humano

human being *s* ser humano

humane [hju'men] *adj* humano (*compasivo, misericordioso; civilizador*)

humanism ['hjumənɪzəm] *s* humanismo

humanist ['hjumənɪst] *adj & s* humanista

humanistic [,hjumə'nɪstɪk] *adj* humanístico

humanitarian [hju,mænɪ'terɪən] *adj & s* humanitario

humanitarianism [hju,mænɪ'tɛrɪənɪzəm] *s* humanitarismo

humanity [hju'mænɪtɪ] *s* (*pl:* **-ties**) humanidad; **the humanities** las humanidades

humanize ['hjumənaɪz] *va* humanizar; *vn* humanizarse

humankind ['hjumən'kaɪnd] *s* género humano

humanly ['hjumənlɪ] *adv* humanamente (*según las fuerzas humanas*)

Humbert ['hʌmbərt] *s* Humberto

humble ['hʌmbəl] o ['ʌmbəl] *adj* humilde; *va* humillar

humblebee ['hʌmbəl,bi] *s* var. de **bumblebee**

humbleness ['hʌmbəlnɪs] o ['ʌmbəlnɪs] *s* humildad

humble pie *s* empanada de menudo de venado; **to eat humble pie** someterse humildemente, reconocer el error y pedir perdón

humbug ['hʌm,bʌg] *s* farsa, patraña; embaucamiento; farsante, patrañero; (*pret & pp:* **-bugged;** *ger:* **-bugging**) *va* embaucar, engaitar

humbuggery ['hʌm,bʌgərɪ] *s* embaucamiento, engaño

humdinger [hʌm'dɪŋər] *s* (slang) persona extraordinaria, cosa formidable

humdrum ['hʌm,drʌm] *adj* monótono; *s* monotonía; charla monótona; machaca (*persona*)

humeral ['hjumərəl] *adj* (anat.) humeral; (anat.) braquial

humeral veil *s* (eccl.) humeral

humerus ['hjumərəs] *s* (*pl:* **-i** [aɪ]) (anat.) húmero; (anat.) brazo (*desde el hombro hasta el codo*)

humic ['hjumɪk] *adj* (chem.) húmico

humid ['hjumɪd] *adj* húmedo

humidification [hju,mɪdɪfɪ'keʃən] *s* humectación

humidifier [hju'mɪdɪ,faɪər] *s* humectador

humidify [hju'mɪdɪfaɪ] (*pret & pp:* **-fied**) *va* humedecer

humidity [hju'mɪdɪtɪ] *s* humedad

humidor ['hjumɪdɔr] *s* bote humectativo (*para tabaco de fumar*); humectador (*en la industria de hilandería*)

humifuse ['hjumɪfjuz] *adj* (bot.) humifuso

humiliate [hju'mɪlɪet] *va* humillar

humiliating [hju'mɪlɪ,etɪŋ] *adj* humillante

humiliation [hju,mɪlɪ'eʃən] *s* humillación

humility [hju'mɪlɪtɪ] *s* (*pl:* **-ties**) humildad

humin ['hjumɪn] *s* (biochem.) humina

humming ['hʌmɪŋ] *adj* zumbrador; (coll.) animado, vivo

hummingbird ['hʌmɪŋ,bʌrd] *s* (orn.) colibrí, pájaro mosca, picaflor

hummock ['hʌmək] *s* mogote, morón; hummock, lomo o mole de hielo

hummocky ['hʌməkɪ] *adj* a modo de mogote; fragoso, escabroso

humor ['hjumər] o ['jumər] *s* humor; humorismo; **bad humor** mal humor; **good humor** buen humor; **out of humor** de mal humor; **to be in the humor for** tener ganas de; *va* seguir el humor a; acomodarse a; manejar suavemente

humoresque [,hjumə'rɛsk] *s* (mus.) juguete, capricho

humorist ['hjumərɪst] o ['jumərɪst] *s* persona chistosa; humorista (*escritor*)

humorous ['hjumərəs] o ['jumərəs] *adj* chistoso, gracioso; humorístico (*escritor, dibujo*); (obs.) humoroso

humour ['hjumər] o ['jumər] *s & va* (Brit.) var. de **humor**

hump [hʌmp] *s* corcova, giba, joroba; montecillo; prominencia; (rail.) lomo, lomo de asno; *va* encorvar; **to hump it** o **to hump oneself** (slang) esforzarse, echar los bofes; *vn* encorvarse; (slang) esforzarse, echar los bofes

humpback ['hʌmp,bæk] *s* corcova, joroba; corcovado, jorobado; (zool.) gubarte

humpbacked ['hʌmp,bækt] *adj* corcovado, jorobado

humph [həm] *interj* ¡bah!; ¡uf!

Humphrey ['hʌmfrɪ] *s* Hunfredo

humpty-dumpty ['hʌmptɪ'dʌmptɪ] *adj* rechoncho

humpy ['hʌmpɪ] *adj* (*comp:* **-ier;** *super:* **-iest**) desigual; giboso

hump yard *s* (rail.) patio de lomo para maniobras por gravedad

humus ['hjuməs] *s* humus, mantillo

Hun [hʌn] *s* huno; (fig.) vándalo

hunch [hʌntʃ] *s* corcova, joroba; (coll.) corazonada; tajada, pedazo; *va* encorvar; mover a empujones o a tirones; *vn* encorvarse; moverse a empujones o a tirones

hunchback ['hʌntʃ,bæk] *s* corcova, joroba; corcovado, jorobado

hunch-backed ['hʌntʃ,bækt] *adj* corcovado, jorobado

hundred ['hʌndrəd] *adj* cien (*antes de substantivo*); ciento; **a hundred** u **one hundred** cien (*antes de substantivo*); ciento; *s* ciento, cien; **a hundred** u **one hundred** ciento, cien; **by the hundred** por cientos, a centenares; **the hundreds** las centenas (*los números 100, 200, 300, etc.*)

Hundred Days *spl* (hist.) Cien Días

hundredfold ['hʌndrəd,fold] *adj & s* céntuplo; *adv* cien veces más

hundred-per-cent ['hʌndrədpər'sɛnt] *adj* cabal, perfecto, puro, incontestable

hundred-per-cent American *s* americano cien por ciento (*americano muy patriótico*)

hundredth ['hʌndrədθ] *adj & s* centésimo

hundredweight ['hʌndrəd,wet] *s* centipondio, quintal
Hundred Years' War *s* guerra de los Cien Años
hung [hʌŋ] *pret & pp de* **hang**
Hungarian [hʌŋ'gɛrɪən] *adj & s* húngaro
Hungary ['hʌŋgərɪ] *s* Hungría
hunger ['hʌŋgər] *s* hambre; *vn* hambrear; **to hunger for** tener hambre de
hunger march *s* marcha del hambre
hunger strike *s* huelga de hambre
hungry ['hʌŋgrɪ] *adj* (*comp:* **-grier;** *super:* **-griest**) hambriento; estéril (*tierra*); **to be hungry** tener hambre; **to go hungry** pasar hambre; **hungry for** hambriento de (*p.ej., riquezas*)
hunk [hʌŋk] *s* (coll.) pedazo grande, buen pedazo
hunky-dory [,hʌŋkɪ'dorɪ] *adj* (coll.) excelente, óptimo
hunt [hʌnt] *s* caza; cacería, montería; partida de caza; busca; **on the hunt for** a caza de; *va* cazar; hacer la batida de (*un terreno*); emplear (*perros o caballos*) en la caza; perseguir; buscar; **to hunt down** cazar y matar, cazar y destruir; buscar (*una cosa*) hasta dar con ella; **to hunt up** rebuscar; buscar y hallar; *vn* cazar; buscar; **to go hunting** ir de caza; **to hunt for** buscar; **to hunt up and down (for)** buscar por todas partes; **to take hunting** llevar de caza
hunter ['hʌntər] *s* cazador; perro o caballo de caza; saboneta (*reloj*)
hunting ['hʌntɪŋ] *adj* cazador; de caza; *s* caza (*acción*); cacería, montería (*arte*); (elec.) movimiento oscilatorio
hunting case *s* caja de saboneta
hunting dog *s* perro de caza; (zool.) perro-hiena
hunting ground *s* cazadero
huntinghorn ['hʌntɪŋ,hɔrn] *s* cuerno de caza
hunting jacket *s* cazadora (*chaqueta*)
hunting knife *s* cuchillo de caza
hunting lodge *s* casa de montería
hunting season *s* tiempo de caza
hunting watch *s* saboneta
huntress ['hʌntrɪs] *s* cazadora (*mujer*)
huntsman ['hʌntsmən] *s* (*pl:* **-men**) cazador, montero; montero mayor
hurdle ['hʌrdəl] *s* cañizo, zarzo; narria (*para llevar los reos al patíbulo*); (sport) valla (*portátil*); (fig.) obstáculo; **hurdles** *spl* (sport) carrera de vallas; *va* cercar con zarzos; saltar por encima de, vencer
hurdler ['hʌrdlər] *s* (sport) corredor en una carrera de vallas
hurdle race *s* (sport) carrera de vallas
hurdy-gurdy ['hʌrdɪ,gʌrdɪ] *s* (*pl:* **-dies**) organillo; (archaic) zanfonía
hurl [hʌrl] *s* lanzamiento; *va* lanzar, arrojar
hurly-burly ['hʌrlɪ,bʌrlɪ] *s* (*pl:* **-ies**) alboroto, tumulto
Huronian [hjʊ'ronɪən] *adj & s* (geol.) huroniense
hurrah [hʊ'rɑ] o [hʊ'rɔ] o **hurray** [hʊ're] *s* viva; *interj* ¡hurra!, ¡viva!; **hurrah for . . . !** ¡viva . . . !; *va* aplaudir, vitorear; *vn* dar vivas
hurricane ['hʌrɪken] *s* huracán; (naut.) huracán; *vn* huracanarse
hurricane deck *s* cubierta superior (*de un vapor de pasajeros*)
hurried ['hʌrɪd] *adj* apresurado; hecho de prisa
hurry ['hʌrɪ] *s* (*pl:* **-ries**) prisa; **to be in a hurry** tener prisa, estar de prisa; **to be in a hurry to** + *inf* tener prisa en o por + *inf;* **what's the hurry?** ¿qué prisa hay? ‖ (*pret & pp:* **-ried**) *va* apresurar, dar prisa a; **to hurry off** hacer marchar de prisa; **to hurry on** apresurar; **to hurry over** pasar rápidamente; hacer con precipitación o ligereza; **to hurry up** apresurar ‖ *vn* apresurarse, darse prisa; ir corriendo; **to hurry after** correr en pos de; **to hurry away** marcharse de prisa, salir precipitadamente; **to hurry back** volver de prisa, apresurarse a volver; **to hurry off** marcharse de prisa; **to hurry on** apresurarse; seguir adelante con mucha prisa; **to hurry to** + *inf* apresurarse a + *inf;* **to hurry up** apresurarse
hurry-scurry o **hurry-skurry** ['hʌrɪ'skʌrɪ] *adj* precipitado, atropellado; *adv* precipitadamente, atropelladamente; *s* precipitación, atropello
hurt [hʌrt] *s* daño; dolor; herida; *adj* ofendido, resentido; (*pret & pp:* **hurt**) *va* dañar, lastimar; herir; perjudicar; doler; ofender, lastimar; *vn* doler
hurtful ['hʌrtfəl] *adj* dañoso, perjudicial
hurtle ['hʌrtəl] *s* choque, fragor; *va* arrojar con violencia; chocar con; dar en o contra con gran estruendo; *vn* arrojarse con violencia; chocar; resonar con gran estruendo; pasar con gran estruendo, moverse con gran estruendo
husband ['hʌzbənd] *s* marido, esposo; *va* economizar, manejar con economía; procurar marido a; ser o pasar por marido de; (archaic) cultivar
husbandman ['hʌzbəndmən] *s* (*pl:* **-men**) granjero, agricultor
husbandry ['hʌzbəndrɪ] *s* granjería; buena dirección, buen gobierno (*de la hacienda o los recursos de uno*); economía
hush [hʌʃ] *s* silencio; *interj* ¡chito!, ¡chitón!; *va* callar; apaciguar; **to hush up** echar tierra a (*p.ej., un escándalo*); *vn* callar o callarse
hushaby ['hʌʃə,baɪ] *interj* ¡ro ro!
hush-hush ['hʌʃ,hʌʃ] *adj* muy secreto
hush money *s* dinero con que se compra el silencio de una persona
husk [hʌsk] *s* cáscara, hollejo, vaina; perfolla (*del maíz*); (fig.) cáscara o capa exterior; *va* descascarar, deshollejar, desvainar; espinochar (*el maíz*)
husking ['hʌskɪŋ] *s* despancación del maíz; minga para la despancación del maíz
husking bee *s* minga para la despancación del maíz
husky ['hʌskɪ] *adj* (*comp:* **-ier;** *super:* **-iest**) cascarudo; ronco; (coll.) fortachón, fornido; *s* (*pl:* **-ies**) (coll.) persona fornida; (*cap.*) *s* (*pl:* **-ies**) esquimal (*individuo; idioma*); perro esquimal
hussar [hʊ'zɑr] *s* (mil.) húsar
Hussite ['hʌsaɪt] *adj & s* husita
Hussitism ['hʌsaɪtɪzəm] *s* husitismo
hussy ['hʌzɪ] o ['hʌsɪ] *s* (*pl:* **-sies**) buena pieza, muchacha descarada; corralera (*mujer desvergonzada*)
hustings ['hʌstɪŋz] *spl* tribuna para discursos electorales; elecciones
hustle ['hʌsəl] *s* prisa; empujón; (coll.) energía, vigor; *va* apresurar, dar prisa a; empujar; echar a empellones; *vn* apresurarse, darse prisa; (coll.) menearse; (coll.) trabajar con gran ahinco
hustler ['hʌslər] *s* (coll.) trafagón, buscavidas
hut [hʌt] *s* casucha, choza
hutch [hʌtʃ] *s* conejera; hucha, arca; cabaña, choza
huzza [hʌ'zɑ] *s* viva; *interj* ¡vítor!; *va* vitorear; *vn* dar vivas
hyacinth ['haɪəsɪnθ] *s* (bot. & mineral.) jacinto
hyacinth bean *s* (bot.) frijol caballero, frijol de Antibo
hyacinthine [,haɪə'sɪnθɪn] o [,haɪə'sɪnθaɪn] *adj* de o del jacinto; adornado con jacintos
hyacinth of Peru *s* (bot.) jacinto estrellado
Hyacinthus [,haɪə'sɪnθəs] *s* (myth.) Jacinto
Hyades ['haɪədiz] o **Hyads** ['haɪædz] *spl* (astr. & myth.) Híadas o Híades
hyaena [haɪ'inə] *s* var. de **hyena**
hyaline ['haɪəlɪn] o ['haɪəlaɪn] *adj* hialino (*parecido al vidrio*); *s* (poet.) cosa vítrea o transparente; ['haɪəlɪn] o ['haɪəlin] *s* (biochem.) hialina
hyaline degeneration *s* (path.) degeneración hialina
hyalite ['haɪəlaɪt] *s* (mineral.) hialita
hyalitis [,haɪə'laɪtɪs] *s* (path.) hialitis
hyaloid ['haɪəlɔɪd] *adj* hialoideo; *s* (anat.) hialoides
hyaloplasm ['haɪəloplæzəm] *s* (biol.) hialoplasma
hybrid ['haɪbrɪd] *adj & s* híbrido
hybridism ['haɪbrɪdɪzəm] *s* hibridismo
hybridization [,haɪbrɪdɪ'zeʃən] *s* hibridación
hybridize ['haɪbrɪdaɪz] *va & vn* hibridar

hydantoin [haɪˈdænto·ɪn] *s* (chem.) hidantoína
hydatid [ˈhaɪdətɪd] *s* (path.) hidátide; *adj* hidatídico
hydnum [ˈhɪdnəm] *s* (bot.) hidno
hydra [ˈhaɪdrə] *s* (*pl:* **-dras** o **-drae** [dri]) hidra (*mal persistente*); (zool.) hidra (*pólipo*); (*cap.*) *s* (astr. & myth.) Hidra
hydracid [haɪˈdræsɪd] *s* (chem.) hidrácido
hydrangea [haɪˈdrendʒə] o [haɪˈdrændʒɪə] *s* (bot.) hortensia, hidrangea
hydrant [ˈhaɪdrənt] *s* boca de agua, boca de riego
hydrargyriasis [,haɪdrɑrdʒɪˈraɪəsɪs] *s* (path.) hidrargirismo
hydrargyrum [haɪˈdrɑrdʒɪrəm] *s* (chem.) hidrargiro
hydrate [ˈhaɪdret] *s* (chem.) hidrato; *va* (chem.) hidratar; *vn* (chem.) hidratarse
hydration [haɪˈdreʃən] *s* (chem.) hidratación
hydraulic [haɪˈdrɔlɪk] *adj* hidráulico; **hydraulics** *ssg* hidráulica
hydraulically [haɪˈdrɔlɪkəlɪ] *adv* hidráulicamente
hydraulic brake *s* freno hidráulico
hydraulic elevator *s* ascensor hidráulico
hydraulic jack *s* gato hidráulico
hydraulic lime *s* cal hidráulica
hydraulic mortar *s* argamasa hidráulica
hydraulic press *s* prensa hidráulica
hydraulic ram *s* ariete hidráulico
hydraulic turbine *s* turbina hidráulica
hydrazide [ˈhaɪdrəzaɪd] o [ˈhaɪdrəzɪd] *s* (chem.) hidracida
hydrazine [ˈhaɪdrəzin] o [ˈhaɪdrəzɪn] *s* (chem.) hidracina
hydric [ˈhaɪdrɪk] *adj* (chem.) hídrico
hydrid [ˈhaɪdrɪd] o **hydride** [ˈhaɪdraɪd] o [ˈhaɪdrɪd] *s* (chem.) hidruro
hydriodic [,haɪdrɪˈɑdɪk] *adj* (chem.) yodhídrico
hydriodic acid *s* (chem.) ácido yodhídrico
hydrobromic [,haɪdrəˈbromɪk] *adj* (chem.) bromhídrico
hydrobromic acid *s* (chem.) ácido bromhídrico
hydrocarbon [,haɪdrəˈkɑrbən] *s* (chem.) hidrocarburo
hydrocele [ˈhaɪdrəsil] *s* (path.) hidrocele
hydrocephalous [,haɪdrəˈsɛfələs] *adj* hidrocéfalo
hydrocephalus [,haɪdrəˈsɛfələs] *s* (path.) hidrocefalía
hydrochlorate [,haɪdrəˈkloret] o [,haɪdrəˈklorɪt] *s* (chem.) clorhidrato
hydrochloric [,haɪdrəˈklorɪk] *adj* (chem.) clorhídrico
hydrochloric acid *s* (chem.) ácido clorhídrico
hydrocyanic [,haɪdrosaɪˈænɪk] *adj* (chem.) cianhídrico
hydrocyanic acid *s* (chem.) ácido cianhídrico
hydrodynamic [,haɪdrədaɪˈnæmɪk] o [,haɪdrədɪˈnæmɪk] *adj* hidrodinámico; **hydrodynamics** *ssg* hidrodinámica
hydroelectric [,haɪdro·ɪˈlɛktrɪk] *adj* hidroeléctrico
hydroelectricity [,haɪdro·ɪ,lɛkˈtrɪsɪtɪ] *s* hidroelectricidad
hydrofluoric [,haɪdrofluˈɑrɪk] o [,haɪdrofluˈɔrɪk] *adj* (chem.) fluorhídrico
hydrofluoric acid *s* (chem.) ácido fluorhídrico
hydrofoil [ˈhaɪdrə,fɔɪl] *s* superficie de reacción hidráulica, plano hidrodinámico; hidroaleta; barco que se desliza sobre hidroaletas
hydrogel [ˈhaɪdrə,dʒɛl] *s* (chem.) hidrogel
hydrogen [ˈhaɪdrədʒən] *s* (chem.) hidrógeno
hydrogenate [ˈhaɪdrədʒənet] *va* (chem.) hidrogenar
hydrogenation [,haɪdrədʒənˈeʃən] *s* (chem.) hidrogenación
hydrogen bomb *s* (phys.) bomba de hidrógeno
hydrogen ion *s* (chem.) hidrogenión, ion hidrógeno, ion de hidrógeno
hydrogenize [ˈhaɪdrədʒənaɪz] *va* var. de **hydrogenate**
hydrogenous [haɪˈdrɑdʒɪnəs] *adj* hidrogenado
hydrogen peroxide *s* (chem.) peróxido de hidrógeno
hydrogen sulfide *s* (chem.) sulfuro de hidrógeno
hydrographer [haɪˈdrɑgrəfər] *s* hidrógrafo
hydrographic [,haɪdrəˈgræfɪk] *adj* hidrográfico
hydrography [haɪˈdrɑgrəfɪ] *s* hidrografía
hydroid [ˈhaɪdrɔɪd] *s* (zool.) hidroide
hydrologist [haɪˈdrɑlədʒɪst] *s* hidrólogo
hydrology [haɪˈdrɑlədʒɪ] *s* hidrología
hydrolysis [haɪˈdrɑlɪsɪs] *s* (*pl:* **-ses** [siz]) (chem.) hidrólisis
hydrolytic [,haɪdrəˈlɪtɪk] *adj* hidrolítico
hydrolyze [ˈhaɪdrəlaɪz] *va* (chem.) hidrolizar; *vn* (chem.) hidrolizarse
hydromancy [ˈhaɪdrə,mænsɪ] *s* hidromancía
hydromantic [,haɪdrəˈmæntɪk] *adj* hidromántico
hydromechanical [,haɪdromɪˈkænɪkəl] *adj* hidromecánico
hydromechanics [,haɪdromɪˈkænɪks] *ssg* hidromecánica
hydromedusa [,haɪdromɪˈdjusə] o [,haɪdromɪˈdusə] *s* (*pl:* **-sae** [si]) (zool.) hidromedusa
hydromel [ˈhaɪdrəmɛl] *s* hidromel
hydrometeor [,haɪdrəˈmitɪər] *s* (meteor.) hidrometeoro
hydrometer [haɪˈdrɑmɪtər] *s* areómetro
hydrometric [,haɪdrəˈmɛtrɪk] o **hydrometrical** [,haɪdrəˈmɛtrɪkəl] *adj* areométrico
hydrometry [haɪˈdrɑmɪtrɪ] *s* areometría
hydropath [ˈhaɪdrəpæθ] *s* hidrópata
hydropathic [,haɪdrəˈpæθɪk] *adj* hidropático
hydropathist [haɪˈdrɑpəθɪst] *s* hidrópata
hydropathy [haɪˈdrɑpəθɪ] *s* hidropatía
hydrophane [ˈhaɪdrəfen] *s* (mineral.) hidrófana
hydrophid [ˈhaɪdrəfɪd] *s* (zool.) hidrófido
hydrophile [ˈhaɪdrəfaɪl] o [ˈhaɪdrəfɪl] o **hydrophilic** [,haɪdrəˈfɪlɪk] *adj* (chem.) hidrófilo
hydrophobe [ˈhaɪdrəfob] *s* hidrófobo
hydrophobia [,haɪdrəˈfobɪə] *s* (path.) hidrofobia
hydrophobic [,haɪdrəˈfobɪk] *adj* hidrofóbico; hidrófobo (*que padece de hidrofobia*)
hydrophone [ˈhaɪdrəfon] *s* hidrófono
hydrophyte [ˈhaɪdrəfaɪt] *s* (bot.) hidrófita
hydropic [haɪˈdrɑpɪk] o **hydropical** [haɪˈdrɑpɪkəl] *adj* hidrópico
hydroplane [ˈhaɪdrəplen] *s* hidroplano (*buque*); (aer.) hidroplano o hidroavión
hydroponic [,haɪdrəˈpɑnɪk] *adj* hidropónico; **hydroponics** *spl* hidroponía
hydrops [ˈhaɪdrɑps] o **hydropsy** [ˈhaɪ,drɑpsɪ] *s* (path.) hidropesía
hydroquinone [,haɪdrəkwɪˈnon] o [,haɪdrəˈkwɪnon] *s* (chem.) hidroquinona
hydrosol [ˈhaɪdrəsɑl] o [ˈhaɪdrəsol] *s* (chem.) hidrosol
hydrosphere [ˈhaɪdrəsfɪr] *s* hidrosfera
hydrostat [ˈhaɪdrəstæt] *s* hidrostato
hydrostatic [,haɪdrəˈstætɪk] *adj* hidrostático; **hydrostatics** *ssg* hidrostática
hydrosulfid [,haɪdrəˈsʌlfɪd] o **hydrosulfide** [,haɪdrəˈsʌlfaɪd] o [,haɪdrəˈsʌlfɪd] *s* (chem.) hidrosulfuro
hydrosulfite [,haɪdrəˈsʌlfaɪt] *s* (chem.) hidrosulfito; (chem.) hidrosulfito sódico (*agente reductor*)
hydrotechny [ˈhaɪdrə,tɛknɪ] *s* hidrotecnia
hydrotherapeutic [,haɪdro,θɛrəˈpjutɪk] *adj* hidroterápico; **hydrotherapeutics** *ssg* hidroterapia
hydrotherapy [,haɪdroˈθɛrəpɪ] *s* var. de **hydrotherapeutics**
hydrothermal [,haɪdrəˈθʌrməl] *adj* hidrotérmico
hydrothorax [,haɪdrəˈθoræks] *s* (path.) hidrotórax
hydrotropism [haɪˈdrɑtrəpɪzəm] *s* (biol.) hidrotropismo
hydrous [ˈhaɪdrəs] *adj* hidratado
hydroxid [haɪˈdrɑksɪd] o **hydroxide** [haɪˈdrɑksaɪd] o [haɪˈdrɑksɪd] *s* (chem.) hidróxido
hydroxyl [haɪˈdrɑksɪl] *s* (chem.) hidroxilo u oxhidrilo
hydroxylamine [haɪ,drɑksɪləˈmin] o [haɪ,drɑksɪlˈæmɪn] *s* (chem.) hidroxilamina
hydroxyl radical *s* (chem.) radical hidroxilo
hydrozoan [,haɪdrəˈzoən] *s* (zool.) hidrozoo; *adj* hidrozoico
hyena [haɪˈinə] *s* (zool.) hiena

Hygeia [haɪ'dʒiə] *s* (myth.) Higía
hygiene ['haɪdʒin] o ['haɪdʒɪin] *s* higiene
hygienic [,haɪdʒɪ'ɛnɪk] o [haɪ'dʒinɪk] *adj* higiénico
hygienist ['haɪdʒɪənɪst] *adj & s* higienista
hygrometer [haɪ'grɑmɪtər] *s* higrómetro
hygrometric [,haɪgrə'mɛtrɪk] *adj* higrométrico
hygrometry [haɪ'grɑmɪtrɪ] *s* higrometría
hygroscope ['haɪgrəskop] *s* higroscopio
hygroscopic [,haɪgrə'skɑpɪk] *adj* higroscópico
hying ['haɪɪŋ] *ger de* **hie**
Hyksos ['hɪksɑs] o ['hɪksos] *spl* (hist.) Hicsos
hyla ['haɪlə] *s* (zool.) rubeta, rana de San Antonio
hylozoism [,haɪlə'zo·ɪzəm] *s* (philos.) hilozoísmo
hymen ['haɪmən] *s* (anat.) himen; (*cap.*) *s* (myth.) Himeneo
hymeneal [,haɪmə'niəl] *adj* nupcial; *s* himeneo (*himno nupcial*)
hymenium [haɪ'minɪəm] *s* (*pl:* **-a** [ə] o **-ums**) (bot.) himenio
hymenopter ['haɪmə,nɑptər] *s* (*pl:* **-tera** [tərə]) (zool.) himenóptero
hymenopterous [,haɪmə'nɑptərəs] *adj* (zool.) himenóptero
Hymettus [haɪ'mɛtəs] *s* Himeto
hymn [hɪm] *s* himno; *va* alabar con himnos; expresar en himnos; *vn* cantar himnos
hymnal ['hɪmnəl] *s* himnario
hymnology [hɪm'nɑlədʒɪ] *s* himnología; himnos
hyoid ['haɪɔɪd] *adj* hioideo; hioides; *s* (anat.) hioides
hyoides [haɪ'ɔɪdiz] *s* (anat.) hioides
hyoscine ['haɪəsin] o ['haɪəsɪn] *s* (trademark) hioscina (*alcaloide*)
hyoscyamine [,haɪə'saɪəmin] o [,haɪə'saɪəmɪn] *s* (chem.) hiosciamina
hyp. abr. de **hypotenuse** y **hypothesis**
hypabyssal [,hɪpə'bɪsəl] *adj* (geol.) hipabisal
hypallage [hɪ'pælədʒi] o [haɪ'pælədʒi] *s* (rhet.) hipálage
Hypatia [haɪ'peʃə] o [haɪ'peʃɪə] *s* Hipatia
hyperacidity [,haɪpərə'sɪdɪtɪ] *s* hiperacidez
hyperacusis [,haɪpərə'kjusɪs] *s* (path.) hiperacusia o hiperacusis
hyperaemia [,haɪpər'imɪə] *s* (path.) var. de **hyperemia**
hyperaesthesia [,haɪpərɪs'θiʒə] o [,haɪpərɪs'θiʒɪə] *s* (path.) hiperestesia
hyperbatic [,haɪpər'bætɪk] *adj* hiperbático
hyperbaton [haɪ'pʌrbətɑn] *s* (*pl:* **-ta** [tə]) (gram.) hipérbaton
hyperbola [haɪ'pʌrbələ] *s* (geom.) hipérbola
hyperbole [haɪ'pʌrbəlɪ] *s* (rhet.) hipérbole
hyperbolic [,haɪpər'bɑlɪk] *adj* (geom. & rhet.) hiperbólico
hyperbolism [haɪ'pʌrbəlɪzəm] *s* (rhet.) hiperbolismo
hyperbolize [haɪ'pʌrbəlaɪz] *va* usar de hipérboles en; *vn* hiperbolizar
hyperboloid [haɪ'pʌrbəlɔɪd] *s* (geom.) hiperboloide
hyperborean [,haɪpər'borɪən] *adj & s* hiperbóreo; (*cap.*) *s* (myth.) hiperbóreo
hyperchlorhydria [,haɪpərklor'haɪdrɪə] *s* (path.) hiperclorhidria
hypercritical [,haɪpər'krɪtɪkəl] *adj* hipercrítico
hyperdulia [,haɪpərdjʊ'laɪə] o [,haɪpərdʊ'laɪə] *s* (theol.) hiperdulía
hyperemia [,haɪpər'imɪə] *s* (path.) hiperemia
hyperesthesia [,haɪpərɪs'θiʒə] o [,haɪpərɪs'θiʒɪə] *s* (path.) hiperestesia
Hyperion [haɪ'pɪrɪən] *s* (myth.) Hiperión
hyperkinesia [,haɪpərkɪ'niʒə] o [,haɪpərkaɪ'niʒə] *s* (path.) hipercinesia
hypermetropia [,haɪpərmɪ'tropɪə] *s* (path.) hipermetropía
Hypermnestra [,haɪpərm'nɛstrə] *s* (myth.) Hipermnestra
hyperopia [,haɪpər'opɪə] *s* (path.) hiperopía
hyperopic [,haɪpər'ɑpɪk] *adj* hiperópico
hyperpituitarism [,haɪpərpɪ'tjuɪtərɪzəm] o [,haɪpərpɪ'tuɪtərɪzəm] *s* (path.) hiperpituitarismo
hyperpnea [,haɪpərp'niə] o [,haɪpər'niə] *s* (path.) hiperpnea
hyperpyrexia [,haɪpərpaɪ'rɛksɪə] *s* (path.) hiperpirexia
hypersensitive [,haɪpər'sɛnsɪtɪv] *adj* extremadamente sensible; (path.) hipersensible
hypersensitivity [,haɪpər,sɛnsɪ'tɪvɪtɪ] *s* exceso de sensibilidad; (path.) hipersensibilidad
hypertension [,haɪpər'tɛnʃən] *s* (path.) hipertensión
hyperthyroidism [,haɪpər'θaɪrɔɪdɪzəm] *s* (path.) hipertiroidismo
hypertonic [,haɪpər'tɑnɪk] *adj* (chem. & physiol.) hipertónico
hypertrophic [,haɪpər'trɑfɪk] *adj* hipertrófico
hypertrophy [haɪ'pʌrtrəfɪ] *s* (biol. & path.) hipertrofia; (*pret & pp:* **-phied**) *vn* hipertrofiarse
hypha ['haɪfə] *s* (*pl:* **-phae** [fi]) (bot.) hifa
hyphen ['haɪfən] *s* guión; *va* unir con guión, separar con guión
hyphenate ['haɪfənet] *va* unir con guión, separar con guión; escribir con guión
hyphenated American *s* (U.S.A.) ciudadano norteamericano de nacimiento extranjero que guarda lealtad a la madre patria y cuya nacionalidad se indica con dos palabras unidas con guión, p.ej., **Anglo-American** anglonorteamericano
hypnale ['hɪpnəli] *s* (chem.) hipnal; (obs.) hipnal (*áspid*)
Hypnos ['hɪpnɑs] *s* (myth.) Hipnos
hypnosis [hɪp'nosɪs] *s* (*pl:* **-ses** [siz]) hipnosis
hypnotic [hɪp'nɑtɪk] *adj* hipnótico; *s* hipnótico; (med.) hipnótico (*medicamento*)
hypnotically [hɪp'nɑtɪkəlɪ] *adv* hipnóticamente
hypnotism ['hɪpnətɪzəm] *s* hipnotismo
hypnotist ['hɪpnətɪst] *s* hipnotista
hypnotization [,hɪpnətɪ'zeʃən] *s* hipnotización
hypnotize ['hɪpnətaɪz] *va* hipnotizar
hypo ['haɪpo] *s* (*pl:* **-pos**) (phot.) hipo (*hiposulfito sódico*); (slang) aguja hipodérmica, inyección hipodérmica, jeringazo
hypoblast ['haɪpəblæst] *s* (embryol.) hipoblasto
hypocaust ['hɪpəkɔst] *s* (archeol.) hipocausto
hypochlorite [,haɪpo'kloraɪt] *s* (chem.) hipoclorito
hypochlorous [,haɪpo'klorəs] *adj* (chem.) hipocloroso
hypochlorous acid *s* (chem.) ácido hipocloroso
hypochondria [,haɪpə'kɑndrɪə] o [,hɪpə'kɑndrɪə] *s* (path.) hipocondría
hypochondriac [,haɪpə'kɑndrɪæk] o [,hɪpə'kɑndrɪæk] *adj & s* hipocondríaco
hypochondrium [,haɪpə'kɑndrɪəm] o [,hɪpə'kɑndrɪəm] *s* (*pl:* **-a** [ə]) (anat.) hipocondrio
hypocoristic [,hɪpəko'rɪstɪk] *adj* hipocorístico
hypocotyl [,haɪpo'kɑtɪl] *s* (bot.) hipocotíleo
hypocrisy [hɪ'pɑkrɪsɪ] *s* (*pl:* **-sies**) hipocresía
hypocrite ['hɪpəkrɪt] *s* hipócrita
hypocritical [,hɪpə'krɪtɪkəl] *adj* hipócrita
hypocycloid [,haɪpə'saɪklɔɪd] *s* (geom.) hipocicloide
hypodermal [,haɪpə'dʌrməl] *adj* (bot.) hipodermo
hypodermic [,haɪpə'dʌrmɪk] *adj* hipodérmico; *s* medicamento hipodérmico; inyección hipodérmica; jeringa hipodérmica
hypodermically [,haɪpə'dʌrmɪkəlɪ] *adv* hipodérmicamente
hypodermic injection *s* inyección hipodérmica
hypodermic needle *s* aguja hipodérmica
hypodermic syringe *s* jeringa hipodérmica
hypogastric [,haɪpə'gæstrɪk] *adj* hipogástrico
hypogastrium [,haɪpə'gæstrɪəm] *s* (*pl:* **-a** [ə]) (anat. & zool.) hipogastrio
hypogene ['hɪpədʒin] *adj* (geol.) hipogénico
hypogeous [,haɪpə'dʒiəs] *adj* (bot. & zool.) hipogeo
hypogeum [,hɪpə'dʒiəm] *s* (*pl:* **-a** [ə]) (arch.) hipogeo
hypoglossal [,haɪpo'glɑsəl] *adj & s* (anat.) hipogloso
hypoid ['haɪpɔɪd] *adj* (mach.) hipoide

hypophosphite [ˌhaɪpoˈfɑsfaɪt] *s* (chem.) hipofosfito
hypophosphoric [ˌhaɪpofɑsˈfɑrɪk] o [ˌhaɪpofɑsˈfɔrɪk] *adj* (chem.) hipofosfórico
hypophosphoric acid *s* (chem.) ácido hipofosfórico
hypophosphorous [ˌhaɪpoˈfɑsfərəs] *adj* (chem.) hipofosforoso
hypophosphorous acid *s* (chem.) ácido hipofosforoso
hypophysis [haɪˈpɑfɪsɪs] *s* (*pl:* **-ses** [siz]) (anat.) hipófisis
hypostasis [haɪˈpɑstəsɪs] *s* (*pl:* **-ses** [siz]) (philos. & theol.) hipóstasis
hypostatic [ˌhaɪpəˈstætɪk] *adj* hipostático
hypostyle [ˈhɪpəstaɪl] o [ˈhaɪpəstaɪl] *adj & s* (arch.) hipóstilo
hyposulfite [ˌhaɪpoˈsʌlfaɪt] *s* (chem.) hiposulfito (*tiosulfato; sal del ácido hiposulfuroso*)
hyposulfurous [ˌhaɪposʌlˈfjurəs] o [ˌhaɪpoˈsʌlfərəs] *adj* (chem.) hiposulfuroso
hyposulfurous acid *s* (chem.) ácido hiposulfuroso
hypotenuse [haɪˈpɑtɪnjus] o [haɪˈpɑtɪnus] *s* (geom.) hipotenusa
hypothalamus [ˌhaɪpəˈθæləməs] *s* (anat.) hipotálamo
hypothec [haɪˈpɑθɛk] *s* (law) hipoteca
hypothecate [haɪˈpɑθɪket] *va* hipotecar
hypothecation [haɪˌpɑθɪˈkeʃən] *s* hipotecación
hypothenuse [haɪˈpɑθɪnjus] o [haɪˈpɑθɪnus] *s* var. de **hypotenuse**
hypothermia [ˌhaɪpoˈθʌrmɪə] *s* (med.) hipotermia
hypothesis [haɪˈpɑθɪsɪs] *s* (*pl:* **-ses** [siz]) hipótesis
hypothesize [haɪˈpɑθɪsaɪz] *va* formar hipótesis de; *vn* formar hipótesis
hypothetic [ˌhaɪpəˈθɛtɪk] o **hypothetical** [ˌhaɪpəˈθɛtɪkəl] *adj* hipotético
hypothyroidism [ˌhaɪpoˈθaɪrɔɪdɪzəm] *s* (path.) hipotiroidismo
hypotonic [ˌhaɪpəˈtɑnɪk] *adj* (chem. & physiol.) hipotónico
hypoxanthine [ˌhaɪpəˈzænθin] o [ˌhaɪpəˈzænθɪn] *s* (chem.) hipoxantina
hypsometer [hɪpˈsɑmɪtər] *s* hipsómetro
hypsometry [hɪpˈsɑmɪtrɪ] *s* hipsometría
hyson [ˈhaɪsən] *s* té verde chino
hyssop [ˈhɪsəp] *s* (bot. & eccl.) hisopo; (Bib.) alcaparra (*Capparis spinosa*)
hyssop loosestrife *s* (bot.) hierba del toro
hysterectomy [ˌhɪstəˈrɛktəmɪ] *s* (*pl:* **-mies**) (surg.) histerectomía
hysteresis [ˌhɪstəˈrisɪs] *s* (phys.) histéresis
hysteria [hɪsˈtɪrɪə] *s* excitación loca; (path.) histeria
hysteric [hɪsˈtɛrɪk] *adj* locamente excitado; (path.) histérico; **hysterics** *spl* paroxismo histérico
hysterical [hɪsˈtɛrɪkəl] *adj* locamente excitado; (path.) histérico
hysterotomy [ˌhɪstəˈrɑtəmɪ] *s* (*pl:* **-mies**) (surg.) histerotomía
hyther [ˈhaɪðər] *s* (biol.) híter
hyzone [ˈhaɪzon] *s* (chem.) hizono

I

I, i [aɪ] *s* (*pl:* **I's, i's** [aɪz]) novena letra del alfabeto inglés
i. abr. de **intransitive** y **island**
I. abr. de **Island, Islands, Isle** y **Isles**
I [aɪ] *pron pers* (*pl:* **we**) yo; **it is I** soy yo; *s* (*pl:* **I's** [aɪz]) (philos.) yo
Ia. abr. de **Iowa**
iamb [ˈaɪæmb] *s* yambo
iambic [aɪˈæmbɪk] *adj* yámbico; *s* yambo; verso yámbico
iambus [aɪˈæmbəs] *s* (*pl:* **-bi** [baɪ] o **-buses**) yambo
ib. abr. de **ibidem**
I beam *s* (constr.) viga I
Iberia [aɪˈbɪrɪə] *s* Iberia
Iberian [aɪˈbɪrɪən] *adj* ibérico, iberio o ibero; *s* ibero
Iberian Peninsula *s* Península Ibérica
Iberism [ˈaɪbərɪzəm] *s* iberismo
Ibero-America [aɪˈbɪroəˈmɛrɪkə] *s* Iberoamérica
Ibero-American [aɪˈbɪroəˈmɛrɪkən] *adj* & *s* iberoamericano
ibex [ˈaɪbɛks] *s* (*pl:* **ibexes** o **ibices** [ˈɪbɪsiz] o [ˈaɪbɪsiz]) (zool.) íbice, cabra montés; (zool.) cabra bezoar (*Capra aegagrus*)
ibid. abr. de **ibidem**
ibidem [ɪˈbaɪdɛm] *adv* (Lat.) ibídem (*en el mismo lugar*)
ibis [ˈaɪbɪs] *s* (*pl:* **ibises** o **ibis**) (orn.) ibis
Ibsenian [ɪbˈsinɪən] *adj* & *s* ibseniano
-ic *suffix adj* -ico, p.ej., **metallic** metálico; **public** público; **volcanic** volcánico; excepto en la terminología química, los sufijos **-ic** e **-ical** son por la mayor parte iguales e intercambiables, p.ej., **hypothetic** o **hypothetical** hipotético; **symbolic** o **symbolical** simbólico; al mismo tiempo, hay algunas palabras que tienen sentido distinto según terminan en **-ic** o **-ical,** v.g., **comic** cómico (*perteneciente a la comedia que no a la tragedia*), p.ej., **comic actor** actor cómico; **comical** cómico (*divertido, gracioso*), p.ej., **comical episode** episodio cómico; **historic** histórico (*importante en la historia*), p.ej., **historic event** acontecimiento histórico; **historical** histórico (*que trata de la historia*), p.ej., **historical novel** novela histórica; (chem.) -ico, p.ej., **cupric** cúprico; **sulfuric** sulfúrico; *suffix s* -ico, p.ej., **domestic** doméstico; **critic** crítico; -ica, p.ej., **arithmetic** aritmética; **music** música; **-ics** *suffix ssg* -ica, p.ej., **physics** física; **politics** política
-cal *suffix adj* -ico, p.ej., **critical** crítico; **logical** lógico; **musical** músico; para la comparación de **-ic** e **-ical,** véase **-ic**
Icarian [aɪˈkɛrɪən] *adj* icáreo o icario
Icarius [aɪˈkɛrɪəs] *s* (myth.) Icario
Icarus [ˈɪkərəs] *s* (myth.) Ícaro
ICBM abr. de **intercontinental ballistic missile**
I.C.C. abr. de **Interstate Commerce Commission**
ice [aɪs] *s* hielo; helado, sorbete; garapiña, costra de azúcar; **to break the ice** dar comienzo a una empresa difícil; romper el hielo (*quebrantar la reserva*); **to cut no ice** (coll.) no surtir efecto, no importar nada; **to skate on thin ice** buscar el peligro; usar de argumentos infundados; *adj* glacial; de hielo; *va* helar; enfriar con hielo; garapiñar (*bañar en el almíbar*); *vn* helarse; **to ice up** (aer.) helarse
ice age *s* (geol.) época glacial, edad del hielo
ice bag *s* bolsa de hielo, bolsa (de caucho) para hielo
iceberg [ˈaɪsˌbʌrg] *s* banquisa, iceberg
iceboat [ˈaɪsˌbot] *s* trineo con vela para deslizarse por el hielo; rompehielos, cortahielos
icebound [ˈaɪsˌbaʊnd] *adj* detenido por el hielo, rodeado de hielo
icebox [ˈaɪsˌbɑks] *s* nevera, fresquera
icebreaker [ˈaɪsˌbrekər] *s* rompehielos, cortahielos
icecap [ˈaɪsˌkæp] *s* manto de hielo, helero; bolsa para hielo
ice cream *s* helado
ice-cream cone [ˈaɪsˈkrim] *s* cornet de helado, cucurucho
ice-cream freezer *s* heladora, sorbetera, garapiñera
ice-cream parlor *s* heladería, salón de refrescos, botillería
ice-cream soda *s* agua gaseosa con helado
ice cube *s* cubito de hielo
iced [aɪst] *adj* helado; garapiñado
ice field *s* banquisa, bancos de hielo
ice hockey *s* hockey sobre patines
icehouse [ˈaɪsˌhaʊs] *s* nevera
Iceland [ˈaɪslənd] *s* Islandia
Icelander [ˈaɪsˌlændər] o [ˈaɪsləndər] *s* islandés
Icelandic [aɪsˈlændɪk] *adj* islandés; *s* islandés (*idioma*)
Iceland moss *s* (bot.) musgo de Islandia
Iceland spar *s* (mineral.) espato de Islandia
iceman [ˈaɪsˌmæn] *s* (*pl:* **-men**) vendedor de hielo, repartidor de hielo
ice pack *s* hielo flotante; aplicación de hielo empaquetado
ice pail *s* enfriadera
ice pick *s* picahielos, punzón para romper hielo
ice plant *s* fábrica de hielo; (bot.) escarchada
ice sheet *s* masa de hielo, manto de hielo
ice skate *s* patín de cuchilla, patín de hielo
ice tray *s* bandejita del hielo
ice-up [ˈaɪsˌʌp] *s* (aer.) formación de hielo
ice water *s* agua helada
ichneumon [ɪkˈnjumən] o [ɪkˈnumən] *s* (zool. & ent.) icneumón; (zool.) meloncillo (*Herpestes ichneumon*)
ichneumon fly *s* (ent.) icneumón
ichnography [ɪkˈnɑgrəfɪ] *s* (arch.) icnografía
ichor [ˈaɪkɔr] *s* (path.) icor (*de una úlcera*); (myth.) sangre de los dioses
ichorous [ˈaɪkərəs] *adj* icoroso
ichthyol [ˈɪkθɪol] o [ˈɪkθɪɑl] *s* (trademark) ictiol
ichthyologic [ˌɪkθɪəˈlɑdʒɪk] o **ichthyological** [ˌɪkθɪəˈlɑdʒɪkəl] *adj* ictiológico
ichthyologist [ˌɪkθɪˈɑlədʒɪst] *s* ictiólogo
ichthyology [ˌɪkθɪˈɑlədʒɪ] *s* ictiología
ichthyophagist [ˌɪkθɪˈɑfədʒɪst] *s* ictiófago
ichthyophagous [ˌɪkθɪˈɑfəgəs] *adj* ictiófago
ichthyosaur [ˈɪkθɪəˌsɔr] *s* (pal.) ictiosauro
ichthyosaurus [ˌɪkθɪəˈsɔrəs] *s* (*pl:* **-ri** [raɪ]) (pal.) var. de **ichthyosaur**
ichthyosis [ˌɪkθɪˈosɪs] *s* (path.) ictiosis
ichthyosism [ˈɪkθɪəsɪzəm] *s* (vet.) ictiosismo
ichu [ˈitʃu] *s* (bot.) icho o ichú
-ician *suffix s* -ico, p.ej., **logician** lógico; **musician** músico
icicle [ˈaɪsɪkəl] *s* carámbano
icing [ˈaɪsɪŋ] *s* costra de azúcar, capa de azúcar; (aer.) formación de hielo
icon [ˈaɪkɑn] *s* icono; (eccl.) icón
iconoclasm [aɪˈkɑnəklæzəm] *s* iconoclasia o iconoclasmo
iconoclast [aɪˈkɑnəklæst] *s* iconoclasta
iconoclastic [aɪˌkɑnəˈklæstɪk] *adj* iconoclasta
iconographic [aɪˌkɑnəˈgræfɪk] o **iconographical** [aɪˌkɑnəˈgræfɪkəl] *adj* iconográfico
iconography [ˌaɪkəˈnɑgrəfɪ] *s* iconografía
iconolater [ˌaɪkəˈnɑlətər] *s* iconólatra
iconolatrous [ˌaɪkəˈnɑlətrəs] *adj* iconólatra
iconolatry [ˌaɪkəˈnɑlətrɪ] *s* iconolatría
iconology [ˌaɪkəˈnɑlədʒɪ] *s* iconología

iconomania [aɪˌkɑnəˈmenɪə] *s* iconomanía
iconoscope [aɪˈkɑnəskop] *s* (trademark) iconoscopio
iconostasion [aɪˌkɑnəˈstesɪɑn] *s* (eccl.) iconostasio
icosahedron [ˌaɪkosəˈhidrən] *s* (*pl:* **-dra** [drə]) (geom.) icosaedro
icteric [ɪkˈtɛrɪk] *adj* ictérico
icterus [ˈɪktərəs] *s* (path.) ictericia
ictus [ˈɪktəs] *s* (*pl:* **ictuses** o **ictus**) (path. & pros.) ictus
icy [ˈaɪsɪ] *adj* (*comp:* **icier;** *super:* **iciest**) helado, frío; resbaladizo; (fig.) frío
id. abr. de **idem**
Id. abr. de **Idaho**
I'd [aɪd] contracción de **I had, I should** y **I would**
id [ɪd] *s* (psychoanal.) ello
Ida. abr. de **Idaho**
idea [aɪˈdiə] *s* idea
ideal [aɪˈdiəl] *adj & s* ideal
idealism [aɪˈdiəlɪzəm] *s* idealismo
idealist [aɪˈdiəlɪst] *adj & s* idealista
idealistic [aɪˌdiəlˈɪstɪk] *adj* idealista; (philos.) idealístico
ideality [ˌaɪdɪˈælɪtɪ] *s* (*pl:* **-ties**) idealidad
idealization [aɪˌdiəlɪˈzeʃən] *s* idealización
idealize [aɪˈdiəlaɪz] *va* idealizar
ideally [aɪˈdiəlɪ] *adv* idealmente
ideation [ˌaɪdɪˈeʃən] *s* ideación
idem [ˈaɪdɛm] *adj & pron* (Lat.) ídem
identic [aɪˈdɛntɪk] o **identical** [aɪˈdɛntɪkəl] *adj* idéntico
identical twins *spl* gemelos homólogos o idénticos
identification [aɪˌdɛntɪfɪˈkeʃən] *s* identificación
identification tag *s* (mil.) disco de identificación, placa de identidad
identify [aɪˈdɛntɪfaɪ] (*pret & pp:* **-fied**) *va* identificar
identity [aɪˈdɛntɪtɪ] *s* (*pl:* **-ties**) identidad
ideogram [ˈɪdɪoˌgræm] o [ˈaɪdɪoˌgræm] *s* ideograma
ideograph [ˈɪdɪoˌgræf] o [ˈaɪdɪoˌgræf] *s* ideografía
ideographic [ˌɪdɪoˈgræfɪk] o [ˌaɪdɪoˈgræfɪk] o **ideographical** [ˌɪdɪoˈgræfɪkəl] o [ˌaɪdɪoˈgræfɪkəl] *adj* ideográfico
ideologic [ˌɪdɪoˈlɑdʒɪk] o [ˌaɪdɪoˈlɑdʒɪk] o **ideological** [ˌɪdɪoˈlɑdʒɪkəl] o [ˌaɪdɪoˈlɑdʒɪkəl] *adj* ideológico
ideologist [ˌaɪdɪˈɑlədʒɪst] o [ˌɪdɪˈɑlədʒɪst] *s* ideólogo
ideology [ˌaɪdɪˈɑlədʒɪ] o [ˌɪdɪˈɑlədʒɪ] *s* (*pl:* **-gies**) ideología
ides [aɪdz] *spl* idus
idiocy [ˈɪdɪəsɪ] *s* (*pl:* **-cies**) idiotez
idioelectric [ˌɪdɪo·ɪˈlɛktrɪk] o **idioelectrical** [ˌɪdɪo·ɪˈlɛktrɪkəl] *adj* idioeléctrico
idiom [ˈɪdɪəm] *s* modismo; idioma, lenguaje, jerga; genio, índole (*de un idioma*); estilo (*de un escritor*)
idiomatic [ˌɪdɪəˈmætɪk] *adj* idiomático
idiosyncrasy [ˌɪdɪoˈsɪŋkrəsɪ] *s* (*pl:* **-sies**) idiosincrasia
idiosyncratic [ˌɪdɪosɪnˈkrætɪk] *adj* idiosincrásico
idiot [ˈɪdɪət] *s* idiota
idiotic [ˌɪdɪˈɑtɪk] *adj* idiota
idiotically [ˌɪdɪˈɑtɪkəlɪ] *adv* estúpidamente, imbécilmente
idioticon [ˌɪdɪˈɑtɪkɑn] *s* idiótico
idle [ˈaɪdəl] *adj* ocioso; **at idle moments** a ratos perdidos; **to run idle** marchar en ralentí o en vacío; *va* (mach.) hacer marchar en ralentí o en vacío; **to idle away** gastar ociosamente (*el tiempo*); *vn* estar ocioso, holgar, haraganear; (mach.) marchar en ralentí o en vacío
idleness [ˈaɪdəlnɪs] *s* ociosidad
idler [ˈaɪdlər] *s* ocioso, haragán; (mach.) polea loca, rueda loca
idol [ˈaɪdəl] *s* ídolo; (fig.) ídolo
idolater [aɪˈdɑlətər] *s* idólatra
idolatress [aɪˈdɑlətrɪs] *s* idólatra
idolatrous [aɪˈdɑlətrəs] *adj* idolátrico, idólatra
idolatry [aɪˈdɑlətrɪ] *s* (*pl:* **-tries**) idolatría
idolization [ˌaɪdəlɪˈzeʃən] *s* idolatría
idolize [ˈaɪdəlaɪz] *va* idolatrar
Idomeneus [aɪˈdɑmɪnjus] o [aɪˈdɑmɪnus] *s* (myth.) Idomeneo
Idumaea o **Idumea** [ˌɪdjuˈmiə] o [ˌaɪdjuˈmiə] *s* (Bib.) Idumea
Idumaean o **Idumean** [ˌɪdjuˈmiən] o [ˌaɪdjuˈmiən] *adj & s* idumeo
idyl o **idyll** [ˈaɪdəl] *s* idilio
idyllic [aɪˈdɪlɪk] *adj* idílico
i.e. abr. de **id est** (Lat.) **that is, that is to say**
-ie *suffix dim* var. de **-y,** p.ej., **doggie** perrito; **Annie** Anita
if [ɪf] *s* hipótesis; *conj* si; **if so** si es así; **if true** si es cierto
igloo [ˈɪglu] *s* iglú
Ignatian [ɪgˈneʃən] *adj & s* ignaciano
Ignatius [ɪgˈneʃəs] *s* Ignacio
igneous [ˈɪgnɪəs] *adj* ígneo
igniferous [ɪgˈnɪfərəs] *adj* ignífero
ignifuge [ˈɪgnɪfjudʒ] *adj & s* ignífugo
ignis fatuus [ˈɪgnɪsˈfætʃuəs] *s* (*pl:* **ignes fatui** [ˈɪgnizˈfætʃuaɪ]) fuego fatuo
ignite [ɪgˈnaɪt] *va* encender; *vn* encenderse
igniter [ɪgˈnaɪtər] *s* encendedor (*persona y dispositivo*)
ignition [ɪgˈnɪʃən] *s* ignición, encendido, inflamación
ignition coil *s* (aut.) bobina de encendido
ignition point *s* punto de inflamación
ignition stroke *s* (aut.) carrera de encendido
ignition switch *s* (aut.) interruptor del encendido
ignivomous [ɪgˈnɪvəməs] *adj* ignívomo
ignoble [ɪgˈnobəl] *adj* innoble
ignominious [ˌɪgnəˈmɪnɪəs] *adj* ignominioso
ignominy [ˈɪgnəmɪnɪ] *s* (*pl:* **-ies**) ignominia
ignoramus [ˌɪgnəˈreməs] *s* ignorante
ignorance [ˈɪgnərəns] *s* ignorancia
ignorant [ˈɪgnərənt] *adj* ignorante
ignore [ɪgˈnor] *va* no hacer caso de; no hacerle caso (*a una persona*); (law) rechazar
Igorot [ˌɪgəˈrot] *adj & s* igorrote
Igorrote [ˌɪgəˈrotɪ] *s* igorrote
iguana [ɪˈgwɑnə] *s* (zool.) iguana
iguanodont [ɪˈgwænədɑnt] *s* (pal.) iguanodonte
IHS abr. de **In Hac (Cruce) Salus** (Lat.) **In this cross salvation; In Hoc Signo Vinces** (Lat.) **In this sign shalt thou conquer;** y **Iesus Hominum Salvator** (Lat.) **Jesus, Saviour of Men**
ikon [ˈaɪkɑn] *s* var. de **icon**
ileac [ˈɪlɪæk] *adj* (anat. & path.) ilíaco
ileocaecal [ˌɪlɪoˈsikəl] *adj* ileocecal
ileum [ˈɪlɪəm] *s* (anat.) íleon
ileus [ˈɪlɪəs] *s* (path.) íleo
ilex [ˈaɪlɛks] *s* (bot.) acebo; (bot.) hierba mate; (bot.) encina
iliac [ˈɪlɪæk] *adj* (anat.) ilíaco; (*cap.*) *adj* (myth.) ilíaco
Iliad [ˈɪlɪəd] *s* Ilíada
Ilian [ˈɪlɪən] *adj* (myth.) iliense
ilicaceous [ˌaɪlɪˈkeʃəs] *adj* (bot.) ilicáceo
Ilion [ˈɪlɪən] *s* (myth.) Ilión
ilium [ˈɪlɪəm] *s* (*pl:* **-a** [ə]) (anat.) ilion; (*cap.*) *s* (myth.) Ilión
ilk [ɪlk] *s* jaez, especie; **of that ilk** (coll.) del mismo nombre; (coll.) de ese jaez, de esa especie
ill. abr. de **illustrated** y **illustration**
Ill. abr. de **Illinois**
I'll [aɪl] contracción de **I shall** y **I will**
ill [ɪl] *adj* (*comp:* **worse;** *super:* **worst**) malo, enfermo; *adv* mal; **to take ill** tomar a mal; caer enfermo; *s* mal, enfermedad
ill-advised [ˈɪlədˈvaɪzd] *adj* malaconsejado, desaconsejado
ill at ease *adj* incómodo, inquieto, corrido, avergonzado
illation [ɪˈleʃən] *s* ilación
illative [ˈɪlətɪv] *adj* ilativo; *s* ilativa
ill-boding [ˈɪlˈbodɪŋ] *adj* nefasto, aciago, ominoso
ill-bred [ˈɪlˈbrɛd] *adj* malcriado
ill breeding *s* mala crianza, malos modales
ill-considered [ˈɪlkənˈsɪdərd] *adj* desconsiderado
ill-disposed [ˈɪldɪsˈpozd] *adj* malintencionado; maldispuesto
illegal [ɪˈligəl] *adj* ilegal
illegality [ˌɪliˈgælɪtɪ] *s* (*pl:* **-ties**) ilegalidad

illegibility [ˌɪlɛdʒɪˈbɪlɪtɪ] *s* (*pl:* **-ties**) ilegibilidad
illegible [ɪˈlɛdʒɪbəl] *adj* ilegible
illegitimacy [ˌɪlɪˈdʒɪtɪməsɪ] *s* ilegitimidad
illegitimate [ˌɪlɪˈdʒɪtɪmɪt] *adj* ilegítimo
ill fame *s* mala fama; reputación de inmoral
ill-fated [ˈɪlˈfetɪd] *adj* aciago, funesto, infausto; malogrado; siniestrado
ill-favored [ˈɪlˈfevərd] *adj* feo, repugnante
ill-featured [ˈɪlˈfitʃərd] *adj* mal agestado, de mala cara
ill-founded [ˈɪlˈfaʊndɪd] *adj* mal fundado
ill-gotten [ˈɪlˈgɑtən] *adj* mal ganado
ill health *s* mala salud
ill humor *s* mal humor
ill-humored [ˈɪlˈhjumərd] *adj* malhumorado
illiberal [ɪˈlɪbərəl] *adj* iliberal
illiberality [ɪˌlɪbəˈrælɪtɪ] *s* iliberalidad
illicit [ɪˈlɪsɪt] *adj* ilícito
illimitable [ɪˈlɪmɪtəbəl] *adj* ilimitable, infinito
illinium [ɪˈlɪnɪəm] *s* (chem.) ilinio
illiteracy [ɪˈlɪtərəsɪ] *s* (*pl:* **-cies**) ignorancia, incultura; analfabetismo; (gram.) barbarismo
illiterate [ɪˈlɪtərɪt] *adj* iliterato; analfabeto; *s* analfabeto
ill-judged [ˈɪlˈdʒʌdʒd] *adj* desconsiderado, imprudente
ill-mannered [ˈɪlˈmænərd] *adj* de malos modales
ill nature *s* mala disposición
ill-natured [ˈɪlˈnetʃərd] *adj* maldispuesto, malicioso
illness [ˈɪlnɪs] *s* enfermedad
illogical [ɪˈlɑdʒɪkəl] *adj* ilógico
ill-omened [ˈɪlˈomənd] *adj* malhadado
ill-spent [ˈɪlˈspɛnt] *adj* malgastado
ill-starred [ˈɪlˈstɑrd] *adj* malhadado
ill-suited [ˈɪlˈsutɪd] o [ˈɪlˈsjutɪd] *adj* inadecuado; incompetente
ill temper *s* mal genio
ill-tempered [ˈɪlˈtɛmpərd] *adj* de mal genio
ill-timed [ˈɪlˈtaɪmd] *adj* intempestivo, inoportuno
ill-treat [ˌɪlˈtrit] *va* maltratar
ill treatment *s* malos tratamientos
ill turn *s* mala jugada; cambio desfavorable
illuminant [ɪˈlumɪnənt] *adj* iluminante; *s* alumbrado
illuminate [ɪˈlumɪnet] *va* iluminar, alumbrar; ilustrar; (f.a.) iluminar, miniar; *vn* hacer luminarias
Illuminati [ɪˌlumɪˈnetaɪ] *spl* iluminados, alumbrados (*secta mística, nacida en España en el siglo XVI*)
illuminating gas *s* gas de alumbrado
illuminating oil *s* aceite de alumbrado
illumination [ɪˌlumɪˈneʃən] *s* iluminación
illuminative [ɪˈlumɪˌnetɪv] *adj* iluminativo
illuminator [ɪˈlumɪˌnetər] *s* iluminador
illumine [ɪˈlumɪn] *va* iluminar; animar, avivar; *vn* iluminarse
Illuminism [ɪˈlumɪnɪzəm] *s* iluminismo
illus. abr. de **illustrated** y **illustration**
ill usage *s* malos tratamientos
ill-use [ˌɪlˈjuz] *va* maltratar
illusion [ɪˈluʒən] *s* ilusión; cendal (*tela*)
illusionist [ɪˈluʒənɪst] *s* ilusionista, prestidigitador
illusive [ɪˈlusɪv] *adj* ilusivo
illusory [ɪˈlusərɪ] *adj* ilusorio
illust. abr. de **illustrated** y **illustration**
illustrate [ˈɪləstret] o [ɪˈlʌstret] *va* ilustrar
illustration [ˌɪləsˈtreʃən] *s* ilustración
illustrative [ɪˈlʌstrətɪv] o [ˈɪləsˌtretɪv] *adj* ilustrativo
illustrator [ˈɪləsˌtretər] *s* ilustrador
illustrious [ɪˈlʌstrɪəs] *adj* ilustre
ill will *s* mala voluntad, odio, inquina
Illyria [ɪˈlɪrɪə] *s* Iliria
Illyrian [ɪˈlɪrɪən] *adj* & *s* ilirio
Illyric [ɪˈlɪrɪk] *adj* ilírico
I'm [aɪm] contracción de **I am**
image [ˈɪmɪdʒ] *s* imagen; **in his own image** a su imagen; **the very image of** la propia estampa de, el vivo retrato de; *va* imaginar; representar; representar con imágenes; reflejar
imagery [ˈɪmɪdʒrɪ] o [ˈɪmɪdʒərɪ] *s* (*pl:* **-ries**) fantasía; imágenes; paisaje
imaginable [ɪˈmædʒɪnəbəl] *adj* imaginable
imaginary [ɪˈmædʒɪˌnɛrɪ] *adj* imaginario
imagination [ˌɪmædʒɪˈneʃən] *s* imaginación
imaginative [ɪˈmædʒɪˌnetɪv] *adj* imaginativo
imagine [ɪˈmædʒɪn] *va* imaginar; *vn* imaginar; (coll.) imaginarse; **to imagine** + *ger* imaginarse + *inf*
imagist [ˈɪmɪdʒɪst] *s* imagista o imaginista (*individuo de un grupo de poetas ingleses y norteamericanos*)
imago [ɪˈmego] *s* (*pl:* **imagos** o **imagines** [ɪˈmædʒɪniz]) (zool.) imago
imam [ɪˈmɑm] *s* imán (*título mahometano*)
imbalm [ɪmˈbɑm] *va* var. de **embalm**
imbecile [ˈɪmbɪsɪl] *adj* & *s* imbécil
imbecility [ˌɪmbɪˈsɪlɪtɪ] *s* (*pl:* **-ties**) imbecilidad
imbed [ɪmˈbɛd] (*pret* & *pp:* **-bedded;** *ger:* **-bedding**) *va* hincar, encajar, empotrar, plantar
imbibe [ɪmˈbaɪb] *va* beber; embeber; embeberse de o en; *vn* beber; (coll.) empinar el codo
imbibition [ˌɪmbɪˈbɪʃən] *s* imbibición
imbricate [ˈɪmbrɪket] o [ˈɪmbrɪkɪt] o **imbricated** [ˈɪmbrɪˌketɪd] *adj* imbricado
imbrication [ˌɪmbrɪˈkeʃən] *s* imbricación
imbroglio [ɪmˈbroljo] *s* (*pl:* **-glios**) embrollo
imbrue [ɪmˈbru] *va* mojar, mojar con sangre, ensangrentar
imbue [ɪmˈbju] *va* imbuir; **to imbue with** imbuir de o en
imitable [ˈɪmɪtəbəl] *adj* imitable
imitate [ˈɪmɪtet] *va* imitar
imitation [ˌɪmɪˈteʃən] *s* imitación; **in imitation of** a imitación de; *adj* imitación, de imitación, p.ej., **imitation jewelry** joyas imitación, joyas de imitación; imitado, p.e., **imitation pearls** perlas imitadas
imitative [ˈɪmɪˌtetɪv] *adj* imitativo; imitador
imitator [ˈɪmɪˌtetər] *s* imitador
immaculate [ɪˈmækjəlɪt] *adj* inmaculado
Immaculate Conception *s* Inmaculada Concepción
immanence [ˈɪmənəns] o **immanency** [ˈɪmənənsɪ] *s* inmanencia
immanent [ˈɪmənənt] *adj* inmanente
Immanuel [ɪˈmænjuəl] *s* (Bib.) Emanuel
immaterial [ˌɪməˈtɪrɪəl] *adj* inmaterial; sin importancia, indiferente
immaterialism [ˌɪməˈtɪrɪəlɪzəm] *s* inmaterialismo
immateriality [ˌɪməˌtɪrɪˈælɪtɪ] *s* inmaterialidad
immature [ˌɪməˈtjʊr] o [ˌɪməˈtʊr] *adj* inmaturo
immaturity [ˌɪməˈtjʊrɪtɪ] o [ˌɪməˈtʊrɪtɪ] *s* inmadurez
immeasurable [ɪˈmɛʒərəbəl] *adj* inmensurable
immeasurably [ɪˈmɛʒərəblɪ] *adv* inmensurablemente
immediacy [ɪˈmidɪəsɪ] *s* inmediación
immediate [ɪˈmidɪɪt] *adj* inmediato
immediately [ɪˈmidɪɪtlɪ] *adv* inmediatamente
immedicable [ɪˈmɛdɪkəbəl] *adj* inmedicable
immemorial [ˌɪmɪˈmorɪəl] *adj* inmemorial o inmemorable
immense [ɪˈmɛns] *adj* inmenso; (slang) excelente
immensely [ɪˈmɛnslɪ] *adv* inmensamente
immensity [ɪˈmɛnsɪtɪ] *s* (*pl:* **-ties**) inmensidad
immensurable [ɪˈmɛnʃʊrəbəl] *adj* inmensurable
immerge [ɪˈmʌrdʒ] *va* inmergir, sumergir; *vn* inmergirse, sumergirse
immerse [ɪˈmʌrs] *va* inmergir, sumergir; bautizar por inmersión
immersion [ɪˈmʌrʃən] o [ɪˈmʌrʒən] *s* inmersión; (astr.) inmersión; bautismo por inmersión
immigrant [ˈɪmɪgrənt] *adj* & *s* inmigrante
immigrate [ˈɪmɪgret] *vn* inmigrar
immigration [ˌɪmɪˈgreʃən] *s* inmigración
immigration quota *s* cuota de inmigración
imminence [ˈɪmɪnəns] o **imminency** [ˈɪmɪnənsɪ] *s* inminencia
imminent [ˈɪmɪnənt] *adj* inminente
immiscible [ɪˈmɪsɪbəl] *adj* inmiscible
immobile [ɪˈmobɪl] o [ɪˈmobil] *adj* inmoble
immobility [ˌɪmoˈbɪlɪtɪ] *s* inmovilidad
immobilization [ɪˌmobɪlɪˈzeʃən] *s* inmovilización

immobilize [ɪ'mobɪlaɪz] *va* inmovilizar
immoderate [ɪ'mɑdərɪt] *adj* inmoderado
immoderation [ɪ,mɑdə'reʃən] *s* inmoderación
immodest [ɪ'mɑdɪst] *adj* inmodesto
immodesty [ɪ'mɑdɪstɪ] *s* inmodestia
immolate ['ɪmolet] *va* inmolar
immolation [,ɪmo'leʃən] *s* inmolación
immolator ['ɪmo,letər] *s* inmolador
immoral [ɪ'mɑrəl] o [ɪ'mɔrəl] *adj* inmoral
immorality [,ɪmə'rælɪtɪ] *s* (*pl:* **-ties**) inmoralidad
immortal [ɪ'mɔrtəl] *adj & s* inmortal
immortality [,ɪmɔr'tælɪtɪ] *s* inmortalidad
immortalize [ɪ'mɔrtəlaɪz] *va* inmortalizar
immortelle [,ɪmɔr'tɛl] *s* (bot.) siempreviva, perpetua
immortification [ɪ,mɔrtɪfɪ'keʃən] *s* inmortificación
immortified [ɪ'mɔrtɪfaɪd] *adj* inmortificado
immovability [ɪ,muvə'bɪlɪtɪ] *s* inmovilidad; impasibilidad
immovable [ɪ'muvəbəl] *adj* inmoble; (fig.) inmoble; impasible, insensible; (law) inmueble; **immovables** *spl* (law) inmuebles, bienes raíces
immovable feast *s* (eccl.) fiesta fija o inmoble
immune [ɪ'mjun] *adj* inmune; **immune to** inmune contra
immunity [ɪ'mjunɪtɪ] *s* (*pl:* **-ties**) inmunidad
immunization [,ɪmjənɪ'zeʃən] o [ɪ,mjunɪ'zeʃən] *s* inmunización
immunize ['ɪmjənaɪz] o [ɪ'mjunaɪz] *va* inmunizar
immunologist [,ɪmjə'nɑlədʒɪst] *s* inmunólogo
immunology [,ɪmjə'nɑlədʒɪ] *s* inmunología
immure [ɪ'mjʊr] *va* emparedar
immurement [ɪ'mjʊrmənt] *s* emparedamiento
immutability [ɪ,mjutə'bɪlɪtɪ] *s* inmutabilidad
immutable [ɪ'mjutəbəl] *adj* inmutable
imp [ɪmp] *s* diablillo; niño travieso
impact ['ɪmpækt] *s* impacto, choque; (fig.) impacto
impacted [ɪm'pæktɪd] *adj* apretado; (dent.) impactado
impaction [ɪm'pækʃən] *s* (dent. & med.) impacción
impair [ɪm'pɛr] *va* empeorar, deteriorar
impairment [ɪm'pɛrmənt] *s* empeoramiento, deterioro
impale [ɪm'pel] *va* empalar; cercar
impalement [ɪm'pelmənt] *s* empalamiento; cercamiento
impalpability [ɪm,pælpə'bɪlɪtɪ] *s* impalpabilidad
impalpable [ɪm'pælpəbəl] *adj* impalpable
impanation [,ɪmpə'neʃən] *s* (theol.) impanación
impanel [ɪm'pænəl] (*pret & pp:* **-eled** o **-elled;** *ger:* **-eling** o **-elling**) *va* inscribir en la lista de los jurados; elegir (*un jurado*)
imparadise [ɪm'pærədaɪs] *va* convertir en un paraíso; colmar de felicidad
imparidigitate [ɪm,pærɪ'dɪdʒɪtet] *adj* (zool.) imparidígito
imparipinnate [ɪm,pærɪ'pɪnet] *adj* (bot.) imparipinado
imparisyllabic [ɪm,pærɪsɪ'læbɪk] *adj* (gram.) imparisílabo o imparisilábico; *s* (gram.) nombre imparisílabo
imparity [ɪm'pærɪtɪ] *s* desigualdad, disparidad
impart [ɪm'pɑrt] *va* decir, hacer saber; imprimir, comunicar
impartial [ɪm'pɑrʃəl] *adj* imparcial
impartiality [,ɪmpɑrʃɪ'ælɪtɪ] *s* imparcialidad
impassability [ɪm,pæsə'bɪlɪtɪ] o [ɪm,pɑsə'bɪlɪtɪ] *s* impracticabilidad
impassable [ɪm'pæsəbəl] o [ɪm'pɑsəbəl] *adj* intransitable, impracticable
impasse [ɪm'pæs] o ['ɪmpæs] *s* callejón sin salida
impassibility [ɪm,pæsɪ'bɪlɪtɪ] *s* impasibilidad
impassible [ɪm'pæsɪbəl] *adj* impasible
impassioned [ɪm'pæʃənd] *adj* ardiente, vehemente
impassive [ɪm'pæsɪv] *adj* impasible
impassivity [,ɪmpæ'sɪvɪtɪ] *s* impasibilidad
impaste [ɪm'pest] *va* (f.a.) empastar
impatience [ɪm'peʃəns] *s* impaciencia
impatient [ɪm'peʃənt] *adj* impaciente

impeach [ɪm'pitʃ] *va* poner en tela de juicio; acusar; (law) residenciar
impeachable [ɪm'pitʃəbəl] *adj* censurable; (law) susceptible de ser residenciado
impeachment [ɪm'pitʃmənt] *s* juicio; acusación; (law) residencia
impearl [ɪm'pʌrl] *va* (poet.) aljofarar
impeccability [ɪm,pɛkə'bɪlɪtɪ] *s* impecabilidad
impeccable [ɪm'pɛkəbəl] *adj* impecable
impecuniosity [,ɪmpɪ,kjunɪ'ɑsɪtɪ] *s* inopia
impecunious [,ɪmpɪ'kjunɪəs] *adj* inope
impedance [ɪm'pidəns] *s* (elec.) impedancia
impedance coil *s* (elec.) bobina de impedancia
impede [ɪm'pid] *va* dificultar, contrariar, estorbar
impediment [ɪm'pɛdɪmənt] *s* impedimento; defecto; (law) impedimento
impedimenta [ɪm,pɛdɪ'mɛntə] *spl* equipajes; (mil.) impedimento
impel [ɪm'pɛl] (*pret & pp:* **-pelled;** *ger:* **-pelling**) *va* impeler, impulsar; **to impel to** + *inf* impeler o impulsar a + *inf*
impend [ɪm'pɛnd] *vn* pender; amenazar, ser inminente
impending [ɪm'pɛndɪŋ] *adj* pendiente; amenazante, inminente
impenetrability [ɪm,pɛnɪtrə'bɪlɪtɪ] *s* impenetrabilidad; impersuasión
impenetrable [ɪm'pɛnɪtrəbəl] *adj* impenetrable; impersuasible
impenitence [ɪm'pɛnɪtəns] *s* impenitencia
impenitent [ɪm'pɛnɪtənt] *adj & s* impenitente
imper. abr. de **imperative**
imperative [ɪm'pɛrətɪv] *adj* imperativo; imperioso, urgente; (gram.) imperativo; *s* imperativo; (gram.) imperativo
imperative mood *s* (gram.) modo imperativo
imperceptibility [,ɪmpər,sɛptɪ'bɪlɪtɪ] *s* imperceptibilidad
imperceptible [,ɪmpər'sɛptɪbəl] *adj* imperceptible
imperceptibly [,ɪmpər'sɛptɪblɪ] *adv* imperceptiblemente
imperf. abr. de **imperfect**
imperfect [ɪm'pʌrfɪkt] *adj* imperfecto; (gram.) imperfecto; *s* (gram.) imperfecto; (gram.) pretérito imperfecto
imperfection [,ɪmpər'fɛkʃən] *s* imperfección, desperfecto
imperfective [,ɪmpər'fɛktɪv] *adj* (gram.) imperfectivo
imperforate [ɪm'pʌrfəret] o [ɪm'pʌrfərɪt] *adj* imperforado; (philately) sin dentar
imperforation [ɪm,pʌrfə'reʃən] *s* imperforación
imperial [ɪm'pɪrɪəl] *adj* imperial; majestuoso, magnífico; *s* perilla; imperial (*sitio con asientos de algunos carruajes encima de la cubierta*)
imperial eagle *s* (orn.) águila imperial
imperial gallon *s* galón inglés
imperialism [ɪm'pɪrɪəlɪzəm] *s* imperialismo
imperialist [ɪm'pɪrɪəlɪst] *s* imperialista
imperialistic [ɪm,pɪrɪə'lɪstɪk] *adj* imperialista
imperialistically [ɪm,pɪrɪə'lɪstɪkəlɪ] *adv* de modo imperialista
imperil [ɪm'pɛrɪl] (*pret & pp:* **-iled** o **-illed;** *ger:* **-iling** o **-illing**) *va* poner en peligro
imperious [ɪm'pɪrɪəs] *adj* imperioso
imperishability [ɪm,pɛrɪʃə'bɪlɪtɪ] *s* inmortalidad, eternidad
imperishable [ɪm'pɛrɪʃəbəl] *adj* imperecedero
imperium [ɪm'pɪrɪəm] *s* (*pl:* **-a** [ə]) imperio, mandato, autoridad; (law) poder
impermanence [ɪm'pʌrmənəns] *s* impermanencia
impermanent [ɪm'pʌrmənənt] *adj* impermanente
impermeability [ɪm,pʌrmɪə'bɪlɪtɪ] *s* impermeabilidad
impermeable [ɪm'pʌrmɪəbəl] *adj* impermeable
impermutable [,ɪmpər'mjutəbəl] *adj* impermutable
impers. abr. de **impersonal**
impersonal [ɪm'pʌrsənəl] *adj* impersonal; (gram.) impersonal, unipersonal
impersonality [ɪm,pʌrsə'nælɪtɪ] *s* impersonalidad; cosa impersonal, fuerza impersonal

impersonally [ɪm'pʌrsənəlɪ] *adv* impersonalmente
impersonate [ɪm'pʌrsənet] *va* hacer el papel de; imitar; personificar
impersonation [ɪm,pʌrsə'neʃən] *s* papel; imitación; personificación
impersonator [ɪm'pʌrsə,netər] *s* representador, actor; imitador; personificador; transformista (*actor que hace mutaciones rápidas*)
impertinence [ɪm'pʌrtɪnəns] *s* impertinencia
impertinency [ɪm'pʌrtɪnənsɪ] *s* (*pl:* **-cies**) var. de **impertinence**
impertinent [ɪm'pʌrtɪnənt] *adj & s* impertinente
imperturbability [,ɪmpər,tʌrbə'bɪlɪtɪ] *s* imperturbabilidad
imperturbable [,ɪmpər'tʌrbəbəl] *adj* imperturbable
impervious [ɪm'pʌrvɪəs] *adj* impervio, impenetrable, impermeable; impersuasible, inflexible
impetigo [,ɪmpɪ'taɪgo] *s* (path.) impétigo
impetuosity [ɪm,pɛtʃu'ɑsɪtɪ] *s* (*pl:* **-ties**) impetuosidad
impetuous [ɪm'pɛtʃuəs] *adj* impetuoso
impetus ['ɪmpɪtəs] *s* ímpetu
imp. gal. abr. de **imperial gallon**
impiety [ɪm'paɪətɪ] *s* (*pl:* **-ties**) impiedad
impinge [ɪm'pɪndʒ] *vn* incidir, chocar; **to impinge on** o **upon** incidir en; pasar los límites de
impingement [ɪm'pɪndʒmənt] *s* choque; infracción, violación
impious ['ɪmpɪəs] *adj* impío
impish ['ɪmpɪʃ] *adj* endiablado, travieso
implacability [ɪm,plekə'bɪlɪtɪ] o [ɪm,plækə'bɪlɪtɪ] *s* implacabilidad
implacable [ɪm'plekəbəl] o [ɪm'plækəbəl] *adj* implacable
implant [ɪm'plænt] *va* plantar; implantar
implantation [,ɪmplæn'teʃən] *s* plantación; implantación
implement ['ɪmplɪmənt] *s* utensilio, instrumento, herramienta; ['ɪmplɪmɛnt] *va* pertrechar; poner por obra, llevar a cabo
implementation [,ɪmplɪmɛn'teʃən] *s* ejecución, cumplimiento
implicate ['ɪmplɪket] *va* implicar, comprometer; enlazar, enredar
implication [,ɪmplɪ'keʃən] *s* indicación, insinuación; implicación, complicidad
implicit [ɪm'plɪsɪt] *adj* implícito; absoluto, ciego
implicitly [ɪm'plɪsɪtlɪ] *adv* implícitamente; absolutamente
implied [ɪm'plaɪd] *adj* implícito
impliedly [ɪm'plaɪɪdlɪ] *adv* implícitamente
implore [ɪm'plor] *va* implorar
implosion [ɪm'ploʒən] *s* implosión; (phonet.) implosión
implosive [ɪm'plosɪv] *adj* (phonet.) implosivo; *s* (phonet.) implosiva
impluvium [ɪm'pluvɪəm] *s* (*pl:* **-via** [vɪə]) impluvio
imply [ɪm'plaɪ] (*pret & pp:* **-plied**) *va* implicar, incluir en esencia, dar a entender
impolite [,ɪmpə'laɪt] *adj* descortés
impolitic [ɪm'pɑlɪtɪk] *adj* imprudente, indiscreto
imponderability [ɪm,pɑndərə'bɪlɪtɪ] *s* imponderabilidad
imponderable [ɪm'pɑndərəbəl] *adj & s* imponderable
import ['ɪmport] *s* importación; artículo importado; importancia; sentido, significación; [ɪm'port] o ['ɪmport] *va* importar; significar; *vn* importar
importance [ɪm'pɔrtəns] *s* importancia
important [ɪm'pɔrtənt] *adj* importante
importation [,ɪmpor'teʃən] *s* importación; artículo importado
importer [ɪm'portər] *s* importador; casa importadora
importunate [ɪm'pɔrtʃənɪt] *adj* importuno
importune [,ɪmpɔr'tjun] o [,ɪmpɔr'tun] *va* importunar
importunity [,ɪmpɔr'tjunɪtɪ] o [,ɪmpɔr'tunɪtɪ] *s* (*pl:* **-ties**) importunidad
impose [ɪm'poz] *va* imponer (*la voluntad de uno, tributos, silencio, etc.*); (print.) imponer; (eccl.) imponer (*las manos*); hacer aceptar; **to impose onself on** o **upon** hacerse aceptar por; *vn* imponerse; **to impose on** o **upon** abusar de, engañar
imposing [ɪm'pozɪŋ] *adj* imponente
imposition [,ɪmpə'zɪʃən] *s* imposición (*p.ej., de la voluntad de uno*); (print.) imposición; (eccl.) imposición; abuso, engaño
impossibility [ɪm,pɑsɪ'bɪlɪtɪ] *s* (*pl:* **-ties**) imposibilidad
impossible [ɪm'pɑsɪbəl] *adj* imposible
impossibly [ɪm'pɑsɪblɪ] *adv* imposiblemente
impost ['ɪmpost] *s* impuesto; (arch.) imposta
impostor [ɪm'pɑstər] *s* impostor
impostress [ɪm'pɑstrɪs] *s* impostora
imposture [ɪm'pɑstʃər] *s* impostura
impotence ['ɪmpətəns] o **impotency** ['ɪmpətənsɪ] *s* impotencia; (path.) impotencia
impotent ['ɪmpətənt] *adj* impotente; (path.) impotente
impound [ɪm'paʊnd] *va* acorralar, encerrar; represar, rebalsar (*agua*); (law) depositar, embargar, secuestrar
impoverish [ɪm'pɑvərɪʃ] *va* empobrecer
impoverishment [ɪm'pɑvərɪʃmənt] *s* empobrecimiento
impower [ɪm'paʊər] *va* facultar, habilitar; autorizar
impracticability [ɪm,præktɪkə'bɪlɪtɪ] *s* (*pl:* **-ties**) impracticabilidad; cosa impracticable
impracticable [ɪm'præktɪkəbəl] *adj* impracticable; intratable
impractical [ɪm'præktɪkəl] *adj* impráctico, impracticable; soñador, utópico
imprecate ['ɪmprɪket] *va* imprecar
imprecation [,ɪmprɪ'keʃən] *s* imprecación
imprecatory ['ɪmprɪkə,torɪ] *adj* imprecatorio
impregnability [ɪm,prɛgnə'bɪlɪtɪ] *s* inexpugnabilidad
impregnable [ɪm'prɛgnəbəl] *adj* inexpugnable
impregnate [ɪm'prɛgnet] *adj* imbuído; *va* empreñar; imbuir; (phys.) impregnar, empapar
impregnation [,ɪmprɛg'neʃən] *s* fecundación; infusión; (phys.) impregnación
impresario [,ɪmprɛ'sɑrio] *s* (*pl:* **-rios**) empresario, empresario de teatro
imprescriptible [,ɪmprɪ'skrɪptɪbəl] *adj* imprescriptible
impress ['ɪmprɛs] *s* impresión; [ɪm'prɛs] *va* imprimir; apretar; impresionar; expropiar, apoderarse de; (mil.) enganchar
impressibility [ɪm,prɛsɪ'bɪlɪtɪ] *s* impresionabilidad
impressible [ɪm'prɛsɪbəl] *adj* impresionable
impression [ɪm'prɛʃən] *s* impresión; (fig.) impresión
impressionability [ɪm,prɛʃənə'bɪlɪtɪ] *s* impresionabilidad
impressionable [ɪm'prɛʃənəbəl] *adj* impresionable
impressionism [ɪm'prɛʃənɪzəm] *s* (paint., lit. & mus.) impresionismo
impressionist [ɪm'prɛʃənɪst] *s* impresionista
impressionistic [ɪm,prɛʃə'nɪstɪk] *adj* impresionista
impressive [ɪm'prɛsɪv] *adv* impresionante
impressment [ɪm'prɛsmənt] *s* expropiación; (mil.) enganche
imprimatur [,ɪmprɪ'metər] *s* imprimátur; aprobación, permiso
imprint ['ɪmprɪnt] *s* impresión; (print.) pie de imprenta; [ɪm'prɪnt] *va* imprimir, estampar
imprison [ɪm'prɪzən] *va* aprisionar, encarcelar
imprisonment [ɪm'prɪzənmənt] *s* encarcelamiento
improbability [ɪm,prɑbə'bɪlɪtɪ] *s* (*pl:* **-ties**) improbabilidad
improbable [ɪm'prɑbəbəl] *adj* improbable
improbably [ɪm'prɑbəblɪ] *adv* improbablemente
impromptu [ɪm'prɑmptju] o [ɪm'prɑmptu] *adv* de improviso; *s* improvisación; (mus.) impromptu
improper [ɪm'prɑpər] *adj* impropio; indecoroso
improper fraction *s* (math.) fracción impropia
impropriety [,ɪmprə'praɪətɪ] *s* (*pl:* **-ties**) in-

conveniencia, indecencia; impropiedad (*especialmente en el lenguaje*)
improve [ɪm'pruv] *va* perfeccionar, mejorar; aprovechar; *vn* perfeccionarse, mejorar, mejorarse; **to improve on** o **upon** perfeccionar, mejorar
improvement [ɪm'pruvmənt] *s* perfeccionamiento, mejoramiento; mejoría (*p.ej., en la salud*); reforma, renovación; aprovechamiento (*empleo útil, p.ej., del tiempo*)
improvidence [ɪm'prɑvɪdəns] *s* imprevisión
improvident [ɪm'prɑvɪdənt] *adj* imprevisor, impróvido
improvisation [,ɪmprəvaɪ'zeʃən] o [,ɪmprɑvɪ'zeʃən] *s* improvisación
improvise ['ɪmprəvaɪz] *va & vn* improvisar
improviser ['ɪmprə,vaɪzər] *s* improvisador
imprudence [ɪm'prudəns] *s* imprudencia
imprudent [ɪm'prudənt] *adj* imprudente
impuberate [ɪm'pjubəret] *adj* impúber o impúbero
impudence ['ɪmpjədəns] *s* impudencia, insolencia
impudent ['ɪmpjədənt] *adj* impudente, insolente
impugn [ɪm'pjun] *va* impugnar; poner en tela de juicio
impugnable [ɪm'pʌgnəbəl] *adj* inexpugnable
impugnation [,ɪmpʌg'neʃən] *s* impugnación
impulse ['ɪmpʌls] *s* impulso; (mech.) impulso
impulse turbine *s* turbina de acción, turbina de impulsión
impulsion [ɪm'pʌlʃən] *s* impulsión
impulsive [ɪm'pʌlsɪv] *adj* impulsivo
impulsiveness [ɪm'pʌlsɪvnɪs] *s* impulsividad
impunity [ɪm'pjunɪtɪ] *s* impunidad
impure [ɪm'pjʊr] *adj* impuro
impurity [ɪm'pjʊrɪtɪ] *s* (*pl:* **-ties**) impureza o impuridad
imputable [ɪm'pjutəbəl] *adj* imputable
imputation [,ɪmpjʊ'teʃən] *s* imputación
impute [ɪm'pjut] *va* imputar
imputer [ɪm'pjutər] *s* imputador
in. abr. de **inch** o **inches**
in [ɪn] *adv* dentro, adentro, hacia adentro; en casa, en su oficina; en posesión; en el poder; en su turno; **to be in** estar en casa, estar en su oficina; **to be in for** estar expuesto a, no poder evitar; **to be in with** gozar del favor de; **in here** aquí dentro; **in there** allí dentro; *adj* interior, de adentro; *prep* en, con, de, durante, dentro de, de aquí a, sobre; por, p.ej., **he traveled in Spain** viajó por España; **in so far as** en tanto que; **in that** en que, por cuanto; *s* rincón, recodo; **ins and outs** recovecos; pormenores minuciosos
inability [,ɪnə'bɪlɪtɪ] *s* inhabilidad, incapacidad
inaccessibility [,ɪnæk,sɛsɪ'bɪlɪtɪ] *s* inaccesibilidad; inasequibilidad
inaccessible [,ɪnæk'sɛsɪbəl] *adj* inaccesible; inasequible
inaccessibly [,ɪnæk'sɛsɪblɪ] *adv* inaccesiblemente; inasequiblemente
inaccuracy [ɪn'ækjərəsɪ] *s* (*pl:* **-cies**) inexactitud, incorrección
inaccurate [ɪn'ækjərɪt] *adj* inexacto, incorrecto
inaction [ɪn'ækʃən] *s* inacción
inactive [ɪn'æktɪv] *adj* inactivo
inactivity [,ɪnæk'tɪvɪtɪ] *s* inactividad
inadaptability [,ɪnə,dæptə'bɪlɪtɪ] *s* inadaptabilidad
inadaptable [,ɪnə'dæptəbəl] *adj* inadaptable
inadequacy [ɪn'ædɪkwəsɪ] *s* insuficiencia, inadecuación
inadequate [ɪn'ædɪkwɪt] *adj* insuficiente, inadecuado
inadmissibility [,ɪnəd,mɪsɪ'bɪlɪtɪ] *s* inadmisibilidad
inadmissible [,ɪnəd'mɪsɪbəl] *adj* inadmisible
inadvertence [,ɪnəd'vʌrtəns] *s* inadvertencia
inadvertency [,ɪnəd'vʌrtənsɪ] *s* (*pl:* **-cies**) var. de **inadvertence**
inadvertent [,ɪnəd'vʌrtənt] *adj* inadvertido
inadvertently [,ɪnəd'vʌrtəntlɪ] *adv* inadvertidamente
inadvisable [,ɪnəd'vaɪzəbəl] *adj* no aconsejable, imprudente
inalienability [ɪn,eljənə'bɪlɪtɪ] *s* inalienabilidad
inalienable [ɪn'eljənəbəl] *adj* inalienable, imprescindible
inamorata [ɪn,æmə'rɑtə] *s* amada, enamorada
inane [ɪn'en] *adj* inane
inanimate [ɪn'ænɪmɪt] *adj* inanimado
inanition [,ɪnə'nɪʃən] *s* inanición
inanity [ɪn'ænɪtɪ] *s* (*pl:* **-ties**) inanidad
inapplicability [ɪn,æplɪkə'bɪlɪtɪ] *s* inaplicación
inapplicable [ɪn'æplɪkəbəl] *adj* inaplicable
inapposite [ɪn'æpəzɪt] *adj* impertinente, inadecuado, inaplicable
inappreciable [,ɪnə'priʃɪəbəl] *adj* inapreciable
inappreciably [,ɪnə'priʃɪəblɪ] *adv* inapreciablemente
inappropriate [,ɪnə'proprɪɪt] *adj* inapropiado, no a propósito
inapt [ɪn'æpt] *adj* inapto
inaptitude [ɪn'æptɪtjud] o [ɪn'æptɪtud] *s* ineptitud
inarticulate [,ɪnɑr'tɪkjəlɪt] *adj* inarticulado; incapaz de expresarse
inartistic [,ɪnɑr'tɪstɪk] *adj* inartístico
inartistically [,ɪnɑr'tɪstɪkəlɪ] *adv* sin arte
inasmuch as [,ɪnəz'mʌtʃæz] *conj* ya que, puesto que; en cuanto, hasta donde
inattention [,ɪnə'tɛnʃən] *s* desatención, inatención
inattentive [,ɪnə'tɛntɪv] *adj* desatento, inatento
inaudible [ɪn'ɔdɪbəl] *adj* inaudible
inaugural [ɪn'ɔgjərəl] *adj* inaugural; *s* oración inaugural, discurso inaugural
inaugurate [ɪn'ɔgjəret] *va* inaugurar
inauguration [ɪn,ɔgjə'reʃən] *s* inauguración; toma de posesión
inauspicious [,ɪnɔ'spɪʃəs] *adj* impropicio, desfavorable
inboard ['ɪn,bord] *adj* (naut.) interior; *adv* (mach.) hacia dentro; (naut.) hacia dentro del casco
inborn ['ɪn,bɔrn] *adj* innato, ingénito
inbound ['ɪn,baʊnd] *adj* entrante
inbred ['ɪn,brɛd] *adj* ínsito, innato; engendrado sin mezcla de familias o razas; ['ɪn,brɛd] o [ɪn'brɛd] *pret & pp de* **inbreed**
inbreed ['ɪn,brid] o [ɪn'brid] (*pret & pp:* **-bred**) *va* engendrar sin mezclar familias ni razas
inbreeding ['ɪn,bridɪŋ] *s* intracruzamiento, generación sin mezcla de familias o razas
inc. abr. de **inclosure, included, including, inclusive, incorporated** y **increase**
Inca ['ɪŋkə] *s* inca; *adj* incaico
incalculable [ɪn'kælkjələbəl] *adj* incalculable
Incan ['ɪŋkən] *adj & s* inca
incandescence [,ɪnkən'dɛsəns] *s* incandescencia
incandescent [,ɪnkən'dɛsənt] *adj* incandescente
incantation [,ɪnkæn'teʃən] *s* conjuro
incapability [,ɪnkepə'bɪlɪtɪ] *s* incapacidad
incapable [ɪn'kepəbəl] *adj* incapaz
incapacitate [,ɪnkə'pæsɪtet] *va* incapacitar, inhabilitar
incapacitation [,ɪnkə,pæsɪ'teʃən] *s* inhabilitación
incapacity [,ɪnkə'pæsɪtɪ] *s* (*pl:* **-ties**) incapacidad
incarcerate [ɪn'kɑrsəret] *va* encarcelar
incarceration [ɪn,kɑrsə'reʃən] *s* encarcelación; (path.) incarceración
incarnadine [ɪn'kɑrnədaɪn] o [ɪn'kɑrnədin] *adj & s* encarnado; *va* volver encarnado
incarnate [ɪn'kɑrnɪt] o [ɪn'kɑrnet] *adj* encarnado (*en forma humana*); [ɪn'kɑrnet] *va* encarnar
incarnation [,ɪnkɑr'neʃən] *s* encarnación; (med.) encarnamiento; (*cap.*) *s* (theol.) encarnación
incase [ɪn'kes] *va* encajonar, encerrar
incasement [ɪn'kesmənt] *s* encajonamiento, encerramiento; caja, cobertura
incautious [ɪn'kɔʃəs] *adj* incauto
incendiarism [ɪn'sɛndɪərɪzəm] *s* incendio malicioso; (fig.) incitación al desorden
incendiary [ɪn'sɛndɪ,ɛrɪ] *adj* incendiario; *s* (*pl:* **-ies**) incendiario
incendiary bomb *s* (mil.) bomba incendiaria
incense ['ɪnsɛns] *s* incienso; (fig.) incienso;

va incensar; (fig.) incensar (*lisonjear*); [ɪn'sɛns] *va* exasperar, encolerizar
incense burner ['insɛns] *s* incensario
incensory ['ɪnsɛn,sorɪ] *s* (*pl:* **-ries**) incensario
incentive [ɪn'sɛntɪv] *adj & s* incentivo
inception [ɪn'sɛpʃən] *s* principio, comienzo
inceptive [ɪn'sɛptɪv] *s* (gram.) verbo incoativo; *adj* incipiente; (gram.) incoativo
incertitude [ɪn'sʌrtɪtjud] o [ɪn'sʌrtɪtud] *s* incertidumbre
incessant [ɪn'sɛsənt] *adj* incesante.
incest ['ɪnsɛst] *s* incesto
incestuous [ɪn'sɛstʃuəs] *adj* incestuoso
inch [ɪntʃ] *s* pulgada; pizca; **by inches** pulgada por pulgada; a poquitos; **every inch** hasta los tuétanos; **inch by inch** pulgada por pulgada; a poquitos; **within an inch of** a dos dedos de; *vn* avanzar a poquitos; **to inch ahead** avanzar a poquitos
inchmeal ['ɪntʃ,mil] *adv* poco a poco; **by inchmeal** poco a poco
inchoate [ɪn'ko·ɪt] o ['ɪnkoet] *adj* incipiente, rudimental
inchoative [ɪn'koətɪv] *adj* incipiente, rudimental; (gram.) incoativo; *s* (gram.) verbo incoativo
inchworm ['ɪntʃ,wʌrm] *s* (zool.) geómetra
incidence ['ɪnsɪdəns] *s* incidencia; extensión (*de los efectos de una cosa*); (geom. & phys.) incidencia
incident ['ɪnsɪdənt] *adj* incidente; *s* incidente, incidencia
incidental [,ɪnsɪ'dɛntəl] *adj* incidente; obvencional; *s* elemento incidental; **incidentals** *spl* gastos menudos
incidentally [,ɪnsɪ'dɛntəlɪ] *adv* incidentalmente, incidentemente; a propósito
incinerate [ɪn'sɪnəret] *va* incinerar
incineration [ɪn,sɪnə'reʃən] *s* incineración
incinerator [ɪn'sɪnə,retər] *s* incinerador
incipience [ɪn'sɪpɪəns] *s* comienzo, principio
incipient [ɪn'sɪpɪənt] *adj* incipiente
incise [ɪn'saɪz] *va* cortar; grabar, tallar
incision [ɪn'sɪʒən] *s* incisión
incisive [ɪn'saɪsɪv] *adj* incisivo; (anat.) incisivo
incisor [ɪn'saɪzər] *s* (anat.) diente incisivo
incisory [ɪn'saɪsərɪ] *adj* incisorio
incitation [,ɪnsaɪ'teʃən] o [,ɪnsɪ'teʃən] *s* incitación
incite [ɪn'saɪt] *va* incitar; **to incite to** + *inf* incitar a + *inf*
incitement [ɪn'saɪtmənt] *s* incitamento
incivility [,ɪnsɪ'vɪlɪtɪ] *s* (*pl:* **-ties**) incivilidad
incl. abr. de **inclosure, including** y **inclusive**
inclemency [ɪn'klɛmənsɪ] *s* (*pl:* **-cies**) inclemencia
inclement [ɪn'klɛmənt] *adj* inclemente
inclination [,ɪnklɪ'neʃən] *s* inclinación
incline ['ɪnklaɪn] o [ɪn'klaɪn] *s* declive, pendiente; [ɪn'klaɪn] *va* inclinar; *vn* inclinarse
inclined [ɪn'klaɪnd] *adj* inclinado; **to be inclined to** + *inf* inclinarse a + *inf*
inclined plane *s* (mech.) plano inclinado
inclinometer [,ɪnklɪ'nɑmɪtər] *s* inclinómetro
inclose [ɪn'kloz] *va* cercar, encerrar, incluir; **to inclose herewith** remitir adjunto (*con una carta*)
inclosure [ɪn'kloʒər] *s* cercamiento, encerramiento, inclusión; cerca, encierro, recinto; cosa inclusa, carta inclusa, copia inclusa
include [ɪn'klud] *va* incluir; **to be included in** figurar en
including [ɪn'kludɪŋ] *prep* incluso
inclusion [ɪn'kluʒən] *s* inclusión; cosa inclusa, carta inclusa
inclusion body *s* (path.) cuerpo de inclusión
inclusive [ɪn'klusɪv] *adj* inclusivo; detallado, completo; **inclusive of** comprensivo de
incog. abr. de **incognito**
incog [ɪn'kɑg] *adj, s & adv* (coll.) var. de **incognito**
incognito [ɪn'kɑgnɪto] *adj* incógnito; *s* (*pl:* **-tos**) incógnito; *adv* de incógnito
incoherence [,ɪnko'hɪrəns] *s* incoherencia
incoherency [,ɪnko'hɪrənsɪ] *s* (*pl:* **-cies**) var. de **incoherence**
incoherent [,ɪnko'hɪrənt] *adj* incoherente
incombustibility [,ɪnkəm,bʌstɪ'bɪlɪtɪ] *s* incombustibilidad
incombustible [,ɪnkəm'bʌstɪbəl] *adj* incombustible; *s* substancia incombustible
income ['ɪnkʌm] *s* renta, utilidad, rédito
income tax *s* impuesto de utilidades, impuesto sobre rentas, impuesto a los réditos
income-tax return ['ɪnkʌm,tæks] *s* declaración de utilidades, declaración de ingresos
incoming ['ɪn,kʌmɪŋ] *adj* entrante; ascendente (*marea*); *s* entrada, llegada
incommensurability [,ɪnkə,mɛnʃərə'bɪlɪtɪ] *s* inconmensurabilidad
incommensurable [,ɪnkə'mɛnʃərəbəl] *adj* inconmensurable
incommensurate [,ɪnkə'mɛnʃərɪt] *adj* desproporcionado; inconmensurable
incommode [,ɪnkə'mod] *va* incomodar, desacomodar
incommodious [,ɪnkə'modɪəs] *adj* incómodo
incommunicability [,ɪnkə,mjunɪkə'bɪlɪtɪ] *s* incomunicabilidad
incommunicable [,ɪnkə'mjunɪkəbəl] *adj* incomunicable; inconversable
incommunicado [,ɪnkə,mjunɪ'kɑdo] *adj* incomunicado
incommunicative [,ɪnkə'mjunɪ,ketɪv] *adj* inconversable, insociable
incomparable [ɪn'kɑmpərəbəl] *adj* incomparable
incompatibility [,ɪnkəm,pætɪ'bɪlɪtɪ] *s* incompatibilidad
incompatible [,ɪnkəm'pætɪbəl] *adj* incompatible; desconforme
incompetence [ɪn'kɑmpɪtəns] o **incompetency** [ɪn'kɑmpɪtənsɪ] *s* incompetencia
incompetent [ɪn'kɑmpɪtənt] *adj* incompetente
incomplete [,ɪnkəm'plit] *adj* incompleto
incompletely [,ɪnkəm'plitlɪ] *adv* incompletamente
incomplex [,ɪnkəm'plɛks] *adj* incomplejo, incomplexo
incomprehensibility [,ɪnkɑmprɪ,hɛnsɪ'bɪlɪtɪ] *s* incomprehensibilidad o incomprensibilidad
incomprehensible [,ɪnkɑmprɪ'hɛnsɪbəl] *adj* incomprehensible o incomprensible
incompressibility [,ɪnkəm,prɛsɪ'bɪlɪtɪ] *s* incompresibilidad
incompressible [,ɪnkəm'prɛsɪbəl] *adj* incompresible
inconceivability [,ɪnkən,sivə'bɪlɪtɪ] *s* inconcebibilidad
inconceivable [,ɪnkən'sivəbəl] *adj* inconcebible
inconceivably [,ɪnkən'sivəblɪ] *adv* inconcebiblemente
inconclusive [,ɪnkən'klusɪv] *adj* inconcluyente
inconel ['ɪŋkənəl] *s* inconel
incongruent [ɪn'kɑŋgruənt] *adj* incongruente
incongruity [,ɪnkən'gruɪtɪ] *s* (*pl:* **-ties**) incongruencia
incongruous [ɪn'kɑŋgruəs] *adj* incongruo
inconsequence [ɪn'kɑnsɪkwɛns] *s* inconsecuencia
inconsequent [ɪn'kɑnsɪkwɛnt] *adj* inconsecuente
inconsequential [ɪn,kɑnsɪ'kwɛnʃəl] *adj* inconsecuente; de poca importancia
inconsiderable [,ɪnkən'sɪdərəbəl] *adj* insignificante
inconsiderate [,ɪnkən'sɪdərɪt] *adj* inconsiderado, desconsiderado
inconsiderateness [,ɪnkən'sɪdərɪtnɪs] *s* inconsideración, desconsideración
inconsistency [,ɪnkən'sɪstənsɪ] *s* (*pl:* **-cies**) inconsistencia, inconsecuencia
inconsistent [,ɪnkən'sɪstənt] *adj* inconsistente, inconsecuente
inconsolable [,ɪnkən'soləbəl] *adj* inconsolable
inconsonant [ɪn'kɑnsənənt] *adj* inconsonante
inconspicuous [,ɪnkən'spɪkjuəs] *adj* poco aparente; poco llamativo
inconstancy [ɪn'kɑnstənsɪ] *s* inconstancia
inconstant [ɪn'kɑnstənt] *adj* inconstante
incontestable [,ɪnkən'tɛstəbəl] *adj* incontestable
incontinence [ɪn'kɑntɪnəns] *s* incontinencia; (path.) incontinencia
incontinent [ɪn'kɑntɪnənt] *adj* incontinente
incontrovertibility [,ɪnkɑntrə,vʌrtɪ'bɪlɪtɪ] *s* incontrovertibilidad
incontrovertible [,ɪnkɑntrə'vʌrtɪbəl] *adj* incontrovertible

inconvenience [ˌɪnkənˈvinjəns] *s* incomodidad, inconveniencia, molestia; *va* incomodar, molestar
inconvenient [ˌɪnkənˈvinjənt] *adj* incómodo, inconveniente, molesto
inconvertibility [ˌɪnkənˌvʌrtɪˈbɪlɪtɪ] *s* inconvertibilidad
inconvertible [ˌɪnkənˈvʌrtɪbəl] *adj* inconvertible
inconvincible [ˌɪnkənˈvɪnsɪbəl] *adj* inconvencible
incoördination [ˌɪnkoˌɔrdɪˈneʃən] *s* incoordinación
incorporate [ɪnˈkɔrpərɪt] *adj* incorporado; [ɪnˈkɔrpəret] *va* incorporar; constituir en sociedad anónima; *vn* incorporarse; constituirse en sociedad anónima
incorporation [ɪnˌkɔrpəˈreʃən] *s* incorporación; constitución en sociedad anónima
incorporator [ɪnˈkɔrpəˌretər] *s* incorporador; fundador de una sociedad anónima
incorporeal [ˌɪnkɔrˈporɪəl] *adj* incorpóreo, incorporal
incorrect [ˌɪnkəˈrɛkt] *adj* incorrecto
incorrectness [ˌɪnkəˈrɛktnɪs] *s* incorrección
incorrigibility [ɪnˌkɑrɪdʒɪˈbɪlɪtɪ] o [ɪnˌkɔrɪdʒɪˈbɪlɪtɪ] *s* incorregibilidad
incorrigible [ɪnˈkɑrɪdʒɪbəl] o [ɪnˈkɔrɪdʒɪbəl] *adj* incorregible
incorrupt [ˌɪnkəˈrʌpt] *adj* incorrupto
incorruptibility [ˌɪnkəˌrʌptɪˈbɪlɪtɪ] *s* incorruptibilidad
incorruptible [ˌɪnkəˈrʌptɪbəl] *adj* incorruptible
increase [ˈɪnkris] *s* aumento; crecida, ascenso (*del agua*); ganancia, interés; hijo, hijos; productos agrícolas; **to be on the increase** ir en aumento; [ɪnˈkris] *va* aumentar; multiplicar; *vn* aumentar; multiplicarse
increasing [ɪnˈkrisɪŋ] *adj* creciente
increasingly [ɪnˈkrisɪŋlɪ] *adv* cada vez más
incredibility [ɪnˌkrɛdɪˈbɪlɪtɪ] *s* incredibilidad
incredible [ɪnˈkrɛdɪbəl] *adj* increíble
incredulity [ˌɪnkrɪˈdjulɪtɪ] o [ˌɪnkrɪˈdulɪtɪ] *s* incredulidad
incredulous [ɪnˈkrɛdʒələs] *adj* incrédulo
increment [ˈɪnkrɪmənt] *s* incremento; (math.) incremento
incriminate [ɪnˈkrɪmɪnet] *va* acriminar, incriminar
incrimination [ɪnˌkrɪmɪˈneʃən] *s* acriminación, incriminación
incriminatory [ɪnˈkrɪmɪnəˌtorɪ] *adj* acriminador
incrust [ɪnˈkrʌst] *va* incrustar; *vn* incrustarse
incrustation [ˌɪnkrʌsˈteʃən] *s* incrustación
incrustive [ɪnˈkrʌstɪv] *adj* incrustante
incubate [ˈɪnkjəbet] *va & vn* incubar
incubation [ˌɪnkjəˈbeʃən] *s* incubación
incubation period *s* (path.) período de incubación
incubator [ˈɪnkjəˌbetər] *s* incubadora
incubus [ˈɪnkjəbəs] *s* (*pl:* **-buses** o **-bi** [baɪ]) íncubo; (med.) íncubo
inculcate [ɪnˈkʌlket] o [ˈɪnkʌlket] *va* inculcar
inculcation [ˌɪnkʌlˈkeʃən] *s* inculcación
inculpable [ɪnˈkʌlpəbəl] *adj* inculpable
inculpate [ɪnˈkʌlpet] o [ˈɪnkʌlpet] *va* inculpar
inculpation [ˌɪnkʌlˈpeʃən] *s* inculpación
incumbency [ɪnˈkʌmbənsɪ] *s* (*pl:* **-cies**) incumbencia
incumbent [ɪnˈkʌmbənt] *adj* incumbente; (bot. & zool.) incumbente; **to be incumbent on** o **upon one** incumbirle a uno; **to be incumbent on one to** + *inf* incumbir a uno + *inf;* *s* titular, posesor; (eccl.) beneficiado
incumber [ɪnˈkʌmbər] *va* embarazar, estorbar; impedir; gravar
incumbrance [ɪnˈkʌmbrəns] *s* embarazo, estorbo; impedimento; gravamen; hijo menor de edad
incunabula [ˌɪnkjuˈnæbjələ] *spl* orígenes; incunables
incur [ɪnˈkʌr] (*pret & pp:* **-curred;** *ger:* **-curring**) *va* incurrir en; contraer (*una deuda*)
incurability [ɪnˌkjurəˈbɪlɪtɪ] *s* incurabilidad
incurable [ɪnˈkjurəbəl] *adj & s* incurable
incurious [ɪnˈkjurɪəs] *adj* indiferente; poco interesante
incursion [ɪnˈkʌrʒən] o [ɪnˈkʌrʃən] *s* incursión, irrupción, invasión
incurve [ˈɪnˌkʌrv] *s* (baseball) curva adentro; [ɪnˈkʌrv] *va* (baseball) encorvar hacia dentro; *vn* (baseball) encorvarse hacia dentro
incus [ˈɪŋkəs] *s* (*pl:* **incudes** [ɪnˈkjudiz]) (anat.) yunque
incuse [ɪnˈkjuz] *adj* incuso
ind. abr. de **independent, indicative** y **industrial**
Ind. abr. de **India, Indian** y **Indiana**
Ind [ɪnd] *s* (poet.) India, Indias
indebted [ɪnˈdɛtɪd] *adj* adeudado; obligado, reconocido
indebtedness [ɪnˈdɛtɪdnɪs] *s* deuda; obligación
indecency [ɪnˈdisənsɪ] *s* (*pl:* **-cies**) indecencia, deshonestidad
indecent [ɪnˈdisənt] *adj* indecente, deshonesto
indecent exposure *s* exhibición impúdica, delito de exhibicionismo
indecipherable [ˌɪndɪˈsaɪfərəbəl] *adj* indescifrable
indecision [ˌɪndɪˈsɪʒən] *s* indecisión
indecisive [ˌɪndɪˈsaɪsɪv] *adj* indeciso
indeclinable [ˌɪndɪˈklaɪnəbəl] *adj* (gram.) indeclinable
indecorous [ɪnˈdɛkərəs] o [ˌɪndɪˈkorəs] *adj* indecoroso
indecorum [ˌɪndɪˈkorəm] *s* indecoro
indeed [ɪnˈdid] *adv* verdaderamente, de veras, claro está; *interj* ¡ de veras!
indef. abr. de **indefinite**
indefatigability [ˌɪndɪˌfætɪgəˈbɪlɪtɪ] *s* infatigabilidad
indefatigable [ˌɪndɪˈfætɪgəbəl] *adj* infatigable
indefeasible [ˌɪndɪˈfizɪbəl] *adj* inabrogable
indefensible [ˌɪndɪˈfɛnsɪbəl] *adj* indefendible
indefinable [ˌɪndɪˈfaɪnəbəl] *adj* indefinible
indefinite [ɪnˈdɛfɪnɪt] *adj* indefinido
indefinite article *s* (gram.) artículo indefinido
indehiscence [ˌɪndɪˈhɪsəns] *s* (bot.) indehiscencia
indehiscent [ˌɪndɪˈhɪsənt] *adj* (bot.) indehiscente
indelibility [ɪnˌdɛlɪˈbɪlɪtɪ] *s* indelebilidad
indelible [ɪnˈdɛlɪbəl] *adj* indeleble
indelible ink *s* tinta indeleble
indelible lead pencil *s* lápiz tinta, lápiz violado de copiar
indelicacy [ɪnˈdɛlɪkəsɪ] *s* (*pl:* **-cies**) indelicadeza
indelicate [ɪnˈdɛlɪkɪt] *adj* indelicado
indemnification [ɪnˌdɛmnɪfɪˈkeʃən] *s* indemnización
indemnify [ɪnˈdɛmnɪfaɪ] (*pret & pp:* **-fied**) *va* indemnizar
indemnity [ɪnˈdɛmnɪtɪ] *s* (*pl:* **-ties**) indemnización; indemnidad (*seguridad contra un daño*)
indemonstrable [ˌɪndɪˈmɑnstrəbəl] o [ɪnˈdɛmənstrəbəl] *adj* indemostrable
indent [ˈɪndɛnt] o [ɪnˈdɛnt] *s* mella, diente, muesca; [ɪnˈdɛnt] *va* mellar, dentar; (print.) sangrar; *vn* mellarse
indentation [ˌɪndɛnˈteʃən] *s* mella, muesca; (print.) sangría
indented [ɪnˈdɛntɪd] *adj* sangrado; (her.) endentado
indention [ɪnˈdɛnʃən] *s* mella; (print.) sangría
indenture [ɪnˈdɛntʃər] *s* escritura, contrato; contrato de aprendizaje, contrato de servidumbre; mella; *va* obligar por contrato
independence *s* [ˌɪndɪˈpɛndəns] *s* independencia
Independence Day *s* (U.S.A.) día de la independencia
independency [ˌɪndɪˈpɛndənsɪ] *s* (*pl:* **-cies**) independencia; país independente
independent [ˌɪndɪˈpɛndənt] *adj* independiente; **independent of** independiente de; *s* independiente
independently [ˌɪndɪˈpɛndəntlɪ] *adv* independientemente; **independently of** independientemente de
indescribable [ˌɪndɪˈskraɪbəbəl] *adj* indescriptible
indestructibility [ˌɪndɪˌstrʌktɪˈbɪlɪtɪ] *s* indestructibilidad
indestructible [ˌɪndɪˈstrʌktɪbəl] *adj* indestructible

indeterminability [ˌɪndɪˌtʌrmɪnəˈbɪlɪtɪ] *s* indeterminabilidad
indeterminable [ˌɪndɪˈtʌrmɪnəbəl] *adj* indeterminable
indeterminate [ˌɪndɪˈtʌrmɪnɪt] *adj* indeterminado
indetermination [ˌɪndɪˌtʌrmɪˈneʃən] *s* indeterminación
indeterminism [ˌɪndɪˈtʌrmɪnɪzəm] *s* indeterminismo
indeterminist [ˌɪndɪˈtʌrmɪnɪst] *adj & s* indeterminista
indeterministic [ˌɪndɪˌtʌrmɪˈnɪstɪk] *adj* indeterminista
indevotion [ˌɪndɪˈvoʃən] *s* indevoción
index [ˈɪndɛks] *s* (*pl:* **indexes** o **indices** [ˈɪndɪsiz]) índice; (print.) manecilla; (math.) índice; (*cap.*) *s* índice de libros prohibidos; (*l.c.*) *va* poner índice a; poner en un índice
index card *s* ficha catalográfica (*de una biblioteca*)
Index Expurgatorius [ɛksˌpʌrgəˈtorɪəs] *s* (eccl.) índice expurgatorio
index finger *s* dedo índice
index of refraction *s* (phys.) índice de refracción
index tab *s* pestaña
India [ˈɪndɪə] *s* la India
India ink *s* tinta china
Indiaman [ˈɪndɪəmən] *s* (*pl:* **-men**) buque de la compañía de las Indias
Indian [ˈɪndɪən] *adj & s* indio
Indian club *s* maza de gimnasia
Indian corn *s* (bot.) panizo de las Indias (*planta y grano*)
Indian cress *s* (bot.) capuchina
Indian Empire *s* Imperio de las Indias
Indian fig *s* (bot.) nopal castellano, penco
Indian file *s* fila india; *adv* en fila india
Indian giver *s* (coll.) dador de toma y daca
Indian heart *s* (bot.) farolillo
Indianism [ˈɪndɪənɪzəm] *s* indianismo
Indianist [ˈɪndɪənɪst] *s* indianista
Indian meal *s* harina de maíz
Indian millet *s* (bot.) alcandía
Indian Ocean *s* océano Índico, mar de las Indias
Indian pipe *s* (bot.) monotropa
Indian reed *s* (bot.) caña de Indias, cañacoro
Indian reservation *s* (U.S.A.) reserva de indios
Indian rice *s* (bot.) arroz de los pieles rojas
Indian shot *s* var. de **Indian reed**
Indian summer *s* veranillo, veranillo de San Martín
Indian Territory *s* Gobernación de los Indios
Indian tobacco *s* (bot.) tabaco indio
Indian turnip *s* (bot.) arisema
Indian yellow *s* amarillo indio
India paper *s* papel de China
India rubber o **india rubber** *s* caucho
indic. abr. de **indicative**
indican [ˈɪndɪkæn] *s* (chem. & biochem.) indicán
indicant [ˈɪndɪkənt] *adj & s* indicante
indicanuria [ˌɪndɪkəˈnjʊrɪə] o [ˌɪndɪkəˈnʊrɪə] *s* (path.) indicanuria
indicate [ˈɪndɪket] *va* indicar
indication [ˌɪndɪˈkeʃən] *s* indicación
indicative [ɪnˈdɪkətɪv] *adj* indicativo; (gram.) indicativo; *s* (gram.) indicativo
indicative mood *s* (gram.) modo indicativo
indicator [ˈɪndɪˌketər] *s* indicador; (chem.) indicador
indicatory [ˈɪndɪkəˌtorɪ] *adj* indicador
indict [ɪnˈdaɪt] *va* (law) acusar, procesar
indictable [ɪnˈdaɪtəbəl] *adj* (law) denunciable, procesable
indiction [ɪnˈdɪkʃən] *s* indicción
indictment [ɪnˈdaɪtmənt] *s* (law) acusación, procesamiento; (law) auto de acusación formulado por el gran jurado
Indies [ˈɪndiz] *spl* Indias
indifference [ɪnˈdɪfərəns] *s* indiferencia
indifferent [ɪnˈdɪfərənt] *adj* indiferente; pasadero, mediano
indifferentism [ɪnˈdɪfərəntɪzəm] *s* indiferentismo
indifferently [ɪnˈdɪfərəntlɪ] *adv* indiferentemente; pasaderamente, medianamente; mal
indigence [ˈɪndɪdʒəns] *s* indigencia
indigenous [ɪnˈdɪdʒɪnəs] *adj* indígena; innato
indigent [ˈɪndɪdʒənt]*adj* indigente; **the indigent** los indigentes
indigestibility [ˌɪndɪˌdʒɛstɪˈbɪlɪtɪ] *s* indigestibilidad
indigestible [ˌɪndɪˈdʒɛstɪbəl] *adj* indigestible o indigerible
indigestion [ˌɪndɪˈdʒɛstʃən] *s* indigestión
indignant [ɪnˈdɪgnənt] *adj* indignado
indignation [ˌɪndɪgˈneʃən] *s* indignación
indignation meeting *s* reunión de protesta
indignity [ɪnˈdɪgnɪtɪ] *s* (*pl:* **-ties**) indignidad (*afrenta, ultraje*)
indigo [ˈɪndɪgo] *s* (*pl:* **-gos** o **-goes**) (bot. & chem.) índigo; añil o índigo (*del espectro solar*); *adj* de añil, azul de añil
indigo bunting *s* (orn.) azulejo
indigo extract *s* extracto de índigo, carmín de índigo
indirect [ˌɪndɪˈrɛkt] o [ˌɪndaɪˈrɛkt] *adj* indirecto
indirect discourse *s* (gram.) estilo indirecto
indirection [ˌɪndɪˈrɛkʃən] *s* rodeo; engaño
indirect lighting *s* iluminación indirecta, alumbrado reflejado
indirect object *s* (gram.) complemento indirecto
indirect tax *s* contribución indirecta
indiscernibility [ˌɪndɪˌzʌrnɪˈbɪlɪtɪ] o [ˌɪndɪˌsʌrnɪˈbɪlɪtɪ] *s* indiscernibilidad
indiscernible [ˌɪndɪˈzʌrnɪbəl] o [ˌɪndɪˈsʌrnɪbəl] *adj* indiscernible
indiscreet [ˌɪndɪsˈkrit] *adj* indiscreto
indiscretion [ˌɪndɪsˈkreʃən] *s* indiscreción
indiscriminate [ˌɪndɪsˈkrɪmɪnɪt] *adj* promiscuo; poco distintivo
indispensability [ˌɪndɪˌspɛnsəˈbɪlɪtɪ] *s* indispensabilidad
indispensable [ˌɪndɪˈspɛnsəbəl] *adj* indispensable, imprescindible
indispose [ˌɪndɪsˈpoz] *va* indisponer
indisposed [ˌɪndɪsˈpozd] *adj* maldispuesto; indispuesto (*algo enfermo*)
indisposition [ˌɪndɪspəˈzɪʃən] *s* desinclinación; indisposición (*enfermedad pasajera*)
indisputability [ɪnˌdɪspjutəˈbɪlɪtɪ] o [ˌɪndɪˌspjutəˈbɪlɪtɪ] *s* indisputabilidad
indisputable [ɪnˈdɪspjutəbəl] o [ˌɪndɪsˈpjutəbəl] *adj* indisputable
indissolubility [ˌɪndɪˌsɑljəˈbɪlɪtɪ] *s* indisolubilidad
indissoluble [ˌɪndɪˈsɑljəbəl] *adj* indisoluble
indistinct [ˌɪndɪˈstɪŋkt] *adj* indistinto
indistinctness [ˌɪndɪˈstɪŋktnɪs] *s* indistinción
indistinguishable [ˌɪndɪˈstɪŋgwɪʃəbəl] *adj* indistinguible
indite [ɪnˈdaɪt] *va* redactar, poner por escrito
indium [ˈɪndɪəm] *s* (chem.) indio
individual [ˌɪndɪˈvɪdʒʊəl] *adj* individual; *s* individuo; (biol.) individuo
individualism [ˌɪndɪˈvɪdʒʊəlɪzəm] *s* individualismo
individualist [ˌɪndɪˈvɪdʒʊəlɪst] *s* individualista
individualistic [ˌɪndɪˌvɪdʒʊəlˈɪstɪk] *adj* individualista
individuality [ˌɪndɪˌvɪdʒʊˈælɪtɪ] *s* (*pl:* **-ties**) individualidad; individuo
individualize [ˌɪndɪˈvɪdʒʊəlaɪz] *va* individualizar
individually [ˌɪndɪˈvɪdʒʊəlɪ] *adv* individualmente
individuate [ˌɪndɪˈvɪdʒʊet] *va* individuar
individuation [ˌɪndɪˌvɪdʒʊˈeʃən] *s* individuación
indivisibility [ˌɪndɪˌvɪzɪˈbɪlɪtɪ] *s* indivisibilidad
indivisible [ˌɪndɪˈvɪzɪbəl] *adj* indivisible
indivision [ˌɪndɪˈvɪʒən] *s* indivisión
Indochina [ˈɪndoˈtʃaɪnə] *s* la Indochina
Indochinese [ˈɪndotʃaɪˈniz] *adj* indochino; *s* (*pl:* **-nese**) indochino
indoctrinate [ɪnˈdɑktrɪnet] *va* adoctrinar, inculcar
indoctrination [ɪnˌdɑktrɪˈneʃən] *s* adoctrinamiento, inculcación
Indo-European [ˈɪndoˌjʊrəˈpiən] *adj & s* indoeuropeo

Indo-Germanic [ˈɪndodʒʌrˈmænɪk] *adj & s* indogermánico
indole [ˈɪndol] *s* (chem.) indol
indolence [ˈɪndələns] *s* indolencia
indolent [ˈɪndələnt] *adj* indolente; (med.) indolente
Indo-Malayan [ˈɪndoməˈleən] *adj* indomalayo
indomitable [ɪnˈdɑmɪtəbəl] *adj* indomable, indómito
indomitably [ɪnˈdɑmɪtəblɪ] *adv* indómitamente
Indonesia [ˌɪndoˈniʃə] o [ˌɪndoˈniʒə] *s* la Indonesia
Indonesian [ˌɪndoˈniʃən] o [ˌɪndoˈniʒən] *adj & s* indonesio
indoor [ˈɪnˌdor] *adj* interior, de puertas adentro
indoor aerial *s* (rad.) antena de interior
indoor games *spl* diversiones caseras
indoors [ˈɪnˈdorz] *adv* dentro, en casa, bajo techado
indophenol [ˌɪndoˈfinol] o [ˌɪndoˈfinɑl] *s* (chem.) indofenol
indorse [ɪnˈdɔrs] *va* endosar; apoyar, aprobar, respaldar
indorsee [ˌɪndɔrˈsi] *s* endosatario
indorsement [ɪnˈdɔrsmənt] *s* endoso; apoyo, aprobación
indorser [ɪnˈdɔrsər] *s* endosante
indoxyl [ɪnˈdɑksɪl] *s* (chem.) indoxilo
indraft o **indraught** [ˈɪnˌdræft] o [ˈɪnˌdrɑft] *s* atracción hacia el interior; aspiración, aire aspirado; corriente entrante
indubitable [ɪnˈdjubɪtəbəl] o [ɪnˈdubɪtəbəl] *adj* indubitable
induce [ɪnˈdjus] o [ɪnˈdus] *va* inducir; causar, producir; (log. & elec.) inducir; **to induce to** + *inf* inducir a + *inf*
inducement [ɪnˈdjusmənt] o [ɪnˈdusmənt] *s* incentivo, atractivo, estímulo
induct [ɪnˈdʌkt] *va* instalar; introducir; iniciar; (mil.) quintar
inductance [ɪnˈdʌktəns] *s* (elec.) inductancia
inductee [ˌɪndʌkˈti] *s* (mil.) quinto
inductile [ɪnˈdʌktɪl] *adj* no dúctil, inflexible
induction [ɪnˈdʌkʃən] *s* instalación; (log. & elec.) inducción; (mil.) quinta
induction coil *s* (elec.) bobina de inducción, carrete de inducción
induction motor *s* (elec.) motor de inducción
inductive [ɪnˈdʌktɪv] *adj* inductivo
inductivity [ˌɪndʌkˈtɪvɪtɪ] *s* inductividad
inductor [ɪnˈdʌktər] *s* instalador; (elec.) inductor
indue [ɪnˈdju] o [ɪnˈdu] *va* dotar, investir; poner, vestir
indulge [ɪnˈdʌldʒ] *va* mimar; gratificar (*p.ej., los deseos de uno*); indulgenciar; *vn* abandonarse; **to indulge in** abandonarse a, entregarse a; permitirse el placer de, darse el lujo de
indulgence [ɪnˈdʌldʒəns] *s* indulgencia; intemperancia, desenfreno
indulgent [ɪnˈdʌldʒənt] *adj* indulgente
indurate [ˈɪndjʊret] o [ˈɪndʊret] *adj* endurecido; (med.) indurado; *va* endurecer; (med.) indurar; *vn* endurecerse
induration [ˌɪndjʊˈreʃən] o [ˌɪndʊˈreʃən] *s* induración; (med.) induración
Indus [ˈɪndəs] *s* Indo
indusium [ɪnˈdjuzɪəm] o [ɪnˈduzɪəm] *s* (bot.) indusio
industrial [ɪnˈdʌstrɪəl] *adj* industrial
industrialism [ɪnˈdʌstrɪəlɪzəm] *s* industrialismo
industrialist [ɪnˈdʌstrɪəlɪst] *s* industrial
industrialization [ɪnˌdʌstrɪəlɪˈzeʃən] *s* industrialización
industrialize [ɪnˈdʌstrɪəlaɪz] *va* industrializar
industrially [ɪnˈdʌstrɪəlɪ] *adv* industrialmente
industrious [ɪnˈdʌstrɪəs] *adj* aplicado, industrioso
industry [ˈɪndəstrɪ] *s* (*pl:* **-tries**) industria; aplicación, laboriosidad
indwelling [ˈɪnˌdwɛlɪŋ] *adj* interior
-ine *suffix adj* -uno, p.ej., **bovine** boyuno; **cervine** cervuno; **leporine** lebruno; **porcine** porcuno
inebriate [ɪnˈibrɪɪt] o [ɪnˈibrɪet] *s* borracho; [ɪnˈibrɪet] *va* embriagar, inebriar
inebriation [ɪnˌibrɪˈeʃən] o **inebriety** [ˌɪnɪˈbraɪətɪ] *s* embriaguez
inedible [ɪnˈɛdɪbəl] *adj* incomible, no comestible
ineffability [ɪnˌɛfəˈbɪlɪtɪ] *s* inefabilidad
ineffable [ɪnˈɛfəbəl] *adj* inefable
ineffaceable [ˌɪnɪˈfesəbəl] *adj* imborrable
ineffective [ˌɪnɪˈfɛktɪv] *adj* ineficaz; incapaz
ineffectual [ˌɪnɪˈfɛktʃʊəl] *adj* ineficaz
inefficacious [ˌɪnɛfɪˈkeʃəs] *adj* ineficaz
inefficacy [ɪnˈɛfɪkəsɪ] *s* ineficacia
inefficiency [ˌɪnɪˈfɪʃənsɪ] *s* ineficiencia; mal rendimiento
inefficient [ˌɪnɪˈfɪʃənt] *adj* ineficiente; de mal rendimiento
inelastic [ˌɪnɪˈlæstɪk] *adj* inelástico
inelasticity [ˌɪnɪlæsˈtɪsɪtɪ] *s* inelasticidad
inelegance [ɪnˈɛlɪgəns] *s* inelegancia
inelegancy [ɪnˈɛlɪgənsɪ] *s* (*pl:* **-cies**) var. de **inelegance**
inelegant [ɪnˈɛlɪgənt] *adj* inelegante
ineligibility [ɪnˌɛlɪdʒɪˈbɪlɪtɪ] *s* inelegibilidad
ineligible [ɪnˈɛlɪdʒɪbəl] *adj* inelegible
ineluctable [ˌɪnɪˈlʌktəbəl] *adj* ineluctable
inept [ɪnˈɛpt] *adj* inepto
ineptitude [ɪnˈɛptɪtjud] o [ɪnˈɛptɪtud] *s* ineptitud
inequality [ˌɪniˈkwɑlɪtɪ] *s* (*pl:* **-ties**) desigualdad
inequitable [ɪnˈɛkwɪtəbəl] *adj* injusto
inequity [ɪnˈɛkwɪtɪ] *s* (*pl:* **-ties**) inequidad, injusticia
ineradicable [ˌɪnɪˈrædɪkəbəl] *adj* inextirpable
inert [ɪnˈʌrt] *adj* inerte
inert gas *s* (chem.) gas inerte
inertia [ɪnˈʌrʃə] *s* inercia; (mech.) inercia; (med.) inercia de la matriz
inertial [ɪnˈʌrʃəl] *adj* inercial
inescapable [ˌɪnɛsˈkepəbəl] *adj* ineludible
inestimability [ɪnˌɛstɪməˈbɪlɪtɪ] *s* inestimabilidad
inestimable [ɪnˈɛstɪməbəl] *adj* inestimable
inevitability [ɪnˌɛvɪtəˈbɪlɪtɪ] *s* inevitabilidad
inevitable [ɪnˈɛvɪtəbəl] *adj* inevitable
inexact [ˌɪnɛgˈzækt] *adj* inexacto
inexcusable [ˌɪnɛksˈkjuzəbəl] *adj* inexcusable, indisculpable
inexhaustibility [ˌɪnɛgˌzɔstɪˈbɪlɪtɪ] *s* (lo) inagotable
inexhaustible [ˌɪnɛgˈzɔstɪbəl] *adj* inagotable
inexistence [ˌɪnɛgˈzɪstəns] *s* inexistencia
inexistent [ˌɪnɛgˈzɪstənt] *adj* inexistente
inexorability [ɪnˌɛksərəˈbɪlɪtɪ] *s* inexorabilidad
inexorable [ɪnˈɛksərəbəl] *adj* inexorable
inexpediency [ˌɪnɛkˈspidɪənsɪ] *s* imprudencia, inconveniencia, inoportunidad
inexpedient [ˌɪnɛkˈspidɪənt] *adj* imprudente, inconveniente, inoportuno
inexpensive [ˌɪnɛkˈspɛnsɪv] *adj* barato
inexperience [ˌɪnɛkˈspɪrɪəns] *s* inexperiencia
inexperienced [ˌɪnɛkˈspɪrɪənst] *adj* inexperto
inexpert [ɪnˈɛkspʌrt] o [ˌɪnɛkˈspʌrt] *adj* inexperto, imperito
inexpiable [ɪnˈɛkspɪəbəl] *adj* inexpiable
inexplicable [ɪnˈɛksplɪkəbəl] *adj* inexplicable
inexpressible [ˌɪnɛkˈsprɛsɪbəl] *adj* inexpresable
inexpressibly [ˌɪnɛkˈsprɛsɪblɪ] *adv* inexpresablemente
inexpressive [ˌɪnɛkˈsprɛsɪv] *adj* inexpresivo
inexpugnability [ˌɪnɛkˌspʌgnəˈbɪlɪtɪ] *s* inexpugnabilidad
inexpugnable [ˌɪnɛkˈspʌgnəbəl] *adj* inexpugnable
inextinguishable [ˌɪnɛkˈstɪŋgwɪʃəbəl] *adj* inextinguible
inextricability [ɪnˌɛkstrɪkəˈbɪlɪtɪ] *s* inextricabilidad
inextricable [ɪnˈɛkstrɪkəbəl] *adj* inextricable
inf. abr. de **infantry** y **infinitive**
Inf. abr. de **Infantry**
infallibility [ɪnˌfælɪˈbɪlɪtɪ] *s* infalibilidad
infallible [ɪnˈfælɪbəl] *adj* infalible
infamous [ˈɪnfəməs] *adj* infame; (law) infamante (*pena*)
infamy [ˈɪnfəmɪ] *s* (*pl:* **-mies**) infamia
infancy [ˈɪnfənsɪ] *s* (*pl:* **-cies**) infancia; (fig.) infancia; (law) minoridad

infant [ˈɪnfənt] *s* nene, infante, criatura; (law) menor; *adj* infantil

infanta [ɪnˈfæntə] *s* infanta

infante [ɪnˈfænte] *s* infante

infanticidal [ɪnˈfæntɪˌsaɪdəl] *adj* infanticida

infanticide [ɪnˈfæntɪsaɪd] *s* infanticidio (*acción*); infanticida (*persona*)

infantile [ˈɪnfəntaɪl] o [ˈɪnfəntɪl] *adj* infantil; aniñado, trivial, infantil

infantile paralysis *s* (path.) parálisis infantil

infantilism [ɪnˈfæntɪlɪzəm] *s* infantilismo

infantine [ˈɪnfəntaɪn] o [ˈɪnfəntɪn] *adj* aniñado, infantil

infant prodigy *s* niño prodigio

infantry [ˈɪnfəntrɪ] *s* (*pl:* **-tries**) infantería

infantryman [ˈɪnfəntrɪmən] *s* (*pl:* **-men**) infante, soldado de infantería

infarct [ɪnˈfɑrkt] *s* (path.) infarto

infarction [ɪnˈfɑrkʃən] *s* (path.) infartación

infatuate [ɪnˈfætʃuet] *adj* apasionado, amartelado; *va* apasionar, amartelar

infatuation [ɪnˌfætʃuˈeʃən] *s* apasionamiento, amartelamiento

infect [ɪnˈfɛkt] *va* infectar, infeccionar, inficionar; influenciar

infection [ɪnˈfɛkʃən] *s* infección

infectious [ɪnˈfɛkʃəs] *adj* infeccioso

infective [ɪnˈfɛktɪv] *adj* infectivo

infectivity [ˌɪnfɛkˈtɪvɪtɪ] *s* infectividad

infelicitous [ˌɪnfɪˈlɪsɪtəs] *adj* infeliz, desgraciado; impropio, desacertado

infelicity [ˌɪnfɪˈlɪsɪtɪ] *s* (*pl:* **-ties**) infelicidad; impropiedad, desacierto

infer [ɪnˈfʌr] (*pret & pp:* **-ferred;** *ger:* **-ferring**) *va* inferir; (coll.) suponer, conjeturar

inference [ˈɪnfərəns] *s* inferencia

inferential [ˌɪnfəˈrɛnʃəl] *adj* ilativo

inferior [ɪnˈfɪrɪər] *adj & s* inferior

inferiority [ɪnˌfɪrɪˈɑrɪtɪ] o [ɪnˌfɪrɪˈɔrɪtɪ] *s* inferioridad

inferiority complex *s* complejo de inferioridad

infernal [ɪnˈfʌrnəl] *adj* infernal; (coll.) infernal (*muy malo, abominable*)

infernal machine *s* máquina infernal

inferno [ɪnˈfʌrno] *s* (*pl:* **-nos**) infierno

infertile [ɪnˈfʌrtɪl] *adj* estéril

infertility [ˌɪnfərˈtɪlɪtɪ] *s* esterilidad

infest [ɪnˈfɛst] *va* infestar

infestation [ˌɪnfɛsˈteʃən] *s* infestación

infidel [ˈɪnfɪdəl] *adj & s* infiel (*a la fe verdadera*)

infidelity [ˌɪnfɪˈdɛlɪtɪ] *s* (*pl:* **-ties**) infidelidad

infield [ˈɪnˌfild] *s* terrenos de una granja más cercanos a las casas; (baseball) losange, cuadro interior

infielder [ˈɪnˌfildər] *s* (baseball) jugador del cuadro interior

infighting [ˈɪnˌfaɪtɪŋ] *s* (box.) (el) cuerpo a cuerpo

infiltrate [ɪnˈfɪltret] *va* infiltrar; infiltrarse en; *vn* infiltrarse

infiltration [ˌɪnfɪlˈtreʃən] *s* infiltración

infin. abr. de **infinitive**

infinite [ˈɪnfɪnɪt] *adj & s* infinito; **the Infinite** el infinito (*Dios*)

infinitely [ˈɪnfɪnɪtlɪ] *adv* infinitamente

infinitesimal [ˌɪnfɪnɪˈtɛsɪməl] *adj* infinitesimal; *s* (math.) infinitésimo

infinitesimal calculus *s* cálculo infinitesimal

infinitesimally small [ˌɪnfɪnɪˈtɛsɪməlɪ] *adj* infinitamente pequeño

infinitive [ɪnˈfɪnɪtɪv] *adj & s* (gram.) infinitivo

infinitude [ɪnˈfɪnɪtjud] o [ɪnˈfɪnɪtud] *s* infinitud

infinity [ɪnˈfɪnɪtɪ] *s* (*pl:* **-ties**) infinidad; (math.) infinito

infirm [ɪnˈfʌrm] *adj* achacoso, enfermizo; inestable; inconstante; débil, flaco

infirmary [ɪnˈfʌrmərɪ] *s* (*pl:* **-ries**) enfermería, sala de enfermos

infirmity [ɪnˈfʌrmɪtɪ] *s* (*pl:* **-ties**) achaque, enfermedad; inestabilidad; inconstancia; debilidad, flaqueza

infix [ˈɪnfɪks] *s* (gram.) interposición; [ɪnˈfɪks] *va* clavar, encajar, empotrar

inflame [ɪnˈflem] *va* inflamar; *vn* inflamarse

inflammability [ɪnˌflæməˈbɪlɪtɪ] *s* inflamabilidad

inflammable [ɪnˈflæməbəl] *adj* inflamable

inflammation [ˌɪnfləˈmeʃən] *s* inflamación; (path.) inflamación

inflammatory [ɪnˈflæməˌtorɪ] *adj* incendiario; (med.) inflamatorio

inflate [ɪnˈflet] *va* inflar; *vn* inflarse

inflation [ɪnˈfleʃən] *s* inflación

inflationary [ɪnˈfleʃənˌɛrɪ] *adj* inflacionista, inflatorio

inflationism [ɪnˈfleʃənɪzəm] *s* inflacionismo

inflationist [ɪnˈfleʃənɪst] *s* inflacionista

inflect [ɪnˈflɛkt] *va* torcer, doblar; modular (*la voz*); (gram.) poner por orden las formas de, declinar (*los nombres, pronombres y adjetivos*), conjugar (*los verbos*); *vn* (gram.) experimentar o sufrir flexión

inflection [ɪnˈflɛkʃən] *s* inflexión; (geom. & gram.) inflexión

inflectional [ɪnˈflɛkʃənəl] *adj* (gram.) flexional

inflexibility [ɪnˌflɛksɪˈbɪlɪtɪ] *s* inflexibilidad

inflexible [ɪnˈflɛksɪbəl] *adj* inflexible

inflict [ɪnˈflɪkt] *va* infligir; **to inflict on** infligir a

infliction [ɪnˈflɪkʃən] *s* imposición; pena, castigo, sufrimiento

inflorescence [ˌɪnfloˈrɛsəns] *s* (bot.) florescencia (*época*); (bot.) inflorescencia (*disposición de las flores; conjunto de flores*)

inflorescent [ˌɪnfloˈrɛsənt] *adj* floreciente

inflow [ˈɪnˌflo] *s* afluencia; [ˌɪnˈflo] *vn* afluir

influence [ˈɪnfluəns] *s* influencia; *va* influenciar, influir sobre; *vn* influir

influence peddler *s* (coll.) vendehumos, persona que comercia en la influencia política

influence peddling *s* (coll.) comercio de la influencia política

influential [ˌɪnfluˈɛnʃəl] *adj* influyente

influenza [ˌɪnfluˈɛnzə] *s* (path.) influenza

influx [ˈɪnflʌks] *s* afluencia

infold [ɪnˈfold] *va* envolver, arrollar, abrazar, estrechar

inform [ɪnˈfɔrm] *va* informar; avisar, enterar; *vn* informar; **to inform against** informar contra

informal [ɪnˈfɔrməl] *adj* informal; familiar

informality [ˌɪnfɔrˈmælɪtɪ] *s* (*pl:* **-ties**) informalidad; sencillez, falta de ceremonia

informant [ɪnˈfɔrmənt] *s* informante

information [ˌɪnfərˈmeʃən] *s* información, informes

informational [ˌɪnfərˈmeʃənəl] *adj* informativo

informative [ɪnˈfɔrmətɪv] *adj* informativo

informed [ɪnˈfɔrmd] *adj* entendido; enterado; **to keep informed (about)** ponerse al corriente (de); **to keep someone informed (about)** poner a alguien al corriente (de)

informer [ɪnˈfɔrmər] *s* informador; delator

infortiate [ɪnˈfɔrʃɪɪt] *s* inforciado

infraction [ɪnˈfrækʃən] *s* infracción

infra dig [ˌɪnfrə ˈdɪg] abr. de **infra dignitatem** [ˌdɪgnɪˈtetɛm] (Lat.) por debajo de la dignidad de uno

infrangible [ɪnˈfrændʒɪbəl] *adj* infrangible

infrared [ˌɪnfrəˈrɛd] *adj & s* infrarrojo

infrequence [ɪnˈfrikwəns] o **infrequency** [ɪnˈfrikwənsɪ] *s* infrecuencia

infrequent [ɪnˈfrikwənt] *adj* infrecuente

infringe [ɪnˈfrɪndʒ] *va* infringir, violar; *vn* invadir; **to infringe on** o **upon** invadir, abusar de

infringement [ɪnˈfrɪndʒmənt] *s* infracción, violación

infuriate [ɪnˈfjurɪet] *va* enfurecer

infuriation [ɪnˌfjurɪˈeʃən] *s* enfurecimiento

infuse [ɪnˈfjuz] *va* infundir

infusibility [ɪnˌfjuzɪˈbɪlɪtɪ] *s* infusibilidad

infusible [ɪnˈfjuzɪbəl] *adj* infusible

infusion [ɪnˈfjuʒən] *s* infusión

infusorian [ˌɪnfjuˈsorɪən] *adj & s* (zool.) infusorio

-ing *suffix adj* -ador, p.ej., **accusing** acusador; -edor, p.ej., **learning** aprendedor; -idor, p.ej., **following** seguidor; -ando, p.ej., **graduating** graduando; -ante, p.ej., **loving** amante; **Spanish-speaking** hispanohablante; -iente, p.ej., **boiling** hirviente; **following** siguiente; -ueño, p.ej., **flattering** halagüeño; **smiling** risueño; *suffix ger* -ando, p.ej., **accusing** acusando; -iendo, p.ej., **learning** aprendiendo; *suffix s* -ado, p.ej., **ironing** planchado;

tamping tamponado; -ería, p.ej., **barbering** barbería; **engineering** ingeniería
ingathering ['ɪn,gæðərɪŋ] *s* cosecha, recolección
ingenerable [ɪn'dʒɛnərəbəl] *adj* ingenerable
ingenious [ɪn'dʒinjəs] *adj* ingenioso
ingénue [ɛ̃ʒe'ny] *s* dama joven ingenua de la escena
ingenuity [,ɪndʒɪ'njuɪtɪ] o [,ɪndʒɪ'nuɪtɪ] *s* (*pl:* **-ties**) ingeniosidad
ingenuous [ɪn'dʒɛnjʊəs] *adj* ingenuo
ingest [ɪn'dʒɛst] *va* injerir
ingestion [ɪn'dʒɛstʃən] *s* ingestión
ingle ['ɪŋgəl] *s* llama, fuego; chimenea, hogar
inglenook ['ɪŋgəl,nʊk] *s* chimenea, rincón de la chimenea
inglorious [ɪn'glorɪəs] *adj* sin fama; afrentoso, ignominioso
ingoing ['ɪn,go·ɪŋ] *adj* entrante, que llega
ingot ['ɪŋgət] *s* lingote
ingraft [ɪn'græft] o [ɪn'grɑft] *va* (hort. & surg.) injertar; (fig.) implantar
ingrain ['ɪn,gren] *s* lana teñida en rama, hilo teñido en rama; *adj* teñido en rama; [ɪn'gren] *va* teñir en rama
ingrained [ɪn'grend] *adj* profundamente arraigado
ingrate ['ɪngret] *s* ingrato
ingratiate [ɪn'greʃɪet] *va* hacer aceptable; **to ingratiate oneself with** congraciarse con
ingratiating [ɪn'greʃɪ,etɪŋ] *adj* congraciador
ingratiation [ɪn,greʃɪ'eʃən] *s* congraciamiento
ingratitude [ɪn'grætɪtjud] o [ɪn'grætɪtud] *s* ingratitud, desagradecimiento
ingredient [ɪn'gridɪənt] *s* ingrediente
ingress ['ɪngrɛs] *s* ingreso, entrada, acceso
ingrowing ['ɪn,gro·ɪŋ] *adj* que crece hacia dentro
ingrowing nail *s* uñero
ingrown ['ɪn,gron] *adj* crecido hacia dentro; introducido en la carne
inguinal ['ɪŋgwɪnəl] *adj* inguinal
ingulf [ɪn'gʌlf] *va* sumir, hundir
ingurgitate [ɪn'gʌrdʒɪtet] *va* ingurgitar
ingurgitation [ɪn,gʌrdʒɪ'teʃən] *s* ingurgitación
inhabit [ɪn'hæbɪt] *va* habitar, poblar
inhabitability [ɪn,hæbɪtə'bɪlɪtɪ] *s* habitabilidad
inhabitable [ɪn'hæbɪtəbəl] *adj* habitable
inhabitant [ɪn'hæbɪtənt] *s* habitante
inhalant [ɪn'helənt] *s* (med.) inhalador; medicamento inhalatorio
inhalation [,ɪnhə'leʃən] *s* aspiración, inspiración; (med.) inhalación; medicamento inhalado
inhale [ɪn'hel] *va* aspirar, inspirar; (med.) inhalar; *vn* aspirar; tragar el humo
inhaler [ɪn'helər] *s* (med.) inhalador; aspirador
inharmonic [,ɪnhɑr'mɑnɪk] *adj* inarmónico
inharmonious [,ɪnhɑr'monɪəs] *adj* poco armonioso, discordante
inhere [ɪn'hɪr] *vn* ser inherente, residir
inherence [ɪn'hɪrəns] *s* inherencia
inherent [ɪn'hɪrənt] *adj* inherente
inherently [ɪn'hɪrəntlɪ] *adv* inherentemente
inherit [ɪn'hɛrɪt] *va & vn* heredar
inheritable [ɪn'hɛrɪtəbəl] *adj* heredable; heredero
inheritance [ɪn'hɛrɪtəns] *s* herencia
inheritance tax *s* impuesto sobre herencias
inheritor [ɪn'hɛrɪtər] *s* heredero
inhibit [ɪn'hɪbɪt] *va* inhibir
inhibition [,ɪnhɪ'bɪʃən] *s* inhibición
inhibitive [ɪn'hɪbɪtɪv] *adj* inhibitivo
inhibitory [ɪn'hɪbɪ,torɪ] *adj* inhibitorio
inhospitable [ɪn'hɑspɪtəbəl] o [,ɪnhɑs'pɪtəbəl] *adj* inhospedable, inhospitable, inhospital o inhospitalario
inhospitality [ɪn,hɑspɪ'tælɪtɪ] *s* inhospitalidad
inhuman [ɪn'hjumən] *adj* inhumano
inhumane [,ɪnhju'men] *adj* inhumano, inhumanitario
inhumanity [,ɪnhju'mænɪtɪ] *s* (*pl:* **-ties**) inhumanidad
inhumation [,ɪnhjʊ'meʃən] *s* inhumación
inhume [ɪn'hjum] *va* inhumar
inimical [ɪn'ɪmɪkəl] *adj* enemigo
inimitable [ɪn'ɪmɪtəbəl] *adj* inimitable
inimitably [ɪn'ɪmɪtəblɪ] *adv* inimitablemente
iniquitous [ɪ'nɪkwɪtəs] *adj* inicuo
iniquity [ɪ'nɪkwɪtɪ] *s* (*pl:* **-ties**) iniquidad
initial [ɪ'nɪʃəl] *adj* inicial; *s* inicial, letra inicial; sigla (*letra inicial usada como abreviatura*); (*pret & pp:* **-tialed** o **-tialled;** *ger:* **-tialing** o **-tialling**) *va* firmar con sus iniciales; marcar (*p.ej., un pañuelo*)
initially [ɪ'nɪʃəlɪ] *adv* al principio
initiate [ɪ'nɪʃɪɪt] o [ɪ'nɪʃɪet] *s & adj* iniciado; [ɪ'nɪʃɪet] *va* iniciar
initiation [ɪ,nɪʃɪ'eʃən] *s* iniciación
initiative [ɪ'nɪʃɪətɪv] o [ɪ'nɪʃɪ,etɪv] *s* iniciativa; **to take the initiative** tomar la iniciativa
initiator [ɪ'nɪʃɪ,etər] *s* iniciador
inject [ɪn'dʒɛkt] *va* inyectar; introducir (*una advertencia*)
injectable [ɪn'dʒɛktəbəl] *adj* inyectable
injection [ɪn'dʒɛkʃən] *s* inyección
injector [ɪn'dʒɛktər] *s* (mach.) inyector
injudicious [,ɪndʒu'dɪʃəs] *adj* indiscreto, imprudente
injunction [ɪn'dʒʌŋkʃən] *s* mandato; (law) entredicho
injure ['ɪndʒər] *va* dañar, averiar; herir, lisiar, lastimar; injuriar, ofender
injurious [ɪn'dʒʊrɪəs] *adj* dañoso, perjudicial; injurioso, ofensivo
injuriously [ɪn'dʒʊrɪəslɪ] *adv* dañosamente, perjudicialmente; injuriosamente, ofensivamente
injury ['ɪndʒərɪ] *s* (*pl:* **-ries**) daño; herida, lesión
injustice [ɪn'dʒʌstɪs] *s* injusticia
ink [ɪŋk] *s* tinta; (zool.) tinta (*de calamar*); *va* entintar
ink eradicator *s* borratintas
inkhorn ['ɪŋk,hɔrn] *s* tintero hecho de cuerno; *adj* pedantesco
inking ['ɪŋkɪŋ] *s* (print.) entintado, tintaje
inkling ['ɪŋklɪŋ] *s* sospecha, indicio, vislumbre; insinuación
ink sac *s* (zool.) bolsa de la tinta
inkstand ['ɪŋk,stænd] *s* tintero; portatintero
inkwell ['ɪŋk,wɛl] *s* tintero
inky ['ɪŋkɪ] *adj* (*comp:* **-ier;** *super:* **-iest**) entintado; negro
inlaid ['ɪn,led] o [ɪn'led] *adj* embutido, taraceado; *pret & pp de* **inlay**
inland ['ɪnlənd] *adj* interior; ['ɪnlənd] o ['ɪn,lænd] *s* interior; *adv* tierra adentro
Inland Sea *s* mar del Japón
in-law ['ɪn,lɔ] *s* (coll.) pariente político
inlay ['ɪn,le] *s* embutido, taraceado; [ɪn'le] o ['ɪn,le] (*pret & pp:* **-laid**) *va* embutir, taracear
inlet ['ɪnlɛt] *s* entrada; ensenada; estuario
inly ['ɪnlɪ] *adj* interior; *adv* interiormente; completamente
inmate ['ɪnmet] *s* residente, asilado, recluso, desvalido; enfermo, enfermo mental; preso, presidiario
inmost ['ɪnmost] *adj* interior, (el) más íntimo, (el) más recóndito
inn [ɪn] *s* posada, mesón, fonda
innate ['ɪnet], [ɪn'net] o [ɪ'net] *adj* innato, ingénito
innatism ['ɪnnetɪzəm] *s* innatismo
inner ['ɪnər] *adj* interior; oculto, secreto
Inner Mongolia *s* la Mogolia Interior
innermost ['ɪnərmost] *adj* interior, (el) más íntimo
innerspring mattress ['ɪnər'sprɪŋ] *s* colchón de muelles interiores
inner tube *s* cámara, tubo interior
innervation [,ɪnər'veʃən] *s* inervación
inning ['ɪnɪŋ] *s* turno, mano, entrada
innkeeper ['ɪn,kipər] *s* posadero, mesonero, fondista
innocence ['ɪnəsəns] *s* inocencia; (bot.) houstonia cerúlea
innocency ['ɪnəsənsɪ] *s* (*pl:* **-cies**) inocencia
innocent ['ɪnəsənt] *adj & s* inocente; (*cap.*) *s* Inocencio
innocuous [ɪ'nɑkjʊəs] *adj* innocuo
innominate [ɪ'nɑmɪnɪt] *adj* innominado
innovate ['ɪnovet] *va* innovar
innovation [,ɪno'veʃən] *s* innovación
innovator ['ɪno,vetər] *s* innovador
innoxious [ɪ'nɑkʃəs] *adj* innocuo

innuendo [ˌɪnjuˈɛndo] *s* (*pl:* **-does**) indirecta, insinuación
innumerability [ɪˌnjumərəˈbɪlɪtɪ] o [ɪˌnumərəˈbɪlɪtɪ] *s* innumerabilidad
innumerable [ɪˈnjumərəbəl] o [ɪˈnumərəbəl] *adj* innumerable
innumerably [ɪˈnjumərəblɪ] o [ɪˈnumərəblɪ] *adv* innumerablemente
inobedience [ˌɪnəˈbidɪəns] *s* desobediencia, inobediencia
inobedient [ˌɪnəˈbidɪənt] *adj* desobediente, inobediente
inobservance [ˌɪnəbˈzʌrvəns] *s* inobservancia
inoculable [ɪnˈɑkjələbəl] *adj* inoculable
inoculant [ɪnˈɑkjələnt] *s* substancia inoculante
inoculate [ɪnˈɑkjəlet] *va* inocular; (coll.) imbuir; *vn* inocular
inoculation [ɪnˌɑkjəˈleʃən] *s* inoculación
inodorous [ɪnˈodərəs] *adj* inodoro
inoffensive [ˌɪnəˈfɛnsɪv] *adj* inofensivo
inofficious [ˌɪnəˈfɪʃəs] *adj* inoficioso; (law) inoficioso
inoperable [ɪnˈɑpərəbəl] *adj* (surg.) inoperable
inoperative [ɪnˈɑpəˌretɪv] o [ɪnˈɑpərətɪv] *adj* inoperante
inopportune [ɪnˌɑpərˈtjun] o [ɪnˌɑpərˈtun] *adj* inoportuno
inordinate [ɪnˈɔrdɪnɪt] *adj* excesivo; desenfrenado
inorganic [ˌɪnɔrˈgænɪk] *adj* inorgánico
inorganic chemistry *s* química inorgánica
inosculate [ɪnˈɑskjəlet] *va* unir por anastomosis; (fig.) unir íntimamente; *vn* anastomosarse
inpatient [ˈɪnˌpeʃənt] *s* enfermo de dentro
input [ˈɪnˌpʊt] *s* gasto, consumo; dinero invertido; (mach.) potencia consumida, energía absorbida; (elec.) entrada; (elec.) circuito de entrada
input transformer *s* (rad.) transformador de entrada
inquest [ˈɪnkwɛst] *s* (law) pesquisa judicial, reconocimiento médico, levantamiento del cadáver
inquietude [ɪnˈkwaɪətjud] o [ɪnˈkwaɪətud] *s* inquietud
inquire [ɪnˈkwaɪr] *va* averiguar, inquirir; *vn* preguntar; **to inquire about, after** o **for** preguntar por; **to inquire into** averiguar, inquirir; **to inquire of** preguntar a
inquiry [ɪnˈkwaɪrɪ] o [ˈɪnkwɪrɪ] *s* (*pl:* **-ies**) encuesta, averiguación; pregunta
inquisition [ˌɪnkwɪˈzɪʃən] *s* inquisición; (*cap.*) *s* Inquisición
inquisitive [ɪnˈkwɪzɪtɪv] *adj* curioso
inquisitor [ɪnˈkwɪzɪtər] *s* inquisidor; (*cap.*) *s* (eccl.) Inquisidor
inquisitorial [ɪnˌkwɪzɪˈtorɪəl] *adj* inquisitorial
in re [ɪnˈri] (Lat.) concerniente a
inroad [ˈɪnˌrod] *s* incursión
inrush [ˈɪnˌrʌʃ] *s* afluencia; irrupción
ins. abr. de **inches, insulated** y **insurance**
insalivate [ɪnˈsælɪvet] *va* (physiol.) insalivar
insalivation [ɪnˌsælɪˈveʃən] *s* (physiol.) insalivación
insalubrious [ˌɪnsəˈlubrɪəs] *adj* insalubre
insane [ɪnˈsen] *adj* insano, loco
insane asylum *s* asilo de locos, manicomio
insanitary [ɪnˈsænɪˌtɛrɪ] *adj* insalubre
insanity [ɪnˈsænɪtɪ] *s* (*pl:* **-ties**) insania, locura
insatiable [ɪnˈseʃəbəl] *adj* insaciable; **insatiable for** insaciable de
insatiably [ɪnˈseʃəblɪ] *adv* insaciablemente
insatiate [ɪnˈseʃɪɪt] *adj* insaciable
inscribe [ɪnˈskraɪb] *va* inscribir; (geom. & fig.) inscribir; dedicar (*una obra literaria*)
inscription [ɪnˈskrɪpʃən] *s* inscripción; dedicatoria
inscrutability [ɪnˌskrutəˈbɪlɪtɪ] *s* inescrutabilidad
inscrutable [ɪnˈskrutəbəl] *adj* inescrutable
insect [ˈɪnsɛkt] *s* insecto
insecticidal [ɪnˈsɛktɪˌsaɪdəl] *adj* insecticida
insecticide [ɪnˈsɛktɪsaɪd] *adj* & *s* insecticida
insectile [ɪnˈsɛktɪl] *adj* insectil
insectivore [ɪnˈsɛktɪvor] *s* (zool.) insectívoro; (bot.) insectívora
insectivorous [ˌɪnsɛkˈtɪvərəs] *adj* insectívoro
insecure [ˌɪnsɪˈkjʊr] *adj* inseguro
insecurity [ˌɪnsɪˈkjʊrɪtɪ] *s* (*pl:* **-ties**) inseguridad
inseminate [ɪnˈsɛmɪnet] *va* sembrar; inseminar
insemination [ɪnˌsɛmɪˈneʃən] *s* inseminación
insensate [ɪnˈsɛnset] *adj* insensible (*que no experimenta sensación; cruel*); insensato (*necio, loco, ciego*)
insensibility [ɪnˌsɛnsɪˈbɪlɪtɪ] *s* insensibilidad; inconsciencia
insensible [ɪnˈsɛnsɪbəl] *adj* insensible; inconsciente
insensitive [ɪnˈsɛnsɪtɪv] *adj* insensible
insentient [ɪnˈsɛnʃɪənt] o [ɪnˈsɛnʃənt] *adj* insensible, inconsciente
inseparability [ɪnˌsɛpərəˈbɪlɪtɪ] *s* inseparabilidad
inseparable [ɪnˈsɛpərəbəl] *adj* & *s* inseparable
insert [ˈɪnsʌrt] *s* inserción; [ɪnˈsʌrt] *va* insertar
insertion [ɪnˈsʌrʃən] *s* inserción; (sew.) entredós; (bot. & zool.) inserción
in-service [ˈɪnˌsʌrvɪs] *adj* (educ.) en período de instrucción, adquiriendo práctica
inset [ˈɪnˌsɛt] *s* inserción, intercalación; [ɪnˈsɛt] o [ˈɪnˌsɛt] (*pret & pp:* **-set;** *ger:* **-setting**) *va* insertar, intercalar, encastrar, embutir
inshore [ˈɪnˈʃor] *adj* cercano a la orilla; *adv* cerca de la orilla; hacia la orilla
inside [ˈɪnˌsaɪd] *s* interior, parte de dentro; forro (*de una prenda de vestir*); **insides** *spl* (coll.) entrañas; **on the inside** (slang) en el secreto de las cosas; *adj* interior; interno; secreto; [ˌɪnˈsaɪd] *adv* dentro, hacia dentro; **to turn inside out** volver al revés; volverse al revés; **inside of** (coll.) dentro de; **inside out** al revés; *prep* dentro de
inside information *s* informes confidenciales
insider [ˌɪnˈsaɪdər] *s* socio, miembro; persona informada, persona enterada
inside story *s* interioridades
inside track *s* (sport) pista interior; (coll.) ventaja, situación favorable
insidious [ɪnˈsɪdɪəs] *adj* insidioso
insight [ˈɪnˌsaɪt] *s* penetración
insignia [ɪnˈsɪgnɪə] *spl* insignias
insignificance [ˌɪnsɪgˈnɪfɪkəns] *s* insignificancia
insignificant [ˌɪnsɪgˈnɪfɪkənt] *adj* insignificante
insincere [ˌɪnsɪnˈsɪr] *adj* insincero
insincerity [ˌɪnsɪnˈsɛrɪtɪ] *s* (*pl:* **-ties**) insinceridad
insinuate [ɪnˈsɪnjʊet] *va* insinuar; **to insinuate oneself** insinuarse
insinuation [ɪnˌsɪnjʊˈeʃən] *s* insinuación
insinuative [ɪnˈsɪnjʊˌetɪv] *adj* insinuativo
insipid [ɪnˈsɪpɪd] *adj* insípido
insipidity [ˌɪnsɪˈpɪdɪtɪ] *s* (*pl:* **-ties**) insipidez
insist [ɪnˈsɪst] *vn* insistir; **to insist on** o **upon** insistir en o sobre; **to insist on** + *ger* insistir en + *inf;* **to insist that** insistir en que + *subj*
insistence [ɪnˈsɪstəns] o **insistency** [ɪnˈsɪstənsɪ] *s* insistencia
insistent [ɪnˈsɪstənt] *adj* insistente; urgente
insnare [ɪnˈsnɛr] *va* entrampar
insobriety [ˌɪnsoˈbraɪətɪ] *s* intemperancia
insofar as [ˌɪnsoˈfɑræz] *conj* en cuanto
insolate [ˈɪnsolet] *va* insolar
insolation [ˌɪnsoˈleʃən] *s* insolación; (med. & meteor.) insolación
insole [ˈɪnˌsol] *s* plantilla
insolence [ˈɪnsələns] *s* insolencia
insolent [ˈɪnsələnt] *adj* insolente
insolubility [ɪnˌsɑljəˈbɪlɪtɪ] *s* insolubilidad
insoluble [ɪnˈsɑljəbəl] *adj* insoluble
insolvable [ɪnˈsɑlvəbəl] *adj* insoluble
insolvency [ɪnˈsɑlvənsɪ] *s* (*pl:* **-cies**) insolvencia
insolvent [ɪnˈsɑlvənt] *adj* insolvente
insomnia [ɪnˈsɑmnɪə] *s* insomnio
insomuch [ˌɪnsoˈmʌtʃ] *adv* de tal modo, hasta tal punto: **insomuch as** ya que, puesto que; **insomuch that** de tal modo que, hasta el punto que
insouciance [ɪnˈsusɪəns] *s* despreocupación
insouciant [ɪnˈsusɪənt] *adj* despreocupado

inspect [ɪn'spɛkt] *va* inspeccionar; intervenir
inspection [ɪn'spɛkʃən] *s* inspección; intervención
inspector [ɪn'spɛktər] *s* inspector
inspiration [,ɪnspɪ'reʃən] *s* inspiración
inspirational [,ɪnspɪ'reʃənəl] *adj* inspirativo; inspirado
inspiratory [ɪn'spaɪrə,torɪ] *adj* (anat.) inspirador, inspiratorio
inspire [ɪn'spaɪr] *va & vn* inspirar; **to inspire to** + *inf* inspirar a +*inf*
inspiring [ɪn'spaɪrɪŋ] *adj* inspirante; emocionante
inspirit [ɪn'spɪrɪt] *va* alentar, animar
inspissate [ɪn'spɪset] *va* espesar; *vn* espesarse
inst. abr. de **instant (present month)**
Inst. abr. de **Institute** y **Institution**
instability [,ɪnstə'bɪlɪtɪ] *s* inestabilidad
instable [ɪn'stebəl] *adj* inestable
install [ɪn'stɔl] *va* instalar
installation [,ɪnstə'leʃən] *s* instalación
installment o **instalment** [ɪn'stɔlmənt] *s* instalación; entrega; **in installments** a plazos; por entregas
installment plan *s* pago a plazos, pago en abonos, compra a plazos
instance ['ɪnstəns] *s* instancia, petición; ocasión; caso, ejemplo; (law) instancia; **at the instance of** a instancia de; **for instance** por ejemplo; *va* citar como ejemplo
instant ['ɪnstənt] *adj* inmediato; urgente; corriente; instantáneo; *s* instante, momento; ocasión; corriente, mes corriente; **the instant** así que, tan pronto como
instantaneous [,ɪnstən'tenɪəs] *adj* instantáneo
instanter [ɪn'stæntər] *adv* al instante
instantly ['ɪnstəntlɪ] *adv* inmediatamente, al instante
instate [ɪn'stet] *va* instalar
instead [ɪn'stɛd] *adv* en lugar de otro; **instead of** en lugar de, en vez de
instep ['ɪnstɛp] *s* empeine (*del pie, la media o el calzado*); parte anterior de la pata trasera (*del caballo*)
instigate ['ɪnstɪget] *va* instigar
instigation [,ɪnstɪ'geʃən] *s* instigación; **at the instigation of** a instigación de
instigator ['ɪnstɪ,getər] *s* instigador
instill o **instil** [ɪn'stɪl] (*pret & pp:* **-stilled**; *ger:* **-stilling**) *va* instilar
instillation [,ɪnstɪ'leʃən] *s* instilación
instinct ['ɪnstɪŋkt] *s* instinto; [ɪn'stɪŋkt] *adj* animado, movido, lleno; **instinct with** animado de
instinctive [ɪn'stɪŋktɪv] *adj* instintivo
institute ['ɪnstɪtjut] o ['ɪnstɪtut] *s* instituto; **institutes** *spl* (law) instituta; *va* instituir
institution [,ɪnstɪ'tjuʃən] o [,ɪnstɪ'tuʃən] *s* institución; (law) institución; uso establecido; (coll.) persona muy conocida, cosa muy conocida
institutional [,ɪnstɪ'tjuʃənəl] o [,ɪnstɪ'tuʃənəl] *adj* institucional
instruct [ɪn'strʌkt] *va* instruir
instruction [ɪn'strʌkʃən] *s* instrucción; **instructions** *spl* instrucciones, indicaciones
instructional [ɪn'strʌkʃənəl] *adj* educacional; de los instructores, para los instructores
instructive [ɪn'strʌktɪv] *adj* instructivo
instructor [ɪn'strʌktər] *s* instructor
instructress [ɪn'strʌktrɪs] *s* instructora
instrument ['ɪnstrumənt] *s* instrumento; (mus.) instrumento; ['ɪnstrumɛnt] o [,ɪnstru'mɛnt] *va* (mus.) instrumentar
instrumental [,ɪnstru'mɛntəl] *adj* instrumental
instrumentalist [,ɪnstru'mɛntəlɪst] *s* instrumentista
instrumentality [,ɪnstrumən'tælɪtɪ] *s* (*pl:* **-ties**) agencia, mediación
instrumentation [,ɪnstrumɛn'teʃən] *s* instrumentación
instrument board *s* tablero de instrumentos
instrument flying *s* (aer.) vuelo por instrumentos
instrument landing *s* (aer.) aterrizaje por instrumentos
instrument maker *s* instrumentista
instrument panel *s* (aut.) tablero de instrumentos, plancha portainstrumentos
insubordinate [,ɪnsə'bɔrdɪnɪt] *adj* insubordinado
insubordination [,ɪnsə,bɔrdɪ'neʃən] *s* insubordinación
insubstantial [,ɪnsəb'stænʃəl] *adj* insubstancial
insubstantiality [,ɪnsəb,stænʃɪ'ælɪtɪ] *s* insubstancialidad
insufferable [ɪn'sʌfərəbəl] *adj* insufrible
insufficiency [,ɪnsə'fɪʃənsɪ] *s* insuficiencia
insufficient [,ɪnsə'fɪʃənt] *adj* insuficiente
insufflate [ɪn'sʌflet] o ['ɪnsəflet] *va* insuflar
insufflation [,ɪnsə'fleʃən] *s* insuflación
insular ['ɪnsələr] o ['ɪnsjulər] *adj* insular; (fig.) de miras estrechas
insularity [,ɪnsə'lærɪtɪ] o [,ɪnsju'lærɪtɪ] *s* insularidad; (fig.) estrechez de miras
insulate ['ɪnsəlet] o ['ɪnsjulet] *va* aislar
insulation [,ɪnsə'leʃən] o [,ɪnsju'leʃən] *s* (elec.) aislamiento, aislación
insulator ['ɪnsə,letər] o ['ɪnsju,letər] *s* aislador
insulin ['ɪnsəlɪn] o ['ɪnsjulɪn] *s* (trademark) insulina; *adj* insulínico
insulin shock *s* (path.) shock insulínico, insulismo
insult ['ɪnsʌlt] *s* insulto; [ɪn'sʌlt] *va* insultar
insulting [ɪn'sʌltɪŋ] *adj* insultante
insuperable [ɪn'supərəbəl] o [ɪn'sjupərəbəl] *adj* insuperable
insupportable [,ɪnsə'portəbəl] *adj* insoportable
insurable [ɪn'ʃurəbəl] *adj* asegurable
insurance [ɪn'ʃurəns] *s* seguro; prima (*que el asegurado paga al asegurador*)
insurance agent *s* agente de seguros
insurance broker *s* corredor de seguros
insurance company *s* compañía de seguros
insurance policy *s* póliza de seguro
insurant [ɪn'ʃurənt] *s* asegurado
insure [ɪn'ʃur] *va* asegurar
insured [ɪn'ʃurd] *adj & s* asegurado
insurer [ɪn'ʃurər] *s* asegurador
insurgence [ɪn'sʌrdʒəns] o **insurgency** [ɪn'sʌrdʒənsɪ] *s* insurrección, sublevación
insurgent [ɪn'sʌrdʒənt] *adj & s* insurgente
insurmountable [,ɪnsər'mauntəbəl] *adj* insuperable
insurrection [,ɪnsə'rɛkʃən] *s* insurrección
insurrectionary [,ɪnsə'rɛkʃən,ɛrɪ] *adj* insurreccional
insurrectionist [,ɪnsə'rɛkʃənɪst] *s* insurrecto
insusceptibility [,ɪnsə,sɛptɪ'bɪlɪtɪ] *s* insusceptibilidad
insusceptible [,ɪnsə'sɛptɪbəl] *adj* insusceptible
int. abr. de **interest, interior, internal, international** y **intransitive**
intact [ɪn'tækt] *adj* intacto, ileso, incólume
intaglio [ɪn'tæljo] o [ɪn'tɑlɪo] *s* (*pl:* **-ios**) entallo; joya entallada
intake ['ɪn,tek] *s* producto; cantidad admitida; admisión
intake manifold *s* múltiple de admisión, colector de admisión
intake stroke *s* (mach.) carrera de admisión o de aspiración
intake valve *s* válvula de admisión
intangibility [ɪn,tændʒɪ'bɪlɪtɪ] *s* intangibilidad; incomprensibilidad
intangible [ɪn'tændʒɪbəl] *adj* intangible; incomprensible
integer ['ɪntɪdʒər] *s* (math.) entero, número entero; todo, cosa entera
integrable ['ɪntɪgrəbəl] *adj* (math.) integrable
integral ['ɪntɪgrəl] *adj* íntegro; (math.) integral; **integral with** solidario de; *s* conjunto, todo; (math.) integral
integral calculus *s* cálculo integral
integral sign *s* (math.) integral
integrant ['ɪntɪgrənt] *adj* integrante
integrate ['ɪntɪgret] *va* integrar; (math.) integrar
integration [,ɪntɪ'greʃən] *s* integración
integrationist [,ɪntɪ'greʃənɪst] *s* partidario de la integración racial
integrator ['ɪntɪ,gretər] *s* integrador

integrity [ɪn'tɛgrɪtɪ] *s* integridad
integument [ɪn'tɛgjəmənt] *s* integumento
intellect ['ɪntəlɛkt] *s* intelecto; intelectual (*persona*)
intellectual [,ɪntə'lɛktʃuəl] *adj & s* intelectual
intellectualism [,ɪntə'lɛktʃuəlɪzəm] *s* intelectualismo
intellectuality [,ɪntə,lɛktʃu'ælɪtɪ] *s* (*pl:* **-ties**) intelectualidad
intellectually [,ɪntə'lɛktʃuəlɪ] *adv* intelectualmente
intelligence [ɪn'tɛlɪdʒəns] *s* inteligencia; información; inteligencia (*información secreta; policía secreta*)
intelligence department *s* departamento de inteligencia, servicio de inteligencia
intelligence quotient *s* cociente intelectual
intelligence test *s* (psychol.) prueba de inteligencia
intelligent [ɪn'tɛlɪdʒənt] *adj* inteligente
intelligentsia [ɪn,tɛlɪ'dʒɛntsɪə] o [ɪn,tɛlɪ'gɛntsɪə] *s* intelectualidad (*conjunto de los intelectuales de un país*)
intelligibility [ɪn,tɛlɪdʒɪ'bɪlɪtɪ] *s* inteligibilidad
intelligible [ɪn'tɛlɪdʒɪbəl] *adj* inteligible
intemperance [ɪn'tɛmpərəns] *s* intemperancia, destemplanza
intemperate [ɪn'tɛmpərɪt] *adj* intemperante; riguroso (*dícese del tiempo*)
intend [ɪn'tɛnd] *va* pensar, proponerse; destinar; querer decir; **to intend to** + *inf* pensar o proponerse + *inf*
intendancy [ɪn'tɛndənsɪ] *s* (*pl:* **-cies**) intendencia
intendant [ɪn'tɛndənt] *s* intendente
intended [ɪn'tɛndɪd] *adj* pensado; (coll.) prometido, prometida; *s* (coll.) prometido, prometida
intense [ɪn'tɛns] *adj* intenso
intensely [ɪn'tɛnslɪ] *adv* intensamente; sobremanera
intensification [ɪn,tɛnsɪfɪ'keʃən] *s* intensificación
intensify [ɪn'tɛnsɪfaɪ] (*pret & pp:* **-fied**) *va* intensar o intensificar; (phot.) reforzar; *vn* intensarse o intensificarse
intensity [ɪn'tɛnsɪtɪ] *s* (*pl:* **-ties**) intensidad
intensive [ɪn'tɛnsɪv] *adj* intensivo
intent [ɪn'tɛnt] *s* intento; acepción, sentido; **to all intents and purposes** virtualmente, en realidad; *adj* atento; resuelto; **intent on** atento a; resuelto a
intention [ɪn'tɛnʃən] *s* intención; acepción, sentido; **intentions** *spl* (coll.) intenciones (*con respecto al matrimonio*)
intentional [ɪn'tɛnʃənəl] *adj* intencional
intentionally [ɪn'tɛnʃənəlɪ] *adv* intencionalmente
inter [ɪn'tʌr] (*pret & pp:* **-terred;** *ger:* **-terring**) *va* enterrar
interact ['ɪntər,ækt] *s* (theat.) entreacto; [,ɪntər'ækt] *vn* obrar recíprocamente
interaction [,ɪntər'ækʃən] *s* interacción
interallied [,ɪntərə'laɪd] *adj* interaliado
inter-American [,ɪntərə'mɛrɪkən] *adj* interamericano
inter-Americanism [,ɪntərə'mɛrɪkənɪzəm] *s* interamericanismo
inter-Andean [,ɪntəræn'diən] *adj* interandino
interborough ['ɪntər,bʌro] *adj* interseccional
interbreed [,ɪntər'brid] (*pret & pp:* **-bred**) *va* entrecruzar; *vn* entrecruzarse
intercadence [,ɪntər'kedəns] *s* (med.) intercadencia
intercalary [ɪn'tʌrkə,lɛrɪ] *adj* intercalar
intercalate [ɪn'tʌrkəlet] *va* intercalar
intercalation [ɪn,tʌrkə'leʃən] *s* intercalación
intercede [,ɪntər'sid] *vn* interceder
intercellular [,ɪntər'sɛljələr] *adj* intercelular
intercept [,ɪntər'sɛpt] *va* interceptar; (geom.) cortar
interception [,ɪntər'sɛpʃən] *s* interceptación o intercepción
interceptor [,ɪntər'sɛptər] *s* interceptor; avión interceptor
intercession [,ɪntər'sɛʃən] *s* intercesión
intercessor [,ɪntər'sɛsər] o ['ɪntər,sɛsər] *s* intercesor
intercessory [,ɪntər'sɛsərɪ] *adj* intercesorio
interchange ['ɪntər,tʃendʒ] *s* intercambio; correspondencia (*en una carretera, el metro, etc.*); [,ɪntər'tʃendʒ] *va* intercambiar; alternar; *vn* intercambiarse; alternarse
interchangeable [,ɪntər'tʃendʒəbəl] *adj* intercambiable
intercollegiate [,ɪntərkə'lidʒɪɪt] *adj* interescolar, intercolegiado, interuniversitario
intercolonial [,ɪntərkə'lonɪəl] *adj* intercolonial
intercolumniation [,ɪntərkə,lʌmnɪ'eʃən] *s* (arch.) intercolumnio
intercom ['ɪntər,kɑm] *s* (slang) intercomunicador, aparato de intercomunicación
intercommunicate [,ɪntərkə'mjunɪket] *vn* intercomunicarse
intercommunication [,ɪntərkə,mjunɪ'keʃən] *s* intercomunicación
interconnect [,ɪntərkə'nɛkt] *va* interconectar
interconnection [,ɪntərkə'nɛkʃən] *s* interconexión
intercontinental [,ɪntər,kɑntɪ'nɛntəl] *adj* intercontinental
intercostal [,ɪntər'kɑstəl] o [,ɪntər'kɔstəl] *adj* (anat.) intercostal; *s* (anat.) músculo intercostal
intercourse ['ɪntərkors] *s* intercambio, comunicación, trato; comercio, cópula; **to have intercourse** juntarse
intercross [,ɪntər'krɔs] o [,ɪntər'krɑs] *va* entrecruzar; *vn* entrecruzarse
intercurrent [,ɪntər'kʌrənt] *adj* (path.) intercurrente
intercutaneous [,ɪntərkju'tenɪəs] *adj* intercutáneo
interdenominational ['ɪntərdɪ,nɑmɪ'neʃənəl] *adj* intersectario, interconfesional
interdental [,ɪntər'dɛntəl] *adj & s* (phonet.) interdental
interdepartmental ['ɪntər,dipɑrt'mɛntəl] *adj* interdepartamental
interdependence [,ɪntərdɪ'pɛndəns] *s* interdependencia
interdependent [,ɪntərdɪ'pɛndənt] *adj* interdependiente
interdict ['ɪntərdɪkt] *s* interdicto, entredicho; [,ɪntər'dɪkt] *va* interdecir
interdiction [,ɪntər'dɪkʃən] *s* interdicción, entredicho
interdigital [,ɪntər'dɪdʒɪtəl] *adj* interdigital
interest ['ɪntərɛst] o ['ɪntrɪst] *s* interés; **interests** *spl* personas interesadas; **to put out at interest** poner a interés; *va* interesar; **to be interested in** interesarse en o por; **to interest someone to** + *inf* interesarle a uno + *inf*
interested ['ɪntərɛstɪd] o ['ɪntrɪstɪd] *adj* interesado
interesting ['ɪntərɛstɪŋ] o ['ɪntrɪstɪŋ] *adj* interesante
interfere [,ɪntər'fɪr] *vn* oponerse; meterse, inmiscuirse; interferir, interponerse; rozarse (*el caballo un pie con el otro*); (phys.) interferir; (sport) parar una jugada; **to interfere in** meterse en; **to interfere with** estorbar, impedir, dificultar
interference [,ɪntər'fɪrəns] *s* oposición; ingerencia; interferencia; intervención; estorbo, impedimento; (phys. & rad.) interferencia
interferential [,ɪntərfɪ'rɛnʃəl] *adj* (phys.) interferencial
interferometer [,ɪntərfɪ'rɑmɪtər] *s* (phys.) interferómetro
interfold [,ɪntər'fold] *va* entrelazar
interfoliate [,ɪntər'folɪet] *va* interfoliar
interfuse [,ɪntər'fjuz] *va* entremezclar; *vn* entremezclarse
interfusion [,ɪntər'fjuʒən] *s* entremezcladura
intergovernmental [,ɪntər,gʌvərn'mɛntəl] *adj* intergubernamental
interim ['ɪntərɪm] *adj* interino; provisional; *s* intervalo, intermedio; **in the interim** entretanto; (*cap.*) *s* (eccl.) ínterin
interior [ɪn'tɪrɪər] *adj & s* interior
interior decoration *s* decoración interior
interj. abr. de **interjection**
interjacent [,ɪntər'dʒesənt] *adj* interyacente
interject [,ɪntər'dʒɛkt] *va* interponer, introducir; *vn* interponerse

interjection [ˌɪntər'dʒɛkʃən] *s* interposición; exclamación; (gram.) interjección
interjectional [ˌɪntər'dʒɛkʃənəl] *adj* interpuesto; exclamativo; (gram.) interjectivo
interknit [ˌɪntər'nɪt] (*pret & pp:* **-knitted** o **-knit;** *ger:* **-knitting**) *va* entrelazar
interlace ['ɪntərˌles] *s* entrelazado; [ˌɪntər'les] *va* entrelazar, entretejer; *vn* entrelazarse, entretejerse
interlard [ˌɪntər'lɑrd] *va* (cook.) mechar; interpolar
interleaf ['ɪntərˌlif] *s* (*pl:* **-leaves**) hoja interfoliada
interleave [ˌɪntər'liv] *va* interfoliar
interlibrary loan [ˌɪntər'laɪˌbrɛrɪ] o [ˌɪntər'laɪbrərɪ] *s* préstamo entre bibliotecas
interline ['ɪntərˌlaɪn] *s* interlínea; [ˌɪntər'laɪn] *va* interlinear; (sew.) entretelar
interlinear [ˌɪntər'lɪnɪər] *adj* interlineal
interlineation [ˌɪntərˌlɪnɪ'eʃən] *s* interlineación
interlining [ˌɪntər'laɪnɪŋ] *s* interlineación; ['ɪntərˌlaɪnɪŋ] *s* (sew.) entretela
interlink [ˌɪntər'lɪŋk] *va* eslabonar
interlock [ˌɪntər'lɑk] *va* trabar, engargantar, enclavijar; *vn* trabarse, engargantarse, enclavijarse
interlocking [ˌɪntər'lɑkɪŋ] *adj* trabado, entrelazado
interlocking system *s* (rail.) enclavamiento
interlocutor [ˌɪntər'lɑkjətər] *s* interlocutor
interlocutory [ˌɪntər'lɑkjəˌtorɪ] *adj* dialogístico; (law) interlocutorio
interlope [ˌɪntər'lop] *vn* traficar sin derecho
interloper ['ɪntərˌlopər] *s* intruso
interlude ['ɪntərlud] *s* intervalo; (theat.) intermedio; (mus.) interludio
interlunar [ˌɪntər'lunər] *adj* interlunar
interlunation [ˌɪntərlu'neʃən] *s* (astr.) interlunio
intermarriage [ˌɪntər'mærɪdʒ] *s* casamiento entre parientes, casamiento entre personas de distintas razas
intermarry [ˌɪntər'mærɪ] (*pret & pp:* **-ried**) *vn* casarse desentendiéndose del parentesco, casarse desentendiéndose de las diferencias de raza; unirse por medio del matrimonio
intermaxillary [ˌɪntər'mæksɪˌlɛrɪ] *adj* intermaxilar
intermeddle [ˌɪntər'mɛdəl] *vn* entrometerse
intermediary [ˌɪntər'midɪˌɛrɪ] *adj* intermediario; *s* (*pl:* **-ies**) intermediario
intermediate [ˌɪntər'midɪɪt] *adj* intermediario, intermedio; *s* intermediario; [ˌɪntər'midɪet] *vn* intermediar
intermediate frequency *s* (rad.) frecuencia intermedia
intermediation [ˌɪntərˌmidɪ'eʃən] *s* mediación, intervención
interment [ɪn'tʌrmənt] *s* entierro
intermezzo [ˌɪntər'mɛtso] o [ˌɪntər'mɛdzo] *s* (*pl:* **-zos** o **-zi** [sɪ] o [zɪ]) intermezzo, intermedio
interminable [ɪn'tʌrmɪnəbəl] *adj* interminable
interminably [ɪn'tʌrmɪnəblɪ] *adv* interminablemente
intermingle [ˌɪntər'mɪŋgəl] *va* entremezclar; *vn* entremezclarse
intermission [ˌɪntər'mɪʃən] *s* intermisión; (path.) intermisión, intermitencia; (theat.) intermedio, entreacto
intermit [ˌɪntər'mɪt] (*pret & pp:* **-mitted;** *ger:* **-mitting**) *va* intermitir
intermittence [ˌɪntər'mɪtəns] o **intermittency** [ˌɪntər'mɪtənsɪ] *s* intermitencia
intermittent [ˌɪntər'mɪtənt] *adj* intermitente
intermix [ˌɪntər'mɪks] *va* entremezclar; *vn* entremezclarse
intermixture [ˌɪntər'mɪkstʃər] *s* entremezcladura
intern ['ɪntʌrn] *s* (médico) interno de hospital; [ɪn'tʌrn] *va* recluir, internar
internal [ɪn'tʌrnəl] *adj* interno
internal-combustion engine [ɪn'tʌrnəlkəm'bʌstʃən] *s* motor de combustión interna, motor de explosión
internally [ɪn'tʌrnəlɪ] *adv* internamente
internal medicine *s* medicina interna
internal revenue *s* rentas internas (*del gobierno*)
international [ˌɪntər'næʃənəl] *adj* internacional; (*cap.*) *s* Internacional (*asociación de obreros*)
international candle *s* (phys.) bujía internacional
international code *s* (telg.) código internacional
International Court *s* Tribunal internacional
international date line *s* línea internacional de cambio de fecha
internationalism [ˌɪntər'næʃənəlɪzəm] *s* internacionalismo
internationalist [ˌɪntər'næʃənəlɪst] *s* internacionalista
internationality ['ɪntərˌnæʃə'nælɪtɪ] *s* internacionalidad
internationalization [ˌɪntərˌnæʃənəlɪ'zeʃən] *s* internacionalización
internationalize [ˌɪntər'næʃənəlaɪz] *va* internacionalizar
international law *s* derecho internacional, derecho de gentes
internationally [ˌɪntər'næʃənəlɪ] *adv* internacionalmente
interne ['ɪntʌrn] *s* (médico) interno de hospital
internecine [ˌɪntər'nisɪn] *adj* sanguinario
internee [ˌɪntʌr'ni] *s* (mil.) internado
internist [ɪn'tʌrnɪst] *s* (med.) internista
internment [ɪn'tʌrnmənt] *s* reclusión, internación, internamiento
internment camp *s* campo de internamiento
internode ['ɪntərˌnod] *s* internodio
internship ['ɪntʌrnʃɪp] *s* residencia (*de un médico*) en un hospital
internuncio [ˌɪntər'nʌnʃɪo] *s* (*pl:* **-cios**) internuncio
interoceanic [ˌɪntərˌoʃɪ'ænɪk] *adj* interoceánico
interocular [ˌɪntər'ɑkjələr] *adj* interocular
interosseous [ˌɪntər'ɑsɪəs] *adj* interóseo
interpage [ˌɪntər'pedʒ] *va* interpaginar
interparietal [ˌɪntərpə'raɪətəl] *adj* (anat.) interparietal
interparliamentary [ˌɪntərˌpɑrlɪ'mɛntərɪ] *adj* interparlamentario
interpellate [ˌɪntər'pɛlet] o [ɪn'tʌrpɪlet] *va* interpelar
interpellation [ˌɪntərpɛ'leʃən] o [ɪnˌtʌrpɪ'leʃən] *s* interpelación
interpenetrate [ˌɪntər'pɛnɪtret] *va* penetrar completamente; *vn* compenetrarse
interpenetration ['ɪntərˌpɛnɪ'treʃən] *s* interpenetración
interphone ['ɪntərˌfon] *s* aparato de intercomunicación
interplanetary [ˌɪntər'plænɪˌtɛrɪ] *adj* interplanetario
interplay ['ɪntərˌple] *s* interacción
interpolate [ɪn'tʌrpəlet] *va* interpolar; (math.) interpolar
interpolation [ɪnˌtʌrpə'leʃən] *s* interpolación
interpose [ˌɪntər'poz] *va* interponer; *vn* interponerse
interposition [ˌɪntərpə'zɪʃən] *s* interposición
interpret [ɪn'tʌrprɪt] *va* interpretar
interpretable [ɪn'tʌrprɪtəbəl] *adj* interpretable
interpretation [ɪnˌtʌrprɪ'teʃən] *s* interpretación
interpretative [ɪn'tʌrprɪˌtetɪv] *adj* interpretativo
interpreter [ɪn'tʌrprɪtər] *s* intérprete
interpretive [ɪn'tʌrprɪtɪv] *adj* interpretativo
interracial [ˌɪntər'reʃəl] *adj* interracial
interregnum [ˌɪntər'rɛgnəm] *s* interregno
interrelated [ˌɪntərrɪ'letɪd] *adj* correlativo
interrelation [ˌɪntərrɪ'leʃən] *s* correlación
interrogate [ɪn'tɛrəget] *va & vn* interrogar
interrogation [ɪnˌtɛrə'geʃən] *s* interrogación
interrogation mark o **point** *s* interrogación o signo de interrogación
interrogative [ˌɪntə'rɑgətɪv] *adj* interrogativo; interrogante; *s* (gram.) interrogativo
interrogator [ɪn'tɛrəˌgetər] *s* interrogante
interrogatory [ˌɪntə'rɑgəˌtorɪ] *adj* interrogante; *s* (*pl:* **-ries**) interrogatorio
interrupt [ˌɪntə'rʌpt] *va* interrumpir
interruption [ˌɪntə'rʌpʃən] *s* interrupción
interscholastic [ˌɪntərskə'læstɪk] *adj* interescolar

intersect [ˌɪntərˈsɛkt] *va* intersecar; *vn* intersecarse
intersection [ˌɪntərˈsɛkʃən] *s* cruce; (geom.) intersección
intersidereal [ˌɪntərsaɪˈdɪrɪəl] *adj* intersideral
interspace [ˈɪntərˌspes] *s* espacio intermedio; [ˌɪntərˈspes] *va* dejar espacio entre; llenar el espacio entre; espaciar
intersperse [ˌɪntərˈspʌrs] *va* entremezclar, intercalar, esparcir
interspersion [ˌɪntərˈspʌrʒən] o [ˌɪntərˈspʌrʃən] *s* entremezcladura, intercalación, esparcimiento
interstage [ˈɪntərˌstedʒ] *adj* (rad.) inter-etapa
interstate [ˈɪntərˌstet] *adj* interestadal
interstellar [ˌɪntərˈstɛlər] *adj* interestelar
interstice [ɪnˈtʌrstɪs] *s* intersticio
interstitial [ˌɪntərˈstɪʃəl] *adj* intersticial
intertribal [ˌɪntərˈtraɪbəl] *adj* entre tribus
intertrigo [ˌɪntərˈtraɪgo] *s* (path.) intertrigo
intertropical [ˌɪntərˈtrɑpɪkəl] *adj* intertropical
intertwine [ˌɪntərˈtwaɪn] *va* entrelazar; *vn* entrelazarse
intertwist [ˌɪntərˈtwɪst] *va* torcer (*uno con otro*); entremezclar; *vn* torcerse uno con otro; entremezclarse
interuniversity [ˌɪntərˌjunɪˈvʌrsɪtɪ] *adj* interuniversitario
interurban [ˌɪntərˈʌrbən] *adj* interurbano
interval [ˈɪntərvəl] *s* intervalo; (mus.) intervalo; **at intervals** de vez en cuando; de trecho en trecho
intervene [ˌɪntərˈvin] *vn* intervenir
intervening [ˌɪntərˈvinɪŋ] *adj* intermedio
intervention [ˌɪntərˈvɛnʃən] *s* intervención
interventionist [ˌɪntərˈvɛnʃənɪst] *adj* & *s* intervencionista
interview [ˈɪntərvju] *s* entrevista, interviú; *va* entrevistarse con
intervocalic [ˌɪntərvoˈkælɪk] *adj* intervocálico
interweave [ˌɪntərˈwiv] (*pret:* **-wove** o **-weaved;** *pp:* **-woven, -wove** o **-weaved**) *va* entretejer
interwove [ˌɪntərˈwov] *pret* & *pp de* **interweave**
interwoven [ˌɪntərˈwovən] *pp de* **interweave**
interzonal [ˌɪntərˈzonəl] o **interzone** [ˌɪntərˈzon] *adj* interzonal
intestacy [ɪnˈtɛstəsɪ] *s* falta de testamento
intestate [ɪnˈtɛstet] o [ɪnˈtɛstɪt] *adj* & *s* intestado
intestinal [ɪnˈtɛstɪnəl] *adj* intestinal
intestinal worm *s* (zool.) lombriz intestinal
intestine [ɪnˈtɛstɪn] *adj* intestino (*interno; doméstico*); *s* (anat.) intestino; **intestines** *spl* (anat.) intestinos
inthrall [ɪnˈθrɔl] *va* encantar, dominar; esclavizar, sojuzgar
inthrone [ɪnˈθron] *va* entronizar
intimacy [ˈɪntɪməsɪ] *s* (*pl:* **-cies**) intimidad
intimate [ˈɪntɪmɪt] *adj* íntimo; *s* amigo íntimo; [ˈɪntɪmet] *va* insinuar; intimar (*hacer saber*)
intimation [ˌɪntɪˈmeʃən] *s* insinuación; intimación (*informe, noticia*)
intimidate [ɪnˈtɪmɪdet] *va* intimidar
intimidation [ɪnˌtɪmɪˈdeʃən] *s* intimidación
intine [ˈɪntɪn] o [ˈɪntaɪn] *s* (bot.) intina
intitle [ɪnˈtaɪtəl] *va* intitular; dar derecho a
into [ˈɪntu] o [ˈɪntʊ] *prep* en, dentro de, hacia el interior de
intolerability [ɪnˌtɑlərəˈbɪlɪtɪ] *s* intolerabilidad
intolerable [ɪnˈtɑlərəbəl] *adj* intolerable
intolerance [ɪnˈtɑlərəns] *s* intolerancia
intolerant [ɪnˈtɑlərənt] *adj* & *s* intolerante
intomb [ɪnˈtum] *va* sepultar
intombment [ɪnˈtummənt] *s* sepultura
intonate [ˈɪntonet] *va* entonar
intonation [ˌɪntoˈneʃən] *s* entonación; (phonet.) entonación
intone [ɪnˈton] *va* entonar; salmodiar
intoxicant [ɪnˈtɑksɪkənt] *adj* embriagador; *s* bebida alcohólica
intoxicate [ɪnˈtɑksɪket] *va* embriagar; (med.) intoxicar, envenenar
intoxicating [ɪnˈtɑksɪˌketɪŋ] *adj* embriagante
intoxication [ɪnˌtɑksɪˈkeʃən] *s* embriaguez; (med.) intoxicación, envenenamiento
intr. abr. de **intransitive**
intractability [ɪnˌtræktəˈbɪlɪtɪ] *s* intratabilidad
intractable [ɪnˈtræktəbəl] *adj* intratable
intrados [ɪnˈtredɑs] *s* (arch.) intradós
intramolecular [ˌɪntrəməˈlɛkjələr] *adj* intramolecular
intramural [ˌɪntrəˈmjurəl] *adj* interior; (anat.) intramural
intramuscular [ˌɪntrəˈmʌskjələr] *adj* intramuscular
intrans. abr. de **intransitive**
intransigence [ɪnˈtrænsɪdʒəns] o **intransigency** [ɪnˈtrænsɪdʒənsɪ] *s* intransigencia
intransigent [ɪnˈtrænsɪdʒənt] *adj* & *s* intransigente
intransitive [ɪnˈtrænsɪtɪv] *adj* (gram.) intransitivo, neutro
intravenous [ˌɪntrəˈvinəs] *adj* intravenoso
intravenously [ˌɪntrəˈvinəslɪ] *adv* por vía intravenosa
intreat [ɪnˈtrit] *va* rogar, suplicar
intrench [ɪnˈtrɛntʃ] *va* atrincherar; establecer firmemente; *vn* atrincherarse; **to intrench on** o **upon** infringir, violar
intrenchment [ɪnˈtrɛntʃmənt] *s* atrincheramiento
intrepid [ɪnˈtrɛpɪd] *adj* intrépido
intrepidity [ˌɪntrɪˈpɪdɪtɪ] *s* intrepidez
intricacy [ˈɪntrɪkəsɪ] *s* (*pl:* **-cies**) intrincación
intricate [ˈɪntrɪkɪt] *adj* intrincado
intrigue [ɪnˈtrig] o [ˈɪntrig] *s* intriga; intriga amorosa; [ɪnˈtrig] *va* intrigar, despertar la curiosidad de; *vn* intrigar; tener intrigas amorosas
intriguer [ɪnˈtrigər] *s* intrigante
intrinsic [ɪnˈtrɪnsɪk] o **intrinsical** [ɪnˈtrɪnsɪkəl] *adj* intrínseco
intrinsically [ɪnˈtrɪnsɪkəlɪ] *adv* intrínsecamente
introd. abr. de **introduction** y **introductory**
introduce [ˌɪntrəˈdjus] o [ˌɪntrəˈdus] *va* introducir; presentar (*una persona a otra*)
introducer [ˌɪntrəˈdjusər] o [ˌɪntrəˈdusər] *s* introductor
introduction [ˌɪntrəˈdʌkʃən] *s* introducción; presentación
introductory [ˌɪntrəˈdʌktərɪ] *adj* introductivo, introductor
introductory offer *s* ofrecimiento de presentación
Introit [ɪnˈtro·ɪt] *s* (eccl.) introito
introrse [ɪnˈtrɔrs] *adj* (bot.) introrso
introspection [ˌɪntrəˈspɛkʃən] *s* introspección
introspective [ˌɪntrəˈspɛktɪv] *adj* introspectivo
introversion [ˌɪntrəˈvʌrʒən] o [ˌɪntrəˈvʌrʃən] *s* introversión
introvert [ˈɪntrəˌvʌrt] *adj* introverso; *s* introvertido
intrude [ɪnˈtrud] *va* imponer (*su opinión a otros*); *vn* entremeterse; estorbar
intruder [ɪnˈtrudər] *s* intruso
intrusion [ɪnˈtruʒən] *s* intrusión
intrusive [ɪnˈtrusɪv] *adj* intruso
intrust [ɪnˈtrʌst] *va* confiar; **to intrust to** confiar a; **to intrust someone with something** confiar algo a alguien
intubation [ˌɪntjəˈbeʃən] *s* (med.) intubación
intuit [ˈɪntjuɪt] o [ˈɪntuɪt] *va* intuir
intuition [ˌɪntʊˈɪʃən] o [ˌɪntjʊˈɪʃən] *s* intuición
intuitional [ˌɪntʊˈɪʃənəl] o [ˌɪntjʊˈɪʃənəl] *adj* intuitivo
intuitionism [ˌɪntʊˈɪʃənɪzəm] o [ˌɪntjʊˈɪʃənɪzəm] *s* intuicionismo
intuitive [ɪnˈtuɪtɪv] o [ɪnˈtjuɪtɪv] *adj* intuitivo
intussusception [ˌɪntəssəˈsɛpʃən] *s* (biol. & path.) intususcepción
inulase [ˈɪnjəles] *s* (biochem.) inulasa
inulin [ˈɪnjəlɪn] *s* (chem.) inulina
inundate [ˈɪnʌndet] *va* inundar
inundation [ˌɪnʌnˈdeʃən] *s* inundación
inure [ɪnˈjur] *va* acostumbrar, endurecer; *vn* redundar; **to inure to** redundar en
inutility [ˌɪnjʊˈtɪlɪtɪ] *s* (*pl:* **-ties**) inutilidad
inv. abr. de **invented, inventor** y **invoice**
in vacuo [ɪnˈvækjuo] (Lat.) en el vacío
invade [ɪnˈved] *va* invadir

invader [ɪn'vedər] *s* invasor
invaginate [ɪn'vædʒɪnet] *va* invaginar; *vn* invaginarse
invagination [ɪn,vædʒɪ'neʃən] *s* invaginación
invalid [ɪn'vælɪd] *adj* inválido (*nulo, de ningún valor*); ['ɪnvəlɪd] *adj & s* inválido (*por enfermo*); *va* incapacitar; matricular en el registro de inválidos
invalidate [ɪn'vælɪdet] *va* invalidar
invalidation [ɪn,vælɪ'deʃən] *s* invalidación
invalid chair *s* sillón para inválidos
invalidism ['ɪnvəlɪdɪzəm] *s* estado de inválido, estado de valetudinario
invalidity [,ɪnvə'lɪdɪtɪ] *s* invalidez
invaluable [ɪn'væljuəbəl] o [ɪn'væljəbəl] *adj* inestimable, inapreciable
invaluably [ɪn'væljuəblɪ] o [ɪn'væljəblɪ] *adv* inestimablemente, inapreciablemente
invar [ɪn'vɑr] *s* (trademark) invar (*aleación*)
invariability [ɪn,verɪə'bɪlɪtɪ] *s* invariabilidad
invariable [ɪn'verɪəbəl] *adj* invariable
invariably [ɪn'verɪəblɪ] *adv* invariablemente
invariant [ɪn'verɪənt] *adj & s* (math.) invariante
invasion [ɪn'veʒən] *s* invasión
invective [ɪn'vɛktɪv] *s* invectiva
inveigh [ɪn've] *vn* prorrumpir en invectivas; **to inveigh against** invectivar
inveigle [ɪn'vegəl] o [ɪn'vigəl] *va* engatusar; **to inveigle into** + *ger* engatusar para que + *subj*
invent [ɪn'vɛnt] *va* inventar
invention [ɪn'vɛnʃən] *s* invención; invento
Invention of the Cross *s* (eccl.) Invención de la Santa Cruz
inventive [ɪn'vɛntɪv] *adj* inventivo
inventiveness [ɪn'vɛntɪvnɪs] *s* inventiva
inventor [ɪn'vɛntər] *s* inventor
inventory ['ɪnvən,torɪ] *s* (*pl:* **-ries**) inventario; existencia; (*pret & pp:* **-ried**) *va* inventariar
inverisimilitude [ɪn,vɛrɪsɪ'mɪlɪtjud] o [,ɪn,vɛrɪsɪ'mɪlɪtud] *s* inverisimilitud
inverness [,ɪnvər'nɛs] *s* macfarlán (*gabán*)
inverse [ɪn'vʌrs] o ['ɪnvʌrs] *adj* inverso
inverse ratio *s* (math.) razón inversa
inversion [ɪn'vʌrʒən] o [ɪn'vʌrʃən] *s* inversión
invert ['ɪnvʌrt] *s* (psychiatry) invertido; [ɪn'vʌrt] *va* invertir
invertase [ɪn'vʌrtes] *s* (biochem.) invertasa
invertebrate [ɪn'vʌrtɪbret] o [ɪn'vʌrtɪbrɪt] *adj & s* invertebrado
inverted exclamation point *s* (gram.) principio de admiración
inverted question mark *s* (gram.) principio de interrogación
invest [ɪn'vɛst] *va* investir (*poner en posesión de una dignidad*); cubrir, envolver; sitiar, cercar; invertir (*dinero*); **to invest with** investir de o con
investigate [ɪn'vɛstɪget] *va* investigar
investigation [ɪn,vɛstɪ'geʃən] *s* investigación
investigator [ɪn'vɛstɪ,getər] *s* investigador
investiture [ɪn'vɛstɪtʃər] *s* investidura; vestidura
investment [ɪn'vɛstmənt] *s* investidura; vestidura; sitio, cerco; inversión (*de dinero*)
investment capital *s* capital de inversión
investment trust *s* sociedad de inversión, sociedad de cartera
investor [ɪn'vɛstər] *s* inversionista
inveteracy [ɪn'vɛtərəsɪ] *s* hábito inveterado
inveterate [ɪn'vɛtərɪt] *adj* inveterado, sempiterno, empedernido
invidious [ɪn'vɪdɪəs] *adj* odioso, abominable, injusto
invigorate [ɪn'vɪgəret] *va* vigorizar
invigorating [ɪn'vɪgə,retɪŋ] *adj* vigorizante
invigoration [ɪn,vɪgə'reʃən] *s* tonificación
invincibility [ɪn,vɪnsɪ'bɪlɪtɪ] *s* invencibilidad
invincible [ɪn'vɪnsɪbəl] *adj* invencible
Invincible Armada *s* Armada Invencible
inviolability [ɪn,vaɪələ'bɪlɪtɪ] *s* inviolabilidad
inviolable [ɪn'vaɪələbəl] *adj* inviolable
inviolate [ɪn'vaɪəlɪt] o [ɪn'vaɪəlet] *adj* inviolado
invisibility [ɪn,vɪzɪ'bɪlɪtɪ] *s* invisibilidad
invisible [ɪn'vɪzɪbəl] *adj* invisible; *s* ser invisible; mundo invisible
invisible ink *s* tinta simpática
invisible mending *s* zurcido invisible
invisibly [ɪn'vɪzɪblɪ] *adv* invisiblemente
invitation [,ɪnvɪ'teʃən] *s* invitación, convite
invite [ɪn'vaɪt] *va* convidar, invitar; **to invite to** + *inf* convidar a + *inf*
inviting [ɪn'vaɪtɪŋ] *adj* incitante, seductor; provocativo; apetitoso (*alimento*)
in vitro ['vaɪtro] (Lat.) en vidrio
invocation [,ɪnvə'keʃən] *s* invocación; conjuro (*p.ej., de diablos*)
invocatory [ɪn'vɑkə,torɪ] *adj* invocatorio
invoice ['ɪnvɔɪs] *s* factura; remesa; **as per invoice** según factura; *va* facturar
invoice price *s* precio de factura
invoke [ɪn'vok] *va* invocar; conjurar (*p.ej., los demonios*)
involucrate [,ɪnvə'lukrɪt] *adj* (bot.) involucrado
involucre ['ɪnvə,lukər] *s* (bot.) involucro
involuntary [ɪn'vɑlən,terɪ] *adj* involuntario
involute ['ɪnvəlut] *adj* intrincado; vuelto hacia dentro; enrollado en espiral; *s* (geom.) involuta
involution [,ɪnvə'luʃən] *s* intrincación; involución, envolvimiento; (biol. & med.) involución; (math.) potenciación, elevación a potencias; (math.) involución (*caso particular de las formas proyectivas superpuestas*)
involve [ɪn'vɑlv] *va* envolver, enrollar; implicar, comprometer; enredar, enmarañar; embeber
involvement [ɪn'vɑlvmənt] *s* envolvimiento; complicación; implicación
invulnerability [ɪn,vʌlnərə'bɪlɪtɪ] *s* invulnerabilidad
invulnerable [ɪn'vʌlnərəbəl] *adj* invulnerable
inward ['ɪnwərd] *adj* interior, interno; *adv* interiormente, hacia dentro
inward-flow turbine ['ɪnwərd'flo] *s* turbina centrípeta
inwardly ['ɪnwərdlɪ] *adv* interiormente; dentro, hacia dentro
inwardness ['ɪnwərdnɪs] *s* esencia, fondo; espiritualidad; sinceridad
inwards ['ɪnwərdz] *adv* interiormente, hacia dentro; *spl* interiores, entrañas
inweave [ɪn'wiv] (*pret:* **-wove**; *pp:* **-woven** o **-wove**) *va* entretejer
inwove [ɪn'wov] *pret & pp de* **inweave**
inwoven [ɪn'wovən] *pp de* **inweave**
inwrap [ɪn'ræp] (*pret & pp:* **-wrapped**; *ger:* **-wrapping**) *va* arropar, envolver
inwreathe [ɪn'rið] *va* enguirnaldar
inwrought ['ɪn,rɔt] *adj* entremezclado; embutido, incrustado
Io ['aɪo] *s* (myth.) Ío
iodate ['aɪədet] *s* (chem.) yodato
iodic [aɪ'ɑdɪk] *adj* yódico
iodid ['aɪədɪd] o **iodide** ['aɪədaɪd] o ['aɪədɪd] *s* (chem.) yoduro
iodin ['aɪədɪn] o **iodine** ['aɪədaɪn], ['aɪədɪn] o ['aɪədin] *s* (chem.) yodo; (pharm.) tintura de yodo
iodism ['aɪədɪzəm] *s* (path.) yodismo
iodoform [aɪ'odəfɔrm] o [aɪ'ɑdəfɔrm] *s* (chem.) yodoformo
iodous [aɪ'odəs] o [aɪ'ɑdəs] *adj* (chem.) yodoso
ion ['aɪən] o ['aɪɑn] *s* (chem. & phys.) ion
Ionia [aɪ'onɪə] *s* Jonia
Ionian [aɪ'onɪən] *adj & s* jonio o jónico
Ionian Islands *spl* islas Jonias
Ionian Sea *s* mar Jonio
ionic [aɪ'ɑnɪk] *adj* (chem. & phys.) iónico; (*cap.*) *adj* jonio, jónico; (arch.) jónico
ionium [aɪ'onɪəm] *s* (chem.) ionio
ionization [,aɪənɪ'zeʃən] *s* ionización
ionization chamber *s* (phys.) cámara de ionización
ionize ['aɪənaɪz] *va* ionizar; *vn* ionizarse
ionosphere [aɪ'ɑnəsfɪr] *s* ionosfera
ion trap *s* (telv.) trampa de iones
iota [aɪ'otə] *s* iota (*letra griega*); ápice, jota
iotacism [aɪ'otəsɪzəm] *s* iotacismo
I.O.U. o **I O U** ['aɪ,o'ju] abr. de **I owe you;** *s* pagaré
ipecac ['ɪpɪkæk] *s* (bot.) ipecacuana (*planta, raíz y medicamento*)
ipecacuanha [,ɪpɪ,kækju'ænə] *s* var. de **ipecac**
Iphigenia [,ɪfɪdʒɪ'naɪə] *s* (myth.) Ifigenia

ipse dixit ['ɪpsɪ'dɪksɪt] *s* (*pl:* **ipse dixits**) afirmación dogmática
I.Q. o **IQ** abr. de **intelligence quotient**
Ir. abr. de **Ireland** y **Irish**
Irak [ɪ'rɑk] *s* var. de **Iraq**
Iran [ɪ'rɑn] o [aɪ'ræn] *s* el Irán
Iranian [aɪ'renɪən] *adj & s* iranés o iranio
Iranian Plateau *s* meseta del Irán
Iraq [ɪ'rɑk] *s* el Irak
Iraqi [ɪ'rɑki] *adj* iraqués; *s* (*pl:* **-qis**) iraqués
irascibility [ɪ,ræsɪ'bɪlɪtɪ] *s* irascibilidad
irascible [ɪ'ræsɪbəl] o [aɪ'ræsɪbəl] *adj* irascible
irate ['aɪret] o [aɪ'ret] *adj* airado
IRBM abr. de **intermediate range ballistic missile**
Ire. abr. de **Ireland**
ire [aɪr] *s* ira, cólera
ireful ['aɪrfəl] *adj* iracundo
Ireland ['aɪrlənd] *s* Irlanda
Irene [aɪ'rin] *s* Irene
iridaceous [,aɪrɪ'deʃəs] *adj* (bot.) iridáceo
iridescence [,ɪrɪ'dɛsəns] *s* iridiscencia, irisación
iridescent [,ɪrɪ'dɛsənt] *adj* iridiscente
iridium [ɪ'rɪdɪəm] o [aɪ'rɪdɪəm] *s* (chem.) iridio
iris ['aɪrɪs] *s* iris, arco iris; (anat. & opt.) iris; (bot.) lirio; (*cap.*) *s* (myth.) Iris; (*l.c.*) *va* irisar
iris diaphragm *s* (opt.) diafragma iris
Irish ['aɪrɪʃ] *adj* irlandés; *s* irlandés (*idioma*); whisky de Irlanda; **the Irish** los irlandeses
Irish Free State *s* Estado Libre de Irlanda
Irish linen *s* irlanda
Irishman ['aɪrɪʃmən] *s* (*pl:* **-men**) irlandés
Irish moss *s* (bot.) musgo de Irlanda
Irish potato *s* patata común
Irish Sea *s* mar de Irlanda
Irish setter *s* perro perdiguero de raza irlandesa
Irish stew *s* guisado de carne con patatas y cebollas
Irish terrier *s* terrier de raza irlandesa
Irishwoman ['aɪrɪʃ,wʊmən] *s* (*pl:* **-women**) irlandesa
iritis [aɪ'raɪtɪs] *s* (path.) iritis
irk [ʌrk] *va* fastidiar, molestar
irksome ['ʌrksəm] *adj* fastidioso, molesto
iron ['aɪərn] *s* hierro; plancha (*para estirar y asentar la ropa*); (golf) hierro; **irons** *spl* hierros, grilletes; **to have too many irons in the fire** tener demasiados asuntos a que atender; **to strike while the iron is hot** a hierro caliente batir de repente, aprovechar la ocasión; *adj* férreo; *va* herrar (*guarnecer de hierro*); aherrojar, poner grilletes a; poner chapas de hierro a; planchar (*la ropa*); **to iron out** (fig.) allanar
iron age *s* (myth. & fig.) siglo de hierro; (*caps.*) *s* (archeol.) edad del hierro
iron-bound ['aɪərn,baʊnd] *adj* unido con hierro, zunchado con hierro; escabroso, rocoso; férreo, duro, inflexible
Iron Chancellor *s* Canciller de hierro (*Bismarck*)
ironclad ['aɪərn,klæd] *adj* acorazado; inabrogable; *s* acorazado
iron constitution *s* constitución de hierro, constitución robusta
iron-core transformer ['aɪərn,kor] *s* (elec.) transformador de núcleo de hierro
Iron Cross *s* cruz de hierro
iron curtain *s* (fig.) telón de acero, cortina de hierro
iron digestion *s* estómago de avestruz
iron fittings *spl* herraje
Iron Gates *spl* Puertas de Hierro (*en el Danubio*)
iron-gray ['aɪərn,gre] *adj* gris obscuro
iron horse *s* (coll.) caballo de hierro (*locomotora*)
ironic [aɪ'rɑnɪk] o **ironical** [aɪ'rɑnɪkəl] *adj* irónico
ironing ['aɪərnɪŋ] *s* planchado
ironing board *s* mesa de planchar, tabla de planchar
iron losses *spl* (elec.) pérdidas magnéticas
iron lung *s* pulmón de hierro
ironmaster ['aɪərn,mæstər] o ['aɪərn,mɑstər] *s* fabricante de hierro
iron mold *s* mancha de orín
ironmonger ['aɪərn,mʌŋgər] *s* (Brit.) quincallero
ironmongery ['aɪərn,mʌŋgərɪ] *s* (Brit.) quincalla; (Brit.) quincallería
iron-nickel alkaline cell ['aɪərn'nɪkəl] *s* (elec.) acumulador de ferro-níquel
iron pyrites *s* pirita de hierro, pirita marcial
ironsides ['aɪərn,saɪdz] *s* acorazado; hombre forzudo; (*cap.*) *spl* caballería de Oliverio Cromwell
ironstone ['aɪərn,ston] *s* mineral de hierro
ironware ['aɪərn,wɛr] *s* ferretería
ironweed ['aɪərn,wid] *s* (bot.) ambrosia; (bot.) verónica
iron will *s* voluntad de hierro, voluntad férrea
iron-willed ['aɪərn'wɪld] *adj* de voluntad férrea
ironwood ['aɪərn,wʊd] *s* (bot.) palo de hierro; (bot.) guapaque; (bot.) cambrón; (bot.) ébano de Ceilán; (bot.) palo santo
ironwork ['aɪərn,wʌrk] *s* herraje; **ironworks** *spl* ferrería, talleres metalúrgicos
ironworker ['aɪərn,wʌrkər] *s* herrero de obra, ferrón; cerrajero (*el que trabaja el hierro en frío*)
ironwort ['aɪərn,wʌrt] *s* (bot.) siderita, samarilla
irony ['aɪrənɪ] *s* (*pl:* **-nies**) ironía
Iroquoian [,ɪrə'kwɔɪən] *adj & s* iroqués
Iroquois ['ɪrəkwɔɪ] o ['ɪrəkwɔɪz] *s* (*pl:* **-quois**) iroqués
irradiance [ɪ'redɪəns] *s* irradiación; lustre, esplendor
irradiate [ɪ'redɪet] *va* irradiar; (med.) tratar con irradiación; *vn* brillar, lucir
irradiation [,ɪredɪ'eʃən] *s* irradiación; brillo, esplendor; (med.) irradiación
irrational [ɪ'ræʃənəl] *adj* irracional; (math.) irracional
irrationality [ɪ,ræʃə'nælɪtɪ] *s* irracionalidad
irreclaimable [,ɪrɪ'kleməbəl] *adj* incorregible, irredimible; inutilizable
irreconcilable [ɪ'rɛkən,saɪləbəl] *adj* irreconciliable: *s* intransigente
irrecoverable [,ɪrɪ'kʌvərəbəl] *adj* irrecuperable; irremediable
irredeemable [,ɪrɪ'diməbəl] *adj* irredimible
Irredentist [,ɪrɪ'dɛntɪst] *s* irredentista
irreducible [,ɪrɪ'djusɪbəl] o [,ɪrɪ'dusɪbəl] *adj* irreducible
irrefragable [ɪ'rɛfrəgəbəl] *adj* irrefragable
irrefutable [ɪ'rɛfjʊtəbəl] o [,ɪrɪ'fjutəbəl] *adj* irrefutable
irregular [ɪ'rɛgjələr] *adj* irregular; (bot., geom., gram. & mil.) irregular; *s* (mil.) irregular
irregularity [ɪ,rɛgjə'lærɪtɪ] *s* (*pl:* **-ties**) irregularidad
irrelevance [ɪ'rɛlɪvəns] *s* inaplicabilidad, impertinencia
irrelevancy [ɪ'rɛlɪvənsɪ] *s* (*pl:* **-cies**) var. de **irrelevance**
irrelevant [ɪ'rɛlɪvənt] *adj* inaplicable, impertinente
irreligion [,ɪrɪ'lɪdʒən] *s* irreligión
irreligious [,ɪrɪ'lɪdʒəs] *adj* irreligioso
irremediable [,ɪrɪ'midɪəbəl] *adj* irremediable
irremissable [,ɪrɪ'mɪsɪbəl] *adj* irremisible
irremovable [,ɪrɪ'muvəbəl] *adj* inamovible, irremovible
irreparable [ɪ'rɛpərəbəl] *adj* irreparable
irreplaceable [,ɪrɪ'plesəbəl] *adj* irreemplazable
irreprehensible [ɪ,rɛprɪ'hɛnsɪbəl] *adj* irreprensible
irrepressible [,ɪrɪ'prɛsɪbəl] *adj* irreprimible, incontenible
irreproachable [,ɪrɪ'protʃəbəl] *adj* irreprochable
irresistible [,ɪrɪ'zɪstɪbəl] *adj* irresistible
irresolute [ɪ'rɛzəlut] *adj* irresoluto
irresolution [,ɪrɛzə'luʃən] *s* irresolución
irrespective [,ɪrɪ'spɛktɪv] *adj* imparcial; **irrespective of** sin hacer caso de, prescindiendo de
irresponsibility [,ɪrɪ,spɑnsɪ'bɪlɪtɪ] *s* irresponsabilidad
irresponsible [,ɪrɪ'spɑnsɪbəl] *adj* irresponsable
irretrievable [,ɪrɪ'trivəbəl] *adj* irrecuperable

irreverence [ɪˈrɛvərəns] *s* irreverencia
irreverent [ɪˈrɛvərənt] *adj* irreverente
irreversible [ˌɪrɪˈvʌrsɪbəl] *adj* irreversible
irrevocability [ɪˌrɛvəkəˈbɪlɪtɪ] *s* irrevocabilidad
irrevocable [ɪˈrɛvəkəbəl] *adj* irrevocable
irrigable [ˈɪrɪgəbəl] *adj* irrigable
irrigate [ˈɪrɪget] *va* irrigar, regar; (med.) irrigar
irrigation [ˌɪrɪˈgeʃən] *s* irrigación, riego; (med.) irrigación
irrigation channel *s* canal de riego
irrigator [ˈɪrɪˌgetər] *s* irrigador
irritability [ˌɪrɪtəˈbɪlɪtɪ] *s* irritabilidad
irritable [ˈɪrɪtəbəl] *adj* irritable
irritant [ˈɪrɪtənt] *adj & s* irritante
irritate [ˈɪrɪtet] *va* irritar
irritation [ˌɪrɪˈteʃən] *s* irritación
irruption [ɪˈrʌpʃən] *s* irrupción
irruptive [ɪˈrʌptɪv] *adj* irruptor
is. abr. de **island**
is [ɪz] *tercera persona del sg del pres de ind de* **be; as is** tal como está
Isaac [ˈaɪzək] *s* Isaac
isabelita [ˌɪzəbəˈlitə] *s* (ichth.) isabelita
Isabella [ˌɪzəˈbɛlə] *s* Isabel
Isabelline [ˌɪzəˈbɛlɪn] o [ˌɪzəˈbɛlaɪn] *adj* isabelino
Isaiah [aɪˈzeə] o [aɪˈzaɪə] *s* (Bib.) Isaías
isallobar [aɪˈsælobɑr] *s* (meteor.) isalóbara
Iscariot [ɪsˈkærɪət] *s* (Bib.) Iscariote
ischial [ˈɪskɪəl] *adj* (anat.) isquiático
ischium [ˈɪskɪəm] *s* (*pl:* **-a** [ə]) (anat.) isquión
Iseult [ɪˈsult] *s* (myth.) Isolda
-ish *suffix adj* -izco, p.ej., **whitish** blanquizco; -ujo, p.ej., **softish** blandujo; -uno, p.ej., **friarish** frailuno; **mannish** hombruno; -uzco, p.ej., **whitish** blancuzco; **blackish** negruzco; *suffix v* -ecer, p.ej., **establish** establecer; **perish** perecer
Ishmael [ˈɪʃmɪəl] *s* (Bib.) Ismael
Ishmaelite [ˈɪʃmɪəlaɪt] *s* ismaelita; (fig.) paria
Isiac [ˈaɪsɪæk] *adj* isíaco
Isidore [ˈɪzɪdor] *s* Isidoro
Isidorian [ˌɪzɪˈdorɪən] *adj* isidoriano
isinglass [ˈaɪzɪŋˌglæs] o [ˈaɪzɪŋˌglɑs] *s* colapez, cola de pescado (*gelatina*); mica
Isis [ˈaɪsɪs] *s* (myth.) Isis
isl. abr. de **island**
Islam [ˈɪsləm] o [ɪsˈlɑm] *s* el Islam
Islamic [ɪsˈlæmɪk] o [ɪsˈlɑmɪk] *adj* islámico
Islamism [ˈɪsləmɪzəm] *s* islamismo
Islamite [ˈɪsləmaɪt] *adj & s* islamista o islamita
Islamize [ˈɪsləmaɪz] *va* islamizar; *vn* islamizar o islamizarse
island [ˈaɪlənd] *s* isla; (fig.) isla (*colina; grupo de árboles*); *adj* isleño; *va* aislar; dar forma de isla a
islander [ˈaɪləndər] *s* isleño
island universe *s* (astr.) universo aislado
isle [aɪl] *s* isleta; isla
Isle of Man *s* Isla de Man
Isle of Pines *s* Isla de Pinos
islet [ˈaɪlɪt] *s* isleta
ism [ˈɪzəm] *s* ismo
isn't [ˈɪzənt] contracción de **is not**
isobar [ˈaɪsobɑr] *s* (chem.) isobaro; (meteor.) isobara, curva o línea isobárica
isobaric [ˌaɪsoˈbærɪk] *adj* isobaro, isobárico
isocheim [ˈaɪsokim] *s* (meteor.) isoquímena
isocheimenal [ˌaɪsoˈkimənəl] *adj* (meteor.) isoquímeno
isochromatic [ˌaɪsokroˈmætɪk] *adj* isocromático
isochronal [aɪˈsɑkrənəl] o **isochronous** [aɪˈsɑkrənəs] *adj* isócrono
isoclinal [ˌaɪsoˈklaɪnəl] *adj* isoclinal; *s* isoclina (*línea*)
Isocrates [aɪˈsɑkrətiz] *s* Isócrates
isodactylous [ˌaɪsoˈdæktɪləs] *adj* isodáctilo
isodynamic [ˌaɪsodaɪˈnæmɪk] o [ˌaɪsodɪˈnæmɪk] *adj* isodinámico
isogloss [ˈaɪsoglɔs] o [ˈaɪsoglɑs] *s* isoglosa
isoglossal [ˌaɪsoˈglɑsəl] *adj* isogloso
isogonic [ˌaɪsoˈgɑnɪk] *adj* isogónico, isógono
isogonic line *s* isógona
isolate [ˈaɪsəlet] o [ˈɪsəlet] *va* aislar
isolation [ˌaɪsəˈleʃən] o [ˌɪsəˈleʃən] *s* aislamiento
isolation hospital *s* hospital de aislamiento
isolationism [ˌaɪsəˈleʃənɪzəm] o [ˌɪsəˈleʃənɪzəm] *s* aislacionismo
isolationist [ˌaɪsəˈleʃənɪst] o [ˌɪsəˈleʃənɪst] *adj & s* aislacionista, insulista
Isolde [ɪˈzɔldə] o [ɪˈsold] *s* var. de **Iseult**
isomer [ˈaɪsomər] *s* (chem.) isómero
isomeric [ˌaɪsoˈmɛrɪk] o **isomerical** [ˌaɪsoˈmɛrɪkəl] *adj* (chem.) isómero o isomérico
isomerism [aɪˈsɑmərɪzəm] *s* (chem.) isomería o isomerismo
isomerous [aɪˈsɑmərəs] *adj* (anat., bot. & chem.) isómero
isometric [ˌaɪsoˈmɛtrɪk] o **isometrical** [ˌaɪsoˈmɛtrɪkəl] *adj* isométrico
isomorphic [ˌaɪsoˈmɔrfɪk] *adj* (biol., chem. & mineral.) isomorfo
isomorphism [ˌaɪsoˈmɔrfɪzəm] *s* (biol., chem. & mineral.) isomorfismo
isomorphous [ˌaɪsoˈmɔrfəs] *adj* isomorfo
isoniazid [ˌaɪsoˈnaɪəzɪd] *s* (pharm.) isoniacida
isoperimetric [ˌaɪsoˌpɛrɪˈmɛtrɪk] o **isoperimetrical** [ˌaɪsoˌpɛrɪˈmɛtrɪkəl] *adj* isoperímetro
isopod [ˈaɪsopɑd] *adj & s* (zool.) isópodo
isoprene [ˈaɪsoprin] *s* (chem.) isopreno
isosceles [aɪˈsɑsəliz] *adj* (geom.) isósceles
isotheral [aɪˈsɑθərəl] *adj* isótero
isothere [ˈaɪsoθɪr] *s* isótera
isotherm [ˈaɪsoθʌrm] *s* isoterma
isothermal [ˌaɪsoˈθʌrməl] *adj* isotermo
isotope [ˈaɪsotop] *s* (chem.) isótopo
isotopic [ˌaɪsoˈtɑpɪk] *adj* isotópico
isotopy [aɪˈsɑtəpɪ] *s* isotopia
isotropic [ˌaɪsoˈtrɑpɪk] *adj* (biol. & phys.) isótropo, isotrópico
isotropous [aɪˈsɑtrəpəs] *adj* isotropo
isotropy [aɪˈsɑtrəpɪ] *s* (biol. & phys.) isotropía
Israel [ˈɪzrɪəl] *s* Israel
Israeli [ɪzˈrelɪ] *adj* israelí; *s* (*pl:* **-lis** [lɪz]) israelí
Israelite [ˈɪzrɪəlaɪt] *adj & s* israelita
issuance [ˈɪʃuəns] *s* emisión
issue [ˈɪʃu] *s* edición, impresión, tirada; entrega, número (*de revista, periódico, etc.*); salida; emisión; flujo; beneficios, producto; réditos; consecuencia, resultado, éxito; punto en disputa, tema de discusión, problema; sucesión, prole; (med.) exutorio; **at issue** en disputa; **to face the issue** afrontar la situación; **to force the issue** forzar la solución, insistir en que se decida el asunto; **to join issue** ponerse a disputar; **to take issue with** estar en desacuerdo con, no estar de acuerdo con; *va* publicar, dar a luz; emitir, poner en circulación; expedir; *vn* salir; **to issue from** provenir de, tener su origen en; **to issue in** dar por resultado
Istanbul [ˌɪstɑnˈbul] *s* Istambul
isthmian [ˈɪsmɪən] *adj* ístmico; istmeño; *s* istmeño
Isthmian games *spl* juegos ístmicos
isthmus [ˈɪsməs] *s* istmo; (anat.) istmo
Isthmus of Corinth *s* istmo de Corinto
Isthmus of Panama *s* istmo de Panamá
Isthmus of Suez *s* istmo de Suez
istle [ˈɪstlɪ] *s* ixtle (*fibra*)
It. abr. de **Italian** y **Italy**
it [ɪt] *pron pers neuter* él, ella; lo, la; le; **this is it** ésta es la fija (*aquello que se teme o espera*); **it is raining** llueve; **it is I** soy yo
ital. abr. de **italic**
Ital. abr. de **Italian** y **Italy**
Italian [ɪˈtæljən] *adj & s* italiano
Italianism [ɪˈtæljənɪzəm] *s* italianismo
Italianize [ɪˈtæljənaɪz] *va* italianizar
Italian millet *s* (bot.) panizo
Italian rye grass *s* (bot.) ballico
Italic [ɪˈtælɪk] *adj* itálico; (*l.c.*) *adj* itálico; (print.) itálico, bastardillo; *s* (print.) letra itálica, bastardilla; **italics** *spl* (print.) letra itálica, bastardilla, letras itálicas
italicize [ɪˈtælɪsaɪz] *va* poner en letra bastardilla; subrayar; dar énfasis a, mediante letras bastardillas
Italy [ˈɪtəlɪ] *s* Italia
itch [ɪtʃ] *s* comezón, picazón; (path.) sarna; (fig.) comezón, prurito; *va* picar, dar comezón a; *vn* picar, sentir o tener comezón; **to itch**

to + *inf* tener prurito por + *inf*, sentir prurito de + *inf*
itch mite *s* (ent.) arador, ácaro de la sarna
itchy ['ɪtʃɪ] *adj* (*comp:* **-ier;** *super:* **-iest**) picante, hormigoso; (path.) sarnoso
itea ['ɪtɪə] *s* (bot.) itea
item ['aɪtəm] *s* ítem, artículo; noticia, suelto; partida (*de una cuenta*); (coll.) detalle
itemize ['aɪtəmaɪz] *va* detallar, especificar, particularizar
iterate ['ɪtəret] *va* iterar
iteration [,ɪtə'reʃən] *s* iteración
iterative ['ɪtə,retɪv] o ['ɪtərətɪv] *adj* iterativo; (gram.) frecuentativo
Ithaca ['ɪθəkə] *s* Ítaca (*isla al oeste de Grecia*)
itineracy [aɪ'tɪnərəsɪ] o [ɪ'tɪnərəsɪ] o **itinerancy** [aɪ'tɪnərənsɪ] o [ɪ'tɪnərənsɪ] *s* peregrinación; predicadores ambulantes; jueces ambulantes
itinerant [aɪ'tɪnərənt] o [ɪ'tɪnərənt] *adj* ambulante; *s* viandante
itinerary [aɪ'tɪnə,rɛrɪ] o [ɪ'tɪnə,rɛrɪ] *s* (*pl:* **-ies**) itinerario; *adj* itinerario
itinerate [aɪ'tɪnəret] o [ɪ'tɪnəret] *va* viajar por; *vn* seguir un itinerario
its [ɪts] *adj poss* su; *pron poss* el suyo
it's [ɪts] contracción de **it is**
itself [ɪt'sɛlf] *pron* mismo; sí, sí mismo; se
I've [aɪv] contracción de **I have**
ivied ['aɪvɪd] *adj* cubierto de hiedra
Iviza [i'viθɑ] *s* Ibiza (*una de las islas Baleares*)
ivory ['aɪvərɪ] *s* (*pl:* **-ries**) marfil; **ivories** *spl* teclas del piano; bolas de billar; dados; (slang) dientes; *adj* ebúrneo, marfileño, marfilino
ivorybill ['aɪvərɪ,bɪl] *s* (orn.) pico de marfil
ivory black *s* negro de marfil
Ivory Coast *s* Costa de Marfil (*África*)
ivory nut *s* nuez de marfil
ivory palm *s* (bot.) tagua
ivory tower *s* (fig.) torre de marfil
ivy ['aɪvɪ] *s* (*pl:* **ivies**) (bot.) hiedra
I.W.W. abr. de **Industrial Workers of the World**
Ixion [ɪks'aɪən] *s* (myth.) Ixión
izzard ['ɪzərd] *s* (dial.) zeda (*letra*); **from A to izzard** de cabo a rabo

J

J, j [dʒe] *s* (*pl:* **J's, j's** [dʒez]) décima letra del alfabeto inglés
j. abr. de **joule**
J. abr. de **Judge** y **Justice**
Ja. abr. de **January**
jab [dʒæb] *s* hurgonazo, pinchazo, piquete; codazo; (box.) golpe inverso; (*pret & pp:* **jabbed;** *ger:* **jabbing**) *va* hurgonear, pinchar; dar un codazo a; *vn* hurgonear, pinchar
jabber ['dʒæbər] *s* jerigonza; chapurreo; *va* decir precipitadamente y de modo poco inteligible; chapurrear (*un idioma*); *vn* farfullar, parlotear; chapurrear
jabot [ʒæ'bo] o ['ʒæbo] *s* chorrera
jacaranda [,dʒækə'rændə] *s* (bot.) abey, jacarandá
jacinth ['dʒesɪnθ] o ['dʒæsɪnθ] *s* (mineral.) jacinto
jack [dʒæk] *s* gato, cric; mozo, sujeto; marinero; asno, burro; liebre muy grande norteamericana; sota o valet (*en los naipes*); boliche; cantillo; torno de asador; jaquemar (*figura que da la hora en un reloj*); sacabotas; (coll.) dinero; (rad. & telp.) jack; (elec.) caja (*de enchufe*); (naut.) yac (*bandera de proa*); (*cap.*) *s* Juanillo; **jacks** *spl* cantillos, juego de los cantillos; **every man jack** todos sin excepción; *va* alzar con el gato; **to jack up** alzar con el gato; (coll.) subir, aumentar (*sueldos, precios, etc.*); (coll.) recordar su obligación a (*una persona*
jackal ['dʒækəl] *s* (zool.) chacal; (fig.) paniaguado
jackanapes ['dʒækəneps] *s* mequetrefe
jackass ['dʒæk,æs] *s* asno, burro; (fig.) asno, burro
jackboot ['dʒæk,but] *s* bota grande y fuerte
jackdaw ['dʒæk,dɔ] *s* (orn.) corneja
jacket ['dʒækɪt] *s* chaqueta; cubierta, envoltura; sobrecubierta (*de un libro encuadernado*); camisa (*de agua*); **to dust one's jacket** (slang) sacudirle el polvo a uno; *va* poner chaqueta a; cubrir con chaqueta; cubrir
Jack Frost *s* el frío (*personificado*)
jackhammer ['dʒæk,hæmər] *s* martillo perforador
jack-in-a-box ['dʒækɪnə,bɑks] o **jack-in-the-box** ['dʒækɪnðə,bɑks] *s* caja de sorpresa (*muñeco en una caja de resorte*)
jack-in-the-pulpit ['dʒækɪnðə'pulpɪt] *s* (bot.) arisema (*Arisema triphyllum*)
Jack Ketch *s* el verdugo
jackknife ['dʒæk,naɪf] *s* (*pl:* **-knives**) navaja de bolsillo; salto de carpa (*que se ejecuta tocándose los pies antes de dar en el agua*)
jack of all trades *s* factótum, dije, hombre apto para muchas cosas
jack-o'-lantern ['dʒækə,læntərn] *s* fuego fatuo; linterna que se hace colocando una vela encendida en una calabaza cortada de modo que remede las facciones humanas
jack plane *s* (carp.) garlopín
jack pot *s* (poker) jugada para la que se necesita tener un par de sotas o algo mejor; **to hit the jack pot** (slang) ponerse las botas
jack rabbit *s* liebre muy grande norteamericana
jackscrew ['dʒæk,skru] *s* gato de tornillo
jacksnipe ['dʒæk,snaɪp] *s* (orn.) becada de los pantanos
jackstone ['dʒæk,ston] *s* cantillo; **jackstones** *spl* cantillos, juego de los cantillos
jackstraw ['dʒæk,strɔ] *s* pajita; **jackstraws** *spl* juego de las pajitas
jack tar o **Jack Tar** *s* marinero
Jacob ['dʒekəb] *s* Jacobo; (Bib.) Jacob
Jacobean [,dʒækə'biən] *adj* de Jacobo I de Inglaterra, del reinado de Jacobo I; *s* escritor u otro personaje del reinado de Jacobo I de Inglaterra
jacobean lily *s* (bot.) flor de lis
Jacobin ['dʒækəbɪn] *adj & s* jacobino
Jacobinic [,dʒækə'bɪnɪk] o **Jacobinical** [,dʒækə'bɪnɪkəl] *adj* jacobínico
Jacobinism ['dʒækəbɪnɪzəm] *s* jacobinismo
Jacobinize ['dʒækəbɪnaɪz] *va* jacobinizar
Jacobite ['dʒækəbaɪt] *s* jacobita
Jacob's ladder *s* (Bib.) escala de Jacob; (naut.) escala de jarcia
Jacob's-ladder ['dʒekəbz'lædər] *s* (bot.) escala de Jacob
Jacqueminot ['dʒækmɪno] *s* rosa de color rojo intenso
jade [dʒed] *s* jamelgo; mujer, mujeruela; verde; (mineral.) jade; *adj* verde; *va* cansar; ahitar, saciar
jaded ['dʒedɪd] *adj* cansado; ahito, saciado
jaeger o **jäger** ['jegər] *s* (orn.) estercorario
Jael ['dʒeəl] *s* (Bib.) Jahel
jag [dʒæg] *s* diente, púa; **to have a jag on** (slang) estar borracho; (*pret & pp:* **jagged;** *ger:* **jagging**) *va* dentar, cortar en dientes; cortar o rasgar en sietes
jagged ['dʒægɪd] *adj* dentado; cortado o rasgado en sietes
jaguar ['dʒægwɑr] *s* (zool.) jaguar
jail [dʒel] *s* cárcel; **to break jail** escaparse de la cárcel; *va* encarcelar
jailbird ['dʒel,bʌrd] *s* encarcelado, preso; malhechor que ha sido encarcelado repetidas veces
jail delivery *s* evasión de la cárcel; acción de sacar todos los presos de una cárcel con motivo de la vista de causa de cada uno
jailer o **jailor** ['dʒelər] *s* carcelero
jalap ['dʒæləp] *s* (bot.) jalapa
jalopy [dʒə'lɑpɪ] *s* (*pl:* **-ies**) (coll.) automóvil viejo y ruinoso
jalousie [,ʒælu'zi] *s* celosía (*enrejado en las ventanas*)
Jam. abr. de **Jamaica**
jam [dʒæm] *s* compota, conserva; apiñadura, apretura; atoramiento; bloqueo, embotellamiento; (coll.) aprieto, situación peliaguda; (*pret & pp:* **jammed;** *ger:* **jamming**) *va* apiñar, apretujar; trabar; atorar; llenar y tapar apretando; machucarse (*p.ej., un dedo*); (naut.) forzar (*un buque*); (rad.) perturbar, sabotear (*un programa*); **to jam on** poner (*el freno*) con violencia; *vn* apiñarse, apretujarse; trabarse, ahorcarse; atorarse
Jamaica [dʒə'mekə] *s* Jamaica; jamaica (*ron*)
Jamaican [dʒə'mekən] *adj & s* jamaicano
Jamaica quassia *s* (bot. & pharm.) cuasia de Jamaica
jamb o **jambe** [dʒæm] *s* (arch.) jamba; (arm.) canillera, greba
jambeau [dʒæm'bo] *s* (*pl:* **-beaux** ['boz]) (arm.) canillera, greba
jamboree [,dʒæmbə'ri] *s* (slang) francachela, jolgorio; congreso de Niños Exploradores
James [dʒemz] *s* Diego, Jacobo, Jaime, Santiago
jamming ['dʒæmɪŋ] *s* (rad.) radioperturbación, interferencia
jam nut *s* tuerca fiadora, contratuerca
jam-packed ['dʒæm'pækt] *adj* (coll.) apretujado, apiñado, atestado
jam session *s* reunión de músicos de jazz para tocar improvisaciones
jam weld *s* soldadura de tope
Jan. abr. de **January**
Jane [dʒen] *s* Juana
jangle ['dʒæŋgəl] *s* cencerreo, sonido discordante; altercado, riña; *va* hacer sonar de ma-

nera discordante; *vn* cencerrear, sonar de manera discordante; altercar, reñir
Janiculum [dʒəˈnɪkjələm] *s* Janículo
Janissary o **janissary** [ˈdʒænɪˌsɛrɪ] *s* (*pl:* **-ies**) var. de **Janizary**
janitor [ˈdʒænɪtər] *s* portero, conserje
janitress [ˈdʒænɪtrɪs] *s* portera
Janizary o **janizary** [ˈdʒænɪˌzɛrɪ] *s* (*pl:* **-ies**) jenízaro
Jansen [ˈdʒænsən] *s* Jansenio
Jansenism [ˈdʒænsənɪzəm] *s* jansenismo
Jansenist [ˈdʒænsənɪst] *adj & s* jansenista
Jansenistic [ˌdʒænsəˈnɪstɪk] *adj* jansenista
January [ˈdʒænjuˌɛrɪ] *s* enero
Janus [ˈdʒenəs] *s* (myth.) Jano
Janus-faced [ˈdʒenəsˌfest] *adj* de doble cara; falso, traidor
Jap. abr. de **Japan** y **Japanese**
Jap [dʒæp] *adj & s* (slang) japonés
Japan [dʒəˈpæn] *s* el Japón; (*l.c.*) *s* laca japonesa; obra japonesa charolada; aceite secante japonés; (*pret & pp:* **-panned;** *ger:* **-panning**) *va* charolar con laca japonesa
Japan current *s* corriente del Japón
Japanese [ˌdʒæpəˈniz] *adj* japonés; *s* (*pl:* **-nese**) japonés
Japanese beetle *s* (ent.) escarabajo japonés
Japanese lantern *s* linterna china o veneciana
Japanese pagoda tree *s* (bot.) sófora
Japanese persimmon *s* (bot.) caqui
Japan globeflower *s* (bot.) mosqueta
jape [dʒep] *s* burla, engaño; *va* burlar, engañar; *vn* burlarse
Japhetic [dʒəˈfɛtɪk] *adj* jafético
japonica [dʒəˈpɑnɪkə] *s* (bot.) rosal de China, rosal japonés; (bot.) membrillero del Japón
jar [dʒɑr] *s* tarro; frasco (*p.ej., de aceitunas*); vaso, recipiente (*de acumulador*); sacudida; ruido desapacible; sorpresa desagradable; discordia; vuelta o giro; **on the jar** entreabierto, entornado; (*pret & pp:* **jarred;** *ger:* **jarring**) *va* sacudir; chocar; traquetear; *vn* sacudirse; traquetear; disputar, reñir; **to jar on** irritar
jardiniere [ˌdʒɑrdɪˈnɪr] *s* jardinera (*mueble*); florero (*vaso o maceta grandes*)
jargon [ˈdʒɑrgən] *s* jerigonza, jerga (*de los individuos de ciertos oficios, grupos, etc.; lenguaje difícil de entender*); (mineral.) jergón; *vn* hablar en jerigonza; charlar, parlotear
jarring [ˈdʒɑrɪŋ] *s* sacudida; discordia; *adj* discordante
Jas. abr. de **James**
jasmine [ˈdʒæsmɪn] o [ˈdʒæzmɪn] *s* (bot.) jazmín; (bot.) jazmín del Cabo; (bot.) jazmín silvestre; (bot.) lirio tricolor
Jason [ˈdʒesən] *s* (myth.) Jasón
jasper [ˈdʒæspər] *s* (mineral.) jaspe; (*cap.*) *s* Gaspar
jaspery [ˈdʒæspərɪ] *adj* jaspeado
jaundice [ˈdʒɔndɪs] o [ˈdʒɑndɪs] *s* (path.) ictericia; (fig.) negro humor, envidia, celos; *va* dar ictericia a; (fig.) avinagrar el genio a, amargar la vida a
jaundiced [ˈdʒɔndɪst] o [ˈdʒɑndɪst] *adj* ictericiado, aliacanado; (fig.) avinagrado
jaunt [dʒɔnt] o [dʒɑnt] *s* caminata, paseo, excursión; *vn* hacer una excursión de recreo
jaunting car *s* tílburi irlandés
jaunty [ˈdʒɔntɪ] o [ˈdʒɑntɪ] *adj* (*comp:* **-tier;** *super:* **-tiest**) airoso, gallardo; elegante, de buen gusto
Javanese [ˌdʒævəˈniz] *adj* javanés; *s* (*pl:* **-nese**) javanés
javelin [ˈdʒævlɪn] o [ˈdʒævəlɪn] *s* (hist. & sport) jabalina
Javel water [ʒəˈvɛl] *s* agua de Javel
jaw [dʒɔ] *s* (anat.) quijada, mandíbula; (mach.) quijada, mordaza; (mach.) mandíbula (*de una trituradora*); (slang) chismes, cháchara; **jaws** *spl* boca (*con la quijada y los dientes*); garganta, desfiladero; garras, p.ej., **into the jaws of death** a o en las garras de la muerte; *va* (slang) reñir, regañar; *vn* (slang) reñir, regañar; (slang) chismear, chacharear
jawbone [ˈdʒɔˌbon] *s* (anat.) quijada, mandíbula; (anat.) quijada inferior, mandíbula inferior
jawbreaker [ˈdʒɔˌbrekər] *s* (slang) trabalenguas; (slang) hinchabocas; (mach.) trituradora de mandíbulas
jaw clutch *s* (mach.) embrague de mordaza
jaw vise *s* tornillo de mordazas
jay [dʒe] *s* (orn.) arrendajo; (slang) tonto, necio
jaywalk [ˈdʒeˌwɔk] *vn* (coll.) cruzar la calle estúpidamente (*desentendiéndose de las ordenanzas municipales*)
jaywalker [ˈdʒeˌwɔkər] *s* peatón imprudente
jazz [dʒæz] *s* (mus.) jazz; (slang) animación, viveza; *adj* de jazz; *va* sincopar, tocar sincopadamente; (slang) animar, dar viveza a
jazz band *s* jazz-band, orquesta de jazz
J.C. abr. de **Jesus Christ** y **Julius Caesar**
jct. abr. de **junction**
Je. abr. de **June**
jealous [ˈdʒɛləs] *adj* celoso; envidioso; cuidadoso, solícito, vigilante
jealousy [ˈdʒɛləsɪ] *s* (*pl:* **-ies**) celosía, celos; celo (*esmero, interés activo*)
Jean [dʒin] *s* Juana; (*l.c.*) [dʒin] o [dʒen] *s* dril; **jeans** *spl* pantalones de dril, guardapolvo de dril
Jeanne d'Arc [ˌʒɑnˈdɑrk] *s* Juana de Arco
Jeannette [dʒəˈnɛt] *s* Juanita
Jebel Musa [ˈdʒɛbəlˈmusɑ] *s* el monte Ábila (*frente a Gibraltar*)
jeep [dʒip] *s* pequeño automóvil militar que se maniobra con gran facilidad y en poco espacio
jeer [dʒɪr] *s* befa, mofa, vaya; *va* befar; *vn* burlarse, mofarse; **to jeer at** befar, burlarse de, mofarse de
jeeringly [ˈdʒɪrɪŋlɪ] *adv* burlándose, con escarnio
Jehoshaphat [dʒɪˈhɑʃəfæt] *s* (Bib.) Josafat
Jehovah [dʒɪˈhovə] *s* Jehová
Jehovah's Witnesses *spl* testigos de Jehová
Jehovism [dʒɪˈhovɪzəm] *s* jehovismo
Jehu [ˈdʒihju] *s* (Bib.) Jehú; **like Jehu** (slang) en carrera desenfrenada, vertiginosamente; (*l.c.*) *s* (hum.) conductor, cochero (*especialmente el que va muy aprisa*)
jejune [dʒɪˈdʒun] *adj* seco, poco alimenticio; (fig.) árido, estéril, aburrido
jejunum [dʒɪˈdʒunəm] *s* (anat.) yeyuno
jelab [dʒəˈlɑb] *s* chilaba
jell [dʒɛl] *s* (coll.) jalea; *vn* (coll.) convertirse en jalea; (fig.) cuajar
jellaba [dʒəˈlɑbə] *s* var. de **jelab**
jellied [ˈdʒɛlɪd] *adj* convertido en jalea
jellify [ˈdʒɛlɪfaɪ] (*pret & pp:* **-fied**) *va* convertir en jalea, hacer gelatinoso; *vn* convertirse en jalea, hacerse gelatinoso
jelly [ˈdʒɛlɪ] *s* (*pl:* **-lies**) jalea; (*pret & pp:* **-lied**) *va* convertir en jalea; *vn* convertirse en jalea
jellyfish [ˈdʒɛlɪˌfɪʃ] *s* (zool.) aguamar, medusa; (coll.) calzonazos
jennet [ˈdʒɛnɪt] *s* jaca chica española
jenny [ˈdʒɛnɪ] *s* (*pl:* **-nies**) máquina de hilar de múltiples husos; hembra (*de ciertos animales*); (*cap.*) *s* nombre abreviado de **Jane**
jenny ass *s* asna, burra
jenny winch *s* grúa ligera de brazos rígidos
jenny wren *s* rey de zarza
jeopard [ˈdʒɛpərd] o **jeopardize** [ˈdʒɛpərdaɪz] *va* arriesgar, exponer, comprometer
jeopardy [ˈdʒɛpərdɪ] *s* riesgo, peligro
Jephthah [ˈdʒɛfθə] *s* (Bib.) Jefté
Jer. abr. de **Jeremiah**
jerboa [dʒərˈboə] *s* (zool.) jerbo
jeremiad [ˌdʒɛrɪˈmaɪæd] *s* jeremiada
Jeremiah [ˌdʒɛrɪˈmaɪə] o **Jeremias** [ˌdʒɛrɪˈmaɪəs] *s* (Bib.) Jeremías; (Bib.) libro de Jeremías
Jeremian [ˌdʒɛrɪˈmaɪən] o **Jeremianic** [ˌdʒɛrɪmaɪˈænɪk] *adj* jeremíaco
Jericho [ˈdʒɛrɪko] *s* (*pl:* **-chos**) Jericó; (fig.) lugar lejano
jerk [dʒʌrk] *s* estirón, tirón, arranque; tic, espasmo muscular; **by jerks** a tirones, a sacudidas; *va* mover de un tirón; arrojar de un tirón; decir de repente; atasajar (*carne*); *vn* avanzar a tirones, avanzar dando tumbos
jerked beef *s* tasajo
jerkin [ˈdʒʌrkɪn] *s* jubón, justillo
jerkwater [ˈdʒʌrkˌwɔtər] o [ˈdʒʌrkˌwɑtər] *adj* (coll.) secundario, accesorio; (coll.) de mala muerte; *s* (coll.) tren de línea secundaria, tren de ferrocarril económico
jerky [ˈdʒʌrkɪ] *adj* (*comp:* **-ier;** *super:* **-iest**)

desigual (*camino; estilo*); **the train was jerky** el tren andaba a tirones
Jerome [dʒəˈrom] o [ˈdʒerəm] *s* Jerónimo
Jeronymite [dʒɪˈrɑnɪmaɪt] *s* jerónimo
Jerry [ˈdʒerɪ] *s* nombre abreviado de **Gerald, Gerard, Jeremiah** y **Jerome**
jerry-built [ˈdʒerɪ,bɪlt] *adj* mal construído, sin solidez ni consistencia
jersey [ˈdʒʌrzɪ] *s* jersey; tejido de punto; (*cap.*) *s* raza jerseyesa, vaca jerseyesa
Jerusalem [dʒɪˈrusələm] *s* Jerusalén
Jerusalem artichoke *s* (bot.) ajipa, aguaturma, patata de caña, pataca
Jerusalem sage *s* (bot.) aguavientos, matagallos
Jerusalem thorn *s* (bot.) cinacina; (bot.) espina santa, espina vera
jess [dʒes] *s* pihuela (*en la pata del halcón*); *va* poner las pihuelas a
jessamine [ˈdʒesəmɪn] *s* var. de **jasmine**
Jesse [ˈdʒesɪ] *s* (Bib.) Jesé
jest [dʒest] *s* broma, chiste; cosa de risa, ridiculez; **in jest** en broma; *vn* bromear; chancearse
jester [ˈdʒestər] *s* bufón, truhán; bromista
Jesu [ˈdʒizju] o [ˈdʒizu] *s* (poet.) Jesús
Jesuit [ˈdʒeʒuɪt] o [ˈdʒezjuɪt] *adj & s* jesuíta; (fig.) jesuíta (*intrigante*)
Jesuitess [ˈdʒeʒuɪtɪs] o [ˈdʒezjuɪtɪs] *s* jesuitisa
Jesuitic [,dʒeʒuˈɪtɪk] o [,dʒezjuˈɪtɪk] o **Jesuitical** [,dʒeʒuˈɪtɪkəl] o [,dʒezjuˈɪtɪkəl] *adj* jesuítico; (*l.c.*) *adj* jesuítico (*solapado*)
Jesuitism [ˈdʒeʒuɪtɪzəm] o [ˈdʒezjuɪtɪzəm] *s* jesuitismo; (*l.c.*) *s* jesuitismo (*disimulo refinado*)
Jesus [ˈdʒizəs] *s* Jesús
Jesus Christ *s* Jesucristo
jet [dʒet] *s* chorro; surtidor (*de fuente*); mechero (*de gas*); avión de chorro, avión a reacción; (mineral.) azabache; *adj* de azabache; azabachado; (*pret & pp:* **jetted**; *ger:* **jetting**) *va* echar o arrojar en chorro; *vn* chorrear, salir en chorro; volar en avión de chorro
jet age *s* era de los aviones de chorro
jet-black [ˈdʒetˈblæk] *adj* azabachado
jet bomber *s* (aer.) bombardero de reacción a chorro
jet coal *s* carbón de llama larga, carbón de bujía
jet engine *s* motor de reacción, aeropropulsor por reacción, motor a chorro
jet fighter *s* (aer.) caza de reacción, cazarreactor
Jethro [ˈdʒeθro] *s* (Bib.) Jetró
jetliner [ˈdʒet,laɪnər] *s* avión de travesía con propulsión a chorro
jet plane *s* (aer.) avión de propulsión a chorro, avión de chorro, avión a reacción
jet-powered [ˈdʒet,pauərd] *adj* propulsado por motor de reacción
jet propulsion *s* propulsión de escape, propulsión a chorro, propulsión por reacción
jetsam [ˈdʒetsəm] *s* (naut.) echazón; cosa desechada por inútil
jet stream *s* chorro del motor de reacción o el motor cohete; (meteor.) viento fuerte y veloz que circunda la tierra a la altura de 10 kilómetros y entre los 30 y 60 grados de latitud
jettison [ˈdʒetɪsən] *s* (naut.) echazón; *va* (naut.) echar al mar (*para aligerar el buque*); desechar, rechazar
jettison gear *s* (aer.) lanzador
jetty [ˈdʒetɪ] *s* (*pl:* **-ties**) malecón, escollera; muelle; *adj* de azabache; azabachado
Jew [dʒu] *s* judío
jewel [ˈdʒuəl] *s* piedra fina; joya, alhaja; rubí (*de un reloj*); (fig.) joya, alhaja (*persona o cosa*); (*pret & pp:* **-eled** o **-elled**; *ger:* **-eling** o **-elling**) *va* adornar con piedras preciosas; engastar con joyas; (fig.) coronar o adornar (*p.ej., de luces*)
jewel case *s* estuche, joyero
jeweler o **jeweller** [ˈdʒuələr] *s* joyero; relojero
jewellery [ˈdʒuəlrɪ] *s* (Brit.) var. de **jewelry**
jewelry [ˈdʒuəlrɪ] *s* joyería, joyas
jewelry store *s* joyería; relojería
jewelweed [ˈdʒuəl,wid] *s* (bot.) hierba de Santa Catalina (*Impatiens biflora e I. pallida*)
Jewess [ˈdʒuɪs] *s* judía
jewfish [ˈdʒu,fɪʃ] *s* (ichth.) cherna, mero, guasa
Jewish [ˈdʒuɪʃ] *adj* judío; ajudiado
Jewry [ˈdʒurɪ] *s* (*pl:* **-ries**) judería (*barrio; raza, pueblo*); Judea
jews'-harp o **jew's-harp** [ˈdʒuz,hɑrp] *s* (mus.) birimbao
Jew's pitch *s* betún de Judea
Jezebel [ˈdʒezəbəl] *s* (Bib.) Jezabel; mujer depravada
jib [dʒɪb] *s* aguilón o pescante (*de una grúa*); (naut.) foque; **cut of one's jib** (coll.) aspecto exterior de uno; (*pret & pp:* **jibbed**; *ger:* **jibbing**) *va* (naut.) virar; *vn* andar a la pierna, plantarse (*un caballo*); (Brit.) resistirse; (naut.) virar
jib boom *s* (naut.) botalón de foque, tormentín
jibe [dʒaɪb] *s* remoque, pulla; *va* (naut.) virar; *vn* mofarse; (naut.) virar; (coll.) concordar (*dos cosas*); **to jibe at** mofarse de
jiffy [ˈdʒɪfɪ] *s* (*pl:* **-fies**) (coll.) periquete, santiamén; **in a jiffy** (coll.) en un periquete, en un santiamén
jig [dʒɪg] *s* giga (*baile y música*); anzuelo de cuchara; gálibo, plantilla; guía, montaje; (min.) criba hidráulica, cribón de vaivén; **the jig is up** (slang) ya se acabó todo, estamos perdidos; (*pret & pp:* **jigged**; *ger:* **jigging**) *va* bailar (*la giga*); mover a saltitos; mover con movimiento de vaivén; (min.) separar por vibración y lavado; *vn* bailar una giga; moverse a saltitos; oscilar en un vaivén continuo; pescar con anzuelo de cuchara
jig bushing *s* (mach.) buje guía
jigger [ˈdʒɪgər] *s* anzuelo de cuchara; rueda de alfarero; jígger (*máquina para teñir*); (elec.) transformador de oscilaciones; (ent.) ácaro; (ent.) garrapata; (ent.) nigua; (golf) jígger; (min.) criba hidráulica, cribón de vaivén; (naut.) aparejuelo (*conjunto de jarcias y velas*); (naut.) contramesana, palo de mesana; (naut.) velamen de contramesana; (coll.) cosilla, dispositivo, chisme, aparato (*cuyo nombre se ignora o se olvida*); (U.S.A.) vasito para medir el licor de un coctel (*onza y media*)
jigger mast *s* (naut.) contramesana, palo de mesana
jiggle [ˈdʒɪgəl] *s* zarandeo, zangoloteo, zangoteo; *va* zarandear, zangolotear, zangotear; *vn* zarandearse, zangolotearse, zangotearse
jig saw *s* sierra de vaivén
jigsaw puzzle [ˈdʒɪg,sɔ] *s* rompecabezas (*figura cortada en trozos menudos que hay que recomponer*)
jihad [dʒɪˈhɑd] *s* guerra santa (*de los musulmanes contra pueblos que profesan distinta religión*); guerra o cruzada en pro de, o contra una religión, un principio, etc.
jill o **Jill** [dʒɪl] *s* muchacha; mujer, esposa; querida
jilt [dʒɪlt] *s* coqueta que da calabazas al galán; *va* dar calabazas a (*un galán*)
Jim [dʒɪm] *s* nombre abreviado de **James**
Jim Crow *s* (offensive) negro
jim-crow [ˈdʒɪm,kro] *s* (mach.) encorvador de rieles
Jim Crow law *s* ley que segrega a los negros de los blancos en lugares y vehículos públicos
jimjams [ˈdʒɪm,dʒæmz] *spl* (slang) nerviosidad; (slang) delírium tremens
jimmy [ˈdʒɪmɪ] *s* (*pl:* **-mies**) palanqueta; (*cap.*) *s* Dieguito; (*l.c.*) (*pret & pp:* **-mied**) *va* forzar con palanqueta; **to jimmy open** abrir con palanqueta
jimson weed o **Jimson weed** [ˈdʒɪmsən] *s* (bot.) hierba hedionda, higuera loca, manzana espinosa
jingle [ˈdʒɪŋgəl] *s* cascabeleo; cascabel; sonaja (*del pandero*); rima infantil; (rad.) anuncio rimado y cantado; *va* hacer sonar; *vn* cascabelear
jinglet [ˈdʒɪŋglɪt] *s* escrupulillo
jingly [ˈdʒɪŋglɪ] *adj* metálico (*sonido*)
jingo [ˈdʒɪŋgo] *adj* jingoísta; *s* (*pl:* **-goes**) (hist.) jingo; jingoísta; **by jingo!** (coll.) ¡caramba!
jingoism [ˈdʒɪŋgo·ɪzəm] *s* jingoísmo
jingoist [ˈdʒɪŋgo·ɪst] *adj & s* jingoísta
jingoistic [,dʒɪŋgoˈɪstɪk] *adj* jingoísta

jinn [dʒɪn] *s* (*pl:* **jinn** o **jinns**) genio (*espíritu fantástico*)
jinni o **jinnee** [dʒɪˈni] *s* (*pl:* **jinn**) var. de **jinn**
jinrikisha o **jinricksha** [dʒɪnˈrɪkʃə] o [dʒɪnˈrɪkʃɔ] *s* jinrikischa (*pequeño carruaje chino y japonés de dos ruedas y tirado por uno o más hombres*)
jinx [dʒɪŋks] *s* (slang) cenizo, gafe (*persona o cosa que trae mala suerte*); *va* (slang) traer mala suerte a
jitney [ˈdʒɪtnɪ] *s* (slang) automóvil de pasaje; (slang) moneda de cinco centavos
jitterbug [ˈdʒɪtərˌbʌg] *s* persona que baila de manera acrobática y entusiasta la música de jazz; (*pret & pp:* **-bugged; *ger:* -bugging**) *vn* bailar de manera acrobática y entusiasta la música de jazz
jitters [ˈdʒɪtərz] *spl* (slang) agitación, inquietud, nerviosidad; **to give the jitters** (slang) poner nervioso, volver loco; **to have the jitters** (slang) ponerse nervioso
jittery [ˈdʒɪtərɪ] *adj* (slang) agitado, inquieto, nervioso, loco
jiujitsu o **jiujutsu** [dʒuˈdʒɪtsu] *s* var. de **jujitsu**
jive [dʒaɪv] *s* (slang) charla y bromas mientras se toca el jazz; jerga de los músicos de jazz; jazz
Jno. abr. de **John**
jo [dʒo] *s* (*pl:* **joes**) (Scotch) amante
Joachim [ˈdʒoəkɪm] *s* Joaquín
Joan [dʒon] *s* Juana
Joan of Arc [ˈdʒon əv ˈɑrk] o [dʒoˈæn əv ˈɑrk] *s* Juana de Arco
job [dʒɑb] *s* obra; trabajo; tarea, quehacer; deber; oficio; destajo; agiotaje (*sobre los fondos públicos*); (print.) remiendo; (coll.) asunto; (coll.) empleo; (slang) robo; (slang) condena, período (*de prisión*); **by the job** a destajo; **on the job** (slang) en su puesto, atento a sus obligaciones; adquiriendo práctica, trabajando de aprendiz; **to be out of a job** estar desocupado, estar sin trabajo; **to lie down on the job** (slang) echarse en el surco, estirar la pierna, no trabajar por pereza o desaliento ‖ *adj* hecho a destajo; alquilado o contratado por tiempo ‖ (*cap.*)[dʒob] *s* (Bib.) Job; (Bib.) libro de Job; (fig.) job (*hombre de mucha paciencia*) ‖ [dʒɑb] (*pret & pp:* **jobbed;** *ger:* **jobbing**) *va* comprar y vender en calidad de corredor; ceder (*un trabajo*) por contrato ‖ *vn* trabajar a destajo; especular con los fondos públicos
job analysis *s* análisis ocupacional
jobber [ˈdʒɑbər] *s* agiotista (*a expensas del erario público*); destajero; (com.) corredor
jobbery [ˈdʒɑbərɪ] *s* agiotaje (*sobre los fondos públicos*)
jobholder [ˈdʒɑbˌholdər] *s* empleado; burócrata
jobless [ˈdʒɑblɪs] *adj* desocupado, sin trabajo
job lot *s* lote suelto de mercancías, mercancías variadas, saldo de mercancías; sarta, letanía
job printer *s* impresor de remiendos
job printing *s* (print.) remiendo
Job's-tears [ˈdʒobzˈtɪrz] *spl* (bot.) lágrimas de David o de Job
job work *s* var. de **job printing**
Jocasta [dʒoˈkæstə] *s* (myth.) Yocasta
jockey [ˈdʒɑkɪ] *s* (sport) jockey; *va* (sport) montar (*un caballo*) en la pista; maniobrar (*para sacar ventaja o ganar un puesto*); embaucar; **to jockey into** + *ger* embaucar para que + *subj*, p.ej., **they jockeyed him into going into the house** le embaucaron para que entrase en la casa
jockstrap [ˈdʒɑkˌstræp] *s* suspensorio (*para sostener el escroto*)
jocose [dʒoˈkos] *adj* jocoso
jocosity [dʒoˈkɑsɪtɪ] *s* (*pl:* **-ties**) jocosidad
jocular [ˈdʒɑkjələr] *adj* jocoso
jocularity [ˌdʒɑkjəˈlærɪtɪ] *s* (*pl:* **-ties**) jocosidad
jocund [ˈdʒɑkənd] o [ˈdʒokənd] *adj* jocundo, alegre
jocundity [dʒoˈkʌndɪtɪ] *s* jocundidad, alegría
jodhpurs [ˈdʒɑdpərz] o [ˈdʒodpʊrz] *spl* pantalones de equitación
Joe [dʒo] *s* Pepe; (*l.c.*) *s* (Scotch) amante
joe-pye weed [ˌdʒoˈpaɪ] *s* (bot.) eupatorio maculado, eupatorio purpúreo
jog [dʒɑg] *s* golpecito, empujoncito, sacudimiento ligero; estímulo (*a la memoria*); trote corto; paso lento; resalte, saliente; muesca cuadrada; (*pret & pp:* **jogged;** *ger:* **jogging**) *va* dar un golpecito a, empujar levemente; sacudir con el codo o la mano; estimular (*la memoria*); *vn* avanzar al trote corto, avanzar con ritmo lento; **to jog along** avanzar al trote corto, avanzar con ritmo lento
joggle [ˈdʒɑgəl] *s* traqueo; ensambladura dentada; muesca o diente (*de una ensambladura dentada*); *va* traquear; ensamblar (*con ensambladura dentada*); *vn* traquear
jog trot *s* trote de perro; (fig.) rutina
John [dʒɑn] *s* Juan; (Bib.) San Juan; (Bib.) el Evangelio según San Juan
John Bull *s* el inglés típico; Inglaterra
John Doe *s* (law) Fulano de Tal
John Dory *s* (*pl:* **John Dorys**) (ichth.) pez de San Pedro
John Hancock [ˈhænkɑk] *s* (coll.) la firma de uno
Johnny [ˈdʒɑnɪ] *s* Juanito
johnnycake [ˈdʒɑnɪˌkek] *s* pan de maíz
Johnny-come-lately [ˈdʒɑnɪˌkʌmˈletlɪ] *s* (coll.) persona recién llegada
Johnny-jump-up [ˈdʒɑnɪˈdʒʌmpˌʌp] *s* (bot.) pensamiento, trinitaria; (bot.) violeta
Johnny on the spot *s* (coll.) el que llega a tiempo a todas partes; (coll.) el que está siempre presente y listo
John of Gaunt [gɔnt] o [gɑnt] *s* Juan de Gante
Johnsonese [ˌdʒɑnsəˈniz] *s* estilo ampuloso y rimbombante
Johnsonian [dʒɑnˈsonɪən] *adj* de Samuel Johnson y sus escritos; ampuloso y rimbombante; castizo; latinizante; difuso, dilatado
John the Baptist *s* San Juan Bautista
join [dʒɔɪn] *s* juntura, costura; *va* ensamblar, juntar, unir; unirse a, asociarse a, reunirse a; incorporarse a, ingresar en; abrazar (*un partido*); hacerse socio de (*una asociación*); alistarse en (*el ejército*); trabar (*batalla*); desaguar en, desembocar en; *vn* juntarse, unirse; confluir (*p.ej., dos ríos*)
joiner [ˈdʒɔɪnər] *s* ensamblador; ebanista; (coll.) persona que tiene la manía de incorporarse a muchas asociaciones
joiner's gage *s* gramil
joinery [ˈdʒɔɪnərɪ] *s* ebanistería (*arte, obras, etc. del ebanista*)
joint [dʒɔɪnt] *s* empalme, juntura (*p.ej., de una cañería*); artículo (*segmento interarticular*); (anat.) articulación, coyuntura; (arch.) junta; (b.b.) cartivana; (b.b.) nervura; (bot. & zool.) articulación; (carp.) ensambladura; (elec.) empalme; (geol.) grieta; tajada (*de carne*); (slang) garito; (slang) fonducho, restaurante de mala muerte; **out of joint** descoyuntado, desencajado; (fig.) en desorden, desbarajustado; **to throw out of joint** descoyuntarse (*p.ej., el brazo*); *adj* común, mutuo, unido, asociado; copartícipe; colectivo; solidario; indiviso; conjunto; *va* articular; unir, juntar; descuartizar (*p.ej., un pollo*); igualar (*los dientes de una sierra*); (carp.) ensamblar
joint account *s* cuenta en participación, cuenta en común
joint author *s* coautor
joint box *s* (elec.) caja de empalme, caja de conexiones
Joint Chiefs of Staff *spl* estado mayor conjunto
joint committee *s* comisión mixta
jointer [ˈdʒɔɪntər] *s* (carp.) ensambladora, juntera; igualador (*de una sierra*)
jointer plane *s* (carp.) garlopa
joint fir *s* (bot.) hierba de las coyunturas, belcho
joint grass *s* (bot.) gramilla; (bot.) equiseto
jointly [ˈdʒɔɪntlɪ] *adv* juntamente, en común
joint owner *s* condueño
joint session *s* sesión plena, sesión conjunta
joint-stock company [ˈdʒɔɪntˈstɑk] *s* (law) sociedad anónima
joint tenant *s* (law) propietario pro indiviso

jointure [ˈdʒɔɪntʃər] *s* (law) bienes parafernales
joist [dʒɔɪst] *s* viga
joke [dʒok] *s* broma, chiste; cosa de reír; bufón, hazmerreír; **no joke** cosa seria; **to tell a joke** contar un chiste o un chascarrillo; **to play a joke (on)** gastar una broma (a); *va* burlarse de, reírse de; **to joke one's way into** conseguir (*p.ej., un empleo*) burla burlando; *vn* bromear, chancear, hablar en broma; **no joking** o **joking aside** burlas aparte, hablando en serio
joke book *s* libro de chistes
joker [ˈdʒokər] *s* bromista, chancero; frase engañadora (*en un documento*); comodín (*naipe*)
jollification [ˌdʒalɪfɪˈkeʃən] *s* regocijo, alborozo
jollity [ˈdʒalɪtɪ] *s* (*pl:* **-ties**) alegría; diversión
jolly [ˈdʒalɪ] *adj* (*comp:* **-lier;** *super:* **-liest**) jovial, alegre; (coll.) agradable, excelente; *adv* (coll.) muy, harto; (*pret & pp:* **-lied**) *va* (coll.) dar vaya a; (coll.) seguir el humor a; (coll.) reírse de; *vn* (coll.) dar vaya
jolly boat *s* (naut.) bote, esquife
Jolly Roger *s* bandera de piratas
jolt [dʒolt] *s* sacudida, sacudión; *va* sacudir, traquear; *vn* traquear, dar saltos
jolty [ˈdʒoltɪ] *adj* (coll.) desigual (*camino*); que da saltos, que va dando tumbos
Jonah [ˈdʒonə] *s* (Bib.) Jonás; (Bib.) el libro de Jonás; (fig.) ave de mal agüero, persona que trae mala suerte
Jonas [ˈdʒonəs] *s* (Bib.) Jonás; (Bib.) el libro de Jonás
Jonathan [ˈdʒanəθən] *s* Jonatás
jongleur [ˈdʒaŋglər] o [ʒõˈglœr] *s* juglar, trovador
jonquil [ˈdʒaŋkwɪl] *s* (bot.) junquillo
Jordan [ˈdʒɔrdən] *s* Jordán (*río*); Jordania (*país*)
Jordan almond *s* almendra de Málaga
Jordanian [dʒɔrˈdenɪən] *adj & s* jordano
jorum [ˈdʒorəm] *s* (coll.) copa grande
Joseph [ˈdʒozəf] *s* José; (*l.c.*) *s* capa de montar de mujer (*del siglo XVIII*)
Josephine [ˈdʒozəfin] *s* Josefa o Josefina
Joseph of Arimathea [ˌærɪməˈθiə] *s* (Bib.) José de Arimatea
Joseph's-coat [ˈdʒozəfsˈkot] *s* (bot.) papagayo
Josephus [dʒoˈsifəs] *s* Josefo
Josh. abr. de **Joshua**
josh [dʒaʃ] *va* (slang) dar broma a, burlarse de; *vn* (slang) dar broma, burlarse
Joshua [ˈdʒaʃʊə] o [ˈdʒaʃəwə] *s* (Bib.) Josué; (Bib.) el libro de Josué
Josiah [dʒoˈsaɪə] *s* (Bib.) Josías
joss [dʒas] *s* dios familiar chino, ídolo chino
joss house *s* templo chino
joss stick *s* pebete (*que queman los chinos en sus templos*)
jostle [ˈdʒasəl] *s* empellón, empujón; *va* empellar, empujar; forzar, meter a empellones; *vn* chocar; avanzar a fuerza de empujones o codazos
jot [dʒat] *s* jota (*cosa mínima*); **I don't care a jot (about)** no se me da un bledo (de); (*pret & pp:* **jotted;** *ger:* **jotting**) *va* escribir aprisa; **to jot down** apuntar
jottings [ˈdʒatɪŋz] *spl* apuntes
joule [dʒul] o [dʒaʊl] *s* (phys.) julio
jounce [dʒaʊns] *s* traqueo, sacudida; *va* traquear, sacudir; *vn* traquear, dar tumbos
journal [ˈdʒʌrnəl] *s* diario (*periódico; apuntes personales*); revista; (com.) libro diario; (naut.) diario de navegación; (mach.) gorrón, muñón
journal bearing *s* (mach.) chumacera
journal box *s* caja de grasa
journalese [ˌdʒʌrnəˈliz] *s* estilo periodístico
journalism [ˈdʒʌrnəlɪzəm] *s* periodismo
journalist [ˈdʒʌrnəlɪst] *s* periodista
journalistic [ˌdʒʌrnəˈlɪstɪk] *adj* periodístico
journey [ˈdʒʌrnɪ] *s* viaje; *vn* viajar
journeyman [ˈdʒʌrnɪmən] *s* (*pl:* **-men**) oficial
joust [dʒʌst], [dʒust] o [dʒaʊst] *s* justa, torneo; *vn* justar
Jove [dʒov] *s* (myth.) Jove; (poet.) Júpiter (*planeta*); **by Jove!** ¡por Dios!
jovial [ˈdʒovɪəl] *adj* jovial
joviality [ˌdʒovɪˈælɪtɪ] *s* jovialidad
Jovian [ˈdʒovɪən] *adj* joviano o jovio
jowl [dʒaʊl] *s* moflete; quijada; barba (*de ave*); papada (*del ganado*); cabeza de pescado aderezada
joy [dʒɔɪ] *s* alegría, regocijo; **to leap with joy** brincar o saltar de gozo; *vn* alegrarse, regocijarse
joyance [ˈdʒɔɪəns] *s* (archaic) alegría, júbilo
joyful [ˈdʒɔɪfəl] *adj* alegre (*persona; noticia*); **joyful over** gozoso con o de
joyless [ˈdʒɔɪlɪs] *adj* sin alegría, triste, lúgubre
joyous [ˈdʒɔɪəs] *adj* alegre (*persona; noticia*)
joyousness [ˈdʒɔɪəsnɪs] *s* alegría, regocijo
joy ride *s* (coll.) paseo alocado en coche (*muchas veces sin permiso del dueño*)
joy-ride [ˈdʒɔɪˌraɪd] (*pret:* **-rode;** *pp:* **-ridden**) *vn* (coll.) dar un paseo alocado en coche (*muchas veces sin permiso del dueño*)
joy stick *s* (aer.) palanca de mando
Jozy [ˈdʒozɪ] *s* Pepa, Pepita
J.P. abr. de **Justice of the Peace**
Jr. abr. de **Junior**
jubbah [ˈdʒʊbə] *s* aljuba
jube [ˈdʒubi] *s* (arch.) jube
jubilance [ˈdʒubɪləns] *s* júbilo, alborozo
jubilant [ˈdʒubɪlənt] *adj* jubiloso, alborozado
Jubilate [ˌdʒubɪˈletɪ] o [ˌdʒubɪˈlatɪ] *s* Salmo que empieza por esta palabra (*XCIX en la Vulgata*); jubilate (*tercer domingo después de Pascua*); (*l.c.*) [ˈdʒubɪlet] *vn* alegrarse, regocijarse
jubilation [ˌdʒubɪˈleʃən] *s* júbilo, regocijo, alborozo
jubilee [ˈdʒubɪli] *s* júbilo (*viva alegría*); aniversario; quincuagésimo aniversario; (hist. & eccl.) jubileo
Jud. abr. de **Judges** y **Judith**
Judaea [dʒuˈdiə] *s* var. de **Judea**
Judah [ˈdʒudə] *s* (Bib.) Judá (*hijo de Jacob; reino; tribu*)
Judahite [ˈdʒudəaɪt] *s* judaíta
Judaic [dʒuˈdeɪk] *adj* judaico
Judaism [ˈdʒudeɪzəm] *s* judaísmo
Judaize [ˈdʒudeaɪz] *va* convertir al judaísmo; hacer conforme al judaísmo; *vn* judaizar
Judas [ˈdʒudəs] *s* (Bib. & fig.) Judas; (Bib.) Epístola de San Judas
Judas Iscariot *s* (Bib.) Judas Iscariote
Judas kiss *s* beso de Judas
Judas tree *s* (bot.) árbol de Judas o de Judea, árbol del amor
Judea [dʒuˈdiə] *s* Judea
Judean [dʒuˈdiən] *adj & s* judío
Judg. abr. de **Judges**
judge [dʒʌdʒ] *s* juez; **to be a good judge of** ser buen juez en; **Judges** *spl* (Bib.) el libro de los Jueces; *va & vn* juzgar; **judging by** o **from** a juzgar por
judge advocate *s* (mil.) auditor de guerra; (nav.) auditor de marina
judgeship [ˈdʒʌdʒʃɪp] *s* judicatura
judgment o **judgement** [ˈdʒʌdʒmənt] *s* juicio; (law) sentencia; (law) apremio (*para compeler a uno al cumplimiento de una cosa*); (log. & theol.) juicio; **the Judgment** o **the Last Judgment** el juicio final, el juicio universal
judgment day *s* día del juicio
judgment seat *s* tribunal
judicatory [ˈdʒudɪkəˌtorɪ] *adj* judicial; *s* (*pl:* **-ries**) tribunal de justicia; judicatura
judicature [ˈdʒudɪkətʃər] *s* judicatura
judicial [dʒuˈdɪʃəl] *adj* judicial; juicioso
judiciary [dʒuˈdɪʃɪˌɛrɪ] *adj* judicial; *s* (*pl:* **-ies**) judicatura (*de una ciudad, país, etc.*); poder judicial
judicious [dʒuˈdɪʃəs] *adj* juicioso
Judith [ˈdʒudɪθ] *s* Judit; (Bib.) el libro de Judit
judo [ˈdʒudo] *s* judo
Judy [ˈdʒudɪ] *s* nombre abreviado de **Judith;** la mujer de Polichinela (*en las funciones de títeres inglesas y norteamericanas*)
jug [dʒʌg] *s* jarra, botija, cántaro; (slang) bote, chirona (*cárcel*); (*pret & pp:* **jugged;** *ger:* **jugging**) *va* (slang) encarcelar
Juggernaut [ˈdʒʌgərnɔt] *s* imagen del dios bramánico Krichna que solían sacar en procesión, colocada en un carro cuyas ruedas aplastaban a los fieles, que así se sacrificaban;

(fig.) objeto de devoción ciega; (fig.) monstruo destructor de los hombres
juggle [ˈdʒʌgəl] *s* juego de manos; trampa; *va* escamotear; falsear, alterar fraudulentamente (*cuentas, documentos, etc.*); *vn* hacer juegos de manos, hacer suertes; hacer trampas
juggler [ˈdʒʌglər] *s* jugador de manos, malabarista; impostor; (obs.) juglar, bufón
jugglery [ˈdʒʌglərɪ] *s* (*pl:* **-ies**) prestidigitación; decepción, fraude
juglandaceous [ˌdʒuglænˈdeʃəs] *adj* (bot.) juglandáceo o juglándeo
Jugoslav o **Jugo-Slav** [ˈjugoˈslɑv] *adj* & *s* var. de **Yugoslav**
Jugoslavia o **Jugo-Slavia** [ˈjugoˈslɑvɪə] *s* var. de **Yugoslavia**
Jugoslavic [ˈjugoˈslɑvɪk] *adj* var. de **Yugoslavic**
jugular [ˈdʒʌgjələr] o [ˈdʒugjələr] *adj* & *s* (anat.) yugular
jugular vein *s* (anat.) vena yugular
Jugurtha [dʒuˈgʌrθə] *s* Yugurta
juice [dʒus] *s* zumo, jugo; (slang) electricidad; (slang) gasolina
juicy [ˈdʒusɪ] *adj* (*comp:* **-ier;** *super:* **-iest**) zumoso, jugoso; (fig.) picante, sabroso; (coll.) lluvioso
jujitsu [dʒuˈdʒɪtsu] *s* jiu-jitsú (*arte japonés de luchar brazo a brazo sin armas*)
jujube [ˈdʒudʒub] *s* (bot.) azufaifo; azufaifa (*fruto*); pastilla de pasta de azufaifas; pastilla
jujutsu [dʒuˈdʒɪtsu] *s* var. de **jujitsu**
juke box [dʒuk] *s* (coll.) tocadiscos tragamonedas
Jul. abr. de **July**
julep [ˈdʒulɪp] *s* julepe (*bebida helada compuesta de whisky o aguardiente, azúcar y hojas de menta*)
Julian [ˈdʒuljən] *adj* juliano; *s* Juliano o Julián
Juliana [ˌdʒulɪˈænə] o [ˌdʒulɪˈɑnə] *s* Juliana
Julian Alps *spl* Alpes julianos
Julian calendar *s* calendario juliano
Julian the Apostate *s* Juliano el Apóstata
julienne [ˌʒulɪˈɛn] *s* sopa juliana; *adj* rajado, en rajas
Juliet [ˈdʒulɪɛt] *s* Julieta
Julius [ˈdʒuljəs] *s* Julio
July [dʒuˈlaɪ] *s* julio
jumble [ˈdʒʌmbəl] *s* masa confusa, revoltijo; bollito delgado en forma de rosca; *va* emburujar, revolver
jumbo [ˈdʒʌmbo] *s* (*pl:* **-bos**) elefante, coloso; *adj* enorme, colosal
jump [dʒʌmp] *s* salto; lanzamiento (*en paracaídas*); **to be always on the jump** (coll.) andar siempre de aquí para allí; **to get** o **to have the jump on** (slang) coger la delantera a, llevar la ventaja a; *va* saltar; hacer saltar (*a un caballo*); comer (*en las damas y el ajedrez*); salir fuera de (*el carril*); saltar a (*un tren*); *vn* saltar; lanzarse (*en paracaídas desde un avión*); saltar espacios (*la máquina de escribir*); **to jump at** saltar sobre; apresurarse a aceptar (*una invitación*); apresurarse a aprovechar (*la oportunidad*); **to jump on** saltar a (*un tren*); (slang) culpar, regañar, criticar; **to jump over** saltar por, pasar de un salto; saltar (*p.ej., la página de un libro*); **to jump to** sacar precipitadamente (*una conclusión*)
jumper [ˈdʒʌmpər] *s* saltador; blusa holgada de obrero; (elec.) alambre de cierre; **jumpers** *spl* traje holgado de juego para niños
jumping bean *s* semilla brincadora
jumping jack *s* títere
jumping-off place [ˈdʒʌmpɪŋˈɔf] o [ˈdʒʌmpɪŋˈɑf] *s* fin del camino, sitio muy remoto
jump seat *s* traspuntín (*de coche*); (aut.) estrapontín
jump spark *s* (elec.) chispa de entrehierro
jump wire *s* (elec.) alambre de cierre
jumpy [ˈdʒʌmpɪ] *adj* (*comp:* **-ier;** *super:* **-iest**) saltón; asustadizo, alborotadizo
jun. abr. de **junior**
Jun. abr. de **June** y **Junior**
junc. abr. de **junction**
juncaceous [dʒʌŋˈkeʃəs] *adj* (bot.) juncáceo
junco [ˈdʒʌŋko] *s* (*pl:* **-cos**) (orn.) junquito, echalumbre
junction [ˈdʒʌŋkʃən] *s* juntura, unión; ensambladura; confluencia (*de dos ríos*); (elec.) caja de empalme; (rail.) empalme
junction box *s* (elec.) caja de empalme, caja de conexiones
juncture [ˈdʒʌŋktʃər] *s* juntura, unión; coyuntura (*sazón, oportunidad*); **at this juncture** en esto, a esta sazón
June [dʒun] *s* junio
June beetle o **bug** *s* (ent.) escarabajo norteamericano que comienza a volar en el mes de junio (*Phyllophaga; Cotinus nitida*)
Juneberry [ˈdʒunˌbɛrɪ] *s* (*pl:* **-ries**) (bot.) guillomo (*arbusto y fruto*)
jungle [ˈdʒʌŋgəl] *s* jungla; selva, matorral impenetrable; maraña, laberinto; (slang) sitio en despoblado y casi siempre cerca de la vía del ferrocarril, donde acampan los vagos
jungle fever *s* (path.) fiebre de los grandes bosques
jungle fowl *s* (orn.) gallo salvaje; (orn.) gallo de los juncales
junior [ˈdʒunjər] *adj* menor, más joven; juvenil; posterior; más nuevo, más reciente; de penúltimo año; hijo, p.ej., **John Jones, Junior** Juan Jones, hijo; *s* menor; estudiante de penúltimo año
junior college *s* (U.S.A.) colegio que comprende los dos primeros años universitarios
junior high school *s* (U.S.A.) escuela intermedia (*entre la primaria y la secundaria*)
junior partner *s* socio menor
juniper [ˈdʒunɪpər] *s* (bot.) enebro común; (bot.) cedro de Virginia
juniper berry *s* enebrina
juniper cedar *s* (bot.) cedro de Virginia
juniper-tar oil [ˈdʒunɪpərˌtɑr] *s* aceite de cada
junk [dʒʌŋk] *s* chatarra, hierro viejo, ropa vieja, etc.; (slang) trastos viejos, baratijas viejas; jarcia trozada (*que se utiliza, p.ej., para estopa*); junco (*embarcación china*); (naut.) carne salada y dura; *va* (slang) echar a la basura; (slang) reducir (*una máquina*) a hierro viejo
junk dealer *s* chatarrero, chapucero
Junker [ˈjuŋkər] *s* aristócrata reaccionario prusiano
junket [ˈdʒʌŋkɪt] *s* manjar de leche, cuajo y azúcar; jira; viaje de recreo; *vn* ir de jira; hacer un viaje de recreo
junkman [ˈdʒʌŋkˌmæn] *s* (*pl:* **-men**) chatarrero, chapucero, hombre que compra y vende hierro viejo, trapos, papeles, etc.; tripulante de junco
junk room *s* trastera, leonera
junk shop *s* (coll.) tienda de trastos viejos
junk yard *s* chatarrería
Juno [ˈdʒuno] *s* (*pl:* **-nos**) (myth.) Juno; (fig.) mujer de belleza imponente
Junoesque [ˌdʒunoˈɛsk] *adj* imponente
junr. o **Junr.** abr. de **junior**
junta [ˈdʒʌntə] *s* junta; cábala, camarilla
junto [ˈdʒʌnto] *s* (*pl:* **-tos**) cábala, camarilla
Jupiter [ˈdʒupɪtər] *s* (astr. & myth.) Júpiter
jural [ˈdʒurəl] *adj* legal; judicial
Jurassic [dʒuˈræsɪk] *adj* & *s* (geol.) jurásico
Jur. D. abr. de **juris doctor** (Lat.) **Doctor of Law**
juridical [dʒuˈrɪdɪkəl] *adj* jurídico
jurisconsult [ˌdʒurɪskənˈsʌlt] o [ˌdʒurɪsˈkɑnsʌlt] *s* jurisconsulto
jurisdiction [ˌdʒurɪsˈdɪkʃən] *s* jurisdicción
jurisdictional [ˌdʒurɪsˈdɪkʃənəl] *adj* jurisdiccional
jurisdictional strike *s* huelga por jurisdicción entre gremios
jurisprudence [ˌdʒurɪsˈprudəns] *s* jurisprudencia
jurisprudent [ˌdʒurɪsˈprudənt] *s* jurisprudente
jurist [ˈdʒurɪst] *s* jurista
juristic [dʒuˈrɪstɪk] *adj* jurídico
juror [ˈdʒurər] *s* jurado (*individuo*)
jury [ˈdʒurɪ] *s* (*pl:* **-ries**) jurado (*grupo*); *adj* (naut.) provisional
jury box *s* tribuna del jurado
juryman [ˈdʒurɪmən] *s* (*pl:* **-men**) jurado (*individuo*)
jury mast *s* (naut.) bandola
jury-rigged [ˈdʒurɪˌrɪgd] *adj* (naut.) de aparejo provisional

Jus. P. abr. de **justice of the peace**
just [dʒʌst] *adj* justo; **the just** los justos; *adv* justo, justamente; hace poco; apenas; casi no; no más que; sólo; (coll.) absolutamente, verdaderamente; **had just** + *pp* acababa de + *inf*, p.ej., **we had just left** acabábamos de marcharnos; **to have just** + *pp* acabar de + *inf*, p.ej., **I have just arrived** acabo de llegar; **just as** como; en el momento en que; lo mismo que; tal como; **just beyond** un poco más allá (de); **just now** ahora mismo; hace poco; **just out** acabado de aparecer, recién publicado; **just** + *pp* acabado de + *inf*, p.ej., **just received** acabado de recibir; *s* justa; *vn* justar
justice ['dʒʌstɪs] *s* justicia; premio merecido; juez; juez de paz; **to bring to justice** aprehender y condenar por justicia; **to do justice to** hacer justicia a; tratar debidamente, apreciar debidamente; **to do oneself justice** no quedar corto, hacerlo (*una persona*) lo mejor que pueda; quedar bien
justice of the peace *s* juez de paz
justiceship ['dʒʌstɪsʃɪp] *s* judicatura
justifiable ['dʒʌstɪ,faɪəbəl] *adj* justificable
justification [,dʒʌstɪfɪ'keʃən] *s* justificación; (print.) justificación
justificatory [dʒʌs'tɪfɪkə,torɪ] *adj* justificativo
justifier ['dʒʌstɪ,faɪər] *s* justificador, justificante
justify ['dʒʌstɪfaɪ] (*pret & pp:* **-fied**) *va* justificar; (print.) justificar
Justinian [dʒʌs'tɪnɪən] *s* Justiniano
Justinian Code *s* código de Justiniano
Justin Martyr ['dʒʌstɪn] *s* San Justino
justle ['dʒʌsəl] *s, va & vn* var. de **jostle**
justly ['dʒʌstlɪ] *adv* justamente
justness ['dʒʌstnɪs] *s* justicia; exactitud
jut [dʒʌt] *s* resalto, saliente, saledizo; (*pret & pp:* **jutted**; *ger:* **jutting**) *vn* resaltar, proyectarse; **to jut out** resaltar, proyectarse
jute [dʒut] *s* (bot.) yute (*planta, fibra y tejido*); (*cap.*) *s* juto
Jutland ['dʒʌtlənd] *s* Jutlandia
Jutlander ['dʒʌtləndər] *s* jutlandés
Jutlandish ['dʒʌtləndɪʃ] *adj* jutlandés
Juturna [dʒu'tʌrnə] *s* (myth.) Yuturna
Juvenal ['dʒuvənəl] *s* Juvenal
juvenescence [,dʒuvə'nɛsəns] *s* rejuvenecimiento
juvenescent [,dʒuvə'nɛsənt] *adj* rejuveneciente
juvenile ['dʒuvənɪl] o ['dʒuvənaɪl] *adj* juvenil; de o para jóvenes o niños; *s* joven, mocito; libro para niños; (theat.) galán joven, galancete
juvenile court *s* tribunal tutelar de menores
juvenile delinquency *s* delincuencia de menores
juvenile lead [lid] *s* (theat.) papel de galancete; (theat.) galancete
juvenilia [,dʒuvə'nɪlɪə] *spl* obras de juventud
juvenility [,dʒuvə'nɪlɪtɪ] *s* juventud, mocedad
juxtapose [,dʒʌkstə'poz] *va* yuxtaponer
juxtaposition [,dʒʌkstəpə'zɪʃən] *s* yuxtaposición
Jy. abr. de **July**
jynx [dʒɪŋks] *s* encanto, hechizo; (orn.) torcecuello

K

K, k [ke] *s* (*pl:* **K's, k's** [kez]) undécima letra del alfabeto inglés
k. abr. de **karat, kilogram** y **kopeck**
K. abr. de **King** y **Knight**
Kaaba ['kɑbə] *s* Caaba (*de la Meca*)
Kaffir o **Kafir** ['kæfər] o ['kɑfər] *adj & s* cafre; (*l.c.*) *s* (bot.) panizo negro, maíz de Guinea
kaffir corn o **kafir corn** *s* (bot.) panizo negro, maíz de Guinea
kaftan ['kæftən] *s* caftán
kaiak ['kaɪæk] *s* var. de **kayak**
kail [kel] *s* var. de **kale**
kaiser ['kaɪzər] *s* emperador
kaki ['kɑki] *s* (*pl:* **-kis**) (bot.) caqui
kale [kel] *s* (bot.) col, berza común (*Brassica oleracea acephala*); (slang) dinero, dinero contante y sonante
kaleidoscope [kə'laɪdəskop] *s* calidoscopio; (fig.) calidoscopio
kaleidoscopic [kə,laɪdə'skɑpɪk] *adj* calidoscópico; (fig.) calidoscópico
kalends ['kælɪndz] *spl* var. de **calends**
kalmia ['kælmɪə] *s* (bot.) calmia
kalsomine ['kælsəmaɪn] *s & va* var. de **calcimine**
Kamerun [,kɑmə'run] *s* var. de **Cameroons**
kamikase [,kɑmɪ'kɑzi] *s* kamikazo (*aviador suicida japonés*)
Kan. abr. de **Kansas**
Kanaka [kə'nækə] o ['kænəkə] *s* hawaiano; polinesio
kangaroo [,kæŋgə'ru] *s* (zool.) canguro
kangaroo court *s* (coll.) tribunal irregular, tribunal desautorizado; (coll.) tribunal fingido
kangaroo rat *s* (zool.) rata canguro
Kans. abr. de **Kansas**
Kantian ['kæntɪən] *adj & s* kantiano
Kantianism ['kæntɪənɪzəm] *s* kantismo
kaolin o **kaoline** ['keəlɪn] *s* caolín
kapok ['kepɑk] *s* capoc, lana de ceiba
karakul ['kærəkəl] *s* var. de **caracul**
karat ['kærət] *s* var. de **carat**
Karelia [kə'rilɪə] *s* Carelia
Karelian [kə'rilɪən] *adj & s* carelio o careliano
karyokinesis [,kærɪokɪ'nisɪs] o [,kærɪokaɪ'nisɪs] *s* (biol.) cariocinesis
karyomitome [,kærɪ'ɑmɪtom] *s* (biol.) cariomitoma
karyoplasm ['kærɪəplæzəm] *s* (biol.) carioplasma
karyosome ['kærɪə,som] *s* (biol.) cariosoma
karyotin [,kærɪ'otɪn] *s* (biol.) cariotina
Kasbah ['kɑzba] *s* var. de **Casbah**
kashmir y **Kashmir** ['kæʃmɪr] *s* var. de **cashmere** y **Cashmere**
katabolism [kə'tæbəlɪzəm] *s* var. de **catabolism**
Katherine ['kæθərɪn] *s* var. de **Catherine**
katydid ['ketɪdɪd] *s* (ent.) saltamontes cuyo macho emite un sonido chillón (*Microcentrum retinervis y Amblycorypha*)
kauri ['kaurɪ] *s* (*pl:* **-ris**) (bot.) kauri
kauri resin *s* resina o copal de kauri
kaury ['kaurɪ] *s* (*pl:* **-ries**) var. de **kauri**
kayak ['kaɪæk] *s* kayak (*embarcación*)
kc. abr. de **kilocycle** o **kilocycles**
K.C. abr. de **King's Counsel** y **Knights of Columbus**
K.C.B. abr. de **Knight Commander of the Bath**
kea ['keə] o ['kiə] *s* (orn.) kea (*Nestor notabilis*)
kedge [kɛdʒ] *s* (naut.) anclote; *va* (naut.) mover con anclote; *vn* (naut.) moverse con anclote
keel [kil] *s* (aer., naut. & bot.) quilla; (poet.) nave; **on an even keel** (naut.) en iguales calados; (fig.) firme, estable; *va* volcar (*una embarcación*) poniéndola quilla arriba; volcar (*cualquier cosa*); *vn* (naut.) dar de quilla; volcarse; **to keel over** (naut.) dar de quilla; volcarse; caerse de repente; (coll.) desmayarse
keelhaul ['kil,hɔl] *va* (naut.) pasar por debajo de la quilla (*por castigo*)
keelson ['kɛlsən] o ['kilsən] *s* (naut.) sobrequilla
keen [kin] *adj* agudo; mordaz; ansioso; entusiasta; **to be keen on** ser muy aficionado a (*p.ej., la lectura*); **I'm not very keen on him** no es santo de mi devoción
keenness ['kinnɪs] *s* agudeza; mordacidad; ansia, entusiasmo
keep [kip] *s* manutención, subsistencia; (fort.) torre del homenaje; **for keeps** (coll.) para guardar; (coll.) para siempre; **to earn one's keep** (coll.) ganarse la vida; **to play for keeps** (coll.) jugar de veras ‖ (*pret & pp:* **kept**) *va* guardar; conservar; quedarse con; tener (*criados, gallinas, huéspedes, etc.*); guardar, cumplir (*su palabra o promesa*); cultivar (*una huerta*); mantener; dirigir (*una escuela, un hotel*); llevar (*cuentas, libros; la anotación en los naipes*); celebrar (*fiestas*); mantenerse firme en (*su puesto, la silla de montar*); detener, hacer tardar (*a una persona*); **to keep away** tener apartado, impedir que venga; **to keep back** retener; reprimir; reservar (*no divulgar*); **to keep down** reprimir, sujetar; reducir (*los gastos*) al mínimo; **to keep from** + *ger* no dejar + *inf*, p.ej., **keep him from eating too much** no le deje comer demasiado; **to keep in** tener encerrado, no dejar salir; **to keep off** tener a distancia; no dejar penetrar (*p.ej., la lluvia*); evitar (*p.ej., el polvo*); **to keep on** no quitarse (*p.ej., el abrigo*); **to keep out** no dejar entrar; no dejar penetrar; **to keep someone informed (about)** poner a alguien al corriente (de); **to keep to oneself** callarse (*algo*) a sí mismo; **to keep up** mantener, conservar; **to keep** + *ger* hacer + *inf*, p.ej., **I am sorry to keep you waiting** siento hacerle esperar ‖ *vn* quedarse, permanecer; mantenerse; conservarse, durar sin dañarse; estarse, p.ej., **keep quiet** estése Vd. quieto; **to keep at** continuar en, empeñarse en (*p.ej., su trabajo*); **to keep away** mantenerse a distancia; no dejarse ver; **to keep away from** no meterse en; no dejarse ver en; no meterse con, evitar todo roce con; no probar (*p.ej., vino*); **to keep from** + *ger* abstenerse de + *inf;* **to keep informed (about)** ponerse al corriente (de); **to keep in with** (coll.) mantener amistad con, no perder el favor de; **to keep off** no acercarse a; no andar por; no pisar (*el césped*); **to keep on** continuar; no caerse de (*p.ej., un caballo*); **to keep on** + *ger* seguir + *ger;* **to keep on with** continuar con; **to keep out** no entrar; **to keep out of** no entrar en; no meterse en; evitar (*peligro*); **to keep to** adherirse estrictamente a; seguir por, llevar (*la derecha, la izquierda*); **to keep to oneself** quedarse a solas, huir de las gentes; **to keep up** continuar; no rezagarse; **to keep up with** ir al paso de; llevar el mismo tren de vida de; llevar adelante, proseguir; **to keep** + *ger* seguir + *ger*
keeper ['kipər] *s* encargado; guarda; guardabosque; archivero; guardián, custodio; protector; cerradero (*de cerrojo*); armadura, culata (*de imán*)
keeping ['kipɪŋ] *s* manutención; guarda, custodia, cuidado, cargo; guardar, p.ej., **the keeping of Lent** el guardar la cuaresma; **in keeping with** de acuerdo con, en armonía con; **in safe keeping** en lugar seguro, en bue-

nas manos; **out of keeping with** en desacuerdo con
keepsake ['kip,sek] *s* recuerdo
keg [kɛg] *s* cuñete; 100 libras de clavos
kelp [kɛlp] *s* (bot.) quelpo; cenizas del quelpo
kelpie o **kelpy** ['kɛlpɪ] *s* (*pl:* **-pies**) trasgo o duende en forma de caballo que mora en las aguas y se ocupa en ahogar a las personas o en darles aviso de que han de morir ahogadas
kelson ['kɛlsən] *s* var. de **keelson**
Kelt [kɛlt] *s* celta; (*l.c.*) *s* (ichth.) salmón zancado
kelter ['kɛltər] *s* var. de **kilter**
Keltic ['kɛltɪk] *adj & s* var. de **Celtic**
Ken. abr. de **Kentucky**
ken [kɛn] *s* alcance de la vista, alcance del saber; **beyond the ken of** fuera del alcance del saber de; (*pret & pp:* **kenned;** *ger:* **kenning**) *va* (archaic) ver, reconocer; *vn* (archaic & Brit. dial.) saber
Kendal green ['kɛndəl] *s* tejido de lana de Kendal (*de color verde*)
kennel ['kɛnəl] *s* perrera; establecimiento donde se crían los perros; jauría; (*pret & pp:* **-neled** o **-nelled;** *ger:* **-neling** o **-nelling**) *va* tener o encerrar en perrera; *vn* guarecerse en perrera
kenning ['kɛnɪŋ] *s* perífrasis poética, nombre metafórico (*en la literatura teutónica antigua*)
keno ['kino] *s* juego casero parecido a la lotería de familia
kentledge ['kɛntlɪdʒ] *s* (naut.) enjunque
kepi ['kɛpɪ] *s* (*pl:* **-is**) (mil.) quepis
kept [kɛpt] *pret & pp de* **keep**
kept woman *s* entretenida
keramic [kɪ'ræmɪk] *adj* var. de **ceramic; keramics** *ssg & spl* var. de **ceramics**
keratin ['kɛrətɪn] *s* (zool.) queratina
keratoconus [,kɛrəto'konəs] *s* (path.) córnea cónica
keratogenous [,kɛrə'tɑdʒɪnəs] *adj* queratógeno
kerb [kʌrb] *s* (Brit.) encintado (*de la acera*)
kerchief ['kʌrtʃɪf] *s* pañuelo
kerchoo [kə'tʃu] *interj* ¡ ah-chis!
kerf [kʌrf] *s* corte; trozo cortado
kermes ['kʌrmiz] *s* quermes (*materia colorante*); (bot.) coscoja; coscojo
kermes mineral *s* (chem.) quermes mineral
kermess ['kʌrmɛs] o **kermis** ['kʌrmɪs] *s* kermese (*fiesta generalmente con propósito caritativo*)
kern [kʌrn] *s* labriego irlandés; (print.) rabillo de ojo que sobresale
kernel ['kʌrnəl] *s* almendra (*de cualquier fruto drupáceo*); grano (*de trigo o maíz*); (fig.) medula o meollo
kerosene ['kɛrəsin] o [,kɛrə'sin] *s* keroseno
kerosene lamp *s* lámpara de petróleo
ker-plunk [kər'plʌŋk] *interj* ¡ pataplún!
kersey ['kʌrzɪ] *s* carsaya, carisea
kestrel ['kɛstrəl] *s* (orn.) cernícalo
ketch [kɛtʃ] *s* queche
ketchup ['kɛtʃəp] *s* var. de **catsup**
ketene ['kitin] *s* (chem.) queteno
ketone ['kiton] *s* (chem.) cetona o quetona
ketose ['kitos] *s* (chem.) quetosa
kettle ['kɛtəl] *s* caldera; cafetera; tetera; calderada (*lo que cabe en una caldera*); **kettle of fish** berenjenal, p.ej., **this is a fine kettle of fish we've got into** en buen berenjenal nos hemos metido
kettledrum ['kɛtəl,drʌm] *s* (mus.) timbal
key [ki] *s* llave; tecla (*de piano, máquina de escribir, etc.*); chaveta, clavija, cuña; (bot.) sámara; (geog.) cayo; (mus.) clave o llave; (mus.) tono; (telg.) manipulador; (fig.) persona o cosa dominante o principal; (fig.) clave o llave (*a un código, problema, secreto, etc.*); (fig.) llave (*lugar estratégico más propicio*); **off key** desafinado; desafinadamente; *adj* clave, llave, dominante; *va* afinar, templar (*con llave*); enchavetar, acuñar; arreglar; **to key up** alentar, excitar
keyboard ['ki,bord] *s* teclado
key fruit *s* (bot.) sámara, fruto alado
keyhole ['ki,hol] *s* ojo de la cerradura, bocallave; agujero para la llave del reloj
keyhole saw *s* sierra de punta, sierra caladora, sierra de calador
key man *s* hombre principal, hombre muy importante
keynote ['ki,not] *s* (mus.) tónica, nota tónica; (fig.) tónica, idea fundamental
keynoter ['ki'notər] *s* (coll.) miembro informante
keynote speech *s* discurso de apertura
keypuncher ['ki,pʌntʃər] *s* perforista
key ring *s* llavero
key seat *s* (mach.) cajera de cuña
key signature *s* (mus.) armadura
key socket *s* (elec.) portalámparas de llave giratoria
keystone ['ki,ston] *s* clave, espinazo (*de un arco*); (fig.) piedra angular
keyway ['ki,we] *s* (mach.) chavetera
Key West *s* Cayo Hueso
key word *s* palabra clave
kg. abr. de **kilogram** o **kilograms**
K.G. abr. de **Knight of the Garter**
khaki ['kɑkɪ] o ['kækɪ] *s* (*pl:* **-kis**) caqui; *adj* caqui
khalif ['kelɪf] o ['kælɪf] *s* var. de **caliph**
khan [kɑn] *s* kan (*título; sitio destinado para el reposo de las caravanas*)
khanate ['kɑnet] *s* kanato
Khartoum o **Khartum** [kɑr'tum] *s* Jartum
khedive [kə'div] *s* jedive
kiang [kɪ'æŋ] *s* (zool.) hemíono
kibe [kaɪb] *s* sabañón ulcerado (*en el talón*)
kibitz ['kɪbɪts] *vn* (coll.) dar consejos molestos a los jugadores
kibitzer ['kɪbɪtsər] *s* (coll.) mirón (*de una partida de juego*); (coll.) entremetido, camasquince
kiblah ['kɪblɑ] *s* alquibla (*punto hacia donde los musulmanes miran cuando rezan*)
kibosh ['kaɪbɑʃ] o [kɪ'bɑʃ] *s* (slang) música celestial; **to put the kibosh on** (slang) desbaratar, imposibilitar
kick [kɪk] *s* puntapié; coz (*de animal*); culatazo (*de arma de fuego*); (slang) queja, protesta; (slang) fuerza (*de una bebida*); (slang) estímulo, efecto estimulador (*de una bebida*); (slang) placer, gusto; **to get a kick out of** (slang) hallar placer en; *va* dar de puntapiés a; dar de coces a; **to kick down** echar abajo a puntapiés; **to kick in** romper a puntapiés; **to kick out** dar la patada a, echar a puntapiés a la calle; echar, despedir; **to kick up** (slang) armar (*p.ej., un bochinche*); *vn* cocear; dar culatazos, patear (*un arma de fuego*); (coll.) cocear, tirar coces, quejarse; **to kick about** (coll.) quejarse de; **to kick off** (football) dar el golpe de salida
kickback ['kɪk,bæk] *s* (coll.) contragolpe; (slang) devolución de cosas robadas; (slang) devolución estipulada de parte de un salario o pago, porcentaje devuelto de un salario o pago
kickoff ['kɪk,ɔf] o ['kɪk,ɑf] *s* (football) saque, golpe de salida, puntapié inicial
kickshaw ['kɪk,ʃɔ] *s* bocado delicado; bagatela, fruslería
kid [kɪd] *s* cabrito; cabritilla (*piel*); (coll.) chico; **kids** *spl* guantes o zapatos de cabritilla; (*pret & pp:* **kidded;** *ger:* **kidding**) *va* (slang) embromar; **to kid oneself** (slang) hacerse ilusiones; *vn* (slang) bromearse; **I was only kidding** (slang) lo decía en broma
kidder ['kɪdər] *s* (slang) bromista
kid-glove ['kɪd'glʌv] *adj* ceremonioso; quisquilloso
kid gloves *spl* guantes de cabritilla; **to handle with kid gloves** tratar con suma cautela y discreción
kidnap ['kɪdnæp] (*pret & pp:* **-naped** o **-napped;** *ger:* **-naping** o **-napping**) *va* secuestrar
kidnaper o **kidnapper** ['kɪd,næpər] *s* secuestrador, ladrón de niños
kidney ['kɪdnɪ] *s* (anat.) riñón; (cook.) riñones; carácter, natural; clase, especie
kidney bean *s* (bot.) judía de España, judía escarlata; (bot.) frijol, habichuela, judía
kidney ore *s* (min.) riñón
kidney stone *s* (path.) cálculo renal
kidskin ['kɪd,skɪn] *s* cabritilla
kill [kɪl] *s* matanza; ataque final (*de la jauría, el ejército, una fiera, etc.*); arroyo, riachuelo; (hunt.) caza, piezas; **for the kill** para dar muerte; para el golpe final; *va* matar (*a una*

persona o animal; el fuego, la luz, el hambre, el tiempo, etc.); ahogar (*un proyecto de ley*); quitar (*el sabor*); impresionar de modo irresistible; *vn* matar
killdee [ˈkɪl,di] o **killdeer** [ˈkɪl,dɪr] *s* (orn.) tildío, chorlito gritón peleador
killer [ˈkɪlər] *s* matador; (zool.) orca
killer whale *s* (zool.) orca
killing [ˈkɪlɪŋ] *s* matanza; (hunt.) caza, piezas; (coll.) gran ganancia; **to make a killing** (coll.) enriquecerse de golpe; *adj* matador; destructivo; quemador (*dícese, p.ej., de una helada*); abrumador (*trabajo*); irresistible; (coll.) de lo más ridículo
kill-joy [ˈkɪl,dʒɔɪ] *s* aguafiestas
kiln [kɪl] o [kɪln] *s* horno; *va* cocer, quemar o secar en horno
kilo [ˈkilo] o [ˈkɪlo] *s* (*pl:* **-los**) kilo o quilo (*kilogramo*); kilómetro o quilómetro
kiloampere [ˈkɪlo,æmpɪr] *s* (elec.) kiloamperio
kilocalorie [ˈkɪlə,kælərɪ] *s* (phys.) kilocaloría
kilocycle [ˈkɪlə,saɪkəl] *s* kilociclo
kilogram o **kilogramme** [ˈkɪləgræm] *s* kilogramo
kilogrammeter [ˈkɪləgræmˈmitər] *s* kilográmetro
kiloliter [ˈkɪlə,litər] *s* kilolitro
kilometer [ˈkɪlə,mitər] o [kɪˈlɑmɪtər] *s* kilómetro
kilometric [,kɪləˈmɛtrɪk] *adj* kilométrico
kiloton [ˈkɪlətʌn] *s* kilotonelada
kilovolt [ˈkɪlə,volt] *s* (elec.) kilovoltio
kilowatt [ˈkɪlə,wɑt] *s* (elec.) kilovatio
kilowatt-hour [ˈkɪlə,wɑtˈaʊr] *s* (*pl:* **kilowatt-hours**) (elec.) kilovatio-hora
kilt [kɪlt] *s* enagüillas; *va* (Scotch) arremangar; plegar
kilter [ˈkɪltər] *s* (coll.) buen estado, buena condición; **to be out of kilter** (coll.) estar descompuesto
kilting [ˈkɪltɪŋ] *s* pliegues solapados
kimono [kɪˈmonə] o [kɪˈmono] *s* (*pl:* **-nos**) quimono
kin [kɪn] *s* parentesco; parentela, familia, deudos; **near of kin** muy allegado; **next of kin** deudo más cercano, deudos más cercanos; **of kin** allegado; *adj* allegado
kinaesthesia [,kɪnɪsˈθiʒə] *s* cinestesia
kind [kaɪnd] *adj* bueno, bondadoso, amable; afectuoso (*saludo*); **to be kind to** ser bueno para con; *s* clase, especie, género, suerte; **a kind of** uno a modo de; **all kinds of** (slang) gran cantidad de; **in kind** en especie; en la misma moneda; **of a kind** de una misma clase; de mala muerte, de poco valor; **of the kind** por el estilo, semejante; **kind of** (coll.) algo, un poco, más bien, casi
kindergarten [ˈkɪndər,gɑrtən] *s* escuela de párvulos, jardín de la infancia
kindergartener o **kindergartner** [ˈkɪndər,gɑrtnər] *s* párvulo (*en las escuelas de párvulos*); parvulista (*maestro o maestra*)
kind-hearted [ˈkaɪndˈhɑrtɪd] *adj* de buen corazón, bondadoso
kindle [ˈkɪndəl] *va* encender; *vn* encenderse
kindliness [ˈkaɪndlɪnɪs] *s* bondad; benignidad
kindling [ˈkɪndlɪŋ] *s* encendimiento; leña
kindling wood *s* leña
kindly [ˈkaɪndlɪ] *adj* (*comp:* **-lier**; *super:* **-liest**) bondadoso; benigno, agradable; *adv* bondadosamente; benignamente, agradablemente; **to not take kindly to** no aceptar de buen grado, no poder sufrir
kindness [ˈkaɪndnɪs] *s* bondad; **have the kindness to** + *inf* tenga Vd. la bondad de + *inf*
kindred [ˈkɪndrɪd] *s* parentesco; parentela, familia; semejanza; *adj* allegado; semejante
kine [kaɪn] *spl* (archaic & dial.) vacas
kinematic [,kɪnɪˈmætɪk] *adj* cinemático; **kinematics** *ssg* cinemática
kinematograph [,kɪnɪˈmætəgræf] [,kɪnɪˈmætəgrɑf] *s* var. de **cinematograph**
kinescope [ˈkɪnɪskop] *s* (trademark) cinescopio
kinesthesia [,kɪnɪsˈθiʒə] *s* cinestesia
kinesthetic [,kɪnɪsˈθɛtɪk] *adj* cinestésico
kinetic [kɪˈnɛtɪk] o [kaɪˈnɛtɪk] *adj* cinético; **kinetics** *ssg* cinética
kinetic energy *s* (phys.) energía cinética, energía viva
kinfolk [ˈkɪn,fok] *spl* (dial.) var. de **kinsfolk**
king [kɪŋ] *s* rey; (cards, chess & fig.) rey; (checkers) dama; **Kings** *spl* (Bib.) el libro de los Reyes (*uno de dos libros del Antiguo Testamento protestante; uno de cuatro libros del Antiguo Testamento católico*)
King Arthur *s* el rey Artús
kingbird [ˈkɪŋ,bʌrd] *s* (orn.) tirano, pecho amarillo
kingbolt [ˈkɪŋ,bolt] *s* pivote central; (rail.) perno pinzote
king crab *s* (zool.) cangrejo bayoneta
kingcraft [ˈkɪŋ,kræft] o [ˈkɪŋ,krɑft] *s* arte de reinar
kingcup [ˈkɪŋ,kʌp] *s* (bot.) hierba velluda; (bot.) botón de oro; (bot.) hierba centella
kingdom [ˈkɪŋdəm] *s* reino
kingfish [ˈkɪŋ,fɪʃ] *s* (ichth.) pez grande comestible (*Menticirrhus nebulosus; Genyonemus lineatus; Sierra cavalla*)
kingfisher [ˈkɪŋ,fɪʃər] *s* (orn.) martín pescador
King James Version *s* traducción de la Biblia que mandó hacer el rey Jacobo de Inglaterra (*1611*)
kinglet [ˈkɪŋlɪt] *s* reyezuelo; (orn.) reyezuelo
kingly [ˈkɪŋlɪ] *adj* (*comp:* **-lier**; *super:* **-liest**) real, regio; noble, digno de un rey; *adv* regiamente; noblemente, con dignidad real
king of arms *s* (her.) rey de armas
king of beasts *s* rey de los animales (*león*)
king of birds *s* rey de las aves (*águila*)
kingpin [ˈkɪŋ,pɪn] *s* bolo de adelante (*en el juego de bolos*); pivote central; (aut.) pivote de dirección; (coll.) persona principal
king post *s* pendolón
king's English *s* inglés castizo
king's evil *s* escrófula
kingship [ˈkɪŋʃɪp] *s* dignidad real; reino (*territorio gobernado por un rey*)
king-size [ˈkɪŋ,saɪz] *adj* de tamaño largo (*cigarrillo*)
king snake *s* (zool.) coralilla
king's ransom *s* riquezas de Creso
King's Speech *s* discurso de la corona
king truss *s* armadura de pendolón
kink [kɪŋk] *s* enroscadura (*de cabo, cuerda, pelo, etc.*); tortícolis (*dolor*); chifladura, manía; *va* enroscar; *vn* enroscarse
kinkajou [ˈkɪŋkədʒu] *s* (zool.) quincayú, martucha
kinky [ˈkɪŋkɪ] *adj* (*comp:* **-ier**; *super:* **-iest**) enroscado, encarrujado
kino [ˈkino] *s* quino
kino gum *s* goma quino
kinsfolk [ˈkɪnz,fok] *spl* parentela, familia, deudos
kinship [ˈkɪnʃɪp] *s* parentesco; correspondencia, semejanza
kinsman [ˈkɪnzmən] *s* (*pl:* **-men**) pariente
kinswoman [ˈkɪnz,wʊmən] *s* (*pl:* **-women**) parienta
kiosk [kɪˈɑsk] o [ˈkaɪɑsk] *s* quiosco (*para vender periódicos, flores, etc.*); [kɪˈɑsk] *s* quiosco (*pabellón de gusto oriental en un jardín*)
kip [kɪp] *s* piel de res pequeña; kilolibra
kipper [ˈkɪpər] *s* macho del salmón durante o después de la época del celo; salmón o arenque acecinados o salados; *va* acecinar (*el salmón o el arenque*)
Kirghiz [kɪrˈgiz] *s* (*pl:* **-ghiz** o **-ghizes**) kirguís
kirk [kʌrk] *s* (Scotch) iglesia; **the Kirk** la iglesia nacional de Escocia (*de la secta presbiteriana*)
kirmess [ˈkʌrmɛs] *s* var. de **kermess**
kirtle [ˈkʌrtəl] *s* (archaic) falda, ropón
kismet [ˈkɪzmɛt] o [ˈkɪsmɛt] *s* destino, sino
kiss [kɪs] *s* beso; roce; pelo, retruco (*en el billar*); merengue, dulce; *va* besar; acariciar (*rozar suavemente*); **to kiss away** borrar con besos (*p.ej., las penas de otra persona*); *vn* besar; besarse; retrucar (*en el billar*)
kisser [ˈkɪsər] *s* besador; (slang) bozo, pico, hocico, rostro
kissing bug *s* (ent.) reduvio
kit [kɪt] *s* equipaje (*del viajero*); pertrechos o equipo (*del soldado*); avíos; herramental, cartera de herramientas; conjunto de piezas ne-

cesarias para construir una radio, un aeromodelo, etc.; balde, cubo, tineta; gatito; pequeño violín; (coll.) juego, lote, grupo; **the whole kit and caboodle** (coll.) la totalidad, el conjunto; (*cap.*) *s* abr. de **Catherine** y **Christopher**
kitchen [ˈkɪtʃən] *s* cocina
kitchenette [ˌkɪtʃəˈnɛt] *s* cocinilla, cocina pequeña
kitchen garden *s* huerto
kitchenmaid [ˈkɪtʃənˌmed] *s* pincha, ayudanta de cocina
kitchen midden [ˈmɪdən] *s* (anthrop.) acumulación de basura (*en o cerca de las viviendas prehistóricas*)
kitchen police *s* (mil.) trabajo de cocina; (mil.) pinches
kitchen range *s* cocina económica
kitchen sink *s* fregadero
kitchenware [ˈkɪtʃənˌwɛr] *s* chirimbolos de cocina, utensilios de cocina
kite [kaɪt] *s* cometa (*juguete*); (orn.) milano; *vn* (coll.) deslizarse rápidamente
kite balloon *s* globo cometa
kith and kin [kɪθ] *spl* deudos y amigos; parientes
kitten [ˈkɪtən] *s* gatito
kittenish [ˈkɪtənɪʃ] *adj* juguetón, retozón; coquetón
kittiwake [ˈkɪtɪwek] *s* (orn.) risa (*especie de gaviota*)
kitty [ˈkɪtɪ] *s* (*pl:* **-ties**) minino, gatito; polla, puesta (*en los juegos de naipes*); **kitty, kitty!** ¡miz, miz!; (*cap.*) *s* nombre abreviado de **Katherine**
kiwi [ˈkiwɪ] *s* (*pl:* **-wis**) (orn.) kiwi
K.K.K. abr. de **Ku Klux Klan**
kl. abr. de **kiloliter**
klaxon [ˈklæksən] *s* claxon
kleptomania [ˌklɛptoˈmenɪə] *s* cleptomanía
kleptomaniac [ˌklɛptoˈmenɪæk] *adj & s* cleptómano
klieg light [klig] *s* lámpara klieg
klystron [ˈklaɪstrən] *s* (trademark) klistrón
km. abr. de **kilometer** o **kilometers**
knack [næk] *s* tino, tranquillo; costumbre, hábito
knapsack [ˈnæpˌsæk] *s* mochila; *adj* de mochila, p.ej., **knapsack spray** pulverizador de mochila
knapweed [ˈnæpˌwid] *s* (bot.) centaura negra
knave [nev] *s* bribón, pícaro; sota (*en los naipes*); (archaic) criado, mozo; (archaic) villano
knavery [ˈnevərɪ] *s* (*pl:* **-ies**) bribonería, picardía, bellaquería
knavish [ˈnevɪʃ] *adj* bribón, pícaro, bellaco
knead [nid] *va* amasar, sobar
knee [ni] *s* (anat.) rodilla; codillo (*de los cuadrúpedos*); rodillera (*p.ej., de los pantalones*); ángulo, codo, escuadra; **to bring to one's knees** rendir, vencer; **to be on the knees of the gods** depender sólo de Dios o de la voluntad divina; **to go down on one's knees** caer de rodillas; **to go down on one's knees to** implorar de rodillas
knee action *s* (aut.) acción de rodilla, acción independiente
knee-action wheel [ˈniˌækʃən] *s* (aut.) rueda con acción de rodilla, rueda independiente
knee brace *s* esquinal
knee breeches *spl* pantalones cortos
kneecap [ˈniˌkæp] *s* (anat.) rótula, choquezuela; rodillera (*abrigo de la rodilla*)
knee-deep [ˈniˈdip] *adj* metido hasta las rodillas
knee-high [ˈniˈhaɪ] *adj* que llega hasta la rodilla
knee-high to a grasshopper *adj* diminuto, liliputiense
kneehole [ˈniˌhol] *s* hueco para introducir cómodamente las piernas
knee jerk *s* (med.) reflejo rotuliano o patelar
kneel [nil] (*pret & pp:* **knelt** o **kneeled**) *vn* arrodillarse; estar arrodillado
kneepad [ˈniˌpæd] *s* rodillera (*abrigo de la rodilla*)
kneepan [ˈniˌpæn] *s* (anat.) rótula, choquezuela
knee swell *s* (mus.) rodillera (*del órgano*)
knell [nɛl] *s* doble, toque a muerto; anuncio, mal agüero; **to toll the knell of** anunciar el fin de; *va* proclamar a toque de campana; convocar o llamar a toque de campana; *vn* doblar, tocar a muerto; sonar tristemente
knelt [nɛlt] *pret & pp de* **kneel**
knew [nju] o [nu] *pret de* **know**
Knickerbocker [ˈnɪkərˌbɑkər] *s* descendiente de los fundadores holandeses de Nueva York; neoyorquino; **knickerbockers** *spl* pantalones de media pierna, calzones cortos
knickers [ˈnɪkərz] *spl* pantalones de media pierna, calzones cortos
knickknack [ˈnɪkˌnæk] *s* baratija, chuchería, bujería
knife [naɪf] *s* (*pl:* **knives**) cuchillo; (mach.) cuchilla; **to go under the knife** (coll.) operarse; *va* acuchillar; (slang) traicionar
knife edge *s* filo de cuchillo; arista, filo; eje de apoyo (*de una balanza*)
knife plug *s* (elec.) clavija a cuchilla
knife sharpener *s* afilador, afilón
knife switch *s* (elec.) interruptor de cuchilla
knifing [ˈnaɪfɪŋ] *s* cuchillada
knight [naɪt] *s* caballero; caballo (*en el ajedrez*); *va* armar caballero
knight-errant [ˈnaɪtˈɛrənt] *s* (*pl:* **knights-errant**) caballero andante
knight-errantry [ˈnaɪtˈɛrəntrɪ] *s* (*pl:* **-ries**) caballería andante; quijotada, acción quijotesca
knighthood [ˈnaɪthʊd] *s* caballería
knightly [ˈnaɪtlɪ] *adj* caballeroso, caballeresco; *adv* caballerosamente, caballerescamente
Knight of the Rueful Countenance *s* Caballero de la triste figura (*Don Quijote*)
Knights of Columbus *spl* caballeros de Colón (*asociación fraternal católica*)
Knight Templar *s* (*pl:* **Knights Templars**) Templario, caballero del Temple; (*pl:* **Knights Templar**) (U.S.A.) caballero templario
knit [nɪt] (*pret & pp:* **knitted** o **knit;** *ger:* **knitting**) *va* trabajar a punto de aguja; enlazar, unir; fruncir (*las cejas*); *vn* hacer calceta, hacer malla; trabarse, unirse; soldarse (*un hueso*)
knit goods *spl* géneros de punto
knitting [ˈnɪtɪŋ] *s* trabajo de punto
knitting machine *s* máquina de hacer media, máquina de hacer punto, máquina para punto
knitting needle *s* aguja de media, aguja de hacer media
knitwear [ˈnɪtˌwɛr] *s* géneros de punto
knob [nɑb] *s* bulto, protuberancia; botón, tirador (*de puerta*); perilla o botón (*de aparato de radio*); colina o montaña redondeada
knobby [ˈnɑbɪ] *adj* (*comp:* **-bier;** *super:* **-biest**) nudoso; redondeado; montañoso
knock [nɑk] *s* golpe; toque, llamada; aldabonazo; golpeteo; pistoneo (*del motor de combustión interna*); (slang) censura, crítica ‖ *va* golpear; golpetear; (slang) censurar, criticar; **to knock down** derribar (*de un golpe, puñetazo, etc.*); vencer; hincar; roblar; rematar (*al mejor postor*); desarmar, desmontar (*un aparato o máquina*); **to knock off** hacer saltar a fuerza de golpes; suspender (*el trabajo*); rebajar (*del precio*); poner fin a; (slang) matar; **to knock out** agotar; (box.) poner fuera de combate; **to knock together** construir, armar o montar precipitadamente ‖ *vn* tocar, llamar; pistonear, golpear (*el motor de combustión interna*); (slang) censurar, criticar; **to knock about** (coll.) andar vagando, vagabundear; **to knock at** tocar a, llamar a (*la puerta*); **to knock against** dar contra, tropezar con; **to knock off** dejar de trabajar; (slang) morir
knockabout [ˈnɑkəˌbaut] *adj* para usos generales; turbulento, tumultuoso; *s* (naut.) yate pequeño (*sin bauprés*)
knockdown [ˈnɑkˌdaun] *adj* abrumador, irresistible; entregado en piezas sueltas (*listo para armarse o montarse*); desarmable; mínimo (*precio a que se venderá una cosa en subasta*); s golpe abrumador; derribo; cosa desmontada, cosa entregada en piezas (*lista para armarse o montarse*)
knocker [ˈnɑkər] *s* llamador; aldaba; (slang) criticón
knock-kneed [ˈnɑkˌnid] *adj* patizambo, zambo
knockout [ˈnɑkˌaut] *s* golpe decisivo, puñeta-

zo decisivo; (box.) (el) fuera de combate, knock-out; (elec.) agujero ciego, destapadero; (slang) real moza

knockout drops *spl* (slang) gotas narcóticas

knoll [nol] *s* mambla, otero; toque de campana; *va* anunciar a toque de campana; *vn* doblar, tocar a muerto

Knossos [ˈnasəs] *s* Cnosos

knot [nat] *s* nudo; lazo (*adorno*); lazo matrimonial; corrillo, grupo; calambre (*de un músculo*); (naut.) nudo; canut (*Calidris canutus*); chorlo rojizo (*Calidris canutus rufus*); (fig.) nudo (*enlace; punto difícil*); **to get a knot in one's throat** hacérsele a uno un nudo en la garganta; (*pret & pp:* **knotted**; *ger:* **knotting**) *va* anudar; fruncir (*las cejas*); *vn* anudarse

knotgrass [ˈnat,græs] o [ˈnat,gras] *s* (bot.) centinodia, sanguinaria mayor

knothole [ˈnat,hol] *s* agujero (*que deja en la madera un nudo al desprenderse*)

knotted [ˈnatɪd] *adj* anudado, nudoso

knotty [ˈnatɪ] *adj* (*comp:* **-tier**; *super:* **-tiest**) nudoso; (fig.) espinoso, difícil

knotty brake *s* (bot.) helecho macho

know [no] *s* (coll.) conocimiento; **to be in the know** (coll.) estar enterado, tener informes secretos; (*pret:* **knew**; *pp:* **known**) *va & vn* saber (*tener conocimiento por medio de la razón*); conocer (*tener conocimiento por medio de los sentidos; entender, reconocer; distinguir*); **to know best** ser el mejor juez, saber lo que más conviene; **to know how to** + *inf* saber + *inf;* **to know it all** (coll.) sabérselo todo; **to know of** saber de, tener noticia de; **to know what one is doing** obrar con conocimiento de causa; **to know what's what** (coll.) saber cuántas son cinco; **to not know what it's all about** (coll.) no saber cuántas son cinco, estar a obscuras; **You ought to know better** Deberías tener vergüenza

knowable [ˈnoəbəl] *adj* conocible

know-how [ˈno,haʊ] *s* destreza, habilidad, maña

knowing [ˈno·ɪŋ] *adj* entendido, inteligente; astuto, sutil; de inteligencia, de complicidad

knowingly [ˈno·ɪŋlɪ] *adv* a sabiendas; con conocimiento de causa

know-it-all [ˈno·ɪt,ɔl] *adj* sabidillo, sabihondo; *s* sabidillo, sabihondo, sábelotodo

knowledge [ˈnalɪdʒ] *s* el saber (*facultad*); conocimiento; conocimientos; **to be a matter of common knowledge** ser notorio; **to have a thorough knowledge of** conocer a fondo; **to my knowledge** según mi leal saber y entender; que yo sepa; **to the best of my knowledge** según mi leal saber y entender; **with full knowledge** con conocimiento de causa; **without my knowledge** sin mi noticia, sin saberlo yo

knowledgeable [ˈnalɪdʒəbəl] *adj* (coll.) conocedor, inteligente

known [non] *pp de* **know**

know-nothing [ˈno,nʌθɪŋ] *s* ignorante; **Know-Nothing** *s* (U.S.A.) partido político que quería alejar del gobierno a todos los individuos de nacimiento extranjero; (U.S.A.) miembro de este partido

knuckle [ˈnʌkəl] *s* nudillo; jarrete (*de la res*); (mach.) junta de charnela; **knuckles** *spl* bóxer; **to rap the knuckles of** dar con la badila en los nudillos a; *vn* tocar con los nudillos en el suelo; **to knuckle down** someterse, darse por vencido; trabajar con ahinco; **to knuckle under** someterse, darse por vencido

knuckle joint *s* (mach.) junta articulada, unión de gozne

knurl [nʌrl] *s* nudo, protuberancia; moleteado, gráfila; *va* moletear, cerrillar (*las piezas de moneda*)

knurly [ˈnʌrlɪ] *adj* (*comp:* **-ier**; *super:* **-iest**) nudoso; moleteado

k.o. abr. de **knockout**

koala [koˈalə] *s* (zool.) coala

kobold [ˈkobald] o [ˈkobold] *s* duende; gnomo

kodak [ˈkodæk] *s* (trademark) kodak; *va & vn* fotografiar con kodak

K. of C. abr. de **Knights of Columbus**

kohl [kol] *s* alcohol (*polvo negro para teñir los párpados y las pestañas*)

kohlrabi [ˈkol,rabɪ] *s* (*pl:* **-bies**) (bot.) colirrábano

kola [ˈkolə] *s* (bot.) árbol de la cola; nuez de cola; (pharm.) nuez de cola

kola nut *s* nuez de cola

kolinsky [koˈlɪnskɪ] *s* (*pl:* **-skies**) (zool.) visón de Siberia (*animal y piel*)

koodoo [ˈkudu] *s* var. de **kudu**

kopeck o **kopek** [ˈkopɛk] *s* copeck (*moneda rusa*)

Koran [koˈran] o [ˈkoræn] *s* Alcorán, Corán

Koranic [koˈrænɪk] *adj* alcoránico

Koranist [koˈrænɪst] *s* alcoranista

Korea [koˈriə] *s* Corea

Korean [koˈriən] *adj & s* coreano

Korea Strait *s* el estrecho de Corea

kosher [ˈkoʃər] *adj* autorizado por la ley judía; (slang) genuino

kotow [ˈkoˈtaʊ] *s & vn* var. de **kowtow**

koumis [ˈkumɪs] *s* var. de **kumiss**

kowtow [ˈkaʊˈtaʊ] o [ˈkoˈtaʊ] *s* homenaje de los chinos (*postrándose con la frente en el suelo*); *vn* arrodillarse y tocar el suelo con la frente (*en señal de homenaje*); doblegarse servilmente, humillarse

K.P. abr. de **Kitchen Police**

kraal [kral] *s* población de hotentotes; corral, redil (*del África austral*)

Kremlin [ˈkrɛmlɪn] *s* Kremlín

kris [kris] *s* var. de **creese**

Kriss Kringle [ˈkrɪs ˈkrɪŋgəl] *s* San Nicolás, Papá Noel

kruller [ˈkrʌlər] *s* var. de **cruller**

krypton [ˈkrɪptan] *s* (chem.) criptón

Kt. abr. de **Knight**

K.T. abr. de **Knight Templar**

kudos [ˈkjudas] *s* (coll.) renombre, gloria

kudu [ˈkudu] *s* (zool.) cudú

Ku-Klux [ˈkju,klʌks] o **Ku Klux Klan** [klæn] *s* asociación secreta norteamericana que combate a los negros, los judíos, los católicos y los extranjeros

kulak [kuˈlak] *s* kulak (*campesino ruso acomodado*)

kumiss [ˈkumɪs] *s* cumís

kümmel [ˈkɪməl] *s* cúmel

kumquat [ˈkʌmkwat] *s* (bot.) kumquat (*naranjo chino: Fortunella japonica; su fruto*)

Kurd [kʌrd] o [kurd] *s* curdo

Kurdish [ˈkʌrdɪʃ] o [ˈkurdɪʃ] *adj* curdo; *s* curdo (*idioma*)

Kurdistan [,kʌrdɪˈstæn] o [,kurdɪˈstan] *s* el Curdistán

Kurile Islands [ˈkurɪl] *spl* islas Curiles

Kurland [ˈkurlənd] *s* var. de **Courland**

kw. abr. de **kilowatt**

K.W.H. abr. de **kilowatt-hour**

Ky. abr. de **Kentucky**

kymograph [ˈkaɪmogræf] o [ˈkaɪmograf] *s* quimógrafo

kyphosis [kaɪˈfosɪs] *s* (path.) cifosis

L

L, l [ɛl] *s* (*pl:* **L's, l's** [ɛlz]) duodécima letra del alfabeto inglés
l. abr. de **liter, line, league, length,** y **lira** o **liras**
L. abr. de **Latin** y **Low**
La. abr. de **Louisiana**
la [lɑ] o [lɔ] *interj* ¡ ah!
Lab. abr. de **Labrador** y **Laborite**
lab [læb] *s* (coll.) laboratorio
Laban ['lebən] *s* (Bib.) Labán
labarum ['læbərəm] *s* (*pl:* **-ra** [rə]) lábaro; (hist.) lábaro
labdanum ['læbdənəm] *s* ládano
label ['lebəl] *s* rótulo, marbete, etiqueta; calificación, epíteto; (b.b.) tejuelo; (her.) lambel; (*pret & pp:* **-beled** o **-belled;** *ger:* **-beling** o **-belling**) *va* rotular, poner marbete o etiqueta a; calificar, apodar
labellum [lə'bɛləm] *s* (*pl:* **-la** [lə]) (bot.) labelo; (ent.) labela
labial ['lebɪəl] *adj & s* labial
labialize ['lebɪəlaɪz] *va* (phonet.) labializar
labiate ['lebɪet] o ['lebɪɪt] *adj* (anat., zool. & bot.) labiado; *s* (bot.) labiada
labile ['lebɪl] *adj* (chem.) lábil
lability [le'bɪlɪtɪ] *s* labilidad
labiodental [,lebɪo'dɛntəl] *adj & s* (phonet.) labiodental
labium ['lebɪəm] *s* (*pl:* **-a** [ə]) labio; (anat., bot. & zool.) labio
labor ['lebər] *s* labor, trabajo; tarea, faena; los obreros (*trabajo en contraposición de capital*); mano de obra (*trabajo de los obreros; remuneración del trabajo*); parto; **labors** *spl* esfuerzos; **to be in labor** estar de parto; *va* desarrollar (*p.ej., un concepto*) con nimiedad; *vn* trabajar; forcejar; estar de parto; trabajar (*un buque*) contra las olas y el viento; moverse penosamente; **to labor under** estar sufriendo (*p.ej., una enfermedad*); tener que luchar contra; **to labor under a mistake** estar equivocado
laboratory ['læbərə,torɪ] *s* (*pl:* **-ries**) laboratorio
labor camp *s* campo de trabajo
Labor Day *s* (U.S.A.) día del trabajo (*primer lunes de septiembre*)
labored ['lebərd] *adj* dificultoso, penoso; forzado; torpe, lento; artificial, premioso
laborer ['lebərər] *s* trabajador, obrero; bracero, jornalero, peón
laborious [lə'borɪəs] *adj* laborioso
Laborite ['lebəraɪt] *s* laborista
labor-management ['lebər'mænɪdʒmənt] *adj* obrero-patronal
labor-saving ['lebər,sevɪŋ] *adj* economizador de trabajo
labors of Hercules *spl* (myth.) trabajos de Hércules
labor turnover *s* número de obreros que se emplean para reemplazar a los que han dejado el trabajo; proporción entre los obreros que trabajan transitoriamente y el número total de obreros (*en una empresa*)
labor union *s* unión de obreros
labour ['lebər] *s, va & vn* (Brit.) var. de **labor**
Labour Party *s* (Brit.) partido laborista, laborismo británico
Labrador ['læbrədər] *s* el Labrador
labradorite ['læbrədɔraɪt] o [,læbrə'dɔraɪt] *s* (mineral.) labradorita
labrum ['lebrəm] o ['læbrəm] *s* (*pl:* **-bra** [brə]) (zool.) labro
laburnum [lə'bʌrnəm] *s* (bot.) lluvia de oro, codeso
labyrinth ['læbɪrɪnθ] *s* laberinto; (anat. & mach.) laberinto; **the Labyrinth** (myth.) el laberinto de Creta
labyrinthine [,læbɪ'rɪnθɪn] *adj* laberíntico
lac [læk] *s* laca (*resina*)
lac dye *s* color de laca (*para usos tintóreos*)
lace [les] *s* encaje; cordón o lazo (*de zapato, corsé, etc.*); galón, galoncillo; *va* adornar con encaje, adornar con randas; atar (*los zapatos, el corsé, etc.*); enlazar, entrelazar; rayar (*con líneas finas*); azotar, dar una paliza a; echar licor a (*p.ej., el café*); *vn* atarse; apretarse mucho el corsé; **to lace into** arremeter contra; poner de oro y azul
lace bug *s* (ent.) chinche de encaje
Lacedaemon [,læsə'dimən] *s* la Lacedemonia
Lacedaemonian [,læsədɪ'monɪən] *adj & s* lacedemón o lacedemonio
laceman ['lesmən] *s* (*pl:* **-men**) encajero
lacerate ['læsəret] *va* lacerar; (fig.) herir (*p.ej., las sensibilidades de una persona*)
laceration [,læsə'reʃən] *s* laceración
lacewing ['les,wɪŋ] *s* (ent.) crisopo
lacewoman ['les,wʊmən] *s* (*pl:* **-women**) encajera
lacework ['les,wʌrk] *s* encaje, obra de encaje
laches ['lætʃɪz] *s* dejadez, flojedad, descuido; (law) culpa lata
Lachesis ['lækɪsɪs] *s* (myth.) Laquesis
lachryma ['lækrɪmə] *s* (*pl:* **-mas** o **-mae** [mi]) lágrima
Lachryma Christi ['krɪstɪ] o ['krɪstaɪ] *s* lácrima cristi (*vino*)
lachrymal ['lækrɪməl] *adj* lagrimal; (anat.) lagrimal; **lachrymals** *spl* (anat.) glándulas lagrimales
lachrymal caruncle *s* (anat.) carúncula lagrimal
lachrymal gland *s* (anat.) glándula lagrimal
lachrymal vase *s* vaso lacrimatorio
lachrymatory ['lækrɪmə,torɪ] *adj* lacrimatorio; lagrimal; *s* (*pl:* **-ries**) lacrimatorio (*vaso*); (hum.) pañuelo
lachrymose ['lækrɪmos] *adj* lacrimoso
lacing ['lesɪŋ] *s* cordón o lazo (*de zapato, corsé, etc.*); galón o galoncillo; paliza, tunda
lacinia [lə'sɪnɪə] *s* (*pl:* **-ae** [i] o **-as**) (bot.) lacinia
laciniate [lə'sɪnɪet] o [lə'sɪnɪɪt] *adj* (bot.) laciniado
lac insect *s* (ent.) cochinilla de la laca
lack [læk] *s* carencia; falta; deficiencia; **to supply the lack** suplir la falta; *va* carecer de; necesitar, faltarle a uno, hacerle a uno falta, p.ej., **I lack money** me falta dinero, me hace falta dinero; *vn* faltar
lackadaisical [,lækə'dezɪkəl] *adj* lánguido, indiferente
lackaday ['lækə,de] *interj* ¡ ay de mí!
lackey ['lækɪ] *s* lacayo; secuaz servil; *va* servir; doblegarse ante
lacking ['lækɪŋ] *adj* defectuoso; carente; falto de; **to be lacking** faltar; **lacking in** carente de, falto de; *prep* sin, no teniendo
lackluster ['læk,lʌstər] *adj* deslustrado, deslucido, inexpresivo
Laconia [lə'konɪə] *s* Laconia
Laconian [lə'konɪən] *adj & s* laconio
laconic [lə'kɑnɪk] *adj* lacónico
laconically [lə'kɑnɪkəlɪ] *adv* lacónicamente
laconism ['lækənɪzəm] *s* laconismo
lacquer ['lækər] *s* laca (*barniz y objeto barnizado; color*); *va* laquear, barnizar con laca
lacquer ware *s* lacas, objetos de laca
lacrimal ['lækrɪməl] *adj* var. de **lachrymal**
lacrosse [lə'krɔs] o [lə'krɑs] *s* (sport) crosse (*juego de pelota del Canadá*); **to play lacrosse** jugar a la crosse
lactam ['læktæm] *s* (biochem.) lactama
lactase ['læktes] *s* (biochem.) lactasa
lactate ['læktet] *s* (chem.) lactato

lactation [læk'teʃən] *s* lactancia
lacteal ['læktɪəl] *adj* lácteo; quilífero; *s* (anat.) vaso quilífero
lacteous ['læktɪəs] *adj* lácteo
lactescence [læk'tɛsəns] *s* lactescencia
lactescent [læk'tɛsənt] *adj* lactescente; (bot.) lactescente
lactic ['læktɪk] *adj* láctico
lactic acid *s* (chem.) ácido láctico
lactiferous [læk'tɪfərəs] *adj* lactífero
lactoflavin [,lækto'flevɪn] *s* lactoflavina
lactometer [læk'tɑmɪtər] *s* lactómetro
lactone ['lækton] *s* (chem.) lactona
lactose ['læktos] *s* (chem.) lactosa
lacuna [lə'kjunə] *s* (*pl:* **-nas** o **-nae** [ni]) laguna, hueco; (anat., bot. & zool.) laguna
lacunar [lə'kjunər] *s* (arch.) lagunar
lacustrine [lə'kʌstrɪn] *adj* lacustre; (geol.) lacustre
lacy ['lesɪ] *adj* (*comp:* **-ier;** *super:* **-iest**) de encaje; etéreo, diáfano
lad [læd] *s* muchacho; (coll.) hombre
ladder ['lædər] *s* escala, escalera; (fig.) escalón; carrera (*en las medias*)
ladder truck *s* carro de escaleras de incendio
laddie ['lædɪ] *s* (Scotch) muchacho
lade [led] (*pret:* **laded;** *pp:* **laden** o **laded**) *va* cargar; sacar, echar fuera, servir (*un líquido*) con cucharón; *vn* tomar cargamento
laden ['ledən] *adj* cargado; *pp de* **lade**
Ladin [lə'din] *s* ladino (*variedad de romancho*)
lading ['ledɪŋ] *s* carga
Ladino [lɑ'dino] *s* (*pl:* **-nos**) ladino (*mestizo hispanohablante; lenguaje híbrido hebreorrománico de ciertos judíos*)
ladle ['ledəl] s cazo, cucharón; (found.) cazo de colada, caldero de colada; *va* sacar o servir con cucharón; llevar en cucharón
lady ['ledɪ] *s* (*pl:* **-dies**) señora; dama
ladybird ['ledɪ,bʌrd] o **ladybug** ['ledɪ,bʌg] *s* (ent.) mariquita, vaca de San Antón
lady bullfighter *s* señorita-torera
Lady Day *s* (eccl.) anunciación (*25 de marzo*)
ladyfinger ['ledɪ,fɪŋgər] *s* melindre, bizcocho de plantilla
lady in waiting *s* camarera (*que sirve a una reina o princesa*)
lady-killer ['ledɪ,kɪlər] *s* (slang) matador de mujeres, ladrón de corazones, tenorio
ladylike ['ledɪ,laɪk] *adj* afeminado; delicado, elegante; **to be ladylike** ser (*una mujer*) muy dama
ladylove ['ledɪ,lʌv] *s* amada, amiga querida
Lady of the Lake *s* Doncella del Lago (*del ciclo bretón del rey Artús*)
lady's-comb ['ledɪz'kom] *s* (bot.) peine de Venus
ladyship ['ledɪʃɪp] *s* señoría (*título y persona*)
lady-slipper ['ledɪ,slɪpər] o **lady's-slipper** ['ledɪz,slɪpər] *s* (bot.) chapín, zapatilla de señorita
lady's maid *s* doncella
lady's man *s* perico entre ellas
lady's-mantle ['ledɪz'mæntəl] *s* (bot.) alquimila, estela
lady's-thumb ['ledɪz'θʌm] *s* (bot.) pesicaria, duraznillo
lag [læg] *s* retraso; (*pret & pp:* **lagged;** *ger:* **lagging**) *vn* retrasarse; quedarse atrás, rezagarse
lagena [lə'dʒinə] *s* (*pl:* **-nae** [ni]) (zool.) lagena
lager ['lɑgər] o **lager beer** *s* cerveza reposada, cerveza de conserva
laggard ['lægərd] *adj & s* rezagado, perezoso
lagniappe o **lagnappe** [læn'jæp] *s* adehala, yapa
lagoon [lə'gun] *s* laguna
lag screw *s* tirafondo
laic ['leɪk] *adj & s* laico
laicization [,leɪsɪ'zeʃən] *s* laicización
laicize ['leɪsaɪz] *va* laicizar
laid [led] *pret & pp de* **lay;** *adj* vergueteado; **laid up** almacenado, guardado; ahorrado; encamado (*por estar enfermo*); (naut.) inactivo
lain [len] *pp de* **lie**
lair [lɛr] *s* cubil, cama
laird [lɛrd] *s* (Scotch) dueño de tierras
laisser faire o **laissez faire** [,lɛse'fɛr] *s* laisser faire (*doctrina según la cual los poderes públicos deben intervenir lo menos posible en los intereses de los particulares y de las asociaciones*)
laissez-faire [,lɛse'fɛr] *adj* de laisser faire
laity ['leɪtɪ] *s* (*pl:* **-ties**) legos
Laius ['leəs] *s* (myth.) Layo
lake [lek] *s* lago; laca (*materia colorante*)
Lake Aral ['ærəl] *s* el lago de Aral
Lake Country o **Lake District** *s* región de los lagos (*en el noroeste de Inglaterra*)
lake dweller *s* hombre lacustre
lake dwelling *s* habitación lacustre
Lake of Constance *s* el lago de Constanza
Lake Ontario [ɑn'tɛrɪo] *s* el lago Ontario
Lake poets *spl* lakistas (*Wordsworth, Coleridge y Southey*)
Lake Superior *s* el lago Superior
lake trout *s* (ichth.) trucha de los lagos
Lam. abr. de **Lamentations**
lama ['lɑmə] *s* lama (*sacerdote del Tibet*)
Lamaism ['lɑməɪzəm] *s* lamaísmo
Lamaist ['lɑməɪst] *adj & s* lamaísta
Lamarckian [lə'mɑrkɪən] *adj & s* lamarquista
Lamarckianism [lə'mɑrkɪənɪzəm] o **Lamarckism** [lə'mɑrkɪzəm] *s* lamarquismo
lamasery ['lɑmə,sɛrɪ] *s* (*pl:* **-ies**) lamasería
lamb [læm] *s* cordero; carne de cordero; piel de cordero; (fig.) cordero (*persona inocente, humilde*); (fig.) nene; **like a lamb** inocente, humilde; inocentemente, humildemente; **the Lamb** el Cordero (*Jesucristo*); *vn* parir (*la oveja*)
lambaste [læm'best] *va* (slang) dar una paliza a, azotar sin piedad; (slang) dar una jabonadura a
lamb chop *s* chuleta de cordero
lambent ['læmbənt] *adj* ondulante, lamiente (*llama*); centelleante (*ingenio, estilo*); suave (*luz*)
Lambert ['læmbərt] *s* Lamberto
lambkin ['læmkɪn] *s* corderito; (fig.) nenito
Lamb of God *s* Cordero de Dios, Divino Cordero
lambrequin ['læmbrəkɪn] *s* lambrequín, guardamalleta; (her.) lambrequín
lambskin ['læm,skɪn] *s* corderina, piel de cordero; corderillo (*adobado con su lana*)
lame [lem] *adj* cojo; molido, lastimado; pobre, débil, frívolo; *va* encojar; *vn* encojarse
lamé [læ'me] *s* lama (*tejido*)
lame duck *s* (coll.) persona incapacitada; (coll.) cosa inútil; (U.S.A.) diputado que no ha sido reelegido y espera el cese venidero
lamella [lə'mɛlə] *s* (*pl:* **-las** o **-lae** [li]) laminilla; (bot.) laminilla
lamellar [lə'mɛlər] o ['læmələr] o **lamellate** ['læməlet] o [lə'mɛlet] *adj* laminar
lamellibranch [lə'mɛlɪbræŋk] *adj & s* (zool.) lamelibranquio
lameness ['lemnɪs] *s* cojera; pobreza, debilidad, imperfección
lament [lə'mɛnt] *s* lamento; elegía; *va* lamentar; *vn* lamentarse
lamentable ['læməntəbəl] *adj* lamentable
lamentably ['læməntəblɪ] *adv* lamentablemente
lamentation [,læmən'teʃən] *s* lamentación; **Lamentations** *spl* (Bib.) Lamentaciones de Jeremías
lamia ['lemɪə] *s* (*pl:* **-as** o **-ae** [i]) (ichth. & myth.) lamia
lamiaceous [,lemɪ'eʃəs] *adj* (bot.) lamiáceo
lamina ['læmɪnə] *s* (*pl:* **-nae** [ni] o **-nas**) lámina; (anat., bot., geol. & zool.) lámina
laminar ['læmɪnər] *adj* laminar
laminate ['læmɪnet] *adj* laminado; *va* laminar
lamination [,læmɪ'neʃən] *s* laminación, laminado
laminose ['læmɪnos] *adj* laminoso
Lammas ['læməs] *s* (archaic) fiesta de la recolección de la cosecha; (eccl.) fiesta de San Pedro encadenado
lammergeier ['læmər,gaɪər] *s* (orn.) águila barbuda
lamp [læmp] *s* lámpara; (poet.) antorcha; (poet.) astro; **lamps** *spl* (slang) ojos
lampadary ['læmpə,derɪ] *s* (*pl:* **-ies**) lampadario (*sacerdote; columna con lámparas*)
lampblack ['læmp,blæk] *s* negro de humo
lamp chimney *s* tubo, tubo de lámpara
lamp cord *s* (elec.) cordón de lámpara

lamp holder *s* (elec.) portalámparas
lamplight [ˈlæmp,laɪt] *s* luz de lámpara
lamplighter [ˈlæmp,laɪtər] *s* farolero; cerilla o rollo de papel (*que sirve para encender lámparas o faroles*)
lampoon [læmˈpun] *s* pasquín, libelo; *va* pasquinar
lampoonist [læmˈpunɪst] *s* escritor de pasquines, libelista
lamppost [ˈlæmp,post] *s* poste de farol
lamprey [ˈlæmprɪ] *s* (ichth.) lamprea
lamp shade *s* pantalla de lámpara
lampwick [ˈlæmp,wɪk] *s* torcida, mecha de lámpara; (bot.) candilera
lanate [ˈlenet] *adj* lanado
Lancastrian [læŋˈkæstrɪən] *adj & s* lancasteriano
lance [læns] o [lɑns] *s* lanza; arpón de pesca; (surg.) lanceta; *va* alancear; (surg.) abrir con lanceta
lance corporal *s* (Brit.) soldado que hace las veces de cabo
Lancelot [ˈlænsəlɑt] o [ˈlɑnsəlɑt] *s* Lanzarote (*de la Mesa redonda*)
lanceolate [ˈlænsɪəlet] *adj* (bot.) lanceolado, alanceado
lancer [ˈlænsər] o [ˈlɑnsər] *s* lancero; **lancers** *spl* lanceros (*baile y música*)
lance rest *s* ristre
lance sergeant *s* (Brit.) cabo que hace las veces de sargento
lancet [ˈlænsɪt] o [ˈlɑnsɪt] *s* (surg.) lanceta; (arch.) ojiva de lanceta
lancet arch *s* (arch.) ojiva de lanceta
lancewood [ˈlæns,wʊd] o [ˈlɑns,wʊd] *s* (bot.) palo de lanza
lancinate [ˈlænsɪnet] *va* lancinar
land [lænd] *s* tierra; **by land** por tierra; **on land, on sea, and in the air** en tierra, mar y aire; **to see how the land lies** medir el terreno, ver el cariz que van tomando las cosas; *adj* terrestre; terral (*viento*); *va* desembarcar; coger (*un pez*); conducir (*un avión*) a tierra; (coll.) conseguir, obtener; *vn* desembarcar, saltar en tierra; arribar, aterrar; ir a dar, ir a parar; aterrizar (*un avión*); **to land on one's feet** caer de pies; **to land on one's head** caer de cabeza
landau [ˈlændɔ] o [ˈlændaʊ] *s* landó
landaulet o **landaulette** [,lændɔˈlɛt] *s* landolé; landolé automóvil
land-based plane [ˈlænd,best] *s* (aer.) avión con base en tierra
land breeze *s* terral
landed [ˈlændɪd] *adj* hacendado; que consiste en tierras; **landed property** bienes raíces
landfall [ˈlænd,fɔl] *s* (naut.) aterrada (*aproximación a tierra, vista de la costa*); (aer.) aterrizaje; costa o tierra vista desde el mar; tierra (*donde uno aborda*); derrumbamiento de tierra; herencia inesperada de tierras
land grant *s* donación de tierras
land-grant college o **university** [ˈlænd,grænt] o [ˈlænd,grɑnt] *s* (U.S.A.) centro docente fundado por el gobierno federal mediante una donación de tierras
landgrave [ˈlænd,grev] *s* landgrave o langrave
landgraviate [lændˈgrevɪɪt] *s* landgraviato
landholder [ˈlænd,holdər] *s* terrateniente
landholding [ˈlænd,holdɪŋ] *s* tenencia de tierra o tierras; *adj* hacendado
landing [ˈlændɪŋ] *s* aterraje (*de buque*); aterraje o aterrizaje (*de avión*); desembarco (*de pasajeros*); desembarcadero (*lugar para desembarcar*); desembarco o descanso (*de escalera*)
landing beacon *s* (aer.) radiofaro de aterrizaje
landing craft *s* (nav.) lancha de desembarco
landing field *s* (aer.) pista de aterrizaje
landing force *s* (nav.) compañía de desembarco
landing gear *s* (aer.) tren de aterrizaje
landing net *s* red con mango (*para sacar del agua un pez cogido en el anzuelo*)
landing place *s* apeadero, desembarcadero; descanso (*de escalera*)
landing ship *s* (nav.) buque de desembarco
landing stage *s* embarcadero flotante
landing strip *s* (aer.) faja de aterrizaje
landlady [ˈlænd,ledɪ] *s* (*pl:* **-dies**) dueña, casera; patrona (*de una casa de huéspedes*); mesonera, posadera
landless [ˈlændlɪs] *adj* sin tierras, que no posee tierras
landlocked [ˈlænd,lɑkt] *adj* cercado de tierra; que no tiene acceso al mar (*dícese de ciertos salmones*)
landlord [ˈlænd,lɔrd] *s* dueño, casero; patrón (*de una casa de huéspedes*); mesonero, posadero
landlubber [ˈlænd,lʌbər] *s* marinero de agua dulce; marinero matalote (*hombre de mar, torpe en su oficio*)
landmark [ˈlænd,mɑrk] *s* mojón (*señal en un camino que sirve de guía*); guía (*accidente del terreno que sirve de guía*); punto culminante, acontecimiento que hace época; (naut.) marca de reconocimiento
land office *s* oficina del catastro
land-office business [ˈlænd,ɔfɪs] o [ˈlænd,ɑfɪs] *s* (coll.) negocio de mucho movimiento
land of make-believe *s* reino de los sueños
Land of Promise *s* (Bib.) Tierra de promisión
Land of the Midnight Sun *s* tierra del sol de medianoche (*Noruega*)
Land of the Rising Sun *s* tierra del sol naciente (*el Japón*)
landowner [ˈlænd,onər] *s* terrateniente
landownership [ˈlænd,onərʃɪp] *s* tenencia de tierra o tierras
land-poor [ˈlænd,pʊr] *adj* rico de tierras y falto de dinero
landscape [ˈlændskep] *s* paisaje; (f.a.) paisaje; *va* ajardinar
landscape architect *s* arquitecto paisajista
landscape gardener *s* arquitecto de jardines, plantista, jardinero, adornista
landscape painter *s* paisajista, pintor paisajista
landscapist [ˈlændskepɪst] *s* paisajista
Land's End *s* Cabo Finisterre (*de la extremidad sudoccidental de Inglaterra*)
landslide [ˈlænd,slaɪd] *s* argayo, derrumbe, corrimiento; (fig.) victoria electoral arrolladora, mayoría de votos abrumadora
landslip [ˈlænd,slɪp] *s* (Brit.) argayo, derrumbe
landsman [ˈlændzmən] *s* (*pl:* **-men**) hombre de tierra; marinero matalote
landward [ˈlændwərd] *adj* de hacia tierra, de la parte de la tierra; *adv* hacia tierra, hacia la costa
landwards [ˈlændwərdz] *adv* hacia tierra, hacia la costa
land wind *s* terral
lane [len] *s* callejuela; carril (*camino muy estrecho*); faja (*de una carretera*); (aer. & naut.) derrotero, ruta, vía
langsyne [ˈlæŋˈsaɪn] *adv* (Scotch) hace mucho tiempo; *s* (Scotch) tiempo de antaño
language [ˈlæŋgwɪdʒ] *s* lenguaje; idioma, lengua (*lenguaje de un pueblo o nación*); jerga (*de un determinado grupo de personas*)
language barrier *s* barrera del idioma
langued [læŋd] *adj* (her.) linguado
langue d'oc [lɑ̃gˈdɑk] *s* lengua de oc, lenguadoque
Languedocian [,læŋgəˈdoʃən] *adj & s* languedociano
langue d'oïl [lɑ̃gdɔˈil] *s* lengua de oíl
languid [ˈlæŋgwɪd] *adj* lánguido
languish [ˈlæŋgwɪʃ] *vn* languidecer; afectar languidez; **to languish for** penar por, suspirar por
languishing [ˈlæŋgwɪʃɪŋ] *adj* lánguido; languescente
languishment [ˈlæŋgwɪʃmənt] *s* languidez; consumimiento; aspecto lánguido, manera lánguida
languor [ˈlæŋgər] *s* languidez
languorous [ˈlæŋgərəs] *adj* lánguido; enervante
langur [lʌŋˈgʊr] *s* (zool.) hanumán, mono sagrado de la India
laniard [ˈlænjərd] *s* var. de **lanyard**
lank [læŋk] *adj* descarnado, larguirucho; lacio (*cabello*)
lanky [ˈlæŋkɪ] *adj* (*comp:* **-ier**; *super:* **-iest**) descarnado, larguirucho
lanner [ˈlænər] *s* lanero (*halcón*)
lanolin [ˈlænəlɪn] o **lanoline** [ˈlænəlɪn] o [ˈlænəlin] *s* lanolina

lansquenet ['lænskənɛt] *s* lansquenete (*lancero de a pie; juego de naipes*)
lantern ['læntərn] *s* linterna; linterna mágica; (arch. & mach.) linterna; (naut.) linterna (*fanal*); (zool.) linterna de Aristóteles
lantern-jawed ['læntərn,dʒɔd] *adj* chupado de cara
lantern pinion *s* (mach.) piñón de linterna
lantern slide *s* diapositiva, tira de vidrio
lantern wheel *s* (mach.) rueda de linterna
lanthanum ['lænθənəm] *s* (chem.) lantano
lanyard ['lænjərd] *s* (naut.) acollador; (arti.) cuerda y gancho de disparo
Laocoön [le'ɑkoɑn] *s* (myth.) Laocoonte
Laodicean [le,ɑdɪ'siən] *adj* tibio e indiferente; *s* persona tibia e indiferente; cristiano tibio e indiferente
Laotian [le'oʃən] *adj & s* laocio, laosiano
lap [læp] *s* regazo; falda; caída, doblez (*de un vestido*); traslapo; lametada; chapaleteo (*de las olas*); (mach.) recubrimiento (*de la válvula de corredera*); (sport) vuelta, etapa (*en las carreras*); **it is in the lap of the gods** eso sólo Dios lo sabe; **to live in the lap of luxury** vivir en el lujo, llevar una vida regalada; (*pret & pp:* **lapped;** *ger:* **lapping**) *va* traslapar; juntar a traslapo; envolver; beber con la lengua; lamer (*el arroyo las arenas*); (sport) llevar una vuelta o más de una vuelta de ventaja a; **to lap up** (slang) aceptar en el acto; *vn* traslapar; traslaparse (*dos o más cosas*); **to lap against** lamer (*el arroyo las arenas*); **to lap over** salir fuera; **to lap over into** extenderse hasta
lapboard ['læp,bord] *s* tabla faldera
lap dog *s* perro faldero
lapel [lə'pɛl] *s* solapa
lapful ['læpfʊl] *s* lo que cabe en el regazo, cabida del regazo
lapidary ['læpɪ,dɛrɪ] *adj* lapidario; *s* (*pl:* **-ies**) lapidario
lapidification [lə,pɪdɪfɪ'keʃən] *s* lapidificación
lapidify [lə'pɪdɪfaɪ] (*pret & pp:* **-fied**) *va* lapidificar; *vn* lapidificarse
lapin ['læpɪn] *s* piel de conejo
lapis lazuli ['læpɪs 'læzjəlaɪ] *s* (mineral.) lapislázuli
Lapland ['læplænd] *s* Laponia
Laplander ['læplændər] *s* lapón (*habitante*)
Lapp [læp] *s* lapón (*habitante; idioma*)
lappet ['læpɪt] *s* caída, doblez, pliegue (*de un vestido*); pliegue (*de una membrana, tegumento, etc.*); lóbulo (*de la oreja*); carúncula (*de algunas aves*)
Lappish ['læpɪʃ] *adj* lapón; *s* lapón (*idioma*)
lap robe *s* manta de coche
lapse [læps] *s* lapso (*curso de tiempo; caída en culpa o error*); recaída; (law) caducidad; *vn* caer en culpa o error; caerse; recaer; decaer, pasar (*p.ej., el entusiasmo*); (law) caducar
lapwing ['læp,wɪŋ] *s* (orn.) ave fría
larboard ['lɑrbərd] o ['lɑrbord] *s* (naut.) babor; *adj* (naut.) de babor
larcenous ['lɑrsənəs] *adj* ratero; de ratería
larceny ['lɑrsənɪ] *s* (*pl:* **-nies**) (law) ratería, hurto
larch [lɑrtʃ] *s* (bot.) alerce, pino salgareño, pino negral
lard [lɑrd] *s* manteca de puerco, cochevira; *va* (cook.) mechar; (fig.) interpolar para dar variedad o aumentar el interés
larder ['lɑrdər] *s* despensa
lares and penates ['lɛrɪz ənd pɛ'netiz] *spl* lares y penates (*dioses domésticos de los romanos*); conjunto de objetos que dan carácter e intimidad a la casa propia u hogar
large [lɑrdʒ] *adj* grande; **at large** en libertad; largamente, con extensión; en general; por el estado entero (*dícese de los diputados que representan una región entera, a distinción de los que representan tan sólo una división política menos grande*); **in large** o **in the large** en grande escala
large-hearted ['lɑrdʒ'hɑrtɪd] *adj* desprendido, magnánimo
large intestine *s* (anat.) intestino grueso
largely ['lɑrdʒlɪ] *adj* grandemente; por la mayor parte
largeness ['lɑrdʒnɪs] *s* grandeza
large periwinkle *s* (bot.) vincapervinca, hierba doncella
large-scale ['lɑrdʒ,skel] *adj* en grande; grande escala, p.ej., **large-scale model** modelo grande escala
largess o **largesse** ['lɑrdʒɛs] *s* largueza (*liberalidad*); dádiva espléndida
largo ['lɑrgo] *s* (*pl:* **-gos**) (mus.) largo
lariat ['lærɪət] *s* lazo (*que sirve para enlazar caballos, toros, etc.*); cuerda o soga (*que sirve para tener atado un animal*)
lark [lɑrk] *s* (orn.) alondra; (orn.) chirlota (*Sturnella magna*); (coll.) parranda, travesuras; **to go on a lark** (coll.) andar de parranda, echar una cana al aire; *vn* (coll.) parrandear, hacer travesuras
larkspur ['lɑrkspʌr] *s* (bot.) consuelda (*Delphinium consolida*); consólida real, espuela de caballero (*Delphinium ajacis*)
La Rochelle [la ro'ʃɛl] *s* La Rochela (*ciudad de Francia*)
larrup ['lærəp] *va* (coll.) zurrar, tundir
larva ['lɑrvə] *s* (*pl:* **-vae** [vi]) (ent.) larva
larval ['lɑrvəl] *adj* larval; (path.) larvado
laryngeal [lə'rɪndʒɪəl] o [,lærɪn'dʒiəl] *adj* laríngeo
laryngitis [,lærɪn'dʒaɪtɪs] *s* (path.) laringitis
laryngologist [,lærɪŋ'gɑlədʒɪst] *s* laringólogo
laryngology [,lærɪŋ'gɑlədʒɪ] *s* laringología
laryngoscope [lə'rɪŋgəskop] *s* laringoscopio
laryngoscopic [lə,rɪŋgə'skɑpɪk] *adj* laringoscópico
laryngoscopy [,lærɪŋ'gɑskəpɪ] *s* laringoscopia
larynx ['lærɪŋks] *s* (*pl:* **larynges** [lə'rɪndʒiz] o **larynxes**) (anat.) laringe
lascar ['læskər] *s* lascar (*marinero de las Indias Orientales*)
lascivious [lə'sɪvɪəs] *adj* lascivo
laserwort ['lesər,wʌrt] *s* (bot.) laserpicio
lash [læʃ] *s* tralla; latigazo (*golpe con el látigo; reprensión áspera*); coletazo; embate (*de las olas del mar*); (anat.) pestaña; *va* atar, trincar; azotar; agitar, sacudir; increpar, reñir; vituperar; *vn* chocar, azotar; lanzarse; pasar como un relámpago; **to lash against** chocar con, azotar; **to lash at** increpar, reñir; vituperar; **to lash down** caer con abundancia (*la lluvia*); **to lash out** dar golpes, dar coces, embestir; desatarse, descomedirse
lashing ['læʃɪŋ] *s* atadura; (naut.) amarra; paliza, zurra; latigazo (*reprensión áspera*)
lass [læs] *s* muchacha; amada, amiga querida
lassie ['læsɪ] *s* muchachita
lassitude ['læsɪtjud] o ['læsɪtud] *s* lasitud
lasso ['læso] o [læ'su] *s* (*pl:* **-sos** o **-soes**) lazo; *va* lazar
last [læst] o [lɑst] *adj* último; pasado; final; **before last** antepasado, p.ej., **the week before last** la semana antepasada; **the last to** + *inf* el último en + *inf;* **last but not least** último en orden pero no en importancia, el último pero no el ínfimo; **last but one** penúltimo; *adv* después de todos los demás; por último; por última vez; *s* última persona; última cosa; fin; horma (*en que se conforman los zapatos*); **at last** por fin; **at long last** al fin y al cabo; **stick to your last!** ¡zapatero, a tus zapatos!; **to breathe one's last** dar el último suspiro; **to see the last of** no volver a ver; **to stick to one's last** atender a sus negocios, no meterse (*uno*) en lo que no le importa; **to the last** hasta el fin; *va* fabricar (*botas, zapatos*) en la horma; *vn* durar; seguir así; p.ej., **this can't last** las cosas no pueden seguir así; resistir; dar buen resultado (*p.ej., una prenda de vestir*)
lasting ['læstɪŋ] o ['lɑstɪŋ] *adj* duradero, perdurable
Last Judgment *s* Juicio Final
lastly ['læstlɪ] o ['lɑstlɪ] *adv* finalmente, por último
last-minute news ['læst'mɪnɪt] o ['lɑst'mɪnɪt] *s* noticias de última hora
last name *s* apellido
last night *adv* anoche
last offices *spl* oficio de difuntos
last quarter *s* cuarto menguante (*de la luna*)
last sleep *s* último sueño (*la muerte*)
last straw *s* colmo, acabóse

Last Supper *s* Cena, última Cena
last will and testament *s* (law) última voluntad
last word *s* última palabra; (coll.) última palabra (*última moda; lo más perfecto que hay*)
lat. abr. de **latitude**
Lat. abr. de **Latin**
latch [lætʃ] *s* picaporte; **on the latch** cerrado con picaporte; *va* cerrar con picaporte
latchet ['lætʃɪt] *s* (archaic) correa de zapato
latchkey ['lætʃ,ki] *s* llavín, picaporte (*llave para abrir el picaporte*); llave de la puerta principal
latchstring ['lætʃ,strɪŋ] *s* cordón de aldaba; **the latchstring is out** ya sabe Vd. que ésta es su casa
late [let] *adj* (*comp:* **later** o **latter;** *super:* **latest** o **last**) tardío; avanzado (*dícese de la hora*); reciente, moderno; fallecido, difunto; de fines de, p.ej., **the late nineteenth-century novel** la novela de fines del siglo diez y nueve; de última hora (*dícese de las noticias*); **to be late** ser tarde; llegar tarde (*una persona*); llegar con retraso (*p.ej., un tren*); **to be late in** + *ger* tardar en + *inf;* **of late** recientemente, últimamente; **later** posterior; *adv* (*comp:* **later;** *super:* **latest** o **last**) tarde; **late in** hacia fines de (*la semana, el año, el siglo, etc.*); **late in life** a una edad avanzada
late-comer ['let,kʌmər] *s* recién llegado; rezagado
lateen [læ'tin] *adj* (naut.) latino
lateen-rigged [læ'tin,rɪgd] *adj* (naut.) que tiene vela latina
lateen sail *s* (naut.) vela latina
lateen yard *s* (naut.) entena
late-lamented ['letlə'mɛntɪd] *adj* fallecido . . . que en paz descanse, p.ej., **the late-lamented professor** el fallecido profesor que en paz descanse
lately ['letlɪ] *adv* recientemente, últimamente
latency ['letənsɪ] *s* estado latente
latent ['letənt] *adj* latente
latent period *s* (path.) latencia
lateral ['lætərel] *adj* lateral; *s* parte lateral; ramal; (min.) galería lateral
laterally ['lætərəlɪ] *adv* lateralmente
lateral pass *s* (football) pase lateral (*lance que consiste en lanzar lateralmente el balón de modo que lo reciba un jugador al otro lado de la zona de juego*)
Lateran ['lætərən] *adj* lateranense; *s* San Juan de Letrán (*basílica*); palacio de Letrán
latex ['letɛks] *s* (*pl:* **latexes** o **latices** ['lætɪsiz]) (bot.) látex
lath [læθ] o [lɑθ] *s* listón; enlistonado; *va* enlistonar
lathe [leð] *s* torno (*para trabajar madera, hierro, etc. con movimiento circular*)
lather ['læθər] o ['lɑθər] *s* (carp.) listonador; ['læðər] *s* espuma de jabón; espuma de sudor; *va* enjabonar; (coll.) tundir, zurrar; *vn* espumar, echar espuma; cubrirse de espuma (*p.ej., un caballo*)
lathery ['læðərɪ] *adj* espumoso, cubierto de espuma
lathing ['læθɪŋ] o ['lɑθɪŋ] o **lathwork** ['læθ,wʌrk] o ['lɑθ,wʌrk] *s* enlistonado
lathy ['læθɪ] o ['lɑθɪ] *adj* en forma de listón; largo y delgado
Latin ['lætɪn] o ['lætən] *adj* latino; *s* latín (*lengua*); latino (*individuo*)
Latin America *s* Latinoamérica, la América Latina
Latin American *s* latinoamericano
Latin-American ['lætɪnə'mɛrɪkən] *adj* latinoamericano
Latin Church *s* Iglesia latina
Latin cross *s* cruz latina
Latinism ['lætɪnɪzəm] *s* latinismo
Latinist ['lætɪnɪst] *s* latinista
Latinity [lə'tɪnɪtɪ] *s* latinidad
Latinization [,lætɪnɪ'zeʃən] *s* latinización
Latinize ['lætɪnaɪz] *va* latinizar; *vn* latinizarse
Latin Quarter *s* Barrio Latino
Latin Rite *s* rito latino
latitude ['lætɪtjud] o ['lætɪtud] *s* latitud; (fig.) latitud (*libertad; clima, región*)
latitudinal [,lætɪ'tjudɪnəl] o [,lætɪ'tudɪnəl] *adj* latitudinal
latitudinarian [,lætɪ,tjudɪ'nɛrɪən] o [,lætɪ,tudɪ'nɛrɪən] *adj & s* latitudinario
latitudinarianism [,lætɪ,tjudɪ'nɛrɪənɪzəm] o [,lætɪ,tudɪ'nɛrɪənɪzəm] *s* latitudinarismo
Latium ['leʃɪəm] *s* el Lacio
latria [lə'traɪə] *s* (theol.) latría
latrine [lə'trin] *s* letrina (*en un campamento, hospital, etc.*)
latten ['lætən] *s* latón en hojas
latter ['lætər] *adj* posterior, más reciente; segundo (*de dos*); **the latter** éste; **the latter part of** la última parte de; fines de (*la semana, el mes, etc.*)
latter-day ['lætər'de] *adj* reciente, moderno; de los últimos días
Latter-day Saint *s* santo de los últimos días (*mormón*)
latterly ['lætərlɪ] *adv* recientemente, últimamente
lattice ['lætɪs] *s* enrejado, celosía; (her.) celosía; (phys.) reja; *va* enrejar; poner celosía a
lattice bridge *s* puente de celosía
lattice girder *s* viga de celosía
latticework ['lætɪs,wʌrk] *s* enrejado, celosía
Latvia ['lætvɪə] *s* Letonia o Latvia
Latvian ['lætvɪən] *adj & s* letón o latvio
laud [lɔd] *s* alabanza, elogio; canción laudatoria; **lauds** o **Lauds** *spl* (eccl.) laudes; *va* alabar, elogiar
laudability [,lɔdə'bɪlɪtɪ] *s* laudabilidad
laudable ['lɔdəbəl] *adj* laudable
laudanum ['lɔdənəm] o ['lɔdnəm] *s* (pharm.) láudano
laudation [lɔ'deʃən] *s* alabanza
laudatory ['lɔdə,torɪ] *adj* laudatorio
laugh [læf] o [lɑf] *s* risa; *va* hacer o llevar a cabo riendo; expresar riendo; **to laugh away** ahogar en risa, olvidar riendo; **to laugh off** tomar a risa; *vn* reír, reírse; (fig.) reír (*p.ej., una corriente de agua*); **to laugh out** reírse a carcajadas
laughable ['læfəbəl] o ['lɑfəbəl] *adj* risible
laughing ['læfɪŋ] o ['lɑfɪŋ] *adj* risueño, reidor; **to be no laughing matter** no ser cosa de juego; *s* risa, reír
laughing gas *s* gas exhilarante, gas hilarante
laughing jackass *s* (orn.) martín cazador
laughingly ['læfɪŋlɪ] o ['lɑfɪŋlɪ] *adv* riendo, entre risas
laughingstock ['læfɪŋ,stɑk] o ['lɑfɪŋ,stɑk] *s* hazmerreír
laughter ['læftər] o ['lɑftər] *s* risa, risas
launch [lɔntʃ] o [lɑntʃ] *s* botadura (*de un buque*); lanzamiento (*de un cohete*); lancha automóvil; (nav.) lancha; *va* lanzar (*un dardo, un cohete, maldiciones, una ofensiva, un producto nuevo*); botar, lanzar (*un buque*); *vn* lanzarse; **to launch forth** u **out** salir, ponerse en marcha
launcher ['lɔntʃər] o ['lɑntʃər] *s* lanzador
launching device *s* instrumento de lanzamiento
launching pad *s* plataforma de lanzamiento
launching silo *s* pozo o silo de lanzamiento
launching site *s* puesto de lanzamiento
launching tower *s* torre de lanzamiento
launder ['lɔndər] o ['lɑndər] *va* lavar y planchar; *vn* resistir bien el lavado
launderer ['lɔndərər] o ['lɑndərər] *s* lavandero
laundress ['lɔndrɪs] o ['lɑndrɪs] *s* lavandera
laundromat ['lɔndrəmæt] o ['lɑndrəmæt] *s* (trademark) lavadero de autoservicio
laundry ['lɔndrɪ] o ['lɑndrɪ] *s* (*pl:* **-dries**) lavadero (*sitio*); lavandería (Am.); lavado de ropas; ropa sucia; ropa lavada y planchada
laundryman ['lɔndrɪmən] o ['lɑndrɪmən] *s* (*pl:* **-men**) lavandero
laundrywoman ['lɔndrɪ,wʊmən] o ['lɑndrɪ,wʊmən] *s* (*pl:* **-women**) lavandera
lauraceous [lɔ'reʃəs] *adj* (bot.) lauráceo
laureate ['lɔrɪɪt] *adj* laureado; *s* laureado; poeta laureado
laureateship ['lɔrɪɪt,ʃɪp] *s* dignidad de poeta laureado
laurel ['lɔrəl] o ['lɑrəl] *s* (bot.) laurel; (bot.) calmia; (bot.) rododendro; hojas de laurel; **laurels** *spl* laurel (*de la victoria*); **to look to one's laurels** no dormirse sobre sus laureles; **to rest** o **to sleep on one's laurels** dormirse sobre sus laureles; (*pret & pp:* **-reled** o

-**relled; *ger:* -reling** o **-relling**) *va* laurear, coronar de laurel
laureled o **laurelled** ['lɔrəld] o ['lɑrəld] *adj* laureado
Laurence ['lɔrəns] o ['lɑrəns] *s* Lorenzo
Laurentian [lɔ'rɛnʃɪən] *adj* laurentino; (geol.) laurentino; *s* (geol.) laurentino
Laurentian Mountains *spl* montes Laurentinos
laurustine ['lɔrəstɪn] *s* (bot.) durillo, barbadija
Lausanne [lo'zæn] *s* Losana
lava ['lɑvə] o ['lævə] *s* lava
lava bed *s* yacimiento de lava
lavabo [lə'vebo] *s* (*pl:* **-boes**) (eccl. & hist.) lavabo; (*cap.*) *s* (eccl.) lavabo (*paño*)
lava field *s* terreno cubierto de lava
lavage ['lævɪdʒ] *s* lavado; (med.) lavado
lavalier, lavaliere o **lavallière** [,lævə'lɪr] *s* pendiente (*que se lleva alrededor del cuello*)
lavatory ['lævə,torɪ] *s* (*pl:* **-ries**) lavabo (*cuarto*); excusado, retrete; lavamanos, lavatorio; (eccl.) lavatorio
lave [lev] *va* (poet.) bañar; *vn* (poet.) bañarse
lavender ['lævəndər] *s* (bot.) alhucema, espliego (*planta y flores y hojas secas*); color de alhucema; *adj* de color de alhucema
lavender cotton *s* (bot.) abrótano hembra
lavender water *s* agua de alhucema, agua de espliego
laver ['levər] *s* (archaic) aguamanil, jofaina
lavish ['lævɪʃ] *adj* pródigo; *va* prodigar
law [lɔ] *s* ley; derecho (*conjunto de leyes; estudio de las leyes*); **the Law** (Bib.) la ley de Moisés; (Bib.) el Antiguo Testamento; **to enter the law** hacerse abogado; **to have the law on** (coll.) iniciar un juicio contra; **to go to law** recurrir a la ley; **to lay down the law** dar órdenes terminantes; decir cuántas son cinco; **to maintain law and order** mantener la paz; **to practice law** ejercer la profesión de abogado; **to read law** estudiar derecho (*en el bufete de un abogado*); **to take the law into one's own hands** hacerse justicia por sí mismo
law-abiding ['lɔə,baɪdɪŋ] *adj* observante de la ley
lawbreaker ['lɔ,brekər] *s* infractor de la ley
lawbreaking ['lɔ,brekɪŋ] *adj* infractor de la ley; *s* infracción de la ley
law court *s* tribunal de justicia
lawful ['lɔfəl] *adj* legal, lícito, legítimo, permitido
lawgiver ['lɔ,gɪvər] *s* legislador
lawless ['lɔlɪs] *adj* ilegal; desaforado, desenfrenado, licencioso; sin leyes
lawmaker ['lɔ,mekər] *s* legislador
lawmaking ['lɔ,mekɪŋ] *adj* legislativo; *s* legislación
lawn [lɔn] *s* césped; linón (*tela*); episcopado anglicano
lawn mower *s* cortacésped, tundidora de césped
lawn tennis *s* (sport) lawn-tennis
law office *s* bufete, despacho de abogado
law of Moses *s* ley de Moisés
law of nations *s* derecho de gentes
law of the jungle *s* ley de la selva
law of the Medes and Persians *s* (Bib.) ley de Media y de Persia (*ley inmutable*)
Lawrence ['lɔrəns] o ['lɑrəns] *s* Lorenzo
law student *s* estudiante de leyes, estudiante de derecho
lawsuit ['lɔ,sut] o ['lɔ,sjut] *s* pleito, litigio, proceso
lawyer ['lɔjər] *s* abogado
lax [læks] *adj* laxo (*flojo; relajado, libre*); descuidado, negligente; vago, indeterminado
laxation [læk'seʃən] *s* laxación
laxative ['læksətɪv] *adj & s* (med.) laxante
laxity ['læksɪtɪ] *s* laxitud, flojedad; descuido, negligencia
lay [le] *s* disposición, situación, orientación; trama (*de un cable o cuerda*); lay (*poema, canción*); *adj* seglar, lego; lego, profano (*que carece de conocimientos en una materia*) ‖ *pret de* **lie** ‖ (*pret & pp:* **laid**) *va* poner, colocar; dejar; acostar en el suelo, dejar en el suelo; tender (*un cable*); echar (*cimientos; la culpa*); situar (*la acción de un drama*); preparar (*el fuego*); asentar (*el polvo; una vía*); poner (*huevos la gallina; la mesa una criada*); formar, proyectar, trazar (*planes*); conjurar (*un fantasma*); alisar (*la lanilla de una tela*); apostar (*dinero*); hacer (*una apuesta*); imponer (*castigos, penas, etc.*); presentar (*reclamaciones*); atribuir (*responsabilidades*); conjurar, exorcizar (*un aparecido*); (naut.) colchar o corchar (*las filásticas de un cordón o los cordones de un cabo*); **to be laid in** ser en, p.ej., **the scene is laid in New York** la escena es en Nueva York; **to lay aside, away** o **by** echar a un lado; ahorrar; **to lay bare** poner al descubierto; **to lay down** afirmar, declarar; dar (*la vida*); guardar, reservar; hacer (*una apuesta*); rendir, deponer (*las armas*); **to lay in** proveerse de, guardar, ahorrar; **to lay low** abatir, derribar; poner fuera de combate, obligar a guardar cama; matar; **to lay off** poner a un lado; despedir (*a obreros*); trazar, marcar (*en el suelo*); **to lay on** descargar (*golpes*); aplicar; distribuir (*agua, gas, etc.*); cobrar (*carnes*); **to lay oneself out** (coll.) hacer un gran esfuerzo; **to lay open** descubrir, revelar; exponer (*p.ej., a un riesgo o peligro*); **to lay out** tender, extender; jalonar; marcar (*una tarea, un trabajo*); disponer, proyectar; gastar; amortajar (*a un difunto*); **to lay over** aplazar; (slang) aventajar, superar; **to lay up** ahorrar; obligar a guardar cama; (naut.) desarmar ‖ *vn* poner (*las gallinas*); apostar; **to lay about** dar palos de ciego; **to lay down** (slang) aflojar, cejar; **to lay for** (coll.) acechar; **to lay off** (slang) parar, cesar; (slang) dejar de trabajar; (slang) dejar de molestar; **to lay on** dar palos de ciego; **to lay over** detenerse durante un viaje; **to lay to** (naut.) estar parado en la dirección del viento
lay brother *s* donado, lego
lay days *spl* (naut.) días de estadía, días de demora
layer ['leər] *s* gallina ponedora; ['leər] o [lɛr] *s* capa, camada; (geol.) capa, estrato; (hort.) acodo, codadura; *va* (hort.) acodar
layerage ['leərɪdʒ] *s* (hort.) acodadura
layer cake *s* bizcocho de varias camadas
layette [le'ɛt] *s* canastilla (*para el niño que ha de nacer*)
lay figure *s* maniquí; (fig.) maniquí
laying ['leɪŋ] *s* colocación; postura (*de huevos*); tendido (*p.ej., de un cable*); capa; primera capa (*de un enlucido*)
laying on of hands *s* (eccl.) imposición de manos
laying top *s* galapo (*usado para formar maromas*)
layman ['lemən] *s* (*pl:* **-men**) seglar, lego; lego, profano (*persona que carece de conocimientos en una materia*)
layoff ['le,ɔf] o ['le,ɑf] *s* despido (*de obreros*); paro forzoso
lay of the land *s* configuración del terreno; (fig.) cariz que van tomando las cosas
layout ['le,aut] *s* disposición, arreglo; trazado; equipo; juego (*de herramientas, instrumentos, etc.*); conjunto de cosas exhibidas; (slang) banquete, festín
layover ['le,ovər] *s* parada intermedia
lay sister *s* donada
lazar ['læzər] *s* (archaic) leproso; (archaic) mendigo enfermo
lazaret o **lazarette** [,læzə'rɛt] *s* var. de **lazaretto**
lazaretto [,læzə'rɛto] *s* (*pl:* **-tos**) lazareto; (naut.) despensa
Lazarus ['læzərəs] *s* Lázaro
laze [lez] *vn* darse al ocio, holgazanear
lazulite ['læzjəlaɪt] *s* (mineral.) lazulita
lazy ['lezɪ] *adj* (*comp:* **-zier;** *super:* **-ziest**) perezoso
lazybones ['lezɪ,bonz] *s* perezoso; **to be a lazybones** tener los huesos cansados
lb. abr. de **pound** o **pounds**
lbs. abr. de **pounds**
l.c. abr. de **lower case** y **loco citato** (Lat.) **in the place cited**
l.c.m. o **L.C.M.** abr. de **least common multiple**
Ld. abr. de **Lord**
lea [li] *s* prado

leach [litʃ] *s* lixiviador; *va* lixiviar; mojar; *vn* lixiviarse
leachy [ˈlitʃɪ] *adj* poroso
lead [lɛd] *s* (chem.) plomo; plomo (*pedazo de plomo; plomada de albañil; bala*); mina (*del lapicero*); (naut.) escandallo; (print.) interlínea, regleta; **leads** *spl* hojas de plomo; armaduras de plomo (*de las vidrieras*) ‖ *adj* de plomo ‖ (*pret & pp:* **leaded**) *va* emplomar; vidriar con esmalte de plomo; (print.) interlinear, regletear ‖ [lid] *s* conducta, dirección, guía; conductor, guía; ejemplo (*de otra persona*); sugestión, indicación (*con la que se guía a otra persona*); delantera, primer lugar; ventaja (*p.ej., en una carrera*); salida (*en los naipes*); traílla; pasadizo libre (*por entre masas de hielo flotante*); primer párrafo (*de un artículo de periódico*); (box.) golpe inicial (*de la ofensiva*); (elec.) conductor; (elec. & mach.) avance; (min.) filón, veta; (rad.) alambre de entrada; (theat.) papel principal; (theat.) primer galán; (theat.) dama; **to take the lead** tomar la delantera ‖ (*pret & pp:* **led**) *va* conducir, llevar; acaudillar, mandar; dirigir (*p.ej., una orquesta*); estar a la cabeza de; llevar (*buena o mala vida*); pasar (*un hilo, soga, etc.*); hacer pasar (*agua, vapor*); influenciar; dar comienzo a; salir con (*cierto naipe*); (elec. & mach.) avanzar, adelantar; **to lead to** + *inf* llevar (*a alguien*) a + *inf* ‖ *vn* enseñar el camino, ir delante; ser el primero, ser el más importante; tener el mando; cabestrear (*seguir sin repugnancia la bestia al que la lleva del cabestro*); (box.) tomar la ofensiva; (cards) salir, ser mano; (mus.) llevar la batuta; **to lead off** comenzar, empezar; **to lead on** enseñar el camino; seguir adelante; **to lead up to** conducir a
lead acetate [lɛd] *s* (chem.) acetato de plomo
lead acid cell [lɛd] *s* (elec.) acumulador de plomo-ácido
lead-burn [ˈlɛd,bʌrn] *va* soldar (*dos piezas de plomo*) con soldadura autógena
lead-burning [ˈlɛd,bʌrnɪŋ] *s* soldadura autógena del plomo
leaden [ˈlɛdən] *adj* de plomo; plúmbeo (*que pesa como el plomo*); plomizo (*de color de plomo*); lóbrego, triste
leaden-eyed [ˈlɛdən,aɪd] *adj* de ojos dormidos
leader [ˈlidər] *s* caudillo, jefe, líder; cabecilla, instigador; guión; guía (*caballo*); director (*p.ej., de una orquesta*); primer violín; sotileza (*parte fina del aparejo de pescar*); artículo que se ofrece a un precio muy vientajoso para despertar el interés de los compradores; artículo de fondo; (min.) guía; **leaders** *spl* (print.) puntos suspensivos
leadership [ˈlidərʃɪp] *s* caudillaje, dirección, jefatura, mando; dotes de mando
lead glance [lɛd] *s* (mineral.) galena
leading [ˈlidɪŋ] *adj* director; primero, principal; preeminente; *s* dirección; [ˈlɛdɪŋ] *s* hojas o tiras de plomo; armaduras de plomo (*de las vidrieras*); (print.) regletas
leading article *s* artículo de fondo
leading block *s* retorno
leading current *s* (elec.) corriente avanzada
leading edge *s* (aer.) borde de entrada o de ataque
leading lady *s* (theat.) dama, primera actriz
leading man *s* (theat.) primer galán, primer actor
leading question *s* pregunta capciosa, pregunta tendenciosa
leading strings *spl* andadores (*para sostener al niño cuando aprende a andar*)
lead-in wire [ˈlid,ɪn] *s* (rad.) alambre de entrada, bajada de antena
lead pencil [lɛd] *s* lápiz (*de grafito*)
lead poisoning [lɛd] *s* (path.) envenenamiento plúmbico
lead tetraethyl [lɛd] *s* var. de **tetraethyl lead**
leadwort [ˈlɛd,wʌrt] *s* (bot.) belesa, dentelaria, hierba del cáncer
leaf [lif] *s* (*pl:* **leaves**) hoja (*de planta, libro, mesa, muelle, puerta plegadiza, etc.; pétalo de flor*); pámpano (*de vid*); trampilla (*hoja de mesa que se levanta como trampa*); **to shake like a leaf** temblar como un azogado; **to take a leaf from the book of** seguir el ejemplo de; **to turn over a new leaf** hacer libro nuevo (*corregir sus vicios*); *va* hojear; *vn* echar hojas; **to leaf through** trashojar
leafage [ˈlifɪdʒ] *s* follaje
leaf bud *s* (bot.) yema
leaf insect *s* (ent.) hojaseca
leafless [ˈliflɪs] *adj* deshojado
leaflet [ˈliflɪt] *s* hojuela, hojilla; hoja suelta, hoja volante
leaf mold *s* (agr.) abono verde
leaf roller *s* (ent.) oruga de arrolladora o torcedora
leaf sewer [ˈsoər] *s* (ent.) arrolladora, torcedora
leafstalk [ˈlif,stɔk] *s* (bot.) pecíolo, rabillo (*de la hoja*)
leafy [ˈlifɪ] *adj* (*comp:* **-ier**; *super:* **-iest**) hojoso, hojudo, frondoso
league [lig] *s* legua (*medida*); liga, sociedad; **in league** asociado; **the League** la Sociedad de las Naciones; *va* asociar; *vn* asociarse, ligarse
League of Nations *s* Sociedad de las Naciones
leaguer [ˈligər] *s* miembro de una liga; (archaic) cerco, sitio; (archaic) real (*campamento de un ejército*); *va* (archaic) cercar, sitiar
Leah [ˈliə] *s* (Bib.) Lía
leak [lik] *s* gotera (*en un techo*); agua, vía de agua (*en un buque*); agujero (*por donde se escapa el agua, gas, vapor*); salida, escape, fuga (*de agua, gas, electricidad, vapor*); filtración (*de dinero*); **to spring a leak** tener un escape; (naut.) empezar a hacer agua; *va* dejar salir, dejar escapar (*el agua, gas, vapor*); *vn* tener fugas; rezumarse (*el agua*); salirse, escaparse (*el agua, gas, vapor*); filtrarse (*dinero*); (naut.) hacer agua; **to leak out** trascender (*un hecho que estaba oculto*); rezumarse (*una especie*)
leakage [ˈlikɪdʒ] *s* salida, escape, fuga; (com.) merma; (elec.) dispersión
leakage conductance *s* (elec.) perditancia
leaky [ˈlikɪ] *adj* (*comp:* **-ier**; *super:* **-iest**) llovedizo (*techo*); agujereado, roto; (naut.) que hace agua; (coll.) indiscreto
lean [lin] *s* molla, carne mollar o magra; inclinación; *adj* mollar, magro; flaco; malo, improductivo; de carestía, p.ej., **lean years** años de carestía; pobre (*mezcla de gasolina*); (*pret & pp:* **leaned** o **leant**) *va* inclinar, ladear, arrimar; *vn* inclinarse, ladearse, arrimarse; (fig.) inclinarse, propender, tender; **to lean against** apoyarse a, arrimarse a, estar arrimado a; **to lean back** retreparse, recostarse; **to lean on** apoyarse en; acodarse sobre; depender de, necesitar el apoyo de; **to lean out (of)** asomarse (a); **to lean over backward** (coll.) extremar la imparcialidad; **to lean toward** inclinarse a o hacia
Leander [lɪˈændər] *s* (myth.) Leandro
leaning [ˈlinɪŋ] *s* inclinación; (fig.) inclinación, propensión, tendencia; *adj* inclinado
Leaning Tower *s* Torre inclinada
leanness [ˈlinnɪs] *s* magrez; flaqueza; improductividad, carestía; pobreza
leant [lɛnt] *pret & pp de* **lean**
lean-to [ˈlin,tu] *adj* colgadizo; *s* (*pl:* **-tos**) colgadizo
leap [lip] *s* salto; **by leaps and bounds** con gran rapidez; **leap in the dark** salto a ciegas, salto en vago; (*pret & pp:* **leaped** o **leapt**) *va* saltar; *vn* saltar; dar un salto (*el corazón de uno*)
leap day *s* día intercalar (*en el año bisiesto y en cualquier calendario*)
leapfrog [ˈlip,frɑg] o [ˈlip,frɔg] *s* fil derecho, juego del salto; **to play leapfrog** jugar a la una la mula
leapt [lɛpt] o [lipt] *pret & pp de* **leap**
leap year *s* año bisiesto
learn [lʌrn] (*pret & pp:* **learned** o **learnt**) *va* aprender; saber (*una noticia*); oír decir; *vn* aprender; **to learn of** saber, tener noticia de; **to learn to** + *inf* aprender a + *inf*
learned [ˈlʌrnɪd] *adj* docto, erudito; (philol.) docto, culto
learned journal *s* publicación periódica científica
learned society *s* sociedad de eruditos
learned word *s* cultismo, voz culta
learned world *s* mundo de la erudición

learner ['lʌrnər] *s* aprendiz, principiante
learning ['lʌrnɪŋ] *s* aprendizaje; erudición
learnt [lʌrnt] *pret & pp de* **learn**
lease [lis] *s* arrendamiento; **to give a new lease on life to** renovar completamente, poner completamente bueno; volver a hacer feliz; *va* arrendar; *vn* arrendarse
leasehold ['lis,hold] *s* arrendamiento; bienes raíces arrendados
leash [liʃ] *s* traílla; pihuela (*para asegurar los pies de los halcones*); lizo; grupo de tres; **to hold in leash** dominar, reprimir; *va* atraillar
least [list] *adj* (el) menor, mínimo, más pequeño; *adv* menos; *s* (lo) menos, p.ej., **that is the least you can do** eso es lo menos que puede Vd. hacer; (el) menor; **at least** o **at the least** al menos, a lo menos o por lo menos; **not in the least** de ninguna manera
least common multiple *s* (math.) mínimo común múltiplo
leastways ['list,wez] *adv* (coll.) var. de **leastwise**
leastwise ['list,waɪz] *adv* por lo menos, a lo menos; de todos modos
leather ['lɛðər] *s* cuero; *adj* de cuero; *va* forrar o guarnecer con cuero; (coll.) zurrar
leatherback ['lɛðər,bæk] *s* (zool.) laúd
leatherette [,lɛðə'rɛt] *s* cuero artificial, imitación cuero
leather goods *spl* artículos de cuero
leathern ['lɛðərn] *adj* de cuero; como de cuero
leatherneck ['lɛðər,nɛk] *s* (slang) soldado de infantería de marina de los EE.UU.
leatheroid ['lɛðərɔɪd] *s* cuero sintético
leathery ['lɛðərɪ] *adj* correoso
leave [liv] *s* permiso; licencia; despedida; **by your leave** con permiso de Vd.; **on leave** de permiso, con licencia; **to give leave to** dar licencia a; **to take leave (of)** despedirse (de) ‖ (*pret & pp:* **left**) *va* dejar; salir de; legar (*por testamento*); **to be left** quedarse; quedar, p.ej., **the letter was left unanswered** la carta quedó sin contestar; **to leave alone** dejar en paz, dejar tranquilo; no meterse con; no probar (*el vino*); **to leave off** dejar, cesar; no ponerse (*una prenda de vestir*); **to leave out** omitir; **to leave things as they are** dejarlo como está; **to leave to** dejar al criterio o elección de; **leave it to me!** ¡déjeme Vd. a mí! ‖ *vn* irse, marcharse; salir (*un tren, vapor, avión, etc.*); **to leave off** cesar, desistir ‖ (*pret & pp:* **leaved**) *vn* echar hojas
leaven ['lɛvən] *s* levadura; (fig.) mezcla, influencia, fuerza; *va* leudar; (fig.) penetrar, transformar, corromper
leavening ['lɛvənɪŋ] *s* levadura
leave of absence *s* licencia
leave-taking ['liv,tekɪŋ] *s* despedida
leavings ['livɪŋz] *spl* desperdicios, sobras; residuos
Lebanese [,lɛbə'niz] *adj* libanés; *s* (*pl:* **-nese**) libanés
Lebanon ['lɛbənən] *s* el Líbano, la República del Líbano
Lebanon Mountains, the el Líbano
Lebensraum ['lebəns,raum] *s* espacio vital (*de una nación*)
lecher ['lɛtʃər] *s* libertino, lujurioso
lecherous ['lɛtʃərəs] *adj* lascivo, lujurioso
lechery ['lɛtʃərɪ] *s* lascivia, lujuria
lecithin ['lɛsɪθɪn] *s* (biochem.) lecitina
lectern ['lɛktərn] *s* atril
lection ['lɛkʃən] *s* lección; (eccl.) lección
lectionary ['lɛkʃə,nɛrɪ] *s* (*pl:* **-ies**) (eccl.) leccionario
lector ['lɛktər] *s* lector
lecture ['lɛktʃər] *s* conferencia; sermoneo; *va* instruir por medio de conferencias; sermonear; *vn* dar una conferencia, dar conferencias
lecturer ['lɛktʃərər] *s* conferenciante
led [lɛd] *pret & pp de* **lead**
Leda ['lidə] *s* (myth.) Leda
ledge [lɛdʒ] *s* repisa; retallo (*en el paramento de un muro*); tongada; cama de roca; arrecife
ledger ['lɛdʒər] *s* libro mayor; losa, lápida; solera
ledger line *s* (mus.) línea suplementaria
lee [li] (naut.) socaire (*abrigo*); (naut.) sotavento; **lees** *spl* heces; *adj* (naut.) de sotavento
leeboard ['li,bord] *s* (naut.) orza de deriva
leech [litʃ] *s* (zool.) sanguijuela; (fig.) sanguijuela (*persona*); (naut.) grátil; (naut.) orilla de popa (*de una cangreja*); (med.) sanguijuela artificial; (archaic) médico; *va* (archaic) curar
leek [lik] *s* (bot.) puerro
leer [lɪr] *s* mirada de reojo (*con intención maligna o lujuriosa*); *va* tentar con mirada de reojo; *vn* echar una mirada o miradas de reojo (*con intención maligna o lujuriosa*)
leery ['lɪrɪ] *adj* (slang) astuto, entendido; (slang) suspicaz, receloso
lee shore *s* costa de sotavento
leeward ['luərd] o ['liwərd] *s* (naut.) sotavento; *adv* (naut.) a sotavento
Leeward Islands ['liwərd] *spl* islas de Sotavento
leeway ['li,we] *s* (naut.) deriva; (aer.) abatimiento; (coll.) libertad de acción, tiempo o dinero de sobra, sitio en que moverse
left [lɛft] *adj* izquierdo; (pol.) de izquierda; *s* izquierda (*mano izquierda*); (box.) zurdazo; (pol.) izquierda; **on** o **to the left** a o por la izquierda; *pret & pp de* **leave**
left field *s* (baseball) jardín izquierdo
left-hand ['lɛft,hænd] *adj* izquierdo; de, con o para la mano izquierda; de movimiento, funcionamiento, etc. hacia la izquierda
left-hand drive *s* (aut.) conducción a izquierda
left-handed ['lɛft'hændɪd] *adj* zurdo; de la mano izquierda; para zurdos; torpe, desmañado; insincero, malicioso; irónico; (mach.) zurdo (*p.ej., tornillo*)
left-handed marriage *s* matrimonio de la mano izquierda
leftish ['lɛftɪʃ] *adj* izquierdizante
leftism ['lɛftɪzəm] *s* izquierdismo
leftist ['lɛftɪst] *adj & s* izquierdista
left jab *s* (box.) inverso de izquierda
leftover ['lɛft,ovər] *adj & s* sobrante; **leftovers** *spl* sobras
left wing *s* ala izquierda (*de un ejército*); (pol.) izquierda
left-wing ['lɛft,wɪŋ] *adj* izquierdista
left-winger ['lɛft,wɪŋər] *s* (coll.) izquierdista
leg. abr. de **legal, legislative** y **legislature**
leg [lɛg] *s* pierna (*de hombre o animal*); pata (*de animal, mesa, silla, etc.*); muslo (*de ave cocida*); caña (*de bota o de media*); pernera (*de pantalón*); pierna (*de un compás de dibujo*); etapa, trecho (*p.ej., de un viaje*); (elec.) circuito derivado; (geom.) cateto; **to be on one's last legs** andar de capa caída; estar al cabo, estar en las últimas; **to give a leg up** ayudar a subir; **to not have a leg to stand on** (coll.) no tener disculpa alguna; no poder aducir razón alguna en defensa de su opinión; **to pull one's leg** (coll.) tomar el pelo a, engañarle a uno; **to shake a leg** (coll.) darse prisa; (coll.) bailar; **to stretch one's legs** estirar o extender las piernas, dar un paseíto; (*pret & pp:* **legged**; *ger:* **legging**) *va* hacer con las piernas; **to leg it** (coll.) caminar, ir a pie, correr; *vn* (coll.) caminar, ir a pie, correr
legacy ['lɛgəsɪ] *s* (*pl:* **-cies**) legado
legal ['ligəl] *adj* legal
legalism ['ligəlɪzəm] *s* rigorismo
legalist ['ligəlɪst] *s* rigorista; legista, legisperito
legalistic [,ligə'lɪstɪk] *adj* legalista
legality [lɪ'gælɪtɪ] *s* (*pl:* **-ties**) legalidad
legalization [,ligəlɪ'zeʃən] *s* legalización
legalize ['ligəlaɪz] *va* legalizar
legally ['ligəlɪ] *adv* legalmente
legal tender *s* curso legal, moneda de curso legal
legate ['lɛgɪt] *s* legado
legatee [,lɛgə'ti] *s* (law) legatario
legation [lɪ'geʃən] *s* legación
leg bail *s* (slang) fuga, evasión; **to give leg bail** (slang) fugarse, escaparse
legend ['lɛdʒənd] *s* leyenda
legendary ['lɛdʒən,dɛrɪ] *adj* legendario
legerdemain [,lɛdʒərdɪ'men] *s* juego de manos, prestidigitación; trapacería
leger line ['lɛdʒər] *s* var. de **ledger line**
legged [lɛgd] o ['lɛgɪd] *adj* que tiene piernas o patas
legging ['lɛgɪŋ] *s* polaina
leggy ['lɛgɪ] *adj* zanquilargo
leghorn ['lɛghɔrn] o ['lɛgərn] *s* sombrero de pa-

ja de Italia; (*cap.*) *s* gallina Leghorn; [ˈlɛghɔrn] *s* Liorna (*ciudad*)
legibility [ˌlɛdʒɪˈbɪlɪtɪ] *s* legibilidad
legible [ˈlɛdʒɪbəl] *adj* legible
legion [ˈlidʒən] *s* legión; **to be legion** constituir legión
legionary [ˈlidʒəˌnɛrɪ] *adj* legionario; *s* (*pl:* **-ies**) legionario
legionnaire [ˌlidʒəˈnɛr] *s* legionario
Legion of Honor *s* legión de Honor
legislate [ˈlɛdʒɪslet] *va* obligar mediante legislación, hacer o llevar a cabo mediante legislación; *vn* legislar
legislation [ˌlɛdʒɪsˈleʃən] *s* legislación
legislative [ˈlɛdʒɪsˌletɪv] *adj* legislativo
legislator [ˈlɛdʒɪsˌletər] *s* legislador
legislature [ˈlɛdʒɪsˌletʃər] *s* cuerpo legislativo, asamblea legislativa
legitim [ˈlɛdʒɪtɪm] *s* (law) legítima
legitimacy [lɪˈdʒɪtɪməsɪ] *s* legitimidad
legitimate [lɪˈdʒɪtɪmɪt] *adj* legítimo; [lɪˈdʒɪtɪmet] *va* legitimar
legitimate drama *s* teatro serio (*a distinción del cine o el melodrama*)
legitimation [lɪˌdʒɪtɪˈmeʃən] *s* legitimación
legitimism [lɪˈdʒɪtɪmɪzəm] *s* legitimismo
legitimist [lɪˈdʒɪtɪmɪst] *adj & s* legitimista
legitimize [lɪˈdʒɪtɪmaɪz] *va* legitimar
legman [ˈlɛgˌmæn] *s* (*pl:* **-men**) (coll.) repórter que anda de un lugar a otro en busca de noticias; (coll.) subordinado que hace mandados y otras tareas
leg of lamb *s* pierna de cordero
leg of mutton *s* pierna de carnero
leg-of-mutton sail [ˈlɛgəvˈmʌtən] *s* (naut.) vela triangular
leg-of-mutton sleeve *s* manga de jamón
legume [ˈlɛgjum] o [lɪˈgjum] *s* (bot.) legumbre (*planta y fruto como garbanzo, haba, etc.*); vaina (*de legumbre*)
legumin [lɪˈgjumɪn] *s* (biochem.) legumina
leguminous [lɪˈgjumɪnəs] *adj* leguminoso
legwork [ˈlɛgˌwʌrk] *s* (coll.) el mucho caminar, como parte esencial de un trabajo o empleo (*especialmente de un repórter o de alguien al servicio de un repórter*)
lehua [leˈhuɑ] *s* (bot.) lehua (*planta y flor de Metrosideros polymorpha*)
lei [ˈle·ɪ] *s* guirnalda hawaiana
leishmaniasis [ˌliʃməˈnaɪəsɪs] o **leishmaniosis** [liʃˌmenɪˈosɪs] *s* (path.) leishmaniosis
leisure [ˈliʒər] o [ˈlɛʒər] *s* ocio, desocupación; **at leisure** libre, desocupado; **at one's leisure** a la conveniencia de uno; **in one's leisure** en sus ratos de ocio, en sus ratos libres; *adj* de ocio; acomodado, desocupado
leisure classes *s* gente acomodada
leisured [ˈliʒərd] o [ˈlɛʒərd] *adj* acomodado, desocupado; lento, pausado, deliberado
leisure hours *spl* horas de ocio, ratos perdidos
leisurely [ˈliʒərlɪ] o [ˈlɛʒərlɪ] *adj* lento, pausado, deliberado; *adv* despacio, sin prisa
leitmotif o **leitmotiv** [ˈlaɪtmoˌtif] *s* (mus.) leitmotiv, tema o motivo conductor
lemming [ˈlɛmɪŋ] *s* (zool.) conejo de Noruega
lemnaceous [lɛmˈneʃəs] *adj* (bot.) lemnáceo
lemniscate [lɛmˈnɪsket] *s* (geom.) lemniscata
lemniscus [lɛmˈnɪskəs] *s* (*pl:* **-nisci** [ˈnɪsaɪ]) lemnisco; (anat.) lemnisco
lemon [ˈlɛmən] *s* (bot.) limonero o limón (*árbol*); limón (*fruto*); (slang) maula; *adj* de limón; limonado (*de color de limón*)
lemonade [ˌlɛmənˈed] *s* limonada
lemon squeezer *s* exprimidor de limón
lemon verbena *s* (bot.) luisa, reina luisa
lemur [ˈlimər] *s* (zool.) lémur; **lemures** [ˈlɛmjəriz] *spl* (myth.) lémures
lend [lɛnd] (*pret & pp:* **lent**) *va* prestar; dar (*p.ej., color*); añadir, aumentar (*p.ej., el interés de un relato*); **to lend itself** o **to lend oneself** prestarse
lending library *s* biblioteca de préstamo
Lend-Lease Act [ˈlɛndˈlis] *s* ley de préstamos y arriendos
length [lɛŋθ] *s* largo, largura; (racing) cuerpo; **at full length** tendido cuan largo es; **at length** por fin, finalmente; largamente, extensamente; **through the length and breadth of the land** hasta los últimos rincones del país; **to go to any length** hacer cuanto esté de su parte, hacer todo lo posible; **to keep at arm's length** mantener a distancia, no querer intimar con; mantenerse a distancia; **to measure one's length** medir el suelo, caer (*uno*) cuan largo es
lengthen [ˈlɛŋθən] *va* alargar; *vn* alargarse
lengthways [ˈlɛŋθwez] o **lengthwise** [ˈlɛŋθwaɪz] *adj* longitudinal; *adv* longitudinalmente
lengthy [ˈlɛŋθɪ] *adj* (*comp:* **-ier**; *super:* **-iest**) largo, prolongado; difuso, prolijo
lenience [ˈlinɪəns] o **leniency** [ˈlinɪənsɪ] *s* clemencia, indulgencia, lenitud
lenient [ˈlinɪənt] *adj* clemente, indulgente; (archaic) lenitivo
Leningrad [ˈlɛnɪngræd] *s* Leningrado
Leninism [ˈlɛnɪnɪzəm] *s* leninismo
Leninist [ˈlɛnɪnɪst] o **Leninite** [ˈlɛnɪnaɪt] *adj & s* leninista
lenitive [ˈlɛnɪtɪv] *adj & s* lenitivo; laxante
lenity [ˈlɛnɪtɪ] *s* (*pl:* **-ties**) lenidad
lens [lɛnz] *s* (opt. & geol.) lente; (anat.) cristalino
Lent [lɛnt] *s* cuaresma; (*l.c.*) *pret & pp de* **lend**
Lenten o **lenten** [ˈlɛntən] *adj* cuaresmal
lenticel [ˈlɛntɪsɛl] *s* (bot.) lentejuela
lenticular [lɛnˈtɪkjələr] *adj* lenticular
lentil [ˈlɛntəl] *s* (bot.) lenteja (*planta y semilla*)
l'envoi o **l'envoy** [lɛnˈvɔɪ] *s* tornada, despedida (*a una composición poética*); epílogo en prosa
Leo [ˈlio] *s* León (*nombre de varón*); (astr.) Leo o León
Leonard [ˈlɛnərd] *s* Leonardo
Leonese [ˌliəˈniz] *adj* leonés; *s* (*pl:* **-nese**) leonés
Leonid [ˈliənɪd] *s* (astr.) leónida
Leonidas [lɪˈɑnɪdəs] *s* Leónidas
leonine [ˈliənaɪn] *adj* leonino
Leonora [ˌliəˈnorə] o **Leonore** [ˈliənor] *s* Leonor
leontiasis [ˌliɑnˈtaɪəsɪs] *s* (path.) leontíasis, leonina
leopard [ˈlɛpərd] *s* (zool.) leopardo; (zool.) jaguar
leopardess [ˈlɛpərdɪs] *s* leopardo hembra
Leopold [ˈliəpold] *s* Leopoldo
leotard [ˈliətɑrd] *s* traje muy ajustado (*de los acróbatas, volatineros y bailadores*)
leper [ˈlɛpər] *s* leproso
lepidolite [lɪˈpɪdolaɪt] o [ˈlɛpɪdolaɪt] *s* (miner-al.) lepidolita
lepidopteron [ˌlɛpɪˈdɑptərɑn] *s* (*pl:* **-a** [ə]) (ent.) lepidóptero
lepidopterous [ˌlɛpɪˈdɑptərəs] *adj* (ent.) lepidóptero
lepidosiren [ˌlɛpɪdoˈsaɪrən] *s* (ichth.) lepidosirena
Lepidus [ˈlɛpɪdəs] *s* Lépido
leporine [ˈlɛpəraɪn] o [ˈlɛpərɪn] *adj* leporino
leprechaun [ˈlɛprəkɔn] *s* (Irish) duende, gnomo
leprosarium [ˌlɛprəˈsɛrɪəm] *s* leprosería
leprosy [ˈlɛprəsɪ] *s* (path.) lepra
leprous [ˈlɛprəs] *adj* leproso; escamoso
leptophyllous [ˌlɛptoˈfɪləs] *adj* (bot.) leptofilo
leptorrhine [ˈlɛptərɪn] *adj* (anthrop.) leptorrino
Lesbian [ˈlɛzbɪən] *adj* lesbiano o lesbio; *s* lesbiano, lesbio; lesbia (*mujer homosexual*)
Lesbianism [ˈlɛzbɪənɪzəm] *s* lesbianismo
lese majesty [ˈlizˈmædʒɪstɪ] *s* delito o crimen de lesa majestad
lesion [ˈliʒən] *s* lesión; (path. & law) lesión
less [lɛs] *adj* menor; *adv* menos; **at less than** en menos que; **the less . . . the less** (o **the more**) mientras menos . . . menos (o más), p.ej., **the less he works the less he earns** mientras menos trabaja menos gana; **less and less** cada vez menos; **less than** menos que; menos de lo que + *verb*; menos de + *numeral*; *prep & s* menos
lessee [lɛsˈi] *s* arrendatario
lessen [ˈlɛsən] *va* disminuir, reducir a menos; quitar importancia a, hacer poco caso de; *vn* disminuirse; amainar (*el viento*)
lesser [ˈlɛsər] *adj* menor, más pequeño
Lesser Antilles *spl* Antillas Menores
lesser bindweed *s* (bot.) correhuela
lesser yellowlegs *s* (orn.) chorlo menor de

patas amarillas, chorlito pardo mayor o patiamarilla
lesson [ˈlɛsən] *s* lección; *va* aleccionar; sermonear, reprender
lessor [ˈlɛsɔr] o [lɛˈsɔr] *s* arrendador
lest [lɛst] *conj* no sea que, para que no, de miedo que
let [lɛt] *s* estorbo, obstáculo; (tennis) let (*servicio en que la pelota roza la red y cae dentro de las líneas límites*); **without let or hindrance** sin estorbo ni obstáculo ‖ (*pret & pp:* **let;** *ger:* **letting**) *va* dejar, permitir; dejar pasar; alquilar, arrendar; sacar (*sangre a un enfermo*); **to be let off** salir bien librado; **to let** se alquila, p.ej., **room to let** se alquila un cuarto; **to let** + *inf* dejar o permitir + *inf;* **to let alone** dejar en paz, dejar tranquilo; **to let be** no meterse con; no tocar; dejar en paz; **to let by** dejar pasar; **to let down** bajar; dejar bajar; dejar caer; desilusionar, traicionar, humillar; dejar plantado, dejar colgado o chasqueado; **to let fly** disparar; (fig.) disparar, soltar (*palabras injuriosas*); **to let go** soltar, desasirse de; dejar, vender; **to let good enough alone** bueno está lo bueno; **to let in** dejar entrar, dejar entrar en; **to let it go at that** no hacer o decir nada más; **to let know** hacer saber, enterar; **to let loose** soltar; **to let off** disparar; (coll.) soltar, dejar libre; **to let on** (coll.) dar a entender; **to let oneself go** entregarse a sus deseos o pasiones; emplear todas sus fuerzas o energías; **to let out** hacer saber, revelar, publicar; dejar salir; dar, soltar (*p.ej., más cuerda*); dar (*un grito*); agrandar, ensanchar (*un vestido que aprieta*); dar en arrendamiento; (coll.) despedir; **to let through** dejar pasar, dejar pasar por; **to let up** dejar subir; dejar incorporarse; dejar levantarse; **let** + *inf* que + *subj,* p.ej., **let him do it if he wants to** que lo haga si quiere; **let alone** sin mencionar; y mucho menos, p.ej., **he cannot speak his own language, let alone a foreign language** no puede hablar su propio idioma y mucho menos un idioma extranjero; **let us** + *inf* vamos a + *inf,* p.ej., **let us eat** vamos a comer, comamos ‖ *vn* alquilarse, arrendarse; **to let down** (coll.) ir más despacio; **to let fly** (slang) desatarse en improperios; **to let go** soltar, desasirse; **to let go of** soltar, desasirse de; **to let on** (coll.) fingir; **to let out** (coll.) despedirse, cerrarse (*p.ej., la escuela*); **to let up** (coll.) cesar, desistir; (coll.) disminuir, moderarse; **to let up on** largar, aflojar
letdown [ˈlɛtˌdaʊn] *s* aflojamiento, relajamiento; desilusión, chasco; humillación
lethal [ˈliθəl] *adj* letal
lethargic [lɪˈθɑrdʒɪk] *adj* letárgico
lethargy [ˈlɛθərdʒɪ] *s* (*pl:* **-gies**) letargo
Lethe [ˈliθɪ] *s* (myth.) Lete o Leteo (*río*); (fig.) olvido
Lethean [lɪˈθiən] *adj* leteo
let's [lɛts] contracción de **let us**
Lett [lɛt] *s* letón (*persona e idioma*)
letter [ˈlɛtər] *s* carta; letra (*del alfabeto*); patente (*para el goce de un empleo o privilegio*); (fig.) letra (*sentido material*); **letters** *spl* letras (*literatura*); **to the letter** a la letra, al pie de la letra; *va* rotular, estampar o marcar con letras
letter box *s* buzón
letter carrier *s* cartero
letter drop *s* buzón (*abertura por donde se echan las cartas*)
lettered [ˈlɛtərd] *adj* rotulado, marcado con letras; que sabe leer y escribir; letrado (*literato*)
letter file *s* guardacartas
letterhead [ˈlɛtərˌhɛd] *s* membrete; memorándum (*papel con membrete*)
lettering [ˈlɛtərɪŋ] *s* inscripción, letras
letter of credit *s* (com.) carta orden de crédito, carta de crédito
letter paper *s* papel de cartas
letter-perfect [ˈlɛtərˈpʌrfɪkt] *adj* que tiene bien aprendido su papel o su lección; exacto, correcto
letter press *s* prensa de copiar cartas
letterpress [ˈlɛtərˌprɛs] *s* (print.) texto impreso (*a distinción de los grabados, etc.*)
letter scales *spl* pesacartas
letters of marque *spl* (naut.) patente de corso o carta de marca
letters patent *ssg & spl* patente de privilegio
Lettish [ˈlɛtɪʃ] *adj* letón; *s* letón (*idioma*)
lettre de cachet [ˈlɛtrə də kɑˈʃɛ] *s* (hist.) carta del rey sellada (*que mandaba prisión o destierro*)
lettuce [ˈlɛtɪs] *s* (bot.) lechuga; lechugas (*hojas que se comen en ensalada*)
letup [ˈlɛtˌʌp] *s* (coll.) calma (*p.ej., en el dolor, los negocios*); **without letup** (coll.) sin cesar
leucine [ˈlusin] o [ˈlusɪn] *s* (biochem.) leucina
leucite [ˈlusaɪt] *s* (mineral.) leucita
leuco base [ˈluko] *s* (chem.) leucobase
leucocyte [ˈlukosaɪt] *s* (physiol.) leucocito
leucocythemia [ˌlukosaɪˈθimɪə] *s* (path.) leucocitemia
leucocytosis [ˌlukosaɪˈtosɪs] *s* (path.) leucocitosis
leucoma [luˈkomə] *s* (path.) leucoma
leucomaine [luˈkomən] o [luˈkomən] *s* (biochem.) leucomaína
leucon [ˈlukɑn] *s* (*pl:* **leucones** [luˈkoniz]) (zool.) leucón
leucopenia [ˌlukəˈpinɪə] *s* (path.) leucopenia
leucoplast [ˈlukəplæst] *s* (bot.) leucoplasto
leucorrhea [ˌlukəˈriə] *s* (path.) leucorrea
leukemia [luˈkimɪə] *s* (path.) leucemia
Lev. abr. de **Leviticus**
Levant [lɪˈvænt] *s* Levante; (*l.c.*) *s* tafilete de Levante
Levantine [lɪˈvæntin] o [ˈlɛvəntin] *adj* levantino; *s* levantino; buque de Levante
Levant morocco *s* tafilete de Levante
levee [ˈlɛvɪ] *s* ribero (*para contener las aguas*); desembarcadero; [ˈlɛvɪ] o [lɛˈvi] *s* besamanos; recepción
level [ˈlɛvəl] *s* nivel; terreno llano, llanura; tramo (*de un canal entre dos esclusas*); **to be on the level** obrar sin engaño, decir la pura verdad; ser la pura verdad; **to find its level** o **to find one's level** hallar su propio nivel; *adj* raso, llano; nivelado; a nivel; (coll.) juicioso, sensato; **one's level best** (coll.) lo mejor que uno puede; **level with** al nivel de, a flor de, a ras de; (*pret & pp:* **-eled** o **-elled;** *ger:* **-eling** o **-elling**) *va* nivelar; arrasar, echar por tierra; apuntar (*un arma de fuego*); (fig.) allanar (*dificultades*); *vn* nivelar; apuntar un arma; dirigir la mente; **to level off** (aer.) nivelarse para aterrizar
level crossing *s* (Brit.) paso a nivel
level-headed [ˈlɛvəlˈhɛdɪd] *adj* juicioso, sensato
leveling o **levelling** [ˈlɛvəlɪŋ] *adj* nivelador; *s* nivelación
leveling rod *s* (surv.) jalón de mira
lever [ˈlɛvər] o [ˈlivər] *s* palanca; (mach. & mech.) palanca; *va & vn* apalancar
leverage [ˈlɛvərɪdʒ] o [ˈlivərɪdʒ] *s* palancada; poder de una palanca; influencia, poder, ventaja
leveret [ˈlɛvərɪt] *s* lebratillo
Levi [ˈlivaɪ] *s* (Bib.) Leví
leviathan [lɪˈvaɪəθən] *s* (Bib. & fig.) leviatán; buque muy grande
levigate [ˈlɛvɪget] *va* pulverizar; pulimentar; levigar (*desleír en agua para separar la parte más leve*)
levigation [ˌlɛvɪˈgeʃən] *s* pulverización; pulimento; levigación
levirate [ˈlɛvɪrɪt] o [ˈlivɪrɪt] *s* (hist.) levirato
levitate [ˈlɛvɪtet] *va* elevar y mantener en el aire (*por medios espiritistas*); *vn* elevarse y flotar en el aire
levitation [ˌlɛvɪˈteʃən] *s* levitación
Levite [ˈlivaɪt] *s* (Bib.) levita
Levitical [lɪˈvɪtɪkəl] *adj* levítico
Leviticus [lɪˈvɪtɪkəs] *s* (Bib.) Levítico
levity [ˈlɛvɪtɪ] *s* (*pl:* **-ties**) levedad, ligereza; frivolidad
levoglucose [ˌlivoˈglukos] *s* (chem.) levoglucosa
levorotatory [ˌlivoˈrotəˌtorɪ] *adj* (chem. & opt.) levógiro
levulin [ˈlɛvjəlɪn] *s* (chem.) levulina
levulinic [ˌlɛvjəˈlɪnɪk] *adj* levulínico
levulinic acid *s* (chem.) ácido levulínico
levulose [ˈlɛvjəlos] *s* (chem.) levulosa

levy ['lɛvɪ] *s* (*pl:* **-ies**) recaudación, exacción (*de tributos, impuestos*); dinero recaudado; (mil.) leva, recluta, enganche; (*pret & pp:* **-ied**) *va* recaudar, exigir (*tributos, impuestos*); hacer (*la guerra*); (law) embargar; (mil.) reclutar, enganchar
lewd [lud] *adj* lascivo, lujurioso; obsceno, indecente
lewdness ['ludnɪs] *s* lascivia, lujuria; obscenidad, indecencia
Lewis ['luɪs] *s* Luis
lewisite ['luɪsaɪt] *s* (mil.) lewisita
lexical ['lɛksɪkəl] *adj* léxico
lexicographer [,lɛksɪ'kɑgrəfər] *s* lexicógrafo
lexicographic [,lɛksɪko'græfɪk] o **lexicographical** [,lɛksɪko'græfɪkəl] *adj* lexicográfico
lexicography [,lɛksɪ'kɑgrəfɪ] *s* lexicografía
lexicologic [,lɛksɪkə'lɑdʒɪk] o **lexicological** [,lɛksɪkə'lɑdʒɪkəl] *adj* lexicológico
lexicologist [,lɛksɪ'kɑlədʒɪst] *s* lexicólogo
lexicology [,lɛksɪ'kɑlədʒɪ] *s* lexicología
lexicon ['lɛksɪkən] *s* léxico o lexicón
Leyden jar ['laɪdən] *s* (elec.) botella de Leiden
L.I. abr. de **Long Island**
liability [,laɪə'bɪlɪtɪ] *s* (*pl:* **-ties**) exposición, riesgo; responsabilidad; obligación; deuda; desventaja; **liabilities** *spl* (com.) pasivo
liability insurance *s* seguro contra responsabilidad civil
liable ['laɪəbəl] *adj* sujeto, expuesto; responsable, obligado
liaison [,lie'zõ] o ['liə,zɑn] *s* enlace, unión; lío, amancebamiento; (mil.) enlace, intercomunicación; (phonet.) enlace de una consonante final con la vocal inicial de la palabra siguiente
liaison officer *s* (mil.) oficial de enlace
liana [lɪ'ɑnə] o [lɪ'ænə] o **liane** [lɪ'ɑn] *s* (bot.) bejuco, liana
liar ['laɪər] *s* mentiroso
Liassic [laɪ'æsɪk] *adj & s* (geol.) liásico
lib. abr. de **librarian, library** y **liber** (Lat.) **book**
libation [laɪ'beʃən] *s* libación; (hum.) libación (*bebida alcohólica*)
libel ['laɪbəl] *s* libelo (*escrito infamatorio*); calumnia, difamación; (*pret & pp:* **-beled** o **-belled**; *ger:* **-beling** o **-belling**) *va* calumniar, difamar
libeler o **libeller** ['laɪbələr] *s* libelista (*autor de un libelo*); calumniador, difamador
libelous o **libellous** ['laɪbələs] *adj* infamador, infamatorio, calumniador
liber ['laɪbər] *s* (bot.) líber
liberal ['lɪbərəl] *adj* liberal; tolerante, de amplias miras; (pol.) liberal; libre (*traducción*); *s* (pol.) liberal
liberal arts *spl* artes liberales *fpl*
liberal education *s* instrucción que consiste en el estudio de las artes liberales
liberalism ['lɪbərəlɪzəm] *s* liberalismo
liberality [,lɪbə'rælɪtɪ] *s* (*pl:* **-ties**) liberalidad
liberalization [,lɪbərəlɪ'zeʃən] *s* liberalización
liberalize ['lɪbərəlaɪz] *va* liberalizar; *vn* liberalizarse
liberal-minded ['lɪbərəl'maɪndɪd] *adj* tolerante, de amplias miras
liberate ['lɪbəret] *va* libertar; (chem.) desprender
liberation [,lɪbə'reʃən] *s* liberación; (chem.) desprendimiento
liberator ['lɪbə,retər] *s* liberador, libertador
Liberian [laɪ'bɪrɪən] *adj & s* liberiano
liberticidal [lɪ,bʌrtɪ'saɪdəl] *adj* liberticida
liberticide [lɪ'bʌrtɪsaɪd] *s* liberticida (*destructor de la libertad*); destrucción de la libertad
libertine ['lɪbərtin] *adj & s* libertino
libertinism ['lɪbərtɪnɪzəm] *s* libertinaje
liberty ['lɪbərtɪ] *s* (*pl:* **-ties**) libertad; (naut.) licencia, permiso; **at liberty** en libertad; libre, desocupado; **to be at liberty to** + *inf* ser libre para + *inf,* tener permiso para + *inf;* **to take the liberty to** + *inf* tomarse la libertad de + *inf;* **to take liberties** tomarse libertades (*propasarse*)
Liberty Bell *s* (U.S.A.) campana de la libertad
liberty cap *s* gorro frigio
liberty-loving ['lɪbərtɪ'lʌvɪŋ] *adj* amante de la libertad
libidinous [lɪ'bɪdɪnəs] *adj* libidinoso
libido [lɪ'bido] o [lɪ'baɪdo] *s* (psychol.) libídine o libido
Libra ['laɪbrə] *s* (astr.) Libra
librarian [laɪ'brɛrɪən] *s* bibliotecario
library ['laɪ,brɛrɪ] o ['laɪbrərɪ] *s* (*pl:* **-ies**) biblioteca
library number *s* signatura
library school *s* escuela de bibliotecarios
library science *s* bibliotecnia, biblioteconomía
libration [laɪ'breʃən] *s* libración; (astr.) libración
librettist [lɪ'brɛtɪst] *s* libretista
libretto [lɪ'brɛto] *s* (*pl:* **-tos**) (mus.) libreto
Libya ['lɪbɪə] *s* la Libia
Libyan ['lɪbɪən] *adj* líbico o libio; *s* libio
Libyan Desert *s* Desierto de Libia
lice [laɪs] *pl de* **louse**
license o **licence** ['laɪsəns] *s* licencia (*permiso; documento en que consta la licencia; libertad abusiva; libertinaje*); *va* licenciar
licensee [,laɪsən'si] *s* concesionario, persona que obtiene licencia
license number *s* número de matrícula
license plate *s* placa de matrícula, chapa de circulación
license-plate light ['laɪsəns'plet] *s* luz de matrícula
license tag *s* var. de **license plate**
licentiate [laɪ'sɛnʃɪɪt] o [laɪ'sɛnʃɪet] *s* licenciado (*el que tiene licencia para ejercer una profesión; el que tiene grado de licenciado*); licencia o licenciatura (*grado*)
licentious [laɪ'sɛnʃəs] *adj* licencioso
licentiousness [laɪ'sɛnʃəsnɪs] *s* libertinaje, licencia
lichee ['litʃi] *s* var. de **litchi**
lichen ['laɪkən] *s* (bot. & path.) liquen
lichenin ['laɪkənɪn] *s* (chem.) liquenina
lichenology [,laɪkə'nɑlədʒɪ] *s* liquenología
lichenous ['laɪkənəs] *adj* liquenoso
lich gate [lɪtʃ] *s* puerta de cementerio de parroquia donde se posa en tierra el féretro mientras se espera a que venga el pastor encargado del entierro
licit ['lɪsɪt] *adj* lícito
lick [lɪk] *s* lamedura; lamedero, salobral; (coll.) zurra; (coll.) velocidad; (coll.) bofetón; (coll.) vestigio; (coll.) pizca; (coll.) limpión; **to give a lick and a promise to** (coll.) hacer aprisa y mal, hacer rápida y superficialmente; *va* lamer; lamerse (*p.ej., los labios*); (fig.) lamer (*dícese de las llamas*); (coll.) zurrar; (coll.) vencer; (coll.) confundir; **to lick clean** lamer hasta dejar limpio
lickerish ['lɪkərɪʃ] *adj* goloso; codicioso; lascivo
lickspittle ['lɪk,spɪtəl] *s* quitapelillos
licorice ['lɪkərɪs] *s* (bot.) orozuz, alcazuz, regaliz; dulce de orozuz, dulce de regaliz
lictor ['lɪktər] *s* (hist.) lictor
lid [lɪd] *s* tapa, tapadera (*de caja, cofre, arca, etc.*); cobertera (*de olla, cazuela, etc.*); (anat.) párpado; (slang) techo (*sombrero*)
lidless ['lɪdlɪs] *adj* sin tapa, sin tapadera; sin párpados; (poet.) vigilante
lie [laɪ] *s* mentira; mentís (*acción de desmentir*); disposición, situación, orientación; **to catch in a lie** coger en una mentira; **to give the lie to** dar un mentís a ‖ (*pret & pp:* **lied**; *ger:* **lying**) *va* conseguir mintiendo; **to lie one's way out of** vencer (*p.ej., una dificultad*) mintiendo ‖ *vn* mentir ‖ (*pret:* **lay**; *pp:* **lain**; *ger:* **lying**) *vn* echarse, acostarse; estar echado; estar situado, hallarse; yacer, estar enterrado; (archaic) pernoctar; **to lie down** echarse, acostarse; **to lie in** depender de; consistir en; corresponder a; estar de parto; **to lie off** (naut.) guardar cierta distancia de; descansar; (slang) contenerse al principio (*de una carrera*); **to lie over** detenerse algún tiempo, esperando la hora o la ocasión de continuar el viaje; aplazarse; quedar en suspenso; **to lie to** (naut.) aguantarse a la capa; **to lie with** tocar a, corresponder a; yacer con (*tener trato carnal con*)
lie detector *s* detector de mentiras

lief [lif] *adv* de buena gana; **I would as lief** + *inf* tanto me da + *inf*
liege [lidʒ] *adj* feudal; vasallo; *s* señor feudal; vasallo
Liége [lɪˈeʒ] *s* Lieja
liege lord *s* señor feudal
liegeman [ˈlidʒmən] *s* (*pl:* **-men**) vasallo; (fig.) fiel secuaz
lien [lin] o [ˈliən] *s* (law) embargo preventivo, derecho de retención
lienteric [ˌlaɪənˈtɛrɪk] *adj* lientérico
lientery [ˈlaɪənˌtɛrɪ] *s* (path.) lientera o lientería
lie of the land *s* var. de **lay of the land**
lieu [lu] *s* lugar; **in lieu of** en lugar de, en vez de
Lieut. abr. de **Lieutenant**
lieutenancy [luˈtɛnənsɪ] *s* (*pl:* **-cies**) lugartenencia; (mil. & nav.) tenencia
lieutenant [luˈtɛnənt] *s* lugarteniente; (mil.) teniente; (nav.) teniente de navío
lieutenant colonel *s* (mil.) teniente coronel
lieutenant commander *s* (nav.) capitán de corbeta
lieutenant general *s* (mil.) teniente general
lieutenant governor *s* (U.S.A.) vicegobernador; (Brit.) lugarteniente del gobernador (*de una colonia o provincia*)
lieutenant junior grade *s* (nav.) alférez de navío
lieve [liv] *adv* var. de **lief**
life [laɪf] *s* (*pl:* **lives**) vida; vigencia (*de una póliza*); **as big as life** de tamaño natural; en persona; **for the life of me** a fe mía, así me maten; **for life** de por vida, por toda la vida; **from life** del natural; **the life and soul of** la alegría de (*p.ej., la fiesta*); **to come to life** volver a la vida; **to depart this life** partir o partirse de esta vida; **to have life** vivir; tener vivacidad; **to put new life into** vigorizar; **to run for one's life** salvarse por los pies, salir huyendo para que no le maten; **to see life** ver mundo; **to take one's own life** quitarse la vida; **to take one's life in one's hands** tomarse la muerte por su mano, jugarse la vida; **to the life** del natural, fielmente; *adj* vital (*perteneciente a la vida*); perpetuo; vitalicio; (f.a.) copiando el modelo vivo
life-and-death struggle [ˈlaɪfənˈdɛθ] *s* lucha a vida o muerte
life annuitant *s* vitalicista
life annuity *s* renta vitalicia
life belt *s* cinturón salvavidas
lifeblood [ˈlaɪfˌblʌd] *s* sangre vital; alma, nervio
lifeboat [ˈlaɪfˌbot] *s* bote de salvamento, bote salvavidas, salvavidas; lancha de auxilio (*en los puertos*)
lifeboat drill *s* (naut.) ejercicios con botes de salvamento
lifeboat station *s* estación de salvamento
life buoy *s* (naut.) boya salvavidas
life expectancy *s* expectación de vida
lifeguard [ˈlaɪfˌgɑrd] *s* empleado de una estación de salvamento
Life Guards *spl* (Brit.) guardia de corps
life imprisonment *s* cadena perpetua
life insurance *s* seguro sobre la vida
life interest *s* (law) usufructo
lifeless [ˈlaɪflɪs] *adj* sin vida, muerto; exánime, desmayado; deslucido, amortiguado
lifelike [ˈlaɪfˌlaɪk] *adj* natural, vivo
life line *s* cuerda salvavidas; cuerda de comunicación (*de una escafandra*); línea de la vida (*en la quiromancía*)
lifelong [ˈlaɪfˌlɔŋ] o [ˈlaɪfˌlɑŋ] *adj* de toda la vida; *adv* durante toda la vida; *s* toda la vida
life net *s* red de salvamento
life of leisure *s* vida de ocio
life of Riley [ˈraɪlɪ] *s* vida regalada
life of the party *s* (coll.) alma de la fiesta, alegría de la fiesta
life preserver *s* salvavidas, chaleco flotador; (Brit.) cachiporra
lifer [ˈlaɪfər] *s* (slang) presidiario de por vida
life raft *s* balsa salvavidas
lifesaver [ˈlaɪfˌsevər] *s* salvador (*persona que salva la vida a otra*); empleado de una estación de salvamento; (coll.) paño de lágrimas, tabla de salvación
lifesaving [ˈlaɪfˌsevɪŋ] *adj* de salvamento; *s* salvamento; servicio de salvavidas
lifesaving gun *s* cañón lanzacabos
life sentence *s* condena a cadena perpetua
life-size [ˈlaɪfˌsaɪz] *adj* de tamaño natural
life span *s* vida (*la duración más larga de una especie animal o vegetal*)
lifetime [ˈlaɪfˌtaim] *s* vida, curso de la vida; *adj* vitalicio
lifework [ˈlaɪfˌwʌrk] *s* trabajo de toda la vida, obra principal de la vida de uno
lift [lɪft] *s* elevación, levantamiento; empuje hacia arriba; tapa (*del tacón del zapato*); altura de aspiración (*de una bomba*); juego de una leva; fuerza de sustentación o fuerza ascensional (*de un avión*); ayuda (*para levantar una carga*); elevación del terreno, repecho; invitación para subir a un coche que pasa; paseo en un coche que pasa; exaltación, estímulo; (Brit.) ascensor; **to give a lift to** ayudar a levantar o a levantarse; invitar (*a un peatón*) a subir a un coche; llevar en un coche; (fig.) reanimar; *va* levantar, elevar; extinguir (*una hipoteca*); quitarse (*el sombrero*); exaltar, estimular; (naut.) izar (*vergas, velas, etc.*); (coll.) robar; (coll.) plagiar; *vn* levantarse, elevarse; disiparse (*las nubes, la niebla, la obscuridad*); aparecer en el horizonte (*la tierra, cuando el navegante se aproxima a la costa*); **to lift at** tratar de levantar
lift bridge *s* puente levadizo
lifter [ˈlɪftər] *s* alzador; aparato de alzamiento; (mach.) leva
lift-off [ˈlɪftˌɔf] o [ˈlɪftˌɑf] *s* despegue vertical
lift pump *s* bomba aspirante
ligament [ˈlɪgəmənt] *s* ligamento; (anat. & zool.) ligamento
ligamentous [ˌlɪgəˈmɛntəs] *adj* ligamentoso
ligate [ˈlaɪget] *va* (surg.) ligar
ligation [laɪˈgeʃən] *s* ligación
ligator [laɪˈgetər] *s* (surg.) ligador
ligature [ˈlɪgətʃər] *s* ligadura; (mus.) ligado, ligadura; (print.) ligado; (surg.) ligadura; *va* ligar
light [laɪt] *adj* ligero, leve, liviano; ligero (*dotado de pocas armas o poca impedimenta; fino, delicado; ágil, rápido; de poca monta; superficial; impertinente; inconstante; alegre; dícese también del alimento, vino, sueño*); claro (*luminoso, brillante; que recibe mucha luz; de color poco subido; dícese tambien de la cerveza*); rubio, blondo; de tez blanca; arenoso (*suelo*); flúido (*aceite*); poco serio (*dícese, p.ej., de la lectura*); (naut.) boyante (*que no cala lo que debe calar*); **light in the head** mareado; tonto, necio; loco; **to be light on one's feet** andar con mucha agilidad; **to make light of** no dar importancia a, no tomar en serio ‖ *adv* ligeramente ‖ *s* luz; lumbre o fuego (*p.ej., para encender el cigarro*); luz o señal (*de tráfico*); luz, claro, hueco (*ventana, tronera u otra abertura en una pared*); lumbrera (*persona insigne*); (fig.) lumbre (*p.ej., del rostro de Dios*); **lights** *spl* bofes, livianos; noticias; conocimientos; (slang) ojos; **according to one's lights** según Dios le da a uno a entender, lo mejor que uno puede; **against the light** al trasluz; **in the light of** a la luz de; **in this light** desde este punto de vista; **to bring to light** sacar a luz, descubrir, revelar; **to cast light on** echar luz sobre; **to come to light** salir a luz, descubrirse; **to see the light** o **to see the light of day** salir a luz, ver la luz; caer en la cuenta; ver el cielo abierto (*descubrir el medio de salir de un apuro*); **to shed** o **throw light on** o **upon** echar luz sobre; **to strike a light** echar una yesca; encender un fósforo ‖ (*pret & pp:* **lighted** o **lit**) *va* encender (*una luz, el fuego, el cigarro, etc.*); alumbrar (*dar luz a*); iluminar (*dar luz a; adornar con muchas luces*); **to light up** iluminar ‖ *vn* encenderse; alumbrarse; bajar (*p.ej., de un coche*); posar (*las aves*); **to light into** (slang) arremeter contra; (slang) poner de oro y azul; **to light out** (slang) salir pitando, poner pies en polvorosa; **to light upon** dar con, tropezar con, hallar por casualidad
light air *s* (naut.) ventolina
light alloy *s* metal ligero de aleación

light-armed ['laɪt'ɑrmd] *adj* armado de armas ligeras, armado de armadura ligera
light breeze *s* (naut.) viento flojito
light bulb *s* ampolleta, bombilla
light-complexioned ['laɪtkəm'plɛkʃənd] *adj* de tez blanca
lighten ['laɪtən] *va* aligerar; alegrar, regocijar; iluminar; *vn* aligerarse; alegrarse, regocijarse; iluminarse; relampaguear; (fig.) iluminarse (*la cara de una persona*)
lighter ['laɪtər] *s* alumbrador; mecha (*para pegar fuego a cohetes, minas, etc.*); encendedor (*p.ej., de cigarrillos*); alijador (*barcaza*); *va* transportar en alijador
lighterage ['laɪtərɪdʒ] *s* alijo; gastos de alijo
lighter-than-air [,laɪtərθən'ɛr] *adj* (aer.) más ligero que el aire
lightface ['laɪt,fes] *s* (print.) tipo común
light-fingered ['laɪt'fɪŋgərd] *adj* largo de uñas, listo de manos
light-foot ['laɪt,fʊt] o **light-footed** ['laɪt'fʊtɪd] *adj* ligero de pies
light-headed ['laɪt'hɛdɪd] *adj* mareado; casquivano, ligero de cascos; delirante
light-hearted ['laɪt'hɑrtɪd] *adj* libre de cuidados, alegre
light heavyweight *s* (box.) peso pesado ligero, peso medio fuerte
light horse *s* (mil.) caballería ligera
light-horseman ['laɪt,hɔrsmən] *s* (*pl:* **-men**) soldado de un cuerpo de caballería ligera
lighthouse ['laɪt,haʊs] *s* faro
lighthouseman ['laɪt,haʊsmən] *s* (*pl:* **-men**) torrero
light infantry *s* infantería ligera
lighting ['laɪtɪŋ] *s* iluminación, alumbrado; encendido, encendimiento
lighting fixtures *spl* artefactos de alumbrado
lightly ['laɪtlɪ] *adv* ligeramente
light meter *s* (phot.) exposímetro
light-minded ['laɪt'maɪndɪd] *adj* tonto, atolondrado
lightness ['laɪtnɪs] *s* ligereza; claridad, blancura, luminosidad
lightning ['laɪtnɪŋ] *s* relámpagos, relampagueo; *vn* relampaguear
lightning arrester *s* pararrayos
lightning bug *s* (ent.) bicho de luz, luciérnaga
lightning rod *s* pararrayos, barra pararrayos
light of the World *s* (theol.) luz del mundo
light opera *s* (mus.) opereta
lightship ['laɪt,ʃɪp] *s* (naut.) buque fanal, buque faro
lightsome ['laɪtsəm] *adj* ligero (*ágil; frívolo*); alegre, festivo
light-struck ['laɪt,strʌk] *adj* velado (*por la acción indebida de la luz*)
lightweight ['laɪt,wet] *s* persona de poco peso; (box.) peso ligero, peso liviano; (coll.) pelele; *adj* ligero; de entretiempo, p.ej., **lightweight coat** abrigo de entretiempo
light-year ['laɪt,jɪr] *s* (astr.) año luz
ligneous ['lɪgnɪəs] *adj* lignario, leñoso
lignify ['lɪgnɪfaɪ] (*pret & pp:* **-fied**) *va* convertir en madera; *vn* lignificarse
lignin ['lɪgnɪn] *s* (bot.) lignina
lignite ['lɪgnaɪt] *s* (mineral.) lignito
lignocellulose [,lɪgnə'sɛljəlos] *s* lignocelulosa
lignum vitae ['lɪgnəm 'vaɪti] *s* (bot.) guayacán o guayaco (*árbol*); palo santo (*madera*)
ligroin ['lɪgro·ɪn] *s* (chem.) ligroína
ligula ['lɪgjələ] *s* (*pl:* **-lae** [li] o **-las**) (anat., bot. & zool.) lígula
ligulate ['lɪgjəlɪt] o ['lɪgjəlet] *adj* ligulado
ligule ['lɪgjul] *s* (bot. & zool.) lígula
Ligurian [lɪ'gjʊrɪən] *adj & s* ligur o ligurino
likable ['laɪkəbəl] *adj* simpático
like [laɪk] *adj* parecido, semejante, p.ej., **a like instance** un ejemplo semejante; **plants with like flowers** plantas con flores semejantes; parecido a, semejante a, p.ej., **this book is like the other one** este libro es semejante al otro; propio de, característico de; (elec.) del mismo nombre (*dícese de los polos de un imán*); **something like** algo así como; **to be like to** + *inf* (archaic & coll.) ser probable que + *subj*, p.ej., **the king is like to die** es probable que muera el rey; **to feel like** + *ger* tener ganas de + *inf;* **to look like** parecerse a; parecer que, p.ej., **it looks like rain** parece que va a llover ‖ *adv* del mismo modo; probablemente, p.ej., **like enough it will rain** probablemente lloverá; **nothing like** ni con mucho; **like mad** como un loco ‖ *prep* como ‖ *conj* (coll.) del mismo modo que; (coll.) que, p.ej., **it looks like he's right** parece que tiene razón ‖ *s* semejante; gusto, preferencia; **and the like** y cosas por el estilo; **the like** o **the likes of him** (coll.) otro semejante; **to give like for like** pagar en la misma moneda ‖ *va* gustar, p.ej., **John did not like these apples** no le gustaron a Juan estas manzanas; gustar de, p.ej., **I like music** gusto de la música; **to like better** o **best** preferir; **to like it in** estar o encontrarse a gusto en (*p.ej., el campo*); **to like to** + *inf* gustarle a uno + *inf*, p.ej., **I like to travel** me gusta viajar; gustar de + *inf*, p.ej., **I like to read** gusto de leer; **to like** (*someone*) **to** + *inf* gustar que + *subj*, p.ej., **I should like him to come to see me** me gustaría que viniese a verme ‖ *vn* querer, p.ej., **as you like** como Vd. quiera; (coll.) por poco, p.ej., **he liked to have died laughing** o **he had like to have died laughing** por poco murió de risa
likeable ['laɪkəbəl] *adj* var. de **likable**
likelihood ['laɪklɪhʊd] *s* probabilidad
likely ['laɪklɪ] *adj* (*comp:* **-lier;** *super:* **-liest**) probable; prometiente, prometedor; **to be likely to** + *inf* ser probable que + *subj*, p.ej., **John is likely to arrive early** es probable que Juan llegue temprano
like-minded ['laɪk'maɪndɪd] *adj* del mismo parecer, de natural semejante
liken ['laɪkən] *va* asemejar, comparar
likeness ['laɪknɪs] *s* parecido, semejanza; retrato; forma, aspecto; **to be a good likeness** tener un gran parecido
likewise ['laɪk,waɪz] *adv* asimismo, igualmente; del mismo modo; lo mismo, p.ej., **the rest did likewise** los demás hicieron lo mismo
liking ['laɪkɪŋ] *s* gusto, preferencia, afición, simpatía; **to be to the liking of** ser del gusto de; **to take a liking for** o **to** tomar el gusto a, aficionarse a
lilac ['laɪlək] *s* (bot.) lila (*arbusto y flor*); lila (*color*); *adj* de color de lila
liliaceous [,lɪlɪ'eʃəs] *adj* (bot.) liliáceo
Lille [lil] *s* Lila
Lilliputian [,lɪlɪ'pjuʃən] *adj & s* liliputiense
lilt [lɪlt] *s* música o canción alegres; paso o movimiento airosos; *va* tocar o cantar (*una melodía*) airosamente
lily ['lɪlɪ] *s* (*pl:* **-ies**) (bot.) azucena; (bot.) lirio de agua, cala; flor de lis (*escudo de armas de Francia*); **to gild the lily** ponerle colores al oro; *adj* de alabastro, blanco; puro, tierno; pálido
lily family *s* (bot.) liliáceas
lily-livered ['lɪlɪ,lɪvərd] *adj* cobarde, pusilánime
lily of the valley *s* (bot.) muguete, lirio de los valles
lily pad *s* hoja de nenúfar
Lima bean ['laɪmə] *s* (bot.) judía de la peladilla, frijol de media luna (*Phaseolus limensis*)
Lima wood ['limə] o ['laɪmə] *s* madera de cesalpínea tintórea
limb [lɪm] *s* miembro (*brazo o pierna*); rama (*de árbol*); vástago (*de una planta o una familia*); brazo (*de cruz; del mar*); (astr., bot. & surv.) limbo; **to be a limb of the devil** u **of Satan** ser maligno; ser la piel o de la piel del diablo; **to be out on a limb** (coll.) estar en un aprieto
limber ['lɪmbər] *s* (arti.) armón, avantrén; *adj* flexible; ágil; *va* poner flexible; agilitar; *vn* ponerse flexible; agilitarse; **to limber up** ponerse flexible; agilitarse; (fig.) humanarse (*hacerse más afable*)
limbo ['lɪmbo] *s* (theol.) limbo; lugar de personas o cosas olvidadas o pasadas de moda; cárcel, prisión
limb of the law *s* policía, guardia; abogado; juez
Limburg ['lɪmbʌrg] *s* Limburgo
Limburger ['lɪmbʌrgər] *s* queso de Limburgo
lime [laɪm] *s* cal; calcio; liga (*materia viscosa*); (bot.) limero agrio (*Citrus aurantifolia*); lima

agria (*fruto*); (bot.) tila o tilo; *va* encalar; (agr.) encalar; untar con liga; coger (*pájaros*) con liga
Limean ['limɪən] *adj & s* limeño
lime burner *s* calero
limekiln ['laɪm,kɪl] o ['laɪm,kɪln] *s* horno de cal, calera
limelight ['laɪm,laɪt] *s* (theat.) haz luminoso del proyector; **to be in the limelight** estar a la vista del público
limen ['laɪmɛn] *s* (*pl:* **-mens** o **-mina** [mɪnə]) (psychol.) umbral
limerick ['lɪmərɪk] *s* quintilla jocosa
limestone ['laɪm,ston] *s* caliza, piedra caliza; *adj* calizo
limewater ['laɪm,wɔtər] o ['laɪm,wɑtər] *s* agua de cal
liminal ['lɪmɪnəl] o ['laɪmɪnəl] *adj* (psychol.) liminal
limit ['lɪmɪt] *s* límite; **to be the limit** (slang) ser el colmo, ser inaguantable; **to go the limit** no dejar piedra por mover, hacer todos los esfuerzos posibles; **to know no limit** no tener límites, ser infinito; *va* limitar; **to limit to** + *ger* limitar a + *inf*
limitation [,lɪmɪ'teʃən] *s* limitación; (law) prescripción
limitative ['lɪmɪ,tetɪv] *adj* limitativo
limited ['lɪmɪtɪd] *adj* limitado; *s* (rail.) tren expreso con tarifa recargada
limited company *s* (com.) sociedad limitada
limited monarchy *s* monarquía constitucional
limiter ['lɪmɪtər] *s* limitador; (elec.) limitacorrientes
limitless ['lɪmɪtlɪs] *adj* ilimitado
limit turbine *s* turbina límite
limn [lɪm] *va* pintar (*un cuadro*); (fig.) pintar (*describir*)
limnology [lɪm'nɑlədʒɪ] *s* limnología
limonene ['lɪmənin] *s* (chem.) limoneno
limonite ['laɪmənaɪt] *s* (mineral.) limonita
limousine ['lɪmə,zin] o [,lɪmə'zin] *s* (aut.) limosina
limp [lɪmp] *s* cojera; paso cojeante; *adj* flojo; flexible; (fig.) blando, sin carácter; *vn* cojear; (fig.) cojear (*un verso*)
limpet ['lɪmpɪt] *s* (zool.) lapa, lápade
limpid ['lɪmpɪd] *adj* diáfano, cristalino; claro
limpidity [lɪm'pɪdɪtɪ] *s* diafanidad; claridad
limpkin ['lɪmpkɪn] *s* (orn.) guariao
limy ['laɪmɪ] *adj* (*comp:* **-ier;** *super:* **-iest**) calizo; pegajoso, viscoso; untado con liga
linage ['laɪnɪdʒ] *s* alineación; (print.) número de líneas
linaloöl [lɪ'næloɔl], [lɪ'næloɑl] o [,lɪnə'lul] *s* (chem.) linalol
linchpin ['lɪntʃ,pɪn] *s* pezonera, sotrozo
linden ['lɪndən] *s* (bot.) tila o tilo
line [laɪn] *s* línea; cuerda, cordel; sedal (*de la caña de pescar*); arruga; renglón (*línea escrita o impresa; ramo de mercancías*); ramo (*de mercancías, de negocios*); surtido; especialidad; manera (*de pensar*); (phys.) raya (*del espectro*); (slang) charla propia (*de una persona*); **lines** *spl* línea (*contorno*); (theat.) papel; versos; riendas; (mil.) línea defensiva, trincheras; **a line** unas líneas (*carta muy breve*); **all along the line** en toda la línea; por todas partes; desde cualquier punto de vista; **in line** alineado; dispuesto, preparado; **in line with** de acuerdo con; **on a line** nivelado, ras con ras; **on the line** en la línea divisoria; ni lo uno ni lo otro; **out of line** desalineado; en desacuerdo; **the line** (geog.) la línea (*el ecuador*); **to bring into line** poner de acuerdo, convencer, persuadir; **to come into line** ponerse de acuerdo, dejarse convencer o persuadir; **to draw the line at** no ir más allá de; **to fall in line** conformarse; formar cola; (mil.) alinearse en su lugar; **to fall into line** ponerse de acuerdo; **to get a line on** (coll.) llegar a conocer; **to get in line** alinearse; ponerse de acuerdo; **to get out of line** salirse de la fila; **to have a line on** (coll.) conocer, estar enterado de; **to read between the lines** leer entre líneas, leer entre renglones; **to stand in line** hacer cola; **to take a line** adoptar una actitud; **to toe the line** ponerse en la raya; obrar como se debe; **to wait in line** hacer cola (*esperar vez formando cola con otras personas*); *va* linear, rayar; arrugar (*p.ej., la cara*); alinear; formar hilera a lo largo de (*p.ej., la acera*); forrar (*p.ej., un vestido*); guarnecer (*un freno*); **to line up** (mach.) alinear; *vn* alinearse; **to line up** ponerse en fila; hacer cola
lineage ['lɪnɪɪdʒ] *s* linaje; alineación; (print.) número de líneas
lineal ['lɪnɪəl] *adj* lineal; hereditario; en línea recta
lineally ['lɪnɪəlɪ] *adv* en línea recta
lineament ['lɪnɪəmənt] *s* lineamento; **lineaments** *spl* lineamentos (*del rostro*)
linear ['lɪnɪər] *adj* lineal
linear equation *s* (alg.) ecuación de primer grado
linearity [,lɪnɪ'ærɪtɪ] *s* linearidad
linear measure *s* medida de longitud; sistema de medidas de longitud
linear perspective *s* perspectiva lineal
line engraving *s* grabado de líneas
lineman ['laɪnmən] *s* (*pl:* **-men**) (elec.) recorredor de la línea; (rail.) guardavía; (surv.) cadenero; (football) jugador de la línea de embestida
linen ['lɪnən] *s* lienzo, lino; hilo de lino; ropa blanca; *adj* de lino
linen draper *s* lencero
linen drapery *s* lencería
line of battle *s* línea de batalla, línea de combate
line of circumvallation *s* (fort.) línea de circunvalación
line of collimation *s* línea de colimación
Line of Demarcation *s* (hist.) línea de demarcación
line of fire *s* (mil.) línea de tiro
line of force *s* (phys.) línea de fuerza
line of incidence *s* línea de incidencia
line of least resistance *s* (fig.) ley del menor esfuerzo; **to follow the line of least resistance** seguir la corriente, no hacer resistencia
line of march *s* recorrido
line of sight *s* (arti. & surv.) línea de mira
line of vision *s* visual
liner ['laɪnər] *s* trazador de líneas; forrador; forro; vapor o avión de travesía; (mach.) forro tubular; (baseball) pelota rasa
line radio *s* (rad.) radiocomunicación por corrientes de alta frecuencia de una red alambrada
linesman ['laɪnzmən] *s* (*pl:* **-men**) (elec.) recorredor de la línea; (sport) juez de línea; (mil.) soldado de línea
line squall *s* (meteor.) línea de turbonada
line-up ['laɪn,ʌp] *s* formación; rueda de presos
ling [lɪŋ] *s* (ichth.) bacalao ling, abadejo largo; (ichth.) lota; (bot.) brezo (*Calluna vulgaris y plantas de los géneros Carex y Erica*)
linger ['lɪŋgər] *vn* estarse, quedarse; demorar, tardar; tardar en marcharse; tardar en morirse; **to linger over** meditar, reflexionar (*una cosa*)
lingerie [,læŋʒə'ri] *s* lencería; lencería fina; ropa blanca de mujer
lingering ['lɪŋgərɪŋ] *adj* prolongado, lento
lingo ['lɪŋgo] *s* (*pl:* **-goes**) idioma; algarabía; jerga (*de los individuos de ciertas profesiones u oficios*)
lingua franca ['lɪŋgwə 'fræŋkə] *s* lengua franca
lingual ['lɪŋgwəl] *adj* lingual; (phonet.) lingual; *s* (phonet.) lingual
linguist ['lɪŋgwɪst] *s* lingüista (*el que estudia la lingüística*); poligloto (*el que sabe varias lenguas*)
linguistic [lɪŋ'gwɪstɪk] *adj* lingüístico; **linguistics** *ssg* lingüística
linguistically [lɪŋ'gwɪstɪkəlɪ] *adv* lingüísticamente
linguistic geography *s* geografía lingüística
liniment ['lɪnɪmənt] *s* linimento
linin ['laɪnɪn] *s* (biol. & chem.) linina
lining ['laɪnɪŋ] *s* forro; guarnición (*de freno*); rayado
link [lɪŋk] *s* eslabón; eslabón de la cadena de Gúnter (*201,2 mm*); hacha de viento; varilla de conexión; meandro de río; (fig.) eslabón;

links *spl* campo de golf; *va* eslabonar; *vn* eslabonarse
linkage [ˈlɪŋkɪdʒ] *s* eslabonamiento; (chem.) enlace; (elec.) acoplamiento inductivo; (mech.) varillaje
linkboy [ˈlɪŋkˌbɔɪ] *s* (hist.) paje de hacha
Linnaean o **Linnean** [lɪˈniən] *adj* linneano
linnet [ˈlɪnɪt] *s* (orn.) pardillo; (orn.) jilguero
linoleum [lɪˈnolɪəm] *s* linóleo
linotype [ˈlaɪnəˌtaɪp] *s* (trademark) linotipia; *va* componer con linotipia
linotyper [ˈlaɪnəˌtaɪpər] o **linotypist** [ˈlaɪnəˌtaɪpɪst] *s* linotipista
linseed [ˈlɪnˌsid] *s* linaza
linseed cake *s* torta de linaza
linseed meal *s* harina de linaza
linseed oil *s* aceite de linaza
linsey [ˈlɪnzɪ] o **linsey-woolsey** [ˈlɪnzɪˈwʊlzɪ] *s* tela basta de lino y lana o de algodón y lana; *adj* de lino y lana, de algodón y lana; basto; ni fu ni fa
linstock [ˈlɪnˌstɑk] *s* botafuego
lint [lɪnt] *s* hilacha; hilas (*para curar las llagas*)
lintel [ˈlɪntəl] *s* (arch.) dintel
lion [ˈlaɪən] *s* (zool.) león; (fig.) león (*hombre audaz y valiente*); (fig.) celebridad muy solicitada; (*cap.*) *s* (astr.) León; **to beard the lion in his den** entrar en el cubil de la fiera (*a desafiar la cólera de un jefe, etc.*); **to put one's head in the lion's mouth** meterse en la boca del lobo
lioness [ˈlaɪənɪs] *s* leona
lion-hearted [ˈlaɪənˌhɑrtɪd] *adj* valiente
lionization [ˌlaɪənɪˈzeʃən] *s* agasajo
lionize [ˈlaɪənaɪz] *va* agasajar
lions' den *s* (Bib.) fosa de los leones
lion's-foot [ˈlaɪənzˌfʊt] *s* (bot.) pie de león
lion's share *s* parte del león
lip [lɪp] *s* labio; labio, pico (*de un jarro*); (mach.) labio; (mus.) boquilla o embocadura; (surg.) labio (*de una herida*); (slang) insolencias; **lips** *spl* (fig.) labios (*palabras*); **to hang on the lips of** estar pendiente de las palabras de; **to keep a stiff upper lip** no desanimarse; **to lick one's lips** lamerse los labios; (*pret & pp:* **lipped**; *ger:* **lipping**) *va* rozar con los labios; besar; lamer; murmurar; (slang) cantar; *vn* chapotear; (mus.) tocar un instrumento de viento
lipase [ˈlaɪpes] o [ˈlɪpes] *s* (biochem.) lipasa
lipoma [lɪˈpomə] *s* (*pl:* **-mata** [mətə] o **-mas**) (path.) lipoma
lip-read [ˈlɪpˌrid] (*pret & pp:* **-read** [ˌrɛd]) *va & vn* leer en los labios
lip reading *s* lectura de los movimientos de los labios, labiolectura
lip service *s* jarabe de pico, homenaje de boca
lipstick [ˈlɪpˌstɪk] *s* lápiz labial, lápiz de labios, barra de labios
liq. abr. de **liquid** y **liquor**
liquate [ˈlaɪkwet] *va* (metal.) licuar
liquation [laɪˈkweʃən] *s* (metal.) licuación
liquefaction [ˌlɪkwɪˈfækʃən] *s* licuefacción, liquidación
liquefiable [ˈlɪkwɪˌfaɪəbəl] *adj* liquidable
liquefy [ˈlɪkwɪfaɪ] (*pret & pp:* **-fied**) *va* liquidar; *vn* liquidarse
liquescence [lɪˈkwɛsəns] *s* licuescencia
liquescent [lɪˈkwɛsənt] *adj* licuescente
liqueur [lɪˈkʌr] *s* licor (*bebida espiritosa preparada por mezcla de azúcar y substancias aromáticas*)
liquid [ˈlɪkwɪd] *adj* líquido; claro, puro (*sonido*); (com.) realizable; (phonet.) líquido; *s* líquido; (phonet.) líquida
liquid air *s* aire líquido
liquidambar [ˈlɪkwɪdˌæmbər] *s* (bot.) liquidámbar (*árbol y líquido*)
liquid ammonia *s* (chem.) amoníaco líquido
liquidate [ˈlɪkwɪdet] *va* liquidar; (slang) matar (*a una persona*); *vn* liquidarse
liquidation [ˌlɪkwɪˈdeʃən] *s* liquidación
liquidator [ˈlɪkwɪˌdetər] *s* liquidador
liquid crystal *s* cristal líquido
liquid fire *s* (mil.) fuego líquido
liquidity [lɪˈkwɪdɪtɪ] *s* liquidez
liquid measure *s* medida para líquidos; sistema de medidas para líquidos
liquor [ˈlɪkər] *s* licor (*bebida espiritosa; cuerpo líquido*); (pharm.) licor
liquorice [ˈlɪkərɪs] *s* var. de **licorice**
Lisbon [ˈlɪzbən] *s* Lisboa
lisle [laɪl] *s* hilo de Escocia
lisp [lɪsp] *s* ceceo; balbuceo; *vn* cecear; balbucear
lisper [ˈlɪspər] *s* zopas
lissome o **lissom** [ˈlɪsəm] *adj* flexible, elástico; ágil, ligero
list [lɪst] lista (*serie de palabras, nombres, etc.*); lista, tira; orilla (*de una tela*); orillo (*orilla basta*); (naut.) ladeo; **lists** *spl* liza (*campo para la lid*); barrera (*de la liza*); **to have a list** (naut.) irse a la banda, recalcar; **to enter the lists** entrar en liza, entrar en la contienda; *va* poner en una lista; hacer una lista de; registrar; alistar; orillar; (naut.) ladear, hacer recalcar; (archaic & poet.) escuchar; *vn* alistarse; (naut.) irse a la banda, recalcar; (archaic & poet.) escuchar; (archaic) querer, antojarse, p.ej., **the wind bloweth where it listeth** el viento sopla donde se le antoja
listel [ˈlɪstəl] *s* (arch.) listel
listen [ˈlɪsən] *vn* escuchar, oír; obedecer; **to listen in** escuchar a hurtadillas (*descolgando el receptor de un teléfono, sin que los interlocutores lo sepan*); escuchar por radio; **to listen to** escuchar, oír; **to listen to reason** meterse en razón
listener [ˈlɪsənər] *s* oyente; radioyente, radioescucha
listening post *s* puesto de escucha
lister [ˈlɪstər] *s* (agr.) arado de pala y vuelos; (agr.) arado sembrador
listerine [ˌlɪstəˈrin] o [ˈlɪstərin] *s* (trademark) listerina
listless [ˈlɪstlɪs] *adj* desatento, descuidado, indiferente
listlessness [ˈlɪstlɪsnɪs] *s* desatención, descuido, indiferencia
list price *s* precio de tarifa, precio de catálogo
lit. abr. de **liter, literature, literal** y **literally**
lit [lɪt] *pret & pp de* **light**
litany [ˈlɪtənɪ] *s* (*pl:* **-nies**) letanía; (fig.) letanía (*enumeración seguida*)
litchi [ˈlitʃi] *s* (bot.) litchi
Lit.D. abr. de **litterarum doctor** (Lat.) **Doctor of Letters**
liter [ˈlitər] *s* litro
literacy [ˈlɪtərəsɪ] *s* desanalfabetismo, capacidad de leer y escribir
literal [ˈlɪtərəl] *adj* literal
literalism [ˈlɪtərəlɪzəm] *s* literalismo
literalist [ˈlɪtərəlɪst] *adj & s* literalista
literalistic [ˌlɪtərəlˈɪstɪk] *adj* literalista
literally [ˈlɪtərəlɪ] *adv* literalmente
literary [ˈlɪtəˌrɛrɪ] *adj* literario; literato
literate [ˈlɪtərɪt] *adj* que sabe leer y escribir; literato; *s* persona que sabe leer y escribir; literato
literati [ˌlɪtəˈretaɪ] o [ˌlɪtəˈrɑtɪ] *spl* literatos
literatim [ˌlɪtəˈretɪm] *adv* (Lat.) al pie de la letra
literature [ˈlɪtərətʃər] *s* literatura; (coll.) impresos, literatura de propaganda
litharge [ˈlɪθɑrdʒ] o [lɪˈθɑrdʒ] *s* (chem.) litargirio
lithe [laɪð] o **lithesome** [ˈlaɪðsəm] *adj* flexible, elástico, ágil
lithia [ˈlɪθɪə] *s* (chem.) litina
lithiasis [lɪˈθaɪəsɪs] *s* (path.) litiasis
lithia water *s* agua de litina
lithic [ˈlɪθɪk] *adj* lítico; (chem.) lítico
lithium [ˈlɪθɪəm] *s* (chem.) litio
lithium hydride *s* (chem.) hidruro de litio
lithoclase [ˈlɪθəkles] *s* (geol.) litoclasa
lithograph [ˈlɪθəgræf] o [ˈlɪθəgrɑf] *s* litografía; *va* litografiar
lithographer [lɪˈθɑgrəfər] *s* litógrafo
lithographic [ˌlɪθəˈgræfɪk] *adj* litográfico
lithography [lɪˈθɑgrəfɪ] *s* litografía
lithoid [ˈlɪθɔɪd] *adj* litoideo
lithologic [ˌlɪθəˈlɑdʒɪk] o **lithological** [ˌlɪθəˈlɑdʒɪkəl] *adj* litológico
lithology [lɪˈθɑlədʒɪ] *s* (geol. & med.) litología
lithomarge [ˈlɪθəmɑrdʒ] *s* (mineral.) litomarga
lithophagous [lɪˈθɑfəgəs] *adj* (zool.) litófago
lithophotography [ˌlɪθəfəˈtɑgrəfɪ] *s* litofotografía

lithopone ['lɪθəpon] *s* litopón
lithosphere ['lɪθəsfɪr] *s* litosfera
lithotomy [lɪ'θɑtəmɪ] *s* (*pl:* **-mies**) (surg.) litotomía
lithotrite ['lɪθətraɪt] *s* (surg.) litotritor
lithotrity [lɪ'θɑtrɪtɪ] *s* (*pl:* **-ties**) (surg.) litotricia
Lithuania [,lɪθʊ'enɪə] o [,lɪθjʊ'enɪə] *s* Lituania
Lithuanian [,lɪθʊ'enɪən] o [,lɪθjʊ'enɪən] *adj & s* lituano
litigable ['lɪtɪgəbəl] *adj* litigioso (*que puede ocasionar un litigio*)
litigant ['lɪtɪgənt] *adj & s* litigante
litigate ['lɪtɪget] *va & vn* litigar
litigation [,lɪtɪ'geʃən] *s* litigación
litigious [lɪ'tɪdʒəs] *adj* litigioso
litmus ['lɪtməs] *s* (chem.) tornasol
litmus paper *s* papel de tornasol
litotes ['laɪtətiz] o ['lɪtətiz] *s* (rhet.) lítote
litre ['litər] s var. de **liter**
Litt. D. abr. de **litterarum doctor** (Lat.) **Doctor of Literature** o **Doctor of Letters**
litter ['lɪtər] *s* litera (*llevada por hombres o caballerías*); camilla (*para la conducción de enfermos o heridos*); desorden, objetos en desorden; tendalera (*desorden de las cosas tendidas por el suelo*); basura (*que se recoge barriendo*); cama o paja (*que se pone en el piso de los establos*); ventregada (*conjunto de animales que nacen de una vez*); **to make a litter** dejarlo todo en desorden; *va* poner o dejar en desorden; esparcir cosas por; parir; preparar la cama de paja a (*los animales en el establo*); **to litter the floor with paper** esparcir desordenadamente papeles por el suelo; *vn* parir
littérateur o **litterateur** [,lɪtərə'tʌr] *s* literato
litterbug ['lɪtər,bʌg] s (coll.) persona que ensucia las calles tirando papeles rotos y desechados
litter case *s* herido que hay que transportar en camilla
little ['lɪtəl] *adj* (*comp:* **less, lesser** o **littler;** *super:* **least** o **littlest**) pequeño; *adv* (*comp:* **less;** *super:* **least**) poco; **little by little** poco a poco; *s* poco; **a little** un poco (de); algo; **in little** en pequeño, en pequeña escala; **not a little** muy; mucho; **to make little of** no dar importancia a, no tomar en serio; **to think little of** tener en poco; no vacilar en
Little America *s* la Pequeña América (*base del almirante Byrd cerca del polo sur en 1929 y 1934*)
Little Bear *s* (astr.) Osa menor
little bustard *s* (orn.) sisón
Little Corporal *s* Cabito (*Napoleón*)
Little Dipper *s* (astr.) Carro menor
Little Dog *s* (astr.) Can menor
little finger *s* dedo auricular, dedo meñique; **to twist around one's little finger** conquistar fácilmente, manejar completamente
little hours *spl* (eccl.) horas menores
littleness ['lɪtəlnɪs] *s* pequeñez
little office *s* (eccl.) oficio parvo
little owl *s* (orn.) mochuelo (*Athene noctua*)
little people *spl* hadas
Little Red Ridinghood ['raɪdɪŋ,hʊd] *s* Caperucita Roja
Little Russian *s* pequeño ruso
little slam *s* (bridge) semibola, pequeño eslam
littoral ['lɪtərəl] *adj & s* litoral
liturgic [lɪ'tʌrdʒɪk] o **liturgical** [lɪ'tʌrdʒɪkəl] *adj* litúrgico
liturgist ['lɪtərdʒɪst] *s* liturgista
liturgy ['lɪtərdʒɪ] *s* (*pl:* **-gies**) liturgia
livable ['lɪvəbəl] *adj* habitable; simpático; llevadero, soportable
live [laɪv] *adj* vivo; ardiente, encendido, en ascua; palpitante, de actualidad; natural (*música; programa*); cargado (*cartucho*); (elec.) cargado; (min.) vivo (*no separado de la cantera*) ‖ [lɪv] *va* llevar (*tal o cual vida*); vivir (*p.ej., una aventura*); obrar en conformidad con, convertir en norma de vida (*una doctrina religiosa, una filosofía, etc.*); **to live down** borrar (*una falta, un error*); **to live out** pasar (*toda la vida*); salir con vida de (*un desastre, una guerra, etc.*); vivir hasta el fin de ‖ *vn* vivir; **to live and learn** vivir para ver; **to live and let live** vivir y dejar vivir; **to live apart** vivir aislado; vivir separados; **to live high** darse buena vida; comer bien; **to live on** seguir viviendo; vivir de (*p.ej., pan*); vivir a expensas de; **to live up to** cumplir (*lo prometido*); vivir en conformidad con; **to live up to one's income** comerse todas sus rentas
liveable ['lɪvəbəl] *adj* var. de **livable**
live axle [laɪv] *s* (mach.) eje vivo
live center [laɪv] *s* (mach.) punta giratoria
livelihood ['laɪvlɪhʊd] *s* vida, subsistencia; **to earn one's livelihood** ganarse la vida
livelong ['lɪv,lɔŋ] o ['lɪv,lɑŋ] *adj* todo; **all the livelong day** todo el santo día
lively ['laɪvlɪ] *adj* (*comp:* **-lier;** *super:* **-liest**) vivo; animado, de mucho bullicio; elástico; alegre, festivo; *adv* vivamente; aprisa
liven ['laɪvən] *va* animar, regocijar; *vn* animarse, regocijarse
live oak [laɪv] *s* (bot.) roble vivo o siempre verde (*Quercus virginiana*)
live program [laɪv] *s* (rad.) programa vivo
liver ['lɪvər] *s* vividor; (anat.) hígado
liver extract *s* extracto de hígado
liveried ['lɪvərɪd] *adj* en librea
Liverpudlian [,lɪvər'pʌdlɪən] *adj* perteneciente a Liverpool; *mf* natural o habitante de Liverpool
liverwort ['lɪvər,wʌrt] *s* (bot.) hepática, hierba del hígado, hierba de la Trinidad
liverwurst ['lɪvər,wʊrst] *s* embutido de hígado
livery ['lɪvərɪ] *s* (*pl:* **-ies**) librea (*traje*); caballeriza; cochera de carruajes de alquiler; pensión de caballos; alquiler de coches, bicicletas, automóviles o embarcaciones; (fig.) librea (*señales características*)
liveryman ['lɪvərɪmən] *s* (*pl:* **-men**) dueño de una cochera de carruajes de alquiler; mozo de cuadra; (obs.) criado de librea
livery stable *s* caballeriza, cochera de carruajes de alquiler
live steam [laɪv] *s* vapor vivo
livestock ['laɪv,stɑk] *s* ganadería, ganado; *adj* ganadero
live weight [laɪv] *s* peso en vivo
live wire [laɪv] *s* (elec.) alambre cargado; (slang) trafagón, pólvora
livid ['lɪvɪd] *adj* lívido
lividity [lɪ'vɪdɪtɪ] *s* lividez
living ['lɪvɪŋ] *s* vida; (eccl.) beneficio; **for a living** para ganarse la vida; **to make a living** ganarse la vida; *adj* vivo, viviente; **the living** los vivos, los vivientes
living death *s* larga agonía, agonía que se prolonga
living quarters *spl* aposentos, habitaciones
living room *s* sala, sala de estar
living space *s* espacio vital (*de una nación*)
living wage *s* jornal suficiente para vivir
Livy ['lɪvɪ] *s* Livio, Tito Livio
lizard ['lɪzərd] *s* (zool.) lagarto; (slang) holgón
ll. abr. de **lines**
llama ['lɑmə] *s* (zool.) llama
llano ['lɑno] *s* (*pl:* **-nos**) llano, llanura
LL.D. abr. de **legum doctor** (Lat.) **Doctor of Laws**
lo [lo] *interj* ¡he aquí!
loach [lotʃ] *s* (ichth.) locha
load [lod] *s* carga; (elec.) carga; (slang) borrachera; **loads** *spl* (coll.) gran cantidad, gran número, muchísmos; **at full load** (elec. & mach.) con plena carga; *va* cargar (*un buque, un carro; un arma de fuego, un horno; los dados; a una persona*); recibir carga de; (ins.) recargar (*el premio*); **to load with** colmar de (*p.ej., mercedes*); agobiar de (*p.ej., tributos*); llenar de (*p.ej., reconvenciones*); *vn* cargar; cargarse; **to load up with** recibir carga de; agobiarse de
load displacement *s* (naut.) desplazamiento con carga
loaded ['lodɪd] *adj* cargado
loaded dice *spl* dados cargados
load factor *s* (elec.) factor de carga
loading ['lodɪŋ] *s* cargamento, embarque; (elec.) carga; (ins.) recargo al premio (*para cubrir ciertos gastos*)
loading coil *s* (elec.) bobina de carga
loading zone *s* zona de carga

load line *s* (naut.) línea de flotación con carga
loadstar ['lod,stɑr] *s* var. de **lodestar**
loadstone ['lod,ston] *s* piedra imán; (fig.) imán
loaf [lof] *s* (*pl:* **loaves**) pan; pilón (*de azúcar*); *vn* haraganear, holgazanear
loafer ['lofər] *s* haragán, holgazán, arrimón
loaf sugar *s* azúcar de pilón, azúcar cubicado
loam [lom] *s* suelo franco; (found.) tierra de moldeo; *va* cubrir o llenar de suelo franco; (found.) revestir con tierra de moldeo, rellenar de tierra de moldeo
loamy ['lomɪ] *adj* franco (*suelo*)
loan [lon] *s* préstamo; empréstito (*préstamo de una empresa o del Estado*); **to hit for a loan** (coll.) dar un sablazo a; *va & vn* prestar
loan shark *s* (coll.) usurero
loan word *s* (philol.) voz extranjera, préstamo lingüístico
loath [loθ] *adj* poco dispuesto, desinclinado; **nothing loath** dispuesto; de buena gana
loathe [loð] *va* abominar, detestar
loathing ['loðɪŋ] *s* abominación, asco, detestación
loathly ['loðlɪ] *adj* (lit.) asqueroso, repugnante; ['loθlɪ] o ['loðlɪ] *adv* de mala gana
loathsome ['loðsəm] *adj* asqueroso, repugnante
lob [lɑb] *s* (tennis) pelota voleada desde muy alto; (cricket) pelota baja, de poca velocidad; (*pret & pp:* **lobbed**; *ger:* **lobbing**) *va* (tennis) volear desde muy alto; (cricket) lanzar en trayectoria baja con poca velocidad
lobar ['lobər] *adj* lobar, lobular
lobar pneumonia *s* (path.) neumonía lobar
lobate ['lobet] *adj* lobado, lobulado
lobation [lo'beʃən] *s* forma lobulada; lóbulo
lobby ['lɑbɪ] *s* (*pl:* **-bies**) salón de entrada, vestíbulo, foyer; cabildero, cabilderos; (*pret & pp:* **-bied**) *va* procurar ganar (*partidarios en una asamblea legislativa*); procurar ganar partidarios para (*un proyecto de ley*); *vn* cabildear
lobbying ['lɑbɪɪŋ] *s* cabildeo
lobbyist ['lɑbɪɪst] *s* cabildero
lobe [lob] *s* lóbulo
lobed [lobd] *adj* lobulado
lobelia [lo'biljə] *s* (bot.) lobelia
lobeliaceous [lo,bilɪ'eʃəs] *adj* (bot.) lobeliáceo
loblolly ['lɑb,lɑlɪ] *s* (*pl:* **-lies**) (bot.) pino del incienso (*Pinus taeda*); pantano; gachas muy espesas
lobotomy [lo'bɑtəmɪ] *s* (surg.) lobotomía
lobscouse ['lɑb,skaus] *s* (naut.) puchero
lobster ['lɑbstər] *s* (zool.) langosta (*Palinurus*); (zool.) bogavante, cabrajo (*Homarus*)
lobster pot *s* langostera
lobster thermidor ['θʌrmɪdɔr] *s* (cook.) langosta a la Termidor
lobular ['lɑbjələr] *adj* lobular
lobulate ['lɑbjəlɪt] o ['lɑbjəlet] *adj* lobulado
lobule ['lɑbjul] *s* lobulillo
local ['lokəl] *adj* local; (med.) local; *s* tren ómnibus (*con paradas en todas las estaciones de la línea*); junta local (*p.ej., de una confederación de trabajadores*); noticia de interés local
local anesthesia *s* anestesia local
local color *s* (lit. & paint.) color local
locale [lo'kæl] *s* lugar (*considerado como teatro de ciertos acontecimientos*)
local government *s* gobierno local
localism ['lokəlɪzəm] *s* localismo
locality [lo'kælɪtɪ] *s* (*pl:* **-ties**) localidad
localization [,lokəlɪ'zeʃən] *s* localización
localize ['lokəlaɪz] *va* localizar
locally ['lokəlɪ] *adv* localmente
local option *s* jurisdicción local (*para determinar si se pueden vender bebidas alcohólicas dentro de sus límites*)
locate ['loket] o [lo'ket] *va* localizar (*descubrir el paradero de*); colocar; establecer; *vn* (coll.) establecerse
location [lo'keʃən] *s* localización; colocación; sitio, localidad; trazado (*p.ej., de una línea férrea*); **on location** (mov.) en exteriores
locative ['lɑkətɪv] *adj & s* (gram.) locativo
loc. cit. abr. de **loco citato** (Lat.) **in the place cited**
loch [lɑk] o [lɑx] *s* (Scotch) lago; (Scotch) ría
lochia ['lokɪə] o ['lɑkɪə] *spl* (obstet.) loquios
lochial ['lokɪəl] *adj* loquial
lock [lɑk] *s* cerradura; traba, retén; esclusa (*de un canal*); llave (*de arma de fuego*); bucle (*de pelo*); mechón; (eng.) cámara intermedia (*entre presiones atmosféricas diferentes*); (sport) presa (*en la lucha*); **locks** *spl* cabellos; **under lock and key** debajo de llave; *va* cerrar con llave; encerrar; enlazar, trabar; acuñar; hacer pasar (*un buque*) por una esclusa; **to lock in** encerrar, poner debajo de llave; **to lock out** cerrar la puerta a, dejar en la calle; dejar sin trabajo (*a los obreros para obligarles a pactar con la empresa*); **to lock up** encerrar, poner debajo de llave; encarcelar; *vn* cerrarse con llave; trabarse; pasar por una esclusa
lockage ['lɑkɪdʒ] *s* construcción de esclusas; servicio de esclusas; movimiento de buques por una esclusa; diferencia de nivel (*en un canal de esclusas*); portazgo (*de esclusa*)
locker ['lɑkər] *s* cerrador; cajón, gaveta, alacena, armario, etc., cerrados con llave
locket ['lɑkɪt] *s* guardapelo, medallón
lockjaw ['lɑk,dʒɔ] *s* (path.) trismo
lock nut *s* contratuerca
lockout ['lɑk,aut] *s* paro, cierre (*de una fábrica u otro establecimiento por los dueños para obligar a los obreros a pactar con la empresa*)
locksmith ['lɑk,smɪθ] *s* cerrajero
lock step *s* marcha en fila apretada
lock stitch *s* (sew.) punto encadenado (*hecho en la máquina de coser*)
lock, stock, and barrel *adv* (coll.) del todo, por completo
lock tender *s* esclusero
lockup ['lɑk,ʌp] *s* cárcel
lock washer *s* arandela de seguridad
loco ['loko] *s* (bot.) loco; (vet.) locoísmo; *adj* (slang) loco; *va* envenenar con el veneno del loco
loco disease *s* (vet.) locoísmo
locomobile [,lokə'mobɪl] *adj & s* locomóvil
locomotion [,lokə'moʃən] *s* locomoción
locomotive [,lokə'motɪv] *adj* locomotor; *s* locomóvil; (rail.) locomotora
locomotor [,lokə'motər] *adj* locomotor; *s* persona, animal o cosa locomotoras
locomotor ataxia *s* (path.) ataxia locomotriz progresiva
locoweed ['loko,wid] *s* (bot.) loco, cascabelito
locular ['lɑkjələr] *adj* locular
loculate ['lɑkjəlet] o ['lɑkjəlɪt] *adj* (bot.) loculado
loculicidal [,lɑkjəlɪ'saɪdəl] *adj* (bot.) loculicida
loculus ['lɑkjələs] *s* (*pl:* **-li** [laɪ]) (bot. & hist.) lóculo
locum tenens ['lokəm 'tinɛnz] *s* interino
locus ['lokəs] *s* (*pl:* **-ci** [saɪ]) sitio, lugar; (geom.) lugar (geométrico)
locust ['lokəst] *s* (ent.) langosta, saltamontes; (ent.) cigarra; (bot.) acacia falsa
locust bean *s* algarroba
locution [lo'kjuʃən] *s* locución
lode [lod] *s* (min.) filón, venero
lodestar ['lod,stɑr] *s* estrella de guía; (astr.) estrella polar; (fig.) norte (*dirección o guía*)
lodestone ['lod,ston] *s* var. de **loadstone**
lodge [lɑdʒ] *s* casa de guarda; casa de campo; casita (*p.ej., de jardinero*); cabaña, choza; madriguera (*de castores o nutrias*); logia (*p.ej., de francmasones*); *va* alojar, hospedar; colocar, depositar; comunicar (*informes*); presentar (*una queja*); conferir (*autoridad*); *vn* alojarse, hospedarse; ir a parar, quedarse, quedar colgado
lodgement ['lɑdʒmənt] *s* var. de **lodgment**
lodger ['lɑdʒər] *s* huésped, inquilino
lodging ['lɑdʒɪŋ] *s* alojamiento, hospedaje; cobijo (*hospedaje sin manutención*); **lodgings** *spl* habitación, aposentos
lodging house *s* casa de huéspedes
lodgment ['lɑdʒmənt] *s* aposento, habitación, alojamiento, casa; cosa depositada; (mil.) posición ganada; (mil.) atrincheramiento hecho rápidamente en terreno recién ganado al enemigo
loess ['loɛs] o ['lo·ɪs] *s* loess, tierra amarilla
loft [lɔft] o [lɑft] *s* desván, sobrado; henal, pajar; galería (*en los teatros e iglesias*); piso al-

to (*en un almacén o edificio de oficinas*); (golf) ángulo de elevación; (golf) elevación; *va* (golf) lanzar en alto
loftiness ['lɔftɪnɪs] o ['lɑftɪnɪs] *s* elevación, altura; eminencia, excelsitud; altivez, orgullo
lofty ['lɔftɪ] o ['lɑftɪ] *adj* (*comp:* **-ier;** *super:* **-iest**) elevado, encumbrado; eminente, excelso; altivo, orgulloso
log. o **log** abr. de **logarithm** o **logarithmic**
log [lɔg] o [lɑg] *s* leño, tronco, troza; (naut.) cuaderno de bitácora; (naut.) barquilla (*de la corredera*); (naut.) corredera (*barquilla y cordel*); (aer.) diario de vuelo; **to sleep like a log** dormir como un leño; *adj* de troncos; (*pret & pp:* **logged;** *ger:* **logging**) *va* cortar en trozos; extraer madera de (*un terreno poblado de árboles*); (naut.) apuntar el nombre de (*un marinero*) en el libro de bordo, junto con el desliz que ha cometido; *vn* extraer madera de un bosque
loganberry ['logən,bɛrɪ] *s* (*pl:* **-ries**) (bot.) frambueso norteamericano (*Rubus loganobaccus*); frambuesa norteamericana
loganiaceous [lo,genɪ'eʃəs] *adj* (bot.) loganiáceo
logarithm ['lɔgərɪðəm] o ['lɑgərɪðəm] *s* (math.) logaritmo
logarithmic [,lɔgə'rɪðmɪk] o [,lɑgə'rɪðmɪk] o **logarithmical** [,lɔgə'rɪðmɪkəl] o [,lɑgə'rɪðmɪkəl] *adj* logarítmico
logbook ['lɔg,bʊk] o ['lɑg,bʊk] *s* (naut.) cuaderno de bitácora; (aer.) libro de vuelo
log cabin *s* cabaña de troncos
log chip *s* (naut.) barquilla
log driver *s* ganchero
log driving *s* flotaje
logger ['lɔgər] o ['lɑgər] *s* maderero, hachero; grúa, cargadora de troncos; tractor
loggerhead ['lɔgər,hɛd] o ['lɑgər,hɛd] *s* majadero, mentecato; (zool.) tortuga de mar; **to be at loggerheads** comerse unos a otros, estar reñidos
loggia ['lodʒə] *s* (arch.) logia
logging ['lɔgɪŋ] o ['lɑgɪŋ] *s* extracción de madera de los bosques
logic ['lɑdʒɪk] *s* lógica
logical ['lɑdʒɪkəl] *adj* lógico
logician [lo'dʒɪʃən] *s* lógico
logistic [lo'dʒɪstɪk] *adj* (mil.) logístico; **logistics** *ssg* (mil.) logística
logistical [lo'dʒɪstɪkəl] *adj* (mil.) logístico
log line *s* (naut.) corredera, cordel de la corredera
logogriph ['lɔgəgrɪf] o ['lɑgəgrɪf] *s* logogrifo
logomachy [lo'gɑməkɪ] *s* (*pl:* **-chies**) logomaquia
logotype ['lɔgətaɪp] o ['lɑgətaɪp] *s* (print.) logotipo
log reel *s* (naut.) carretel
logroll ['lɔg,rol] o ['lɑg,rol] *va* lograr que se apruebe (*un proyecto de ley*) mediante un intercambio de favores políticos; *vn* trocar favores políticos, seguir el sistema de hoy por ti y mañana por mí
logrolling ['lɔg,rolɪŋ] o ['lɑg,rolɪŋ] *s* intercambio de favores políticos, sistema de hoy por ti y mañana por mí; arrastre cooperativo de maderos en los bosques
log ship *s* var. de **log chip**
logwood ['lɔg,wʊd] o ['lɑg,wʊd] *s* campeche, palo campeche; (bot.) campeche (*árbol*)
logy ['logɪ] *adj* (*comp:* **-gier;** *super:* **-giest**) torpe, lerdo
loin [lɔɪn] *s* ijada, lomo; lomo (*carne de lomo del animal*); **to gird up one's loins** ceñirse los riñones (*disponerse para la acción*)
loincloth ['lɔɪn,klɔθ] o ['lɔɪn,klɑθ] *s* taparrabo
Loire [lwɑr] *s* Loira
loiter ['lɔɪtər] *va;* **to loiter away** malgastar (*el tiempo*); *vn* holgazanear, rezagarse, perder el tiempo
loiterer ['lɔɪtərər] *s* holgazán, rezagado
loll [lɑl] *va* colgar flojamente hacia fuera, sacar (*la lengua*) fuera de la boca; *vn* colgar flojamente hacia fuera; arrellanarse, repantigarse, estar recostado con indolencia
Lollard ['lɑlərd] *s* lolardo
lollipop ['lɑlɪpɑp] *s* paleta (*dulce con un palito que sirve de mango*)
Lombard ['lɑmbɑrd] o ['lɑmbərd] *adj & s* lombardo
Lombardy ['lɑmbərdɪ] *s* Lombardía
Lombardy poplar *s* (bot.) álamo de Italia, chopo lombardo
Lombrosian [lɑm'brozɪən] *adj* lombrosiano
loment ['lomɛnt] *s* (bot.) lomento
lomentaceous [,lomən'teʃəs] *adj* (bot.) lomentáceo
lon. abr. de **longitude**
London ['lʌndən] *s* Londres; *adj* londinense
Londoner ['lʌndənər] *s* londinense
lone [lon] *adj* solo, solitario; único; (hum.) sin cónyuge, soltero, viudo
lone hand *s* (cards) mano jugada sin intervención de compañero; (fig.) lobo solitario
loneliness ['lonlɪnɪs] *s* soledad
lonely ['lonlɪ] *adj* (*comp:* **-lier;** *super:* **-liest**) solitario; soledoso
lonesome ['lonsəm] *adj* solitario (*lugar o ambiente*); solo y triste, soledoso
lone wolf *s* (fig.) lobo solitario
long. abr. de **longitude**
long [lɔŋ] o [lɑŋ] *adj* (*comp:* **longer** ['lɔŋgər] o ['lɑŋgər]; *super:* **longest** ['lɔŋgɪst] o ['lɑŋgɪst]) largo; de largo, p.ej., **two feet long** dos pies de largo; (com.) alcista; (phonet.) largo; **to be long (in)** + *ger* tardar en + *inf;* **to be not long for this world** estar cercano a la muerte; *adv* (*comp:* **longer** ['lɔŋgər] o ['lɑŋgər]; *super:* **longest** ['lɔŋgɪst] o ['lɑŋgɪst]) largamente, mucho tiempo, largo tiempo; **all night long** (durante) toda la noche; **as long as** mientras; con tal de que; puesto que; **before long** dentro de poco; **how long** cuánto tiempo; cuándo; **no longer** ya no; **so long!** (coll.) ¡hasta luego!; **so long as** con tal de que; **long ago** hace mucho tiempo; **long before** mucho antes; **longer** más tiempo; **long since** desde hace mucho tiempo; *vn* anhelar, suspirar; **to long for** anhelar por; **to long to** + *inf* anhelar + *inf*
longboat ['lɔŋ,bot] o ['lɑŋ,bot] *s* (naut.) lancha
longbow ['lɔŋ,bo] o ['lɑŋ,bo] *s* arco (*disparado a mano*); **to draw the longbow** mentir por la barba (*al narrar cuentos de aventuras extraordinarias*)
longcloth ['lɔŋ,klɔθ] o ['lɑŋ,klɑθ] *s* tejido de algodón muy fino
long-distance ['lɔŋ'dɪstəns] o ['lɑŋ'dɪstəns] *adj* (telp.) de larga distancia, interurbano; *s* (telp.) central (*oficina o mujer*) de llamadas a larga distancia
long-distance call *s* (telp.) llamada a larga distancia
long-distance flight *s* (aer.) vuelo a distancia
long dozen *s* docena del fraile (*trece*)
long-drawn ['lɔŋ,drɔn] o ['lɑŋ,drɔn] *adj* muy prolongado, prolijo
longeron ['lɑndʒərən] *s* (aer.) larguero
longevity [lɑn'dʒɛvɪtɪ] *s* longevidad
longevous [lɑn'dʒivəs] *adj* longevo
long face *s* (coll.) cara triste, cara inquieta
long green *s* (slang) papel moneda (*de los EE.UU.*)
longhair ['lɔŋ,hɛr] o ['lɑŋ,hɛr] *adj* (slang) de o por la música clásica; (slang) aficionado a la música clásica; *s* (slang) aficionado a la música clásica
longhand ['lɔŋ,hænd] o ['lɑŋ,hænd] *s* escritura ordinaria (*a distinción de la taquigrafía*)
long-headed ['lɔŋ'hɛdɪd] o ['lɑŋ'hɛdɪd] *adj* dolicocéfalo; (fig.) astuto, sagaz, precavido
longhorn ['lɔŋ,hɔrn] o ['lɑŋ,hɔrn] *s* res vacuna de cuernos largos
longing ['lɔŋɪŋ] o ['lɑŋɪŋ] *s* anhelo; *adj* anhelante
Longinus [lɑn'dʒaɪnəs] *s* Longino
longish ['lɔŋɪʃ] o ['lɑŋɪʃ] *adj* algo largo, un poco largo
longitude ['lɑndʒɪtjud] o ['lɑndʒɪtud] *s* longitud
longitudinal [,lɑndʒɪ'tjudɪnəl] o [,lɑndʒɪ'tudɪnəl] *adj* longitudinal
longitudinally [,lɑndʒɪ'tjudɪnəlɪ] o [,lɑndʒɪ'tudɪnəlɪ] *adj* longitudinalmente
long-lived ['lɔŋ'laɪvd], ['lɑŋ'laɪvd], ['lɔŋ'lɪvd] o ['lɑŋ'lɪvd] *adj* duradero, de larga vida
long measure *s* medida de longitud

long moss *s* (bot.) caballo de rey
Longobard ['lɑŋgobɑrd] *adj & s* longobardo
Long Parliament *s* (hist.) Parlamento Largo
long-playing record ['lɔŋ'pleɪŋ] o ['lɑŋ-'pleɪŋ] *s* disco de larga duración
long primer ['prɪmər] *s* (print.) entredós
long-range ['lɔŋ'rendʒ] o ['lɑŋ'rendʒ] *adj* de gran alcance, de largo alcance
longshore ['lɔŋ,ʃor] o ['lɑŋ,ʃor] *adj* de la costa; del muelle, de los muelles
longshoreman ['lɔŋ,ʃormən] o ['lɑŋ,ʃormən] *s* (*pl:* **-men**) estibador
long-sighted ['lɔŋ'saɪtɪd] o ['lɑŋ'saɪtɪd] *adj* présbita; previsor, precavido
long-standing ['lɔŋ,stændɪŋ] o ['lɑŋ,stændɪŋ] *adj* existente desde hace mucho tiempo
long-suffering ['lɔŋ'sʌfərɪŋ] o ['lɑŋ'sʌfərɪŋ] *adj* longánimo, sufrido; *s* longanimidad
long suit *s* (cards) palo fuerte; (fig.) fuerte
long-tailed titmouse ['lɔŋ,teld] o ['lɑŋ,teld] *s* (orn.) chamarón
long-term ['lɔŋ,tʌrm] o ['lɑŋ,tʌrm] *adj* (com.) a largo plazo
long ton *s* tonelada larga o gruesa (*2240 libras o 1016,06 kilogramos*)
long-tongued ['lɔŋ'tʌŋd] o ['lɑŋ'tʌŋd] *adj* de lengua larga; longílocuo, largo de lengua
long wave *s* (rad.) onda larga
long-wave ['lɔŋ,wev] o ['lɑŋ,wev] *adj* (rad.) de onda larga
longways ['lɔŋwez] o ['lɑŋwez] *adv* a lo largo, longitudinalmente
long-winded ['lɔŋ'wɪndɪd] o ['lɑŋ'wɪndɪd] *adj* de buenos pulmones; (fig.) palabrero, difuso, verboso
longwise ['lɔŋwaɪz] o ['lɑŋwaɪz] *adv* var. de **longways**
look [lʊk] *s* mirada; búsqueda; aspecto, apariencia; cara, aire; **looks** *spl* aspecto, apariencia; **to have a look (of)** tener un aire (de), p.ej., **to have an unfriendly look** tener un aire hostil; **to take a look at** echar una mirada a ‖ *va* expresar con la mirada; representar (*p.ej., la edad que uno tiene*); **to look over** examinar; **to look the part** vestir el cargo; **to look through** hojear, p.ej., **I didn't have time to look the book through** no tuve tiempo de hojear el libro; **to look up** buscar (*p.ej., en el diccionario*); ir a visitar, venir a ver ‖ *vn* mirar; buscar; parecer; **to look about** mirar alrededor; **to look after** mirar por, cuidar de; ocuparse en; **to look alike** parecerse; **to look at** mirar; **to look back** mirar hacia atrás; (fig.) mirar el pasado; **to look back on** o **upon** recordar, evocar; **to look down on** o **upon** mirar por encima del hombro; **to look for** buscar; creer, p.ej., **I look for rain** creo que va a llover; **to look forward to** esperar con placer anticipado, anticipar con placer; **to look ill** tener mala cara; **to look in** hacer una visita breve; **to look in on** pasar por la casa o la oficina de; **to look into** averiguar, examinar, estudiar; **to look like** parecerse a; tener trazas de; **to look on** mirar, p.ej., **he stood awhile looking on** estuvo un rato mirando; **to look on as** tener por, p.ej., **I look on him as a fool** lo tengo por muy tonto; **to look oneself** parecer el mismo; tener buena cara; **to look out** mirar por (*p.ej., la ventana*); tener cuidado; **to look out for** mirar por, cuidar de, defender; guardarse de; **to look out of** mirar por (*p.ej., la ventana*); **to look out on** dar a, p.ej., **the house looks out on the ocean** la casa da al mar; **to look through** mirar por (*p.ej., la ventana*); hojear (*p.ej., un libro*); **to look to** mirar por, cuidar de; ocuparse en; acudir a (*una persona en busca de ayuda*); **to look towards** dar a, p.ej., **the house looks towards the ocean** la casa da al mar; **to look up** (coll.) mejorar; (coll.) sentirse mejor, mejorar de salud; **to look up to** admirar, mirar con respeto; **to look well** tener buena cara; estar bien, ir bien; **look out!** ¡cuidado!, ¡ojo!
looker-on [,lʊkər'ɑn] o [,lʊkər'ɔn] *s* (*pl:* **lookers-on**) mirón, espectador
look-in ['lʊk,ɪn] *s* mirada, mirada adentro; (slang) oportunidad, parte de una empresa
looking glass *s* espejo
lookout ['lʊk,aʊt] *s* vigilancia; vigilante; vista, perspectiva; atalaya (*hombre o torre*); (coll.) cuidado (*asunto que está a cargo de uno*); **to be on the lookout (for)** estar a la mira (de); estar a la expectativa (de)
loom [lum] *s* telar; (elec.) tubo fibroso flexible; (naut.) guión (*de remo*); vislumbre; *va* tejer en un telar; *vn* vislumbrarse; amenazar, parecer inevitable
loon [lun] *s* bobo, mequetrefe; (orn.) zambullidor (*Gavia immer*)
loony ['lunɪ] *adj* (*comp:* **-ier;** *super:* **-iest**) (slang) loco; *s* (*pl:* **-ies**) (slang) loco
loop [lup] *s* lazo; curva cerrada o casi cerrada; vuelta (*p.ej., de un cabo*); meandro (*p.ej., de un río*); recoveco (*p.ej., de un camino*); onda, bucle; presilla (*para asegurar un botón*); (aer.) rizo; (bact.) asa; (elec.) circuito cerrado; (rail.) ramal cerrado; **to loop the loop** (aer.) hacer o rizar el rizo; *va* hacer lazos en; doblar formando curva cerrada; enlazar; asegurar con una presilla; *vn* formar lazo o lazos; andar formando arcos (*los geómetras*); (aer.) hacer el rizo
loop aerial o **loop antenna** *s* (rad.) antena de cuadro
loophole ['lup,hol] *s* aspillera, saetera, portillo; (fig.) callejuela, evasiva, efugio
loose [lus] *adj* flojo (*p.ej., vestido, diente, tornillo, vientre*); suelto (*p.ej., ajuste, hilo, alambre, remache, animal, lengua, vientre*); desmenuzado (*dícese de la tierra*); sueltos (*papeles sin encuadernar*); a granel, sin envase; loco (*dícese de una polea*); libre (*traducción*); poco exacto; relajado (*dícese de la vida, la moral, etc.*); fácil, frágil (*p.ej., mujer*); (paint.) bien manejado; **to become loose** aflojarse, desatarse; **to break loose** desatarse; ponerse en libertad; **to cast loose** desatar, soltar; **to cut loose** cortar las amarras de; separarse; huir, ponerse en libertad; (coll.) echar una cana al aire; **to let, set** o **turn loose** soltar; *adv* flojamente; libremente; *s* relajamiento (*en la moral*); **to be on the loose** (coll.) ser libre, estar sin trabas; (coll.) estar de juerga; *va* soltar, poner en libertad; desatar, desencadenar
loose end *s* cabo suelto; **at loose end** sin empleo; **at loose ends** desarreglado
loose-jointed ['lus'dʒɔɪntɪd] *adj* de articulaciones flojas; de movimientos sueltos
loose-leaf notebook ['lus,lif] *s* cuaderno de hojas sueltas, cuaderno de hojas cambiables
loosen ['lusən] *va* desatar, aflojar, desapretar; desasir; aflojar, laxar (*el vientre*); *vn* desatarse, aflojarse, desapretarse
looseness ['lusnɪs] *s* flojedad; soltura; relajamiento (*en la moral*)
loosestrife ['lus,straɪf] *s* (bot.) lisimaquia; (bot.) salicaria
loose-tongued ['lus'tʌŋd] *adj* largo de lengua, suelto de lengua
loot [lut] *s* botín, presa; *va & vn* saquear, robar
lop [lɑp] (*pret & pp:* **lopped;** *ger:* **lopping**) *va* desmochar; podar; *vn* colgar; agitarse
lope [lop] *s* medio galope; paso largo; *vn* correr a medio galope; correr a paso largo
lop-eared ['lɑp,ɪrd] *adj* de orejas caídas
lophobranch ['lofəbræŋk] o ['lɑfəbræŋk] *adj & s* (ichth.) lofobranquio
lopsided ['lɑp'saɪdɪd] *adj* más pesado de un lado que de otro, ladeado, sesgado; asimétrico, desproporcionado, patituerto; (fig.) maniático
loquacious [lo'kweʃəs] *adj* locuaz
loquacity [lo'kwæsɪtɪ] *s* locuacidad
loquat ['lokwɑt] o ['lokwæt] *s* (bot.) níspero del Japón
loran ['lɔrən] o ['lorən] *s* (naut.) lorán
lord [lɔrd] *s* señor (*de un estado feudal; amo, dueño*); (Brit.) lord; (hum. & poet.) marido; **Lord** *s* Señor (*Dios, Jesucristo*); (Brit.) lord (*título*); **our Lord** nuestro Señor; **the Lords** los lores (*la Cámara alta del Parlamento británico*); **to die in the Lord** morir en el Señor; **to rest in the Lord** descansar en el Señor; **to sleep in the Lord** dormir en el Señor; *va* investir con la dignidad de lord; **to lord it over** imponerse a, dominar despóticamente; *vn* mandar despóticamente
Lord Chamberlain *s* (Brit.) camarero mayor
lordling ['lɔrdlɪŋ] *s* hidalguillo, señorito
lordly ['lɔrdlɪ] *adj* (*comp:* **-lier;** *super:* **-liest**)

señoril; espléndido, magnífico; altivo; despótico, imperioso; *adv* señorilmente; magníficamente; altivamente; imperiosamente
Lord Mayor *s* alcalde de la ciudad de Londres
Lord of hosts *s* Señor de los ejércitos
lordosis [lɔr'dosɪs] *s* (path.) lordosis
Lord's Anointed, The el ungido del Señor
Lord's Day, the el domingo
lordship ['lɔrdʃɪp] *s* señoría, excelencia; señorío
Lord's Prayer *s* oración dominical, padrenuestro
lords spiritual *spl* (Brit.) lores espirituales (*brazo eclesiástico en la Cámara alta*)
Lord's Supper *s* Cena, Cena del Señor; sagrada comunión
lords temporal *spl* (Brit.) lores temporales (*brazo de nobles en la Cámara alta*)
lore [lor] *s* ciencia popular, saber popular; ciencia, saber
lorgnette [lɔrn'jɛt] *s* impertinente o impertinentes; gemelos de teatro
lorgnon [lɔr'njõ] *s* gafas; lentes de nariz
lorica [lo'raɪkə] *s* (*pl:* **-cae** [si]) (arm. & zool.) loriga
loris ['lorɪs] *s* (*pl:* **-ris**) (zool.) loris
lorn [lɔrn] *adj* abandonado, desamparado; (archaic) arruinado, perdido
Lorraine [lo'ren] *s* Lorena
Lorrainer [lə'renər] *s* lorenés
Lorrainese [,lɑre'niz] *adj* lorenés
lorry ['lɑrɪ] o ['lɔrɪ] *s* (*pl:* **-ries**) (Brit.) vagoneta; (Brit.) carro de plataforma; (Brit.) autocamión
lory ['lorɪ] *s* (*pl:* **-ries**) (orn.) loro
lose [luz] (*pret & pp:* **lost**) *va* perder; hacer perder, p.ej., **that lost him the battle** eso le hizo perder la batalla; tener la culpa de que se pierda, p.ej., **he lost the game** él tuvo la culpa de que se perdiera el partido; no lograr salvar (*el médico al enfermo*); **to lose oneself** perderse, errar el camino; ensimismarse, abismarse (*p.ej., en la lectura*); confundirse; **to lose to** perder (*p.ej., el mercado*) en beneficio de; *vn* perder, tener una pérdida; ser o quedar vencido; retrasarse (*un reloj*)
loser ['luzər] *s* perdidoso
losing ['luzɪŋ] *adj* perdidoso; **losings** *spl* pérdidas, dinero perdido
loss [lɔs] o [lɑs] *s* pérdida; **to be at a loss** estar perplejo, no saber qué hacer; **to be at a loss to** + *inf* no saber cómo + *inf;* **to sell at a loss** vender con pérdida
loss of face *s* desprestigio, pérdida de prestigio
lost [lɔst] o [lɑst] *pret & pp de* **lose;** *adj* perdido; perplejo; **lost in** abismado en, embebido en; **lost to** perdido para; insensible a; inaccesible a
lost-and-found department ['lɔstənd'faʊnd] o ['lɑstənd'faʊnd] *s* oficina de objetos perdidos, departamento de cosas olvidadas
lost motion *s* movimiento perdido
lost sheep *s* (fig.) oveja perdida
lot [lɑt] *s* solar, parcela (*para construir una casa*); suerte; lote (*parte, porción*); grupo (*de personas*); (coll.) gran cantidad, gran número; (coll.) individuo, sujeto, tipo; **a lot** (coll.) mucho; (coll.) muchos; **a lot of** (coll.) mucho, muchos; **by lots** echando suertes; **to draw** o **to cast lots** echar suertes; **to cast** o **to throw in one's lot with** compartir la suerte de; **to fall to one's lot** caerle a uno en suerte; **lots of** (coll.) mucho, muchos; (*pret & pp:* **lotted;** *ger:* **lotting**) *va* repartir; asignar; dividir echando suertes, escoger echando suertes; *vn* echar suertes
loth [loθ] *adj* var. de **loath**
Lothario [lo'θerɪo] *s* (*pl:* **-os**) tenorio, libertino
lotiform ['lotɪfɔrm] *adj* lotiforme
lotion ['loʃən] *s* (pharm.) loción
lotos ['lotəs] *s* var. de **lotus**
lottery ['lɑtərɪ] *s* (*pl:* **-ies**) lotería
lottery wheel *s* rueda de lotería
lotto ['lɑto] *s* lotería (*juego casero*)
lotus ['lotəs] *s* (bot., arch. & myth.) loto
lotus-eater ['lotəs,itər] *s* lotófago; persona indolente y soñadora
loud [laʊd] *adj* alto; ruidoso; fuerte, recio; (coll.) chillón, llamativo; (coll.) charro, cursi; (coll.) apestoso, maloliente; *adv* ruidosamente; alto, en voz alta
loudish ['laʊdɪʃ] *adj* un poco alto, algo fuerte
loudspeaker ['laʊd'spikər] *s* (rad.) altavoz, altoparlante
lough [lɑk] o [lɑx] *s* (Irish) lago; (Irish) ría
Louis ['luɪ] o ['luɪs] *s* Luis
Louisa [lu'izə] o **Louise** [lu'iz] *s* Luisa
Louisiana [lu,izɪ'ænə] o [,luɪzɪ'ænə] *s* la Luisiana
Louisianan [lu,izɪ'ænən] o [,luɪzɪ'ænən] *adj & s* luisianense
Louis Napoleon ['luɪ] *s* Luis Napoleón
Louis Phillipe ['luɪ fɪ'lip] *s* Luis Felipe
lounge [laʊndʒ] *s* canapé ancho y cómodo; salón de tertulia, salón social; paso lento y perezoso; haraganería; *va* gastar ociosamente; *vn* pasearse perezosamente, repantigarse a su sabor, recostarse cómodamente, estar arrimado a la pared, un farol, etc.
lour [laʊr] *s* ceño; *vn* fruncir el entrecejo, poner mala cara; encapotarse o nublarse (*el cielo*)
Lourdes [lurd] *s* Lurdes
louse [laʊs] *s* (*pl:* **lice**) (ent.) piojo
lousewort ['laʊs,wʌrt] *s* (bot.) gallarito (*Pedicularis sylvatica*)
lousy ['laʊzɪ] *adj* (*comp:* **-ier;** *super:* **-iest**) piojoso; (slang) asqueroso, sucio; (slang) colmado (*p.ej., de riquezas*)
lout [laʊt] *s* patán
loutish ['laʊtɪʃ] *adj* patán
Louvain [lu'ven] *s* Lovaina
louver ['luvər] *s* lumbrera (*abertura por donde entran el aire y la luz*); persiana; tabla de persiana; (aut.) persiana de ventilación
louver boards *spl* tablas pluviales
Louvre ['luvrə] *s* Luvre (*museo*)
lovable ['lʌvəbəl] *adj* amable
lovage ['lʌvɪdʒ] *s* (bot.) ligústico; (bot.) levístico
love [lʌv] *s* amor; (tennis) cero, nada; (coll.) preciosidad, p.ej., **it's a love of a cottage** la casita es una preciosidad; (*cap.*) *s* Amor (*Cupido*); **for love** por amor, por placer; **for the love of** por el amor de; **not for love or money** ni a tiros, por nada del mundo; **to be in love (with)** estar enamorado (de); **to fall in love (with)** enamorarse (de); **to make love** hacer el amor; **to make love to** cortejar, galantear; *va* amar, querer, tener cariño a; gustar de (*p.ej., la música*); *vn* amar; enamorarse
loveable ['lʌvəbəl] *adj* var. de **lovable**
love affair *s* amores, amorío
love apple *s* tomate
lovebird ['lʌv,bʌrd] *s* (orn.) inseparable (*Agapornis*); (orn.) pupuí (*Psittacus*)
love child *s* hijo del amor
love feast *s* ágape
love-in-a-mist ['lʌvɪnə'mɪst] *s* (bot.) ajenuz, arañuela
love-in-idleness ['lʌvɪn'aɪdəlnɪs] *s* (bot.) pensamiento, trinitaria
love knot *s* nudo o lazo de amor
loveless ['lʌvlɪs] *adj* desamorado (*que no siente amor*); abandonado, sin amor
love-lies-bleeding ['lʌvlaɪz'blidɪŋ] *s* (bot.) amaranto rojo
loveliness ['lʌvlɪnɪs] *s* hermosura, belleza; preciosidad, exquisitez; (coll.) gracia, encanto
lovelock ['lʌv,lɑk] *s* tirabuzón (*rizo de cabello*); (archaic) rizo largo con lazo de cinta
lovelorn ['lʌv,lɔrn] *adj* suspirando de amor, herido de amor
lovely ['lʌvlɪ] *adj* (*comp:* **-lier;** *super:* **-liest**) hermoso, bello; precioso, exquisito; (coll.) gracioso, encantador
love-maker ['lʌv,mekər] *s* galanteador
love-making ['lʌv,mekɪŋ] *adj* galanteador; *s* galanteo
love match *s* matrimonio por amor
love potion *s* filtro, filtro de amor
lover ['lʌvər] *s* aficionado (*p.ej., a la caza*); amigo (*p.ej., del trabajo*); amante; **lovers** *spl* amantes (*hombre y mujer que se aman*)
love seat *s* confidente
lovesick ['lʌv,sɪk] *adj* enfermo de amor
lovesickness ['lʌv,sɪknɪs] *s* mal de amor

love song *s* canción de amor
loving [ˈlʌvɪŋ] *adj* afectuoso, cariñoso, amoroso
loving cup *s* copa de la amistad
loving-kindness [ˌlʌvɪŋˈkaɪndnɪs] *s* bondad infinita, misericordia
low [lo] *adj* bajo; abatido; gravemente enfermo; malo (*dícese de la dieta, la opinión, etc.*); escotado; muerto; lento (*fuego*); (phonet.) abierto; **to feel low** sentirse abatido; **to lay low** dejar tendido, derribar; matar; **to lie low** (coll.) mantenerse oculto, no dejarse ver; (coll.) no chistar; *adv* bajo; bajamente; *s* punto bajo, lugar bajo; (el) precio más bajo, precio mínimo; mugido; (aut.) primera marcha, primera velocidad; (meteor.) depresión; *vn* mugir (*la vaca*)
low area *s* área de baja presión barométrica
lowborn [ˈloˌbɔrn] *adj* de humilde cuna, plebeyo, mal nacido
lowboy [ˈloˌbɔɪ] *s* cómoda baja sostenida por patas cortas
lowbred [ˈloˌbrɛd] *adj* grosero, palurdo
lowbrow [ˈloˌbraʊ] *adj* (slang) ignorante; (slang) de o para gente ignorante o sin cultura; *s* (slang) ignorante
Low Church *s* baja iglesia (*rama no conservadora de la Iglesia anglicana*)
Low-Church [ˈloˈtʃʌrtʃ] *adj* no ritualista
Low-Churchman [ˌloˈtʃʌrtʃmən] *s* (*pl:* **-men**) protestante episcopal no ritualista
low comedy *s* comedia bufa, farsa
low-cost housing [ˈloˈkɔst] o [ˈloˈkɑst] *s* habitación popular, casas baratas
Low Countries *spl* Países Bajos (*Bélgica, Holanda y Luxemburgo*)
low-country [ˈloˌkʌntrɪ] *adj* de los Países Bajos
low-down [ˈloˈdaʊn] *adj* (coll.) bajo, vil; [ˈloˌdaʊn] *s* (slang) informes confidenciales, hechos verdaderos
lower [ˈloər] *adj* más bajo; inferior; *va & vn* bajar; [ˈlaʊər] *s* ceño; *vn* fruncir el entrecejo, poner mala cara; encapotarse o nublarse (*el cielo*)
lower berth [ˈloər] *s* litera baja
Lower California [ˈloər] *s* Baja California
lower case [ˈloər] *s* (print.) letra de caja baja
lower-case [ˈloərˌkes] *adj* (print.) de caja baja
lowerclassman [ˈloərˈklæsmən] o [ˈloərˈklɑsmən] *s* (*pl:* **-men**) estudiante de los dos primeros años
Lower House [ˈloər] *s* Cámara baja
lowering [ˈlaʊərɪŋ] *adj* ceñoso, ceñudo; encapotado, nublado
lower lip [ˈloər] *s* labio inferior
lowermost [ˈloərmost] *adj* (el) más bajo
lower regions [ˈloər] *spl* infiernos
lower world [ˈloər] *s* tierra; mundo subterráneo, infiernos
low frequency *s* (elec.) baja frecuencia
low-frequency [ˈloˈfrikwənsɪ] *adj* (elec.) de baja frecuencia
low gear *s* (aut.) primera marcha, primera velocidad
Low German *s* bajoalemán
Low-German [ˈloˈdʒʌrmən] *adj* bajoalemán
lowland [ˈlolənd] *adj* de tierra baja; *s* tierra baja; **Lowlands** *spl* Tierra Baja (*de Escocia*)
Lowlander [ˈloləndər] *s* natural de la Tierra Baja de Escocia
Low Latin *s* bajo latín
lowliness [ˈlolɪnɪs] *s* humildad
lowly [ˈlolɪ] *adj* (*comp:* **-lier;** *super:* **-liest**) humilde, de baja condición; *adv* humildemente
Low Mass *s* (eccl.) misa rezada
low-minded [ˈloˈmaɪndɪd] *adj* vil, ruin
low-necked [ˈloˈnɛkt] *adj* escotado
low-pass filter [ˈloˌpæs] o [ˈloˌpɑs] *s* (elec.) filtro paso inferior, filtro de paso bajo
low-pitched [ˈloˈpɪtʃt] *adj* de poco declive, poco pendiente; grave (*sonido*)
low-pressure [ˈloˈprɛʃər] *adj* de baja presión
low relief *s* bajo relieve
low shoe *s* zapato inglés (*zapato bajo que se cierra con cordones*)
low speed *s* baja velocidad
low-speed [ˈloˌspid] *adj* de baja velocidad
low-spirited [ˈloˈspɪrɪtɪd] *adj* abatido, desanimado
low spirits *spl* abatimiento, desanimación
Low Sunday *s* domingo de cuasimodo
low tension *s* (elec.) baja tensión
low-tension [ˈloˈtɛnʃən] *adj* (elec.) de baja tensión
low tide *s* bajamar, marea baja; (fig.) punto más bajo
low visibility *s* (aer.) poca visibilidad
low-voltage [ˈloˈvoltɪdʒ] *adj* (elec.) de bajo voltaje, de baja tensión
low water *s* estiaje (*por causa de la sequía*); marea baja; nivel mínimo (*p.ej., de un río*)
low-water mark [ˈloˈwɔtər] o [ˈloˈwɑtər] *s* línea de aguas mínimas, línea de bajamar; (fig.) punto más bajo
loxodrome [ˈlɑksədrom] *s* (naut.) loxodromia
loxodromic [ˌlɑksəˈdrɑmɪk] o **loxodromical** [ˌlɑksəˈdrɑmɪkəl] *adj* (naut.) loxodrómico
loyal [ˈlɔɪəl] *adj* leal
loyalist [ˈlɔɪəlɪst] *s* legitimista; (*cap.*) *s* realista (*en la guerra de la Independencia de los EE.UU.*); leal, gubernamental, republicano (*en la guerra civil de España*)
loyalty [ˈlɔɪəltɪ] *s* (*pl:* **-ties**) lealtad
lozenge [ˈlɑzɪndʒ] *s* pastilla, tableta; (geom. & her.) losange
lozengy [ˈlɑzɪndʒɪ] *adj* (her.) losangeado o losanjado
LP abr. de **long-playing;** *s* disco de larga duración, disco microsurco
L.S.D. o **l.s.d.** abr. de **pounds, shillings, and pence**
Lt. abr. de **Lieutenant**
Ltd. o **ltd.** abr. de **limited**
lubber [ˈlʌbər] *s* palurdo; marinero matalote
lubberly [ˈlʌbərlɪ] *adj* palurdo; *adv* palurdamente
lubricant [ˈlubrɪkənt] *adj & s* lubricante
lubricate [ˈlubrɪket] *va* lubricar
lubrication [ˌlubrɪˈkeʃən] *s* lubricación
lubricator [ˈlubrɪˌketər] *s* lubricador (*persona y aparato*)
lubricious [luˈbrɪʃəs] *adj* lúbrico (*libidinoso*)
lubricity [luˈbrɪsɪtɪ] *s* (*pl:* **-ties**) lubricidad
lubricous [ˈlubrɪkəs] *adj* lúbrico (*resbaladizo; libidinoso*); inconstante, incierto
Lucan [ˈlukən] *s* Lucano
lucence [ˈlusəns] o **lucency** [ˈlusənsɪ] *s* brillantez; translucidez
lucent [ˈlusənt] *adj* luciente; translúcido
lucerne [luˈsʌrn] *s* (bot.) mielga; (*cap.*) *s* Lucerna
Lucia [ˈluʃɪə] o [ˈluʃə] *s* Lucía
Lucian [ˈluʃɪən] o [ˈluʃən] *s* Luciano
lucid [ˈlusɪd] *adj* luciente; cristalino; lúcido (*claro en el razonamiento, estilo, etc.*); (med.) lúcido (*intervalo*)
lucidity [luˈsɪdɪtɪ] *s* lucidez; doble vista; (psychol.) lucidez
lucifer [ˈlusɪfər] *s* fósforo de fricción; (*cap.*) *s* Lucifer (*príncipe de los ángeles rebeldes; Venus, lucero del alba*)
luciferase [luˈsɪfəres] *s* (biochem.) luciferasa
Luciferian [ˌlusɪˈfɪrɪən] *adj* luciferino
luciferin [luˈsɪfərɪn] *s* (biochem.) luciferina
lucifugous [luˈsɪfjəgəs] *adj* (biol.) lucífugo
luck [lʌk] *s* suerte (*buena o mala*); suerte, buena suerte; **down on one's luck** (coll.) de mala suerte, de malas; **for luck** para que traiga buena suerte; **in luck** de buena suerte, de buenas; **out of luck** de mala suerte, de malas; **to bring luck** traer buena suerte; **to try one's luck** meter la mano en el cántaro, probar fortuna; **worse luck** desgraciadamente
luckily [ˈlʌkɪlɪ] *adv* afortunadamente
luckless [ˈlʌklɪs] *adj* desafortunado, malaventurado
lucky [ˈlʌkɪ] *adj* (*comp:* **-ier;** *super:* **-iest**) afortunado; de buen agüero; **to be lucky** tener buena suerte
lucky hit *s* (coll.) golpe de fortuna
lucrative [ˈlukrətɪv] *adj* lucrativo
lucre [ˈlukər] *s* (el) vil metal (*raíz de muchos males*)
Lucrece [luˈkris] o [ˈlukris] o **Lucretia** [luˈkriʃə] *s* Lucrecia
Lucretius [luˈkriʃəs] *s* Lucrecio
lucubrate [ˈlukjəbret] *va & vn* lucubrar

lucubration [ˌlukjəˈbreʃən] *s* lucubración
Lucullian [luˈkʌlɪən] *adj* opíparo, magnífico
Lucullus [luˈkʌləs] *s* Lúculo
Lucy [ˈlusɪ] *s* Lucía
ludicrous [ˈludɪkrəs] *adj* absurdo, ridículo
lues [ˈluiz] *s* (path.) lúes (*sífilis*)
luff [lʌf] *s* (naut.) orza; (naut.) orilla de proa (*de una cangreja*); (naut.) aparejo de combés; *vn* (naut.) orzar
lug [lʌg] *s* orejeta; estirón, esfuerzo; (naut.) vela al tercio; (*pret & pp:* **lugged**; *ger:* **lugging**) *va* arrastrar, tirar con fuerza de; (coll.) traer a colación (*especies inoportunas en una conversación*); *vn* tirar con fuerza
luggage [ˈlʌgɪdʒ] *s* equipaje
luggage rack *s* red de equipaje
lugger [ˈlʌgər] *s* (naut.) lugre
lugsail [ˈlʌgsəl] o [ˈlʌgˌsel] *s* (naut.) vela al tercio
lugubrious [luˈgjubrɪəs] *adj* lúgubre
lugworm [ˈlʌgˌwʌrm] *s* (zool.) arenícola
Luke [luk] *s* Lucas; (Bib.) San Lucas; (Bib.) el Evangelio según San Lucas
lukewarm [ˈlukˌwɔrm] *adj* tibio; (fig.) tibio
lull [lʌl] *s* momento de silencio, momento de calma; *va* calmar, adormecer, arrullar; *vn* calmarse; amainar (*el viento*)
lullaby [ˈlʌləbaɪ] *s* (*pl:* **-bies**) arrullo, canción de cuna
Lullian [ˈlʌlɪən] *adj* luliano o lulista
Lullianist [ˈlʌlɪənɪst] o **Lullist** [ˈlʌlɪst] *s* luliano o lulista
lumbago [lʌmˈbego] *s* (path.) lumbago
lumbar [ˈlʌmbər] *adj* lumbar; *s* (anat.) vértebra, arteria o nervio lumbares
lumber [ˈlʌmbər] *s* madera aserrada, madera de construcción; trastos viejos; *va* amontonar trastos viejos en, no dejar sitio para moverse en; *vn* cortar y aserrar madera, explotar los bosques; andar o moverse pesadamente; avanzar con ruido sordo
lumbering [ˈlʌmbərɪŋ] *adj* pesado, que se mueve pesadamente; *s* explotación de bosques maderables, extracción de madera
lumberjack [ˈlʌmbərˌdʒæk] *s* leñador, hachero
lumberman [ˈlʌmbərmən] *s* (*pl:* **-men**) maderero; leñador
lumber room *s* trastera, leonera
lumberyard [ˈlʌmbərˌjɑrd] *s* corral de madera, almacén de maderas, madereria
lumbrical [ˈlʌmbrɪkəl] *adj* (anat.) lumbrical
lumen [ˈlumɛn] *s* (*pl:* **-mina** [mɪnə] o **-mens**) (anat., bot. & phys.) lumen
lumen-hour [ˈlumɛnˈaʊr] *s* (phys.) lumen hora
luminal [ˈlumɪnəl] *s* (trademark) luminal
luminary [ˈlumɪˌnɛrɪ] *s* (*pl:* **-ies**) luminar; (fig.) luminar (*persona*)
luminescence [ˌlumɪˈnɛsəns] *s* luminiscencia
luminescent [ˌlumɪˈnɛsənt] *adj* luminiscente
luminiferous [ˌlumɪˈnɪfərəs] *adj* luminífero
luminosity [ˌlumɪˈnɑsɪtɪ] *s* (*pl:* **-ties**) luminosidad; cuerpo luminoso
luminous [ˈlumɪnəs] *adj* luminoso
lummox [ˈlʌməks] *s* (coll.) chapucero estúpido, persona torpe y estúpida
lump [lʌmp] *s* terrón; borujo; bulto, chichón, hinchazón; conjunto, todo; (coll.) bodoque; (coll.) persona espalduda; **in the lump** en grueso, por junto; **to get a lump in one's throat** hacérsele a uno un nudo en la garganta; *adj* en terrón, en terrones; global; *va* aterronar; aborujar; producir protuberancias en; combinar; agrupar; (coll.) aguantar, tragar (*cosa vejatoria*); *vn* aterronarse; aborujarse; abultar; andar con pasos pesados
lumpish [ˈlʌmpɪʃ] *adj* aterronado; torpe, pesado, estúpido, hobachón
lump sugar *s* azúcar en terrón
lump sum *s* suma total, cantidad gruesa
lumpy [ˈlʌmpɪ] *adj* (*comp:* **-ier**; *super:* **-iest**) aterronado; borujoso; torpe, pesado; agitado (*p.ej., mar*)
lunacy [ˈlunəsɪ] *s* (*pl:* **-cies**) locura
luna moth [ˈlunə] *s* (ent.) actias luna
lunar [ˈlunər] *adj* lunar
lunar caustic *s* cáustico lunar, piedra infernal (*nitrato de plata*)
lunar month *s* mes lunar
lunar year *s* año lunar
lunate [ˈlunet] *adj* lunado
lunatic [ˈlunətɪk] *adj* loco; de locos; necio; *s* loco
lunatic asylum *s* manicomio
lunatic fringe *s* minoría fanática (*en lo político, social, religioso, etc.*)
lunation [luˈneʃən] *s* (astr.) lunación
lunch [lʌntʃ] *s* almuerzo, merienda; colación, refacción; *vn* almorzar, merendar; tomar una colación
lunch basket *s* fiambrera
lunch cloth *s* mantelito
luncheon [ˈlʌntʃən] *s* almuerzo, merienda; almuerzo de ceremonia; *vn* almorzar, merendar
luncheonette [ˌlʌntʃəˈnɛt] *s* cantina
lunchroom [ˈlʌntʃˌrum] o [ˈlʌntʃˌrʊm] *s* restaurante
lune [lun] *s* media luna; (geom.) lúnula
lunette [luˈnɛt] *s* luneta (*adorno en forma de media luna*); (arch.) luneto o luneta; (fort.) luneta
lung [lʌŋ] *s* (anat.) pulmón
lunge [lʌndʒ] *s* arremetida, embestida; estocada; *vn* arremeter, embestir; dar una estocada; **to lunge at** arremeter contra
lungwort [ˈlʌŋˌwʌrt] *s* (bot.) pulmonaria
lunule [ˈlunjul] *s* (anat. & zool.) lúnula
Lupercalia [ˌlupərˈkelɪə] *spl* (hist.) lupercales
lupine [ˈlupaɪn] *adj* lupino; [ˈlupɪn] *s* (bot.) lupino, altramuz
lupus [ˈlupəs] *s* (path.) lupus
lurch [lʌrtʃ] *s* sacudida, tumbo, balanceo brusco; (naut.) bandazo; **to leave in the lurch** dejar colgado, abandonar en la estacada; *vn* dar una sacudida, dar sacudidas, dar un tumbo; (naut.) dar un bandazo
lurcher [ˈlʌrtʃər] *s* ladronzuelo, ratero; cazador furtivo; (Brit.) perro de caza
lure [lʊr] *s* cebo; señuelo; (fig.) señuelo, aliciente; *va* atraer con cebo; atraer con señuelo; (fig.) atraer, tentar, seducir; **to lure away** llevarse con señuelo; desviar (*p.ej., de su deber*); **to lure someone into** tentar a uno a que entre en; **to lure someone into** + *ger* tentar a uno a que + *subj*
lurid [ˈlʊrɪd] *adj* ardiente; asombroso, sensacional; espeluznante
lurk [lʌrk] *vn* acechar, estar oculto, moverse furtivamente
luscious [ˈlʌʃəs] *adj* delicioso, exquisito; rico, dulce y sabroso
lush [lʌʃ] *adj* jugoso, lozano; abundante; lujuriante
Lusitanian [ˌlusɪˈtenɪən] *adj & s* lusitano
Lusitanism [ˈlusɪtənɪzəm] *s* lusitanismo
lust [lʌst] *s* deseo vehemente, deseo desordenado; codicia; lujuria; *vn* codiciar; lujuriar; **to lust after** o **for** codiciar; apetecer contacto carnal con
luster [ˈlʌstər] *s* lustre, brillo; viso (*de ciertas telas*); porcelana con visos de azulejo; tela lustrosa de lana y algodón; (fig.) lustro (*fama, gloria*)
lustful [ˈlʌstfəl] *adj* lujurioso, lúbrico
lustral [ˈlʌstrəl] *adj* lustral
lustrate [ˈlʌstret] *va* lustrar
lustration [lʌsˈtreʃən] *s* lustración; (hum.) lavación, lavatorio
lustre [ˈlʌstər] *s* var. de **luster**
lustrous [ˈlʌstrəs] *adj* lustroso
lustrum [ˈlʌstrəm] *s* (*pl:* **-trums** o **-tra** [trə]) lustro (*cinco años*); (hist.) lustro
lusty [ˈlʌstɪ] *adj* (*comp:* **-ier**; *super:* **-iest**) robusto, lozano, fuerte
lute [lut] *s* (mus.) laúd; (chem.) lodo (*para cerrar junturas, tapar grietas, etc.*); *va* (chem.) enlodar
lutecium [luˈtiʃɪəm] *s* (chem.) lutecio
luteolin [ˈlutɪəlɪn] *s* (chem.) luteolina
luteous [ˈlutɪəs] *adj* lúteo
Luther [ˈluθər] *s* Lutero
Lutheran [ˈluθərən] *adj & s* luterano
Lutheranism [ˈluθərənɪzəm] *s* luteranismo
lux [lʌks] *s* (*pl:* **luces** [ˈlusiz]) (phys.) lux
luxate [ˈlʌkset] *va* luxar
luxation [lʌkˈseʃən] *s* luxación
Luxemburg [ˈlʌksəmbʌrg] *s* Luxemburgo
luxuriance [lʌgˈʒʊrɪəns] o [lʌkˈʃʊrɪəns] o **luxuriancy** [lʌgˈʒʊrɪənsɪ] o [lʌkˈʃʊrɪənsɪ] *s* lozanía

luxuriant [lʌgˈʒurɪənt] o [lʌkˈʃurɪənt] *adj* lozano, lujuriante; de ornamentación recargada
luxuriate [lʌgˈʒurɪet] o [lʌkˈʃurɪet] *vn* crecer con lozanía; entregarse al lujo; lozanear (*deleitarse*)
luxurious [lʌgˈʒurɪəs] o [lʌkˈʃurɪəs] *adj* lujoso
luxury [ˈlʌkʃərɪ] *s* (*pl:* **-ries**) lujo; lujuria (*concupiscencia de la carne*); *adj* de lujo
lycanthrope [ˈlaɪkənθrop] o [laɪˈkænθrop] *s* licántropo
lycanthropy [laɪˈkænθrəpɪ] *s* licantropía
lyceum [laɪˈsiəm] *s* liceo
lych gate [lɪtʃ] *s* var. de **lich gate**
lychnis [ˈlɪknɪs] *s* (bot.) licnis
Lycia [ˈlɪʃɪə] *s* Licia
Lycian [ˈlɪʃɪən] *adj & s* licio
lycopodium [ˌlaɪkəˈpodɪəm] *s* (bot.) licopodio
Lycurgus [laɪˈkʌrgəs] *s* Licurgo
lyddite [ˈlɪdaɪt] *s* lidita (*explosivo*)
Lydia [ˈlɪdɪə] *s* Lidia
Lydian [ˈlɪdɪən] *adj* lidio; (mus.) lidio; (fig.) blando, afeminado, voluptuoso; *s* lidio
lye [laɪ] *s* lejía
lying [ˈlaɪɪŋ] *s* el mentir; *adj* mentiroso; *ger de* **lie**
lying-in [ˈlaɪɪŋˈɪn] *s* parto
lying-in hospital *s* hospital de parturientas, casa de maternidad
lymph [lɪmf] *s* (anat. & physiol.) linfa
lymphadenitis [lɪmˌfædɪˈnaɪtɪs] *s* (path.) linfadenitis
lymphangiitis [lɪmˌfændʒɪˈaɪtɪs] *s* (path.) linfangitis
lymphatic [lɪmˈfætɪk] *adj* linfático; (fig.) linfático; *s* (anat.) vaso linfático
lymph gland o **node** *s* (anat.) ganglio o nódulo linfático
lymphocyte [ˈlɪmfəsaɪt] *s* (anat.) linfocito
lyncean [lɪnˈsiən] *adj* linceo
lynch [lɪntʃ] *va* linchar
lynching [ˈlɪntʃɪŋ] *s* linchamiento
lynch law *s* ley de Lynch, justicia de la soga
lynchpin [ˈlɪntʃˌpɪn] *s* var. de **linchpin**
lynx [lɪŋks] *s* (*pl:* **lynxes** o **lynx**) (zool.) lince; (*cap.*) *s* (astr.) Lince
lynx-eyed [ˈlɪŋksˌaɪd] *adj* de ojos linces
Lyonese [ˌlaɪəˈniz] *adj* lionés; *s* (*pl:* **-ese**) lionés
lyonnaise [ˌlaɪəˈnez] *adj* (cook.) a la lionesa, p.ej., **lyonnaise potatoes** patatas a la lionesa
Lyonnesse [ˌlaɪəˈnɛs] *s* región fabulosa de Inglaterra que se supone hundida en el mar
Lyons [ˈlaɪənz] *s* León de Francia, Lyón
Lyra [ˈlaɪrə] *s* (astr.) Lira
lyrate [ˈlaɪret] *adj* lirado; (bot.) lirado
lyre [laɪr] *s* (mus.) lira; (*cap.*) *s* (astr.) Lira
lyrebird [ˈlaɪrˌbʌrd] *s* (orn.) ave lira
lyric [ˈlɪrɪk] *adj* lírico; (theat.) lírico (*músico, operístico*); *s* poema lírico; (coll.) letra (*de una canción*)
lyrical [ˈlɪrɪkəl] *adj* lírico
lyricism [ˈlɪrɪsɪzəm] *s* lirismo
Lysander [laɪˈsændər] *s* Lisandro
Lysenkoism [lɪˈsɛŋko·ɪzəm] *s* lisencoísmo
lysin [ˈlaɪsɪn] o **lysine** [ˈlaɪsin] o [ˈlaɪsɪn] *s* (biochem.) lisina
Lysippus [laɪˈsɪpəs] *s* Lisipo
lysol [ˈlaɪsol] o [ˈlaɪsɑl] *s* (trademark) lisol
lyssophobia [ˌlɪsəˈfobɪə] *s* (psychopath.) lisofobia
lythraceous [lɪˈθreʃəs] o [laɪˈθreʃəs] *adj* (bot.) litráceo

M

M, m [ɛm] *s* (*pl:* **M's, m's** [ɛmz]) décimotercera letra del alfabeto inglés
m. abr. de **mark, married, masculine, meter, midnight, mile, minim, minute, month** y **moon**
M. abr. de **midnight** y **Monday**
M.A. abr. de **Magister Artium** (Lat.) **Master of Arts**
ma [mɑ] *s* (coll.) mamá
ma'am [mæm] o [mɑm] *s* (coll.) señora
macabre [mə'kɑbər] *adj* macábrico o macabro
macaco [mə'keko] *s* (*pl:* **-cos**) (zool.) maquí
macadam [mə'kædəm] *s* macadam o macadán
macadamize [mə'kædəmaɪz] *va* macadamizar
macaque [mə'kɑk] *s* (zool.) macaco
macaroni [,mækə'ronɪ] *s* (*pl:* **-nis** o **-nies**) *s* macarrones
macaronic [,mækə'rɑnɪk] *adj* macarrónico; *s* macarronea
macaroon [,mækə'run] *s* almendrado, mostachón, macarrón
Macassar oil [mə'kæsər] *s* aceite de Macasar
macaw [mə'kɔ] *s* (orn.) ara, aracanga
Maccabaeus [,mækə'biəs] *s* (Bib.) Macabeo
Maccabean [,mækə'biən] *adj* de los macabeos
Maccabees ['mækəbiz] *spl* (Bib.) macabeos
maccaboy o **maccoboy** ['mækəbɔɪ] *s* macuba (*tabaco aromático*)
mace [mes] *s* maza; macero; macia o macis (*especia*); *va* macear
macebearer ['mes,bɛrər] *s* macero
macédoine [,mæse'dwɑn] *s* macedonia (*ensalada; mezcla, mezcolanza*)
Macedon ['mæsɪdɑn] *s* Macedonia (*antigua*)
Macedonia [,mæsɪ'donɪə] *s* Macedonia
Macedonian [,mæsɪ'donɪən] *adj* & *s* macedonio
macer ['mesər] *s* var. de **macebearer**
macerate ['mæsəret] *va* macerar; *vn* macerarse
macerater ['mæsə,retər] *s* macerador
maceration [,mæsə'reʃən] *s* maceración
Mach [mɑk] *s* (aer.) número Mach
machete [mɑ'tʃete] o [mə'ʃɛt] *s* machete
Mache unit ['mɑxə] *s* (phys.) mache
Machiavelli [,mækɪə'vɛlɪ] *s* Maquiavelo
Machiavellian o **Machiavelian** [,mækɪə'vɛlɪən] *adj* maquiavelista; maquiavélico (*astuto, engañador*); *s* maquiavelista
Machiavellianism [,mækɪə'vɛlɪənɪzəm] o **Machiavellism** [,mækɪə'vɛlɪzəm] *s* maquiavelismo
machicolate [mə'tʃɪkəlet] *va* aspillerar
machicolation [mə,tʃɪkə'leʃən] *s* (fort.) matacán (*balcón*); aspillera (*abertura*)
machinate ['mækɪnet] *va* & *vn* maquinar
machination [,mækɪ'neʃən] *s* maquinación
machinator ['mækɪ,netər] *s* maquinador
machine [mə'ʃin] *s* máquina; coche, automóvil; avión; camarilla (*de políticos*); (lit. & theat.) máquina; *va* trabajar a máquina
machine age *s* edad de la máquina
machine gun *s* ametralladora
machine-gun [mə'ʃin,gʌn] (*pret & pp:* **-gunned;** *ger:* **-gunning**) *va* ametrallar
machine gunner *s* ametrallador
machine-made [mə'ʃin,med] *adj* hecho a máquina, labrado mecánicamente
machinery [mə'ʃinərɪ] *s* (*pl:* **-ies**) maquinaria; (fig.) maquinaria (*p.ej., del gobierno*)
machine screw *s* tornillo para metales
machine shop *s* taller mecánico, taller de maquinaria
machine tool *s* máquina-herramienta
machine translation *s* traducción automática
machinist [mə'ʃinɪst] *s* mecánico; maquinista; (naut.) segundo maquinista; (theat.) tramoyista
macintosh ['mækɪntɑʃ] *s* var. de **mackintosh**
mackerel ['mækərəl] *s* (ichth.) caballa, escombro
mackerel sky *s* cielo aborregado
mackinaw ['mækɪnɔ] *s* manta gruesa de lana con listas de varios colores; chaquetón de mucho abrigo
mackintosh ['mækɪntɑʃ] *s* impermeable; tela impermeabilizada
mackle ['mækəl] *s* (print.) maculatura (*mancha*); *va* (print.) macular, repintar; *vn* (print.) macularse, repintarse
macle ['mækəl] *s* (mineral.) macla
macramé ['mækrəme] *s* macramé
macrobiotic [,mækrəbaɪ'ɑtɪk] *adj* macrobiótico; **macrobiotics** *ssg* macrobiótica
macrocosm ['mækrəkɑzəm] *s* macrocosmo
macrocyte ['mækrəsaɪt] *s* (path.) macrocito
macrogamete [,mækrogə'mit] *s* (biol.) macrogameto
macromolecule [,mækro'mɑlɪkjul] *s* macromolécula
macron ['mekrɑn] o ['mækrɑn] *s* (gram.) raya que se pone sobre las vocales para indicar su largura
macrophysics [,mækro'fɪzɪks] *ssg* macrofísica
macrosmatic [,mækrɑz'mætɪk] *adj* (zool.) macrosmático
macruran [mə'krurən] *adj* & *s* (zool.) macruro
macula ['mækjələ] *s* (*pl:* **-lae** [li]) (anat., astr. & path.) mácula
macule ['mækjul] *s*, *va* & *vn* var. de **mackle**
mad [mæd] *adj* (*comp:* **madder;** *super:* **maddest**) loco; enojado, furioso; rabioso (*perro*); necio, tonto; muy aficionado; **like mad** como un loco; con todas sus fuerzas; **to be mad about** tener locura por, ser muy aficionado a; **to drive mad** volver loco, enloquecer; **to go mad** volverse loco, enloquecer; rabiar (*un perro*); **mad as a hatter** o **mad as a March hare** loco de atar
madam ['mædəm] *s* (*pl:* **madams** o **mesdames** [me'dɑm]) señora
madame ['mædəm] o [mɑ'dɑm] *s* (*pl:* **mesdames** [me'dɑm]) (Fr.) madama
madapollam [,mædə'pɑləm] *s* madapolán
madcap ['mæd,kæp] *adj* & *s* alocado
madden ['mædən] *va* enojar, poner furioso; enloquecer
madder ['mædər] *s* (bot.) rubia (*planta y raíz*); (chem.) rojo de rubia
madding ['mædɪŋ] *adj* irritante; furioso, loco
made [med] *adj* hecho, fabricado; inventado; llegado (*a la meta del éxito completo*); *pret & pp de* **make**
Madeira [mə'dɪrə] *s* madera, vino de Madera
Madeleine ['mædəlɪn] *s* var. de **Magdalen**
mademoiselle [,mædəmə'zɛl] *s* (*pl:* **mesdemoiselles** [medmwɑ'zɛl]) (Fr.) madamisela
made-to-order ['medtə'ɔrdər] *adj* hecho a la medida; hecho especialmente para el comprador
made-up ['med'ʌp] *adj* hecho, completo; compuesto; ficticio; postizo; pintado (*rostro*)
Madge [mædʒ] *s* nombre abreviado de **Margaret**
madhouse ['mæd,haus] *s* casa de locos, manicomio; (fig.) casa de locos, gallinero
madly ['mædlɪ] *adv* locamente; furiosamente; neciamente; desesperadamente
madman ['mæd,mæn] o ['mædmən] *s* (*pl:* **-men**) loco
madness ['mædnɪs] *s* locura; furia, rabia; (path.) rabia
Madonna [mə'dɑnə] *s* Madona; (f.a.) Madona
Madonna lily *s* (bot.) azucena
madras ['mædrəs] o [mə'dræs] *s* madrás
madrepore ['mædrɪpor] *s* (zool.) madrépora

madreporic [ˌmædrɪˈpɔrɪk] o [ˌmædrɪˈpɑrɪk] *adj* madrepórico
madrigal [ˈmædrɪgəl] *s* madrigal; (mus.) madrigal
Madrilenian [ˌmædrɪˈlinɪən] *adj* & *s* madrileño
madwort [ˈmædˌwʌrt] *s* (bot.) raspilla (*Asperugo procumbens*); (bot.) camelina
Maecenas [mɪˈsinəs] *s* Mecenas; (fig.) mecenas
maelstrom [ˈmelstrəm] *s* remolino; (fig.) remolino
maenad [ˈminæd] *s* (hist. & fig.) ménade
maestro [ˈmaɪstro] o [mɑˈɛstro] *s* (*pl:* **-tros** o **-tri** [tri]) maestro (*en cualquier arte*)
Maffia o **Mafia** [ˈmɑfɪɑ] *s* maffia
mag. abr. de **magazine**
magazine [ˈmægəzin] o [ˌmægəˈzin] *s* revista; almacén; cámara (*para cartuchos*); polvorín; (naut.) santabárbara; (phot.) almacén
Magdalen [ˈmægdələn] o [ˈmægdəlɛn] *s* Magdalena
Magdalene [ˈmægdəlin] o [ˌmægdəˈlini] *s* (Bib.) Santa María Magdalena; (*l.c.*) *s* (fig.) magdalena (*mujer penitente*)
Magdalenian [ˌmægdəˈlinɪən] *adj* (geol.) magdaleniense
Magdeburg hemispheres [ˈmægdəbʌrg] *spl* (phys.) hemisferios de Magdeburgo
mage [medʒ] *s* (archaic) mágico
Magellan [məˈdʒɛlən] *s* Magallanes
Magellanic [ˌmædʒəˈlænɪk] *adj* magallánico
magenta [məˈdʒɛntə] *s* magenta
maggot [ˈmægət] *s* (zool.) cresa; antojo, capricho
maggoty [ˈmægətɪ] *adj* agusanado, gusaniento; caprichoso
Magi [ˈmedʒaɪ] *spl* magos (*de la religión zoroástrica*); Reyes Magos
Magian [ˈmedʒɪən] *adj* & *s* mago; (*l.c.*) *adj* & *s* mago (*mágico*)
magic [ˈmædʒɪk] *adj* mágico; *s* magia; prestidigitación; **as if by magic** como por encanto
magical [ˈmædʒɪkəl] *adj* mágico
magic carpet *s* alfombra mágica
magician [məˈdʒɪʃən] *s* mágico; prestidigitador
magic lantern *s* linterna mágica
magic square *s* cuadrado mágico
magisterial [ˌmædʒɪsˈtɪrɪəl] *adj* magistral; de magistrado
magistracy [ˈmædʒɪstrəsɪ] *s* (*pl:* **-cies**) magistratura
magistral [ˈmædʒɪstrəl] *adj* magistral; (fort. & pharm.) magistral; *s* (metal.) magistral
magistrate [ˈmædʒɪstret] o [ˈmædʒɪstrɪt] *s* magistrado; juez
magma [ˈmægmə] *s* (*pl:* **-mata** [mətə] o **-mas**) magma; (geol. & pharm.) magma
Magna Charta o **Magna Carta** [ˈmægnə ˈkɑrtə] *s* Carta Magna
magnanimity [ˌmægnəˈnɪmɪtɪ] *s* (*pl:* **-ties**) magnanimidad
magnanimous [mægˈnænɪməs] *adj* magnánimo
magnate [ˈmægnet] *s* magnate
magnesia [mægˈniʃə] o [mægˈniʒə] *s* (chem.) magnesia; magnesio
magnesian [mægˈniʃən] o [mægˈniʒən] *adj* magnesiano
magnesic [mægˈnisɪk] *adj* magnésico
magnesite [ˈmægnɪsaɪt] *s* (mineral.) magnesita
magnesium [mægˈniʃɪəm] o [mægˈniʒɪəm] *s* (chem.) magnesio
magnesium bronze *s* bronce de magnesio
magnesium light *s* luz de magnesio
magnet [ˈmægnɪt] *s* (mineral., phys. & fig.) imán
magnetic [mægˈnɛtɪk] *adj* magnético; atrayente, cautivador
magnetic curves *spl* espectro magnético
magnetic field *s* campo magnético
magnetic flux *s* flujo magnético
magnetic moment *s* (phys.) momento magnético
magnetic needle *s* aguja imanada o magnética
magnetic pole *s* polo magnético
magnetic storm *s* (phys.) borrasca magnética, tempestad magnética
magnetic tape *s* cinta magnética
magnetism [ˈmægnɪtɪzəm] *s* magnetismo; magnetismo personal, don de gentes
magnetite [ˈmægnɪtaɪt] *s* (mineral.) magnetita
magnetization [ˌmægnɪtɪˈzeʃən] *s* magnetización
magnetize [ˈmægnɪtaɪz] *va* magnetizar; atraer, cautivar, fascinar
magneto [mægˈnito] *s* (*pl:* **-tos**) magneto
magnetoelectric [mægˌnito·ɪˈlɛktrɪk] *adj* magnetoeléctrico
magnetometer [ˌmægnɪˈtɑmɪtər] *s* magnetómetro
magneton [ˈmægnɪtɑn] *s* (phys.) magnetón
magnetophone [mægˈnitofon] *s* (phys.) magnetófono
magnetosphere [mægˈnitəsfɪr] *s* magnetosfera
magnetron [ˈmægnɪtrɑn] *s* (rad.) magnetrón
magnific [mægˈnɪfɪk] o **magnifical** [mægˈnɪfɪkəl] *adj* magnificente; grandílocuo
Magnificat [mægˈnɪfɪkæt] *s* magníficat
magnification [ˌmægnɪfɪˈkeʃən] *s* (opt.) magnificación; ampliación (*copia ampliada*); exageración
magnificence [mægˈnɪfɪsəns] *s* magnificencia
magnificent [mægˈnɪfɪsənt] *adj* magnífico
magnifico [mægˈnɪfɪko] *s* (*pl:* **-coes**) caballero noble de Venecia; personaje ilustre
magnifier [ˈmægnɪˌfaɪər] *s* magnificador; exagerador; vidrio de aumento
magnify [ˈmægnɪfaɪ] (*pret & pp:* **-fied**) *va* (opt.) magnificar; exagerar; (archaic) magnificar (*alabar, ensalzar*)
magnifying glass *s* lupa, vidrio de aumento, lente de aumento
magniloquence [mægˈnɪləkwəns] *s* grandilocuencia; jactancia
magniloquent [mægˈnɪləkwənt] *adj* grandílocuo; jactancioso
magnitude [ˈmægnɪtjud] o [ˈmægnɪtud] *s* magnitud; (astr. & math.) magnitud
magnolia [mægˈnolɪə] *s* (bot.) magnolia
magnum [ˈmægnəm] *s* botella de dos litros
magnum opus *s* obra maestra
magpie [ˈmægpaɪ] *s* (orn.) urraca; charlador; regañón
maguey [ˈmægwe] *s* (bot.) pita, maguey
Magus [ˈmegəs] *s* (*pl:* **-gi** [dʒaɪ]) Rey Mago
Magyar [ˈmægjɑr] *adj* & *s* magiar
maharaja o **maharajah** [ˌmɑhəˈrɑdʒə] *s* maharajá
mahatma [məˈhɑtmə] o [məˈhætmə] *s* mahatma; (theosophy) mahatma
Mahdi [ˈmɑdi] *s* (*pl:* **-dis**) mehedí
mah-jongg o **mah-jong** [ˈmɑˈdʒɑŋ] *s* mah-jong (*juego chino parecido al dominó*)
mahlstick [ˈmɑlˌstɪk] o [ˈmɔlˌstɪk] *s* (paint.) tiento
mahogany [məˈhɑgənɪ] *s* (*pl:* **-nies**) (bot.) caoba; *adj* de caoba; de color de caoba
Mahomet [məˈhɑmɪt] *s* var. de **Mohammed**
Mahometan [məˈhɑmɪtən] *adj* & *s* var. de **Mohammedan**
Mahometanism [məˈhɑmɪtənɪzəm] *s* var. de **Mohammedanism**
Mahon stock [məˈhon] *s* (bot.) mahonesa
mahout [məˈhaʊt] *s* naire, cornaca
maid [med] *s* criada, moza; doncella (*mujer virgen; criada que se ocupa en los menesteres domésticos ajenos a la cocina*); soltera
maiden [ˈmedən] *s* doncella; *adj* virginal; de soltera; virgen; primero
maidenhair [ˈmedənˌhɛr] *s* (bot.) cabello de Venus
maidenhead [ˈmedənˌhɛd] *s* doncellez; (anat.) himen
maidenhood [ˈmedənhud] *s* doncellez
maiden lady *s* soltera, solterona
maidenly [ˈmedənlɪ] *adj* virginal; pudoroso
maiden name *s* apellido de soltera
maiden speech *s* primer discurso (*de un orador*)
maiden voyage *s* primera travesía
maid in waiting *s* dama
maid of all work *s* criada para todo, moza de servicio
maid of honor *s* dama, menina; doncella, menina; doncella de honor (*de una boda*)
Maid of Orleans *s* Doncella de Orleáns

maidservant ['med,sʌrvənt] *s* sirvienta, criada
mail [mel] *s* correspondencia; correo; vapor correo, paquebote; malla (*de la armadura*); cota (*de malla*); armadura; **by return mail** a vuelta de correo; *adj* del correo; postal; *va* enviar por correo; echar al correo; armar (*especialmente con cota de malla*)
mailbag ['mel,bæg] *s* valija; correo
mailboat ['mel,bot] *s* vapor correo, paquebote
mailbox ['mel,bɑks] *s* buzón
mail car *s* (rail.) carro correo, coche-correo
mail carrier *s* cartero
mail chute *s* buzón tubular
mail coach *s* diligencia (*que lleva correo*)
mailed fist *s* puño armado
mailing list *s* lista de direcciones (*de clientes*)
mailing permit *s* porte concertado
mailman ['mel,mæn] *s* (*pl:* **-men**) cartero
mail order *s* pedido postal
mail-order house ['mel,ɔrdər] *s* casa de pedidos postales; casa de ventas por correo
mailplane ['mel,plen] *s* avión-correo
mail train *s* tren correo
maim [mem] *va* estropear, mutilar, lisiar
Maimonides [maɪ'mɑnɪdiz] *s* Maimónides
main [men] *s* cañería, cañería maestra; (poet.) mar, océano; (archaic) tierra firme, continente; **in the main** mayormente, en su mayor parte; *adj* principal; maestro; mayor
main clause *s* (gram.) proposición dominante
main course *s* plato fuerte, plato principal; (naut.) vela mayor
main deck *s* (naut.) cubierta principal
main highway *s* carretera principal
mainland ['men,lænd] o ['menlənd] *s* tierra firme, continente
main line *s* (rail.) línea principal, tronco
mainly ['menlɪ] *adv* mayormente, en su mayor parte
mainmast ['menməst], ['men,mæst] o ['men,mɑst] *s* (naut.) palo mayor
main office *s* casa central, oficina central
mainsail ['mensəl] o ['men,sel] *s* (naut.) vela mayor
mainsheet ['men,ʃit] *s* (naut.) escota mayor
mainspring ['men,sprɪŋ] *s* (horol.) muelle real; (fig.) causa principal, origen
mainstay ['men,ste] *s* (naut.) estay mayor; (fig.) sostén principal
main street *s* calle mayor
maintain [men'ten] *va* mantener
maintenance ['mentɪnəns] *s* mantenimiento; modesto pasar; conservación, gastos de conservación, gastos de entretenimiento
maintenance costs *spl* gastos de conservación
maintenance of way *s* (rail.) conservación de la vía
maintop ['men,tɑp] *s* (naut.) cofa mayor o de gavia
maintopgallant ['mentə'gælənt] o ['men,tɑp'gælənt] *s* (naut.) mastelero de galope mayor, masterillo de mayor; (naut.) juanete mayor; (naut.) verga de juanete mayor
maintopmast [,men'tɑpməst] *s* (naut.) mastelero de mayor
maintopsail [,men'tɑpsəl] *s* (naut.) gavia, vela de gavia
main track *s* (rail.) vía principal
main-traveled o **main-travelled** ['men,trævəld] *adj* de mucho tránsito
main yard *s* (naut.) verga mayor
Mainz [maɪnts] *s* Maguncia
maître d'hôtel ['mɛtrədo'tɛl] *s* mayordomo; jefe de comedor; salsa de mantequilla, perejil picado y jugo de limón
maize [mez] *s* (bot.) maíz (*planta y grano*); color de maíz
Maj. abr. de **Major**
majestic [mə'dʒɛstɪk] o **majestical** [mə'dʒɛstɪkəl] *adj* majestuoso
majesty ['mædʒɪstɪ] *s* (*pl:* **-ties**) majestad; (*cap.*) *s* Majestad (*título*)
majolica [mə'dʒɑlɪkə] *s* mayólica
major ['medʒər] *adj* mayor; principal, importante; mayor de edad; (log. & mus.) mayor; *s* mayor de edad; (mil.) comandante; (educ.) asignatura o curso de especialización; (mus.) acorde, escala o intervalo mayor; *vn* (coll.) especializarse (*en una asignatura o curso*)
major axis *s* eje principal
Majorca [mə'dʒɔrkə] *s* Mallorca
Majorcan [mə'dʒɔrkən] *adj & s* mallorquín
major-domo [,medʒər'domo] *s* (*pl:* **-mos**) mayordomo
major general *s* (mil.) general de división
majority [mə'dʒɑrɪtɪ] o [mə'dʒɔrɪtɪ] *s* (*pl:* **-ties**) mayoría; (mil.) comandancia; *adj* de la mayoría, mayoritario
major key *s* (mus.) tono mayor
major orders *spl* (eccl.) órdenes mayores
major premise *s* (log.) premisa mayor
major scale *s* (mus.) escala mayor
major surgery *s* cirugía mayor
make [mek] *s* hechura; corte (*de un vestido*); marca; modelo; constitución; natural, carácter; producción total; **on the make** (slang) buscando provecho ‖ (*pret & pp:* **made**) *va* hacer; ganar (*dinero; una baza; el mayor número de tantos*); dar (*dinero una empresa*); dar (*una vuelta*); pronunciar (*un discurso*); coger (*un tren*); cometer (*un error*); adquirir (*buena reputación*); llegar a (*la meta, el puerto, etc.*); cerrar (*un circuito*); hacer (*p.ej., cien kilómetros por hora*); poner (*a uno, p.ej., nervioso*); inventar; calcular; ser causa del éxito de; ser, p.ej., **he will make a good doctor** será un buen médico; servir de; **to make** + *inf* hacer + *inf*, p.ej., **I made him leave at once** le hice salir en seguida; **to make believe** hacer creer; **to make do** hacer servir; **to make into** convertir en; **to make known** hacer saber, declarar; dar a conocer; **to make of** pensar de, sacar de, p.ej., **what do you make of this?** ¿qué saca Vd. de esto?; **to make oneself known** darse a conocer; **to make or break** hacer la fortuna o ser la ruina de; **to make out** descifrar, entender; distinguir, vislumbrar; hacer (*la cuenta que uno debe pagar*); escribir (*una receta*); llenar (*un cheque*); declarar (*peor de lo que se creía*); **to make over** rehacer (*un traje*); convertir; (com.) transferir; **to make up** juntar, reunir; preparar; confeccionar (*un medicamento*); componer; integrar; inventar (*un cuento, una disculpa*); recobrar (*el tiempo perdido*); pagar, compensar; (print.) ajustar, compaginar; este verbo, seguido de un adjetivo, se traduce a veces por un verbo activo que corresponda al adjetivo, p.ej., **to make tired** cansar; **to make sick** enfermar ‖ *vn* estar (*p.ej., seguro*); **to make to** + *inf* hacer ademán de + *inf*, dar un paso para + *inf;* **to make after** perseguir; **to make as if** fingir que, hacer como que; **to make away with** llevarse; deshacerse de; matar; **to make believe** fingir, p.ej., **he made believe he was dead** fingió estar muerto; **to make for** ir hacia; abalanzarse para coger, embestir contra; hacer, p.ej., **his presence made for a pleasant day** su presencia hizo el día agradable; contribuir a (*p.ej., la paz*); **to make of** (coll.) mostrar cariño a; **to make off** largarse; **to make off with** hacerse con, irse con, llevarse; **to make out** arreglárselas, desenvolverse; **to make toward** dirigirse a, encaminarse a; **to make up** maquillarse; componerse (*hacer las paces*); **to make up for** suplir; compensar por (*una pérdida*); **to make up to** (coll.) querer congraciarse con
make and break *s* (elec.) dispositivo de ruptura y contacto
make-believe ['mekbɪ,liv] *adj* simulado; *s* simulación, artificio, pretexto; simulador
maker ['mekər] *s* constructor; fabricante; (*cap.*) *s* Hacedor
makeshift ['mek,ʃɪft] *s* expediente; tapagujeros (*persona*); *adj* provisional, de fortuna
make-up ['mek,ʌp] *s* composición, constitución; cosméticos; (theat.) maquillaje; (print.) imposición
make-up man *s* (theat.) experto en maquillaje, maquillador
makeweight ['mek,wet] *s* contrapeso (*para completar el peso de carne, pescado, etc.*); (fig.) suplente
making ['mekɪŋ] *s* hechura; fabricación; causa del éxito (*de una persona*); material necesario (*para hacer alguna cosa*); madera (*p.ej., de estudiante, médico*); **makings** *spl* elementos,

materiales; **in the making** sin terminar, no acabado de hacer; **while in the making** mientras se está haciendo
Malacca cane [mə'lækə] *s* rotén (*bastón*)
Malachi ['mæləkaɪ] o **Malachias** [,mælə'kaɪəs] *s* (Bib.) Malaquías
malachite ['mæləkaɪt] *s* (mineral.) malaquita
malacology [,mælə'kɑlədʒɪ] *s* malacología
malacopterygian [,mælə,kɑptə'rɪdʒɪən] *adj & s* (zool.) malacopterigio
malacostracan [,mælə'kɑstrəkən] *adj & s* (zool.) malacostráceo
maladjusted [,mælə'dʒʌstɪd] *adj* mal ajustado; inadaptado, mal adaptado, desequilibrado
maladjustment [,mælə'dʒʌstmənt] *s* mal ajuste; mala adaptación, desequilibrio
maladminister [,mæləd'mɪnɪstər] *va* administrar inepta, ineficaz o fraudulentamente
maladministration [,mæləd,mɪnɪs'treʃən] *s* administración inepta, ineficaz o fraudulenta
maladroit [,mælə'drɔɪt] *adj* torpe, desmañado
malady ['mælədɪ] *s* (*pl:* **-dies**) mal, enfermedad
malaise [mæ'lez] *s* malestar, indisposición
malanders ['mæləndərz] *spl* (vet.) ajuagas
malapert ['mæləpʌrt] *adj* descarado, insolente
malapropism ['mæləprɑpɪzəm] *s* despropósito
malapropos [,mælæprə'po] *adj* no a propósito; *adv* fuera de propósito
malar ['melər] *adj & s* (anat.) malar
malaria [mə'lɛrɪə] *s* (path.) malaria, paludismo
malarial [mə'lɛrɪəl] o **malarious** [mə'lɛrɪəs] *adj* palúdico; enfermo de paludismo
malarky [mə'lɑrkɪ] *s* (slang) habla necia e insincera
Malay ['mele] o [mə'le] *adj & s* malayo
Malaya [mə'leə] *s* Malaya
Malayan [mə'leən] *adj & s* malayo
Malay Archipelago *s* archipiélago Malayo
Malay Peninsula *s* península Malaya o península de Malaca
Malaysia [mə'leʒə] o [mə'leʃə] *s* la Malasia
Malaysian [mə'leʒən] o [mə'leʃən] *adj & s* malasio
Malay States *spl* Estados Malayos
malcontent ['mælkən,tɛnt] *adj & s* malcontento
male [mel] *adj* masculino; macho, p.ej., **a male weasel** una comadreja macho; varón, p.ej., **male child** hijo varón; (bot.) masculino; (bot. & mach.) macho; *s* macho; varón
malediction [,mælɪ'dɪkʃən] *s* maldición
malefaction [,mælɪ'fækʃən] *s* delito
malefactor ['mælɪ,fæktər] *s* malhechor
male fern *s* (bot.) helecho macho
maleficence [mə'lɛfɪsəns] *s* maleficencia
maleficent [mə'lɛfɪsənt] *adj* maléfico (*que hace daño*)
male nurse *s* enfermero
malevolence [mə'lɛvələns] *s* malevolencia
malevolent [mə'lɛvələnt] *adj & s* malévolo
malfeasance [mæl'fizəns] *s* corrupción, venalidad
malformation [,mælfɔr'meʃən] *s* malformación, deformidad
malformed [mæl'fɔrmd] *adj* malhecho, contrahecho
malfunction [mæl'fʌŋkʃən] *s* malfuncionamiento
malic ['mælɪk] o ['melɪk] *adj* málico
malic acid *s* (chem.) ácido málico
malice ['mælɪs] *s* malicia, mala voluntad; (law) dolo penal, intención delictuosa; **to bear malice** guardar rencor
malicious [mə'lɪʃəs] *adj* malicioso (*malo, maligno*)
malign [mə'laɪn] *adj* maligno; (path.) maligno; *va* calumniar
malignance [mə'lɪgnəns] o **malignancy** [mə'lɪgnənsɪ] *s* malignidad
malignant [mə'lɪgnənt] *adj* maligno; (path.) maligno
malignity [mə'lɪgnɪtɪ] *s* (*pl:* **-ties**) malignidad
maline [mə'lin] *s* tela de Malinas
Malines [mə'linz] *s* Malinas; (*l.c.*) *s* tela de Malinas; encaje de Malinas
malinger [mə'lɪŋgər] *vn* hacerse el enfermo, fingirse enfermo
malingerer [mə'lɪŋgərər] *s* simulador (*persona que finge padecer una enfermedad*)
malingering [mə'lɪŋgərɪŋ] *s* simulación (*fingimiento de una enfermedad*)
malison ['mælɪzən] o ['mælɪsən] *s* (archaic) maldición
mall [mɔl] o [mæl] *s* alameda, paseo de árboles
mallard ['mælərd] *s* (orn.) pato silvestre, pato real, ánade salvaje
malleability [,mælɪə'bɪlɪtɪ] *s* maleabilidad; docilidad
malleable ['mælɪəbəl] *adj* maleable; dócil, manejable
malleolar [mə'liələr] *adj* (anat.) maleolar
malleolus [mə'liələs] *s* (*pl:* **-li** [laɪ]) (anat.) maléolo
mallet ['mælɪt] *s* mazo (*martillo de madera*); (sport) mallete (*en el croquet y el polo*)
malleus ['mælɪəs] *s* (*pl:* **-i** [aɪ]) (anat.) martillo (*del oído*)
mallow ['mælo] *s* (bot.) malva
malmsey ['mɑmzɪ] *s* malvasía (*vino*)
malnutrition [,mælnju'trɪʃən] o [,mælnu'trɪʃən] *s* desnutrición
malodor [mæl'odər] *s* olor muy malo
malodorous [mæl'odərəs] *adj* maloliente
malpighiaceous [mæl,pɪgɪ'eʃəs] *adj* (bot.) malpigiáceo
Malpighian corpuscle [mæl'pɪgɪən] *s* (anat.) corpúsculo de Malpighi
malpractice [mæl'præktɪs] *s* malpraxis; procedimientos ilegales o criminales; mala conducta
malt [mɔlt] *s* malta *m*; (coll.) cerveza; *va* hacer germinar (*la cebada*); preparar con malta
maltase ['mɔltes] *s* (biochem.) maltasa
malted milk *s* leche preparada con malta
Maltese [mɔl'tiz] *adj* maltés; *s* (*pl:* **-tese**) maltés
Maltese cat *s* gato maltés
Maltese cross *s* cruz de Malta
malt extract *s* extracto de malta
malthouse ['mɔlt,haʊs] *s* cámara de germinación (*de la cebada, para la fabricación de la cerveza*)
Malthusian [mæl'θuʒən] *adj & s* maltusiano
Malthusianism [mæl'θuʒənɪzəm] *s* maltusianismo
maltose ['mɔltos] *s* (chem.) maltosa
maltreat [mæl'trit] *va* maltratar
maltreatment [mæl'tritmənt] *s* maltratamiento, malos tratos
maltster ['mɔltstər] *s* fermentador de cebada; vendedor de malta
malt sugar *s* azúcar de malta
malvaceous [mæl'veʃəs] *adj* (bot.) malváceo
malvasia [,mælvə'siə] *s* malvasía (*uva y vino*)
malversation [,mælvər'seʃən] *s* malversación
malvoisie ['mælvɔɪzɪ] *s* var. de **malmsey**
mama ['mɑmə] o [mə'mɑ] *s* mama o mamá
mambo ['mɑmbo] *s* mambo (*música y baile*); *vn* bailar el mambo
mameluke ['mæməluk] *s* mameluco (*esclavo*); (*cap.*) *s* mameluco (*soldado*)
Mamie ['memɪ] *s* nombre abreviado de **Margaret**
mamma ['mæmə] *s* (*pl:* **-mae** [mi]) (anat.) mama; ['mɑmə] o [mə'mɑ] *s* mama o mamá
mammal ['mæməl] *s* (zool.) mamífero
mammalian [mæ'melɪən] *adj & s* (zool.) mamífero
mammary ['mæmərɪ] *adj* mamario
mammary gland *s* (anat.) glándula mamaria
mammee [mɑ'me] o [mɑ'mi] *s* (bot.) mamey
mammilla [mə'mɪlə] *s* (*pl:* **-lae** [li]) (anat. & bot.) mamelón
mammillary ['mæmɪ,lɛrɪ] *adj* mamilar
Mammon o **mammon** ['mæmən] *s* (Bib.) mammón
mammoth ['mæməθ] *s* (pal.) mamut; *adj* gigantesco
mammy ['mæmɪ] *s* (*pl:* **-mies**) nodriza negra; negra vieja; mamá
Man. abr. de **Manitoba**
man [mæn] *s* (*pl:* **men**) hombre; pieza (*en el ajedrez*); pieza o peón (*en el juego de las damas*); **a man** uno, p.ej., **a man must keep his word** uno debe cumplir su palabra; **as a man** desde el punto de vista humano; **as one**

man unánimemente; **no man** nadie; **to a man** todos, sin faltar uno solo; **to become man** humanarse (*el Verbo divino*); **to be one's own man** no depender de nadie; estar sobre sí; **man alive!** ¡hombre!; **man and boy** desde la primera mocedad; **man and wife** marido y mujer; (*pret & pp:* **manned;** *ger:* **manning**) *va* proveer de gente armada, guarnecer (*una fortaleza*); tripular (*una embarcación, un coche, etc.*); servir (*los cañones*); preparar, p.ej., **to man oneself** prepararse (*p.ej., para resistir un golpe*)
man about town *s* hombre aficionado a los bulevares, hombre de mucho mundo
manacle [ˈmænəkəl] *s* manilla; **manacles** *spl* esposas; (fig.) estorbo; *va* poner manilla a, poner esposas a; (fig.) estorbar
manage [ˈmænɪdʒ] *va* manejar; (equit.) manejar (*un caballo*); *vn* manejarse; **to manage to** + *inf* ingeniarse a + *inf;* **to manage to get along** ingeniarse a vivir; arreglárselas
manageability [ˌmænɪdʒəˈbɪlɪtɪ] *s* manejabilidad
manageable [ˈmænɪdʒəbəl] *adj* manejable
management [ˈmænɪdʒmənt] *s* dirección, gerencia, manejo; organización industrial, gestión científica, taylorismo; la parte patronal, la empresa, los dirigentes, los patronos
manager [ˈmænɪdʒər] *s* director; gerente; empresario; persona económica; (sport) manager
managerial [ˌmænəˈdʒɪrɪəl] *adj* directorial, administrativo
Manasseh [məˈnæsə] *s* (Bib.) Manasés
man-at-arms [ˈmænətˈɑrmz] *s* (*pl:* **men-at-arms**) hombre de guerra (*militar*); hombre de armas (*jinete armado de todas piezas*)
manatee [ˌmænəˈti] *s* (zool.) manatí
manchet [ˈmæntʃɪt] *s* (archaic) pan candeal
man-child [ˈmænˌtʃaɪld] *s* (*pl:* **men-children**) niño varón
manchineel [ˌmæntʃɪˈnil] *s* (bot.) manzanillo (*árbol*)
manchineel apple *s* manzanilla de Indias (*fruto*)
Manchu [mænˈtʃu] o [ˈmæntʃu] *adj* manchú; *s* (*pl:* **-chus**) manchú
Manchurian [mænˈtʃʊrɪən] *adj & s* manchuriano
manciple [ˈmænsɪpəl] *s* administrador o mayordomo (*p.ej., de un colegio*)
Mancunian [mænˈkjunɪən] *adj* perteneciente a Mánchester; *s* natural o habitante de Mánchester (*Inglaterra*)
mandamus [mænˈdeməs] *s* (law) despacho
mandarin [ˈmændərɪn] *adj* mandarín; *s* mandarín; (bot.) mandarino (*árbol*); mandarina (*fruto*); (*cap.*) *s* mandarina (*lengua*)
mandarin duck *s* (orn.) pato mandarín
mandarin orange *s* naranja mandarina
mandarin porcelain *s* porcelana mandarina
mandatary [ˈmændəˌtɛrɪ] *s* (*pl:* **-ies**) (law & dipl.) mandatario
mandate [ˈmændet] *s* mandato; (law & dipl.) mandato; (pol.) voluntad manifiesta (*de los votantes*); *va* asignar por mandato
mandator [mænˈdetər] *s* (law) mandante
mandatory [ˈmændəˌtorɪ] *adj* obligatorio, preceptivo; conferido por mandato; *s* (*pl:* **-ries**) mandatario
mandible [ˈmændɪbəl] *s* (anat. & zool.) mandíbula
mandibular [mænˈdɪbjələr] *adj* mandibular
mandolin [ˈmændəlɪn] *s* (mus.) mandolina
mandragora [mænˈdrægərə] *s* (bot.) mandrágora
mandrake [ˈmændrek] *s* (bot.) mandrágora; (bot.) podofilo
mandrake apple *s* limón silvestre, manzana de mayo
mandrel o **mandril** [ˈmændrəl] *s* (mach.) mandril
mandrill [ˈmændrɪl] *s* (zool.) mandril
mane [men] *s* crin (*del caballo*); melena (*del león; de una persona*)
man-eater [ˈmænˌitər] *s* caníbal; (zool.) jaquetón (*tiburón*)
manège [məˈnɛʒ] o [məˈneʒ] *s* (equit.) manejo (*arte*); (equit.) picadero (*sitio*); (equit.) marcha o aires (*del caballo adiestrado*)
manes o **Manes** [ˈmeniz] *spl* manes
maneuver [məˈnuvər] *s* maniobra; (fig.) maniobra; *va* hacer maniobrar; ejecutar con maniobras, lograr con maniobras; dirigir las maniobras de; *vn* maniobrar; (fig.) maniobrar
maneuverability [məˌnuvərəˈbɪlɪtɪ] *s* maniobrabilidad
maneuverable [məˈnuvərəbəl] *adj* maniobrable
man Friday *s* criado fidelísimo
manful [ˈmænfəl] *adj* varonil
manganese [ˈmæŋgənis] o [ˈmæŋgəniz] *s* (chem.) manganeso
manganese steel *s* acero al manganeso
manganic [mænˈgænɪk] *adj* mangánico
manganic acid *s* (chem.) ácido mangánico
manganite [ˈmæŋgənaɪt] *s* (chem.) manganita
manganous [ˈmæŋgənəs] o [mænˈgænəs] *adj* manganoso
mange [mendʒ] *s* sarna
mangel-wurzel [ˈmæŋgəlˌwʌrzəl] *s* (bot.) remolacha forrajera
manger [ˈmendʒər] *s* pesebre
mangle [ˈmæŋgəl] *s* (mach.) mangle; *va* prensar con mangle; destrozar, lacerar; echar a perder, estropear
mango [ˈmæŋgo] *s* (*pl:* **-goes** o **-gos**) (bot.) mango
mangonel [ˈmæŋgənɛl] *s* mangano o mandrón
mangosteen [ˈmæŋgəstin] *s* (bot.) mangostán (*árbol*); mangosto (*fruto*)
mangrove [ˈmæŋgrov] *s* (bot.) mangle
mangy [ˈmendʒɪ] *adj* (*comp:* **-gier;** *super:* **-giest**) sarnoso; (fig.) roñoso, sucio
manhandle [ˈmænˌhændəl] *va* mover a brazo (*sin máquinas*); maltratar
manhole [ˈmænˌhol] *s* buzón, caja de registro (*en las calles*); agujero de hombre (*en una caldera*)
manhole cover *s* tapa de registro
manhood [ˈmænhʊd] *s* virilidad; masculinidad; hombres
man-hour [ˈmænˈaʊr] *s* (*pl:* **man-hours**) hora-hombre (*obra de una hora hecha por un solo hombre*)
man hunt *s* caza al hombre, persecución de un criminal
mania [ˈmenɪə] *s* manía; (psychopath.) manía
maniac [ˈmenɪæk] *adj & s* maníaco
maniacal [məˈnaɪəkəl] *adj* maníaco
manic [ˈmenɪk] o [ˈmænɪk] *adj* (psychopath.) maníaco
manic-depressive insanity [ˈmænɪkdɪˈprɛsɪv] *s* (psychopath.) manía-melancolía, locura de doble forma, psicosis maníacodepresiva
Manichean [ˌmænɪˈkiən] *adj & s* maniqueo
Manicheanism [ˌmænɪˈkiənɪzəm] o **Manicheism** [ˈmænɪˌkiɪzəm] *s* maniqueísmo
manichord [ˈmænɪkərd] *s* (mus.) manicordio o monacordio
manicure [ˈmænɪkjʊr] *s* manicura (*cuidado de las manos y las uñas*); manicuro o manicura (*persona*); *va* hacer la manicura a, hacer (*las manos o las uñas*)
manicurist [ˈmænɪˌkjʊrɪst] *s* manicuro o manicura (*persona*)
manifest [ˈmænɪfɛst] *adj* manifiesto; *s* (naut.) manifiesto; *va* manifestar
manifestant [ˌmænɪˈfɛstənt] *s* manifestante
manifestation [ˌmænɪfɛsˈteʃən] *s* manifestación
manifesto [ˌmænɪˈfɛsto] *s* (*pl:* **-toes**) manifiesto, proclama
manifold [ˈmænɪfold] *adj* múltiple, variado, multiforme; *s* copia, ejemplar; (mach.) múltiple; *va* hacer o sacar varias copias de
manikin [ˈmænɪkɪn] *s* maniquí; enano
manila [məˈnɪlə] *s* cáñamo de Manila; papel de Manila
Manila hemp *s* cáñamo de Manila
Manila paper *s* papel de Manila
Manila rope *s* cuerda de cáñamo, cuerda de abacá
manilla [məˈnɪlə] *s* cáñamo de Manila; papel de Manila; malilla (*segunda carta en valor*)
man in the moon *s* cara o cuerpo de hombre imaginarios en la luna llena; persona imaginaria
man in the street *s* hombre de la calle (*ciudadano típico*)

manioc ['mænɪɑk] *s* (bot.) mandioca (*planta y harina*)
maniple ['mænɪpəl] *s* (hist. & eccl.) manípulo
manipulate [mə'nɪpjəlet] *va* manipular
manipulation [mə,nɪpjə'leʃən] *s* manipulación
manipulative [mə'nɪpjə,letɪv] *adj* de manipulación
manipulator [mə'nɪpjə,letər] *s* manipulador
manito ['mænɪto] o **manitou** ['mænɪtu] *s* espíritu, fetiche (*objeto de culto de los pieles rojas*)
mankind [,mæn'kaɪnd] *s* humanidad, raza humana; ['mæn,kaɪnd] *s* sexo masculino, hombres
manlike ['mæn,laɪk] *adj* varonil; hombruno, masculino
manliness ['mænlɪnɪs] *s* virilidad; masculinidad
manly ['mænlɪ] *adj* (*comp:* **-lier;** *super:* **-liest**) varonil; masculino
man-made ['mæn,med] *adj* hecho por el hombre
man midwife *s* comadrón, partero
manna ['mænə] *s* (Bib.) maná; (bot.) maná (*líquido que fluye del Fraxinus ornus y otros vegetales*); cosa llovida del cielo; **like manna from heaven** como llovido del cielo
manna ash *s* (bot.) orno
manna grass *s* (bot.) hierba del maná
manna sugar *s* manita
manned spacecraft o **spaceship** [mænd] *s* astronave tripulada
mannequin ['mænɪkɪn] *s* maniquí (*armazón de figura humana, que usan los sastres y costureras*); maniquí, modelo (*mujer que sirve para probar prendas de vestir*)
manner ['mænər] *s* manera; (f.a. & lit.) manera (*p.ej., de Rafael*); **manners** *spl* modales, maneras; costumbres; **by all manner of means** de todos modos, sin falta; **by no manner of means** de ninguna manera; **in a manner of speaking** como quien dice, como si dijéramos; **in the manner of** a la manera de; **to the manner born** avezado desde la cuna
mannered ['mænərd] *adj* amanerado; de modales (*buenos o malos*)
mannerism ['mænərɪzəm] *s* costumbre, hábito (*p.ej., de rascarse la oreja*); amaneramiento; (f.a. & lit.) manierismo
mannerless ['mænərlɪs] *adj* descortés
mannerly ['mænərlɪ] *adj* cortés, urbano; *adv* cortésmente, urbanamente
Mannie ['mænɪ] *s* Manolo
mannikin ['mænɪkɪn] *s* var. de **manikin**
mannish ['mænɪʃ] *adj* hombruno
mannitol ['mænɪtɑl] o ['mænɪtol] *s* (chem.) manita
mannose ['mænos] *s* (chem.) manosa
manoeuvre [mə'nuvər] *s, va & vn* var. de **maneuver**
Man of Destiny *s* hombre del destino (*Napoleón*)
man of distinction *s* hombre de distinción
Man of Galilee, the el Galileo
man of God *s* santo, profeta; hombre de iglesia (*clérigo*)
man of his word *s* hombre de palabra
man of letters *s* hombre de letras
man of means *s* hombre de dinero
man of parts *s* hombre de buenas prendas, hombre de talento
man of property *s* hombre de fondos
man of repute *s* hombre de fama
Man of Sorrows *s* Hombre de los Dolores, Varón de Dolores (*Jesucristo*)
man of straw *s* hombre de suposición
man of the hour *s* hombre del momento
man of the world *s* hombre de mundo
man-of-war [,mænəv'wɔr] *s* (*pl:* **men-of-war**) acorazado, buque de guerra
man-of-war bird *s* (orn.) fragata, rabihorcado
manometer [mə'nɑmɪtər] *s* manómetro
manometric [,mænə'mɛtrɪk] *adj* manométrico
manometric capsule *s* (phys.) cápsula manométrica
manometric flame *s* (phys.) llama manométrica
man on horseback *s* caudillo revolucionario
manor ['mænər] *s* feudo; finca solariega, señorío
manor house *s* casa solariega
manorial [mə'norɪəl] *adj* señorial; solariego
man overboard *interj* ¡hombre al agua!, ¡hombre a la mar!
man power *s* mano de obra, potencial humano; (mil.) fuerzas disponibles
manrope ['mæn,rop] *s* (naut.) guardamancebo
mansard ['mænsɑrd] *s* mansarda; piso de mansarda
mansard roof *s* mansarda
manse [mæns] *s* rectoría
manservant ['mæn,sʌrvənt] *s* (*pl:* **menservants**) criado
mansion ['mænʃən] *s* hotel, palacio, casa magnífica; casa solariega
manslaughter ['mæn,slɔtər] *s* (law) homicidio criminal pero sin premeditación
mantel ['mæntəl] *s* manto (*de chimenea*); mesilla, repisa de chimenea
mantelet ['mæntəlɛt] o ['mæntlɪt] *s* manteleta (*esclavina*); (mil.) mantelete
mantelletta [,mæntə'lɛtə] *s* (eccl.) mantelete
mantelpiece ['mæntəl,pis] *s* mesilla, repisa de chimenea
mantilla [mæn'tɪlə] *s* mantilla (*prenda*)
mantis ['mæntɪs] *s* (*pl:* **-tises** o **-tes** [tiz]) (ent.) mantis religiosa
mantis crab *s* (zool.) esquila
mantissa [mæn'tɪsə] *s* (math.) mantisa
mantle ['mæntəl] *s* manto (*vestido amplio a modo de capa*); capa (*p.ej., de nieve*); camiseta o manguito (*del alumbrado de gas*); (zool.) manto; *va* vestir con manto; cubrir, tapar; encubrir, ocultar; *vn* ponerse encendido (*dícese, p.ej., de las mejillas*); extenderse (*el color encendido de las mejillas*); cubrirse de algas (*las aguas estancadas*)
mantling ['mæntlɪŋ] *s* mesilla, repisa de chimenea; rubor, sonrojo; (her.) mantelete
mantua ['mæntʃuə] o ['mæntuə] *s* manto
Mantuan ['mæntʃuən] o ['mæntuən] *adj & s* mantuano
Mantuan Swan *s* cisne de Mantua (*Virgilio*)
manual ['mænjuəl] *adj* manual; *s* manual (*libro*); (mus.) teclado manual (*de órgano*); (mil.) ejercicio, p.ej., **manual of arms** ejercicio de armas
manual alphabet *s* abecedario manual
manually ['mænjuəlɪ] *adv* manualmente
manual training *s* instrucción en artes y oficios
manubrium [mə'njubrɪəm] o [mə'nubrɪəm] *s* (*pl:* **-a** [ə] o **-ums**) (anat., bot. & zool.) manubrio
manufactory [,mænjə'fæktərɪ] *s* (*pl:* **-ries**) manufactura, fábrica (*establecimiento*)
manufacture [,mænjə'fæktʃər] *s* fabricación; manufactura (*obra fabricada*); *va* manufacturar, fabricar; (fig.) fabricar
manufacturer [,mænjə'fæktʃərər] *s* fabricante
manufacturing [,mænjə'fæktʃərɪŋ] *adj* manufacturero; *s* fabricación
manumission [,mænjə'mɪʃən] *s* (law) manumisión
manumit [,mænjə'mɪt] (*pret & pp:* **-mitted;** *ger:* **-mitting**) *va* (law) manumitir
manumitter [,mænjə'mɪtər] *s* manumisor
manure [mə'njur] o [mə'nur] *s* estiércol; *va* estercolar
manuscript ['mænjəskrɪpt] *adj & s* manuscrito
Manx [mæŋks] *adj* manés; *s* manés (*idioma*); *spl* maneses
Manx cat *s* gato manés
Manxman ['mæŋksmən] *s* (*pl:* **-men**) manés
many ['mɛnɪ] *adj* (*comp:* **more;** *super:* **most**) muchos; *pron* muchos; *s* gran número; **a good many** un buen número; **a great many** un gran número; **as many as** tantos como; hasta, p.ej., **as many as ten** hasta diez; **how many** cuántos; **one too many for** la ruina de; **so many** tantos; **the many** los más; la plebe, la gente menuda; **too many** demasiados; de más, de sobra, p.ej., **one too many** uno de más, uno de sobra; **twice as many as** dos veces más que; **many a** muchos, p.ej., **many a time** muchas veces; **many another**

muchos otros; **many more** muchos más; **many of** muchos de; **many people** mucha gente

many-colored [ˈmɛnɪˌkʌlərd] *adj* multicolor

manyplies [ˈmɛnɪˌplaɪz] *s* (zool.) omaso

manyroot [ˈmɛnɪˌrut] o [ˈmɛnɪˌrʊt] *s* (bot.) saltaperico

many-sided [ˈmɛnɪˌsaɪdɪd] *adj* multilátero; (fig.) de muchas habilidades, de gran curiosidad intelectual, polifacético

manzanita [ˌmænzəˈnitə] *s* (bot.) manzanita

Maori [ˈmɑorɪ] *adj* maorí; *s* (*pl:* **-ris**) maorí

map [mæp] *s* mapa; plano (*p.ej., de una ciudad*); (*pret & pp:* **mapped;** *ger:* **mapping**) *va* trazar el mapa de; indicar en el mapa; planear, trazar el plan de; **to map out** planear, trazar el plan de

maple [ˈmepəl] *s* (bot.) arce

maple sugar *s* azúcar de arce

maple syrup *s* jarabe de arce

maquette [mɑˈkɛt] *s* maqueta

maqui [ˈmɑkɪ] *s* (bot.) maqui

Mar. abr. de **March**

mar [mɑr] (*pret & pp:* **marred;** *ger:* **marring**) *va* desfigurar, estropear, echar a perder

marabou [ˈmærəbu] *s* (orn.) marabú (*ave y adorno*)

maraschino [ˌmærəˈskino] *s* marrasquino

maraschino cherries *spl* guindas en conserva con sabor a marrasquino

marasmus [məˈræzməs] *s* (path.) marasmo

Marathon [ˈmærəθɑn] *s* Maratón; (*l.c.*) *s* (sport) maratón, carrera de maratón

marathon race *s* (sport) carrera de maratón

maraud [məˈrɔd] *va* merodear por; *vn* merodear

marauder [məˈrɔdər] *s* merodeador, merodista

marauding [məˈrɔdɪŋ] *adj* merodeador; *s* merodeo

maravedi [ˌmærəˈvedɪ] *s* maravedí

marble [ˈmɑrbəl] *s* mármol; canica (*bolita*); **marbles** *ssg* canica (*juego*); *adj* marmóreo; *va* marmolizar; crispir, jaspear; *vn* marmolizarse

marcasite [ˈmɑrkəsaɪt] *s* (mineral.) marcasita

marcel [mɑrˈsɛl] *s* ondulado Marcel; (*pret & pp:* **-celled;** *ger:* **-celling**) *va* rizar (*el cabello*) a la Marcel

Marcella [mɑrˈsɛlə] *s* Marcela

Marcellus [mɑrˈsɛləs] *s* Marcelo

marcescence [mɑrˈsɛsəns] *s* (bot.) marcescencia

marcescent [mɑrˈsɛsənt] *adj* (bot.) marcescente

march [mɑrtʃ] *s* marcha; (mil. & mus.) marcha; (fig.) marcha (*progreso*); marca (*frontera; territorio*); **on the march** en marcha; **to steal a march on someone** ganarle a uno por la mano; (*cap.*) *s* marzo; *adj* marzal; (*l.c.*) *va* hacer marchar; llevar (*a una persona*) a donde tiene pocas ganas de ir; *vn* marchar; (mil.) marchar

marchioness [ˈmɑrʃənɪs] *s* marquesa

marchland [ˈmɑrtʃˌlænd] *s* terreno fronterizo

marchpane [ˈmɑrtʃˌpen] *s* mazapán

marconigram [mɑrˈkonɪgræm] *s* marconigrama

Marcus [ˈmɑrkəs] *s* Marco

Mardi gras [ˈmɑrdɪ ˈgrɑ] *s* martes de carnaval

mare [mɛr] *s* yegua; asna

marekanite [ˌmærɪˈkænaɪt] *s* (mineral.) marecanita

mare's-nest [ˈmɛrzˌnɛst] *s* parto de los montes

mare's-tail [ˈmɛrzˌtel] *s* (bot.) corregüela hembra; (bot.) cola de caballo, equiseto; rabos de gallo (*cirro o nube cirrosa*)

Margaret [ˈmɑrgərɪt] *s* Margarita

margarin [ˈmɑrdʒərɪn] o [ˈmɑrgərɪn] o **margarine** [ˈmɑrdʒərin] o [ˈmɑrgərin] *s* margarina

margarite [ˈmɑrgəraɪt] *s* (mineral.) margarita

marge [mɑrdʒ] *s* (poet.) margen

margent [ˈmɑrdʒənt] *s* (archaic) margen

margin [ˈmɑrdʒɪn] *s* margen; reserva (*para futuras contingencias*); excedente, sobrante; ganancia bruta; doble (*fianza que pide el corredor al comprador en las operaciones de bolsa*); (ins.) recargo al premio (*para cubrir ciertos gastos*)

marginal [ˈmɑrdʒɪnəl] *adj* marginal; (bot.) marginado

marginalia [ˌmɑrdʒɪˈnelɪə] o [ˌmɑrdʒɪˈneljə] *spl* notas marginales, apostillas

marginally [ˈmɑrdʒɪnəlɪ] *adv* al margen

marginal note *s* nota marginal

marginal stop *s* marginador, fijamárgenes (*de una máquina de escribir*)

margin of error *s* margen de error

margin of safety *s* margen de seguridad

margin release *s* tecla de escape, soltador del margen, llave de salto (*de una máquina de escribir*)

margrave [ˈmɑrgrev] *s* margrave

margraviate [mɑrˈgrevɪɪt] *s* margraviato

margravine [ˈmɑrgrəvin] *s* margravina

marguerite [ˌmɑrgəˈrit] *s* (bot.) margarita; (*cap.*) *s* Margarita

Marian [ˈmærɪən] o [ˈmɛrɪən] *adj* mariano; *s* Mariana

Marianne [ˌmɛrɪˈæn] *s* Mariana

Marie [məˈri] *s* María

marigold [ˈmærɪgold] *s* (bot.) maravilla, flamenquilla; (bot.) clavelón (*Targetes erecta*)

marigraph [ˈmærɪgræf] o [ˈmærɪgrɑf] *s* mareógrafo

marihuana o **marijuana** [ˌmɑrɪˈhwɑnə] *s* (bot.) mariguana (*Cannabis sativa*); mariguana falsa o maraquiana (*Nicotiana glauca*)

marimba [məˈrɪmbə] *s* (mus.) marimba

marinade [ˌmærɪˈned] *s* escabeche; [ˈmærɪned] *va* escabechar, marinar

marinate [ˈmærɪnet] *va* escabechar, marinar

marine [məˈrin] *adj* marino, marítimo; *s* marina de guerra; marina mercante; marina (*cuadro o pintura*); infantería de marina; infante de marina, soldado de infantería de marina; **tell that to the marines** (coll.) a otro perro con ese hueso, cuénteselo a su abuela

marine code *s* código de señales marítimas

Marine Corps *s* (U.S.A.) infantería de marina

mariner [ˈmærɪnər] *s* marino, marinero

Marion [ˈmærɪən] o [ˈmɛrɪən] *s* Mariana (*nombre de mujer*); Mariano (*nombre de varón*)

marionette [ˌmærɪəˈnɛt] *s* marioneta, títere, figurilla

marish [ˈmærɪʃ] *adj* (archaic & poet.) pantanoso; *s* (archaic & poet.) pantano

Marist [ˈmɛrɪst] *adj & s* (eccl.) marista

marital [ˈmærɪtəl] *adj* marital

marital status *s* estado civil

maritime [ˈmærɪtaɪm] o [ˈmærɪtɪm] *adj* marítimo

Maritime Provinces *spl* Provincias Marítimas (*del Canadá*)

Marius [ˈmɛrɪəs] *s* Mario

marjoram [ˈmɑrdʒərəm] *s* (bot.) orégano; (bot.) mejorana (*Majorana hortensis*)

mark [mɑrk] *s* marca; señal; huella; mancha; marbete, etiqueta; fin, propósito; calificación, nota (*en un examen*); blanco (*a que se tira*); signo (*señal de cruz que se usa en vez de la firma de uno*); marco (*moneda; peso*); meta; (sport) raya (*que indica el punto desde el que se ha de partir en una carrera*); (archaic) marca (*distrito fronterizo*); (*cap.*) *s* Marcos; (Bib.) Marcos; (Bib.) el Evangelio según San Marcos; **of mark** célebre, importante; **to be beside the mark** no venir al caso; **to come up to the mark** alcanzar lo que era de esperar, ser completamente satisfactorio; **to hit the mark** dar en el blanco; poner el dedo en la llaga; **to leave one's mark** dejar memoria de sí; **to make one's mark** hacerse un hombre de provecho; llegar a ser célebre; **to miss the mark** errar el tiro; **to shoot beside the mark** errar el tiro; no atinar en el punto de la dificultad; **to toe the mark** ponerse en la raya; obrar como se debe **|** *va* marcar, señalar; indicar (*p.ej., disgusto*); distinguir; advertir, notar, poner atención a; marcar (*los tantos en un juego*); indicar el precio de, con lápiz o etiqueta; dar nota o notas a (*un alumno*); calificar (*un examen*); **to mark down** apuntar, poner por escrito; marcar a un precio más bajo; rebajar el precio de; **to mark off** u **out** indicar, señalar; separar con un guión o con una raya; **to mark out for** escoger para **|** *vn* poner atención; dar notas (*el maestro*); quedarse marcado

markdown [ˈmarkˌdaʊn] *s* precio reducido
marked [markt] *adj* marcado
marked man *s* hombre sospechoso; futura víctima
marker [ˈmarkər] *s* marcador; mojón; ficha (*en los juegos*); (sport) marcador (*instrumento para señalar el terreno de juego en el tenis, etc.; aparato para señalar los tantos del billar, etc.*)
marker light *s* (aer.) luz de balizaje
market [ˈmarkɪt] *s* mercado; bolsa; **to bear the market** jugar a la baja; **to be in the market for** querer comprar; **to bull the market** jugar al alza; **to lose one's market** perder la clientela; **to play the market** jugar a la bolsa o en bolsa; **to put on the market** lanzar al mercado; *va* vender; llevar o enviar al mercado; hallar mercado para; comprar en el mercado; *vn* comerciar
marketability [ˌmarkɪtəˈbɪlɪtɪ] *s* comercialidad
marketable [ˈmarkɪtəbəl] *adj* comerciable, vendible
market basket *s* cesta para compras
marketeer [ˌmarkɪˈtɪr] *s* placero
marketing [ˈmarkɪtɪŋ] *s* mercadotecnia, mercología; *adj* mercológico
market place *s* plaza del mercado
market price *s* precio corriente o de plaza
market value *s* valor en plaza
marking [ˈmarkɪŋ] *s* marca, señal, signo; pinta (*mancha; adorno en forma de mancha*); coloración; marchamo o marchamos (*de aduana*)
marking gauge *s* gramil
marksman [ˈmarksmən] *s* (*pl:* **-men**) tirador; **to be a good marksman** ser un buen tiro
marksmanship [ˈmarksmənʃɪp] *s* puntería
markup [ˈmarkˌʌp] *s* aumento de precio; margen de ganancia, margen de utilidad; direcciones en un manuscrito para el impresor
marl [marl] *s* marga; *va* margar; (naut.) trincafiar
marlin [ˈmarlɪn] *s* (ichth.) aguja (*pez del género Makaira*)
marline [ˈmarlɪn] *s* (naut.) merlín, trincafía
marlinespike o **marlinspike** [ˈmarlɪnˌspaɪk] *s* (naut.) burel, pasador
marlpit [ˈmarlˌpɪt] *s* almarga, marguera
marly [ˈmarlɪ] *adj* (*comp:* **-ier;** *super:* **-iest**) margoso
marmalade [ˈmarməled] *s* mermelada; mermelada de naranjas
marmalade tree *s* (bot.) zapote chico
marmoreal [marˈmorɪəl] *adj* marmóreo
marmoset [ˈmarməzɛt] *s* (zool.) tití
marmot [ˈmarmət] *s* (zool.) marmota
maroon [məˈrun] *adj* marrón (*castaño obscuro*); *s* marrón (*castaño obscuro; esclavo fugitivo, negro descendiente de esclavos fugitivos en las Antillas y la Guayana Holandesa; bomba de anuncio*); *va* dejar abandonado, aislar (*p.ej., en una isla desierta*)
marplot [ˈmarˌplat] *s* aguafiestas
marque [mark] *s* (naut.) licencia oficial para el corso
marquee [marˈki] *s* gran tienda de campaña; marquesina (*sobre la puerta de un hotel, etc.*)
marquess [ˈmarkwɪs] *s* marqués
marquetry [ˈmarkətrɪ] *s* (*pl:* **-tries**) marquetería (*taracea*)
marquis [ˈmarkwɪs] *s* marqués
marquisate [ˈmarkwɪzɪt] *s* marquesado
marquise [marˈkiz] *s* marquesa; marquesina (*sobre la puerta de un hotel, etc.*)
marquisette [ˌmarkɪˈzɛt] o [ˌmarkwɪˈzɛt] *s* tejido fino de mallas cuadradas
marriage [ˈmærɪdʒ] *s* matrimonio; maridaje (*vida de casados; unión o conformidad*)
marriageability [ˌmærɪdʒəˈbɪlɪtɪ] *s* nubilidad
marriageable [ˈmærɪdʒəbəl] *adj* casadero, núbil
marriage bed *s* cama de recién casados
marriage license *s* licencia de matrimonio
marriage portion *s* dote
marriage rate *s* nupcialidad
marriage settlement s capitulaciones
married [ˈmærɪd] *adj* casado; conyugal; (fig.) maridado
married life *s* vida conyugal
marrons [ˈmærənz] *spl* marrones (*castañas confitadas*)
marrow [ˈmæro] *s* (anat. & fig.) médula
marrowbone [ˈmæroˌbon] *s* hueso medular; **marrowbones** *spl* (hum.) rodillas; huesos cruzados (*símbolo de la muerte*)
marrowfat [ˈmæroˌfæt] *s* guisante de semilla grande
marrowy [ˈmærəwɪ] *adj* medular, meolludo
marry [ˈmærɪ] *interj* (archaic) ¡por mi fe!, ¡válgame Dios!; (*pret & pp:* **-ried**) *va* casar; casar con o casarse con; (fig.) maridar (*unir, enlazar*); **to get married to** casar con o casarse con; *vn* casar o casarse; **to marry into** emparentar con (*p.ej., una familia rica*); **to marry the second time** casarse en segundas nupcias
Mars [marz] *s* (astr. & myth.) Marte
Marseillaise [ˌmarsəˈlez] *s* Marsellesa (*himno patriótico francés*)
Marseilles [marˈselz] *s* Marsella; (*l.c.*) *s* tela tupida de algodón dibujada en relieve
marsh [marʃ] *s* pantano
marshal [ˈmarʃəl] *s* (mil.) mariscal; cursor de procesiones; maestro de ceremonias; magistrado de audiencias; (U.S.A.) oficial de justicia; (*pret & pp:* **-shaled** o **-shalled;** *ger:* **-shaling** o **-shalling**) *va* conducir con solemnidad ceremonial; ordenar (*p.ej., los hechos de un argumento*)
marsh gas *s* gas de los pantanos
marsh harrier *s* (orn.) arpella, buzo de los pantanos, busardo, borní
marsh mallow *s* (bot.) malvavisco
marshmallow [ˈmarʃˌmælo] *s* pastilla o bombón de malvavisco; pastilla o bombón de merengue blando
marsh marigold *s* (bot.) hierba centella
marsh warbler *s* (orn.) arandillo, curruca de los pantanos
marshy [ˈmarʃɪ] *adj* (*comp:* **-ier;** *super:* **-iest**) pantanoso; palustre
marsupial [marˈsupɪəl] o [marˈsjupɪəl] *adj* & *s* (zool.) marsupial
marsupium [marˈsupɪəm] o [marˈsjupɪəm] *s* (*pl:* **-a** [ə]) (zool.) bolsa (*de la hembra de los marsupiales*)
Marsyas [ˈmarsɪæs] *s* (myth.) Marsias
mart [mart] *s* emporio, centro comercial
marteline [ˈmartəlɪn] *s* martellina
marten [ˈmartən] *s* (zool.) marta (*Martes martes*); (zool.) garduña (*Martes foina*)
Martha [ˈmarθə] *s* Marta
martial [ˈmarʃəl] *adj* marcial; (*cap.*) *s* Marcial
martial law *s* ley marcial; **to be under martial law** estar en estado de guerra
Martian [ˈmarʃən] *adj* & *s* marciano
martin [ˈmartɪn] *s* (orn.) avión; (*cap.*) *s* Martín
martinet [ˌmartɪˈnɛt] o [ˈmartɪnɛt] *s* ordenancista
martingale [ˈmartɪŋgel] *s* amarra, gamarra; (naut.) moco del bauprés
Martinique [ˌmartɪˈnik] *s* la Martinica
Martinmas [ˈmartɪnməs] *s* día de San Martín
martlet [ˈmartlɪt] *s* (orn.) avión; (her.) merleta
martyr [ˈmartər] *s* mártir; *va* martirizar
martyrdom [ˈmartərdəm] *s* martirio
martyrize [ˈmartəraɪz] *va* martirizar
martyrology [ˌmartəˈralədʒɪ] *s* (*pl:* **-gies**) martirologio
marvel [ˈmarvəl] *s* maravilla; (*pret & pp:* **-veled** o **-velled;** *ger:* **-veling** o **-velling**) *vn* maravillarse; **to marvel at** maravillarse con o de
marvel-of-Peru [ˈmarvələvpəˈru] *s* (bot.) arrebolera, dondiego
marvelous o **marvellous** [ˈmarvələs] *adj* maravilloso
Marxian [ˈmarksɪən] *adj* & *s* marxista
Marxism [ˈmarksɪzəm] *s* marxismo
Marxist [ˈmarksɪst] *adj* & *s* var. de **Marxian**
Mary [ˈmɛrɪ] *s* María
Mary Magdalene *s* (Bib.) Santa María Magdalena
marzipan [ˈmarzɪpæn] *s* mazapán
masc. abr. de **masculine**
mascara [mæsˈkærə] *s* preparación para teñir las pestañas
mascle [ˈmæskəl] *s* (her.) macle
mascot [ˈmæskat] *s* mascota
masculine [ˈmæskjəlɪn] *adj* masculino; hom-

bruno; (gram.) masculino; *s* (gram.) masculino (*género*); (gram.) palabra masculina
masculine rhyme *s* (pros.) rima masculina
masculinity [ˌmæskjəˈlɪnɪtɪ] *s* masculinidad, hombradía
maser [ˈmezər] *s* (electron.) dispositivo amplificador que sirve para captar microondas emitidas por objetos celestes lejanos, y también para generar radiaciones electromagnéticas y especialmente rayos de luz
mash [mæʃ] *s* masa (*mezcla espesa y blanda*); harina o afrecho amasado con agua caliente; masa de cebada (*para la elaboración de la cerveza*); *va* majar, machacar; bracear (*la cerveza*)
mashed potatoes *spl* patatas majadas, puré de patatas
masher [ˈmæʃər] *s* mano (*útil de cocina en forma de maza*); (coll.) galanteador atrevido
mashie o **mashy** [ˈmæʃɪ] *s* (*pl:* **-ies**) (golf) mashie
mashie niblick *s* (golf) mashie-morder
mask [mæsk] o [mɑsk] *s* máscara; mascarilla (*p.ej., de un cadáver*); máscaras, mascarada; máscara (*persona*); (phot.) desvanecedor; (arch.) mascarón; (fig.) máscara; **to take off one's mask** (fig.) quitarse la máscara; *va* enmascarar; (phot.) desvanecer; *vn* enmascararse
masked ball *s* baile de máscaras
masking tape *s* cinta para cubrir
masochism [ˈmæzəkɪzəm] *s* (path.) masoquismo
masochist [ˈmæzəkɪst] *s* masoquista
masochistic [ˌmæzəˈkɪstɪk] *adj* masoquista
mason [ˈmesən] *s* albañil; (*cap.*) *s* masón
Mason and Dixon's Line [ˈdɪksənz] *s* frontera entre Pensilvania y Maryland y antes considerada como la línea divisoria entre el norte y el sur de los EE.UU.
mason bee *s* (ent.) albañila, abeja albañila
mason bird *s* pájaro que hace el nido de barro
masoned [ˈmesənd] *adj* (her.) mazonado
Masonic o **masonic** [məˈsɑnɪk] *adj* masónico
masonite [ˈmesənaɪt] *s* (mineral.) masonita; (trademark) masonita
masonry [ˈmesənrɪ] *s* (*pl:* **-ries**) albañilería; (*cap.*) *s* masonería
mason wasp *s* (ent.) avispa de barro
masque [mæsk] o [mɑsk] *s* zarzuela antigua; máscaras, baile de máscaras
masquerade [ˌmæskəˈred] o [ˌmɑskəˈred] *s* mascarada; máscara (*traje; disfraz*); farsa; *vn* enmascararse; ser farsante
masquerade ball *s* baile de máscaras
masquerader [ˌmæskəˈredər] o [ˌmɑskəˈredər] *s* máscara (*persona*)
Mass. abr. de **Massachusetts**
mass [mæs] *s* masa; gran cantidad; bulto informe (*que se vislumbra, p.ej., entre la niebla*); macizo; mole (*cosa de gran bulto*); gran mancha (*de color en una pintura*); (phys.) masa; (eccl. & mus.) misa; **in the mass** en masa; **the masses** las masas; **to hear mass** oír misa; **to say mass** decir o cantar misa; *adj* en masa, p.ej., **mass inoculation** la inoculación en masa; (phys.) másico; *va* juntar en masa; juntar, reunir; enmasar (*tropas*); *vn* juntarse en masa; juntarse, reunirse
massacre [ˈmæsəkər] *s* carnicería, matanza, destrozo; *va* hacer destrozo de, degollar
massage [məˈsɑʒ] *s* masaje; *va* masar
mass defect *s* (phys.) defecto de masa
masseter [mæˈsitər] *s* (anat.) masetero
masseur [mæˈsœr] *s* masajista (*hombre*)
masseuse [mæˈsœz] *s* masajista (*mujer*)
mass formation *s* (mil.) formación en masa
massicot [ˈmæsɪkɑt] *s* masicote
massive [ˈmæsɪv] *adj* macizo, de gran mole
mass media *spl* medios de comunicación en grande escala (*periódicos, libros en rústica, radio, televisión, cine*)
mass meeting *s* mitin popular
mass number *s* (phys.) número másico
mass production *s* fabricación en serie, producción en masa o en serie
mass ratio *s* razón de masas
mass spectrograph *s* (phys.) espectrógrafo de masa o de masas
massy [ˈmæsɪ] *adj* (*comp:* **-ier;** *super:* **-iest**) var. de **massive**
mast [mæst] o [mɑst] *s* (naut.) mástil; palo (*p.ej., de una bandera*); (elec.) poste; (rad.) torre; (agr.) fabuco, bellota; **before the mast** como marinero; **to spend a mast** (naut.) perder un palo
master [ˈmæstər] o [ˈmɑstər] *s* patrón, dueño; amo, señor; amo (*de un perro*); maestro; perito; señorito (*título de cortesía que se da a un muchacho*); pintura o estatua de uno de los grandes maestros; (educ.) maestro; (educ.) grado de maestro; (law) juez auxiliar; (naut.) maestre; **the Master** Jesucristo; *adj* maestro; magistral; de maestro; *va* dominar, vencer; adiestrarse en, llegar a ser maestro o perito en
master-at-arms [ˈmæstərətˈɑrmz] o [ˈmɑstərətˈɑrmz] *s* (*pl:* **masters-at-arms**) (naut.) cabo de mar encargado de la policía y de los prisioneros
master bedroom *s* alcoba del jefe de familia, alcoba de respeto
master blade *s* hoja maestra (*de un muelle*)
master builder *s* arquitecto; aparejador, maestro de obras
master clock *s* reloj magistral
master controller *s* (elec.) combinador principal
masterdom [ˈmæstərdəm] o [ˈmɑstərdəm] *s* maestría; dominio
masterful [ˈmæstərfəl] o [ˈmɑstərfəl] *adj* dominante, imperioso; perito, experto, de maestro
master hand *s* perito; pericia de maestro
master key *s* llave maestra, llave de paso
masterly [ˈmæstərlɪ] o [ˈmɑstərlɪ] *adj* magistral; *adv* magistralmente
master mason *s* maestro albañil; masón de grado tres
master mechanic *s* maestro mecánico
mastermind [ˈmæstərˌmaɪnd] o [ˈmɑstərˌmaɪnd] *s* mente directora; *va* dirigir con gran acierto
master of ceremonies *s* maestro de ceremonias; animador (*de un café cantante*)
masterpiece [ˈmæstərˌpis] o [ˈmɑstərˌpis] *s* obra maestra
master's degree *s* maestría, grado de maestro
mastership [ˈmæstərʃɪp] o [ˈmɑstərʃɪp] *s* maestría; magisterio; dominio
mastersingers [ˈmæstərˌsɪŋərz] o [ˈmɑstərˌsɪŋərz] *spl* maestros cantores
master stroke *s* golpe maestro
masterwork [ˈmæstərˌwʌrk] o [ˈmɑstərˌwʌrk] *s* obra maestra; desempeño magistral
masterwort [ˈmæstərˌwʌrt] o [ˈmɑstərˌwʌrt] *s* (bot.) imperatoria; (bot.) astrancia mayor
mastery [ˈmæstərɪ] o [ˈmɑstərɪ] *s* (*pl:* **-ies**) maestría; dominio (*p.ej., de un idioma extranjero*)
masthead [ˈmæstˌhɛd] o [ˈmɑstˌhɛd] *s* (naut.) tope; membrete editorial (*de una revista, periódico, etc.*)
mastic [ˈmæstɪk] *s* mástique; (bot.) charneca, lentisco, almácigo
masticate [ˈmæstɪket] *va* masticar; (tech.) masticar (*p.ej., el caucho*)
mastication [ˌmæstɪˈkeʃən] *s* masticación; (tech.) masticación
masticator [ˈmæstɪˌketər] *s* mascador; masticador (*instrumento*)
masticatory [ˈmæstɪkəˌtorɪ] *adj* masticatorio; *s* (*pl:* **-ries**) masticatorio
mastic tree *s* (bot.) charneca, lentisco, almácigo; (bot.) ácana (*Sideroxylon mastichodendron*)
mastiff [ˈmæstɪf] o [ˈmɑstɪf] *s* mastín
mastitis [mæsˈtaɪtɪs] *s* (path.) mastitis
mastman [ˈmæstmən] o [ˈmɑstmən] *s* (naut.) gaviero
mastodon [ˈmæstədɑn] *s* (pal.) mastodonte
mastoid [ˈmæstɔɪd] *adj & s* (anat.) mastoides
mastoidectomy [ˌmæstɔɪˈdɛktəmɪ] *s* (*pl:* **-mies**) (surg.) mastoidectomía
mastoiditis [ˌmæstɔɪˈdaɪtɪs] *s* (path.) mastoiditis
masturbate [ˈmæstərbet] *vn* masturbarse
masturbation [ˌmæstərˈbeʃən] *s* masturbación
masurium [məˈsurɪəm] o [məˈsjurɪəm] *s* (chem.) masurio
mat [mæt] *s* estera; ruedo o esterilla (*que se coloca debajo de una fuente caliente*); felpudo

(*p.ej., de puerta*); borde de cartón (*alrededor de un cuadro y dentro del marco*); colchoncillo (*de gimnasio*); greña; entretejimiento; superficie mate; *adj* mate (*no pulido*); (*pret & pp:* **matted**; *ger:* **matting**) *va* esterar; enmarañar, entretejer, enredar; matar, deslustrar (*el brillo de un metal*); *vn* enmarañarse, entretejerse, enredarse
matador ['mætədər] *s* (taur.) matador, espada; (cards) matador
match [mætʃ] *s* fósforo; mecha; igual; compañero; pareja (*conjunto de dos personas o cosas*); partido (*casamiento que elegir*); (sport) match, partido; **to be a good match** ser un buen partido; **to be a match for** hacer juego con; poder con, poder vencer; **to meet one's match** hallar la horma de su zapato; *va* igualar; aparear; emparejar; medir (*sus fuerzas*); hacer juego con, responder a, p.ej., **the chair matches the table** la silla responde a la mesa; **to match someone for the drinks** jugar a uno las bebidas; *vn* hacer juego, ser parejos; **to match** a juego, p.ej., **a handkerchief to match** un pañuelo a juego
matchbox ['mætʃ,bɑks] *s* fosforera, cerillera
matchless ['mætʃlɪs] *adj* sin igual, incomparable
matchlock ['mætʃ,lɑk] *s* mosquete; llave de mosquete
matchmaker ['mætʃ,mekər] *s* fabricante de fósforos; casamentero; promotor de partidos de boxeo, de lucha, de carreras, etc.
matchmaking ['mætʃ,mekɪŋ] *s* fabricación de fósforos; actividad de casamentero; promoción de partidos de boxeo, de lucha, de carreras, etc.; *adj* casamentero
matchwood ['mætʃ,wʊd] *s* madera para hacer fósforos; astillas, fragmentos de madera
mate [met] *s* compañero; hermano o compañero (*p.ej., de un zapato*); cónyuge, esposo; ayudante; macho (*de una hembra*); hembra (*de un macho*); (naut.) piloto; (chess) mate; *va* aparear; casar; (chess) dar jaque mate a; **to be well mated** hacer una buena pareja; *vn* aparearse; casarse; acoplarse
maté o **mate** ['mɑte] *s* (bot.) mate o hierba mate; mate (*hojas e infusión*)
mater ['metər] o ['mɑtər] *s* (coll.) madre
material [mə'tɪrɪəl] *adj* material; importante; *s* material; materia; tela, género; **materials** *spl* materiales; efectos (*de escritorio*); avíos (*de fumar*)
materialism [mə'tɪrɪəlɪzəm] *s* materialismo
materialist [mə'tɪrɪəlɪst] *s* materialista
materialistic [mə,tɪrɪə'lɪstɪk] *adj* materialista
materialistically [mə,tɪrɪə'lɪstɪkəlɪ] *adv* como materialista
materialization [mə,tɪrɪəlɪ'zeʃən] *s* realización; encarnación (*de un espíritu*); materialización (*de las ideas*)
materialize [mə'tɪrɪəlaɪz] *va* realizar, convertir en realidad, dar forma a; dotar de forma visible (*a un espíritu*); materializar (*p.ej., una idea*); *vn* realizarse; tomar forma visible (*un espíritu*)
materially [mə'tɪrɪəlɪ] *adv* materialmente; notablemente
materia medica [mə'tɪrɪə 'mɛdɪkə] *s* materia médica (*cuerpos de los cuales se sacan los medicamentos; parte de la terapéutica*)
matériel [mə,tɪrɪ'ɛl] *s* material (*conjunto de objetos necesarios para un servicio*); (mil.) material
maternal [mə'tʌrnəl] *adj* materno; maternal (*propio del cariño de madre*)
maternity [mə'tʌrnɪtɪ] *s* maternidad; (med.) maternidad (*casa de maternidad*); *adj* de maternidad
maternity hospital *s* casa de maternidad
math. abr. de **mathematics**
mathematical [,mæθɪ'mætɪkəl] *adj* matemático
mathematically [,mæθɪ'mætɪkəlɪ] *adv* matemáticamente
mathematical pendulum *s* péndulo matemático
mathematician [,mæθɪmə'tɪʃən] *s* matemático
mathematics [,mæθɪ'mætɪks] *ssg* matemática o matemáticas
Matilda [mə'tɪldə] *s* Matilde
matinal ['mætɪnəl] *adj* matinal, matutino
matinée o **matinee** [,mætɪ'ne] o ['mætɪne] *s* matinée (*función de tarde*)
mating season *s* época de celo
matins ['mætɪnz] *spl* (eccl.) maitines; oración matinal (*en la Iglesia anglicana*); (poet.) canto matinal (*p.ej., de pájaros*)
matrass ['mætrəs] *s* matraz
matriarch ['metrɪɑrk] *s* matriarca
matriarchal [,metrɪ'ɑrkəl] *adj* matriarcal
matriarchy ['metrɪɑrkɪ] *s* (*pl:* **-chies**) matriarcado
matricidal [,metrɪ'saɪdəl] o [,mætrɪ'saɪdəl] *adj* matricida
matricide ['metrɪsaɪd] o ['mætrɪsaɪd] *s* matricidio (*acción*); matricida (*persona*)
matriculate [mə'trɪkjəlɪt] *adj & s* matriculado; [mə'trɪkjəlet] *va* matricular; *vn* matricularse
matriculation [mə,trɪkjə'leʃən] *s* matrícula
matrimonial [,mætrɪ'monɪəl] *adj* matrimonial
matrimonially [,mætrɪ'monɪəlɪ] *adv* matrimonialmente
matrimony ['mætrɪ,monɪ] *s* (*pl:* **-nies**) matrimonio; vida matrimonial
matrix ['metrɪks] o ['mætrɪks] *s* (*pl:* **matrices** ['metrɪsiz] o ['mætrɪsiz] o **matrixes**) matriz (*útero; molde; impresión de disco de fonógrafo*); (anat., biol., math. & geol.) matriz
matron ['metrən] *s* matrona; ama de llaves (*en un colegio, etc.*); carcelera, matrona
matronly ['metrənlɪ] *adj* matronal; respetable; algo gruesa
matron of honor *s* dama de honor (*de una boda*)
Matt. abr. de **Matthew**
matte [mæt] *s* (metal.) mata
matter ['mætər] *s* materia; motivo (*p.ej., de queja*); (path.) materia (*pus*); correspondencia o impresos (*enviados por correo*); (print.) material (*preparado para la prensa*); **a matter of** cosa de u obra de (*p.ej., diez minutos*); **for that matter** en cuanto a eso; **in a matter of** en cosa de; **in the matter** al respecto; **in the matter of** en materia de; **no matter** no importa; **no matter how** de cualquier modo; **no matter when** cuando quiera; **no matter where** dondequiera; **to be of no matter** no tener importancia; **to go into the matter** entrar en materia; **what is the matter?** ¿qué hay?, ¿qué pasa?; **what is the matter with him?** ¿qué tiene?, ¿qué le pasa?; *vn* importar; supurar
Matterhorn, the ['mætərhɔrn] el monte Cervino
matter of course *s* cosa de cajón; **as a matter of course** por rutina
matter of fact *s* hecho positivo, hecho evidente; **as a matter of fact** en honor a la verdad, en realidad
matter-of-fact ['mætərəv,fækt] *adj* prosaico, de poca imaginación
matter of form *s* cosa de pura fórmula; **as a matter of form** por fórmula
Matthew ['mæθju] *s* Mateo; (Bib.) San Mateo; (Bib.) el Evangelio según San Mateo
Matthias [mə'θaɪəs] *s* Matías
matting ['mætɪŋ] *s* estera
mattock ['mætək] *s* zapapico, azadón de peto o de pico
mattress ['mætrɪs] *s* colchón; (hyd.) colchón de ramaje
maturate ['mætʃʊret] o ['mætjʊret] *va & vn* madurar
maturation [,mætʃʊ'reʃən] o [,mætjʊ'reʃən] *s* maduración
mature [mə'tjʊr] o [mə'tʊr] *adj* maduro; (com.) vencido, pagadero; (fig.) muy bien elaborado, preparado cuidadosamente; *va* madurar; elaborar o preparar cuidadosamente; *vn* madurar; (com.) vencer
maturity [mə'tjʊrɪtɪ] o [mə'tʊrɪtɪ] *s* madurez; perfección; (com.) vencimiento
matutinal [mə'tjutɪnəl] o [mə'tutɪnəl] *adj* matutinal, matutino

matzo ['mɑtso] *s* (*pl:* **matzos** o **matzoth** ['mɑtsoθ]) galleta de pan sin levadura
maudlin ['mɔdlɪn] *adj* sensiblero; chispo y lloroso
mauger o **maugre** ['mɔgər] *prep* (archaic) a pesar de
maul [mɔl] *s* machota, mazo; *va* aporrear, maltratar
maulstick ['mɔl,stɪk] *s* (paint.) tiento
maunder ['mɔndər] *vn* parlotear; andar como atontado
maundy ['mɔndɪ] *s* (eccl.) mandato, lavatorio
Maundy Thursday *s* Jueves Santo
Maurice ['mɔrɪs] o ['mɑrɪs] *s* Mauricio (*nombre de varón*)
Mauritius [mɔ'rɪʃəs] o [mɔ'rɪʃɪəs] *s* la isla Mauricio o la isla de Mauricio
Mauser o **mauser** ['mauzər] *s* (trademark) máuser
mausoleum [,mɔsə'liəm] *s* (*pl:* **-ums** o **-a** [ə]) mausoleo
mauve [mov] *adj* de color de malva; *s* color de malva
maverick ['mævərɪk] *s* animal sin marca de hierro; becerro separado de su madre; disidente
mavis ['mevɪs] *s* (orn.) malvís; (orn.) cagaaceite
mavourneen o **mavournin** [mə'vʊrnin] *s* (Irish) vida mía
maw [mɔ] *s* buche (*de las aves*); vejiga de aire (*de los peces*); fauces (*de un animal devorador*)
mawkish ['mɔkɪʃ] *adj* empalagoso; sensiblero
max. abr. de **maximum**
maxilla [mæk'sɪlə] *s* (*pl:* **-lae** [li]) (anat. & zool.) maxila
maxillary ['mæksɪ,lɛrɪ] *adj* maxilar; *s* (*pl:* **-ies**) (anat.) maxilar
maxim ['mæksɪm] *s* máxima
Maximilian [,mæksɪ'mɪljən] *s* Maximiliano
maximum ['mæksɪməm] *adj* máximo; *s* (*pl:* **-mums** o **-ma** [mə]) máximo o máximum
maxwell ['mækswɛl] *s* (elec.) maxvelio
May [me] *s* mayo (*mes*); (*l.c.*) *v aux* poder, p.ej., **it may be** puede ser; **may I sit down?** ¿puedo sentarme?; **may you be happy!** ¡que seas feliz!
Maya ['mɑjə] o **Mayan** ['mɑjən] *adj* & *s* maya
May apple *s* (bot.) podofilo; limón silvestre, manzana de mayo (*fruto*)
maybe ['mebɪ] *adv* quizá, tal vez
May Day *s* primero de mayo; fiesta del primero de mayo
Mayfair ['me,fɛr] *s* la alta sociedad londinense
Mayflower ['me,flaʊər] *s* (bot. Brit.) primavera, cala, majuelo, hierba centella, etc.; (bot. U.S.A.) anemona, epigea rastrera, hepática, etc.
May fly *s* (ent.) mosca de mayo, mosca de un día
mayhap [,me'hæp] o ['mehæp] *adv* (archaic) quizá, tal vez
mayhem ['mehɛm] o ['meəm] *s* (law) mutilación criminal
Maying ['meɪŋ] *s* festejos del mes de mayo; **to go a-Maying** irse a la fiesta de mayo
mayonnaise [,meə'nez] *s* mayonesa, mahonesa
mayor ['meər] o [mɛr] *s* alcalde; intendente municipal (Am.)
mayoralty ['meərəltɪ] o ['mɛrəltɪ] *s* (*pl:* **-ties**) alcaldía; intendencia (Am.)
mayoress ['meərɪs] o ['mɛrɪs] *s* alcaldesa
Maypole o **maypole** ['me,pol] *s* mayo (*árbol adornado de cintas*)
Maypole dance *s* danza de cintas
May queen *s* maya (*joven que preside la fiesta de mayo*)
Maytide ['me,taid] o **Maytime** ['me,taɪm] *s* mes de mayo
mayweed ['me,wid] *s* (bot.) magarzuela, manzanilla hedionda; (bot.) matricaria
Mazdaism o **Mazdeism** ['mæzdəɪzəm] *s* mazdeísmo
Mazdaist o **Mazdeist** ['mæzdəɪst] *s* mazdeísta
Mazdean ['mæzdɪən] o [mæz'diən] *adj* mazdeísta
maze [mez] *s* laberinto
mazourka o **mazurka** [mə'zʌrkə] o [mə'zʊrkə] *s* (mus.) mazurca
mazy ['mezɪ] *adj* (*comp:* **-zier;** *super:* **-ziest**) laberíntico
M.C. abr. de **Master of Ceremonies** y **Member of Congress**
Md. abr. de **Maryland**
M.D. abr. de **Doctor of Medicine**
mdse. abr. de **merchandise**
Me. abr. de **Maine**
ME. abr. de **Middle English**
M.E. abr. de **Master of Engineering, Mechanical Engineer, Methodist Episcopal, Middle English** y **Mining Engineer**
me [mi] *pron pers* me; mí; **with me** conmigo, p.ej., **he came with me** vino conmigo
mead [mid] *s* aloja; (poet.) prado
meadow ['mɛdo] *s* henar; pradera, prado, vega
meadow crowfoot *s* (bot.) hierba velluda
meadow foxtail *s* (bot.) cola de zorra
meadowland ['mɛdo,lænd] *s* pradera
meadow lark *s* (orn.) chirlota, sabanero, triguero
meadow sage *s* (bot.) tarrago
meadowsweet ['mɛdo,swit] *s* (bot.) ulmaria, reina de los prados
meadowy ['mɛdo·ɪ] o ['mɛdəwɪ] *adj* pradeño, praderoso
meager o **meagre** ['migər] *adj* magro, flaco; pobre, escaso
meal [mil] *s* comida; harina
mealtime ['mil,taɪm] *s* hora de comer
mealy ['milɪ] *adj* (*comp:* **-ier;** *super:* **-iest**) panoso, harinoso; enharinado; pálido; meloso; poco sincero, falso
mealy-mouthed ['milɪ'mauðd] o ['milɪ'mauθt] *adj* meloso; poco sincero, falso
mean [min] *adj* medio; mediano; mezquino, tacaño; sórdido, innoble; pobre, inferior; humilde, obscuro; andrajoso, raído; vil, ruin; insignificante; mal intencionado (*dícese de las caballerías*); (coll.) malo, de mal genio, desconsiderado; (coll.) avergonzado, corrido, indigno; (coll.) indispuesto; **no mean** famoso, excelente ‖ *s* medio; promedio o término medio; (math.) media; **means** *ssg o spl* medio o medios; manera, modo; **means** *spl* bienes de fortuna, dinero, p.ej., **a man of means** un hombre de dinero; **by all means** por todos los medios posibles; sin falta; sí, por cierto; **by any means** de cualquier modo que sea; **by means of** por medio de; **by no means** de ningún modo, en ningún caso; **by some means** de alguna manera; **by this means** por este medio, de este modo; **means to an end** paso dado para lograr un fin ‖ (*pret & pp:* **meant**) *va* querer decir, significar; **to mean to** + *inf* pensar + *inf* ‖ *vn* tener intenciones (*buenas o malas*), p.ej., **he means well** tiene buenas intenciones; **to mean well by** favorecer, querer ayudar
meander [mɪ'ændər] *s* meandro; (f.a.) meandro; *vn* serpentear; vagar
meander line *s* (surv.) línea de meandro
meandrous [mɪ'ændrəs] *adj* meándrico
meaning ['minɪŋ] *adj* significativo; *s* significado, sentido
meaningful ['minɪŋfəl] *adj* significativo
meaningless ['minɪŋlɪs] *adj* sin sentido; insensato
meanness ['minnɪs] *s* mezquindad, tacañería; pobreza; humildad, obscuridad; vileza, ruindad; maldad; acción indigna
mean noon *s* (astr.) mediodía medio
mean sun *s* (astr.) sol medio
meant [mɛnt] *pret & pp de* **mean**
meantime ['min,taɪm] *adv* entretanto, mientras tanto; *s* ínterin, medio tiempo; **in the meantime** entretanto, mientras tanto
mean time *s* (astr.) tiempo medio
meanwhile ['min,hwaɪl] *adv* & *s* var. de **meantime**
measles ['mizəlz] *s* (path.) sarampión; (path.) rubéola; (vet.) roña de los cerdos
measly ['mizlɪ] *adj* (*comp:* **-slier;** *super:* **-sliest**) sarampioso; (slang) mezquino, insignificante, despreciable
measurable ['mɛʒərəbəl] *adj* medible, mensurable
measurably ['mɛʒərəblɪ] *adv* mediblemente; perceptiblemente
measure ['mɛʒər] *s* medida; gestión, paso;

(mus.) compás; (pros.) medida; (pros.) pie (*del verso*); (law) ley, proyecto de ley; **beyond measure** con exceso, a más no poder; **in a measure** en parte, hasta cierto punto; **in great measure** en gran parte; **to take measures** tomar las medidas necesarias; **to take one's measure** tomarle a uno las medidas, medir a uno con la vista; **to tread a measure** bailar; *va* medir; recorrer (*cierta distancia*); **to measure off** medir; **to measure out** medir; distribuir, repartir; *vn* medir

measured ['mɛʒərd] *adj* regular, uniforme; deliberado, hecho con reflexión; rítmico

measureless ['mɛʒərlɪs] *adj* inmensurable, inmenso

measurement ['mɛʒərmənt] *s* medida; medición

measuring worm *s* (zool.) geómetra

meat [mit] *s* carne (*de animal o de la fruta*); vianda, alimento; comida; materia (*para la reflexión*); meollo (*p.ej., de un libro*); *adj* cárnico

meat ball *s* albóndiga

meat chopper *s* picadora de carne

meat day *s* día de carne

meat fly *s* mosca de la carne

meat grinder *s* máquina de picar carne

meathook ['mit,hʊk] *s* garabato de carnicero

meat market *s* carnicería

meat packing s preparación o conservación de la carne congelada

meat pie *s* pastel de carne

meatus [mɪ'etəs] *s* (*pl:* **-tuses** o **-tus**) (anat.) meato

meaty ['mitɪ] *adj* (*comp:* **-ier;** *super:* **-iest**) carnoso (*de carne; que tiene consistencia de carne*); jugoso, substancioso

mecca o **Mecca** ['mɛkə] *s* Meca (*sitio a que se dirigen muchas personas*); (*cap.*) *s* La Meca (*ciudad*)

Meccan ['mɛkən] *adj & s* mecano

mechanic [mɪ'kænɪk] *s* mecánico; **mechanics** *ssg* mecánica (*parte de la física*); mecanismo; *spl* técnica (*de un arte o ciencia*)

mechanical [mɪ'kænɪkəl] *adj* mecánico, maquinal; (fig.) maquinal

mechanical drawing *s* dibujo mecánico

mechanical engineer *s* ingeniero mecánico

mechanical engineering *s* ingeniería mecánica

mechanically [mɪ'kænɪkəlɪ] *adv* mecánicamente; (fig.) maquinalmente

mechanical pencil *s* portaminas

mechanical toy *s* juguete de movimiento

mechanician [,mɛkə'nɪʃən] *s* mecánico

mechanism ['mɛkənɪzəm] *s* mecanismo; (biol. & philos.) mecanicismo

mechanist ['mɛkənɪst] *s* (biol. & philos.) mecanicista

mechanistic [,mɛkə'nɪstɪk] *adj* mecánico; (biol. & philos.) mecanicista

mechanization [,mɛkənɪ'zeʃən] *s* mecanización; (econ.) maquinismo

mechanize ['mɛkənaɪz] *va* mecanizar

mechanotherapy [,mɛkano'θɛrəpɪ] *s* mecanoterapia

Mechlin ['mɛklɪn] *s* Malinas; encaje de Malinas

meconium [mɪ'konɪəm] *s* meconio

med. abr. de **medicinal, medicine, medieval** y **medium**

medal ['mɛdəl] *s* medalla

medalist o **medallist** ['mɛdəlɪst] *s* medallista; persona condecorada con una medalla

medallion [mɪ'dæljən] *s* medallón

meddle ['mɛdəl] *vn* entremeterse

meddler ['mɛdlər] *s* entremetido

meddlesome ['mɛdəlsəm] *adj* entremetido

meddling ['mɛdlɪŋ] *adj* entremetido; *s* intromisión

Mede [mid] *s* medo

mediaeval [,midɪ'ivəl] o [,mɛdɪ'ivəl] *adj* var. de **medieval**

medial ['midɪəl] *adj* medianero; intermedio; (phonet.) medial, interior

medially ['midɪəlɪ] *adv* en el centro

medial strip *s* faja central o divisora (*de la carretera*)

median ['midɪən] *adj* medio, intermedio; (bot. & zool.) medial o mediano; *s* punto medio (*en una serie*); número medio (*en una serie*); (anat.) mediano; (geom.) mediana; (*cap.*) *adj & s* medo

median barrier *s* barrera o valla central (*de la carretera*)

median strip *s* var. de **medial strip**

mediastinum [,midɪæs'taɪnəm] *s* (*pl:* **-na** [nə]) (anat.) mediastino

mediate ['midɪɪt] *adj* mediato; ['midɪet] *va* dirimir (*una contienda*); arreglar (*paces*); reconciliar; servir de mediador para efectuar (*un resultado*), entregar (*un regalo*), comunicar (*informes, etc.*); *vn* mediar

mediation [,midɪ'eʃən] *s* mediación; (astr., dipl. & mus.) mediación

mediator ['midɪ,etər] *s* mediador

mediatorial [,midɪə'torɪəl] o **mediatory** ['midɪə,torɪ] *adj* mediador

medic ['mɛdɪk] *s* (bot.) mielga; médico; (coll.) estudiante de medicina

medicable ['mɛdɪkəbəl] *adj* medicable

medical ['mɛdɪkəl] *adj* médico; de medicina, p.ej., **medical student** estudiante de medicina

medicament [mə'dɪkəmənt] o ['mɛdɪkəmənt] *s* medicamento

medicaster ['mɛdɪ,kæstər] *s* medicastro

medicate ['mɛdɪket] *va* medicinar (*a un enfermo*); impregnar (*p.ej., una venda*) con una substancia medicinal

medication [,mɛdɪ'keʃən] *s* medicación; impregnación de una venda con una substancia medicinal

medicinal [mɛ'dɪsɪnəl] *adj* medicinal

medicinally [mɛ'dɪsɪnəlɪ] *adv* medicinalmente

medicine ['mɛdɪsɪn] *s* medicina (*ciencia y arte*); medicina o medicamento (*remedio*); talismán (*entre los pieles rojas*); **to take one's medicine** echar el pecho al agua; hacer (*uno*) a la fuerza lo que no quiere

medicine ball *s* pelota medicinal

medicine cabinet *s* armario botiquín

medicine dance *s* danza sagrada (*entre los pieles rojas*)

medicine kit *s* botiquín

medicine man *s* exorcista, curandero (*entre los pieles rojas*)

medico ['mɛdɪko] *s* (*pl:* **-cos**) (slang) médico, cirujano, estudiante de medicina

medicochirurgical [,mɛdɪkokaɪ'rʌrdʒɪkəl] *adj* médicoquirúrgico

medicolegal [,mɛdɪko'ligəl] *adj* médicolegal

medieval [,midɪ'ivəl] o [,mɛdɪ'ivəl] *adj* medieval

medieval history *s* la historia medieval o media

medievalism [,midɪ'ivəlɪzəm] o [,mɛdɪ'ivəlɪzəm] *s* medievalismo

medievalist [,midɪ'ivəlɪst] o [,mɛdɪ'ivəlɪst] *s* medievalista

mediocre ['midɪ,okər] o [,midɪ'okər] *adj* mediano, mediocre

mediocrity [,midɪ'ɑkrɪtɪ] *s* (*pl:* **-ties**) mediocridad; medianía o mediocridad (*persona*)

meditate ['mɛdɪtet] *va & vn* meditar

meditation [,mɛdɪ'teʃən] *s* meditación

meditative ['mɛdɪ,tetɪv] *adj* meditativo

Mediterranean [,mɛdɪtə'renɪən] *adj & s* Mediterráneo

Mediterranean Sea *s* mar Mediterráneo

medium ['midɪəm] *adj* mediano, intermedio; a medio cocer, a medio asar; *s* (*pl:* **-ums** o **-a** [ə]) medio; medio o médium (*en el espiritismo*); (bot. & bact.) medio; (paint.) aceite; **through the medium of** por medio de

mediumistic [,midɪə'mɪstɪk] *adj* mediúmnico

medium of exchange *s* mediador de cambio

medium-range ['midɪəm'rendʒ] *adj* de alcance medio

medium-sized ['midɪəm'saɪzd] *adj* de tamaño mediano

medium steel *s* acero mediano o intermedio

medlar ['mɛdlər] *s* (bot.) níspero (*árbol y fruto*); níspola (*fruto*)

medley ['mɛdlɪ] *s* mezcolanza, revoltijo; (mus.) popurrí

medulla [mɪ'dʌlə] *s* (*pl:* **-lae** [li]) (anat. & bot.) medula; (anat.) medula oblonga u oblongada

medulla oblongata [,ɑblɑŋ'getə] *s* (anat.) medula oblonga u oblongada

medullary ['mɛdə,lɛrɪ] o [mɪ'dʌlərɪ] *adj* medular

medusa [mɪˈdjusə] o [mɪˈdusə] *s* (*pl:* **-sas** o **-sae** [si]) (zool.) medusa; (*cap.*) *s* (*pl:* **-sas**) (myth.) Medusa
meed [mid] *s* (poet.) galardón
meek [mik] *adj* manso, dócil, humilde
meekness [ˈmiknɪs] *s* mansedumbre, docilidad, humildad
meerschaum [ˈmɪrʃəm] o [ˈmɪrʃɔm] *s* (mineral.) espuma de mar; pipa de espuma de mar
meet [mit] *s* concurso de deportistas; concurrencia de gente (*en un lugar de luchas atléticas*); lugar de reunión; *adj* conveniente; (*pret & pp:* **met**) *va* encontrar, encontrarse con; conocer; ir a recibir; ir a esperar; satisfacer (*un pedido*); pagar, honrar (*una letra*); conformarse a (*los deseos de uno*); hacer frente a (*gastos*); cumplir (*obligaciones*); refutar (*acusaciones*); responder a (*reparos*); verse cara a cara con, batirse con; recibir (*la mirada de otra persona*); tener que aguantar (*desprecio*); tener (*mala suerte*); empalmar con (*otro tren u ómnibus*); hallar (*la muerte*); *vn* encontrarse; reunirse; conocerse; luchar, batirse; **till we meet again** hasta más ver; **to meet with** encontrarse con; reunirse con; empalmar con; tener (*un accidente*)
meeting [ˈmitɪŋ] *s* junta, sesión; asamblea, reunión; encuentro; congregación; confluencia (*de dos ríos o caminos*); desafío, duelo
meeting house *s* iglesia; iglesia de los disidentes; iglesia de los cuáqueros
meeting of the minds *s* concierto de voluntades, voluntad común
meetly [ˈmitlɪ] *adv* convenientemente
megacycle [ˈmɛgəˌsaɪkəl] *s* (rad.) megaciclo
megalith [ˈmɛgəlɪθ] *s* (archeol.) megalito
megalithic [ˌmɛgəˈlɪθɪk] *adj* megalítico
megalocephalous [ˌmɛgəloˈsɛfələs] *adj* megalocéfalo
megalomania [ˌmɛgəloˈmenɪə] *s* (psychopath.) megalomanía
megalomaniac [ˌmɛgəloˈmenɪæk] *s* megalómano
megalomaniacal [ˌmɛgəloməˈnaɪəkəl] *adj* megalómano
megalosaur [ˈmɛgələˌsɔr] *s* (pal.) megalosaurio
megaphone [ˈmɛgəfon] *s* megáfono, portavoz
megathere [ˈmɛgəθɪr] *s* (pal.) megaterio
megaton [ˈmɛgətʌn] *s* megatón, megatonelada
megohm [ˈmɛgˌom] *s* (elec.) megohmio
megrim [ˈmigrɪm] *s* (path.) hemicránea, jaqueca; (archaic) antojo, capricho; **megrims** *spl* hipocondría
Mekka [ˈmɛkə] *s* var. de **Mecca**
melancholia [ˌmɛlənˈkolɪə] *s* (path.) melancolía
melancholic [ˌmɛlənˈkɑlɪk] *adj* melancólico; (path.) melancólico
melancholy [ˈmɛlənˌkɑlɪ] *adj* melancólico; *s* (*pl:* **-ies**) melancolía
Melanesia [ˌmɛləˈniʃə] o [ˌmɛləˈniʒə] *s* la Melanesia
Melanesian [ˌmɛləˈniʃən] o [ˌmɛləˈniʒən] *adj & s* melanesio
mélange [meˈlɑ̃ʒ] *s* mezcolanza
melanite [ˈmɛlənaɪt] *s* (mineral.) melanita
melanoma [ˌmɛləˈnomə] *s* (*pl:* **-mata** [mətə]) (path.) melanoma
melanosis [ˌmɛləˈnosɪs] *s* (path.) melanosis
melaphyre [ˈmɛləfaɪr] *s* (geol.) meláfiro
Melbourne [ˈmɛlbərn] *s* Melburna
Melchior [ˈmɛlkɪɔr] *s* Melchor
Meleager [ˌmɛlɪˈedʒər] *s* (myth.) Meleagro
melee o **mêlée** [ˈmele] o [ˈmɛle] *s* refriega, reyerta
meliaceous [ˌmilɪˈeʃəs] *adj* (bot.) meliáceo
melic [ˈmɛlɪk] *adj* mélico
melilot [ˈmɛlɪlɑt] *s* (bot.) meliloto
melinite [ˈmɛlɪnaɪt] *s* melinita
meliorate [ˈmiljəret] *va* mejorar; *vn* mejorarse
melioration [ˌmiljəˈreʃən] *s* mejoramiento
mellifluence [mɛˈlɪfluəns] *s* melifluencia
mellifluent [mɛˈlɪfluənt] o **mellifluous** [mɛˈlɪfluəs] *adj* melifluo
mellow [ˈmɛlo] *adj* maduro, sazonado; suave, meloso; margoso; melodioso; añejo (*vino*); *va* madurar; suavizar; *vn* madurarse; suavizarse
melodeon [mɪˈlodɪən] *s* (mus.) melodión
melodic [mɪˈlɑdɪk] *adj* melódico; **melodics** *ssg* teoría de la melodía
melodically [mɪˈlɑdɪkəlɪ] *adv* melódicamente
melodious [mɪˈlodɪəs] *adj* melodioso
melodist [ˈmɛlədɪst] *s* melodista
melodrama [ˈmɛləˌdrɑmə] o [ˈmɛləˌdræmə] *s* melodrama; acción, literatura, discurso y escrito melodramáticos
melodramatic [ˌmɛlədrəˈmætɪk] *adj* melodramático
melodramatically [ˌmɛlədrəˈmætɪkəlɪ] *adv* melodramáticamente
melody [ˈmɛlədɪ] *s* (*pl:* **-dies**) melodía
melon [ˈmɛlən] *s* melón (*fruto*); **to cut a melon** (slang) repartir ganancias extraordinarias
Melpomene [mɛlˈpɑmɪnɪ] *s* (myth.) Melpómene
melt [mɛlt] *s* derretimiento; (found.) hornada; *va* derretir; fundir (*metales*); disolver (*azúcar*); disipar; ablandar, aplacar; **to melt down** fundir; disolver; *vn* derretirse; fundirse; disolverse; disiparse, desaparecer; ablandarse, aplacarse; **to melt away** desvanecerse; **to melt into** convertirse gradualmente en; deshacerse en (*p.ej., lágrimas*)
melting point *s* punto de fusión
melting pot *s* crisol; (fig.) país o ciudad de mucha inmigración
melton [ˈmɛltən] *s* meltón
member [ˈmɛmbər] *s* miembro
membered [ˈmɛmbərd] *adj* (her.) membrado
member nation *s* (*pl:* **member nations**) nación miembro
membership [ˈmɛmbərʃɪp] *s* asociación; personal (*de un club, etc.*); número de miembros o socios
membranaceous [ˌmɛmbrəˈneʃəs] *adj* membranáceo
membrane [ˈmɛmbren] *s* (bot. & zool.) membrana
membranous [ˈmɛmbrənəs] *adj* membranoso
memento [mɪˈmɛnto] *s* (*pl:* **-tos** o **-toes**) recordatorio, prenda de recuerdo; (*cap.*) *s* (eccl.) memento
Memnon [ˈmɛmnɑn] *s* (myth.) Memnón; estatua de Memnón en Tebas
memo [ˈmɛmo] *s* (*pl:* **-os**) (coll.) apunte, membrete; (coll.) memorándum
memoir [ˈmɛmwɑr] *s* biografía; memoria; **memoirs** *spl* memorias
memorabilia [ˌmɛmərəˈbɪlɪə] *spl* cosas memorables
memorable [ˈmɛmərəbəl] *adj* memorable
memorandum [ˌmɛməˈrændəm] *s* (*pl:* **-dums** o **-da** [də]) memorándum; apunte
memorial [mɪˈmorɪəl] *adj* conmemorativo; *s* memoráculo, monumento conmemorativo; memorial (*escrito en que se pide un favor*)
memorial arch *s* arco triunfal
Memorial Day *s* (U.S.A.) día de recordación de los caídos (*30 de mayo*)
memorialize [mɪˈmorɪəlaɪz] *va* conmemorar; dirigir un memorial a
memorize [ˈmɛməraɪz] *va* aprender de memoria, memorizar
memory [ˈmɛmərɪ] *s* (*pl:* **-ries**) memoria; **in memory of** en memoria de; **to commit to memory** encomendar a la memoria; **within my memory** que yo recuerde; **within the memory of man** que la historia registra
memory book *s* libro de recuerdos
Memphis [ˈmɛmfɪs] *s* Menfis
men [mɛn] *pl de* **man**
menace [ˈmɛnɪs] *s* amenaza; *va & vn* amenazar
menad [ˈminæd] *s* var. de **maenad**
ménage o **menage** [meˈnɑʒ] *s* casa, hogar; cuidado de la casa, economía doméstica
menagerie [məˈnædʒərɪ] o [məˈnæʒərɪ] *s* colección de fieras y de animales raros; casa de fieras
Mencius [ˈmɛnʃɪəs] *s* Mencio
mend [mɛnd] *s* compostura; remiendo; mejora; **to be on the mend** ir mejorando; *va* componer, remendar, reparar; reformar, mejorar; *vn* mejorar o mejorarse
mendacious [mɛnˈdeʃəs] *adj* mendaz; falso
mendacity [mɛnˈdæsɪtɪ] *s* (*pl:* **-ties**) mendacidad; mentira

mendelevium [ˌmɛndɪˈlivɪəm] *s* (chem.) mendelevio
Mendelian [mɛnˈdilɪən] *adj* mendeliano
Mendelianism [mɛnˈdilɪənɪzəm] o **Mendelism** [ˈmɛndəlɪzəm] *s* mendelismo
mendicancy [ˈmɛndɪkənsɪ] *s* mendicidad
mendicant [ˈmɛndɪkənt] *adj & s* mendicante
mendicity [mɛnˈdɪsɪtɪ] *s* var. de **mendicancy**
mending [ˈmɛndɪŋ] *s* remiendo, zurcido
mending tape *s* cinta de remendar
Menelaus [ˌmɛnəˈleəs] *s* (myth.) Menelao
menfolk [ˈmɛnˌfok] *spl* hombres
menhaden [mɛnˈhedən] *s* (*pl:* **-den**) (ichth.) menhaden (*Brevoortia tyrannus*)
menhaden oil *s* aceite de menhaden
menhir [ˈmɛnhɪr] *s* (archeol.) menhir
menial [ˈminɪəl] *adj* bajo, servil; *s* criado, doméstico
meningeal [mɪˈnɪndʒɪəl] *adj* meníngeo
meninges [mɪˈnɪndʒiz] *spl* (anat.) meninges
meningitis [ˌmɛnɪnˈdʒaɪtɪs] *s* (path.) meningitis
meningococcus [mɪˌnɪŋgəˈkɑkəs] *s* (*pl:* **-cocci** [ˈkɑksaɪ]) (bact.) meningococo
meniscus [mɪˈnɪskəs] *s* (*pl:* **meniscuses** o **menisci** [mɪˈnɪsaɪ]) media luna; (anat., opt. & phys.) menisco
menispermaceous [ˌmɛnɪspərˈmeʃəs] *adj* (bot.) menispermáceo
Mennonite [ˈmɛnənaɪt] *adj & s* menonita
menopause [ˈmɛnəpɔz] *s* (physiol.) menopausia
menorrhagia [ˌmɛnəˈredʒɪə] *s* (path.) menorragia
menses [ˈmɛnsiz] *spl* menstruo
men's furnishings *spl* artículos para caballeros
Menshevik [ˈmɛnʃəvɪk] *s* (*pl:* **Mensheviks** o **Mensheviki** [ˌmɛnʃəˈvikɪ]) menchevique
men's room *s* lavabo de caballeros, reservado para hombres
menstrual [ˈmɛnstruəl] *adj* mensual; (physiol.) menstrual
menstruate [ˈmɛnstruet] *vn* menstruar
menstruation [ˌmɛnstruˈeʃən] *s* menstruación
menstruous [ˈmɛnstruəs] *adj* menstruoso
menstruum [ˈmɛnstruəm] *s* (*pl:* **-ums** o **-a** [ə]) (chem.) menstruo
mensurability [ˌmɛnʃərəˈbɪlɪtɪ] *s* mensurabilidad
mensurable [ˈmɛnʃərəbəl] *adj* mensurable
mensural [ˈmɛnʃərəl] *adj* mensural
mensuration [ˌmɛnʃəˈreʃən] *s* mensuración
mental [ˈmɛntəl] *adj* mental
mental age *s* (psychol.) edad mental
mental arithmetic *s* cálculo mental
mental deficiency *s* debilidad mental
mental disease *s* enfermedad mental
mental healer *s* curador mental
mental healing *s* curación por el espíritu
mental health *s* estado mental; buen estado mental
mental hygiene *s* higiene mental
mental illness *s* enfermedad mental
mentality [mɛnˈtælɪtɪ] *s* (*pl:* **-ties**) mentalidad
mentally [ˈmɛntəlɪ] *adv* mentalmente
mental reservation *s* reserva mental
mental test *s* prueba mental
menthol [ˈmɛnθɑl] *s* (chem.) mentol
mentholated [ˈmɛnθəˌletɪd] *adj* mentolado
mention [ˈmɛnʃən] *s* mención; **to make mention of** hacer mención de; *va* mencionar; **don't mention it** no hay de qué; **not to mention** sin contar; además de
mentor [ˈmɛntər] *s* mentor; (*cap.*) *s* (myth.) Mentor
menu [ˈmɛnju] o [ˈmenju] *s* menú; comida
meow [mɪˈaʊ] *s* maullido; *vn* maullar
Mephistopheles [ˌmɛfɪsˈtɑfəliz] *s* Mefistófeles
Mephistophelian [ˌmɛfɪstəˈfilɪən] *adj* mefistofélico
mephitic [mɪˈfɪtɪk] *adj* mefítico
mephitis [mɪˈfaɪtɪs] *s* mefitis
mercantile [ˈmʌrkəntɪl] o [ˈmʌrkəntaɪl] *adj* mercantil
mercantile marine *s* marina mercante
mercantile system *s* sistema mercantil
mercantilism [ˈmʌrkəntɪlɪzəm] o [ˈmʌrkəntaɪlɪzəm] *s* mercantilismo
mercantilist [ˈmʌrkəntɪlɪst] o [ˈmʌrkəntaɪlɪst] *adj & s* mercantilista
Mercator's chart [mərˈketərz] *s* (geog.) carta de Mercátor
Mercator's projection *s* (geog.) proyección de Mercátor
Mercedarian [ˌmʌrsɪˈdɛrɪən] *s* mercedario
Mercedes [mərˈsidiz] *s* Mercedes (*nombre de mujer*)
mercenary [ˈmʌrsəˌnɛrɪ] *adj* (mil. & fig.) mercenario; *s* (*pl:* **-ies**) (mil.) mercenario
mercer [ˈmʌrsər] *s* (Brit.) mercader de telas de seda
mercerize [ˈmʌrsəraɪz] *va* mercerizar
merchandise [ˈmʌrtʃəndaɪz] *s* mercancías; *va* comerciar o traficar en; *vn* comerciar o traficar
merchant [ˈmʌrtʃənt] *adj* mercante; *s* comerciante
merchantable [ˈmʌrtʃəntəbəl] *adj* comerciable
merchantman [ˈmʌrtʃəntmən] *s* (*pl:* **-men**) buque mercante
merchant marine *s* marina mercante
merchant prince *s* comerciante rico, magnate del comercio
merchant tailor *s* sastre comerciante
merchant vessel *s* buque mercante
Mercian [ˈmʌrʃɪən] o [ˈmʌrʃən] *adj & s* merciano
merciful [ˈmʌrsɪfəl] *adj* misericordioso
merciless [ˈmʌrsɪlɪs] *adj* desapiadado, despiadado
mercurial [mərˈkjʊrɪəl] *adj* mercurial; vivo, despierto; veleidoso, inconstante; (*cap.*) *adj* (astr. & myth.) mercurial; (*l.c.*) *s* (pharm.) mercurial
mercurialism [mərˈkjʊrɪəlɪzəm] *s* (path.) mercurialismo
mercuric [mərˈkjʊrɪk] *adj* (chem.) mercúrico
mercuric chloride *s* (chem.) cloruro mercúrico
mercuric oxide *s* (chem.) óxido mercúrico, óxido de mercurio
mercurochrome [mərˈkjʊrəˌkrom] *s* (trademark) mercurocromo
mercurous [mərˈkjʊrəs] o [ˈmʌrkjərəs] *adj* (chem.) mercurioso
mercury [ˈmʌrkjərɪ] *s* (*pl:* **-ries**) (chem.) mercurio; columna de mercurio (*del termómetro*); (*cap.*) *s* (astr. & myth.) Mercurio
mercury-arc lamp [ˈmʌrkjərɪˌɑrk] *s* var. de **mercury-vapor lamp**
mercury chloride *s* var. de **mercuric chloride**
mercury fulminate *s* (chem.) fulminato mercúrico
mercury-vapor lamp [ˈmʌrkjərɪˌvepər] *s* (elec.) lámpara de vapor de mercurio
mercy [ˈmʌrsɪ] *s* (*pl:* **-cies**) misericordia; merced, beneficio, favor; **to be at the mercy of** estar a la merced de
mercy killing *s* eutanasia
mercy seat *s* propiciatorio; trono de Dios
mere [mɪr] *adj* mero; nada más que; *s* (poet. & dial.) lago
merely [ˈmɪrlɪ] *adv* meramente
meretricious [ˌmɛrɪˈtrɪʃəs] *adj* postizo, de oropel
merganser [mərˈgænsər] *s* (orn.) pato sierra (*Mergus merganser*); (orn.) serrata (*Mergus serrator*)
merge [mʌrdʒ] *va* fusionar, enchufar (*dos negocios*); *vn* fusionarse, enchufarse; convergir (*p.ej., dos caminos*); **to merge into** convertirse gradualmente en
merger [ˈmʌrdʒər] *s* fusión de empresas, amalgamación comercial
mericarp [ˈmɛrɪkɑrp] *s* (bot.) mericarpio
meridian [məˈrɪdɪən] *adj* meridiano; mayor, sumo, más elevado; *s* meridiano; altura meridiana; (fig.) auge, cumbre
meridional [məˈrɪdɪənəl] *adj & s* meridional
meringue [məˈræŋ] *s* merengue
merino [məˈrino] *adj* merino; *s* (*pl:* **-nos**) merino (*carnero; lana; tejido*)
meristem [ˈmɛrɪstɛm] *s* (bot.) meristemo

merit ['mɛrɪt] *s* mérito, merecimiento; **merits** *spl* (law) méritos; *va & vn* merecer
meritorious [,mɛrɪ'torɪəs] *adj* meritorio
merl o **merle** [mʌrl] *s* (poet.) mirlo
merlin ['mʌrlɪn] *s* (orn.) esmerejón, neblí; (orn). halcón palumbario; (*cap.*) *s* Merlín
merlon ['mʌrlən] *s* (fort.) merlón, almena
mermaid ['mʌr,med] *s* sirena; (fig.) ninfa marina (*mujer muy experta en la natación*)
merman ['mʌr,mæn] *s* (*pl:* **-men**) tritón; (fig.) tritón (*hombre muy experto en la natación*)
Merovingian [,mɛro'vɪndʒɪən] *adj & s* merovingio
merriment ['mɛrɪmənt] *s* alegría, regocijo, alborozo
merry ['mɛrɪ] *adj* (*comp:* **-rier;** *super:* **-riest**) alegre, regocijado, alborozado; **to make merry** alegrarse, regocijarse
merry-andrew [,mɛrɪ'ændru] *s* matachín, bufón
Merry Christmas *interj* ¡Felices Pascuas!, ¡Felices Navidades!
merry-go-round ['mɛrɪgo,raʊnd] *s* tiovivo, caballitos; fiesta continua; **merry-go-round of parties** serie ininterrumpida de fiestas o tertulias
merrymaker ['mɛrɪ,mekər] *s* fiestero; parrandista
merrymaking ['mɛrɪ,mekɪŋ] *adj* fiestero; jaranero; *s* regocijo, alborozo; jarana
merrythought ['mɛrɪ,θɔt] *s* hueso de la suerte
mésalliance [me'zælɪəns] o [meza'ljɑ̃s] *s* matrimonio con una persona de clase inferior
mescal [mɛs'kæl] *s* (bot.) mescal (*planta y bebida*)
meseems [mi'simz] *vn* (archaic) me parece
mesencephalon [,mɛsɛn'sɛfəlɑn] *s* (pl: **-la** [lə]) (anat.) mesencéfalo
mesenchyme ['mɛsɛŋkɪm] *s* (embryol.) mesénquima
mesenteric [,mɛsən'tɛrɪk] *adj* mesentérico
mesenteritis [mɛ,sɛntə'raɪtɪs] *s* (path.) mesenteritis
mesentery ['mɛsən,tɛrɪ] *s* (*pl:* **-ies**) (anat.) mesenterio
mesh [mɛʃ] *s* malla (*de una red*); red; (mach.) engrane; **meshes** *spl* red, celada; **in mesh** en toma, engranados; *va* enredar; (mach.) engranar; *vn* enredarse; (mach.) engranar
mesh bag *s* bolsa o saquillo de malla
mesial ['mizɪəl] o ['mɛsɪəl] *adj* mediano
mesitylene [mɪ'sɪtɪlin] o ['mɛsɪtɪ,lin] *s* (chem.) mesitileno
mesmerian [mɛs'mɪrɪən] o [mɛz'mɪrɪən] *adj & s* mesmeriano
mesmeric [mɛs'mɛrɪk] o [mɛz'mɛrɪk] *adj* mesmeriano
mesmerism ['mɛsmərɪzəm] o ['mɛzmərɪzəm] *s* mesmerismo
mesmerist ['mɛsmərɪst] o ['mɛzmərɪst] *s* mesmerista
mesmerize ['mɛsməraɪz] o ['mɛzməraɪz] *va* hipnotizar
mesoblast ['mɛsəblæst] o ['misəblæst] *s* (embryol.) mesoblasto
mesocarp ['mɛsəkɑrp] o ['misəkɑrp] *s* (bot.) mesocarpio
mesocephalic [,mɛsosɪ'fælɪk] o [,misosɪ'fælɪk] *adj* (anthrop.) mesocéfalo
mesoderm ['mɛsədʌrm] o ['misədʌrm] *s* (embryol.) mesodermo
mesogastrium [,mɛsə'gæstrɪəm] o [,misə'gæstrɪəm] *s* (anat. & zool.) mesogastrio
meson ['misɑn] *s* (phys.) mesón
mesophyll ['mɛsəfɪl] o ['misəfɪl] *s* (bot.) mesofilo
mesophyte ['mɛsəfaɪt] o ['misəfaɪt] *s* (bot.) mesófita
mesorrhine ['mɛsəraɪn] o ['misəraɪn] *adj* (anthrop.) mesorrino
mesosphere ['mɛzəsfɪr] *s* mesosfera
mesothorax [,mɛsə'θoræks] o [,misə'θoræks] *s* (*pl:* **-raxes** o **-races** [rəsiz]) (zool.) mesotórax
mesothorium [,mɛsə'θorɪəm] o [,mɛzə'θorɪəm] *s* (chem.) mesotorio
mesotron ['mɛsətrɑn] o ['misətrɑn] *s* (phys.) mesotrón
Mesozoic [,mɛsə'zo·ɪk] o [,misə'zo·ɪk] *adj & s* (geol.) mesozoico

mesquite [mɛs'kit] o ['mɛskit] *s* (bot.) mezquite
mess [mɛs] *s* fregado (*enredo*); lío, revoltijo; asco, suciedad; cochinadas; rancho (*comida para muchos; grupo de soldados que comen juntos*); cantidad; plato; bazofia; **to be in a mess** estar aviado; **to get into a mess** hacerse un lío; **to make a mess of** ensuciar; echarlo todo a rodar; *va* ensuciar; desarreglar; echar a perder, estropear; *vn* hacer rancho, comer; **to mess about** o **around** perder el tiempo, ocuparse en fruslerías
message ['mɛsɪdʒ] *s* mensaje; recado; buena nueva, palabras inspiradas
messaline [,mɛsə'lin] o ['mɛsəlin] *s* tela parecida al raso
messenger ['mɛsəndʒər] *s* mensajero; mandadero; precursor, presagio
mess hall *s* sala de rancho, salón comedor
Messiah [mə'saɪə] *s* (Bib. & fig.) Mesías
Messiahship [mə'saɪəʃɪp] *s* mesiazgo
Messianic [,mɛsɪ'ænɪk] *adj* mesiánico
Messianism [mə'saɪənɪzəm] *s* mesianismo
mess kit *s* utensilios de rancho
messmate ['mɛs,met] *s* comensal; compañero de rancho
mess of pottage *s* plato de lentejas, cosa de poco valor, nada
Messrs. ['mɛsərz] *pl de* **Mr.**
mess table *s* mesa de rancho
messuage ['mɛswɪdʒ] *s* (law) casería (*casa y edificios dependientes*)
messy ['mɛsɪ] *adj* (*comp:* **-ier;** *super:* **-iest**) sucio; desarreglado, desaliñado
mestizo [mɛs'tizo] *s* (*pl:* **-zos** o **-zoes**) mestizo
met. abr. de **metropolitan**
met [mɛt] *pret & pp de* **meet**
metabolic [,mɛtə'bɑlɪk] *adj* (physiol. & zool.) metabólico
metabolism [mə'tæbəlɪzəm] *s* (physiol.) metabolismo
metabolize [mə'tæbəlaɪz] *va* transformar por metabolismo; *vn* transformarse por metabolismo
metacarpal [,mɛtə'kɑrpəl] *adj & s* (anat.) metacarpiano
metacarpus [,mɛtə'kɑrpəs] *s* (*pl:* **-pi** [paɪ]) (anat.) metacarpo
metacenter [,mɛtə'sɛntər] *s* metacentro
metachromatism [,mɛtə'kromətɪzəm] *s* (physical chem.) metacromatismo
metachronism [mɪ'tækrənɪzəm] *s* metacronismo
metagenesis [,mɛtə'dʒɛnɪsɪs] *s* (biol.) metagénesis
metal ['mɛtəl] *s* metal; vidrio en fusión; (her.) metal; (Brit.) grava (*piedra machacada para caminos*); (fig.) ánimo, brío; *adj* metálico; *va* metalizar
metalepsis [,mɛtə'lɛpsɪs] *s* (*pl:* **-ses** [siz]) (rhet.) metalepsis
metaline ['mɛtəlɪn] o ['mɛtəlin] *s* metalina (*aleación*)
metalization [,mɛtəlɪ'zeʃən] *s* metalización
metalize ['mɛtəlaɪz] *va* metalizar
metallic [mɪ'tælɪk] *adj* metálico
metalliferous [,mɛtə'lɪfərəs] *adj* metalífero
metalline ['mɛtəlɪn] o ['mɛtəlaɪn] *adj* metálico; que contiene sales metálicas
metallographic [mɪ,tælə'græfɪk] *adj* metalográfico
metallography [,mɛtə'lɑgrəfɪ] *s* metalografía
metalloid ['mɛtəlɔɪd] *s* (chem.) metaloide (*elemento no metálico*); (chem.) metaloide muy semejante a los metales (*antimonio, arsénico, bismuto, silicio, telurio, etc.*)
metallotherapy [mɪ,tælo'θɛrəpɪ] *s* metaloterapia
metallurgic [,mɛtə'lʌrdʒɪk] o **metallurgical** [,mɛtə'lʌrdʒɪkəl] *adj* metalúrgico
metallurgist ['mɛtə,lʌrdʒɪst] *s* metalúrgico o metalurgista
metallurgy ['mɛtə,lʌrdʒɪ] *s* metalurgia
metal polish *s* limpiametales
metalwork ['mɛtəl,wʌrk] *s* metalistería; objetos de metalistería
metalworker ['mɛtəl,wʌrkər] *s* metalario, metalista
metalworking ['mɛtəl,wʌrkɪŋ] *s* metalistería
metamere ['mɛtəmɪr] *s* (zool.) metámero

metameric [,mɛtə'mɛrɪk] *adj* (chem. & zool.) metámero
metamorphic [,mɛtə'mɔrfɪk] *adj* metamórfico
metamorphism [,mɛtə'mɔrfɪzəm] *s* metamorfismo
metamorphose [,mɛtə'mɔrfoz] o [,mɛtə'mɔrfos] *va* metamorfosear; *vn* metamorfosearse
metamorphosis [,mɛtə'mɔrfəsɪs] *s* (*pl:* **-ses** [siz]) metamorfosis
metaphase ['mɛtəfez] *s* (biol.) metafase
metaphony [mɪ'tæfənɪ] *s* (phonet.) metafonía
metaphor ['mɛtəfər] o ['mɛtəfɔr] *s* metáfora; **to mix metaphors** mezclar las metáforas
metaphorical [,mɛtə'fɑrɪkəl] o [,mɛtə'fɔrɪkəl] *adj* metafórico
metaphrase ['mɛtəfrez] *s* metafrasis
metaphysical [,mɛtə'fɪzɪkəl] *adj* metafísico
metaphysician [,mɛtəfɪ'zɪʃən] *s* metafísico
metaphysics [,mɛtə'fɪzɪks] *ssg* metafísica
metaplasm ['mɛtəplæzəm] *s* (biol.) metaplasma; (gram.) metaplasmo
metaprotein [,mɛtə'protiɪn] o [,mɛtə'protin] *s* (biochem.) metaproteína
metasomatism [,mɛtə'somətɪzəm] *s* (geol.) metasomatismo
metastasis [mɪ'tæstəsɪs] *s* (*pl:* **-ses** [siz]) (path.) metástasis
metatarsal [,mɛtə'tɑrsəl] *adj & s* (anat.) metatarsiano
metatarsus [,mɛtə'tɑrsəs] *s* (*pl:* **-si** [saɪ]) (anat. & zool.) metatarso
metathesis [mɪ'tæθɪsɪs] *s* (*pl:* **-ses** [siz]) (philol.) metátesis
metathorax [,mɛtə'θoræks] *s* (*pl:* **-raxes** o **-races** [rəsiz]) (zool.) metatórax
metazoan [,mɛtə'zoən] *s* (zool.) metazoo
mete [mit] *s* confín, límite; mojón; *va* repartir; (poet.) medir
metempsychosis [mɪ,tɛmpsɪ'kosɪs] *s* (*pl:* **-ses** [siz]) metempsicosis
metencephalon [,mɛtɛn'sɛfəlɑn] *s* (*pl:* **-la** [lə]) (anat.) metencéfalo
meteor ['mitɪər] *s* estrella fugaz, bólido, meteorito; meteoro (*fenómeno atmosférico*)
meteoric [,mitɪ'ɑrɪk] o [,mitɪ'ɔrɪk] *adj* meteórico; (fig.) meteórico
meteoric stone *s* piedra meteórica
meteorite ['mitɪəraɪt] *s* meteorito
meteorologic [,mitɪərə'lɑdʒɪk] o **meteorological** [,mitɪərə'lɑdʒɪkəl] *adj* meteorológico
meteorologist [,mitɪə'rɑlədʒɪst] *s* meteorologista
meteorology [,mitɪə'rɑlədʒɪ] *s* meteorología
meter ['mitər] *s* metro (*unidad; verso*); (mus.) compás, tiempo; (mach.) contador, medidor; *va* medir (*con contador o medidor*)
metering ['mitərɪŋ] *s* medición
meter reader *s* lector (*del contador*)
Meth. abr. de **Methodist**
methacrylate [mɪ'θækrɪlet] *s* (chem.) metacrilato
methacrylic [,mɛθə'krɪlɪk] *adj* metacrílico
methacrylic acid *s* (chem.) ácido metacrílico
methane ['mɛθen] *s* (chem.) metano
methanol ['mɛθənol] o ['mɛθənɑl] *s* (chem.) metanol
metheglin [mə'θɛglɪn] *s* aloja
methinks [mɪ'θɪŋks] (*pret:* **methought**) *vn* (archaic) me parece
methionine [mɪ'θaɪənin] o [mɪ'θaɪənɪn] *s* (biochem.) metionina
method ['mɛθəd] *s* método; **there's method in his madness** es más cuerdo de lo que parece
methodic [mɪ'θɑdɪk] o **methodical** [mɪ'θɑdɪkəl] *adj* metódico
Methodism ['mɛθədɪzəm] *s* metodismo
Methodist ['mɛθədɪst] *adj & s* metodista
methodize ['mɛθədaɪz] *va* metodizar
methodology [,mɛθə'dɑlədʒɪ] *s* (*pl:* **-gies**) metodología
methought [mɪ'θɔt] *pret de* **methinks**
Methuselah [mɪ'θuzələ] o [mɪ'θjuzələ] *s* (Bib. & fig.) Matusalén; **to be as old as Methuselah** vivir más años que Matusalén
methyl ['mɛθɪl] *s* (chem.) metilo
methyl alcohol *s* alcohol metílico
methylamine [,mɛθɪlə'min] o [,mɛθɪ'læmɪn] *s* (chem.) metilamina
methylate ['mɛθɪlet] *s* (chem.) metilato; *va* combinar con metilo o con alcohol metílico
methylene ['mɛθɪlin] *s* (chem.) metileno
methylene blue *s* azul de metileno
methylic [mɪ'θɪlɪk] *adj* (chem.) metílico
methyl orange *s* anaranjado de metilo
methyl violet *s* violeta de metilo
meticulous [mɪ'tɪkjələs] *adj* minucioso, meticuloso
métier [me'tje] *s* oficio, profesión; fuerte (*aptitud especial de una persona*)
metol ['mitol] o ['mitɑl] *s* (chem.) metol
Metonic cycle [mɪ'tɑnɪk] *s* (astr.) ciclo de Metón
metonym ['mɛtənɪm] *s* (rhet.) palabra o expresión metonímicas
metonymic [,mɛtə'nɪmɪk] o **metonymical** [,mɛtə'nɪmɪkəl] *adj* metonímico
metonymy [mɪ'tɑnɪmɪ] *s* (rhet.) metonimia
me-tooer ['mi'tuər] *s* (slang) persona que sigue al que triunfa o se pone de su parte; (slang) exitista (Am.)
metope ['mɛtəpɪ] o ['mɛtop] *s* (arch.) métopa
metre ['mitər] *s* metro (*unidad; verso*); (mus.) compás, tiempo
metric ['mɛtrɪk] *adj* métrico; **metrics** *spl* métrica
metrical ['mɛtrɪkəl] *adj* métrico
metrically ['mɛtrɪkəlɪ] *adv* métricamente
metric horsepower *s* (mech.) caballo de fuerza, caballo de vapor (*736 vatios*)
metric system *s* sistema métrico
metric ton *s* tonelada métrica (*de peso*)
metrist ['mitrɪst] o ['mɛtrɪst] *s* metrista
metritis [mɪ'traɪtɪs] *s* (path.) metritis
metrology [mɪ'trɑlədʒɪ] *s* metrología
metronome ['mɛtrənom] *s* (mus..) metrónomo
metronomic [,mɛtrə'nɑmɪk] *adj* metronómico
metropolis [mɪ'trɑpəlɪs] *s* metrópoli; (eccl.) metrópoli
metropolitan [,mɛtrə'pɑlɪtən] *adj* metropolitano; *s* ciudadano de una gran ciudad; (eccl.) metropolitano
metrorrhagia [,mitrə'redʒɪə] o [,mɛtrə'redʒɪə] *s* (path.) metrorragia
mettle ['mɛtəl] *s* ánimo, brío; **on one's mettle** dispuesto a hacer grandes esfuerzos
mettlesome ['mɛtəlsəm] *adj* animoso, brioso
Meuse [mjuz] *s* Mosa
mew [mju] *s* jaula; halconera; maullido; (orn.) gaviota; **mews** *spl* caballeriza construída alrededor de un corral; *va* enjaular; encerrar; esconder; **to mew up** tener escondido; *vn* maullar
mewl [mjul] *vn* lloriquear
Mex. abr. de **Mexican** y **Mexico**
Mexican ['mɛksɪkən] *adj & s* mejicano
Mexican bean beetle *s* (ent.) tortuguilla de frijol, conchuela
Mexican poppy *s* (bot.) argemone mejicana, chicalote
Mexico ['mɛksɪko] *s* Méjico
Mexico City *s* Ciudad de Méjico
mezereon [mɪ'zɪrɪən] *s* (bot.) lauréola hembra
mezzanine ['mɛzənin] *s* entresuelo
mezzo ['mɛtso] o ['mɛzo] *adj* (mus.) medio, a media voz, entre fuerte y piano
mezzo-soprano ['mɛtsosə'præno] o ['mɛtsosə'prɑno] *s* (*pl:* **-os**) mezzo-soprano
mezzotint ['mɛtsotɪnt] o ['mɛzotɪnt] *s* grabado al humo o a media tinta; *va* grabar al humo o a media tinta
mfg. abr. de **manufacturing**
mfr. abr. de **manufacturer**
mg. abr. de **milligram** o **milligrams**
Mgr. abr. de **Manager, Monseigneur** y **Monsignor**
mho [mo] *s* (elec.) mho
mi. abr. de **mile** o **miles**
mi [mi] *s* (mus.) mi
miaow o **miaou** [mɪ'aʊ] *s & vn* var. de **meow**
miasma [maɪ'æzmə] o [mɪ'æzmə] *s* (*pl:* **-mas** o **-mata** [mətə]) miasma
miasmal [maɪ'æzməl] o [mɪ'æzməl] o **miasmatic** [,maɪæz'mætɪk] *adj* miasmático
mica ['maɪkə] *s* (mineral.) mica
micaceous [maɪ'keʃəs] *adj* micáceo
Micah ['maɪkə] *s* (Bib.) Miqueas
mica schist *s* micacita, micasquisto
mice [maɪs] *pl de* **mouse**

micellar [mɪ'sɛlər] *adj* micelar
micelle [mɪ'sɛl] *s* (biol. & chem.) micela
Mich. abr. de **Michaelmas** y **Michigan**
Michael ['maɪkəl] *s* Miguel
Michaelmas ['mɪkəlməs] *s* fiesta de San Miguel
Michaelmastide ['mɪkəlməs,taɪd] *s* sanmiguelada
Michelangelo [,maɪkəl'ændʒəlo] *s* Miguel Ángel
Michigan ['mɪʃɪgən] *s* Michigán
Mickey Mouse ['mɪkɪ] *s* el ratón Miguelito
mickle ['mɪkəl] *adj & adv* (Scotch) mucho
microanalysis [,maɪkroə'nælɪsɪs] *s* (*pl:* **-ses** [siz]) (chem.) microanálisis
microbarograph [,maɪkro'bærəgræf] o [,maɪkro'bærəgrɑf] *s* microbarógrafo
microbe ['maɪkrob] *s* microbio
microbial [maɪ'krobɪəl] *adj* microbiano
microbic [maɪ'krobɪk] *adj* micróbico
microbiological [,maɪkro,baɪə'lɑdʒɪkəl] *adj* microbiológico
microbiologist [,maɪkrobaɪ'ɑlədʒɪst] *s* microbiólogo
microbiology [,maɪkrobaɪ'ɑlədʒɪ] *s* microbiología
microcard ['maɪkrəkɑrd] *s* microficha
microcephalic [,maɪkrosɪ'fælɪk] *adj* (anthrop. & path.) microcéfalo
microchemistry [,maɪkro'kɛmɪstrɪ] *s* microquímica
microcline ['maɪkrəklaɪn] *s* (mineral.) microclina
micrococcus [,maɪkrə'kɑkəs] *s* (*pl:* **-cocci** ['kɑksaɪ]) (bact.) micrococo
microcopy ['maɪkrə,kɑpɪ] *s* (*pl:* **-ies**) microcopia
microcosm ['maɪkrokɑzəm] *s* microcosmo
microcyte ['maɪkrəsaɪt] *s* (path.) microcito
microdissection [,maɪkrodɪ'sɛkʃən] *s* microdisección
microdont ['maɪkrodɑnt] *adj & s* microdonte
microfarad [,maɪkro'færæd] *s* (elec.) microfaradio
microfilm ['maɪkrəfɪlm] *s* microfilm, micropelícula; *va* microfilmar
microgamete [,maɪkrogə'mit] *s* (biol.) microgameto
microgram ['maɪkrogræm] *s* microgramo
micrography [maɪ'krɑgrəfɪ] *s* micrografía
microgroove ['maɪkrəgruv] *s* microsurco; (trademark) disco microsurco
microinch ['maɪkro,ɪntʃ] *s* micropulgada
micrometer [maɪ'krɑmɪtər] *s* micrómetro
micrometer caliper *s* pálmer, calibre micrométrico
micrometer screw *s* tornillo micrométrico
micrometric [,maɪkro'mɛtrɪk] o **micrometrical** [,maɪkro'mɛtrɪkəl] *adj* micrométrico
micrometry [maɪ'krɑmɪtrɪ] *s* micrometría
micromillimeter [,maɪkro'mɪlɪ,mitər] *s* micromilímetro
micromotion ['maɪkro,moʃən] *s* micromovimiento
micron ['maɪkrɑn] *s* (*pl:* **-crons** o **-cra** [krə]) micra o micrón
Micronesia [,maɪkro'niʃə] o [,maɪkro'niʒə] *s* la Micronesia
Micronesian [,maɪkro'niʃən] o [,maɪkro'niʒən] *adj & s* micronesio
microörganism [,maɪkro'ɔrgənɪzəm] *s* (bact.) microorganismo
microphone ['maɪkrəfon] *s* micrófono
microphotograph [,maɪkro'fotəgræf] o [,maɪkro'fotəgrɑf] *s* microfotografía
microphotography [,maɪkrofə'tɑgrəfɪ] *s* microfotografía
microphysics [,maɪkro'fɪzɪks] *ssg* microfísica
microphyte ['maɪkrəfaɪt] *s* (bot.) micrófito
micropyle ['maɪkrəpaɪl] *s* (bot. & zool.) micrópilo
microscope ['maɪkrəskop] *s* microscopio
microscopic [,maɪkrə'skɑpɪk] o **microscopical** [,maɪkrə'skɑpɪkəl] *adj* microscópico
microscopically [,maɪkrə'skɑpɪkəlɪ] *adv* microscópicamente
microscopist [maɪ'krɑskəpɪst] o ['maɪkrə,skopɪst] *s* microscopista
microscopy [maɪ'krɑskəpɪ] o ['maɪkrə,skopɪ] *s* microscopia
microseism ['maɪkrosaɪzəm] *s* microsismo
microsome ['maɪkrəsom] *s* (biol.) microsoma
microsporangium [,maɪkrospo'rændʒɪəm] *s* (*pl:* **-a** [ə]) (bot.) microsporangio
microspore ['maɪkrəspor] *s* (bot.) microspora
microsporous [,maɪkrə'sporəs] *adj* microsporo
microtome ['maɪkrətom] *s* micrótomo
microwave ['maɪkro,wev] *s* (phys.) microonda
micturition [,mɪktʃə'rɪʃən] *s* micción, micturición
mid [mɪd] *adj* medio, p.ej., **in mid afternoon** a media tarde
mid o **'mid** [mɪd] *prep* (poet.) entre, en medio de
Midas ['maɪdəs] *s* (myth.) Midas
midbrain ['mɪd,bren] *s* (anat.) mesencéfalo
midchannel [,mɪd'tʃænəl] *s* medio del canal, río o pasadizo marítimo
midcontinent [,mɪd'kɑntɪnənt] *s* centro del continente
midday ['mɪd,de] *s* mediodía; *adj* de mediodía
middle ['mɪdəl] *s* centro, medio; cintura (*del hombre*); **middles** *spl* (agr.) caballones, lomos; **about the middle of** a mediados de; **in the middle of** en medio de; a medio, p.ej., **in the middle of the afternoon** a media tarde; **from the middle of** desde en medio de; *adj* medio; intermedio; de en medio, p.ej., **the middle room** el cuarto de en medio
middle age *s* mediana edad; **Middle Ages** *spl* Edad Media
middle-aged ['mɪdəl,edʒd] *adj* de mediana edad
Middle America *s* Méjico y la América Central, la parte central de las Américas
middle class *s* clase media, burguesía
middle-class ['mɪdəl,klæs] o ['mɪdəl,klɑs] *adj* aburguesado, de la clase media
middle distance *s* (paint.) segundo término
middle ear *s* (anat.) oído medio
Middle East *s* Oriente Medio
Middle Eastern *adj* medio-oriental
Middle English *s* el inglés medio
middle finger *s* dedo cordial, dedo de en medio, dedo del corazón
Middle High German *s* el medio altoalemán
middleman ['mɪdəl,mæn] *s* (*pl:* **-men**) (com.) intermediario
middlemost ['mɪdəlmost] *adj* más céntrico, más cercano al centro
middle passage *s* travesía que hacían los traficantes en negros de África a las Antillas
middle term *s* (log.) término medio
middle voice *s* (gram.) voz media
middleweight ['mɪdəl,wet] *s* persona de peso medio; (box.) peso mediano o medio
Middle West *s* mediooeste, llanura central (*de los EE.UU.*)
middling ['mɪdlɪŋ] *adj* mediano, regular; *adv* (coll.) medianamente; **fairly middling** (coll.) así, así; **middlings** *spl* acemite; productos de tamaño regular, o de calidad o precio intermedios; clase de algodón que sirve de base a las cotizaciones
middy ['mɪdɪ] *s* (*pl:* **-dies**) (coll.) aspirante de marina; marinera (*blusa de niño*)
middy blouse *s* marinera (*blusa de niño*)
midge [mɪdʒ] *s* (ent.) mosca pequeñita, díptero; enano
midget ['mɪdʒɪt] *s* enano
Midianite ['mɪdɪənaɪt] *s* (Bib.) madianita
midiron ['mɪd,aɪərn] *s* (golf) mazo de hierro que se emplea cuando hay que dar a la bola un salto bastante grande
midland ['mɪdlənd] *s* interior, región central (*de un país*); *adj* del interior, de tierra adentro
midleg ['mɪd,lɛg] *s* media pierna; (ent.) pata intermedia, pata del mesotórax; *adv* hasta la media pierna
midmost ['mɪdmost] *adj* var. de **middlemost**
midnight ['mɪd,naɪt] *s* medianoche; *adj* de medianoche; **to burn the midnight oil** quemarse las cejas
midnight sun *s* sol de medianoche
midrange ['mɪd,rendʒ] *s* medio alcance; gama intermedia (*de los sonidos audibles*)
midrib ['mɪd,rɪb] *s* (bot.) nervio medial o principal

midriff ['mɪdrɪf] *s* (anat.) diafragma; traje que deja descubierta parte del diafragma
midship ['mɪd,ʃɪp] *adj* del o en el medio del buque; **midships** *adv* en medio del buque
midship frame *s* (naut.) cuaderna maestra
midshipman ['mɪd,ʃɪpmən] *s* (*pl:* **-men**) aspirante de marina, cadete de la escuela naval; guardia marina (*en un buque naval*); (archaic) mandadero de a bordo
midshipmite ['mɪd,ʃɪpmaɪt] *s* (hum.) guardia marina de estatura pequeña
midst [mɪdst] *s* centro, medio; **in the midst of** entre, en medio de; en lo más recio de
midst o **'midst** [mɪdst] *prep* (poet.) var. de **amidst**
midstream ['mɪd,strim] *s* medio de una corriente o río; **in midstream** en pleno río
midsummer ['mɪd,sʌmər] *s* pleno verano; (Brit.) fines de junio, solsticio de verano; *adj* en pleno verano
mid-Victorian ['mɪdvɪk'torɪən] *adj* chapado a la antigua; austero, rígido; *s* contemporáneo de la reina Victoria en la época media de su reinado
midway ['mɪd,we] *s* mitad del camino; avenida central (*p.ej., de una exposición*); *adj* situado a mitad del camino; *adv* a mitad del camino
midweek ['mɪd,wik] *s* mediados de la semana; (*cap.*) *s* (Quaker) miércoles
Midwest ['mɪd'wɛst] *s* mediooeste, llanura central (*de los EE.UU.*)
Midwestern [,mɪd'wɛstərn] *adj* del mediooeste (*de los EE.UU.*)
Midwesterner [,mɪd'wɛstərnər] *s* habitante del mediooeste (*de los EE.UU.*)
midwife ['mɪd,waɪf] *s* (*pl:* **-wives**) comadrona, partera
midwifery ['mɪd,waɪfrɪ] *s* partería
midwinter ['mɪd,wɪntər] *s* pleno invierno; (Brit.) fines de diciembre, solsticio de invierno; *adj* en pleno invierno
midyear ['mɪd,jɪr] *adj* de mediados del año; *s* (coll.) examen de mediados del año, examen de entre semestres
mien [min] *s* porte, aspecto, semblante, talante
miff [mɪf] *s* (coll.) desavenencia, disgusto; *va* disgustar, ofender; *vn* amoscarse
might [maɪt] *s* fuerza, poderío; **with might and main** con todas sus fuerzas, a más no poder; *v aux* podría, ser posible, p.ej., **he might come this evening** es posible que venga esta tarde
mightily ['maɪtɪlɪ] *adv* poderosamente; (coll.) muchísimo
mightiness ['maɪtɪnɪs] *s* fuerza, poderío; grandeza
mightn't ['maɪtənt] contracción de **might not**
mighty ['maɪtɪ] *adj* (*comp:* **-ier;** *super:* **-iest**) fuerte, potente, poderoso; grandísimo; *adv* (coll.) muy, p.ej., **it's mighty hard** es muy difícil; (coll.) mucho, p.ej., **it's mighty hot** hace mucho calor
mignon ['mɪnjɑn] *adj* lindo, primoroso
mignonette [,mɪnjə'nɛt] *s* (bot.) reseda, miñoneta
migraine ['maɪgren] o [mɪ'gren] *s* (path.) migraña, hemicránea
migrant ['maɪgrənt] *adj* migratorio; *s* peregrino, nómada; planta o animal migratorios
migrate ['maɪgret] *vn* emigrar
migration [maɪ'greʃən] *s* migración
migratory ['maɪgrə,torɪ] *adj* migratorio
mihrab ['mirəb] *s* mihrab
mikado [mɪ'kɑdo] *s* (*pl:* **-dos**) micado
mike [maɪk] *s* (slang) micrófono; (*cap.*) *s* Miguelito
mil. abr. de **military** y **militia**
mil [mɪl] *s* milipulgada
milady o **miladi** [mɪ'ledɪ] *s* (*pl:* **-dies**) miladi
Milan [mɪ'læn] o ['mɪlən] *s* Milán
Milanese [,mɪlə'niz] *adj* milanés; *s* (*pl:* **-nese**) milanés
milch [mɪlk] *adj* lechero
milch cow *s* vaca lechera, vaca de leche
mild [maɪld] *adj* suave, manso; dulce; templado; leve, ligero
mildew ['mɪldju] o ['mɪldu] *s* (agr.) mildiú; enmohecimiento, moho; *va* enmohecer; *vn* enmohecerse
mildly ['maɪldlɪ] *adv* suavemente, mansamente; dulcemente; algo, un poco
mildness ['maɪldnɪs] *s* suavidad, mansedumbre; dulzura; templanza (*del clima*)
mile [maɪl] *s* milla inglesa
mileage ['maɪlɪdʒ] *s* número de millas, recorrido en millas; gastos de viaje (*que se pagan a tanto por milla*)
mileage ticket *s* billete kilométrico
milepost ['maɪl,post] *s* poste miliar
Milesian [maɪ'liʃən] o [maɪ'liʒən] *adj & s* milesio
Milesian tales *spl* fábulas milesias
milestone ['maɪl,ston] *s* piedra miliaria; (fig.) piedra miliar; **to be a milestone** hacer época
Miletus [maɪ'litəs] *s* Mileto
milfoil ['mɪlfɔɪl] *s* (bot.) milefolio
miliary ['mɪlɪ,ɛrɪ] o ['mɪljərɪ] *adj* miliar; (path.) miliar
milieu [mi'ljø] *s* medio, ambiente
militancy ['mɪlɪtənsɪ] *s* belicosidad; actitud o política belicosas
militant ['mɪlɪtənt] *adj* militante, aguerrido, belicoso; *s* militante, partidario aguerrido
militarism ['mɪlɪtərɪzəm] *s* militarismo
militarist ['mɪlɪtərɪst] *adj* militarista; *s* militarista; estratégico
militarization [,mɪlɪtərɪ'zeʃən] *s* militarización
militarize ['mɪlɪtəraɪz] *va* militarizar
military ['mɪlɪ,tɛrɪ] *adj* militar; *s* (los) militares
Military Academy *s* (U.S.A.) Academia General Militar
military police *s* policía militar
military service *s* servicio militar
militate ['mɪlɪtet] *vn* militar; **to militate against** militar contra
militia [mɪ'lɪʃə] *s* milicia
militiaman [mɪ'lɪʃəmən] *s* (*pl:* **-men**) miliciano
milk [mɪlk] *s* leche; **to cry over spilt milk** lamentar lo irremediable; *va* ordeñar; extraer; chupar; *vn* dar leche
milk-and-water ['mɪlkənd'wɔtər] o ['mɪlkənd'wɑtər] *adj* débil, sin carácter
milk can *s* lechera (*vasija*)
milk crust *s* (path.) lactumen
milk diet *s* régimen lácteo
milker ['mɪlkər] *s* ordeñador; ordeñadora, máquina de ordeñar; vaca, cabra, etc. lecheras
milk fever *s* (path.) fiebre láctea
milking ['mɪlkɪŋ] *s* ordeño
milking machine *s* ordeñadora
milk leg *s* (path.) flebitis de las venas de la pierna
milkmaid ['mɪlk,med] *s* lechera
milkman ['mɪlk,mæn] *s* (*pl:* **-men**) lechero
milk of human kindness *s* compasión, humanidad
milk of lime *s* lechada de cal
milk of magnesia *s* (pharm.) leche de magnesia
milk pail *s* ordeñadero
milk powder *s* leche en polvo
milk shake *s* batido de leche
milk snake *s* (zool.) culebrilla norteamericana (*Lampropeltis triangulum*)
milksop ['mɪlk,sɑp] *s* marica, calzonazos
milk sugar *s* azúcar de leche
milk thistle *s* (bot.) cardo lechero, arzolla
milk tooth *s* diente de leche
milk vetch *s* (bot.) astrágalo
milkweed ['mɪlk,wid] *s* (bot.) algodoncillo
milk-white ['mɪlk,hwaɪt] *adj* blanco como la leche
milkwort ['mɪlk,wʌrt] *s* (bot.) lechera amarga, polígala
milky ['mɪlkɪ] *adj* (*comp:* **-ier;** *super:* **-iest**) lechoso; apocado, tímido, débil
Milky Way *s* (astr.) Vía láctea
mill [mɪl] *s* molino; fábrica, taller; hilandería (*de tejidos*); ingenio (*de azúcar*); aserradero; (U.S.A.) milésima (*de dólar*); (slang) pendencia a puñetazos; **to go through the mill** (coll.) entrenarse rigurosamente; (coll.) aprender por experiencia; **to put through the mill** (coll.) poner a prueba; (coll.) someter a

un entrenamiento riguroso; *va* moler; machacar, triturar; fabricar; cerrillar o acordonar (*monedas*); fresar; batir (*chocolate*); *vn* hormiguear, arremolinarse (*una muchedumbre*); (slang) luchar a puñetazos; **to mill about** o **around** moverse en círculos
millclapper ['mɪl,klæpər] *s* tarabilla, cítola; (dial.) tarabilla, charlador, parlanchín
milldam ['mɪl,dæm] *s* presa de molino; represa de molino
millenarian [,mɪlɪ'nɛrɪən] *adj & s* milenario
mill end *s* retazo de hilandería
millenium [mɪ'lɛnɪəm] *s* (*pl:* **-ums** o **-a** [ə]) milenario, milenio
millennial [mɪ'lɛnɪəl] *adj* milenario
millepede ['mɪlɪpid] *s* (zool.) milípedo
millepore ['mɪlɪpor] *s* (zool.) milépora
miller ['mɪlər] *s* molinero; (ent.) mariposa nocturna de alas empolvadas; (mach.) fresa
miller's-thumb ['mɪlərz'θʌm] *s* (ichth.) coto
millesimal [mɪ'lɛsɪməl] *adj & s* milésimo
millet ['mɪlɪt] *s* (bot.) mijo o millo; (bot.) panizo
mill hand *s* molinero, obrero de molino; hilandero
milliammeter [,mɪlɪ'æm,mitər] *s* (elec.) miliamperímetro
milliampere [,mɪlɪ'æmpɪr] *s* (elec.) miliamperio
milliard ['mɪljərd] *s* mil millones
milliary ['mɪlɪ,ɛrɪ] *adj* miliario
millibar ['mɪlɪbɑr] *s* milibar
millicurie [,mɪlɪ'kjuri] o [,mɪlɪkju'ri] *s* (phys.) milicurie
milligram o **milligramme** ['mɪlɪgræm] *s* miligramo
milliliter ['mɪlɪ,litər] *s* mililitro
millimeter ['mɪlɪ,mitər] *s* milímetro
millimicron ['mɪlɪ,maɪkrɑn] *s* (*pl:* **-cra** [krə]) milimicrón
milliner ['mɪlɪnər] *s* modista de sombreros, sombrerero, sombrerera
millinery ['mɪlɪ,nɛrɪ] o ['mɪlɪnərɪ] *s* sombreros de señora; confección de sombreros de señora; venta de sombreros de señora
millinery shop *s* sombrerería (*de la modista de sombreros de señora*)
milling ['mɪlɪŋ] *s* molienda; acordonamiento; cordoncillo; fabricación; fresado
milling machine *s* fresadora
million ['mɪljən] *s* millón; *adj* millón de, millones de, p.ej., **two million inhabitants** dos millones de habitantes
millionaire [,mɪljən'ɛr] *adj & s* millonario
millionfold ['mɪljən,fold] *adj* multiplicado por un millón; *adv* millón de veces
millionth ['mɪljənθ] *adj & s* millonésimo
millipede ['mɪlɪpid] *s* var. de **millepede**
millivolt ['mɪlɪ,volt] *s* (elec.) milivoltio
millpond ['mɪl,pɑnd] *s* represa de molino
millrace ['mɪl,res] *s* caz; corriente del caz
millstone ['mɪl,ston] *s* muela de molino; (fig.) peso agobiador, carga agobiadora
mill wheel *s* rueda de molino
millwork ['mɪl,wʌrk] *s* carpintería mecánica, materiales prefabricados de construcción; trabajo de taller, de fábrica o de molino
millwright ['mɪl,raɪt] *s* montador de ejes, poleas, transmisiones, etc.; fabricante de molinos
milord [mɪ'lɔrd] *s* milord
milt [mɪlt] *s* (ichth.) lecha (*licor seminal y bolsa que lo contiene*); (anat.) bazo
Miltiades [mɪl'taɪədiz] *s* Milcíades
Miltonian [mɪl'tonɪən] o **Miltonic** [mɪl'tɑnɪk] *adj* miltoniano
mimbar ['mɪmbɑr] *s* almimbar (*púlpito en la mezquita*)
mime [maɪm] *s* mimo; *va* remedar; *vn* actuar de mimo, hacer el bufón
mimeograph ['mɪmɪə,græf] o ['mɪmɪə,grɑf] *s* (trademark) ciclostilo, mimeógrafo; *va* mimeografiar
mimesis [mɪ'misɪs] o [maɪ'misɪs] *s* (rhet., biol. & path.) mímesis
mimetic [mɪ'mɛtɪk] o [maɪ'mɛtɪk] *adj* imitativo; fingido; (biol. & mineral.) mimético
mimic ['mɪmɪk] *adj* mímico; fingido; *s* remedador; (*pret & pp:* **-icked;** *ger:* **-icking**) *va* imitar; remedar (*especialmente por burla*)
mimicry ['mɪmɪkrɪ] *s* (*pl:* **-ries**) mímica, remedo; (biol.) mimicria
mimosaceous [,mɪmə'seʃəs] o [,maɪmə'seʃəs] *adj* (bot.) mimosáceo
min. abr. de **minimum** y **minute** o **minutes**
minacious [mɪ'neʃəs] *adj* amenazador
minaret [,mɪnə'rɛt] o ['mɪnərɛt] *s* alminar, minarete
minatory ['mɪnə,torɪ] *adj* amenazador
mince [mɪns] *s* picadillo; *va* desmenuzar; picar (*carne*); andar con rodeos al hablar de; hacer remilgadamente; decir remilgadamente; **not to mince matters** hablar con toda franqueza, no tener pelos en la lengua; *vn* andar remilgadamente; hablar remilgadamente
mincemeat ['mɪns,mit] *s* cuajado (*carne picada con frutas*); **to make mincemeat of** hacer pedazos
mince pie *s* pastel de carne picada con frutas
mincing ['mɪnsɪŋ] *adj* remilgado; andando remilgadamente
mind [maɪnd] *s* mente, espíritu; juicio; ánimo; parecer; persona de gran entendimiento; **to bear in mind** tener presente; **to be in one's right mind** estar en sus cabales, estar en su juicio; **to be of one mind** estar de acuerdo (*dos o más personas*); **to be on one's mind** preocuparle a uno; **to be out of one's mind** estar fuera de juicio; **to bring** o **to call to mind** traer a las mientes; **to change one's mind** cambiar o mudar de opinión o de parecer; **to come to mind** venir a las mientes; **to go out of one's mind** volverse loco; **to have a mind to** + *inf* estar en ánimo de + *inf*, estar por + *inf;* **to have half a mind to** + *inf* inclinarse a + *inf;* **to have in mind** tener en mente, tener pensado; acordarse de; pensar en; **to have in mind to** + *inf* pensar en + *inf;* **to have on one's mind** preocuparse con; **to keep in mind** tener presente; **to know one's mind** saber lo que uno quiere; **to lose one's mind** perder el juicio; **to make up one's mind** resolverse; **to my mind** en mi opinión, a mi parecer; **to pass out of mind** caer en el olvido; **to put in mind** recordar; **to read minds** leer mentes, adivinar el pensamiento ajeno; **to say whatever comes into one's mind** decir lo que se le viene a la boca; **to set one's mind on** desear con vehemencia; **to set one's mind on** + *ger* resolverse a + *inf;* **to slip one's mind** escaparse de la memoria; **to speak one's mind** decir su parecer, hablar en plata, hablar con franqueza; **with one mind** unánimemente ‖ *va* acordarse de; tener en cuenta; fijarse en; meterse en; obedecer, guiarse por; cuidar, estar al cuidado de (*p.ej., un niño*); sentir molestia por; **do you mind the smoke?** ¿le molesta el humo?; **mind your own business** no se meta Vd. en lo que no le toca ‖ *vn* tener cuidado; fijarse; tener inconveniente; **never mind** no se moleste Vd., no importa; **now mind** fíjese Vd.
minded ['maɪndɪd] *adj* inclinado, dispuesto
mindful ['maɪndfəl] *adj* atento, cuidadoso; **mindful of** atento a, cuidadoso de
mindless ['maɪndlɪs] *adj* estúpido, sin inteligencia; poco atento
mind reader *s* adivinador del pensamiento ajeno
mind reading *s* adivinación del pensamiento
mind's eye *s* imaginación
mine [maɪn] *adj poss* (archaic) mi; *pron poss* mío; el mío; **a friend of mine** un amigo mío; *s* mina; (mil., nav. & fig.) mina; **to work a mine** beneficiar una mina; *va* minar; extraer (*carbón, mineral, etc.*); beneficiar (*un terreno*); (mil., nav. & fig.) minar; *vn* minar; abrir minas; dedicarse a la minería
mine detector *s* detector de minas
mine field *s* (mil. & nav.) campo de minas
mine layer *s* (nav.) buque portaminas, minador
miner ['maɪnər] *s* minero; (mil.) minador
mineral ['mɪnərəl] *adj & s* mineral
mineral green *s* verdemontaña (*mineral y color*)
mineralization [,mɪnərəlɪ'zeʃən] *s* mineralización
mineralize ['mɪnərəlaɪz] *va* mineralizar; *vn* buscar minerales
mineral jelly *s* jalea mineral (*petrolato crudo*)

mineral kingdom *s* reino mineral
mineralogical [ˌmɪnərəˈlɑdʒɪkəl] *adj* mineralógico
mineralogically [ˌmɪnərəˈlɑdʒɪkəlɪ] *adv* mineralógicamente
mineralogist [ˌmɪnəˈrælədʒɪst] *s* mineralogista
mineralogy [ˌmɪnəˈrælədʒɪ] *s* mineralogía
mineral oil *s* aceite mineral
mineral pitch *s* brea mineral (*asfalto*)
mineral right *s* (law) derecho al subsuelo, derecho para explotar yacimientos minerales
mineral water *s* agua mineral, agua mineromedicinal
mineral wool *s* lana de escoria, lana mineral
Minerva [mɪˈnʌrvə] *s* (myth.) Minerva
minestrone [ˌmɪnɛˈstrone] *s* sopa de legumbres y fideos
mine sweeper *s* (nav.) dragaminas, barreminas
mine thrower *s* (mil.) lanzaminas
mingle [ˈmɪŋgəl] *va* mezclar, confundir; *vn* mezclarse, confundirse; asociarse
miniature [ˈmɪnɪətʃər] o [ˈmɪnɪtʃər] *s* miniatura; modelo pequeño; **in miniature** en miniatura; *adj* miniatura; miniaturesco, diminuto
miniaturist [ˈmɪnɪətʃərɪst] o [ˈmɪnɪtʃərɪst] miniaturista
miniaturization [ˌmɪnɪətʃərɪˈzeʃən] o [ˌmɪnɪtʃərɪˈzeʃən] *s* miniaturización
miniaturize [ˈmɪnɪətʃəraiz] o [ˈmɪnɪtʃəraɪz] *va* miniaturizar
Minié ball [ˈmɪnɪe] o [ˈmɪnɪ] *s* bala Minié
minim [ˈmɪnɪm] *s* cantidad muy pequeña; mínima; (mus.) mínima; (pharm.) minim
minimal [ˈmɪnɪməl] *adj* mínimo
minimization [ˌmɪnɪmɪˈzeʃən] *s* reducción al mínimo; paliación; minimización, empequeñecimiento, menosprecio
minimize [ˈmɪnɪmaɪz] *va* reducir al mínimo; paliar; minimizar, empequeñecer, menospreciar
minimum [ˈmɪnɪməm] *adj* mínimo; *s* (*pl:* **-mums** o **-ma** [mə]) mínimo o mínimum
minimum wage *s* jornal mínimo
mining [ˈmaɪnɪŋ] *adj* minero; *s* mineraje, minería; (nav.) minado (*p.ej., de un puerto*)
mining engineer *s* ingeniero de minas
minion [ˈmɪnjən] *s* paniaguado; privado, valido; (print.) miñona; *adj* lindo, primoroso
minion of the law *s* esbirro, polizonte
minister [ˈmɪnɪstər] *s* ministro; (pol., dipl. & eccl.) ministro; *va & vn* ministrar
Minister of Foreign Affairs *s* (Brit.) ministro de Asuntos Exteriores
minister of the Gospel *s* ministro del santo Evangelio (*pastor protestante*)
ministerial [ˌmɪnɪsˈtɪrɪəl] *adj* ministerial; administrativo; ministrante
minister plenipotentiary *s* (*pl:* **ministers plenipotentiary**) ministro plenipotenciario
minister without portfolio *s* ministro sin cartera
ministral [ˈmɪnɪstrəl] *adj* ministerial
ministrant [ˈmɪnɪstrənt] *adj & s* ministrador, ministrante
ministration [ˌmɪnɪˈstreʃən] *s* ayuda, solicitud, suministración; (eccl.) ministerio
ministry [ˈmɪnɪstrɪ] *s* (*pl:* **-tries**) ministerio
minitrack [ˈmɪnɪˌtræk] *s* sistema electrónico para el rastreo de los satélites terrestres mediante radioondas captadas por una cadena mundial de radiorreceptoras
minium [ˈmɪnɪəm] *s* (chem.) minio
miniver [ˈmɪnɪvər] *s* piel de forro blanca o blanca con motas negras; (zool.) gris, ardilla de Siberia; (zool.) armiño en su piel blanca de invierno; (Brit.) piel blanca
mink [mɪŋk] *s* (zool.) visón; piel de visón
mink coat *s* abrigo de visón
Minn. abr. de **Minnesota**
minnesinger [ˈmɪnəˌsɪŋər] *s* trovador alemán
minnow [ˈmɪno] *s* pececillo; (ichth.) foxino; (ichth.) ciprino
Minoan [mɪˈnoən] *adj* minoico
minor [ˈmaɪnər] *adj* menor; de menor importancia; menor de edad; (log. & mus.) menor; *s* menor de edad; (educ.) asignatura o curso secundario; (mus.) acorde, escala o intervalo menor; *vn* (coll.) seguir una asignatura o curso secundario
Minorca [mɪˈnɔrkə] *s* Menorca
Minorcan [mɪˈnɔrkən] *adj & s* menorquín
minority [mɪˈnɑrɪtɪ] o [mɪˈnɔrɪtɪ] *s* (*pl:* **-ties**) minoría; *adj* minoritario
minor key *s* (mus..) tono menor
minor orders *spl* (eccl.) órdenes menores
minor premise *s* (log.) premisa menor
minor scale *s* (mus.) escala menor
minor surgery *s* cirugía menor
Minos [ˈmaɪnɑs] *s* (myth.) Minos
Minotaur [ˈmɪnətɔr] *s* (myth.) Minotauro
minster [ˈmɪnstər] *s* santuario de monasterio; catedral
minstrel [ˈmɪnstrəl] *s* ministril (*criado que con música y canto divertía a su señor*); trovador; juglar; (U.S.A.) cómico disfrazado de negro
minstrel show *s* función de cómicos disfrazados de negro
minstrelsy [ˈmɪnstrəlsɪ] *s* (*pl:* **-sies**) juglaría, poesía o música trovadorescas, cancionero; compañía de juglares o trovadores
mint [mɪnt] *s* (bot.) hierbabuena, menta; pastilla o bombón de menta; casa de moneda; dineral, montón de dinero; sinnúmero; fuente inagotable; *adj* sin usar, no usado; *va* acuñar; (fig.) inventar
mintage [ˈmɪntɪdʒ] *s* acuñación; moneda acuñada; derechos de cuño; sello, señal
mint block *s* (philately) cuadrito sin usar
mint julep *s* julepe (*bebida helada compuesta de whisky, azúcar y hojas de menta*)
minuend [ˈmɪnjʊɛnd] *s* (math.) minuendo
minuet [ˌmɪnjʊˈɛt] *s* minué o minuete (*baile y música*)
minus [ˈmaɪnəs] *s* menos (*signo*); *adj* menos; *prep* menos; falto de, sin
minus sign *s* signo menos
minute [maɪˈnjut] o [maɪˈnut] *adj* menudo, diminuto; minucioso; [ˈmɪnɪt] *s* minuto (*de hora; de grado*); instante, momento; **minutes** *spl* acta (*de una junta*); **up to the minute** al corriente; de última hora; *va* minutar; levantar acta de
minute gun [ˈmɪnɪt] *s* cañón que se dispara de minuto en minuto (*en señal de luto o de alarma*)
minute hand [ˈmɪnɪt] *s* minutero
minutely [maɪˈnjutlɪ] o [maɪˈnutlɪ] *adv* menudamente, minuciosamente
minuteman [ˈmɪnɪtˌmæn] *s* (*pl:* **-men**) (U.S.A.) miliciano de la Revolución
minuteness [maɪˈnjutnɪs] o [maɪˈnutnɪs] *s* menudencia, minuciosidad
minutiae [mɪˈnjuʃɪi] o [mɪˈnuʃɪi] *spl* minucias, detalles minuciosos
minx [mɪŋks] *s* moza descarada, coqueta
Miocene [ˈmaɪosin] *adj & s* (geol.) mioceno
miquelet [ˈmɪkəlɛt] *s* miquelete
miracle [ˈmɪrəkəl] *s* milagro; dechado (*p.ej., de paciencia*); (theat.) auto, milagro
miracle play *s* auto, milagro
miraculous [mɪˈrækjələs] *adj* milagroso
mirage [mɪˈrɑʒ] *s* (opt. & fig.) espejismo, miraje
mire [maɪr] *s* lodo, lodazal; *va* enlodar; dar con (*p.ej., caballos*) en un atolladero; *vn* atollarse, atascarse
mirk [mʌrk] *s* var. de **murk**
mirky [ˈmʌrkɪ] *adj* (*comp:* **-ier**; *super:* **-iest**) var. de **murky**
mirror [ˈmɪrər] *s* espejo; (aut.) retrovisor; *va* reflejar
mirth [mʌrθ] *s* alegría, regocijo, risa, hilaridad
mirthful [ˈmʌrθfəl] *adj* alegre, regocijado, reidor
mirthless [ˈmʌrθlɪs] *adj* abatido, triste, tétrico
miry [ˈmaɪrɪ] *adj* (*comp:* **-ier**; *super:* **-iest**) lodoso; pantanoso; sucio
misadventure [ˌmɪsədˈvɛntʃər] *s* desgracia, contratiempo
misalignment [ˌmɪsəˈlaɪnmənt] *s* desalineamiento
misalliance [ˌmɪsəˈlaɪəns] *s* alianza mal hecha; matrimonio con una persona de clase inferior
misanthrope [ˈmɪsənθrop] *s* misántropo

misanthropic [ˌmɪsənˈθrɑpɪk] *adj* misantrópico
misanthropist [mɪsˈænθrəpɪst] *s* var. de **misanthrope**
misanthropy [mɪsˈænθrəpɪ] *s* misantropía
misapplication [ˌmɪsæplɪˈkeʃən] *s* aplicación errada; mal uso
misapply [ˌmɪsəˈplaɪ] (*pret & pp:* **-plied**) *va* aplicar mal; hacer mal uso de
misapprehend [ˌmɪsæprɪˈhɛnd] *va* entender mal
misapprehension [ˌmɪsæprɪˈhɛnʃən] *s* equivocación; mala inteligencia
misappropriate [ˌmɪsəˈproprɪet] *va* malversar; hacer mal uso de
misappropriation [ˌmɪsəˌproprɪˈeʃən] *s* malversación; mal uso
misbecome [ˌmɪsbɪˈkʌm] (*pret:* **-came;** *pp:* **-come**) *va* no convenir a, no ser propio de, ser indigno de
misbegotten [ˌmɪsbɪˈgɑtən] *adj* bastardo
misbehave [ˌmɪsbɪˈhev] *vn* conducirse mal, portarse mal
misbehavior [ˌmɪsbɪˈhevjər] *s* mala conducta, mal comportamiento
misbelief [ˌmɪsbɪˈlif] *s* error, opinión errónea; creencia heterodoxa
misbelieve [ˌmɪsbɪˈliv] *va* dudar, no creer; *vn* estar en error, tener opiniones erróneas; tener creencias heterodoxas
misbeliever [ˌmɪsbɪˈlivər] *s* persona equivocada; heterodoxo
misbrand [mɪsˈbrænd] *va* herrar falsamente; marcar falsamente
misc. abr. de **miscellaneous** y **miscellany**
miscalculate [mɪsˈkælkjəlet] *va & vn* calcular mal
miscalculation [ˌmɪskælkjəˈleʃən] *s* cálculo errado; desacierto
miscall [mɪsˈkɔl] *va* errar el nombre de
miscarriage [mɪsˈkærɪdʒ] *s* aborto, malparto; fracaso, malogro; extravío (*p.ej., de una carta*)
miscarry [mɪsˈkærɪ] (*pret & pp:* **-ried**) *vn* salir mal, malograrse; extraviarse (*p.ej., una carta*); abortar
miscegenation [ˌmɪsɪdʒɪˈneʃən] *s* miscegenación
miscellaneous [ˌmɪsəˈlenɪəs] *adj* misceláneo
miscellany [ˈmɪsəˌlenɪ] *s* (*pl:* **-nies**) miscelánea (*mezcla; obra*); **miscellanies** *spl* miscelánea (*obra*)
mischance [mɪsˈtʃæns] o [mɪsˈtʃɑns] *s* desgracia, infortunio, mala suerte
mischief [ˈmɪstʃɪf] *s* daño, mal; diablura; travesura; malicia; diablillo, persona traviesa
mischief-maker [ˈmɪstʃɪfˌmekər] *s* camorrista, cizañador
mischievous [ˈmɪstʃɪvəs] *adj* dañoso, malo; travieso; malicioso; enredador
miscible [ˈmɪsɪbəl] *adj* miscible
misconceive [ˌmɪskənˈsiv] *va & vn* entender mal
misconception [ˌmɪskənˈsɛpʃən] *s* concepto erróneo; mala interpretación
misconduct [mɪsˈkɑndʌkt] *s* mala conducta; desorden, desbarajuste; [ˌmɪskənˈdʌkt] *va* administrar mal; **to misconduct oneself** conducirse mal, portarse mal
misconstruction [ˌmɪskənˈstrʌkʃən] *s* mala interpretación
misconstrue [ˌmɪskənˈstru] o [mɪsˈkɑnstru] *va* interpretar mal
miscount [mɪsˈkaunt] *s* cuenta errónea; *va & vn* contar mal
miscreant [ˈmɪskrɪənt] *adj* vil, ruin; (archaic) hereje; *s* pillo, sinvergüenza; (archaic) hereje
miscreated [ˌmɪskriˈetɪd] *adj* contrahecho, mal formado
miscue [mɪsˈkju] *s* (billiards) pifia; (coll.) pifia, descuido; *vn* (billiards) pifiar; (theat.) equivocarse de apunte
misdate [mɪsˈdet] *s* fecha falsa o equivocada; *va* fechar falsa o equivocadamente
misdeal [ˈmɪsˌdil] *s* repartición errónea (*de naipes*); [mɪsˈdil] (*pret & pp:* **-dealt**) *va & vn* dar mal, repartir mal
misdeed [mɪsˈdid] o [ˈmɪsˌdid] *s* malhecho, infracción
misdemean [ˌmɪsdɪˈmin] *vn* portarse mal; (law) cometer un delito menor
misdemeanor [ˌmɪsdɪˈminər] *s* mala conducta; culpa; (law) delito de menor cuantía
misdid [mɪsˈdɪd] *pret de* **misdo**
misdirect [ˌmɪsdɪˈrɛkt] o [ˌmɪsdaɪˈrɛkt] *va* dirigir erradamente; extraviar, hacer perder el camino a
misdirection [ˌmɪsdɪˈrɛkʃən] o [ˌmɪsdaɪˈrɛkʃən] *s* mala dirección, instrucciones erradas
misdo [mɪsˈdu] (*pret* **-did;** *pp:* **-done**) *va* hacer mal
misdoing [mɪsˈduɪŋ] *s* maldad, perversidad
misdone [mɪsˈdʌn] *pp de* **misdo**
mise en scène [mizɑ̃ˈsɛn] *s* (Fr.) puesta en escena
misemploy [ˌmɪsɛmˈplɔɪ] *va* emplear mal
miser [ˈmaɪzər] *s* avaro, verrugo
miserable [ˈmɪzərəbəl] *adj* miserable; (coll.) indispuesto, en mala salud
Miserere [ˌmɪzəˈrɪrɪ] o [ˌmɪzəˈrɛrɪ] *s* (eccl. & mus.) miserere; (*l.c.*) *s* (arch.) misericordia, coma
misericord [ˌmɪzərɪˈkɔrd] o [mɪˈzɛrɪkɔrd] *s* misericordia (*puñal*); (arch.) misericordia, coma (*ménsula*); (eccl.) misericordia (*sala; dispensación*)
miserly [ˈmaɪzərlɪ] *adj* mísero, avariento
misery [ˈmɪzərɪ] *s* (*pl:* **-ies**) miseria; (dial.) dolor, sufrimiento
misfeasance [mɪsˈfizəns] *s* (law) acción mala; (law) abuso de autoridad, fraude
misfire [mɪsˈfaɪr] *s* falla de tiro; falla de encendido; mechazo; *vn* no dar fuego; fallar; dar mechazo
misfit [ˈmɪsˌfɪt] *s* vestido o traje mal cortados; cosa que no encaja bien o que no sienta bien; persona desequilibrada, persona reñida con su ambiente; [mɪsˈfɪt] (*pret & pp:* **-fitted;** *ger:* **-fitting**) *va* cortar mal; encajar mal, sentar mal; *vn* encajar mal, sentar mal
misfortune [mɪsˈfɔrtʃən] *s* desventura
misgive [mɪsˈgɪv] (*pret:* **-gave;** *pp:* **-given**) *va* hacer dudar o recelar, dar mala espina a; *vn* temer, recelar
misgiving [mɪsˈgɪvɪŋ] *s* duda, recelo, ansiedad
misgovern [mɪsˈgʌvərn] *va* desgobernar; administrar mal, manejar mal
misgovernment [mɪsˈgʌvərnmənt] *s* desgobierno; mala administración, mal manejo
misguide [mɪsˈgaɪd] *va* dirigir mal; aconsejar mal; descarriar
misguided [mɪsˈgaɪdɪd] *adj* errado, erróneo; mal aconsejado; descarriado
mishandle [mɪsˈhændəl] *va* manejar mal; maltratar
mishap [ˈmɪshæp] o [mɪsˈhæp] *s* accidente, percance
mishear [mɪsˈhɪr] (*pret & pp:* **-heard**) *va* oír mal
misinform [ˌmɪsɪnˈfɔrm] *va* informar mal, dar informes erróneos o falsos a
misinformation [ˌmɪsɪnfərˈmeʃən] *s* informes erróneos o falsos
misinterpret [ˌmɪsɪnˈtʌrprɪt] *va* interpretar mal
misinterpretation [ˌmɪsɪnˌtʌrprɪˈteʃən] *s* mala interpretación
misjudge [mɪsˈdʒʌdʒ] *va & vn* juzgar mal o injustamente
misjudgment o **misjudgement** [mɪsˈdʒʌdʒmənt] *s* juicio errado o injusto
mislay [mɪsˈle] (*pret & pp:* **-laid**) *va* colocar mal; extraviar, perder
mislead [mɪsˈlid] (*pret & pp:* **-led**) *va* extraviar; descarriar; engañar
misleading [mɪsˈlidɪŋ] *adj* engañoso; de falsas apariencias
mismanage [mɪsˈmænɪdʒ] *va* manejar mal, administrar mal
mismanagement [mɪsˈmænɪdʒmənt] *s* mal manejo, mala administración
mismatch [mɪsˈmætʃ] *s* unión o ayuntamiento mal hechos; casamiento desigual o mal hecho; *va* unir mal, emparejar mal, hermanar mal
mismate [mɪsˈmet] *va & vn* emparejar mal, hermanar mal; casar mal
misname [mɪsˈnem] *va* llamar por mal nombre, equivocar el nombre de
misnomer [mɪsˈnomər] *s* mal nombre, nombre inapropiado; nombre erróneo
misogamic [ˌmɪsoˈgæmɪk] *adj* misógamo

misogamist [mɪ'sɑgəmɪst] *s* misógamo
misogamy [mɪ'sɑgəmɪ] *s* misogamia
misogynist [mɪ'sɑdʒɪnɪst] *s* misógino
misogynous [mɪ'sɑdʒɪnəs] *adj* misógino
misogyny [mɪ'sɑdʒɪnɪ] *s* misoginia
misoneism [,mɪso'niɪzəm] *s* misoneísmo
misoneist [,mɪso'niɪst] *s* misoneísta
mispickel ['mɪs,pɪkəl] *s* (mineral.) mispíquel
misplace [mɪs'ples] *va* colocar mal o fuera de su lugar; (coll.) extraviar, perder; dar (*amor o confianza*) a quien no lo merece
misplacement [mɪs'plesmənt] *s* colocación de una cosa fuera de su lugar; extravío, pérdida
misplay [mɪs'ple] *s* mala jugada; *va & vn* jugar mal
misprint ['mɪs,prɪnt] *s* errata de imprenta; [mɪs'prɪnt] *va* imprimir mal, imprimir con erratas
misprision [mɪs'prɪʒən] *s* (law) delito (*especialmente de funcionario público*); (coll.) ocultación de un delito
misprize [mɪs'praɪz] *va* menospreciar; desestimar
mispronounce [,mɪsprə'naʊns] *va* pronunciar mal
mispronunciation [,mɪsprə,nʌnsɪ'eʃən] o [,mɪsprə,nʌnʃɪ'eʃən] *s* pronunciación errada o inexacta
misquotation [,mɪskwo'teʃən] *s* cita falsa o equivocada
misquote [mɪs'kwot] *va* citar falsa o equivocadamente
misread [mɪs'rid] (*pret & pp:* **-read** ['rɛd]) *va* leer mal; entender o interpretar mal
misrepresent [,mɪsrɛprɪ'zɛnt] *va* exponer o alegar falsamente; falsificar (*los hechos*); describir engañosamente
misrepresentation [,mɪsrɛprɪzɛn'teʃən] *s* exposición falsa; falsificación; descripción falsa
misrule [mɪs'rul] *s* confusión, desorden; desgobierno; *va* desgobernar
Miss. abr. de **Mississippi**
miss [mɪs] *s* falta; tiro errado; malogro, fracaso; muchacha, jovencita; (*cap.*) señorita; **a miss is as good as a mile** lo mismo da librarse por poco que por mucho; *va* echar de menos (*a una persona*); hacer falta, p.ej., **I have missed you very much** Vd. me ha hecho mucha falta; errar (*el blanco; la vocación*); perder (*el tren, la función, la oportunidad*); librarse de (*p.ej., la muerte*); no comprender, no entender; no ver; omitir; no dar con, no hallar; no encontrar; no lograr coger u obtener; escapársele a uno, p.ej., **I missed what you said** se me escapó lo que dijo Vd.; **to miss** + *ger* por poco + *ind*, p.ej., **the car just missed running over me** el coche por poco me atropella; *vn* errar el blanco; malograrse, no surtir efecto; fallar
missal ['mɪsəl] *s* (eccl.) misal
missel thrush ['mɪsəl] *s* (orn.) cagaaceite, charla
misshape [mɪs'ʃep] (*pret:* **-shaped;** *pp:* **-shaped** o **-shapen**) *va* deformar
misshapen [mɪs'ʃepən] *adj* deforme, contrahecho; *pp de* **misshape**
missile ['mɪsɪl] *adj* arrojadizo; *s* arma arrojadiza; proyectil
missileer [,mɪsɪl'ɪr] *s* var. de **missileman**
missile gap *s* inferioridad del proyectil, desventaja en el desarrollo del proyectil
missileman ['mɪsɪlmən] *s* (*pl:* **-men**) perito en materia de proyectiles dirigidos
missilery ['mɪsɪlrɪ] *s* ciencia de los proyectiles dirigidos
missing ['mɪsɪŋ] *adj* desaparecido; ausente; **to be missing** faltar, hacer falta; haber desaparecido
missing link *s* eslabón perdido, hombre mono
missing persons *spl* desaparecidos
mission ['mɪʃən] *s* misión; casa de misión; **missions** *spl* misiones, propagación de la fe
missionary ['mɪʃən,ɛrɪ] *adj* misional; misionero (*p.ej., espíritu*); *s* (*pl:* **-ies**) misionario; propagandista; (eccl.) misionario o misionero
mission furniture *s* muebles al estilo de las misiones californianas (*pesados y de roble ahumado*)
missis o **missus** ['mɪsɪz] *s* (coll.) esposa, mujer; (coll.) ama de casa
missish ['mɪsɪʃ] *adj* relamido, remilgado
Mississippi [,mɪsɪ'sɪpɪ] *s* Misisipí (*río y estado*)
missive ['mɪsɪv] *adj* misivo; *s* misiva
Missouri [mɪ'zʊrɪ] o [mɪ'zʊrə] *s* Misurí (*río y estado*); **from Missouri** (slang) escéptico, difícil de engañar
misspeak [mɪs'spik] (*pret:* **-spoke;** *pp:* **-spoken**) *va* decir, pronunciar o hablar mal o erróneamente
misspell [mɪs'spɛl] (*pret & pp:* **-spelled** o **-spelt**) *va & vn* deletrear o escribir mal
misspelling [mɪs'spɛlɪŋ] *s* falta de ortografía
misspend [mɪs'spɛnd] (*pret & pp:* **-spent**) *va* malgastar, desbaratar
misspent [mɪs'spɛnt] *adj* malgastado, desbaratado; *pret & pp de* **misspend**
misspoke [mɪs'spok] *pret de* **misspeak**
misspoken [mɪs'spokən] *pp de* **misspeak**
misstate [mɪs'stet] *va* relatar mal o falsamente
misstatement [mɪs'stetmənt] *s* relato inexacto o falso
misstep [mɪs'stɛp] *s* paso falso; resbalón (*en un delito o culpa*)
missy ['mɪsɪ] *s* (*pl:* **-ies**) (coll.) señorita, hija mía
mist [mɪst] *s* niebla, neblina; llovizna; velo (*p.ej., de lágrimas*); *va* empañar, velar; *vn* lloviznar; empañarse, velarse
mistakable [mɪs'tekəbəl] *adj* confundible, equívoco
mistake [mɪs'tek] *s* error, equivocación; culpa; decisión poco acertada; **and no mistake** sin duda alguna; **by mistake** por descuido; **to make a mistake** equivocarse; (*pret:* **-took;** *pp:* **-taken**) *va* entender mal, interpretar mal; confundir; tomar (*por otro; por lo que no es*); **to be mistaken for** equivocarse con; *vn* errar, equivocarse
mistaken [mɪs'tekən] *adj* errado, erróneo; equivocado; desacertado; *pp de* **mistake**
mistaken identity *s* identificación equivocada
mistakenly [mɪs'tekənlɪ] *adv* por error, equivocadamente
mister ['mɪstər] *s* señor; (*cap.*) *s* señor (*tratamiento de cortesía*); (*l.c.*) *va* (coll.) dar tratamiento de señor a
mistime [mɪs'taɪm] *va* hacer o decir a deshora; equivocarse al decir la hora, el día, el año, etc. de; cronometrar mal
mistimed [mɪs'taɪmd] *adj* inoportuno, intempestivo
mistletoe ['mɪsəlto] *s* (bot.) muérdago (*Viscum album*); (bot.) cabellera, visco (*Phoradendron*); (bot.) loranto
mistook [mɪs'tʊk] *pret de* **mistake**
mistral ['mɪstrəl] o [mɪs'trɑl] *s* mistral (*viento*)
mistranslate [,mɪstræns'let] o [mɪs'trænslet] *va* traducir mal o erróneamente
mistranslation [,mɪstræns'leʃən] *s* traducción errónea
mistreat [mɪs'trit] *va* maltratar
mistreatment [mɪs'tritmənt] *s* maltratamiento, malos tratos
mistress ['mɪstrɪs] *s* ama de casa; señora; perita; maestra de escuela; moza, querida, manceba; (archaic) amada; (archaic & dial.) señora, señorita (*tratamiento de cortesía*); (fig.) señora (*país que gobierna, p.ej., los mares*); (*cap.*) ['mɪsɪz] *s* señora (*tratamiento de cortesía que se da a una mujer casada*)
Mistress of the Seas *s* señora de los mares (*Inglaterra*)
mistrial [mɪs'traɪəl] *s* (law) pleito o juicio viciado de nulidad
mistrust [mɪs'trʌst] *s* desconfianza; *va* desconfiar de; *vn* desconfiar
mistrustful [mɪs'trʌstfəl] *adj* desconfiado
misty ['mɪstɪ] *adj* (*comp:* **-ier;** *super:* **-iest**) brumoso, nebuloso, neblinoso; empañado; vago, indistinto
misunderstand [,mɪsʌndər'stænd] (*pret & pp:* **-stood**) *va & vn* entender mal, no comprender
misunderstanding [,mɪsʌndər'stændɪŋ] *s* malentendido; desavenencia
misunderstood [,mɪsʌndər'stud] *adj* no bien comprendido; insuficientemente apreciado o estimado; *pret & pp de* **misunderstand**

misusage [mɪsˈjusɪdʒ] o [mɪsˈjuzɪdʒ] *s* mal uso, mal empleo; maltratamiento
misuse [mɪsˈjus] *s* mal uso, mal empleo; uso erróneo o impropio; [mɪsˈjuz] *va* emplear mal; maltratar
misword [mɪsˈwʌrd] *va* expresar mal, expresar con palabras impropias
mite [maɪt] *s* pizca; óbolo; (zool.) mita, garrapata
miter [ˈmaɪtər] *s* mitra (*p.ej., de obispo; cargo o dignidad de obispo*); (carp.) inglete; (carp.) junta a inglete, ensambladura de inglete; *va* conferir una mitra a, elevar al obispado; (carp.) cortar ingletes en; (carp.) juntar con junta a inglete
miter box *s* (carp.) caja de ingletes, caja de cortar al sesgo
mitered [ˈmaɪtərd] *adj* mitrado; (carp.) con junta o juntas a inglete
miter joint *s* (carp.) junta a inglete, ensambladura de inglete
miter sill *s* busco, batiente de esclusa
Mithras [ˈmɪθræs] *s* (myth.) Mitra
Mithridates [ˌmɪθrɪˈdetiz] *s* Mitrídates
mitigate [ˈmɪtɪget] *va* mitigar; *vn* mitigarse
mitigation [ˌmɪtɪˈgeʃən] *s* mitigación
mitigative [ˈmɪtɪˌgetɪv] *adj* mitigativo
mitigator [ˈmɪtɪˌgetər] *s* mitigador
mitosis [mɪˈtosɪs] *s* (biol.) mitosis
mitotic [mɪˈtɑtɪk] *adj* mitósico
mitral [ˈmaɪtrəl] *adj* mitral; (anat.) mitral
mitral cell *s* (anat.) célula mitral
mitral insufficiency *s* (path.) insuficiencia mitral
mitral valve *s* (anat.) válvula mitral
mitre [ˈmaɪtər] *s & va* var. de **miter**
mitt [mɪt] *s* mitón (*guante que deja los dedos al descubierto*); guante con sólo el pulgar separado; guante de béisbol
mitten [ˈmɪtən] *s* guante con sólo el pulgar separado; **mittens** *spl* (slang) guantes de boxeo; **to get the mitten** recibir calabazas; **to give the mitten to** dar calabazas a
mix [mɪks] *s* mezcla; (coll.) embrollo, enredo, lío; *va* mezclar; hacer o confeccionar (*hormigón*); amasar (*una torta, un bollo*); aderezar (*ensalada*); confeccionar mezclando; **to get mixed up in** mojar en; **to get mixed with** tener que ver con; **to mix up** equivocar (*confundir completamente*); *vn* mezclarse; asociarse; granjearse amigos; entrecruzarse
mixed [mɪkst] *adj* mixto; mezclado; variados (*p.ej., bombones*); (coll.) confundido
mixed chorus *s* coro mixto
mixed company *s* reunión de personas de ambos sexos
mixed drinks *spl* bebidas mezcladas
mixed feeling *s* concepto vacilante
mixed-flow turbine [ˈmɪkstˌflo] *s* turbina mixta
mixed marriage *s* matrimonio mixto (*es decir, entre personas de distintas razas o religiones*)
mixed metaphore *s* metáfora incoherente
mixed number *s* (math.) número mixto
mixed train *s* (rail.) tren mixto
mixer [ˈmɪksər] *s* mezclador; mezcladora, hormigonera; persona sociable; **to be a good mixer** tener don de gentes
mixtilineal [ˌmɪkstɪˈlɪnɪəl] *adj* mixtilíneo
mixture [ˈmɪkstʃər] *s* mixtura
mix-up [ˈmɪksˌʌp] *s* (coll.) bullaje, bullanga; (coll.) lío, enredo; (coll.) equívoco
mizzen [ˈmɪzən] *s* (naut.) mesana (*vela; mástil*)
mizzenmast [ˈmɪzənməst], [ˈmɪzənˌmæst] o [ˈmɪzənˌmɑst] *s* (naut.) palo de mesana
mm. abr. de **millimeter** o **millimeters**
mnemonic [niˈmɑnɪk] *adj* mnemónico; **mnemonics** *ssg* mnemónica; *spl* figuras o caracteres mnemónicos
Mnemosyne [niˈmɑsɪni] *s* (myth.) Mnemosina o Mnemósine
mnemotechnics [ˌnimoˈtɛknɪks] *ssg* mnemotécnica
mnemotechny [ˈnimoˌtɛknɪ] *s* mnemotecnia
mo. abr. de **month** o **months**
Mo. abr. de **Missouri**
M.O. o **m.o.** abr. de **money order**
Moabite [ˈmoəbaɪt] *adj & s* moabita
moan [mon] *s* gemido; *va* expresar con gemidos; *vn* gemir
moat [mot] *s* (fort.) foso; *va* fosar
mob [mɑb] *s* gentío, muchedumbre; chusma, populacho; muchedumbre airada; (*pret & pp:* **mobbed;** *ger:* **mobbing**) *va* atropellar, asaltar, apoderarse de
mobcap [ˈmɑbˌkæp] *s* toca de mujer
mobile [ˈmobɪl] o [ˈmobil] *adj* móvil
mobile unit *s* (rad.) unidad móvil
mobility [moˈbɪlɪtɪ] *s* movilidad
mobilization [ˌmobɪlɪˈzeʃən] *s* movilización
mobilize [ˈmobɪlaɪz] *va* movilizar; *vn* movilizar o movilizarse
mobster [ˈmɑbstər] *s* (slang) bandido, malhechor
moccasin [ˈmɑkəsɪn] *s* mocasín o mocasina; (zool.) mocasín, víbora de agua
moccasin flower *s* (bot.) zapatilla de señorita
Mocha [ˈmokə] *s* moca, café de moca; piel de Moka (*que se usa para guantes*)
mock [mɑk] *s* burla, mofa, escarnio; hazmerreír; cosa despreciable; *adj* falso, fingido, simulado; *va* burlarse de, mofarse de, escarnecer; remedar; despreciar, hacer poco caso de; engañar, decepcionar; *vn* mofarse; **to mock at** mofarse de
mock cypress *s* (bot.) ayuga, mirabel
mockery [ˈmɑkərɪ] *s* (*pl:* **-ies**) burla, mofa, escarnio; hazmerreír; mal remedo; desprecio, negación (*p.ej., de la justicia*)
mock-heroic [ˌmɑkhɪˈro·ɪk] *adj* heroicocómico; *s* obra heroicocómica
mockingbird [ˈmɑkɪŋˌbʌrd] *s* (orn.) burlón, sinsonte
mock moon *s* (meteor.) paraselene
mock orange *s* (bot.) jeringuilla, celinda
mock privet *s* (bot.) olivillo
mock turtle soup *s* sopa de cabeza de ternera (*a imitación de la de tortuga*)
mock-up [ˈmɑkˌʌp] *s* maqueta, modelo (*generalmente en tamaño natural*)
modal [ˈmodəl] *adj* modal
modal auxiliary *s* (gram.) auxiliar modal
modality [moˈdælɪtɪ] *s* modalidad
mode [mod] *s* modo, manera; moda; (gram. & mus.) modo
model [ˈmɑdəl] *s* modelo; *adj* modelo, p.ej., **model city** ciudad modelo; (*pret & pp:* **-eled** o **-elled;** *ger:* **-eling** o **-elling**) *va* modelar; **to model after** planear según, construir a imitación de; *vn* modelar; modelarse; servir de modelo
model airplane *s* aeromodelo
model airplane builder *s* aeromodelista
model airplane building *s* aeromodelismo
modeling o **modelling** [ˈmɑdəlɪŋ] *s* modelado
model sailing *s* navegación de modelos a vela
moderate [ˈmɑdərɪt] *adj & s* moderado; [ˈmɑdəret] *va* moderar; *vn* moderarse
moderate breeze *s* (naut.) viento bonancible
moderate gale *s* (naut.) viento frescachón
moderately [ˈmɑdərɪtlɪ] *adv* moderadamente
moderation [ˌmɑdəˈreʃən] *s* moderación; **in moderation** con moderación
moderator [ˈmɑdəˌretər] *s* moderador; árbitro; presidente (*de una asamblea*); (mach., phys. & chem.) moderador
modern [ˈmɑdərn] *adj & s* moderno
Modern English *s* el inglés moderno
modern history *s* la historia moderna
modernism [ˈmɑdərnɪzəm] *s* modernismo; neologismo
modernist [ˈmɑdərnɪst] *adj* modernista; *s* modernista; neólogo
modernistic [ˌmɑdərˈnɪstɪk] *adj* modernista
modernity [moˈdʌrnɪtɪ] *s* (*pl:* **-ties**) modernidad; cosa moderna
modernization [ˌmɑdərnɪˈzeʃən] *s* modernización
modernize [ˈmɑdərnaɪz] *va* modernizar; *vn* modernizarse
modern languages *spl* lenguas modernas, lenguas vivas
Modern Spanish *s* el español moderno
modest [ˈmɑdɪst] *adj* modesto; moderado; sencillo
modestly [ˈmɑdɪstlɪ] *adv* modestamente
modesty [ˈmɑdɪstɪ] *s* (*pl:* **-ties**) modestia
modicum [ˈmɑdɪkəm] *s* cantidad módica
modifiable [ˈmɑdɪˌfaɪəbəl] *adj* modificable
modification [ˌmɑdɪfɪˈkeʃən] *s* modificación

modifier ['mɑdɪ,faɪər] *s* modificador; (gram.) modificante
modify ['mɑdɪfaɪ] (*pret & pp:* **-fied**) *va* modificar; *vn* modificarse
modillion [mo'dɪljən] *s* (arch.) modillón
modish ['modɪʃ] *adj* de moda, elegante
modiste [mo'dist] *s* modista
modular ['mɑdʒələr] *adj* modular
modulate ['mɑdʒəlet] *va & vn* modular
modulation [,mɑdʒə'leʃən] *s* modulación
modulator ['mɑdʒə,letər] *s* modulador; (rad.) modulador
module ['mɑdʒul] *s* módulo (*de una medalla o moneda*); (arch., hyd. & mach.) módulo
modulus ['mɑdʒələs] *s* (*pl:* **-li** [laɪ]) módulo (*norma*); (phys.) módulo
modus ['modəs] *s* (*pl:* **-di** [daɪ]) *s* modo
modus operandi [,ɑpə'rændaɪ] *s* modo de proceder
modus vivendi [vɪ'vɛndaɪ] *s* modo de vivir; convenio provisional
mofette [mo'fɛt] *s* mofeta (*de las minas o de la actividad volcánica*)
mogul [mo'gʌl] o ['mogʌl] *s* magnate; locomotora mogol; (*cap.*) *s* mogol
mohair ['mohɛr] *s* moer o mohair
Mohammed [mo'hæmɪd] *s* Mahoma
Mohammedan [mo'hæmɪdən] *adj & s* mahometano
Mohammedanism [mo'hæmɪdənɪzəm] *s* mahometismo
Mohammedanize [mo'hæmɪdənaɪz] *va* mahometizar
Mohican [mo'hikən] *adj & s* mohicano
moiety ['mɔɪətɪ] *s* (*pl:* **-ties**) mitad; parte, porción
moil [mɔɪl] *s* afán, trabajo penoso; confusión, alboroto; *vn* afanarse, trabajar sin descanso
moire [mwɑr] *s* muaré
moiré [mwɑ're] o [mo're] *adj & s* muaré
moist [mɔɪst] *adj* húmedo; mojado
moisten ['mɔɪsən] *va* humedecer, mojar; *vn* humedecerse, mojarse
moistener ['mɔɪsənər] *s* mojador (*persona; tacita con agua para mojar sellos o para mojarse la punta de los dedos*); humectador (*para humedecer los efectos engomados*)
moisture ['mɔɪstʃər] *s* humedad
mol [mol] *s* (chem.) mol
molal ['moləl] *adj* (chem.) molal
molar ['molər] *adj* (anat., phys. & path.) molar; *s* (anat.) molar, diente molar
molasses [mə'læsɪz] *s* melaza
molasses candy *s* melcocha
molasses grass *s* (bot.) zacategordura
mold [mold] *s* molde; cosa moldeada; forma (*dada por el molde*); carácter, índole; mantillo (*tierra vegetal*); (bot.) moho; (archaic) tierra; *va* moldear; enmohecer; **to mold oneself on** amoldarse por; *vn* enmohecerse
Moldavian [mɑl'devɪən] *adj & s* moldavo
moldboard ['mold,bord] *s* vertedera u orejera (*del arado*)
molder ['moldər] *s* moldeador; *va* convertir en polvo, consumir; *vn* convertirse en polvo, consumirse
molding ['moldɪŋ] *s* moldeado; vaciado; moldura; (elec.) cajetín
molding board *s* tabla para amasar pan
molding cutter *s* cuchilla de moldurar
molding machine *s* (carp.) moldeador; (fund.) moldeadora
molding sand *s* arena de molde, arena de fundición
mold loft *s* (naut.) sala de gálibos
moldy ['moldɪ] *adj* (*comp:* **-ier**; *super:* **-iest**) mohoso; rancio, pasado
mole [mol] *s* rompeolas; dársena; lunar; (path.) mola; (zool.) topo; (hist.) mola (*harina de cebada usada en los sacrificios*)
mole cricket *s* (ent.) cortón, alacrán cebollero
molecular [mə'lɛkjələr] *adj* molecular
molecular weight *s* (phys.) peso molecular
molecule ['mɑlɪkjul] *s* (chem. & phys.) molécula
molehill ['mol,hɪl] *s* topinera o topera; (fig.) pamplina, cosa de poca monta
moleskin ['mol,skɪn] *s* piel de topo; molesquina; **moleskins** *spl* pantalones de molesquina
molest [mo'lɛst] *va* molestar, incomodar; faltar al respeto a (*una mujer*)
molestation [,molɛs'teʃən] o [,mɑləs'teʃən] *s* molestia, vejación
moll [mɑl] *s* (slang) golfa, ladrona; (slang) ramera; (slang) manceba de gángster
mollification [,mɑlɪfɪ'keʃən] *s* apaciguamiento, mitigación
mollify ['mɑlɪfaɪ] (*pret & pp:* **-fied**) *va* apaciguar, mitigar
mollusc o **mollusk** ['mɑləsk] *s* (zool.) molusco
Molly ['mɑlɪ] *s* Mariquita
mollycoddle ['mɑlɪ,kɑdəl] *s* mantecón, marica; *va* mimar, consentir
Moloch ['molɑk] *s* (Bib.) Moloc; (*l.c.*) *s* (zool.) moloc, diablo punzante
molt [molt] *s* muda (*de pluma o pellejo*); *va* mudar (*la pluma, el pellejo*); *vn* mudar la pluma, mudar el pellejo
molten ['moltən] *adj* derretido; fundido, vaciado
mol. wt. abr. de **molecular weight**
moly ['molɪ] *s* (*pl:* **-lies**) (myth.) hierba moli; (bot.) ajo silvestre (*Allium moly*)
molybdate [mo'lɪbdet] *s* (chem.) molibdato
molybdenite [mo'lɪbdɪnaɪt] o [,mɑlɪb'dinaɪt] *s* (mineral.) molibdenita
molybdenous [mo'lɪbdɪnəs] o [,mɑlɪb'dinəs] *adj* (chem.) molibdenoso
molybdenum [mo'lɪbdɪnəm] o [,mɑlɪb'dinəm] *s* (chem.) molibdeno
molybdenum steel *s* acero al molibdeno
molybdic [mo'lɪbdɪk] *adj* (chem.) molíbdico
moment ['momənt] *s* momento; (mech.) momento; **at any moment** de un momento a otro; **for the moment** por ahora, por lo presente; **in a moment** en un momento
momentarily ['momən,tɛrɪlɪ] *adv* momentáneamente; de un momento a otro
momentary ['momən,tɛrɪ] *adj* momentáneo
momently ['momәntlɪ] *adv* a cada momento; de un momento a otro; momentáneamente
moment of inertia *s* (mech.) momento de inercia
momentous [mo'mɛntəs] *adj* grave, trascendental
momentously [mo'mɛntəslɪ] *adv* gravemente, grandemente
momentum [mo'mɛntəm] *s* (*pl:* **-tums** o **-ta** [tə]) ímpetu; (mech.) cantidad de movimiento
Momus ['moməs] *s* (myth.) Momo; criticón, reparón
Mon. abr. de **Monday**
monachal ['mɑnəkəl] *adj* monacal
monachism ['mɑnəkɪzəm] *s* monaquismo
monad ['mɑnæd] o ['monæd] *s* (biol., chem., philos. & zool.) mónada
monadelphous [,mɑnə'dɛlfəs] *adj* (bot.) monadélfico
monadism ['mɑnədɪzəm] o ['monədɪzəm] *s* (philos.) monadismo
monandrous [mo'nændrəs] *adj* monándrico; (bot.) manandro
monandry [mo'nændrɪ] *s* monandria; (bot.) monandria
monarch ['mɑnərk] *s* monarca; (ent.) mariposa (*Danaus menippe*)
monarchal [mə'nɑrkəl] *adj* monárquico
monarchial [mə'nɑrkɪəl], **monarchic** [mə'nɑrkɪk] o **monarchical** [mə'nɑrkɪkəl] *adj* monárquico; monarquista
monarchism ['mɑnərkɪzəm] *s* monarquismo
monarchist ['mɑnərkɪst] *adj & s* monarquista
monarchistic [,mɑnər'kɪstɪk] *adj* monarquista
monarchy ['mɑnərkɪ] *s* (*pl:* **-chies**) monarquía
monasterial [,mɑnəs'tɪrɪəl] *adj* monasterial
monastery ['mɑnəs,tɛrɪ] *s* (*pl:* **-ies**) monasterio
monastic [mə'næstɪk] *adj* monástico; *s* monje
monastical [mə'næstɪkəl] *adj* monástico
monasticism [mə'næstɪsɪzəm] *s* monacato, monaquismo
monazite ['mɑnəzaɪt] *s* (mineral.) monacita
Monday ['mʌndɪ] *s* lunes
monecious [mo'niʃəs] *adj* var. de **monoecious**
Monegasque [,mɑnə'gɑsk] *adj & s* monegasco
Monel metal [mo'nɛl] *s* (trademark) metal monel

monetary ['mɑnɪ,tɛrɪ] o ['mʌnɪ,tɛrɪ] *adj* monetario; pecuniario
monetization [,mɑnɪtɪ'zeʃən] o [,mʌnɪtɪ'zeʃən] *s* monetización
monetize ['mɑnɪtaɪz] o ['mʌnɪtaɪz] *va* monetizar
money ['mʌnɪ] *s* dinero; **to make money** ganar dinero; dar dinero (*una empresa*); **your money or your life** la bolsa o la vida
moneybag ['mʌnɪ,bæg] *s* monedero, talega para dinero; **moneybags** *spl* (coll.) talegas (*riquezas*); *ssg* (coll.) tacaño, ricacho
money belt *s* faja para llevar moneda
money broker *s* numulario, cambista
moneychanger ['mʌnɪ,tʃendʒər] *s* cambista
moneyed ['mʌnɪd] *adj* adinerado, dineroso
moneyer ['mʌnɪər] *s* monedero
moneylender ['mʌnɪ,lɛndər] *s* prestamista
money-maker ['mʌnɪ,mekər] *s* acaudalador; manantial de beneficios
money of account *s* moneda imaginaria
money order *s* giro postal
money's worth *s* valor; **to get one's money's worth out of** sacar el valor de
moneywort ['mʌnɪ,wʌrt] *s* (bot.) hierba de la moneda
monger ['mʌŋgər] *s* tratante, traficante
Mongol ['mɑŋgɑl] o ['mɑŋgəl] *adj & s* mogol
Mongolia [mɑŋ'golɪə] *s* la Mogolia
Mongolian [mɑŋ'golɪən] *adj & s* mogol
Mongolian idiocy *s* idiotez mogólica
Mongolian pheasant *s* (orn.) faisán de Mogolia
Mongolism ['mɑŋgəlɪzəm] *s* mogolismo
Mongoloid ['mɑŋgəlɔɪd] *adj & s* mogoloide
mongoose o **mongoos** ['mɑŋgus] *s* (*pl:* **-gooses**) (zool.) mangosta
mongrel ['mʌŋgrəl] o ['mɑŋgrəl] *adj* mestizo; *s* mestizo; perro mestizo, perro cruzado
moniker ['mɑnɪkər] *s* signo de identificación de un vagabundo; (slang) apodo
moniliform [mo'nɪlɪfɔrm] *adj* moniliforme; (bot. & zool.) moniliforme
monism ['mɑnɪzəm] o ['monɪzəm] *s* (philos.) monismo
monist ['mɑnɪst] o ['monɪst] *adj & s* monista
monistic [mo'nɪstɪk] *adj* monista
monition [mo'nɪʃən] *s* admonición
monitor ['mɑnɪtər] *s* monitor; (hyd., naut. & rad.) monitor; (zool.) varano; *va* (rad.) controlar (*la señal*); (rad.) escuchar (*radiotransmisiones*)
monitorial [,mɑnɪ'torɪəl] *adj* monitorio
monitorship ['mɑnɪtər,ʃɪp] *s* cargo de monitor
monitory ['mɑnɪ,torɪ] *adj* monitorio; *s* (*pl:* **-ries**) monitorio
monk [mʌŋk] *s* monje
monkey ['mʌŋkɪ] *s* (zool.) mono; (zool.) mono pequeño (*con cola*); (fig.) mono (*persona que hace gestos monescos*); (fig.) mona (*persona que imita a las demás*); **to make a monkey of** tomar el pelo a; *va* imitar, remedar; mofarse de; *vn* tontear, hacer payasadas; **to monkey around** haraganear; **to monkey with** manosear, ajar
monkey business *s* (slang) conducta estrafalaria, tretas, trampas
monkey chatter *s* (rad.) mezcla de señales
monkey flower *s* (bot.) mímulo; (bot.) linaria
monkey jacket *s* capote de piloto; (slang) smoking
monkey puzzle *s* (bot.) pehuén, pino araucano
monkeyshine ['mʌŋkɪ,ʃaɪn] *s* (slang) monada, diablura, payasada
monkey wrench *s* llave inglesa; **to throw a monkey wrench into the works** (coll.) hacer fracasar el proyecto, echarlo todo a rodar
monkhood ['mʌŋkhud] *s* monacato; frailería, los monjes
monkish ['mʌŋkɪʃ] *adj* frailengo; (scornful) frailuno
monk seal *s* (zool.) foca fraile
monkshood ['mʌŋks,hud] *s* (bot.) cogulla de fraile, napelo
monoatomic [,mɑnoə'tɑmɪk] *adj* monoatómico
monobasic [,mɑnə'besɪk] *adj* (chem.) monobásico
monocarpellary [,mɑnə'kɑrpə,lɛrɪ] *adj* (bot.) monocarpelar
Monoceros [mə'nɑsərəs] *s* (astr.) Monócero
monocerous [mə'nɑsərəs] *adj* monócero
monochord ['mɑnəkɔrd] *s* (mus.) monocordio; armonía, concordia
monochroic [,mɑnə'kro·ɪk] *adj* monocroico
monochromatic [,mɑnəkro'mætɪk] *adj* monocromático
monochrome ['mɑnəkrom] *adj & s* monocromo
monochromy ['mɑnə,kromɪ] *s* monocromía
monocle ['mɑnəkəl] *s* monóculo
monocled ['mɑnəkəld] *adj* con monóculo
monoclinic [,mɑnə'klɪnɪk] *adj* (cryst.) monoclínico
monocotyledon [,mɑnə,kɑtɪ'lidən] *s* (bot.) monocotiledón
monocular [mə'nɑkjələr] *adj* monocular; monóculo (*que tiene un solo ojo*)
monoculture [,mɑnə'kʌltʃər] *s* (agr.) monocultura
monoculus [mə'nɑkjələs] *s* (surg.) monóculo
monodic [mə'nɑdɪk] *adj* monódico
monody ['mɑnədɪ] *s* (*pl:* **-dies**) (mus.) monodia; elegía, canto fúnebre
monoecious [mo'niʃəs] *adj* (bot.) monoico
monogamic [,mɑnə'gæmɪk] *adj* monogámico
monogamist [mə'nɑgəmɪst] *adj & s* monógamo
monogamistic [mə,nɑgə'mɪstɪk] *adj* monogamista
monogamous [mə'nɑgəməs] *adj* monógamo
monogamy [mə'nɑgəmɪ] *s* monogamia; (zool.) monogamia
monogenism [mə'nɑdʒɪnɪzəm] *s* (anthrop.) monogenismo
monogenist [mə'nɑdʒɪnɪst] *s* monogenista
monogram ['mɑnəgræm] *s* monograma
monograph ['mɑnəgræf] o ['mɑnəgrɑf] *s* monografía
monographer [mə'nɑgrəfər] *s* monografista
monographic [,mɑnə'græfɪk] *adj* monográfico
monogynous [mə'nɑdʒɪnəs] *adj* (bot.) monógino
monolith ['mɑnəlɪθ] *s* monolito
monolithic [,mɑnə'lɪθɪk] *adj* monolítico
monolog ['mɑnəlɔg] o ['mɑnəlɑg] *s* var. de **monologue**
monologist ['mɑnə,lɔgɪst] o ['mɑnə,lɑgɪst] *s* var. de **monologuist**
monologue ['mɑnəlɔg] o ['mɑnəlɑg] *s* monólogo
monologuist ['mɑnə,lɔgɪst] o ['mɑnə,lɑgɪst] *s* monologuista; hablador que no deja meter baza a los demás
monomania [,mɑnə'menɪə] *s* monomanía
monomaniac [,mɑnə'menɪæk] *s* monomaníaco
monomaniacal [,mɑnəmə'naɪəkəl] *adj* monomaníaco
monometallic [,mɑnəmɪ'tælɪk] *adj* (chem.) monometálico; monometalista
monometallism [,mɑnə'mɛtəlɪzəm] *s* monometalismo
monometallist [,mɑnə'mɛtəlɪst] *adj & s* monometalista
monomial [mo'nomɪəl] *adj* (alg. & biol.) que consta de un solo término; *s* (alg.) monomio
monopetalous [,mɑnə'pɛtələs] *adj* (bot.) monopétalo
monophase ['mɑnəfez] *adj* (elec.) monofásico
monophonic [,mɑnə'fɑnɪk] *adj* monofónico
monophyllous [,mɑnə'fɪləs] *adj* (bot.) monofilo
Monophysite [mə'nɑfɪsaɪt] *s* (rel.) monofisita
monoplane ['mɑnəplen] *s* monoplano
monoplegia [,mɑnə'plidʒɪə] *s* (path.) monoplejía
monopolist [mə'nɑpəlɪst] *s* monopolista
monopolistic [mə,nɑpə'lɪstɪk] *adj* monopolizador
monopolization [mə,nɑpəlɪ'zeʃən] *s* monopolización
monopolize [mə'nɑpəlaɪz] *va* monopolizar; acaparar (*p.ej., la conversación*)
monopoly [mə'nɑpəlɪ] *s* (*pl:* **-lies**) monopolio
monopteral [mə'nɑptərəl] *adj* (arch.) monóptero

monorail ['mɑnərel] *s* monorriel; línea de monorriel
monorhymed ['mɑnəraɪmd] *adj* monorrimo
monosaccharide [ˌmɑnə'sækəraɪd] o [ˌmɑnə'sækərɪd] *s* (chem.) monosacárido
monosepalous [ˌmɑnə'sɛpələs] *adj* (bot.) monosépalo
monospermous [ˌmɑnə'spʌrməs] *adj* (bot.) monospermo
monostrophe [mə'nɑstrəfɪ] o ['mɑnəstrof] *s* monóstrofe
monosyllabic [ˌmɑnəsɪ'læbɪk] *adj* monosílabo (*de una sola sílaba*); monosilábico
monosyllable ['mɑnəˌsɪləbəl] *s* monosílabo
monotheism ['mɑnəˌθiɪzəm] *s* monoteísmo
monotheist ['mɑnəˌθiɪst] *adj & s* monoteísta
monotheistic [ˌmɑnəθi'ɪstɪk] *adj* monoteísta
monotone ['mɑnəton] *adj* monótono; *s* monotonía
monotonous [mə'nɑtənəs] *adj* monótono
monotony [mə'nɑtənɪ] *s* monotonía
monotreme ['mɑnətrim] *adj & s* (zool.) monotrema
monotype ['mɑnətaɪp] *s* (biol.) especie única; (trademark) monotipia; carácter de monotipia; *va* componer con monotipia
monotyper ['mɑnəˌtaɪpər] *s* monotipista
monovalent [ˌmɑnə'velənt] *adj* (chem. & bact.) monovalente
monoxide [mə'nɑksaɪd] *s* (chem.) monóxido
Monroe Doctrine [mən'ro] *s* doctrina de Monroe
Monroeism [mən'ro·ɪzəm] *s* monroísmo
monseigneur o **Monseigneur** [ˌmɑnsen'jœr] *s* (*pl:* **Messeigneurs** [ˌmɛsen'jœr]) monseñor
monsignor o **Monsignor** [mɑn'sinjər] *s* (*pl:* **Monsignors** o **Monsignori** [ˌmɔnsi'njori]) (eccl.) monseñor
monsoon [mɑn'sun] *s* monzón
monsoonal [mɑn'sunəl] *adj* monzónico
monster ['mɑnstər] *s* monstruo; *adj* monstruoso
monstrance ['mɑnstrəns] *s* (eccl.) custodia, ostensorio
monstrosity [mɑn'strɑsɪtɪ] *s* (*pl:* **-ties**) monstruosidad
monstrous ['mɑnstrəs] *adj* monstruoso; *adv* (coll.) monstruosamente
mons Veneris [mɑnz'vɛnərɪs] *s* (anat.) monte de Venus
Mont. abr. de **Montana**
montage [mɑn'tɑʒ] *s* montaje
montane ['mɑnten] *adj* montano
montan wax ['mɑntæn] *s* cera montana
Mont Blanc [mɑnt'blæŋk] *s* el monte Blanco
monte ['mɑntɪ] *s* monte (*juego de naipes*)
Montenegrin [ˌmɑntɪ'nigrɪn] *adj & s* montenegrino
month [mʌnθ] *s* mes
monthly ['mʌnθlɪ] *adj* mensual; *adv* mensualmente; *s* (*pl:* **-lies**) revista mensual; **monthlies** *spl* reglas
monument ['mɑnjəmənt] *s* monumento; mojón (*para fijar linderos*)
monumental [ˌmɑnjə'mɛntəl] *adj* monumental
moo [mu] *s* mugido (*de la vaca*); *vn* mugir (*la vaca*)
mooch [mutʃ] *va* (slang) robar; (slang) pedir de gorra; *vn* (slang) andar a sombra de tejado
mood [mud] *s* humor, genio; (gram.) modo; **moods** *spl* arranques de cólera, ataques de melancolía; **to be in a bad mood** estar de mal talante; **to be in a good mood** estar de buen talante; **to be in the mood to** + *inf* estar en disposición de + *inf*
moody ['mudɪ] *adj* (*comp:* **-ier**; *super:* **-iest**) caprichoso, veleidoso; caviloso; triste, hosco
moon [mun] *s* luna; **to bark** o **to bay at the moon** ladrar a la luna; *vn* estar viendo visiones, andar como alma en pena
moonbeam ['munˌbim] *s* rayo lunar
mooncalf ['munˌkæf] o ['munˌkɑf] *s* bobo, tonto, imbécil; (path.) mola (*tumor del útero*)
moon-faced ['munˌfest] *adj* mofletudo, carirredondo
moonlight ['munˌlaɪt] *s* claror de luna, luz de la luna; *adj* iluminado por la luna; de luz lunar
moonlighting ['munˌlaɪtɪŋ] *s* (coll.) multiempleo
moonlit ['munˌlɪt] *adj* iluminado por la luna
moonrise ['munˌraɪz] *s* salida de la luna
moonsail ['munˌsel] *s* (naut.) monterilla
moonshine ['munˌʃaɪn] *s* luz de la luna; cháchara, pamplinas; (coll.) licor destilado ilegalmente
moonshiner ['munˌʃaɪnər] *s* (coll.) fabricante de licor ilegal; (coll.) traficante nocturno ilegal
moon shot *s* lanzamiento a la Luna
moonstone ['munˌston] *s* (mineral.) piedra de la luna
moonstruck ['munˌstrʌk] *adj* aturdido; enloquecido
moonwort ['munˌwʌrt] *s* (bot.) botriquio, lunaria menor; (bot.) hierba de la plata
moony ['munɪ] *adj* (*comp:* **-ier**; *super:* **-iest**) lunar; lunado; alelado; desatento, indiferente
moor [mʊr] *s* brezal, páramo; (*cap.*) *s* moro; (*l.c.*) *va* (naut.) amarrar; *vn* (naut.) echar las amarras, echar las anclas
moorage ['mʊrɪdʒ] *s* (naut.) amarradura; (naut.) amarradero; (naut.) derechos de puerto
moor cock *s* (orn.) lagópedo de Escocia
moorfowl ['mʊrˌfaʊl] *s* (orn.) lagópedo de Escocia
moor hen *s* (orn.) hembra del lagópedo de Escocia; (orn.) polla
mooring ['mʊrɪŋ] *s* (naut.) amarradura; **moorings** *spl* (naut.) amarras; (naut.) amarradero
mooring mast *s* (aer.) antena o poste de amarre (*de un dirigible*)
Moorish ['mʊrɪʃ] *adj* moro
Moorish arch *s* (arch.) arco arábigo
moorland ['mʊrˌlænd] o ['mʊrlənd] *s* brezal
moose [mus] *s* (*pl:* **moose**) (zool.) alce de América
moot [mut] *adj* opinable, discutible; dudoso, indeciso; *s* junta, reunión; *va* discutir judicialmente; proponer para la discusión
moot court *s* (law) tribunal ad hoc (*en las escuelas de derecho*)
mop [mɑp] *s* mueca; espesura, cabellera espesa; aljofifa, estropajo; (*pret & pp:* **mopped**; *ger:* **mopping**) *va* aljofifar; enjugarse o secarse (*la frente con un pañuelo*); **to mop up** (mil.) acabar con (*el resto del enemigo*); (mil.) limpiar (*un terreno conquistado*) de combatientes dispersos; (slang) acabar con; (Brit.) beber; *vn* hacer muecas; **to mop and mow** hacer muecas
mopboard ['mɑpˌbord] *s* rodapié
mope [mop] *s* apático, melancólico; *vn* andar abatido, entregarse a la melancolía
mopish ['mopɪʃ] *adj* abatido, melancólico
moppet ['mɑpɪt] *s* (coll.) chiquillo; (coll.) muñeca
moquette [mo'kɛt] *s* moqueta
moraceous [mo'reʃəs] *adj* (bot.) moráceo
moraine [mə'ren] *s* (geol.) morena
moral ['mɑrəl] o ['mɔrəl] *adj* moral; *s* moraleja (*p.ej., de una fábula*); **morals** *spl* moral (*ciencia de la conducta; conducta*)
moral certainty *s* certidumbre moral
morale [mə'ræl] o [mə'rɑl] *s* moral (*p.ej., de las tropas*)
moralist ['mɑrəlɪst] o ['mɔrəlɪst] *s* moralizador; moralista
moralistic [ˌmɑrə'lɪstɪk] o [ˌmɔrə'lɪstɪk] *adj* moralizador
morality [mə'rælɪtɪ] *s* (*pl:* **-ties**) moralidad; (lit.) moralidad
morality play *s* (lit.) moralidad
moralize ['mɑrəlaɪz] o ['mɔrəlaɪz] *va* moralizar; deducir la moral de; *vn* moralizar
moralizer ['mɑrəˌlaɪzər] o ['mɔrəˌlaɪzər] *s* moralizador
morally ['mɑrəlɪ] o ['mɔrəlɪ] *adv* moralmente
moral philosophy *s* filosofía moral
morals charge *s* acusación por delito sexual, acusación por inmoralidades
moral support *s* ayuda moral
moral victory *s* derrota que, por razones morales, no lo es, sino victoria
morass [mə'ræs] *s* pantano; (fig.) pantano (*dificultad, estorbo*)
moratorium [ˌmɑrə'torɪəm] o [ˌmɔrə'torɪəm] *s* (*pl:* **-ums** o **-a** [ə]) moratoria

moratory ['mɑrə,torɪ] o ['mɔrə,torɪ] *adj* moratorio
Moravian [mo'revɪən] *adj* moravo; *s* moravo; hermano moravo
moray ['more] o [mo're] *s* (ichth.) morena
morbid ['mɔrbɪd] *adj* morboso; malsano; horrible, espantoso
morbidity [mɔr'bɪdɪtɪ] *s* morbosidad
morbific [mɔr'bɪfɪk] o **morbifical** [mɔr'bɪfɪkəl] *adj* morbífico
mordacious [mɔr'deʃəs] *adj* mordaz
mordacity [mɔr'dæsɪtɪ] *s* mordacidad
mordancy ['mɔrdənsɪ] *s* mordacidad
mordant ['mɔrdənt] *adj* mordaz; *s* mordiente
Mordecai ['mɔrdɪkaɪ] *s* (Bib.) Mardoqueo
mordent ['mɔrdənt] *s* (mus.) mordente
more [mor] *adj, adv & s* más; **any more** ya no; **at more than** en más de + *numeral;* **neither more nor less** ni más ni menos; **no more** no más; ya no; se acabó; **no more, no less** ni más ni menos; **the more the merrier** cuanto más mejor, cuantos más mejor; **the more . . . the more** (o **the less**) cuanto más . . . tanto más (o menos) o mientras más . . . más (o menos), p.ej., **the more he has the more he wants** cuanto más tiene tanto más desea o mientras más tiene más desea; **more and more** más y más, cada vez más; **more or less** más o menos; poco más o menos; **more than** más que; más de lo que + *verb;* más de + *numeral*
moreen [mə'rin] *s* filipichín
morel [mə'rɛl] o ['mɑrɛl] *s* (bot.) múrgula, morilla
moreover [mor'ovər] *adv* además, por otra parte
mores ['moriz] *spl* costumbres, usos tradicionales
Moresque [mo'rɛsk] *adj* moro; (arch.) árabe; *s* (arch.) estilo árabe
morganatic [,mɔrgə'nætɪk] *adj* morganático
morganatically [,mɔrgə'nætɪkəlɪ] *adv* morganáticamente
morganatic marriage *s* matrimonio morganático
Morgan le Fay ['mɔrgən lə 'fe] *s* (myth.) Morgana
morgue [mɔrg] *s* depósito de cadáveres (*no identificados*)
moribund ['mɑrɪbʌnd] o ['mɔrɪbʌnd] *adj & s* moribundo
morin ['morɪn] *s* (chem.) morina
morion ['morɪɑn] *s* morrión
Morisco [mə'rɪsko] *adj* morisco, moro; *s* (*pl:* **-cos** o **-coes**) moro; moro de España; morisco (*en Méjico, descendiente de mulato y española o de mulata y español*)
Mormon ['mɔrmən] *adj* mormónico; *s* mormón; (*l.c.*) *s* (zool.) mormón
Mormonism ['mɔrmənɪzəm] *s* mormonismo
morn [mɔrn] *s* (poet.) mañana
morning ['mɔrnɪŋ] *s* mañana; (fig.) aurora (*principios*); **the morning after** (coll.) la mañana después de la juerga; *adj* matinal, de la mañana, de mañana
morning coat *s* chaqué
morning dress *s* traje de mañana
morning-glory ['mɔrnɪŋ,glorɪ] *s* (*pl:* **-ries**) (bot.) dondiego de día
morning sickness *s* (path.) vómitos del embarazo
morning star *s* lucero del alba; (bot.) pegarropa; (mil.) mangual
Moro ['moro] *s* (*pl:* **-ros**) moro (*malayo mahometano de las Islas Filipinas y su idioma*)
Moroccan [mə'rɑkən] *adj & s* marroquí o marroquín
Morocco [mə'rɑko] *s* Marruecos; (*l.c.*) *s* marroquí o marroquín (*tafilete*)
moron ['morɑn] *s* morón; (coll.) imbécil
morose [mə'ros] *adj* malhumorado, triste, lóbrego
morphea [mɔr'fiə] *s* (path.) morfea
morpheme ['mɔrfim] *s* (gram.) morfema
Morpheus ['mɔrfjus] o ['mɔrfɪəs] *s* (myth.) Morfeo
morphia ['mɔrfɪə] o **morphine** ['mɔrfin] *s* (chem.) morfina
morphinism ['mɔrfɪnɪzəm] *s* (path.) morfinismo
morphogenesis [,mɔrfə'dʒɛnɪsɪs] *s* morfogénesis
morphogenic [,mɔrfə'dʒɛnɪk] *adj* (embryol.) morfógeno
morphologic [,mɔrfə'lɑdʒɪk] o **morphological** [,mɔrfə'lɑdʒɪkəl] *adj* morfológico
morphology [mɔr'fɑlədʒɪ] *s* (biol. & gram.) morfología
Morris ['mɔrɪs] o ['mɑrɪs] *s* Mauricio; (*l.c.*) *s* mojiganga
morris chair *s* poltrona de espaldar ajustable
morris dance *s* mojiganga
morrow ['mɑro] o ['mɔro] *s* (archaic) mañana (*parte del día hasta mediodía*); mañana (*día que sigue al de hoy*); día siguiente; **on the morrow** en el día de mañana; el día siguiente
Morse code [mɔrs] *s* (telg.) alfabeto Morse
morsel ['mɔrsəl] *s* pedazo, fragmento; bocado
mort [mɔrt] *s* (hunt.) toque de muerte (*que se hace sonar al morir la res*); (dial.) gran cantidad, gran número
mortal ['mɔrtəl] *adj & s* mortal
mortality [mɔr'tælɪtɪ] *s* mortalidad (*calidad de mortal; número proporcional de defunciones*); mortandad (*muertes causadas por epidemia, guerra, etc.*)
mortally ['mɔrtəlɪ] *adv* mortalmente
mortal sin *s* pecado mortal
mortar ['mɔrtər] *s* mortero (*vasija; argamasa*); (arti.) mortero; *va* argamasar; enlucir
mortarboard ['mɔrtər,bord] *s* esparavel; gorro estudiantil cuadrado, birrete
mortgage ['mɔrgɪdʒ] *s* hipoteca; *va* hipotecar; (fig.) vender (*p.ej., el alma al diablo*)
mortgagee [,mɔrgɪ'dʒi] *s* acreedor hipotecario
mortgager o **mortgagor** ['mɔrgɪdʒər] *s* deudor hipotecario
mortice ['mɔrtɪs] *s & va* var. de **mortise**
mortician [mɔr'tɪʃən] *s* funerario, empresario de pompas fúnebres
mortification [,mɔrtɪfɪ'keʃən] *s* mortificación; humillación
mortify ['mɔrtɪfaɪ] (*pret & pp:* **-fied**) *va* mortificar; humillar; *vn* mortificarse (*un tejido u órgano del cuerpo*)
mortise ['mɔrtɪs] *s* (carp.) muesca, mortaja; *va* (carp.) enmuescar, amortajar
mortise-and-tenon joint ['mɔrtɪsənd'tɛnən] *s* (carp.) ensambladura de caja y espiga
mortise gauge *s* (carp.) gramil para mortajas
mortise lock *s* cerradura recercada, cerradura embutida
mortiser ['mɔrtɪsər] *s* (carp.) machihembradora (*máquina*)
mortmain ['mɔrtmen] *s* (law) manos muertas
mortuary ['mɔrtʃu,ɛrɪ] *adj* mortuorio; *s* (*pl:* **-ies**) depósito de cadáveres
morula ['mɔrjulə] o ['mɔrulə] *s* (*pl:* **-lae** [li]) (embryol.) mórula
mos. abr. de **months**
Mosaic [mo'zeɪk] *adj* mosaico (*perteneciente a Moisés*); (*l.c.*) *adj* mosaico; *s* (aer., f.a., & telv.) mosaico
mosaic disease *s* (plant path.) enfermedad del mosaico
mosaic gold *s* oro mosaico o musivo
Mosaic law *s* ley mosaica
Mosaism ['mozeɪzəm] *s* mosaísmo
Moscow ['mɑskaʊ] o ['mɑsko] *s* Moscú
Moselle [mo'zɛl] *s* Mosela
Moses ['mozɪz] o ['mozɪs] *s* Moisés
Moslem ['mɑzləm] o ['mɑsləm] *adj* musulmán, muslim; *s* (*pl:* **-lems** o **-lem**) musulmán, muslim
mosque [mɑsk] *s* mezquita
mosquito [məs'kito] *s* (*pl:* **-toes** o **-tos**) (ent.) mosquito
mosquito fleet *s* (slang) escuadrilla (*de barcos pequeños*)
mosquito hawk *s* (orn.) chotacabras; (ent.) caballito del diablo
mosquito net *s* mosquitero
moss [mɔs] o [mɑs] *s* (bot.) musgo; *va* cubrir de musgo
moss agate *s* (mineral.) ágata musgosa
mossback ['mɔs,bæk] o ['mɑs,bæk] *s* (slang) fósil (*persona de ideas anticuadas*)
moss-grown ['mɔs,gron] o ['mɑs,gron] *adj* musgoso; (fig.) fósil, anticuado

moss rose *s* (bot.) rosa musgosa
mossy ['mɔsɪ] o ['mɑsɪ] *adj* (*comp:* **-ier;** *super:* **-iest**) musgoso
most [most] *adj* más, p.ej., **the one who works hardest earns most money** el que más trabaja gana más dinero; la mayor parte de, los más de, casi todos; *adv* más, p.ej., **this tooth hurts most** esta muela duele más; **she is the most beautiful girl I know** es la muchacha más hermosa que conozco; muy, sumamente, de lo más; (coll.) casi, p.ej., **the work is most finished** el trabajo está casi terminado; *s* la mayor parte, el mayor número, los más; **at most** o **at the most** a lo más, cuando más; **to make the most of** sacar el mejor partido de; **most of** la mayor parte de, el mayor número de, los más
most favored nation *s* (dipl.) (la) nación más favorecida
Most High, the el Altísimo, el Excelso (*Dios*)
mostly ['mostlɪ] *adv* por la mayor parte, principalmente; casi, p.ej., **the work is mostly finished** el trabajo está casi terminado
mote [mot] *s* mota de polvo
motel [mo'tɛl] *s* motel, parador de turismo
motet [mo'tɛt] *s* (mus.) motete
moth [mɔθ] o [mɑθ] *s* (*pl:* **moths** [mɔðz], [mɑðz], [mɔθs] o [mɑθs]) (ent.) polilla; (ent.) mariposa nocturna
moth ball *s* bola de alcanfor, bola de naftalina (*para la polilla*)
moth-ball fleet ['mɔθ,bɔl] o ['mɑθ,bɔl] *s* (nav.) flota en conserva, flota en naftalina
moth-eaten ['mɔθ,itən] o ['mɑθ,itən] *adj* apolillado; (fig.) anticuado
mother ['mʌðər] *s* madre; tía (*tratamiento que se da a las mujeres ancianas*); *adj* madre, p.ej., **mother plant** planta madre; maternal, p.ej., **mother love** amor maternal; materno, p.ej., **mother tongue** lengua materna; metropolitano; *va* servir de madre a; reconocer por hijo; ser origen, causa o fuente de; reconocerse o declararse autor de
Mother Carey's chicken ['kɛrɪz] *s* (orn.) petrel de la tempestad
mother church *s* la santa madre iglesia; iglesia metropolitana
mother country *s* madre patria (*estado que ha formado una colonia y que la gobierna*); patria (*lugar de nacimiento*)
mother earth *s* madre tierra
Mother Goose *s* supuesta autora o narradora de una colección de cuentos infantiles (en España: *Cuentos de Calleja*)
motherhood ['mʌðərhʊd] *s* maternidad; madres, conjunto de madres
Mother Hubbard ['hʌbərd] *s* bata suelta (*de mujer*)
mother-in-law ['mʌðərɪn,lɔ] *s* (*pl:* **mothers-in-law**) suegra
motherland ['mʌðər,lænd] *s* patria
motherless ['mʌðərlɪs] *adj* huérfano de madre, sin madre
mother liquid o **liquor** *s* aguas madres
mother lode *s* (min.) veta principal
motherly ['mʌðərlɪ] *adj* maternal; *adv* maternalmente
Mother of God *s* (eccl.) madre de Dios
mother-of-pearl ['mʌðərəv'pʌrl] *s* nácar; *adj* nacarado
Mother's Day *s* (U.S.A.) día de la madre o de las madres
mother ship *s* (nav.) buque madre
mother superior *s* superiora
mother tongue *s* lengua materna; lengua madre o matriz (*la de que se han derivado otras*)
mother wit *s* inteligencia natural; chispa, ingenio
motherwort ['mʌðər,wʌrt] *s* (bot.) agripalma
moth hole *s* apolilladura
mothy ['mɔθɪ] o ['mɑθɪ] *adj* (*comp:* **-ier;** *super:* **-iest**) apolillado
motif [mo'tif] *s* (f.a. & mus.) motivo; (fig.) idea dominante
motile ['motɪl] *adj* movible
motility [mo'tɪlɪtɪ] *s* (biol.) motilidad
motion ['moʃən] *s* movimiento; moción (*en junta deliberante*); seña, indicación; (mus.) movimiento; **in motion** en movimiento; en marcha; **to make a motion** hacer o presentar una moción; *va* indicar a (*una persona*) con la mano, la cabeza, etc., p.ej., **he motioned me to sit down** me indicó con la mano que me sentara; *vn* hacer señas
motionless ['moʃənlɪs] *adj* inmoble
motion picture *s* película cinematográfica
motion-picture ['moʃən,pɪktʃər] *adj* cinematográfico
motion-picture camera *s* cámara cinematográfica
motivate ['motɪvet] *va* motivar
motivation [,motɪ'veʃən] *s* motivación
motive ['motɪv] *adj* motivo; motor; *s* motivo; (f.a. & mus.) motivo
motive power *s* potencia motora o motriz, fuerza motriz; conjunto de locomotoras de un ferrocarril
motley ['mɑtlɪ] *adj* abigarrado; mezclado, variado; *s* mezcla confusa; traje abigarrado de payaso
motor ['motər] *adj* motor; (anat.) motor; *s* motor; motor eléctrico; automóvil; *vn* ir, pasear o viajar en automóvil
motor block *s* bloque de cilindros
motorboat ['motər,bot] *s* autobote, gasolinera
motorbus ['motər,bʌs] *s* autobús, ómnibus automóvil
motorcade ['motər,ked] *s* caravana de automóviles
motorcar ['motər,kɑr] *s* automóvil; (rail.) autocarril
motor coach *s* coche motor, autobús
motor converter *s* (elec.) motor-convertidor
motorcycle ['motər,saɪkəl] *s* motocicleta
motorcyclist ['motər,saɪklɪst] *s* motociclista
motor drive *s* (elec.) grupo motopropulsor
motor-driven ['motər,drɪvən] *adj* (elec.) motopropulsor
motordrome ['motər,drom] *s* motódromo
motor generator *s* (elec.) grupo de motor y generador, motor-generador
motoring ['motərɪŋ] *s* motorismo, automovilismo
motorist ['motərɪst] *s* motorista, automovilista
motorization [,motərɪ'zeʃən] *s* motorización
motorize ['motəraɪz] *va* motorizar
motor launch *s* lancha automóvil
motor lorry *s* (Brit.) autocamión
motorman ['motərmən] *s* (*pl:* **-men**) conductor (*de un tranvía o de una locomotora eléctrica*)
motor sailer *s* (naut.) motovelero
motor scooter *s* motoneta
motor ship *s* motonave
motor truck *s* autocamión, camión automóvil
motor van *s* (Brit.) autocamión
motor vehicle *s* vehículo motor
mottle ['mɑtəl] *s* mancha o veta de color; color moteado o veteado; *va* abigarrar, jaspear, motear
motto ['mɑto] *s* (*pl:* **-toes** o **-tos**) lema, divisa
mouflon o **moufflon** ['muflɑn] *s* (zool.) musmón
mould [mold] *s, va & vn* var. de **mold**
moulder ['moldər] *s, va & vn* var. de **molder**
moulding ['moldɪŋ] *s* var. de **molding**
mouldy ['moldɪ] *adj* (*comp:* **-ier;** *super:* **-iest**) var. de **moldy**
mound [maʊnd] *s* montón de tierra o piedras; montecillo, montículo; (baseball) lomita, montículo; *va* amontonar; encerrar con terraplenes de defensa
mount [maʊnt] *s* monte; montura (*cabalgadura*); montadura (*p.ej., de una joya*); soporte; papel de soporte; cartón o tela (*en que está pegada una fotografía*); (mach.) montaje; (arti.) montajes; *va* subir (*una escalera, una cuesta, etc.*); subir a (*p.ej., la plataforma*); escalar (*p.ej., una muralla*); montar (*subir a; armar; preparar para la exhibición; engastar*); (mach.) montar; (naut.) montar (*tantos o cuantos cañones*); (mil.) montar (*la guardia*); poner a caballo; proveer de caballos; pegar (*vistas, pruebas, etc.*); *vn* montar; montarse; aumentar (*p.ej., precios, deudas*)
mountain ['maʊntən] *s* montaña; (fig.) montón (*cosas puestas unas encima de otras; cantidad abundante*); **to make a mountain out**

of a molehill hacer de una pulga un camello o un elefante; *adj* montañés; montañoso
mountain ash *s* (bot.) serbal; (bot.) serbal de los cazadores; (bot.) alfitonia
mountain chain *s* cadena de montañas
mountain climber *s* montañero, alpinista
mountain climbing *s* montañismo, alpinismo
mountain cranberry *s* (bot.) arándano encarnado
mountain damson *s* (bot.) aceitillo (*Simarouba amara*)
mountain dew *s* (slang) whisky de Escocia; (slang) whisky de contrabando
mountaineer [,maʊntə'nɪr] *s* montañés; alpinista, montañero; *vn* dedicarse al alpinismo
mountaineering [,maʊntə'nɪrɪŋ] *s* alpinismo, montañismo; *adj* montañero
mountain goat *s* (zool.) cabra de las Montañas Rocosas (*Oreamnos montanus*)
mountain laurel *s* (bot.) calmia
mountain lion *s* (zool.) puma, león de América
mountainous ['maʊntənəs] *adj* montañoso; inmenso
mountain parsley *s* (bot.) oreoselino, perejil de monte
mountain railroad o **railway** *s* ferrocarril de cremallera
mountain range *s* cordillera, sierra
mountain sheep *s* (zool.) carnero cimarrón de las Montañas Rocosas
mountain sickness *s* mal de altura, mal de las montañas
Mountain time *s* (U.S.A.) hora legal correspondiente al meridiano 105°
mountaintop ['maʊntən,tɑp] *s* cumbre de la montaña
mountebank ['maʊntɪbæŋk] *s* saltabanco
mounted ['maʊntɪd] *adj* montado (*a caballo, de a caballo; armado; engastado*)
mounting ['maʊntɪŋ] *s* montura (*de una piedra preciosa, arma, telescopio, etc.*); montaje (*de una máquina*); papel de soporte; papel o tela (*en que está pegada una fotografía*)
mourn [morn] *va* llorar (*la muerte de una persona*); lamentar (*una desgracia*); *vn* lamentarse; vestir de luto
mourner ['mornər] *s* doliente; penitente; plañidera
mourners' bench *s* banco de los penitentes (*en ciertas solemnidades religiosas*)
mournful ['mornfəl] *adj* dolorido, triste; lúgubre
mourning ['mornɪŋ] *adj* de luto; *s* luto; **to be in mourning** estar de luto
mourning band *s* crespón fúnebre
mourning bride *s* (bot.) viuda
mourning dove *s* (orn.) paloma triste
mourning widow *s* (bot.) viuda
mouse [maʊs] *s* (*pl:* **mice**) (zool.) ratón; (naut.) barrilete; [maʊz] *va* cazar o coger (*ratones*); husmear; (naut.) amarrar; *vn* cazar o coger ratones; andar al acecho; andar a hurtadillas
mouse-ear ['maʊs,ɪr] *s* (bot.) pelosilla, vellosilla
mousehole ['maʊs,hol] *s* ratonera; pequeño agujero
mouser ['maʊzər] *s* desmurador, gato desmurador; husmeador
mousetrap ['maʊs,træp] *s* ratonera (*trampa*)
mousing ['maʊzɪŋ] *s* (naut.) barrilete
mousse [mus] *s* mousse, manjar de crema batida y gelatina
mousseline [mus'lin] *s* (Fr.) muselina
mousseline de laine [də 'lɛn] *s* (Fr.) muselina de lana
mousseline de soie [də 'swɑ] *s* (Fr.) muselina de China
moustache [məs'tæʃ], [məs'tɑʃ] o ['mʌstæʃ] *s* var. de **mustache**
mousy ['maʊsɪ] *adj* (*comp:* **-ier;** *super:* **-iest**) ratonesco; infestado de ratones; que huele a ratones; (fig.) silencioso
mouth [maʊθ] *s* (*pl:* **mouths** [maʊðz]) boca; embocadura, desembocadura (*de un río*); tragante (*de un horno de cuba*); mueca; expresión (*de un concepto*); **by mouth** por vía bucal; **down in the mouth** abatido, cariacontecido; **to be born with a silver spoon in one's mouth** nacer de pie; **to laugh on the other** o **wrong side of one's mouth** convertir la risa en llanto; **to make one's mouth water** hacerle a uno la boca agua; **to not open one's mouth** no decir esta boca es mía; [maʊð] *va* tomar en la boca, asir con los dientes; cariciar o tocar con la boca; articular (*palabras*) con rimbombancia; *vn* hablar con rimbombancia
mouther ['maʊðər] *s* parlón
mouthful ['maʊθfʊl] *s* bocado; (slang) abundancia de palabras
mouth organ *s* (mus.) armónica de boca; (mus.) flauta de Pan
mouthpiece ['maʊθ,pis] *s* boquilla (*de un instrumento de música, de una herramienta, etc.*); bocado (*de freno*); (fig.) portavoz
mouthwash ['maʊθ,wɑʃ] *s* enjuague, enjuagadientes
mouthy ['maʊðɪ] o ['maʊθɪ] *adj* (*comp:* **-ier;** *super:* **-iest**) deslenguado, vocinglero, ampuloso
movable ['muvəbəl] *adj* movible; mueble; (astrol.) movible; *s* mueble; **movables** *spl* bienes muebles
movable feast *s* (eccl.) fiesta movible
move [muv] *s* movimiento; paso; mudanza (*de una casa a otra*); acción, gestión; **on the move** en movimiento; **to get a move on** (coll.) menearse, darse prisa; **to make a move** dar un paso; tomar medidas; hacer una jugada; *va* mover; evacuar, exonerar (*el vientre*); proponer; conmover, enternecer; **to move someone to** + *inf* mover a alguien a + *inf;* **to move up** adelantar (*una fecha*); *vn* moverse; caminar; desplazarse (*un viajante, los planetas, etc.*); circular; mudarse, mudar de casa; trasladarse (*p.ej., a otra ciudad*); hacer una jugada; hacer una moción; venderse, tener salida (*una mercancía*); moverse, evacuarse, exonerarse (*el vientre*); girar (*una puerta*); **to move about** moverse de acá para allá, desplazarse; **to move along** ir a gran velocidad; **to move away** apartarse; marcharse; mudar de casa; **to move forward** avanzar; **to move in** instalarse; instalarse en; alternar con, frecuentar (*p.ej., la buena sociedad*); **to move off** alejarse
moveable ['muvəbəl] *adj* & *s* var. de **movable**
movement ['muvmənt] *s* movimiento; evacuación (*del vientre*); aparato de relojería; (f.a. & lit.) movimiento; (mus.) movimiento (*velocidad del compás*); (mus.) tiempo (*cada una de las divisiones de una sonata, sinfonía, etc.*)
mover ['muvər] *s* movedor; móvil; autor (*de una moción*); empleado de una casa de mudanzas
movie ['muvɪ] *s* (coll.) película, cinta; (coll.) sala de proyección, local cinematográfico; **movies** *spl* (coll.) cine
movie-goer ['muvɪ,goər] *s* (coll.) aficionado al cine
movie house *s* (coll.) cineteatro
movieland ['muvɪ,lænd] *s* (coll.) tierra del ensueño del cine; (coll.) cinelandia, centro principal de la producción cinematográfica
moving ['muvɪŋ] *adj* movedor; móvil; conmovedor; *s* movimiento; mudanza (*de una casa a otra*)
moving coil *s* (elec.) bobina móvil
moving day *s* día de mudanza
moving part *s* (mach.) órgano móvil
moving picture *s* var. de **motion picture**
moving spirit *s* alma (*de una empresa*)
moving staircase o **stairway** *s* escalera automática, móvil o rodante
moving van *s* carro de mudanza
mow [mo] o [maʊ] *s* mueca; [maʊ] *s* granero; henal; montón de heno o de gavillas dentro del granero; [mo] (*pret:* **mowed;** *pp:* **mowed** o **mown**) *va* segar (*el heno, el campo*); **to mow down** segar; matar (*soldados*) con fuego graneado; *vn* segar
mower ['moər] *s* segador; segadora mecánica, guadañadora
mowing ['mo·ɪŋ] *s* siega; prado de guadaña; *adj* segador
mowing machine *s* segadora mecánica, guadañadora
Mozarab [mo'zærəb] *s* mozárabe
Mozarabic [mo'zærəbɪk] *adj* mozárabe
mozzetta [mo'zɛtə] *s* (eccl.) muceta
M.P. o **MP** abr. de **Member of Parliament,**

Metropolitan Police, Military Police y **Mounted Police**
mph o **m.p.h.** abr. de **miles per hour**
Mr. o **Mr** ['mɪstər] *s* (*pl:* **Messrs.** ['mɛsərz]) señor (*tratamiento*)
Mrs. ['mɪsɪz] *s* señora (*tratamiento*)
ms., Ms. o **MS.** abr. de **manuscript**
M.S. o **M.Sc.** abr. de **Master of Science**
Msgr. abr. de **Monsignor**
mss., Mss. o **MSS.** abr. de **manuscripts**
mt. abr. de **mountain**
Mt. abr. de **Mount**
mtn. abr. de **mountain**
mts. abr. de **mountains**
much [mʌtʃ] *adj* (*comp:* **more;** *super:* **most**) mucho; **as much . . . as** tanto . . . como; **to be much of a** ser todo un; **too much** demasiado; *adv* (*comp:* **more;** *super:* **most**) mucho; casi, p.ej., **much the same** casi lo mismo; muy, p.ej., **much surprised** muy asombrado; **as much** tanto; otro tanto; **as much as** tanto como; **as much more** otro tanto más; **too much** demasiado; **however much** por mucho que; **how much** cuánto; **so much** tanto; **so much the better** tanto mejor; **very much** muchísimo; muy, p.ej., **very much annoyed** muy enojado; **much more** mucho más; *s* mucho; **not much of a** de poca cuantía, p.ej., **not much of a person** una persona de poca cuantía; **not much to look at** de mal aspecto, poco imponente; **to make much of** tener en mucho, dar mucha importancia a
muchness ['mʌtʃnɪs] *s* abundancia, gran cantidad; **much of a muchness** (coll.) casi lo mismo
mucilage ['mjusɪlɪdʒ] *s* mucilago
mucilaginous [,mjusɪ'lædʒɪnəs] *adj* mucilaginoso
mucin ['mjusɪn] *s* (biochem.) mucina
muck [mʌk] *s* estiércol húmedo; (min.) zafra; (coll.) porquería, asquerosidad; *va* estercolar; (coll.) ensuciar
mucker ['mʌkər] *s* (min.) zafrero; (slang) grosero
muck-rake ['mʌk,rek] *vn* (coll.) exponer ruindades
muck-raker ['mʌk,rekər] *s* (coll.) expositor de ruindades
mucky ['mʌkɪ] *adj* (*comp:* **-ier;** *super:* **-iest**) podrido, estercolizo; puerco, sucio
mucoid ['mjukɔɪd] *s* (biochem.) mucoide
mucosa [mju'kosə] *s* (*pl:* **-sae** [si]) (anat.) mucosa
mucosity [mju'kɑsɪtɪ] *s* mucosidad
mucous ['mjukəs] *adj* mucoso
mucous membrane *s* (anat.) membrana mucosa
mucronate ['mjukronɪt] o ['mjukronet] *adj* mucronato
mucus ['mjukəs] *s* moco, mucosidad
mud [mʌd] *s* fango, barro, lodo; (fig.) fango; **to sling mud at** (fig.) llenar de fango
muddle ['mʌdəl] *s* embrollo, confusión; *va* embrollar, confundir; atontar, aturdir; achispar; *vn* obrar confusamente; **to muddle through** salir del paso a duras penas; acertar de puro cachazudo
muddlehead ['mʌdəl,hɛd] *s* farraguista
muddleheaded ['mʌdəl,hɛdɪd] *adj* atontado, confuso, estúpido
muddy ['mʌdɪ] *adj* (*comp:* **-dier;** *super:* **-diest**) fangoso, barroso; turbio; (*pret & pp:* **-died**) *va* enturbiar; *vn* enturbiarse
mud eel *s* (ichth.) anguila de barro
mudguard ['mʌd,gɑrd] *s* guardabarros
mud hen *s* (orn.) polla, fúlica americana
mudhole ['mʌd,hol] *s* ciénaga, lodazal
mud puppy *s* (zool.) necturo; (zool.) ajolote; (zool.) salamandra gigante norteamericana
mudsill ['mʌd,sɪl] *s* madero de construcción colocado en el suelo como cimiento
mudslinger ['mʌd,slɪŋər] *s* (fig.) lanzador de lodo
mud turtle *s* (zool.) tortuga de río; (zool.) jicotea; (zool.) chiquigao, tortuga lagarto
mud volcano *s* (geol.) volcán de lodo
muezzin [mju'ɛzɪn] *s* almuecín o almuédano
muff [mʌf] *s* manguito; chapucería, torpeza; (baseball) falta que consiste en dejar caer torpemente la pelota; *va* chafallar, frangollar; (baseball) dejar escapar (*la pelota*)
muffin ['mʌfɪn] *s* bollo, mollete, panecillo
muffle ['mʌfəl] *s* ruido sordo o amortiguado; amortiguador de sonido; tambor de polea; mufla (*de un horno*); *va* amortiguar (*un ruido*); enfundar (*un tambor*); embozar, arropar; envolver en paños la cabeza de
muffle furnace *s* horno de mufla
muffler ['mʌflər] *s* bufanda; amortiguador de ruido; (aut.) silencioso, silenciador
mufti ['mʌftɪ] *s* (*pl:* **-tis**) traje de paisano; muftí (*jurisconsulto musulmán*)
mug [mʌg] *s* vaso con asa, pichel; (slang) hocico (*de un persona*); (slang) mueca; (*pret & pp:* **mugged;** *ger:* **mugging**) *va* (slang) fotografiar; (slang) sofocar poniendo el brazo alrededor del cuello; *vn* (slang) hacer muecas
muggy ['mʌgɪ] *adj* (*comp:* **-gier;** *super:* **-giest**) bochornoso, húmedo y sofocante
mugwort ['mʌg,wʌrt] *s* (bot.) artemisa
mugwump ['mʌg,wʌmp] *s* votante independiente (*sin alianzas de partido*); (U.S.A.) republicano rebelde (*de los que en las elecciones de 1884 negaron el voto al candidato oficial del partido republicano*)
Muhammad [mʊ'hæməd] *s* var. de **Mohammed**
mulatto [mjʊ'læto] o [mə'læto] *adj* mulato; *s* (*pl:* **-toes**) mulato
mulberry ['mʌl,bɛrɪ] *s* (*pl:* **-ries**) (bot.) morera (*Morus alba*); (bot.) moreda o moral (*Morus nigra*); mora (*fruto*); morado, color morado; *adj* morado
mulch [mʌltʃ] *s* (hort.) estiércol, paja y hojas; *va* (hort.) cubrir con estiércol, paja y hojas
mulct [mʌlkt] *s* multa; *va* multar; defraudar
mule [mjul] *s* mulo; babucha; hiladora mecánica alternativa; (coll.) persona terca
mule chair *s* artolas
mule deer *s* (zool.) ciervo mulo
muleteer [,mjulə'tɪr] *s* mulatero, arriero
mulish ['mjulɪʃ] *adj* terco, obstinado
mull [mʌl] *s* muselina clara; *va* calentar (*vino*) con especias; *vn* reflexionar; **to mull over** reflexionar sobre
mullein o **mullen** ['mʌlɪn] *s* (bot.) gordolobo
muller ['mʌlər] *s* moleta
mullet ['mʌlɪt] *s* (ichth.) mújol, céfalo
mulligan ['mʌlɪgən] *s* (slang) olla, puchero
mulligatawny [,mʌlɪgə'tɔnɪ] *s* sopa de arroz y carne sazonada con cari
mullion ['mʌljən] *s* (arch.) parteluz (*de una ventana*); (arch.) montante (*de una puerta*)
mullioned ['mʌljənd] *adj* (arch.) dividido por montantes
mulse [mʌls] *s* vino mulso
multicellular [,mʌltɪ'sɛljələr] *adj* multicelular
multicolored ['mʌltɪ,kʌlərd] *adj* multicolor
multidentate [,mʌltɪ'dɛntet] *adj* multidentado
multifarious [,mʌltɪ'fɛrɪəs] *adj* múltiple
multiflorous [,mʌltɪ'florəs] *adj* (bot.) multifloro
multifold ['mʌltɪfold] *adj* múltiple
multiform ['mʌltɪfɔrm] *adj* multiforme
multigraph ['mʌltɪgræf] o ['mʌltɪgrɑf] *s* (trademark) multígrafo; *va* multigrafiar
multilateral [,mʌltɪ'lætərəl] *adj* multilátero (*de muchos lados*); multilateral (*pacto, alianza*)
multimillionaire [,mʌltɪ,mɪljə'nɛr] *s* multimillonario
multipara [mʌl'tɪpərə] *s* (*pl:* **-rae** [ri]) multípara
multiparous [mʌl'tɪpərəs] *adj* multípara
multiphase ['mʌltɪfez] *adj* (elec.) polifásico
multiple ['mʌltɪpəl] *adj* múltiplo; (elec. & math.) múltiplo; *s* (elec. & math.) múltiplo; **in multiple** (elec.) en múltiplo
multiple-lens camera ['mʌltɪpəl'lɛnz] *s* (phot.) cámara múltiple
multiple sclerosis *s* (path.) esclerosis múltiple, esclerosis en placas
multiplet ['mʌltɪplɪt] *s* (phys.) multiplete
multiplex ['mʌltɪplɛks] *adj* múltiple; (rad. & telg.) múltiplex
multipliable ['mʌltɪ,plaɪəbəl] *adj* multiplicable
multiplicand [,mʌltɪplɪ'kænd] *s* (math.) multiplicando

multiplication [ˌmʌltɪplɪˈkeʃən] *s* multiplicación
multiplication table *s* tabla de multiplicación, tabla de multiplicar
multiplicity [ˌmʌltɪˈplɪsɪtɪ] *s* (*pl:* **-ties**) multiplicidad
multiplier [ˈmʌltɪˌplaɪər] *s* multiplicador; (math.) multiplicador
multiply [ˈmʌltɪplaɪ] (*pret & pp:* **-plied**) *va* multiplicar; *vn* multiplicarse
multipolar [ˌmʌltɪˈpolər] o **multipole** [ˈmʌltɪpol] *adj* (anat. & elec.) multipolar
multistage [ˈmʌltɪstedʒ] *adj* de etapas múltiples, multiseccional
multistory [ˈmʌltɪˌstorɪ] *adj* de varios pisos
multitude [ˈmʌltɪtjud] o [ˈmʌltɪtud] *s* multitud
multitudinous [ˌmʌltɪˈtjudɪnəs] o [ˌmʌltɪˈtudɪnəs] *adj* numeroso; múltiple
multivalence [ˌmʌltɪˈveləns] o [mʌlˈtɪvələns] *s* (bact. & chem.) polivalencia
multivalent [ˌmʌltɪˈvelənt] o [mʌlˈtɪvələnt] *adj* (bact. & chem.) polivalente
multivalve [ˈmʌltɪˌvælv] *adj* multivalvo
mum [mʌm] *adj* callado; **to keep mum** estar en muda; **to keep mum about** callar; **mum's the word!** ¡punto en boca!, ¡que se guarde silencio!; *interj* ¡a callar!, ¡chitón!
mumble [ˈmʌmbəl] *s* mascujada; *va & vn* mascujar (*decir o hablar entre dientes; mascar mal*)
mumbo jumbo [ˈmʌmbo ˈdʒʌmbo] *s* (*pl:* **mumbo jumbos**) fetiche, coco; conjuro; (*caps.*) *s* genio tutelar (*entre los negros del Gambia*)
mummer [ˈmʌmər] *s* máscara (*persona*); cómico, histrión
mummery [ˈmʌmərɪ] *s* (*pl:* **-ies**) mojiganga; (fig.) mojiganga (*burla, hipocresía*)
mummification [ˌmʌmɪfɪˈkeʃən] *s* momificación
mummify [ˈmʌmɪfaɪ] (*pret & pp:* **-fied**) *va* momificar; *vn* momificarse
mummy [ˈmʌmɪ] *s* (*pl:* **-mies**) momia
mumps [mʌmps] *s* (path.) papera, parótidas
munch [mʌntʃ] *va* ronzar
mundane [ˈmʌnden] *adj* mundano
municipal [mjuˈnɪsɪpəl] *adj* municipal
municipality [mjuˌnɪsɪˈpælɪtɪ] *s* (*pl:* **-ties**) municipio
municipalization [mjuˌnɪsɪpəlɪˈzeʃən] *s* municipalización
municipalize [mjuˈnɪsɪpəlaɪz] *va* municipalizar
munificence [mjuˈnɪfɪsəns] *s* munificencia
munificent [mjuˈnɪfɪsənt] *adj* munífico
muniment [ˈmjunɪmənt] *s* apoyo, defensa; **muniments** *spl* (law) documentos probatorios, privilegios
munition [mjuˈnɪʃən] *s* munición; *adj* de municiones; *va* municionar
munition dump *s* depósito de municiones
mural [ˈmjurəl] *adj* mural; *s* pintura mural, decoración mural
mural crown *s* (hist.) corona mural
murder [ˈmʌrdər] *s* asesinato, homicidio; **murder will out** el homicidio no se encubre; toda culpa a su tiempo ha de saberse; *va* asesinar; chafallar, chapucear (*cualquier trabajo*); despachurrar, destripar (*un discurso*); cantar o tocar bárbaramente
murderer [ˈmʌrdərər] *s* asesino
murderess [ˈmʌrdərɪs] *s* asesina
murderous [ˈmʌrdərəs] *adj* asesino; mortal; sanguinario
murex [ˈmjurɛks] *s* (*pl:* **-rexes** o **-rices** [rɪsiz]) (zool.) múrice; múrice (*color de púrpura*)
muriate [ˈmjurɪet] o [ˈmjurɪɪt] *s* (chem.) muriato
muriatic [ˌmjurɪˈætɪk] *adj* muriático
muriatic acid *s* (chem.) ácido muriático
murine [ˈmjuraɪn] o [ˈmjurɪn] *adj & s* (zool.) murino
murk [mʌrk] *s* obscuridad, tinieblas; *adj* (poet.) obscuro, tenebroso
murky [ˈmʌrkɪ] *adj* (*comp:* **-ier**; *super:* **-iest**) lóbrego; calinoso, espeso
murmur [ˈmʌrmər] *s* murmullo; (med.) murmullo (*p.ej., del corazón*); *va & vn* murmurar
murrain [ˈmʌrɪn] *s* (vet.) ántrax; (vet.) fiebre aftosa; **a murrain on you!** (archaic) ¡maldito seas!
murrhine [ˈmʌrɪn] o [ˈmʌraɪn] *adj* múrrino
murther [ˈmʌrðər] *s & va* (dial.) var. de **murder**
mus. abr. de **museum** y **music**
musaceous [mjuˈzeʃəs] *adj* (bot.) musáceo
muscadine [ˈmʌskədɪn] o [ˈmʌskədaɪn] *s* (bot.) vid y uva del sur de los Estados Unidos (*Vitis rotundifolia*)
muscardine [ˈmʌskərdɪn] o [ˈmʌskərdin] *s* (zool.) muscardina
muscarine [ˈmʌskərin] o [ˈmʌskərɪn] *s* (chem.) muscarina
muscat [ˈmʌskæt] o **muscatel** [ˌmʌskəˈtɛl] *s* moscatel (*uva o vino*)
muscle [ˈmʌsəl] *s* (anat.) músculo; (fig.) fuerza muscular; **not to move a muscle** mantenerse inmóvil; *vn* (coll.) avanzar o entrar por fuerza
muscle-bound [ˈmʌsəlˌbaund] *adj* con agujetas en los músculos
muscovado [ˌmʌskoˈvedo] *adj & s* mascabado
muscovite [ˈmʌskəvaɪt] *s* (mineral.) moscovita; (*cap.*) *adj & s* moscovita
Muscovitic [ˌmʌskəˈvɪtɪk] *adj* moscovítico
Muscovy [ˈmʌskəvɪ] *s* Moscovia
Muscovy duck *s* (orn.) pato almizclado
muscular [ˈmʌskjələr] *adj* muscular (*perteneciente a los músculos*); musculoso (*que tiene muchos músculos o músculos abultados*)
muscular dystrophy *s* (path.) distrofia muscular progresiva
muscularity [ˌmʌskjəˈlærɪtɪ] *s* carnadura, musculatura, fuerza muscular
musculature [ˈmʌskjələtʃər] *s* musculatura
muse [mjuz] *s* musa; (*cap.*) *s* (myth.) Musa; (*l.c.*) *va* decir pausadamente, midiendo bien las palabras; *vn* meditar, reflexionar; **to muse on** contemplar
musette bag [mjuˈzɛt] *s* morral, mochila
museum [mjuˈziəm] *s* museo
museum beetle *s* (ent.) antreno, polilla de los museos de historia natural
mush [mʌʃ] *s* gachas; (coll.) sensiblería; marcha por la tundra nevada con un trineo tirado por perros; *vn* caminar por la tundra nevada con un trineo tirado por perros
mushroom [ˈmʌʃrum] o [ˈmʌʃrum] *s* (bot.) hongo, seta; cosa que aparece de la noche a la mañana; *adj* fungoideo; que aparece de la noche a la mañana; *vn* aparecer de la noche a la mañana; tomar la forma de hongo; esparcirse o crecer rápidamente; aplastarse; **to mushroom into** convertirse en poco tiempo en
mushroom head *s* (mach.) cabeza de hongo
mushroom valve *s* (mach.) válvula anular, válvula tipo hongo
mushy [ˈmʌʃɪ] *adj* (*comp:* **-ier**; *super:* **-iest**) mollar, pulposo; (coll.) sobón, sensiblero; (coll.) baboso (*para con las mujeres*); **to be mushy** (coll.) hacerse unas gachas
music [ˈmjuzɪk] *s* música; **to face the music** (coll.) hacer frente a las consecuencias; **to set to music** poner en música
musical [ˈmjuzɪkəl] *adj* musical, músico; aficionado a la música; *s* (coll.) ópera bufa, zarzuela; (coll.) velada musical, concierto casero
musical comedy *s* ópera bufa, zarzuela
musicale [ˌmjuzɪˈkæl] *s* velada musical, concierto casero
musically [ˈmjuzɪkəlɪ] *adv* musicalmente
music box *s* caja de música
music cabinet *s* musiquero
music hall *s* salón de conciertos; (Brit.) teatro de variedades, café-concierto
musician [mjuˈzɪʃən] *s* músico
musicianly [mjuˈzɪʃənlɪ] *adj* entendido en música; artístico (*respecto de las cosas de música*)
musicianship [mjuˈzɪʃənʃɪp] *s* musicalidad
music lover *s* melómano
music of the spheres *s* música mundana (*armonía que guardan los cuerpos celestes en su movimiento*)
musicographer [ˌmjuzɪˈkɑgrəfər] *s* musicógrafo
musicological [ˌmjuzɪkəˈlɑdʒɪkəl] *adj* musicológico
musicologist [ˌmjuzɪˈkɑlədʒɪst] *s* musicólogo

musicology [ˌmjuzɪˈkɑlədʒɪ] *s* musicología
music paper *s* papel de música
music rack *s* atril
musing [ˈmjuzɪŋ] *adj* pensativo, meditativo; *s* meditación, contemplación
musk [mʌsk] *s* almizcle; olor o perfume de almizcle
musk beetle *s* (ent.) macuba
musk deer *s* (zool.) almizclero, cabra de almizcle
muskellunge [ˈmʌskəlʌndʒ] *s* (ichth.) sollo norteamericano (*Esox masquinongy*)
musket [ˈmʌskɪt] *s* mosquete
musketeer [ˌmʌskɪˈtɪr] *s* mosquetero
musketry [ˈmʌskɪtrɪ] *s* mosquetería (*tropa; descarga*); mosquetes
muskmelon [ˈmʌskˌmɛlən] *s* (bot.) melón
musk ox *s* (zool.) buey almizclado
muskrat [ˈmʌskˌræt] *s* (zool.) almizclera, rata almizclera
musk rose *s* (bot.) rosa almizcleña
musky [mʌskɪ] *adj* almizcleño, almizclado
Muslem o **Muslim** [ˈmʌzləm] o [ˈmʌsləm] *adj & s* muslim o muslime
muslin [ˈmʌzlɪn] *s* muselina; *adj* de muselina
muss [mʌs] *s* (coll.) desaliño, desorden, confusión; *va* (coll.) desaliñar, desarreglar (*el pelo*); (coll.) chafar (*p.ej., la ropa*)
mussel [ˈmʌsəl] *s* (zool.) mejillón
Mussulman [ˈmʌsəlmən] *adj* musulmán; *s* (*pl:* **-mans**) musulmán
mussy [ˈmʌsɪ] *adj* (*comp:* **-ier;** *super:* **-iest**) (coll.) desaliñado, ajado
must [mʌst] *s* mosto (*zumo de la uva antes de fermentar*); moho; cosa indispensable; *va* enmohecer; *vn* enmohecerse; *v aux* deber, tener que; deber de; **he must be ill** estará enfermo; **he must have been ill** habrá estado enfermo
mustache [məsˈtæʃ], [məsˈtɑʃ] o [ˈmʌstæʃ] *s* bigote o bigotes
mustachio [məsˈtɑʃo] *s* (*pl:* **-chios**) var. de **mustache**
mustachioed [məsˈtɑʃod] *adj* abigotado, bigotudo, amostachado
mustang [ˈmʌstæŋ] *s* mustango
mustard [mʌstərd] *s* (bot.) mostaza; mostaza (*polvo o salsa*)
mustard gas *s* gas mostaza
mustard oil *s* aceite de mostaza; (chem.) esencia de mostaza
mustard plaster *s* sinapismo, cataplasma de mostaza
mustard seed *s* semilla de mostaza; mostacilla (*munición*)
muster [ˈmʌstər] *s* asamblea, reunión; (mil.) asamblea; (mil.) matrícula de revista; (mil.) número de oficiales y soldados en la matrícula de revista; **to pass muster** pasar revista; ser aceptable, ser aceptado; *va* llamar a asamblea; juntar o reunir para pasar revista; tomar (*resolución, ánimo, etc.*); ascender a, importar; **to muster in** (mil.) alistar; **to muster out** (mil.) dar de baja, dar la licencia absoluta a; **to muster up** tomar (*resolución, ánimo, etc.*); *vn* juntarse
muster roll *s* (mil.) lista de revista
musty [ˈmʌstɪ] *adj* (*comp:* **-tier;** *super:* **-tiest**) mohoso; que huele a cerrado; anticuado, pasado de moda
mutability [ˌmjutəˈbɪlɪtɪ] *s* mutabilidad
mutable [ˈmjutəbəl] *adj* mudable
mutant [ˈmjutənt] *s* (biol.) mutante
mutarotation [ˌmjutəroˈteʃən] *s* (chem.) mutarrotación
mutate [ˈmjutet] *va* mudar; *vn* sufrir mutación
mutation [mjuˈteʃən] *s* mutación; (biol. & phonet.) mutación
mutational [mjuˈteʃənəl] *adj* mutacional
mutch [mʌtʃ] *s* (Scotch) gorra de mujer o de niño
mute [mjut] *adj* mudo; (phonet.) mudo (*que no se pronuncia; oclusivo*); *s* mudo; (phonet.) letra muda; (phonet.) consonante muda; (mus.) sordina; *va* poner sordina a, ajustar la sordina a
mutilate [ˈmjutɪlet] *va* mutilar
mutilation [ˌmjutɪˈleʃən] *s* mutilación
mutilator [ˈmjutɪˌletər] *s* mutilador
mutineer [ˌmjutɪˈnɪr] *s* amotinado; *vn* amotinarse
mutinous [ˈmjutɪnəs] *adj* amotinado
mutiny [ˈmjutɪnɪ] *s* (*pl:* **-nies**) motín; (*pret & pp:* **-nied**) *vn* amotinarse
mutism [ˈmjutɪzəm] *s* mutismo
mutt [mʌt] *s* (slang) perro, perro cruzado; (slang) bobo, tonto
mutter [ˈmʌtər] *s* murmullo; *va & vn* murmurar
mutton [ˈmʌtən] *s* carnero (*carne*)
mutton chop *s* chuleta de carnero; (fig.) barba de boca de hacha
mutual [ˈmjutʃuəl] *adj* mutuo; (coll.) común
mutual aid *s* socorros mutuos
mutual benefit society *s* mutualidad, montepío
mutual conductance *s* (elec.) conductancia mutua
mutual fund *s* sociedad inversionista mutualista
mutual inductance *s* (elec.) inductancia mutua
mutual induction *s* (elec.) inducción mutua
mutual insurance *s* seguro mutuo
mutualism [ˈmjutʃuəlɪzəm] *s* mutualismo
mutuality [ˌmjutʃuˈælɪtɪ] *s* mutualidad
mutual savings bank *s* caja mutua de ahorros
mutule [ˈmjutʃul] *s* (arch.) mútulo
mutuum [ˈmjutʃuəm] *s* (*pl:* **-a** [ə]) (law) mutuo
muzzle [ˈmʌzəl] *s* hocico; bozal (*frenillo que se pone en el hocico*); boca (*de un arma de fuego*); *va* abozalar; (fig.) amordazar, imponer silencio a
muzzleloader [ˈmʌzəlˌlodər] *s* arma de antecarga
muzzleloading [ˈmʌzəlˌlodɪŋ] *adj* de antecarga
muzzy [ˈmʌzɪ] *adj* (*comp:* **-zier;** *super:* **-ziest**) (coll.) confuso, atontado; (coll.) lóbrego; (coll.) borroso
my [maɪ] *adj poss* mi; *interj* ¡hombre!
myalgia [maɪˈældʒɪə] *s* (path.) mialgia
myasthenia [ˌmaɪæsˈθinɪə] *s* (path.) miastenia
mycelium [maɪˈsilɪəm] *s* (*pl:* **-a** [ə]) (bot.) micelio
Mycenae [maɪˈsini] *s* Micenas
Mycenaean [ˌmaɪsɪˈniən] *adj* micénico
mycologic [ˌmaɪkəˈlɑdʒɪk] o **mycological** [ˌmaɪkəˈlɑdʒɪkəl] *adj* micológico
mycologist [maɪˈkɑlədʒɪst] *s* micólogo
mycology [maɪˈkɑlədʒɪ] *s* micología
mycosis [maɪˈkosɪs] *s* (path.) micosis
mydriasis [mɪˈdraɪəsɪs] o [maɪˈdraɪəsɪs] *s* (path.) midriasis
mydriatic [ˌmɪdrɪˈætɪk] *adj & s* midriático
myelencephalon [ˌmaɪəlɛnˈsɛfəlɑn] *s* (anat.) mielencéfalo
myelin [ˈmaɪəlɪn] *s* (anat.) mielina
myelitis [ˌmaɪəˈlaɪtɪs] *s* (path.) mielitis
myna [ˈmaɪnə] *s* (orn.) estornino de los pastores
myocarditis [ˌmaɪokɑrˈdaɪtɪs] *s* (path.) miocarditis
myocardium [ˌmaɪoˈkɑrdɪəm] *s* (anat.) miocardio
myoglobin [ˌmaɪoˈglobɪn] *s* (biochem.) mioglobina
myograph [ˈmaɪəgræf] o [ˈmaɪəgrɑf] *s* miógrafo
myology [maɪˈɑlədʒɪ] *s* miología
myoma [maɪˈomə] *s* (*pl:* **-mata** [mətə] o **-mas**) (path.) mioma
myope [ˈmaɪop] *s* miope
myopia [maɪˈopɪə] *s* (path.) miopía
myopic [maɪˈɑpɪk] *adj* miope; (fig.) miope
myosis [maɪˈosɪs] *s* (path.) miosis
myosotis [ˌmaɪəˈsotɪs] *s* (bot.) miosotis
myriad [ˈmɪrɪəd] *s* miríada (*diez mil; número muy grande*); *adj* miríada de; vario, múltiple
myriapod [ˈmɪrɪəˌpɑd] *adj & s* (zool.) miriópodo
myricaceous [ˌmɪrɪˈkeʃəs] *adj* (bot.) miricáceo
myristicaceous [mɪˌrɪstɪˈkeʃəs] *adj* (bot.) miristicáceo
myrmecologist [ˌmʌrmɪˈkɑlədʒɪst] *s* mirmecólogo
myrmecology [ˌmʌrmɪˈkɑlədʒɪ] *s* mirmecología
myrmecophagous [ˌmʌrmɪˈkɑfəgəs] *adj* mirmecófago

myrmecophile ['mʌrmɪko,faɪl] o ['mʌrmɪko,fɪl] *s* (ent.) mirmecófilo
myrmecophilous [,mʌrmɪ'kɑfɪləs] *adj* mirmecófilo
myrmidon ['mʌrmɪdɑn] *s* secuaz fiel; esbirro; (*cap.*) *s* (myth.) Mirmidón
myrobalan [maɪ'rɑbələn] *s* (bot.) mirobálano (*árbol y fruto*)
myrrh [mʌr] *s* mirra
myrrhed [mʌrd] *adj* mirrado
myrrhic ['mʌrɪk] o ['mɪrɪk] *adj* mirrino
myrtaceous [mʌr'teʃəs] *adj* (bot.) mirtáceo
myrtle ['mʌrtəl] *s* (bot.) arrayán, mirto; (bot.) pervinca, brusela
myself [maɪ'sɛlf] *pron pers* yo mismo; me; mí, mí mismo; **with myself** conmigo
mystagogue ['mɪstəgɔg] o ['mɪstəgɑg] *s* (hist.) mistagogo
mysterious [mɪs'tɪrɪəs] *adj* misterioso
mystery ['mɪstərɪ] *s* (*pl:* **-ies**) misterio; (theat.) auto, misterio; (archaic) oficio, mester; (archaic) gremio
mystery play *s* auto, misterio
mystic ['mɪstɪk] *adj & s* místico
mystical ['mɪstɪkəl] *adj* místico
mysticism ['mɪstɪsɪzəm] *s* misticismo
mystification [,mɪstɪfɪ'keʃən] *s* misterio; confusión, perplejidad, mixtificación
mystify ['mɪstɪfaɪ] (*pret & pp:* **-fied**) *va* rodear de misterio; confundir, dejar perplejo, mixtificar
myth. abr. de **mythology**
myth [mɪθ] *s* mito
mythic ['mɪθɪk] o **mythical** ['mɪθɪkəl] *adj* mítico
mythological [,mɪθə'lɑdʒɪkəl] *adj* mitológico
mythologically [,mɪθə'lɑdʒɪkəlɪ] *adv* mitológicamente
mythologist [mɪ'θɑlədʒɪst] *s* mitológico, mitologista o mitólogo
mythology [mɪ'θɑlədʒɪ] *s* (*pl:* **-gies**) mitología
Mytilene [,mɪtɪ'linɪ] *s* Mitilene
myxedema [,mɪksɪ'dimə] *s* (path.) mixedema
myxomatosis [,mɪksomə'tosɪs] *s* (vet.) mixomatosis
myxomycete [,mɪksomaɪ'sit] *s* (bot.) mixomiceto

N

N, n [ɛn] *s* (*pl:* **N's, n's** [ɛnz]) décimocuarta letra del alfabeto inglés; (*l.c.*) *s* (alg.) n (*número indeterminado*)
n. abr. de **neuter, new, nominative, noon, north, northern, noun** y **number**
N. abr. de **Nationalist, Navy, New, Noon, Norse, North, Northern** y **November**
N abr. de **North** y **Northern**
N.A. abr. de **National Army** y **North America**
nab [næb] (*pret & pp:* **nabbed;** *ger:* **nabbing**) *va* (slang) coger, agarrar; (slang) prender, poner preso
nabob [ˈnebɑb] *s* nabab o nababo
Naboth [ˈnebɑθ] *s* (Bib.) Nabot
nacelle [næˈsɛl] *s* (aer.) barquilla o nacela
nacre [ˈnekər] *s* nácar
nadir [ˈnedər] o [ˈnedɪr] *s* (astr. & fig.) nadir
nag [næg] *s* caballo; caballejo, jaco; pequeño caballo de silla; (*pret & pp:* **nagged;** *ger:* **nagging**) *va* importunar regañando; *vn* regañar, ser regañón; **to nag at** importunar regañando
Nahum [ˈnehəm] *s* (Bib.) Nahúm
naiad o **Naiad** [ˈneæd] o [ˈnaɪæd] *s* (myth.) náyade; (fig.) nadadora
nail [nel] *s* uña (*del dedo*); clavo (*para asegurar una cosa a otra*); **on the nail** en seguida, en el acto; **to bite one's nails** comerse las uñas; **to hit the nail on the head** dar en el clavo; *va* clavar (*asegurar con clavos; fijar, p. ej., los ojos, la atención*); tachonar (*adornar con tachones*); poner término a (*p.ej., una mentira*); **to nail down** o **to nail up** clavar, cerrar con clavos
nailbrush [ˈnel,brʌʃ] *s* cepillo para las uñas
nail claw *s* arrancaclavos, sacaclavos
nail clippers o **nail cutters** *spl* cortaúñas
nail extractor *s* arrancaclavos, sacaclavos
nail file *s* lima de uñas, lima para las uñas
nail hole *s* clavera; uña (*en la hoja de un cortaplumas*)
nail polish *s* esmalte para las uñas, laca de uñas
nail puller *s* cazaclavos
nail scissors *ssg* o *spl* tijeras para las uñas
nailset [ˈnel,sɛt] *s* contrapunzón
nail works *s* fábrica de clavos
nainsook [ˈnensʊk] o [ˈnænsʊk] *s* nansú
naïve o **naive** [nɑˈiv] *adj* cándido, sencillo, ingenuo
naïveté [nɑ,ivˈte] *s* candidez, sencillez, ingenuidad
naja [ˈnedʒə] *s* (zool.) naja
naked [ˈnekɪd] *adj* desnudo; **to go naked** ir desnudo; **to strip naked** desnudar; desnudarse; **with the naked eye** a simple vista
nakedness [ˈnekɪdnɪs] *s* desnudez
namby-pamby [ˈnæmbɪˈpæmbɪ] *adj* melindroso; *s* (*pl:* **-bies**) melindroso (*persona*); melindres (*delicadeza*)
name [nem] *s* nombre; fama, reputación; linaje, raza; **by name** de nombre; **in the name of** a nombre de, en nombre de; **in name only** tan sólo en el nombre; **to answer to the name of** atender (*p.ej., un perro*) por; **to call names** poner como un trapo (*a una persona*); **to go by the name of** ser conocido por el nombre de; **to make a name for oneself** darse a conocer, hacerse un nombre; **what is your name?** ¿cómo se llama Vd.?; **my name is** me llamo; *va* nombrar; designar; fijar (*el precio de una cosa*)
nameless [ˈnemlɪs] *adj* innominado, sin nombre, anónimo; obscuro; nefando
namely [ˈnemlɪ] *adv* a saber
name plate *s* placa, letrero con nombre; placa de fabricante
namesake [ˈnem,sek] *s* homónimo, tocayo
Nancy [ˈnænsɪ] *s* Anita
nandu [ˈnændu] *s* (orn.) ñandú
nankeen o **nankin** [nænˈkin] *s* mahón o nanquín; **nankeens** *spl* pantalones de mahón
nanny goat [ˈnænɪ] *s* (coll.) cabra
Naomi [neˈomɪ] o [ˈneomɪ] (Bib.) Noemí
nap [næp] *s* lanilla, flojel (*pelillo que tiene el paño*); siesta, sueñecillo; **against the nap** a contrapelo, a pospelo; **to take a nap** descabezar un sueñecillo; (*pret & pp:* **napped;** *ger:* **napping**) *vn* dormir un rato; estar desprevenido; **to catch napping** coger desprevenido
napalm [ˈnepɑm] *s* (mil.) gelatina incendiaria
nape [nep] *s* nuca; **nape of the neck** nuca
Naperian [neˈpɪrɪən] *adj* var. de **Napierian**
napery [ˈnepərɪ] *s* mantelería
Naphtali [ˈnæftəlaɪ] *s* (Bib.) Naftalí o Neftalí
naphtha [ˈnæfθə] *s* nafta
naphthalene o **naphthaline** [ˈnæfθəlin] o **naphthalin** [ˈnæfθəlɪn] *s* (chem.) naftalina
naphthol [ˈnæfθɑl] *s* (chem.) naftol
Napierian [neˈpɪrɪən] *adj* neperiano
napkin [ˈnæpkɪn] *s* servilleta (*para aseo en la mesa*); pañal (*de los niños de teta*)
napkin ring *s* servilletero
Naples [ˈnepəlz] *s* Nápoles
Napoleon [nəˈpolɪən] *s* Napoleón; (*l.c.*) *s* napoleón (*moneda*); pastelito de crema y hojaldre
Napoleonic [nə,polɪˈɑnɪk] *adj* napoleónico
Napoleonic code *s* código napoleónico
Narbonne [nɑrˈbɑn] *s* Narbona
narceine [ˈnɑrsɪin] *s* (chem.) narceína
narcissism [nɑrˈsɪsɪzəm] *s* (psychoanal.) narcisismo
narcissus [nɑrˈsɪsəs] *s* (bot.) narciso; (*cap.*) *s* (myth.) Narciso
narcosis [nɑrˈkosɪs] *s* narcosis
narcotic [nɑrˈkɑtɪk] *s & adj* narcótico, estupefaciente
narcotine [ˈnɑrkətin] *s* (chem.) narcotina
narcotism [ˈnɑrkətɪzəm] *s* narcotismo
narcotize [ˈnɑrkətaɪz] *va* narcotizar
nard [nɑrd] *s* (bot. & pharm.) nardo
nares [ˈnɛriz] *spl* (anat.) narices, ventanas de la nariz
narghile o **nargile** [ˈnɑrgɪlɪ] *s* narguile
narratable [næˈretəbəl] *adj* narrable
narrate [næˈret] *va* narrar
narration [næˈreʃən] *s* narración
narrative [ˈnærətɪv] *adj* narrativo; *s* narrativa (*relato; habilidad en narrar*)
narrator [næˈretər] *s* narrador
narrow [ˈnæro] *adj* estrecho, angosto; intolerante; minucioso; estricto (*sentido de una palabra*); **in narrow circumstances** alcanzado, falto de recursos; **to have a narrow escape** escapar por un pelo; *s* garganta, desfiladero; **narrows** *spl* angostura, paso estrecho; *va* enangostar, estrechar, encoger, disminuir; *vn* enangostarse, estrecharse, encogerse, reducirse
narrow gauge *s* vía estrecha, trocha angosta
narrow-gauge [ˈnæro,gedʒ] *adj* de vía angosta o estrecha, de trocha angosta; intolerante
narrow-minded [ˈnæroˈmaɪndɪd] *adj* intolerante, poco liberal (en las ideas), de miras estrechas
narrow-mindedness [ˈnæroˈmaɪndɪdnɪs] *s* intolerancia, falta de liberalidad (en las ideas)
narrowness [ˈnæronɪs] *s* estrechez
narrow squeak *s* (coll.) escapada en una tabla
narwhal [ˈnɑrwəl] *s* (zool.) narval
nasal [ˈnezəl] *adj & s* nasal
nasality [neˈzælɪtɪ] *s* nasalidad
nasalization [,nezəlɪˈzeʃən] *s* nasalización; gangueo
nasalize [ˈnezəlaɪz] *va* nasalizar; *vn* ganguear

nasal vowel *s* vocal nasal
nascent ['næsənt] o ['nesənt] *adj* naciente; (chem.) naciente
nastic ['næstɪk] *adj* (plant path.) nástico
nastiness ['næstɪnɪs] o ['nɑstɪnɪs] *s* suciedad, asquerosidad; molestia; desvergüenza
nasturtium [nə'stʌrʃəm] *s* (bot.) capuchina, espuela de galán
nasty ['næstɪ] o ['nɑstɪ] *adj* (*comp:* **-tier;** *super:* **-tiest**) sucio, asqueroso; desagradable; desvergonzado; amenazador; terrible, horrible
nat. abr. de **national, native** y **natural**
natal ['netəl] *adj* natal
natality [ne'tælɪtɪ] *s* nacimiento; natalidad
natant ['netənt] *adj* natátil; (bot.) natátil
natatorial [,netə'torɪəl] *adj* natatorio
natatorium [,netə'torɪəm] *s* (*pl:* **-ums** o **-a** [ə]) piscina de natación
natatory ['netə,torɪ] *adj* natatorio
Nathan ['neθən] *s* (Bib.) Natán
Nathanael [nə'θænɪəl] *s* (Bib.) Natanael
nation ['neʃən] *s* nación
national ['næʃənəl] *adj & s* nacional
national anthem *s* himno nacional
national flag *s* bandera o pabellón nacional
national guard *s* milicia nacional, guardia nacional
national holiday *s* fiesta nacional
nationalism ['næʃənəlɪzəm] *s* nacionalismo
nationalist ['næʃənəlɪst] *adj & s* nacionalista
nationalistic [,næʃənəl'ɪstɪk] *adj* nacionalista
nationality [,næʃən'ælɪtɪ] *s* (*pl:* **-ties**) nacionalidad, naturalidad
nationalization [,næʃənəlɪ'zeʃən] *s* nacionalización
nationalize ['næʃənəlaɪz] *va* nacionalizar
National Socialist Party *s* partido nacionalsocialista
nation-wide ['neʃən,waɪd] *adj* por toda la nación, de toda la nación
native ['netɪv] *adj* nativo; indígena; materno (*idioma*); **to go native** vivir como los indígenas; *s* natural; indígena
native-born ['netɪv,bɔrn] *adj* indígena
native land *s* patria
nativity [nə'tɪvɪtɪ] *s* (*pl:* **-ties**) nacimiento, natividad; (astr.) horóscopo; (*cap.*) *s* natividad (*festividad en que se celebra el nacimiento de Jesucristo, de la Virgen María o de San Juan Bautista*); (f.a.) pintura de la natividad
natl. abr. de **national**
Nato ['neto] *s* la O.T.A.N. (*la Organización para el Tratado del Atlántico Norte*)
natrolite ['nætrəlaɪt] o ['netrəlaɪt] *s* (mineral.) natrolita
natron ['netrɑn] *s* (mineral.) natrón
nattiness ['nætɪnɪs] *s* elegancia, garbo
natty ['nætɪ] *adj* (*comp:* **-tier;** *super:* **-tiest**) elegante, garboso
natural ['nætʃərəl] *adj* natural; (mus.) natural; *s* imbécil; (coll.) cosa de éxito certero; (mus.) tono natural, nota natural; (mus.) becuadro (*signo*); (mus.) tecla blanca (*del piano*)
natural gas *s* gas natural, gas combustible natural
natural history *s* historia natural
naturalism ['nætʃərəlɪzəm] *s* naturalismo
naturalist ['nætʃərəlɪst] *s* naturalista
naturalistic [,nætʃərə'lɪstɪk] *adj* naturalista
naturalization [,nætʃərəlɪ'zeʃən] *s* naturalización
naturalization papers *spl* carta de naturaleza
naturalize ['nætʃərəlaɪz] *va* naturalizar; *vn* naturalizarse (*vivir como los naturales de un país extranjero*)
natural law *s* ley natural
naturally ['nætʃərəlɪ] *adv* naturalmente; por supuesto
natural magnet *s* imán natural
naturalness ['nætʃərəlnɪs] *s* naturalidad
natural philosophy *s* filosofía natural
natural religion *s* religión natural
natural resources *spl* recursos naturales
natural rights *spl* derechos naturales
natural science *s* ciencia natural
natural selection *s* (biol.) selección natural
natural sign *s* (mus.) becuadro
nature ['netʃər] *s* naturaleza; **from nature** (f.a.) del natural; **in the nature of** algo como
nature study *s* historia natural
naturopathy [,netʃər'ɑpəθɪ] *s* naturopatía
naught [nɔt] *s* nada; cero; **to bring to naught** anular, invalidar, destruir; **to come to naught** reducirse a nada, frustrarse
naughtiness ['nɔtɪnɪs] *s* desobediencia, picardía; desvergüenza
naughty ['nɔtɪ] *adj* (*comp:* **-tier;** *super:* **-tiest**) desobediente, pícaro; desvergonzado; verde (*cuento*)
nausea ['nɔʃɪə] o ['nɔsɪə] *s* náusea (*mareo, basca; repugnancia, asco grande*)
nauseate ['nɔʃɪet] o ['nɔsɪet] *va* dar náuseas a (*marear, dar bascas a; dar asco a*); *vn* nausear, marearse
nauseating ['nɔʃɪ,etɪŋ] o ['nɔsɪ,etɪŋ] *adj* nauseabundo, asqueroso
nauseous ['nɔʃɪəs] o ['nɔsɪəs] *adj* nauseabundo
Nausicaä [nɔ'sɪkeə] *s* (myth.) Nausica
nautical ['nɔtɪkəl] *adj* náutico, naval
nautical day *s* singladura (*intervalo de 24 horas, contadas de mediodía a mediodía*)
nautical mile *s* milla marina
nautics ['nɔtɪks] *ssg* náutica; *spl* deportes acuáticos
nautilus ['nɔtɪləs] *s* (*pl:* **-luses** o **-li** [laɪ]) (zool.) nautilo
nav. abr. de **naval** y **navigation**
naval ['nevəl] *adj* naval, naval militar
Naval Academy *s* (U.S.A.) Escuela Naval Militar
naval air base *s* base aeronaval
naval base *s* base naval
naval officer *s* oficial de marina
naval station *s* apostadero
Navarre [nə'vɑr] *s* Navarra
Navarrese [,nɑvɑ'riz] *adj* navarro; *s* (*pl:* **-rese**) navarro
nave [nev] *s* (arch.) nave central, nave principal; cubo (*de una rueda*)
navel ['nevəl] *s* ombligo; (fig.) centro, medio
navel orange *s* navel, naranja umbilicada, naranja de ombligo
navicert ['nævɪsʌrt] *s* (Brit.) pasavante
navicula [nə'vɪkjələ] *s* (*pl:* **-lae** [li]) (bot.) navícula; (eccl.) naveta (*para ministrar el incienso*)
navicular [nə'vɪkjələr] *adj* navicular; *s* (anat.) navicular
navigability [,nævɪgə'bɪlɪtɪ] *s* navegabilidad (*de un río*); buen gobierno (*de un buque*)
navigable ['nævɪgəbəl] *adj* navegable (*dícese de un río, canal, etc.*); marinero, de buen gobierno
navigate ['nævɪget] *va & vn* navegar
navigation [,nævɪ'geʃən] *s* navegación
navigator ['nævɪ,getər] *s* navegador o navegante; oficial de derrota; tratado de náutica; (Brit.) peón
navvy ['nævɪ] *s* (*pl:* **-vies**) (Brit.) peón, bracero
navy ['nevɪ] *s* (*pl:* **-vies**) marina de guerra, flota de guerra, armada; marina (*conjunto de personas que sirven en la marina de guerra*); (archaic & poet.) armada (*reunión de buques*); color azul obscuro; *adj* azul obscuro
navy bean *s* (bot.) frijol blanco común
navy blue *s* azul de mar, azul marino
navy-blue ['nevɪ'blu] *adj* azul de mar, azul marino
navy chaplain *s* capellán de la armada, capellán de navío
navy yard *s* arsenal de puerto
nawab [nə'wɔb] *s* nabab o nababo
nay [ne] *s* no, voto negativo; *adv* y aun, más aún; (obs.) no
Nazarene [,næzə'rin] *adj & s* nazareno; **the Nazarene** el Nazareno o el Divino Nazareno
Nazareth ['næzərəθ] o ['næzərɪθ] *s* Nazaret
Nazi ['nɑtsɪ] o ['nætsɪ] *adj* nazi o nacista; *s* (*pl:* **-zis**) nazi o nacista
Nazify ['nɑtsɪfaɪ] o ['nætsɪfaɪ] (*pret & pp:* **-fied**) *va* nazificar
Nazism ['nɑtsɪzəm] o ['nætsɪzəm] o **Naziism** ['nɑtsɪɪzəm] o ['nætsɪɪzəm] *s* nazismo
n.b. abr. de **nota bene** (Lat.) **note well, observe carefully**
N.B. abr. de **New Brunswick** y **nota bene** (Lat.) **note well, observe carefully**
N-bomb ['ɛn,bɑm] *s* bomba de neutrones

N.C. abr. de **North Carolina**

N.C.O. abr. de **noncommissioned officer**

N.D. o **N. Dak.** abr. de **North Dakota**

n.e. o **NE** abr. de **northeast** y **northeastern**

N.E. abr. de **New England, northeast** y **northeastern**

Neanderthal man [nɪ'ændərtɑl] *s* (anthrop.) hombre de Neanderthal

neap [nip] *s* marea muerta

Neapolitan [,niə'pɑlɪtən] *adj & s* napolitano

Neapolitan ice cream *s* arlequín

Neapolitan medlar *s* (bot.) acerolo (*arbusto*); acerola (*fruto*)

neap tide *s* marea muerta

near [nɪr] *adj* próximo, cercano; íntimo; tacaño; imitado; literal; **near** + *ger* cercano a + *inf; adv* cerca; íntimamente; **to come near** acercarse; acercarse a; *prep* cerca de; hacia, por; **to come near** + *ger* estar para + *inf*, estar en poco que + *subj; va* acercarse a; *vn* acercarse

near beer *s* cerveza sin alcohol

nearby ['nɪr,baɪ] *adj* próximo, cercano; *adv* cerca

Near East *s* Cercano Oriente, Próximo Oriente

nearly ['nɪrlɪ] *adv* casi; de cerca; íntimamente; tacañamente; por poco, p.ej., **he nearly fell** por poco se cae

nearness ['nɪrnɪs] *s* proximidad; intimidad

near-sighted ['nɪr'saɪtɪd] *adj* miope

nearsightedness ['nɪr'saɪtɪdnɪs] *s* miopía

neat [nit] *adj* pulcro, aseado; pulido; primoroso, diestro; puro, sin mezcla; *ssg* res vacuna; *spl* ganado vacuno

neath o **'neath** [niθ] *prep* (poet.) var. de **beneath**

neatherd ['nit,hʌrd] *s* vaquero

neatness ['nitnɪs] *s* pulcritud, aseo, esmero; pulidez; primor, habilidad

neat's-foot oil ['nits,fʊt] *s* aceite de pie de buey

neb [nɛb] *s* pico (*del ave*); punta, extremidad; boca, nariz; hocico

Nebuchadnezzar [,nɛbjəkəd'nɛzər] *s* (Bib.) Nabucodonosor

nebula ['nɛbjələ] *s* (*pl:* **-lae** [li] o **-las**) (astr.) nebulosa

nebular ['nɛbjələr] *adj* (astr.) nebular, nebuloso

nebular hypothesis *s* (astr.) hipótesis nebular, hipótesis de Laplace

nebulization [,nɛbjəlɪ'zeʃən] *s* nebulización

nebulize ['nɛbjəlaɪz] *va & vn* nebulizar

nebulosity [,nɛbjə'lɑsɪtɪ] *s* (*pl:* **-ties**) nebulosidad; (astr.) nebulosa

nebulous ['nɛbjələs] *adj* nebuloso (*nubloso, brumoso, neblinoso, confuso*); (astr.) nebuloso

necessarily ['nɛsɪ,sɛrɪlɪ] *adv* necesariamente

necessary ['nɛsɪ,sɛrɪ] *adj* necesario; *s* (*pl:* **-ies**) cosa necesaria, cosa indispensable

necessitate [nɪ'sɛsɪtet] *va* necesitar

necessitous [nɪ'sɛsɪtəs] *adj* necesitado

necessity [nɪ'sɛsɪtɪ] *s* (*pl:* **-ties**) necesidad; **of necessity** de o por necesidad; **under the necessity of** en la necesidad de

neck [nɛk] *s* cuello (*del cuerpo, prenda de vestir, columna, vasija, diente, etc.*); gollete (*de botella*); mástil (*de violín o guitarra*); istmo, península; estrecho; **to break one's neck** (coll.) deslomarse, matarse trabajando; **to stick one's neck out** (coll.) descubrir el cuerpo (*exponerse a las malas resultas de un negocio*); **to win by a neck** ganar con poca ventaja; **neck and neck** parejos; **neck or nothing** a toda costa; *vn* (slang) acariciarse (*dos enamorados*)

neckband ['nɛk,bænd] *s* tirilla (*de camisa*)

neckcloth ['nɛk,klɔθ] o ['nɛk,klɑθ] *s* corbata, pañuelo de cuello

neckerchief ['nɛkərtʃɪf] *s* pañuelo de cuello, pañoleta (*de forma triangular*)

neckguard ['nɛk,gɑrd] *s* cubrenuca

necklace ['nɛklɪs] *s* collar (*usado como adorno*)

necklet ['nɛklɪt] *s* collar

neckpiece ['nɛk,pis] *s* cuello de pieles

necktie ['nɛk,taɪ] *s* corbata

necktie pin *s* alfiler de corbata

neckwear ['nɛk,wɛr] *s* prendas para el cuello

necrology [nɛ'krɑlədʒɪ] *s* necrología

necromancer ['nɛkro,mænsər] *s* necromántico o nigromántico

necromancy ['nɛkro,mænsɪ] *s* necromancia o nigromancia

necromantic [,nɛkro'mæntɪk] *adj* necromántico o nigromántico

necropolis [nɛ'krɑpəlɪs] *s* necrópolis

necrosis [nɛ'krosɪs] *s* (*pl:* **-ses** [siz]) (path. & bot.) necrosis

nectar ['nɛktər] *s* (myth., bot. & fig.) néctar

nectareous [nɛk'terɪəs] *adj* nectáreo

nectarine ['nɛktərɪn] *adj* nectarino; [,nɛktə'rin] o ['nɛktərɪn] *s* bruñón (*melocotón*)

nectary ['nɛktərɪ] *s* (*pl:* **-ries**) (bot.) nectario

née o **nee** [ne] *adj* nacida o de soltera, p.ej., **Mary Wilson, née Miller** María Wilson, nacida Miller o María Wilson, de soltera Miller

need [nid] *s* necesidad; requisito; **to be in need** estar necesitado; **to be in need of** estar necesitado de; **to have need of** necesitar, tener necesidad de; **to have need to** + *inf* deber, necesitar, tener necesidad de + *inf; va* necesitar; **to need** + *inf* deber, tener que + *inf;* **if need be** si fuere necesario; *vn* estar necesitado; ser necesario

needful ['nidfəl] *adj* necesario; **the needful** lo necesario; (slang) el dinero

needle ['nidəl] *s* aguja (*con que se cose; del fonógrafo; obelisco*); **to look for a needle in a haystack** buscar una aguja en un pajar; *va* coser con aguja; aguijar, incitar; (coll.) añadir alcohol a (*cerveza o vino*)

needle bath *s* ducha en alfileres

needlecase ['nidəl,kes] *s* alfiletero

needlefish ['nidəl,fɪʃ] *s* (ichth.) aguja

needleful ['nidəlfʊl] *s* hebra

needle gun *s* fusil de aguja (*de Dreyse*)

needle point *s* bordado al pasado; encaje de mano

needle scratch *s* arañar de la aguja (*del fonógrafo*)

needless ['nidlɪs] *adj* innecesario, inútil

needle valve *s* válvula de aguja

needlewoman ['nidəl,wʊmən] *s* (*pl:* **-women**) costurera

needlework ['nidəl,wʌrk] *s* costura, labor, bordado

needn't ['nidənt] contracción de **need not**

needs [nidz] *adv* necesariamente, forzosamente

needy ['nidɪ] *adj* (*comp:* **-ier;** *super:* **-iest**) necesitado, indigente; **the needy** los necesitados

ne'er [nɛr] *adv* (poet.) var. de **never**

ne'er-do-well ['nɛrdu,wɛl] *adj & s* holgazán, perdido

nefarious [nɪ'fɛrɪəs] *adj* nefario

negate [nɪ'get] o ['niget] *va* negar; anular, invalidar

negation [nɪ'geʃən] *s* negación

negative ['nɛgətɪv] *adj* negativo; *s* negativa; (math.) término negativo; (elec.) electricidad negativa, borne negativo; (gram.) negación; (phot.) negativa o negativo; *va* desaprobar; inutilizar, anular

negativism ['nɛgətɪvɪzəm] *s* negativismo

negatron ['nɛgətrɑn] *s* (chem.) negatrón

neglect [nɪ'glɛkt] *s* negligencia, descuido, abandono; *va* descuidar, abandonar; **to neglect oneself** dejarse, descuidarse de sí mismo; **to neglect to** + *inf* dejar de, olvidarse de + *inf*

neglectful [nɪ'glɛktfəl] *adj* negligente, descuidado

négligé [negli'ʒe] o **negligee** [,nɛglɪ'ʒe] o ['nɛglɪʒe] *s* traje de casa, bata de mujer

negligence ['nɛglɪdʒəns] *s* negligencia, descuido

negligent ['nɛglɪdʒənt] *adj* negligente, descuidado

negligible ['nɛglɪdʒɪbəl] *adj* insignificante, imperceptible

negotiability [nɪ,goʃɪə'bɪlɪtɪ] *s* negociabilidad

negotiable [nɪ'goʃɪəbəl] *adj* negociable; transitable

negotiate [nɪ'goʃɪet] *va* negociar; (coll.) vencer, salvar; *vn* negociar

negotiation [nɪ,goʃɪ'eʃən] *s* negociación

negotiator [nɪ'goʃɪ,etər] *s* negociador

Negress ['nigrɪs] *s* (offensive) negra

Negrito [nɪ'grito] *s* (*pl:* **-tos** o **-toes**) negrito (*individuo de una raza parecida a la de los*

negros, de estatura muy pequeña y de color pardo muy obscuro)
Negro ['nigro] o **negro** *s* (*pl:* **-groes**) negro; *adj* negro
Negroid ['nigrɔɪd] *adj* negroide o negroideo
negus ['nigəs] *s* carraspada, sangría; (*cap.*) *s* Negus (*emperador de Abisinia*)
Neh. abr. de **Nehemiah**
Nehemiah [,niə'maɪə] *s* (Bib.) Nehemías
neigh [ne] *s* relincho; *vn* relinchar
neighbor ['nebər] *s* vecino; prójimo (*cualquier hombre respecto de otro*); *adj* vecino; *va* ser vecino de, colindar con; ser amigo de; *vn* estar cercano; tener relaciones amistosas
neighborhood ['nebərhud] *s* vecindad; **in the neighborhood of** (coll.) cerca de, casi
neighboring ['nebərɪŋ] *adj* vecino, colindante
neighborly ['nebərlɪ] *adj* buen vecino, amable
neighbour ['nebər] *s, adj, va & vn* (Brit.) var. de **neighbor**
neither ['niðər] o ['naɪðər] *pron indef* ninguno (de los dos); ni uno ni otro, ni lo uno ni lo otro; *adj indef* ninguno . . . (de los dos); **neither one** ninguno de los dos; *conj* ni; tampoco; ni . . . tampoco; **neither . . . nor** ni . . . ni
nelumbo [nɪ'lʌmbo] *s* (*pl:* **-bos**) (bot.) nelumbio
nemathelminth [,nɛmə'θɛlmɪnθ] *s* (zool.) nematelminto
nematocyst ['nɛmətəsɪst] *s* (zool.) nematocisto
nematode ['nɛmətod] *s* (zool.) nematoda
Nemean [nɪ'miən] o ['nimɪən] *adj* nemeo
Nemean games *spl* fiestas nemeas
Nemean lion *s* (myth.) león de Nemea
nemesis ['nɛmɪsɪs] *s* (*pl:* **-ses** [siz]) justo castigo; castigador; (*cap.*) *s* (myth.) Némesis
Neo-Catholic ['niə'kæθəlɪk] *adj & s* neocatólico
Neo-Catholicism ['niəkə'θɑlɪsɪzəm] *s* neocatolicismo
neoclassic [,niə'klæsɪk] *adj* neoclásico
neoclassicism [,niə'klæsɪsɪzəm] *s* neoclasicismo
neoclassicist [,niə'klæsɪsɪst] *s* neoclásico
neodymium [,nio'dɪmɪəm] *s* (chem.) neodimio
Neo-Latin [,niə'lætɪn] o [,niə'lætən] *adj* neolatino
neolithic [,nio'lɪθɪk] *adj* neolítico
neologism [ni'ɑlədʒɪzəm] *s* neologismo
neologist [ni'ɑlədʒɪst] *s* neologista o neólogo
neology [ni'ɑlədʒɪ] *s* neología
neomycin [,nio'maɪsɪn] *s* (pharm.) neomicina
neon ['niɑn] *s* (chem.) neón o neo
neon light *s* lámpara neón, lámpara de neo
neophyte ['niofaɪt] *s* neófito
neoplasm ['niəplæzəm] *s* (path.) neoplasia o neoplasma
Neo-Platonism o **Neoplatonism** [,nio'pletənɪzəm] *s* neoplatonicismo
neoprene ['niəprin] *s* neopreno
neosalvarsan [,nio'sælvərsæn] *s* (trademark) neosalvarsán
Neo-Scholasticism ['niəskə'læstɪsɪzəm] *s* neoescolasticismo
neoteny [nɪ'ɑtənɪ] *s* (biol.) neotenia
Neo-Thomism ['nio'tomɪzəm] o ['nio'θomɪzəm] *s* neotomismo
neoytterbium [,nio·ɪ'tʌrbɪəm] *s* (chem.) neoiterbio
Neozoic [,nio'zo·ɪk] *adj* neozoico
Nepal [nɪ'pɔl] *s* el Nepal
Nepalese [,nɛpə'liz] *adj* nepalés; *s* (pl: **-lese**) nepalés
nepenthe [nɪ'pɛnθɪ] *s* nepente (*bebida mágica*); (bot.) nepente
nephew ['nɛfju] o ['nɛvju] *s* sobrino
nephoscope ['nɛfəskop] *s* nefoscopio
nephralgia [nɪ'frældʒɪə] *s* (path.) nefralgia
nephrectomy [nɪ'frɛktəmɪ] *s* (*pl:* **-mies**) (surg.) nefrectomía
nephridium [nɪ'frɪdɪəm] *s* (*pl:* **-a** [ə]) (embryol.) nefridio
nephrite ['nɛfraɪt] *s* (mineral.) nefrita
nephritic [nɪ'frɪtɪk] *adj* nefrítico
nephritis [nɪ'fraɪtɪs] *s* (path.) nefritis
nephrolith ['nɛfrəlɪθ] *s* (path.) nefrolito
nephrotomy [nɪ'frɑtəmɪ] *s* (*pl:* **-mies**) (surg.) nefrotomía
Nepos ['nipɑs] o ['nɛpɑs] *s* Nepote
nepotism ['nɛpətɪzəm] *s* nepotismo
Neptune ['nɛptʃun] o ['nɛptjun] *s* (myth. & astr.) Neptuno
Neptunian [nɛp'tʃunɪən] o [nɛp'tjunɪən] *adj* neptúneo; (geol.) neptúnico
neptunium [nɛp'tʃunɪəm] o [nɛp'tjunɪəm] *s* (chem.) neptunio
Nereid o **nereid** ['nɪrɪɪd] *s* (myth.) nereida
Nereus ['nɪrus] *s* (myth.) Nereo
Nero ['nɪro] *s* Nerón
nerol ['nɪrəl] *s* (chem.) nerol
neroli oil ['nɛrəlɪ] o ['nɪrəlɪ] *s* (chem.) aceite de nerolí
nerval ['nʌrvəl] *adj* nerval
nervation [nʌr'veʃən] *s* nervadura o nerviación
nerve [nʌrv] *s* (anat. & bot.) nervio; (ent.) nervadura; (fig.) nervio; (slang) descaro; **nerves** *spl* excitabilidad nerviosa; **to get on one's nerves** enojar, crispar o irritar los nervios a; **to strain every nerve** esforzarse lo sumo posible; *va* animar, alentar
nerve cell *s* (anat.) neurona; (anat.) célula nerviosa
nerve center *s* (anat.) centro nervioso
nerve fiber *s* (anat.) fibra nerviosa
nerveless ['nʌrvlɪs] *adj* sin nervios; enervado; cobarde
nerve pulp *s* (anat.) pulpa (*de los dientes*)
nerve-racking ['nʌrv,rækɪŋ] *adj* irritante, exasperante
nerve tonic *s* tónico nervioso
nervine ['nʌrvin] o ['nʌrvaɪn] *adj & s* nervino
nervous ['nʌrvəs] *adj* nervioso
nervous breakdown *s* crisis nerviosa, colapso nervioso
nervousness ['nʌrvəsnɪs] *s* nerviosidad, nerviosismo
nervous prostration *s* prostración nerviosa, agotamiento nervioso
nervous shudder *s* muerte chiquita
nervous system *s* (anat.) sistema nervioso
nervure ['nʌrvjʊr] *s* (bot. & ent.) nervadura
nervy ['nʌrvɪ] *adj* (*comp:* **-ier;** *super:* **-iest**) nervioso (*fuerte, vigoroso*); atrevido, audaz; (slang) descarado
nescience ['nɛʃəns] o ['nɛʃɪəns] *s* nesciencia
-ness *suffix s* -ería, p.ej., **childishness** niñería; **foolishness** tontería; -ez, p.ej., **haughtiness** altivez; **ripeness** madurez; **smallness** pequeñez; -eza, p.ej., **bigness** grandeza; **lightness** ligereza; **cleanliness** limpieza; -or, p.ej., **bitterness** amargor; **sweetness** dulzor; -ura, p.ej., **bitterness** amargura; **smoothness** lisura; los nombres que terminan en **-ness** se pueden traducir generalmente al español con el adjetivo correspondiente, precedido por **lo,** p.ej., **the pleasantness of her smile** lo agradable de su sonrisa
Nessus ['nɛsəs] *s* (myth.) Neso
nest [nɛst] *s* nido; nidal (*donde la gallina pone sus huevos*); nidada (*pajarillos en el nido*); juego (*de mesitas, cajones, etc.*); (fig.) nido (*de ladrones, de ametralladoras, etc.*); **to feather one's nest** hacer todo para enriquecerse; *va* colocar en un nido; encajar formando juego; *vn* anidar; buscar nidos
nest egg *s* nidal; (fig.) peculio, ahorros, reserva, buena hucha
nestle ['nɛsəl] *va* anidar, abrigar, poner en un nido; apretar, arrimar afectuosamente; *vn* anidar; estar abrigado como en un nido; arrimarse cómodamente; **to nestle up to** arrimarse a
nestling ['nɛstlɪŋ] *s* pajarillo en el nido
Nestor ['nɛstər] *s* (myth.) Néstor
Nestorian [nɛs'torɪən] *adj & s* nestoriano
net [nɛt] *s* red; (com.) precio neto, peso neto, ganancia líquida; *adj* neto, líquido; (*pret & pp:* **netted;** *ger:* **netting**) *va* enredar, tejer; coger con red; cubrir con red; (com.) producir (*cierta ganancia líquida*)
nether ['nɛðər] *adj* inferior, más bajo
Netherlander ['nɛðər,lændər] o ['nɛðərləndər] *s* neerlandés (*persona*)
Netherlandish ['nɛðər,lændɪʃ] o ['nɛðərləndɪʃ] *adj* neerlandés; *s* neerlandés (*idioma*)
Netherlands, The ['nɛðərləndz] los Países Bajos (*Holanda*)

nethermost ['nɛðərmost] *adj* (el) más bajo
nether world *s* infierno; (el) otro mundo
netting ['nɛtɪŋ] *s* red
nettle ['nɛtəl] *s* (bot.) ortiga; *va* irritar, provocar
nettle rash *s* (path.) urticaria
nettle tree *s* (bot.) almez
network ['nɛt,wʌrk] *s* red
neume [njum] o [num] *s* (mus.) neuma
neuralgia [nju'rældʒə] o [nʊ'rældʒə] *s* (path.) neuralgia
neurasthenia [,njʊrəs'θinɪə] o [,nʊrəs'θinɪə] *s* (path.) neurastenia
neurasthenic [,njʊrəs'θɛnɪk] o [,nʊrəs'θɛnɪk] *adj & s* neurasténico
neurectomy [njʊ'rɛktəmɪ] o [nʊ'rɛktəmɪ] *s* (*pl:* **-mies**) (surg.) neurectomía
neuritis [njʊ'raɪtɪs] o [nʊ'raɪtɪs] *s* (path.) neuritis
neuroglia [njʊ'rɑglɪə] o [nʊ'rɑglɪə] *s* (anat.) neuroglia
neurological [,njʊrə'lɑdʒɪkəl] o [,nʊrə'lɑdʒɪkəl] *adj* neurológico
neurologist [njʊ'rɑlədʒɪst] o [nʊ'rɑlədʒɪst] *s* neurólogo
neurology [njʊ'rɑlədʒɪ] o [nʊ'rɑlədʒɪ] *s* neurología
neuron ['njʊrɑn] o ['nʊrɑn] o **neurone** ['njʊron] o ['nʊron] *s* (anat.) neurona
neuropath ['njʊrəpæθ] o ['nʊrəpæθ] *s* neurópata
neuropathic [,njʊrə'pæθɪk] o [,nʊrə'pæθɪk] *adj* neuropático
neuropathy [njʊ'rɑpəθɪ] o [nʊ'rɑpəθɪ] *s* neuropatía
neuropsychiatry [,njʊrosaɪ'kaɪətrɪ] o [,nʊrosaɪ'kaɪətrɪ] *s* neuropsiquiatría
neurosis [njʊ'rosɪs] o [nʊ'rosɪs] *s* (*pl:* **-ses** [siz]) (path.) neurosis
neurosurgery [,njʊrə'sʌrdʒərɪ] o [,nʊrə'sʌrdʒərɪ] *s* cirugía nerviosa, neurocirugía
neurosurgical [,njʊrə'sʌrdʒɪkəl] o [,nʊrə'sʌrdʒɪkəl] *adj* neuroquirúrgico
neurotic [njʊ'rɑtɪk] o [nʊ'rɑtɪk] *adj & s* neurótico
neut. abr. de **neuter**
neuter ['njutər] o ['nutər] *adj* neutro; *s* (gram.) género neutro
neutral ['njutrəl] o ['nutrəl] *adj* neutral (*que no es de un partido ni de otro*); neutro (*que no es de un color ni de otro*); (bot., chem., elec., phonet. & zool.) neutro; *s* neutral; (aut.) punto muerto, punto neutral
neutralism ['njutrəlɪzəm] o ['nutrəlɪzəm] *s* neutralismo
neutralist ['njutrəlɪst] o ['nutrəlɪst] *adj & s* neutralista
neutrality [nju'trælɪtɪ] o [nu'trælɪtɪ] *s* neutralidad
neutralization [,njutrəlɪ'zeʃən] o [,nutrəlɪ'zeʃən] *s* neutralización
neutralize ['njutrəlaɪz] o ['nutrəlaɪz] *va* neutralizar
neutrino [nju'trino] o [nu'trino] *s* (*pl:* **-nos**) (phys.) neutrino
neutron ['njutrɑn] o ['nutrɑn] *s* (phys.) neutrón
neutron bomb *s* (phys.) bomba de neutrones, bomba neutrónica
Nev. abr. de **Nevada**
never ['nɛvər] *adv* nunca; de ningún modo, ni . . . siquiera; **never fear** no hay cuidado; **never mind** no importa
nevermore [,nɛvər'mor] *adv* nunca más
nevertheless [,nɛvərðə'lɛs] *adv* sin embargo, no obstante, a pesar de eso
new [nju] o [nu] *adj* nuevo
new arrival *s* recién llegado; recién nacido
newborn ['nju,bɔrn] o ['nu,bɔrn] *adj* recién nacido; renacido
New Castile *s* Castilla la Nueva
Newcastle ['nju,kæsəl] o ['nu,kæsəl] *s;* **to carry coals to Newcastle** echar agua al mar, llevar hierro a Vizcaya, cargar leña para el monte
newcomer ['nju,kʌmər] o ['nu,kʌmər] *s* recién venido, recién llegado
New Covenant *s* (Bib.) Nuevo Testamento
New Deal *s* (pol.) nuevo trato (*política de Franklin D. Roosevelt*)
New Delhi ['dɛlɪ] *s* Nueva Delhi
newel ['njuəl] o ['nuəl] *s* nabo (*de una escalera de caracol*); alma, núcleo (*que termina la barandilla de una escalera*)
New England *s* la Nueva Inglaterra
newfangled ['nju,fæŋgəld] o ['nu,fæŋgəld] *adj* de última moda, recién inventado
new-fashioned ['nju,fæʃənd] o ['nu,fæʃənd] *adj* de última moda
Newfoundland ['njufənd,lænd] o ['nufənd,lænd] *s* Terranova (*isla y provincia*); [nju'faʊndlənd] o [nu'faʊndlənd] *s* Terranova (*perro*)
New Granada [grə'nɑdə] *s* la Nueva Granada
New Guinea *s* la Nueva Guinea
New Hampshire ['hæmpʃɪr] *s* Nuevo Hampshire
New Hebrides *spl* Nuevas Hébridas
newish ['njuɪʃ] o ['nuɪʃ] *adj* algo nuevo, bastante nuevo
New Jersey *s* Nueva Jersey
new look *s* nuevo aspecto (*especialmente de las modas por el año de 1947*)
newly ['njulɪ] o ['nulɪ] *adv* nuevamente; **newly** + *pp* recién + *pp*
newlywed ['njulɪ,wɛd] o ['nulɪ,wɛd] *s* desposado, recién casado
New Mexican *adj & s* neomejicano, nuevomejicano
New Mexico *s* Nuevo Méjico
new moon *s* novilunio, luna nueva
newness ['njunɪs] o ['nunɪs] *s* novedad; falta de práctica
New Order *s* (pol.) Orden Nuevo
New Orleans ['ɔrlɪənz] *s* Nueva Orleáns
news [njuz] o [nuz] *ssg* noticias; **a news item** una noticia
news agency *s* agencia de noticias
news beat *s* anticipación de una noticia (*por un periódico*)
newsboy ['njuz,bɔɪ] o ['nuz,bɔɪ] *s* vendedor de periódicos
newscast ['njuz,kæst], ['njuz,kɑst], ['nuz,kæst] o ['nuz,kɑst] *s* (rad.) noticiario; *va* radiar (*noticias, sucesos*); *vn* radiar noticias
newscaster ['njuz,kæstər], ['njuz,kɑstər], ['nuz,kæstər] o ['nuz,kɑstər] *s* cronista de radio, reportero radiofónico
news coverage *s* reportaje
newsdealer ['njuz,dilər] o ['nuz,dilər] *s* vendedor de periódicos
newshawk ['njuz,hɔk] o ['nuz,hɔk] *s* (coll.) cazanoticias
newsletter ['njuz,lɛtər] o ['nuz,lɛtər] *s* circular noticiera
newsmagazine ['nuz,mægəzin] o ['nuz,mægəzin] *s* revista de noticias
newsman ['njuzmən] o ['nuzmən] *s* (*pl:* **-men**) noticiero
newsmonger ['njuz,mʌŋgər] o ['nuz,mʌŋgər] *s* portanuevas, gacetista
New South Wales *s* la Nueva Gales del Sur
New Spain *s* la Nueva España (*el Méjico de los conquistadores españoles*)
newspaper ['njuz,pepər] o ['nuz,pepər] *s* periódico; *adj* periodístico
newspaper clipping *s* recorte de periódico
newspaperman ['njuz,pepər,mæn] o ['nuz,pepər,mæn] *s* (*pl:* **-men**) periodista
newspaper wrapper *s* faja
news photographer *s* reportero gráfico
newsprint ['njuz,prɪnt] o ['nuz,prɪnt] *s* papel de periódico, papel para periódicos, papel-prensa
newsreel ['njuz,ril] o ['nuz,ril] *s* película noticiera, actualidades, noticiario cinematográfico
newsroom ['njuz,rum] o ['nuz,rum] *s* redacción de un periódico (*oficina u oficinas*); tienda de periódicos; sala de lectura de periódicos
newsstand ['njuz,stænd] o ['nuz,stænd] *s* quiosco de periódicos
New Style *s* estilo nuevo (*calendario*)
newsweekly ['njuz,wiklɪ] o ['nuz,wiklɪ] *s* (*pl:* **-lies**) semanario de noticias
newsworthy ['njuz,wʌrðɪ] o ['nuz,wʌrðɪ] *adj* de gran actualidad, de interés periodístico
newsy ['njuzɪ] o ['nuzɪ] *s* (*pl:* **-ies**) (coll.) chiquillo vendedor de periódicos; *adj* (*comp:* **-ier**; *super:* **-iest**) (coll.) informativo

newt [njut] o [nut] *s* (zool.) tritón, salamandra acuática
New Testament *s* Nuevo Testamento
Newtonian [nju'tonɪən] o [nu'tonɪən] *adj* neutoniano
New World *s* Nuevo Mundo
new-world ['nju,wʌrld] o ['nu,wʌrld] *adj* del Nuevo Mundo
new year *s* año nuevo; (*cap.*) *s* el día de año nuevo
New Year's *s* el día de año nuevo
New Year's card *s* tarjeta de felicitación de Año Nuevo
New Year's Day *s* el día de año nuevo
New Year's Eve *s* la víspera de año nuevo, la noche vieja
New Year's gift *s* regalo de año nuevo
New York [jɔrk] *s* Nueva York; *adj* neoyorquino
New Yorker ['jɔrkər] *s* neoyorquino
New Zealand ['zilənd] *s* Nueva Zelanda; *adj* neocelandés
New Zealander ['ziləndər] *s* neocelandés
next [nɛkst] *adj* próximo, siguiente; venidero, que viene; de al lado; **next door** la casa de al lado, en la casa de al lado; **next door to** en la casa siguiente de; casi; **next of kin** pariente(s) más cercano(s); **next time** la próxima vez; *adv* luego, después, inmediatamente después; la próxima vez; **to come next** venir después, ser el que sigue; **next to** junto a; después de; el primero después de; **the next best** lo mejor después de eso; **next to nothing** casi nada
next-door ['nɛkst,dor] *adj* siguiente, de al lado
nexus ['nɛksəs] *s* nexo
N.F. abr. de **Newfoundland** y **Norman French**
n.g. abr. de **no good**
N.G. abr. de **National Guard** y **no good**
N.H. abr. de **New Hampshire**
N.I. abr. de **Northern Ireland**
niacin ['naɪəsɪn] *s* (chem.) niacina
Niagara Falls [naɪ'ægərə] *spl* las cataratas del Niágara
nib [nɪb] *s* pico (*del ave*); punta (*de la pluma de escribir*); gavilán (*cada uno de los dos lados de la punta de la pluma*)
nibble ['nɪbəl] *s* mordisco; *va* mordiscar; *vn* picar; **to nibble at** picar de o en
Nibelung ['nibəlʊŋ] *s* (myth.) nibelungo
niblick ['nɪblɪk] *s* (golf) niblick
nibs [nɪbz] *s* (hum.) personaje; **his nibs** (hum.) su Señoría
Nicaea [naɪ'siə] *s* Nicea
Nicaragua [,nɪkə'rɑgwə] *s* Nicaragua
Nicaraguan [,nɪkə'rɑgwən] *adj & s* nicaragüense o nicaragüeño
niccolite ['nɪkəlaɪt] *s* (mineral.) niquelina
nice [naɪs] *adj* fino, sutil, delicado; primoroso, pulido, refinado; dengoso, melindroso; atento, cortés, culto; escrupuloso, esmerado; simpático, agradable; complaciente; decoroso, conveniente; preciso, satisfactorio; bien, bueno; **nice and** (coll.) muy, mucho; (coll.) -ito, p.ej., **nice and early** tempranito; (*cap.*) [nis] *s* Niza
nicely ['naɪslɪ] *adv* con precisión; escrupulosamente; satisfactoriamente; (coll.) muy bien
Nicene [naɪ'sin] o ['naɪsin] *adj & s* niceno, de Nicea
Nicene Council *s* concilio de Nicea
Nicene Creed *s* Símbolo de Nicea
nicety ['naɪsətɪ] *s* (*pl:* **-ties**) precisión; sutileza; finura; **to a nicety** con la mayor precisión
niche [nɪtʃ] *s* hornacina, nicho; (fig.) colocación conveniente
Nicholas ['nɪkələs] *s* Nicolás
nichrome ['naɪkrom] *s* nicromo
nick [nɪk] *s* mella, muesca; (print.) cran; (*cap.*) *s* nombre abreviado de **Nicholas; in the nick of time** en el momento crítico; *va* mellar, hacer muescas en; cortar; acertar
nickel ['nɪkəl] *s* (chem.) níquel; (U.S.A.) moneda de cinco centavos; *va* niquelar
nickel-cadmium battery ['nɪkəl'kædmɪəm] *s* (elec.) acumulador níquel-cadmio
nickel plate *s* niqueladura
nickel-plate ['nɪkəl,plet] *va* niquelar
nickel silver *s* metal blanco, melchor
nickel steel *s* aceroníquel, acero al níquel
nicknack ['nɪk,næk] *s* chuchería, friolera
nickname ['nɪk,nem] *s* apodo; *va* apodar
Nicol prism ['nɪkəl] *s* (opt.) prisma de Nicol
nicotine ['nɪkətin] *s* nicotina
nicotinic [,nɪkə'tɪnɪk] *adj* nicotínico
nicotinic acid *s* (chem.) ácido nicotínico
niece [nis] *s* sobrina
niello [nɪ'ɛlo] *s* (*pl:* **-li** [lɪ]) niel; *va* nielar
Nietzschean ['nitʃɪən] *adj & s* nietzscheano
Nietzscheanism ['nitʃɪənɪzəm] o **Nietzscheism** ['nitʃɪɪzəm] *s* nietzschismo
nifty ['nɪftɪ] *adj* (*comp:* **-tier;** *super:* **-tiest**) (slang) elegante; (slang) excelente
Niger ['naɪdʒər] *s* Níger (*río*); colonia del Níger
Nigeria [naɪ'dʒɪrɪə] *s* Nigeria
niggard ['nɪgərd] *adj & s* tacaño
niggardly ['nɪgərdlɪ] *adj* tacaño; *adv* tacañamente
nigger ['nɪgər] *s* (offensive) negro; (offensive) defecto mecánico; (offensive) **nigger in the woodpile** (coll.) gato encerrado
niggle ['nɪgəl] *va* trampear; burlar, engañar; esmerarse en; recargar con adornos; *vn* ocuparse en fruslerías; agitarse, menearse; ser melindroso
nigh [naɪ] *adj, adv & prep* (archaic & dial.) var. de **near**
night [naɪt] *s* noche; **at** o **by night** de noche o por la noche; **to make a night of it** (coll.) divertirse hasta muy entrada la noche
night blindness *s* ceguera nocturna
night-blooming cereus ['naɪt,blumɪŋ] *s* (bot.) pitahaya
night bolt *s* pestillo de golpe
nightcap ['naɪt,kæp] *s* gorro de dormir; trago antes de acostarse, sosiega
night clothes *spl* traje de dormir
night club *s* cabaret, café cantante, café-concierto
nightdress ['naɪt,drɛs] *s* camisa de dormir, camisón
night driving *s* (aut.) conducción de noche
nightfall ['naɪt,fɔl] *s* anochecer, caída de la noche; **at nightfall** al anochecer
nightgown ['naɪt,gaʊn] *s* camisa de dormir, camisón
nighthawk ['naɪt,hɔk] *s* (orn.) chotacabras, chotacabras norteamericano; trasnochador, anochecedor
night heron *s* (orn.) martín del río, martinete
nightingale ['naɪtəngel] *s* (orn.) ruiseñor
nightjar ['naɪt,dʒɑr] *s* (orn.) chotacabras
night lamp *s* lamparilla o luz de noche
night latch *s* cerradura de resorte
night letter *s* carta telegráfica nocturna, telegrama nocturno
night life *s* vida nocturna
night light *s* lamparilla o luz de noche
nightlong ['naɪt,lɔŋ] o ['naɪt,lɑŋ] *adj* de toda la noche; *adv* durante toda la noche
nightly ['naɪtlɪ] *adj* nocturno; de cada noche; *adv* cada noche; de noche, por la noche
nightmare ['naɪt,mɛr] *s* pesadilla; (fig.) pesadilla
nightmarish ['naɪt,mɛrɪʃ] *adj* de pesadilla; espeluznante, horroroso
night owl *s* buho nocturno, lechuza nocturna; (coll.) anochecedor, noctámbulo, trasnochador
night piece *s* (f.a.) cuadro nocturno, escena nocturna
night school *s* escuela de noche, escuela nocturna
nightshade ['naɪt,ʃed] *s* (bot.) dulcamara; (bot.) hierba mora
night shift *s* turno de noche
nightshirt ['naɪt,ʃʌrt] *s* camisón, camisa de dormir
night spot *s* (coll.) var. de **night club**
night table *s* mesilla de noche
nighttime ['naɪt,taɪm] *s* noche; **in the nighttime** de noche; *adj* nocturno
nightwalker ['naɪt,wɔkər] *s* vagabundo nocturno, noctámbulo; ladrón nocturno; ramera callejera nocturna; somnámbulo; lombriz nocturna
night watch *s* sereno; guardia de noche, ronda de noche; (mil.) vigilia

night watchman *s* vigilante nocturno; sereno (*vigilante que vela de noche por la seguridad del vecindario*)
nihilism ['naɪɪlɪzəm] *s* nihilismo
nihilist ['naɪɪlɪst] *s* nihilista
nihilistic [,naɪɪl'ɪstɪk] *adj* nihilista
nil [nɪl] *s* nada
Nile [naɪl] *s* Nilo
nimble ['nɪmbəl] *adj* ágil, ligero; vivo, listo
nimbly ['nɪmblɪ] *adv* ágilmente; vivamente
nimbus ['nɪmbəs] *s* (*pl:* **-buses** o **-bi** [baɪ]) nimbo
Nimrod ['nɪmrɑd] *s* (Bib. & fig.) Nemrod
nincompoop ['nɪnkəmpup] *s* badulaque, necio, bobo, papirote
nine [naɪn] *adj* nueve; **nine days' wonder** prodigio de unos días; *s* nueve; equipo de beisbol; **the Nine** (myth.) las nueve musas; **nine o'clock** las nueve
ninefold ['naɪn,fold] *adj* nueve veces mayor; de nueve partes; *adv* nueve veces
nine hundred *adj & s* novecientos
nine hundredth *adj & s* noningentésimo
ninepins ['naɪn,pɪnz] *s* juego de bolos
nineteen ['naɪn'tin] *adj & s* diecinueve o diez y nueve
nineteenth ['naɪn'tinθ] *adj* décimonono; diecinueveavo; *s* décimonono; diecinueveavo; diecinueve (*en las fechas*)
ninetieth ['naɪntɪɪθ] *adj & s* nonagésimo, noventavo
ninety ['naɪntɪ] *adj* noventa; *s* (*pl:* **-ties**) noventa
Nineveh ['nɪnəvə] *s* Nínive
Ninevite ['nɪnəvaɪt] *s* ninivita
ninny ['nɪnɪ] *s* (*pl:* **-nies**) mentecato, bobo
ninth [naɪnθ] *adj* nono, noveno; *s* nono, noveno; nueve (*en las fechas*)
Niobe ['naɪəbɪ] *s* (myth.) Níobe
niobium [naɪ'obɪəm] *s* (chem.) niobio
nip [nɪp] *s* pellizco, mordisco; helada, escarcha, quemadura; traguito; **nip and tuck** a quién ganará; (*pret & pp:* **nipped;** *ger:* **nipping**) *va* pellizcar, mordiscar; helar, escarchar, quemar; (slang) asir, coger, robar; **to nip in the bud** atajar en el principio; *vn* beborrotear
nipa palm ['nipə] o ['naɪpə] *s* (bot.) nipa
nipper ['nɪpər] *s* pinza grande (*del cangrejo*); pala (*del caballo*); (coll.) chiquillo; **nippers** *spl* tenazas, cortaalambre, alicates de corte
nipple ['nɪpəl] *s* pezón (*de las hembras*); tetilla (*de los machos; del biberón*); (mach.) entrerrosca, tubo roscado de unión
nipplewort ['nɪpəl,wʌrt] *s* (bot.) lámpsana
Nippon [nɪ'pɑn] o ['nɪpɑn] *s* el Japón
Nipponese [,nɪpə'niz] *adj* nipón; *s* (*pl:* **-ese**) nipón
nippy ['nɪpɪ] *adj* (*comp:* **-pier;** *super:* **-piest**) mordaz, picante; frío, helado; (Brit.) ágil, ligero
nirvana o **Nirvana** [nɪr'vɑnə] *s* el nirvana
Nisei ['ni'se] *s* (*pl:* **-sei** o **-seis**) persona nacida en los EE.UU. de padres japoneses
nit [nɪt] *s* piojito; liendre (*huevecillo del piojo*)
niter ['naɪtər] *s* nitro (*nitrato potásico*); nitro de Chile (*nitrato sódico*)
niton ['naɪtɑn] *s* (chem.) nitón
nitrate ['naɪtret] *s* nitrato; nitrato de potasio o nitrato de sodio (*empleados como abono*); *va* (chem.) nitrar
nitration [naɪ'treʃən] *s* (chem.) nitración
nitre ['naɪtər] *s* var. de **niter**
nitric ['naɪtrɪk] *adj* (chem.) nítrico
nitric acid *s* (chem.) ácido nítrico
nitride ['naɪtraɪd] o ['naɪtrɪd] *s* (chem.) nitruro
nitrification [,naɪtrɪfɪ'keʃən] *s* nitrificación
nitrify ['naɪtrɪfaɪ] (*pret & pp:* **-fied**) *va* nitrar; nitrificar (*por la acción de bacterias*); abonar con nitratos
nitrile ['naɪtrɪl] o ['naɪtril] *s* (chem.) nitrilo
nitrite ['naɪtraɪt] *s* (chem.) nitrito
nitrobacteria [,naɪtrobæk'tɪrɪə] *spl* (agr.) nitrobacterias
nitrobenzene [,naɪtro'benzin] o [,naɪtroben'zin] *s* (chem.) nitrobenceno o nitrobencina
nitrocellulose [,naɪtro'sɛljəlos] *s* nitrocelulosa
nitrogen ['naɪtrədʒən] *s* (chem.) nitrógeno
nitrogen cycle *s* ciclo del nitrógeno
nitrogen fixation *s* (chem.) fijación del nitrógeno
nitrogenous [naɪ'trɑdʒɪnəs] *adj* nitrogenado
nitroglycerin o **nitroglycerine** [,naɪtro'glɪsərɪn] *s* nitroglicerina
nitrolic [naɪ'trɑlɪk] *adj* (chem.) nitrólico
nitrolime ['naɪtro,laɪm] *s* nitrocal
nitrometer [naɪ'trɑmɪtər] *s* nitrómetro
nitrosyl [naɪ'trosɪl], [,naɪtrə'sil] o ['naɪtrəsɪl] *s* (chem.) nitrosilo
nitrous ['naɪtrəs] *adj* (chem.) nitroso
nitrous oxide *s* (chem.) óxido nitroso
nitty ['nɪtɪ] *adj* lendroso
nitwit ['nɪt,wɪt] *s* (slang) bobalicón
nix [nɪks] *s* (myth.) espíritu de las aguas; *adv* (slang) nexo (*no*)
nixie ['nɪksɪ] *s* (myth.) ondina
N.J. abr. de **New Jersey**
N.M. o **N. Mex.** abr. de **New Mexico**
no. abr. de **number**
No. abr. de **north** y **northern**
no [no] *adj indef* ninguno; **with no** sin; **no admittance** no se permite la entrada; **no matter** no importa; **no parking** se prohibe estacionarse; **no smoking** se prohibe fumar; **no thoroughfare** prohibido el paso; **no use** inútil; *adv* no; **no good** de ningún valor; vil, ruin; **no longer** ya no; **no sooner** no bien
Noah ['noə] *s* (Bib.) Noé
Noah's Ark *s* arca de Noé
nob [nɑb] *s* (slang) cabeza; (slang) persona de viso
nobby ['nɑbɪ] *adj* (*comp:* **-bier;** *super:* **-biest**) (slang) elegante; (slang) excelente
nobelium [no'bilɪəm] *s* (chem.) nobelio
Nobel prizes [no'bɛl] *spl* premios Nóbel
nobiliary [no'bɪlɪ,ɛrɪ] *adj* nobiliario
nobiliary particle *s* partícula nobiliaria
nobility [no'bɪlɪtɪ] *s* (*pl:* **-ties**) nobleza
noble ['nobəl] *adj & s* noble
nobleman ['nobəlmən] *s* (*pl:* **-men**) noble, hidalgo
nobleness ['nobəlnɪs] *s* nobleza
noblewoman ['nobəl,wumən] *s* (*pl:* **-women**) mujer noble, hidalga
nobody ['nobɑdɪ] *s* (*pl:* **-ies**) nadie (*persona insignificante*); *pron indef* nadie, ninguno; **nobody but** nadie más que; **nobody else** nadie más, ningún otro
noctambulation [nɑk,tæmbjə'leʃən] *s* noctambulación
noctambulism [nɑk'tæmbjəlɪzəm] *s* noctambulismo
nocturnal [nɑk'tʌrnəl] *adj* nocturno
nocturnally [nɑk'tʌrnəlɪ] *adv* nocturnalmente; cada noche
nocturne ['nɑktʌrn] *s* (mus.) nocturno; (paint.) escena nocturna
nod [nɑd] *s* inclinación de cabeza; seña con la cabeza; cabezada (*del que duerme sentado*); (*pret & pp:* **nodded;** *ger:* **nodding**) *va* inclinar (*la cabeza*); indicar con una inclinación de cabeza; *vn* inclinar la cabeza; cabecear; dormitar
nodal ['nodəl] *adj* nodal
noddle ['nɑdəl] *s* (coll.) cabeza
noddy ['nɑdɪ] *s* (*pl:* **-dies**) bobalicón; (orn.) golondrina de mar
node [nod] *s* bulto, protuberancia; nudo, enredo, trama; (astr., med. & phys.) nodo; (bot.) nudo
nodular ['nɑdʒələr] *adj* nodular; (bot.) tuberculoso
nodule ['nɑdʒul] *s* nódulo; (bot.) tubérculo; (anat., geol. & min.) nódulo
noël [no'ɛl] o ['noɛl] *s* villancico de Navidad
noggin ['nɑgɪn] *s* tacita, cubilete; octavo de litro
nohow ['no,hau] *adv* (coll.) de ninguna manera
noise [nɔɪz] *s* ruido; *va* divulgar
noiseless ['nɔɪzlɪs] *adj* silencioso, sin ruido
noisemaker ['nɔɪz,mekər] *s* persona ruidosa, parrandista; matraca
noise suppressor *s* (rad.) silenciador de ruidos
noisome ['nɔɪsəm] *adj* apestoso; nocivo
noisy ['nɔɪzɪ] *adj* (*comp:* **-ier;** *super:* **-iest**) ruidoso, estrepitoso
nol-pros [,nɑl'prɑs] (*pret & pp:* **-prossed;** *ger:* **-prossing**) *va* (law) abandonar (*la acción o parte de ella*)
nom. abr. de **nominative**

nomad ['nomæd] o ['namæd] *adj & s* nómada
nomadic [no'mædɪk] *adj* nómada
nomadism ['nomædɪzəm] o ['namædɪzəm] *s* nomadismo
no man's land *s* terreno sin reclamar; (mil.) tierra de nadie
nomenclature ['nomən,kletʃər] o [no'mɛnklətʃər] *s* nomenclatura
nominal ['namɪnəl] *adj* nominal; módico (*p.ej., precio*)
nominalism ['namɪnəlɪzəm] *s* nominalismo
nominalist ['namɪnəlɪst] *s* nominalista
nominally ['namɪnəlɪ] *adv* nominalmente
nominate ['namɪnet] *va* nominar; poner para candidato, elegir candidato
nomination [,namɪ'neʃən] *s* nominación; propuesta, postulación (*de un candidato*); **to put in nomination** poner para candidato
nominative ['namɪnətɪv] o ['namɪ,netɪv] *adj* nominativo (*que lleva el nombre del propietario*); (gram.) nominativo; *s* (gram.) nominativo
nominator ['namɪ,netər] *s* nombrador; proponedor
nominee [,namɪ'ni] *s* nómino, propuesto (*para un cargo o empleo*)
nonacceptance [,nanæk'sɛptəns] *s* falta de aceptación
nonage ['nanɪdʒ] o ['nonɪdʒ] *s* minoridad, minoría de edad; infancia
nonagenarian [,nanədʒɪ'nɛrɪən] o [,nonədʒɪ'nɛrɪən] *adj & s* nonagenario, noventón
nonaggression [,nanə'grɛʃən] *s* no agresión
nonagon ['nanəgan] *s* (geom.) nonágono o eneágono
nonalcoholic [,nanælkə'hɔlɪk] o [,nanælkə'halɪk] *adj* no alcohólico
nonappearance [,nanə'pɪrəns] *s* (law) no comparencia, contumacia
nonattendance [,nanə'tɛndəns] *s* falta de asistencia
nonbelligerency [,nanbə'lɪdʒərənsɪ] *s* no beligerancia
nonbelligerent [,nanbə'lɪdʒərənt] *adj & s* no beligerante
nonbreakable [nan'brekəbəl] *adj* irrompible
non-Catholic [nan'kæθəlɪk] *adj* acatólico
nonce [nans] *s* tiempo presente; **for the nonce** por el momento
nonce word *s* palabra para el caso
nonchalance ['nanʃələns] o [,nanʃə'lans] *s* descuido, indiferencia
nonchalant ['nanʃələnt] o [,nanʃə'lant] *adj* descuidado, indiferente
nonclerical [nan'klɛrɪkəl] *adj* no oficinesco
noncom. abr. de **noncommissioned officer**
noncom ['nan,kam] *s* (coll.) clase, suboficial
noncombatant [nan'kambətənt] *adj & s* no combatiente
noncommissioned officer [,nankə'mɪʃənd] *s* clase, suboficial
noncommittal [,nankə'mɪtəl] *adj* evasivo, reticente
noncommitted [,nankə'mɪtɪd] *adj* no comprometido, no empeñado
noncompliance [,nankəm'plaɪəns] *s* falta de cumplimiento
non compos mentis ['nan'kampəs'mɛntɪs] *adj* falto de juicio, loco
nonconducting [,nankən'dʌktɪŋ] *adj* no conductor, mal conductor
nonconductor [,nankən'dʌktər] *s* mal conductor
nonconformance [,nankən'fɔrməns] *s* desconformidad
nonconformist [,nankən'fɔrmɪst] *s* disidente
nonconformity [,nankən'fɔrmɪtɪ] *s* desconformidad, disidencia
nondelivery [,nandɪ'lɪvərɪ] *s* falta de entrega
nondescript ['nandɪskrɪpt] *adj* indefinido, inclasificable
none [non] *s* nona; **nones** *spl* (hist.) nonas; (eccl.) nona; [nʌn] *pron indef* nadie, ninguno, ningunos; **none of** ninguno de (*p.ej., los libros*); nada de (*p.ej., la leche*); **none other** ningún otro; *adv* nada, de ninguna manera; **none the less** sin embargo, no obstante
nonentity [nan'ɛntɪtɪ] *s* (*pl:* **-ties**) cosa inexistente; nulidad (*persona*)
nonessential [,nanɛ'sɛnʃəl] *adj & s* no esencial
nonesuch ['nʌn,sʌtʃ] *s* persona sin par, cosa sin igual
non-Euclidean [,nanju'klɪdɪən] *adj* no euclidiano
non-Euclidean geometry *s* geometría no euclidiana
nonexistence [,nanɛg'zɪstəns] *s* inexistencia; cosa inexistente
nonexistent [,nanɛg'zɪstənt] *adj* inexistente
nonferrous [nan'fɛrəs] *adj* no ferroso
nonfiction [nan'fɪkʃən] *s* literatura no novelesca
nonfulfillment [,nanfʊl'fɪlmənt] *s* incumplimiento
noninflammable [,nanɪn'flæməbəl] *adj* ininflamable
noninterference [,nanɪntər'fɪrəns] *s* no interferencia
nonintervention [,nanɪntər'vɛnʃən] *s* (dipl.) no intervención
nonintoxicating [,nanɪn'taksɪ,ketɪŋ] *adj* no embriagante
nonjuror [nan'dʒʊrər] *s* no jurante
nonmember [nan'mɛmbər] *s* no asociado, no miembro
nonmetal ['nan,mɛtəl] *s* (chem.) metaloide
nonmetallic [,nanmɪ'tælɪk] *adj* (chem.) metaloideo; no metálico
nonmoral [nan'marəl] o [nan'mɔrəl] *adj* amoral
nonpareil [,nanpə'rɛl] *s* persona sin par, cosa sin igual; (print.) nomparell; *adj* sin par, sin igual
nonpartisan or **nonpartizan** [nan'partɪzən] *adj* independiente, imparcial
nonpayment [nan'pemənt] *s* falta de pago
nonperformance [,nanpər'fɔrməns] *s* falta de ejecución
nonplus ['nanplʌs] o [nan'plʌs] *s* estupefacción; (*pret & pp:* **-plused** o **-plussed;** *ger:* **-plusing** o **-plussing**) *va* dejar estupefacto, dejar perplejo, dejar pegado a la pared
nonproductive [,nanprə'dʌktɪv] *adj* no productivo
nonprofit [nan'prafɪt] *adj* sin beneficio, no comercial
nonquota [nan'kwotə] *adj* no cuota
nonrefillable [,nanri'fɪləbəl] *adj* irrellenable
nonrenewable [,nanrɪ'njuəbəl] o [,nanrɪ'nuəbəl] *adj* no renovable
nonresidence [nan'rɛzɪdəns] *s* no residencia
nonresident [nan'rɛzɪdənt] *adj & s* transeúnte
nonresidential [nan,rɛzɪ'dɛnʃəl] *adj* comercial
nonresistance [,nanrɪ'zɪstəns] *s* no resistencia; obediencia pasiva
nonresistant [,nanrɪ'zɪstənt] *adj* no resistente
nonscientific [nan,saɪən'tɪfɪk] *adj* no científico
nonsectarian [,nansɛk'tɛrɪən] *adj* no sectario
nonsense ['nansɛns] *s* disparate, tontería
nonsensical [nan'sɛnsɪkəl] *adj* disparatado, tonto
non seq. abr. de **non sequitur**
non sequitur [nan'sɛkwɪtər] *s* non séquitur (*conclusión falsa*)
nonshatterable [nan'ʃætərəbəl] *adj* inastillable
nonskid ['nan'skɪd] *adj* antideslizante, antiderrapante, antirresbaladizo
nonstop ['nan,stap] *adj & adv* sin parar, sin escala
nonstop flight *s* (aer.) vuelo sin parar
nonsubscriber [,nansəb'skraɪbər] *s* no abonado
nonsuit ['nan,sut] o ['nan,sjut] *s* (law) absolución de la instancia; *va* (law) absolver de la instancia
nonsupport [,nansə'port] *s* falta de mantenimiento, incumplimiento de la obligación de alimentos
nontaxable [nan'tæksəbəl] *adj* no sujeto a impuesto
nonunion [nan'junjən] *adj* no agremiado
nonviolence [nan'vaɪələns] *s* no violencia
nonvoter [nan'votər] *s* no votante

noodle ['nudəl] *s* tallarín; (slang) tonto, mentecato; (slang) cabeza
noodle soup *s* sopa de pastas
nook [nʊk] *s* rinconcito, escondrijo
noon [nun] o **noonday** ['nun,de] *s* mediodía; **at broad** o **high noon** en pleno mediodía; *adj* meridiano, de mediodía
no one o **no-one** ['no,wʌn] *pron indef* nadie, ninguno; **no one else** nadie más, ningún otro
nooning ['nunɪŋ] *s* mediodía; almuerzo; siesta
noontide ['nun,taɪd] o **noontime** ['nun,taɪm] *s* mediodía
noose [nus] *s* lazo corredizo; dogal (*para ahorcar a un reo*); trampa; *va* lazar, coger con lazo corredizo; coger en una trampa
nor [nɔr] *conj* ni; **neither . . . nor** ni . . . ni
Nordic ['nɔrdɪk] *adj & s* nórdico
Norfolk Island pine ['nɔrfək] *s* (bot.) araucaria
norm [nɔrm] *s* norma, pauta
normal ['nɔrməl] *adj* normal; *s* estado normal, nivel normal
normalcy ['nɔrməlsɪ] *s* normalidad
normality [nɔr'mælɪtɪ] *s* normalidad
normalize ['nɔrməlaɪz] *va* normalizar
normally ['nɔrməlɪ] *adv* normalmente
normal school *s* escuela normal
Norman ['nɔrmən] *adj & s* normando
Norman Conquest *s* conquista de Inglaterra por los normandos, conquista normanda
Normandy ['nɔrməndɪ] *s* Normandía
Normanesque [,nɔrmən'ɛsk] *adj* (arch.) normando
Norman French *s* normánico
Norn [nɔrn] *s* (myth.) Norna
Norse [nɔrs] *adj* nórdico; noruego; *ssg* nórdico (*antiguo idioma escandinavo*); noruego (*idioma de Noruega*); *spl* nórdicos; noruegos
Norseman ['nɔrsmən] *s* (*pl:* **-men**) normando (*antiguo escandinavo*)
Norse mythology *s* mitología nórdica
north [nɔrθ] *s* norte; *adj* septentrional, del norte; *adv* al norte
North Africa *s* Noráfrica, el África del Norte
North African *adj & s* norteafricano
North America *s* Norteamérica, la América del Norte
North American *adj & s* norteamericano
North Cape *s* el cabo Norte
North Carolina [,kærə'laɪnə] *s* la Carolina del Norte
North Dakota [də'kotə] *s* el Dakota del Norte
northeast [,nɔrθ'ist] *adj* nordeste, nordestal; *s* nordeste; *adv* al nordeste, hacia el nordeste
northeaster [,nɔrθ'istər] *s* nordeste (*viento*); nordestada (*viento fuerte*)
northeasterly [,nɔrθ'istərlɪ] *adj* nordestal; *adv* hacia el nordeste; desde el nordeste
northeastern [,nɔrθ'istərn] *adj* nordeste, nordestal
northeastward [,nɔrθ'istwərd] *adj* que va hacia el nordeste; *s* nordeste; *adv* hacia el nordeste
northeastwardly [,nɔrθ'istwərdlɪ] *adj* que va hacia el nordeste; *adv* hacia el nordeste
northeastwards [,nɔrθ'istwərdz] *adv* hacia el nordeste
norther ['nɔrðər] *s* norte, nortada (*viento*)
northerly ['nɔrðərlɪ] *adj* septentrional; que viene desde el norte; que va hacia el norte; *adv* desde el norte; hacia el norte
northern ['nɔrðərn] *adj* septentrional, norteño, nórtico
northerner ['nɔrðərnər] *s* septentrional, habitante del norte
Northern Hemisphere *s* hemisferio boreal
Northern Ireland *s* la Irlanda Septentrional, la Irlanda del Norte
northern lights *spl* aurora boreal
northernmost ['nɔrðərnmost] *adj* (el) más septentrional
northern phalarope *s* (orn.) chorlito de mar apizarrado
North Island *s* la Isla de Norte (*Nueva Zelanda*)
North Korea *s* la Corea del Norte
North Korean *adj & s* norcoreano
northland ['nɔrθlənd] *s* región septentrional; (*cap.*) *s* región boreal; Península escandinava
northlander ['nɔrθləndər] *s* septentrional
North Magnetic Pole *s* polo norte magnético
Northman ['nɔrθmən] *s* (*pl:* **-men**) normando (*antiguo escandinavo*); escandinavo
north-northeast ['nɔrθ,nɔrθ'ist] *s* nornordeste o nornoreste
north-northwest ['nɔrθ,nɔrθ'wɛst] *s* nornoroeste o nornorueste
North Pole *s* polo norte
North Sea *s* mar del Norte
North Star *s* estrella del Norte
northward ['nɔrθwərd] *adj* que va hacia el norte; *s* norte; *adv* hacia el norte
northwardly ['nɔrθwərdlɪ] *adj* que va hacia el norte; *adv* hacia el norte
northwards ['nɔrθwərdz] *adv* hacia el norte
northwest [,nɔrθ'wɛst] *adj & s* noroeste; *adv* al noroeste, hacia el noroeste
northwester [,nɔrθ'wɛstər] *s* noroeste (*viento*); noroestada (*viento fuerte*)
northwesterly [,nɔrθ'wɛstərlɪ] *adj* noroeste; *adv* hacia el noroeste; desde el noroeste
northwestern [,nɔrθ'wɛstərn] *adj* noroeste, nordoccidental
Northwest Passage *s* paso del Noroeste
Northwest Territories *spl* Territorios del Noroeste (*del Canadá*)
northwestward [,nɔrθ'wɛstwərd] *adj* que va hacia el noroeste; *s* noroeste; *adv* hacia el noroeste
northwestwardly [,nɔrθ'wɛstwərdlɪ] *adj* que va hacia el noroeste; *adv* hacia el noroeste
northwestwards [,nɔrθ'wɛstwərdz] *adv* hacia el noroeste
north wind *s* norte, aquilón
Norway ['nɔrwe] *s* Noruega
Norway lobster *s* (zool.) cigala
Norway rat *s* (zool.) rata de alcantarilla
Norwegian [nɔr'widʒən] *adj & s* noruego
nos. abr. de **numbers**
nose [noz] *s* nariz; (aer.) proa; **to blow one's nose** sonarse las narices; **to count noses** averiguar cuántas personas hay; **to follow one's nose** seguir todo derecho; avanzar guiándose por el instinto; **to hold one's nose** tabicarse las narices; **to lead by the nose** tener agarrado por las narices; **to look down one's nose at** (coll.) mirar por encima del hombro; **to pay through the nose** pagar un precio escandaloso; **to pick one's nose** hurgarse las narices; **to poke one's nose into** meter las narices en, meter el hocico en; **to speak through the nose** ganguear; **to thumb one's nose at** (coll.) señalar (*a una persona*) poniendo el pulgar sobre la nariz en son de burla; (coll.) tratar con sumo desprecio; **to turn up one's nose at** mirar con desprecio; **under the nose of** en las narices de, en las barbas de ‖ *va* husmear, olfatear; restregar la nariz contra; descubrir, averiguar; **to nose out** huronear; vencer con poca ventaja ‖ *vn* ventear; **to nose about** curiosear; **to nose over** (aer.) capotar; **to nose up** encabritarse (*un buque, un avión, etc.*)
nose bag *s* morral, cebadera
noseband ['noz,bænd] *s* sobarba, muserola
nosebleed ['noz,blid] *s* hemorragia nasal
nose cone *s* cono de proa (*de un cohete*)
nose count *s* (coll.) recuento del número de personas
nose dive *s* (aer.) descenso de cabeza, descenso de picado; (fig.) descenso precipitado
nose-dive ['noz,daɪv] *vn* (aer.) descender de cabeza, picar; (fig.) descender precipitadamente
nosegay ['nozge] *s* ramillete
nose glasses *spl* anteojos de nariz, lentes
nosepiece ['noz,pis] *s* sobarba, muserola; ventalle (*del yelmo*); portaobjetivo (*del microscopio*)
nose ring *s* nariguera
nose wheel *s* (aer.) rueda de proa
nosey ['nozɪ] *adj* var. de **nosy**
no-show ['no'ʃo] *s* (coll.) pasajero no presentado (*pasajero que deja de notificar la empresa que no va a ocupar la plaza reservada*)
nosing ['nozɪŋ] *s* vuelo de huella (*de escalera*); serpenteo, movimiento de lanzadera (*de locomotora*); tajamar (*de puente*); arista (*de moldura*)
nostalgia [nɑ'stældʒə] *s* nostalgia

nostalgic [nɑ'stældʒɪk] *adj* nostálgico
nostril ['nɑstrɪl] *s* nariz, ventana (*de la nariz*)
nostrum ['nɑstrəm] *s* remedio de charlatán; panacea
nosy ['nozɪ] *adj* (*comp:* **-ier;** *super:* **-iest**) (coll.) husmeador, curioso
not [nɑt] *adv* no; **to think not** creer que no; **why not?** ¿cómo no?; **not at all** de ningún modo, nada; **not yet** todavía no
notability [,notə'bɪlɪtɪ] *s* (*pl:* **-ties**) notabilidad
notable ['notəbəl] *adj* notable; *s* notable, notabilidad
notably ['notəblɪ] *adv* notablemente
notarial [no'tɛrɪəl] *adj* notarial
notarize ['notəraɪz] *va* abonar con fe notarial, dar fe notarial de
notary ['notərɪ] *s* (*pl:* **-ries**) notario
notary public *s* (*pl:* **notaries public**) notario
notation [no'teʃən] *s* notación
notch [nɑtʃ] *s* muesca, mella, corte; (U.S.A.) paso, desfiladero; (coll.) grado; *va* hacer muescas en, mellar; anotar con cortes; señalar (*los tantos*)
note [not] *s* nota, apunte; esquela, cartita; marca, señal; (com.) pagaré, vale; (com.) billete (*de banco*); (mus.) figura (*que fija la duración del sonido*); (mus.) nota; canto, melodía; acento, voz; **of note** notable; **to compare notes** hacer intercambio de opiniones; **to make a note of** apuntar; **to strike the right note** hacer o decir lo que conviene; **to take note of** tomar nota de; **to take notes** tomar notas; *va* notar, apuntar; marcar, señalar
notebook ['not,bʊk] *s* cuaderno, libro de apuntes
noted ['notɪd] *adj* conocido, afamado
note paper *s* papel de cartas, papel para esquelas
noteworthy ['not,wʌrðɪ] *adj* notable, digno de notarse
nothing ['nʌθɪŋ] *s* nada, cero; nadería, friolera; *pron indef* nada; **for nothing** gratis, de balde; inútilmente; **that's nothing to me** eso nada me importa; **to make nothing of** no hacer caso de; no aprovecharse de; no entender; despreciar; **to think nothing of** no hacer caso de; tener por fácil; despreciar; **nothing doing** (slang) ni por pienso; **nothing else** nada más; *adv* de ninguna manera, nada; **nothing daunted** sin temor alguno; **nothing less** no menos; **nothing less than** de todo punto; **nothing like** ni con mucho
nothingness ['nʌθɪŋnɪs] *s* nada, inexistencia; nadería, friolera; insignificancia; inconsciencia, falta de conocimiento
notice ['notɪs] *s* atención, reparo, advertencia; aviso, noticia; letrero; reseña, mención; llamada; notificación; **on short notice** con poco tiempo de aviso; **to escape one's notice** pasarle inadvertido a uno, escapársele a uno; **to give notice (that)** dar noticia (de que); **to serve notice (that)** hacer saber (que); **to take notice (of)** notar, observar, reparar; *va* notar, observar, reparar, reparar en; mencionar
noticeable ['notɪsəbəl] *adj* sensible, perceptible; notable
noticeably ['notɪsəblɪ] *adv* perceptiblemente
notification [,notɪfɪ'keʃən] *s* notificación
notify ['notɪfaɪ] (*pret & pp:* **-fied**) *va* notificar, avisar; **to notify a person of something** notificar a una persona una cosa
notion ['noʃən] *s* noción; capricho; **notions** *spl* mercería (*alfileres, cintas, etc.*); **to have a notion to** + *inf* pensar + *inf*, tener ganas de + *inf*
notional ['noʃənəl] *adj* especulativo; imaginario; imaginativo, caprichoso
notochord ['notəkɔrd] *s* (biol.) notocordio
notoriety [,notə'raɪɪtɪ] *s* (*pl:* **-ties**) notoriedad; mala reputación; notabilidad (*persona*)
notorious [no'torɪəs] *adj* notorio; de historia, de mala reputación
Notre Dame [,notrə'dɑm] *s* Nuestra Señora; Nuestra Señora de París
no-trump ['no'trʌmp] *adj & s* sin triunfo; **a no-trump hand** un sin triunfo
notwithstanding [,nɑtwɪð'stændɪŋ] o [,nɑtwɪθ'stændɪŋ] *adv* no obstante; *conj* a pesar de que; *prep* a pesar de
nougat ['nugət] o ['nugɑ] *s* turrón, nuégado
nought [nɔt] *s* var. de **naught**
noumenon ['numɪnɑn] o ['naʊmɪnɑn] *s* (*pl:* **-na** [nə]) (philos.) nóumeno
noun [naʊn] *s* nombre, substantivo; *adj* substantivo
nourish ['nʌrɪʃ] *va* nutrir, alimentar; abrigar (*pensamientos, esperanzas, etc.*)
nourishing ['nʌrɪʃɪŋ] *adj* nutritivo
nourishment ['nʌrɪʃmənt] *s* nutrimento, alimento
nouveau riche [nuvo'riʃ] *s* (*pl:* **nouveaux riches** [nuvo'riʃ]) nuevo rico
Nov. abr. de **November**
nova ['novə] *s* (*pl:* **-vae** [vi] o **-vas**) (astr.) nova
Nova Scotia ['novə'skoʃə] *s* la Nueva Escocia
Nova Scotian ['novə'skoʃən] *adj & s* neoescocés
novate [no'vet] o ['novet] *va* (law) novar
novation [no'veʃən] *s* (law) novación
novel ['nɑvəl] *s* novela; novelística (*literatura novelesca*); *adj* nuevo, insólito, original
novelette [,nɑvəl'ɛt] *s* novela corta
novelist ['nɑvəlɪst] *s* novelista
novelistic [,nɑvəl'ɪstɪk] *adj* novelesco
novelize ['nɑvəlaɪz] *va* novelizar, novelar
novelty ['nɑvəltɪ] *s* (*pl:* **-ties**) novedad, innovación; **novelties** *spl* bisutería, baratijas
November [no'vɛmbər] *s* noviembre
novena [no'vinə] *s* (*pl:* **-nae** [ni]) (eccl.) novena
novice ['nɑvɪs] *s* novicio, principiante; (eccl.) novicio
noviciate o **novitiate** [no'vɪʃɪɪt] *s* noviciado, aprendizaje; (eccl.) noviciado
novocaine ['novəken] *s* (trademark) novocaína
now [naʊ] *s* actualidad; *adv* ahora, ahora mismo; ya; entonces; **from now on** de ahora en adelante; **how now?** ¿cómo?; **just now** hace un momento; **now and again** o **now and then** de vez en cuando; **now . . . now** ora . . . ora, ya . . . ya; **now that** ya que; **now then** ahora bien; *interj* ¡vamos!
nowadays ['naʊə,dez] *s* actualidad; *adv* hoy en día
noway ['nowe] o **noways** ['nowez] *adv* de ningún modo
nowhere ['nohwɛr] *adv* en ninguna parte, a ninguna parte; **nowhere else** en ninguna otra parte
nowise ['nowaɪz] *adv* de ningún modo
noxious ['nɑkʃəs] *adj* nocivo
nozzle ['nɑzəl] *s* boquerel (*de la manguera*); rallo o roseta (*de la regadera*); cubo (*del candelero*); (slang) nariz
N.S. abr. de **Nova Scotia** y **New Style**
N.S.W. abr. de **New South Wales**
N.T. abr. de **New Testament** y **Northern Territory**
nth [ɛnθ] *adj* (math.) n^{mo} (*enésimo*); **to the nth degree** (math.) elevado a la potencia n; (fig.) a lo sumo posible, lo último de potencia
nt. wt. abr. de **net weight**
nuance [nju'ɑns] o ['njuɑns] *s* matiz
nub [nʌb] *s* protuberancia; pedazo; (coll.) meollo; **the nub of the question** lo más esencial
nubbin ['nʌbɪn] *s* pedazo; mazorca imperfecta; fruto mal desarrollado
Nubian ['njubɪən] o ['nubɪən] *adj & s* nubiense
Nubian Desert *s* desierto de Nubia
nubile ['njubɪl] o ['nubɪl] *adj* núbil
nubility [nju'bɪlɪtɪ] o [nu'bɪlɪtɪ] *s* nubilidad
nuclear ['njuklɪər] o ['nuklɪər] *adj* nuclear, nucleario
nuclear fission *s* (phys.) fisión nuclear
nuclear force *s* (mil.) fuerza nuclear
nuclear fusion *s* (phys.) fusión nuclear
nuclear physics *ssg* física nuclear
nuclear-powered ['njuklɪər'paʊərd] o ['nuklɪər'paʊərd] *adj* accionado por la energía nuclear
nuclear reactor *s* (phys.) reactor nuclear
nuclear test ban *s* proscripción de las pruebas nucleares
nuclease ['njuklɪes] o ['nuklɪes] *s* (biochem.) nucleasa
nucleate ['njuklɪet] o ['nuklɪet] *adj* nucleario; (bot.) nucleado; *va* agregar formando núcleo; *vn* formar núcleo

nucleic [nju'kliɪk] o [nu'kliɪk] *adj* nucleico o nucleínico
nucleic acid *s* (biochem.) ácido nucleico o nucleínico
nuclein ['njuklɪɪn] o ['nuklɪɪn] *s* (biochem.) nucleína
nucleolus [nju'kliələs] o [nu'kliələs] *s* (*pl:* **-li** [laɪ]) (biol.) nucléolo
nucleon ['njuklɪɑn] o ['nuklɪɑn] *s* (phys.) nucleón
nucleonic [,njuklɪ'ɑnɪk] o [,nuklɪ'ɑnɪk] *adj* nucleónico; **nucleonics** *ssg* nucleónica
nucleus ['njuklɪəs] o ['nuklɪəs] *s* (*pl:* **-i** [aɪ] o **-uses**) núcleo; (anat., biol., chem. & phys.) núcleo
nude [njud] o [nud] *adj* desnudo; *s* (f.a.) desnudo; **the nude** el desnudo; **in the nude** desnudo
nudge [nʌdʒ] *s* codazo suave; *va* dar un codazo suave a, empujar suavemente
nudism ['njudɪzəm] o ['nudɪzəm] *s* nudismo
nudist ['njudɪst] o ['nudɪst] *s* nudista
nudity ['njudɪtɪ] o ['nudɪtɪ] *s* (*pl:* **-ties**) desnudez
nugatory ['njugə,torɪ] o ['nugə,torɪ] *adj* insignificante, ineficaz
nugget ['nʌgɪt] *s* pedazo; pepita (*p.ej., de oro*); (fig.) preciosidad
nuisance ['njusəns] o ['nusəns] *s* molestia, estorbo, incomodidad; persona o cosa fastidiosa; **to commit a nuisance** orinar, depositar inmundicias
nuisance tax *s* impuesto indirecto y fastidioso
null [nʌl] *adj* nulo; **null and void** nulo, írrito
nullification [,nʌlɪfɪ'keʃən] *s* anulación, invalidación
nullify ['nʌlɪfaɪ] (*pret & pp:* **-fied**) *va* anular, invalidar
nullity ['nʌlɪtɪ] *s* (*pl:* **-ties**) nulidad
Num. abr. de **Numbers**
Numantia [nju'mænʃɪə] o [nu'mænʃɪə] *s* Numancia
numb [nʌm] *adj* entumecido; *va* entumecer
number ['nʌmbər] *s* número; (gram.) número; **numbers** *spl* muchos; (poet. & mus.) números; **Numbers** *spl* (Bib.) los Números; **a number of** varios; **beyond number** muchísimos; **to look out for number one** mirar por el número uno (*sí mismo*); **without number** sin número; *va* numerar; ascender a; **his days are numbered** tiene sus días contados o sus horas contadas; **to be numbered among** hallarse entre
numberless ['nʌmbərlɪs] *adj* innumerable
numbers game o **pool** *s* quiniela en que se apuesta a ciertas cifras de las carreras de caballos o de otros acontecimientos cotidianos
numbness ['nʌmnɪs] *s* entumecimiento
numerable ['njumərəbəl] o ['numərəbəl] *adj* numerable
numeral ['njumərəl] o ['numərəl] *adj* numeral; *s* número
numerary ['njumə,rɛrɪ] o ['numə,rɛrɪ] *adj* numerario
numerate ['njuməret] o ['numəret] *va* numerar; enumerar
numeration [,njumə'reʃən] o [,numə'reʃən] *s* numeración
numerator ['njumə,retər] o ['numə,retər] *s* numerador; (math.) numerador
numeric [nju'mɛrɪk] o [nu'mɛrɪk] o **numerical** [nju'mɛrɪkəl] o [nu'mɛrɪkəl] *adj* numérico
numerically [nju'mɛrɪkəlɪ] o [nu'mɛrɪkəlɪ] *adv* numéricamente
numerous ['njumərəs] o ['numərəs] *adj* numeroso
Numidian [nju'mɪdɪən] o [nu'mɪdɪən] *adj* númida, numídico; *s* númida
Numidian crane *s* (orn.) grulla de Numidia
numismatic [,njumɪz'mætɪk] o [,numɪz'mætɪk] *adj* numismático; **numismatics** *ssg* numismática
numismatist [nju'mɪzmətɪst] o [nu'mɪzmətɪst] *s* numismático
numskull ['nʌm,skʌl] *s* bodoque, mentecato
nun [nʌn] *s* monja, religiosa
nunciature ['nʌnʃɪətʃər] *s* nunciatura
nuncio ['nʌnʃɪo] *s* (*pl:* **-os**) nuncio o nuncio apostólico
nuncupative will ['nʌŋkjə,petɪv] *s* (law) testamento nuncupativo
nunnery ['nʌnərɪ] *s* (*pl:* **-ies**) convento de monjas
nun's veiling *s* velo de monja
nuptial ['nʌpʃəl] *adj* nupcial; **nuptials** *spl* nupcias
nuptial mass *s* misa de esposos, misa de velaciones
nurse [nʌrs] *s* enfermera; nodriza, ama de cría; niñera; protector, fomentador; **male nurse** enfermero; *va* amamantar; criar; alimentar; cuidar (*a una persona enferma*); tratar de curarse de (*p.ej., un resfriado*); cebar, fomentar (*p.ej., un sentimiento de odio*); acariciar, mimar; **to nurse at the breast** criar a los pechos; *vn* amamantarse; ser enfermera, servir de enfermera
nurseling ['nʌrslɪŋ] *s* var. de **nursling**
nursemaid ['nʌrs,med] *s* niñera
nursery ['nʌrsərɪ] *s* (*pl:* **-ies**) cuarto de los niños, cuarto de juegos; (agr.) semillero, criadero, plantel; (fig.) semillero
nurserymaid ['nʌrsərɪ,med] *s* var. de **nursemaid**
nurseryman ['nʌrsərɪmən] *s* (*pl:* **-men**) cultivador de semillero
nursery rhymes *spl* versos para niños
nursery school *s* escuela materna (*para niños muy pequeños*)
nursery tales *spl* cuentos para niños
nursing ['nʌrsɪŋ] *s* oficio de enfermera
nursing bottle *s* biberón
nursing home *s* clínica de reposo
nursling ['nʌrslɪŋ] *s* cría, niño de teta
nurture ['nʌrtʃər] *s* crianza, educación; alimentación, nutrimento; *va* criar, educar; alimentar, nutrir; acariciar (*p.ej., una esperanza*)
nut [nʌt] *s* nuez; (mach.) tuerca; diapasón (*del violín, etc.*); (slang) cabeza; (slang) estrafalario, tonto, necio; **a hard nut to crack** (coll.) hueso duro de roer, rompecabezas
nutation [nju'teʃən] o [nu'teʃən] *s* (astr. & bot.) nutación
nut-brown ['nʌt,braʊn] *adj* marrón, castaño, avellanado; tostado
nutcracker ['nʌt,krækər] *s* cascanueces; (orn.) cascanueces, nucifraga
nut-driver ['nʌt,draɪvər] *s* aprietatuercas
nutgall ['nʌt,gɔl] *s* (bot.) agalla, abogalla
nuthatch ['nʌt,hætʃ] *s* (orn.) trepatroncos
nutmeat ['nʌt,mit] *s* gajo de nuez
nutmeg ['nʌt,mɛg] *s* (bot.) mirística (*árbol*); nuez de especia, nuez moscada (*semilla*)
nutria ['njutrɪə] o ['nutrɪə] *s* (zool.) coipo; piel de coipo
nutrient ['njutrɪənt] o ['nutrɪənt] *adj* nutritivo; *s* nutrimento
nutriment ['njutrɪmənt] o ['nutrɪmənt] *s* nutrimento
nutrition [nju'trɪʃən] o [nu'trɪʃən] *s* nutrición, nutrimento; (biol.) nutrición
nutritional [nju'trɪʃənəl] o [nu'trɪʃənəl] *adj* alimenticio
nutritious [nju'trɪʃəs] o [nu'trɪʃəs] *adj* nutricio, nutritivo, alimentoso
nutritive ['njutrɪtɪv] o ['nutrɪtɪv] *adj* nutritivo; alimenticio
nutshell ['nʌt,ʃɛl] *s* cáscara de nuez; **in a nutshell** en pocas palabras
nutty ['nʌtɪ] *adj* (*comp:* **-tier;** *super:* **-tiest**) abundante en nueces; que sabe a nueces; (slang) loco; **nutty about** (slang) loco por (*p.ej., los deportes*)
nux vomica ['nʌks 'vɑmɪkə] *s* (bot.) nuez vómica (*árbol y semilla*)
nuzzle ['nʌzəl] *va* hozar, hocicar; *vn* hocicar; arrimarse cómodamente; arroparse bien
n.w., N.W. o **NW** abr. de **northwest**
N.Y. abr. de **New York State**
N.Y.C. abr. de **New York City**
nyctalopia [,nɪktə'lopɪə] *s* nictalopía
nylon ['naɪlɑn] *s* (trademark) nilón; **nylons** *spl* medias de nilón
nymph [nɪmf] *s* (myth., ent. & fig.) ninfa
nymphomania [,nɪmfə'menɪə] *s* (path.) ninfomanía
nystagmus [nɪs'tægməs] *s* (path.) nistagmo
N.Z. abr. de **New Zealand**

O

O, o [o] *s* (*pl:* **O's, o's** [oz]) décimaquinta letra del alfabeto inglés
O. abr. de **Ohio**
O *interj* ¡Oh!; ¡oye!; ¡ay!, p.ej., **O, how pretty she is!** ¡Ay qué linda!; **O that . . .!** ¡Ojalá que . . .!
oaf [of] *s* tonto, zoquete; niño contrahecho
oafish [ˈofɪʃ] *adj* tonto, torpe, pesado
oak [ok] *s* (bot.) roble
oak apple *s* gran agalla de roble
oaken [ˈokən] *adj* de roble, hecho de roble
oak gall *s* agalla de roble, nuez de agallas, bugalla
oak moss *s* (bot.) musgo de roble
oakum [ˈokəm] *s* (naut.) estopa, estopa de calafatear
oar [or] *s* remo; remero; **to lie** o **rest on one's oars** aguantar los remos, cesar de remar; aflojar en el trabajo, dormirse sobre sus laureles; **to put in one's oar** meter su cuchara; *va* conducir remando o a remo; *vn* remar, bogar
oarless [ˈorlɪs] *adj* sin remos; que no conoce el remo
oarlock [ˈor,lɑk] *s* (naut.) escalamera, chumacera
oarsman [ˈorzmən] *s* (*pl:* **-men**) remero
OAS *s* OEA (*Organización de Estados Americanos*)
oasis [oˈesɪs] u [ˈoəsɪs] *s* (*pl:* **-ses** [siz]) oasis
oat [ot] *s* (bot.) avena; (poet.) avena (*flauta rústica*); **oats** *spl* avena (*granos*); **to feel one's oats** (slang) estar fogoso y brioso; (slang) estar muy pagado de sí mismo; **to sow one's wild oats** correrla, pasar las mocedades
oatcake [ˈot,kek] *s* torta de harina de avena
oaten [ˈotən] *adj* hecho de harina de avena, hecho de paja de avena
oat field *s* avenal
oath [oθ] *s* (*pl:* **oaths** [oðz] u [oθs]) juramento; **on oath** bajo juramento; **to take oath** prestar juramento
oatmeal [ˈot,mil] *s* harina de avena; gachas de avena
ob. abr. de **obiit** (Lat.) **died**
obbligato [,ɑblɪˈgɑto] *adj* (mus.) obligado; *s* (*pl:* **-tos**) (mus.) obligado
obduracy [ˈɑbdjʊrəsɪ] o [ˈɑbdjərəsɪ] *s* obduración
obdurate [ˈɑbdjʊrɪt] o [ˈɑbdjərɪt] *adj* obstinado, terco; empedernido
obedience [oˈbidɪəns] *s* obediencia
obedient [oˈbidɪənt] *adj* obediente
obeisance [oˈbesəns] u [oˈbisəns] *s* saludo respetuoso; homenaje, respeto
obelisk [ˈɑbəlɪsk] *s* obelisco
obese [oˈbis] *adj* obeso
obesity [oˈbisɪtɪ] u [oˈbɛsɪtɪ] *s* obesidad
obey [oˈbe] *va & vn* obedecer
obfuscate [ɑbˈfʌsket] o [ˈɑbfəsket] *va* ofuscar
obfuscation [,ɑbfəsˈkeʃən] *s* ofuscación
obiter dictum [ˈɑbɪtər ˈdɪktəm] *s* (*pl:* **obiter dicta**) dictamen de carácter incidental
obituary [oˈbɪtʃʊ,ɛrɪ] *adj* necrológico; *s* (*pl:* **-ies**) obituario; (eccl.) obituario
obj. abr. de **object, objection** y **objective**
object [ˈɑbdʒɪkt] *s* objeto; mamarracho (*persona o cosa ridícula*); (gram.) objeto, complemento; **with the object of** al objeto de; [əbˈdʒɛkt] *va* objetar; *vn* hacer objeciones; **to object to** hacer objeciones a, oponerse a; sentir disgusto por
object ball *s* mingo
object glass *s* (opt.) objetivo, lente objetiva
objection [əbˈdʒɛkʃən] *s* objeción; **to have no objections to make** no tener nada que objetar; **to raise an objection to** poner reparo a
objectionable [əbˈdʒɛkʃənəbəl] *adj* que da lugar a objeciones; desagradable; censurable, reprensible
objective [əbˈdʒɛktɪv] *adj* objetivo; (gram.) objetivo; *s* objetivo (*fin, intento*); (opt.) objetivo
objectivity [,ɑbdʒɛkˈtɪvɪtɪ] *s* objetividad
object lesson *s* lección práctica; lección de cosas
objector [əbˈdʒɛktər] *s* objetante
object pronoun *s* pronombre complementario
object teaching *s* enseñanza objetiva
objet d'art [ɔbʒe ˈdɑr] *s* objeto de arte
objurgate [ˈɑbdʒərget] *va* increpar, reconvenir
objurgation [,ɑbdʒərˈgeʃən] *s* increpación, reconvención, obyurgación
objurgatory [əbˈdʒʌrgə,torɪ] *adj* increpador
obl. abr. de **oblique** y **oblong**
oblate [ˈɑblet] o [ɑbˈlet] *adj* (geom.) achatado por los polos; (eccl.) oblato; *s* (eccl.) oblato
oblation [ɑbˈleʃən] *s* oblación; (eccl.) oblata (*especialmente la que se da a la fábrica de la iglesia*)
obligate [ˈɑblɪget] *va* obligar; **to obligate oneself to** + *inf* obligarse a + *inf*
obligation [,ɑblɪˈgeʃən] *s* obligación; **to be under obligation to** correr obligación a
obligato [,ɑblɪˈgɑto] *adj & s* var. de **obbligato**
obligatory [əˈblɪgə,torɪ] o [ˈɑblɪgə,torɪ] *adj* obligatorio
oblige [əˈblaɪdʒ] *va* obligar; complacer; **much obliged** muchas gracias; **to be obliged for** estar agradecido por; **to be obliged to** + *inf* estar obligado a + *inf;* **to oblige to** + *inf* obligar a + *inf*
obligee [,ɑblɪˈdʒi] *s* obligado
obliging [əˈblaɪdʒɪŋ] *adj* complaciente, condescendiente, servicial
oblique [əˈblik] *adj* oblicuo; indirecto, evasivo, torcido; [əˈblaɪk] *vn* (mil.) oblicuar
obliquity [əbˈlɪkwɪtɪ] *s* (*pl:* **-ties**) oblicuidad; aberración, extravío
obliquity of the ecliptic *s* (astr.) oblicuidad de la eclíptica
obliterate [əˈblɪtəret] *va* borrar; arrasar, destruir; obliterar (*un sello de correo*); (med.) obliterar
obliteration [ə,blɪtəˈreʃən] *s* borradura; arrasamiento, destrucción; (med.) obliteración
oblivion [əˈblɪvɪən] *s* olvido
oblivious [əˈblɪvɪəs] *adj* olvidadizo, desatento, inconsciente; que causa olvido
oblong [ˈɑblɔŋ] o [ˈɑblɑŋ] *adj* oblongo, cuadrilongo; *s* cuadrilongo
obloquy [ˈɑbləkwɪ] *s* (*pl:* **-quies**) deshonra, baldón; censura, calumnia
obnoxious [əbˈnɑkʃəs] *adj* detestable, ofensivo, odioso
oboe [ˈobo] *s* (mus.) oboe
oboist [ˈobo·ɪst] *s* (mus.) oboe, oboísta (*músico*)
obreptitious [,ɑbrɛpˈtɪʃəs] *adj* obrepticio
obs. abr. de **obsolete**
obscene [ɑbˈsin] *adj* obsceno
obscenity [ɑbˈsɛnɪtɪ] o [ɑbˈsinɪtɪ] *s* (*pl:* **-ties**) obscenidad
obscurant [ɑbˈskjʊrənt] *adj & s* var. de **obscurantist**
obscurantism [ɑbˈskjʊrəntɪzəm] *s* obscurantismo
obscurantist [ɑbˈskjʊrəntɪst] *adj & s* obscurantista
obscuration [,ɑbskjʊˈreʃən] *s* obscurecimiento
obscure [əbˈskjʊr] *adj* obscuro; (phonet.) relajado, neutro; *va* obscurecer

obscurity [əb'skjurɪtɪ] *s* (*pl:* **-ties**) obscuridad
obsecrate ['absɪkret] *va* rogar, suplicar
obsecration [,absɪ'kreʃən] *s* obsecración
obsequies ['absɪkwɪz] *spl* exequias
obsequious [əb'sikwɪəs] *adj* obsequioso, servil, rastrero
observable [əb'zʌrvəbəl] *adj* observable
observably [əb'zʌrvəblɪ] *adv* perceptiblemente, notablemente
observance [əb'zʌrvəns] *s* observancia
observant [əb'zʌrvənt] *adj* observador
observation [,abzər'veʃən] *s* observación; observancia; **to escape observation** no ser observado; **to keep under observation** vigilar
observational [,abzər'veʃənəl] *adj* de la observación, observacional
observation balloon *s* globo de observación
observation car *s* (rail.) vagón-mirador
observatory [əb'zʌrvə,torɪ] *s* (*pl:* **-ries**) observatorio
observe [əb'zʌrv] *va* observar (*guardar, cumplir; examinar con atención; advertir, reparar; atisbar*); guardar (*una fiesta; silencio*)
observer [əb'zʌrvər] *s* observador
observing [əb'zʌrvɪŋ] *adj* observador
obsess [əb'sɛs] *va* obsesionar, causar obsesión a
obsession [əb'sɛʃən] *s* obsesión
obsidian [ab'sɪdɪən] *s* (mineral.) obsidiana
obsolescence [,absə'lɛsəns] *s* caída en desuso
obsolescent [,absə'lɛsənt] *adj* arcaizante, algo anticuado; **to be obsolescent** irse haciendo anticuado, ir cayendo en desuso
obsolete ['absəlit] *adj* anticuado, caído en desuso, desusado; (biol.) rudimentario
obstacle ['abstəkəl] *s* obstáculo
obstacle race *s* carrera de obstáculos
obstetric [ab'stɛtrɪk] *adj* obstétrico; **obstetrics** *ssg* obstetricia
obstetrical [ab'stɛtrɪkəl] *adj* obstétrico
obstetrician [,abstɛ'trɪʃən] *s* obstétrico, médico partero
obstinacy ['abstɪnəsɪ] *s* (*pl:* **-cies**) obstinación
obstinate ['abstɪnɪt] *adj* obstinado
obstreperous [əb'strɛpərəs] *adj* estrepitoso, turbulento, desmandado
obstruct [əb'strʌkt] *va* obstruir
obstruction [əb'strʌkʃən] *s* obstrucción
obstructionism [əb'strʌkʃənɪzəm] *s* obstruccionismo
obstructionist [əb'strʌkʃənɪst] *adj & s* obstruccionista
obstructive [əb'strʌktɪv] *adj* obstructivo
obtain [əb'ten] *va* obtener; *vn* existir, prevalecer
obtainable [əb'tenəbəl] *adj* obtenible
obtainment [əb'tenmənt] *s* obtención
obtrude [əb'trud] *va* imponer (*sus opiniones*); extender; *vn* entremeterse
obtrusion [əb'truʒən] *s* imposición; entremetimiento
obtrusive [əb'trusɪv] *adj* entremetido, intruso
obturate ['abtjəret] *va* obturar
obturation [,abtjə'reʃən] *s* obturación
obturator ['abtjə,retər] *s* obturador; (phot. & surg.) obturador
obtuse [əb'tjus] o [əb'tus] *adj* obtuso; (fig.) obtuso
obtuse angle *s* (geom.) ángulo obtuso
obverse [ab'vʌrs] o ['abvʌrs] *adj* obverso; complementario; ['abvʌrs] *s* anverso; frente; complemento
obviate ['abvɪet] *va* obviar
obviation [,abvɪ'eʃən] *s* evitación
obvious ['abvɪəs] *adj* obvio
ocarina [,akə'rinə] *s* (mus.) ocarina
occasion [ə'keʒən] *s* ocasión; **on occasion** de vez en cuando; **on the occasion of** con ocasión de; **on several occasions** en varias ocasiones; **to improve the occasion** aprovechar la ocasión; *va* ocasionar
occasional [ə'keʒənəl] *adj* raro, poco frecuente; alguno que otro; de circunstancia
occasionally [ə'keʒənəlɪ] *adv* ocasionalmente (*de vez en cuando*)
occident ['aksɪdənt] *s* occidente; (*cap.*) *s* Occidente
occidental [,aksɪ'dɛntəl] *adj* occidental; (*cap.*) *adj & s* occidental
Occidentalize [,aksɪ'dɛntəlaɪz] *va* occidentalizar
occipital [ak'sɪpɪtəl] *adj* occipital; *s* (anat.) occipital, hueso occipital
occipital bone *s* (anat.) hueso occipital
occiput ['aksɪpət] *s* (*pl:* **occipita** [ak'sɪpɪtə]) (anat.) occipucio
occlude [a'klud] *va* obstruir; obscurecer; (chem. & dent.) ocluir; *vn* (dent.) ocluirse
occlusal [a'klusəl] *adj* (anat. & dent.) oclusal
occlusion [a'kluʒən] *s* obstrucción; obscurecimiento; (chem., dent., med. & phonet.) oclusión
occlusive [a'klusɪv] *adj* oclusivo; *s* (phonet.) oclusiva
occult [a'kʌlt] o ['akʌlt] *adj* oculto (*misterioso; sobrenatural*)
occultation [,akʌl'teʃən] *s* ocultación; (astr.) ocultación
occultism [a'kʌltɪzəm] o ['akəltɪzəm] *s* ocultismo
occultist [a'kʌltɪst] o ['akəltɪst] *s* ocultista
occult sciences *spl* ciencias ocultas
occupancy ['akjəpənsɪ] *s* ocupación, tenencia
occupant ['akjəpənt] *s* ocupante; inquilino
occupation [,akjə'peʃən] *s* ocupación; inquilinato
occupational [,akjə'peʃənəl] *adj* ocupacional
occupational disease *s* enfermedad profesional, enfermedad de ocupación
occupational therapy *s* sistema terapéutico que consiste en la enseñanza de artes y oficios
occupy ['akjəpaɪ] (*pret & pp:* **-pied**) *va* ocupar; habitar (*p.ej., cierta casa*)
occur [ə'kʌr] (*pret & pp:* **-curred;** *ger:* **-curring**) *vn* ocurrir, acontecer, suceder; encontrarse (*p.ej., una palabra en un escrito*); ocurrir (*venir a la mente*); **to occur to one to** + *inf* ocurrírsele a uno + *inf*
occurrence [ə'kʌrəns] *s* acontecimiento; aparición, caso
ocean ['oʃən] *s* océano; (fig.) océano (*vasta extensión de cualquier cosa*); (fig.) mar (*gran cantidad*), p.ej., **oceans of work** la mar de trabajo
Oceania [,oʃɪ'ænɪə] *s* la Oceanía
oceanic [,oʃɪ'ænɪk] *adj* oceánico
Oceanica [,oʃɪ'ænɪkə] *s* var. de **Oceania**
Oceanids [o'siənɪdz] *spl* (myth.) Oceánidas
ocean liner *s* buque transoceánico
oceanographer [,oʃən'agrəfər] *s* oceanógrafo
oceanographic [,oʃənə'græfɪk] u **oceanographical** [,oʃənə'græfɪkəl] *adj* oceanográfico
oceanography [,oʃən'agrəfɪ] *s* oceanografía
Oceanus [o'siənəs] *s* (myth.) Océano
ocellate ['asəlet] u [o'sɛlet] *adj* ocelado
ocellus [o'sɛləs] *s* (*pl:* **-li** [laɪ]) (zool.) ocelo (*ojo simple de los anélidos; mancha redonda en las plumas de ciertas aves*)
ocelot ['osəlat] o ['asəlat] *s* (zool.) ocelote
ocher u **ochre** ['okər] *s* (mineral.) ocre; *adj* ocroso
ocherous ['okərəs] *adj* ocroso
o'clock [ə'klak] *adv* por el reloj; **it is one o'clock** es la una; **it is two o'clock** son las dos; **what o'clock is it?** ¿qué hora es?
Oct. abr. de **October**
octagon ['aktəgan] o ['aktəgən] *s* octágono
octagonal [ak'tægənəl] *adj* octagonal, octágono
octahedral [,aktə'hidrəl] *adj* octaédrico
octahedron [,aktə'hidrən] *s* (*pl:* **-drons** o **-dra** [drə]) (geom.) octaedro
octane ['akten] *s* (chem.) octano
octane number o **rating** *s* (chem.) índice de octano
octastyle ['aktəstaɪl] *adj* (arch.) octóstilo
octave ['aktɪv] o ['aktev] *s* (mus., pros. & eccl.) octava
Octavian [ak'tevɪən] *s* Octaviano
Octavius [ak'tevɪəs] *s* Octavio
octavo [ak'tevo] o [ak'tavo] *adj* en octavo; *s* (*pl:* **-vos**) libro en octavo
octet u **octette** [ak'tɛt] *s* (mus.) octeto; (pros.) octava; grupo de ocho
octillion [ak'tɪljən] *s* (Brit.) octillón
October [ak'tobər] *s* octubre
octogenarian [,aktodʒɪ'nɛrɪən] *adj & s* octogenario
octopus ['aktəpəs] *s* (*pl:* **-puses** o **-pi** [paɪ]) (zool.) pulpo; (fig.) organización monopolizadora con grandes facultades para hacer daño

octoroon [ˌɑktəˈrun] *s* octavo (*hijo de cuarterón y blanca o de cuarterona y blanco*)
octosyllabic [ˌɑktosɪˈlæbɪk] *adj* octosilábico, octosílabo
octosyllable [ˈɑktoˌsɪləbəl] *s* octosílabo (*verso*)
octroi [ɑkˈtrwɑ] *s* fielato (*oficina*); consumos (*impuestos*)
octuple [ˈɑktjʊpəl] o [ˈɑktʊpəl] *adj & s* óctuple; *va* octuplicar; *vn* octuplicarse
ocular [ˈɑkjələr] *adj* ocular; *s* (opt.) ocular
oculist [ˈɑkjəlɪst] *s* oculista
O.D. abr. de **officer of the day** y **olive drab**
odalisque u **odalisk** [ˈodəlɪsk] *s* odalisca
odd [ɑd] *adj* suelto; impar (*número*); dispar (*que no hace juego*); libre, de ocio; sobrante; extraño, raro, singular; y pico o y tantos, p.ej., **two hundred odd** doscientos y pico; **odds** *ssg o spl* ventaja (*en las apuestas*); apuesta desigual; puntos de ventaja; **at odds** de monos, riñendo; **by all odds** muy probablemente, sin duda alguna; **it makes no odds** lo mismo da; **the odds are** lo probable es; la ventaja es de; **to be at odds** estar de punta, estar encontrados; **to be at odds with** estar de punta con, estar encontrado con; **to set at odds** enemistar, malquistar
oddish [ˈɑdɪʃ] *adj* algo raro, algo singular
oddity [ˈɑdɪtɪ] *s* (*pl:* **-ties**) rareza, cosa rara, ente singular
odd jobs *spl* extraños empleos, pequeñas tareas
odd lot *s* (com.) lote inferior al centenar
oddly [ˈɑdlɪ] *adv* extrañamente, singularmente
oddment [ˈɑdmənt] *s* sobra, pedazo, retal
odd number *s* número impar, número non
odds and ends *spl* trozos sobrantes, pedacitos varios, despojos, cajón de sastre
ode [od] *s* oda
Odessa [oˈdɛsə] *s* Odesa
odeum [oˈdiəm] *s* (*pl:* **-a** [ə]) odeón
Odin [ˈodɪn] *s* (myth.) Odín
odious [ˈodɪəs] *adj* odioso, abominable
odium [ˈodɪəm] *s* odio (*que una persona se conquista*); oprobio; **to bring into odium** hacer aborrecido (*a uno*); **to bring odium upon a person** hacer que una persona sea odiada
Odoacer [ˌodoˈesər] *s* Odoacro
odometer [oˈdɑmɪtər] *s* odómetro
odontoblast [oˈdɑntəblæst] *s* (anat.) odontoblasto
odontocete [oˈdɑntəsit] *adj & s* (zool.) odontoceto
odontological [oˌdɑntəˈlɑdʒɪkəl] *adj* odontológico
odontologist [ˌodɑnˈtɑlədʒɪst] *s* odontólogo
odontology [ˌodɑnˈtɑlədʒɪ] *s* odontología
odor [ˈodər] *s* olor; **to be in bad odor** tener mala fama
odoriferous [ˌodəˈrɪfərəs] *adj* odorífero
odorless [ˈodərlɪs] *adj* inodoro
odor of sanctity *s* olor de santidad
odorous [ˈodərəs] *adj* oloroso
odour [ˈodər] *s* (Brit.) var. de **odor**
Odysseus [oˈdɪsus] u [oˈdɪsɪəs] *s* (myth.) Odiseo
Odyssey [ˈɑdɪsɪ] *s* (myth.) Odisea; (*l.c.*) *s* (fig.) odisea
O.E. abr. de **Old English**
oecumenical [ˌɛkjʊˈmɛnɪkəl] *adj* var. de **ecumenical**
Oedipus [ˈɛdɪpəs] o [ˈidɪpəs] *s* (myth.) Edipo
Oedipus complex *s* (psychoanal.) complejo de Edipo
oenometer [iˈnɑmɪtər] *s* enómetro
Oenone [iˈnonɪ] *s* (myth.) Enona
o'er [or] *adv & prep* (poet.) var. de **over**
oersted [ˈʌrstɛd] *s* (elec.) oerstedio
oesophagus [iˈsɑfəgəs] *s* (*pl:* **-gi** [dʒaɪ]) var. de **esophagus**
of [ɑv] o [əv] *prep* de, p.ej., **the top of the mountain** la cima de la montaña; a: **to smell of** oler a; **to taste of** saber a; con: **to dream of** soñar con; en; **to think of** pensar en; menos: **a quarter of two** las dos menos cuarto; por: **of a summer morning** por una mañana de verano
off. abr. de **office, officer** y **official**
off [ɔf] o [ɑf] *adj* malo, p.ej., **off day** día malo; poco probable, errado (*p.ej., en las cuentas*); en marcha; más distante, más lejano; libre, sin trabajo; quitado; apagado; cortado (*dícese, p.ej., de electricidad*); de descuento, de rebaja; de la parte del mar; de la derecha (*dícese de un caballo o buey en la yunta*); **to be . . . off** faltar para, p.ej., **the wedding is two days off** faltan dos días para la boda; *adv* fuera, a distancia, lejos; **far off** muy lejos; **to be off** ponerse en marcha, marcharse en seguida, haberse marchado; **off and on** unas veces sí y otras no, de vez en cuando; **off in the distance** allá lejos; **off of** (coll.) de; (coll.) a expensas de; *prep* fuera de (*p.ej., el camino*); de, desde; al lado de, a nivel de; (naut.) frente a, a la altura de, cerca de; libre de; **to be off** faltar a, p.ej., **a button is off his coat** a su chaqueta le falta un botón; *interj* ¡fuera!; **off with you!** ¡fuera de aquí!, ¡márchate!
offal [ˈɑfəl] u [ˈɔfəl] *s* carniza (*desecho de la carne*); basura, desperdicios
offbeat [ˈɔfˈbit] o [ˈɑfˈbit] *adj* (slang) insólito, chocante, original
off-chance [ˈɔfˌtʃæns], [ˈɔfˌtʃɑns], [ˈɑfˌtʃæns] o [ˈɑfˌtʃɑns] *s* posibilidad poco probable, posibilidad remota; **on the off-chance that** pensando que tal vez
off-color [ˈɔfˌkʌlər] o [ˈɑfˌkʌlər] *adj* desteñido; (fig.) verde, subido de color
offend [əˈfɛnd] *va & vn* ofender
offender [əˈfɛndər] *s* ofensor
offense [əˈfɛns] *s* ofensa; **to take offense (at)** ofenderse (de)
offenseless [əˈfɛnslɪs] *adj* inofensivo
offensive [əˈfɛnsɪv] *adj* ofensivo; *s* ofensiva; **on the offensive** en la ofensiva; **to take the offensive** tomar la ofensiva
offer [ˈɔfər] o [ˈɑfər] *s* ofrecimiento, oferta; *va* ofrecer; rezar (*oraciones*); oponer (*resistencia*); **to offer to** + *inf* ofrecerse a + *inf;* intentar + *inf; vn* ofrecerse
offering [ˈɔfərɪŋ] o [ˈɑfərɪŋ] *s* ofrecimiento; ofrenda (*en el culto divino*); oferta (*don, dádiva*)
offertory [ˈɔfərˌtorɪ] o [ˈɑfərˌtorɪ] *s* (*pl:* **-ries**) (eccl.) ofrenda; (eccl.) música o canto que acompaña la recaudación de la ofrenda en las iglesias protestantes; (eccl.) ofertorio (*parte de las misa y su antífona*)
offhand [ˈɔfˈhænd] o [ˈɑfˈhænd] *adj* hecho de improviso; brusco, desenvuelto; *adv* de corrido, de improviso, sin pensarlo; bruscamente
offhanded [ˈɔfˈhændɪd] o [ˈɑfˈhændɪd] *adj* hecho de improviso; brusco, desenvuelto
office [ˈɔfɪs] o [ˈɑfɪs] *s* oficina; oficio, función; cargo, ministerio; bufete (*de abogado*); consultorio (*de médico*); (eccl.) oficio; **offices** *spl* (Brit.) oficinas (*piezas bajas de las casas que sirven para ciertos menesteres domésticos*); **to be in office** estar en funciones; **to take office** entrar en funciones; **good offices** buenos oficios; *adj* oficinesco
office boy *s* mandadero
office building *s* edificio de oficinas
office force *s* personal o gente de la oficina
officeholder [ˈɔfɪsˌholdər] o [ˈɑfɪsˌholdər] *s* funcionario, empleado público
office hours *spl* horas de oficina; horas de consulta (*de un médico*)
office manager *s* jefe de oficina
officer [ˈɔfɪsər] o [ˈɑfɪsər] *s* jefe, director; dignatario; oficial (*del ejército, de una orden, sociedad, etc.*); funcionario; agente de policía; *va* mandar; proveer de jefes, proveer de oficiales
officer of the day *s* (mil.) jefe de día
office seeker *s* aspirante, pretendiente
office supplies *spl* artículos para escritorio, suministros para oficinas
office work *s* trabajo de oficina
official [əˈfɪʃəl] *adj* oficial; *s* jefe, director; funcionario; oficial (*p.ej., de una sociedad*)
officialdom [əˈfɪʃəldəm] *s* las autoridades, los círculos oficiales
officialism [əˈfɪʃəlɪzəm] *s* costumbres oficiales; formalismo
officially [əˈfɪʃəlɪ] *adv* oficialmente
officiant [əˈfɪʃɪənt] *s* (eccl.) oficiante
officiate [əˈfɪʃɪet] *vn* (eccl.) oficiar; **to officiate as** oficiar de
officinal [əˈfɪsɪnəl] *adj* (pharm.) oficinal; *s* (pharm.) medicamento oficinal
officious [əˈfɪʃəs] *adj* oficioso; (dipl.) oficioso
offing [ˈɔfɪŋ] o [ˈɑfɪŋ] *s* (naut.) largo, alta

mar; lontananza; **in the offing** (naut.) a lo largo, mar afuera; bastante cerca, en perspectiva
offish ['ɔfɪʃ] o ['ɑfɪʃ] *adj* huraño, arisco
off-peak ['ɔf,pik] o ['ɑf,pik] *adj* (elec.) de las horas de menos carga, en horas de valle
off-peak heater *s* (elec.) termos de acumulación
off-peak load *s* (elec.) carga en horas de valle
offprint ['ɔf,prɪnt] o ['ɑf,prɪnt] *s* sobretiro
offscourings ['ɔf,skaurɪŋz] o ['ɑf,skaurɪŋz] *spl* inmundicias; hez, gente vil
offset ['ɔf,sɛt] o ['ɑf,sɛt] *s* compensación; ramal; (arch.) retallo; (hort.) acodo; (mach.) codo; (print.) offset; (top.) línea perpendicular a otra principal y que se extiende a un punto exterior; *adj* (print.) de offset; [,ɔf'sɛt] o [,ɑf'sɛt] (*pret & pp:* **-set;** *ger:* **-setting**) *va* componer; oponer; (print.) imprimir por offset; *vn* imprimir por offset
offshoot ['ɔf,ʃut] o ['ɑf,ʃut] *s* retoño, renuevo; ramal
offshore ['ɔf,ʃor] o ['ɑf,ʃor] *adj* (naut.) terral, que sopla de tierra; (naut.) que se encuentra a lo largo; *adv* (naut.) a lo largo
offshore fishing *s* pesca de bajura
offshore islands *spl* islas costeras
offside ['ɔf,saɪd] o ['ɑf,saɪd] *adj* (sport) entre los del bando contrario; (sport) fuera de juego; **to be offside** (sport) hacer una jugada estando la pelota fuera de juego
offspring ['ɔf,sprɪŋ] o ['ɑf,sprɪŋ] *s* sucesión, descendencia; hijo; (fig.) producto, resultado
off-stage ['ɔf,stedʒ] o ['ɑf,stedʒ] *adj* (theat.) de entre bastidores
off-the-record ['ɔfðə'rɛkərd] o ['ɑfðə'rɛkərd] *adj* extraoficial, confidencial
oft [ɔft] o [ɑft] *adv* (poet.) var. de **often**
often ['ɔfən] o ['ɑfən] *adv* a menudo, muchas veces; **as often as** siempre que; **how often** cada cuánto, p.ej., **how often does the train stop here?** ¿cada cuánto pára el tren aquí?; cuántas veces; **not often** pocas veces, rara vez
oftentimes ['ɔfən,taɪmz] o ['ɑfən,taɪmz] *adv* var. de **often**
ofttimes ['ɔft,taɪmz] o ['ɑft,taɪmz] *adv* (poet.) var. de **often**
ogee [o'dʒi] u ['odʒi] *s* (arch.) cimacio, gola
ogee arch *s* (arch.) arco conopial
ogival [o'dʒaɪvəl] *adj* ojival; (arch.) ojival
ogive ['odʒaɪv] u [o'dʒaɪv] *s* (arch.) ojiva
ogle ['ogəl] *s* mirada torpe, mirada de amor; *va* ojear; echar miradas torpes a, echar miradas de amor a; *vn* mirar amorosamente
Ogpu ['ɑgpu] *s* Guepeu (*policía política soviética*)
ogre ['ogər] *s* ogro; (fig.) ogro (*persona*)
ogreish ['ogərɪʃ] *adj* de ogro
ogress ['ogrɪs] *s* ogra u ogresa
ogrish ['ogrɪʃ] *adj* var. de **ogreish**
oh u **Oh** [o] *interj* var. de **O**
ohm [om] *s* (elec.) ohmio
ohmic ['omɪk] *adj* óhmico
ohmmeter ['om,mitər] *s* (elec.) ohmímetro
oho [o'ho] *interj* ¡ ajá!
oïdium [o'ɪdɪəm] *s* (*pl:* **-a** [ə]) (bot. & plant path.) oídio
oil [ɔɪl] *s* aceite; petróleo; color al óleo; óleo, pintura al óleo; **to burn the midnight oil** quemarse las cejas; **to pour oil on the fire** echar aceite en el fuego; **to pour oil on troubled waters** mojar la pólvora, aplacar las pasiones; **to strike oil** encontrar una capa de petróleo; (fig.) enriquecerse de súbito; *va* aceitar; hacer liso, suave o agradable; lisonjear; untar (*corromper, sobornar*); *vn* desleírse (*p.ej., la manteca*); proveerse de petróleo (*un buque*)
oil beetle *s* (ent.) aceitera, carraleja
oilbird ['ɔɪl,bʌrd] *s* (orn.) guácharo, papagayo de noche
oil burner *s* quemador de petróleo
oil cake *s* torta de borujo
oilcan ['ɔɪl,kæn] *s* aceitera
oilcloth ['ɔɪl,klɔθ] u ['ɔɪl,klɑθ] *s* encerado, hule
oil color *s* color al óleo; (paint.) pintura al óleo
oil cup *s* (mach.) aceitera, copilla de aceite, caja de aceite
oiler ['ɔɪlər] *s* aceitador (*obrero*); aceitera (*vasija*); buque petrolero
oil field *s* campo de petróleo
oil filler *s* llenador de aceite
oil gas *s* gas de aceite
oil gauge *s* indicador de aceite, indicador del nivel de aceite
oil gun *s* bomba de mano para lubricación
oil hole *s* agujero de engrase, orificio de engrase
oil line *s* conducto del aceite, cañería de lubricación
oil of vitriol *s* aceite de vitriolo
oil of wintergreen *s* aceite de gaulteria
oil painting *s* pintura al óleo, cuadro al óleo
oil pan *s* (aut.) colector de aceite
oilpaper ['ɔɪl,pepər] *s* papel encerado e impermeable
oil pump *s* bomba de aceite
oilskin ['ɔɪl,skɪn] *s* hule; **oilskins** *spl* traje de hule
oilstone ['ɔɪl,ston] *s* asperón de grano fino
oil stove *s* estufa o cocina de aceite
oil tanker *s* buque petrolero, buque tanque para petróleo
oil well *s* pozo de petróleo; (mach.) cubeta de aceite
oily ['ɔɪlɪ] *adj* (*comp:* **-ier;** *super:* **-iest**) aceitoso; liso, resbaladizo; zalamero
ointment ['ɔɪntmənt] *s* ungüento
O.K. u **OK** ['o'ke] *s* (coll.) aprobación; *adj* (coll.) aprobado, conforme; *adv* (coll.) está bien, muy bien, V.°B.° (*visto bueno*); (*pret & pp:* **O.K.'d** u **OK'd;** *ger:* **O.K.'ing** u **OK'ing**) *va* (coll.) aprobar
okapi [o'kɑpɪ] *s* (zool.) okapi
okay ['o'ke] *s, adj, adv & va* var. de **O.K.**
Okla. abr. de **Oklahoma**
okra ['okrə] *s* (bot.) quingombó (*planta y fruto*)
old [old] *adj* viejo; antiguo; añejo (*dícese, p.ej., del vino*); **of old** de antaño, antiguamente; **how old do you think he is?** ¿qué edad le echa Vd.?; **how old is . . .?** ¿cuántos años tiene . . .?; **to be . . . years old** tener . . . años; **older woman** señora de edad
old age *s* ancianidad, vejez; **to die of old age** morir de viejo
old bachelor *s* solterón
Old Bailey ['belɪ] *s* tribunal supremo de lo criminal en Londres
old boy *s* viejo; graduado; **the Old Boy** (slang) el Diablo
Old Castile *s* Castilla la Vieja
old-clothesman ['old'kloðz,mæn] *s* (*pl:* **-men**) ropavejero
old country *s* madre patria (*de los emigrantes o sus descendientes*)
Old Dominion *s* el estado de Virginia, EE.UU.
olden ['oldən] *adj* (poet.) antiguo
Old English *s* el inglés antiguo; (print.) letra gótica
olden times *spl* (poet.) tiempos antiguos
old-fashioned ['old'fæʃənd] *adj* chapado a la antigua; anticuado, fuera de moda
old fogey u **old fogy** *s* persona un poco ridícula por sus ideas o costumbres atrasadas
old-fogey u **old-fogy** ['old,fogɪ] *adj* atrasado, anticuado, fuera de moda
Old French *s* el francés antiguo
Old Glory *s* la bandera de los EE.UU.
Old Guard *s* (U.S.A.) bando conservador del partido republicano
old hand *s* perito, practicón, veterano
Old Harry *s* el Diablo
Old High German *s* el antiguo altoalemán
oldish ['oldɪʃ] *adj* algo viejo
old-line ['old,laɪn] *adj* conservador, tradicional; (com.) bien establecido, establecido desde hace muchos años
old maid *s* solterona
old-maidish [,old'medɪʃ] *adj* que parece u obra como solterona, melindroso, remilgado
old man *s* viejo; tío; (mach.) abrazadera de taladrar; (theol.) hombre viejo; (theat.) barba
Old Man of the Mountain *s* (hist.) viejo de la montaña
old master *s* (paint.) grande maestro; obra (de pintura) de un grande maestro
old moon *s* luna menguante
Old Nick *s* el Diablo
Old Norse *s* el nórdico antiguo

old salt *s* lobo de mar
Old Saxon *s* el sajón antiguo
old school *s* gente chapada a la antigua, gente de ideas anticuadas
Old Spanish *s* el español antiguo
oldster ['oldstər] *s* (coll.) viejo o vieja; (Brit.) guardia marina que lo es por lo menos desde hace cuatro años
Old Style *s* estilo antiguo (*calendario*)
Old Testament *s* Antiguo Testamento
old-time ['old,taɪm] *adj* del tiempo viejo, como en el tiempo viejo
old-timer ['old'taɪmər] *s* (coll.) antiguo residente, antiguo concurrente; (coll.) veterano (*en cualquier profesión o ejercicio*); (coll.) persona chapada a la antigua
oldwife ['old,waɪf] *s* (*pl:* **-wives**) (ichth.) cochino
old wives' tale *s* cuento de viejas
old-womanish [,old'wʊmənɪʃ] *adj* de vieja, remilgado
Old World *s* viejo mundo
old-world ['old,wʌrld] *adj* prehistórico; del tiempo viejo, de los tiempos antiguos; del viejo mundo
oleaceous [,olɪ'eʃəs] *adj* (bot.) oleáceo
oleaginous [,olɪ'ædʒɪnəs] *adj* oleaginoso
oleander [,olɪ'ændər] *s* (bot.) adelfa, baladre
oleaster [,olɪ'æstər] *s* (bot.) cinamomo (*Elaeagnus angustifolia*)
oleate ['olɪet] *s* (chem.) oleato
olecranon [o'lɛkrənɑn] u [,olə'krenɑn] *s* (anat.) olécranon
oleic [o'liɪk] u ['olɪɪk] *adj* (chem.) oleico
oleic acid *s* (chem.) ácido oleico
oleiferous [,olɪ'ɪfərəs] *adj* (bot.) oleífero
olein ['olɪɪn] *s* (chem.) oleína
oleo ['olɪo] *s* var. de **oleomargarin**
oleograph ['olɪə,græf] u ['olɪə,grɑf] *s* oleografía
oleomargarin [,olɪo'mɑrdʒərɪn] u [,olɪo'mɑrgərɪn] u **oleomargarine** [,olɪo'mɑrdʒərin] u [,olɪo'mɑrgərin] *s* oleomargarina
oleometer [,olɪ'ɑmɪtər] *s* oleómetro
oleoresin [,olɪo'rɛzɪn] *s* oleorresina
olfaction [ɑl'fækʃən] *s* olfacción
olfactory [ɑl'fæktərɪ] *adj* olfativo u olfatorio
olfactory nerve *s* (anat.) nervio olfativo
Olga ['ɑlgə] *s* Olga
oligarch ['ɑlɪgɑrk] *s* oligarca
oligarchic [,ɑlɪ'gɑrkɪk] u **oligarchical** [,ɑlɪ'gɑrkɪkəl] *adj* oligárquico
oligarchy ['ɑlɪ,gɑrkɪ] *s* (*pl:* **-chies**) oligarquía
oligist ['ɑlɪdʒɪst] *s* (mineral.) oligisto
Oligocene ['ɑlɪgosin] *adj & s* (geol.) oligoceno
olivaceous [,ɑlɪ'veʃəs] *adj* oliváceo
olive ['ɑlɪv] *s* (bot.) olivo, aceituno (*árbol*); aceituna (*fruto*); oliva (*color*); (anat.) oliva; *adj* aceitunado, aceitunil; verde plateado (*color de las hojas del olivo*)
olive branch *s* ramo de olivo; oliva (*paz*); hijo, vástago
olive drab *s* color oliváceo; tela de lana de color oliváceo (*que sirve para hacer los uniformes del ejército de los EE.UU.*)
olive fly *s* (ent.) mosca de la aceituna, mosca del olivo
olive grove *s* olivar
olive oil *s* aceite, aceite de oliva
Oliver ['ɑlɪvər] *s* Oliverio; Oliveros (*amigo de Roldán*)
Olives, Mount of el monte de los Olivos
Olivet, Mount ['ɑlɪvɛt] el monte Olivete
olivine ['ɑlɪvin] o [,ɑlɪ'vin] *s* (mineral.) olivino
olla-podrida [,ɑləpo'dridə] *s* (cook.) olla podrida; (fig.) mescolanza
ology ['ɑlədʒɪ] *s* (*pl:* **-gies**) ciencia, ramo del saber
Olympia [o'lɪmpɪə] *s* (geog.) Olimpia
Olympiad u **olympiad** [o'lɪmpɪæd] *s* Olimpíada
Olympian [o'lɪmpɪən] *adj* olímpico; *s* dios griego, dios del paganismo; concurrente en los Juegos olímpicos
Olympian games *spl* (hist.) Juegos olímpicos
Olympic [o'lɪmpɪk] *adj* olímpico; **Olympics** *spl* Olímpicos (*Juegos olímpicos de la Grecia antigua y los modernos*)
Olympic games *spl* (hist.) Juegos olímpicos; Juegos olímpicos (*modernos*)
Olympus, Mount [o'lɪmpəs] *s* (geog., myth. & fig.) el Olimpo
Olynthus [o'lɪnθəs] *s* Olinto
omasum [o'mesəm] *s* (*pl:* **-sa** [sə]) (zool.) omaso
omber ['ɑmbər] *s* hombre (*juego de naipes*)
omega [o'mɛgə], [o'migə] u ['omɛgə] *s* omega; fin
omelet u **omelette** ['ɑməlɛt] o ['ɑmlɪt] *s* tortilla (de huevos)
omen ['omən] *s* agüero; *va* ominar, presagiar
omental [o'mɛntəl] *adj* omental
omentum [o'mɛntəm] *s* (*pl:* **-ta** [tə]) (anat.) omento
omicron ['ɑmɪkrɑn] *s* ómicron
ominous ['ɑmɪnəs] *adj* ominoso
omission [o'mɪʃən] *s* omisión
omit [o'mɪt] (*pret & pp:* **omitted;** *ger:* **omitting**) *va* omitir; **to omit** + *ger* omitir + *inf*
ommatidium [,ɑmə'tɪdɪəm] *s* (*pl:* **-a** [ə]) (zool.) omatidio
omnibus ['ɑmnɪbʌs] o ['ɑmnɪbəs] *s* ómnibus; *adj* general; colecticio (*tomo*)
omnifarious [,ɑmnɪ'fɛrɪəs] *adj* de todo género
omnipotence [ɑm'nɪpətəns] *s* omnipotencia
omnipotent [ɑm'nɪpətənt] *adj* omnipotente
omnipresence [,ɑmnɪ'prɛzəns] *s* omnipresencia
omnipresent [,ɑmnɪ'prɛzənt] *adj* omnipresente
omniscience [ɑm'nɪʃəns] *s* omnisciencia
omniscient [ɑm'nɪʃənt] *adj* omnisciente
omnium-gatherum [,ɑmnɪəm'gæðərəm] *s* maremagno, mescolanza
omnivorous [ɑm'nɪvərəs] *adj* omnívoro
Omphale ['ɑmfəli] *s* (myth.) Onfala
on [ɑn] u [ɔn] *adj* puesto, p.ej., **with his hat on** con el sombrero puesto; principiando; en funcionamiento; encendido; conectado; **the deal is on** ya está concertado el trato; **the game is on** ya están jugando; **the race is on** allá van los corredores; **what is on at the theater this evening?** ¿qué representan esta noche? ‖ *adv* adelante; encima; **and so on** y así sucesivamente, y cosas así; **come on!** ¡anda, anda!; **farther on** más allá, más adelante; **later on** más tarde, después; **to be on to a person** (coll.) conocerle a una persona el juego; **to have on** tener puesto, llevar; **to . . . on** seguir + *ger*, p.ej., **he played on** siguió tocando; **on and on** sin cesar, sin parar, continuamente ‖ *prep* en, sobre, encima de; a, p.ej., **on foot** a pie; **on my arrival** a mi llegada; bajo, p.ej., **on my responsibility** bajo mi responsabilidad; contra, p.ej., **an attack on liberty** un ataque contra la libertad; de, p.ej., **on good authority** de buena tinta; **on a journey** de viaje; hacia, p.ej., **to march on the capital** marchar hacia la capital; por, p.ej., **on all sides** por todos lados; tras, p.ej., **defeat on defeat** derrota tras derrota; **on** + *ger* al + *inf*, p.ej., **on arriving** al llegar
onager ['ɑnədʒər] *s* (zool.) onagro
Onan ['onən] *s* (Bib.) Onán
onanism ['onənɪzəm] *s* onanismo
once [wʌns] *s* vez, una vez, p.ej., **this once** esta vez; **once is enough** basta con una vez; *adj* antiguo, que fué, p.ej., **a once friend of ours** uno amigo que fué de nosotros; *adv* una vez; antes, p.ej., **once so happy** antes tan feliz; alguna vez, p.ej., **if this once becomes known** si esto llega a saberse alguna vez; **all at once** de súbito, de repente; **at once** en seguida; a la vez, en el mismo momento; **for once** una vez por lo menos; **once and again** repetidas veces; **once for all** una vez por todas, definitivamente; **once in a while** de vez en cuando, de tarde en tarde; **once more** otra vez; más una vez; **once or twice** varias veces; **once upon a time there was** érase una vez, érase que se era; *conj* una vez que
once-over ['wʌns,ovər] *s* (slang) examen rápido, vistazo; **to give a thing the once-over** (coll.) examinar una cosa superficialmente
oncology [ɑŋ'kɑlədʒɪ] *s* oncología
oncoming ['ɑn,kʌmɪŋ] *adj* próximo, que viene; *s* aproximación, llegada

ondograph ['ɑndəgræf] o ['ɑndəgrɑf] *s* ondógrafo
one [wʌn] *adj* un, uno; un tal, p.ej., **one Smith** un tal Smith; único, p.ej., **one price** precio único; *s* uno; *pron* uno, p.ej., **one does not know what to do here** uno no sabe qué hacer aquí; se, p.ej., **how does one go to the station?** ¿cómo se va a la estación?; **I for one** yo por lo menos; **it's all one and the same** es lo mismo; **it's all one and the same to me** me es indiferente; **my little one** mi chiquito; **of one another** el uno del otro, los unos de los otros, p.ej., **we took leave of one another** nos despedimos el uno del otro; **the blue book and the red one** el libro azul y el rojo; **the one and only** el único; **the one that** el que, la que; **this one** éste; **that one** ése, aquél; **to make one** unir; casar; ser uno (*dícese de un grupo*); **we are one** somos unos; **one and all** todos; **one another** se, p.ej., **they greeted one another** se saludaron; uno a otro, unos a otros, p.ej., **they looked at one another** se miraron uno a otro; **one by one** uno a uno; **one o'clock** la una; **one or two** unos pocos; **one's** su, el . . . de uno
one-act ['wʌn,ækt] *adj* de un acto
one-celled ['wʌn,sɛld] *adj* (biol.) unicelular
one-horse ['wʌn,hɔrs] *adj* de un solo caballo, tirado por un solo caballo; (coll.) insignificante, de poca monta
oneiromancy [o'naɪrə,mænsɪ] *s* oniromancía
one-man ['wʌn,mæn] *adj* hecho por un solo hombre; de un solo hombre; para un solo hombre; apegado a un solo hombre
one line *s* (aut.) paso único
oneness ['wʌnnɪs] *s* unidad (*indivisión; singularidad; conformidad, unión*)
one-piece ['wʌn'pis] *adj* de una pieza
onerous ['ɑnərəs] *adj* oneroso; (law) oneroso
oneself [,wʌn'sɛlf] *pron* uno mismo; sí, sí mismo; se; **to be oneself** tener dominio de sí mismo; conducirse con naturalidad; **to come to oneself** volver en sí; **to say to oneself** decir para sí; **to talk to oneself** hablar consigo mismo; **to oneself** para sus adentros
one-sided ['wʌn'saɪdɪd] *adj* de un solo lado; injusto, parcial; desigual; desequilibrado, desproporcionado; unilateral
one's self *pron* var. de **oneself**
one-step ['wʌn,stɛp] *s* baile de salón con música al compás de dos por cuatro; (*pret & pp:* **-stepped;** *ger:* **-stepping**) *vn* bailar el one-step
one-time ['wʌn,taɪm] *adj* antiguo
one-track ['wʌn,træk] *adj* de carril único; (coll.) con un solo interés
one-way ['wʌn,we] *adj* de una sola dirección, unidireccional; (rail.) sencillo, de ida sólo
one-way street *s* calle de dirección única
onion ['ʌnjən] *s* (bot.) cebolla (*planta y bulbo*); **to know one's onions** (slang) saber más que Merlín
onion set *s* (bot.) cebollino
onionskin ['ʌnjən,skɪn] *s* papel de seda, papel cebolla
onlooker ['ɑn,lʊkər] *s* mirón, espectador, circunstante
onlooking ['ɑn,lʊkɪŋ] *adj* mirón, espectador; *s* asistencia (*a un acontecimiento*)
only ['onlɪ] *adj* solo, único; *adv* sólo, solamente, únicamente; no . . . más que; **if only . . .!** ¡ojalá . . .!; **only too** muy, muchísimo; **not only . . . but also** no sólo . . . sino también; **only when** solamente cuando; *conj* sólo que, pero; **only that** sólo que, pero
only-begotten ['onlɪbɪ'gɑtən] *adj* unigénito
onomancy ['ɑnə,mænsɪ] *s* onomancía
onomastic [,ɑnə'mæstɪk] *adj* onomástico
onomatology [,ɑnəmə'tɑlədʒɪ] *s* onomatología
onomatopoeia [,ɑnə,mætə'piə] *s* onomatopeya
onomatopoeic [,ɑnə,mætə'piɪk] u **onomatopoetic** [,ɑnə,mætəpo'ɛtɪk] *adj* onomatopéyico
onrush ['ɑn,rʌʃ] *s* arremetida, embestida; arranque, fuerza impetuosa
onset ['ɑn,sɛt] *s* arremetida, embestida; principio (*de una enfermedad*)
onshore ['ɑn,ʃor] *adj & adv* en tierra; hacia la tierra
onside ['ɑn,saɪd] *adj* (sport) legal, permitido; *adv* (sport) legalmente, según las reglas
onslaught ['ɑn,slɔt] *s* ataque furioso, embestida violenta
Ont. abr. de **Ontario**
onto ['ɑntu] *prep* a, en, sobre
ontogeny [ɑn'tɑdʒɪnɪ] *s* (biol.) ontogenia
ontological [,ɑntə'lɑdʒɪkəl] *adj* ontológico
ontological argument *s* (philos.) argumento ontológico
ontologism [ɑn'tɑlədʒɪzəm] *s* (theol.) ontologismo
ontology [ɑn'tɑlədʒɪ] *s* ontología
onus ['onəs] *s* carga, obligación, responsabilidad
onward ['ɑnwərd] *adj* hacia adelante; (fig.) de progreso; *adv* adelante, hacia adelante
onwards ['ɑnwərdz] *adv* adelante, hacia adelante
onyx ['ɑnɪks] *s* (mineral.) ónice u ónix
oöcyte ['oosaɪt] *s* (biol.) oocito
oögonium [,oo'gonɪəm] *s* (*pl:* **-a** [ə] o **-ums**) (bot.) oogonio
oölite ['oolaɪt] *s* (mineral.) oolito
oölitic [,oo'lɪtɪk] *adj* oolítico
oölogy [o'ɑlədʒɪ] *s* oología
oomiak ['umɪæk] *s* barca de la mujer (*de los esquimales*)
oöphorectomy [,oofə'rɛktəmɪ] *s* (*pl:* **-mies**) (surg.) ooforectomía
oöphoritis [,oofə'raɪtɪs] *s* (path.) ooforitis
oösphere ['oosfɪr] *s* (bot.) oosfera
oöspore ['oospor] *s* (bot.) oósporo
oösporous [o'ɑspərəs] *adj* (bot.) oósporo
ooze [uz] *s* chorro suave; rezumo; rezumadero; cieno, limo, lama; *va* rezumar (*humedad*); *vn* rezumar o rezumarse; manar suavemente (*p.ej., la sangre de una herida*); agotarse poco a poco
oozy ['uzɪ] *adj* rezumoso; cenagoso
op. abr. de **opera, operation, opus** y **opposite**
opacity [o'pæsɪtɪ] *s* (*pl:* **-ties**) opacidad; obscuridad (*del estilo*); estupidez
opal ['opəl] *s* (mineral.) ópalo
opalesce [,opə'lɛs] *vn* tener reflejos opalinos, irisar
opalescence [,opə'lɛsəns] *s* opalescencia
opalescent [,opə'lɛsənt] *adj* opalescente
opaline ['opəlin] u ['opəlaɪn] *adj* opalino
opaque [o'pek] *adj* opaco; obscuro (*estilo*); estúpido; *s* cosa opaca, substancia opaca
op. cit. abr. de **opere citato** (Lat.) **in the work cited**
ope [op] *adj, va & vn* (poet.) var. de **open**
open ['opən] *adj* abierto; descubierto, destapado; sin tejado; despejado; vacante; libre (*hora*); público, para todos; claro, ralo (*tejido*); extendido, desplegado (*p.ej., periódico*); templado, sin heladas (*invierno*); libre de hielo; discutible, pendiente; susceptible, expuesto; notorio, conocido o sabido de todos; liberal (*mano*); franco, abierto; (mus.) no pisado (*dícese de una cuerda*); (mus.) de cuerda no pisada (*dícese de una nota de violín*); (mil. & phonet.) abierto; (hunt.) legal (*temporada*); **to break open** o **to crack open** abrir con violencia, abrir por la fuerza; **to throw open** abrir de par en par; **open to** accesible a; expuesto a ‖ *s* abertura; claro (*en un bosque*); **in the open** al aire libre; a campo raso, al raso; en el campo; a alta mar; en alta mar; abiertamente, al descubierto ‖ *va* abrir; destapar (*una botella*); desbullar (*la ostra*); **to open up** abrir; descubrir (*p.ej., a la vista*) ‖ *vn* abrir o abrirse; estrenarse (*un drama*); expresar una opinión; llegar a ser receptivo; **to open into** desembocar en (*dícese de una calle, un río, etc.*); **to open on** dar a; **to open up** descubrirse, presentarse; descubrir el pecho
open-air ['opən,ɛr] *adj* al aire libre, a cielo abierto
open-and-shut ['opənənd'ʃʌt] *adj* (coll.) claro, manifiesto, incontestable
open circuit *s* (elec.) circuito abierto
open city *s* ciudad abierta
open country *s* campo raso
open door *s* (dipl.) puerta abierta
opener ['opənər] *s* abridor (*persona o cosa*); (baseball) primero de una serie de partidos
open-eyed ['opən,aɪd] *adj* alerta, vigilante;

con ojos asombrados; hecho con los ojos abiertos
open face *s* cara franca; muestra de reloj sin tapa
open-faced ['opən,fest] *adj* con la cara descubierta; de cara o mirada franca; sin tapa
open-handed ['opən'hændɪd] *adj* maniabierto, liberal
open-hearted ['opən'hɑrtɪd] *adj* franco, sincero
open-hearth furnace ['opən,hɑrθ] *s* horno de hogar abierto, horno Siemens-Martin
open-hearth process *s* procedimiento de solera abierta, procedimiento Siemens-Martin
open-hearth steel *s* acero al hogar abierto
open house *s* coliche; **to keep open house** agasajar o recibir a todos, gustar de tener siempre convidados en casa, tener mesa
opening ['opənɪŋ] *s* abertura; apertura (*de la escuela, el teatro, etc.*); claro (*en un bosque*); hueco, vacante (*empleo sin proveer*); hueco (*de cordón o hilera de coches*); ocasión (*p.ej., para decir algo*); (chess) apertura; (phonet.) abertura
opening night *s* (theat.) noche de estreno
opening number *s* primer número (*de un programa*)
opening price *s* primer curso, precio de apertura (*en la Bolsa*)
open letter *s* carta abierta
open market *s* mercado público
open-minded ['opən'maɪndɪd] *adj* receptivo, razonable, imparcial
open-mouthed ['opən,maʊðd] u ['opən,maʊθt] *adj* boquiabierto; voraz; clamoroso; ancho de boca
openness ['opənnɪs] *s* abertura, franqueza, sinceridad; imparcialidad, liberalidad; publicidad
open plumbing *s* tuberías descubiertas
open port *s* puerto abierto al comercio extranjero; puerto cuyas aguas no se hielan durante todo el año
open question *s* cuestión discutible o pendiente
open secret *s* secreto a voces, secreto conocido de todos
open sesame *interj* ¡sésamo ábrete! o ¡ábrete, sésamo! (*fórmula mágica*)
open shop *s* taller franco
open trolley car *s* jardinera
openwork ['opən,wʌrk] *s* calado
opera ['ɑpərə] *s* (mus.) ópera
operable ['ɑpərəbəl] *adj* operable; (surg.) operable
opéra bouffe ['ɑpərə'buf] u [ɔpera'buf] *s* ópera bufa
opera glasses *spl* gemelos de teatro
opera hat *s* clac, sombrero de muelles
opera house *s* teatro de la ópera
opera singer *s* operista, cantante de opera
operate ['ɑpəret] *va* actuar, hacer funcionar; efectuar, producir; dirigir, manejar; explotar; *vn* funcionar; operar (*p.ej., un medicamento*); (com., mil., nav. & surg.) operar; **to operate on** producir efecto en; (surg.) operar (*p.ej., una hernia; a un niño*); **to operate on someone for something** (surg.) operar a uno de una cosa
operatic [,ɑpə'rætɪk] *adj* operístico
operatically [,ɑpə'rætɪkəlɪ] *adv* en la ópera; a modo de ópera
operating expenses *spl* gastos ordinarios, gastos de explotación
operating room *s* (surg.) quirófano
operating table *s* (surg.) mesa operatoria
operation [,ɑpə'reʃən] *s* operación; funcionamiento; explotación; **in operation** funcionando; en uso, vigente
operational [,ɑpə'reʃənəl] *adj* operacional, de operación
operative ['ɑpə,retɪv] o ['ɑpərətɪv] *adj* operador, operativo; (surg.) operatorio; *s* operario; detective
operator ['ɑpə,retər] *s* operador, maquinista; (surg. & telg.) operador; (telp.) operador, telefonista; (com.) explotador, empresario; (com.) agente, corredor de bolsa
operculum [o'pʌrkjələm] *s* (*pl:* **-la** [lə] o **-lums**) (bot. & zool.) opérculo
operetta [,ɑpə'rɛtə] *s* (mus.) opereta
Ophelia [o'filjə] *s* Ofelia
ophidian [o'fɪdɪən] *adj & s* (zool.) ofidio
Ophir ['ofər] *s* (Bib.) Ofir
ophite ['ɑfaɪt] u ['ofaɪt] *s* (mineral.) ofita
ophthalmia [ɑf'θælmɪə] *s* (path.) oftalmía
ophthalmic [ɑf'θælmɪk] *adj* oftálmico
ophthalmological [ɑf,θælmə'lɑdʒɪkəl] *adj* oftalmológico
ophthalmologist [,ɑfθæl'mɑlədʒɪst] *s* oftalmólogo
ophthalmology [,ɑfθæl'mɑlədʒɪ] *s* oftalmología
ophthalmoscope [ɑf'θælməskop] *s* oftalmoscopio
ophthalmoscopy [,ɑfθæl'mɑskəpɪ] *s* oftalmoscopia
opiate ['opɪɪt] u ['opɪet] *s* opiata; calmante; *adj* opiáceo, opiático (*opiado; soporífero; calmante*)
opine [o'paɪn] *vn* opinar
opinion [ə'pɪnjən] *s* opinión; **in my opinion** a mi parecer; **to be of the opinion that** ser de opinión que; **to have a high opinion of** tener buen concepto de; **to have a high opinion of oneself** ser muy pagado de sí mismo
opinionated [ə'pɪnjə,netɪd] u **opinionative** [ə'pɪnjə,netɪv] *adj* porfiado (en su parecer), dogmático
opium ['opɪəm] *s* (pharm.) opio
opium den *s* fumadero de opio
opium poppy *s* (bot.) adormidera
Opium War *s* guerra del opio
opopanax [ə'pɑpənæks] *s* (pharm.) opopónaco
opossum [ə'pɑsəm] *s* (zool.) zarigüeya
opponent [ə'ponənt] *adj* contrario; (anat.) oponente; *s* contrario, opositor; contrincante, opositor
opportune [,ɑpər'tjun] o [,ɑpər'tun] *adj* oportuno
opportunism [,ɑpər'tjunɪzəm] o [,ɑpər'tunɪzəm] *s* oportunismo
opportunist [,ɑpər'tjunɪst] o [,ɑpər'tunɪst] *s* oportunista
opportunistic [,ɑpərtjʊ'nɪstɪk] o [,ɑpərtʊ'nɪstɪk] *adj* oportunista
opportunity [,ɑpər'tjunɪtɪ] o [,ɑpər'tunɪtɪ] *s* (*pl:* **-ties**) oportunidad, ocasión; **to seize the opportunity** aprovechar la oportunidad
opposable [ə'pozəbəl] *adj* oponible
oppose [ə'poz] *va* oponerse a; **to oppose something to something else** oponer una cosa a otra
opposing [ə'pozɪŋ] *adj* opuesto; contrario
opposite ['ɑpəzɪt] *adj* opuesto; de enfrente, p.ej., **the house opposite** la casa de enfrente; (bot.) opuesto; *prep* enfrente de, p.ej., **he was seated opposite me** estaba sentado enfrente de mí; *s* contrario
opposite number *s* igual, doble (*en otro sistema u organización correspondiente*)
opposition [,ɑpə'zɪʃən] *s* oposición
oppress [ə'prɛs] *va* oprimir
oppression [ə'prɛʃən] *s* opresión
oppressive [ə'prɛsɪv] *adj* opresivo; sofocante, bochornoso
oppressor [ə'prɛsər] *s* opresor
opprobrious [ə'probrɪəs] *adj* oprobioso
opprobrium [ə'probrɪəm] *s* oprobio
oppugn [ɑ'pjun] *va* opugnar (*oponerse a; contradecir*)
opsonin ['ɑpsonɪn] *s* (bact.) opsonina
opt [ɑpt] *vn* optar
optative ['ɑptətɪv] *adj* optativo; (gram.) optativo; *s* (gram.) optativo (*modo*); (gram.) verbo optativo
optic ['ɑptɪk] *adj* óptico; *s* (coll.) ojo; **optics** *ssg* óptica
optical ['ɑptɪkəl] *adj* óptico
optical axis *s* (opt. & cryst.) eje óptico
optical illusion *s* ilusión de óptica
optical square *s* (surv.) escuadra de reflexión
optician [ɑp'tɪʃən] *s* óptico
optic nerve *s* (anat.) nervio óptico
optic thalamus *s* (anat.) tálamo óptico
optimism ['ɑptɪmɪzəm] *s* optimismo
optimist ['ɑptɪmɪst] *s* optimista
optimistic [,ɑptɪ'mɪstɪk] *adj* optimista
optimistically [,ɑptɪ'mɪstɪkəlɪ] *adv* con optimismo
optimum ['ɑptɪməm] *adj* óptimo, más favora-

ble; *s* (*pl:* **-mums** o **-ma** [mə]) cantidad óptima, grado óptimo, punto óptimo

option [ˈɑpʃən] *s* opción; (com.) opción

optional [ˈɑpʃənəl] *adj* facultativo, optativo, potestativo

optometer [ɑpˈtɑmɪtər] *s* optómetro

optometrist [ɑpˈtɑmɪtrɪst] *s* optometrista

optometry [ɑpˈtɑmɪtrɪ] *s* optometría

opulence [ˈɑpjələns] *s* opulencia

opulent [ˈɑpjələnt] *adj* opulento

opus [ˈopəs] *s* (*pl:* **opera** [ˈɑpərə]) (mus.) opus (*obra*)

opuscule [oˈpʌskjul] *s* opúsculo

or [ɔr] *conj* o, u; de otro modo

orach [ˈɔrətʃ] o [ˈɑrətʃ] *s* (bot.) orzaga

oracle [ˈɑrəkəl] u [ˈɔrəkəl] *s* oráculo; (fig.) oráculo (*persona sabia y autorizada; respuesta que da tal persona*)

oracular [oˈrækjələr] *adj* de oráculo; fatídico; sentencioso; ambiguo, misterioso; sabio

oral [ˈorəl] *adj* oral

orally [ˈorəlɪ] *adv* oralmente

orang [oˈræŋ] *s* var. de **orang-outang**

orange [ˈɑrɪndʒ] u [ˈɔrɪndʒ] *s* naranja (*fruto*); (bot.) naranjo (*árbol*); *adj* naranjado (*color*); naranjero

orangeade [ˌɑrɪndʒˈed] u [ˌɔrɪndʒˈed] *s* naranjada

orange blossom *s* azahar

Orange Free State *s* Estado Libre de Orange

orange grove *s* naranjal

orange jessamine *s* (bot.) boj de China

orange juice *s* zumo de naranja

Orangeman [ˈɑrɪndʒmən] u [ˈɔrɪndʒmən] *s* (*pl:* **-men**) orangista

orange pekoe *s* té negro de Ceilán o la India

orangery [ˈɑrɪndʒrɪ] u [ˈɔrɪndʒrɪ] *s* (*pl:* **-ries**) invernadero para naranjos

orange squeezer *s* exprimidera de naranjas

orange stick *s* limpiaúñas

orange tree *s* (bot.) naranjo

orang-outang [oˈræŋʊˌtæŋ] u **orang-utan** [oˈræŋʊˌtæn] *s* (zool.) orangután

orate [oˈret] u [ˈoret] *vn* (coll.) perorar

oration [oˈreʃən] *s* oración (*discurso*)

orator [ˈɑrətər] u [ˈɔrətər] *s* orador

oratorical [ˌɑrəˈtɑrɪkəl] u [ˌɔrəˈtɔrɪkəl] *adj* oratorio

oratorio [ˌɑrəˈtorɪo] u [ˌɔrəˈtorɪo] *s* (*pl:* **-os**) (mus.) oratorio

oratory [ˈɑrəˌtorɪ] u [ˈɔrəˌtorɪ] *s* (*pl:* **-ries**) oratoria; oratorio (*capilla*)

orb [ɔrb] *s* orbe; (poet.) ojo; *va* redondear; (poet.) encerrar, englobar; *vn* redondearse

orbicular [ɔrˈbɪkjələr] u **orbiculate** [ɔrˈbɪkjəlet] *adj* orbicular

orbit [ˈɔrbɪt] *s* (anat., astr., phys. & fig.) órbita; **to go into orbit** entrar en órbita; *va* poner en órbita; moverse en órbita alrededor de; *vn* moverse en órbita

orbital [ˈɔrbɪtəl] *adj* orbital

orchard [ˈɔrtʃərd] *s* huerto (*de árboles frutales*)

orchestra [ˈɔrkɪstrə] *s* (mus.) orquesta; (theat.) orquesta (*lugar destinado para los músicos*); (theat.) platea

orchestral [ɔrˈkɛstrəl] *adj* orquestal

orchestra seat *s* butaca de orquesta, butaca de platea

orchestrate [ˈɔrkɪstret] *va* orquestar

orchestration [ˌɔrkɪsˈtreʃən] *s* orquestación

orchid [ˈɔrkɪd] *s* (bot.) orquídea; *adj* purpurino

orchidaceous [ˌɔrkɪˈdeʃəs] *adj* orquidáceo

orchis [ˈɔrkɪs] *s* (bot.) órquide

orchitis [ɔrˈkaɪtɪs] *s* (path.) orquitis

Orcus [ˈɔrkəs] *s* (myth.) Orco

ordain [ɔrˈden] *va* ordenar (*poner en orden*); constituir; destinar; (eccl.) ordenar; **to ordain as a priest** ordenar de sacerdote; *vn* mandar, disponer

ordeal [ɔrˈdil] u [ˈɔrdɪəl] *s* prueba rigurosa o penosa; (hist.) ordalías, juicio de Dios

order [ˈɔrdər] *s* orden *m* (*sucesión metódica de las cosas; disposición metódica; paz, tranquilidad; clase, categoría*); orden *f* (*mandato; cuerpo de personas unidas por una regla común o por una distinción honorífica*); (arch., biol., gram. & math.) orden *m*; (com.) pedido; (com.) giro, libranza; (eccl.) orden *m* (*sexto sacramento*); (eccl.) orden *f* (*instituto religioso; grado del ministerio sacerdotal*); (law) provisión; (mil.) orden *f* (*mandato*); (mil.) descanso de armas; (mil.) orden *m* (*formación de la tropa*); (theol.) orden *f* (*cada uno de los nueve grados de los espíritus angélicos*); placa (*insignia de una orden*); tarea, p.ej., **a big order** una tarea peliaguda; estado, p.ej., **in good order** en buen estado; **by order of** por orden de; **in short order** pronto, en seguida; **in order** en orden; por su orden (*sucesivamente*); funcionando; en regla; conveniente, proporcionado; **in orders** revestido de funciones sacerdotales; **in order that** para que, a fin de que; **in order to** + *inf* para + *inf*; **on that order** de esa clase; **on the order of** a modo de; **out of order** desarreglado, descompuesto; mal colocado; fuera de orden (*dícese de una moción*); **till further orders** hasta nueva orden; **to call to order** abrir, llamar al orden; **to get out of order** descomponerse; **to give an order** dar una orden; (com.) hacer un pedido; **to put in order** poner en orden; componer; **to take orders** obedecer; (eccl.) ordenarse; **to the order of** (com.) a la orden de; **to order** por encargo especial; a la medida ‖ *va* ordenar; mandar; encargar, pedir (*p.ej., un coche, mercancías*); mandar hacer (*p.ej., un traje*); (eccl.) ordenar; **to order around** mandar para acá y para allá; dominar, ser muy mandón con; **to order away** despedir, mandar (*a uno*) que se marche; **to order in** mandar entrar; **to order out** mandar salir; **to order to** + *inf* mandar + *inf*, mandar que + *subj*

order blank *s* (com.) hoja de pedidos

orderly [ˈɔrdərlɪ] *adj* ordenado, gobernoso; tranquilo, obediente; *adv* ordenadamente; *s* (*pl:* **-lies**) asistente en un hospital; (mil.) ordenanza

order of the day *s* orden *m* del día (*en una asamblea*); (mil.) orden *f* del día; **to be the order of the day** estar a la orden del día (*eso es, a la moda, en boga*)

Order of the Garter *s* (Brit.) orden *f* de la Jarretera

ordinal [ˈɔrdɪnəl] *adj* ordinal; *s* ordinal; (eccl.) ordo

ordinal number *s* número ordinal

ordinance [ˈɔrdɪnəns] *s* ordenanza (*ley*); (arch.) ordenación; (eccl.) rito, ceremonia

ordinarily [ˈɔrdɪˌnɛrɪlɪ] *adv* ordinariamente

ordinary [ˈɔrdɪˌnɛrɪ] *adj* ordinario; *s* (*pl:* **-ies**) fonda, posada; comedor de una fonda o posada; ordinario (*juez; obispo*); (eccl.) ordinario de la misa; **in ordinary** residente; al servicio; **out of the ordinary** extraordinario, fuera de lo común

ordinate [ˈɔrdɪnɪt] u [ˈɔrdɪnet] *s* (geom.) ordenada

ordination [ˌɔrdɪˈneʃən] *s* (eccl.) ordenación

ordnance [ˈɔrdnəns] *s* (mil.) artillería, cañones; (mil.) pertrechos de guerra

ordnance department *s* (mil.) servicio de municionamiento

Ordovician [ˌɔrdoˈvɪʃən] *adj & s* (geol.) ordoviciense

ordure [ˈɔrdjʊr] u [ˈɔrdʒər] *s* excremento, inmundicia; suciedad (*dicho deshonesto*)

Ore. abr. de **Oregon**

ore [or] *s* mena, mineral metalífero

Oread u **oread** [ˈorɪæd] *s* (myth.) oréade

Orestes [oˈrɛstiz] *s* (myth.) Orestes

organ [ˈɔrgən] *s* (mus., physiol. & fig.) órgano

organdy u **organdie** [ˈɔrgəndɪ] *s* (*pl:* **-dies**) organdí

organ-grinder [ˈɔrgənˌgraɪndər] *s* organillero

organic [ɔrˈgænɪk] *adj* orgánico

organically [ɔrˈgænɪkəlɪ] *adv* orgánicamente

organic chemistry *s* química del carbono, química orgánica

organicism [ɔrˈgænɪsɪzəm] *s* (biol., med. & philos.) organicismo

organicist [ɔrˈgænɪsɪst] *adj & s* organicista

organism [ˈɔrgənɪzəm] *s* organismo; (biol.) organismo

organist [ˈɔrgənɪst] *s* (mus.) organista

organization [ˌɔrgənɪˈzeʃən] *s* organización

organize [ˈɔrgənaɪz] *va* organizar; *vn* organizarse

organizer [ˈɔrgəˌnaɪzər] *s* organizador

organ loft *s* (mus.) tribuna del órgano

organography [ˌɔrgəˈnɑgrəfɪ] *s* organografía
organology [ˌɔrgəˈnɑlədʒɪ] *s* organología
organotherapy [ˌɔrgənoˈθɛrəpɪ] *s* organoterapia
organ pipe *s* (mus.) tubo de órgano
organ stop *s* (mus.) registro de órgano
orgasm [ˈɔrgæzəm] *s* (physiol.) orgasmo
orgasmic [ɔrˈgæzmɪk] u **orgastic** [ɔrˈgæstɪk] *adj* orgástico
orgeat [ˈɔrʒæt] *s* horchata
orgiastic [ˌɔrdʒɪˈæstɪk] *adj* orgiástico
orgy [ˈɔrdʒɪ] *s* (*pl:* **-gies**) orgía; **orgies** *spl* orgías (*de la antigua Grecia*)
oriel [ˈorɪəl] *s* (arch.) camón, mirado
Orient [ˈorɪənt] *s* Oriente; (*l.c.*) *s* oriente (*brillo de las perlas*); (poet.) oriente (*donde nace el Sol*); *adj* naciente; (poet.) resplandeciente; (poet.) oriental, de oriente; [ˈorɪɛnt] *va* orientar; *vn* orientarse
oriental [ˌorɪˈɛntəl] *adj* oriental; (*cap.*) *adj* & *s* oriental
Orientalism u **orientalism** [ˌorɪˈɛntəlɪzəm] *s* orientalismo
Orientalist u **orientalist** [ˌorɪˈɛntəlɪst] *s* orientalista
Orientalize [ˌorɪˈɛntəlaɪz] *va* orientalizar
orientate [ˈorɪɛntet] *va* orientar; *vn* orientarse; mirar hacia el este
orientation [ˌorɪɛnˈteʃən] *s* orientación
orifice [ˈɑrɪfɪs] u [ˈɔrɪfɪs] *s* orificio
oriflamme [ˈɑrɪflæm] u [ˈɔrɪflæm] *s* oriflama
orig. abr. de **original** y **originally**
Origen [ˈɑrɪdʒɪn] u [ˈɔrɪdʒɪn] *s* Orígenes
origin [ˈɑrɪdʒɪn] u [ˈɔrɪdʒɪn] *s* origen
original [əˈrɪdʒɪnəl] *adj* original; originario; *s* original
originality [əˌrɪdʒɪˈnælɪtɪ] *s* originalidad
originally [əˈrɪdʒɪnəlɪ] *adv* originalmente
original sin *s* (theol.) pecado original
originate [əˈrɪdʒɪnet] *va* originar; *vn* originarse
origination [əˌrɪdʒɪˈneʃən] *s* creación, invención; origen
originative [əˈrɪdʒɪˌnetɪv] *adj* creador, inventivo
originator [əˈrɪdʒɪˌnetər] *s* creador, inventor
oriole [ˈorɪol] *s* (orn.) oriol, oropéndola
Orion [oˈraɪən] *s* (astr.) Orión
orison [ˈɑrɪzən] u [ˈɔrɪzən] *s* (archaic & poet.) oración
Orkney Islands [ˈɔrknɪ] *spl* Órcadas
Orleanist [ˈɔrlɪənɪst] *adj* & *s* Orleanista
orlop [ˈɔrlɑp] *s* (naut.) sollado
ormolu [ˈɔrməlu] *s* similor; oro molido (*para dorar el bronce*); bronce dorado
ornament [ˈɔrnəmənt] *s* ornamento; ornamentación; **ornaments** *spl* (eccl.) ornamentos; [ˈɔrnəmɛnt] *va* ornamentar
ornamental [ˌɔrnəˈmɛntəl] *adj* ornamental; (hort.) de adorno
ornamentation [ˌɔrnəmɛnˈteʃən] *s* ornamentación
ornate [ɔrˈnet] u [ˈɔrnet] *adj* ornado, muy ornado; florido (*estilo*)
ornery [ˈɔrnərɪ] *adj* (dial.) ordinario, común; (dial.) feo; (dial.) terco, displicente; (dial.) vil, ruin
ornithological [ˌɔrnɪθəˈlɑdʒɪkəl] *adj* ornitológico
ornithologist [ˌɔrnɪˈθɑlədʒɪst] *s* ornitólogo
ornithology [ˌɔrnɪˈθɑlədʒɪ] *s* ornitología
ornithomancy [ˈɔrnɪθəˌmænsɪ] *s* ornitomancía
ornithorhyncus [ˌɔrnɪθəˈrɪŋkəs] *s* (zool.) ornitorrinco
orobanchaceous [ˌɑrobæŋˈkeʃəs] *adj* (bot.) orobancáceo
orogenic [ˌɔrəˈdʒɛnɪk] o [ˌɑrəˈdʒɛnɪk] *adj* orogénico
orogeny [oˈrɑdʒənɪ] *s* orogenia
orographic [ˌɔrəˈgræfɪk] u **orographical** [ˌɔrəˈgræfɪkəl] *adj* orográfico
orography [oˈrɑgrəfɪ] *s* orografía
orology [oˈrɑlədʒɪ] *s* orología
orometer [oˈrɑmɪtər] *s* orómetro
orotund [ˈorətʌnd] o [ˈɑrətʌnd] *adj* rotundo (*sonoro*); rimbombante
orotundity [ˌorəˈtʌndɪtɪ] o [ˌɑrəˈtʌndɪtɪ] *s* rotundidad; rimbombancia
orphan [ˈɔrfən] *adj* & *s* huérfano; *va* dejar huérfano
orphanage [ˈɔrfənɪdʒ] *s* orfanato, asilo de huérfanos; orfandad (*estado*)
orphan asylum *s* asilo de huérfanos
orphanhood [ˈɔrfənhʊd] *s* orfandad
Orphean [ɔrˈfiən] *adj* órfico
Orpheus [ˈɔrfjus] u [ˈɔrfɪəs] *s* (myth.) Orfeo
orphic [ˈɔrfɪk] *adj* místico, oracular; (*cap.*) *adj* órfico; místico, oracular; dulce y suave al oído
Orphic hymns *spl* poesías órficas
Orphic mysteries *spl* fiestas órficas
orphrey [ˈɔrfrɪ] *s* orifrés
orpiment [ˈɔrpɪmənt] *s* (mineral.) oropimente
orpine u **orpin** [ˈɔrpɪn] *s* (bot.) hierba callera, telefio
orrery [ˈɑrərɪ] u [ˈɔrərɪ] *s* (*pl:* **-ies**) orrery, planetario
orris [ˈɑrɪs] u [ˈɔrɪs] *s* (bot.) lirio de Florencia; rizoma de lirio de Florencia; (pharm.) esencia de lirio de Florencia
orrisroot [ˈɑrɪsˌrut] u [ˈɔrɪsˌrut] *s* rizoma de lirio de Florencia
orthicon [ˈɔrθɪkɑn] *s* orticón
orthochromatic [ˌɔrθokroˈmætɪk] *adj* (phot.) ortocromático
orthoclase [ˈɔrθəkles] u [ˈɔrθəklez] *s* (mineral.) ortosa
orthodontia [ˌɔrθoˈdɑnʃɪə] *s* ortodoncia
orthodox [ˈɔrθədɑks] *adj* ortodoxo
Orthodox Church *s* Iglesia ortodoxa
orthodoxy [ˈɔrθəˌdɑksɪ] *s* ortodoxia
orthoëpic [ˌɔrθoˈɛpɪk] *adj* ortoépico
orthoëpist [ɔrˈθo·ɪpɪst] u [ˈɔrθoɛpɪst] *s* ortólogo
orthoëpy [ɔrˈθo·ɪpɪ] u [ˈɔrθoɛpɪ] *s* ortoepia u ortología
orthogenesis [ˌɔrθoˈdʒɛnɪsɪs] *s* (biol.) ortogénesis
orthognathous [ɔrˈθɑgnəθəs] *adj* ortognato
orthogonal [ɔrˈθɑgənəl] *adj* ortogonal
orthographer [ɔrˈθɑgrəfər] *s* ortógrafo
orthographic [ˌɔrθoˈgræfɪk] u **orthographical** [ˌɔrθoˈgræfɪkəl] *adj* ortográfico
orthography [ɔrˈθɑgrəfɪ] *s* (*pl:* **-phies**) (gram. & geom.) ortografía
orthopaedic u **orthopedic** [ˌɔrθoˈpidɪk] *adj* ortopédico; **orthopedics** *ssg* ortopedia
orthopedist [ˌɔrθoˈpidɪst] *s* ortopedista, ortopédico
orthophony [ɔrˈθɑfənɪ] *s* ortofonía
orthopteran [ɔrˈθɑptərən] *s* (ent.) ortóptero
orthopterous [ɔrˈθɑptərəs] *adj* (ent.) ortóptero
orthorhombic [ˌɔrθoˈrɑmbɪk] *adj* (cryst.) ortorrómbico
orthotropism [ɔrˈθɑtrəpɪzəm] *s* (bot.) ortotropismo
orthotropous [ɔrˈθɑtrəpəs] *adj* (bot.) ortótropo
ortolan [ˈɔrtələn] *s* (orn.) hortelano; (orn.) chambergo
oryx [ˈorɪks] *s* (zool.) órix
O.S. abr. de **Old Style**
os [ɑs] *s* (*pl:* **ossa** [ˈɑsə]) (anat.) hueso; (*pl:* **ora** [ˈorə]) (anat.) orificio
Osage orange [ˈosedʒ] *s* (bot.) maclura (*planta y fruto*)
Oscan [ˈɑskən] *adj* & *s* osco
oscillate [ˈɑsɪlet] *vn* oscilar; (phys.) oscilar
oscillation [ˌɑsɪˈleʃən] *s* oscilación
oscillator [ˈɑsɪˌletər] *s* oscilador; (rad.) oscilador
oscillatory [ˈɑsɪləˌtorɪ] *adj* oscilatorio
oscillogram [əˈsɪləgræm] *s* (phys.) oscilograma
oscillograph [əˈsɪləgræf] o [əˈsɪləgrɑf] *s* (phys.) oscilógrafo
oscilloscope [əˈsɪləskop] *s* (phys.) osciloscopio
oscine [ˈɑsɪn] o [ˈɑsaɪn] *adj* (orn.) oscino; *s* (orn.) oscina
osculate [ˈɑskjəlet] *va* besar; (geom.) tocar por osculación; *vn* besarse; (geom.) ser osculador
osculation [ˌɑskjəˈleʃən] *s* ósculo (*beso*); (geom.) osculación
osculatory [ˈɑskjələˌtorɪ] *adj* osculatorio; (geom.) osculador
osculatrix [ˌɑskjəˈletrɪks] *s* (geom.) osculatriz

osculum [ˈɑskjələm] *s* (*pl:* **-la** [lə]) (zool.) ósculo (*de las esponjas*)
osier [ˈoʒər] *s* mimbre; (bot.) mimbrera, sauce mimbrero; (bot.) cornejo
osiery [ˈoʒərɪ] *s* (*pl:* **-ies**) mimbreral; artículos hechos de mimbre
Osiris [oˈsaɪrɪs] *s* (myth.) Osiris
Osmanli [ɑsˈmænlɪ] *adj* osmanlí; *s* (*pl:* **-lis**) osmanlí
osmium [ˈɑzmɪəm] *s* (chem.) osmio
osmosis [ɑsˈmosɪs] *s* (chem. & physiol.) ósmosis
osmotic [ɑsˈmɑtɪk] *adj* osmótico
osmotic pressure *s* presión osmótica
osprey [ˈɑsprɪ] *s* (orn.) halieto, guincho
Ossa, Mount [ˈɑsə] el monte Osa
osseous [ˈɑsɪəs] *adj* óseo
Ossian [ˈɑʃən] o [ˈɑsɪən] *s* Osián
Ossianic [ˌɑʃɪˈænɪk] o [ˌɑsɪˈænɪk] *adj* osiánico
Ossianism [ˈɑʃənɪzəm] o [ˈɑsɪənɪzəm] *s* osianismo
ossicle [ˈɑsɪkəl] *s* (anat.) osículo
ossification [ˌɑsɪfɪˈkeʃən] *s* osificación
ossifrage [ˈɑsɪfrɪdʒ] *s* (orn.) osífraga
ossify [ˈɑsɪfaɪ] (*pret & pp:* **-fied**) *va* osificar; *vn* osificarse; volverse muy conservador
osteitis [ˌɑstɪˈaɪtɪs] *s* (path.) osteítis
ostensible [ɑsˈtɛnsɪbəl] *adj* aparente, pretendido, supuesto
ostension [ɑsˈtɛnʃən] *s* (eccl.) ostensión
ostensive [ɑsˈtɛnsɪv] *adj* ostensivo
ostentation [ˌɑstɛnˈteʃən] *s* ostentación
ostentatious [ˌɑstɛnˈteʃəs] *adj* ostentativo; ostentoso
osteoblast [ˈɑstɪəblæst] *s* (anat.) osteoblasto
osteolite [ˈɑstɪəˌlaɪt] *s* (mineral.) osteolita
osteological [ˌɑstɪəˈlɑdʒɪkəl] *adj* osteológico
osteologist [ˌɑstɪˈɑlədʒɪst] *s* osteólogo
osteology [ˌɑstɪˈɑlədʒɪ] *s* osteología
osteoma [ˌɑstɪˈomə] *s* (*pl:* **-mas** o **-mata** [mətə]) (path.) osteoma
osteomalacia [ˌɑstɪəməˈleʃɪə] *s* (path.) osteomalacia
osteomyelitis [ˌɑstɪoˌmaɪəˈlaɪtɪs] *s* (path.) osteomielitis
osteopath [ˈɑstɪəpæθ] *s* osteópata
osteopathic [ˌɑstɪəˈpæθɪk] *adj* osteopático
osteopathist [ˌɑstɪˈɑpəθɪst] *s* osteópata
osteopathy [ˌɑstɪˈɑpəθɪ] *s* osteopatía
osteotomy [ˌɑstɪˈɑtəmɪ] *s* (*pl:* **-mies**) (surg.) osteotomía
ostiary [ˈɑstɪˌɛrɪ] *s* (*pl:* **-ies**) (eccl.) ostiario
ostler [ˈɑslər] *s* establero, mozo de cuadra, mozo de paja y cebada; (rail.) encargado de la locomotora al fin del recorrido
ostracism [ˈɑstrəsɪzəm] *s* ostracismo
ostracize [ˈɑstrəsaɪz] *va* desterrar; excluir del trato de las gentes
ostrich [ˈɑstrɪtʃ] *s* (orn.) avestruz; (orn.) avestruz de América o de la pampa
Ostrogoth [ˈɑstrogɑθ] *adj & s* ostrogodo
Oswego tea [ɑsˈwigo] *s* (bot.) té de Pensilvania
O.T. abr. de **Old Testament**
otacoustic [ˌotəˈkustɪk] u [ˌotəˈkaustɪk] *adj* otacústico
otalgia [oˈtældʒɪə] *s* (path.) otalgia
otalgic [oˈtældʒɪk] *adj* otálgico
Othello [oˈθɛlo] *s* Otelo
other [ˈʌðər] *adj & pron indef* otro; *adv* otramente; **above all others** más que ningún otro; el mejor de todos; **the other day** el otro día; **the other one** el otro; **other than** otra cosa que
otherwise [ˈʌðərˌwaɪz] *adj* diferente; *adv* otramente, de otra manera; en otras circunstancias; fuera de eso; *conj* si no, de otro modo
other world *s* otro mundo (*vida eterna*)
otherworldly [ˈʌðərˌwʌrldlɪ] *adj* ultramundano, alejado de este mundo
otiose [ˈoʃɪos] u [ˈotɪos] *adj* ocioso
otitis [oˈtaɪtɪs] *s* (path.) otitis
otocyst [ˈotəsɪst] *s* (zool.) otocisto
otolaryngology [ˌotoˌlærɪŋˈgɑlədʒɪ] *s* otolaringología
otologist [oˈtɑlədʒɪst] *s* otólogo
otology [oˈtɑlədʒɪ] *s* otología
otorhinolaryngologist [ˌotəˌraɪnəˌlærɪŋˈgɑlədʒɪst] *s* otorrinolaringólogo
otorhinolaryngology [ˌotəˌraɪnəˌlærɪŋˈgɑlədʒɪ] *s* otorrinolaringología
otosclerosis [ˌotəsklɪˈrosɪs] *s* (path.) otosclerosis
otoscope [ˈotəskop] *s* otoscopio
otoscopy [oˈtɑskəpɪ] *s* otoscopia
ottava rima [oˈtɑvɑ ˈrimɑ] *s* (pros.) octava rima
otter [ˈɑtər] *s* (zool.) nutria; (zool.) nutria marina; piel de nutria
Otto [ˈɑto] *s* Otón
Ottoman [ˈɑtəmən] *adj* otomano; *s* (*pl:* **-mans**) otomano; (*l.c.*) *s* otomana (*sofá*); escañuelo con cojín; otomán (*tejido de seda*)
Ottoman Empire *s* Imperio otomano
ou [au] *interj* ¡ax!
oubliette [ˌublɪˈɛt] *s* mazmorra; pozo profundo en una mazmorra
ouch [autʃ] *interj* ¡ax!
ought [ɔt] *s* algo, alguna cosa; (coll.) cero, nada; **for ought I know** por lo que yo sepa; *v aux* se emplea para formar el modo potencial, p.ej., **he ought to go at once** debiera salir en seguida; **he ought to have gone at once** debiera haber ido en seguida
ouija [ˈwidʒə] *s* (trademark) tabla de escritura espiritista
ounce [auns] *s* onza; pizca
our [aur] *adj poss* nuestro
Our Lady *s* Nuestra Señora
ours [aurz] *pron poss* nuestro; el nuestro; **a friend of ours** un amigo nuestro
ourself [aurˈsɛlf] *pron pers* nosotros, nos (*usado por un autor, rey, etc., por ficción en vez de "mí" o "me"*)
ourselves [aurˈsɛlvz] *pron pers* nosotros mismos; nos, p.ej., **we enjoyed ourselves** nos divertimos
-ous *suffix adj* -oso, p.ej., **famous** famoso; **marvelous** maravilloso; (chem.) -oso, p.ej., **nitrous** nitroso; **sulfurous** sulfuroso
ousel [ˈuzəl] *s* var. de **ouzel**
oust [aust] *va* echar fuera, desposeer; desahuciar (*al inquilino*)
ouster [ˈaustər] *s* desposeimiento; desahucio
out [aut] *adv* afuera, fuera; al aire libre; hasta el fin; con confianza; con energía; **out and away** con mucho; **out and out** completamente; **out for** buscando; **out of** de; entre; de entre (*las manos de uno*); fuera de (*p.ej., la ciudad*); más allá de; por (*p.ej., caridad, miedo*); sin (*p.ej., dinero, trabajo*); sobre, p.ej., **in nine out of ten cases** en nueve casos sobre diez; (cards) fallo a (*un palo*); **out to** + *inf* esforzándose por + *inf; adj* fuera; fuera de juego; fuera de su sitio; echado, sacado; acabado, concluído; apagado; existente; equivocado; perdidoso; exterior; poco común (*tamaño*); divulgado; publicado; *prep* por (*p.ej., la ventana*); allá en (*p.ej., la avenida*); **out that way** por allá; *interj* ¡fuera de aquí!; *s* cesante; saliente, detalle; (print.) omisión por descuido; (baseball) jugador fuera de juego; **to be at outs** u **on the outs** estar de monos; **to be at outs** u **on the outs with** estar mal con; *va* expeler; desposeer; apagar; divulgar; (slang) poner fuera de combate; (slang) matar; (tenis) volear (*la pelota*) fuera de la pista; *vn* salir; escaparse; descubrirse; **to out with** (coll.) divulgar, revelar
out-and-out [ˈautəndˌaut] *adj* perfecto, verdadero, rematado
outbalance [autˈbæləns] *va* pesar más que; aventajar, sobreexceder
outbid [autˈbɪd] (*pret:* **-bid;** *pp:* **-bid** o **-bidden;** *ger:* **-bidding**) *va* licitar más que (*otra persona*); (bridge) sobrepasar
outboard [ˈautˌbord] *adj & adv* fuera de borda
outboard motor *s* motor fuera de borda, motor de fuera
outbound [ˈautˌbaund] *adj* saliente, de salida
outbrave [autˈbrev] *va* arrostrar; aventajar en valentía
outbreak [ˈautˌbrek] *s* tumulto, motín; arranque (*de ira*); estallido (*p.ej., de una guerra*); brote (*de una epidemia*)
outbuild [autˈbɪld] (*pret & pp:* **-built**) *va* hacer construcciones más imponentes o mejores que las de
outbuilding [ˈautˌbɪldɪŋ] *s* dependencia accesoria

outburst ['aʊt,bʌrst] *s* explosión, arranque; **outburst of laughter** carcajada
outcast ['aʊt,kæst] o ['aʊt,kɑst] *adj* desterrado, excluído, rechazado; *s* paria
outclass [aʊt'klæs] o [aʊt'klɑs] *va* aventajar, ser muy superior a
outcome ['aʊt,kʌm] *s* resultado
outcrop ['aʊt,krɑp] *s* (min.) crestón, afloramiento; [aʊt'krɑp] (*pret & pp:* **-cropped; *ger:* -cropping**) *vn* asomar; (min.) aflorar
outcry ['aʊt,kraɪ] *s* (*pl:* **-cries**) grito; gritería, clamoreo; subasta, venta pública
outcurve ['aʊt,kʌrv] *s* (baseball) curva fuera
outdated [aʊt'detɪd] *adj* fuera de moda, anticuado
outdid [aʊt'dɪd] *pret de* **outdo**
outdistance [aʊt'dɪstəns] *va* dejar atrás, distanciar, rezagar
outdo [aʊt'do] (*pret:* **-did;** *pp:* **-done**) *va* exceder; **to outdo oneself** excederse a sí mismo
outdone [aʊt'dʌn] *pp de* **outdo**
outdoor ['aʊt,dor] *adj* al aire libre; fuera del hospital
outdoors [,aʊt'dorz] *adv* al aire libre, fuera de casa; *s* aire libre, campo raso
outer ['aʊtər] *adj* exterior, externo
Outer Mongolia *s* la Mogolia Exterior
outermost ['aʊtərmost] *adj* extremo, último; (el) más exterior
outer space s espacio exterior; espacio extraatmosférico
outface [aʊt'fes] *va* intimidar mirando con ceño, dominar con los ojos; arrostrar
outfield ['aʊt,fild] *s* (baseball) jardín
outfielder ['aʊt,fildər] *s* (baseball) jardinero
outfit ['aʊtfɪt] *s* equipo (*de ropas, etc.; de obreros, etc.*); traje (*completo*); juego de herramientas; cuerpo (*de soldados*); (com.) compañía; ajuar (*de novia*); (*pret & pp:* **-fitted;** *ger:* **-fitting**) *va* equipar
outfitter ['aʊt,fɪtər] *s* habilitador; abastecedor; armador
outflank [aʊt'flæŋk] *va* (mil.) flanquear; (fig.) burlar (*a un contrario*)
outflow ['aʊt,flo] *s* efusión, derrame, flujo; (fig.) efusión
outgeneral [aʊt'dʒɛnərəl] (*pret & pp:* **-aled** o **-alled;** *ger:* **-aling** o **-alling**) *va* exceder en táctica militar; vencer por medio de evoluciones geniales
outgo ['aʊt,go] *s* (*pl:* **-goes**) gasto
outgoing ['aʊt,go·ɪŋ] *adj* saliente, de salida; exteriorista (*p.ej., índole, naturaleza*); *s* salida
outgrew [aʊt'gru] *pret de* **outgrow**
outgrow [aʊt'gro] (*pret:* **-grew;** *pp:* **-grown**) *va* crecer más que; ser ya grande para; ser ya viejo para; ser ya más apto que; dejar (*las cosas de los niños; a los amigos de la niñez, etc.*); *vn* extenderse
outgrowth ['aʊt,groθ] *s* excrecencia, bulto; nacimiento (*p.ej., de las hojas en la primavera*); consecuencia, resultado
outguess [aʊt'gɛs] *va* burlar a fuerza de ingenio; llevar la ventaja a
outhouse ['aʊt,haʊs] *s* dependencia accesoria; letrina situada fuera de la casa
outing ['aʊtɪŋ] *s* caminata, excursión al campo
outing flannel *s* moletón
outlander ['aʊt,lændər] *s* extranjero; forastero
outlandish [aʊt'lændɪʃ] *adj* estrafalario; de aspecto extranjero; de acento extranjero
outlast [aʊt'læst] o [aʊt'lɑst] *va* durar más que; sobrevivir a
outlaw ['aʊt,lɔ] *s* forajido, bandido; prófugo, proscrito; *va* privar de la protección de las leyes; proscribir; declarar ilegal
outlawry ['aʊt,lɔrɪ] *s* (*pl:* **-ries**) bandolerismo; privación de la protección de las leyes; proscripción
outlay ['aʊt,le] *s* desembolso; [aʊt'le] (*pret & pp:* **-laid**) *va* desembolsar
outlet ['aʊtlɛt] *s* salida; desaguadero; orificio de salida; (elec.) caja de enchufe, toma, receptáculo tomacorriente; (com. & fig.) salida
outlet box *s* (elec.) caja de salida, caja de enchufe
outline ['aʊt,laɪn] *s* contorno; trazado; esquema; esbozo, bosquejo; compendio; **in outline** en silueta; a grandes rasgos, en sus líneas generales; *va* contornar; trazar; trazar el esquema de; esbozar, bosquejar; compendiar
outlive [aʊt'lɪv] *va* sobrevivir a; durar más que
outlook ['aʊt,lʊk] *s* perspectiva; expectativa; concepto de la vida, punto de vista; atalaya
outlying ['aʊt,laɪɪŋ] *adj* remoto, circundante, de las afueras
outmaneuver u **outmanoeuvre** [,aʊtmə'nuvər] *va* ser mejor estratega que; vencer por ser mejor estratega
outmatch [aʊt'mætʃ] *va* aventajar, exceder, mostrarse superior a
outmoded [aʊt'modɪd] *adj* fuera de moda, anticuado
outmost ['aʊtmost] *adj* var. de **outermost**
outnumber [aʊt'nʌmbər] *va* exceder en número, ser más que, ser más numeroso que
out-of-date ['aʊtəv'det] *adj* fuera de moda, anticuado
out-of-door ['aʊtəv'dor] *adj* al aire libre
out-of-doors ['aʊtəv'dorz] *adj* al aire libre; *adv* afuera, fuera de la casa, al aire libre; *s* aire libre, campo raso
out-of-print ['aʊtəv'prɪnt] *adj* agotado
out-of-the-way ['aʊtəvðə'we] *adj* remoto, en sitio apartado; poco usual, poco común
outpatient ['aʊt,peʃənt] *s* enfermo de fuera (*enfermo no hospitalizado que recibe cuidados de un dispensario*)
outpoint [aʊt'pɔɪnt] *va* (sport) exceder en el número de tantos ganados; (naut.) ceñir más el viento que
outpost ['aʊt,post] *s* (mil.) avanzada; (mil.) puesto avanzado; (mil.) fortín de la frontera; (fig.) avanzada; (fig.) portaestandarte
outpour ['aʊt,por] *s* chorro, chorreo; [aʊt'por] *va* verter; hacer salir profusamente; *vn* chorrear; salir profusamente
outpouring ['aʊt,porɪŋ] *s* chorro, efusión; (fig.) efusión
output ['aʊt,pʊt] *s* producción, rendimiento; capacidad; (mech.) rendimiento de trabajo, efecto útil; (elec.) salida; (elec.) circuito de salida
output stage *s* (rad.) etapa de salida
output transformer *s* (rad.) transformador de salida
outrage ['aʊtredʒ] *s* atrocidad; violación; ultraje; *va* maltratar, violentar; violar; ultrajar; escandalizar
outrageous [aʊt'redʒəs] *adj* atroz; violento; ultrajoso
outran [aʊt'ræn] *pret de* **outrun**
outrank [aʊt'ræŋk] *va* exceder en rango o grado, ser de categoría superior a
outré [u'tre] o ['utre] *adj* extremoso, extravagante, raro
outreach [aʊt'ritʃ] *va* pasar más allá de, exceder; extender; *vn* extenderse
outridden [aʊt'rɪdən] *pp de* **outride**
outride [aʊt'raɪd] (*pret:* **-rode;** *pp:* **-ridden**) *va* galopar más que; manejar el caballo mejor que; (naut.) correr (*un temporal*)
outrider ['aʊt,raɪdər] *s* volante, carretista; (Brit.) viajante de comercio
outrigger ['aʊt,rɪgər] *s* (naut.) botalón, botavara, tangón; (naut.) balancín (*de una canoa*); (naut.) portarremos exterior; (naut.) bote con portarremos exteriores
outright ['aʊt,raɪt] *adj* cabal, completo, total; franco, sincero, sin rodeos; hacia adelante; *adv* enteramente; de una vez; abiertamente, sin rodeos; luego, en seguida
outrode [aʊt'rod] *pret de* **outride**
outrun [aʊt'rʌn] (*pret:* **-ran;** *pp:* **-run;** *ger:* **-running**) *va* dejar atrás; correr más aprisa que; exceder; pasar los límites de
outsell [aʊt'sɛl] (*pret & pp:* **-sold**) *va* vender más, más caro o más aprisa que; venderse más, más caro o más aprisa que
outset ['aʊt,sɛt] *s* principio; **at the outset** o **from the outset** al principio, a los principios, de primero
outshine [aʊt'ʃaɪn] (*pret & pp:* **outshone**) *va* brillar más que, exceder en brillantez; (fig.) eclipsar
outshone [aʊt'ʃon] *pret & pp de* **outshine**
outshoot ['aʊt,ʃut] *s* saliente; ramal; [aʊt'ʃut] (*pret & pp:* **-shot**) *va* ser mejor tirador que; tirar más lejos que; *vn* extenderse, sobresalir
outshot [aʊt'ʃɑt] *pret & pp de* **outshoot**

outside ['aut'saɪd] *adj* exterior; superficial; ajeno, de otras personas; más liberal, más optimista; (el) máximo (*precio*); *s* exterior; apariencia; **at the outside** a lo más, a lo sumo; **on the outside** por fuera; *adv* fuera, afuera; **outside of** fuera de; *prep* fuera de; más allá de; (coll.) a excepción de
outsider [,aut'saɪdər] *s* forastero; intruso; (sport) caballo que no figura entre los favoritos
outsize ['aut,saɪz] *s* prenda hecha de tamaño extraordinario; *adj* de tamaño extraordinario
outskirts ['aut,skʌrts] *spl* afueras
outsold [aut'sold] *pret & pp de* **outsell**
outspoken ['aut'spokən] *adj* boquifresco, franco
outspread ['aut,sprɛd] *adj* extendido; [aut'sprɛd] (*pret & pp:* **-spread**) *va* extender; *vn* extenderse
outstanding [aut'stændɪŋ] *adj* saliente, saledizo; destacado, distinguido, sobresaliente; prominente; (com.) pendiente, sin pagar, sin cobrar
outstay [aut'ste] (*pret & pp:* **-stayed** o **-staid**) *va* quedarse más tiempo que; quedarse más tiempo de lo que permite (*la cortesía o la licencia que uno tiene*)
outstretched ['aut,strɛtʃt] *adj* extendido, abierto
outstrip [aut'strɪp] (*pret & pp:* **-stripped;** *ger:* **-stripping**) *va* pasar, dejar atrás; aventajar, adelantar, adelantarse de
outtalk [aut'tɔk] *va* hablar más que, ser más hablador que
outvote [aut'vot] *va* vencer en las elecciones; disponer de más votantes que
outward ['autwərd] *adj* exterior, externo; *adv* exteriormente, hacia fuera
outward-flow turbine ['autwərd'flo] *s* turbina centrífuga
outwardly ['autwərdlɪ] *adv* exteriormente; superficialmente; al parecer; fuera, hacia fuera
outwards ['autwərdz] *adv* exteriormente, hacia fuera
outwear [aut'wɛr] (*pret:* **-wore;** *pp:* **-worn**) *va* durar más que; gastar, romper por uso excesivo; curarse de (*penas*) con el tiempo
outweigh [aut'we] *va* pesar más que; contrapesar, compensar
outwit [aut'wɪt] (*pret & pp:* **-witted;** *ger:* **-witting**) *va* burlar, sobrepujar en astucia, ser más listo que
outwore [aut'wor] *pret de* **outwear**
outwork ['aut,wʌrk] *s* (fort.) obra exterior; [aut'wʌrk] *va* trabajar más o más aprisa que
outworn ['aut,worn] *adj* ajado, usado, desgastado; anticuado, viejo; [aut'worn] *pp de* **outwear**
ouzel ['uzəl] *s* (orn.) mirlo; (orn.) mirlo de agua
oval ['ovəl] *adj* oval, ovalado; *s* óvalo
ovally ['ovəlɪ] *adv* en figura de óvalo, de modo que forma óvalo
ovarian [o'vɛrɪən] *adj* ovárico
ovariotomy [o,vɛrɪ'ɑtəmɪ] *s* (*pl:* **-mies**) (surg.) ovariotomía
ovaritis [,ovə'raɪtɪs] *s* (path.) ovaritis
ovary ['ovərɪ] *s* (*pl:* **-ries**) (anat. & bot.) ovario
ovate ['ovet] *adj* aovado, ovado
ovation [o'veʃən] *s* ovación
oven ['ʌvən] *s* horno
ovenbird ['ʌvən,bʌrd] *s* (orn.) hornero; (orn.) seiuro
over ['ovər] *adv* encima, por encima; al otro lado, a la otra orilla; hacia abajo; al revés; patas arriba; otra vez, de nuevo; de añadidura; acá, p.ej., **hand over the money** déme acá el dinero; allá, p.ej., **over in Europe** allá en Europa; **to be all over** haber pasado, haberse acabado; **over again** una vez más; **over against** enfrente de; a distinción de; en contraste con; **over and over** una y otra vez, repetidas veces; **over here** acá; **over there** allá; *adj* superior, de más autoridad; adicional; excesivo; acabado, concluído; *prep* sobre, encima de, por encima de; por (*un terreno o país*); de un extremo a otro de; al otro lado de; más allá de; desde (*un sitio elevado*); más de (*cierto número*); acerca de; por causa de; durante; **over and above** además de, en exceso de; *s* exceso
overabundance [,ovərə'bʌndəns] *s* sobreabundancia
overact [,ovər'ækt] *va* exagerar (*un papel*)
overactive [,ovər'æktɪv] *adj* demasiado activo
overall ['ovər,ɔl] *adj* cabal, completo; extremo, total; **overalls** *spl* pantalones de trabajo; polainas impermeables
overarch [,ovər'ɑrtʃ] *va* abovedar; *vn* formar bóveda
overate [,ovər'et] *pret de* **overeat**
overawe [,ovər'ɔ] *va* imponer respeto a, intimidar
overbalance [,ovər'bæləns] *s* exceso de peso o valor; falta de equilibrio; *va* pesar más que; valer más que; llevar la ventaja a; derribar
overbear [,ovər'bɛr] (*pret:* **-bore;** *pp:* **-borne**) *va* dominar, oprimir; no hacer caso de; echar por tierra, derribar
overbearing [,ovər'bɛrɪŋ] *adj* altanero, despótico, imperioso
overbid [,ovər'bɪd] (*pret:* **-bid;** *pp:* **-bid** o **-bidden;** *ger:* **-bidding**) *va* ofrecer más de lo que vale (*un objeto*); licitar más que (*otra persona*); *vn* (bridge) declarar demasiado
overblown ['ovər,blon] *adj* deshojado, marchito, pasado; lleno (*de cosas traídas por el viento*)
overboard ['ovər,bord] *adj* al agua; **man overboard!** ¡hombre al agua!; **to throw overboard** arrojar, echar o tirar por la borda; (coll.) arrojar, echar o tirar (*p.ej., a un amigo, las ambiciones de uno, los escrúpulos de uno*) por la borda
overbore [,ovər'bor] *pret de* **overbear**
overborne [,ovər'born] *pp de* **overbear**
overburden [,ovər'bʌrdən] *va* cargar de modo excesivo
overcame [,ovər'kem] *pret de* **overcome**
overcapitalization ['ovər,kæpɪtəlɪ'zeʃən] *s* supercapitalización
overcapitalize [,ovər'kæpɪtəlaɪz] *va* supercapitalizar
overcast ['ovər,kæst] u ['ovər,kɑst] *adj* nublado, encapotado; (sew.) sobrehilado; *s* cielo encapotado; (sew.) sobrehilado; (*pret & pp:* **-cast**) *va* nublar; (sew.) sobrehilar; *vn* nublarse
overcharge ['ovər,tʃɑrdʒ] *s* cargo excesivo, recargo de precio; sobrecarga; (elec.) carga excesiva; [,ovər'tʃɑrdʒ] *va* estafar, hacer pagar mucho más del valor, cargar demasiado en la cuenta a; cargar . . . de más, p.ej., **you have overcharged me one dollar** me ha cargado Vd. un dólar de más; sobrecargar; (elec.) poner una carga excesiva a
overcloud [,ovər'klaud] *va* anublar; *vn* anublarse
overcoat ['ovər,kot] *s* abrigo, gabán, sobretodo
overcome [,ovər'kʌm] (*pret:* **-came;** *pp:* **-come**) *va* vencer; rendir; superar (*dificultades*)
overconfidence [,ovər'kɑnfɪdəns] *s* confianza excesiva
overcritical [,ovər'krɪtɪkəl] *adj* hipercrítico
overcrowd [,ovər'kraud] *va* atestar, apiñar; poblar con exceso
overcrowding [,ovər'kraudɪŋ] *s* exceso de habitantes
overcup oak ['ovər,kʌp] *s* (bot.) roble de hojas aliradas
overdevelop [,ovərdɪ'vɛləp] *va* desarrollar demasiado; (phot.) revelar demasiado
overdid [,ovər'dɪd] *pret de* **overdo**
overdo [,ovər'du] (*pret:* **-did;** *pp:* **-done**) *va* exagerar; agobiar; asurar, requemar; *vn* cansarse mucho, excederse en el trabajo
overdone [,ovər'dʌn] *pp de* **overdo**
overdose ['ovər,dos] *s* dosis excesiva; [,ovər'dos] *va* dar una dosis excesiva a
overdraft ['ovər,dræft] u ['ovər,drɑft] *s* (com.) sobregiro, giro en descubierto
overdraw [,ovər'drɔ] (*pret:* **-drew;** *pp:* **-drawn**) *va & vn* (com.) sobregirar
overdress ['ovər,drɛs] *s* sobreveste; [,ovər'drɛs] *va* engalanar o ataviar con exceso; *vn* engalanarse o ataviarse con exceso
overdrew [,ovər'dru] *pret de* **overdraw**

overdrive ['ovər,draɪv] *s* (aut.) sobremarcha, velocidad sobremultiplicada
overdue ['ovər'dju] u ['ovər'du] *adj* atrasado (*p.ej., en el pago de una cuenta, en llegar al tiempo debido*); vencido y no pagado
overeat [,ovər'it] (*pret:* **-ate;** *pp:* **-eaten**) *va & vn* comer con exceso
overemphasize [,ovər'ɛmfəsaɪz] *va* acentuar demasiado, acentuar demasiado la importancia de
overestimate ['ovər'ɛstɪmɪt] *s* apreciación o estimación excesiva; presupuesto excesivo; [,ovər'ɛstɪmet] *va* avaluar o estimar en valor excesivo; tener un concepto demasiado favorable de; **to overestimate one's strength** creerse (*uno*) más fuerte de lo que es
overexcite [,ovərɛk'saɪt] *va* sobreexcitar
overexcitement [,ovərɛk'saɪtmənt] *s* sobrexcitación
overexert [,ovərɛg'zʌrt] *va* ejercer de modo excesivo; **to overexert oneself** darse demasiado trabajo, hacer esfuerzo excesivo
overexertion [,ovərɛg'zʌrʃən] *s* esfuerzo excesivo
overexpand [,ovərɛks'pænd] *va* ensanchar o extender con exceso; *vn* ensancharse o extenderse con exceso
overexpose [,ovərɛks'poz] *va* sobreexponer; (phot.) sobreexponer
overexposure [,ovərɛks'poʒər] *s* sobreexposición; (phot.) sobreexposición
overfed [,ovər'fɛd] *pret & pp de* **overfeed**
overfeed [,ovər'fid] (*pret & pp:* **-fed**) *va* sobrealimentar; *vn* sobrealimentarse
overfill [,ovər'fɪl] *va* sobrellenar
overflow ['ovər,flo] *s* desbordamiento, rebosamiento; derrames; rebosadero, caño de reboso; [,ovər'flo] *vn* desbordar, rebosar; **to overflow with joy** rebosar de alegría
overflowing [,ovər'flo·ɪŋ] *s* desbordamiento, rebosamiento; **to overflowing** a rebosar, hasta derramarse; en suma abundancia; *adj* desbordante
overflow pipe *s* caño de reboso
overgrew [,ovər'gru] *pret de* **overgrow**
overgrow [,ovər'gro] (*pret:* **-grew;** *pp:* **-grown**) *va* cubrir, entapizar; crecer más que; ser ya grande para; ser ya viejo para; ser ya más apto que; dejar (*las cosas de los niños; a los amigos de la niñez, etc.*); *vn* crecer con demasiada rapidez
overgrown [,ovər'gron] *adj* demasiado grande para su edad; **overgrown boy** muchachón; *pp de* **overgrow**
overgrowth ['ovər,groθ] *s* crecimiento excesivo; maleza, vegetación exuberante
overhand ['ovər,hænd] *adj* (sew.) sobrehilado; (sport) voleado por lo alto; *adv* (sew.) con costura sobrehilada; por lo alto; palma abajo; *va* (sew.) sobrehilar
overhang ['ovər,hæŋ] *s* alcance, proyección; alero (*del tejado*); vuelo (*de cualquier fábrica*); [,ovər'hæŋ] (*pret & pp:* **-hung**) *va* sobresalir por encima de, estar pendiente o colgando sobre, salir fuera del nivel de; amenazar; *vn* estar pendiente, estar colgando
overhaul [,ovər'hɔl] *va* examinar, registrar, revisar; ir alcanzando, alcanzar; componer, rehabilitar, reacondicionar
overhead [,ovər'hɛd] *adv* por encima de la cabeza; en lo alto, arriba; ['ovər,hɛd] *adj* de arriba; aéreo, elevado; general, de conjunto; *s* gastos generales
overhead railway *s* (Brit.) ferrocarril aéreo
overhead valve *s* válvula en la culata
overhear [,ovər'hɪr] (*pret & pp:* **-heard**) *va* oír por casualidad; acertar a oír, alcanzar a oír
overheard [,ovər'hʌrd] *pret & pp de* **overhear**
overheat [,ovər'hit] *va* recalentar; *vn* recalentarse
overhung [,ovər'hʌŋ] *pret & pp de* **overhang**
overindulge [,ovərɪn'dʌldʒ] *va* mimar demasiado; dedicarse con exceso a; tomar con exceso; *vn* darse demasiada buena vida
overindulgence [,ovərɪn'dʌldʒəns] *s* exceso, excesos; indulgencia o lenidad excesiva
overjoy [,ovər'dʒɔɪ] *va* arrebatar de alegría; **to be overjoyed** no caber de contento
overladen [,ovər'ledən] *adj* sobrecargado
overlaid [,ovər'led] *pret & pp de* **overlay**
overlain [,ovər'len] *pp de* **overlie**
overland ['ovər,lænd] u ['ovərlənd] *adj & adv* por tierra, por vía terrestre
overlap ['ovər,læp] *s* solapadura; solapo; imbricación; [,ovər'læp] (*pret & pp:* **-lapped;** *ger:* **-lapping**) *va* solapar, traslapar; *vn* solapar, traslapar; traslaparse (*dos o más cosas*); suceder (*dos hechos*) en parte al mismo tiempo
overlay ['ovər,le] *s* capa sobrepuesta; hoja sobrepuesta; incrustación; [,ovər'le] (*pret & pp:* **-laid**) *va* cubrir; sobrecargar; incrustar; *pret de* **overlie**
overleap [,ovər'lip] *va* saltar por encima de
overlie [,ovər'laɪ] (*pret:* **-lay;** *pp:* **-lain;** *ger:* **-lying**) *va* descansar sobre; sofocar (*a un niño*) echándosele encima
overload ['ovər,lod] *s* sobrecarga; [,ovər'lod] *va* sobrecargar
overlong ['ovər'lɔŋ] u ['ovər'lɑŋ] *adj* demasiado largo; *adv* mucho tiempo, demasiado tiempo
overlook [,ovər'lʊk] *va* dominar con la vista; pasar por alto, no hacer caso de; perdonar, tolerar; espiar, vigilar; cuidar de, dirigir; dar a, p.ej., **the window overlooks the garden** la ventana da al jardín
overlord ['ovər,lɔrd] *s* jefe supremo; [,ovər'lɔrd] *va* dominar despóticamente, imponerse a
overlordship ['ovər,lɔrdʃɪp] *s* jefatura suprema
overly ['ovərlɪ] *adv* (coll.) excesivamente, demasiado
overlying [,ovər'laɪɪŋ] *ger de* **overlie**
overman ['ovərmən] *s* (*pl:* **-men**) capataz; árbitro; ['ovər,mæn] *s* sobrehombre
overmaster [,ovər'mæstər] u [,ovər'mɑstər] *va* dominar, sojuzgar
overmatch [,ovər'mætʃ] *va* sobrepujar
overmodulation ['ovər,mɑdʒə'leʃən] *s* (rad.) sobremodulación
overmuch ['ovər'mʌtʃ] *s* demasía, exceso; *adj & adv* demasiado
overnice ['ovər'naɪs] *adj* melindroso, remilgado
overnight [,ovər'naɪt] *adv* toda la noche; de la tarde a la mañana, durante la noche; **to stay overnight** pasar la noche; ['ovər,naɪt] *adj* de noche; de una sola noche; de la noche anterior; *s* la noche anterior
overnight bag *s* maletín, saco de noche (*para viajes cortos*)
overpaid [,ovər'ped] *pret & pp de* **overpay**
overpass ['ovər,pæs] u ['ovər,pɑs] *s* viaducto; [,ovər'pæs] u [,ovər'pɑs] (*pret & pp:* **-passed** o **-past**) *va* atravesar, salvar; aventajar, exceder; pasar por alto, no hacer caso de
overpay [,ovər'pe] (*pret & pp:* **-paid**) *va* pagar con exceso
overpayment [,ovər'pemənt] *s* pago excesivo, exceso de pago
overpeopled [,ovər'pipəld] *adj* excesivamente poblado
overplay [,ovər'ple] *va* (theat.) exagerar (*un papel*); aventajar, exceder; vencer
overplus ['ovərplʌs] *s* sobrante, superávit
overpopulate [,ovər'pɑpjəlet] *va* superpoblar
overpopulation ['ovər,pɑpjə'leʃən] *s* superpoblación
overpower [,ovər'paʊər] *va* dominar, supeditar, subyugar; colmar, dejar estupefacto
overpowering [,ovər'paʊərɪŋ] *adj* abrumador, arrollador, irresistible
overproduction [,ovərprə'dʌkʃən] *s* superproducción, sobreproducción
overproud ['ovər'praʊd] *adj* orgulloso en exceso
overran [,ovər'ræn] *pret de* **overrun**
overrate [,ovər'ret] *va* exagerar el valor de, apreciar o valuar en más de lo que vale (*una persona o cosa*)
overreach [,ovər'ritʃ] *va* ir más allá de, extenderse más allá de; engañar con astucias; **to overreach oneself** aventurarse más allá de sus fuerzas, pasarse de listo; *vn* ir más allá de lo necesario, extenderse demasiado; alcanzarse (*un caballo*)
overridden [,ovər'rɪdən] *pp de* **override**

override [ˌovərˈraɪd] (*pret:* **-rode;** *pp:* **-ridden**) *va* recorrer; atropellar; desentenderse de, no hacer caso de; anular, invalidar; fatigar, reventar (*p.ej., un caballo*)
overripe [ˈovərˈraɪp] *adj* demasiado maduro, pachucho, papandujo
overrode [ˌovərˈrod] *pret de* **override**
overrule [ˌovərˈrul] *va* anular, invalidar; vencer, triunfar de; (law) denegar
overrun [ˌovərˈrʌn] (*pret:* **-ran;** *pp:* **-run;** *ger:* **-running**) *va* cubrir enteramente; infestar; exceder; **to overrun one's time** quedarse más de lo justo; hablar más de lo justo
oversaw [ˌovərˈsɔ] *pret de* **oversee**
overscore [ˈovərˌskor] *s* (bridge) exceso sobre lo declarado; [ˌovərˈskor] *va* poner una virgulilla o raya sobre; *vn* (bridge) ganar sobre lo declarado
oversea [ˈovərˌsi] *adj* de ultramar; [ˌovərˈsi] *adv* allende los mares, en ultramar
overseas [ˈovərˌsiz] *adj* var. de **oversea;** [ˌovərˈsiz] *adv* var. de **oversea**
oversee [ˌovərˈsi] (*pret:* **-saw;** *pp:* **-seen**) *va* dirigir, superentender, fiscalizar
overseer [ˈovərˌsiər] *s* director, superintendente
oversell [ˌovərˈsɛl] (*pret & pp:* **-sold**) *va* excederse en la venta de; vender (*efectos no disponibles*)
overset [ˈovərˌsɛt] *s* vuelco; [ˌovərˈsɛt] (*pret & pp:* **-set;** *ger:* **-setting**) *va* volcar; (fig.) derrocar; *vn* volcar
overshadow [ˌovərˈʃædo] *va* sombrear; (fig.) eclipsar
overshoe [ˈovərˌʃu] *s* chanclo, zapatón
overshoot [ˌovərˈʃut] (*pret & pp:* **-shot**) *va* tirar por encima de o más allá de; **to overshoot oneself** o **to overshoot the mark** pasar de la raya, excederse; *vn* pasar de la raya, excederse
overshot [ˈovərˌʃɑt] *adj* que tiene saliente la mandíbula superior; de corriente alta; [ˌovərˈʃɑt] *pret & pp de* **overshoot**
overshot water wheel *s* rueda (hidráulica) de corriente alta o de cajones
overside [ˈovərˌsaɪd] *adj* (naut.) por la borda, por encima de la regala; [ˌovərˈsaɪd] *adv* (naut.) por la borda, por encima de la regala
oversight [ˈovərˌsaɪt] *s* inadvertencia, descuido; vigilancia, cuidado
oversize [ˈovərˌsaɪz] *s* tamaño extra; cosa de tamaño extra; *adj* extragrande, de tamaño extra
overskirt [ˈovərˌskʌrt] *s* sobrefalda (*falda corta*); refajo
oversleep [ˌovərˈslip] (*pret & pp:* **-slept**) *vn* dormir demasiado tarde, no despertar
oversold [ˌovərˈsold] *pret & pp de* **oversell**
overspread [ˌovərˈsprɛd] (*pret & pp:* **-spread**) *va* extenderse sobre
overstate [ˌovərˈstet] *va* exagerar
overstatement [ˌovərˈstetmənt] *s* exageración
overstay [ˌovərˈste] (*pret & pp:* **-stayed** o **-staid**) *va* quedarse más tiempo de lo que permite (*la licencia que uno tiene*)
overstep [ˌovərˈstɛp] (*pret & pp:* **-stepped;** *ger:* **-stepping**) *va* exceder, traspasar
overstock [ˈovərˌstɑk] *s* surtido excesivo; existencias excesivas; [ˌovərˈstɑk] *va* abarrotar; **to be overstocked with** tener existencias excesivas de
overstrung [ˈovərˈstrʌŋ] *adj* demasiado impresionable, demasiado excitable
overstuff [ˌovərˈstʌf] *va* atestar; rellenar (*un cojín, almohada, etc.*)
oversubscribe [ˌovərsəbˈskraɪb] *va* contribuir más de lo pedido a (*p.ej., una recaudación de carácter benéfico*); subscribir (*un empréstito*) en exceso de lo disponible
oversubscription [ˌovərsəbˈskrɪpʃən] *s* contribución en exceso de lo pedido; subscripción en exceso de lo disponible
oversupply [ˈovərsəˌplaɪ] *s* (*pl:* **-plies**) provisión excesiva; [ˌovərsəˈplaɪ] (*pret & pp:* **-plied**) *va* proveer en exceso
overt [ˈovʌrt] u [oˈvʌrt] *adj* abierto, manifiesto; premeditado
overtake [ˌovərˈtek] (*pret:* **-took;** *pp:* **-taken**) *va* alcanzar; sobrepasar; sorprender; sobrevenir a
overtask [ˌovərˈtæsk] u [ˌovərˈtɑsk] *va* atarear demasiado, oprimir con trabajo
overtax [ˌovərˈtæks] *va* oprimir con tributos; agotar (*las fuerzas de uno*); exceder los límites de (*p.ej., la credulidad de uno*)
over-the-counter [ˈovərðəˈkaʊntər] *adj* vendido directamente al comprador (*y no en el mercado bursátil*); vendido en tienda al por mayor
overthrew [ˌovərˈθru] *pret de* **overthrow**
overthrow [ˈovərˌθro] *s* derrocamiento (*p.ej., del gobierno*); trastorno (*p.ej., de los proyectos de uno*); [ˌovərˈθro] (*pret:* **-threw;** *pp:* **-thrown**) *va* derrocar; trastornar
overtime [ˈovərˌtaɪm] *adj & adv* en exceso de las horas regulares; *s* tiempo suplementario, horas extraordinarias de trabajo; [ˌovərˈtaɪm] *va* (phot.) sobreexponer
overtone [ˈovərˌton] *s* armónico; **overtones** *spl* insinuación
overtook [ˌovərˈtʊk] *pret de* **overtake**
overtop [ˌovərˈtɑp] (*pret & pp:* **-topped;** *ger:* **-topping**) *va* descollar sobre; sobresalir entre
overtrain [ˌovərˈtren] *va* (sport) sobrentrenar; *vn* (sport) sobrentrenarse
overtrump [ˈovərˌtrʌmp] *s* contrafallo; [ˌovərˈtrʌmp] *va & vn* contrafallar
overture [ˈovərtʃər] *s* insinuación, proposición; (mus.) obertura
overturn [ˈovərˌtʌrn] *s* vuelco; (com.) movimiento de mercancías; [ˌovərˈtʌrn] *va* volcar; trastornar; derrocar (*el gobierno*); *vn* volcar; trastornarse
overwatch [ˌovərˈwɔtʃ] *va* vigilar; cansar a fuerza de vigilias
overweening [ˌovərˈwinɪŋ] *adj* arrogante, presuntuoso
overweigh [ˌovərˈwe] *va* pesar más que; contrapesar, compensar; prevalecer contra; oprimir
overweight [ˈovərˌwet] *adj* excesivamente gordo o grueso; *s* sobrepeso; exceso de peso; peso de añadidura; [ˌovərˈwet] *va* sobrecargar; abrumar con trabajo, responsabilidades, etc.
overwhelm [ˌovərˈhwɛlm] *va* abrumar; inundar; anonadar; colmar (*p.ej., de favores, regalos*)
overwhelming [ˌovərˈhwɛlmɪŋ] *adj* abrumador, arrollador, irresistible
overwork [ˈovərˌwʌrk] *s* trabajo excesivo, exceso de trabajo; trabajo fuera de las horas regulares; [ˌovərˈwʌrk] (*pret & pp:* **-worked** o **-wrought**) *va* hacer trabajar demasiado; oprimir con trabajo; *vn* darse con exceso al trabajo, trabajar demasiado
overworked [ˌovərˈwʌrkt] *adj* atrabajado
overwrite [ˌovərˈraɪt] (*pret:* **-wrote;** *pp:* **-written**) *va* escribir sobre (*una superficie*); escribir encima de; escribir acerca de; refundir; escribir en un estilo acicalado; [ˈovərˌraɪt] *va* (com.) garantizar comisión a (*un representante general*) sobre ventas hechas por un agente regional
overwrought [ˌovərˈrɔt] *adj* atrabajado, abrumado de trabajo; sobrexcitado; muy ornamentado, recargado de ornamentación; *pret & pp de* **overwork**
oviculum [oˈvɪkjələm] *s* (*pl:* **-la** [lə]) (arch.) ovículo
Ovid [ˈɑvɪd] *s* Ovidio
oviduct [ˈovɪdʌkt] *s* (anat.) oviducto
oviform [ˈovɪfɔrm] *adj* oviforme
ovine [ˈovaɪn] u [ˈovɪn] *adj & s* ovino
oviparous [oˈvɪpərəs] *adj* ovíparo
oviposit [ˌovɪˈpɑzɪt] *vn* desovar
ovipositor [ˌovɪˈpɑzɪtər] *s* (zool.) oviscapto
ovoid [ˈovɔɪd] *adj* ovoide, ovoideo; *s* cuerpo ovoideo
ovolo [ˈovəlo] *s* (*pl:* **-li** [li]) (arch.) óvolo
ovoviviparous [ˌovovaɪˈvɪpərəs] *adj* ovovivíparo
ovular [ˈovjələr] *adj* ovular
ovulation [ˌovjəˈleʃən] *s* (biol.) ovulación
ovule [ˈovjul] *s* (biol. & bot.) óvulo
ovum [ˈovəm) *s* (*pl:* **ova** [ˈovə]) (biol.) huevo
ow [aʊ] *interj* ¡ax!
owe [o] *va* deber; *vn* tener deudas
owing [ˈo·ɪŋ] *adj* adeudado; debido, pagadero; **owing to** debido a, por causa de

owl [aʊl] *s* (orn.) búho, lechuza, mochuelo
owlet [ˈaʊlɪt] *s* búho, lechuza o mochuelo pequeños; hijuelo del búho, la lechuza o el mochuelo
owlish [ˈaʊlɪʃ] *adj* de búho; que se da aires de sabio
own [on] *adj* propio, p.ej., **my own brother** mi propio hermano; *s* suyo, lo suyo; **on one's own** (coll.) por su propia cuenta, sin depender de nadie; por su cabeza (*sin tomar consejo*); (coll.) de su cabeza (*de su propio ingenio o invención*); **to come into one's own** entrar en posesión de lo suyo; tener el éxito merecido, recibir el honor merecido; **to have nothing of one's own** no tener (*uno*) nada que pueda llamar suyo; **to hold one's own** no aflojar, no cejar, mantenerse firme; *va* poseer; reconocer; *vn* confesar; **to own up** (coll.) confesar de plano; **to own up to** (coll.) confesar de plano (*una culpa, un delito, etc.*)
owner [ˈonər] *s* amo, dueño, poseedor, propietario
ownership [ˈonərʃɪp] *s* posesión, propiedad
owner's license *s* (aut.) permiso de circulación
ox [ɑks] *s* (*pl:* **oxen**) (zool.) buey; **to work like an ox** trabajar como un buey
oxalate [ˈɑksəlet] *s* (chem.) oxalato
oxalic [ɑksˈælɪk] *adj* oxálico
oxalic acid *s* (chem.) ácido oxálico
oxalidaceous [ɑks,ælɪˈdeʃəs] *adj* (bot.) oxalidáceo
oxalis [ˈɑksəlɪs] *s* (bot.) aleluya, acedera menor, acederilla
oxazine [ˈɑksəzin] o [ˈɑksəzɪn] *s* (chem.) oxacina
oxbow [ˈɑks,bo] *s* collera de yugo; recodo de un río; terreno encerrado en un recodo de río
oxcart [ˈɑks,kɑrt] *s* carreta de bueyes
oxen [ˈɑksən] *pl de* **ox**
oxeye [ˈɑks,aɪ] *s* (bot.) hierba amarilla; (bot.) margarita mayor; (bot.) ojo de buey; (bot.) rudbequia
ox-eyed [ˈɑks,aɪd] *adj* de ojos rasgados, de ojos grandes
oxeye daisy *s* (bot.) hierba amarilla; (bot.) margarita mayor
oxford [ˈɑksfərd] *s* oxford (*tela*); zapato de estilo Oxford; color negro agrisado
Oxford gray *s* color negro agrisado
Oxfordian [ɑksˈfordɪən] *adj & s* oxfordiano; (geol.) oxfordiense
Oxford movement *s* movimiento religioso de Oxford
oxheart [ˈɑks,hɑrt] *s* cereza de color casi negro y de forma de corazón
oxhide [ˈɑks,haɪd] *s* cuero de buey
oxid [ˈɑksɪd] *s* var. de **oxide**
oxidase [ˈɑksɪdes] o [ˈɑksɪdez] *s* (biochem.) oxidasa
oxidation [,ɑksɪˈdeʃən] *s* oxidación
oxide [ˈɑksaɪd] *s* (chem.) óxido
oxide blue *s* azul de cobalto
oxide of iron *s* (chem.) óxido de hierro
oxide yellow *s* óxido amarillo
oxidimetry [,ɑksɪˈdɪmɪtrɪ] *s* oxidimetría
oxidizable [ˈɑksɪ,daɪzəbəl] *adj* oxidable
oxidization [,ɑksɪdɪˈzeʃən] *s* var. of **oxidation**
oxidize [ˈɑksɪdaɪz] *va* oxidar; *vn* oxidarse
oxidizer [ˈɑksɪ,daɪzər] *s* (chem.) oxidante
oxidizing flame *s* (chem.) llama oxidante
oxime [ˈɑksim] o [ˈɑksɪm] *s* (chem.) oxima
oxlip [ˈɑks,lɪp] *s* (bot.) hierba de San Pablo mayor
oxman [ˈɑksmən] *s* (*pl:* **-men**) boyero
Oxonian [ɑksˈonɪən] *adj & s* oxoniense
oxonium [ɑksˈonɪəm] *s* (chem.) oxonio
oxozone [ˈɑksozon] *s* (chem.) oxozono
oxpecker [ˈɑks,pɛkər] *s* (orn.) espulgabueyes, picabueyes
oxtail soup [ˈɑks,tel] *s* sopa de cola de buey
oxtongue [ˈɑks,tʌŋ] *s* (bot.) lengua de buey
oxyacetylene [,ɑksɪəˈsɛtɪlin] *adj* oxiacetilénico
oxyacetylene torch *s* soplete oxiacetilénico
oxyacetylene welding *s* soldadura oxiacetilénica
oxyblepsia [,ɑksɪˈblɛpsɪə] *s* oxiblepsia
oxybromide [,ɑksɪˈbromaɪd] o [,ɑksɪˈbromɪd] *s* (chem.) oxibromuro
oxychloride [,ɑksɪˈkloraɪd] o [,ɑksɪˈklorɪd] *s* (chem.) oxicloruro
oxycyanide [,ɑksɪˈsaɪənaɪd] o [,ɑksɪˈsaɪənɪd] *s* (chem.) oxicianuro
oxygen [ˈɑksɪdʒən] *s* (chem.) oxígeno
oxygenate [ˈɑksɪdʒənet] *va* (chem.) oxigenar
oxygenation [,ɑksɪdʒəˈneʃən] *s* oxigenación
oxygen-hydrogen welding [ˈɑksɪdʒənˈhaɪdrədʒən] *s* soldadura oxhídrica
oxygenize [ˈɑksɪdʒənaɪz] *va* oxigenar
oxygen mask *s* máscara de oxígeno
oxygen tent *s* (med.) tienda de oxígeno, cámara de oxígeno
oxyhemoglobin [,ɑksɪ,himəˈglobɪn] *s* (biochem.) oxihemoglobina
oxyhydrogen [,ɑksɪˈhaɪdrədʒən] *adj* (chem.) oxhídrico; *s* (chem.) gas oxhídrico
oxyhydrogen torch *s* soplete oxhídrico
oxymel [ˈɑksɪmɛl] *s* (pharm.) ojimel
oxyntic [ɑksˈɪntɪk] *adj* oxíntico
oxysulfide [,ɑksɪˈsʌlfaɪd] o [,ɑksɪˈsʌlfɪd] *s* (chem.) oxisulfuro
oxytocic [,ɑksɪˈtosɪk] o [,ɑksɪˈtɑsɪk] *adj & s* (med.) oxitócico
oxytone [ˈɑksɪton] *adj & s* (phonet.) oxítono
oyez u **oyes** [ˈojɛs] u [oˈjɛs] *interj* (law) ¡oíd! (*voz de los ujieres*)
oyster [ˈɔɪstər] *s* (zool.) ostra; (slang) chiticalla (*persona muy callada*); *adj* ostrero
oyster bed *s* ostrero, ostral
oyster catcher *s* (orn.) ostrero
oyster cocktail *s* ostras de entremés, ostras en su concha
oyster crab *s* (zool.) pinotero
oyster cracker *s* galletita salada
oyster culture *s* ostricultura
oysterer [ˈɔɪstərər] *s* ostrero
oyster farm *s* ostrero, ostral, criadero ostrícola
oyster farmer *s* ostricultor
oyster fork *s* desbullador
oysterhouse [ˈɔɪstər,haʊs] *s* ostrería
oyster knife *s* abreostras
oysterman [ˈɔɪstərmən] *s* (*pl:* **-men**) ostrero
oyster opener *s* desbullador (*persona*)
oyster plant *s* (bot.) salsifí; (bot.) mertensia marítima
oyster plover *s* var. de **oyster catcher**
oyster rake *s* raño
oyster shell *s* desbulla, concha de ostra
oyster soup *s* sopa de ostras
oyster tree *s* (bot.) mangle
oysterwoman [ˈɔɪstər,wʊmən] *s* (*pl:* **-women**) ostrera
oz. abr. de **ounce** u **ounces**
ozena [oˈzinə] *s* (path.) ocena
ozocerite [oˈzokəraɪt] u [,ozoˈsɪraɪt] *s* (mineral.) ozocerita u ozoquerita
ozone [ˈozon] *s* (chem.) ozono; (coll.) aire fresco; **to get some ozone** (coll.) tomar el fresco
ozone layer *s* (meteor.) capa de ozono, ozonosfera
ozone paper *s* (chem.) papel de ozono
ozonide [ˈozonaɪd] u [ˈozonɪd] *s* (chem.) ozonuro
ozoniferous [,ozoˈnɪfərəs] *adj* ozonífero
ozonization [,ozonɪˈzeʃən] *s* ozonización
ozonize [ˈozonaɪz] *va* ozonizar; *vn* ozonizarse
ozonolysis [,ozoˈnɑlɪsɪs] *s* (chem.) ozonolisis
ozonometer [,ozoˈnɑmɪtər] *s* ozonómetro
ozonoscope [oˈzonəskop] *s* ozonoscopio
ozonosphere [oˈzonəsfɪr] *s* ozonosfera
ozostomia [,ozɑsˈtomɪə] *s* ozostomía
ozs. abr. de **ounces**

P

P, p [pi] *s* (*pl:* **P's, p's** [piz]) décimasexta letra del alfabeto inglés; **mind your P's and Q's!** ¡tenga Vd. cuidado!, ¡ande Vd. con cuidado con lo que dice!
p. abr. de **page** y **participle**
p.a. abr. de **participial adjective, per annum** y **press agent**
Pa. abr. de **Pennsylvania**
P.A. abr. de **Passenger Agent, Post Adjutant, power of attorney** y **Purchasing Agent**
pa [pɑ] *s* (coll.) papá
pabulum [ˈpæbjələm] *s* pábulo
Pac. abr. de **Pacific**
pace [pes] *s* paso; aire (*manera de andar del caballo*); portante (*manera de andar del caballo en la cual mueve a un tiempo la mano y el pie del mismo lado*); **at a slow pace** a paso lento; **to keep pace with** ir, andar o avanzar al mismo paso que; **to put through one's paces** poner (*a uno*) a prueba; dar (*a uno*) ocasión de lucirse; **to set the pace** llevar el tren, establecer el paso; dar el ejemplo; **to set the pace for** marcar la pauta a; *va* establecer el paso para; medir a pasos; recorrer a pasos; **to pace the floor** pasearse desesperadamente por la habitación; *vn* andar a pasos regulares; amblar (*andar al paso portante*)
pacemaker [ˈpes,mekər] *s* establecedor del paso; ejemplo; (med.) marcapaso (*regulador del latido cardíaco*)
pacer [ˈpesər] *s* establecedor del paso; persona que anda a pasos regulares; caballo amblador
pacha [pəˈʃɑ] o [ˈpæʃə] *s* var. de **pasha**
pachyderm [ˈpækɪdʌrm] *s* (zool.) paquidermo; (fig.) tronco (*persona insensible*)
pachysandra [,pækɪˈsændrə] *s* (bot.) paquisandra
pacific [pəˈsɪfɪk] *adj* pacífico; (*cap.*) *adj & s* Pacífico (*océano*)
pacifically [pəˈsɪfɪkəlɪ] *adv* pacíficamente
pacification [,pæsɪfɪˈkeʃən] *s* pacificación
pacificatory [pəˈsɪfɪkə,torɪ] *adj* pacificador
Pacific Coast *s* Costa del Pacífico
Pacific Ocean *s* océano Pacífico
Pacific time *s* (U.S.A.) hora legal correspondiente al meridiano 120°
pacifier [ˈpæsɪ,faɪər] *s* pacificador; chupete (*para los niños*)
pacifism [ˈpæsɪfɪzəm] *s* pacifismo
pacifist [ˈpæsɪfɪst] *adj & s* pacifista
pacifistic [,pæsɪˈfɪstɪk] *adj* pacifista
pacify [ˈpæsɪfaɪ] (*pret & pp:* **-fied**) *va* pacificar
pack [pæk] *s* lío, fardo; paquete; cantidad empaquetada; perrada, jauría; manada; cuadrilla; pandilla (*de malhechores*); saco, sarta, montón (*p.ej., de mentiras*); baraja (*de naipes*); cajetilla (*de cigarrillos*); témpano (*de hielo flotante*); mochila, morral (*de los caminantes*); (med.) compresa; *va* empaquetar; embaular; encajonar; hacer (*el baúl, la maleta*); conservar en latas; apretar, atestar, llenar; cargar (*una acémila*); escoger o nombrar de modo fraudulento, llenar de partidarios (*p.ej., un jurado*); (coll.) llevar a cuestas; (mach.) empaquetar; **to be packed in** estar o ir como sardinas en banasta; **to pack down** apretar, comprimir; apisonar; **to pack in** empaquetar (*gente en un local*); **to pack up** empaquetar; *vn* empaquetarse; encajonarse; empaquetarse fácilmente; hacer el baúl, hacer la maleta; consolidarse, endurecerse, formar masa compacta; **to pack up** liar el petate, hacer la pacotilla
package [ˈpækɪdʒ] *s* paquete; *va* empaquetar
pack animal *s* acémila, animal de carga
packer [ˈpækər] *s* empaquetador, embaulador; empaquetadora (*máquina*); portador; dueño de una fábrica de conservas alimenticias
packet [ˈpækɪt] *s* paquete; paquebote
packet boat *s* paquebote
pack horse *s* caballo de carga
packing [ˈpækɪŋ] *s* empaque, embalaje; envase; preparación de conservas alimenticias; (mach.) estopa, empaquetadura o guarnición; relleno (*para hacer impermeable al agua*)
packing box *s* caja de embalaje o de embalar; (mach.) prensa estopa
packing case *s* caja de embalaje o de embalar
packing effect *s* (phys.) efecto de empaquetamiento
packing house *s* frigorífico, fábrica para envasar o enlatar comestibles
packing slip *s* hoja de embalaje
packman [ˈpækmən] *s* (*pl:* **-men**) buhonero
pack mule *s* mula de carga
pack needle *s* aguja de embalar, aguja saquera
pack rat *s* (zool.) rata norteamericana (*Neotoma cinerea*)
packsaddle [ˈpæk,sædəl] *s* albarda
packthread [ˈpæk,θred] *s* bramante
pack train *s* recua
pact [pækt] *s* pacto
paction [ˈpækʃən] *s* pacto
pad [pæd] *s* cojincillo; almohadilla; sillín; bloc (*de papel*); tampón (*para entintar sellos*); pisada (*ruido*); jaca, caballo de camino; hoja (*de planta acuática*); peto, plastrón; pata (*de perro, zorra, etc.*); eminencia hipotenar (*del pie de ciertos animales*); plataforma (*de lanzamiento de cohete*); (*pret & pp:* **padded;** *ger:* **padding**) *va* rellenar (*p.ej., con algodón*); acolchar; meter mucho ripio en (*un escrito*); *vn* andar, caminar; caminar despacio y pesadamente; andar con un trotecito ligero
padding [ˈpædɪŋ] *s* relleno; (fig.) relleno, ripio (*en un escrito, discurso o verso*)
paddle [ˈpædəl] *s* canalete, zagual; pala (*de una rueda*); paseo en embarcación impulsada con canalete; palo (*para apalear a una persona, la ropa, etc.*); batidor; *va* impulsar con canalete; apalear; **to paddle one's own canoe** (coll.) bastarse a sí mismo; *vn* remar con canalete; remar suavemente; chapotear, guachapear
paddle box *s* caja que cubre la parte superior de la rueda de paletas
paddlefish [ˈpædəl,fɪʃ] *s* (ichth.) pez hoja
paddle wheel *s* rueda de paletas
paddle-wheel steamer [ˈpædəl,hwil] *s* buque de ruedas, vapor de ruedas
paddock [ˈpædək] *s* dehesa; pesaje, cercado para caballos de carrera (*en los hipódromos*)
paddy [ˈpædɪ] *s* (*pl:* **-dies**) arroz; arroz sin cosechar; palay, arroz con cáscara; (*cap.*) *s* irlandés; nombre abreviado de **Patrick**
paddy wagon *s* (slang) camión de policía
paddywhack [ˈpædɪ,hwæk] *s* (U.S.A. coll.) paliza; (Brit. coll.) mal genio, cólera
padlock [ˈpæd,lɑk] *s* candado; *va* cerrar con candado; condenar (*una habitación*)
padre [ˈpɑdrɪ] *s* padre (*especialmente sacerdote*); (mil.) páter
paean [ˈpiən] *s* canto triunfal, himno de gloria; (hist.) peán
pagan [ˈpegən] *adj & s* pagano
pagandom [ˈpegəndəm] *s* gentilidad
paganism [ˈpegənɪzəm] *s* paganismo
paganize [ˈpegənaɪz] *va & vn* paganizar
page [pedʒ] *s* página; paje; escudero; botones; (fig.) página; *va* paginar; buscar llamando (*en un hotel, club, etc.*)
pageant [ˈpædʒənt] *s* fiesta pública, espectáculo público, pompa; representación al aire libre en una serie de cuadros; boato, bambolla
pageantry [ˈpædʒəntrɪ] *s* (*pl:* **-ries**) pompa; boato, bambolla
page proof *s* (print.) pruebas de planas

pagination [ˌpædʒɪˈneʃən] *s* paginación
pagoda [pəˈgodə] *s* pagoda
paid [ped] *adj* asalariado; pagado; hecho efectivo; *pret & pp de* **pay**
paid-up [ˈpedˈʌp] *adj* terminado de pagar, libre
pail [pel] *s* balde, cubo
pailful [ˈpelfʊl] *s* balde, cubo (*contenido*)
paillasse [pælˈjæs] o [ˈpæljæs] *s* colchón de paja, jergón
pain [pen] *s* dolor; **pains** *spl* esmero, trabajo; dolores de parto; **on pain of** so pena de; **to be in pain** estar con dolor, tener dolores; **to take pains** esmerarse; **to take pains to** + *inf* poner mucho cuidado en + *inf;* **to take pains not to** + *inf* guardarse de + *inf; va & vn* doler
pained [pend] *adj* apenado, afligido
painful [ˈpenfəl] *adj* doloroso; penoso
painkiller [ˈpen,kɪlər] *s* (coll.) remedio contra el dolor
painless [ˈpenlɪs] *adj* indoloro, sin dolor; fácil, sin trabajo
pain reliever *s* calmante del dolor
painstaking [ˈpenz,tekɪŋ] *adj* esmerado
paint [pent] *s* pintura; colorete (*afeite*); *va* pintar; *vn* pintar, ser pintor; pintarse, repintarse
paintbox [ˈpent,bɑks] *s* caja de colores, caja de pinturas
paintbrush [ˈpent,brʌʃ] *s* brocha, pincel
painted lady *s* (bot.) judía de España, judía escarlata
painter [ˈpentər] *s* pintor; (naut.) rejera, amarra; (zool.) puma
Painter's Easel *s* (astr.) Caballete del pintor
painting [ˈpentɪŋ] *s* pintura
paint remover *s* sacapintura, quitapintura
pair [pɛr] *s* par; (pol.) par de diputados apareados para abstenerse de votar; (pol.) convenio para abstenerse de votar; parejas (*dos naipes iguales*); *va* aparear, parear; **to pair off** aparear; *vn* aparearse; **to pair off** aparearse; (pol.) aparearse (*dos diputados*) para abstenerse de votar
pair of glasses *s* gafas; **a pair of glasses** unas gafas
pair of mustaches *s* bigotes
pair of scissors *s* tijeras
pair of spectacles *s* anteojos, gafas
pair of suspenders *s* tirantes
pair of trousers *s* pantalones
paisley [ˈpezlɪ] *s* tela de Paisley; prenda de tela de Paisley
pajamas [pəˈdʒɑməz] o [pəˈdʒæməz] *spl* pijama
Pakistan [ˈpækɪstæn] o [ˈpɑkɪstɑn] *s* el Paquistán
Pakistani [ˌpækɪˈstænɪ] o [ˌpɑkɪˈstɑnɪ] *adj & s* pakistano o pakistaní
pal [pæl] *s* (slang) compañero; (*pret & pp:* **palled;** *ger:* **palling**) *vn* (slang) ser compañeros; **to pal around with** (slang) ser compañero de
palace [ˈpælɪs] *s* palacio
paladin [ˈpælədɪn] *s* paladín
palaestra [pəˈlɛstrə] *s* palestra
palankeen o **palanquin** [ˌpælənˈkin] *s* palanquín
palatable [ˈpælətəbəl] *adj* sabroso, apetitoso
palatal [ˈpælətəl] *adj* palatal; (phonet.) palatal; *s* (phonet.) palatal
palatalization [ˌpælətəlɪˈzeʃən] *s* palatalización
palatalize [ˈpælətəlaɪz] *va* palatalizar; *vn* palatalizarse
palate [ˈpælɪt] *s* (anat.) paladar; (fig.) paladar (*gusto; gastrónomo*)
palatial [pəˈleʃəl] *adj* magnífico, suntuoso
palatinate [pəˈlætɪnet] o [pəˈlætɪnɪt] *s* palatinado; (*cap.*) *s* Palatinado
palatine [ˈpælətaɪn] *adj* palatino; *s* señor palatino, conde palatino; (*cap.*) *adj & s* palatino; **the Palatine** el Palatino
Palatine Hill *s* monte Palatino
palaver [pəˈlævər] o [pəˈlɑvər] *s* plática, conferencia; charla, palabrería; parlamento entre exploradores y bárbaros; lisonja, zalamería; *vn* charlar; parlamentar (*exploradores y bárbaros*); lagotear
pale [pel] *adj* pálido; *s* estaca; palizada; (her.) palo; límite, término; **outside the pale of** fuera de los límites de; *va* empalizar; *vn* palidecer
paleface [ˈpel,fes] *s* rostropálido (*así llamaban los pieles rojas a los de piel blanca*)
paleness [ˈpelnɪs] *s* palidez
paleobotany [ˌpelɪoˈbɑtənɪ] *s* paleobotánica
paleographer [ˌpelɪˈɑgrəfər] *s* paleógrafo
paleographic [ˌpelɪoˈgræfɪk] *adj* paleográfico
paleography [ˌpelɪˈɑgrəfɪ] *s* paleografía
paleolithic [ˌpelɪoˈlɪθɪk] *adj* paleolítico
paleontologist [ˌpelɪɑnˈtɑlədʒɪst] *s* paleontólogo
paleontology [ˌpelɪɑnˈtɑlədʒɪ] *s* paleontología
Paleozoic [ˌpelɪoˈzo·ɪk] *adj & s* (geol.) paleozoico
Palestine [ˈpælɪstaɪn] *s* Palestina
Palestinian [ˌpælɪsˈtɪnɪən] *adj & s* palestino
palette [ˈpælɪt] *s* (paint.) paleta
palette knife *s* espátula
palfrey [ˈpɔlfrɪ] *s* palafrén
Pali [ˈpɑlɪ] *adj & s* pali
palimpsest [ˈpælɪmpsɛst] *s* palimpsesto
palindrome [ˈpælɪndrom] *s* palíndromo, capicúa
paling [ˈpelɪŋ] *s* estaca; estacada
palingenesis [ˌpælɪnˈdʒɛnɪsɪs] *s* palingenesia
palingenetic [ˌpælɪndʒɪˈnɛtɪk] *adj* palingenésico
palinode [ˈpælɪnod] *s* palinodia
palisade [ˈpælɪsed] *s* estaca; estacada, empalizada; acantilado; *va* encerrar con estacada o empalizada
palisander [ˌpælɪˈsændər] *s* (bot.) palisandro
palish [ˈpelɪʃ] *adj* paliducho
pall [pɔl] *s* paño de ataúd, paño mortuorio; capa (*p.e.j., de humo*); (eccl.) palia; hijuela (*para cubrir el cáliz*); *va* hartar, saciar; quitar el sabor a; *vn* perder el sabor; **to pall on** hartar, saciar, dejar de gustar a
palladium [pəˈledɪəm] *s* (*pl:* **-a** [ə]) (chem.) paladio; paladión (*defensa, sostén*); (*cap.*) *s* (myth.) Paladión
Pallas [ˈpæləs] *s* (myth.) Palas
Pallas Athene *s* (myth.) Palas Atenea
pallbearer [ˈpɔl,bɛrər] *s* acompañante de un cadáver; portaféretro, portador del féretro
pallet [ˈpælɪt] *s* jergón; paleta o llana (*de alfarero*); (mach.) uña (*de un trinquete*); (paint.) paleta
palliate [ˈpælɪet] *va* paliar
palliation [ˌpælɪˈeʃən] *s* paliación
palliative [ˈpælɪ,etɪv] *adj & s* paliativo
pallid [ˈpælɪd] *adj* pálido
pallium [ˈpælɪəm] *s* (*pl:* **-ums** o **-a** [ə]) (anat., eccl. & hist.) palio; (eccl.) palia
pall-mall [ˈpɛlˈmɛl] *s* mallo (*juego y terreno*)
pallor [ˈpælər] *s* palidez, palor
palm [pɑm] *s* palma (*de la mano*); palmo (*medida*); (bot.) palma (*árbol y hoja*); (fig.) palma; **to bear the palm** o **to carry off the palm** llevarse la palma; **to grease the palm of** (slang) untar la mano a; **to have an itching palm** (coll.) ser cicatero, ser pesetero; **to yield the palm to** reconocer por vencedor; *va* esconder en la mano; escamotear (*una carta*); **to palm something off on someone** encajarle una cosa a uno
palmaceous [pælˈmeʃəs] *adj* (bot.) palmáceo
palma Christi [ˈpælmə ˈkrɪstaɪ] *s* (bot.) palmacristi
palmary [ˈpælmərɪ] *adj* principal, supremo
palmate [ˈpælmet] *adj* palmeado; (bot. & zool.) palmeado
palmation [pælˈmeʃən] *s* disposición o estructura palmeada; forma o parte palmeada
Palm Beach *s* (trademark) palmiche (*tela*)
palmer [ˈpɑmər] *s* palmero (*peregrino de Tierra Santa*); peregrino; fullero, tahur
palmer worm *s* (ent.) polilla del manzano
palmetto [pælˈmɛto] *s* (*pl:* **-tos** o **-toes**) (bot.) palmito
palmiped [ˈpælmɪpɛd] *adj & s* (zool.) palmípedo
palmist [ˈpɑmɪst] *s* quiromántico
palmistry [ˈpɑmɪstrɪ] *s* quiromancía
palmitate [ˈpælmɪtet] *s* (chem.) palmitato
palm leaf *s* palma, hoja de la palmera
palm oil *s* aceite de palma; (slang) propina; (slang) soborno

Palm Sunday *s* día de ramos, domingo de ramos
palm wax *s* cera de palma
palmy ['pɑmɪ] *adj* (*comp:* **-ier;** *super:* **-iest**) abundante en palmeras; sombreado por palmeras; floreciente, próspero, glorioso
palp [pælp] *s* palpo
palpability [,pælpə'bɪlɪtɪ] *s* palpabilidad
palpable ['pælpəbəl] *adj* palpable
palpate ['pælpet] *va* (med.) palpar
palpation [pæl'peʃən] *s* (med.) palpación
palpebral ['pælpɪbrəl] *adj* palpebral
palpitate ['pælpɪtet] *vn* palpitar
palpitation [,pælpɪ'teʃən] *s* palpitación
palpus ['pælpəs] *s* (*pl:* **-pi** [paɪ]) palpo
palsy ['pɔlzɪ] *s* (*pl:* **-sies**) (path.) perlesía; (*pret & pp:* **-sied**) *va* paralizar
palter ['pɔltər] *vn* hablar u obrar sin sinceridad; regatear; estafar, petardear
paltry ['pɔltrɪ] *adj* (*comp:* **-trier;** *super:* **-triest**) vil, ruin, mezquino, baladí
paly ['pelɪ] *adj* (poet.) algo pálido; (her.) palado
Pamela ['pæmələ] *s* Pamela
pampa ['pæmpə] *s* pampa; **the Pampas** La Pampa
pampas grass *s* (bot.) carrizo de las pampas
pampean [pæm'piən] *adj & s* pampero
pamper ['pæmpər] *va* mimar, consentir
pamphlet ['pæmflɪt] *s* folleto
pamphleteer [,pæmflɪ'tɪr] *s* folletista; *vn* publicar folletos, lanzar folletos
Pamphylia [pæm'fɪlɪə] *s* Panfilia
pan [pæn] *s* cacerola, cazuela, sartén; caldera, perol; cubeta (*usada, p.ej., en la fotografía*); cazoleta (*de arma de fuego*); (min.) gamella; capa arcillosa y dura debajo de terreno blando; (*cap.*) *s* (myth.) Pan; (*l.c.*) (*pret & pp:* **panned;** *ger:* **panning**) *va* cocer, freír; separar (*el oro*) en la gamella; (coll.) criticar ásperamente; *vn* separar el oro en la gamella; dar oro; **to pan out** (coll.) resultar; **to pan out well** (coll.) tener éxito, dar buen resultado
panacea [,pænə'siə] *s* panacea
panache [pə'næʃ] o [pə'nɑʃ] *s* penacho
Panama ['pænəmɑ] o [,pænə'mɑ] *s* Panamá; (*l.c.*) *s* panamá (*sombrero*)
Panama Canal *s* canal de Panamá
Panama Canal Zone *s* Zona del Canal
Panama hat *s* panamá
Panamanian [,pænə'menɪən] o [,pænə'mɑnɪən] *adj & s* panameño
Pan-American [,pænə'mɛrɪkən] *adj* panamericano
Pan-Americanism [,pænə'mɛrɪkənɪzəm] *s* panamericanismo
Pan American Union *s* Unión panamericana
Pan-Arabian [,pænə'rebɪən] *adj* panarábico
Panathenaea [,pænæθɪ'niə] *spl* (hist.) Panateneas
pancake ['pæn,kek] *s* panqueque, hojuela; (aer.) aterrizaje hecho de plano; *vn* (aer.) aterrizar de plano, desplomarse
Pancake Day *s* martes de Carnaval
pancake landing *s* (aer.) aterrizaje en desplome, aterrizaje aplastado
Pancake Tuesday *s* var. de **Pancake Day**
panchromatic [,pænkro'mætɪk] *adj* pancromático
pancreas ['pænkrɪəs] *s* (anat.) páncreas
pancreatic [,pænkrɪ'ætɪk] *adj* pancreático
pancreatic juice *s* (physiol.) jugo pancreático
pancreatin ['pænkrɪətɪn] o ['pæŋkrɪətɪn] *s* (biochem.) pancreatina
panda ['pændə] *s* (zool.) panda
pandanaceous [,pændə'neʃəs] *adj* (bot.) pandanáceo
pandect ['pændɛkt] *s* digesto; **pandects** *spl* recopilación (*de leyes*); **Pandects** *spl* Pandectas
pandemic [pæn'dɛmɪk] *adj* pandémico; *s* pandemia
pandemonium [,pændɪ'monɪəm] *s* pandemónium o pandemonio; alboroto diabólico, gresca de todos los demonios
pander ['pændər] *s* alcahuete; *vn* alcahuetear; **to pander to** gratificar
Pandora [pæn'dorə] *s* (myth.) Pandora
Pandora's box *s* caja de Pandora
pandowdy [pæn'daudɪ] *s* (*pl:* **-dies**) pastel de manzana hecho en vasija honda
pane [pen] *s* cristal, vidrio, hoja de vidrio
panegyric [,pænɪ'dʒɪrɪk] *s* panegírico
panegyrical [,pænɪ'dʒɪrɪkəl] *adj* panegírico
panegyrist [,pænɪ'dʒɪrɪst] o ['pænɪ,dʒɪrɪst] *s* panegirista
panegyrize ['pænɪdʒɪraɪz] *va* panegirizar
panel ['pænəl] *s* panel, entrepaño, cuarterón; tabla (*cuadro pintado en una tabla*); pequeño grupo de personas en discusión cara al público; (aut. & elec.) tablero, panel; (law) lista (*de personas que pueden servir como jurados o para algún otro fin*); (mach.) tablero, plancha; (sew.) paño; (*pret & pp:* **-eled** o **-elled;** *ger:* **-eling** o **-elling**) *va* adornar con cuarterones, labrar en cuarterones; artesonar (*un techo o bóveda*)
panelboard ['pænəl,bord] *s* cuadro de mandos
panel discussion *s* coloquio ante un auditorio
paneling o **panelling** ['pænəlɪŋ] *s* entrepaños, cuarterones; artesonado (*de un techo o bóveda*)
panelist ['pænəlɪst] *s* coloquiante ante un auditorio
panel lights *spl* (aut.) luces del tablero
panentheism [,pæn'ɛnθiɪzəm] *s* (theol.) panenteísmo
pane of glass *s* hoja de vidrio
panetella [[pænə'tɛlə] *s* panetela (*cigarro*)
pang [pæŋ] *s* dolor agudo; punzada (*de remordimiento*); agonía (*de la muerte*)
pangenesis [pæn'dʒɛnɪsɪs] *s* (biol.) pangénesis
Pan-German [,pæn'dʒʌrmən] *adj* pangermanista; *s* (*pl:* **-mans**) pangermanista
Pan-Germanic [,pændʒər'mænɪk] *adj* pangermanista
Pan-Germanism [,pæn'dʒʌrmənɪzəm] *s* pangermanismo
pangolin [pæŋ'golɪn] *s* (zool.) pangolín
panhandle ['pæn,hændəl] *s* mango de sartén; (U.S.A.) faja angosta de territorio de un estado que entra en el de otro; *vn* (slang) mendigar, pedir limosna
panhandler ['pæn,hændlər] *s* (slang) mendigo, pordiosero
Panhellenic o **panhellenic** [,pænhɛ'lɛnɪk] o [,pænhɛ'linɪk] *adj* panhelénico
Panhellenism [pæn'hɛlənɪzəm] *s* panhelenismo
panic ['pænɪk] *adj & s* pánico; (*pret & pp:* **-icked;** *ger:* **-icking**) *va* sobrecoger de pánico; *vn* sobrecogerse de pánico
panic grass *s* (bot.) mijo común
panicky ['pænɪkɪ] *adj* pánico; asustadizo
panicle ['pænɪkəl] *s* (bot.) panícula, panoja
panicled ['pænɪkəld] *adj* (bot.) apanojado
panic-stricken ['pænɪk,strɪkən] *adj* muerto de miedo, paralizado de pánico, sobrecogido de terror
paniculate [pə'nɪkjəlet] *adj* (bot.) paniculado
panification [,pænɪfɪ'keʃən] *s* panificación
Pan-Islamic [,pænɪs'læmɪk] o [,pænɪs'lɑmɪk] *adj* panislamista
Pan-Islamism [,pæn'ɪsləmɪzəm] *s* panislamismo
Pan-Islamist [,pæn'ɪsləmɪst] *s* panislamista
panjandrum [pæn'dʒændrəm] *s* (hum.) persona de campanillas; (hum.) ceremonia exagerada
pannicular [pə'nɪkjələr] *adj* panicular
panniculus [pə'nɪkjələs] *s* (anat.) panículo
pannier ['pænɪər] *s* serón, cuévano; tontillo
pannikin ['pænɪkɪn] *s* cacillo; cubilete, copa
panocha [pə'notʃə] *s* panocha (*azúcar, melcocha*)
panoplied ['pænəplɪd] *adj* armado de pies a cabeza
panoply ['pænəplɪ] *s* (*pl:* **-plies**) panoplia; traje ceremonial
panorama [,pænə'ræmə] o [,pænə'rɑmə] *s* panorama
panoramic [,pænə'ræmɪk] *adj* panorámico
panoramically [,pænə'ræmɪkəlɪ] *adv* panorámicamente
Panpipe ['pæn,paɪp] *s* (mus.) flauta de Pan
Pan-Slav [,pæn'slɑv] o **Pan-Slavic** [,pæn'slɑvɪk] *adj* paneslavista
Pan-Slavism [,pæn'slɑvɪzəm] *s* paneslavismo
Pan's pipes *s* (mus.) flauta de Pan
pansy ['pænzɪ] *s* (*pl:* **-sies**) (bot.) pensamiento
pant [pænt] *s* jadeo; palpitación; resoplido (*de*

una máquina de vapor); **pants** *spl* (coll.) pantalones; **to wear the pants** (coll.) calzarse o ponerse los pantalones; *vn* jadear: palpitar; **to pant for** anhelar, desear con vehemencia
Pantagruelian [ˌpæntəgruˈɛlɪən] o **Pantagruelic** [ˌpæntəgruˈɛlɪk] *adj* pantagruélico
pantalets o **pantalettes** [ˌpæntəˈlɛts] *spl* pantalones de mujer que asomaban debajo de la falda
pantaloon [ˌpæntəˈlun] *s* bufón, gracioso; **pantaloons** *spl* pantalones
pantechnicon [pænˈtɛknɪkən] *s* (Brit.) camión de mudanzas; (Brit.) almacén o depósito de muebles
pantheism [ˈpænθiɪzəm] *s* panteísmo
pantheist [ˈpænθiɪst] *s* panteísta
pantheistic [ˌpænθiˈɪstɪk] *adj* panteístico
pantheistically [ˌpænθiˈɪstɪkəlɪ] *adv* según la doctrina del panteísmo
pantheon [ˈpænθɪɑn] o [pænˈθiən] *s* panteón
panther [ˈpænθər] *s* (zool.) pantera; (zool.) puma
panties [ˈpæntɪz] *spl* braguitas
pantile [ˈpænˌtaɪl] *s* teja romana, teja de cimacio; teja canalón
pantograph [ˈpæntəgræf] o [ˈpæntəgrɑf] *s* pantógrafo; (elec.) pantógrafo
pantomime [ˈpæntəmaɪm] *s* pantomima; *va* expresar o representar por arte pantomímico
pantomimic [ˌpæntəˈmɪmɪk] *adj* pantomímico
pantomimist [ˈpæntəˌmaɪmɪst] *s* pantomimo
pantothenic [ˌpæntəˈθɛnɪk] *adj* pantoténico
pantothenic acid *s* (biochem.) ácido pantoténico
pantry [ˈpæntrɪ] *s* (*pl:* **-tries**) despensa
pantywaist [ˈpæntɪˌwest] *s* (slang) alfeñique, santito; *adj* (slang) afeminado, aniñado
panzer [ˈpænzər] *adj* (mil.) armado, blindado
pap [pæp] *s* papilla o papas
papa [ˈpɑpə] o [pəˈpɑ] *s* papá
papable [ˈpepəbəl] *adj* papable
papacy [ˈpepəsɪ] *s* (*pl:* **-cies**) papado, pontificado
papain [pəˈpeɪn] o [ˈpepəɪn] *s* (biochem.) papaína
papal [ˈpepəl] *adj* papal
papal nuncio *s* nuncio, nuncio apostólico
Papal States *spl* Estados pontificios
papaveraceous [pəˌpævəˈreʃəs] *adj* (bot.) papaveráceo
papaw [ˈpɔpɔ] o [pəˈpɔ] *s* (bot.) asimina; (bot.) papayo; papaya (*fruto*)
papaya [pəˈpɑjə] *s* (bot.) papayo; papaya (*fruto*)
paper [ˈpepər] *s* papel; periódico; papel o paño (*p.ej., de agujas*); *va* empapelar
paperback [ˈpepərˌbæk] *s* libro en rústica
paper blockade *s* bloqueo en el papel
paper-bound [ˈpepərˌbaʊnd] *adj* en rústica
paper clip *s* abrazadera para papeles, sujetapapeles
paper cone *s* cucurucho
paper cup *s* vaso de papel
paper-cup dispenser [ˈpepərˌkʌp] *s* portavasos de papel
paper cutter *s* cortapapeles; guillotina
paper finger *s* aprietapapeles (*de la máquina de escribir*)
paper flower *s* flor de mano, flor artificial
paper hanger *s* empapelador, papelista, pegador
paper knife *s* cortapapeles
paper mill *s* fábrica de papel
paper money *s* papel moneda
paper mulberry *s* (bot.) papelero
paper nautilus *s* (zool.) argonauta
paper profits *spl* ganancias no realizadas sobre valores no vendidos
paper tape *s* cinta perforada
paperweight [ˈpepərˌwet] *s* pisapapeles
paper work *s* preparación o comprobación de escritos (*archivos, avisos, exámenes de alumnos, etc.*)
papery [ˈpepərɪ] *adj* parecido al papel, fino o delgado como el papel
papier-mâché [ˈpepərməˈʃe] *s* cartón piedra; *adj* de cartón piedra
papilionaceous [pəˌpɪlɪəˈneʃəs] *adj* (bot.) papilionáceo
papilla [pəˈpɪlə] *s* (*pl:* **-lae** [li]) (anat. & bot.) papila
papillary [ˈpæpɪˌlɛrɪ] o [pəˈpɪlərɪ] *adj* papilar
papilloma [ˌpæpɪˈlomə] *s* (*pl:* **-mata** [mətə] o **-mas**) (path.) papiloma
papillose [ˈpæpɪlos] *adj* lleno de papilas
papion [ˈpepɪɑn] *s* (zool.) papión
papist [ˈpepist] *adj* & *s* (scornful) papista
papistic [peˈpɪstɪk] o [pəˈpɪstɪk] o **papistical** [peˈpɪstɪkəl] o [pəˈpɪstɪkəl] *adj* (scornful) papístico
papistry [ˈpepɪstrɪ] *s* (scornful) papismo
pappus [ˈpæpəs] *s* (*pl:* **-pi** [paɪ]) (bot.) papo, vilano
pappy [ˈpæpɪ] *adj* (*comp:* **-pier;** *super:* **-piest**) mollar, jugoso; *s* (*pl:* **-pies**) (slang) papá
paprika [pæˈprikə] o [ˈpæprɪkə] *s* pimentón
Papua [ˈpæpjʊə] *s* la Papuasia
Papuan [ˈpæpjʊən] *adj* & *s* papú
papule [ˈpæpjʊl] *s* (path.) pápula
papulose [ˈpæpjəlos] *adj* papuloso
papyraceous [ˌpæpɪˈreʃəs] *adj* papiráceo
papyrus [pəˈpaɪrəs] *s* (*pl:* **-ri** [raɪ]) (bot.) papiro; papiro (*lámina del tallo de esta planta; hoja de papiro escrita*)
par. abr. de **paragraph, parallel, parenthesis** y **parish**
par [pɑr] *adj* a la par; nominal; normal; *s* (com.) paridad; (com.) valor nominal; (golf) norma de perfección; **above par** (com.) sobre la par; (com.) con beneficio, con premio; **at par** (com.) a la par; **below par** o **under par** (com.) bajo la par; (com.) con pérdida, con quebranto; (coll.) indispuesto; **to be on a par with** correr parejas con
parable [ˈpærəbəl] *s* parábola
parabola [pəˈræbələ] *s* (geom.) parábola
parabolic [ˌpærəˈbɑlɪk] *adj* parabólico; (geom.) parabólico
paraboloid [pəˈræbəlɔɪd] *s* (geom.) paraboloide
Paracelsus [ˌpærəˈsɛlsəs] *s* Paracelso
paracentesis [ˌpærəsɛnˈtisɪs] *s* (surg.) paracentesis
parachronism [pæˈrækrənɪzəm] *s* paracronismo
parachute [ˈpærəʃut] *s* paracaídas; *vn* lanzarse en paracaídas; **to parachute to safety** salvarse en paracaídas
parachute jump *s* salto en paracaídas
parachutist [ˈpærəˌʃutɪst] *s* paracaidista
Paraclete [ˈpærəklit] *s* paráclito
parade [pəˈred] *s* desfile; paseo; ostentación; **parade rest** (mil.) en su lugar descanso; *va* ostentar, pasear (*p.ej., una bandera*); (mil.) convocar a una revista; *vn* desfilar, pasar por las calles; (mil.) formar en parada
parade ground *s* (mil.) plaza de armas
paradichlorobenzene [ˌpærədaɪˌkloroˈbɛnzin] *s* (chem.) paradiclorobenceno
paradigm [ˈpærədɪm] o [ˈpærədaɪm] *s* (gram. & fig.) paradigma
paradise [ˈpærədaɪs] *s* paraíso; (slang) paraíso (*en el teatro*); (hort.) manzano enano de San Juan o del paraíso
paradisiacal [ˌpærədɪˈsaɪəkəl] *adj* paradisíaco
paradox [ˈpærədɑks] *s* paradoja; persona o cosa incomprensibles
paradoxical [ˌpærəˈdɑksɪkəl] *adj* paradójico
paraffin [ˈpærəfɪn] o **paraffine** [ˈpærəfɪn] o [ˈpærəfin] *s* parafina
paragoge [ˌpærəˈgodʒɪ] *s* (gram.) paragoge
paragogic [ˌpærəˈgɑdʒɪk] *adj* paragógico
paragon [ˈpærəgɑn] *s* dechado; (print.) parangona
paragraph [ˈpærəgræf] o [ˈpærəgrɑf] *s* párrafo; suelto o gacetilla (*en un periódico*); *va* dividir en párrafos; escribir sueltos o gacetillas sobre
paragrapher [ˈpærəˌgræfər] o [ˈpærəˌgrɑfər] *s* gacetillero
paragraphia [ˌpærəˈgræfɪə] *s* (path.) paragrafía
Paraguay [ˈpærəgwe] o [ˈpærəgwaɪ] *s* el Paraguay
Paraguayan [ˌpærəˈgweən] o [ˌpærəˈgwaɪən] *adj* & *s* paraguayano o paraguayo
Paraguay tea *s* (bot.) hierba del Paraguay
parakeet [ˈpærəkit] *s* (orn.) perico, periquito

paraldehyde [pə'rældɪhaɪd] *s* (chem.) paraldehído
Paralipomena [,pærəlɪ'pɑmɪnə] *spl* (Bib.) paralipómenos; (*l.c.*) *spl* cosas omitidas u olvidadas
paralipsis [,pærə'lɪpsɪs] *s* (*pl:* **-ses** [siz]) (rhet.) paralipsis
parallactic [,pærə'læktɪk] *adj* paraláctico
parallax ['pærəlæks] *s* paralaje
parallel ['pærəlɛl] *adj* paralelo; (elec.) en paralelo; **to run parallel to** andar o ir en línea paralela a; *s* (geom. & fort.) paralela; (geom.) plano paralelo; (geog. & fig.) paralelo; **parallels** *spl* (print.) doble raya vertical; **in parallel** (elec.) en paralelo; (*pret & pp:* **-leled** o **-lelled;** *ger:* **-leling** o **-lelling**) *va* ser paralelo a; poner en dirección paralela; correr parejas con; hallar una cosa semejante a; paralelizar (*hacer la comparación entre*)
parallel bars *spl* (sport) paralelas, barras paralelas
parallelepiped [,pærə,lɛlɪ'paɪpɪd] o **parallelepipedon** [,pærə,lɛlɪ'pɪpɪdɑn] *s* (geom.) paralelepípedo
parallel-flow turbine ['pærəlɛl'flo] *s* turbina paralela
parallelism ['pærəlɛlɪzəm] *s* paralelismo
parallel motion *s* (mach.) mecanismo de movimiento paralelo; (mus.) movimiento paralelo
parallelogram [,pærə'lɛləgræm] *s* (geom.) paralelogramo
parallelogram law *s* (mech.) regla del paralelogramo
parallel postulate *s* (math.) postulado de las paralelas
paralogism [pə'rælədʒɪzəm] *s* paralogismo
paralogize [pə'rælədʒaɪz] *vn* paralogizarse
paralysis [pə'rælɪsɪs] *s* (*pl:* **-ses** [siz]) (path. & fig.) parálisis
paralysis agitans ['ædʒɪtænz] *s* (path.) parálisis agitante
paralytic [,pærə'lɪtɪk] *adj & s* paralítico
paralyzation [,pærəlɪ'zeʃən] *s* paralización
paralyze ['pærəlaɪz] *va* paralizar; (fig.) paralizar
paramagnetic [,pærəmæg'nɛtɪk] *adj* paramagnético
paramagnetism [,pærə'mægnɪtɪzəm] *s* paramagnetismo
paramecium [,pærə'miʃɪəm] o [,pærə'misɪəm] *s* (*pl:* **-a** [ə]) (zool.) paramecio
parameter [pə'ræmɪtər] *s* (math.) parámetro
paramount ['pærəmaʊnt] *adj* capital, supremo, principalísimo
paramour ['pærəmʊr] *s* querido o querida
paranoia [,pærə'nɔɪə] *s* (path.) paranoia
paranoiac [,pærə'nɔɪæk] *adj & s* paranoico
parapet ['pærəpɛt] *s* parapeto; (fort.) parapeto
paraphernalia [,pærəfər'neliə] *spl* bienes personales, trastos, atavíos; (law) bienes parafernales
paraphrase ['pærəfrez] *s* paráfrasis; *va* parafrasear
paraphrast ['pærəfræst] *s* parafraste
paraphrastic [,pærə'fræstɪk] *adj* parafrástico
paraphrastically [,pærə'fræstɪkəlɪ] *adv* parafrásticamente
paraplegia [,pærə'plidʒɪə] *s* (path.) paraplejía
paraplegic [,pærə'plɛdʒɪk] o [,pærə'plidʒɪk] *adj & s* parapléjico
parapsychology [,pærəsaɪ'kɑlədʒɪ] *s* parapsicología
parasang ['pærəsæŋ] *s* parasanga
parasceve ['pærəsiv] *s* parasceve
paraselene [,pærəsɪ'linɪ] *s* (*pl:* **-nae** [ni]) (meteor.) paraselene
parasite ['pærəsaɪt] *s* (biol. & fig.) parásito
parasitic [,pærə'sɪtɪk] o **parasitical** [,pærə'sɪtɪkəl] *adj* parasítico o parasitario
parasiticide [,pærə'sɪtɪsaɪd] *adj & s* parasiticida
parasitism ['pærə,saɪtɪzəm] *s* parasitismo
parasitological [,pærə,saɪtə'lɑdʒɪkəl] *adj* parasitológico
parasitologist [,pærəsaɪ'tɑlədʒɪst] *s* parasitólogo
parasitology [,pærəsaɪ'tɑlədʒɪ] *s* parasitología
parasol ['pærəsɔl] o ['pærəsɑl] *s* quitasol, parasol
parasympathetic [,pærə,sɪmpə'θɛtɪk] *adj & s* (anat. & physiol.) parasimpático
parasynthesis [,pærə'sɪnθɪsɪs] *s* (gram.) parasíntesis
parathyroid [,pærə'θaɪrɔɪd] *adj & s* (anat.) paratiroides
parathyroid glands *spl* (anat.) glándulas paratiroides
paratrooper ['pærə,trupər] *s* (mil.) paracaidista
paratroops ['pærətrups] *spl* (mil.) tropas paracaidistas
paratyphoid [,pærə'taɪfɔɪd] *adj* paratifoide
paratyphoid fever *s* (path.) fiebre paratifoidea
parboil ['pɑrbɔɪl] *va* sancochar; calentar con exceso
parbuckle ['pɑr,bʌkəl] *s* tiravira
Parcae ['pɑrsi] *spl* (myth.) Parcas
parcel ['pɑrsəl] *s* paquete, lío, atado; solar, lote; hatajo (*p.ej., de embustes*); pandilla (*p.ej., de embusteros*); (*pret & pp:* **-celed** o **-celled;** *ger:* **-celing** o **-celling**) *va* empaquetar, embalar; parcelar (*el terreno*); **to parcel out** repartir
parceling o **parcelling** ['pɑrsəlɪŋ] *s* parcelación (*del terreno*); (naut.) entreforro, fajadura
parcel post *s* paquetes postales (*servicio*)
parch [pɑrtʃ] *va* tostar; abrasar; agostar (*las plantas*); *vn* tostarse; abrasarse, sufrir con el calor
parcheesi o **parchesi** [pɑr'tʃizɪ] *s* parchesí
parchment ['pɑrtʃmənt] *s* pergamino; pergamino de imitación
parchment paper *s* papel pergamino
pard [pɑrd] *s* (slang) compadre, amigote; (archaic) pardo, leopardo
pardi o **pardie** [pɑr'di] *interj* (archaic) en verdad, por cierto
pardon ['pɑrdən] *s* perdón; indulto (*gracia concedida, p.ej., por el Estado*); **I beg your pardon** dispense Vd.; *va* perdonar, dispensar; **pardon me** dispense Vd.
pardonable ['pɑrdənəbəl] *adj* perdonable
pardonably ['pɑrdənəblɪ] *adv* disculpablemente
pardon board *s* junta de perdones
pardoner ['pɑrdənər] *s* perdonador; (eccl.) perdonador
pare [pɛr] *va* mondar (*fruta*); pelar (*patatas*); cortar (*callos, uñas, etc.*); despalmar (*la palma córnea de los animales*); adelgazar, sacar de espesor; reducir (*p.ej., gastos*)
paregoric [,pærɪ'gɑrɪk] o [,pærɪ'gɔrɪk] *adj* paregórico, calmante; *s* (pharm.) elixir paregórico, tintura compuesta de alcanfor
paren. abr. de **parenthesis**
parenchyma [pə'rɛŋkɪmə] *s* (anat. & bot.) parénquima
parenchymatous [,pærɛŋ'kɪmətəs] *adj* parenquimatoso
parent ['pɛrənt] *s* padre o madre; autor, fuente, origen; **parents** *spl* padres (*padre y madre*); *adj* madre, principal
parentage ['pɛrəntɪdʒ] *s* paternidad o maternidad; abolengo, linaje
parental [pə'rɛntəl] *adj* parental, de padre y madre
parent company *s* compañía matriz
parenteral [pæ'rɛntərəl] *adj* parenteral
parenthesis [pə'rɛnθɪsɪs] *s* (*pl:* **-ses** [siz]) (gram. & fig.) paréntesis; **in parentheses** dentro de un paréntesis o entre paréntesis
parenthesize [pə'rɛnθɪsaɪz] *va* poner entre paréntesis; insertar entre paréntesis; interrumpir (*un discurso*) con muchos paréntesis
parenthetic [,pærən'θɛtɪk] o **parenthetical** [,pærən'θɛtɪkəl] *adj* parentético; explicativo; digresivo
parenthetically [,pærən'θɛtɪkəlɪ] *adv* por paréntesis
parenthood ['pɛrənthʊd] *s* paternidad o maternidad
paresis [pə'risɪs] o ['pærɪsɪs] *s* (path.) paresia o paresis
paretic [pə'rɛtɪk] o [pə'ritɪk] *adj & s* parético

par excellence [pɑr ˈɛksəlɑns] o [pɑr ɛksɛˈlɑ̃s] (Fr.) por excelencia
parfait [pɑrˈfe] *s* helado hecho sin agitación, de crema batida muy dulce
parget [ˈpɑrdʒɪt] *s* enlucido; molduras de yeso; *va* enlucir; adornar con molduras de yeso
parheliacal [ˌpɑrhɪˈlaɪəkəl] *adj* parhélico
parheliacal ring *s* (meteor.) círculo parhélico
parhelic [pɑrˈhilɪk] *adj* var. de **parheliacal**
parhelic circle *s* var. de **parheliacal ring**
parhelion [pɑrˈhilɪən] *s* (*pl:* **-a** [ə]) (meteor.) parhelio
pariah [pəˈraɪə] o [ˈpɑrɪə] *s* paria
Parian [ˈpɛrɪən] *adj* pario; *s* pario; porcelana paria
parietal [pəˈraɪətəl] *adj* parietal; interior; (anat., bot. & zool.) parietal; *s* (anat.) parietal
pari-mutuel [ˈpærɪˈmjutʃʊəl] *s* apuesta mutua; totalizador, aparato para registro de apuestas mutuas
paring [ˈpɛrɪŋ] *s* peladura, raspadura; cáscara; **parings** *spl* espalmadura, despalmadura (*del casco de los animales*)
paring knife *s* cuchillo para mondar
paripinnate [ˌpærɪˈpɪnet] *adj* (bot.) paripinado
Paris [ˈpærɪs] *s* París; (myth.) Paris
Paris green *s* verde de París, verde de Schweinfurt
parish [ˈpærɪʃ] *s* parroquia; jurisdicción o subdivisión (*del estado de Luisiana, EE.UU.*); (Brit.) distrito civil; *adj* parroquial
parishioner [pəˈrɪʃənər] *s* parroquiano, feligrés
Parisian [pəˈrɪʒən] *adj & s* parisiense
parisyllabic [ˌpærɪsɪˈlæbɪk] *adj* parisilábico o parisílabo
parity [ˈpærɪtɪ] *s* paridad
park [pɑrk] *s* parque; (mil.) parque; (Brit.) parque (*destinado a las fieras*); *va* (aut.) estacionar (*p.ej., en la calle por poco tiempo*); (aut.) aparcar, parquear (*p.ej., en una estación de aparcamiento por un largo plazo*); (mil.) aparcar, parquear; (coll.) colocar, dejar; *vn* (aut.) estacionar; (aut.) aparcar, parquear
parka [ˈpɑrkə] *s* especie de zamarra de los esquimales; chaqueta de lana con capucha (*que llevan los esquiadores y otros deportistas*)
Parker Kalon screw [ˈpɑrkər ˈkelɑn] *s* (trademark) tornillo Parker (*especie de tornillo que labra la rosca por sí mismo*)
parking [ˈpɑrkɪŋ] *s* terreno poblado de árboles y plantas; césped (*y a veces árboles*) plantado entre las dos vías de la carretera o por los dos lados de ella; (aut.) estacionamiento; (aut. & mil.) aparcamiento; **no parking** se prohibe estacionarse
parking brake *s* (aut.) freno de estacionamiento
parking light *s* (aut.) luz de estacionamiento, población o situación
parking lot *s* (aut.) parque, parque de estacionamiento
parking meter *s* (aut.) reloj de estacionamiento
parking station *s* (aut.) estación de aparcamiento
parking ticket *s* aviso de multa (*por estacionar un auto indebidamente*)
Parkinson's disease [ˈpɑrkɪnsənz] *s* (path.) enfermedad de Parkinson, parálisis agitante
parkleaves [ˈpɑrkˌlivz] *s* (bot.) todabuena
parkway [ˈpɑrkˌwe] *s* gran vía adornada con árboles
parlance [ˈpɑrləns] *s* lenguaje
parley [ˈpɑrlɪ] *s* parlamento; *vn* parlamentar
parliament [ˈpɑrlɪmənt] *s* parlamento
parliamentarian [ˌpɑrlɪmɛnˈtɛrɪən] *s* parlamentario; (*cap.*) *s* (hist.) Parlamentario
parliamentarism [ˌpɑrlɪˈmɛntərɪzəm] *s* parlamentarismo
parliamentary [ˌpɑrlɪˈmɛntərɪ] *adj* parlamentario
parlor [ˈpɑrlər] *s* sala; parlatorio, locutorio; salón (*p. ej., de belleza*); *adj* de gabinete
parlor car *s* (rail.) coche-salón
parlor games *spl* diversiones de salón, juegos de sociedad
parlous [ˈpɑrləs] *adj* (archaic & dial.) peligroso; (archaic & dial.) terrible, enorme; (archaic & dial.) astuto; *adv* (archaic & dial.) enormemente, sumamente
Parmenides [pɑrˈmɛnɪdiz] *s* Parménides
Parmesan [ˌpɑrmɪˈzæn] *adj* parmesano; *s* parmesano (*natural; queso*)
Parmesan cheese *s* queso parmesano
Parnassian [pɑrˈnæsɪən] *adj* parnasiano
Parnassus [pɑrˈnæsəs] *s* parnaso (*colección de poesías*); el Parnaso; **Mount Parnassus** el monte Parnaso; **to try to climb Parnassus** hacer pinos en poesía
parochial [pəˈrokɪəl] *adj* parroquial; estrecho, limitado
parochialism [pəˈrokɪəlɪzəm] *s* parroquialidad; estrechez de miras, intolerancia
parochial school *s* escuela parroquial
parodist [ˈpærədɪst] *s* parodista
parody [ˈpærədɪ] *s* (*pl:* **-dies**) parodia; (*pret & pp:* **-died**) *va* parodiar
parole [pəˈrol] *s* palabra de honor; libertad bajo palabra, remisión condicional de la pena, régimen de libertad provisional; **on parole** bajo el régimen de libertad provisional; *va* dejar libre bajo palabra
parolee [pəˌroˈli] *s* delincuente bajo el régimen de libertad vigilada
paronomasia [ˌpærənoˈmeʒɪə] *s* paronomasia
paronym [ˈpærənɪm] *s* parónimo
paronymous [pəˈrɑnɪməs] *adj* parónimo
paronymy [pəˈrɑnɪmɪ] *s* paronimia
paroquet [ˈpærəkɛt] *s* var. de **parakeet**
parotid [pəˈrɑtɪd] *adj* (anat.) parotídeo; *s* (anat.) parótida
parotitic [ˌpærəˈtɪtɪk] *adj* (path.) parotídeo
paroxysm [ˈpærəksɪzəm] *s* paroxismo; (path.) paroxismo
paroxysmal [ˌpærəkˈsɪzməl] *adj* paroxismal
paroxytone [pærˈɑksɪton] *adj & s* (phonet.) paroxítono
parquet [pɑrˈke] o [pɑrˈkɛt] *s* entarimado; (theat.) platea; (*pret & pp:* **-queted** [ˈked] o [ˈkɛtɪd]; *ger:* **-queting** [ˈkeɪŋ] o [ˈkɛtɪŋ]) *va* entarimar
parquet circle *s* (theat.) anfiteatro debajo de la galería
parquetry [ˈpɑrkɪtrɪ] *s* mosaico de madera, obra de entarimado
parr [pɑr] *s* (ichth.) alevín, esguín
parrakeet [ˈpærəkit] *s* var. de **parakeet**
parral o **parrel** [ˈpærəl] *s* (naut.) racamenta o racamento
parricidal [ˌpærɪˈsaɪdəl] *adj* parricida
parricide [ˈpærɪsaɪd] *s* parricidio (*acción*); parricida (*persona*)
parrot [ˈpærət] *s* (orn.) papagayo, loro; (fig.) papagayo; *va* repetir o imitar como loro
parrot disease o **parrot fever** *s* (path.) psitacosis
parrot fish *s* (ichth.) pez-papagayo
parry [ˈpærɪ] *s* (*pl:* **-ries**) parada, quite; (fig.) defensa; (*pret & pp:* **-ried**) *va* parar; (fig.) defenderse de
parry of o **in carte** o **quarte** [kɑrt] *s* (fencing) parada en cuarta
parry of o **in prime** *s* (fencing) parada en primera
parry of o **in seconde** [sɪˈkɑnd] *s* (fencing) parada en segunda
parry of o **in tierce** *s* (fencing) parada en tercera
parse [pɑrs] *va* analizar (*una oración*) gramaticalmente; describir (*una palabra*) gramaticalmente
Parsee o **Parsi** [ˈpɑrsi] *s* parsi
Parseeism [ˈpɑrsiɪzəm] *s* parsismo
Parsic [ˈpɑrsɪk] *adj* parsi
parsimonious [ˌpɑrsɪˈmonɪəs] *adj* parsimonioso
parsimony [ˈpɑrsɪˌmonɪ] *s* parsimonia
parsley [ˈpɑrslɪ] *s* (bot.) perejil (*planta y hojas*)
parsnip [ˈpɑrsnɪp] *s* (bot.) chirivía (*planta y raíz*)
parson [ˈpɑrsən] *s* cura, párroco; clérigo; pastor protestante
parsonage [ˈpɑrsənɪdʒ] *s* rectoría
part. abr. de **participle** y **particular**
part [pɑrt] *s* parte; pieza (*de una máquina*); (theat. & mus.) parte; raya (*en los cabellos*); **parts** *spl* partes, prendas, dotes; partes, partes

vergonzosas; **foreign parts** países extranjeros; **for my (his) part** por mi (su) parte; **for the most part** por lo general, por la mayor parte; **in good part** en buena parte (*sin ofenderse*); **in part** en parte; **on the part of** de la parte de; **to do one's part** cumplir con su obligación; **to look the part** vestir el cargo; **to take part in** tomar parte en; **to take the part of** tomar el partido de, defender; desempeñar el papel de; **part and parcel** parte esencial, elemento esencial, parte inseparable; *va* dividir, partir, separar; **to part company** separarse; **to part the hair** hacerse la raya; *vn* separarse; **to part from** separarse de, despedirse de; **to part with** deshacerse de, abandonar; despedirse de; *adj* parcial; *adv* parte, en parte

partake [pɑrˈtek] (*pret:* **-took;** *pp:* **-taken**) *va* compartir; comer; beber; *vn* participar; **to partake in** participar en; **to partake of** participar de; tener algo de; comer; beber; **will you partake?** ¿gusta Vd.?

parterre [pɑrˈtɛr] *s* parterre (*de jardín*); (theat.) anfiteatro debajo de la galería

parthenogenesis [ˌpɑrθɪnoˈdʒɛnɪsɪs] *s* (biol.) partenogénesis

parthenogenetic [ˌpɑrθɪnodʒɪˈnɛtɪk] *adj* partenogenético

Parthenon [ˈpɑrθɪnɑn] *s* Partenón

Parthia [ˈpɑrθɪə] *s* Partia

Parthian [ˈpɑrθɪən] *adj & s* parto

Parthian shot *s* la flecha del parto

partial [ˈpɑrʃəl] *adj* parcial; aficionado

partial eclipse *s* (astr.) eclipse parcial

partiality [ˌpɑrʃɪˈælɪtɪ] *s* (*pl:* **-ties**) parcialidad; afición

partially [ˈpɑrʃəlɪ] *adv* parcialmente

participant [pɑrˈtɪsɪpənt] *adj & s* partícipe

participate [pɑrˈtɪsɪpet] *vn* participar; **to participate in** participar en

participation [pɑrˌtɪsɪˈpeʃən] *s* participación

participator [pɑrˈtɪsɪˌpetər] *s* partícipe

participial [ˌpɑrtɪˈsɪpɪəl] *adj* participial

participially [ˌpɑrtɪˈsɪpɪəlɪ] *adv* a modo de participio

participle [ˈpɑrtɪsɪpəl] *s* (gram.) participio

particle [ˈpɑrtɪkəl] *s* partícula; (eccl. & gram.) partícula; (chem. & phys.) corpúsculo, partícula

parti-colored [ˈpɑrtɪˌkʌlərd] *adj* abigarrado, jaspeado; (fig.) diversificado, variado

particular [pərˈtɪkjələr] *adj* particular; difícil, exigente, quisquilloso; esmerado; minucioso, detallado; **that particular book** ese libro y no otro; *s* particular (*punto, asunto*); **in particular** en particular

particularity [pərˌtɪkjəˈlærɪtɪ] *s* (*pl:* **-ties**) particularidad; quisquillosidad; esmero; minuciosidad

particularization [pərˌtɪkjələrɪˈzeʃən] *s* particularización

particularize [pərˈtɪkjələraɪz] *va & vn* particularizar

particularly [pərˈtɪkjələrlɪ] *adv* particularmente; minuciosamente, detalladamente

partile [ˈpɑrtɪl] o [ˈpɑrtaɪl] *adj* (astrol.) partil

parting [ˈpɑrtɪŋ] *s* partida; separación, punto de separación; **to come to the parting of the ways** llegar al momento de separarse, no poder permanecer más tiempo asociados; *adj* de despedida; que declina (*dícese del día*)

parting strip *s* (carp.) listón separador; faja central o divisora (*del camino*)

partisan [ˈpɑrtɪzən] *adj & s* partidario, partidista; (mil.) partisano

partisanship [ˈpɑrtɪzənʃɪp] *s* parcialidad, partidismo

partition [pɑrˈtɪʃən] *s* partición, distribución; división; parte, porción; tabique; *va* repartir; dividir en cuartos, aposentos, etc.; tabicar

partitive [ˈpɑrtɪtɪv] *adj* partitivo; (gram.) partitivo; *s* (gram.) palabra partitiva, caso partitivo

partizan [ˈpɑrtɪzən] *adj & s* var. de **partisan**

partner [ˈpɑrtnər] *s* compañero; cónyuge (*marido o mujer*); pareja (*compañero o compañera en los bailes*); (com.) socio

partnership [ˈpɑrtnərʃɪp] *s* asociación; consorcio, vida en común; (com.) sociedad, asociación comercial

part of speech *s* (gram.) parte de la oración, parte del discurso

partook [pɑrˈtʊk] *pret de* **partake**

part owner *s* condueño

partridge [ˈpɑrtrɪdʒ] *s* (orn.) perdiz; (orn.) perdiz pardilla; (orn.) perdiz blanca; (orn.) colín de Virginia; (orn.) bonasa americana

partridgeberry [ˈpɑrtrɪdʒˌbɛrɪ] *s* (*pl:* **-ries**) (bot.) planta rubiácea norteamericana (*Mitchella repens*); (bot.) gaulteria del Canadá

part-time [ˈpɑrtˌtaɪm] *adj* por horas, parcial

parturient [pɑrˈtjʊrɪənt] o [pɑrˈtʊrɪənt] *adj* parturiente; prolífico, lleno (*p.ej., de ideas*)

parturition [ˌpɑrtjʊˈrɪʃən] o [ˌpɑrtʃʊˈrɪʃən] *s* parturición

part way *adv* en parte; parte de la distancia

party [ˈpɑrtɪ] *s* (*pl:* **-ties**) *s* convite, reunión, fiesta, tertulia, recepción; partida (*de campo, caza, pesca, etc.; de gente armada*); grupo; (pol.) partido; parte, cómplice, interesado; (law) parte; (coll.) persona, individuo; **to be a party to** tener parte en, estar interesado en; **to join the party** agregarse a la partida; afiliarse al partido; *adj* de partido; de gala

party boss *s* jefe de partido (comunista)

party-colored [ˈpɑrtɪˌkʌlərd] *adj* var. de **parti-colored**

party girl *s* chica de vida alegre

party-goer [ˈpɑrtɪˌgoər] *s* tertuliano; fiestero

party line *s* linde o lindero (*entre dos inmuebles*); (telp.) línea compartida; línea del partido (*política del partido comunista*)

party liner *s* secuaz del partido comunista

party politics *ssg* política de partido

party wall *s* medianería, pared medianera

party wire *s* (telp.) línea compartida

par value *s* (com.) valor nominal, valor a la par

parvenu [ˈpɑrvənju] o [ˈpɑrvənu] *adj & s* advenedizo

paschal [ˈpæskəl] *adj* pascual

paschal candle *s* (eccl.) cirio pascual

paschal lamb *s* cordero pascual

pasha [pəˈʃɑ] o [ˈpæʃə] *s* bajá

pasqueflower [ˈpæskˌflaʊər] *s* (bot.) pulsatila

pasquinade [ˌpæskwɪˈned] *s* pasquín; *va* pasquinar

pass. abr. de **passenger** y **passive**

pass [pæs] o [pɑs] *s* paso; pase (*permiso; billete gratuito; movimiento de las manos en el mesmerismo*); aprobación (*en un examen*); nota de aprobado ‖ (*pret:* **passed;** *pp:* **passed** o **past**) *va* pasar; pasar de largo (*una luz roja*); aprobar (*un proyecto de ley; un examen; a un alumno*); ser aprobado en (*un examen*); dejar atrás; cruzarse con; expresar (*una opinión*); pronunciar (*una sentencia*); dar (*la palabra*); dejar sin protestar; no pagar (*un dividendo*); evacuar; **to pass along** o **around** pasar de uno a otro; **to pass by** no fijarse en, pasar por alto, no hacer caso de; **to pass each other** cruzarse; **to pass off** colar, pasar, hacer aceptar (*p.ej., moneda falsa*); disimular (*p.ej., una ofensa con una risa*); **to pass on** pasar, transmitir; **to pass out** distribuir; **to pass over** omitir, pasar por alto; excusar; desdeñar; dejar sin protestar; postergar (*a un empleado*); **to pass over in silence** pasar en silencio; **to pass through** pasar por, hacer pasar por ‖ *vn* pasar; pasarse (*introducirse*); aprobar; **to bring to pass** llevar a cabo; **to come to pass** suceder; **to let pass** no hacer caso de; **to pass along** pasar de largo; pasar por (*p.ej., la calle*); **to pass as** pasar por; **to pass away** pasar; **to pass beyond** pasar de, ir más allá de; **to pass by** pasar, pasar de largo; pasar cerca de; **to pass for** pasar por; **to pass off** pasar (*una enfermedad, una tempestad, etc.*); tener lugar; **to pass on** pasar; formar juicio sobre; **to pass out** salir; (slang) desmayarse; **to pass over** atravesar, pasar por; **to pass over to** pasarse a (*p.ej., el enemigo*); **to pass through** atravesar, pasar por

passable [ˈpæsəbəl] o [ˈpɑsəbəl] *adj* pasadero; corriente (*moneda*); promulgable (*ley*)

passably [ˈpæsəblɪ] o [ˈpɑsəblɪ] *adv* pasaderamente

passacaglia [ˌpɑssɑˈkɑljɑ] *s* (mus.) pasacalle

passage [ˈpæsɪdʒ] *s* paso, pasaje; transcurso (*del tiempo*); lance, encuentro personal; intercambio (*p.ej., de confidencias*); evacuación (*del vientre*); (mus.) pasaje
passage at u **of arms** *s* combate, lucha
passageway [ˈpæsɪdʒ,we] *s* pasillo, pasadizo; callejón, pasaje
passant [ˈpæsənt] *adj* (her.) pasante
passbook [ˈpæs,bʊk] o [ˈpɑs,bʊk] *s* cartilla, libreta de banco
passementerie [pæsˈmɛntrɪ] *s* pasamanería
passenger [ˈpæsəndʒər] *s* pasajero
passenger car *s* (rail.) coche de viajeros; (aut.) coche de paseo o de turismo
passenger engine *s* (rail.) locomotora de viajeros
passenger miles *spl* (rail. & aer.) millas-pasajeros, pasajeros-milla
passenger pigeon *s* (orn.) paloma emigrante
passe partout [,pæs pɑrˈtu] *s* paspartú, marco de vidrio y cartón; papel engomado que sirve para pegar el vidrio al cartón; llave maestra
passer-by [ˈpæsərˈbaɪ] o [ˈpɑsərˈbaɪ] *s* (*pl:* **passers-by**) transeúnte
passifloraceous [,pæsɪfloˈreʃəs] *adj* (bot.) pasifloráceo
passing [ˈpæsɪŋ] o [ˈpɑsɪŋ] *adj* pasajero; corriente; de aprobado; *s* paso (*acción de pasar; trance de la muerte*); aprobación (*en un examen*); **in passing** de paso, al pasar; *adv* (archaic) muy, sumamente
passing bell *s* toque de difuntos
passion [ˈpæʃən] *s* pasión; (*cap.*) *s* (rel. & f.a.) Pasión; **to have a passion for** tener pasión por
passional [ˈpæʃənəl] *adj* pasional
passionate [ˈpæʃənɪt] *adj* apasionado; ardiente, vehemente; colérico
passionflower [ˈpæʃən,flaʊər] *s* (bot.) pasionaria (*planta*); granadilla (*flor*)
passionfruit [ˈpæʃən,frut] *s* granadilla
passionless [ˈpæʃənlɪs] *adj* sin pasión, frío
Passion Play *s* drama de la Pasión
Passion Sunday *s* domingo de lázaro o de pasión
Passion Week *s* semana de pasión
passive [ˈpæsɪv] *adj* pasivo; (gram.) pasivo; *s* (gram.) voz pasiva, verbo pasivo, construcción pasiva
passive immunity *s* (immun.) inmunidad pasiva
passively [ˈpæsɪvlɪ] *adv* pasivamente; (gram.) pasivamente
passive resistance *s* resistencia pasiva
passive voice *s* (gram.) voz pasiva
passivity [pæˈsɪvɪtɪ] *s* pasividad
passkey [ˈpæs,ki] o [ˈpɑs,ki] *s* llave de paso; llavín
Passover [ˈpæs,ovər] o [ˈpɑs,ovər] *s* pascua (*de los hebreos*)
passport [ˈpæs,port] o [ˈpɑs,port] *s* pasaporte; (fig.) pasaporte
password [ˈpæs,wʌrd] o [ˈpɑs,wʌrd] *s* santo y seña
past [pæst] o [pɑst] *adj* pasado; último; que fué, p.ej., **past president** presidente que fué; acabado, concluído; (gram.) pasado; **he has been here for some years past** está aquí desde hace algunos años; *adv* más allá; por delante; *prep* más allá de; más de; por delante de; fuera de; después de, p.ej., **past two o'clock** después de las dos; **past belief** increíble; **past cure** incurable; **past hope** sin esperanza; **past recovery** incurable, sin remedio; *s* pasado; (gram.) pasado; *pp de* **pass**
past absolute *s* (gram.) pretérito indefinido (*pasado absoluto*)
paste [pest] *s* pasta (*masa blanda para hacer pasteles, etc.*); engrudo; (mineral. & ceramics) pasta; *va* engrudar, pegar con engrudo; (slang) pegar (*golpear*); **to paste together** juntar con engrudo
pasteboard [ˈpest,bord] *s* cartón; (slang) naipe
pastel [pæsˈtɛl] o [ˈpæstɛl] *s* pastel (*lápiz*); pastel, pintura al pastel; matiz suave de un color; ensayo breve; *adj* claro, suave (*matiz*)
pastelist [ˈpæstɛlɪst] o [pæsˈtɛlɪst] *s* pastelista
paster [ˈpestər] *s* engrudador; papel engomado
pastern [ˈpæstərn] *s* cuartilla
pasteurization [,pæstərɪˈzeʃən] *s* pasterización
pasteurize [ˈpæstəraɪz] *va* pasterizar
pasteurized milk *s* leche pasterizada
pastil [ˈpæstɪl] o **pastille** [pæsˈtil] *s* pastilla; pastel (*lápiz; pasta de que se forman los pasteles*)
pastime [ˈpæs,taɪm] o [ˈpɑs,taɪm] *s* pasatiempo
past master *s* ex maestre, maestre que fué (*de una logia*); maestro sobresaliente, experto
pastor [ˈpæstər] o [ˈpɑstər] *s* pastor (*eclesiástico*)
pastoral [ˈpæstərəl] o [ˈpɑstərəl] *adj* pastoral; *s* (eccl. & mus.) pastoral; (lit.) pastoral (*drama*); (lit.) pastorela (*composición lírica*)
pastorale [,pæstəˈrɑlɪ] *s* (*pl:* **-li** [li] o **-les**) (mus.) pastoral
pastorally [ˈpæstərəlɪ] o [ˈpɑstərəlɪ] *adv* pastoralmente, pastorilmente
pastorate [ˈpæstərɪt] o [ˈpɑstərɪt] *s* rectorado, curato; clero, pastores
pastose [pæsˈtos] o [ˈpæstos] *adj* (paint.) pastoso
pastourelle [,pɑs,tʊˈrɛl] *s* (lit.) pastorela
past participle *s* (gram.) participio pasivo o de pretérito
past perfect *s* (gram.) pluscuamperfecto
pastry [ˈpestrɪ] *s* (*pl:* **-tries**) pastelería
pastry cook *s* pastelero, repostero
pastry shop *s* pastelería
pastry tube *s* carretilla, pintadera
pasturage [ˈpæstʃərɪdʒ] o [ˈpɑstʃərɪdʒ] *s* pasto (*pasturaje, pastura, pastoreo*)
pasture [ˈpæstʃər] o [ˈpɑstʃər] *s* pasto, pastura, dehesa; *va* apacentar, pastorear; pacer
pasty [ˈpestɪ] *adj* (*comp:* **-ier**; *super:* **-iest**) pastoso; flojo, fofo, pálido; [ˈpæstɪ] o [ˈpɑstɪ] *s* (*pl:* **-ies**) (Brit.) pastel de carne o pescado
pat [pæt] *adj* bueno, apto; *adv* a propósito; firme; **to have** o **to know pat** (coll.) saber al dedillo; **to stand pat** (coll.) mantenerse firme; *s* golpecito, palmadita; ruido de pasos ligeros; pastelillo (*p.ej., de mantequilla*); (*cap.*) *s* nombre abreviado de **Patricia**; (*l.c.*) (*pret & pp:* **patted**; *ger:* **patting**) *va* dar golpecitos a, dar palmaditas a; formar a golpecitos de la mano; acariciar con la mano; **to pat on the back** elogiar, cumplimentar; *vn* andar con un trotecito ligero
patagium [pəˈtedʒɪəm] *s* (*pl:* **-a** [ə]) (zool.) patagio
Patagonian [,pætəˈgonɪən] *adj* & *s* patagón
patch [pætʃ] *s* remiendo; parche; terreno, pedazo de terreno; mancha; lunar postizo; *va* remendar; **to patch up** componer (*una desavenencia*); arreglar o componer lo mejor posible (*una cosa descompuesta*); chafallar, hacer aprisa y mal
patchouli [ˈpætʃʊlɪ] o [pəˈtʃulɪ] *s* (bot.) pachulí
patch pocket *s* bolsillo de parche
patch test *s* (med.) alergodiagnóstico con parches de lino o papel secante
patchwork [ˈpætʃ,wʌrk] *s* labor u obra de retacitos; chapucería; cuadros (*p.ej., de sembrados y bosques vistos desde un avión*)
patchwork quilt *s* colcha de retacitos
patchy [ˈpætʃɪ] *adj* (*comp:* **-ier**; *super:* **-iest**) muy remendado; desigual, irregular
pate [pet] *s* mollera
pâté [pɑˈte] *s* pastel de carne o pescado; pasta de carne
pâté de foie gras [də fwɑ ˈgrɑ] *s* pasta o pastelillo de hígado de ganso
patella [pəˈtɛlə] *s* (*pl:* **-las** o **-lae** [li]) (anat.) rótula, patela; (archeol.) patela; (bot.) patélula; (zool.) patela
patellar [pəˈtɛlər] *adj* (anat.) rotular, rotuliano, patelar
patellar reflex *s* (med.) reflejo rotuliano o patelar
paten [ˈpætən] *s* platillo u hoja de metal; (eccl.) patena
patency [ˈpetənsɪ] o [ˈpætənsɪ] *s* evidencia, claridad
patent [ˈpetənt] o [ˈpætənt] *adj* patente; abierto; [ˈpætənt] *adj* patentado; de patente; *s* patente, patente de invención; propiedad industrial; **to take out a patent** obtener una pa-

tente; **patent applied for** se ha solicitado patente; *va* patentar
patent agent ['pætənt] *s* agente de patentes
patentee [,pætən'ti] *s* poseedor de patente
patent law ['pætənt] *s* ley de patentes
patent leather ['pætənt] *s* charol
patently ['petəntlɪ] o ['pætəntlɪ] *adv* patentemente; abiertamente
patent medicine ['pætənt] *s* medicamento de patente, específico
patent office ['pætənt] *s* oficina de patentes
patent rights ['pætənt] *s* derechos de patente
paterfamilias [,petərfə'mɪlɪəs] *s* (*pl:* **patresfamilias** [,petrizfə'mɪlɪəs]) *s* cabeza de familia; (Roman law) páter familias
paternal [pə'tʌrnəl] *adj* paterno; paternal (*propio del cariño de padre*)
paternalism [pə'tʌrnəlɪzəm] *s* paternalismo
paternalistic [pə,tʌrnə'lɪstɪk] *adj* paternal
paternity [pə'tʌrnɪtɪ] *s* paternidad
paternoster ['petər'nɑstər] o ['pætər'nɑstər] *s* padrenuestro, paternóster
path [pæθ] o [pɑθ] *s* senda, sendero; curso, trayectoria; órbita (*de un astro*)
pathetic [pə'θɛtɪk] o **pathetical** [pə'θɛtɪkəl] *adj* patético
pathetically [pə'θɛtɪkəlɪ] *adv* patéticamente
pathetic fallacy *s* atribución de los sentimientos humanos a la naturaleza inanimada
pathfinder ['pæθ,faɪndər] o ['pɑθ,faɪndər] *s* baquiano; explorador
pathless ['pæθlɪs] o ['pɑθlɪs] *adj* sin caminos, no hollado, desconocido
pathogenesis [,pæθə'dʒɛnɪsɪs] o **pathogeny** [pə'θɑdʒɪnɪ] *s* patogénesis o patogenia
pathogenic [,pæθə'dʒɛnɪk] *adj* patógeno (*que produce enfermedades*); patogénico
pathogenic organism *s* (biol.) organismo patógeno
pathologic [,pæθə'lɑdʒɪk] o **pathological** [,pæθə'lɑdʒɪkəl] *adj* patológico
pathologist [pə'θɑlədʒɪst] *s* patólogo
pathology [pə'θɑlədʒɪ] *s* (*pl:* **-gies**) patología
pathos ['peθɑs] *s* patetismo
pathway ['pæθ,we] o ['pɑθ,we] *s* var. de **path**
patience ['peʃəns] *s* paciencia; solitario (*juego de naipes*); **to get out of patience** perder la paciencia
patient ['peʃənt] *adj* paciente; *s* paciente, enfermo; (gram.) paciente
patin ['pætən] *s* var. de **paten**
patina ['pætɪnə] *s* pátina
patine ['pætən] *s* var. de **paten**
patio ['pɑtɪo] *s* (*pl:* **-os**) patio; (metal.) patio, incorporadero
patio process *s* (metal.) método del patio
patois ['pætwɑ] *s* (*pl:* **patois** ['pætwɑz]) patuá o patués
patriarch ['petrɪɑrk] *s* patriarca
patriarchal [,petrɪ'ɑrkəl] *adj* patriarcal
patriarchate ['petrɪɑrkɪt] *s* patriarcado
patriarchy ['petrɪɑrkɪ] *s* (*pl:* **-chies**) patriarcado
patrician [pə'trɪʃən] *adj & s* patricio
patriciate [pə'trɪʃɪet] *s* patriciado
patricidal [,pætrɪ'saɪdəl] *adj* parricida
patricide ['pætrɪsaɪd] *s* parricidio (*acción*); parricida (*persona*)
Patrick ['pætrɪk] *s* Patricio
patrimonial [,pætrɪ'monɪəl] *adj* patrimonial
patrimony ['pætrɪ,monɪ] *s* (*pl:* **-nies**) patrimonio
patriot ['petrɪət] o ['pætrɪət] *s* patriota
patriotic [,petrɪ'ɑtɪk] o [,pætrɪ'ɑtɪk] *adj* patriótico
patriotically [,petrɪ'ɑtɪkəlɪ] o [,pætrɪ'ɑtɪkəlɪ] *adv* patrióticamente
patriotism ['petrɪətɪzəm] o ['pætrɪətɪzəm] *s* patriotismo
patristic [pə'trɪstɪk] *adj* patrístico; **patristics** *ssg* patrística
Patroclus [pə'trokləs] *s* (myth.) Patroclo
patrol [pə'trol] *s* ronda; (aer., mil. & nav.) patrulla; (*pret & pp:* **-trolled;** *ger:* **-trolling**) *va & vn* rondar; (aer., mil. & nav.) patrullar
patrolman [pə'trolmən] *s* (*pl:* **-men**) rondador, guardia municipal, vigilante de policía
patrology [pə'trɑlədʒɪ] *s* patrología
patrol wagon *s* camión de policía, coche de patrulla
patron ['petrən] o ['pætrən] *adj* tutelar, patrocinador; *s* parroquiano; patrocinador, patrono; (eccl.) patrono
patronage ['petrənɪdʒ] o ['pætrənɪdʒ] *s* trato, clientela; patrocinio; aire protector; prebendas, favores políticos; prestigio político
patronal ['petrənəl] o ['pætrənəl] *adj* patronal
patroness ['petrənɪs] o ['pætrənɪs] *s* parroquiana; patrocinadora; madrina; (eccl.) santa patrona
patronize ['petrənaɪz] o ['pætrənaɪz] *va* ser parroquiano de (*un tendero*); comprar de costumbre en (*una tienda*); patrocinar; tratar con aire protector
patronizing ['petrə,naɪzɪŋ] o ['pætrə,naɪzɪŋ] *adj* que trata con aire protector a inferiores; protector (*aire, conducta, etc.*)
patron saint *s* patrón, santo titular
patronymic [,pætrə'nɪmɪk] *adj & s* patronímico
patroon [pə'trun] *s* encomendero holandés en las colonias norteamericanas
patten ['pætən] *s* almadreña, chanclo, zueco
patter ['pætər] *s* golpeteo (*p.ej., de las pisaditas de un niño*); chapaleteo (*de la lluvia*); charla, parloteo; jerga (*lenguaje especial*); *va* repetir rápidamente y sin pensar; murmurar (*p.ej., el padrenuestro*); *vn* golpetear; charlar, parlotear
pattern ['pætərn] *s* patrón, modelo; *va* modelar; **to pattern after** ajustar al modelo de; **to pattern oneself after** imitar, seguir en todo el ejemplo de
patternmaker ['pætərn,mekər] *s* carpintero modelista
patternmaking ['pætərn,mekɪŋ] *s* carpintería de modelos, modelaje
patty ['pætɪ] *s* (*pl:* **-ties**) pastelito; pastilla
patty pan *s* tortera para hacer pastelitos
P.A.U. abr. de **Pan American Union**
paucity ['pɔsɪtɪ] *s* corto número; falta, escasez, insuficiencia
Paul [pɔl] *s* Pablo
pauldron ['pɔldrən] *s* (arm.) hombrera
Pauline ['pɔlaɪn] *adj* paulino; [pɔ'lin] *s* Paulina
Paulinist ['pɔlɪnɪst] *adj & s* paulinista
Paul Jones [dʒonz] *s* bolanchera (*danza*)
paulownia [pɔ'lonɪə] *s* (bot.) paulonia
paunch [pɔntʃ] *s* panza; (zool.) panza (*de los rumiantes*)
paunchy ['pɔntʃɪ] *adj* panzudo
pauper ['pɔpər] *s* pobre, indigente
pauperism ['pɔpərɪzəm] *s* pauperismo
pauperize ['pɔpəraɪz] *va* depauperar
pause [pɔz] *s* pausa; (gram. & mus.) pausa; **to give pause to** dar que pensar a; *vn* hacer pausa, detenerse brevemente; vacilar
pavan o **pavane** ['pævən] *s* pavana (*danza y música*)
pave [pev] *va* pavimentar; **to pave the way for** preparar el terreno a, abrir el camino a
pavement ['pevmənt] *s* pavimento
pavilion [pə'vɪljən] *s* pabellón; (anat. & arch.) pabellón; *va* cobijar o proveer de pabellón
paving ['pevɪŋ] *s* pavimentación; pavimento
paving block *s* adoquín
paw [pɔ] *s* pata; garra, zarpa; (coll.) mano (*del hombre*); *va* dar zarpazos a, restregar con las uñas; golpear (*el suelo los caballos*); (coll.) manosear; (coll.) sobar (*manosear con demasiada familiaridad*); *vn* piafar (*el caballo*)
pawl [pɔl] *s* (mach.) trinquete; (naut.) linguete
pawl bitt *s* (naut.) bita de linguete
pawn [pɔn] *s* peón (*de ajedrez*); (fig.) instrumento (*en manos de otra persona*); (fig.) víctima; prenda; **in pawn** en prenda; *va* empeñar, dar en prenda
pawnbroker ['pɔn,brokər] *s* prestamista
pawnshop ['pɔn,ʃɑp] *s* empeño, casa de empeños, monte de piedad
pawn ticket *s* papeleta de empeño
pawpaw ['pɔpɔ] *s* var. de **papaw**
pax [pæks] *s* (eccl.) paz (*ceremonia y patena*)
pay [pe] *s* paga, sueldo; galardón, recompensa; fuente de sueldos; castigo merecido; **bad pay** mala paga (*persona*); **good pay** buena paga (*persona*); **in the pay of** al servicio de; **poor pay** mala paga (*persona*) ‖ (*pret & pp:* **paid**)

va pagar; prestar o poner (*atención*); dar (*cumplidos*); dar (*dinero una actividad comercial*); dar dinero a, dar grandes ingresos a, ser provechoso a; pagar en la misma moneda, pagar con creces; sufrir (*el castigo de una ofensa*); hacer (*una visita*); cubrir (*los gastos*); **to pay back** devolver; pagar en la misma moneda; **to pay for** pagar, p.ej., **I will pay him for it** se lo pagaré; recompensar, p.ej., **I will pay him well for it** se lo recompensaré muy bien; **to pay off** pagar y despedir (*a un empleado*); pagar todo lo adeudado a; vengarse de; redimir (*una hipoteca*); **to pay out** desembolsar ‖ *vn* pagar; ser provechoso, valer la pena; (naut.) virar a sotavento; **to pay for** pagar, pagar por (*una cosa*); **to pay up** pagar todo lo adeudado; **pay as you enter** pague a la entrada; **pay as you go** pagar el impuesto de utilidades con descuentos anticipados; **pay as you leave** pague a la salida ‖ (*pret & pp:* **payed**) *va* (naut.) ir dando (*cuerda*); **to pay away** u **out** (naut.) ir dando (*cuerda*)

payable [ˈpeəbəl] *adj* pagadero

pay boost *s* (coll.) aumento de salario

paycheck [ˈpe,tʃək] *s* cheque en pago del sueldo; sueldo

payday [ˈpe,de] *s* día de pago

pay dirt *s* (min.) grava provechosa, terreno aurífero

payee [peˈi] *s* (com.) portador, tenedor (*p.ej., de un giro*)

pay envelope *s* sobre con el jornal; jornal, salario

payer [ˈpeər] *s* pagador

paying teller *s* pagador (*de un banco*)

pay load *s* carga útil

paymaster [ˈpe,mæstər] o [ˈpe,mɑstər] *s* pagador, contador, habilitado

paymaster's office *s* pagaduría

payment [ˈpemənt] *s* pago; castigo; **to make payment** efectuar el pago

paynim o **Paynim** [ˈpenɪm] *adj & s* (archaic) gentil, pagano; (archaic) sarraceno, mahometano

pay-off [ˈpe,ɔf] o [ˈpe,ɑf] *s* paga; (coll.) arreglo, resultado

payola [peˈolə] *s* (slang) pago clandestino por un servicio comercial, pago por un servicio ilícito

pay roll *s* nómina, hoja de paga; paga (*de todos los empleados u obreros*)

pay station *s* teléfono público

payt. abr. de **payment**

pc. abr. de **piece**

p.c. abr. de **percent** y **post card**

pd. abr. de **paid**

p.d. abr. de **per diem** y **potential difference**

P.D. abr. de **Police Department** y **per diem**

P.E. abr. de **Protestant Episcopal**

pea [pi] *s* (bot.) guisante (*planta y semilla*); **as like as two peas** parecidos como dos gotas de agua

peace [pis] *s* paz; **to hold** o **keep one's peace** callar; **to keep the peace** mantener la paz; **to make peace with** hacer las paces con

peaceable [ˈpisəbəl] *adj* pacífico

peaceful [ˈpisfəl] *adj* tranquilo, pacífico

peaceful penetration *s* (pol.) penetración pacífica

peace-loving [ˈpisˈlʌvɪŋ] *adj* amante de la paz

peacemaker [ˈpis,mekər] *s* pacificador, iris de paz

peace offensive *s* ofensiva de paz

peace offering *s* sacrificio propiciatorio; prenda de paz

peace officer *s* agente del orden público, guardia municipal

peace of mind *s* serenidad del espíritu

peace pipe *s* pipa ceremonial (*de los pieles rojas*)

peach [pitʃ] *s* (bot.) melocotonero, duraznero; melocotón, durazno (*fruto*); (slang) persona o cosa admirables; (slang) real moza; color de melocotón; *adj* de color de melocotón; *vn* (slang) cantar; **to peach on** (slang) denunciar, hacerse delator de

peachy [ˈpitʃɪ] *adj* (*comp:* **-ier**; *super:* **-iest**) de melocotón; (slang) estupendo, magnífico

pea coal *s* antracita de ½ a 1 y 1/16 pulgada

peacock [ˈpi,kɑk] *s* (orn.) pavo real, pavón; (fig.) pinturero; (*cap.*) *s* (astr.) Pavón

peacock blue *s* verde azulado

peacock butterfly *s* (ent.) ojo de pavo real (*Vanessa io*)

peacock fish *s* (ichth.) papagayo, loro de mar

peafowl [ˈpi,faul] *s* (orn.) pavo real o pava real

pea green *s* verde claro

peahen [ˈpi,hɛn] *s* (orn.) pava real

pea jacket *s* chaqueta de marinero

peak [pik] *s* cima, cumbre, pico; punta, extremo; máximo, punto culminante; visera (*de gorra*); cresta (*de una curva*); (elec.) pico; (naut). penol (*de la verga*); (naut.) pico (*de vela*); *va* (naut.) enarbolar, levantar (*una verga contra el mástil*)

peaked [pikt] *adj* afilado (*dícese de la nariz, el rostro, etc.*); [ˈpikɪd] *adj* enjuto, delgado

peak factor *s* (elec.) factor de punta, factor de cresta

peak load *s* (elec.) carga de punta

peak traffic *s* afluencia máxima, movimiento máximo

peal [pil] *s* fragor, estruendo; repique (*de campanas*); juego de campanas; *va* lanzar (*un mensaje*) con repiqueteo sonoro; *vn* repicar; resonar

peal of laughter *s* carcajada

peal of thunder *s* trueno

peanut [ˈpi,nʌt] *s* (bot.) cacahuete, aráquida, maní (*planta y fruto*)

peanut brittle *s* guirlache o crocante de cacahuetes

peanut butter *s* manteca de cacahuete

peanut candy *s* var. de **peanut brittle**

peanut oil *s* aceite de cacahuete

peanut vendor *s* cacahuetero, manicero

pear [pɛr] *s* (bot.) peral; pera (*fruto*)

pearl [pʌrl] *s* margarita, perla; color de perla; flujo o murmullo (*del agua al correr*); (fig.) perla (*persona o cosa*); (pharm. & f.a.) perla; inversión de la puntada al tejer; guarnición rizada de tela, encaje o cinta; **to cast pearls before swine** echar margaritas a los cerdos o los puercos; *adj* perlino, aperlado; granoso, granular; *va* aljofarar; tejer invirtiendo la puntada; bordar u orlar con guarnición rizada; *vn* aljofararse; pescar perlas

pearlash [ˈpʌrl,æʃ] *s* cenizas de perla

pearl barley *s* cebada perlada

pearl button *s* botón de madreperla

pearl gray *s* color de perla, gris de perla

pearl oyster *s* (zool.) madreperla, ostra perlera

pearly [ˈpʌrlɪ] *adj* (*comp:* **-ier**; *super:* **-iest**) aperlado; nacarado; aljofarado

pearly nautilus *s* (zool.) nautilo

pearmain [ˈpɛrmen] *s* (bot.) pero

pear-shaped [ˈpɛr,ʃept] *adj* piriforme

peart [pɪrt] *adj* (dial.) alegre, jovial, vivo

peasant [ˈpɛzənt] *adj & s* campesino, rústico, labrador

peasantry [ˈpɛzəntrɪ] *s* paisanaje, gente del campo

peascod o **peasecod** [ˈpiz,kɑd] *s* vaina de los guisantes

peashooter [ˈpi,ʃutər] *s* cerbatana, bodoquera

pea soup *s* sopa de guisantes, puré de guisantes; (coll.) neblina espesa y amarillenta

peat [pit] *s* turba

peat bog *s* turbal o turbera

peaty [ˈpitɪ] *adj* turboso

peavey [ˈpivɪ] *s* palanca puntiaguda con gancho

peavy [ˈpivɪ] *s* (*pl:* **-vies**) var. de **peavey**

pebble [ˈpɛbəl] *s* china, guija; *va* agranelar (*cuero*)

pebbly [ˈpɛblɪ] *adj* guijoso

pecan [pɪˈkɑn] o [pɪˈkæn] *s* (bot.) pacana, nuez encarcelada (*árbol y fruto*)

peccadillo [,pɛkəˈdɪlo] *s* (*pl:* **-loes** o **-los**) pecadillo, pecado leve

peccary [ˈpɛkərɪ] *s* (*pl:* **-ries**) (zool.) pecarí, baquira

peck [pɛk] *s* medida de áridos (*nueve litros*); gran cantidad, montón; picotazo; (coll.) beso dado de mala gana; **a peck of trouble** mil dificultades, la mar de disgustos; *va* picotear; **to peck holes in** horadar a picotazos; *vn* picotear; (coll.) rezongar; (coll.) comer melin-

drosamente; **to peck at** (coll.) comer melindrosamente; querer picar, hacer un amago a (*otra ave*) con el pico; censurar constantemente
pecker ['pɛkər] *s* picoteador; rezongador; persona que come melindrosamente
pecten ['pɛktən] *s* (zool.) pectén, peine
pectin ['pɛktɪn] *s* (chem.) pectina
pectinate ['pɛktɪnet] *adj* pectinado
pectineus [pɛk'tɪnɪəs] *s* (anat.) pectíneo
pectinibranchian [,pɛktɪnɪ'bræŋkɪən] *adj* (zool.) pectinibranquio
pectoral ['pɛktərəl] *adj* pectoral; *s* pectoral; (pharm.) pectoral
pectoral cross *s* (eccl.) pectoral
peculate ['pɛkjəlet] *va & vn* malversar
peculation [,pɛkjə'leʃən] *s* peculado
peculator ['pɛkjə,letər] *s* malversador
peculiar [pɪ'kjuljər] *adj* peculiar; singular; excéntrico
peculiarity [pɪ,kjulɪ'ærɪtɪ] *s* (*pl:* **-ties**) peculiaridad; singularidad; excentricidad, rasgo característico
peculiarly [pɪ'kjuljərlɪ] *adv* peculiarmente; singularmente; excéntricamente
pecuniary [pɪ'kjunɪ,ɛrɪ] *adj* pecuniario
pedagog ['pɛdəgɑg] *s* var. de **pedagogue**
pedagogic [,pɛdə'gɑdʒɪk] o **pedagogical** [,pɛdə'gɑdʒɪkəl] *adj* pedagógico
pedagogically [,pɛdə'gɑdʒɪkəlɪ] *adv* pedagógicamente
pedagogue ['pɛdəgɑg] *s* pedagogo; dómine, pedante
pedagogy ['pɛdə,godʒɪ] o ['pɛdə,gɑdʒɪ] *s* pedagogía
pedal ['pɛdəl] o ['pidəl] *adj* del pie; ['pɛdəl] *s* pedal; (mus.) pedal; (*pret & pp:* **-aled** o **-alled;** *ger:* **-aling** o **-alling**) *va* impulsar pedaleando; *vn* pedalear
pedal board *s* (mus.) pedalero
pedal brake *s* freno de pedal, freno de pie
pedal keyboard *s* (mus.) pedalero, teclado pedalero
pedant ['pɛdənt] *s* pedante
pedantic [pɪ'dæntɪk] *adj* pedantesco
pedantically [pɪ'dæntɪkəlɪ] *adv* pedantescamente
pedantry ['pɛdəntrɪ] *s* (*pl:* **-ries**) pedantería
pedate ['pɛdet] *adj* (bot.) pedato
peddle ['pɛdəl] *va* ir vendiendo de puerta en puerta; traer y llevar (*chismes*); vender (*favores*); *vn* ser buhonero, vender menudencias por las calles
peddler ['pɛdlər] *s* buhonero
pederast ['pɛdəræst] o ['pidəræst] *s* pederasta
pederasty ['pɛdə,ræstɪ] o ['pidə,ræstɪ] *s* pederastia
pedestal ['pɛdɪstəl] *s* pedestal; (mus.) cubeta (*del arpa*)
pedestal box *s* (mach.) caja de engrase
pedestal lamp *s* lámpara de pie
pedestal table *s* velador
pedestrian [pɪ'dɛstrɪən] *adj* pedestre; (fig.) pedestre; *s* peatón
pedestrianism [pɪ'dɛstrɪənɪzəm] *s* pedestrismo
pediatric [,pidɪ'ætrɪk] o [,pɛdɪ'ætrɪk] *adj* pediátrico; **pediatrics** *ssg* pediatría
pediatrician [,pidɪə'trɪʃən] o [,pɛdɪə'trɪʃən] *s* pediatra
pedicel ['pɛdɪsəl] *s* (bot. & zool.) pedicelo
pedicle ['pɛdɪkəl] *s* (bot.) pedículo
pedicular [pɪ'dɪkjələr] *adj* pedicular
pedicure ['pɛdikjʊr] *s* pedicuro (*persona*); quiropedia
pedigree ['pɛdɪgri] *s* árbol genealógico, linaje; ascendencia
pedigreed ['pɛdɪgrid] *adj* de pura raza
pediment ['pɛdɪmənt] *s* (arch.) frontón
pedipalpus [,pɛdɪ'pælpəs] *s* (*pl:* **-pi** [paɪ]) (zool.) pedipalpo
pedlar ['pɛdlər] *s* var. de **peddler**
pedometer [pɪ'dɑmɪtər] *s* podómetro
peduncle [pɪ'dʌŋkəl] *s* (anat., bot. & zool.) pedúnculo
peduncular [pɪ'dʌŋkjələr] *adj* peduncular
pedunculate [pɪ'dʌŋkjəlet] *adj* pedunculado
peek [pik] *s* mirada rápida y furtiva; **to take a peek at** echar una mirada rápida y furtiva a; *vn* mirar, mirar a hurtadillas
peel [pil] *s* cáscara, corteza, hollejo, telilla; pala (*de horno*); (print.) colgador; **a piece of lemon peel** una cascarita de limón; *va* pelar; **to keep one's eyes peeled** (slang) estar ojo alerta; **to peel off** pelar, arrancar pelando; *vn* pelarse; desconcharse; (slang) desnudarse
peeling ['pilɪŋ] *s* peladura
peen [pin] *s* peña (*del martillo*)
peep [pip] *s* mirada por una rendija o a hurtadillas; rendija (*por la cual se mira*); pío (*de la cría del ave*); **at the peep of day** al despuntar el día; *va* asomar; **to peep out** asomar; descubrir (*un secreto*); *vn* mirar por una rendija o a hurtadillas; asomar; piar (*los pollos*)
peeper ['pipər] *s* atisbador, mirador; mirón; (coll.) ojo; (zool.) rubeta
peephole ['pip,hol] *s* atisbadero, mirilla, ventanillo
Peeping Tom *s* el mirón Tom; mirón
peep show *s* mundonuevo; (slang) vistas sicalípticas
peer [pɪr] *s* par; *vn* mirar fijando la vista de cerca; asomar, aparecer; **to peer at** mirar con fijeza, mirar con ojos de miope; **to peer into** mirar hacia lo interior de, mirar lo que hay dentro de
peerage ['pɪrɪdʒ] *s* paría; guía de la nobleza
peeress ['pɪrɪs] *s* paresa
peerless ['pɪrlɪs] *adj* sin par, incomparable
peeve [piv] *s* cojijo; *va* (coll.) enojar, irritar
peevish ['pivɪʃ] *adj* cojijoso, displicente
peevishness ['pivɪʃnɪs] *s* displicencia, quejumbre
peg [pɛg] *s* clavija, claveta, estaquilla; escarpia, colgador; grado; (Brit.) trago, traguito; **to take down a peg** bajar los humos a, obligar a guardar más moderación o más cortesía; (*pret & pp:* **pegged;** *ger:* **pegging**) *va* enclavijar; marcar o señalar con clavijas; (com.) fijar, estabilizar (*precios*); (coll.) lanzar (*una pelota*); (surv.) jalonar; *vn* trabajar con ahinco; **to peg away** afanarse, trabajar con ahinco; **to peg away at** afanarse en
Pegasus ['pɛgəsəs] *s* (myth. & astr.) Pegaso
pegbox ['pɛg,bɑks] *s* (mus.) clavijero (*p.ej., de la guitarra*)
Peggy ['pɛgɪ] *s* nombre abreviado de **Margaret**
peg ladder *s* escalera de papagayo
peg leg *s* pata de palo; (slang) pata de palo (*persona*)
pegmatite ['pɛgmətaɪt] *s* (petrog.) pegmatita
peg top *s* peonza; **peg tops** *spl* pantalones anchos de caderas y perniles ajustados
peg-top ['pɛg,tɑp] *adj* en forma de peonza
P.E.I. abr. de **Prince Edward Island**
peignoir [pen'wɑr] o ['penwɑr] *s* peinador, bata de señora
Peiping ['pe'pɪŋ] *s* Peipín
Peiraeus [paɪ'riəs] *s* el Pireo
pejorative ['pidʒə,retɪv] o [pɪ'dʒɔrətɪv] *adj* (gram.) despectivo, peyorativo
pekin ['pi'kɪn] *s* pequín; (*cap.*) *s* Pequín
Pekinese [,pikɪ'niz] *adj* pekinés; *s* (*pl:* **-ese**) pekinés (*natural de Pequín; perro*)
Pekingese [,pikɪŋ'iz] *adj & s* var. de **Pekinese**
pekoe ['pico] *s* té de Pékoë
pelage ['pɛlɪdʒ] *s* pelaje
pelagic [pɪ'lædʒɪk] *adj* pelágico
Pelasgian [pɪ'læzdʒɪən] *adj & s* pelasgo
Pelée, Mount [pə'le] el monte Pelado
pelerine [,pɛlə'rin] *s* esclavina, pelerina
Peleus ['piljus] o ['pilɪəs] *s* (myth.) Peleo
pelf [pɛlf] *s* dinero mal ganado, riquezas mal ganadas
pelican ['pɛlɪkən] *s* (orn.) pelícano
Pelion ['pilɪən] *s* el Pelión; **to heap Pelion upon Ossa** levantar el Pelión sobre el Osa, superponer el Pelión al Osa
pelisse [pə'lis] *s* pelliza
pellagra [pə'legrə] o [pə'lægrə] *s* (path.) pelagra
pellagrous [pə'legrəs] o [pə'lægrəs] *adj* pelagroso
pellet ['pɛlɪt] *s* pelotilla, pella; píldora; bolita; perdigón
pellicle ['pɛlɪkəl] *s* película
pellicular [pə'lɪkjələr] *adj* pelicular

pellitory ['pelɪ,torɪ] *s* (*pl:* **-ries**) (bot. & pharm.) pelitre; (bot.) caracolera
pell-mell ['pel'mel] *adj* confuso, tumultuoso; *adv* atropelladamente; **to run pell-mell** salir pitando, salvarse por pies; *s* batahola, confusión, desorden
pellucid [pə'lusɪd] *adj* diáfano; claro, evidente
Peloponnesian [,peləpə'niʃən] o [,peləpə'niʒən] *adj & s* peloponense
Peloponnesian War *s* guerra del Peloponeso
Peloponnesos o **Peloponnesus** [,peləpə'nisəs] *s* Peloponeso
Pelops ['pilɑps] *s* (myth.) Pélope
pelota [pe'lotə] *s* (sport) pelota vasca
pelt [pelt] *s* pellejo; golpe violento; golpeo violento; velocidad; (hum.) pellejo (*de una persona*); *va* golpear violentamente; apedrear; tirar; *vn* golpear violentamente; caer con fuerza (*el granizo, la lluvia, etc.*); apresurarse
peltry ['peltrɪ] *s* (*pl:* **-ries**) pellejería, corambre; pellejo
pelvic ['pelvɪk] *adj* pelviano
pelvimeter [pel'vɪmɪtər] *s* pelvímetro
pelvis ['pelvɪs] *s* (*pl:* **-ves** [viz]) (anat.) pelvis
pemmican ['pemɪkən] *s* penmicán
pemphigus ['pemfɪgəs] o [pem'faɪgəs] *s* (path.) pénfigo
pen. abr. de **peninsula**
pen [pen] *s* pluma; corral, redil; (fig.) pluma; **to live by one's pen** vivir de la pluma; (*pret & pp:* **penned;** *ger:* **penning**) *va* escribir (*con pluma*); redactar; (*pret & pp:* **penned** o **pent;** *ger:* **penning**) *va* acorralar, encerrar
penal ['pinəl] *adj* penal; penable
penal code *s* código penal
penalize ['pinəlaɪz] o ['penəlaɪz] *va* penar (*un acto, a una persona*); (sport) aplicar una sanción a
penal servitude *s* pena de trabajos forzados, pena de reclusión
penalty ['penəltɪ] *s* (*pl:* **-ties**) pena; (sport) sanción (*que se aplica a ciertas faltas del juego*); (law) penalidad; recargo (*que paga el contribuyente moroso*); **under penalty of** so pena de
penance ['penəns] *s* penitencia; **to do penance** hacer penitencia
penates o **Penates** [pe'netiz] *spl* penates
pence [pens] *spl* peniques
penchant ['penʃənt] *s* afición, inclinación, tendencia
pencil ['pensəl] *s* lápiz; lápiz de color; pincel fino; (fig.) pincel (*modo de pintar*); haz (*de rayos, de luz, etc.*); (*pret & pp:* **-ciled** o **-cilled;** *ger:* **-ciling** o **-cilling**) *va* escribir con lápiz, marcar con lápiz; (med.) pincelar
pencil sharpener *s* sacapuntas, afilalápices
pendant o **pendent** ['pendənt] *adj* pendiente; sobresaliente; (fig.) pendiente; *s* pinjante, medallón; pendiente (*arete*); araña (*de luces*); (arch.) pinjante
pendentive [pen'dentɪv] *s* (arch.) pechina
pending ['pendɪŋ] *adj* pendiente; *prep* hasta; durante
pendragon o **Pendragon** [pen'drægən] *s* jefe supremo de los antiguos británicos
pendulous ['pendʒələs] *adj* colgante, pendiente; oscilante
pendulum ['pendʒələm] o ['pendjələm] *s* péndulo; péndola (*de un reloj*)
pendulum bob *s* lenteja
Penelope [pɪ'neləpɪ] *s* (myth.) Penélope
peneplain ['pinɪ,plen] *s* (geol.) penillanura
penetrability [,penɪtrə'bɪlɪtɪ] *s* penetrabilidad
penetrable ['penɪtrəbəl] *adj* penetrable
penetrate ['penɪtret] *va & vn* penetrar
penetrating ['penɪ,tretɪŋ] *adj* penetrante; (fig.) penetrante
penetration [,penɪ'treʃən] *s* penetración; (fig.) penetración
penetrative ['penɪ,tretɪv] *adj* penetrante, penetrativo
penguin ['peŋgwɪn] *s* (orn.) pingüino, pájaro bobo
penholder ['pen,holdər] *s* portaplumas (*mango*); plumero (*caja*)
penicillin [,penɪ'sɪlɪn] *s* (pharm.) penicilina
peninsula [pə'nɪnsələ] o [pə'nɪnsjulə] *s* península
peninsular [pə'nɪnsələr] o [pə'nɪnsjulər] *adj & s* peninsular
penis ['pinɪs] *s* (*pl:* **-nes** [niz] o **-nises**) (anat.) pene
penitence ['penɪtəns] *s* penitencia
penitent ['penɪtənt] *adj & s* penitente
penitential [,penɪ'tenʃəl] *adj* penitencial; *s* (eccl.) penitencial
penitentially [,penɪ'tenʃəlɪ] *adv* de modo penitencial; por vía de penitencia
penitential psalms *spl* (Bib.) salmos penitenciales
penitentiary [,penɪ'tenʃərɪ] *adj* penitencial; penable; penitenciario; *s* (*pl:* **-ries**) penitenciaría, presidio; (eccl.) penitenciaría (*tribunal*); (eccl.) penitenciario (*presbítero*)
penknife ['pen,naɪf] *s* (*pl:* **-knives**) navaja, cortaplumas
penman ['penmən] *s* (*pl:* **-men**) pendolista; escritor
penmanship ['penmənʃɪp] *s* caligrafía; letra (*de una persona*)
Penn. o **Penna.** abr. de **Pennsylvania**
penna ['penə] *s* (*pl:* **-nae** [ni]) (orn.) pena
pen name *s* seudónimo
pennant ['penənt] *s* gallardete
pennate ['penet] *adj* pennado
penniless ['penɪlɪs] *adj* pelón, sin dinero
penninervate [,penɪ'nʌrvet] (bot.) penninervio
pennon ['penən] *s* pendón
Pennsylvania [,pensɪl'venɪə] *s* Pensilvania
Pennsylvania Dutch *spl* descendientes de los colonizadores alemanes en Pensilvania; *ssg* dialecto alemán hablado en Pensilvania
Pennsylvanian [,pensɪl'venɪən] *adj & s* pensilvano
penny ['penɪ] *s* (*pl:* **-nies**) (U.S.A.) centavo; **a pretty penny** (coll.) un dineral, un ojo de la cara; **to turn an honest penny** ganar honradamente algún dinero; (*pl:* **pence**) (Brit.) penique
pennyroyal [,penɪ'rɔɪəl] *s* (bot.) poleo
pennyweight ['penɪ,wet] *s* peso de 24 granos
penny-wise ['penɪ'waɪz] *adj* tacaño; **penny-wise and pound-foolish** tacaño en lo pequeño, derrochador en lo grande
pennyworth ['penɪ,wʌrθ] *s* valor de un penique; pizca, pequeña cantidad
penological [,pinə'lɑdʒɪkəl] *adj* penológico
penologist [pi'nɑlədʒɪst] *s* penologista o penólogo
penology [pi'nɑlədʒɪ] *s* penología
pen pal *s* (coll.) amigo por correspondencia
pen point *s* punta de la pluma; plumilla or puntilla (*de la plumafuente*)
pensile ['pensɪl] *adj* pensil
pension ['penʃən] *s* pensión, jubilación; *va* pensionar, jubilar
pensioner ['penʃənər] *s* pensionado, pensionista, alimentista
pension fund *s* caja de jubilaciones
pensive ['pensɪv] *adj* pensativo; melancólico
penstock ['pen,stɑk] *s* (hyd.) tubo en carga; (hyd.) compuerta de esclusa; (hyd.) canal de carga
pent [pent] *adj* acorralado, encerrado; *pret & pp de* **pen**
pentacle ['pentəkəl] *s* pentaclo
pentadactyl o **pentadactyle** [,pentə'dæktɪl] *adj* pentadáctilo
pentagon ['pentəgɑn] *s* (geom.) pentágono; **the Pentagon** el Pentágono (*edificio del Ministerio de Defensa en Wáshington*)
pentagonal [pen'tægənəl] *adj* pentagonal
pentahedron [,pentə'hidrən] *s* (*pl:* **-drons** o **-dra** [drə]) (geom.) pentaedro
pentamerous [pen'tæmərəs] *adj* (bot. & zool.) pentámero
pentameter [pen'tæmɪtər] *adj & s* pentámetro
pentane ['penten] *s* (chem.) pentano
pentarchy ['pentɑrkɪ] *s* (*pl:* **-chies**) pentarquía
pentasyllabic [,pentəsɪ'læbɪk] *adj* pentasílabo
Pentateuch ['pentətjuk] o ['pentətuk] *s* (Bib.) Pentateuco
pentathlon [pen'tæθlɑn] *s* (sport) péntatlo
pentatonic [,pentə'tɑnɪk] *adj* pentatónico
pentavalent [,pentə'velənt] o [pen'tævələnt] (chem.) pentavalente

Pentecost ['pɛntɪkɑst] o ['pɛntɪkɔst] *s* Pentecostés
Pentecostal o **pentecostal** [,pɛntɪ'kɑstəl] o [,pɛntɪ'kɔstəl] *adj* de Pentecostés
penthouse ['pɛnt,haʊs] *adj* colgadizo; *s* colgadizo; alpende; casa de azotea
pentode ['pɛntod] *s* (elec.) pentodo o péntodo
pentosan ['pɛntəsæn] *s* (chem.) pentosana
pentose ['pɛntos] *s* (chem.) pentosa
pent roof *s* tejado colgadizo
pent-up ['pɛnt,ʌp] *adj* contenido, reprimido
penult ['pinʌlt] o [pɪ'nʌlt] *s* (phonet.) penúltima
penultimate [pɪ'nʌltɪmɪt] *adj* penúltimo; *s* (phonet.) penúltima
penumbra [pɪ'nʌmbrə] *s* (*pl:* **-brae** [bri] o **-bras**) penumbra
penurious [pɪ'njʊrɪəs] o [pɪ'nʊrɪəs] *adj* tacaño, mezquino
penury ['pɛnjərɪ] *s* pobreza, miseria; penuria (*escasez*)
penwiper ['pɛn,waɪpər] *s* limpiaplumas
peonage ['piənɪdʒ] *s* condición de peón; esclavitud económica de los peones
peony ['piənɪ] *s* (*pl:* **-nies**) (bot.) peonía
people ['pipəl] *spl* gente; personas, p.ej., **a hundred people** un centenar de personas; gente del pueblo, gente común; se, p.ej., **people say** se dice; **my people** los míos; mi familia; mis allegados; *ssg* (*pl:* **peoples**) pueblo, nación, raza; *va* poblar
pep [pɛp] *s* (slang) brío, ánimo, vigor; **to be full of pep** (slang) estar muy jaque; (*pret & pp:* **pepped;** *ger:* **pepping**) *va* (slang) animar; **to pep up** (slang) animar, dar vigor a
peplum ['pɛpləm] *s* (*pl:* **-lums** o **-la** [lə]) (hist.) peplo; faldillas
pepo ['pipo] *s* (bot.) pepónide
pepper ['pɛpər] *s* (bot.) pimentero (*Piper nigrum*); (bot.) pimiento (*Capsicum*); pimienta (*condimento*); pimentero (*vasija*); *va* sazonar con pimienta; acribillar; salpicar; motear
pepper-and-salt ['pɛpərənd'sɔlt] *adj* mezclado de negro y blanco
pepperbox ['pɛpər,bɑks] *s* pimentero
peppercorn ['pɛpər,kɔrn] *s* grano de pimienta; chuchería, bagatela
pepper cress *s* (bot.) mastuerzo
peppergrass ['pɛpər,græs] o ['pɛpər,grɑs] *s* (bot.) mastuerzo; (bot.) sabelección, lepidio
peppermint ['pɛpərmɪnt] *s* (bot.) menta piperita; esencia de menta; pastilla de menta
peppermint drop *s* pastilla de menta
pepper pot *s* sopa de callos, carne y legumbres condimentada con pimientos, ají, etc.
pepper tree *s* (bot.) turbinto, pimentero falso
peppery ['pɛpərɪ] *adj* que tiene mucha o demasiada pimienta; picante, mordaz; enojado, de malas pulgas
peppy ['pɛpɪ] *adj* (*comp:* **-pier;** *super:* **-piest**) (slang) brioso, animoso, vigoroso
pepsin ['pɛpsɪn] *s* (biochem.) pepsina
pep talk *s* (slang) palabras para alentar y confortar
peptic ['pɛptɪk] *adj* péptico; *s* substancia péptica
peptic ulcer *s* (path.) úlcera péptica
peptide ['pɛptaɪd] o ['pɛptɪd] *s* (biochem.) péptido
peptize ['pɛptaɪz] *va* (chem.) peptizar
peptone ['pɛpton] *s* (biochem.) peptona
per [pʌr] *prep* por; **as per** según
peradventure [,pʌrəd'vɛntʃər] *s* duda, incertidumbre; **beyond peradventure** sin posibilidad de duda
perambulate [pər'æmbjəlet] *va* recorrer andando; recorrer para inspeccionar; *vn* pasearse
perambulation [pər,æmbjə'leʃən] *s* visita de inspección; paseo
perambulator [pər'æmbjə,letər] *s* paseante; cochecillo de niño
per annum [pər 'ænəm] por año, al año
perborate [pər'boret] *s* (chem.) perborato
percale [pər'kel] o [pər'kæl] *s* percal
percaline [,pʌrkə'lin] *s* percalina
per capita [pər 'kæpɪtə] por cabeza, por persona
perceive [pər'siv] *va* percibir
per cent o **percent** [pər'sɛnt] por ciento
percentage [pər'sɛntɪdʒ] *s* porcentaje; (slang) provecho, ventaja
percentile [pər'sɛntɪl] *s* percentil
per centum [pər 'sɛntəm] var. de **per cent**
percept ['pʌrsɛpt] *s* percepción (*efecto de percibir; objeto percibido*)
perceptibility [pər,sɛptɪ'bɪlɪtɪ] *s* perceptibilidad
perceptible [pər'sɛptɪbəl] *adj* perceptible
perceptibly [pər'sɛptɪblɪ] *adv* perceptiblemente
perception [pər'sɛpʃən] *s* percepción; comprensión, penetración
perceptive [pər'sɛptɪv] *adj* perceptivo (*que tiene virtud de percibir*)
perceptual [pər'sɛptʃʊəl] *adj* perceptivo (*perteneciente a la percepción*)
Perceval ['pʌrsɪvəl] *s* var. de **Percival**
perch [pʌrtʃ] *s* percha, varilla, rama (*en la que posa un ave*); pescante (*del cochero*); sitio o posición elevada; medida de longitud que equivale a 5,18 metros; medida de área que equivale a 23,3 metros cuadrados; (ichth.) perca; *va* colocar o situar en un sitio algo elevado; *vn* posar (*un ave*); sentarse en un sitio algo elevado, encaramarse
perchance [pər'tʃæns] o [pər'tʃɑns] *adv* (archaic & poet.) quizá, por ventura
Percheron ['pʌrtʃərɑn] o ['pʌrʃərɑn] *adj & s* percherón
perchlorate [pər'kloret] *s* (chem.) perclorato
perchloric [pər'klorɪk] *adj* perclórico
perchloric acid *s* (chem.) ácido perclórico
perchloride [pər'kloraɪd] o [pər'klorɪd] o **perchlorid** [pər'klorɪd] *s* (chem.) percloruro
percipient [pər'sɪpɪənt] *adj & s* perceptor
Percival o **Percivale** ['pʌrsɪvəl] *s* Perceval
percolate ['pʌrkəlet] *va* infiltrarse por entre los poros de; *vn* infiltrarse
percolation [,pʌrkə'leʃən] *s* infiltración
percolator ['pʌrkə,letər] *s* colador; cafetera filtradora
percuss [pər'kʌs] *va* percutir
percussion [pər'kʌʃən] *s* percusión; (med.) percusión
percussion cap *s* cápsula fulminante
percussion hammer *s* martillo neumático; (med.) martillo percusor
percussion instrument *s* (mus.) instrumento de percusión
percussion lock *s* llave de percusión
percussor [pər'kʌsər] *s* (med.) percusor
Percy ['pʌrsɪ] *s* nombre abreviado de **Percival**
per diem [pər 'daɪəm] (Lat.) por día; *s* cantidad que se da cada día
perdition [pər'dɪʃən] *s* perdición; infierno
peregrinate ['pɛrɪgrɪnet] *va* recorrer; *vn* peregrinar
peregrination [,pɛrɪgrɪ'neʃən] *s* peregrinación
peregrine o **peregrin** ['pɛrɪgrɪn] *adj* extranjero; *s* (orn.) halcón peregrino
peregrine falcon *s* (orn.) halcón peregrino
peremptory [pə'rɛmptərɪ] o ['pɛrəmp,torɪ] *adj* perentorio; autoritario, imperioso
perennial [pə'rɛnɪəl] *adj* perenne; (bot.) perenne, vivaz; *s* (bot.) planta vivaz
perennially [pə'rɛnɪəlɪ] *adv* perennemente
perf. abr. de **perfect** y **perforated**
perfect ['pʌrfɪkt] *adj* perfecto; (gram.) perfecto; *s* (gram.) perfecto; (gram.) pretérito perfecto; [pər'fɛkt] o ['pʌrfɪkt] *va* perfeccionar
perfect cadence *s* (mus.) cadencia perfecta
perfectibility [pər,fɛktɪ'bɪlɪtɪ] *s* perfectibilidad
perfectible [pər'fɛktɪbəl] *adj* perfectible
perfection [pər'fɛkʃən] *s* perfección; **to perfection** a la perfección
perfectionist [pər'fɛkʃənɪst] *s* perfeccionista
perfective [pər'fɛktɪv] *adj* perfectivo
perfectly ['pʌrfɪktlɪ] *adv* perfectamente
perfecto [pər'fɛkto] *s* (*pl:* **-tos**) cigarro puro afilado en los dos extremos
perfect participle *s* (gram.) participio pasivo o de pretérito
perfect rhyme *s* (pros.) rima perfecta
perfervid [pər'fʌrvɪd] *adj* fervidísimo
perfidious [pər'fɪdɪəs] *adj* pérfido
perfidy ['pʌrfɪdɪ] *s* (*pl:* **-dies**) perfidia

perfoliate [pər'folɪɪt] o [pər'folɪet] *adj* (bot.) perfoliado
perforate ['pʌrfəret] *adj* perforado; *va* perforar
perforated ['pʌrfə,retɪd] *adj* (philately) dentado
perforation [,pʌrfə'reʃən] *s* perforación; trepado (*línea de puntos taladrados, p.ej., en los sellos de correo*)
perforator ['pʌrfə,retər] *s* perforador; perforadora; (telg.) perforador
perforce [pər'fors] *adv* por fuerza, necesariamente
perform [pər'fɔrm] *va* ejecutar; (theat.) representar; *vn* ejecutar; funcionar (*p.ej., una máquina*)
performance [pər'fɔrməns] *s* actuación, ejecución; interpretación, presentación, representación; funcionamiento; (theat.) función; (sport) performance
performer [pər'fɔrmər] *s* ejecutante; actor, representante; acróbata
perfume ['pʌrfjum] o [pər'fjum] *s* perfume; [pər'fjum] *va* perfumar
perfumer [pər'fjumər] *s* perfumero o perfumista
perfumery [pər'fjumərɪ] *s* (*pl:* **-ies**) perfumería; perfume, perfumes
perfunctory [pər'fʌŋktərɪ] *adj* hecho sin cuidado, hecho a la ligera, perfunctorio; indiferente, negligente
Pergamum ['pʌrgəməm] *s* Pérgamo
pergola ['pʌrgələ] *s* pérgola
perhaps [pər'hæps] *adv* acaso, tal vez, quizá
peri ['pɪrɪ] *s* (*pl:* **-ris**) (myth.) peri
perianth ['perɪænθ] *s* (bot.) periantio
pericardiac [,perɪ'kardɪæk] o **pericardial** [,perɪ'kardɪəl] *adj* pericardíaco
pericarditis [,perɪkar'daɪtɪs] *s* (path.) pericarditis
pericardium [,perɪ'kardɪəm] *s* (*pl:* **-a** [ə]) (anat.) pericardio
pericarp ['perɪkarp] *s* (bot.) pericarpio
Pericles ['perɪkliz] *s* Pericles
pericranium [,perɪ'krenɪəm] *s* (*pl:* **-a** [ə]) (anat.) pericráneo; (hum.) cabeza
peridot ['perɪdat] *s* (mineral.) peridoto
perigee ['perɪdʒi] *s* (astr.) perigeo
perigyny [pə'rɪdʒɪnɪ] *s* (bot.) periginia
perihelion [,perɪ'hilɪən] *s* (*pl:* **-a** [ə]) (astr.) perihelio
peril ['perəl] *s* peligro; (*pret & pp:* **-iled** o **-illed;** *ger:* **-iling** o **-illing**) *va* poner en peligro
perilous ['perɪləs] *adj* peligroso
perimeter [pə'rɪmɪtər] *s* perímetro
perimysium [,perɪ'mɪʒɪəm] o [,perɪ'mɪzɪəm] *s* (anat.) perimisio
perineal [,perɪ'niəl] *adj* perineal
perineum [,perɪ'niəm] *s* (*pl:* **-a** [ə]) (anat.) perineo
perineurium [,perɪ'njurɪəm] o [,perɪ'nurɪəm] *s* (*pl:* **-a** [ə]) (anat.) perineurio
period ['pɪrɪəd] *s* período; (gram.) punto; (sport) división (*de ciertos juegos*); hora (*de clase*)
period costume *s* traje de época
period furniture *s* muebles de estilo
periodic [,pɪrɪ'adɪk] *adj* periódico; (lit.) oratorio; [,pʌraɪ'adɪk] *adj* (chem.) peryódico
periodical [,pɪrɪ'adɪkəl] *adj* periódico; *s* periódico, revista periódica, publicación periódica
periodically [,pɪrɪ'adɪkəlɪ] *adv* periódicamente; de vez en cuando
periodic fraction *s* (math.) fracción periódica
periodicity [,pɪrɪə'dɪsɪtɪ] *s* (*pl:* **-ties**) periodicidad
periodic law *s* (chem.) ley periódica
periodic motion *s* (phys.) movimiento periódico
periodic system *s* (chem.) sistema periódico
periodic table *s* (chem.) tabla periódica, cuadro del sistema periódico
periodide [pər'aɪədaɪd] o [pər'aɪədɪd] *s* (chem.) peryoduro
periodontal [,perɪə'dantəl] *adj* periodontal
perioeci [,perɪ'isaɪ] *spl* periecos
perioecic [,perɪ'isɪk] *adj* perieco
periosteum [,perɪ'astɪəm] *s* (*pl:* **-a** [ə]) (anat.) periostio
periostitis [,perɪas'taɪtɪs] *s* (path.) periostitis
peripatetic [,perɪpə'tetɪk] *adj & s* paseante; (*cap.*) *adj & s* peripatético
peripheral [pə'rɪfərəl] *adj* periférico
periphery [pə'rɪfərɪ] *s* (*pl:* **-ies**) periferia
periphrase ['perɪfrez] *s* perífrasi; *va* expresar con perífrasis; *vn* perifrasear
periphrasis [pə'rɪfrəsɪs] *s* (*pl:* **-ses** [siz]) perífrasi o perífrasis
periphrastic [,perɪ'fræstɪk] *adj* perifrástico
peripteral [pə'rɪptərəl] *adj* (arch.) períptero
periscian [pɪ'rɪʃɪən] o [pɪ'rɪsɪən] *adj* periscio
periscii [pɪ'rɪʃɪaɪ] o [pɪ'rɪsɪaɪ] *spl* periscios
periscope ['perɪskop] *s* periscopio
periscopic [,perɪ'skapɪk] *adj* periscópico
perish ['perɪʃ] *vn* perecer; averiarse (*echarse a perder*); **perish the thought!** ¡no lo permita Dios!
perishable ['perɪʃəbəl] *adj* perecedero; averiable, deleznable; **perishables** *spl* artículos perecederos
perishable goods *spl* artículos perecederos
perissodactyl o **perissodactyle** [pɪ,rɪsə'dæktɪl] *adj & s* (zool.) perisodáctilo
peristalsis [,perɪ'stælsɪs] *s* (*pl:* **-ses** [siz]) (physiol.) peristalsis o peristaltismo
peristaltic [,perɪ'stæltɪk] *adj* peristáltico
peristome ['perɪstom] *s* (bot.) perístoma
peristyle ['perɪstaɪl] *s* (arch.) peristilo
peritoneal [,perɪtə'niəl] *adj* peritoneal
peritoneum o **peritonaeum** [,perɪtə'niəm] *s* *s* (*pl:* **-a** [ə]) (anat.) peritoneo
peritonitis [,perɪtə'naɪtɪs] *s* (path.) peritonitis
periwig ['perɪwɪg] *s* perico (*pelo postizo*)
periwinkle ['perɪ,wɪŋkəl] *s* (bot.) pervinca; (zool.) litorina, bígaro
perjure ['pʌrdʒər] *va* hacer (*a una persona*) quebrantar el juramento; **to perjure oneself** perjurarse
perjured ['pʌrdʒərd] *adj* perjuro
perjurer ['pʌrdʒərər] *s* perjuro
perjury ['pʌrdʒərɪ] *s* (*pl:* **-ries**) perjurio
perk [pʌrk] *va* alzar (*la cabeza*); aguzar (*las orejas*); **to perk out** o **up** engalanar; *vn* pavonearse; engalanarse; **to perk up** reanimarse, sentirse mejor
perky ['pʌrkɪ] *adj* (*comp:* **-ier;** *super:* **-iest**) airoso, gallardo
perlite ['pʌrlaɪt] *s* (metal. & petrog.) perlita
permafrost ['pʌrmə,frɔst] o ['pʌrmə,frast] *s* suelo helado de modo permanente, en las regiones polares
permalloy [,pʌrm'ælɔɪ] *s* (trademark) permaleación, permaloy
permanence ['pʌrmənəns] *s* permanencia
permanency ['pʌrmənənsɪ] *s* (*pl:* **-cies**) permanencia; persona, cosa o posición permanentes
permanent ['pʌrmənənt] *adj* permanente; *s* (coll.) permanente, ondulación permanente
Permanent Court of Arbitration *s* Tribunal Permanente de Arbitraje
Permanent Court of International Justice *s* Tribunal Permanente de Justicia Internacional
permanent magnetism *s* (phys.) magnetismo permanente
permanent tenure *s* inamovilidad
permanent wave *s* ondulación permanente
permanent way *s* (rail.) material fijo
permanganate [pər'mæŋganet] *s* (chem.) permanganato
permanganic [,pʌrmæŋ'gænɪk] *adj* permangánico
permanganic acid *s* (chem.) ácido permangánico
permeability [,pʌrmɪə'bɪlɪtɪ] *s* permeabilidad
permeable ['pʌrmɪəbəl] *adj* permeable
permeance ['pʌrmɪəns] *s* (elec.) permeancia
permeate ['pʌrmɪet] *va & vn* penetrar
permeation [,pʌrmɪ'eʃən] *s* penetración (*al través de los poros*)
Permian ['pʌrmɪən] *adj & s* (geol.) pérmico
permissible [pər'mɪsɪbəl] *adj* permisible
permission [pər'mɪʃən] *s* permisión, permiso
permissive [pər'mɪsɪv] *adj* permisivo; permisible
permit ['pʌrmɪt] *s* permiso; (com.) cédula de

aduana; [pər'mɪt] (*pret & pp:* **-mitted; *ger:* -mitting**) *va* permitir; **to permit to** + *inf* permitir + *inf*, permitir que + *subj*
permutable [pər'mjutəbəl] *adj* permutable
permutation [ˌpʌrmjə'teʃən] *s* permutación; (math.) permutación
permute [pər'mjut] *va* permutar
pernicious [pər'nɪʃəs] *adj* pernicioso
pernicious anemia *s* (path.) anemia perniciosa
pernickety [pər'nɪkɪtɪ] *adj* (coll.) descontentadizo, quisquilloso
perorate ['pɛrəret] *vn* perorar
peroration [ˌpɛrə'reʃən] *s* peroración
peroxide [pər'ɑksaɪd] o **peroxid** [pər'ɑksɪd] *s* (chem.) peróxido; (chem.) peróxido de hidrógeno
peroxide blonde *s* (slang) rubia oxigenada
peroxyacid [pərˌɑksɪ'æsɪd] *s* (chem.) peroxiácido
perpend ['pʌrpənd] *s* (mas.) perpiaño; (pər'pɛnd] *va & vn* (archaic) considerar, reflexionar
perpendicular [ˌpʌrpən'dɪkjələr] *adj & s* perpendicular
perpendicularity [ˌpʌrpənˌdɪkjə'lærɪtɪ] *s* perpendicularidad
perpetrate ['pʌrpɪtret] *va* perpetrar
perpetration [ˌpʌrpɪ'treʃən] *s* perpetración
perpetrator ['pʌrpɪˌtretər] *s* perpetrador
perpetual [pər'pɛtʃuəl] *adj* perpetuo
perpetually [pər'pɛtʃuəlɪ] *adv* perpetuamente
perpetual motion *s* movimiento continuo o movimiento perpetuo
perpetuate [pər'pɛtʃuet] *va* perpetuar
perpetuation [pərˌpɛtʃu'eʃən] *s* perpetuación
perpetuity [ˌpʌrpɪ'tjuɪtɪ] o [ˌpʌrpɪ'tuɪtɪ] *s* (*pl:* **-ties**) perpetuidad; **in perpetuity** perpetuamente, para siempre
Perpignan [pɛrpi'njɑ̃] *s* Perpiñán
perplex [pər'plɛks] *va* dejar perplejo; embrollar, enredar
perplexed [pər'plɛkst] *adj* perplejo
perplexity [pər'plɛksɪtɪ] *s* (*pl:* **-ties**) perplejidad; problema
perquisite ['pʌrkwɪzɪt] *s* obvención, adehala
per se [pər 'si] por sí mismo, en sí mismo, esencialmente
persecute ['pʌrsɪkjut] *va* perseguir
persecution [ˌpʌrsɪ'kjuʃən] *s* persecución; *adj* persecutorio
persecutor ['pʌrsɪˌkjutər] *s* perseguidor
Perseid ['pʌrsɪɪd] *s* (astr.) Perseida
Persephone [pər'sɛfənɪ] *s* (myth.) Perséfone
Perseus ['pʌrsjus] o ['pʌrsɪəs] *s* (myth. & astr.) Perseo
perseverance [ˌpʌrsɪ'vɪrəns] *s* perseverancia
persevere [ˌpʌrsɪ'vɪr] *vn* perseverar; **to persevere in** + *ger* perseverar en + *inf*
persevering [ˌpʌrsɪ'vɪrɪŋ] *adj* perseverante
Persian ['pʌrʒən] o ['pʌrʃən] *adj & s* persa
Persian Gulf *s* golfo Pérsico
Persian lamb *s* oveja caracul; caracul (*piel*)
persicary ['pʌrsɪˌkɛrɪ] *s* (*pl:* **-ies**) (bot.) persicaria, duraznillo
persiflage ['pʌrsɪflɑʒ] *s* burla fina, parloteo festivo
persimmon [pər'sɪmən] *s* (bot.) placaminero; (bot.) caqui
persist [pər'sɪst] o [pər'zɪst] *vn* persistir; **to persist in** + *ger* persistir en + *inf*
persistence [pər'sɪstəns] o [pər'zɪstəns] o **persistency** [pər'sɪstənsɪ] o [pər'zɪstənsɪ] *s* persistencia; porfía; pertinacia (*p.ej., de una enfermedad*)
persistent [pər'sɪstənt] o [pər'zɪstənt] *adj* persistente; porfiado; pertinaz (*enfermedad*)
person ['pʌrsən] *s* persona; (gram. & theol.) persona; **clean about one's person** cuidadoso en su aseo personal; **in the person of** en la persona de; **no person** nadie
personable ['pʌrsənəbəl] *adj* bien parecido, presentable
personage ['pʌrsənɪdʒ] *s* personaje; persona; (theat.) personaje
persona grata [pər'sonə 'gretə] *s* (*pl:* **personae gratae** [pər'soni 'greti]) persona grata
personal ['pʌrsənəl] *adj* personal; de uso personal; mueble, mobilario (*dícese, p.ej., de los bienes*); **to become personal** personalizarse, pasar a hacer alusiones de carácter personal; **to make a personal appearance** aparecer en persona; *s* nota de sociedad; remitido (*en un periódico*)
personal a *s* la preposición **a** con el complemento directo de persona
personal effects *spl* bienes de uso personal
personal equation *s* ecuación personal
personal estate *s* bienes muebles
personality [ˌpʌrsə'nælɪtɪ] *s* (*pl:* **-ties**) personalidad
personality cult *s* culto a la personalidad
personalization [ˌpʌrsənəlɪ'zeʃən] *s* personalización
personalize ['pʌrsənəlaɪz] *va* personalizar
personally ['pʌrsənəlɪ] *adv* personalmente; en particular; como cosa personal
personal pronoun *s* pronombre personal
personal property *s* bienes muebles
personalty ['pʌrsənəltɪ] *s* (*pl:* **-ties**) bienes muebles
personate ['pʌrsənɪt] o ['pʌrsənet] *adj* (bot.) personada (*corola*); ['pʌrsənet] *va* fingir ser, hacerse pasar por; representar, hacer el papel de; *vn* hacer un papel
personation [ˌpʌrsə'neʃən] *s* personificación; representación (*de un papel*); usurpación del nombre de otra persona
personification [pərˌsɑnɪfɪ'keʃən] *s* personificación
personify [pər'sɑnɪfaɪ] (*pret & pp:* **-fied**) *va* personificar
personnel [ˌpʌrsə'nɛl] *s* personal
perspective [pər'spɛktɪv] *adj* perspectivo; *s* perspectiva
perspicacious [ˌpʌrspɪ'keʃəs] *adj* perspicaz
perspicacity [ˌpʌrspɪ'kæsɪtɪ] *s* perspicacia; (archaic) perspicacia (*agudeza de la vista*)
perspicuity [ˌpʌrspɪ'kjuɪtɪ] *s* perspicuidad
perspicuous [pər'spɪkjuəs] *adj* perspicuo
perspiration [ˌpʌrspɪ'reʃən] *s* transpiración
perspire [pər'spaɪr] *va & vn* transpirar, sudar
persuade [pər'swed] *va* persuadir; **to persuade to** + *inf* persuadir a + *inf*, persuadir a que + *subj*
persuasible [pər'swesɪbəl] *adj* fácil de convencer
persuasion [pər'sweʒən] *s* persuasión; persuasiva; secta, creencia religiosa; creencia fuerte; (hum.) clase, especie
persuasive [pər'swesɪv] *adj* persuasivo
pert [pʌrt] *adj* atrevido, descarado; (coll.) animado, vivo
pertain [pər'ten] *vn* pertenecer; **pertaining to** perteneciente a
pertinacious [ˌpʌrtɪ'neʃəs] *adj* pertinaz
pertinacity [ˌpərtɪ'næsɪtɪ] *s* pertinacia
pertinence ['pʌrtɪnəns] o **pertinency** ['pʌrtɪnənsɪ] *s* pertinencia
pertinent ['pʌrtɪnənt] *adj* pertinente
perturb [pər'tʌrb] *va* perturbar
perturbation [ˌpʌrtər'beʃən] *s* perturbación
Peru [pə'ru] *s* el Perú
Perugia [pɛ'rudʒɑ] *s* Perusa
peruke [pə'ruk] *s* peluquín
perusal [pə'ruzəl] *s* lectura, lectura cuidadosa
peruse [pə'ruz] *va* leer, leer con atención
Peruvian [pə'ruvɪən] *adj & s* peruano
Peruvian bark *s* (pharm.) quina, cascarilla
pervade [pər'ved] *va* penetrar, esparcirse por, extenderse por
pervasion [pər'veʒən] *s* penetración, esparcimiento
pervasive [pər'vesɪv] *adj* penetrante
perverse [pər'vʌrs] *adj* perverso; avieso, díscolo; contumaz; (psychopath.) pervertido
perverseness [pər'vʌrsnɪs] *s* perversidad
perversion [pər'vʌrʒən] o [pər'vʌrʃən] *s* perversión; (psychopath.) perversión
perversity [pər'vʌrsɪtɪ] *s* (*pl:* **-ties**) perversidad; indocilidad; contumacia
pervert ['pʌrvərt] *s* renegado, apóstata; (psychopath.) pervertido; [pər'vʌrt] *va* pervertir; emplear mal (*los talentos que uno tiene*)
pervious ['pʌrvɪəs] *adj* permeable; fácil de convencer
pesky ['pɛskɪ] *adj* (*comp:* **-kier;** *super:* **-kiest**) (coll.) molesto, cargante
pessary ['pɛsərɪ] *s* (*pl:* **-ries**) (med.) pesario
pessimism ['pɛsɪmɪzəm] *s* pesimismo
pessimist ['pɛsɪmɪst] *s* pesimista
pessimistic [ˌpɛsɪ'mɪstɪk] *adj* pesimista

pessimistically [ˌpɛsɪˈmɪstɪkəlɪ] *adv* con pesimismo
pest [pɛst] *s* peste; insecto nocivo; (fig.) plaga (*infortunio, contratiempo, etc.*); (fig.) machaca (*persona fastidiosa*)
Pestalozzian [ˌpɛstəˈlɑtsɪən] *adj* (educ.) pestaloziano
pester [ˈpɛstər] *va* molestar, importunar
pesthouse [ˈpɛstˌhaus] *s* lazareto, hospital de contagiosos
pestiferous [pɛsˈtɪfərəs] *adj* pestífero; (coll.) engorroso, molesto
pestilence [ˈpɛstɪləns] *s* pestilencia
pestilent [ˈpɛstɪlənt] *adj* mortífero; pestilente; engorroso, molesto
pestilential [ˌpɛstɪˈlɛnʃəl] *adj* pestilencial; pestilencioso
pestle [ˈpɛsəl] o [ˈpɛstəl] *s* mano de almirez o mortero; *va* majar
pet [pɛt] *s* animal mimado, animal casero; niño mimado; favorito; fanfurriña, enojo pasajero; *adj* mimado; domesticado; favorito; (*pret & pp:* **petted;** *ger:* **petting**) *va* acariciar, mimar; *vn* (slang) besuquearse
petal [ˈpɛtəl] *s* (bot.) pétalo
petaled o **petalled** [ˈpɛtəld] *adj* que tiene pétalos
petard [pɪˈtɑrd] *s* petardo
petcock [ˈpɛtˌkɑk] *s* llave de desagüe, llave de purga
Pete [pit] *s* Perico
Peter [ˈpitər] *s* Pedro; **to rob Peter to pay Paul** desnudar a un santo para vestir a otro; (*l.c.*) *vn* (coll.) agotarse; **to peter out** (coll.) agotarse, acabarse
Peter Pan *s* (lit.) el niño que no quiso crecer, héroe de la famosa comedia infantil de James Barrie
Peter's pence *spl* los diezmos de San Pedro
Peter the Great *s* Pedro el Grande
Peter the Hermit *s* Pedro el Ermitaño
petiolate [ˈpɛtɪolet] *adj* peciolado
petiole [ˈpɛtɪol] *s* (bot. & zool.) pecíolo
petit [ˈpɛtɪ] *adj* (law) menor
petite [pəˈtit] *adj* pequeña, chiquita
petition [pɪˈtɪʃən] *s* petición; instancia, memorial, solicitud; *va* suplicar; dirigir una instancia o memorial a, solicitar
petitionary [pɪˈtɪʃəˌnɛrɪ] *adj* petitorio
petitio principii [pɪˈtɪʃɪo prɪnˈsɪpɪaɪ] *s* (log.) petición de principio
petit jury *s* (law) jurado de juicio
pet name *s* nombre de cariño, sobrenombre familiar
Petrarch [ˈpitrɑrk] *s* Petrarca
Petrarchism [ˈpitrɑrkɪzəm] *s* petrarquismo
petrel [ˈpɛtrəl] *s* (orn.) petrel
Petri dish [ˈpetri] *s* caja o disco de Petri
petrifaction [ˌpɛtrɪˈfækʃən] o **petrification** [ˌpɛtrɪfɪˈkeʃən] *s* petrificación
Petrified Forest *s* Bosque Petrificado
petrify [ˈpɛtrɪfaɪ] (*pret & pp:* **-fied**) *va* petrificar; *vn* petrificarse
petrochemical [ˌpɛtrəˈkɛmɪkəl] *adj* petroquímico; *s* producto petroquímico
Petrograd [ˈpɛtrogræd] *s* Petrogrado
petrography [pɪˈtrɑgrəfɪ] *s* petrografía
petrol [ˈpɛtrəl] *s* (Brit.) gasolina; (*pret & pp:* **-rolled;** *ger:* **-rolling**) *va* (Brit.) limpiar con gasolina
petrolatum [ˌpɛtroˈletəm] *s* (pharm.) petrolato
petroleum [pɪˈtrolɪəm] *s* petróleo
petroleum jelly *s* petrolato, parafina blanda
petroliferous [ˌpɛtrəˈlɪfərəs] *adj* petrolífero
petrology [pɪˈtrɑlədʒɪ] *s* petrología
petronel [ˈpɛtrənəl] *s* pistola de caballería
petrous [ˈpɛtrəs] *adj* petroso; (anat.) petroso
pet shop *s* pajarería (*tienda donde se venden pájaros y otros animales domésticos*)
petticoat [ˈpɛtɪkot] *s* enaguas; (slang) falda (*mujer, muchacha, moza*); *adj* (slang) de mujer, de mujeres
pettifogger [ˈpɛtɪˌfɑgər] *s* picapleitos, trapacista
pettifoggery [ˈpɛtɪˌfɑgərɪ] *s* (*pl:* **-ies**) trapacería
pettifogging [ˈpɛtɪˌfɑgɪŋ] *adj* trapacero; *s* trapacería
pettish [ˈpɛtɪʃ] *adj* malhumorado, enojadizo
petty [ˈpɛtɪ] *adj* (*comp:* **-tier;** *super:* **-tiest**) insignificante, menor, pequeño; mezquino; intolerante
petty cash *s* caja de menores, efectivo para gastos menores
petty jury *s* var. de **petit jury**
petty larceny *s* (law) ratería, hurto
petty officer *s* (nav.) suboficial
petty treason *s* traición menor
petulance [ˈpɛtjələns] o **petulancy** [ˈpɛtjələnsɪ] *s* mal humor
petulant [ˈpɛtjələnt] *adj* malhumorado, enojadizo
petunia [pɪˈtjunɪe] o [pɪˈtunɪə] *s* (bot.) petunia
pew [pju] *s* banco de iglesia; *interj* ¡ fo!
pewee [ˈpiwi] *s* (orn.) aguador
pewit [ˈpiwɪt] *s* (orn.) gaviota de cabeza negra; (orn.) ave fría
pewter [ˈpjutər] *s* peltre; vajilla de peltre; *adj* de peltre
pewterer [ˈpjutərər] *s* peltrero
pf. abr. de **pfennig** y **preferred**
Pfc. abr. de **private first class**
pfd. abr. de **preferred**
pfg. abr. de **pfennig**
Pg. abr. de **Portugal** y **Portuguese**
Phaedra [ˈfidrə] *s* (myth.) Fedra
Phaethon [ˈfeɪθɑn] *s* (myth.) Faetón
phaeton o **phaëton** [ˈfeɪtən] *s* faetón
phagocyte [ˈfægəsaɪt] *s* (physiol.) fagocito
phagocytosis [ˌfægəsaɪˈtosɪs] *s* fagocitosis
phalangeal [fəˈlændʒɪəl] *adj* falangiano
phalanger [fəˈlændʒər] *s* (zool.) falangero
phalangette [ˌfælənˈdʒɛt] *s* (anat.) falangeta
phalanstery [ˈfælənˌstɛrɪ] *s* (*pl:* **-ies**) falansterio
phalanx [ˈfelæŋks] o [ˈfælæŋks] *s* (*pl:* **phalanxes** o **phalanges** [feˈlændʒiz]) falange; (anat. & zool.) falange
phalarope [ˈfælərop] *s* (orn.) falárope
phallic [ˈfælɪk] *adj* fálico
phallicism [ˈfælɪsɪzəm] o **phallism** [ˈfælɪzəm] *s* falismo
phallin [ˈfælɪn] *s* (biochem.) falina
phallus [ˈfæləs] *s* (*pl:* **-li** [laɪ]) falo
phanerogam [ˈfænərəˌgæm] *s* (bot.) fanerógama
phanerogamous [ˌfænəˈrɑgəməs] *adj* (bot.) fanerógamo
phantasm [ˈfæntæzəm] *s* fantasma
phantasmagoria [fænˌtæzməˈgorɪə] *s* fantasmagoría
phantasmagorial [fænˌtæzməˈgorɪəl] o **phantasmagoric** [fænˌtæzməˈgɔrɪk] o [fænˌtæzməˈgɑrɪk] *adj* fantasmagórico
phantasmal [fænˈtæzməl] *adj* fantasmal
phantasy [ˈfæntəsɪ] o [ˈfæntəzɪ] *s* (*pl:* **-sies**) var. de **fantasy**
phantom [ˈfæntəm] *s* fantasma; *adj* fantasmal
phantom circuit *s* (elec.) circuito fantasma
Pharaoh [ˈfɛro] o [ˈfɛreo] *s* Faraón
Pharaonic [ˌfɛreˈɑnɪk] *adj* faraónico
pharisaic [ˌfærɪˈseɪk] *adj* farisaico; (*cap.*) *adj* farisaico
pharisaical [ˌfærɪˈseɪkəl] *adj* farisaico
pharisaism [ˈfærɪseɪzəm] *s* farisaísmo; (*cap.*) *s* farisaísmo
pharisee [ˈfærɪsi] *s* fariseo; (*cap.*) *s* fariseo
phariseeism [ˈfærɪsiɪzəm] *s* var. de **pharisaism**
pharmaceutic [ˌfɑrməˈsutɪk] o [ˌfɑrməˈsjutɪk] *adj* farmacéutico; **pharmaceutics** *ssg* farmacéutica, farmacia
pharmaceutical [ˌfɑrməˈsutɪkəl] o [ˌfɑrməˈsjutɪkəl] *adj* farmacéutico
pharmacist [ˈfɑrməsɪst] *s* farmacéutico
pharmacognosy [ˌfɑrməˈkɑgnəsɪ] *s* farmacognosia
pharmacologist [ˌfɑrməˈkɑlədʒɪst] *s* farmacólogo
pharmacology [ˌfɑrməˈkɑlədʒɪ] *s* farmacología
pharmacopoeia [ˌfɑrməkoˈpiə] *s* farmacopea
pharmacy [ˈfɑrməsɪ] *s* (*pl:* **-cies**) farmacia
pharyngeal [fəˈrɪndʒɪəl] o [ˌfærɪnˈdʒiəl] *adj* faríngeo
pharyngitis [ˌfærɪnˈdʒaɪtɪs] *s* (path.) faringitis
pharyngoscope [fəˈrɪŋgəskop] *s* faringoscopio

pharyngoscopy [ˌfærɪŋˈgɑskəpɪ] *s* faringoscopia
pharynx [ˈfærɪŋks] *s* (*pl:* **pharynxes** o **pharynges** [fəˈrɪndʒiz]) (anat.) faringe
phase [fez] *s* fase; (astr., biol., elec. & phys.) fase; **in phase** (elec.) en fase; **out of phase** (elec.) fuera de fase; *va* (elec.) poner en fase; (coll.) inquietar, molestar
phase lag *s* (elec.) retraso de fase, corrimiento de fase
phase modulation *s* (rad.) modulación de fase
phaseolin [fəˈsiəlɪn] *s* (biochem.) faseolina
phase rule *s* (physical chem.) ley de las fases
phase shift *s* (elec.) decalaje
phase splitter *s* (elec.) divisor de fase
Ph.B. abr. de **Bachelor of Philosophy**
Ph.D. abr. de **Doctor of Philosophy**
pheasant [ˈfɛzənt] *s* (orn.) faisán
phelloderm [ˈfɛlədʌrm] *s* (bot.) felodermo
phellogen [ˈfɛlədʒən] *s* (bot.) felógeno
phenacetin [fɪˈnæsɪtɪn] *s* (pharm.) fenacetina
phenakistoscope [ˌfɛnəˈkɪstəskop] *s* fenaquistiscopio
Phenicia [fɪˈnɪʃə] *s* var. de **Phoenicia**
phenix [ˈfinɪks] *s* var. de **phoenix**
phenobarbital [ˌfinoˈbɑrbɪtæl] o [ˌfinoˈbɑrbɪtɔl] *s* (pharm.) fenobarbital
phenocryst [ˈfinəkrɪst] o [ˈfɛnəkrɪst] *s* (geol.) fenocristal
phenol [ˈfinol] o [ˈfinɑl] *s* (chem.) fenol
phenology [fɪˈnɑlədʒɪ] *s* fenología
phenolphthalein [ˌfinɑlˈθælin] *s* (chem.) fenolftaleína
phenomenal [fɪˈnɑmɪnəl] *adj* fenomenal; (fig.) fenomenal
phenomenalism [fɪˈnɑmənəlɪzəm] *s* (philos.) fenomenalismo
phenomenally [fɪˈnɑmɪnəlɪ] *adv* fenomenalmente
phenomenology [fɪˌnɑməˈnɑlədʒɪ] *s* (philos.) fenomenología
phenomenon [fɪˈnɑmɪnɑn] *s* (*pl:* **-na** [nə]) fenómeno; (philos.) fenómeno
phenothiazine [ˌfinəˈθaɪəzin] *s* (chem.) fenotiacina
phenotype [ˈfinətaɪp] *s* (biol.) fenotipo
phenyl [ˈfɛnɪl] o [ˈfinɪl] *s* (chem.) fenilo
phenylene [ˈfɛnɪlin] o [ˈfinɪlin] *s* (chem.) fenileno
phew [fju] *interj* ¡puf!; ¡anda!; ¡zape!
phial [ˈfaɪəl] *s* frasco, frasco pequeño
Phidian [ˈfɪdɪən] *adj* de Fidias
Phidias [ˈfɪdɪəs] *s* Fidias
Phil. abr. de **Philip, Philippians** y **Philippine**
Phila. abr. de **Philadelphia**
Philadelphia [ˌfɪləˈdɛlfɪə] *s* Filadelfia
Philadelphian [ˌfɪləˈdɛlfɪən] *adj & s* filadelfiano
philander [fɪˈlændər] *s* galanteador, tenorio; (zool.) filandro; *vn* galantear
philanderer [fɪˈlændərər] *s* galanteador, tenorio
philanthropic [ˌfɪlənˈθrɑpɪk] o **philanthropical** [ˌfɪlənˈθrɑpɪkəl] *adj* filantrópico
philanthropist [fɪˈlænθrəpɪst] *s* filántropo
philanthropy [fɪˈlænθrəpɪ] *s* filantropía
philatelic [ˌfɪləˈtɛlɪk] *adj* filatélico
philatelist [fɪˈlætəlɪst] *s* filatelista
philately [fɪˈlætəlɪ] *s* filatelia
Philemon [fɪˈlimən] *s* (myth.) Filemón; (Bib.) Epístola de San Pablo a Filemón
philharmonic [ˌfɪlhɑrˈmɑnɪk] *adj* filarmónico; *s* filarmónico; sociedad filarmónica
philhellene [fɪlˈhɛlin] *adj & s* filheleno
Philip [ˈfɪlɪp] *s* Felipe; Filipo (*p.ej., de Macedonia*)
Philippi [fɪˈlɪpaɪ] *s* Filipos
Philippian [fɪˈlɪpɪən] *adj & s* filipense; **Philippians** *spl* (Bib.) Epístola de San Pablo a los Filipenses
philippic [fɪˈlɪpɪk] *s* filípica; (*cap.*) *s* (hist.) Filípica (*de Demóstenes; de Cicerón*)
Philippine [ˈfɪlɪpin] *adj* filipino; **Philippines** *spl* Filipinas (*islas*)
Philippine Islands *spl* Islas Filipinas
Philistine [fɪˈlɪstin], [ˈfɪlɪstin] o [ˈfɪlɪstaɪn] *adj & s* (Bib. & fig.) filisteo
Philistinism [fɪˈlɪstɪnɪzəm] o [ˈfɪlɪstɪnɪzəm] *s* filisteísmo
Phillips screw [ˈfɪlɪps] *s* tornillo patente Phillips
philologian [ˌfɪləˈlodʒɪən] *s* filólogo
philological [ˌfɪləˈlɑdʒɪkəl] *adj* filológico
philologist [fɪˈlɑlədʒɪst] *s* filólogo
philology [fɪˈlɑlədʒɪ] *s* filología
philomel o **Philomel** [ˈfɪləmɛl] *s* (poet.) filomela o filomena (*ruiseñor*)
Philomela [ˌfɪləˈmilə] *s* (myth.) Filomela; (*l.c.*) *s* (poet.) filomela o filomena (*ruiseñor*)
philopena [ˌfɪləˈpinə] *s* juego de prendas que se inicia compartiendo una nuez; la nuez; la prenda
philosopher [fɪˈlɑsəfər] *s* filósofo
philosopher's stone *s* piedra filosofal
philosophic [ˌfɪləˈsɑfɪk] o **philosophical** [ˌfɪləˈsɑfɪkəl] *adj* filosófico
philosophize [fɪˈlɑsəfaɪz] *vn* filosofar
philosophy [fɪˈlɑsəfɪ] *s* (*pl:* **-phies**) filosofía
philter o **philtre** [ˈfɪltər] *s* filtro (*bebida mágica*); *va* hechizar con filtro
phimosis [faɪˈmosɪs] *s* (path.) fimosis
Phineas [ˈfɪnɪəs] *s* Fineas
phlebitis [flɪˈbaɪtɪs] *s* (path.) flebitis
phlebosclerosis [ˌflɛbosklɪˈrosɪs] *s* (path.) flebosclerosis
phlebotomist [flɪˈbɑtəmɪst] *s* flebotomiano
phlebotomy [flɪˈbɑtəmɪ] *s* flebotomía
phlegm [flɛm] *s* (physiol. & fig.) flema
phlegmatic [flɛgˈmætɪk] o **phlegmatical** [flɛgˈmætɪkəl] *adj* flemático
phlegmon [ˈflɛgmɑn] *s* (path.) flemón
phlegmonous [ˈflɛgmənəs] *adj* flemonoso
phlegmy [ˈflɛmɪ] *adj* flemoso
phloem o **phloëm** [ˈfloɛm] *s* (bot.) floema
phlogistic [floˈdʒɪstɪk] *adj* (path. & old chem.) flogístico
phlogiston [floˈdʒɪstɑn] *s* (old chem.) flogisto
phlogopite [ˈflɑgəpaɪt] *s* (mineral.) flogopita
phlorizin [ˈflɔrɪzɪn] o [fləˈraɪzɪn] *s* (chem.) floricina
phlox [flɑks] *s* (bot.) cambrina, simpática, flox
phlyctena [flɪkˈtinə] *s* (*pl:* **-nae** [ni]) (path.) flictena
phobia [ˈfobɪə] *s* fobia
Phocian [ˈfoʃən] *adj & s* focense
Phocis [ˈfosɪs] *s* la Fócida
phoebe [ˈfibɪ] *s* (orn.) aguador; (*cap.*) *s* (myth.) Febe; (poet.) Febe (*la luna*)
Phoebus [ˈfibəs] *s* (myth.) Febo; (poet.) Febo (*el sol*)
Phoenicia [fɪˈnɪʃə] *s* Fenicia
Phoenician [fɪˈnɪʃən] *adj & s* fenicio
phoenix [ˈfinɪks] *s* (myth. & fig.) fénix
phone [fon] *s* (coll.) teléfono; (phonet.) fon; **to come** o **to go to the phone** acudir al teléfono, ponerse al aparato; *va & vn* (coll.) telefonear
phone call *s* llamada telefónica
phoneme [ˈfonim] *s* (phonet.) fonema
phonemic [foˈnimɪk] *adj* fonémico; **phonemics** *ssg* fonémica
phonet. abr. de **phonetics**
phonetic [foˈnɛtɪk] *adj* fonético; **phonetics** *ssg* fonética
phonetically [foˈnɛtɪkəlɪ] *adv* fonéticamente
phonetician [ˌfonɪˈtɪʃən] *s* fonetista
phoney [ˈfonɪ] *adj* (*comp:* **-nier**; *super:* **-niest**) var. de **phony**; *s* var. de **phony**
phonic [ˈfonɪk] *adj* fónico; **phonics** *ssg* fónica; *spl* sistema fónico, basado en la ortografía ordinaria, que se emplea para enseñar a pronunciar y a leer a los niños
phonogram [ˈfonəgræm] *s* fonograma
phonograph [ˈfonəgræf] o [ˈfonəgrɑf] *s* fonógrafo; *adj* fonográfico
phonographic [ˌfonəˈgræfɪk] *adj* fonográfico
phonographically [ˌfonəˈgræfɪkəlɪ] *adv* fonográficamente
phonograph record *s* disco de fonógrafo
phonography [foˈnɑgrəfɪ] *s* fonografía
phonolite [ˈfonəlaɪt] *s* (mineral.) fonolita
phonologic [ˌfonəˈlɑdʒɪk] o **phonological** [ˌfonəˈlɑdʒɪkəl] *adj* fonológico
phonologist [foˈnɑlədʒɪst] *s* fonólogo
phonology [foˈnɑlədʒɪ] *s* fonología
phonoscope [ˈfonəskop] *s* fonoscopio
phony [ˈfonɪ] *adj* (*comp:* **-nier**; *super:* **-niest**) (slang) falso, contrahecho; *s* (*pl:* **-nies**) (slang) farsa; (slang) farsante

phosgene ['fɑsdʒin] *s* (chem.) fosgeno
phosphate ['fɑsfet] *s* (chem. & agr.) fosfato
phosphatic [fɑs'fætɪk] *adj* fosfático
phosphatize ['fɑsfətaɪz] *va* fosfatar
phosphaturia [,fɑsfə'tjʊrɪə] o [,fɑsfə'tʊrɪə] *s* (path.) fosfaturia
phosphene ['fɑsfin] *s* (physiol.) fosfeno
phosphide ['fɑsfaɪd] o ['fɑsfɪd] *s* (chem.) fosfuro
phosphine ['fɑsfin] o ['fɑsfɪn] *s* (chem.) fosfina
phosphite ['fɑsfaɪt] *s* (chem.) fosfito
phosphonium [fɑs'fonɪəm] *s* (chem.) fosfonio
Phosphor ['fɑsfər] *s* (poet.) Fósforo (*estrella matutina*)
phosphorate ['fɑsfəret] *va* fosforar
phosphor bronze *s* (trademark) bronce fosforoso
phosphoresce [,fɑsfə'rɛs] *vn* fosforecer
phosphorescence [,fɑsfə'rɛsəns] *s* fosforescencia
phosphorescent [,fɑsfə'rɛsənt] *adj* fosforescente
phosphoric [fɑs'fɑrɪk] o [fɑs'fɔrɪk] *adj* (chem.) fosfórico
phosphoric acid *s* (chem.) ácido fosfórico
phosphorite ['fɑsfəraɪt] *s* (mineral.) fosforita
phosphoroscope [fɑs'fɑrəskop] o [fɑs'fɔrəskop] *s* fosforoscopio
phosphorous ['fɑsfərəs] o [fɑs'forəs] *adj* (chem.) fosforoso
phosphorous acid *s* (chem.) ácido fosforoso
phosphorus ['fɑsfərəs] *s* (*pl:* **-ri** [raɪ]) (chem.) fósforo; (*cap.*) *s* (poet.) Fósforo (*estrella matutina*)
phosphureted o **phosphuretted** ['fɑsfjə,rɛtɪd] *adj* (chem.) fosfurado
phot [fɑt] o [fot] *s* (phys.) fotio
photic ['fotɪk] *adj* fótico
photo ['foto] *s* (*pl:* **-tos**) (coll.) foto; *va* (coll.) fotografiar
photoactinic [,fotoæk'tɪnɪk] *adj* fotoactínico
photocell ['foto,sɛl] *s* (elec.) fotocelda o fotocélula
photochemical [,foto'kɛmɪkəl] *adj* fotoquímico
photochemistry [,foto'kɛmɪstrɪ] *s* fotoquímica
photochrome ['fotokrom] *s* fotocromo
photochromy ['foto,kromɪ] *s* fotocromía
photoconductivity [,foto,kɑndʌk'tɪvɪtɪ] *s* (elec.) fotoconductividad
photocopy ['foto,kɑpɪ] *s* (*pl:* **-ies**) fotocopia
photodisintegration [,fotodɪs,ɪntɪ'greʃən] *s* (phys.) fotodesintegración
photodynamic [,fotodaɪ'næmɪk] o [,fotodɪ'næmɪk] *adj* fotodinámico; **photodynamics** *ssg* fotodinámica
photoelectric [,foto·ɪ'lɛktrɪk] *adj* fotoeléctrico
photoelectric cell *s* célula fotoeléctrica
photoelectron [,foto·ɪ'lɛktrɑn] *s* (physical chem.) fotoelectrón
photoengrave [,fotoɛn'grev] *va* fotograbar
photoengraver [,fotoɛn'grevər] *s* fotograbador
photoengraving [,fotoɛn'grevɪŋ] *s* fotograbado
photo finish *s* (sport) llegada de caballos o corredores a la meta con tan poca diferencia que hay que determinar al vencedor mediante el fotofija
photofinishing [,foto'fɪnɪʃɪŋ] *s* (phot.) revelado e impresión
photoflash lamp ['fotə,flæʃ] *s* (phot.) relámpago fotogénico eléctrico
photogen ['fotodʒɛn] *s* (chem.) fotógeno
photogene ['fotodʒin] *s* fotógeno (*impresión visual que dura después que la imagen propia ha cesado de ser visible*); (chem.) fotógeno
photogenic [,foto'dʒɛnɪk] *adj* (biol. & phot.) fotogénico
photogrammetric [,fotogrə'mɛtrɪk] o **photogrammetrical** [,fotogrə'mɛtrɪkəl] *adj* fotogramétrico
photogrammetry [,foto'græmɪtrɪ] *s* fotogrametría
photograph ['fotəgræf] o ['fotəgrɑf] *s* fotografía (*imagen, retrato*); *va & vn* fotografiar; **to photograph well** ser fotogénico
photographer [fə'tɑgrəfər] *s* fotógrafo
photographic [,fotə'græfɪk] *adj* fotográfico
photographically [,fotə'græfɪkəlɪ] *adv* fotográficamente
photography [fə'tɑgrəfɪ] *s* fotografía (*arte*)
photogravure [,fotogrə'vjʊr] o [,foto'grevjər] *s* huecograbado
photojournalism [,foto'dʒʌrnəlɪzəm] *s* fotoperiodismo
photokinesis [,fotokɪ'nisɪs] *s* (physiol.) fotocinesis
photokinetic [,fotokɪ'nɛtɪk] *adj* fotocinético
photolithograph [,foto'lɪθəgræf] o [,foto'lɪθəgrɑf] *s* fotolitografía; *va* fotolitografiar
photolithography [,fotolɪ'θɑgrəfɪ] *s* fotolitografía
photolysis [fo'tɑlɪsɪs] *s* fotólisis
photomechanical [,fotomɪ'kænɪkəl] *adj* fotomecánico
photometer [fo'tɑmɪtər] *s* fotómetro
photometry [fo'tɑmɪtrɪ] *s* fotometría
photomicrography [,fotomaɪ'krɑgrəfɪ] *s* fotomicrografía
photomontage [,fotomɑn'tɑʒ] *s* fotomontaje
photon ['fotɑn] *s* (phys.) fotón
photo-offset [,foto'ɔf,sɛt] o [,foto'ɑf,sɛt] *s* foto-offset
photophobia [,foto'fobɪə] *s* (path.) fotofobia
photoplay ['foto,ple] *s* fotodrama, drama cinematográfico
photoprint ['foto,prɪnt] *s* fotocalco
photoprocess ['foto,prɑsɛs] o ['foto,prosɛs] *s* procedimiento fotomecánico
photoreconnaissance [,fotorɪ'kɑnɪsəns] *s* fotorreconocimiento
photorelief [,fotorɪ'lif] *s* fotografía en relieve, fotorrelieve
photosensitive [,foto'sɛnsɪtɪv] *adj* fotosensitivo
photospectroscope [,foto'spɛktrəskop] *s* fotospectroscopio
photosphere ['foto,sfɪr] *s* (astr.) fotosfera
photostat ['fotostæt] *s* (trademark) fotóstato; *va & vn* fotostatar
photostatic [,foto'stætɪk] *adj* fotostático
photosynthesis [,foto'sɪnθɪsɪs] *s* (bot. & chem.) fotosíntesis
phototaxis [,foto'tæksɪs] *s* (biol.) fototactismo o fototaxis
phototelegraph [,foto'tɛlɪgræf] o [,foto'tɛlɪgrɑf] *s* fototelégrafo; *va & vn* fototelegrafiar
phototelegraphy [,fototɪ'lɛgrəfɪ] *s* fototelegrafía
phototherapeutics [,foto,θɛrə'pjutɪks] o **phototherapy** [,foto'θɛrəpɪ] *s* fototerapia
phototropism [fo'tɑtrəpɪzəm] *s* (biol.) fototropismo
phototube ['fotətjub] o ['fotətub] *s* (elec.) fototubo
phototype ['fototaɪp] *s* fototipo
phototypography [,fototaɪ'pɑgrəfɪ] *s* fototipografía
phototypy ['foto,taɪpɪ] o [fo'tɑtəpɪ] *s* fototipia
photovoltaic [,fotovɑl'teɪk] *adj* fotovoltaico
photozincography [,fotozɪŋ'kɑgrəfɪ] *s* fotocincografía
phrase [frez] *s* frase; (mus.) frase musical; *va* frasear; (mus.) frasear
phraseology [,frezɪ'ɑlədʒɪ] *s* (*pl:* **-gies**) fraseología
phrasing ['frezɪŋ] *s* fraseo; (mus.) fraseo
phratry ['fretrɪ] *s* (*pl:* **-tries**) fratría
phreatic [frɪ'ætɪk] *adj* freático
phrenetic [frɪ'nɛtɪk] *adj* frenético
phrenetically [frɪ'nɛtɪkəlɪ] *adv* frenéticamente
phrenic ['frɛnɪk] *adj* frénico; (anat.) frénico
phrenitis [frɪ'naɪtɪs] *s* (path.) frenitis
phrenological [,frɛnə'lɑdʒɪkəl] *adj* frenológico
phrenologist [frɪ'nɑlədʒɪst] *s* frenólogo
phrenology [frɪ'nɑlədʒɪ] *s* frenología
phrenopathy [frɪ'nɑpəθɪ] *s* (path.) frenopatía
phrensy ['frɛnzɪ] *s* (*pl:* **-sies**) var. de **frenzy**
Phrygia ['frɪdʒɪə] *s* Frigia
Phrygian ['frɪdʒɪən] *adj & s* frigio
PHS. abr. de **Public Health Service**
phthalein ['θælin], ['θælɪɪn], ['fθælin] o ['fθælɪɪn] *s* (chem.) ftaleína

phthalic ['θælɪk] o ['fθælɪk] *adj* (chem.) ftálico
phthalin ['θælɪn] o ['fθælɪn] *s* (chem.) ftalina
phthiocol ['θaɪəkol] o [θaɪəkəl] *s* (biochem.) ftiocol
phthisic ['tɪzɪk] *s* (path.) tisis
phthisical ['tɪzɪkəl] *adj* tísico
phthisis ['θaɪsɪs] *s* (path.) tisis
phycology [faɪ'kɑlədʒɪ] *s* ficología
phylactery [fɪ'læktərɪ] *s* (*pl:* **-ies**) filacteria; (f.a.) filacteria
Phyllis ['fɪlɪs] *s* Filis
phyllite ['fɪlaɪt] *s* (mineral.) filita
phyllium ['fɪlɪəm] *s* (ent.) filio
phyllode ['fɪlod] *s* (bot.) filodio
phyllomania [,fɪlo'menɪə] *s* (bot.) filomanía
phyllophagous [fɪ'lɑfəgəs] *adj* filófago
phyllopod ['fɪləpɑd] *adj & s* (zool.) filópodo
phyllotaxis [,fɪlə'tæksɪs] *s* (bot.) filotaxia
phylloxera [,fɪlɑk'sɪrə] o [fɪ'lɑksərə] *s* (*pl:* **-rae** [ri]) (ent.) filoxera
phylogenesis [,faɪlo'dʒenɪsɪs] *s* (biol.) filogénesis
phylogenetic [,faɪlodʒɪ'netɪk] o **phylogenic** [,faɪlo'dʒenɪk] *adj* filogénico
phylogeny [faɪ'lɑdʒɪnɪ] *s* (*pl:* **-nies**) (biol.) filogenia
phylum ['faɪləm] *s* (*pl:* **-la** [lə]) (biol.) filo o fílum
phys. abr. de **physical, physician, physics, physiological** y **physiology**
physic ['fɪzɪk] *s* medicamento; purgante; **physics** *ssg* física; (*pret & pp:* **-icked**; *ger:* **-icking**) *va* purgar; medicinar; curar
physical ['fɪzɪkəl] *adj* físico
physical chemistry *s* química física
physical culture *s* cultura física
physical education *s* educación física
physical fitness *s* buena salud
physical geography *s* geografía física
physically ['fɪzɪkəlɪ] *adv* físicamente
physical science *s* ciencia física
physical therapy *s* terapia física
physician [fɪ'zɪʃən] *s* médico
physicist ['fɪzɪsɪst] *s* físico
physic nut *s* (bot.) piñón, piñón de Indias
physicochemical [,fɪzɪko'kemɪkəl] *adj* físicoquímico
physicochemist [,fɪzɪko'kemɪst] *s* físicoquímico
physicochemistry [,fɪzɪko'kemɪstrɪ] *s* físicoquímica
physiocracy [,fɪzɪ'ɑkrəsɪ] *s* fisiocracia
physiocrat ['fɪzɪəkræt] *s* fisiócrata
physiocratic [,fɪzɪə'krætɪk] *adj* fisiócrata; fisiocrático
physiognomic [,fɪzɪɑg'nɑmɪk] o [,fɪzɪə'nɑmɪk] o **physiognomical** [,fɪzɪɑg'nɑmɪkəl] o [,fɪzɪə'nɑmɪkəl] *adj* fisonómico
physiognomist [,fɪzɪ'ɑgnəmɪst] o [,fɪzɪ'ɑnəmɪst] *s* fisonomista
physiognomy [,fɪzɪ'ɑgnəmɪ] o [,fɪzɪ'ɑnəmɪ] *s* fisionomía
physiographer [,fɪzɪ'ɑgrəfər] *s* fisiógrafo
physiographic [,fɪzɪə'græfɪk] *adj* fisiográfico
physiography [,fɪzɪ'ɑgrəfɪ] *s* fisiografía
physiological [,fɪzɪə'lɑdʒɪkəl] *adj* fisiológico
physiological chemistry *s* química fisiológica
physiologically [,fɪzɪə'lɑdʒɪkəlɪ] *adv* fisiológicamente
physiologist [,fɪzɪ'ɑlədʒɪst] *s* fisiólogo
physiology [,fɪzɪ'ɑlədʒɪ] *s* fisiología
physiotherapy [,fɪzɪo'θerəpɪ] *s* fisioterapia
physique [fɪ'zik] *s* físico (*exterior, talle, constitución de una persona*)
physostigmine [,faɪso'stɪgmin] o [,faɪso'stɪgmɪn] *s* (chem.) fisostigmina
phytin ['faɪtɪn] *s* (chem.) fitina
phytogeography [,faɪtodʒɪ'ɑgrəfɪ] *s* fitogeografía
phytographer [faɪ'tɑgrəfər] *s* fitógrafo
phytographic [,faɪtə'græfɪk] o **phytographical** [,faɪtə'græfɪkəl] *adj* fitográfico
phytography [faɪ'tɑgrəfɪ] *s* fitografía
phytolaccaceous [,faɪtolə'keʃəs] *adj* (bot.) fitolacáceo
phytology [faɪ'tɑlədʒɪ] *s* fitología
phytopathology [,faɪtopə'θɑlədʒɪ] *s* (bot. & med.) fitopatología
phytophagous [faɪ'tɑfəgəs] *adj* (zool.) fitófago
phytoplankton [,faɪto'plæŋktən] *s* (biol.) fitoplancton
phytotomy [faɪ'tɑtəmɪ] *s* fitotomía
P.I. abr. de **Philippine Islands**
pi [paɪ] *s* (print.) pastel; (math.) pi; mezcolanza; (*pret & pp:* **pied**; *ger:* **piing**) *va* (print.) empastelar
pia mater ['paɪə'metər] *s* (anat.) piamáter
pian [pɪ'æn] o [pjɑn] *s* (path.) pian
pianist [pɪ'ænɪst] o ['piənɪst] *s* pianista
piano [pɪ'æno] *s* (*pl:* **-os**) piano; *adj* pianístico; [pɪ'ɑno] *adj* (mus.) suave; *adv* (mus.) suavemente
pianoforte [pɪ,æno'fɔrtɪ] o [pɪ'ænofort] *s* (mus.) pianoforte
pianola [,piə'nolə] *s* (trademark) pianola, autopiano; *adj* (slang) fácil, fácil de ejecutar
piano stool *s* taburete de piano
piano tuner *s* afinador de pianos
piano wire *s* cuerda de piano
piaster o **piastre** [pɪ'æstər] *s* piastra
piazza [pɪ'æzə] *s* plaza; (arch.) pórtico, galería
pibroch ['pibrɑk] *s* (Scotch) música marcial o fúnebre que se toca con la gaita
pica ['paɪkə] *s* (print.) cícero; (path. & vet.) pica
Picard ['pɪkərd] *adj & s* picardo
Picardy ['pɪkərdɪ] *s* la Picardía
picarel [,pɪkə'rel] *s* (ichth.) mena
picaresque [,pɪkə'resk] *adj* picaresco
picaroon [,pɪkə'run] *s* pícaro; pirata; buque de piratas; *vn* piratear
picayune [,pɪkə'jun] *adj* de poca monta, mezquino; *s* medio real; persona insignificante; bagatela, friolera
piccadilly [,pɪkə'dɪlɪ] *s* (*pl:* **-lies**) cuello de pajarita, foque (*cuello almidonado*)
piccalilli ['pɪkə,lɪlɪ] *s* legumbres en escabeche
piccolo ['pɪkəlo] *s* (mus.) (*pl:* **-los**) flautín
piccoloist ['pɪkəlo·ɪst] *s* flautín (*músico*)
piceous ['pɪsɪəs] o ['paɪsɪəs] *adj* píceo; inflamable
pick [pɪk] *s* pico; punzón; cosecha, recolección; (mus.) plectro; flor (*lo más excelente*) ‖ *va* escoger; recoger (*p.ej., flores*); recolectar (*p.ej., algodón*); picar; cavar con un pico; romper (*el hielo*) con un punzón; picotear; escarbarse, mondarse, limpiarse (*los dientes*); descañonar, desplumar (*un ave*); rascarse (*una cicatriz, una pequeña herida, un grano*); roer (*un hueso*); mondar (*las frutas*); falsear, forzar (*una cerradura*); armar (*una pendencia*); (mus.) herir (*las cuerdas de un instrumento*); puntear (*p.ej., la guitarra*); buscar (*defectos*); separar las fibras de (*p.ej., la estopa*); **to pick off** ir matando con tiros sucesivos; **to pick one's way (through)** andar con mucho tiento (por entre); **to pick out** entresacar; ver (*una cosa que no se destaca de otras*); descifrar; **to pick pockets** hurtar de los bolsillos; **to pick someone to pieces** (coll.) no dejarle a uno un hueso sano; **to pick up** recoger; recobrar (*ánimo, velocidad*); hallar o conseguir por casualidad; aprender con la práctica; aprender de oídas; invitar a subir a un coche; entablar conversación con (*sin presentación previa*); captar (*una señal de radio*) ‖ *vn* picar; comer sin gana, comer melindrosamente; escoger esmeradamente; ratear; **to pick at** tirar de; comer sin gana, comer melindrosamente; (coll.) tomarla con, criticar, regañar; **to pick on** escoger, elegir; (coll.) criticar, regañar; (coll.) molestar, hostilizar; **to pick over** (coll.) ir revolviendo y examinando; preparar para el uso; **to pick up** (coll.) ir mejor, sentirse mejor, restablecerse; recobrar velocidad
pickaback ['pɪkə,bæk] *adv* a cuestas, en hombros
pickaninny ['pɪkə,nɪnɪ] *s* (*pl:* **-nies**) (offensive) negrito, niño negro; niñito
pickax o **pickaxe** ['pɪk,æks] *s* piqueta, zapapico
picker ['pɪkər] *s* recogedor; escardador; escogedor; (mach.) palanca de tiro; (mach.) sacalanzadera
pickerel ['pɪkərəl] *s* (ichth.) sollo norteamericano (*Esox niger y Esox vermiculatus*)

pickerelweed [ˈpɪkərəl,wid] *s* (bot.) flor de la laguna
picket [ˈpɪkɪt] *s* piquete (*estaca clavada en la tierra*); (mil.) piquete; piquete de huelguistas; *va* cercar con piquetes o estacas; atar (*un animal*) a una estaca; estacionar piquetes de huelguistas cerca de, poner un cordón de piquetes a; *vn* servir de piquete de huelguistas
picket fence *s* cerca de estacas
picket line *s* línea de vigilantes huelguistas
pickings [ˈpɪkɪŋz] *spl* lo recogido; lo robado, lo pillado; residuos
pickle [ˈpɪkəl] *s* encurtido; escabeche, salmuera; (metal.) baño químico para limpiar metales; (coll.) apuro, aprieto; **to get into a pickle** (coll.) meterse en un berenjenal; *va* encurtir; escabechar; (metal.) limpiar con baño químico
picklock [ˈpɪk,lɑk] *s* ganzúa (*garfio; ladrón*)
pick-me-up [ˈpɪkmi,ʌp] *s* (coll.) tentempié; (coll.) trago fortificante
pickpocket [ˈpɪk,pɑkɪt] *s* carterista, ratero
pickup [ˈpɪk,ʌp] *s* recolección; recobro (*de un motor*); aceleración (*de un automóvil*); (slang) mejora; (coll.) persona conocida por casualidad y sin presentación; (elec.) pick-up, fonocaptor
pickup truck *s* camioneta de reparto
picky [ˈpɪkɪ] *adj* melindroso en el comer
picnic [ˈpɪknɪk] *s* jira, partida de campo, comida campestre; (slang) rato agradable, cosa fácil; (*pret & pp:* **-nicked; *ger:* -nicking**) *vn* hacer una comida campestre, merendar en el campo
picnicker [ˈpɪknɪkər] *s* merendante en el campo, excursionista
picot [ˈpiko] *s* piquillo, puntilla; (*pret & pp:* **-coted** [kod]; *ger:* **-coting** [ko·ɪŋ] *va* adornar o guarnecer con piquillos
picrate [ˈpɪkret] *s* (chem.) picrato
picric [ˈpɪkrɪk] *adj* pícrico
picric acid *s* (chem.) ácido pícrico
Pict [pɪkt] *s* picto
Pictish [ˈpɪktɪʃ] *adj* picto
pictograph [ˈpɪktəgræf] o [ˈpɪktəgrɑf] *s* pictografía
pictographic [,pɪktəˈgræfɪk] *adj* pictográfico
pictorial [pɪkˈtorɪəl] *adj* pictórico; gráfico; ilustrado; *s* revista ilustrada
pictorially [pɪkˈtorɪəlɪ] *adv* pictóricamente; con ilustraciones
picture [ˈpɪktʃər] *s* cuadro, pintura; imagen; retrato; ilustración; fotografía; lámina, grabado; película; (fig.) retrato, cuadro; estado general (*de un enfermo*); cuadro completo, visión de conjunto; **picture of despair** cuadro de desolación; **picture of health** salud personificada; *va* dibujar; pintar; describir; representarse; **to picture to oneself** representarse
picture book *s* libro con láminas
picture frame *s* marco
picture gallery *s* galería de pinturas
picture hat *s* pamela
picture house *s* cine, teatro cine
picture page *s* noticiario gráfico (*de un periódico*)
picture palace *s* (Brit.) cine, teatro cine
picture post card *s* tarjeta postal ilustrada, tarjeta postal con vistas fotográficas
picture puzzle *s* var. de **jigsaw puzzle**
picture show *s* exhibición de pinturas; cine
picture signal *s* (telv.) videoseñal
picturesque [,pɪktʃəˈrɛsk] *adj* pintoresco
picturesqueness [,pɪktʃəˈrɛsknɪs] *s* carácter pintoresco
picture tube *s* (telv.) tubo de imagen, tubo de televisión
picture writing *s* pictografía
piddle [ˈpɪdəl] *vn* emplearse en bagatelas; (coll.) orinar
piddling [ˈpɪdlɪŋ] *adj* de poca monta, insignificante
piddock [ˈpɪdək] *s* (zool.) julán
pidgin English [ˈpɪdʒɪn] *s* lengua franca usada en China entre los extranjeros y los indígenas
pie [paɪ] *s* pastel; (orn.) picaza, urraca; (print.) pastel; mezcolanza; (*pret & pp:* **pied; *ger:* pieing**) *va* (print.) empastelar
pie à la mode [mod] *s* pastel servido con helado encima
piebald [ˈpaɪ,bɔld] *adj & s* picazo (*caballo*)
piece [pis] *s* pedazo (*fragmento; casco, p.ej., de botella rota; retazo, p.ej., de tela*); pieza (*de una máquina o artefacto; obra dramática; composición suelta de música; cañón; figura que sirve para jugar a las damas, el ajedrez, etc.; moneda*); lote, parcela (*de terreno*); (dial.) rato; (dial.) corta distancia; **a piece of advice** un consejo; **a piece of baggage** un bulto; **a piece of folly** una tontería; **a piece of furniture** un mueble; **a piece of money** una moneda; **a piece of work** un trabajo; **of a piece with** de la misma clase que, lo mismo que; de acuerdo con; **to break to pieces** despedazar, hacer pedazos; despedazarse; **to cut to pieces** desmenuzar; destrozar (*p.ej., un ejército*); **to fall to pieces** desbaratarse, caer en ruina; **to fly to pieces** romperse en mil pedazos; **to give one a piece of one's mind** decirle a uno cuántas son cinco, decirle a uno su parecer con toda franqueza; **to go to pieces** desvencijarse; darse a la desesperación; ir al desastre (*p.ej., un negocio*); sufrir un ataque de nervios; perder por completo la salud; **to pick someone to pieces** (coll.) no dejarle a uno un hueso sano; **to speak one's piece** (coll.) decir su parecer, hablar con franqueza; **to take to pieces** desarmar; refutar punto por punto; *va* juntar las piezas de; formar juntando piezas; remendar; **to piece out** completar a pedacitos; *vn* (coll.) comer a deshora
pièce de résistance [,pjɛs də rezisˈtɑ̃s] *s* plato principal; lo principal, lo más importante
piecemeal [ˈpis,mil] *adj* hecho a bocaditos; fragmentario; *adv* a bocaditos; en pedazos; a remiendos
piece of eight *s* doblón de a ocho (*antigua moneda de oro española*)
piece wage *s* remuneración por rendimiento
piecework [ˈpis,wʌrk] *s* destajo, trabajo a destajo
pieceworker [ˈpis,wʌrkər] *s* destajero
pie crust *s* pasta de pastel
pied [paɪd] *adj* abigarrado; de o con traje abigarrado; pintado, manchado (*pájaro*); pío, remendado (*animal*)
Piedmont [ˈpidmɑnt] *s* el Piamonte; llanura del sureste de los EE.UU.
Piedmontese [,pidmɑnˈtiz] *adj* piamontés; *s* (*pl:* **-tese**) piamontés
pier [pɪr] *s* muelle; estribo, sostén (*de puente*); pila, pilastre (*de varias obras de ingeniería*); rompeolas; (arch.) entrepaño (*espacio de pared entre dos huecos*)
pierce [pɪrs] *va* agujerear, horadar, taladrar; atravesar, traspasar; picar, pinchar, punzar; (fig.) traspasar (*de dolor*); *vn* penetrar, entrar a la fuerza
piercing [ˈpɪrsɪŋ] *adj* penetrante, agudo, desgarrador
pier glass *s* espejo de cuerpo entero
Pierian [paɪˈɪrɪən] *adj* pierio
Pierian spring *s* fuente pieria
pier table *s* consola
pietism [ˈpaɪətɪzəm] *s* piedad, devoción; mojigatería; (*cap.*) *s* pietismo
pietist [ˈpaɪətɪst] *s* beato; (*cap.*) *s* pietista
pietistic [,paɪəˈtɪstɪk] *adj* beato
piety [ˈpaɪətɪ] *s* (*pl:* **-ties**) piedad, devoción
piezoelectric [paɪ,izo·ɪˈlɛktrɪk] *adj* piezoeléctrico
piezoelectricity [paɪ,izo·ɪ,lɛkˈtrɪsɪtɪ] *s* piezoelectricidad
piezometer [,paɪɪˈzɑmɪtər] *s* piezómetro
piffle [ˈpɪfəl] *s* (coll.) disparates, música celestial
pig [pɪg] *s* (zool.) cerdo; puerco, cochino (*cerdo domesticado*); lechón; carne de puerco; (metal.) lingote; (coll.) marrano (*hombre sucio e indecente*); **to buy a pig in a poke** cerrar un trato a ciegas
pigeon [ˈpɪdʒən] *s* (orn.) paloma; (slang) bobalicón
pigeon breast *s* (path.) pecho de pichón
pigeon hawk *s* (orn.) halcón palumbario
pigeonhole [ˈpɪdʒən,hol] *s* hornilla, casilla de paloma; casilla; *va* encasillar; clasificar y retener en la memoria; dar carpetazo a

pigeon house *s* palomar
pigeon-toed ['pɪdʒən,tod] *adj* con los pies torcidos hacia dentro
pigeonwing ['pɪdʒən,wɪŋ] *s* figura de danza en forma de ala de paloma; figura que hacen los patinadores en forma de ala de paloma
piggery ['pɪgərɪ] *s* (*pl:* **-ies**) pocilga
piggish ['pɪgɪʃ] *adj* cochino; glotón, voraz
piggy ['pɪgɪ] *s* (*pl:* **-gies**) lechón, lechoncillo; *adj* glotón
piggyback ['pɪgɪ,bæk] *adv* a cuestas, en hombros
piggybacking ['pɪgɪ,bækɪŋ] *s* transporte de semi-remolques cargados, en vagones de plataforma
pig-headed ['pɪg,hɛdɪd] *adj* terco, cabezudo
pig iron *s* arrabio, hierro colado en barras
piglet ['pɪglɪt] o **pigling** ['pɪglɪŋ] *s* lechón, lechoncillo
pigment ['pɪgmənt] *s* pigmento; *va* pigmentar; *vn* pigmentarse
pigmentary ['pɪgmən,tɛrɪ] *adj* pigmentario
pigmentation [,pɪgmən'teʃən] *s* (biol.) pigmentación
pigmy ['pɪgmɪ] *adj* var. de **pygmy;** *s* (*pl:* **-mies**) var. de **pygmy**
pignut ['pɪg,nʌt] *s* (bot.) pacanero; pacana (*fruto*)
pigpen ['pɪg,pɛn] *s* pocilga; (fig.) corral de vacas (*paraje sucio o destartalado*)
pigskin ['pɪg,skɪn] *s* piel de cerdo, pellejo de cerdo; (coll.) silla de montar; (coll.) balón (*con que se juega al fútbol*)
pigsty ['pɪg,staɪ] *s* (*pl:* **-sties**) pocilga
pigtail ['pɪg,tel] *s* coleta, trenza; andullo (*de tabaco*)
pigweed ['pɪg,wid] *s* (bot.) cenizo, quelite; (bot.) quenopodio; (bot.) mercolina; (bot.) amaranto
pika ['paɪkə] *s* (zool.) ochotona
pike [paɪk] *s* pica; punta (*p.ej., de flecha*); escarpia; carretera; peaje; camino de barrera; (ichth.) lucio; *va* herir o matar con la pica; *vn* (coll.) irse, salir corriendo; **to pike along** (coll.) seguir su camino
pikeman ['paɪkmən] *s* (*pl:* **-men**) piquero
piker ['paɪkər] *s* (slang) cicatero; (slang) persona de poco fuste; (slang) cobarde
Pike's Peak *s* el pico de Pike (*en las Montañas Rocosas*)
pikestaff ['paɪk,stæf] o ['paɪk,stɑf] *s* (*pl:* **-staves** [,stevz]) asta de pica; báculo herrado
pilaf o **pilaff** [pɪ'lɑf] *s* pilav (*manjar oriental*)
pilaster [pɪ'læstər] *s* (arch.) pilastra
Pilate ['paɪlət] *s* Pilatos
pilau o **pilaw** [pɪ'lɔ] *s* var. de **pilaf**
pilchard ['pɪltʃərd] *s* (ichth.) sardina
pile [paɪl] *s* pila, montón; mole; conjunto apretado (*p.ej., de edificios*); pilote; lanilla, pelusa; lana; pira; (coll.) caudal, fortuna; (coll.) montón (*número considerable*); (elec., her. & phys.) pila; **piles** *mpl* (path.) almorranas; **to make a pile** (coll.) hacerse su agosto, enriquecerse; *va* apilar; **to pile on** echar encima; **to pile one thing on another** superponer una cosa a otra; **to pile up** apilar, amontonar; **to pile with** cubrir con, cargar de; *vn* apilarse; **to pile in** o **into** entrar atropelladamente en; entrar todos en (*un recinto pequeño*); subir todos a (*p.ej., un automóvil*); **to pile up** apilarse; acumularse
piled [paɪld] *adj* de mucho pelillo, de mucha lanilla
pile driver *s* martinete
pile dwelling *s* vivienda lacustre sostenida por pilares
pilewort ['paɪl,wʌrt] *s* (bot.) celidonia menor
pilfer ['pɪlfər] *va & vn* ratear
pilgrim ['pɪlgrɪm] *s* peregrino, romero
pilgrimage ['pɪlgrɪmɪdʒ] *s* peregrinación, romería
piling ['paɪlɪŋ] *s* pilotaje (*conjunto de pilotes*)
pill [pɪl] *s* píldora; (slang) pelota; (slang) chinche, posma (*persona molesta*); mal trago, sinsabor; **to gild the pill** dorar la píldora
pillage ['pɪlɪdʒ] *s* pillaje; *va & vn* pillar
pillar ['pɪlər] *s* pilar; (fig.) pilar (*persona*); **from pillar to post** de Herodes a Pilatos; *va* proveer de pilares, sostener con pilares
pillared ['pɪlərd] *adj* con pilares; de forma columnar
Pillars of Hercules *spl* columnas de Hércules
pillbox ['pɪl,bɑks] *s* caja para píldoras; (mil.) fortín armado de ametralladoras
pillory ['pɪlərɪ] *s* (*pl:* **-ries**) picota; (*pret & pp:* **-ried**) *va* empicotar; poner a la vergüenza, poner en ridículo
pillow ['pɪlo] *s* almohada; cojín; mundillo; (mach.) cojinete; (naut.) almohada (*de las jarcias*); (naut.) tragante, descanso (*del bauprés*); *va* poner sobre una almohada; soportar, servir de almohada a
pillow block *s* (mach.) chumacera
pillowcase ['pɪlo,kes] *s* almohada, funda de almohada
pillow lace *s* encaje de bolillos
pillow sham *s* paño bordado (*para cubrir almohadas*)
pillowslip ['pɪlo,slɪp] *s* var. de **pillowcase**
pillowy ['pɪləwɪ] *adj* blando, suave
pilocarpine [,paɪlo'kɑrpin] o [,paɪlo'kɑrpɪn] *s* (chem.) pilocarpina
pilose ['paɪlos] *adj* piloso
pilosity [paɪ'lɑsɪtɪ] *s* pilosidad
pilot ['paɪlət] *s* piloto; práctico (*de puerto*); (rail.) trompa, delantera; mechero encendedor (*de una cocina de gas*); *va* pilotar; conducir (*servir de guía a*)
pilotage ['paɪlətɪdʒ] *s* (naut. & aer.) pilotaje
pilot balloon *s* globo piloto
pilot biscuit o **bread** *s* (naut.) galleta
pilot chute *s* paracaídas piloto
pilot engine *s* (rail.) máquina piloto
pilot fish *s* (ichth.) piloto
pilot house *s* (naut.) timonera
pilot light *s* lámpara testigo, lámpara de comprobación, lámpara piloto; mechero encendedor (*de una cocina de gas*)
pilot plant *s* instalación piloto
Piltdown man ['pɪlt,daʊn] *s* (anthrop.) hombre de Piltdown
pimento [pɪ'mɛnto] *s* (*pl:* **-tos**) (bot.) pimienta; pimienta inglesa (*fruto seco y molido*); pimiento dulce
pimiento [pɪ'mjɛnto] *s* (*pl:* **-tos**) pimiento dulce
pimola [pɪ'molə] *s* aceituna rellena con un taco de pimiento dulce
pimp [pɪmp] *s & vn* var. de **pander**
pimpernel ['pɪmpərnɛl] *s* (bot.) murajes
pimple ['pɪmpəl] *s* grano (*en la piel*)
pimpled ['pɪmpəld] *adj* var. de **pimply**
pimply ['pɪmplɪ] *adj* (*comp:* **-plier;** *super:* **-pliest**) granujoso
pin [pɪn] *s* alfiler; prendedero; clavija; ficha o clavillo (*para sujetar las hojas de las tijeras*); bolo (*del juego de bolos*); asta (*de la bandera que marca cada agujero en el juego de golf*); botón (*de manubrio*); (mach.) gorrón; (naut.) cabilla; (coll.) pierna; **to be on pins and needles** estar en espinas; (*pret & pp:* **pinned;** *ger:* **pinning**) *va* asegurar o prender con un alfiler o con alfileres; clavar, fijar, sujetar; coger y sujetar; **to pin down** sujetar con alfileres; obligar (*a una persona*) a que diga la verdad; **to pin one's faith on** tener puesta su esperanza en; **to pin something on someone** (coll.) acusarle o culparle a uno de una cosa; **to pin up** recoger y apuntar con alfileres, arremangar; fijar en la pared con alfileres
pinacoid ['pɪnəkɔɪd] *s* (cryst.) pinacoide
pinafore ['pɪnə,for] *s* delantal de niña
pinaster [paɪ'næstər] o [pɪ'næstər] *s* (bot.) pinastro, pino rodeno
pinball ['pɪn,bɔl] *s* billar romano, bagatela
pincase ['pɪn,kes] *s* alfiletero, cañutero
pince-nez ['pæns,ne] *s* lentes de nariz, lentes de pinzas
pincer movement *s* (mil.) movimiento de pinzas
pincers ['pɪnsərz] *ssg* o *spl* pinzas (*instrumento; órgano prensil del cangrejo, etc.*); (mil.) movimiento de pinzas
pinch [pɪntʃ] *s* pellizco; apretón; polvo, p.ej., **pinch of snuff** polvo de rapé; aprieto, apuro; tormento (*p.ej., del hambre*); (slang) arresto; (slang) hurto, robo; **in a pinch** en un aprieto; en caso necesario; *va* pellizcar; cogerse

(*los dedos*) en una puerta; apretar, p.ej., **this shoe pinches me** este zapato me aprieta; atenacear; restringir; contraer (*el frío la cara de uno*); adelgazar (*el dolor, el hambre a una persona*); limitar los gastos de; (slang) arrestar, prender; (slang) hurtar, robar; *vn* apretar; economizar, privarse de lo necesario
pinchbeck ['pɪntʃ,bɛk] *s* similor; falsificación; *adj* de similor; falsificado
pinchers ['pɪntʃərz] *ssg* o *spl* var. de **pincers**
pinch-hit ['pɪntʃ,hɪt] (*pret & pp:* **-hit;** *ger:* **-hitting**) *vn* (baseball) batear de emergente; (fig.) substituir a otro en un apuro
pinch hitter *s* (baseball) bateador emergente
pincushion ['pɪn,kʊʃən] *s* acerico
Pindar ['pɪndər] *s* Píndaro
Pindaric [pɪn'dærɪk] *adj* pindárico
pindling ['pɪndlɪŋ] *adj* (coll.) enteco, enfermizo
Pindus ['pɪndəs] *s* Pindo
pine [paɪn] *s* (bot.) pino; *vn* languidecer; **to pine for** penar por
pineal ['pɪnɪəl] *adj* pineal
pineal body o **gland** *s* (anat.) glándula pineal
pineapple ['paɪn,æpəl] *s* (bot.) ananás, piña (*planta y fruto*)
pine cone *s* piña
pine marten *s* (zool.) marta
pine needle *s* pinocha; **pine needles** *spl* alhumajo
pinery ['paɪnərɪ] *s* (*pl:* **-ies**) pinar; piñal
pine tar *s* alquitrán de madera
piney ['paɪnɪ] *adj* var. de **piny**
pinfeather ['pɪn,fɛðər] *s* cañón (*pluma del ave no desarrollada*)
pinfold ['pɪn,fold] *s* corral de concejo; *va* encerrar en corral de concejo
ping [pɪŋ] *s* silbido de bala; *vn* silbar como una bala
ping-pong ['pɪŋ,pɑŋ] *s* (trademark) ping-pong, tenis de mesa, tenis de salón
pinguin ['pɪŋgwɪn] *s* (bot.) piña de ratón, piñuela, maya
pinhead ['pɪn,hɛd] *s* cabecilla de alfiler; cosa muy pequeña o insignificante; (slang) bobalicón
pinhole ['pɪn,hol] *s* agujero que hace un alfiler; agujero para espiga o clavija
pinion ['pɪnjən] *s* (mach. & orn.) piñón; (orn.) ala; (orn.) remera; *va* cortar las alas a (*un ave*); maniatar
pinion gear *s* (aut.) piñón diferencial
pink [pɪŋk] *adj* rosado, sonrosado; *s* color de rosa; estado perfecto; comunistoide; (bot.) clavel, clavellina; *va* herir levemente con daga, espada, etc.; adornar; (sew.) ondear, ojetear, picar
pinkeye ['pɪŋk,aɪ] *s* (path.) conjuntivitis catarral aguda
pinking shears ['pɪŋkɪŋ] *spl* tijeras picafestones
pinkish ['pɪŋkɪʃ] *adj* rosado claro, que tira a rosado
pin money *s* alfileres, dinero para alfileres
pinna ['pɪnə] *s* (*pl:* **-nae** [ni] o **-nas**) (orn.) pluma; (orn.) ala; (zool.) aleta (*de pez o foca*); (anat.) pabellón del oído; (bot.) folíolo
pinnace ['pɪnɪs] *s* (naut.) pinaza; (naut.) bote
pinnacle ['pɪnəkəl] *s* pináculo, cumbre; (arch.) pináculo; (fig.) pináculo, cumbre
pinnate ['pɪnet] *adj* (bot.) pinado
pinnatifid [pɪ'nætɪfɪd] *adj* (bot.) pinatífido
pinniped ['pɪnɪpɛd] *adj & s* (zool.) pinnípedo
pin oak *s* (bot.) roble de los pantanos
Pinocchio [pɪ'nɔkɪo] *s* Pinocho
pinochle o **pinocle** ['pi,nʌkəl] *s* pinocle (*juego de naipes*)
piñon ['pɪnjən] o ['pinjon] *s* (bot.) pino piñón; piñón (*fruto*)
pinpoint ['pɪn,pɔɪnt] *s* punta de alfiler; *adj* exacto, preciso; *va & vn* apuntar con precisión
pinpoint bombing *s* (aer.) bombardeo de precisión
pinprick ['pɪn,prɪk] *s* alfilerazo
pint [paɪnt] *s* pinta (*medida*)
pintail ['pɪn,tel] *s* (orn.) pato cuellilargo; (orn.) ganga
pin-tailed sand grouse ['pɪn,teld] *s* (orn.) ganga
pintle ['pɪntəl] *s* gorrón; perno de un gozne; (naut.) pinzote, macho de timón
pinto ['pɪnto] *adj* pintado; *s* (*pl:* **-tos**) caballo pintado; pinto (*frijol*)
pint pot *s* olla con capacidad de pinta
pint-size ['paɪnt,saɪz] o **pint-sized** ['paɪnt,saɪzd] *adj* diminuto
pinup girl ['pɪn,ʌp] *s* fotografía o dibujo artístico de una muchacha linda; muchacha modelo para tal fotografía
pinwheel ['pɪn,hwil] *s* rueda de fuego, rueda giratoria (*de fuegos artificiales*); molino de viento, rehilandera (*juguete de niño*)
pinworm ['pɪn,wʌrm] *s* (zool.) lombriz de los niños
piny ['paɪnɪ] *adj* (*comp:* **-ier;** *super:* **-iest**) pinoso
pioneer [,paɪə'nɪr] *s* pionero (*explorador, colonizador; primer promotor*); (mil.) zapador; *va* preparar el camino a; iniciar, promover; abrir o explorar (*el camino*); *vn* abrir nuevos caminos, explorar
pious ['paɪəs] *adj* pío, piadoso; mojigato
pip [pɪp] *s* pepita (*simiente*); (vet.) pepita; punto (*en un naipe, dado, etc.*); (coll.) enfermedad pasajera; (*pret & pp:* **pipped;** *ger:* **pipping**) *va* romper (*el cascarón el polluelo*); *vn* piar, pipiar
pipe [paɪp] *s* caño, conducto, tubo; cañería; pipa (*para fumar tabaco*); fumarada (*tabaco que cabe en la pipa*); (mus.) caramillo, zampoña, pipa, flauta de Pan; (mus.) cañón (*de órgano*); silbo, nota aflautada, voz atiplada; pipa, tonel; (naut.) pito o silbato del contramaestre; **pipes** *spl* (mus.) gaita; *va* conducir por medio de tubos o cañerías; proveer de tuberías o cañerías; instalar tubos o cañerías en; decir o pronunciar con voz atiplada; cantar con voz atiplada; llamar con silbatos; (sew.) adornar con cordoncillos; *vn* tocar el caramillo; hablar o cantar con voz atiplada; tocar su pito (*el contramaestre*); **to pipe down** (slang) callarse; **to pipe up** comenzar a tocar; (slang) comenzar a hablar
pipe bender *s* curvatubos
pipe clamp *s* sujetatubos
pipe clay *s* albero, tierra de pipa
pipe-clay ['paɪp,kle] *va* blanquear o limpiar con albero
pipe cleaner *s* desobturador de pipa, limpiapipas
pipe cutter *s* cortatubos (*herramienta*)
pipe dream *s* (coll.) idea o esperanza imposibles, castillo en el aire
pipe fitter *s* cañero, montador de tuberías
pipe fitting *s* instalación de tuberías; **pipe fittings** *spl* accesorios para tubería, accesorios de cañería
pipeful ['paɪpfʊl] *s* fumarada (*tabaco que cabe en la pipa*)
pipe hanger *s* portacaño
pipe line *s* cañería, tubería; oleoducto; fuente de informes confidenciales
pipe-line ['paɪp,laɪn] *va* conducir por medio de un oleoducto; proveer de un oleoducto
pipe of peace *s* pipa de paz
pipe organ *s* (mus.) órgano
piper ['paɪpər] *s* flautista; gaitero; **to pay the piper** pagar los vidrios rotos
piperaceous [,pɪpə'reʃəs] *adj* (bot.) piperáceo
piperine ['pɪpərin] o ['pɪpərɪn] *s* (chem.) piperina
pipestem ['paɪp,stɛm] *s* boquilla de pipa de fumar
pipe thread *s* rosca de tubería
pipe tobacco *s* tabaco de pipa
pipette [paɪ'pɛt] o [pɪ'pɛt] *s* pipeta
pipe wrench *s* llave para tubos, llave de caño
piping ['paɪpɪŋ] *s* cañería, tubería; canalización; materia para la fabricación de tubos; notas de flauta; música de gaita; notas aflautadas; silbido, sonido agudo; (sew.) cordoncillo; figuras hechas con azúcar en un bollo; *adj* aflautado, agudo
piping hot *adj* muy caliente, hirviendo; **to be piping hot** estar que quema
pipit ['pɪpɪt] *s* (orn.) bisbita
pipkin ['pɪpkɪn] *s* ollita
pippin ['pɪpɪn] *s* camuesa (*manzana*); (slang) real moza

pipsissewa [pɪp'sɪsɪwə] *s* (bot.) quimafila
pipy ['paɪpɪ] *adj* (*comp:* **-ier;** *super:* **-iest**) tubular; agudo, chillón
piquancy ['pikənsɪ] *s* picante
piquant ['pikənt] *adj* picante
pique [pik] *s* pique, resentimiento; **in a pique** resentido; *va* picar, enojar, provocar; despertar, excitar; **to be piqued at** tener un pique con; **to pique oneself on** o **upon** enorgullecerse de
piqué [pɪ'ke] *s* piqué (*tela*)
piquet [pɪ'kɛt] *s* séptimo, juego de los ciento
piracy ['paɪrəsɪ] *s* (*pl:* **-cies**) piratería; publicación fraudulenta
Piraeus [paɪ'riəs] *s* el Pireo
piragua [pɪ'rɑgwə] o [pɪ'rægwə] *s* var. de **pirogue**
pirate ['paɪrɪt] *s* pirata; *va* robar, pillar; publicar fraudulentamente; *vn* piratear
piratical [paɪ'rætɪkəl] *adj* pirático
pirogue [pɪ'rog] *s* piragua
pirouette [,pɪru'ɛt] *s* pirueta; *vn* piruetear
piscatorial [,pɪskə'torɪəl] o **piscatory** ['pɪskə,torɪ] *adj* piscatorio
Pisces ['pɪsiz] *spl* (astr.) Piscis
piscina [pɪ'saɪnə] o [pɪ'sinə] *s* (*pl:* **-nae** [ni]) (eccl.) piscina
piscivorous [pɪ'sɪvərəs] *adj* piscívoro
pish [pɪʃ] *interj* ¡bah!; *vn* refunfuñar
pisiform ['paɪsɪfɔrm] *adj* pisiforme; (anat.) pisiforme
Pisistratus [paɪ'sɪstrətəs] *s* Pisístrato
pismire ['pɪs,maɪr] *s* (ent.) hormiga
pistachio [pɪs'tɑʃɪo] o [pɪs'tæʃɪo] *s* (*pl:* **-os**) (bot.) alfóncigo (*árbol y fruto*); (bot.) pistachero (*árbol*); pistacho (*almendra*); sabor a pistacho; color de pistacho
pistil ['pɪstɪl] *s* (bot.) pistilo
pistillate ['pɪstɪlet] *adj* (bot.) pistilado
pistol ['pɪstəl] *s* pistola (*arma de fuego*)
pistole [pɪs'tol] *s* pistola (*moneda*)
piston ['pɪstən] *s* (mach.) émbolo, pistón; (mus.) pistón
piston assembly *s* conjunto del émbolo
piston displacement *s* cilindrada
piston pin *s* eje o pasador de émbolo
piston pump *s* bomba de émbolo
piston ring *s* anillo de émbolo, aro de émbolo
piston rod *s* vástago de émbolo
piston stroke *s* carrera del émbolo
piston valve *s* válvula de émbolo
pit [pɪt] *s* hoyo; cárcava, hoya; cacaraña, hoyuelo (*en la piel*); trampa; hueso (*de ciertas frutas*); cancha, reñidero (*para peleas de gallos, etc.*); boca (*del estómago*); fosa común (*de muchos cadáveres*); pozo (*de tirador*); (aut.) fosa; (com.) bolsa (*dedicada a un solo producto*); abismo, infierno; (min.) pozo; (Brit.) foso, parte posterior del patio; (Brit.) mosqueteros (*personas que veían la comedia de pie desde la parte posterior del patio*); (fig.) escollo (*peligro latente*); (*pret & pp:* **pitted;** *ger:* **pitting**) *va* marcar con hoyos; dejar hoyoso (*el rostro*); poner en un hoyo; deshuesar (*p.ej., una ciruela*); **to pit one person against another** oponer una persona a otra
pitapat ['pɪtə,pæt] *s* latido rápido; sonido de un trotecito ligero; *adv* con latido rápido; con un trotecito ligero
pitch [pɪtʃ] *s* pez *f* (*substancia negra y pegajosa*); echada, lanzamiento; cosa lanzada; pelota lanzada; cabezada (*de un barco*); pendiente (*de un tejado*); elevación (*de un arco de puente*); declive, grado de inclinación; paso (*de hélice, tornillo, etc.*); distancia (*p.ej., entre remaches*); (elec.) paso (*p.ej., de un arrollamiento*); (mus.) tono, altura; (fig.) grado, extremo; *va* echar, lanzar; elevar (*el heno*) con la horquilla, lanzar (*el heno*) al camión; armar o plantar (*una tienda de campaña*); embrear; cantear (*una piedra*); (mus.) graduar el tono de; *vn* caerse, caer de cabeza; fijarse, instalarse; bajar en declive, inclinarse; (naut.) cabecear; **to pitch about** agitarse, sacudirse; **to pitch in** (coll.) poner manos a la obra; (coll.) comenzar a comer; **to pitch into** (coll.) arremeter contra, desatarse contra; (coll.) regañar, reprender; **to pitch on** o **upon** escoger, elegir
pitch accent *s* acento de altura
pitchblende ['pɪtʃ,blɛnd] *s* (mineral.) pechblenda
pitch-dark ['pɪtʃ'dɑrk] *adj* negro u obscuro como la pez
pitched battle *s* batalla campal
pitcher ['pɪtʃər] *s* jarra; (baseball) lanzador
pitcherful ['pɪtʃərfʊl] *s* jarra (*lo que cabe en esta vasija*)
pitcher plant *s* (bot.) planta cazadora de insectos (*Sarracenia y Darlingtonia*)
pitchfork ['pɪtʃ,fɔrk] *s* (agr.) horca, horquilla; **to rain pitchforks** (coll.) caer o llover chuzos, llover a cántaros; *va* amontonar o elevar (*heno*) con la horquilla
pitchman ['pɪtʃmən] *s* (*pl:* **-men**) (slang) buhonero (*con un puesto en las ferias y verbenas*)
pitch pine *s* (bot.) pino tea
pitch pipe *s* (mus.) diapasón
pitchstone ['pɪtʃ,ston] *s* vidrio volcánico
pitchy ['pɪtʃɪ] *adj* (*comp:* **-ier;** *super:* **-iest**) peceño
piteous ['pɪtɪəs] *adj* lastimero, lastimoso
pitfall ['pɪt,fɔl] *s* (hunt.) trampa, callejo; (fig.) escollo
pith [pɪθ] *s* (bot.) médula; (fig.) fuerza, vigor; (fig.) médula
pit head *s* (min.) boca de pozo
pithecanthropus [,pɪθɪkæn'θropəs] *s* (*pl:* **-pi** [paɪ]) (anthrop.) pitecántropo
pithy ['pɪθɪ] *adj* (*comp:* **-ier;** *super:* **-iest**) medular; meduloso; enérgico, expresivo, vivo
pitiable ['pɪtɪəbəl] *adj* enternecedor, lamentable; despreciable
pitiably ['pɪtɪəblɪ] *adv* lamentablemente; de modo despreciable
pitiful ['pɪtɪfʊl] lastimero, lastimoso; compasivo; despreciable
pitiless ['pɪtɪlɪs] *adj* desapiadado, empedernido, incompasivo
pitometer [pɪ'tɑmɪtər] *s* (hyd.) pitómetro
pitpit ['pɪt,pɪt] *s* (orn.) pitpit, azucarero
pittance ['pɪtəns] *s* jornal miserable; recursos insuficientes; ración de hambre
pitter ['pɪtər] *s* deshuesadora
pitter-patter ['pɪtər,pætər] *s* chapaleteo (*de la lluvia*); golpeteo suave o ligero; *adv* con chapaleteo; con golpeteo suave o ligero
Pittsburgh ['pɪtsbʌrg] *s* Pitsburgo
pituitary [pɪ'tjuɪ,tɛrɪ] o [pɪ'tuɪ,tɛrɪ] *adj* pituitario
pituitary body *s* (anat.) cuerpo pituitario
pituitary gland *s* (anat.) glándula pituitaria
pituitary membrane *s* (anat.) membrana pituitaria
pituitous [pɪ'tjuɪtəs] o [pɪ'tuɪtəs] *adj* pituitoso
pity ['pɪtɪ] *s* (*pl:* **-ies**) piedad, compasión, lástima; **for pity's sake!** ¡por piedad!, ¡por Dios!; **it is a pity (that)** es lástima (que); **to have** o **to take pity on** tener piedad de, apiadarse de, compadecer; **what a pity!** ¡qué lástima!; (*pret & pp:* **-ied**) *va* apiadarse de, compadecer
pityriasis [,pɪtɪ'raɪəsɪs] *s* (path.) pitiríasis
Pius ['paɪəs] *s* Pío
pivot ['pɪvət] *s* pivote, gorrón, eje de rotación; (fig.) eje, punto fundamental; *va* montar sobre un pivote; colocar por medio de un pivote; proveer de pivote; *vn* pivotar; **to pivot on** girar sobre; depender de
pivotal ['pɪvətəl] *adj* céntrico; fundamental
pixilated ['pɪksɪ,letɪd] *adj* chiflado; (slang) borracho
pixy o **pixie** ['pɪksɪ] *s* (*pl:* **-ies**) duende, hada
pizzle ['pɪzəl] *s* vergajo
pk. abr. de **park, peak** y **peck**
pkg. abr. de **package**
pl. abr. de **place** y **plural**
placable ['plekəbəl] o ['plækəbəl] *adj* placable
placard ['plækɑrd] *s* cartel; [plə'kɑrd] o ['plækɑrd] *va* llenar de carteles; fijar carteles en; fijar (*un anuncio*) en sitio público; publicar por medio de carteles
placate ['pleket] *va* aplacar
place [ples] *s* sitio, lugar; puesto; local (*de un establecimiento*); distrito; parte; (arith.) lugar; (arith.) decimal; calle o plaza de poca extensión; **in place** en su sitio; a propósito, oportuno; **in the first place** en primer lugar; **in the next place** luego, después; **in no place**

en ninguna parte; **in place of** en lugar de, en vez de; **out of place** fuera de su lugar; impropio, inconveniente, fuera de propósito; **to give place** ceder, hacer lugar; **to hold one's place** no cejar, no perder terreno; **to know one's place** quedarse en su lugar, mirarse a sí, ser respetuoso; **to look for a place to live** buscar piso; **to take place** tener lugar; *va* poner, colocar; acordarse bien de; dar colocación o empleo a; (com.) prestar a interés; *vn* (sport) colocarse (*un caballo en las carreras*)
placebo [plə'sibo] *s* (*pl:* **-bos** o **-boes**) (eccl. & med.) placebo
place card *s* tarjeta (*que indica la colocación de uno en la mesa*)
place in the sun *s* la igualdad, su porción de los bienes de este mundo, su porción de gloria
place kick *s* (football) puntapié que se da a la pelota después de colocarla en tierra
place-kick ['ples,kɪk] *vn* (football) patear la pelota después de colocarla en tierra
placement ['plesmənt] *s* colocación; (football) colocación de la pelota en tierra para patearla
placement test *s* (educ.) examen selectivo
place name *s* nombre de lugar, topónimo
placenta [plə'sɛntə] *s* (*pl:* **-tae** [ti] o **-tas**) (anat., bot. & zool.) placenta
placental [plə'sɛntəl] *adj* placentario; *s* (zool.) placentario
place of business *s* establecimiento, local de negocios
place of refuge *s* asilo, refugio
place of worship *s* templo, edificio de culto
placer ['plæsər] *s* (min.) placer; (min.) lavadero de oro
placer mining *s* minería de lavado
placid ['plæsɪd] *adj* plácido
placidity [plə'sɪdɪtɪ] *s* placidez
placket ['plækɪt] *s* abertura en la parte superior de la falda o las enaguas; bolsillo (de falda)
plagiarism ['pledʒɪərɪzəm] o ['pledʒərɪzəm] *s* plagio
plagiarist ['pledʒɪərɪst] o ['pledʒərɪst] *s* plagiario
plagiarize ['pledʒɪəraɪz] o ['pledʒəraɪz] *va* plagiar
plagioclase ['pledʒɪə,kles] *s* (mineral.) plagioclasa
plagiostome ['pledʒɪə,stom] *adj* & *s* (ichth.) plagiostomo
plagiotropic [,pledʒɪə'trɑpɪk] *adj* (bot.) plagiotropo
plagiotropism [,pledʒɪ'ɑtrəpɪzəm] *s* (bot.) plagiotropismo
plague [pleg] *s* plaga; peste; *va* plagar, apestar, infestar; atormentar, molestar
plaguey o **plaguy** ['plegɪ] *adj* (coll.) enfadoso, molesto
plaice [ples] *s* (ichth.) platija
plaid [plæd] *s* tartán (*tela*); cuadros a la escocesa; plaid (*manta*); *adj* listado a la escocesa
plaided ['plædɪd] *adj* listado a la escocesa; con manta de tartán
plain [plen] *adj* llano; feo, sin atractivo; ordinario; solo, natural, puro; sencillo; **in plain English** sin rodeos; **in plain sight** o **view** en plena vista; *s* llano, llanura; *vn* (archaic & dial.) quejarse
plain chant *s* canto llano
plain clothes *spl* traje de calle, traje de paisano
plain-clothes man ['plen'kloz] o ['plen'kloðz] *s* agente de policía que no lleva uniforme, agente de policía que lleva traje de calle
plain dealing *s* trato sincero, buena fe
plain knitting *s* punto de media
plainness ['plennɪs] *s* llaneza; fealdad
plain omelet *s* tortilla a la francesa
plain sailing *s* navegación libre y serena; acción desembarazada
plainsman ['plenzmən] *s* (*pl:* **-men**) llanero
plain song *s* canto llano
plain speaking *s* franqueza
plain-spoken ['plen'spokən] *adj* franco, sincero, brusco, directo
plaint [plent] *s* quejido, lamento; (law) querella; (archaic & dial.) plañido
plaintiff ['plentɪf] *s* (law) demandante
plaintive ['plentɪv] *adj* quejumbroso, lastimero
plait [plæt] o [plet] *s* trenza; *va* trenzar; [plæt] o [plit] *s* pliegue; *va* plegar
plan [plæn] *s* plan (*intento, proyecto*); plan, plano (*representación gráfica*); **to change one's plans** cambiar de proyecto; (*pret & pp:* **planned;** *ger:* **planning**) *va* planear, planificar; **to plan to** + *inf* proponerse + *inf; vn* hacer proyectos
planchette [plæn'ʃɛt] *s* tabla de escritura espiritista
plane [plen] *adj* plano; *s* plano; (aer.) plano o ala; aeroplano, avión; (carp.) cepillo; garlopa (*cepillo grande*); (bot.) plátano de oriente; (bot.) plátano de occidente; (fig.) nivel (*grado de elevación moral, etc.*); *va* acepillar, cepillar; **to plane down** reducir con el cepillo el espesor de; **to plane off** o **away** quitar con el cepillo; *vn* viajar en aeroplano; (aer.) planear; (naut.) elevarse (*el barco*) al ser impulsado por el motor
plane cell *s* (aer.) célula (*de avión*)
plane geometry *s* geometría plana
plane of incidence *s* (opt.) plano de incidencia
planer ['plenər] *s* acepillador; acepilladora (*máquina*); (print.) tamborilete
planer tree *s* (bot.) planera
plane sickness *s* (aer.) mareo del aire, mal de vuelo
planet ['plænɪt] *s* (astr. & astrol.) planeta
plane table *s* (surv.) plancheta
planetarium [,plænɪ'tɛrɪəm] *s* (*pl:* **-a** [ə]) planetario
planetary ['plænɪ,tɛrɪ] *adj* planetario; errante, inconstante; mundano, terrestre; (mach.) planetario
planetesimal [,plænɪ'tɛsɪməl] *adj* & *s* planetesimal
planetoid ['plænɪtɔɪd] *s* (astr.) planetoide
plane tree *s* (bot.) plátano de oriente; (bot.) plátano de occidente
plane trigonometry *s* trigonometría plana
planimeter [plə'nɪmɪtər] *s* planímetro
planimetric [,plænɪ'mɛtrɪk] o **planimetrical** [,plænɪ'mɛtrɪkəl] *adj* planimétrico
planimetry [plə'nɪmɪtrɪ] *s* planimetría
planing mill *s* taller de cepillado; cepilladora
planish ['plænɪʃ] *va* aplanar
planisphere ['plænɪsfɪr] *s* planisferio
plank [plæŋk] *s* tabla gruesa, tablón; artículo de un programa político; **to walk the plank** lanzarse al mar (*pena de muerte que imponían los piratas a sus víctimas*); *va* entablar, entarimar; asar a la brasa en una tabla; **to plank down** (coll.) colocar firmemente; (coll.) arrojar con alguna violencia (*sobre una mesa, un mostrador, etc.*); **to plank out** (coll.) pagar o desembolsar sin vacilación
planking ['plæŋkɪŋ] *s* entablación; tablaje; maderamen de cubierta, tablazón de buque
plank-sheer ['plæŋk,ʃɪr] *s* (naut.) regala
plankton ['plæŋktən] *s* (biol.) plankton o plancton
planned economy *s* economía dirigida o planificada
planned parenthood *s* natalidad dirigida, procreación planeada
planner ['plænər] *s* proyectista
plano-concave [,pleno'kɑnkev] *adj* planocóncavo
plano-convex [,pleno'kɑnvɛks] *adj* planoconvexo
plant [plænt] o [plɑnt] *s* (bot.) planta; fábrica, taller; grupo motor (*de un automóvil*); plantel (*establecimiento de educación*); (slang) proyecto para engañar; *va* plantar; sembrar (*semillas*); inculcar (*doctrinas*); (slang) plantar (*golpes*); (slang) ocultar (*géneros robados*)
plantaginaceous [,plæntədʒɪ'neʃəs] *adj* (bot.) plantagináceo
plantain ['plæntɪn] *s* (bot.) plátano (*Musa paradisiaca y fruto*); (bot.) llantén (*Plantago major*)
plantation [plæn'teʃən] *s* plantío; plantación
planter ['plæntər] o ['plɑntər] *s* plantador; plantadora (*máquina*)
plantigrade ['plæntɪgred] *adj* & *s* (zool.) plantígrado

plantlet ['plæntlɪt] o ['plɑntlɪt] *s* plantilla, planta rudimentaria
plant louse *s* (ent.) pulgón
plant pathology *s* patología vegetal
plant physiology *s* fisiología vegetal
plaque [plæk] *s* placa
plaquette [plæ'kɛt] *s* (anat.) plaqueta
plash [plæʃ] *s* salpicadura; chapoteo; mancha; charco; *va* salpicar; chapotear; manchar; entretejer (*ramas*); hacer o podar (*un seto vivo*) entretejiendo ramas; *vn* chapotear, caer con ruido
plashy ['plæʃɪ] *adj* (*comp:* **-ier;** *super:* **-iest**) cenagoso, pantanoso; salpicado, manchado
plasm ['plæzəm] *s* var. de **plasma**
plasma ['plæzmə] *s* (anat., phys. & physiol.) plasma *m;* (biol.) protoplasma; (mineral.) plasma *f;* suero (*de la leche*)
plasmatic [plæz'mætɪk] o **plasmic** ['plæzmɪk] *adj* plasmático
plasmochin ['plæzməkɪn] *s* (pharm.) plasmoquina
plasmodium [plæz'modɪəm] *s* (*pl:* **-a** [ə]) (biol.) plasmodio
plasmolysis [plæz'mɑlɪsɪs] *s* (physiol.) plasmólisis
plasmoquine ['plæzməkwaɪn] *s* var. de **plasmochin**
plasmosome ['plæzməsom] *s* (biol.) plasmosoma
plaster ['plæstər] o ['plɑstər] *s* yeso; argamasa; enlucido (*capa de yeso*); (pharm.) emplasto; *va* enyesar; argamasar; enlucir; emplastar; embadurnar, untar; pegar (*anuncios, carteles*); **to plaster down** pegar (*p.ej., el pelo al cráneo*)
plasterboard ['plæstər,bord] o ['plɑstər,bord] *s* cartón de yeso y fieltro
plaster cast *s* (surg.) vendaje enyesado
plasterer ['plæstərər] o ['plɑstərər] *s* yesero, enlucidor, revocador
plastering ['plæstərɪŋ] o ['plɑstərɪŋ] *s* enlucimiento; enlucido, enyesado
plastering trowel *s* llana de enlucir
plaster of Paris *s* yeso de París
plastic ['plæstɪk] *adj* plástico; *s* plástico (*cuerpo*); plástica (*arte de plasmar*)
plastic bomb *s* bomba de plástico
plasticine ['plæstɪsin] *s* (trademark) arcilla de modelar, plastilina
plasticity [plæs'tɪsɪtɪ] *s* plasticidad
plasticize ['plæstɪsaɪz] *va* plastificar; *vn* plastificarse
plastic surgery *s* cirugía plástica
plastic wood *s* (trademark) madera plástica
plastron ['plæstrən] *s* pechera; (arm. & zool.) peto; (fencing) plastrón
plat [plæt] *s* plan, plano o mapa; parcela, solar; trenza; (*pret & pp:* **platted;** *ger:* **platting**) *va* trazar el plano o mapa de, trasladar al papel; trenzar
platan ['plætən] *s* var. de **plane tree**
platanaceous [,plætə'neʃəs] *adj* (bot.) platanáceo
plate [plet] *s* plato; vajilla de oro, vajilla de plata; cubierto; placa, chapa (*de metal, cristal, etc.*); escudete; lámina; clisé; dentadura postiza, base de la dentadura postiza; pecho delgado (*carne de vaca*); (arch.) viga horizontal; (baseball) puesto meta, puesto del batter; (anat., elec., phot., rad. & zool.) placa; (mach.) plato; *va* chapear; blindar; platear, dorar, niquelar (*por la galvanoplastia*); (print.) clisar
plateau [plæ'to] *s* meseta
plate circuit *s* (rad.) circuito de placa
plate current *s* (rad.) corriente de placa
plateful ['pletfʊl] *s* plato (*lo que contiene un plato*)
plate glass *s* vidrio o cristal cilindrado
plateholder ['plet,holdər] *s* (phot.) almacén de placas, portaplacas, chasis
platen ['plætən] *s* platina, rodillo
plater ['pletər] *s* (sport) caballo que no gana carreras
plateresque [,plætə'rɛsk] *adj* (arch.) plateresco
platform ['plæt,fɔrm] *s* plataforma; andén; cargadero; tribuna (*de orador*); (geog.) plataforma; (fig.) plataforma (*programa político*)
platform car *s* (rail.) plataforma
platform carriage *s* carro fuerte
Platine ['plætaɪn] *adj* rioplatense
plating ['pletɪŋ] *s* galvanoplastia; capa metálica; blindaje
platiniridium [,plætɪnɪ'rɪdɪəm] *s* platiniridio
platinocyanide [,plætɪno'saɪənaɪd] o [,plætɪno'saɪənɪd] *s* (chem.) platinocianuro
platinoid ['plætɪnɔɪd] *s* platinoide
platinotype ['plætɪnə,taɪp] *s* (phot.) platinotipia
platinum ['plætɪnəm] *s* (chem.) platino
platinum black *s* negro de platino
platinum blonde *s* rubia platino
platitude ['plætɪtjud] o ['plætɪtud] *s* perogrullada, trivialidad; falta de gracia
platitudinous [,plætɪ'tjudɪnəs] o [,plætɪ'tudɪnəs] *adj* trivial, falto de gracia
Plato ['pleto] *s* Platón
Platonic [plə'tɑnɪk] *adj* platónico
Platonic love *s* amor platónico
Platonism ['pletənɪzəm] *s* platonismo
Platonist ['pletənɪst] *s* platonista
platoon [plə'tun] *s* (mil.) pelotón; grupo (*de personas*)
platter ['plætər] *s* fuente, platón; (slang) disco de fonógrafo
platyhelminth [,plætɪ'hɛlmɪnθ] *s* (zool.) platelminto
platypus ['plætɪpəs] *s* (*pl:* **-puses** o **-pi** [paɪ]) (zool.) ornitorrinco
platyrrhine ['plætɪraɪn] o ['plætɪrɪn] *adj & s* (zool.) platirrino
plaudit ['plɔdɪt] *s* aplauso
plausibility [,plɔzɪ'bɪlɪtɪ] *s* especiosidad; (coll.) credibilidad
plausible ['plɔzɪbəl] *adj* especioso, aparente; bien hablado; (coll.) creíble
Plautine ['plɔtaɪn] o ['plɔtɪn] *adj* plautino
Plautus ['plɔtəs] *s* Plauto
play [ple] *s* juego; jugada (*lance de juego*); pieza, obra dramática; juego (*de aguas, de colores, de luces, etc.*); (mach.) juego; **at play** jugando; **to be full of play** ser retozón, ser travieso; **to come into play** entrar en juego; **to give full play to** dar rienda suelta a ‖ *va* jugar (*p.ej., un naipe, una partida de juego*); jugar a (*p.ej., los naipes*); jugar con (*un contrario*); dar (*un chasco*); hacer (*una mala jugada*); dirigir (*agua, una manguera*); hacer o desempeñar (*un papel*); hacer o desempeñar el papel de; representar (*una obra dramática, un film*); dar representaciones en (*una ciudad*); apostar por (*un caballo*); darse al juego en (*las carreras de caballo*); dejar que se canse (*un pez que ha picado en el anzuelo*); gastar (*una broma*); (mus.) tocar (*un instrumento, una pieza, un disco de fonógrafo*); **to be played out** estar agotado; estar estropeado por el uso, estar inservible; **to play back** retocar (*un disco de fonógrafo*); **to play someone false** engañarle a uno; **to play up** ensalzar, dar bombo a ‖ *vn* jugar; representar, desempeñar un papel; correr (*una fuente*); rielar (*la luz en la superficie del agua*); vagar (*p.ej., una sonrisa por los labios*); hacerse el (o la), p.ej., **to play sick** hacerse el enfermo; **to play on** continuar jugando; continuar tocando; aprovecharse de, valerse de; agitar (*emociones*) por provecho propio; (mus.) tocar (*un instrumento*); **to play out** cansarse, rendirse; agotarse; acabarse; **to play safe** tomar sus precauciones; **to play up to** hacer la rueda a, halagar servilmente
playable ['pleəbəl] *adj* servible; (theat.) representable
play-act ['ple,ækt] *vn* (coll.) actuar, hacer un papel; (coll.) hacer la comedia
playback ['ple,bæk] *s* (elec.) lectura (*de una grabación fonográfica acabada de registrar*); (elec.) aparato de lectura
playback head *s* cabeza de lectura (*del magnetófono*)
playbill ['ple,bɪl] *s* cartel; programa (*de una pieza dramática*)
playboy ['ple,bɔɪ] *s* (slang) amante de los placeres, niño bonito
player ['pleər] *s* jugador; actor; ejecutante; autopiano
player piano *m* autopiano
playfellow ['ple,fɛlo] *s* compañero de juego
playful ['plefəl] *adj* juguetón; dicho en broma

playfulness ['plefəlnɪs] *s* travesura, retozo; jovialidad
playgoer ['ple,goər] *s* aficionado al teatro, persona que frecuenta el teatro
playground ['ple,graʊnd] *s* patio de recreo, campo de juego
playhouse ['ple,haʊs] *s* casita de juguete para niños, casita de muñecas; teatro
playing card *s* naipe
playing field *s* campo de deportes, terreno de juego
playlet ['plelɪt] *s* (theat.) juguete cómico, paso de comedia
playmate ['ple,met] *s* compañero de juego
play-off ['ple,ɔf] o ['ple,ɑf] *s* (sport) partido de desempate
play on words *s* juego de palabras, retruécano
play pen *s* parque, corralito plegable (*para bebés*)
playroom ['ple,rum] o ['ple,rʊm] *s* cuarto de juegos
plaything ['ple,θɪŋ] *s* juguete; (fig.) juguete
playtime ['ple,taɪm] *s* hora de recreo, hora de juego
playwright ['ple,raɪt] *s* autor dramático, dramaturgo
plaza ['plɑzə] o ['plæzə] *s* plaza
plea [pli] *s* ruego, súplica; disculpa, excusa; (law) contestación a la demanda
pleach [plitʃ] *va* entretejer (*p.ej., ramas de árboles*)
plead [plid] (*pret & pp:* **pleaded** o **pled**) *va* alegar; (law) defender (*una causa*); *vn* suplicar; argumentar; abogar; (law) abogar; **to plead against** abogar contra; **to plead for** abogar por; **to plead guilty** (law) confesarse culpable; **to plead not guilty** (law) negar la acusación, declararse inocente; **to plead with** suplicar; **to plead with someone for something** rogarle a uno que conceda algo
pleader ['plidər] *s* suplicante; (law) abogado
pleadings ['plidɪŋz] *spl* (law) alegatos
pleasance ['plɛzəns] *s* parque, jardín de recreo; (archaic) placer
pleasant ['plɛzənt] *adj* agradable; simpático
pleasantness ['plɛzəntnɪs] *s* agradabilidad
pleasantry ['plɛzəntrɪ] *s* (*pl:* **-ries**) chanza, chiste, dicho gracioso
please [pliz] *va & vn* gustar; **as you please** como Vd. quiera; **if you please** si quiere, si me hace el favor; **to be pleased to** + *inf* alegrarse de + *inf*, complacerse en + *inf;* **to be pleased with** estar satisfecho de o con; **to be pleased with oneself** estar satisfecho de sí mismo; **to do as one pleases** hacer su voluntad; **to please oneself** darse gusto, no hacer más que lo que se le antoja; **please God** si Dios lo quiere; **please** + *inf* tenga Vd. la bondad de + *inf*, hágame Vd. el favor de + *inf*, sírvase + *inf*
pleasing ['plizɪŋ] *adj* agradable, grato
pleasurable ['plɛʒərəbəl] *adj* agradable
pleasure ['plɛʒər] *s* placer, goce, deleite, gusto; **what is your pleasure?** ¿en qué puedo servirle?, ¿qué es lo que Vd. desea?; **with pleasure** con mucho gusto
pleasure boat *s* bote de recreo
pleasure car *s* (aut.) coche de paseo, coche de deporte
pleasure seeker *s* persona que anda tras los placeres, amigo de los placeres
pleasure trip *s* viaje de recreo, viaje de placer
pleat [plit] *s* pliegue, plisado; *va* plegar, plisar
pleating ['plitɪŋ] *s* plisado
plebe [plib] *s* (mil.) cadete de primer año (*en la Academia Militar de los EE.UU.*); (nav.) guardia marina de primer año (*en la Academia Naval de los EE.UU.*)
plebeian [plɪ'biən] *adj & s* plebeyo
plebeianism [plɪ'biənɪzəm] *s* plebeísmo
plebiscite ['plɛbɪsaɪt] o ['plɛbɪsɪt] *s* plebiscito
plebs [plɛbz] *s* (*pl:* **plebes** ['plibiz]) plebe; (hist.) plebe
plectognath ['plɛktɑgnæθ] *adj & s* (zool.) plectognato
plectrum ['plɛktrəm] *s* (*pl:* **-trums** o **-tra** [trə]) (mus.) plectro
pled [plɛd] *pret & pp de* **plead**
pledge [plɛdʒ] *s* promesa; voto (*promesa que se hace a Dios*); prenda; brindis; **as a pledge of** en prenda de; **to take the pledge** comprometerse a no catar bebidas alcohólicas; *va* prometer; empeñar; dar (*la palabra*); brindar por; **to pledge to secrecy** exigir promesa de secreto o silencio a
pledgee [plɛdʒ'i] *s* depositario
Pleiad ['pliæd] o ['plaɪæd] *s* (*pl:* **Pleiades** ['pliədiz] o ['plaɪədiz]) Pléyade; **Pleiades** *spl* (myth. & astr.) Pléyades
Pleiocene ['plaɪəsin] *adj & s* var. de **Pliocene**
Pleistocene ['plaɪstəsin] *adj & s* (geol.) pleistoceno
plenary ['plinərɪ] o ['plɛnərɪ] *adj* plenario
plenary indulgence *s* (eccl.) indulgencia plenaria
plenary session *s* sesión plenaria
plenipotentiary [,plɛnɪpə'tɛnʃɪ,ɛrɪ] o [,plɛnɪpə'tɛnʃərɪ] *adj* plenipotenciario; *s* (*pl:* **-ies**) plenipotenciario
plenitude ['plɛnɪtjud] o ['plɛnɪtud] *s* plenitud
plenteous ['plɛntɪəs] o **plentiful** ['plɛntɪfəl] *adj* abundante, copioso
plenty ['plɛntɪ] *s* copia, abundancia; cantidad suficiente; *adj* suficiente; *adv* (coll.) completamente, muy
plenum ['plinəm] *s* (*pl:* **-nums** o **-na** [nə]) pleno
plenum chamber *s* cámara de pleno
pleochroism [plɪ'ɑkro·ɪzəm] *s* (cryst.) pleocroísmo
pleonasm ['pliənæzəm] *s* pleonasmo; palabra o frase superfluas
pleonastic [,pliə'næstɪk] *adj* pleonástico
plesiosaur ['plisɪə,sɔr] *s* (pal.) plesiosauro
plethora ['plɛθərə] *s* plétora; (path.) plétora
plethoric [plɛ'θɑrɪk], [plɛ'θɔrɪk] o ['plɛθərɪk] *adj* pletórico; (fig.) ampuloso, hinchado
plethysmograph [plɪ'θɪzmogræf] o [plɪ'θɪzmogrɑf] *s* (physiol.) pletismógrafo
pleura ['plʊrə] *s* (*pl:* **-rae** [ri]) (anat. & zool.) pleura
pleural ['plʊrəl] *adj* pleural
pleurisy ['plʊrɪsɪ] *s* (path.) pleuresía
pleuritic [plʊ'rɪtɪk] *adj* pleurítico
pleuritis [plʊ'raɪtɪs] *s* (path.) pleuritis
pleurodont ['plʊrədɑnt] *adj* (zool.) pleurodonto
pleuronectid [,plʊrə'nɛktɪd] *adj & s* (ichth.) pleuronecto
pleuropneumonia [,plʊronju'monɪə] o [,plʊronu'monɪə] *s* (path.) pleuroneumonía
plexiglass ['plɛksɪ,glæs] o ['plɛksɪ,glɑs] *s* (trademark) plexiglás
plexus ['plɛksəs] *s* (*pl:* **-uses** o **-us**) (anat. & zool.) plexo
pliability [,plaɪə'bɪlɪtɪ] *s* flexibilidad, docilidad
pliable ['plaɪəbəl] *adj* flexible, plegable, dócil
pliancy ['plaɪənsɪ] *s* flexibilidad, docilidad
pliant ['plaɪənt] *adj* flexible; manejable, sumiso
plicate ['plaɪket] *adj* plegado (*en forma de abanico*)
pliers ['plaɪərz] *ssg* o *spl* alicates, pinzas
plight [plaɪt] *s* estado, situación; apuro, aprieto; promesa, compromiso solemne; *va* empeñar o dar (*su palabra*); prometer en matrimonio; **to plight one's troth** prometer fidelidad; dar palabra de casamiento, contraer esponsales
Plimsoll line o **mark** ['plɪmsɑl] o ['plɪmsəl] *s* (naut.) marca Plimsoll (*línea de carga máxima*)
plinth [plɪnθ] *s* (arch.) plinto
Pliny ['plɪnɪ] *s* Plinio
Pliny the Elder *s* Plinio el Antiguo
Pliny the Younger *s* Plinio el Joven
Pliocene ['plaɪəsin] *adj & s* (geol.) pliocénico
plod [plɑd] (*pret & pp:* **plodded;** *ger:* **plodding**) *va* recorrer (*un camino*) pausada y pesadamente; *vn* caminar pausada y pesadamente; trabajar laboriosamente; **to plod away at** dedicarse laboriosamente a, ocuparse laboriosamente en
plodder ['plɑdər] *s* persona que camina pausada y pesadamente; persona que trabaja con más aplicación que talento; estudiante más aplicado que brillante
plop [plɑp] *s* paf (*ruido de la caída de un objeto plano que cae sin violencia al agua*); *adv* dejando oír un paf; (*pret & pp:* **plopped;** *ger:*

plopping) *va* arrojar dejando oír un paf; **to plop down** arrojar sobre el mostrador; *vn* dejar oír un paf; caer dejando oír un paf
plot [plɑt] *s* complot, conspiración; argumento, trama (*de una novela, etc.*); parcela, solar; plano, mapa; cuadro de flores; cuadro de hortalizas; (*pret & pp:* **plotted;** *ger:* **plotting**) *va* fraguar, tramar, urdir, maquinar; dividir en parcelas o solares; trazar el plano de; trazar, tirar (*líneas*); *vn* conspirar
Plotinus [plo'taɪnəs] *s* Plotino
plotter ['plɑtər] *s* conjurado, conspirador; maquinador
plough [plaʊ] *s, va & vn* var. de **plow**
plover ['plʌvər] o ['plovər] *s* (orn.) chorlito
plow [plaʊ] *s* arado; quitanieve, barredora de nieve; *va* arar; surcar; quitar o barrer (*la nieve*); **to plow back** reinvertir (*ganancias*); **to plow under** cubrir arando; **to plow up** arrancar con un arado; romper (*p.ej., un pavimento*) como con un arado; *vn* arar; avanzar como un arado
plowboy ['plaʊ,bɔɪ] *s* yuguero; gañancico
plowland ['plaʊ,lænd] *s* tierra labrantía; tierra labrada
plowman ['plaʊmən] *s* (*pl:* **-men**) arador, labrador, yuguero; gañán
plowshare ['plaʊ,ʃɛr] *s* reja de arado
plowshare bone *s* (anat.) vómer
plowstaff ['plaʊ,stæf] o ['plaʊ,stɑf] *s* abéstola, aguijada
plowtail ['plaʊ,tel] *s* esteva o estevas
ploy [plɔɪ] *s* maniobra, manejo, artimaña; *vn* (mil.) pasar del orden abierto al compacto
pluck [plʌk] *s* ánimo, coraje, valor; asadura; tirón; *va* arrancar, coger; herir, puntear (*las cuerdas de un instrumento con los dedos*); desplumar (*un ave*); (coll.) dar calabazas a (*en un examen*); (slang) estafar, robar; *vn* tirar, dar un tirón; **to pluck up** recobrar ánimo, envalentonarse
plucky ['plʌkɪ] *adj* (*comp:* **-ier;** *super:* **-iest**) animoso, valiente
plug [plʌg] *s* taco, tarugo; boca de agua; tableta de tabaco; (slang) chistera; (elec.) tapón fusible; (elec.) clavija, toma, ficha; (aut.) bujía; (coll.) rocín, penco; (slang) elogio incidental; (*pret & pp:* **plugged;** *ger:* **plugging**) *va* atarugar; (slang) pegar; (slang) taladrar con una bala; calar (*un melón*); **to plug in** (elec.) enchufar; *vn* (coll.) trabajar con ahinco; **to plug along** (coll.) trabajar con ahinco
plug fuse *s* (elec.) tapón fusible
plugger ['plʌgər] *s* (coll.) trabajador diligente, estudiante diligente; (dent.) orificador
plug hat *s* (slang) chistera, sombrero de copa alta
plug-in ['plʌg,ɪn] *adj* enchufable
plug tobacco *s* tabaco torcido
plug-ugly ['plʌg,ʌglɪ] *s* (*pl:* **-lies**) (slang) bullanguero, matón
plum [plʌm] *s* (bot.) ciruelo; ciruela (*fruto*); pasa (*en un bollo, etc.*); confite; la cosa mejor; turrón, pingüe destino; *adj* morado
plumage ['plumɪdʒ] *s* plumaje
plumb [plʌm] *s* plomada; **in plumb** a plomo; **out of plumb** fuera de plomo; *adj* vertical; (coll.) completo; *adv* a plomo, verticalmente; (coll.) completamente; (coll.) directamente; *va* aplomar; sondear
plumbaginaceous [plʌm,bædʒɪ'neʃəs] *adj* (bot.) plumbagináceo
plumbago [plʌm'bego] *s* plombagina
plumb bob *s* plomada, perpendículo
plumber ['plʌmər] *s* cañero, instalador de cañería, plomero
plumbery ['plʌmərɪ] *s* (*pl:* **-ies**) plomería
plumbic ['plʌmbɪk] *adj* plúmbeo; (chem.) plúmbico
plumbing ['plʌmɪŋ] *s* plomería; instalación sanitaria; conjunto de cañerías; sondeo
plumbing fixtures *spl* artefactos o efectos sanitarios
plumb line *s* cuerda de plomada
plum cake *s* pastel aderezado con pasas de Corinto y ron
plume [plum] *s* pluma (*de ave*); penacho; *va* emplumar; componerse (*las plumas*); **to plume oneself on** enorgullecerse de
plume grass *s* (bot.) carricera, vulpino
plumelet ['plumlɪt] *s* plumilla
plummet ['plʌmɪt] *s* plomada; *vn* caer a plomo, precipitarse
plumose ['plumos] *adj* plumoso
plump [plʌmp] *s* (coll.) caída pesada; (coll.) ruido sordo; *adj* rechoncho, regordete; brusco, directo, franco; *adv* de golpe, de sopetón; francamente, sin rodeos; *va* engordar; hinchar; *vn* engordar; hincharse; caer a plomo, desplomarse, dejarse caer pesadamente
plum pudding *s* pudín inglés con pasas de Corinto, piel de limón, huevos, ron, etc.
plum tree *s* (bot.) ciruelo
plumule ['plumjul] *s* (bot.) plúmula; (orn.) plumón
plumy ['plumɪ] *adj* plumoso; empenachado
plunder ['plʌndər] *s* pillaje, saqueo; botín; *va* pillar, saquear
plunge [plʌndʒ] *s* zambullida; caída a plomo; tumbo, sacudida violenta; salto; corcovo (*de un animal encorvando el lomo*); baño en agua fría; piscina natatoria; cabeceo (*de un buque*); *va* zambullir; sumergir; hundir (*p.ej., un puñal*); *vn* zambullirse; sumergirse; abismarse, hundirse (*p.ej., en la tristeza*); caer a plomo; dar un tumbo, empezar a dar tumbos; arrojarse, precipitarse; corcovear (*un animal encorvando el lomo*); cabecear (*un buque*); (slang) entregarse al juego, entregarse a las especulaciones
plunger ['plʌndʒər] *s* zambullidor; (mach.) émbolo buzo; obús (*de una válvula de neumático*); persona impetuosa; (slang) jugador o especulador desenfrenado
plunk [plʌŋk] *s* (coll.) golpe seco; (coll.) ruido seco; *adv* (coll.) con un golpe seco; (coll.) con un ruido de golpe seco; *va* puntear (*p.ej., la guitarra*); (coll.) arrojar, empujar o dejar caer pesadamente; **to plunk down** (coll.) arrojar pesadamente; *vn* sonar o caer con un ruido de golpe seco
pluperfect ['plu,pʌrfɪkt] o [,plu'pʌrfɪkt] *adj & s* (gram.) pluscuamperfecto
plupf. abr. de **pluperfect**
plur. abr. de **plural**
plural ['plʊrəl] *adj & s* (gram.) plural
plurality [plʊ'rælɪtɪ] *s* (*pl:* **-ties**) pluralidad
pluralize ['plʊrəlaɪz] *va* pluralizar
plurally ['plʊrəlɪ] *adv* en el plural
plus [plʌs] *s* más (*signo*); añadidura; *adj* más; y pico; **to be plus** (coll.) tener además, tener por añadidura; *prep* más
plus fours *spl* pantalones holgados de media pierna
plush [plʌʃ] *s* felpa; *adj* afelpado; (slang) lujoso, suntuoso
plushy ['plʌʃɪ] *adj* (*comp:* **-ier;** *super:* **-iest**) felpudo
plus sign *s* signo más
Plutarch ['plutɑrk] *s* Plutarco
Pluto ['pluto] *s* (myth. & astr.) Plutón
plutocracy [plu'tɑkrəsɪ] *s* (*pl:* **-cies**) plutocracia
plutocrat ['plutəkræt] *s* plutócrata
plutocratic [,plutə'krætɪk] *adj* plutocrático
Plutonian [plu'tonɪən] *adj* plutoniano
plutonic [plu'tɑnɪk] *adj* (geol.) plutónico; (*cap.*) *adj* (myth. & geol.) plutónico
plutonium [plu'tonɪəm] *s* (chem.) plutonio
Plutus ['plutəs] *s* (myth.) Pluto
pluvial ['pluvɪəl] *adj* pluvial
pluviometer [,pluvɪ'ɑmɪtər] *s* pluviómetro
pluvious ['pluvɪəs] *adj* pluvioso
ply [plaɪ] *s* (*pl:* **plies**) capa o doblez (*de una tela, manguera, etc.*); cordón (*de un cable*); (*pret & pp:* **plied**) *va* manejar (*la aguja, un instrumento, etc.*); ejercer (*un oficio*); batir (*el agua con los remos*); no dejar descansar, no dar descanso a; trabajar con ahinco en; acosar, importunar; navegar por (*un río*); *vn* estar en movimiento incesante, funcionar constantemente; avanzar, moverse; (naut.) barloventear; **to ply between** hacer el servicio entre
plywood ['plaɪ,wʊd] *s* chapeado, madera contrachapada, madera laminada
p.m. abr. de **post meridiem** (Lat.) **after noon** y **post mortem**
P.M. abr. de **post meridiem** (Lat.) **after noon, Postmaster** y **Provost Marshal**

pneumatic [nju'mætɪk] o [nu'mætɪk] *adj* neumático; **pneumatics** *ssg* neumática
pneumatically [nju'mætɪkəlɪ] o [nu'mætɪkəlɪ] *adv* neumáticamente
pneumatic drill *s* perforadora de aire comprimido
pneumococcus [ˌnjumə'kakəs] o [ˌnumə'kakəs] *s* (*pl:* **-cocci** ['kaksaɪ]) (bact.) neumococo
pneumonia [nju'monɪə] o [nu'monɪə] *s* (path.) pulmonía o neumonía; **an attack of pneumonia** o **a case of pneumonia** una pulmonía; **to get pneumonia** coger una pulmonía
pneumonic [nju'manɪk] o [nu'manɪk] *adj* neumónico
pneumothorax [ˌnjumo'θoræks] o [ˌnumo'θoræks] *s* (path. & med.) neumotórax
P.O. abr. de **post office**
poach [potʃ] *va* coger en vedado; (cook.) escalfar (*huevos*); *vn* cazar o pescar en vedado
poached egg *s* huevo escalfado
poacher ['potʃər] *s* cazador furtivo, pescador furtivo
pock [pak] *s* hoyuelo (*en la piel*)
pocket ['pakɪt] *s* bolsillo, faltriquera; cavidad; talega (*saco de lienzo basto*); tronera (*de la mesa de billar*); (aer.) bolsa de aire, vacío; (mil.) bolsón; (min.) depósito de pepitas de oro, cueva mineralizada; **in pocket** con ganancia; **out of pocket** perdidoso; **to pick pockets** hurtar de los bolsillos; *va* embolsar; tragarse (*injurias*); disimular (*emociones*); apropiarse (*ganancias sin tener derecho a ellas*)
pocket battleship *s* acorazado de bolsillo
pocket billiards *ssg* trucos (*juego*)
pocketbook ['pakɪtˌbʊk] *s* portamonedas, cartera; bolsa (*de mujer*)
pocketful ['pakɪtfʊl] *s* bolsillo, lo que cabe en el bolsillo
pocket handkerchief *s* pañuelo de bolsillo o de mano
pocketknife ['pakɪtˌnaɪf] *s* (*pl:* **-knives** [ˌnaɪvz]) navaja, cortaplumas
pocket money *s* alfileres, dinero de bolsillo
pocket veto *s* (U.S.A.) veto indirecto o implícito (*que consiste en no firmar el Presidente una ley dentro del plazo legal*)
pockmark ['pakˌmark] *s* var. de **pock**
pock-marked ['pakˌmarkt] *adj* apedreado, picado de viruelas, varioloso, picoso
pod [pad] *s* (bot.) vaina; (*pret & pp:* **podded;** *ger:* **podding**) *vn* (bot.) criar vainas; llenarse, henchirse
podgy ['padʒɪ] *adj* (*comp:* **-ier;** *super:* **-iest**) gordinflón, rechoncho
podiatrist [po'daɪətrɪst] *s* podíatra
podiatry [po'daɪətrɪ] *s* podiatría
podium ['podɪəm] *s* (*pl:* **-a** [ə]) (arch.) podio; (anat. & zool.) pie; (bot.) pecíolo; estrado (*de director de orquesta*)
podophyllin [ˌpadə'fɪlɪn] *s* (pharm.) podofilino
podophyllotoxin [ˌpadəˌfɪlə'taksɪn] *s* (chem.) podofilotoxina
podophyllum [ˌpadə'fɪləm] *s* podofilo
poem ['po·ɪm] *s* poema; (fig.) poesía (*cosa muy hermosa*)
poesy ['po·ɪsɪ] o ['po·ɪzɪ] *s* (*pl:* **-sies**) (archaic) poesía; (obs.) poema
poet ['po·ɪt] *s* poeta
poetaster ['po·ɪtˌæstər] *s* poetastro
poetess ['po·ɪtɪs] *s* poetisa
poetic [po'ɛtɪk] *adj* poético; **poetics** *ssg* poética
poetical [po'ɛtɪkəl] *adj* poético
poetic justice *s* justicia ideal
poetic license *s* licencia poética
poetic vein *s* numen poético
poetize ['po·ɪtaɪz] *va & vn* poetizar
poet laureate *s* (*pl:* **poets laureate**) poeta laureado
poetry ['po·ɪtrɪ] *s* poesía
pogrom ['pogram] *s* pogrom, levantamiento contra los judíos
poignancy ['pɔɪnənsɪ] o ['pɔɪnjənsɪ] *s* picante; viveza, intensidad
poignant ['pɔɪnənt] o ['pɔɪnjənt] *adj* picante; vivo, intenso
poikilothermal [ˌpɔɪkɪlo'θʌrməl] *adj* (zool.) poiquilotermo
poilu ['pwalu] *s* soldado francés
poinsettia [pɔɪn'sɛtɪə] *s* (bot.) flor de la Pascua, pastora
point [pɔɪnt] *s* punta (*de espada, lápiz, tierra*); punto; pico (*de la pluma de escribir*); puntilla (*de la plumafuente*); gracia (*del chiste*); rasgo, peculiaridad; propósito; tanto o punto (*unidad de cuenta en los juegos*); (coll.) indirecta, insinuación; (elec.) punta; (print. & math.) punto; (naut.) cuarta (*de la rosa náutica*); (hunt.) punta (*del perro de caza*); (Brit.) aguja (*riel*); **at the point of** a punto de; **at the point of death** a punto de morir, en artículo de muerte; **beside the point** fuera de propósito; **from the point of view of** bajo el punto de vista de; **in point** a propósito; **in point of** por lo que toca a; **in point of fact** en realidad; **just the point** lo que importa; **to a certain point** hasta cierto punto; **to be beside the point** no venir al caso; **to be on the point of** estar a punto de; **to carry one's point** salirse con la suya; **to come** o **to get to the point** venir al caso o al grano, llegar al punto fundamental; **to get the point** caer en la cuenta; **to make a point of** hacer hincapié de; **to make a point of** + *ger* insistir en + *inf*, no dejar de + *inf*, esmerarse en + *inf;* **to speak to the point** hablar al caso; **to strain** o **stretch a point** exceder el límite; excederse haciendo concesiones, hacer una excepción; **to the point** a propósito; **up to a certain point** hasta cierto punto ‖ *va* aguzar, sacar punta a; apuntar (*p.ej. un arma de fuego*); señalar, señalar con el dedo; puntuar; rejuntar, resanar (*una pared*); reforzar; puntar (*las letras hebreas y árabes*); (hunt.) parar (*la caza*); **to point one's finger at** señalar con el dedo; **to point a gun at** apuntar con el fusil; **to point off** indicar con un punto o con puntos; **to point out** señalar, indicar, hacer notar; **to point up** poner de realce o de relieve, destacar ‖ *vn* apuntar; apostemarse; pararse (*el perro de muestra*); **to point at** apuntar; apuntar o señalar con el dedo; **to point to** señalar; indicar, pronosticar
point-blank ['pɔɪntˌblæŋk] *adj & adv* a quema ropa; **to ask a question point-blank** hacer una pregunta a quema ropa
pointed ['pɔɪntɪd] *adj* puntiagudo; picante; directo, acentuado
pointedly ['pɔɪntɪdlɪ] *adv* directamente, enfáticamente; a propósito
pointer ['pɔɪntər] *s* indicador; puntero; manecilla del reloj; perro de muestra; fiel (*de la balanza*); (coll.) indicación, dirección
point lace *s* encaje de punto, puntas
pointless ['pɔɪntlɪs] *adj* sin punta; sin sentido, insubstancial; sin tantos
point of honor *s* punto de honor, pundonor
point of order *s* cuestión de procedimiento
point of view *s* punto de vista
poise [pɔɪz] *s* equilibrio, aplomo, serenidad, balance; *va* equilibrar; sopesar; considerar; *vn* equilibrarse; estar suspendido; cernerse
poison ['pɔɪzən] *s* veneno, ponzoña; (fig.) ponzoña; *adj* venenoso, ponzoñoso; *va* envenenar
poisoner ['pɔɪzənər] *s* envenenador
poison gas *s* (mil.) gas tóxico, gas de guerra
poison hemlock *s* (bot.) cicuta, cicuta mayor
poisoning ['pɔɪzənɪŋ] *s* envenenamiento
poison ivy *s* (bot.) hiedra venenosa, chechén, tosiguero
poison oak *s* (bot.) hiedra venenosa, chechén; (bot.) zumaque venenoso
poisonous ['pɔɪzənəs] *adj* venenoso
poison-pen letter ['pɔɪzənˌpɛn] *s* paulina (*carta ofensiva anónima*)
poison sumac *s* (bot.) zumaque venenoso
poke [pok] *s* empuje, empujón; codazo; hurgonazo; tardón; papalina de ala abovedada; (bot.) hierba carmín, grana encarnada; *va* empujar; hacer (*un agujero*) a empujones; abrirse (*paso*) a empujones, abrirse (*paso*) a fuerza de codazos; atizar, hurgar; introducir, meter; **to poke fun at** burlarse de; **to poke one's nose into** entremeterse en; **to poke someone in the ribs** darle a uno un codazo en las costillas; *vn* fisgar, husmear; andar perezosamente; **to poke along** andar perezosamente; **to poke**

around fisgar, husmear; andar buscando algo; **to poke into** hurgar en

pokeberry ['pok,bɛrɪ] *s* (*pl:* **-ries**) (bot.) hierba carmín, grana encarnada (*planta y baya*)

poke bonnet *s* papalina de ala abovedada

poker ['pokər] *s* hurgón; tardón; póker o pócar (*juego de naipes*)

poker face *s* (coll.) cara de jugador de póker (*cara impasible*); **to keep a poker face** (coll.) disfrazar la expresión del rostro

pokeweed ['pok,wid] *s* (bot.) hierba carmín, grana encarnada

poky o **pokey** ['pokɪ] *adj* (*comp:* **-ier;** *super:* **-iest**) roncero, lerdo, perezoso, tardo; insignificante; desaliñado

polacre [po'lɑkər] *s* (naut.) polacra

Poland ['polənd] *s* Polonia

polar ['polər] *adj* polar

polar bear *s* (zool.) oso blanco

polar cap *s* casquete polar (*del planeta Marte*)

polarimeter [,polə'rɪmɪtər] *s* polarímetro

Polaris [po'lɛrɪs] *s* (astr.) la estrella polar, la polar norte

polariscope [po'lærɪskop] *s* polariscopio

polarity [po'lærɪtɪ] *s* polaridad

polarization [,polərɪ'zeʃən] *s* polarización

polarize ['poləraɪz] *va* polarizar

polarizer ['polə,raɪzər] *s* (opt.) polarizador

polaroid ['polərɔɪd] *s* (trademark) polaroide

polaroid lenses *spl* lentes polarizantes

pole [pol] *s* pértiga; poste, piquete, jalón; asta (*de bandera*); botador (*para mover los barcos*); (astr., geog., biol., elec. & math.) polo; medida lineal equivalente a 5,03 metros; medida de superficie equivalente a 25,2 metros cuadrados; (*cap.*) *s* polaco; (*l.c.*) *va* finear, impeler (*una embarcación*) con botador; *vn* silgar, singar

poleax o **poleaxe** ['pol,æks] *s* hachuela de mano; jifero

polecat ['pol,kæt] *s* (zool.) turón, veso (*Putorius putorius*); (zool.) mofeta (*Mephitis*); (zool.) vormela (*Putorius sarmaticus*)

pole gap *s* (phys.) entrehierro, entrehierro polar (*del ciclotrón*)

polemic [po'lɛmɪk] *adj* polémico; *s* polémica (*controversia*); polemista; **polemics** *ssg* polémica (*arte*)

polemical [po'lɛmɪkəl] *adj* polémico

polemist ['pɑlɪmɪst] *s* polemista

polemoniaceous [,pɑlɪ,monɪ'eʃəs] *adj* (bot.) polemoniáceo

polenta [po'lɛntə] *s* polenta

pole piece *s* parhilera; (elec.) pieza polar

pole pitch *s* (elec.) paso polar, distancia interpolar

polestar ['pol,stɑr] *s* (astr.) estrella polar; (fig.) norte (*guía*); (fig.) miradero (*centro de interés*)

pole vault *s* (sports) salto con garrocha, salto con pértiga

police [pə'lis] *s* policía; (mil.) limpieza; *va* poner o mantener servicio de policía en; (mil.) limpiar

police action *s* (int. law) acción de policía

police car *s* coche de policía

police court *s* tribunal de policía

police dog *s* perro policía

police force *s* cuerpo de policía, servicio de policía

police headquarters *s* jefatura de policía

policeman [pə'lismən] *s* (*pl:* **-men**) policía, agente o guardia de policía, guardia urbano

police record *s* ficha

police state *s* estado-policía, estado policial

police station *s* oficina de policía, prefectura

policewoman [pə'lis,wʊmən] *s* (*pl:* **-women**) mujer policía

policy ['pɑlɪsɪ] *s* (*pl:* **-cies**) política; (ins.) póliza; (U.S.A.) lotería

policyholder ['pɑlɪsɪ,holdər] *s* asegurado, tenedor de una póliza

policy of encirclement *s* política de cerco, política de acorralamiento

policy racket *s* var. de **numbers game**

polio ['polɪo] *s* (coll.) polio (*poliomielitis*)

poliomyelitis [,pɑlɪo,maɪə'laɪtɪs] *s* (path.) poliomielitis

Polish ['polɪʃ] *adj* polaco; *spl* polacos; *ssg* polaco (*idioma*); (*l.c.*) ['pɑlɪʃ] *s* pulimento (*acción o efecto; ingrediente*); cera de lustrar; bola, betún, crema; elegancia, pulidez; cultura, urbanidad; *va* pulir; embolar, dar bola, betún o brillo a (*los zapatos*); (fig.) pulir; **to polish off** (coll.) terminar de prisa, acabar con, sin más ni más; (slang) engullir; **to polish up** mejorar, perfeccionar; *vn* pulirse

Polish Corridor ['polɪʃ] *s* Corredor Polaco

polished ['pɑlɪʃt] *adj* pulido, terso, brillante; cortés, distinguido, urbano

polisher ['pɑlɪʃər] *s* pulidor; pulidora (*máquina*)

polishing wax *s* cera de lustrar

polishing wheel *s* rueda de bruñir, muela pulidora

Politburo [pɑ'lɪt,bjʊrɑ] *s* Politburó

polite [pə'laɪt] *s* cortés; culto

politeness [pə'laɪtnɪs] *s* cortesía; cultura

Politian [po'lɪʃən] *s* Policiano

politic ['pɑlɪtɪk] *adj* prudente, sagaz; astuto, ladino; político; **politics** *ssg* o *spl* política

political [pə'lɪtɪkəl] *adj* político

political economy *s* economía política

political science *s* ciencia política

politician [,pɑlɪ'tɪʃən] *s* político; politiquero (*político de propósitos ruines*)

polity ['pɑlɪtɪ] *s* (*pl:* **-ties**) gobierno; estado

polka ['polkə] *s* (mus.) polca; *vn* polcar

polka dot ['pokə] *s* punto (*en un diseño de puntos*); diseño de puntos

poll [pol] *s* encuesta; votación; nómina, lista electoral; cabeza; **polls** *spl* colegio electoral, urnas electorales; **to go to the polls** ir a las urnas, acudir a los comicios; **to take a poll** hacer una encuesta; *va* dar (*un voto*); recibir (*votos*); encuestar (*la opinión pública*); recibir en la urna los votos de; podar, desmochar (*un árbol*); descornar; trasquilar; *vn* votar

pollack ['pɑlək] *s* (ichth.) gado (*de los géneros Pollachius y Theragra*)

pollard ['pɑlərd] *s* árbol desmochado; res descornada; *va* acotar, desmochar (*un árbol*); descornar

pollen ['pɑlən] *s* (bot.) polen

pollinate ['pɑlɪnet] *va* polinizar

pollination [,pɑlɪ'neʃən] *s* polinización

polling booth *s* cabina o caseta de votar

polling place *s* urnas electorales, lugar donde se vota

pollinic [pə'lɪnɪk] o **pollinical** [pə'lɪnɪkəl] *adj* polínico

polliniferous [,pɑlɪ'nɪfərəs] *adj* polinífero

pollinium [pə'lɪnɪəm] *s* (*pl:* **-a** [ə]) (bot.) polinio

pollinosis [,pɑlɪ'nosɪs] *s* (path.) polinosis

polliwog ['pɑlɪwɑg] *s* (zool.) renacuajo; (slang) persona que atraviesa el ecuador en un barco por primera vez

pollock ['pɑlək] *s* var. de **pollack**

poll tax *s* capitación

pollute [pə'lut] *va* contaminar, ensuciar, corromper

pollution [pə'luʃən] *s* contaminación, corrupción; (path.) polución

Pollux ['pɑləks] *s* (myth. & astr.) Pólux

Polly ['pɑlɪ] *s* Mariquita

pollywog ['pɑlɪwɑg] *s* var. de **polliwog**

polo ['polo] *s* (sport) polo

polonaise [,pɑlə'nez] o [,polə'nez] *s* polonesa (*prenda de vestir*); (mus.) polonesa

polonium [pə'lonɪəm] *s* (chem.) polonio

polo player *s* polista, jugador de polo

polo shirt *s* pulóver con cuello abotonado

poltergeist ['poltər,gaɪst] *s* espíritu que golpea y mueve mesas y otros objetos para indicar su presencia

poltroon [pɑl'trun] *s* cobarde

poltroonery [pɑl'trunərɪ] *s* cobardía

poly ['pɑlɪ] *s* (*pl:* **-lies**) (bot.) polio

polyandrous [,pɑlɪ'ændrəs] *adj* poliándrico; (bot.) poliandro

polyandry ['pɑlɪ,ændrɪ] *s* poliandria; (bot.) poliandria

polyanthus [,pɑlɪ'ænθəs] *s* (bot.) hierba de San Pablo mayor; (bot.) narciso de manojo

polyarchy ['pɑlɪ,ɑrkɪ] *s* poliarquía

polybasic [,pɑlɪ'besɪk] *adj* (chem.) polibásico

polybasite [,pɑlɪ'besaɪt] o [pə'lɪbəsaɪt] *s* (mineral.) polibasita

polycarpic [,pɑlɪ'kɑrpɪk] o **polycarpous** [,pɑlɪ'kɑrpəs] *adj* (bot.) policárpico

polychromatic [ˌpɑlɪkroˈmætɪk] *adj* policromo
polychrome [ˈpɑlɪkrom] *adj* policromo; *s* combinación de varios colores; obra policroma; *va* policromar
polychromy [ˈpɑlɪˌkromɪ] *s* policromía
polyclinic [ˌpɑlɪˈklɪnɪk] *s* policlínica
Polydorus [ˌpɑlɪˈdorəs] *s* (myth.) Polidoro
polyethylene [ˌpɑlɪˈɛθɪlin] (chem) polietileno
polygamist [pəˈlɪgəmɪst] *s* polígamo
polygamous [pəˈlɪgəməs] *adj* polígamo
polygamy [pəˈlɪgəmɪ] *s* poligamia
polygenism [pəˈlɪdʒɪnɪzəm] *s* poligenismo
polyglot [ˈpɑlɪglɑt] *adj & s* poligloto; *s* libro poligloto; Biblia poliglota
polygon [ˈpɑlɪgɑn] *s* (geom.) polígono
polygonal [pəˈlɪgənəl] *adj* poligonal
polygraph [ˈpɑlɪgræf] o [ˈpɑlɪgrɑf] *s* polígrafo (*autor; aparato multicopista*); (med.) polígrafo
polygraphy [pəˈlɪgrəfɪ] *s* poligrafía
polyhedral [ˌpɑlɪˈhidrəl] *adj* poliédrico
polyhedron [ˌpɑlɪˈhidrən] *s* (*pl:* **-drons** o **-dra** [drə]) (geom.) poliedro
Polyhymnia [ˌpɑlɪˈhɪmnɪə] *s* (myth.) Polimnia
polymer [ˈpɑlɪmər] *s* (chem.) polímero
polymeric [ˌpɑlɪˈmɛrɪk] *adj* polímero
polymerism [ˈpɑlɪmərɪzəm] o [pəˈlɪmərɪzəm] *s* polimería
polymerization [ˌpɑlɪmərɪˈzeʃən] o [pəˌlɪmərɪˈzeʃən] *s* polimerización
polymerize [ˈpɑlɪməraɪz] o [pəˈlɪməraɪz] *va* polimerizar; *vn* polimerizarse
polymorphic [ˌpɑlɪˈmɔrfɪk] *adj* var. de **polymorphous**
polymorphism [ˌpɑlɪˈmɔrfɪzəm] *s* polimorfismo
polymorphous [ˌpɑlɪˈmɔrfəs] *adj* polimorfo
Polynesia [ˌpɑlɪˈniʃə] o [ˌpɑlɪˈniʒə] *s* la Polinesia
Polynesian [ˌpɑlɪˈniʃən] o [ˌpɑlɪˈniʒən] *adj & s* polinesio
polyneuritis [ˌpɑlɪnjuˈraɪtɪs] o [ˌpɑlɪnuˈraɪtɪs] *s* (path.) polineuritis
polynomial [ˌpɑlɪˈnomɪəl] *adj* polinómico; *s* (alg.) polinomio
polynuclear [ˌpɑlɪˈnjuklɪər] o [ˌpɑlɪˈnuklɪər] *adj* polinuclear
polyp [ˈpɑlɪp] *s* (zool. & path.) pólipo
polypary [ˈpɑlɪˌpɛrɪ] *s* (*pl:* **-ies**) (zool.) polipero
polypetalous [ˌpɑlɪˈpɛtələs] *adj* (bot.) polipétalo
polyphagia [ˌpɑlɪˈfedʒɪə] *s* (path.) polifagía
polyphase [ˈpɑlɪfez] *adj* (elec.) polifásico
Polyphemus [ˌpɑlɪˈfiməs] *s* (myth.) Polifemo
polyphone [ˈpɑlɪfon] *s* (phonet.) letra polífona, símbolo polífono
polyphonic [ˌpɑlɪˈfɑnɪk] *adj* polifónico
polyphony [pəˈlɪfənɪ] *s* (mus. & phonet.) polifonía
polyphyletic [ˌpɑlɪfaɪˈlɛtɪk] *adj* polifilético
polypody [ˈpɑlɪˌpodɪ] *s* (*pl:* **-dies**) (bot.) polipodio
polypus [ˈpɑlɪpəs] *s* (*pl:* **-pi** [paɪ]) (path.) pólipo
polysemous [ˌpɑlɪˈsiməs] *adj* polisémico o polisemo
polysemy [ˈpɑlɪˌsimɪ] *s* polisemia
polystyle [ˈpɑlɪstaɪl] *adj & s* (arch.) polistilo
polystylous [ˌpɑlɪˈstaɪləs] *adj* (bot.) polistilo
polystyrene [ˌpɑlɪˈstaɪrin] o [ˌpɑlɪˈstɪrin] *s* (chem.) polistireno
polysyllabic [ˌpɑlɪsɪˈlæbɪk] *adj* polisílabo, polisilábico
polysyllable [ˈpɑlɪˌsɪləbəl] *s* polisílabo
polysyndeton [ˌpɑlɪˈsɪndətən] *s* (rhet.) polisíndeton
polysynthetic [ˌpɑlɪsɪnˈθɛtɪk] *adj* polisintético
polytechnic [ˌpɑlɪˈtɛknɪk] *adj* politécnico; *s* escuela politécnica
polytheism [ˈpɑlɪθiɪzəm] *s* politeísmo
polytheist [ˈpɑlɪθiɪst] *s* politeísta
polytheistic [ˌpɑlɪθiˈɪstɪk] *adj* politeísta
polytonal [ˌpɑlɪˈtonəl] *adj* politonal
polytonality [ˌpɑlɪtoˈnælɪtɪ] *s* (mus.) politonalidad
polyuria [ˌpɑlɪˈjurɪə] *s* (path.) poliuria
polyvalence [ˌpɑlɪˈveləns] o [pəˈlɪvələns] *s* (bact. & chem.) polivalencia
polyvalent [ˌpɑlɪˈvelənt] o [pəˈlɪvələnt] *adj* (bact. & chem.) polivalente
pomace [ˈpʌmɪs] *s* bagazo de manzanas; bagazo
pomaceous [poˈmeʃəs] *adj* (bot.) pomáceo
pomade [pəˈmed] o [pəˈmɑd] *s* pomada
pomander [poˈmændər] o [ˈpomændər] *s* poma, bola aromática
pomatum [poˈmetəm] o [poˈmɑtəm] *s* var. de **pomade**
pome [pom] *s* (bot.) pomo
pomegranate [ˈpɑmˌgrænɪt], [pɑmˈgrænɪt] o [ˈpʌmˌgrænɪt] *s* (bot.) granado; granada (*fruto*)
pomelo [ˈpɑməlo] *s* (*pl:* **-los**) (bot.) pomelo
Pomeranian [ˌpɑməˈrenɪən] *adj* pomeranio o pomerano; *s* pomeranio o pomerano; perro pomerano
pomfret [ˈpɑmfrɪt] *s* (ichth.) castañola
pommel [ˈpʌməl] o [ˈpɑməl] *s* pomo (*de la guarnición de la espada*); perilla (*del arzón*); (*pret & pp:* **-meled** o **-melled;** *ger:* **-meling** o **-melling**) *va* apuñear, aporrear
pomology [poˈmɑlədʒɪ] *s* pomología
pomp [pɑmp] *s* pompa
pompadour [ˈpɑmpədor] o [ˈpɑmpədur] *s* copete
pompano [ˈpɑmpəno] *s* (*pl:* **-nos**) (ichth.) pampanito
Pompeian [pɑmˈpeən] *adj & s* pompeyano
Pompeii [pɑmˈpe] o [pɑmˈpe·i] *s* Pompeya
Pompey [ˈpɑmpɪ] *s* Pompeyo
pompon [ˈpɑmpɑn] *s* pompón
pomposity [pɑmˈpɑsɪtɪ] *s* (*pl:* **-ties**) pomposidad
pompous [ˈpɑmpəs] *adj* pomposo
poncho [ˈpɑntʃo] *s* (*pl:* **-chos**) capote de monte, poncho
pond [pɑnd] *s* estanque, charco; vivero; (hum.) charco (*mar, océano*)
ponder [ˈpɑndər] *va* ponderar, considerar con particular cuidado; *vn* meditar, pensar con cuidado; **to ponder on** u **over** ponderar, considerar con particular cuidado
ponderable [ˈpɑndərəbəl] *adj* ponderable; (fig.) ponderable
ponderosity [ˌpɑndəˈrɑsɪtɪ] *s* ponderosidad; pesadez
ponderous [ˈpɑndərəs] *adj* ponderoso; pesado
pond lily *s* (bot.) ninfea, nenúfar
pondweed [ˈpɑndˌwid] *s* (bot.) acaxaxán, zacatillo
pone [pon] *s* pan de maíz
pongee [pɑnˈdʒi] *s* tela suave de seda
poniard [ˈpɑnjərd] *s* puñal; *va* apuñalar
pontederiaceous [ˌpɑntɪˌdɪrɪˈeʃəs] *adj* (bot.) pontederiáceo
Pontic [ˈpɑntɪk] *adj* póntico
pontifex [ˈpɑntɪfɛks] *s* (*pl:* **pontifices** [pɑnˈtɪfɪsiz]) (hist. & eccl.) pontífice
pontiff [ˈpɑntɪf] *s* (hist. & eccl.) pontífice; sumo sacerdote; Sumo Pontífice
pontifical [pɑnˈtɪfɪkəl] *adj* pontifical, pontificio; *s* pontifical (*libro litúrgico*); **pontificals** *spl* pontificales
pontificate [pɑnˈtɪfɪkɪt] o [pɑnˈtɪfɪket] *s* pontificado; [pɑnˈtɪfɪket] *vn* pontificar; hablar con ampulosidad
pontil [ˈpɑntɪl] *s* var. de **punty**
Pontine Marshes [ˈpɑntɪn] o [ˈpɑntaɪn] *spl* Pantanos Pontinos
Pontius [ˈpɑnʃəs] o [ˈpɑntɪəs] *s* Poncio
pontlevis [pɑntˈlɛvɪs] *s* puente levadizo
pontonier [ˌpɑntəˈnɪr] *s* (mil.) pontonero
pontoon [pɑnˈtun] *s* pontón; flotador (*de hidroavión*)
pontoon bridge *s* puente de barcas, puente de pontones
Pontus [ˈpɑntəs] *s* (myth.) Ponto; **the Pontus** el Ponto (*país*)
Pontus Euxinus [jukˈsaɪnəs] *s* Ponto Euxino (*antiguo nombre del mar Negro*)
pony [ˈponɪ] *s* (*pl:* **-nies**) jaca, caballito; (coll.) traducción usada ilícitamente en las lecciones o exámenes; pequeño vaso (*para licor alcohólico*); (*pret & pp:* **-nied**) *va & vn* (coll.) traducir con clave o ayuda; (slang) pagar; **to pony up** (slang) pagar

pony engine *s* pequeña locomotora de maniobras
pony express *s* sistema de correo utilizando hombres a caballo
pooch [putʃ] *s* (coll.) perro
poodle [ˈpudəl] *s* perro de lanas
pooh [pu] *interj* ¡bah!, ¡qué va!
pooh-pooh [ˌpuˈpu] *va* negar importancia a; *vn* mofar; *interj* ¡bah!, ¡qué va!
pooh-pooh theory *s* (philol.) teoría de las expresiones afectivas
pool [pul] *s* cuerpo de agua estancado; charco (*en el pavimento*); piscina; hoya (*en un río*); trucos (*juego*); polla o puesta (*en ciertos juegos*); mancomunidad, combinación de intereses con un propósito común; caudales unidos para un fin; *va* mancomunar
poolroom [ˈpulˌrum] o [ˈpulˌrʊm] *s* sala de trucos; sala de apuestas
pool table *s* mesa de trucos
poop [pup] *s* (naut.) popa; (naut.) toldilla (*cubierta*); *va* (naut.) embarcar (*agua*) por la popa
poop deck *s* (naut.) toldilla
poop royal *s* (naut.) chopeta
poor [pʊr] *adj* pobre; malo; **the poor** los pobres; **poor as a church mouse** más pobre que las ratas o una rata; **poor in spirit** pobre de espíritu
poor box *s* caja de limosnas, cepillo
poor farm *s* granja o finca sostenida por la caridad pública donde se recluye a los menesterosos
poorhouse [ˈpʊrˌhaus] *s* asilo de pobres, casa de caridad
poor law *s* ley acerca de los menesterosos
poorly [ˈpʊrlɪ] *adj* (coll.) malo, enfermo; *adv* pobremente; mal
poor rate *s* diezmos pagados para el socorro de los menesterosos
Poor Richard *s* el buenhombre Ricardo (*seudónimo de Benjamín Franklin*)
poor-spirited [ˈpʊrˈspɪrɪtɪd] *adj* cobarde, pusilánime
poor thing *s* pobrecito o pobrecita
poor white *s* pobre de la raza blanca (*en el sur de los EE.UU.*)
pop. abr. de **popular** y **population**
pop [pɑp] *s* estallido, taponazo; bebida gaseosa; *interj* ¡paf!; (*pret & pp:* **popped;** *ger:* **popping**) *va* disparar; hacer estallar; hacer (*una pregunta*); **to pop the question** (coll.) hacer una declaración de amor; *vn* estallar (*como un cohete*); reventarse; suceder de repente; **to pop at** tirar a; **to pop in and out** entrar y salir súbita e inesperadamente; **to pop up** aparecer súbita o inesperadamente
pop concert *s* concierto popular
popcorn [ˈpɑpˌkɔrn] *s* rosetas, palomitas
pope o **Pope** [pop] s papa
popedom [ˈpopdəm] *s* papado
Pope Joan *s* Juana la papisa, la papisa Juana
popery [ˈpopərɪ] *s* (scornful) papismo
popess [ˈpopɪs] *s* papisa
popeyed [ˈpɑpˌaɪd] *adj* de ojos saltones
popgun [ˈpɑpˌgʌn] *s* tirabala, taco
popinjay [ˈpɑpɪndʒe] *s* pisaverde, galancete; (orn.) pito real
popish [ˈpopɪʃ] *adj* (scornful) papista, católico
poplar [ˈpɑplər] *s* (bot.) álamo
poplin [ˈpɑplɪn] *s* popelina
popliteal [pɑpˈlɪtɪəl] *adj* (anat.) poplíteo
popover [ˈpɑpˌovər] *s* panecillo hueco de masa muy fina
popper [ˈpɑpər] *s* persona o cosa que produce un estallido; canasto de alambre o cacerola de metal donde se tuesta el maíz
poppet [ˈpɑpɪt] *s* (mach.) válvula de disco con movimiento vertical
poppy [ˈpɑpɪ] *s* (*pl:* **-pies**) (bot.) amapola, ababa
poppycock [ˈpɑpɪˌkɑk] *s* (coll.) necedad, tontería; *interj* ¡necedades!, ¡tonterías!
popsicle [ˈpɑpsɪkəl] *s* polo (*pequeño sorbete en el extremo de un palito*)
populace [ˈpɑpjəlɪs] *s* populacho
popular [ˈpɑpjələr] *adj* popular
popular etymology *s* etimología popular
popularity [ˌpɑpjəˈlærɪtɪ] *s* popularidad
popularization [ˌpɑpjələrɪˈzeʃən] *s* popularización, vulgarización
popularize [ˈpɑpjələraɪz] *va* popularizar, vulgarizar
popularly [ˈpɑpjələrlɪ] *adv* popularmente
populate [ˈpɑpjəlet] *va* poblar
population [ˌpɑpjəˈleʃən] *s* población
Populism [ˈpɑpjəlɪzəm] *s* populismo
Populist [ˈpɑpjəlɪst] *s* populista
populous [ˈpɑpjələs] *adj* populoso
populousness [ˈpɑpjələsnɪs] *s* (lo) populoso
porbeagle [ˈpɔrˌbigəl] *s* (ichth.) tiburón (*Lamna nasus*)
porcelain [ˈpɔrsəlɪn] o [ˈpɔrslɪn] *s* porcelana
porcelain crab *s* (zool.) liebre de mar o liebre marina
porch [portʃ] *s* porche, pórtico, cobertizo
porcine [ˈpɔrsaɪn] o [ˈpɔrsɪn] *adj* porcino
porcupine [ˈpɔrkjəpaɪn] *s* (zool.) puerco espín
pore [por] *s* poro; *vn* mirar con mirada intensa y sostenida; **to pore over** meditar (*un asunto*) cuidadosamente; estudiar larga y detenidamente
porgy [ˈpɔrgɪ] *s* (*pl:* **-gies**) (ichth.) pagro
poricidal [ˌporɪˈsaɪdəl] *adj* (bot.) poricida
pork [pork] *s* carne de cerdo, carne de puerco; (slang) dinero del estado usado para conferir favores políticos
pork barrel *s* (slang) política que sigue un diputado para conseguir beneficios para la región que representa, asegurándose así los votos; fondos votados por los diputados para el cumplimiento de esta política
pork chop *s* chuleta de puerco
porker [ˈporkər] *s* cerdo, cerdo cebado
porky [ˈporkɪ] *adj* porcuno; gordo
pornographer [pɔrˈnɑgrəfər] *s* pornógrafo
pornographic [ˌpɔrnəˈgræfɪk] *adj* pornográfico
pornography [pɔrˈnɑgrəfɪ] *s* pornografía
porosity [poˈrɑsɪtɪ] *s* porosidad
porous [ˈporəs] *adj* poroso
porous plaster *s* parche poroso
porphyritic [ˌpɔrfɪˈrɪtɪk] *adj* porfídico
porphyry [ˈpɔrfɪrɪ] *s* (*pl:* **-ries**) pórfido
porpoise [ˈpɔrpəs] *s* (zool.) marsopa, puerco de mar
porraceous [pəˈreʃəs] *adj* porráceo
porridge [ˈpɑrɪdʒ] o [ˈpɔrɪdʒ] *s* gachas
porringer [ˈpɑrɪndʒər] o [ˈpɔrɪndʒər] *s* escudilla
port [port] *s* puerto; (naut.) portilla; (nav.) tronera; (naut.) babor; (mach.) lumbrera; porte; oporto, vino de Oporto; **to put into port** entrar a puerto; *adj* portuario; *vn* (naut.) virar hacia el lado de babor
portable [ˈportəbəl] *adj* portátil
portable typewriter *s* máquina de escribir portátil
portage [ˈportɪdʒ] *s* porteo (*acción de llevar por tierra y a cuestas barcos, provisiones, etc., de una corriente de agua a otra*); porte; *va* portear
portal [ˈportəl] *s* portada; boca o portal (*de túnel*)
portal vein *s* (anat.) vena porta
Port Arthur *s* Puerto Arturo
Port-au-Prince [ˌportoˈprɪns] *s* Puerto Príncipe
port authority *s* autoridad portuaria, autoridad del puerto
portcullis [portˈkʌlɪs] *s* (fort.) rastrillo
Porte [port] *s* Puerta (*Turquía*)
porte-cochere o **porte-cochère** [ˈportkoˈʃɛr] *s* puerta cochera
porte-monnaie [ˌportməˈne] o [ˈportˌmʌnɪ] *s* portamonedas
portend [porˈtɛnd] *va* presagiar, anunciar de antemano
portent [ˈportɛnt] *s* presagio, augurio
portentous [porˈtɛntəs] *adj* amenazante, ominoso; portentoso, extraordinario
porter [ˈportər] *s* mozo de servicio (*en trenes y hoteles*); portero, conserje; pórter (*cerveza de color obscuro y sabor amargo*)
porterage [ˈportərɪdʒ] *s* oficio o trabajo de mozo de servicio; portería; porte (*lo que se paga por el transporte*)

porterhouse ['portər,haʊs] o **porterhouse steak** s biftec de filete
porter's lodge s portería, conserjería
portfolio [port'folɪo] s (*pl:* **-os**) cartera (*estuche para papeles; empleo de ministro; valores comerciales*)
porthole ['port,hol] s (naut.) porta, portilla; (nav.) tronera
Portia ['porʃɪə] o ['porʃə] s Porcia
portico ['portɪko] s (*pl:* **-coes** o **-cos**) pórtico
portiere o **portière** [por'tjɛr] s antepuerta, portier
portion ['porʃən] s porción; dote; *va* dividir, repartir; dotar
Portland cement ['portlənd] s cemento pórtland
portly ['portlɪ] *adj* (*comp:* **-lier;** *super:* **-liest**) corpulento; grave, majestuoso
portmanteau [port'mænto] s (*pl:* **-teaus** o **-teaux** [toz]) portamanteo
portmanteau word s palabra de enchufamiento
port of call s (naut.) escala
Port of Spain s Puerto de España (*en la isla de la Trinidad*)
Porto Rican ['porto 'rikən] *adj & s* var. de **Puerto Rican**
Porto Rico ['porto 'riko] s var. de **Puerto Rico**
portrait ['portret] o ['portrɪt] s retrato
portraitist ['portretɪst] s retratista
portrait painter s pintor retratista
portraiture ['portrɪtʃər] s acción de retratar; retrato
portray [por'tre] *va* retratar; (fig.) retratar
portrayal [por'treəl] s representación gráfica; descripción acertada, retrato
portress ['portrɪs] s portera
Portugal ['portʃəgəl] s Portugal
Portuguese ['portʃəgiz] *adj* portugués; s (*pl:* **-guese**) portugués
Portuguese East Africa s el África Oriental Portuguesa
Portuguese Guinea s la Guinea Portuguesa
Portuguese India s la India Portuguesa
Portuguese West Africa s el África Occidental Portuguesa
portulaca [,portʃə'lækə] s (bot.) verdolaga
port wine s vino de Oporto
pose [poz] s pose (*postura del cuerpo; afectación*); *va* colocar en cierta postura; formular, hacer, proponer, plantear (*una pregunta, cuestión, etc.*); confundir; *vn* posar (*para retratarse; como modelo*); fachendear; **to pose as** dárselas de, hacerse pasar por
Poseidon [po'saɪdən] s (myth.) Poseidón
poser ['pozər] s presuntuoso; problema de difícil comprensión
poseur [po'zʌr] s poseur (*persona afectada, persona que emplea afectación con el propósito de causar sensación*)
posh [pɑʃ] *adj* (slang) elegante, gracioso; (slang) lujoso, suntuoso
posit ['pɑzɪt] *va* colocar, disponer; (philos.) aceptar como hecho, proponer como principio
position [pə'zɪʃən] s posición; empleo, puesto; opinión; **to be in a position to** + *inf* estar en condiciones de + *inf*
positive ['pɑzɪtɪv] *adj* positivo; s (math.) término positivo; (elec.) electricidad positiva, borne positivo; (gram.) positivo; (phot.) positiva o positivo
positivism ['pɑzɪtɪvɪzəm] s positivismo
positivist ['pɑzɪtɪvɪst] s positivista
positivistic [,pɑzɪtɪ'vɪstɪk] *adj* positivista
positron ['pɑzɪtrɑn] s (phys.) positrón
posology [pə'sɑlədʒɪ] s (med.) posología
posse ['pɑsɪ] s grupo de hombres llamados a las armas por el jefe local para ayudarle a ejercer su autoridad
possess [pə'zɛs] *va* poseer
possession [pə'zɛʃən] s posesión
possessive [pə'zɛsɪv] *adj* posesivo; deseoso de poseer; (gram.) posesivo; s (gram.) posesivo
possessor [pə'zɛsər] s poseedor, posesor
possessory [pə'zɛsərɪ] *adj* posesorio
posset ['pɑsɪt] s bebida caliente hecha con leche, licor y especias
possibility [,pɑsɪ'bɪlɪtɪ] s (*pl:* **-ties**) posibilidad; persona o cosa posibles
possible ['pɑsɪbəl] *adj* posible
possibly ['pɑsɪblɪ] *adv* posiblemente; tal vez
possum ['pɑsəm] s (zool.) zarigüeya; **to act** o **play possum** (coll.) fingir estar dormido, hacer la mortecina, hacer o hacerse el muerto
post [post] s poste; puesto; cargo, destino; correo; casa de postas; cartero; casa de correos; buzón; (mil.) apostadero, puesto militar; (mil.) campamento, guarnición; *adv* por la posta, a toda prisa; *va* fijar (*carteles*); poner en lista; echar al correo; apostar, situar; enterar, tener al corriente; nombrar (*a una persona*) para desempeñar un cargo determinado; (com.) pasar (*un asiento*) del libro diario al libro mayor; **post no bills** se prohíbe fijar carteles; *vn* correr la posta; viajar en posta
postage ['postɪdʒ] s porte, franqueo
postage stamp s sello de correo; estampilla, timbre (Am.)
postal ['postəl] *adj* postal; s postal (*tarjeta*)
postal car s (rail.) coche de correos
postal card s tarjeta postal
postal permit s franqueo concertado
postal savings bank s caja postal de ahorros
postboy ['post,bɔɪ] s cartero; postillón
postbox ['post,bɑks] s buzón
post card s tarjeta postal
post chaise s silla de posta
postdate ['post,det] s posfecha; [,post'det] *va* posfechar; seguir, acontecer después de
postdiluvian [,postdɪ'luvɪən] *adj* postdiluviano
posted ['postɪd] *adj* con postes o pilares; (coll.) enterado, al corriente
poster ['postər] s cartel, cartelón, letrero; fijador de carteles; caballo de posta
poste restante [,post rɛs'tɑnt] s (Fr.) lista de correos
posterior [pɑs'tɪrɪər] *adj* posterior; s nalgas
posteriority [pɑs,tɪrɪ'ɔrɪtɪ] o [pɑs,tɪrɪ'ɑrɪtɪ] s posterioridad
posterity [pɑs'tɛrɪtɪ] s posteridad
postern ['postərn] s portillo, postigo; (fort.) poterna
Post Exchange s (U.S.A.) cantina y tienda de variedades para los militares en los campamentos
postfix ['postfɪks] s (gram.) posfijo
postgraduate [post'grædʒuɪt] *adj & s* postgraduado
posthaste ['post'hest] *adv* por la posta, a toda prisa
posthole ['post,hol] s agujero de poste
posthole digger s barrena para practicar hoyos en la colocación de postes, cavador de agujeros de poste
post horse s caballo de posta
posthouse ['post,haʊs] s posta, casa de postas
posthumous ['pɑstʃuməs] *adj* póstumo
posthumously ['pɑstʃuməslɪ] *adv* póstumamente
posthypnotic [,posthɪp'nɑtɪk] *adj* posthipnótico
postiche [pɔs'tiʃ] *adj* postizo
postilion o **postillion** [pos'tɪljən] o [pɑs'tɪljən] s postillón
postimpressionism [,postɪm'prɛʃənɪzəm] s postimpresionismo
postimpressionist [,postɪm'prɛʃənɪst] s postimpresionista
postliminy [post'lɪmɪnɪ] s (law) postliminio
postlude ['postlud] s (mus.) postludio
postman ['postmən] s (*pl:* **-men**) cartero
postmark ['post,mɑrk] s matasellos, timbre de correos (*que marca la fecha, hora y lugar de salida o recibo del correo*); *va* matasellar, timbrar (*el correo*)
postmaster ['post,mæstər] o ['post,mɑstər] s administrador de correos
postmaster general s (*pl:* **postmasters general**) director general de correos
postmastership ['post,mæstərʃɪp] o ['post,mɑstərʃɪp] s administración de correos
postmeridian [,postmə'rɪdɪən] *adj* postmeridiano
post meridiem [,post mə'rɪdɪəm] (Lat.) por la tarde
postmistress ['post,mɪstrɪs] s administradora de correos
post-mortem [,post'mɔrtəm] *adj* posterior a la muerte; s autopsia, examen de un cadáver

postnatal [post'netəl] *adj* postnatal
post-obit [,post'obɪt] o [,post'ɑbɪt] *adj* válido después de la muerte de una persona
post office *s* casa de correos
post-office box ['post,ɑfɪs] *s* apartado de correos, casilla postal
post-office branch *s* estafeta, sucursal de correos
post-office savings bank *s* var. de **postal savings bank**
postoperative [post'ɑpə,retɪv] o [post'ɑpərətɪv] *adj* postoperatorio
postorbital [post'ɔrbɪtəl] *adj* postorbital
postpaid ['post,ped] *adj* con porte pagado, franco de porte
postpalatal [post'pælətəl] *adj & s* (phonet.) postpalatal
postpone [post'pon] *va* aplazar
postponement [post'ponmənt] *s* aplazamiento
postprandial [post'prændɪəl] *adj* postprandial
postprandial speech *s* discurso de sobremesa
postrider ['post,raɪdər] *s* corredor de posta
post road *s* camino de postas; ruta por donde pasa el correo
postscript ['postskrɪpt] *s* posdata (*a una carta*); suplemento a un escrito
posttonic [post'tɑnɪk] *adj* (phonet.) postónico
postulant ['pɑstʃələnt] *s* (rel.) postulante, postulanta
postulate ['pɑstʃəlɪt] *s* postulado; ['pɑstʃəlet] *va* postular, pedir, solicitar; (eccl.) postular; admitir sin pruebas
postulation [,pɑstʃə'leʃən] *s* postulación, petición; (eccl.) postulación; admisión sin pruebas
postulator ['pɑstʃə,letər] *s* (eccl.) postulador
posture ['pɑstʃər] *s* postura; *va* poner en una postura o en posturas; *vn* adoptar una postura
posturer ['pɑstʃərər] *s* poseur; contorsionista
postwar ['post,wɔr] *adj* de la postguerra
posy ['pozɪ] *s* (*pl:* **-sies**) flor; ramillete de flores; verso grabado en una sortija
pot [pɑt] *s* pote, tiesto; caldera, olla, puchero (*de cocina*); puesta (*en el juego*); bebida alcohólica; (found.) crisol de horno; (coll.) cantidad considerable de dinero; vaso de noche, orinal; **to go to pot** (coll.) fracasar, tronarse, arruinarse; **to keep the pot boiling** (coll.) ganar el pan de cada día; (coll.) mantener las cosas en marcha; (*pret & pp:* **potted;** *ger:* **potting**) *va* plantar en tiestos o macetas; cocer y conservar en olla; conservar en botes o marmitas; disparar contra; (coll.) ganar, apoderarse de; *vn* disparar; beber cerveza, empinar el codo
potable ['potəbəl] *adj* potable; *s* cosa que puede beberse
potash ['pɑt,æʃ] *s* (chem.) potasa
potassic [pə'tæsɪk] *adj* potásico
potassium [pə'tæsɪəm] *s* (chem.) potasio
potassium bromide *s* (chem.) bromuro de potasio
potassium carbonate *s* (chem.) carbonato de potasio
potassium chlorate *s* (chem.) clorato de potasio
potassium cyanide *s* (chem.) cianuro de potasio
potassium hydroxide *s* (chem.) hidróxido de potasio
potassium nitrate *s* (chem.) nitrato de potasio
potassium permanganate *s* (chem.) permanganato de potasio
potation [po'teʃən] *s* potación
potato [pə'teto] *s* (*pl:* **-toes**) (bot.) patata (*planta y tubérculo*); papa (Am.); (bot.) batata (*Ipomoea batatas*); (coll.) nulidad, persona o cosa insignificante
potato beetle o **bug** *s* (ent.) chinche de la patata, chaquetudo, escarabajo patatero
potato blight *s* plaga de la patata
potato chip *s* rebanada de patata frita
potato omelet *s* tortilla a la española
potbellied ['pɑt,belɪd] *adj* barrigón, panzudo
potbelly ['pɑt,belɪ] *s* (*pl:* **-lies**) barriga, panza; persona panzuda
potboiler ['pɑt,bɔɪlər] *s* obra artística o literaria hecha con el solo propósito de ganar dinero
potboy ['pɑt,bɔɪ] *s* mozo de servicio de una fonda o taberna; lavaplatos
pot cheese *s* requesón
pot companion *s* compañero de taberna
potency ['potənsɪ] *s* (*pl:* **-cies**) potencia
potent ['potənt] *adj* potente
potentate ['potəntet] *s* potentado
potent cross *s* (her.) cruz potenzada
potential [pə'tenʃəl] *adj* potencial; (gram.) potencial; *s* potencial; (elec., gram., math. & phys.) potencial
potential energy *s* (phys.) energía potencial
potential function *s* (math.) función potencial
potentiality [pə,tenʃɪ'ælɪtɪ] *s* (*pl:* **-ties**) potencialidad
potentially [pə'tenʃəlɪ] *adv* potencialmente
potential mood *s* (gram.) modo potencial
potentilla [,potən'tɪlə] *s* (bot.) potentila
potentiometer [pə,tenʃɪ'ɑmɪtər] *s* (elec.) potenciómetro
pothanger ['pɑt,hæŋər] *s* llares
pother ['pɑðər] *s* agitación, confusión, barahunda; nube de polvo o humo asfixiante; *va* agitar, confundir, molestar; *vn* agitarse, confundirse, molestarse
potherb ['pɑt,ʌrb] o ['pɑt,hʌrb] *s* hortaliza, verdura; hierba que se emplea para sazonar
potholder ['pɑt,holdər] *s* portaollas
pothole ['pɑt,hol] *s* bache, hoyo redondo (*en el camino*); (geol.) marmita de gigante
pothook ['pɑt,hʊk] *s* garabato (*gancho; letra mal hecha*)
pothouse ['pɑt,haʊs] *s* cervecería, taberna
pothunter ['pɑt,hʌntər] *s* persona que caza para obtener alimento sin preocuparse por las reglas de la caza; persona que toma parte en concursos, contiendas y torneos con el solo propósito de ganar premios
potion ['poʃən] *s* poción
pot lead [lɛd] *s* grafito
potlid ['pɑt,lɪd] *s* cobertera, tapadera
potluck ['pɑt,lʌk] *s* comida sin preparación ni cumplidos, lo que haya de comer; **to take potluck** hacer penitencia
potpie ['pɑt,paɪ] *s* pastelón de carne; estofado con bollos de harina
potpourri [popu'ri] o [pɑt'pʊrɪ] *s* mezcolanza aromática de pétalos secos y especias; (mus.) popurrí
pot roast *s* asado hecho en marmita
potsherd ['pɑt,ʃʌrd] *s* tiesto, casco (*pedazo roto*)
pot shot *s* tiro a corta distancia; tiro en contra de las reglas del juego limpio
pottage ['pɑtɪdʒ] *s* potaje
potted ['pɑtɪd] *adj* cocido y conservado en botes u ollas; de maceta, p.ej., **potted plants** plantas de maceta; (slang) borracho
potter ['pɑtər] *s* alfarero; *vn* ocuparse en fruslerías
potter's clay *s* arcilla figulina, barro de alfarería
potter's field *s* cementerio de los pobres, hoyanca
potter's wheel *s* rueda o torno de alfarero
pottery ['pɑtərɪ] *s* (*pl:* **-ies**) alfarería; cacharros (de alfarería)
pottle ['pɑtəl] *s* azumbre (*medida*); licor alcohólico; (Brit.) cesto para frutas
pot-valiant ['pɑt,væljənt] *adj* valiente por el licor que le anima
pouch [paʊtʃ] *s* bolsa, saquillo; bolsa (*del canguro*); valija; petaca; cartuchera; *va* embolsar; formar una bolsa en; fruncir; *vn* formar una bolsa; hacer pucheros; deglutir, saciarse
poulard [pu'lɑrd] *s* polla capona que se ceba para comerla
poulterer ['poltərər] *s* pollero
poultice ['poltɪs] *s* cataplasma; *va* poner una cataplasma a
poultry ['poltrɪ] *s* aves de corral
poultry dealer *s* recovero
pounce [paʊns] *s* grasilla, arenilla (*para secar escritos*); carbón molido que se usa para traspasar dibujos picados a otra tela o papel; golpe súbito, zarpada; zarpa de ave de rapiña; *va* alisar, preparar o rociar (*una superficie*) con

grasilla o arenilla; estarcir con arenilla; *vn* entrar súbita e inesperadamente; **to pounce at, on** o **upon** saltar sobre, precipitarse sobre
pounce bag *s* cisquero
pounce box *s* cajita de polvos de arenilla
pouncet box ['paunsɪt] *s* cajita agujereada para perfumes
pound [paund] *s* libra (*peso*); golpazo, martilleo; corral de concejo (*para encerrar animales descarriados*); *va* golpear, golpetear, martillar; machacar, moler; encerrar en el corral de concejo; bombardear incesantemente; (fig.) desempedrar (*pasear mucho por*); *vn* golpear, golpetear
poundage ['paundɪdʒ] *s* impuesto, comisión, etc. exigida por cada libra esterlina o cada libra de peso
poundal ['paundəl] *s* (phys.) poundal
poundcake ['paund,kek] *s* pastel en que entra una libra de cada ingrediente; ponqué
pounder ['paundər] *s* martillador; machaca; persona o cosa que pesa determinado número de libras o que está relacionada con determinado número de libras, p.ej., **a ten-pounder** un cañón de a diez; **a five-pounder** un pescado de cinco libras
pound-foolish ['paund'fulɪʃ] *adj* incapaz de guardar o manejar grandes sumas de dinero
poundkeeper ['paund,kipər] *s* guardián de corral de concejo
pound net *s* red de pesca, nasa de pescar
pound sterling *s* libra esterlina
pour [por] *s* lluvia torrencial; *va* vaciar, verter, derramar; hacer fluir; hacer salir profusamente; **to pour out** verter (*p.ej., agua*); *vn* fluir rápidamente; llover a torrentes; **to pour into** entrar a montones en; **to pour out** salir a chorros; salir a montones; **to pour out of** inclinar para vaciar, verter (*un recipiente*); salir a montones de (*p.ej., el teatro*)
pourboire [pur'bwɑr] *s* propina
pourparler [pur'pɑrlɪ] *s* coloquio, conferencia
pout [paut] *s* mala cara, mal gesto, puchero; (ichth.) gado; (ichth.) zoarce; *vn* poner mala cara, hacer gesto de enojo y desagrado, hacer pucheros
pouter ['pautər] *s* persona que hace pucheros, persona que pone cara de enfado; (orn.) paloma buchona
poverty ['pɑvərtɪ] *s* pobreza
poverty-stricken ['pɑvərtɪ,strɪkən] *adj* extremadamente pobre
POW abr. de **prisoner of war**
powder ['paudər] *s* polvo; polvos (*de tocador*); pólvora (*mezcla explosiva*); *va* pulverizar; empolvar, polvorear; *vn* hacerse polvo; empolvarse
powder blue *s* azul pálido
powdered milk *s* leche en polvo
powdered sugar *s* azúcar en polvo
powder flask *s* polvorín
powder horn *s* chifle
powder magazine *s* (naut.) santabárbara
powder maker *s* polvorista
powder monkey *s* mozo que antiguamente iba en los barcos de guerra para ocuparse de transportar la pólvora a los cañones
powder puff *s* borla para empolvarse
powder room *s* cuarto tocador, cuarto de aseo
powdery ['paudərɪ] *adj* polvoriento, polvoroso; empolvado; deleznable, quebradizo
power ['pauər] *s* poder, poderío, potencia; (math., mech., opt. & phys.) potencia; (fig.) energía; **Powers** *spl* potestades (*sexta orden de los ángeles*); **in power** en el poder; **the Great Powers** las grandes potencias; **the powers that be** las autoridades, los que mandan; **to the best of one's power** cuanto esté en el poder de uno; *va* accionar, impulsar
power amplifier *s* (rad.) amplificador de poder o de potencia
power behind the throne *s* poder oculto
powerboat ['pauər,bot] *s* autobote, bote automóvil, gasolinera
power brake *s* (aut.) servofreno
power company *s* empresa de fuerza motriz
power cord *s* (elec.) cordón de alimentación
power dive (aer.) picado con motor
power drill *s* taladradora de fuerza
power factor *s* (elec.) factor de potencia
powerful ['pauərfəl] *adj* poderoso
powerhouse ['pauər,haus] *s* (elec.) estación generadora, central eléctrica; (slang) manantial de fuerza, persona llena de energía, fuerza arrolladora
powerless ['pauərlɪs] *adj* impotente
power line *s* (elec.) línea de fuerza; (elec.) sector de distribución (*en las ciudades*)
power mower *s* motosegadora
power of attorney *s* (law) poder
power of the keys *s* (eccl.) llaves de la iglesia
power pack *s* (rad.) fuente surtidora, fuente de alimentación, fuente de poder
power plant *s* (elec.) estación generadora, central eléctrica; (aut.) grupo motor; (aer.) grupo motopropulsor
power play *s* maniobra ofensiva concentrada
power politics *ssg* o *spl* política de poder
power reactor *s* (phys.) reactor generador de energía
power saw *s* motosierra
power shovel *s* excavadora
power station *s* (elec.) estación generadora, central eléctrica
power steering *s* (aut.) servodirección
power stroke *s* carrera motriz
power supply *s* (rad.) suministro de potencia
power tool *s* herramienta motriz
power transformer *s* (elec.) transformador de fuerza
power transmission *s* (elec.) transmisión de energía
power tube *s* (rad.) válvula de fuerza o de poder
powwow ['pau,wau] *s* ceremonia de los indios norteamericanos que consiste en bailes y fiestas para ahuyentar las enfermedades y tener éxito en las empresas; conferencia acerca de o con los indios norteamericanos; conferencia; curandero indio; santiguadera; *vn* conferenciar
pox [pɑks] *s* enfermedad que afecta la piel creando una erupción de pústulas; sífilis
pozzolana [,pɑtsə'lɑnɑ] o **pozzuolana** [,pɑtswə'lɑnɑ] *s* (geol.) puzolana
pp. abr. de **pages, past participle** y **pianissimo**
p.p. abr. de **parcel post, past participle** y **postpaid**
ppr. o **p.pr.** abr. de **present participle**
pr. abr. de **pair, present** y **price**
P.R. abr. de **Puerto Rico**
practicability [,præktɪkə'bɪlɪtɪ] *s* factibilidad
practicable ['præktɪkəbəl] *adj* practicable
practical ['præktɪkəl] *adj* práctico
practicality [,præktɪ'kælɪtɪ] *s* (*pl:* **-ties**) espíritu práctico; cosa práctica
practical joke *s* burla de consecuencias
practically ['præktɪkəlɪ] *adv* prácticamente; casi, poco más o menos
practical nurse *s* enfermera práctica (*que ejerce la profesión sin haber terminado el curso oficial*)
practice ['præktɪs] *s* práctica; ensayo; ejercicio (*p.ej., de la medicina*); **in practice** en la práctica; **to make a practice of** + *inf* acostumbrar + *inf; va* practicar; ejercitar (*p.ej., caridad*); ejercer (*una profesión*); hacer ejercicios en, estudiar (*p.ej., el piano*); tener por costumbre; **to practice** + *ger* ensayarse a + *inf;* **to practice what one preaches** predicar con el ejemplo; *vn* ejercitarse; ejercer; practicar la medicina; ensayarse; entrenarse; conducirse; **to practice as** ejercer de (*p.ej., abogado*)
practiced ['præktɪst] *adj* práctico
practician [præk'tɪʃən] *s* practicón
practise ['præktɪs] *s, va & vn* var. de **practice**
practitioner [præk'tɪʃənər] *s* profesional; práctico (*médico*)
praedial ['pridɪəl] *adj* predial
praefect ['prifɛkt] *s* var. de **prefect**
praefloration [,priflo'reʃən] *s* (bot.) prefloración
praefoliation [,prifolɪ'eʃən] *s* (bot.) prefoliación
praenomen [pri'nomɛn] *s* (*pl:* **-nomina** ['nɑmɪnə]) prenombre
praetor ['pritər] o ['pritɔr] *s* pretor

praetorian [priˈtorɪən] *adj & s* pretoriano
pragmatic [prægˈmætɪk] o **pragmatical** [prægˈmætɪkəl] *adj* pragmático; dogmático, engreído; oficioso, entremetido; activo, ocupado; práctico
pragmatic sanction *s* sanción pragmática o pragmática sanción
pragmatism [ˈprægmətɪzəm] *s* (philos.) pragmatismo; dogmatismo; oficiosidad; positivismo
pragmatist [ˈprægmətɪst] *adj & s* (philos.) pragmatista
Prague [prɑg] o [preg] *s* Praga
prairie [ˈprɛrɪ] *s* llanura, pampa, pradera
prairie chicken *s* (orn.) gallina de las praderas
prairie dog *s* (zool.) ardilla ladradora, perro de las praderas
prairie schooner *s* carromato de cuatro ruedas y toldo, que se usaba para viajar en el oeste de los EE.UU. antes del ferrocarril transcontinental
prairie wolf *s* (zool.) coyote
praise [prez] *s* alabanza, elogio; elogios; **to heap praises on** amontonar alabanzas sobre; **to sing the praise** o **the praises of** alabar o elogiar con efusión y entusiasmo; *va* alabar, elogiar; **to praise to the skies** poner sobre las estrellas, poner por las nubes
praiseworthy [ˈprezˌwʌrðɪ] *adj* laudable, elogiable
Prakrit [ˈprɑkrɪt] *s* prácrito
praline [ˈprɑlin] *s* almendra garapiñada, almendra confitada, pacana garapiñada
pram [præm] *s* (coll.) cochecillo de niño
prance [præns] o [prɑns] *s* cabriola; trenzado; *vn* cabriolar; trenzar; pavonearse al caminar
prancer [ˈprænsər] o [ˈprɑnsər] *s* caballo trenzador
prandial [ˈprændɪəl] *adj* prandial
prank [præŋk] *s* travesura, picardía; broma; *va* adornar con exceso; *vn* adornarse con exceso, sobrecargarse en el vestir
prankish [ˈpræŋkɪʃ] *adj* travieso, pícaro
prankster [ˈpræŋkstər] *s* (coll.) bromista
prase [prez] *s* (mineral.) prasio
praseodymium [ˌprezɪoˈdɪmɪəm] *s* (chem.) praseodimio
prate [pret] *s* charla, parloteo; *vn* charlar, parlotear
prater [ˈpretər] *s* charlatán
pratique [præˈtik] *s* (naut.) libre plática
prattle [ˈprætəl] *s* charla, parloteo; charla necia y sin sentido (*imitando a los niños en la pronunciación*); *vn* charlar, parlotear; hablar como los niños
prattler [ˈprætlər] *s* charlatán, parlanchín
prawn [prɔn] *s* (zool.) camarón (*Palaemon*); (zool.) langostín (*Peneus*); (zool.) gamba, quisquilla (*Pandalus*)
Praxiteles [præksˈɪtəliz] *s* Praxiteles
pray [pre] *va* implorar, rogar, suplicar; rezar (*una oración*); *vn* orar, rezar; **to pray for** orar por; **pray** + *inf* sírvase + *inf*, p.ej., **pray tell me** sírvase decirme
prayer [prɛr] *s* oración, rezo; ruego, súplica; oficio (*rezo diario*); **to say one's prayers** decir sus oraciones; [ˈpreər] *s* rezador
prayer book [prɛr] *s* devocionario, oracional
prayerful [ˈprɛrfəl] *adj* rezador, devoto
prayerless [ˈprɛrlɪs] *adj* sin rezo; que no reza
prayer meeting [prɛr] *s* reunión para orar y alabar a Dios
prayer rug [prɛr] *s* alfombra de rezo
praying mantis *s* (ent.) mantis religiosa, predicador, rezadora
preach [pritʃ] *va* predicar; aconsejar (*p.ej., la paciencia*); *vn* predicar
preacher [ˈpritʃər] *s* predicador; pastor espiritual; sermoneador
preachify [ˈpritʃɪfaɪ] (*pret & pp:* **-fied**) *vn* predicar o sermonear molestamente
preaching [ˈpritʃɪŋ] *s* predicación; sermón, sermoneo
preachment [ˈpritʃmənt] *s* prédica, sermón, arenga
preachy [ˈpritʃɪ] *adj* (*comp:* **-ier**; *super:* **-iest**) (coll.) inclinado a predicar, moralizador
preadamic [ˌpriəˈdæmɪk] *adj* preadamítico
preadamite [priˈædəmaɪt] *s* preadamita
preadaptation [ˌpriædæpˈteʃən] *s* (biol.) preadaptación
preamble [ˈpriˌæmbəl] *s* preámbulo
preamplifier [priˈæmplɪˌfaɪər] *s* (rad.) preamplificador
prearrange [ˌpriəˈrendʒ] *va* arreglar de antemano
prearrangement [ˌpriəˈrendʒmənt] *s* arreglo previo
prebend [ˈprɛbənd] *s* prebenda; prebendado
prebendary [ˈprɛbənˌdɛrɪ] *s* (*pl:* **-ies**) prebendado
Pre-Cambrian [ˌpriˈkæmbrɪən] *adj & s* (geol.) precámbrico
precarious [prɪˈkɛrɪəs] *adj* precario
precariousness [prɪˈkɛrɪəsnɪs] *s* precariedad
precaution [prɪˈkɔʃən] *s* precaución
precautionary [prɪˈkɔʃənˌɛrɪ] *adj* precaucionado, precavido
precautious [prɪˈkɔʃəs] *adj* precavido
precede [priˈsid] *va & vn* preceder
precedence [priˈsidəns] o [ˈprɛsɪdəns] *s* precedencia
precedency [priˈsidənsɪ] o [ˈprɛsɪdənsɪ] *s* (*pl:* **-cies**) var. de **precedence**
precedent [priˈsidənt] o [ˈprɛsɪdənt] *adj* precedente; [ˈprɛsɪdənt] *s* precedente
preceding [priˈsidɪŋ] *adj* precedente
precentor [prɪˈsɛntər] *s* chantre
precept [ˈprisɛpt] *s* precepto
preceptive [prɪˈsɛptɪv] *adj* preceptivo
preceptor [prɪˈsɛptər] *s* preceptor
preceptorial [ˌprisɛpˈtorɪəl] *adj* preceptoral
preceptress [prɪˈsɛptrɪs] *s* preceptora
precession [priˈsɛʃən] *s* precedencia; (mech.) precesión
precessional [priˈsɛʃənəl] *adj* de la precesión de los equinoccios, causado por la precesión de los equinoccios
precession of the equinoxes *s* (astr.) precesión de los equinoccios
precinct [ˈprisɪŋkt] *s* barriada, recinto; distrito electoral
preciosity [ˌprɛʃɪˈɑsɪtɪ] *s* (*pl:* **-ties**) (lit.) preciosismo
precious [ˈprɛʃəs] *adj* precioso; caro, amado; (coll.) considerable; *adv* (coll.) muy, p.ej., **precious little** muy poco
preciously [ˈprɛʃəslɪ] *adv* preciosamente; extremadamente; con mucho cuidado
precious stone *s* piedra preciosa
precipice [ˈprɛsɪpɪs] *s* precipicio
precipitance [prɪˈsɪpɪtəns] o **precipitancy** [prɪˈsɪpɪtənsɪ] *s* precipitación
precipitant [prɪˈsɪpɪtənt] *adj* precipitado; *s* (chem.) precipitante
precipitate [prɪˈsɪpɪtɪt] o [prɪˈsɪpɪtet] *adj* precipitado; *s* (chem.) precipitado; [prɪˈsɪpɪtet] *va* precipitar; (chem.) precipitar; *vn* precipitarse; (chem.) precipitarse
precipitation [prɪˌsɪpɪˈteʃən] *s* precipitación; (chem., meteor. & fig.) precipitación
precipitin [prɪˈsɪpɪtɪn] *s* (immun.) precipitina
precipitous [prɪˈsɪpɪtəs] *adj* empinado, escarpado; precipitoso, precipitado
precipitron [prɪˈsɪpɪtrɑn] *s* (trademark) precipitrón
precise [prɪˈsaɪs] *adj* preciso; escrupuloso, meticuloso
precision [prɪˈsɪʒən] *s* precisión
precision bombing *s* (aer.) bombardeo de precisión
precision instrument *s* instrumento de precisión, aparato de precisión
preclude [prɪˈklud] *va* excluir, imposibilitar
preclusion [prɪˈkluʒən] *s* exclusión, evitación
precocious [prɪˈkoʃəs] *adj* precoz
precocity [prɪˈkɑsɪtɪ] *s* precocidad
precognition [ˌprikɑgˈnɪʃən] *s* precognición
pre-Columbian [ˌprikəˈlʌmbɪən] *adj* precolombino
preconceive [ˌprikənˈsiv] *va* preconcebir
preconception [ˌprikənˈsɛpʃən] *s* preconcepción
preconcert [ˌprikənˈsʌrt] *va* concertar de antemano
precontract [priˈkɑntrækt] *s* contrato previo; [ˌprikənˈtrækt] o [priˈkɑntrækt] *va & vn* contratar de antemano
precool [priˈkul] *va* preenfriar
precordial [priˈkɔrdʒəl] o [priˈkɔrdjəl] *adj* (anat.) precordial

precursor [pri'kʌrsər] *s* precursor
precursory [pri'kʌrsərɪ] *adj* precursor
pred. abr. de **predicate**
predacious [prɪ'deʃəs] o **predatory** ['prɛdə,torɪ] *adj* rapaz; predador, predator, depredador
predeceased [,pridɪ'sist] *adj* predifunto, premuerto
predecessor ['prɛdɪ,sɛsər] o [,prɛdɪ'sɛsər] *s* predecesor
predestinarian [pri,dɛstɪ'nɛrɪən] *adj & s* predestinaciano, predestinador
predestinate [pri'dɛstɪnɪt] *s* (theol.) predestinado; [pri'dɛstɪnet] *va* predestinar
predestination [pri,dɛstɪ'neʃən] *s* predestinación; (theol.) predestinación
predestine [pri'dɛstɪn] *va* predestinar
predeterminate [,pridɪ'tʌrmɪnɪt] *adj* predeterminado
predetermination [,pridɪ,tʌrmɪ'neʃən] *s* predeterminación
predetermine [,pridɪ'tʌrmɪn] *va* predeterminar
predial ['pridɪəl] *adj* predial
predicable ['prɛdɪkəbəl] *adj* predicable; *s* (log.) predicable
predicament [prɪ'dɪkəmənt] *s* trance apurado, situación difícil; (log.) predicamento
predicant ['prɛdɪkənt] *adj & s* predicante
predicate ['prɛdɪkɪt] *s* predicado; ['prɛdɪket] *va & vn* predicar
predication [,prɛdɪ'keʃən] *s* aserción, afirmación
predicative ['prɛdɪ,ketɪv] *adj* predicativo
predict [prɪ'dɪkt] *va* predecir
predictable [prɪ'dɪktəbəl] *adj* pronosticable
prediction [prɪ'dɪkʃən] *s* predicción
predictive [prɪ'dɪktɪv] *adj* profético
predictor [prɪ'dɪktər] *s* predictor; (aer.) predictor
predigest [,pridɪ'dʒɛst] o [,pridaɪ'dʒɛst] *va* predigerir
predigestion [,pridɪ'dʒɛstʃən] o [,pridaɪ'dʒɛstʃən] *s* predigestión
predilection [,pridɪ'lɛkʃən] o [,prɛdɪ'lɛkʃən] *s* predilección
predispose [,pridɪs'poz] *va* predisponer
predisposition [,pridɪspə'zɪʃən] *s* predisposición
predominance [prɪ'dɑmɪnəns] *s* predominancia
predominant [prɪ'dɑmɪnənt] *adj* predominante
predominate [prɪ'dɑmɪnet] *va & vn* predominar
predomination [prɪ,dɑmɪ'neʃən] *s* predominación
preëlection [,priɪ'lɛkʃən] *s* preelección; *adj* preelectoral
preëminence [pri'ɛmɪnəns] *s* preeminencia
preëminent [pri'ɛmɪnənt] *adj* preeminente
preëminently [pri'ɛmɪnəntlɪ] *adv* preeminentemente
preëmpt [pri'ɛmpt] *va* asegurarse de (*una cosa*) antes que nadie; apropiarse (*terreno*) con el derecho de comprarlo antes que nadie
preëmption [pri'ɛmpʃən] *s* preempción
preëmptor [pri'ɛmptər] o [pri'ɛmptɔr] *s* comprador por derecho de prioridad
preen [prin] *va* arreglarse (*las plumas*) con el pico; **to preen oneself** atildarse, componerse, vestirse cuidadosamente
preëngage [,priɛn'gedʒ] *va* contratar o comprometer de antemano
preëstablish [,priɛs'tæblɪʃ] *va* establecer de antemano
preëxist [,priɛg'zɪst] *vn* preexistir
preëxistence [,priɛg'zɪstəns] *s* preexistencia
preëxistent [,priɛg'zɪstənt] *adj* preexistente
pref. abr. de **preface, preferred** y **prefix**
prefabricate [pri'fæbrɪket] *va* prefabricar
preface ['prɛfɪs] *s* prefacio; *va* introducir, empezar; decir a modo de introducción; prologar
prefatorial [,prɛfə'torɪəl] o **prefatory** ['prɛfə,torɪ] *adj* introductor, preliminar; como prefacio
prefect ['prifɛkt] *s* prefecto
prefecture ['prifɛktʃər] *s* prefectura
prefer [prɪ'fʌr] (*pret & pp:* **-ferred;** *ger:* **-ferring**) *va* preferir; presentar; promover; **to prefer to** + *inf* preferir + *inf*
preferable ['prɛfərəbəl] *adj* preferible
preferably ['prɛfərəblɪ] *adv* preferiblemente
preference ['prɛfərəns] *s* preferencia
preferential [,prɛfə'rɛnʃəl] *adj* preferente
preferential tariff *s* aranceles preferenciales
preferential voting *s* votación en la cual el elector indica un segundo candidato en caso de que el de su primera elección sea derrotado
preferment [prɪ'fʌrmənt] *s* preferencia; ascenso, promoción; dignidad
preferred stock *s* (com.) acción preferente, acciones preferentes
prefiguration [,prifɪgjə'reʃən] *s* prefiguración
prefigure [pri'fɪgjər] *va* prefigurar; representarse de antemano
prefix ['prifɪks] *s* (gram.) prefijo; [pri'fɪks] *va* prefijar; (gram.) prefijar
preformation [,prifɔr'meʃən] *s* preformación
pregnable ['prɛgnəbəl] *adj* expugnable
pregnancy ['prɛgnənsɪ] *s* (*pl:* **-cies**) preñez, embarazo
pregnant ['prɛgnənt] *adj* preñado; fértil; (fig.) preñado
preheat [pri'hit] *va* precalentar, calentar previamente
prehensile [prɪ'hɛnsɪl] *adj* prensil
prehension [prɪ'hɛnʃən] *s* prensión
prehistoric [,prihɪs'tɑrɪk] o [,prihɪs'tɔrɪk] o **prehistorical** [,prihɪs'tɑrɪkəl] o [,prihɪs'tɔrɪkəl] *adj* prehistórico
prehistorically [,prihɪs'tɑrɪkəlɪ] o [,prihɪs'tɔrɪkəlɪ] *adv* prehistóricamente
prehistory [pri'hɪstərɪ] *s* prehistoria
preignition [,priɪg'nɪʃən] *s* preignición
prejudge [pri'dʒʌdʒ] *va* prejuzgar
prejudgment o **prejudgement** [pri'dʒʌdʒmənt] *s* prejuicio
prejudice ['prɛdʒədɪs] *s* prejuicio, preocupación; perjuicio (*daño*); **to the prejudice of** con perjuicio de; **without prejudice** (law) sin detrimento de sus propios derechos; *va* predisponer, prevenir; perjudicar (*dañar*)
prejudicial [,prɛdʒə'dɪʃəl] *adj* perjudicial
prejudicially [,prɛdʒə'dɪʃəlɪ] *adv* perjudicialmente
prelacy ['prɛləsɪ] *s* (*pl:* **-cies**) prelacía
prelate ['prɛlɪt] *s* prelado
prelature ['prɛlətʃər] *s* prelatura
pre-Lenten [pri'lɛntən] *adj* carnavalesco
prelim. abr. de **preliminary**
preliminary [prɪ'lɪmɪ,nɛrɪ] *adj* preliminar; *s* (*pl:* **-ies**) preliminar
prelude ['prɛljud], ['prilud] o ['priljud] *s* preludio; (mus.) preludio; *va* preludiar; *vn* preludiar; (mus.) preludiar
premarital [pri'mærɪtəl] *adj* premarital
premature [,primə'tjur] o [,primə'tur] *adj* prematuro
prematurely [,primə'tjurlɪ] o [,primə'turlɪ] *adv* prematuramente
premedical [pri'mɛdɪkəl] *adj* premédico
premeditate [pri'mɛdɪtet] *va* premeditar
premeditated [pri'mɛdɪ,tetɪd] *adj* premeditado
premeditation [,primɛdɪ'teʃən] *s* premeditación
premier ['primɪər] o ['prɛmjər] *adj* primero; principal, superior; [prɪ'mɪr] o ['primɪər] *s* primer ministro, jefe del estado, presidente del consejo
première [prə'mjɛr] o [prɪ'mɪr] *s* estreno; actriz principal
premiership [prɪ'mɪrʃɪp] o ['primɪər,ʃɪp] *s* jefatura del estado, presidencia del consejo
premise ['prɛmɪs] *s* (law & log.) premisa; **premises** *spl* predio, local; **major premise** (log.) premisa mayor; **minor premise** (log.) premisa menor; *va* sentar o establecer como premisa; *vn* establecer una premisa
premium ['primɪəm] *s* premio; (ins.) prima; **at a premium** a premio; en gran demanda, muy solicitado
premolar [pri'molər] *adj & s* (anat.) premolar
premonish [prɪ'mɑnɪʃ] *va* advertir, prevenir
premonition [,primə'nɪʃən] *s* advertencia; presentimiento
premonitory [prɪ'mɑnɪ,torɪ] *adj* premonitorio

Premonstratensian [prɪ,mɑnstrə'tɛnʃən] *adj & s* (eccl.) premonstratense
prenatal [pri'netəl] *adj* prenatal
preoccupancy [pri'ɑkjəpənsɪ] *s* (*pl:* **-cies**) preocupación
preoccupation [pri,ɑkjə'peʃən] *s* preocupación
preoccupied [pri'ɑkjəpaɪd] *adj* preocupado
preoccupy [pri'ɑkjəpaɪ] (*pret & pp:* **-pied**) *va* preocupar
preordain [,priɔr'den] *va* preordinar
preordination [,priɔrdɪ'neʃən] *s* preordinación
prep. abr. de **preparatory** y **preposition**
prepaid [pri'ped] *adj* pagado por adelantado; con porte pagado; *pret & pp de* **prepay**
prepalatal [pri'pælətəl] *adj & s* (phonet.) prepalatal
preparation [,prɛpə'reʃən] *s* preparación
preparative [prɪ'pærətɪv] *adj & s* preparativo
preparatory [prɪ'pærə,torɪ] *adj* preparatorio
preparatory school *s* escuela preparatoria
prepare [prɪ'pɛr] *va* preparar, prevenir; *vn* prepararse, prevenirse; **to prepare against** prevenirse a o contra; **to prepare to** + *inf* prepararse a o para + *inf*
preparedness [prɪ'pɛrɪdnɪs] o [prɪ'pɛrdnɪs] *s* preparación; preparación militar, armamentismo
prepay [prɪ'pe] (*pret & pp:* **-paid**) pagar por adelantado
prepayment [prɪ'pemənt] *s* pago adelantado
prepense [prɪ'pɛns] *adj* premeditado; **with malice prepense** (law) con malicia y premeditación
preponderance [prɪ'pɑndərəns] *s* preponderancia
preponderant [prɪ'pɑndərənt] *adj* preponderante
preponderate [prɪ'pɑndəret] *vn* preponderar
preposition [,prɛpə'zɪʃən] *s* preposición
prepositional [,prɛpə'zɪʃənəl] *adj* preposicional
prepositionally [,prɛpə'zɪʃənəlɪ] *adv* de manera preposicional, como preposición
prepositive [pri'pɑzɪtɪv] *adj* prepositivo; *s* (gram.) partícula prepositiva
prepossess [,pripə'zɛs] *va* preocupar, predisponer favorablemente
prepossessing [,pripə'zɛsɪŋ] *adj* agradable, simpático
prepossession [,pripə'zɛʃən] *s* preocupación, predisposición favorable
preposterous [prɪ'pɑstərəs] *adj* absurdo, ridículo
preposterously [prɪ'pɑstərəslɪ] *adv* absurdamente, ridículamente
prepotency [pri'potənsɪ] *s* (*pl:* **-cies**) prepotencia
prepotent [pri'potənt] *adj* prepotente
prep school [prɛp] *s* (slang) escuela preparatoria
prepuce ['pripjus] *s* (anat.) prepucio
Pre-Raphaelite [,pri'ræfɪəlaɪt] [,pri'refɪəlaɪt] *adj & s* prerrafaelista
Pre-Raphaelitism [,pri'ræfɪə,laɪtɪzəm] o [,pri'refɪə,laɪtɪzəm] *s* prerrafaelismo
prerecorded [,prirɪ'kɔrdɪd] *adj* (rad. & telv.) grabado anteriormente, grabado de antemano
prerequisite [pri'rɛkwɪzɪt] *adj* necesario de antemano; *s* requisito previo, requisito prescrito de antemano
prerogative [prɪ'rɑgətɪv] *adj* privilegiado; *s* prerrogativa
preromanticism [,priro'mæntɪsɪzəm] *s* prerromanticismo
pres. abr. de **present**
Pres. abr. de **Presbyterian** y **President**
presage ['prɛsɪdʒ] *s* presagio; [prɪ'sedʒ] *va* presagiar
presbyope ['prɛzbɪop] o ['prɛsbɪop] *s* presbiope
presbyopia [,prɛzbɪ'opɪə] o [,prɛsbɪ'opɪə] *s* (path.) presbiopía
presbyopic [,prɛzbɪ'ɑpɪk] o [,prɛsbɪ'ɑpɪk] *adj* presbiope
presbyte ['prɛzbaɪt] o ['prɛsbaɪt] *s* présbita
presbyter ['prɛzbɪtər] o ['prɛsbɪtər] *s* presbítero
Presbyterian [,prɛzbɪ'tɪrɪən] o [,prɛsbɪ'tɪrɪən] *adj & s* presbiteriano
Presbyterianism [,prɛzbɪ'tɪrɪənɪzəm] o [,prɛsbɪ'tɪrɪənɪzəm] *s* presbiterianismo
presbytery ['prɛzbɪ,tɛrɪ] o ['prɛsbɪ,tɛrɪ] *s* (*pl:* **-ies**) presbiterio
presbytia [prɛz'bɪtɪə] o [prɛs'bɪtɪə] *s* (path.) presbicia
presbytic [prɛz'bɪtɪk] o [prɛs'bɪtɪk] *adj* présbita
preschool ['pri,skul] *adj* preescolar
prescience ['priʃɪəns] o ['prɛʃɪəns] *s* presciencia
prescient ['priʃɪənt] o ['prɛʃɪənt] *adj* presciente
prescribe [prɪ'skraɪb] *va & vn* prescribir; (pharm.) recetar
prescript [prɪ'skrɪpt] o ['priskrɪpt] *adj* prescrito; ['priskrɪpt] *s* regla, precepto
prescriptible [prɪ'skrɪptɪbəl] *adj* prescriptible
prescription [prɪ'skrɪpʃən] *s* prescripción; (law & med.) prescripción; (pharm.) receta
prescriptive [prɪ'skrɪptɪv] *adj* directivo; sancionado por la costumbre; adquirido o establecido por prescripción
preselector [,prisɪ'lɛktər] *s* (telp.) preselector
presence ['prɛzəns] *s* presencia; **in the presence of** en presencia de; **saving your presence** con excusas por haber dicho (o hecho) esto en su presencia
presence chamber *s* salón de recepciones, salón donde recibe un soberano u otra persona de alto rango
presence of mind *s* presencia de ánimo
present ['prɛzənt] *adj* presente (*que está aquí*); presente, actual; *s* presente, regalo; (gram.) presente; **at present** al presente, actualmente; **by these presents** por las presentes, por las escrituras presentes; **for the present** por lo presente; [prɪ'zɛnt] *va* presentar; **to present arms** (mil.) presentar armas; **to present oneself** presentarse; **to present with** obsequiar con
presentable [prɪ'zɛntəbəl] *adj* presentable; bien apersonado
presentation [,prɛzən'teʃən] o [,prizən'teʃən] *s* presentación; **on presentation** (com.) a presentación
presentation copy *s* ejemplar de cortesía con dedicatoria del autor
present-day ['prɛzənt,de] *adj* de hoy en día
presentiment [prɪ'zɛntɪmənt] *s* presentimiento
presently ['prɛzəntlɪ] *adv* luego, dentro de poco
presentment [prɪ'zɛntmənt] *s* presentación; retrato; representación teatral; (law) acusación por el gran jurado
present participle *s* (gram.) participio activo o de presente
present perfect *s* (gram.) pretérito perfecto
preservation [,prɛzər'veʃən] *s* conservación; preservación
preservative [prɪ'zʌrvətɪv] *adj & s* preservativo
preserve [prɪ'zʌrv] *s* conserva, confitura, compota; vedado; *va* conservar; preservar, proteger; *vn* hacer conservas
preserved fruit *s* dulce de almíbar
preserve jar *s* bote de conservas
preserver [prɪ'zʌrvər] *s* preservador
preside [prɪ'zaɪd] *vn* presidir; **to preside over** presidir
presidency ['prɛzɪdənsɪ] *s* (*pl:* **-cies**) presidencia
president ['prɛzɪdənt] *s* presidente; rector (*de una universidad*)
president-elect ['prɛzɪdəntɪ'lɛkt] *s* presidente electo
presidential [,prɛzɪ'dɛnʃəl] *adj* presidencial
presidium [prɪ'sɪdɪəm] *s* presidio
press [prɛs] *s* apretón, empujón, presión; prisa, urgencia; apiñamiento, muchedumbre; prensa (*máquina para prensar, comprimir o imprimir; conjunto de periódicos o periodistas*); imprenta (*acción o arte de imprimir*); pliegue (*de una prenda planchada*); armario; **in press** en prensa; **to have a good** (o **bad**) **press** tener buena (o mala) prensa; **to go to**

press entrar en prensa; *va* apretar; prensar; planchar (*la ropa*); apresurar; abrumar, acosar, instar; insistir en; abrazar; imprimir (*discos de fonógrafo*); **to press into service** poner a trabajar; **to press one's point** insistir en su punto de vista; *vn* pesar, ejercer presión; urgir; apiñarse; apresurarse; **to press forward** avanzar, adelantarse; **to press through the crowd** abrirse paso por entre la multitud
press agent *s* agente de publicidad
pressboard [ˈprɛsˌbord] *s* cartón prensado
press box *s* tribuna de la prensa
press conference *s* entrevista de prensa, conferencia de prensa
press gang *s* (mil.) levadores; (nav.) ronda de matrícula
pressing [ˈprɛsɪŋ] *adj* apremiante, urgente; *s* planchado (*de la ropa*)
pressing boards *spl* (b.b.) tablillas de encuadernar
pressman [ˈprɛsmən] *s* (*pl:* **-men**) prensador; (print.) prensista
pressmark [ˈprɛsˌmɑrk] *s* marca de biblioteca; *va* poner marca de biblioteca en
press proof *s* (print.) prueba de impresión
press release *s* comunicado de prensa
pressroom [ˈprɛsˌrum] o [ˈprɛsˌrʊm] *s* salón de prensas, taller de imprenta
pressure [ˈprɛʃər] *s* presión; opresión; urgencia; tensión de nervios; (elec.) tensión, fuerza electromotriz; **to exert pressure on** ejercer presión sobre
pressure cooker *s* cocina de presión, olla a o de presión
pressure gage o **pressure gauge** *s* manómetro, indicador de presión
pressure group *s* minoría que ejerce influencia en los cuerpos legislativos
pressure suit *s* traje a presión
pressure tunnel *s* (aer.) túnel a presión
pressurize [ˈprɛʃəraɪz] *va* (aer.) sobrecargar, sobrecomprimir, presurizar
presswork [ˈprɛsˌwʌrk] *s* impresión, tirada; trabajo de impresor; chapas de madera encoladas y prensadas
prester [ˈprɛstər] *s* (obs.) sacerdote
Prester John *s* el Preste Juan
prestidigitation [ˌprɛstɪˌdɪdʒɪˈteʃən] *s* prestidigitación
prestidigitator [ˌprɛstɪˈdɪdʒɪˌtetər] *s* prestidigitador
prestige [prɛsˈtiʒ] o [ˈprɛstɪdʒ] *s* prestigio
presumable [prɪˈzuməbəl] o [prɪˈzjuməbəl] *adj* presumible
presumably [prɪˈzuməblɪ] o [prɪˈzjuməblɪ] *adv* probablemente, verosímilmente
presume [prɪˈzum] o [prɪˈzjum] *va* presumir; suponer, dar por sentado; **to presume to** + *inf* tomar la libertad de + *inf; vn* suponer; **to presume on** o **upon** abusar de
presumedly [prɪˈzumɪdlɪ] o [prɪˈzjumɪdlɪ] *adv* supuestamente
presumption [prɪˈzʌmpʃən] *s* presunción; pretensión; (law) presunción
presumptive [prɪˈzʌmptɪv] *adj* presuntivo; presunto (*supuesto*)
presumptively [prɪˈzʌmptɪvlɪ] *adv* presuntivamente
presumptuous [prɪˈzʌmptʃʊəs] *adj* confianzudo, desenvuelto
presuppose [ˌprisəˈpoz] *va* presuponer
presupposition [ˌprisʌpəˈzɪʃən] *s* presuposición
pret. abr. de **preterit**
pretence [prɪˈtɛns] o [ˈpritɛns] *s* var. de **pretense**
pretend [prɪˈtɛnd] *va* aparentar, fingir (*alegría, dolor, etc.*); **to pretend to** + *inf* fingir + *inf*, aparentar que + *ind;* **to pretend to be** fingirse, p.ej., **to pretend to be a friend** fingirse amigo; *vn* fingir; **to pretend to** pretender (*p.ej., el trono*)
pretended [prɪˈtɛndɪd] *adj* pretendido
pretender [prɪˈtɛndər] *s* pretendiente
pretense [prɪˈtɛns] o [ˈpritɛns] *s* pretensión; fingimiento; presunción; **under false pretenses** con falsas apariencias, con apariencias fingidas; **under pretense of** so pretexto de
pretension [prɪˈtɛnʃən] *s* pretensión
pretentious [prɪˈtɛnʃəs] *adj* pretencioso, aparatoso; ambicioso, vasto
preterit o **preterite** [ˈprɛtərɪt] *adj & s* (gram.) pretérito
preterition [ˌprɛtəˈrɪʃən] *s* preterición; (law & rhet.) preterición
pretermission [ˌpritərˈmɪʃən] *s* pretermisión
pretermit [ˌpritərˈmɪt] (*pret & pp:* **-mitted;** *ger:* **-mitting**) *va* pretermitir
preternatural [ˌpritərˈnætʃərəl] *adj* preternatural
pretext [ˈpritɛkst] *s* pretexto; *va* pretextar
pretonic [priˈtɑnɪk] *adj* (gram.) pretónico
pretor [ˈpritər] o [ˈpritɔr] *s* var. de **praetor**
pretorian [priˈtorɪən] *adj & s* var. de **praetorian**
prettify [ˈprɪtɪfaɪ] (*pret & pp:* **-fied**) *va* embellecer
pretty [ˈprɪtɪ] *adj* (*comp:* **-tier;** *super:* **-tiest**) bonito, lindo; bello; (scornful) bueno, grande; (coll.) bueno, bastante, considerable; *adv* algo, bastante; **sitting pretty** (slang) en buena posición; (slang) acomodado; *s* (*pl:* **-ties**) persona linda, cosa linda
pretty penny *s* (coll.) dineral, ojo de la cara
pretzel [ˈprɛtsəl] *s* galleta tostada hecha en forma de rosquilla y polvoreada con sal
prevail [prɪˈvel] *vn* prevalecer; **to be prevailed on** o **upon to** + *inf* dejarse persuadir a + *inf;* **to prevail against** u **over** prevalecer sobre, triunfar de; **to prevail on, upon** o **with** persuadir
prevailing [prɪˈvelɪŋ] *adj* prevaleciente, reinante, imperante; común, corriente
prevalence [ˈprɛvələns] *s* frecuencia, uso corriente, boga, costumbre
prevalent [ˈprɛvələnt] *adj* común, corriente, en boga
prevaricate [prɪˈværɪket] *vn* mentir, usar de lenguaje ambiguo para engañar; (law) prevaricar
prevarication [prɪˌværɪˈkeʃən] *s* mentira, lenguaje ambiguo; (law) prevaricación
prevaricator [prɪˈværɪˌketər] *s* mentiroso; (law) prevaricador
prevent [prɪˈvɛnt] *va* impedir, estorbar; **to prevent from** + *ger* impedir + *inf* o impedir que + *subj; vn* obstar
preventable [prɪˈvɛntəbəl] *adj* evitable
preventative [prɪˈvɛntətɪv] *adj & s* var. de **preventive**
preventer [prɪˈvɛntər] *s* (naut.) contraamura
preventible [prɪˈvɛntɪbəl] *adj* var. de **preventable**
prevention [prɪˈvɛnʃən] *s* prevención; estorbo, obstáculo
preventive [prɪˈvɛntɪv] *adj* impeditivo, preventivo; profiláctico, preservativo; *s* preservativo
preventive medicine *s* medicina profiláctica, medicina preventiva
preview [ˈpriˌvju] *s* vista anticipada, inspección previa; (mov.) avance; (mov.) preestreno; [priˈvju] o [ˈpriˌvju] *va* ver de antemano, inspeccionar de antemano
previous [ˈprivɪəs] *adj* previo, anterior; *adv* previamente; **previous to** antes de
previously [ˈprivɪəslɪ] *adv* previamente, anteriormente
previous question *s* petición que se hace en una asamblea legislativa para saber si se ha de hacer una votación para dar término al debate
prevision [priˈvɪʒən] *s* previsión
previsional [priˈvɪʒənəl] *adj* previsor
prewar [ˈpriˌwɔr] *adj* prebélico, de antes de la guerra, de preguerra
prey [pre] *s* presa; víctima; **to be prey to** ser presa de; *vn* cazar; **to prey on** o **upon** apresar y devorar; pillar, robar; tener preocupado, tener en zozobra, agobiar
Priam [ˈpraɪəm] *s* (myth.) Príamo
priapism [ˈpraɪəpɪzəm] *s* (path.) priapismo
Priapus [praɪˈepəs] *s* (myth.) Príapo
price [praɪs] *s* precio; **at any price** a toda costa; de cualquier manera; **beyond** o **without price** tan valioso que no puede comprarse; **to set a price on someone's head** poner a precio la cabeza de uno; *va* apreciar, esti-

mar, fijar el precio de, poner precio a; averiguar el precio de
price ceiling *s* precio tope
price control *s* control de precios, intervención de los precios
price cutting *s* reducción de precios (*a un nivel inferior a la tarifa establecida*)
price fixing *s* fijación de precios, tarificación; acuerdo secreto para la fijación de precios
price freezing *s* congelación de precios
priceless [ˈpraɪslɪs] *adj* inapreciable, sin precio; (coll.) divertido, absurdo; **to be priceless** no tener precio
price list *s* lista de precios
price mark *s* marbete o etiqueta (*que expresa el precio de un artículo*)
price stabilization *s* estabilización de precios
price war *s* guerra de precios
prick [prɪk] *s* espiche (*arma o instrumento puntiagudo*); púa (*punta aguda*); agujerillo (*hecho con una punta aguda*); pinchazo, punzada (*herida; dolor*); aguijón; **to kick against the pricks** tener rebeldía que sólo es motivo de sufrimiento, cocear contra el aguijón; *va* pinchar; marcar con agujerillos; punzar (*herir*); dar una punzada a; clavar o enclavar (*a las caballerías*); **to prick up** aguzar (*p.ej., las orejas*); *vn* causar una punzada; sentir una punzada; sentir comezón; erguirse; picarse (*el vino*)
pricket [ˈprɪkɪt] *s* candelero que termina en punta aguda donde se clava la bujía; gamo de un año de edad
prickle [ˈprɪkəl] *s* espina, pincho, púa; pinchazo, punzada; *va* causar una punzada a; *vn* sentir una punzada
prickly [ˈprɪklɪ] *adj* (*comp:* **-lier;** *super:* **-liest**) espinoso, puado, lleno de púas; agudo, punzante
prickly heat *s* (path.) salpullido causado por exceso de calor
prickly pear *s* (bot.) chumbera, higuera chumba, higuera de tuna; higo chumbo, higo de tuna (*fruto*)
prickly poppy *s* (bot.) adormidera espinosa
pride [praɪd] *s* orgullo; arrogancia, altivez; *va* enorgullecer; **to pride oneself on** o **upon** enorgullecerse de; **to pride oneself on** + *ger* enorgullecerse de + *inf*
prideful [ˈpraɪdfəl] *adj* orgulloso
Pride's Purge *s* (hist.) la purificación de Pride
prie-dieu [priˈdjœ] *s* reclinatorio
prier [ˈpraɪər] *s* hurón (*persona que todo lo averigua*)
priest [prist] *s* sacerdote
priestcraft [ˈprist,kræft] o [ˈprist,krɑft] *s* trapisondas eclesiásticas
priestess [ˈpristɪs] *s* sacerdotisa
priesthood [ˈpristhʊd] *s* sacerdocio; clero
priestly [ˈpristlɪ] *adj* (*comp:* **-lier;** *super:* **-liest**) sacerdotal
priest-ridden [ˈprist,rɪdən] *adj* abarrotado de curas
prig [prɪg] *s* pedante, presuntuoso, mojigato
priggery [ˈprɪgərɪ] *s* (*pl:* **-ies**) pedantería, presuntuosidad, mojigatería
priggish [ˈprɪgɪʃ] *adj* pedante, presuntuoso, mojigato
prim [prɪm] *adj* (*comp:* **primmer;** *super:* **primmest**) estirado, relamido
primacy [ˈpraɪməsɪ] *s* (*pl:* **-cies**) primacía
prima donna [ˈprimə ˈdɑnə] *s* (*pl:* **prima donnas**) (mus.) prima donna (*la cantante principal en una ópera*)
prima-facie [ˈpraɪməˈfeʃɪi] *adj* (law) suficiente para justificar la presunción del hecho
primage [ˈpraɪmɪdʒ] *s* (naut.) capa, quintalada
primal [ˈpraɪməl] *adj* primitivo; básico, principal
primarily [ˈpraɪmɛrɪlɪ] o [ˈpraɪmərɪlɪ] *adv* primariamente (*en primer lugar; principalmente*)
primary [ˈpraɪmɛrɪ] o [ˈpraɪmərɪ] *adj* primario; *s* (*pl:* **-ries**) (lo) principal; color primario; elección preliminar para nombrar candidatos para las elecciones generales; reunión de electores para nombrar candidatos para las elecciones generales; (orn.) pluma primaria; (elec.) primario (*arrollamiento*)
primary accent *s* (phonet.) acento primario
primary cell *s* (elec.) elemento primario
primary coil *s* (elec.) carrete primario
primary colors *spl* colores primarios
primary education *s* enseñanza primaria
primary election *s* elección preliminar para nombrar candidatos para las elecciones generales
primary feather *s* (orn.) pluma primaria
primary planet *s* (astr.) planeta primario
primary point *s* (com.) lugar de distribución del grano
primary school *s* escuela de primera enseñanza
primary union *s* (surg.) unión de primera intención
primate [ˈpraɪmet] *s* (eccl.) primado; (zool.) primate
primateship [ˈpraɪmetʃɪp] *s* primacía
primatial [praɪˈmeʃəl] *adj* primacial
prime [praɪm] *adj* primero, principal; básico; primo (*excelente, de primera calidad*); (arith.) primo; (print.) marcado con virgulilla; *s* flor, juventud, primavera; alba, aurora; (la) flor y nata; (arith.) número primo; (eccl.) prima; (phys.) minuto (*de un grado*); (print.) virgulilla; **prime of life** edad viril, flor de edad; *va* preparar, instruir, informar de antemano; cebar (*un arma de fuego, una bomba, un carburador*); poner la primera capa o la primera mano a; poner virgulilla a; **to be primed for an examination** (coll.) ir bien empollado
prime meridian *s* primer meridiano
prime minister *s* primer ministro
prime mover *s* fuente de fuerza; máquina motriz; palanca (*de una empresa*); (philos.) primer motor
prime number *s* (arith.) número primo
primer [ˈpraɪmər] *s* persona que ceba un arma; persona que cubre con una primera mano de pintura; cápsula detonante, cebador; [ˈprɪmər] *s* cartilla
primeval [praɪˈmivəl] *adj* prístino
prime vertical *s* (astr.) primer vertical
priming [ˈpraɪmɪŋ] *s* preparación; cebo; (mas. & paint.) primera capa
primipara [praɪˈmɪpərə] *s* (*pl:* **-rae** [ri]) (obstet.) primípara
primitive [ˈprɪmɪtɪv] *adj* primitivo; *s* (f.a.) primitivo
primogenitor [,praɪmoˈdʒɛnɪtər] *s* progenitor
primogeniture [,praɪmoˈdʒɛnɪtʃər] *s* primogenitura
primordial [praɪˈmɔrdɪəl] *adj* primordial
primp [prɪmp] *va* acicalar, engalanar; *vn* acicalarse, engalanarse
primrose [ˈprɪm,roz] *s* (bot.) primavera; (bot.) primavera de la China; (bot.) hierba del asno; color amarillo claro; *adj* de color amarillo claro; alegre, florido
primrose path *s* sendero alfombrado de flores, sendero fácil y agradable; vida dada a los placeres de los sentidos
primula [ˈprɪmjʊlə] *s* (bot.) primavera
primulaceous [,prɪmjəˈleʃəs] *adj* (bot.) primuláceo
prin. abr. de **principal**
prince [prɪns] *s* príncipe; **to live like a prince** portarse como un príncipe
Prince Albert *s* gabán largo y cruzado
prince consort *s* príncipe consorte
princedom [ˈprɪnsdəm] *s* principado
Prince Edward Island *s* la Isla del príncipe Eduardo
princeling [ˈprɪnslɪŋ] *s* principito
princely [ˈprɪnslɪ] *adj* (*comp:* **-lier;** *super:* **-liest**) principesco
Prince of Darkness *s* príncipe de las tinieblas (*demonio*)
Prince of Peace *s* (Bib.) príncipe de paz (*Jesucristo*)
prince of the blood *s* príncipe de la sangre
Prince of the Church *s* príncipe de la Iglesia (*cardenal*)
Prince of Wales *s* príncipe de Gales
prince royal *s* hijo mayor de un soberano
princess [ˈprɪnsɪs] *s* princesa
princesse dress [prɪnˈsɛs] o [ˈprɪnsɪs] *s* princesa
princess royal *s* hija mayor de un soberano
principal [ˈprɪnsɪpəl] *adj* principal; *s* principal, jefe; director (*de una escuela*); (com. &

law) principal; criminal; (arch.) jamba de fuerza
principal clause *s* (gram.) proposición dominante
principality [ˌprɪnsɪˈpælɪtɪ] *s* (*pl:* **-ties**) principado; **principalities** *spl* (rel.) principados
principally [ˈprɪnsɪpəlɪ] *adv* por lo general; principalmente
principal parts *spl* (gram.) partes principales
principalship [ˈprɪnsɪpəlˌʃɪp] *s* dirección; dirección de una escuela
principate [ˈprɪnsɪpet] *s* supremacía; principado
principle [ˈprɪnsɪpəl] *s* principio; (chem.) principio; **in principle** en principio; **on principle** por principio
principled [ˈprɪnsɪpəld] *adj* escrupuloso, de principios
prink [prɪŋk] *va & vn* var. de **primp**
print [prɪnt] *s* tipo, letra de molde; estampa; grabado, lámina; estampado (*tejido*); diseño (*estampado*); impresión; tirada, edición; (phot.) impresión; **in print** en letra de molde; impreso, publicado; **out of print** agotado; *va* imprimir; estampar; hacer imprimir; publicar; escribir en letra de molde, escribir en caracteres de imprenta; (phot.) tirar, imprimir; (fig.) imprimir o grabar (*en la memoria*); *vn* imprimir; ser impresor
printable [ˈprɪntəbəl] *adj* imprimible
printed circuit *s* (elec.) circuito impreso
printed matter *s* impresos
printer [ˈprɪntər] *s* impresor
printer's devil *s* aprendiz de imprenta
printer's ink *s* tinta de imprenta
printer's mark *s* (print.) pie de imprenta
printing [ˈprɪntɪŋ] *s* impresión; caracteres impresos; tirada, edición; letras de mano imitación de las impresas; (phot.) tiraje
printing frame *s* (phot.) marco de imprimir, prensa
printing press *s* prensa de imprenta
print shop *s* imprenta; estampería
prior [ˈpraɪər] *adj* anterior; *adv* anteriormente; **prior to** antes de; *s* prior
priorate [ˈpraɪərɪt] o [ˈpraɪəret] *s* priorato
prioress [ˈpraɪərɪs] *s* priora
priority [praɪˈɑrɪtɪ] o [praɪˈɔrɪtɪ] *s* (*pl:* **-ties**) prioridad
priory [ˈpraɪərɪ] *s* (*pl:* **-ries**) priorato
prise [praɪz] *va* levantar o mover por fuerza
prism [ˈprɪzəm] *s* (geom., opt. & cryst.) prisma
prismatic [prɪzˈmætɪk] *adj* prismático
prismatic colors *spl* colores prismáticos
prism binocular *s* anteojo prismático
prison [ˈprɪzən] *s* cárcel, prisión; *va* encarcelar
prison camp *s* campamento para prisioneros, campo de prisioneros
prisoner [ˈprɪzənər] o [ˈprɪznər] *s* preso; (mil.) prisionero; **to take prisoner** coger preso a; (mil.) hacer prisionero
prisoner of war *s* prisionero de guerra
prisoner's base *s* rescate (*juego de muchachos*)
prison reform *s* reforma penitenciaria
prison van *s* coche celular
prissy [ˈprɪsɪ] *adj* (*comp:* **-sier;** *super:* **-siest**) (coll.) remilgado, melindroso, estirado
pristine [ˈprɪstin] o [ˈprɪstaɪn] *adj* prístino
prithee [ˈprɪðɪ] *interj* (archaic) ¡te ruego!
privacy [ˈpraɪvəsɪ] *s* (*pl:* **-cies**) aislamiento, retiro; secreto, reserva; **to have no privacy** no poder estar a solas, no poder retirarse de la vista del público
private [ˈpraɪvɪt] *adj* particular; privado, íntimo; confidencial, secreto; retirado; *s* soldado raso; **privates** *spl* partes pudendas; **in private** privadamente; en secreto
private enterprise *s* empresa privada (*dirección y control de la industria por personas privadas*)
privateer [ˌpraɪvəˈtɪr] *s* (naut.) corsario (*embarcación; marino*); *vn* (naut.) corsear
privateering [ˌpraɪvəˈtɪrɪŋ] *adj* (naut.) corsario; *s* (naut.) corso
privateersman [ˌpraɪvəˈtɪrzmən] *s* (*pl:* **-men**) (naut.) corsario
private first class *s* soldado de primera, aspirante a cabo
private hospital *s* clínica, casa de salud
private individual *s* particular
private life *s* vida privada
private line *s* línea (telefónica) particular
privately [ˈpraɪvɪtlɪ] *adv* privadamente; secretamente
private property *s* propiedad privada, bienes particulares
private sale *s* venta directa (*sin licitación y sin corredor*)
private view *s* (f.a.) día de inauguración
privation [praɪˈveʃən] *s* privación
privative [ˈprɪvətɪv] *adj* privativo; (gram.) privativo; *s* (gram.) prefijo privativo, sufijo privativo
privet [ˈprɪvɪt] *s* (bot.) aligustre, ligustro; *adj* ligustrino
privilege [ˈprɪvɪlɪdʒ] *s* privilegio; *va* privilegiar
privily [ˈprɪvɪlɪ] *adv* privadamente, secretamente
privy [ˈprɪvɪ] *s* (*pl:* **-ies**) privada, letrina; *adj* privado; **privy to** enterado secretamente de
privy council *s* consejo privado
privy seal *s* (Brit.) sello pequeño
prize [praɪz] *s* premio; presa; botín; **to take the prize** llevarse el premio; (fig.) llevarse la mapa; *adj* premiado; digno de premio; dado como premio; *va* apreciar, estimar; tasar; levantar o mover por fuerza
prize court *s* tribunal de presas marítimas
prize crew *s* (naut.) tripulación encargada de llevar a puerto la nave apresada
prize fight *s* partido de boxeo profesional
prize fighter *s* boxeador profesional
prize fighting *s* boxeo profesional
prizeman [ˈpraɪzmən] *s* (*pl:* **-men**) laureado, premiado
prize money *s* premio en metálico; (box.) bolsa; (naut.) parte de presa
prize ring *s* cuadrilátero de boxeo
prize winner *s* ganador del premio
pro [pro] *prep* en pro de; *s* (*pl:* **pros**) razón en favor; voto afirmativo; (coll.) deportista profesional; **the pros and the cons** el pro y el contra
proa [ˈproə] *s* prao (*embarcación malaya*)
pro-Ally [ˌproəˈlaɪ] o [ˌproˈælaɪ] *adj & s* aliadófilo
probabilism [ˈprɑbəbɪlɪzəm] *s* (philos.) probabilismo
probability [ˌprɑbəˈbɪlɪtɪ] *s* (*pl:* **-ties**) probabilidad; acontecimiento probable; (meteor.) tiempo probable; **in all probability** según toda probabilidad
probable [ˈprɑbəbəl] *adj* probable
probably [ˈprɑbəblɪ] *adv* probablemente
probang [ˈprobæŋ] *s* (surg.) sonda esofágica
probate [ˈprobet] *adj* (law) testamentario; *s* (law) prueba legal de la autenticidad de un testamento; (law) copia auténtica de un testamento; *va* (law) probar por proceso legal la autenticidad de (*un testamento*)
probate court *s* (law) tribunal encargado de probar la autenticidad de testamentos
probation [proˈbeʃən] *s* probación; libertad vigilada; **to put on probation** dar el azul a
probational [proˈbeʃənəl] o **probationary** [proˈbeʃəˌnerɪ] *adj* probatorio; de libertad vigilada; tutelar
probationer [proˈbeʃənər] *s* persona que está a prueba; liberto, delincuente puesto bajo vigilancia
probationership [proˈbeʃənərˌʃɪp] *s* período de prueba, condición del que está a prueba
probation officer *s* (law) agente de vigilancia (*de los delincuentes juveniles*)
probative [ˈprobətɪv] o [ˈprɑbətɪv] *adj* probatorio
probe [prob] *s* sonda; encuesta, indagación; (surg.) sonda; *va* indagar; (surg.) sondar, tentar
probity [ˈprobɪtɪ] o [ˈprɑbɪtɪ] *s* probidad
problem [ˈprɑbləm] *s* problema
problematic [ˌprɑbləˈmætɪk] o **problematical** [ˌprɑbləˈmætɪkəl] *adj* problemático
problematically [ˌprɑbləˈmætɪkəlɪ] *adv* problemáticamente
proboscidian [ˌprobəˈsɪdɪən] *adj & s* (zool.) proboscidio

proboscis [pro'basɪs] *s* (*pl:* **-boscises** o **-boscides** ['basɪdiz]) *s* (zool. & ent.) probóscide; (hum.) trompa (*nariz del hombre*)
proboscis monkey *s* (zool.) nasica
procedure [pro'sidʒər] *s* procedimiento
proceed [pro'sid] *vn* proceder; **to proceed against** proceder contra; **to proceed from** proceder de; **to proceed to** + *inf* proceder a + *inf;* **to proceed to blows** ir a las manos; **proceeds** ['prosidz] *spl* producto, ganancia
proceeding [pro'sidɪŋ] *s* procedimiento; **proceedings** *spl* actas; (law) procedimiento
process ['prasɛs] o ['prosɛs] *s* procedimiento; proceso (*transcurso del tiempo*); (anat. & biol.) proceso; (law) comparendo; **in process** haciéndose; **in the process of time** andando el tiempo, con el tiempo; *adj* de elaboración; fotomecánico; *va* preparar o tratar mediante un procedimiento especial; (law) procesar
procession [pro'sɛʃən] *s* procesión
processional [pro'sɛʃənəl] *adj* procesional; *s* procesional, libro procesional
proclaim [pro'klem] *va* proclamar
proclamation [,praklə'meʃən] *s* proclamación
proclitic [pro'klɪtɪk] *adj & s* (gram.) proclítico
proclivity [pro'klɪvɪtɪ] *s* (*pl:* **-ties**) inclinación, propensión
Procne ['praknɪ] *s* (myth.) Procne o Progne
procommunist [pro'kamjənɪst] *adj & s* filocomunista
proconsul [pro'kansəl] *s* procónsul
proconsular [pro'kansələr] o [pro'kansjələr] *adj* proconsular
proconsulate [pro'kansəlɪt] o [pro'kansjəlɪt] o **proconsulship** [pro'kansəlʃɪp] *s* proconsulado
procrastinate [pro'kræstɪnet] *va* procrastinar, diferir de un día para otro; *vn* tardar, ser moroso, no decidirse
procrastination [pro,kræstɪ'neʃən] *s* tardanza; falta de decisión
procrastinator [pro'kræstɪ,netər] *s* tardador; persona que no se decide pronto
procreate ['prokrɪet] *va* procrear
procreation [,prokrɪ'eʃən] *s* procreación
procreative ['prokrɪ,etɪv] *adj* procreador, procreante
procreator ['prokrɪ,etər] *s* procreador
Procrustean [pro'krʌstɪən] *adj* de Procusto
Procrustes [pro'krʌstiz] *s* (myth.) Procustes o Procusto
proctology [prak'talədʒɪ] *s* proctología
proctor ['praktər] *s* (educ.) censor; (law) procurador
proctorial [prak'torɪəl] *adj* del guardián de la disciplina
proctorship ['praktərʃɪp] *s* (educ.) cargo u oficio del censor; (law) procuración
proctoscope ['praktəskop] *s* proctoscopio
procumbent [pro'kʌmbənt] *adj* boca abajo; (bot.) procumbente
procurable [pro'kjʊrəbəl] *adj* asequible
procurator ['prakjə,retər] *s* procurador
procure [pro'kjʊr] *va* conseguir, obtener; causar, ocasionar; solicitar y obtener (*mujeres*) para casas de prostitución; *vn* alcahuetear
procurement [pro'kjʊrmənt] *s* consecución, obtención
procurer [pro'kjʊrər] *s* alcahuete
procuress [pro'kjʊrɪs] *s* alcahueta
Procyon ['prosɪan] *s* (astr.) Proción
prod [prad] *s* empuje; aguijada, pincho; (*pret & pp:* **prodded;** *ger:* **prodding**) *va* aguijar, pinchar; (fig.) aguijar, pinchar
prodigal ['pradɪgəl] *adj* pródigo; *s* pródigo; (law) pródigo
prodigality [,pradɪ'gælɪtɪ] *s* (*pl:* **-ties**) prodigalidad
prodigal son *s* hijo pródigo
prodigious [pro'dɪdʒəs] *adj* prodigioso, maravilloso; enorme, inmenso
prodigy ['pradɪʒɪ] *s* (*pl:* **-gies**) prodigio
prodromal ['pradrəməl] *adj* prodrómico
prodrome ['prodrom] *s* (path.) pródromo
produce ['prodjus] o ['produs] *s* producción, producto; productos agrícolas; [pro'djus] o [pro'dus] *va* producir; presentar (*p.ej., un drama*) al público; (geom.) prolongar (*p.ej., una línea*)
producer [pro'djusər] o [pro'dusər] *s* productor; gasógeno; (theat.) realizador
producer gas *s* gas pobre
producers' goods *spl* bienes de producción
product ['pradəkt] *s* producto; (chem. & math.) producto
production [pro'dʌkʃən] *s* producción
productive [pro'dʌktɪv] *adj* productivo
productivity [,prodʌk'tɪvɪtɪ] *s* productividad
proem ['proɛm] *s* proemio
proemial [pro'imɪəl] *adj* proemial
Prof. abr. de **Professor**
profanation [,prafə'neʃən] *s* profanación
profanatory [pro'fænə,torɪ] *adj* profanador
profane [pro'fen] *adj* profano; injurioso (*lenguaje*); *s* profano; *va* profanar
profanity [pro'fænɪtɪ] *s* (*pl:* **-ties**) profanidad; blasfemia
profess [pro'fɛs] *va & vn* profesar
professed [pro'fɛst] *adj* alegado, declarado, imputado; (rel.) profeso; *s* (rel.) profeso
professedly [pro'fɛsɪdlɪ] *adv* declaradamente; concedidamente; supuestamente
profession [pro'fɛʃən] *s* profesión
professional [pro'fɛʃənəl] *adj & s* profesional
professionalism [pro'fɛʃənəlɪzəm] *s* profesionalismo
professionalize [pro'fɛʃənəlaɪz] *va* hacer profesional; *vn* hacerse profesional
professorate [pro'fɛsərɪt] *s* profesorado
professor [pro'fɛsər] *s* catedrático, profesor; (coll.) profesor, maestro
professorial [,profɛ'sorɪəl] o [,prafɪ'sorɪəl] *adj* profesoral
professorship [pro'fɛsərʃɪp] *s* profesorado
proffer ['prafər] *s* oferta, propuesta; *va* ofrecer, proponer
proficiency [pro'fɪʃənsɪ] *s* (*pl:* **-cies**) pericia, destreza, habilidad
proficient [pro'fɪʃənt] *adj* perito, diestro, hábil; *s* perito
profile ['profaɪl] *s* perfil; contorno; bosquejo biográfico conciso y vivo; *va* perfilar
profit ['prafɪt] *s* provecho, beneficio, utilidad, ganancia; **at a profit** con ganancia; *va* servir, ser de utilidad a; *vn* sacar provecho, ganar; adelantar, mejorar; **to profit by** aprovechar, sacar provecho de
profitable ['prafɪtəbəl] *adj* provechoso
profitably ['prafɪtəblɪ] *adv* provechosamente
profit and loss *s* (com.) ganancias y pérdidas
profiteer [,prafɪ'tɪr] *s* logrero, usurero, explotador; *vn* logrear, explotar, usurear
profit sharing *s* participación en los beneficios, división de los beneficios entre dueño y empleados
profit squeeze *s* (coll.) var. de **cost-price squeeze**
profligacy ['praflɪgəsɪ] *s* libertinaje; prodigalidad
profligate ['praflɪgɪt] *adj & s* libertino; pródigo
pro forma [pro 'fɔrmə] *adv* (Lat.) por mera forma; *adj* (com.) simulado
pro forma invoice *s* factura simulada
profound [pro'faʊnd] *adj* profundo
profundity [pro'fʌndɪtɪ] *s* (*pl:* **-ties**) profundidad
profuse [pro'fjus] *adj* profuso; pródigo
profusion [pro'fjuʒən] *s* profusión
progenitor [pro'dʒɛnɪtər] *s* progenitor
progeniture [pro'dʒɛnɪtʃər] *s* engendramiento; prole
progeny ['pradʒɪnɪ] *s* (*pl:* **-nies**) prole
pro-German [,pro'dʒʌrmən] *adj* pro-alemán; *s* (*pl:* **-mans**) pro-alemán
progesterone [pro'dʒɛstəron] *s* (biochem.) progesterona
proglottid [pro'glatɪd] *s* (zool.) proglotis
prognathism ['pragnəθɪzəm] o [prag'neθɪzəm] *s* prognatismo
prognathous ['pragnəθəs] o [prag'neθəs] *adj* prognato
prognosis [prag'nosɪs] *s* (*pl:* **-ses** [siz]) pronóstico (*especialmente de una enfermedad*)
prognostic [prag'nastɪk] *adj* pronosticador; *s* pronóstico
prognosticate [prag'nastɪket] *va* pronosticar
prognostication [prag,nastɪ'keʃən] *s* pronosticación

prognosticator [prɑg'nɑstɪ,ketər] *s* pronosticador
program o **programme** ['prograem] *s* programa; *adj* de programa; programático; (*pret & pp:* **-gramed** o **-grammed;** *ger:* **-graming** o **-gramming**) *va* programar
programing o **programming** ['programɪŋ] *s* programación
program music *s* música de programa
progress ['prɑgrɛs] o ['progrɛs] *s* progreso; progresos (*de una enfermedad, de un alumno, etc.*); **to make progress** hacer progresos; [pro'grɛs] *vn* progresar
progression [pro'grɛʃən] *s* progresión; (math.) progresión
progressive [pro'grɛsɪv] *adj* progresivo; (gram.) durativo; (pol.) progresista; *s* (pol.) progresista
prohibit [pro'hɪbɪt] *va* prohibir
prohibition [,pro·ɪ'bɪʃən] *s* prohibición
prohibitionist [,pro·ɪ'bɪʃənɪst] *adj & s* prohibicionista
prohibitive [pro'hɪbɪtɪv] *adj* prohibitivo
prohibitory [pro'hɪbɪ,torɪ] *adj* prohibitorio
project ['prɑdʒɛkt] *s* proyecto; [pro'dʒɛkt] *va* proyectar (*una bala; un film; un plan; una sombra*); hacer resaltar o sobresalir; (geom.) proyectar; *vn* resaltar, sobresalir
project administrator *s* proyectista
projectile [pro'dʒɛktɪl] *adj* arrojadizo; arrojador; *s* proyectil
projection [pro'dʒɛkʃən] *s* proyección; saliente, resalte
projection machine *s* (mov.) proyector
projective [pro'dʒɛktɪv] *adj* proyectivo
projective geometry *s* geometría proyectiva
projector [pro'dʒɛktər] *s* proyector (*aparato*); proyectista (*persona*)
prolan ['prolæn] *s* (biochem.) prolán
prolapse [pro'læps] o **prolapsus** [pro'læpsəs] *s* (path.) prolapso
prolate ['prolet] *adj* (geom.) alargado en la dirección del diámetro polar
prolegomenon [,prolɪ'gɑmɪnɑn] *s* (*pl:* **-na** [nə]) prolegómeno
prolepsis [pro'lɛpsɪs] *s* (*pl:* **-ses** [siz]) (rhet.) prolepsis
proletarian [,prolɪ'tɛrɪən] *adj & s* proletario
proletarianize [,prolɪ'tɛrɪənaɪz] *va* proletarizar
proletariat [,prolɪ'tɛrɪət] *s* proletariado
proliferate [pro'lɪfəret] *va* (biol.) multiplicar (*células, tejidos, etc.*); *vn* (biol.) proliferar (*células, tejidos, etc.*); proliferar
proliferation [pro,lɪfə'reʃən] *s* proliferación
proliferous [pro'lɪfərəs] *adj* (bot.) prolífero
prolific [pro'lɪfɪk] *adj* prolífico
prolificacy [pro'lɪfɪkəsɪ] *s* prolificación
prolifically [pro'lɪfɪkəlɪ] *adv* prolíficamente
proline ['prolin] o ['prolɪn] *s* (biochem.) prolina
prolix ['prolɪks] o [pro'lɪks] *adj* difuso, verboso
prolixity [pro'lɪksɪtɪ] *s* difusión, verbosidad
prolocutor [pro'lɑkjətər] *s* portavoz; presidente (*de una asamblea*)
prologue o **prolog** ['prolɔg] o ['prolɑg] *s* prólogo
prologuize ['prolɔgaɪz] o ['prolɑgaɪz] *vn* prologar
prolong [pro'lɔŋ] o [pro'lɑŋ] *va* prolongar
prolongation [,prolɔŋ'geʃən] o [,prolɑŋ'geʃən] *s* prolongación
prolonge [pro'lɑndʒ] *s* (arti.) prolonga
prom [prɑm] *s* (U.S.A.) baile de gala bajo los auspicios de los alumnos de una clase colegial o universitaria
promenade [,prɑmɪ'ned] o [,prɑmɪ'nɑd] *s* paseo; baile de gala; *vn* pasear o pasearse
promenade concert *s* concierto durante el cual la gente pasea o baila
promenade deck *s* (naut.) cubierta de paseo
Promethean [pro'miθɪən] *adj* de Prometeo
Prometheus [pro'miθus] o [pro'miθɪəs] *s* (myth.) Prometeo
promethium [pro'miθɪəm] *s* (chem.) prometio
prominence ['prɑmɪnəns] *s* prominencia; eminencia
prominent ['prɑmɪnənt] *adj* prominente; eminente
prominently ['prɑmɪnəntlɪ] *adv* prominentemente; eminentemente
promiscuity [,prɑmɪs'kjuɪtɪ] o [,promɪs'kjuɪtɪ] *s* promiscuidad
promiscuous [pro'mɪskjuəs] *adj* promiscuo
promiscuous intercourse *s* promiscuidad
promise ['prɑmɪs] *s* promesa; (fig.) promesa (*señal que hace esperar un bien*); **to give promise** prometer; *va & vn* prometer; **to promise to** + *inf* prometer + *inf*
Promised Land *s* (Bib.) Tierra de promisión; (*l.c.*) *s* (fig.) tierra de promisión
promising ['prɑmɪsɪŋ] *adj* prometedor, prometiente
promissory ['prɑmɪ,sorɪ] *s* promisorio
promissory note *s* pagaré
promontory ['prɑmən,torɪ] *s* (*pl:* **-ries**) promontorio; (anat.) promontorio
promote [prə'mot] *va* promover; fomentar
promoter [prə'motər] *s* promotor; fomentador
promotion [prə'moʃən] *s* promoción; fomento
prompt [prɑmpt] *adj* pronto, puntual; listo, dispuesto; *va* incitar, mover; inspirar, sugerir; soplar; (theat.) apuntar; **to prompt someone to** + *inf* mover a alguien a + *inf*
promptbook ['prɑmpt,bʊk] *s* (theat.) apunte
prompter ['prɑmptər] *s* (theat.) apuntador
prompter's box *s* (theat.) concha
promptitude ['prɑmptɪtjud] o ['prɑmptɪtud] *s* prontitud, puntualidad
promptly ['prɑmptlɪ] *adv* pronto, puntualmente
promptness ['prɑmptnɪs] *s* prontitud, puntualidad
promulgate [pro'mʌlget] o ['prɑməlget] *va* promulgar
promulgation [,promʌl'geʃən] o [,prɑməl'geʃən] *s* promulgación
promulgator [pro'mʌlgetər] o ['prɑməl,getər] *s* promulgador
pron. abr. de **pronoun** y **pronunciation**
pronation [pro'neʃən] *s* (physiol.) pronación
pronator [pro'netər] *s* (anat.) pronador
prone [pron] *adj* postrado boca abajo; extendido sobre el suelo; dispuesto, propenso
proneness ['pronnɪs] *s* postración; disposición, propensión
pronephros [pro'nɛfrɑs] *s* (embryol.) pronefros
prong [prɔŋ] o [prɑŋ] *s* punta (*de tenedor, horquilla, etc.*); *va* hincar con punta, traspasar
prongbuck ['prɔŋ,bʌk] o ['prɑŋ,bʌk] *s* (zool.) berrendo; (zool.) gacela del sur de África (*Antidorcas marsupialis*)
pronged [prɔŋd] o [prɑŋd] *adj* provisto de puntas o dientes
pronghorn ['prɔŋ,hɔrn] o ['prɑŋ,hɔrn] *s* (zool.) berrendo
pronominal [pro'nɑmɪnəl] *adj* pronominal
pronominally [pro'nɑmɪnəlɪ] *adv* pronominalmente
pronoun ['pronaʊn] *s* pronombre
pronounce [prə'naʊns] *va* pronunciar
pronounceable [prə'naʊnsəbəl] *adj* pronunciable
pronounced [prə'naʊnst] *adj* marcado, definido, decidido
pronouncement [prə'naʊnsmənt] *s* declaración, manifiesto; decisión, opinión
pronouncing [prə'naʊnsɪŋ] *adj* pronunciador, de pronunciación
pronto ['prɑnto] *adv* (coll.) pronto, en seguida
pronunciamento [prə,nʌnsɪə'mɛnto] *s* (*pl:* **-tos**) proclama, manifiesto
pronunciation [prə,nʌnsɪ'eʃən] o [prə,nʌnʃɪ'eʃən] *s* pronunciación
proof [pruf] *s* prueba; graduación normal de las bebidas alcohólicas; (law, math., phot. & print.) prueba; **to be proof against** ser o estar a prueba de; **to put to the proof** poner a prueba; *adj* de prueba; a prueba de; de graduación normal (*dícese de las bebidas alcohólicas*)
proof plane *s* (phys.) plano de prueba
proofread ['pruf,rid] (*pret & pp:* **-read** [,rɛd]) *va* (print.) corregir (*pruebas*), corregir prueba de
proofreader ['pruf,ridər] *s* (print.) corrector de pruebas

proofreading [ˈpruf,ridɪŋ] *s* (print.) corrección de pruebas
proof sheet *s* (print.) pliego de prueba
proof spirit *s* licor de prueba
prop [prɑp] *s* apoyo, sostén, puntal; riostra; rodrigón (*para sostener una planta*); (min.) entibo; **props** *spl* (theat.) accesorios; (*pret & pp:* **propped;** *ger:* **propping**) *va* apoyar, sostener, apuntalar; poner un rodrigón a; (min.) entibar
propaganda [,prɑpəˈgændə] *s* propaganda; *adj* propagandístico
propagandism [,prɑpəˈgændɪzəm] *s* propagandismo
propagandist [,prɑpəˈgændɪst] *adj & s* propagandista
propagate [ˈprɑpəget] *va* propagar; *vn* propagarse
propagation [,prɑpəˈgeʃən] *s* propagación
propagative [ˈprɑpə,getɪv] *adj* propagativo
propagator [ˈprɑpə,getər] *s* propagador
propane [ˈpropen] *s* (chem.) propano
proparoxytone [,propærˈɑksɪton] *adj & s* (phonet.) proparoxítono
propel [proˈpɛl] (*pret & pp:* **-pelled;** *ger:* **-pelling**) *va* propulsar, impeler hacia adelante
propellant [proˈpɛlənt] *s* propulsante
propellent [proˈpɛlənt] *adj & s* propulsor
propeller [proˈpɛlər] *s* propulsor
propensity [proˈpɛnsɪtɪ] *s* (*pl:* **-ties**) propensión
proper [ˈprɑpər] *adj* propio, conveniente; decente, decoroso; exacto, justo; propio, p.ej., **China proper** China propia; (coll.) excelente
proper fraction *s* (math.) fracción propia
properly [ˈprɑpərlɪ] *adv* propiamente, convenientemente; decentemente, decorosamente; exactamente; **properly speaking** hablando en términos precisos
proper noun *s* (gram.) nombre propio
propertied [ˈprɑpərtɪd] *adj* propietario; adinerado
property [ˈprɑpərtɪ] *s* (*pl:* **-ties**) propiedad; **properties** *spl* (theat.) accesorios
property line *s* línea de edificación
property man *s* (theat.) encargado de los accesorios
property owner *s* propietario de bienes raíces
prophecy [ˈprɑfɪsɪ] *s* (*pl:* **-cies**) profecía
prophesy [ˈprɑfəsaɪ] (*pret & pp:* **-sied**) *va & vn* profetizar
prophet [ˈprɑfɪt] *s* profeta; **the Prophet** el Profeta (*Mahoma*); **the Prophets** (Bib.) las Profecías
prophetess [ˈprɑfɪtɪs] *s* profetisa
prophetic [proˈfɛtɪk] *adj* profético
prophetically [proˈfɛtɪkəlɪ] *adv* proféticamente
prophylactic [,profɪˈlæktɪk] o [,prɑfɪˈlæktɪk] *adj & s* profiláctico
prophylaxis [,profɪˈlæksɪs] o [,prɑfɪˈlæksɪs] *s* profilaxis
propinquity [proˈpɪŋkwɪtɪ] *s* propincuidad
propitiate [proˈpɪʃɪet] *va* propiciar
propitiation [pro,pɪʃɪˈeʃən] *s* propiciación
propitiatory [proˈpɪʃɪə,torɪ] *adj* propiciatorio
propitious [proˈpɪʃəs] *adj* propicio
propolis [ˈprɑpəlɪs] *s* propóleos, aleda, cera aleda
proponent [proˈponənt] *s* proponedor; defensor, patrocinador
proportion [prəˈporʃən] *s* proporción; (math.) proporción; **proportions** *spl* proporciones (*tamaño; dimensiones*); **in proportion as** a medida que; **in proportion to** a medida de; **out of proportion** desproporcionado; *va* proporcionar
proportionable [prəˈporʃənəbəl] *adj* proporcionable
proportional [prəˈporʃənəl] *adj* proporcional; *s* (math.) número o cantidad proporcional
proportionality [prə,porʃəˈnælɪtɪ] *s* proporcionalidad
proportionally [prəˈporʃənəlɪ] *adv* proporcionalmente
proportional representation *s* (pol.) representación proporcional
proportionate [prəˈporʃənɪt] *adj* proporcionado
proportionately [prəˈporʃənɪtlɪ] *adv* proporcionadamente
proportioned [prəˈporʃənd] *adj* proporcionado
proportionment [prəˈporʃənmənt] *s* (el) proporcionar
proposal [prəˈpozəl] *s* propuesta; oferta de matrimonio
propose [prəˈpoz] *va* proponer; *vn* proponer; proponer matrimonio; **to propose to** pedir la mano a; **to propose to** + *inf* proponer o proponerse + *inf*
proposition [,prɑpəˈzɪʃən] *s* proposición; (coll.) empresa; (coll.) asunto, cosa, problema; (coll.) sujeto, tipo
propound [prəˈpaʊnd] *va* proponer (*una adivinanza, problema, teoría, etc.*)
proprietary [prəˈpraɪə,tɛrɪ] *adj* propietario; patentado (*aplícase a las medicinas de patente*); *s* (*pl:* **-ies**) propietario; grupo de propietarios; posesión
proprietor [prəˈpraɪətər] *s* propietario
proprietorship [prəˈpraɪətər,ʃɪp] *s* propiedad, posesión
proprietress [prəˈpraɪətrɪs] *s* propietaria
propriety [prəˈpraɪətɪ] *s* (*pl:* **-ties**) corrección, conducta decorosa; conveniencia; **proprieties** *spl* cánones sociales, convenciones
propulsion [proˈpʌlʃən] *s* propulsión
propulsive [proˈpʌlsɪv] *adj* propulsor
propyl [ˈpropɪl] *s* (chem.) propilo
pro rata [pro ˈretə] *adv* a prorrateo, a prorrata
prorate [ˈpro,ret] *s* prorrata; [proˈret] o [ˈpro,ret] *va* prorratear
prorogation [,proroˈgeʃən] *s* prorrogación
prorogue [proˈrog] *va* prorrogar
prosaic [proˈzeɪk] *adj* prosaico; (fig.) prosaico
prosaically [proˈzeɪkəlɪ] *adv* prosaicamente
proscenium [proˈsinɪəm] *s* proscenio
proscribe [proˈskraɪb] *va* proscribir
proscription [proˈskrɪpʃən] *s* proscripción
proscriptive [proˈskrɪptɪv] *adj* proscriptor
prose [proz] *s* prosa; *adj* prosaico, prosístico
prosector [proˈsɛktər] *s* prosector
prosecute [ˈprɑsɪkjut] *va* (law) procesar; desempeñar (*un cargo*); llevar a cabo
prosecution [,prɑsɪˈkjuʃən] *s* (law) procesamiento; (law) parte actora, parte acusadora; prosecución
prosecutor [ˈprɑsɪ,kjutər] *s* (law) fiscal; (law) acusador, demandante
proselyte [ˈprɑsəlaɪt] *s* prosélito; *va* convertir de una creencia u opinión a otra; *vn* ganar prosélitos
proselytism [ˈprɑsəlaɪtɪzəm] o [ˈprɑsəlɪtɪzəm] *s* proselitismo
proselytize [ˈprɑsəlaɪtaɪz] o [ˈprɑsəlɪtaɪz] *va* convertir de una creencia u opinión a otra; *vn* ganar prosélitos
prosenchyma [prɑsˈɛŋkɪmə] *s* (bot.) prosénquima
prose poem *s* poema en prosa
Proserpina [proˈsʌrpɪnə] o **Proserpine** [proˈsʌrpɪni] o [ˈprɑsərpaɪn] *s* (myth.) Proserpina
prose writer *s* prosista
prosimian [proˈsɪmɪən] *adj & s* (zool.) prosimiano
prosit [ˈprosɪt] o [ˈprozɪt] *interj* (Lat.) ¡salud!
proslavery [proˈslevərɪ] *adj* esclavista
prosodist [ˈprɑsədɪst] *s* persona diestra en el arte métrica
prosody [ˈprɑsədɪ] *s* métrica
prosopopoeia [pro,sopəˈpiə] *s* (rhet.) prosopopeya
prospect [ˈprɑspɛkt] *s* perspectiva, vista; expectativa, esperanza; probabilidad de éxito; cliente o comprador probable; **in prospect** anticipado, esperado; *va* prospectar (*un terreno*); *vn* prospectar; **to prospect for** buscar (*p.ej., oro, petróleo*)
prospective [prəˈspɛktɪv] *adj* anticipado, esperado, probable
prospector [ˈprɑspɛktər] *s* prospector (*explorador de minas, petróleo*); gambusino (Am.)
prospectus [prəˈspɛktəs] *s* prospecto
prosper [ˈprɑspər] *va & vn* prosperar
prosperity [prɑsˈpɛrɪtɪ] *s* (*pl:* **-ties**) prosperidad

prosperous ['prɑspərəs] *adj* próspero; prosperado (*rico*)
prostate ['prɑstet] *s* (anat.) próstata; *adj* prostático
prostatectomy [,prɑstə'tɛktəmɪ] *s* (surg.) prostatectomía
prostate gland *s* (anat.) glándula prostática
prosthesis ['prɑsθɪsɪs] *s* (gram.) prótesis o próstesis; (surg.) prótesis
prosthetic [prɑs'θɛtɪk] *adj* (gram.) protético o prostético; (surg.) protético
prostitute ['prɑstɪtjut] o ['prɑstɪtut] *s* prostituta; persona que prostituye su talento y habilidad por dinero; *va* prostituir
prostitution [,prɑstɪ'tjuʃən] o [,prɑstɪ'tuʃən] *s* prostitución
prostrate ['prɑstret] *adj* postrado; postrado boca abajo, postrado en el suelo; *va* postrar; **to prostrate oneself** postrarse
prostration [prɑs'treʃən] *s* postración
prostyle ['prostaɪl] *s* (arch.) próstilo
prosy ['prozɪ] *adj* (*comp:* **-ier**; *super:* **-iest**) prosaico
Prot. abr. de **Protestant**
protactinium [,protæk'tɪnɪəm] *s* (chem.) var. de **protoactinium**
protagonist [pro'tægənɪst] *s* protagonista
Protagoras [pro'tægərəs] *s* Protágoras
protasis ['prɑtəsɪs] *s* (gram.) prótasis
protean ['protɪən] o [pro'tiən] *adj* proteico (*que cambia de formas o de ideas*); (*cap.*) *adj* (myth.) proteico
protect [prə'tɛkt] *va* proteger
protection [prə'tɛkʃən] *s* protección; pasaporte, salvoconducto
protectionism [prə'tɛkʃənɪzəm] *s* proteccionismo
protectionist [prə'tɛkʃənɪst] *adj* & *s* proteccionista
protective [prə'tɛktɪv] *adj* protector
protective coloration *s* (biol.) homocromía, mimetismo
protective custody *s* custodia preventiva
protective tariff *s* protección aduanera, tarifa proteccionista
protector [prə'tɛktər] *s* protector; (sport) coraza
protectorate [prə'tɛktərɪt] *s* protectorado
protectory [prə'tɛktərɪ] *s* (*pl:* **-ries**) asilo (*para la protección de menores*)
protectress [prə'tɛktrɪs] *s* protectora o protectriz
protégé ['protəʒe] *s* ahijado, protegido
protégée ['protəʒe] *s* ahijada, protegida
proteid ['protiɪd] *s* (biochem.) proteido; *adj* (biochem.) proteico
protein ['protiɪn] o ['protin] *s* (biochem.) proteína
pro tem. abr. de **pro tempore**
pro tempore [pro'tɛmpərɪ] *adv* (Lat.) interinamente
pro-tempore [pro'tɛmpərɪ] *adj* interino
Proterozoic [,prɑtəro'zo·ɪk] *adj* & *s* (geol.) proterozoico
protest ['protɛst] *s* protesta; (com.) protesto; (law) protesta; **under protest** de mala gana, haciendo objeciones; [pro'tɛst] *va* protestar, declarar enérgicamente; protestar de, contra o por (*mostrar disconformidad con*); (com.) prostestar; *vn* protestar
protestant ['prɑtɪstənt] o [pro'tɛstənt] *adj* & *s* protestante; (*cap.*) ['prɑtɪstənt] *adj* & *s* protestante
Protestantism ['prɑtɪstəntɪzəm] *s* protestantismo
protestation [,prɑtɛs'teʃən] *s* protestación
Proteus ['protjus] o ['protɪəs] *s* (myth. & fig.) Proteo
prothallium [pro'θælɪəm] *s* (*pl:* **-a** [ə]) (bot.) protalo
prothesis ['prɑθɪsɪs] *s* (gram.) prótesis o próstesis; (surg.) prótesis
prothetic [pro'θɛtɪk] *adj* (gram.) protético o prostético; (surg.) protético
prothonotary [pro'θɑnə,tɛrɪ] o [,proθə'notərɪ] *s* (*pl:* **-ies**) escribano principal (*de un tribunal*); (eccl.) protonotario
prothorax [pro'θoræks] *s* (*pl:* **-raxes** o **-races** [rəsiz]) (ent.) protórax
protium ['protɪəm] o ['proʃɪəm] *s* (chem.) procio
protoactinium [,protoæk'tɪnɪəm] *s* (chem.) protoactinio
protocol ['protəkɑl] *s* protocolo; *va* protocolar
protogine ['protədʒɪn] o ['protədʒin] *s* (geol.) protógina
protomartyr [,proto'mɑrtər] *s* protomártir
proton ['protɑn] *s* (phys. & chem.) protón
protonema [,protə'nimə] *s* (*pl:* **-mata** [mətə]) (bot.) protonema
protoplasm ['protəplæzəm] *s* (biol.) protoplasma
protoplasmic [,protə'plæzmɪk] *adj* protoplásmico
prototype ['protətaɪp] *s* prototipo
protozoan [,protə'zoən] *adj* & *s* (zool.) protozoario o protozoo
protozoölogy [,protəzo'ɑlədʒɪ] *s* protozoología
protozoön [,protə'zoɑn] *s* (*pl:* **-a** [ə]) (zool.) protozoo
protract [pro'trækt] *va* prolongar; (surv.) dibujar con la escala y el transportador
protractile [pro'træktɪl] *adj* protráctil
protraction [pro'trækʃən] *s* prolongación; (surv.) dibujo hecho con la escala y el transportador
protractor [pro'træktər] *s* prolongador; (surv.) transportador
protrude [pro'trud] *va* empujar hacia afuera, sacar fuera; *vn* resaltar, sobresalir
protrusion [pro'truʒən] *s* avanzamiento hacia afuera; saliente, resalte
protrusive [pro'trusɪv] *adj* saliente, protuberante
protuberance [pro'tjubərəns] o [pro'tubərəns] *s* protuberancia
protuberant [pro'tjubərənt] o [pro'tubərənt] *adj* protuberante
proud [praʊd] *adj* orgulloso; soberbio
proud flesh *s* (path.) carnosidad, bezo
prov. abr. de **provincialism**
Prov. abr. de **Provence, Provençal, Proverbs, Province** y **Provost**
provable ['pruvəbəl] *adj* comprobable, demostrable
prove [pruv] (*pret:* **proved**; *pp:* **proved** o **proven**) *va* probar; *vn* resultar; **to prove to be** venir a ser; resultar, salir
Provençal [,provən'sɑl] *adj* & *s* provenzal
Provence [pro'vɑns] *s* la Provenza
provender ['prɑvəndər] *s* forraje; (coll.) comida
prover ['pruvər] *s* probador, ensayador
proverb ['prɑvərb] *s* proverbio; ejemplo típico, ejemplo notorio; **Proverbs** *spl* (Bib.) Proverbios, Libro de los Proverbios
proverbial [pro'vʌrbɪəl] *adj* proverbial
proverbially [pro'vʌrbɪəlɪ] *adv* proverbialmente
provide [prə'vaɪd] *va* proporcionar; suministrar; *vn* precaverse; prepararse; disponer, estipular; **to provide against** precaverse contra o de; **to provide for** proveer a; asegurarse (*el porvenir*); proveer lo necesario para (*p.ej., la educación de un hijo*)
provided [prə'vaɪdɪd] *conj* a condición (de) que, con tal (de) que
providence ['prɑvɪdəns] *s* providencia; (*cap.*) *s* Providencia
provident ['prɑvɪdənt] *adj* providente
providential [,prɑvɪ'dɛnʃəl] *adj* providencial
provider [prə'vaɪdər] *s* proveedor
providing [prə'vaɪdɪŋ] *conj* var. de **provided**
province ['prɑvɪns] *s* provincia; competencia
provincial [prə'vɪnʃəl] *adj* provincial (*perteneciente a la provincia*); provinciano (*campesino; perteneciente a una provincia en contraposición a la capital*); intolerante; *s* provinciano; (eccl.) provincial
provincialism [prə'vɪnʃəlɪzəm] *s* provincialismo; intolerancia
provinciality [prə,vɪnʃɪ'ælɪtɪ] *s* (*pl:* **-ties**) provincialismo; provincianismo
proving ground *s* campo de ensayos
provision [prə'vɪʒən] *s* provisión; condición, estipulación; **provisions** *spl* provisiones; **to make provision for** providenciar; asegurar el porvenir de (*p.ej., la familia de uno*); ase-

gurarse (*el porvenir*); proveer lo necesario para (*p. ej., la educación de un hijo*); *va* aprovisionar
provisional [prə'vɪʒənəl] *adj* provisional
provisionally [prə'vɪʒənəlɪ] *adv* provisionalmente
proviso [prə'vaɪzo] *s* (*pl:* **-sos** o **-soes**) condición, estipulación, salvedad
provisory [prə'vaɪzərɪ] *adj* condicional, provisorio
provitamin [pro'vaɪtəmɪn] *s* (biochem.) provitamina
provocation [,prɑvə'keʃən] *s* provocación
provocative [prə'vɑkətɪv] *adj* provocativo; *s* provocación
provoke [prə'vok] *va* provocar; **to provoke to** + *inf* provocar a + *inf*
provoking [prə'vokɪŋ] *adj* provocador (*irritante*)
provost ['prɑvəst] *s* preboste; (eccl.) prepósito; (educ.) preboste (*jefe educacional en algunas universidades norteamericanas*)
provost marshal ['provo] *s* (mil.) capitán preboste; (nav.) oficial de vigilancia
provostship ['prɑvəstʃɪp] *s* prebostazgo; (eccl.) prepositura
prow [praʊ] *s* (naut.) proa
prowess ['praʊɪs] *s* proeza; destreza
prowl [praʊl] *s* ronda en busca de presa o pillaje, vagabundeo; *vn* rondar en busca de presa o pillaje, cazar al acecho, vagabundear, rodar
prowler ['praʊlər] *s* rondador; ladrón
proximal ['prɑksɪməl] *adj* (anat.) proximal
proximate ['prɑksɪmɪt] *adj* próximo
proximately ['prɑksɪmɪtlɪ] *adv* próximamente
proximity [prɑk'sɪmɪtɪ] *s* proximidad
proximity fuse *s* espoleta de proximidad por radio
proximo ['prɑksɪmo] *adv* del o en el mes que viene
proxy ['prɑksɪ] *s* (*pl:* **-ies**) poder; apoderado, poderhabiente; **by proxy** por poderes
prude [prud] *s* mojigato, gazmoño
prudence ['prudəns] *s* prudencia
prudent ['prudənt] *adj* prudente
prudential [pru'dɛnʃəl] *adj* prudencial
prudery ['prudərɪ] *s* (*pl:* **-ies**) mojigatería, gazmoñería
prudish ['prudɪʃ] *adj* mojigato, gazmoño
prune [prun] *s* ciruela pasa; *va* escamondar, podar; (fig.) escamondar
pruning hook o **knife** *s* podadera
prurience ['prʊrɪəns] o **pruriency** ['prʊrɪənsɪ] *s* lascivia
prurient ['prʊrɪənt] *adj* lascivo; anheloso
pruriginous [prʊ'rɪdʒɪnəs] *adj* pruriginoso
prurigo [prʊ'raɪgo] *s* (path.) prurigo
pruritus [prʊ'raɪtəs] *s* (path.) prurito
Prussia ['prʌʃə] *s* Prusia
Prussian ['prʌʃən] *adj* & *s* prusiano
Prussian blue *s* azul de Prusia
Prussianism ['prʌʃənɪzəm] *s* prusianismo
prussiate ['prʌʃɪet] o ['prʌsɪet] *s* (chem.) prusiato
prussic ['prʌsɪk] *adj* prúsico
prussic acid *s* (chem.) ácido prúsico
pry [praɪ] *s* (*pl:* **pries**) palanca, alzaprima; persona entremetida; (*pret* & *pp:* **pried**) *va* alzaprimar; conseguir con gran dificultad; **to pry open** forzar (*p.ej., una tapa*) con la alzaprima o palanca; **to pry out of** arrancar (*p.ej., un secreto*) a (*una persona*); *vn* entremeterse; **to pry into** meterse en, entremeterse en
pryer ['praɪər] *s* var. de **prier**
prying ['praɪɪŋ] *adj* curioso, entremetido
prythee ['prɪðɪ] *interj* (archaic) ¡ te ruego!
Ps. abr. de **Psalm** o **Psalms**
P.S. abr. de **postscript** y **Privy Seal**
psalm [sɑm] *s* salmo; **the Psalms** (Bib.) los Salmos
psalmbook ['sɑm,bʊk] *s* libro de Salmos versificados
psalmist ['sɑmɪst] *s* salmista; **the Psalmist** el Salmista
psalmody ['sɑmədɪ] o ['sælmədɪ] *s* (*pl:* **-dies**) salmodia; salmos
Psalter ['sɔltər] *s* Salterio
psaltery ['sɔltərɪ] *s* (*pl:* **-ies**) (mus.) salterio
pseudo ['sudo] o ['sjudo] *adj* supuesto, falso, fingido
pseudohermaphroditism [,sudohʌr'mæfrədaɪtɪzəm] o [,sjudohʌr'mæfrədaɪtɪzəm] *s* seudohermafroditismo
pseudomorphism [,sudə'mɔrfɪzəm] o [,sjudə'mɔrfɪzəm] *s* (mineral.) seudomorfismo
pseudonym ['sudənɪm] o ['sjudənɪm] *s* seudónimo
pseudonymous [su'dɑnɪməs] o [sju'dɑnɪməs] *adj* seudónimo
pseudopod ['sudəpɑd] o ['sjudəpɑd] *s* (zool.) seudópodo
pseudopodium [,sudə'podɪəm] o [,sjudə'podɪəm] *s* (*pl:* **-a** [ə]) var. de **pseudopod**
pshaw [ʃɔ] *interj* ¡ pche!
psilosis [saɪ'losɪs] *s* (path.) psilosis (*caída del pelo; esprue*)
psittacism ['sɪtəsɪzəm] *s* psitacismo
psittacosis [,sɪtə'kosɪs] *s* (path.) psitacosis
psoas ['soəs] *s* (anat.) psoas
psoriasis [so'raɪəsɪs] *s* (path.) soriasis
P.S.T. abr. de **Pacific Standard Time**
pst [pst] *interj* ¡ chis, chis!, ¡ ce!
psych. abr. de **psychology** y **psychological**
psychasthenia [,saɪkæs'θinɪə] *s* (path.) psicastenia
psyche ['saɪkɪ] *s* psiquis (*alma, inteligencia*); (*cap.*) *s* (myth.) Psiquis
psychiatric [,saɪkɪ'ætrɪk] *adj* psiquiátrico
psychiatrist [saɪ'kaɪətrɪst] *s* psiquíatra
psychiatry [saɪ'kaɪətrɪ] *s* psiquiatría
psychic ['saɪkɪk] *adj* psíquico; mediúmnico; *s* médium
psychical ['saɪkɪkəl] *adj* var. de **psychic**
psychoanalysis [,saɪkoə'nælɪsɪs] *s* psicoanálisis
psychoanalyst [,saɪko'ænəlɪst] *s* psicoanalista
psychoanalytic [,saɪko,ænə'lɪtɪk] o **psychoanalytical** [,saɪko,ænə'lɪtɪkəl] *adj* psicoanalítico
psychoanalytically [,saɪko,ænə'lɪtɪkəlɪ] *adv* psicoanalíticamente
psychoanalyze [,saɪko'ænəlaɪz] *va* psicoanalizar
psychodynamic [,saɪkodaɪ'næmɪk] *adj* psicodinámico; **psychodynamics** *ssg* psicodinámica
psychognosis [saɪ'kɑgnəsɪs] *s* psicognostia
psychologic [,saɪkə'lɑdʒɪk] o **psychological** [,saɪkə'lɑdʒɪkəl] *adj* psicológico
psychologically [,saɪkə'lɑdʒɪkəlɪ] *adv* psicológicamente
psychological moment *s* momento psicológico
psychological warfare *s* guerra psicológica
psychologist [saɪ'kɑlədʒɪst] *s* psicólogo
psychology [saɪ'kɑlədʒɪ] *s* psicología
psychometric [,saɪko'mɛtrɪk] *adj* psicométrico; **psychometrics** *ssg* psicometría
psychometry [saɪ'kɑmɪtrɪ] *s* psicometría
psychoneurosis [,saɪkonjʊ'rosɪs] o [,saɪkonʊ'rosɪs] *s* (*pl:* **-ses** [siz]) (path.) psiconeurosis
psychopath ['saɪkopæθ] *s* psicópata
psychopathic [,saɪko'pæθɪk] *adj* psicopático
psychopathology [,saɪkopə'θɑlədʒɪ] *s* psicopatología
psychopathy [saɪ'kɑpəθɪ] *s* psicopatía
psychophysics [,saɪko'fɪzɪks] *ssg* psicofísica
psychosis [saɪ'kosɪs] *s* (*pl:* **-ses** [siz]) (path.) psicosis; (psychol.) estado mental
psychosomatic [,saɪkoso'mætɪk] *adj* psicosomático
psychotherapy [,saɪko'θɛrəpɪ] *s* psicoterapia
psychrometer [saɪ'krɑmɪtər] *s* psicrómetro
pt. abr. de **part, pint** o **pints** y **point**
ptarmigan ['tɑrmɪgən] *s* (orn.) perdiz blanca
pteridophyte ['tɛrɪdo,faɪt] *s* (bot.) pteridófita o teridófita
pterodactyl [,tɛro'dæktɪl] *s* (pal.) pterodáctilo
Ptolemaic [,tɑlɪ'meɪk] *adj* ptolemaico; *s* partidario de Tolomeo
Ptolemaic system *s* (astr.) sistema de Tolomeo
Ptolemy ['tɑlɪmɪ] *s* Tolomeo
ptomaine o **ptomain** ['tomen] *s* (biochem.) ptomaína o tomaína
ptomaine poisoning *s* envenenamiento ptomaínico
pts. abr. de **parts, pints** y **points**

ptyalin ['taɪəlɪn] *s* (path.) ptialina
ptyalism ['taɪəlɪzəm] *s* (path.) ptialismo
pub [pʌb] *s* (Brit. slang) taberna
puberty ['pjubərtɪ] *s* pubertad
pubes ['pjubiz] *s* (anat.) pubis (*parte inferior del vientre; vello que la cubre*); *pl de* **pubis**
pubescence [pju'bɛsəns] *s* pubescencia
pubescent [pju'bɛsənt] *adj* pubescente
pubic ['pjubɪk] *adj* púbico
pubis ['pjubɪs] *s* (*pl:* **-bes** [biz]) (anat.) pubis (*parte del hueso coxal*)
public ['pʌblɪk] *adj* público; *s* público; **in public** en público
public-address system ['pʌblɪkə'drɛs] *s* sistema amplificador de discursos públicos
publican ['pʌblɪkən] *s* (hist.) publicano; (Brit.) tabernero
publication [,pʌblɪ'keʃən] *s* publicación
public charge *s* carga pública
public conveyance *s* vehículo de servicio público, vehículo de transporte urbano
public debt *s* deuda pública
public enemy *s* enemigo público
public health *s* higiene pública
public house *s* posada, hotel; (Brit.) taberna
publicist ['pʌblɪsɪst] *s* publicista
publicity [pʌb'lɪsɪtɪ] *s* publicidad; *adj* publicitario
publicize ['pʌblɪsaɪz] *va* publicar
public library *s* biblioteca municipal
publicly ['pʌblɪklɪ] *adv* públicamente
public official *s* funcionario público
public opinion *s* opinión pública
public relations *spl* relaciones públicas
public school *s* (U.S.A.) escuela pública; (Brit.) internado privado con dote
public servant *s* funcionario público
public speaking *s* elocución, oratoria
public spirit *s* celo patriótico del buen ciudadano
public-spirited ['pʌblɪk'spɪrɪtɪd] *adj* cívico, patriótico
public square *s* plaza; plaza de armas (Am.)
public thoroughfare *s* vía pública
public toilet *s* quiosco de necesidad
public utility *s* empresa de servicio público; **public utilities** *spl* acciones emitidas por empresas de servicio público
public works *spl* obras públicas
publish ['pʌblɪʃ] *va* publicar; (eccl.) publicar
publisher ['pʌblɪʃər] *s* editor
publishing house *s* casa editorial
puccoon [pə'kun] *s* (bot.) litospermo; (bot.) sanguinaria del Canadá
puce [pjus] *adj* de color castaño rojizo; *s* color castaño rojizo
puck [pʌk] *s* duende malicioso; (sport) disco de caucho
pucker ['pʌkər] *s* pliegue mal hecho; frunce; *va* plegar mal; fruncir; *vn* plegarse mal
puckish ['pʌkɪʃ] *adj* travieso, juguetón
pudding ['pʊdɪŋ] *s* pudín; chorizo
pudding stone *s* (geol.) pudinga
puddle ['pʌdəl] *s* aguazal, charco; mezcla de arcilla húmeda y arena en una pasta; *va* mojar, enlodar, enfangar; hacer una pasta de (*arcilla húmeda y arena*); tapar u obstruir con una mezcla de arcilla húmeda y arena; (found.) pudelar
puddler ['pʌdlər] *s* (found.) pudelador
puddling ['pʌdlɪŋ] *s* (found.) pudelación; arcilla pastosa
puddling furnace *s* horno de pudelar
puddly ['pʌdlɪ] *adj* encharcado
pudency ['pjudənsɪ] *s* pudicicia
pudgy ['pʌdʒɪ] *adj* (*comp:* **-ier**; *super:* **-iest**) gordinflón, rechoncho
pueblo ['pwɛblo] *s* (*pl:* **-los**) (U.S.A.) pueblo indio
puerile ['pjuərɪl] *adj* pueril
puerility [,pjuə'rɪlɪtɪ] *s* (*pl:* **-ties**) puerilidad
puerperal [pju'ʌrpərəl] *adj* puerperal
puerperal fever *s* (path.) fiebre puerperal
puerperium [,pjuər'pɪrɪəm] *s* (obstet.) puerperio
Puerto Rican ['pwɛrto 'rikən] *adj & s* puertorriqueño
Puerto Rico ['pwɛrto 'riko] *s* Puerto Rico
puff [pʌf] *s* resoplido, soplo vivo; bocanada (*de humo*); bullón (*de vestido*); borla de polvos; pastelillo de crema o jalea; masa redonda y suave; alabanza exagerada; ráfaga, ventolera; *va* soplar; hinchar; alabar exageradamente; *vn* soplar; resollar; echar bocanadas (*p.ej., una chimenea*); hincharse; enorgullecerse exageradamente
puff adder *s* (zool.) víbora puff
puffball ['pʌf,bɔl] *s* (bot.) bejín, cuesco de lobo
puffer ['pʌfər] *s* soplador; (ichth.) pez globo; (ichth.) diodón; (ichth.) tamboril
puffin ['pʌfɪn] *s* (orn.) frailecillo (*Fratercula arctica*)
puffing adder *s* (zool.) heterodón
puff paste *s* pasta de harina muy fina que se usa para hacer pasteles y tortas, hojaldre
puff sleeve *s* manga de bullón
puffy ['pʌfɪ] *adj* (*comp:* **-ier**; *super:* **-iest**) hinchado; que viene en bocanadas; corto de resuello; (fig.) hinchado, engreído; (fig.) campanudo
pug [pʌg] *s* doguino, perro carlín
pugilism ['pjudʒɪlɪzəm] *s* pugilismo o pugilato
pugilist ['pjudʒɪlɪst] *s* púgil o pugilista
pugilistic [,pjudʒɪ'lɪstɪk] *adj* de pugilato, pugilístico
pugnacious [pʌg'neʃəs] *adj* pugnaz, belicoso
pugnacity [pʌg'næsɪtɪ] *s* pugnacidad, belicosidad
pug nose *s* nariz roma y levantada
pug-nosed ['pʌg,nozd] *adj* braco
puissance ['pjuɪsəns], [pju'ɪsəns] o ['pwɪsəns] *s* fuerza grande, pujanza
puissant ['pjuɪsənt], [pju'ɪsənt] o ['pwɪsənt] *adj* fuerte, pujante
puke [pjuk] *s* (slang) vómito; *va & vn* (slang) vomitar
pulchritude ['pʌlkrɪtjud] o ['pʌlkrɪtud] *s* belleza, hermosura
pule [pjul] *vn* gemir, quejarse, llorar con voz débil (*como hacen los niños*)
pull [pʊl] *s* tirón, estirón; chupada (*p.ej., a un cigarro*); tirador (*de una puerta*); cuerda (*con que se tira de una cosa*); esfuerzo penoso o prolongado; (slang) enchufe, buenas aldabas; (fig.) tirón (*atracción*) ‖ *va* tirar de; arrancar, coger; rasgar; estirar, dislocar, torcer (*p.ej., un ligamento*); chupar; beber; reservar (*p.ej., las fuerzas*); (print.) sacar (*una impresión o prueba*); (slang) llevar a cabo; (slang) arrestar; **to pull apart** separar por tracción; romper en dos; **to pull down** demoler, derribar; bajar (*p.ej., la cortinilla*); abatir, degradar, humillar; **to pull in** cobrar (*una cuerda o soga*); **to pull off** (slang) llevar a cabo; **to pull oneself together** componerse, recobrar la calma; **to pull out** arrancar, sacar; **to pull through** sacar de un aprieto, sacar de una enfermedad; **to pull up** arrancar, desarraigar; detener, parar ‖ *vn* moverse despacio, moverse con esfuerzo; remar; **to pull apart** romperse por tracción; **to pull at** tirar de (*p.ej., su corbata*); chupar (*p.ej., un cigarro*); **to pull for** (slang) apoyar, ayudar; **to pull for oneself** tirar por su lado; **to pull in** detenerse; llegar (*un tren*) a la estación; **to pull on** tirar de; **to pull out** partir; partir (*un tren*) de la estación; **to pull through** salir a flote; recobrar la salud; **to pull up** moverse hacia adelante; detenerse, pararse; arrimarse (*p.ej., un auto a la acera*); **pull** tirad (*indicación en una puerta*)
pull chain *s* (elec.) cadenilla de tiro, tirador
pull cord *s* (elec.) tirador
pulldevil ['pʊl,dɛvəl] *s* potera
puller ['pʊlər] *s* tirador, extractor, arrancador; (slang) atracción
pullet ['pʊlɪt] *s* polla (*gallina joven*)
pulley ['pʊlɪ] *s* polea; sistema de poleas; polea de transmisión
Pullman car ['pʊlmən] *s* coche Pullman
pull-over ['pʊl,ovər] *s* pulóver (*chaleco de punto de media que se pone comenzando por la cabeza*)
pull socket *s* (elec.) portalámparas de cadena
pullulate ['pʌljəlet] *vn* pulular
pulmonary ['pʌlmə,nɛrɪ] *adj* pulmonar
pulmonate ['pʌlmənet] o ['pʌlmənɪt] *adj* pulmonado
pulmotor ['pʌl,motər] o ['pʊl,motər] *s* pulmotor
pulp [pʌlp] *s* pulpa; pasta (*para hacer papel*);

(anat.) bulbo (*de diente*); *va* hacer pulpa (*una cosa*)
pulpit ['pulpɪt] *s* púlpito; (fig.) púlpito
pulpit glasses *spl* anteojos de predicador
pulpwood ['pʌlp,wud] *s* madera de pulpa; madera hecha pulpa para hacer papel
pulpy ['pʌlpɪ] *adj* (*comp:* **-ier;** *super:* **-iest**) pulposo
pulque ['pulkɪ] *s* pulque
pulsate ['pʌlset] *vn* pulsar; vibrar
pulsatile ['pʌlsətɪl] *adj* pulsátil
pulsation [pʌl'seʃən] *s* pulsación; (phys. & physiol.) pulsación
pulsative ['pʌlsətɪv] *adj* pulsativo
pulse [pʌls] *s* pulso; legumbres (*garbanzos, habas, lentejas*); **to feel** o **take the pulse of** tomar el pulso a; *vn* pulsar
pulsimeter [pʌl'sɪmɪtər] *s* pulsímetro
pulsometer [pʌl'sɑmɪtər] *s* pulsómetro; pulsímetro
pulverizable ['pʌlvə,raɪzəbəl] *adj* pulverizable
pulverization [,pʌlvərɪ'zeʃən] *s* pulverización
pulverize ['pʌlvəraɪz] *va* pulverizar; *vn* pulverizarse
puma ['pjumə] *s* (zool.) puma
pumice ['pʌmɪs] *s* piedra pómez; *va* apomazar
pumice stone *s* piedra pómez
pummel ['pʌməl] (*pret & pp:* **-meled** o **-melled;** *ger:* **-meling** o **-melling**) *va* apuñear, aporrear
pump [pʌmp] *s* bomba; servilla, zapatilla; *va* elevar (*agua*) por medio de una bomba; sacar (*agua*) por medio de una bomba; llenar de aire por medio de una bomba; mover de arriba para abajo (*como el guimbalete de una bomba*); sonsacar; tirar de la lengua a; **to pump up** hinchar, inflar (*el neumático*); *vn* trabajar elevando agua por medio de una bomba; moverse de arriba para abajo
pump box *s* cuerpo de bomba; émbolo de bomba
pump dale *s* (naut.) dala, adala
pumper ['pʌmpər] *s* bombero; ganzúa, sonsacador
pumpernickel ['pʌmpər,nɪkəl] *s* pan de centeno entero
pump handle *s* guimbalete
pump house *s* casa de bombas
pumping station *s* estación de bombas, estación elevadora
pumpkin ['pʌmpkɪn] o ['pʌŋkɪn] *s* (bot.) calabaza común; (coll.) cachazudo; **some pumpkins** (coll.) persona de muchas campanillas
pump piston *s* émbolo de bomba
pump-priming ['pʌmp,praɪmɪŋ] *s* (econ.) inyección económica (*por parte del gobierno*)
pun [pʌn] *s* retruécano, equívoco, juego de palabras; (*pret & pp:* **punned;** *ger:* **punning**) *vn* jugar del vocablo, decir equívocos
punch [pʌntʃ] *s* puñetazo; punzón; sacabocado; perforación; ponche (*bebida*); (coll.) empuje, fuerza, vigor; **to pull one's punches** (box.) moderar los puñetazos; (slang) moderar el ataque; (*cap.*) *s* Polichinela; **pleased as Punch** muy satisfecho; (*l.c.*) *va* pegar con los puños; punzonar; picar, taladrar, perforar (*p.ej., un billete*)
Punch-and-Judy show ['pʌntʃənd'dʒudɪ] *s* función de títeres en la cual Polichinela se pelea con su mujer
punch bowl *s* ponchera
punch card *s* tarjeta perforada
punch-drunk ['pʌntʃ,drʌnk] *adj* atontado (*p.ej,. por una tunda de golpes*); completamente aturdido
punched card [pʌntʃt] *s* var. de **punch card**
punched tape *s* cinta perforada
puncheon ['pʌntʃən] *s* pipa, tonel; punzón; pie derecho; pedazo de un tronco dividido por la mitad y con la superficie pulida rudamente
punchinello [,pʌntʃɪ'nɛlo] *s* (*pl:* **-los** o **-loes**) polichinela, pulchinela
punching bag *s* (sport) boxibalón
punch line *s* broche de oro, colofón del artículo (*frase que sintetiza el escrito*)
punch press *s* (mach.) prensa punzonadora
punctilio [pʌŋk'tɪlɪo] *s* (*pl:* **-os**) puntillo, pundonor
punctilious [pʌŋk'tɪlɪəs] *adj* puntilloso, pundonoroso
punctual ['pʌŋktʃuəl] *adj* puntual
punctuality [,pʌŋktʃu'ælɪtɪ] *s* puntualidad
punctually ['pʌŋktʃuəlɪ] *adv* puntualmente
punctuate ['pʌŋktʃuet] *va* puntuar; acentuar, destacar; interrumpir; *vn* puntuar
punctuation [,pʌŋktʃu'eʃən] *s* puntuación
punctuation mark *s* signo de puntuación
puncture ['pʌŋktʃər] *s* puntura; (aut.) pinchazo, picadura, perforación; (surg.) punción; **to have a puncture** tener un neumático pinchado; *va* pinchar, picar, perforar; (surg.) puncionar; *vn* ser pinchado
puncture-proof ['pʌŋktʃər,pruf] *adj* (aut.) imperforable, a prueba de pinchazos
pundit ['pʌndɪt] *s* erudito, sabio
pungency ['pʌndʒənsɪ] *s* picante; estímulo, vivacidad
pungent ['pʌndʒənt] *adj* picante; estimulante, vivaz
Punic ['pjunɪk] *adj* púnico; (fig.) púnico
Punic Wars *spl* guerras púnicas
punish ['pʌnɪʃ] *va* castigar; (coll.) maltratar
punishable ['pʌnɪʃəbəl] *adj* castigable, punible
punishment ['pʌnɪʃmənt] *s* castigo; (coll.) maltrato
punitive ['pjunɪtɪv] o **punitory** ['pjunɪ,torɪ] *adj* punitivo
Punjab [pʌn'dʒɑb] o ['pʌndʒɑb] *s* Penyab
punk [pʌŋk] *s* yesca, pebete; hupe; (slang) pillo, gamberro; *adj* (slang) malo, de mala calidad
punster ['pʌnstər] *s* vocablista, equivoquista
punt [pʌnt] *s* batea, pontón (*barco chato*); (football) puntapié dado al balón en el aire; *va* impeler (*un barco*) con un botador; (football) dar un puntapié a (*el balón*) antes que llegue al suelo; *vn* pasear o pescar en una batea; jugar por dinero; apostar contra el banquero
punter ['pʌntər] *s* hombre que impele un barco con el botador; (football) jugador que da un puntapié al balón en el aire; jugador que apuesta contra el banquero
punty ['pʌntɪ] *s* (*pl:* **-ties**) puntel
puny ['pjunɪ] *adj* (*comp:* **-nier;** *super:* **-niest**) encanijado, débil; insignificante, mezquino
pup [pʌp] *s* var. de **puppy**
pupa ['pjupə] *s* (*pl:* **-pae** [pi]) (ent.) pupa, ninfa
pupal ['pjupəl] *adj* (ent.) pupal
puparium [pju'pɛrɪəm] *s* (ent.) pupario
pupil ['pjupəl] *s* alumno; (anat.) pupila
pupillary ['pjupɪ,lɛrɪ] *adj* pupilar (*perteneciente al pupilo o huérfano*); (anat.) pupilar
Pupin system [pju'pin] *s* (elec.) pupinización
puppet ['pʌpɪt] *s* títere; muñeca pequeña; (fig.) maniquí; (mach.) muñeca
puppeteer [,pʌpɪ'tɪr] *s* titiritero
puppet government *s* gobierno títere, gobierno de monigotes
puppet regime *s* régimen títere
puppet show *s* función de títeres
puppy ['pʌpɪ] *s* (*pl:* **-pies**) cachorro; pisaverde
puppyish ['pʌpɪɪʃ] *adj* de cachorro; fatuo
puppy love *s* (coll.) primeros amores
pup tent *s* (mil.) tienda de abrigo
pur [pʌr] *s* ronroneo; (*pret & pp:* **purred;** *ger:* **purring**) *va* decir murmurando; *vn* ronronear (*el gato; el avión*)
purblind ['pʌr,blaɪnd] *adj* cegato; miope, falto de comprensión
purchasable ['pʌrtʃəsəbəl] *adj* comprable; sobornable
purchase ['pʌrtʃəs] *s* compra; agarre firme; **you have no purchase** Vd. no tiene donde agarrarse; *va* comprar
purchaser ['pʌrtʃəsər] *s* comprador
purchasing power *s* poder adquisitivo, poder de adquisición (*del dinero*)
pure [pjur] *adj* puro
pure-blooded ['pjur,blʌdɪd] *adj* castizo, de sangre pura
purée [pju're] o ['pjure] *s* puré
pure line *s* (biol.) linaje puro
pureness ['pjurnɪs] *s* pureza
purfle ['pʌrfəl] *s* orla; *va* orlar
purgation [pʌr'geʃən] *s* purgación

purgative [ˈpʌrgətɪv] *adj* purgativo o purgante; *s* purgante
purgatorial [ˌpʌrgəˈtorɪəl] *adj* purgatorio
purgatory [ˈpʌrgəˌtorɪ] *s* (*pl:* **-ries**) (theol. & fig.) purgatorio
purge [pʌrdʒ] *s* purgación; purgante; *va* purgar; *vn* purgarse
purification [ˌpjurɪfɪˈkeʃən] *s* purificación
purify [ˈpjurɪfaɪ] (*pret & pp:* **-fied**) *va* purificar; *vn* purificarse
Purim [ˈpjurɪm] o [ˈpurɪm] *s* (rel.) Purim
purine [ˈpjurin] o [ˈpjurɪn] *s* (chem.) purina
purism [ˈpjurɪzəm] *s* casticismo, purismo
purist [ˈpjurɪst] *adj* purista; *s* casticista, purista
puristic [pjuˈrɪstɪk] *adj* purista
puritan [ˈpjurɪtən] *adj & s* puritano; (*cap.*) *adj & s* puritano
puritanic [ˌpjurɪˈtænɪk] o **puritanical** [ˌpjurɪˈtænɪkəl] *adj* puritano
Puritanism [ˈpjurɪtənɪzəm] *s* puritanismo
purity [ˈpjurɪtɪ] *s* pureza
purl [pʌrl] *s* flujo y murmullo; inversión de la puntada al tejer; guarnición rizada de tela, encaje o cinta; *va* tejer invirtiendo la puntada; bordar u orlar con guarnición rizada; *vn* fluir murmurando
purlieu [ˈpʌrlu] *s* terreno contiguo a un bosque; territorio lindante; jurisdicción; guarida, nidal; **purlieus** *spl* alrededores, inmediaciones
purlin o **purline** [ˈpʌrlɪn] *s* (carp.) correa
purloin [pərˈlɔɪn] *va & vn* robar, hurtar
purple [ˈpʌrpəl] *s* púrpura; *adj* purpúreo; *va* purpurar; *vn* purpurear
purple loosestrife *s* (bot.) salicaria
purple martin *s* (orn.) golondrina purpúrea
purplish [ˈpʌrplɪʃ] *adj* algo purpúreo
purport [ˈpʌrport] *s* significado, idea principal; [pərˈport] o [ˈpʌrport] *va* significar, querer decir; **to purport to** + *inf* pretender + *inf*
purpose [ˈpʌrpəs] *s* intención, propósito; fin, objeto; **for the purpose** al efecto; **for what purpose?** ¿con qué fin?; **on purpose** adrede, de propósito; **to good purpose** con buenos resultados; **to little purpose** con pocos resultados; **to no purpose** sin resultado; **to serve one's purpose** servir para el caso; *va* proponer, proyectar; proponerse
purposeful [ˈpʌrpəsfəl] *adj* porfiador; intencional; que obra con propósito
purposeless [ˈpʌrpəslɪs] *adj* sin propósito, sin fin determinado
purposely [ˈpʌrpəslɪ] *adv* adrede, de propósito
purposive [ˈpʌrpəsɪv] *adj* intencional; funcional; que obra con propósito
purr [pʌr] *s, va & vn* var. de **pur**
purse [pʌrs] *s* bolsa; colecta (*recaudación con fin caritativo*); *va* fruncir (*p.ej., los labios*)
purse crab *s* (zool.) cobo
purse-proud [ˈpʌrsˌpraud] *adj* envanecido por tener mucho dinero, orgulloso por ser rico
purser [ˈpʌrsər] *s* (naut.) contador de navío, comisario de a bordo
purse strings *spl* cordones de la bolsa
purslane [ˈpʌrslen] o [ˈpʌrslɪn] *s* (bot.) verdolaga
pursuance [pərˈsuəns] o [pərˈsjuəns] *s* prosecución
pursuant [pərˈsuənt] o [pərˈsjuənt] *adj* consiguiente; *adv* conforme; **pursuant to** conforme a, de acuerdo con
pursue [pərˈsu] o [pərˈsju] *va* perseguir; proseguir; seguir (*una carrera*)
pursuit [pərˈsut] o [pərˈsjut] *s* persecución; prosecución; busca o búsqueda (*p.ej., de la felicidad*); empleo, ocupación, oficio
pursuit plane *s* (aer.) caza, avión de caza
pursuivant [ˈpʌrswɪvənt] *s* persevante; acompañante, secuaz
pursy [ˈpʌrsɪ] *adj* (*comp:* **-sier;** *super:* **-siest**) obeso; asmático; flojo, holgado; fruncido, plegado
purulence [ˈpjurələns] o [ˈpjurjələns] o **purulency** [ˈpjurələnsɪ] o [ˈpjurjələnsɪ] purulencia
purulent [ˈpjurələnt] o [ˈpjurjələnt] *adj* purulento
purvey [pərˈve] *va* abastecer, proveer, suministrar
purveyance [pərˈveəns] *s* abastecimiento, proveimiento, suministro
purveyor [pərˈveər] *s* abastecedor, proveedor
purview [ˈpʌrvju] *s* alcance
pus [pʌs] *s* pus
push [puʃ] *s* empuje, empujón; (fig.) empuje (*fuerza, vigor*); *va* empujar; extender (*p.ej., conquistas*); **to push around** (coll.) tratar a empujones; **to push aside** hacer a un lado; **to push away** empujar, rechazar; apartar con la mano; **to push back** echar atrás: **to push through** forzar (*p.ej., una resolución*); *vn* empujar, moverse o apresurarse dando empujones; **to push ahead** adelantarse dando empujones; avanzar; **to push off** irse, salir; comenzar; apartarse de la orilla dando empujones; **to push on** avanzar, seguir adelante; **push** empujad (*indicación en una puerta*)
pushball [ˈpuʃˌbəl] *s* (sport) juego en que se emplea una pelota pesada y de grandes dimensiones que se empuja con cualquier parte del cuerpo excepto las manos
push button *s* pulsador, botón de llamada, botón interruptor
push-button control [ˈpuʃˌbʌtən] *s* mando por botón
push-button starter *s* (aut.) botón de arranque
push-button tuning *s* (rad.) sintonización de botón
push-button war *s* guerra por botón
pushcart [ˈpuʃˌkɑrt] *s* carretilla de mano
push drill *s* taladro de empuje
pusher [ˈpuʃər] *s* empujador; (coll.) persona emprendedora; (aer.) avión que lleva el motor propulsor en la parte de atrás
pusher engine *s* (rail.) locomotora de empuje
pushing [ˈpuʃɪŋ] *adj* emprendedor; entremetido, agresivo
push-over [ˈpuʃˌovər] *s* (slang) cosa muy fácil de hacer; (slang) persona muy fácil de dominar
pushpin [ˈpuʃˌpɪn] *s* crucillo (*juego de los alfileres*); chinche (*clavito*)
push-pull [ˈpuʃˈpul] *adj* (rad.) simétrico, de contrafase, de empuja-tira, de tira y empuje
push-pull amplification *s* (rad.) amplificación en disposición simétrica, contrafase
pusillanimity [ˌpjusɪləˈnɪmɪtɪ] *s* pusilanimidad
pusillanimous [ˌpjusɪˈlænɪməs] *adj* pusilánime
puss [pus] *s* gato; liebrecilla; chica, muchacha; (slang) cara, boca
Puss in Boots *s* El gato con botas
pussy [ˈpusɪ] *s* (*pl:* **-ies**) michito, gatito (*pequeño gato*); (bot.) amento
pussyfoot [ˈpusɪˌfut] *s* (*pl:* **-foots**) (slang) persona que anda a paso de gato, persona de evasivas; *vn* (slang) moverse a paso de gato, andar con cautela, no declararse
pussy willow *s* (bot.) sauce norteamericano de amentos muy sedosos (*Salix discolor*)
pustular [ˈpʌstʃələr] *adj* pustuloso
pustulation [ˌpʌstʃəˈleʃən] *s* pustulación
pustule [ˈpʌstʃul] *s* (bot. & path.) pústula
put [put] *s* echada; (com.) privilegio u opción de venta dentro de un plazo determinado por un precio estipulado ‖ (*pret & pp:* **put;** *ger:* **putting**) *va* poner, colocar; exponer, expresar; proponer para ser discutido; hacer (*una pregunta*); estimar, valuar; poner en ejercicio; imponer (*impuestos, multas*); arrojar, echar, lanzar; **to put across** llevar a cabo; hacer aceptar; **to put aside** poner aparte; rechazar; ahorrar (*dinero*); **to put away** guardar (*p.ej., en un cajón*); ahorrar (*dinero*); **to put by** ahorrar (*dinero*); **to put down** anotar, apuntar; sofocar (*una insurrección*); rebajar (*los precios*); **to put forth** echar, producir; extender; dar a luz; ejercer, emplear; proponer; **to put in** introducir en; interponer (*palabras*); pasar (*el tiempo*); **to put off** posponer, dejar para más tarde; deshacerse de; hacer guardar; **to put on** ponerse (*la ropa*); calzarse (*las botas*); poner en escena; llevar (*p.ej., un drama a la pantalla*); accionar (*p.ej., un freno*); fingir; atribuir; cargar (*impuestos*); **to put oneself out** incomodarse, molestarse; desvivirse, afanarse; **to put out** poner en la

calle; extender (*la mano*); sacar (*p.ej., un ojo*); apagar (*un fuego, la luz*); dar a luz, publicar; plantar; decepcionar, frustrar; (sport) sacar fuera de la partida; **to put over** (slang) llevar a cabo; **to put through** llevar a cabo; **to put to it** forzar a seguir un camino difícil, causar dificultad a; **to put up** mostrar, ofrecer; construir, edificar; poner a un lado; poner en el sitio acostumbrado; abrir (*un paraguas*); conservar (*fruta, legumbres, etc.*); hospedar; (coll.) incitar; (slang) proyectar con malicia; **put it here!** (coll.) ¡dame esa mano! ‖ *vn* dirigirse; **to put about** (naut.) cambiar de rumbo; **to put in** (naut.) entrar a puerto; **to put on** fingir; **to put up** parar, hospedarse; **to put up with** aguantar, tolerar

putamen [pju'temɪn] *s* (*pl:* **-tamina** ['tæmɪnə]) (bot.) putamen (*cuesco, huesco, núcleo*)

putative ['pjutətɪv] *adj* reputado, supuesto; putativo

putative marriage *s* (canon law) matrimonio putativo

putlog ['pʌt,lɔg] o ['pʌt,lɑg] *s* (carp.) almojaya

putlog hole *s* mechinal

put-out ['put,aut] *adj* contrariado, enojado, ofendido

putrefaction [,pjutrɪ'fækʃən] *s* putrefacción

putrefactive [,pjutrɪ'fæktɪv] *adj* putrefactivo

putrefy ['pjutrɪfaɪ] (*pret & pp:* **-fied**) *va* pudrir; *vn* pudrirse

putrescence [pju'trɛsəns] *s* pudrición, putrefacción

putrescent [pju'trɛsənt] *adj* putrescente

putrescible [pju'trɛsɪbəl] *adj* putrescible

putrescine [pju'trɛsin] o [pju'trɛsɪn] *s* (biochem.) putrescina

putrid ['pjutrɪd] *adj* pútrido; corrompido, perverso

putridity [pju'trɪdɪtɪ] *s* putridez; podredumbre

Putsch [putʃ] *s* intentona de sublevación; insurrección, sublevación

putt [pʌt] *s* (golf) golpe que hace meterse la pelota en el agujero o cerca de él; *va* (golf) golpear (*la pelota*) con cuidado para que corra a meterse en el agujero o cerca de él

puttee [pə'ti] o ['pʌtɪ] *s* polaina (*de cuero o paño*)

putter ['pʌtər] *vn* trabajar sin orden ni sistema; **to putter around** ocuparse en fruslerías, temporizar

putting green *s* (golf) campo de juego nivelado que circunda cada agujero

putty ['pʌtɪ] *s* (*pl:* **-ties**) masilla; (*pret & pp:* **-tied**) *va* enmasillar

putty knife *s* cuchillo de enmasillar, cuchillo de vidriero, espátula

putty powder *s* polvos de estaño, cenizas de estaño

put-up ['put,ʌp] *adj* (coll.) proyectado y preparado de antemano, premeditado con malicia

puzzle ['pʌzəl] *s* enigma; acertijo, rompecabezas; *va* confundir, poner perplejo; **to puzzle out** descifrar, desenredar; *vn* estar confundido, estar perplejo; **to puzzle over** tratar de resolver, tratar de descifrar

puzzlement ['pʌzəlmənt] *s* confusión, perplejidad

puzzler ['pʌzlər] *s* quisicosa (*objeto de pregunta muy dudosa*)

puzzling ['pʌzlɪŋ] *adj* enigmático

Pvt. abr. de **Private**

PW abr. de **prisoner of war**

pwt. abr. de **pennyweight**

PX ['pi'ɛks] *s* var. de **Post Exchange**

pyaemia [paɪ'imɪə] *s* (path.) pioemia

pycnostyle ['pɪknostaɪl] *s* (arch.) picnóstilo

pyemia [paɪ'imɪə] *s* var. de **pyaemia**

Pygmalion [pɪg'melɪən] *s* (myth.) Pigmalión

pygmy ['pɪgmɪ] *adj* pigmeo; *s* (*pl:* **-mies**) pigmeo

pyjamas [pɪ'dʒɑməz] o [pɪ'dʒæməz] *spl* var. de **pajamas**

pylon ['paɪlɑn] *s* pilón

pyloric [paɪ'lɑrɪk] o [paɪ'lɔrɪk] *adj* pilórico

pylorus [paɪ'lorəs] *s* (*pl:* **-ri** [raɪ]) (anat.) píloro

pyogenic [,paɪə'dʒɛnɪk] *adj* piogénico

pyorrhea o **pyorrhoea** [,paɪə'riə] *s* (path.) piorrea

pyramid ['pɪrəmɪd] *s* pirámide; **the Pyramids** las Pirámides; *va* dar forma de pirámide a; aumentar (*su dinero*) comprando o vendiendo al crédito y empleando las ganancias para comprar o vender más; *vn* tener forma de pirámide

pyramidal [pɪ'ræmɪdəl] *adj* piramidal

Pyramus ['pɪrəməs] *s* (myth.) Píramo

pyran ['paɪræn] o [paɪ'ræn] *s* (chem.) pirano

pyre [paɪr] *s* pira

Pyrenean [,pɪrɪ'niən] *adj* pirenaico

Pyrenees ['pɪrɪniz] *spl* Pirineos

pyretic [paɪ'rɛtɪk] *adj* pirético

pyretology [,paɪrɪ'tɑlədʒɪ] *s* piretología

pyrex ['paɪrɛks] *s* (trademark) cristal que resiste el calor del horno

pyrexia [paɪ'rɛksɪə] *s* (path.) pirexia

pyribenzamine [,pɪrɪ'bɛnzəmin] o [,pɪrɪ'bɛnzəmɪn] *s* (pharm.) piribenzamina

pyridine ['pɪrɪdin] o ['pɪrɪdɪn] *s* (chem.) piridina

pyriform ['pɪrɪfɔrm] *adj* piriforme

pyrites [paɪ'raɪtiz], [pɪ'raɪtiz] o ['paɪraɪts] *s* (mineral.) pirita

pyrogallic [,paɪro'gælɪk] *adj* pirogálico

pyrogallol [,paɪro'gælol] o [,paɪro'gælɑl] *s* (chem.) pirogalol

pyrography [paɪ'rɑgrəfɪ] *s* pirograbado

pyrolusite [,paɪrə'lusaɪt] o [paɪ'rɑljəsaɪt] *s* (mineral.) pirolusita

pyromancy ['paɪro,mænsɪ] *s* piromancía

pyromania [,paɪro'menɪə] *s* piromanía

pyrometer [paɪ'rɑmɪtər] *s* (phys.) pirómetro

pyrophorus [paɪ'rɑfərəs] *s* (*pl:* **-ri** [raɪ]) (chem.) piróforo

pyroscope ['paɪrəskop] *s* (phys.) piroscopio

pyrosis [paɪ'rosɪs] *s* (path.) pirosis

pyrosphere ['paɪrosfɪr] *s* pirosfera

pyrotechnic [,paɪro'tɛknɪk] *adj* pirotécnico; **pyrotechnics** *spl* pirotecnia

pyrotechnical [,paɪro'tɛknɪkəl] *adj* pirotécnico

pyrotechnist [,paɪro'tɛknɪst] *s* pirotécnico

pyroxene ['paɪrɑksin] *s* (mineral.) piroxena

pyroxylin o **pyroxyline** [paɪ'rɑksɪlɪn] *s* piroxilina

Pyrrha ['pɪrə] *s* (myth.) Pirra

pyrrhic ['pɪrɪk] *adj* pírrico; (*cap.*) *adj* pírrico

Pyrrhic victory *s* triunfo pírrico, victoria pírrica

Pyrrhonism ['pɪrənɪzəm] *s* pirronismo

Pyrrhus ['pɪrəs] *s* Pirro

pyrrole [pɪ'rol] o ['pɪrol] *s* (chem.) pirrol

Pythagoras [pɪ'θægərəs] *s* Pitágoras

Pythagorean [pɪ,θægə'riən] *adj & s* pitagórico

Pythian ['pɪθɪən] *adj* pitio

Pythian games *spl* juegos pitios

Pythias ['pɪθɪəs] *s* (myth.) Pitias

python ['paɪθɑn] o ['paɪθən] *s* (zool.) pitón; (*cap.*) *s* (myth.) Pitón

pythoness ['paɪθənɪs] *s* pitonisa

pyuria [paɪ'jurɪə] *s* (path.) piuria

pyx [pɪks] *s* (eccl.) píxide, copón; (Brit.) caja que se guarda en la casa de moneda para conservar especímenes para probarlos en peso y pureza

pyxidium [pɪks'ɪdɪəm] *s* (*pl:* **-a** [ə]) (bot.) pixidio

Q

Q, q [kju] *s* (*pl:* **Q's, q's** [kjuz]) décimaséptima letra del alfabeto inglés
Q. abr. de **quarto, queen, question** y **quire**
Q.E.D. abr. de **quod erat demonstrandum** (Lat.) **which was to be proved**
Q.M. abr. de **quartermaster**
Q.M.G. abr. de **Quartermaster General**
qr. abr. de **quarter** y **quire**
qt. abr. de **quantity** y **quart** o **quarts**
qts. abr. de **quarts**
qu. abr. de **quart, quarter, quarterly, queen, query** y **question**
quack [kwæk] *s* graznido del pato; charlatán; medicastro, curandero; ignorante que se las echa de tener conocimientos en una materia; *adj* falso; *vn* parpar (*el pato*)
quackery ['kwækərɪ] *s* (*pl:* **-ies**) charlatanismo
quacksalver ['kwæk,sælvər] *s* medicastro, curandero
quad [kwɑd] *s* (print.) cuadratín; (coll.) plaza cuadrangular, patio cuadrangular (*en las universidades*)
quadragenarian [,kwɑdrədʒɪ'nɛrɪən] *adj & s* cuadragenario
Quadragesima [,kwɑdrə'dʒɛsɪmə] *s* (eccl.) cuadragésima
Quadragesimal [,kwɑdrə'dʒɛsɪməl] *adj* cuadragesimal
quadrangle ['kwɑd,ræŋgəl] *s* cuadrángulo; plaza cuadrangular, patio cuadrangular
quadrangular [kwɑd'ræŋgjələr] *adj* cuadrangular
quadrant ['kwɑdrənt] *s* (astr. & geom.) cuadrante
quadrat ['kwɑdræt] *s* (print.) cuadratín
quadrate ['kwɑdret] o ['kwɑdrɪt] *adj & s* cuadrado; ['kwɑdret] *va* cuadrar; *vn* cuadrar (*conformarse*)
quadratic [kwɑ'drætɪk] *adj* (alg.) de segundo grado, cuadrático; **quadratics** *spl* ramo del álgebra que trata de las ecuaciones de segundo grado
quadratic equation *s* (alg.) ecuación de segundo grado, ecuación cuadrática
quadrature ['kwɑdrətʃər] *s* (astr., elec. & math.) cuadratura
quadrature of the circle *s* (math.) cuadratura del círculo
quadrennial [kwɑd'rɛnɪəl] *adj & s* cuadrienal
quadrennially [kwɑd'rɛnɪəlɪ] *adv* cada cuatro años
quadriceps ['kwɑdrɪsɛps] *s* (anat.) cuadríceps
quadriga [kwɑd'raɪgə] *s* (*pl:* **-gae** [dʒi]) (hist.) cuadriga
quadrilateral [,kwɑdrɪ'lætərəl] *adj & s* cuadrilátero
quadrille [kwə'drɪl] *adj* cuadriculado; *s* cuadrícula; cuadrilla (*baile*); (taur.) cuadrilla; *va* cuadricular; *vn* bailar una cuadrilla; cuadrillar (Am.)
quadrille ruling *s* cuadrícula
quadrillion [kwɑd'rɪljən] *s* (Brit.) cuatrillón
quadrinomial [,kwɑdrɪ'nomɪəl] *s* (alg.) cuadrinomio
quadripartite [,kwɑdrɪ'pɑrtaɪt] *adj* cuadripartido, cuatripartito
quadrivium [kwɑd'rɪvɪəm] *s* cuadrivio (*en la edad media, las cuatro artes matemáticas*)
quadroon [kwɑd'run] *s* cuarterón
quadrumanous [kwɑd'rumənəs] *adj* (zool.) cuadrúmano
quadruped ['kwɑdrupɛd] *adj & s* cuadrúpedo
quadrupedal [kwɑd'rupədəl] *adj* cuadrupedal
quadruple ['kwɑdrupəl] o [kwɑd'rupəl] *adj & s* cuádruple; *adv* cuatro veces; cuatro veces mayor; *va* cuadruplicar; *vn* cuadruplicarse
quadruplet ['kwɑdruplɛt] o [kwɑd'ruplɛt] *s* grupo de cuatro; cuatrillizo (*cada uno de los cuatro hijos de un mismo parto*)
quadruplicate [kwɑd'ruplɪkɪt] o [kwɑd'ruplɪket] *adj* cuadruplicado; [kwɑd'ruplɪket] *va* cuadruplicar
quadruplication [kwɑd,ruplɪ'keʃən] *s* cuadruplicación
quaestor ['kwɛstər] o ['kwistər] *s* cuestor
quaestorship ['kwɛstərʃɪp] o ['kwistərʃɪp] *s* cuestura
quaff [kwɑf] o [kwæf] *s* trago grande; *va & vn* beber en gran cantidad
quagga ['kwægə] *s* (zool.) cuaga
quaggy ['kwægɪ] *adj* (*comp:* **-gier**; *super:* **-giest**) pantanoso; blando como lodo
quagmire ['kwæg,maɪr] o ['kwɑg,maɪr] *s* cenagal; (coll.) cenagal (*negocio de difícil salida*)
quahog ['kwɔhɑg] o [kwə'hɑg] *s* (zool.) almeja redonda (*Venus mercenaria*)
quail [kwel] *s* (orn.) codorniz; *vn* acobardarse, cejar por temor
quaint [kwent] *adj* curioso, raro; afectado, rebuscado; fantástico, singular
quake [kwek] *s* temblor, terremoto; *vn* temblar
Quaker ['kwekər] *adj & s* cuáquero
Quakeress ['kwekərɪs] *s* cuáquera
Quakerish ['kwekərɪʃ] *adj* parecido a los cuáqueros; de cuáquero
Quakerism ['kwekərɪzəm] *s* cuaquerismo
quaker-lady ['kwekər,ledɪ] *s* (*pl:* **-dies**) (bot.) houstonia cerúlea
Quaker meeting *s* reunión de cuáqueros; (coll.) reunión en que hay poca conversación
quaking bog *s* tremadal
quaking grass *s* (bot.) tembladera, zarcillitos
qualifiable ['kwɑlɪ,faɪəbəl] *adj* calificable
qualification [,kwɑlɪfɪ'keʃən] *s* calificación; capacidad, idoneidad; requisito
qualified ['kwɑlɪfaɪd] *adj* calificado
qualifier ['kwɑlɪ,faɪər] *s* calificador; (gram.) calificativo
qualify ['kwɑlɪfaɪ] (*pret & pp:* **-fied**) *va* calificar; capacitar, habilitar; *vn* capacitarse, habilitarse
qualitative ['kwɑlɪ,tetɪv] *adj* cualitativo
qualitative analysis *s* (chem.) análisis cualitativo
quality ['kwɑlɪtɪ] *s* (*pl:* **-ties**) calidad; cualidad (*característica de una persona o cosa*); (dial.) gente de categoría; (phonet.) timbre; **in quality of** en calidad de; *adj* (coll.) de calidad, p.ej., **quality goods** mercancías de calidad
qualm [kwɑm] *s* escrúpulo de conciencia; duda, inquietud; basca (*malestar de estómago*)
qualmish ['kwɑmɪʃ] *adj* escrupuloso; bascoso
quandary ['kwɑndərɪ] *s* (*pl:* **-ries**) incertidumbre, perplejidad
quantify ['kwɑntɪfaɪ] (*pret & pp:* **-fied**) *va* cuantificar
quantimeter [kwɑn'tɪmɪtər] *s* cuantímetro
quantitative ['kwɑntɪ,tetɪv] *adj* cuantitativo
quantitative analysis *s* (chem.) análisis cuantitativo
quantity ['kwɑntɪtɪ] *s* (*pl:* **-ties**) cantidad
quantum ['kwɑntəm] *s* (*pl:* **-ta** [tə]) (phys.) quántum o cuanto; *adj* (phys.) cuántico
quantum mechanics *ssg* (phys.) mecánica cuántica
quantum theory *s* (phys.) teoría de los cuanta, teoría cuántica
quarantine ['kwɑrəntin] o ['kwɔrəntin] *s* cuarentena; estación de cuarentena; *va* poner en cuarentena
quarrel ['kwɑrəl] o ['kwɔrəl] *s* disputa, riña, pelea; cuadrillo (*saeta de cuatro aristas*); pe-

queño vidrio (*de vidriera*); cincel de albañil; **to have no quarrel with** no estar en desacuerdo con; **to pick a quarrel with** tomarse con; (*pret & pp:* **-reled** o **-relled;** *ger:* **-reling** o **-relling**) *vn* disputar, reñir, pelear
quarrelsome [ˈkwɑrəlsəm] o [ˈkwɔrəlsəm] *adj* pendenciero
quarrier [ˈkwɑrɪər] o [ˈkwɔrɪər] *s* cantero, picapedrero
quarry [ˈkwɑrɪ] o [ˈkwɔrɪ] *s* (*pl:* **-ries**) cantera, pedrera; caza, presa; rombo (*de vidrio, loza, teja, etc.*); (*pret & pp:* **-ried**) *va* sacar (*piedras*) de una cantera; sacar como de una cantera
quart [kwɔrt] *s* cuarto de galón
quartan [ˈkwɔrtən] *s* (path.) cuartana; *adj* cuartanal
quarter [ˈkwɔrtər] *adj* cuarto; *s* cuarto; trimestre; moneda de 25 centavos; pierna y partes adyacentes; calcañar; (astr.) cuarto de luna; (mil.) cuartel (*buen trato a los vencidos*); (naut.) cuadra; región, lugar; fuente, origen; **quarters** *spl* morada, vivienda; local; (aer.) compartimiento (*de tripulación*); (mil.) cuarteles; **at close quarters** pegados, muy cerca; **from all quarters** de todas partes; **to give no quarter to** no dar cuartel a; **to take up quarters at** alojarse en; (mil.) acuartelarse en; *va* cuartear; descuartizar; alojar, hospedar; (her. & mil.) acuartelar; *vn* alojarse, hospedarse; (mil.) acuartelarse
quarterback [ˈkwɔrtərˌbæk] *s* (football) uno de cuatro jugadores que juegan detrás de la línea
quarter day *s* (Brit.) día en que empieza un trimestre; (Brit.) día en que se paga un trimestre
quarterdeck [ˈkwɔrtərˌdɛk] *s* (naut.) alcázar
quartered [ˈkwɔrtərd] *adj* dividido en cuartos; aserrado en cuartos (*para mostrar la veta*); alojado, hospedado; (mil.) acuartelado; (her.) cuartelado
quartered oak *s* roble aserrado en cuartos
quarter-hour [ˈkwɔrtərˈaʊr] *s* cuarto de hora; **on the quarter-hour** al cuarto en punto, cada cuarto de hora
quartering [ˈkwɔrtərɪŋ] *s* división en cuartos; acuartelamiento; (her.) acuartelamiento; (her.) cuartel
quarterly [ˈkwɔrtərlɪ] *adj* trimestral; *adv* trimestralmente; (her.) en cruz; *s* (*pl:* **-lies**) publicación o revista trimestral
quartermaster [ˈkwɔrtərˌmæstər] o [ˈkwɔrtərˌmɑstər] *s* (mil.) comisario; (nav.) cabo de brigadas
quartermaster corps *s* (mil.) cuerpo de administración militar, intendencia
quartern [ˈkwɔrtərn] *s* cuarterón (*cuarta parte*)
quarter note *s* (mus.) negra, semínima
quarter round *s* cuarto bocel
quartersaw [ˈkwɔrtərˌsɔ] (*pret:* **-sawed;** *pp:* **-sawed** o **-sawn**) *va* aserrar (*un tronco*) longitudinalmente en cruz y luego en tablas
quarter section *s* terreno, por lo general, cuadrado, que tiene 160 acres
quarter sessions *spl* tribunal que se reúne trimestralmente
quarterstaff [ˈkwɔrtərˌstæf] o [ˈkwɔrtərˌstɑf] *s* (*pl:* **-staves** [ˌstevz]) pica (*lanza larga*)
quartet o **quartette** [kwɔrˈtɛt] (mus.) cuarteto; cuarteto (*grupo de cuatro*)
quarto [ˈkwɔrto] *adj* en cuarto; *s* (*pl:* **-tos**) libro en cuarto
quartz [kwɔrts] *s* (mineral.) cuarzo; (min.) quijo (*mineral de oro o plata*)
quartz glass *s* vidrio de cuarzo
quartziferous [kwɔrtˈsɪfərəs] *adj* cuarcífero
quartzite [ˈkwɔrtsaɪt] *s* (mineral.) cuarcita
quartz lamp *s* lámpara de cuarzo
quartzose [ˈkwɔrtsos] o **quartzous** [ˈkwɔrtsəs] *adj* cuarzoso
quartz plate *s* (elec.) placa de cuarzo
quartz sand *s* arena cuarzosa
quash [kwɑʃ] *va* sofocar, reprimir; anular, invalidar
quasi [ˈkwesaɪ] o [ˈkwɑsɪ] *adv* cuasi
quasi contract *s* (law) cuasicontrato
Quasimodo [ˌkwæsɪˈmodo] *s* (eccl.) cuasimodo, domingo de cuasimodo
quassia [ˈkwɑʃə] *s* (bot. & pharm.) cuasia
quaternary [kwɑˈtʌrnərɪ] *adj* cuaternario; (chem.) cuaternario; *s* (*pl:* **-ries**) cuaternario; (*cap.*) *adj & s* (geol.) cuaternario
quatrain [ˈkwɑtren] *s* cuarteto (*verso*)
quatrefoil [ˈkætərˌfɔɪl] o [ˈkætrəˌfɔɪl] *s* (bot.) hoja cuadrifoliada, flor cuadrifoliada; (arch.) cuadrifolio
quaver [ˈkwevər] *s* temblor, estremecimiento, vibración; (mus.) trémolo, trino; (mus.) corchea; *vn* temblar, estremecerse, vibrar; (mus.) trinar
quavery [ˈkwevərɪ] *adj* tembloroso, trémulo, vibrante
quay [ki] *s* muelle, desembarcadero
Que. abr. de **Quebec**
quean [kwin] *s* prostituta; moza o mujer atrevida y descocada; (Scotch) moza, muchacha
queasy [ˈkwizɪ] *adj* (*comp:* **-sier;** *super:* **-siest**) bascoso; nauseabundo; fastidioso, delicado; remilgado
queen [kwin] *s* reina; dama o reina (*en el ajedrez*); dama (*naipe que corresponde al caballo*); abeja reina, abeja maestra; (fig.) reina; *vn* ser reina; conducirse como reina
Queen Anne *s* Ana Estuardo
Queen Anne's lace *s* (bot.) dauco, zanahoria silvestre
queen bee *s* abeja maestra, abeja reina; (slang) marimandona, la que lleva la voz cantante
queen cell *s* maestril, realera
queen consort *s* esposa del rey
queendom [ˈkwindəm] *s* dominio de la reina; dignidad de reina
queen dowager *s* reina viuda
queenhood [ˈkwinhʊd] *s* dignidad de reina
queenly [ˈkwinlɪ] *adj* (*comp:* **-lier;** *super:* **-liest**) de reina, propio de una reina; como reina; como de reina
queen mother *s* reina madre
Queen of Sheba *s* reina de Sabá
queen olive *s* aceituna de la reina, aceituna gordal
queen post *s* péndola
queen regent *s* reina regente (*durante la ausencia del rey*); reina reinante
queen regnant *s* reina reinante
queen's English *s* inglés castizo
queen's ware *s* loza inglesa de color de crema
queer [kwɪr] *adj* curioso, raro; estrambótico, estrafalario; indispuesto, aturdido; (coll.) sospechoso, misterioso; (slang) falso; **queer in the head** (coll.) chiflado; *va* (slang) echar a perder; (slang) comprometer
queer fish *s* estrafalario
quell [kwɛl] *va* sofocar, reprimir; mitigar (*una pena o dolor*)
quench [kwɛntʃ] *va* apagar; templar (*el acero*)
quenched gap *s* (elec.) entrehierro de chispa amortiguada
quenching bath *s* (metal.) baño para templar
quenchless [ˈkwɛntʃlɪs] *adj* inextinguible
quercine [ˈkwʌrsɪn] o [ˈkwʌrsaɪn] *adj* (bot.) cercíneo o quercíneo
quercitrin [ˈkwʌrsɪtrɪn] *s* (chem.) quercitrina
quercitron [ˈkwʌrsɪtrən] *s* (bot.) cuercitrón o quercitrón (*árbol, corteza y colorante*)
quern [kwʌrn] *s* molinillo de mano
querulous [ˈkwɛrələs] o [ˈkwɛrjələs] *adj* querelloso, quejoso; cojijoso
query [ˈkwɪrɪ] *s* (*pl:* **-ries**) pregunta; signo de interrogación; duda, incertidumbre; (*pret & pp:* **-ried**) *va* preguntar, interrogar; marcar con signo de interrogación; dudar, expresar duda acerca de; *vn* hacer preguntas; expresar duda
ques. abr. de **question**
quest [kwɛst] *s* búsqueda; demanda (*p.ej., del Santo Grial*); **in quest of** en busca de; *va & vn* buscar
question [ˈkwɛstʃən] *s* pregunta; cuestión (*objeto de discusión*); proposición; **beside the question** que no viene al caso; **beyond question** fuera de duda; **in question** en cuestión; **out of the question** imposible, indiscutible, impensable; **to ask a question** hacer una pregunta; **to be a question of** tratarse de, ser cuestión de; **to call in question** (law) emplazar; (law) recusar; poner en duda; poner en tela de juicio; **without question** sin

duda; *va* interrogar; preguntar; cuestionar, poner en tela de juicio; *vn* interrogar, hacer preguntas
questionable ['kwɛstʃənəbəl] *adj* cuestionable
question mark *s* (gram.) interrogación, signo de interrogación, punto interrogante
questionnaire [,kwɛstʃən'ɛr] *s* cuestionario
quetzal [kɛt'sɑl] *s* (orn.) quezal
queue [kju] *s* coleta; cola (*hilera de personas*); *vn* hacer cola
quibble ['kwɪbəl] *s* sutileza, subterfugio; *vn* sutilizar, emplear subterfugios
quibbler ['kwɪblər] *s* sutilizador
quick [kwɪk] *adj* rápido, veloz; ágil, vivo; despierto, listo, penetrante; súbito; fácil de convertir en efectivo; **quick on the draw** u **on the trigger** agudo, listo, vivo, impetuoso; *adv* aprisa, pronto; rápidamente, velozmente; *s* carne viva; (lo) más hondo del ser, (lo) más profundo del alma; **the quick** los vivos; **the quick and the dead** los vivos y los muertos; **to cut** o **to sting to the quick** herir en lo vivo, tocar en la herida
quick-acting ['kwɪk'æktɪŋ] *adj* de acción rápida
quick assets *spl* (com.) disponibilidades, activo disponible
quick-break switch ['kwɪk,brek] *s* (elec.) interruptor de ruptura brusca
quick-burning ['kwɪk'bʌrnɪŋ] *adj* de quema rápida
quick-change artist ['kwɪk,tʃendʒ) *s* (theat.) transformista
quick-change gear *s* (mach.) engranaje de cambio rápido
quicken ['kwɪkən] *va* acelerar, avivar; aguzar, animar; *vn* acelerarse, avivarse; aguzarse, animarse
quick-freeze ['kwɪk'friz] (*pret:* **-froze;** *pp:* **-frozen**) *va* congelar rápidamente
quick grass *s* (bot.) grama del norte
quicklime ['kwɪk,laɪm] *s* cal viva
quick lunch *s* servicio rápido, servicio de la barra
quickly ['kwɪklɪ] *adv* aprisa, pronto; rápidamente, velozmente
quickness ['kwɪknɪs] *s* rapidez, velocidad; agilidad, viveza; penetración, sagacidad
quick return *s* (mach.) retroceso rápido
quicksand ['kwɪk,sænd] *s* arena movediza
quickset ['kwɪk,sɛt] *s* arbusto vivo; seto vivo; *adj* hecho de arbustos vivos
quick-setting ['kwɪk'sɛtɪŋ] *adj* de fraguado rápido
quicksilver ['kwɪk,sɪlvər] *s* azogue; *va* azogar
quickstep ['kwɪk,stɛp] *s* pasacalle; marcha escrita en compás acelerado; paso acelerado
quick-tempered ['kwɪk'tɛmpərd] *adj* vivo de genio, irascible
quick time *s* (mil.) paso redoblado, paso forzado
quick trick *s* (cards) baza rápida
quick-witted ['kwɪk'wɪtɪd] *adj* despierto, listo, perspicaz
quid [kwɪd] *s* mascada de tabaco; (*pl:* **quid**) (Brit. slang) libra esterlina
quiddity ['kwɪdɪtɪ] *s* (*pl:* **-ties**) esencia, quid; quisquilla, sutileza
quidnunc ['kwɪd,nʌŋk] *s* correveidile, curioso
quiescence [kwaɪ'ɛsəns] *s* quietud, reposo; (gram.) quiescencia
quiescent [kwaɪ'ɛsənt] *adj* quieto, reposado; (gram.) quiescente
quiet ['kwaɪət] *adj* quieto; silencioso, callado; (com.) encalmado (*mercado*); **to keep quiet** estarse callado; *adv* quietamente; calladamente; *s* quietud; silencio; **on the quiet** a las calladas, de callada; *va* aquietar; *vn* aquietarse
quietism ['kwaɪətɪzəm] *s* quietismo
quietist ['kwaɪətɪst] *adj & s* quietista
quietness ['kwaɪətnɪs] *s* quietud; silencio
quietude ['kwaɪətjud] o ['kwaɪətud] *s* quietud
quietus [kwaɪ'itəs] *s* golpe decisivo; muerte
quill [kwɪl] *s* pluma de ave; cañón de pluma; púa (*del erizo, puerco espín, etc.*)
quill driver *s* (scornful) cagatintas
quillwort ['kwɪl,wʌrt] *s* (bot.) isoete; (bot.) eupatorio purpúreo
quilt [kwɪlt] *s* edredón; *va* acolchar
quilting ['kwɪltɪŋ] *s* trabajo de acolchado; género acolchado; material para edredones
quilting bee *s* grupo de damas reunidas para hacer edredones
quince [kwɪns] *s* (bot.) membrillo (*árbol y fruto*)
quincunx ['kwɪnkʌŋks] *s* (hort.) quincunce; **in a quincunx** o **in quincunxes** a o al tresbolillo
quinin ['kwɪnɪn] o **quinine** ['kwaɪnaɪn] o [kwɪ'nin] *s* (chem.) quinina
quinoline ['kwɪnəlin] *s* (chem.) quinoleína o quinolina
quinquagenarian [,kwɪnkwədʒɪ'nɛrɪən] *adj & s* quincuagenario
Quinquagesima [,kwɪnkwə'dʒɛsɪmə] *s* (eccl.) quincuagésima
quinquennial [kwɪn'kwɛnɪəl] *adj* quinquenal
quinquennium [kwɪn'kwɛnɪəm] *s* (*pl:* **-a** [ə]) quinquenio
quinquereme ['kwɪnkwɪrim] *s* quinquerreme
quinsy ['kwɪnzɪ] *s* (path.) esquinencia, cinanquia
quint [kwɪnt] *s* (coll.) quintillizo
quintal ['kwɪntəl] *s* quintal
quinte [kæ̃t] *s* (fencing) quinta
quintessence [kwɪn'tɛsəns] *s* quintaesencia
quintessential [,kwɪntɛ'sɛnʃəl] *adj* quintaesenciado
quintet o **quintette** [kwɪn'tɛt] *s* (mus.) quinteto; quinteto (*grupo de cinco*)
quintile ['kwɪntɪl] o ['kwɪntaɪl] *s* quintilo
Quintilian [kwɪn'tɪljən] *s* Quintiliano
quintillion [kwɪn'tɪljən] *s* (U.S.A.) trillón; (Brit.) quintillón
quintuple ['kwɪntjupəl], ['kwɪntupəl], [kwɪn'tjupəl] o [kwɪn'tupəl] *adj & s* quíntuplo; *adv* cinco veces; cinco veces mayor; *va* quintuplicar; *vn* quintuplicarse
quintuplet ['kwɪntjuplɛt], ['kwɪntuplɛt], [kwɪn'tjuplɛt] o [kwɪn'tuplɛt] *s* grupo de cinco; quintillizo
quintuplication [kwɪn,tjuplɪ'keʃən] o [kwɪn,tuplɪ'keʃən] *s* quintuplicación
quip [kwɪp] *s* agudeza, ocurrencia; pulla, chufleta; sutileza, subterfugio; (*pret & pp:* **quipped;** *ger:* **quipping**) *va* decir en son de burla; *vn* burlarse, echar pullas
quipster ['kwɪpstər] *s* chistoso, pullista
quire [kwaɪr] *s* mano de papel; (b.b.) alzado
Quirinal ['kwɪrɪnəl] *adj* quirinal; *s* Quirinal
quirk [kwʌrk] *s* rareza (*acción caprichosa*); agudeza, ocurrencia; sutileza, subterfugio; vuelta repentina; rasgo (*en la escritura*)
quirt [kwʌrt] *s* látigo con mango corto y correa de cuero crudo retorcido
quisling ['kwɪzlɪŋ] *s* quisling (*traidor a la patria*)
quit [kwɪt] *adj* libre, descargado, sin obligaciones; **quits** *adj* en paz, corrientes (*por medio del pago o venganza*); **to be quits** estar desquitados; **to cry quits** pedir treguas; (*pret & pp:* **quit** o **quitted;** *ger:* **quitting**) *va* dejar; pagar (*una deuda*); **to quit** + *ger* dejar de + *inf; vn* irse, marcharse; parar; (coll.) dejar de trabajar
quitch [kwɪtʃ] o **quitch grass** *s* (bot.) grama del norte
quitclaim ['kwɪt,klem] *s* (law) renuncia; *va* (law) renunciar (*p.ej., una herencia*)
quite [kwaɪt] *adv* absolutamente, enteramente; verdaderamente; (coll.) bastante, muy
quitrent ['kwɪt,rɛnt] *s* (feud.) censo que se pagaba en dinero en vez de trabajo
quittance ['kwɪtəns] *s* quitanza; pago, retorno
quitter ['kwɪtər] *s* remolón, persona que deja fácilmente lo empezado, persona que se da fácilmente por vencida; desertor (*de una causa*)
quiver ['kwɪvər] *s* temblor, estremecimiento; aljaba, carcaj; *vn* temblar, estremecerse
quiverleaf ['kwɪvər,lif] *s* (bot.) alamillo
qui vive [ki'viv] (Fr.) ¿quién vive?; **to be on the qui vive** estar alerta
Quixote ['kwɪksət] *s* (fig.) quijote (*hombre quijotesco*)
quixotic [kwɪks'ɑtɪk] *adj* quijotesco
quixotically [kwɪks'ɑtɪkəlɪ] *adv* quijotescamente

quixotism ['kwɪksətɪzəm] *s* quijotismo; quijotada (*acto*)
quixotry ['kwɪksətrɪ] *s* quijotería
quiz [kwɪz] *s* (*pl:* **quizzes**) examen escrito u oral; broma pesada; bromista; (*pret & pp:* **quizzed;** *ger:* **quizzing**) *va* examinar; interrogar; burlarse de; mirar con aire burlón
quiz game *s* torneo de preguntas y respuestas
quiz master *s* (rad. & telv.) animador de un programa de preguntas y respuestas
quiz program *s* (rad. & telv.) programa de preguntas y respuestas, torneo radiofónico
quiz section *s* (educ.) clase dedicada a preguntas y respuestas, grupo de práctica
quizzical ['kwɪzɪkəl] *adj* curioso, raro; cómico; burlón, gracioso
quizzing glass *s* monóculo con mango
quodlibet ['kwadlɪbɛt] *s* cuodlibeto; (mus.) fantasía, miscelánea
quodlibetic [,kwadlɪ'bɛtɪk] o **quodlibetical** [,kwadlɪ'bɛtɪkəl] *adj* cuodlibético
quoin [kɔɪn] o [kwɔɪn] *s* esquina; piedra angular; cuña; (print.) cuña; *va* (print.) acuñar
quoin post *s* poste de quicio, poste de esclusa
quoit [kwɔɪt] o [kɔɪt] *s* herrón, tejo; **quoits** *ssg* hito (*juego de tejos*)
quondam ['kwandæm] *adj* antiguo, de otro tiempo
Quonset hut ['kwansɪt] *s* cobertizo de metal semicilíndrico
quorum ['kworəm] *s* quórum
quot. abr. de **quotation**
quota ['kwotə] *s* cuota
quotable ['kwotəbəl] *adj* citable
quota system *s* sistema de cuotas
quotation [kwo'teʃən] *s* cita (*de un texto*); (com.) cotización
quotation marks *spl* comillas
quote [kwot] *s* (coll.) cita; (coll.) cotización; **quotes** *spl* (coll.) comillas; **close quote** fin de la cita; *va & vn* citar; cotizar; **quote** cito
quoteworthy ['kwot,wʌrðɪ] *adj* digno de citarse
quoth [kwoθ] *1ª y 3ª personas del sg del pret* (archaic) dije, dijo
quotha ['kwoθə] *interj* (archaic) ¡no digas!, ¡vaya!
quotidian [kwo'tɪdɪən] *adj* cotidiano; *s* fiebre cotidiana
quotient ['kwoʃənt] *s* (math.) cociente
quo warranto [kwo wa'rænto] *s* (law) notificación legal por la cual se pregunta a una persona con qué derecho tiene ciertos privilegios y franquicias; (law) proceso legal emprendido contra tal persona
q.v. abr. de **quod vide** (Lat.) **which see**
qy. abr. de **query**

R

R, r [ɑr] *s* (*pl:* **R's, r's** [ɑrz]) décimoctava letra del alfabeto inglés; **the three R's (reading, 'riting, and 'rithmetic)** lectura, escritura y aritmética
r. abr. de **railroad, railway, road, rod, ruble** y **rupee**
R. abr. de **railroad, railway, Regina** (Lat.) **Queen, Republican, response, Rex** (Lat.) **King, River** y **Royal**
R.A. abr. de **Rear Admiral, Royal Academy** y **Royal Artillery**
rabbet ['ræbɪt] *s* (carp.) barbilla, rebajo, muesca; (carp.) embarbillado; *va* (carp.) embarbillar, rebajar; (carp.) cortar una muesca en
rabbi ['ræbaɪ] *s* (*pl:* **-bis** o **-bies**) rabino
rabbinic [rə'bɪnɪk] o **rabbinical** [rə'bɪnɪkəl] *adj* rabínico; **Rabbinic** *s* lengua rabínica
rabbinism ['ræbɪnɪzəm] *s* rabinismo
rabbinist ['ræbɪnɪst] *s* rabinista
rabbit ['ræbɪt] *s* (zool.) conejo
rabble ['ræbəl] *s* canalla, chusma; multitud turbulenta; (found.) hurgón
rabble rouser *s* populachero, alborotapueblos
rabble-rousing ['ræbəl,raʊzɪŋ] *adj* populachero
Rabelaisian [,ræbə'lezɪən] *adj & s* rabelesiano
rabic ['ræbɪk] *adj* (med. & vet.) rábico
rabid ['ræbɪd] *adj* rabioso
rabies ['rebiz] o ['rebɪiz] *s* (path.) rabia
raccoon [ræ'kun] *s* (zool.) mapache, oso lavador; piel de mapache
race [res] *s* raza; buena casta, buen abolengo; carrera; sabor o gusto particular (*del vino*); certamen (*que sugiere una carrera*); movimiento progresivo; corriente de agua fuerte y veloz; caz (*para tomar y conducir el agua*); **to run a race** correr una carrera; *va* competir con, en una carrera; hacer correr de prisa; acelerar (*un motor*) al máximo, hacer funcionar (*un motor*) a velocidad excesiva; **I'll race you to the corner** a ver quién llega primero a la esquina; *vn* correr de prisa; correr en una carrera; competir en una carrera; embalarse (*un motor*); (naut.) regatear
race course *s* pista de carreras; **autódromo**
race hatred *s* odio de razas
race horse *s* caballo de carreras
raceme [ræ'sim] *s* (bot.) racimo
racemose ['ræsɪmos] *adj* (bot.) racimoso
racer ['resər] *s* corredor; caballo de carreras; auto de carrera
race riot *s* disturbio racista, motín entre gentes de razas distintas
race suicide *s* suicidio de la raza
race track *s* carrera, pista de carreras, hipódromo
race wire service *s* servicio telegráfico y telefónico de noticias turfistas
Rachel ['retʃəl] *s* Raquel
rachialgia [,rekɪ'ældʒɪə] *s* (path.) raquialgia
rachidian [rə'kɪdɪən] *adj* raquídeo
rachis ['rekɪs] *s* (*pl:* **rachises** o **rachides** ['rækɪdiz] o ['rekɪdiz]) (anat. & bot.) raquis; cañón de pluma
rachitic [rə'kɪtɪk] *adj* raquítico
rachitis [rə'kaɪtɪs] *s* (path.) raquitis
rachitome ['rekɪtom] *s* (surg.) raquítomo
rachitomy [rə'kɪtəmɪ] *s* (surg.) raquitomía
racial ['reʃəl] *adj* racial
racing car *s* (aut.) coche de carreras
racing form *s* programa de las carreras de caballos
racism ['resɪzəm] *s* racismo
racist ['resɪst] *adj & s* racista
rack [ræk] *s* estante; percha (*en que se cuelga la ropa*); red de equipaje (*en los trenes*); pesebre; astillero; armero; rambla (*para estirar los paños*); paso fino (*del caballo*); nube pasajera que el viento arrastra en girones; recorrido de una tempestad; destrucción, ruina; dolor, tormento; caballete (*en que se daba tormento*); vestigio; (mach.) cremallera; **on the rack** en gran dolor, en gran sufrimiento; **to go to rack and ruin** caer en un estado de ruina total; **rack and pinion** cremallera y piñón; *va* estirar, forzar; atormentar; torturar en el caballete; despedazar; agobiar, oprimir; **to rack off** trasegar (*el vino*); **to rack one's brains** calentarse la cabeza, devanarse los sesos; *vn* caminar (*el caballo*) a paso fino
rack-and-pinion jack ['rækənd'pɪnjən] *s* gato de cremallera
racket ['rækɪt] *s* (sport) raqueta; raqueta (*para andar por la nieve*); alboroto, baraúnda; esfuerzo, pena, trabajo; (slang) trapisonda, trapacería; **rackets** *ssg* juego parecido al tenis que se juega en una cancha rodeada de paredes altas; **to raise a racket** armar un alboroto
racketeer [,rækɪ'tɪr] *s* trapisondista, trapacista; *vn* trapacear
rack rail *s* carril de cremallera
rack railway *s* ferrocarril de cremallera
raconteur [,rækɑn'tʌr] *s* cuentista
racoon [ræ'kun] *s* var. de **raccoon**
racquet ['rækɪt] *s* (sport) raqueta; raqueta (*para andar por la nieve*); **racquets** *ssg* var. de **rackets**
racy ['resɪ] *adj* (*comp:* **-ier**; *super:* **-iest**) espiritoso, vivo de genio; chispeante; que tiene aroma, fragancia, sabor especial; picante (*algo libre*)
rad. abr. de **radical**
radar ['redɑr] *s* (elec.) radar
radar-controlled ['redɑrkən'trold] *adj* mandado por radar
radarscope ['redɑrskop] *s* radarscopio o radaroscopio
radar screen *s* antena de radar
raddle ['rædəl] *s* almagre; *va* pintar o marcar con almagre; pintar (*el rostro*); entrelazar
radial ['redɪəl] *adj* radial
radial engine *s* motor radial
radial-flow turbine ['redɪəl,flo] *s* turbina radial
radian ['redɪən] *s* (math.) radián
radiance ['redɪəns] o **radiancy** ['redɪənsɪ] *s* brillo, resplandor; (phys.) radiación
radiant ['redɪənt] *adj* radiante, resplandeciente; (phys.) radiante; (fig.) radiante (*alegre, sonriente*); *s* (astr.) radiante
radiant energy *s* (phys.) energía radiante
radiant-panel heat ['redɪənt,pænəl] *s* calefacción a panel radiante
radiate ['redɪet] *adj* radiado; (bot. & zool.) radiado; *s* (zool.) radiado; *va* radiar; difundir (*p.ej., felicidad*); *vn* radiar, irradiar; extenderse de un punto central
radiation [,redɪ'eʃən] *s* radiación
radiation sickness *s* (path.) enfermedad de radiación, mal de rayos
radiator ['redɪ,etər] *s* radiador
radiator cap *s* (aut.) tapón de radiador
radical ['rædɪkəl] *adj* radical; (bot., chem., math., philol. & pol.) radical; *s* raíz, principio fundamental; (chem., math., philol. & pol.) radical
radical-changing verb ['rædɪkəl'tʃendʒɪŋ] *s* (gram.) verbo que cambia la vocal de la raíz
radicalism ['rædɪkəlɪzəm] *s* radicalismo
radical sign *s* (math.) signo de radicación
radicle ['rædɪkəl] *s* (bot.) radícula
radio ['redɪo] *s* (*pl:* **-os**) radio (*emisión; aparato*); (coll.) radiograma; **on the radio** en la radio; *adj* de radio; *va* **radiar, radiodifundir**

radioactive [ˌredɪoˈæktɪv] *adj* radiactivo
radioactive carbon *s* (phys.) radiocarbono
radioactivity [ˌredɪoækˈtɪvɪtɪ] *s* radiactividad
radio amateur *s* radioaficionado
radio announcer *s* locutor de la radio
radioastronomy [ˌredɪoəˈstrɑnəmɪ] *s* radioastronomía
radio beacon *s* radiofaro
radio beam *s* haz del radiofaro
radiobiology [ˌredɪobaɪˈɑlədʒɪ] *s* radiobiología
radiobroadcasting [ˌredɪoˈbrɔdˌkæstɪŋ] o [ˌredɪoˈbrɔdˌkɑstɪŋ] *s* radiodifusión
radiobroadcasting station *s* radiodifusora, radioemisora
radiochemistry [ˌredɪoˈkɛmɪstrɪ] *s* radioquímica
radio commentator *s* comentarista de la radio
radio compass *s* radiobrújula
radioelement [ˌredɪoˈɛlɪmənt] *s* (chem.) radioelemento
Radio Free Europe *s* Radio Europa Libre
radio frequency *s* (rad.) radiofrecuencia
radio-frequency [ˌredɪoˈfrikwənsɪ] *adj* (rad.) de radiofrecuencia
radiogoniometer [ˌredɪoˌgonɪˈɑmɪtər] *s* radiogoniómetro
radiogoniometry [ˌredɪoˌgonɪˈɑmɪtrɪ] *s* radiogoniometría
radiogram [ˈredɪoˌgræm] *s* radiograma
radiograph [ˈredɪoˌgræf] o [ˈredɪoˌgrɑf] *s* radiografía; *va* radiografiar
radiographic [ˌredɪoˈgræfɪk] *adj* radiográfico
radiography [ˌredɪˈɑgrəfɪ] *s* radiografía
radioisotope [ˌredɪoˈaɪsotop] *s* radioisótopo
radiolarian [ˌredɪoˈlɛrɪən] *s* (zool.) radiolario
radio listener *s* radioyente, radioescucha
radiolocation [ˌredɪoloˈkeʃən] *s* radiolocalización
radiologist [ˌredɪˈɑlədʒɪst] *s* radiólogo
radiology [ˌredɪˈɑlədʒɪ] *s* radiología
radiometer [ˌredɪˈɑmɪtər] *s* radiómetro
radiometry [ˌredɪˈɑmɪtrɪ] *s* radiometría
radio network *s* red de emisoras, red radioemisora, cadena de radiodifusoras
radio newscaster *s* cronista de radio
radiopaque [ˌredɪoˈpek] *adj* radiopaco
radiophone [ˈredɪoˌfon] *s* (phys.) radiófono; (rad.) radioteléfono
radiophonic [ˌredɪoˈfɑnɪk] *adj* radiofónico
radiophonograph [ˌredɪoˈfonəgræf] o [ˌredɪoˈfonəgrɑf] *s* radiofonógrafo, radiogramófono
radiophony [ˌredɪˈɑfənɪ] *s* (phys. & rad.) radiofonía
radiophoto [ˌredɪoˈfoto] *s* (*pl:* **-tos**) radiofoto; *adj* de radiofoto
radio receiver *s* radiorreceptor, radiorreceptora
radio repairs *spl* radiorreparaciones
radioscopy [ˌredɪˈɑskəpɪ] *s* radioscopia
radiosensitive [ˌredɪoˈsɛnsɪtɪv] *adj* radiosensitivo
radio set *s* aparato de radio; radiorreceptor
radiosonde [ˈredɪoˌsɑnd] *s* (meteor.) radiosonda
radio spectrum *s* (phys.) espectro de radio, espectro electromagnético
radio station *s* radioestación, estación emisora
radiotelegraph [ˌredɪoˈtɛlɪgræf] o [ˌredɪoˈtɛlɪgrɑf] *s* radiotelégrafo; *va* radiotelegrafiar
radiotelegraphy [ˌredɪotɪˈlɛgrəfɪ] *s* radiotelegrafía
radiotelephone [ˌredɪoˈtɛlɪfon] *s* radioteléfono; *va* radiotelefonear
radiotelephony [ˌredɪotɪˈlɛfənɪ] *s* radiotelefonía
radio telescope *s* radiotelescopio
radiotherapy [ˌredɪoˈθɛrəpɪ] *s* radioterapia
radiothermy [ˈredɪoˌθʌrmɪ] *s* radiotermia
radiothorium [ˌredɪoˈθorɪəm] *s* (chem.) radiotorio
radio transmitter *s* radiotransmisor
radiotron [ˈredɪətrɑn] *s* (trademark) radiotrón
radio tube *s* lámpara termoiónica, tubo radiógeno, tubo de radio
radio wave *s* onda de radio, radioonda
radish [ˈrædɪʃ] *s* (bot.) rábano
radium [ˈredɪəm] *s* (chem.) radio
radius [ˈredɪəs] *s* (*pl:* **-i** [aɪ] o **-uses**) (anat. & geom.) radio; radio (*p.ej., de acción*); **within a radius of** en . . . a la redonda, p.ej., **within a radius of five kilometers** en cinco kilómetros a la redonda
radix [ˈredɪks] *s* (*pl:* **radices** [ˈrædɪsiz] o [ˈredɪsiz] o **radixes**) (bot. & gram.) raíz; (math.) base (*para un sistema de números*)
radome [ˈredom] *s* (electron.) cúpula protectora de la antena
radon [ˈredɑn] *s* (chem.) radón
radula [ˈrædʒʊlə] *s* (*pl:* **-lae** [li]) (zool.) rádula
R.A.F. abr. de **Royal Air Force**
raffia [ˈræfɪə] *s* (bot.) rafia (*palmera y fibra*)
raffle [ˈræfəl] *s* rifa; *va & vn* rifar
raft [ræft] o [rɑft] *s* balsa, armadía; (coll.) gran número; *va* convertir en balsa; transportar en balsa; pasar en balsa
rafter [ˈræftər] o [ˈrɑftər] *s* par (*de un cuchillo de armadura*); cabrio, contrapar
rag [ræg] *s* trapo; (slang) fisga (*burla*); **rags** *spl* trapos (*prendas de vestir*); andrajos, harapos; **to be in rags** estar en andrajos; **to chew the rag** (slang) dar la lengua; (*pret & pp:* **ragged**; *ger:* **ragging**) *va* (slang) regañar; (slang) hacer fisga a
ragamuffin [ˈrægəˌmʌfɪn] *s* pelagatos; golfo, chiquillo haraposo
rag baby o **rag doll** *s* muñeca de trapo
rage [redʒ] *s* rabia; ardor, entusiasmo; violencia; boga, moda; **to be all the rage** estar en boga, estar de moda, hacer furor; **to fly into a rage** montar en cólera, montar en furor; *vn* arrebatarse; entusiasmarse
ragged [ˈrægɪd] *adj* andrajoso, harapiento, haraposo; áspero, desigual, raspado; cortado en dientes
raglan [ˈræglən] *s* raglán
ragman [ˈrægˌmæn] *s* (*pl:* **-men**) andrajero, trapero
ragout [ræˈgu] *s* (cook.) guisado
ragpicker [ˈrægˌpɪkər] *s* andrajero, trapero
ragtag [ˈrægˌtæg] *s* chusma, populacho; **ragtag and bobtail** canalla, gentuza
ragtime [ˈrægˌtaɪm] *s* (coll.) ritmo musical con acentos irregulares; (coll.) música popular de acentos irregulares
ragweed [ˈrægˌwid] *s* (bot.) ambrosía
ragwort [ˈrægˌwʌrt] *s* (bot.) hierba de Santiago
rah [rɑ] *interj* ¡ viva!, ¡ hurra!
raid [red] *s* ataque inesperado; invasión, incursión; *va* atacar inesperadamente; invadir; capturar (*p.ej., la policía un garito*)
raider [ˈredər] *s* invasor; buque corsario
rail [rel] *s* carril, riel; barandilla; guardalado (*p.ej., de un puente*); apoyo para los pies (*en un bar*); listón de madera; (naut.) obra muerta; (orn.) rascón, ralo acuático; bance (*para cerrar un portillo*); (carp.) peinazo (*p.ej., de una puerta*); **rails** *spl* títulos o valores de ferrocarril; **by rail** por ferrocarril; **off the rails** descarrilado; *adj* ferroviario; *va* poner barandilla a; **to rail off** cercar con barandilla; *vn* quejarse amargamente; **to rail at** injuriar, ultrajar
rail car *s* automotriz
rail center *s* centro ferroviario
rail chair *s* (rail.) cojinete
rail fence *s* cerca hecha de palos horizontales
railhead [ˈrelˌhɛd] *s* término de vía de un ferrocarril en construcción; cabeza de carril; (mil.) estación ferroviaria de víveres y municiones
railing [ˈrelɪŋ] *s* barandilla, pasamano
raillery [ˈrelərɪ] o [ˈrælərɪ] *s* (*pl:* **-ies**) burla, chanza, zumba
railroad [ˈrelˌrod] *s* ferrocarril; *adj* ferroviario; *va* enviar por ferrocarril; llevar o transportar por ferrocarril; (coll.) llevar a cabo con demasiada precipitación; (slang) encarcelar falsamente; *vn* trabajar en el ferrocarril, ser ferrocarrilero
railroad car *s* coche o vagón ferroviario
railroad crossing *s* paso a nivel
railroader [ˈrelˌrodər] *s* ferrocarrilero, ferroviario
railroading [ˈrelˌrodɪŋ] *s* construcción y manejo de ferrocarriles; trabajo en el ferrocarril; (coll.) ejecución demasiado apresurada
railway [ˈrelˌwe] *s* ferrocarril; *adj* ferroviario
raiment [ˈremənt] *s* prendas de vestir
rain [ren] *s* lluvia; (fig.) lluvia; **the rains** la época de las lluvias; *va* llover (*enviar como llu-*

via); *vn* llover; **it is raining** llueve; **to rain on** llover sobre; **rain or shine** llueva o no, con buen o mal tiempo
rainbow ['ren,bo] *s* arco iris; *adj* irisado
rainbow trout *s* (ichth.) trucha arco iris
rain check *s* billete que se devuelve a los espectadores de un espectáculo al aire libre en caso de lluvia
rain cloud *s* nube de lluvia
raincoat ['ren,kot] *s* impermeable, chubasquero
raindrop ['ren,drɑp] *s* gota de lluvia
rainfall ['ren,fɔl] *s* lluvia repentina; precipitación acuosa
rain gage o **gauge** *s* pluviómetro
rainproof ['ren,pruf] *adj* impermeable, a prueba de lluvia
rainstorm ['ren,stɔrm] *s* tempestad de lluvia
rain water *s* agua lluvia, agua llovediza
rainy ['renɪ] *adj* (*comp:* **-ier**; *super:* **-iest**) lluvioso
rainy day *s* día lluvioso; tiempo futuro de posible necesidad; **to save up for a rainy day** ahorrar dinero para asegurarse el porvenir
rainy season *s* estación de las lluvias
raise [rez] *s* aumento; alza, subida; *va* levantar; criar (*a niños, animales*); cultivar (*plantas*); reunir (*dinero*); suscitar (*una duda*); resucitar (*a los muertos*); avistar, columbrar; dejarse (*barba, bigote*); poner (*una objeción*); plantear (*una pregunta*); aumentar; aumentar fraudulentamente el valor de (*un cheque*); levantar (*tropas; un sitio*); (math.) elevar (*a potencias*)
raised [rezd] *adj* saliente, en relieve, de realce
raiser ['rezər] *s* criador (*p.ej., de ganado*); cultivador (*p.ej., de legumbres*)
raisin ['rezən] *s* pasa (*uva seca*)
raison d'être ['rezɔn 'dɛtrə] *s* razón de ser
rajah o **raja** ['rɑdʒə] *s* rajá
rake [rek] *s* rastro, rastrillo; rastrilladora (*rastro montado sobre dos ruedas*); raqueta (*de la mesa de juego*); calavera, libertino; desviación de la vertical; *va* rastrillar; escudriñar; atizar, avivar; barrer (*p.ej., una línea de soldados con una ametralladora*); **to rake together** acumular (*p.ej., dinero*); *vn* rastrear
rake-off ['rek,ɔf] o ['rek,ɑf] *s* (slang) dinero u otra cosa obtenida ilícitamente
rakish ['rekɪʃ] *adj* airoso, gallardo; listo, vivo; libertino
râle [rɑl] *s* estertor
rally ['rælɪ] *s* (*pl:* **-lies**) reunión popular, reunión política; recuperación, recobro; (tennis) acción de pegar la pelota de un lado para otro repetidas veces; (*pret & pp:* **-lied**) *va* reunir; reanimar; recobrar (*la fuerza, la salud, el ánimo*); ridiculizar, embromar; *vn* reunirse; reunirse y rehacerse; recobrarse (*p.ej., los precios en la Bolsa*); recobrar la fuerza, la salud, el ánimo; **to rally to the side of** acudir a, ir en socorro de
Ralph [rælf] *s* Rodolfo
ram [ræm] *s* (zool.) carnero; pisón; (naut.) espolón; (naut.) buque con espolón; émbolo de percusión (*de una bomba*); ariete hidráulico; (*cap.*) *s* (astr.) Aries; (*l.c.*) (*pret & pp:* **rammed**; *ger:* **ramming**) *va* dar contra, pegar contra, chocar en (*p.ej., un camión*); atestar, rellenar; apisonar; (naut.) atacar con espolón; *vn* chocar; **to ram into** chocar en
Ramadan [,ræmə'dɑn] *s* el Ramadán
ramble ['ræmbəl] *s* paseo; *vn* pasear; divagar (*andar a la ventura; hablar apartándose del asunto*); serpentear (*p.ej., un río*); extenderse serpenteando (*como hacen las enredaderas*)
rambler ['ræmblər] *s* paseador, vagabundo; divagador; (bot.) rosal de enredadera
rambling ['ræmblɪŋ] *adj* divagador; encantado (*dícese de una casa grande*); *s* divagación
rambunctious [ræm'bʌŋkʃəs] *adj* (slang) revoltoso, inmanejable; (slang) alborotado, turbulento
ramekin o **ramequin** ['ræmɪkɪn] *s* quesadilla; pequeña cazuela para quesadillas
Rameses ['ræmɪsiz] *s* Ramsés
ramie ['ræmɪ] *s* (bot.) ramio; ramina (*fibra*)
ramification [,ræmɪfɪ'keʃən] *s* ramificación
ramify ['ræmɪfaɪ] (*pret & pp:* **-fied**) *va* ramificar; *vn* ramificarse
ram-jet engine ['ræm,dʒɛt] *s* (aer.) motor autorreactor, estatorreactor, pulsorreactor
rammer ['ræmər] *s* pisón; baqueta de fusil
rammish ['ræmɪʃ] *adj* carneruno; maloliente; libidinoso
ramose ['remos] o [rə'mos] *adj* ramoso
ramous ['reməs] *adj* ramoso; ramiforme
ramp [ræmp] *s* rampa; *vn* moverse con violencia; saltar o precipitarse con furia; pararse en las patas traseras con la mano abierta y las garras tendidas
rampage ['ræmpedʒ] *s* alboroto; **to go on a rampage** alborotar, comportarse como un loco; [ræm'pedʒ] o ['ræmpedʒ] *vn* alborotar, comportarse como un loco
rampancy ['ræmpənsɪ] *s* exuberancia, extravagancia; violencia, desenfreno
rampant ['ræmpənt] *adj* exuberante, extravagante; violento, desenfrenado; (her.) rampante
rampant arch *s* (arch.) arco por tranquil, arco en rampa
rampart ['ræmpɑrt] *s* (fort.) terraplén; muralla; defensa, amparo
rampion ['ræmpɪən] *s* (bot.) rapónchigo
ramrod ['ræm,rɑd] *s* baqueta, atacador
ramshackle ['ræm,ʃækəl] *adj* desvencijado, destartalado
ran [ræn] *pret de* **run**
ranch [ræntʃ] *s* hacienda, granja; hacendados; *vn* trabajar en una hacienda; dirigir una hacienda
rancher ['ræntʃər] *s* hacendado
ranchman ['ræntʃmən] *s* (*pl:* **-men**) hacendado
rancid ['rænsɪd] *adj* rancio
rancidity [ræn'sɪdɪtɪ] *s* rancidez, ranciedad
rancor ['ræŋkər] *s* rencor
rancorous ['ræŋkərəs] *adj* rencoroso
Randolph ['rændɑlf] *s* Randolfo
random ['rændəm] *adj* casual, fortuito, sin proyectar; **at random** al azar, a la ventura
ranee ['rɑnɪ] *s* raní
rang [ræŋ] *pret de* **ring**
range [rendʒ] *s* escala (*p.ej., de velocidades, precios*); fila, hilera, ringlera; alcance; divagación; línea de tiro; campo de tiro; terreno de pasto; cordillera; línea de dirección; campo de actividad; autonomía (*p.ej., de un buque o avión*); cocina económica, hornillo; extensión (*de la voz*); serie o gama (*de colores*); clase, orden; **at close range** a quema ropa; **within range** a tiro; **within range of** al alcance de; *va* alinear; recorrer (*un terreno, el bosque*); ir a lo largo de (*la costa*); arreglar, ordenar; *vn* variar, fluctuar (*entre ciertos límites*); extenderse; divagar, errar; ponerse en fila; **to range over** recorrer
range finder *s* telémetro
range pole *s* (surv.) jalón
ranger ['rendʒər] *s* guardamayor de bosque; recorredor; perro ventor
Rangoon [ræŋ'gun] *s* Rangún
rangy ['rendʒɪ] *adj* (*comp:* **-ier**; *super:* **-iest**) ágil; de patas largas y fino de ancas; ancho, espacioso
rani ['rɑnɪ] *s* (*pl:* **-nis**) raní
rank [ræŋk] *s* fila; (mil.) grado, empleo; categoría, rango; condición, posición; distinción; **the ranks** los soldados de fila; el pueblo, la gente común; **to break ranks** (mil.) romper filas; **to close ranks** estrechar las distancias; (mil.) cerrar las filas; **to reduce to the ranks** degradar; **to rise from the ranks** llegar a oficial (*de soldado raso*); *adj* lozano, exuberante; denso, espeso; grosero; maloliente; excesivo, extremado; incorregible, rematado; indecente, vulgar; *va* alinear; ordenar; tener posición o grado más alto que; *vn* tener (cierta) posición o grado; ocupar el último grado; **to rank high** ocupar alta posición; ser tenido en alta estima; sobresalir; **to rank low** ocupar baja posición; **to rank with** estar al nivel de; tener el mismo grado que
rank and file *spl* soldados de fila; pueblo, gente común
rankle ['ræŋkəl] *va* enconar, agriar; *vn* enconarse
ransack ['rænsæk] *va* registrar, escudriñar; robar, saquear
ransom ['rænsəm] *s* rescate; *va* rescatar; redimir (*del pecado*)

rant [rænt] *s* lenguaje alborotado y retumbante; *vn* despotricar, delirar, hablar a gritos
ranula [ˈrænjələ] *s* (path. & vet.) ránula
ranunculaceous [rəˌnʌŋkjəˈleʃəs] *adj* (bot.) ranunculáceo
ranunculus [rəˈnʌŋkjələs] *s* (*pl:* **-luses** o **-li** [laɪ]) (bot.) ranúnculo
rap [ræp] *s* golpe corto y seco; taque (*ruido de golpe con que se llama a una puerta*); (slang) crítica mordaz; (coll.) bledo; **I don't care a rap** (coll.) no se me da un bledo de ello; **to take the rap** (slang) pagar la multa, sufrir las consecuencias; (*pret & pp:* **rapped;** *ger:* **rapping**) *va* golpear con golpe corto y seco; decir vivamente; (slang) criticar mordazmente; *vn* golpear con golpe corto y seco; **to rap at the door** tocar a la puerta
rapacious [rəˈpeʃəs] *adj* rapaz
rapaciousness [rəˈpeʃəsnɪs] *s* rapacidad
rapacity [rəˈpæsɪtɪ] *s* rapacidad
rape [rep] *s* rapto; estupro, violación; (bot.) naba; *va* raptar; estuprar, violar
rape oil *s* aceite de colza
rapeseed [ˈrepˌsid] *s* semillas de colza
Raphael [ˈræfɪəl] o [ˈrefɪəl] *s* Rafael
Raphaelesque [ˌræfɪəˈlɛsk] *adj* rafaelesco
raphania [rəˈfenɪə] *s* (path.) rafania
raphe [ˈrefi] *s* (*pl:* **-phae** [fi]) (anat. & bot.) rafe
rapid [ˈræpɪd] *adj* rápido; **rapids** *spl* rápidos (*de un río*)
rapid-fire [ˈræpɪdˈfaɪr] *adj* de tiro rápido; hecho vivamente
rapidity [rəˈpɪdɪtɪ] *s* rapidez
rapid transit *s* transporte rápido de viajeros
rapier [ˈrepɪər] *s* estoque, espadín
rapine [ˈræpɪn] *s* rapiña
rapping [ˈræpɪŋ] *s* (el) golpear (*de los espíritus*)
rapport [ræˈport] o [rɑˈpɔr] *s* relación, conformidad; **en rapport** de acuerdo
rapprochement [rɑprɔʃˈmɑ̃] *s* acercamiento, aproximación
rapscallion [ræpˈskæljən] *s* canalla, golfo, pícaro
rapt [ræpt] *adj* arrebatado, extático, transportado; absorto
Raptores [ræpˈtoriz] *spl* (zool.) rapaces
raptorial [ræpˈtorɪəl] *adj* predador; propio para asir y retener la presa; rapaz
rapture [ˈræptʃər] *s* rapto, éxtasis
rapturous [ˈræptʃərəs] *adj* extático
rare [rɛr] *adj* raro; poco usado (*dícese de una palabra o locución*); (cook.) poco asado
rare bird *s* mirlo blanco, rara avis
rarebit [ˈrɛrbɪt] o [ˈræbɪt] *s* var. de **Welsh rabbit**
rare earth *s* (chem.) tierra rara
raree show [ˈrɛri] *s* mundonuevo; espectáculo
rarefaction [ˌrɛrɪˈfækʃən] *s* rarefacción
rarefy [ˈrɛrɪfaɪ] (*pret & pp:* **-fied**) *va* enrarecer, rarefacer; *vn* enrarecerse, rarefacerse
rare gas *s* (chem.) gas raro
rarely [ˈrɛrlɪ] *adv* raramente, rara vez; excelentemente; extremadamente
rareness [ˈrɛrnɪs] *s* rareza
rarity [ˈrɛrɪtɪ] *s* (*pl:* **-ties**) rareza; (phys.) raridad
rascal [ˈræskəl] *s* bellaco, bribón, pícaro
rascality [ræsˈkælɪtɪ] *s* (*pl:* **-ties**) bellaquería, bribonada, picardía
rascally [ˈræskəlɪ] *adj* bellaco, bribón, pícaro
rase [rez] *va* var. de **raze**
rash [ræʃ] *adj* temerario; *s* brote (*erupción cutánea*)
rasher [ˈræʃər] *s* torrezno (*lonja de tocino*)
rashness [ˈræʃnɪs] *s* temeridad
rasp [ræsp] o [rɑsp] *s* escofina; sonido de escofina, ronquido; *va* escofinar; irritar, molestar; decir con voz ronca; *vn* hacer sonido áspero
raspberry [ˈræzˌbɛrɪ] o [ˈrɑzˌbɛrɪ] *s* (*pl:* **-ries**) (bot.) frambueso, sangüeso; frambuesa, sangüesa (*fruto*)
raspberry bush *s* (bot.) frambueso, sangüeso
rat [ræt] *s* (zool.) rata; (coll.) postizo; (slang) canalla; (slang) desertor; (slang) esquirol; (slang) soplón; **to smell a rat** olerse una trama, sospechar una intriga; (*pret & pp:* **ratted;** *ger:* **ratting**) *vn* cazar ratas; (slang) portarse como un canalla; (slang) soplar, delatar
ratable [ˈretəbəl] *adj* tasable, valuable; (Brit.) sujeto a impuestos o contribuciones
ratan [ræˈtæn] *s* var. de **rattan**
rat-a-tat [ˌrætəˈtæt] *interj* ¡ta, ta!, ¡tras, tras!
ratcatcher [ˈrætˌkætʃər] *s* cazarratas (*persona y animal*)
ratch [rætʃ] o **ratchet** [ˈrætʃɪt] *s* (mach.) rueda de trinquete, barra de trinquete; (mach.) trinquete (*garfio*); (mach.) mecanismo de trinquete
ratchet brace *s* berbiquí de trinquete
ratchet drill *s* taladro de trinquete
ratchet jack *s* cric de cremallera
ratchet screwdriver *s* destornillador de trinquete
ratchet wheel *s* rueda de trinquete
ratchet wrench *s* llave de trinquete
rate [ret] *s* razón (*cantidad medida por otra cosa tomada como unidad*); tipo (*p.ej., de interés*); velocidad; tarifa; clase, calidad; manera, modo; (Brit.) impuesto local; **at any rate** de todos modos; **at the rate of** a razón de; **at that rate** de ese modo, en ese caso; **at the same rate** al mismo ritmo; *va* valuar; estimar, juzgar; clasificar; regañar; *vn* ser considerado, ser tenido; estar clasificado; regañar
rateable [ˈretəbəl] *adj* var. de **ratable**
ratel [ˈretəl] o [ˈrɑtəl] *s* (zool.) ratel
rate of climb *s* (aer.) velocidad ascensional
rate of exchange *s* tipo de cambio
ratepayer [ˈretˌpeər] *s* (Brit.) contribuyente
rather [ˈræðər] o [ˈrɑðər] *adv* algo, un poco; bastante; antes, más bien; mejor dicho; por el contrario; muy, mucho; **had rather** preferiría; **would have rather** hubiera preferido; **rather than** antes que, más bien que; *interj* ¡ya lo creo!
rathskeller [ˈrɑtsˌkɛlər] *s* taberna o restaurante de sótano
ratification [ˌrætɪfɪˈkeʃən] *s* ratificación
ratify [ˈrætɪfaɪ] (*pret & pp:* **-fied**) *va* ratificar
ratiné [ˌrætɪˈne] *s* ratina (*tela*)
rating [ˈretɪŋ] *s* grado, clase, rango; justiprecio; clasificación; (Brit.) marinero
ratio [ˈreʃo] o [ˈreʃɪo] *s* (*pl:* **-tios**) (math.) razón; (math.) cociente
ratiocinate [ˌræʃɪˈɑsɪnet] *vn* raciocinar
ratiocination [ˌræʃɪˌɑsɪˈneʃən] *s* raciocinación
ration [ˈreʃən] o [ˈræʃən] *s* ración; (mil.) ración; *va* racionar; (mil.) racionar
rational [ˈræʃənəl] *adj* racional; (math.) racional; *s* (eccl.) racional
rationale [ˌræʃənˈɑlɪ] *s* razón fundamental; exposición razonada
rationalism [ˈræʃənəlɪzəm] *s* racionalismo
rationalist [ˈræʃənəlɪst] *s* racionalista
rationalistic [ˌræʃənəˈlɪstɪk] *adj* racionalista
rationality [ˌræʃəˈnælɪtɪ] *s* (*pl:* **-ties**) racionalidad; ademán o uso razonables
rationalization [ˌræʃənəlɪˈzeʃən] *s* acción de hacer racional; busca de excusas; (com. & math.) racionalización
rationalize [ˈræʃənəlaɪz] *va* hacer racional; cohonestar; (math.) racionalizar; *vn* buscar excusas
ration book *s* cartilla de racionamiento
rationing [ˈreʃənɪŋ] o [ˈræʃənɪŋ] *s* racionamiento
Ratisbon [ˈrætɪsbɑn] *s* Ratisbona
ratite [ˈrætaɪt] *adj* (orn.) corredor; *s* (orn.) corredora
ratline o **ratlin** [ˈrætlɪn] *s* (naut.) flechaste
ratoon [ræˈtun] *s* (agr.) retoño; (agr.) soca (*retoño de la caña de azúcar*)
ratsbane [ˈrætsˌben] *s* veneno para matar las ratas; trióxido de arsénico
rattail file [ˈrætˌtel] *s* lima de cola de rata
rattan [ræˈtæn] *s* (bot.) rota, roten; caña de la rota; roten (*bastón*)
ratter [ˈrætər] *s* cazador de ratas
rattle [ˈrætəl] *s* carraca, matraca; sonajero (*de niño*); matraqueo; traqueteo (*de una cosa que se transporta*); baraúnda; estertor (*del que agoniza*); anillos o discos de la punta de la cola de la serpiente de cascabel; *va* traquetear; atortolar, confundir; **to rattle off** decir rápida-

mente; *vn* traquetear; moverse o funcionar con traqueteo; hablar rápida y tontamente
rattlebrain ['rætəl,bren] *s* cascabel, casquivano
rattlepate ['rætəl,pet] *s* casquivano, charlador necio
rattler ['rætlər] *s* (zool.) serpiente de cascabel; (coll.) tren de carga rápido
rattlesnake ['rætəl,snek] *s* (zool.) serpiente de cascabel
rattletrap ['rætəl,træp] *s* trasto viejo; coche destartalado; (slang) tarabilla, parlanchín; (slang) boca; **rattletraps** *spl* chucerías, fruslerías
rattling ['rætlɪŋ] *adj* que traquetea, ruidoso; vivo, alegre; (coll.) enorme, extraordinario; *adv* (coll.) muy, sumamente
rattly ['rætlɪ] *adj* ruidoso, que traquetea
rattrap ['ræt,træp] *s* ratonera (*para cazar ratas*); trance apurado, atolladero
ratty ['rætɪ] *adj* (*comp:* **-tier;** *super:* **-tiest**) de ratas, como ratas; lleno de ratas; (slang) vil, ruin
raucous ['rɔkəs] *adj* ronco
rauwolfia [rɔ'wʊlfɪə] *s* (bot.) rauwulfia; (pharm.) rauwulfina
ravage ['rævɪdʒ] *s* estrago, destrucción, ruina; *va* estragar, destruir, arruinar
rave [rev] *vn* desvariar, delirar, disparatar; bramar, enfurecerse; **to rave about** hacerse lenguas de, deshacerse en elogios de
ravehook ['rev,hʊk] *s* (naut.) descalcador
ravel ['rævəl] *s* hilacha sin destorcer; (*pret & pp:* **-eled** o **-elled;** *ger:* **-eling** o **-elling**) *va* deshilar, destorcer; desenredar; enredar, confundir; *vn* deshilarse, destorcerse; desenredarse; enredarse
ravelin ['rævlɪn] *s* (fort.) revellín
raveling o **ravelling** ['rævəlɪŋ] *s* hilacha
raven ['revən] *s* (orn.) cuervo; (*cap.*) *s* (astr.) Cuervo; (*l.c.*) *adj* negro y lustroso (*como el plumaje del cuervo*)
ravening ['rævənɪŋ] *adj* voraz
ravenous ['rævənəs] *adj* voraz, hambriento, famélico; rapaz
ravin ['rævɪn] *s* var. de **rapine**
ravine [rə'vin] *s* hondonada, cañón
raving ['revɪŋ] *s* desvarío, delirio; *adj* desvariado, delirante; (coll.) extraordinario
ravioli [,rɑvɪ'olɪ] o [,rævɪ'olɪ] *spl* (cook.) rabioles
ravish ['rævɪʃ] *va* encantar, entusiasmar; raptar; violar (*a una mujer*)
ravishing ['rævɪʃɪŋ] *adj* encantador, pasmoso
ravishment ['rævɪʃmənt] *s* encanto, transporte; rapto; violación (*de una mujer*)
raw [rɔ] *adj* crudo; principiante, inexperto; ulceroso, en carne viva; crudo (*día, tiempo*); (slang) injusto, severo; *s* carne viva; llaga, úlcera
raw-boned ['rɔ,bond] *adj* descarnado, demacrado
raw cotton *s* algodón en rama
raw deal *s* (slang) mala pasada; **to give someone a raw deal** (slang) jugarle a uno una mala pasada
rawhide ['rɔ,haɪd] *s* cuero en verde; látigo hecho de cuero en verde; *va* azotar con látigo de cuero en verde
raw material *s* primera materia, materia prima
raw silk *s* seda en rama
raw sugar *s* azúcar amarillo, azúcar sin refinar
raw umber *s* tierra de sombra cruda
ray [re] *s* rayo (*de luz*); raya (*línea fina*); (bot.) bráctea; (zool.) radio; (ichth.) raya; (fig.) vislumbre; *va* radiar; tratar con rayos; *vn* irradiar; extenderse de un punto central
Raymond ['remənd] *s* Ramón, Raimundo
rayon ['reɑn] *s* rayón
raze [rez] *va* arrasar, asolar
razor ['rezər] *s* navaja de afeitar
razorback ['rezər,bæk] *s* (zool.) puerco cimarrón; (zool.) rorcual; sierra, cordillera
razor blade *s* hoja u hojita de afeitar
razor clam *s* (zool.) mango de cuchillo, muergo
razor strop *s* asentador, suavizador
razz [ræz] *s* (slang) irrisión; *va* (slang) mofarse de
razzia ['ræzɪə] *s* razzia

R.C. abr. de **Red Cross, Reserve Corps** y **Roman Catholic**
r-colored vowel ['ɑr,kʌlərd] *s* (phonet.) vocal de colorido de r
rd. abr. de **road** y **rod** o **rods**
R.D. abr. de **Rural Delivery**
reach [ritʃ] *s* alcance; estirón; extensión; extensión de un canal entre dos compuertas; extensión de un río entre dos recodos; (naut.) bordada; **beyond reach (of)** u **out of reach (of)** fuera del alcance (de); **within reach** al alcance de la mano; a tiro; **within reach of** al alcance de; *va* alcanzar; estirar; alargar, extender; pasar o entregar con la mano; ponerse en contacto con; llegar a; influenciar; cumplir (*cierto número de años*); *vn* alcanzar; alargar o extender la mano o el brazo; extenderse; (naut.) navegar de bolina; **to reach after** o **for** esforzarse por coger; echar mano a; **to reach into** meter la mano en; penetrar en
reachable ['ritʃəbəl] *adj* alcanzadizo
react [rɪ'ækt] *vn* reaccionar
re-act [ri'ækt] *va* volver a representar (*una escena, un drama*)
reactance [rɪ'æktəns] *s* (elec.) reactancia
reaction [rɪ'ækʃən] *s* reacción
reactionary [rɪ'ækʃən,ɛrɪ] *adj* reaccionario; *s* (*pl:* **-ies**) reaccionario
reaction turbine *s* turbina de reacción
reactive [rɪ'æktɪv] *adj* reactivo
reactor [rɪ'æktər] *s* (elec. & phys.) reactor
read [rid] (*pret & pp:* **read** [rɛd]) *va* leer; recitar (*poesía*); rezar; interpretar (*atribuir cierto fin a*); estudiar (*derecho*); leer en, adivinar (*el pensamiento ajeno*); **to read out of** despedir de (*p.ej., un partido político*); **to read over** recorrer, repasar (*un escrito*); *vn* leer; rezar, p.ej., **this page reads thus** esta página reza así; leerse, p.ej., **this book reads easily** este libro se lee con facilidad; **to read about** leer sobre; **to read between the lines** leer entre líneas; **to read of** leer acerca de; aprender o saber leyendo; **to read on** seguir leyendo; **to read up on** informarse por la lectura acerca de; [rɛd] *adj* leído (*enterado mediante la lectura*)
readable ['ridəbəl] *adj* leíble, legible; ameno, interesante (*libro*)
readapt [,riə'dæpt] *va* readaptar
readdress [,riə'drɛs] *va* volver a dirigir (*una carta*); poner nueva dirección a (*una carta*)
reader ['ridər] *s* lector; libro de lectura
readily ['rɛdɪlɪ] *adv* pronto; fácilmente, sin esfuerzo; de buena gana
readiness ['rɛdɪnɪs] *s* preparación; disposición; propensión; agilidad, destreza; disponibilidad; vivacidad (*de ingenio*)
reading ['ridɪŋ] *adj* lector; de lectura, para leer; *s* lectura; recitación, declamación; lectura o lección (*interpretación de un pasaje*)
reading book *s* libro de lectura
reading desk *s* atril
reading glass *s* lente para leer, vidrio de aumento; **reading glasses** *spl* anteojos para la lectura
reading lamp *s* lámpara de sobremesa
reading material *s* material de lectura
reading room *s* gabinete de lectura; sala de lectura
readjustment [,riə'dʒʌstmənt] *s* reajuste, reacomodo
readmit [,riəd'mɪt] (*pret & pp:* **-mitted;** *ger:* **-mitting**) *va* readmitir
ready ['rɛdɪ] *adj* (*comp:* **-ier;** *super:* **-iest**) listo, preparado, pronto; dispuesto; propenso; ágil, diestro; disponible; vivo; **to make ready** preparar; prepararse; (*pret & pp:* **-ied**) *va* preparar; *vn* prepararse
ready cash *s* dinero a la mano, fondos disponibles, dinero contante y sonante
ready-made ['rɛdɪ,med] *adj* hecho, confeccionado, p.ej., **a ready-made suit** un traje hecho
ready-made clothes *spl* ropa hecha
ready-made clothier *s* ropero, confeccionista
ready-made clothing *s* ropa hecha
ready-mixed paint ['rɛdɪ,mɪkst] *s* pintura preparada o hecha
ready money *s* dinero contante

reaffirm [ˌriəˈfʌrm] *va* reafirmar
reaffirmation [ˌriæfərˈmeʃən] *s* reafirmación
reagent [rɪˈedʒənt] *s* (chem.) reactivo
real [ˈriəl] *adj* real; auténtico; inmueble
real estate *s* bienes raíces
real-estate [ˈriəlɪˌstet] *adj* inmobiliario
real-estate broker *s* corredor de bienes raíces
realgar [rɪˈælgər] *s* (mineral.) rejalgar
real image *s* (phys.) imagen real
realism [ˈriəlɪzəm] *s* realismo
realist [ˈriəlɪst] *s* realista
realistic [ˌriəˈlɪstɪk] *adj* realista
realistically [ˌriəˈlɪstɪkəlɪ] *adv* de manera realista
reality [rɪˈælɪtɪ] *s* (*pl:* **-ties**) realidad; **in reality** en realidad
realization [ˌriəlɪˈzeʃən] *s* comprensión; realización; adquisición (*de dinero*)
realize [ˈriəlaɪz] *va* darse cuenta de, hacerse cargo de; realizar; hacer aparecer real; adquirir (*ganancias*); reportar (*ganancias*); *vn* realizar (*vender bienes rápidamente*)
really [ˈriəlɪ] *adv* realmente
realm [rɛlm] *s* reino
realtor [ˈriəltɔr] o [ˈriəltər] *s* corredor de bienes raíces
realty [ˈriəltɪ] *s* bienes raíces, bienes inmuebles
real wages *spl* salario real
ream [rim] *s* resma; **reams** *spl* (coll.) montones; *va* escariar
reamer [ˈrimər] *s* escariador; exprimidor (*para extraer el jugo de las frutas*)
reanimate [riˈænɪmet] *va* reanimar; *vn* reanimarse
reap [rip] *va* segar; cosechar; *vn* cosechar
reaper [ˈripər] *s* segador; segadora, máquina segadora
reaping machine *s* máquina segadora
reappear [ˌriəˈpɪr] *vn* reaparecer
reappearance [ˌriəˈpɪrəns] *s* reaparición
reappoint [ˌriəˈpɔɪnt] *va* volver a nombrar
reappointment [ˌriəˈpɔɪntmənt] *s* nuevo nombramiento
reapportion [ˌriəˈporʃən] *s* volver a prorratear
reapportionment [ˌriəˈporʃənmənt] *s* nuevo prorrateo
rear [rɪr] *adj* posterior, trasero; de atrás; de retaguardia; *s* parte posterior, parte de atrás; espalda; fondo (*de una sala*); cola (*de una fila, de un automóvil*); retaguardia; (slang) culo, trasero; **at** o **in the rear of** detrás de; al fondo de; *va* alzar, levantar; edificar, erigir; criar, educar; *vn* encabritarse, suspenderse (*un caballo*)
rear admiral *s* contraalmirante
rear axle *s* eje trasero
rear-axle housing [ˈrɪrˈæksəl] *s* (aut.) caja de puente trasero
rear-end [ˈrɪrˌɛnd] *adj* de cola, p.ej., **rear-end collision** colisión de cola
rear guard *s* retaguardia
rearm [riˈɑrm] *va* rearmar; *vn* rearmarse
rearmament [riˈɑrməmənt] *s* rearme
rearmost [ˈrɪrmost] *adj* último de atrás, último de todos
rearrange [ˌriəˈrendʒ] *va* volver a arreglar o disponer; (mus.) volver a adaptar
rearrangement [ˌriəˈrendʒmənt] *s* nuevo arreglo, nueva disposición; (mus.) nueva adaptación
rear-view mirror [ˈrɪrˈvju] *s* (aut.) retrovisor, espejo de retrovisión
rearward [ˈrɪrwərd] *adj* postrero, último; *adv* hacia atrás
rear wheel *s* (aut.) rueda trasera
rear window *s* (aut.) luneta, luneta posterior
reason [ˈrizən] *s* razón; **by reason of** a causa de, en virtud de; **in all reason** con razón; **in reason** dentro de lo razonable; **out of reason** fuera de razón; **to bring to reason** meter en razón; **to listen to reason** meterse en razón; **to stand to reason** ser razonable; *va & vn* razonar
reasonable [ˈrizənəbəl] *adj* razonable
reasonably [ˈrizənəblɪ] *adv* razonablemente
reasoner [ˈrizənər] *s* razonador
reasoning [ˈrizənɪŋ] *adj* razonador; *s* razonamiento
reason of state *s* razón de estado
reassemble [ˌriəˈsɛmbəl] *va* volver a reunir; (mach.) volver a armar o montar; *vn* volver a reunirse
reassess [ˌriəˈsɛs] *va* volver a amillarar; volver a apreciar, volver a estimar
reassessment [ˌriəˈsɛsmənt] *s* nuevo amillaramiento; nueva apreciación, nueva estimación
reassume [ˌriəˈsum] o [ˌriəˈsjum] *va* reasumir
reassumption [ˌriəˈsʌmpʃən] *s* reasunción
reassurance [ˌriəˈʃurəns] *s* afirmación reiterada, certeza restablecida; nueva confianza
reassure [ˌriəˈʃur] *va* volver a asegurar; tranquilizar
reassuring [ˌriəˈʃurɪŋ] *adj* tranquilizador
reattach [ˌriəˈtætʃ] *va* reatar
reawaken [ˌriəˈwekən] *va* volver a despertar; *vn* volver a despertarse
rebaptize [ˌribæpˈtaɪz] *va* rebautizar
rebate [ˈribet] o [rɪˈbet] *s* rebaja; *va* rebajar
rebec o **rebeck** [ˈribɛk] *s* (mus.) rabel
Rebecca [rɪˈbɛkə] *s* Rebeca
rebel [ˈrɛbəl] *adj & s* rebelde; [rɪˈbɛl] (*pret & pp:* **-belled;** *ger:* **-belling**) *vn* rebelarse
rebellion [rɪˈbɛljən] *s* rebelión
rebellious [rɪˈbɛljəs] *adj* rebelde
rebind [ˈriˌbaɪnd] *s* libro reencuadernado; [riˈbaɪnd] (*pret & pp:* **-bound**) *va* reatar; (sew.) ribetear; (b.b.) reencuadernar
rebinding [riˈbaɪndɪŋ] *s* (b.b.) reencuadernación
rebirth [ˈriˌbʌrθ] o [riˈbʌrθ] *s* renacimiento
rebore [riˈbor] *va* rectificar, retaladrar (*un cilindro*)
reborn [riˈbɔrn] *adj* renacido
rebound [ˈriˌbaund] o [rɪˈbaund] *s* rebote, repercusión; [rɪˈbaund] *vn* rebotar, repercutir; [riˈbaund] *adj* reatado; reencuadernado; *pret & pp de* **rebind**
rebroadcast [riˈbrɔdkæst] o [riˈbrɔdkɑst] *s* retransmisión; (*pret & pp:* **-cast** o **-casted**) *va* retransmitir
rebuff [rɪˈbʌf] *s* rechazo, desaire; *va* rechazar, desairar
rebuild [riˈbɪld] (*pret & pp:* **-built**) *va* reconstruir, reedificar
rebuke [rɪˈbjuk] *s* reprensión; *va* reprender
rebus [ˈribəs] *s* jeroglífico; (her.) armas parlantes
rebush [riˈbuʃ] *va* rellenar (*los cojinetes*) con metal blanco
rebut [rɪˈbʌt] (*pret & pp:* **-butted;** *ger:* **-butting**) *va* rebatir, refutar (*un argumento*)
rebuttal [rɪˈbʌtəl] *s* rebatimiento, refutación
rebutter [rɪˈbʌtər] *s* (law) dúplica, contrarréplica
rec. abr. de **receipt, recipe, record** y **recorder**
recalcitrance [rɪˈkælsɪtrəns] o **recalcitrancy** [rɪˈkælsɪtrənsɪ] *s* obstinación, terquedad
recalcitrant [rɪˈkælsɪtrənt] *adj* recalcitrante
recalescence [ˌrikəˈlɛsəns] *s* (metal.) recalescencia
recall [rɪˈkɔl] o [ˈrikɔl] *s* aviso, llamada (*para hacer volver*); recordación; revocación, anulación; retirada (*de un diplomático*); deposición de un funcionario público por votación popular; [rɪˈkɔl] *va* hacer volver, mandar volver; recordar; revocar, anular; retirar (*a un diplomático*); deponer
recant [rɪˈkænt] *va* retractar; *vn* retractarse
recantation [ˌrikænˈteʃən] *s* retractación, recantación
recap [ˈriˌkæp] o [riˈkæp] (*pret & pp:* **-capped;** *ger:* **-capping**) *va* recauchutar (*un neumático*)
recapitalization [riˌkæpɪtəlɪˈzeʃən] *s* recapitalización
recapitalize [riˈkæpɪtəlaɪz] *va* recapitalizar
recapitulate [ˌrikəˈpɪtʃəlet] *va & vn* recapitular
recapitulation [ˌrikəˌpɪtʃəˈleʃən] *s* recapitulación
recapture [riˈkæptʃər] *s* recobro; recordación; represa (*de una embarcación de los enemigos*); *va* recobrar; recordar (*a la memoria*); represar (*una embarcación*)
recast [ˈriˌkæst] o [ˈriˌkɑst] *s* refundición; reconstrucción (*p.ej., de una frase*); [riˈkæst] o

[ri'kɑst] (*pret & pp:* **-cast**) *va* refundir; reconstruir (*p.ej., una frase*)
recd. o **rec'd.** abr. de **received**
recede [rɪ'sid] *vn* retroceder; deprimirse; retirarse
receipt [rɪ'sit] *s* recepción; recibo; recibí; receta, fórmula; **receipts** *spl* entradas, ingresos; **on receipt of** al recibo de; **to acknowledge receipt of** acusar recibo de; **to be in receipt of a letter** obrar una carta en mi (nuestro) poder, p.ej., **I am in receipt of your letter** obra en mi poder su carta; **receipt in full** finiquito; *va* poner el recibí a (*una cuenta*)
receivable [rɪ'sivəbəl] *adj* recibidero; por cobrar, p.ej., **bills receivable** cuentas por cobrar
receive [rɪ'siv] *va* recibir; receptar (*cosas que son materia de delito*); **received payment** recibí; *vn* recibir; comulgar; (rad.) recibir; (sport) ser restador
receiver [rɪ'sivər] *s* receptor; recipiente; (telg., telp. & rad.) receptor; (telp.) receptor telefónico, auricular; (rad.) estación receptora; auricular de casco, receptor de cabeza; (phys.) recipiente (*de la máquina neumática*); receptador (*de cosas que son materia de delito*); (law) síndico (*en un concurso de acreedores o en una quiebra*); (law) receptor (*que hace cobranzas*); (sport) restador
receivership [rɪ'sivərʃɪp] *s* (law) sindicatura; (law) receptoría
receiving set *s* (telg., telp. & rad.) receptor, aparato receptor
receiving teller *s* recibidor (*de un banco*)
recency ['risənsɪ] *s* novedad, (lo) reciente
recension [rɪ'sɛnʃən] *s* recensión
recent ['risənt] *adj* reciente; **the recent past** el pasado próximo; (*cap.*) *adj* (geol.) holoceno, diluvial
recently ['risəntlɪ] *adv* recientemente; recién, p.ej., **recently arrived** recién llegado
receptacle [rɪ'sɛptəkəl] *s* receptáculo; recipiente (*vasija*); (bot.) receptáculo; (elec.) receptáculo, caja de contacto
receptacle plate *s* (elec.) escudete de receptáculo
receptacle plug *s* (elec.) clavija o ficha de receptáculo
reception [rɪ'sɛpʃən] *s* recepción
reception center *s* (mil.) centro de recepción
reception hall *s* sala de recepción, sala de recibo
receptionist [rɪ'sɛpʃənɪst] *s* (coll.) persona encargada de recibir visitantes a la entrada de una oficina, consultorio, etc.
receptive [rɪ'sɛptɪv] *adj* receptivo
receptivity [,risɛp'tɪvɪtɪ] *s* receptividad
receptor [rɪ'sɛptər] *s* receptador (*p.ej., de delincuentes*); (physiol.) receptor
recess [rɪ'sɛs] o ['risɛs] *s* intermisión, tregua; descanso; recreo, hora de recreo; hueco, nicho; depresión; retiro, escondrijo; [rɪ'sɛs] *va* ahuecar; empotrar; deprimir; hacer un nicho en; apartar, retirar; *vn* (coll.) tomar una recreación; (coll.) prorrogarse, suspenderse
recess hour *s* hora de recreo
recession [rɪ'sɛʃən] *s* retroceso; retirada; baja; depresión (*p.ej., de una pared*); contracción económica; procesión que vuelve a la sacristía; [ri'sɛʃən] *s* restitución; cesión de bienes a un propietario anterior
recessional [rɪ'sɛʃənəl] *s* himno que se canta al retirarse el sacerdote y el coro a la sacristía; *adj* cantado o tocado al retirarse el sacerdote y el coro a la sacristía; (geol.) de retroceso
recessive [rɪ'sɛsɪv] *adj* regresivo; (biol.) recesivo
recessive character *s* (biol.) carácter recesivo
recharge [ri'tʃɑrdʒ] *s* (elec.) recarga; carga de recambio (*p.ej., de extintor*); *va* recargar; (elec.) recargar
recheck [ri'tʃɛk] *s* nueva comprobación o verificación; *va* volver a comprobar o verificar
recherché [rəʃɛr'ʃe] o [rə'ʃɛrʃe] *adj* muy buscado, solicitado; esmerado, exquisito; alambicado, rebuscado
recidivism [rɪ'sɪdɪvɪzəm] *s* recidivismo
recidivist [rɪ'sɪdɪvɪst] *s* recidivista
recipe ['rɛsɪpɪ] *s* fórmula, receta, receta de cocina
recipient [rɪ'sɪpɪənt] *adj & s* recibidor; recipiente
reciprocal [rɪ'sɪprəkəl] *adj* recíproco; (gram.) recíproco; *s* cosa recíproca; (math.) recíproca
reciprocally [rɪ'sɪprəkəlɪ] *adv* recíprocamente
reciprocate [rɪ'sɪprəket] *va* intercambiar, trocar; corresponder a (*p.ej., la amistad de una persona*); reciprocar, hacer corresponder; (mach.) dar movimiento alternativo o de vaivén a; *vn* alternar; reciprocarse, corresponder; (mach.) tener movimiento alternativo o de vaivén
reciprocating [rɪ'sɪprə,ketɪŋ] *adj* alternativo, de vaivén; de movimiento alternativo
reciprocating engine *s* máquina de movimiento alternativo
reciprocation [rɪ,sɪprə'keʃən] *s* intercambio; reciprocación, correspondencia; alternación
reciprocity [,rɛsɪ'prɑsɪtɪ] *s* reciprocidad; (com.) reciprocidad (*entre dos naciones*)
recital [rɪ'saɪtəl] *s* narración; (mus.) recital
recitation [,rɛsɪ'teʃən] *s* recitación; narración
recitative ['rɛsɪ,tetɪv] o [rɪ'saɪtətɪv] *adj* recitativo; [,rɛsɪtə'tiv] *adj* (mus.) recitativo; *s* (mus.) recitado
recite [rɪ'saɪt] *va* recitar; narrar
reck [rɛk] *va* preocuparse por; *vn* preocuparse; (archaic) importar
reckless ['rɛklɪs] *adj* atolondrado, inconsiderado, temerario
recklessness ['rɛklɪsnɪs] *s* atolondramiento, inconsideración, temeridad
reckon ['rɛkən] *va* calcular; considerar, estimar; (coll.) calcular (*pensar, conjeturar*); *vn* calcular; **to reckon on** contar con; **to reckon with** tener en cuenta, tomar en serio
reckoning ['rɛkənɪŋ] *s* cálculo, cómputo; cuenta; arreglo o ajuste de cuentas; (naut.) estima; **to be out of one's reckoning** estar lejos de la cuenta, engañarse en el cálculo
reclaim [ri'klem] *va* reclamar (*lo que pertenece a uno*); [rɪ'klem] *va* hacer utilizable; hacer labrantío (*un terreno*); ganar (*terreno*) a la mar; recuperar (*materiales usados*); conducir o guiar (*a los que hacen mala vida*); (law) reclamar; *vn* reclamar (*protestar*)
reclamation [,rɛklə'meʃən] *s* utilización (*de materiales usados*); recuperación; reclamación (*protesta*); (law) reclamación
recline [rɪ'klaɪn] *va* reclinar; *vn* reclinarse
reclining [rɪ'klaɪnɪŋ] *adj* reclinable
reclothe [ri'kloð] *va* volver a vestir
recluse [rɪ'klus] *adj* solitario; [rɪ'klus] o ['rɛklus] *s* solitario, ermitaño
reclusion [rɪ'kluʒən] *s* reclusión, encierro
recognition [,rɛkəg'nɪʃən] *s* reconocimiento; (dipl.) reconocimiento
recognizable ['rɛkəg,naɪzəbəl] *adj* reconocible
recognizance [rɪ'kɑgnɪzəns] o [rɪ'kɑnɪzəns] *s* (law) obligación (*escritura en que uno se obliga a cumplir un acto determinado*); (law) suma que uno tiene que perder por incumplimiento de una obligación
recognize ['rɛkəgnaɪz] *va* reconocer
recoil [rɪ'kɔɪl] *s* reculada; reculada, culatazo (*de un arma de fuego*); *vn* recular, apartarse; recular (*un arma de fuego*); reaccionar
recollect [,rɛkə'lɛkt] *va & vn* recordar
re-collect [,rikə'lɛkt] *va* recoger, reunir; recobrar; **to re-collect oneself** componerse, recobrar la calma; *vn* reunirse, volver a juntarse
recollection [,rɛkə'lɛkʃən] *s* recordación; recolección, recogimiento
recommence [,rikə'mɛns] *va* recomenzar
recommend [,rɛkə'mɛnd] *va* recomendar
recommendation [,rɛkəmɛn'deʃən] *s* recomendación
recommendatory [,rɛkə'mɛndə,torɪ] *adj* recomendatorio
recommender [,rɛkə'mɛndər] *s* recomendante
recommit [,rikə'mɪt] (*pret & pp:* **-mitted;** *ger:* **-mitting**) *va* volver a confiar, volver a entregar; volver a cometer; volver a someter; volver a comprometer; volver a internar
recommitment [,rikə'mɪtmənt] o **recommittal** [,rikə'mɪtəl] *s* nueva comisión; nueva internación; nuevo compromiso

recompense ['rɛkəmpɛns] *s* recompensa; *va* recompensar
recompose [,rikəm'poz] *va* recomponer
recomposition [,rikampə'zɪʃən] *s* recomposición
reconcilable ['rɛkən,saɪləbəl] *adj* reconciliable
reconcile ['rɛkənsaɪl] *va* reconciliar; (eccl.) reconciliar; **to become reconciled** reconciliarse (*dos o más personas*); **to reconcile oneself** resignarse, someterse
reconcilement ['rɛkən,saɪlmənt] o **reconciliation** [,rɛkən,sɪlɪ'eʃən] *s* reconciliación
reconciliatory [,rɛkən'sɪlɪə,torɪ] *adj* reconciliador
recondite ['rɛkəndaɪt] o [rɪ'kandaɪt] *adj* recóndito
recondition [,rikən'dɪʃən] *va* reacondicionar
reconnaissance [rɪ'kanɪsəns] *s* (mil.) reconocimiento
reconnoiter o **reconnoitre** [,rɛkə'nɔɪtər] o [,rikə'nɔɪtər] *va & vn* (mil.) reconocer
reconquer [ri'kaŋkər] *va* reconquistar
reconquest [ri'kaŋkwɛst] *s* reconquista; *va* reconquistar
reconsider [,rikən'sɪdər] *va* reconsiderar
reconsideration [,rikən,sɪdə'reʃən] *s* reconsideración
reconstituent [,rikən'stɪtjuənt] *adj & s* reconstituyente
reconstitute [ri'kanstɪtjut] o [ri'kanstɪtut] *va* reconstituir
reconstitution [ri,kanstɪ'tjuʃən] o [ri,kanstɪ'tuʃən] *s* reconstitución
reconstruct [,rikən'strʌkt] *va* reconstruir
reconstruction [,rikən'strʌkʃən] *s* reconstrucción
reconstructive [,rikən'strʌktɪv] *adj* reconstructor; reconstructivo
reconvene [,rikən'vin] *va* convocar de nuevo; *vn* convenir de nuevo, volver a juntarse o reunirse
reconvention [,rikən'vɛnʃən] *s* (law) reconvención
reconversion [,rikən'vʌrʒən] o [,rikən'vʌrʃən] *s* reconversión
reconvert [,rikən'vʌrt] *va* reconvertir
reconveyance [,rikən'veəns] *s* devolución; escritura de traspaso al poseedor anterior
record ['rɛkərd] *s* registro; anotación; ficha, historia personal; protocolo (*de un notario*); disco (fonográfico); cilindro (fonográfico); (educ.) expediente académico; (sport) record, plusmarca; **records** *spl* anales, memorias; archivo; **off the record** confidencialmente; **on record** registrado; **to break a record** batir un record; superar precedentes; **to make a record** establecer un record; grabar un disco; *adj* máximo; notable, sin precedentes; [rɪ'kɔrd] *va* registrar; asentar; inscribir; protocolar; grabar (*un disco fonográfico*); grabar en disco fonográfico
record breaker *s* (sport) plusmarquista
record changer *s* cambiadiscos, tocadiscos automático
recorder [rɪ'kɔrdər] *s* registrador; contador, indicador; grabador, grabadora o registrador (*de fonógrafo*); juez recopilador
recorder of deeds *s* registrador de la propiedad
recordership [rɪ'kɔrdərʃɪp] *s* cargo u oficio de registrador
record holder *s* (sport) recordman
recording [rɪ'kɔrdɪŋ] *adj* registrador; magnetofónico (*alambre o cinta*); *s* registro; grabación o grabado (*de discos fonográficos*)
recording head *s* cabeza de registro o cabeza grabadora
recording secretary *s* secretario escribiente, secretario de actas
recording tape *s* cinta magnetofónica
record library *s* discoteca
record player *s* tocadiscos
re-count ['rikaunt] o [ri'kaunt] *s* recuento; [ri'kaunt] *va* recontar
recount [rɪ'kaunt] *va* recontar, referir
recoup [rɪ'kup] *va* recobrar; resarcir; **to recoup oneself** recobrarse; *vn* recobrarse
recourse [rɪ'kors] o ['rikors] *s* recurso; paño de lágrimas; **to have recourse to** recurrir a
recover [rɪ'kʌvər] *va* recobrar; recuperar; libertar, rescatar; (law) reivindicar; **to recover oneself** contenerse; recobrar el equilibrio; *vn* recobrarse; recobrarse de la enfermedad, recobrar la salud; (law) ganar un pleito
re-cover [ri'kʌvər] *va* recubrir
recovery [rɪ'kʌvərɪ] *s* (*pl:* **-ies**) recobro; recuperación; (law) reivindicación; **past recovery** sin remedio
recreancy ['rɛkrɪənsɪ] *s* pusilanimidad; deslealtad, traición
recreant ['rɛkrɪənt] *adj & s* cobarde; traidor
recreate ['rɛkrɪet] *va* recrear (*divertir*); *vn* recrearse
re-create [,rikri'et] *va* recrear (*crear o producir de nuevo*)
recreation [,rɛkrɪ'eʃən] *s* recreación, recreo
recreational [,rɛkrɪ'eʃənəl] *adj* de recreación
recreation hall *s* salón de recreo
recreative ['rɛkrɪ,etɪv] *adj* recreativo
recrement ['rɛkrɪmənt] *s* (physiol.) recremento
recriminate [rɪ'krɪmɪnet] *va* recriminar (*una acusación*); recriminar contra (*un acusador*); *vn* recriminar
recrimination [rɪ,krɪmɪ'neʃən] *s* recriminación
recriminative [rɪ'krɪmɪ,netɪv] o **recriminatory** [rɪ'krɪmɪnə,torɪ] *adj* recriminatorio
recross [ri'krɔs] o [ri'kras] *va* recruzar; *vn* recruzarse
recrudescence [,rikru'dɛsəns] *s* recrudescencia
recrudescent [,rikru'dɛsənt] *adj* recrudescente
recruit [rɪ'krut] *s* recluta; *va* reclutar; reforzar con reclutas, proveer de reclutas; aumentar o mantener el número de; restablecer, rehacer; abastecer; *vn* alistar reclutas; ganar reclutas; restablecerse, rehacerse, reponerse
recruitment [rɪ'krutmənt] *s* reclutamiento
rect. abr. de **receipt, rector** y **rectory**
rectal ['rɛktəl] *adj* rectal
rectangle ['rɛktæŋgəl] *s* (geom.) rectángulo
rectangular [rɛk'tæŋgjələr] *adj* rectangular
rectification [,rɛktɪfɪ'keʃən] *s* rectificación
rectifier ['rɛktɪ,faɪər] *s* rectificador; (chem. & elec.) rectificador
rectify ['rɛktɪfaɪ] (*pret & pp:* **-fied**) rectificar; (chem. & elec.) rectificar
rectilinear [,rɛktɪ'lɪnɪər] *adj* rectilíneo
rectinerved ['rɛktɪ,nʌrvd] *adj* (bot.) rectinervio
rectitude ['rɛktɪtjud] o ['rɛktɪtud] *s* rectitud, probidad, corrección
recto ['rɛkto] *s* (*pl:* **-tos**) (print.) recto
rectocele ['rɛktəsil] *s* (path.) rectocele
rector ['rɛktər] *s* rector
rectorate ['rɛktərɪt] *s* rectorado
rectory ['rɛktərɪ] *s* (*pl:* **-ries**) casa del rector; (Brit.) rectoría
rectrix ['rɛktrɪks] *s* (*pl:* **rectrices** [rɛk'traɪsiz]) (orn.) rectriz
rectum ['rɛktəm] *s* (*pl:* **-ta** [tə]) (anat.) recto
rectus ['rɛktəs] *s* (*pl:* **-ti** [taɪ]) (anat.) recto (*músculo*)
recumbency [rɪ'kʌmbənsɪ] *s* reclinación
recumbent [rɪ'kʌmbənt] *adj* reclinado
recuperate [rɪ'kjupəret] *va* recuperar; restablecer, reponer; *vn* recuperarse, recobrarse
recuperation [rɪ,kjupə'reʃən] *s* recuperación; restablecimiento
recuperative [rɪ'kjupə,retɪv] *adj* recuperativo
recuperator [rɪ'kjupə,retər] *s* (mach.) recuperador
recur [rɪ'kʌr] (*pret & pp:* **-curred;** *ger:* **-curring**) *vn* volver a ocurrir, repetirse; volver (*a un asunto*); volver a presentarse (*a la memoria*)
recurrence [rɪ'kʌrəns] *s* repetición
recurrent [rɪ'kʌrənt] *adj* repetido; periódico; (anat., math. & path.) recurrente
recurve [rɪ'kʌrv] *va* recorvar; *vn* recorvarse
recusancy ['rɛkjuzənsɪ] o [rɪ'kjuzənsɪ] *s* recusación; (hist.) falta de sumisión a la Iglesia anglicana por parte de un católico
recusant ['rɛkjuzənt] o [rɪ'kjuzənt] *adj & s* recusante; (hist.) no conformista (*con el anglicanismo*)
recuse [rɪ'kjuz] *va* (law) recusar
red [rɛd] *adj* (*comp:* **redder;** *super:* **reddest**)

rojo; ruboroso; enrojecido, inflamado; tinto (*vino*); *s* rojo, color rojo; **in the red** (coll.) endeudado; **to see red** (coll.) enfurecerse, echar chispas; (*cap.*) *adj & s* rojo (*comunista*)
redact [rɪˈdækt] *va* redactar
redaction [rɪˈdækʃən] *s* redacción
redan [rɪˈdæn] *s* (fort.) rediente
red ant *s* (ent.) hormiga roja (*Formica rufa*)
redbait [ˈrɛd‚bet] *va* motejar (*a uno*) de rojo o comunista
redbird [ˈrɛd‚bʌrd] *s* (orn.) cardenal; (orn.) piranga
red-blooded [ˈrɛd‚blʌdɪd] *adj* fuerte, valiente, vigoroso
red brass *s* latón rojo
redbreast [ˈrɛd‚brɛst] *s* (orn.) petirrojo
redbud [ˈrɛd‚bʌd] *s* (bot.) árbol del amor
redcap [ˈrɛd‚kæp] *s* (Brit.) policía militar; (U.S.A.) mozo de estación (*que suele llevar gorra roja*); (orn.) jilguero
red cedar *s* (bot.) cedro rojo, cedro de Virginia
red cell *s* (physiol.) hematíe, glóbulo rojo
red cent *s* (coll.) centavo; **to be not worth a red cent** (coll.) no valer un pito
red clover *s* (bot.) trébol rojo
redcoat [ˈrɛd‚kot] *s* soldado inglés
red corpuscle *s* (physiol.) glóbulo rojo
red cross *s* cruz roja; (*caps.*) *s* Cruz Roja
redd [rɛd] (*pret & pp:* **redd** o **redded**) *va* (coll. & dial.) asear, poner en orden
red deer *s* (zool.) ciervo común; ciervo de Virginia (*cuando ostenta su pelaje rojizo de verano*)
redden [ˈrɛdən] *va* enrojecer; *vn* enrojecerse
reddish [ˈrɛdɪʃ] *adj* rojizo
red dogwood *s* (bot.) sanguiñuelo, sanapudio blanco, cornejo hembra
redeem [rɪˈdim] *va* redimir; cumplir (*una promesa*); compensar
redeemable [rɪˈdiməbəl] *adj* redimible
redeemer [rɪˈdimər] *s* redentor; (*cap.*) *s* Redentor
redemption [rɪˈdɛmpʃən] *s* redención
redemptive [rɪˈdɛmptɪv] o **redemptory** [rɪˈdɛmptərɪ] *adj* redentor
redevelop [‚ridɪˈvɛləp] *va* desarrollar de nuevo; (phot.) volver a revelar; *vn* desarrollarse de nuevo
redevelopment [‚ridɪˈvɛləpmənt] *s* nuevo desarrollo
red-eyed [ˈrɛd‚aɪd] *adj* con los ojos inyectados
red fire *s* fuego rojo (*compuesto de estroncio*)
red flag *s* bandera roja; provocación
red fox *s* (zool.) zorra roja; zorro rojo (*piel*)
red-haired [ˈrɛd‚hɛrd] *adj* pelirrojo
red-handed [ˈrɛdˈhændɪd] *adj* con las manos ensangrentadas; en flagrante
red hat *s* capelo (*sombrero rojo de los cardenales; dignidad de cardenal*)
redhead [ˈrɛd‚hɛd] *s* pelirrojo; (orn.) pato de cabeza colorada (*Nyroca americana*)
redheaded [ˈrɛd‚hɛdɪd] *adj* pelirrojo; de cabeza roja; colérico
red heat *s* calor rojo; **to a red heat** al rojo
red herring *s* arenque seco y ahumado; (fig.) artificio para distraer la atención del asunto de que se trata
red-hot [ˈrɛdˈhɑt] *adj* calentado al rojo, candente; ardiente, entusiasta; nuevo, fresco
redingote [ˈrɛdɪŋgot] *s* redingote
redintegrate [rɛdˈɪntɪgret] *va* reintegrar; *vn* reintegrarse
redintegration [rɛd‚ɪntɪˈgreʃən] *s* reintegración
redirect [‚ridɪˈrɛkt] o [‚ridaɪˈrɛkt] *adj* (law) del segundo interrogatorio de un testigo por su abogado después de las repreguntas; *va* volver a dirigir
rediscount [riˈdɪskaʊnt] *s* redescuento; *va* redescontar
rediscount rate *s* tipo de redescuento
rediscover [‚ridɪsˈkʌvər] *va* redescubrir
rediscovery [‚ridɪsˈkʌvərɪ] *s* (*pl:* **-ies**) redescubrimiento
redistribute [‚ridɪsˈtrɪbjut] *va* redistribuir
redistribution [‚ridɪstrɪˈbjuʃən] *s* redistribución
redistrict [riˈdɪstrɪkt] *va* volver a dividir en distritos
red lead [lɛd] *s* rojo de plomo
red-letter [ˈrɛd‚lɛtər] *adj* marcado con letra roja; (fig.) feliz, memorable
red light *s* luz roja; (fig.) señal amonestadora
red-light district [ˈrɛdˈlaɪt] *s* barrio de los lupanares
red man *s* piel roja (*indio norteamericano*)
red mullet *s* (ichth.) salmonete
redness [ˈrɛdnɪs] *s* rojez; inflamación
redo [ˈriˈdu] *s* repetición; refundición; reforma; (*pret:* **-did;** *pp:* **-done**) *va* repetir, rehacer; refundir; reformar
red oak *s* (bot.) roble rojo
red ocher *s* (mineral.) ocre rojo, almagre
redolence [ˈrɛdələns] *s* fragancia, perfume
redolent [ˈrɛdələnt] *adj* fragante, perfumado; **redolent of** que huele a (*que despide un fuerte olor de; que hace pensar en*)
redouble [riˈdʌbəl] *va* redoblar; (bridge) decir recontra a; *vn* redoblarse; (bridge) decir recontra; volver atrás
redoubt [rɪˈdaʊt] *s* (fort.) reducto
redoubtable [rɪˈdaʊtəbəl] *adj* formidable, temible
redound [rɪˈdaʊnd] *vn* redundar; **to redound to** redundar en
redowa [ˈrɛdəwə] o [ˈrɛdəvə] *s* redova
red pepper *s* pimentón
red periwinkle *s* (bot.) dominica, flor de príncipe
redpoll [ˈrɛd‚pol] *s* (orn.) pajarel, pardillo
redraft [ˈri‚dræft] o [ˈri‚drɑft] *s* nuevo dibujo, diseño o plan; nuevo borrador, nueva copia; (com.) resaca; [riˈdræft] o [riˈdrɑft] *va* volver a dibujar; hacer un nuevo borrador de; volver a trazar
redress [rɪˈdrɛs] o [ˈridrɛs] *s* reparación, resarcimiento; corrección, enmienda; alivio, remedio; equilibrio; [rɪˈdrɛs] *va* reparar, resarcir; corregir, enmendar; aliviar, remediar; equilibrar (*una balanza*)
Red Ridinghood [ˈraɪdɪŋ‚hʊd] *s* Caperucita Roja
red sandalwood *s* (bot.) sándalo rojo
Red Sea *s* mar Rojo
red shift *s* (phys.) desviación hacia el rojo del espectro
redskin [ˈrɛd‚skɪn] *s* piel roja (*indio norteamericano*)
red snapper *s* (ichth.) huachinango
red squirrel *s* (zool.) ardilla roja de Norteamérica
redstart [ˈrɛd‚stɑrt] *s* (orn.) colirrojo (*Phoenicurus phoenicurus*); (orn.) candelita
red tape *s* balduque; (fig.) formalismo, expedienteo, papeleo
redtop [ˈrɛd‚tɑp] *s* (bot.) agróstide
reduce [rɪˈdjus] o [rɪˈdus] *va* reducir; (chem., math., surg. & phot.) reducir; (mil.) degradar; *vn* reducirse; reducir peso
reducer [rɪˈdjusər] o [rɪˈdusər] *s* reductor; (chem. & phot.) reductor; (mach.) reducción (*para unir dos tubos o árboles de calibres diferentes*)
reducible [rɪˈdjusɪbəl] o [rɪˈdusɪbəl] *adj* reducible
reducing agent *s* (chem.) agente reductor
reducing exercises *spl* ejercicios físicos para adelgazar o para reducir peso
reducing flame *s* (chem.) llama reductora
reductase [rɪˈdʌktes] o [rɪˈdʌktez] *s* (biochem.) reductasa
reductio ad absurdum [rɪˈdʌkʃɪo æd æbˈsʌrdəm] *s* reducción al absurdo
reduction [rɪˈdʌkʃən] *s* reducción
redundance [rɪˈdʌndəns] *s* var. de **redundancy**
redundancy [rɪˈdʌndənsɪ] *s* (*pl:* **-cies**) redundancia
redundant [rɪˈdʌndənt] *adj* redundante
reduplicate [rɪˈdjuplɪket] o [rɪˈduplɪket] *adj* reduplicado; (bot.) reduplicado; *va* reduplicar
reduplication [rɪ‚djuplɪˈkeʃən] o [rɪ‚duplɪˈkeʃən] *s* reduplicación; (gram.) reduplicación
red valerian *s* (bot.) milamores
red wine *s* vino tinto
redwing [ˈrɛd‚wɪŋ] *s* (orn.) tordo alirrojo; (orn.) arrocero (*Agelaius phoeniceus*)
red-winged blackbird [ˈrɛd‚wɪŋd] *s* (orn.) arrocero

redwood ['rɛd,wʊd] *s* (bot.) secoya; madera de secoya
reëcho [ri'ɛko] *s* (*pl:* **-oes**) eco repetido; *va* repetir el eco de; repetir como eco; *vn* responder el eco; resonar
reed [rid] *s* (bot.) carrizo (*Phragmites communis*); (bot.) caña (*Arundo donax*); caña; flecha o saeta de caña; (mus.) instrumento de lengüeta; peine (*de los telares*); *adj* (mus.) de lengüeta
reedbird ['rid,bʌrd] *s* (orn.) chambergo
reed instrument *s* (mus.) instrumento de lengüeta
reëdit [ri'ɛdɪt] *va* refundir
reed mace *s* (bot.) espadaña
reed organ *s* (mus.) órgano de lengüetas
reed pipe *s* (mus.) tubo de lengüeta
reëducate [ri'ɛdʒəket] o [ri'ɛdʒuket] *va* reeducar
reëducation [,riɛdʒə'keʃən] o [,riɛdʒu'keʃən] *s* reeducación
reedy ['ridɪ] *adj* (*comp:* **-ier;** *super:* **-iest**) lleno de cañas; hecho de caña o cañas; agudo, de tono delgado y agudo
reef [rif] *s* arrecife, escollo; (min.) veta, filón; (naut.) parte de la vela que se puede aferrar con rizos; **to let out the reef** (naut.) largar rizos; **to take in the reef** (naut.) tomar rizos; *va* arrizar; **to reef one's sails** (fig.) aflojar en un empeño
reef band *s* (naut.) faja de rizos
reefer ['rifər] *s* (naut.) el que arriza las velas; chaquetón; (slang) pitillo de mariguana
reef knot *s* (naut.) nudo llano, nudo de rizos
reef point *s* (naut.) rizo
reek [rik] *s* vaho; *va* ahumar; despedir; oler a; *vn* vahear, humear; estar bañado en sudor; estar mojado con sangre; **to reek of** o **with** oler a
reel [ril] *s* carrete; tambor; carretel; devanadera; rollo; broca; baile escocés o virginiano muy vivo; película o cinta (*de cine*); tambaleo; **off the reel** (coll.) fácil y prestamente; *va* aspar (*en carretel*); tirar de (*un pez*) haciendo girar el carretel; devanar, enrollar; hacer tambalear; **to reel off** decir o narrar fácil y prestamente; *vn* tambalear, dar vueltas; cejar (*andar hacia atrás, p.ej., el enemigo*)
reëlect [,riɪ'lɛkt] *va* reelegir
reëlection [,riɪ'lɛkʃən] *s* reelección
reëligible [ri'ɛlɪdʒɪbəl] *adj* reelegible
reëmbark [,riɛm'bɑrk] *va* reembarcar; *vn* reembarcar o reembarcarse
reënact [,riɛn'ækt] *va* volver a decretar; volver a promulgar; volver a desempeñar el papel de; reproducir, volver a representar; *vn* volver a actuar, volver a desempeñar un papel
reënactment [,riɛn'æktmənt] *s* ley o estatuto nuevo; nueva promulgación; nueva representación
reënforce [,riɛn'fors] *va* var. de **reinforce**
reënforcement [,riɛn'forsmənt] *s* var. de **reinforcement**
reënlist [,riɛn'lɪst] *va* reenganchar; *vn* reengancharse
reënlistment [,riɛn'lɪstmənt] *s* reenganche
reënter [ri'ɛntər] *va* reentrar en; volver a asentar; volver a matricular; volver a matricularse en; *vn* reentrar, reingresar; volver a matricularse
reëntering [ri'ɛntərɪŋ] *adj* (math. & mil.) entrante
reëntry [ri'ɛntrɪ] *s* (*pl:* **-tries**) reingreso, nueva entrada; vuelta a la atmósfera terrestre
reëntry permit *s* permiso de regreso
reëstablish [,riɛs'tæblɪʃ] *va* restablecer
reëstablishment [,riɛs'tæblɪʃmənt] *s* restablecimiento
reeve [riv] (*pret & pp:* **rove** o **reeved**) *va* (naut.) pasar en un ojal, jareta, etc.; (naut.) asegurar (*p.ej., un cabo*); (naut.) asegurar con cabo; *vn* (naut.) laborear
reëxamination [,riɛg,zæmɪ'neʃən] *s* reexaminación
reëxamine [,riɛg'zæmɪn] *va* reexaminar
reëxport [ri'ɛksport] *s* reexportación; [,riɛks'port] o [ri'ɛksport] *va* reexportar
ref. abr. de **referee, reference, referred, reformation, reformed** y **reformer**

refection [rɪ'fɛkʃən] *s* refacción o refección (*alimento*)
refectory [rɪ'fɛktərɪ] *s* (*pl:* **-ries**) refectorio
refer [rɪ'fʌr] (*pret & pp:* **-ferred;** *ger:* **-ferring**) *va* referir; *vn* referirse
referee [,rɛfə'ri] *s* (sport) árbitro; (law) juez árbitro; *va & vn* arbitrar
reference ['rɛfərəns] *s* referencia; persona a quien se puede acudir para referencias; **in** o **with reference to** en cuanto a, respecto de; **to make reference to** hacer alusión a
reference frame *s* var. de **frame of reference**
reference library *s* biblioteca de consulta
reference mark *s* (print.) llamada
reference work *s* obra de consulta
referendum [,rɛfə'rɛndəm] *s* (*pl:* **-da** [də]) referéndum
refill ['rifɪl] *s* relleno; [ri'fɪl] *va* rellenar
refillable [ri'fɪləbəl] *adj* rellenable
refine [rɪ'faɪn] *va* refinar; *vn* refinarse; sutilizar; **to refine on** o **upon** mejorar; aventajar, superar
refined [rɪ'faɪnd] *adj* refinado; fino, cortés, sutil; esmerado, exacto
refinement [rɪ'faɪnmənt] *s* refinamiento (*acción de refinar; buen gusto; perfeccionamiento*); sutileza
refiner [rɪ'faɪnər] *s* refinador
refinery [rɪ'faɪnərɪ] *s* (*pl:* **-ies**) refinería
refit [ri'fɪt] (*pret & pp:* **-fitted;** *ger:* **-fitting**) *va* componer, reparar, restaurar
reflect [rɪ'flɛkt] *va* reflejar; echar, traer consigo; *vn* reflejar o reflexionar; **to reflect on** o **upon** reflexionar en o sobre; tachar, notar
reflecting telescope *s* telescopio de espejo
reflection [rɪ'flɛkʃən] *s* reflexión; reflejo (*imagen*); tacha, reproche; (physiol.) reflejo
reflective [rɪ'flɛktɪv] *adj* reflexivo; (fig.) reflexivo
reflector [rɪ'flɛktər] *s* reflector
reflex ['riflɛks] *adj & s* reflejo; (physiol.) reflejo; [rɪ'flɛks] *va* replegar
reflexible [rɪ'flɛksɪbəl] *adj* reflexible
reflexive [rɪ'flɛksɪv] *adj & s* (gram.) reflexivo (*pronombre o verbo*)
refloat [ri'flot] *va* poner a flote nuevamente; *vn* flotar nuevamente
refluent ['rɛfluənt] *adj* refluente
reflux ['riflʌks] *s* reflujo
reforest [ri'fɑrɪst] o [ri'fɔrɪst] *va* volver a repoblar (*un monte*)
reforestation [,rifɑrɪs'teʃən] o [,rifɔrɪs'teʃən] *s* reforestación, nueva repoblación (*de un monte*)
reform [rɪ'fɔrm] *s* reforma; *va* reformar; *vn* reformarse
re-form [ri'fɔrm] *va* reformar; *vn* reformarse
reformation [,rɛfər'meʃən] *s* reformación; (*cap.*) *s* (hist.) Reforma
reformative [rɪ'fɔrmətɪv] *adj* reformativo
reformatory [rɪ'fɔrmə,torɪ] *adj* reformatorio; *s* (*pl:* **-ries**) reformatorio
reformed [rɪ'fɔrmd] *adj* reformado: (*cap.*) *adj & s* reformado
reformer [rɪ'fɔrmər] *s* reformador
reformist [rɪ'fɔrmɪst] *adj & s* reformista
reform school *s* casa de correción, reformatorio
refract [rɪ'frækt] *va* refractar; determinar la condición refractiva de (*un ojo*); determinar el poder refractor de (*un lente*)
refraction [rɪ'frækʃən] *s* (phys. & opt.) refracción; determinación de la condición refractiva del ojo
refractive [rɪ'fræktɪv] *adj* refractivo
refractive index *s* (opt.) índice de refracción
refractometer [,rifræk'tɑmɪtər] *s* refractómetro
refractor [rɪ'fræktər] *s* (opt.) refractor
refractory [rɪ'fræktərɪ] *adj* refractario
refrain [rɪ'fren] *s* estribillo; *vn* abstenerse, refrenarse; **to refrain from** abstenerse de
refrangibility [rɪ,frændʒɪ'bɪlɪtɪ] *s* refrangibilidad
refrangible [rɪ'frændʒɪbəl] *adj* refrangible
refresh [rɪ'frɛʃ] *va* refrescar; **to refresh the memory** refrescar la memoria; *vn* refrescarse
refresher course [rɪ'frɛʃər] *s* curso de repaso

refreshing [rɪˈfrɛʃɪŋ] *adj* refrescante; alentador, confortante
refreshment [rɪˈfrɛʃmənt] *s* refrescadura (*acción*); refresco (*alimento o bebida*)
refrigerant [rɪˈfrɪdʒərənt] *adj & s* refrigerante
refrigerate [rɪˈfrɪdʒəret] *va* refrigerar
refrigeration [rɪˌfrɪdʒəˈreʃən] *s* refrigeración
refrigeration coil *s* serpentín de refrigeración
refrigerator [rɪˈfrɪdʒəˌretər] *s* refrigerador, heladera, nevera
refrigerator car *s* (rail.) carro o vagón frigorífico
refringency [rɪˈfrɪndʒənsɪ] *s* refringencia
refringent [rɪˈfrɪndʒənt] *adj* refringente
refuel [riˈfjuəl] *va* reaprovisionar de combustible; *vn* reaprovisionarse de combustible
refuge [ˈrɛfjudʒ] *s* refugio; expediente, subterfugio; **to take refuge** refugiarse
refugee [ˌrɛfjuˈdʒi] *s* refugiado
refulgence [rɪˈfʌldʒəns] *s* refulgencia
refulgent [rɪˈfʌldʒənt] *adj* refulgente
refund [ˈrifʌnd] *s* reembolso; [rɪˈfʌnd] *va* reembolsar; [riˈfʌnd] *va* consolidar
refurbish [riˈfʌrbɪʃ] *va* restaurar, retocar, repulir
refurnish [riˈfʌrnɪʃ] *va* amueblar de nuevo
refusal [rɪˈfjuzəl] *s* denegación, negativa; opción exclusiva
refuse [ˈrɛfjus] *s* basura, desecho; hez, zupia; [rɪˈfjuz] *va* rehusar; rechazar, no querer aceptar; **to refuse to** + *inf* negarse a + *inf*, rehusar + *inf*
refutation [ˌrɛfjʊˈteʃən] *s* refutación
refute [rɪˈfjut] *va* refutar
reg. abr. de **register, registered, registrar, registry, regular** y **regularly**
regain [rɪˈgen] *va* recobrar, recuperar; volver a alcanzar
regal [ˈrigəl] *adj* regio
regale [rɪˈgel] *va* regalar; **to regale oneself** regalarse
regalement [rɪˈgelmənt] *s* regalamiento
regalia [rɪˈgelɪə] *s* cigarro de regalía; *spl* regalías (*derechos o privilegios pertenecientes al rey*); insignias reales; insignias o distintivos (*de una asociación, orden, etc.*); galas, trajes de lujo
regalism [ˈrigəlɪzəm] *s* regalismo
regalist [ˈrigəlɪst] *s* regalista
regality [rɪˈgælɪtɪ] *s* (*pl:* **-ties**) realeza; soberanía; reino
regard [rɪˈgɑrd] *s* mirada; consideración; respeto; respecto, relación; **regards** *spl* recuerdos; **in** o **with regard to** en cuanto a, respecto a o de; **without regard to** sin considerar, sin hacer caso de; **without any regard for** sin miramientos por; *va* mirar; considerar; tocar a, referirse a; **as regards** en cuanto a; *vn* mirar
regardful [rɪˈgɑrdfəl] *adj* atento; mirado, respetuoso
regarding [rɪˈgɑrdɪŋ] *prep* tocante a, respecto a o de
regardless [rɪˈgɑrdlɪs] *adj* desatento, descuidado, indiferente; *adv* (coll.) pese a quien pese, cueste lo que cueste; **regardless of** sin hacer caso de; a pesar de
regatta [rɪˈgætə] *s* regata
regency [ˈridʒənsɪ] *s* (*pl:* **-cies**) regencia
regeneracy [rɪˈdʒɛnərəsɪ] *s* regeneración
regenerate [rɪˈdʒɛnərɪt] *adj* regenerado; [rɪˈdʒɛnəret] *va* regenerar; *vn* regenerarse
regeneration [rɪˌdʒɛnəˈreʃən] *s* regeneración
regenerative [rɪˈdʒɛnəˌretɪv] *adj* regenerativo
regenerative braking *s* (elec.) frenaje de regeneración
regenerative furnace *s* horno de regeneración
regenerator [rɪˈdʒɛnəˌretər] *s* regenerador; (mach.) regenerador
regent [ˈridʒənt] *adj* regente; *s* regente; miembro de una junta directiva
regentship [ˈridʒəntʃɪp] *s* regencia
regicidal [ˌrɛdʒɪˈsaɪdəl] *adj* regicida
regicide [ˈrɛdʒɪsaɪd] *s* regicidio (*acción*); regicida (*persona*)
regild [riˈgɪld] *va* volver a dorar
regime o **régime** [reˈʒim] o **regimen** [ˈrɛdʒɪmɛn] *s* régimen
regiment [ˈrɛdʒɪmənt] *s* (mil.) regimiento; [ˈrɛdʒɪmɛnt] *va* regimentar
regimental [ˌrɛdʒɪˈmɛntəl] *adj* regimental; **regimentals** *spl* uniforme militar
regimentation [ˌrɛdʒɪmɛnˈteʃən] *s* regimentación
Reginald [ˈrɛdʒɪnəld] *s* Reginaldo
region [ˈridʒən] *s* región
regional [ˈridʒənəl] *adj* regional
regionalism [ˈridʒənəlɪzəm] *s* regionalismo
regionalist [ˈridʒənəlɪst] *adj & s* regionalista
register [ˈrɛdʒɪstər] *s* registro; registrador (*aparato*); registro parroquial; reja regulable de calefacción; índice, tabla de materias; (mus.) extensión (*de la voz, de un instrumento*); (naut.) matrícula; (print.) registro; *va* registrar; manifestar, dar a conocer; certificar; (print.) registrar; *vn* registrarse; inscribirse
registered letter *s* carta certificada
registered nurse *s* (U.S.A.) enfermera titulada
registrable [ˈrɛdʒɪstrəbəl] *adj* registrable
registrar [ˈrɛdʒɪstrɑr] o [ˌrɛdʒɪˈstrɑr] *s* registrador, archivero
registration [ˌrɛdʒɪˈstreʃən] *s* registro, inscripción; matrícula
registration fee *s* derechos de matrícula
registry [ˈrɛdʒɪstrɪ] *s* (*pl:* **-tries**) registro
regnant [ˈrɛgnənt] *adj* reinante
regress [ˈrigrɛs] *s* retroceso; (astr.) retrogradación; (eccl.) regreso; [rɪˈgrɛs] *vn* retroceder; (astr.) retrogradar
regression [rɪˈgrɛʃən] *s* regresión
regressive [rɪˈgrɛsɪv] *adj* regresivo
regret [rɪˈgrɛt] *s* pesar, sentimiento; pesadumbre, remordimiento; **regrets** *spl* excusas (*que se envían para rehusar una invitación*); (*pret & pp:* **-gretted;** *ger:* **-gretting**) *va* sentir, lamentar; lamentar la pérdida de; arrepentirse de; **to regret to** + *inf* sentir + *inf*
regretful [rɪˈgrɛtfəl] *adj* pesaroso; deplorable
regrettable [rɪˈgrɛtəbəl] *adj* lamentable
regrettably [rɪˈgrɛtəblɪ] *adv* lamentablemente
regroup [riˈgrup] *va* reagrupar; *vn* reagruparse
Regt. abr. de **regent** y **regiment**
regular [ˈrɛgjələr] *adj* regular; (bot., eccl., geom., gram. & mil.) regular; (coll.) cabal, completo, verdadero; *s* obrero permanente; parroquiano regular; (eccl. & mil.) regular; **regulars** *spl* (mil.) tropas regulares
regularity [ˌrɛgjəˈlærɪtɪ] *s* regularidad
regularization [ˌrɛgjələrɪˈzeʃən] *s* regularización
regularize [ˈrɛgjələraɪz] *va* regularizar
regulate [ˈrɛgjəlet] *va* regular; graduar (*p.ej., un grifo*)
regulation [ˌrɛgjəˈleʃən] *s* regulación; regla, ordenanza; *adj* regular; de regla, de ordenanza
regulative [ˈrɛgjəˌletɪv] *adj* regulativo
regulator [ˈrɛgjəˌletər] *s* regulador; (mach. & elec.) regulador
regulatory [ˈrɛgjələˌtorɪ] *adj* regulador
regulus [ˈrɛgjələs] *s* (*pl:* **-luses** o **-li** [laɪ]) régulo; (chem. & metal.) régulo; (*cap.*) *s* (astr.) Régulo
regurgitate [riˈgʌrdʒɪtet] *va* volver a arrojar (*un líquido*); vomitar sin esfuerzo; *vn* regurgitar
regurgitation [riˌgʌrdʒɪˈteʃən] *s* regurgitación
rehabilitate [ˌrihəˈbɪlɪtet] *va* rehabilitar
rehabilitation [ˌrihəˌbɪlɪˈteʃən] *s* rehabilitación
rehandle [riˈhændəl] *va* manejar de nuevo
rehash [ˈrihæʃ] *s* rehacimiento; repetición (*p.ej., de viejos argumentos*); refundición, refrito (*especialmente de una obra dramática*); [riˈhæʃ] *va* rehacer; repetir una y otra vez
rehearsal [rɪˈhʌrsəl] *s* ensayo; repetición detallada
rehearse [rɪˈhʌrs] *va* ensayar; repetir detalladamente; *vn* ensayarse; **to rehearse** + *ger* ensayarse a + *inf*
reheat [riˈhit] *va* recalentar
reign [ren] *s* reino; reinado; dominio, imperio; **in the reign of** durante el reinado de; *vn* reinar
reignite [ˌriɪgˈnaɪt] *va* reencender; *vn* reencenderse
Reign of Terror *s* (hist.) Terror

reimburse [ˌriɪm'bʌrs] *va* reembolsar
reimbursement [ˌriɪm'bʌrsmənt] *s* reembolso
reimport [ri'ɪmport] *s* reimportación; [ˌriɪm'port] o [ri'ɪmport] *va* reimportar
reimportation [ˌriɪmpor'teʃən] *s* reimportación
reimpression [ˌriɪm'prɛʃən] *s* reimpresión
rein [ren] *s* rienda; **to draw rein** tener las riendas; detener el paso, parar; **to give rein to** aflojar las riendas a; **to give free rein to** dar rienda suelta a; **to take the reins** tomar las riendas; **with free rein** a rienda suelta; *va* dirigir por medio de riendas; contener, gobernar, refrenar; *vn* obedecer a las riendas; detener el paso
reincarnate [ˌriɪn'kɑrnet] *va* reencarnar
reincarnation [ˌriɪnkɑr'neʃən] *s* reencarnación
reindeer ['renˌdɪr] *s* (zool.) reno
reinfect [ˌriɪn'fɛkt] *va* reinfectar
reinfection [ˌriɪn'fɛkʃən] *s* reinfección
reinflate [ˌriɪn'flet] *va* reinflar
reinforce [ˌriɪn'fors] *va* reforzar
reinforced concrete *s* cemento armado, hormigón armado
reinforcement [ˌriɪn'forsmənt] *s* refuerzo; **reinforcements** *spl* (mil.) refuerzos
reinoculate [ˌriɪn'ɑkjəlet] *va* reinocular; *vn* reinocularse
reinoculation [ˌriɪnˌɑkjə'leʃən] *s* reinoculación
reinstall [ˌriɪn'stɔl] *va* reinstalar
reinstate [ˌriɪn'stet] *va* reinstalar; renovar
reinstatement [ˌriɪn'stetmənt] *s* reinstalación; renovación
reinsurance [ˌriɪn'ʃurəns] *s* reaseguro
reinsure [ˌriɪn'ʃur] *va* reasegurar
reinvest [ˌriɪn'vɛst] *va* reinvertir
reinvestment [ˌriɪn'vɛstmənt] *s* reinversión
reiterate [ri'ɪtəret] *va* reiterar
reiteration [riˌɪtə'reʃən] *s* reiteración
reiterative [ri'ɪtəˌretɪv] *adj* reiterativo
reject [rɪ'dʒɛkt] *va* rechazar; arrojar (*vomitar*)
rejection [rɪ'dʒɛkʃən] *s* rechazamiento; vómito; **rejections** *spl* excremento
rejoice [rɪ'dʒɔɪs] *va* regocijar; *vn* regocijarse
rejoicing [rɪ'dʒɔɪsɪŋ] *s* regocijo
rejoin [ri'dʒɔɪn] *va* volver a juntar o unir; volver a juntarse con, volver a la compañía de; [rɪ'dʒɔɪn] *va* contestar; *vn* contestar; (law) duplicar
rejoinder [rɪ'dʒɔɪndər] *s* contestación; (law) contrarréplica
rejuvenate [rɪ'dʒuvɪnet] *va* rejuvenecer; *vn* rejuvenecerse
rejuvenation [rɪˌdʒuvɪ'neʃən] *s* rejuvenecimiento
rekindle [ri'kɪndəl] *va* reencender; *vn* reencenderse
rel. abr. de **relating, relative, relatively, religion** y **religious**
relaid [ri'led] *pret & pp de* **relay**
relapse [rɪ'læps] *s* recaída; *vn* recaer
relate [rɪ'let] *va* relacionar; contar, relatar; *vn* relacionarse
related [rɪ'letɪd] *adj* relacionado
relation [rɪ'leʃən] *s* relación; narración, relato; pariente; parentesco; **relations** *spl* cópula; **in relation to** o **with relation to** respecto de
relational [rɪ'leʃənəl] *adj* que expresa relación; de parentesco
relationship [rɪ'leʃənʃɪp] *s* relación; parentesco
relative ['rɛlətɪv] *adj* relativo; (gram.) relativo; *s* deudo, pariente; (gram.) relativo
relative clause *s* (gram.) oración de relativo
relative humidity *s* (meteor.) humedad relativa
relatively ['rɛlətɪvlɪ] *adv* relativamente
relativism ['rɛlətɪvɪzəm] *s* relativismo
relativity [ˌrɛlə'tɪvɪtɪ] *s* relatividad; (phys.) relatividad
relator [rɪ'letər] *s* relator
relax [rɪ'læks] *va* relajar; esparcir, desahogar; *vn* relajar (*aflojarse; hacerse menos severo*); esparcirse, desahogarse, despreocuparse
relaxation [ˌrilæks'eʃən] *s* relajación; esparcimiento, desahogo, despreocupación
relaxation of tension *s* disminución de la tirantez internacional
relaxative [rɪ'læksətɪv] *adj & s* relajante
relaxedly [rɪ'læksɪdlɪ] *adv* relajadamente; desahogadamente
relaxing [rɪ'læksɪŋ] *adj* despreocupante
relay ['rile] o [rɪ'le] *s* relevo, remuda; parada, posta (*de caballos*); (mil. & sport) relevo; (sport) carrera de relevos o de equipos; (elec.) relai o relais; (*pret & pp:* **-layed**) *va* transmitir relevándose; enviar por la posta; transmitir con un relais; retransmitir (*una emisión*); reexpedir (*un radiotelegrama*); [ri'le] (*pret & pp:* **-laid**) *va* volver a colocar
relay race *s* (sport) carrera de relevos o de equipos
release [rɪ'lis] *s* liberación; excarcelación; alivio; finiquito; desprendimiento; (mach.) escape, disparador; (law) cesión; (law) acta o escritura de cesión; permiso de publicación, venta, etc.; obra o pieza lista para la publicación, venta, etc.; (aer.) lanzamiento; *va* soltar; aliviar; relevar; (law) ceder; permitir la publicación, venta, etc. de; (aut.) soltar (*el embrague, el freno*); (aer.) lanzar (*una bomba*)
re-lease [ri'lis] *va* arrendar de nuevo
relegate ['rɛlɪget] *va* relegar
relegation [ˌrɛlɪ'geʃən] *s* relegación
relent [rɪ'lɛnt] *vn* ablandarse, aplacarse
relentless [rɪ'lɛntlɪs] *adj* implacable
relevance ['rɛlɪvəns] o **relevancy** ['rɛlɪvənsɪ] *s* pertinencia
relevant ['rɛlɪvənt] *adj* pertinente
reliability [rɪˌlaɪə'bɪlɪtɪ] *s* confiabilidad
reliable [rɪ'laɪəbəl] *adj* confiable, fidedigno
reliable sources *spl* fuentes fidedignas
reliably [rɪ'laɪəblɪ] *adv* de un modo confiable
reliance [rɪ'laɪəns] *s* confianza
reliant [rɪ'laɪənt] *adj* confiado
relic ['rɛlɪk] *s* reliquia
relict [rɪ'lɪkt] *adj* (biol.) relicto; ['rɛlɪkt] *s* (biol.) reliquia, forma relicta; viuda; **relicts** *spl* restos mortales
relief [rɪ'lif] *s* relevación; alivio; caridad; relieve (*labor que resalta sobre un plano*); (fort.) relieve; (mil.) relevo; **in relief** en relieve; **on relief** viviendo de socorro, recibiendo manutención gratuita
relief map *s* mapa en relieve
relieve [rɪ'liv] *va* relevar; aliviar; auxiliar (*a los necesitados*); (mil.) relevar
relievo [rɪ'livo] *s* (*pl:* **-vos**) relieve
relight [ri'laɪt] *va* reencender
religion [rɪ'lɪdʒən] *s* religión
religiosity [rɪˌlɪdʒɪ'ɑsɪtɪ] *s* religiosidad; beatería
religious [rɪ'lɪdʒəs] *adj* religioso; *s* religioso; *spl* religiosos
reline [ri'laɪn] *va* reforrar, revestir; (aut.) reforrar (*los frenos*)
relinquish [rɪ'lɪŋkwɪʃ] *va* abandonar, dejar, renunciar
relinquishment [rɪ'lɪŋkwɪʃmənt] *s* abandono, dejación, renuncia
reliquary ['rɛlɪˌkwɛrɪ] *s* (*pl:* **-ies**) relicario
relique ['rɛlɪk] o [rɛ'lik] *s* var. de **relic**
relish ['rɛlɪʃ] *s* buen sabor, gusto; condimento, sazón; dejo, gustillo, saborcillo; entremés; *va* saborear; gustar de; comer o beber con placer; *vn* saber bien; agradar, gustar
relive [ri'lɪv] *va* volver a llevar (*tal o cual vida*); repasar en la memoria (*un tiempo pasado*); *vn* renacer, volver a la vida
reload [ri'lod] *va* recargar, volver a cargar
reluctance [rɪ'lʌktəns] *s* renuencia, aversión; (elec.) reluctancia; **with reluctance** de mala gana
reluctancy [rɪ'lʌktənsɪ] *s* renuencia, aversión
reluctant [rɪ'lʌktənt] *adj* renuente, maldispuesto
reluctivity [ˌrɛlək'tɪvɪtɪ] *s* (elec.) reluctividad
relume [ri'lum] *va* reencender
rely [rɪ'laɪ] (*pret & pp:* **-lied**) *vn* depender, confiar; **to rely on** depender de, confiar en
remade [ri'med] *pret & pp de* **remake**
remain [rɪ'men] *vn* permanecer, quedarse; restar; continuar; **to remain to be** + *pp* quedar por + *inf*, p.ej., **more than half of the railroad remains to be built** aún queda más de la mitad del ferrocarril por construir;

remains *spl* desechos, residuos, restos; restos mortales; obra póstuma
remainder [rɪˈmendər] *s* resto, restante, residuo; (math.) resta, resto o residuo; libro casi invendible; *va* saldar (*libros que ya no se venden*)
remake [riˈmek] (*pret & pp:* **-made**) *va* rehacer
remand [rɪˈmænd] o [rɪˈmɑnd] *va* reencarcelamiento; persona reencarcelada; *va* reencarcelar
remanent magnetism [ˈrɛmənənt] *s* (phys.) magnetismo remanente
remark [rɪˈmɑrk] *s* observación, nota; *va & vn* observar, notar; **to remark on** o **upon** aludir a, comentar
remarkable [rɪˈmɑrkəbəl] *adj* notable, extraordinario
remarkably [rɪˈmɑrkəblɪ] *adv* notablemente, extraordinariamente
remarriage [riˈmærɪdʒ] *s* segundas (o terceras, etc.) nupcias
remarry [riˈmærɪ] (*pret & pp:* **-ried**) *vn* volver a casarse
remediable [rɪˈmidɪəbəl] *adj* remediable
remediably [rɪˈmidɪəblɪ] *adv* remediablemente
remedial [rɪˈmidɪəl] *adj* remediador
remediless [ˈrɛmɪdɪlɪs] *adj* irremediable, sin remedio
remedy [ˈrɛmɪdɪ] *s* (*pl:* **-dies**) remedio; (*pret & pp:* **-died**) *va* remediar
remember [rɪˈmɛmbər] *va* acordarse de, recordar; **to remember to** + *inf* acordarse de + *inf*, recordar + *inf*, p.ej., **he remembered to do it** se acordó de hacerlo, recordó hacerlo; **to remember** + *ger* acordarse de + *perf inf*, recordar + *perf inf*, p.ej., **he remembered doing it** se acordaba de haberlo hecho, recordaba haberlo hecho; **remember me to your brother** recuerdos a su hermano, déle Vd. a su hermano recuerdos o memorias de mi parte; *vn* acordarse, recordar; **if I remember correctly** si mal no me acuerdo, si mal no recuerdo
remembrance [rɪˈmɛmbrəns] *s* recuerdo; **remembrances** *spl* recuerdos, saludos
remembrancer [rɪˈmɛmbrənsər] *s* recordatorio, recordativo
remiges [ˈrɛmɪdʒiz] *spl* (orn.) rémiges, remeras
remind [rɪˈmaɪnd] *va* recordar; **to remind someone of something** recordar algo a alguien; **to remind to** + *inf* recordar que + *subj*, p.ej., **remind him to write** recuérdele Vd. que escriba
reminder [rɪˈmaɪndər] *s* recordatorio, recordativo
Remington gun [ˈrɛmɪŋtən] *s* rémington
reminisce [ˌrɛmɪˈnɪs] *vn* contar sus recuerdos, entregarse a los recuerdos
reminiscence [ˌrɛmɪˈnɪsəns] *s* reminiscencia; (philos.) reminiscencia
reminiscent [ˌrɛmɪˈnɪsənt] *adj* recordativo; evocador
remiss [rɪˈmɪs] *adj* descuidado, negligente
remissible [rɪˈmɪsɪbəl] *adj* remisible
remission [rɪˈmɪʃən] *s* remisión
remission of sins *s* remisión de los pecados
remissness [rɪˈmɪsnɪs] *s* descuido, negligencia
remit [rɪˈmɪt] (*pret & pp:* **-mitted;** *ger:* **-mitting**) *va* remitir; devolver, restituir; reencarcelar; *vn* remitir dinero; remitir o remitirse
remittal [rɪˈmɪtəl] *s* remisión
remittance [rɪˈmɪtəns] *s* remesa
remittent [rɪˈmɪtənt] *adj* remitente
remnant [ˈrɛmnənt] *adj* remanente; *s* remanente, resto; retal, retazo; saldo (*resto de mercancías*)
remodel [riˈmɑdəl] (*pret & pp:* **-eled** o **-elled;** *ger:* **-eling** o **-elling**) *va* modelar de nuevo; rehacer, reconstruir; convertir, transformar
remonetize [riˈmɑnɪtaɪz] o [riˈmʌnɪtaɪz] *va* volver a monetizar
remonstrance [rɪˈmɑnstrəns] *s* protesta, reconvención
remonstrant [rɪˈmɑnstrənt] *adj & s* protestante
remonstrate [rɪˈmɑnstret] *vn* protestar; **to remonstrate with** reconvenir
remonstration [ˌrimɑnˈstreʃən] o [ˌrɛmɑnˈstreʃən] *s* protesta, reconvención
remonstrative [rɪˈmɑnstrətɪv] *adj* protestante
remonstrator [rɪˈmɑnstretər] *s* protestante
remora [ˈrɛmərə] *s* (ichth.) rémora
remorse [rɪˈmɔrs] *s* remordimiento
remote [rɪˈmot] *adj* remoto
remote control *s* comando a distancia, telecontrol, control remoto
remotely [rɪˈmotlɪ] *adv* remotamente
remount [riˈmaʊnt] *s* caballo de remonta; remonta (*conjunto de caballos*); *va* volver a subir (*p.ej., una escalera*); (mil.) remontar; *vn* volver a subir
removal [rɪˈmuvəl] *s* sacamiento; remoción; mudanza, traslado; eliminación; deposición (*de un empleo*)
remove [rɪˈmuv] *s* grado, paso, escalón; mudanza; *va* remover; quitar de en medio, apartar matando; *vn* removerse
removed [rɪˈmuvd] *adj* distante, apartado; **first cousin once removed** hijo de primo carnal
remunerate [rɪˈmjunəret] *va* remunerar
remuneration [rɪˌmjunəˈreʃən] *s* remuneración
remunerative [rɪˈmjunəˌretɪv] *adj* remunerativo
Remus [ˈriməs] *s* (myth.) Remo
renaissance [ˌrɛnəˈsɑns] o [rɪˈnesəns] *s* renacimiento; (*cap.*) *s* Renacimiento
renal [ˈrinəl] *adj* renal
rename [riˈnem] *va* volver a nombrar, dar nuevo nombre a
Renard [ˈrɛnərd] *s* var. de **Reynard**
renascence [rɪˈnæsəns] *s* renacimiento; (*cap.*) *s* Renacimiento
renascent [rɪˈnæsənt] *adj* renaciente
rencounter [rɛnˈkaʊntər] *s* altercado, refriega; encuentro fortuito
rend [rɛnd] (*pret & pp:* **rent**) *va* desgarrar; hender, rajar; arrancar; estremecer (*un ruido el aire*)
render [ˈrɛndər] *va* rendir (*gracias, obsequios, homenaje*); prestar, suministrar (*p.ej., ayuda*); pagar (*p.ej., un tributo*); desempeñar (*un papel*); traducir (*p.ej., sentimientos*); verter (*de un idioma a otro*); derretir (*cera, manteca, etc.*); extraer o clarificar derritiendo; extraer la grasa o el sebo a; dar la primera capa de enlucido a; volver, poner; hacer (*p.ej., justicia*); (mus.) ejecutar
rendezvous [ˈrɑndəvu] *s* (*pl;* **-vous** [vuz]) cita; encuentro, reunión (*en el espacio*); (*pret & pp:* **-voused** [vud]; *ger:* **-vousing** [vuɪŋ]) *va* reunir a una cita; *vn* reunirse a una cita
rendition [rɛnˈdɪʃən] *s* rendición; traducción; (mus.) ejecución
renegade [ˈrɛnɪged] *adj & s* renegado; traidor; desertor
renege [rɪˈnɪg] *s* renuncio; *va* renunciar; *vn* renunciar; (coll.) volverse atrás, no cumplir su promesa
renegotiation [ˌrinɪˌgoʃɪˈeʃən] *s* renegociación
renew [rɪˈnju] o [rɪˈnu] *va* renovar; *vn* renovarse; obtener o conceder una renovación o extensión de contrato, cuenta, etc.
renewable [rɪˈnjuəbəl] o [rɪˈnuəbəl] *adj* renovable
renewal [rɪˈnjuəl] o [rɪˈnuəl] *s* renovación
renewedly [rɪˈnjuɪdlɪ] o [rɪˈnuɪdlɪ] *adv* de nuevo, otra vez
reniform [ˈrɛnɪfɔrm] o [ˈrinɪfɔrm] *adj* reniforme
rennet [ˈrɛnɪt] *s* cuajo
rennet bag *s* (zool.) cuajar
rennin [ˈrɛnɪn] *s* (biochem.) quimosina
renomination [riˌnɑmɪˈneʃən] *s* nueva nominación, nuevo nombramiento
renounce [rɪˈnaʊns] *va* renunciar (*p.ej., una herencia, un ofrecimiento, un derecho*); renunciar a (*un proyecto*); desconocer; *vn* renunciar
renouncement [rɪˈnaʊnsmənt] *s* renunciación; desconocimiento
renovate [ˈrɛnovet] *va* renovar; reformar (*p.ej., una tienda, una casa*)
renovation [ˌrɛnoˈveʃən] *s* renovación; reforma
renovator [ˈrɛnoˌvetər] *s* renovador

renown [rɪˈnaʊn] *s* renombre
renowned [rɪˈnaʊnd] *adj* renombrado
rent [rɛnt] *s* alquiler, arriendo; renta de la tierra; desgarro, rasgón; cisma, desavenencia; **for rent** se alquila; *adj* desgarrado, rasgado; andrajoso, haraposo; *va* alquilar, arrendar; *vn* alquilarse, arrendarse; *pret & pp de* **rend**
rentable [ˈrɛntəbəl] *adj* arrendable
rental [ˈrɛntəl] *s* alquiler, arriendo
rent control *s* control de alquileres
renter [ˈrɛntər] *s* inquilino, arrendatario
rent roll *s* lista de rentas
renumber [riˈnʌmbər] *va* volver a numerar, corregir la numeración de
renunciation [rɪˌnʌnsɪˈeʃən] o [rɪˌnʌnʃɪˈeʃən] *s* renunciación, renunciamiento; desconocimiento
reopen [riˈopən] *va* reabrir; *vn* reabrirse
reopening [riˈopənɪŋ] *s* reapertura
reorganization [ˌriɔrgənɪˈzeʃən] *s* reorganización
reorganize [riˈɔrgənaɪz] *va* reorganizar; *vn* reorganizarse
reorient [riˈorɪɛnt] *va* reorientar
rep. abr. de **report, reported, reporter, representative** y **republic**
Rep. abr. de **Republic** y **Republican**
rep [rɛp] *s* reps (*tela*); (slang) reputación
repack [riˈpæk] *va* reempacar; (mach.) reempaquetar
repaid [rɪˈped] *pret & pp de* **repay**
repaint [riˈpent] *s* repinte; *va & vn* repintar
repair [rɪˈpɛr] *s* reparación; remonta (*de las botas*); **in repair** en buen estado; **in bad repair** en mal estado; **in good repair** en buen estado; *va* reparar; remontar (*botas*); *vn* dirigirse; volver
repairable [rɪˈpɛrəbəl] *adj* var. de **reparable**
repairman [rɪˈpɛrˌmæn] o [rɪˈpɛrmən] *s* (*pl:* **-men**) reparador, mecánico
repair service *s* servicio de reparaciones
repair shop *s* taller de reparaciones
repaper [riˈpepər] *va* empapelar de nuevo
reparable [ˈrɛpərəbəl] *adj* reparable
reparation [ˌrɛpəˈreʃən] *s* reparación
reparative [rɪˈpærətɪv] *adj* reparativo
repartee [ˌrɛpɑrˈti] *s* respuesta viva y bien sentada; agudeza y gracia en responder
repartition [ˌripɑrˈtɪʃən] o [ˌripərˈtɪʃən] *s* reparto; *va* repartir
repass [riˈpæs] o [riˈpɑs] *va* repasar; hacer repasar; volver a aprobar (*un proyecto de ley*); *vn* repasar
repast [rɪˈpæst] o [rɪˈpɑst] *s* comida, comilona
repatriate [riˈpetrɪet] *s* repatriado; *va* repatriar
repatriation [riˌpetrɪˈeʃən] *s* repatriación
repave [riˈpev] *va* repavimentar
repay [rɪˈpe] (*pret & pp:* **-paid**) *va* reembolsar; resarcir; compensar
repayable [rɪˈpeəbəl] *adj* reembolsable; resarcible; compensable
repayment [rɪˈpemənt] *s* reembolso; resarcimiento; compensación
repeal [rɪˈpil] *s* abrogación, revocación; *va* abrogar, revocar
repeat [rɪˈpit] *s* repetición; (mus.) repetición; *va* repetir; **to repeat oneself** repetirse; *vn* repetir; (path.) repetir; (U.S.A.) volver a votar en la misma elección (*ilegalmente*)
repeatedly [rɪˈpitɪdlɪ] *adv* repetidamente
repeater [rɪˈpitər] *s* repetidor; rifle de repetición; reloj de repetición; (U.S.A.) persona que vota más de una vez en una elección; (telp.) repetidor
repeating decimal *s* (math.) fracción decimal periódica
repeating rifle *s* rifle de repetición
repeating watch *s* reloj de repetición
repel [rɪˈpɛl] (*pret & pp:* **-pelled;** *ger:* **-pelling**) *va* rechazar; repugnar
repellent [rɪˈpɛlənt] *adj* repulsivo; (med.) repercusivo; *s* tela impermeable; (med.) repercusivo
repent [rɪˈpɛnt] *va* arrepentirse de; *vn* arrepentirse; **to repent having** + *pp* arrepentirse de haber + *pp*
repentance [rɪˈpɛntəns] *s* arrepentimiento
repentant [rɪˈpɛntənt] *adj* arrepentido; de arrepentimiento
repeople [riˈpipəl] *va* repoblar
repercussion [ˌripərˈkʌʃən] *s* repercusión
repertoire [ˈrɛpərtwɑr] *s* repertorio
repertory [ˈrɛpərˌtorɪ] *s* (*pl:* **-ries**) repertorio
repertory theater *s* teatro de repertorio
repetend [ˈrɛpɪtɛnd] o [ˌrɛpɪˈtɛnd] *s* (math.) período
repetition [ˌrɛpɪˈtɪʃən] *s* repetición
repetitious [ˌrɛpɪˈtɪʃəs] *adj* repetidor
repetitive [rɪˈpɛtɪtɪv] *adj* reiterativo
rephrase [riˈfrez] *va* volver a expresar o formular; expresar o formular de modo diferente
repine [rɪˈpaɪn] *vn* apurarse, afligirse, quejarse
replace [rɪˈples] *va* reponer; reemplazar
replaceable [rɪˈplesəbəl] *adj* reemplazable
replacement [rɪˈplesmənt] *s* reposición; reemplazo; repuesto; pieza de repuesto; (mil.) soldado reemplazante
replacement center *s* (mil.) centro de substitución
replant [riˈplænt] o [riˈplɑnt] *va* replantar; resembrar
replenish [rɪˈplɛnɪʃ] *va* llenar, henchir; rellenar, rehenchir; reaprovisionar; colmar de inspiración
replenishment [rɪˈplɛnɪʃmənt] *s* henchimiento; relleno; reaprovisionamiento
replete [rɪˈplit] *adj* repleto
repletion [rɪˈpliʃən] *s* repleción
replevin [rɪˈplɛvɪn] *s* (law) reivindicación; (law) auto de desembargo; *va* (law) reivindicar
replevy [rɪˈplɛvɪ] (*pret & pp:* **-ied**) *va* (law) reivindicar
replica [ˈrɛplɪkə] *s* (f.a.) réplica; (mus.) repetición; segunda edición (*persona o cosa muy semejante a otra*)
reply [rɪˈplaɪ] *s* (*pl:* **-plies**) contestación, respuesta; (*pret & pp:* **-plied**) *va* contestar, responder; *vn* contestar, responder; (law) replicar
reply coupon *s* cupón-respuesta
report [rɪˈport] *s* relato; informe; denuncia; detonación, tiro; rumor; reputación; *va* relatar; informar acerca de, redactar un informe acerca de; denunciar; **to report out** devolver o presentar (*p.ej., un proyecto de ley*) con dictamen o informes; *vn* hacer un relato; redactar un informe; ser repórter; presentarse; **to report on** notificar
reportable [rɪˈportəbəl] *adj* digno de ser relatado
report card *s* certificado escolar
reportedly [rɪˈportɪdlɪ] *adv* según se informa
reporter [rɪˈportər] *s* relator; repórter o reportero (*de un periódico*)
reporting [rɪˈpɔrtɪŋ] *s* reportaje
reportorial [ˌrɛpərˈtorɪəl] *adj* reporteril
repose [rɪˈpoz] *s* descanso; *va* descansar; poner (*confianza*); *vn* descansar
reposeful [rɪˈpozfəl] *adj* reposado
repository [rɪˈpɑzɪˌtorɪ] *s* (*pl:* **-ries**) almacén, depósito, repositorio; depositario (*persona*); mina o almacén (*de información*); filón
repossess [ˌripəˈzɛs] *va* recobrar; **to repossess of** o **in** restaurar en la posesión de
repossession [ˌripəˈzɛʃən] *s* recobro
repoussé [rəpuˈse] *adj & s* repujado
repp [rɛp] *s* reps (*tela*)
reprehend [ˌrɛprɪˈhɛnd] *va* reprender
reprehensible [ˌrɛprɪˈhɛnsɪbəl] *adj* reprensible
reprehension [ˌrɛprɪˈhɛnʃən] *s* reprensión
represent [ˌrɛprɪˈzɛnt] *va* representar
re-present [ˌriprɪˈzɛnt] *va* volver a presentar
representation [ˌrɛprɪzɛnˈteʃən] *s* representación
representative [ˌrɛprɪˈzɛntətɪv] *adj* representativo; *s* representante
repress [rɪˈprɛs] *va* reprimir
repressible [rɪˈprɛsɪbəl] *adj* reprimible
repression [rɪˈprɛʃən] *s* represión; (psychoanal.) represión
repressive [rɪˈprɛsɪv] *adj* represivo
reprieve [rɪˈpriv] *s* suspensión temporal de un castigo, suspensión temporal de la pena de

muerte; respiro, alivio temporal; *va* suspender temporalmente el castigo de, suspender temporalmente la pena de muerte de; aliviar temporalmente

reprimand ['rɛprɪmænd] o ['rɛprɪmɑnd] *s* reprimenda; *va* reconvenir, reprender

reprint ['ri,prɪnt] *s* reimpresión; tirada aparte; [ri'prɪnt] *va* reimprimir

reprisal [rɪ'praɪzəl] *s* represalia o represalias; **to make reprisals** tomar represalias

reproach [rɪ'protʃ] *s* reproche; oprobio; *va* reprochar; oprobiar; **to reproach someone for something** reprochar algo a alguien

reproachable [rɪ'protʃəbəl] *adj* reprochable

reproachful [rɪ'protʃfəl] *adj* reprochador, reprensor

reproachless [rɪ'protʃlɪs] *adj* irreprochable

reprobate ['rɛprobet] *adj & s* malvado; (theol.) réprobo; *va* reprobar

reprobation [,rɛpro'beʃən] *s* reprobación

reproduce [,riprə'djus] o [,riprə'dus] *va* reproducir; *vn* reproducirse

reproducer [,riprə'djusər] o [,riprə'dusər] *s* reproductor; (mach. & elec.) reproductor

reproducible [,riprə'djusɪbəl] o [,riprə'dusɪbəl] *adj* reproductible

reproduction [,riprə'dʌkʃən] *s* reproducción

reproductive [,riprə'dʌktɪv] *adj* reproductor

reproof [rɪ'pruf] *s* reprobación

reprovable [rɪ'pruvəbəl] *adj* reprobable

reproval [rɪ'pruvəl] *s* reprobación

reprove [rɪ'pruv] *va* reprobar

reptile ['rɛptɪl] *adj & s* (zool. & fig.) reptil

reptilian [rɛp'tɪlɪən] *adj* (zool. & fig.) reptil; *s* (zool.) reptil

Repub. abr. de **Republic** y **Republican**

republic [rɪ'pʌblɪk] *s* república; **The Republic** la República de Platón

republican [rɪ'pʌblɪkən] *adj & s* republicano

republicanism [rɪ'pʌblɪkənɪzəm] *s* republicanismo

republication [,ripʌblɪ'keʃən] *s* nueva publicación

republic of letters *s* república de las letras o república literaria

republish [ri'pʌblɪʃ] *va* volver a publicar

repudiate [rɪ'pjudɪet] *va* repudiar; no reconocer (*p.ej., una deuda*)

repudiation [rɪ,pjudɪ'eʃən] *s* repudiación; desconocimiento (*p.ej., de una deuda*)

repugnance [rɪ'pʌgnəns] o **repugnancy** [rɪ'pʌgnənsɪ] *s* repugnancia

repugnant [rɪ'pʌgnənt] *adj* repugnante

repulse [rɪ'pʌls] *s* repulsión, rechazo; *va* repeler, rechazar

repulsion [rɪ'pʌlʃən] *s* repulsión; (phys.) repulsión; (fig.) repulsión (*antipatía*)

repulsive [rɪ'pʌlsɪv] *adj* (phys. & fig.) repulsivo; feúcho

repurchase [ri'pʌrtʃəs] *s* recompra; *va* recomprar

reputable ['rɛpjətəbəl] *adj* bien reputado, de buena reputación; castizo (*vocablo*)

reputation [,rɛpjə'teʃən] *s* reputación; buena reputación

repute [rɪ'pjut] *s* reputación; buena reputación; **by repute** según la opinión común; *va* reputar

reputed [rɪ'pjutɪd] *adj* supuesto; **highly reputed** bien reputado

reputedly [rɪ'pjutɪdlɪ] *adv* según la opinión común

request [rɪ'kwɛst] *s* petición, solicitud; **at the request of** a petición de; **by request** a petición; **on** o **upon request** a pedido, a solicitud; *va* pedir; **to request something from someone** pedir algo a alguien; **to request someone to do something** pedir a alguien que haga algo

requiem o **Requiem** ['rikwɪɛm] o ['rɛkwɪɛm] *s* réquiem (*misa y música*)

requiem mass *s* misa de réquiem

requiescat [,rɛkwɪ'ɛskæt] *s* oración o voto por un difunto

require [rɪ'kwaɪr] *va* requerir, exigir

requirement [rɪ'kwaɪrmənt] *s* requisito; necesidad

requisite ['rɛkwɪzɪt] *adj & s* requisito

requisition [,rɛkwɪ'zɪʃən] *s* demanda, exacción; demanda de extradición; (mil.) requisición; *va* demandar, exigir; (mil.) requisar

requital [rɪ'kwaɪtəl] *s* compensación, retorno

requite [rɪ'kwaɪt] *va* corresponder a (*los beneficios, el amor, etc.*); corresponder con (*el bienhechor*); **to requite a person for his efforts** compensar a una persona sus esfuerzos

reran [ri'ræn] *pret de* **rerun**

reread [ri'rid] (*pret & pp:* **-read** ['rɛd]) *va* releer

rerebrace ['rɪr,bres] *s* (arm.) brafonera

reredos ['rɪrdɑs] *s* (eccl.) retablo

reroute [ri'rut] o [ri'raʊt] *va* reencaminar

rerun ['ri,rʌn] *s* nueva exhibición de una película; (telv.) programa grabado repetido; [ri'rʌn] (*pret:* **-ran;** *pp;* **-run;** *ger:* **-running**) *va* volver a exhibir (*una película*)

resale ['ri,sel] o [ri'sel] *s* reventa

rescind [rɪ'sɪnd] *va* rescindir

rescission [rɪ'sɪʒən] *s* rescisión

rescript ['riskrɪpt] *s* rescripto; refundición

rescue ['rɛskjʊ] *s* salvación; liberación; rescate; liberación violenta de un preso; recuperación ilegal de una cosa retenida por la autoridad; **to go to the rescue of** acudir al socorro de; *va* salvar, librar; libertar; rescatar; libertar violenta e ilegalmente; recobrar violenta e ilegalmente

rescue party *s* pelotón de salvamento

rescuer ['rɛskjʊər] *s* salvador

reseal [ri'sil] *va* resellar

research [rɪ'sʌrtʃ] o ['risʌrtʃ] *s* investigación; *vn* investigar

researcher [rɪ'sʌrtʃər] o ['risʌrtʃər] *s* investigador

research professor *s* profesor o catedrático investigador

reseat [ri'sit] *va* volver a sentar; poner un asiento o fondo nuevo a (*una silla*)

resect [rɪ'sɛkt] *va* (surg.) resecar

resection [rɪ'sɛkʃən] *s* resección

resedaceous [,rɛsɪ'deʃəs] *adj* (bot.) resedáceo

resell [ri'sɛl] (*pret & pp:* **-sold**) *va* revender

reseller [ri'sɛlər] *s* revendedor

resemblance [rɪ'zɛmbləns] *s* parecido, semejanza

resemble [rɪ'zɛmbəl] *va* asemejarse a, parecerse a

resent [rɪ'zɛnt] *va* resentirse de o por

resentful [rɪ'zɛntfəl] *adj* resentido

resentment [rɪ'zɛntmənt] *s* resentimiento

reserpine ['rɛsərpɪn], ['rɛsərpin], [rə'sʌrpɪn] o [rə'sʌrpin] *s* (pharm.) reserpina

reservation [,rɛzər'veʃən] *s* reservación; reserva; **without reservation** sin reserva

reserve [rɪ'zʌrv] *adj* (mil.) reservista; *s* reserva; (com. & mil.) reserva; *va* reservar

reserve bank *s* (U.S.A.) banco de reserva

reserved [rí'zʌrvd] *adj* reservado

reservedly [rɪ'zʌrvɪdlɪ] *adv* reservadamente

reserve officer *s* (mil.) oficial de complemento, oficial de reserva

reservist [rɪ'zʌrvɪst] *s* (mil.) reservista

reservoir ['rɛzərvwɑr] *s* depósito, reservorio; embalse, pantano; (fig.) mina; (fig.) fondo (*p.ej., de sabiduría*)

reset ['ri,sɛt] *s* nuevo engaste, nueva montadura; reducción (*de un hueso dislocado*); (print.) recomposición; [ri'sɛt] (*pret & pp:* **-set;** *ger:* **-setting**) *va* volver a engastar o a montar; volver a encajar (*un hueso dislocado*); (print.) recomponer (*un texto*); (print.) volver a disponer (*los tipos*)

resettle [ri'sɛtəl] *va* volver a arreglar; volver a determinar; volver a colonizar; llegar a un nuevo acuerdo sobre; *vn* volver a arreglarse; volver a determinarse; restablecerse; hacer nuevo asiento (*un edificio*); llegar a un nuevo acuerdo

resettlement [ri'sɛtəlmənt] *s* nuevo arreglo; nueva determinación; nueva colonización; restablecimiento; nuevo acuerdo

reshape [ri'ʃep] *va* reformar

reship [ri'ʃɪp] (*pret & pp:* **-shipped;** *ger:* **-shipping**) *va* reembarcar; reenviar, reexpedir; *vn* reembarcarse

reshipment [ri'ʃɪpmənt] *s* reembarco (*de personas*); reembarque (*de mercancías*); reenvío, reexpedición

reshuffle [riˈʃʌfəl] *s* nueva barajadura; recomposición; *va* volver a barajar; mezclar y revolver otra vez
reside [rɪˈzaɪd] *vn* residir
residence [ˈrɛsɪdəns] *s* residencia; (educ.); residencia
residency [ˈrɛzɪdənsɪ] *s* (*pl:* **-cies**) residencia
resident [ˈrɛzɪdənt] *adj* residente; (orn.) no migratorio; *s* residente; médico interno, médico residente
residential [ˌrɛzɪˈdɛnʃəl] *adj* residencial
residual [rɪˈzɪdʒuəl] *adj* residual
residual magnetism *s* var. de **remanent magnetism**
residuary [rɪˈzɪdʒuˌɛrɪ] *adj* residual
residue [ˈrɛzɪdju] o [ˈrɛzɪdu] *s* resto, residuo
residuum [rɪˈzɪdʒuəm] *s* (*pl:* **-a** [ə]) residuo
resign [rɪˈzaɪn] *va* dimitir, resignar, renunciar; **to resign command to another person** resignar el mando en otra persona; **to resign oneself** resignarse; **to resign oneself to** + *inf* resignarse a + *inf; vn* dimitir; separarse (*p.ej., de un club*); resignarse
resignation [ˌrɛzɪgˈneʃən] *s* dimisión, renuncia; resignación
resigned [rɪˈzaɪnd] *adj* resignado
resignedly [rɪˈzaɪnɪdlɪ] *adv* resignadamente
resilience [rɪˈzɪlɪəns] o **resiliency** [rɪˈzɪlɪənsɪ] *s* elasticidad; alegría, viveza; (mech.) resiliencia
resilient [rɪˈzɪlɪənt] *adj* elástico; alegre, vivo
resin [ˈrɛzɪn] *s* resina; *va* tratar con resina, aplicar una capa de resina a
resinate [ˈrɛzɪnet] *s* (chem.) resinato
resinoid [ˈrɛzɪnɔɪd] *adj* resinoide, resinoideo; *s* resinoide; gomorresina
resinous [ˈrɛzɪnəs] *adj* resinoso
resist [rɪˈzɪst] *va* resistir (*la tentación*); resistir a (*la violencia; la risa*); **to resist** + *ger* resistir a + *inf; vn* resistirse
resistance [rɪˈzɪstəns] *s* resistencia; (elec.) resistencia; **to offer resistance** oponer resistencia
resistance box *s* (elec.) caja de resistencias
resistance coil *s* (elec.) bobina o carrete de resistencia
resistance movement *s* movimiento de resistencia
resistant [rɪˈzɪstənt] *adj* resistente
resistibility [rɪˌzɪstɪˈbɪlɪtɪ] *s* resistibilidad
resistible [rɪˈzɪstɪbəl] *adj* resistible
resistive [rɪˈzɪstɪv] *adj* resistivo
resistivity [ˌrizɪsˈtɪvɪtɪ] *s* resistencia; (elec.) resistividad
resistless [rɪˈzɪstlɪs] *adj* irresistible
resistor [rɪˈzɪstər] *s* (elec.) resistor
resnatron [ˈrɛznətrɑn] *s* (elec.) resnatrón
resold [riˈsold] *pret & pp de* **resell**
resole [riˈsol] *va* sobresolar (*un zapato*)
resoluble [ˈrɛzəlubəl] *adj* resoluble
resolute [ˈrɛzəlut] *adj* resuelto
resolution [ˌrɛzəˈluʃən] *s* resolución; **good resolutions** buenos propósitos
resolvable [rɪˈzɑlvəbəl] *adj* resoluble
resolve [rɪˈzɑlv] *s* resolución; *va* resolver; *vn* resolverse; **to resolve on** o **upon** resolverse por; **to resolve to** + *inf* resolverse a + *inf*
resolved [rɪˈzɑlvd] *adj* resuelto
resonance [ˈrɛzənəns] *s* resonancia
resonant [ˈrɛzənənt] *adj* resonante
resonate [ˈrɛzənet] *vn* resonar
resonator [ˈrɛzəˌnetər] *s* resonador
resorb [rɪˈsɔrb] *va* resorber
resorcin [rɛˈzɔrsɪn] o **resorcinol** [rɛˈzɔrsɪnɑl] *s* (chem.) resorcina
resorption [rɪˈsɔrpʃən] *s* resorción
resort [rɪˈzɔrt] *s* concurrencia; recreo; lugar muy frecuentado; estación (*p.ej., de verano*); recurso; **as a last resort** como último recurso; **to have resort to** recurrir a; *vn* concurrir; recurrir; **to resort to** recurrir a
resound [rɪˈzaʊnd] *va* hacer resonar; cantar, celebrar; *vn* resonar
resource [rɪˈsors] o [ˈrisors] *s* recurso
resourceful [rɪˈsorsfəl] *adj* despejado, ingenioso, listo
respect [rɪˈspɛkt] *s* respeto (*veneración*); respecto (*relación, concepto*); **respects** *spl* recuerdos, saludos; **in that respect** bajo ese respecto; **in respect of** respecto a o de; **in respect that** puesto que, ya que; **to pay one's respects to** ofrecer sus respetos a; **with respect to** respecto a o de; *va* respetar (*venerar*); respectar (*tocar*)
respectability [rɪˌspɛktəˈbɪlɪtɪ] *s* respetabilidad
respectable [rɪˈspɛktəbəl] *adj* respetable; **at a respectable distance** a respetable distancia
respectful [rɪˈspɛktfəl] *adj* respetuoso
respectfully [rɪˈspɛktfəlɪ] *adv* respetuosamente; **respectfully yours** de Vd. atento y seguro servidor
respecting [rɪˈspɛktɪŋ] *prep* con respecto a, respecto de
respective [rɪˈspɛktɪv] *adj* respectivo
respectively [rɪˈspɛktɪvlɪ] *adv* respectivamente
respell [riˈspɛl] (*pret & pp:* **-spelled** o **-spelt**) *va* volver a deletrear; transcribir (*en letras de otro alfabeto*)
respiration [ˌrɛspɪˈreʃən] *s* respiración
respirator [ˈrɛspɪˌretər] *s* respirador; máscara respiratoria
respiratory [rɪˈspaɪrəˌtorɪ] o [ˈrɛspɪrəˌtorɪ] *adj* respiratorio
respire [rɪˈspaɪr] *va & vn* respirar
respite [ˈrɛspɪt] *s* respiro; suspensión (*especialmente de la pena de muerte*); **without respite** sin respirar; *va* dar treguas a; aplazar, diferir; dar suspensión a
resplendence [rɪˈsplɛndəns] o **resplendency** [rɪˈsplɛndənsɪ] *s* resplandor
resplendent [rɪˈsplɛndənt] *adj* resplandeciente
respond [rɪˈspɑnd] *vn* responder
respondent [rɪˈspɑndənt] *adj* respondedor; *s* respondedor; (law) demandado (*especialmente en pleito de divorcio*)
response [rɪˈspɑns] *s* respuesta; (eccl.) respuesta que da la congregación a las palabras del oficiante; (eccl.) responsorio; (rad.) respuesta
responsibility [rɪˌspɑnsɪˈbɪlɪtɪ] *s* (*pl:* **-ties**) responsabilidad
responsible [rɪˈspɑnsɪbəl] *adj* responsable; de confianza, p.ej., **a responsible position** un puesto de confianza; **responsible for** responsable de
responsive [rɪˈspɑnsɪv] *adj* responsivo; sensible
responsory [rɪˈspɑnsərɪ] *s* (*pl:* **-ries**) (eccl.) responsorio
rest [rɛst] *s* descanso; reposo (*falta de movimiento*); descansadero; paz (*de los muertos*); (mach.) luneta; (mus.) pausa; resto (*lo que queda*); (billiards & pool) diablo; **at rest** en reposo (*sin movimiento*); tranquilo; dormido; en paz (*muerto*); **the rest** lo demás, lo restante; los demás; **to come to rest** venir a parar; **to lay to rest** enterrar; **without rest** sin descanso; *va* descansar; parar; poner (*p.ej., confianza*); (law) terminar la presentación de pruebas en (*un pleito*); *vn* descansar; residir, estar, hallarse; (law) terminar la presentación de pruebas; **to rest assured** estar seguro, tener la seguridad; **to rest from** descansar de (*p.ej., fatigas*); **to rest on** descansar en o sobre, estribar en
restate [riˈstet] *va* volver a declarar; volver a exponer; volver a formular; volver a plantear (*p.ej., un problema*)
restatement [riˈstetmənt] *s* nueva declaración; nueva exposición
restaurant [ˈrɛstərənt] o [ˈrɛstərɑnt] *s* restaurante
restaurateur [ˌrɛstərɑˈtʌr] *s* dueño de un restaurante, fondista
rest cure *s* cura de reposo
restful [ˈrɛstfəl] *adj* descansado, reposado, tranquilo
restharrow [ˈrɛstˌhæro] *s* (bot.) detienebuey
resting place *s* lugar de descanso; última morada; descansadero (*de escalera*)
restitution [ˌrɛstɪˈtjuʃən] o [ˌrɛstɪˈtuʃən] *s* restitución
restive [ˈrɛstɪv] *adj* intranquilo; rebelón
restless [ˈrɛstlɪs] *adj* intranquilo; insomne
restlessness [ˈrɛstlɪsnɪs] *s* intranquilidad; insomnio

restock [ri'stɑk] *va* reaprovisionar; repoblar (*p.ej., un acuario*)
restoration [,rɛstə'reʃən] *s* restauración
restorative [rɪ'storətɪv] *adj & s* restaurativo
restore [rɪ'stor] *va* restaurar; devolver
restorer [rɪ'storər] *s* restaurador
restrain [rɪ'stren] *va* refrenar; aprisionar, encerrar
restrainedly [rɪ'strenɪdlɪ] o [rɪ'strendlɪ] *adv* comedidamente
restraint [rɪ'strent] *s* restricción; freno; comedimiento
restraint of trade *s* limitación de la libre competencia
restrict [rɪ'strɪkt] *va* restringir
restriction [rɪ'strɪkʃən] *s* restricción
restrictive [rɪ'strɪktɪv] *adj* restrictivo; (gram.) restrictivo
restring [ri'strɪŋ] (*pret & pp:* **-strung**) *va* volver a enhebrar o ensartar; volver a atar con cuerdas; volver a proveer de cuerdas; volver a tender (*un alambre*); volver a encordar (*un violín, una raqueta*)
restringent [rɪ'strɪndʒənt] *adj & s* restringente
rest room *s* sala de descanso; excusado, retrete; (theat.) saloncillo
restrung [ri'strʌŋ] *pret & pp de* **restring**
result [rɪ'zʌlt] *s* resultado; **as a result of** de resultas de; *vn* resultar; **to result from** resultar de; **to result in** dar por resultado, parar en
resultant [rɪ'zʌltənt] *adj* resultante; *s* resultado; (mech.) resultante
resume [rɪ'zum] o [rɪ'zjum] *va* reasumir; reanudar (*el viaje, el vuelo, etc.*); volver a tomar (*asiento*); *vn* continuar; recomenzar; recomenzar a hablar
résumé [,rɛzu'me] o [,rɛzju'me] *s* resumen
resumption [rɪ'zʌmpʃən] *s* reasunción; renovación; continuación
resurface [ri'sʌrfɪs] *va* volver a allanar o alisar; dar nueva superficie a; *vn* volver a emerger (*un submarino*)
resurge [rɪ'sʌrdʒ] *vn* resurgir
resurgence [rɪ'sʌrdʒəns] *s* resurgimiento
resurrect [,rɛzə'rɛkt] *va & vn* resucitar
resurrection [,rɛzə'rɛkʃən] *s* resurrección; (*cap.*) *s* (theol.) Resurrección
resuscitate [rɪ'sʌsɪtet] *va & vn* resucitar
resuscitation [rɪ,sʌsɪ'teʃən] *s* resucitación
resuscitative [rɪ'sʌsɪ,tetɪv] *adj* resucitador
ret [rɛt] (*pret & pp:* **retted;** *ger:* **retting**) *va* enriar
retable [rɪ'tebəl] *s* (eccl.) retablo
retail ['ritel] *s* venta al por menor; **at retail** al por menor; *adj* al por menor, p.ej., **retail price** precio al por menor; **retail trade** comercio al por menor; *va* detallar, vender al por menor; repetir (*p.ej., calumnias*); *vn* vender al por menor; venderse al por menor
retailer ['ritelər] *s* revendedor, detallista, comerciante al por menor
retain [rɪ'ten] *va* retener; contratar (*a un abogado*) pagándole honorarios anticipados
retainer [rɪ'tenər] *s* criado, dependiente; adherente, partidario; (law) ajuste con un abogado; cantidad que se da a un abogado en virtud de ajuste; (law) retención
retaining wall *s* muro de retención
retake ['ri,tek] *s* nueva toma (*p.ej., de vistas cinematográficas*); [ri'tek] (*pret:* **-took;** *pp:* **-taken**) *va* volver a tomar
retaliate [rɪ'tælɪet] *vn* vengarse, desquitarse; **to retaliate on** o **upon** desquitarse con, represaliar
retaliation [rɪ,tælɪ'eʃən] *s* venganza, desquite, represalia
retaliative [rɪ'tælɪ,etɪv] o **retaliatory** [rɪ'tælɪə,torɪ] *adj* vengador; vengativo
retard [rɪ'tɑrd] *s* retardo; *va* retardar; atrasar o retrasar (*un reloj*); *vn* retardarse; atrasarse o retrasarse (*un reloj*)
retardation [,ritɑr'deʃən] *s* retardación
retarded [rɪ'tɑrdɪd] *adj* atrasado; **mentally retarded** mentalmente atrasado
retaught [ri'tɔt] *pret & pp de* **reteach**
retch [rɛtʃ] *va* vomitar; *vn* arquear, esforzarse por vomitar
retching ['rɛtʃɪŋ] *s* esfuerzo de vómito
ret'd. abr. de **returned**
reteach [ri'titʃ] (*pret & pp:* **-taught**) *va* volver a enseñar
retell [ri'tɛl] (*pret & pp:* **-told**) *va* volver a decir; recontar (*volver a relatar; volver a sumar o adicionar*); dar nueva versión de
retention [rɪ'tɛnʃən] *s* retención
retentive [rɪ'tɛntɪv] *adj* retentivo
retentivity [,ritɛn'tɪvɪtɪ] *s* retención; (phys.) retentividad
retiarius [,riʃɪ'ɛrɪəs] *s* (*pl:* **-i** [aɪ]) (hist.) reciario
reticence ['rɛtɪsəns] *s* reserva (*inclinación a guardar silencio*); (rhet.) reticencia
reticent ['rɛtɪsənt] *adj* reservado (*inclinado a guardar silencio*)
reticle ['rɛtɪkəl] *s* (opt.) retículo
reticular [rɪ'tɪkjələr] *adj* reticular
reticulate [rɪ'tɪkjəlet] o [rɪ'tɪkjəlɪt] *adj* reticulado; [rɪ'tɪkjəlet] *va* disponer en forma de red; marcar con líneas que forman red; *vn* formar red, tener figura de red
reticulation [rɪ,tɪkjə'leʃən] *s* reticulación; malla (*del tejido de la red*)
reticule ['rɛtɪkjul] *s* retícula (*bolsillito de mano*); (opt.) retícula; (*cap.*) *s* (astr.) Retícula
reticulum [rɪ'tɪkjələm] *s* (*pl:* **-la** [lə]) retículo; (anat. & bot.) retículo; (zool.) redecilla, retículo
retina ['rɛtɪnə] *s* (anat.) retina
retinal ['rɛtɪnəl] *adj* retiniano
retinitis [,rɛtɪ'naɪtɪs] *s* (path.) retinitis
retinue ['rɛtɪnju] *s* comitiva, séquito
retire [rɪ'taɪr] *va* retirar; jubilar (*a un empleado*); (baseball) retirar (*a un batter o equipo*); *vn* retirarse; jubilarse; recogerse (*retirarse a dormir*); (mil.) retirarse
retired [rɪ'taɪrd] *adj* retirado; jubilado
retirement [rɪ'taɪrmənt] *s* retiro; jubilación (*de un empleado*); (mil.) retirada (*retroceso en buen orden*)
retirement annuity *s* jubilación, pensión de retiro
retiring [rɪ'taɪrɪŋ] *adj* reservado; retraído, tímido; dimitente
retold [ri'told] *pret & pp de* **retell**
retook [ri'tuk] *pret de* **retake**
retool [ri'tul] *vn* instalar nuevas máquinas-herramientas
retorsion [rɪ'tɔrʃən] *s* retorsión; (law) retorsión
retort [rɪ'tɔrt] *s* réplica, respuesta pronta y aguda; (chem.) retorta; *va* rebatir, redargüir (*un argumento*); devolver (*un insulto u ofensa*); *vn* replicar
retort stand *s* portarretorta
retouch [ri'tʌtʃ] *va* retocar; (phot.) retocar
retrace [rɪ'tres] *va* repasar; volver a seguir las huellas de; **to retrace one's steps** volver sobre sus pasos
re-trace [ri'tres] *va* volver a trazar
retract [rɪ'trækt] *va* retraer; retractar o retractarse de (*lo que se ha dicho*); *vn* retraerse; retractarse
retractable [rɪ'træktəbəl] *adj* retractable; (aer.) replegable, retráctil
retractation [,ritræk'teʃən] *s* retractación
retractile [rɪ'træktɪl] *adj* retráctil
retraction [rɪ'trækʃən] *s* retracción; retractación (*de lo que se ha dicho*)
retractive [rɪ'træktɪv] *adj* retractor
retractor [rɪ'træktər] *s* (surg.) retractor; (anat.) músculo retractor
retranslate [,ritræns'let] o [ri'trænslet] *va* retraducir
retread ['ri,trɛd] *s* neumático recauchutado; neumático ranurado; [ri'trɛd] (*pret & pp:* **-treaded**) *va* recauchutar (*un neumático*); volver a ranurar (*un neumático*); (*pret:* **-trod;** *pp:* **-trod** o **-trodden**) *va* desandar; *vn* volverse atrás
retreat [rɪ'trit] *s* retiro; retraimiento (*habitación retirada*); refugio; manicomio; casa para alcohólicos; (eccl.) retiro; (mil.) retirada, retreta; (mil.) retreta (*toque*); **in full retreat** en plena retirada; **to beat a retreat** retraerse, retirarse; (mil.) batirse o marchar en retirada, emprender la retirada; *vn* retraerse, retirarse; deprimirse; (aer.) inclinarse hacia atrás

retrench [rɪ'trɛntʃ] *va* cercenar; (mil.) atrincherar; *vn* recogerse (*moderarse en los gastos*)
retrenchment [rɪ'trɛntʃmənt] *s* cercenadura; (mil.) atrincheramiento
retrial [ri'traɪəl] *s* reensayo; (law) revista; nuevo proceso
retribution [,rɛtrɪ'bjuʃən] *s* justo castigo; (theol.) juicio final
retributive [rɪ'trɪbjətɪv] o **retributory** [rɪ'trɪbjə,torɪ] *adj* castigador; justiciero
retrieval [rɪ'trivəl] *s* recobro; reparación; (hunt.) cobra
retrieve [rɪ'triv] *va* cobrar; reparar (*p.ej., un daño*); desquitarse de (*una pérdida, una derrota*); (hunt.) cobrar, portar; *vn* (hunt.) cobrar, portar
retriever [rɪ'trivər] *s* perro cobrador, perro traedor
retroactive [,rɛtro'æktɪv] *adj* retroactivo
retroactivity [,rɛtroæk'tɪvɪtɪ] *s* retroactividad
retrocede [,rɛtro'sid] *va* hacer retrocesión de; *vn* retroceder
retrocession [,rɛtro'sɛʃən] *s* retrocesión
retrochoir ['rɛtro,kwaɪr] *s* (arch.) trascoro
retrod [ri'trɑd] *pret & pp de* **retread**
retrodden [ri'trɑdən] *pp de* **retread**
retrofiring [,rɛtro'faɪrɪŋ] *s* retrodisparo
retroflex ['rɛtroflɛks] *adj* desviado hacia atrás
retroflexion [,rɛtro'flɛkʃən] *s* retroflexión; (path.) retroflexión
retrogradation [,rɛtrogrə'deʃən] *s* retrogradación; (astr.) retrogradación
retrograde ['rɛtrogred] *adj* retrógrado; *vn* retroceder, volver atrás; decaer, degenerar; (astr.) retrogradar
retrogress ['rɛtrogrɛs] *vn* retroceder; empeorar
retrogression [,rɛtro'grɛʃən] *s* retrogresión; empeoramiento
retrogressive [,rɛtro'grɛsɪv] *adj* regresivo, retrógrado
retrorocket [,rɛtro'rɑkɪt] *s* retrocohete
retrospect ['rɛtrospɛkt] *s* retrospección; consideración de lo pasado; **in retrospect** retrospectivamente; *va* recorrer en la memoria
retrospection [,rɛtro'spɛkʃən] *s* retrospección; consideración de lo pasado
retrospective [,rɛtro'spɛktɪv] *adj* retrospectivo; retroactivo
retroussé [,rɛtru'se] o [rə'truse] *adj* arremangado
retroversion [,rɛtro'vʌrʃən] *s* (path.) retroversión
retry [ri'traɪ] (*pret & pp:* **-tried**) *va* reensayar; rever (*un caso legal*); (law) procesar de nuevo (*a una persona*)
retting ['rɛtɪŋ] *s* enriamiento
return [rɪ'tʌrn] *s* vuelta; devolución; recompensa; respuesta; informe, noticia; ganancia, provecho; rédito; resultado (*de las elecciones*); reportaje (*de las elecciones*); declaración (*de impuestos*); **in return** en cambio; en recompensa; en resarcimiento; **many happy returns of the day** feliz cumpleaños, que cumpla muchos más; *adj* repetido; de vuelta; **by return mail** a vuelta de correo; *va* volver, devolver; rendir; dar en cambio; corresponder a (*un favor*); dar (*un fallo, una respuesta, las gracias*); anunciar oficialmente; elegir (*a cuerpo legislativo*); restar (*la pelota*); devolver (*un naipe del palo que acaba de jugar el compañero*); **to return to** + *inf* volver a, regresar a + *inf; vn* volver; responder
returnable [rɪ'tʌrnəbəl] *adj* restituíble; (law) devolutivo
return address *s* dirección del remitente
return game *s* (sport) desquite, juego de desquite
return ticket *s* billete de vuelta; billete de ida y vuelta
return trip *s* viaje de vuelta
retuse [rɪ'tjus] o [rɪ'tus] *adj* (bot.) retuso
Reuben ['rubɪn] *s* (Bib.) Rubén
reunification [ri,junɪfɪ'keʃən] *s* reunificación
reunify [ri'junɪfaɪ] (*pret & pp:* **-fied**) *va* reunificar
reunion [ri'junjən] *s* reunión; (*cap.*) *s* la Isla de la Reunión
reunite [,rijʊ'naɪt] *va* reunir; *vn* reunirse

rev. abr. de **revenue, reverse, review, revised, revision** y **revolution**
Rev. abr. de **Revelation** y **Reverend**
rev [rɛv] *s* (coll.) revolución; (*pret & pp:* **revved;** *ger:* **revving**) *va* (coll.) cambiar la velocidad de; **to rev up** (coll.) acelerar; *vn* (coll.) acelerarse
revaccinate [ri'væksɪnet] *va* revacunar
revaccination [,rivæksɪ'neʃən] *s* revacunación
revaluation [,rivælju'eʃən] *s* nueva valoración; (econ.) revaloración
revalue [ri'væljʊ] *va* revalorizar
revamp [ri'væmp] *va* renovar, componer, remendar
revanchist [rɪ'vɑntʃɪst] *adj & s* revanchista
reveal [rɪ'vil] *va* revelar
revealed religion *s* (theol.) religión revelada
revealment [rɪ'vilmənt] *s* revelamiento
reveille ['rɛvəlɪ] *s* (mil.) diana, toque de diana
revel ['rɛvəl] *s* jarana, regocijo tumultuoso; (*pret & pp:* **-eled** o **-elled;** *ger:* **-eling** o **-elling**) *vn* jaranear; deleitarse; **to revel in** deleitarse en
revelation [,rɛvə'leʃən] *s* revelación; (*cap.*) *s* (Bib.) libro de la Revelación
reveler o **reveller** ['rɛvələr] *s* jaranero
revelry ['rɛvəlrɪ] *s* (*pl:* **-ries**) jarana, diversión tumultuosa
revenant ['rɛvənənt] *s* persona que vuelve; espectro, aparecido
revenge [rɪ'vɛndʒ] *s* venganza; *va* vengar; **to be revenged** o **to revenge oneself** vengarse; *vn* vengarse
revengeful [rɪ'vɛndʒfəl] *adj* vengativo
revenue ['rɛvənju] o ['rɛvənu] *s* renta, rédito; rentas públicas
revenue cutter *s* (naut.) escampavía
revenue officer *s* agente fiscal
revenue stamp *s* sello fiscal
reverberant [rɪ'vʌrbərənt] *adj* reverberante
reverberate [rɪ'vʌrbəret] *va* reflejar; *vn* reverberar
reverberation [rɪ,vʌrbə'reʃən] *s* reverberación
reverberatory [rɪ'vʌrbərə,torɪ] *adj* reverberatorio
reverberatory furnace *s* horno de reverbero
revere [rɪ'vɪr] *va* reverenciar, venerar
reverence ['rɛvərəns] *s* reverencia; (*cap.*) *s* Reverencia (*título*); (*l.c.*) *va* reverenciar
reverend ['rɛvərənd] *adj* reverendo; *s* (coll.) clérigo, eclesiástico, pastor
reverent ['rɛvərənt] *adj* reverente
reverential [,rɛvə'rɛnʃəl] *adj* reverencial
reverie ['rɛvərɪ] *s* ensueño, ensueños
revers [rə'vɪr] o [rə'vɛr] *s* (*pl:* **revers** [rə'vɪrz] o [rə'vɛrz]) (sew.) solapa
reversal [rɪ'vʌrsəl] *s* inversión; cambio (*p.ej., de opinión*); (law) revocación
reverse [rɪ'vʌrs] *adj* invertido; contrario; de marcha atrás; *s* revés; contrario; contramarcha, marcha atrás, mecanismo de marcha atrás; (fig.) revés, contratiempo; **in reverse** en marcha atrás; **quite the reverse** todo lo contrario; **to put a car in reverse** invertir la marcha de un coche; *va* invertir; dar vuelta a; poner en marcha atrás; dar contravapor a (*una máquina de vapor*); (law) revocar; **to reverse oneself** cambiar de opinión, contradecirse; **to reverse the charges** (telp.) cobrar al número llamado; (telg.) cobrar al destinatario; *vn* invertirse; cambiarse al sentido opuesto (*en los bailes*)
reverse gear *s* (aut.) (engranaje de) marcha atrás
reversely [rɪ'vʌrslɪ] *adv* al revés
reverse pedal *s* pedal de marcha atrás
reverser [rɪ'vʌrsər] *s* (elec.) inversor
reverse turn *s* (aer.) cambio de dirección hacia atrás
reversibility [rɪ,vʌrsɪ'bɪlɪtɪ] *s* reversibilidad
reversible [rɪ'vʌrsɪbəl] *adj* reversible
reversible lock *s* cerradura que cierra por ambos lados
reversible reaction *s* (chem.) reacción reversible
reversion [rɪ'vʌrʒən] o [rɪ'vʌrʃən] *s* reversión; (biol. & law) reversión; (law) futura
reversional [rɪ'vʌrʒənəl] o [rɪ'vʌrʃənəl] o **re-**

versionary [rɪˈvʌrʒəˌnɛrɪ] o [rɪˈvʌrʃəˌnɛrɪ] *adj* de reversión, de la reversión
revert [rɪˈvʌrt] *vn* revertir, recudir; (biol.) saltar atrás; (law) revertir
revery [ˈrɛvərɪ] *s* (*pl:* **-ies**) var. de **reverie**
revet [rɪˈvɛt] (*pret & pp:* **-vetted;** *ger:* **-vetting**) *va* revestir (*un muro, un terraplén, etc.*)
revetment [rɪˈvɛtmənt] *s* revestimiento
revictual [riˈvɪtəl] (*pret & pp:* **-ualed** o **-ualled;** *ger:* **-ualing** o **-ualling**) *va* reavituallar; *vn* reavituallarse
review [rɪˈvju] *s* revista (*reexaminación; reconocimiento; publicación periódica*); reseña, revista (*de un libro*); repaso (*de una lección*); (mil.) revista, reseña; (theat.) revista; *va* rever, revisar; reseñar (*un libro*); repasar (*una lección*); (mil.) revistar
reviewer [rɪˈvjuər] *s* revisor; revistero, crítico
revile [rɪˈvaɪl] *va* ultrajar, vilipendiar
revilement [rɪˈvaɪlmənt] *s* ultraje, vilipendio
revise [rɪˈvaɪz] *s* revisión; refundición; (print.) segunda prueba; *va* rever, revisar; refundir (*un libro*); enmendar
Revised Version *s* versión enmendada de la Biblia (*de 1881 y 1885*)
revision [rɪˈvɪʒən] *s* revisión; refundición (*de un libro*); enmienda
revisionism [rɪˈvɪʒənɪzəm] *s* revisionismo
revisionist [rɪˈvɪʒənɪst] *adj & s* revisionista
revisory [rɪˈvaɪzərɪ] *adj* revisor
revitalize [riˈvaɪtəlaɪz] *va* revitalizar
revival [rɪˈvaɪvəl] *s* resucitación; reanimación; restablecimiento; renacimiento; despertamiento religioso; servicios especiales destinados a despertar el interés por la religión; (theat.) reestreno, reposición
revivalist [rɪˈvaɪvəlɪst] *s* predicador que dirige servicios especiales para despertar el sentimiento religioso
Revival of Learning *s* Renacimiento literario, Renacimiento humanista
revive [rɪˈvaɪv] *va* revivir; (theat.) reestrenar; *vn* revivir; volver en sí, recordar
revivification [rɪˌvɪvɪfɪˈkeʃən] *s* revivificación
revivify [rɪˈvɪvɪfaɪ] (*pret & pp:* **-fied**) *va* revivificar
revocable [ˈrɛvəkəbəl] *adj* revocable
revocation [ˌrɛvəˈkeʃən] *s* revocación
revocatory [ˈrɛvəkəˌtorɪ] *adj* revocatorio
revoke [rɪˈvok] *s* renuncio (*en algunos juegos de naipes*); *va* revocar; *vn* renunciar
revolt [rɪˈvolt] *s* rebelión; *va* dar o causar asco a; repugnar, indignar; *vn* rebelarse; sentir asco
revolting [rɪˈvoltɪŋ] *adj* asqueroso, repugnante; abominable, odioso; rebelde, insurrecto
revolution [ˌrɛvəˈluʃən] *s* revolución
revolutionary [ˌrɛvəˈluʃənˌɛrɪ] *adj* revolucionario; *s* (*pl:* **-ies**) revolucionario
Revolutionary War *s* (U.S.A.) guerra de la Independencia
revolutionist [ˌrɛvəˈluʃənɪst] *s* revolucionario
revolutionize [ˌrɛvəˈluʃənaɪz] *va* revolucionar
revolve [rɪˈvɑlv] *va* hacer girar; revolver (*en la mente*); *vn* girar; (astr.) revolverse (*un astro en su órbita*)
revolver [rɪˈvɑlvər] *s* revólver
revolving [rɪˈvɑlvɪŋ] *adj* giratorio; rotativo
revolving bookcase *s* giratoria
revolving door *s* puerta giratoria
revolving fund *s* fondo rotativo
revue [rɪˈvju] *s* (theat.) revista
revulsion [rɪˈvʌlʃən] *s* cambio repentino, reacción fuerte (*sobre todo en los sentimientos o las ideas*); (med.) revulsión
revulsive [rɪˈvʌlsɪv] *adj & s* revulsivo
Rev. Ver. abr. de **Revised Version**
reward [rɪˈwɔrd] *s* premio, recompensa; hallazgo, p.ej., **five dollars reward** cinco dólares de hallazgo; *va* premiar, recompensar, gratificar
rewarding [rɪˈwɔrdɪŋ] *adj* provechoso, útil, valioso
rewind [riˈwaɪnd] (*pret & pp:* **-wound**) *va* rebobinar, redevanar
rewire [riˈwaɪr] *va* reatar con alambre; cambiar el alambre a; reinstalar alambre conductor en; telegrafiar de nuevo; *vn* telegrafiar de nuevo
reword [riˈwʌrd] *va* volver a formular; formular en otras palabras; repetir
rewrite [ˈriˌraɪt] *s* (U.S.A.) artículo preparado para la publicación; [riˈraɪt] (*pret* **-wrote;** *pp:* **-written**) *va* escribir de nuevo; refundir (*un escrito*); (U.S.A.) preparar (*un escrito o relato de otra persona*) para la publicación
Reynard [ˈrɛnərd] o [ˈrenɑrd] *s* maese Renarte
R.F. o **r.f.** abr. de **radio frequency**
R.F.D. abr. de **Rural Free Delivery**
R.H. abr. de **Royal Highlanders** y **Royal Highness**
Rhadamanthus [ˌrædəˈmænθəs] *s* (myth.) Radamanto
Rhaetia [ˈriʃɪə] *s* la Recia
Rhaetian [ˈriʃən] *adj & s* rético
Rhaetian Alps *spl* Alpes réticos
Rhaeto-Romanic [ˌritoroˈmænɪk] *adj & s* retorromano
rhamnaceous [ræmˈneʃəs] *adj* (bot.) ramnáceo
rhapsodic [ræpˈsɑdɪk] o **rhapsodical** [ræpˈsɑdɪkəl] *adj* rapsódico; extático, locamente entusiasmado
rhapsodist [ˈræpsədɪst] *s* (hist.) rapsoda; (lit.) rapsodista; persona que se expresa con extravagante entusiasmo
rhapsodize [ˈræpsədaɪz] *va* recitar con extravagante entusiasmo; *vn* expresarse con extravagante entusiasmo
rhapsody [ˈræpsədɪ] *s* (*pl:* **-dies**) (mus. & lit.) rapsodia; expresión o escritura caracterizadas por extravagante entusiasmo
rhatany [ˈrætənɪ] *s* (*pl:* **-nies**) (bot.) ratania (*planta y raíz*)
rhea [ˈriə] *s* (orn.) ñandú o avestruz de la pampa; (*cap.*) *s* (myth.) Rea
Rheingold [ˈraɪnˌgold] *s* (myth.) el oro del Rin
Rhenish [ˈrɛnɪʃ] *adj* renano; *s* vino del Rin
rhenium [ˈrinɪəm] *s* (chem.) renio
rheometer [riˈɑmɪtər] *s* reómetro
rheophore [ˈriofor] *s* (elec.) reóforo
rheostat [ˈriostæt] *s* (elec.) reóstato
rhesus [ˈrisəs] *s* (zool.) macaco de la India
rhetor [ˈritər] o [ˈritɔr] *s* rétor; orador
rhetoric [ˈrɛtərɪk] *s* retórica
rhetorical [rɪˈtɑrɪkəl] o [rɪˈtɔrɪkəl] *adj* retórico
rhetorically [rɪˈtɑrɪkəlɪ] o [rɪˈtɔrɪkəlɪ] *adv* retóricamente
rhetorical question *s* comunicación
rhetorician [ˌrɛtəˈrɪʃən] *s* retórico
rheum [rum] *s* (path.) reuma, corrimiento; (path.) catarro; (poet.) lágrimas
rheumatic [ruˈmætɪk] *adj & s* reumático; **rheumatics** *spl* (dial.) reumatismo
rheumatic fever *s* (path.) fiebre reumática
rheumatism [ˈrumətɪzəm] *s* (path.) reumatismo
rheumatoid [ˈrumətɔɪd] *adj* reumatoideo
rheumatoid arthritis *s* (path.) artritis reumatoidea
rheumy [ˈrumɪ] *adj* catarroso; húmedo y frío
Rh factor *s* (biochem.) factor Rh
rhinal [ˈraɪnəl] *adj* rinal
Rhine [raɪn] *s* Rin
Rhinegold [ˈraɪnˌgold] *s* var. de **Rheingold**
Rhineland [ˈraɪnˌlænd] *s* Renania
rhinencephalon [ˌraɪnɛnˈsɛfəlɑn] *s* (*pl:* **-la** [lə]) (anat.) rinencéfalo
Rhine Province *s* Provincia del Rin
rhinestone [ˈraɪnˌston] *s* diamante de imitación hecho de vidrio
Rhine wine *s* vino del Rin
rhinitis [raɪˈnaɪtɪs] *s* (path.) rinitis
rhino [ˈraɪno] *s* (*pl:* **-nos**) (coll.) rinoceronte; (Brit.) dinero
rhinoceros [raɪˈnɑsərəs] *s* (zool.) rinoceronte
rhinoceros hornbill *s* (orn.) cálao rinoceronte
rhinoplasty [ˈraɪnoˌplæstɪ] *s* (surg.) rinoplastia
rhinoscope [ˈraɪnəskop] *s* rinoscopio
rhinoscopy [raɪˈnɑskəpɪ] *s* rinoscopia
rhizoid [ˈraɪzɔɪd] *adj* rizoide; *s* (bot.) rizoide
rhizome [ˈraɪzom] *s* (bot.) rizoma
rhizophagous [raɪˈzɑfəgəs] *adj* (zool.) rizófago

rhizophoraceous [ˌraɪzəfəˈreʃəs] *adj* (bot.) rizoforáceo
rhizopod [ˈraɪzopɑd] *s* (zool.) rizópodo
rhizotomy [raɪˈzɑtəmɪ] *s* (*pl:* **-mies**) (surg.) rizotomía
Rhodes [rodz] *s* Rodas
Rhodesia [roˈdiʒə] *s* la Rodesia
Rhodian [ˈrodɪən] *adj & s* rodio o rodano
rhodium [ˈrodɪəm] *s* (chem.) rodio
rhododendron [ˌrodəˈdɛndrən] *s* (bot.) rododendro
rhodophyceous [ˌrodəˈfaɪʃəs] *adj* (bot.) rodofíceo
rhodopsin [roˈdɑpsɪn] *s* (physiol.) rodopsina
rhodora [roˈdorə] *s* (bot.) rodora
rhomb [rɑm] o [rɑmb] *s* (geom.) rombo
rhombencephalon [ˌrɑmbɛnˈsɛfəlɑn] *s* (anat.) rombencéfalo
rhombic [ˈrɑmbɪk] *adj* (geom.) rombal; (cryst.) rómbico
rhombohedron [ˌrɑmbəˈhidrən] *s* (*pl:* **-dra** [drə]) (geom.) romboedro
rhomboid [ˈrɑmbɔɪd] *adj* romboidal; *s* (geom.) romboide
rhomboidal [rɑmˈbɔɪdəl] *adj* romboidal
rhombus [ˈrɑmbəs] *s* (*pl:* **-buses** o **-bi** [baɪ]) (geom.) rombo
rhonchus [ˈrɑŋkəs] *s* (*pl:* **-chi** [kaɪ]) estertor
Rhone o **Rhône** [ron] *s* Ródano; *adj* rodánico
rhopalic [roˈpælɪk] *adj* (pros.) ropálico
rhotacism [ˈrotəsɪzəm] *s* (philol.) rotacismo
rhubarb [ˈrubɑrb] *s* (bot. & pharm.) ruipóntico (*Rheum rhaponticum*); (bot. & pharm.) ruibarbo (*Rheum palmatum y Rheum officinale*); (cook.) ruipóntico; (slang) disputa, pendencia
rhumb [rʌm] o [rʌmb] *s* (naut.) rumbo de la aguja, cuarta (*de la rosa náutica*)
rhumb line *s* (naut.) loxodromia
rhyme [raɪm] *s* rima; **without rhyme or reason** sin ton ni son; *va & vn* rimar
rhymer [ˈraɪmər] *s* rimador
rhymester [ˈraɪmstər] *s* rimador (*poeta de mediano valor*)
rhynchocephalian [ˌrɪŋkosɪˈfelɪən] *adj & s* rincocéfalo
rhyolite [ˈraɪolaɪt] *s* (mineral.) riolita
rhythm [ˈrɪðəm] *s* ritmo
rhythmic [ˈrɪðmɪk] *adj* rítmico; **rhythmics** *ssg* rítmica
rhythmical [ˈrɪðmɪkəl] *adj* rítmico
rhyton [ˈraɪtɑn] *s* (*pl:* **-ta** [tə]) (archeol.) ritón
R.I. abr. de **Royal Institute** y **Rhode Island**
rialto [rɪˈælto] (*pl:* **-tos**) mercado; (*cap.*) *s* puente del Rialto (*de Venecia*); centro teatral de Nueva York
rib [rɪb] *s* costilla; (anat., bot. & naut.) costilla; varilla (*del abanico, paraguas, etc.*); cuerda (*de neumático*); (sew.) canilla, vivo; (zool.) nervio (*del ala de los insectos*); (fig.) costilla (*mujer propia*); (*pret & pp:* **ribbed;** *ger:* **ribbing**) *va* proveer de costillas; (sew.) hacer vivos en; (slang) tomar el pelo a
ribald [ˈrɪbəld] *adj* grosero y obsceno (*especialmente en el lenguaje*); *s* persona grosera y obscena
ribaldry [ˈrɪbəldrɪ] *s* lenguaje grosero y obsceno
riband o **ribband** [ˈrɪbənd] *s* (archaic) var. de **ribbon**
ribbed [rɪbd] *adj* acostillado; acanalado, rayado; nervudo
ribbing [ˈrɪbɪŋ] *s* costillaje; varillaje; nervadura
ribbon [ˈrɪbən] *s* cinta; *va* encintar; *vn* extenderse como cinta, serpentear
ribboned [ˈrɪbənd] *adj* encintado
riboflavin [ˌraɪboˈflevɪn] *s* (biochem.) riboflavina
ribwort [ˈrɪbˌwʌrt] *s* (bot.) lancéola
rice [raɪs] *s* (bot.) arroz (*planta y fruto*); *va* pasar por una hilera
ricebird [ˈraɪsˌbʌrd] *s* (orn.) chambergo; (orn.) pájaro conirrostro de Malasia (*Munia oryzivora*)
rice field *s* arrozal
rice paper *s* papel de paja de arroz
rice powder *s* polvos de arroz
rice pudding *s* arroz con leche
ricer [ˈraɪsər] *s* hilera
rich [rɪtʃ] *adj* rico; vivo (*color*); sonoro (*dícese de la voz*); azucarado o condimentado; generoso (*vino*); (coll.) divertido, entretenido; (coll.) ridículo; **the rich** los ricos; **to strike it rich** descubrir un buen filón, tener un golpe de fortuna; **riches** *spl* riqueza
Richard [ˈrɪtʃərd] *s* Ricardo
Richard Coeur de Lion [ˈkʌr də ˈliən] *s* Ricardo, Corazón de León
richly [ˈrɪtʃlɪ] *adv* ricamente; abundantemente, completamente
richness [ˈrɪtʃnɪs] *s* riqueza; viveza (*de color*); sonoridad (*de la voz*); crasitud, suculencia
rick [rɪk] *s* montón de paja, heno, grano, etc. al raso y frecuentemente bardado; *va* hacer montones de (*paja, heno, grano, etc.*)
rickets [ˈrɪkɪts] *s* (path.) raquitis
rickettsia [rɪˈkɛtsɪə] *s* (*pl:* **-ae** [i]) (bact.) rickettsia
rickety [ˈrɪkɪtɪ] *adj* (path.) raquítico; tambaleante, vacilante; destartalado, desvencijado
ricksha [ˈrɪkʃɔ] o [ˈrɪkʃɑ] o **rickshaw** [ˈrɪkʃɔ] *s* rikscha (*pequeño carruaje chino y japonés de dos ruedas y tirado por uno o más hombres*)
ricochet [ˌrɪkəˈʃe] o [ˌrɪkəˈʃɛt] *s* rebote; (*pret & pp:* **-cheted** [ˈʃed] o **-chetted** [ˈʃɛtɪd]; *ger:* **-cheting** [ˈʃeɪŋ] o **-chetting** [ˈʃɛtɪŋ]) *vn* rebotar
ricochet fire *s* (gun.) fuego de rebote
rid [rɪd] (*pret & pp:* **rid** o **ridded;** *ger:* **ridding**) *va* desembarazar, librar; **to be rid of** estar libre de; **to get rid of** desembarazarse de, deshacerse de; matar; **to rid oneself of** desembarazarse de, deshacerse de
riddance [ˈrɪdəns] *s* supresión, libramiento; **good riddance!** ¡adiós, gracias! (*¡de buena me he librado!*)
ridden [ˈrɪdən] *pp de* **ride**
riddle [ˈrɪdəl] *s* acertijo, adivinanza; enigma (*persona o cosa difíciles de comprender*); garbillo, criba gruesa; *va* adivinar; solucionar; garbillar, cribar; acribillar; **to riddle with bullets** acribillar a balazos; **to riddle with questions** acribillar a preguntas; *vn* hablar enigmáticamente
ride [raɪd] *s* paseo; **to thumb a ride** pedir ser llevado en automóvil indicando la dirección con el pulgar ‖ (*pret:* **rode;** *pp:* **ridden**) *va* montar (*un caballo, una bicicleta, los hombros de una persona, etc.*); recorrer a caballo; flotar sobre (*las olas*); hender o surcar (*las olas*); correr a caballo en (*una carrera*); luchar felizmente contra; cabalgar (*cubrir el caballo u otro animal a su hembra*); dominar, tiranizar; (coll.) llevar, transportar; (coll.) llevar a horcajadas; (coll.) burlarse de; (coll.) molestar criticando o poniendo en ridículo; **to ride down** revolcar, atropellar; rendir, vencer; alcanzar (*a una persona*) andando a caballo; **to ride out** luchar felizmente con (*una tempestad*); aguantar o soportar con buen éxito (*una desgracia*) ‖ *vn* montar; pasear en coche o carruaje; montar en bicicleta; flotar (*en la superficie del agua o en el aire*); marchar, funcionar; rodar (*alrededor del eje*); **to let ride** (slang) dejar correr; **to ride in** entrar a caballo; entrar en coche; **to ride out** salir a caballo; salir en coche; **to take riding** llevar de paseo
rider [ˈraɪdər] *s* caballero, jinete; pasajero; (law) aditamento a un documento; (law) cláusula añadida a un proyecto de ley; (naut.) sobreplán
ridge [rɪdʒ] *s* espinazo; caballete (*del tejado; de tierra entre dos surcos*); cordoncillo (*de un tejido*); cordillera; arista, intersección (*de dos planos*); *va* formar caballetes, cordoncillos, etc. en; cubrir o marcar con caballetes, cordoncillos, etc.; *vn* estar marcado con caballetes, cordoncillos, etc.
ridgeband [ˈrɪdʒˌbænd] *s* sufra
ridgepole [ˈrɪdʒˌpol] *s* parhilera
ridge purlin *s* (carp.) correa de cumbrera
ridgy [ˈrɪdʒɪ] *adj* (*comp:* **-ier;** *super:* **-iest**) acanalado, alomado, rugoso; cerril
ridicule [ˈrɪdɪkjul] *s* irrisión; **to expose to ridicule** poner en ridículo; *va* ridiculizar
ridiculous [rɪˈdɪkjələs] *adj* ridículo
riding academy *s* escuela de equitación

riding boot *s* bota de montar
riding breeches *spl* pantalones de equitación
riding crop *s* látigo de montar
riding habit *s* traje de montar
riding master *s* maestro de equitación
riding saddle *s* silla de montar
riding whip *s* fusta
Rif [rɪf], **Er** [ɛr] El Rif
rife [raɪf] *adj* frecuente, común, corriente, general; abundante, lleno; **rife with** abundante en, lleno de
Riff [rɪf] *s* rifeño
Riffian [ˈrɪfɪən] *adj & s* rifeño
riffle [ˈrɪfəl] *s* recial; rizo (*de agua*); *va* peinar (*la baraja*)
riffraff [ˈrɪf,ræf] *s* bahorrina; *adj* ruin, vil; de ningún valor
rifle [ˈraɪfəl] *s* rifle, fusil; *va* rayar (*un rifle*); hurtar, robar; escudriñar y robar; desnudar, despojar
rifleman [ˈraɪfəlmən] *s* (*pl:* **-men**) tirador armado de rifle; riflero (*soldado*)
rifle pit *s* pozo para rifleros
rifle range *s* tiro de rifle
rifling [ˈraɪflɪŋ] *s* rayado (*de un rifle*)
rift [rɪft] *s* raja, abertura; desavenencia, desacuerdo; *va* rajar; *vn* rajarse
rifty [ˈrɪftɪ] *adj* rajado
rig [rɪg] *s* (naut.) aparejo; equipaje; aparejos; (coll.) traje, traje extraño y poco conveniente; carruaje con caballo o caballos; mala partida, mala jugada; timo, robo, engaño; (*pret & pp:* **rigged;** *ger:* **rigging**) *va* (naut.) aparejar, enjarciar; equipar; (coll.) vestir, vestir de una manera extraña y poco conveniente; aprestar, disponer; improvisar; arreglar o manejar de una manera artificiosa o fraudulenta
rigadoon [,rɪgəˈdun] *s* rigodón (*danza y música*)
rigger [ˈrɪgər] *s* (naut.) aparejador; (aer.) montador
rigging [ˈrɪgɪŋ] *s* (naut.) aparejo; avíos, equipo, todo género de instrumentos
right [raɪt] *adj* derecho; verdadero; conveniente; favorable; sano, normal; bien, p.ej., **his work is right** su trabajo está bien; que se busca, p.ej., **this is the right house** ésta es la casa que se busca; que se necesita, p.ej., **this is the right train** éste es el tren que se necesita; que debe, p.ej., **he is going the right way** sigue el camino que debe; (pol.) de derecha; correcto; señalado; correspondiente; (geom.) rectángulo; **to be right** tener razón; **to be all right** estar bien; estar bien de salud; **right or wrong** con razón o sin ella, bueno o malo, a tuertas o a derechas ‖ *adv* derechamente; directamente; correctamente; exactamente; convenientemente; favorablemente; en orden, en buen estado; a la derecha, hacia la derecha; completamente; (coll.) muy; (archaic) muy, p.ej., **right honorable** muy honorable; mismo, p.ej., **right here** aquí mismo; **right now** ahora mismo; **right in Spain** en España mismo; **right from Seville** desde Sevilla mismo; **all right** muy bien; **right afterwards** acto seguido; **right along** sin cesar, sin interrupción; **right away** en seguida; **right off** en seguida ‖ *interj* ¡bien!, ¡bueno!; **right about!** (mil.) ¡derecha! ‖ *s* derecho (*justicia, razón*); derecha (*mano derecha*); (box.) derechazo; (com.) derecho de subscribirse a la compra de acciones o bonos; (com.) certificado que da derecho a comprar acciones o bonos; (pol.) derecha; **by right** o **by rights** según derecho; **on the right** a la derecha; **to be in the right** tener razón; **to have the right to** tener derecho a; **to the right** a la derecha; **to rights** (coll.) en orden ‖ *va* enderezar; corregir, rectificar; hacer justicia a; deshacer (*un entuerto*); (naut.) adrizar ‖ *vn* enderezarse; (naut.) adrizarse
rightabout-face [ˈraɪtə,bautˈfes] *s* media vuelta a la derecha; *vn* dar media vuelta a la derecha
right-and-left [ˈraɪtəndˈlɛft] *adj* derecho e izquierdo; *adv* a diestra y siniestra; a diestro y siniestro (*sin tino, sin orden*)
right angle *s* ángulo recto
right-angled [ˈraɪtˈæŋgəld] *adj* rectangular
right ascension *s* (astr.) ascensión recta
righteous [ˈraɪtʃəs] *adj* recto, justo; virtuoso
righteousness [ˈraɪtʃəsnɪs] *s* rectitud, justicia; virtud
right field *s* (baseball) jardín derecho
rightful [ˈraɪtfəl] *adj* justo; legítimo
rightfully [ˈraɪtfəlɪ] *adv* justamente; legítimamente; a justo título
right-hand [ˈraɪt,hænd] *adj* derecho; de, con o para la mano derecha; de movimiento, funcionamiento, etc. hacia la derecha
right-hand drive *s* (aut.) conducción a derecha
right-handed [ˈraɪtˈhændɪd] *adj* que usa la mano derècha; con o para la mano derecha; para los que usan la mano derecha; de movimiento hacia la derecha
right-hand man *s* mano derecha, brazo derecho
rightism [ˈraɪtɪzəm] *s* derechismo
rightist [ˈraɪtɪst] *adj & s* derechista
right jab *s* (box.) inverso de derecha
rightly [ˈraɪtlɪ] *adv* derechamente; correctamente; con razón; convenientemente; **rightly or wrongly** con razón o sin ella; **rightly so** a justo título
right mind *s* entero juicio
right-minded [ˈraɪtˈmaɪndɪd] *adj* honrado, recto
rightness [ˈraɪtnɪs] *s* derechura
righto [ˈraɪto] *interj* (coll.) ¡muy bien!, ¡con mucho gusto!
right of assembly *s* derecho de reunión
right of asylum *s* derecho de asilo
right of search o **right of visit** *s* (int. law) derecho de visita
right of way *s* derecho de tránsito o de paso; (law) servidumbre de paso; (rail.) servidumbre de vía
right shoulder arms *interj* (mil.) ¡arma al hombro!
rights of man *spl* derechos del hombre
right to work *s* libertad de trabajo
right triangle *s* (geom.) triángulo rectángulo
right wing *s* ala derecha (*de un ejército*); (pol.) derecha
right-wing [ˈraɪt,wɪŋ] *adj* derechista
right-winger [ˈraɪt,wɪŋər] *s* (coll.) derechista
rigid [ˈrɪdʒɪd] *adj* rígido
rigidity [rɪˈdʒɪdɪtɪ] *s* rigidez
rigmarole [ˈrɪgmərol] *s* galimatías
rigor [ˈrɪgər] *s* rigor; (path. & physiol.) rigor
rigorism [ˈrɪgərɪzəm] *s* rigorismo
rigorist [ˈrɪgərɪst] *s* rigorista
rigor mortis [ˈraɪgɔr ˈmɔrtɪs] o [ˈrɪgər ˈmɔrtɪs] *s* rigor de la muerte, rigidez cadavérica
rigorous [ˈrɪgərəs] *adj* riguroso
rile [raɪl] *va* (coll.) exasperar, irritar con exceso
rill [rɪl] *s* arroyuelo o riachuelo; *vn* correr (*el agua*) en un arroyuelo o riachuelo
rim [rɪm] *s* canto, borde; llanta (*de la rueda*); (aut.) aro (*de neumático*); (*pret & pp:* **rimmed;** *ger:* **rimming**) *va* proveer de un canto o borde; correr alrededor del canto de; cercar, rodear
rime [raɪm] *s* rima; escarcha; **without rime or reason** sin ton ni son; *va* rimar; cubrir con escarcha; *vn* rimar
rimer [ˈraɪmər] *s* var. de **rhymer**
rimester [ˈraɪmstər] *s* var. de **rhymester**
rim lock *s* cerradura guarnecida al revés
rimy [ˈraɪmɪ] *adj* (*comp:* **-ier;** *super:* **-iest**) escarchado
rind [raɪnd] *s* corteza; *va* descortezar
rinderpest [ˈrɪndər,pɛst] *s* (vet.) fiebre biliosa hematúrica, ictericia hematúrica
ring [rɪŋ] *s* anillo; sortija; círculo; corona (*de un vaso, copa, etc.*); reborde (*de una moneda*); círculo de goma (*para tarros de frutas*); anilla (*que se emplea en la gimnasia*); argolla (*que se pone en la nariz a un animal*); arena (*para carreras, juegos deportivos, etc.*); circo (*para ejercicios ecuestres o acrobáticos*); (taur.) redondel; cuadrilátero o ruedo (*para el boxeo*); boxeo, pugilato; corro (*de gente*); cuadrilla (*grupo de personas*); pandilla (*grupo de personas con un fin censurable o ilícito*); ojera (*bajo el párpado inferior*); (naut.) arganeo (*de la caña del ancla*); (chem.) núcleo; campanada (*toque de campana; sonido de reloj*); campanilleo; tañido; tintineo (*de choque de*

copas, de campanilla, timbre, etc.); llamada (*aviso acústico*); (fig.) tono (*carácter, espíritu*); **the rings of Saturn** (astr.) los anillos de Saturno; **to be in the ring (for)** ser candidato (a); **to run rings around** dar cien vueltas a, vencer completamente ‖ *adj* anular ‖ (*pret & pp:* **ringed**) *va* cercar, rodear; anillar; quitar a (*un árbol*) una tira circular de corteza; (sport); meter el herrón o la herradura en (*el clavo*); (sport) meter (*el herrón o la herradura*) en el clavo ‖ *vn* anillarse; formar círculo o corro ‖ (*pret:* **rang** o **rung**; *pp:* **rung**) *va* sonar; tañer, repicar; tocar; llamar o convocar repicando o tocando campanas; llamar al timbre; anunciar o celebrar con repique de campanas; entonar (*las alabanzas de una persona*); dar (*las horas la campana del reloj*); llamar por teléfono; **to ring in** (coll.) introducir con maña o fraudulentamente; **to ring up** llamar por teléfono; marcar (*una compra*) con el timbre ‖ *vn* sonar (*una campana, un timbre, el teléfono*); campanear; campanillear; repicar; tintinear (*el choque de copas, una campanilla*); llamar; resonar, retumbar; ser celebrado, tener fama; zumbar (*los oídos*); (fig.) sonar (*tener cierta apariencia*); **to ring for** llamar, llamar al timbre; **to ring off** terminar una llamada por teléfono; **to ring up** llamar por teléfono

ring-around-a-rosy [ˈrɪŋəˌraʊndəˈrozɪ] *s* corro, juego del corro

ringbolt [ˈrɪŋˌbolt] *s* perno con anillo, cáncamo de argolla

ringdove [ˈrɪŋˌdʌv] *s* (orn.) paloma torcaz; (orn.) tórtola (*Streptopelia risoria*)

ringed [rɪŋd] *adj* anillado; que lleva anillo; que lleva anillo de matrimonio; casado

ringer [ˈrɪŋər] *s* campanero; dispositivo de llamada; impulsador de campanilla de teléfono; herrón o herradura metida en el clavo; (slang) jugador que toma parte en una competencia atlética representándose falsamente; (slang) segunda edición (*persona o cosa que se parece mucho a otra*)

ring finger *s* dedo anular, dedo médico

ring formation *s* (chem.) ciclización

ringing [ˈrɪŋɪŋ] *s* anillamiento; campaneo; repique; tintineo; retintín o silbido (*de oídos*); *adj* resonante, retumbante

ringleader [ˈrɪŋˌlidər] *s* cabecilla

ringlet [ˈrɪŋlɪt] *s* anillejo; rizo

ringleted [ˈrɪŋlɪtɪd] *adj* rizado

ringmaster [ˈrɪŋˌmæstər] o [ˈrɪŋˌmɑstər] *s* hombre encargado de los ejercicios ecuestres y acrobáticos de un circo

Ring of the Nibelung *s* Anillo del Nibelungo

ring shake *s* acebolladura

ringside [ˈrɪŋˌsaɪd] *s* lugar junto al cuadrilátero de boxeo; lugar desde el cual se puede ver de cerca

ringworm [ˈrɪŋˌwʌrm] *s* (path.) tiña

rink [rɪŋk] *s* patinadero

rinse [rɪns] *s* enjuague, aclaración; *va* enjuagar, aclarar

riot [ˈraɪət] *s* alboroto, desorden, tumulto; regocijos ruidosos, orgía; exhibición brillante (*de colores*); **to read the riot act** mandar que cese la agitación; reprender vehementemente, protestar vehementemente; **to run riot** desenfrenarse; crecer lozanamente (*las plantas*)

rioter [ˈraɪətər] *s* alborotador; jaranero, libertino

riotous [ˈraɪətəs] *adj* alborotado, desenfrenado, bullicioso; desenfrenado, libertino

riot squad *s* pelotón de asalto, escuadra de choque

R.I.P. abr. de **Requiescat** (o **Requiescant**) **in pace** (Lat.) **May he** o **she** (o **they**) **rest in peace**

rip [rɪp] *s* rasgón; (sew.) descosido; corriente rápida hecha por la marea; agua que se ha puesto revuelta por la confluencia de corrientes o mareas; (coll.) holgazán; (coll.) jamelgo; (*pret & pp:* **ripped**; *ger:* **ripping**) *va* rasgar, desgarrar; (sew.) descoser; (carp.) aserrar (*la madera*) al hilo; **to rip off** quitar rasgando; arrebatar, quitar violentamente; **to rip open** abrir desgarrando; abrir violentamente; **to rip out** arrancar o sacar desgarrando; arrancar o sacar violentamente; (coll.) decir con violencia; **to rip up** rasgar, desgarrar; desarraigar con violencia; *vn* rasgarse, desgarrarse; (coll.) adelantar o moverse de prisa o con violencia; **to rip out with** (coll.) decir con violencia

riparian [rɪˈpɛrɪən] o [raɪˈpɛrɪən] *adj & s* ribereño

rip cord *s* (aer.) cabo de desgarre; (aer.) cuerda de apertura

ripe [raɪp] *adj* maduro; rosado, colorado; hecho, acabado; dispuesto, preparado, pronto; madurado (*divieso, tumor*); negro (*dícese de una aceituna*)

ripen [ˈraɪpən] *va & vn* madurar

ripeness [ˈraɪpnɪs] *s* madurez

riposte [rɪˈpost] *s* (fencing) estocada que se da después de parar; (fig.) respuesta pronta y aguda; *vn* (fencing) reparar y dar la estocada a un mismo tiempo; (fig.) responder con viveza

rip panel *s* (aer.) faja de desgarre

ripper [ˈrɪpər] *s* rasgador; descosedor

ripping [ˈrɪpɪŋ] *s* rasgadura, desgarro; *adj* (slang) espléndido, excelente, magnífico

ripple [ˈrɪpəl] *s* rizo, temblor, ondulación; murmullo; *va* rizar; *vn* rizarse; correr con rizos u olas pequeñas; murmurar

ripplet [ˈrɪplɪt] *s* rizo pequeño (*de agua*)

ripply [ˈrɪplɪ] *adj* rizado; murmullante

riprap [ˈrɪpˌræp] *s* ripio; muro hecho con ripio; (*pret & pp:* **-rapped**; *ger:* **-rapping**) *va* reforzar con ripio; construir con ripio

rip-roaring [ˈrɪpˈrorɪŋ] *adj* (slang) alborozado, bullicioso

ripsaw [ˈrɪpˌsɔ] *s* sierra de hilar o hender; *va* aserrar al hilo

rise [raɪz] *s* subida (*p.ej., de la temperatura, de precios, de un pez a la superficie del agua para coger cebo; cuesta ascendiente*); elevación (*p.ej., del terreno, de la voz*); salida (*de un astro*); ascenso (*en un empleo*); altura (*de peldaño*); montea (*de arco*); nacimiento (*de un manantial*); crecida; (mach.) levantamiento (*de una válvula*); (slang) réplica mordaz; **to get a rise out of** (slang) sacar una réplica mordaz a; **to give rise to** dar origen a; (*pret:* **rose**; *pp:* **risen**) *vn* levantarse; subir; salir (*un astro*); asomar (*p.ej., un peligro*); brotar (*un manantial, una planta*); resucitar; ganar (*en la estimación de uno*); **to rise above** alzarse por encima de; mostrarse superior a; **to rise early** madrugar; **to rise to** ser capaz de, sentirse con fuerzas para

risen [ˈrɪzən] *pp de* **rise**

riser [ˈraɪzər] *s* contrahuella, contraescalón (*frente del peldaño*); **early riser** madrugador; **late riser** dormilón

risibility [ˌrɪzɪˈbɪlɪtɪ] *s* (*pl:* **-ties**) risibilidad; **risibilities** *spl* ganas de reírse, reideras

risible [ˈrɪzɪbəl] *adj* risible; **risibles** *spl* reideras

rising [ˈraɪzɪŋ] *adj* ascendiente; naciente; creciente; saliente (*Sol*); venidero; (phonet.) creciente (*diptongo*)

risk [rɪsk] *s* riesgo; **at the risk of** + *ger* a riesgo de + *inf;* **to run** o **take a risk** correr riesgo; **to run** o **take the risk of** + *ger* correr riesgo de + *inf;* *va* arriesgar; arriesgarse en (*una empresa dudosa*); **to risk** + *ger* arriesgarse a + *inf*

risky [ˈrɪskɪ] *adj* (*comp:* **-ier**; *super:* **-iest**) arriesgado; escabroso

risqué [rɪsˈke] *adj* escabroso

rissole [ˈrɪsol] o [riˈsɔl] *s* (cook.) risol (*torta tostada hecha de carne picada o pescado, huevos, migas de pan y otros ingredientes*)

rite [raɪt] *s* rito

ritornel o **ritornelle** [ˌrɪtərˈnɛl] *s* (mus.) retornelo

ritual [ˈrɪtʃʊəl] *adj & s* ritual

ritualism [ˈrɪtʃʊəlɪzəm] *s* ritualismo

ritualist [ˈrɪtʃʊəlɪst] *adj & s* ritualista

ritualistic [ˌrɪtʃʊəlˈɪstɪk] *adj* ritualista

ritually [ˈrɪtʃʊəlɪ] *adv* según el ritual

ritual murder *s* asesinato ritual

riv. abr. de **river**

rival [ˈraɪvəl] *adj & s* rival; (*pret & pp:* **-valed** o **-valled**; *ger:* **-valing** o **-valling**) *va* rivalizar con

rivalry [ˈraɪvəlrɪ] *s* (*pl:* **-ries**) rivalidad

rivalship ['raɪvəlʃɪp] *s* rivalidad
rive [raɪv] (*pret:* **rived;** *pp:* **rived** o **riven**) *va* rajar; *vn* rajarse
riven ['rɪvən] *adj* rajado; *pp de* **rive**
river ['rɪvər] *s* río; (fig.) río (*p.ej., de sangre*); **down the river** río abajo; **up the river** río arriba; *adj* fluvial
river basin *s* cuenca de río
river bed *s* cauce
river front *s* orilla del río
river-god ['rɪvər,gad] *s* dios del río
riverhead ['rɪvər,hɛd] *s* nacimiento de un río
river horse *s* (zool.) caballo marino (*hipopótamo*)
riverside ['rɪvər,saɪd] *s* ribera; *adj* ribereño
rivet ['rɪvɪt] *s* roblón, remache; *va* remachar; clavar (*p.ej., los ojos en una persona*)
riveter ['rɪvɪtər] *s* remachador; remachadora (*máquina*)
rivulet ['rɪvjəlɪt] *s* riachuelo
rm. abr. de **ream** y **room**
rms. abr. de **reams** y **rooms**
R.N. abr. de **registered nurse** y **Royal Navy**
roach [rotʃ] *s* (ent.) cucaracha; (ichth.) leucisco
road [rod] *s* camino; (naut.) rada; **in the road** estorbando el paso; incomodando; **to be on the road** viajar de lugar en lugar (*en el ejercicio de un empleo*); **to get out of the road** quitarse de en medio; **to take to the road** (archaic) hacerse salteador de caminos
road agent *s* (U.S.A.) salteador de caminos
roadbed ['rod,bɛd] *s* firme; (rail.) infraestructura; (rail.) capa de balastro
roadblock ['rod,blak] *s* (mil.) barricada; (fig.) obstáculo
roadhouse ['rod,haʊs] *s* posada en el camino, venta
road laborer *s* peón caminero
road map *s* mapa itinerario
road metal *s* grava, piedra triturada para caminos
road roller *s* cilindro de caminos, apisonador
road runner *s* (orn.) correcamino
road scraper *s* traílla
road service *s* (aut.) auxilio en carretera
roadside ['rod,saɪd] *s* borde del camino, borde de la carretera
roadside inn *s* posada en el camino, venta
road sign *s* señal de carretera, poste indicador
roadstead ['rod,stɛd] *s* (naut.) rada
roadster ['rodstər] *s* caminante; caballo de campo; (aut.) roadster, coche de caja abierta y de dos plazas
roadway ['rod,we] *s* camino, vía
roam [rom] *s* vagabundeo; *va* vagar por, recorrer a la ventura; *vn* vagar, andar errante
roan [ron] *adj* roano; *s* color roano; caballo roano
roar [ror] *s* rugido, bramido; *va* decir a gritos; **to roar oneself hoarse** ponerse ronco gritando; *vn* rugir, bramar; reírse a carcajadas
roast [rost] *s* asado; carne para asar; variedad de café tostado; (coll.) fiesta en que se comen manjares asados directamente al o en el fuego; (coll.) burla o censura severa, despellejadura; *adj* asado; tostado (*café*); *va* asar; tostar (*café*); (coll.) burlarse de, mofarse de, despellejar; *vn* asarse; tostarse (*café*)
roast beef *s* rosbif
roaster ['rostər] *s* asador; tostador; pollo o lechón propio para asar
roast of beef *s* carne de vaca asada o para asar
rob [rab] (*pret & pp:* **robbed;** *ger:* **robbing**) *va* robar; **to rob someone of something** o **to rob something from someone** robarle algo a alguien; **to rob Peter to pay Paul** desnudar a un santo para vestir a otro; *vn* robar; (*cap.*) *s* nombre abreviado de **Robert**
robber ['rabər] *s* robador, ladrón
robbery ['rabərɪ] *s* (*pl:* **-ies**) robo
robe [rob] *s* manto; abrigo; toga, túnica (*del letrado, juez, etc.*); traje talar (*del sacerdote*); manta (*de coche*); traje, vestido (*de mujer*); *va* vestir; *vn* vestirse
Robert ['rabərt] *s* Roberto
robin ['rabɪn] *s* (orn.) petirrojo; (orn.) primavera (*Turdus migratorius*)
robin's-egg blue ['rabɪnz,ɛg] *s* color azul verdoso
robot ['robat] o ['rabət] *s* robot; (fig.) robot (*persona*)
robot bomb *s* (mil.) bomba volante, bomba cohete
robust [ro'bʌst] *adj* robusto; arduo, vigoroso; grosero
robustious [ro'bʌstʃəs] *adj* (archaic & hum.) robusto; (archaic & hum.) alborotado, ruidoso, grosero
roc [rak] *s* (myth.) roc o rocho (*ave*)
rocambole ['rakəmbol] *s* (bot.) rocambola
Rochelle salt [ro'ʃɛl] *s* (pharm.) sal de la Rochela
rochet ['ratʃɪt] *s* (eccl.) roquete
rock [rak] *s* roca; escollo (*a flor de agua*); (coll.) piedra (*que se tira*); (slang) diamante, piedra preciosa; (orn.) paloma zorita; (ichth.) pez anadromo (*Roccus saxatilis*); mecedura; (*cap.*) *s* Peñón (*de Gibraltar*); **on the rocks** (coll.) arruinado, quebrado, en pobreza extrema; (coll.) con sólo trocitos de hielo, sobre hielo (*dícese de ciertas bebidas alcohólicas*); *adj* de roca, formado de rocas; entre las rocas; *va* mecer; acunar; arrullar; calmar, sosegar; sacudir; **to rock the boat** mover el barco de un modo temerario; (fig.) perturbar la armonía; **to rock to sleep** arrullar, adormecer meciendo; *vn* mecerse; sacudirse
rock bottom *s* el fondo, lo más profundo
rock-bottom ['rak,batəm] *adj* (el) mínimo, (el) más bajo
rock-bound ['rak,baʊnd] *adj* rodeado de rocas; inaccesible
rock candy *s* azúcar cande, azúcar candi
rock crystal *s* cristal de roca
rock dove *s* (orn.) paloma zorita
rocker ['rakər] *s* mecedora (*silla*); arco (*de mecedora o cuna*); (mach.) eje de balancín; (mach.) balancín
rocker arm *s* (mach.) balancín
rockershaft ['rakər,ʃæft] o ['rakər,ʃaft] *s* (mach.) eje de balancín
rocket ['rakɪt] *s* cohete; (bot.) roqueta, ruca; (bot.) juliana, violeta; *vn* subir como un cohete, lucirse y desaparecer; alcanzar gran altura rápida y súbitamente
rocket bomb *s* bomba cohete
rocketeer [,rakɪ'tɪr] *s* cohetero
rocket gun *s* (mil.) cañón cohete
rocket larkspur *s* (bot.) espuela de caballero
rocket launcher *s* (mil.) lanzacohetes
rocket motor *s* motor cohete
rocket plane *s* (aer.) avión cohete
rocket-powered ['rakɪt,paʊərd] *adj* propulsado por cohetes
rocket propulsion *s* propulsión a cohete
rocketry ['rakɪtrɪ] *s* cohetería
rocket salad *s* (bot.) roqueta, ruca
rocket ship *s* aeronave cohete
rock garden *s* jardín entre rocas
Rockies ['rakɪz] *spl* Montañas Rocosas o Roqueñas
rocking chair *s* mecedora, sillón de hamaca
rocking horse *s* caballo mecedor
rock of ages *s* Cristo; la fe de Cristo
Rock of Gibraltar *s* peñón de Gibraltar
rock ptarmigan *s* (orn.) perdiz blanca
rock-ribbed ['rak,rɪbd] *adj* que tiene costillas de roca; fuerte, inflexible
rockrose ['rak,roz] *s* (bot.) estepa
rock salt *s* sal de compás, sal gema
rockshaft ['rak,ʃæft] o ['rak,ʃaft] *s* (mach.) eje de balancines; (min.) pozo de relleno
rockweed ['rak,wid] *s* (bot.) fuco
rock wool *s* lana mineral
rocky ['rakɪ] *adj* (*comp:* **-ier;** *super:* **-iest**) roqueño; despiadado, inflexible; (slang) que bambolea; (slang) débil, poco firme
Rocky Mountains *spl* Montañas Rocosas o Roqueñas
Rocky Mountain spotted fever *s* (path.) fiebre purpúrea de las Montañas Rocosas
rococo [ro'koko] o ['rokəko] *adj & s* (f.a.) rococó
rod [rad] *s* vara; varilla; barra; vara buscadora; vara de medir; caña de pescar; medida inglesa de longitud que equivale a cinco yardas y media; (anat.) bastoncillo (*de la retina*); (bact.)

bastoncito; (mach.) vástago; (surv.) jalón; vara alta (*autoridad*); opresión, tiranía; (Bib.) linaje, raza, vástago; (slang) revólver, pistola; **to spare the rod** excusar la vara (*no castigar a un niño*)
rode [rod] *pret de* **ride**
rodent [ˈrodənt] *adj & s* (zool.) roedor
rodeo [roˈdeo] o [ˈrodɪo] *s* (*pl:* **-os**) rodeo (*recogida de los ganados; espectáculo de los vaqueros norteamericanos*)
Roderick [ˈrɑdərɪk] *s* Rodrigo
rodman [ˈrɑdmən] *s* (*pl:* **-men**) (surv.) portamira
rodomontade [ˌrɑdəmɑnˈted] o [ˌrɑdəmɑnˈtɑd] *s* rodomontada, fanfarronada; *adj* fanfarrón; *vn* fanfarronear
roe [ro] *s* (zool.) corzo; hueva (*masa de huevecillos de ciertos peces*)
roebuck [ˈroˌbʌk] o **roe deer** *s* (zool.) corzo
roentgenogram [ˈrɛntgənəˌgræm] *s* roentgenograma
roentgenologist [ˌrɛntgəˈnɑlədʒɪst] *s* roentgenólogo
roentgenology [ˌrɛntgəˈnɑlədʒɪ] *s* roentgenología
roentgenotherapy [ˌrɛntgənoˈθɛrəpɪ] *s* roentgenoterapia
Roentgen rays [ˈrɛntgən] *spl* (phys.) rayos Roentgen
rogation [roˈgeʃən] *s* (hist.) rogación; (eccl.) rogativa; **rogations** *spl* (eccl.) rogativas (*especialmente las que caen en los tres días antes de la Ascensión*)
rogatory [ˈrogəˌtorɪ] *adj* rogatorio
Roger [ˈrɑdʒər] *s* Rogelio
rogue [rog] *s* bribón, pícaro; elefante u otro animal bravo que vive separado del rebaño
roguery [ˈrogərɪ] *s* (*pl:* **-ies**) bribonería, picardía; travesura, diablura
rogues' gallery *s* colección de retratos de malhechores para uso de la policía
roguish [ˈrogɪʃ] *adj* bribón, pícaro; travieso, retozón
roil [rɔɪl] *va* enturbiar; irritar, vejar
roily [ˈrɔɪlɪ] *adj* enturbiado; irritado, vejado
roister [ˈrɔɪstər] *vn* jaranear; fanfarronear
roisterer [ˈrɔɪstərər] *s* jaranero; fanfarrón
roisterous [ˈrɔɪstərəs] *adj* jaranero; fanfarrón
Roland [ˈrolənd] *s* Rolando, Roldán
rôle o **role** [rol] *s* papel; **to play a rôle** desempeñar un papel
roll [rol] *s* rollo; rodillo; rodadura; echada (*de los dados*); panecillo; ondulación; bamboleo; balance (*del barco*); redoble (*del tambor*); retumbo (*p.ej., del trueno*); rol, lista; (slang) fajo (*de papel moneda*); **to call the roll** pasar lista; **to strike off the rolls** excluir de la lista de miembros ‖ *va* arrollar; envolver; hacer rodar; empujar sobre rodillos; empujar hacia adelante; rodillar; cilindrar; laminar; entintar con rodillo; liar (*un cigarrillo*); mover (*p.ej., el cuerpo*) de un lado a otro; mover o menear (*los ojos*) de uno a otro lado, mover (*los ojos*) hacia arriba, poner (*los ojos*) en blanco; tocar redobles con (*el tambor*); hacer resonar; vibrar (*la voz*); pronunciar (*la r*) vibrando la lengua; meditar cuidadosamente, pesar detenidamente; **to roll one's own** hacérselos o liárselos (*liarse sus propios cigarrillos*); (slang) arreglárselas bien solo; **to roll the bones** (slang) echar o tirar los dados, jugar a los dados; **to roll the eye over** echar una mirada a; **to roll the eyes** poner los ojos en blanco; **to roll up** arrollar; arremangar (*p.ej., las mangas*); amontonar (*p.ej., fortuna*) ‖ *vn* rodar; bambolear o bambolearse; balancear o balancearse (*un barco*); ondear; girar; moverse (*los ojos*) de uno a otro lado, moverse (*los ojos*) hacia arriba; retumbar (*el trueno*); redoblar (*un tambor*); **to roll in** entrar rodando; entrar bamboleándose; avanzar ondeando (*el agua*); (coll.) arroparse en la cama; (coll.) nadar en (*p.ej., dinero*); **to roll out** salir bamboleándose; (slang) levantarse desarropándose; **to roll up** arrollar; llegar en vehículo; amontonarse (*p.ej., dinero*)
roll call *s* lista, (el) pasar lista
rolled oats *spl* copos de avena
roller [ˈrolər] *s* rodillo; tambor; ruedecilla (*de un mueble*); rueda (*de patines*); venda (*para cubrir una herida*); ola larga y creciente; (orn.) pichón volteador; (orn.) canario de canto sostenido
roller bearing *s* cojinete de rodillos
roller blind *s* cortina de resorte
roller coaster *s* montaña rusa
roller mill *s* molino de cilindros, trituradora de cilindros
roller skate *s* patín de ruedas
roller-skate [ˈrolərˌsket] *vn* patinar con patines de ruedas
roller towel *s* toalla sin fin, toalla continua
roll film *s* (phot.) película en carretes
rollick [ˈrɑlɪk] *vn* jugetear, retozar, divertirse de manera turbulenta
rollicking [ˈrɑlɪkɪŋ] o **rollicksome** [ˈrɑlɪksəm] *adj* juguetón, retozón, alegre, turbulento
rolling [ˈrolɪŋ] *adj* rodante; rodadero; girante; retumbante; undulante u ondulado; doblegado, plegado; *s* rodadura; bamboleo; balanceo; retumbo; undulación; redoble (*del tambor*)
rolling barrage *s* (mil.) cortina de fuego rodante
rolling kitchen *s* (mil.) cocina rodante
rolling mill *s* laminadero, taller de laminación; laminador, tren de laminadores
rolling pin *s* hataca, rodillo, rodillo de pastelero
rolling stock *s* (rail.) material móvil, material rodante
rolling stone *s* (fig.) piedra movediza
roll sulfur *s* azufre cañón, azufre en canuto
roll-top desk [ˈrolˌtɑp] *s* escritorio norteamericano
roly-poly [ˈrolɪˈpolɪ] *adj* regordete, rechoncho; *s* (*pl:* **-lies**) persona regordeta; pudín en forma de rollo, cocido, horneado o sometido a la acción del vapor
Rom. abr. de **Roman, Romance** y **Romans** (Bib.)
rom o **Rom** [rʌm] *s* rom, hombre o muchacho gitano
Romaean [roˈmiən] *adj* romeo (*griego bizantino*)
Romaic [roˈmeɪk] *adj & s* romaico
romaine [roˈmen] *s* lechuga romana
Roman [ˈromən] *adj & s* romano; **Romans** *spl* (Bib.) Epístola a los romanos; (*l.c.*) *adj* (print.) redondo; *s* (print.) letra redonda
Roman candle *s* vela romana
Roman Catholic *adj & s* católico romano
Roman Catholicism *s* catolicismo romano
Romance [roˈmæns] o [ˈromæns] *adj* romance o románico (*neolatino*); (*l.c.*) *s* romance (*libro o novela de caballerías*); cuento de aventuras; cuento de amor, cuento de enamorados; (lo) pintoresco (*p.ej., de la historia*); interés en las aventuras, el amor o lo pintoresco; intriga amorosa; ficción, invención; (mus.) romanza; [roˈmæns] *vn* contar o escribir romances, contar o escribir cuentos de aventuras o de amor; pensar o hablar de un modo romántico o fantástico; exagerar; mentir
romance of chivalry *s* libro de caballerías
romancer [roˈmænsər] *s* romancero; visionario; embustero
Roman Curia *s* Curia romana
Roman Empire *s* Imperio romano
Romanesque [ˌromənˈɛsk] *adj & s* (arch.) románico
Romanic [roˈmænɪk] *adj* románico (*neolatino*)
Romanism [ˈromənɪzəm] *s* romanismo; (offensive) romanismo (*la religión católica*)
Romanist [ˈromənɪst] *s* romanista; (offensive) romanista (*persona que profesa la religión católica*)
Romanization [ˌromənɪˈzeʃən] *s* romanización; conversión al catolicismo
Romanize [ˈromənaɪz] *va* romanizar; convertir al catolicismo; *vn* romanizarse; convertirse al catolicismo
Roman law *s* derecho romano
Roman nose *s* nariz aguileña
Roman numeral *s* número romano
Roman rite *s* rito romano
Romansh [roˈmænʃ] o [roˈmɑnʃ] *s* romanche o rumanche
romantic [roˈmæntɪk] *adj* romántico; encantado (*sitio*); *s* romántico
romantically [roˈmæntɪkəlɪ] *adv* románticamente

romanticism [ro'mæntɪsɪzəm] *s* romanticismo
romanticist [ro'mæntɪsɪst] *s* romántico
romanticize [ro'mæntɪsaɪz] *va* hacer romántico; *vn* ser romántico, hablar o escribir de un modo romántico
Romantic Movement *s* Romanticismo
Romany ['rɑmənɪ] *adj* romany; *s* (*pl:* **-nies**) romany
Rom. Cath. abr. de **Roman Catholic**
Rome [rom] *s* Roma
Rome-Berlin axis ['rombʌr'lɪn] *s* eje Roma-Berlín
romp [rɑmp] *s* trisca, retozo; saltabardales; *vn* triscar, corretear
rompers ['rɑmpərz] *spl* traje holgado de juego para niños
Romulus ['rɑmjələs] *s* (myth.) Rómulo
rondeau ['rɑndo] o [rɑn'do] *s* rondó o rondeau
rondel ['rɑndəl] *s* rondel
rondo ['rɑndo] o [rɑn'do] *s* (*pl:* **-dos**) (mus.) rondó
rood [rud] *s* crucifijo; cruz en que murió Cristo
rood screen *s* (arch.) jube
roof [ruf] o [rʊf] *s* tejado (*cubierta de un edificio*); techo (*de paja, bálago, etc.*); azotea (*cubierta llana de un edificio*); imperial (*de un coche*); paladar (*de la boca*); techo interior, cielo raso; cubierta; bóveda (*del cielo*); (fig.) techo (*domicilio, morada*); **to raise the roof** (slang) poner el grito en el cielo; *va* techar
roofer ['rufər] o ['rʊfər] *s* constructor de techos o tejados, techador
roof garden *s* pérgola; azotea de baile y diversión
roofing ['rufɪŋ] o ['rʊfɪŋ] *s* material para techos
roofless ['ruflɪs] o ['rʊflɪs] *adj* sin techo; mostrenco
rooftree ['ruf,tri] o ['rʊf,tri] *s* cumbrera o parhilera; tejado; (fig.) techo (*domicilio*)
rook [rʊk] *s* (orn.) chova, grajo, cuervo merendero; embustero; torre, roque (*en el ajedrez*); *va & vn* trampear
rookery ['rʊkərɪ] *s* (*pl:* **-ies**) bosque grajero; criadero de focas, grullas, aves marinas, etc.; casa o habitación baja y escuálida; vecindario bajo y escuálido
rookie ['rʊkɪ] *s* (slang) bisoño, novato
room [rum] o [rʊm] *s* aposento, cuarto, habitación, pieza; espacio, sitio, lugar; ocasión; **to make room** abrir paso, hacer lugar, despejar la vía; **there is no room for doubt** no cabe duda; **there is no more room** no cabe(n) más; *vn* alojarse, hospedarse
room and board *s* pensión completa
roomer ['rumər] o ['rʊmər] *s* inquilino
roomful ['rumfʊl] o ['rʊmfʊl] *s* cuarto lleno; gente en un cuarto, cosas en un cuarto
rooming house *s* casa donde se alquilan cuartos
roommate ['rum,met] o ['rʊm,met] *s* compañero de cuarto
room service *s* servicio de los cuartos, servicio de restaurante en las habitaciones de un hotel
roomy ['rumɪ] o ['rʊmɪ] *adj* (*comp:* **-ier;** *super:* **-iest**) amplio, espacioso, holgado
roorback ['rʊrbæk] *s* (U.S.A.) libelo contra un candidato, que se circula por su efecto político
roost [rust] *s* percha de gallinero; gallinero; lugar de descanso; **to rule the roost** mandar, tener el mando y el palo (*especialmente en la casa de uno*); *vn* descansar (*las aves*) en la percha; estar alojado; pasar la noche
rooster ['rustər] *s* gallo
roosterfish ['rustər,fɪʃ] *s* (ichth.) papagayo
root [rut] o [rʊt] *s* raíz; (bot., gram. & math.) raíz; (anat.) raigón (*del diente*); (mus.) base, nota fundamental; **to get to the root of** profundizar; **to take root** echar raíces; *va* plantar firmemente; hocicar u hozar; desarraigar; **to root out** o **up** desarraigar; *vn* arraigar; hocicar u hozar; **to root about** andar buscando; **to root for** (slang) aplaudir o gritar ruidosamente por el éxito de
rootage ['rutɪdʒ] o ['rʊtɪdʒ] *s* arraigo
root and branch *adv* por completo
root beer *s* bebida no alcohólica hecha de extractos de varias raíces
root canal *s* (anat. & dent.) conducto radicular
rooter ['rutər] o ['rʊtər] *s* hozador (*animal*); (slang) hincha (*entusiasta que aplaude o grita ruidosamente por el éxito de un jugador, equipo, etc.*)
root hair *s* (bot.) pelos absorbentes
rootlet ['rutlɪt] o ['rʊtlɪt] *s* raicilla
rootstock ['rut,stɑk] o ['rʊt,stɑk] *s* (bot.) rizoma
rooty ['rutɪ] o ['rʊtɪ] *adj* (*comp:* **-ier;** *super:* **-iest**) lleno de raíces; radicoso
rope [rop] *s* cuerda; dogal (*para ahorcar a un reo*); lazo (*para coger animales*); muerte en la horca; masa fibrosa y viscosa; **to be at the end of one's rope** estar sin recursos, andar o estar en las últimas; no saber qué hacer; **to give a person rope** (coll.) dar libertad de acción a una persona, dejar que una persona actúe u obre libremente; **to jump** o **to skip rope** saltar a la comba; **to know the ropes** conocer la jarcia o las cuerdas de un buque; (slang) saber cuántas son cinco, saber todas las tretas; *va* atar o amarrar con una cuerda; cercar con cuerdas, rodear con soga; **to rope in** (slang) embaucar o engañar con arte y maña; **to rope off** cercar con cuerdas, rodear con soga; *vn* hacer madeja (*un licor*)
ropedancer ['rop,dænsər] o ['rop,dɑnsər] *s* bailarín de cuerda
rope ladder *s* escala de cuerda
rope railway *s* alambrecarril
ropewalk ['rop,wɔk] *s* cordelería
ropewalker ['rop,wɔkər] *s* volatinero; bailarín de cuerda
ropeway ['rop,we] *s* cablecarril, teleférico
ropy ['ropɪ] *adj* (*comp:* **-ier;** *super:* **-iest**) correoso, fibroso, viscoso; de cuerda, como una cuerda
Roquefort ['rokfərt] *s* queso de Roquefort
roquet [ro'ke] (*pret & pp:* **-queted** ['ked]; *ger:* **-queting** ['keɪŋ]) *va & vn* (croquet) enrocar
roquette [ro'kɛt] *s* (bot.) roqueta
rorqual ['rɔrkwəl] *s* (zool.) rorcual
rosaceous [ro'zeʃəs] *adj* rosáceo; (bot.) rosáceo
Rosalie ['rɑzəlɪ] o ['rozəlɪ] *s* Rosalía
Rosalind ['rɑzəlɪnd] o ['rɑzəlaɪnd] *s* Rosalinda
rosary ['rozərɪ] *s* (*pl:* **-ries**) rosario; macizo de rosales; jardín de rosales
rose [roz] *s* rosa (*flor*); (bot.) rosal (*planta*); rosa (*color; lazo de cintas; piedra preciosa; perfume*); roseta (*de una regadera*); mujer muy hermosa; (arch.) rosa o rosetón; **under the rose** secretamente; *adj* rosado, de color de rosa; *va* hacer rosado; *pret de* **rise**
rose acacia *s* (bot.) acacia rosa
roseate ['roziet] o ['rozɪɪt] *adj* róseo, rosado; alegre, jovial, vivo
rosebay ['roz,be] *s* (bot.) adelfa, baladre, rododafne; (bot.) rododendro
rose beetle *s* (ent.) macrodáctilo; (ent.) cetoína dorada
rosebud ['roz,bʌd] *s* pimpollo, capullo de rosa
rose bug *s* (ent.) macrodáctilo
rosebush ['roz,bʊʃ] *s* (bot.) rosal
rose chafer *s* (ent.) cetoína dorada
rose-colored ['roz,kʌlərd] *adj* róseo, rosado; alegre, jovial, vivo; **to see everything in rose-colored spectacles** verlo todo de color de rosa
rose diamond *s* diamante rosa
rose geranium *s* (bot.) geranio de rosa
rose hip *s* (bot.) cinarrodón, eterio
rose leaf *s* pétalo de rosa
roselle [ro'zɛl] o **rosella** [ro'zɛlə] *s* (bot.) agrio, jamaica, viña
rose mallow *s* (bot.) malva rósea; (bot.) amor al uso, flor de la vida
rosemary ['roz,mɛrɪ] *s* (*pl:* **-ies**) (bot.) romero
rose of China *s* (bot.) rosa de China, tulipán (*Hibiscus rosa-sinensis*)
rose of Jericho *s* (bot.) rosa de Jericó
rose of Sharon ['ʃɛrən] *s* (bot.) rosa de Siria; (bot.) hipericón; (Bib.) flor del campo
roseola [ro'ziələ] *s* (path.) roséola; (path.) rubéola
Rosetta stone [ro'zɛtə] *s* piedra de Roseta

rosette [ro'zɛt] *s* rosa (*lazo de cintas*); (arch.) rosetón; (metal.) roseta
rose water *s* agua de rosas
rose window *s* (arch.) rosetón
rosewood ['roz,wʊd] *s* palo de rosa; (bot.) palisandro; (bot.) leño de Botany
Rosicrucian [,rozɪ'kruʃən] *adj & s* rosicruciano o rosacruz
rosily ['rozɪlɪ] *adv* con color de rosa; alegremente
rosin ['rɑzɪn] *s* colofonia, brea seca; resina; *va* frotar con colofonia
Rosinante [,rɑzɪ'næntɪ] *s* rocinante (*rocín matalón*)
rosolio [rə'zoljo] *s* rosoli
roster ['rɑstər] *s* catálogo, lista, registro; horario escolar, horas de clase; (mil.) lista o reglamento que indica los deberes de los oficiales
rostral ['rɑstrəl] *adj* rostral
rostral column *s* columna rostral
rostrate ['rɑstret] *adj* rostrado
rostrum ['rɑstrəm] *s* (*pl:* **-trums** o **-tra** [trə]) *s* tribuna; (anat., naut. & zool.) rostro
rosy ['rozɪ] *adj* (*comp:* **-ier;** *super:* **-iest**) rosado; sonrosado; alegre
rot [rɑt] *s* podredumbre; (bot.) úlcera; (vet.) comalía, morriña; (slang) tontería; (*pret & pp:* **rotted;** *ger:* **rotting**) *va* pudrir; enriar; *vn* pudrirse
Rotarian [ro'terɪən] *adj & s* rotario
rotary ['rotərɪ] *adj* rotatorio, rotativo
rotary press *s* (print.) rotativa, prensa rotativa
rotate ['rotet] o [ro'tet] *va* hacer girar; alternar; *vn* girar, rodar; alternar
rotation [ro'teʃən] *s* rotación; **in rotation** por turno
rotational [ro'teʃənəl] *adj* rotatorio
rotation of crops *s* rotación de cosechas o de cultivos
rotator ['rotetər] o [ro'tetər] *s* (*pl:* **rotators**) persona o cosa que da vueltas; (*pl:* **rotatores** [,rotə'toriz]) (anat.) rotador
rotatory ['rotə,torɪ] *adj* rotatorio
rote [rot] *s* rutina, repetición maquinal; **by rote** de memoria; maquinalmente
rotgut ['rɑt,gʌt] *s* (slang) matarratas
rotifer ['rotɪfər] *s* (zool.) rotífero
rotiferous [ro'tɪfərəs] *adj* rotífero
rotogravure [,rotəgrə'vjʊr] o [,rotə'grevjʊr] *s* rotograbado
rotor ['rotər] *s* (mach. & elec.) rotor
rotor ship *s* (naut.) buque a rotores
rotten ['rɑtən] *adj* podrido; fétido; viciado (*aire*); poco firme, en mal estado; despreciable; corrompido, no honrado; (slang) vil, ruin
rotten borough *s* (Brit.) pueblo antes de 1832 que, a pesar de sus pocos votantes, tuvo el derecho de representación en el Parlamento
rottenness ['rɑtənnɪs] *s* podredumbre; fetidez
rottenstone ['rɑtən,ston] *s* (mineral.) trípol; *va* tripolizar
rotter ['rɑtər] *s* (slang) sinvergüenza
rotular ['rɑtʃələr] *adj* rotular
rotulian [ro'tjulɪən] *adj* rotuliano
rotund [ro'tʌnd] *adj* redondo de cuerpo; rotundo (*lenguaje*)
rotunda [ro'tʌndə] *s* rotonda o rotunda
rotundity [ro'tʌndɪtɪ] *s* (*pl:* **-ties**) redondez de cuerpo; rotundidad; cosa redonda
rouble ['rubəl] *s* var. de **ruble**
roué [ru'e] *s* libertino
Rouen [ru'ɑn] *s* Ruán
rouge [ruʒ] *s* arrebol, alconcilla, colorete; colcótar, rojo de pulir; *va* arrebolar, pintar; *vn* arrebolarse, pintarse
rough [rʌf] *adj* áspero; borrascoso, tempestuoso; agitado (*mar*); peludo, velludo; chapucero, tosco; aproximativo; alborotado, turbulento; brutal; bruto; (phonet.) aspirado; *s* brutal, matón; terreno áspero, maleza; cosa áspera o tosca; **in the rough** en bruto (*sin pulimento*); *va* poner áspero; tratar ásperamente; bosquejar o trazar rudamente; labrar toscamente; **to rough it** vivir sin comodidades, hacer vida campestre; *vn* ponerse áspero
roughage ['rʌfɪdʒ] *s* material áspero o grosero; alimento o forraje poco digeribles
rough-and-ready ['rʌfənd'rɛdɪ] *adj* tosco pero eficaz; desenvuelto; vigoroso pero poco fino
rough-and-tumble ['rʌfənd'tʌmbəl] *adj* desordenado, violento; *s* lucha o pelea desordenada y violenta
roughcast ['rʌf,kæst] o ['rʌf,kɑst] *s* modelo tosco; mezcla gruesa, mortero grueso; (*pret & pp:* **-cast**) *va* bosquejar; dar a (*la pared*) una capa de mezcla gruesa
rough copy *s* borrador
rough diamond *s* diamante en bruto; (fig.) diamante en bruto
rough draft *s* bosquejo; borrador
rough-dry [,rʌf'draɪ] *adj* seco y sin planchar; (*pret & pp:* **-dried**) *va* secar (*ropa*) sin planchar
roughen ['rʌfən] *va* poner áspero o tosco; *vn* ponerse áspero o tosco
rough-hew [,rʌf'hju] (*pret:* **-hewed;** *pp:* **-hewed** o **-hewn**) *va* desbastar; modelar toscamente
roughhouse ['rʌf,haʊs] *s* (slang) trapatiesta, conducta bulliciosa; *va* (slang) molestar o perturbar por conducta bulliciosa; *vn* (slang) conducirse de un modo bullicioso; **to start roughhousing** armar una trapatiesta
roughing-in ['rʌfɪŋ'ɪn] *s* capa de mezcla gruesa; instalación de tubos, conductos, cajas de salida, etc. (*dentro de los pisos y paredes*)
roughish ['rʌfɪʃ] *adj* algo áspero
roughly ['rʌflɪ] *adv* ásperamente; toscamente; aproximadamente; turbulentamente; brutalmente
roughneck ['rʌf,nɛk] *s* (slang) canalla
roughness ['rʌfnɪs] *s* aspereza, tosquedad; rigor (*del tiempo*); agitación (*del mar*); chapucería; brutalidad
roughrider ['rʌf,raɪdər] *s* domador de caballos; hombre acostumbrado a montar caballos indómitos; soldado irregular a caballo; **Roughriders** *spl* regimiento de caballería voluntario norteamericano, organizado por Teodoro Roosevelt, que tomó parte en la guerra entre España y los Estados Unidos
roughshod ['rʌf,ʃɑd] *adj* herrado con ramplones (*que impiden resbalar*); **to ride** o **run roughshod over** traer a redopelo, tratar sin miramiento
rough sketch *s* bosquejo; borrador
roulade [ru'lɑd] *s* (mus.) trino; rebanada de carne arrollada, con relleno de carne picada
roulette [ru'lɛt] *s* ruleta (*juego; ruedecilla con puntas*)
Roumania [ru'menɪə] *s* var. de **Rumania**
Roumanian [ru'menɪən] *adj & s* var. de **Rumanian**
round [raʊnd] *adj* redondo; rechoncho; rotundo (*categórico; sonoro*); franco; fuerte, vigoroso; (phonet.) redondeado ‖ *adv* redondamente; alrededor; acá y allá; de boca en boca, de una persona a otra; de un lado para otro; por todas partes; **round about** en contorno ‖ *prep* alrededor de, en torno de; por todos lados de; a la vuelta de (*p.ej., la esquina*); cerca de, cosa de, como; acá y allá en; a todas las partes de; **to come** o **to get round** sobrepujar en astucia a; engatusar ‖ *s* redondo (*cosa redonda o circular*); camino, circuito, ruta; recorrido (*de un policía*); jira (*viaje circular*); redondez; revolución; serie, rutina; ronda (*de cigarros o bebidas*); salva (*de muchas armas de fuego a un tiempo; de aplausos*); disparo o tiro (*de un arma de fuego*); cartucho con bala; corro, círculo (*de personas*); rodaja de carne de vaca; (box.) asalto o suerte; canción corta cantada por varias voces, que empiezan a intervalos sucesivos; danza en que los bailadores se mueven en círculo; **rounds** *spl* recorrido (*de un policía*); **to go the round** ir de boca en boca; ir de mano en mano ‖ *va* redondear; doblar (*una esquina, un promontorio*); cercar, circundar, rodear; (phonet.) redondear; **to round in** (naut.) halar; **to round off** u **out** redondear; acabar, completar, perfeccionar; **to round up** juntar, recoger ‖ *vn* redondearse; girar; **to round off** u **out** redondearse; **to round to** (naut.) orzar
roundabout ['raʊndə,baʊt] *adj* indirecto, ambagioso; *s* modo indirecto, curso indirecto; chaqueta; tío vivo
round dance *s* baile que ejecutan las parejas con movimiento circular
roundel ['raʊndəl] *s* figura redonda; (arch.) nicho, panel o ventana circular; rondel; rondó

roundelay ['raʊndəle] *s* melodía que se canta en rueda; baile en círculo
rounder ['raʊndər] *s* (coll.) pródigo, malgastador; (coll.) criminal habitual, borrachín habitual, catavinos
roundheaded ['raʊnd'hɛdɪd] *adj* de cabeza redondeada; de cabeza de hongo (*dícese de un tornillo*)
roundhouse ['raʊnd,haʊs] *s* (rail.) cocherón, casa de máquinas, depósito de locomotoras; (naut.) chupeta, toldilla
rounding ['raʊndɪŋ] *s* redondeamiento; (phonet.) redondeamiento
roundish ['raʊndɪʃ] *adj* redondete
roundly ['raʊndlɪ] *adv* redondamente
roundness ['raʊndnɪs] *s* redondez
round number *s* número redondo
round robin *s* petición firmada en rueda o con las firmas en rueda; competencia atlética en la cual varios equipos o jugadores compiten en una serie de partidos, cada equipo o jugador compitiendo con cada uno de los demás
round-shouldered ['raʊnd'ʃoldərd] *adj* cargado de espaldas
roundsman ['raʊndzmən] *s* (*pl:* **-men**) rondador de policía
round steak *s* tajada de carne de vaca
Round Table *s* (myth.) Mesa Redonda (*en que tenían asiento el rey Artús y sus caballeros*); (myth.) Tabla Redonda (*caballeros del rey Artús*)
round-table discussion ['raʊnd,tebəl] *s* discusión de mesa redonda
round tower *s* torre redonda aislada con remate cónico
round trip *s* viaje de ida y vuelta, viaje redondo
round-trip ticket ['raʊnd'trɪp] *s* billete de ida y vuelta
roundup ['raʊnd,ʌp] *s* rodeo (*del ganado mayor*); redada (*de criminales*); reunión (*p.ej., de viejos amigos*)
roundworm ['raʊnd,wʌrm] *s* (zool.) ascáride
roup [rup] *s* ronquera; catarro de las aves domésticas
rouse [raʊz] *va* despertar; excitar, provocar; levantar (*la caza*); *vn* despertarse, despabilarse, animarse
rouser ['raʊzər] *s* despertador; excitador; (coll.) cosa extraordinaria, fenómeno
rousing ['raʊzɪŋ] *adj* conmovedor; activo, animado, vigoroso; (coll.) extraordinario
Roussillon, the [ro'sɪljən] o [rusi'jõ] el Rosellón
rout [raʊt] *s* derrota; derrota completa, fuga desordenada; comitiva, séquito; canalla, gentuza; alboroto, tumulto; *va* derrotar; derrotar completamente, poner en fuga desordenada; arrancar hozando; arrojar, echar o hacer salir con violencia; *vn* hozar
route [rut] o [raʊt] *s* ruta; itinerario; *va* encaminar
routine [ru'tin] *adj* rutinario; *s* rutina
routinist [ru'tinɪst] *s* rutinero
rove [rov] *s* madeja de algodón, lana o seda tirada; arandela de remache; *va* torcer (*el hilo*) antes de encanillarlo; *vn* andar errante, errar, vagar; *pret & pp de* **reeve**
rover ['rovər] *s* vagabundo; pirata; buque de piratas; (croquet) corsario (*jugador*); (croquet) corsaria (*bola*)
row [ro] *s* fila, hilera; crujía (*de casas*); remadura; paseo en bote de remos; **in a row** seguidos, p.ej., **five hours in a row** cinco horas seguidas; [raʊ] *s* (coll.) camorra, pendencia, riña; (coll.) alboroto, bullicio; **to raise a row** (coll.) armar camorra; [ro] *va* conducir o transportar en un bote de remos; mover o impeler remando; manejar (*el remo*); competir con (*una persona*) en una regata a remo; competir en (*una regata a remo*); *vn* remar; **to row hard** hacer fuerza de remos; [raʊ] *va* (coll.) regañar, reñir; *vn* (coll.) armar camorra, pelearse
rowan ['roən] o ['raʊən] *s* (bot.) serbal de los cazadores
rowboat ['ro,bot] *s* bote, bote de remos
rowdy ['raʊdɪ] *adj* (*comp:* **-dier**; *super:* **-diest**) gamberro; *s* (*pl:* **-dies**) gamberro
rowdyish ['raʊdɪɪʃ] *adj* gamberro
rowdyism ['raʊdɪɪzəm] *s* gamberrismo
rowel ['raʊəl] *s* rodaja (*de espuela*); (vet.) sedal; (*pret & pp:* **-eled** o **-elled**; *ger:* **-eling** o **-elling**) *va* espolear con la rodaja; (vet.) poner sedal a
rower ['roər] *s* remero
row house [ro] *s* casa de una fila de casas seguidas
rowing ['ro·ɪŋ] *s* (sport) remo
rowlock ['rolɑk] o ['rʌlək] *s* (naut.) escalamera, chumacera; (mas.) sardinel
royal ['rɔɪəl] *adj* real; *s* tamaño de papel, de 19 por 24 pulgadas para escribir y de 20 por 25 para imprenta; (naut.) sobrejuanete
Royal Air Force College *s* (Brit.) Academia General del Aire
royal fern *s* (bot.) helecho real
royal flush *s* flux real
royalism ['rɔɪəlɪzəm] *s* realismo
royalist ['rɔɪəlɪst] *s* realista
royalistic [,rɔɪə'lɪstɪk] *adj* realista
Royal Military College *s* (Brit.) Academia General Militar
Royal Naval College *s* (Brit.) Escuela Naval Militar
royal palm *s* (bot.) palma real, palmiche
royalty ['rɔɪəltɪ] *s* (*pl:* **-ties**) realeza; personaje real, personajes reales; derechos (*pagados a un autor o inventor*)
r.p.m. abr. de **revolutions per minute**
R.R. abr. de **railroad** y **Right Reverend**
R.S.F.S.R. abr. de **Russian Socialist Federated Soviet Republic**
R.S.V.P. abr. de **répondez s'il vous plaît** (Fr.) **please answer** sírvase enviar respuesta
Rt. Hon. abr. de **Right Honorable**
Rt. Rev. abr. de **Right Reverend**
rub [rʌb] *s* roce, frotación; rozadura (*de la piel*); sarcasmo; obstáculo, estorbo; busilis; desigualdad (*de la superficie*); **there's the rub** ahí está el busilis; (*pret & pp:* **rubbed**; *ger:* **rubbing**) *va* restregar, frotar; pasar la mano sobre la superficie de; limpiar, fregar o pulir frotando o rascando; irritar frotando; **to rub away** quitar frotando; **to rub down** amasar; almohazar (*un caballo*); **to rub elbows with** rozarse mucho con; **to rub it in** (slang) reiterar demasiado una cosa desagradable; **to rub in** hacer penetrar por los poros frotando; **to rub off** quitar o limpiar frotando; **to rub out** borrar; (slang) asesinar; **to rub the right way** apaciguar, sosegar; **to rub the wrong way** contrariar, irritar; *vn* restregar, frotar; restregarse, frotarse; **to rub along, on** o **through** ir viviendo con apuros o con trabajo; **to rub off** quitarse o limpiarse frotando; borrarse
rub-a-dub ['rʌbə,dʌb] *s* rataplán, tantarantán
rubber ['rʌbər] *s* caucho, goma; goma de borrar; chanclo, zapato de goma; jugada final que decide un empate; (bridge) robre; *adj* de caucho, de goma; *vn* (slang) estirar el cuello o volver la cabeza para ver, mirar estirando el cuello o volviendo la cabeza
rubber band *s* liga de goma
rubber cement *s* cemento de goma
rubber-covered ['rʌbər,kʌvərd] *adj* cauchotado
rubber dam *s* (dent.) dique de caucho o goma
rubber heel *s* tacón de goma
rubber hose *s* manguera de goma
rubberize ['rʌbəraɪz] *va* engomar, cauchotar
rubberneck ['rʌbər,nɛk] *s* (slang) turista que trata de verlo todo; *vn* (slang) estirar el cuello o volver la cabeza para ver, mirar estirando el cuello o volviendo la cabeza
rubberoid ['rʌbərɔɪd] *s* ruberoide
rubber plant *s* (bot.) árbol del caucho (*planta que produce caucho; planta de adorno*)
rubber plantation *s* cauchal
rubber stamp *s* sello de goma, cajetín; estampilla (*de la firma de una persona*); (coll.) persona que aprueba sin reflexionar
rubber-stamp [,rʌbər'stæmp] *va* estampar con un sello de goma; estampillar (*con la firma de una persona*); (coll.) aprobar sin reflexionar
rubbery ['rʌbərɪ] *adj* elástico (*como el caucho*)
rubbing alcohol *s* alcohol para fricciones

rubbish [ˈrʌbɪʃ] *s* basura, desecho, desperdicios; disparate, necedad, tontería
rubble [ˈrʌbəl] *s* ripio; mampostería; desecho; disparate; *va* ripiar
rubblework [ˈrʌbəl,wʌrk] *s* mampostería
rubdown [ˈrʌb,daun] *s* amasamiento o masaje
rube [rub] *s* (slang) campesino, rústico, aldeano
rubefacient [,rubɪˈfeʃənt] *adj & s* (med.) rubefaciente
rubefaction [,rubɪˈfækʃən] *s* rubefacción
rubescent [ruˈbɛsənt] *adj* rubescente
rubiaceous [,rubɪˈeʃəs] *adj* (bot.) rubiáceo
rubican [ˈrubɪkən] *adj* rubicán
rubicel [ˈrubɪsɛl] *s* (mineral.) rubicela
Rubicon [ˈrubɪkɑn] *s* Rubicón; **to cross the Rubicon** pasar el Rubicón
rubicund [ˈrubɪkʌnd] *adj* rubicundo
rubicundity [,rubɪˈkʌndɪtɪ] *s* rubicundez
rubidium [ruˈbɪdɪəm] *s* (chem.) rubidio
ruble [ˈrubəl] *s* rublo
rubric [ˈrubrɪk] *s* rúbrica
rubrical [ˈrubrɪkəl] *adj* escrito o impreso de color rojo; marcado con encarnado; de rúbrica
rubricate [ˈrubrɪket] *va* rubrificar, poner de color rojo; proveer de rúbricas; dirigir con rúbricas
rubrician [ruˈbrɪʃən] *s* rubriquista
ruby [ˈrubɪ] *s* (*pl:* **-bies**) rubí; (horol.) rubí; *adj* de color de rubí
ruby silver *s* (mineral.) plata roja
ruby spinel *s* (mineral.) rubí espinela
ruche [ruʃ] *s* (sew.) lechuga de encaje o de malla
ruching [ˈruʃɪŋ] *s* (sew.) guarnición que consiste en lechugas de encaje o malla
ruck [rʌk] *s* vulgo; arruga; *va* arrugar; *vn* arrugarse
rucksack [ˈrʌk,sæk] o [ˈrʊk,sæk] *s* barjuleta, mochila
ruckus [ˈrʌkəs] o **ruction** [ˈrʌkʃən] *s* (coll.) alboroto, bullicio, tumulto
rudder [ˈrʌdər] *s* timón, gobernalle; veleta (*de molino de viento*)
ruddle [ˈrʌdəl] *s* almagre; *va* marcar con almagre
ruddy [ˈrʌdɪ] *adj* (*comp:* **-dier;** *super:* **-diest**) rubicundo, coloradote
ruddy turnstone *s* (orn.) playero turco
rude [rud] *adj* rudo; inculto, salvaje
rudeness [ˈrudnɪs] *s* rudeza; incultura
rudiment [ˈrudɪmənt] *s* rudimento
rudimental [,rudɪˈmɛntəl] *adj* rudimental
rudimentary [,rudɪˈmɛntərɪ] *adj* rudimentario
Rudolph [ˈrudɑlf] *s* Rodolfo
rue [ru] *s* (bot.) ruda; *va* sentir o lamentar; *vn* arrepentirse
rueful [ˈrufəl] *adj* lamentable
ruff [rʌf] *s* (sew.) lechuguilla; (cards) fallada; collar (*de plumas o de pelo de distinto color alrededor del cuello*); arrebato de cólera; (ichth.) acerina; (orn.) combatiente; *va* (cards) fallar
ruffed grouse [rʌft] *s* (orn.) bonasa americana (*Bonasa umbellus*)
ruffian [ˈrʌfɪən] *adj* grosero y brutal; *s* hombre grosero y brutal
ruffianism [ˈrʌfɪənɪzəm] *s* conducta grosera y brutal, brutalidad
ruffianly [ˈrʌfɪənlɪ] *adj* grosero y brutal
ruffle [ˈrʌfəl] *s* arruga; (sew.) volante; enojo, molestia; confusión, desorden; redoble (*del tambor*); *va* arrugar; (sew.) fruncir un volante en; (sew.) adornar o guarnecer con volante; erizar (*las plumas*); agitar, descomponer; enojar, molestar; confundir; barajar (*los naipes*); redoblar (*el tambor*); *vn* arrugarse; enojarse, molestarse
rufous [ˈrufəs] *adj* rufo, rojizo, rojizo parduzco
rug [rʌg] *s* alfombra; alfombrilla; manta (*de coche, de viaje, etc.*)
Rugby [ˈrʌgbɪ] *s* (sport) rugby (*clase de fútbol*)
rugged [ˈrʌgɪd] *adj* áspero, rugoso; fuerte, recio, vigoroso; rudo, tempestuoso
rugosity [ruˈgɑsɪtɪ] *s* rugosidad
Ruhmkorff coil [ˈrumkɔrf] *s* (phys.) carrete de Ruhmkorff, carrete de inducción
Ruhr [rʊr] *s* Ruhr; región del Ruhr
ruin [ˈruɪn] *s* ruina; *va* arruinar; *vn* arruinarse
ruination [,ruɪˈneʃən] *s* arruinamiento
ruinous [ˈruɪnəs] *adj* ruinoso
rule [rul] *s* regla; código; autoridad, mando, poder; regla de imprenta; (law) fallo o decisión (*de un tribunal*); **as a rule** por regla general; **to be the rule** ser de regla; **to make it a rule to** + *inf* hacerse una regla de + *inf; va* gobernar, mandar, regir; dirigir, guiar; contener, moderar, reprimir; reglar (*marcar con rayas o líneas*); (law) decidir según leyes o reglas; **to rule out** excluir, rechazar, no admitir; *vn* gobernar, mandar, regir; prevalecer, estar en boga; **to rule over** gobernar, mandar, regir
rule of law *s* régimen de justicia
rule of three *s* (math.) regla de oro, regla de proporción, regla de tres
rule of thumb o **rule o' thumb** *s* regla empírica; método empírico
ruler [ˈrulər] *s* gobernante; regla (*para trazar líneas*)
ruling [ˈrulɪŋ] *adj* gobernante, dirigente, imperante; *s* fallo o decisión de un tribunal o juez; rayado (*de papel*)
ruling pen *s* tiralíneas
rum [rʌm] *s* ron, aguardiente de caña; (U.S.A.) aguardiente (*cualquier licor alcohólico*); *adj* (slang) extraño, singular
Rumania [ruˈmenɪə] *s* Rumania
Rumanian [ruˈmenɪən] *adj & s* rumano
rumba [ˈrʌmbə] *s* rumba (*baile y música*)
rumble [ˈrʌmbəl] *s* retumbo; rugido (*de las tripas*); compartimiento posterior (*de un vehículo*); asiento situado detrás de un carruaje (*para los criados*); (aut.) asiento trasero descubierto; (slang) riña entre pandillas; *va* expresar o pronunciar con un sonido sordo y prolongado; *vn* retumbar; avanzar o moverse retumbando
rumble seat *s* (aut.) asiento trasero descubierto
rumen [ˈrumɛn] *s* (*pl:* **-mina** [mɪnə]) (zool.) rumen; bolo alimenticio
ruminant [ˈrumɪnənt] *adj* (zool. & fig.) rumiante; *s* (zool.) rumiante
ruminate [ˈrumɪnet] *va & vn* rumiar; (fig.) rumiar
rumination [,rumɪˈneʃən] *s* rumia, rumiación
ruminative [ˈrumɪ,netɪv] *adj* rumiante, rumión
rummage [ˈrʌmɪdʒ] *s* búsqueda desordenada; *va* buscar revolviéndolo todo; descubrir, sacar a luz; *vn* buscar revolviéndolo todo; alborotar
rummage sale *s* venta de prendas usadas (*con el fin de recoger fondos para obras caritativas*)
rummy [ˈrʌmɪ] *adj* (*comp:* **-mier;** *super:* **-miest**) (slang) extraño, raro, singular; *s* rummy (*juego de naipes*); (slang) borracho
rumor [ˈrumər] *s* rumor; *va* rumorear; **it is rumored that** se rumorea que
rumormongering [ˈrumər,mʌŋgərɪŋ] *s* (el) propalar rumores
rump [rʌmp] *s* anca, nalga; rabadilla u obispillo (*de ave*); (cook.) cuarto trasero (*p.ej., de vaca*); resto, residuo
rumple [ˈrʌmpəl] *s* arruga; *va* arrugar, ajar, chafar; *vn* arrugarse
rumpot [ˈrʌmpɑt] *s* (slang) cuba, pellejo, odre (*borracho*)
rumpus [ˈrʌmpəs] *s* (coll.) batahola, la de San Quintín; (coll.) alboroto, tumulto; **to raise a rumpus** (coll.) armar la de San Quintín
rumrunner [ˈrʌm,rʌnər] *s* importador contrabandista de licores alcohólicos
run [rʌn] *s* carrera; curso; corrida; adelantamiento, progreso; clase, género, tipo; libertad de ir y venir a voluntad; carrera (*en las medias*); curso (*de un líquido*); arroyo; migración (*de peces*); terreno de pasto; tubo, caño; descarga de mercancías de contrabando; asedio (*de un banco por los depositantes*); serie (*de representaciones teatrales; de repetidos éxitos*); (baseball & mus.) carrera; (naut.) racel; **a run for one's money** competencia fuerte; satisfacción por sus esfuerzos; **day's run** (naut.) singladura; **in the long run** a la larga; **on the run** a escape, apresurándose; en fuga desordenada; **the common run of people** el común de las gentes; **the general run of** la generalidad de; **to be on the run** darse a la fuga; ceder; volverse atrás; **to have a long run** (theat.) permanecer en cartel du-

rante mucho tiempo; **to have** o **to get the run of** hallar el secreto de, hallar el modo de hacer; tener libertad de ir y venir por ‖ (*pret:* **ran;** *pp:* **run;** *ger:* **running**) *va* correr; dirigir o manejar; trazar o tirar (*una línea*); hacer entrar; introducir o pasar (*mercancías de contrabando*); introducir por fuerza; derretir o fundir (*un metal*); exhibir (*un cine*); proyectar (*una película cinematográfica*); hacer (*mandados*); tener como candidato; gobernar (*un país, una ciudad*); burlar o violar (*un bloqueo*); tener (*calentura*); **to run down** cazar y matar, cazar y destruir; derribar; atropellar (*p.ej., a un peatón*); (coll.) denigrar, desacreditar, desprestigiar; **to run in** (print.) insertar, poner de seguido, sin párrafo; (slang) meter en la cárcel; **to run off** tocar (*una pieza de música*); tirar, imprimir; **to run through** traspasar (*p.ej., con una espada*); **to run up** (coll.) aumentar (*p.ej., gastos*) ‖ *vn* correr; rodar (*sobre ruedas*); apresurarse, darse prisa; trepar (*la vid*); ir y venir, hacer viajes (*un vapor*); supurar (*una llaga*); colar (*un líquido*); correrse (*un color o tinte*); continuar, seguir; ocurrir, suceder; presentar su candidatura; andar, marchar, funcionar; rezar (*decirse un escrito*); desenfrenarse; derretirse o fundirse; migrar (*los peces*); deshilarse (*las medias*); estar en fuerza; **to run about** correr de lugar en lugar; **to run across** dar con, tropezar con; **to run after** seguir, rondar; anhelar por; **to run against** chocar, topar; oponerse a (*otro aspirante a un cargo político*); **to run along** correr; correr a lo largo de; **to run around with** asociarse con; tener amores con; **to run away** correr, huir; desbocarse (*un caballo*); **to run away with** arrebatar; fugarse con; ganar (*p.ej., un campeonato*) fácilmente; **to run back** correr hacia atrás; remontarse; **to run behind** correr detrás; atrasarse; **to run down** escurrir, gotear (*un líquido*); dejar de funcionar; descargarse (*un acumulador*); soltarse (*un muelle*); distenderse (*el muelle del reloj*); acabarse la cuerda, p.ej., **the watch ran down** se acabó la cuerda; agotarse; deteriorarse; **to run dry** secarse (*p.ej., un pozo*); funcionar en seco (*p.ej., engranajes*); **to run empty** marchar desalquilado (*p.ej., un autobús*); **to run flat** (aut.) rodar desinflado, marchar con un neumático deshinchado; **to run for** presentar su candidatura a; **to run for it** correr para librarse; **to run in** entrar al pasar; **to run in the blood** estar en la sangre; **to run in the family** venir de familia; **to run into** dar con, tropezar con; chocar con, topar con; **to run off the road** desviarse de la carretera; **to run off the track** descarrilar (*un tren*); **to run on** continuar; **to run out** salir; expirar, terminar; acabarse; agotarse; **to run out of** no tener más, acabársele a uno, p.ej., **I have run out of money** se me ha acabado el dinero; **to run out on** (coll.) dejar colgado; **to run over** atropellar (*p.ej., a un peatón*); recorrer; registrar a la ligera; pasar por encima; leer rápidamente; rebosar (*un líquido*); **to run through** disipar rápidamente (*una fortuna*); estar difundido en; registrar a la ligera; **to run up and down** correr de una parte a otra; subir y bajar corriendo; **to run with** abundar en; estar empapado de

runabout [ˈrʌnəˌbaut] *s* coche pequeño de dos asientos; carruaje pequeño; autobote pequeño; callejero

runagate [ˈrʌnəget] *s* (archaic) fugitivo; (archaic) vagabundo

runaround [ˈrʌnəˌraund] *s* desviación, vía de paso; (path.) panadizo; (print.) líneas acortadas para intercalar una ilustración; (slang) trato evasivo; **to give the runaround** (slang) tratar evasivamente

runaway [ˈrʌnəˌwe] *s* fugitivo; caballo desbocado; fuga o huída; (sport) partida ganada fácilmente; *adj* fugitivo; desbocado (*caballo*); (sport) ganado fácilmente

runaway marriage *s* casamiento que sigue a una fuga

runcinate [ˈrʌnsɪnet] o [ˈrʌnsɪnɪt] *adj* (bot.) runcinado

rundle [ˈrʌndəl] *s* escalón; rueda

rundown [ˈrʌnˌdaun] *s* informe detallado

run-down [ˈrʌnˈdaun] *adj* desmantelado; inculto; desmedrado, desmirriado; distendido (*muelle de un reloj*); descargado (*acumulador*)

rune [run] *s* runa (*carácter*); escrito rúnico; poema escandinavo escrito en runas; misterio, magia

rung [rʌŋ] *s* escalón; travesaño de silla; radio o rayo (*de rueda*); *pret & pp de* **ring**

runic [ˈrunɪk] *adj* rúnico o runo

run-in [ˈrʌnˌɪn] *s* (print.) palabra o palabras insertadas en un párrafo; (slang) encuentro, riña

runlet [ˈrʌnlɪt] o **runnel** [ˈrʌnəl] *s* arroyuelo

runner [ˈrʌnər] *s* corredor; caballo de carreras; mensajero; maquinista, operador; cuchilla (*de un patín*); patín (*de un trineo*); agente, factor; pasacaminos (*alfombra larga y angosta*); tapete, camino (*de mesa*); pasador (*de contrabando*); carrera (*en las medias*); (bot.) brote rastrero

runner-up [ˈrʌnərˈʌp] *s* (*pl:* **runners-up**) (sport) subcampeón, jugador o equipo clasificado después del campeón

running [ˈrʌnɪŋ] *adj* corriente; corredor (*caballo*); corredizo (*lazo*); trepador; continuo; repetido continuamente; cursivo (*dícese de la escritura*); supurante; seguido, p.ej., **four times running** cuatro veces seguidas; en marcha; (sport) lanzado (*dícese de la salida de una carrera*); *s* carrera, corrida; administración, dirección; marcha, funcionamiento; flujo; **to be in the running** tener esperanzas o posibilidades de ganar; **to be out of the running** no tener esperanzas ni posibilidades de ganar

running board *s* (aut.) estribo

running expenses *spl* gastos corrientes

running gear *s* rodamientos

running head *s* var. de **running title**

running knot *s* lazo corredizo

running mate *s* caballo establecedor del paso (*en una carrera de caballos*); (U.S.A.) compañero de candidatura, candidato a la vicepresidencia (*respecto del candidato a la presidencia*); (coll.) compañero

running start *s* (sport) salida lanzada

running title *s* titulillo (*título de página*)

running water *s* agua viva; agua corriente

runny [ˈrʌnɪ] coladizo; supurante (*llaga*)

run-off [ˈrʌnˌɔf] o [ˈrʌnˌɑf] *s* agua de desagüe; (sport) carrera decisiva o final

run-of-mine coal [ˈrʌnəvˈmaɪn] *s* carbón tal como sale de la mina

runproof [ˈrʌnˌpruf] *adj* indesmallable

runt [rʌnt] *s* enano, hombrecillo; redrojo; animal achaparrado

runty [ˈrʌntɪ] *adj* enano; achaparrado

runway [ˈrʌnˌwe] *s* cauce (*de un arroyo*); vía; senda trillada; (aer.) pista de aterrizaje

rupee [ruˈpi] *s* rupia

Rupert [ˈrupərt] *s* Ruperto

rupestrian [ruˈpɛstrɪən] *adj* rupestre

rupia [ˈrupɪə] *s* (path.) rupia

rupture [ˈrʌptʃər] *s* ruptura, rompimiento; (path.) quebradura; (fig.) ruptura (*cesación de relaciones*); *va* romper; causar una hernia en; *vn* romperse; padecer hernia

rural [ˈrurəl] *adj* rural

rural free delivery *s* distribución gratuita del correo en el campo

ruralist [ˈrurəlɪst] *s* rurícola

ruralize [ˈrurəlaɪz] *va* hacer rural; *vn* hacerse rural; rusticar

Rus. abr. de **Russia** y **Russian**

ruse [ruz] *s* astucia

rush [rʌʃ] *s* acometida, ataque; precipitación, prisa grande; demanda extraordinaria; agolpamiento de gente; friolera, bagatela; (bot.) junco (*planta y tallo*); (U.S.A.) lucha entre dos grupos de estudiantes; **with a rush** de repente; *adj* urgente; juncoso; *va* acometer o atacar con violencia o prisa; empujar con violencia o prisa; despachar con prontitud; (slang) cortejar insistentemente (*a una muchacha*); (slang) solicitar insistentemente a (*los estudiantes de primer año*) para que se inscriban en una sociedad estudiantil; **to rush through** ejecutar de prisa; *vn* lanzarse, precipitarse; venir de prisa, ir de prisa; actuar

con prontitud; **to rush about** dar vueltas de un lado para otro; **to rush forward** lanzarse, precipitarse; **to rush in** entrar precipitadamente; **to rush out** salir precipitadamente; **to rush through** lanzarse a través de, lanzarse por entre
rush-bottomed chair ['rʌʃ'bɑtəmd] *s* silla de junco
rush hour *s* hora de tránsito intenso, hora de aglomeración
rushlight ['rʌʃ,laɪt] *s* vela con pábilo de junco
rushlike ['rʌʃ,laɪk] *adj* juncoso
rush order *s* pedido urgente
rushy ['rʌʃɪ] *adj* (*comp:* **-ier;** *super:* **-iest**) juncoso; juncino
rusk [rʌsk] *s* galleta dulce; pedazo de pan tostado en el horno
Russ [rʌs] *adj* ruso; *s* (*pl:* **Russ**) ruso
russet ['rʌsɪt] *adj* canelo; *s* color de canela; paño burdo canelo; variedad de manzana de color de canela
Russia ['rʌʃə] *s* Rusia; (*l.c.*) *s* piel de Rusia
Russia leather *s* piel de Rusia
Russian ['rʌʃən] *adj* & *s* ruso
Russian Church *s* Iglesia rusa
Russianization [,rʌʃənɪ'zeʃən] *s* rusificación
Russianize ['rʌʃənaɪz] *va* rusificar
Russian olive *s* (bot.) cinamomo
Russian Revolution *s* Revolución rusa
Russian Socialist Federated Soviet Republic *s* República Federativa Socialista Soviética Rusa
Russian thistle *s* (bot.) barrilla pestífera
Russian Turkestan *s* el Turquestán Ruso
Russian turnip *s* (bot.) col de Laponia
Russian wolfhound *s* galgo ruso
Russo-Japanese [,rʌso,dʒæpə'niz] *adj* rusojaponés
Russophile ['rʌsofaɪl] *adj* & *s* rusófilo
Russophobe ['rʌsofob] *adj* & *s* rusófobo
Russophobia [,rʌso'fobɪə] *s* rusofobia
rust [rʌst] *s* orín, moho, herrumbre; (bot.) roña, roya; inacción, ociosidad; influencia dañosa; color rojizo o anaranjado; *adj* rojizo, anaranjado; *va* aherrumbrar; hacer entrar la roya en (*una planta*); *vn* aherrumbrarse; tener la roya (*una planta*); deteriorarse por falta de uso
rustic ['rʌstɪk] *adj* rústico; sencillo, sin artificio; *s* rústico
rustically ['rʌstɪkəlɪ] *adv* rústicamente
rusticate ['rʌstɪket] *va* enviar al campo, desterrar al campo; (Brit.) suspender temporalmente (*a un alumno de la universidad*); *vn* rusticar
rustication [,rʌstɪ'keʃən] *s* destierro al campo; rusticación; (Brit.) suspensión temporal de la universidad
rusticity [rʌs'tɪsɪtɪ] *s* rusticidad; vida campestre
rustle ['rʌsəl] *s* susurro, crujido; *va* hacer susurrar, hacer crujir; hurtar (*ganado*); *vn* susurrar, crujir; (slang) proceder con energía, trabajar con ahinco
rustler ['rʌslər] *s* (slang) buscavidas; (coll.) ladrón de ganado, cuatrero
rustless ['rʌstlɪs] *adj* sin herrumbre, inoxidable; a prueba de herrumbre
rustproof ['rʌst,pruf] *adj* a prueba de herrumbre
rustre ['rʌstər] *s* (her.) rustro
rusty ['rʌstɪ] *adj* (*comp:* **-ier;** *super:* **-iest**) oxidado, mohoso, herrumbroso; rojizo; raído, usado; (bot.) herrumbroso; **to be rusty** estar oxidado, desusado, empolvado, p.ej., **my French is rusty** mi francés está oxidado, mi francés se ha oxidado; estar remoto (*estar uno casi olvidado de una cosa que aprendió*)
rut [rʌt] *s* rodada, bache; hábito arraigado, rutina; celo; brama (*época de celo*); **in rut** en celo; (*pret* & *pp:* **rutted; ***ger:* **rutting**) *va* hacer rodadas en, surcar; *vn* estar en celo
rutabaga [,rutə'begə] *s* (bot.) rutabaga
rutaceous [ru'teʃəs] *adj* (bot.) rutáceo
Ruth [ruθ] *s* Rut
Ruthenia [ru'θinɪə] *s* Rutenia
Ruthenian [ru'θinɪən] *adj* & *s* ruteno
ruthenium [ru'θinɪəm] *s* (chem.) rutenio
ruthless ['ruθlɪs] *adj* despiadado, cruel
rutile ['rutil] o ['rutaɪl] *s* (mineral.) rutilo
rutin ['rutɪn] *s* (chem.) rutina
rutty ['rʌtɪ] *adj* (*comp:* **-tier;** *super:* **-tiest**) lleno de rodadas, surcado
R.V. abr. de **Revised Version**
Ry. abr. de **railway**
rye [raɪ] *s* (bot.) centeno; whisky de centeno
rye grass *s* (bot.) ballico perenne; (bot.) cizaña vivaz
rye whiskey *s* whisky de centeno

S

S, s [ɛs] *s* (*pl:* **S's, s's** ['ɛsɪz]) décimonona letra del alfabeto inglés
s. abr. de **second, shilling, shillings, singular** y **south**
S. abr. de **Saint, Saturday, September, South** y **southern**
S abr. de **South**
-'s desinencia del posesivo singular, p.ej., **the girl's book** el libro de la muchacha; contracción de **is,** p.ej., **he's here** él está aquí; de **has,** p.ej., **she's gone** ella ha ido; de **us** en **let's,** p.ej., **let's go** vámonos
-s' desinencia del posesivo plural, p.ej., **a girls' school** una escuela de muchachas
S.A. abr. de **Salvation Army, South Africa, South America** y **South Australia**
Saar [sɑr] *s* Sarre (*río*); Sarre o territorio del Sarre
Saar Basin *s* territorio del Sarre
Saarland ['sɑrlænd] *s* Sarre o territorio del Sarre
Saarlander ['sɑrlændər] *s* sarrés
sabadilla [ˌsæbə'dɪlə] *s* (bot.) cebadilla (*planta y semillas*)
Sabaean [sə'biən] *adj & s* sabeo
Sabaeanism [sə'biənɪzəm] *s* sabeísmo
Sabbatarian [ˌsæbə'tɛrɪən] *adj* sabatario; dominical; *s* sabatario (*persona que guarda la fiesta del sábado*); partidario de guardar santamente el domingo
Sabbatarianism [ˌsæbə'tɛrɪənɪzəm] *s* sabatismo; observancia estricta del descanso dominical
Sabbath ['sæbəθ] *s* sábado (*de los judíos*); domínica (*de los cristianos*); **to keep the Sabbath** guardar el domingo, observar el descanso dominical; *adj* sabático; dominical
sabbatic [sə'bætɪk] o **sabbatical** [sə'bætɪkəl] *adj* sabático; dominical; de descanso
sabbatical year *s* (Jewish hist.) año sabático; (U.S.A.) año de licencia (*concedido a un profesor universitario*)
sabella [sə'bɛlə] *s* (zool.) sabela
saber ['sebər] *s* sable; *va* golpear con sable, herir a sablazos, matar a sablazos
saber-toothed tiger ['sebərˌtuθt] *s* (pal.) maquerodo
Sabine ['sebaɪn] *adj & s* sabino
sable ['sebəl] *s* (zool.) marta cebellina; marta cebellina (*piel*); (her.) sable; **sables** *spl* vestidos de luto; *adj* negro
sabot ['sæbo] o [sɑ'bo] *s* zueco
sabotage ['sæbətɑʒ] *s* sabotaje; *va & vn* sabotear
saboteur [ˌsæbə'tʌr] *s* saboteador
sabre ['sebər] *s & va* var. de **saber**
sabulous ['sæbjələs] *adj* sabuloso
saburra [sə'bʌrə] *s* saburra
saburral [sə'bʌrəl] *adj* saburral
sac [sæk] *s* (anat., bot. & zool.) saco
saccharification [səˌkærɪfɪ'keʃən] *s* sacarificación
saccharify [sə'kærɪfaɪ] (*pret & pp:* **-fied**) *va* sacarificar
saccharimeter [ˌsækə'rɪmɪtər] *s* sacarímetro
saccharimetry [ˌsækə'rɪmɪtrɪ] *s* sacarimetría
saccharin ['sækərɪn] *s* (chem.) sacarina
saccharine ['sækərɪn] o ['sækəraɪn] *adj* sacarino; (fig.) azucarado; *s* (chem.) sacarina
saccharoid ['sækərɔɪd] *adj* sacaroideo
saccharose ['sækəros] *s* (chem.) sacarosa
saccule ['sækjul] *s* (anat.) sáculo
sacerdotal [ˌsæsər'dotəl] *adj* sacerdotal
sacerdotalism [ˌsæsər'dotəlɪzəm] *s* sistema sacerdotal; clericalismo
sachem ['setʃəm] *s* cacique
sachet ['sæʃe] o [sæ'ʃe] *s* saquito de perfumes; polvo oloroso
sack [sæk] *s* saco; americana, saco; vino blanco generoso; (mil.) saco, saqueo; (slang) despedida (*de un empleado*); **to hold the sack** (coll.) quedarse con la carga en las costillas; *va* ensacar; saquear; (slang) despedir (*a un empleado*)
sackbut ['sækˌbʌt] *s* sacabuche (*instrumento o músico*)
sackcloth ['sækˌklɔθ] o ['sækˌklɑθ] *s* harpillera; cilicio (*usado para la penitencia*); **in sackcloth and ashes** en hábito de penitencia; en señal de arrepentimiento o humildad
sack coat *s* saco, americana
sacker ['sækər] *s* ensacador; saqueador
sackful ['sækfʊl] *s* saco
sacking ['sækɪŋ] *s* tela de saco, harpillera
sacque [sæk] *s* saco (*prenda de vestir holgada*); bata (*vestido holgado de mujer*)
sacral ['sekrəl] *adj* (anat.) sacro
sacrament ['sækrəmənt] *s* sacramento; sacramento del altar (*eucaristía*); juramento solemne
sacramental [ˌsækrə'mɛntəl] *adj & s* sacramental
Sacramentarian [ˌsækrəmɛn'tɛrɪən] *adj & s* sacramentario
sacred ['sekrɪd] *adj* sagrado
Sacred College *s* (eccl.) colegio de cardenales
sacred cow *s* vaca sagrada (*persona o cosa inmunes a la crítica*)
sacred ear o **sacred earflower** ['ɪrˌflaʊər] *s* flor de la oreja
sacred music *s* música sagrada o sacra
sacrifice ['sækrɪfaɪs] *s* sacrificio; **at a sacrifice** con pérdida; *va* sacrificar; malvender; *vn* sacrificar; sacrificarse
Sacrifice of the Mass *s* sacrificio de la misa, sacrificio del altar
sacrificial [ˌsækrɪ'fɪʃəl] *adj* sacrificador, sacrificatorio; de sacrificio
sacrificially [ˌsækrɪ'fɪʃəlɪ] *adv* por sacrificio
sacrilege ['sækrɪlɪdʒ] *s* sacrilegio
sacrilegious [ˌsækrɪ'lɪdʒəs] o [ˌsækrɪ'lidʒəs] *adj* sacrílego
sacristan ['sækrɪstən] *s* sacristán
sacristy ['sækrɪstɪ] *s* (*pl:* **-ties**) sacristía
sacroiliac [ˌsekro'ɪlɪæk] *adj* (anat.) sacroilíaco
sacroiliac joint *s* (anat.) sínfisis sacroilíaca
sacrosanct ['sækrosæŋkt] *adj* sacrosanto
sacrosanctity [ˌsækro'sæŋktɪtɪ] *s* (lo) sacrosanto
sacrum ['sekrəm] *s* (*pl:* **-cra** [krə]) (anat.) sacro
sad [sæd] *adj* (*comp:* **sadder;** *super:* **saddest**) triste; (slang) malo; (dial.) pesado (*al paladar*)
sadden ['sædən] *va* entristecer; *vn* entristecerse
saddle ['sædəl] *s* silla de montar; sillín (*de bicicleta*); cincha (*del arnés*); cuarto trasero (*de una res*); paso, puerto (*entre dos montañas*); **in the saddle** en el poder; listo; *va* ensillar; **to saddle on** o **upon** cargar en; **to saddle with** gravar con, echar a cuestas a
saddleback ['sædəlˌbæk] *s* ensillada (*collado*)
saddle-backed ['sædəlˌbækt] *adj* ensillado
saddlebags ['sædəlˌbægz] *spl* alforjas, bizazas
saddle blanket *s* sudadero
saddlebow ['sædəlˌbo] *s* arzón delantero, fuste delantero
saddlecloth ['sædəlˌklɔθ] o ['sædəlˌklɑθ] *s* sudadero
saddle horse *s* caballo de silla
saddler ['sædlər] *s* sillero, talabartero
saddlery ['sædlərɪ] *s* (*pl:* **-ies**) talabartería; guarniciones de caballería

saddle strap *s* ación
saddle tree [ˈsædəl,tri] *s* arzón, fuste
Sadducee [ˈsædʒəsi] o [ˈsædjusi] *s* saduceo
Sadduceeism [ˈsædʒəsiɪzəm] o [ˈsædjusiɪzəm] *s* saduceísmo
sadiron [ˈsæd,aɪərn] *s* plancha pesada
sadism [ˈsædɪzəm] o [ˈsedɪzəm] *s* sadismo
sadist [ˈsædɪst] o [ˈsedɪst] *s* sádico
sadistic [sæˈdɪstɪk] o [seˈdɪstɪk] *adj* sádico
sadness [ˈsædnɪs] *s* tristeza
sad sack *s* (slang) soldado raso, manso y torpe; (slang) persona inadaptada y ridícula
safari [səˈfɑrɪ] *s* (*pl:* **-ris**) safari
safe [sef] *s* caja fuerte, caja de caudales; caja; alacena, despensa; *adj* seguro, ileso, salvo; cierto, digno de confianza; innocuo; intacto; sin peligro, a salvo; hecho cuidadosamente; **safe and sound** sano y salvo; **safe from** a salvo de
safeblower [ˈsef,bloər] *s* ladrón dinamitero de cajas fuertes
safebreaker [ˈsef,brekər] *s* ladrón que abre cajas fuertes por la fuerza
safe-conduct [ˈsefˈkɑndʌkt] *s* salvoconducto
safe-deposit box [ˈsefdɪˈpɑzɪt] *s* caja de seguridad
safeguard [ˈsef,gɑrd] *s* salvaguardia, medida de seguridad; *va* salvaguardar
safekeeping [ˈsef,kipɪŋ] *s* custodia, protección
safely [ˈseflɪ] *adv* seguramente; a salvo, felizmente
safety [ˈseftɪ] *s* (*pl:* **-ties**) seguridad; confianza; innocuidad; salud pública; **to parachute to safety** salvarse en paracaídas; **to reach safety** ponerse a salvo, llegar a lugar seguro; *adj* de seguridad
safety belt *s* cinturón de seguridad (*de reparadores de líneas telegráficas*); (aer. & aut.) correa de seguridad; (naut.) cinturón salvavidas
safety bolt *s* cerrojo de seguridad
safety curtain *s* (theat.) telón de seguridad, telón contra incendios
safety film *s* (phot.) película de seguridad
safety fuse *s* espoleta de seguridad; (elec.) fusible de seguridad
safety glass *s* vidrio de seguridad
safety island *s* isla de seguridad, burladero
safety lamp *s* lámpara de seguridad
safety mask *s* máscara de seguridad
safety match *s* fósforo de seguridad
safety nut *s* tuerca de seguridad
safety pin *s* imperdible, alfiler de seguridad
safety rail *s* guardarriel
safety razor *s* máquina de afeitar, maquinilla de seguridad
safety stop *s* mecanismo de detención automático
safety valve *s* válvula de seguridad
safety zone *s* zona de seguridad, burladero
safflower [ˈsæ,flauər] *s* (bot.) alazor; flores de alazor
saffron [ˈsæfrən] *s* (bot.) azafrán; azafrán (*estigma y color*); *adj* azafranado; *va* azafranar (*teñir; poner azafrán en*)
saffroned [ˈsæfrənd] *adj* azafranado
sag [sæg] *s* combadura, comba; flecha (*p.ej., de un cable*); baja (*p.ej., de los precios*); (*pret & pp:* **sagged;** *ger:* **sagging**) *vn* combarse; ceder, doblegarse, aflojar; bajar (*los precios*)
saga [ˈsɑgə] *s* saga
sagacious [səˈgeʃəs] *adj* sagaz
sagacity [səˈgæsɪtɪ] *s* (*pl:* **-ties**) sagacidad
sagamore [ˈsægəmor] *s* cacique
sagapenum [,sægəˈpinəm] *s* sagapeno
sagathy [ˈsægəθɪ] *s* sagatí
sage [sedʒ] *adj* sabio, grave, solemne, cuerdo; *s* sabio; (bot.) salvia; (bot.) artemisa
sagebrush [ˈsedʒ,brʌʃ] *s* (bot.) artemisa
sagittal [ˈsædʒɪtəl] *adj* sagital; (anat. & zool.) sagital
Sagittarius [,sædʒɪˈterɪəs] *s* (astr.) Sagitario
sagittate [ˈsædʒɪtet] *adj* (bot.) sagitado
sago [ˈsego] *s* (*pl:* **-gos**) sagú (*fécula*); (bot.) sagú
sago palm *s* (bot.) sagú
saguaro [səˈgwɑro] *s* (*pl:* **-ros**) (bot.) saguaro
Sahara [səˈherə] o [səˈhɑrə] *s* Sahara; *adj* sahárico
Sahara Desert *s* Desierto de Sahara
Sahib [ˈsɑ·ɪb] *s* Sahib (*señor, amo—tratamiento que dan los habitantes de la India a los europeos*)
said [sɛd] *pret & pp de* **say**
sail [sel] *s* vela; barco de vela; brazo (*del molino de viento*); paseo en barco de vela, viaje en barco de vela; **in sail** en barco de vela; **to make sail** alzar velas; **to set sail** hacerse a la vela; empezar un viaje en una embarcación; **to take in sail** apocar las velas; (fig.) recoger velas; **under full sail** a vela llena; **under sail** con las velas alzadas; *va* gobernar (*un barco de vela*); navegar (*un mar, río, etc.*); *vn* navegar, navegar a la vela; salir, salir del puerto, salir de viaje; deslizarse, flotar, volar; **to sail along** volar, ir muy de prisa; **to sail along the coast** costear; **to sail back** tomar puerto; **to sail into** (slang) atacar, azotar; (slang) regañar, reñir
sailboat [ˈsel,bot] *s* buque de vela, barco de vela, velero
sailcloth [ˈsel,klɔθ] o [ˈsel,klɑθ] *s* (naut.) lona, paño
sailer [ˈselər] *s* velero; **good sailer** barco marinero
sailfish [ˈsel,fɪʃ] *s* (ichth.) aguja de mar, pez vela
sailing [ˈselɪŋ] *s* navegación; paseo en barco de vela; salida (*de un buque*)
sailing orders *spl* últimas instrucciones (*dadas al capitán de un buque*)
sailing vessel *s* buque velero
sail loft *s* velería
sailmaker [ˈsel,mekər] *s* velero
sail needle *s* aguja capotera
sailor [ˈselər] *s* marinero, marino; canotié; (nav.) marino (*que no tiene categoría de oficial*); *adj* marinero, marinesco
sailor-fashion [ˈselər,fæʃən] *adv* a la marinera
sailoring [ˈselərɪŋ] *s* marinería
sailorly [ˈselərlɪ] *adj* marinesco
sailplane [ˈsel,plen] *s* (aer.) velero
sainfoin [ˈsenfɔɪn] o [ˈsænfɔɪn] *s* (bot.) pipirigallo, esparceta
saint [sent] *s & adj* santo; *va* (eccl.) canonizar; **Saint** se abrevia **St.** en la toponimia, y tales palabras se encuentran alfabetizadas bajo **St.**
Saint Agnes's Eve *s* vigilia del día de Santa Inés (*20 de enero*)
Saint Andrew's cross *s* cruz de San Andrés
Saint-Andrew's-cross [sentˈændruzˈkrɔs] o [sentˈændruzˈkrɑs] *s* (bot.) arrayanilla
Saint Anthony's fire *s* (path.) fuego de San Antón, fuego de San Marcial
Saint Bernard [bərˈnɑrd] *s* perro de San Bernardo
sainted [ˈsentɪd] *adj* santo; bendito, canonizado
sainthood [ˈsenthud] *s* santidad
Saint James the Greater *s* Santiago el Mayor
Saint James the Less *s* Santiago el Menor
saintliness [ˈsentlɪnɪs] *s* santidad
saintly [ˈsentlɪ] *adj* santo
Saint Patrick's Day *s* día de San Patricio (*17 de marzo*)
saintship [ˈsentʃɪp] *s* santidad
Saint-Simonian [,sentsaɪˈmonɪən] *adj & s* sansimoniano
Saint-Simonianism [,sentsaɪˈmonɪənɪzəm] *s* sansimonismo
Saint-Simonist [sentˈsaɪmənɪst] *s* sansimoniano
Saint Swithin's Day [ˈswɪðɪnz] *s* día de San Swithin (*que corresponde al día de San Regalado por la tradición que sostiene que si llueve este día, lo hace 40 días seguidos*)
Saint Valentine's Day *s* día de San Valentín (*14 de febrero, día en que en los países del norte se ofrecen felicitaciones y regalos los amantes en señal de cariño y amor*)
Saint Vitus's dance [ˈvaɪtəsɪz] *s* (path.) baile de San Vito
sake [sek] *s* motivo; respeto, bien, amor; **for his sake** por su bien; **for the sake of** por, por motivo de, por amor a; **for your own sake** por su propio bien
saker [ˈsekər] *s* (orn. & arti.) sacre

salaam [sə'lɑm] *s* zalema; *va* saludar con zalema, hacer zalema a
salability [,selə'bɪlɪtɪ] *s* facilidad de venta, salida
salable ['seləbəl] *adj* venable, vendible
salacious [sə'leʃəs] *adj* salaz
salacity [sə'læsɪtɪ] *s* salacidad
salad ['sæləd] *s* ensalada; hortaliza, verdura
salad bowl *s* ensaladera
salad days *spl* ingenuidad juvenil
salad dressing *s* aderezo, aliño
Saladin ['sælədɪn] *s* Saladino
salad oil *s* aceite de comer
salamander ['sælə,mændər] *s* salamandra (*estufa*); (zool. & myth.) salamandra; (zool.) tuza; (fig.) pirófago
Salamis ['sæləmɪs] *s* Salamina
sal ammoniac [sæl] *s* sal amoníaca, sal amoníaco
salaried ['sælərɪd] *adj* a sueldo; retribuído (*empleo*)
salary ['sælərɪ] *s* (*pl:* **-ries**) sueldo
salary scale *s* escala de sueldos
salary worker *s* persona que trabaja a sueldo
sale [sel] *s* venta; almoneda, subasta; demanda, mercado; **for sale, on sale** de venta, en venta; se vende(n)
saleable ['seləbəl] *adj* var. de **salable**
salep ['sælɛp] *s* salep
saleratus [,sælə'retəs] *s* bicarbonato de sosa, bicarbonato de potasa, salerato
salesclerk ['selz,klʌrk] *s* vendedor, dependiente de tienda
sales commission *s* comisión de ventas
salesgirl ['selz,gʌrl] *s* vendedora, dependienta de tienda
Salesian [sə'liʃən] *adj* & *s* salesiano (*de las órdenes fundadas por Dom Bosco*); salesa (*de la orden de la Visitación de Nuestra Señora*)
saleslady ['selz,ledɪ] *s* (*pl:* **-dies**) (coll.) vendedora
salesman ['selzmən] *s* (*pl:* **-men**) vendedor, dependiente de tienda
sales manager *s* gerente de ventas
salesmanship ['selzmənʃɪp] *s* venta, ocupación de vendedor; arte de vender
salespeople ['selz,pipəl] *spl* vendedores
salesperson ['selz,pʌrsən] *s* vendedor
salesroom ['selz,rum] o ['selz,rʊm] *s* salón de ventas; salón de exhibición
sales talk *s* argumento para inducir a comprar
sales tax *s* impuesto sobre ventas
saleswoman ['selz,wʊmən] *s* (*pl:* **-women**) vendedora, dependienta de tienda
Salian ['selɪən] *adj* & *s* salio
Salic ['sælɪk] o ['selɪk] *adj* sálico
salicaceous [,sælɪ'keʃəs] *adj* (bot.) salicáceo
salicin ['sælɪsɪn] *s* (chem.) salicina
Salic law *s* ley sálica
salicylate ['sælɪ,sɪlet] o [sə'lɪsɪlet] *s* (chem.) salicilato
salicylic [,sælɪ'sɪlɪk] *adj* (chem.) salicílico
salicylic acid *s* (chem.) ácido salicílico
salience ['selɪəns] o **saliency** ['selɪənsɪ] *s* énfasis; saliente (*parte que sobresale*)
salient ['selɪənt] *adj* saliente; sobresaliente; (her.) empinado
saliferous [sə'lɪfərəs] *adj* salífero
salifiable [,sælɪ'faɪəbəl] *adj* (chem.) salificable
salification [,sælɪfɪ'keʃən] *s* (chem.) salificación
salify ['sælɪfaɪ] (*pret* & *pp:* **-fied**) *va* (chem.) salificar
saline ['selaɪn] *adj* salino; *s* saladar; substancia salina
salinity [sə'lɪnɪtɪ] *s* salinidad
saliva [sə'laɪvə] *s* saliva
salivary ['sælɪ,vɛrɪ] *adj* salival
salivary gland *s* (anat.) glándula salival
salivate ['sælɪvet] *va* hacer salivar; *vn* salivar
salivation [,sælɪ'veʃən] *s* salivación
salivous [sə'laɪvəs] *adj* salivoso
sallet ['sælɪt] *s* (arm.) celada
sallow ['sælo] *adj* cetrino; *s* (bot.) sauce cabruno; *va* poner cetrino
sallowish ['sælo·ɪʃ] *adj* algo cetrino
Sallust ['sæləst] *s* Salustio
sally ['sælɪ] *s* (*pl:* **-lies**) paseo, viaje; ímpetu, arranque; salida, ocurrencia, humorada; (arch.) saledizo, vuelo; (mil.) salida; (*pret* & *pp:* **-lied**) *vn* salir, hacer una salida; ir de paseo, ir de viaje; **to sally forth** avanzar, avanzar con denuedo; (*cap.*) *s* Sara
salmagundi [,sælmə'gʌndɪ] *s* salpicón; mescolanza, olla podrida
salmi ['sælmɪ] *s* guisado de caza asado, salmorejo
salmon ['sæmən] *s* salmón (*color*); (ichth.) salmón; (ichth.) salmón de California (*Oncorhynchus tschawytscha*); *adj* salmonado (*de color parecido al de la carne del salmón*)
salmon pink *s* salmón, rojo amarillento
salmon trout *s* (ichth.) trucha salmonada
salol ['sælol] o ['sælɑl] *s* (trademark) salol
Salome [sə'lomɪ] *s* (Bib.) Salomé
salon [sæ'lɑn] *s* salón
saloon [sə'lun] *s* cantina, taberna; salón (*p.ej., de un buque*)
saloon deck *s* (naut.) cubierta de salón
saloonkeeper [sə'lun,kipər] *s* tabernero
salpa ['sælpə] *s* (zool.) salpa
salsify ['sælsɪfɪ] *s* (bot.) salsifí
salt [sɔlt] *s* sal; purgante de sal; salero; (coll.) marinero; **salts** *spl* sales medicinales; **to not be worth one's salt** no valer uno el pan que come; *adj* salado; *va* salar; marinar (*el pescado*); salgar (*el ganado*); (min.) poner mineral en (*una mina*) para hacer creer que es productiva; (fig.) avivar, aguzar; **to salt away** o **down** conservar con sal; (slang) ahorrar, guardar para uso futuro
saltant ['sæltənt] o ['sɔltənt] *adj* saltante; (her.) empinado
salt cedar *s* (bot.) taray
saltcellar ['sɔlt,sɛlər] *s* salero
salted peanuts *spl* saladillos
salter ['sɔltər] *s* salador (*de carne o pescado*); salinero (*persona que prepara o vende la sal*)
salt-free diet ['sɔlt'fri] *s* régimen desclorurado
salthouse ['sɔlt,haʊs] *s* salero, salín
saltier ['sæltɪr] *s* (her.) sotuer
saltine [sɔl'tin] *s* galletita salada
salting ['sɔltɪŋ] *s* saladura, salazón
saltish ['sɔltɪʃ] *adj* salobre, sabroso
salt lick *s* salero, lamedero
salt mackerel *s* caballa marinada
salt marsh *s* saladar, salina
salt of sorrel *s* sal de acederas
salt of the earth, the lo mejor del mundo, de lo mejor del mundo; (Bib.) la sal de la tierra
saltpeter o **saltpetre** [,sɔlt'pitər] *s* nitro o salitre (*nitrato potásico*); nitro de Chile (*nitrato sódico*)
saltpetrous [,sɔlt'pitrəs] *adj* salitrado, salitral, salitroso
salt pit *s* hoyo salobre, saladar
salt rheum *s* (coll.) eczema
salt shaker *s* salero
salt water *s* agua salada
salt-water ['sɔlt,wɔtər] o ['sɔlt,wɑtər] *adj* de agua salada; marino
saltworks ['sɔlt,wʌrks] *ssg* o *spl* salina
saltwort ['sɔlt,wʌrt] *s* (bot.) barrilla
salty ['sɔltɪ] *adj* (*comp:* **-ier**; *super:* **-iest**) salado; (fig.) salado, saleroso
salubrious [sə'lubrɪəs] *adj* salubre
salubrity [sə'lubrɪtɪ] *s* salubridad
salutary ['sæljə,tɛrɪ] o ['sælju,tɛrɪ] *adj* saludable
salutation [,sæljə'teʃən] o [,sælju'teʃən] *s* saludo, salutación
salutatorian [sə,lutə'torɪən] *s* (U.S.A.) graduando que pronuncia el discurso de salutación (*en las ceremonias de graduación*)
salutatory [sə'lutə,torɪ] *s* (*pl:* **-ries**) (U.S.A.) discurso de salutación; *adj* (U.S.A.) de salutación
salute [sə'lut] *s* saludo; (mil.) saludo; *va* saludar; (mil.) saludar; alcanzar, llegar a
Salv. abr. de **Salvador**
Salvador ['sælvədɔr] *s* var. de **El Salvador**
Salvadoran [,sælvə'dorən] o **Salvadorian** [,sælvə'dorɪən] *adj* & *s* salvadoreño
salvage ['sælvɪdʒ] *s* salvamento; *va* salvar; recobrar
salvarsan ['sælvərsæn] *s* (trademark) salvarsán
salvation [sæl'veʃən] *s* salvación
Salvation Army *s* ejército de Salvación

Salvationist [sælˈveʃənɪst] *s* salutista
salve [sæv] o [sɑv] *s* ungüento; (fig.) ungüento, alivio; *va* curar con ungüento; preservar, proteger; aliviar; salvar (*buque, carga, etc.*)
salver [ˈsælvər] *s* bandeja
salvia [ˈsælvɪə] *s* (bot.) salvia
salvo [ˈsælvo] *s* (*pl:* **-vos** o **-voes**) salva
sal volatile [ˌsælvəˈlætɪlɪ] *s* sal volátil
S.Am. abr. de **South America** y **South American**
Sam [sæm] *s* nombre abreviado de **Samuel**
samara [ˈsæmərə] o [səˈmɛrə] *s* (bot.) sámara
Samaritan [səˈmærɪtən] *adj & s* samaritano
samarium [səˈmɛrɪəm] *s* (chem.) samario
sambuke [ˈsæmbjuk] *s* (mus.) sambuca
same [sem] *adj & pron indef* mismo; **all the same** a pesar de todo; **it is all the same to me** lo mismo me da; **just the same** lo mismo, sin embargo; **much the same** casi lo mismo; **same . . . as** mismo . . . que
sameness [ˈsemnɪs] *s* igualdad, indentidad; monotonía
Samian [ˈsemɪən] *adj & s* samio
samisen [ˈsæmɪsɛn] *s* (mus.) samisén
samite [ˈsæmaɪt] o [ˈsemaɪt] *s* jamete
samlet [ˈsæmlɪt] *s* (ichth.) salmoncillo, esguín
Samoan [səˈmoən] *adj & s* samoano
Samos [ˈsemɑs] *s* Samos
Samothrace [ˈsæmoθres] *s* Samotracia
Samothracian [ˌsæmoˈθreʃən] *adj & s* samotracio
samovar [ˈsæməvɑr] o [ˌsæməˈvɑr] *s* samovar
samp [sæmp] *s* maíz molido grueso
sampan [ˈsæmpæn] *s* sampán
samphire [ˈsæmfaɪr] *s* (bot.) empetro, hinojo marino
sample [ˈsæmpəl] *s* muestra; *va* catar, probar
sample copy *s* ejemplar muestra
sampler [ˈsæmplər] *s* catador, probador; dechado, marcador (*pedazo de tela con diferentes estilos de labor*)
sampling [ˈsæmplɪŋ] *s* catadura, probadura; (statistics) muestreo
Samson [ˈsæmsən] *s* (Bib. & fig.) Sansón
Samuel [ˈsæmjʊəl] *s* Samuel
samurai [ˈsæmʊraɪ] *s* samurai
sanative [ˈsænətɪv] *adj* sanativo
sanatorium [ˌsænəˈtorɪəm] *s* (*pl:* **-ums** o **-a** [ə]) sanatorio
sanatory [ˈsænəˌtorɪ] *adj* sanativo
sanbenito [ˌsænbəˈnito] *s* sambenito
sanctification [ˌsæŋktɪfɪˈkeʃən] *s* santificación
sanctify [ˈsæŋktɪfaɪ] (*pret & pp:* **-fied**) *va* santificar
sanctimonious [ˌsæŋktɪˈmonɪəs] *adj* santurrón
sanctimony [ˈsæŋktɪˌmonɪ] *s* santurronería
sanction [ˈsæŋkʃən] *s* sanción; *va* sancionar (*aprobar; confirmar*)
sanctity [ˈsæŋktɪtɪ] *s* (*pl:* **-ties**) santidad
sanctuary [ˈsæŋktʃʊˌɛrɪ] *s* (*pl:* **-ies**) santuario; sanctasanctórum; asilo, refugio; **to take sanctuary** acogerse a sagrado
sanctum [ˈsæŋktəm] *s* lugar sagrado; asilo, refugio
sanctum sanctorum [sæŋkˈtorəm] *s* sanctasanctórum; asilo, lugar retirado
Sanctus [ˈsæŋktəs] *s* (eccl. & mus.) Sanctus
Sanctus bell *s* (eccl.) campanilla con la que toca a Sanctus el acólito
sand [sænd] *s* arena; (slang) valentía, resolución; dinero; **sands** *spl* arenal; (fig.) momentos de la vida; *va* enarenar; polvorear con arena; lijar con papel de lija
sandal [ˈsændəl] *s* sandalia; abarca (*sandalia rústica*); alpargata (*de cáñamo o de esparto*); cacle, guarache, huarache (Am.); zapatilla; chanclo bajito de goma ligera; tira o correa para asegurar la zapatilla; cendal; (bot.) sándalo
sandaled o **sandalled** [ˈsændəld] *adj* calzado con sandalias; abarcado
sandalwood [ˈsændəlˌwʊd] *s* (bot.) sándalo; *adj* sandalino
sandarac [ˈsændəræk] *s* sandáraca (*resina; rejalgar*); (bot.) tuya articulada
sandbag [ˈsændˌbæg] *s* saco de arena; (fort.) saco terrero; (*pret & pp:* **-bagged**; *ger:* **-bagging**) *va* obstruir con sacos de arena; atacar o golpear con sacos de arena
sandbank [ˈsændˌbæŋk] *s* banco de arena
sand bar *s* barra de arena
sandblast [ˈsændˌblæst] o [ˈsændˌblɑst] *s* soplador de arena; chorro de arena; *va* limpiar con o por medio de chorro de arena, moler por chorro de arena
sandbox [ˈsændˌbɑks] *s* caja para arena; salvadera; (rail.) arenero
sandbox tree *s* (bot.) jabillo, árbol del diablo
sand dollar *s* (zool.) equinaracnio
sand dome *s* (rail.) cúpula de arena
sand dune *s* duna, médano
sander [ˈsændər] *s* arenadora (*p.ej., de locomotora*); soplador de arena; lijador; lijadora (*máquina*)
sanderling [ˈsændərlɪŋ] *s* (orn.) chorlito
sand flea *s* (ent.) nigua
sand fly *s* (ent.) jijene
sandglass [ˈsændˌglæs] o [ˈsændˌglɑs] *s* reloj de arena
sand hill *s* colina de arena, médano
sandhog [ˈsændˌhɑg] o [ˈsændˌhɔg] *s* obrero que cava arena; obrero que trabaja en cámaras de sumersión
sand hopper *s* (zool.) pulga de mar
sanding block *s* taco de alisar
sand launce [læns] o [lɑns] *s* (ichth.) cebo de fango
sand lot *s* (U.S.A.) campo o terreno en una ciudad o cerca de ella que se usa para el béisbol y otros deportes
sandman [ˈsændˌmæn] *s* genio de la fábula que da sueño a los niños
San Domingo [sændoˈmɪŋgo] *s* var. de **Santo Domingo**
sandpaper [ˈsændˌpepər] *s* papel de lija; *va* lijar
sandpaper tree *s* (bot.) vacabuey
sandpiper [ˈsændˌpaɪpər] *s* (orn.) caballero de vientre blanco, lavandera (*Tringoides hypoleucus*)
sand pit *s* hoyo de arena; mina de arena
sand shoe *s* (Brit.) playera (*calzado*)
sandstone [ˈsændˌston] *s* (mineral.) arenisca, piedra arenisca
sandstorm [ˈsændˌstɔrm] *s* tempestad de arena
sand viper *s* (zool.) heterodón; (zool.) víbora cornuda
sand wasp *s* (ent.) amófilo
sandwich [ˈsændwɪtʃ] *s* emparedado; *va* intercalar
Sandwich Islands *spl* islas Sandwich
sandwich man *s* anunciador ambulante que lleva dos cartelones colgados uno por delante y otro por detrás
sandwort [ˈsændˌwʌrt] *s* (bot.) arenaria
sandy [ˈsændɪ] *adj* (*comp:* **-ier**; *super:* **-iest**) arenoso, arenisco; rufo (*pelo*); inconstante, cambiante, movible
sane [sen] *adj* cuerdo, sensato; sano (*p.ej., principio*)
sang [sæŋ] *pret de* **sing**
sangaree [ˌsæŋgəˈri] *s* sangría
sang-froid [sɑ̃ˈfrwɑ] *s* sangre fría
sangsue [ˈsæŋsju] *s* sanguijuela
sanguinary [ˈsæŋgwɪnˌɛrɪ] *adj* sanguinario; sangriento
sanguine [ˈsæŋgwɪn] *adj* confiado, esperanzado, optimista; coloradote; sanguinario; *s* sanguina (*lápiz rojo; dibujo hecho con lápiz rojo*)
sanguineous [sæŋˈgwɪnɪəs] *adj* sanguíneo; confiado, optimista
Sanhedrim [ˈsænhɪdrɪm] o **Sanhedrin** [ˈsænhɪdrɪn] *s* sanedrín
sanicle [ˈsænɪkəl] *s* (bot.) sanícula
sanidine [ˈsænɪdɪn] o [ˈsænɪdin] *s* (mineral.) sanidina
sanies [ˈsenɪiz] *s* (path.) sanie o sanies
sanious [ˈsenɪəs] *adj* (path.) sanioso
sanitarian [ˌsænɪˈtɛrɪən] *adj* sanitario; *s* perito de sanidad
sanitarium [ˌsænɪˈtɛrɪəm] *s* (*pl:* **-ums** o **-a** [ə]) sanatorio
sanitary [ˈsænɪˌtɛrɪ] *adj* sanitario
sanitary cordon *s* cordón sanitario
sanitary corps *s* cuerpo de sanidad
sanitary napkin *s* compresa higiénica, paño higiénico

sanitation [ˌsænɪˈteʃən] *s* sanidad (*métodos sanitarios*); saneamiento (*acción de dar condiciones de salubridad a un terreno, edificio, etc.*)
sanity [ˈsænɪtɪ] *s* cordura, sensatez
San Jose scale [ˈsæn hoˌze] *s* (ent.) cochinilla de San José
San Juan Hill [sæn ˈhwɑn] *s* la loma de San Juan
sank [sæŋk] *pret de* **sink**
San Salvador [sæn ˈsælvədɔr] *s* San Salvador (*isla de las Bahamas; capital de la républica de El Salvador*)
Sanscrit [ˈsænskrɪt] *adj & s* sánscrito
sansevieria [ˌsænsɪvɪˈɪrɪə] *s* (bot.) sanseviera
Sanskrit [ˈsænskrɪt] *adj & s* sánscrito
Sanskritist [ˈsænskrɪtɪst] *s* sanscritista
Santa Claus [ˈsæntəklɔz] o [ˈsæntɪklɔz] *s* San Nicolás, el Papá Noel (*que en los países del norte ocupa el lugar de los Reyes Magos*)
santalaceous [ˌsæntəˈleʃəs] *adj* (bot.) santaláceo
Santo Domingo [ˈsæntodoˈmɪŋgo] *s* Santo Domingo (*antiguo nombre de la República Dominicana; nombre de su capital*)
santonica [sænˈtɑnɪkə] *s* (bot.) santónico; (pharm.) semencontra
santonin [ˈsæntənɪn] *s* (pharm.) santonina
Saône [son] *s* Saona
sap [sæp] *s* savia (*de las plantas*); (bot.) sámago; (fort.) zapa; (slang) necio, tonto; (fig.) savia; (*pret & pp:* **sapped;** *ger:* **sapping**) *va* zapar, socavar; atacar por medio de una zapa; agotar, consumir, desgastar; *vn* hacer trabajos de zapa, cavar una zapa
sap green *s* verdevejiga
saphead [ˈsæpˌhɛd] *s* (coll.) cabeza de chorlito
saphenous [səˈfinəs] *adj* (anat.) safeno
sapid [ˈsæpɪd] *adj* sápido; interesante, sabroso
sapidity [səˈpɪdɪtɪ] *s* sapidez; interés, sabor
sapience [ˈsepɪəns] o **sapiency** [ˈsepɪənsɪ] *s* sapiencia
sapient [ˈsepɪənt] *adj* sapiente
sapindaceous [ˌsæpɪnˈdeʃəs] *adj* (bot.) sapindáceo
sapless [ˈsæplɪs] *adj* seco, sin savia; débil, falto de vigor
sapling [ˈsæplɪŋ] *s* árbol muy joven; jovenzuelo, mozuelo
sapodilla [ˌsæpəˈdɪlə] *s* (bot.) zapote (*árbol y fruto*)
saponaceous [ˌsæpəˈneʃəs] *adj* saponáceo
saponifiable [səˈpɑnɪˌfaɪəbəl] *adj* saponificable
saponification [səˌpɑnɪfɪˈkeʃən] *s* saponificación
saponify [səˈpɑnɪfaɪ] (*pret & pp:* **-fied**) *va* saponificar; *vn* saponificarse
saponin [ˈsæpənɪn] *s* (chem.) saponina
saponite [ˈsæpənaɪt] *s* (mineral.) saponita
sapor [ˈsepər] o [ˈsepɔr] *s* sabor
saporific [ˌsæpəˈrɪfɪk] *adj* saporífero
sapotaceous [ˌsæpəˈteʃəs] *adj* (bot.) sapotáceo
sapper [ˈsæpər] *s* (mil.) zapador
Sapphic [ˈsæfɪk] *adj & s* sáfico
Sapphira [səˈfaɪrə] *s* (Bib.) Safira
sapphire [ˈsæfaɪr] *s* zafiro; *adj* zafirino
Sappho [ˈsæfo] *s* Safo
sappy [ˈsæpɪ] *adj* (*comp:* **-pier;** *super:* **-piest**) jugoso, lleno de savia; fuerte, enérgico; (slang) necio, tonto, estúpido; (slang) sensiblero
saprophagous [səˈprɑfəgəs] *adj* (zool.) saprófago
saprophyte [ˈsæprofaɪt] *s* (biol.) saprófito
saprophytic [ˌsæproˈfɪtɪk] *adj* (bot.) saprófito
sapsucker [ˈsæpˌsʌkər] *s* (orn.) pequeño picamaderos norteamericano
sapwood [ˈsæpˌwud] *s* sámago, alborno, madera alburente
saraband [ˈsærəbænd] *s* (mus.) zarabanda
Saracen [ˈsærəsən] *adj & s* sarraceno
Saracenic [ˌsærəˈsɛnɪk] o **Saracenical** [ˌsærəˈsɛnɪkəl] *adj* sarracénico
Saragossa [ˌsærəˈgɑsə] *s* Zaragoza
Sarah [ˈsɛrə] *s* Sara
Saratoga trunk [ˌsærəˈtogə] *s* baúl mundo
sarcasm [ˈsɑrkæzəm] *s* sarcasmo
sarcastic [sɑrˈkæstɪk] *adj* sarcástico
sarcastically [sɑrˈkæstɪkəlɪ] *adv* sarcásticamente
sarcenet [ˈsɑrsnɛt] *s* tafetán de Florencia
sarcina [ˈsɑrsɪnə] *s* (*pl:* **-nae** [ni]) (bact.) sarcina
sarcocarp [ˈsɑrkokɑrp] *s* (bot.) sarcocarpio
sarcocele [ˈsɑrkosil] *s* (path.) sarcocele
sarcocolla [ˌsɑrkoˈkɑlə] *s* sarcocola (*goma*)
sarcolemma [ˌsɑrkoˈlɛmə] *s* (anat.) sarcolema
sarcology [sɑrˈkɑlədʒɪ] *s* sarcología
sarcoma [sɑrˈkomə] *s* (path.) sarcoma
sarcophagus [sɑrˈkɑfəgəs] *s* (*pl:* **-gi** [dʒaɪ] o **-guses**) sarcófago
sard [sɑrd] *s* sardio
Sardanapalian [ˌsɑrdənəˈpelɪən] *adj* sardanapalesco
Sardanapalus [ˌsɑrdənəˈpeləs] *s* Sardanápalo
sardine [sɑrˈdin] *s* (ichth.) sardina; sardio (*piedra, joya*); **packed like sardines** como sardinas en banasta o en lata
Sardinia [sɑrˈdɪnɪə] *s* Cerdeña
Sardinian [sɑrˈdɪnɪən] *adj & s* sardo
sardius [ˈsɑrdɪəs] *s* sardio
sardonic [sɑrˈdɑnɪk] *adj* burlón, sarcástico
sardonically [sɑrˈdɑnɪkəlɪ] *adv* sarcásticamente
sardonyx [ˈsɑrdənɪks] *s* (mineral.) sardónice
sargasso [sɑrˈgæso] *s* (bot.) sargazo
Sargasso Sea *s* mar de Sargazos
sargo [ˈsɑrgo] *s* (*pl:* **-gos**) (ichth.) sargo
sark [sɑrk] *s* (Scotch) camisa
sarsaparilla [ˌsɑrsəpəˈrɪlə] *s* (bot.) zarzaparrilla (*arbusto, extracto y bebida*)
sarsenet [ˈsɑrsnɛt] *s* var. de **sarcenet**
sartorial [sɑrˈtorɪəl] *adj* de sastre, de sastrería; (anat.) sartorio
sash [sæʃ] *s* (sew.) banda, echarpe, faja; fajín (*insignia*); (carp.) marco de ventana; *va* proveer de marcos
sash bar *s* (arch.) parteluz
sash chain *s* cadena para contrapesos de ventana, cadena para hojas de ventana
sash cord *s* cuerda para contrapesos de ventana
sash lift *s* manija para ventana de guillotina, levantaventana
sash plane *s* cepillo rebajador
sash tool *s* brocha para pintar marcos de ventana
sash weight *s* contrapeso de ventana
sash window *s* ventana de guillotina
sassafras [ˈsæsəfræs] *s* (bot.) sasafrás (*árbol y corteza de las raíces*)
Sat. abr. de **Saturday**
sat [sæt] *pret & pp de* **sit**
Satan [ˈsetən] *s* Satán o Satanás
satanic o **Satanic** [seˈtænɪk] *adj* satánico
satanically [seˈtænɪkəlɪ] *adv* satánicamente
satchel [ˈsætʃəl] *s* maletín; cartapacio (*de los muchachos de escuela*)
sate [set] *va* saciar, hartar, hastiar
sateen [sæˈtin] *s* satén
sateless [ˈsetlɪs] *adj* insaciable
satellite [ˈsætəlaɪt] *s* (astr. & fig.) satélite; *adj* satélite, satelitario
satellite country *s* país satélite
satellite pinion *s* (mach.) satélite
satiable [ˈseʃɪəbəl] o [ˈseʃəbəl] *adj* saciable
satiate [ˈseʃɪɪt] o [ˈseʃɪet] *adj* ahito, harto; [ˈseʃɪet] *va* saciar
satiation [ˌseʃɪˈeʃən] *s* saciedad
satiety [səˈtaɪətɪ] *s* saciedad
satin [ˈsætən] *s* raso; *adj* satinado; *va* satinar (*p.ej., el papel*)
satinet o **satinette** [ˌsætɪˈnɛt] *s* rasete
satinwood [ˈsætənˌwud] *s* madera satinada de las Indias; doradillo, satín
satiny [ˈsætənɪ] *adj* arrasado, satinado
satire [ˈsætaɪr] *s* sátira
satiric [səˈtɪrɪk] o **satirical** [səˈtɪrɪkəl] *adj* satírico
satirist [ˈsætɪrɪst] *s* satírico
satirize [ˈsætɪraɪz] *va & vn* satirizar
satisfaction [ˌsætɪsˈfækʃən] *s* satisfacción; **to the satisfaction of** a satisfacción de
satisfactory [ˌsætɪsˈfæktərɪ] *adj* satisfactorio
satisfy [ˈsætɪsfaɪ] (*pret & pp:* **-fied**) *va & vn* satisfacer
satrap [ˈsetræp] o [ˈsætræp] *s* sátrapa
satrapy [ˈsetrəpɪ] o [ˈsætrəpɪ] *s* (*pl:* **-ies**) satrapía
saturable [ˈsætʃərəbəl] *adj* saturable
saturate [ˈsætʃəret] *va* saturar

saturation [ˌsætʃəˈreʃən] *s* saturación
saturation bombing *s* (aer.) bombardeo de saturación
saturation current *s* (phys.) corriente de saturación
saturation point *s* punto de saturación
saturator [ˈsætʃəˌretər] *s* saturador
Saturday [ˈsætərdɪ] o [ˈsætərde] *s* sábado; *adj* sabatino
Saturn [ˈsætərn] *s* (myth. & astr.) Saturno
saturnalia [ˌsætərˈnelɪə] *ssg* o *spl* saturnal (*orgía desenfrenada*); (*cap.*) *ssg* saturnales (*fiestas en honor de Saturno*)
saturnalian [ˌsætərˈnelɪən] *adj* desenfrenado; (*cap.*) *adj* saturnal
Saturnian [səˈtʌrnɪən] *adj* saturniano (*perteneciente a Saturno; perteneciente a una forma poética en uso entre los romanos*); feliz, dichoso
saturnine [ˈsætərnaɪn] *adj* saturnino
saturnism [ˈsætərnɪzəm] *s* (path.) saturnismo
satyr [ˈsætər] o [ˈsetər] *s* (myth.) sátiro; sátiro (*hombre lascivo*)
sauce [sɔs] *s* salsa; crema (*p.ej., de chocolate*); compota; jugo (*de caramelo*); gracia, viveza; (coll.) insolencia; (coll.) lenguaje descomedido; *va* condimentar, sazonar; (coll.) ser insolente con, desvergonzarse con
saucebox [ˈsɔsˌbɑks] *s* (coll.) insolente, descarado
saucepan [ˈsɔsˌpæn] *s* cacerola
saucer [ˈsɔsər] *s* platillo
saucer-eyed [ˈsɔsərˌaɪd] *adj* de ojos de platillo
saucisson [ˌsosiˈsõ] *s* (fort. & mil.) salchicha, salchichón
saucy [ˈsɔsɪ] *adj* (*comp:* **-cier;** *super:* **-ciest**) insolente, descarado; gracioso, vivo
Saudi Arabia [sɑˈudɪ əˈrebɪə] *s* la Arabia Saudita
sauerkraut [ˈsaʊrˌkraʊt] *s* chucruta
Saul [sɔl] *s* (Bib.) Saúl; (Bib.) Saulo (*nombre de San Pablo antes de su conversión*)
saunter [ˈsɔntər] *s* paseo; paso tranquilo y alegre; *vn* pasearse; pasearse con paso tranquilo y alegre
saurian [ˈsɔrɪən] *adj & s* (zool.) saurio
sausage [ˈsɔsɪdʒ] *s* salchicha
sauté [soˈte] *adj* (cook.) salteado; *va* (cook.) saltear
savage [ˈsævɪdʒ] *adj & s* salvaje
savageness [ˈsævɪdʒnɪs] *s* salvajismo
savagery [ˈsævɪdʒrɪ] *s* (*pl:* **-ries**) salvajería, salvajismo
savanna o **savannah** [səˈvænə] *s* sabana
savant [ˈsævənt] *s* sabio, erudito
save [sev] *prep* (lit.) salvo, excepto; *conj* (lit.) a no ser que; *va* salvar (*p.ej., una vida, un alma, un edificio del incendio*); ahorrar (*dinero*); guardar, conservar; amparar, proteger; **God save the Queen!** ¡Dios guarde a la Reina!; **to save face** salvar las apariencias; **to save oneself the trouble** ahorrarse la molestia; **to save one's eyes** cuidarse la vista; *vn* economizar
save-all [ˈsevˌɔl] *s* adminículo; alcancía; pantalones de trabajo; delantal de niño
saveloy [ˈsævəlɔɪ] *s* salchicha seca y bien sazonada
savin o **savine** [ˈsævɪn] *s* (bot. & pharm.) sabina
saving [ˈsevɪŋ] *adj* ahorrativo, económico; calificativo; *prep* salvo, excepto; con el debido respeto a; **saving your presence** con excusas por mi conducta en su presencia; **savings** *spl* ahorros, economías
saving clause *s* (law) cláusula que contiene una salvedad
saving grace *s* mérito especial
savings account *s* cuenta de ahorros
savings and loan association *s* sociedad de ahorros y préstamos
savings bank *s* banco de ahorros, caja de ahorros
savior [ˈsevjər] *s* salvador
Saviour [ˈsevjər] *s* Salvador
savoir-faire [sævwɑrˈfɛr] *s* maña, habilidad, destreza
savoir-vivre [sævwɑrˈvivrə] *s* mundo, trato de gentes
savor [ˈsevər] *s* sabor; *va* saborear; *vn* heder; oler; **to savor of** oler a, saber a
savory [ˈsevərɪ] *adj* (*comp:* **-ier;** *super:* **-iest**) sabroso; salado, picante; fragante; *s* (*pl:* **-ies**) (bot.) ajedrea de jardín; (bot.) tomillo real; (Brit.) digestivo
savour [ˈsevər] *s, va & vn* (Brit.) var. de **savor**
savoy [səˈvɔɪ] *s* col de Saboya; (*cap.*) *s* la Saboya
Savoyard [səˈvɔɪərd] *adj* saboyano; *s* saboyano; partidario de las operetas de Gilbert y Sullivan
savvy [ˈsævɪ] *s* (slang) comprensión; (*pret & pp:* **-vied**) *va & vn* (slang) comprender
saw [sɔ] *s* sierra; refrán, dicho, proverbio; (*pret:* **sawed;** *pp:* **sawed** o **sawn**) *va* aserrar, serrar; *vn* serrar; serrarse; moverse de atrás para delante como una sierra; *pret de* **see**
sawbuck [ˈsɔˌbʌk] *s* cabrilla, borrico, burro
sawdust [ˈsɔˌdʌst] *s* aserrín, serrín
sawfish [ˈsɔˌfɪʃ] *s* (ichth.) sierra, pez sierra
sawfly [ˈsɔˌflaɪ] *s* (*pl:* **-flies**) (ent.) mosca de sierra
sawhorse [ˈsɔˌhɔrs] *s* cabrilla, borrico, burro
sawings [ˈsɔ·ɪŋz] *spl* aserraduras
sawmill [ˈsɔˌmɪl] *s* aserradero, serrería
sawn [sɔn] *pp de* **saw**
saw set *s* triscador
sawyer [ˈsɔjər] *s* aserrador
Saxe-Coburg-Gotha [ˈsæksˈkobʌrgˈgoθə] *s* Sajonia-Coburgo-Gotha
saxhorn [ˈsæksˌhɔrn] *s* (mus.) bombardón
saxifragaceous [ˌsæksɪfrəˈgeʃəs] *adj* (bot.) saxifragáceo
saxifrage [ˈsæksɪfrɪdʒ] *s* (bot.) saxífraga
Saxon [ˈsæksən] *adj & s* sajón
Saxony [ˈsæksənɪ] *s* Sajonia
saxophone [ˈsæksəfon] *s* (mus.) saxofón
saxophonist [ˈsæksəˌfonɪst] *s* saxofonista
saxtuba [ˈsæksˌtjubə] o [ˈsæksˌtubə] *s* (mus.) bombardón
say [se] *s* decir; **to have one's say** decir su parecer; (*pret & pp:* **said**) *va* decir; **I should say so!** ¡ya lo creo!; **it is said** se dice; **no sooner said than done** dicho y hecho; **that is to say** es decir, esto es; **to go without saying** caerse de su peso; **to say nothing of** eso sin tomar en cuenta; **to say over again** repetir, volver a decir; **to say the least** por lo menos; **to say to oneself** decir para sí; **say when** (coll.) Vd. dirá
saying [ˈseɪŋ] *s* refrán, proverbio; **as the saying goes** como dice el refrán
says [sɛz] *tercera persona del sg del pres de ind de* **say**
say-so [ˈseˌso] *s* (coll.) voz no confirmada, rumor sin fundamento; (coll.) decir, autoridad
sb. abr. de **substantive**
S.B. abr. de **Scientiarum Baccalaureus** (Lat.) **Bachelor of Science**
'sblood [zblʌd] *interj* (archaic) ¡sangre de Cristo!
sc. abr. de **scene, science, scruple** y **scilicet** (Lat.) **to wit, namely**
S.C. abr. de **Sanitary Corps, Signal Corps, South Carolina, Staff Corps** y **Supreme Court**
scab [skæb] *s* costra, postilla; (vet.) roña; (bot.) escabro; esquirol (*obrero que substituye a un huelguista*); (slang) golfo, bribón; (*pret & pp:* **scabbed;** *ger:* **scabbing**) *vn* formar costra; trabajar como esquirol
scabbard [ˈskæbərd] *s* vaina, funda
scabble [ˈskæbəl] *va* desbastar
scabby [ˈskæbɪ] *adj* (*comp:* **-bier;** *super:* **-biest**) costroso, postilloso, tiñoso, roñoso; (coll.) vil, ruin
scabies [ˈskebɪiz] o [ˈskebiz] *s* (path.) sarna, escabiosis
scabiosa [ˌskebɪˈosə] *s* var. de **scabious**
scabious [ˈskebɪəs] *adj* escabioso; *s* (bot.) escabiosa; (bot.) viuda de jardín, escabiosa de Indias (*Scabiosa atropurpurea*)
scabrous [ˈskebrəs] *adj* escabroso
scads [skædz] *spl* (slang) montones
scaffold [ˈskæfəld] *s* andamio; cadalso (*para dar pena de muerte a un criminal*); *va* proveer de andamio; proveer de cadalso; sostener por medio de un andamio

scaffolding [ˈskæfəldɪŋ] *s* andamiada o andamiaje
scalawag [ˈskæləwæg] *s* (coll.) tuno, bribón, golfo
scald [skɔld] *s* escaldadura; *va* escaldar
scale [skel] *s* escama; (bot.) escama; balanza; platillo de balanza; escala (*p.ej., de un mapa*); (mus.) escala; (ent.) cóccido; **scales** *spl* balanza; **Scales** *spl* (astr.) Balanza; **on a scale of** en escala de (*p.ej., 1 por 100*); **on a large scale** en grande escala; **on a small scale** en pequeña escala; **to tip the scales** inclinar la balanza; **to turn the scales** decidir, determinar; **to scale** según escala; *va* escamar; descortezar, descostrar; cubrir con escamas; pesar; escalar, subir, trepar; medir con escala; graduar; reducir de acuerdo con una escala; tirar (*una piedra*) de manera que corte la superficie del agua; *vn* descamarse; descortezarse, descostrarse; cubrirse de escamas; formarse escamas, formarse incrustaciones; subir, trepar
scale fern *s* (bot.) doradilla
scale insect *s* (ent.) cóccido
scale model *s* maqueta o modelo a escala
scalene [skeˈlin] o [ˈskelin] *adj* (geom. & anat.) escaleno
scalenohedron [ske,linoˈhidrən] *s* (cryst.) escalenoedro
scalenus [skeˈlinəs] *s* (anat.) escaleno, músculo escaleno
scaling [ˈskelɪŋ] *s* escamadura (*acción de quitar las escamas*); escalamiento (*acción de entrar por medio de escalas; medición por escala*)
scaling ladder *s* escala de sitio
scallion [ˈskæljən] *s* chalote, escalluna; (bot.) puerro; (bot.) cebolleta
scallop [ˈskɑləp] o [ˈskæləp] *s* (zool.) concha de peregrino; concha de peregrino, pechina, venera (*que llevaban los peregrinos*); concha (*en que se sirve el pescado*); (sew.) festón; *va* hornear a la crema y con pan rallado; cocer (*p.ej., ostras*) en su concha; festonear
scalloping [ˈskɑləpɪŋ] o [ˈskæləpɪŋ] *s* festón bordado, borde adornado con festones
scallop shell *s* concha de peregrino, pechina, venera
scalp [skælp] *s* cuero cabelludo; (fig.) trofeo; *va* escalpar; comprar y revender (*p.ej., billetes de teatro*)
scalpel [ˈskælpəl] *s* (surg.) escalpelo
scalper [ˈskælpər] *s* revendedor de billetes de teatro
scaly [ˈskelɪ] *adj* (*comp:* **-ier;** *super:* **-iest**) escamoso; (coll.) vil, ruin, mezquino
scammony [ˈskæmənɪ] *s* (bot. & pharm.) escamonea
scamp [skæmp] *s* golfo, bribón; *va* hacer descuidada y chapuceramente
scamper [ˈskæmpər] *s* huída precipitada, carrera rápida; *vn* escaparse precipitadamente, correr rápidamente; **to scamper away** escaparse precipitadamente, correr rápidamente
scampish [ˈskæmpɪʃ] *adj* bribón
scan [skæn] (*pret & pp:* **scanned;** *ger:* **scanning**) *va* escudriñar; escandir (*versos*); (telv.) explorar; (coll.) dar un vistazo a
Scand. abr. de **Scandinavia** y **Scandinavian**
scandal [ˈskændəl] *s* escándalo; campanada (*suceso ruidoso*)
scandalize [ˈskændəlaɪz] *va* escandalizar
scandalmonger [ˈskændəl,mʌŋgər] *s* maldiciente, murmurador
scandalous [ˈskændələs] *adj* escandaloso; maldiciente, murmurador
Scandinavia [,skændɪˈnevɪə] *s* Escandinavia
Scandinavian [,skændɪˈnevɪən] *adj & s* escandinavo
scandium [ˈskændɪəm] *s* (chem.) escandio
scanning disk *s* (telv.) disco explorador
scansion [ˈskænʃən] *s* escansión
scant [skænt] *adj* escaso, limitado, insuficiente; mero, solo, apenas suficiente; escaso, p.ej., **a scant half-hour** media hora escasa; **scant of** escaso de; *va* reducir, limitar, escatimar
scantling [ˈskæntlɪŋ] *s* (carp.) cuartón; cuartones
scanty [ˈskæntɪ] *adj* (*comp:* **-ier;** *super:* **-iest**) escaso, limitado, insuficiente, poco suficiente; ligero (*dícese de la ropa*)

scape [skep] *s* (arch., bot. & zool.) escapo
'scape o **scape** [skep] *s, va & vn* (archaic) var. de **escape**
scapegoat [ˈskep,got] *s* (Bib.) cabrón-emisario; cabeza de turco, víctima propiciatoria, víctima inocente
scapegrace [ˈskep,gres] *s* pícaro, truhán, bribón
scaphoid [ˈskæfɔɪd] *s* (anat.) escafoides
scapula [ˈskæpjələ] *s* (*pl:* **-lae** [li] o **-las**) (anat.) escápula, omóplato
scapular [ˈskæpjələr] *adj* escapular; *s* escapulario; pluma escapular; (surg.) vendaje para el omóplato
scar [skɑr] *s* cicatriz, señal; paraje rocoso, escollo; (fig.) cicatriz; (*pret & pp:* **scarred;** *ger:* **scarring**) *va* señalar; *vn* cicatrizarse
scarab [ˈskærəb] *s* (ent. & f.a.) escarabajo
scarabaeus [,skærəˈbiəs] *s* (*pl:* **-i** [aɪ]) var. de **scarab**
scaramouch [ˈskærə,maʊtʃ] o [ˈskærə,muʃ] *s* fanfarrón; truhán, bribón
scarce [skɛrs] *adj* escaso, raro; **to make oneself scarce** (coll.) no dejarse ver, hacerse el perdidizo
scarcely [ˈskɛrslɪ] *adv* apenas; probablemente no; ciertamente no; **scarcely ever** raramente
scarcity [ˈskɛrsɪtɪ] *s* (*pl:* **-ties**) escasez, carestía, rareza
scare [skɛr] *s* susto, alarma; *va* asustar, espantar; **to scare away** espantar, ahuyentar; **to scare up** (coll.) juntar, recoger (*dinero*); **scared stiff** muerto de miedo
scarecrow [ˈskɛr,kro] *s* espantajo (*figura; persona; cosa que infunde temor*); espantapájaros (*figura*)
scarf [skɑrf] *s* (*pl:* **scarfs** o **scarves**) bufanda, chal; pañuelo para el cuello; chalina (*corbata de caídas largas*); tapete (*adorno o protección de los muebles*); *s* (*pl:* **scarfs**) (carp.) ensambladura francesa; *va* unir con ensambladura francesa
scarfpin [ˈskɑrf,pɪn] *s* alfiler de corbata
scarfskin [ˈskɑrf,skɪn] *s* epidermis
scarification [,skærɪfɪˈkeʃən] *s* (agr. & surg.) escarificación
scarificator [ˈskærɪfɪ,ketər] *s* (surg.) escarificador
scarifier [ˈskærɪ,faɪər] *s* (agr. & surg.) escarificador
scarify [ˈskærɪfaɪ] (*pret & pp:* **-fied**) *va* (agr. & surg.) escarificar; criticar severamente
scarious [ˈskɛrɪəs] *adj* (bot.) escarioso
scarlatina [,skɑrləˈtinə] *s* (path.) escarlatina; (path.) escarlatina de forma benigna
scarlet [ˈskɑrlɪt] *adj* escarlata; *s* escarlata (*color y tela*)
scarlet fever *s* (path.) escarlata
scarlet lychnis *s* (bot.) cruz de Malta
scarlet oak *s* (bot.) coscoja, roble escarlata
scarlet runner *s* (bot.) judía de España, judía escarlata
scarlet tanager *s* (orn.) piranga
scarp [skɑrp] *s* escarpa, declive; (fort.) escarpa; *va* escarpar; *vn* hacer escarpa, tener escarpa
scary [ˈskɛrɪ] *adj* (*comp:* **-ier;** *super:* **-iest**) (coll.) asustadizo; (coll.) espantoso
scat [skæt] *interj* ¡zape!
scathe [skeð] *va* (archaic & dial.) hacer daño a; abrasar; criticar acerbamente
scatheless [ˈskeðlɪs] *adj* sano y salvo, ileso
scathing [ˈskeðɪŋ] *adj* acerbo, duro
scatological [,skætəˈlɑdʒɪkəl] *adj* escatológico
scatology [skəˈtɑlədʒɪ] *s* escatología
scatter [ˈskætər] *s* esparcimiento, dispersión; *va* esparcir, dispersar
scatterbrain [ˈskætər,bren] *s* (coll.) cabeza de chorlito
scatterbrained [ˈskætər,brend] *adj* (coll.) alegre de cascos, casquivano
scattered [ˈskætərd] *adj* esparcido; irregular, intermitente; despeinado; divagador
scattering [ˈskætərɪŋ] *s* esparcimiento, dispersión; pequeño número, pequeña cantidad
scaup [skɔp] o **scaup duck** *s* (orn.) coquinero
scaur [skɔr] *s* paraje rocoso; roca a flor del agua
scavenge [ˈskævɪndʒ] *va* limpiar, barrer

scavenger ['skævɪndʒər] *s* basurero; animal que se alimenta de carroña; *vn* recoger la basura
scenario [sɪ'nɛrɪo] o [sɪ'nɑrɪo] *s* (*pl:* **-os**) (mov. & theat.) guión
scenarist [sɪ'nɛrɪst] o [sɪ'nɑrɪst] *s* (mov.) guionista
scene [sin] *s* escena (*en literatura, arte, teatro y cine*); vista, paisaje; arrebato, escándalo, demostración de pasión; **behind the scenes** (theat. & fig.) entre bastidores; **to make a scene** dar un espectáculo, causar escándalo
scenery ['sinərɪ] *s* (*pl:* **-ies**) paisaje; (theat.) decoraciones
scene shifter *s* tramoyista
scenic ['sinɪk] o ['sɛnɪk] *adj* escénico (*perteneciente a la escena*); pintoresco; gráfico
scenographer [si'nɑgrəfər] *s* escenógrafo
scenography [si'nɑgrəfɪ] *s* escenografía
scent [sɛnt] *s* olor; perfume; olfato; rastro, pista; *va* oler; perfumar; rastrear; sospechar
scentless ['sɛntlɪs] *adj* inodoro; sin olfato
scepter ['sɛptər] *s* cetro; *va* proveer de cetro
sceptered ['sɛptərd] *adj* que lleva cetro; regio, imperial
sceptic ['skɛptɪk] *adj & s* escéptico
sceptical ['skɛptɪkəl] *adj* escéptico
scepticism ['skɛptɪsɪzəm] *s* escepticismo
sceptre ['sɛptər] *s & va* var. de **scepter**
Schaffhausen [,ʃɑf'hauzən] *s* Escafusa
schappe ['ʃɑpə] *s* sedalina
schedule ['skɛdʒʊl] *s* lista, cuadro, catálogo; plan, programa; horario (*p.ej., de los trenes*); *va* catalogar; proyectar; fijar la hora de, fijar el tiempo de
Scheherazade [ʃə,hɛrə'zɑdə] *s* Scherezada
Scheldt [skɛlt] *s* Escalda (*río*)
schema ['skimə] *s* (*pl:* **-mata** [mətə]) esquema; (philos.) esquema
schematic [ski'mætɪk] *adj* esquemático
scheme [skim] *s* esquema; plan, proyecto, designio; ardid, treta; *va & vn* proyectar, tramar
schemer ['skimər] *s* proyectista; intrigante
scheming ['skimɪŋ] *adj* astuto, mañoso, intrigante
Schick test [ʃɪk] *s* (med.) prueba de Schick
schilling ['ʃɪlɪŋ] *s* chelín austríaco
schism ['sɪzəm] *s* cisma; facción cismática, secta cismática
schismatic [sɪz'mætɪk] *adj & s* cismático
schismatical [sɪz'mætɪkəl] *adj* cismático
schist [ʃɪst] *s* (geol.) esquisto
schistose ['ʃɪstos] o **schistous** ['ʃɪstəs] *adj* esquistoso
schizocarp ['skɪzokɑrp] *s* (bot.) esquizocarpio
schizomycete [,skɪzomaɪ'sit] *s* (bot.) esquizomiceto
schizophrenia [,skɪzo'frinɪə] *s* (path.) esquizofrenia
schizophrenic [,skɪzo'frɛnɪk] *adj & s* esquizofrénico
schmaltz [ʃmɑlts] *s* (slang) sensiblería
schnapps o **schnaps** [ʃnɑps] *s* ginebra de Holanda; aguardiente
schnorkel o **schnorkle** ['ʃnɔrkəl] *s* var. de **snorkel**
scholar ['skɑlər] *s* escolar (*estudiante*); sabio, erudito; becario (*estudiante que disfruta una beca*)
scholarly ['skɑlərlɪ] *adj* erudito; *adv* eruditamente
scholarship ['skɑlərʃɪp] *s* erudición; beca (*plaza gratuita en una escuela o universidad*)
scholastic [skə'læstɪk] *adj & s* escolástico
scholastically [skə'læstɪkəlɪ] *adv* escolásticamente
scholasticism [skə'læstɪsɪzəm] *s* escolasticismo; (philos.) escolasticismo
scholiast ['skolɪæst] *s* escoliador o escoliasta
scholiastic [,skolɪ'æstɪk] *adj* de los escoliastas
scholium ['skolɪəm] *s* (*pl:* **-a** [ə]) escolio
school [skul] *s* escuela; facultad (*de la universidad*); banco o cardume (*de peces*); **in school** en la escuela; *adj* de escuela, para escuela, escolar; *va* enseñar, instruir, adiestrar, disciplinar; *vn* nadar (*los peces*) en bancos
school age *s* edad escolar
school board *s* junta de instrucción pública
schoolbook ['skul,bʊk] *s* libro escolar
schoolboy ['skul,bɔɪ] *s* alumno de escuela
school day *s* día lectivo
schoolfellow ['skul,fɛlo] *s* condiscípulo, compañero de escuela
schoolgirl ['skul,gʌrl] *s* alumna de escuela
schoolhouse ['skul,haʊs] *s* escuela (*edificio*)
schooling ['skulɪŋ] *s* instrucción, enseñanza; experiencia; coste de la instrucción escolar
schoolman ['skulmən] *s* (*pl:* **-men**) maestro; (philos.) escolástico
schoolmarm ['skul,mɑrm] *s* (coll.) maestra de escuela
schoolmaster ['skul,mæstər] o ['skul,mɑstər] *s* maestro de escuela
schoolmate ['skul,met] *s* condiscípulo, compañero de escuela
schoolmistress ['skul,mɪstrɪs] *s* maestra de escuela
school of thought *s* escuela (*doctrina, sistema*); (coll.) punto de vista, modo de ver
schoolroom ['skul,rum] o ['skul,rʊm] *s* aula, sala de clase
school ship *s* buque escuela
schoolteacher ['skul,titʃər] *s* maestro de escuela
schoolyard ['skul,jɑrd] *s* patio de recreo de la escuela
school year *s* año escolar, año lectivo
school zone *s* zona escolar
schooner ['skunər] *s* (naut.) goleta; (U.S.A.) carromato de cuatro ruedas y con toldo; (coll.) vaso grande de cerveza
schooner-rigged ['skunər,rɪgd] *adj* (naut.) de velas cangrejas
schottische ['ʃɑtɪʃ] *s* chotis (*baile y música*)
schwa [ʃwɑ] *s* (phonet.) e relajada
sci. abr. de **science** y **scientific**
sciatic [saɪ'ætɪk] *adj* ciático
sciatica [saɪ'ætɪkə] *s* (path.) ciática
sciatic nerve *s* (anat.) nervio ciático
science ['saɪəns] *s* ciencia; (*cap.*) *s* ciencia cristiana
science fiction *s* novela científica, novela de divulgación científica
scientific [,saɪən'tɪfɪk] *adj* científico
scientifically [,saɪən'tɪfɪkəlɪ] *adv* científicamente
scientific management *s* gestión científica, organización científica del trabajo
scientism ['saɪəntɪzəm] *s* cientismo
scientist ['saɪəntɪst] *s* científico, hombre de ciencia, sabio; (*cap.*) *s* adepto de la ciencia cristiana
scil. abr. de **scilicet** (Lat.) **to wit, namely**
scimitar o **scimiter** ['sɪmɪtər] *s* cimitarra
scintilla [sɪn'tɪlə] *s* centella, chispa; partícula, vestigio
scintillate ['sɪntɪlet] *vn* centellear, chispear
scintillation [,sɪntɪl'eʃən] *s* centelleo
scintillation counter *s* (phys.) centellador, contador de centelleo
sciolism ['saɪəlɪzəm] *s* erudición superficial, pseudoerudición
sciolist ['saɪəlɪst] *s* erudito superficial, pseudoerudito
scion ['saɪən] *s* (hort. & fig.) vástago
Scipio ['sɪpɪo] *s* Escipión
scirrhous ['skɪrəs] o ['sɪrəs] *adj* escirroso
scirrhus ['skɪrəs] o ['sɪrəs] *s* (*pl:* **-rhi** [raɪ] o **-rhuses**) (path.) escirro
scission ['sɪʒən] o ['sɪʃən] *s* escisión
scissor ['sɪzər] *va* cortar con tijeras; **scissors** *ssg* o *spl* tijeras
scissors-grinder ['sɪzərz'graɪndər] *s* afilador de tijeras; (orn.) chotacabras
scissors kick *s* (swimming) golpe de tijera
sclerenchyma [sklɪ'rɛŋkɪmə] *s* (bot.) esclerénquima
scleroderma [,sklɪro'dʌrmə] *s* (path.) esclerodermia
scleroma [sklɪ'romə] *s* (*pl:* **-mata** [mətə]) (path.) escleroma
sclerometer [sklɪ'rɑmɪtər] *s* esclerómetro
sclerosis [sklɪ'rosɪs] *s* (*pl:* **-ses** [siz]) (path. & bot.) esclerosis
sclerotic [sklɪ'rɑtɪk] *adj* (anat.) esclerótico; (path.) escleroso; *s* (anat.) esclerótica
sclerotitis [,sklɪro'taɪtɪs] *s* (path.) esclerotitis
sclerotium [sklɪ'roʃɪəm] *s* (*pl:* **-a** [ə]) (bot.) esclerocio

sclerotomy [sklɪˈrɑtəmɪ] *s* (*pl:* **-mies**) (surg.) esclerotomía
sclerous [ˈsklɪrəs] *adj* escleroso
scoff [skɔf] o [skɑf] *s* mofa, burla; *vn* mofarse, burlarse; **to scoff at** mofarse de, burlarse de
scoffer [ˈskɔfər] o [ˈskɑfər] *s* mofador, burlador
scoffingly [ˈskɔfɪŋlɪ] o [ˈskɑfɪŋlɪ] *adv* con mofa y escarnio
scold [skold] *s* regañón, regañona; *va & vn* regañar
scolex [ˈskolɛks] *s* (*pl:* **scoleces** [skoˈlisiz]) (zool.) escólex
scoliosis [ˌskolɪˈosɪs] o [ˌskɑlɪˈosɪs] *s* (path.) escoliosis
scollop [ˈskɑləp] *s & va* var. de **scallop**
scolopendra [ˌskɑloˈpɛndrə] *s* (zool.) escolopendra
sconce [skɑns] *s* defensa, cobertizo; baluarte, fortín; (coll.) cabeza; (coll.) agudeza, inteligencia; candelabro de pared, candelero de pared; *va* defender, cubrir; fortificar con baluarte
scone [skon] o [skɑn] *s* bizcocho chato cocido en una plancha metálica
scoop [skup] *s* cuchara (*de excavadora; cualquier instrumento en forma de cuchara*); paleta (*utensilio de cocina*); achicador (*para extraer el agua*); cucharada, palada, paletada (*porción recogida de una vez*); hueco (*lugar ahuecado con la cuchara, etc.*); (coll.) buena ganancia; (slang) primera publicación de una noticia; *va* sacar con pala, paleta o cuchara; achicar (*agua*); ahuecar; **to scoop out** ahuecar, vaciar
scoopful [ˈskupfʊl] *s* cucharada, palada, paletada
scoop net *s* esparavel, manga
scoot [skut] *s* (coll.) carrera precipitada; *vn* (coll.) correr precipitadamente
scooter [ˈskutər] *s* monopatín o patinete (*plancha montada sobre ruedas*); motoneta; lancha rápida; velero que se desliza rápidamente por el hielo o el agua; (orn.) negreta; *vn* correr en monopatín o patinete; deslizar
scope [skop] *s* alcance, extensión; oportunidad; indicador visual
scopolamine [skoˈpɑləmin] o [ˌskopoˈlæmɪn] *s* (chem.) escopolamina
scops owl [skɑps] *s* (orn.) buharro, corneja
scorbutic [skɔrˈbjutɪk] *adj & s* escorbútico
scorbutus [skɔrˈbjutəs] *s* (path.) escorbuto
scorch [skɔrtʃ] *s* chamusco (*quemadura leve*); *va* chamuscar; abrasar (*secar, marchitar*); criticar acerbamente; *vn* chamuscarse; abrasarse; (coll.) correr muy rápidamente
scorched-earth policy [ˈskɔrtʃtˈʌrθ] *s* (mil.) política de tierra abrasada
scorcher [ˈskɔrtʃər] *s* (coll.) día de mucho calor; (coll.) reproche acerbo; (coll.) jinete o biciclista que va a toda velocidad
scorching [ˈskɔrtʃɪŋ] *adj* abrasador; acerbo, duro, mordaz
score [skor] *s* cuenta, tantos (*en un juego*); nota (*en un examen*); muesca, entalladura; línea, raya; (mus.) partitura; veintena; **on that score** a ese respecto; **on the score of** a título de, con motivo de; **to keep score** tantear, apuntar los tantos; **to pay off a score** o **to settle a score** desquitarse de un agravio; *va* anotar (*los tantos*); ganar, tantear (*tantos*); señalar, rayar; (mus.) instrumentar; criticar severamente, regañar acerbamente; **to score a cylinder** (aut.) rayar un cilindro; **to score a point** ganar un punto; *vn* ganar tantos; marcar los tantos; hacer rayas, hacer señales
score board *s* pizarrón anotador, cuadro indicador, marcador
score card *s* anotador
score keeper *s* tanteador
scoria [ˈskorɪə] *s* (*pl:* **-ae** [i]) escoria; (petrog.) escoria
scoriaceous [ˌskorɪˈeʃəs] *adj* escoriáceo
scorify [ˈskorɪfaɪ] (*pret & pp:* **-fied**) *va* escorificar
scorn [skɔrn] *s* desprecio, desdén; **to cast scorn upon** denigrar; *va & vn* despreciar, desdeñar; **to scorn to** + *inf* no dignarse + *inf*
scornful [ˈskɔrnfəl] *adj* desdeñoso
scorpene [ˈskɔrpin] *s* (ichth.) escorpina, raño
Scorpio [ˈskɔrpɪo] *s* (astr.) Escorpión
scorpion [ˈskɔrpɪən] *s* (ent.) alacrán, escorpión; escorpión (*azote; ballesta de los antiguos*)
scorpion grass *s* (bot.) alacranera
Scot. abr. de **Scotch, Scotland** y **Scottish**
scot [skɑt] *s* escote; (*cap.*) *s* escocés
scotch [skɑtʃ] *s* corte, incisión; marca, señal; calce, cuña; obstáculo, impedimento; (*cap.*) *adj* escocés; *s* escocés (*dialecto; whisky*); *spl* escoceses; (*l.c.*) *va* cortar; marcar; herir ligeramente; calzar; detener, frustrar; engalgar (*una rueda*)
Scotch-Irish [ˈskɑtʃˈaɪrɪʃ] *adj* de descendencia irlandesa y escocesa
Scotchman [ˈskɑtʃmən] *s* (*pl:* **-men**) escocés
Scotch pine *s* (bot.) pino albar
Scotch tape *s* (trademark) cinta adhesiva transparente
Scotch terrier *s* perro escocés
Scotch thistle *s* (bot.) acantio, cardo borriqueño, toba
Scotch whiskey *s* whisky escocés
scoter [ˈskotər] *s* (orn.) negreta, pato negro
scot-free [ˈskɑtˈfri] *adj* impune
scotia [ˈskoʃɪə] o [ˈskoʃə] *s* (arch.) escocia, nacela; (*cap.*) [ˈskoʃə] *s* (poet.) Escocia
Scotism [ˈskotɪzəm] *s* escotismo
Scotland [ˈskɑtlənd] *s* Escocia
Scotland Yard *s* cuerpo de detectives de Londres
Scots [skɑts] *adj* escocés; *ssg* escocés (*dialecto*); *spl* escoceses
Scotsman [ˈskɑtsmən] *s* (*pl:* **-men**) escocés
Scotticism [ˈskɑtɪsɪzəm] *s* acento del habla escocesa
Scottish [ˈskɑtɪʃ] *adj* escocés; *ssg* escocés (*dialecto*); *spl* escoceses
scoundrel [ˈskaʊndrəl] *s* pícaro, bribón
scoundrelly [ˈskaʊndrəlɪ] *adj* pícaro, bribón
scour [skaʊr] *s* fregado, estregamiento; *va* fregar, estregar (*frotar con fuerza para limpiar*); escurar (*el paño*); purgar; limpiar con un chorro de agua; formar (*un cauce el agua corriente*); recorrer rápidamente, explorar detenidamente; batir (*el monte*)
scourge [skʌrdʒ] *s* azote, flagelo; *va* azotar; flagelar
Scourge of God, the el azote de Dios (*Atila*)
scouring [ˈskaʊrɪŋ] *s* fregadura; **scourings** *spl* residuo de la fregadura; pulpa inservible que se saca al grano; (fig.) escoria, canalla
scout [skaʊt] *s* (mil.) escucha, explorador; niño explorador, niña exploradora; exploración, reconocimiento; (slang) tipo, individuo, sujeto; *va* explorar, reconocer (*un territorio*); observar (*al enemigo*); negarse a creer, burlarse de; *vn* explorar, reconocer; **to scout at** mofarse de; **to scout for** (coll.) buscar
scouting [ˈskaʊtɪŋ] *s* exploración, reconocimiento; actividades de los niños exploradores
scoutmaster [ˈskaʊtˌmæstər] o [ˈskaʊtˌmɑstər] *s* jefe de tropa de niños exploradores
scow [skaʊ] *s* (U.S.A.) lanchón de carga
scowl [skaʊl] *s* ceño, semblante ceñudo; *vn* mirar con ceño, poner mal gesto
scrabble [ˈskræbəl] *s* pataleo; garrapatos (*mala escritura*); *va* arañar; garrapatear (*escribir mal*); *vn* patalear; garrapatear
scrag [skræg] *s* persona delgada y pellejuda, animal delgado y pellejudo; (slang) pescuezo; (*pret & pp:* **scragged;** *ger:* **scragging**) *va* (slang) ahorcar, torcer el pescuezo a
scraggly [ˈskræglɪ] *adj* (*comp:* **-glier;** *super:* **-gliest**) áspero, dentado, harapiento, desgreñado
scraggy [ˈskrægɪ] *adj* (*comp:* **-gier;** *super:* **-giest**) áspero, nudoso; flaco, delgado, huesoso
scram [skræm] (*pret & pp:* **scrammed;** *ger:* **scramming**) *vn* (slang) largarse, salir de naja
scramble [ˈskræmbəl] *s* lucha, contienda; arrebatiña; trepa; *va* arrebatar; recoger de prisa, recoger con confusión; revolver; hacer un revoltillo de (*huevos*); trepar; (rad.) invertir o cambiar de otra manera el espectro de frecuencias de (*una señal*) de modo que no pueda ser recobrada sino por el aparato receptor que tenga la clave electrónica; *vn* luchar; trepar
scrambled eggs *spl* revoltillo, huevos revueltos

scrannel ['skrænəl] *adj* delgado, descarnado; chillón, rechinante
scrap [skræp] *s* pedazo, fragmento, migaja; desecho, metal viejo, chatarra; (slang) riña, contienda, camorra; **scraps** *spl* sobras (*de la mesa*); ripios, desperdicios; parte seca de la grasa animal, chicharrón; *adj* desechado, viejo; (*pret & pp:* **scrapped**; *ger:* **scrapping**) *va* desechar, descartar, echar a la basura; despedazar; reducir a hierro viejo; *vn* (slang) reñir, pelear
scrapbook ['skræp,bʊk] *s* álbum de recortes, libro de recuerdos
scrape [skrep] *s* raspadura; raspazo (*lugar que se ha raspado*); aprieto, enredo; reverencia hecha con un pie echado hacia atrás; *va* raspar; arañar (*recoger con mucho afán*); **to scrape acquaintance** trabar amistad; **to scrape together, to scrape up** arañar; *vn* raspar; rascar (*tocar un instrumento de cuerda y arco haciendo un sonido de raspadura*); hacer una reverencia echando el pie hacia atrás; arreglárselas, desenvolverse en un aprieto; amontonar dinero poco a poco; **to scrape along** ir tirando; **to scrape through** aprobar justo
scraper ['skrepər] *s* raedera, raspador; arañador (*de dinero; del violín*); rascatripas (*del violín*); desuellacaras (*barbero malo*); limpiabarros, estregadera (*para estregar los pies*)
scrap heap *s* montón de cachivaches, montón de desechos
scrap iron *s* hierro de desecho, desecho de hierro, chatarra
scrapple ['skræpəl] *s* pasta (frita) de harina de maíz con pedazos de carne de puerco
scrappy ['skræpɪ] *adj* (*comp:* **-pier**; *super:* **-piest**) fragmentario, inconexo, misceláneo; (slang) peleador
scratch [skrætʃ] *s* arañazo, rasguño; (coll.) garrapato; (sport) línea de partida; prueba de valor; (billiards) bambarria, chiripa; **to be up to scratch** estar en buena condición; **to start from scratch** empezar sin nada, empezar sin ventaja, empezar desde el principio; *va* arañar, rasguñar; (coll.) garrapatear; borrar, raspar (*lo escrito*); (sport) borrar (*un corredor o caballo*); **to scratch out** borrar; sacar (*ojos*) con las uñas; *vn* arañar, rasguñar; (coll.) garrapatear; raspear (*una pluma al escribir*); juntar dinero con gran dificultad
scratch hit *s* (baseball) golpe por casualidad o por chamba
scratch pad *s* cuadernillo de apuntes
scratch test *s* medida de dureza al rayado; (med.) reacción de la escarificación
scratchy ['skrætʃɪ] *adj* (*comp:* **-ier**; *super:* **-iest**) arañador, raspador; áspero, irregular
scrawl [skrɔl] *s* garrapatos; *va & vn* garrapatear
scrawny ['skrɔnɪ] *adj* (*comp:* **-nier**; *super:* **-niest**) descarnado, huesudo
screak [skrik] *s* chirrido, rechinamiento; *vn* chirriar, rechinar
scream [skrim] *s* chillido, alarido, grito; (slang) persona o cosa muy divertidas; *va* vociferar; *vn* chillar, gritar; reírse a gritos
screamer ['skrimər] *s* chillón, gritón; (slang) persona sobresaliente, cosa sobresaliente; (slang) persona muy divertida, escrito muy divertido; (orn.) anhima, palamedea; (orn.) chajá (*Chauna chavaria*)
screaming ['skrimɪŋ] *s* chillido, alarido, grito; *adj* chillón, gritón; llamativo; cómico, chistoso, divertidísimo; (slang) excelente
screech [skritʃ] *s* chillido; *vn* chillar
screech owl *s* (orn.) corneja, buharro; (orn.) lechuza, lechuza norteamericana; profeta del mal
screechy ['skritʃɪ] *adj* (*comp:* **-ier**; *super:* **-iest**) chillón
screed [skrid] *s* tirada; diatriba; (mas.) maestra
screen [skrin] *s* mampara, biombo; pantalla (*delante de la chimenea*); alambrera (*para evitar que las moscas se introduzcan en las habitaciones*); tamiz (*para pasar arena, carbón, etc.*); retícula, trama (*para obtener fotograbados*); (mov., phys. & telv.) pantalla; (fig.) pantalla (*cine, arte del cine*); **to put on the screen** llevar a la pantalla, llevar al celuloide; *va* defender, proteger; cubrir, ocultar; cinematografiar; rodar, proyectar (*una película*); adaptar para el cine; tamizar (*p.ej., arena*); dividir, separar
screen grid *s* (rad.) rejilla blindada
screen-grid tube ['skrin'grɪd] *s* (rad.) válvula de rejilla blindada, válvula de rejilla-pantalla
screenings ['skrinɪŋz] *spl* residuos de criba, desperdicios de criba
screen play ['skrin,ple] *s* cinedrama
screw [skru] *s* tornillo; rosca (*filete; vuelta espiral*); tuerca (*pieza taladrada en que se encaja el tornillo*); hélice (*de un vapor*); tacaño; **to have a screw loose** (slang) faltarle a uno un tornillo, tener flojos los tornillos; **to put the screws on** apretar los tornillos a; *va* atornillar; enroscar (*torcer en forma de tornillo*); obligar; obtener por fuerza; **to screw from** u **out of** sonsacar; **to screw up** torcer (*el rostro*); **to screw up courage** animarse, cobrar ánimo; *vn* atornillarse; enroscarse
screwball ['skru,bɔl] *adj & s* (slang) extravagante, excéntrico, estrafalario
screw bolt *s* perno roscado
screw conveyor *s* transportador de tornillo sin fin
screwdriver ['skru,draɪvər] *s* destornillador
screw eye *s* armella
screwhead ['skru,hɛd] *s* cabeza de tornillo
screw jack *s* gato de tornillo
screw key *s* desvolvedor
screw propeller *s* hélice
screw tap *s* macho de terraja
screw thread *s* filete de tornillo
scribal error ['skraɪbəl] *s* error de escribiente
scribble ['skrɪbəl] *s* garrapatos; *va & vn* garrapatear
scribbler ['skrɪblər] *s* garrapateador; mal escritor, autorzuelo despreciable
scribe [skraɪb] *s* escriba (*intérprete de la ley entre los judíos*); amanuense; escribiente; autor, escritor; *va* arañar, rayar; trazar con punzón
scriber ['skraɪbər] *s* punzón de trazar
scrim [skrɪm] *s* tejido de algodón o lino ligero y basto
scrimmage ['skrɪmɪdʒ] *s* lucha, pelea; (football) jugada en que, los equipos estando juntos, se lanza la pelota hacia atrás
scrimp [skrɪmp] *va* escatimar; **to scrimp someone for food** escatimar a uno la comida; *vn* escatimar
scrimpy ['skrɪmpɪ] *adj* (*comp:* **-ier**; *super:* **-iest**) escaso, escatimoso
scrip [skrɪp] *s* cédula, documento; vale, abonaré
script [skrɪpt] *s* escritura, letra cursiva; (print.) plumilla inglesa; manuscrito; texto, palabras (*de un drama, cine, etc.*); (rad. & telv.) guión; (law) escritura
scriptorium [skrɪp'torɪəm] *s* (*pl:* **-ums** o **-a** [ə]) escritorio
scriptural o **Scriptural** ['skrɪptʃərəl] *adj* bíblico
scripturally ['skrɪptʃərəlɪ] *adv* conforme a la Biblia
scripture ['skrɪptʃər] *s* escrito sagrado; (*cap.*) *s* Escritura; **Scriptures** *spl* Escrituras; **Holy Scriptures** Sagradas Escrituras
scriptwriter ['skrɪpt,raɪtər] *s* guionista
scrivener ['skrɪvnər] *s* (archaic) escribano; (archaic) escribiente
scrod [skrɑd] *s* (ichth.) cría del abadejo común
scrofula ['skrɑfjələ] *s* (path.) escrófula
scrofulous ['skrɑfjələs] *adj* escrofuloso
scroll [skrol] *s* rollo de papel, rollo de pergamino; (arch.) voluta
scroll saw *s* sierra de calar, sierra para contornear
scrollwork ['skrol,wʌrk] *s* dibujo de volutas, adornos de voluta, obra con volutas
scrotal ['skrotəl] *adj* escrotal
scrotum ['skrotəm] *s* (*pl:* **-ta** [tə] o **-tums**) (anat.) escroto
scrub [skrʌb] *s* monte bajo; persona de poca altura; (sport) jugador no oficial, no adiestrado; fregado; *adj* achaparrado; (sport) no ofi-

cial, no adiestrado; (*pret & pp:* **scrubbed;** *ger:* **scrubbing**) *va* fregar, restregar
scrubbing brush *s* cepillo de fregar, estregadera
scrubby ['skrʌbɪ] *adj* (*comp:* **-bier;** *super:* **-biest**) achaparrado, bajo, pequeño; vil, miserable, despreciable; erizado, mal afeitado
scrub oak *s* (bot.) chaparro
scrub woman *s* fregona
scruff [skrʌf] *s* nuca; piel que cubre la nuca; capa, superficie; espuma, escoria
scrumptious ['skrʌmpʃəs] *adj* (slang) elegante, magnífico
scrunch [skrʌntʃ] *s* (coll.) crujido; *va & vn* (coll.) ronzar
scruple ['skrupəl] *s* escrúpulo; (pharm.) escrúpulo; cantidad ínfima; *va* tener escrúpulos acerca de; *vn* escrupulizar
scrupulosity [ˌskrupjə'lɑsɪtɪ] *s* (*pl:* **-ties**) escrupulosidad
scrupulous ['skrupjələs] *adj* escrupuloso
scrutinize ['skrutɪnaɪz] *va* escrutar, escudriñar
scrutiny ['skrutɪnɪ] *s* (*pl:* **-nies**) escrutinio, escudriñamiento
scud [skʌd] *s* carrera rápida; salpicaduras de agua que lleva el viento; nube correo; (*pret & pp:* **scudded;** *ger:* **scudding**) *vn* correr rápidamente, deslizarse precipitadamente
scuff [skʌf] *s* rascadura; desgaste; *va* rascar; desgastar; arrastrar (*los pies*); *vn* rascarse; desgastarse; arrastrar los pies
scuffle ['skʌfəl] *s* sarracina, lucha; *vn* luchar, forcejear; arrastrar los pies
scull [skʌl] *s* espadilla; remo; bote; *va* impulsar con espadilla; *vn* cinglar, remar con espadilla
sculler ['skʌlər] *s* bote de espadilla; remero de bote
scullery ['skʌlərɪ] *s* (*pl:* **-ies**) espetera, sollastría; trascocina
scullery maid *s* fregona
scullion ['skʌljən] *s* (archaic) sollastre (*mozo de cocina; pícaro*)
sculpin ['skʌlpɪn] *s* (ichth.) coto; individuo despreciable
sculptor ['skʌlptər] *s* escultor
sculptress ['skʌlptrɪs] *s* escultora
sculptural ['skʌlptʃərəl] *adj* escultural
sculpture ['skʌlptʃər] *s* escultura; *va & vn* esculpir
sculptured ['skʌlptʃərd] *adj* esculpido, ornado de esculturas
sculpturesque [ˌskʌlptʃə'rɛsk] *adj* escultural
scum [skʌm] *s* espuma, nata; (fig.) escoria, canalla, gente baja; (*pret & pp:* **scummed;** *ger:* **scumming**) *va & vn* espumar
scummy ['skʌmɪ] *adj* (*comp:* **-mier;** *super:* **-miest**) espumoso; vil, ruin
scup [skʌp] *s* (ichth.) pagro
scupper ['skʌpər] *s* imbornal; (naut.) imbornal o embornal
scuppernong ['skʌpərnɑŋ] *s* moscatel norteamericano
scurf [skʌrf] *s* caspa; costra
scurfy ['skʌrfɪ] *adj* (*comp:* **-ier;** *super:* **-iest**) casposo; costroso
scurrility [skə'rɪlɪtɪ] *s* (*pl:* **-ties**) procacidad, insolencia, grosería
scurrilous ['skʌrɪləs] *adj* procaz, insolente, grosero, chocarrero
scurry ['skʌrɪ] *s* fuga, carrera precipitada; ventolera, remolino; ráfaga, nevisca; (*pret & pp:* **-ried**) *va* poner en fuga, hacer correr; *vn* echar a correr, escabullirse; **to scurry around** menearse; **to scurry off** escabullirse; **to scurry through** pasar precipitadamente por; hacer de prisa, leer de prisa, terminar rápidamente
scurvy ['skʌrvɪ] *s* (path.) escorbuto; *adj* (*comp:* **-vier;** *super:* **-viest**) vil, ruin, despreciable
scurvy grass *s* (bot.) coclearia, hierba de las cucharas
scut [skʌt] *s* rabito
Scutari ['skutɑrɪ] *s* Escútari
scutate ['skjutet] *adj* escutiforme
scutch [skʌtʃ] *s* agramadera; agramaduras; martillo cortador de ladrillos; *va* agramar
scutcheon ['skʌtʃən] *s* var. de **escutcheon**
scutch grass *s* (bot.) grama; (bot.) grama del norte
scute [skjut] *s* (zool.) escudo
scutellate ['skjutəlet] o [skju'tɛlet] *adj* (bot., zool. & orn.) escutelado
scutellum [skju'tɛləm] *s* (*pl:* **-la** [lə]) (bot. & zool.) escutelo
scutiform ['skjutɪfɔrm] *adj* escutiforme
scuttle ['skʌtəl] *s* cubo, balde; escotillón; (naut.) escotilla; abertura, agujero; fuga, paso acelerado; *va* (naut.) barrenar, dar barreno a; (naut.) agujerear la cubierta de; *vn* echar a correr, correr con precipitación
scuttlebutt ['skʌtəlˌbʌt] *s* (naut.) pipa o tonel de agua de beber; (naut.) fuente de beber; (slang) runrún, chismes
scutum ['skjutəm] *s* (*pl:* **-ta** [tə]) (zool.) escudo
scybalum ['sɪbələm] *s* (*pl:* **-la** [lə]) (path.) esquíbala
Scylla ['sɪlə] *s* (geog. & myth.) Escila; **to be between Scylla and Charybdis** estar entre Escila y Caribdis
scythe [saɪð] *s* guadaña, dalla; *va* guadañar
Scythia ['sɪθɪə] *s* la Escitia
Scythian ['sɪθɪən] *adj* escita, escítico; *s* escita
S. Dak. abr. de **South Dakota**
'sdeath [zdɛθ] *interj* (archaic) ¡ vive Dios!
S.E. o **SE** abr. de **southeast**
sea [si] *s* mar; fig.) mar (*p.ej., de lágrimas*); **at sea** en el mar; perplejo, confuso; **beyond the sea** allende el mar; **by the sea** a la orilla del mar; **by sea** por mar; **in the open sea** en pleno mar; **to follow the sea** ser marinero; **to go to sea** hacerse marinero; emprender un viaje por mar; **to put to sea** hacerse a la mar
sea anemone *s* (zool.) anemone de mar
sea bass [bæs] *s* (ichth.) serrano, perca de mar
sea bird *s* ave marina, ave de mar
seaboard ['siˌbord] *s* costa del mar, litoral; playa; *adj* costanero, costero
sea-born ['siˌbɔrn] *adj* nacido en el mar, nacido del mar, que sale del mar
sea-borne ['siˌborn] *adj* transportado por mar
sea bread *s* galleta, bizcocho (*de marinero*)
sea bream *s* (ichth.) besugo
sea breeze *s* brisa de mar
sea calf *s* (zool.) becerro marino
sea coal *s* (archaic) carbón de piedra
seacoast ['siˌkost] *s* litoral, costa marítima
sea cow *s* (zool.) manatí; (zool.) ternera marina (*morsa*)
sea cucumber *s* (zool.) cohombro de mar
sea daffodil *s* (bot.) nardo marítimo, amormío
sea dog *s* (zool.) foca; (zool.) perro de mar; marinero viejo, lobo de mar
sea eagle *s* (orn.) águila marina; (orn.) quebrantahuesos
sea elephant *s* (zool.) foca de trompa, elefante marino
seafarer ['siˌfɛrər] *s* marinero; navegante
seafaring ['siˌfɛrɪŋ] *adj* marinero; navegante; *s* marinería; navegación
sea foam *s* espuma de mar
seafood ['siˌfud] *s* pescado de mar, mariscos
seafowl ['siˌfaul] *s* ave de mar
seagirt ['siˌgʌrt] *adj* cercado por el mar
seagoing ['siˌgo·ɪŋ] *adj* de alta mar, de la navegación marítima
sea goose *s* (orn.) barnacla
sea grape *s* (bot.) cocobolo, uvero
sea green *s* verdemar
sea gull *s* (orn.) gaviota
sea hare *s* (zool.) liebre de mar o liebre marina
sea hedgehog *s* (zool.) apancora
sea hog *s* (zool.) puerco de mar
sea horse *s* (ichth.) caballito de mar; (ichth. & zool.) caballo marino; (her.) monstruo mitad caballo y mitad pez
sea kale *s* (bot.) col marina
sea king *s* rey del mar (*pirata noruego de la Edad Media*)
seal [sil] *s* sello; (zool.) foca; (zool.) león marino; **to set one's seal to** poner el sello a; aprobar; **seals** *spl* sellos (*símbolo de la autoridad*); *va* sellar; cerrar herméticamente; decidir irrevocablemente; lacrar; **to seal in** cerrar herméticamente; *vn* cazar focas
sea lavender *s* (bot.) acelga silvestre, limonio
sealed-in ['sildˌɪn] *adj* hermético
sea legs *spl* pie marino
sealer ['silər] *s* sellador; cierre hermético; ca-

zador de focas; embarcación en que se cazan focas
sealery ['silərɪ] *s* (*pl:* **-ies**) caza de focas; lugar donde se cazan focas
sea level *s* nivel del mar
sea lily *s* (zool.) lirio de mar (*crinoideo*)
sealing wax *s* lacre; **to seal with sealing wax** lacrar
sea lion *s* (zool.) león marino
seal ring *s* sortija con sello, anillo sigilar
sealskin ['sil,skɪn] *s* piel de foca
seam [sim] *s* costura; metido (*tela sobrante en las costuras de una prenda de ropa*); costurón (*cicatriz o línea semejante en la piel*); arruga (*pliegue en la piel*); grieta, juntura; (min.) filón, veta; *va* coser; señalar con cicatrices; arrugar; *vn* agrietarse
seaman ['simən] *s* (*pl:* **-men**) marinero; (nav.) marino (*que no tiene categoría de oficial*)
seamanlike ['simən,laɪk] o **seamanly** ['simənlɪ] *adj* de buen marinero
seamanship ['simənʃɪp] *s* náutica, marinería
seamark ['si,mark] *s* línea de límite de la marea; (naut.) marca de reconocimiento
sea mew *s* (orn.) gaviota
sea mile *s* milla náutica
seamless ['simlɪs] *adj* inconsútil, sin costura
sea monster *s* monstruo marino
seamstress ['simstrɪs] *s* costurera; modistilla
seamy ['simɪ] *adj* (*comp:* **-ier;** *super:* **-iest**) con costuras; basto; ruin, miserable
séance ['seɑns] *s* sesión, reunión; sesión de espiritistas
Sea of Galilee *s* mar de Galilea
Sea of Japan *s* mar del Japón
Sea of Marmara o **Marmora** ['mɑrmərə] *s* mar de Mármara
Sea of Tiberias [taɪ'bɪrɪəs] *s* lago de Tiberíades
sea otter *s* (zool.) lataz
sea pink *s* (bot.) césped de Olimpo, estátice
seaplane ['si,plen] *s* hidroplano
seaport ['si,port] *s* puerto, puerto de mar
sea power *s* potencia naval
sea purse *s* cáscara córnea del huevo de la raya
sear [sɪr] *s* chamusco, socarra; gacheta (*de un arma de fuego*); *adj* seco, marchito; raído, gastado; *va* chamuscar, socarrar; cauterizar; endurecer; *vn* chamuscarse, socarrarse; endurecerse; marchitarse
search [sʌrtʃ] *s* busca, búsqueda; pesquisa, indagación; **in search of** en busca de; *va* buscar; explorar, averiguar; registrar; **to search out** buscar; examinar; descubrir buscando; *vn* buscar; **to search after** buscar; explorar, averiguar; preguntar por; **to search for** buscar; **to search into** indagar, investigar
searching ['sʌrtʃɪŋ] *adj* escrutador; agudo, penetrante, minucioso
searching party *s* grupo de personas que se envían en busca de alguien
searchlight ['sʌrtʃ,laɪt] *s* reflector, proyector; luz de un proyector
search warrant *s* (law) orden de allanamiento, auto de registro domiciliario
sea robber *s* pirata, corsario
sea robin *s* (ichth.) rubio volador
sea room *s* espacio para maniobrar sin peligro
sea rover *s* pirata, corsario
sea salt *s* sal marina
seascape ['siskep] *s* vista del mar; (paint.) marina
seascapist ['si,skepɪst] *s* marinista
sea serpent *s* monstruo marino; (zool.) hidrófido
sea shell *s* concha marina, caracol marino
seashore ['si,ʃor] *s* ribera del mar, playa
seasick ['si,sɪk] *adj* mareado
seasickness ['si,sɪknɪs] *s* mareo
seaside ['si,saɪd] *s* ribera del mar, orilla del mar, playa; *adj* costanero; de playa, de mar
sea snake *s* (zool.) hidrófido
season ['sizən] *s* estación (*una de las cuatro partes del año*); temporada (*espacio de tiempo formando un conjunto; tiempo en que un lugar está más frecuentado*); sazón (*tiempo oportuno; tiempo de madurez*); **for a season** durante una temporada; **in good season** con tiempo; **in season** a su tiempo; en sazón; con tiempo; **in season and out of season** en tiempo y a destiempo; **out of season** fuera de sazón; a destiempo; **to dress according to the season** vestir con la estación; *va* sazonar; curar (*la madera*); acostumbrar; moderar, templar; *vn* sazonarse; curarse (*p.ej., la madera*); acostumbrarse
seasonable ['sizənəbəl] *adj* oportuno, tempestivo, conveniente
seasonal ['sizənəl] *adj* estacional
seasoning ['sizənɪŋ] *s* aliño, aderezo, condimento; sal, chiste; cura (*de la madera*)
season ticket *s* billete de abono
sea squirt *s* (zool.) ascidia
seat [sit] *s* asiento; fondillos (*de los calzones o pantalones*); morada, residencia; sitio, lugar, paraje; sede (*p.ej., del gobierno*); escaño (*en las Cortes*); teatro, (*p.ej., de una guerra*); centro (*p.ej., de la erudición*); batalla (*de la silla de montar*); **to take a seat** tomar asiento; *va* sentar; tener asientos para, tener cabida para; poner asiento a (*una silla*); ajustar (*una válvula*) en su asiento; echar fondillos a (*pantalones*); arraigar, fijar, establecer, afianzar; **to seat oneself** sentarse; **to be seated** estar sentado; sentarse; estar situado
seat belt *s* cinturón de asiento
seat cover *s* funda de asiento
seating capacity *s* aforo, cabida, número de asientos
Seato ['sito] *s* la O.T.A.S.E. (*la Organización del Tratado del Sudeste Asiático*)
sea trout *s* (ichth.) trucha marina, trucha de mar
sea urchin *s* (zool.) erizo de mar
sea wall *s* dique marítimo
seaward ['siwərd] *s* dirección hacia el mar; *adj* dirigido hacia el mar; *adv* hacia el mar
seawards ['siwərdz] *adv* hacia el mar
seaway ['si,we] *s* ruta marítima; mar ancha, alta mar; mar gruesa, mar alborotada; avance de una embarcación por mar; vía de agua interior para buques de alta mar
seaweed ['si,wid] *s* plantas marinas; algas; (bot.) alga marina
sea wind *s* viento que sopla del mar
seaworthy ['si,wʌrðɪ] *adj* marinero, en condiciones de navegar
sebaceous [sɪ'beʃəs] *adj* sebáceo
sebaceous gland *s* (anat.) glándula sebácea
Sebastian [sɪ'bæstʃən] *s* Sebastián
sebesten [sɪ'bɛstən] *s* (bot.) sebestén (*árbol y fruto*)
sec. abr. de **secant, second, secondary, secretary, section** y **sector**
SEC abr. de **Securities and Exchange Commission**
secant ['sikənt] *adj & s* (geom. & trig.) secante
secede [sɪ'sid] *vn* separarse, retirarse
secession [sɪ'sɛʃən] *s* secesión
secessionism [sɪ'sɛʃənɪzəm] *s* secesionismo
secessionist [sɪ'sɛʃənɪst] *adj & s* secesionista
seckel ['sɛkəl] *s* pera pequeña de color rojizo
seclude [sɪ'klud] *va* recluir
secluded [sɪ'kludɪd] *adj* recluso; solitario, retirado
seclusion [sɪ'kluʒən] *s* reclusión, soledad
seclusive [sɪ'klusɪv] *adj* solitario; exclusivo
second ['sɛkənd] *adj* segundo; **to be second to none** ser sin segundo, no ir en zaga a nada, no ir en zaga a nadie; **to play second fiddle** desempeñar un papel secundario; *s* segundo; artículo de segunda calidad; padrino (*p.ej., en un certamen, desafío*); segundante (*en el boxeo*); (mus.) segunda; (aut.) segunda (velocidad); dos (*en las fechas*); *adv* en segundo lugar; *va* secundar; apoyar (*una moción en junta deliberante*)
Second Advent *s* segundo advenimiento, segunda venida (*de Jesucristo*)
secondary ['sɛkən,dɛrɪ] *adj* secundario; *s* (*pl:* **-ies**) (elec.) secundario
secondary accent *s* (phonet.) acento secundario
secondary cell *s* (elec.) elemento secundario
secondary coil *s* (elec.) carrete secundario
secondary feather *s* (orn.) pluma secundaria
secondary school *s* escuela de segunda enseñanza

second base *s* (baseball) segunda base *f* (*puesto*); (baseball) segunda base *m* (*jugador*)
second baseman *s* (baseball) segunda base *m* (*jugador*)
second best *s* (el) mejor después del primero
second childhood *s* segunda niñez
second-class ['sɛkənd,klæs] o ['sɛkənd,klɑs] *adj* de segunda clase; de clase inferior
second-class matter *s* correspondencia de segunda clase
seconder ['sɛkəndər] *s* persona que apoya una moción
second hand *s* segundero (*de reloj*)
second-hand ['sɛkənd,hænd] *adj* de segunda mano, de ocasión
second-hand bookshop *s* librería de viejo
second-hand dealer *s* prendero
second-hand shop *s* prendería
second lieutenant *s* (mil.) alférez, subteniente
second nature *s* segunda naturaleza
second person *s* (gram.) segunda persona
second-rate ['sɛkənd,ret] *adj* de segundo orden; de calidad inferior, de menor cuantía
second-run wine ['sɛkənd,rʌn] *s* vino de segunda
second sight *s* doble vista, segunda vista
seconds pendulum *s* péndulo de segundos
second violin *s* segundo violín
second wind [wɪnd] *s* nuevo aliento
secrecy ['sikrəsɪ] *s* (*pl:* **-cies**) secreto; **in secrecy** en secreto
secret ['sikrɪt] *adj* secreto; *s* secreto; (eccl.) secreta (*oración*); **in secret** en secreto
secret agent *s* agente secreto, agente de la policía secreta
secretarial [,sɛkrɪ'tɛrɪəl] *adj* de secretario, para secretarios
secretariat o **secretariate** [,sɛkrɪ'tɛrɪɪt] *s* secretaría
secretary ['sɛkrɪ,tɛrɪ] *s* (*pl:* **-ies**) secretario; secreter, escritorio
secretary bird *s* (orn.) secretario, serpentario
Secretary of State *s* (U.S.A.) ministro de Asuntos Exteriores
secretaryship ['sɛkrɪ,tɛrɪʃɪp] *s* secretaría
secret ballot *s* voto secreto
secrete [sɪ'krit] *va* esconder, encubrir; (physiol.) secretar
secretin [sɪ'kritɪn] *s* (biochem.) secretina
secretion [sɪ'kriʃən] *s* (physiol.) secreción
secretive [sɪ'kritɪv] *adj* callado, reservado; (physiol.) secretorio
secretory [sɪ'kritərɪ] *adj* (physiol.) secretorio; *s* órgano secretorio, glándula secretoria
secret service *s* servicio secreto; servicio de espionaje
secret society *s* sociedad secreta
secs. abr. de **seconds** y **sections**
sect. abr. de **section**
sect [sɛkt] *s* secta
sectarian [sɛk'tɛrɪən] *adj* & *s* sectario
sectarianism [sɛk'tɛrɪənɪzəm] *s* sectarismo
sectary ['sɛktərɪ] *adj* sectario; *s* (*pl:* **-ries**) sectario
sectile ['sɛktɪl] *adj* sectil
section ['sɛkʃən] *s* sección; (arch., geom. & mil.) sección; región (*de un país*); barrio (*de una ciudad*); (rail.) distrito, tramo; *va* seccionar
sectional ['sɛkʃənəl] *adj* seccional; regional, local
sectionalism ['sɛkʃənəlɪzəm] *s* regionalismo
sectionalize ['sɛkʃənəlaɪz] *va* dividir en secciones; (U.S.A.) dividir según los intereses locales
sectionally ['sɛkʃənəlɪ] *adv* en secciones, por secciones; en una región
section foreman *s* (rail.) capataz de tramo
section gang *s* (rail.) cuadrilla de tramo
section hand *s* (rail.) peón ferrocarrilero
sector ['sɛktər] *s* sector; (geom., math. & mil.) sector
secular ['sɛkjələr] *adj* secular; *s* seglar
secularism ['sɛkjələrɪzəm] *s* secularismo
secularist ['sɛkjələrɪst] *s* secularista
secularity [,sɛkjə'lærɪtɪ] *s* secularidad
secularization [,sɛkjələrɪ'zeʃən] *s* secularización
secularize ['sɛkjələraɪz] *va* secularizar
secure [sɪ'kjʊr] *adj* seguro; *va* asegurar; obtener, conseguir; *vn* asegurarse
security [sɪ'kjʊrɪtɪ] *s* (*pl:* **-ties**) seguridad; segurador (*persona*); **securities** *spl* valores, obligaciones, títulos
Security Council *s* Consejo de Seguridad
security risk *s* riesgo a la seguridad nacional (*persona*)
secy. o **sec'y.** abr. de **secretary**
sedan [sɪ'dæn] *s* silla de manos; (aut.) sedán
sedan chair *s* silla de manos
sedate [sɪ'det] *adj* sentado, sosegado, tranquilo
sedation [sɪ'deʃən] *s* (med.) sedación
sedative ['sɛdətɪv] *adj* & *s* (med.) sedativo
sedentary ['sɛdən,tɛrɪ] *adj* sedentario
sedge [sɛdʒ] *s* (bot.) juncia
sedged [sɛdʒd] *adj* júnceo; hecho de juncias
sedge warbler *s* (orn.) saltamimbres
sedgy ['sɛdʒɪ] *adj* júnceo; abundante en juncias
sediment ['sɛdɪmənt] *s* sedimento; *va* sedimentar; *vn* sedimentarse
sedimental [,sɛdɪ'mɛntəl] *adj* sedimentario
sedimentary [,sɛdɪ'mɛntərɪ] *adj* sedimentario; (geol.) sedimentario
sedimentation [,sɛdɪmɛn'teʃən] *s* sedimentación
sedimentation test *s* (physiol.) velocidad de sedimentación globular
sedition [sɪ'dɪʃən] *s* sedición
seditionary [sɪ'dɪʃə,nɛrɪ] *adj* & *s* sedicioso
seditious [sɪ'dɪʃəs] *adj* sedicioso
seduce [sɪ'djus] o [sɪ'dus] *va* seducir
seducement [sɪ'djusmənt] o [sɪ'dusmənt] *s* seducción
seducer [sɪ'djusər] o [sɪ'dusər] *s* seductor
seducible [sɪ'djusɪbəl] o [sɪ'dusɪbəl] *adj* seducible
seduction [sɪ'dʌkʃən] *s* seducción
seductive [sɪ'dʌktɪv] *adj* seductivo
sedulity [sɪ'djulɪtɪ] o [sɪ'dulɪtɪ] *s* diligencia, cuidado
sedulous ['sɛdjələs] *adj* diligente, cuidadoso
sedum ['sidəm] *s* (bot.) hierba callera (*Sedum telephium*); (bot.) uva de gato (*Sedum acre*)
see [si] *s* (eccl.) sede; (*pret:* **saw**; *pp:* **seen**) *va* ver; recibir; acompañar (*a casa, a la puerta, etc.*); (poker) aceptar (*una apuesta*) apostando una cantidad igual; (poker) aceptar la apuesta de (*un jugador*) apostando una cantidad igual; **to see** + *inf* ver + *inf*, p.ej., **I saw the train go by** ví pasar el tren; **to see** + *pp* ver + *inf*, p.ej.,**I saw the criminal hanged** ví ahorcar al criminal; **to see off** ir a despedir (*a una persona*); **to see out** llevar a cabo; (coll.) aventajar, beber más que; **to see through** llevar a cabo; ayudar en un trance difícil; *vn* ver; **let's see** a ver, veamos; **to see about** + *ger* ver de + *inf;* **to see after** cuidar, cuidar de; buscar; **to see into** conocer el juego de; **to see that** atender a que, ver que; **to see through** conocer el juego de; **to see to** atender a; tener cuidado de; **to see to it that** atender a que, ver que; **see here!** ¡mire Vd.!
seed [sid] *s* simiente; **to go to seed** dar semilla; dar en grana; echarse a perder; *adj* seminal; *va* sembrar; despepitar (*quitar las semillas de*); *vn* sembrar; dejar caer semillas
seedcake ['sid,kek] *s* torta de semillas aromáticas
seed capsule *s* (bot.) pericarpio
seedcase ['sid,kes] *s* (bot.) pericarpio
seed coat *s* (bot.) tegumento seminal, cubierta de la semilla
seed corn *s* maíz para sembrar
seeder ['sidər] *s* sembrador; sembradora (*máquina*); máquina de despepitar
seeding ['sidɪŋ] *s* siembra, sementera; caída de semilla
seed-lac ['sid,læk] *s* laca en grano
seed leaf *s* (bot.) cotiledón
seedling ['sidlɪŋ] *s* planta de semilla; árbol de pie; arbolito que no pasa de tres pies de alto
seed oysters *spl* ostras muy jóvenes
seed pearl *s* perlita, aljófar
seed plant *s* planta de semilla
seedsman ['sidzmən] *s* (*pl:* **-men**) sembrador; vendedor de semillas
seedtime ['sid,taɪm] *s* siembra
seed vessel *s* (bot.) pericarpio

seedy ['sidɪ] *adj* (*comp:* **-ier;** *super:* **-iest**) lleno de granos; (coll.) raído, andrajoso
seeing ['siɪŋ] *adj* vidente; *s* vista, visión; (el) ver; *conj* visto que
Seeing Eye dog *s* perro-lazarillo
seek [sik] (*pret & pp:* **sought**) *va* buscar; recorrer buscando; procurar; dirigirse a; **to seek a person's life** tratar de matar a una persona; *vn* buscar; **to seek after** tratar de obtener; solicitar; **to seek to** + *inf* esforzarse por + *inf*
seem [sim] *vn* parecer; **I still seem to hear the music** todavía me parece oír la música
seeming ['simɪŋ] *adj* aparente; *s* apariencia
seemingly ['simɪŋlɪ] *adv* aparentemente, al parecer
seemly ['simlɪ] *adj* (*comp:* **-lier;** *super:* **-liest**) decente, decoroso, correcto; bien parecido; *adv* decentemente, decorosamente, correctamente
seen [sin] *pp de* **see**
seep [sip] *vn* percolarse, rezumarse, escurrirse, filtrar
seepage ['sipɪdʒ] *s* percolación, filtración
seer [sɪr] *s* vidente, profeta
seeress ['sɪrɪs] *s* vidente, profetisa
seersucker ['sɪr,sʌkər] *s* sirsaca
seesaw ['si,sɔ] *s* balancín, columpio de tabla; vaivén (*movimiento*); *adj* de balancín; *vn* columpiarse (*en el balancín*); alternar; vacilar
seethe [sið] *va* empapar, embeber; (pharm.) elijar; *vn* hervir; (fig.) hervir
segment ['sɛgmənt] *s* segmento; *va* dividir en segmentos
segmental [sɛg'mɛntəl] *adj* segmental; (arch. & zool.) segmental
segmental arch *s* (arch.) arco escarzano
segmentally [sɛg'mɛntəlɪ] *adv* en segmentos
segmentary ['sɛgmən,tɛrɪ] *adj* segmentario
segmentation [,sɛgmən'teʃən] *s* segmentación
sego ['sigo] *s* (*pl:* **-gos**) (bot.) ayatito
sego lily *s* (bot.) ayatito
segregate ['sɛgrɪget] o ['sɛgrɪgɪt] *adj* segregado; ['sɛgrɪget] *va* segregar
segregation [,sɛgrɪ'geʃən] *s* segregación
segregationist [,sɛgrɪ'geʃənɪst] *s* segregacionista
segregative ['sɛgrɪ,getɪv] *adj* segregativo
Seidlitz powder ['sɛdlɪts] *s* polvos de Seidlitz
seigneur [sin'jʌr] *s* señor (*feudal*)
seignior ['sinjər] *s* señor
seigniorage ['sinjərɪdʒ] *s* señoreaje
seigniory ['sinjərɪ] *s* (*pl:* **-ies**) señorío (*en la época feudal*)
seignorial [sin'jorɪəl] o [sin'jɔrɪəl] señoril
Seine [sen] *s* Sena; (*l.c.*) *s* red barredera; *va & vn* pescar con red barredera
seism ['saɪzəm] *s* sismo o seísmo
seismic ['saɪzmɪk] *adj* sísmico
seismogram ['saɪzməgræm] *s* sismograma
seismograph ['saɪzməgræf] o ['saɪzməgrɑf] *s* sismógrafo
seismographic [,saɪzmə'græfɪk] o **seismographical** [,saɪzmə'græfɪkəl] *adj* sismográfico
seismography [saɪz'mɑgrəfɪ] *s* sismografía
seismologic [,saɪzmə'lɑdʒɪk] o **seismological** [,saɪzmə'lɑdʒɪkəl] *adj* sismológico
seismologist [saɪz'mɑlədʒɪst] *s* sismologista
seismology [saɪz'mɑlədʒɪ] *s* sismología
seismometer [saɪz'mɑmɪtər] *s* sismómetro
seize [siz] *va* asir, agarrar, coger; comprender; embargar, secuestrar; aprovecharse de (*una oportunidad*); apoderarse de; atar, prender, sujetar; *vn* agarrar, coger; **to seize on** o **upon** asir de repente, coger de repente; apoderarse de
seizin ['sizən] *s* (law) posesión, toma de posesión
seizing ['sizɪŋ] *s* agarro, captura; atadura, ligadura, aferramiento; cuerda
seizure ['siʒər] *s* asimiento, prendimiento, prisión; captura, presa, toma; embargo, secuestro; ataque (*de una enfermedad*)
selachian [sɪ'lekɪən] *adj & s* (ichth.) selacio
seldom ['sɛldəm] *adv* raramente, rara vez
select [sɪ'lɛkt] *adj* selecto, escogido; *va* seleccionar
selectee [sɪ,lɛk'ti] *s* (mil.) quinto
selection [sɪ'lɛkʃən] *s* selección; trozo escogido; (com.) surtido
selective [sɪ'lɛktɪv] *adj* selectivo; (rad.) selectivo
selective service *s* servicio militar obligatorio
selectivity [sɪ,lɛk'tɪvɪtɪ] *s* (rad.) selectividad
selectman [sɪ'lɛktmən] *s* (*pl:* **-men**) concejal, miembro del ayuntamiento, miembro del concejo municipal
selector [sɪ'lɛktər] *s* escogedor; (telp.) selector (*órgano del teléfono automático*)
Selene [sɛ'lini] *s* (myth.) Selene
selenide ['sɛlɪnaɪd] o ['sɛlɪnɪd] *s* (chem.) seleniuro
selenite ['sɛlɪnaɪt] o [sɛ'linaɪt] *s* (mineral.) selenita
selenium [sɛ'linɪəm] *s* (chem.) selenio
selenium cell *s* (elec.) célula de selenio
selenium rectifier *s* (elec.) rectificador de selenio
selenographer [,sɛlɪ'nɑgrəfər] o **selenographist** [,sɛlɪ'nɑgrəfɪst] *s* selenógrafo
selenography [,sɛlɪ'nɑgrəfɪ] *s* selenografía
self [sɛlf] *adj* mismo; *pron* sí mismo; *s* (*pl:* **selves**) uno mismo; **all by one's self** sin ayuda de nadie; **one's other self** su otro yo; **the self** el yo, el propio yo
self-abasement [,sɛlfə'besmənt] *s* rebajamiento de sí mismo
self-abhorrence [,sɛlfæb'hɑrəns] o [,sɛlfæb'hɔrəns] *s* aborrecimiento de sí mismo
self-abnegation [,sɛlf,æbnɪ'geʃən] *s* abnegación
self-absorption [,sɛlfæb'sɔrpʃən] o [,sɛlfæb'zɔrpʃən] *s* ensimismamiento
self-abuse [,sɛlfə'bjus] *s* abuso de sí mismo; masturbación
self-acting [,sɛlf'æktɪŋ] *adj* automático
self-addressed [,sɛlfə'drɛst] *adj* dirigido a sí mismo
self-analysis [,sɛlfə'nælɪsɪs] *s* autoanálisis
self-appointed [,sɛlfə'pɔɪntɪd] *adj* designado por sí mismo
self-assertion [,sɛlfə'sʌrʃən] *s* agresividad
self-assertive [,sɛlfə'sʌrtɪv] *adj* agresivo
self-assurance [,sɛlfə'ʃurəns] *s* confianza en sí mismo
self-assured [,sɛlfə'ʃurd] *adj* seguro de sí
self-centered o **self-centred** [,sɛlf'sɛntərd] *adj* egocéntrico, concentrado en sí mismo
self-cleaning [,sɛlf'klinɪŋ] *adj* autolimpiador
self-colored [,sɛlf'kʌlərd] *adj* de color uniforme; de color natural
self-command [,sɛlfkə'mænd] o [,sɛlfkə'mɑnd] *s* dominio sobre sí mismo
self-communion [,sɛlfkə'mjunjən] *s* comunión consigo mismo
self-complacence [,sɛlfkəm'plesəns] o **self-complacency** [,sɛlfkəm'plesənsɪ] *s* complacencia en sí mismo
self-conceit [,sɛlfkən'sit] *s* presunción, arrogancia, vanagloria
self-confidence [,sɛlf'kɑnfɪdəns] *s* confianza en sí mismo
self-conscious [,sɛlf'kɑnʃəs] *adj* consciente de sí, cohibido, apocado, tímido
self-consciousness [,sɛlf'kɑnʃəsnɪs] *s* conciencia de sí, apocamiento, timidez; autoconciencia
self-consequence [,sɛlf'kɑnsɪkwens] *s* conciencia de su propia importancia
self-consistent [,sɛlfkən'sɪstənt] *adj* consecuente
self-contained [,sɛlfkən'tend] *adj* callado, reservado, silencioso; dueño de sí mismo; independiente, autónomo, completo en sí mismo
self-contradiction ['sɛlf,kɑntrə'dɪkʃən] *s* proposición que envuelve contradicción
self-control [,sɛlfkən'trol] *s* dominio de sí mismo, señorío de sí mismo
self-controlled [,sɛlfkən'trold] *adj* dueño de sí mismo; automático
self-cooling [,sɛlf'kulɪŋ] *adj* enfriado automáticamente; *s* autoenfriamiento
self-criticism [,sɛlf'krɪtɪsɪzəm] *s* autocrítica
self-deception [,sɛlfdɪ'sɛpʃən] *s* autoengaño
self-defeating [,sɛlfdɪ'fitɪŋ] *adj* contraproducente
self-defense [,sɛlfdɪ'fɛns] *s* autodefensa; **in self-defense** en defensa propia
self-denial [,sɛlfdɪ'naɪəl] *s* abnegación

self-destruction [ˌsɛlfdɪsˈtrʌkʃən] *s* autodestrucción
self-determination [ˈsɛlfdɪˌtʌrmɪˈneʃən] *s* (pol.) autodeterminación o autodeterminismo
self-devotion [ˌsɛlfdɪˈvoʃən] *s* sacrificio de sí mismo
self-discipline [ˌsɛlfˈdɪsɪplɪn] *s* autodisciplina, disciplina de sí mismo
self-educated [ˌsəlfˈɛdjəˌketɪd] *adj* autodidacto
self-effacement [ˌsɛlfɪˈfesmənt] *s* modestia, recogimiento
self-employed [ˌsɛlfɛmˈplɔɪd] *adj* que trabaja por su propia cuenta
self-esteem [ˌsɛlfɛsˈtim] *s* amor propio, respeto de sí mismo
self-evident [ˌsɛlfˈɛvɪdənt] *adj* patente, manifiesto, evidente por sí mismo
self-examination [ˈsɛlfɛgˌzæmɪˈneʃən] *s* autocrítica
self-existent [ˌsɛlfɛgˈzɪstənt] *adj* existente por sí mismo
self-explanatory [ˌsɛlfɛksˈplænəˌtorɪ] *adj* que se explica por sí mismo
self-expression [ˌsɛlfɛksˈprɛʃən] *s* expresión de la personalidad propia
self-filling [ˌsɛlfˈfɪlɪŋ] *adj* que se llena automáticamente
self-governing [ˌsɛlfˈgʌvərnɪŋ] *adj* autónomo
self-government [ˌsɛlfˈgʌvərnmənt] *s* autogobierno, autonomía; dominio sobre sí mismo
selfheal [ˈsɛlfˌhil] *s* (bot.) sanícula; (bot.) hierba de las heridas
self-help [ˌsɛlfˈhɛlp] *s* ayuda de sí mismo, ayuda propia
selfhood [ˈsɛlfhud] *s* individualidad; personalidad; egoísmo
self-ignition [ˌsɛlfɪgˈnɪʃən] *s* encendido automático; autoencendido
self-importance [ˌsɛlfɪmˈpɔrtəns] *s* altivez, arrogancia, imperio
self-important [ˌsɛlfɪmˈpɔrtənt] *adj* altivo, arrogante, imperioso
self-imposed [ˌsɛlfɪmˈpozd] *adj* que uno se impone a sí mismo
self-improvement [ˌsɛlfɪmˈpruvmənt] *s* perfeccionamiento de sí mismo
self-inductance [ˌsɛlfɪnˈdʌktəns] *s* (elec.) autoinductancia
self-induction [ˌsɛlfɪnˈdʌkʃən] *s* (elec.) autoinducción
self-induction coil *s* (elec.) self
self-indulgence [ˌsɛlfɪnˈdʌldʒəns] *s* desenfreno, falta de sobriedad, intemperancia
self-inflicted [ˌsɛlfɪnˈflɪktɪd] *adj* que uno se ha infligido a sí mismo
self-instruction [ˌsɛlfɪnˈstrʌkʃən] *s* autoenseñanza
self-interest [ˌsɛlfˈɪntərɛst] o [ˌsɛlfˈɪntrɪst] *s* interés personal, egoísmo
selfish [ˈsɛlfɪʃ] *adj* egoísta
selfishness [ˈsɛlfɪʃnɪs] *s* egoísmo
self-knowledge [ˌsɛlfˈnɑlɪdʒ] *s* conocimiento de sí mismo
selfless [ˈsɛlflɪs] *adj* generoso, desinteresado
self-liquidating [ˌsɛlfˈlɪkwɪˌdetɪŋ] *adj* que se liquida por sí mismo, autoamortizable
self-loading [ˌsɛlfˈlodɪŋ] *adj* autocargador
self-locking [ˌsɛlfˈlɑkɪŋ] *adj* autocerrador
self-love [ˌsɛlfˈlʌv] *s* amor propio, egoísmo
self-made man [ˈsɛlfˌmed] *s* hijo de sus propias obras, hombre que ha logrado éxito por sus propios esfuerzos
self-moving [ˌsɛlfˈmuvɪŋ] *adj* automotor
self-opinionated [ˌsɛlfəˈpɪnjəˌnetɪd] *adj* orgulloso, vanidoso; porfiado en su parecer
self-pity [ˌsɛlfˈpɪtɪ] *s* compasión de sí mismo
self-pollinate [ˌsɛlfˈpɑlɪnet] *va* (bot.) autopolinizar
self-pollination [ˈsɛlfˌpɑlɪˈneʃən] *s* (bot.) autopolinización
self-pollution [ˌsɛlfpəˈluʃən] *s* polución voluntaria
self-portrait [ˌsɛlfˈportret] *s* autorretrato
self-possessed [ˌsɛlfpəˈzɛst] *adj* sereno, dueño de sí mismo
self-possession [ˌsɛlfpəˈzɛʃən] *s* serenidad, dominio sobre sí mismo, tranquilidad del ánimo
self-preservation [ˈsɛlfˌprɛzərˈveʃən] *s* propia conservación
self-propagating [ˌsɛlfˈprɑpəˌgetɪŋ] *adj* autopropagado
self-propelled [ˌsɛlfproˈpɛld] *adj* autopropulsado, de propulsión automática
self-propelling [ˌsɛlfproˈpɛlɪŋ] *adj* autopropulsor
self-propulsion [ˌsɛlfproˈpʌlʃən] *s* autopropulsión
self-protection [ˌsɛlfprəˈtɛkʃən] *s* autoprotección
self-recording [ˌsɛlfrɪˈkɔrdɪŋ] *adj* autorregistrador
self-regulating [ˌsɛlfˈrɛgjəˌletɪŋ] *adj* autorregulador
self-reliance [ˌsɛlfrɪˈlaɪəns] *s* confianza en sí mismo
self-reliant [ˌsɛlfrɪˈlaɪənt] *adj* confiado en sí mismo
self-reproach [ˌsɛlfrɪˈprotʃ] *s* culpa que uno se echa a sí mismo
self-respect [ˌsɛlfrɪˈspɛkt] *s* decoro, dignidad, respeto de sí mismo
self-respecting [ˌsɛlfrɪˈspɛktɪŋ] *adj* decoroso, lleno de dignidad
self-restraint [ˌsɛlfrɪˈstrent] *s* dominio sobre sí mismo
self-righteous [ˌsɛlfˈraɪtʃəs] *adj* santurrón
self-sacrifice [ˌsɛlfˈsækrɪfaɪs] *s* sacrificio de sí mismo
selfsame [ˈsɛlfˌsem] *adj* mismísimo
self-satisfaction [ˈsɛlfˌsætɪsˈfækʃən] *s* satisfacción de sí mismo
self-satisfied [ˌsɛlfˈsætɪsfaɪd] *adj* satisfecho de sí
self-sealing [ˌsɛlfˈsilɪŋ] *adj* autotaponador
self-seeker [ˌsɛlfˈsikər] *s* egoísta
self-seeking [ˌsɛlfˈsikɪŋ] *adj* egoísta; *s* egoísmo
self-service [ˈsɛlfˈsʌrvɪs] *s* autoservicio; *adj* de autoservicio
self-starter [ˌsɛlfˈstɑrtər] *s* (aut.) arrancador automático, arranque automático
self-starting [ˌsɛlfˈstɑrtɪŋ] *adj* de arranque automático
self-styled [ˌsɛlfˈstaɪld] *adj* llamado por sí mismo
self-sufficiency [ˌsɛlfsəˈfɪʃənsɪ] *s* confianza desmedida en sí mismo; autosuficiencia
self-sufficient [ˌsɛlfsəˈfɪʃənt] *adj* excesivamente confiado en sí mismo; autosuficiente
self-support [ˌsɛlfsəˈport] *s* mantenimiento económico propio
self-sustaining [ˌsɛlfsəsˈtenɪŋ] *adj* que se gana la vida; autosostenido, automantenido
self-tapping screw [ˌsɛlfˈtæpɪŋ] *s* tornillo que labra la rosca por sí mismo
self-taught [ˌsɛlfˈtɔt] *adj* autodidacto
self-will [ˌsɛlfˈwɪl] *s* voluntariedad
self-willed [ˌsɛlfˈwɪld] *adj* obstinado, terco
self-winding clock [ˌsɛlfˈwaɪndɪŋ] *s* reloj de cuerda automática, reloj de autocuerda
sell [sɛl] *s* (slang) estafa, engaño; *va* vender; (slang) hacer aceptar (*p.ej., una idea, un sistema*); **to sell out** realizar, saldar; (slang) vender, traicionar; **to sell someone on something** (slang) hacer aceptar una cosa a una persona, convencer a una persona del valor de una cosa; *vn* venderse, estar de venta; ser aceptado; **to sell for** correr a o por, venderse en (*tantos dólares*); **to sell off** bajar (*el mercado de valores*); **to sell out** venderlo todo, realizar
seller [ˈsɛlər] *s* vendedor
seller's market *s* mercado del vendedor
selling race *s* carrera a reclamar, carrera de ventas
sellout [ˈsɛlˌaut] *s* (slang) saldo, realización; (slang) traición; (slang) función de teatro para la que están vendidos todos los asientos
seltzer [ˈsɛltsər] *s* agua de seltz
selvage o **selvedge** [ˈsɛlvɪdʒ] *s* orillo, vendo, borde; (min.) salbanda
Sem. abr. de **Seminary** y **Semitic**
semantic [sɪˈmæntɪk] *adj* semántico; **semantics** *ssg* semántica
semanticist [sɪˈmæntɪsɪst] *s* semantista
semaphore [ˈsɛməfor] *s* semáforo; *va & vn* comunicar por medio de un semáforo
semaphoric [ˌsɛməˈfɑrɪk] o **semaphorical** [ˌsɛməˈfɑrɪkəl] *adj* semafórico

semasiological [sɪ,mesɪə'lɑdʒɪkəl] *adj* semasiológico
semasiology [sɪ,mesɪ'ɑlədʒɪ] *s* semasiología
semblance ['sɛmbləns] *s* simulacro, apariencia, imagen
semeiology [,simaɪ'ɑlədʒɪ] *s* semiología
semeiotic [,simaɪ'ɑtɪk] o **semeiotical** [,simaɪ'ɑtɪkəl] *adj* semiótico; **semeiotics** *ssg* semiótica
Semele ['sɛməli] *s* (myth.) Semele
semen ['simɛn] (bot. & physiol.) semen
semester [sɪ'mɛstər] *s* semestre; *adj* semestral
semester hour *s* (educ.) hora semestral
semiannual [,sɛmɪ'ænjʊəl] *adj* semianual
semiarid [,sɛmɪ'ærɪd] *adj* semiárido
semiautomatic [,sɛmɪ,ɔtə'mætɪk] *adj* semiautomático
semibreve ['sɛmɪ,briv] *s* (mus.) semibreve
semicadence [,sɛmɪ'kedəns] *s* (mus.) semicadencia
semicentennial [,sɛmɪsɛn'tɛnɪəl] *adj* & *s* cincuentenario
semicircle ['sɛmɪ,sʌrkəl] *s* semicírculo
semicircular [,sɛmɪ'sʌrkjələr] *adj* semicircular
semicircular arch *s* (arch.) arco de medio punto
semicircular canal *s* (anat.) canal semicircular
semicivilized [,sɛmɪ'sɪvɪlaɪzd] *adj* semicivilizado
semicoke ['sɛmɪ'kok] *s* semicoque
semicolon ['sɛmɪ,kolən] *s* (gram.) punto y coma
semiconductor [,sɛmɪkən'dʌktər] *s* (elec.) semiconductor
semiconscious [,sɛmɪ'kɑnʃəs] *adj* semiconsciente
semiconsonant [,sɛmɪ'kɑnsənənt] *s* semiconsonante
semiconsonantal [,sɛmɪ,kɑnsə'næntəl] *adj* semiconsonante
semicylindrical [,sɛmɪsɪ'lɪndrɪkəl] *adj* semicilíndrico
semidaily [,sɛmɪ'delɪ] *adv* dos veces al día
semideponent [,sɛmɪdɪ'ponənt] *adj* (gram.) semideponente
semidetached [,sɛmɪdɪ'tætʃt] *adj* semiseparado
semideveloped [,sɛmɪdɪ'vɛləpt] *adj* desarrollado incompletamente, a medio desarrollar
semidiameter [,sɛmɪdaɪ'æmɪtər] *s* (astr. & geom.) semidiámetro
semi-Diesel engine [,sɛmɪ'dizəl] *s* semidiesel
semidivine [,sɛmɪdɪ'vaɪn] *adj* semidivino
semielliptical [,sɛmɪ·ɪ'lɪptɪkəl] *adj* semielíptico
semifinal [,sɛmɪ'faɪnəl] *adj* & *s* (sport) semifinal
semifluid [,sɛmɪ'fluɪd] *adj* semiflúido
semilearned [,sɛmɪ'lʌrnɪd] *adj* (philol.) semiculto
semiliquid [,sɛmɪ'lɪkwɪd] *adj* & *s* semilíquido
semilunar [,sɛmɪ'lunər] *adj* semilunar
semimonthly [,sɛmɪ'mʌnθlɪ] *adj* quincenal; *adv* quincenalmente; *s* (*pl:* **-lies**) periódico quincenal, revista quincenal
seminal ['sɛmɪnəl] *adj* seminal; (fig.) primigenio, primordial
seminar ['sɛmɪnɑr] o [,sɛmɪ'nɑr] *s* seminario
seminarist ['sɛmɪ,nɛrɪst] *s* seminarista
seminary ['sɛmɪ,nɛrɪ] *s* (*pl:* **-ies**) seminario
semination [,sɛmɪ'neʃən] *s* sembradura; propagación, diseminación
seminiferous [,sɛmɪ'nɪfərəs] *adj* seminífero
Seminole ['sɛmɪnol] *adj* & *s* semínola
semiofficial [,sɛmɪə'fɪʃəl] *adj* semioficial
semiology [,simaɪ'ɑlədʒɪ] *s* var. de **semeiology**
semiotic [,simaɪ'ɑtɪk] *adj* var. de **semeiotic**
semipedal [sɪ'mɪpɪdəl] o [,sɛmɪ'pidəl] *adj* semipedal
Semi-Pelagian [,sɛmɪpɪ'ledʒɪən] *adj* & *s* semipelagiano
Semi-Pelagianism [,sɛmɪpɪ'ledʒɪənɪzəm] *s* semipelagianismo
semipermeable [,sɛmɪ'pʌrmɪəbəl] *adj* semipermeable
semipopular [,sɛmɪ'pɑpjələr] *adj* semipopular
semiprecious [,sɛmɪ'prɛʃəs] *adj* semiprecioso, fino
semiquaver ['sɛmɪ,kwevər] *s* (mus.) semicorchea
Semiramis [sə'mɪrəmɪs] *s* Semíramis
semirigid [,sɛmɪ'rɪdʒɪd] *adj* (aer.) semirrígido
semiskilled [,sɛmɪ'skɪld] *adj* medio mecánico
semisolid [,sɛmɪ'sɑlɪd] *adj* & *s* semisólido
Semite ['sɛmaɪt] o ['simaɪt] *s* semita
Semitic [sɪ'mɪtɪk] *adj* semítico; *s* semita (*individuo*); lengua semítica; semítico (*grupo de lenguas*)
Semitism ['sɛmɪtɪzəm] o ['simɪtɪzəm] *s* semitismo
Semitist ['sɛmɪtɪst] o ['simɪtɪst] *s* semitista
semitone ['sɛmɪ,ton] *s* (mus.) semitono
semitrailer ['sɛmɪ,trelər] *s* semi-remolque
semitropical [,sɛmɪ'trɑpɪkəl] *adj* semitropical
semivocalic [,sɛmɪvo'kælɪk] *adj* semivocal
semivowel ['sɛmɪ,vaʊəl] *s* semivocal
semiweekly [,sɛmɪ'wiklɪ] *adj* bisemanal; *adv* bisemanalmente; *s* (*pl:* **-lies**) periódico bisemanal, revista bisemanal
semiyearly [,sɛmɪ'jɪrlɪ] *adj* semestral; *adv* semestralmente
semolina [,sɛmə'linə] *s* sémola
sempiternal [,sɛmpɪ'tʌrnəl] *adj* sempiterno
sempstress ['sɛmpstrɪs] *s* var. de **seamstress**
Sen. o **sen.** abr. de **Senate, Senator** y **Senior**
senate ['sɛnɪt] *s* senado
senator ['sɛnətər] *s* senador
senatorial [,sɛnə'torɪəl] *adj* senatorial
senatorship ['sɛnətərʃɪp] *s* senaduría
senatus consultum [sɪ'netəskən'sʌltəm] *s* (*pl:* **senatus consulta**) senadoconsulto
send [sɛnd] (*pret & pp:* **sent**) *va* enviar, mandar; remitir, expedir; lanzar (*una bola, flecha, etc.*); poner (*un telegrama*); **to send away** despedir; despachar; **to send back** reenviar, devolver; **to send down** enviar abajo; mandar bajar; **to send packing** despedir con cajas destempladas; **to send up** enviar arriba; mandar subir; (coll.) enviar a la cárcel; **to send word** mandar recado; **to send to** + *inf* enviar a + *inf; vn* (rad.) transmitir; **to send for** enviar por, enviar a buscar
sendal ['sɛndəl] *s* cendal
sender ['sɛndər] *s* remitente; (telg.) transmisor
sending ['sɛndɪŋ] *s* remisión; (telg.) transmisión
sending key *s* (telg.) manipulador
send-off ['sɛnd,ɔf] o ['sɛnd,ɑf] *s* (coll.) empujón; (coll.) despedida afectuosa
Senegal [,sɛnɪ'gɔl] *s* el Senegal
Senegalese [,sɛnɪgɔ'liz] *adj* senegalés; *s* (*pl:* **-ese**) senegalés
senescence [sɪ'nɛsəns] *s* senescencia
senescent [sɪ'nɛsənt] *adj* senescente
seneschal ['sɛnɪʃəl] *s* senescal
senile ['sinaɪl] o ['sinɪl] *adj* senil
senility [sɪ'nɪlɪtɪ] *s* senilidad
senior ['sinjər] *adj* mayor, de mayor edad; viejo; del último año; padre, p.ej., **John Jones, Senior,** Juan Jones, padre; *s* mayor; socio más antiguo; alumno del último año
seniority [sin'jɑrɪtɪ] o [sin'jɔrɪtɪ] *s* antigüedad, ancianidad; prioridad, precedencia
senna ['sɛnə] *s* (bot. & pharm.) sen
Sennacherib [sə'nækərɪb] *s* Senaquerib
sennight ['sɛnaɪt] *s* (archaic) semana
sennit ['sɛnɪt] *s* (naut.) cajeta
sensation [sɛn'seʃən] *s* sensación; **to cause a sensation** hacer sensación
sensational [sɛn'seʃənəl] *adj* sensacional
sensationalism [sɛn'seʃənəlɪzəm] *s* sensacionalismo; (philos.) sensacionalismo, sensacionismo, sensualismo
sensationalist [sɛn'seʃənəlɪst] *s* persona que causa sensación; (philos.) sensacionalista, sensacionista
sense [sɛns] *s* sentido; opinión; (geom. & mech.) sentido; **in a sense** en cierto sentido; **to be out of one's senses** haber perdido el juicio; **to come to one's senses** volver en sí; recobrar el sentido común; **to make sense** tener sentido, ser razonable; **to make sense out of** comprender, explicarse; *va* intuir, sentir, sospechar; (coll.) comprender
senseless ['sɛnslɪs] *adj* falto de sentido, sin

sentido; desmayado, inconsciente; insensato, necio
sense of guilt *s* cargo de conciencia
sense of humor *s* sentido del humor
sense organ *s* órgano sensorio
sensibility [ˌsɛnsɪˈbɪlɪtɪ] *s* (*pl:* **-ties**) sensibilidad; susceptibilidad; **sensibilities** *spl* sentimientos delicados
sensible [ˈsɛnsɪbəl] *adj* sensato, cuerdo; sensible
sensitive [ˈsɛnsɪtɪv] *adj* sensible; susceptible; sensitivo, sensorio; (phot. & rad.) sensible; (phot.) sensibilizado
sensitiveness [ˈsɛnsɪtɪvnɪs] *s* sensibilidad; susceptibilidad; (phot. & rad.) sensibilidad
sensitive plant *s* (bot.) sensitiva, mimosa vergonzosa
sensitivity [ˌsɛnsɪˈtɪvɪtɪ] *s* (*pl:* **-ties**) sensibilidad; susceptibilidad; (phot. & rad.) sensibilidad
sensitization [ˌsɛnsɪtɪˈzeʃən] *s* sensibilización
sensitize [ˈsɛnsɪtaɪz] *va* sensibilizar; (phot.) sensibilizar
sensorial [sɛnˈsorɪəl] *adj* sensorio
sensorium [sɛnˈsorɪəm] *s* (*pl:* **-ums** o **-a** [ə]) sensorio
sensory [ˈsɛnsərɪ] *adj* sensorio
sensual [ˈsɛnʃʊəl] *adj* sensual
sensualism [ˈsɛnʃʊəlɪzəm] *s* sensualismo; (philos.) sensualismo
sensualist [ˈsɛnʃʊəlɪst] *adj* & *s* sensualista; (philos.) sensualista
sensuality [ˌsɛnʃʊˈælɪtɪ] *s* (*pl:* **-ties**) sensualidad
sensualize [ˈsɛnʃʊəlaɪz] *va* hacer sensual; *vn* volverse sensual
sensually [ˈsɛnʃʊəlɪ] *adv* sensualmente
sensuous [ˈsɛnʃʊəs] *adj* sensual; voluptuoso
sent [sɛnt] *pret & pp de* **send**
sentence [ˈsɛntəns] *s* frase, oración; sentencia; (law) sentencia; *va* sentenciar, condenar
sentential [sɛnˈtɛnʃəl] *adj* (gram.) oracional
sententious [sɛnˈtɛnʃəs] *adj* sentencioso
sentience [ˈsɛnʃəns] *s* sensibilidad
sentient [ˈsɛnʃənt] *adj* sensitivo, sensible; *s* ser sensitivo; conciencia
sentiment [ˈsɛntɪmənt] *s* sentimiento
sentimental [ˌsɛntɪˈmɛntəl] *adj* sentimental
sentimentalism [ˌsɛntɪˈmɛntəlɪzəm] *s* sentimentalismo
sentimentalist [ˌsɛntɪˈmɛntəlɪst] *s* sentimentalista
sentimentality [ˌsɛntɪmɛnˈtælɪtɪ] *s* (*pl:* **-ties**) sentimentalismo
sentimentalize [ˌsɛntɪˈmɛntəlaɪz] *va* hacer sentimental; tratar sentimentalmente; *vn* obrar sentimentalmente, afectar sentimiento
sentinel [ˈsɛntɪnəl] *s* centinela; **to stand sentinel** estar de centinela, hacer centinela
sentry [ˈsɛntrɪ] *s* (*pl:* **-tries**) centinela
sentry box *s* garita de centinela
Seoul [seˈul] o [sol] *s* Seúl
sepal [ˈsipəl] o [ˈsɛpəl] *s* (bot.) sépalo
separable [ˈsɛpərəbəl] *adj* separable
separably [ˈsɛpərəblɪ] *adv* separablemente
separate [ˈsɛpərɪt] *adj* separado; suelto; [ˈsɛpəret] *va* separar; *vn* separarse
separately [ˈsɛpərɪtlɪ] *adv* separadamente
separation [ˌsɛpəˈreʃən] *s* separación
separatism [ˈsɛpərɪtɪzəm] *s* separatismo
separatist [ˈsɛpərɪtɪst] *adj* & *s* separatista
separative [ˈsɛpəˌretɪv] *adj* separativo
separator [ˈsɛpəˌretər] *s* separador (*persona; máquina*); (elec.) separador (*de las placas de un acumulador*)
Sephardic [sɪˈfɑrdɪk] *adj* sefardí o sefardita
Sephardim [sɪˈfɑrdɪm] *spl* sefardíes
sepia [ˈsipɪə] *s* sepia (*pez, tinta, pigmento, color, estampado*); *adj* sepia, a la sepia
sepia paper *s* (phot.) papel sepia
sepoy [ˈsipɔɪ] *s* cipayo
seps [sɛps] *s* (zool.) eslizón, sepedón
sepsis [ˈsɛpsɪs] *s* (path.) sepsis
Sept. abr. de **September**
septal [ˈsɛptəl] *adj* septal
September [sɛpˈtɛmbər] *s* septiembre
septenary [ˈsɛptɪˌnɛrɪ] *adj* septenario; *s* (*pl:* **-ies**) septena; septenio
septennial [sɛpˈtɛnɪəl] *adj* que dura siete años; que ocurre una vez en siete años
septentrional [sɛpˈtɛntrɪənəl] *adj* septentrional
septet o **septette** [sɛpˈtɛt] *s* septena; (mus.) septeto
septfoil [ˈsɛptˌfɔɪl] *s* (bot.) siéteenrama
septic [ˈsɛptɪk] *adj* séptico
septicemia o **septicaemia** [ˌsɛptɪˈsimɪə] *s* (path.) septicemia
septicidal [ˌsɛptɪˈsaɪdəl] *adj* (bot.) septicida
septic tank *s* fosa séptica, pozo séptico
septifragal [sɛpˈtɪfrəgəl] *adj* (bot.) septífrago
septillion [sɛpˈtɪljən] *s* (U.S.A.) cuatrillón; (Brit.) septillón
septimole [ˈsɛptɪmol] *s* (mus.) septillo
septuagenarian [ˌsɛptʃʊədʒɪˈnɛrɪən] *adj* & *s* septuagenario
septuagenary [ˌsɛptʃʊˈædʒɪˌnɛrɪ] *adj* septuagenario; *s* (*pl:* **-ies**) septuagenario
Septuagesima [ˌsɛptʃʊəˈdʒɛsɪmə] o **Septuagesima Sunday** *s* (eccl.) septuagésima
Septuagint [ˈsɛptuədʒɪnt] o [ˈsɛptʃʊədʒɪnt] *s* (Bib.) versión de los Setenta
septum [ˈsɛptəm] *s* (*pl:* **-ta** [tə]) (anat.) septo
septuple [ˈsɛptʊpəl], [ˈsɛptjʊpəl], [sɛpˈtupəl] o [sɛpˈtjupəl] *adj* & *s* séptuplo; *va* septuplicar
septuplication [sɛpˌtuplɪˈkeʃən] o [sɛpˌtjuplɪˈkeʃən] *s* septuplicación
sepulcher [ˈsɛpəlkər] *s* sepulcro; (arch.) sepulcro; *va* sepultar en sepulcro
sepulchral [sɪˈpʌlkrəl] *adj* sepulcral; (fig.) sepulcral
sepulture [ˈsɛpəltʃər] *s* sepultura (*acción y lugar*); *va* sepultar
seq. abr. de **sequentia** (Lat.) **the following**
sequel [ˈsikwəl] *s* resultado, secuela; continuación; capítulo final (*de un cuento*)
sequela [sɪˈkwilə] *s* (*pl:* **-lae** [li]) secuaz, secuaces; secuela; (med.) secuela
sequence [ˈsikwəns] *s* sucesión, orden de sucesión; resultado, consecuencia; secansa, runfla, escalera (*en los naipes*); (eccl., mov. & mus.) secuencia
sequent [ˈsikwənt] *adj* subsiguiente; consecutivo; consiguiente; *s* resultado, consecuencia
sequential [sɪˈkwenʃəl] *adj* consecutivo; consiguiente
sequester [sɪˈkwɛstər] *va* apartar, alejar, segregar; (law) secuestrar
sequestration [ˌsikwɛsˈtreʃən] *s* apartamiento; retiro, reclusión; (law) secuestro
sequestrum [sɪˈkwɛstrəm] *s* (*pl:* **-tra** [trə]) (med.) secuestro
sequin [ˈsikwɪn] *s* lentejuela; cequí (*moneda*)
sequoia [sɪˈkwɔɪə] *s* (bot.) secoya
seraglio [sɛˈræljo] *s* (*pl:* **-ios**) serrallo
serape [sɛˈrɑpe] *s* sarape
seraph [ˈsɛrəf] *s* (*pl:* **-aphs** o **-aphim** [əfɪm]) (Bib. & theol.) serafín
seraphic [sɪˈræfɪk] *adj* seráfico
seraphim [ˈsɛrəfɪm] *pl de* **seraph**
Serb [sʌrb] *adj* & *s* servio
Serbia [ˈsʌrbɪə] *s* Servia
Serbian [ˈsʌrbɪən] *adj* & *s* var. de **Serb**
Serbo-Croatian [ˌsʌrbokroˈeʃən] *adj* & *s* servocroata
sere [sɪr] *adj* seco, marchito; gastado
serenade [ˌsɛrəˈned] *s* serenata; *va* dar serenata a; *vn* dar serenatas
serendipity [ˌsɛrənˈdɪpɪtɪ] *s* don de acertar sin buscar
serene [sɪˈrin] *adj* sereno
serenity [sɪˈrɛnɪtɪ] *s* (*pl:* **-ties**) serenidad; (*cap.*) *s* Serenidad (*título*)
serf [sʌrf] *s* siervo de la gleba
serfdom [ˈsʌrfdəm] *s* servidumbre de la gleba
serge [sʌrdʒ] *s* sarga
sergeancy [ˈsɑrdʒənsɪ] *s* (*pl:* **-cies**) sargentía
sergeant [ˈsɑrdʒənt] *s* (mil.) sargento; alguacil
sergeant-at-arms [ˈsɑrdʒəntətˈɑrmz] *s* (*pl:* **sergeants-at-arms**) oficial de orden
sergeant major *s* (*pl:* **sergeant majors**) (mil.) sargento auxiliar del ayudante, suboficial
sergt. abr. de **sergeant**
serial [ˈsɪrɪəl] *adj* serial; publicado por entregas; (rad.) seriado; *s* cuento por entregas, novela por entregas; (rad.) serial, drama en episodios
serially [ˈsɪrɪəlɪ] *adv* en serie, por series; por entregas

serial number *s* número de serie
seriate ['sɪrɪet] *adj* serial
seriatim [ˌsɪrɪ'etɪm] o [ˌsɛrɪ'etɪm] *adv* en serie
sericulture ['sɛrɪˌkʌltʃər] *s* sericicultura, sericultura
sericulturist [ˌsɛrɪ'kʌltʃərɪst] *s* sericicultor, sericultor
series ['sɪrɪz] *s* serie; *adj* (elec.) en serie
series-wound ['sɪrɪzˌwaʊnd] *adj* (elec.) arrollado en serie
serif ['sɛrɪf] *s* (print.) trazo fino de adorno (*de una letra*)
serin ['sɛrɪn] *s* (orn.) verdecillo
seriocomic [ˌsɪrɪo'kɑmɪk] *adj* jocoserio
serious ['sɪrɪəs] *adj* serio
seriously ['sɪrɪəslɪ] *adv* seriamente
seriousness ['sɪrɪəsnɪs] *s* seriedad
serjeant ['sɑrdʒənt] *s* var. de **sergeant**
sermon ['sʌrmən] *s* sermón; (fig.) sermón
sermonize ['sʌrmənaɪz] *va & vn* sermonear
sermonizing ['sʌrməˌnaɪzɪŋ] *adj* sermoneador; *s* sermoneo
Sermon on the Mount *s* (Bib.) sermón de la Montaña
serology [sɪ'rɑlədʒɪ] *s* serología
seroon [sə'run] *s* churla
serosity [sɪ'rɑsɪtɪ] *s* (med. & physiol.) serosidad
serotinous [sɪ'rɑtɪnəs] *adj* (bot.) serondo o serótino
serous ['sɪrəs] *adj* seroso
serous membrane *s* (anat.) membrana serosa
serpent ['sʌrpənt] *s* serpiente; buscapiés, carretilla (*cohete*); (mus.) serpentón (*instrumento de viento*); (fig.) serpiente (*persona traidora; el demonio*); (*cap.*) *s* (astr.) Serpiente
Serpent Bearer *s* (astr.) Serpentario
serpentine ['sʌrpəntin] *s* (mineral.) serpentina; ['sʌrpəntin] o ['sʌrpəntaɪn] *adj* serpentino; *vn* serpentear
serpiginous [sər'pɪdʒɪnəs] *adj* serpiginoso
serpigo [sər'paɪgo] *s* (path.) serpigo
serrate ['sɛret] o **serrated** ['sɛretɪd] *adj* serrado
serration [sɛ'reʃən] *s* endentadura
serratus [sɛ'retəs] *s* (anat.) serrato
serried ['sɛrɪd] *adj* apretado
serrulate ['sɛrjəlet] *adj* dentelado
serum ['sɪrəm] *s* (*pl:* **-rums** o **-ra** [rə]) (biol. & med.) suero; suero de la leche
serum therapy *s* seroterapia
serval ['sʌrvəl] *s* (zool.) serval
servant ['sʌrvənt] *s* criado, servidor, sirviente
servant girl *s* muchacha de servir
servant problem *s* crisis del servicio doméstico
serve [sʌrv] *s* (tennis) servicio, saque; *va* servir; abastecer, proporcionar; maniobrar (*un cañón*); cubrir (*a la hembra*); cumplir (*una condena*); (law) entregar (*una citación*); (naut.) aforrar (*un cable*); (tennis) servir; **to serve right** merecerlo bien, p.ej., **it serves me right** bien me lo merezco; *vn* servir; (tennis & mil.) servir; **to serve as** servir de
server ['sʌrvər] *s* criado, servidor; mozo de comedor, mozo de café; (tennis) sacador, servidor; (eccl.) acólito; bandeja
Servia ['sʌrvɪə] *s* var. de **Serbia**
Servian ['sʌrvɪən] *adj & s* var. de **Serbian**
service ['sʌrvɪs] *s* servicio; (naut.) forro de cable; (law) entrega; **at your service** para servir a Vd.; **in service** funcionando; **out of service** descompuesto; **the service** el ejército; la marina; la aviación; **the services** las fuerzas armadas; **to be of service (to)** servir; *va* instalar; mantener, reparar
serviceability [ˌsʌrvɪsə'bɪlɪtɪ] *s* utilidad; estabilidad; complacencia
serviceable ['sʌrvɪsəbəl] *adj* servible, útil; duradero; servicial, complaciente
serviceberry ['sʌrvɪsˌbɛrɪ] *s* (*pl:* **-ries**) (bot.) guillomo (*arbusto y fruto*); (bot.) serbal (*árbol*); serba (*fruto*)
service ceiling *s* (aer.) techo de servicio
service dress *s* (mil. & nav.) uniforme diario
service entrance *s* entrada para el servicio
service line (tennis) línea de saque o servicio; (tennis) línea de fondo
serviceman ['sʌrvɪsˌmæn] *s* (*pl:* **-men**) empleado de servicio, reparador, mecánico; (mil.) militar
service record *s* hoja de servicios
service station *s* estación de servicio, taller de reparaciones, gasolinera
service stripe *s* galón de servicio
service tree *s* (bot.) acafresna, serbal
serviette [ˌsʌrvɪ'ɛt] *s* servilleta
servile ['sʌrvɪl] *adj* servil
servility [sər'vɪlɪtɪ] *s* (*pl:* **-ties**) servilismo
serving ['sʌrvɪŋ] *s* porción (*de un alimento*)
serving mallet *s* (naut.) maceta de aforrar
serving table *s* pequeño aparador, mesa para el servicio de los manjares
servitor ['sʌrvɪtər] *s* servidor; secuaz, partidario
servitude ['sʌrvɪtjud] o ['sʌrvɪtud] *s* servidumbre; trabajos forzados; (law) servidumbre
servo brake ['sʌrvo] *s* servofreno
servo control *s* (aer.) servocontrol
servomechanism [ˌsʌrvo'mɛkənɪzəm] *s* servomecanismo
servomotor [ˌsʌrvo'motər] *s* (mach.) servomotor
sesame ['sɛsəmɪ] *s* (bot.) sésamo, ajonjolí; sésamo (*palabra mágica*); **open sesame** sésamo ábrete
sesamoid ['sɛsəmɔɪd] o **sesamoidal** [ˌsɛsə'mɔɪdəl] *adj* sesamoideo
sesquialtera [ˌsɛskwɪ'æltərə] *s* (mus.) sesquiáltera (*intervalo; juego de órgano*)
sesquialteral [ˌsɛskwɪ'æltərəl] *adj* sesquiáltero
sesquicentennial [ˌsɛskwɪsɛn'tɛnɪəl] *adj & s* sesquicentenario
sesquipedalian [ˌsɛskwɪpɪ'delɪən] *adj* sesquipedal (*de pie y medio de largo; excesivamente largo*); que emplea palabras sesquipedales; *s* palabra sesquipedal
sessile ['sɛsɪl] *adj* (bot.) sésil, sentado
session ['sɛʃən] *s* sesión; período escolar; **to be in session** sesionar
sessional ['sɛʃənəl] *adj* de una sesión; de cada sesión
sestet [sɛs'tɛt] *s* (mus.) sexteto; dos tercetos (*de un soneto*)
set [sɛt] *s* juego (*de libros, sillas, etc.*); tren (*p.ej., de engranajes*); aderezo (*p.ej., de diamantes*); pareja (*p.ej., de caballos*); partida (*de tenis*); servicio (*de mesa*); equipo; grupo, clase; batería (*de utensilios de cocina*); (mov.) plató; (rad., telg. & telp.) aparato; (theat.) decoración; colocación, disposición; porte, postura; caída, ajuste (*de una prenda de vestir*); dirección, tendencia; vuelta; muestra (*del perro en acecho de la caza*); planta de transplantar; pie de árbol; triscamiento de los dientes (*de una sierra*); endurecimiento (*de la cola*); fraguado (*del cemento o yeso*); **set of artificial teeth** caja de dientes postizos, dentadura artificial; **set of dishes** servicio de mesa, vajilla; **set of teeth** dentadura ‖ *adj* resuelto, determinado; inflexible, obstinado; fijo, firme, sólido; meditado, estudiado; **set price** precio fijo; ‖ (*pret & pp:* **set;** *ger:* **setting**) *va* poner; asentar, colocar; establecer, instalar; arreglar, preparar; adornar; apostar; poner (*un reloj*) en hora; reenvidar (*en el juego de bridge*); poner, meter, pegar (*fuego*); fijar, determinar (*el precio*); expresar, escribir; poner a empollar (*una gallina*); montar, engastar (*una piedra preciosa*); cuajar (*un líquido*); encasar (*un hueso dislocado*); disponer (*los tipos*); triscar, trabar (*los dientes de la sierra*); armar, colocar (*una trampa*); fijar (*el peinado*); poner (*la mesa*); **to be set** perder (*en el juego de bridge*); **to set afire** poner fuego a, pegar fuego a; **to set an example** dar ejemplo; **to set apart** o **aside** reservar, poner a un lado; **to set back** parar, detener; poner obstáculos a; hacer retroceder; atrasar o retrasar (*p.ej., un reloj*); **to set down** deponer, depositar; poner por escrito; atribuir; **to set forth** exponer, dar a conocer; **to set off** hacer estallar, hacer saltar; poner de relieve; **to set on** azuzar; **to set one's jaws** apretar las quijadas; **to set one's heart on** tener la esperanza puesta en; **to set one's teeth** apretar los dientes; **to set out** sacar y disponer; **to set right** enmendar, corregir; **to set sail** hacerse a la vela; **to set someone against** poner a una persona mal con; **to set store by** dar mucha importancia a; **to set to music** poner música a; **to set**

up levantar, construir; armar, montar; comenzar, emprender; ensalzar; regocijar; (print.) componer; **to set up shop** poner tienda; **to set up the drinks** (coll.) convidar a beber ‖ *vn* ponerse (*dícese del Sol, la Luna, etc.*); cuajarse (*un líquido*); endurecerse (*la cola*); fraguar (*el cemento, el yeso*); empollar (*una gallina*); estar de muestra (*un perro de caza*); caer, sentar (*una prenda de vestir*); tender; **to set about** + *ger* ponerse a + *inf;* **to set forth** ponerse en camino; **to set in** aparecer, comenzar, declararse; fluir (*la marea*); **to set off** salir, partir; **to set out** ponerse en camino; emprender un negocio; **to set out for** salir para, partir para; **to set out to** + *inf* ponerse a + *inf;* **to set to work** poner manos a la obra; **to set upon** atacar, acometer
setaceous [sɪˈteʃəs] *adj* cerdoso; setáceo
setback [ˈsɛtˌbæk] *s* revés, contrariedad; (arch.) retraqueo
set-in [ˈsɛtˌɪn] *adj* empotrado
setoff [ˈsɛtˌɔf] o [ˈsɛtˌɑf] *s* salida, partida; adorno; compensación
setscrew [ˈsɛtˌskru] *s* tornillo de presión
settee [sɛˈti] *s* canapé, sofá; banco (*con respaldo y brazos*)
settee bed *s* canapé cama, sofá cama
setter [ˈsɛtər] *s* (print.) compositor, cajista; sétter (*perro de muestra*)
setting [ˈsɛtɪŋ] *s* armadura, marco; engaste, montadura; fraguado (*del cemento*); puesta, ocaso (*p.ej., del Sol*); (theat.) puesta en escena, decoración; (theat.) escena
setting-up exercises [ˈsɛtɪŋˈʌp] *spl* ejercicios sin aparatos, gimnasia sueca
settle [ˈsɛtəl] *s* banco largo; *va* asentar, colocar; asegurar, fijar; acabar; componer, conciliar; templar, moderar, calmar; determinar, decidir; hacer compacto; solidificar; hacer depositar; matar (*el polvo*); dar una profesión a; casar; poblar, colonizar; ajustar, arreglar (*cuentas*); **to settle on** o **upon** dar en dote, dar en propiedad; *vn* asentarse (*un líquido, un edificio*); arraigar, establecerse; componerse; templarse, moderarse, calmarse; hacerse compacto; solidificarse; **to settle down** irse lentamente a fondo (*un buque*); aflojar el paso; formalizarse; **to settle down to work** ponerse seriamente a trabajar; **to settle on** fijar, señalar (*p.ej., una fecha*); escoger
settlement [ˈsɛtəlmənt] *s* establecimiento; composición; determinación, decisión; colonización; colonia; caserío, poblado; pago, arreglo, ajuste (*de cuentas*); casa de beneficencia; (law) asignación, traspaso (*de bienes*)
settlement house *s* casa de beneficencia
settlement worker *s* persona que se consagra al servicio de una casa de beneficiencia
settler [ˈsɛtlər] *s* fundador; colono, poblador; (coll.) fin, golpe de gracia
settling [ˈsɛtlɪŋ] *s* asiento, sentamiento; colonización; **settlings** *spl* heces, zurrapas
set-to [ˈsɛtˌtu] *s* (*pl:* **-tos**) (coll.) lucha, combate, disputa
setup [ˈsɛtˌʌp] *s* porte, postura; disposición (*p.ej., de las partes de una máquina*); (coll.) organización; (slang) invitación a beber, bebida
setwall [ˈsɛtwɔl] *s* (bot.) valeriana
seven [ˈsɛvən] *adj* siete; *s* siete; **seven o'clock** las siete
seven deadly sins *spl* siete pecados capitales
sevenfold [ˈsɛvənˌfold] *adj & s* séptuplo; *adv* siete veces
Seven Hills *spl* siete colinas (*de Roma*)
seven hundred *adj & s* setecientos
seven seas *spl* todos los mares del mundo
seventeen [ˈsɛvənˈtin] *adj & s* diecisiete o diez y siete
seventeenth [ˈsɛvənˈtinθ] *adj* décimoséptimo; diecisieteavo; *s* décimoséptimo; diecisieteavo; diecisiete (*en las fechas*)
seventeen-year locust [ˈsɛvənˌtinˌjɪr] *s* (ent.) cigarra norteamericana cuya larva vive hasta diecisiete años (*Cicada septendecim*)
seventh [ˈsɛvənθ] *adj* séptimo; *s* séptimo; siete (*en las fechas*); (mus.) séptima
seventh day *s* sábado, el séptimo día de la semana
seventh-day [ˈsɛvənθˌde] *adj* sabatino
Seventh-Day Adventist *s* adventista del séptimo día
seventh heaven *s* séptimo cielo; (coll.) séptimo cielo (*felicidad suprema*); **to be in seventh heaven** (coll.) estar en sus glorias
seventieth [ˈsɛvəntɪɪθ] *adj & s* septuagésimo; setentavo
seventy [ˈsɛvəntɪ] *adj* setenta; *s* (*pl:* **-ties**) setenta
Seven Wonders of the World *spl* siete maravillas del mundo
Seven Years' War *s* guerra de los Siete Años
sever [ˈsɛvər] *va* separar, desunir; romper (*relaciones*); *vn* separarse, desunirse
several [ˈsɛvərəl] *adj* varios, diversos; distintos, respectivos; *spl* varios; algunos
severally [ˈsɛvərəlɪ] *adv* separadamente; respectivamente
severalty [ˈsɛvərəltɪ] *s* (*pl:* **-ties**) singularidad; (law) posesión privativa
severance [ˈsɛvərəns] *s* separación; ruptura (*p.ej., de las relaciones diplomáticas*)
severance pay *s* indemnización por despido
severe [sɪˈvɪr] *adj* severo; riguroso (*tiempo*); violento, recio
severity [sɪˈvɛrɪtɪ] *s* (*pl:* **-ties**) severidad; rigor; violencia
Severn [ˈsɛvərn] *s* Severna
Seville [səˈvɪl] o [ˈsɛvɪl] *s* Sevilla
Sevillian [səˈvɪljən] *adj & s* sevillano
sew [so] (*pret:* **sewed;** *pp:* **sewed** o **sewn**) *va & vn* coser
sewage [ˈsuɪdʒ] o [ˈsjuɪdʒ] *s* aguas de albañal, aguas fecales
sewage disposal *s* depuración de aguas fecales
sewer [ˈsuər] o [ˈsjuər] *s* albañal, cloaca, alcantarilla; mayordomo de comedor, jefe de los mozos; *va* alcantarillar; [ˈsoər] *s* persona que cose, costurera, sastre, etc.; (ent.) arrolladora, torcedora
sewerage [ˈsuərɪdʒ] o [ˈsjuərɪdʒ] *s* desagüe; alcantarillado (*sistema*); aguas de albañal
sewer gas [ˈsuər] o [ˈsjuər] *s* gas cloacal
sewing [ˈso·ɪŋ] *s* costura; *adj* de coser, para coser
sewing basket *s* cesta de costura, canastilla de la costura
sewing bee *s* reunión para hacer costura
sewing circle *s* círculo de costura
sewing machine *s* máquina de coser
sewing press *s* (b.b.) telar
sewn [son] *pp de* **sew**
sex [sɛks] *s* sexo; **the fair sex** o **the gentle sex** el bello sexo; **the sterner sex** o **the stronger sex** el sexo feo o el sexo fuerte; **the weaker sex** el sexo débil; *adj* sexual
sexagenarian [ˌsɛksədʒɪˈnɛrɪən] *adj & s* sexagenario
sexagenary [sɛksˈædʒɪˌnɛrɪ] *adj* sexagenario; *s* (*pl:* **-ies**) sexagenario
Sexagesima [ˌsɛksəˈdʒɛsɪmə] o **Sexagesima Sunday** *s* (eccl.) sexagésima
sexagesimal [ˌsɛksəˈdʒɛsɪməl] *adj* sexagesimal
sexangle [ˈsɛksˌæŋgəl] *s* (geom.) sexángulo
sex appeal *s* atracción sexual; atracción o encanto femenino
sex chromosome *s* (biol.) cromosoma sexual
sexennial [sɛksˈɛnɪəl] *adj* sexenal
sex hygiene *s* higiene sexual
sex-linkage [ˈsɛksˌlɪŋkɪdʒ] *s* (biol.) herencia ligada al sexo
sex-linked [ˈsɛksˌlɪŋkt] *adj* (biol.) ligado al sexo
sexologist [sɛksˈɑlədʒɪst] *s* sexólogo
sexology [sɛksˈɑlədʒɪ] *s* sexología
sext [sɛkst] *s* (eccl.) sexta
sextain [ˈsɛksten] *s* sextilla
sextan [ˈsɛkstən] *adj* sextano; *s* (path.) fiebre sextana
sextant [ˈsɛkstənt] *s* (math.) sexta parte del círculo; sextante (*instrumento*); (*cap.*) *s* (astr.) Sextante
sextet o **sextette** [sɛksˈtɛt] *s* grupo de seis; (mus.) sexteto
sextile [ˈsɛkstɪl] *adj* (astrol.) sextil
sextillion [sɛksˈtɪljən] *s* (Brit.) sextillón
sexton [ˈsɛkstən] *s* sacristán
sextuple [ˈsɛkstupəl], [ˈsɛkstjupəl], [sɛks-

'tupəl] o [sɛks'tjupəl] *adj & s* séxtuplo; *va* sextuplicar; *vn* sextuplicarse

sextuplet ['sɛkstʊplɛt], ['sɛkstjʊplɛt], [sɛks'tuplɛt] o [sɛks'tjuplɛt] *s* grupo de seis; uno de seis nacidos a un tiempo; (mus.) seisillo

sextuplication [sɛks,tuplɪ'keʃən] o [sɛks,tjʊplɪ'keʃən] *s* sextuplicación

sexual ['sɛkʃʊəl] *adj* sexual

sexual intercourse *s* comercio sexual

sexuality [,sɛkʃʊ'ælɪtɪ] *s* sexualidad

sexy ['sɛksɪ] *adj* (*comp:* **-ier;** *super:* **-iest**) (slang) sicalíptico

sfumato [sfu'mɑto] *adj* (paint.) esfumado

s.g. abr. de **specific gravity**

sgraffito [zgrɑf'fito] *s* (f.a.) esgrafiado

Sgt. abr. de **Sergeant**

shabby ['ʃæbɪ] *adj* (*comp:* **-bier;** *super:* **-biest**) raído, usado, gastado; andrajoso, desaseado; vil, ruin

shabby-genteel ['ʃæbɪdʒɛn'til] *adj* pobre pero de aspecto digno

shack [ʃæk] *s* choza, casucha

shackle ['ʃækəl] *s* grillete, grillo; maniota (*con que se ata un animal*); (fig.) traba, impedimento; **shackles** *spl* grillos, cadenas, esposas; *va* poner grilletes a, poner esposas a; encadenar; (fig.) trabar, poner obstáculos a

shackle bolt *s* perno de horquilla, bulón de grillete

shad [ʃæd] *s* (ichth.) sábalo

shadberry ['ʃæd,bɛrɪ] *s* (*pl:* **-ries**) (bot.) cornillo, cornijuelo, guillomo; (bot.) níspero del Canadá (*arbusto y fruto*)

shadblossom ['ʃæd,blɑsəm] *s* flor de níspero del Canadá

shadbush ['ʃæd,bʊʃ] *s* (bot.) cornillo, cornijuelo, guillomo; (bot.) níspero del Canadá

shaddock ['ʃædək] *s* (bot.) pamplemusa (*árbol y fruto*)

shade [ʃed] *s* sombra; pantalla (*de lámpara*); cortina, visillo, estor (*de una ventana*); cortina de resorte; matiz (*diferencia muy pequeña*); **in the shade** o **into the shade** a la sombra; (fig.) en condición inferior; **the shades** las tinieblas; las sombras (*de los muertos*); *va* sombrear; obscurecer; rebajar ligeramente (*el precio*); (f.a.) sombrear; *vn* cambiar poco a poco

shadeless ['ʃedlɪs] *adj* privado de sombra

shade tree *s* árbol de sombra

shad fly *s* (ent.) cachipolla

shading ['ʃedɪŋ] *s* sombreo; sombreado; matiz; ligera rebaja (*en los precios*)

shadow ['ʃædo] *s* sombra; (fig.) sombra (*vestigio; espectro; amparo, protección; parte obscura; persona que sigue a otra por todas partes*); aspecto triste; **in the shadow of** dentro de la sombra de; muy cerca de; **the shadows** las tinieblas; *va* sombrear; representar o indicar vagamente; simbolizar; acechar, espiar, seguir (*a una persona*) como su propia sombra; (f.a.) sombrear, matizar; entristecer; **to shadow forth** representar vagamente, representar de un modo profético

shadowboxing ['ʃædo,bɑksɪŋ] *s* (sport) boxeo con un adversario imaginario

shadowgraph ['ʃædo,græf] o ['ʃædo,grɑf] *s* radiografía; sombras chinescas

shadowless ['ʃædolɪs] *adj* sin sombra

shadow play *s* (theat.) sombras chinescas

shadowy ['ʃædo·ɪ] o ['ʃædəwɪ] *adj* sombroso; vago, ligero, indefinido; imaginario, quimérico; simbólico

shady ['ʃedɪ] *adj* (*comp:* **-ier;** *super:* **-iest**) sombrío, umbroso; (coll.) sospechoso; (coll.) deshonroso, de mala fama; (coll.) verde (*cuento*); **on the shady side of** más allá de (*cierta edad*); **to keep shady** (slang) no dejarse ver

shaft [ʃæft] o [ʃɑft] *s* dardo, flecha, saeta; astil (*de flecha; de pluma*); mango (*p.ej., de martillo*); rayo (*de luz*); vara alcándara, limonera, fuste (*de un coche o carro*); pozo (*de mina; de ascensor*); caña, fuste (*de columna*); asta (*de una bandera*); (mach.) árbol, eje; (bot.) tallo, vástago; (bot.) pezón, pedúnculo; (fig.) dardo (*para ridiculizar a una persona*)

shaft furnace *s* horno de cuba

shag [ʃæg] *s* pelo áspero y lanudo; lana áspera; felpa; tripe (*tejido*); picadura de tabaco muy ordinario

shagbark ['ʃæg,bɑrk] *s* (bot.) nuez dura

shaggy ['ʃægɪ] *adj* (*comp:* **-gier;** *super:* **-giest**) peludo, velludo, hirsuto; lanudo; afelpado; áspero

shagreen [ʃə'grin] *s* chagrín; lija, zapa; *adj* achagrinado

shah [ʃɑ] *s* chah

shake [ʃek] *s* sacudida, sacudimiento; (coll.) temblor, terremoto; (coll.) apretón de manos; (slang) instante, momento; grieta, hendedura; (mus.) trino; (coll.) batido (*de leche*); **no great shakes** (coll.) poco extraordinario, poco importante; (*pret:* **shook;** *pp:* **shaken**) *va* sacudir; arrojar con una sacudida; agitar; volver (*la cabeza*) de un lado a otro (*en señal de negación*); hacer temblar; estrechar, apretar (*la mano a uno*); hacer ondear; perturbar, inquietar; (slang) zafarse de; **to shake down** bajar sacudiendo; hacer depositar; poner en condiciones de funcionar; (slang) sacar dinero a; **to shake off** sacudir; arrojar con una sacudida; dar esquinazo a, zafarse de; **to shake up** agitar, sacudir con violencia; cambiar bruscamente, trastornar; reorganizar; *vn* sacudirse, agitarse; ondear, bambolearse; temblar; (mus.) trinar; (fig.) agitarse, perturbarse, inquietarse; **to shake with cold** tiritar de frío; **shake!** (coll.) ¡vengan esos cinco!, ¡estrechémoslas!, ¡choque Vd. esos cinco!

shakedown ['ʃek,daʊn] *s* cama improvisada; prueba, ensayo; (slang) concusión, exacción de dinero por compulsión

shakedown cruise *s* (nav.) crucero de ensayo (*para comprobar la nave o aclimatar al personal*)

shaken ['ʃekən] *pp de* **shake**

shaker ['ʃekər] *s* sacudidor; agitador (*aparato*); espolvoreador (*utensilio*)

Shakespearian o **Shakesperian** [ʃek'spɪrɪən] *adj & s* shakespeariano o shakespiriano

shake-up ['ʃek,ʌp] *s* profunda conmoción; cambio de personal, reorganización completa

shako ['ʃæko] o ['ʃeko] *s* (*pl:* **-os**) chacó

Shaksperian [ʃek'spɪrɪən] *adj & s* var. de **Shakespearian**

shaky ['ʃekɪ] *adj* (*comp:* **-ier;** *super:* **-iest**) trémulo, vacilante; débil; falto de crédito, indigno de confianza

shale [ʃel] *s* pizarra

shale oil *s* aceite de pizarra bituminosa, aceite esquistoso

shall [ʃæl] (*cond:* **should**) *v aux* se emplea para formar (1) el futuro de ind, p.ej., **I shall arrive** llegaré; (2) el futuro perfecto de ind, p.ej., **I shall have arrived** habré llegado; y (3) el modo potencial, p.ej., **what shall he do?** ¿qué ha de hacer?, ¿qué debe hacer?

shalloon [ʃæ'lun] *s* chalón

shallop ['ʃæləp] *s* chalupa

shallot [ʃə'lɑt] *s* (bot.) chalote

shallow ['ʃælo] *adj* bajo, poco profundo; (fig.) superficial, frívolo; *s* bajo, bajío; *va* hacer menos profundo; *vn* hacerse menos profundo

shaly ['ʃelɪ] *adj* pizarreño

sham [ʃæm] *s* fingimiento, pretexto, engaño, falsificación; farsante; cubierta de adorno; *adj* fingido, falso; postizo; (*pret & pp:* **shammed;** *ger:* **shamming**) *va & vn* fingir

shaman ['ʃɑmən] o ['ʃæmən] *s* chamán; hechicero

sham battle *s* simulacro de combate

shamble ['ʃæmbəl] *s* bamboleo; **shambles** *spl* o *ssg* matadero, degolladero; matanza, carnicería, lugar de gran matanza; **to leave a shambles** dejar (*un sitio*) arruinado, en desorden; *vn* andar bamboleándose

shame [ʃem] *s* vergüenza; deshonra; **for shame!** ¡qué vergüenza! **to be a shame** ser una mala vergüenza; **to bring shame upon** deshonrar; **to put to shame** avergonzar; superar, aventajar; **what a shame!** ¡qué lástima!; **shame on you!** ¡qué vergüenza!, ¡eso está feo para Vd.!; *va* avergonzar; deshonrar

shamefaced ['ʃem,fest] *adj* vergonzoso; tímido

shameful ['ʃemfəl] *adj* vergonzoso

shameless ['ʃemlɪs] *adj* desvergonzado, descarado

shammer [ˈʃæmər] *s* fingidor, impostor
shammy [ˈʃæmɪ] *s* (*pl:* **-mies**) gamuza (*animal y piel*)
shampoo [ʃæmˈpu] *s* champú, lavado de la cabeza; *va* lavar (*la cabeza*); lavar la cabeza a
shamrock [ˈʃæmrɑk] *s* (bot.) trébol irlandés; (bot.) trébol blanco; (bot.) acedera menor (*Oxalis acetosella*); (bot.) lupulina (*Medicago lupulina*)
shanghai [ˈʃæŋhaɪ] o [ʃæŋˈhaɪ] (*pret & pp:* **-haied;** *ger:* **-haiing**) *va* embarcar emborrachando, embarcar narcotizando; llevarse con violencia, llevarse con engaño
Shangrila [ˈʃæŋgrɪˈlɑ] *s* Jauja (*país maravilloso*)
shank [ʃæŋk] *s* caña o cañilla de la pierna; pierna (*de un animal*); zanca (*de un ave*); astil, caña, fuste; mango, vástago; caña (*del ancla*); enfranque (*de la suela del zapato*); (print.) árbol; remate, extremidad; **to go** o **to ride on shank's mare** caminar en coche de San Francisco
shan't [ʃænt] o [ʃɑnt] contracción de **shall not**
shantung [ʃænˈtʌŋ] *s* shantung
shanty [ˈʃæntɪ] *s* (*pl:* **-ties**) cabaña pobre o ruda, chabola, choza; (naut.) saloma
shape [ʃep] *s* forma; (iron mfg.) perfil; **in bad shape** (coll.) arruinado, descompuesto; (coll.) muy malo, muy enfermo; **out of shape** deformado; descompuesto, desarreglado; **to lick into shape** (coll.) preparar (*una cosa*) para que pueda hacer su servicio; **to put into shape** ordenar, poner en orden; **to take shape** tomar forma; *va* formar; definir, determinar; dirigir; idear, dibujar; *vn* formarse; **to shape up** formarse; desarrollarse bien
shapeless [ˈʃeplɪs] *adj* informe
shapely [ˈʃeplɪ] *adj* (*comp:* **-lier;** *super:* **-liest**) bien formado, bien hecho, esbelto
shard [ʃɑrd] *s* fragmento, tiesto, casco; élitro (*de los coleópteros*)
share [ʃɛr] *s* parte, porción; reja (*del arado*); (com.) acción; **on shares** participando en los riesgos y la ganancia; **to go shares** participar; *va* repartir; tener parte en, usar juntos de, poseer en común; *vn* participar, tener parte
sharecropper [ˈʃɛrˌkrɑpər] *s* aparcero, mediero
shareholder [ˈʃɛrˌholdər] *s* (com.) accionista
shark [ʃɑrk] *s* (ichth.) tiburón; estafador, gato; (slang) experto, perito
sharkskin [ˈʃɑrkˌskɪn] *s* lija, zapa; tejido de algodón o rayón (*para trajes*)
sharp [ʃɑrp] *adj* agudo, afilado; anguloso; fuerte, pronunciado (*dícese de una curva o pendiente*); nítido (*dícese de una fotografía*); rápido, veloz (*dícese del paso de una persona*); fogoso, violento; fuerte, vehemente; atento, despierto; picante, mordaz; penetrante; vivo, listo; fino (*oído*); (phonet.) sordo; (mus.) sostenido; (slang) elegante; **sharp features** facciones bien marcadas; **sharp taste** sabor acre; **sharp temper** genio áspero; **sharp tuning** (rad.) sintonía afilada; **sharp turn** vuelta repentina; *adv* agudamente; en punto, p.ej., **at three o'clock sharp** a las tres en punto; *s* (mus.) sostenido; estafador; (coll.) experto, perito; **sharps** *spl* parte del trigo a la que hay que dar la segunda molienda
sharpen [ˈʃɑrpən] *va* aguzar, afilar, sacar punta a; *vn* afilarse
sharpener [ˈʃɑrpənər] *s* aguzador, afilador; máquina de afilar
sharper [ˈʃɑrpər] *s* fullero, caballero de industria
sharpie [ˈʃɑrpɪ] *s* embarcación de fondo plano con una o dos velas triangulares
sharpness [ˈʃɑrpnɪs] *s* agudeza; angulosidad; nitidez; rapidez, velocidad; fuerza, violencia
sharp-nosed [ˈʃɑrpˌnozd] *adj* de nariz puntiaguda; de finísimo olfato
sharp-set [ˈʃɑrpˌsɛt] *adj* famélico, hambriento; ávido, ansioso; de borde afilado
sharpshooter [ˈʃɑrpˌʃutər] *s* tirador certero; (mil.) tirador distinguido
sharp-sighted [ˈʃɑrpˌsaɪtɪd] *adj* de vista penetrante; listo, perspicaz
sharp-witted [ˈʃɑrpˌwɪtɪd] *adj* penetrante, perspicaz
shatter [ˈʃætər] *va* romper, hacer astillas, hacer pedazos, romper de un golpe; destruir, destrozar; quebrantar (*la salud*); agitar, perturbar; *vn* romperse, hacerse pedazos; **shatters** *spl* fragmentos, pedazos
shatterproof [ˈʃætərˈpruf] *adj* inastillable
shattery [ˈʃætərɪ] *adj* saltadizo
shave [ʃev] *s* afeitado; raedura; rascador; rebanada delgada; **to have a close shave** (coll.) escapar en una tabla; (*pret:* **shaved;** *pp:* **shaved** o **shaven**) *va* afeitar (*la cara*); raer, raspar; rebanar (*en porciones muy delgadas*); rozar (*raer la superficie de; pasar tocando la superficie de; cortar muy justo*); (carp.) cepillar, alisar, rascar; (taur.) afeitar (*las astas del toro*); *vn* afeitarse; estafar, ser duro en un negocio
shaveling [ˈʃevlɪŋ] *s* jovenzuelo; (scornful) fraile, monje
shaven [ˈʃevən] *pp de* **shave**
shaver [ˈʃevər] *s* barbero; máquina de afeitar; alisador, rascador; (coll.) muchachito
Shavian [ˈʃevɪən] *adj & s* shaviano
shaving [ˈʃevɪŋ] *s* afeitado; viruta (*de madera, metal, etc.*)
shaving brush *s* brocha de afeitar, escobilla de afeitar o de barba
shaving cream *s* crema de afeitar
shaving foam *s* espuma de afeitar
shaving soap *s* jabón de afeitar, jabón para la barba
shawl [ʃɔl] *s* chal, mantón
shawm [ʃɔm] *s* (mus.) caramillo
shay [ʃe] *s* (coll.) silla volante (*coche ligero*)
she [ʃi] *pron pers* (*pl:* **they**) ella; *s* (*pl:* **shes**) hembra
sheaf [ʃif] *s* (*pl:* **sheaves**) gavilla; *va* agavillar
shear [ʃɪr] *s* esquileo, trasquila; lana que se ha esquilado; hoja de la tijera; **shears** *spl* tijeras grandes; cizallas (*para cortar metales*); grúa de tijera; (*pret:* **sheared;** *pp:* **sheared** o **shorn**) *va* esquilar, trasquilar (*las ovejas*); cortar con tijeras, cizallar, cortar con cizallas; quitar cortando, cortar muy cerca; romper o cortar por fuerza del cizallamiento
shearwater [ˈʃɪrˌwɔtər] o [ˈʃɪrˌwɑtər] *s* (orn.) pufino, fardela del Atlántico; (orn.) pico tijera, meauca (*Rhynchops*)
sheatfish [ˈʃitˌfɪʃ] *s* (ichth.) siluro
sheath [ʃiθ] *s* (*pl:* **sheaths** [ʃiðz]) vaina; envoltura, cubierta, estuche; (bot.) vaina
sheathe [ʃið] *va* envainar; enfundar; embonar (*el casco de un buque*)
sheathing [ˈʃiðɪŋ] *s* forro, revestimiento; enfundadura; entablado, entarimado; (naut.) embono
sheathing board *s* cartón de yeso
sheathing nail *s* clavo de entablar
sheath knife *s* cuchillo encerrado en una vaina
sheave [ʃiv] *s* roldana; *va* agavillar
Sheba [ˈʃibə] *s* Sabá; **Queen of Sheba** reina de Sabá
shebang [ʃəˈbæŋ] *s* (slang) equipo, apresto; **the whole shebang** (coll.) la totalidad, el todo
she'd [ʃid] contracción de **she had** y de **she would**
shed [ʃɛd] *s* cobertizo; vertiente (*de agua*); (*pret & pp:* **shed;** *ger:* **shedding**) *va* verter, derramar; largar, desprenderse de; dar, echar, esparcir (*luz*); mudar (*la pluma, el pellejo, etc.*); *vn* pelechar (*los animales*)
shedder [ˈʃɛdər] *s* derramador; cangrejo o langosta que comienza a mudar el caparazón; cangrejo que acaba de mudar el caparazón
shedding [ˈʃɛdɪŋ] *s* vertimiento, derramamiento; desprendimiento; esparcimiento (*de luz*); muda (*p.ej., de plumas*)
sheen [ʃin] *s* lustre, brillo, resplandor; prensado (*lustre de los tejidos prensados*)
sheeny [ˈʃinɪ] *adj* lustroso, brillante
sheep [ʃip] *s* (*pl:* **sheep**) carnero; oveja (*hembra*); badana (*piel*); tonto, simplón, papanatas; **to make sheep's eyes** mirar con ojos de carnero degollado; *adj* ovejero
sheep botfly *s* (ent.) estro o moscardón de carnero

sheepcote ['ʃip,kot] o ['ʃip,kɑt] *s* aprisco, redil, ovil
sheep dog *s* perro de pastor, perro ovejero
sheepfold ['ʃip,fold] *s* aprisco, redil, ovil
sheephook ['ʃip,hʊk] *s* cayada, cayado
sheepish ['ʃipɪʃ] *adj* avergonzado, corrido; tonto, tímido, pulsilánime
sheepman ['ʃip,mæn] *s* (*pl:* **-men**) dueño y criador de ganado lanar; pastor
sheep range *s* pasto de ovejas
sheepshead ['ʃips,hɛd] *s* cabeza de oveja; papanatas, simplón; (ichth.) sargo, salema
sheepshearer ['ʃip,ʃɪrər] *s* esquilador (*persona*); esquiladora (*máquina*)
sheepskin ['ʃip,skɪn] *s* zalea (*cuero que conserva la lana*); badana (*piel curtida*); (coll.) diploma
sheep sorrel *s* (bot.) acederilla
sheep tick *s* (ent.) mosca del carnero
sheepwalk ['ʃip,wɔk] *s* pasto de ovejas, dehesa de ovejas
sheer [ʃɪr] *s* (naut.) desviación (*de un buque de su rumbo*); (naut.) arrufadura (*curvatura*); *adj* fino, delgado, ligero; puro, sin mezcla; cabal, completo; casi transparente; escarpado; *adv* cabalmente, completamente; de un golpe, directamente; en cuesta; *va* desviar; *vn* desviarse
sheet [ʃit] *s* sábana (*para la cama*); hoja (*de papel, metal, etc.*); hoja impresa; diario, periódico; extensión (de agua); (naut.) escota; (poet.) vela (*de navío*); **to be** o **to have a sheet in the wind** (slang) estar entre dos velas, estar chispado, estar borrachuelo; **sheet of paper** papel; **sheets** *spl* espacio a proa o a popa de bote abierto; *va* ensabanar; proveer de sábana; *vn* extenderse en hojas
sheet anchor *s* (naut.) ancla de la esperanza; (fig.) áncora de salvación
sheeting ['ʃitɪŋ] *s* lencería para sábanas; encofrado (*revestimiento de planchas*); cobertura de placas, laminado
sheet iron *s* palastro, hierro laminado
sheet lightning *s* fucilazo, relámpago difuso
sheet metal *s* metal laminado, metal en láminas
sheet music *s* música en hojas sueltas
Sheffield plate ['ʃɛfild] *s* plateado de Sheffield
sheik o **sheikh** [ʃik] *s* jeque; (slang) galanteador irresistible, sultán
sheikdom ['ʃikdəm] *s* principado (de jeque)
shekel ['ʃɛkəl] *s* siclo; **shekels** *spl* (slang) dinero
sheldrake ['ʃɛl,drek] *s* (orn.) tadorna; (orn.) pato canelo; (orn.) pato sierra
shelf [ʃɛlf] *s* (*pl:* **shelves**) estante, anaquel, entrepaño; bajío, banco de arena; roca subyacente; **on the shelf** arrinconado, desechado, olvidado; en prenda
shelflist ['ʃɛlf,lɪst] *s* catálogo topográfico (*de una biblioteca*)
shelf warmer *s* artículo de venta morosa, artículo invendible
she'll [ʃil] contracción de **she shall** y de **she will**
shell [ʃɛl] *s* cáscara (*de huevo, nuez, etc.*); concha, caparazón (*p.ej., de crustáceo*); vaina (*de legumbre*); cubierta, corteza; armazón, esqueleto; bomba, proyectil; cápsula (*para cartuchos*); cuerpo (*p.ej., de caldera*); (sport) piragua, yola; **to come out of one's shell** salir del carapacho o de la concha; **to retire into one's shell** meterse en su carapacho o en su concha; *va* descascarar; desvainar; desgranar (*p.ej., guisantes*); cañonear, bombardear; **to shell out** (coll.) entregar (*dinero*); *vn* descascararse; desconcharse; **to shell out** (coll.) entregar el dinero, pagar
shellac [ʃə'læk] o ['ʃɛlæk] *s* laca, goma laca; (*pret & pp:* **-lacked;** *ger:* **-lacking**) *va* barnizar con goma laca
shellacking [ʃə'lækɪŋ] *s* (slang) paliza, zurra; (slang) derrota
shellback ['ʃɛl,bæk] *s* (slang) lobo de mar; (slang) persona que ha atravesado el ecuador en un barco
shellbark ['ʃɛl,bɑrk] *s* (bot.) nuez dura
sheller ['ʃɛlər] *s* descascarador; desgranador; descascaradora (*máquina*)
shellfire ['ʃɛl,faɪr] *s* cañoneo, fuego de bomba
shellfish ['ʃɛl,fɪʃ] *s* marisco, mariscos
shellfishery ['ʃɛl,fɪʃərɪ] *s* (*pl:* **-ies**) marisqueo
shell hole *s* (mil.) embudo
shellproof ['ʃɛl,pruf] *adj* a prueba de bomba
shell shock *s* conmoción psiconeurótica del soldado, neurosis de guerra
shelly ['ʃɛlɪ] *adj* (*comp:* **-ier;** *super:* **-iest**) conchado, conchudo
shelter ['ʃɛltər] *s* abrigo, amparo, refugio, resguardo, asilo; **to take shelter** abrigarse, refugiarse; *va* abrigar, amparar, proteger, guarecer; *vn* abrigarse, refugiarse, guarecerse
shelter tent *s* (mil.) tienda de abrigo
shelve [ʃɛlv] *va* poner sobre un estante o anaquel; proveer de estantes o anaqueles; arrinconar, desechar, dejar a un lado; diferir indefinidamente; *vn* estar en declive
shelving ['ʃɛlvɪŋ] *s* anaquelería, estantería; material para anaqueles o estantes
Shemite ['ʃɛmaɪt] *s* var. de **semite**
shenanigans [ʃɪ'nænɪgənz] *spl* (coll.) artificios, embustes
sheol ['ʃiol] *s* (coll.) infierno, báratro
shepherd ['ʃɛpərd] *s* pastor; (fig.) pastor; *va* pastorear (*a las ovejas o los fieles*)
shepherd dog *s* perro de pastor, perro ovejero
shepherd god *s* dios de los pastores (*el dios Pan*)
shepherdess ['ʃɛpərdɪs] *s* pastora
Shepherd kings *spl* reyes pastores
shepherd's pipe *s* zampoña
shepherd's-purse ['ʃɛpərdz,pʌrs] *s* (bot.) bolsa de pastor, zurrón de pastor, pan y quesillo
sherbet ['ʃʌrbət] *s* sorbete
sherd [ʃʌrd] *s* var. de **shard**
shereef o **sherif** [ʃɛ'rif] *s* jerife
sheriff ['ʃɛrɪf] *s* oficial de justicia inglés o norteamericano
sherifian [ʃɛ'rifɪən] *adj* jerifiano
sherry ['ʃɛrɪ] *s* (*pl:* **-ries**) jerez, vino de Jerez
sherry cobbler *s* bebida compuesta de agua y vino de Jerez con azúcar, limón, naranja y pedacitos de hielo (*sírvese con pajas*)
sherry reception *s* vino (*reunión donde se ofrece vino de Jerez*)
she's [ʃiz] contracción de **she is** y de **she has**
shew [ʃo] *s, va & vn* var. de **show**
shewbread ['ʃo,brɛd] *s* (Bib.) panes de la proposición
shibboleth ['ʃɪbəlɛθ] *s* lema, santo y seña; habla, jerga; rasgo distintivo
shield [ʃild] *s* escudo; (bot., zool., her. & fig.) escudo; (elec.) blindaje; sobaquera (*con que se resguarda del sudor la parte del vestido correspondiente al sobaco*); *va* amparar, defender, escudar; (elec.) blindar
shield-bearer ['ʃild,bɛrər] *s* escudero
shift [ʃɪft] *s* cambio; tanda (*grupo de obreros*); turno (*orden del trabajo*); maña, subterfugio, fraude; **to make shift** ayudarse, ingeniarse, componérselas; ingeniarse a duras penas; hacer lo posible; *va* cambiar; deshacerse de; **to shift gears** cambiar de marcha; **to shift the blame** echar la culpa a otro; **to shift the blame on** echar la culpa a; *vn* cambiar, cambiar de puesto; mañear, tergiversar; ayudarse, ingeniarse; **to shift for oneself** ayudarse, ingeniarse
shifting engine *s* (rail.) locomotora de maniobras
shift key *s* tecla de cambio, tecla de mayúsculas, palanca de mayúsculas
shiftless ['ʃɪftlɪs] *adj* inútil, galbanoso
shifty ['ʃɪftɪ] *adj* (*comp:* **-ier;** *super:* **-iest**) ingenioso; tramoyista; huyente (*vistazo*)
shill [ʃɪl] *s* (slang) cómplice de un fullero
shillalah o **shillelagh** [ʃɪ'lelə] o [ʃɪ'lelɪ] *s* palo, cachiporra
shilling ['ʃɪlɪŋ] *s* chelín
shilly-shally ['ʃɪlɪ,ʃælɪ] *adj* irresoluto; *adv* irresolutamente; (*pret & pp:* **-lied**) *vn* estar irresoluto, no saber qué hacer
shily ['ʃaɪlɪ] *adv* tímidamente
shim [ʃɪm] *s* cuña, calza; (*pret & pp:* **shimmed;** *ger:* **shimming**) *va* acuñar, calzar
shimmer ['ʃɪmər] *s* luz trémula, débil resplandor; *vn* rielar
shimmery ['ʃɪmərɪ] *adj* trémulo, resplandeciente

shimmy [ˈʃɪmɪ] *s* (*pl:* **-mies**) shimmy (*baile*); (coll.) camisa de mujer; vibración excesiva; (aut.) abaniqueo (*de las ruedas delanteras*); (*pret & pp:* **-mied**) *vn* bailar el shimmy; vibrar; (aut.) bambolear
shin [ʃɪn] *s* (anat.) espinilla; (*pret & pp:* **shinned;** *ger:* **shinning**) *va & vn* trepar; **to shin up** trepar
shinbone [ˈʃɪn,bon] *s* (anat.) tibia, espinilla
shindig [ˈʃɪndɪg] *s* (slang) juerga, fiesta ruidosa
shindy [ˈʃɪndɪ] *s* (*pl:* **-dies**) (slang) alboroto, zacapela; (slang) juerga, fiesta ruidosa
shine [ʃaɪn] *s* luz, brillo; lustre, bruñido; buen tiempo; (coll.) lustre (*que se da al calzado*); (slang) simpatía; (slang) alboroto; (slang) travesura; **to take a shine to** (slang) tomar simpatía por; (*pret & pp:* **shined**) *va* (coll.) embetunar, embolar, limpiar (*el calzado*); bruñir, pulir; dar lustre a, poner lustroso; (*pret & pp:* **shone**) *va* hacer brillar, abrillantar; *vn* lucir, brillar, resplandecer; hacer sol, hacer buen tiempo; (fig.) brillar, lucir (*distinguirse, sobresalir*); **to shine up to** (slang) tratar de conquistar la amistad de
shiner [ˈʃaɪnər] *s* cosa que brilla; limpiabotas; (ichth.) pececillo plateado; (slang) ojo; (slang) ojo morado; (slang) guinea o soberano (*monedas inglesas*)
shingle [ˈʃɪŋgəl] *s* ripia (*usada como una teja para cubrir el tejado de las casas*); tejamaní (Am.); pelo a la garçonne; (coll.) letrero de oficina; guijo, guijarro, cascajo; guijarral (*playa u otro terreno*); **to hang out one's shingle** (coll.) abrir una oficina; (coll.) abrir un consultorio médico; **shingles** *spl* (path.) zona; *va* cubrir con ripias; cortar (*el pelo*) a la garçonne; cinglar (*el hierro*); *vn* ripiar
shingly [ˈʃɪŋglɪ] *adj* guijarroso, cascajoso
shin guard *s* (sport) espinillera
shining [ˈʃaɪnɪŋ] *adj* brillante, luciente; (fig.) brillante, distinguido
shinny [ˈʃɪnɪ] *s* (*pl:* **-nies**) cachava (*juego y palo*); (*pret & pp:* **-nied**) *vn* (coll.) trepar valiéndose de las espinillas
Shinto [ˈʃɪnto] *s* sintoísmo; sintoísta; *adj* sintoísta
Shintoism [ˈʃɪnto·ɪzəm] *s* sintoísmo
Shintoist [ˈʃɪnto·ɪst] *adj & s* sintoísta
shiny [ˈʃaɪnɪ] *adj* (*comp:* **-ier;** *super:* **-iest**) brillante, lustroso; glaseado (*p.ej., papel*); brilloso (*que brilla por el mucho uso*)
-ship *suffix s* -ato, p.ej., **deanship** decanato; **generalship** generalato; -ción p.ej., **horsemanship** equitación; **scholarship** erudición; -ía, p.ej., **chancellorship** cancillería; **lordship** señoría; **secretaryship** secretaría
ship [ʃɪp] *s* nave, buque, barco, navío; nave aérea, aeronave; tripulación; (*pret & pp:* **shipped;** *ger:* **shipping**) *va* embarcar; enviar, remitir; armar (*p.ej., los remos*); **to ship water** embarcar agua; *vn* embarcarse (*ir a bordo de un buque; aceptar un empleo a bordo de un buque*); **to ship on** tripular (*ir de tripulación en*)
ship biscuit *s* galleta, pan de marinero
shipboard [ˈʃɪp,bord] *s* bordo; **on shipboard** a bordo
ship bread *s* var. de **ship biscuit**
shipbuilder [ˈʃɪp,bɪldər] *s* arquitecto naval, ingeniero naval; constructor de buques
shipbuilding [ˈʃɪp,bɪldɪŋ] *s* arquitectura naval; construcción de buques; *adj* armador
ship canal *s* canal de navegación
ship carpenter *s* carpintero de ribera
ship chandler *s* abastecedor de buques
shipload [ˈʃɪp,lod] *s* cargamento completo de un buque
shipman [ˈʃɪpmən] *s* (*pl:* **-men**) capitán de buque, patrón
shipmaster [ˈʃɪp,mæstər] o [ˈʃɪp,mɑstər] *s* capitán de buque, patrón
shipmate [ˈʃɪp,met] *s* camarada de a bordo
shipment [ˈʃɪpmənt] *s* embarque (*por agua*); envío, remesa
ship money *s* (Brit.) impuesto de guerra para la construcción de buques
ship of the desert *s* nave del desierto (*camello*)
ship of the line *s* navío de línea, navío de alto bordo
ship of war *s* navío de guerra
shipowner [ˈʃɪp,onər] *s* naviero, armador
shipper [ˈʃɪpər] *s* embarcador (*en una embarcación*); expedidor, remitente
shipping [ˈʃɪpɪŋ] *s* embarque; envío, remesa; navegación; marina, flota
shipping clerk *s* dependiente encargado de envíos y transportes de mercancías
shipping memo *s* nota de remisión
shipping room *s* local de donde se hacen envíos
shipplane [ˈʃɪp,plen] *s* avión de cubierta
ship-rigged [ˈʃɪp,rɪgd] *adj* (naut.) aparejado con velas cuadradas y tres mástiles
shipshape [ˈʃɪp,ʃep] *adj & adv* en buen orden
ship's husband *s* director de una empresa naviera; encargado de un buque en el puerto
shipside [ˈʃɪp,saɪd] *adj & adv* al costado del buque; *s* zona de embarque y desembarque; muelle
ship's papers *spl* documentación del buque
ship's time *s* hora local del buque
shipworm [ˈʃɪp,wʌrm] *s* (zool.) broma, tiñuela
shipwreck [ˈʃɪp,rɛk] *s* naufragio; barco náufrago; (fig.) naufragio; *va* hacer naufragar; *vn* naufragar; (fig.) naufragar
shipwright [ˈʃɪp,raɪt] *s* carpintero de ribera, carpintero de navío
shipyard [ˈʃɪp,jɑrd] *s* astillero
shire [ʃaɪr] *s* (Brit.) condado
shirk [ʃʌrk] *s* persona que evita trabajar; *va* evitar (*el trabajo*); faltar a (*un deber*); *vn* evitar trabajar; faltar a sus obligaciones, escurrir el hombro
shirr [ʃʌr] *s* (sew.) frunce; *va* (sew.) fruncir; cocer (*huevos*) en un plato chato con crema o pan rallado
shirred egg *s* huevo al plato
shirring [ˈʃʌrɪŋ] *s* (sew.) frunce
shirt [ʃʌrt] *s* camisa; camiseta (*ropa interior*); **to keep one's shirt on** (slang) quedarse sereno, no perder la paciencia; **to lose one's shirt** (slang) perder hasta la camisa
shirtband [ˈʃɪrt,bænd] *s* cuello de camisa, tira del cuello de la camisa de hombre
shirt front *s* pechera de camisa
shirting [ˈʃʌrtɪŋ] *s* tela para camisas de hombre
shirt sleeve *s* manga de camisa; **in shirt sleeves** en camisa, en mangas de camisa
shirt-sleeve [ˈʃʌrt,sliv] *adj* (coll.) sencillo, directo
shirttail [ˈʃʌrt,tel] *s* pañal, faldón
shirtwaist [ˈʃʌrt,west] *s* blusa (*de mujer*)
shivaree [,ʃɪvəˈri] *s* cantaleta, cencerrada
shiver [ˈʃɪvər] *s* tiritón, estremecimiento, temblor; *va* estrellar, hacer astillas; *vn* tiritar, estremecerse; estrellarse, hacerse pedazos
shivery [ˈʃɪvərɪ] *adj* estremecido, trémulo; estremecedor; frío; friolento (*sensible al frío*); quebradizo, saltadizo
shoal [ʃol] *s* bajo, bajío, banco de arena; muchedumbre, gran cantidad; *adj* bajo, poco profundo; *vn* disminuir en profundidad; reunirse en gran número
shoaly [ˈʃolɪ] *adj* bajo, poco profundo, vadoso
shoat [ʃot] *s* cochinillo, gorrino
shock [ʃɑk] *s* choque (*encuentro violento y repentino*); temblor de tierra; (elec.) sacudida; (med. & fig.) choque; (path.) choque (*depresión profunda*); sobresalto (*conmoción nerviosa o mental repentina*); (coll.) parálisis; (agr.) tresnal, hacina; greña (*de pelo*); *va* chocar; sobresaltar (*asustar, alterar profundamente*); dar una sacudida eléctrica a; chocar, escandalizar (*causar extrañeza, enfado, etc.*); (agr.) hacinar; *vn* chocar
shock absorber *s* amortiguador
shock-headed [ˈʃɑk,hedɪd] *adj* greñudo
shocking [ˈʃɑkɪŋ] *adj* chocante, escandalizador
shockproof [ˈʃɑk,pruf] *adj* a prueba de sacudidas
shock therapy o **treatment** *s* shockterapia, convulsoterapia
shock troops *spl* (mil.) tropas de asalto
shock wave *s* (aer.) onda de choque
shod [ʃɑd] *pret & pp de* **shoe**
shoddy [ˈʃɑdɪ] *s* lana mecánica sin fieltrar; caedura de lana; paño burdo de lana; imitación, ostentación vulgar; *adj* (*comp:* **-dier;** *super:*

-diest) hecho de lana desechada; falso, de imitación
shoe [ʃu] *s* bota, botina (*calzado que sube más arriba del tobillo*); zapato (*calzado que no pasa del tobillo*); cubierta (*de un neumático*); zapata (*de un freno; del carruaje eléctrico para sacar la corriente del tercer carril*); regatón (*remate de metal*); **in the shoes of** en el pellejo de; **to die with one's shoes on** morir al pie del cañón; **to put on one's shoes** calzarse; **where the shoe pinches** donde está el busilis; (*pret & pp:* **shod**) *va* calzar; herrar (*un caballo*); poner regatón a; *vn* calzarse
shoebill [ˈʃuˌbɪl] *s* (orn.) picozapato
shoeblack [ˈʃuˌblæk] *s* limpiabotas
shoe blacking *s* betún, bola
shoehorn [ˈʃuˌhɔrn] *s* calzador
shoelace [ˈʃuˌles] *s* cordón de zapato, lazo de zapato
shoe leather *s* cuero para zapatos; correjel
shoemaker [ˈʃuˌmekər] *s* zapatero; zapatero remendón
shoemaking [ˈʃuˌmekɪŋ] *s* zapatería
shoe mender *s* zapatero remendón
shoe polish *s* betún, bola
shoeshine [ˈʃuˌʃaɪn] *s* brillo, lustre; limpiabotas
shoe store *s* zapatería
shoestring [ˈʃuˌstrɪŋ] *s* agujeta, cordón de zapato, lazo de zapato; pequeña cantidad de dinero; **on a shoestring** con muy poco dinero
shoe tree *s* horma
shogun [ˈʃogun] *s* shogún
shogunate [ˈʃogunet] *s* shogunado
shone [ʃon] o [ʃɑn] *pret & pp de* **shine**
shoo [ʃu] *interj* ¡ox! (*para espantar las aves de corral*); *va & vn* oxear
shook [ʃʊk] *pret de* **shake**
shoot [ʃut] *s* renuevo, retoño, pimpollo, vástago; conducto inclinado; tolva (*para agua, granos, carbón, etc.*); tiro; tiro al blanco, certamen de tiradores; lanzamiento (*de un cohete al espacio*) ‖ (*pret & pp:* **shot**) *va* tirar, disparar (*un arma*); herir o matar con arma de fuego, herir o matar con arma arrojadiza; fusilar (*ejecutar con descarga de fusilería*); fotografiar; rodar, filmar; echar (*los dados*); descargar, verter, vaciar de golpe; medir la altura de (*p.ej., el Sol*); **to shoot craps** jugar a los dados; **to shoot down** derribar (*un avión*); **to shoot the rapids** bajar por los rápidos, salvar los rápidos; **to shoot to death** matar a tiros; **to shoot trouble** buscar desperfectos, localizar averías; **to shoot up** (slang) destrozar echando balas a diestra y siniestra ‖ *vn* tirar; nacer, brotar, germinar; lanzarse, precipitarse, moverse rápidamente; punzar (*dícese de un dolor, una llaga, etc.*); **to shoot at** tirar a; (coll.) hacer tiro a (*desear, ambicionar*); **to shoot up** nacer, brotar; moverse rápidamente hacia arriba
shooter [ˈʃutər] *s* tirador; (coll.) arma de fuego, revólver
shooting [ˈʃutɪŋ] *s* tiro; caza con escopeta; fusilería; cañoneo; rodaje (*de un cine o film*)
shooting box *s* (Brit.) pabellón de caza
shooting gallery *s* galería de tiro al blanco, galería de tirar al blanco
shooting match *s* certamen de tiro al blanco; (slang) totalidad, conjunto, todo
shooting pain *s* punzada
shooting season *s* tiempo de caza
shooting star *s* estrella fugaz, estrella filante; (bot.) sarapico
shooting war *s* guerra verdadera
shop [ʃɑp] *s* tienda; taller (*oficina de trabajo manual*); **to set up shop** abrir tienda; emprender un negocio; **to shut up shop** cerrar, alzar o levantar tienda; desistir de una empresa; **to talk shop** hablar de su oficio, hablar del propio trabajo (*fuera de tiempo*); (*pret & pp:* **shopped;** *ger:* **shopping**) *vn* ir de compras, ir de tiendas; **to go shopping** ir de compras, ir de tiendas; **to send shopping** mandar a la compra; **to shop around** ir de tienda en tienda buscando gangas
shopgirl [ˈʃɑpˌgʌrl] *s* muchacha de tienda, dependienta
shopkeeper [ˈʃɑpˌkipər] *s* tendero
shoplifter [ˈʃɑpˌlɪftər] *s* ratero de tiendas, mechera
shoplifting [ˈʃɑpˌlɪftɪŋ] *s* ratería en las tiendas (*por parte de personas que se fingen parroquianos*)
shopman [ˈʃɑpmən] *s* (*pl:* **-men**) tendero; vendedor, mancebo de tienda
shopper [ˈʃɑpər] *s* comprador
shopping center *s* agrupación de tiendas, con parque para automóviles
shopping district *s* barrio comercial
shopwalker [ˈʃɑpˌwɔkər] *s* (Brit.) vigilante de almacén
shopwindow [ˈʃɑpˌwɪndo] *s* escaparate; vidriera (Am.)
shopwork [ˈʃɑpˌwʌrk] *s* trabajo de taller
shopworn [ˈʃɑpˌworn] *adj* desgastado con el trajín de la tienda
shore [ʃor] *s* orilla, ribera; costa, playa; (min.) entibo, ademe; (naut.) escora; **in shore** muy cerca de la tierra; **off shore** a lo largo de la costa; **on shore** en tierra; **shores** *spl* (poet.) clima, región; *va* apuntalar; (min.) entibar; (naut.) escorar
shore dinner *s* comida de mariscos
shore leave *s* (naut.) permiso para ir a tierra
shoreless [ˈʃorlɪs] *adj* sin costa; ilimitado
shore line *s* línea de la playa; línea de barcos costeros
shore patrol *s* (naut.) patrulla en tierra
shoreward [ˈʃorwərd] *adj & adv* hacia la playa
shoring [ˈʃorɪŋ] *s* apuntalamiento; puntales
shorn [ʃorn] *adj* esquilado; mocho, pelado; **shorn of** privado de, despojado de; *pp de* **shear**
short [ʃɔrt] *adj* corto (*en espacio, tiempo y cantidad*); breve (*en tiempo*); bajo (*de cuerpo*); poco (*tiempo*); (fig.) corto, sucinto, lacónico; brusco, seco; friable, quebradizo; (com.) que vende sin posesión; (phonet.) breve; **for short** para abreviar, para ser más breve; **in a short time** en breve, dentro de poco; **in short** en fin; **in short order** prontamente; **on short notice** con poco tiempo de aviso; **to be short of** estar escaso de; no responder a; estar lejos de; **short of breath** corto de resuello ‖ *adv* brevemente; sucintamente, lacónicamente; bruscamente; corto; (com.) sin posesión; **to cut short** interrumpir bruscamente; acabar bruscamente; **to fall short** ser insuficiente; **to fall short of** no alcanzar, no llegar a; **to run short** ser insuficiente; **to run short of** acabársele a uno, p.ej., **I am running short of gasoline** se me acaba la gasolina; **to sell short** (com.) vender al descubierto; **to stop short** parar de repente ‖ *s* (mov.) cortometraje, cinta de corto metraje; (com.) persona que vende al descubierto; (com.) venta al descubierto; (com.) valores vendidos al descubierto; (elec.) cortocircuito; **shorts** *spl* calzones cortos; calzoncillos; mezcla de salvado y harina basta ‖ *va* (elec.) poner en cortocircuito ‖ *vn* (elec.) ponerse en cortocircuito
shortage [ˈʃɔrtɪdʒ] *s* déficit; escasez, carestía, falta
shortbread [ˈʃɔrtˌbrɛd] *s* torta dulce y friable hecha con manteca
shortcake [ˈʃɔrtˌkek] *s* torta de frutas
short-change [ˌʃɔrtˈtʃendʒ] *va* (coll.) no devolver la vuelta debida a; (coll.) estafar, engañar
short circuit *s* (elec.) cortocircuito
short-circuit [ˌʃɔrtˈsʌrkɪt] *va* (elec.) cortocircuitar; *vn* (elec.) cortocircuitarse
shortcoming [ˈʃɔrtˌkʌmɪŋ] *s* defecto, desperfecto
short-commons [ˈʃɔrtˈkɑmənz] *spl* ración escasa, comida insuficiente
short cut *s* atajo; (fig.) atajo
shorten [ˈʃɔrtən] *va* acortar; hacer más friable con grasa; *vn* acortarse
shortening [ˈʃɔrtənɪŋ] o [ˈʃɔrtnɪŋ] *s* acortamiento; grasa para hacer la pastelería más friable
shorthand [ˈʃɔrtˌhænd] *s* taquigrafía; **to take shorthand** escribir al dictado; *adj* taquigráfico
short-handed [ˈʃɔrtˈhændɪd] *adj* escaso de mano de obra, escaso de ayudantes
shorthand-typist [ˈʃɔrtˌhændˈtaɪpɪst] *s* taquimecanógrafo, taquimeca
shorthorn [ˈʃɔrtˌhɔrn] *s* ganado vacuno de cuernos cortos

shortish [ˈʃɔrtɪʃ] *adj* algo corto, algo pequeño
short-legged [ˈʃɔrtˌlɛgɪd] o [ˈʃɔrtˌlɛgd] *adj* de piernas cortas
short-lived [ˈʃɔrtˈlaɪvd] o [ˈʃɔrtˈlɪvd] *adj* de breve vida, de breve duración
shortly [ˈʃɔrtlɪ] *adv* luego, en breve; en pocas palabras; descortésmente; **shortly after** poco tiempo después; **shortly after** + *ger* a poco de + *inf*
short money *s* (com.) dinero prestado a corto plazo
shortness [ˈʃɔrtnɪs] *s* cortedad, brevedad; escasez, insuficiencia; friabilidad
short-range [ˈʃɔrtˌrendʒ] *adj* de poco alcance
short sale *s* (com.) venta al descubierto, venta a plazo
short shrift *s* tiempo muy breve para confesarse; breve tregua; **to make short shrift of** despachar de prisa, enviar noramala
short-sighted [ˈʃɔrtˈsaɪtɪd] *adj* miope, corto de vista; falto de perspicacia, falto de previsión
shortstop [ˈʃɔrtˌstɑp] *s* (baseball) medio (*jugador que está entre la segunda y tercera bases*); guardabosque, torpedero (Am.)
short story *s* cuento
short suit *s* (cards) fallo
short-tempered [ˈʃɔrtˈtɛmpərd] *adj* de mal genio
short-term [ˈʃɔrtˌtʌrm] *adj* (com.) a corto plazo
short ton *s* tonelada corta o menor (*2000 libras o 907,2 kilogramos*)
short-waisted [ˈʃɔrtˈwestɪd] *adj* corto de talle
short wave *s* (rad.) onda corta
short-wave [ˈʃɔrtˌwev] *adj* (rad.) de onda corta
short-winded [ˈʃɔrtˈwɪndɪd] *adj* corto de resuello
short-witted [ˈʃɔrtˈwɪtɪd] *adj* corto de alcances
shot [ʃɑt] *s* tiro, disparo; balazo (*golpe de bala y herida*); alcance (*distancia*); golpe, tirada, jugada (*en ciertos juegos*); lanzamiento (*de un cohete al espacio*); (min.) barreno; (phot.) instantánea, fotografía; escote (*parte que hay que pagar*); tentativa, conjetura; (sport) pesa (*bola de metal muy pesada*); (slang) dosis, jeringazo, trago; (fig.) tiro (*tirador; indirecta desfavorable contra una persona*); perdigones (*granos de plomo*); munición; **like a shot** como una bala; **long shot** esfuerzo por hacer algo muy difícil; **not by a long shot** ni con mucho, ni por pienso; **to be a good shot** ser un buen tiro, tener buena puntería; **to put the shot** (sport) tirar la pesa; **to start like a shot** salir disparado; **to take a shot at** disparar un tiro a; hacer una tentativa de; **within pistol shot** a tiro de pistola; *adj* tornasolado; **shot through with** cargado de; (*pret & pp:* **shotted;** *ger:* **shotting**) *va* cargar con perdigones, cargar con munición; tornasolar (*un tejido*); *pret & pp de* **shoot**
shote [ʃot] s var. de **shoat**
shotgun [ˈʃɑtˌgʌn] *s* escopeta
shot-put [ˈʃɑtˌpʊt] *s* (sport) tiro de la pesa
should [ʃʊd] *v aux* se emplea para formar (1) el condicional presente, p.ej., **if I should wait for him, I should miss the train** si yo le esperase, perdería el tren; (2) el condicional pasado, p.ej., **if I had waited for him, I should have missed the train** si yo le hubiese esperado, habría perdido el tren; y (3) el modo potencial, p.ej., **he should go at once** debiera salir en seguida; **he should have gone at once** debiera haber salido en seguida
shoulder [ˈʃoldər] *s* hombro; brazuelo (*de res muerta*); (print.) hombro; saliente (*de un bastión; de un camino*); hombrera (*de una prenda de vestir*); **across the shoulder** en bandolera; **on the shoulders of** a hombros de; **straight from the shoulder** con toda franqueza; **to have broad shoulders** tener buenas espaldas; **to put one's shoulders to the wheel** arrimar el hombro; **to square one's shoulders** enderezar los hombros, cuadrarse; **to turn a cold shoulder to** volver las espaldas a, negarse al trato de; **shoulder to shoulder** hombro a hombro; *va* llevar a hombros, cargar sobre los hombros, echar sobre las espaldas; cargar con (*el fusil*); tomar sobre sí, hacerse responsable de; aceptar con resignación; empujar con los hombros para abrirse paso; **shoulder arms** (mil.) armas al hombro
shoulder blade *s* (anat.) escápula, omóplato
shoulder knot *s* dragona
shoulder padding *s* hombrera
shoulder strap *s* (mil.) charretera; presilla (*p.ej., de ropa interior*)
shouldn't [ˈʃʊdənt] contracción de **should not**
shout [ʃaʊt] *s* voz, grito; alboroto, gritería; *va* vocear, gritar; **to shout down** hacer sentar a gritos, hacer callar haciendo mucho alboroto; *vn* dar voces, gritar; alborotar
shove [ʃʌv] *s* empujón; *va* empujar; *vn* dar empujones, avanzar a empujones; **to shove off** alejarse de la costa; (slang) salir, ponerse en marcha
shovel [ˈʃʌvəl] *s* pala; palada (*cantidad que se recoge en una pala de una vez*); sombrero de teja; (*pret & pp:* **-eled** o **-elled;** *ger:* **-eling** o **-elling**) *va* traspalar; construir con pala; espalar (*p.ej., la nieve*); abrir con pala; limpiar con pala; echar en grandes cantidades; *vn* trabajar con pala
shovelboard [ˈʃʌvəlˌbord] *s* var. de **shuffleboard**
shoveler o **shoveller** [ˈʃʌvələr] *s* paleador; (orn.) espátula; (orn.) pato cuchareta, ánade cucharetero (*Spatula clypeata*)
shovelful [ˈʃʌvəlfʊl] *s* palada
shovel hat *s* sombrero de teja
show [ʃo] *s* exhibición, exposición, muestra; espectáculo; (coll.) función (*en el teatro*); sesión (*cada representación de un drama o película*); ostentación; falsa apariencia; prueba, demostración; indicación, signo, señal; apariencia, exterior; alarde (*p.ej., de confianza*); (coll.) ocasión, oportunidad; (slang) equipo, apresto; (coll.) tercer puesto en una carrera; espectáculo ridículo; hazmerreír; **to be the whole show** (coll.) ser el todo; **to make a show of** hacer gala de; **to steal the show from** robar la obra a (*otro actor*) ‖ (*pret:* **showed;** *pp:* **shown** o **showed**) *va* mostrar, enseñar; probar, demostrar; marcar (*p.ej., la hora*); acompañar (*p.ej., a la puerta*); **to show off** hacer alarde de; **to show up** hacer subir; (coll.) desenmascarar ‖ *vn* mostrarse, aparecer, asomar; salir (*p.ej., la combinación*); (coll.) llegar en tercer puesto en una carrera; (theat.) actuar; (theat.) representarse; **to show off** alardear, fachendear; **to show up** destacarse; (coll.) presentarse, dejarse ver
show bill *s* cartel
show biz [bɪz] *s* (slang) var. de **show business**
showboat [ˈʃoˌbot] *s* barco teatro, buque teatro
showbread [ˈʃoˌbrɛd] *s* var. de **shewbread**
show business *s* comercio de los espectáculos; ocupación de actor, empresario, etc.
showcase [ˈʃoˌkes] *s* vitrina, vitrina de exposición
showdown [ˈʃoˌdaʊn] *s* cartas boca arriba; (coll.) revelación forzosa, arreglo terminante
shower [ˈʃaʊər] *s* ducha; aguacero, chaparrón; reunión o fiesta para obsequiar con regalos a una novia próxima a casarse; (fig.) rociada (*p.ej., de balas*); *va* regar; **to shower with favors** colmar de favores; *vn* llover
shower bath *s* ducha, baño de ducha
showery [ˈʃaʊərɪ] *adj* chubascoso, lluvioso
show girl *s* (theat.) corista
showiness [ˈʃo·ɪnɪs] *s* vistosidad, aparatosidad; cursería
showing [ˈʃo·ɪŋ] *s* demostración; exhibición
showman [ˈʃomən] *s* (*pl:* **-men**) director de espectáculos, empresario de teatro, empresario de circo
showmanship [ˈʃomənʃɪp] *s* habilidad para presentar espectáculos; teatralidad
show-off [ˈʃoˌɔf] o [ˈʃoˌɑf] *s* ostentación; (coll.) pinturero, persona muy ostentosa
show of hands *s* votación por manos levantadas
show of strength *s* demostración de fuerza, despliegue de poder

showpiece ['ʃo,pis] *s* objeto expuesto a la vista; objeto de arte sobresaliente
show place *s* sitio o edificio que se exhibe al público por su belleza o lujo
showroom ['ʃo,rum] o ['ʃo,rʊm] *s* sala de muestras, sala de exhibición
show window *s* escaparate de tienda; vidriera (Am.)
showy ['ʃo·ɪ] *adj* (*comp:* **-ier;** *super:* **-iest**) vistoso, ostentoso, aparatoso; cursi
shrank [ʃræŋk] *pret de* **shrink**
shrapnel ['ʃræpnəl] *s* granada de metralla; metralla
shred [ʃrɛd] *s* triza, jirón, tira; pizca, fragmento; **to be in shreds** estar hecho trizas, estar raído, estar andrajoso; **to tear to shreds** hacer trizas; (*pret & pp:* **shredded** o **shred;** *ger:* **shredding**) *va* hacer trizas, hacer tiras, desmenuzar; deshilar (*carne*)
shrew [ʃru] *s* arpía, mujer regañona, fierecilla; (zool.) musaraña
shrewd [ʃrud] *adj* astuto; vivo, listo, despierto
shrewdness ['ʃrudnɪs] *s* astucia; viveza
shrewish ['ʃruɪʃ] *adj* regañona, de mal genio
shrewmouse ['ʃru,maʊs] *s* (*pl:* **-mice** [,maɪs]) (zool.) musaraña
shriek [ʃrik] *s* chillido, grito agudo; risotada chillona; *vn* chillar
shrievalty ['ʃrivəltɪ] *s* (*pl:* **-ties**) cargo y jurisdicción de sheriff
shrift [ʃrɪft] *s* confesión
shrike [ʃraɪk] *s* (orn.) alcaudón, verdugo
shrill [ʃrɪl] *adj* chillón, agudo y penetrante; *s* chillido; *vn* chillar
shrilly ['ʃrɪllɪ] *adv* de manera chillona, con un ruido agudo y penetrante
shrimp [ʃrɪmp] *s* (zool.) camarón; (zool.) crustáceo del género *Crangon;* (fig.) renacuajo (*hombrecillo; persona muy pequeña*)
shrimpfish ['ʃrɪmp,fɪʃ] *s* (ichth.) centrisco, chocha de mar
shrine [ʃraɪn] *s* relicario; sepulcro de santo; santuario; lugar sagrado (*por ciertos recuerdos, por su historia, etc.*); *va* guardar en un relicario
shrink [ʃrɪŋk] *s* contracción, encogimiento; (*pret:* **shrank** o **shrunk;** *pp:* **shrunk** o **shrunken**) *va* contraer, encoger; **to shrink on** montar en caliente, zunchar en caliente; *vn* contraerse, encogerse; moverse hacia atrás; rehuirse, acobardarse, retirarse
shrinkable ['ʃrɪŋkəbəl] *adj* contráctil, que se puede contraer o encoger
shrinkage ['ʃrɪŋkɪdʒ] *s* contracción, encogimiento; disminución, reducción; merma, pérdida
shrive [ʃraɪv] (*pret:* **shrove** o **shrived;** *pp:* **shriven** o **shrived**) *va* imponer la penitencia a, dar la absolución a; confesar; oír en confesión; **to shrive oneself** confesarse y hacer penitencia; *vn* confesarse; oír al penitente
shrivel ['ʃrɪvəl] (*pret & pp:* **-eled** o **-elled;** *ger:* **-eling** o **-elling**) *va* arrugar, marchitar, fruncir; *vn* arrugarse, marchitarse, fruncirse; **to shrivel up** avellanarse; consumirse
shriven ['ʃrɪvən] *pp de* **shrive**
shroud [ʃraʊd] *s* mortaja, sudario; cubierta, velo; cuerda de suspensión (*del paracaídas*); (naut.) obenque; *va* amortajar; cubrir, velar
shroud line *s* cuerda de suspensión (*del paracaídas*)
shrove [ʃrov] *pret de* **shrive**
Shrove Monday *s* lunes de carnaval
Shrove Sunday *s* domingo de carnaval
Shrovetide ['ʃrov,taɪd] *s* carnestolendas
Shrove Tuesday *s* martes de carnaval
shrub [ʃrʌb] *s* (bot.) arbusto; ponche (*bebida*)
shrubbery ['ʃrʌbərɪ] *s* (*pl:* **-ies**) arbustos; plantío de arbustos
shrubby ['ʃrʌbɪ] *adj* (*comp:* **-bier;** *super:* **-biest**) arbustivo
shrug [ʃrʌg] *s* encogimiento de hombros; (*pret & pp:* **shrugged;** *ger:* **shrugging**) *va* contraer; **to shrug one's shoulders** encogerse de hombros; *vn* encogerse de hombros
shrunk [ʃrʌŋk] *pret & pp de* **shrink**
shrunken ['ʃrʌŋkən] *adj* mermado, encogido, arrugado, seco; *pp de* **shrink**
sh-sh [ʃʃ] *interj* ¡chitón!
shuck [ʃʌk] *s* cáscara, vaina, hollejo; *va* descascarar, descortezar; quitar la concha a (*una ostra*)
shudder ['ʃʌdər] *s* estremecimiento; *vn* estremecerse
shuffle ['ʃʌfəl] *s* arrastramiento de pies; barajadura (*de naipes*); turno de barajar; movimiento rápido de un lado a otro; evasiva, mala jugada; recomposición; *va* mezclar, mezclar desordenadamente, revolver; arrastrar (*los pies*); barajar (*naipes*); **to shuffle off** deshacerse de; *vn* caminar arrastrando los pies; bailar arrastrando los pies; moverse rápidamente de un lado a otro; barajar; esquivarse por medio de jugarretas; **to shuffle along** ir arrastrando los pies; ir tirando; **to shuffle off** irse arrastrando los pies
shuffleboard ['ʃʌfəl,bord] *s* juego de tejo; mesa de tejo
shun [ʃʌn] (*pret & pp:* **shunned;** *ger:* **shunning**) *va* esquivar, evitar, apartarse de
shunt [ʃʌnt] *s* desviación; (elec.) derivación; (rail.) aguja, cambio de vía; *va* desviar; apartar, deshacerse de; (rail.) desviar; (elec.) poner en derivación
shunt-wound ['ʃʌnt,waʊnd] *adj* (elec.) arrollado en derivación
shut [ʃʌt] *adj* cerrado; (phonet.) cerrado; (*pret & pp:* **shut;** *ger:* **shutting**) *va* cerrar, tapar; **to shut down** cerrar (*p.ej., una fábrica*); **to shut in** encerrar; **to shut off** cortar (*electricidad, gas, agua*); **to shut out** impedir la entrada de, cerrar la puerta a; (sport) no permitir a (*el equipo enemigo*) ganar tantos; **to shut up** cerrar bien, tapar; acorralar, aprisionar; (coll.) hacer callar; **to shut up shop** cerrar, alzar o levantar tienda; desistir de una empresa; *vn* cerrarse; **to shut down** parar; **to shut down on** o **upon** (coll.) reprimir, suprimir; **to shut up** (coll.) callarse la boca
shut-down ['ʃʌt,daʊn] *s* cierre, cesación de trabajo
shut-in ['ʃʌt,ɪn] *adj* recluso; (psychopath.) aislado; *s* recluso, valetudinario que vive encerrado en su casa o el hospital
shut-out ['ʃʌt,aʊt] *s* cierre para impedir la entrada; (sport) triunfo en que el contrario no gana un solo tanto
shutter ['ʃʌtər] *s* cerrador; persiana, celosía; contraventana (*para el exterior de las vidrieras*); cierre metálico (*de escaparate*); (phot.) obturador
shuttle ['ʃʌtəl] *s* lanzadera; *vn* ir y venir acompasadamente; hacer viajes cortos de ida y vuelta
shuttlecock ['ʃʌtəl,kɑk] *s* volante
shuttle service *s* servicio de ida y vuelta entre dos estaciones cercanas
shuttle train *s* tren que hace viajes cortos de ida y vuelta
shy [ʃaɪ] *adj* (*comp:* **shyer** *o* **shier;** *super:* **shyest** o **shiest**) tímido, recatado, arisco; asustadizo; cauteloso, prudente; escaso, pobre; (slang) adeudado; **to be shy a dollar** (slang) faltarle a uno un dólar; **to be shy on** (slang) estar escaso de; **to fight shy of** evitar, tratar de evitar; *s* (*pl:* **shies**) echada; respingo; (*pret & pp:* **shied**) *va* arrojar, lanzar; *vn* esquivarse, hacerse a un lado; respingar, espantarse; **to shy at** retroceder ante, respingar al ver, espantarse con; **to shy away** alejarse asustado
shyly ['ʃaɪlɪ] *adv* tímidamente
shyness ['ʃaɪnɪs] *s* timidez, recato; miedo; cautela, prudencia, reserva
shyster ['ʃaɪstər] *s* (coll.) abogado trampista
S.I. abr. de **Staten Island**
si [si] *s* (mus.) si
Siam [saɪ'æm] o ['saɪæm] *s* Siam
Siamese [,saɪə'miz] *adj* siamés; *s* (*pl:* **-mese**) siamés
Siamese twins *spl* hermanos siameses
sib [sɪb] *adj* emparentado; *s* parentela; pariente; hermano, hermana
Siberia [saɪ'bɪrɪə] *s* Siberia
Siberian [saɪ'bɪrɪən] *adj & s* siberiano
Siberian sable *s* (zool.) marta cebellina
sibilance ['sɪbɪləns] o **sibilancy** ['sɪbɪlənsɪ] *s* calidad sibilante

sibilant ['sɪbɪlənt] *adj* sibilante; *s* sonido sibilante; letra sibilante
sibilate ['sɪbɪlet] *vn* silbar
sibling ['sɪblɪŋ] *s* hermano, hermana
sibyl ['sɪbɪl] *s* sibila
sibylline ['sɪbɪlaɪn] o ['sɪbɪlɪn] *adj* sibilino; (fig.) sibilino
Sibylline Books *spl* Libros sibilinos
sic [sɪk] *va* (*pret & pp:* **sicked;** *ger:* **sicking**) atacar; azuzar, abijar (*a un perro*)
Sicanian [sɪ'kenɪən] *adj* sicano
siccative ['sɪkətɪv] *adj & s* secante
Sicilian [sɪ'sɪljən] *adj & s* siciliano
Sicilian Vespers *spl* (hist.) Vísperas sicilianas
Sicily ['sɪsɪlɪ] *s* Sicilia
sick [sɪk] *adj* enfermo; nauseado; pálido, demacrado; cansado, agotado; **the sick** los enfermos; **to be sick of** estar cansado de, estar harto de; **to be sick at one's stomach** tener náuseas; **to take sick** caer enfermo; **sick and tired of** (coll.) harto y cansado de; **sick at heart** afligido de corazón, angustiado; *va* var. de **sic**
sick bay *s* (naut.) enfermería
sickbed ['sɪk,bɛd] *s* lecho de enfermo
sick call *s* visita del médico o clérigo a un enfermo; (mil.) toque de visita médica
sicken ['sɪkən] *va & vn* enfermar
sickening ['sɪkənɪŋ] *adj* nauseabundo; achacoso; repelente
sick headache *s* (path.) jaqueca con náuseas
sickish ['sɪkɪʃ] *adj* enfermucho; nauseabundo
sickle ['sɪkəl] *s* hoz
sick leave *s* licencia por enfermo
sickly ['sɪklɪ] *adj* (*comp:* **-lier;** *super:* **-liest**) enfermizo; pálido, demacrado; apestado
Sick Man of Europe, the el enfermo de Europa (*Turquía*)
sickness ['sɪknɪs] *s* enfermedad; náusea
sick nurse *s* enfermera
sickroom ['sɪk,rum] o ['sɪk,rʊm] *s* cuarto del enfermo
side [saɪd] *s* lado; cara (*de un sólido; de un disco de fonógrafo*); falda (*de una colina*); orilla, margen; facción, partido; campo (*en algún desafío*); bando (*en el bridge*); (geom.) lado; (naut.) costado; **by the side of** al lado de; **on all sides** por todos lados, por todas partes; **on the side** (slang) por añadidura; **the other side of the picture** el revés de la medalla; **to split one's sides** desternillarse de risa; **to take sides** tomar partido; **to take sides with** tomar el partido de, ponerse al lado de; **side by side** juntos, lado a lado; *adj* lateral; de lado; indirecto, oblicuo; secundario; suplementario; *va* echar a un lado; poner costados a; *vn* tomar partido; **to side with** declararse por
side arms *spl* armas de cinto
sidebands ['saɪd,bændz] *spl* (rad.) bandas laterales
sideboard ['saɪd,bord] *s* aparador; adral, tablar (*de un carro*)
sideburns ['saɪd,bʌrnz] *spl* patillas
sidecar ['saɪd,kɑr] *s* cochecito lateral de una motocicleta
side chain *s* (chem.) cadena lateral
side dish *s* plato de entrada
side door *s* puerta lateral; puerta excusada o falsa
side effect *s* (med.) efecto secundario perjudicial de ciertos medicamentos
side face *s* perfil
side glance *s* mirada de soslayo, mirada de través
side issue *s* cuestión secundaria
side-kick ['saɪd,kɪk] *s* (slang) a látere
side light *s* luz lateral; detalle incidental, información incidente
side line *s* línea lateral; negocio accesorio, actividad suplementaria; (tennis) línea de lado; **side lines** *spl* (sport) sitio fuera de las líneas; **on the side lines** sin participar, sin tomar parte
sidelock ['saɪd,lɑk] *s* tufo
sidelong ['saɪd,lɔŋ] o ['saɪd,lɑŋ] *adj* lateral; *adv* lateralmente
side meat *s* tocino, tocino salado
sidenote ['saɪd,not] *s* (print.) ladillo
sidepiece ['saɪd,pis] *s* pieza lateral, parte lateral
sidereal [saɪ'dɪrɪəl] *adj* sidéreo
siderite ['sɪdəraɪt] *s* (mineral.) siderosa, siderita
siderosis [,sɪdə'rosɪs] *s* (path.) siderosis
siderurgical [,sɪdər'ʌrdʒɪkəl] *adj* siderúrgico
siderurgy ['sɪdər,ʌrdʒɪ] *s* siderurgia
sidesaddle ['saɪd,sædəl] *s* sillón, silla de mujer; *adv* a asentadillas, a mujeriegas
side show *s* feria, espectáculo de atracciones, espectáculo del circo; asunto de importancia secundaria
sideslip ['saɪd,slɪp] *s* resbalamiento lateral (*de un neumático*); deslizamiento lateral (*de un avión*); (*pret & pp:* **-slipped;** *ger:* **-slipping**) *vn* resbalar hacia un lado; deslizar hacia un lado
sidesplitting ['saɪd,splɪtɪŋ] *adj* desternillante
side step *s* paso hacia un lado; escalón para subir a un carruaje, embarcación, etc.; (box.) esquivada lateral
side-step ['saɪd,stɛp] (*pret & pp:* **-stepped;** *ger:* **-stepping**) *va* evitar, evadir, esquivar; *vn* dar un paso hacia un lado, hacerse a un lado, esquivarse; retirarse
sideswipe ['saɪd,swaɪp] *s* (coll.) rozadura, tocamiento oblicuo; *va* (coll.) rozar, tocar oblicuamente
sidetrack ['saɪd,træk] *s* (rail.) vía muerta, desviadero, apartadero; *va* desviar (*un tren*); echar a un lado, hacer desviar
side view *s* vista de perfil, vista de lado
sidewalk ['saɪd,wɔk] *s* acera; banqueta, vereda (Am.)
sidewalk café *s* terraza (*café en la acera*)
sidewall ['saɪd,wɔl] *s* (aut.) flanco (*de un neumático*)
sideward ['saɪdwərd] *adj* oblicuo, sesgado; *adv* de lado, hacia un lado
sidewards ['saɪdwərdz] *adv* de lado, hacia un lado
sideway ['saɪd,we] *s* vereda; callejuela; acera; *adj* oblicuo, sesgado; *adv* de lado, oblicuamente; al través; hacia un lado
sideways ['saɪd,wez] *adj* oblicuo, sesgado; *adv* de lado, oblicuamente; al través; hacia un lado
side-wheel ['saɪd,hwil] *adj* de ruedas laterales (*dícese de un barco de vapor*)
side-wheeler ['saɪd,hwilər] *s* (coll.) vapor de ruedas laterales
side whiskers *spl* patillas
sidewinder ['saɪd,waɪndər] *s* (zool.) cerasta, víbora cornuda; (slang) puñetazo fuerte dado de lado; (mil.) proyectil antiaéreo de propulsante sólido (*aire-aire*)
sidewise ['saɪd,waɪz] *adj* oblicuo, sesgado; *adv* de lado, oblicuamente, sesgadamente; al través; hacia un lado
siding ['saɪdɪŋ] *s* (rail.) vía muerta, desviadero, apartadero; entablado de los costados
sidle ['saɪdəl] *vn* ir de lado, moverse de lado y furtivamente; **to sidle up** acercarse de lado para no ser visto
Sidonian [saɪ'donɪən] *adj & s* sidonio
siege [sidʒ] *s* sitio, cerco; (coll.) paso interminable; **to lay siege to** (mil.) poner sitio o cerco a; (fig.) asediar (*p.ej., al corazón de una mujer*); **to raise the siege** (mil.) alzar el cerco, levantar el sitio
siege artillery *s* artillería de sitio
Siege Perilous *s* Silla peligrosa (*en la mesa redonda del rey Artús*)
Siegfried ['sigfrid] *s* Sigfrido
Sienese [,siə'niz] *adj* sienés; *s* (*pl:* **-ese**) sienés
sienna [sɪ'ɛnə] *s* siena, tierra de siena
sierra [sɪ'ɛrə] *s* sierra (*cadena de montes y peñascos cortados*); (ichth.) pintada, sierra
siesta [sɪ'ɛstə] *s* siesta; *vn* sestear
Sieva bean ['sivə] *s* (bot.) frijol iztagapa; chilipuca (*semilla*)
sieve [sɪv] *s* cedazo, tamiz; persona que no sabe guardar secretos; *va* cerner, tamizar
sieve cell *s* (bot.) célula cribosa
sieve disk o **plate** *s* (bot.) placa acribillada
sieve tissue *s* (bot.) tejido criboso
sieve tube o **vessel** *s* (bot.) tubo criboso
sift [sɪft] *va* cerner, cribar; escudriñar, examinar; *vn* servirse de un cedazo; caer de un cedazo, caer como de un cedazo

sifter ['sɪftər] *s* cribador; cedazo, criba, tamiz
sigh [saɪ] *s* suspiro; **to breathe a sigh of relief** respirar, cobrar aliento; *va* decir con suspiros; lamentar; *vn* suspirar; **to sigh for** suspirar por
sight [saɪt] *s* vista, visión; cosa digna de verse; (coll.) espantajo; (coll.) horror, atrocidad; mira (*de arma de fuego, telescopio, etc.*); opinión, juicio; (coll.) gran cantidad, montón; (com.) vista, p.ej., **thirty days sight** treinta días vista; **at first sight** al primer contacto; **at sight** a primera vista; a libro abierto (*dícese de una traducción*); (com.) a la vista; **in sight** visible; **in sight of** a la vista de; **on sight** a primera vista; **out of sight** fuera del alcance de la vista; por las nubes (*dícese de los precios*); **out of sight of** sin ver; sin ser visto por; **to catch sight of** avistar, alcanzar a ver; **to come into sight** aparecer; asomar; **to heave in sight** (naut.) aparecer en el horizonte; **to keep out of sight** no dejar ver; no dejarse ver; **to know by sight** conocer de vista; **to lose sight of** perder de vista; **to not be able to stand the sight of** no poder ver ni en pintura; **to see the sights** visitar los puntos de interés; **sight unseen** sin haberlo visto; *va* avistar, alcanzar con la vista; descubrir con un instrumento óptico, localizar con la vista por medio de un instrumento; *vn* apuntar con una mira; dirigir una visual
sight draft *s* (com.) giro a la vista, letra a la vista
sightless ['saɪtlɪs] *adj* ciego; invisible
sightly ['saɪtlɪ] *adj* (*comp:* **-lier;** *super:* **-liest**) vistoso, hermoso
sight-read ['saɪt,rid] (*pret & pp:* **-read** [,rɛd]) *va* leer a libro abierto; (mus.) ejecutar a la primera lectura; *vn* leer a libro abierto; (mus.) repentizar
sight reader *s* lector a libro abierto; (mus.) repentista
sight reading *s* lectura a libro abierto (*de un idioma extranjero*); (mus.) ejecución a la primera lectura
sightseeing ['saɪt,siɪŋ] *s* excursionismo, turismo, visita de puntos de interés; **to go sightseeing** ir a ver los puntos de interés
sightseeing bus *s* autocar, ómnibus de excursión
sightseer ['saɪt,siər] *s* excursionista, turista
sigma ['sɪgmə] *s* sigma
sigmoid ['sɪgmɔɪd] *adj* sigmoideo
sign [saɪn] *s* signo (*p.ej., de la lluvia*); (astr., math., med., mus. & print.) signo; señal, marca, huella, vestigio; letrero, muestra; **to show signs of** dar muestras de, tener trazas de; **sign of the cross** señal de la cruz; *va* firmar; contratar, hacer firmar; ceder, traspasar mediante escritura; **to sign away** u **over** firmar el traspaso de, firmar la cesión de; **to sign up** ajustar (*para un trabajo o servicio*); *vn* firmar; **to sign off** (rad.) terminar la transmisión; **to sign up** (coll.) firmar el contrato
signal ['sɪgnəl] *s* señal; (rad.) señal; *adj* señalado, notable; (*pret & pp:* **-naled** o **-nalled;** *ger:* **-naling** o **-nalling**) *va* señalar, hacer saber por medio de señales; *vn* hacer señales
signal code *s* código de señales
signal corps *s* (mil.) cuerpo de señales
signal flag *s* bandera de señales
signalize ['sɪgnəlaɪz] *va* distinguir, singularizar
signally ['sɪgnəlɪ] *adv* señaladamente, notablemente
signalman ['sɪgnəl,mæn] *s* (*pl:* **-men**) hombre de señal, señalero; (rail.) guardavía, (rail.) semaforista
signal strength *s* (rad.) fuerza de señal
signal tower *s* torre de señales
signatory ['sɪgnə,torɪ] *adj* signatario, firmante; *s* (*pl:* **-ries**) signatario, firmante
signature ['sɪgnətʃər] *s* firma; (print.) signatura; (print.) pliego con signatura; **over one's signature** bajo su firma
signboard ['saɪn,bord] *s* letrero, cartelón, muestra; (fig.) muestra
signer ['saɪnər] *s* firmante, signatario
signet ['sɪgnɪt] *s* sello; signáculo
signet ring *s* sortija de sello, anillo sigilar
significance [sɪg'nɪfɪkəns] *s* significación
significant [sɪg'nɪfɪkənt] *adj* significativo
signification [,sɪgnɪfɪ'keʃən] *s* significación
significative [sɪg'nɪfɪ,ketɪv] *adj* significativo
signify ['sɪgnɪfaɪ] (*pret & pp:* **-fied**) *va & vn* significar
sign language *s* lenguaje de los signos, dactilología
sign manual *s* firma rubricada, firma de propio puño; sello de individualidad
signory ['sinjərɪ] *s* (*pl:* **-ries**) señorío (*mando; dominio feudal*); señoría (*gobierno de ciertas ciudades italianas medievales; república italiana medieval*)
sign painter *s* pintor de muestras
signpost ['saɪn,post] *s* hito, poste de guía
Sikh [sik] *s* sij
silage ['saɪlɪdʒ] *s* ensilaje
silence ['saɪləns] *s* silencio; **in silence** en silencio; *interj* ¡silencio!; *va* acallar, silenciar, imponer silencio a; (mil.) apagar el fuego de; (mil.) apagar (*el fuego del enemigo*)
silencer ['saɪlənsər] *s* silenciero (*persona*); silenciador (*aparato para armas de fuego, motores de explosión, etc.*)
silent ['saɪlənt] *adj* silencioso; (phonet.) mudo
silent movie *s* (coll.) cine mudo
silent partner *s* (com.) socio comanditario
Silenus [saɪ'linəs] *s* (myth.) Sileno
Silesian [sɪ'liʃən] o [saɪ'liʃən] *adj & s* silesiano o silesio
silex ['saɪlɛks] *s* (mineral.) sílex; (chem.) sílice
silhouette [,sɪlu'ɛt] *s* silueta; **in silhouette** en silueta; *va* siluetar
silica ['sɪlɪkə] *s* (chem.) sílice
silicate ['sɪlɪket] o ['sɪlɪkɪt] *s* (chem.) silicato
siliceous [sɪ'lɪʃəs] *adj* silíceo
silicic [sɪ'lɪsɪk] *adj* (chem.) silícico
silicide ['sɪlɪsaɪd] o ['sɪlɪsɪd] *s* (chem.) siliciuro
silicious [sɪ'lɪʃəs] *adj* var. de **siliceous**
silicle ['sɪlɪkəl] *s* (bot.) silícula
silicon ['sɪlɪkən] *s* (chem.) silicio
silicone ['sɪlɪkon] *s* (chem.) silicón
silicosis [,sɪlɪ'kosɪs] *s* (path.) silicosis
silique [sɪ'lik] o ['sɪlɪk] *s* (bot.) silicua
siliquose ['sɪlɪkwos] o **siliquous** ['sɪlɪkwəs] *adj* (bot.) silicuoso
silk [sɪlk] *s* seda; **to hit the silk** (slang) lanzarse en paracaídas; *adj* sedeño
silkaline [,sɪlkə'lin] *s* sedalina
silk-cotton tree ['sɪlk'kɑtən] *s* (bot.) capoquero
silken ['sɪlkən] *adj* sedeño; asedado; vestido de seda
silk hat *s* sombrero de copa
silk-stocking ['sɪlk,stɑkɪŋ] *adj* aristocrático; *s* aristócrata
silkworm ['sɪlk,wʌrm] *s* gusano de seda
silky ['sɪlkɪ] *adj* (*comp:* **-ier;** *super:* **-iest**) sedoso
sill [sɪl] *s* travesaño, solera; umbral (*de puerta*); antepecho (*de ventana*)
sillabub ['sɪləbʌb] *s* postre hecho de nata, huevos, vino y azúcar
silliness ['sɪlɪnɪs] *s* necedad, tontería
silly ['sɪlɪ] *adj* (*comp:* **-lier;** *super:* **-liest**) necio, tonto; (coll.) patidifuso
silo ['saɪlo] *s* (*pl:* **-los**) (agr.) silo; *va* (agr.) asilar
Siloam [sɪ'loəm] o [saɪ'loəm] *s* (Bib.) Siloé
silt [sɪlt] *s* cieno, sedimento; *va* obstruir con cieno, obstruir con sedimentos; *vn* obstruirse con cieno, obstruirse con sedimentos
silty ['sɪltɪ] *adj* (*comp:* **-ier;** *super:* **-iest**) cenagoso, sedimentoso
Silurian [sɪ'lurɪən] *adj & s* (geol.) siluriano o silúrico
silva ['sɪlvə] *s* árboles de un país; tratado sobre los árboles de un país
silvan ['sɪlvən] *adj* var. de **sylvan;** (*cap.*) *s* Silvano
silver ['sɪlvər] *s* (chem.) plata; plata (*moneda o monedas*); plateado (*color*); *adj* plateado; de plata; argentino (*dícese de la voz*); elocuente; *va* platear; azogar (*un espejo*); *vn* platearse
silver age *s* (myth.) edad de plata, siglo de plata

silver fir *s* (bot.) abeto blanco, abeto de hojas de tejo o abeto plateado
silverfish ['sɪlvər,fɪʃ] *s* (ent.) pez de plata; (ichth.) pez de colores
silver foil *s* hoja de plata
silver fox *s* (zool.) zorro plateado
silver gilt *s* plata dorada
silver leaf *s* hoja de plata
silver lining *s* aspecto agradable de una condición desgraciada o triste
silver-mounted ['sɪlvər,maʊntɪd] *adj* montado en plata; adornado de plata
silver nitrate *s* (chem.) nitrato de plata
silver pheasant *s* (orn.) faisán plateado
silver plate *s* plateado; plato de plata; vajilla de plata
silver-plated ['sɪlvər'pletɪd] *adj* argentado, plateado
silver plating *s* plateado, plateadura
silver screen *s* pantalla plateada; (fig.) pantalla (*el cine*)
silversmith ['sɪlvər,smɪθ] *s* platero, orfebre
silver-tongue ['sɪlvər,tʌŋ] *s* (coll.) pico de oro
silver-tongued ['sɪlvər'tʌŋd] *adj* elocuente, con el pico de oro
silverware ['sɪlvər,wɛr] *s* plata, vajilla de plata
silver wedding *s* bodas de plata
silvery ['sɪlvərɪ] *adj* argénteo, argentino
Silvester [sɪl'vɛstər] *s* Silvestre
Simeon ['sɪmɪən] *s* Simeón
simian ['sɪmɪən] *adj* símico; *s* (zool.) simio
similar ['sɪmɪlər] *adj* similar, semejante
similarity [,sɪmɪ'lærɪtɪ] *s* (*pl:* **-ties**) semejanza
simile ['sɪmɪlɪ] *s* (rhet.) símil
similitude [sɪ'mɪlɪtjud] o [sɪ'mɪlɪtud] *s* similitud; símil, comparación; imagen, copia
similor ['sɪmɪlər] *s* similor
simitar ['sɪmɪtər] *s* var. de **scimitar**
simmer ['sɪmər] *va* cocer a fuego lento; *vn* cocer a fuego lento; (fig.) estar a punto de estallar; **to simmer down** (coll.) reducirse lentamente; (coll.) tranquilizarse lentamente
simoleon [sɪ'molɪən] *s* (slang) dólar
Simon ['saɪmən] *s* Simón
simoniacal [,saɪmə'naɪəkəl] *adj* simoníaco
Simoniz ['saɪmənaɪz] *s* (trademark) simonización; *va* simonizar
simon-pure ['saɪmən'pjʊr] *adj* auténtico, puro, genuino, verdadero
simony ['sɪmənɪ] o ['saɪmənɪ] *s* simonía
simoom [sɪ'mum] o **simoon** [sɪ'mun] *s* simún
simp [sɪmp] *s* (slang) bobo, mentecato
simper ['sɪmpər] *s* sonrisa boba; *va* decir con sonrisa boba, decir con bobería; *vn* sonreír bobamente
simple ['sɪmpəl] *adj* simple; *s* simple (*bobo, mentecato; persona mansa e incauta; planta medicinal*); cosa o idea simples; persona de humilde alcurnia; (eccl.) fiesta simple; (pharm.) simple
simple engine *s* máquina de simple expansión
simple equation *s* (alg.) ecuación de primer grado
simple fraction *s* (math.) fracción incompleja
simple-hearted ['sɪmpəl'hɑrtɪd] *adj* inocente, ingenuo
simple interest *s* interés simple
simple machine *s* mecanismo elemental
simple-minded ['sɪmpəl'maɪndɪd] *adj* estúpido, ignorante; candoroso; idiota, imbécil
simpleness ['sɪmpəlnɪs] *s* simplicidad
simple sentence *s* (gram.) oración simple
simple substance *s* (chem.) cuerpo simple (*elemento*)
simpleton ['sɪmpəltən] *s* bobo, mentecato
simplicity [sɪm'plɪsɪtɪ] *s* (*pl:* **-ties**) simplicidad; simpleza (*bobería, necedad*)
simplification [,sɪmplɪfɪ'keʃən] *s* simplificación
simplify ['sɪmplɪfaɪ] (*pret & pp:* **-fied**) *va* simplificar
Simplon tunnel ['sɪmplɑn] *s* túnel del Simplón
simply ['sɪmplɪ] *adv* simplemente, sencillamente; solamente
simulacrum [,sɪmjə'lekrəm] *s* (*pl:* **-cra** [krə] o **-crums**) simulacro
simulate ['sɪmjəlɪt] o ['sɪmjəlet] *adj* simulado; ['sɪmjəlet] *va* simular
simulation [,sɪmjə'leʃən] *s* simulación
simulative ['sɪmjə,letɪv] *adj* simulador
simultaneity [,saɪməltə'niɪtɪ] o [,sɪməltə'niɪtɪ] *s* simultaneidad
simultaneous [,saɪməl'tenɪəs] o [,sɪməl'tenɪəs] *adj* simultáneo
simultaneous equation *s* (alg.) ecuación simultánea
simultaneously [,saɪməl'tenɪəslɪ] o [,sɪməl'tenɪəslɪ] *adv* simultáneamente
sin [sɪn] *s* pecado; (*pret & pp:* **sinned;** *ger:* **sinning**) *vn* pecar
Sinai ['saɪnaɪ] o ['saɪnɪaɪ] *s* el Sinaí (*península*); **Mount Sinai** el monte Sinaí
sinapism ['sɪnəpɪzəm] *s* sinapismo
since [sɪns] *adv* desde entonces, después; **long since** hace mucho tiempo; *prep* desde; después de; **since when?** ¿desde cuándo?; *conj* desde que; después (de) que; ya que, puesto que
sincere [sɪn'sɪr] *adj* sincero
sincerity [sɪn'sɛrɪtɪ] *s* (*pl:* **-ties**) sinceridad
sine [saɪn] *s* (trig.) seno
sinecure ['saɪnɪkjʊr] o ['sɪnɪkjʊr] *s* sinecura
sinecurist ['saɪnɪ,kjʊrɪst] o ['sɪnɪ,kjʊrɪst] *s* sinecurista
sine curve *s* (math.) curva senoidal
sine die ['saɪnɪ'daɪi] (Lat.) hasta nueva orden, indefinidamente
sine qua non ['saɪnɪkwe'nɑn] *s* (Lat.) condición sin la cual no se hará una cosa, condición indispensable
sinew ['sɪnju] *s* tendón; (fig.) fibra, nervio, vigor; (fig.) fuente de energía y vigor
sine wave *s* (phys.) onda senoidal
sinewy ['sɪnjəwɪ] *adj* nervoso, nervudo; fuerte, vigoroso
sinful ['sɪnfəl] *adj* pecador; pecaminoso (*dícese del acto, la intención, etc.*)
sing. abr. de **singular**
sing [sɪŋ] *s* silbido, zumbido (*p.ej., de un proyectil*); canto; cantata; (*pret:* **sang** o **sung;** *pp:* **sung**) *va* cantar; **to sing to sleep** arrullar, adormecer cantando; *vn* cantar; chillar (*p.ej., los oídos*)
Singapore ['sɪŋgəpor], ['sɪŋəpor] o [,sɪŋgə'por] *s* Singapur
singe [sɪndʒ] *s* chamusquina, socarra; (*ger:* **singeing**) *va* chamuscar, socarrar; quemar ligeramente, quemar las puntas de; sollamar (*un ave*); perjudicar, dañar
singer ['sɪŋər] *s* cantante; vocalista (*p.ej., en un café cantante*); pájaro cantor
Singhalese [,sɪŋgə'liz] *adj* cingalés; *s* (*pl:* **-lese**) cingalés
singing ['sɪŋɪŋ] *s* canto; chillido (*en los oídos*)
singing school *s* escuela de canto
single ['sɪŋgəl] *adj* uno; único, solo; simple; particular; individual (*p.ej., cuarto en un hotel*); suelto (*ejemplar*); soltero; de soltero; sincero, honrado; (bot.) sencillo; (naut.) single; *s* simple, individuo; (baseball) sencillo; **singles** *spl* (tennis) juego de simples o individuales; *va* escoger, elegir; singularizar; **to single out** separar, entresacar; singularizar, señalar con especialidad; *vn* andar (*un caballo*) a paso fino; (baseball) pasar a primera base
single-acting ['sɪŋgəl'æktɪŋ] *adj* (mach.) de simple efecto
single bed *s* cama camera
single blessedness *s* estado de soltero o soltera
single-breasted ['sɪŋgəl'brɛstɪd] *adj* sin cruzar, de una hilera de botones, de un solo pecho
single-cut file ['sɪŋgəl,kʌt] *s* lima de picadura sencilla
single entry *s* (com.) partida simple
single-eyed ['sɪŋgəl,aɪd] *adj* tuerto; clarividente; justo, honrado
single file *s* fila india; **in single file** uno tras otro, de uno en uno, de reata
single-foot ['sɪŋgəl,fʊt] *s* paso fino (*de un caballo*); *vn* caminar (*un caballo*) a paso fino
single-handed ['sɪŋgəl'hændɪd] *adj* de una mano; para una persona; sin ayuda
single-hearted ['sɪŋgəl'hɑrtɪd] *adj* sincero, sin doblez; con un solo propósito
single life *s* vida de soltero
single line *s* (aut.) paso único

single-minded ['sɪŋgəl'maɪndɪd] *adj* con un solo propósito; ingenuo, sincero
singleness ['sɪŋgəlnɪs] *s* unidad; sencillez, llaneza; sinceridad, honradez; soltería
single-phase ['sɪŋgəl'fez] *adj* (elec.) monofásico
single-pole switch ['sɪŋgəl'pol] *s* (elec.) interruptor unipolar
single room *s* habitación individual, cuarto para una persona
single-seater ['sɪŋgəl'sitər] *s* (aer.) monoplaza, avión de una plaza
single-space ['sɪŋgəl'spes] *adj* a un solo espacio, escrito a un solo espacio
single-stage ['sɪŋgəl'stedʒ] *adj* de etapa única
singlestick ['sɪŋgəl,stɪk] *s* (fencing) bastón; esgrima del bastón; *vn* esgrimir el bastón
singlet ['sɪŋglɪt] *s* camiseta
single tax *s* impuesto único
single-throw switch ['sɪŋgəl'θro] *s* (elec.) interruptor de una caída
singleton ['sɪŋgəltən] *s* (bridge) única carta de un palo
single-track ['sɪŋgəl,træk] *adj* de vía única, de vía sencilla; (coll.) de cortos alcances, de intereses limitados
singletree ['sɪŋgəl,tri] *s* balancín
singsong ['sɪŋ,sɔŋ] o ['sɪŋ,sɑŋ] *s* salmodia, sonsonete, acento cantante; *adj* monótono; *va & vn* salmodiar
singular ['sɪŋgjələr] *adj* singular; (gram.) singular; *s* (gram.) singular
singularity [,sɪŋgjə'lærɪtɪ] *s* (*pl:* **-ties**) singularidad
Sinhalese [,sɪnhə'liz] *adj & s* var. de **Singhalese**
Sinic ['sɪnɪk] *adj* sínico
sinister ['sɪnɪstər] *adj* siniestro (*que está a la mano izquierda; malintencionado; funesto*); (her.) siniestro
sinistral ['sɪnɪstrəl] *adj* siniestro
sinistrorse ['sɪnɪstrɔrs] *adj* (bot.) sinistrorso
sink [sɪŋk] *s* fregadero (*de la cocina*); sumidero, desaguadero; área pantanosa; lugar de vicio y mal vivir; (*pret:* **sank** o **sunk;** *pp:* **sunk**) *va* hundir, sumergir; echar a pique; abrir, cavar (*un pozo*); hincar (*p.ej., los dientes*); enterrar (*un poste*); bajar (*la voz; el precio*); calar (*un cajón hidráulico*); invertir (*mucho dinero*); invertir (*mucho dinero*) perdiéndolo todo; ocultar, suprimir; *vn* hundirse; irse a pique; sumirse (*el agua en la tierra*); sentarse (*p.ej., un edificio*); hundirse (*p.ej., el Sol en el horizonte*); dejarse caer (*en una silla*); descender, desaparecer; menguar, disminuir; decaer (*un enfermo; una llama*)
sinkable ['sɪŋkəbəl] *adj* hundible, sumergible
sinker ['sɪŋkər] *s* plomo (*de las redes de pesca*)
sinkhole ['sɪŋk,hol] *s* agujero de desagüe; hoyo de aguas sucias; lugar de vicio y mal vivir
sinking fund *s* fondo de amortización
sinless ['sɪnlɪs] *adj* impecable, inmaculado, exento de pecado
sinner ['sɪnər] *s* pecador
Sino-American [,saɪnoə'merɪkən] o [,sɪnoə'merɪkən] *adj* chinoamericano
Sino-Japanese [,saɪno,dʒæpə'niz] o [,sɪno,dʒæpə'niz] *adj* sinojaponés
Sinological [,saɪnə'lɑdʒɪkəl] o [,sɪnə'lɑdʒɪkəl] *adj* sinológico
Sinologist [saɪ'nɑlədʒɪst] o [sɪ'nɑlədʒɪst] *s* sinólogo
Sinology [saɪ'nɑlədʒɪ] o [sɪ'nɑlədʒɪ] *s* sinología
sinuate ['sɪnjʊet] *adj* sinuoso; (bot.) festoneado
sinuosity [,sɪnjʊ'ɑsɪtɪ] *s* (*pl:* **-ties**) sinuosidad
sinuous ['sɪnjʊəs] *adj* sinuoso
sinus ['saɪnəs] *s* (anat., bot., zool. & path.) seno
sinusitis [,saɪnə'saɪtɪs] *s* (path.) sinusitis
sinusoid ['saɪnəsɔɪd] *s* (math.) sinusoide
sinusoidal [,saɪnə'sɔɪdəl] *adj* sinusoidal
Sion ['saɪən] *s* var. de **Zion**
sip [sɪp] *s* sorbo, trago; (*pret & pp:* **sipped;** *ger:* **sipping**) *va & vn* sorber, beber a tragos
siphon ['saɪfən] *s* sifón; *va* sacar con sifón, trasegar con sifón; pasar a través de un sifón
siphon bottle *s* sifón
siphonogam ['saɪfənəgæm] *s* (bot.) sifonógama
siphonogamic [,saɪfənə'gæmɪk] *adj* (bot.) sifonógamo
sir [sʌr] *s* señor; (*cap.*) *s* sir (*tratamiento honorífico en Inglaterra*)
sire [saɪr] *s* padre, semental; caballo padre; sire (*tratamiento dado primero a los señores y luego sólo al rey*); (poet.) padre, antecesor; (obs.) señor; *va* engendrar
siren ['saɪrən] *s* (aut., phys., myth. & fig.) sirena
sirenian [saɪ'rinɪən] *adj & s* (zool.) sirenio
Sirian ['sɪrɪən] *adj* (astr.) siríaco
Sirius ['sɪrɪəs] *s* (astr.) Sirio
sirloin ['sʌrlɔɪn] *s* solomillo
sirocco [sɪ'rɑko] *s* (*pl:* **-cos**) siroco
sirrah ['sɪrə] *s* (archaic) señoritingo
sirup ['sɪrəp] o ['sʌrəp] *s* var. de **syrup**
sirupy ['sɪrəpɪ] o ['sʌrəpɪ] *adj* var. de **syrupy**
sis [sɪs] *s* (coll.) hermanita
sisal ['saɪsəl] o ['sɪsəl] *s* (bot.) sisal, henequén; cáñamo sisal
sisal hemp *s* cáñamo sisal
sissify ['sɪsɪfaɪ] (*pret & pp:* **-fied**) *va* (coll.) afeminar
sissy ['sɪsɪ] *s* (*pl:* **-sies**) (coll.) hermanita, pequeñita; (coll.) afeminado, maricón, santito
sister ['sɪstər] *s* hermana; *adj* hermano, p.ej., **sister language** lengua hermana; gemelo, p.ej., **sister ship** buque gemelo
sisterhood ['sɪstərhʊd] *s* hermandad, cofradía de mujeres
sister-in-law ['sɪstərɪn,lɔ] *s* (*pl:* **sisters-in-law**) cuñada, hermana política; concuñada
sisterly ['sɪstərlɪ] *adj* como hermana, como hermanas
Sister of Charity o **Sister of Mercy** *s* hermana de la caridad
Sistine ['sɪstin] o ['sɪstɪn] *adj* sixtino
Sistine Chapel *s* Capilla sixtina
sistrum ['sɪstrəm] *s* (*pl:* **-trums** o **-tra** [trə]) (mus.) sistro
Sisyphus ['sɪsɪfəs] *s* (myth.) Sísifo
sit [sɪt] *va* (*pret & pp:* **sat;** *ger:* **sitting**) sentar; montar (*un caballo*); empollar (*huevos*); **to sit out** aguantar hasta el fin; permanecer sentado durante; permanecer más tarde que (*otra persona*); *vn* estar sentado; sentarse; posarse (*el ave sobre una rama*); echarse (*un ave sobre los huevos*); reunirse, celebrar junta; descansar; sentar (*bien o mal un vestido*); **to sit down** sentarse; **to sit in** tomar parte en; **to sit on** o **upon** tomar asiento en (*p.ej., una junta*); tomar parte en; (slang) hacer callar, poner en su lugar; (slang) desairar; **to sit still** estarse quieto; **to sit tight** (coll.) mantenerse firme en su puesto; (coll.) callarse, ocultarse; **to sit up** permanecer sentado; incorporarse (*el que estaba echado*); velar, quedarse en vela; **to sit up and take notice** (coll.) despabilarse
sit-down strike ['sɪt,daʊn] *s* huelga de sentados, huelga de brazos caídos
site [saɪt] *s* sitio, paraje, lugar, local
sit-in ['sɪt,ɪn] *s* huelga de brazos caídos; ocupación de asientos en un local sólo para blancos en protesta contra la discriminación racial
sitology [saɪ'tɑlədʒɪ] *s* sitología
sitter ['sɪtər] *s* persona sentada, pasajero sentado; modelo de pintor o fotógrafo; ave clueca, gallina clueca
sitting ['sɪtɪŋ] *adj* sentado; *s* sentada; estadía (*p.ej., ante un pintor*); **at one sitting** de una sentada
sitting duck *s* pato sentado en el agua (*fácil de matar a tiro de escopeta*); (coll.) blanco de fácil alcance
sitting room *s* sala, sala de estar
situate ['sɪtʃʊet] *va* situar
situation [,sɪtʃʊ'eʃən] o [,sɪtʃə'weʃən] *s* situación; puesto, colocación
situs ['saɪtəs] *s* sitio, situación
sitz bath [sɪts] *s* baño de asiento
six [sɪks] *adj* seis; *s* seis; **at sixes and sevens** en confusión; en desacuerdo; **six o'clock** las seis
sixfold ['sɪks,fold] *adj & s* séxtuplo; *adv* seis veces
six hundred *adj & s* seiscientos

sixpence ['sɪkspəns] *s* seis peniques
sixpenny ['sɪks,pɛnɪ] o ['sɪkspənɪ] *adj* de seis peniques; mezquino, insignificante; de dos pulgadas
sixshooter ['sɪks,ʃutər] *s* revólver de seis tiros
sixteen ['sɪks'tin] *adj & s* dieciséis o diez y seis
sixteenth ['sɪks'tinθ] *adj* décimosexto; dieciseisavo; *s* décimosexto; dieciseisavo; dieciséis (*en las fechas*)
sixteenth note *s* (mus.) semicorchea
sixth [sɪksθ] *adj* sexto; *s* sexto; seis (*en las fechas*); (mus.) sexta
sixthly ['sɪksθlɪ] *adv* en sexto lugar
sixth sense *s* sexto sentido
sixtieth ['sɪkstɪɪθ] *adj & s* sexagésimo; sesentavo
Sixtus ['sɪkstəs] *s* Sixto (*nombre de varios papas*)
sixty ['sɪkstɪ] *adj* sesenta; *s* (*pl:* **-ties**) sesenta
sixty-four dollar question ['sɪkstɪ'for] *s* (la) pregunta principal y más difícil (*de un programa de radio o televisión*)
sixty-fourth note ['sɪkstɪ'forθ] *s* (mus.) semifusa
sizable ['saɪzəbəl] *adj* considerable, bastante grande
size [saɪz] *s* tamaño; dimensiones; talla (*de una persona, un vestido*); extensión; diámetro (*de un tubo, alambre, etc.*); apresto (*para empapelar, pintar, etc.*); sisa, cola de retazo (*de los doradores*); (coll.) verdadera situación o condición; **of a size** del mismo tamaño; *va* clasificar según el tamaño; medir el tamaño de; aprestar (*para empapelar*); sisar, encolar; **to size up** enfocar (*un problema*); medir con la vista (*a una persona*)
sizeable ['saɪzəbəl] *adj* var. de **sizable**
size stick *s* cartabón, marco (*para medir la longitud del pie*)
sizing ['saɪzɪŋ] *s* apresto (*para empapelar, pintar, etc.*); sisa, cola de retazo
sizy ['saɪzɪ] *adj* glutinoso, pegajoso, viscoso
sizz [sɪz] *s* silbido, siseo; *vn* silbar, sisear
sizzle ['sɪzəl] *s* siseo (*de la manteca al freírse*); *vn* sisear
S.J. abr. de **Society of Jesus**
S.J.D. abr. de **Scientiae Juridicae Doctor** (Lat.) **Doctor of Juridical Science**
skald [skɔld] o [skɑld] *s* escaldo (*bardo de la Escandinavia antigua*)
skate [sket] *s* patín; (ichth.) raya; (slang) adefesio, tipo; (slang) caballejo, rocín; *vn* patinar; **to skate on thin ice** buscar el peligro; usar de argumentos infundados; **to skate over** mencionar muy por encima, pasar por alto
skatemobile ['sketmo,bil] *s* patinete montado sobre patines
skater ['sketər] *s* patinador
skating ['sketɪŋ] *s* patinaje
skating rink *s* patinadero, pista de patinar
skedaddle [skɪ'dædəl] *vn* (coll.) huir precipitadamente
skee [ski] *s & vn* var. de **ski**
skein [sken] madeja; enredo, maraña; bandada de aves silvestres
skeletal ['skɛlɪtəl] *adj* esquelético
skeleton ['skɛlɪtən] *s* esqueleto; (fig.) esqueleto (*sujeto muy flaco; bosquejo*); *adj* esquelético; reducido
skeletonize ['skɛlɪtənaɪz] *va* reducir a un esqueleto; preparar el esqueleto de; bosquejar; reducir
skeleton key *s* llave maestra
skeptic ['skɛptɪk] *adj & s* escéptico
skeptical ['skɛptɪkəl] *adj* escéptico
skepticism ['skɛptɪsɪzəm] *s* escepticismo
sketch [skɛtʃ] *s* boceto, croquis, dibujo; bosquejo, esbozo, esquicio; drama corto, pieza corta; *va* hacer el bosquejo de, dibujar; bosquejar, esbozar, esquiciar
sketchbook ['skɛtʃ,buk] *s* libro de bocetos; libro de bosquejos
sketchy ['skɛtʃɪ] *adj* (*comp:* **-ier;** *super:* **-iest**) bosquejado; incompleto, fragmentario; galopeado
skew [skju] *s* esviaje, curso oblicuo, posición oblicua, desviación de la línea recta; *adj* oblicuo, sesgado; *va* sesgar; falsear, tergiversar; *vn* torcerse, ponerse al sesgo
skewback ['skju,bæk] *s* (arch.) salmer
skewer ['skjuər] *s* (cook.) broqueta; *va* espetar; sujetar por medio de broquetas; traspasar con aguja o estaquilla
ski [ski] o [ʃi] *s* (*pl:* **skis** o **ski**) esquí; *vn* esquiar
skid [skɪd] *s* resbalón, deslizamiento (*de un coche*); patinaje, patinazo (*de una rueda*); calzo; galga (*palo que sirve de freno*); (naut.) varadera; (aer.) esquí, patín; **to be on the skids** (slang) ir decayendo; ir fatalmente hacia un desastre; (*pret & pp:* **skidded;** *ger:* **skidding**) *va* calzar; *vn* resbalar, deslizarse (*un coche*); patinar (*una rueda*)
skid chain *s* cadena para impedir el patinaje
skiddy ['skɪdɪ] *adj* (coll.) resbaladizo; (coll.) resbalador
skid road *s* camino de arrastre; camino con trozas transversales
skid row [ro] *s* barrio de mala vida
skier ['skiər] o ['ʃiər] *s* esquiador
skiff [skɪf] *s* esquife
skiing ['skiɪŋ] o ['ʃiɪŋ] *s* esquiismo
skijoring [ski'dʒorɪŋ] *s* esquí remolcado
ski jump *s* salto de esquí; cancha de esquiar; trampolín
skill [skɪl] *s* pericia, destreza, habilidad
skilled [skɪld] *adj* experto, práctico, hábil, diestro; de experto
skillet ['skɪlɪt] *s* sartén; cacerola de mango largo
skillful o **skilful** ['skɪlfəl] *adj* experto, hábil, diestro, primoroso; de experto, de perito
skim [skɪm] *s* nata, escoria; (*pret & pp:* **skimmed;** *ger:* **skimming**) *va* desnatar, escoriar, espumar; rasar, rozar; tocar ligeramente, examinar ligeramente; *vn* deslizar; rozar; **to skim over** pasar rasando, pasar a la ligera; examinar ligeramente
ski mask *s* pasamontaña
skimmer ['skɪmər] *s* espumador; espumadera (*paleta cóncava*); canotié; (orn.) rayador, picotijera
skim milk *s* leche desnatada
skim-milk ['skɪm'mɪlk] *adj* débil, flojo, de inferior calidad
skimp [skɪmp] *s* escatimar, escasear; chapucear; *vn* economizar, apretarse; chapucear
skimpy ['skɪmpɪ] *adj* (*comp:* **-ier;** *super:* **-iest**) escaso; tacaño, mezquino
skin [skɪn] *s* piel; pellejo (*receptáculo para líquidos*); forro de acero (*de una nave*); (coll.) pillo, tramposo; (coll.) tacaño, avaro; **in** o **with a whole skin** ileso, sano y salvo; **to be nothing but skin and bones** estar hecho una oblea, estar en los huesos; **to get soaked to the skin** calarse hasta los huesos; **to save one's skin** salvar el pellejo; (*pret & pp:* **skinned;** *ger:* **skinning**) *va* pelar, desollar; escoriarse (*el codo*); (coll.) timar; cubrir de piel; **to skin alive** (coll.) desollar vivo (*hacer pagar más de lo justo*); torturar, martirizar; regañar severamente; vencer completamente; *vn* perder la piel; cubrirse de piel, cubrirse de pellejo; cicatrizarse; (slang) escabullirse
skin-deep ['skɪn'dip] *adj* superficial; *adv* superficialmente
skin diver *s* submarinista
skin diving *s* submarinismo
skin effect *s* (elec.) efecto pelicular
skinflint ['skɪn,flɪnt] *s* avaro, escasero
skinful ['skɪnful] *s* contenido de un pellejo; (coll.) hartazgo, panzada; (coll.) hartazgo de bebida
skin game *s* (slang) fullería
skin grafting *s* (surg.) injerto cutáneo
skink [skɪŋk] *s* (zool.) escinco
skinner ['skɪnər] *s* desollador; peletero
skinny ['skɪnɪ] *adj* (*comp:* **-nier;** *super:* **-niest**) flaco, magro, seco, enjuto; pellejudo
skin-tight ['skɪn'taɪt] *adj* ajustado al cuerpo
skip [skɪp] *s* salto; (*pret & pp:* **skipped;** *ger:* **skipping**) *va* saltar; *vn* saltar; saltar espacios (*la máquina de escribir*); irse precipitadamente; moverse saltando; (coll.) escabullirse
skip bombing *s* (aer.) bombardeo de rebote
skip distance *s* (rad.) distancia de la zona intermedia de mala recepción o silencio

skipjack ['skɪp,dʒæk] *s* (ichth.) pez saltador; (ent.) cucuyo
ski pole *s* bastón de esquiar
skipper ['skɪpər] *s* saltador; jefe, caudillo; patrón (*de barco*); gusano del queso; (ent.) hesperia; *va* patronear (*un barco*)
skipping rope *s* comba, saltador
skip-stop ['skɪp,stɑp] *adj* (*tren*) que salta ciertas estaciones, (*ascensor*) que salta ciertos pisos
skirmish ['skʌrmɪʃ] *s* escaramuza; *vn* escaramuzar
skirmisher ['skʌrmɪʃər] *s* escaramuzador
skirmish line *s* (mil.) línea de escaramuza
skirret ['skɪrɪt] *s* (bot.) escaravia
skirt [skʌrt] *s* falda; borde, orilla; oreja de cuero (*de la silla de montar*); (slang) falda (*mujer*); *va* proveer de falda; proveer de borde u orilla; bordear, seguir el borde o la orilla de; mantenerse fuera del alcance de, moverse a lo largo de; *vn* moverse al borde, estar al margen
skirting ['skʌrtɪŋ] *s* material para faldas
ski stick *s* var. de **ski pole**
skit [skɪt] *s* boceto satírico, boceto burlesco, paso cómico, pasillo
skitter ['skɪtər] *va* hacer saltar (*el anzuelo*) ligeramente sobre la superficie del agua; *vn* saltar ligeramente, deslizarse saltando
skittish ['skɪtɪʃ] *adj* caprichoso; asustadizo; tímido
skittles ['skɪtəlz] *s* juego de bolos
skive [skaɪv] *s* disco para pulir diamantes; *va* pulir (*diamantes*); raspar (*cueros*); cortar (*cueros*) en capas finas
Skr. abr. de **Sanskrit**
skua ['skjuə] *s* (orn.) estercorario
skulduggery [skʌl'dʌgərɪ] *s* (coll.) trampa, embuste
skulk [skʌlk] *s* remolón; *vn* remolonear; moverse en la sombra, acechar sin ser visto
skull [skʌl] *s* cráneo, calavera; cabeza; cerebro
skull and crossbones *spl* calavera y dos huesos cruzados, calavera con dos tibias cruzadas (*insignia en la bandera de los piratas y ahora señal del veneno y peligro de muerte*)
skullcap ['skʌl,kæp] *s* casquete; (anat.) sincipucio, coronilla
skunk [skʌŋk] *s* (zool.) mofeta; (zool.) zorrillo, mapurite (Am.); (coll.) canalla (*persona*)
skunk cabbage *s* (bot.) simplocarpo
sky [skaɪ] *s* (*pl:* **skies**) cielo; (paint.) cielo; **out of a clear sky** de buenas a primeras, inesperadamente; **to praise to the skies** poner por las nubes, poner en el cielo
sky blue *s* azul celeste
sky-blue ['skaɪ'blu] *adj* celeste
sky diving *s* (sport) paracaidismo
skyey ['skaɪɪ] *adj* celeste, etéreo
sky-high ['skaɪ'haɪ] *adj & adv* tan alto como el cielo; por las nubes
skylark ['skaɪ,lɑrk] *s* (orn.) alondra; *vn* jaranear, juguetear, triscar
skylight ['skaɪ,laɪt] *s* tragaluz
skyline ['skaɪ,laɪn] *s* línea del horizonte, línea de los edificios contra el cielo
sky pilot *s* (slang) clérigo, capellán
skyrocket ['skaɪ,rɑkɪt] *s* cohete; *vn* subir como un cohete, lucirse y desaparecer; alcanzar gran altura rápida y súbitamente; elevarse súbitamente (*los precios*)
skysail ['skaɪsəl] o ['skaɪ,sel] *s* (naut.) periquito, sosobre
skyscraper ['skaɪ,skrepər] *s* rascacielos
skyward ['skaɪwərd] *adj* que se dirige hacia el cielo; *adv* hacia el cielo
skywards ['skaɪwərdz] *adv* hacia el cielo
skywriting ['skaɪ,raɪtɪŋ] *s* escritura aérea
slab [slæb] *s* losa; tabla, tablón, plancha; tajada gruesa (*p.ej., de carne*); costero (*tabla inmediata a la corteza*)
slabber ['slæbər] *s, va & vn* var. de **slobber**
slack [slæk] *adj* flojo; tardo, lento, perezoso; negligente, descuidado; inactivo; *s* flojedad; estado flojo; inactividad; estación muerta, temporada inactiva; cisco (*polvo de carbón*); aguas represadas; **slacks** *spl* pantalones flojos o sueltos; *va* aflojar; apagar (*la cal*); *vn* atrasarse; descuidarse; **to slack off** aflojar; **to slack up** aflojar el paso
slacken ['slækən] *va* aflojar; atrasar; disminuir; descuidar; apagar (*la cal*); *vn* aflojarse; atrasarse; aflojar, dejarse ir
slacker ['slækər] *s* haragán, perezoso; (mil.) prófugo
slackness ['slæknɪs] *s* flojedad; negligencia; inactividad
slack rope *s* cuerda floja
slack water *s* (naut.) repunte de la marea; aguas semiestancadas
slag [slæg] *s* escoria; (*pret & pp:* **slagged;** *ger:* **slagging**) *va* convertir en escoria; *vn* formarse escoria; hacerse escoria
slaggy ['slægɪ] *adj* escoriáceo
slain [slen] *pp de* **slay**
slake [slek] *va* aplacar, calmar; apagar (*la cal*); *vn* aflojar, dejarse ir; apagarse (*la cal*)
slalom ['slɑlom] *s* eslalom
slam [slæm] *s* golpe; portazo; (coll.) crítica acerba; (bridge) bola, slam; (*pret & pp:* **slammed;** *ger:* **slamming**) *va* cerrar de golpe; mover, golpear o empujar estrepitosamente; (coll.) criticar acerbamente; *vn* cerrarse de golpe
slam-bang ['slæm'bæŋ] *adv* (coll.) de golpe y porrazo
slander ['slændər] *s* calumnia, difamación; *va* calumniar, difamar
slanderer ['slændərər] *s* calumniador, difamador
slanderous ['slændərəs] *adj* calumnioso, difamatorio
slang [slæŋ] *s* vulgarismo; jerga (*lenguaje especial de un grupo*)
slangy ['slæŋɪ] *adj* (*comp:* **-ier;** *super:* **-iest**) que emplea vulgarismos; lleno de vulgarismos
slant [slænt] *s* inclinación; parecer, punto de vista; *va* inclinar, sesgar; tergiversar, deformar (*p.ej., una noticia*); *vn* inclinarse, sesgarse
slantways ['slænt,wez] *adv* inclinadamente, sesgadamente
slantwise ['slænt,waɪz] *adj* inclinado, sesgado; *adv* inclinadamente, sesgadamente
slap [slæp] *s* palmada, manazo; bofetada (*golpe en la cara*); regaño, recriminación; insulto, desaire; (coll.) prueba, ensayo; *adv* directamente; súbitamente; (*pret & pp:* **slapped;** *ger:* **slapping**) *va* dar una palmada a, dar un manazo a; dar una bofetada a; poner con fuerza y ruidosamente
slapdash ['slæp,dæʃ] *s* trabajo descuidado, chapucería; *adj* descuidado, chapucero; *adv* con descuido, apresuradamente
slap in the back *s* espaldarazo
slapjack ['slæp,dʒæk] *s* torta frita en la sartén
slapstick ['slæp,stɪk] *s* paleta de payaso o cómico; comedia de golpe y porrazo, comedia de payasadas; *adj* de golpe y porrazo, de payasadas
slash [slæʃ] *s* tajo, tajada; cuchillada; azote; claro en un bosque; montón de hojas y ramas secas; (sew.) cuchillada; *va* acuchillar; dar un tajo a; hacer fuerte rebaja de (*precios, sueldos, etc.*); azotar; criticar acerbamente; cortar extensamente; acuchillar (*una prenda de vestir*)
slat [slæt] *s* hoja, lámina, tablilla
slate [slet] *s* pizarra; negro azulado, color de pizarra; candidatura, lista de candidatos; **to have a clean slate** tener las manos limpias; **to wipe the slate clean** empezar de nuevo; *adj* negro azulado, color pizarra; *va* empizarrar, cubrir de pizarra; poner en la lista de candidatos
slate pencil *s* pizarrín
slater ['sletər] *s* pizarrero; (zool.) cochinilla de humedad, cochinilla de tierra
slate roof *s* empizarrado
slattern ['slætərn] *s* mujer desaliñada
slatternly ['slætərnlɪ] *adj* desaliñado
slaty ['sletɪ] *adj* (*comp:* **-ier;** *super:* **-iest**) pizarreño
slaughter ['slɔtər] *s* matanza, carnicería; *va* matar; carnear (Am.)
slaughter house *s* matadero
slaughter of the innocents *s* degollación de los inocentes
slaughterous ['slɔtərəs] *adj* mortífero, destructivo
Slav [slɑv] o [slæv] *adj & s* eslavo
slave [slev] *s & adj* esclavo; *vn* trabajar como esclavo
Slave Coast *s* Costa de los Esclavos

slave driver *s* negrero; (fig.) negrero, persona despótica que agobia de trabajo a otra
slaveholder [ˈslev,holdər] *s* dueño de esclavos
slaveholding [ˈslev,holdɪŋ] *adj* que posee esclavos; *s* posesión de esclavos
slave labor *s* trabajo de esclavos; trabajadores forzados
slaver [ˈslevər] *s* negrero; barco negrero; [ˈslævər] *s* baba; *va* babosear; *vn* babear
slavery [ˈslevərɪ] *s* esclavitud
slave trade *s* trata de esclavos, tráfico de esclavos
slavey [ˈslevɪ] *s* (coll.) criada, fregona
Slavic [ˈslɑvɪk] o [ˈslævɪk] *adj* eslavo; *s* eslavo (*idioma*)
slavish [ˈslevɪʃ] *adj* servil; esclavizado
Slavonia [sləˈvonɪə] *s* Eslavonia
Slavonian [sləˈvonɪən] *adj* & *s* eslavonio; eslavo
Slavonic [sləˈvɑnɪk] *adj* eslavo; eslavonio; *s* eslavo
slaw [slɔ] *s* ensalada de col cortada muy fina
slay [sle] (*pret:* **slew;** *pp:* **slain**) *va* matar
slayer [ˈsleər] *s* matador, asesino
sleave [sliv] *s* hilacha; *va* deshilachar
sleazy [ˈslizɪ] o [ˈslezɪ] *adj* (*comp:* **-zier;** *super:* **-ziest**) débil, ligero, tenue
sled [slɛd] *s* luge, trineo; (*pret* & *pp:* **sledded;** *ger:* **sledding**) *va* llevar en trineo; *vn* ir en trineo
sledding [ˈslɛdɪŋ] *s* transportación en trineo, uso del trineo; **hard sledding** camino dificultoso, circunstancias poco favorables; **smooth sledding** circunstancias favorables
sledge [slɛdʒ] *s* acotillo; trineo; *va* transportar en trineo; *vn* ir o pasear en trineo
sledge hammer *s* acotillo; cosa fuerte y aplastante
sledge-hammer [ˈslɛdʒ,hæmər] *adj* fuerte y aplastante; *va* & *vn* golpear con fuerza con acotillo o como si fuera con acotillo
sleek [slik] *adj* liso y brillante, alisado y suave; mañoso, zalamero; *va* alisar y pulir; suavizar
sleep [slip] *s* sueño; **to be overcome with sleep** caerse de sueño; **to go to sleep** dormirse; dormirse o morirse (*entorpecerse un miembro*); **to put to sleep** adormecer, dormir; matar por anestesia (*p.ej., a un perro enfermo*); **to read someone to sleep** adormecerle a uno leyendo; **to talk to sleep** adormecer hablando; (*pret* & *pp:* **slept**) *va* pasar durmiendo; **to sleep away** pasar durmiendo; **to sleep off** dormir (*p.ej., una borrachera*); *vn* dormir; **to sleep over** trasnochar, dormir sobre
sleeper [ˈslipər] *s* durmiente (*persona; traviesa de la vía férrea*); coche-cama, coche-dormitorio
sleeper seat *s* (aer. & rail.) butacama
sleepiness [ˈslipɪnɪs] *s* somnolencia
sleeping [ˈslipɪŋ] *adj* durmiente; de dormir, para dormir
sleeping bag *s* saco para dormir (*a la intemperie*)
Sleeping Beauty *s* la Bella durmiente del bosque
sleeping car *s* coche-cama, coche-dormitorio, vagón cama
sleeping partner *s* (com.) socio comanditario
sleeping pill *s* píldora para dormir
sleeping powder *s* polvos calmantes, polvos para dormir
sleeping sickness *s* (path.) enfermedad del sueño
sleepless [ˈsliplɪs] *adj* insomne, desvelado; despierto, vivo; sin dormir; pasado en vela
sleeplessness [ˈsliplɪsnɪs] *s* insomnio, desvelo
sleepwalker [ˈslip,wɔkər] *s* sonámbulo
sleepwalking [ˈslip,wɔkɪŋ] *s* sonambulismo; *adj* sonámbulo
sleepy [ˈslipɪ] *adj* (*comp:* **-ier;** *super:* **-iest**) soñoliento; **to be sleepy** tener sueño
sleepyhead [ˈslipɪ,hɛd] *s* dormilón
sleet [slit] *s* cellisca, nevisca; *vn* cellisquear, neviscar
sleety [ˈslitɪ] *adj* (*comp:* **-ier;** *super:* **-iest**) de cellisca; lleno de cellisca, cubierto de cellisca
sleeve [sliv] *s* manga; (mach.) manguito; **to laugh in** o **up one's sleeve** reírse interiormente, reírse para sí; **up one's sleeve** en reserva
sleeveless [ˈslivlɪs] *adj* sin mangas
sleigh [sle] *s* trineo; *va* transportar en trineo; *vn* pasearse en trineo
sleigh bell *s* cascabel
sleighing [ˈsleɪŋ] *s* paseo en trineo; estado de las carreteras que permite ir en trineo sobre ellas
sleigh ride *s* paseo en trineo
sleight [slaɪt] *s* destreza, pericia, habilidad; ardid, artificio
sleight of hand *s* juego de manos, prestidigitación
slender [ˈslɛndər] *adj* delgado, flaco; escaso, insuficiente
slept [slɛpt] *pret* & *pp de* **sleep**
sleuth [sluθ] *s* sabueso (*perro y detective*); *vn* andar espiando, andar acechando, seguir un rastro o una huella
sleuthhound [ˈsluθ,haʊnd] *s* sabueso; (coll.) sabueso (*detective*)
slew [slu] *s* ciénaga; vuelta rápida; (coll.) montón, gran cantidad; *va* volver, torcer; *vn* volverse, torcerse; *pret de* **slay**
slice [slaɪs] *s* rebanada, tajada; gajo (*p.ej., de naranja*); trozo, pedazo; (cook.) estrelladera, pala; *va* rebanar, tajar; cortar; dividir
slice bar *s* limpiaparrilla
sliced peaches *spl* melocotones en tajadas
slicer [ˈslaɪsər] *s* rebanador (*persona o máquina*)
slicing machine *s* rebanador o rebanadora
slick [slɪk] *s* lugar aceitoso y lustroso (*en el agua*); *adj* liso y brillante; aceitoso y lustroso; meloso, suave, pulido; (coll.) astuto, mañoso; *adv* directamente; (coll.) astutamente, con maña; *va* alisar, pulir
slickenside [ˈslɪkən,saɪd] *s* (geol.) espejo de falla, superficie de deslizamiento
slicker [ˈslɪkər] *s* impermeable; (coll.) embaucador, galafate
slid [slɪd] *pret* & *pp de* **slide**
slidden [ˈslɪdən] *pp de* **slide**
slide [slaɪd] *s* resbalón; resbaladero; derrumbamiento; derrumbamiento de tierra; alud; portaobjeto, plaquilla de vidrio (*para microscopio*); desliz (*superficie lisa*); diapositiva, transparencia; cursor, reglilla (*de regla de cálculo*); (mus.) tubo en forma de U; (mus.) grupeto (*de notas*); (mus.) trasporte; (mach.) cursor; *adj* de cursor; (*pret* & *pp:* **slid;** *pp:* **slid** o **slidden**) *va* deslizar, hacer resbalar; *vn* deslizar, resbalar; **to let slide** dejar pasar, no hacer caso de, no ocuparse de; **to slide over** pasar ligeramente, recorrer superficialmente
slide caliper *s* pie de rey
slide fastener *s* cierre cremallera
slide rule *s* nonio, regla de cálculo
slide valve *s* (mach.) corredera, distribuidor, válvula corrediza
sliding [ˈslaɪdɪŋ] *s* deslizamiento; *adj* corredizo; móvil, graduado
sliding contact *s* (elec.) cursor
sliding door *s* puerta de corredera
sliding scale *s* (econ.) escala móvil (*p.ej., de salarios*); regla de cálculo
slight [slaɪt] *s* descuido, desatención; desaire, menosprecio; *adj* delgado; sutil, delicado; leve, ligero; pequeño, insignificante; escaso; *va* descuidar, desatender; desairar, menospreciar
slily [ˈslaɪlɪ] *adv* var. de **slyly**
slim [slɪm] *adj* (*comp:* **slimmer;** *super:* **slimmest**) delgado; leve, débil, pequeño
slime [slaɪm] *s* légamo; baba (*de las culebras, los peces, etc.*); porquería
slimmish [ˈslɪmɪʃ] *adj* algo delgado
slimy [ˈslaɪmɪ] *adj* (*comp:* **-ier;** *super:* **-iest**) legamoso, pecinoso; baboso, viscoso; puerco, sucio
sling [slɪŋ] *s* honda (*para tirar piedras*); cabestrillo (*para sostener el brazo lastimado*); hondazo, tirada de honda, golpe dado con una honda; (naut.) braga; (naut.) eslinga; **slings** *spl* grátil (*parte central de la verga*); (*pret* & *pp:* **slung**) *va* lanzar con una honda; lanzar, tirar; poner en cabestrillo; colgar flojamente; (naut.) embragar; (naut.) eslingar
slinger [ˈslɪŋər] *s* hondero; lanzador, pedrero; cargador que emplea eslinga

slingshot [ˈslɪŋ,ʃɑt] *s* honda, tirador
slink [slɪŋk] (*pret & pp:* **slunk**) *vn* andar furtivamente; **to slink away** escurrirse, escabullirse
slip [slɪp] *s* resbalón, desliz; falta, error, desliz; lapso; embarcadero; grada (*plano inclinado, donde se construyen los barcos*); funda (*de muebles, de almohada*); papeleta, pedazo de papel; sarmiento (*para transplantar*); combinación (*prenda de vestir*); huída, evasión; traílla (*de perro*); (min. & geol.) dislocación; persona joven y menuda de cuerpo; **to give the slip to** escaparse de, burlar la vigilancia de ‖ (*pret & pp:* **slipped;** *ger:* **slipping**) *va* deslizar; dejar escapar; pasar por alto; soltar (*un perro*); poner rápidamente; quitar rápidamente; dislocarse (*un hueso*); decir inadvertidamente; eludir, evadir; **to slip off** (coll.) quitarse de prisa; **to slip on** (coll.) ponerse de prisa; **to slip one over on** (coll.) jugar una mala pasada a; **to slip one's mind** olvidársele a uno ‖ *vn* escurrirse; borrarse de la memoria; deslizarse; tropezar; errar, equivocarse; (coll.) declinar, deteriorarse; **to let slip** dejar pasar; decir inadvertidamente; **to slip away** escurrirse, escabullirse; **to slip by** pasar inadvertido; pasar rápidamente (*p.ej., el tiempo*); **to slip out of one's hands** escurrirse de entre las manos; **to slip through** colarse; **to slip through one's fingers** írsele a uno de entre las manos; **to slip up** (coll.) equivocarse, errar
slipcase [ˈslɪp,kes] *s* estuche (*para guardar libros*)
slip cover *s* funda
slip knot *s* nudo corredizo
slip of the pen *s* error de pluma
slip of the tongue *s* error de lengua
slip-on [ˈslɪp,ɑn] *s* prenda de vestir que se pone por la cabeza; prenda de vestir de quitaipón
slipper [ˈslɪpər] *s* zapatilla, babucha
slippered [ˈslɪpərd] *adj* calzado con zapatillas
slippering [ˈslɪpərɪŋ] *s* pantuflazo
slippery [ˈslɪpərɪ] *adj* deslizadizo, resbaladizo; astuto, zorro; **to be as slippery as an eel** escurrirse como una anguila
slippery elm (bot.) olmo norteamericano (*Ulmus fulva*); corteza de *Ulmus fulva* empleada como demulcente
slipshod [ˈslɪp,ʃɑd] *adj* en chancletas; desaseado, desaliñado; arrastrando los pies
slipslop [ˈslɪp,slɑp] *s* (coll.) aguachirle
slip stream *s* (aer.) viento de la hélice
slip-up [ˈslɪp,ʌp] *s* (coll.) error, equivocación
slit [slɪt] *s* raja, hendedura; cortada, incisión; (*pret & pp:* **slit;** *ger:* **slitting**) *va* rajar, hender; cortar
slit-eyed [ˈslɪt,aɪd] *adj* de ojos almendrados
slither [ˈslɪðər] *s* desliz súbito e irregular; *vn* rodar, deslizarse, culebrear
slit skirt *s* falda hendida, falda de tubo (*con abertura*)
sliver [ˈslɪvər] *s* raja (*de madera*); fibra de algodón o lana en hebras; *va* cortar en rajas; separar en hebras
slob [slɑb] *s* (slang) sujeto desaseado, sujeto desmañado
slobber [ˈslɑbər] *s* baba; sensiblería; *va* babosear; *vn* babear; hablar con sensiblería
slobbery [ˈslɑbərɪ] *adj* baboso; húmedo
sloe [slo] *s* (bot.) endrino (*arbusto*); endrina (*fruto*)
sloe-colored [ˈslo,kʌlərd] *adj* endrino
sloe-eyed [ˈslo,aɪd] *adj* de ojos endrinos
sloe gin *s* ginebra de endrinas
slog [slɑg] *s* golpetazo; (*pret & pp:* **slogged;** *ger:* **slogging**) *va* golpear; *vn* (coll.) afanarse, trabajar con ahinco
slogan [ˈslogən] *s* lema, mote; grito de combate, grito de guerra
sloop [slup] *s* (naut.) balandra
slop [slɑp] *s* mojadura, líquido derramado en el suelo; zupia, gacha; **slops** *spl* agua sucia; ropa barata y mal hecha; pantalones holgados; (naut.) pacotilla; (*pret & pp:* **slopped;** *ger:* **slopping**) *va* derramar, salpicar, ensuciar, enlodar; *vn* derramarse; chapotear (*con los pies*); **to slop over** derramarse; (slang) hacer demostraciones excesivas de entusiasmo
slope [slop] *s* cuesta, pendiente; declive (*grado de inclinación*); vertiente (*de un continente*); *va* inclinar; cortar al sesgo; *vn* inclinarse; desviarse
sloppy [ˈslɑpɪ] *adj* (*comp:* **-pier;** *super:* **-piest**) mojado y sucio; desgalichado (*p.ej., en el vestir*); chapucero (*en el trabajo*)
slopshop [ˈslɑp,ʃɑp] *s* bazar de ropa barata, tienda de pacotilla
slosh [slɑʃ] *s* fango; nieve sucia; (coll.) aguachirle; *vn* chapotear; vagabundear
slot [slɑt] *s* ranura (*en que se introduce una moneda*); pista; (*pret & pp:* **slotted;** *ger:* **slotting**) *va* hacer una ranura en; seguir la pista de
sloth [sloθ] o [slɔθ] *s* pereza; (zool.) perezoso
sloth bear *s* (zool.) oso bezudo
slothful [ˈsloθfəl] o [ˈslɔθfəl] *adj* perezoso
slot machine *s* tragamonedas, tragaperras, distribuidor automático, máquina sacaperras
slot meter *s* limitador de corriente, contador automático
slotting machine *s* ranuradora
slouch [slaʊtʃ] *s* postura relajada, postura floja; persona desaseada y torpe de movimientos; **to walk with a slouch** andar con los hombros caídos y la cabeza inclinada; *va* agachar, doblar hacia abajo; *vn* agacharse, encorvarse; andar caído de hombros; **to slouch in a chair** repantigarse
slouch hat *s* sombrero gacho
slouch pocket *s* bolsillo inclinado
slouchy [ˈslaʊtʃɪ] *adj* (*comp:* **-ier;** *super:* **-iest**) relajado, flojo; desaseado; inclinado, encorvado
slough [slaʊ] *s* cenagal, fangal; estado de abandono moral; [slu] *s* ciénaga; ensenada de río; (U.S.A.) charca; [slʌf] *s* camisa, piel que muda la serpiente; (path.) escara; *va* mudar, echar de sí; *vn* caerse, desprenderse
slough of despond [slaʊ] *s* abatimiento profundo
sloughy [ˈslaʊɪ] *adj* (*comp:* **-ier;** *super:* **-iest**) cenagoso, fangoso; [ˈslʌfɪ] *adj* de escara
Slovak [ˈslovæk] o [sloˈvæk] *adj & s* eslovaco
Slovakia [sloˈvɑkɪə] o [sloˈvækɪə] *s* Eslovaquia
Slovakian [sloˈvɑkɪən] o [sloˈvækɪən] *adj & s* var. de **Slovak**
sloven [ˈslʌvən] *s* persona desaseada; *adj* desaseado, abandonado
Slovene [sloˈvin] o [ˈslovin] *adj & s* esloveno
Slovenia [sloˈvinɪə] *s* Eslovenia
Slovenian [sloˈvinɪən] *adj & s* var. de **Slovene**
slovenly [ˈslʌvənlɪ] *adj* (*comp:* **-lier;** *super:* **-liest**) desaseado, desaliñado, abandonado; *adv* desaliñadamente
slow [slo] *adj* lento; atrasado (*dícese del reloj*); tardío; lerdo, tardo, torpe (*para comprender*); aburrido; *adv* lentamente, despacio; *va* retardar; atrasar (*p.ej., un reloj*); *vn* retardarse, ir más despacio; atrasarse (*p.ej., un reloj*)
slowdown [ˈslo,daʊn] *s* huelga de brazos caídos (*actitud de los obreros cuando trabajan a ritmo lento*)
slow-drying [ˈsloˈdraɪɪŋ] *adj* de secado lento
slow match *s* mecha tardía
slow-motion [ˈslo,moʃən] *adj* a cámara lenta, al ralentí
slow-moving [ˈsloˈmuvɪŋ] *adj* tardo, lento, de marcha lenta; (com.) de venta morosa, de morosa salida
slowness [ˈslonɪs] *s* lentitud; torpeza
slow-witted [ˈsloˈwɪtɪd] *adj* lerdo, tardo, torpe
slowworm [ˈslo,wʌrm] *s* (zool.) lución
sludge [slʌdʒ] *s* lodo, cieno, fango; sedimento fangoso; pedazos de hielo flotantes
slue [slu] *s* ciénaga; ensenada de río; vuelta rápida; *va* volver, torcer; *vn* volverse, torcerse
slug [slʌg] *s* (coll.) porrazo, puñetazo; (coll.) trago (*de aguardiente*); (gun.) posta; ficha; lingote, pedazo de metal; (print.) lingote; (print.) línea de linotipia; (zool.) babosa; (*pret & pp:* **slugged;** *ger:* **slugging**) *va* aporrear, apuñear
slugabed [ˈslʌgə,bɛd] *s* aficionado a quedarse en la cama
sluggard [ˈslʌgərd] *adj & s* haragán, perezoso, pachón

sluggish [ˈslʌgɪʃ] *adj* inactivo, tardo, indolente; haragán, perezoso, pachorrudo
sluggishness [ˈslʌgɪʃnɪs] *s* inactividad, indolencia, pereza, pachorra
sluice [slus] *s* presa; compuerta; muralla, dique; canal; *va* dar paso a, abriendo la compuerta; limpiar, dejando entrar el agua; (min.) lavar (*el oro*); lanzar (*maderos*) por un canal o corriente de agua; *vn* salir el agua a borbotones
sluice gate *s* compuerta de presa
slum [slʌm] *s* barrio bajo; **the slums** los barrios bajos, los barrios de indigentes; (*pret & pp:* **slummed;** *ger:* **slumming**) *vn* visitar los barrios bajos
slumber [ˈslʌmbər] *s* sueño, sueño ligero, sueño tranquilo; inactividad; *va* pasar (*el tiempo*) durmiendo; *vn* dormir; dormitar; permanecer inactivo
slumberous [ˈslʌmbərəs] o **slumbrous** [ˈslʌmbrəs] *adj* soñoliento; tranquilo, calmo; inactivo
slum clearance *s* eliminación de los barrios bajos
slummer [ˈslʌmər] *s* visitante de los barrios bajos; habitante de los barrios bajos
slumming [ˈslʌmɪŋ] *s* visita a los barrios bajos
slump [slʌmp] *s* hundimiento, desplome; fracaso; (com.) baja repentina (*de precios, valores, etc.*); *vn* hundirse, desplomarse; fracasar; bajar repentinamente (*los precios, valores, etc.*)
slung [slʌŋ] *pret & pp de* **sling**
slung shot *s* rompecabezas (*arma ofensiva*)
slunk [slʌŋk] *pret & pp de* **slink**
slur [slʌr] *s* farfulla, pronunciación indistinta; borrón, mancha (*en la reputación*); reparo crítico, observación crítica; (mus.) ligado; (*pret & pp:* **slurred;** *ger:* **slurring**) *va* pasar por encima, suprimir, ocultar, pasar ligeramente; pronunciar indistintamente, comerse (*sonidos, sílabas*); farfullar, decir precipitadamente; (mus.) ligar; (mus.) marcar con un ligado; manchar la reputación de, insultar, despreciar, menospreciar
slush [slʌʃ] *s* fango muy blando; agua nieve fangosa, nieve a medio derretir; grasa; sentimentalismo tonto
slush fund *s* (slang) fondos que se usan para el soborno, especialmente en el comercio de la influencia política
slushy [ˈslʌʃɪ] *adj* (*comp:* **-ier** *super:* **-iest**) fangoso; lleno de nieve a medio derretir; sentimental
slut [slʌt] *s* perra; mala mujer, prostituta; mujer sucia
sluttish [ˈslʌtɪʃ] *adj* desaliñado, sucio; malo, inmoral
sly [slaɪ] *adj* (*comp:* **slyer** o **slier;** *super:* **slyest** o **sliest**) secreto, furtivo; astuto, socarrón; travieso; **on the sly** a hurtadillas, a escondidas
slyly [ˈslaɪlɪ] *adv* secretamente, furtivamente; astutamente
smack [smæk] *s* dejo, gustillo, saborcillo; pizca, pequeña cantidad; manotada, palmada; golpe; chasquido (*de látigo*); beso sonado; (naut.) queche; *adv* violentamente; directamente; *va* dar una manotada a; golpear; hacer chasquidos con (*p.ej., un látigo*); besar sonoramente; **to smack one's lips** chuparse los labios; *vn* **to smack of** saber a, oler a; (fig.) oler a
smacking [ˈsmækɪŋ] *adj* vivo, fuerte
small [smɔl] *adj* pequeño, chico; bajo; pobre, obscuro, humilde; insignificante; (print.) minúsculo; **to come out on the small end** salir perdiendo, llevarse lo peor; *adv* en miniatura; en pedazos menudos; en tono bajo y suave; tímidamente; **to feel small** sentirse pequeño o insignificante; **to sing small** ponerse modesto y humilde; *s* parte más estrecha (*p.ej., de la espalda*)
smallage [ˈsmɔlɪdʒ] *s* apio silvestre
small arms *spl* armas ligeras
small beer *s* cerveza floja; bagatela; persona de poca monta
small boy *s* chico, chico travieso
small capital *s* versalilla o versalita
small change *s* suelto, dinero menudo
small circle *s* (astr. & geom.) círculo menor
small clothes *spl* calzones
small fry *s* gente menuda, chiquillos; gentecilla de poco más o menos
small hours *spl* primeras horas de la mañana
small intestine *s* (anat.) intestino delgado
smallish [ˈsmɔlɪʃ] *adj* algo pequeño, pequeñito
small letter *s* letra minúscula
small-minded [ˈsmɔlˈmaɪndɪd] *adj* tacaño, mezquino; malo, bajo, ruin; intolerante, poco liberal (*en las ideas*)
smallness [ˈsmɔlnɪs] *s* pequeñez; (fig.) pequeñez
small of the back *s* parte más estrecha de la espalda
small potatoes *ssg* persona o cosa insignificante; *spl* personas o cosas insignificantes
smallpox [ˈsmɔlˌpɑks] *s* (path.) viruela
small print *s* tipo menudo, cuerpo pequeño
small talk *s* charladuría, charlas frívolas, palique
small-time [ˈsmɔlˈtaɪm] *adj* (slang) insignificante, de poca monta
small-town [ˈsmɔlˈtaʊn] *adj* lugareño, apegado a cosas lugareñas
smalt [smɔlt] *s* esmalte (*pigmento y color*)
smaltite [ˈsmɔltaɪt] *s* (mineral.) esmaltina
smart [smɑrt] *adj* listo, vivo, inteligente; agudo, penetrante, punzante; aseado; majo, elegante; astuto, ladino; fatuo, presuntuoso, sabihondo; (coll.) grande, considerable; *s* escozor; dolor vivo; *va* escocer en (*p.ej., la lengua*); *vn* escocer; sufrir, padecer; sentir irritación en el ánimo
smart aleck *s* (coll.) fatuo, presuntuoso, sabihondo
smarten [ˈsmɑrtən] *va* abrillantar, hermosear; avivar, animar; *vn* avivarse, animarse
smartness [ˈsmɑrtnɪs] *s* vivacidad, inteligencia, agudeza; astucia; elegancia, buen tono; fatuidad, presunción
smart set *s* gente chic, gente de buen tono
smartweed [ˈsmɑrtˌwid] *s* (bot.) pimienta de agua
smash [smæʃ] *s* rotura violenta, ruido de una rotura violenta; fracaso, ruina; quiebra, bancarrota; (coll.) choque o tope violento; (coll.) golpe violento; **to go to smash** hacerse pedazos; arruinarse; *va* romper con fuerza; hacer pedazos; arruinar, destrozar; aplastar; (tenis) volear (*la pelota*) con un golpe rápido y fuerte; *vn* romperse con fuerza; hacerse pedazos; arruinarse, destrozarse; aplastarse; **to smash into** topar con, chocar con
smash hit *s* (coll.) éxito rotundo
smash-up [ˈsmæʃˌʌp] *s* colisión violenta; ruina, desastre; quiebra, bancarrota
smatter [ˈsmætər] o **smattering** [ˈsmætərɪŋ] *s* barniz, tintura, migaja (*noción superficial de algo*)
smear [smɪr] *s* embarradura; (bact.) frotis; (fig.) mancha, desdoro; *va* embarrar, untar, manchar; (fig.) manchar, desdorar; *vn* embarrarse, untarse, mancharse
smear campaign *s* campaña de calumnias
smearcase [ˈsmɪrˌkes] *s* naterón, názula, requesón
smear word *s* palabra muy insultante, palabra desprestigiadora
smeary [ˈsmɪrɪ] *adj* (*comp:* **-ier;** *super:* **-iest**) manchado, graso, grasiento
smectic [ˈsmɛktɪk] *adj* esmético
smell [smɛl] *s* olor (*bueno o malo*); olfato (*sentido*); perfume, fragancia; hedor; traza, vestigio, señal; (*pret & pp:* **smelled** o **smelt**) *va* oler; olfatear, cazar olfateando; (fig.) olfatear, husmear; **to smell up** (coll.) dar mal olor a; *vn* oler; heder, oler mal; **to smell of** oler a
smeller [ˈsmɛlər] *s* oledor; (coll.) nariz
smelling bottle *s* redomilla para sales aromáticas
smelling salts *spl* sales aromáticas
smelly [ˈsmɛlɪ] *adj* (*comp:* **-ier;** *super:* **-iest**) hediondo
smelt [smɛlt] *s* (ichth.) esperinque, eperlano; *va & vn* (found.) fundir (*minerales*); *pret & pp de* **smell**
smelter [ˈsmɛltər] *s* fundidor; fundición (*fábrica*)

smelting furnace *s* horno de fundición
smilax ['smaɪlæks] *s* (bot.) zarzaparrilla; (bot.) mirsífilo
smile [smaɪl] *s* sonrisa; *va* expresar con una sonrisa; tener (*una sonrisa*); *vn* sonreír o sonreírse
smiling ['smaɪlɪŋ] *adj* risueño; (fig.) risueño
smilingly ['smaɪlɪŋlɪ] *adv* con cara risueña, con una sonrisa, sonriendo
smirch [smʌrtʃ] *s* tiznón; (fig.) deshonra; *va* tiznar; (fig.) tiznar
smirk [smʌrk] *s* sonrisa fatua y afectada; *vn* sonreír fatua y afectadamente
smit [smɪt] *pp de* **smite**
smite [smaɪt] (*pret:* **smote;** *pp:* **smitten** o **smit**) *va* golpear o herir súbitamente y con fuerza; caer con fuerza sobre; apenar, afligir; castigar
smith [smɪθ] *s* forjador, herrero
smithereens [,smɪðə'rinz] *spl* (coll.) añicos; **to tear to smithereens** (coll.) hacer añicos
smithy ['smɪθɪ] *s* (*pl:* **-ies**) herrería
smitten ['smɪtən] *adj* herido, afligido; impresionado; muy enamorado; *pp de* **smite**
smock [smɑk] *s* bata (*ropa talar para el trabajo de clínica, laboratorio, taller, etc.*); (archaic) camisa de mujer; *va* adornar con frunces que forman dibujo
smock frock *s* blusa de obrero
smocking ['smɑkɪŋ] *s* adorno de frunces que forman un dibujo
smog [smɑg] *s* (coll.) mezcla de humo y niebla
smoke [smok] *s* humo; tabaco; **to go up in smoke** irse todo en humo; **to have a smoke** echar un cigarro o cigarrillo; *va* ahumar; cecinar; fumar (*p.ej., cigarros*); pasar (*el tiempo*) fumando; **to smoke out** ahuyentar con humo; dar humazo a; descubrir; *vn* humear; fumar; hacer humo (*una chimenea dentro de la habitación*)
smokebox ['smok,bɑks] *s* caja de humos
smoked glasses *spl* gafas ahumadas
smokehouse ['smok,haus] *s* ahumadero
smokeless ['smoklɪs] *adj* sin humo
smokeless powder *s* pólvora sin humo
smoker ['smokər] *s* fumador; fumadero (*local*); (rail.) coche fumador, vagón de fumar; reunión o recepción de fumadores
smoke rings *spl* anillos de humo; **to blow smoke rings** sacar humo formando anillos
smoke screen *s* cortina de humo, niebla artificial
smokestack ['smok,stæk] *s* chimenea
smoke tree *s* (bot.) fustete
smoking ['smokɪŋ] *adj* fumante; *s* (el) fumar; **no smoking** prohibido fumar, se prohíbe fumar
smoking car *s* (rail.) coche fumador, vagón de fumar
smoking jacket *s* batín
smoking room *s* fumadero, saloncito para fumadores
smoky ['smokɪ] *adj* (*comp:* **-ier;** *super:* **-iest**) humeante; humoso, ahumado
smolder ['smolder] *s* fuego lento, sin llama y con mucho humo; *vn* arder en rescoldo (*arder sin llama y con mucho humo*); (fig.) estar latente, existir sin manifestarse al exterior, expresar una ira latente; (fig.) resquemarse (*resentirse sin manifestarlo*)
smolt [smolt] *s* (ichth.) cría del salmón que baja al mar
smooth [smuð] *adj* liso, terso, suave; plano, llano; igual, parejo; afable, blando, meloso; melifluo y sagaz; flúido y fácil (*dícese del estilo*); (phonet.) suave; **smooth as butter** como manteca; *adv* lisamente, suavemente; llanamente; afablemente, blandamente; *va* alisar, suavizar, allanar; facilitar; **to smooth away** quitar (*p.ej., obstáculos*) suavemente; **to smooth down** ablandar, calmar; **to smooth over** atenuar, limar
smoothbore ['smuð,bor] *adj* de ánima lisa; *s* arma de ánima lisa
smooth-faced ['smuð,fest] *adj* barbilampiño; bien afeitado; liso; de aspecto y palabras agradables
smooth hound *s* (ichth.) musola, cazón
smoothie ['smuðɪ] *s* var. de **smoothy**
smoothness ['smuðnɪs] *s* lisura, tersura; suavidad, blandura; llanura
smooth-spoken ['smuð,spokən] *adj* meloso, lisonjero
smooth-tongued ['smuð,tʌŋd] *adj* suave y blando en sus palabras; adulador, lisonjero
smoothy ['smuðɪ] *s* (*pl:* **-ies**) (coll.) galante (*hombre obsequioso con las damas*); (coll.) elegante, hombre distinguido; (coll.) adulador, lisonjero
smote [smot] *pret de* **smite**
smother ['smʌðər] *s* humareda, polvareda, nube; sofocación; *va* sofocar, ahogar; (cook.) ahogar, estofar; suprimir, ocultar; contener, reprimir; *vn* sofocarse; estar latente
smothery ['smʌðərɪ] *adj* sofocante; polvoroso, humoso
smoulder ['smoldər] *s & vn* var. de **smolder**
smudge [smʌdʒ] *s* fumigación, humareda; tiznón, mancha hecha con tizne; *va* tiznar, manchar con tizne; ahumar, fumigar (*p.ej., una huerta*)
smudge pot *s* vasija nebulizadora (*para proteger las tierras de cultivo contra las heladas*)
smudgy ['smʌdʒɪ] *adj* (*comp:* **-ier;** *super:* **-iest**) tiznado
smug [smʌg] *adj* (*comp:* **smugger;** *super:* **smuggest**) presumido, relamido; farisaico, pagado de sí mismo; compuesto, pulcro
smuggle ['smʌgəl] *va* meter de contrabando; **to smuggle in** meter o pasar de contrabando; **to smuggle out** sacar de contrabando; *vn* contrabandear
smuggler ['smʌglər] *s* contrabandista; barco contrabandista
smuggling ['smʌglɪŋ] *s* contrabando
smut [smʌt] *s* tizne, tiznón; suciedad; sitio sucio; obscenidad, indecencia, dicho obsceno o indecente; (agr.) carbón, tizón, tizoncillo; (*pret & pp:* **smutted;** *ger:* **smutting**) *va* tiznar; (agr.) atizonar; *vn* tiznarse; (agr.) atizonarse
smutch [smʌtʃ] *s* mancha, tiznón; *va* manchar, tiznar
smutty ['smʌtɪ] *adj* (*comp:* **-tier;** *super:* **-tiest**) tiznado, manchado; verde, obsceno, indecente; (agr.) atizonado
Smyrna ['smʌrnə] *s* Esmirna
snack [snæk] *s* bocadillo, tentempié; parte, porción
snack bar *s* bar o puesto público (*donde no se sirven comidas formales sino bocadillos, dulces, helados, refrescos, etc.*); cantina (*en las estaciones*)
snaffle ['snæfəl] *s* bridón del bocado; *va* contener por medio del bridón del bocado
snafu [snæ'fu] o ['snæfu] *adj* (slang) caótico; *s* (slang) caos, confusión, desorden; *va* (slang) confundir, enmarañar
snag [snæg] *s* tocón; raigón (*de un diente*); tropiezo, obstáculo; **to strike** o **hit a snag** tropezar con un obstáculo; (*pret & pp:* **snagged;** *ger:* **snagging**) *va* arrancar (*troncos*) del fondo del río; encontrar (*un tronco sumergido*); impedir, obstruir, enredar
snaggletooth ['snægəl,tuθ] *s* (*pl:* **-teeth**) sobrediente
snaggle-toothed ['snægəl,tuθt] *adj* que tiene sobredientes, que tiene dientes rotos o sobresalientes
snaggy ['snægɪ] *adj* (*comp:* **-gier;** *super:* **-giest**) nudoso; lleno de troncos, lleno de tocones; sobresaliente; rugoso, desigual
snail [snel] *s* (zool.) caracol; (zool.) babosa; (fig.) posma
snailflower ['snel,flauər] *s* (bot.) caracol real
snail-paced ['snel,pest] *adj* lento como una tortuga, lento como un caracol
snail's pace *s* paso de tortuga, paso de caracol; **at a snail's pace** a paso de tortuga, a paso de caracol
snake [snek] *s* culebra, serpiente; buscapiés, carretilla (*cohete*); (fig.) serpiente (*persona*); *va* arrastrar tirando de; (coll.) sacudir; *vn* culebrear, serpentear; (coll.) sacudirse, moverse a tirones
snakebird ['snek,bʌrd] *s* (orn.) anhinga
snake charmer *s* encantador de serpientes
snake in the grass *s* peligro insospechado, peligro desconocido; amigo pérfido, amigo desleal
snakeroot ['snek,rut] o ['snek,rʊt] *s* (bot.)

serpentaria de Virginia; (bot.) polígala de Virginia
snakeskin ['snek,skɪn] *s* piel de serpiente
snakeweed ['snek,wid] *s* (bot.) bistorta; (bot.) serpentaria de Virginia
snaky ['snekɪ] *adj* (*comp:* **-ier;** *super:* **-iest**) serpentino, tortuoso; lleno de serpientes; astuto y traidor
snap [snæp] *s* estallido, chasquido; castañetazo (*de los dedos*); mordedura, mordisco; discurso corto y mordaz; movimiento rápido; corto período (*p.ej., de frío agudo*); broche de presión; galletita; disparo rápido sin apuntar; instantánea; ganga, cosa fácil; **not a snap** nada, de ninguna manera ‖ *adj* rápido, hecho de repente ‖ (*pret & pp:* **snapped;** *ger:* **snapping**) *va* asir, cerrar, etc. de golpe; fotografiar instantáneamente; tomar (*una instantánea*); castañetear (*los dedos*); chasquear (*p.ej., el látigo*); **to snap one's fingers at** tratar con desprecio, burlarse de; **to snap up** asir, agarrar; aceptar con avidez, comprar con avidez; cortar la palabra a ‖ *vn* estallar, chasquear; saltar; exclamar; moverse rápidamente; chispear (*los ojos*); (fig.) estallar (*de fatiga*); **to snap at** querer morder; asir (*una oportunidad*); **to snap back at** tirar una mordida a; dar una respuesta grosera a; **to snap off** soltarse; **to snap out of it** (slang) cambiarse repentinamente; **to snap shut** cerrarse de golpe
snapdragon ['snæp,drægən] *s* (bot.) dragón, boca de dragón; (bot.) linaria, pajarita
snap fastener *s* corchete de presión
snap hook *s* mosquetón
snap judgment *s* decisión atolondrada
snap-on ['snæp,ɑn] *s* (aut.) abrazadera
snapper ['snæpər] *s* mordedor; (zool.) chiquiguao, chopontil (*tortuga*); (ichth.) cubera, pargo criollo, pargo colorado
snapping beetle *s* (ent.) elatérido (*p.ej., cucuyo, atóo, cardióforo, campilo, corimbites*)
snapping turtle *s* (zool.) chiquiguao, chopontil
snappish ['snæpɪʃ] *adj* propenso a morder; arisco, mordaz; respondón; irritable
snappy ['snæpɪ] *adj* (*comp:* **-pier;** *super:* **-piest**) crepitante; mordaz; (coll.) elegante, garboso; (coll.) fuerte, enérgico; acre y picante (*p.ej., queso*)
snapshot ['snæp,ʃɑt] *s* instantánea; disparo rápido sin apuntar; (*pret & pp:* **-shotted;** *ger:* **-shotting**) *va* tomar una instantánea de
snap switch *s* (elec.) interruptor de resorte
snare [snɛr] *s* lazo, trampa; bordón, tirante, timbre (*de un tambor*); *va* tender lazos a, coger con trampa; (fig.) hacer caer en el lazo
snare drum *s* caja clara, tambor con tirantes de cuerda
snarl [snɑrl] *s* gruñido; regaño; maraña; greña, pelo enmarañado; *va* decir con un gruñido; enmarañar, enredar; *vn* gruñir; regañar; enmarañarse, enredarse
snarly ['snɑrlɪ] *adj* (*comp:* **-ier;** *super:* **-iest**) gruñón; regañón; enredoso, enredado
snatch [snætʃ] *s* arrebatamiento; trocito, pedacito; ratito; **by snatches** a ratos; *va & vn* arrebatar; **to snatch at** tratar de asir o agarrar; **to snatch from** arrebatar a
snatch block *s* (naut.) pasteca
snatchy ['snætʃɪ] *adj* irregular, intermitente
snath [snæθ] o **snathe** [sneð] *s* mango de guadaña
sneak [snik] *s* entrada furtiva; sujeto solapado; *adj* furtivo; *va* mover a hurtadillas; robar; **to sneak in** introducir a hurtadillas; **to sneak out** llevarse (*algo*) a hurtadillas; *vn* andar furtivamente, moverse a hurtadillas; **to sneak in** entrarse a hurtadillas; **to sneak out** salirse a hurtadillas; **to sneak out of** evitar disimuladamente
sneaker ['snikər] *s* sujeto ruin y solapado; (coll.) zapato ligero de lona con suela de goma
sneaking ['snikɪŋ] *adj* husmeador; solapado; vil, bajo, ruin; oculto, secreto
sneak thief *s* ratero, descuidero
sneaky ['snikɪ] *adj* (*comp:* **-ier;** *super:* **-iest**) husmeador; solapado, socarrón; vil, despreciable
sneer [snɪr] *s* expresión de burla y desprecio; *va* decir o expresar con burla y desprecio; *vn* hablar con desprecio, hacer un gesto de desprecio, echar una mirada de desprecio; **to sneer at** mofarse de
sneering ['snɪrɪŋ] *adj* burlador y despreciativo
sneeze [sniz] *s* estornudo; *vn* estornudar; **to sneeze at** (coll.) despreciar, menospreciar, burlarse de
snell [snɛl] *s* hilo con que se ata el anzuelo al sedal
snick [snɪk] *s* tijeretada; golpe seco; ruido rápido y agudo; pelota golpeada; *va* tijeretear; golpear con fuerza; hacer que (*una cosa*) produzca un ruido como de golpe seco; *vn* producir un ruido como de golpe seco
snicker ['snɪkər] *s* risita medio contenida, risa tonta; *vn* reírse tontamente
snide [snaɪd] *adj* (slang) socarrón y malicioso
sniff [snɪf] *s* husmeo, venteo; sorbo por las narices; *va* husmear, ventear; sorber por las narices; (fig.) husmear, averiguar; sospechar; *vn* ventear; **to sniff at** husmear; menospreciar
sniffle ['snɪfəl] *s* resuello fuerte y repetido; **the sniffles** ataque de resoplidos; *vn* resollar fuerte y repetidamente
sniffy ['snɪfɪ] *adj* (*comp:* **-ier;** *super:* **-iest**) (coll.) estirado, desdeñoso
snifter ['snɪftər] *s* copa para aguardiente; (slang) trago de licor
snigger ['snɪgər] *s & vn* var. de **snicker**
snip [snɪp] *s* tijeretada; recorte, retazo; pedacito; (coll.) persona pequeña o insignificante; (coll.) sastre; **snips** *spl* tijeras para cortar el metal; (*pret & pp:* **snipped;** *ger:* **snipping**) *va* tijeretear; **to snip off** recortar, cortar de un tijeretazo
snipe [snaɪp] *s* (orn.) agachadiza, becacín; *vn* paquear, tirar desde un apostadero, tirar desde un escondite; **to snipe at** paquear, tirar desde un apostadero contra
snipe eel *s* (ichth.) anguila agachadiza
sniper ['snaɪpər] *s* paco, tirador escondido, tirador emboscado
sniping ['snaɪpɪŋ] *s* paqueo
snippet ['snɪpɪt] *s* recorte; (coll.) persona pequeña o insignificante
snippy ['snɪpɪ] *adj* (*comp:* **-pier;** *super:* **-iest**) compuesto de recortes; (coll.) arrogante, desdeñoso; (coll.) brusco, acre
snitch [snɪtʃ] *va & vn* (slang) soplar, ratear, escamotear
snivel ['snɪvəl] *s* gimoteo, lloriqueo; moqueo; moquita; (*pret & pp:* **-eled** o **-elled;** *ger:* **-eling** o **-elling**) *vn* gimotear, lloriquear; moquear
snob [snɑb] *s* esnob (*persona con pretensiones sociales*)
snobbery ['snɑbərɪ] *s* (*pl:* **-ies**) esnobismo
snobbish ['snɑbɪʃ] *adj* esnob
snobbishness ['snɑbɪʃnɪs] *s* esnobismo
snood [snud] *s* cintillo (*alrededor de la cabeza*); red llevada sobre la cabeza; *va* atar (*el cabello*) con un cintillo; recoger (*el cabello*) con una red
snooded ['snudɪd] *adj* atado con un cintillo; recogido con una red
snook [snuk] *s* (ichth.) róbalo
snoop [snup] *s* (coll.) curioso, buscavidas; *vn* (coll.) curiosear, ventear
snooper ['snupər] *s* (coll.) curioso, buscavidas
snoopy ['snupɪ] *adj* (coll.) curioso, entremetido, furtivo
snoot [snut] *s* (slang) cara, narices
snooty ['snutɪ] *adj* (*comp:* **-ier;** *super:* **-iest**) (slang) esnob
snooze [snuz] *s* (coll.) siestecita, sueñecito; *vn* (coll.) dormitar, echar una siestecita
snore [snor] *s* ronquido; *va* pasar roncando; *vn* roncar
snorkel ['snɔrkəl] *s* tubo snorkel o respiradero (*de submarino*)
snort [snɔrt] *s* bufido; *va* decir o expresar con un bufido; *vn* bufar
snot [snɑt] *s* (slang) mocarro
snotty ['snɑtɪ] *adj* (coll.) mocoso; (coll.) sucio, asqueroso; (slang) fachedón, engreído, huraño
snout [snaʊt] *s* hocico; morro (*cosa parecida a un hocico de animal*); (coll.) hocico (*de una persona*)
snout beetle *s* (ent.) rincóforo
snouted ['snaʊtɪd] *adj* hocicudo

snow [sno] *s* nieve; nevada; (telv.) nieve (*aspecto moteado*); (poet.) nieve (*blancura*); (slang) nieve (*cocaína, heroína*); *va* cubrir u obstruir con nieve; dejar caer como nieve; **to snow in** encerrar mediante la nieve; **to snow under** cubrir u obstruir con nieve; (coll.) derrotar completamente (*a un candidato*); *vn* nevar
snowball ['sno,bɔl] *s* bola de nieve; (bot.) bola de nieve; *va* lanzar bolas de nieve a; *vn* aumentar rápidamente (*como una bola de nieve que rueda*)
snowbank ['sno,bæŋk] *s* banco de nieve
snowbell ['sno,bɛl] *s* (bot.) estoraque norteamericano
snowberry ['sno,bɛrɪ] *s* (*pl:* **-ries**) (bot.) bolitas de nieve; (bot.) aceitillo, oreja de ratón, sueldaconsuelda
snowbird ['sno,bʌrd] *s* (orn.) pinzón de las nieves; (orn.) junquito; (orn.) echalumbre
snow-blind ['snow,blaɪnd] *adj* deslumbrado o cegado por los reflejos de la nieve
snow blindness *s* deslumbramiento debido a la nieve
snow-bound ['sno,baʊnd] *adj* detenido o aprisionado por la nieve
snow bunting *s* (orn.) pinzón de las nieves
snow-capped ['sno,kæpt] *adj* coronado de nieve
snow-clad ['sno,klæd] *adj* cubierto de nieve
snowdrift ['sno,drɪft] *s* ventisquero; nieve movida por el viento
snowdrop ['sno,drɑp] *s* (bot.) campanilla de invierno
snowfall ['sno,fɔl] *s* nevada
snow fence *s* valla paranieves
snowflake ['sno,flek] *s* ampo, copo de nieve; (orn.) pinzón de las nieves; (bot.) campanilla
snow flurry *s* nevisca
snow ice *s* hielo producido por la congelación del agua nieve
snowiness ['sno·ɪnɪs] *s* blancura de nieve
snow line o **limit** *s* límite de las nieves perpetuas
snow man *s* figura de nieve
snowplow ['sno,plaʊ] *s* quitanieve, barredora de nieve, expulsanieves
snowshed ['sno,ʃɛd] *s* guardanieve
snowshoe ['sno,ʃu] *s* raqueta de nieve; *vn* andar sobre la nieve llevando raquetas
snowslide ['sno,slaɪd] *s* alud; caída de un alud
snowstorm ['sno,stɔrm] *s* nevasca, fuerte nevada
Snow White *s* Blanca Nieves
snow-white ['sno,hwaɪt] *adj* blanco como la nieve
snowy ['sno·ɪ] *adj* (*comp:* **-ier;** *super:* **-iest**) nevoso
snowy owl *s* (orn.) lechuza blanca
snub [snʌb] *s* desaire; parada brusca; (*pret & pp:* **snubbed;** *ger:* **snubbing**) *va* desairar; parar bruscamente
snubber ['snʌbər] *s* persona arrogante; tambor de frenaje; (aut.) amortiguador
snubby ['snʌbɪ] *adj* (*comp:* **-bier;** *super:* **-biest**) respingón
snub-nosed ['snʌb,nozd] *adj* nacho, de nariz respingona
snuff [snʌf] *s* tabaco rapé, tabaco en polvo; costra, moco (*de la mecha de una vela*); **up to snuff** (slang) difícil de engañar; (slang) en buena condición; *va* husmear, olfatear; aspirar, sorber por la nariz; despabilar (*una candela*); **to snuff out** apagar, extinguir
snuffbox ['snʌf,bɑks] *s* tabaquera
snuffer ['snʌfər] *s* despabilador; **snuffers** *spl* despabiladeras, despabilador, apagavelas
snuffle ['snʌfəl] *s* gangueo; **the snuffles** ataque de gangueo; *vn* ganguear; husmear, ventear
snuffy ['snʌfɪ] *adj* (*comp:* **-ier;** *super:* **-iest**) tabacoso; desagradable, descortés
snug [snʌg] *adj* (*comp:* **snugger;** *super:* **snuggest**) cómodo, abrigado; apañado, ajustado; bien aparejado (*dícese de una embarcación*); muy ceñido (*dícese de una prenda de vestir*); escondido; acomodado; **snug as a bug in a rug** como un pez en el agua; *adv* cómodamente; ajustadamente; a escondidas; bastante pero sin holgura; (*pret & pp:* **snugged;** *ger:* **snugging**) *va* acomodar; apañar, ajustar; aparejar; esconder; hacer suficiente pero no abundante
snuggery ['snʌgərɪ] *s* (*pl:* **-ies**) casa cómoda y bien arreglada; sitio cómodo y bien arreglado; posición cómoda y a propósito
snuggle ['snʌgəl] *va* apretar, arrimar; *vn* apretarse, arrimarse; dormir bien abrigado; **to snuggle up to** arrimarse a
snugness ['snʌgnɪs] *s* comodidad, bienestar, holgura
So. abr. de **south**
so [so] *s* (mus.) sol; *adv* así; tan + *adj* o *adv;* por tanto, por consiguiente; también; **and so** así pues; también, lo mismo; **and so on** y así sucesivamente; **or so** más o menos; **to think so** creer que sí; **so as to** + *inf* para + *inf;* **so far** hasta aquí; hasta ahora; **so long** (coll.) hasta la vista; **so many** tantos; **so much** tanto; **so so** tal cual; así así; **so that** de modo que, de suerte que, así que; para que; con tal de que; **so to speak** por decirlo así; *conj* así que; *interj* ¡ bien!; ¿ verdad?
soak [sok] *s* mojada, empapamiento; (coll.) potista, borrachín; *va* empapar, remojar; absorber, embeber; (slang) aporrear, castigar severamente; (slang) hacer pagar un precio o precios exorbitantes; **to soak up** absorber, embeber; (fig.) entender; **soaked to the skin** calado hasta los huesos; *vn* empaparse, remojarse; calarse; (coll.) beber mucho, emborracharse; **to soak into** penetrar, filtrarse en
soakage ['sokɪdʒ] *s* remojo; líquido rezumado
so-and-so ['soənd,so] *s* (*pl:* **-sos**) fulano, fulano de tal; tal; tal cosa; *adj* bien arreglado
soap [sop] *s* jabón; *va* jabonar
soapberry ['sop,bɛrɪ] *s* (*pl:* **-ries**) (bot.) jaboncillo
soapbox ['sop,bɑks] *s* caja de jabón; caja vacía empleada como tribuna en la calle; *vn* hablar en la calle desde una tribuna improvisada
soapbox orator *s* orador de plazuela
soapbox oratory *s* oratoria de barricada
soap bubble *s* burbuja de jabón, pompa de jabón
soap dish *s* jabonera
soap flakes *spl* copos de jabón
soapmaker ['sop,mekər] *s* jabonero
soap opera *s* (coll.) drama radiofónico transmitido en una serie de programas de temas doméstico-sentimentales, serial lacrimógeno
soap powder *s* jabón en polvo, polvo de jabón
soapstone ['sop,ston] *s* (mineral.) esteatita; jabón de sastre
soapsuds ['sop,sʌdz] *spl* jabonaduras
soapwort ['sop,wʌrt] *s* (bot.) jabonera, saponaria
soapy ['sopɪ] *adj* (*comp:* **-ier;** *super:* **-iest**) jabonoso
soar [sor] *vn* encumbrarse, subir muy alto, volar a gran altura; aspirar, pretender; (aer.) planear
sob [sɑb] *s* sollozo; suspiro (*p.ej., del viento*); *adj* (slang) sentimental; (*pret & pp:* **sobbed;** *ger:* **sobbing**) *va* decir o expresar sollozando; **to sob oneself to sleep** adormecerse sollozando; *vn* sollozar; suspirar (*el viento*)
sober ['sobər] *adj* sobrio, moderado; no embriagado; grave, serio; cuerdo, sensato; sereno, tranquilo; apagado (*color*); *va* poner sobrio; desemborrachar; **to sober down** calmar, sosegar; **to sober up** desemborrachar; *vn* volverse sobrio; **to sober down** calmarse, sosegarse; **to sober up** desemborracharse
sober-minded ['sobər'maɪndɪd] *adj* cuerdo, sensato, de mente serena, dueño de sí
soberness ['sobərnɪs] *s* sobriedad; seriedad; cordura; serenidad
sobriety [so'braɪətɪ] *s* (*pl:* **-ties**) sobriedad, moderación; gravedad, seriedad; cordura, sensatez; serenidad
sobriquet ['sobrɪke] *s* apodo
sob sister *s* (slang) periodista llorona
sob story *s* (slang) historia de lagrimitas
soc. o **Soc.** abr. de **society**
socage o **soccage** ['sɑkɪdʒ] *s* (feud.) ocupación de una tierra por prestación de trabajo pero sin servicio militar
so-called ['so,kɔld] *adj* llamado, así llamado; supuesto
soccer ['sɑkər] *s* (sport) fútbol asociación

soccer pool *s* quiniela (*apuesta mutua de fútbol*)
sociability [ˌsoʃəˈbɪlɪtɪ] *s* (*pl:* **-ties**) sociabilidad
sociable [ˈsoʃəbəl] *adj* sociable; *s* tertulia; sociable (*coche*)
social [ˈsoʃəl] *adj* social; sociable; socialista; de la buena sociedad; *s* reunión social
social climber *s* ambicioso de figurar
social evil *s* prostitución
social hygiene *s* higiene social
socialism [ˈsoʃəlɪzəm] *s* socialismo
socialist [ˈsoʃəlɪst] *adj & s* socialista
socialistic [ˌsoʃəˈlɪstɪk] *adj* socialista
socialistically [ˌsoʃəˈlɪstɪkəlɪ] *adv* según el socialismo
socialite [ˈsoʃəlaɪt] *s* (coll.) personaje de la buena sociedad
sociality [ˌsoʃɪˈælɪtɪ] *s* (*pl:* **-ties**) sociabilidad (*calidad de sociable; índole sociable; tendencia del hombre a la vida social*)
socialization [ˌsoʃəlɪˈzeʃən] *s* socialización
socialize [ˈsoʃəlaɪz] *va* socializar
socialized medicine *s* medicina social
social register *s* guía social, registro de la buena sociedad
social science *s* ciencia social
social security *s* seguro social, retiro obrero, previsión social
social service *s* servicio social
social work *s* auxilio social
social worker *s* persona que se consagra al auxilio social
society [səˈsaɪətɪ] *s* (*pl:* **-ties**) sociedad; compañía (*trato*); buena sociedad, mundo elegante; **to be in society** hallarse en sociedad
society editor *s* cronista de la vida social
Society Islands *spl* islas de la Sociedad
Society of Jesus *s* Compañía de Jesús
sociological [ˌsosɪəˈlɑdʒɪkəl] o [ˌsoʃɪəˈlɑdʒɪkəl] *adj* sociológico
sociologically [ˌsosɪəˈlɑdʒɪkəlɪ] o [ˌsoʃɪəˈlɑdʒɪkəlɪ] *adv* según la sociología
sociologist [ˌsosɪˈɑlədʒɪst] o [ˌsoʃɪˈɑlədʒɪst] *s* sociólogo
sociology [ˌsosɪˈɑlədʒɪ] o [ˌsoʃɪˈɑlədʒɪ] *s* sociología
sock [sɑk] *s* calcetín; zueco (*zapato ligero; comedia*); (slang) golpe fuerte; *adv* (slang) derecho, bien; *va* (slang) pegar, golpear con fuerza
socket [ˈsɑkɪt] *s* cuenca (*de los ojos*); alvéolo (*de un diente*); cañón (*de un candelero*); cubo (*de un candelero; de una llave de caja*); (elec.) portalámparas; (rad.) portaválvula, zócalo
socket wrench *s* llave de cubo, llave de caja
socle [ˈsɑkəl] o [ˈsokəl] *s* (arch.) zócalo
Socrates [ˈsɑkrətiz] *s* Sócrates
Socratic [soˈkrætɪk] *adj* socrático
sod [sɑd] *s* césped; terrón de césped; **under the sod** bajo la tierra; (*pret & pp:* **sodded;** *ger:* **sodding**) *va* cubrir de césped, encespedar
soda [ˈsodə] *s* (chem.) sosa, soda; soda (*bebida refrescante*)
soda ash *s* cenizas de sosa
soda cracker *s* galletita un poco salada, muy friable y sin azúcar ni grasa
soda fountain *s* fuente de sodas (*aparato o mostrador con grifos para servir gaseosas y sodas*)
soda jerk *s* (slang) mozo que sirve en la fuente de sodas
soda lime *s* cal sodada
sodality [soˈdælɪtɪ] *s* (*pl:* **-ties**) amistad íntima; hermandad; cofradía
soda water *s* agua gaseosa
sodden [ˈsɑdən] *adj* empapado, saturado; lerdo, estúpido
sodium [ˈsodɪəm] *s* (chem.) sodio; *adj* sódico o de sodio, p.ej., **sodium chloride** cloruro sódico o cloruro de sodio
sodium bicarbonate *s* (chem.) bicarbonato sódico
sodium carbonate *s* (chem.) carbonato sódico
sodium cyanide *s* (chem.) cianuro sódico
sodium hydrosulfite *s* (chem.) hidrosulfito sódico (*agente reductor*)
sodium hydroxide *s* (chem.) hidróxido de sodio
sodium hyposulfite *s* (chem.) hiposulfito de sodio ($S_2O_4Na_2$); (chem. & phot.) hiposulfito de sodio ($S_2O_3Na_2$)
sodium nitrate *s* (chem.) nitrato sódico
Sodom [ˈsɑdəm] *s* (Bib.) Sodoma
Sodomite [ˈsɑdəmaɪt] *s* sodomita; (*l.c.*) *s* sodomita
sodomy [ˈsɑdəmɪ] *s* sodomía
soever [soˈɛvər] *adv* de cualquier modo; de cualquier clase; en cualquier caso
sofa [ˈsofə] *s* sofá
soffit [ˈsɑfɪt] *s* (arch.) sofito
Sofia [soˈfiə] *s* Sofía (*ciudad*)
soft [sɔft] o [sɑft] *adj* blando, muelle; delicado; suave; flojo; flexible (*dícese, p.ej., de un sombrero*); dulce (*metal*); tierno (*dícese de la soldadura*); torpe, estúpido; (phonet.) sonoro; (phonet.) sibilante; (phys.) blando (*rayo; tubo al vacío*); (coll.) fácil; (coll.) fácil de tratar; *adv* blandamente; delicadamente; suavemente; flojamente; *interj* ¡quedo!, ¡sin ruido!, ¡poco a poco!
softball [ˈsɔftˌbɔl] o [ˈsɑftˌbɔl] béisbol que se juega con pelota blanda; pelota blanda
soft-boiled egg [ˈsɔftˈbɔɪld] o [ˈsɑftˈbɔɪld] *s* huevo pasado por agua
soft coal *s* hulla grasa
soft collar *s* cuello blando
soft drink *s* bebida no alcohólica, refresco
soften [ˈsɔfən] o [ˈsɑfən] *va* ablandar; afeminar; **to soften up** ablandar (*por medio del bombardeo*); *vn* ablandarse; afeminarse
softening of the brain *s* (path.) reblandecimiento cerebral
soft-hearted [ˈsɔftˈhɑrtɪd] o [ˈsɑftˈhɑrtɪd] *adj* de buen corazón
softish [ˈsɔftɪʃ] o [ˈsɑftɪʃ] *adj* blandujo
softness [ˈsɔftnɪs] o [ˈsɑftnɪs] *s* blandura; suavidad; dulzura; flojedad; debilidad (*de carácter*); (coll.) facilidad
soft palate *s* (anat.) paladar blando, velo del paladar
soft pedal *s* (mus.) pedal suave, pedal celeste
soft-pedal [ˌsɔftˈpɛdəl] o [ˌsɑftˈpɛdəl] *va* (mus.) disminuir la intensidad de, por medio del pedal suave; (slang) moderar; *vn* (mus.) disminuir la intensidad por medio del pedal suave; (slang) moderar
soft sell *s* (coll.) método mañoso e indirecto de anunciar o vender mercancías
soft-shelled crab [ˈsɔftˌʃɛld] o [ˈsɑftˌʃɛld] *s* cangrejo después de la muda
soft-shelled turtle *s* (zool.) trióníx espinífero
soft soap *s* jabón blando o graso; (coll.) lisonja, adulación
soft-soap [ˌsɔftˈsop] o [ˌsɑftˈsop] *va* (coll.) enjabonar, dar jabón a
soft-spoken [ˈsɔftˈspokən] o [ˈsɑftˈspokən] *adj* de voz suave; dicho con voz suave
soft spot *s* (coll.) afición, simpatía; (coll.) sentimentalismo; (coll.) flaqueza
soft steel *s* acero dulce o suave
soft water *s* agua blanda, agua suave, agua delgada
softwood [ˈsɔftˌwʊd] o [ˈsɑftˌwʊd] *s* árbol conífero; madera de árbol conífero; madera blanda
softy [ˈsɔftɪ] o [ˈsɑftɪ] *s* (*pl:* **-ies**) (coll.) mollejón; (coll.) inocentón
soggy [ˈsɑgɪ] *adj* (*comp:* **-gier;** *super:* **-giest**) empapado, remojado
soil [sɔɪl] *s* suelo, tierra; país, región; mancha; (fig.) mancha, deshonra; *va* manchar, ensuciar; (fig.) manchar, deshonrar; viciar, corromper; *vn* mancharse, ensuciarse; (fig.) mancharse, deshonrarse
soilage [ˈsɔɪlɪdʒ] *s* ensuciamiento; (agr.) pasto verde para el ganado
soil conservation *s* conservación de suelos
soil pipe *s* tubo de desagüe sanitario, cañería de arcilla vitrificada
soiree o **soirée** [swɑˈre] *s* sarao, verbena, velada
sojourn [ˈsodʒʌrn] *s* estancia, permanencia; [ˈsodʒʌrn] o [soˈdʒʌrn] *vn* estarse, residir por una temporada
sol. abr. de **soluble** y **solution**
Sol. abr. de **Solomon** y **Solicitor**
sol [sɑl] o [sol] *s* (chem. & mus.) sol; (*cap.*) [sɑl] *s* el Sol; (myth.) Sol

solace ['sɑlɪs] *s* solaz, consuelo; *va* solazar, consolar
solan ['solən] *s* (orn.) alcatraz, planga
solanaceous [ˌsɑlə'neʃəs] *adj* (bot.) solanáceo
solanine ['sɑlənin] o ['solənin] *s* (chem.) solanina
solar ['solər] *adj* solar
solarium [so'lɛrɪəm] *s* (*pl:* **-a** [ə]) solana
solar plexus ['plɛksəs] *s* (anat.) plexo solar
solar protuberances *spl* (astr.) protuberancias solares
solar system *s* sistema solar
solar year *s* año solar
sold [sold] *pret & pp de* **sell**
solder ['sɑdər] *s* soldadura; *va* soldar
soldering ['sɑdərɪŋ] *s* soldadura
soldering iron *s* soldador, estañador, cautín
soldering paste *s* pasta para soldar
soldier ['soldʒər] *s* soldado (*militar sin graduación*); militar (*el que forma parte del ejército*); *vn* militar, servir como soldado; holgazanear; fingirse enfermo
soldierly ['soldʒərlɪ] *adj* soldadesco, militar
soldier of fortune *s* aventurero militar
soldiery ['soldʒərɪ] *s* (*pl:* **-ies**) soldadesca
sold on *adj* (slang) convencido del valor o el mérito de
sold out *adj* agotado; **the theater is sold out** todas las localidades están vendidas; **we are sold out of those neckties** se nos han agotado esas corbatas
sole [sol] *s* planta (*del pie*); suela (*del calzado*); palma (*del casco del caballo*); base, fondo; (ichth.) lenguado; (ichth.) sol, suela, lenguita (*Symphurus plagiusa*); *adj* solo, único; exclusivo; *va* solar
solecism ['sɑlɪsɪzəm] *s* solecismo; desacierto, patochada
sole leather *s* cuero de suela, solería
solely ['sollɪ] *adv* solamente, únicamente
solemn ['sɑləm] *adj* solemne
solemnity [sə'lɛmnɪtɪ] *s* (*pl:* **-ties**) solemnidad
solemnization [ˌsɑləmnɪ'zeʃən] *s* solemnización
solemnize ['sɑləmnaɪz] *va* solemnizar
solenoid ['solɪnɔɪd] *s* (elec.) solenoide
soleus ['solɪəs] *s* (anat.) sóleo
sol-fa [ˌsol'fɑ] *s* (mus.) solfa; *va & vn* solfear
sol-faist [ˌsol'fɑ·ɪst] *s* (mus.) solfista
solfeggio [sɑl'fɛdʒo] *s* (*pl:* **-gios**) (mus.) solfeo
solicit [sə'lɪsɪt] *va* solicitar; intentar seducir, intentar corromper; *vn* hacer una solicitud, hacer una petición
solicitation [səˌlɪsɪ'teʃən] *s* solicitación; incitación, tentación, seducción; tentativa de corrupción
solicitor [sə'lɪsɪtər] *s* solicitador; (law) procurador
solicitor general *s* (*pl:* **solicitors general**) (U.S.A.) subsecretario de justicia; (U.S.A.) procurador general del Estado; (Brit.) subfiscal de la corona
solicitous [sə'lɪsɪtəs] *adj* solícito, ansioso
solicitude [sə'lɪsɪtjud] o [sə'lɪsɪtud] *s* solicitud, ansiedad
solid ['sɑlɪd] *adj* sólido; denso; todo; unánime; impreso sin interlíneas; escrito en una sola palabra; (fig.) sólido, macizo (*p.ej., argumento*); **a solid hour** una hora entera; *s* sólido
solidarity [ˌsɑlɪ'dærɪtɪ] *s* (*pl:* **-ties**) solidaridad
solid geometry *s* geometría del espacio
solidification [səˌlɪdɪfɪ'keʃən] *s* solidificación
solidify [sə'lɪdɪfaɪ] (*pret & pp:* **-fied**) *va* solidificar; *vn* solidificarse
solidity [sə'lɪdɪtɪ] *s* (*pl:* **-ties**) solidez
Solid South *s* (U.S.A.) conjunto de los estados del Sur (*considerado como unidad política por su apoyo al partido Democrático*)
solid state *s* (phys.) estado sólido
solid-state physics ['sɑlɪd'stet] *ssg* física del estado sólido
solid tire *s* (aut.) macizo
soliloquize [sə'lɪləkwaɪz] *vn* soliloquiar
soliloquy [sə'lɪləkwɪ] *s* (*pl:* **-quies**) soliloquio
solipsism ['sɑlɪpsɪzəm] *s* (philos.) solipsismo
solitaire ['sɑlɪter] *s* solitario (*juego y diamante*); sortija solitario
solitary ['sɑlɪˌtɛrɪ] *adj* solitario; *s* (*pl:* **-ies**) solitario
solitary confinement *s* celda de castigo, aislamiento penal, incomunicación
solitary sandpiper *s* (orn.) chorlito de manchas acaneladas
solleret ['sɑlərɛt] o [ˌsɑlə'rɛt] *s* escarpadura (*de las armaduras antiguas*)
solmization [ˌsɑlmɪ'zeʃən] *s* (mus.) solfa
solo ['solo] *s* (*pl:* **-los**) (mus.) solo; *adj* (mus.) solista; a solas, hecho a solas
soloist ['solo·ɪst] *s* solista
Solomon ['sɑləmən] *s* Salomón; (fig.) Salomón
Solomonic [ˌsɑlə'mɑnɪk] *adj* salomónico
Solomon Islands *spl* islas Salomón
Solomon's seal *s* sello de Salomón
Solomon's-seal ['sɑləmənzˌsil] *s* (bot.) sello de Salomón
Solon ['solɑn] *s* Solón; (fig.) Solón
solstice ['sɑlstɪs] *s* (astr.) solsticio
solstitial [sɑl'stɪʃəl] *adj* solsticial
solubility [ˌsɑljə'bɪlɪtɪ] *s* solubilidad
soluble ['sɑljəbəl] *adj* soluble
solute ['sɑljut] o ['solut] *s* (chem.) soluto
solution [sə'luʃən] *s* solución
solution of continuity *s* solución de continuidad
solvable ['sɑlvəbəl] *adj* soluble
solve [sɑlv] *va* resolver, solucionar; adivinar (*un enigma*)
solvency ['sɑlvənsɪ] *s* (*pl:* **-cies**) solvencia
solvent ['sɑlvənt] *adj* solvente; (chem.) solvente; *s* (chem.) solvente
Solyman ['sɑlɪmən] *s* Solimán
soma ['somə] *s* (*pl:* **-mata** [mətə]) (biol.) soma
Somali [so'mɑlɪ] *s* (*pl:* **-li** o **-lis**) somalí
Somaliland [so'mɑlɪˌlænd] *s* la Somalía
somatic [so'mætɪk] *adj* somático
somatology [ˌsomə'tɑlədʒɪ] *s* somatología
somber o **sombre** ['sɑmbər] *adj* sombrío
sombrero [sɑm'brɛro] *s* (*pl:* **-ros**) sombrero jarano
some [sʌm] *adj indef* algún; un poco de; unos; (coll.) grande, bueno, famoso, p.ej., **some crackpot** famoso tarambana; *pron indef pl* algunos; *adv* (coll.) algo; (coll.) muy, mucho
somebody ['sʌmˌbɑdɪ] *pron indef* alguien; **somebody else** algún otro, otra persona; *s* (*pl:* **-ies**) personaje
someday ['sʌmde] *adv* algún día
somehow ['sʌmhaʊ] *adv* de algún modo, de alguna manera; **somehow or other** de un modo u otro
someone ['sʌmwʌn] *pron indef* alguien; **someone else** algún otro, otra persona
somersault ['sʌmərˌsɔlt] o **somerset** ['sʌmərˌsɛt] *s* salto mortal; **to turn a somersault** dar un salto mortal; *vn* dar un salto mortal, dar saltos mortales
something ['sʌmθɪŋ] *s* alguna cosa, algo; cosa de importancia, cosa de suposición; **something else** otra cosa; *adv* algo, un poco
sometime ['sʌmtaɪm] *adj* antiguo, de otro tiempo; *adv* alguna vez, en algún tiempo; antiguamente, en otro tiempo
sometimes ['sʌmtaɪmz] *adv* a veces, a las veces, algunas veces
someway ['sʌmwe] *adv* de algún modo
somewhat ['sʌmhwɑt] *adv* algo, un poco; *s* alguna cosa, algo, un poco
somewhere ['sʌmhwɛr] *adv* en alguna parte, a alguna parte; en algún tiempo; **somewhere else** en otra parte, a otra parte
somewhile ['sʌmhwaɪl] *adv* a veces; alguna vez; antiguamente, en otro tiempo
somewhither ['sʌmhwɪðər] *adv* hacia alguna parte
somnambulism [sɑm'næmbjəlɪzəm] *s* sonambulismo
somnambulist [sɑm'næmbjəlɪst] *s* sonámbulo
somnambulistic [sɑmˌnæmbjə'lɪstɪk] *adj* sonámbulo
somniferous [sɑm'nɪfərəs] *adj* somnífero; soñoliento
somnolence ['sɑmnələns] *s* somnolencia o soñolencia
somnolent ['sɑmnələnt] *adj* soñoliento
Somnus ['sɑmnəs] *s* (myth.) el Sueño
son [sʌn] *s* hijo; **the Son** el Hijo (*Jesucristo*)
sonance ['sonəns] *s* sonoridad

sonant [ˈsonənt] *adj* sonante; (phonet.) sonoro; *s* (phonet.) sonora
sonar [ˈsonɑr] *s* sonar
sonata [səˈnɑtə] *s* (mus.) sonata
sonatina [ˌsɑnəˈtinə] *s* (mus.) sonatina
song [sɔŋ] o [sɑŋ] *s* canción, canto; bagatela; **for a song** muy barato; **to sing the same old song** volver a la misma canción
songbird [ˈsɔŋˌbʌrd] o [ˈsɑŋˌbʌrd] *s* ave canora; (fig.) cantora, cantatriz
songless [ˈsɔŋlɪs] o [ˈsɑŋlɪs] *adj* sin canto
Song of Solomon *s* (Bib.) Cantares de Salomón
Song of Songs *s* (Bib.) Cantar de los Cantares
songster [ˈsɔŋstər] o [ˈsɑŋstər] *s* cantor, cantante; cancionista; ave canora
songstress [ˈsɔŋstrɪs] o [ˈsɑŋstrɪs] *s* cantora, cantatriz; cancionista; poetisa; ave canora
song thrush *s* (orn.) malvís, tordo alirrojo
sonic [ˈsɑnɪk] *adj* sónico
sonic barrier *s* barrera del sonido, barrera sónica
sonic boom *s* estallido que da un avión al atravesar la barrera sónica
sonic depth finder *s* sonda acústica
soniferous [soˈnɪfərəs] *adj* sonoro, sonante
son-in-law [ˈsʌnɪnˌlɔ] *s* (*pl:* **sons-in-law**) yerno
sonnet [ˈsɑnɪt] *s* soneto
sonneteer [ˌsɑnɪˈtɪr] *s* sonetista; poetastro; *vn* sonetear, sonetizar
sonny [ˈsʌnɪ] *s* (*pl:* **-nies**) hijito
Son of God *s* Hijo de Dios (*Jesucristo*)
Son of Man *s* Hijo del Hombre (*Jesucristo*)
sonometer [soˈnɑmɪtər] *s* sonómetro
sonorant [soˈnorənt] *s* (phonet.) sonante
sonority [səˈnɑrɪtɪ] o [səˈnɔrɪtɪ] *s* (*pl:* **-ties**) sonoridad
sonorous [səˈnorəs] *adj* sonoro, resonante
soon [sun] *adv* pronto, en breve; temprano; de buena gana; **soon after** poco después, poco después de; **as soon as** así que, luego que, tan pronto como; **as soon as possible** cuanto antes, lo más pronto posible; **had sooner** preferiría; **how soon?** ¿cuándo?; **sooner or later** tarde o temprano
soot [sʊt] o [sut] *s* hollín; *va* manchar o cubrir de hollín, ensuciar con hollín
soothe [suð] *va* calmar, sosegar, aliviar
soothsayer [ˈsuθˌseər] *s* adivino
soothsaying [ˈsuθˌseɪŋ] *s* adivinación, adivinanza
sooty [ˈsʊtɪ] o [ˈsutɪ] *adj* (*comp:* **-ier;** *super:* **-iest**) holliniento
sop [sɑp] *s* sopa (*pan u otra cosa empapada en un líquido*); regalo (*para acallar, apaciguar o sobornar*); persona muy mojada, cosa muy mojada; (*pret & pp:* **sopped;** *ger:* **sopping**) *va* empapar, ensopar; **to sop up** absorber
Sophia [soˈfaɪə] o [ˈsofɪə] *s* Sofía (*nombre de mujer*)
sophism [ˈsɑfɪzəm] *s* sofisma
sophist [ˈsɑfɪst] *s* sofista; sabio, filósofo
sophistic [səˈfɪstɪk] o **sophistical** [səˈfɪstɪkəl] *adj* sofista; sofístico
sophisticate [səˈfɪstɪket] *s* mundano, hombre mundano; *va* hacer mundano; envolver en sofisterías; engañar; *vn* valerse de sofismas
sophisticated [səˈfɪstɪˌketɪd] *adj* mundano, falto de simplicidad; engañoso, fraudulento
sophistication [səˌfɪstɪˈkeʃən] *s* mundanería, falta de simplicidad; sofistería
sophistry [ˈsɑfɪstrɪ] *s* sofistería
Sophoclean [ˌsɑfəˈkliən] *adj* sofocleo
Sophocles [ˈsɑfəkliz] *s* Sófocles
sophomore [ˈsɑfəmor] *s* estudiante de segundo año
sophomoric [ˌsɑfəˈmɑrɪk] o [ˌsɑfəˈmɔrɪk] *adj* de los estudiantes de segundo año; engreído e ignorante
soporiferous [ˌsopəˈrɪfərəs] o [ˌsɑpəˈrɪfərəs] *adj* soporífero
soporific [ˌsopəˈrɪfɪk] o [ˌsɑpəˈrɪfɪk] *adj* soporífero, soporífico; soporoso; *s* soporífero
sopping [ˈsɑpɪŋ] *adj* empapado; **sopping wet** hecho una sopa
soppy [ˈsɑpɪ] *adj* (*comp:* **-pier;** *super:* **-piest**) empapado; lluvioso
soprano [səˈpræno] o [səˈprɑno] *s* (*pl:* **-os**) soprano; *adj* de soprano, para soprano

sorb [sɔrb] *s* (bot.) serbal; serba (*fruto*)
Sorbonne [sɔrˈbɑn] *s* Sorbona
sorcerer [ˈsɔrsərər] *s* hechicero, brujo
sorceress [ˈsɔrsərɪs] *s* hechicera, bruja
sorcery [ˈsɔrsərɪ] *s* (*pl:* **-ies**) hechicería, brujería, sortilegio
sordid [ˈsɔrdɪd] *adj* sórdido
sore [sor] *s* llaga, úlcera; pena, dolor, disgusto, aflicción; **to open an old sore** renovar la herida; *adj* enrojecido, inflamado; dolorido; susceptible, irritable; (coll.) sentido, picado, resentido; penoso; fuerte, vehemente; **to be sore at** (coll.) estar enojado con
sore ears *spl* mal o dolor de oídos
sore eyes *spl* dolor de ojos
sorehead [ˈsorˌhɛd] *s* (coll.) persona resentida
sorely [ˈsorlɪ] *adv* penosamente; con urgencia
soreness [ˈsornɪs] *s* dolor, inflamación; amargura de una pena
sore throat *s* mal o dolor de garganta
sorghum [ˈsɔrgəm] *s* (bot.) alcandía, sorgo, zahína
sorority [səˈrɑrɪtɪ] o [səˈrɔrɪtɪ] *s* (*pl:* **-ties**) hermandad (*de mujeres; de estudiantas*)
sorosis [səˈrosɪs] *s* (bot.) sorosis
sorrel [ˈsɑrəl] o [ˈsɔrəl] *adj* alazán; *s* (bot.) acedera; alazán (*color y caballo de este color*)
sorrow [ˈsɑro] o [ˈsɔro] *s* dolor, pesar, pena; arrepentimiento; *vn* dolerse, apenarse, sentir pena; arrepentirse; **to sorrow for** añorar
sorrowful [ˈsɑrofəl] o [ˈsɔrofəl] *adj* doloroso, pesaroso, afligido, penoso
sorry [ˈsɑrɪ] o [ˈsɔrɪ] *adj* (*comp:* **-rier;** *super:* **-riest**) pesaroso, afligido, apenado; arrepentido; malo, pésimo; despreciable, ridículo; **to be** o **feel sorry** sentir; arrepentirse; **to be** o **feel sorry for** compadecer; **to be sorry to** + *inf* sentir + *inf*
sort [sɔrt] *s* clase, especie; tipo; modo, manera; (print.) tipo; **a sort of** uno a modo de; **of sorts** de varias clases; de poco valor, de mala muerte; **out of sorts** de mal humor; indispuesto; incómodo; **sort of** (coll.) algo, en cierta medida; *va* clasificar, separar; escoger; entresacar; *vn* asociarse; concordar, estar de acuerdo
sortie [ˈsɔrtɪ] *s* (mil.) salida, surtida
sorus [ˈsorəs] *s* (*pl:* **-ri** [[raɪ]) (bot.) soro
S O S [ˈɛsˌoˈɛs] *s* (rad.) S O S (*señal de peligro*); (coll.) llamada de auxilio
so-so [ˈsoˌso] *adj* mediano, regular, talcualillo; *adv* así así, tal cual
sot [sɑt] *s* borracho
soteriology [səˌtɪrɪˈɑlədʒɪ] *s* (theol.) soteriología
sottish [ˈsɑtɪʃ] *adj* embrutecido por la mucha bebida, hecho una uva
sotto voce [ˈsɑto ˈvotʃe] a sovoz, en voz baja
soubrette [suˈbrɛt] *s* (theat.) camarera o confidenta de comedia; (theat.) doncella coquetona
soubriquet [ˈsubrɪke] *s* var. de **sobriquet**
Soudan [suˈdæn] *s* var. de **Sudan**
soufflé [suˈfle] o [ˈsufle] *s* flan, soufflé
sough [sʌf] o [saʊ] *s* susurro, suspiro, murmullo; *vn* susurrar, suspirar, murmullar
sought [sɔt] *pret & pp de* **seek**
soul [sol] *s* alma; **upon my soul!** ¡por vida mía!
soulful [ˈsolfəl] *adj* conmovedor, sentimental
soulless [ˈsollɪs] *adj* desalmado
sound [saʊnd] *s* sonido; ruido; tañido (*de las campanas*); (surg.) sonda, tienta; (geog.) estrecho, brazo de mar; vejiga natatoria (*de los peces*); **within sound of** al alcance de; *adj* sano; profundo (*dícese, p.ej., del sueño*); sólido, firme; puro; perfecto; solvente; sonoro; **sound of mind** en su juicio cabal; *adv* profundamente; *va* sonar; tocar (*p.ej., campanas*); tantear, sondear; auscultar (*p.ej., los pulmones*); entonar (*p.ej., alabanzas*); (surg.) sondar, tentar; **to sound the call to arms** tocar llamada; *vn* sonar, resonar; sondar; sumergirse (*una ballena*); parecer; **to sound like** sonar como (*p.ej., un trueno*)
sound barrier *s* (aer.) barrera del sonido
soundboard [ˈsaʊndˌbord] *s* secreto, caja de resonancia (*de un instrumento musical*); tornavoz (*para dirigir el sonido hacia el público*); (fig.) caja de resonancia

sound effects *spl* (mov. & rad.) efectos sonoros
sounder ['saundər] *s* sonador; sondeador; (telg.) resonador
sound film *s* film sonoro, película sonora
sounding ['saundɪŋ] *adj* sonante, resonante; *s* sondeo; **soundings** *spl* sondas
sounding balloon *s* globo sonda
sounding board *s* var. de **soundboard**
sounding line *s* (naut.) sondaleza
soundless ['saundlɪs] *adj* silencioso; insondable
soundly ['saundlɪ] *adv* sanamente; profundamente; a fondo; sólidamente; violentamente
soundproof ['saund'pruf] *adj* antisonoro; *va* insonorizar
soundproofing ['saund'prufɪŋ] *s* aislación de sonido
sound track *s* (mov.) huella de sonido, banda sonora, pista sonora
sound wave *s* (phys.) onda sonora
soup [sup] *s* sopa; **in the soup** (slang) en apuros, en aprietos
soup dish *s* plato sopero
soup kitchen *s* comedor de beneficencia, dispensario de alimentos (*para los pobres*); (mil.) cocina de campaña
soup ladle *s* cucharón
soup spoon *s* cuchara de sopa
soup tureen *s* sopera
soupy ['supɪ] *adj* (*comp:* **-ier;** *super:* **-iest**) parecido a la sopa; brumoso
sour [saur] *adj* agrio; (fig.) agrio, acre, desapacible; *va* agriar; *vn* agriarse; malearse (*la tierra*)
source [sors] *s* fuente
source book *s* texto original; colección de textos originales
source material *s* fuentes originales
sour cherry *s* (bot.) guindo (*árbol*); guinda (*fruto*)
sourdough ['saur,do] *s* (coll.) explorador en el Canadá y Alaska
sour grapes *spl* agraz; (fig.) las uvas verdes (*de la fábula "La zorra y las uvas" de Esopo, es decir, algo que se finge despreciar porque no se puede conseguir*); **sour grapes!** ¡están verdes las uvas!
sour gum *s* (bot.) tupelo
sourish ['saurɪʃ] *adj* agrete
sourness ['saurnɪs] *s* agrura
sourpuss ['saur,pus] *s* (slang) cascarrabias, vinagre (*persona*)
souse [saus] *s* zambullida, chapuz; salmuera; adobo; escabeche; cabeza, patas y orejas de cerdo en escabeche; (slang) borrachín; *va* zambullir, chapuzar; adobar; escabechar; verter; **to get soused** (slang) emborracharse; *vn* zambullirse; (slang) embriagarse habitualmente
soutache ['sutæʃ] o [su'tæʃ] *s* trencilla
soutane [su'tɑn] *s* sotana
south [sauθ] *s* sur, mediodía; *adj* meridional, del sur; *adv* al sur
South Africa *s* Sudáfrica; la Unión Sudafricana
South African *adj & s* sudafricano
South America *s* Sudamérica, la América del Sur
South American *adj & s* sudamericano
South Australia *s* la Australia Meridional
South Carolina [,kærə'laɪnə] *s* la Carolina del Sur
South China Sea *s* mar de la China Meridional
South Dakota [də'kotə] *s* el Dakota del Sur
southeast [,sauθ'ist] *adj* sudeste, sudestal; *s* sudeste; *adv* al sudeste, hacia el sudeste
Southeast Asia *s* el Asia sudoriental, el Sudeste Asiático, el Sudeste de Asia
southeaster [,sauθ'istər] *s* sudeste (*viento*); sudestada (*viento fuerte*)
southeasterly [,sauθ'istərlɪ] *adj* sudestal; *adv* hacia el sudeste; desde el sudeste
southeastern [,sauθ'istərn] *adj* sudeste, suroriental
southeastward [,sauθ'istwərd] *adj* que va hacia el sudeste; *s* sudeste; *adv* hacia el sudeste
southeastwardly [,sauθ'istwərdlɪ] *adj* que va hacia el sudeste; *adv* hacia el sudeste
southeastwards [,sauθ'istwərdz] *adv* hacia el sudeste
souther ['sauðər] *s* sur (*viento*)
southerly ['sʌðərlɪ] *adj* meridional; que viene desde el sur; que va hacia el sur; *adv* desde el sur; hacia el sur
southern ['sʌðərn] *adj* meridional
Southern Cross *s* (astr.) Cruz del Sur
southerner ['sʌðərnər] *s* meridional, habitante del sur
Southern Hemisphere *s* hemisferio austral
southernmost ['sʌðərnmost] *adj* (el) más meridional
southernwood ['sʌðərn,wud] *s* (bot.) abrótano
southing ['sauðɪŋ] *s* movimiento hacia el sur; diferencia de latitud sur
South Island *s* la Isla del Sur (*Nueva Zelanda*)
South Korea *s* la Corea del Sur
South Korean *adj & s* surcoreano
southland ['sauθlənd] o ['sauθ,lænd] *s* región meridional
southlander ['sauθləndər] o ['sauθ,lændər] *s* meridional
South Magnetic Pole *s* polo sur magnético
southpaw ['sauθ,pɔ] *adj & s* (sport & slang) zurdo
South Pole *s* polo sur
southron ['sʌðrən] *adj & s* meridional
South Sea Islander *s* oceánico
South Sea Islands *spl* la Oceanía
South Seas *spl* Grande Océano (*el Pacífico Sur*); mares del sur (*al sur del ecuador*)
south-southeast ['sauθ,sauθ'ist] *s* sudsudeste
south-southwest ['sauθ,sauθ'wɛst] *s* sudsudoeste
southward ['sauθwərd] *adj* que va hacia el sur; *s* sur; *adv* hacia el sur
southwardly ['sauθwərdlɪ] *adj* que va hacia el sur; *adv* hacia el sur
southwards ['sauθwərdz] *adv* hacia el sur
southwest [,sauθ'wɛst] *adj & s* sudoeste; *adv* al sudoeste, hacia el sudoeste
Southwest Africa *s* el África del Sudoeste
southwester [,sauθ'wɛstər] *s* sudoeste (*viento*); sudoestada (*viento fuerte*); sueste (*sombrero impermeable*)
southwesterly [,sauθ'wɛstərlɪ] *adj* sudoeste; *adv* hacia el sudoeste; desde el sudoeste
southwestern [,sauθ'wɛstərn] *adj* sudoeste
southwestward [,sauθ'wɛstwərd] *adj* que va hacia el sudoeste; *s* sudoeste; *adv* hacia el sudoeste
southwestwardly [,sauθ'wɛstwərdlɪ] *adj* que va hacia el sudoeste; *adv* hacia el sudoeste
southwestwards [,sauθ'wɛstwərdz] *adv* hacia el sudoeste
south wind *s* austro, noto
souvenir [,suvə'nɪr] o ['suvənɪr] *s* recuerdo, memoria
souvenir sheet *s* (philately) hoja-bloque
sou'wester [,sau'wɛstər] *s* var. de **southwester**
sovereign ['sɑvrɪn] o ['sʌvrɪn] *adj* soberano; *s* soberano (*rey; moneda*); soberana (*reina*)
sovereignly ['sɑvrɪnlɪ] o ['sʌvrɪnlɪ] *adv* soberanamente; eficazmente
sovereignty ['sɑvrɪntɪ] o ['sʌvrɪntɪ] *s* (*pl:* **-ties**) soberanía
soviet ['sovɪɛt] *s* soviet; *adj* soviético
sovietism ['sovɪɛtɪzəm] *s* sovietismo
sovietization [,sovɪ,ɛtɪ'zeʃən] *s* sovietizacíon
sovietize ['sovɪɛtaɪz] *va* sovietizar
Soviet Russia *s* la Rusia Soviética
Soviet Union *s* Unión Soviética
sow [sau] *s* puerca; (found.) galápago (*lingote*); (found.) fosa, reguera; [so] (*pret:* **sowed;** *pp:* **sown** o **sowed**) *va* sembrar; **to sow with mines** plagar de minas; *vn* sembrar
sowbread ['sau,brɛd] *s* (bot.) pamporcino
sow bug [sau] *s* (zool.) cochinilla de humedad
sower ['soər] *s* sembrador
sown [son] *pp de* **sow**
sow thistle [sau] *s* (bot.) cerraja
soy [sɔɪ] *s* (bot.) soja; semilla de soja; (cook.) salsa de soja
soybean ['sɔɪ,bin] *s* (bot.) soja; semilla de soja
sp. abr. de **special, species, specific, specimen** y **spelling**
Sp. abr. de **Spain, Spaniard** y **Spanish**
spa [spɑ] *s* caldas, manantial de agua mineral; balneario

space [spes] *s* espacio; (mus. & print.) espacio; **in the space of** por espacio de (*p.ej., un año*); *adj* espacial; de espacios; *va* espaciar; (print.) espaciar; (print.) regletear
space age *s* era del espacio
space bar o **space key** *s* tecla de espacios, llave espacial, espaciador
space charge *s* (elec.) carga de espacio, carga interespacial
spacecraft ['spes,kræft] o ['spes,krɑft] *s* var. de **spaceship**
space exploration *s* exploración del espacio
space flight *s* vuelo espacial
space helmet *s* casco espacial, escafandra espacial
space-lattice ['spes,lætɪs] *s* (physical chem.) estructura del cristal (*ordenamiento de los átomos de un cristal mediante la aplicación de los rayos X*)
spaceless ['speslɪs] *adj* infinito; que no ocupa espacio
spaceman ['spes,mæn] *s* (*pl:* **-men**) navegador del espacio; visitante a la Tierra del espacio exterior
space mark *s* (print.) signo para indicar el espaciado
space medicine *s* medicina del espacio
space probe *s* sondaje del espacio
spacer ['spesər] *s* (print.) espaciador; (telg.) separador
space race *s* carrera espacial
space science *s* ciencia del espacio
spaceship ['spes,ʃɪp] *s* nave del espacio, nave espacial, astronave
space suit *s* traje espacial
space-time continuum ['spes,taɪm] *s* (phys.) continuo espacio tiempo, continuo espaciotemporal
space travel *s* viajes por el espacio, astronavegación
space vehicle *s* vehículo espacial
spacing ['spesɪŋ] *s* espaciamiento
spacious ['speʃəs] *adj* espacioso
spade [sped] *s* laya; (mil.) zapa; pique (*naipe que corresponde a la espada*); **spades** *spl* piques (*palo que corresponde al de espadas*); **to call a spade a spade** llamar al pan pan y al vino vino; *va* layar; *vn* layar; (mil.) zapar
spadework ['sped,wʌrk] *s* trabajo hecho con la laya; (fig.) trabajo preliminar y fundamental
spadix ['spedɪks] *s* (*pl:* **spadixes** o **spadices** [spe'daɪsiz]) (bot.) espádice
spaghetti [spə'gɛtɪ] *s* macarrones delgados; (elec.) tubería aisladora
spahi o **spahee** ['spɑhi] *s* espahí
Spain [spen] *s* España
spake [spek] (archaic) *pret de* **speak**
spall [spɔl] *s* lasca, astilla de piedra; *va* romper (*piedras*) con la almádena
span [spæn] *s* palmo, llave de la mano; extensión completa; (arch.) ojo; pareja (*de caballos*); (aer.) envergadura; (*pret & pp:* **spanned;** *ger:* **spanning**) *va* medir a palmos; atravesar, extenderse sobre, abrazar
spandrel ['spændrəl] *s* (arch.) enjuta, embecadura
spangle ['spæŋgəl] *s* lentejuela; *va* estrellar; adornar con lentejuelas; *vn* brillar, resplandecer
Spaniard ['spænjərd] *s* español o española
spaniel ['spænjəl] *s* perro de aguas; persona rastrera que sirve de instrumento a otra
Spanish ['spænɪʃ] *adj* español; *spl* españoles; *ssg* español (*idioma*)
Spanish American *adj & s* hispanoamericano (*de la América española*)
Spanish-American ['spænɪʃə'mɛrɪkən] *adj* hispanoamericano (*perteneciente a España y América o España y los Estados Unidos*)
Spanish-American War *s* guerra hispanoamericana
Spanish Armada *s* Armada Invencible
Spanish bayonet *s* (bot.) bayoneta
Spanish broom *s* (bot.) retama de China, retama de olor, gayomba
Spanish dagger *s* (bot.) bayoneta
Spanish fir *s* (bot.) pinsapo
Spanish fly *s* (ent.) abadejo, mosca de España, cantárida
Spanish Guinea *s* la Guinea Española
Spanish Inquisition *s* Inquisición de España
Spanish mackerel *s* (ichth.) caballa con manchas parduscas por los lados (*Scomberomorus maculatus*)
Spanish Main *s* Costa Firme, Tierra Firme; mar Caribe
Spanish-Moroccan ['spænɪʃmə'rɑkən] *adj* hispanomarroquí
Spanish Morocco *s* el Marruecos Español
Spanish moss *s* (bot.) barba española
Spanish n *s* la letra eñe
Spanish omelet *s* tortilla de tomate
Spanish onion *s* cebolla grande de sabor dulce
Spanish oyster plant *s* (bot.) cardillo, tagarnina
Spanish paprika *s* (bot.) asnaucho
Spanish plum *s* (bot.) jocotal (*árbol*); jocote (*fruto*)
Spanish-speaking ['spænɪʃ'spikɪŋ] *adj* hispanohablante, de habla española
spank [spæŋk] *s* azote, manotada; *va* azotar, manotear; *vn* correr rápidamente, galopar
spanker ['spæŋkər] *s* (coll.) cosa muy grande, hermosa o extraordinaria; (coll.) caballo muy veloz; (naut.) cangreja de popa
spanker boom *s* (naut.) verga de popa
spanker gaff *s* (naut.) cangrejo, pico de cangrejo
spanking ['spæŋkɪŋ] *s* azote, manotada; *adj* rápido, veloz; fuerte; (coll.) muy grande, muy hermoso, extraordinario
spanless ['spænlɪs] *adj* que no se puede medir, atravesar o abrazar
spanner ['spænər] *s* llave de tuercas, llave de manguera
spar [spɑr] *s* (naut.) mástil, verga, palo; (aer.) viga mayor; (mineral.) espato; boxeo; combate de gallos a espolonazos; riña, pelea; (*pret & pp:* **sparred;** *ger:* **sparring**) *va* proveer de mástiles, vergas o palos; *vn* reñir, pelear; boxear; luchar a espolonazos (*los gallos*)
spar deck *s* (naut.) cubierta de guindaste
spare [spɛr] *adj* sobrante, de repuesto; libre, disponible; flaco, enjuto, delgado; escaso; sobrio, frugal; *va* pasar sin, pasarse sin; perdonar; exonerar; salvar, guardar; ahorrar; **to have . . . to spare** tener de sobra, p.ej., **they have money to spare** tienen dinero de sobra; **to have no time to spare** no tener tiempo que perder; **to spare oneself** ahorrarse esfuerzo; *vn* economizar; ser clemente
spare bed *s* cama de sobra
spare hours *spl* horas de recreo, horas de ocio
spare money *s* dinero de reserva
spare parts *spl* piezas de recambio o de repuesto
sparerib ['spɛr,rɪb] *s* costilla de cerdo con poca carne
spare room *s* cuarto del huésped, habitación del forastero
spare time *s* tiempo desocupado
spare tire *s* neumático de repuesto, goma de recambio
spare wheel *s* rueda de recambio
sparing ['spɛrɪŋ] *adj* económico; escaso
spark [spɑrk] *s* chispa; (coll.) galán, cortejador; (coll.) petimetre; (fig.) centellita (*p.ej., de verdad*); *va* (coll.) galantear, cortejar (*a una mujer*); *vn* chispear; (coll.) ser galante
spark arrester *s* parachispas; (elec.) parachispas; (rail.) chispero
spark coil *s* bobina de chispas, bobina de encendido
sparker ['spɑrker] *s* artificio chispero; bujía, encendedor; (elec.) apagachispas, parachispas; (slang) galán, enamorado
spark gap *s* (elec.) entrehierro (*del carrete de inducción*); (elec.) espacio de chispa (*de la bujía de encendido*)
sparkish ['spɑrkɪʃ] *adj* galante, elegante
sparkle ['spɑrkəl] *s* chispita, destello; viveza, alegría; chispa (*diamante muy pequeño*); *va* hacer chispear; *vn* chispear; ser vivaz, ser alegre; espumar, ser efervescente, ser espumoso
spark lead [lid] *s* (mach.) avance del encendido
sparkler ['spɑrklər] *s* piedra preciosa muy brillante, diamante; fuegos artificiales que echan chispitas; ojo muy brillante
sparklet ['spɑrklɪt] *s* chispa, centella; (trademark) cápsula metálica, llena de ácido carbó-

nico líquido y con la cual se pueden fabricar bebidas gaseosas en la mesa
sparkling ['spɑrklɪŋ] *adj* chispeante, centelleante; espumante, espumoso (*vino*); **gaseoso** (*agua*)
spark plug *s* bujía
sparrow ['spæro] *s* (orn.) gorrión, pardal
sparrow hawk *s* (orn.) gavilán, cernícalo
sparse [spɑrs] *adj* esparcido, disperso; escaso, poco abundante; ralo (*dícese del pelo*)
sparsity ['spɑrsɪtɪ] *s* dispersión; escasez; raleza
Sparta ['spɑrtə] *s* Esparta
Spartacus ['spɑrtəkəs] *s* Espártaco
Spartan ['spɑrtən] *adj & s* espartano; (fig.) espartano
Spartanism ['spɑrtənɪzəm] *s* severidad de espartano
spasm ['spæzəm] *s* (path.) espasmo; ataque súbito y violento, esfuerzo súbito y de breve duración
spasmodic [spæz'mɑdɪk] *adj* espasmódico; irregular, intermitente
spasmodically [spæz'mɑdɪkəlɪ] *adv* espasmódicamente; irregularmente, intermitentemente
spastic ['spæstɪk] *adj* espástico
spasticity [spæs'tɪsɪtɪ] *s* (path.) espasticidad
spat [spæt] *s* manotada, bofetada; palmadita; riña, disputa; botín, polaina corta; ostra joven; masa de ostras jóvenes; (*pret & pp:* **spatted;** *ger:* **spatting**) *va* dar una manotada a; golpear ligeramente; *vn* reñir, disputar; desovar (*las ostras*); *pret & pp de* **spit**
spate [spet] *s* (Brit.) avenida (*de agua*); (Brit.) chaparrón; gran cantidad; torrente de palabras; emoción intensa
spathe [speð] *s* (bot.) espata
spathic ['spæθɪk] *adj* (mineral.) espático
spatial ['speʃəl] *adj* espacial
spatter ['spætər] *s* salpicadura; *va* salpicar; (fig.) manchar; *vn* chorrear; chapotear
spatterdash ['spætər,dæʃ] *s* polaina larga
spatterdock ['spætər,dɑk] *s* (bot.) nenúfar amarillo
spatula ['spætʃələ] *s* espátula; (cook. & paint.) espátula
spatulamancy ['spætʃələ,mænsɪ] *s* espatulomancía
spatulate ['spætʃəlet] *adj* espatulado
spavin ['spævɪn] *s* (vet.) esparaván
spavined ['spævɪnd] *adj* que tiene esparaván
spawn [spɔn] *s* (ichth.) freza; pececillos; producto, resultado; prole; germen, fuente; (bot.) micelio; *va* engendrar, producir; *vn* frezar (*los peces*); producir en abundancia
spawning ['spɔnɪŋ] *s* freza, desove
spawning time *s* freza, desove
spay [spe] *va* sacar los ovarios a (*un animal*)
spaying ['speɪŋ] *s* castración femenina
S.P.C.A. abr. de **Society for the Prevention of Cruelty to Animals**
speak [spik] (*pret:* **spoke;** *pp:* **spoken**) *va* hablar (*un idioma*); decir (*la verdad*); *vn* hablar; **so to speak** por decirlo así; **to know to speak to** conocer de pocas palabras; **to not speak to** negar o quitar el habla a, no hablar con (*por haber reñido*); **to speak for** hablar por, hablar en favor de; pedir, solicitar; representar; **to speak out** elevar la voz, osar hablar, hablar alto; **to speak well for** demostrar el mérito de; **to speak well of** hablar bien de; **speaking!** ¡al habla! (*contestación telefónica*)
speakeasy ['spik,izɪ] *s* (*pl:* **-ies**) (slang) taberna clandestina
speaker ['spikər] *s* hablante; orador; presidente (*p.ej., de una asamblea legislativa*); (rad.) altavoz
Speaker of the House *s* (U.S.A.) presidente de la Cámara de Representantes
speakership ['spikərʃɪp] *s* presidencia de una asamblea legislativa
speaking ['spikɪŋ] *s* habla; elocuencia; *adj* hablante; viviente; **to be on speaking terms** hablarse
speaking tube *s* tubo acústico
spear [spɪr] *s* lanza; arpón (*para pescar*); hoja (*de hierba*); *va* alancear, herir con lanza; *vn* brotar
spearhead ['spɪr,hɛd] *s* punta de lanza; (fig.) punta de lanza
spearman ['spɪrmən] *s* (*pl:* **-men**) lancero
spearmint ['spɪr,mɪnt] *s* (bot.) menta verde, menta romana
spec. abr. de **special**
special ['spɛʃəl] *adj* especial; *s* tren especial
special delivery *s* correspondencia urgente, correo urgente, entrega inmediata
special-delivery ['spɛʃəldɪ'lɪvərɪ] *adj* urgente, de urgencia
specialism ['spɛʃəlɪzəm] *s* especialización
specialist ['spɛʃəlɪst] *adj & s* especialista
speciality [,spɛʃɪ'ælɪtɪ] *s* (*pl:* **-ties**) especialidad
specialization [,spɛʃəlɪ'zeʃən] *s* especialización
specialize ['spɛʃəlaɪz] *va* especializar; especificar; *vn* especializar o especializarse
specially ['spɛʃəlɪ] *adv* especialmente
special pleading *s* (law) alegación parcial
specialty ['spɛʃəltɪ] *s* (*pl:* **-ties**) especialidad
specie ['spiʃɪ] *s* efectivo, numerario, metálico
species ['spiʃɪz] *s* (*pl:* **-cies**) especie; (eccl.) especies sacramentales; **the species** la especie humana
specif. abr. de **specifically**
specific [spɪ'sɪfɪk] *adj & s* específico
specifically [spɪ'sɪfɪkəlɪ] *adv* específicamente; especificadamente
specification [,spɛsɪfɪ'keʃən] *s* especificación; presupuesto o plan detallado (*de un edificio*)
specificative [spɪ'sɪfɪ,ketɪv] *adj* especificativo
specific gravity *s* (phys.) peso específico
specific heat *s* calor específico
specify ['spɛsɪfaɪ] (*pret & pp:* **-fied**) *va* especificar; designar en el presupuesto
specimen ['spɛsɪmən] *s* espécimen; (coll.) tipo (*persona estrafalaria*)
speciosity [,spiʃɪ'ɑsɪtɪ] *s* (*pl:* **-ties**) especiosidad
specious ['spiʃəs] *adj* especioso (*engañoso*)
speck [spɛk] *s* manchita; partícula, pizca; *va* manchar, salpicar de manchas
speckle ['spɛkəl] *s* mota, punto; *va* motear, puntear
specs [spɛks] *spl* (coll.) anteojos, gafas
spectacle ['spɛktəkəl] *s* espectáculo; **spectacles** *spl* anteojos, gafas
spectacle case *s* funda de gafas
spectacled ['spɛktəkəld] *adj* que lleva anteojos o gafas
spectacular [spɛk'tækjələr] *adj* espectacular, aparatoso, ostentoso
spectator ['spɛktetər] o [spɛk'tetər] *s* espectador
specter ['spɛktər] *s* espectro
spectral ['spɛktrəl] *adj* espectral; (phys.) espectral
spectrograph ['spɛktrəgræf] o ['spɛktrəgrɑf] *s* espectrógrafo
spectroscope ['spɛktrəskop] *s* espectroscopio
spectroscopic [,spɛktrə'skɑpɪk] *adj* espectroscópico
spectroscopy [spɛk'trɑskəpɪ] *s* espectroscopia
spectrum ['spɛktrəm] *s* (*pl:* **-tra** [trə] o **-trums**) (phys.) espectro
spectrum analysis *s* análisis espectral
specular ['spɛkjələr] *adj* especular
specular iron *s* (mineral.) hierro especular
speculate ['spɛkjəlet] *vn* especular; (com.) especular
speculation [,spɛkjə'leʃən] *s* especulación; (com.) especulación
speculative ['spɛkjə,letɪv] *adj* especulativo; arriesgado, aventurado
speculator ['spɛkjə,letər] *s* especulador
speculum ['spɛkjələm] *s* (*pl:* **-la** [lə] o **-lums**) *s* espejo; (med. & surg.) espéculo
sped [spɛd] *pret & pp de* **speed**
speech [spitʃ] *s* habla (*facultad de hablar; manera de hablar; idioma, lenguaje; arenga, discurso*); conferencia; parlamento (*de un actor*)
speech clinic *s* clínica de la palabra, clínica para la corrección de defectos del habla
speech correction *s* rehabilitación del habla, corrección de defectos del habla
speechify ['spitʃɪfaɪ] (*pret & pp:* **-fied**) *vn* (hum. & scornful) arengar, perorar
speechless ['spitʃlɪs] *adj* sin habla; mudo, silencioso; estupefacto

speed [spid] *s* velocidad; velocidad máxima; (aut.) marcha, velocidad (*de los engranajes*); **at full speed** a toda velocidad; **to make speed** marchar a gran velocidad; (*pret & pp:* **sped**) *va* apresurar, dar prisa a; despedir, despachar; ayudar, favorecer; *vn* apresurarse, darse prisa; adelantar, progresar; ir con exceso de velocidad, exceder la velocidad permitida
speedboat ['spid,bot] *s* lancha de gran velocidad, lancha de carreras
speeder ['spidər] *s* persona o cosa que anda a gran velocidad; automovilista que excede la velocidad permitida
speeding ['spidɪŋ] *s* exceso de velocidad
speed king *s* (aut.) as del volante
speed limit *s* velocidad permitida, velocidad máxima
speedometer [spi'dɑmɪtər] *s* velocímetro; (aut.) taquímetro y cuentakilómetros unidos
speed record *s* marca de velocidad
speed-up ['spid,ʌp] *s* aumento de producción; (coll.) aceleración; (aut.) acelerada (*del motor*)
speedway ['spid,we] *s* vía de tráfico rápido; carretera para carreras
speedwell ['spidwɛl] *s* (bot.) verónica
speedy ['spidɪ] *adj* (*comp:* **-ier;** *super:* **-iest**) veloz, rápido; pronto, vivo
speleologist [,spilɪ'ɑlədʒɪst] *s* espeleólogo
speleology [,spilɪ'ɑlədʒɪ] *s* espeleología
spell [spɛl] *s* encanto, hechizo; turno, tanda, revezo; rato, poco tiempo; temporada (*p.ej., de buen tiempo*); **by spells** a ratos; **to cast a spell on** encantar, hechizar; **under a spell** bajo el poder de un encanto; (*pret & pp:* **spelled** o **spelt**) *va* deletrear; descifrar; indicar, significar; **to spell it out to someone** (coll.) decírselo a uno deletreando; **to spell out** (coll.) explicar detalladamente; *vn* deletrear; (*pret & pp:* **spelled**) *va* relevar, revezar, reemplazar
spellbind ['spɛl,baɪnd] (*pret & pp:* **-bound**) *va* fascinar (*especialmente con su oratoria*)
spellbinder ['spɛl,baɪndər] *s* (coll.) orador fascinante, orador persuasivo
spellbinding ['spɛl,baɪndɪŋ] *adj* fascinante, persuasivo
spellbound ['spɛl,baʊnd] *pret & pp de* **spellbind**
speller ['spɛlər] *s* deletreador (*persona*); abecedario, silabario; cartilla de deletrear
spelling ['spɛlɪŋ] *s* deletreo; ortografía; grafía
spelling bee *s* concurso o certamen de ortografía
spelt [spɛlt] *s* (bot.) espelta; *pret & pp de* **spell**
spelter ['spɛltər] *s* peltre
spelunker [spɪ'lʌŋkər] *s* aficionado a la espeleología, espeleólogo de afición
spencer ['spɛnsər] *s* chaqueta corta de punto
spend [spɛnd] (*pret & pp:* **spent**) *va* gastar; pasar (*una hora, un día, etc.*); **to spend a mast** (naut.) perder un palo; *vn* gastar dinero; consumirse
spender ['spɛndər] *s* gastador
spending money *s* dinero para gastos menudos
spendthrift ['spɛnd,θrɪft] *s & adj* gastador, derrochador, pródigo
Spenserian [spɛn'sɪrɪən] *adj* spenseriano
spent [spɛnt] *adj* gastado; pasado; consumido, agotado; *pret & pp de* **spend**
sperm [spʌrm] *s* esperma; espermatozoo; (zool.) cachalote; esperma de ballena
spermaceti [,spʌrmə'sɛtɪ] o [,spʌrmə'sitɪ] *s* espermaceti
spermatic [spər'mætɪk] *adj* espermático
spermatic cord *s* (anat.) cordón espermático
spermatophyte ['spʌrmətə,faɪt] *s* (bot.) espermatofita
spermatorrhea [,spʌrmətə'riə] (path.) espermatorrea
spermatozoön [,spʌrmətə'zoɑn] *s* (*pl:* **-zoa** ['zoə]) (zool.) espermatozoo
spermogonium [,spʌrmə'gonɪəm] *s* (*pl:* **-a** [ə]) (bot.) espermogonio
sperm oil *s* aceite de esperma
sperm whale *s* (zool.) cachalote
spew [spju] *va & vn* vomitar
sp. gr. abr. de **specific gravity**
sphacelate ['sfæsəlet] *vn* (path.) esfacelarse
sphacelus ['sfæsələs] *s* (path.) esfacelo
sphagnum ['sfægnəm] *s* (*pl:* **-na** [nə]) (bot.) esfágnea
sphene [sfin] *s* (mineral.) esfena o esfeno
sphenoid ['sfinɔɪd] *s* (anat.) esfenoides
sphenoidal [sfɪ'nɔɪdəl] *adj* esfenoidal
sphere [sfɪr] *s* (geom.) esfera; (astr.) astro; (astr.) esfera celeste; (fig.) esfera (*ambiente, círculo*); (poet.) esfera (*cielo*)
sphere of influence *s* (dipl.) esfera de influencia
spherical ['sfɛrɪkəl] *adj* esférico
spherical trigonometry *s* trigonometría esférica
spherical vault *s* (arch.) bóveda de casquete esférico
sphericity [sfɪ'rɪsɪtɪ] *s* (*pl:* **-ties**) esfericidad
spheroid ['sfɪrɔɪd] *s* (geom.) esferoide
spheroidal [sfɪ'rɔɪdəl] *adj* esferoidal
spherometer [sfɪ'rɑmɪtər] *s* (phys.) esferómetro
spherule ['sfɛrʊl] *s* esférula
sphincter ['sfɪŋktər] *s* (anat.) esfínter
sphinx [sfɪŋks] *s* (*pl:* **sphinxes** o **sphinges** ['sfɪndʒiz]) esfinge; (fig.) esfinge (*personaje impenetrable*)
sphragistic [sfrə'dʒɪstɪk] *adj* esfragístico; **sphragistics** *ssg* esfragística
sphygmograph ['sfɪgməgræf] o ['sfɪgməgrɑf] *s* (physiol.) esfigmógrafo
spica ['spaɪkə] *s* (*pl:* **-cae** [si]) (archeol. & surg.) espiga; (*cap.*) *s* (astr.) espiga de la Virgen
spicate ['spaɪket] *adj* (bot.) espigado
spice [spaɪs] *s* especia; sainete, picante; aroma, fragancia; punta, pequeña cantidad; (fig.) sainete; *va* especiar; dar gusto o picante a
spiceberry ['spaɪs,bɛrɪ] *s* (*pl:* **-ries**) (bot.) gaulteria o té del Canadá
spice box *s* especiero
spicebush ['spaɪs,bʊʃ] *s* (bot.) benjoin
Spice Islands *spl* islas de las Especias
spicery ['spaɪsərɪ] *s* (*pl:* **-ies**) especiería (*conjunto de especias*); aroma, picante
spiciform ['spaɪsɪfɔrm] *adj* (bot.) espiciforme
spiciness ['spaɪsɪnɪs] *s* picante, aroma; (fig.) picante; (fig.) sicalipsis
spick-and-span ['spɪkənd'spæn] *adj* flamante; bien arreglado; impecablemente limpio
spicular ['spɪkjələr] o **spiculate** ['spɪkjəlet] *adj* espicular
spicule ['spɪkjul] *s* aguja (*p.ej., de hielo*); (anat., bot. & zool.) espícula
spicy ['spaɪsɪ] *adj* (*comp:* **-ier;** *super:* **-iest**) especiado; aromático, picante; (fig.) sabroso, picante; (fig.) sicalíptico
spider ['spaɪdər] *s* (ent. & mach.) araña; trébedes (*cazo con pies*); sartén de mango largo
spider crab *s* (zool.) araña de mar
spider lines *spl* retículo
spider monkey *s* (zool.) mono araña
spider web *s* tela de araña, telaraña
spiderwort ['spaɪdər,wʌrt] *s* (bot.) pasajera
spidery ['spaɪdərɪ] *adj* de araña; lleno de arañas; semejante a una telaraña; largo y delgado
spiel [spil] *s* (slang) arenga, discurso; *vn* (slang) arengar, hacer un discurso
spiffy ['spɪfɪ] *adj* (*comp:* **-ier;** *super:* **-iest**) (slang) guapo, elegante
spigot ['spɪgət] *s* grifo; espiche (*taco para tapar un agujero*)
spike [spaɪk] *s* perno (*clavo muy largo*); alcayata, escarpia; espigón (*cosa puntiaguda*); (bot.) espiga; *va* empernar; sujetar con alcayatas o escarpias; herir con un clavo; clavar (*un cañón*); acabar, poner fin a; inutilizar
spikelet ['spaɪklɪt] *s* (bot.) espiguita o espiguilla
spikenard ['spaɪknərd] o ['spaɪknɑrd] *s* (bot.) espicanardo; (bot.) aralia; nardo (*de los antiguos*)
spiky ['spaɪkɪ] *adj* espigado; erizado, puntiagudo
spile [spaɪl] *s* pilote; espiche; caño para sacar el azúcar del arce azucarero; *va* proveer de pilote; proveer de espiche; poner espiche a; afirmar con pilotes; cerrar con tarugo
spilikin ['spɪlɪkɪn] *s* pajita o astilla (*que se usan en ciertos juegos*); **spilikins** *spl* juego de pajitas
spill [spɪl] *s* derramamiento; líquido derramado; (coll.) vuelco, caída; astilla; alegrador (*tira de papel para encender*); (*pret & pp:* **spilled** o **spilt**) *va* derramar, verter; esparcir; (coll.)

volcar, hacer caer; (naut.) hacer relingar, quitarle el viento a (*una vela*); **to spill the beans** (slang) revelar el secreto; *vn* derramarse, verterse
spillikin ['spɪlɪkɪn] *s* var. de **spilikin**
spillway ['spɪl,we] *s* derramadero, vertedero, canal de desagüe
spilt [spɪlt] *pret & pp de* **spill**
spin [spɪn] *s* vuelta, giro muy rápido; (coll.) paseo en coche, bicicleta, etc.; (phys.) giro electrónico; (aer.) barrena; **to go into a spin** (aer.) entrar en barrena; (*pret & pp:* **spun;** *ger:* **spinning**) *va* hacer dar vueltas, hacer girar; hilar (*lino, el capullo, etc.*); bailar (*un trompo*); **to spin out** alargar, extender, prolongar; **to spin yarns** contar cuentos increíbles; *vn* dar vueltas, girar; hilar; bailar (*dícese del trompo*); (coll.) correr rápidamente; (aer.) entrar en barrena
spinach ['spɪnɪtʃ] o ['spɪnɪdʒ] *s* (bot.) espinaca; espinacas (*hojas que se comen*)
spinal ['spaɪnəl] *adj* espinal
spinal anesthesia *s* (med.) anestesia espinal
spinal column *s* (anat.) espina dorsal, columna vertebral
spinal cord *s* (anat.) médula espinal
spindle ['spɪndəl] *s* huso; eje; (carp.) mazorca (*de un balustre*); *vn* crecer muy alto y delgado
spindle-legged ['spɪndəl,lɛgɪd] o ['spɪndəl,lɛgd] *adj* zanquilargo, zanquivano
spindlelegs ['spɪndəl,lɛgz] *spl* piernas largas y delgadas; *ssg* (coll.) zanquivano
spindle-shanked ['spɪndəl,ʃæŋkt] *adj* var. de **spindle-legged**
spindleshanks ['spɪndəl,ʃæŋks] *spl & ssg* var. de **spindlelegs**
spindle tree *s* (bot.) bonetero
spindling ['spɪndlɪŋ] *adj* largo y delgado; flaco y demasiado alto
spindly ['spɪndlɪ] *adj* (*comp:* **-dlier;** *super:* **-dliest**) largo y delgado; flaco y demasiado alto
spindrift ['spɪn,drɪft] *s* (naut.) rocío (*de las olas*)
spine [spaɪn] *s* espina, púa; cordoncillo; loma, cerro; (anat., bot. & zool.) espina; (anat.) espina, espinazo; (b.b.) lomo; (fig.) valor, ánimo
spined [spaɪnd] *adj* espinoso
spinel [spɪ'nɛl] o ['spɪnəl] *s* (mineral.) espinela
spineless ['spaɪnlɪs] *adj* sin espinas; sin espinazo; sin firmeza de carácter
spinet ['spɪnɪt] *s* (mus.) espineta
spinnaker ['spɪnəkər] *s* (naut.) spinnaker (*vela grande triangular de un yate, opuesta a la vela mayor*)
spinnaker boom *s* (naut.) botalón del spinnaker
spinner ['spɪnər] *s* hilador, hilandero; máquina de hilar
spinneret ['spɪnəret] *s* (zool.) hilera
spinney ['spɪnɪ] *s* (Brit.) bosquete (*para cazar*)
spinning ['spɪnɪŋ] *s* hila (*acción*); hilandería (*arte*); *adj* hilador
spinning frame *s* hilandería
spinning jenny *s* máquina de hilar de múltiples husos
spinning machine *s* máquina hiladora, máquina de hilar
spinning wheel *s* torno de hilar
spin-off ['spɪn,af] o ['spɪn,ɔf] *s* (com.) traspaso de ciertas actividades de una compañía a otra compañía nueva e independiente, recibiendo los accionistas originales acciones de la nueva compañía libres de impuestos
spinose ['spaɪnos] *adj* espinoso
spinous ['spaɪnəs] *adj* espinoso; espíneo
Spinozism [spɪ'nozɪzəm] *s* espinosismo
Spinozist [spɪ'nozɪst] *s* espinosista
spinster ['spɪnstər] *s* solterona, doncellueca; hilandera
spinsterhood ['spɪnstərhud] *s* soltería de mujer
spintight ['spɪn,taɪt] *s* (trademark) aprietatuercas
spinule ['spaɪnjul] o ['spɪnjul] *s* espínula
spiny ['spaɪnɪ] *adj* (*comp:* **-ier;** *super:* **-iest**) espinoso; puntiagudo; (fig.) espinoso (*enmarañado, difícil*)
spiny lobster *s* (zool.) langosta
spiraea [spaɪ'riə] *s* (bot.) espirea
spiracle ['spaɪrəkəl] o ['spɪrəkəl] *s* (zool.) espiráculo
spiral ['spaɪrəl] *adj & s* espiral; (*pret & pp:* **-raled** o **-ralled;** *ger:* **-raling** o **-ralling**) *va* mover formando espiras; torcer en espiral; *vn* moverse formando espiras; dar vueltas como una espiral; (aer.) volar en espiral
spiral nebula *s* (astr.) nebulosa espiral
spiral staircase *s* escalera de caracol, escalera espiral
spirant ['spaɪrənt] *adj & s* (phonet.) espirante
spire [spaɪr] *s* (arch.) aguja, chapitel; peñasco, cúspide, cima; espira; espiral; (geom. & zool.) espira; tallo (*de hierba*); *vn* crecer hacia arriba en forma espiral; rematar en punta; germinar
spirea [spaɪ'riə] *s* var. de **spiraea**
spirillum [spaɪ'rɪləm] *s* (*pl:* **-la** [lə]) (bact.) espirilo
spirit ['spɪrɪt] *s* espíritu; humor, temple; personaje; licor; **spirits** *spl* humor, genio; espíritu, brío, vivacidad; espíritu (*solución alcohólica*); licor; **out of spirits** triste, abatido, desalentado; **the Spirit** Dios; el Espíritu Santo; **to break the spirit of** desalentar; reprimir, sujetar; **to keep up one's spirits** no desalentarse, no desanimarse; *va* alentar, animar; **to spirit away** llevarse misteriosamente
spirited ['spɪrɪtɪd] *adj* espiritoso, fogoso
spiritism ['spɪrɪtɪzəm] *s* espiritismo
spirit lamp *s* lámpara de alcohol
spiritless ['spɪrɪtlɪs] *adj* apocado, tímido, sin ánimo
spirit level *s* nivel de burbuja, nivel de aire
spiritual ['spɪrɪtʃuəl] *adj* espiritual; *s* espiritual (*tonada religiosa de los negros*)
spiritual director *s* director espiritual
spiritualism ['spɪrɪtʃuəlɪzəm] *s* espiritismo; espiritualismo (*contrario de materialismo*)
spiritualist ['spɪrɪtʃuəlɪst] *s* espiritista; espiritualista
spiritualistic [,spɪrɪtʃuə'lɪstɪk] *adj* espiritista; espiritualista
spiritualistic séance *s* sesión de espiritistas
spirituality [,spɪrɪtʃu'ælɪtɪ] *s* (*pl:* **-ties**) espiritualidad
spiritualization [,spɪrɪtʃuəlɪ'zeʃən] *s* espiritualización
spiritualize ['spɪrɪtʃuəlaɪz] *va* espiritualizar
spirituel [,spɪrɪtʃu'ɛl] *adj* ingenioso, agudo, gracioso; etéreo, espiritual
spirituelle [,spɪrɪtʃu'ɛl] *adj fem de* **spirituel**
spirituous ['spɪrɪtʃuəs] *adj* espiritoso o espirituoso
spirituous liquors *spl* licores espirituosos
spirochete ['spaɪrokit] *s* (bact.) espiroqueta
spirogyra [,spaɪro'dʒaɪrə] *s* (bot.) espirogira
spirometer [spaɪ'rɑmɪtər] *s* espirómetro
spirt [spʌrt] *s, va & vn* var. de **spurt**
spiry ['spaɪrɪ] *adj* espiral, acaracolado; afilado, puntiagudo; con muchos chapiteles
spit [spɪt] *s* saliva, esputo; espuma (*de un insecto*); llovizna; nevisca; asador, espetón; punta o lengua de tierra; **the spit of** o **the spit and image of** la segunda edición de, el retrato de; (*pret & pp:* **spat** o **spit;** *ger:* **spitting**) *va* escupir; **to spit forth** escupir (*p.ej., metralla*); *vn* escupir; lloviznar; neviscar; fufar (*el gato*); (*pret & pp:* **spitted;** *ger:* **spitting**) *va* espetar
spitball ['spɪt,bɔl] *s* pelotilla de papel mascado; (baseball) curva conseguida mojando la pelota con saliva
spitchcock ['spɪtʃ,kɑk] *s* anguila tajada y asada o frita; *va* tajar y asar o freír; maltratar
spit curl *s* (coll.) caracol (*rizo aplastado sobre la sien*)
spite [spaɪt] *s* despecho, rencor, inquina, mala voluntad; molestia, fastidio; **in spite of** a pesar de, a despecho de; **out of spite** por despecho; *va* despechar, picar, molestar
spiteful ['spaɪtfəl] *adj* despechado, rencoroso
spitfire ['spɪt,faɪr] *s* fierabrás; mujer de mal genio; artificio que echa chispas y fuego
spittle ['spɪtəl] *s* saliva, esputo
spittoon [spɪ'tun] *s* escupidera
spitz [spɪts] *s* perro de Pomerania, perro lulú
spiv [spɪv] *s* (Brit. coll.) estraperlista muy guapo, galafate, gorrón, parásito

splanchnic ['splæŋknɪk] *adj* esplácnico
splash [splæʃ] *s* salpicadura, rociada; chapoteo; mancha; **to make a splash** (coll.) hacer impresión, llamar la atención; *va* salpicar; chapotear; manchar; *vn* chapotear, caer con ruido; salpicar; moverse o caer golpeando el agua
splashboard ['splæʃ,bord] *s* alero, guardafango (*de un carruaje*)
splasher ['splæʃər] *s* salpicador; salpicadero
splash lubrication *s* lubricación al chapoteo o al barboteo
splashy ['splæʃɪ] *adj* (*comp:* **-ier;** *super:* **-iest**) fangoso, lodoso; (coll.) llamativo
splat [splæt] *s* pieza central y vertical del respaldo de una silla
splatter ['splætər] *s, va & vn* var. de **spatter**
splay [sple] *s* bisel, chaflán; alféizar; extensión, expansión; *adj* ancho, extendido, desplegado; torpe, sin gracia; *va* biselar, achaflanar; extender; *vn* extenderse, extenderse sin gracia
splayed arch *s* (arch.) arco abocinado
splayfoot ['sple,fut] *s* (*pl:* **-feet**) pie aplastado y torcido; (path.) pie contrahecho, pie zambo
splay-footed ['sple,futɪd] *adj* que tiene los pies aplastados y torcidos; torpe, sin gracia
spleen [splin] *s* (anat.) baso; mal humor; (archaic) esplín (*tristeza profunda*); **to vent one's spleen** descargar la bilis
spleenish ['splinɪʃ] *adj* bilioso, malhumorado, irritable
spleenwort ['splin,wʌrt] *s* (bot.) asplenio
splendent ['splɛndənt] *adj* esplendente
splendid ['splɛndɪd] *adj* espléndido
splendiferous [splɛn'dɪfərəs] *adj* (coll.) espléndido, magnífico
splendor ['splɛndər] *s* esplendor
splenectomy [splɪ'nɛktəmɪ] *s* (*pl:* **-mies**) (surg.) esplenectomía
splenetic [splɪ'nɛtɪk] *adj* esplénico; (fig.) bilioso, malhumorado, irritable
splenetically [splɪ'nɛtɪkəlɪ] *adv* rencorosamente, de mal humor
splenic ['splɛnɪk] o ['splinɪk] *adj* esplénico
splenitis [splɪ'naɪtɪs] *s* (path.) esplinitis
splice [splaɪs] *s* empalme, junta; *va* empalmar, juntar; (slang) casar
spline [splaɪn] *s* tira flexible, tira flexible para dibujar curvas; ranura para una cuña; cuña; *va* ranurar; proveer de cuña
splint [splɪnt] *s* astilla, tablilla; launa (*de las armaduras antiguas*); (surg.) cabestrillo, tablilla; (vet.) sobrehueso (*tumor y hueso*); **in a splint** (surg.) entablillado; *va* (surg.) entablillar
splint bone *s* (vet.) sobrehueso; (anat.) peroné
splinter ['splɪntər] *s* astilla; esquirla (*de piedra, cristal; de hueso*); *va* astillar; *vn* astillarse, hacerse astillas
splinter group *s* grupo disidente
splintery ['splɪntərɪ] *adj* astilloso
split [splɪt] *s* fractura, división; (slang) porción; (coll.) media botella; dulce de fruta fresca, helado, jarabe y nueces; caída acrobática con las piernas en línea recta; *adj* hendido, partido; dividido; (*pret & pp:* **split;** *ger:* **splitting**) *va* partir, dividir; **to split one's sides with laughter** desternillarse de risa; *vn* partirse, dividirse a lo largo; **to split away (from)** separarse (de); **my head is splitting** me duele terriblemente la cabeza; **to split up** (coll.) separarse, desavenirse (*dos o más personas*); **to split with** (coll.) desavenirse con, romper con
split fee *s* dicotomía (*entre médicos*)
split infinitive *s* (gram.) infinitivo partido (*infinitivo inglés en el que se interponen una o más palabras entre la preposición* **to** *y el verbo*)
split-level house ['splɪt'lɛvəl] *s* casa con pisos contiguos construídos en niveles distintos
split peas *spl* guisantes majados
split personality *s* personalidad desdoblada
split phase *s* (elec.) fase partida
split second *s* fracción de segundo
splitter ['splɪtər] *s* partidor, hendedor, divisor; persona quisquillosa
splitter wheel *s* disco abridor (*para facilitar el paso de la sierra*)
split ticket *s* (pol.) candidatura dividida, voto dividido (*entre candidatos de dos o más partidos*)
splitting ['splɪtɪŋ] *s* hendimiento, fractura, división; escisión (*del átomo*); *adj* partidor; fuerte, violento; enloquecedor (*dolor de cabeza*)
split-up ['splɪt,ʌp] *s* (com.) división de las acciones de una empresa en nuevas acciones de menor valor; (coll.) desunión, desavenencia
splotch [splɑtʃ] *s* borrón, mancha grande; *va* manchar, salpicar
splotchy ['splɑtʃɪ] *adj* (*comp:* **-ier;** *super:* **-iest**) lleno de borrones o manchas
splurge [splʌrdʒ] *s* (coll.) fachenda, ostentación; *vn* (coll.) fachendear, hacer ostentación
splutter ['splʌtər] *s* chisporroteo; farfulla (*manera de hablar*); *va* farfullar; *vn* chisporrotear; farfullar
spodumene ['spɑdʒumin] *s* (mineral.) espodumeno
spoil [spɔɪl] *s* despojo, botín, presa; **spoils** *spl* robo, botín, presa; empleos repartidos entre los vencedores; (*pret & pp:* **spoiled** o **spoilt**) *va* echar a perder, estropear, deteriorar; mimar; amargar (*una tertulia, una velada*); **to spoil of** despojar de; *vn* echarse a perder, estropearse; **to spoil for, to be spoiling for** (coll.) ansiar, anhelar
spoiled [spɔɪld] *adj* consentido (*dícese de un niño*)
spoiler ['spɔɪlər] *s* corruptor; consentidor; despojador
spoilsman ['spɔɪlzmən] *s* (*pl:* **-men**) individuo del partido vencedor que toma un empleo público como recompensa
spoils system *s* sistema de acaparamiento de los cargos públicos por el partido victorioso en las elecciones
spoilt [spɔɪlt] *pret & pp de* **spoil**
spoke [spok] *s* radio o rayo (*de rueda*); freno; escalón (*de escalera*); **to put a spoke in one's wheel** ponerle trabas a uno; *pret de* **speak**
spoken ['spokən] *pp de* **speak**
spokeshave ['spok,ʃev] *s* rebajador de radios (*de ruedas*)
spokesman ['spoksmən] *s* (*pl:* **-men**) vocero, portavoz
spokesmanship ['spoksmənʃɪp] *s* vocería
spokewise ['spok,waɪz] *adv* como un radio de rueda, como radios de rueda
spoliation [,spolɪ'eʃən] *s* expoliación, despojo
spondaic [spɑn'deɪk] espondaico
spondee ['spɑndi] *s* espondeo
spondulics [spɑn'dulɪks] *ssg* (slang) cuartos, plata
spondyl o **spondyle** ['spɑndɪl] *s* (anat.) espóndil o espóndilo
spondylitis [,spɑndɪ'laɪtɪs] *s* (path.) espondilitis
sponge [spʌndʒ] *s* esponja; (fig.) esponja (*gorrón, parásito*); **to throw up** (o **in**) o **to toss up** (o **in**) **the sponge** (coll.) tirar la esponja (*darse por vencido*); *va* limpiar con esponja; borrar; absorber; *vn* recoger o pescar esponjas; ser absorbente; **to sponge on** (coll.) vivir a costa de (*otra persona*)
sponge cake *s* bizcocho muy ligero, pastaflora
sponger ['spʌndʒər] *s* persona que limpia con esponja; máquina para humedecer las telas antes de plancharlas; embarcación que va a la pesca de esponjas; (fig.) esponja (*gorrón, parásito*)
sponge rubber *s* caucho esponjoso
spongin ['spʌndʒɪn] *s* (biochem.) espongina
spongy ['spʌndʒɪ] *adj* (*comp:* **-gier;** *super:* **-giest**) esponjoso
sponson ['spɑnsən] *s* barbeta lateral de un buque de guerra; plataforma triangular detrás o delante de la rueda de paletas de un barco de vapor; cámara de aire (*en la borda de una canoa*); flotador (*de un hidroavión*)
sponsor ['spɑnsər] *s* patrocinador; padrino, madrina; (rad. & telv.) patrocinador; **to stand sponsor for** apadrinar; *va* patrocinar; apadrinar; (rad. & telv.) patrocinar
sponsorial [spɑn'sorɪəl] *adj* patrocinador
sponsorship ['spɑnsərʃɪp] *s* patrocinio; padrinazgo; (rad. & telv.) patrocinio

spontaneity [ˌspɑntəˈniɪtɪ] *s* (pl: **-ties**) espontaneidad
spontaneous [spɑnˈtenɪəs] *adj* espontáneo; (bot. & biol.) espontáneo
spontaneous combustion *s* combustión espontánea, inflamación espontánea
spontaneous generation *s* (biol.) generación espontánea
spontoon [spɑnˈtun] *s* espontón
spoof [spuf] *s* (slang) engaño; (slang) broma; *va* (slang) engañar; *vn* (slang) bromear
spook [spuk] *s* (coll.) aparecido, espectro
spooky [ˈspukɪ] *adj* (*comp:* **-ier;** *super:* **-iest**) (coll.) semejante a un fantasma; (coll.) visitado por fantasmas; (coll.) horripilante
spool [spul] *s* carrete; canilla (*de una máquina de tejer*); *va* devanar; encanillar
spoon [spun] *s* cuchara; **born with a silver spoon in one's mouth** nacido de pie; *va* cucharear; dar forma de cuchara a; *vn* (slang) besuquearse (*los enamorados*)
spoonbill [ˈspunˌbɪl] *s* (orn.) espátula; (orn.) cucharón, ajaja; (ichth.) pez hoja
spoondrift [ˈspunˌdrɪft] *s* var. de **spindrift**
spoonerism [ˈspunərɪzəm] *s* contrepetterie o contrepèterie (*lapsus linguae en forma de metátesis entre vocablos, que produce un resultado absurdo*)
spoonful [ˈspunfʊl] *s* cucharada
spoon hook *s* anzuelo de cuchara
spoony [ˈspunɪ] *adj* (*comp:* **-ier;** *super:* **-iest**) (coll.) sobón; *s* (*pl:* **-ies**) (coll.) sobón, galán meloso
spoor [spʊr] *s* pista de un animal salvaje; *va* seguir la pista de
sporadic [spəˈrædɪk] o **sporadical** [spəˈrædɪkəl] *adj* esporádico
sporangium [spoˈrændʒɪəm] *s* (*pl:* **-a** [ə]) (bot.) esporangio
spore [spor] *s* (biol.) espora
sporidium [spoˈrɪdɪəm] *s* (*pl:* **-a** [ə]) (bot.) esporidio
sporocarp [ˈsporəkɑrp] *s* (bot.) esporocarpo
sporophyll o **sporophyl** [ˈsporəfɪl] *s* (bot.) esporofila
sporophyte [ˈsporəfaɪt] *s* (bot.) esporofito
sporozoan [ˌsporəˈzoən] *adj & s* (zool.) esporozoo
sporran [ˈspɑrən] o [ˈspɔrən] *s* escarcela de los montañeses de Escocia
sport [sport] *s* deporte; deportista; juguete (*persona o cosa dominada por algún poder*); hazmerreír; (coll.) jugador, tahur; (coll.) buen perdedor (*en el juego*); (coll.) buen compañero, tipo; (coll.) majo, guapo; (biol.) mutación; **to make sport of** reirse de, burlarse de; *adj* deportivo; *va* (coll.) lucir (*p.ej., un traje nuevo*); *vn* divertirse; estar de burla; juguetear
sport clothes *spl* var. de **sportswear**
sport coat *s* americana sport
sport fan *s* (slang) aficionado al deporte
sportful [ˈsportfəl] *adj* juguetón
sporting [ˈsportɪŋ] *adj* deportista; deportivo; honrado, leal; temerario; arriesgado
sporting chance *s* (coll.) riesgo de buen perdedor
sporting goods *spl* artículos de deporte
sporting house *s* (coll.) casa de juego; (coll.) casa de rameras
sportive [ˈsportɪv] *adj* juguetón; alegre, festivo
sports *adj* deportivo
sports car *s* coche deportivo
sportscaster [ˈsportsˌkæstər] o [ˈsportsˌkɑstər] *s* (rad. & telv.) locutor deportivo
sport shirt *s* camisa sport
sportsman [ˈsportsmən] *s* (*pl:* **-men**) deportista; persona muy honrada; persona temeraria
sportsmanlike [ˈsportsmənˌlaɪk] *adj* de deportista; leal y honrado
sportsmanship [ˈsportsmənʃɪp] *s* pericia en los deportes; lealtad y honradez; nobleza, magnanimidad, grandeza
sports news *s* noticiario deportivo
sportswear [ˈsportsˌwɛr] *s* trajes de sport, trajes deportivos
sportswoman [ˈsportsˌwʊmən] *s* (*pl:* **-women**) deportista *f*
sports writer *s* cronista deportivo
sporty [ˈsportɪ] *adj* (*comp:* **-ier;** *super:* **-iest**) (coll.) alegre, brillante; (coll.) disipado, libertino; (coll.) magnánimo; (coll.) elegante, guapo
sporulation [ˌspɑrjəˈleʃən] o [ˌspɔrjəˈleʃən] *s* (biol.) esporulación
sporule [ˈspɑrjul] o [ˈspɔrjul] *s* (bot.) espórula
spot [spɑt] *s* mancha; sitio, lugar; (coll.) poquito; **in spots** aquí y allí; en algunos respectos; **on the spot** sobre el terreno, allí mismo; al punto; (slang) en dificultad; (slang) destinado a ser matado; **to hit the spot** (coll.) tener razón; (coll.) dar satisfacción; **to put on the spot** poner en un aprieto; *adj* disponible; contante; (*pret & pp:* **spotted;** *ger:* **spotting**) *va* manchar; esparcir, diseminar; (coll.) descubrir, encontrar, reconocer; *vn* mancharse, tener manchas
spot cash *s* dinero contante
spotless [ˈspɑtlɪs] *adj* inmaculado, sin manchas
spotlight [ˈspɑtˌlaɪt] *s* proyector orientable; (aut.) faro piloto, faro giratorio; luz concentrada; atención del público
spot remover [rɪˈmuvər] *s* quitamanchas (*persona y substancia*)
spotted [ˈspɑtɪd] *adj* manchado; moteado
spotted fever *s* (path.) tifus exantemático; (path.) fiebre purpúrea de las Montañas Rocosas
spotted hyena *s* (zool.) hiena manchada
spotted sandpiper *s* (orn.) chorlo manchado, chorlito playero manchado
spotter [ˈspɑtər] *s* vigilante secreto; atalayador, observador; situador
spotty [ˈspɑtɪ] *adj* (*comp:* **-tier;** *super:* **-tiest**) manchado; irregular
spot-weld [ˈspɑtˌwɛld] *va* soldar por puntos
spot welding *s* soldadura por puntos
spousal [ˈspaʊzəl] *adj* nupcial; *s* nupcias; **spousals** *spl* nupcias
spouse [spaʊz] o [spaʊs] *s* cónyuge, consorte
spout [spaʊt] *s* canalón (*para el agua del tejado*); pico (*de cafetera, jarra, etc.*); chorro; **up the spout** (slang) en prenda; (slang) acabado, arruinado; *va* echar en chorro; declamar; *vn* chorrear; declamar; soplar (*echar agua la ballena*)
sprain [spren] *s* torcedura, esguince; *va* torcer, torcerse (*p.ej., una cuerda, un tendón*)
sprang [spræŋ] *pret de* **spring**
sprat [spræt] *s* (ichth.) pequeño arenque (*Clupea sprattus*)
sprawl [sprɔl] *s* postura floja; *vn* arrellanarse
spray [spre] *s* rociada; espuma (*del mar*); rociador, pulverizador; ramita; *va & vn* rociar
sprayer [ˈspreər] *s* rociador, pulverizador, vaporizador
spray gun *s* pistola pulverizadora
spray nozzle *s* espumadera, lanza regadera
spread [sprɛd] *s* extensión; amplitud, anchura; intervalo; diferencia; difusión; colcha, sobrecama, cubrecama; mantel, tapete; (coll.) festín, banquete; envergadura (*de las alas de las aves*); (aer.) envergadura; (*pret & pp:* **spread**) *va* extender; difundir, propagar; untar, dar una capa a; esparcir, desparramar; escalonar; abrir, separar; poner (*la mesa*); **to spread oneself** (coll.) echar el resto; (coll.) tratar de impresionar, tratar de ganarse la buena voluntad; (coll.) lucirse, fachendear, jactarse; *vn* extenderse; difundirse, propagarse; desparramarse; abrirse, separarse
spread eagle *s* figura de águila con las alas abiertas (*emblema de los EE.UU.*); bocón, fanfarrón; fanfarronería, chovinismo
spread-eagle [ˈsprɛdˌigəl] *adj* con las alas abiertas (*como un águila*); (coll.) fanfarrón; (coll.) patriotero; *va* (naut.) atar con brazos y piernas extendidas (*para flagelar*)
spread-eagleism [ˈsprɛdˌigəlɪzəm] *s* (coll.) patriotería
spreader [ˈsprɛdər] *s* esparcidor; divulgador; distribuidora de abono
spree [spri] *s* juerga, parranda; borrachera; **to go on a spree** ir de juerga; coger una borrachera
sprig [sprɪg] *s* ramita; (scornful) jovenzuelo
sprightly [ˈspraɪtlɪ] *adj* (*comp:* **-lier;** *super:* **-liest**) vivo, alegre, animado

spring [sprɪŋ] *s* primavera (*estación del año*); muelle, resorte (*pieza elástica de metal*); ballesta (*muelle de coche*); fuente, manantial; surtidor (*de petróleo*); salto, brinco; abertura, grieta; tensión, tirantez; (arch.) arranque ‖ *adj* de muelle, de resorte; primaveral; de fuente, de manantial ‖ (*pret:* **sprang** o **sprung;** *pp:* **sprung**) *va* soltar (*un muelle o resorte*); torcer, combar, encorvar; hacer saltar (*una trampa, una mina*); **to spring something on someone** embocarle o soltarle a uno una cosa (*p.ej., una mala noticia*) ‖ *vn* saltar, brincar; moverse rápidamente o de golpe; saltar de golpe a un lado o atrás; brotar, nacer, proceder; torcerse, combarse, encorvarse; **to spring at** abalanzarse sobre; **to spring back** saltar hacia atrás; **to spring to one's feet** levantarse de un salto; **to spring forth** precipitarse; brotar; **to spring forward** arrojarse; **to spring up** levantarse de un salto; brotar, nacer; presentarse a la vista
springal [ˈsprɪŋəl] o **springald** [ˈsprɪŋəld] *s* joven, muchacho
spring beauty *s* (bot.) claytonia
springboard [ˈsprɪŋ,bord] *s* trampolín; (fig.) trampolín
springbok [ˈsprɪŋ,bɑk] *s* (zool.) gacela del sur de África (*Antidorcas marsupialis*)
spring bolt *s* pestillo de golpe
spring chicken *s* polluelo; (coll.) pollita, p.ej., **she's no longer a spring chicken** ya no es una pollita
springe [sprɪndʒ] *s* lazo, trampa; *va* coger con un lazo o trampa
springer [ˈsprɪŋər] *s* saltador; perro ojeador; (arch.) imposta; (zool.) gacela del sur de África
spring fever *s* (hum.) ataque primaveral, galbana
springhalt [ˈsprɪŋ,hɔlt] *s* (vet.) cojera de caballo
spring hook *s* mosquetón
springhouse [ˈsprɪŋ,haʊs] *s* enfriadero sobre un manantial
springlet [ˈsprɪŋlɪt] *s* fuentezuela
spring lock *s* cerradura de golpe o de muelle
spring mattress *s* colchón de muelles, somier
springtail [ˈsprɪŋ,tel] *s* (ent.) tisanuro
springtide [ˈsprɪŋ,taɪd] *s* primavera
spring tide *s* (naut.) aguas vivas; corriente o torrente muy impetuoso
springtime [ˈsprɪŋ,taɪm] *s* primavera
spring water *s* agua manantial, agua de manantial
spring wheat *s* trigo de primavera
springy [ˈsprɪŋɪ] *adj* (*comp:* **-ier;** *super:* **-iest**) elástico; lleno de manantiales
sprinkle [ˈsprɪŋkəl] *s* rociada; llovizna; poquito, pizca; *va* rociar, regar; salpicar, sembrar; espolvorear (*p.ej., azúcar*); *vn* rociar; lloviznar, gotear (*llover a gotas espaciadas*)
sprinkler [ˈsprɪŋklər] *s* rociadera o regadera
sprinkler system *s* instalación de rociadura automática (*para la extinción de incendios*)
sprinkling [ˈsprɪŋklɪŋ] *s* rociada, rociadura; pequeña cantidad
sprinkling can *s* regadera
sprint [sprɪnt] *s* (sport) embalaje, carrera corta de velocidad; *vn* (sport) embalarse, lanzarse, correr a toda velocidad sobre un recorrido muy corto
sprinter [ˈsprɪntər] *s* (sport) corredor de velocidad a pequeñas distancias
sprit [sprɪt] *s* (naut.) botavara, verga de abanico
sprite [spraɪt] *s* duende, trasgo
spritsail [ˈsprɪtsəl] o [ˈsprɪt,sel] *s* (naut.) cebadera
sprocket [ˈsprɑkɪt] *s* diente de rueda de cadena; rueda de cadena
sprocket wheel *s* rueda de cadena
sprout [spraʊt] *s* (bot.) retoño, renuevo, brote; **sprouts** *spl* (bot.) bretones; *va* hacer brotar o germinar; (coll.) quitar los brotes o botones a; *vn* brotar o germinar, echar renuevos; crecer rápidamente
spruce [sprus] *s* (bot.) abeto del Norte, abeto falso, abeto rojo, pícea; *adj* garboso, apuesto, elegante; *va* ataviar, componer; *vn* ataviarse, componerse; **to spruce up** emperifollarse
sprue [spru] *s* (path.) esprue, psilosis; (found.) bebedero
sprung [sprʌŋ] *pret & pp de* **spring**
spry [spraɪ] *adj* (*comp:* **spryer** o **sprier;** *super:* **spryest** o **spriest**) activo, vivo, listo, ágil
spt. abr. de **seaport**
spud [spʌd] *s* (agr.) escarda; escoplo (*para quitar la corteza a los árboles*); (coll.) patata
spue [spju] *va & vn* var. de **spew**
spume [spjum] *s* espuma; *vn* espumar
spumy [ˈspjumɪ] *adj* (*comp:* **-ier;** *super:* **-iest**) espumoso, espumajoso
spun [spʌn] *pret & pp de* **spin**
spun glass *s* vidrio hilado, cristal hilado
spunk [spʌŋk] *s* (coll.) corazón, coraje, valor, ánimo; yesca; *vn* encenderse; **to spunk up** (coll.) dar prueba de valor
spunky [ˈspʌŋkɪ] *adj* (*comp:* **-ier;** *super:* **-iest**) (coll.) vivo, valiente, animado; (coll.) enfadadizo
spun silk *s* seda cardada e hilada
spun yarn *s* (naut.) meollar
spur [spʌr] *s* espuela; gusanillo (*rosca puntiaguda en que terminan las barrenas*); espolón (*del gallo; de una montaña; de un buque de guerra*); (carp.) espolón; (rail.) ramal corto; (fig.) espuela (*estímulo*); **on the spur of the moment** impulsivamente, sin la reflexión debida; **to win one's spurs** distinguirse; cobrar buena fama sin ayuda ajena; (*pret & pp:* **spurred;** *ger:* **spurring**) *va* espolear; proveer de espuelas; **to spur on** (fig.) espolear; *vn* cabalgar muy aprisa; apretar el paso
spurgall [ˈspʌr,gɔl] *s* espoleadura
spurge [spʌrdʒ] *s* (bot.) euforbio
spur gear *s* (mach.) rueda dentada recta; engranaje de ruedas dentadas rectas
spurge flax *s* (bot.) torvisco
spurge laurel *s* (bot.) lauréola
spurious [ˈspjʊrɪəs] *adj* espurio
spurn [spʌrn] *s* desdén, menosprecio; coz; *va* desdeñar, menospreciar; rechazar a puntapiés; *vn* cocear
spurred [spʌrd] *adj* con espuelas; con espolones
spurry [ˈspʌrɪ] *s* (bot.) esparcilla
spur stone *s* guardacantón
spurt [spʌrt] *s* chorro repentino; arranque; esfuerzo extraordinario y breve; *va* hacer salir a borbotones, hacer salir en chorro; *vn* salir a borbotones, salir en chorro; hacer un esfuerzo extraordinario y breve
spur track (rail.) ramal corto
spur wheel *s* (mach.) engranaje de ruedas dentadas rectas
sputnik [ˈspʊtnɪk] o [ˈspʌtnɪk] *s* sputnik (*satélite artificial ruso*)
sputter [ˈspʌtər] *s* farfulla (*manera de hablar*); ruido del que farfulla; palabras pronunciadas atropelladamente; chisporroteo; *va* farfullar; escupir farfullando; *vn* farfullar; chisporrotear
sputum [ˈspjutəm] *s* (*pl:* **-ta** [tə]) esputo
spy [spaɪ] *s* (*pl:* **spies**) espía; (*pret & pp:* **spied**) *va* espiar; columbrar, divisar; *vn* espiar; **to spy on** espiar
spyglass [ˈspaɪ,glæs] o [ˈspaɪ,glɑs] *s* catalejo
sq. abr. de **square**
squab [skwɑb] *s* (orn.) pichón, pichoncillo; (orn.) pollo, pollito; sofá, canapé; cojín; *adj* acabado de nacer (*dícese de las aves*); regordete, rechoncho
squabble [ˈskwɑbəl] *s* riña, reyerta; *vn* reñir, disputar
squabby [ˈskwɑbɪ] *adj* regordete, rechoncho
squad [skwɑd] *s* escuadra; (mil.) escuadra
squadron [ˈskwɑdrən] *s* (nav.) escuadra; (aer.) escuadrilla; (mil.) escuadrón (*de caballería*)
squalid [ˈskwɑlɪd] *adj* escuálido
squall [skwɔl] *s* grupada; chubasco; ráfaga de viento; (coll.) riña; (coll.) chubasco (*adversidad*); chillido; *vn* chillar
squally [ˈskwɔlɪ] *adj* (*comp:* **-ier;** *super:* **-iest**) chubascoso; ventoso; (coll.) amenazador
squalor [ˈskwɑlər] *s* escualor, escualidez
squama [ˈskwemə] *s* (*pl:* **-mae** [mi]) (anat. & biol.) escama
squamate [ˈskwemet] *adj* escamoso

squamose [ˈskwemos] o **squamous** [ˈskweməs] *adj* escamoso
squander [ˈskwɑndər] *va* malgastar, despilfarrar
square [skwɛr] *s* (geom. & math.) cuadrado; (carp.) escuadra; (mil.) cuadro; manzana (*de casas*); plaza; casilla o escaque (*del tablero de ajedrez o damas*); **to be on the square** (coll.) obrar en buena fe ‖ *adj* cuadrado, p.ej., **eight square inches** ocho pulgadas cuadradas; en cuadro, de lado, p.ej., **eight inches square** ocho pulgadas en cuadro u ocho pulgadas de lado; rectangular; en ángulo recto; justo, recto, equitativo; saldado; leal, honrado; claro y directo; sólido, fuerte; (coll.) abundante, completo; **to get square with** (coll.) hacérselas pagar a ‖ *adv* en cuadro; en forma de rectángulo; en ángulo recto; lealmente, honradamente ‖ *va* cuadrar; (math.) cuadrar; (carp.) escuadrar; dividir en cuadros; ajustar, nivelar, conformar; (slang) cohechar, sobornar; **to square oneself** compensar un dicho o hecho; pagar con las misma moneda ‖ *vn* cuadrarse, ajustarse, conformarse; (coll.) saldar cuentas; **to square away** (naut.) bracear en cuadro; **to square off** (coll.) colocarse en posición de defensa
square dance *s* danza de figuras
square deal *s* (coll.) trato equitativo, juego limpio
square-faced [ˈskwɛr,fest] *adj* de cara cuadrada
square-headed [ˈskwɛrˈhɛdɪd] *adj* de cabeza cuadrada; de cabeza de diamante (*tuerca*)
square knot *s* nudo llano, nudo derecho
square meal *s* (coll.) comida abundante
square measure *s* medida cuadrada o de superficie
square piano *s* piano cuadrado
square-rigger [ˈskwɛr,rɪgər] *s* (naut.) buque de cruz
square root *s* (math.) raíz cuadrada
square sail *s* (naut.) vela de cruz
square shooter *s* (coll.) persona leal y honrada
square-toed [ˈskwɛr,tod] *adj* con los dedos de los pies gruesos y cortos; de ideas anticuadas
squarish [ˈskwɛrɪʃ] *adj* casi cuadrado
squash [skwɑʃ] *s* (bot.) calabaza (*planta y fruto*); aplastamiento, despachurramiento; *va* aplastar, despachurrar, apabullar; apiñar, apretar; poner fin a, por la fuerza; confutar (*un argumento*); acallar con un argumento, respuesta, etc.; *vn* aplastarse; apiñarse, apretarse
squashy [ˈskwɑʃɪ] *adj* (*comp:* **-ier;** *super:* **-iest**) aplastado; mojado y blando, lodoso; fácil de aplastar
squat [skwɑt] *s* posición del que está en cuclillas; *adj* en cuclillas; rechoncho; (*pret & pp:* **squatted** o **squat;** *ger:* **squatting**) *va* hacer acuclillarse; *vn* acuclillarse, agacharse, acurrucarse; sentarse en el suelo, estar sentado en el suelo; establecerse en terreno ajeno sin derecho; establecerse en un terreno público para crear un derecho
squatter [skwɑtər] *s* advenedizo, intruso, colono usurpador; colono que se establece en un terreno público para crear un derecho
squatty [ˈskwɑtɪ] *adj* (*comp:* **-tier;** *super:* **-tiest**) rechoncho, regordete
squaw [skwɔ] *s* india norteamericana; mujer, esposa, muchacha
squawk [skwɔk] *s* graznido; (slang) queja en voz chillona; *va* (slang) decir en voz chillona; *vn* graznar; (slang) quejarse en voz chillona
squaw man *s* blanco casado con india
squeak [skwik] *s* chillido; chirrido; **narrow squeak** (coll.) escapada en una tabla; *va* decir con un chillido; hacer chirriar; *vn* dar chillidos; chirriar
squeaky [ˈskwikɪ] *adj* (*comp:* **-ier;** *super:* **-iest**) chillón; chirriador, chirriante
squeal [skwil] *s* alarido, chillido; *va* proferir con un alarido o chillido; *vn* dar un alarido o chillido; (slang) soplar, delatar; **to squeal on** (slang) soplar, delatar (*a una persona*)
squealer [ˈskwilər] *s* chillador; (slang) soplón
squealing [ˈskwilɪŋ] *s* (rad.) aullido
squeamish [ˈskwimɪʃ] *adj* delicado, escrupuloso, remilgado; excesivamente modesto
squeegee [ˈskwidʒi] *s* alisador o enjugador de goma (*para secar superficies mojadas*); (*pret & pp:* **-geed;** *ger:* **-geeing**) *va* secar con alisador o enjugador de goma
squeeze [skwiz] *s* estrujón, apretón, abrazo fuerte; apiñamiento; impresión; (coll.) forzosa (*presión de hacer algo*); **to put the squeeze on someone** (coll.) poner a uno las peras a cuatro o a ocho, meter en prensa a uno, hacer a uno la forzosa; *va* estrujar, apretar; exprimir; agobiar, oprimir, estrujar; **to squeeze in** meter a estrujones; *vn* tupirse; **to squeeze through** abrirse paso a estrujones por entre, pasar apretadamente a través de
squeezer [ˈskwizər] *s* exprimidera
squelch [skwɛltʃ] *s* (coll.) tapaboca; *va* apabullar, despachurrar; *vn* chapotear, andar chapoteando
squib [skwɪb] *s* buscapiés, carretilla; cohete que falla con un sonido crepitante; pasquín, escrito satírico; (*pret & pp:* **squibbed;** *ger:* **squibbing**) *va* arrojar; salpicar; pasquinar; *vn* soltar carretillas; estallar; divulgar pasquinadas
squid [skwɪd] *s* (zool.) calamar; (zool.) flecha de mar, calamar volante
squid-jigger [ˈskwɪd,dʒɪgər] *s* guadañeta
squill [skwɪl] *s* (bot.) escila, esquila, cebolla albarrana; (zool.) esquila
squint [skwɪnt] *s* mirada bizca; mirada de soslayo, mirada furtiva; bizquera, estrabismo; propensión, tendencia; *adj* bizco, bisojo; de soslayo, de mal ojo; *va* hacer torcer la vista a; achicar (*los ojos*); *vn* bizquear; torcer la vista; tener los ojos medio cerrados; andar o correr oblicuamente; tener una tendencia indirecta; mirar de mal ojo
squint-eyed [ˈskwɪnt,aɪd] *adj* bizco, bisojo; malévolo, sospechoso
squire [skwaɪr] *s* (feud.) escudero; (Brit.) terrateniente de antigua heredad; (U.S.A.) juez de paz, juez local; asistente, sirviente; acompañante (*de una señora*); *va* asistir o servir como escudero; acompañar (*a una señora*); *vn* ser escudero; ser acompañante
squireen [skwaɪˈrin] *s* terrateniente de poca monta
squirm [skwʌrm] *s* retorcimiento; *vn* retorcerse; **to squirm out of** escaparse de (*p.ej., un aprieto*) haciendo muchas fuerzas
squirmy [ˈskwɪrmɪ] *adj* (*comp:* **-ier;** *super:* **-iest**) retorcido, retorciéndose
squirrel [ˈskwʌrəl] *s* (zool.) ardilla; petigrís (*piel*)
squirrel-cage motor [ˈskwʌrəl,kedʒ] *s* (elec.) motor de jaula de ardilla
squirt [skwʌrt] *s* chorro, chisguete; jeringazo; (coll.) mono, presuntuoso; *va* arrojar a chorros; *vn* salir a chorros
squirting cucumber *s* (bot.) cohombrillo amargo, pepinillo del diablo
Sr. abr. de **senior** y de **Sir**
S.R.O. abr. de **standing room only**
S.S. abr. de **Secretary of State, Straits Settlements, steamship** y **Sunday school**
St. abr. de **Saint, Strait** y **Street**
stab [stæb] *s* puñalada; (coll.) tentativa; **stab in the back** puñalada (de traidor) por la espalda; **to make a stab at** (slang) esforzarse por hacer; (*pret & pp:* **stabbed;** *ger:* **stabbing**) *va* apuñalar; traspasar; **to stab to death** escabechar; *vn* apuñalar, dar de puñaladas
Stabat Mater [ˈstɑbɑt ˈmɑtər] o [ˈstebæt ˈmetər] *s* (eccl. & mus.) stábat máter
stability [stəˈbɪlɪtɪ] *s* (*pl:* **-ties**) estabilidad
stabilization [,stebɪlɪˈzeʃən] o [,stæbɪlɪˈzeʃən] *s* estabilización
stabilize [ˈstebɪlaɪz] o [ˈstæbɪlaɪz] *va* estabilizar
stabilizer [ˈstebɪ,laɪzər] o [ˈstæbɪ,laɪzər] *s* estabilizador (*persona o aparato*)
stable [ˈstebəl] *adj* estable; *s* establo, cuadra, caballeriza; caballos de carrera de un particular; *va* poner o guardar en un establo, cuadra o caballeriza; *vn* estar colocado en un establo, cuadra o caballeriza
stable boy [ˈstebəl,bɔɪ] *s* mozo de caballerías, mozo de cuadra

stable fly *s* (ent.) mosca picadora de los establos
stableman [ˈstebəl,mæn] *s* (*pl:* **-men**) establero
stably [ˈsteblɪ] *adv* establemente
staccato [stəˈkɑto] *s* (*pl:* **-tos**) (mus.) staccato
stack [stæk] *s* niara, hacina, rimero; pila, montón; (mil.) pabellón de fusiles; estantería, depósito (*de libros en una biblioteca*); cañón de chimenea; cuba (*del alto horno*); (coll.) montón, gran número; *va* amontonar, apilar; hacinar; florear (*el naipe*); **to have the cards stacked against one** estar en una situación desventajosa
staddle [ˈstædəl] *s* resalvo
stadholder [ˈstæd,holdər] *s* estatúder
stadholderate [ˈstæd,holdəret] **stadholdership** [ˈstæd,holdərʃɪp] *s* estatuderato
stadia [ˈstedɪə] *s* (surv.) estadia
stadia hairs *spl* (surv.) hilos taquimétricos
stadia rod *s* (surv.) mira taquimétrica
stadium [ˈstedɪəm] *s* (*pl:* **-ums** o **-a** [ə]) estadio
stadtholder [ˈstæt,holdər] *s* var. de **stadholder**
staff [stæf] o [stɑf] *s* (*pl:* **staves** [stevz] o **staffs**) bastón; apoyo, sostén; (mus.) pentágrama; *s* (*pl:* **staffs**) personal; (mil.) estado mayor; *va* proveer de personal, nombrar personal para
staff officer *s* (mil.) oficial de estado mayor
staff tree *s* (bot.) celastro
stag [stæg] *s* (zool.) ciervo; varón; varón solo (*no acompañado de mujeres*); *adj* exclusivo para hombres
stag beetle *s* (ent.) ciervo volante
stage [stedʒ] *s* escena; estrado; andamio, tablado; cadalso; teatro (*de cualquier suceso*); etapa, jornada, posta; descansadero, parada; fase, estadio; diligencia (*coche*); portaobjeto (*del microscopio*); (rad.) etapa, escalón; **by easy stages** a pequeñas etapas; lentamente; **on the stage** sobre la escena, en el teatro; **to go on the stage** hacerse actor; *va* poner en escena, representar; preparar, organizar; *vn* ser apropiado al teatro; viajar en diligencia
stagecoach [ˈstedʒ,kotʃ] *s* diligencia
stagecraft [ˈstedʒ,kræft] o [ˈstedʒ,krɑft] *s* arte teatral
stage door *s* (theat.) entrada de los artistas
stage effect *s* efecto escénico
stage fright *s* miedo al público, trac
stagehand [ˈstedʒ,hænd] *s* tramoyista, metemuertos, metesillas
stage manager *s* (theat.) director de escena
stager [ˈstedʒər] *s* hombre experimentado; (coll.) caballo de diligencia
stage setting *s* (theat.) arreglo de escena; (theat.) aparato escénico
stage-struck [ˈstedʒ,strʌk] *adj* loco por el teatro
stage whisper *s* susurro en voz alta
stagger [ˈstægər] *s* vacilación, tambaleo; (aer.) decalaje; **staggers** *ssg* (vet.) modorra, vértigo; *va* hacer vacilar, hacer tambalear; hacer titubear; sorprender; asustar; escalonar (*las horas de trabajo*); *vn* vacilar, tambalear, hacer eses al andar; titubear; sorprenderse; asustarse; conmoverse mucho
staggering [ˈstægərɪŋ] *adj* tambaleante; derribador; sorprendente; espantoso
staghound [ˈstæg,haʊnd] *s* sabueso
staging [ˈstedʒɪŋ] *s* andamiada; (theat.) representación; viajes en diligencia
staging area *s* (mil.) zona de embarco
stagnancy [ˈstægnənsɪ] *s* estancación o estancamiento
stagnant [ˈstægnənt] *adj* estancado, estadizo; (fig.) estancado, inactivo, paralizado
stagnate [ˈstægnet] *va* estancar; *vn* estancarse
stagnation [stægˈneʃən] *s* estancación o estancamiento; (fig.) estancamiento
stag party *s* tertulia de hombres solos
stagy [ˈstedʒɪ] *adj* (*comp:* **-ier**; *super:* **-iest**) teatral
staid [sted] *adj* grave, serio, formal
stain [sten] *s* mancha; tinte, tintura; materia colorante; *va* manchar; teñir; colorar; *vn* mancharse; hacer manchas
stained glass *s* vidrio de color
stained-glass window [ˈstend,glæs] o [ˈstend,glɑs] *s* vidriera de colores, vitral (en color)
stainless [ˈstenlɪs] *adj* inoxidable, inmanchable; inmaculado
stainless steel *s* acero inoxidable
stair [stɛr] *s* escalón (*peldaño de escalera*); escalera; **stairs** *spl* escalera; **below stairs** abajo, al o en el piso bajo; en la cocina, en las viviendas de escalera abajo
staircase [ˈstɛr,kes] *s* escalera, caja de la escalera
stairway [ˈstɛr,we] *s* escalera
stair well *s* hueco de escalera
stake [stek] *s* estaca; telero (*de un carro*); puesta, posta; rodrigón (*para sostener plantas*); bigorneta; premio del vencedor; **at stake** en juego; en gran peligro; **to die at the stake** morir en la hoguera; **to have much at stake** irle a uno mucho en una cosa; **to pull up stakes** (coll.) irse; (coll.) mudar de casa; *va* estacar; atar a una estaca; rodrigar (*plantas*); apostar; arriesgar, aventurar; **to stake all** jugarse el todo por el todo; **to stake off** o **to stake out** estacar, señalar con estacas
stakeholder [ˈstek,holdər] *s* el que guarda las apuestas y paga al que gana
stake truck *s* camión de plataforma con teleros
Stakhanovism [stəˈxɑnəvɪzəm] *s* stajanovismo
Stakhanovite [stəˈxɑnəvaɪt] *adj & s* stajanovista
stalactite [stəˈlæktaɪt] o [ˈstæləktaɪt] *s* estalactita
stalagmite [stəˈlægmaɪt] o [ˈstæləgmaɪt] *s* estalagmita
stale [stel] *adj* añejo, rancio, viejo; anticuado; viciado (*aire*); mohoso (*chiste*); *va* añejar, enranciar; *vn* añejarse, enranciarse
stalemate [ˈstel,met] *s* mate ahogado (*en el ajedrez*); estancación; **to reach a stalemate** llegar a un punto muerto; *va* dar mate ahogado a; estancar, paralizar
Stalingrad [ˈstɑlɪn,grɑd] *s* Stalingrado
Stalinism [ˈstɑlɪnɪzəm] *s* stalinismo
Stalinist [ˈstɑlɪnɪst] *adj & s* stalinista
stalk [stɔk] *s* (bot.) tallo; (bot., anat. & zool.) pedúnculo; (el) cazar al acecho; paso majestuoso; (obs.) paso furtivo; *va* cazar al acecho; acechar, espiar; *vn* cazar al acecho; andar con paso majestuoso; andar con paso altivo; (obs.) andar con paso furtivo; **to stalk out** salir con paso airado
stalking-horse [ˈstɔkɪŋ,hɔrs] *s* caballo o figura que representa un caballo que usan los cazadores al acecho para esconderse; (pol.) candidato que sirve para encubrir la candidatura de otra persona; disfraz, pretexto, máscara
stall [stɔl] *s* establo, pesebre; puesto (*para la venta*); caseta (*de una feria*); (Brit.) butaca; (slang) pretexto; *va* encerrar en un establo; estancar, poner trabas a; parar (*un motor*); **to stall off** (coll.) eludir, evitar; *vn* estar o vivir en un establo; atascarse, atollarse; pararse (*un motor*); (slang) eludir para engañar o demorar; **to stall for time** (slang) tardar para ganar tiempo
stall-fed [ˈstɔl,fɛd] *adj* cebado o engordado en un establo
stallion [ˈstæljən] *s* caballo padre, caballo semental
stalwart [ˈstɔlwərt] *s* persona fornida; partidario leal; *adj* fornido, forzudo; valiente; leal, constante
Stambul o **Stamboul** [stɑmˈbul] *s* Estambul
stamen [ˈstemən] *s* (bot.) estambre
stamina [ˈstæmɪnə] *s* fuerza, nervio, vigor, resistencia
staminate [ˈstæmɪnet] *adj* (bot.) estaminado (*que sólo tiene estambres*); (bot.) estaminífero
staminode [ˈstæmɪnod] *s* var. de **staminodium**
staminodium [,stæmɪˈnodɪəm] *s* (*pl:* **-dia** [dɪə]) (bot.) estaminodio o estaminodo
stammer [ˈstæmər] *s* balbuceo, tartamudeo; *va* balbucear (*p.ej., excusas*); *vn* balbucear o balbucir; tartamudear
stamp [stæmp] *s* sello; estampilla (*sello con letrero para estampar*); marca, impresión, rastro; pisón; cuño, troquel (*para estampar las monedas, etc.*); tipo, clase, calaña; *va* hollar, pisotear; imprimir, estampar; sellar; troquelar; pa-

tear; indicar, señalar; poner el sello a; bocartear (*el mineral*); **to stamp out** apagar pateando; extinguir con la fuerza; suprimir; *vn* patalear
Stamp Act *s* (hist.) ley del Timbre
stampede [stæmˈpid] *s* estampida; movimiento precipitado y unánime; *va* hacer huir en desorden; provocar a pánico, provocar a obrar impulsivamente; *vn* huir en desorden; obrar por común impulso
stamping grounds *spl* (slang) guarida (*sitio frecuentado por una persona*)
stamp mill *s* (min.) bocarte
stamp pad *s* tampón
stamp-vending machine [ˈstæmp,vɛndɪŋ] *s* máquina expendedora de sellos
stance [stæns] *s* (sport) postura, planta
stanch [stɑntʃ] *adj* firme, fuerte; leal, constante; estanco; *va* estancar; restañar (*la sangre de una herida*); *vn* apagarse; restañarse
stanchion [ˈstænʃən] *s* puntal, montante, pie derecho; cornadiza (*en las vaquerías*); *va* proveer de puntales, montantes o pies derechos; sujetar a puntales
stand [stænd] *s* parada; estancia (*entre dos etapas*); postura, posición; resistencia; tribuna, estrado; sostén, soporte, pie, pedestal; puesto, quiosco ‖ (*pret & pp:* **stood**) *va* poner derecho, colocar verticalmente; tolerar, soportar, resistir; (coll.) aguantar (*a una persona*); (coll.) sufragar (*un gasto*); **to stand off** tener a raya; **to stand on end** poner de punta; **to stand one's ground** mantenerse firme, mantenerse en su puesto ‖ *vn* estar, estar situado; estar parado; estacionarse; estar de pie, estar derecho; ponerse de pie, levantarse; resultar; navegar; mostrar la caza (*un perro*); persistir; mantenerse; quedarse; surgir, nacer; pararse; **to stand aloof** mantenerse apartado; **to stand apart** o **aside** apartarse, mantenerse apartado; **to stand back of** colocarse detrás de; garantizar, respaldar; **to stand by** mantenerse a corta distancia; estar alerta; (rad. & telv.) esperar la continuación de un programa interrumpido; apoyar, defender; **to stand for** significar, representar; apoyar, defender; apadrinar; mantener (*p.ej., una opinión*); presentarse como candidato de; (coll.) tolerar; navegar hacia; **to stand forth** destacarse; **to stand in** (coll.) tener buenas aldabas, estar en buenas relaciones; **to stand in for** substituir (*a una persona*); **to stand in line** hacer cola; **to stand in the way** cerrar el paso; estorbar; **to stand off** apartarse, quedar a distancia; **to stand on** depender de, basarse en; pedir con insistencia; **to stand on end** ponerse de punta; erizarse, encresparse (*el pelo*); **to stand out** sobresalir; resaltar, destacarse; no ceder; **to stand to reason** ser lógico, ser razonable; **to stand up** ponerse de pie, levantarse; durar, conservarse; **to stand up for** apoyar, defender; **to stand up to** hacer resueltamente frente a
standard [ˈstændərd] *s* patrón; norma, regla establecida; bandera, estandarte; emblema, símbolo; (bot.) árbol o arbusto de tronco o tallo alto y derecho; *adj* normal; corriente, regular; legal; clásico
standardbearer [ˈstændərd,bɛrər] *s* abanderado o portaestandarte; jefe (*de un movimiento*); (orn.) chotacabras africano
standard broadcasting *s* difusión normal
standard candle *s* (phys.) bujía normal o patrón
standard gauge *s* (rail.) vía normal
standard gold *s* oro de ley
standardization [,stændərdɪˈzeʃən] *s* normalización, estandardización
standardize [ˈstændərdaɪz] *va* normalizar, estandardizar
standard keyboard *s* teclado universal (*de la máquina de escribir*)
standard meter *s* metro patrón
standard of living *s* nivel de vida
standard time *s* hora legal
stand-by [ˈstænd,baɪ] *s* (*pl:* **-bys**) adherente fiel, recurso seguro, paño de lágrimas
standee [stænˈdi] *s* (coll.) espectador que asiste de pie
stand-in [ˈstænd,ɪn] *s* (mov.) doble; (coll.) buenas aldabas
standing [ˈstændɪŋ] *s* posición, condición; reputación; duración; parada; **in good standing** en posición acreditada; **of long standing** de mucho tiempo, de antigua fecha; **of standing** de prestigio; *adj* derecho, en pie; de pie; permanente, estable, fijo; parado, inmóvil; encharcado, estancado; vigente
standing army *s* ejército permanente
standing committee *s* comisión permanente
standing rigging *s* (naut.) jarcia de firme, jarcia muerta
standing room *s* sitio para estar de pie
stand-off [ˈstænd,ɔf] o [ˈstænd,ɑf] *s* reserva, aislamiento; empate; *adj* retraído, reservado, indiferente
stand-offish [,stændˈɔfɪʃ] o [,stændˈɑfɪʃ] *adj* retraído, reservado, indiferente, huraño
standpat [ˈstænd,pæt] *adj & s* (coll.) conservador
standpatter [ˈstænd,pætər] *s* (coll.) conservador
standpipe [ˈstænd,paɪp] *s* columna de alimentación, columna de alimentación de agua
standpoint [ˈstænd,pɔɪnt] *s* punto de vista
standstill [ˈstænd,stɪl] *s* parada, detención, alto; descanso, inactividad; **to come to a standstill** cesar, pararse
stand-up [ˈstænd,ʌp] *adj* derecho; estando de pie, p.ej., **a stand-up meal** una comida de pie
stanhope [ˈstænhop] o [ˈstænəp] *s* cabriolé ligero
stank [stæŋk] *pret de* **stink**
stannate [ˈstænet] *s* (chem.) estannato
stannic [ˈstænɪk] *adj* (chem.) estánnico
stannous [ˈstænəs] *adj* (chem.) estannoso
stanza [ˈstænzə] *s* estancia, estrofa
stapedius [stəˈpidɪəs] *s* (anat.) estapedio
stapes [ˈstepiz] *s* (anat.) estribo
staphylococcus [,stæfɪləˈkɑkəs] *s* (*pl:* **-cocci** [ˈkɑksaɪ]) (bact.) estafilococo
staphyloma [,stæfɪˈlomə] *s* (*pl:* **-mata** [mətə]) (path.) estafiloma
staple [ˈstepəl] *s* grapa (*para clavar; para sujetar papeles*); artículo o producto principal; materia prima; fibra textil; *adj* primero, principal; corriente, reconocido, establecido; *va* sujetar con grapas; clasificar (*hebras textiles*) según su longitud
stapler [ˈsteplər] *s* surtidor de lanas; engrapador, cose-papeles
star [stɑr] *s* astro (*cuerpo celeste*); estrella (*cualquier astro, a excepción del Sol y la Luna; figura con que se representa una estrella; cosa que tiene esta figura*); estrellón (*fuego artificial*); (mov. & theat.) estrella (*mujer u hombre*); (elec.) estrella; (print.) estrella o asterisco; (fig.) estrella o astro (*persona que sobresale*); (fig.) as (*p.ej., de fútbol*); (fig.) estrella (*hado, destino; pelos blancos en la frente del caballo*); **to see stars** (coll.) ver las estrellas; **to thank one's lucky stars** estar agradecido por su buena suerte; *adj* estelar; principal; sobresaliente; (*pret & pp:* **starred**; *ger:* **starring**) *va* estrellar, adornar o señalar con estrellas; marcar con asterisco; presentar como estrella (*a un actor o una actriz*); *vn* ser la estrella; ser el astro; lucirse; sobresalir
star apple *s* (bot.) caimito (*árbol y fruto*)
starboard [ˈstɑrbərd] o [ˈstɑrbord] *s* (naut.) estribor; *adj* de estribor; *adv* a estribor; *va & vn* volver a estribor
star boarder *s* huésped principal o predilecto (*en una casa de huéspedes*)
starch [stɑrtʃ] *s* almidón, fécula; entono, arrogancia; (slang) fuerza, vigor; *va* almidonar
Star Chamber *s* (Brit. hist.) cámara estrellada; tribunal secreto y arbitrario
starchy [ˈstɑrtʃɪ] *adj* (*comp:* **-ier**; *super:* **-iest**) feculento, feculoso; almidonado; (fig.) tieso, entonado
star connection *s* (elec.) conexión en estrella
stardom [ˈstɑrdəm] *s* (theat.) estrellato (*categoría o condición de estrella*); actores eminentes
star drill *s* barrena de filo en cruz, taladro estrella

star dust *s* nebulosas; partículas de meteoritos; (coll.) encanto
stare [stɛr] *s* mirada fija; *va* mirar fijamente, mirar de hito en hito, clavar la vista en; **to stare down** o **to stare out of countenance** desconcertar mirando fijamente, avergonzar con la mirada; **to stare one in the face** darle a uno en la cara, estar a la vista, saltar a la vista; deber acontecer; *vn* mirar fijamente, fijar estrechamente la mirada
starfish [ˈstɑr,fɪʃ] *s* (zool.) estrella de mar
star gauge *s* (gun.) calibrador de ánima
stargaze [ˈstɑr,gez] *vn* mirar las estrellas; ser distraído, soñar despierto
stargazer [ˈstɑr,gezər] *s* el que mira las estrellas; astrólogo; astrónomo; (ichth.) uranóscopo
stargazing [ˈstɑr,gezɪŋ] *s* observación de las estrellas; abstracción, ensimismamiento
staring [ˈstɛrɪŋ] *adj* mirando fijamente; llamativo, vistoso
stark [stɑrk] *adj* completo, cabal, puro; tieso, rígido; duro, severo; *adv* completamente, enteramente; rígidamente, severamente
stark-naked [ˈstɑrkˈnekɪd] *adj* en pelota, en cueros
starless [ˈstɑrlɪs] *adj* sin estrellas
starlet [ˈstɑrlɪt] *s* estrellita
starlight [ˈstɑr,laɪt] *s* luz de las estrellas; *adj* estrellado
starlike [ˈstɑr,laɪk] *adj* estrellado; brillante como una estrella
starling [ˈstɑrlɪŋ] *s* (orn.) estornino; (orn.) trupial
starlit [ˈstɑr,lɪt] *adj* iluminado por las estrellas
Star of Bethlehem *s* estrella de Belén
star-of-Bethlehem [ˈstɑrəvˈbɛθlɪəm] *s* (bot.) leche de gallina, estrella de Belén
star-of-night [ˈstɑrəvˈnaɪt] *s* (bot.) copey
star polygon *s* (geom.) estrella poligonal
starred [stɑrd] *adj* estrellado; (theat.) presentado como estrella; afortunado
starry [ˈstɑrɪ] *adj* (*comp:* **-rier**; *super:* **-riest**) estrellado; brillante, rutilante
starry-eyed [ˈstɑrɪ,aɪd] *adj* soñador, quimérico
Stars and Bars *spl* (hist.) bandera de la Confederación de los estados del Sur de Norteamérica
Stars and Stripes *spl* estrellas y listas, barras y estrellas, franjas y estrellas (*bandera de los EE.UU.*)
star sapphire *s* zafiro asteriado, zafiro de ojo de gato
star shell *s* (mil.) bomba luminosa
star shower *s* lluvia de estrellas
star-spangled [ˈstɑr,spæŋgəld] *adj* estrellado
Star-Spangled Banner *s* bandera estrellada (*bandera de los EE.UU.*)
start [stɑrt] *s* principio, comienzo; salida, partida; lugar de partida; ventaja (*en una carrera*); sobresalto; respingo (*de un caballo*); arranque (*de un coche, tren, etc.*); (sport) salida; **to give a start** sobresaltar; **to give a start to** poner en marcha; hacer que empiece a funcionar; ayudar (*a un joven*) a establecerse en los negocios; **to make a fresh start** volver a empezar; *va* principiar, empezar; poner en marcha, hacer andar; hacer arrancar; dar la señal de partida a; entablar (*una conversación*); levantar (*la caza*); *vn* principiar, empezar; sobresaltar; nacer, provenir; aflojarse; ponerse en marcha; arrancar; **starting with** a partir de; **to start after** salir en busca de; **to start in, out** o **up** principiar, empezar; ponerse en marcha; **to start to** + *inf* principiar a + *inf*, empezar a + *inf;* ponerse a + *inf;* echarse a (*reír, llorar, correr*)
starter [ˈstɑrtər] *s* iniciador; primero (*de una serie*); (aut.) arranque, motor de arranque; (elec.) encebador, encendedor (*de tubos fluorescentes*); (sport) stárter, juez de salida
star thistle *s* (bot.) cardo estrellado, calcitrapa
starting [ˈstɑrtɪŋ] *s* puesta en marcha
starting crank *s* manivela de arranque
starting motor *s* motor de arranque
starting point *s* punto de partida
starting post *s* (sport) poste o línea de partida
startle [ˈstɑrtəl] *s* susto; *va* asustar, sorprender, sobrecoger; *vn* asustarse, sorprenderse, sobrecogerse
startling [ˈstɑrtlɪŋ] *adj* alarmante, asombroso, sorprendente
starvation [stɑrˈveʃən] *s* hambre, inanición
starvation diet *s* régimen de hambre
starvation wages *spl* salario de hambre
starve [stɑrv] *va* hambrear; hacer morir de hambre; obligar mediante el hambre; **to starve out** hacer rendirse por hambre; *vn* hambrear; morir de hambre; (coll.) tener hambre; **to starve for** sufrir por la falta de
starveling [ˈstɑrvlɪŋ] *adj & s* hambrón
starving [ˈstɑrvɪŋ] *adj* hambriento, famélico
stash [stæʃ] *va* ocultar, guardar en lugar seguro
stat. abr. de **statuary, statute** y **statue**
statable [ˈstetəbəl] *adj* enunciable, formulable
state [stet] *s* estado; fausto, pompa, ceremonia; **to lie in state** estar expuesto en capilla ardiente, estar de cuerpo presente (*el cadáver de un muerto*); **to live in state** gastar mucho lujo; **to ride in state** pasear en carruaje de lujo; *adj* de estado, del estado; estatal (*del Estado*); público; de gala, de lujo; *va* declarar, afirmar; exponer, manifestar; formular; plantear (*p.ej., un problema*)
statecraft [ˈstet,kræft] o [ˈstet,krɑft] *s* política, arte de gobernar
stated [ˈstetɪd] *adj* fijo, establecido; dicho
statehood [ˈstethʊd] *s* estatidad
Statehouse o **statehouse** [ˈstet,haʊs] *s* (U.S.A.) edificio del Estado (*en que tiene reuniones la legislatura de uno de los estados de los EE.UU.*)
stateless [ˈstetlɪs] *adj* apátrida
stateliness [ˈstetlɪnɪs] *s* majestuosidad
stately [ˈstetlɪ] *adj* (*comp:* **-lier**; *super:* **-liest**) imponente, majestuoso
statement [ˈstetmənt] *s* declaración; exposición, informe, relación; (com.) estado de cuentas
state of mind *s* estado de ánimo
state of siege *s* estado de sitio
State rights *spl* var. de **States' rights**
stateroom [ˈstet,rum] o [ˈstet,rʊm] *s* (naut.) camarote; (rail.) compartimiento particular
state room *s* sala para las ceremonias
state secret *s* secreto de estado
state's evidence *s* (law) testimonio aducido por el procurador del Estado en un juicio criminal; testimonio de un cómplice o de cómplices; **to turn state's evidence** (law) atestar en un juicio en contra de un cómplice o de cómplices, convertirse en testigo del estado
States-General [ˈstetsˈdʒɛnərəl] *s* (hist.) estados generales (*de Francia*); parlamento de los Países Bajos
stateside [ˈstet,saɪd] *adj* (coll.) estadounidense; *adv* (coll.) a o en los Estados Unidos; **a o en** la parte continental de los Estados Unidos
statesman [ˈstetsmən] *s* (*pl:* **-men**) estadista, hombre de estado
statesmanlike [ˈstetsmən,laɪk] *adj* de estadista, propio de estadista
statesmanly [ˈstetsmənlɪ] *adj* de estadista, digno de un estadista
statesmanship [ˈstetsmənʃɪp] *s* habilidad de estadista
state socialism *s* socialismo del estado
States' rights *spl* (U.S.A.) derechos de los Estados
state-wide [ˈstet,waɪd] *adj* por todo el estado, de todo el estado
static [ˈstætɪk] *adj* estático; (rad.) atmosférico; *s* (rad.) parásitos atmosféricos; **statics** *ssg* (mech.) estática
static electricity *s* electricidad estática
static machine *s* (elec.) máquina electrostática
station [ˈsteʃən] *s* estación; condición, situación; (astr. & eccl.) estación; *va* estacionar, apostar, colocar
station agent *s* (rail.) jefe de estación
stationary [ˈsteʃən,ɛrɪ] *adj* estacionario
station break *s* (rad.) descanso, intermedio
stationer [ˈsteʃənər] *s* papelero; (archaic) estacionario (*librero*)
stationery [ˈsteʃən,ɛrɪ] *s* efectos de escritorio
stationery store *s* papelería
station house *s* paradero; estación de ferrocarril; cuartelillo de policía

station identification *s* (rad. & telv.) indicativo de la emisora
stationmaster [ˈsteʃən,mæstər] o [ˈsteʃən,mɑstər] *s* (rail.) jefe de estación
stations of the cross *spl* (eccl.) estaciones, estaciones de la cruz
station wagon *s* rubia, coche rural
statism [ˈstetɪzəm] *s* estatismo
statist [ˈstetɪst] *adj* estatista; *s* estatista; estadístico
statistic [stəˈtɪstɪk] *adj* estadístico; **statistics** *ssg* estadística (*ciencia*); *spl* estadística o estadísticas
statistical [stəˈtɪstɪkəl] *adj* estadístico
statistician [,stætɪsˈtɪʃən] *s* estadístico
statocyst [ˈstætəsɪst] *s* (zool.) estatocisto
statolith [ˈstætəlɪθ] *s* (zool.) estatolito
stator [ˈstetər] *s* (mach. & elec.) estator
statoscope [ˈstætəskop] *s* (phys.) estatoscopio o estatóscopo
statuary [ˈstætʃʊ,ɛrɪ] *adj* estatuario; *s* (*pl:* **-ies**) estatuario (*persona*); estatuaria (*arte*); estatuas
statue [ˈstætʃʊ] *s* estatua; *va* estatuar
Statue of Liberty *s* estatua de la Libertad
statuesque [,stætʃʊˈɛsk] *adj* escultural
statuette [,stætʃʊˈɛt] *s* figurilla, estatuita
stature [ˈstætʃər] *s* estatura, talla; habilidad, carácter
status [ˈstetəs] *s* estado, condición; situación social, profesional o legal; categoría (*distinción, elevada condición*)
status quo [kwo] *s* statu quo (*la situación presente; la situación de antes*)
status seeker *s* persona que trata de adquirir categoría
status seeking *s* esfuerzo por adquirir categoría
status symbol *s* símbolo de categoría social
statute [ˈstætʃʊt] *s* estatuto, ley
statute mile *s* milla ordinaria (*5280 pies*)
statute of limitations *s* (law) ley de la prescripción
statutory [ˈstætʃʊ,torɪ] *adj* estatutario, legal
St. Augustine [sent ˈɔgəstin] *s* San Agustín (*ciudad de la Florida*)
staunch [stɔntʃ] o [stɑntʃ] *adj, va & vn* var. de **stanch**
staurolite [ˈstɔrəlaɪt] *s* (mineral.) estaurolita
stave [stev] *s* duela (*de barril*); palo, bastón; peldaño (*de escala*); estrofa; (mus.) pentagrama; (*pret & pp:* **staved** o **stove**) *va* romper, destrozar; desfondar; romper las duelas a; proveer de duelas; **to stave off** impedir, evitar, diferir; *vn* romperse, destrozarse, desfondarse
staves [stevz] *pl de* **staff** y de **stave**
stavesacre [ˈstevzekər] *s* (bot.) estafisagria, albarraz
stay [ste] *s* morada, permanencia, estancia; parada, detención, suspensión; (law) dilación, prórroga; paciencia, resistencia; (naut.) estay; varilla o ballena (*de corsé*); apoyo, sostén; **stays** *spl* corsé; **in stays** (naut.) en la virada; *va* asentar, fijar, fundar; apoyar, sostener; soportar, tolerar; aplazar, detener; esperar; poner freno a; *vn* quedar, quedarse, permanecer; hospedarse; habitar; parar, pararse, detenerse; esperar; resistir; (naut.) virar o cambiar de rumbo o bordada; **to stay away** quedarse apartado, quedarse fuera; **to stay in** quedarse en casa; **to stay out** quedarse fuera; **to stay up** velar, no acostarse
stay-at-home [ˈsteət,hom] *adj & s* hogareño; acaserado (Am.)
staying power *s* resistencia, fortaleza, aguante
staysail [ˈstesəl] o [ˈste,sel] *s* (naut.) vela de estay
St. Croix [sent ˈkrɔɪ] *s* Santa Cruz (*isla*)
S.T.D. abr. de **Sacrae Theologiae Doctor** (Lat.) **Doctor of Sacred Theology**
stead [stɛd] *s* lugar; **in his stead** en su lugar, en lugar de él; **to stand in good stead** ser ventajoso, ser de provecho, ayudar, servir
steadfast [ˈstɛdfæst] o [ˈstɛdfɑst] *adj* resuelto; constante; fijo
steadfastness [ˈstɛdfæstnɪs] o [ˈstɛdfɑstnɪs] *s* resolución; constancia; fijeza
steadiness [ˈstɛdɪnɪs] *s* constancia, fijeza, seguridad; uniformidad; resolución; seriedad
steady [ˈstɛdɪ] *adj* (*comp:* **-ier;** *super:* **-iest**) constante, fijo, firme, seguro; regular, uniforme; resuelto; asentado, serio; (com.) en calma (*dícese de la Bolsa*); (naut.) estable, en calma; (*pret & pp:* **-ied**) *va* estabilizar, reforzar; calmar (*los nervios*); *vn* estabilizarse; calmarse
steady state *s* (phys.) régimen permanente
steak [stek] *s* lonja o tajada (*de carne o pescado*); biftec
steal [stil] *s* (coll.) robo, hurto; (*pret:* **stole;** *pp:* **stolen**) *va* robar, hurtar; atraer, cautivar; *vn* robar, hurtar; **to steal away** escabullirse; **to steal into** meterse a hurtadillas en; **to steal out of** salirse a escondidas de; **to steal upon** aproximarse sin ruido a
stealth [stɛlθ] *s* cautela, recato; **by stealth** a hurtadillas, a escondidas
stealthy [ˈstɛlθɪ] *adj* (*comp:* **-ier;** *super:* **-iest**) astuto, taimado; secreto, furtivo, clandestino
steam [stim] *s* vapor, vapor de agua; vaho; (coll.) potencia, energía; **to blow off steam** dejar escapar vapor; (coll.) desfogarse, desahogarse, soltar la lengua; **to get up steam** dar presión; **to let off steam** descargar vapor; (fig.) desahogarse; **under steam** bajo presión; *adj* de vapor; *va* cocer al vapor; dar un baño de vapor a, saturar de vapor; empañar (*p.ej., las ventanas*); **to get steamed up** empañarse (*p.ej., un vidrio, un cristal*); (coll.) excitarse, animarse; (slang) emborracharse; *vn* emitir vapor, echar vapor; evaporarse; marchar o funcionar a vapor; **to steam ahead** avanzar, adelantar por medio de vapor; (fig.) hacer grandes progresos; **to steam away** salir (*la locomotora, el buque de vapor*)
steamboat [ˈstim,bot] *s* vapor, buque de vapor
steam boiler *s* caldera de vapor
steam box o **chest** *s* caja o cámara de vapor
steam dome *s* (rail.) cúpula de toma de vapor
steam engine *s* máquina de vapor
steamer [ˈstimər] *s* vapor, buque de vapor; automóvil de vapor
steamer rug *s* manta de viaje
steamer trunk *s* baúl de camarote
steam fitter *s* tubero, cañero, montador de calderas de vapor
steam heat *s* calefacción por vapor
steaming [ˈstimɪŋ] *adj* vaporoso; humeante; *adv* **steaming hot** intensamente caliente
steam organ *s* (mus.) órgano de vapor
steam power plant *s* estación termoeléctrica, central térmica
steam roller *s* apisonadora (*movida a vapor*); (coll.) fuerza arrolladora
steam-roller [ˈstim,rolər] *adj* (coll.) arrollador; *va* allanar y afirmar (*la carretera*) con apisonadora; (coll.) aplastar con fuerza arrolladora
steamship [ˈstim,ʃɪp] *s* vapor, buque de vapor
steam shovel *s* pala mecánica de vapor, máquina excavadora de vapor
steam table *s* plancha caliente
steamtight [ˈstim,taɪt] *adj* a prueba de vapor
steam turbine *s* turbina de vapor
steamy [ˈstimɪ] *adj* (*comp:* **-ier;** *super:* **-iest**) vaporoso; humeante; empañado; (coll.) muy excitado
steapsin [stɪˈæpsɪn] *s* (biochem.) esteapsina
stearate [ˈstiəret] *s* (chem.) estearato
stearic [stɪˈærɪk] o [ˈstɪrɪk] *adj* (chem.) esteárico
stearic acid *s* (chem.) ácido esteárico
stearin [ˈstiərɪn] o [ˈstɪrɪn] *s* (chem.) estearina
stearoptene [,stiəˈrɑptin] *s* (chem.) estearopteno
steatite [ˈstiətaɪt] *s* (mineral.) esteatita
steatitic [,stiəˈtɪtɪk] *adj* (mineral.) esteatitoso
steatopygia [,stiətoˈpaɪdʒɪə] o [,stiətoˈpɪdʒɪə] *s* (anthrop.) esteatopigia
stedfast [ˈstɛdfæst] o [ˈstɛdfɑst] *adj* var. de **steadfast**
steed [stid] *s* caballo; corcel; caballo de combate; caballo de carrera
steel [stil] *s* acero; ballena de acero; eslabón (*hierro acerado para sacar fuego de un pedernal; cilindro de acero para afilar cuchillas*); (fig.) acero (*fuerza; valor*); *adj* acerado; (fig.) frío, duro; *va* acerar; (fig.) acerar; **to steel oneself** (fig.) acerarse, acorazarse

steel blue *s* azul acerado
steel mill *s* acería, fábrica de acero
steel wool *s* virutillas de acero, estopa de acero
steelwork [ˈstil,wʌrk] *s* artículos, partes, instrumentos de acero; montaje de acero; **steelworks** *ssg* o *spl* fábrica de acero
steelworker [ˈstil,wʌrkər] *s* herrero de obra; obrero en una fábrica de acero
steely [ˈstilɪ] *adj* (*comp:* **-ier**; *super:* **-iest**) acerado; (fig.) fuerte, inflexible, duro
steelyard [ˈstiljɑrd] o [ˈstiljərd] *s* romana
steenbok [ˈstin,bɑk] o [ˈsten,bɑk] *s* (zool.) antílope africano
steep [stip] *adj* escarpado, empinado; (coll.) alto, excesivo (*precio*); *s* cuesta empinada; empapamiento, remojo; (found.) brasca; *va* empapar, remojar, poner en infusión; **steeped in** absorbido en; lleno de; *vn* (coll.) empaparse, estar en infusión
steeple [ˈstipəl] *s* aguja, campanario (*de iglesia*)
steeplebush [ˈstipəl,bʊʃ] *s* (bot.) espirea norteamericana (*Spiraea tomentosa*)
steeplechase [ˈstipəl,tʃes] *s* carrera del campanario, carrera (de caballos) de obstáculos
steeplejack [ˈstipəl,dʒæk] *s* (coll.) reparador de altas chimeneas, torres, etc.
steer [stɪr] *s* buey (*de cualquier edad*); novillo; *va* guiar, conducir, gobernar; *vn* gobernar, p.ej., **this boat does not steer well** este buque no gobierna bien; conducirse; **to steer clear of** (coll.) evitar, eludir
steerage [ˈstɪrɪdʒ] *s* dirección; (naut.) proa, entrepuente
steerage passenger *s* (naut.) pasajero de proa
steerageway [ˈstɪrɪdʒ,we] *s* (naut.) empuje del buque necesario para gobernar
steering column *s* (aut.) columna de dirección
steering committee *s* comisión de iniciativas
steering gear *s* mecanismo de dirección
steering knuckle *s* (aut.) charnela de dirección, muñón de dirección
steering wheel *s* (naut.) rueda del timón; (aut.) volante o volante de dirección
steersman [ˈstɪrzmən] *s* (*pl:* **-men**) piloto, timonero; conductor (*de automóvil*)
steeve [stiv] *s* (naut.) lanzamiento
stegomyia [,stɛgəˈmaɪə] *s* (ent.) estegomía
stegosaurus [,stɛgəˈsɔrəs] *s* (*pl:* **-ri** [raɪ]) (pal.) estegosauro
stein [staɪn] *s* pichel para cerveza
steinbok [ˈstaɪn,bɑk] *s* (zool.) antílope africano; (zool.) íbice
stele [ˈstilɪ] *s* (*pl:* **-lae** [li] o **-les**) (arch. & bot.) estela
stellar [ˈstɛlər] *adj* estelar, estelario
stellate [ˈstɛlet] *adj* estrellado
St. Elmo's fire o **St. Elmo's light** [ˈɛlmoz] *s* fuego de Santelmo
stem [stɛm] *s* (bot.) tallo, vástago; (bot.) pedúnculo; pie (*de una copa*); cañón (*de una pipa; de una pluma*); (mach.) varilla, vástago; fuste (*de una columna*); tija o espiga (*de una llave*); botón (*de un reloj de bolsillo*); (naut.) roda, tajamar; (gram.) tema; **from stem to stern** de proa a popa; (*pret & pp:* **stemmed**; *ger:* **stemming**) *va* desgranar, despalillar; estancar, represar; detener, refrenar; hacer frente a; embestir con la proa; **to stem the tide** rendir la marea; **to stem the torrent** detener el torrente; *vn* provenir, nacer; **to stem from** provenir de, originarse en, traer su origen de
stemless [ˈstɛmlɪs] *adj* sin vástago; (bot.) sin tallo, sin pedúnculo; que no se puede desgranar
stemma [ˈstɛmə] *s* (*pl:* **-mas** o **-mata** [mətə]) (zool.) estema (*ojo simple de los insectos*)
stemmed [stɛmd] *adj* (bot.) con tallo, con pedúnculo; desgranado
stemmer [ˈstɛmər] *s* máquina de despalillar
stemple [ˈstɛmpəl] *s* (min.) estemple
stemson [ˈstɛmsən] *s* (naut.) contrabranque, contrarroda
stem-winder [ˈstɛm,waɪndər] *s* (coll.) remontuar
stem-winding [ˈstɛm,waɪndɪŋ] *adj* de remontuar
stench [stɛntʃ] *s* hedor, hediondez
stencil [ˈstɛnsəl] *s* patrón picado; estarcido (*dibujo*); (*pret & pp:* **-ciled** o **-cilled**; *ger:* **-ciling** o **-cilling**) *va* estarcir
stenocardia [,stɛnəˈkɑrdɪə] *s* (path.) estenocardia
stenograph [ˈstɛnəgræf] o [ˈstɛnəgrɑf] *s* escritura taquigráfica; máquina para taquigrafiar; *va & vn* estenografiar, taquigrafiar
stenographer [stəˈnɑgrəfər] *s* estenógrafo
stenographic [,stɛnəˈgræfɪk] *adj* estenográfico
stenographically [,stɛnəˈgræfɪkəlɪ] *adv* estenográficamente
stenography [stəˈnɑgrəfɪ] *s* estenografía
stenosis [stɪˈnosɪs] *s* (path.) estenosis
stenotype [ˈstɛnətaɪp] *s* (trademark) máquina estenotipiadora o de estenotipiar; estenotipia (*letra o grupo de letras*)
stenotypy [ˈstɛnə,taɪpɪ] *s* estenotipia
Stentor [ˈstɛntɔr] *s* (myth.) Estentor; (*l.c.*) *s* persona con voz estentórea
stentorian [stɛnˈtorɪən] *adj* estentóreo
step [stɛp] *s* paso; escalón, grada, peldaño; grado; medida, gestión; (mus.) intervalo; (naut.) carlinga; estribo (*de un coche*); **steps** *spl* escalera de mano; **in step** llevando el paso; de acuerdo; (elec.) en fase; **out of step** no llevando el paso; en desacuerdo; **to break step** romper paso; **to take steps** dar pasos; tomar medidas, gestionar; **to watch one's step** mirarse en ello, ser prudente, proceder con cautela, andarse con tiento; **step by step** paso a paso ‖ (*pret & pp:* **stepped**; *ger:* **stepping**) *va* escalonar, colocar de trecho en trecho; plantar (*el pie*); **to step down** reducir, disminuir; **to step off** medir a pasos; **to step up** elevar, aumentar ‖ *vn* dar un paso, dar pasos; andar, caminar, ir; (coll.) andar de prisa; **to step aside** hacerse a un lado; retirarse; **to step back** dar un paso atrás; volver hacia atrás, retroceder; **to step down** bajar; dimitir; **to step in** entrar; (coll.) visitar al pasar; tomar parte (en); **to step lively** darse prisa; **to step on** pisar; **to step on it** (coll.) acelerar la marcha, darse prisa; (coll.) pisar fuertemente el acelerador, apretar el acelerador a fondo; **to step on the starter** pisar el arranque; **to step out** salir; bajar (*de un coche*); apretar el paso; entregarse al lujo, los placeres o los vicios; andar de parranda; **to step up** subir; avanzar
stepbrother [ˈstɛp,brʌðər] *s* medio hermano, hermanastro
stepchild [ˈstɛp,tʃaɪld] *s* (*pl:* **-children**) hijastro, alnado
stepdaughter [ˈstɛp,dɔtər] *s* hijastra
step-down transformer [ˈstɛp,daʊn] *s* (elec.) transformador reductor
stepfather [ˈstɛp,fɑðər] *s* padrastro
stephanite [ˈstɛfənaɪt] *s* (mineral.) estefanita, plata agria
Stephen [ˈstivən] *s* Esteban
step-in [ˈstɛp,ɪn] *adj* que se pone comenzando por los pies (*dícese de ciertas prendas de vestir*); **step-ins** *spl* bragas (*pantalones de mujer*)
stepladder [ˈstɛp,lædər] *s* escala, escalera doble, escalera de tijera
stepmother [ˈstɛp,mʌðər] *s* madrastra; (dial.) padrastro (*de las uñas*)
stepparent [ˈstɛp,pɛrənt] *s* padrastro o madrastra
steppe [stɛp] *s* estepa
stepping stone *s* estriberón, pasadera; escalón (*para la realización de un deseo*); escabel (*para medrar*)
stepsister [ˈstɛp,sɪstər] *s* media hermana, hermanastra
stepson [ˈstɛp,sʌn] *s* hijastro
step terrace *s* parata
step-up transformer [ˈstɛp,ʌp] *s* (elec.) transformador elevador
stercoraceous [,stʌrkəˈreʃəs] *adj* estercóreo
sterculiaceous [stʌr,kjulɪˈeʃəs] *adj* (bot.) esterculiáceo
stere [stɪr] *s* estéreo
stereo [ˈstɛrɪo] o [ˈstɪrɪo] *adj* (coll.) estereofónico; (coll.) estereoscópico; *s* (*pl:* **-os**) (coll.) música estereofónica, disco estereofónico, radiodifusión estereofónica; (coll.) fotografía estereoscópica
stereobate [ˈstɛrɪəbet] *s* (arch.) estereóbato

stereo camera *s* verascopio, cámara estereoscópica
stereochemical [ˌstɛrɪo'kɛmɪkəl] *s* estereoquímico
stereochemistry [ˌstɛrɪo'kɛmɪstrɪ] *s* estereoquímica
stereochromy ['stɛrɪəˌkromɪ] *s* estereocromía
stereogram ['stɛrɪəˌgræm] *s* estereograma
stereographic [ˌstɛrɪə'græfɪk] o **stereographical** [ˌstɛrɪə'græfɪkəl] *adj* estereográfico
stereography [ˌstɛrɪ'ɑgrəfɪ] *s* estereografía
stereoisomerism [ˌstɛrɪoaɪ'sɑmərɪzəm] *s* (chem.) estereoisomería
stereometry [ˌstɛrɪ'ɑmɪtrɪ] *s* estereometría
stereophonic [ˌstɛrɪə'fɑnɪk] *adj* estereofónico
stereophony [ˌstɛrɪ'ɑfənɪ] *s* estereofonía
stereophotography [ˌstɛrɪəfə'tɑgrəfɪ] *s* estereofotografía
stereopsis [ˌstɛrɪ'ɑpsɪs] *s* esteriopsis
stereopticon [ˌstɛrɪ'ɑptɪkən] *s* estereóptico
stereoscope ['stɛrɪəˌskop] *s* estereoscopio
stereoscopic [ˌstɛrɪə'skɑpɪk] *adj* estereoscópico
stereoscopically [ˌstɛrɪə'skɑpɪkəlɪ] *adv* estereoscópicamente
stereoscopy [ˌstɛrɪ'ɑskəpɪ] *s* estereoscopia
stereotomy [ˌstɛrɪ'ɑtəmɪ] *s* estereotomía
stereotropism [ˌstɛrɪ'ɑtrəpɪzəm] *s* (biol.) estereotropismo
stereotype ['stɛrɪəˌtaɪp] *s* estereotipo; estereotipia; *va* estereotipar; (fig.) estereotipar
stereotyped ['stɛrɪəˌtaɪpt] *adj* estereotipado; (fig.) estereotipado (*fijo e invariable; gastado, trillado*)
stereotypy ['stɛrɪəˌtaɪpɪ] *s* estereotipia
stereo viewer *s* verascopio (*estereoscopio para diapositivas*)
stereovision ['stɛrɪoˌvɪʒən] o ['stɪrɪoˌvɪʒən] *s* estereovisión
sterile ['stɛrɪl] *adj* estéril
sterility [stə'rɪlɪtɪ] *s* (*pl:* **-ties**) esterilidad
sterilization [ˌstɛrɪlɪ'zeʃən] *s* esterilización
sterilize ['stɛrɪlaɪz] *va* esterilizar
sterilizer ['stɛrɪˌlaɪzər] *s* esterilizador (*persona y aparato*)
sterling ['stʌrlɪŋ] *s* libras esterlinas; plata de ley; vajilla de plata; *adj* fino, de ley; verdadero, genuino, puro, excelente
sterling area o **bloc** *s* área de la libra esterlina
sterling silver *s* plata de ley
stern [stʌrn] *s* (naut.) popa; *adj* severo, austero; firme, decidido
sternal ['stʌrnəl] *adj* (anat.) esternal
stern chase *s* (naut.) caza en que una nave persigue a otra marchando en la estela de ésta
stern chaser *s* (naut.) guardatimón
stern fast *s* (naut.) codera
stern gallery *s* (naut.) galería de popa
sternmost ['stʌrnmost] *adj* (naut.) popel
sternpost ['stʌrnˌpost] *s* (naut.) codaste
stern sheets *spl* (naut.) cámara a popa
sternum ['stʌrnəm] *s* (*pl:* **-na** [nə] o **-nums**) (anat.) esternón
sternutative [stər'njutətɪv] o [stər'nutətɪv] *adj* estornutativo o estornutatorio
sternward ['stʌrnwərd] o **sternwards** ['stʌrnwərdz] *adv* (naut.) a popa, hacia la popa
sternway ['stʌrnˌwe] *s* (naut.) cía
stern-wheeler ['stʌrnˌhwilər] *s* bote de rueda de paletas a popa
stertor ['stʌrtər] *s* estertor
stertorous ['stʌrtərəs] *adj* estertoroso
stet [stɛt] *s* (print.) indicación de no suprimir lo ya cancelado; (*pret & pp:* **stetted**; *ger:* **stetting**) *va* (print.) marcar para que no se suprima
stethoscope ['stɛθəskop] *s* (med.) estetoscopio
stethoscopic [ˌstɛθə'skɑpɪk] *adj* estetoscópico
stethoscopy [stɛ'θɑskəpɪ] *s* (med.) estetoscopia
stevedore ['stivədor] *s* (naut.) estibador
stew [stju] o [stu] *s* guisado, estofado; **to be in a stew** (coll.) estar apurado; *va* guisar, estofar; *vn* abrasarse; (coll.) estar apurado, estar preocupado; **to stew in one's own juice** cocer en su propia salsa, freír en su aceite
steward ['stjuərd] o ['stuərd] *s* administrador; mayordomo, senescal; despensero; camarero (*de buque o avión*)
stewardess ['stjuərdɪs] o ['stuərdɪs] *s* mayordoma; camarera (*de buque o avión*); azafata, aeromoza (*de avión*)
stewardship ['stjuərdʃɪp] o ['stuərdʃɪp] *s* administración; mayordomía
stewed fruit *s* compota de frutas
stewed tomatoes *spl* puré de tomates
stewpan ['stjuˌpæn] o ['stuˌpæn] *s* cazuela, cacerola
St. George's Channel *s* el canal de San Jorge
St. Gotthard [sent 'gɑtərd] *s* San Gotardo (*montaña, cuello y túnel*)
St. Helena [sent hɛ'linə] *s* Santa Elena (*isla y colonia inglesas en el Atlántico Meridional*)
sthenic ['sθɛnɪk] *adj* (med.) esténico
stibine ['stɪbin] o ['stɪbɪn] *s* (chem.) estibina
stibium ['stɪbɪəm] *s* (chem.) estibio
stibonium [stɪ'bonɪəm] *s* (chem.) estibonio
stick [stɪk] *s* palillo, palito; vara, bastón; barra (*de dinamita*); (aer.) mango de escoba, palanca de mando; (naut.) mástil, verga; (coll.) bodoque; (coll.) dosis de licor muy fuerte que se añade a una bebida; (print.) componedor; (print.) texto contenido en el componedor; puñalada, estocada; parada, demora; pegadura; **sticks** *spl* (coll.) monte, afueras del poblado ‖ (*pret & pp:* **sticked**) *va* proveer de palo, sostener con un palo; (print.) componer, colocar (*letras*) en el componedor ‖ (*pret & pp:* **stuck**) *va* picar, punzar; apuñalar; clavar, hincar; poner, meter; parar, detener; pegar; (coll.) confundir, aturrullar; **to stick out** asomar (*la cabeza*); sacar (*la lengua*); **to stick up** (slang) atracar, asaltar (*para robar*); **to stick one's hands up** alzar las manos (*en señal de sumisión*) ‖ *vn* estar prendido, estar hincado; pegarse; agarrarse (*la pintura*); encastillarse (*p.ej., una ventana*); asomarse; resaltar, sobresalir; continuar, persistir; permanecer; atascarse; quedarse parado; dudar, vacilar; **to stick around** (slang) quedarse, demorarse; **to stick at** persistir en; sentir escrúpulo por; **to stick at it** persistir; **to stick out** salir (*p.ej., el pañuelo del bolsillo*); sobresalir, proyectarse; velar (*un escollo, peñasco, etc.*); resultar evidente; (coll.) perseverar hasta el fin; **to stick to** aferrarse a, con o en (*p.ej., una opinión*); **to stick together** (coll.) quedarse unidos, no abandonarse; **to stick to one's guns** mantenerse firme, no cejar; **to stick up** destacarse; estar de punta (*el pelo*); **to stick up for** (coll.) defender
sticker ['stɪkər] *s* etiqueta engomada, marbete engomado; punta, espina; fijador; persona perseverante; (coll.) misterio, problema arduo
sticking plaster *s* esparadrapo
stick-in-the-mud ['stɪkɪnðəˌmʌd] *adj & s* perezoso, tardón; conservador, chapado a la antigua
stick-lac ['stɪkˌlæk] *s* laca en palo o en rama
stickle ['stɪkəl] *vn* porfiar o disputar por menudencias, sentir escrúpulos por menudencias
stickleback ['stɪkəlˌbæk] *s* (ichth.) espinoso
stickler ['stɪklər] *s* rigorista; problema arduo
stickpin ['stɪkˌpɪn] *s* alfiler de corbata
sticktight ['stɪkˌtaɪt] *s* (bot.) bidente
stick-up ['stɪkˌʌp] *s* (slang) atraco, asalto
sticky ['stɪkɪ] *adj* (*comp:* **-ier**; *super:* **-iest**) pegajoso; (coll.) bochornoso; (coll.) húmedo, mojado; (coll.) azucarado, sentimental; (coll.) difícil
stiff [stɪf] *adj* tieso; anquilosado (*músculo*); entorpecido, entumecido; arduo, difícil; (coll.) excesivo (*precio*); (fig.) tieso, ceremonioso, severo; *s* (slang) cadáver; (slang) persona tiesa y afectada
stiff collar *s* cuello almidonado
stiffen ['stɪfən] *va* atiesar; endurecer; espesar; (elec.) aumentar la inductancia de; *vn* atiesarse; endurecerse; espesarse; arrecirse (*de frío*); (fig.) obstinarse
stiffening ['stɪfənɪŋ] *s* atiesamiento; atiesador (*lo que pone tieso*)
stiff-jointed ['stɪfˌdʒɔɪntɪd] *adj* de junturas rígidas
stiff neck *s* tortícolis (*dolor*); obstinación; persona obstinada
stiff-necked ['stɪfˌnɛkt] *adj* terco, obstinado

stiffness ['stɪfnɪs] *s* tiesura; (fig.) tiesura
stiff shirt *s* camisola
stifle ['staɪfəl] *s* (vet.) babilla; *va* ahogar, sofocar; apagar, suprimir; *vn* ahogarse, sofocarse
stifle joint *s* (vet.) babilla
stifling ['staɪflɪŋ] *adj* ahogado, sofocante, bochornoso
stigma ['stɪgmə] *s* (*pl:* **-mas** o **-mata** [mətə]) (bot., hist., path., zool. & fig.) estigma; **stigmata** *spl* estigmas (*señales de las llagas de Jesucristo*)
stigmatic [stɪg'mætɪk] *adj* estigmático; manchado; deforme; (opt.) anastigmático; *s* (eccl.) estigmático (*persona que presenta los estigmas de Jesucristo*)
stigmatism ['stɪgmətɪzəm] *s* (opt. & path.) estigmatismo
stigmatization [ˌstɪgmətɪ'zeʃən] *s* estigmatización
stigmatize ['stɪgmətaɪz] *va* estigmatizar
St.-Ignatius's-bean [sentɪg'neʃəsɪz'bin] *s* haba de San Ignacio
stile [staɪl] *s* escalera para atravesar una empalizada, tapia, etc.; torniquete; (arch.) montante
stiletto [stɪ'leto] *s* (*pl:* **-tos**) estilete, puñal
still [stɪl] *adj* inmóvil; quieto, tranquilo; callado, silencioso; bajo, suave; no espumoso; **to hold still** estarse quieto o callado; *adv* tranquilamente; silenciosamente; todavía, aún; *conj* sin embargo, con todo; *s* alambique, destiladera; destilería; vista fija, fotografía de lo inmóvil; (poet.) silencio; *va* acallar, hacer callar; amortiguar; calmar; *vn* callar; calmarse
stillbirth ['stɪlˌbʌrθ] *s* parto muerto
stillborn ['stɪlˌbɔrn] *adj* nacido muerto
still hunt *s* caza al acecho; empeño secreto o escondido; indagación clandestina; (pol.) solicitación clandestina de votos
still-hunt ['stɪlˌhʌnt] *va & vn* cazar al acecho, sin perros
still life *s* (*pl:* **still lifes** o **still lives**) (paint.) bodegón, naturaleza muerta
still-life ['stɪlˌlaɪf] *adj* de naturaleza muerta
stillness ['stɪlnɪs] *s* inmovilidad; tranquilidad, silencio
Stillson wrench ['stɪlsən] *s* llave Stillson, llave para tubos
stilly ['stɪlɪ] *adj* (*comp:* **-ier;** *super:* **-iest**) (poet.) quieto, silencioso, calmo; ['stɪllɪ] *adv* quietamente, silenciosamente
stilt [stɪlt] *s* zanco; pilote (*en el agua*); (orn.) cigoñuela
stilted ['stɪltɪd] *adj* elevado; tieso, hinchado, pomposo
stilted arch *s* (arch.) arco peraltado
Stilton cheese ['stɪltən] *s* queso Stilton
stilt sandpiper *s* (orn.) chorlito palmeado de pico largo
stimulant ['stɪmjələnt] *adj & s* estimulante
stimulate ['stɪmjəlet] *va & vn* estimular; **to stimulate to** + *inf* estimular a + *inf*, estimular a que + *subj*
stimulation [ˌstɪmjə'leʃən] *s* estímulo, excitación
stimulative ['stɪmjəˌletɪv] *adj* estimulador; *s* estímulo
stimulus ['stɪmjələs] *s* (*pl:* **-li** [laɪ]) estímulo
sting [stɪŋ] *s* picadura; picazón (*dolor*); estímulo; (bot. & zool.) aguijón; (*pret & pp:* **stung**) *va* picar, pinchar, punzar; aguijonear, espolear; **to sting to the quick** herir en lo vivo; *vn* picar
stingaree ['stɪŋəri] *s* (ichth.) pastinaca
stingbull ['stɪŋˌbul] *s* (ichth.) pez víbora, araña
stinger ['stɪŋər] *s* aguijón, púa (*de un animal o planta*); (coll.) dicho mordaz
stinginess ['stɪndʒɪnɪs] *s* ahorratividad, tacañería, mezquindad; escasez
sting ray *s* (ichth.) pastinaca
stingy ['stɪndʒɪ] *adj* (*comp:* **-gier;** *super:* **-giest**) avariento, mezquino, tacaño; escaso, poco; ['stɪŋɪ] *adj* (*comp:* **-ier;** *super:* **-iest**) picante, punzante; aguijonado
stink [stɪŋk] *s* hedor, mal olor; **to raise a stink** (slang) armar una trapisonda; (*pret:* **stank** o **stunk;** *pp:* **stunk**) *va* dar mal olor a, hacer oler mal; **to stink out** ahuyentar con humo o vapores hediondos; *vn* heder, oler muy mal; (fig.) tener muy mala reputación; **to stink in one's nostrils** repugnar muchísmo; **to stink of** (slang) poseer (*p.ej., dinero*) en un grado que da asco
stink bomb *s* bomba fétida
stinkbug ['stɪŋkˌbʌg] *s* (ent.) chinche de jardín
stinker ['stɪŋkər] *s* pebete (*cosa hedionda*); persona hedionda; (orn.) petrel gigante; (slang) sinvergüenza, canalla
stinking camomile *s* (bot.) manzanilla fétida o hedionda
stinking iris *s* (bot.) lirio hediondo, íride
stint [stɪnt] *s* límite, restricción; ahorro; tarea, faena; *va* limitar, restringir; *vn* ser económico, ahorrar con mezquindad
stipe [staɪp] *s* (bot. & zool.) estipe
stipel ['staɪpəl] *s* (bot.) estipulilla
stipend ['staɪpɛnd] *s* estipendio; *va* estipendiar
stipendiary [staɪ'pɛndɪˌɛrɪ] *adj* estipendiario; *s* (*pl:* **-ies**) estipendiario
stipple ['stɪpəl] *s* graneo, punteado; *va & vn* granear, puntear
stippling ['stɪplɪŋ] *s* graneo, punteado
stipular ['stɪpjələr] *adj* (bot.) estipular
stipulate ['stɪpjəlet] *adj* (bot.) estipulado; *va* estipular
stipulation [ˌstɪpjə'leʃən] *s* estipulación
stipule ['stɪpjul] *s* (bot.) estípula
stir [stʌr] *s* agitación, movimiento, meneo; alboroto, tumulto; empuje, hurgonada; **to create a stir** hacer o meter ruido; (*pret & pp:* **stirred;** *ger:* **stirring**) *va* mover, agitar; revolver; excitar, emocionar, conmover; atizar o avivar (*el fuego*); remover (*un líquido*); **to stir up** revolver; despertar; excitar, conmover; fomentar, suscitar (*discordias, rebeliones, etc.*); *vn* moverse, bullirse, agitarse; tener lugar; (coll.) estar levantado
stirps [stʌrps] *s* (*pl:* **stirpes** ['stʌrpiz]) estirpe; progenitor
stirring ['stʌrɪŋ] *adj* activo, despierto; conmovedor, emocionante
stirrup ['stʌrəp] o ['stɪrəp] *s* estribo
stirrup bone *s* (anat.) estribo
stirrup cup *s* trago de partida, copa de despedida
stirrup pump *s* (Brit.) bomba de mano
stirrup strap *s* ación
stitch [stɪtʃ] *s* punto, puntada; pedazo de tela; (coll.) pizca, poquito; punzada, dolor punzante; **to be in stitches** (coll.) desternillarse de risa; *va* coser, bastear, hilvanar, unir, puntear, dar puntadas en; *vn* coser, bordar
stithy ['stɪðɪ] o ['stɪθɪ] *s* (*pl:* **-ies**) yunque; herrería
St. John Lateran *s* San Juan de Letrán (*iglesia*)
St.-John's-wort [sent'dʒɑnzˌwʌrt] *s* (bot.) hierba de San Juan
St. Lawrence [sent 'lɔrəns] o [sent 'lɑrəns] *s* San Lorenzo (*río*)
stoat [stot] *s* (zool.) armiño de verano; (zool.) comadreja
stock [stɑk] *s* surtido, existencias; capital comercial; acciones, valores; caldo (*de carne*); ganado; tronco (*p.ej., de árbol*); cepo (*del yunque*); cepa (*de tronco de árbol*); palo, madero; leño; mango, manija; culata, caja (*de fusil*); (naut.) cepo (*del ancla*); materias primas; alzacuello; familia, estirpe; (bot.) patrón (*en que se injerta una rama*); (bot.) injerto; (bot.) alhelí; (mach.) terraja; (theat.) programa, repertorio; (fig.) tronco (*persona torpe*); **stocks** *spl* cepo, corma (*castigo*); (naut.) astillero, grada de construcción; potro (*para sujetar los caballos para herrarlos*); **in stock** en existencia, en almacén; **on the stocks** en preparación; (naut.) en vía de construcción; **out of stock** agotado; **to take stock** hacerse el inventario; **to take stock in** (coll.) interesarse en, sentir interés por; dar importancia a; (coll.) confiar en; (com.) comprar acciones de ‖ *adj* común, regular; consagrado; banal, vulgar; (theat.) de repertorio; bursátil; ganadero, del ganado ‖ *va* surtir, abastecer; tener en existencias, tener existencias de; encepar; acumular, acopiar; sembrar hierba en; poblar (*un estanque, una colmena, etc.*)

stockade [sta'ked] *s* estacada, empalizada, palanquera; *va* empalizar
stockbreeder ['stak,bridər] *s* criador de ganado
stockbroker ['stak,brokər] *s* bolsista, corredor de bolsa, agente de bolsa, agente de cambio
stockbrokerage ['stak,brokərɪdʒ] o **stockbroking** ['stak,brokɪŋ] *s* correduría de bolsa
stock car *s* (rail.) vagón para el ganado; (aut.) coche de serie
stock company *s* (com.) sociedad anónima; (theat.) teatro de repertorio
stock dividend *s* dividendo en acciones
stock dove *s* (orn.) paloma brava o silvestre
stock exchange *s* bolsa
stock farm *s* hacienda de ganado
stockfish ['stak,fɪʃ] *s* pescado aplastado y secado al aire sin salar
stockholder ['stak,holdər] *s* accionista, tenedor de acciones
stockholder of record *s* accionista que como tal figura en el libro-registro de la compañía
Stockholm ['stakhom] *s* Estocolmo
stockinet [,stakɪ'nɛt] *s* elástica, tela de punto
stocking ['stakɪŋ] *s* media; **in one's stocking feet** con medias pero sin zapatos
stock in trade *s* artículos que se venden en una tienda; existencias de un comercio; útiles, herramienta; recursos
stockjobber ['stak,dʒabər] *s* corredor de bolsa; agente de corredores de bolsa
stockman ['stak,mæn] *s* (*pl:* **-men**) ganadero; almacenero, almacenista
stock market *s* bolsa, mercado de valores; **to play the stock market** jugar en bolsa, jugar a la bolsa
stockpile ['stak,paɪl] *s* reserva de materias primas; acopio de materiales estratégicos; *va* acumular, reunir (*materias primas*); hacer acopio de (*materiales estratégicos*); *vn* acumular, reunir materias primas; hacer acopio de materiales estratégicos
stockpiling ['stak,paɪlɪŋ] *s* almacenaje de reservas; acumulación de materiales estratégicos
stock raising *s* ganadería
stockroom ['stak,rum] o ['stak,rʊm] *s* almacén; sala de exposición para los viajantes en los hoteles
stock split *s* (com.) división de las acciones de una empresa en nuevas acciones de menor valor
stock-still ['stak'stɪl] *adj* completamente inmóvil
stocktaking ['stak,tekɪŋ] *s* (el) inventariar
stocky ['stakɪ] *adj* (*comp:* **-ier;** *super:* **-iest**) bajo, grueso y fornido
stockyard ['stak,jard] *s* corral de concentración de ganado
stodgy ['stadʒɪ] *adj* (*comp:* **-ier;** *super:* **-iest**) pesado, indigesto, aburrido; repleto, muy lleno, rollizo
stogie o **stogy** ['stogɪ] *s* (*pl:* **-gies**) cigarro barato, largo y delgado
stoic ['sto·ɪk] *adj & s* estoico; (*cap.*) *adj & s* estoico
stoical ['sto·ɪkəl] *adj* estoico
stoicheiology [,stɔɪkɪ'alədʒɪ] *s* var. de **stoichiology**
stoicheiometry [,stɔɪkɪ'amɪtrɪ] *s* var. de **stoichiometry**
stoichiology [,stɔɪkɪ'alədʒɪ] *s* estequiología
stoichiometry [,stɔɪkɪ'amɪtrɪ] *s* estequiometría
stoicism ['sto·ɪsɪzəm] *s* estoicismo; (*cap.*) *s* estoicismo
stoke [stok] *va* atizar, avivar (*el fuego*); cebar, alimentar (*un horno*); *vn* atizar el fuego; cebar el horno; (fig.) comer
stokehold ['stok,hold] *s* (naut.) cuarto de calderas; (naut.) boca del horno
stokehole ['stok,hol] *s* boca del horno; plataforma del fogonero
stoker ['stokər] *s* fogonero; alimentador de hogar (*aparato*)
stole [stol] *s* estola; *pret de* **steal**
stolen ['stolən] *pp de* **steal**
stolen base *s* (baseball) base robada
stolid ['stalɪd] *adj* impasible, insensible
stolidity [stə'lɪdɪtɪ] *s* (*pl:* **-ties**) impasibilidad, insensibilidad
stolon ['stolan] *s* (bot. & zool.) estolón
stoma ['stomə] *s* (*pl:* **stomata** ['stomətə] o ['stamətə]) (anat., bot. & zool.) estoma
stomach ['stʌmək] *s* (anat.) estómago; barriga, vientre; apetito; deseo, inclinación; **to turn the stomach** revolver el estómago, dar asco; *va* tragar (*recibir en el estómago; aguantar, tolerar*)
stomacher ['stʌməkər] *s* peto
stomachic [sto'mækɪk] *adj* estomacal; *s* (med.) estomacal
stomach pump *s* bomba estomacal
stomate ['stomet] *adj* provisto de estoma o estomas; *s* (bot.) estoma
stomatic [sto'mætɪk] *adj* estomático (*perteneciente a la boca*)
stomatitis [,stomə'taɪtɪs] *s* (path.) estomatitis
stomatology [,stomə'talədʒɪ] *s* estomatología
stomatoplasty ['stomətə,plæstɪ] *s* estomatoplastia
stone [ston] *s* piedra; hueso (*de la fruta*); (path.) piedra o cálculo; (path.) mal de piedra; (Brit.) 14 libras (*peso*); **to cast the first stone** lanzar la primera piedra; **to leave no stone unturned** no dejar piedra por mover; *va* revestir de piedra; lapidar, apedrear; deshuesar
Stone Age *s* (archeol.) edad de piedra
stone-blind ['ston'blaɪnd] *adj* completamente ciego
stone-broke ['ston'brok] *adj* (slang) arrancado, sin blanca
stone bruise *s* contusión producida por una piedra bajo la planta del pie; (aut.) rotura superficial (*de un neumático*) producida por una piedra
stonechat ['ston,tʃæt] *s* (orn.) culiblanco
stonecrop ['ston,krap] *s* (bot.) pan de cuco
stone crusher *s* quebradora de roca, trituradora
stone curlew *s* (orn.) alcaraván
stonecutter ['ston,kʌtər] *s* cantero, picapedrero; máquina de labrar piedras
stone-deaf ['ston'dɛf] *adj* sordo como una tapia
stone fruit *s* (bot.) drupa, fruta de hueso
stone marten *s* (zool.) garduña
stonemason ['ston,mesən] *s* albañil; cantero
stone pine *s* (bot.) pino piñonero (*Pinus pinea*); (bot.) pino cembro
stone's throw *s* tiro de piedra; **within a stone's throw** a tiro de piedra
stoneware ['ston,wɛr] *s* gres
stonework ['ston,wʌrk] *s* cantería, obra de sillería
stoneworker ['ston,wʌrkər] *s* cantero, picapedrero
stoneyard ['ston,jard] *s* cantería
stony ['stonɪ] *adj* (*comp:* **-ier;** *super:* **-iest**) pedregoso; pétreo; empedernido, duro
stony-hearted ['stonɪ,hartɪd] *adj* de corazón empedernido
stood [stʊd] *pret & pp de* **stand**
stooge [studʒ] *s* (slang) preguntador apostado en el auditorio para hacer preguntas preparadas de antemano a un comediante que las contesta de manera divertida para el público; (slang) paniaguado, hombre de paja
stool [stul] *s* escabel, banquillo; planta madre; grupo de vástagos; añagaza, señuelo; cimillo (*palo a que se ata el señuelo*); inodoro, sillico, retrete; cámara, evacuación de vientre; solera o repisa de ventana; *vn* brotar, echar tallos; obrar, hacer del cuerpo, exonerar el vientre
stool pigeon *s* cimbel (*ave*); soplón, espía
stoop [stup] *s* inclinación, encorvada; dignación; descenso rápido; escalinata de entrada; *va* inclinar, bajar; *vn* doblarse, inclinarse, encorvarse; andar encorvado; humillarse, rebajarse; bajar rápidamente sobre la presa; **to stoop to** + *inf* rebajarse a + *inf*
stoop-shouldered ['stup'ʃoldərd] *adj* cargado de espaldas
stop [stap] *s* parada, alto, pausa; estada, estancia; detención; fin, cesación, suspensión; cerradura, tapadura; obstáculo, impedimento; freno; tope, retén, paleta, fiador; (mus.) llave, traste (*de guitarra*); (mus.) registro (*de órgano*); (gram.) punto; (phonet.) oclusión; (phonet.) consonante oclusiva; punto (*en los tele-*

gramas); **to put a stop to** poner fin a ‖ (*pret & pp:* **stopped;** *ger:* **stopping**) *va* parar, detener; acabar, terminar; estorbar, obstruir; interceptar, interrumpir, suspender; cerrar, tapar; rechazar (*un golpe*); retener (*un sueldo o parte de él*); (sport) poner fuera de combate; **to stop up** tapar, obstruir, cegar ‖ *vn* parar, pararse, detenerse; quedarse, permanecer; hospedarse, alojarse; acabarse, terminarse; **to stop** + *ger* cesar de, dejar de + *inf;* **to stop at** pararse en, hospedarse en; **to stop at nothing** no pararse en escrúpulos; **to stop off** quedarse un poco; **to stop over** quedarse un poco; detenerse durante un viaje; **to stop short** pararse de sopetón, detenerse de golpe; **to stop to** + *inf* detenerse a + *inf*

stopcock [ˈstɑpˌkɑk] *s* llave de cierre, llave de paso

stope [stop] *s* (min.) grada, obra en escalones; *va & vn* (min.) excavar en escalones

stopgap [ˈstɑpˌgæp] *s* tapadero; substituto provisional; *adj* provisional

stop light *s* luz de parada, luz de paro

stop-loss order [ˈstɑpˌlɔs] o [ˈstɑpˌlɑs] *s* orden a un corredor de Bolsa para que compre o venda al ser alcanzada determinada cotización

stopover [ˈstɑpˌovər] *s* (rail.) parada intermedia, billete de parada intermedia

stoppage [ˈstɑpɪdʒ] *s* parada, detención; cesación; interrupción, interceptación; suspensión; obstrucción; obstáculo; resistencia; retención (*de un sueldo o parte de él*); embargo por el vendedor de mercancías en tránsito; (path.) obstrucción

stop payment *s* orden a un banco de detener el pago de un cheque

stopper [ˈstɑpər] *s* tapón; tapador; taco, tarugo; (naut.) boza; *va* entaponar

stopple [ˈstɑpəl] *s* tapón; *va* entaponar

stop sign o **stop signal** *s* señal de alto, señal de parada

stop watch *s* reloj de segundos muertos, cronómetro

storage [ˈstorɪdʒ] *s* almacenaje, depósito; (aut.) pupilaje

storage battery *s* (elec.) acumulador

storage space *s* espacio de almacenaje

storax [ˈstoræks] *s* (bot.) estoraque (*árbol y bálsamo*)

store [stor] *s* tienda; almacén; provisión, repuesto; **I know what is in store for you** sé lo que le espera a Vd.; **to have in store** tener guardado, tener reservado; **to set store by** dar mucha importancia a, confiarse en; *va* abastecer; tener guardado, tener en reserva, almacenar; **to store away** acumular

storehouse [ˈstorˌhaʊs] *s* almacén, depósito; (fig.) mina (*p.ej., de sabiduría*)

storekeeper [ˈstorˌkipər] *s* guardaalmacén; tendero; (naut.) pañolero

storeroom [ˈstorˌrum] o [ˈstorˌrʊm] *s* cuarto de almacenar; (naut.) despensa, pañol de víveres

storey [ˈstorɪ] *s* piso

storied [ˈstorɪd] *adj* celebrado en la historia; (f.a.) historiado (*cuadro, dibujo, etc.*); de (*tantos*) pisos, p.ej., **two-storied house** casa de dos pisos

storiette [ˌstorɪˈɛt] *s* cuentecillo

stork [stɔrk] *s* (orn.) cigüeña; **to have a visit from the stork** (fig.) recibir a la cigüeña

stork's-bill [ˈstɔrkzˌbɪl] *s* (bot.) geranio; (bot.) pico de cigüeña

storm [stɔrm] *s* tormenta, tempestad, borrasca; huracán, vendaval; (mil.) asalto; (naut.) borrasca; (fig.) tempestad, agitación, tumulto; **to take by storm** tomar por asalto; *va* asaltar; *vn* tempestear, haber tormenta, haber tempestad; (fig.) tempestear (*rabiar, impacientarse*); (fig.) precipitarse

storm cellar *s* sótano que sirve de asilo durante las tempestades

storm center *s* centro de la tempestad, zona de presión mínima; (fig.) centro de la agitación

storm cloud *s* nubarrón

storm door *s* contrapuerta, guardapuerta, cancel

storm hood *s* pasamontaña

storm troops *spl* tropas de asalto

storm window *s* sobrevidriera

stormy [ˈstɔrmɪ] *adj* (*comp:* **-ier;** *super:* **-iest**) borrascoso, tempestuoso; (fig.) borrascoso, turbulento, violento

stormy petrel *s* (orn.) petrel de la tempestad; (fig.) persona pendenciera, persona que anuncia el mal

story [ˈstorɪ] *s* (*pl:* **-ries**) historia, historieta, cuento, anécdota; trama, enredo, argumento; (coll.) mentira, embuste; piso, alto; (*pret & pp:* **-ried**) *va* historiar

storyteller [ˈstorɪˌtɛlər] *s* narrador; (coll.) mentiroso, embustero

storytelling [ˈstorɪˌtɛlɪŋ] *s* narración de cuentos; (coll.) mentira, impostura, embustes

stoup [stup] *s* copa, frasco; (eccl.) pila de agua bendita

stout [staʊt] *adj* corpulento, gordo, robusto, fornido; animoso, valiente; leal; terco, obstinado; *s* cerveza obscura fuerte

stout-hearted [ˈstaʊtˌhɑrtɪd] *adj* valiente, intrépido

stoutness [ˈstaʊtnɪs] *s* corpulencia, gordura, robustez; ánimo, valor; obstinación

stove [stov] *s* estufa (*para calentar*); hornillo, cocina de gas, cocina eléctrica; invernáculo, estufa; horno cerámico; cuarto de secar; *pret & pp de* **stave**

stovepipe [ˈstovˌpaɪp] *s* tubo de estufa, tubo de hornillo; (coll.) chistera, chimenea (*sombrero*)

stow [sto] *va* meter, guardar, esconder; (naut.) estibar, arrumar; (slang) acabar con; *vn* (naut.) estar arrumado; **to stow away** esconderse en un barco o avión, embarcarse clandestinamente

stowage [ˈsto·ɪdʒ] *s* (naut.) estiba, arrumaje; (naut.) bodega

stowaway [ˈstoəˌwe] *s* polizón, pasajero clandestino, llovido

St. Peter's *s* San Pedro de Roma (*basílica*)

St. Petersburg [sent ˈpitərzbʌrg] *s* San Petersburgo

str. abr. de **strait** y **steamer**

strabismal [strəˈbɪzməl] o **strabismic** [strəˈbɪzmɪk] *adj* estrábico

strabismus [strəˈbɪzməs] *s* (path.) estrabismo

Strabo [ˈstrebo] *s* Estrabón

strabotomy [strəˈbɑtəmɪ] *s* (*pl:* **-mies**) (surg.) estrabotomía

straddle [ˈstrædəl] *s* separación de las piernas, esparrancamiento; *va* montar a horcajadas; (coll.) favorecer a ambos lados en (*un pleito, controversia, etc.*); *vn* ponerse a horcajadas; esparrancarse; (coll.) favorecer a ambos lados

Stradivarius [ˌstrædɪˈvɛrɪəs] *s* Estradivario; estradivario (*violín*)

strafe [strɑf] o [stref] *s* (slang) bombardeo violento; *va* (slang) bombardear violentamente

straggle [ˈstrægəl] *vn* vagar, errar; extraviarse, andar perdido; separarse; estar esparcido

straggler [ˈstræglər] *s* extraviado; rezagado; rama extendida; objeto aislado

straggly [ˈstræglɪ] *adj* dispersado por todas partes, desordenado

straight [stret] *adj* derecho; recto; erguido; lacio (*cabello*); seguido, continuo; sincero, honrado; exacto, correcto; decidido, intransigente; solo (*p.ej., whisky*); en orden; **to set a person straight** mostrar el camino a una persona; mostrar a una persona el modo de proceder; dar consejo a una persona; *adv* derecho, derechamente; sin interrupción; sinceramente, con franqueza; exactamente; en seguida; **to go straight** (coll.) enmendarse; **to talk straight from the shoulder** hablar con toda franqueza; **straight ahead** todo derecho, todo seguido; *s* rectitud; recta (*de un camino*); (poker) escalera

straight angle *s* ángulo derecho

straight-arm [ˈstretˌɑrm] *va* (football) rechazar (*al adversario*) tendiendo los brazos

straight away *adv* luego, en seguida

straightaway [ˈstretəˌwe] *s* derechera, parte recta de un camino; (rail.) recta; *adj* derecho, directo, en línea recta

straightedge [ˈstretˌɛdʒ] *s* regla de borde recto

straighten [ˈstretən] *va* enderezar; arreglar, poner en orden; *vn* enderezarse; **to straighten up** enderezarse

straight face *s* cara seria
straightforward [ˌstret'fɔrwərd] *adj* franco, sincero; honrado; derecho, recto, en línea recta; *adv* en derechura
straightforwards [ˌstret'fɔrwərdz] *adv* en derechura
straight grain *s* veta recta, fibra derecha
straight-grained ['stretˌgrend] *adj* veteado en línea recta
straight line *s* recta, línea recta
straight man *s* (coll.) actor cuyas preguntas, hechas con cara seria, ponen de relieve los chistes de un actor cómico
straight off *adv* luego, en seguida
straight-out ['stretˌaut] *adv* (coll.) cabal, completo, entero
straight ticket *s* (pol.) candidatura completa
straightway ['stretˌwe] *adv* luego, inmediatamente
strain [stren] *s* tensión, tirantez; esfuerzo muy grande; agotamiento, fatiga excesiva; torcedura (*de un músculo*); (mach.) deformación; aire, melodía; cepa (*de una familia o linaje*); raza, linaje, rasgo racial; vena, genio; traza, huella, rastro; clase (*de plantas o animales*); *va* estirar, tender con fuerza, poner tirante, hacer fuerza a; torcer o torcerse (*p.ej., la muñeca*); forzar (*los nervios, la vista, etc.*); apretar, exprimir; deformar; colar, tamizar; *vn* esforzarse, hacer un esfuerzo excesivo; deformarse; colarse, tamizarse; filtrarse; exprimirse (*un jugo*); poner dificultades, resistirse; **to strain at** hacer grandes esfuerzos por
strained [strend] *adj* forzado (*dícese, p.ej., de una risa*); tirante (*dícese de las relaciones de amistad*)
strainer ['strenər] *s* colador
strait [stret] *s* (geog.) estrecho; **straits** *spl* (geog.) estrecho; aprieto, apuro; **to be in dire straits** estar en el mayor apuro, hallarse en gran estrechez
straiten ['stretən] *va* estrechar, contraer, rodear; apremiar, embarazar; **in straitened circumstances** estrecho de medios
strait jacket *s* camisa de fuerza
strait-laced ['stretˌlest] *adj* gazmoño, estrecho de conciencia
Strait of Dover *s* Paso de Calais
Strait of Gibraltar *s* estrecho de Gibraltar
Strait of Magellan *s* estrecho de Magallanes
Straits Settlements *spl* Establecimientos de los Estrechos (*Malaca*)
strake [strek] *s* (naut.) traca
stramonium [strə'monɪəm] *s* (bot.) estramonio; (pharm.) daturina
strand [strænd] *s* playa, ribera; hebra, filamento; torón, ramal (*de cuerda, cable, etc.*); hilo (*de perlas*); pelo; (poet.) tierra lejana; *va* deshebrar, deshilar; trenzar, retorcer (*cuerda, cable, etc.*); zurcir (*una media o calceta*); dejar perdido o desamparado; (naut.) varar; *vn* andar perdido o desamparado; (naut.) varar, encallar
stranded ['strændɪd] *adj* encallado (*buque*); desprovisto, desamparado; en cordones, trenzado, retorcido (*dícese de la cuerda, cable o alambre*)
strange [strendʒ] *adj* extraño; esquivo, retraído; nuevo, desconocido; novel, no acostumbrado
strangeness ['strendʒnɪs] *s* extrañeza, rareza; esquivez; novedad; maravilla
stranger ['strendʒər] *s* forastero; visitador; intruso; desconocido; principiante; **to be no stranger to** no ser ignorante de, no desconocer
strangle ['stræŋgəl] *va* estrangular; reprimir, suprimir; *vn* estrangularse
strangle hold *s* (sport) collar de fuerza; (fig.) aprieto, opresión, dominio completo
strangulate ['stræŋgjəlet] *va* (path. & surg.) estrangular
strangulated hernia *s* (path.) hernia estrangulada
strangulation [ˌstræŋgjə'leʃən] *s* estrangulación; (path. & surg.) estrangulación
strangullion [stræŋ'gʌljən] *s* (vet.) estrangol
strangury ['stræŋgjərɪ] *s* (path.) estangurria o estranguria
S trap *s* sifón en S
strap [stræp] *s* correa (*de cuero*); banda, tira (*de tela, metal, etc.*); trabilla (*debajo del zapato*); asentador (*para afilar las navajas*); (*pret & pp:* **strapped;** *ger:* **strapping**) *va* atar o liar con correa, banda o tira; azotar con una correa; fajar, vendar; asentar (*una navaja*)
straphanger ['stræpˌhæŋər] *s* (coll.) pasajero colgado (*pasajero agarrado a las anillas de soporte*)
strap iron *s* fleje, flejes
strapped [stræpt] *adj* (slang) alcanzado
strapper ['stræpər] *s* atador; mozo de cuadra; asentador; (coll.) persona alta y fuerte; (slang) mentira enorme
strapping ['stræpɪŋ] *adj* (coll.) alto y fuerte; (coll.) enorme, grandísimo
Strasbourg o **Strassburg** ['stræsbʌrg] *s* Estrasburgo
stratagem ['strætədʒəm] *s* estratagema
strategic [strə'tidʒɪk] *adj* estratégico; **strategics** *ssg* estrategia
strategical [strə'tidʒɪkəl] *adj* estratégico
strategist ['strætɪdʒɪst] *s* estratega
strategy ['strætɪdʒɪ] *s* (*pl:* **-gies**) estrategia
stratification [ˌstrætɪfɪ'keʃən] *s* estratificación
stratify ['strætɪfaɪ] (*pret & pp:* **-fied**) *va* estratificar; *vn* estratificarse
stratigraphic [ˌstrætɪ'græfɪk] o **stratigraphical** [ˌstrætɪ'græfɪkəl] *adj* estratigráfico
stratigraphy [strə'tɪgrəfɪ] *s* estratigrafía
stratocruiser ['strætoˌkruzər] *s* transaéreo estratosférico
strato-cumulus [ˌstreto'kjumjələs] *s* (*pl:* **-li** [laɪ]) (meteor.) estratocúmulo
stratoliner ['strætoˌlaɪnər] *s* transaéreo estratosférico
stratosphere ['strætəsfɪr] o ['stretəsfɪr] *s* estratosfera
stratospheric [ˌstrætəs'fɛrɪk] o [ˌstretəs'fɛrɪk] *adj* estratosférico
stratovision ['strætəˌvɪʒən] *s* estratovisión
stratum ['stretəm] o ['strætəm] *s* (*pl:* **-ta** [tə] o **-tums**) (anat. & geol.) estrato; clase, categoría (*de la sociedad*)
stratus ['stretəs] *s* (*pl:* **-ti** [taɪ]) (meteor.) estrato
straw [strɔ] *s* paja; pajita (*para beber*); chispazo (*indicación*); **I don't care a straw** no se me da un bledo; **to be the last straw** ser el colmo; **to catch at a straw** obrar con desesperación; *adj* pajizo; baladí, de poca importancia; falso, ficticio
straw ballot *s* var. de **straw vote**
strawberry ['strɔˌbɛrɪ] *s* (*pl:* **-ries**) (bot.) fresa (*planta y fruto*)
strawberry patch *s* fresal
strawberry shortcake *s* torta de fresa, ponqué de fresa
strawberry tomato *s* (bot.) tomate de invierno
strawberry tree *s* (bot.) madroño; (bot.) bonetero
strawboard ['strɔˌbord] *s* cartón de paja
straw hat *s* sombrero de paja; canotié (*el de copa plana y baja*)
straw man *s* figura de paja; testaferro; testigo falso; persona de poca monta
straw vote *s* voto informativo
strawy ['strɔ·ɪ] *adj* (*comp:* **-ier;** *super:* **-iest**) pajizo; baladí
stray [stre] *adj* perdido, extraviado; disperso, aislado, suelto; (elec.) parásito; *s* vagabundo; animal perdido o extraviado; **strays** *spl* (rad.) ruidos parásitos; *vn* perderse, extraviarse
streak [strik] *s* raya, lista; vena, veta; traza, rasgo; rayo (*de luz*); (coll.) tiempo muy breve; racha (*de fortuna*); **like a streak** (coll.) como un rayo; *va* rayar, listar; abigarrar; *vn* rayarse; (coll.) andar o pasar como un rayo
streaky ['strikɪ] *adj* (*comp:* **-ier;** *super:* **-iest**) rayado, listado, veteado; abigarrado; desigual, irregular
stream [strim] *s* corriente; río, arroyo; flujo, chorro; torrente (*de personas*); desfile (*de autos*); **against the stream** contra la corriente; *va* arrojar, derramar; hacer ondear; (min.) lavar con un chorro de agua; *vn* correr, manar (*un líquido*); chorrear; ondear, flotar; correr rápidamente; **to stream out** salir a torrentes
streamer ['strimər] *s* flámula; cinta ondeante; rayo de luz, faja de luz; cola o cabellera de co-

meta; extensión de la corona solar (*durante los eclipses de Sol*); título que ocupa todo el ancho del periódico
streamlet [ˈstrimlɪt] *s* arroyuelo; hilo de agua
streamline [ˈstrim,laɪn] *s* línea aerodinámica; *adj* aerodinámico; *va* aerodinamizar, hacer aerodinámico
streamlined [ˈstrim,laɪnd] *adj* aerodinámico, perfilado
streamliner [ˈstrim,laɪnər] *s* tren aerodinámico de lujo
street [strit] *s* calle; *adj* callejero
street Arab *s* pillete de calle
streetcar [ˈstrit,kɑr] *s* tranvía
street cleaner *s* basurero; barredera (*aparato*)
street cleaning *s* limpieza de calles, servicio de riego
street clothes *spl* traje de calle
street floor *s* piso bajo
street lamp *s* farol (de la calle)
street lighting *s* alumbrado público
street railway *s* tranvía, ferrocarril urbano
street sprinkler *s* carricuba, carro de riego, regadera
street sweeper *s* barredera, raspadora
streetwalker [ˈstrit,wɔkər] *s* cantonera, carrerista, prostituta de calle
strength [strɛŋθ] *s* fuerza; intensidad; (mil.) número (*de soldados o fuerzas militares*); (com.) tendencia a la subida; **by main strength** con todas sus fuerzas; **on the strength of** fundándose en; confiando en
strengthen [ˈstrɛŋθən] *va* fortificar, reforzar, fortalecer; confirmar, corroborar; *vn* fortificarse, reforzarse, fortalecerse
strenuous [ˈstrɛnjuəs] *adj* estrenuo, vigoroso; arduo, difícil, activo
streptococcic [,strɛptəˈkɑksɪk] *adj* estreptocócico
streptococcus [,strɛptəˈkɑkəs] *s* (*pl:* **-cocci** [ˈkɑksaɪ]) (bact.) estreptococo
streptomycin [,strɛptoˈmaɪsɪn] *s* (pharm.) estreptomicina
streptotrichin [strɛpˈtɑtrɪkɪn] *s* (pharm.) estreptotricina
stress [strɛs] *s* tensión, fuerza, esfuerzo; compulsión; importancia; acento; (mech.) tensión (*resistencia molecular a fuerzas exteriores*); **to lay stress on** o **upon** hacer hincapié en; *va* someter a esfuerzo, ejercer coerción sobre; hacer hincapié en; acentuar
stress accent *s* acento prosódico
stretch [strɛtʃ] *s* estiramiento, estirón; trecho (*distancia de lugar o tiempo*); tramo (*de carretera*); tensión, extensión; esfuerzo (*de la imaginación*); (slang) condena (*extensión de la pena*); **at a stretch** de un tirón, p.ej., **three hours at a stretch** tres horas de un tirón; *va* estirar; alargar, extender; tender; forzar, violentar; (fig.) estirar (*el dinero*); **to stretch a point** hacer una concesión; **to stretch oneself** desperezarse; *vn* estirarse; alargarse, extenderse; tenderse; desperezarse; **to stretch out** echarse
stretcher [ˈstrɛtʃər] *s* ensanchador (*para los guantes*); camilla (*para los heridos y enfermos*); (mas.) soga; (mach.) tensor, estirador; (paint.) bastidor
stretcher-bearer [ˈstrɛtʃər,bɛrər] *s* camillero
stretchy [ˈstrɛtʃɪ] *adj* (coll.) estirable, extensible; (coll.) propenso a desperezarse
strew [stru] (*pret:* **strewed;** *pp:* **strewed** o **strewn**) *va* esparcir, derramar; sembrar, salpicar; polvorear
strewn [strun] *pp de* **strew**
stria [ˈstraɪə] *s* (*pl:* **-ae** [i]) estría; (arch. & med.) estría
striated [ˈstraɪetɪd] *adj* estriado
striation [straɪˈeʃən] *s* estriación
stricken [ˈstrɪkən] *adj* herido; afligido; inhabilitado; rasado (*con el rasero*); **stricken in age** o **in years** debilitado por los años; *pp de* **strike**
strickle [ˈstrɪkəl] *s* rasero; escantillón; *va* rasar
strict [strɪkt] *adj* estricto, riguroso
strictness [ˈstrɪktnɪs] *s* rigor, severidad, exactitud
stricture [ˈstrɪktʃər] *s* crítica severa, censura; (path.) estrictura, estenosis
stridden [ˈstrɪdən] *pp de* **stride**
stride [straɪd] *s* zancada, trancada, tranco; **to hit one's stride** alcanzar la actividad o velocidad acostumbrada; **to make great** o **rapid strides** avanzar a grandes pasos; **to take in one's stride** hacer sin esfuerzo, hacer con mucha desenvoltura; (*pret:* **strode;** *pp:* **stridden**) *va* pasar a zancadas, cruzar de un tranco; montar a horcajadas; *vn* dar zancadas, andar a trancos, caminar a paso largo
stridence [ˈstraɪdəns] o **stridency** [ˈstraɪdənsɪ] *s* estridencia, estridor
strident [ˈstraɪdənt] *adj* estridente
stridor [ˈstraɪdər] *s* (path.) estridor
stridulant [ˈstrɪdʒələnt] *adj* estriduloso
stridulate [ˈstrɪdʒəlet] *vn* estridular
stridulation [,strɪdʒəˈleʃən] *s* estridulación; (zool.) estridulación
stridulous [ˈstrɪdʒələs] *adj* estriduloso; (path.) estriduloso
strife [straɪf] *s* contienda, refriega; rivalidad, emulación
strike [straɪk] *s* golpe; huelga; (min.) descubrimiento repentino; golpe de fortuna; hembra (*de una cerradura*); rasero; (baseball) golpe (*pelota que pasa sobre el puesto meta y entre el hombro y la rodilla del batter*); acto de tragar el anzuelo; (bowling) pleno; **to go on strike** ir a la huelga, ponerse en huelga ‖ (*pret:* **struck;** *pp:* **struck** *o* **stricken**) *va* golpear; pulsar (*una tecla*); herir, percutir; topar, dar con; acuñar (*monedas*); echar (*raíces*); frotar, rayar o encender (*un fósforo*); (min.) descubrir repentinamente; cerrar (*un trato*), hacer (*un pacto*); (naut.) arriar (*las velas*); rasar, nivelar; coger con el anzuelo; arponear; dar (*la hora*); afligir, herir; impresionar; tomar o asumir (*una postura*); quitar de un golpe; borrar, cancelar; **to strike a snag** encontrar un obstáculo; **to strike camp** batir tiendas; **to strike for a loan** dar un sablazo a; **to strike it rich** descubrir un buen filón, tener un golpe de fortuna; **to strike off** quitar de golpe; borrar; deducir; impresionar; (print.) tirar; **to strike one's attention** atraer la atención; **to strike one's fancy** antojársele a uno; **to strike out** borrar, tachar, cancelar; (baseball) hacer golpear mal la pelota tres veces; **to strike up** trabar (*conversación, amistad*); entablar (*una conversación*); empezar a cantar, empezar a tocar; **to strike with terror** sobrecoger de terror ‖ *vn* dar, sonar (*una campana, un reloj*); encenderse (*un fósforo*); declararse o estar en huelga; agarrarse, fijarse; echar raíces; tragar o coger el anzuelo; (mil.) dar el asalto; **to strike at** tratar de golpear; acometer; **to strike out** ponerse en marcha, echar camino adelante; (baseball) golpear mal la pelota tres veces
strikebreaker [ˈstraɪk,brekər] *s* rompehuelgas, esquirol
striker [ˈstraɪkər] *s* golpeador; huelguista; (mach.) percutor
striking [ˈstraɪkɪŋ] *adj* percutor; impresionante, llamativo, sorprendente; en huelga
striking mechanism *s* sonería (*del reloj*)
striking power *s* potencia de choque, poder ofensivo
striking range *s* alcance agresivo
string [strɪŋ] *s* cuerdecilla; hilo o hebra fuerte; sarta (*de perlas; de mentiras*); hebra (*de habichuelas*); (arch.) limón; (mus.) cuerda; lazo; (coll.) condición (*de una concesión*); **strings** *spl* (mus.) instrumentos de cuerda; **on a string** en su poder; **to have two strings to one's bow** tener dos cuerdas en su arco; **to pull strings** ejercer su influencia secretamente; utilizar apoyos secretos; (*pret & pp:* **strung**) *va* enhebrar, ensartar; atar con cuerdas; proveer de cuerdas; colgar de una cuerda; tender (*un cable, un alambre*); encordar (*un violín, una raqueta*); templar (*un violín*); desfibrar, quitar las fibras a; extender, colocar en fila; (slang) hacer fisga a; **to string along** (slang) traer al retortero; **to string up** (coll.) ahorcar
string bean *s* (bot.) habichuela, judía; habichuela verde, judía verde
stringcourse [ˈstrɪŋ,kors] *s* (arch.) cordón

stringed instrument *s* (mus.) instrumento de cuerda
stringency ['strɪndʒənsɪ] *s* (*pl:* **-cies**) rigor, severidad; fuerza de persuasión; (com.) tirantez
stringent ['strɪndʒənt] *adj* riguroso, severo, estricto; convincente; (com.) tirante
stringer ['strɪŋər] *s* encordador; ensartador; (carp.) riostra; (rail.) durmiente longitudinal
stringhalt ['strɪŋ,hɔlt] *s* (vet.) ancado
stringhalted ['strɪŋ,hɔltɪd] *adj* (vet.) ancado
string orchestra *s* orquesta de cuerdas
stringpiece ['strɪŋ,pis] *s* riostra
string quartet *s* (mus.) cuarteto de cuerdas
string tie *s* corbatín angosto
stringy ['strɪŋɪ] *adj* (*comp:* **-ier;** *super:* **-iest**) fibroso, filamentoso; correoso, duro; viscoso
strip [strɪp] *s* tira; lámina (*de metal*); faja (*de tierra*); (*pret & pp:* **stripped;** *ger:* **stripping**) *va* desnudar; despojar, desmantelar, robar; desforrar; deshacer (*la cama*); estropear (*el engranaje, un tornillo*); ordeñar hasta agotar; desvenar (*tabaco*); descortezar; **to strip of** despojar de; **to strip down** desguarnecer; *vn* desnudarse; despojarse; descortezarse
stripe [straɪp] *s* raya, lista, banda; gaya; cinta, franja; (mil. & nav.) galón; tipo, índole; latigazo; *va* rayar, listar; gayar
striped [straɪpt] o ['straɪpɪd] *adj* rayado, a rayas
striped hyena *s* (zool.) hiena rayada
striped mullet *s* (ichth.) mújol
stripling ['strɪplɪŋ] *s* rapagón, mozuelo
strip mining *s* mineraje a tajo abierto
stripped-down ['strɪpt,daʊn] *adj* desguarnecido
stripteaser ['strɪp'tizər] *s* desnudista *f*
strive [straɪv] (*pret:* **strove;** *pp:* **striven**) *vn* esforzarse; hacer lo posible; luchar; **to strive to** + *inf* esforzarse por + *inf*
striven ['strɪvən] *pp de* **strive**
strobile ['strɑbɪl] *s* (bot. & zool.) estróbilo
stroboscope ['strɑbəskop] *s* estroboscopio
strode [strod] *pret de* **stride**
stroke [strok] *s* golpe; campanada (*de un reloj o campana*); plumada; pincelada; brochada; brazada (*en la natación*); jugada; caricia (*hecha con la mano*); raya; raquetazo; (mach.) embolada, carrera; palada, remada; primer remero; ataque de parálisis, apoplejía; buen éxito inesperado; golpe (*de fortuna*); rasgo (*de ingenio*); **at one stroke** de un golpe, de una sola vez; **at the stroke of** al dar las (*p.ej., tres*); **to keep stroke** remar al compás (*dos o más bogadores*); **to not do a stroke of work** no dar golpe, no levantar paja del suelo; **with one fell stroke** de un plumazo; **stroke of fortune** golpe de fortuna; **stroke of wit** chiste, agudeza; *va* frotar suavemente, acariciar con la mano; rayar
stroke oar *s* primer remero, bogavante
stroll [strol] *s* paseo; **to take a stroll** dar un paseo; *va* pasearse por; **to stroll the streets** callejear; *vn* pasear, pasearse; vagar, errar, callejear
stroller ['strolər] *s* paseante; vagabundo; cómico ambulante; andaderas, cochecito para niños
stroma ['stromə] *s* (*pl:* **-mata** [mətə]) (anat., biol. & bot.) estroma
Stromboli ['strɔmbɔli] *s* Estrómboli
strong [strɔŋ] o [strɑŋ] *adj* (*comp:* **stronger** ['strɔŋgər] o ['strɑŋgər]; *super:* **strongest** ['strɔŋgɪst] o ['strɑŋgɪst]) fuerte, resistente; intenso; firme (*mercado*); violento; enérgico; marcado; celoso, acérrimo; picante; rancio; (gram.) fuerte (*vocal; verbo*); ascendiendo a, p.ej., **a thousand strong** ascendiendo a mil; *adv* fuertemente, vigorosamente
strong-arm ['strɔŋ,ɑrm] o ['strɑŋ,ɑrm] *adj* (coll.) violento; *va* (coll.) usar violencia contra
strongbox ['strɔŋ,bɑks] o ['strɑŋ,bɑks] *s* cofre fuerte, caja de caudales
strong breeze *s* (naut.) viento fresco
strong drink *s* bebida alcohólica, bebida fuerte
strong gale *s* (naut.) viento muy duro
stronghold ['strɔŋ,hold] o ['strɑŋ,hold] *s* fuerte, fortaleza; plaza fuerte
strong man *s* hércules; (coll.) promotor, alma (*el que da aliento y fuerza a una cosa*)
strongman ['strɔŋ,mæn] o ['strɑŋ,mæn] *s* (*pl:* **-men**) hombre fuerte (*dictador*)
strong-minded ['strɔŋ'maɪndɪd] o ['strɑŋ'maɪndɪd] *adj* de inteligencia vigorosa; independiente; hombruna (*dícese de una mujer*)
strontia ['strɑnʃɪə] *s* (chem.) estronciana
strontianite ['strɑnʃɪənaɪt] *s* (mineral.) estroncianita
strontium ['strɑnʃɪəm] *s* (chem.) estroncio
strop [strɑp] *s* suavizador; (*pret & pp:* **stropped;** *ger:* **stropping**) *va* suavizar (*una navaja*)
strophe ['strofɪ] *s* estrofa
strophic ['strɑfɪk] o ['strofɪk] *adj* estrófico
strove [strov] *pret de* **strive**
struck [strʌk] *pret & pp de* **strike**
structural ['strʌktʃərəl] *adj* estructural
structure ['strʌktʃər] *s* estructura; construcción
struggle ['strʌgəl] *s* lucha; esfuerzo, forcejeo; *vn* luchar; esforzarse, forcejear; **to struggle to** + *inf* luchar por + *inf*
struggle for existence *s* lucha por la vida o por la existencia
strum [strʌm] *s* cencerreo; (*pret & pp:* **strummed;** *ger:* **strumming**) *va* arañar (*un instrumento músico*) sin arte; *vn* cencerrear
struma ['strumə] *s* (*pl:* **-mae** [mi]) *s* (path.) estruma (*escrófula; bocio*); (bot.) apófisis
strumous ['struməs] *adj* estrumoso
strumpet ['strʌmpɪt] *s* ramera, prostituta
strung [strʌŋ] *pret & pp de* **string**
strut [strʌt] *s* (carp.) tornapunta, riostra, jabalcón; contoneo, pavoneo; (*pret & pp:* **strutted;** *ger:* **strutting**) *vn* contonearse, pavonearse
strychnin ['strɪknɪn] o **strychnine** ['strɪknɪn], ['strɪknaɪn] o ['strɪknin] *s* (chem.) estricnina
St. Sophia [sent so'faɪə] *s* Santa Sofía (*mezquita*)
St. Thomas [sent 'tɑməs] *s* Santo Tomás (*isla*)
Stuart, Mary ['stjuərt] o ['stuərt] María Estuardo
stub [stʌb] *s* trozo, fragmento; colilla (*de cigarro*); zoquete (*de madera no labrada*); tocón (*de un árbol cortado*); cepa (*de árbol*); pluma de escribir corta y de punta gruesa; talón (*de un cheque*); *adj* embotado; (*pret & pp:* **stubbed;** *ger:* **stubbing**) *va* rozar, limpiar, arrancar los tocones de; desarraigar; aplastar; **to stub off** embotar; **to stub one's toe** dar un tropezón
stub axle *s* (aut.) mangueta
stubble ['stʌbəl] *s* (agr.) rastrojo; *va* (agr.) rastrojar
stubbly ['stʌblɪ] *adj* lleno de rastrojo; cerdoso, hirsuto
stubborn ['stʌbərn] *adj* terco, testarudo, obstinado; porfiado, cabezón; intratable
stubbornness ['stʌbərnnɪs] *s* terquedad, testarudez, obstinación; porfía
stubby ['stʌbɪ] *adj* (*comp:* **-bier;** *super:* **-biest**) cachigordete; corto, grueso y cerdoso; lleno de troncos, lleno de tocones
stub nail *s* clavo de herrar viejo
stub-pointed ['stʌb,pɔɪntɪd] *adj* mocho
stucco ['stʌko] *s* (*pl:* **-coes** o **-cos**) estuco; *va* estucar
stuccowork ['stʌko,wʌrk] *s* estuco, obra de estuco
stuck [stʌk] *pret & pp de* **stick**
stuck-up ['stʌk,ʌp] *adj* (coll.) tieso, estirado, espetado, orgulloso
stud [stʌd] *s* tachón; botón de camisa; montante, pie derecho, poste de tabique; refuerzo de eslabón; perno prisionero, espárrago; clavo de adorno; yeguada (*rebaño; establecimiento*); caballeriza; caballada; caballo padre; **at stud** destinado a padrear; *adj* semental; (*pret & pp:* **studded;** *ger:* **studding**) *va* tachonar
stud bolt *s* perno prisionero, espárrago
studbook ['stʌd,bʊk] *s* registro genealógico de caballos, libro de oro de los caballos de pura sangre
studding ['stʌdɪŋ] *s* montantes de tabique; madera para construir montantes
studdingsail ['stʌdɪŋsəl] o ['stʌdɪŋ,sel] *s* (naut.) ala

student ['stjudənt] o ['studənt] *s* estudiante; investigador
student body *s* estudiantado
student lamp *s* quinqué
stud farm *s* acaballadero
studhorse ['stʌd,hɔrs] *s* caballo padre, caballo semental
studied ['stʌdɪd] *adj* estudiado (*afectado*); premeditado, hecho adrede
studio ['stjudɪo] o ['studɪo] *s* (*pl:* **-os**) taller, estudio; (mov. & rad.) estudio
studious ['stjudɪəs] o ['studɪəs] *adj* estudioso; asiduo, solícito
study ['stʌdɪ] *s* (*pl:* **-ies**) estudio; meditación profunda; solicitud; **to be in a brown study** estar absorto en la meditación; (*pret & pp:* **-ied**) *va* estudiar; *vn* estudiar; **to study to** + *inf* esforzarse por + *inf*
study hall *s* sala de estudio o de lectura
stuff [stʌf] *s* materia, material; tela, género, paño; cosa o cosas; efectos, muebles, baratijas, bagatelas; medicina; fruslerías; índole, carácter; *va* rellenar, atestar, colmar; atascar, tapar, cerrar; embutir; atracar (*de comida*); (cook.) rellenar; meter sin orden, llenar sin orden; disecar (*un animal muerto para conservar su apariencia*); *vn* atracarse, hartarse
stuffed olives *spl* aceitunas rellenas
stuffed shirt *s* (slang) tragavirotes
stuffing ['stʌfɪŋ] *s* relleno
stuffing box *s* caja de estopas, prensaestopas
stuffing nut *s* (mach.) tuerca del prensaestopas
stuffy ['stʌfɪ] *adj* (*comp:* **-ier;** *super:* **-iest**) sofocante, mal ventilado; aburrido, sin interés; cerrado, tapado; (coll.) etiquetero, relamido; (coll.) picajoso
Stuka ['stukə] o ['ʃtukə] *s* stuka (*avión alemán de combate en picado*)
stultification [,stʌltɪfɪ'keʃən] *s* posición ridícula, apariencia estulta; descrédito
stultify ['stʌltɪfaɪ] (*pret & pp:* **-fied**) *va* poner en ridículo, hacer parecer ridículo; quitar importancia a; **to stultify oneself** ponerse en ridículo
stumble ['stʌmbəl] *s* tropiezo, tropezón, traspié; desatino, desliz; *va* hacer tropezar, hacer dar un traspié; confundir; extraviar; *vn* tropezar, dar un traspié; errar; moverse a tropezones, hablar a tropezones; **to stumble on** o **upon** tropezar con
stumbling block *s* tropezadero, escollo
stumbly ['stʌmblɪ] *adj* tropezoso
stump [stʌmp] *s* cepa (*tronco próximo a las raíces*); tocón (*tronco que queda de un árbol*); muñón (*p.ej., de brazo cortado*); raigón (*de muela*); colilla (*de cigarro*); fragmento, resto; rabo (*de una cola*); paso pesado; (coll.) desafío, reto; (slang) pierna; (f.a.) esfumino; tribuna pública; **up a stump** perplejo, en un apuro; *va* arrancar los tocones de; cortar, amputar; (coll.) confundir, dejar confuso, dejar sin habla; (coll.) desafiar; recorrer pronunciando discursos políticos; (f.a.) esfumar; *vn* cojear, renquear; pronunciar discursos políticos
stump puller *s* destroncadora
stump speaker *s* orador callejero
stump speech *s* arenga electoral
stumpy ['stʌmpɪ] *adj* (*comp:* **-ier;** *super:* **-iest**) lleno de tocones; cachigordete, achaparrado
stun [stʌn] (*pret & pp:* **stunned:** *ger:* **stunning**) *va* aturdir, atolondrar, dejar pasmado
stung [stʌŋ] *pret & pp de* **sting**
stunk [stʌŋk] *pret & pp de* **stink**
stunner ['stʌnər] *s* golpe que aturde; (coll.) cosa pasmosa, persona maravillosa
stunning ['stʌnɪŋ] *adj* aturdidor; (coll.) brutal (*pasmoso, estupendo, pistonudo, elegante, hermoso, lujoso*)
stunsail ['stʌnsəl] *s* var. de **studdingsail**
stunt [stʌnt] *s* atrofia, falta de crecimiento o desarrollo; engendro (*animal, planta u otra cosa*); (coll.) suerte acrobática, maniobra sensacional; (coll.) faena, hazaña, proeza, recurso (*para lograr un fin*); (coll.) anuncio de reclamo; (aer.) vuelo acrobático; *va* atrofiar, impedir el crecimiento o desarrollo de; (coll.) hacer suertes con; *vn* (coll.) hacer suertes acrobáticas, hacer maniobras sensacionales; (aer.) lucirse haciendo maniobras acrobáticas
stunt man *s* (mov.) doble que hace suertes peligrosas
stupe [stjup] o [stup] *s* (med.) fomento, compresa pequeña
stupefacient [,stjupɪ'feʃənt] o [,stupɪ'feʃənt] *adj & s* estupefaciente
stupefaction [,stjupɪ'fækʃən] o [,stupɪ'fækʃən] *s* estupefacción
stupefy ['stjupɪfaɪ] o ['stupɪfaɪ] (*pret & pp:* **-fied**) *va* dejar estupefacto, pasmar; causar estupor a
stupendous [stju'pɛndəs] o [stu'pɛndəs] *adj* estupendo; enorme
stupid ['stjupɪd] o ['stupɪd] *adj & s* estúpido
stupidity [stju'pɪdɪtɪ] o [stu'pɪdɪtɪ] *s* (*pl:* **-ties**) estupidez
stupor ['stjupər] o ['stupər] *s* estupor
sturdiness ['stʌrdɪnɪs] *s* fuerza, robustez; firmeza, tenacidad
sturdy ['stʌrdɪ] *adj* (*comp:* **-dier;** *super:* **-diest**) fuerte, robusto, fornido; firme, tenaz
sturgeon ['stʌrdʒən] *s* (ichth.) esturión
stutter ['stʌtər] *s* tartamudeo; *va* decir tartamudeando; *vn* tartamudear
St. Vincent [sent 'vɪnsənt] *s* San Vicente (*isla*)
sty [staɪ] *s* (*pl:* **sties**) pocilga, zahurda; (path.) orzuelo
Stygian ['stɪdʒɪən] *adj* estigio, estigioso
style [staɪl] *s* estilo; moda; elegancia; título, epíteto; (bot. & print.) estilo; modelo, p.ej., **latest style** último modelo; **in style** de moda; **in the style of** al estilo de; **to live in great style** vivir en gran lujo; *va* adaptar a la moda, cortar a la moda; nombrar, intitular
stylebook ['staɪl,buk] *s* (print.) libro de ejemplos de impresión y modelos de ortografía, etc.
stylet ['staɪlɪt] *s* estilete; (surg.) estilete
stylish ['staɪlɪʃ] *adj* de moda, elegante
stylist ['staɪlɪst] *s* estilista
stylistic [staɪ'lɪstɪk] *adj* estilístico; **stylistics** *ssg* estilística
stylite ['staɪlaɪt] *s* estilita
stylize ['staɪlaɪz] *va* estilizar
stylograph ['staɪləgræf] o ['staɪləgrɑf] *s* estilógrafo
stylographic [,staɪlə'græfɪk] *adj* estilográfico
styloid ['staɪlɔɪd] *adj* (anat.) estiloides
stylus ['staɪləs] *s* estilo; aguja (*de fonógrafo*)
stymie ['staɪmɪ] *s* (golf) condición en que una pelota se encuentra entre la del adversario y el agujero; (*pret & pp:* **-mied;** *ger:* **-mieing**) *va* (golf) estorbar con una pelota entre la del adversario y el agujero; (fig.) frustrar
stymy ['staɪmɪ] *s* (*pl:* **-mies**) var. de **stymie;** (*pret & pp:* **-mied**) *va* var. de **stymie**
styptic ['stɪptɪk] *adj & s* estíptico
styptic pencil *s* lápiz estíptico
styracaceous [,staɪrə'keʃəs] *adj* (bot.) estiracáceo
styrene ['staɪrin] o ['stɪrin] *s* (chem.) estireno
Styria ['stɪrɪə] *s* Estiria
Styx [stɪks] *s* (myth.) Estigia
suasion ['sweʒən] *s* persuasión
suasive ['swesɪv] *adj* suasorio, persuasor
suave [swɑv] o [swev] *adj* suave; afable, fino, zalamero, pulido
suavity ['swævɪtɪ] o ['swɑvɪtɪ] *s* (*pl:* **-ties**) suavidad; afabilidad, finura
sub. abr. de **subscription, substitute** y **suburban**
sub [sʌb] *s & adj* (coll.) substituto; (coll.) submarino; (coll.) subordinado; (coll.) subalterno; (*pret & pp:* **subbed;** *ger:* **subbing**) *va* (coll.) atacar o hundir con submarino; *vn* (coll.) ser substituto; **to sub for** (coll.) hacer las veces de
subacetate [sʌb'æsɪtet] *s* (chem.) subacetato
subacid [sʌb'æsɪd] *adj* (chem.) subácido
subagent [sʌb'edʒənt] *s* subagente
subaltern [səb'ɔltərn] o ['sʌbəltərn] *adj & s* subalterno
subantarctic [,sʌbænt'ɑrktɪk] *adj* subantártico
subaquatic [,sʌbə'kwætɪk] o [,sʌbə'kwɑtɪk] *adj* subacuático
subaqueous [sʌb'ekwɪəs] o [sʌb'ækwɪəs] *adj* subácueo
subarctic [sʌb'ɑrktɪk] *adj* subártico
subarid [sʌb'ærɪd] *adj* medianamente árido
subatom [sʌb'ætəm] *s* (chem. & phys.) subátomo
subatomic [,sʌbə'tɑmɪk] *adj* subatómico

subcellar ['sʌb,sɛlər] *s* sótano inferior
subchaser ['sʌb,tʃesər] *s* cazasubmarinos
subclass ['sʌb,klæs] o ['sʌb,klɑs] *s* (biol.) subclase
subclavian [sʌb'kleviən] *adj* (anat.) subclavio
subcommittee ['sʌbkə,mɪtɪ] *s* subcomisión
subconscious [sʌb'kɑnʃəs] *adj* subconsciente; *s* subconsciencia
subconsciousness [sʌb'kɑnʃəsnɪs] *s* subconsciencia
subcontinent [sʌb'kɑntɪnənt] *s* subcontinente
subcontract [sʌb'kɑntrækt] *s* subcontrato; [sʌb'kɑntrækt] o [,sʌbkən'trækt] *va & vn* subcontratar
subcontractor [sʌb'kɑntræktər] o [,sʌbkən'træktər] *s* subcontratista
subcostal [sʌb'kɑstəl] *adj* (anat. & zool.) subcostal
subcritical [sʌb'krɪtɪkəl] *adj* subcrítico
subcutaneous [,sʌbkju'tenɪəs] *adj* subcutáneo
subdeacon [sʌb'dikən] *s* subdiácono
subdeaconry [sʌb'dikənrɪ] *s* subdiaconato
subdean ['sʌb,din] *s* subdecano
subdeb [sʌb'dɛb] *s* (coll.) tobillera, chica muy joven, ya casi en edad de ponerse de largo
subdelirium [,sʌbdɪ'lɪrɪəm] *s* (path.) subdelirio
subdivide [,sʌbdɪ'vaɪd] o ['sʌbdɪ,vaɪd] *va* subdividir; *vn* subdividirse
subdivision [,sʌbdɪ'vɪʒən] o ['sʌbdɪ,vɪʒən] *s* subdivisión
subdominant [sʌb'dɑmɪnənt] *s* (mus.) subdominante
subdouble [sʌb'dʌbəl] *adj* (math.) subduplo
subdue [səb'dju] o [səb'du] *va* subyugar, sojuzgar; dominar, sujetar; amansar, suavizar; mejorar (*tierras*)
subereous [su'bɪrɪəs] o [sju'bɪrɪəs] *adj* suberoso
suberin ['subərɪn] o ['sjubərɪn] *s* (biochem.) suberina
subfamily [sʌb'fæmɪlɪ] o ['sʌb,fæmɪlɪ] *s* (*pl:* **-lies**) (biol.) subfamilia
subgenus [sʌb'dʒinəs] o ['sʌb,dʒinəs] *s* (*pl:* **-genera** ['dʒɛnərə] o **-genuses**) (biol.) subgénero
subgroup ['sʌb,grup] *s* subgrupo
subhead ['sʌb,hɛd] *s* subtítulo; subdirector
subheading ['sʌb,hɛdɪŋ] *s* subtítulo
subhuman [sʌb'hjumən] *adj* inferior a lo humano; casi humano
subindex [sʌb'ɪndɛks] *s* (*pl:* **-dices** [dɪsiz]) subíndice
subj. abr. de **subject, subjective** y **subjunctive**
subjacent [sʌb'dʒesənt] *adj* subyacente
subject ['sʌbdʒɪkt] *s* asunto, materia; objeto (*de un experimento*); (mus.) tema; súbdito (*persona sujeta a la autoridad de un superior*); (gram., med., philos., psychol. & log.) sujeto; *adj* súbdito; sujeto; [səb'dʒɛkt] *va* sujetar, someter
subject index *s* índice de materias
subjection [səb'dʒɛkʃən] *s* sujeción
subjective [səb'dʒɛktɪv] *adj* subjetivo
subjectivism [səb'dʒɛktɪvɪzəm] *s* (philos.) subjetivismo
subjectivity [,sʌbdʒɛk'tɪvɪtɪ] *s* subjetividad
subject matter *s* asunto, materia, objeto
subject pronoun *s* pronombre sujeto
subjoin [səb'dʒɔɪn] *va* añadir, adjuntar
subjugate ['sʌbdʒəget] *va* subyugar
subjugation [,sʌbdʒə'geʃən] *s* subyugación
subjugator ['sʌbdʒə,getər] *s* subyugador
subjunctive [səb'dʒʌŋktɪv] *adj & s* (gram.) subjuntivo
subkingdom [sʌb'kɪŋdəm] o ['sʌb,kɪŋdəm] *s* (biol.) subreino
sublease ['sʌb,lis] *s* subarriendo; [,sʌb'lis] o ['sʌb,lis] *va & vn* subarrendar
sublet [sʌb'lɛt] o ['sʌb,lɛt] (*pret & pp:* **-let;** *ger:* **-letting**) *va & vn* subarrendar, realquilar
sublieutenant [,sʌblu'tɛnənt] *s* subteniente
sublimate ['sʌblɪmet] *adj* sublimado; *s* (chem.) sublimado; *va* sublimar
sublimation [,sʌblɪ'meʃən] *s* sublimación
sublime [sə'blaɪm] *adj* sublime; **the sublime** lo sublime; *va* sublimar
Sublime Porte [port] *s* Sublime Puerta (*Turquía*)
subliminal [sʌb'lɪmɪnəl] o [sʌb'laɪmɪnəl] *adj & s* (psychol.) subliminar
sublimity [səb'lɪmɪtɪ] *s* (*pl:* **-ties**) sublimidad
sublingual [sʌb'lɪŋgwəl] *adj* (anat.) sublingual
sublunar [sʌb'lunər] o **sublunary** ['sʌblu,nɛrɪ] o [sʌb'lunərɪ] *adj* sublunar
submachine gun [,sʌbmə'ʃin] *s* subfusil ametrallador
submarginal [sʌb'mɑrdʒɪnəl] *adj* submarginal; improductivo
submarine ['sʌbmə,rin] *adj & s* submarino; *va* (coll.) atacar o hundir con un submarino
submaxilla [,sʌbmæks'ɪlə] *s* (*pl:* **-lae** [li]) (anat. & zool.) mandíbula submaxilar
submaxillary [sʌb'mæksɪ,lɛrɪ] *adj* submaxilar; *s* (*pl:* **-ies**) mandíbula submaxilar; glándula submaxilar
submaxillary gland *s* (anat.) glándula submaxilar
submerge [səb'mʌrdʒ] *va* sumergir; *vn* sumergirse
submergence [səb'mʌrdʒəns] *s* sumersión
submerse [səb'mʌrs] *va & vn* var. de **submerge**
submersible [səb'mʌrsɪbəl] *adj* sumergible, hundible; *s* sumergible (*buque*)
submersion [səb'mʌrʒən] o [səb'mʌrʃən] *s* sumersión
submicroscopic [,sʌbmaɪkrə'skɑpɪk] *adj* submicroscópico
submission [səb'mɪʃən] *s* sumisión
submissive [səb'mɪsɪv] *adj* sumiso
submit [səb'mɪt] (*pret & pp:* **-mitted;** *ger:* **-mitting**) *va* someter (*razones, reflexiones, etc.; un negocio*); proponer, permitirse decir; *vn* someterse
submultiple [sʌb'mʌltɪpəl] *adj & s* (math.) submúltiplo
subnormal [sʌb'nɔrməl] *adj* subnormal; *s* (geom.) subnormal
suborbital [sʌb'ɔrbɪtəl] *adj* suborbital
suborder ['sʌb,ɔrdər] o [sʌb'ɔrdər] *s* suborden
subordinate [səb'ɔrdɪnɪt] *adj* subordinado; (gram.) subordinado (*aplícase a la oración*); (gram.) subordinante (*aplícase a la conjunción*); [səb'ɔrdɪnet] *va* subordinar
subordinating conjunction *s* (gram.) conjunción subordinante
subordination [səb,ɔrdɪ'neʃən] *s* subordinación
suborn [sə'bɔrn] *va* sobornar
subornation [,sʌbɔr'neʃən] *s* soborno
subornation of perjury *s* (law) soborno de testigo
subplot ['sʌb,plɑt] *s* trama secundaria
subpoena o **subpena** [sʌb'pinə] o [sə'pinə] *s* (law) comparendo; *va* (law) mandar comparecer
sub rosa [sʌb 'rozə] *adv* en secreto, en confianza
subsatellite [sʌb'sætəlaɪt] *s* subsatélite
subscapular [sʌb'skæpjələr] *adj* (anat.) subscapular
subscribe [səb'skraɪb] *va* subscribir; *vn* subscribir; subscribirse, abonarse; **to subscribe for** o **to** subscribir (*un número de acciones u obligaciones*); subscribirse a, abonarse a (*una publicación periódica*); **to subscribe to** subscribir (*una opinión o dictamen*)
subscriber [səb'skraɪbər] *s* subscriptor; abonado
subscription [səb'skrɪpʃən] *s* subscripción; firma; abono (*p.ej., a una revista*)
subsection ['sʌb,sɛkʃən] o [sʌb'sɛkʃən] *s* subdivisión
subsequence ['sʌbsɪkwəns] *s* subsecuencia, posterioridad; acontecimiento subsiguiente
subsequent ['sʌbsɪkwənt] *adj* subsecuente o subsiguiente, posterior
subserve [səb'sʌrv] *va* adelantar, ayudar
subservience [səb'sʌrvɪəns] o **subserviency** [səb'sʌrvɪənsɪ] *s* servilismo; subordinación; utilidad
subservient [səb'sʌrvɪənt] *adj* servil; subordinado; útil
subside [səb'saɪd] *vn* apaciguarse, calmarse; cesar, acabarse; bajar (*el nivel de un líquido*); hundirse, irse al fondo; (coll.) caer
subsidence [səb'saɪdəns] o ['sʌbsɪdəns] *s* apaciguamiento, calma; cesación; bajada; hundimiento, sumersión
subsidiary [səb'sɪdɪ,ɛrɪ] *adj* subsidiario, auxi-

liar; afiliado; *s* (*pl:* **-ies**) suplemento; (com.) filial
subsidiary company *s* (com.) filial
subsidize [ˈsʌbsɪdaɪz] *va* subsidiar, subvencionar; comprar la ayuda de; sobornar
subsidy [ˈsʌbsɪdɪ] *s* (*pl:* **-dies**) subsidio, subvención
subsist [səbˈsɪst] *va* alimentar, mantener; *vn* subsistir
subsistence [səbˈsɪstəns] *s* subsistencia; (philos.) subsistencia
subsistent [səbˈsɪstənt] *adj* subsistente
subsoil [ˈsʌbˌsɔɪl] *s* subsuelo
subsonic [sʌbˈsɑnɪk] *adj* subsónico
subspecies [ˈsʌbˌspiʃɪz] o [sʌbˈspiʃɪz] *s* (*pl:* **-cies**) (biol.) subespecie
subst. abr. de **substantive** y **substitute**
substance [ˈsʌbstəns] *s* substancia; **in substance** en substancia
substandard [sʌbˈstændərd] o [ˈsʌbˌstændərd] *adj* inferior al nivel normal, inferior a la norma
substantial [səbˈstænʃəl] *adj* substancial; substancioso; fuerte, sólido; rico, acomodado; **to be in substantial agreement** estar de acuerdo en substancia
substantiality [səbˌstænʃɪˈælɪtɪ] *s* (*pl:* **-ties**) substancialidad; fuerza, solidez; opulencia, riqueza
substantiate [səbˈstænʃɪet] *va* verificar, comprobar, establecer; dar cuerpo a
substantiation [səbˌstænʃɪˈeʃən] *s* verificación, comprobación; incorporación
substantival [ˌsʌbstænˈtaɪvəl] *adj* (gram.) substantivo
substantive [ˈsʌbstəntɪv] *adj* substantivo; (gram.) substantivo; *s* (gram.) substantivo
substantivize [ˈsʌbstəntɪvaɪz] *va* (gram.) substantivar
substation [ˈsʌbˌsteʃən] *s* dependencia; (elec.) subcentral, subestación
substitute [ˈsʌbstɪtjut] o [ˈsʌbstɪtut] *adj* substitutivo, sucedáneo; *s* substituto (*persona*); substitutivo, sucedáneo; (mil.) reemplazo (*hombre que sirve en lugar de otro*); **beware of substitutes** desconfíe de substitutivos; *va* poner (*a una persona o cosa*) en lugar de otra, p.ej., **we substituted margarine for butter** pusimos (o usamos) margarina en lugar de mantequilla; *vn* actuar de substituto; **to substitute for** substituir (*a una persona o cosa*), p.ej., **John substituted for Peter** Juan substituyó a Pedro
substitution [ˌsʌbstɪˈtjuʃən] o [ˌsʌbstɪˈtuʃən] *s* empleo o uso de una persona o cosa en lugar de otra; (alg., chem. & law) substitución; (coll.) imitación fraudulenta
substitutional [ˌsʌbstɪˈtjuʃənəl] o [ˌsʌbstɪˈtuʃənəl] *adj* substituidor, sucedáneo
substitutive [ˈsʌbstɪˌtjutɪv] o [ˈsʌbstɪˌtutɪv] *adj* substitutivo
substrate [ˈsʌbstret] *s* substrato; (biochem.) substrato
substratum [sʌbˈstretəm] o [sʌbˈstrætəm] *s* (*pl:* **-ta** [tə] o **-tums**) substrato
substructure [ˈsʌbˌstrʌktʃər] o [sʌbˈstrʌktʃər] *s* subestructura
subsume [səbˈsum] o [səbˈsjum] *va* subsumir
subsumption [səbˈsʌmpʃən] *s* subsumpción
subtenancy [sʌbˈtɛnənsɪ] *s* (*pl:* **-cies**) subarriendo
subtenant [sʌbˈtɛnənt] *s* subarrendatario
subtend [səbˈtɛnd] *va* (geom. & bot.) subtender
subterfuge [ˈsʌbtərfjudʒ] *s* subterfugio, escapatoria
subterranean [ˌsʌbtəˈrenɪən] *adj* subterráneo; *s* subterráneo (*lugar o espacio*); habitante subterráneo
subterraneous [ˌsʌbtəˈrenɪəs] *adj* subterráneo
subtile [ˈsʌtəl] o [ˈsʌbtɪl] *adj* sutil; astuto
subtility [sʌbˈtɪlɪtɪ] o **subtilty** [ˈsʌtəltɪ] o [ˈsʌbtɪltɪ] *s* (*pl:* **-ties**) sutileza o sutilidad
subtitle [ˈsʌbˌtaɪtəl] *s* subtítulo; *va* subtitular
subtle [ˈsʌtəl] *adj* sutil; astuto; insidioso
subtlety [ˈsʌtəltɪ] *s* (*pl:* **-ties**) sutileza o sutilidad; astucia; distinción sutil
subtly [ˈsʌtlɪ] *adv* sutilmente; astutamente; insidiosamente
subtract [səbˈtrækt] *va & vn* substraer o sustraer
subtraction [səbˈtrækʃən] *s* substracción o sustracción
subtrahend [ˈsʌbtrəhɛnd] *s* (math.) substraendo
subtreasury [ˈsʌbˌtrɛʒərɪ] o [sʌbˈtrɛʒərɪ] *s* (*pl:* **-ies**) subtesorería
subtropical [sʌbˈtrɑpɪkəl] *adj* subtropical
subtropics [ˈsʌbˌtrɑpɪks] o [sʌbˈtrɑpɪks] *spl* subtrópicos
suburb [ˈsʌbʌrb] *s* suburbio, arrabal; **the suburbs** las afueras, los alrededores, los barrios externos
suburban [səˈbʌrbən] *adj & s* suburbano
suburbanite [səˈbʌrbənaɪt] *s* suburbano
subvention [sʌbˈvɛnʃən] *s* subvención
subversion [sʌbˈvʌrʒən] o [sʌbˈvʌrʃən] *s* subversión
subversive [sʌbˈvʌrsɪv] *adj* subversivo; *s* subversor
subvert [sʌbˈvʌrt] *va* subvertir
subway [ˈsʌbˌwe] *s* galería subterránea; paso subterráneo; ferrocarril subterráneo, metro
succeed [səkˈsid] *va* suceder (*a una persona o cosa*), p.ej., **autumn succeeds summer** el otoño sucede al verano; *vn* tener buen éxito, salir bien; **to succeed in** tener éxito en, salir bien en; **to succeed in** + *ger* conseguir o lograr + *inf;* **to succeed to** suceder a (*p.ej., la corona*)
succeeding [səkˈsidɪŋ] *adj* subsiguiente; sucesor
success [səkˈsɛs] *s* buen éxito; éxito, resultado; persona o cosa que tiene buen éxito; **to make a success of** tener éxito en
successful [səkˈsɛsfəl] *adj* próspero, feliz; logrado; acertado; **to be successful** tener buen éxito
succession [səkˈsɛʃən] *s* sucesión; **in succession** uno tras otro, seguidos
successive [səkˈsɛsɪv] *adj* sucesivo
successor [səkˈsɛsər] *s* sucesor
succinct [səkˈsɪŋkt] *adj* sucinto
succinic [səkˈsɪnɪk] *adj* succínico
succor [ˈsʌkər] *s* socorro; *va* socorrer
succory [ˈsʌkərɪ] *s* var. de **chicory**
succotash [ˈsʌkətæʃ] *s* guiso de maíz tierno y habas
succubus [ˈsʌkjəbəs] *s* (*pl:* **-bi** [baɪ] o **-buses**) súcubo, demonio súcubo
succulence [ˈsʌkjələns] *s* suculencia
succulency [ˈsʌkjələnsɪ] *s* (*pl:* **-cies**) var. de **succulence**
succulent [ˈsʌkjələnt] *adj* suculento
succumb [səˈkʌm] *vn* sucumbir
succuss [səˈkʌs] *va* sacudir; (med.) sacudir (*a un paciente para descubrir la presencia de un líquido*)
succussation [ˌsʌkəˈseʃən] o **succussion** [səˈkʌʃən] *s* sucusión
such [sʌtʃ] *adj indef & pron indef* tal, semejante; **as such** como tal; **one such** un tal; **such a** tal, semejante; **such a** + *adj* un tan + *adj;* **such and such** tal o cual; **such as** quienes, los que
suchlike [ˈsʌtʃˌlaɪk] *adj indef* tal, semejante; *pron indef* tales personas, tales cosas
suck [sʌk] *s* chupada; mamada; *va & vn* chupar; aspirar (*el aire*); mamar
sucker [ˈsʌkər] *s* chupador; mamón, mamantón; (bot.) serpollo, pimpollo; (bot.) mamón, chupón; (ichth.) catostomo; (mach.) chupón (*émbolo*); (mach.) válvula de bomba; (mach.) caño de bomba; (zool.) ventosa; (coll.) primo, bobo; *va* (bot.) cortar los chupones de; *vn* (bot.) echar chupones
suckle [ˈsʌkəl] *va* lactar; criar, educar; *vn* lactar
suckling [ˈsʌklɪŋ] *adj & s* mamón, mamantón
sucrose [ˈsukros] o [ˈsjukros] *s* (chem.) sacarosa
suction [ˈsʌkʃən] *s* succión; *adj* aspirante
suction cup *s* copa de succión
suction pump *s* bomba aspirante
suctorial [sʌkˈtorɪəl] *adj* suctorio
Sudan [suˈdæn] *s* Sudán
Sudanese [ˌsudəˈniz] *adj* sudanés; *s* (*pl:* **-nese**) sudanés
Sudan grass (bot.) hierba del Sudán, sorgo del Sudán
sudatorium [ˌsudəˈtorɪəm] o [ˌsjudəˈtorɪəm] *s* (*pl:* **-a** [ə]) sudadero; (hist.) sudatorio

sudatory [ˈsudəˌtorɪ] o [ˈsjudəˌtorɪ] *adj* sudatorio
sudden [ˈsʌdən] *adj* súbito, repentino; **all of a sudden** de repente
suddenness [ˈsʌdənnɪs] *s* rapidez, precipitación, brusquedad
Sudeten [suˈdetən] *spl* sudetas o sudetes (*naturales*); montes Sudetes
Sudetenland [suˈdetənˌlænd] *s* región de los Sudetes
sudoriferous [ˌsudəˈrɪfərəs] o [ˌsjudəˈrɪfərəs] *adj* sudorífero
sudorific [ˌsudəˈrɪfɪk] o [ˌsjudəˈrɪfɪk] *adj & s* sudorífico
sudoriparous [ˌsudəˈrɪpərəs] o [ˌsjudəˈrɪpərəs] *adj* (anat.) sudoríparo
suds [sʌdz] *spl* jabonaduras; (slang) espuma, cerveza
sudsy [ˈsʌdzɪ] *adj* espumoso, jabonoso
sue [su] o [sju] *va* demandar; pedir; (law) procesar; **to sue out** (law) rogar y obtener; *vn* (law) poner pleito, entablar juicio; **to sue for damages** demandar por daños y perjuicios; **to sue for peace** pedir la paz
suede [swed] *s* suecia, gamuza, ante
suet [ˈsuɪt] o [ˈsjuɪt] *s* sebo
Suetonius [swɪˈtonɪəs] *s* Suetonio
suety [ˈsuɪtɪ] o [ˈsjuɪtɪ] *adj* seboso; sebáceo
Suevian [ˈswivɪən] *adj & s* suevo
Suez Canal [suˈɛz] o [ˈsuɛz] *s* canal de Suez
suffer [ˈsʌfər] *va* sufrir, padecer; *vn* sufrir, padecer; **to suffer from** padecer de, adolecer de; (fig.) adolecer de
sufferable [ˈsʌfərəbəl] *adj* sufrible
sufferance [ˈsʌfərəns] *s* sufrimiento, tolerancia; paciencia; **on sufferance** por tolerancia
sufferer [ˈsʌfərər] *s* sufridor; doliente; víctima
suffering [ˈsʌfərɪŋ] *s* sufrimiento, dolencia; *adj* doliente
suffice [səˈfaɪs] *va* satisfacer; ser suficiente a o para; *vn* bastar, ser suficiente
sufficiency [səˈfɪʃənsɪ] *s* (*pl:* **-cies**) suficiencia
sufficient [səˈfɪʃənt] *adj* suficiente
suffix [ˈsʌfɪks] *s* (gram.) sufijo; [səˈfɪks] *va* añadir como sufijo
suffocate [ˈsʌfəket] *va* sofocar; *vn* sofocarse
suffocation [ˌsʌfəˈkeʃən] *s* sofocación
suffocative [ˈsʌfəˌketɪv] *adj* sofocante
suffragan [ˈsʌfrəgən] *adj* sufragáneo; *s* obispo sufragáneo
suffragan bishop *s* obispo sufragáneo
suffrage [ˈsʌfrɪdʒ] *s* sufragio; aprobación, voto favorable; (eccl.) sufragio
suffragette [ˌsʌfrəˈdʒɛt] *s* (coll.) sufragista (*mujer*)
suffragist [ˈsʌfrədʒɪst] *s* sufragista
suffuse [səˈfjuz] *va* difundir, bañar, llenar
suffusion [səˈfjuʒən] *s* difusión, baño; (path.) sufusión
Sufi [ˈsufɪ] *s* (*pl:* **-fis** [fɪz]) sufí
Sufism [ˈsufɪzəm] *s* sufismo
sugar [ˈʃugər] *s* azúcar; *adj* azucarero; *va* azucarar; (fig.) azucarar; *vn* formar azúcar; **to sugar off** hacer el azúcar de arce; (slang) salirse a hurtadillas
sugar beet *s* (bot.) remolacha azucarera
sugar bowl *s* azucarero
sugarbush [ˈʃugərˌbuʃ] *s* bosquecillo de arces del azúcar
sugar cane *s* (bot.) caña de azúcar
sugar-coat [ˈʃugərˌkot] *va* azucarar; endulzar, dorar (*lo desagradable*)
sugar-coating [ˈʃugərˌkotɪŋ] *s* capa de azúcar, garapiña; dorado (*de lo desagradable*)
sugar daddy *s* (slang) viejo verde que prodiga regalos a las chicas
sugar loaf *s* pan de azúcar (*cono de azúcar; sombrero; colina*)
sugar-loaf [ˈʃugərˌlof] *adj* de forma de pan de azúcar, cónico
sugar maple *s* (bot.) arce del azúcar
sugar mill *s* ingenio de azúcar
sugar of lead [lɛd] *s* (chem.) azúcar de plomo
sugar of milk *s* azúcar de leche
sugarplum [ˈʃugərˌplʌm] *s* confite, dulce
sugar tongs *spl* tenacillas (*para coger terrones de azúcar*)
sugary [ˈʃugərɪ] *adj* azucarado
suggest [səgˈdʒɛst] *va* sugerir; sugestionar (*por hipnosis*); **to suggest** + *ger* sugerir + *inf*
suggestible [səgˈdʒɛstɪbəl] *adj* sugerible (*cosa*); sugestionable (*persona*)
suggestion [səgˈdʒɛstʃən] *s* sugerencia; (psychol.) sugestión; sombra, traza ligera
suggestive [səgˈdʒɛstɪv] *adj* sugestivo; sicalíptico, sugestivo de lo indecente
suicidal [ˌsuɪˈsaɪdəl] o [ˌsjuɪˈsaɪdəl] *adj* suicida
suicide [ˈsuɪsaɪd] o [ˈsjuɪsaɪd] *s* suicidio (*acción*); suicida (*persona*); **to commit suicide** suicidarse
suint [ˈsuɪnt] o [swɪnt] *s* suarda (*grasa de la lana*)
suit [sut] o [sjut] *s* juego (*de cosas relacionadas entre sí*); traje, terno; traje sastre (*de mujer*); súplica, petición; cortejo, galanteo; palo (*de la baraja*); (law) pleito, proceso; **to follow suit** servir del palo; seguir el ejemplo de otro, seguir la corriente; **suit of armor** armadura completa; *va* adaptar, ajustar, acomodar; adaptarse a; proveer de traje o trajes; sentar, ir o venir bien a; favorecer; satisfacer; **to suit oneself** hacer (*uno*) lo que guste; *vn* convenir, ser a propósito
suitability [ˌsutəˈbɪlɪtɪ] o [ˌsjutəˈbɪlɪtɪ] *s* conveniencia, adaptabilidad
suitable [ˈsutəbəl] o [ˈsjutəbəl] *adj* conveniente, apropiado, satisfactorio, adecuado
suitably [ˈsutəblɪ] o [ˈsjutəblɪ] *adv* convenientemente, apropiadamente, a propósito
suitcase [ˈsutˌkes] o [ˈsjutˌkes] *s* maleta, valija
suite [swit] *s* séquito, comitiva; juego (*de cosas relacionadas entre sí*); serie; crujía (*de piezas*); habitación salón (*en un hotel*); (mus.) suite
suiting [ˈsutɪŋ] o [ˈsjutɪŋ] *s* tela para trajes, corte de traje
suit of clothes *s* traje completo (*de hombre*)
suitor [ˈsutər] o [ˈsjutər] *s* suplicante; galán, cortejador, enamorado; (law) demandante, parte actora
sulcus [ˈsʌlkəs] *s* (*pl:* **-ci** [saɪ]) surco; (anat.) cisura
Suleiman [ˌsuleˈmɑn] *s* var. de **Solyman**
sulfadiazine [ˌsʌlfəˈdaɪəzin] o [ˌsʌlfəˈdaɪəzɪn] *s* (pharm.) sulfadiacina
sulfa drugs [ˈsʌlfə] *spl* (pharm.) medicamentos sulfas
sulfanilamide [ˌsʌlfəˈnɪləmaɪd] o [ˌsʌlfəˈnɪləmɪd] *s* (pharm.) sulfanilamida
sulfapyridine [ˌsʌlfəˈpɪrɪdin] o [ˌsʌlfəˈpɪrɪdɪn] *s* (pharm.) sulfapiridina
sulfarsphenamine [ˌsʌlfɑrsfɛnəˈmin] o [ˌsʌlfɑrsfəˈnæmɪn] *s* (pharm.) sulfarsfenamina
sulfas [ˈsʌlfəz] *spl* (pharm.) sulfas
sulfate [ˈsʌlfet] *s* (chem.) sulfato; *va* sulfatar; (elec.) sulfatar
sulfathiazole [ˌsʌlfəˈθaɪəzol] *s* (pharm.) sulfatiazol
sulfation [sʌlˈfeʃən] *s* sulfatación; (elec.) sulfatación
sulfhydric acid [sʌlfˈhaɪdrɪk] *s* (chem.) ácido sulfhídrico
sulfid [ˈsʌlfɪd] o **sulfide** [ˈsʌlfaɪd] o [ˈsʌlfɪd] *s* (chem.) sulfuro
sulfite [ˈsʌlfaɪt] *s* (chem.) sulfito
sulfonal [ˈsʌlfənæl] o [ˌsʌlfəˈnæl] *s* (pharm.) sulfonal
sulfonamide [sʌlˈfɑnəmaɪd] o [sʌlˈfɑnəmɪd] *s* (chem.) sulfonamida
sulfur [ˈsʌlfər] *s* (chem.) azufre; véase **sulphur**
sulfurate [ˈsʌlfjəret] o [ˈsʌlfəret] *va* sulfurar (*combinar con el azufre*); azufrar (*echar azufre sobre; sahumar con azufre*)
sulfuration [ˌsʌlfjəˈreʃən] o [ˌsʌlfəˈreʃən] *s* sulfuración; azuframiento
sulfur dioxide *s* (chem.) dióxido de azufre
sulfuret [ˈsʌlfjərɪt] *s* (chem.) sulfuro; [ˈsʌlfjərɛt] (*pret & pp:* **-reted** o **-retted;** *ger:* **-reting** o **-retting**) *va* azufrar; sulfurar
sulfuric [sʌlˈfjurɪk] *adj* sulfúrico, sulfúreo; (chem.) sulfúrico
sulfuric acid *s* (chem.) ácido sulfúrico
sulfur mine *s* azufrera
sulfurous [ˈsʌlfərəs] *adj* sulfuroso, sulfúreo; [ˈsʌlfərəs] o [sʌlˈfjurəs] *adj* (chem.) sulfuroso
sulfurous acid *s* (chem.) ácido sulfuroso

sulk [sʌlk] *s* enfurruñamiento, murria; *vn* enfurruñarse
sulky [ˈsʌlkɪ] *adj* (*comp:* **-ier;** *super:* **-iest**) enfurruñado, murrio, resentido; *s* (*pl:* **-ies**) coche de dos ruedas y un solo asiento
Sulla [ˈsʌlə] *s* Sila (*general romano*)
sulla clover [ˈsʌlə] o [ˈsʊlə] *s* (bot.) zulla
sullen [ˈsʌlən] *adj* hosco, malhumorado, taciturno, resentido, triste
sullenness [ˈsʌlənnɪs] *s* hosquedad, mal humor, resentimiento, tristeza
sully [ˈsʌlɪ] *s* (*pl:* **-lies**) mancha, tacha; (*pret & pp:* **-lied**) *va* manchar, empañar
sulphadiazine [ˌsʌlfəˈdaɪəzin] o [ˌsʌlfəˈdaɪəzɪn] *s* var. de **sulfadiazine**
sulpha drugs [ˈsʌlfə] *spl* var. de **sulfa drugs**
sulphanilamide [ˌsʌlfəˈnɪləmaɪd] o [ˌsʌlfəˈnɪləmɪd] *s* var. de **sulfanilamide**
sulphapyridine [ˌsʌlfəˈpɪrɪdin] o [ˌsʌlfəˈpɪrɪdɪn] *s* var. de **sulfapyridine**
sulphas [ˈsʌlfəz] *spl* var. de **sulfas**
sulphate [ˈsʌlfet] *s & va* var. de **sulfate**
sulphathiazole [ˌsʌlfəˈθaɪəzol] *s* var. de **sulfathiazole**
sulphid [ˈsʌlfɪd] o **sulphide** [ˈsʌlfaɪd] o [ˈsʌlfɪd] *s* var. de **sulfid** o **sulfide**
sulphite [ˈsʌlfaɪt] *s* var. de **sulfite**
sulphur [ˈsʌlfər] *s* (chem.) azufre; color de azufre; *adj* azufrado; *va* azufrar
sulphurate [ˈsʌlfjəret] o [ˈsʌlfəret] *va* var. de **sulfurate**
sulphureous [sʌlˈfjʊrɪəs] *adj* sulfúreo
sulphuret [ˈsʌlfjərɪt] *s* var. de **sulfuret;** [ˈsʌlfjərɛt] (*pret & pp:* **-reted** o **-retted;** *ger:* **-reting** o **-retting**) *va* var. de **sulfuret**
sulphuric [sʌlˈfjʊrɪk] *adj* var. de **sulfuric**
sulphurize [ˈsʌlfjəraɪz] *va* azufrar
sulphurous [ˈsʌlfərəs] *adj* sulfuroso, sulfúreo; infernal; ardiente, abrasador; [ˈsʌlfərəs] o [sʌlˈfjʊrəs] *adj* (chem.) sulfuroso
sulphury [ˈsʌlfərɪ] o [ˈsʌlfrɪ] *adj* sulfúreo, azufroso
sulphydric acid [sʌlˈfaɪdrɪk] *s* (chem.) ácido sulfhídrico
sultan [ˈsʌltən] *s* sultán
sultana [sʌlˈtænə] o [sʌlˈtɑnə] *s* sultana; (orn.) calamón; uva sultanina; pasa sultanina
sultanate [ˈsʌltənet] *s* sultanato
sultaness [ˈsʌltənɪs] o [sʌlˈtɑnɪs] *s* sultana
sultanic [sʌlˈtænɪk] *adj* sultánico
sultry [ˈsʌltrɪ] *adj* (*comp:* **-trier;** *super:* **-triest**) bochornoso
Sulu [ˈsulu] *s* joloano
Suluan [suˈluən] *adj & s* joloano
Sulu Archipelago *s* archipiélago de Sulú o Joló
sum [sʌm] *s* suma; (coll.) problema de aritmética; (*pret & pp:* **summed;** *ger:* **summing**) *va* sumar; **to sum up** sumar, resumir, compendiar; *vn* sumar; **to sum to** ascender a
sumac o **sumach** [ˈʃumæk] o [ˈsumæk] *s* (bot.) zumaque; hojas de zumaque secas
Sumatran [suˈmɑtrən] *adj & s* sumatrino
Sumerian [suˈmɪrɪən] o [sjuˈmɪrɪən] *adj & s* sumerio
summarization [ˌsʌmərɪˈzeʃən] *s* resumen, recapitulación
summarize [ˈsʌməraɪz] *va* resumir, recapitular
summary [ˈsʌmərɪ] *adj* sumario; *s* (*pl:* **-ries**) sumario, resumen
summation [sʌmˈeʃən] *s* adición; recapitulación; suma, total
summer [ˈsʌmər] *s* verano, estío; viga maestra; sotabanco (*piedra*); dintel; abril (*es decir, año*), p.ej., **to have seen fifteen summers** tener quince abriles; *adj* veraniego, estival; *va* preservar o mantener durante el verano; *vn* veranear
summer camp *s* campamento de veraneo
summer colony *s* colonia veraniega
summerhouse [ˈsʌmərˌhaʊs] *s* cenador, glorieta
summer house *s* casa para veranear, casa de verano
summering [ˈsʌmərɪŋ] *adj* veraneante; *s* veraneo
summer resort *s* lugar de veraneo, estación de verano
summersault [ˈsʌmərˌsɔlt] *s & vn* var. de **somersault**
summer sausage *s* salchicha cruda seca, salchicha cruda ahumada
summer savory *s* (bot.) ajedrea de jardín
summer school *s* escuela de verano
summer solstice *s* (astr.) solsticio de verano
summer squash *s* calabaza (*variedad de Cucurbita Pepo que se come en el verano*)
summertime [ˈsʌmərˌtaɪm] *s* verano, estío
summer wheat *s* trigo de primavera
summery [ˈsʌmərɪ] *adj* veraniego, estival
summing up *s* recapitulación, resumen
summit [ˈsʌmɪt] *s* cima, cumbre; sumidad
summit conference *s* conferencia en la cumbre
summitry [ˈsʌmɪtrɪ] *s* reuniones en la cumbre, esfuerzo por resolver los problemas internacionales mediante conferencias en la cumbre
summon [ˈsʌmən] *va* llamar, convocar; (law) emplazar, citar; evocar
summoner [ˈsʌmənər] *s* (law) emplazador; (law) ujier
summons [ˈsʌmənz] *s* (*pl:* **-monses**) orden, señal; (law) emplazamiento, citación; *va* (coll.) emplazar, citar
sump [sʌmp] *s* sumidero; (mach.) colector de aceite
sumpter [ˈsʌmptər] *s* acémila
sumptuary [ˈsʌmptʃʊˌɛrɪ] *adj* suntuario
sumptuary laws *spl* leyes suntuarias
sumptuous [ˈsʌmptʃʊəs] *adj* suntuoso
Sun. abr. de **Sunday**
sun [sʌn] *s* sol; año solar; **from sun to sun** de sol a sol; **to have a place in the sun** ocupar su puesto en el mundo; **under the sun** debajo del sol, en este mundo; (*pret & pp:* **sunned;** *ger:* **sunning**) *va* asolear; *vn* asolearse
sun bath *s* baño de sol
sunbeam *s* [ˈsʌnˌbim] *s* rayo de sol
sunbird [ˈsʌnˌbʌrd] *s* (orn.) suimanga; (orn.) pájaro sol, tigana (*Eurypyga helias*)
sun bittern *s* (orn.) tigana, pájaro sol
sunbonnet [ˈsʌnˌbɑnɪt] *s* papalina
sunburn [ˈsʌnˌbʌrn] *s* quemadura de sol, solanera; (*pret & pp:* **-burned** o **-burnt**) *va* quemar al sol, tostar al sol; *vn* quemarse al sol, tostarse al sol
sunburnt [ˈsʌnˌbʌrnt] *adj* requemado, bronceado
sunburst [ˈsʌnˌbʌrst] *s* resplandor repentino del sol en medio de las nubes; broche en forma de sol
sundae [ˈsʌndɪ] *s* helado con frutas, jarabes o nueces
Sunda Islands [ˈsʌndə] *spl* islas de la Sonda
sun dance *s* danza del sol
Sunda Strait [ˈsʌndə] *s* estrecho de la Sonda
Sunday [ˈsʌndɪ] *s* domingo; *adj* dominical; dominguero (*que se usa en domingo*)
Sunday best *s* (coll.) trapos de cristianar, ropa dominguera
Sunday law *s* ley del descanso dominical
Sunday's child *s* niño nacido de pies, niño mimado de la fortuna
Sunday school *s* escuela dominical, doctrina dominical
sunder [ˈsʌndər] *s* separación; **in sunder** en dos, en partes; *va* separar; romper; *vn* separarse; romperse
sundew [ˈsʌnˌdju] o [ˈsʌnˌdu] *s* (bot.) rocío de sol, rosolí, drosera
sundial [ˈsʌnˌdaɪəl] *s* reloj de sol, cuadrante solar
sundog [ˈsʌnˌdɔg] o [ˈsʌnˌdɑg] *s* parhelio; arco iris incompleto
sundown [ˈsʌnˌdaʊn] *s* puesta del sol
sun-dried [ˈsʌnˌdraɪd] *adj* secado al sol
sundries [ˈsʌndrɪz] *spl* artículos diversos
sundry [ˈsʌndrɪ] *adj* varios, diversos
sunfast [ˈsʌnˌfæst] o [ˈsʌnˌfɑst] *adj* inalterable al sol
sunfish [ˈsʌnˌfɪʃ] *s* (ichth.) luna, pez luna; (ichth.) pomotio
sunflower [ˈsʌnˌflaʊər] *s* (bot.) girasol
sung [sʌŋ] *pret & pp de* **sing**
sunglasses [ˈsʌnˌglæsɪz] o [ˈsʌnˌglɑsɪz] *spl* gafas para sol, gafas de sol
sunglow [ˈsʌnˌglo] *s* arrebol
sun god *s* dios del sol, divinidad solar
sunk [sʌŋk] *pret & pp de* **sink**

sunken ['sʌŋkən] *adj* hundido, sumido
sun lamp *s* (med.) lámpara de rayos ultravioletas, lámpara de cuarzo
sunless ['sʌnlɪs] *adj* nublado, sin sol
sunlight ['sʌn,laɪt] *s* luz del sol
sunlit ['sʌn,lɪt] *adj* iluminado por el sol
sunn [sʌn] *s* var. de **sunn hemp**
Sunna o **Sunnah** ['sʊnə] *s* zuna
sunn hemp *s* (bot.) cáñamo de Bengala
sunny ['sʌnɪ] *adj* (*comp:* **-nier;** *super:* **-niest**) de sol; asoleado, bañado de sol; brillante, resplandeciente; alegre, risueño; **to be sunny** hacer sol
sunny side *s* sol, lado del sol; (fig.) lado bueno, lado favorable
sun parlor *s* solana, mirador
sun porch *s* solana
sunproof ['sʌn,pruf] *adj* a prueba de sol
sunrise ['sʌn,raɪz] *s* salida del sol, orto del sol
sunroom ['sʌn,rum] o ['sʌn,rʊm] *s* solana
sunset ['sʌn,sɛt] *s* puesta del sol, ocaso del sol
sunshade ['sʌn,ʃed] *s* quitasol, sombrilla; toldo, marquesina; visera contra el sol
sunshine ['sʌn,ʃaɪn] *s* día, claridad del sol; alegría, contento; **in the sunshine** al sol
sunshine roof *s* (aut.) techo corredizo
sunshiny ['sʌn,ʃaɪnɪ] *adj* (*comp:* **-ier;** *super:* **-iest**) lleno de sol; brillante, resplandeciente; alegre, risueño
sunspot ['sʌn,spɑt] *s* mancha solar, mácula solar
sun spurge *s* (bot.) lechetrezna
sunstroke ['sʌn,strok] *s* (path.) insolación
sun-up ['sʌn,ʌp] *s* salida o nacimiento del sol
sunward ['sʌnwərd] *adj* que va hacia el sol; *adv* hacia el sol
sunwards ['sʌnwərdz] *adv* hacia el sol
sunwise ['sʌn,waɪz] *adj & adv* con el sol (*en su aparente movimiento diurno*)
sup. abr. de **superior, superlative, supine** y **supplement**
sup [sʌp] *s* sorbo; (*pret & pp:* **supped;** *ger:* **supping**) *va* sorber; dar de cenar a; *vn* cenar
super ['supər] o ['sjupər] *s* (coll.) figurante, comparsa; (coll.) superintendente; *adj* (coll.) súper, archi (*excelente, muy bueno*)
superable ['supərəbəl] o ['sjupərəbəl] *adj* superable
superabound [,supərə'baʊnd] o [,sjupərə'baʊnd] *vn* sobreabundar o superabundar
superabundance [,supərə'bʌndəns] o [,sjupərə'bʌndəns] *s* sobreabundancia o superabundancia
superabundant [,supərə'bʌndənt] o [,sjupərə'bʌndənt] *adj* sobreabundante o superabundante
superadd [,supər'æd] o [,sjupər'æd] *va* sobreañadir
superannuate [,supər'ænjʊet] o [,sjupər'ænjʊet] *va* inhabilitar; jubilar (*por motivo de ancianidad o enfermedad*); *vn* inhabilitarse; jubilarse
superannuated [,supər'ænjʊ,etɪd] o [,sjupər'ænjʊ,etɪd] *adj* inhabilitado; jubilado; añejo, anticuado, fuera de moda
superannuation [,supər,ænjʊ'eʃən] o [,sjupər,ænjʊ'eʃən] *s* inhabilitación; jubilación
superb [su'pʌrb] o [sju'pʌrb] *adj* soberbio, estupendo, magnífico
superbomb ['supər,bɑm] o ['sjupər,bɑm] superbomba
supercargo ['supər,kɑrgo] o ['sjupər,kɑrgo] *s* (*pl:* **-goes** o **-gos**) (naut.) sobrecargo
supercharge [,supər'tʃɑrdʒ] o [,sjupər'tʃɑrdʒ] *va* sobrealimentar
supercharger ['supər,tʃɑrdʒər] o ['sjupər,tʃɑrdʒər] *s* (mach.) compresor de sobrealimentación, superalimentador
superciliary [,supər'sɪlɪ,ɛrɪ] o [,sjupər'sɪlɪ,ɛrɪ] *adj* (anat.) superciliar
supercilious [,supər'sɪlɪəs] o [,sjupər'sɪlɪəs] *adj* arrogante, altanero, desdeñoso
supercolumniation *s* [,supərkə,lʌmnɪ'eʃən] o [,sjupərkə,lʌmnɪ'eʃən] *s* (arch.) superposición de columnas
superconductivity [,supər,kɑndʌk'tɪvɪtɪ] o [,sjupər,kɑndʌk'tɪvɪtɪ] *s* superconductividad
superconductor [,supərkən'dʌktər] o [,sjupərkən'dʌktər] *s* (elec.) superconductor
superdominant [,supər'dɑmɪnənt] o [,sjupər'dɑmɪnənt] *s* (mus.) superdominante
superego [,supər'igo], [,supər'ɛgo], [,sjupər'igo] o [,sjupər'ɛgo] *s* (psychoanal.) super-yo
superelevation [,supər,ɛlɪ'veʃən] o [,sjupər,ɛlɪ'veʃən] *s* (rail.) peralte
supereminent [,supər'ɛmɪnənt] o [,sjupər'ɛmɪnənt] *adj* supereminente
supererogation [,supər,ɛro'geʃən] o [,sjupər,ɛro'geʃən] *s* supererogación
supererogatory [,supərɪ'rɑgə,torɪ] o [,sjupərɪ'rɑgə,torɪ] *adj* supererogatorio
superfetation [,supərfɪ'teʃən] o [,sjupərfɪ'teʃən] *s* superfetación
superficial [,supər'fɪʃəl] o [,sjupər'fɪʃəl] *adj* superficial
superficiality [,supər,fɪʃɪ'ælɪtɪ] o [,sjupər,fɪʃɪ'ælɪtɪ] *s* (*pl:* **-ties**) superficialidad
superficiary [,supər'fɪʃɪ,ɛrɪ] o [,sjupər'fɪʃɪ,ɛrɪ] *adj* (law) superficiaro
superficies [,supər'fɪʃiiz] o [,sjupər'fɪʃiiz] *s* (*pl:* **-cies**) superficie
superfine ['supər,faɪn] o ['sjupər,faɪn] *adj* superfino
superfluity [,supər'fluɪtɪ] o [,sjupər'fluɪtɪ] *s* (*pl:* **-ties**) superfluidad
superfluous [sʊ'pʌrfluəs] o [sjʊ'pʌrfluəs] *adj* superfluo
superfort ['supər,fɔrt] o ['sjupər,fɔrt] o **superfortress** ['supər,fɔrtrɪs] o ['sjupər,fɔrtrɪs] *s* (aer.) superfortaleza
superheat [,supər'hit] o [,sjupər'hit] *va* recalentar, sobrecalentar
superheater [,supər'hitər] o [,sjupər'hitər] *s* recalentador de vapor
superheterodyne [,supər'hɛtərədaɪn] o [,sjupər'hɛtərədaɪn] *adj & s* (rad.) superheterodino
superhighway [,supər'haɪ,we] o [,sjupər'haɪ,we] *s* supercarretera
superhuman [,supər'hjumən] o [,sjupər'hjumən] *adj* sobrehumano
superhumeral [,supər'hjumərəl] o [,sjupər'hjumərəl] *s* (eccl.) superhumeral
superimpose [,supərɪm'poz] o [,sjupərɪm'poz] *va* sobreponer
superincumbent [,supərɪn'kʌmbənt] o [,sjupərɪn'kʌmbənt] *adj* superyacente
superinduce [,supərɪn'djus] o [,sjupərɪn'djus] *va* sobreañadir
superinduction [,supərɪn'dʌkʃən] o [,sjupərɪn'dʌkʃən] *s* sobreañadidura
superintend [,supərɪn'tɛnd] o [,sjupərɪn'tɛnd] *va* superentender
superintendence [,supərɪn'tɛndəns] o [,sjupərɪn'tɛndəns] *s* superintendencia
superintendency [,supərɪn'tɛndənsɪ] o [,sjupərɪn'tɛndənsɪ] *s* (*pl:* **-cies**) var. de **superintendence**
superintendent [,supərɪn'tɛndənt] o [,sjupərɪn'tɛndənt] *s* superintendente
superior [sə'pɪrɪər] o [sʊ'pɪrɪər] *adj* superior; sereno, indiferente; arrogante; *s* superior; superiora
superioress [sə'pɪrɪərɪs] o [sʊ'pɪrɪərɪs] *s* superiora
superiority [sə,pɪrɪ'ɑrɪtɪ] o [sʊ,pɪrɪ'ɑrɪtɪ] *s* superioridad; serenidad, indiferencia; arrogancia
superl. abr. de **superlative**
superlative [sə'pʌrlətɪv] o [sʊ'pʌrlətɪv] *adj* superlativo; (gram.) superlativo; *s* (gram.) superlativo; **to talk in superlatives** exagerar
superman ['supər,mæn] o ['sjupər,mæn] *s* (*pl:* **-men**) sobrehombre, superhombre
supermarket ['supər,mɑrkɪt] o ['sjupər,mɑrkɪt] *s* supermercado
supermundane [,supər'mʌnden] o [,sjupər'mʌnden] *adj* sobremundano o supramundano
supernal [su'pʌrnəl] o [sju'pʌrnəl] *adj* superno, excelso, celestial
supernatant [,supər'netənt] o [,sjupər'netənt] *adj* sobrenadante
supernatural [,supər'nætʃərəl] o [,sjupər'nætʃərəl] *adj* sobrenatural
supernaturalism [,supər'nætʃərəlɪzəm] o [,sjupər'nætʃərəlɪzəm] *s* sobrenaturalismo
supernumerary [,supər'numə,rɛrɪ] o [,sjupər'njumə,rɛrɪ] *adj* supernumerario; *s* (*pl:* **-ies**) supernumerario; (theat.) figurante, comparsa

superorganic [ˌsupərɔrˈgænɪk] o [ˌsjupərɔrˈgænɪk] *adj* sobreorgánico
superphosphate [ˌsupərˈfɑsfet] o [ˌsjupərˈfɑsfet] *s* (chem. & agr.) superfosfato
superpose [ˌsupərˈpoz] o [ˌsjupərˈpoz] *va* sobreponer, superponer
superposition [ˌsupərpəˈzɪʃən] o [ˌsjupərpəˈzɪʃən] *s* superposición; (geom.) superposición
superpower [ˈsupərˌpaʊər] o [ˈsjupərˌpaʊər] *s* (dipl. & elec.) superpotencia
superproduction [ˌsupərprəˈdʌkʃən] o [ˌsjupərprəˈdʌkʃən] *s* superproducción
superregeneration [ˌsupərrɪˌdʒɛnəˈreʃən] o [ˌsjupərrɪˌdʒɛnəˈreʃən] *s* (rad.) superreacción, superregeneración
superregenerative [ˌsupərrɪˈdʒɛnəˌretɪv] o [ˌsjupərrɪˈdʒɛnəˌretɪv] *adj* (rad.) superregenerativo
supersaturate [ˌsupərˈsætʃəret] o [ˌsjupərˈsætʃəret] *va* sobresaturar
supersaturation [ˌsupərˌsætʃəˈreʃən] o [ˌsjupərˌsætʃəˈreʃən] *s* (chem.) sobresaturación
superscribe [ˌsupərˈskraɪb] o [ˌsjupərˈskraɪb] *va* sobrescribir
superscript [ˈsupərskrɪpt] o [ˈsjupərskrɪpt] *adj* sobrescrito; *s* (math.) índice sobrescrito
superscription [ˌsupərˈskrɪpʃən] o [ˌsjupərˈskrɪpʃən] *s* sobrescrito; (pharm.) superscripción
supersede [ˌsupərˈsid] o [ˌsjupərˈsid] *va* reemplazar, substituir; desalojar; (law) sobreseer
supersensible [ˌsupərˈsɛnsɪbəl] o [ˌsjupərˈsɛnsɪbəl] *adj* suprasensible
supersensitive [ˌsupərˈsɛnsɪtɪv] o [ˌsjupərˈsɛnsɪtɪv] *adj* supersensible
supersonic [ˌsupərˈsɑnɪk] o [ˌsjupərˈsɑnɪk] *adj* supersónico; **supersonics** *ssg* supersónica
superspy [ˈsupərˌspaɪ] o [ˈsjupərˌspaɪ] *s* (*pl:* **-spies**) superespía
superstate [ˈsupərˌstet] o [ˈsjupərˌstet] *s* superestado
superstition [ˌsupərˈstɪʃən] o [ˌsjupərˈstɪʃən] *s* superstición
superstitious [ˌsupərˈstɪʃəs] o [ˌsjupərˈstɪʃəs] *adj* supersticioso
superstructure [ˈsupərˌstrʌktʃər] o [ˈsjupərˌstrʌktʃər] *s* superstructura o superestructura
supertax [ˈsupərˌtæks] o [ˈsjupərˌtæks] *s* sobretasa, impuesto adicional
supervene [ˌsupərˈvin] o [ˌsjupərˈvin] *vn* sobrevenir
supervention [ˌsupərˈvɛnʃən] o [ˌsjupərˈvɛnʃən] *s* sobrevenida o superveniencia
supervise [ˈsupərvaɪz] o [ˈsjupərvaɪz] *va* superentender, supervisar
supervision [ˌsupərˈvɪʒən] o [ˌsjupərˈvɪʒən] *s* superintendencia, supervisión
supervisor [ˈsupərˌvaɪzər] o [ˈsjupərˌvaɪzər] *s* superintendente, supervisor
supervisory [ˌsupərˈvaɪzərɪ] o [ˌsjupərˈvaɪzərɪ] *adj* vigilante, supervisor, de superintendente
supervoltage [ˌsupərˈvoltɪdʒ] o [ˌsjupərˈvoltɪdʒ] *s* (phys.) supervoltaje
supination [ˌsupɪˈneʃən] o [ˌsjupɪˈneʃən] *s* supinación; (anat. & physiol.) supinación
supinator [ˌsupɪˈnetər] o [ˌsjupɪˈnetər] *s* (anat.) supinador
supine [suˈpaɪn] o [sjuˈpaɪn] *adj* supino; [ˈsupaɪn] o [ˈsjupaɪn] *s* (gram.) supino
supp. abr. de **supplement**
supper [ˈsʌpər] *s* cena; **to eat supper** tomar la cena, cenar
suppl. abr. de **supplement**
supplant [səˈplænt] *va* reemplazar, substituir; suplantar (*con malas artes*)
supple [ˈsʌpəl] *adj* flexible; dócil, servil; *va* hacer flexible; hacer dócil o servil; *vn* volverse flexible; volverse dócil o servil
supplement [ˈsʌplɪmənt] *s* suplemento (*lo que se añade para completar; parte que se añade a un diccionario, periódico u otro escrito*); (trig.) suplemento; [ˈsʌplɪmɛnt] *va* suplir, completar
supplemental [ˌsʌplɪˈmɛntəl] *adj* suplemental
supplementary [ˌsʌplɪˈmɛntərɪ] *adj* suplementario; (geom.) suplementario
suppliance [ˈsʌplɪəns] *s* súplica, suplicación
suppliant [ˈsʌplɪənt] o **supplicant** [ˈsʌplɪkənt] *adj & s* suplicante
supplicate [ˈsʌplɪket] *va & vn* suplicar
supplication [ˌsʌplɪˈkeʃən] *s* súplica, suplicación
supplicator [ˈsʌplɪˌketər] *s* suplicante
supplicatory [ˈsʌplɪkəˌtorɪ] *adj* suplicatorio
supply [səˈplaɪ] *s* (*pl:* **-plies**) suministro, provisión, aprovisionamiento; surtido, repuesto; suplente, substituto; oferta, existencia; **supplies** *spl* pertrechos; provisiones, víveres; artículos, efectos, materiales; **to be in short supply** escasear, ir a menos; (*pret & pp:* **-plied**) *va* abastecer, suministrar, proveer, aprovisionar; reemplazar; [ˈsʌplɪ] *adv* flexiblemente; dócilmente
supply and demand [səˈplaɪ] *spl* oferta y demanda
support [səˈport] *s* apoyo, soporte, sostén; sustento; *va* apoyar, soportar, sostener; sustentar; aguantar; (theat.) hacer el papel de; (theat.) acompañar (*a un actor principal*)
supportable [səˈportəbəl] *adj* soportable
supporter [səˈportər] *s* defensor, mantenedor, partidario; apoyo, soporte, sostén; tirante (*para medias*); suspensorio (*para sostener el escroto*); faja medical; (her.) tenante (*del escudo*)
suppose [səˈpoz] *va* suponer; creer; **to be supposed to** + *inf* deber + *inf*, p.ej., **he is supposed to arrive by three o'clock** debe llegar para las tres; **to be supposed to be** tener fama de (ser); **suppose we take a walk?** ¿qué será si damos un paseo?; **to suppose so** suponer que sí
supposed [səˈpozd] *adj* supuesto
supposedly [səˈpozɪdlɪ] *adv* según lo que se supone
supposition [ˌsʌpəˈzɪʃən] *s* suposición, creencia, opinión
suppositional [ˌsʌpəˈzɪʃənəl] *adj* supositivo, hipotético
supposititious [səˌpɑzɪˈtɪʃəs] *adj* supositicio (*fingido*); supositivo
suppository [səˈpɑzɪˌtorɪ] *s* (*pl:* **-ries**) supositorio
suppress [səˈprɛs] *va* suprimir
suppresser [səˈprɛsər] *s* var. de **suppressor**
suppressible [səˈprɛsɪbəl] *adj* suprimible
suppression [səˈprɛʃən] *s* supresión
suppressive [səˈprɛsɪv] *adj* supresivo
suppressor [səˈprɛsər] *s* supresor; eliminador (*de ruidos, de parásitos atmosféricos, etc.*)
suppurate [ˈsʌpjəret] *vn* supurar
suppuration [ˌsʌpjəˈreʃən] *s* supuración
suppurative [ˈsʌpjəˌretɪv] *adj* supurativo; supurante; *s* supurativo
supranational [ˌsuprəˈnæʃənəl] o [ˌsjuprəˈnæʃənəl] *adj* supranacional
supraorbital [ˌsuprəˈɔrbɪtəl] o [ˌsjuprəˈɔrbɪtəl] *adj* (anat.) supraorbital
suprarenal [ˌsuprəˈrinəl] o [ˌsjuprəˈrinəl] *adj* (anat.) suprarrenal; *s* (anat.) glándula suprarrenal
supraspinous [ˌsuprəˈspaɪnəs] o [ˌsjuprəˈspaɪnəs] *adj* supraspinoso
supraspinous fossa *s* (anat.) supraspina
supremacy [səˈprɛməsɪ], [sʊˈprɛməsɪ] o [sjʊˈprɛməsɪ] *s* supremacía
supreme [səˈprim], [sʊˈprim] o [sjʊˈprim] *adj* supremo; **supreme moment** momento supremo, hora suprema (*muerte*); **supreme sacrifice** sacrificio supremo
Supreme Being *s* Ser Supremo
Supreme Court *s* Tribunal Supremo; Corte Suprema (Am.)
supt. o **Supt.** abr. de **superintendent**
surah [ˈsʊrə] *s* surá (*tejido*)
sural [ˈsjʊrəl] *adj* (anat.) sural
surcease [sʌrˈsis] *s* (archaic) cesación
surcharge [ˈsʌrˌtʃɑrdʒ] *s* sobrecarga; (philately) sobrecarga; [ˌsʌrˈtʃɑrdʒ] o [ˈsʌrˌtʃɑrdʒ] *va* sobrecargar; (philately) sobrecargar
surcingle [ˈsʌrˌsɪŋgəl] *s* sobrecincha
surcoat [ˈsʌrˌkot] *s* gabán, sobretodo; sobrevesta (*sobre la armadura*)
surd [sʌrd] *adj* (math. & phonet.) sordo; *s* (math.) número sordo; (phonet.) sonido sordo, consonante sorda
sure [ʃʊr] *adj* seguro; **for sure** seguramente,

sin duda; **to be sure** seguramente, sin duda; **to be sure to** + *inf* no dejar de + *inf;* **to make sure** asegurar; asegurarse, cerciorarse; *adv* (coll.) seguramente; **sure enough** efectivamente
sure-fire [ˈʃʊrˌfaɪr] *adj* (slang) seguro, de éxito seguro
sure-footed [ˈʃʊrˈfʊtɪd] *adj* de pie firme
sure thing *s* (slang) sacabocados; *adv* (slang) seguramente; *interj* (slang) ¡claro!, ¡seguro!
surety [ˈʃʊrtɪ] o [ˈʃʊrɪtɪ] *s* (*pl:* **-ties**) seguridad, fiador
suretyship [ˈʃʊrtɪʃɪp] o [ˈʃʊrɪtɪʃɪp] *s* seguridad, fianza
surf [sʌrf] *s* cachones, olas que rompen en la playa
surface [ˈsʌrfɪs] *s* superficie; *adj* superficial; *va* alisar, allanar; recubrir; cepillar (*madera*); emplastecer (*para pintar*); *vn* emerger (*un submarino*)
surface mail *s* correo por vía ordinaria
surface tension *s* (phys.) tensión superficial
surfbird [ˈsʌrfˌbʌrd] *s* (orn.) afriza, chorlo de las playas
surfboard [ˈsʌrfˌbord] *s* (sport) patín de mar
surfboat [ˈsʌrfˌbot] *s* (naut.) bote que puede resistir a las marejadas fuertes
surf duck *s* (orn.) negreta
surfeit [ˈsʌrfɪt] *s* exceso; hastío, hartura; empacho, indigestión; *va* atracar, hastiar, hartar; encebadar (*las bestias*); *vn* atracarse, hartarse; encebadarse
surf-riding [ˈsʌrfˌraɪdɪŋ] *s* (sport) patinaje sobre las olas
surfy [ˈsʌrfɪ] *adj* agitado, espumoso, undoso
surge [sʌrdʒ] *s* oleada; (elec.) sobretensión; *va* hacer undular; (naut.) aflojar, lascar, soltar poco a poco; *vn* agitarse, undular
surgeon [ˈsʌrdʒən] *s* cirujano
surgeonfish [ˈsʌrdʒənˌfɪʃ] *s* (ichth.) cirujano
Surgeon General *s* (*pl:* **Surgeons General**) médico mayor, jefe de la sanidad militar o naval
surgery [ˈsʌrdʒərɪ] *s* (*pl:* **-ies**) cirugía; gabinete de cirujano, sala de operaciones
surgical [ˈsʌrdʒɪkəl] *adj* quirúrgico
surgy [ˈsʌrdʒɪ] *adj* (*comp:* **-ier;** *super:* **-iest**) agitado, onduloso
surly [ˈsʌrlɪ] *adj* (*comp:* **-lier;** *super:* **-liest**) áspero, rudo, hosco, insolente
surmise [sʌrˈmaɪz] o [ˈsʌrmaɪz] *s* conjetura, suposición; [sʌrˈmaɪz] *va & vn* conjeturar, suponer
surmount [sərˈmaʊnt] *va* levantarse sobre; coronar; aventajar, sobrepujar; superar
surmullet [sərˈmʌlɪt] *s* (ichth.) mullo, salmonete
surname [ˈsʌrˌnem] *s* apellido; sobrenombre (*nombre que se añade al apellido*); *va* apellidar; sobrenombrar, dar un sobrenombre a
surpass [sərˈpæs] o [sərˈpɑs] *va* sobrepasar, aventajar
surpassing [sərˈpæsɪŋ] o [sərˈpɑsɪŋ] *adj* sobresaliente, extraordinario, incomparable
surplice [ˈsʌrplɪs] *s* (eccl.) sobrepelliz
surpliced [ˈsʌrplɪst] *adj* con sobrepelliz
surplus [ˈsʌrplʌs] *s* exceso, demasía, sobrante; (com.) superávit; *adj* sobrante, de sobra, excedente
surplusage [ˈsʌrplʌsɪdʒ] *s* exceso, demasía, sobrante; superfluidades (*palabras*)
surplus property *s* excedentes
surprisal [sərˈpraɪzəl] *s* sorpresa
surprise [sərˈpraɪz] *s* sorpresa; **to take by surprise** coger o tomar por sorpresa; *adj* inesperado, improviso; *va* sorprender; **to be surprised at** estar sorprendido de
surprise attack *s* ataque por sorpresa
surprise package *s* sorpresa
surprise party *s* reunión improvisada para felicitar a alguien
surprising [sərˈpraɪzɪŋ] *adj* sorprendente, sorpresivo
surrealism [səˈriəlɪzəm] *s* surrealismo
surrealist [səˈriəlɪst] *adj & s* surrealista
surrealistic [səˌriəlˈɪstɪk] *adj* surrealista
surrender [səˈrɛndər] *s* rendición, entrega; dejación, abandono; sumisión; *va* rendir, entregar; dejar, abandonar; *vn* rendirse, entregarse
surrender value *s* (ins.) valor de rescate
surreptitious [ˌsʌrɛpˈtɪʃəs] *adj* subrepticio
surrey [ˈsʌrɪ] *s* birlocho
surrogate [ˈsʌrəget] *s* substituto; (eccl.) vicario; (law) juez de testamentarías
surround [səˈraʊnd] *va* cercar, rodear, circundar; (mil.) sitiar
surrounding [səˈraʊndɪŋ] *adj* circundante, circunvecino; **surroundings** *spl* alrededores, contornos; ambiente, medio
surtax [ˈsʌrtæks] *s* impuesto adicional sobre rentas que pasan de cierta cantidad
surveillance [sərˈveləns] o [sərˈveljəns] *s* vigilancia
survey [ˈsʌrve] *s* examen, reconocimiento, inspección, estudio; medición, agrimensura, plano; levantamiento de planos; encuesta (*p.ej., de opinión*); bosquejo (*p.ej., de literatura*); [sʌrˈve] o [ˈsʌrve] *va* examinar, reconocer, inspeccionar, estudiar; medir; levantar el plano de; *vn* levantar el plano
surveying [sʌrˈveɪŋ] *s* agrimensura, planimetría
surveyor [sʌrˈveər] *s* examinador, inspector; sobrestante, vigilante; agrimensor, topógrafo; vista, inspector de aduanas
surveyorship [sʌrˈveərʃɪp] *s* agrimensura, empleo de agrimensor
surveyor's measure *s* sistema de medidas usado por los agrimensores (*la unidad es la cadena de 66 pies de largo, hecha de eslabones de 7,92 pulgadas de largo*)
survival [sərˈvaɪvəl] *s* supervivencia
survival of the fittest *s* (biol.) supervivencia de los más aptos
survive [sərˈvaɪv] *va* sobrevivir a (*otra persona, un desastre*); *vn* sobrevivir
surviving [sərˈvaɪvɪŋ] *adj* sobreviviente
survivor [sərˈvaɪvər] *s* sobreviviente
Susan [ˈsjuzən] o [ˈsuzən] *s* Susana
susceptibility [səˌsɛptɪˈbɪlɪtɪ] *s* (*pl:* **-ties**) susceptibilidad; impresionabilidad; (elec.) susceptibilidad
susceptible [səˈsɛptɪbəl] *adj* susceptible; enamoradizo
suspect [ˈsʌspɛkt] o [səsˈpɛkt] *s* sospechoso; *adj* sospechado; [səsˈpɛkt] *va & vn* sospechar
suspend [səsˈpɛnd] *va* suspender; **to suspend payment** suspender pagos; *vn* dejar de obrar, dejar de funcionar; suspender pagos
suspenders [səsˈpɛndərz] *spl* tirantes (*de pantalón*)
suspense [səsˈpɛns] *s* suspensión; duda, incertidumbre; ansiedad; indecisión, irresolución; **in suspense** en suspenso (*pendiente de alguna resolución*); en la incertidumbre
suspension [səsˈpɛnʃən] *s* suspensión; (rhet.) suspensión
suspension bridge *s* puente colgante, puente de suspensión
suspension of arms *s* suspensión de armas
suspension points *spl* puntos suspensivos
suspensive [səsˈpɛnsɪv] *adj* suspensivo; indeciso, irresoluto
suspensory [səsˈpɛnsərɪ] *adj* suspensorio; *s* (*pl:* **-ries**) suspensorio
suspicion [səsˈpɪʃən] *s* sospecha, suspicacia; sombra, traza ligera; **above suspicion** superior a la sospecha, por encima de toda sospecha; **on suspicion** por ser sospechado; **under suspicion** sospechado
suspicious [səsˈpɪʃəs] *adj* sospechoso
suspiration [ˌsʌspɪˈreʃən] *s* suspiro; respiración muy larga
suspire [səsˈpaɪr] *va* expresar con un suspiro; *vn* (poet.) suspirar, respirar con fuerza
sustain [səsˈten] *va* sostener, sustentar; apoyar, defender; confirmar, probar; sufrir (*p.ej., un daño, una pérdida*)
sustaining program *s* (rad. & telv.) programa sin patrocinador
sustenance [ˈsʌstɪnəns] *s* sustento, alimentos, subsistencia; sostenimiento
sutler [ˈsʌtlər] *s* vivandero
suture [ˈsutʃər] o [ˈsjutʃər] *s* costura; (anat., bot., surg. & zool.) sutura; *va* unir mediante sutura
suzerain [ˈsuzəren] o [ˈsjuzəren] *adj* soberano, supremo; *s* (feud.) suzerano; (dipl.) estado que ejerce la soberanía sobre otro
suzerainty [ˈsuzərentɪ] o [ˈsjuzərentɪ] *s*

(feud.) suzeranía; (dipl.) soberanía de un estado sobre otro
svelte [svɛlt] *adj* sutil, flexible, delgado, esbelto
s.w., S.W. o **SW** abr. de **southwest**
swab [swɑb] *s* escobón, estropajo, aljofifa, esponja; (surg.) algodón, esponja, tapón de algodón; (naut.) lampazo; (gun.) escobillón; (slang) patán; (*pret & pp:* **swabbed;** *ger:* **swabbing**) *va* limpiar, fregar; (surg.) limpiar con algodón; (naut.) lampacear
swabber [ˈswɑbər] *s* escobón; (surg.) algodón, esponja, tapón de algodón; (naut.) lampazo; (naut.) lampacero
Swabia [ˈswebɪə] *s* Suabia
Swabian [ˈswebɪən] *adj & s* suabo
swaddle [ˈswɑdəl] *s* faja, pañal; *va* fajar, envolver, empañar
swaddling clothes *spl* envoltura, pañales, mantillas
swag [swæg] *s* (slang) robo, hurto, botín; (f.a.) guirnalda
swage [swedʒ] *s* estampa, tas; *va* estampar, forjar en estampa, formar en el yunque
swagger [ˈswægər] *s* fanfarronada; contoneo, paso jactancioso; *adj* (coll.) muy elegante; *va* intimidar; decir fanfarroneando; *vn* fanfarronear; contonearse
swagger stick *s* bastón ligero de paseo
swain [swen] *s* zagal; (slang) amante, enamorado
swale [swel] *s* pantano, prado
swallow [ˈswɑlo] *s* trago, deglución; tragadero; (orn.) golondrina; *va* tragar, deglutir; (fig.) tragar o tragarse (*cosas inverosímiles; cosas repulsivas o vejatorias*); (fig.) suprimir, retractar, desdecir; engullir (*paparruchas*); *vn* tragar, deglutir
swallow-tail [ˈswɑlo,tel] *s* frac; (carp.) cola de milano
swallow-tailed coat [ˈswɑlo,teld] *s* frac
swallowwort [ˈswɑlo,wʌrt] *s* (bot.) golondrinera, celidonia
swam [swæm] *pret de* **swim**
swamp [swɑmp] *s* pantano, marisma; *va* sumergir, encharcar, inundar; abrumar (*p.ej., de trabajo*); *vn* sumergirse, hundirse
swampland [ˈswɑmp,lænd] *s* pantanal
swamp oak *s* (bot.) roble blanco de California (*Quercus lobata*); (bot.) casuarina; (bot.) roble de los pantanos (*Quercus palustris*); (bot.) viminaria
swampy [ˈswɑmpɪ] *adj* (*comp:* **-ier;** *super:* **-iest**) pantanoso
swan [swɑn] *s* (orn.) cisne; (fig.) cisne (*poeta*); (*cap.*) *s* (astr.) Cisne
swan dive *s* salto de ángel
swank [swæŋk] *s* (coll.) jactancia, ostentación, elegancia vistosa; *adj* (slang) vistoso, ostentoso, elegante; *vn* (coll.) fanfarronear, pavonearse
swan knight *s* (myth.) caballero del cisne
swanky [ˈswæŋkɪ] *adj* (*comp:* **-ier;** *super:* **-iest**) (slang) brioso, vistoso, ostentoso, elegante
swan mussel *s* (zool.) almeja de los estanques
swanneck [ˈswɑn,nɛk] *s* cuello de cisne
swan's-down [ˈswɑnz,daʊn] *s* plumón de cisne; moletón, paño de vicuña
swanskin [ˈswɑn,skɪn] *s* piel de cisne; moletón, lanilla
swan song *s* canto del cisne
swap [swɑp] *s* (coll.) trueque, cambalache; (*pret & pp:* **swapped;** *ger:* **swapping**) *va & vn* (coll.) trocar, cambalachear
sward [swɔrd] *s* césped
swarm [swɔrm] *s* enjambre; (fig.) enjambre; *va* enjambrar; trepar; *vn* enjambrar; trepar; volar o moverse en enjambres; hormiguear (*una multitud de gente o animales*)
swarming [ˈswɔrmɪŋ] *adj* hormigueante; *s* enjambrazón (*de abejas*)
swart [swɔrt] *adj* var. de **swarthy**
swarthy [ˈswɔrðɪ] o [ˈswɔrθɪ] *adj* (*comp:* **-ier;** *super:* **-iest**) moreno, atezado, carinegro
swash [swɑʃ] *s* chorretada, golpe de agua; ruido del agua movida; canalizo; *va* salpicar; *vn* chapotear; hacer ruido (*el agua*); baladronear, hacer ruido
swashbuckler [ˈswɑʃ,bʌklər] *s* espadachín, valentón, matón, matasiete
swashbuckling [ˈswɑʃ,bʌklɪŋ] *adj* fanfarrón, jactancioso; *s* fanfarronada, jactancia
swash plate *s* (mach.) placa oscilante
swastika [ˈswɑstɪkə] o [ˈswæstɪkə] *s* svástica
swat [swɑt] *s* (coll.) golpe violento; (*pret & pp:* **swatted;** *ger:* **swatting**) *va* (coll.) golpear con fuerza; (coll.) aporrear, aplastar (*una mosca*)
swatch [swɑtʃ] *s* muestra de tela, cuero, etc.; muestrario
swath [swɔθ] o [swɑθ] *s* guadañada; ringlera de hierba o mies acabada de segar; faja, tira; **to cut a swath** hacer gran papel
swathe [sweð] *s* envoltura; vendaje; guadañada; ringlera de hierba o mies acabada de segar; *va* envolver, fajar; atar, liar; vendar
sway [swe] *s* sacudimiento, oscilación, vaivén; inclinación, ladeo; imperio, mando, dominio; **to hold sway** tener dominio; **to hold sway over** dominar; *va* sacudir, hacer oscilar; conmover; disuadir; dominar, gobernar; *vn* inclinarse, ladearse; desviarse; oscilar; tambalear, flaquear
swayback [ˈswe,bæk] *s* corcova con prominencia anterior; *adj* deslomado, derrengado
sway-backed [ˈswe,bækt] *adj* deslomado, derrengado
swear [swɛr] (*pret:* **swore;** *pp:* **sworn**) *va* jurar; juramentar; prestar (*juramento*); **to swear in** tomar juramento a, hacer prestar juramento; **to swear off** jurar renunciar a; **to swear out** obtener mediante juramento; *vn* jurar; **to swear at** decir juramentos a, maldecir; **to swear by** jurar por; poner toda su confianza en; **to swear to** prestar juramento a; declarar bajo juramento; **to swear to** + *inf* jurar + *inf*, p.ej., **he swore to tell the truth** juró decir la verdad
sweat [swɛt] *s* sudor; (coll.) sudor, trasudor; (*pret & pp:* **sweat** o **sweated**) *va* sudar (*agua por los poros; la ropa*); hacer sudar; (slang) hacer sudar (*es decir, hacer dar a disgusto*); (slang) someter a un interrogatorio brutal para arrancar informes o una confesión; (metal.) fundir, soldar, calentar hasta la fusión; **to sweat it out** (slang) aguantarlo hasta el fin; *vn* sudar; (coll.) sudar (*trabajar con fatiga*)
sweatband [ˈswɛt,bænd] *s* badana del forro del sombrero, tafilete
sweater [ˈswɛtər] *s* sudante (*persona*); suéter
sweat gland *s* (anat.) glándula sudorípara
sweatily [ˈswɛtɪlɪ] *adv* con sudor
sweat shirt s (sport) pulóver de mangas largas
sweatshop [ˈswɛt,ʃɑp] *s* taller donde hacen sudar al obrero todo lo que puede rendir por un salario de miseria
sweaty [ˈswɛtɪ] *adj* (*comp:* **-ier;** *super:* **-iest**) sudoriento, sudoroso; (fig.) penoso, laborioso
Swed. abr. de **Sweden** y **Swedish**
Swede [swid] *s* sueco
Sweden [ˈswidən] *s* Suecia
Swedish [ˈswidɪʃ] *adj* sueco; *spl* suecos; *ssg* sueco (*idioma*)
Swedish clover *s* (*bot.*) trébol sueco
Swedish turnip *s* (bot.) nabo de Suecia
sweep [swip] *s* barrido; soplo (*del viento*); extensión; alcance; barrendero; deshollinador; remo largo y pesado; cigoñal (*de pozo*); (sport) carrera que decide las apuestas; (*pret & pp:* **swept**) *va* barrer; arrastrar, arrebatar; tocar, rozar; recorrer con la mirada, los dedos, etc.; *vn* barrer; pasar o moverse rápidamente; pasar arrasando; extenderse; precipitarse; andar con paso majestuoso
sweepback [ˈswip,bæk] *s* (aer.) flecha
sweeper [ˈswipər] *s* barrendero (*persona*); barredera (*máquina para barrer las calles*); barredera de alfombra; (nav.) dragaminas
sweep generator *s* (telv.) generador de barrido
sweeping [ˈswipɪŋ] *adj* arrebatador; comprensivo, extenso, vasto; *s* barredura; **sweepings** *spl* barreduras
sweep second hand *s* segundero central
sweepstake [ˈswip,stek] *s* ganancia por una persona de todas las apuestas; **sweepstakes** *ssg & spl* lotería en la cual una persona gana todas las apuestas; carrera que decide todas las apuestas; premio en las carreras de caballos
sweet [swit] *s* persona querida; dulzura; **sweets**

spl dulces, golosinas; *adj* dulce; oloroso; fresco; bueno, fértil; querido; lindo; amable; **to be sweet on** (coll.) estar enamorado de; *adv* dulcemente; **to smell sweet** tener buen olor
sweet alyssum *s* (bot.) alhelicillo
sweet basil *s* (bot.) albahaca
sweet bay *s* (bot.) laurel; (bot.) magnolia
sweetbread ['swit,brɛd] *s* lechecillas, mollejas
sweetbriar o **sweetbrier** ['swit,braɪər] *s* (bot.) eglantina (*Rosa eglanteria*)
sweet cicely *s* (bot.) perifollo oloroso
sweet cider *s* sidra dulce
sweet clover *s* (bot.) trébol oloroso
sweet corn *s* maíz tierno, maíz de grano dulce
sweeten ['switən] *va* endulzar, azucarar; suavizar; purificar; *vn* endulzarse, azucararse; suavizarse
sweetening ['switənɪŋ] *s* dulcificación; (cook.) dulcificante
sweet fern *s* (bot.) polipodio común; (bot.) perifollo oloroso
sweet flag *s* (bot.) ácoro, iris amarillo
sweet gale *s* (bot.) mirto de Brabante
sweet gum *s* (bot.) ocozol
sweetheart ['swit,hɑrt] *s* enamorado o enamorada; querida, amiga querida; galán, cortejo
sweetie ['switɪ] *s* (coll.) var. de **sweetheart**
sweeting ['switɪŋ] *s* camuesa (*manzana*)
sweetish ['switɪʃ] *adj* algo dulce
sweet marjoram *s* (bot.) mejorana
sweetmeats ['swit,mits] *spl* confitura, confites, dulces
sweetness ['switnɪs] *s* dulzura; suavidad
sweet oil *s* aceite de oliva
sweet pea *s* (bot.) guisante de olor
sweet pepper *s* (bot.) pimiento dulce
sweet pepper bush *s* (bot.) cletra
sweet potato *s* batata, camote; (coll.) ocarina
sweet scabious *s* (bot.) escabiosa de Indias
sweet-scented ['swit,sɛntɪd] *adj* oloroso, perfumado
sweet sixteen *s* los dieciséis abriles
sweetsop ['swit,sɑp] *s* (bot.) chirimoyo del Senegal; chirimoya del Senegal (*fruto*)
sweet spirit of niter *s* (pharm.) espíritu de nitro dulce
sweet-tempered ['swit'tɛmpərd] *adj* complaciente, de carácter dulce
sweet tooth *s* gusto por los dulces
sweet-toothed ['swit,tuθt] *adj* goloso
sweet william o **sweet William** *s* (bot.) clavel de ramillete, clavel de San Isidro, minutisa
swell [swɛl] *s* hinchazón; entumecimiento; oleada, marejada; oleaje; mar tendida, mar de fondo o de leva; ondulación del terreno; (mus.) reguladores; (mus.) pedal de expresión (*del órgano*); (coll.) persona muy elegante; *adj* (coll.) muy elegante; (slang) de órdago, magnífico, excelente; (*pret:* **swelled**; *pp:* **swelled** o **swollen**) *va* hinchar, inflar (*con aire*); abultar, aumentar, acrecentar; elevar, levantar; (mus.) aumentar gradualmente la fuerza de; (fig.) hinchar, engreír; *vn* hincharse; inflarse; abultarse, aumentar, crecer; elevarse, levantarse; (mus.) aumentar gradualmente en fuerza; (fig.) hincharse, engreírse; embravecerse (*el mar*)
swelled head *s* entono, soberbia; **to have a swelled head** estar muy pagado de sí mismo
swelling ['swɛlɪŋ] *s* hinchazón; bulto, chichón, protuberancia
swelter ['swɛltər] *s* calor abrumador; sudor abundante; *va* abrumar, sofocar; sudar, hacer sudar; *vn* abrumarse, sofocarse de calor; chorrear de sudor
swept [swɛpt] *pret & pp de* **sweep**
sweptback wing ['swɛpt,bæk] *s* var. de **backswept wing**
swerve [swʌrv] *s* desvío brusco; *va* desviar; *vn* desviarse, torcer, cambiar repentinamente de dirección
swift [swɪft] *adj* veloz, rápido; pronto, presto; repentino; vivo, activo; *adv* velozmente, rápidamente; *s* (orn.) vencejo (*Apus apus*); (orn.) salangana (*Collocalia esculenta*)
swift-footed ['swɪft'futɪd] *adj* ligero, veloz, de paso rápido
swiftly ['swɪftlɪ] *adv* velozmente, rápidamente; pronto
swiftness ['swɪftnɪs] *s* velocidad, rapidez; prontitud
swig [swɪg] *s* (coll.) tragantada; (*pret & pp:* **swigged**; *ger:* **swigging**) *va & vn* (coll.) beber a grandes tragos
swill [swɪl] *s* bazofia; basura, inmundicia; tragantada; *va* lavar, inundar de agua; beber a grandes tragos; llenar; emborrachar; *vn* chapotear, salpicar; beber a grandes tragos; emborracharse
swim [swɪm] *s* natación; nadada (Am.); distancia recorrida nadando; vahido, desmayo; (ichth.) vejiga natatoria, nadadera de pez; **the swim** (coll.) la corriente (*p.ej., de los negocios*); (*pret:* **swam**; *pp:* **swum**; *ger:* **swimming**) *va* pasar a nado; hacer nadar o flotar; *vn* nadar; deslizarse, escurrirse; padecer vahidos; dar vueltas (*la cabeza*); **to go swimming** ir a nadar, ir a bañarse; **to swim across** atravesar a nado
swimmer ['swɪmər] *s* nadador
swimmeret ['swɪmərɛt] *s* (zool.) pleópodo
swimming ['swɪmɪŋ] *s* natación; vahido, vértigo; *adj* nadante; lleno de lágrimas
swimmingly ['swɪmɪŋlɪ] *adv* lisamente, sin tropiezo, sin dificultad
swimming pool *s* piscina, piscina natatoria
swimming suit *s* traje de baño, traje de natación
swimwear ['swɪm,wɛr] *s* ropa de natación, trajes de natación
swindle ['swɪndəl] *s* estafa, timo; *va & vn* estafar, timar
swindler ['swɪndlər] *s* estafador, timador
swine [swaɪn] *s* cerdo, puerco; (fig.) puerco, cochino; *spl* ganado de cerda
swineherd ['swaɪn,hʌrd] *s* porquero, porquerizo
swing [swɪŋ] *s* oscilación, balance, vaivén; columpio; hamaca; anchura, libertad de acción; alcance; turno, período; jira; fuerza, ímpetu; vuelta; (boxing) golpe lateral, golpe de lado; (mus. & poet.) ritmo constantemente repetido; **in full swing** en plena marcha, en pleno vigor; (*pret & pp:* **swung**) *va* blandir (*p.ej., un arma*); menear (*los brazos*); hacer oscilar, hacer dar vueltas a; colgar (*una cosa*) para que oscile; columpiar; manejar con éxito; *vn* oscilar; balancearse, bambolear; columpiarse; estar colgado; dar una vuelta; **to swing open** abrirse de pronto (*una puerta*)
swing drawbridge *s* puente giratorio
swingeing ['swɪndʒɪŋ] *adj* (coll.) muy grande, extraordinario
swinging boom *s* (naut.) tangón
swinging door *s* batiente oscilante
swingle ['swɪŋgəl] *s* espadilla; *va* espadillar
swingletree ['swɪŋgəl,tri] *s* var. de **singletree**
swing music *s* música de baile de ritmo repetido y con improvisaciones
swing shift *s* (coll.) turno desde las quince hasta medianoche
swinish ['swaɪnɪʃ] *adj* porcuno; (fig.) puerco, cochino
swipe [swaɪp] *s* (coll.) golpe fuerte; *va* (coll.) dar un golpe fuerte a; (slang) hurtar, robar
swirl [swʌrl] *s* remolino, torbellino; vuelta, movimiento giratorio; *va* hacer girar; *vn* remolinar, arremolinarse; girar
swish [swɪʃ] *s* silbido, zumbido; chasquido (*p. ej., de látigo*); crujido (*de un vestido*); *va* chasquear (*p.ej., el látigo*); *vn* moverse produciendo un silbido o zumbido; chasquear; crujir (*un vestido*)
Swiss [swɪs] *adj & ssg* suizo; *spl* suizos
Swiss chard *s* (bot.) acelga
Swiss cheese *s* queso suizo, Gruyère
Swiss Guards *spl* guardia suiza
Swiss mountain pine *s* (bot.) pino negro
Swiss pine *s* (bot.) pino cembro
switch [swɪtʃ] *s* varilla, bastoncillo, latiguillo; golpe, latigazo; coletazo; cabellera, trenza o moño postizo, añadido (*de mujer*); (elec.) llave; (elec.) interruptor; (elec.) conmutador; (rail.) agujas; desviación, conmutación, cambio; *va* azotar, fustigar; (elec.) conmutar; (rail.) desviar; **to switch off** (elec.) cortar, desconectar; **to switch on** (elec.) cerrar (*el*

circuito); poner, encender (*la luz, la radio, etc.*); *vn* cambiarse, moverse; desviarse
switchback [ˈswɪtʃˌbæk] *s* (rail.) pendiente de vaivén; deslizador circular, montaña rusa
switchboard [ˈswɪtʃˌbord] *s* (elec. & telp.) cuadro de distribución
switching engine *s* (rail.) locomotora de maniobras
switchman [ˈswɪtʃmən] *s* (*pl:* **-men**) (rail.) guardagujas, agujetero
switch plate *s* (elec.) placa de interruptor, placa de llave
switch tender *s* (rail.) guardagujas, agujetero
switch tower *s* (rail.) garita o torre de control
switchyard [ˈswɪtʃˌjɑrd] *s* (rail.) patio de maniobras
Switzerland [ˈswɪtsərlənd] *s* Suiza
swivel [ˈswɪvəl] *s* eslabón giratorio; torniquete (*de silla giratoria*); enganche giratorio; (gun.) colisa; (*pret & pp:* **-eled** o **-elled;** *ger:* **-eling** o **-elling**) *va* hacer girar sobre un eje; enganchar con un eslabón giratorio; *vn* girar sobre un eje
swivel chair *s* silla giratoria
swivel gun *s* colisa
swob [swɑb] *s* var. de **swab;** (*pret & pp:* **swobbed;** *ger:* **swobbing**) *va* var. de **swab**
swollen [ˈswolən] *adj* hinchado; crecido; **swollen with pride** hinchado de orgullo; *pp de* **swell**
swoon [swun] *s* desmayo, deliquio; *vn* desmayarse, desvanecerse
swoop [swup] *s* arremetida, descenso súbito; *va* arrebatar, coger al vuelo; *vn* bajar rápidamente, precipitarse; abatirse (*el ave de rapiña*)
swop [swɑp] *s* var. de **swap;** (*pret & pp:* **swopped;** *ger:* **swopping**) *va & vn* var. de **swap**
sword [sord] *s* espada; **at swords' points** enemistados a sangre y fuego; **the sword** el poder de la espada; **to cross swords** luchar, reñir; **to draw the sword** tirar de la espada, desnudar la espada; **to measure swords** medir las espadas; **to put to the sword** pasar al filo de la espada; **to sheathe the sword** envainar la espada
sword-and-cloak [ˈsordəndˈklok] *adj* de capa y espada
sword arm *s* brazo derecho
sword bayonet *s* bayoneta espada, sable-bayoneta
sword bean *s* (bot.) caraota grande (*Canavalia gladiata*)
swordbearer [ˈsordˌbɛrər] *s* paje que llevaba la espada al caballero
sword belt *s* cinturón
sword cane *s* bastón de estoque
sword dance *s* danza de espadas
sword fern *s* (bot.) cola de quetzal
swordfish [ˈsordˌfɪʃ] *s* (ichth.) pez espada
sword handler *s* (taur.) mozo de estoques
sword knot *s* borla de espada
sword lily *s* (bot.) estoque
swordman [ˈsordmən] *s* (*pl:* **-men**) var. de **swordsman**
Sword of Damocles *s* espada de Dámocles
swordplay [ˈsordˌple] *s* esgrima; danza de espadas
sword rattling *s* fanfarronería
sword side *s* lado del padre, varones de la familia
swordsman [ˈsordzmən] *s* (*pl:* **-men**) espada; esgrimidor
swordsmanship [ˈsordzmənʃɪp] *s* esgrima, habilidad en el manejo de la espada
sword swallower [ˈswɑloər] *s* tragasable
sword thrust *s* estocada, golpe de espada
swore [swor] *pret de* **swear**
sworn [sworn] *pp de* **swear**
sworn enemy *s* enemigo jurado
swum [swʌm] *pp de* **swim**
swung [swʌŋ] *pret & pp de* **swing**
Sybarite [ˈsɪbəraɪt] *adj & s* sibarita
Sybaritic [ˌsɪbəˈrɪtɪk] *adj* sibarítico
sybaritism [ˈsɪbəraɪtɪzəm] *s* sibaritismo
sycamore [ˈsɪkəmor] *s* (bot.) sicómoro; (bot.) plátano; (bot.) falso plátano, arce blanco
sycamore fig *s* (bot.) sicómoro
sycamore maple *s* (bot.) falso plátano, arce blanco
sycon [ˈsaɪkɑn] *s* (zool.) sicón
syconium [saɪˈkonɪəm] *s* (bot.) sicono
sycophancy [ˈsɪkəfənsɪ] *s* adulación, servilismo; parasitismo
sycophant [ˈsɪkəfənt] *s* adulador; parásito; (hist.) sicofanta (*denunciador; impostor*)
sycophantic [[ˌsɪkəˈfæntɪk] *adj* adulatorio; parasítico
sycosis [saɪˈkosɪs] *s* (path.) sicosis (*afección de la piel*)
syenite [ˈsaɪənaɪt] *s* (mineral.) sienita
syll. abr. de **syllable** y **syllabus**
syllabary [ˈsɪləˌbɛrɪ] *s* (*pl:* **-ies**) silabario
syllabic [sɪˈlæbɪk] *adj* silábico
syllabicate [sɪˈlæbɪket] *va* silabear
syllabication [sɪˌlæbɪˈkeʃən] o **syllabification** [sɪˌlæbɪfɪˈkeʃən] *s* silabeo
syllabify [sɪˈlæbɪfaɪ] (*pret & pp:* **-fied**) *va* silabear
syllabize [ˈsɪləbaɪz] *va* var. de **syllabify**
syllable [ˈsɪləbəl] *s* sílaba; *va* silabear
syllabub [ˈsɪləbʌb] *s* var. de **sillabub**
syllabus [ˈsɪləbəs] *s* (*pl:* **-buses** *o* **-bi** [baɪ]) sílabo
syllepsis [sɪˈlɛpsɪs] *s* (*pl:* **-ses** [siz]) (rhet.) silepsis
syllogism [ˈsɪlədʒɪzəm] *s* silogismo
syllogistic [ˌsɪləˈdʒɪstɪk] *adj* silogístico
syllogize [ˈsɪlədʒaɪz] *va* deducir mediante silogismos; *vn* silogizar
sylph [sɪlf] *s* (myth.) silfo, sílfide; (fig.) sílfide
sylva [ˈsɪlvə] *s* var. de **silva**
sylvan [ˈsɪlvən] *adj* selvoso, selvático
sylvanite [ˈsɪlvənaɪt] *s* (mineral.) silvanita
Sylvia [ˈsɪlvɪə] *s* Silvia
sylviculture [ˌsɪlvɪˈkʌltʃər] *s* silvicultura
sylvite [ˈsɪlvaɪt] *s* (mineral.) silvina
Sylvanus [sɪlˈvenəs] *s* Silvano
sym. abr. de **symbol, symmetrical, symphony** y **symptom**
symbiont [ˈsɪmbaɪɑnt] o [ˈsɪmbɪɑnt] *s* (biol.) simbión o simbiota
symbiosis [ˌsɪmbaɪˈosɪs] o [ˌsɪmbɪˈosɪs] *s* (biol.) simbiosis
symbiotic [ˌsɪmbaɪˈɑtɪk] o [ˌsɪmbɪˈɑtɪk] *adj* (biol.) simbiótico
symbol [ˈsɪmbəl] *s* símbolo; *va* simbolizar
symbolic [sɪmˈbɑlɪk] o **symbolical** [sɪmˈbɑlɪkəl] *adj* simbólico
symbolism [ˈsɪmbəlɪzəm] *s* simbolismo
symbolist [ˈsɪmbəlɪst] *s* simbolista
symbolistic [ˌsɪmbəlˈɪstɪk] *adj* simbolístico
symbolization [ˌsɪmbəlɪˈzeʃən] *s* simbolización
symbolize [ˈsɪmbəlaɪz] *va* simbolizar
symmetric [sɪˈmɛtrɪk] o **symmetrical** [sɪˈmɛtrɪkəl] *adj* simétrico
symmetrically [sɪˈmɛtrɪkəlɪ] *adv* simétricamente
symmetrize [ˈsɪmɪtraɪz] *va* simetrizar
symmetry [ˈsɪmɪtrɪ] *s* (*pl:* **-tries**) simetría
sympathectomy [ˌsɪmpəˈθɛktəmɪ] *s* (surg.) simpaticectomía
sympathetic [ˌsɪmpəˈθɛtɪk] *adj* simpático (*p.ej., sentimiento*); compasivo; (anat., mus., phys. & physiol.) simpático; **sympathetic to** o **toward** favorablemente dispuesto a o hacia
sympathetically [ˌsɪmpəˈθɛtɪkəlɪ] *adv* simpáticamente; compasivamente
sympathetic ink *s* tinta simpática
sympathetic nervous system *s* (anat. & physiol.) gran simpático, sistema nervioso simpático, sistema del gran simpático
sympathetic strike *s* huelga para ayuda a otros huelguistas
sympathize [ˈsɪmpəθaɪz] *vn* simpatizar, compadecerse; **to sympathize with** compadecer, compadecerse de; comprender
sympathizer [ˈsɪmpəˌθaɪzər] *s* simpatizador; partidario
sympathy [ˈsɪmpəθɪ] *s* (*pl:* **-thies**) simpatía; compasión, conmiseración; **to be in sympathy with** estar de acuerdo con, ser partidario de; **to extend one's sympathies to** dar el pésame a
sympetalous [sɪmˈpɛtələs] *adj* (bot.) simpétalo
symphonic [sɪmˈfɑnɪk] *adj* sinfónico
symphonic poem *s* (mus.) poema sinfónico

symphonious [sɪm'fonɪəs] *adj* armonioso
symphonist ['sɪmfənɪst] *s* sinfonista
symphony ['sɪmfənɪ] *s* (*pl:* **-nies**) sinfonía
symphony orchestra *s* orquesta sinfónica o gran orquesta
symphysis ['sɪmfɪsɪs] *s* (*pl:* **-ses** [siz]) (anat. & zool.) sínfisis
sympodium [sɪm'podɪəm] *s* (*pl:* **-a** [ə]) (bot.) simpodio
symposium [sɪm'pozɪəm] *s* (*pl:* **-a** [ə]) coloquio; colección de artículos sobre un mismo tema; (hist.) simposio
symptom ['sɪmptəm] *s* (med. & fig.) síntoma
symptomatic [ˌsɪmptə'mætɪk] *adj* sintomático
symptomatology [ˌsɪmptəmə'tɑlədʒɪ] *s* sintomatología
syn. abr. de **synonym** y **synonymous**
synaeresis [sɪ'nɛrɪsɪs] *s* sinéresis
synaesthesia [ˌsɪnɛs'θiʒə] o [ˌsɪnɛs'θiʒɪə] *s* var. de **synesthesia**
synagogue ['sɪnəgɑg] *s* sinagoga
synalepha o **synaloepha** [ˌsɪnə'lifə] *s* sinalefa
synapse [sɪ'næps] *s* (physiol.) sinapsis
synapsis [sɪ'næpsɪs] *s* (*pl:* **-ses** [siz]) (biol. & physiol.) sinapsis
synarthrosis [ˌsɪnɑr'θrosɪs] *s* (anat.) sinartrosis
sync [sɪŋk] *s* (coll.) sincronización (*en la cinematografía y la telecomunicación*); (*pret & pp:* **synced** [sɪŋkt]; *ger:* **syncing** ['sɪŋkɪŋ]) *va & vn* (coll.) sincronizar
syncarp ['sɪnkɑrp] *s* (bot.) sincarpo
syncarpous [sɪn'kɑrpəs] *adj* (bot.) sincárpeo
synchromesh ['sɪŋkroˌmɛʃ] *s* (aut.) engranaje sincronizado; (aut.) cambio de velocidades sincronizado
synchronal ['sɪŋkrənəl] *adj* var. de **synchronous**
synchronic [sɪn'krɑnɪk] *adj* sincrónico
synchronism ['sɪŋkrənɪzəm] *s* sincronismo; cuadro sincrónico
synchronization [ˌsɪŋkrənɪ'zeʃən] *s* sincronización
synchronize ['sɪŋkrənaɪz] *va & vn* sincronizar
synchronizer ['sɪŋkrəˌnaɪzər] *s* sincronizador
synchronoscope [sɪn'krɑnəskop] *s* (elec.) sincronoscopio
synchronous ['sɪŋkrənəs] *adj* síncrono; (elec.) síncrono
synchronous converter *s* (elec.) convertidor sincrónico
synchronous motor *s* (elec.) motor sincrónico
synchronous speed *s* (elec.) velocidad de sincronismo
synchrony ['sɪŋkrənɪ] o ['sɪnkrənɪ] *s* sincronía
synchrotron ['sɪŋkrətrɑn] *s* (phys.) sincrotrón
synchro unit ['sɪŋkro] *s* (elec.) motor sincronizador
synclastic [sɪn'klæstɪk] *adj* (math.) sinclástico
synclinal [sɪn'klaɪnəl] o ['sɪŋklɪnəl] *adj* sinclinal; (geol.) sinclinal
syncline ['sɪŋklaɪn] *s* (geol.) sinclinal
syncopal ['sɪŋkəpəl] *adj* sincopal
syncopate ['sɪŋkəpet] *va* (mus. & phonet.) sincopar
syncopated ['sɪŋkəˌpetɪd] *adj* sincopado
syncopation [ˌsɪŋkə'peʃən] *s* (mus. & phonet.) síncopa
syncope ['sɪŋkəpɪ] *s* (mus. & phonet.) síncopa; (path. & phonet.) síncope
syncretic [sɪn'krɛtɪk] *adj* sincrético
syncretism ['sɪŋkrətɪzəm] *s* sincretismo
syncrisis ['sɪŋkrɪsɪs] *s* (rhet.) sincrisis
syndactyl o **syndactyle** [sɪn'dæktɪl] *adj & s* sindáctilo
syndesmosis [ˌsɪndɛs'mosɪs] *s* (*pl:* **-ses** [siz]) (anat.) sindesmosis
syndic ['sɪndɪk] *s* síndico
syndical ['sɪndɪkəl] *adj* sindical
syndicalism ['sɪndɪkəlɪzəm] *s* sindicalismo
syndicalist ['sɪndɪkəlɪst] *adj & s* sindicalista
syndicate ['sɪndɪkɪt] o ['sɪndɪket] *s* sindicato; ['sɪndɪket] *va* sindicar; dirigir mediante un sindicato; publicar mediante un sindicato; *vn* sindicarse
syndication [ˌsɪndɪ'keʃən] *s* sindicación
syndrome ['sɪndrəmi] o ['sɪndrom] *s* (path.) síndrome
synecdoche [sɪ'nɛkdəkɪ] (rhet.) sinécdoque
syneresis [sɪ'nɛrɪsɪs] *s* var. de **synaeresis**
synergy ['sɪnərdʒɪ] *s* sinergia
synesthesia [ˌsɪnɛs'θiʒə] o [ˌsɪnɛs'θiʒɪə] *s* (physiol. & psychol.) sinestesia
syngamy ['sɪŋgəmɪ] *s* (biol.) singamia
syngenesious [ˌsɪndʒɪ'niʃəs] *adj* (bot.) singenésico
syngenesis [sɪn'dʒɛnɪsɪs] *s* (biol.) singénesis
synizesis [ˌsɪnɪ'zisɪs] *s* (gram., biol. & path.) sinizesis
synod ['sɪnəd] *s* sínodo; (astr. & astrol.) sínodo
synodal ['sɪnədəl] *adj* sinodal
synodic [sɪ'nɑdɪk] o **synodical** [sɪ'nɑdɪkəl] *adj* sinódico; (astr.) sinódico
synonym ['sɪnənɪm] *s* sinónimo
synonymity [ˌsɪnə'nɪmɪtɪ] *s* sinonimia
synonymous [sɪ'nɑnɪməs] *adj* sinónimo
synonymy [sɪ'nɑnɪmɪ] *s* (*pl:* **-mies**) sinonimia; (rhet.) sinonimia
synop. abr. de **synopsis**
synopsis [sɪ'nɑpsɪs] *s* (*pl:* **-ses** [siz]) sinopsis
synoptic [sɪ'nɑptɪk] o **synoptical** [sɪ'nɑptɪkəl] *adj* sinóptico
synorchism [sɪ'nɔrkɪzəm] *s* (path.) sinorquismo
synovia [sɪ'novɪə] *s* (anat.) sinovia
synovial [sɪ'novɪəl] *adj* sinovial
synovitis [ˌsɪnə'vaɪtɪs] *s* (path.) sinovitis
syntactic [sɪn'tæktɪk] o **syntactical** [sɪn'tæktɪkəl] *adj* sintáctico
syntax ['sɪntæks] *s* sintaxis
synthesis ['sɪnθɪsɪs] *s* (*pl:* **-ses** [siz]) síntesis
synthesize ['sɪnθɪsaɪz] *va* sintetizar
synthetic [sɪn'θɛtɪk] o **synthetical** [sɪn'θɛtɪkəl] *adj* sintético
synthetically [sɪn'θɛtɪkəlɪ] *adv* sintéticamente
synthetic rubber *s* caucho sintético
syntonic [sɪn'tɑnɪk] o **syntonical** [sɪn'tɑnɪkəl] *adj* (elec.) sintónico
syntonin ['sɪntənɪn] *s* (biochem.) sintonina
syntony ['sɪntənɪ] *s* (elec.) sintonía
syphilide ['sɪfɪlɪd] *s* (path.) sifílide
syphilis ['sɪfɪlɪs] *s* (path.) sífilis
syphilitic [ˌsɪfɪ'lɪtɪk] *adj & s* sifilítico
syphilologist [ˌsɪfɪ'lɑlədʒɪst] *s* sifilólogo
syphilology [ˌsɪfɪ'lɑlədʒɪ] *s* sifilología
syphilosis [ˌsɪfɪ'losɪs] *s* (path.) sifilosis
syphon ['saɪfən] *s & va* var. de **siphon**
syr. abr. de **syrup**
Syracusan [ˌsɪrə'kjuzən] *adj & s* siracusano
Syracuse ['sɪrəkjus] *s* Siracusa
Syria ['sɪrɪə] *s* Siria
Syriac ['sɪrɪæk] *adj & s* siríaco (*dialecto*)
Syrian ['sɪrɪən] *adj & s* sirio
syringa [sɪ'rɪŋgə] *s* (bot.) jeringuilla, celinda
syringe ['sɪrɪndʒ] o [sɪ'rɪndʒ] *s* jeringa; (med.) jeringa, jeringuilla; (med.) jeringa, mangueta (*para echar ayudas*); *va* jeringar
syringin [sɪ'rɪndʒɪn] *s* (chem.) siringina
syringomyelia [sɪˌrɪŋgomaɪ'ilɪə] *s* (path.) siringomielia
syringotomy [ˌsɪrɪŋ'gɑtəmɪ] *s* (surg.) siringotomía
syrinx ['sɪrɪŋks] *s* (*pl:* **syringes** [sɪ'rɪndʒiz] o **syrinxes**) (anat.) trompa de Eustaquio; siringa (*zampoña, flauta de Pan*); siringe (*órgano cantor de los pájaros*)
syrt [sʌrt] *s* sirte
syrtis ['sʌrtɪs] *s* (*pl:* **-tes** [tiz]) sirte
syrup ['sɪrəp] o ['sʌrəp] *s* almíbar; jarabe (*almíbar con zumos refrescantes o medicinales*)
syrupy ['sɪrəpɪ] o ['sʌrəpɪ] *adj* almibarado; espeso como jarabe
syssarcosis [ˌsɪsɑr'kosɪs] *s* (anat.) sisarcosis
Syst. abr. de **system**
systaltic [sɪs'tæltɪk] *adj* sistáltico
system ['sɪstəm] *s* sistema
systematic [ˌsɪstə'mætɪk] *adj* sistemático; **systematics** *ssg* sistemática
systematical [ˌsɪstə'mætɪkəl] *adj* var. de **systematic**
systematically [ˌsɪstə'mætɪkəlɪ] *adv* sistemáticamente

systematization [ˌsɪstəmətɪˈzeʃən] *s* sistematización
systematize [ˈsɪstəmətaɪz] *va* sistematizar
systematology [ˌsɪstəməˈtɑlədʒɪ] *s* sistematología
systemic [sɪsˈtɛmɪk] *adj* (anat. & physiol.) sistemático
systemize [ˈsɪstəmaɪz] *va* var. de **systematize**
systole [ˈsɪstəlɪ] *s* (gram., biol. & physiol.) sístole
systolic [sɪsˈtɑlɪk] *adj* sistólico
systyle [ˈsɪstaɪl] *s* (arch.) sístilo
syzygy [ˈsɪzɪdʒɪ] *s* (*pl:* **-gies**) (astr.) sicigia

T

T, t [ti] *s* (*pl:* **T's, t's** [tiz]) vigésima letra del alfabeto inglés
t. abr. de **teaspoon, temperature, tempore, tenor, tense, territory, time, ton** o **tons, town** y **transitive**
T. abr. de **Territory, Testament** y **Tuesday**
tab [tæb] *s* apéndice; marbete; lengüeta; (coll.) cuenta; (aer.) aleta compensadora; **to keep tab on** (coll.) verificar, tener a la vista; **to pick up the tab** (coll.) pagar la cuenta
tabard [ˈtæbərd] *s* tabardo
tabasco [təˈbæsko] *s* (trademark) tabasco
tabby [ˈtæbɪ] *adj* atigrado; *s* (*pl:* **-bies**) gato atigrado; gata; solterona; chismosa maldiciente; tabí, tafetán
tabernacle [ˈtæbərˌnækəl] *s* tabernáculo; templo, santuario; (*cap.*) *s* (Bib.) Tabernáculo
table [ˈtebəl] *s* mesa; tabla (*lista, cuadro o catálogo, etc.*); (arch.) tablero; (anat.) tabla; **on the table** sobre la mesa del presidente; **to clear the table** alzar o levantar la mesa; **to help at table** servir en la mesa; **to set the table** poner la mesa; **to turn the tables** volver las tornas; **under the table** completamente emborrachado; **tables of the law** (Bib.) tablas de la ley; *va* poner sobre la mesa; poner índice a; disponer en una tabla; dar carpetazo a, aplazar la discusión de
tableau [ˈtæblo] *s* (*pl:* **-leaus** o **-leaux** [loz]) cuadro vivo; espectáculo
tablecloth [ˈtebəlˌklɔθ] o [ˈtebəlˌklɑθ] *s* mantel; tela para manteles
table cover *s* carpeta, cubierta de mesa, sobremesa, tapete
table d'hôte [ˈtɑbəlˈdot] *s* mesa redonda; comida a precio fijo
table lamp *s* lámpara de mesa
tableland [ˈtebəlˌlænd] *s* meseta; planicie
table linen *s* mantelería
table manners *spl* modales que uno tiene en la mesa
table of contents *s* índice de materias, tabla de materias
table oil *s* aceite de comer
table rapping *s* (el) golpear (*de los espíritus*)
tables of the law *spl* (Bib.) tablas de la ley
tablespoon [ˈtebəlˌspun] *s* cuchara de sopa, cuchara grande
tablespoonful [ˈtebəlˌspunfʊl] *s* cucharada de sopa, cucharada grande
tablet [ˈtæblɪt] *s* tableta, comprimido, pastilla; lápida, placa; taco o bloc de papel
table talk *s* conversación de sobremesa
table tennis *s* tenis de mesa, tenis de salón
table tilting, tipping o **turning** *s* movimientos de las mesas (*atribuídos a los espíritus*)
table top *s* tablero
tableware [ˈtebəlˌwɛr] *s* servicio, artículos para la mesa
tabloid [ˈtæblɔɪd] *adj* condensado, conciso, breve; *s* diario ilustrado de noticias condensadas y sensacionales; (pharm.) tableta, pastilla
taboo [təˈbu] *s* tabú; *adj* prohibido; *va* prohibir
tabor [ˈtebər] *s* tamboril
taboret o **tabouret** [ˈtæbərɛt] *s* taburete (*asiento*); bastidor de bordar; (mus.) tamborilete
tabu [təˈbu] *s, adj & va* var. de **taboo**
tabular [ˈtæbjələr] *adj* tabular
tabulate [ˈtæbjəlet] *va* tabular, poner en forma de tabla
tabulation [ˌtæbjəˈleʃən] *s* tabulación
tabulator [ˈtæbjəˌletər] *s* tabulador
tabulator key *s* tecla tabulatoria, tecla del tabulador
tacamahac [ˈtækəməˌhæk] *s* (bot.) tacamaca (*árbol y resina*)
tachistoscope [təˈkɪstəskop] *s* taquistoscopio
tachometer [təˈkɑmɪtər] *s* tacómetro
tachycardia [ˌtækɪˈkɑrdɪə] *s* (path.) taquicardia
tachygraph [ˈtækɪgræf] o [ˈtækɪgrɑf] *s* taquigrafía; taquígrafo
tachygrapher [tæˈkɪgrəfər] *s* taquígrafo
tachygraphic [ˌtækɪˈgræfɪk] o **tachygraphical** [ˌtækɪˈgræfɪkəl] *adj* taquigráfico
tachygraphy [tæˈkɪgrəfɪ] *s* taquigrafía
tachylyte [ˈtækɪlaɪt] *s* (mineral.) taquilita
tachymeter [tæˈkɪmɪtər] *s* taquímetro; (surv.) taquímetro
tachymetric [ˌtækɪˈmɛtrɪk] *adj* taquimétrico
tachymetry [tæˈkɪmɪtrɪ] *s* taquimetría
tachysterol [təˈkɪstərol] *s* (biochem.) taquisterol
tacit [ˈtæsɪt] *adj* tácito
tacitly [ˈtæsɪtlɪ] *adv* tácitamente
taciturn [ˈtæsɪtərn] *adj* taciturno
taciturnity [ˌtæsɪˈtʌrnɪtɪ] *s* taciturnidad
Tacitus [ˈtæsɪtəs] *s* Tácito
tack [tæk] *s* tachuela, puntilla; (sew.) hilván; (naut.) bordada, virada; (naut.) amura; cambio de dirección; política, línea de conducta; alimento; *va* clavar con tachuelas; (sew.) coser, hilvanar; unir, añadir; *vn* (naut.) virar, cambiar de bordada; cambiar de política, cambiar de línea de conducta
tackle [ˈtækəl] *s* aparejo, avíos, enseres; polea, poleame; (football) atajo y agarrada; (football) atajador; *va* asir, agarrar; atacar, embestir; abordar (*un problema*); (football) atajar
tacky [ˈtækɪ] *adj* (*comp:* **-ier;** *super:* **-iest**) pegajoso; (coll.) mal vestido, desaseado, descuidado
tact [tækt] *s* tacto, discreción
tactful [ˈtæktfəl] *adj* discreto, político
tactical [ˈtæktɪkəl] *adj* táctico
tactically [ˈtæktɪkəlɪ] *adv* tácticamente
tactician [tækˈtɪʃən] *s* táctico
tactics [ˈtæktɪks] *spl* táctica; *ssg* (mil.) táctica
tactile [ˈtæktɪl] o [ˈtæktaɪl] *adj* táctil; tangible, palpable
tactility [tækˈtɪlɪtɪ] *s* tactilidad; tangibilidad
tactless [ˈtæktlɪs] *adj* indiscreto
tactual [ˈtæktʃʊəl] *adj* tactivo, táctil
tactually [ˈtæktʃʊəlɪ] *adv* mediante el tacto; respecto al tacto
tadpole [ˈtædˌpol] *s* (zool.) renacuajo
ta'en [ten] (poet.) var. de **taken**
taenia [ˈtinɪə] *s* (*pl:* **-ae** [i]) (anat., arch. & zool.) tenia
taeniacide [ˈtinɪəˌsaɪd] *s* (med.) tenicida
taeniafuge [ˈtinɪəˌfjudʒ] *adj & s* (med.) tenífugo
taeniasis [tiˈnaɪəsɪs] *s* (path.) teniasis
taffeta [ˈtæfɪtə] *s* tafetán; *adj* de tafetán; muy delicado; florido (*estilo*)
taffrail [ˈtæfrel] *s* (naut.) coronamiento; (naut.) pasamano de la borda a popa
taffy [ˈtæfɪ] *s* melcocha, arropía; (coll.) lisonja
tag [tæg] *s* marbete, etiqueta; cola, rabito, pingajo; copo, mechón; vedija; herrete; sentencia o cita que se añade a una composición literaria; (theat.) palabra o frase de efecto contenida en un discurso; **to play tag** jugar al tócame tú; (*pret & pp:* **tagged;** *ger:* **tagging**) *va* pegar un marbete a; marcar con marbete o etiqueta; proveer de etiqueta o etiquetas; (coll.) perseguir, seguir los pasos de; añadir para producir efecto; alcanzar, tocar (*como en un juego de niños*); *vn* (coll.) seguir de cerca; **to tag after** (coll.) seguir de cerca
Tagalog [tɑˈgɑlɑg] *s* tagalo
tag day *s* (U.S.A.) día de cartelas (*día en que se solicitan en las calles contribuciones para obras de caridad, poniendo una cartela o flor en el ojal del contribuyente*)

tag end *s* cabo flojo; retal, retazo
tagrag [ˈtæg,ræg] *s* canalla; harapo, andrajo
Tagus [ˈtegəs] *s* Tajo
Tahitian [tɑˈhitɪən] *adj & s* taitiano
tail [tel] *s* cola; (fig.) cola (*de un cometa, una chaqueta*); trenza (*de pelo*); **tails** *spl* (coll.) cruz (*de una moneda*); (coll.) frac; **to turn tail** volver la espalda, mostrar los talones; **with his tail between his legs** con el rabo entre las piernas; **tails, you lose** cruz y pierde Vd.; *adj* de cola; *va* proveer de cola; seguir como una cola; añadir; atar, juntar; *vn* formar cola; llegar al fin; disminuir poco a poco; **to tail after** seguir de cerca, pisar los talones a
tail assembly *s* (aer.) empenaje, planos de cola
tailboard [ˈtel,bord] *s* tabla en la parte posterior de un carro, camión, etc., que se puede bajar o quitar para cargar o descargar
tail end *s* cola, parte de atrás; conclusión; **at the tail end** al final
tail fin *s* (aer.) plano de deriva
tail gunner *s* (aer.) artillero de cola
tailing [ˈtelɪŋ] *s* (mas.) entrega, tizón; **tailings** *spl* desechos, restos; (min.) colas
tail lamp o **tail light** *s* farol de cola, farol trasero
tailor [ˈtelər] *s* sastre; *va* entallar (*un traje*); proveer de trajes o vestidos; *vn* ser sastre
tailorbird [ˈtelər,bʌrd] *s* (orn.) sutora, pájaro sastre
tailoring [ˈtelərɪŋ] *s* sastrería, costura
tailor-made [ˈtelər,med] *adj* hecho por sastre, hecho con corte de sastre
tailpiece [ˈtel,pis] *s* apéndice, cabo; (arch.) viga que entra en una pared sostenida por un sillar o tizón; (mus.) cordal (*de un instrumento de cuerda*); (print.) florón, marmosete
tail plane *s* (aer.) plano de cola
tailrace [ˈtel,res] *s* cauce de salida, caz de descarga; (min.) canal que arrastra el agua con el material de desecho
tail skid *s* (aer.) patín de cola
tail spin *s* (aer.) barrena picada
tailstock [ˈtel,stɑk] *s* (mach.) contrapunta
tail wind *s* (aer.) viento de cola, viento trasero; (naut.) viento en popa
tain [ten] *s* hoja de estaño
taint [tent] *s* mancha; corrupción, infección; *va* manchar; corromper, viciar; *vn* mancharse; corromperse, viciarse
take [tek] *s* toma; presa, redada; (mov.) toma; (slang) entradas, ingresos ‖ (*pret:* **took;** *pp:* **taken**) *va* tomar; quedarse con; coger; llevarse; llevar; aceptar; arrebatar, quitar; comer (*una pieza, en el juego de ajedrez y en el de damas*); cobrar, percibir; ganar; aguantar, tolerar; deducir, substraer; soportar; cautivar, deleitar; tener, sentir; saltar por encima de; dar (*un salto, un paso, un paseo*); hacer (*un viaje; ejercicio*); seguir (*un consejo; una asignatura*); sacar (*fotografías*); necesitar; usar, calzar (*cierto tamaño de zapatos*); estudiar (*p.ej., historia, francés, matemáticas*); echar (*una siesta*); tomar (*un tren, tranvía, etc.*); sufrir (*un examen*); **to take amiss** llevar a mal, tomar en mala parte; **to take apart** descomponer, desarmar, desmontar; **to take away** llevarse; quitar; **to take back** recibir devuelto; devolver; retractar, desdecirse de; **to take down** bajar; descolgar; poner por escrito; tomar nota de; desmontar; tragar; (coll.) quitar los humos a, humillar; **to take for** considerar, suponer, tomar por, p.ej., **I took you for someone else** le tomé a Vd. por otra persona; **to take from** quitar a; restar de; **to take in** acoger, admitir; recibir (*en su casa, en la sociedad, etc.*); abarcar; comprender; ganar (*dinero*); visitar (*los puntos de interés*); cazar (*captarse la voluntad de, con halagos y engaños*); meter (*p.ej., las costuras de una prenda de vestir*); **to take it out on** (coll.) desquitarse a costa de, desahogarse riñendo (*a una persona*); **to take it that** suponer que; **to take it upon oneself to** + *inf* encargarse de + *inf;* **to take off** quitarse (*p.ej., el sombrero*); descontar; (coll.) imitar, parodiar; **to take on** tomar, contratar; empezar; cargar con, tomar sobre sí; desafiar; **to take out** sacar; pasear (*a un niño, un caballo*); llevar fuera, poner fuera; omitir; obtener; quitar; extraer, separar; (bridge) sacar (*al compañero*); escoltar (*a una muchacha*); (coll.) tener amores con (*una muchacha*); para la calle, p.ej., **give me a sandwich to take out** me da un sandwich para la calle; **to take over** tomar posesión de; tomar la dirección de; **to take seriously** tomar en serio; **to take up** subir; apretar, atiesar; levantar; coger, prender; recoger; absorber; amortiguar; rebajar, disminuir; emprender, comenzar; tomar, estudiar; ocupar, llenar (*un espacio*); tomar posesión de; pagar; consultar (*un asunto*); **to take upon oneself** tomar sobre sí, encargarse de ‖ *vn* arraigar, prender; cuajar; tomar posesión; actuar, obrar; salir, resultar; tomar (*por la derecha, por la izquierda*); adherirse; pegar; darse, dedicarse; (coll.) tener éxito; **to take after** parecerse a, ser semejante a; seguir el ejemplo de; **to take off** levantarse; salir; (aer.) despegar; **to take on** (coll.) excitarse, quejarse; **to take to** aficionarse a, tomar cariño a; dedicarse a; dirigirse a; **to take to** + *ger* ponerse a + *inf;* **to take up with** (coll.) relacionarse con, estrechar amistad con; (coll.) vivir con; **to take well** (coll.) sacar buen retrato
take-down [ˈtek,daʊn] *adj* desmontable; *s* desmontaje; mecanismo de desmontar; rifle desmontable; (coll.) humillación
take-home pay [ˈtekˈhom] *s* salario menos impuestos, etc.
taken [ˈtekən] *pp de* **take**
take-in [ˈtek,ɪn] *s* (coll.) abuso, engaño
take-off [ˈtek,ɑf] *s* salto; raya de donde se salta; (coll.) imitación burlesca, parodia; (mach.) toma de fuerza; (aer.) despegue
take-out [ˈtek,aʊt] *s* (bridge) sacada
take-out bid *s* (bridge) declaración de sacada
take-over [ˈtek,ovər] *s* toma
take-up [ˈtek,ʌp] *s* apretadura; apretador; atesador (*p.ej., de correa*); tensor; canal de llamas ascendente; (sew.) frunce
taking [ˈtekɪŋ] *adj* atractivo, encantador; (coll.) contagioso; *s* toma; toma de posesión; **takings** *spl* ingresos
talbot [ˈtɔlbət] *s* perro de San Huberto
talc [tælk] *s* (mineral.) talco; (*pret & pp:* **talcked** o **talced** [tælkt]; *ger:* **talcking** o **talcing** [ˈtælkɪŋ]) *va* tratar con talco, aplicar talco a
talcose [ˈtælkos] o [tælˈkos] o **talcous** [ˈtælkəs] *adj* talcoso
talcum [ˈtælkəm] *s* (mineral.) talco; talco en polvo
talcum powder *s* talco en polvo; polvos de talco, polvos blancos faciales
tale [tel] *s* cuento (*relato; enredo; mentira*); cuenta; **to tell tales** contar cuentos
talebearer [ˈtel,bɛrər] *s* cuentista, chismoso
talebearing [ˈtel,bɛrɪŋ] *adj* cuentista, chismoso; *s* chismería
talent [ˈtælənt] *s* talento; gente de talento
talented [ˈtæləntɪd] *adj* talentoso
talent scout *s* buscador de nuevas figuras (*para la televisión, el cine, etc.*)
talesman [ˈtelizmən] o [ˈtelzmən] *s* (*pl:* **-men**) (law) jurado suplente
taleteller [ˈtel,tɛlər] *s* var. de **talebearer**
talion [ˈtælɪən] *s* talión
talipot [ˈtælɪpɑt] *s* (bot.) palmera de sombrilla
talisman [ˈtælɪsmən] o [ˈtælɪzmən] *s* (*pl:* **-mans**) talismán
talismanic [,tælɪsˈmænɪk] o [,tælɪzˈmænɪk] *adj* talismánico
talk [tɔk] *s* charla, plática (*conversación; conferencia, discurso*); fábula, comidilla (*p.ej., de la ciudad*); **to cause talk** dar que hablar; *va* hablar (*cierto idioma; disparates*); hablar de; convencer hablando; **to be talked out** (coll.) haber hablado hasta no poder más; **to talk down** tapar la boca a, hacer callar hablando más o en voz más alta; **to talk into** + *ger* persuadir a + *inf;* **to talk out of** conseguir hablando a; **to talk out of** + *ger* disuadir de + *inf;* **to talk over** convencer o persuadir discutiendo; **to talk up** ensalzar; *vn* hablar; parlar (*p.ej., el loro*); **to talk back** replicar, responder con malos modales; **to talk on** discutir (*un asunto*); hablar sin parar; continuar hablando; **to talk over** discutir; **to talk to**

(coll.) reprender; **to talk up** elevar la voz, osar hablar, hablar alto
talkative [ˈtɔkətɪv] *adj* hablador, locuaz
talked-about [ˈtɔktəˌbaʊt] *adj* sonado
talker [ˈtɔkər] *s* hablador; orador; parlón, charlatán
talkie [ˈtɔkɪ] *s* (coll.) cine hablado, cine parlante
talking doll *s* muñeca parlante
talking film *s* (mov.) película hablada
talking machine *s* máquina parlante
talking picture *s* cine hablado, cine parlante
talking point *s* (slang) argumento (*para inducir a comprar*)
talking-to [ˈtɔkɪŋˌtu] *s* (*pl:* **-tos**) (coll.) reprensión, rapapolvo
tall [tɔl] *adj* alto; (coll.) exagerado, extraordinario
tallish [ˈtɔlɪʃ] *adj* un poco alto
tallith [ˈtælɪθ] *s* taled
tallow [ˈtælo] *s* sebo; *va* ensebar
tallowy [ˈtælo·ɪ] o [ˈtæləwɪ] *adj* seboso
tally [ˈtælɪ] *s* (*pl:* **-lies**) tara o tarja (*palo partido en dos donde se marca con muescas las ventas*); muesca en una tarja; cuenta; unidad (*en un cómputo hecho por grupos*); etiqueta, rótulo; contraparte; duplicado; (*pret & pp:* **-lied**) *va* marcar, notar; tarjar; echar la cuenta de; ajustar, acomodar; *vn* echar una cuenta; concordar, corresponder, conformarse
tallyho [ˈtælɪˌho] *s* (*pl:* **-hos**) coche de cuatro caballos; grito de cazador de zorras; [ˌtælɪˈho] *interj* grito del cazador
tally sheet *s* hoja en que se anota una cuenta, especialmente en una elección
Talmudic [tælˈmʌdɪk] *adj* talmúdico
Talmudist [ˈtælmədɪst] *s* talmudista
talon [ˈtælən] *s* garra; (arch.) talón (*moldura*); **talons** *spl* dedos o manos rapaces
talus [ˈteləs] *s* (*pl:* **-li** [laɪ]) (anat.) astrágalo; (*pl:* **-luses**) *s* talud; (geol.) talud detrítico
tam [tæm] *s* boina escocesa
tamale [təˈmɑlɪ] *s* tamal (*manjar mejicano*)
tamarack [ˈtæmərӕk] *s* (bot.) alerce americano (*Larix laricina*)
tamaricaceous [ˌtæmərɪˈkeʃəs] *adj* (bot.) tamaricáceo
tamarin [ˈtæmərɪn] *s* (zool.) saguino
tamarind [ˈtæmərɪnd] *s* (bot.) tamarindo (*árbol y fruto*)
tamarisk [ˈtæmərɪsk] *s* (bot.) tamariz o tamarisco
tambo [ˈtæmbo] *s* (theat.) var. de **end man;** [ˈtɑmbo] *s* tambo (Am.)
tambour [ˈtæmbʊr] *s* tambor; (sew.) tambor (*para hacer bordados*); *va & vn* bordar a tambor
tambourine [ˌtæmbəˈrin] *s* (mus.) pandereta; (orn.) tamboreta
tame [tem] *adj* amansado, domesticado; dócil, sumiso; aburrido, insípido; *va* amansar, domesticar; someter, avasallar; suavizar
tameless [ˈtemlɪs] *adj* indomable; indómito
Tamerlane [ˈtæmərlen] *s* Tamerlán
Tamil [ˈtæməl] *adj & s* tamul
tammy [ˈtæmɪ] *s* (*pl:* **-mies**) estameña
tam-o'-shanter [ˈtæməˈʃæntər] *s* boina escocesa
tamp [tæmp] *va* atacar (*un barreno*); apisonar
tamper [ˈtæmpər] *s* apisonador (*persona*); pisón; *vn* entremeterse; **to tamper with** manosear, tocar ajando; tratar de forzar (*una cerradura*); falsificar (*un documento*); corromper
tampion [ˈtæmpɪən] *s* (arm.) tapabocas; (mus.) tapón de cañón de órgano
tampon [ˈtæmpɑn] *s* (surg.) tapón; *va* (surg.) taponar
tamponage [ˈtæmpənɪdʒ] o **tamponment** [ˈtæmpənmənt] *s* (surg.) taponamiento
tan o **tan.** abr. de **tangent**
tan [tæn] *adj* requemado, tostado; de color; de color de canela; marrón; *s* casca (*corteza que se usa para curtir*); tanino; (*pret & pp:* **tanned;** *ger:* **tanning**) *va* curtir, adobar, zurrar; quemar, tostar; (coll.) zurrar, dar una paliza a
tanager [ˈtænədʒər] *s* (orn.) tángara
tanbark [ˈtænˌbɑrk] *s* casca
tandem [ˈtændəm] *s* tándem; *adj & adv* en tándem
tang [tæŋ] *s* sabor u olor fuerte y picante; dejo, gustillo; espiga o cola (*de un formón, lima, etc.*); tañido (*sonido vibrante*); *va* hacer retiñir; *vn* retiñir
tangency [ˈtændʒənsɪ] *s* tangencia
tangent [ˈtændʒənt] *adj* tangente; (geom.) tangente; *s* (geom., trig. & mus.) tangente; **to fly off** o **go off at a tangent** cambiar de repente, tomar súbitamente nuevo rumbo
tangential [tænˈdʒɛnʃəl] *adj* tangencial; divergente; apenas contiguo
Tangerine [ˌtændʒəˈrin] *adj & s* tangerino; (*l.c.*) *s* mandarina (*fruto*)
tangibility [ˌtændʒɪˈbɪlɪtɪ] *s* tangibilidad
tangible [ˈtændʒɪbəl] *adj* tangible; **tangibles** *spl* bienes materiales
tangibly [ˈtændʒɪblɪ] *adv* tangiblemente
Tangier [tænˈdʒɪr] *s* Tánger
tangle [ˈtæŋgəl] *s* enredo, maraña, lío; *va* enredar, enmarañar; *vn* enredarse, enmarañarse
tangly [ˈtæŋglɪ] *adj* enredado, enmarañado
tango [ˈtæŋgo] *s* (*pl:* **-gos**) tango (*baile y música*); *vn* bailar el tango
tangram [ˈtæŋgræm] *s* jugete chino que consiste en un cuadrado dividido en siete piezas de forma variada, tales que con ellas dispuestas de varias maneras se puedan formar diversas figuras
tangy [ˈtæŋɪ] *adj* fuerte y picante
tank [tæŋk] *s* tanque; cisterna; (aut.) depósito; (mil.) tanque, carro de combate; (rail.) ténder; (slang) barriga; (slang) bodega (*hombre que bebe mucho*); *va* almacenar o poner en tanques; *vn* **to tank up** (slang) emborracharse
tankage [ˈtæŋkɪdʒ] *s* cabida de un tanque; depósito en tanques; precio del depósito en tanques; (agr.) residuos animales que se emplean como abono o alimento para los animales
tankard [ˈtæŋkərd] *s* jarro grande con asa y tapa
tank car *s* (rail.) carro cuba, vagón cisterna, vagón tanque
tank engine *s* (rail.) locomotora-ténder
tanker [ˈtæŋkər] *s* (naut.) barco tanque, buque cisterna; (aer.) avión nodriza
tanker plane *s* (aer.) aeroplano-nodriza, avión-nodriza
tank farming *s* quimicultura, cultivo hidropónico
tank locomotive *s* (rail.) locomotora-ténder
tank truck *s* camión cisterna, camión tanque
tannate [ˈtænet] *s* (chem.) tanato
tanner [ˈtænər] *s* noquero, curtidor
tannery [ˈtænərɪ] *s* (*pl:* **-ies**) tenería, curtiduría
tannic [ˈtænɪk] *adj* (chem.) tánico
tannic acid *s* (chem.) ácido tánico
tannin [ˈtænɪn] *s* (chem.) tanino
tanning [ˈtænɪŋ] *s* curtido, curtimiento; quemadura o tostadura (*del cutis por el sol*); (coll.) zurra, paliza
tansy [ˈtænzɪ] *s* (*pl:* **-sies**) (bot.) tanaceto, hierba lombriguera
tantalate [ˈtæntəlet] *s* (chem.) tantalato
tantalic [tænˈtælɪk] *adj* (chem.) tantálico
tantalic acid *s* (chem.) ácido tantálico
tantalite [ˈtæntəlaɪt] *s* (mineral.) tantalita
tantalization [ˌtæntəlɪˈzeʃən] *s* exasperación, tentación sin satisfacción posible
tantalize [ˈtæntəlaɪz] *va* exasperar, atormentar mostrando lo que no se puede conseguir
tantalum [ˈtæntələm] *s* (chem.) tántalo o tantalio
tantalus [ˈtæntələs] *s* frasquera; (*cap.*) *s* (myth.) Tántalo
tantamount [ˈtæntəˌmaʊnt] *adj* equivalente
tantara [tænˈtærə] o [ˈtæntərə] *s* toque de trompeta, cuerno de caza, etc.
tantivy [tænˈtɪvɪ] *adj* rápido, veloz; *adv* a galope tendido; *interj* (hunt.) ¡a galope!; *s* (*pl:* **-ies**) galopada
tantrum [ˈtæntrəm] *s* berrinche, rabieta
Taoism [ˈtaʊɪzəm] *s* taoísmo
Taoist [ˈtaʊɪst] *adj & s* taoísta
tap [tæp] *s* golpecito, palmadita; canilla, espita; grifo; remiendo del tacón (*de un calzado*); calidad o clase (*de vino*); (elec.) toma; (mach.) macho de terraja; (coll.) taberna, mostrador de taberna; **taps** *spl* silencio (*toque que manda que cada cual se acueste*); **on tap** sacado del

barril, servido al grifo; listo, a mano; (*pret & pp:* **tapped;** *ger:* **tapping**) *va* dar golpecitos o palmaditas a o en; poner la espita a; sacar o tomar (*quitando la espita*); sangrar (*un árbol*); (surg.) sajar; remontar, remendar el tacón de; unir, hacer comunicar; (elec.) hacer una derivación en; intervenir (*un teléfono*); (mach.) aterrajar; *vn* dar golpecitos, golpear ligeramente
tap dance *s* zapateo, zapateado
tap-dance [ˈtæpˌdæns] o [ˈtæpˌdɑns] *vn* zapatear
tape [tep] *s* cinta; (sport) cinta tendida para marcar el final de una carrera; *va* proveer de cinta o cintas; medir con cinta; (coll.) grabar en cinta magnetofónica
tapeline [ˈtepˌlaɪn] *s* cinta de medir
tape measure *s* cinta de medir, cinta métrica
taper [ˈtepər] *s* cerilla, velita larga y delgada; ahusamiento; *adj* ahusado; *va* ahusar; *vn* ahusarse; ir disminuyendo
tape recorder *s* grabador o grabadora de cinta, magnetófono
tape recording *s* grabación sobre cinta
tapestry [ˈtæpɪstrɪ] *s* (*pl:* **-tries**) tapiz; (*pret & pp:* **-tried**) *va* entapizar, tapizar
tapeworm [ˈtepˌwʌrm] *s* solitaria, lombriz solitaria
tapioca [ˌtæpɪˈokə] *s* tapioca
tapir [ˈtepər] *s* (zool.) tapir, danta
tapis [ˈtæpɪ] o [ˈtæpɪs] *s* (obs.) tapiz; **on** o **upon the tapis** sobre el tapete
tapper [ˈtæpər] *s* macito (*de un timbre, descohesor, etc.*); (telg.) manipulador; instrumento de aterrajar
tappet [ˈtæpɪt] *s* (mach.) botador; (aut.) alzaválvulas, taqué
tappet rod *s* varilla levantaválvula, varilla empujadora
taproom [ˈtæpˌrum] o [ˈtæpˌrʊm] *s* bodegón, taberna
taproot [ˈtæpˌrut] o [ˈtæpˌrʊt] *s* (bot.) raíz central o maestra
tapster [ˈtæpstər] *s* mozo de taberna
tap water *s* agua corriente, agua de grifo
tap wrench *s* volvedor de machos
tar [tɑr] *s* alquitrán; (coll.) marinero; *adj* alquitranado; (*pret & pp:* **tarred;** *ger:* **tarring**) *va* alquitranar; **to tar and feather** embrear y emplumar, untar de brea y cubrir de plumas (*por castigo*)
tarantella [ˌtærənˈtɛlə] *s* tarantela (*baile y música*)
tarantula [təˈræntʃələ] *s* (zool.) tarántula
tarboosh [tɑrˈbuʃ] *s* fez (*gorro turco rojo*)
tardigrade [ˈtɑrdɪgred] *adj* (zool.) tardígrado
tardily [ˈtɑrdɪlɪ] *adv* tardíamente
tardiness [ˈtɑrdɪnɪs] *s* tardanza
tardy [ˈtɑrdɪ] *adj* (*comp:* **-dier;** *super:* **-diest**) tardío
tare [tɛr] *s* tara (*rebaja en el peso*); (bot.) arveja o veza; (Bib.) cizaña; *va* tarar
tarente [təˈrɛnte] *s* (zool.) estelión
targe [tɑrdʒ] *s* (archaic) tarja (*escudo*)
target [ˈtɑrgɪt] *s* blanco; (rail.) placa de señal; (phys.) blanco (*foco de emisión*); (surv.) corredera; (fig.) blanco (*de la burla*), objeto (*de risa, críticas, etc.*); (obs.) tarja, rodela
target area *s* zona a batir
target practice *s* tiro al blanco
tariff [ˈtærɪf] *s* tarifa; arancel; *adj* arancelario
tarlatan [ˈtɑrlətən] *s* tarlatana
tarmac [ˈtɑrmæk] *s* (trademark) tarmac; (aer.) tarmac (*frente a un hangar*)
tarn [tɑrn] *s* lago pequeño de montaña
tarnish [ˈtɑrnɪʃ] *s* deslustre; *va* deslustrar; *vn* deslustrarse
taro [ˈtɑro] *s* (*pl:* **-ros**) (bot.) taro, colocasia
tar paper *s* papel alquitranado, cartón alquitranado o embreado
tarpaulin [tɑrˈpɔlɪn] *s* alquitranado; encerado; abrigo o sombrero impermeables hechos de encerado
Tarpeia [tɑrˈpiə] *s* Tarpeya
Tarpeian [tɑrˈpiən] *adj* tarpeyo
Tarpeian Rock *s* roca Tarpeya
tarpon [ˈtɑrpɑn] *s* (ichth.) tarpón
Tarquin [ˈtɑrkwɪn] *s* Tarquino
tarragon [ˈtærəgɑn] *s* (bot.) dragoncillo, estragón
tarry [ˈtɑrɪ] *adj* alquitranado, embreado; [ˈtærɪ] (*pret & pp:* **-ried**) *va* (archaic) esperar; *vn* detenerse, pararse, quedarse; esperar; tardar
tarry-fingered [ˈtɑrɪˈfɪŋgərd] *adj* largo de uñas
tarsal [ˈtɑrsəl] *adj* tarsiano; *s* (anat. & zool.) tarso
tarsier [ˈtɑrsɪər] *s* (zool.) mago
tarsus [ˈtɑrsəs] *s* (*pl:* **-si** [saɪ]) (anat. & zool.) tarso; (*cap.*) *s* Tarso
tart [tɑrt] *adj* acre, agrio; (fig.) áspero, mordaz; *s* tarta
tartan [ˈtɑrtən] *s* tartán; dibujo escocés; (naut.) tartana; *adj* de tartán; hecho de tartán
tartar [ˈtɑrtər] *s* (chem.) tártaro; tártaro o sarro (*de los dientes*); mujer regañona; **to catch a tartar** meterse con uno muy fuerte; (*cap.*) *adj & s* tártaro
Tartarean [tɑrˈtɛrɪən] *adj* tartáreo
tartar emetic *s* (chem.) tártaro emético
tartare sauce [ˈtɑrtər] *s* salsa tártara
tartaric [tɑrˈtærɪk] o [tɑrˈtɑrɪk] *adj* tártrico
tartaric acid *s* (chem.) ácido tártrico
tartarize [ˈtɑrtəraɪz] *va* tartarizar
Tartarus [ˈtɑrtərəs] *s* (myth.) Tártaro (*infierno*)
Tartary [ˈtɑrtərɪ] *s* Tartaria
tartlet [ˈtɑrtlɪt] *s* tarta o pastel pequeño
tartrate [ˈtɑrtret] *s* (chem.) tartrato
task [tæsk] o [tɑsk] *s* tarea; **to bring** o **take to task** llamar a capítulo; *va* atarear; abrumar, exigir demasiado de; acusar, tachar
task force *s* (mil. & nav.) agrupación de fuerzas para una misión especial
taskmaster [ˈtæskˌmæstər] o [ˈtɑskˌmɑstər] *s* persona que señala las tareas, amo, superintendente; ordenancista
Tasmanian [tæzˈmenɪən] *adj & s* tasmanio
Tasmanian wolf *s* (zool.) lobo marsupial
tassel [ˈtæsəl] *s* borla; (bot.) penacho (*inflorescencia macho, especialmente del maíz*); (*pret & pp:* **-seled** o **-selled;** *ger:* **-seling** o **-selling**) *va* adornar con borlas; hacer borlas de; *vn* echar penachos (*el maíz*)
tassel hyacinth *s* (bot.) jacinto de penacho
taste [test] *s* gusto, sabor; sorbo, trago; muestra, ejemplar; gusto, buen gusto; **in bad taste** de mal gusto; **in good taste** de buen gusto; **to acquire a taste for** tomar gusto a; **to have a taste for** tener gusto a; **to taste** a gusto, a sabor; **to the king's** o **queen's taste** perfectamente; *va* gustar; probar; *vn* saber; **to taste like** u **of** saber a
taste bud *s* (anat.) papila del gusto
tasteful [ˈtestfəl] *adj* de buen gusto, elegante
tasteless [ˈtestlɪs] *adj* desabrido, insípido; de mal gusto
taster [ˈtestər] *s* catador, probador; catavino (*taza*)
tasty [ˈtestɪ] *adj* (*comp:* **-ier;** *super:* **-iest**) (coll.) sabroso; (coll.) de buen gusto
tat [tæt] (*pret & pp:* **tatted;** *ger:* **tatting**) *vn* (sew.) hacer frivolité
Tatar [ˈtɑtər] *adj & s* tártaro, tátaro
tatouay [ˈtætue] o [ˌtɑtuˈaɪ] *s* (zool.) tatú
tatter [ˈtætər] *s* andrajo, harapo, guiñapo; *va* hacer andrajos
tatterdemalion [ˌtætərdɪˈmeljən] o [ˌtætərdɪˈmæljən] *s* zaparrastroso, guiñapo
tattered [ˈtætərd] *adj* andrajoso, haraposo
tatting [ˈtætɪŋ] *s* (sew.) frivolité
tattle [ˈtætəl] *s* charla; chismografía; *va* descubrir (*secretos*) charlando; *vn* charlar; chismear
tattler [ˈtætlər] *s* charlador; chismoso; (orn.) sarapico
tattletale [ˈtætəlˌtel] *s* cuentista, chismoso; *adj* revelador
tattoo [tæˈtu] *s* tatuaje; (mil.) retreta, toque de retreta; retreta (*fiesta nocturna en la cual las tropas recorren las calles*); *va* tatuar o tatuarse (*p.ej., el brazo o algo en el brazo*)
taught [tɔt] *pret & pp de* **teach**
taunt [tɔnt] o [tɑnt] *s* dicterio; mofa, pulla; *va* reprochar o provocar con insultos; **to taunt a person into doing something** conseguir con insultos que una persona haga algo
taupe [top] *adj & s* gris obscuro amarillento

taurine ['tɔraɪn] o ['tɔrɪn] *adj* taurino; *s* (chem.) taurina
Taurus ['tɔrəs] *s* (astr. & geog.) Tauro
taut [tɔt] *adj* tieso, tirante; aseado, bien arreglado
tautog [tɔ'tɑg] *s* (ichth.) tautoga
tautological [,tɔtə'lɑdʒɪkəl] *adj* tautológico
tautology [tɔ'tɑlədʒɪ] *s* tautología
tautomer ['tɔtəmər] *s* (chem.) tautómero
tautomerism [tɔ'tɑmərɪzəm] *s* (chem.) tautomería
tavern ['tævərn] *s* taberna; mesón, posada
taw [tɔ] *s* bolita de mármol; juego de las bolitas de mármol; línea desde donde se tiran las bolitas de mármol
tawdry ['tɔdrɪ] *adj* cursi, charro, vistoso
tawny ['tɔnɪ] *adj* (*comp:* **-nier;** *super:* **-niest**) leonado
tawny owl *s* (orn.) cárabo
tax [tæks] *s* impuesto, contribución; esfuerzo; *va* poner impuestos a (*una persona*); poner impuestos sobre (*la propiedad*); abrumar, someter a esfuerzo excesivo; agotar (*la paciencia de uno*); censurar, reprender; (law) tasar (*las costas*); (coll.) cobrar
taxable ['tæksəbəl] *adj* imponible; sujeto a impuesto
taxation [tæk'seʃən] *s* impuestos, contribuciones; imposición de contribuciones; (law) tasación de costas
tax collector *s* recaudador de impuestos
tax cut *s* reducción de impuestos
tax evader *s* burlador de impuestos
tax-exempt ['tæksɪg,zɛmpt] *adj* exento de impuesto
tax-free ['tæks,fri] *adj* libre de impuesto
taxi ['tæksɪ] *s* (*pl:* **-is**) taxi; (*pret & pp:* **-ied;** *ger:* **-iing** o **-ying**) *va* (aer.) carretear; *vn* ir en taxi; (aer.) carretear, correr por tierra, taxear
taxicab ['tæksɪ,kæb] *s* taxi
taxi dancer *s* taxi (*muchacha empleada para bailar con los clientes en salas de baile y cabarets*)
taxidermal [,tæksɪ'dʌrməl] *adj* taxidérmico
taxidermist ['tæksɪ,dʌrmɪst] *s* taxidermista
taxidermy ['tæksɪ,dʌrmɪ] *s* taxidermia
taxi driver *s* taxista, conductor de taxi
taxilight ['tæksɪ,laɪt] *s* (aer.) luz de rodaje
taximeter ['tæksɪ,mitər] *s* taxímetro
taxiplane ['tæksɪ,plen] *s* (aer.) avioneta de alquiler
taxis ['tæksɪs] *s* (biol.) tactismo, taxia o taxis; (surg.) taxis
taxi service *s* servicio de taxis; (aer.) servicio regular de aviones de alquiler
taxi stand *s* parada de taxis
taxiway ['tæksɪ,we] *s* (aer.) pista de rodaje
taxonomic [,tæksə'nɑmɪk] *adj* taxonómico
taxonomist [tæks'ɑnəmɪst] *s* taxonomista
taxonomy [tæks'ɑnəmɪ] *s* taxonomía
taxpayer ['tæks,peər] *s* contribuyente
tax rate *s* tipo (*porcentaje*) de impuesto, tipo impositivo
t.b. abr. de **tuberculosis**
tbs. o **tbsp.** abr. de **tablespoon** o **tablespoons**
tea [ti] *s* (bot.) té; té (*hoja seca; bebida; reunión por la tarde*); tisana (*bebida medicinal*); caldo de carne
tea bag *s* muñeca
tea ball *s* huevo del té, bolita (perforada) para té; bolsita de té
teaboard ['ti,bord] *s* bandeja para servir el té
tea caddy *s* bote para té
teacart ['ti,kɑrt] *s* mesita de té con ruedas
teach [titʃ] (*pret & pp:* **taught**) *va* enseñar; dar (*una lección*); (coll.) dar una lección a (*una persona para que comprenda la falta que ha cometido*); **to teach how to** + *inf* o **to teach to** + *inf* enseñar a + *inf;* **to teach someone something** enseñar algo a alguien; *vn* enseñar
teachability [,titʃə'bɪlɪtɪ] *s* docilidad
teachable ['titʃəbəl] *adj* dócil, educable, enseñable
teacher ['titʃər] *s* maestro, instructor; (fig.) maestra (*p.ej., la desgracia*)
teacher's pet *s* alumno mimado
teaching ['titʃɪŋ] *adj* docente; *s* enseñanza; doctrina
teaching staff *s* personal docente
tea cozy *s* cubretetera
teacup ['ti,kʌp] *s* taza de té, taza para té
teacupful ['tɪkʌpfʊl] *s* taza de té
tea dance *s* té bailable
teahouse ['ti,haʊs] *s* salón de té, sitio donde se vende y sirve té y refrescos
teak [tik] *s* (bot.) teca (*árbol y madera*)
teakettle ['ti,kɛtəl] *s* tetera
teakwood ['tik,wʊd] *s* teca (*madera*)
teal [til] *s* (orn.) pato chiquito; (orn.) cerceta, trullo
tea leaf *s* hoja de té
team [tim] *s* atelaje, tiro, tronco; yunta (*de bueyes*); (sport) equipo; *va* enyugar, uncir, enganchar juntos; acarrear, transportar o conducir con un tronco; *vn* conducir un tronco; ser tronquista; **to team up** asociarse, unirse; formar un equipo
teammate ['tim,met] *s* compañero de equipo, equipier
teamster ['timstər] *s* tronquista; carretero; camionista
teamwork ['tim,wʌrk] *s* solidaridad, cooperación; espíritu de equipo
tea party *s* reunión para tomar el té
teapot ['ti,pɑt] *s* tetera
tear [tɪr] *s* lágrima; **in tears** en llanto; **to burst into tears** romper a llorar; **to fill with tears** arrasarse (*los ojos*) de o en lágrimás; **to hold back one's tears** beberse las lágrimas; **to laugh away one's tears** convertir las lágrimas en risas; **to move to tears** mover a lágrimas ‖ [tɛr] *s* rasgón, desgarro; raja, hendedura; precipitación, prisa; (slang) borrachera ‖ [tɛr] (*pret:* **tore;** *pp:* **torn**) *va* rasgar, desgarrar; rajar; lacerar; herir; arrancar; acongojar, afligir; mesarse (*los cabellos*); **to tear apart** romper en dos; **to tear down** derribar (*un edificio*); desarmar (*una máquina*); **to tear oneself away** (coll.) irse o separarse de mala gana; **to tear open** abrir rasgando; **to tear out** arrancar; **to tear up** romper (*un papel*) ‖ *vn* rasgarse, desgarrarse; lacerarse; correr, precipitarse; **to tear along** correr a toda velocidad
tear bomb [tɪr] *s* bomba lacrimógena
teardrop ['tɪr,drɑp] *s* lágrima
tearful ['tɪrfəl] *adj* lacrimoso
tear gas [tɪr] *s* gas lacrimógeno
tear-jerker ['tɪr,dʒʌrkər] *s* (slang) drama o cine que arranca lágrimas
tear-off ['tɛr,ɔf] o ['tɛr,ɑf] *adj* exfoliador
tearoom ['ti,rum] o ['ti,rʊm] *s* salón de té
tear sheet [tɛr] *s* hoja del anunciante
teary ['tɪrɪ] *adj* lloroso
tease [tiz] *s* embromador; broma continua; *va* embromar, fastidiar, azuzar; cardar (*el paño*)
teasel ['tizəl] *s* (bot.) cardencha; (bot.) cardo de cardadores; carda (*cabeza del tallo de la cardencha; instrumento para cardar*); (*pret & pp:* **-seled** o **-selled;** *ger:* **-seling** o **-selling**) *va* cardar, rebotar (*el paño*)
teaser ['tizər] *s* embromador; broma continua; (coll.) rompecabezas, problema difícil
tea set *s* servicio para té
teaspoon ['ti,spun] *s* cucharilla o cucharita
teaspoonful ['tispunfʊl] *s* cucharada pequeña o de café, cucharadita
teat [tit] *s* teta; pezón (*extremidad de la teta*)
tea time *s* hora de té
tea wagon *s* var. de **teacart**
teazel ['tizəl] *s* var. de **teasel;** (*pret & pp:* **-zeled** o **-zelled;** *ger:* **-zeling** o **-zelling**) *va* var. de **teasel**
tech. abr. de **technical** y **technology**
technetium [tɛk'niʃɪəm] *s* (chem.) tecnetio
technic ['tɛknɪk] *adj* técnico; *s* técnica (*ciencia de un arte; habilidad*); término técnico; **technics** *ssg* técnica (*ciencia de un arte*); *spl* técnica (*habilidad*)
technical ['tɛknɪkəl] *adj* técnico
technicality [,tɛknɪ'kælɪtɪ] *s* (*pl:* **-ties**) tecnicismo (*término técnico*); tecnicidad (*carácter técnico*); cosa técnica, procedimiento técnico
technically ['tɛknɪkəlɪ] *adv* técnicamente
technician [tɛk'nɪʃən] *s* técnico
technicolor ['tɛknɪ,kʌlər] *s* (trademark) tecnicolor

technique [tɛk'nik] *s* técnica (*método; habilidad*)
technocracy [tɛk'nɑkrəsɪ] *s* tecnocracia
technocrat ['tɛknəkræt] *s* tecnócrata
technocratic [,tɛknə'krætɪk] *adj* tecnocrático
technologic [,tɛknə'lɑdʒɪk] o **technological** [,tɛknə'lɑdʒɪkəl] *adj* tecnológico
technologist [tɛk'nɑlədʒɪst] *s* tecnólogo
technology [tɛk'nɑlədʒɪ] *s* tecnología
techy ['tɛtʃɪ] *adj* (*comp:* **-ier;** *super:* **-iest**) (coll.) cosquilloso, picajón
tectonic [tɛk'tɑnɪk] *adj* tectónico; **tectonics** *ssg* tectónica
ted [tɛd] (*pret & pp:* **tedded;** *ger:* **tedding**) *va* henear; esparcir; disipar
tedder ['tɛdər] *s* heneador (*persona o aparato*)
Teddy ['tɛdɪ] *s* nombre abreviado de **Theodore**
Teddy bear *s* oso de juguete, oso de trapo
Te Deum [ti'diəm] *s* tedeum
tedious ['tidɪəs] o ['tidʒəs] *adj* tedioso
tedium ['tidɪəm] *s* tedio
tee [ti] *s* (sport) hito (*p.ej., en el juego de tejos*); (golf) tee (*punto de saque*); te (*empalme para tubos en forma de T*); *va* (golf) colocar (*la pelota*) en el tee; **to tee off** (golf) golpear (*la pelota*) desde el tee
teem [tim] *vn* hormiguear, abundar; llover a cántaros; **to teem with** abundar en, hervir de
teeming ['timɪŋ] *adj* hormigueante; torrencial (*lluvia*)
teen age [tin] *s* edad de 13 a 19 años
teen-ager ['tin,edʒər] *s* joven de 13 a 19 años de edad
teens [tinz] *spl* números ingleses que terminan en **-teen** (de 13 a 19); edad de 13 a 19 años; **to be in one's teens** tener de 13 a 19 años
teeny ['tinɪ] *adj* (*comp:* **-nier;** *super:* **-niest**) (coll.) diminuto, menudo, pequeñito
teepee ['tipi] *s* var. de **tepee**
teeter ['titər] *s* vaivén, balanceo; columpio; *vn* balancear, oscilar; estar temblando
teeth [tiθ] *pl de* **tooth**
teethe [tið] *vn* endentecer
teething ['tiðɪŋ] *s* dentición
teething ring *s* chupador
teetotal [ti'totəl] *adj* teetotalista; (coll.) absoluto, completo
teetotaler o **teetotaller** [ti'totələr] *s* teetotalista
teetotalism [ti'totəlɪzəm] *s* teetotalismo (*templanza que excluye por completo las bebidas alcohólicas*)
teetotum [ti'totəm] *s* perinola
tegmen ['tɛgmɛn] *s* (*pl:* **-mina** [mɪnə]) (bot. & zool.) tegmen
tegula ['tɛgjələ] *s* (*pl:* **-lae** [li]) (zool.) tégula
tegular ['tɛgjələr] *adj* tegular
tegument ['tɛgjəmənt] *s* (anat., bot. & zool.) tegumento
tegumentary [,tɛgjə'mɛntərɪ] *adj* tegumentario
te-hee [ti'hi] *s* risita entre dientes; *vn* reírse entre dientes; *interj* ¡ ji, ji!
tektite ['tɛktaɪt] *s* (geol.) tectita
tel. abr. de **telegram, telegraph** y **telephone**
telamon ['tɛləmɑn] *s* (*pl:* **telamones** [,tɛlə'moniz]) (arch.) telamón
telangiectasis [tɛl,ændʒɪ'ɛktəsɪs] *s* (*pl:* **-ses** [siz]) (path.) telangiectasia
telautograph [tɛl'ɔtəgræf] o [tɛl'ɔtəgrɑf] *s* telautógrafo
telecamera [,tɛlɪ'kæmərə] *s* cámara televisora
telecast ['tɛlɪ,kæst] o ['tɛlɪ,kɑst] *s* teledifusión; (*pret & pp:* **-cast** o **-casted**) *va & vn* teledifundir
telecommunication [,tɛlɪkə,mjunɪ'keʃən] *s* telecomunicación
teledu ['tɛlɪdu] *s* (zool.) tejón teledu
telega [tɛ'lɛgə] *s* telega
telegony [tɪ'lɛgənɪ] *s* (biol.) telegonía
telegram ['tɛlɪgræm] *s* telegrama
telegraph ['tɛlɪgræf] o ['tɛlɪgrɑf] *s* telégrafo; *va & vn* telegrafiar
telegraph code *s* código telegráfico
telegrapher [tɪ'lɛgrəfər] *s* telegrafista
telegrapher's cramp *s* calambre de los telegrafistas
telegraphic [,tɛlɪ'græfɪk] *adj* telegráfico
telegraphically [,tɛlɪ'græfɪkəlɪ] *adv* telegráficamente
telegraph pole *s* poste telegráfico
telegraphy [tɪ'lɛgrəfɪ] *s* telegrafía
telekinesis [,tɛlɪkɪ'nisɪs] *s* telequinesia
telelectric [,tɛlɪ'lɛktrɪk] *adj* teleléctrico
Telemachus [tɪ'lɛməkəs] *s* (myth.) Telémaco
telemechanic [,tɛlɪmɪ'kænɪk] *adj* telemecánico; **telemechanics** *ssg* telemecánica
telemeter [tɪ'lɛmɪtər] *s* telémetro; *va & vn* telemetrar
telemetric [,tɛlɪ'mɛtrɪk] *adj* telemétrico
telemetry [tɪ'lɛmɪtrɪ] *s* telemetría
telencephalon [,tɛlɛn'sɛfəlɑn] *s* (anat.) telencéfalo
teleological [,tɛlɪə'lɑdʒɪkəl] o [,tilɪə'lɑdʒɪkəl] *adj* teleológico
teleology [,tɛlɪ'ɑlədʒɪ] o [,tilɪ'ɑlədʒɪ] *s* teleología
teleost ['tɛlɪɑst] o ['tilɪɑst] *adj & s* (ichth.) teleósteo
telepathic [,tɛlɪ'pæθɪk] *adj* telepático
telepathically [,tɛlɪ'pæθɪkəlɪ] *adv* telepáticamente
telepathist [tɪ'lɛpəθɪst] *s* telepatista
telepathy [tɪ'lɛpəθɪ] *s* telepatía
telephone ['tɛlɪfon] *s* teléfono; *va & vn* telefonear
telephone book *s* libro de teléfonos
telephone booth *s* locutorio, cabina telefónica
telephone call *s* llamada telefónica
telephone directory *s* anuario telefónico, guía telefónica
telephone exchange *s* estación telefónica, central de teléfonos
telephone girl *s* señorita telefonista
telephone message *s* telefonema, despacho telefónico
telephone number *s* número de teléfono
telephone operator *s* telefonista
telephone receiver *s* receptor telefónico
telephone switchboard *s* cuadro de control telefónico
telephone table *s* mesita portateléfono
telephonic [,tɛlɪ'fɑnɪk] *adj* telefónico
telephony [tɪ'lɛfənɪ] *s* telefonía
telephote ['tɛlɪfot] *s* (elec.) telefoto *m*
telephoto [,tɛlɪ'foto] *adj* telefotográfico; *s* telefoto *f* (*imagen*); telefotógrafo (*aparato*); lente telefotográfico
telephotograph [,tɛlɪ'fotəgræf] o [,tɛlɪ'fotəgrɑf] *s* telefotografía; *va & vn* telefotografiar
telephotographic [,tɛlɪ,fotə'græfɪk] *adj* telefotográfico
telephotography [,tɛlɪfə'tɑgrəfɪ] *s* telefotografía
telephoto lens *s* lente telefotográfico, teleobjetivo
teleprinter ['tɛlɪ,prɪntər] *s* teleimpresor
teleprompter ['tɛlɪ,prɑmptər] *s* (trademark) apuntador automático (*para ayudar a un actor u orador*)
teleran ['tɛlɪræn] *s* (elec.) telerán
telescope ['tɛlɪskop] *s* telescopio; catalejo (*anteojo de larga vista*); *va* telescopar; acortar; *vn* telescoparse
telescope word *s* var. de **portmanteau word**
telescopic [,tɛlɪ'skɑpɪk] *adj* telescópico
telescopically [,tɛlɪ'skɑpɪkəlɪ] *adv* telescópicamente
Telescopium [,tɛlɪ'skopɪəm] *s* (astr.) Telescopio
telescopy [tɪ'lɛskəpɪ] *s* arte de hacer o manejar el telescopio
telestereoscope [,tɛlɪ'stɛrɪə,skop] *s* telestereoscopio
telesthesia [,tɛlɪs'θiʒə] o [,tɛlɪs'θiʒɪə] *s* telestesia
telethermometer [,tɛlɪθər'mɑmɪtər] *s* teletermómetro
teletype ['tɛlɪtaɪp] *s* (trademark) teletipo; *va* transmitir por teletipo
teletyper ['tɛlɪ,taɪpər] *s* teletipista
teletypewriter [,tɛlɪ'taɪp,raɪtər] *s* teletipia
teleview ['tɛlɪ,vju] *va & vn* ver por televisión
televiewer ['tɛlɪ,vjuər] *s* televidente, telespectador
televise ['tɛlɪvaɪz] *va* televisar
television ['tɛlɪ,vɪʒən] *s* televisión
television camera *s* cámara televisora

television screen *s* pantalla televisora
television set *s* televisor, telerreceptor
telfordize ['tɛlfərdaɪz] *va* recubrir con pavimento télford
telford pavement *s* pavimento télford (*superficie compuesta de una mezcla de piedras grandes y pequeñas y una capa dura de grava*)
tell [tɛl] (*pret & pp:* **told**) *va* decir; contar (*narrar; computar*); determinar; conocer, distinguir; **to tell someone off** (coll.) decirle a uno cuántas son cinco; **to tell someone to** + *inf* decirle a uno que + *subj; vn* hablar; surtir efecto; **to tell on** dejarse ver en (*p.ej., la salud de uno*); (coll.) denunciar, contar chismes de
tellable ['tɛləbəl] *adj* decible
teller ['tɛlər] *s* narrador, relator; cajero (*de un banco*); escrutador (*de votos*)
telling ['tɛlɪŋ] *adj* eficaz; *s* narración; **there is no telling** no es posible decir
telltale ['tɛl,tel] *s* soplón, chismoso; indicio, señal; reloj registrador; (naut.) axiómetro; *adj* revelador; indicador
tellurate ['tɛljəret] *s* (chem.) telurato
telluric [tɛ'lʊrɪk] *adj* telúrico; (chem.) telúrico
telluride ['tɛljəraɪd] o ['tɛljərɪd] *s* (chem.) telururo
tellurite ['tɛljəraɪt] *s* (chem.) telurito; (mineral.) telurita
tellurium [tɛ'lʊrɪəm] *s* (chem.) telurio
tellurous ['tɛljərəs] *adj* (chem.) teluroso
telly ['tɛlɪ] *s* (*pl:* **-lies**) (Brit.) televisión
telolecithal [,tɛlə'lɛsɪθəl] *adj* (embryol.) telolecito
telophase ['tɛləfez] *s* (biol.) telofase
telpher ['tɛlfər] *adj & s* teleférico; *va* teleferar
telpherage ['tɛlfərɪdʒ] *s* teleferaje
temblor [tɛm'blor] *s* temblor de tierra
temerarious [,tɛmə'rɛrɪəs] *adj* temerario
temerity [tɪ'mɛrɪtɪ] *s* temeridad
temper ['tɛmpər] *s* temple (*natural, genio; dureza del acero*); mal genio, cólera; punto (*de una mezcla*); **to fly into a temper** montar en cólera; **to keep one's temper** dominar su mal genio; **to lose one's temper** perder la paciencia, encolerizarse; *va* templar; (mus.) templar; *vn* templarse
tempera ['tɛmpərə] *s* (paint.) temple (*procedimiento*)
temperament ['tɛmpərəmənt] *s* temperamento (*naturaleza particular de un individuo*); disposición, genialidad; (mus.) temperamento
temperamental [,tɛmpərə'mɛntəl] *adj* temperamental; original, genial
temperance ['tɛmpərəns] *s* templanza; *adj* de templanza, p.ej., **temperance society** sociedad de templanza
temperate ['tɛmpərɪt] *adj* templado (*en comer y beber; en clima*)
temperately ['tɛmpərɪtlɪ] *adv* templadamente
temperate zone *s* zona templada
temperature ['tɛmpərətʃər] *s* temperatura; (path.) temperatura (*fiebre*)
tempered ['tɛmpərd] *adj* templado; (mus.) templado
tempest ['tɛmpɪst] *s* tempestad; *va* agitar violentamente
tempest in a teapot *s* más el ruido que las nueces
tempestuous [tɛm'pɛstʃʊəs] *adj* tempestuoso; (fig.) tempestuoso
Templar ['tɛmplər] *s* Templario, caballero del Temple; (U.S.A.) caballero templario
template ['tɛmplɪt] *s* var. de **templet**
temple ['tɛmpəl] *s* templo; templén (*de un telar*); gafa (*enganche con que se afianzan los anteojos en las sienes*); (anat.) sien
templet ['tɛmplɪt] *s* plantilla; (constr.) solera; (naut.) gálibo
tempo ['tɛmpo] *s* (*pl:* **-pos** o **-pi** [pi]) (mus.) tiempo; (fig.) ritmo (*p.ej., de la vida*)
temporal ['tɛmpərəl] *adj* temporal; (anat. & gram.) temporal
temporal bone *s* (anat.) hueso temporal
temporality [,tɛmpə'rælɪtɪ] *s* (*pl:* **-ties**) temporalidad; cosa temporal; **temporalities** *spl* (eccl.) temporalidades
temporally ['tɛmpərəlɪ] *adv* temporalmente (*en el orden de lo temporal o terreno*)
temporarily ['tɛmpə,rɛrɪlɪ] *adv* temporalmente (*por algún tiempo*)
temporary ['tɛmpə,rɛrɪ] *adj* temporal, temporáneo, temporario
temporization [,tɛmpərɪ'zeʃən] *s* contemporización
temporize ['tɛmpəraɪz] *vn* contemporizar, temporizar
tempt [tɛmpt] *va* tentar; **to tempt a person into a house** tentar a una persona a que entre en una casa; **to tempt someone to** + *inf* tentar a uno a + *inf*, tentar a uno a que + *subj*
temptation [tɛmp'teʃən] *s* tentación
tempter ['tɛmptər] *s* tentador; **the Tempter** el tentador (*el diablo*)
tempting ['tɛmptɪŋ] *adj* tentador
temptress ['tɛmptrɪs] *s* tentadora
ten [tɛn] *adj* diez; *s* diez; **ten o'clock** las diez; **the tens** las decenas (*los números 10, 20, 30, etc.*)
tenability [,tɛnə'bɪlɪtɪ] o [,tinə'bɪlɪtɪ] *s* defendibilidad
tenable ['tɛnəbəl] o ['tinəbəl] *adj* defendible
tenace ['tɛnes] *s* (bridge) tenaza (*reina y as o rey y sota*)
tenacious [tɪ'neʃəs] *adj* tenaz
tenacity [tɪ'næsɪtɪ] *s* tenacidad; (phys.) tenacidad
tenaculum [tɪ'nækjələm] *s* (*pl:* **-la** [lə]) (surg.) tenáculo
tenaille [tɛ'nel] *s* (fort.) tenaza
tenancy ['tɛnənsɪ] *s* (*pl:* **-cies**) tenencia; propiedad arrendada
tenant ['tɛnənt] *s* arrendatario, inquilino; morador, residente; *va* arrendar, alquilar
tenant farmer *s* colono
tenantry ['tɛnəntrɪ] *s* (*pl:* **-ries**) arrendatarios, inquilinos; tenencia; propiedad arrendada
tench [tɛntʃ] *s* (ichth.) tenca
Ten Commandments *spl* (Bib.) diez mandamientos
tend [tɛnd] *va* cuidar, vigilar; servir; *vn* tender; dirigirse; **to tend to** atender a (*p.ej., los negocios*); **to tend to** + *inf* tender a + *inf*
tendance ['tɛndəns] *s* atención, cuidado
tendency ['tɛndənsɪ] *s* (*pl:* **-cies**) tendencia
tendentious [tɛn'dɛnʃəs] *adj* tendencioso
tender ['tɛndər] *s* oferta; (naut.) alijador, falúa; (naut.) nodriza; (rail.) ténder; *adj* tierno; dolorido; *va* ofrecer; tender
tenderfoot ['tɛndər,fʊt] *s* (*pl:* **-foots** o **-feet**) *s* recién llegado (*en condiciones de vida muy ásperas*); principiante, novato
tender-hearted ['tɛndər'hartɪd] *adj* compasivo, tierno de corazón
tenderloin ['tɛndər,lɔɪn] *s* filete (*de carne de vaca o cerdo*); (*cap.*) *s* barrio de mala vida (*en las grandes ciudades*)
tenderness ['tɛndərnɪs] *s* ternura, terneza; sensibilidad
tendinous ['tɛndɪnəs] *adj* tendinoso
tendon ['tɛndən] *s* (anat.) tendón
tendril ['tɛndrɪl] *s* (bot.) zarcillo, tijereta; rizo (*de pelo*)
Tenebrae ['tɛnɪbri] *spl* (eccl.) tinieblas
tenebrous ['tɛnɪbrəs] *adj* tenebroso
tenement ['tɛnɪmənt] *s* habitación, vivienda; aposento; casa de vecindad
tenement house *s* casa de vecindad
tenesmus [tə'nɛzməs] o [tə'nɛsməs] *s* (path.) tenesmo, pujo
tenet ['tɛnɪt] o ['tinɪt] *s* credo, dogma, principio
tenfold ['tɛn,fold] *adj & s* décuplo; *adv* diez veces
Tenn. abr. de **Tennessee**
tennis ['tɛnɪs] *s* (sport) tenis; *adj* tenístico
tennis ball *s* pelota de tenis
tennis court *s* (sport) campo de tenis, cancha de tenis
tennis player *s* tenista
tenon ['tɛnən] *s* (carp.) espiga, almilla; *va* (carp.) espigar, despatillar, desquijerar; (carp.) ensamblar con espiga
tenor ['tɛnər] *s* tenor, carácter, curso, tendencia; (mus.) tenor (*persona; voz; instrumento*); *adj* (mus.) de tenor, para el tenor
tenotomy [tɪ'nɑtəmɪ] *s* (*pl:* **-mies**) (surg.) tenotomía

tenpenny ['tɛn,pɛnɪ] o ['tɛnpənɪ] *adj* de diez peniques, que vale diez peniques
tenpenny nail *s* clavo de tres pulgadas
tenpins ['tɛn,pɪnz] *ssg* juego de bolos en que se juega con diez bolos de madera dispuestos en triángulo; *spl* los diez bolos
tense [tɛns] *adj* tenso, tieso; tenso (*dícese de una persona o de una situación dramática*); tirante (*dícese de las relaciones de amistad próximas a romperse*); *s* (gram.) tiempo; *va* estirar
tenseness ['tɛnsnɪs] *s* tensión, tirantez
tensible ['tɛnsɪbəl] *adj* tensible
tensile ['tɛnsɪl] o ['tɛnsaɪl] *adj* tensor; de tensión; dúctil, flexible
tensile strength *s* (phys.) resistencia a la tensión
tension ['tɛnʃən] *s* tensión; (mech.) tracción; esfuerzo mental, ansia, congoja; tirantez (*de amistad, de relaciones diplomáticas próximas a romperse*); tensor, regulador de la tensión (*dispositivo*)
tensional ['tɛnʃənəl] *adj* de tensión
tensity ['tɛnsɪtɪ] *s* tensión
tenson ['tɛnsən] *s* (lit.) tensón o tensión
tensor ['tɛnsər] o ['tɛnsɔr] *s* (anat.) tensor
ten-strike ['tɛn,straɪk] *s* (sport) golpe con que se derriban todos los bolos (*en el juego de diez bolos*); (coll.) golpe o jugada muy difícil y de mucho éxito
tent [tɛnt] *s* tienda, tienda de campaña; (surg.) lechino, tapón; *va* acampar bajo tiendas; (surg.) tener abierto con tapón; *vn* acampar bajo una tienda
tentacle ['tɛntəkəl] *s* (bot. & zool.) tentáculo
tentacular [tɛn'tækjələr] *adj* tentacular
tentative ['tɛntətɪv] *adj* tentativo
tent caterpillar *s* (ent.) falsa lagarta
tenter ['tɛntər] *s* tendedor, bastidor; escarpia o alcayata (*de tendedor*); *va* enramblar; *vn* enramblarse
tenterhook ['tɛntər,hʊk] *s* escarpia o alcayata (*de tendedor*); **on tenterhooks** en ascuas, ansioso
tenth [tɛnθ] *adj* décimo; *s* décimo; diez (*en las fechas*); (mus.) décima
tenuity [tɛ'njuɪtɪ] *s* tenuidad; raridad (*p.ej., del aire*)
tenuous ['tɛnjʊəs] *adj* tenue; raro (*poco denso*)
tenure ['tɛnjər] *s* tenencia; ejercicio (*de un cargo*); inamovilidad (*de un cargo*)
tepee ['tipi] *s* tipi (*tienda de los indios norteamericanos*)
tepid ['tɛpid] *adj* tibio; (fig.) tibio
tepidity [tɪ'pɪdɪtɪ] *s* tibieza; (fig.) tibieza
ter. abr. de **territory**
teratological [,tɛrətə'lɑdʒɪkəl] *adj* teratológico
teratology [,tɛrə'tɑlədʒɪ] *s* teratología
terbium ['tʌrbɪəm] *s* (chem.) terbio
tercel ['tʌrsəl] *s* (orn.) halcón macho, terzuelo
tercentenary [tʌr'sɛntə,nɛrɪ] *adj* de trescientos años; *s* (*pl:* **-ies**) tricentenario
tercet ['tʌrsɪt] *s* terceto; (mus.) tresillo
terebinth ['tɛrɪbɪnθ] *s* (bot.) terebinto, albotín
teredo [tɛ'rido] *s* (*pl:* **-dos**) (zool.) teredo
Terence ['tɛrəns] *s* Terencio
tergiversate ['tʌrdʒɪvər,set] *vn* tergiversar
tergiversation [,tʌrdʒɪvər'seʃən] *s* tergiversación
tergiversator ['tʌrdʒɪvər,setər] *s* tergiversador
term [tʌrm] *s* término; condena, período (*de prisión*); semestre, período escolar; período o mandato (*p.ej., del presidente de los EE.UU.*); (arch., log. & math.) término; **terms** *spl* términos (*expresiones, palabras; relaciones mutuas*); condiciones; **to be on good terms with** estar en buenos términos con; **to bring to terms** imponer condiciones a; someter, vencer; **to come to terms** ponerse de acuerdo; someterse; *va* llamar, nombrar
termagancy ['tʌrməgənsɪ] *s* mal genio (*de mujer*)
termagant ['tʌrməgənt] *adj* regañona, de mal genio; *s* mujer regañona, mujer de mal genio
terminability [,tʌrmɪnə'bɪlɪtɪ] *s* terminabilidad
terminable ['tʌrmɪnəbəl] *adj* terminable
terminal ['tʌrmɪnəl] *adj* terminal; *s* término, fin; (elec.) terminal; (rail.) estación de cabeza, estación de fin de línea
terminally ['tʌrmɪnəlɪ] *adv* al final, finalmente
terminate ['tʌrmɪnet] *va & vn* terminar
termination [,tʌrmɪ'neʃən] *s* terminación; (gram.) terminación, desinencia
terminative ['tʌrmɪ,netɪv] *adj* terminativo
terminological [,tʌrmɪnə'lɑdʒɪkəl] *adj* terminológico
terminology [,tʌrmɪ'nɑlədʒɪ] *s* (*pl:* **-gies**) terminología
term insurance *s* seguro a plazo fijo
terminus ['tʌrmɪnəs] *s* (*pl:* **-ni** [naɪ] o **-nuses**) término; (rail.) estación de cabeza, estación extrema; (*cap.*) *s* (myth.) Término
termite ['tʌrmaɪt] *s* (ent.& fig.) termita
term of service *s* período de servicio
tern [tʌrn] *s* (orn.) gaviotín (*Sterna hirundo*); (orn.) golondrina de mar (*Hydrochelidon*)
ternary ['tʌrnərɪ] *adj* ternario
ternate ['tʌrnet] *adj* ternario; (bot.) ternado
terpene ['tʌrpin] *s* (chem.) terpeno
terpineol [tər'pɪniol] o [tər'pɪnɪɑl] *s* (chem.) terpineol
Terpsichore [tərp'sɪkərɪ] *s* (myth.) Terpsícore
terpsichorean [,tʌrpsɪkə'riən] *adj* de Terpsícore
terr. abr. de **terrace** y **territory**
terrace ['tɛrəs] *s* terraplén; terraza; azotea, terrado; hilera de casas dispuestas a lo largo de una serie de gradas o terraplenes; *va* terraplenar
terra cotta ['tɛrə 'kɑtə] *s* terracota; color rojo oscuro
terra firma ['tɛrə 'fʌrmə] *s* tierra firme; **on terra firma** sobre suelo firme
terrain [tɛ'ren] o ['tɛren] *s* terreno; (geol.) terreno
terra incognita ['tɛrə ɪn'kɑgnɪtə] *s* tierra desconocida
terra japonica ['tɛrə dʒə'pɑnɪkə] *s* (pharm.) tierra japónica
terramycin [,tɛrə'maɪsɪn] *s* (pharm.) terramicina
terrane [tɛ'ren] o ['tɛren] *s* (geol.) terreno
terrapin ['tɛrəpɪn] *s* (zool.) terrapene
terraqueous [tɛr'ekwɪəs] *adj* terráqueo
terrazzo [tɛ'rɑtso] *s* piso veneciano
terreplein ['tɛr,plen] *s* (fort.) terraplén
terrestrial [tə'rɛstrɪəl] *adj* terrestre
terrestrial globe *s* globo terráqueo o terrestre (*la Tierra; mapa de la Tierra en forma de bola*)
terrestrial magnetism *s* magnetismo terrestre
terret ['tɛrɪt] *s* anillo de collera, portarriendas
terrible ['tɛrɪbəl] *adj* terrible; (coll.) muy malo, muy desagradable
terribly ['tɛrɪblɪ] *adv* terriblemente; (coll.) muy, excesivamente
terrier ['tɛrɪər] *s* terrier
terrific [tə'rɪfɪk] *adj* terrífico; (coll.) brutal (*extraordinariamente grande, intenso, lujoso, hermoso, excelente, etc.*)
terrifically [tə'rɪfɪkəlɪ] *adv* terriblemente; (coll.) enormemente, extraordinariamente
terrify ['tɛrɪfaɪ] (*pret & pp:* **-fied**) *va* aterrorizar
territorial [,tɛrɪ'torɪəl] *adj* territorial; (*cap.*) *s* (Brit.) soldado territorial
territoriality [,tɛrɪ,torɪ'ælɪtɪ] *s* territorialidad
territorially [,tɛrɪ'torɪəlɪ] *adv* territorialmente
territory ['tɛrɪ,torɪ] *s* (*pl:* **-ries**) territorio
terror ['tɛrər] *s* terror
terrorism ['tɛrərɪzəm] *s* terrorismo
terrorist ['tɛrərɪst] *adj & s* terrorista
terroristic [,tɛrə'rɪstɪk] *adj* de terrorismo, de terrorista
terrorization [,tɛrərɪ'zeʃən] *s* terror, terrorismo
terrorize ['tɛrəraɪz] *va* aterrorizar
terror-stricken ['tɛrər,strɪkən] *adj* aterrorizado
terry cloth ['tɛrɪ] *s* albornoz
terse [tʌrs] *adj* breve, sucinto, vivo
tertian ['tʌrʃən] *adj* terciano; *s* (path.) terciana

tertiary [ˈtʌrʃɪˌɛrɪ] o [ˈtʌrʃərɪ] *adj* terciario; (*cap.*) *adj* (geol.) terciario; *s* (*pl:* **-ies**) (geol.) terciario
Tertullian [tərˈtʌlɪən] *s* Tertuliano
terza rima [ˈtɛrtsɑ ˈrimɑ] *s* (pros.) tercia rima
tessellate [ˈtɛsəlet] *adj* teselado; *va* formar con teselas
tessera [ˈtɛsərə] *s* (*pl:* **-ae** [i]) tesela; (hist.) tésera
Test. abr. de **Testament**
test [tɛst] *s* prueba, ensayo; examen; (educ. & psychol.) test; (zool.) testa; *va* probar, poner a prueba; examinar
testa [ˈtɛstə] *s* (*pl:* **-tae** [ti]) (bot. & zool.) testa
testacean [tɛsˈteʃən] *adj* & *s* (zool.) testáceo
testacy [ˈtɛstəsɪ] *s* estado de testado
testament [ˈtɛstəmənt] *s* testamento; (*cap.*) *s* Testamento
testamentary [ˌtɛstəˈmɛntərɪ] *adj* testamentario
testate [ˈtɛstet] *adj* testado
testator [tɛsˈtetər] o [ˈtɛstetər] *s* testador
testatrix [tɛsˈtetrɪks] *s* (*pl:* **-trices** [trɪsiz]) testadora
test ban *s* proscripción de las pruebas nucleares
tester [ˈtɛstər] *s* probador, ensayador; baldaquín, dosel
test flight *s* (aer.) vuelo de ensayo o de prueba
testicle [ˈtɛstɪkəl] *s* (anat.) testículo
testicular [tɛsˈtɪkjələr] *adj* testicular
testify [ˈtɛstɪfaɪ] (*pret* & *pp:* **-fied**) *va* & *vn* testificar
testimonial [ˌtɛstɪˈmonɪəl] *adj* de recomendación; de homenaje; *s* recomendación, certificado; homenaje
testimony [ˈtɛstɪˌmonɪ] *s* (*pl:* **-nies**) testimonio; (Bib.) testimonio; **testimonies** *spl* Sagradas Escrituras; **in testimony whereof** en testimonio de lo cual
testing bench *s* banco de pruebas
testing grounds *spl* campo de prueba
testis [ˈtɛstɪs] *s* (*pl:* **-tes** [tiz]) (anat.) teste
test of strength *s* prueba de fuerza
testosterone [tɛsˈtɑstəron] *s* (biochem.) testosterona
test pilot *s* (aer.) piloto de pruebas
test tube *s* probeta, tubo de ensayo
testudinal [tɛsˈtjudɪnəl] o [tɛsˈtudɪnəl] *adj* (zool.) testudinal
testudinous [tɛsˈtjudɪnəs] o [tɛsˈtudɪnəs] *adj* testudíneo
testudo [tɛsˈtjudo] o [tɛsˈtudo] *s* (*pl:* **-dines** [dɪniz]) (hist.) testudo
testy [ˈtɛstɪ] *adj* (*comp:* **-tier;** *super:* **-tiest**) enojadizo, picajoso, quisquilloso
tetanic [tɪˈtænɪk] *adj* tetánico
tetanize [ˈtɛtənaɪz] *va* tetanizar
tetanus [ˈtɛtənəs] *s* (path.) tétanos
tetany [ˈtɛtənɪ] *s* (path.) tetania
tetartohedral [tɪˌtɑrtoˈhidrəl] *adj* (cryst.) tetartoédrico
tetartohedron [tɪˌtɑrtoˈhidrən] *s* (cryst.) tetartoedro
tetchy [ˈtɛtʃɪ] *adj* (*comp:* **-ier;** *super:* **-iest**) pelilloso, enojadizo
tête-à-tête [ˈtetəˈtet] *s* conversación a solas entre dos; confidente (*mueble*); *adj* de persona a persona; *adv* a solas, cara a cara
tête-bêche [tɛtˈbɛʃ] *adj* (philately) capiculado
tether [ˈtɛðər] *s* traba, atadura; **at the end of one's tether** al límite de las posibilidades o paciencia de uno; *va* apersogar
tetrachlorid [ˌtɛtrəˈklorɪd] o **tetrachloride** [ˌtɛtrəˈkloraɪd] o [ˌtɛtrəˈklorɪd] *s* (chem.) tetracloruro
tetrachord [ˈtɛtrəkɔrd] *s* (mus.) tetracordio
tetrachordal [ˌtɛtrəˈkɔrdəl] *adj* (mus.) tetracordal
tetracycline [ˌtɛtrəˈsaɪklɪn] *s* (pharm.) tetraciclina
tetradymite [tɛˈtrædɪmaɪt] *s* (mineral.) tetradimita
tetraethyl lead [ˌtɛtrəˈɛθɪl lɛd] *s* (chem.) tetraetilo de plomo
tetragon [ˈtɛtrəgɑn] *s* (geom.) tetrágono
tetragonal [tɛˈtrægənəl] *adj* tetragonal
tetrahedral [ˌtɛtrəˈhidrəl] *adj* tetraédrico
tetrahedron [ˌtɛtrəˈhidrən] *s* (*pl:* **-drons** o **-dra** [drə]) (geom.) tetraedro
tetralogy [tɛˈtrælədʒɪ] *s* (*pl:* **-gies**) (theat.) tetralogía
tetrameter [tɛˈtræmɪtər] *adj* & *s* tetrámetro
tetrapetalous [ˌtɛtrəˈpɛtələs] *adj* (bot.) tetrapétalo
tetrarch [ˈtɛtrɑrk] *s* tetrarca
tetrarchy [ˈtɛtrɑrkɪ] *s* (*pl:* **-chies**) tetrarquía
tetrasyllabic [ˌtɛtrəsɪˈlæbɪk] *adj* tetrasílabo o tetrasilábico
tetrasyllable [ˌtɛtrəˈsɪləbəl] *s* tetrasílabo
tetravalent [ˌtɛtrəˈvelənt] o [tɛˈtrævələnt] *adj* (chem.) tetravalente
tetrode [ˈtɛtrod] *s* (elec.) tetrodo
tetroxide [tɛˈtrɑksaɪd] o [tɛˈtrɑksɪd] *s* (chem.) tetróxido
tetryl [ˈtɛtrɪl] *s* tetrilo
tetter [ˈtɛtər] *s* (path.) empeine, herpes, culebrilla
Teucer [ˈtjusər] o [ˈtusər] *s* (myth.) Teucro
Teucrian [ˈtjukrɪən] o [ˈtukrɪən] *adj* & *s* teucro
Teuton [ˈtjutən] o [ˈtutən] *adj* & *s* teutón
Teutonic [tjuˈtɑnɪk] o [tuˈtɑnɪk] *adj* teutónico; *s* teutónico (*idioma*)
Tex. abr. de **Texas**
Texan [ˈtɛksən] *adj* & *s* tejano
Texas [ˈtɛksəs] *s* Tejas
Texas fever *s* (vet.) fiebre de Tejas
text [tɛkst] *s* texto; lema, tema
textbook [ˈtɛkstˌbʊk] *s* libro de texto
textile [ˈtɛkstɪl] o [ˈtɛkstaɪl] *adj* textil; *s* textil (*materia que puede tejerse*); tejido
textual [ˈtɛkstʃʊəl] *adj* textual
textual criticism *s* crítica textual
textualist [ˈtɛkstʃʊəlɪst] *s* textualista
textually [ˈtɛkstʃʊəlɪ] *adv* textualmente
textural [ˈtɛkstʃərəl] *adj* textural
textura [ˈtɛkstʃər] *s* textura; (fig.) textura (*estructura*)
Th. abr. de **Thomas** y **Thursday**
T.H. abr. de **Territory of Hawaii**
Thaddeus [ˈθædɪəs] *s* Tadeo
Thai [ˈtɑ·i] o [taɪ] *adj* & *s* tailandés
Thailand [ˈtaɪlənd] *s* Tailandia
thalamic [θəˈlæmɪk] *adj* talámico
thalamus [ˈθæləməs] *s* (*pl:* **-mi** [maɪ]) (anat.) tálamo
thalassic [θəˈlæsɪk] *adj* talásico
Thales [ˈθeliz] *s* Tales
Thalia [θəˈlaɪə] *s* (myth.) Talía
thallium [ˈθælɪəm] *s* (chem.) talio
thallophyte [ˈθælofaɪt] *s* (bot.) talófita
thallophytic [ˌθæloˈfɪtɪk] *adj* talofítico
thallus [ˈθæləs] *s* (*pl:* **-li** [laɪ] o **-luses**) (bot.) talo
thalweg [ˈtɑlˌvex] *s* vaguada
Thames [tɛmz] *s* Támesis
than [ðæn] *conj* que, p.ej., **he is richer than I** es más rico que yo; **than** + *numeral* de + *numeral*, p.ej., **more than twenty** más de veinte; **than** + *verb* de lo que + *verb*, p.ej., **he writes better than he speaks** escribe mejor de lo que habla; **than** + *verb with direct object understood* del (de la, de los, de las) que, p.ej., **they sent us more coffee than we ordered** nos enviaron más café del que pedimos; *prep* **than which** o **than whom** comparado con el cual
thane [θen] *s* (Brit. hist.) caballero, gentilhombre; (Scottish hist.) barón, señor
thank [θæŋk] *s* (archaic) gracia; **thanks** *spl* gracias; agradecimiento, gratitud; **thanks to** gracias a (*merced a, por intervención de*); **thanks** *interj* ¡gracias!; *va* agradecer, dar las gracias a; **to have oneself to thank** tener la culpa, ser responsable; **to thank someone for something** agradecerle a uno una cosa; **to thank someone to** + *inf* agradecerle a uno (que) + *subj*, p.ej., **we will thank you to fill out the enclosed card** le agradeceremos llene la adjunta tarjeta
thankful [ˈθæŋkfəl] *adj* agradecido
thankfully [ˈθæŋkfəlɪ] *adv* con agradecimiento
thankfulness [ˈθæŋkfəlnɪs] *s* agradecimiento, gratitud
thankless [ˈθæŋklɪs] *adj* ingrato (*desagradecido; que no corresponde al trabajo que cuesta*)
thanksgiving [θæŋksˈgɪvɪŋ] *s* acción de gracias; (*cap.*) *s* (U.S.A.) día de acción de gracias

Thanksgiving Day *s* (U.S.A.) día de acción de gracias, día de gracias
that [ðæt] *adj dem* (*pl:* **those**) ese; aquel; *pron dem* (*pl:* **those**) ése; aquél; eso; aquello; **at that** (coll.) sin más; (coll.) considerándolo todo; **in that** porque; **upon that** sobre eso; luego; **that's that** (coll.) así es; *pron rel* que, quien, el cual, el que; en que, cuando; *adv* tan; **that far** tan lejos; hasta allí; **that much** tanto; *conj* que; para que; **so that** de modo que; para que
thatch [θætʃ] *s* paja, barda, bálago; techo de paja o bálago; (coll.) pelo (*de la cabeza*); *va* cubrir de paja, bardar, poner un techo de paja a
thatched roof *s* techo de paja o bálago
thaumaturge ['θɔmətʌrdʒ] *s* taumaturgo
thaumaturgic [,θɔmə'tʌrdʒɪk] o **thaumaturgical** [,θɔmə'tʌrdʒɪkəl] *adj* taumatúrgico
thaumaturgy ['θɔmə,tʌrdʒɪ] *s* taumaturgia
thaw [θɔ] *s* deshielo, derretimiento; (fig.) ablandamiento, enternecimiento; *va* deshelar, derretir; *vn* deshelarse, derretirse; (fig.) ablandarse, enternecerse
the [ðə], [ðɪ] o [ði] *art def* el; el más a propósito; [ðə] o [ðɪ] *adv* cuanto, p.ej., **the more the merrier** cuanto más mejor; **the more . . . the more** cuanto más . . . tanto más
theaceous [θi'eʃəs] *adj* (bot.) teáceo
theanthropism [θi'ænθrəpɪzəm] *s* teantropía
theater ['θiətər] *s* teatro; (fig.) teatro (*p.ej., de una guerra*)
theater-in-the-round ['θiətərɪnðə'raʊnd] *s* teatro circular
theater of war *s* (mil.) teatro de la guerra
theatre ['θiətər] *s* var. de **theater**
theatric [θɪ'ætrɪk] *adj* teatral
theatrical [θɪ'ætrɪkəl] *adj* teatral; **theatricals** *spl* funciones teatrales; asuntos teatrales; modales artificiales o exagerados
theatricalism [θɪ'ætrɪkəlɪzəm] *s* teoría y método dramático; calidad teatral, estilo teatral
theatricality [θɪ,ætrɪ'kælɪtɪ] *s* teatralidad
thebaine ['θibəin], [θɪ'bein] o [θɪ'beɪn] *s* (chem.) tebaína
Theban ['θibən] *adj & s* tebano o tebeo
Thebes [θibz] *s* Tebas (*de Egipto; de Grecia*)
theca ['θikə] *s* (*pl:* **-cae** [si]) (anat. & bot.) teca
thé dansant [tedɑ̃'sɑ̃] *s* (*pl:* **thés dansants** [tedɑ̃'sɑ̃]) té baile, té bailable
thee [ði] *pron pers* (archaic, poet. & Bib.) te; ti; (en el lenguaje familiar entre los cuáqueros) tú; **with thee** contigo
theelin [θilɪn] *s* (biochem.) teelina
theft [θɛft] *s* hurto, robo
thegn [θen] *s* var. de **thane**
thein ['θiɪn] o **theine** ['θiin] o ['θiɪn] *s* (chem.) teína
their [ðɛr] *adj poss* su; el (o su) . . . de ellos
theirs [ðɛrz] *pron poss* el suyo, el de ellos
theism ['θiɪzəm] *s* teísmo
theist ['θiɪst] *s* teísta
theistic [θi'ɪstɪk] *adj* teísta
them [ðɛm] *pron pers* los; ellos; **to them** les; a ellos
thematic [θi'mætɪk] *adj* temático
theme [θim] *s* tema; (mus.) tema
theme song *s* (mus.) tema central; (rad.) sintonía
Themistocles [θɪ'mɪstəkliz] *s* Temístocles
themselves [ðɛm'sɛlvz] *pron pers* ellos mismos; se; sí, sí mismos; **with themselves** consigo
then [ðɛn] *s* aquel tiempo; *adj* de entonces; *adv* entonces (*en aquel tiempo*); después, luego, en seguida; además, también; **but then** pero al mismo tiempo, pero por otro lado; **by then** para entonces; **from then on** desde entonces, de allí en adelante; **then and there** ahí mismo, al momento
thenar ['θinɑr] *adj & s* (anat.) tenar
thence [ðɛns] *adv* desde allí; desde entonces; por eso, por esa razón
thenceforth [,ðɛns'forθ] o **thenceforward** [,ðɛns'fɔrwərd] *adv* de allí en adelante; desde entonces
theobromine [,θiə'bromin] o [,θiə'bromɪn] *s* (chem.) teobromina
theocracy [θi'ɑkrəsɪ] *s* (*pl:* **-cies**) teocracia
theocrat ['θiəkræt] *s* teócrata
theocratic [,θiə'krætɪk] *adj* teocrático
Theocritus [θi'ɑkrɪtəs] *s* Teócrito
theodicy [θi'ɑdɪsɪ] *s* (*pl:* **-cies**) teodicea
theodolite [θi'ɑdəlaɪt] *s* teodolito
Theodore ['θiədor] *s* Teodoro
Theodoric [θi'ɑdərɪk] *s* Teodorico
Theodosius [,θiə'doʃɪəs] *s* Teodosio
theogonic [,θiə'gɑnɪk] *adj* teogónico
theogony [θi'ɑgənɪ] *s* (*pl:* **-nies**) teogonía
theologian [,θiə'lodʒɪən] *s* teólogo
theological [,θiə'lɑdʒɪkəl] *adj* teológico
theologically [,θiə'lɑdʒɪkəlɪ] *adv* teológicamente
theologize [θi'ɑlədʒaɪz] *va* hacer teológico; discurrir teológicamente sobre; *vn* teologizar
theologue ['θiəlɔg] o ['θiəlɑg] *s* (coll.) teólogo (*estudiante*)
theology [θi'ɑlədʒɪ] *s* (*pl:* **-gies**) teología
Theophilus [θi'ɑfɪləs] *s* Teófilo
Theophrastus [,θiə'fræstəs] *s* Teofrasto
theorem ['θiərəm] *s* teorema
theoretic [,θiə'rɛtɪk] o **theoretical** [,θiə'rɛtɪkəl] *adj* teórico
theoretically [,θiə'rɛtɪkəlɪ] *adv* teóricamente
theoretician [,θiərə'tɪʃən] *s* teórico
theorist ['θiərɪst] *s* teorizante; teórico
theorize ['θiəraɪz] *vn* teorizar
theory ['θiərɪ] *s* (*pl:* **-ries**) teoría
theory of knowledge *s* (philos.) teoría del conocimiento
theosophic [,θiə'sɑfɪk] o **theosophical** [,θiə'sɑfɪkəl] *adj* teosófico
theosophist [θi'ɑsəfɪst] *s* teósofo
theosophy [θi'ɑsəfɪ] *s* teosofía
therapeutic [,θɛrə'pjutɪk] *adj* terapéutico; **therapeutics** *ssg* terapéutica
therapeutical [,θɛrə'pjutɪkəl] *adj* terapéutico
therapeutically [,θɛrə'pjutɪkəlɪ] *adv* terapéuticamente
therapeutist [,θɛrə'pjutɪst] *s* terapeuta
therapist ['θɛrəpɪst] *s* terapeuta
therapy ['θɛrəpɪ] *s* (*pl:* **-pies**) terapia
there [ðɛr] *adv* ahí, allí, allá; **all there** (coll.) despierto, vigilante, vivo; **to not be all there** (coll.) no estar en sus cabales; **there is** o **there are** hay; aquí tiene Vd.; usado enfáticamente con un verbo, se omite en la traducción al español, p.ej., **there appeared a man dressed in black** apareció un hombre vestido de negro; *interj* ¡ eso es!, ¡ mira!, ¡ vaya!
thereabout ['ðɛrə,baʊt] o **thereabouts** ['ðɛrə,baʊts] *adv* por ahí, por allí; cerca, aproximadamente
thereafter [ðɛr'æftər] o [ðɛr'ɑftər] *adv* después de eso, de allí en adelante; conforme, en conformidad
thereat [ðɛr'æt] *adv* entonces, en eso; en aquel lugar; por eso, por esa razón
thereby [ðɛr'baɪ] o ['ðɛrbaɪ] *adv* con eso; así, de tal modo; cerca de ahí, por allí cerca
therefor [ðɛr'fɔr] *adv* para esto, para eso
therefore ['ðɛrfor] *adv* por lo tanto, por consiguiente
therefrom [ðɛr'frɑm] o [ðɛr'frʌm] *adv* de eso, de ahí, de allí
therein [ðɛr'ɪn] *adv* en esto, en eso; en ese respecto
thereinto [ðɛr'ɪntu] o [,ðɛrɪn'tu] *adv* dentro de esto, dentro de eso
thereof [ðɛr'ɑv] *adv* de esto, de eso
thereon [ðɛr'ɑn] o [ðɛr'ɔn] *adv* en eso, sobre eso, encima de eso; en seguida
there's [ðɛrz] contracción de **there is** y **there has**
Theresa [tə'risə] o [tə'rɛsə] *s* Teresa
thereto [ðɛr'tu] *adv* a eso; además, además de eso
theretofore [,ðɛrtu'for] *adv* antes de eso, hasta entonces
thereunder [ðɛr'ʌndər] *adv* bajo eso, debajo de eso; debajo, por debajo
thereupon [,ðɛrə'pɑn] o [,ðɛrə'pɔn] *adv* sobre eso, encima de eso; por eso, por consiguiente; al momento, en seguida
therewith [ðɛr'wɪð] o [ðɛr'wɪθ] *adv* con esto, con eso; luego, en seguida
therewithal [,ðɛrwɪð'ɔl] *adv* con esto, con eso; a más, además
therianthropic [,θɪrɪæn'θrɑpɪk] *adj* terianthrópico

theriomorphic [,θɪrɪə'mɔrfɪk] o **theriomorphous** [,θɪrɪə'mɔrfəs] *adj* teriomórfico
therm [θʌrm] *s* (phys.) termia o termio
thermae ['θʌrmi] *spl* termas
thermal ['θʌrməl] *adj* termal
thermal barrier *s* barrera térmica
thermalize ['θʌrməlaɪz] o **thermatize** ['θʌrmətaɪz] *va* (phys.) termatizar
thermesthesia [,θʌrmɪs'θiʒə] o [,θʌrmɪs'θiʒɪə] *s* (physiol.) termoestesia
thermic ['θʌrmɪk] *adj* térmico
thermion ['θʌrm,aɪən] o ['θʌrmɪən] *s* (phys.) termión
thermionic [,θʌrmaɪ'ɑnɪk] o [,θʌrmɪ'ɑnɪk] *adj* termiónico; **thermionics** *ssg* termiónica
thermistor [θər'mɪstər] *s* (elec.) termistor
thermit ['θʌrmɪt] o **thermite** ['θʌrmaɪt] *s* (trademark) termita
thermobarograph [,θʌrmo'bærəgræf] o [,θʌrmo'bærəgrɑf] *s* termobarógrafo
thermobarometer [,θʌrmobə'rɑmɪtər] *s* termobarómetro
thermocautery [,θʌrmo'kɔtərɪ] *s* termocauterio
thermochemical [,θʌrmo'kɛmɪkəl] *adj* termoquímico
thermochemistry [,θʌrmo'kɛmɪstrɪ] *s* termoquímica
thermocouple ['θʌrmo,kʌpəl] *s* (elec.) termopar, par térmico
thermodynamic [,θʌrmodaɪ'næmɪk] o [,θʌrmodɪ'næmɪk] *adj* termodinámico; **thermodynamics** *ssg* termodinámica
thermoelectric [,θʌrmo·ɪ'lɛktrɪk] o **thermoelectrical** [,θʌrmo·ɪ'lɛktrɪkəl] *adj* termoeléctrico
thermoelectric couple *s* (elec.) par termoeléctrico
thermoelectricity [,θʌrmo·ɪ,lɛk'trɪsɪtɪ] *s* termoelectricidad
thermoelectromotive [,θʌrmo·ɪ,lɛktro'motɪv] *adj* termoelectromotor
thermoelement [,θʌrmo'ɛlɪmənt] *s* (elec.) termoelemento
thermofission [,θʌrmo'fɪʃən] *s* (phys.) termofisión
thermofusion [,θʌrmo'fjuʒən] *s* (phys.) termofusión
thermogenesis [,θʌrmo'dʒɛnɪsɪs] *s* (physiol.) termogénesis
thermogenetic [,θʌrmodʒɪ'nɛtɪk] *adj* termógeno
thermograph ['θʌrməgræf] o ['θʌrməgrɑf] *s* termógrafo
thermolabile [,θʌrmo'lebɪl] *adj* (biochem.) termolábil
thermology [θər'mɑlədʒɪ] *s* termología
thermolysis [θər'mɑlɪsɪs] *s* (chem. & physiol.) termólisis
thermometer [θər'mɑmɪtər] *s* termómetro
thermometric [,θʌrmo'mɛtrɪk] *adj* termométrico
thermometry [θər'mɑmɪtrɪ] *s* termometría
thermomotive [,θʌrmo'motɪv] *adj* termomotor
thermonuclear [,θʌrmo'njuklɪər] o [,θʌrmo'nuklɪər] *adj* termonuclear
thermopile ['θʌrməpaɪl] *s* (phys.) termopila
thermoplastic [,θʌrmə'plæstɪk] *adj* termoplástico
Thermopylae [θər'mɑpɪli] *s* las Termópilas
thermos bottle ['θʌrməs] *s* termos, botella termos
thermoscope ['θʌrməskop] *s* termoscopio
thermosiphon [,θʌrmo'saɪfən] *s* termosifón
thermostat ['θʌrməstæt] *s* termóstato
thermostatic [,θʌrmə'stætɪk] *adj* termostático
thermostatically [,θʌrmə'stætɪkəlɪ] *adv* mediante un termóstato
thermotropism [θər'mɑtrəpɪzəm] *s* (biol.) termotropismo
Thersites [θər'saɪtiz] *s* (myth.) Tersites
thesaurus [θɪ'sɔrəs] *s* (*pl:* **-ri** [raɪ]) tesoro; tesauro o tesoro (*catálogo, diccionario, etc.*)
these [ðiz] *pl de* **this**
Theseus ['θisus] o ['θisɪəs] *s* (myth.) Teseo
thesis ['θisɪs] *s* (*pl:* **-ses** [siz]) tesis; (mus.) tesis
thesis play *s* pieza de tesis
Thespian ['θɛspɪən] *adj* de Tespis; dramático, trágico; *s* actor dramático o trágico
Thespis ['θɛspɪs] *s* Tespis
Thess. abr. de **Thessalonians**
Thessalian [θɛ'selɪən] *adj & s* tesaliano
Thessalonian [,θɛsə'lonɪən] *adj & s* tesalonicense; **Thessalonians** *spl* (Bib.) Epístola a los Tesalonicenses (*cada una de dos*)
Thessalonica [,θɛsəlo'naɪkə] o [,θɛsə'lɑnɪkə] *s* (hist.) Tesalónica
Thessaly ['θɛsəlɪ] *s* la Tesalia
Thetis ['θitɪs] *s* (myth.) Tetis
theurgic [θi'ʌrdʒɪk] o **theurgical** [θi'ʌrdʒɪkəl] *adj* teúrgico
theurgist ['θiʌrdʒɪst] *s* teurgo
theurgy ['θiʌrdʒɪ] *s* (*pl:* **-gies**) teurgia
thews [θuz] o [θjuz] *spl* músculos; fuerza muscular
they [ðe] *pron pers* ellos
they'd [ðed] contracción de **they had** y **they would**
they'll [ðel] contracción de **they will** y **they shall**
they're [ðɛr] contracción de **they are**
they've [ðev] contracción de **they have**
thiamine ['θaɪəmin] o ['θaɪəmɪn] *s* (biochem.) tiamina
thiazole ['θaɪəzol] *s* (chem.) tiazol
Thibetan [tɪ'bɛtən] *adj & s* var. de **Tibetan**
thick [θɪk] *adj* espeso, grueso, denso; de espesor, p.ej., **three inches thick** de tres pulgadas de espesor; abundante; cubierto, lleno; brumoso, nebuloso; torpe, estúpido; basto, burdo, grosero; (coll.) íntimo; (coll.) insoportable, insolente; **to be thick with** (coll.) tener mucha intimidad con; *adv* espesamente, densamente; abundantemente; **to lay it on thick** (coll.) exagerar en los reproches o las alabanzas; **to talk thick** tener la lengua gorda; *s* espesor, grueso; **the thick of** lo más denso de (*p.ej., la multitud*); lo más reñido de (*p.ej., el combate*); **through thick and thin** a toda prueba, por las buenas y las malas
thicken ['θɪkən] *va* espesar; *vn* espesarse; complicarse (*el enredo*)
thickener ['θɪkənər] *s* espesador
thickening ['θɪkənɪŋ] *adj* espesativo; *s* espesamiento; espesante, espesador
thicket ['θɪkɪt] *s* espesura, soto, matorral
thickhead ['θɪk,hɛd] *s* (coll.) cabeza dura (*persona*)
thick-headed ['θɪk'hɛdɪd] *adj* (coll.) torpe, estúpido
thick-knee ['θɪk,ni] *s* (orn.) alcaraván
thickly ['θɪklɪ] *adv* espesamente, densamente; abundantemente; repetidamente; muy, sumamente
thickness ['θɪknɪs] *s* espesura (*calidad*); espesor (*dimensión; densidad de un flúido*); lo más denso; lo más reñido; capa, estrato
thick-set ['θɪk,sɛt] *adj* denso, muy poblado; grueso, rechoncho; *s* espesura, soto, matorral; seto espeso
thick-skinned ['θɪk'skɪnd] *adj* de pellejo espeso; duro, insensible
thick-witted ['θɪk'wɪtɪd] *adj* torpe, estúpido, imbécil
thief [θif] *s* (*pl:* **thieves**) ladrón
thieve [θiv] *vn* hurtar, robar
thievery ['θivərɪ] *s* (*pl:* **-ies**) hurto, robo, latrocinio
thieves' Latin *s* caló o jerga de los ladrones
thievish ['θivɪʃ] *adj* engatado, ratero, rapaz
thigh [θaɪ] *s* (anat.) muslo
thighbone ['θaɪ,bon] *s* (anat.) fémur
thigmotaxis [,θɪgmə'tæksɪs] *s* (biol.) tigmotaxia
thigmotropism [θɪg'mɑtrəpɪzəm] *s* (biol.) tigmotropismo
thill [θɪl] *s* limonera o lanza
thimble ['θɪmbəl] *s* dedal; (mach.) manguito; (naut.) guardacabo
thimbleberry ['θɪmbəl,bɛrɪ] *s* (*pl:* **-ries**) (bot.) frambueso norteamericano (*Rubus occidentalis, R. parviflorus y R. argutus*); frambuesa (*fruto*)
thimbleful ['θɪmbəlfʊl] *s* dedal (*cantidad que cabe en un dedal*)
thimblerig ['θɪmbəl,rɪg] *s* fullería hecha jugando con tres tacitas y un guisante; (*pret &*

pp: **-rigged;** *ger:* **-rigging**) *va & vn* engañar con la fullería de tres tacitas y un guisante; engañar
thin [θɪn] *adj* (*comp:* **thinner;** *super:* **thinnest**) delgado, tenue, flaco; fino (*paño, papel, suela de zapato, etc.*); ralo (*pelo*); aguado (*caldo*); transparente; claro, ligero, escaso; *adv* delgadamente; ligeramente; poco; (*pret & pp:* **thinned;** *ger:* **thinning**) *va* adelgazar, enflaquecer; enrarecer; aclarar; aguar; desleír (*los colores*); *vn* adelgazarse; enflaquecerse; enrarecerse
thine [ðaɪn] *adj poss* (archaic & poet.) tu; *pron poss* (archaic & poet.) tuyo; el tuyo
thing [θɪŋ] *s* cosa; **of all things!** ¡qué sorpresa!; **the thing** lo que está de moda; lo debido, lo importante; **to be the real thing** estar muy de veras; **to know a thing or two** (coll.) saber cuántas son cinco; (coll.) tener experiencia; **to make a good thing of** (coll.) sacar provecho de; **to not know the first thing about** no saber nada de; **to see things** ver visiones, padecer alucinaciones; **to tell someone a thing or two** (coll.) decirle a uno dos gracias
thing-in-itself [ˌθɪŋɪnɪtˈsɛlf] *s* (philos.) cosa en sí
thingumbob [ˈθɪŋəmbɑb] *s* (coll.) cosa, negocillo (*cosa cuyo nombre se ha olvidado o no se quiere pronunciar*)
think [θɪŋk] (*pret & pp:* **thought**) *va* pensar; acordarse de; **to think it over** pensarlo; **to think nothing of** tener en poco; creer fácil; no dar importancia a; **to think of** pensar de (*tener cierta opinión de*); **to think out** imaginar, idear, descubrir, resolver; **to think up** imaginar; inventar (*p.ej., una excusa*); *vn* pensar; **to think aloud** pensar en alta voz, expresar lo que uno piensa; **to think ill of** tener mala opinión de; **to think not** creer que no; **to think of** pensar en (*tener el pensamiento concentrado en*); pensar (*un número, un naipe, etc.*); **to think out loud** pensar en alta voz, expresar lo que uno piensa; **to think over** pensar detenidamente; **to think so** creer que sí; **to think twice** pensar dos veces; **to think well of** tener buena opinión de; **you think so!** (iron.) ¡que te crees tú eso!
thinkable [ˈθɪŋkəbəl] *adj* pensable, concebible
thinker [ˈθɪŋkər] *s* pensador
thinking [ˈθɪŋkɪŋ] *adj* pensante; pensador (*meditabundo*); *s* pensamiento; parecer
thinner [ˈθɪnər] *s* diluente
thinnish [ˈθɪnɪʃ] *adj* flacucho; algo ralo
thin-skinned [ˈθɪnˈskɪnd] *adj* de pellejo delgado; sensible, susceptible
thiocyanate [ˌθaɪoˈsaɪənet] *s* (chem.) tiocianato
thiocyanic [ˌθaɪosaɪˈænɪk] *adj* tiociánico
thiocyanic acid *s* (chem.) ácido tiociánico
thionic [θaɪˈɑnɪk] *adj* tiónico
thionic acid *s* (chem.) ácido tiónico
thiophene [ˈθaɪəfin] *s* (chem.) tiofeno
thiosinamine [ˌθaɪəsɪˈnæmɪn] *s* (chem.) tiosinamina
thiosulfate [ˌθaɪoˈsʌlfet] *s* (chem.) tiosulfato
thiosulfuric [ˌθaɪosʌlˈfjʊrɪk] *adj* tiosulfúrico
thiosulfuric acid *s* (chem.) ácido tiosulfúrico
thiourea [ˌθaɪojʊˈriə] o [ˌθaɪoˈjʊrɪə] *s* (chem.) tiourea
third [θʌrd] *adj* tercero; *s* tercero; tercio (*una de tres partes iguales*); tres (*en las fechas*); (mus.) tercera; (aut.) tercera (velocidad)
third base *s* (baseball) tercera base *f* (*puesto*); (baseball) tercera base *m* (*jugador*)
third baseman *s* (baseball) tercera base *m* (*jugador*)
third-class [ˈθʌrdˌklæs] o [ˈθʌrdˌklɑs] *adj* de tercera clase
third degree *s* (coll.) interrogatorio de un preso, hecho de una manera brutal, interrogatorio bajo tortura
thirdly [ˈθʌrdlɪ] *adv* en tercer lugar
third person *s* (gram.) tercera persona
third rail *s* (rail.) tercer carril
third-rate [ˈθʌrdˌret] *adj* de tercer orden; de mala calidad, de última clase
thirst [θʌrst] *s* sed; (fig.) sed; *vn* tener sed; **to thirst for** tener sed de; (fig.) tener sed de
thirsty [ˈθʌrstɪ] *adj* (*comp:* **-ier;** *super:* **-iest**) sediento; **to be thirsty** tener sed; **to be thirsty for** tener sed de
thirteen [ˈθʌrˈtin] *adj & s* trece
thirteenth [ˈθʌrˈtinθ] *adj* décimotercero o décimotercio; trezavo; *s* decimotercero o décimotercio; trezavo; trece (*en las fechas*)
thirtieth [ˈθʌrtɪɪθ] *adj* trigésimo; treintavo; *s* trigésimo; treintavo; treinta (*en las fechas*)
thirty [ˈθʌrtɪ] *adj* treinta; *s* (*pl:* **-ties**) treinta; **thirty all** (tennis) treinta iguales
thirty-second note [ˈθʌrtɪˈsɛkənd] *s* (mus.) fusa
thirty-twomo [ˌθʌrtɪˈtuˌmo] *adj* en treintaidosavo; *s* libro en treintaidosavo
Thirty Years' War *s* guerra de los Treinta Años
this [ðɪs] *adj dem* (*pl:* **these**) este; *pron dem* (*pl:* **these**) éste; esto; *adv* tan
Thisbe [ˈθɪzbɪ] *s* (myth.) Tisbe
thistle [ˈθɪsəl] *s* (bot.) cardo
thistledown [ˈθɪsəlˌdaʊn] *s* borrilla de cardo
thistly [ˈθɪslɪ] *adj* lleno de cardos; espinoso
thither [ˈθɪðər] o [ˈðɪðər] *adj* más lejano, al otro lado; *adv* allá, hacia allá, para allá
thitherward [ˈθɪðərwərd] o [ˈðɪðərwərd] *adv* allá, hacia allá, para allá
tho o **tho'** [ðo] *adv & conj* var. de **though**
thole [θol] o **tholepin** [ˈθolˌpɪn] *s* (naut.) escálamo o tolete
Thomas [ˈtɑməs] *s* Tomás
Thomism [ˈtomɪzəm] o [ˈθomɪzəm] *s* tomismo
Thomist [ˈtomɪst] o [ˈθomɪst] *adj & s* tomista
thong [θɔŋ] o [θɑŋ] *s* correa, tira de cuero
thoracic [θoˈræsɪk] *adj* torácico
thoracic duct *s* (anat.) conducto torácico
thorax [ˈθoræks] *s* (*pl:* **-raxes** o **-races** [rəsiz]) (anat. & zool.) tórax
thoric [ˈθɑrɪk] o [ˈθorɪk] *adj* (chem.) tórico
thorite [ˈθoraɪt] *s* (mineral.) torita
thorium [ˈθorɪəm] *s* (chem.) torio
thorn [θɔrn] *s* espina; (bot.) espino u oxcicanto; (bot.) endrino; (fig.) espina (*ansia, tormento*); **thorn in the flesh** o **side** espina en el dedo, motivo de continuo enojo
thorn apple *s* (bot.) manzana espinosa, higuera loca
thornback [ˈθɔrnˌbæk] *s* (ichth.) raya espinosa; (zool.) centolla
thorny [ˈθɔrnɪ] *adj* (*comp:* **-ier;** *super:* **-iest**) espinoso; (fig.) espinoso
thoro [ˈθʌro] *adj* var. de **thorough**
thoron [ˈθorɑn] *s* (chem.) torón
thorough [ˈθʌro] *adj* cabal, completo; cuidadoso, concienzudo
thoroughbred [ˈθʌroˌbrɛd] *adj* de pura raza o sangre; bien nacido, bien educado; *s* pura sangre *m*; persona bien nacida, persona bien educada
thoroughfare [ˈθʌroˌfɛr] *s* carretera, vía pública; tránsito, pasaje; **no thoroughfare** se prohíbe el paso
thoroughgoing [ˈθʌroˌgo·ɪŋ] *adj* cabal, completo, esmerado, perfecto
thoroughly [ˈθʌrolɪ] *adv* a fondo
thoroughness [ˈθʌronɪs] *s* entereza, perfección, minuciosidad
thoroughwort [ˈθʌroˌwʌrt] *s* (bot.) eupatorio
thorp [θɔrp] *s* (archaic) aldea
those [ðoz] *pl de* **that**
thou [ðaʊ] *pron pers* (archaic, poet. & Bib.) tú; *va & vn* (archaic) tutear
though [ðo] *adv* sin embargo; *conj* aun cuando, aunque, bien que, si bien; **as though** como si
thought [θɔt] *s* pensamiento; consideración; (coll.) pizca, muy poco; *pret & pp de* **think**
thought control *s* control del pensamiento
thoughtful [ˈθɔtfəl] *adj* pensativo; atento, considerado
thoughtfulness [ˈθɔtfəlnɪs] *s* atención, consideración, solicitud
thoughtless [ˈθɔtlɪs] *adj* irreflexivo; descuidado; inconsiderado
thought transference *s* transmisión del pensamiento
thousand [ˈθaʊzənd] *adj & s* mil; **a thousand** u **one thousand** mil
Thousand and One Nights, The las Mil y una noches
thousandfold [ˈθaʊzəndˌfold] *adj* multiplicado por mil; *adv* mil veces más

Thousand Islands, the las Mil Islas
thousandth ['θaʊzəndθ] *adj & s* milésimo
Thrace [θres] *s* la Tracia
Thracian ['θreʃən] *adj & s* traciano o tracio
thrall [θrɔl] *s* esclavo; esclavitud, servidumbre
thralldom o **thraldom** ['θrɔldəm] *s* esclavitud, servidumbre
thrash [θræʃ] *va* (agr.) trillar; azotar, zurrar; **to thrash out** decidir después de una discusión cabal; **to thrash over** discutir repetidas veces; *vn* (agr.) trillar; dar vueltas, sacudirse, menearse
thrasher ['θræʃər] *s* (agr.) trillador; (agr.) trilladora mecánica; (orn.) cuicacoche; (ichth.) raposa de mar, zorra de mar
thread [θrɛd] *s* hilo; (mach.) filete o rosca; (zool.) hilo (*de la araña*); (fig.) hilo (*de un discurso, de la vida, etc.*); **to hang by a thread** estar colgado de un hilo; **to lose the thread of** perder el hilo de; *va* enhebrar; ensartar (*p.ej., cuentas*); (mach.) aterrajar, filetear; **to thread one's way through** serpentear por, abrirse camino por; *vn* (cook.) formar filamentos; serpentear, abrirse camino
threadbare ['θrɛd,bɛr] *adj* raído; andrajoso; gastado, viejo
threadworm ['θrɛd,wʌrm] *s* (zool.) lombriz de los niños (*Oxyuris vermicularis*); (zool.) filaria
thready ['θrɛdɪ] *adj* filiforme; fibroso, correoso, viscoso; débil, tenue (*voz*); (med.) débil (*pulso*)
threat [θrɛt] *s* amenaza
threaten ['θrɛtən] *va & vn* amenazar; **to threaten to** + *inf* amenazar + *inf* o amenazar con + *inf*
threatening ['θrɛtənɪŋ] *adj* amenazador, amenazante
three [θri] *adj* tres; *s* tres; **three o'clock** las tres
three-banded armadillo ['θri,bændɪd] *s* (zool.) armadillo de tres fajas, apar
three-color process ['θri,kʌlər] *s* tricromía, procedimiento tricromo
three-cornered ['θri'kɔrnərd] *adj* triangular; ternario; tricornio, de tres picos (*sombrero*)
three-D ['θri'di] *adj* (coll.) tridimensional; *s* (coll.) película cinematográfica tridimensional, cinestéreo, estereocinema
three-decker ['θri'dɛkər] *s* (naut.) navío de tres puentes; cosa que tiene tres capas, partes, pisos, etc.; (coll.) novela de tres tomos, novela muy larga
three-dimensional ['θridɪ'mɛnʃənəl] *adj* tridimensional
three-element vacuum tube ['θri,ɛlɪmənt] *s* (rad.) tubo al vacío de tres electrodos
threefold ['θri,fold] *adj & s* triple; *adv* tres veces más
three-four time ['θri'for] *s* (mus.) compás de tres por cuatro
three hundred *adj & s* trescientos
three-mile limit ['θri,maɪl] *s* (int. law) límite de tres millas
threepence ['θrɛpəns] o ['θrɪpəns] *s* suma de tres peniques; moneda de tres peniques
threepenny ['θrɛpənɪ], ['θrɪpənɪ] o ['θri,pɛnɪ] *adj* de tres peniques; barato, vil, ruin
three-phase ['θri,fez] *adj* (elec.) trifásico
three-ply ['θri,plaɪ] *adj* de tres capas
three-point landing ['θri,pɔɪnt] *s* (aer.) aterrizaje sobre tres puntos
three R's [ɑrz] *spl* lectura, escritura y aritmética
threescore ['θri'skor] *adj* tres veintenas de, sesenta
threesome ['θrisəm] *s* grupo de tres personas; grupo de tres jugadores; juego de tres jugadores
three-square file ['θri'skwɛr] *s* lima triangular
three-way cock ['θri,we] *s* grifo de tres vías
three-way switch *s* (elec.) conmutador de tres terminales
three-wire ['θri,waɪr] *adj* (elec.) trifilar
Three Wise Men *spl* Reyes Magos
threnody ['θrɛnədɪ] *s* (*pl:* **-dies**) treno (*canto fúnebre*)
threonine ['θriənin] o ['θriənɪn] *s* (biochem.) treonina
thresh [θrɛʃ] *va* (agr.) trillar; **to thresh out** decidir después de una discusión cabal; **to thresh over** discutir repetidas veces; *vn* (agr.) trillar; dar vueltas, sacudirse, menearse
thresher ['θrɛʃər] *s* (agr.) trillador; (agr.) trilladora; (ichth.) raposa de mar, zorra de mar
thresher shark *s* (ichth.) raposa de mar, zorra de mar
threshing floor *s* era
threshing machine *s* máquina trilladora
threshold ['θrɛʃold] *s* umbral; (psychol. & fig.) umbral, limen; **to be on the threshold of** estar en los umbrales de; **to cross the threshold** atravesar los umbrales
threw [θru] *pret de* **throw**
thrice [θraɪs] *adv* tres veces; muy, sumamente, repetidamente
thrift [θrɪft] *s* economía, parquedad; (bot.) estátice, césped de Olimpo
thriftiness ['θrɪftɪnɪs] *s* economía, parquedad
thriftless ['θrɪftlɪs] *adj* manirroto, malgastador
thrifty ['θrɪftɪ] *adj* (*comp:* **-ier**; *super:* **-iest**) económico, parco; floreciente, próspero
thrill [θrɪl] *s* emoción viva; *va* emocionar, conmover; *vn* emocionarse, conmoverse
thriller ['θrɪlər] *s* persona o cosa emocionante; cuento o pieza de teatro espeluznante
thrilling ['θrɪlɪŋ] *adj* emocionante; espeluznante
thrippence ['θrɪpəns] *s* var. de **threepence**
thrips [θrɪps] *s* (ent.) tripso
thrive [θraɪv] (*pret:* **throve** o **thrived**; *pp:* **thriven** o **thrived**) *vn* medrar, prosperar
thriven ['θrɪvən] *pp de* **thrive**
thro' o **thro** [θru] *adj, adv & prep* var. de **through**
throat [θrot] *s* garganta; (bot.) garganta; (arch.) goterón; (fig.) garganta (*de un río, una vasija, etc.*); **to clear one's throat** aclarar la voz; **to cut one's throat** degollarle a uno; desacreditarle a uno; degollarse; desacreditarse; **to jump down one's throat** enfadarse violentamente contra una persona; **to stick in one's throat** clavársele a uno en la garganta (*p.ej., una espina*); ser difícil de decir
throatband ['θrot,bænd] *s* ahogadero
throated ['θrotɪd] *adj* que tiene garganta; que tiene cierta garganta, p.ej., **white-throated** de garganta blanca
throatful ['θrotfʊl] *s* gargantada (*trago*)
throatlatch ['θrot,lætʃ] *s* var. de **throatband**
throatwort ['θrot,wʌrt] *s* (bot.) hermosilla
throaty ['θrotɪ] *adj* (*comp:* **-ier**; *super:* **-iest**) gutural, ronco
throb [θrɑb] *s* latido, palpitación, pulsación; (*pret & pp:* **throbbed**; *ger:* **throbbing**) *vn* latir, palpitar, pulsar
throbbing ['θrɑbɪŋ] *adj* palpitante
throe [θro] *s* dolor, congoja; **throes** *spl* angustia, agonía; esfuerzo penoso
thrombin ['θrɑmbɪn] *s* (biochem.) trombina
thrombocyte ['θrɑmbosaɪt] *s* (physiol.) trombocito
thrombosis [θrɑm'bosɪs] *s* (path.) trombosis
thrombus ['θrɑmbəs] *s* (*pl:* **-bi** [baɪ]) (path.) trombo
throne [θron] *s* trono; **thrones** *spl* (eccl.) tronos; *va* entronizar
throne room *s* salón del trono
throng [θrɔŋ] o [θrɑŋ] *s* gentío, tropel, muchedumbre; *va* apretar, atestar; *vn* agolparse, apiñarse
throstle ['θrɑsəl] *s* (orn.) malvís, tordo alirrojo; (mach.) telar continuo
throttle ['θrɑtəl] *s* garganta, gaznate; (mach.) válvula de estrangulación, válvula reguladora; regulador (*de locomotora*); acelerador (*de automóvil*); *va* ahogar, sofocar; impedir, suprimir; (mach.) estrangular; (mach.) regular; **to throttle down** reducir la velocidad de
through [θru] *adj* de paso; directo, sin paradas, con pocas paradas; acabado, terminado; **to be through with** haber acabado con; no querer ocuparse más de; *adv* a través, de un lado a otro, de parte a parte; desde el principio hasta el fin; completamente; **through and through** de punta a cabo; de todo en todo, hasta los tuétanos; *prep* por, a través de; me-

diante, por medio de; a causa de; por entre; durante todo; todo lo largo de
throughout [θru'aut] *adv* en todas partes; por todas partes; en todo, en todos respectos; desde el principio hasta el fin; *prep* en todo; durante todo; a lo largo de
throughway ['θru,we] *s* carretera troncal, carretera de acceso limitado
throve [θrov] *pret de* **thrive**
throw [θro] *s* echada, tirada, lance; riesgo, ventura; capita, bufanda, chal; cobertor o colcha ligera ‖ (*pret:* **threw;** *pp:* **thrown**) *va* arrojar, echar, lanzar; disparar; lanzar (*p.ej., la jabalina*); dirigir, lanzar (*p.ej., una mirada*); tirar (*los dados*); derribar; desarzonar; proyectar (*una sombra*); dar a luz, parir; dar forma a (*las vasijas de barro*); perder con premeditación (*un juego, una carrera*); torcer (*hilo*); tender (*un puente*); **to throw away** tirar; malgastar; perder, no aprovechar; **to throw back** rechazar; **to throw down** echar por tierra, derribar; **to throw in** añadir, dar de más; **to throw off** desechar, deshacerse de; (coll.) producir (*p.ej., poesías*) con desenvoltura; **to throw on** echarse (*una prenda de vestir*); **to throw oneself at** asediar (*p.ej., una mujer a un hombre*); **to throw out** botar, arrojar, desechar; echar a la calle; **to throw over** abandonar, dejar; **to throw up** abandonar, dejar; renunciar; levantar rápidamente; echar en cara; (coll.) vomitar ‖ *vn* arrojar, echar, lanzar; **to throw back** parecerse a un antepasado, retroceder a un tipo anterior; **to throw up** vomitar
throwback ['θro,bæk] *s* salto atrás, retroceso; (biol.) reversión; (mov.) escena retrospectiva
thrower ['θroər] *s* tirador, lanzador; torcedor de seda
thrown [θron] *pp de* **throw**
thru [θru] *adj, adv & prep* var. de **through**
thrum [θrʌm] *s* rasgueo; hilo basto, hilo destorcido; **thrums** *spl* cadillos; (*pret & pp:* **thrummed;** *ger:* **thrumming**) *va* rasguear sin arte (*un instrumento de cuerda*); golpear ociosamente; repetir de modo monótono; *vn* zangarrear; teclear
thrush [θrʌʃ] *s* (orn.) tordo; (orn.) arandillo, malvís; (path.) ubrera; (vet.) higo
thrust [θrʌst] *s* empuje; acometida; cuchillada, estocada, puñalada; (phys.) empuje; (*pret & pp:* **thrust**) *va* empujar; acometer; atravesar, traspasar; clavar, hincar; imponer (*una tarea a una persona*); *vn* dar un empujón; abrirse paso por fuerza
thrust fault *s* (geol.) falla acostada
Thucydides [θu'sɪdɪdiz] o [θju'sɪdɪdiz] *s* Tucídides
thud [θʌd] *s* baque, ruido sordo; (*pret & pp:* **thudded;** *ger:* **thudding**) *va & vn* golpear con ruido sordo
thug [θʌg] *s* malhechor, ladrón, asesino
thuja ['θudʒə] *s* (bot.) tuya
Thule ['θulɪ] o ['θjulɪ] *s* Tule
thulium ['θulɪəm] o ['θjulɪəm] *s* (chem.) tulio
thumb [θʌm] *s* pulgar, dedo gordo; **all thumbs** (coll.) desmañado, chapucero, torpe; **to twiddle one's thumbs** menear ociosamente los pulgares; no hacer nada, estar ocioso; **under the thumb of** bajo la férula de, bajo el zapato de; **thumbs down** con el pulgar vuelto hacia abajo (*en señal de desaprobación*); **thumbs up** con el pulgar vuelto hacia arriba (*en señal de aprobación*); *va* manosear sin cuidado; ensuciar con los dedos; **to thumb a ride** pedir ser llevado en automóvil indicando la dirección con el pulgar; **to thumb one's nose at** (coll.) señalar (*a una persona*) poniendo el pulgar sobre la nariz en son de burla; (coll.) tratar con sumo desprecio; *vn* zangarrear; **to thumb through** hojear (*un libro*) con el pulgar
thumb index *s* índice recortado, índice en el corte
thumbnail ['θʌm,nel] *s* uña del pulgar; cosa muy pequeña o breve; *adj* muy pequeño, muy pequeño pero completo, en miniatura
thumb notch *s* uñero
thumb nut *s* tuerca de orejetas; tuerca moleteada
thumbprint ['θʌm,prɪnt] *s* impresión del pulgar; *va* marcar con impresión del pulgar
thumbscrew ['θʌm,skru] *s* tornillo de mariposa, tornillo de orejas; empulgueras (*instrumento para dar tormento*)
thumbstall ['θʌm,stɔl] *s* funda para el pulgar
thumbtack ['θʌm,tæk] *s* chinche, chincheta
thump [θʌmp] *s* golpazo, porrazo, trastazo; *va* dar un golpe pesado a; golpear, aporrear; *vn* dar un porrazo; caer con golpe pesado; andar con pasos pesados; latir (*el corazón*) con golpes pesados
thumping ['θʌmpɪŋ] *adj* (coll.) pesado, enorme
thunder ['θʌndər] *s* trueno; estruendo (*p.ej., de aplausos*); amenaza, denunciación; **to steal one's thunder** robar la idea o el método de uno; *va* fulminar (*censuras, amenazas, etc.*); arrojar o lanzar con estruendo; expresar con estruendo; *vn* tronar; **it is thundering** truena; **to thunder along** pasar con estruendo; **to thunder at** tronar contra
thunder and lightning *s* rayos y truenos
thunderbolt ['θʌndər,bolt] *s* rayo; (fig.) rayo
thunderclap ['θʌndər,klæp] *s* tronido
thundercloud ['θʌndər,klaud] *s* nube cargada de electricidad
thunderer ['θʌndərər] *s* tronador; **the Thunderer** Júpiter tonante o tronante
thunderhead ['θʌndər,hɛd] *s* cúmulo (*que se resuelve en lluvia con truenos*)
thundering ['θʌndərɪŋ] *adj* tronador; tronitoso, estrepitoso; (coll.) enorme, extraordinario
thunderous ['θʌndərəs] *adj* tronante, tronitoso
thundershower ['θʌndər,ʃauər] *s* chubasco con truenos
thundersquall ['θʌndər,skwɔl] *s* ráfaga o racha de viento, acompañada de lluvia y truenos
thunderstorm ['θʌndər,stɔrm] *s* tronada, tempestad de truenos
thunderstruck ['θʌndər,strʌk] *adj* atónito, estupefacto, pasmado
Thur. abr. de **Thursday**
thurible ['θurɪbəl] o ['θjurɪbəl] *s* (eccl.) turíbulo
thurifer ['θurɪfər] o ['θjurɪfər] *s* (eccl.) turiferario
thurify ['θurɪfaɪ] o ['θjurɪfaɪ] (*pret & pp:* **-fied**) *va & vn* turificar
Thuringia [θu'rɪndʒɪə] o [θju'rɪndʒɪə] *s* Turingia
Thuringian [θu'rɪndʒɪən] o [θju'rɪndʒɪən] *adj & s* turingiano
Thursday ['θʌrzdɪ] *s* jueves
thus [ðʌs] *adv* así; **thus far** hasta aquí, hasta ahora
thwack [θwæk] *s* golpe, porrazo; sequete; *va* golpear, pegar; dar un golpe seco a
thwart [θwɔrt] *s* riostra (*de una canoa*); bancada, banco de remeros; *adj* transversal, oblicuo; *adv* de través; *va* desbaratar, impedir, frustrar
thy [ðaɪ] *adj poss* (archaic & poet.) tu
thylacine ['θaɪləsaɪn] o ['θaɪləsɪn] *s* (zool.) lobo marsupial
thyme [taɪm] *s* (bot.) tomillo
thymelaeaceous [,θɪmɪlɪ'eʃəs] *adj* (bot.) timeleáceo
thymic ['taɪmɪk] *adj* tímico (*perteneciente al tomillo*); ['θaɪmɪk] *adj* tímico (*perteneciente al timo*)
thymol ['θaɪmɑl] *s* (chem.) timol
thymus ['θaɪməs] *s* (anat.) timo; *adj* tímico
thymus gland *s* (anat.) timo
thyroid ['θaɪrɔɪd] *adj* tiroides; *s* (anat.) tiroides (*glándula, cartílago*); (pharm.) tiroidina
thyroidectomy [,θaɪrɔɪ'dɛktəmɪ] *s* (*pl:* **-mies**) (surg.) tiroidectomía
thyroid extract *s* (pharm.) tiroidina
thyroid gland *s* (anat.) glándula tiroides
thyroxin [θaɪ'rɑksɪn] o **thyroxine** [θaɪ'rɑksin] *s* (biochem.) tiroxina
thyrse [θʌrs] *s* (bot.) tirso
thyrsus ['θʌrsəs] *s* (*pl:* **-si** [saɪ]) (bot. & myth.) tirso
thyself [ðaɪ'sɛlf] *pron* (archaic & poet.) tú mismo; ti mismo; te, ti
tiara [taɪ'ɛrə] o [tɪ'ɑrə] *s* tiara; diadema (*adorno femenino de cabeza*)
Tiber ['taɪbər] *s* Tíber
Tiberius [taɪ'bɪrɪəs] *s* Tiberio
Tibet [tɪ'bɛt] o ['tɪbɛt] *s* el Tibet
Tibetan [tɪ'bɛtən] *adj & s* tibetano

tibia ['tɪbɪə] *s* (*pl:* **-ae** [i] o **-as**) (anat. & mus.) tibia
tibial ['tɪbɪəl] *adj* tibial
tic [tɪk] *s* (path.) tic
tic douloureux [,dulu'ru] *s* (path.) tic doloroso de la cara
tick [tɪk] *s* tictac; contramarca, contraseña; (coll.) instante, momento; cutí, terliz; funda (*de almohada o colchón*); (coll.) crédito; (ent.) garrapata, mosca borriquera, pito; **on tick** (coll.) al fiado; *va* marcar, notar o contar con un tictac como el del reloj; marcar, poner una contraseña a; *vn* hacer tictac; latir (*el corazón*)
ticker ['tɪkər] *s* teleimpresor; (slang) reloj; (slang) corazón
ticker tape *s* cinta de teleimpresor
ticket ['tɪkɪt] *s* billete; localidad, entrada; papeleta de empeño; talón; marbete; (coll.) aviso de multa (*por estacionar un auto indebidamente*); (U.S.A.) candidatura; **that's the ticket** (coll.) eso es, eso es lo que se necesita; *va* poner marbete a
ticket agent *s* taquillero
ticket collector *s* revisor
ticket office *s* taquilla, despacho de billetes
ticket of leave *s* (Brit.) libertad bajo palabra
ticket-of-leave man ['tɪkɪtəv'liv] *s* (Brit.) penado libre bajo palabra
ticket scalper *s* revendedor de billetes
ticket window *s* ventanilla, taquilla
tick fever *s* (path.) fiebre de garrapatas; (vet.) fiebre de Tejas
ticking ['tɪkɪŋ] *s* cutí, terliz
tickle ['tɪkəl] *s* cosquillas; cosquilleo; *va* cosquillear; gustar, divertir; *vn* cosquillear; tener o sentir cosquillas
tickler ['tɪklər] *s* persona que cosquillea; libro borrador o de apuntes; (coll.) problema difícil
tickler coil *s* (rad.) bobina de regeneración
ticklish ['tɪklɪʃ] *adj* cosquilloso; picajoso, quisquilloso, cosquilloso; difícil, delicado; inseguro, inestable
tick-tack-toe [,tɪktæk'to] *s* juego, parecido al tres en raya, en el cual dos jugadores ponen su señal alternativamente en uno de nueve espacios de una figura de líneas cruzadas, cada jugador intentando llenar primero tres espacios seguidos
tick-tock ['tɪk,tɑk] *s* tictac (*del reloj*)
tidal ['taɪdəl] *adj* de marea
tidal wave *s* ola de marea; (fig.) ola (*p.ej., de indignación popular*)
tidbit ['tɪd,bɪt] *s* buen bocado, bocado rico, bocadito
tiddledywinks ['tɪdəldɪ,wɪŋks] o **tiddlywinks** ['tɪdlɪ,wɪŋks] *s* juego de la pulga, juego que consiste en hacer saltar un disco en una taza
tide [taɪd] *s* (naut.) marea; temporada; corriente; **to go with the tide** seguir la corriente; **to turn the tide** hacer cambiar las cosas; cambiar el curso (*p.ej., de la batalla*); **the tide turned** dió vuelta la tortilla; *va* llevar, hacer flotar; **to tide over** ayudar un poco; superar (*una dificultad*); *vn* levantarse (*la superficie de las aguas del mar*); navegar o flotar con la marea
tide-driven power plant ['taɪd,drɪvən] *s* usina mareamotriz
tide gate *s* compuerta de marea
tideland ['taɪd,lænd] *s* terreno inundado por la marea, estero
tide power *s* hulla azul
tidewater ['taɪd,wɔtər] o ['taɪd,wɑtər] *s* agua de marea; orilla del mar; *adj* costanero
tideway ['taɪd,we] *s* canal de marea; corriente de marea
tidings ['taɪdɪŋz] *spl* noticias, informes
tidy ['taɪdɪ] *s* (*pl:* **-dies**) pañito bordado, cubierta de respaldar; *adj* (*comp:* **-dier;** *super:* **-diest**) aseado, limpio, pulcro, ordenado; (*pret & pp:* **-died**) *va* asear, limpiar, arreglar, poner en orden; *vn* asearse; poner las cosas en orden
tie [taɪ] *s* atadura; lazo, nudo; corbata; empate (*en elecciones, juegos, etc.*); tirante, estay; (mus.) ligado; (rail.) traviesa; (fig.) lazo, vínculo; **ties** *spl* zapatos bajos de lazos; **to tie a tie** hacer una corbata; (*pret & pp:* **tied;** *ger:* **tying**) *va* atar, liar; enlazar; hacer (*la corbata*); confinar, limitar; empatar (*p.ej., una elección*); empatársela a (*una persona*); (mus.) ligar; **to be tied up** estar ocupado; **to tie down** confinar, limitar; **to tie up** atar; envolver; obstruir (*el tráfico*); (com.) embargar; *vn* atar; empatar o empatarse
tieback ['taɪ,bæk] *s* alzapaño (*tira de tela o cordonería*)
tie bar *s* barra tirante, varilla de tensión; (rail.) barra separadora (*de las dos agujas de cambio*)
tie beam *s* tirante, viga tensora
tiepin ['taɪ,pɪn] *s* alfiler de corbata
tier ['taɪər] *s* atador; (dial.) delantal de niña atado con cintas; [tɪr] *s* fila, ringlera; tonga; (theat.) fila de palcos; *va* formar en filas o tongas
tierce [tɪrs] *s* tercerola (*barril*); tercera o tercia (*tres cartas del mismo palo*); (eccl.) tercia; (mus.) tercera; posición de mano en tercera (*en la esgrima*)
tie rod *s* barra tirante, varilla de tensión; (aut.) biela, barra de acoplamiento de dirección
tie-up ['taɪ,ʌp] *s* enlace, unión; parada o paralización (*causada por una huelga u otros motivos*); bloqueo, embotellamiento (*del tráfico*)
tiff [tɪf] *s* riña ligera, quimera; pique, resentimiento; *vn* reñir; picarse, irritarse
tiffin ['tɪfɪn] *s* (Brit.) almuerzo; *va* (Brit.) dar de almorzar a; *vn* (Brit.) almorzar
tiger ['taɪgər] *s* tigre; (fig.) tigre (*persona muy cruel*)
tiger beetle *s* (ent.) cicindela
tiger cat *s* (zool.) gato montés, ocelote, serval; gato doméstico atigrado
tiger-eye ['taɪgər,aɪ] *s* ojo de gato (*piedra*)
tigerflower ['taɪgər,flaʊər] *s* (bot.) flor de un día, flor de la maravilla
tigerish ['taɪgərɪʃ] *adj* atigrado, tigrino, feroz
tiger lily *s* (bot.) azucena atigrada
tiger moth *s* (ent.) artia
tiger's-eye ['taɪgərz,aɪ] *s* var. de **tiger-eye**
tiger shark *s* (ichth.) pez zorro; (ichth.) alecrín
tight [taɪt] *adj* apretado, estrecho; tieso, tirante; bien cerrado, hermético; estanco; ajustado, ceñido; compacto, denso; fijo, firme, sólido; complicado, difícil; duro, severo; (com.) escaso, difícil de obtener; (paint.) mal manejado; (sport) casi igual; (coll.) agarrado, tacaño; (slang) borracho; (dial.) aseado, pulido; *adv* firmemente; **to hold tight** mantener fijo; agarrarse bien; **to sit tight** (coll.) estarse quieto; (coll.) tener la misma postura; **tights** *spl* traje de malla (*p.ej., de los acróbatas*)
tighten ['taɪtən] *va* apretar; atiesar, estirar; *vn* apretarse; atiesarse, estirarse
tight-fisted ['taɪt'fɪstɪd] *adj* agarrado, tacaño
tight-fitting ['taɪt'fɪtɪŋ] *adj* ceñido, muy ajustado
tight-lipped ['taɪt'lɪpt] *adj* que tiene los labios apretados; callado, silencioso, hermético
tightrope ['taɪt,rop] *s* cuerda tirante; *vn* andar en la cuerda tirante
tight squeeze *s* (coll.) brete, aprieto
tightwad ['taɪt,wɑd] *s* (slang) cicatero
tigress ['taɪgrɪs] *s* tigresa
tigrish ['taɪgrɪʃ] *adj* var. de **tigerish**
tike [taɪk] *s* var. de **tyke**
til [tɪl] o [til] *s* (bot.) ajonjolí; (bot.) til (*de las Canarias*); [til] *s* (phonet.) tilde
tilbury ['tɪlbərɪ] *s* (*pl:* **-ries**) tílburi
tile [taɪl] *s* azulejo; baldosa (*para solar*); teja (*para cubrir por fuera los techos*); tubo de barro cocido, canal de barro cocido; (coll.) chistera, sombrero de copa; *va* azulejar; embaldosar; tejar
tilefish ['taɪl,fɪʃ] *s* (ichth.) lofolátilo
tile kiln *s* tejar, tejería
tiler ['taɪlər] *s* azulejero; tejero
tile roof *s* tejado (de tejas)
tiliaceous [,tɪlɪ'eʃəs] *adj* (bot.) tiliáceo
tiling ['taɪlɪŋ] *s* azulejos; baldosas; tejas; azulejería; embaldosado
till [tɪl] *s* cajón o gaveta del dinero; *prep* hasta; *conj* hasta que; *va* labrar, cultivar
tillable ['tɪləbəl] *adj* labrantío
tillage ['tɪlɪdʒ] *s* cultivo, labranza; agricultura; tierra labrada; cosecha

tiller ['tɪlər] *s* agricultor, labrador; palanca, mango; (naut.) barra o caña del timón; (hort.) sierpe
tilt [tɪlt] *s* inclinación; declive; tienda, entaladura; justa, torneo; martinete de báscula; lanzada; **at tilt** en posición inclinada; dando una lanzada; **full tilt** a toda velocidad; *va* inclinar, volcar; asestar (*una lanza*); acometer; forjar o martillar con martinete; entoldar; *vn* inclinarse; justar, tornear; luchar; **to tilt at** luchar con, arremeter contra; protestar contra
tilth [tɪlθ] *s* cultivo, labranza; tierra labrada; capa cultivable (*de un terreno*)
tilt hammer *s* martinete de báscula
tiltyard ['tɪlt,jɑrd] *s* palestra, lugar de una justa o torneo
Tim. abr. de **Timothy**
timbal ['tɪmbəl] *s* (mus.) timbal; membrana del aparato estridulante (*de los cicádidos*)
timbale ['tɪmbəl] *s* (cook.) timbal
timber ['tɪmbər] *s* madera de construcción; maderaje; viga, madero; bosque, árboles de monte; (naut.) cuaderna; *va* enmaderar
timber hitch *s* (naut.) vuelta de braza
timberland ['tɪmbər,lænd] *s* tierras maderables
timber line *s* altura o límite de la vegetación, límite del bosque maderable
timber wolf *s* (zool.) lobo norteamericano (*Canis lupus lycaon*)
timbre ['tɪmbər] o ['tæmbər] *s* (her., phonet. & phys.) timbre
timbrel ['tɪmbrəl] *s* (mus.) adufe, pandereta
time [taɪm] *s* tiempo; hora, p.ej., **time to go to bed** hora de acostarse; vez, p.ej., **that was the last time I saw him** ésa era la última vez que le ví; rato, p.ej., **he had a nice time** pasó un buen rato; plazo; horas de trabajo; sueldo; tiempo de parir, término del embarazo; hora, última hora; (phot.) tiempo de exposición; **against time** esforzándose por acabar antes de cierto tiempo; **at no time** ninguna vez; **at the same time** a un tiempo; a la vez; todavía, sin embargo; **at the time of** en tiempo de; **at the wrong time** fuera de tiempo; **at times** a tiempos, a veces; **behind time** atrasado; **behind the times** anticuado, fuera de moda; **between times** en los intervalos; **for some time (past)** de algún tiempo a esta parte; **for the time being** por el momento, por ahora; **from time to time** de tiempo en tiempo; **in due time** a su tiempo, en su día; **in good time** en tiempo; pronto; **in no time** en muy poco tiempo, en un abrir y cerrar de ojos; **in time** con tiempo; (mus.) a compás; **in time to** + *inf* a tiempo para + *inf;* **on time** a la hora (debida); con puntualidad; a plazo; **to bide one's time** esperar la hora propicia, tomarse tiempo; **to do time** (coll.) cumplir una condena; **to have a good time** darse buen tiempo, divertirse; **to have no time for** no poder tolerar; **to keep time** contar el tiempo; andar bien (*un reloj*); (mus.) llevar el compás; **to kill time** matar el tiempo; **to know how to tell time** saber o conocer el reloj; **to lose time** atrasarse (*el reloj*); **to make time** ganar tiempo, avanzar con rapidez; **to mark time** hacer tiempo; trabajar en vano; (mil.) marcar el paso; **to pass the time away** matar el tiempo; **to pass the time of day** saludarse (*dos personas*); **to pass the time of day with** saludar, dar los buenos días a; **to take one's time** no darse prisa, ir despacio; **to tell the time** decir la hora, p.ej., **tell me the time** dígame la hora; **to tell time** decir la hora (*p.ej., el reloj de sol*); **to waste time** gastar o perder el tiempo; **what time is it?** ¿qué hora es?; **within a short time** al poco tiempo; **time after time** o **time and again** repetidas veces; **times** (math.) por (*multiplicado por*); *adj* de tiempo, del tiempo; a plazo; *va* calcular el tiempo de; medir el tiempo de; hacer a tiempo oportuno; regular; hacer a compás; (mach.) graduar la distribución de; (sport) cronometrar
time bomb *s* bomba-reloj, bomba a reloj
timecard ['taɪm,kɑrd] *s* hoja de presencia, tarjeta registradora (*de la hora de llegada y salida*); horario
time clock *s* reloj registrador
time-consuming ['taɪmkən,sumɪŋ] o ['taɪmkən,sjumɪŋ] *adj* que toma mucho tiempo
time-delay relay ['taɪmdɪ'le] *s* (elec.) relai de retardo
time draft *s* (com.) letra de cambio a plazo, orden de pago a plazo
time exposure *s* (phot.) pose
time fuse *s* espoleta de tiempos
time-honored ['taɪm,ɑnərd] *adj* consagrado, tradicional
time immemorial *s* tiempo inmemorable; (law) tiempo inmemorial
timekeeper ['taɪm,kipər] *s* listero, apuntador, alistador de tiempo; reloj, cronómetro; (mus.) marcador de tiempo; (sport) cronometrador, juez de tiempo
timeless ['taɪmlɪs] *adj* eterno, infinito; sin fecha, sin limitación de tiempo; intemporal
timely ['taɪmlɪ] *adj* (*comp:* **-lier;** *super:* **-liest**) oportuno
time off *s* permiso, asueto
time out *s* (coll.) descanso, intermisión
time out of mind *s* tiempo inmemorable
timepiece ['taɪm,pis] *s* reloj, cronómetro
timer ['taɪmər] *s* contador de tiempo; (mach.) distribuidor del encendido
timesaver ['taɪm,sevər] *s* economizador de tiempo
timeserver ['taɪm,sʌrvər] *s* contemporizador
timeserving ['taɪm,sʌrvɪŋ] *adj* contemporizador; *s* contemporización
time signal *s* señal horaria
time signature *s* (mus.) signatura
time switch *s* (elec.) interruptor de reloj, interruptor horario
timetable ['taɪm,tebəl] *s* guía, horario, itinerario
timework ['taɪm,wʌrk] *s* trabajo a jornal
timeworn ['taɪm,worn] *adj* traqueado, gastado por el tiempo
time zone *s* huso horario
timid ['tɪmɪd] *adj* tímido
timidity [tɪ'mɪdɪtɪ] *s* timidez
timing ['taɪmɪŋ] *s* medida del tiempo; regulación del tiempo; puesta a punto; selección del momento oportuno (*para producir un efecto deseado*); (aut.) regulación del encendido; (aut.) regulación de la distribución; (mus.) regulación del compás (*ritmo*); (sport) cronometraje; (theat.) sincronización; (theat.) velocidad de la acción
timing gears *spl* (mach.) distribución, engranaje de distribución, mando de las válvulas
timocracy [taɪ'mɑkrəsɪ] *s* (*pl:* **-cies**) timocracia
timocratic [,taɪmə'krætɪk] o **timocratical** [,taɪmə'krætɪkəl] *adj* timocrático
timorous ['tɪmərəs] *adj* temeroso, tímido
timothy ['tɪməθɪ] *s* (bot.) fleo; (*cap.*) Timoteo; (Bib.) Epístola de San Pablo a Timoteo (*cada una de dos*)
timpano ['tɪmpəno] *s* (*pl:* **-ni** [ni]) (mus.) atabal, tímpano
tin [tɪn] *s* (chem.) estaño; hojalata, hoja de lata; lata (*envase*); *adj* de estaño; de hojalata; pobre, inferior; (*pret & pp:* **tinned;** *ger:* **tinning**) *va* estañar; recubrir de estaño; (Brit.) enlatar, conservar en latas
tinamou ['tɪnəmu] *s* (orn.) tinamú
tincal ['tɪŋkɑl] o ['tɪŋkəl] *s* tincal
tin can *s* lata, envase de hojalata
tinctorial [tɪŋk'torɪəl] *adj* tintóreo
tincture ['tɪŋktʃər] *s* (pharm.) tintura; (her.) esmalte; (fig.) tintura (*noticia superficial*); *va* tinturar; (fig.) tinturar
tin cup *s* taza de hojalata
tinder ['tɪndər] *s* yesca; mecha
tinderbox ['tɪndər,bɑks] *s* lumbres, yescas, yesquero; (fig.) persona muy excitable
tine [taɪn] *s* púa (*p.ej., de tenedor*)
tinea ['tɪnɪə] *s* (path.) tiña
tin foil *s* hojuela de estaño, papel de estaño
ting [tɪŋ] *s* tintín; *va* hacer tintinear; *vn* tintinear
ting-a-ling ['tɪŋə,lɪŋ] *s* tilín
tinge [tɪndʒ] *s* matiz, tinte; dejo, gustillo; (*ger:* **tingeing** o **tinging**) *va* matizar, teñir; dar gusto o sabor a
tingle ['tɪŋgəl] *s* comezón, hormigueo; *va* pro-

ducir comezón u hormigueo a; *vn* sentir comezón u hormigueo; zumbar (*los oídos*); estremecerse (*p.ej., de entusiasmo*)
tin hat *s* (coll.) yelmo de acero, casco de acero
tinker [ˈtɪŋkər] *s* calderero remendón; chapucero, chafallón; chapuz, chafallo; *va* remendar chapuceramente; chafallar; *vn* ocuparse vanamente; **to tinker at** o **with** ocuparse vanamente con o en
tinker's damn o **dam** *s* (slang) cosa de ningún valor; **to not be worth a tinker's damn** (slang) no valer un pito; **to not care a tinker's damn** (slang) no importarle a uno un pito
tinkle [ˈtɪŋkəl] *s* retintín; *va* hacer retiñir; marcar con un retintín; *vn* retiñir
tinman [ˈtɪnmən] *s* (*pl:* **-men**) var. de **tinsmith**
tinner [ˈtɪnər] *s* minero de estaño; estañero; hojalatero; (Brit.) envasador de latas
tinnitus [tɪˈnaɪtəs] *s* (path.) zumbido de oídos
tinny [ˈtɪnɪ] *adj* (*comp:* **-nier;** *super:* **-niest**) de estaño; que tintina como los objetos de estaño o de hojalata; que sabe a estaño; débil, endeble
tin-pan alley [ˈtɪn,pæn] *s* barrio, especialmente en la ciudad de Nueva York, donde se publica la mayor parte de la música popular; conjunto de compositores de música popular
tin plate *s* hojalata
tin-plate [ˈtɪn,plet] *va* estañar
tin roof *s* tejado de hojalata
tinsel [ˈtɪnsəl] *s* oropel; (fig.) oropel; lentejuelas o tiritas de hoja de estaño (*que se usan como ornamento, p.ej., para el árbol de Navidad*); lama, restaño, brocadillo; *adj* de oropel; (*pret & pp:* **-seled** o **-selled;** *ger:* **-seling** o **-selling**) *va* oropelar
tinsmith [ˈtɪn,smɪθ] *s* estañero; hojalatero
tin soldier *s* soldadito de plomo (*juguete*)
tint [tɪnt] *s* tinte, matiz; media tinta; *va* teñir, matizar, colorar ligeramente
tintinnabulation [,tɪntɪ,næbjəˈleʃən] *s* campanilleo
tintype [ˈtɪn,taɪp] *s* (phot.) ferrotipo
tinware [ˈtɪn,wɛr] *s* objetos de hojalata
tin wedding *s* décimo aniversario (*del matrimonio*)
tinwork [ˈtɪn,wʌrk] *s* estañadura; hojalatería
tiny [ˈtaɪnɪ] *adj* (*comp:* **-nier;** *super:* **-niest**) diminuto, menudo, pequeñito
tip [tɪp] *s* extremo, extremidad; herrete, casquillo; punta (*p.ej., de la lengua*); puntera (*del zapato*); embocadura (*de cigarrillo*); inclinación, ladeo; palmadita, golpecito; propina (*gratificación*); soplo (*informe dado en secreto*); (*pret & pp:* **tipped;** *ger:* **tipping**) *va* herretear, poner herrete o casquillo a; inclinar, ladear; golpear ligeramente; volcar; dar propina a; informar por debajo de cuerda; tocar (*el sombrero*) con los dedos; quitarse (*el sombrero en señal de cortesía*); **to tip in** (print.) encañonar (*un pliego*); **to tip off** (coll.) informar por debajo de cuerda; (coll.) advertir; **to tip over** volcar; *vn* dar una propina o propinas; inclinarse, ladearse; **to tip over** volcarse
tipcart [ˈtɪp,kɑrt] *s* volquete
tip-in [ˈtɪp,ɪn] *s* (print.) pliego encañonado
tip-off [ˈtɪp,ɔf] o [ˈtɪp,ɑf] *s* (coll.) informe dado por debajo de cuerda; (coll.) advertencia
tipped [tɪpt] *adj* aboquillado (*cigarrillo*); herreteado
tippet [ˈtɪpɪt] *s* palatina; esclavina
tipping [ˈtɪpɪŋ] *s* costumbre de dar propinas
tipple [ˈtɪpəl] *s* bebida alcohólica; volcadero; *va* beber a menudo y en poca cantidad; *vn* beborrotear
tippler [ˈtɪplər] *s* bebedor
tipstaff [ˈtɪp,stæf] o [ˈtɪp,stɑf] *s* vara de justicia; ministril, alguacil de vara
tipster [ˈtɪpstər] *s* (coll.) individuo que vende informes secretos, especialmente a los jugadores
tipsy [ˈtɪpsɪ] *adj* (*comp:* **-sier;** *super:* **-siest**) vacilante; achispado
tipsy cake *s* bizcocho borracho
tiptoe [ˈtɪp,to] *s* punta del pie; puntas de los pies; **on tiptoe** de puntillas; alerta, sobre aviso; furtivamente; (*pret & pp:* **-toed;** *ger:* **-toeing**) *vn* andar de puntillas
tiptop [ˈtɪp,tɑp] *s* cumbre, cima; *adj* al punto más alto; (coll.) superior, excelente
tirade [ˈtaɪred] o [tɪˈred] *s* diatriba, invectiva
tire [taɪr] *s* neumático, llanta de goma; llanta o calce (*cerco metálico de las ruedas*); *va* cansar; aburrir, fastidiar; poner llantas o neumáticos a; *vn* cansarse; aburrirse, fastidiarse
tire chain *s* cadena de llanta, cadena antirresbaladiza
tired [taɪrd] *adj* cansado, rendido
tire gauge *s* indicador de presión de neumáticos, medidor para neumáticos
tire iron *s* (aut.) desmontable
tireless [ˈtaɪrlɪs] *adj* incansable, infatigable
tire pressure *s* presión de inflado
tire pump *s* bomba para inflar neumáticos
tire rack *s* (aut.) portaneumático
tiresome [ˈtaɪrsəm] *adj* cansado, aburrido, pesado
tire spreader *s* ensanchador de neumáticos
Tirol, the [tɪˈrol] o [ˈtɪrɑl] var. de **the Tyrol**
'tis [tɪz] contracción de **it is**
tissue [ˈtɪʃu] *s* tejido fino, gasa, tisú; (biol.) tejido; papel de seda; (fig.) tejido (*p.ej., de mentiras*)
tissue culture *s* (bact.) cultivo de tejidos
tissue paper *s* papel de seda
tit [tɪt] *s* teta; pezón (*extremidad de la teta*); (orn.) paro, herrerillo; **tit for tat** pata es la traviesa, guájete por guájete, ojo por ojo
titan [ˈtaɪtən] *s* titán; (*cap.*) *s* (myth.) Titán; *adj* titánico
titanate [ˈtaɪtənet] *s* (chem.) titanato
titan crane *s* (mach.) titán
Titania [tɪˈtenɪə] *s* Titania
titanic [taɪˈtænɪk] *adj* titánico; (chem.) titánico; (*cap.*) *adj* (myth.) titánico
titanite [ˈtaɪtənaɪt] *s* (mineral.) titanita
titanium [taɪˈtenɪəm] o [tɪˈtenɪəm] *s* (chem.) titanio o titano
titbit [ˈtɪt,bɪt] *s* var. de **tidbit**
titer [ˈtaɪtər] *s* (chem., immun. & physiol.) título
tithable [ˈtaɪðəbəl] *adj* diezmable
tithe [taɪð] *s* décimo (*décima parte*); diezmo (*impuesto pagado a la iglesia*); impuesto muy pequeño; pizca; *va* diezmar
tither [ˈtaɪðər] *s* diezmero
tithing [ˈtaɪðɪŋ] *s* diezmo; recaudación o pago del diezmo; (Brit.) pequeña división administrativa, formada por diez familias de vecinos
Tithonus [tɪˈθonəs] *s* (myth.) Titono
Titian [ˈtɪʃən] *s* El Ticiano; *adj* castaño rojizo, rubio rojizo
titillate [ˈtɪtɪlet] *va* titilar (*cosquillear*)
titillation [,tɪtɪˈleʃən] *s* titilación
titivate [ˈtɪtɪvet] *va* (coll.) ataviar, vestir con mucha elegancia; *vn* (coll.) ataviarse, vestirse con mucha elegancia
titlark [ˈtɪt,lɑrk] *s* (orn.) bisbita
title [ˈtaɪtəl] *s* título; (sport) campeonato; *va* titular, intitular
titled [ˈtaɪtəld] *adj* titulado
title deed *s* (law) título de propiedad
titleholder [ˈtaɪtəl,holdər] *s* titulado; (sport) campeón
title page *s* portada, frontispicio
title rôle *s* (theat.) papel principal (*el que corresponde al título de la obra*)
titmouse [ˈtɪt,maus] *s* (*pl:* **-mice**) (orn.) paro; (orn.) paro carbonero, herrerillo
Titoism [ˈtito·ɪzəm] *s* titoísmo
Titoist [ˈtito·ɪst] *adj & s* titoísta
titrate [ˈtaɪtret] o [ˈtɪtret] *va & vn* (chem.) titrar o titular
titration [taɪˈtreʃən] o [tɪˈtreʃən] *s* (chem.) titración o titulación
titter [ˈtɪtər] *s* risita ahogada o disimulada; *vn* reír a medias, reír con disimulo
tittivate [ˈtɪtɪvet] *va & vn* (coll.) var. de **titivate**
tittle [ˈtɪtəl] *s* ápice (*pequeño signo; parte mínima*)
tittle-tattle [ˈtɪtəl,tætəl] *s* charla, chismes; *vn* charlar, chismear
titular [ˈtɪtʃələr] *adj* titular; nominal (*que sólo tiene el nombre de un cargo sin poder real*)
Titus [ˈtaɪtəs] *s* Tito; (Bib.) Epístola de San Pablo a Tito
tmesis [ˈtmisɪs] *s* (rhet.) tmesis
tn. abr. de **ton**

TNT o **T.N.T.** abr. de **trinitrotoluene**
to [tu], [tʊ] o [tə] *adv* hacia adelante; **to and fro** alternativamente; yendo y viniendo; **to come to** volver en sí; *prep* a, p.ej., **he is going to Buenos Aires** va a Buenos Aires; **they gave something to the beggar** dieron algo al pobre; **we are learning to dance** aprendemos a bailar; para, p.ej., **he is reading to himself** lee para sí; por, p.ej., **work to do** trabajo por hacer; hasta, p.ej., **to a certain extent** hasta cierto punto; en, p.ej., **from door to door** de puerta en puerta; con, p.ej., **kind to her** amable con ella; según, p.ej., **to my way of thinking** según mi modo de pensar; menos, p.ej., **five minutes to ten** las diez menos cinco
toad [tod] *s* (zool.) sapo; (zool.) rana
toadeater ['tod,itər] *s* adulador servil
toadfish ['tod,fɪʃ] *s* (ichth.) sapo
toadflax ['tod,flæks] *s* (bot.) linaria
toadstone ['tod,ston] *s* estelión, estelón
toadstool ['tod,stul] *s* (bot.) agárico, seta; seta venenosa
toady ['todɪ] *s* (*pl:* **-ies**) adulador servil; (*pret & pp:* **-ied**) *va & vn* adular servilmente
toadyism ['todɪɪzəm] *s* adulación servil
to-and-fro ['tuənd'fro] *adj* alternativo, de vaivén
toast [tost] *s* tostadas; brindis; **a piece of toast** una tostada; *va* tostar; brindar a o por; *vn* tostarse; brindar
toaster ['tostər] *s* tostador; brindador
toastmaster ['tost,mæstər] o ['tost,mɑstər] *s* brindador; el que presenta a los oradores en un banquete
Tob. abr. de **Tobit**
tobacco [tə'bæko] *s* (*pl:* **-cos**) (bot.) tabaco; tabaco (*hojas secas*)
tobacco dove *s* (orn.) paloma tojosa
tobaccoism [tə'bæko·ɪzəm] *s* (path.) tabaquismo
tobacco mosaic *s* (plant path.) mosaico del tabaco
tobacconist [tə'bækənɪst] *s* tabaquero, estanquero
tobacco pipe *s* pipa para fumar
tobacco pouch *s* petaca
tobacco worm *s* (zool.) larva de la esfinge
Tobias [to'baɪəs] *s* Tobías
Tobit ['tobɪt] *s* Tobías; (Bib.) Libro de Tobías
toboggan [tə'bɑgən] *s* tobogán; *vn* deslizarse en tobogán; (com.) caer, precipitarse, disminuir en valor súbitamente
toboggan slide *s* pista para tobogán
Toby ['tobɪ] *s* (*pl:* **-bies**) vaso o pichel con asa, en forma de un hombre que lleva un gabán y un sombrero de tres picos; (slang) cigarro largo, delgado y barato
toccata [tə'kɑtə] *s* (mus.) tocata
tocologist [to'kɑlədʒɪst] *s* tocólogo
tocology [to'kɑlədʒɪ] *s* tocología
tocopherol [to'kɑfərol] o [to'kɑfərɑl] *s* (biochem.) tocoferol
tocsin ['tɑksɪn] *s* campana de alarma; campanada de alarma
today o **to-day** [tʊ'de] *adv & s* hoy
toddle ['tɑdəl] *s* tambaleo, pasillos inciertos; *vn* tambalear, andar con pasillos inciertos; hacer pinitos; andar, caminar; bailar; (slang) dar un paseo
toddler ['tɑdlər] *s* persona que anda con pasillos inciertos; niño que hace pinitos
toddy ['tɑdɪ] *s* (*pl:* **-dies**) ponche; vino de palmera
to-do [tʊ'du] *s* (coll.) confusión, alboroto, alharaca
toe [to] *s* dedo del pie; punta del pie; puntera (*remiendo a la media; refuerzo de cuero del zapato*); lumbre (*de la herradura*); pesuño (*de los animales de pata hendida*); **on one's toes** alerta; **to tread on the toes of** estorbar, ofender; (*pret & pp:* **toed**; *ger:* **toeing**) *va* tocar o alcanzar con la punta del pie; echar punteras a; (carp.) clavar oblicuamente; (carp.) clavar con clavos hincados oblicuamente; **to toe the line** o **the mark** ponerse a la raya; obrar como se debe; *vn* golpear con las puntas de los pies; **to toe in** andar con las puntas de los pies hacia adentro; (aut.) convergir (*las ruedas*)
toe dancer *s* bailarina clásica
toenail ['to,nel] *s* uña del dedo del pie; (carp.) clavo oblicuo; *va* (carp.) clavar oblicuamente
toffee o **toffy** ['tɔfɪ] o ['tɑfɪ] *s* melcocha, arropía
tog [tɑg] *s* (coll.) prenda de vestir; **togs** *spl* (coll.) ropa, vestidos; (*pret & pp:* **togged**; *ger:* **togging**) *va* (coll.) vestir, engalanar, acicalar
toga ['togə] *s* (hist.) toga
together [tʊ'geðər] *adv* juntos; juntamente; en común; a un tiempo, al mismo tiempo; sin interrupción; de acuerdo; **to get together** acopiar; reunir; reunirse; ponerse de acuerdo; **to go together** ir juntos; ser novios; armonizar entre sí; **together with** junto con
toggery ['tɑgərɪ] *s* (coll.) ropa, vestidos
toggle ['tɑgəl] *s* cazonete de aparejo; fiador atravesado; palanca acodillada; *va* asegurar con cazonete; proveer de cazonete
toggle bolt *s* tornillo de fiador
toggle chain *s* cadena de ajuste, cadena con fiador y anillo
toggle joint *s* junta de codillo
toggle plate *s* placa de articulación
toggle press *s* prensa de palanca acodillada
toggle switch *s* (elec.) interruptor a palanca, interruptor de rótula
toil [tɔɪl] *s* afán, fatiga; faena, obra laboriosa; **toils** *spl* red, lazo; *vn* afanarse, fatigarse; moverse con fatiga
toiler ['tɔɪlər] *s* trabajador
toilet ['tɔɪlɪt] *s* tocador (*mesa con espejo*); utensilio de tocador, juego de tocador; tocado, atavío; traje; retrete, inodoro, excusado; (surg.) limpiadura de una herida; **to make one's toilet** asearse, acicalarse
toilet articles *spl* artículos de tocador
toilet bowl *s* cubeta del inodoro
toilet paper *s* papel higiénico
toilet powder *s* polvos de tocador
toiletry ['tɔɪlɪtrɪ] *s* (*pl:* **-ries**) artículos de tocador
toilet service *s* juego de tocador
toilet soap *s* jabón de olor, jabón de tocador
toilet tank *s* tanque o depósito del inodoro
toilette [tɔɪ'lɛt] o [twɑ'lɛt] *s* atavío; traje, vestido (*de mujer*)
toilet water *s* agua de tocador
toilsome ['tɔɪlsəm] *s* fatigoso, laborioso, penoso
toilworn ['tɔɪl,worn] *adj* rendido por la fatiga
token ['tokən] *s* señal, símbolo; prenda, recuerdo; prueba, muestra; tanto, ficha o medalla (*usada como moneda*); **by the same token** por el mismo motivo; además; **in token of** en señal de
token payment *s* pago nominal
told [told] *pret & pp de* **tell; all told** todo incluído, en junto
Toledan [tə'lidən] *adj & s* toledano
Toledo [tə'lido] *s* (*pl:* **-dos**) arma toledana, hoja toledana
tolerable ['tɑlərəbəl] *adj* tolerable; mediano, regular
tolerably ['tɑlərəblɪ] *adv* tolerablemente; medianamente
tolerance ['tɑlərəns] *s* tolerancia; (mach. & med.) tolerancia; tolerancia, permiso (*en el monedaje*)
tolerant ['tɑlərənt] *adj* tolerante
tolerate ['tɑləret] *va* tolerar
toleration [,tɑlə'reʃən] *s* tolerancia, tolerantismo
tolerationism [,tɑlə'reʃənɪzəm] *s* tolerantismo
toll [tol] *s* doble (*de las campanas*); peaje, portazgo; pontazgo; maquila (*de molinero*); (telp.) tarifa; impuesto, derecho; derechos de paso (*por un canal*); baja, mortalidad (*número de víctimas*); *va* cobrar o pagar como peaje; imponer peaje a; tocar a muerto (*una campana*); tocar a muerto para; llamar con toque de difuntos; *vn* doblar
toll bar *s* barrera de peaje
toll bridge *s* puente de peaje
toll call *s* (telp.) llamada a larga distancia
tollgate ['tol,get] *s* barrera de peaje
tollkeeper ['tol,kipər] *s* peajero, portazguero
Toltec ['tɑltɛk] *adj & s* tolteca
tolu [to'lu] *s* (pharm.) bálsamo de Tolú
toluene ['tɑljʊin] *s* (chem.) tolueno
toluic [tə'luɪk] o ['tɑljʊɪk] *adj* (chem.) toluico

toluidine [tə'luɪdin] o [tə'luɪdɪn] *s* (chem.) toluidina
toluol ['tɑljʊɑl] *s* (chem.) toluol
tolyl ['tɑlɪl] *s* (chem.) tolilo
tom o **Tom** [tɑm] *s* macho del gato, del pavo y de algún otro animal; (*cap.*) *s* nombre abreviado de **Thomas**
tomahawk ['tɑməhɔk] *s* tomahawk; **to bury the tomahawk** envainar la espada, hacer la paz; *va* herir o matar con tomahawk
tomato [tə'meto] o [tə'mɑto] *s* (*pl:* **-toes**) (bot.) tomatera o tomate (*planta*); tomate (*fruto*); *adj* tomatero
tomato tree *s* (bot.) árbol del tomate
tomb [tum] *s* tumba, sepulcro; (fig.) muerte; *va* sepultar
tombac ['tɑmbæk] *s* tombac
tomboy ['tɑm,bɔɪ] *s* moza retozona, muchacha traviesa
tombstone ['tum,ston] *s* piedra o lápida sepulcral
tomcat ['tɑm,kæt] *s* gato (*macho*)
tomcod ['tɑm,kɑd] *s* (ichth.) microgado, pez escarchada
Tom, Dick, and Harry *s* fulano, zutano y mengano
tome [tom] *s* tomo; libro grueso
tomentose [tə'mɛntos] o ['tomɛntos] *adj* tomentoso
tomentum [tə'mɛntəm] *s* (*pl:* **-ta** [tə]) (bot.) tomento
tomfool [,tɑm'ful] *s* necio, payaso
tomfoolery [,tɑm'fulərɪ] *s* (*pl:* **-ies**) necedad, payasada
tommy o **Tommy** ['tɑmɪ] *s* (*pl:* **-mies**) soldado raso inglés
Tommy gun *s* (slang) pistola ametralladora (*de la marca Thompson*)
tommyrot ['tɑmɪ,rɑt] *s* (slang) mentecatería, música celestial
tomorrow o **to-morrow** [tʊ'mɑro] o [tʊ'mɔro] *adv* & *s* mañana; **the day after tomorrow** pasado mañana
Tom Thumb *s* Pulgarcito (*enano de los cuentos de hadas*)
tomtit ['tɑm,tɪt] *s* (orn.) herrerillo, trepatroncos; (orn.) coletero, rey de zarza
tom-tom ['tɑm,tɑm] *s* tantán
ton [tʌn] *s* tonelada; (naut.) tonelada; **tons** *spl* (coll.) montones
tonal ['tonəl] *adj* tonal
tonality [to'nælɪtɪ] *s* (*pl:* **-ties**) (mus. & f.a.) tonalidad
tone [ton] *s* tono; (f.a., mus., phonet. & physiol.) tono; **to change one's tone** mudar de tono; **to lower one's tone** bajar el tono; *va* entonar (*el cuerpo*); (mus. & paint.) entonar; (phot.) entonar, virar; **to tone down** suavizar el tono de; **to tone up** elevar el tono de; *vn* armonizar; **to tone down** moderarse; **to tone in with** armonizar con; **to tone up** reforzarse
tone arm *s* brazo sonoro, brazo para fonógrafo
tone color *s* (mus.) timbre
tone control *s* (rad.) regulación del tono
tone-deaf ['ton,dɛf] *adj* duro de oído
tone deafness *s* sordera musical
tone poem *s* (mus.) poema sinfónico
tong [tɔŋ] o [tɑŋ] *s* asociación secreta china; **tongs** *spl* tenazas; tenazas de rizar; tenacillas (*p.ej., para azúcar*); *va* asir, sujetar o arrancar con tenazas; *vn* emplear tenazas, trabajar con tenazas
Tongking ['tɑŋ'kɪŋ] *s* var. de **Tonkin**
tongue [tʌŋ] *s* (anat.) lengua; vara o lanza (*de carro*); tarabilla (*de la hebilla de la correa*); lengüeta de balanza; (carp. & mus.) lengüeta; (fig.) lengua (*idioma; badajo de campana; lengua de un animal usada como alimento*); (fig.) lengua (*de tierra, de fuego, de zapato*); **to give tongue** (hunt.) comenzar a ladrar; **to hold one's tongue** morderse la lengua; **to stick one's tongue out at** sacar la lengua a; *va* lamer; (carp.) sacar lengüeta a (*una tabla*); (carp.) ensamblar a lengüeta y ranura; (mus.) producir (*tonos*) con la lengua; *vn* extenderse (*p.ej., una lengua de tierra*); echar llamas; (mus.) producir tonos con la lengua
tongue and groove *s* (carp.) lengüeta y ranura
tongue-and-groove joint ['tʌŋənd'gruv] *s* (carp.) ensambladura de lengüeta y ranura
tongue depressor *s* (med.) depresor de la lengua
tonguefish ['tʌŋ,fɪʃ] *s* (ichth.) lengüita
tongue-lashing ['tʌŋ,læʃɪŋ] *s* (coll.) latigazo (*reprensión áspera*)
tongue-tied ['tʌŋ,taɪd] *adj* mudo, con la lengua atada; que tiene impedimento al hablar
tongue twister *s* trabalenguas
tonic ['tɑnɪk] *adj* tónico; *s* (med.) tónico; (mus. & phonet.) tónica
tonic accent *s* acento tónico
tonicity [to'nɪsɪtɪ] *s* tonicidad
tonight o **to-night** [tʊ'naɪt] *adv* & *s* esta noche
tonite ['tonaɪt] *s* tonita
tonka bean ['tɑŋkə] *s* (bot.) sarapia; haba tonca (*semilla de la sarapia*)
Tonkin ['tɑn'kɪn] *s* el Tonquín
tonnage ['tʌnɪdʒ] *s* tonelaje
tonneau [tʌ'no] *s* (*pl:* **-neaus** o **-neaux** ['noz]) (aut.) compartimiento posterior
tonometer [to'nɑmɪtər] *s* tonómetro
tonsil ['tɑnsəl] *s* (anat.) tonsila, amígdala
tonsillar ['tɑnsɪlər] *adj* tonsilar
tonsillectomy [,tɑnsɪ'lɛktəmɪ] *s* (*pl:* **-mies**) (surg.) tonsilectomía, amigdalotomía
tonsillitis [,tɑnsɪ'laɪtɪs] *s* (path.) tonsilitis, amigdalitis
tonsorial [tɑn'sorɪəl] *adj* barberil
tonsure ['tɑnʃər] *s* (eccl.) tonsura; *va* (eccl.) tonsurar
tontine ['tɑntin] o [tɑn'tin] *s* tontina; *adj* de tontina
tony ['tonɪ] *adj* (*comp:* **-ier;** *super:* **-iest**) (slang) aristocrático, elegante; (*cap.*) *s* Antoñito
too [tu] *adv* también; demasiado; **it is too bad** es lástima; **only too** muy; **too bad!** ¡qué lástima!; **too many** demasiados; **too much** demasiado
took [tʊk] *pret de* **take**
tool [tul] *s* herramienta; (fig.) instrumento; *adj* herramental; *va* trabajar con herramienta; adornar con una herramienta; (b.b.) filetear; *vn* instalar máquinas-herramientas
tool bag *s* bolsa de herramientas
toolbox ['tul,bɑks] *s* caja de herramientas
tool cabinet *s* armario para herramientas
tool chest *s* caja de herramientas
toolholder ['tul,holdər] *s* portaherramientas
tooling ['tulɪŋ] *s* trabajo hecho con herramienta; (b.b.) fileteado
tool kit *s* juego de herramientas
toolmaker ['tul,mekər] *s* tallador de herramientas, herrero de herramientas
toolmaking ['tul,mekɪŋ] *s* talladura de herramientas
tool steel *s* acero de herramientas
toot [tut] *s* sonido breve (*de la bocina, el pito, etc.*); *va* sonar; *vn* sonar la bocina, tocar el cuerno, pitar
tooth [tuθ] *s* (*pl:* **teeth**) (anat.) diente; diente (*de sierra, rastrillo, peine, etc.*); **armed to the teeth** armado hasta los dientes; **by the skin of one's teeth** por poco, por milagro; **in the teeth of** en la cara de; a despecho de; **to cast in one's teeth** darle o echarle en cara a uno; **to cut teeth** endentecer; **to fight tooth and nail** luchar a brazo partido, luchar encarnizadamente; **to set one's teeth** apretar los dientes (*preparar a resistir*); **to show one's teeth** enseñar o mostrar los dientes; **to throw in one's teeth** darle o echarle en cara a uno; *va* dentar (*formar dientes en*); *vn* endentar
toothache ['tuθ,ek] *s* dolor de muelas
toothbrush ['tuθ,brʌʃ] *s* cepillo para los dientes
toothed [tuθt] o [tuðd] *adj* dentado; dentellado
tooth edge *s* dentera
toothing ['tuθɪŋ] *s* (mas.) adaraja
toothing plane *s* (carp.) cepillo dentado
toothless ['tuθlɪs] *adj* desdentado, desmolado
tooth mark *s* dentellada
tooth paste *s* pasta dentífrica
toothpick ['tuθ,pɪk] *s* palillo, mondadientes
tooth powder *s* polvo dentífrico
toothsome ['tuθsəm] *adj* gustoso, sabroso

toothwort ['tuθ,wʌrt] *s* (bot.) madrona, hierba de la madre, dentaria
toothy ['tuθɪ] *adj* (*comp:* **-ier; super: -iest**) que tiene dientes grandes, que muestra sus dientes; hambriento, voraz; (coll.) gustoso, sabroso
top [tɑp] *s* ápice (*extremo superior*); cabeza; cima (*de una montaña, un árbol; tallo de ciertas verduras*); cumbre (*de montaña; punto culminante*); copa (*de un árbol*); fuelle (*de un carruaje*); parche (*de un tambor*); tapa (*de un cilindro, un barril, una caja*); remate (*de un tejado*); principio (*de una página*); cabecera (*de un río*); coronilla (*de la cabeza*); coronamiento (*de un muro*); tablero (*de una mesa*); copete (*de una bota; adorno en la parte superior de un mueble*); cabeza, jefe; colmo (*último grado*); tope (*máximo*); camiseta (*del traje de baño*); peón, peonza, trompo (*juguete*); mapa (*lo que sobresale en algo*); galopo (*usado para formar maromas*); (aut.) capota; (naut.) cofa; (dial.) copete, moño; **at the top of** a la cabeza de (*p.ej., la clase*); **at the top of one's voice** a voz en grito; **from top to bottom** de arriba abajo; de alto a bajo; completamente; **from top to toe** de pies a cabeza; **on top** con el mayor éxito, victorioso; **on top of** encima de, en lo alto de; **on top of the world** en el tejado del mundo (*en el polo norte*); (coll.) en el colmo de la riqueza, la felicidad, etc.; **over the top** (mil.) al ataque, saliendo de las trincheras; **the tops** (slang) la flor de la canela; **to sleep like a top** dormir como un leño; *adj* cimero; máximo; último (*piso*); (él) más alto; tope (*precio*); alto; superior; superficial (*que está en la superficie*); (*pret & pp:* **topped;** *ger:* **topping**) *va* coronar, rematar; llegar a la cima de; cubrir; aventajar, superar; descopar (*p.ej., un árbol*); **to top off** rematar, terminar; (naut.) embicar (*una verga*); *vn* predominar, ser excelente; encumbrarse
topaz ['topæz] *s* topacio
top billing *s* (theat.) cabecera de cartel
top boot *s* bota de campaña; bota con vueltas
topcoat ['tɑp,kot] *s* abrigo, sobretodo; abrigo de entretiempo
top-drawer ['tɑp,drɔr] *adj* (coll.) de las altas clases, de primer rango
top-dress ['tɑp,drɛs] *va* recebar; (agr.) estercolar la superficie de
top-dressing ['tɑp,drɛsɪŋ] *s* recebo; (agr.) estercoladura aplicada a la superficie
tope [top] *va & vn* beber con exceso
toper ['topər] *s* borrachín
topflight ['tɑp,flaɪt] *adj* sobresaliente, destacado, más eminente
topgallant [tə'gælənt] *s* (naut.) juanete; *adj* (naut.) de juanete; [,tɑp'gælənt] *s* ápice, cumbre; cosa sobresaliente; *adj* sobresaliente
topgallant mast [tə'gælənt] *s* (naut.) mastelerillo
topgallant sail [tə'gælənt] *s* (naut.) juanete
top hat *s* chistera, sombrero de copa
top-heavy ['tɑp,hɛvɪ] *adj* demasiado pesado por arriba, más pesado arriba que abajo; (com.) que tiene capitalización inflada; (naut.) alteroso
tophus ['tofəs] *s* (*pl:* **-phi** [faɪ]) (path.) tofo
topiary ['topɪ,ɛrɪ] *adj* topiario; *s* (*pl:* **-ies**) topiaria
topic ['tɑpɪk] *s* asunto, tema, materia, tópico
topical ['tɑpɪkəl] *adj* corriente; del asunto; (med.) tópico
topknot ['tɑp,nɑt] *s* moño (*de pelo, de cintas; de plumas de algunas aves*)
toplofty ['tɑp,lɔftɪ] o ['tɑp,lɑftɪ] *adj* (coll.) copetudo, vanidoso
topman ['tɑpmən] *s* (*pl:* **-men**) (naut.) gaviero
topmast ['tɑpməst], ['tɑp,mæst] o ['tɑp,mɑst] *s* (naut.) mastelero
topmost ['tɑpmost] *adj* (el) más alto
top notch *s* (coll.) colmo, disloque
top-notch ['tɑp'nɑtʃ] *adj* superior, sobresaliente, de primera clase
top-notcher ['tɑp'nɑtʃər] *s* (coll.) persona sobresaliente, cosa sobresaliente
top of the morning *s* primeras horas de la mañana; (Irish) buenos días
topographer [tə'pɑgrəfər] *s* topógrafo
topographic [,tɑpə'græfɪk] o **topographical** [,tɑpə'græfɪkəl] *adj* topográfico
topographically [,tɑpə'græfɪkəlɪ] *adv* topográficamente
topography [tə'pɑgrəfɪ] *s* (*pl:* **-phies**) topografía
topology [tə'pɑlədʒɪ] *s* (anat. & math.) topología
toponym ['tɑpənɪm] *s* topónimo
toponymic [,tɑpə'nɪmɪk] *adj* toponímico; **toponymics** *ssg* toponimia
toponymy [tə'pɑnɪmɪ] *s* (*pl:* **-mies**) toponimia; (anat.) toponimia
topper ['tɑpər] *s* (coll.) persona o cosa de primera clase; (coll.) chistera, sombrero de copa
topping ['tɑpɪŋ] *adj* sobresaliente; (coll.) sobresaliente, de primera clase; *s* copete, moño; **toppings** *spl* desmocho (*p.ej., de los árboles*)
topping lift *s* (naut.) perigallo
topple ['tɑpəl] *va* derribar, volcar; *vn* derribarse, volcarse; caerse, venirse abajo
topsail ['tɑpsəl] o ['tɑp,sel] *s* (naut.) gavia
top-secret ['tɑp'sikrɪt] *adj* extremadamente secreto
top sergeant *s* (coll.) primer sargento
topsides ['tɑp,saɪdz] *spl* (naut.) borda (*parte superior del costado*)
topsoil ['tɑp,sɔɪl] *s* capa superficial del suelo
topsy-turvy ['tɑpsɪ'tʌrvɪ] *adj* desbarajustado, desordenado; *adv* en cuadro, patas arriba; *s* desbarajuste, desorden
top-timber ['tɑp,tɪmbər] *s* (naut.) barraganete
toque [tok] *s* toca
torah ['torə] *s* tora (*de los judíos*); **the Torah** la Tora
torch [tɔrtʃ] *s* antorcha; antorcha a soplete, lámpara de soldar; lámpara de bolsillo; **to carry a** o **the torch for** (slang) amar (*a una persona*) desesperadamente
torchbearer ['tɔrtʃ,berər] *s* portahachón, hachero; (fig.) adicto, partidario, defensor
torchlight ['tɔrtʃ,laɪt] *s* luz de antorcha
torchlight procession *s* desfile de portahachones
torch singer *s* cantante de canciones de amor no correspondido
torch song *s* canción lenta y melancólica de amor no correspondido
torchwood ['tɔrtʃ,wud] *s* (bot.) amírida, ñámbar
tore [tor] *pret de* **tear**
toreador ['tɔrɪədɔr] *s* toreador
toric ['tɑrɪk] *adj* tórico
toric lens *s* lente tórica
torment ['tɔrmɛnt] *s* tormento; [tɔr'mɛnt] *va* atormentar
tormenter o **tormentor** [tɔr'mɛntər] *s* atormentador
torn [torn] *pp de* **tear**
tornado [tɔr'nedo] *s* (*pl:* **-does** o **-dos**) (meteor.) tornado, tromba terrestre; (fig.) explosión violenta
toroid ['torɔɪd] *s* (geom.) toroide
torpedo [tɔr'pido] *s* (*pl:* **-does**) (nav., ichth. & rail.) torpedo; *va* (nav. & fig.) torpedear
torpedo boat *s* (nav.) torpedero, lancha torpedera
torpedo-boat destroyer [tɔr'pido,bot] *s* (nav.) cazatorpedero, contratorpedero
torpedoist [tɔr'pido·ɪst] *s* torpedista
torpedo tube *s* (nav.) tubo lanzatorpedos
torpid ['tɔrpɪd] *adj* torpe; entorpecido; aletargado; indiferente, insensible
torpidity [tɔr'pɪdɪtɪ] o **torpor** ['tɔrpər] *s* torpeza; entorpecimiento; letargo; indiferencia, insensibilidad
torque [tɔrk] *s* (mech.) esfuerzo de rotación, par motor; torques (*collar*)
torque arm *s* (aut.) brazo de par
torque converter *s* (aut.) convertidor de par
torrefaction [,tɑrɪ'fækʃən] o [,tɔrɪ'fækʃən] *s* torrefacción
torrefy ['tɑrɪfaɪ] o ['tɔrɪfaɪ] (*pret & pp:* **-fied**) *va* abrasar, asar, tostar
torrent ['tɑrənt] o ['tɔrənt] *s* torrente (*corriente de aguas impetuosas*); chaparrón violento; (fig.) torrente
torrential [tɑ'rɛnʃəl] o [tɔ'rɛnʃəl] *adj* torrencial
torrid ['tɑrɪd] o ['tɔrɪd] *adj* tórrido

torridity [tɑˈrɪdɪtɪ] o [təˈrɪdɪtɪ] *s* extremo calor
torrid zone *s* zona tórrida
torsion [ˈtɔrʃən] *s* torsión; (mech.) torsión
torsional [ˈtɔrʃənəl] *adj* torsional
torsion balance *s* (phys.) balanza de torsión
torsion pendulum *s* péndulo de torsión
torso [ˈtɔrso] *s* (*pl:* **-sos**) torso; (f.a.) torso
tort [tɔrt] *s* (law) agravio indemnizable en juicio civil (*excepto infracción de contrato*)
torticollis [ˌtɔrtɪˈkɑlɪs] *s* (path.) tortícolis
tortoise [ˈtɔrtəs] *s* (zool.) tortuga, tortuga de tierra
tortoise beetle *s* (ent.) cásida
tortoise shell *s* carey, concha
tortoise-shell [ˈtɔrtəsˌʃɛl] *adj* de carey, de concha; abigarrado como el carey o la concha
tortuosity [ˌtɔrtʃʊˈɑsɪtɪ] *s* (*pl:* **-ties**) tortuosidad
tortuous [ˈtɔrtʃʊəs] *adj* tortuoso; (fig.) tortuoso (*solapado*); (fig.) torcido (*que no obra con rectitud*)
torture [ˈtɔrtʃər] *s* tortura; *va* torturar; torcer, forzar, violentar
torturous [ˈtɔrtʃərəs] *adj* torturador
torulus [ˈtɑrʊləs] *s* (*pl:* **-li** [laɪ]) (ent.) tórulo
torus [ˈtorəs] *s* (*pl:* **-ri** [raɪ]) (arch.) torés; (anat., bot. & math.) toro
tory [ˈtorɪ] *s* (*pl:* **-ries**) conservador; (*cap.*) *s* tory
Toryism [ˈtorɪɪzəm] *s* torismo
tosh [tɑʃ] *s* (slang) música celestial
toss [tɔs] o [tɑs] *s* echada; alcance de una echada; agitación, meneo; *va* echar (*de una parte a otra*); arrojar ligeramente; arrojar de un tirón; lanzar al aire; agitar, menear; mantear; levantar airosamente (*la cabeza*); echar a cara o cruz; lanzar (*p.ej., un comentario*); **to toss aside** echar a un lado; **to toss off** hacer muy rápidamente; tragar de un golpe; *vn* agitarse, menearse; jugar a cara y cruz; **to toss and turn** revolverse, dar vueltas (*en la cama*)
toss-up [ˈtɔsˌʌp] o [ˈtɑsˌʌp] *s* cara y cruz; (coll.) probabilidad igual
tot [tɑt] *s* párvulo; trago; total; (coll.) adición; (*pret & pp:* **totted**; *ger:* **totting**) *va & vn* (coll.) sumar
total [ˈtotəl] *adj & s* total; (*pret & pp:* **-taled** o **-talled**; *ger:* **-taling** o **-talling**) *va* sumar; ascender a; formar un total de
total abstinence *s* abstinencia de bebidas alcohólicas
total eclipse *s* (astr.) eclipse total
totalitarian [toˌtælɪˈtɛrɪən] *adj & s* totalitario
totalitarianism [toˌtælɪˈtɛrɪənɪzəm] *s* totalitarismo
totality [toˈtælɪtɪ] *s* (*pl:* **-ties**) totalidad
totalization [ˌtotəlɪˈzeʃən] *s* totalización
totalize [ˈtotəlaɪz] *va* totalizar
totalizer [ˈtotəˌlaɪzər] *s* totalizador
totally [ˈtotəlɪ] *adv* totalmente
total war *s* guerra total
tote [tot] *va* (coll.) cargar, llevar, acarrear
totem [ˈtotəm] *s* tótem
totemic [toˈtɛmɪk] *adj* totémico
totemism [ˈtotəmɪzəm] *s* totemismo
totem pole *s* pilar totémico
tother [ˈtʌðər] (dial.) contracción de **the other**
totipalmate [ˌtotɪˈpælmɪt] o [ˌtotɪˈpælmet] *adj* (zool.) totipalmo
totter [ˈtɑtər] *s* tambaleo; *vn* tambalearse; amenazar ruina, estar para desplomarse
tottery [ˈtɑtərɪ] *adj* tambaleante, vacilante; ruinoso
toucan [tʊˈkɑn] o [ˈtukən] *s* (orn.) tucán
touch [tʌtʃ] *s* toque; tacto, tiento; pulsación (*del pianista o dactilógrafo*); tacto (*del piano, el pianista, la máquina de escribir, el dactilógrafo*); pizca, poquito; ramo (*de una enfermedad*); (paint.) toque; **by touch** al tacto; **out of touch with** no al corriente de; sin relaciones con; **to get in touch with** ponerse en comunicación o contacto con; **to keep in touch with** mantenerse en comunicación o contacto con; **to lose one's touch** perder el tiento; *va* tocar; conmover, enternecer; igualar, compararse con; tocar (*con la piedra de toque*); (slang) pedir prestado a; (slang) robar; **to not touch** no catar (*p.ej., vino*); **to touch off** descargar; provocar; representar con la mayor precisión; acabar; **to touch up** retocar; estimular; *vn* tocar; **to touch at** tocar en (*un puerto*); **to touch down** (aer.) aterrizar; **to touch on** o **upon** tocar
touch-and-go [ˈtʌtʃəndˈgo] *adj* difícil, arriesgado; hecho de prisa, incompleto
touchback [ˈtʌtʃˌbæk] *s* (football) acción de tocar el suelo con el balón detrás de su propia meta
touchdown [ˈtʌtʃˌdaʊn] *s* (football) jugada que consiste en tocar el suelo con el balón detrás de la meta del adversario; tantos ganados con tal jugada
touched [tʌtʃt] *adj* tocado (*echado a perder; medio loco*); **touched in the head** (coll.) tocado de la cabeza
touchhole [ˈtʌtʃˌhol] *s* fogón, oído del cañón
touching [ˈtʌtʃɪŋ] *adj* conmovedor, enternecedor; *prep* tocante a, en lo que toca a
touch-me-not [ˈtʌtʃmiˌnɑt] *s* (bot.) hierba de Santa Catalina; (bot.) cohombrillo amargo; persona altanera y esquiva
touchstone [ˈtʌtʃˌston] *s* (mineral. & fig.) piedra de toque
touch typewriting *s* escritura al tacto, mecanografía al tacto
touchwood [ˈtʌtʃˌwʊd] *s* yesca
touchy [ˈtʌtʃɪ] *adj* (*comp:* **-ier**; *super:* **-iest**) quisquilloso, enojadizo
tough [tʌf] *adj* correoso, estropajoso; tenaz; difícil; malvado; alborotador, pendenciero; malo (*dícese de la suerte*); *s* alborotador, pendenciero, bribón
toughen [ˈtʌfən] *va* hacer correoso, endurecer; hacer tenaz; dificultar; *vn* ponerse correoso, endurecerse; hacerse tenaz; hacerse difícil
toughness [ˈtʌfnɪs] *s* correosidad; tenacidad; dificultad; maldad
Toulon [tuˈlɑn] *s* Tolón
Toulouse [tuˈluz] *s* Tolosa
toupee [tuˈpe] o [tuˈpi] *s* tupé
tour [tʊr] *s* jira, paseo, vuelta; viaje largo; **on tour** de viaje; **the grand tour** un viaje por los países principales de Europa; **to make a tour** hacer un viaje; **to make a tour of** recorrer; *va* viajar por, recorrer; *vn* viajar por distracción o diversión
Touraine [tʊˈren] *s* la Turena
tour de force [tʊrdəˈfɔrs] *s* juego de destreza
touring [ˈtʊrɪŋ] *s* turismo; *adj* turístico
touring car *s* turismo, coche de turismo
tourist [ˈtʊrɪst] *adj* turístico; *s* turista
tourist camp *s* campamento de turismo
tourist class *s* (aer. & naut.) clase turista
tourmalin [ˈtʊrməlɪn] o **tourmaline** [ˈtʊrməlɪn] o [ˈtʊrməlin] *s* (mineral.) turmalina
tournament [ˈtʊrnəmənt] o [ˈtʌrnəmənt] *s* torneo; (sport) torneo
tourney [ˈtʊrnɪ] o [ˈtʌrnɪ] *s* torneo, justa; *vn* tornear, justar
tourniquet [ˈtʊrnɪkɛt] o [ˈtʌrnɪke] *s* (surg.) torniquete
Tours [tʊr] *s* Turs
tousle [ˈtaʊzəl] *s* enredo de cabello, maraña; *va* enmarañar, despeinar
tout [taʊt] *s* (coll.) solicitante; (coll.) espía de las carreras de caballos (*especialmente el que busca y vende informes confidenciales*); *va* (coll.) solicitar; (coll.) importunar, molestar; (coll.) buscar, husmear o dar (*informes confidenciales sobre carreras de caballos*); (coll.) decir mil bienes de; *vn* (coll.) solicitar clientes, destinos, etc.; (coll.) espiar y obtener informes confidenciales sobre carreras de caballos
tow [to] *s* remolque (*acción; vehículo remolcado; cabo o sirga*); estopa; **to take a tow** hacerse remolcar, ir remolcado; **to take in tow** dar remolque a, llevar o tomar a remolque; *adj* de estopa; *va* remolcar
towage [ˈto·ɪdʒ] *s* remolque; derechos de remolque
toward [tord] o [təˈwɔrd] o **towards** [tordz] o [təˈwɔrdz] *prep* hacia; cerca de; tocante a; para con
towboat [ˈtoˌbot] *s* remolcador
towel [ˈtaʊəl] *s* toalla; (*pret & pp:* **-eled** o **-elled**; *ger:* **-eling** o **-elling**) *va* secar con toalla

toweling o **towelling** ['tauəlɪŋ] *s* género o tela para toallas
towel rack *s* toallero
tower ['tauər] *s* torre; *vn* encumbrarse
tower clock *s* reloj de torre
towering ['tauərɪŋ] *adj* elevado, muy alto; sobresaliente; muy grande; muy violento
Tower of Babel *s* torre de Babel
towery ['tauərɪ] *adj* torreado; muy alto
towhead ['to,hɛd] *s* persona de pelo rubio muy pálido
towheaded ['to,hɛdɪd] *adj* de pelo rubio muy pálido
towhee ['tauhi] o ['tohi] *s* (orn.) tarenga, luis, totochil
towing service *s* (aut.) servicio de grúa, servicio de remolque
towline ['to,laɪn] *s* cable de remolque; (naut.) sirga; (naut.) estacha (*atada al arpón ballenero*)
town [taun] *s* población, pueblo; **in town** a la ciudad, en la ciudad; al centro de la ciudad, en el centro de la ciudad; **to go to town** (slang) tener gran éxito; **to paint the town red** (slang) correrla, ir de parranda
town clerk *s* escribano municipal
town council *s* concejo municipal
town crier *s* pregonero público, voceador
town hall *s* casa de ayuntamiento
town house *s* casa de ciudad, casa en la ciudad
townhouse ['taun,haus] *s* (Brit.) casa de ayuntamiento
town meeting *s* reunión de los habitantes de una población; reunión de los electores de una ciudad (*en la Nueva Inglaterra*)
townsfolk ['taunz,fok] *spl* vecinos del pueblo
township ['taunʃɪp] *s* municipio, sexmo, término municipal; subdivisión de un partido; terreno de seis millas en cuadro
townsman ['taunzmən] *s* (*pl:* **-men**) ciudadano, vecino; conciudadano, paisano
townspeople ['taunz,pipəl] *spl* vecinos del pueblo
town talk *s* comidilla o hablillas del pueblo
towpath ['to,pæθ] o ['to,pɑθ] *s* camino de sirga
tow plane *s* (aer.) avión de remolque
towrope ['to,rop] *s* cable de remolque
tow target *s* (aer.) blanco remolcado
tow truck *s* camión-grúa, grúa-remolque
toxaemia [tɑks'imɪə] *s* var. de **toxemia**
toxalbumin [,tɑksæl'bjumɪn] *s* (biochem.) toxialbúmina
toxemia [tɑks'imɪə] *s* (path.) toxemia
toxemic [tɑks'imɪk] *adj* toxémico
toxic ['tɑksɪk] *adj* & *s* tóxico
toxicity [tɑks'ɪsɪtɪ] *s* (*pl:* **-ties**) toxicidad
toxicogenic [,tɑksɪkə'dʒɛnɪk] *adj* toxicogénico o toxicógeno
toxicological [,tɑksɪkə'lɑdʒɪkəl] *adj* toxicológico
toxicologist [,tɑksɪ'kɑlədʒɪst] *s* toxicólogo
toxicology [,tɑksɪ'kɑlədʒɪ] *s* toxicología
toxicosis [,tɑksɪ'kosɪs] *s* (*pl:* **-ses** [siz]) (path.) toxicosis
toxin ['tɑksɪn] *s* (bact.) toxina
toxiphobia [,tɑksɪ'fobɪə] *s* (psychopath.) toxofobia
toy [tɔɪ] *s* juguete; bagatela; dije, bujería; *adj* de jugar; de adorno; muy pequeño; miniatura (*perro*); *vn* jugar; divertirse; **to toy with** jugar con (*una persona; los sentimientos de una persona*); acariciar (*una idea*); comer melindrosamente (*p.ej., el desayuno*)
toy bank *s* alcancía, hucha
toy dog *s* perrillo, perro miniatura
toyon ['tojən] *s* (bot.) tollón
toyshop ['tɔɪ,ʃɑp] *s* juguetería
toy soldier *s* soldadito de plomo, soldado de juguete
toy train *s* tren de juguete
tp. abr. de **township**
tr. abr. de **transitive, transpose** y **treasurer**
trabecula [trə'bɛkjələ] *s* (*pl:* **-lae** [li]) (anat. & bot.) trabécula
trace [tres] *s* huella, rastro; indicio, señal; trazo (*delineación*); calco (*obtenido por contacto del original*); tirante (*de los arreos de una caballería*); pizca; (geom.) traza; **to kick over the traces** rebelarse; **without leaving a trace** sin dejar rastro; *va* rastrear; trazar (*p.ej., una curva; los rasgos de una persona o cosa*); calcar; localizar; recorrer (*p.ej., un circuito eléctrico en falla*); averiguar el paradero de; remontar al origen de
traceable ['tresəbəl] *adj* trazable
tracer ['tresər] *s* trazador; calcador; encargado de buscar los objetos extraviados; cédula de investigación (*para encontrar los objetos extraviados*); (chem. & phys.) trazador; *adj* (chem. & phys.) trazador
tracer bullet *s* bala trazante o trazadora
tracer element *s* (phys.) radioelemento trazador
tracery ['tresərɪ] *s* (*pl:* **-ies**) (arch.) tracería
trachea ['trekɪə] o [trə'kiə] *s* (*pl:* **-ae** [i]) (anat., bot. & zool.) tráquea
tracheal ['trekɪəl] o [trə'kiəl] *adj* traqueal
tracheid ['trekɪɪd] *s* (bot.) traqueida
tracheitis [,trekɪ'aɪtɪs] *s* (path.) traqueítis
tracheotomy [,trekɪ'ɑtəmɪ] *s* (*pl:* **-mies**) (surg.) traqueotomía
trachoma [trə'komə] *s* (path.) tracoma
trachomatous [trə'kɑmətəs] o [trə'komətəs] *adj* tracomatoso
trachyte ['trekaɪt] o ['trækaɪt] *s* (geol.) traquita
tracing ['tresɪŋ] *s* trazo; calco; *adj* de trazar; de calcar
tracing paper *s* papel de calcar
track [træk]] *s* huella (*que deja el pie; vestigio*); rodada, carril (*que dejan las ruedas al pasar*); estela (*que deja un barco*); vía (*del ferrocarril, los tranvías*); camino, senda; trayectoria (*p.ej., de un avión, un huracán*); llanta de oruga (*de un tractor*); sucesión (*de ideas, acontecimientos, etc.*); derrota (*rumbo que sigue un barco*); (sport) carreras y saltos; (sport) pista (*por donde corren los caballos*); (fig.) camino (*método, procedimiento*); **in one's tracks** allí mismo; **off the track** desviado; descarrilado; **on the right track** en el buen camino; **on the track** en el rastro; **to get off the track** descarrilar; (fig.) descarrilar, salirse del asunto; **to jump the track** descarrilar, salirse fuera del carril; **to keep track of** no olvidar; no perder la cuenta de; no perder de vista; **to lose track of** olvidar; perder de vista; **to make tracks** correr, irse muy de prisa; *va* rastrear, seguir la huella o la pista de; atravesar; manchar pisando, dejar pisadas en; llevar (*p.ej., barro*) con los pies; **to track down** averiguar el origen de; atrapar, seguir y capturar
trackage ['trækɪdʒ] *s* (rail.) sistema de vías; (rail.) derecho para uso de vía; remolque
trackhound ['træk,haund] *s* perro rastrero
tracking ['trækɪŋ] *adj* rastreador; *s* rastreo (*p.ej., de un satélite*)
tracking antenna *s* antena de rastreo
tracking station *s* estación de rastreo
trackless ['træklɪs] *adj* sin rastro; sin caminos, sin tránsito; sin carriles
trackless trolley *s* filobús, trolebús
track meet *s* (sport) concurso de carreras y saltos
track tank *s* (rail.) atarjea de alimentación
trackwalker ['træk,wɔkər] *s* (rail.) guardavía, recorredor de vía
tract [trækt] *s* espacio (*de terreno, de tiempo*); folleto (*especialmente el de propaganda religiosa o política*); (anat.) sistema (*de órganos*)
tractability [,træktə'bɪlɪtɪ] *s* docilidad
tractable ['træktəbəl] *adj* tratable; maleable, dúctil
tractile ['træktɪl] o ['træktaɪl] *adj* dúctil
traction ['trækʃən] *s* tracción; adherencia (*de las ruedas*); (physiol.) contracción
traction company *s* empresa de tranvías
traction engine *s* máquina de tracción
traction wheel *s* rueda de tracción
tractive ['træktɪv] *adj* tractivo, de tracción
tractor ['træktər] *s* tractor; (aer.) hélice de tracción; (aer.) avión de tracción
tractor-trailer ['træktər'trelər] *s* tractocamión, semi-remolque
trade [tred] *s* comercio; contratación, trato, negocio; trueque, canje; oficio; parroquia, clientela; trata (*p.ej., de mujeres*); **the trades** los vientos alisios; *va* trocar, cambiar; **to trade**

in dar como parte del pago; **to trade off** deshacerse de, trocando; *vn* comerciar; comprar; **to trade in** comerciar en; **to trade on** aprovecharse de, explotar
trade binding *s* (b.b.) encuadernación mecánica
trade-in ['tred,ɪn] *s* cosa dada como pago o pago parcial en la compra de otra; trueque
trademark ['tred,mɑrk] *s* marca de fábrica, marca registrada, marca privativa
trade name *s* nombre de fábrica; razón social
trader ['tredər] *s* comerciante, traficante; negociador; trocador; (naut.) buque mercante
trade school *s* escuela de artes y oficios
tradesman ['tredzmən] *s* (*pl:* **-men**) tendero; comerciante; (Brit.) artesano
tradespeople ['tredz,pipəl] *s* tenderos; comerciantes; (Brit.) gente del oficio
trades union o **trade union** *s* sindicato, gremio de obreros
trade unionism *s* sindicalismo
trade unionist *s* sindicalista
trade winds *spl* vientos alisios
trading account *s* cuenta de compraventa
trading post *s* factoría
trading stamp *s* sello de premio, sello de descuento (*que se da al comprador como aliciente*)
tradition [trə'dɪʃən] *s* tradición
traditional [trə'dɪʃənəl] *adj* tradicional
traditionalism [trə'dɪʃənəlɪzəm] *s* tradicionalismo
traditionally [trə'dɪʃənəlɪ] *adv* tradicionalmente
traditionary [trə'dɪʃən,ɛrɪ] *adj* var. de **traditional**
traduce [trə'djus] o [trə'dus] *va* calumniar
traducer [trə'djusər] o [trə'dusər] *s* calumniador
traducianism [trə'djuʃənɪzəm] o [trə'duʃənɪzəm] *s* (theol.) traducianismo
traffic ['træfɪk] *s* tráfico (*comercio; tránsito, circulación de personas y vehículos*); trata (*p.ej., de mujeres*); (*pret & pp:* **-ficked;** *ger:* **-ficking**) *vn* traficar
traffic circle *s* glorieta de tráfico, círculo de tráfico
traffic control *s* regulación de tráfico
traffic court *s* juzgado de tráfico
traffic jam *s* bloqueo, embotellamiento, tapón de tráfico
trafficker ['træfɪkər] *s* traficante
traffic light *s* luz de tráfico, semáforo
traffic manager *s* (com.) jefe de expediciones; (rail.) jefe de tráfico
traffic sign o **signal** *s* señal de tráfico, señal urbana
traffic ticket *s* aviso de multa (*por estacionar un auto indebidamente*)
tragacanth ['trægəkænθ] *s* (bot.) tragacanto (*árbol y goma*)
tragedian [trə'dʒidɪən] *s* trágico (*autor; actor*)
tragedienne o **tragédienne** [trə,dʒidɪ'ɛn] *s* trágica (*actriz*)
tragedy ['trædʒɪdɪ] *s* (*pl:* **-dies**) tragedia
tragic ['trædʒɪk] o **tragical** ['trædʒɪkəl] *adj* trágico
tragically ['trædʒɪkəlɪ] *adv* trágicamente
tragicomedy [,trædʒɪ'kɑmədɪ] *s* (*pl:* **-dies**) tragicomedia
tragicomic [,trædʒɪ'kɑmɪk] o **tragicomical** [,trædʒɪ'kɑmɪkəl] *adj* tragicómico
tragus ['tregəs] *s* (*pl:* **-gi** [dʒaɪ]) (anat.) trago
trail [trel] *s* huella, pista, rastro; sendero, vereda (*p.ej., que cruza un yermo*); estela (*de humo, de polvo, de un cometa, cohete, etc.*); cola (*de vestido*); (arti.) gualdera; *va* arrastrar (*llevar por el suelo*); rastrear, seguir la pista de; cazar siguiendo la pista; andar detrás de; pisar (*la hierba*) hasta formar una senda; llevar (*p.ej., barro*) con los pies; (mil.) bajar (*el arma*); *vn* arrastrar (*moverse como las serpientes; colgar, p.ej., un vestido, hasta tocar en el suelo*); rezagarse, ir rezagado; arrastrarse, trepar (*una planta*); **to trail off** desaparecer poco a poco, desvanecerse (*p.ej., el humo*)
trail blazer *s* explorador, iniciador, pionero
trailer ['trelər] *s* persona o animal que sigue la pista; remolque vivienda, vivienda remolque, autocasa, coche-habitación, casa en ruedas, casa rodante (*que se acopla a un auto*); acoplado, remolque, carretón de remolque; camión acoplado; tranvía acoplado; (bot.) planta rastrera; (mov.) anuncio de próximas atracciones
trailer camp *s* campamento para coches-habitaciones
trailer court *s* parque de remolques viviendas
trailing arbutus *s* (bot.) epigea rastrera
trailing edge *s* (aer.) borde de salida
trail rope *s* arrastradera (*de globo aerostático*); (mil.) prolonga
trail spade *s* (arti.) espolón
train [tren] *s* tren (*serie, p.ej., de ondas*); cola (*de un vestido*); hilo (*del pensamiento*); reguero de pólvora; (rail.) tren; *va* adiestrar; apuntar (*un arma*); guiar (*las plantas*); (sport) entrenar; *vn* adiestrarse; (sport) entrenarse
trainband ['tren,bænd] *s* (Brit. hist.) banda armada
trained dog *s* perro maestro
trained nurse *s* enfermera graduada
trainee [tre'ni] *s* persona que se entrena; (mil.) recluta
trainer ['trenər] *s* amaestrador; (sport) entrenador; (aer.) avión de entrenamiento
training ['trenɪŋ] *s* instrucción, preparación; adiestramiento; (sport) entrenamiento
training camp *s* (mil.) campamento de instrucción militar, campo de entrenamiento
training school *s* escuela práctica; reformatorio
training ship *s* (nav.) buque escuela
trainload ['tren,lod] *s* carga de un tren completo
trainman ['trenmən] *s* (*pl:* **-men**) (rail.) ferroviario; (rail.) guardafrenos
train oil *s* aceite de ballena u otro pescado
train wrecker *s* descarrilador de trenes
trait [tret] *s* rasgo, característica; golpe, toque
traitor ['tretər] *s* traidor
traitorous ['tretərəs] *adj* traidor, traicionero
traitress ['tretrɪs] *s* traidora
Trajan ['tredʒən] *s* Trajano
trajectory [trə'dʒɛktərɪ] *s* (*pl:* **-ries**) trayectoria
tram [træm] *s* trama (*seda para tramar*); (Brit.) tranvía; (min.) vagoneta; (mach.) calibre de alineación
tramcar ['træm,kɑr] *s* (Brit.) tranvía
trammel ['træməl] *s* impedimento, obstáculo; traba, manea, maniota; red (*para cazar o pescar*); trasmallo; garabato de chimenea; (*pret & pp:* **-meled** o **-melled;** *ger:* **-meling** o **-melling**) *va* impedir, estorbar; trabar, poner trabas a
trammel net *s* trasmallo
tramontane [trə'mɑnten] o ['træmənten] *adj* tramontano
tramp [træmp] *s* vagabundo; marcha pesada, paso pesado; pataleo; paseo largo; vapor volandero; *va* pisar con fuerza; recorrer a pie; *vn* patullar; andar o viajar a pie; vagar; vagabundear
trample ['træmpəl] *s* pisoteo; *va* pisotear; *vn* patullar; **to trample on** o **upon** pisotear, hollar
trampoline ['træmpəlɪn] *s* trampolín de acróbata o gimnasta
tramp steamer *s* vapor volandero, buque trampa
tramway ['træm,we] *s* vía aérea, funicular aéreo; (Brit.) tranvía
trance [træns] o [trɑns] *s* rapto, arrobamiento; trance, estado hipnótico; ensimismamiento; *va* encantar, enajenar
tranquil ['træŋkwɪl] *adj* tranquilo
tranquilize ['træŋkwɪlaɪz] *va* tranquilizar; *vn* tranquilizar; tranquilizarse
tranquilizer ['træŋkwɪ,laɪzər] *s* (med.) tranquilizador
tranquillity o **tranquility** [træŋ'kwɪlɪtɪ] *s* tranquilidad
trans. abr. de **transactions, transitive** y **transportation**
transact [træn'zækt] o [træns'ækt] *va* tramitar, llevar a cabo
transaction [træn'zækʃən] o [træns'ækʃən] *s* tramitación; transacción; **transactions** *spl* actas (*de una sociedad erudita*)
transactor [træn'zæktər] o [træns'æktər] *s* tramitador

transalpine [træns'ælpɪn] o [træns'ælpaɪn] *adj* transalpino
trans-Andean [,trænsæn'diən] o [træns'ændɪən] *adj* transandino
transatlantic [,trænsət'læntɪk] *adj & s* transatlántico
Transcaucasia [,trænskɔ'keʒə] o [,trænskɔ'keʃə] *s* la Transcaucasia
transceiver [træn'sivər] *s* (rad.) transceptor
transcend [træn'sɛnd] *va* exceder, sobrepujar, superar; *vn* sobresalir
transcendence [træn'sɛndəns] *s* excelencia, superioridad; (philos.) trascendencia
transcendent [træn'sɛndənt] *adj* excelente, superior; (philos. & theol.) trascendente
transcendental [,trænsɛn'dɛntəl] *adj* sobresaliente; sobrenatural, metafísico; idealista, espiritual; obscuro, incomprensible, vago; (philos. & math.) trascendental
transcendentalism [,trænsɛn'dɛntəlɪzəm] *s* (philos.) transcendentalismo
transcendentalist [,trænsɛn'dɛntəlɪst] *s* transcendentalista
transcontinental [,trænskɑntɪ'nɛntəl] *adj* transcontinental
transcribe [træn'skraɪb] *va* transcribir; (mus. & rad.) transcribir
transcript ['trænskrɪpt] *s* trasunto, traslado; (educ.) certificado de estudios, copia del expediente académico, hoja de estudios
transcription [træn'skrɪpʃən] *s* transcripción; (mus. & rad.) transcripción
transducer [træns'djusər] o [træns'dusər] *s* (phys.) transductor
transect [træn'sɛkt] *va* cruzar de un lado a otro, dividir cruzando
transept ['trænsɛpt] *s* (arch.) crucero, transepto; (arch.) brazo del crucero
transfer ['trænsfər] *s* traslado; transbordo; (rail.) vía de transferencia, estación de transferencia; contraseña o billete de transferencia; transporte, reporte (*de litografía*); (law) transferencia; [træns'fʌr] o ['trænsfər] (*pret & pp:* **-ferred;** *ger:* **-ferring**) *va* trasladar, transferir; transbordar; transportar, reportar (*una prueba litográfica a la piedra*); (law) transferir; *vn* cambiar de tren, tranvía, etc.
transferable [træns'fʌrəbəl] o ['trænsfərəbəl] *adj* transferible
transfer agent *s* (com.) agente de transferencias
transference [træns'fʌrəns] o ['trænsfərəns] *s* transferencia
transferor [træns'fʌrər] *s* (law) transferidor
transferrer [træns'fʌrər] *s* transferidor
transfer table *s* (rail.) carro transbordador
transfiguration [træns,fɪgjə'reʃən] *s* transfiguración; (*cap.*) *s* (Bib. & eccl.) Transfiguración
transfigure [træns'fɪgjər] *va* transfigurar
transfix [træns'fɪks] *va* traspasar, espetar; dejar atónito o confuso (*por maravilla, dolor, etc.*)
transfixion [træns'fɪkʃən] *s* transfixión; (surg.) transfixión
transform [træns'fɔrm] *va* transformar; (elec., math. & phys.) transformar; *vn* transformarse
transformation [,trænsfər'meʃən] *s* transformación (*acción o efecto de transformar; peluca*)
transformative [træns'fɔrmətɪv] *adj* transformativo
transformer [træns'fɔrmər] *s* transformador; (elec.) transformador
transformism [træns'fɔrmɪzəm] *s* (biol.) transformismo
transformist [træns'fɔrmɪst] *adj & s* transformista
transfuse [træns'fjuz] *va* transfundir; (med.) hacer una transfusión de (*p.ej., sangre*); (med.) hacer una transfusión a (*una persona*)
transfuser [træns'fjuzər] *s* transfusor
transfusion [træns'fjuʒən] *s* transfusión; (med.) transfusión de sangre
transfusionist [træns'fjuʒənɪst] *s* (med.) transfusionista
transgress [træns'grɛs] *va* violar, quebrantar, traspasar; exceder, traspasar (*p.ej., los límites de la prudencia*); *vn* cometer transgresión; prevaricar, pecar
transgression [træns'grɛʃən] *s* transgresión; prevaricación, pecado
transgressor [træns'grɛsər] *s* transgresor; prevaricador, pecador
tranship [træn'ʃɪp] (*pret & pp:* **-shipped;** *ger:* **-shipping**) *va* var. de **transship**
transhipment [træn'ʃɪpmənt] *s* var. de **transshipment**
transiency ['trænʃənsɪ] *s* transitoriedad
transient ['trænʃənt] *adj* pasajero, transitorio; transeúnte; de tránsito; *s* transeúnte; (elec.) corriente momentánea
transistor [træn'sɪstər] *s* (elec.) transistor
transistorize [træn'sɪstəraɪz] *va* transistorizar
transit ['trænsɪt] o ['trænzɪt] *s* tránsito; (astr. & surv.) tránsito; **in transit** de o en tránsito; *va* atravesar; (surv.) invertir; *vn* transitar
transition [træn'zɪʃən] *s* transición
transitional [træn'zɪʃənəl] *adj* transitivo, de transición
transitive ['trænsɪtɪv] *adj* transitivo; (gram.) transitivo; *s* (gram.) verbo transitivo
transitory ['trænsɪ,torɪ] *adj* transitorio
transit visa *s* visado de tránsito
Trans-Jordan [træns'dʒɔrdən] o **Transjordania** [,trænsdʒɔr'denɪə] *s* la Transjordania
translatable [træns'letəbəl] *adj* traducible
translate [træns'let] o ['trænslet] *va* traducir (*de una lengua a otra*); trasladar (*de un lugar a otro*); (mech. & telg.) trasladar; (fig.) enajenar, extasiar; *vn* traducir; traducirse
translation [træns'leʃən] *s* traducción; (mech. & telg.) traslación
translator [træns'letər] o ['trænsletər] *s* traductor; (telg. & telp.) traslator
transliterate [træns'lɪtəret] *va* transcribir (*letras, palabras, etc.*)
transliteration [træns,lɪtə'reʃən] *s* transcripción
translucence [træns'lusəns] o **translucency** [træns'lusənsɪ] *s* translucidez
translucent [træns'lusənt] *adj* translúcido
transmarine [,trænsmə'rin] *adj* transmarino
transmigrate [træns'maɪgret] o ['trænsmɪgret] *vn* transmigrar
transmigration [,trænsmaɪ'greʃən] o [,trænsmɪ'greʃən] *s* transmigración
transmissibility [træns,mɪsɪ'bɪlɪtɪ] *s* transmisibilidad
transmissible [træns'mɪsɪbəl] *adj* transmisible
transmission [træns'mɪʃən] *s* transmisión; (aut.) cambio de marchas o cambio de velocidades
transmission gear *s* (aut.) engranaje de transmisión
transmission-gear box [træns'mɪʃən,gɪr] *s* (aut.) caja de cambio de marchas, caja de velocidades
transmit [træns'mɪt] (*pret & pp:* **-mitted;** *ger:* **-mitting**) *va & vn* transmitir
transmittal [træns'mɪtəl] *s* transmisión
transmitter [træns'mɪtər] *s* transmisor; (rad., telg. & telp.) transmisor
transmitting set *s* (rad.) aparato transmisor
transmitting station *s* (rad.) estación transmisora
transmogrify [træns'mɑgrɪfaɪ] (*pret & pp:* **-fied**) *va* (hum.) transformar como por encanto, modificar como por encanto, modificar con una rapidez sorprendente
transmutable [træns'mjutəbəl] *adj* transmutable
transmutation [,trænsmju'teʃən] *s* transmutación; (alchem. & chem.) transmutación; (biol.) transformismo
transmute [træns'mjut] *va* transmutar; *vn* transmutar; transmutarse
transoceanic [,trænsoʃɪ'ænɪk] *adj* transoceánico
transom ['trænsəm] *s* (carp.) travesaño; montante (*hueco cuadrilongo sobre una puerta*); (naut.) yugo de popa
transonic [træn'sɑnɪk] *adj* transónico
transpacific [,trænspə'sɪfɪk] *adj* transpacífico
transpadane ['trænspə,den] o [træns'peden] *adj* transpadano
transparence [træns'pɛrəns] *s* transparencia

transparency [træns'pɛrənsɪ] *s* (*pl:* **-cies**) transparencia; transparente (*figura en un papel translúcido*)
transparent [træns'pɛrənt]] *adj* transparente; (fig.) transparente
transpiration [,trænspɪ'reʃən] *s* transpiración; (bot. & physiol.) transpiración
transpire [træns'paɪr] *va* transpirar; *vn* transpirar; (fig.) transpirar (*dejarse conocer una cosa secreta*); (coll.) acontecer, tener lugar
transplant ['trænsplænt] o ['trænsplɑnt] *s* trasplante; [træns'plænt] o [træns'plɑnt] *va* trasplantar; (surg.) trasplantar; *vn* trasplantarse
transplantable [træns'plæntəbəl] o [træns'plɑntəbəl] *adj* trasplantable
transplantation [,trænsplæn'teʃən] *s* trasplante, trasplantación
transplanter [træns'plæntər] o [træns'plɑntər] *s* trasplantador (*persona o instrumento*)
transpolar [træns'polər] *adj* traspolar
transport ['trænsport] *s* transporte; (aer., naut. & fig.) transporte; deportado, desterrado; [træns'port] *va* transportar; deportar, desterrar; (fig.) transportar
transportable [træns'portəbəl] *adj* transportable; pasible o digno de deportación o destierro
transportation [,trænspor'teʃən] *s* transporte; deportación, destierro; (U.S.A.) pasaje, billete (*de viaje*); (U.S.A.) coste del transporte, precio de viaje
transport worker *s* transportista
transposal [træns'pozəl] *s* transposición
transpose [træns'poz] *va* transponer; (alg.) transponer; (mus.) transportar
transposition [,trænspə'zɪʃən] *s* transposición; (mus.) transposición
trans-Pyrenean [,trænspɪrɪ'niən] *adj* transpirenaico
transship [træns'ʃɪp] (*pret & pp:* **-shipped;** *ger:* **-shipping**) *va* transbordar
transshipment [træns'ʃɪpmənt] *s* transbordo
trans-Siberian [,trænssaɪ'bɪrɪən] *adj* transiberiano
transubstantial [,trænsəb'stænʃəl] *adj* transubstancial
transubstantiate [,trænsəb'stænʃɪet] *va* transubstanciar; *vn* transubstanciarse
transubstantiation [,trænsəb,stænʃɪ'eʃən] *s* transubstanciación
transuranic [,trænsjʊ'rænɪk] *adj* (chem.) transuránico
transurethral [,trænsjʊ'riθrəl] *adj* transuretral
transversal [træns'vʌrsəl] *adj* transversal; *s* (geom.) línea transversal
transverse [træns'vʌrs] o ['trænsvərs] *adj* transverso; *s* transverso; (geom.) eje transverso
transvestite [træns'vɛstaɪt] *adj & s* transvestido
transvestitism [træns'vɛstɪtɪzəm] *s* transvestismo o transvestitismo
Transylvania [,trænsɪl'venɪə] *s* la Transilvania
Transylvanian [,trænsɪl'venɪən] *adj & s* transilvano
trap [træp] *s* trampa; bombillo, sifón (*tubo doblemente acodado*); coche ligero de dos ruedas; (sport) lanzaplatos, lanzadiscos (*para disparar pichones de barro*); (geol.) trap; (slang) boca; **traps** *spl* (mus.) instrumentos de percusión; (coll.) equipaje, efectos personales; **to fall into the trap** caer en el lazo o la trampa; **to spring a trap** hacer saltar una trampa; (*pret & pp:* **trapped;** *ger:* **trapping**) *va* entrampar; atrapar (*a un ladrón*); proveer o tapar con bombillo; adornar, enjaezar; *vn* entrampar
trap door *s* escotillón, trampa; (theat.) escotillón, pescante
trapeze [trə'piz] *s* (sport) trapecio; (geom.) trapezoide
trapeze performer *s* trapecista
trapezial [trə'pizɪəl] *adj* trapecial; (geom.) trapezoidal
trapezium [trə'pizɪəm] *s* (*pl:* **-ums** o **-a** [ə]) (anat.) trapecio; (geom.) trapezoide
trapezius [trə'pizɪəs] *s* (anat.) trapecio
trapezohedron [,træpɪzo'hidrən] *s* (cryst.) trapezoedro
trapezoid ['træpɪzɔɪd] *s* (anat.) trapezoide; (geom.) trapecio
trapezoidal [,træpɪ'zɔɪdəl] *adj* (geom.) trapecial
trapper ['træpər] *s* cazador de alforja, trampero
trappings ['træpɪŋz] *spl* jaeces (*de los caballos*); adornos, atavíos
Trappist ['træpɪst] *adj & s* trapense
trapshooter ['træp,ʃutər] *s* tirador al vuelo
trapshooting ['træp,ʃutɪŋ] *s* tiro al vuelo, tiro de pichón
trash [træʃ] *s* broza (*despojo de las plantas*); basura, desecho; cachivaches; disparates; gentuza
trash can *s* basurero (*recipiente*)
trash collection *s* recogida de basuras
trashy ['træʃɪ] *adj* (*comp:* **-ier;** *super:* **-iest**) baladí, fútil; vil, despreciable
Trasteverine [trɑs'tevərɪn] *adj & s* transtiberino
trauma ['trɔmə] *s* (*pl:* **-mata** [mətə] o **-mas**) (path. & psychopath.) trauma
traumatic [trɔ'mætɪk] *adj* traumático
traumaticine [trɔ'mætɪsin] o [trɔ'mætɪsɪn] *s* (pharm.) traumaticina
traumatism ['trɔmətɪzəm] *s* (path.) traumatismo
travail ['trævel] o ['trævəl] *s* afán, labor, pena; dolores de parto; *vn* afanarse; estar de parto
travel ['trævəl] *s* viaje; circulación, tráfico; (mach.) recorrido; (*pret & pp:* **-eled** o **-elled;** *ger:* **-eling** o **-elling**) *va* hacer viajar; viajar por; recorrer; *vn* viajar; andar, correr
travel agency *s* agencia de viajes
travel bureau *s* oficina de turismo
traveled o **travelled** ['trævəld] *adj* que ha viajado mucho; muy recorrido por los viajeros
traveler o **traveller** ['trævələr] *s* viajero; (com.) viajante
traveler's check *s* cheque de viajeros
traveler's-joy ['trævələrz'dʒɔɪ] *s* (bot.) hierba de pordioseros
traveler's tree *s* (bot.) árbol del viajero, ravenala
traveling o **travelling** ['trævəlɪŋ] *adj* viajante; de viaje, para viajar
traveling crane *s* grúa corredera o corrediza, grúa de puente
traveling expenses *spl* gastos de viaje
traveling fellowship *s* bolsa de viaje, beca de viaje
traveling salesman *s* viajante, agente viajero
travelog o **travelogue** ['trævəlɔg] o ['trævəlɑg] *s* conferencia sobre viajes
traverse ['trævərs] o [trə'vʌrs] *s* paso, pasaje; travesía (*distancia*); travesío (*lugar*); (arch.) través; (arch.) galería que cruza una iglesia; (carp.) travesaño; (fort.) traversa, través; camino oblicuo o en zigzag; (naut.) ruta oblicua, bordada oblicua; (geom.) línea transversal; (surv.) línea quebrada; (law) objeción legal; obstáculo, oposición; través, revés (*desgracia*); *adj* travieso, transversal; *adv* de través, transversalmente; *va* atravesar, cruzar; pasar por, recorrer; hacer dar vueltas o rodar; estorbar, impedir; (arti.) mover o volver lateralmente; (fig.) escudriñar, examinar con cuidado; (law) negar, oponerse a; *vn* atravesarse; hacer vaivén; rodar, girar
traverse circle *s* (arti.) círculo recorrido por la cureña al girar
traverse drill *s* taladro de ajuste lateral, taladro ranurador
traverser [trə'vʌrsər] *s* (rail.) carro transbordador
traverse table *s* (surv.) cuadro de latitudes y desviaciones; (rail.) carro transbordador
travertin ['trævərtɪn] o **travertine** ['trævərtɪn] o ['trævərtin] *s* (mineral.) travertino
travesty ['trævɪstɪ] *s* (*pl:* **-ties**) parodia; (*pret & pp:* **-tied**) *va* parodiar
trawl [trɔl] *s* red barredera, jábega; palangre sostenido por boyas; *va & vn* pescar a la rastra; pescar con palangre
trawler ['trɔlər] *s* jabeguero; barco para la pesca a la rastra; palangrero (*persona y barco*)

trawling ['trɔlɪŋ] *s* pesca a la rastra
trawl line *s* espinal
tray [tre] *s* bandeja; batea (*p.ej., de baúl*); (chem. & phot.) cubeta
tray cloth *s* cubrebandeja
treacherous ['trɛtʃərəs] *adj* traicionero, traidor; incierto, poco seguro
treachery ['trɛtʃərɪ] *s* (*pl:* **-ies**) traición
treacle ['trikəl] *s* (Brit.) melaza
tread [trɛd] *s* pisada; huella, peldaño, grada (*de escalera*); barrote o escalón (*de escala*); suela (*del zapato, del estribo*); horquilla (*de los zancos*); galladura, prendedura (*en la yema del huevo*); (aut.) huella, rodamiento, banda de rodamiento; (aut.) distancia transversal entre las ruedas; (rail.) cara de las ruedas; (rail.) superficie de rodadura; (rail.) entrevía; (*pret:* **trod;** *pp:* **trodden** o **trod**) *va* pisar; pisotear; trillar; apoyar el pie en (*p.ej., un pedal*); abrumar, agobiar, oprimir; seguir (*p.ej., el paso de una persona*); *vn* andar, caminar; poner el pie; **to tread on** pisar; seguir de cerca
treadle ['trɛdəl] *s* pedal; *va* hacer funcionar con pedal; *vn* pedalear
treadmill ['trɛd,mɪl] *s* rueda de andar; (fig.) noria (*cosa en que, sin adelantar nada, se anda como dando vueltas*)
treas. abr. de **treasurer** y **treasury**
treason ['trizən] *s* traición
treasonable ['trizənəbəl] o **treasonous** ['trizənəs] *adj* traicionero, traidor
treasure ['trɛʒər] *s* tesoro; (fig.) tesoro (*persona o cosa de mucho precio*); *va* atesorar; apreciar mucho, considerar o guardar como un tesoro
treasure house *s* tesoro (*lugar de riquezas*)
treasurer ['trɛʒərər] *s* tesorero
treasurership ['trɛʒərər,ʃɪp] *s* tesorería
treasure-trove ['trɛʒər'trov] *s* tesoro hallado
treasury ['trɛʒərɪ] *s* (*pl:* **-ies**) tesorería; tesoro; (fig.) tesoro (*enciclopedia; persona que sabe mucho*); (*cap.*) *s* (Brit.) ministerio de Hacienda
Treasury Department *s* (U.S.A.) ministerio de Hacienda
treasury note *s* (U.S.A.) bono del ministerio de hacienda
treat [trit] *s* convite; regalo; convidada (*invitación a beber*); *va* tratar; regalar; convidar; curar (*un enfermo*); **to treat as** tratar (*a una persona*) de (*p.ej., amigo*); tomar (*una cosa*) de (*p.ej., broma*); *vn* tratar; regalar; convidar; **to treat of** tratar de
treatise ['tritɪs] *s* tratado (*escrito, libro*)
treatment ['tritmənt] *s* tratamiento
treaty ['tritɪ] *s* (*pl:* **-ties**) tratado (*pacto*)
Trebizond ['trɛbɪzɑnd] *s* Trebisonda
treble ['trɛbəl] *adj* triple; sobreagudo; (mus.) atiplado; (mus.) de tiple; *s* (mus.) tiple; *va* triplicar; *vn* triplicarse
treble clef *s* (mus.) clave de sol
trebly ['trɛblɪ] *adv* tres veces, triplicadamente
tree [tri] *s* árbol; (archaic) horca (*para ahorcar a los condenados*); (archaic) cruz (*en que murió Jesucristo*); **to bark up the wrong tree** ir descaminado, quejarse sin razón; **up a tree** (coll.) arrinconado, en un aprieto, entre la espada y la pared; *va* proveer de puntal u otro apoyo de madera; ahuyentar por un árbol; estirar sobre la horma (*de zapatero*); (coll.) poner en aprieto; *vn* ramificarse; huir por un árbol
tree-dozer ['tri,dozər] *s* tumbadora
tree fern *s* (bot.) helecho arbóreo
tree frog *s* (zool.) rana arbórea; (zool.) rubeta, rana de San Antonio
tree heath *s* (bot.) brezo albarino, blanco o castellano
treeless ['trilɪs] *adj* sin árboles
treenail ['tri,nel] o ['trɛnəl] *s* clavija, taruguillo de madera
tree of heaven *s* (bot.) árbol del cielo, barniz del Japón
tree of knowledge of good and evil *s* árbol de la ciencia del bien y del mal
tree of life *s* (Bib. & bot.) árbol de la vida
tree surgeon *s* cirujano de los árboles
tree surgery *s* cirugía de los árboles
tree toad *s* (zool.) rubeta, rana de San Antonio
treetop ['tri,tɑp] *s* copa, cima de árbol
tréflé cross [,tre'fle] *s* (her.) cruz trebolada
trefoil ['trifɔɪl] *s* (bot. & arch.) trébol
trefoil arch *s* (arch.) arco trebolado
trek [trɛk] *s* jornada; migración; (*pret & pp:* **trekked;** *ger:* **trekking**) *vn* viajar; emigrar; viajar en carromato
trellis ['trɛlɪs] *s* enrejado, espaldera; *va* proveer de enrejado o espaldera; entrelazar, entretejer; fijar sobre una espaldera
trelliswork ['trɛlɪs,wʌrk] *s* enrejado, espaldera
trematode ['trɛmətod] o ['trimətod] *s* (zool.) tremátodo
tremble ['trɛmbəl] *s* temblor; estremecimiento; *vn* temblar; tiritar; estremecerse
trembler ['trɛmblər] *s* temblador; (rel.) temblador (*cuáquero*); (elec.) temblador
trembly ['trɛmblɪ] *adj* tembloroso, trémulo
tremendous [trɪ'mɛndəs] *adj* tremendo; (coll.) tremendo (*muy grande*)
tremolite ['trɛməlaɪt] *s* (mineral.) tremolita
tremolo ['trɛməlo] *s* (*pl:* **-los**) (mus.) trémolo
tremor ['trɛmər] o ['trimər] *s* temblor; conmoción, estremecimiento; (path.) temblor
tremulous ['trɛmjələs] *adj* trémulo; tímido, temeroso
trenail ['tri,nel] o ['trɛnəl] *s* var. de **treenail**
trench [trɛntʃ] *s* foso, zanja; acequia, cauce; (mil.) trinchera; *va* hacer fosos o zanjas en; atrincherar; hacer trincheras en; *vn* abrirse camino (*p.ej., un torrente*); hacer trincheras; invadir; **to trench on** o **upon** lindar con, tocar; invadir, pasar los límites de
trenchancy ['trɛntʃənsɪ] *s* agudeza; mordacidad; energía
trenchant ['trɛntʃənt] *adj* agudo; incisivo, mordaz, punzante; enérgico; bien definido, bien delineado
trench coat *s* trinchera
trencher ['trɛntʃər] *s* (hist.) tajadero, plato trinchero
trencherman ['trɛntʃərmən] *s* (*pl:* **-men**) comilón; gorrón, parásito, pegote; **to be a good trencherman** tener buen diente
trench fever *s* (path.) fiebre de las trincheras
trench foot *s* (path.) pie de trinchera, micetoma del pie
trench gun o **mortar** *s* (arti.) mortero de trinchera
trench mouth *s* (path.) estomatitis ulcerosa epidémica
trench warfare *s* guerra de trincheras
trend [trɛnd] *s* dirección, curso, tendencia; *vn* dirigirse, tender
Trent [trɛnt] *s* Trento
trepan [trɪ'pæn] *s* (min. & surg.) trépano; (*pret & pp:* **-panned;** *ger:* **-panning**) *va* (mach. & surg.) trepanar
trepanation [,trɛpə'neʃən] *s* trepanación
trepang [trɪ'pæŋ] *s* (zool.) holoturia; holoturias desecadas
trephine [trɪ'faɪn] o [trɪ'fin] *s* (surg.) trefina; *va* (surg.) trefinar
trepidation [,trɛpɪ'deʃən] *s* miedo, terror; trepidación (*vibración*); (path.) trepidación (*clonus del pie*)
trespass ['trɛspəs] *s* entrada sin derecho; infracción, violación; pecado, culpa; *vn* entrar sin derecho; abusar; pecar; **no trespassing** prohibida la entrada, prohibido el paso; **to trespass against** pecar contra; **to trespass on** entrar o meterse sin derecho en; infringir, violar; abusar de (*p.ej., la paciencia de uno*)
trespasser ['trɛspəsər] *s* intruso; infractor, violador; pecador
tress [trɛs] *s* trenza; bucle, rizo
trestle ['trɛsəl] *s* caballete; puente o viaducto de caballetes
trestle bridge *s* puente de caballetes
trestletree ['trɛsəl,tri] *s* (naut.) bao de los palos
trestlework ['trɛsəl,wʌrk] *s* construcción, estructura u obra de caballetes; castillejo (*andamio*)
Treves [trivz] *s* Tréveris
trey [tre] *s* tres (*naipe, dado o ficha de dominó con tres señales*)
triad ['traɪæd] *s* tríada; (mus.) acorde de tres sonidos
triadelphous [,traɪə'dɛlfəs] *adj* (bot.) triadelfo

trial [ˈtraɪəl] *s* ensayo, prueba, experimento; aflicción, desgracia, mortificación; (law) juicio, proceso, vista de una causa; **on trial** a prueba, puesto a prueba; (law) en juicio; **to bring to trial, to put on trial** (law) encausar, poner en tela de juicio; **to stand trial** (law) ser procesado; *adj* de ensayo, de prueba
trial and error *s* tanteo, método de tanteos
trial balance *s* (com.) balance de prueba, cotejo del déficit y superávit en una cuenta
trial balloon *s* globo sonda; (fig.) globo sonda (*anuncio hecho para probar la opinión pública*); **to send up a trial balloon** (fig.) lanzar un globo sonda
trial by jury *s* (law) juicio por jurado
trial jury *s* (law) jurado procesal
trial order *s* (com.) pedido de ensayo
trial run *s* marcha de ensayo
triandrous [traɪˈændrəs] *adj* (bot.) triandro
triangle [ˈtraɪˌæŋgəl] *s* (geom., mus. & fig.) triángulo; escuadra (*del delineante*); (*cap.*) *s* (astr.) Triángulo
triangular [traɪˈæŋgjələr] *adj* triangular
triangulate [traɪˈæŋgjəlet] *adj* triangulado; *va* triangular
triangulation [traɪˌæŋgjəˈleʃən] *s* triangulación
Triassic [traɪˈæsɪk] *adj & s* (geol.) triásico
triatomic [ˌtraɪəˈtɑmɪk] *adj* (chem.) triatómico
triaxial [traɪˈæksɪəl] *adj* triaxial
tribade [ˈtrɪbəd] *s* tríbada
tribadism [ˈtrɪbədɪzəm] *s* tribadismo
tribal [ˈtraɪbəl] *adj* tribal
tribally [ˈtraɪbəlɪ] *adv* según la tribu; en tribus
tribasic [traɪˈbesɪk] *adj* (chem.) tribásico
tribe [traɪb] *s* tribu
tribesman [ˈtraɪbzmən] *s* (*pl:* **-men**) miembro de una tribu
tribrach [ˈtraɪbræk] o [ˈtrɪbræk] *s* (pros.) tribraquio
tribulation [ˌtrɪbjəˈleʃən] *s* tribulación
tribunal [trɪˈbjunəl] o [traɪˈbjunəl] *s* tribunal; (fig.) tribunal (*de la opinión pública, de la conciencia, etc.*)
tribunate [ˈtrɪbjənɪt] o [ˈtrɪbjənet] *s* tribunado
tribune [ˈtrɪbjun] *s* tribuna (*plataforma elevada desde donde hablan los oradores*); (arch.) tribuna; (hist.) tribuno; tribuno (*demagogo*)
tribuneship [ˈtrɪbjunʃɪp] *s* tribunado
tributary [ˈtrɪbjəˌtɛrɪ] *adj* tributario; *s* (*pl:* **-ies**) tributario
tribute [ˈtrɪbjut] *s* tributo
trice [traɪs] *s* tris (*momento, instante*); **in a trice** en un periquete, en dos trancos; *va* (naut.) izar, izar y liar
tricentennial [ˌtraɪsɛnˈtɛnɪəl] *adj* de trescientos años; *s* tricentenario
triceps [ˈtraɪsɛps] *s* (anat.) tríceps
trichiasis [trɪˈkaɪəsɪs] *s* (path.) triquíasis
trichina [trɪˈkaɪnə] *s* (*pl:* **-nae** [ni]) (zool.) triquina
trichinosis [ˌtrɪkɪˈnosɪs] *s* (path.) triquinosis
trichinous [ˈtrɪkɪnəs] *adj* triquinoso
trichite [ˈtrɪkaɪt] *s* (petrog.) triquita
trichloride [traɪˈkloraɪd] o [traɪˈklorɪd] *s* (chem.) tricloruro
trichology [trɪˈkɑlədʒɪ] *s* tricología
trichotomic [ˌtrɪkəˈtɑmɪk] *adj* tricotómico
trichotomous [traɪˈkɑtəməs] *adj* tricótomo
trichotomy [traɪˈkɑtəmɪ] *s* tricotomía
trichroic [traɪˈkro·ɪk] *adj* tricroico
trichromatic [ˌtraɪkroˈmætɪk] *adj* tricromático
trichromatism [traɪˈkromətɪzəm] *s* tricromatismo
tricipital [traɪˈsɪpɪtəl] *adj* tríceps, tricípite
trick [trɪk] *s* maña (*habilidad; jugada, embuste; hábito; vicio*); suerte, truco; ilusión; burla, chasco; arte, artificio; travesura; turno, tanda; baza (*número de naipes recogidos por el que gana*); (dial.) chiquito o chiquita; **to be up to one's old tricks** hacer de las suyas; **to do** o **to turn the trick** resolver el problema, dar en el clavo; **to play a dirty trick on** hacer una mala jugada a, hacer un flaco servicio a; *adj* ingenioso; pulcro, acicalado; acrobático; *va* trampear; burlar, engañar; ataviar, vestir; vestir de una manera extraña; **to trick into** + *ger* lograr con engaños que (*una persona*) + *subj;* **to trick out** ataviar, vestir; vestir de una manera extraña; *vn* trampear; mañear; hacer suertes; travesear
trickery [ˈtrɪkərɪ] *s* (*pl:* **-ies**) trampería, malas mañas
trickle [ˈtrɪkəl] *s* hilo, chorro delgado, goteo; *va* verter gota a gota; *vn* escurrir, gotear; entrar, salir, pasar gradual e irregularmente
trickster [ˈtrɪkstər] *s* tramposo, embustero
tricksy [ˈtrɪksɪ] *adj* tramposo; engañoso, ilusorio; juguetón, retozón, travieso; garboso, apuesto, elegante
tricktrack [ˈtrɪkˌtræk] *s* chaquete
tricky [ˈtrɪkɪ] *adj* (*comp:* **-ier;** *super:* **-iest**) tramposo, engañoso; difícil, intrincado; delicado, p.ej., **a tricky situation** una situación delicada; vicioso (*animal*)
triclinic [traɪˈklɪnɪk] *adj* (cryst.) triclínico
triclinium [traɪˈklɪnɪəm] *s* (*pl:* **-a** [ə]) (hist.) triclinio
tricolor [ˈtraɪˌkʌlər] *adj* tricolor; *s* bandera tricolor
tricolor tube *s* (telv.) tubo tricolor
tricorn [ˈtraɪkɔrn] *adj & s* tricornio
tricot [ˈtriko] *s* tricot, tejido de punto
tricotine [ˌtrɪkəˈtin] *s* tela asargada de lana
trictrac [ˈtrɪkˌtræk] *s* var. de **tricktrack**
tricuspid [traɪˈkʌspɪd] *adj* tricúspide; (anat.) tricúspide; *s* (anat.) muela tricúspide
tricuspid valve *s* (anat.) válvula tricúspide
tricycle [ˈtraɪsɪkəl] *s* triciclo
trident [ˈtraɪdənt] *adj* tridente; *s* tridente; (hist. & myth.) tridente
tridentate [traɪˈdɛntet] *adj* tridente
tridimensional [ˌtraɪdɪˈmɛnʃənəl] *adj* tridimensional
tried [traɪd] *adj* probado, fiel, seguro
triennial [traɪˈɛnɪəl] *adj* trienal; *s* trienio; tercer aniversario
triennially [traɪˈɛnɪəlɪ] *adv* trienalmente
triennium [traɪˈɛnɪəm] *s* (*pl:* **-ums** o **-a** [ə]) trienio
trifacial [traɪˈfeʃəl] *adj* trifacial
trifid [ˈtraɪfɪd] *adj* trífido
trifle [ˈtraɪfəl] *s* bagatela, friolera, nadería, fruslería; baratija, pizca; dulce de bizcocho borracho, crema, conserva de fruta y nata batida; *va* malgastar; **to trifle away** malgastar; *vn* retozar, travesear; chancear, hablar sin seriedad; **to trifle with** manosear; jugar con, burlarse de
trifler [ˈtraɪflər] *s* persona frívola; chancero, burlón
trifling [ˈtraɪflɪŋ] *adj* frívolo, fútil, ligero; insignificante, sin importancia
trifocal [traɪˈfokəl] *adj* trifocal; *s* lente trifocal; **trifocals** *spl* anteojos trifocales
trifoliate [traɪˈfolɪɪt] o [traɪˈfolɪet] *adj* (bot.) trifoliado
trifoliolate [traɪˈfolɪəlet] *adj* (bot.) trifoliolado
trifolium [traɪˈfolɪəm] *s* (bot.) trifolio
triforium [traɪˈforɪəm] *s* (*pl:* **-a** [ə]) (arch.) triforio
triform [ˈtraɪˌfɔrm] *adj* triforme
trifurcate [traɪˈfʌrkɪt] o [traɪˈfʌrket] *adj* trifurcado; [traɪˈfʌrket] *va* trifurcar; *vn* trifurcarse
trifurcation [ˌtraɪfərˈkeʃən] *s* trifurcación
trig. abr. de **trigonometric** y **trigonometry**
trig [trɪg] *adj* acicalado, elegante; estirado, relamido; firme, fuerte, sano; *s* calzo; (*pret & pp:* **trigged;** *ger:* **trigging**) *va* acicalar; calzar (*una rueda*)
trigeminal [traɪˈdʒɛmɪnəl] *adj* trigémino
trigeminal nerve *s* (anat.) trigémino
trigeminous [traɪˈdʒɛmɪnəs] *adj* trigémino
trigger [ˈtrɪgər] *s* disparador, gatillo (*de pistola, etc.*); (mach.) disparador
triggerfish [ˈtrɪgərˌfɪʃ] *s* (ichth.) pez ballesta
trigger-happy [ˈtrɪgərˌhæpɪ] *adj* de gatillo alegre, demasiado propenso a tirar; pendenciero
trigger mechanism *s* mecanismo de disparo, mecanismo gatillo
triglyph [ˈtraɪglɪf] *s* (arch.) tríglifo
trigon [ˈtraɪgɑn] *s* (astrol. & geom.) trígono; (mus.) trigón
trigonal [ˈtrɪgənəl] *adj* trigonal; (cryst.) trigonal
trigonometer [ˌtrɪgəˈnɑmɪtər] *s* trigonómetra

trigonometric [ˌtrɪgənəˈmɛtrɪk] o **trigonometrical** [ˌtrɪgənəˈmɛtrɪkəl] *adj* trigonométrico
trigonometrically [ˌtrɪgənəˈmɛtrɪkəlɪ] *adv* trigonométricamente
trigonometry [ˌtrɪgəˈnɑmɪtrɪ] *s* trigonometría
trigraph [ˈtraɪgræf] o [ˈtraɪgrɑf] *s* grupo de tres letras que representa un solo sonido
trihedral [traɪˈhidrəl] *adj* triedro
trihedron [traɪˈhidrən] *s* (*pl:* **-drons** o **-dra** [drə]) (geom.) triedro
trilateral [traɪˈlætərəl] *adj* trilátero
trilingual [traɪˈlɪŋgwəl] *adj* trilingüe
triliteral [traɪˈlɪtərəl] *adj* trilítero
trilithon [ˈtrɪlɪθɑn] *s* (archeol.) trilito
trill [trɪl] *s* gorjeo; trino, trinado; (phonet.) vibración; (phonet.) consonante vibrante; *va* decir o cantar gorjeando; (phonet.) pronunciar con vibración; *vn* gorjear; trinar; gotear
trillion [ˈtrɪljən] *s* (U.S.A.) billón (*un millón de millones*); (Brit.) trillón (*un millón de billones*)
trillium [ˈtrɪlɪəm] *s* (bot.) trilio
trilobate [traɪˈlobet] *adj* trilobado
trilobite [ˈtraɪləbaɪt] *s* (pal.) trilobites
trilocular [traɪˈlɑkjələr] *adj* trilocular
trilogy [ˈtrɪlədʒɪ] *s* trilogía
trim [trɪm] *s* estado, condición; buen estado, buena condición; adorno, atavío; traje, vestido, equipo; aseo, compostura; (naut.) asiento, disposición marinera (*de un buque*); (naut.) orientación; (constr.) chambrana (*adorno alrededor de las puertas y ventanas*); **out of trim** en mal estado; (naut.) mal estivado; *adj* (*comp:* **trimmer;** *super:* **trimmest**) acicalado, compuesto, bonito, elegante; (*pret & pp:* **trimmed;** *ger:* **trimming**) *va* ajustar, adaptar; arreglar, componer, pulir; adornar, decorar; enguirnaldar (*el árbol de Navidad*); recortar (*para dar forma a*); despabilar (*una lámpara o vela*); cambiar, mudar; (agr.) podar, mondar; (carp.) acepillar, alisar, desbastar; (naut.) balancear, equilibrar; (naut.) orientar (*las velas*); (naut.) disponer para la navegación; (coll.) derrotar, vencer; (coll.) regañar, reprender; *vn* nadar entre dos aguas, balancearse entre dos opiniones; (naut.) orientarse (*un buque*)
trimerous [ˈtrɪmərəs] *adj* trímero
trimester [traɪˈmɛstər] *s* trimestre
trimestral [traɪˈmɛstrəl] o **trimestrial** [traɪˈmɛstrɪəl] *adj* trimestral
trimeter [ˈtrɪmɪtər] *adj & s* trímetro
trimmer [ˈtrɪmər] *s* guarnecedor; contemporizador; máquina de recortar; (carp.) cabio; (rad.) condensador de ajuste, condensador compensador
trimming [ˈtrɪmɪŋ] *s* guarnición, adorno; orla, franja, ribete; desbastadura; (coll.) paliza, zurra; (coll.) reprensión; (coll.) derrota; **trimmings** *spl* accesorios, arrequives; recortes
trimonthly [traɪˈmʌnθlɪ] *adj* trimestral
trinal [ˈtraɪnəl] *adj* trino
trine [traɪn] *adj* trino; (astrol.) trino; (*cap.*) *s* (theol.) Trinidad
Trinitarian [ˌtrɪnɪˈtɛrɪən] *adj & s* creyente en la Trinidad; (eccl.) trinitario; (*l.c.*) *adj* ternario
trinitrocresol [traɪˌnaɪtroˈkrisol] o [traɪˌnaɪtroˈkrisɑl] *s* (chem.) trinitrocresol
trinitrotoluene [traɪˌnaɪtroˈtɑljuin] *s* (chem.) trinitrotolueno
trinitrotoluol [traɪˌnaɪtroˈtɑljuol] o [traɪˌnaɪtroˈtɑljuɑl] *s* (chem.) trinitrotoluol
trinity [ˈtrɪnɪtɪ] *s* (*pl:* **-ties**) trinca; (*cap.*) *s* (theol.) Trinidad
Trinity Sunday *s* domingo de la santísima Trinidad
trinket [ˈtrɪŋkɪt] *s* dije, chuchería; baratija, bujería
trinomial [traɪˈnomɪəl] *adj* (alg., bot. & zool.) de tres términos; *s* (alg.) trinomio; (bot. & zool.) nombre de tres términos
trio [ˈtrio] *s* (*pl:* **-os**) trío; (mus.) trío
triode [ˈtraɪod] *s* (electron.) triodo
triolet [ˈtraɪolɛt] o [ˈtriolɛt] *s* composición poética de ocho versos con dos rimas
trioxide [traɪˈɔksaɪd] o [traɪˈɔksɪd] *s* (chem.) trióxido
trip [trɪp] *s* viaje; excursión, recorrido; tropiezo; desliz; traspié, zancadilla; paso o movimiento ágil, rápido y ligero; (mach.) trinquete, escape, disparo; (*pret & pp:* **tripped;** *ger:* **tripping**) *va* trompicar, echar la zancadilla a; detener, estorbar, estorbar el paso a; inclinar, volcar; ejecutar con agilidad (*p.ej., un baile*); coger en falta; coger en una mentira; (mach.) disparar, soltar; (naut.) levar (*el ancla*); **to trip the light fantastic** bailar con agilidad; *vn* ir aprisa, ir con paso rápido y ligero; brincar, saltar, correr; tropezar; viajar; **to trip over** tropezar en
triparted [traɪˈpɑrtɪd] *adj* tripartido
tripartite [traɪˈpɑrtaɪt] *adj* tripartito
tripartition [ˌtraɪpɑrˈtɪʃən] *s* tripartición
tripe [traɪp] *s* callos, mondongo, ventrón; (slang) barbaridad, disparate, música celestial
tripetalous [traɪˈpɛtələs] *adj* (bot.) tripétalo
triphammer [ˈtrɪpˌhæmər] *s* martillo de caída, martillo pilón
triphenylmethane [traɪˌfɛnɪlˈmɛθen] o [traɪˌfinɪlˈmɛθen] *s* (chem.) trifenilmetano
triphthong [ˈtrɪfθɔŋ] o [ˈtrɪfθɑŋ] *s* triptongo
tripinnate [traɪˈpɪnet] *adj* (bot.) tripinado
triplane [ˈtraɪˌplen] *s* (aer.) triplano
triple [ˈtrɪpəl] *adj* triple; *s* triple; (baseball) golpe con que el bateador gana la tercera base; *va* triplicar; *vn* triplicarse; (baseball) hacer (*el bateador*) un golpe tal que gane la tercera base
Triple Alliance *s* Triple Alianza o (la) Tríplice
triple crown *s* tiara del papa
triple-nerved [ˈtrɪpəlˈnʌrvd] *adj* (bot.) trinervado
triple play *s* (baseball) jugada que pone fuera de juego a tres jugadores
triplet [ˈtrɪplɪt] *s* trillizo (*cada uno de tres hermanos nacidos de un mismo parto*); terceto (*combinación de tres versos*); (mus.) terceto, tresillo
triple time *s* (mus.) compás ternario
triplex [ˈtrɪplɛks] o [ˈtraɪplɛks] *adj* triple; *s* cosa triple; (mus.) compás ternario
triplicate [ˈtrɪplɪkɪt] *adj* triplicado; *s* triplicado; **in triplicate** por triplicado; [ˈtrɪplɪket] *va* triplicar
triplication [ˌtrɪplɪˈkeʃən] *s* triplicación
triplicity [trɪˈplɪsɪtɪ] *s* triplicidad
triply [ˈtrɪplɪ] *adv* tres veces
tripod [ˈtraɪpɑd] *s* (hist.) trípode; trípode (*para instrumentos geodésicos, fotográficos, etc.*)
tripoli [ˈtrɪpəlɪ] *s* (mineral.) trípol
Tripolitan [trɪˈpɑlɪtən] *adj & s* tripolino o tripolitano
tripper [ˈtrɪpər] *s* corredor; andarín; saltarín; persona que trompica; (mach.) disparador
tripping [ˈtrɪpɪŋ] *adj* ágil, rápido, ligero; (mach.) disparador
triptych [ˈtrɪptɪk] *s* tríptico
trireme [ˈtraɪrim] *s* (hist.) trirreme
trisect [traɪˈsɛkt] *va* trisecar
trisection [traɪˈsɛkʃən] *s* trisección
trismus [ˈtrɪzməs] o [ˈtrɪsməs] *s* (path.) trismo
trispermous [traɪˈspʌrməs] *adj* (bot.) trispermo
Tristan [ˈtrɪstən] o **Tristram** [ˈtrɪstrəm] *s* (myth.) Tristán
trisulcate [traɪˈsʌlket] o [traɪˈsʌlkɪt] *adj* trisulco
trisulfide [traɪˈsʌlfaɪd] o [traɪˈsʌlfɪd] *s* (chem.) trisulfuro
trisyllabic [ˌtrɪsɪˈlæbɪk] o [ˌtraɪsɪˈlæbɪk] *adj* trisílabo
trisyllable [trɪˈsɪləbəl] o [traɪˈsɪləbəl] *s* trisílabo
trite [traɪt] *adj* gastado, trillado, trivial
tritium [ˈtrɪtɪəm] o [ˈtrɪʃɪəm] *s* (chem.) tritio
triton [ˈtraɪtən] *s* (zool.) tritón; (*cap.*) *s* (myth.) Tritón
tritone [ˈtraɪˌton] *s* (mus.) tritono
triturate [ˈtrɪtʃəret] *s* cosa triturada; *va* triturar
trituration [ˌtrɪtʃəˈreʃən] *s* trituración
triumph [ˈtraɪəmf] *s* triunfo; **in triumph** en triunfo; *vn* triunfar; **to triumph over** triunfar de

triumphal [traɪ'ʌmfəl] *adj* triunfal
triumphal arch *s* arco triunfal
triumphant [traɪ'ʌmfənt] *adj* triunfante
triumvir [traɪ'ʌmvər] *s* triunviro
triumviral [traɪ'ʌmvərəl] *adj* triunviral
triumvirate [traɪ'ʌmvərɪt] *s* triunvirato
triune ['traɪjun] *adj* trino y uno (*que es tres y uno al mismo tiempo*); *s* tríada; (*cap.*) *s* (theol.) Trinidad
triunity [traɪ'junɪtɪ] *s* condición o estado de trino y uno
trivalence [traɪ'veləns] o ['trɪvələns] o **trivalency** [traɪ'velənsɪ] o ['trɪvələnsɪ] *s* (chem.) trivalencia
trivalent [traɪ'velənt] o ['trɪvələnt] *adj* (chem.) trivalente
trivalve ['traɪ,vælv] *adj* trivalvo
trivet ['trɪvɪt] *s* trébedes; platillo con tres pies
trivia ['trɪvɪə] *spl* bagatelas, trivialidades
trivial ['trɪvɪəl] *adj* trivial, insignificante
triviality [,trɪvɪ'ælɪtɪ] *s* (*pl:* **-ties**) trivialidad
trivium ['trɪvɪəm] *s* trivio (*en la edad media, las tres primeras artes liberales*)
triweekly [traɪ'wiklɪ] *adj* trisemanal (*que se repite tres veces por semana o cada tres semanas*); *adv* trisemanalmente; *s* (*pl:* **-lies**) periódico o revista trisemanal
trocar ['trokɑr] *s* (surg.) trocar
trochaic [tro'keɪk] *adj* & *s* trocaico
trochanter [tro'kæntər] *s* (anat., ent. & zool.) trocánter
troche ['trokɪ] *s* (pharm.) trocisco
trochee ['troki] *s* troqueo
trochilus ['trɑkɪləs] *s* (*pl:* **-li** [laɪ]) troquilo
trochlea ['trɑklɪə] *s* (*pl:* **-ae** [i]) (anat.) tróclea
trochlear ['trɑklɪər] *adj* (anat.) troclear; (bot.) troclearío
trochoid ['trokɔɪd] *adj* trocoideo; *s* (geom.) trocoide
trod [trɑd] *pret & pp de* **tread**
trodden ['trɑdən] *pp de* **tread**
troglodyte ['trɑglədaɪt] *s* troglodita; mono antropomorfo; (fig.) troglodita (*hombre bárbaro y cruel*); (fig.) ermitaño, solitario
troglodytic [,trɑglə'dɪtɪk] o **troglodytical** [,trɑglə'dɪtɪkəl] *adj* troglodítico
troika ['trɔɪkə] *s* troica
Troilus ['tro·ɪləs] o ['trɔɪləs] *s* (myth.) Troilo
Trojan ['trodʒən] *adj* troyano; *s* troyano; **to work like a Trojan** trabajar con gran ánimo y esfuerzo
Trojan horse *s* caballo de Troya
Trojan War *s* (myth.) guerra de Troya
troll [trol] *s* rodadura; cantar que se entona en partes sucesivas; repetición, rutina; carrete (*de la caña de pescar*); cebo (*para la pesca*); gnomo, enano, gigante; *va* cantar con voz abultada; cantar en sucesión; pescar a la cacea; pescar a la cacea en (*p.ej., un lago*); atraer, seducir; *vn* cantar o tocar alegremente; pescar a la cacea; hablar rápidamente
trolley ['trɑlɪ] *s* corredera elevada; (elec.) polea o arco de trole; (elec.) tranvía; volquete; (Brit.) carretilla; **off one's trolley** (slang) destornillado, chiflado
trolley bus *s* trolebús, ómnibus-tranvía
trolley car *s* coche o carruaje de tranvía
trolley line *s* línea de tranvías, red de tranvías
trolley pole *s* trole
trolley wire *s* cable conductor (*del tranvía eléctrico*)
trolling ['trolɪŋ] *s* cacea, pesca a la cacea
trollop ['trɑləp] *s* cochina (*mujer sucia y desaliñada*); mujer de mala vida
trombone ['trambon] o [trɑm'bon] *s* trombón (*instrumento y el que lo toca*)
trombonist ['trɑmbonɪst] o [trɑm'bonɪst] *s* trombón (*músico*)
trommel ['trɑməl] *s* (metal.) trómel
trompe [trɑmp] *s* (found.) trompa
troop [trup] *s* tropa; compañía (*de actores*); tropa de 32 niños exploradores; (mil.) escuadrón (*de caballería*); **troops** *spl* (mil.) tropas; *va* reunir en tropa; *vn* agruparse, juntarse; marcharse, marcharse en tropel; marchar en orden militar
troop carrier *s* (aer.) avión de transporte de tropas
trooper ['trupər] *s* soldado de caballería; corcel de guerra; (mil.) transporte (*buque*); agente de policía montado; **to swear like a trooper** jurar como un carretero
troopship ['trup,ʃɪp] *s* (mil.) transporte
troostite ['trustaɪt] *s* (metal.) troostita
tropaeolin [tro'piəlɪn] *s* (chem.) tropeolina
tropaeolum [tro'piələm] *s* (*pl:* **-lums** o **-la** [lə]) (bot.) tropeolea
trope [trop] *s* (mus. & rhet.) tropo
tropeine ['tropɪin] o ['tropɪɪn] *s* (chem.) tropeína
trophic ['trɑfɪk] *adj* (physiol.) trófico
trophied ['trofɪd] *adj* adornado, cargado o cubierto de trofeos
trophoplasm ['trɑfəplæzəm] *s* (biol.) trofoplasma
trophy ['trofɪ] *s* (*pl:* **-phies**) trofeo; recuerdo
tropic ['trɑpɪk] *adj* tropical; *s* (astr. & geog.) trópico; **tropics** o **Tropics** *spl* zona tropical
tropical ['trɑpɪkəl] *adj* tropical; (rhet.) trópico
tropical year *s* (astr.) año trópico
tropic bird *s* (orn.) rabijunco, contramaestre
tropic of Cancer *s* trópico de Cáncer
tropic of Capricorn *s* trópico de Capricornio
tropine ['tropin] o ['tropɪn] *s* (chem.) tropina
tropism ['tropɪzəm] *s* (biol.) tropismo
tropistic [tro'pɪstɪk] *adj* del tropismo
tropologic [,trɑpə'lɑdʒɪk] o **tropological** [,trɑpə'lɑdʒɪkəl] *adj* tropológico
tropology [tro'pɑlədʒɪ] *s* (*pl:* **-gies**) tropología
troposphere ['trɑpəsfɪr] *s* (meteor.) troposfera o tropoesfera
trot [trɑt] *s* trote; paso o movimiento vivo o apresurado; niñito; (slang) traducción interlineal que usan los estudiantes para ahorrarse trabajo; (*pret & pp:* **trotted;** *ger:* **trotting**) *va* hacer trotar; pasar al trote por encima de; **to trot out** (slang) sacar para mostrar o enseñar; *vn* trotar
troth [trɔθ] o [troθ] *s* fe; verdad; esponsales; **in troth** en verdad; **to plight one's troth** prometer fidelidad; dar palabra de casamiento, contraer esponsales
trotline ['trɑt,laɪn] *s* palangre
Trotskyism ['trɑtskɪɪzəm] *s* trotskismo
Trotskyite ['trɑtskɪaɪt] *adj* & *s* trotskista
trotter ['trɑtər] *s* trotón; pie de cerdo o carnero (*usado como alimento*)
troubadour ['trubədor] o ['trubədʊr] *s* trovador; *adj* trovadoresco
trouble ['trʌbəl] *s* apuro, dificultad; confusión, estorbo, embarazo; conflicto; inquietud, preocupación; pena, molestia, aflicción; avería, falla, pana (*de índole mecánica*); mal, enfermedad; **that's the trouble** ahí está el busilis, ahí está el tope; **the trouble is that . . .** lo malo es que . . .; **to be in trouble** estar en un aprieto o apuro; **to be looking for trouble** buscar tres (o cinco) pies al gato, buscar camorra; **to get into trouble** enredarse, meterse en líos; **to go to the trouble to** + *inf* darse la molestia de + *inf;* **to put oneself to the trouble to** + *inf* o **to take the trouble to** + *inf* tomarse la molestia de + *inf;* **to shoot trouble** localizar averías; **not to be worth the trouble** no valer la pena; **what's the trouble?** ¿qué sucede?, ¿qué hay?; *va* apurar; confundir, estorbar, embarazar; disturbar; inquietar, preocupar; apenar, afligir; molestar, incomodar; dar que hacer a; **may I trouble you?** ¿me hace Vd. el favor?; **to be troubled with** padecer de; **to trouble oneself** molestarse; *vn* apurarse; inquietarse, preocuparse; molestarse, darse molestia, incomodarse; **to trouble to** + *inf* molestarse en + *inf*
trouble-free ['trʌbəl,fri] *adj* libre de disturbios; exento de averías
trouble lamp *s* lámpara de socorro, lámpara de inspección
troublemaker ['trʌbəl,mekər] *s* perturbador, camorrista
trouble shooting *s* investigación de fallas o panas, localización de averías, comprobación de averías
troublesome ['trʌbəlsəm] *adj* molesto, pesado, gravoso, dificultoso; impertinente; perturbador; camorrista

troublous ['trʌbləs] *adj* agitado, inquieto; molesto
trough [trɔf] o [trɑf] *s* artesa (*p.ej., para amasar pan*); pesebre; abrevadero, camellón; canal (*curso de agua excavado artificialmente; conducto de las aguas del tejado*); abismo (*de una onda*); seno (*entre dos ondas*); (meteor.) mínimo de presión; (coll.) borrachín
trounce [traʊns] *va* zurrar; castigar; (coll.) vencer decisivamente
troupe [trup] *s* compañía de actores o de circo
trouper ['trupər] *s* miembro de una compañía teatral; viejo actor
troupial ['trupɪəl] *s* (orn.) trupial
trousers ['traʊzərz] *spl* pantalones; **to wear the trousers** calzarse o ponerse los calzones o los pantalones (*dícese de la mujer que supedita al marido*)
trousseau [tru'so] ['truso] *s* (*pl:* **-seaux** ['soz] o [soz] o **-seaus**) ajuar, equipo de novia, canastilla, joyas
trout [traʊt] *s* (ichth.) trucha
trout fishing *s* pesca de la trucha
trout stream *s* arroyo en que abunda la trucha
trouvère [tru'vɛr] *s* trovero
trow [tro] o [traʊ] *va & vn* (archaic) creer, pensar; (archaic) esperar
trowel ['traʊəl] *s* paleta, llana, trulla, desplantador
Troy [trɔɪ] *s* Troya
troy weight *s* peso troy (*cuya unidad es la libra de doce onzas, que equivale a 373,24 gramos*)
truancy ['truənsɪ] *s* (*pl:* **-cies**) ausencia de la clase sin permiso; haraganería
truant ['truənt] *adj* haragán; *s* haragán; novillero (*muchacho que no asiste a la clase*); **to play truant** hacer novillos
truant officer *s* vigilante escolar
truce [trus] *s* tregua
truck [trʌk] *s* carro; vagoneta; camión, camioneta; autocamión; carretilla (*carro pequeño de mano*); ruedecilla; remate de asta o mástil; cambio, permuta, trueque; efectos para vender o trocar, baratijas, zupias, hojarasca; pago del salario en especie; (rail.) bogie, carretón (*de locomotora, coche, etc.*); (Brit.) furgón de plataforma; (U.S.A.) hortalizas para el mercado; (coll.) desechos, desperdicios; (coll.) negocio, relaciones; *va* acarrear, transportar en carro, vagoneta, camión, etc.; cambiar, permutar, trocar; traficar en; *vn* conducir un carro, vagoneta, camión, etc.; ser carretero, conductor de camión, etc.
truckage ['trʌkɪdʒ] *s* acarreo; camionaje
truck driver *s* camionista, conductor de camión
trucker ['trʌkər] *s* carretero; camionista, conductor de camión; verdulero
truck garden *s* huerto de hortalizas (*para el mercado*)
truckle ['trʌkəl] *s* ruedecilla; carriola; *va* mover sobre ruedecillas; *vn* rodar sobre ruedecillas; someterse servilmente
truckle bed *s* carriola
truckload ['trʌk,lod] *s* carga de un carro; carga de un camión
truckman ['trʌkmən] *s* (*pl:* **-men**) carretero; conductor de camión; baratador
truculence ['trʌkjələns] o ['trukjələns] o **truculency** ['trʌkjələnsɪ] o ['trukjələnsɪ] *s* truculencia
truculent ['trʌkjələnt] o ['trukjələnt] *adj* truculento
trudge [trʌdʒ] *s* marcha, paseo; marcha penosa; *va* recorrer con pena y trabajo; *vn* caminar, ir a pie; marchar con pena y trabajo; **to trudge along** marchar con pena y trabajo
trudgen stroke ['trʌdʒən] *s* brazada a la marinera
true [tru] *adj* (*comp:* **truer** ['truər]; *super:* **truest** ['truɪst]) verdadero; exacto; constante, uniforme; fiel, leal; alineado; a plomo, a nivel; **to come true** hacerse realidad; **to run true to form** obrar como era de esperarse; **true to life** conforme con la realidad; *adv* verdaderamente; exactamente; propiamente, naturalmente; *s* ajuste, posición debida o correcta; **in true** alineado; **out of true** desalineado; **the true** lo verdadero; *va* alinear, rectificar; **to true up** alinear, rectificar
true bill *s* (law) acto acusatorio formulado por el gran jurado como base del procesamiento de un acusado, por haberse encontrado indicios suficientes de culpabilidad
true-blue ['tru'blu] *adj* fiel, leal, constante
true copy *s* copia fiel
true course *s* (naut.) rumbo verdadero
true-hearted ['tru,hɑrtɪd] *adj* fiel, leal, sincero
truelove ['tru,lʌv] *s* fiel amante; enamorado o enamorada; (bot.) hierba de París
truelove knot o **true-lover's knot** ['tru'lʌvərz] *s* lazo de amor
true ribs *spl* (anat.) costillas verdaderas
true time *s* (astr.) tiempo (solar) verdadero
truffle ['trʌfəl] o ['trufəl] *s* (bot.) trufa
truism ['truɪzəm] *s* perogrullada, verdad trillada, truísmo
trull [trʌl] *s* prostituta, mujer de mala vida
truly ['trulɪ] *adv* verdaderamente; efectivamente; fielmente; **truly yours** su seguro servidor, de Vd. atto. y S.S.
trump [trʌmp] *s* triunfo (*en los juegos de naipes*); (coll.) persona muy simpática, buen chico, buena chica; (archaic & poet.) trompa, toque de trompa; (Scotch & Irish) trompa gallega; **no trump** sin triunfo; *va* matar con un triunfo; aventajar, sobrepujar; (archaic & poet.) tocar (*la trompa*); (archaic & poet.) anunciar a son de trompa; **to trump up** forjar, inventar (*para engañar*); *vn* triunfar (*jugar del palo de triunfo*); (archaic & poet.) tocar la trompa
trumpery ['trʌmpərɪ] *s* (*pl:* **-ies**) hojarasca, oropel, relumbrón; baratija, bujería; necedad, tontería; *adj* de oropel; inútil, sin valor; necio, tonto
trumpet ['trʌmpɪt] *s* trompeta; toque de trompeta; trompetilla o trompeta acústica; trompeta o trompetero (*músico*); **to blow one's own trumpet** cantar sus propias alabanzas; *va* anunciar con trompetas, pregonar a son de trompeta; abocinar; *vn* trompetear; barritar (*el elefante*)
trumpet creeper *s* (bot.) jazmín trompeta
trumpeter ['trʌmpɪtər] *s* trompetero, trompeta; (fig.) pregonero; (orn.) agamí, pájaro trompeta
trumpet flower *s* (bot.) jazmín trompeta; (bot.) madreselva; (bot.) trompetilla
trumpet honeysuckle *s* (bot.) madreselva
trumpet vine *s* var. de **trumpet creeper**
truncate ['trʌŋket] *adj* truncado; *va* truncar
truncation [trʌŋ'keʃən] *s* truncamiento; (cryst.) truncadura
truncheon ['trʌntʃən] *s* cachiporra; bastón de mando; *va* zurrar con cachiporra
trundle ['trʌndəl] *s* rodadura; ruedecilla; ruedecilla de mueble; carriola; *va* hacer rodar; *vn* rodar
trundle bed *s* carriola
trunk [trʌŋk] *s* tronco (*del cuerpo humano o animal, del árbol, de una familia, del ferrocarril, etc.*); baúl; cofre de equipajes, portaequipaje (*del automóvil*); trompa (*del elefante*); vivero; (anat. & arch.) tronco; **trunks** *spl* taparrabo (*usado como traje de baño, etc.*); *adj* troncal; principal
trunk hose *spl* trusas
trunk line *s* (rail.) línea troncal; (telp.) línea principal
trunk piston *s* (mach.) émbolo de tronco
trunnion ['trʌnjən] *s* (arti.) muñón
truss [trʌs] *s* armadura; braguero (*para contener las hernias*); haz, paquete, lío; (Brit.) 60 libras de heno; (Brit.) 36 libras de paja; (hort.) mazorca, racimo; (naut.) troza; *va* armar; empaquetar, liar; espetar; apretar (*barriles*); (naut.) aferrar (*las velas*); (archaic) apretar (*el vestido*); (archaic) atar (*cordones, cintas, etc.*); (archaic) arreglar o componer (*el cabello*); *vn* (archaic) irse, marcharse
trust [trʌst] *s* confianza; esperanza (*persona o cosa en que se confía*); cargo, custodia; depósito; crédito; obligación; (law) fideicomiso; (econ.) trust, cartel; **in trust** en confianza; en depósito; **on trust** a crédito, al fiado; haciendo confianza; *va* confiar; confiar en; vender a crédito a; *vn* confiar; fiar (*vender sin tomar el precio al contado*); **to trust in** fiarse a o de

trust buster *s* (slang) fiscal anticartel
trust company *s* banco fideicomisario, banco de depósitos
trustee [trʌsˈti]] *s* administrador, comisario; regente (universitario); fideicomisario; depositario
trusteeship [trʌsˈtiʃɪp] *s* cargo de administrador, fideicomisario, depositario, etc.; fideicomiso (*de la ONU*)
trustful [ˈtrʌstfəl] o **trusting** [ˈtrʌstɪŋ] *adj* confiado
trustworthiness [ˈtrʌst,wʌrðɪnɪs] *s* confiabilidad
trustworthy [ˈtrʌst,wʌrðɪ] *adj* confiable, fidedigno
trusty [ˈtrʌstɪ] *adj* (*comp:* **-ier;** *super:* **-iest**) fiel, honrado, leal, seguro; *s* (*pl:* **-ies**) persona fiel, segura, digna de confianza; (U.S.A.) preso que se ha merecido algunos privilegios
truth [truθ] *s* (*pl:* **truths** [truðz] o [truθs]) verdad; **in truth** a la verdad, en verdad
truthful [ˈtruθfəl] *adj* verídico, veraz
truthfulness [ˈtruθfəlnɪs] *s* veracidad
try [traɪ] *s* (*pl:* **tries**) intento, ensayo, prueba; (*pret & pp:* **tried**) *va* intentar, ensayar, probar; comprobar, verificar; exasperar, irritar; cansar, fatigar; forzar (*p.ej., la vista, los nervios*); (law) procesar; (law) ver (*un pleito*); refinar o purificar derritiendo o hirviendo; **to try on** probarse (*una prenda de vestir*); **to try out** someter a prueba; refinar o purificar derritiendo o hirviendo; *vn* ensayar, probar; esforzarse; tratar; **to be trying to** + *inf* querer + *inf, p.ej.,* **it is trying to rain** quiere llover; **to try out** (sport) presentarse como competidor; **to try to** + *inf* tratar de + *inf,* intentar + *inf*
trying [ˈtraɪɪŋ] *adj* penoso; molesto, cansado, difícil de soportar
tryout [ˈtraɪ,aut] *s* (coll.) experimento, prueba, prueba de competencia
trypaflavine [,trɪpəˈflevɪn] o [,trɪpəˈflevin] *s* (pharm.) tripaflavina
trypanosome [ˈtrɪpənəsom] *s* (zool.) tripanosoma
tryparsamide [,trɪpɑrˈsæmɪd] o [trɪpˈɑrsəmɪd] *s* (trademark) triparsamida
trypsin [ˈtrɪpsɪn] *s* (biochem.) tripsina
tryptic [ˈtrɪptɪk] *adj* (physiol.) tríptico
tryptophan [ˈtrɪptəfæn] o **tryptophane** [ˈtrɪptəfen] *s* (biochem.) triptófano
trysail [ˈtraɪsəl] o [ˈtraɪ,sel] *s* (naut.) vela mayor de capa
try square *s* escuadra de comprobación
tryst [trɪst] o [traɪst] *s* cita; lugar de cita; *va* dar una cita a; *vn* acudir a una cita
trysting place *s* lugar de cita
tsar [tsɑr] *s* var. de **czar**
tsarevitch [ˈtsɑrɪvɪtʃ] *s* var. de **czarevitch**
tsarina [tsɑˈrinə] *s* var. de **czarina**
tsetse [ˈtsɛtsɪ] *s* (ent.) tsetsé
tsetse fly *s* (ent.) mosca tsetsé
tsp. abr. de **teaspoon**
T square *s* te, regla T
Tu. abr. de **Tuesday**
tub [tʌb] *s* tina, cuba; artesón; (coll.) baño; (coll.) cuba (*persona de mucho vientre*); (coll.) carcamán, trompo (*buque malo y pesado*); (*pret & pp:* **tubbed;** *ger:* **tubbing**) *va* entinar, encubar; bañar en bañera; *vn* bañarse, bañarse en bañera
tuba [ˈtjubə] o [ˈtubə] *s* (mus.) tuba
Tubal-cain [ˈtjubəl,ken] o [ˈtubəl,ken] *s* (Bib.) Tubalcaín
tubbing [ˈtʌbɪŋ] *s* baño
tubby [ˈtʌbɪ] *adj* (*comp:* **-bier;** *super:* **-biest**) rechoncho; sordo (*ruido*)
tube [tjub] o [tub] *s* tubo; túnel; (coll.) ferrocarril subterráneo; (anat.) tubo, trompa; (elec. & rad.) tubo; cámara (*de un neumático*); *va* entubar; meter en un tubo; proveer de tubos; dar forma de tubo a
tubeless [ˈtjublɪs] o [ˈtublɪs] *adj* sin tubo; (aut.) sin cámara
tuber [ˈtjubər] o [ˈtubər] *s* (anat. & bot.) tubérculo
tubercle [ˈtjubərkəl] o [ˈtubərkəl] *s* (anat., bot., path. & zool.) tubérculo
tubercle bacillus *s* (bact.) bacilo de Koch
tubercular [tjuˈbʌrkjələr] o [tuˈbʌrkjələr] *adj* tubercular; tuberculoso; *s* tuberculoso (*persona que padece tuberculosis*)
tubercularization [tju,bʌrkjələrɪˈzeʃən] o [tu,bʌrkjələrɪˈzeʃən] *s* tuberculización
tuberculin [tjuˈbʌrkjəlɪn] o [tuˈbʌrkjəlɪn] *s* (bact.) tuberculina
tuberculosis [tju,bʌrkjəˈlosɪs] o [tu,bʌrkjəˈlosɪs] *s* (path.) tuberculosis
tuberculous [tjuˈbʌrkjələs] o [tuˈbʌrkjələs] *adj* tuberculoso
tuberose [ˈtjub,roz] o [ˈtub,roz] *s* (bot.) tuberosa
tuberosity [,tjubəˈrɑsɪtɪ] o [,tubəˈrɑsɪtɪ] *s* (*pl:* **-ties**) tuberosidad
tuberous [ˈtjubərəs] o [ˈtubərəs] *adj* tuberoso
tube tester *s* (rad.) probador de válvulas
tubeworks [ˈtjub,wʌrks] o [ˈtub,wʌrks] *spl* tubería
tubicolous [tjuˈbɪkələs] o [tuˈbɪkələs] *adj* (zool.) tubícola
tubing [ˈtjubɪŋ] o [ˈtubɪŋ] *s* tubería; material para tubos; trozo de tubo
Tübingen [ˈtybɪŋən] *s* Tubinga
tubular [ˈtjubjələr] o [ˈtubjələr] *adj* tubular
tubular boiler *s* caldera tubular
tubulate [ˈtjubjəlet] o [ˈtubjəlet] *adj* tubular; tubulado
tubulation [,tjubjəˈleʃən] o [,tubjəˈleʃən] *s* tubulación
tubule [ˈtjubjul] o [ˈtubjul] *s* tubito
tubulous [ˈtjubjələs] o [ˈtubjələs] *adj* (bot.) tubuloso
tubulure [ˈtjubjələr] o [ˈtubjələr] *s* (chem.) tubulura
tuck [tʌk] *s* pliegue o doblez (horizontal), alforza; (b.b.) cartera; (coll.) energía, vivacidad; (slang) banquete, festín; (slang) dulce, confitura; (slang) ganas de comer; (naut.) arca de popa; *va* echar un pliegue (horizontal) a, alforzar; doblar (*como para encubrir*); arremangar; apretar; arropar; **to tuck away** encubrir, ocultar; (slang) comer o beber vorazmente; **to tuck in** arropar, enmantar; remeter (*p.ej., la ropa de cama*); **to tuck up** arremangar (*un vestido*); guarnecer (*la cama*); *vn* alforzar
tucker [ˈtʌkər] *s* alforzador; alforzador de la máquina de coser; escote, pañoleta; *va* (coll.) agotar, cansar
Tues. abr. de **Tuesday**
Tuesday [ˈtjuzdɪ] o [ˈtuzdɪ] *s* martes
tufa [ˈtjufə] o [ˈtufə] *s* (geol.) toba (*piedra caliza porosa*)
tufaceous [tjuˈfeʃəs] o [tuˈfeʃəs] *adj* toboso
tuff [tʌf] *s* (geol.) toba (*piedra volcánica*)
tuft [tʌft] *s* copete (*de plumas, cabellos, etc.*); moño; borla; manojo, racimo, ramillete; grupo de árboles o arbustos; *va* empenachar; poner borlas a; *vn* crecer formando mechones
tufted [ˈtʌftɪd] *adj* copetudo; empenachado
tufthunter [ˈtʌft,hʌntər] *s* ambicioso de figurar, zalamero
tufting needle *s* aguja colchonera
tug [tʌg] *s* estirón, tirón; esfuerzo; remolcador (*barco*); tirante (*correa*); (*pret & pp:* **tugged;** *ger:* **tugging**) *va* arrastrar, tirar con fuerza de; remolcar (*un barco*); *vn* tirar con fuerza; esforzarse, luchar
tugboat [ˈtʌg,bot] *s* remolcador
tug of war *s* (sport) lucha de la cuerda; (fig.) lucha suprema, lucha decisiva
Tuileries [ˈtwilərɪz] o [twilˈri] *spl* Tullerías
tuition [tjuˈɪʃən] o [tuˈɪʃən] *s* enseñanza; precio de la enseñanza, cuota
tuitional [tjuˈɪʃənəl] o [tuˈɪʃənəl] *adj* de enseñanza; del precio de la enseñanza
tularemia [,tuləˈrimɪə] *s* (path.) tularemia
tule [ˈtulɛ] *s* (bot.) junco de laguna, tule
tule goose *s* (orn.) ánsar, guanana prieta
tulip [ˈtjulɪp] o [ˈtulɪp] *s* (bot.) tulipán (*planta, raíz bulbosa y flor*)
tulip tree *s* (bot.) tulipanero o tulipero
tulipwood [ˈtjulɪp,wud] o [ˈtulɪp,wud] *s* madera del tulipero; (bot.) palo de rosa (*árbol y madera*)
tulle [tul] *s* tul
Tully [ˈtʌlɪ] *s* Tulio
tumble [ˈtʌmbəl] *s* caída; voltereta; confusión,

desorden; **to take a tumble** rodar, caerse; *va* derribar, derrocar, volcar; revolver; arrojar, tirar; ajar, arrugar; desarreglar, trastornar; *vn* caer o caerse; voltear; derribarse, derrocarse, volcarse; brincar, dar saltos, precipitarse; echarse (*en la cama*); (slang) caer, comprender; **to tumble down** desplomarse, hundirse, venir abajo
tumblebug ['tʌmbəl,bʌg] *s* (ent.) escarabajo pelotero o bolero
tumble-down ['tʌmbəl,daʊn] *adj* destartalado, destrozado, desvencijado
tumbler ['tʌmblər] *s* vaso (*para beber*); volteador, volatinéro; dominguillo, tentemozo (*juguete*); rodete, fiador (*p.ej., de la cerradura*); seguro de escopeta; (orn.) pichón volteador
tumbler switch *s* (elec.) interruptor de volquete
tumbleweed ['tʌmbəl,wid] *s* (bot.) planta rodadora
tumbrel o **tumbril** ['tʌmbrəl] *s* chirrión; carro de artillería
tumefaction [,tjumɪ'fækʃən] o [,tumɪ'fækʃən] *s* tumefacción
tumefy ['tjumɪfaɪ] o ['tumɪfaɪ] (*pret & pp:* **-fied**) *va* tumefacer; *vn* tumefacerse
tumescence [tju'mɛsəns] o [tu'mɛsəns] *s* tumescencia
tumescent [tju'mɛsənt] o [tu'mɛsənt] *adj* tumescente
tumid ['tjumɪd] o ['tumɪd] *adj* túmido; (fig.) túmido
tumor ['tjumər] o ['tumər] *s* (path.) tumor
tumorous ['tjumərəs] o ['tumərəs] *adj* tumoroso
tumular ['tjumjələr] o ['tumjələr] *adj* tumulario
tumult ['tjumʌlt] o ['tumʌlt] *s* tumulto
tumultuary [tju'mʌltʃʊ,ɛrɪ] o [tu'mʌltʃʊ,ɛrɪ] *adj* tumultuario
tumultuous [tju'mʌltʃʊəs] o [tu'mʌltʃʊəs] *adj* tumultuoso
tumulus ['tjumjələs] o ['tumjələs] *s* (*pl:* **-luses** o **-li** [laɪ]) túmulo
tun [tʌn] *s* tonel, barril; tonelada (*medida que equivale a 252 galones*); (*pret & pp:* **tunned;** *ger:* **tunning**) *va* entonelar, embarrilar
tuna ['tunə] *s* (ichth.) atún; (bot.) tuna
tunable ['tjunəbəl] o ['tunəbəl] *adj* armonioso, melodioso; cantable; afinado, templado; que se puede templar; (rad.) sintonizable
tuna fishery *s* atunara, almadraba
tundra ['tʌndrə] o ['tʊndrə] *s* tundra
tune [tjun] o [tun] *s* tonada, aire; armonía; tono (*manera de actuar o hablar*); (rad.) sintonía; **in tune** afinado; afinadamente; **out of tune** desafinado; desafinadamente; **to change one's tune** o **to sing a different tune** mudar de tono; **to the tune of** (coll.) por la suma de; *va* acordar, afinar; armonizar; (rad.) sintonizar; **to tune in** (rad.) sintonizar; **to tune out** (rad.) desintonizar; **to tune up** ajustar, poner a punto; poner a tono (*un motor de automóvil*); (mus.) acordar; *vn* armonizar; **to tune up** (coll.) empezar a cantar, llorar, etc.
tuneable ['tjunəbəl] o ['tunəbəl] *adj* var. de **tunable**
tuneful ['tjunfəl] o ['tunfəl] *adj* armonioso, melodioso
tuneless ['tjunlɪs] o ['tunlɪs] *adj* discorde, disonante
tuner ['tjunər] o ['tunər] *s* (mus.) afinador (*persona*); (rad.) sintonizador
tung oil [tʌŋ] *s* aceite de tung
tungstate ['tʌŋstet] *s* (chem.) tungstato
tungsten ['tʌŋstən] *s* (chem.) tungsteno
tungsten steel *s* acero al tungsteno
tungstic ['tʌŋstɪk] *adj* (chem.) túngstico
tunic ['tjunɪk] o ['tunɪk] *s* túnica; (anat., bot. & zool.) túnica; (eccl.) tunicela
tunicate ['tjunɪket] o ['tunɪket] *adj* tunicado; *s* (zool.) tunicado
tunicle ['tjunɪkəl] o ['tunɪkəl] *s* (eccl.) tunicela
tuning ['tjunɪŋ] o ['tunɪŋ] *s* afinación; armonización; (rad.) sintonización
tuning coil *s* (rad.) bobina sintonizadora, bobina de sintonía
tuning condenser *s* (rad.) condensador de sintonía, condensador sintonizador
tuning dial *s* (rad.) cuadrante de sintonización
tuning fork *s* (mus.) diapasón
tuning hammer o **key** *s* (mus.) afinador, martillo, templador
tuning knob *s* (rad.) botón de sintonización, perilla sintonizadora
Tunis ['tjunɪs] o ['tunɪs] *s* Túnez (*ciudad*)
Tunisia [tju'nɪʃɪə] o [tu'nɪʃɪə] *s* Túnez (*país*)
Tunisian [tju'nɪʃɪən] o [tu'nɪʃɪən] *adj & s* tunecino
tunnel ['tʌnəl] *s* túnel; (min.) galería; (*pret & pp:* **-neled** o **-nelled;** *ger:* **-neling** o **-nelling**) *va* atravesar por túnel; construir un túnel a través de o debajo de; *vn* construir o perforar un túnel
tunnel disease *s* (path.) anemia de los túneles; (path.) enfermedad de los cajones de aire comprimido
tunny ['tʌnɪ] *s* (*pl:* **-nies**) (ichth.) atún
tupelo ['tupɪlo] *s* (*pl:* **-los**) (bot.) tupelo
tuppence ['tʌpəns] *s* var. de **twopence**
tuque [tjuk] o [tuk] *s* gorra de punto de los canadienses
Turanian [tjʊ'renɪən] o [tʊ'renɪən] *adj & s* turanio
turban ['tʌrbən] *s* turbante
turbaned ['tʌrbənd] *adj* tocado con turbante
turbid ['tʌrbɪd] *adj* turbio
turbidimeter [,tʌrbɪ'dɪmɪtər] *s* turbidímetro
turbidimetric [,tʌrbɪdɪ'mɛtrɪk] *adj* turbidimétrico
turbidity [tʌr'bɪdɪtɪ] *s* turbiedad
turbinate ['tʌrbɪnet] o ['tʌrbɪnɪt] *adj* turbinado (*que afecta la figura de un cono inverso*); (anat.) turbinado; *s* concha espiral; (anat.) hueso turbinado
turbine ['tʌrbɪn] o ['tʌrbaɪn] *s* turbina
turbine-electric ['tʌrbɪnɪ'lɛktrɪk] o ['tʌrbaɪnɪ'lɛktrɪk] *adj* turboeléctrico
turbit ['tʌrbɪt] *s* (orn.) paloma de corbata
turboblower ['tʌrbo,bloər] *s* turbosoplador
turbocompressor [,tʌrbokəm'prɛsər] *s* turbocompresor
turbodynamo [,tʌrbo'daɪnəmo] *s* (*pl:* **-mos**) turbodínamo
turbofan ['tʌrbo,fæn] *s* turboventilador
turbogenerator ['tʌrbo'dʒɛnə,retər] *s* turbogenerador
turbojet ['tʌrbo,dʒɛt] *s* turborreactor, motor de turborreacción; avión de turborreacción
turbomotor ['tʌrbo,motər] *s* turbomotor
turbo-prop bomber ['tʌrbo,prɑp] *s* (aer.) bombardero turbohélice
turbo-propeller engine [,tʌrbopro'pɛlər] o **turbo-prop engine** ['tʌrbo,prɑp] *s* (aer.) turbohélice, motor de turbohélice
turbopump ['tʌrbo,pʌmp] *s* turbobomba
turbo-ram-jet [,tʌrbo'ræm'dʒɛt] *s* (aer.) turborreactor a postcombustión
turbosupercharger ['tʌrbo'supər,tʃɑrdʒər] o ['tʌrbo'sjupər,tʃɑrdʒər] *s* turbosupercargador
turbot ['tʌrbət] *s* (ichth.) rodaballo
turboventilator ['tʌrbo'vɛntɪ,letər] *s* turboventilador
turbulence ['tʌrbjələns] o **turbulency** ['tʌrbjələnsɪ] *s* turbulencia
turbulent ['tʌrbjələnt] *adj* turbulento
Turco ['tʌrko] *s* (*pl:* **-cos**) (mil.) turco (*tirador argelino*)
tureen [tʊ'rin] o [tjʊ'rin] *s* sopera
turf [tʌrf] *s* (*pl:* **turfs** o **turves**) césped (*hierba menuda*); tepe, terrón de tierra (*con césped*); turba; hipódromo; carreras de caballos
turfman ['tʌrfmən] *s* (*pl:* **-men**) turfista
turfy ['tʌrfɪ] *adj* (*comp:* **-ier;** *super:* **-iest**) encespedado; turboso; turfista
turgescence [tʌr'dʒɛsəns] *s* turgescencia
turgescent [tʌr'dʒɛsənt] *s* turgescente
turgid ['tʌrdʒɪd] *adj* (path. & fig.) turgente
turgidity [tʌr'dʒɪdɪtɪ] *s* turgencia
Turin ['tjʊrɪn] o ['tʊrɪn] *s* Turín
turion ['tjʊrɪɑn] o ['tʊrɪɑn] *s* (bot.) turión
Turk. abr. de **Turkey** y **Turkish**
Turk [tʌrk] *s* turco; (offensive) persona bárbara y feroz
Turkestan [,tʌrkə'stæn] o [,tʌrkə'stɑn] *s* el Turquestán
turkey ['tʌrkɪ] *s* (orn.) pavo; (*cap.*) *s* Turquía; **to talk turkey** (coll.) no tener pelos en la lengua
turkey buzzard *s* (orn.) aura, gallinazo

turkey cock *s* pavo (*macho*); persona vanagloriosa
turkey gobbler *s* (coll.) pavo (*macho*)
turkey hen *s* pava
Turkey in Asia *s* la Turquía de Asia, la Turquía Asiática
Turkey in Europe *s* la Turquía de Europa, la Turquía Europea
turkey oak *s* (bot.) roble rojo; (bot.) roble ahorquillado; **Turkey oak** *s* (bot.) rebollo (*Quercus cerris*)
Turkey red *s* rojo turco; tela de algodón de color rojo turco
Turkic languages [ˈtʌrkɪk] *spl* (philol.) idiomas turcos
Turkish [ˈtʌrkɪʃ] *adj* turco; *s* turco (*idioma*)
Turkish bath *s* baño turco
Turkish Empire *s* Imperio otomano
Turkish towel *s* toalla rusa
Turkmen Soviet Socialist Republic, the [ˈtʌrkmɛn] el Turkmenistán
Turkoman [ˈtʌrkomən] *s* (*pl:* **-mans**) turcomano
Turkomanic [ˌtʌrkoˈmænɪk] *adj* turcomano
Turkophile [ˈtʌrkofaɪl] *adj & s* turcófilo
Turkophobe [ˈtʌrkofob] *adj & s* turcófobo
Turk's-cap lily [ˈtʌrks ˌkæp] *s* (bot.) martagón
Turk's-head [ˈtʌrks ˌhɛd] *s* tortera con tubo central; deshollinador, escobón; (bot.) melón de costa; (naut.) cabeza de turco
turmeric [ˈtʌrmərɪk] *s* (bot.) cúrcuma (*planta y raíz*)
turmeric paper *s* (chem.) papel de cúrcuma
turmoil [ˈtʌrmɔɪl] *s* alboroto, disturbio, tumulto
turn [tʌrn] *s* vuelta; ocasión, oportunidad; fase; proceder, comportamiento; aspecto, figura, forma; estilo; expresión; vahido, vértigo, desvanecimiento; ensayo, prueba; exigencia; inclinación, propensión; giro (*de la frase*); turno (*alternativa entre dos o más personas*); espira (*de una hélice o una espiral*); (coll.) sacudida, susto; (elec.) espira (*de un rollo de alambre*); (mus.) grupeto; **turns** *spl* (coll.) reglas (*de la mujer*); **at every turn** a cada paso, en todo momento; **at the turn of** a la vuelta de; **bad turn** mala pasada; **by turns** por turnos; **good turn** favor, servicio; **in turn** por turno; **one good turn deserves another** bien con bien se paga; **out of turn** fuera de turno; **to a turn** exactamente; con suma perfección; **to be one's turn** tocarle a uno, p.ej., **it's your turn** le toca a Vd.; **to have a turn for** tener habilidad en, tener inclinación a; **to take a turn** dar una vuelta; cambiar de aspecto; **to take a turn for the better** estar mejorando; **to take a turn for the worse** estar empeorando; **to take turns** turnar, alternar; **to wait one's turn** aguardar turno, esperar vez ‖ *va* volver; dar vuelta a (*p.ej., una llave*); trastornar; torcer (*p.ej., el tobillo*); doblar (*la esquina, la calle*); aplicar, emplear, utilizar; dirigir (*p.ej., los ojos*); agriar; tornear (*labrar al torno*); pasar, sobrepasar; tener (*p.ej., veinte años cumplidos*); (elec.) dar vuelta a (*un interruptor*); **to turn against** predisponer en contra de; **to turn around** volver (*hacer girar*); voltear (*poner al revés*); torcer, dar otro sentido a (*las palabras de una persona*); **to turn aside** desviar; **to turn away** desviar; despachar, despedir; **to turn back** devolver; hacer retroceder; retrasar (*el reloj*); **to turn down** doblar o plegar hacia abajo; invertir; rechazar, rehusar; bajar (*p.ej., el gas*); **to turn in** doblar o plegar hacia adentro; entregar; **to turn into** volver en, p.ej., **he turned the water into wine** volvió el agua en vino; plantar (*a una persona*) en (*p.ej., la calle*); **to turn off** desviar; despedir; hacer, ejecutar; apagar (*la luz, la radio*); cortar (*el agua, gas, etc.*); cerrar (*la llave del agua, gas, etc.; la radio, la televisión*); interrumpir (*la corriente eléctrica*); **to turn on** encender (*la luz*); poner (*la luz, la radio, etc.*); abrir la llave de (*p.ej., el agua, gas*); abrir (*la llave del agua, gas, etc.*); establecer (*la corriente eléctrica*); **to turn out** echar; despedir; sacar hacia afuera; echar al campo (*a los animales*); volver al revés; apagar (*la luz*); hacer, ejecutar, fabricar, producir; **to turn over** entregar; invertir, volcar; doblar, plegar; considerar, revolver; hacer girar (*el motor de un automóvil*); hojear (*un libro*); pasar (*las hojas de un libro*); **to turn to** enderezar (*a una persona*) a o hacia; **to turn up** doblar o plegar hacia arriba; levantar; arremangar; revolver (*la tierra*); volver (*un naipe*); abrir la llave de (*p.ej., el gas*); abrir (*la llave del gas, etc.*); poner más alto o más fuerte (*la radio*) ‖ *vn* volver, p.ej., **the road turns to the right** el camino vuelve hacia la derecha; virar (*un automóvil, un avión, etc.*); girar (*moverse circularmente*); volverse (*inclinar, p.ej., la conversación a determinados asuntos; hacerse, ponerse, resultar; agriarse ciertos licores; mudar de opinión*); doblarse, plegarse; dar vueltas (*la cabeza*); cambiar (*el viento*); **to turn about** dar vuelta, dar una vuelta completa; cambiar de frente; mudar de opinión; voltearse; **to turn against** cobrar aversión a; rebelarse contra; **to turn around** dar vuelta, dar una vuelta completa; **to turn aside** o **away** desviarse; alejarse; **to turn back** volver, regresar; retroceder; **to turn down** doblarse hacia abajo; invertirse; **to turn in** doblarse hacia adentro, replegarse; entrar, dar la vuelta y entrar; recogerse, volver a casa; (coll.) recogerse, acostarse; **to turn into** entrar en; convertirse en; **to turn off** desviarse, cambiar de camino; **to turn on** volverse contra; depender de; versar sobre; ocuparse de; **to turn out** salir a la calle; dejarse ver; acontecer; venir a ser; resultar, salir, p.ej., **he will turn out a good doctor** saldrá un buen médico; (coll.) levantarse (*salir de cama*); **to turn out badly** salir mal; **to turn out right** acabar bien; **to turn out to be** venir a ser; resultar, salir; **to turn out well** salir bien; **to turn over** volcar, derribarse (*un vehículo*); cambiar de posición; **to turn over and over** dar repetidas vueltas; **to turn to** acudir a; recurrir a, dirigirse a; redundar en; convertirse en; **to turn to and fro** volver de un lado a otro; **to turn up** doblarse hacia arriba; levantarse; acontecer; acudir, aparecer, dejarse ver; **to turn upon** volverse contra; depender de; versar sobre; ocuparse en
turnbuckle [ˈtʌrn ˌbʌkəl] *s* tensor roscado, tornillo tensor; torniquete (*para mantener abiertas las hojas de las ventanas*)
turncoat [ˈtʌrn ˌkot] *s* tránsfuga, apóstata, renegado
turndown [ˈtʌrn ˌdaʊn] *s* rechazamiento; *adj* doblado hacia abajo, caído (*cuello*)
turner [ˈtʌrnər] *s* volvedor; torneador; tornero (*obrero que labra al torno*); gimnasta, volatinero
turning [ˈtʌrnɪŋ] *adj* giratorio, rotatorio; *s* vuelta; giro, viraje; tornería; invención (*de una frase*); **turnings** *spl* torneaduras; piezas torneadas
turning point *s* punto de transición, punto decisivo, punto crucial; (surv.) punto de cambio (*en la nivelación*)
turnip [ˈtʌrnɪp] *s* (bot.) nabo (*planta y raíz*); (bot.) colinabo o rutabaga; (slang) calentador (*reloj de bolsillo*); (slang) tipo, sujeto; (coll.) tonto, necio
turnkey [ˈtʌrn ˌki] *s* llavero de una cárcel, carcelero
turn of life *s* (physiol.) menopausia
turn of mind *s* natural, inclinación, propensión
turnout [ˈtʌrn ˌaʊt] *s* concurrencia; entrada (*número de personas que asisten a un espectáculo*); apartadero (*para dejar pasar otros automóviles, trenes, etc.*); producción (*cantidad producida*); equipaje; carruaje de lujo; (coll.) huelga; (coll.) huelguista
turnover [ˈtʌrn ˌovər] *s* vuelco; cambio de personal; movimiento de mercancías; ciclo de compra y venta; (cook.) pastel con repulgo; *adj* doblado hacia abajo
turnpike [ˈtʌrn ˌpaɪk] *s* carretera de peaje, camino de portazgo, autopista de portazgo; barrera de portazgo
turn signals *spl* (aut.) señales de dirección, indicadores de dirección
turnspit [ˈtʌrn ˌspɪt] *s* persona o perro que da vueltas al asador

turnstile ['tʌrn,staɪl] *s* torniquete
turnstone ['tʌrn,ston] *s* (orn.) revuelvepiedras
turntable 'tʌrn,tebəl] *s* placa giratoria, plataforma giratoria (*de ferrocarril*); placa giratoria, plato giratorio (*de gramófono*)
turpentine ['tʌrpəntaɪn] *s* trementina; esencia de trementina
turpeth ['tʌrpɪθ] *s* (bot.) turbit; (pharm.) turbino
turpitude ['tʌrpɪtjud] o ['tʌrpɪtud] *s* torpeza, infamia, vileza
turquoise ['tʌrkɔɪz] o ['tʌrkwɔɪz] *s* (mineral.) turquesa
turquoise blue *s* azul turquesa
turret ['tʌrɪt] *s* torrecilla; (arch.) torreón; (arti.) torre; (hist.) torre móvil; (nav.) torreta
turreted ['tʌrɪtɪd] *adj* torreado; (zool.) turriculado
turret lathe *s* torno revolvedor, torno de torrecilla
turtle ['tʌrtəl] *s* (zool.) tortuga; **to turn turtle** derribarse patas arriba; volcar (*un coche*); zozobrar (*un buque*)
turtleback ['tʌrtəl,bæk] *s* caparazón de tortuga; (naut.) cubierta de caparazón
turtledove ['tʌrtəl,dʌv] *s* (orn.) tórtola; (fig.) tórtolo (*persona enamorada*)
Tuscan ['tʌskən] *adj & s* toscano
Tuscany ['tʌskənɪ] *s* la Toscana
Tusculum ['tʌskjələm] *s* Túsculo
tush [tʌʃ] *s* colmillo; *interj* ¡ bah!
tusk [tʌsk] *s* colmillo (*p.ej., del elefante*); *va* herir con los colmillos; cavar o rasgar con los colmillos
tusker ['tʌskər] *s* animal colmilludo
tussah ['tʌsə] *s* tusor (*seda*); (ent.) anterea
tussle ['tʌsəl] *s* agarrada, riña; *vn* agarrarse, asirse, reñir
tussock ['tʌsək] *s* montecillo de hierbas crecientes
tussock moth *s* (ent.) lagarta, monja
tut [tʌt] *interj* ¡ bah!
tutelage ['tjutɪlɪdʒ] o ['tutɪlɪdʒ] *s* tutela; enseñanza, instrucción
tutelar ['tjutɪlər] o ['tutɪlər] *adj* tutelar
tutelary ['tjutɪ,lɛrɪ] o ['tutɪ,lɛrɪ] *adj* tutelar; *s* (*pl:* **-ies**) divinidad tutelar, santo tutelar, genio tutelar, numen tutelar
tutor ['tjutər] o ['tutər] *s* (law) tutor; preceptor; maestro particular; (Brit.) guardián de la disciplina; *va* ser tutor de; enseñar; dar enseñanza particular a; tratar con severidad; *vn* ser tutor; dar lecciones particulares; (coll.) tomar lecciones particulares
tutorial [tju'torɪəl] o [tu'torɪəl] *adj* tutelar; preceptoral
tutorship ['tjutərʃɪp] o ['tutərʃɪp] *s* tutela; preceptorado
tutsan ['tʌtsən] *s* (bot.) todasana, todabuena
tutti-frutti ['tutɪ'frutɪ] *s* helado de varias frutas; conserva de varias frutas; *adj* hecho con varias frutas
tutty ['tʌtɪ] *s* atutía, tucía
tuxedo [tʌk'sido] *s* (*pl:* **-dos**) smoking
tuyère [twi'jer] o [twɪr] *s* (found.) tobera
TV abr. de **television**
twaddle ['twɑdəl] *s* charla, habladuría; tonterías, disparates; *va* decir tontamente; *vn* charlar, decir tonterías
twain [twen] *adj & s* (archaic & poet.) dos
twang [twæŋ] *s* tañido (*de un instrumento músico*); timbre nasal; *va* tocar con un tañido; arrojar con un sonido agudo; decir con timbre nasal; tirar (*una flecha*); *vn* producir un sonido agudo; hablar por la nariz, hablar con voz nasal
'twas [twɑz] o [twʌz] contracción de **it was**
tweak [twik] *s* pellizco retorcido; *va* pellizcar retorciendo; *vn* dar un pellizco retorcido
tweed [twid] *s* mezcla de lana; traje de mezcla de lana; **tweeds** *spl* ropa de mezcla de lana
tweedledum and tweedledee [,twidəl'dʌm ənd ,twidəl'di] *spl* dos cosas entre las cuales no hay diferencia; **it's tweedledum and tweedledee** llámele Vd. hache, da lo mismo perro que gato
tweedy ['twidɪ] *adj* de mezcla de lana; aficionado a la ropa de mezcla de lana; directo, franco, prosaico
'tween [twin] *prep* (poet.) var. de **between**
tweet [twit] *s* pío; *vn* piar
tweeter ['twitər] *s* (rad.) altavoz para altas audiofrecuencias, altavoz agudos
tweezers ['twizərz] *spl* pinzas, tenacillas, bruselas
twelfth [twɛlfθ] *adj* duodécimo; dozavo; *s* duodécimo; dozavo; doce (*en las fechas*)
Twelfth-day ['twɛlfθ,de] *s* var. de **Twelfth-tide**
Twelfth-night ['twɛlfθ,naɪt] *s* día de Reyes, Epifanía; víspera del día de Reyes
Twelfth-tide ['twɛlfθ,taɪd] *s* día de Reyes, Epifanía
twelve [twɛlv] *adj* doce; *s* doce; **twelve o'clock** las doce; **the Twelve** (Bib.) los doce apóstoles (*de Jesucristo*)
Twelve Apostles *spl* (Bib.) doce apóstoles (*de Jesucristo*)
twelvefold ['twɛlv,fold] *adj* doce veces mayor o más; de doce partes; *adv* doce veces más
twelvemo ['twɛlvmo] *adj* en dozavo; *s* (*pl:* **-mos**) libro en dozavo
twelvemonth ['twɛlv,mʌnθ] *s* año (*doce meses*)
Twelve Tables *spl* doce tablas (*antigua ley romana*)
twentieth ['twɛntɪɪθ] *adj* vigésimo; veintavo; *s* vigésimo; veintavo; veinte (*en las fechas*)
twenty ['twɛntɪ] *adj* veinte; *s* (*pl:* **-ties**) veinte
twentyfold ['twɛntɪ,fold] *adj* veinte veces mayor o más; de veinte partes; *adv* veinte veces más
twenty-one ['twɛntɪ'wʌn] *s* veintiuna (*juego de naipes*)
'twere [twʌr] contracción de **it were**
twice [twaɪs] *adv* dos veces; **twice as large as** dos veces más grande que
twice-told ['twaɪs,told] *adj* dicho dos veces; trillado, sabido
twiddle ['twɪdəl] *s* vuelta ligera; *va* menear o revolver ociosamente; *vn* ocuparse de tonterías; girar; temblar
twig [twɪg] *s* ramito; varilla de virtudes, **twigs** *spl* leña menuda
twilight ['twaɪ,laɪt] *s* crepúsculo; *adj* crepuscular
twilight sleep *s* (med.) sueño crepuscular (*narcosis obstétrica parcial*)
twill [twɪl] *s* tela cruzada; cruzado (*dibujo de tela*); *va* cruzar (*la tela*)
'twill [twɪl] contracción de **it will**
twin [twɪn] *adj & s* gemelo; **the Twins** (astr.) los Gemelos; (*pret & pp:* **twinned;** *ger:* **twinning**) *va* parir (*gemelos*); parear; emparejar; *vn* parir gemelos; nacer gemelo; emparejarse
twin beds *spl* camas gemelas
Twin Cities *spl* ciudades gemelas (*Saint Paul y Minneápolis, EE.UU.*)
twin-cylinder ['twɪn'sɪlɪndər] *adj* de dos cilindros, de cilindros gemelos
twine [twaɪn] *s* bramante, guita; enroscadura; retorcedura; *va* enroscar; retorcer; *vn* enroscarse; retorcerse
twinflower ['twɪn,flaʊər] *s* (bot.) té de Suecia
twinge [twɪndʒ] *s* punzada; *va* causar un dolor agudo a; *vn* sentir una punzada
twin-jet plane ['twɪn'dʒɛt] *s* (aer.) avión birreactor
twinkle ['twɪŋkəl] *s* centelleo; pestañeo; movimiento muy rápido; instante; *va* hacer centellear; abrir y cerrar (*los ojos*) rápidamente; *vn* centellear; pestañear; moverse rápidamente
twinkling ['twɪŋklɪŋ] *s* centelleo; pestañeo; movimiento muy rápido; instante; **in the twinkling of an eye** en un abrir y cerrar de ojos
twin lead [lid] *s* (telv.) alambre gemelo
twin-motor ['twɪn'motər] *adj* (aer.) bimotor
twin-screw ['twɪn'skru] *adj* (naut.) de dos hélices, de doble hélice
twirl [twʌrl] *s* vuelta, giro; rasgo (*trazado con la pluma*); *va* hacer girar; (baseball) arrojar (*la pelota*); *vn* girar, dar vueltas; hacer piruetas
twist [twɪst] *s* torcedura; enroscadura; curva, recodo; giro, vuelta; torzal; rosca (*de pan*); rollo de tabaco; propensión, prejuicio; sesgo (*de la mente*); *va* torcer; retorcer; enroscar;

hacer girar; entrelazar; desviar; (baseball) arrojar (*la pelota*) haciéndola dar vueltas; (fig.) torcer (*dar diverso sentido a*); *vn* torcerse; retorcerse; enroscarse; dar vueltas; entrelazarse; desviarse; serpentear; **to twist and turn** dar vueltas (*en la cama, por no poder dormir*)

twister [ˈtwɪstər] *s* torcedor (*persona y aparato*); torcedero (*aparato*); (baseball) pelota arrojada con efecto; (meteor.) tromba, tornado

twit [twɪt] *s* reprensión; advertencia recordativa; (*pret & pp:* **twitted;** *ger:* **twitting**) *va* reprender; reprender (*a uno*) recordando algo desagradable o poniéndole en ridículo; **to twit with** reprender (*a uno*) recordando (*p.ej., un error o estupidez*)

twitch [twɪtʃ] *s* estirón repentino; crispadura; ligero temblor; acial (*instrumento para oprimir el hocico de las bestias para sujetarlas*); *va* arrancar; mover de un tirón; *vn* crisparse; temblar (*p.ej., los párpados*); dar un tirón

twitter [ˈtwɪtər] *s* gorjeo (*de los pájaros*); risita sofocada; excitación, inquietud; *vn* gorjear (*los pájaros*); reír sofocadamente; agitarse, temblar de inquietud

'twixt [twɪkst] *prep* (poet. & dial.) var. de **betwixt**

two [tu] *adj* dos; *s* dos; **in two** en dos; **to put two and two together** atar cabos, sacar la conclusión evidente; **two o'clock** las dos; **two of a kind** tal para cual

two-bagger [ˈtuˌbægər] *s* (baseball) doblete (*golpe con que el bateador gana la segunda base*)

two-base hit [ˈtuˌbes] *s* var. de **two-bagger**

two-by-four [ˈtubaɪˌfor] *adj* de dos por cuatro (*pulgadas, pies, etc.*); (coll.) pequeño, insignificante; *s* madero de dos por cuatro pulgadas

two-cycle [ˈtuˌsaɪkəl] *adj* (mach.) de dos tiempos; *s* (mach.) ciclo de dos tiempos

two-cylinder [ˈtuˌsɪlɪndər] *adj* (mach.) de dos cilindros, bicilíndrico; **a two-cylinder motor** un dos cilindros

two-edged [ˈtuˌɛdʒd] *adj* de dos filos

two-faced [ˈtuˌfest] *adj* de dos caras; (fig.) de dos caras (*doble, falso*)

two-fisted [ˈtuˌfɪstɪd] *adj* de dos puños; (coll.) fuerte, vigoroso, valiente

two-fold [ˈtuˌfold] *adj* doble; *adv* dos veces

two-four [ˈtuˈfor] *adj* (mus.) de dos por cuatro

two-handed [ˈtuˌhændɪd] *adj* de dos manos; para dos manos; ambidextro

two hundred *adj & s* doscientos

two-part [ˈtuˌpɑrt] *adj* de dos partes

two-part time *s* (mus.) compás a dos tiempos

twopence [ˈtʌpəns] *s* dos peniques; moneda de dos peniques

two-penny [ˈtʌpənɪ] *adj* de dos peniques; despreciable, sin valor

two-phase [ˈtuˌfez] *adj* (elec.) bifásico

two-ply [ˈtuˌplaɪ] *adj* de dos capas; de dos tramas; de dos hilos o hebras

twosome [ˈtusəm] *s* pareja; pareja de jugadores; juego de dos

two-step [ˈtuˌstɛp] *s* paso doble (*baile y música*)

two-stroke cycle [ˈtuˌstrok] *s* (mach.) ciclo de dos tiempos

two-time [ˈtuˌtaɪm] *va* (slang) engañar en amor, ser infiel a (*una persona del otro sexo*)

'twould [twʊd] contracción de **it would**

two-way [ˈtuˌwe] *adj* de dos sentidos o direcciones

two-way radio *s* equipo emisor y receptor, aparato receptor y transmisor

two-way switch *s* (elec.) cada uno de dos conmutadores de tres terminales

two-way valve *s* (mach.) válvula de dos pasos

two-wire [ˈtuˌwaɪr] *adj* (elec.) bifilar

tycoon [taɪˈkun] *s* taicún (*señor feudal del Japón*); (coll.) magnate

tying [ˈtaɪɪŋ] *ger de* **tie**

tyke [taɪk] *s* (coll.) chiquillo, niño travieso; perro, gozque; (archaic & dial.) patán

tympan [ˈtɪmpən] *s* tambor; (arch.) tímpano; (print.) tímpano

tympanic [tɪmˈpænɪk] *adj* (anat. & med.) timpánico

tympanic antrum *s* (anat.) antro timpánico

tympanic membrane *s* (anat.) membrana timpánica

tympanist [ˈtɪmpənɪst] *s* atabalero

tympanites [ˌtɪmpəˈnaɪtiz] *s* (path.) timpanitis (*hinchazón producida por gases*)

tympanitic [ˌtɪmpəˈnɪtɪk] *adj* timpanítico

tympanitis [ˌtɪmpəˈnaɪtɪs] *s* (path.) timpanitis (*inflamación del tímpano del oído*)

tympanum [ˈtɪmpənəm] *s* (*pl:* **-nums** o **-na** [nə]) (arch. & anat.) tímpano

type [taɪp] *s* tipo; (print.) tipo; (print.) letra (*conjunto de letras o tipos*); letras impresas, letras escritas a máquina; tipo (*figura de una moneda o medalla*); (physiol.) grupo; *va* escribir a máquina, mecanografiar; imprimir; representar, simbolizar; (med.) determinar el grupo de (*un espécimen de sangre*); *vn* escribir a máquina

type bar *s* línea de linotipia; palanca portatipos (*de la máquina de escribir*)

type face *s* forma de letra, estilo de letra

type founder *s* fundidor de letra

type founding *s* fundición de letras de imprenta

type gauge *s* tipómetro

type genus *s* (biol.) género tipo

type metal *s* metal de imprenta

typescript [ˈtaɪpˌskrɪpt] *s* material escrito a máquina

typesetter [ˈtaɪpˌsɛtər] *s* (print.) cajista; (print.) máquina de componer

typesetting [ˈtaɪpˌsɛtɪŋ] *s* (print.) composición; *adj* (print.) para componer tipos

typewrite [ˈtaɪpˌraɪt] (*pret:* **-wrote;** *pp:* **-written**) *va & vn* escribir a máquina, mecanografiar

typewriter [ˈtaɪpˌraɪtər] *s* máquina de escribir; mecanógrafo o mecanógrafa, dactilógrafo o dactilógrafa

typewriter ribbon *s* cinta para máquinas de escribir

typewriting [ˈtaɪpˌraɪtɪŋ] *s* mecanografía o dactilografía; trabajo hecho con máquina de escribir

typewritten [ˈtaɪpˌrɪtən] *adj* escrito a máquina; *pp de* **typewrite**

typewrote [ˈtaɪpˌrot] *pret de* **typewrite**

typhoid [ˈtaɪfɔɪd] *adj* tifoideo; *s* (path.) fiebre tifoidea

typhoidal [taɪˈfɔɪdəl] *adj* tifoideo

typhoid bacillus *s* (bact.) bacilo tífico

typhoid fever (path.) fiebre tifoidea

typhoon [taɪˈfun] *s* tifón

typhous [ˈtaɪfəs] *adj* tífico

typhus [ˈtaɪfəs] *s* (path.) tifus

typical [ˈtɪpɪkəl] *adj* típico

typically [ˈtɪpɪkəlɪ] *adv* típicamente

typification [ˌtɪpɪfɪˈkeʃən] *s* simbolización

typify [ˈtɪpɪfaɪ] (*pret & pp:* **-fied**) *va* simbolizar; ser ejemplo o modelo de

typing [ˈtaɪpɪŋ] *s* mecanografía o dactilografía; trabajo hecho con máquina de escribir

typist [ˈtaɪpɪst] *s* mecanógrafo o mecanógrafa, dactilógrafo o dactilógrafa

typographer [taɪˈpɑgrəfər] *s* tipógrafo

typographic [ˌtaɪpəˈgræfɪk] o **typographical** [ˌtaɪpəˈgræfɪkəl] *adj* tipográfico

typographical error *s* error de máquina

typographically [ˌtaɪpəˈgræfɪkəlɪ] *adv* tipográficamente

typography [taɪˈpɑgrəfɪ] *s* tipografía

typolithography [ˌtaɪpəlɪˈθɑgrəfɪ] *s* tipolitografía

typometry [taɪˈpɑmɪtrɪ] *s* (print.) tipometría

tyrannic [tɪˈrænɪk] o [taɪˈrænɪk] o **tyrannical** [tɪˈrænɪkəl] o [taɪˈrænɪkəl] *adj* tiránico

tyrannicidal [tɪˌrænɪˈsaɪdəl] *adj* tiranicida

tyrannicide [tɪˈrænɪsaɪd] o [taɪˈrænɪsaɪd] *s* tiranicidio (*acción*); tiranicida (*persona*)

tyrannize [ˈtɪrənaɪz] *va & vn* tiranizar

tyrannous [ˈtɪrənəs] *adj* tirano

tyranny [ˈtɪrənɪ] *s* (*pl:* **-nies**) tiranía

tyrant [ˈtaɪrənt] *s* tirano

Tyre [taɪr] *s* Tiro

Tyrian [ˈtɪrɪən] *adj & s* tirio

Tyrian purple *s* púrpura de Tiro

tyro [ˈtaɪro] *s* (*pl:* **-ros**) tirón, novicio
Tyrol, the [tɪˈrol] o [ˈtɪrɑl] el Tirol
Tyrolean [tɪˈrolɪən] *adj & s* var. de **Tyrolese**
Tyrolese [ˌtɪroˈliz] *adj* tirolés; *s* (*pl:* **-lese**) tirolés
tyrosinase [ˈtaɪrosɪˌnes] o [ˈtɪrosɪˌnes] *s* (biochem.) tirosinasa
tyrosine [ˈtaɪrəsin] o [ˈtɪrəsin] *s* (biochem.) tirosina
tyrothricin [ˌtaɪrəˈθraɪsɪn] o [ˌtaɪrəˈθrɪsɪn] *s* (pharm.) tirotricina
Tyrrhenian [tɪˈrinɪən] *adj* tirreno
Tyrrhenian Sea *s* mar Tirreno
tzar [tsɑr] *s* var. de **czar**
tzarevitch [ˈtsɑrɪvɪtʃ] *s* var. de **czarevitch**
tzarina [tsɑˈrinə] *s* var. de **czarina**
tzetze [ˈtsɛtsɪ] *s* var. de **tsetse**
tzigane [ˌtsiˈgɑn] *adj & s* gitano (*de Hungría*)

U

U, u [ju] *s* (*pl:* **U's, u's** [juz]) vigésima primera letra del alfabeto inglés
U. abr. de **University**
Ubiquitarian [ju,bɪkwɪ'tɛrɪən] *adj & s* (eccl.) ubiquitario
ubiquitous [ju'bɪkwɪtəs] *adj* ubicuo
ubiquity [ju'bɪkwɪtɪ] *s* ubicuidad
U-boat ['ju,bot] *s* submarino, submarino alemán
U bolt *s* perno en U
u.c. abr. de **upper case**
udder ['ʌdər] *s* ubre
udometer [ju'dɑmɪtər] *s* udómetro
ugh [ʊ] o [ʌ] *interj* ¡puf!, ¡buf!
ugliness ['ʌglɪnɪs] *s* fealdad; (coll.) malhumor
ugly ['ʌglɪ] *adj* (*comp:* **-lier;** *super:* **-liest**) feo; (coll.) malhumorado, pendenciero
ugly duckling *s* niño poco prometedor que sale un adulto interesante; **the Ugly Duckling** el Patito Feo
UHF abr. de **ultrahigh frequency**
uhlan ['ulɑn] o [u'lɑn] *s* (mil.) ulano
U.K. abr. de **United Kingdom**
ukase [ju'kes] *s* ucase
Ukraine ['jukren] o [ju'kren] *s* Ucrania
Ukrainian [ju'krenɪən] *adj & s* ucranio
ulcer ['ʌlsər] *s* (path.) úlcera; (fig.) llaga
ulcerate ['ʌlsəret] *va* ulcerar; *vn* ulcerarse
ulceration [,ʌlsə'reʃən] *s* ulceración
ulcerous ['ʌlsərəs] *adj* ulceroso
ulema [,ulə'mɑ] *s* ulema
uliginose [ju'lɪdʒɪnos] o **uliginous** [ju'lɪdʒɪnəs] *adj* uliginoso
ulitis [ju'laɪtɪs] *s* (path.) ulitis
ulluco [u'juko] *s* (bot.) ulluco (*tubérculo comestible de Sudamérica semejante a la patata*)
ulmaceous [ʌl'meʃəs] *adj* (bot.) ulmáceo
ulna ['ʌlnə] *s* (*pl:* **-nae** [ni] o **-nas**) (anat.) ulna
ulnar ['ʌlnər] *adj* ulnar
ulster ['ʌlstər] *s* úlster
ult. abr. de **ultimo** (Lat.) **in the past month**
ulterior [ʌl'tɪrɪər] *adj* ulterior; escondido, oculto
ultima ['ʌltɪmə] *s* (gram.) última sílaba
ultimate ['ʌltɪmɪt] *adj* último, final; fundamental, esencial; sumo, extremo
ultimately ['ʌltɪmɪtlɪ] *adv* últimamente, por último
ultima Thule *s* última Tule
ultimatum [,ʌltɪ'metəm] *s* (*pl:* **-tums** o **-ta** [tə]) ultimátum
ultimo ['ʌltɪmo] *adv* del mes próximo pasado, en el mes próximo pasado
ultra ['ʌltrə] *s* ultraísta, extremista; *adj* extremo, excesivo; *prep* ultra
ultrahigh frequency [,ʌltrə'haɪ] *s* (rad.) frecuencia ultraelevada
ultraliberal [,ʌltrə'lɪbərəl] *adj & s* ultraliberal
ultramarine [,ʌltrəmə'rin] *adj* ultramarino; *s* ultramar, azul de ultramar, azul ultramarino
ultramarine blue *s* azul de ultramar, azul ultramarino
ultramicroscope [,ʌltrə'maɪkrəskop] *s* ultramicroscopio
ultramicroscopic [,ʌltrə,maɪkrə'skɑpɪk] *adj* ultramicroscópico
ultramicroscopy [,ʌltrəmaɪ'krɑskəpɪ] o [,ʌltrə'maɪkrə,skopɪ] *s* ultramicroscopia
ultramodern [,ʌltrə'mɑdərn] *adj* ultramoderno
ultramontane [,ʌltrə'mɑnten] *adj & s* ultramontano
ultramontanism [,ʌltrə'mɑntənɪzəm] *s* ultramontanismo
ultramundane [,ʌltrə'mʌnden] *adj* ultramundano
ultraradical [,ʌltrə'rædɪkəl] *adj* ultrarradical
ultrarapid [,ʌltrə'ræpɪd] *adj* ultrarrápido
ultrared [,ʌltrə'rɛd] *adj* ultrarrojo
ultrasonic [,ʌltrə'sɑnɪk] *adj* ultrasónico; **ultrasonics** *ssg* ultrasónica
ultratropical [,ʌltrə'trɑpɪkəl] *adj* ultratropical
ultraviolet [,ʌltrə'vaɪəlɪt] *adj* (phys.) ultraviolado o ultravioleta
ultraviolet rays *spl* (phys.) rayos ultravioletas
ultravirus [,ʌltrə'vaɪrəs] *s* ultravirus
ultrazodiacal [,ʌltrəzo'daɪəkəl] *adj* (astr.) ultrazodiacal
ululant ['juljələnt] o ['ʌljələnt] *adj* ululante
ululate ['juljəlet] o ['ʌljəlet] *vn* ulular
ululation [,juljə'leʃən] o [,ʌljə'leʃən] *s* ululación
Ulysses [jʊ'lɪsiz] *s* (myth.) Ulises
umbel ['ʌmbəl] *s* (bot.) umbela
umbellar ['ʌmbələr] o **umbellate** ['ʌmbəlet] *adj* umbelado, umbeliforme
umbelliferous [,ʌmbə'lɪfərəs] *adj* umbelífero
umber ['ʌmbər] *s* tierra de sombra; *adj* de color ocre obscuro
umbilical [ʌm'bɪlɪkəl] *adj* umbilical
umbilical cord *s* (anat.) cordón umbilical
umbilicate [ʌm'bɪlɪkɪt] *adj* umbilicado
umbilicus [ʌm'bɪlɪkəs] o [,ʌmbɪ'laɪkəs] *s* (*pl:* **-ci** [saɪ]) (anat.) ombligo
umbo ['ʌmbo] *s* (*pl:* **umbones** [ʌm'boniz] o **umbos**) umbón (*del escudo*); (anat. & zool.) umbo
umbra ['ʌmbrə] *s* (*pl:* **-brae** [bri]) sombra; (astr.) región sombra, cono de sombra; (astr.) núcleo (*de las manchas solares*); (ichth.) ombrina, ombrina barbuda
umbrage ['ʌmbrɪdʒ] *s* sombra, umbría; resentimiento; **to take umbrage at** resentirse por
umbrageous [ʌm'bredʒəs] *adj* umbroso, sombroso; resentido
umbra tree *s* (bot.) ombú
umbrella [ʌm'brɛlə] *s* paraguas; (zool.) umbrela; (mil.) sombrilla protectora
umbrella man *s* paragüero
umbrella stand *s* paragüero
umbrella tree *s* (bot.) magnolia tripétala
Umbria ['ʌmbrɪə] *s* la Umbría
Umbrian ['ʌmbrɪən] *adj & s* umbro
umiak ['umɪæk] *s* barca de la mujer (*de los esquimales*)
umlaut ['ʊmlaʊt] *s* (phonet.) metafonía; diéresis; *va* modificar por metafonía; escribir con diéresis
umpire ['ʌmpaɪr] *s* árbitro; (sport) árbitro; *va & vn* arbitrar; (sport) arbitrar
UMT abr. de **Universal Military Training**
un- *prefix* in-, p.ej., **uncertain** incierto; **unhappy** infeliz; **unheard-of** inaudito; des-, p.ej., **unequal** desigual; **unfortunate** desgraciado; **unbutton** desabotonar; **unhook** desenganchar; anti-, p.ej., **uneconomic** antieconómico; **unscientific** anticientífico; **unsportsmanlike** antideportivo; poco, p.ej., **unintelligent** poco inteligente
UN ['ju'ɛn] *s* ONU (*organización de las Naciones Unidas*)
unabashed [,ʌnə'bæʃt] *adj* desvergonzado
unable [ʌn'ebəl] *adj* incapaz, inhábil; imposibilitado; **to be unable to** + *inf* no poder + *inf;* **to be unable to make up one's mind** no acabar de decidirse
unabridged [,ʌnə'brɪdʒd] *adj* no abreviado, íntegro, completo
unaccented [ʌn'æksɛntɪd] o [,ʌnæk'sɛntɪd] *adj* inacentuado
unacceptable [,ʌnæk'sɛptəbəl] *adj* inaceptable
unaccompanied [,ʌnə'kʌmpənɪd] *adj* sin acompañamiento

unaccountable [ˌʌnəˈkaʊntəbəl] *adj* inexplicable; irresponsable
unaccountably [ˌʌnəˈkaʊntəblɪ] *adv* inexplicablemente; irresponsablemente
unaccounted-for [ˌʌnəˈkaʊntɪdˌfɔr] *adj* no explicado; no hallado
unaccustomed [ˌʌnəˈkʌstəmd] *adj* no acostumbrado; desacostumbrado
unadaptability [ˌʌnəˌdæptəˈbɪlɪtɪ] *s* inadaptabilidad
unadaptable [ˌʌnəˈdæptəbəl] *adj* inadaptable
unadoptable [ˌʌnəˈdɑptəbəl] *adj* inadoptable
unadulterated [ˌʌnəˈdʌltəˌretɪd] *adj* no adulterado, puro
unadvised [ˌʌnədˈvaɪzd] *adj* desaconsejado, desatentado
unadvisedly [ˌʌnədˈvaɪzɪdlɪ] *adv* inconsideradamente, imprudentemente
unaffected [ˌʌnəˈfɛktɪd] *adj* inafectado
unafraid [ˌʌnəˈfred] *adj* desaprensivo, sin miedo
unaligned [ˌʌnəˈlaɪnd] *adj* no comprometido, no empeñado
unallowable [ˌʌnəˈlaʊəbəl] *adj* inadmisible
unalterability [ʌnˌɔltərəˈbɪlɪtɪ] *s* inalterabilidad
unalterable [ʌnˈɔltərəbəl] *adj* inalterable
unalterably [ʌnˈɔltərəblɪ] *adv* inalterablemente
unaltered [ʌnˈɔltərd] *adj* inalterado
unambiguous [ˌʌnæmˈbɪgjʊəs] *adj* inequívoco
un-American [ˌʌnəˈmɛrɪkən] *adj* antiamericano, antinorteamericano
unanalyzable [ʌnˈænəˌlaɪzəbəl] *adj* inanalizable
unanimism [jʊˈnænɪmɪzəm] *s* unanimismo
unanimity [ˌjunəˈnɪmɪtɪ] *s* unanimidad
unanimous [jʊˈnænɪməs] *adj* unánime
unanswerable [ʌnˈænsərəbəl] o [ʌnˈɑnsərəbəl] *adj* incontestable
unanswered [ʌnˈænsərd] o [ʌnˈɑnsərd] *adj* por contestar; no correspondido
unappealable [ˌʌnəˈpiləbəl] *adj* inapelable
unappetizing [ʌnˈæpɪˌtaɪzɪŋ] *adj* poco apetitoso
unappreciative [ˌʌnəˈpriʃɪˌetɪv] *adj* ingrato, desagradecido
unapprehensive [ʌnˌæprɪˈhɛnsɪv] *adj* desaprensivo
unapproachable [ˌʌnəˈprotʃəbəl] *adj* inaccesible, inabordable; sin igual
unapt [ʌnˈæpt] *adj* inepto, inhábil; improbable; inadecuado
unarm [ʌnˈɑrm] *va* desarmar
unarmed [ʌnˈɑrmd] *adj* desarmado, inerme; (biol.) inerme
unascertainable [ʌnˌæsərˈtenəbəl] *adj* inaveriguable
unasked [ʌnˈæskt] o [ʌnˈɑskt] *adj* no solicitado; sin pedir; no convidado
unassembled [ˌʌnəˈsɛmbəld] *adj* desarmado, desmontado
unassimilable [ˌʌnəˈsɪmɪləbəl] *adj* inasimilable
unassuming [ˌʌnəˈsumɪŋ] o [ˌʌnəˈsjumɪŋ] *adj* modesto, sin pretensiones
unattached [ˌʌnəˈtætʃt] *adj* suelto; libre; no prometido; (law) no embargado; (mil. & nav.) de reemplazo
unattainable [ˌʌnəˈtenəbəl] *adj* inasequible, inalcanzable
unattended [ˌʌnəˈtɛndɪd] *adj* desatendido; inasistido
unattractive [ˌʌnəˈtræktɪv] *adj* sin atractivo, desairado
unauthorized [ʌnˈɔθəraɪzd] *adj* desautorizado
unavailable [ˌʌnəˈveləbəl] *adj* indisponible
unavailing [ˌʌnəˈvelɪŋ] *adj* vano, inútil, ineficaz
unavoidable [ˌʌnəˈvɔɪdəbəl] *adj* inevitable
unaware [ˌʌnəˈwɛr] *adj* inconsciente; **to be unaware of** estar ajeno de; *adv* de improviso; sin saberlo
unawares [ˌʌnəˈwɛrz] *adv* de improviso; sin saberlo; **to catch somebody unawares** coger a una persona desprevenida
unbacked [ʌnˈbækt] *adj* sin ayuda; sin respaldo; sin domar; sin apuesta
unbaked [ʌnˈbekt] *adj* no cocido; no maduro
unbalance [ʌnˈbæləns] *s* desequilibrio; *va* desequilibrar; trastornar
unbalanced [ʌnˈbælənst] *adj* desequilibrado; (fig.) desequilibrado
unbandage [ʌnˈbændɪdʒ] *va* desvendar
unbar [ʌnˈbɑr] (*pret & pp:* **-barred;** *ger:* **-barring**) *va* desatrancar
unbearable [ʌnˈbɛrəbəl] *adj* inaguantable, intolerable
unbearably [ʌnˈbɛrəblɪ] *adv* inaguantablemente, intolerablemente
unbeatable [ʌnˈbitəbəl] *adj* imbatible
unbeaten [ʌnˈbitən] *adj* no batido; no pisado, no trillado; invicto, insuperado, imbatido
unbecoming [ˌʌnbɪˈkʌmɪŋ] *adj* impropio, indecoroso; que sienta mal
unbeknown [ˌʌnbɪˈnon] *adj* (coll.) no sabido, no conocido; **unbeknown to me** (coll.) sin saberlo yo
unbelief [ˌʌnbɪˈlif] *s* descreimiento
unbeliever [ˌʌnbɪˈlivər] *s* descreído
unbelieving [ˌʌnbɪˈlivɪŋ] *adj* descreído
unbelt [ʌnˈbɛlt] *va* desceñir
unbend [ʌnˈbɛnd] (*pret & pp:* **-bent** o **-bended**) *va* enderezar, desencorvar; aflojar, soltar; (naut.) desenvergar; *vn* enderezarse; suavizarse, ponerse afable
unbending [ʌnˈbɛndɪŋ] *adj* inflexible, inconquistable, poco afable
unbent [ʌnˈbɛnt] *pret & pp de* **unbend**
unbiased o **unbiassed** [ʌnˈbaɪəst] *adj* imparcial, despreocupado
unbidden [ʌnˈbɪdən] *adj* no convidado; espontáneo
unbind [ʌnˈbaɪnd] (*pret & pp:* **-bound**) *va* desatar
unbleached [ʌnˈblitʃt] *adj* crudo, sin blanquear
unblessed o **unblest** [ʌnˈblɛst] *adj* no bendecido; maldito; desgraciado; malo, infame
unblushing [ʌnˈblʌʃɪŋ] *adj* desvergonzado
unbodied [ʌnˈbɑdɪd] *adj* incorpóreo
unbolt [ʌnˈbolt] *va* desempernar; desatrancar
unbolted [ʌnˈboltɪd] *adj* desatrancado; sin cerner
unbonnet [ʌnˈbɑnɪt] *va* quitar el bonete o el sombrero a; *vn* descubrirse
unbonneted [ʌnˈbɑnɪtɪd] *adj* sin bonete, sin sombrero
unborn [ʌnˈbɔrn] *adj* no nacido aún, venidero, futuro
unbosom [ʌnˈbuzəm] *va* confesar; **to unbosom oneself** desahogarse, abrir su pecho; **to unbosom oneself of** desahogarse de; *vn* desahogarse, abrir su pecho
unbound [ʌnˈbaʊnd] *adj* desatado, suelto, libre; (b.b.) sin encuadernar; *pret & pp de* **unbind**
unbounded [ʌnˈbaʊndɪd] *adj* ilimitado; desenfrenado
unbowed [ʌnˈbaʊd] *adj* no inclinado; no domado
unbraid [ʌnˈbred] *va* destrenzar, destejer
unbreakable [ʌnˈbrekəbəl] *adj* irrompible
unbred [ʌnˈbrɛd] *adj* malcriado
unbridle [ʌnˈbraɪdəl] *va* desembridar
unbridled [ʌnˈbraɪdəld] *adj* desembridado; desenfrenado
unbroken [ʌnˈbrokən] *adj* intacto, entero; no interrumpido; no adiestrado, no domado, cerrero
unbuckle [ʌnˈbʌkəl] *va* deshebillar; desatar
unburden [ʌnˈbʌrdən] *va* descargar; aliviar; **to unburden oneself of** aliviarse de; desahogarse de
unburied [ʌnˈbɛrɪd] *adj* insepulto
unburned [ʌnˈbʌrnd] o **unburnt** [ʌnˈbʌrnt] *adj* incombusto
unbusinesslike [ʌnˈbɪznɪsˌlaɪk] *adj* poco práctico, descuidado
unbutton [ʌnˈbʌtən] *va* desabotonar
uncage [ʌnˈkedʒ] *va* sacar de la jaula; libertar
uncalled-for [ʌnˈkɔldˌfɔr] *adj* no buscado; gratuito, inmerecido; insolente
uncanceled [ʌnˈkænsəld] *adj* sin cancelar (*dícese de los sellos de correo*)
uncanny [ʌnˈkænɪ] *adj* misterioso, espectral; fantástico
uncap [ʌnˈkæp] (*pret & pp:* **-capped;** *ger:* **-capping**) *va* destapar; *vn* descubrirse
uncared-for [ʌnˈkɛrdˌfɔr] *adj* abandonado, descuidado, desamparado
unceasing [ʌnˈsisɪŋ] *adj* incesante

unceremonious [ˌʌnsɛrɪˈmonɪəs] *adj* inceremonioso
uncertain [ʌnˈsʌrtən] *adj* incierto
uncertainty [ʌnˈsʌrtəntɪ] *s* (*pl:* **-ties**) incertidumbre
unchain [ʌnˈtʃen] *va* desencadenar
unchangeable [ʌnˈtʃendʒəbəl] *adj* incambiable
uncharitable [ʌnˈtʃærɪtəbəl] *adj* poco caritativo, duro
uncharted [ʌnˈtʃartɪd] *adj* inexplorado
unchaste [ʌnˈtʃest] *adj* incasto
unchastity [ʌnˈtʃæstɪtɪ] *s* incontinencia
unchecked [ʌnˈtʃɛkt] *adj* no verificado; no refrenado, inestorbado; desenfrenado
unchristian [ʌnˈkrɪstʃən] *adj* no cristiano; anticristiano; impropio, indecoroso
unchurch [ʌnˈtʃʌrtʃ] *va* expulsar de la iglesia, excomulgar
uncial [ˈʌnʃɪəl] o [ˈʌnʃəl] *adj & s* uncial
unciform [ˈʌnsɪfɔrm] *adj* unciforme; *s* (anat.) unciforme
uncinate [ˈʌnsɪnet] *adj* uncinado
uncircumcised [ʌnˈsʌrkəmsaɪzd] *adj* incircunciso
uncircumscribed [ʌnˈsʌrkəmskraɪbd] *adj* incircunscripto
uncivil [ʌnˈsɪvɪl] *adj* incivil
uncivilized [ʌnˈsɪvɪlaɪzd] *adj* incivilizado, inculto
unclad [ʌnˈklæd] *adj* no vestido, desnudo
unclaimed [ʌnˈklemd] *adj* sin reclamar
unclaimed letter *s* carta rechazada, carta sobrante
unclasp [ʌnˈklæsp] o [ʌnˈklɑsp] *va* desabrochar; *vn* desabrocharse
unclassifiable [ʌnˈklæsɪˌfaɪəbəl] *adj* inclasificable
unclassified [ʌnˈklæsɪfaɪd] *adj* no clasificado; no clasificado como secreto
uncle [ˈʌŋkəl] *s* tío; (coll.) tío (*hombre entrado en edad*); (slang) prestamista
unclean [ʌnˈklin] *adj* sucio
uncleanly [ʌnˈklɛnlɪ] *adj* (*comp:* **-lier**; *super:* **-liest**) sucio; [ʌnˈklinlɪ] *adv* suciamente
uncleanness [ʌnˈklinnɪs] *s* suciedad
unclench [ʌnˈklɛntʃ] *va* desasir, desagarrar, soltar
Uncle Sam *s* el tío Sam
uncloak [ʌnˈklok] *va* desencapotar; *vn* desencapotarse
unclog [ʌnˈklɑg] (*pret & pp:* **-clogged**; *ger:* **-clogging**) *va* desatrancar, desatancar
unclose [ʌnˈkloz] *va* desencerrar
unclothe [ʌnˈkloð] *va* desarropar
unclouded [ʌnˈklaudɪd] *adj* despejado, sin nubes
uncoated [ʌnˈkotɪd] *adj* sin capa (*p.ej., de pintura*)
uncoil [ʌnˈkɔɪl] *va* desarrollar, desenrollar
uncollectible [ˌʌnkəˈlɛktɪbəl] *adj* incobrable
uncombed [ʌnˈkomd] *adj* despeinado
uncomfortable [ʌnˈkʌmfərtəbəl] *adj* incómodo; con malestar
uncommercial [ˌʌnkəˈmʌrʃəl] *adj* no comercial; no comerciante
uncommitted [ˌʌnkəˈmɪtɪd] *adj* no cometido; no comprometido, no empeñado
uncommon [ʌnˈkɑmən] *adj* poco común, raro
uncommonly [ʌnˈkɑmənlɪ] *adv* raramente; extraordinariamente
uncommunicative [ˌʌnkəˈmjunɪˌketɪv] *adj* poco comunicativo, inconversable
uncompromising [ʌnˈkɑmprəˌmaɪzɪŋ] *adj* inflexible, intransigente
unconcern [ˌʌnkənˈsʌrn] *s* indiferencia, despreocupación
unconcerned [ˌʌnkənˈsʌrnd] *adj* indiferente, despreocupado
unconcernedly [ˌʌnkənˈsʌrnɪdlɪ] *adv* indiferentemente, sin preocuparse
unconditional [ˌʌnkənˈdɪʃənəl] *adj* incondicional
unconditionally [ˌʌnkənˈdɪʃənəlɪ] *adv* incondicionalmente
unconditioned [ˌʌnkənˈdɪʃənd] *adj* incondicional; natural, no adquirido
unconducive [ˌʌnkənˈdjusɪv] o [ˌʌnkənˈdusɪv] *adj* inconducente
unconfessed [ˌʌnkənˈfɛst] *adj* inconfeso
unconformity [ˌʌnkənˈfɔrmɪtɪ] *s* (*pl:* **-ties**) disconformidad
uncongealable [ˌʌnkənˈdʒiləbəl] *adj* incongelable
uncongealed [ˌʌnkənˈdʒild] *adj* incongelado
uncongenial [ˌʌnkənˈdʒinɪəl] *adj* antipático; incompatible; desagradable
uncongeniality [ˌʌnkənˌdʒinɪˈælɪtɪ] *s* antipatía; incompatibilidad; desagrado
unconnected [ˌʌnkəˈnɛktɪd] *adj* inconexo; desconectado
unconquerable [ʌnˈkɑŋkərəbəl] *adj* inconquistable
unconquered [ʌnˈkɑŋkərd] *adj* invicto
unconscionable [ʌnˈkɑnʃənəbəl] *adj* desrazonable, desmedido, excesivo, inmoral
unconscionably [ʌnˈkɑnʃənəblɪ] *adv* desrazonablemente, desmedidamente, con exceso, inmoralmente
unconscious [ʌnˈkɑnʃəs] *adj* inconsciente; desmayado; ignorante; no intencional; **the unconscious** lo inconsciente
unconsciousness [ʌnˈkɑnʃəsnɪs] *s* inconsciencia
unconstitutional [ˌʌnkɑnstɪˈtjuʃənəl] o [ˌʌnkɑnstɪˈtuʃənəl] *adj* inconstitucional
unconstitutionality [ˌʌnkɑnstɪˌtjuʃənˈælɪtɪ] o [ˌʌnkɑnstɪˌtuʃənˈælɪtɪ] *s* inconstitucionalidad
uncontaminated [ˌʌnkənˈtæmɪˌnetɪd] *adj* incontaminado
uncontrollable [ˌʌnkənˈtroləbəl] *adj* ingobernable
uncontrolled [ˌʌnkənˈtrold] *adj* incontrolado
unconventional [ˌʌnkənˈvɛnʃənəl] *adj* informal, despreocupado, original
unconventionality [ˌʌnkənˌvɛnʃənˈælɪtɪ] *s* informalidad, despreocupación, originalidad
uncooked [ʌnˈkukt] *adj* crudo, sin cocer
uncork [ʌnˈkɔrk] *va* destapar, descorchar
uncorrupted [ˌʌnkəˈrʌptɪd] *adj* incorrupto
uncountable [ʌnˈkauntəbəl] *adj* incontable
uncounted [ʌnˈkauntɪd] *adj* no contado; innumerable
uncouple [ʌnˈkʌpəl] *va* desatraillar (*los perros*); desacoplar, desenganchar; desaparejar
uncourteous [ʌnˈkʌrtɪəs] *adj* descortés
uncourtly [ʌnˈkortlɪ] *adj* grosero, rústico, inurbano
uncouth [ʌnˈkuθ] *adj* tosco, rústico; extraño, raro
uncover [ʌnˈkʌvər] *va* descubrir; *vn* descubrirse (*quitarse el sombrero*)
uncreated [ˌʌnkriˈetɪd] *adj* increado
uncrown [ʌnˈkraun] *va* destronar
uncrowned [ʌnˈkraund] *adj* sin corona
unction [ˈʌŋkʃən] *s* unción; efusión o entusiasmo poco sinceros, fervor fingido
unctuous [ˈʌŋktʃuəs] *adj* untuoso; (fig.) zalamero
uncultivated [ʌnˈkʌltɪˌvetɪd] *adj* inculto (*no cultivado; tosco, rústico*)
uncultured [ʌnˈkʌltʃərd] *adj* inculto (*tosco, rústico*)
uncurl [ʌnˈkʌrl] *va* desrizar; *vn* desrizarse
uncut [ʌnˈkʌt] *adj* sin cortar; sin labrar; intonso (*libro o revista*)
undamaged [ʌnˈdæmɪdʒd] *adj* indemne, ileso, intacto
undamped [ʌnˈdæmpt] *adj* no humedecido; no refrenado; (phys.) no amortiguado
undated [ʌnˈdetɪd] *adj* sin fecha; sin acontecimientos notables
undaunted [ʌnˈdɔntɪd] *adj* impávido, denodado
undecagon [ʌnˈdɛkəgɑn] *s* (geom.) undecágono, endecágono
undeceive [ˌʌndɪˈsiv] *va* desengañar
undecided [ˌʌndɪˈsaɪdɪd] *adj* indeciso
undeclinable [ˌʌndɪˈklaɪnəbəl] *adj* indeclinable; (gram.) indeclinable
undefeated [ˌʌndɪˈfitɪd] *adj* invicto
undefended [ˌʌndɪˈfɛndɪd] *adj* indefenso
undefensible [ˌʌndɪˈfɛnsɪbəl] *adj* indefendible
undefiled [ˌʌndɪˈfaɪld] *adj* impoluto, inmaculado
undefinable [ˌʌndɪˈfaɪnəbəl] *adj* indefinible
undefined [ˌʌndɪˈfaɪnd] *adj* indefinido
undelivered [ˌʌndɪˈlɪvərd] *adj* sin entregar

undelivered letter *s* carta rechazada, carta sobrante
undemonstrable [ˌʌndɪˈmɑnstrəbəl] o [ʌnˈdemənstrəbəl] *adj* indemostrable
undemonstrative [ˌʌndɪˈmɑnstrətɪv] *adj* reservado, callado, poco expresivo
undeniable [ˌʌndɪˈnaɪəbəl] *adj* innegable, inconcuso; excelentísimo
undeniably [ˌʌndɪˈnaɪəblɪ] *adv* innegablemente
undenominational [ˌʌndɪˌnɑmɪˈneʃənəl] *adj* no sectario
undependable [ˌʌndɪˈpendəbəl] *adj* no confiable
under- *prefix* sub-, p.ej., **underdeveloped** subdesarrollado; **underlying** subyacente; infra-, p.ej., **underconsumption** infraconsumo; **underworld** inframundo; des-, p.ej., **underfed** desnutrido; menos-, p.ej., **underrate** menospreciar; bajo, p.ej., **underneath** parte baja; inferior, p.ej., **underpass** paso inferior
under [ˈʌndər] *adj* inferior; interior (*ropa*); *adv* debajo; más abajo; **to bring under** dominar, someter; **to go under** fracasar; hundirse; **to keep under** oprimir; *prep* bajo; debajo de; inferior a; **under arms** sobre las armas; **under full sail** (naut.) a vela llena; **under lock and key** bajo llave; **under oath** bajo juramento; **under penalty of death** so pena de muerte; **under sail** (naut.) a la vela; **under separate cover** bajo cubierta separada, por separado; **under steam** bajo presión; **under the hand and seal of** firmado y sellado por; **under the necessity of** en la necesidad de; **under one's nose** (coll.) en las barbas de uno; **under way** en camino; principiando
underage [ˈʌndərˌedʒ] *adj* menor de edad; no de la edad a propósito
underbid [ˌʌndərˈbɪd] (*pret & pp:* **-bid;** *ger:* **-bidding**) *va* ofrecer menos que
underbodice [ˈʌndərˌbɑdɪs] *s* cubrecorsé
underbred [ˌʌndərˈbred] *adj* de raza impura; vulgar, rudo
underbrush [ˈʌndərˌbrʌʃ] *s* maleza
undercarriage [ˈʌndərˌkærɪdʒ] *s* carro inferior; (aer.) tren de aterrizaje
undercharge [ˈʌndərˌtʃɑrdʒ] *s* cargo insuficiente, precio insuficiente; [ˌʌndərˈtʃɑrdʒ] *va* hacer pagar menos del valor, no cargar bastante en la cuenta a; cargar . . . de menos, p.ej., **you have undercharged me one dollar** me ha cargado Vd. un dólar de menos
underclassman [ˌʌndərˈklæsmən] o [ˌʌndərˈklɑsmən] *s* (*pl:* **-men**) alumno universitario de los dos primeros años
underclothes [ˈʌndərˌkloz] *spl* o **underclothing** [ˈʌndərˌkloðɪŋ] *s* ropa interior
undercoat [ˈʌndərˌkot] *s* chaqueta interior; pelaje corto; capa de fondo, primera mano (*de pintura*)
underconsumption [ˈʌndərkənˈsʌmpʃən] *s* infraconsumo
undercover [ˌʌndərˈkʌvər] *adj* secreto, confidencial
undercurrent [ˈʌndərˌkʌrənt] *s* corriente submarina, corriente subfluvial; (fig.) tendencia oculta, tendencia obscura
undercut [ˈʌndərˌkʌt] *adj* socavado; *s* socava, socavación; filete, solomillo; [ˌʌndərˈkʌt] (*pret & pp:* **-cut;** *ger:* **-cutting**) *va* socavar
underdevelop [ˌʌndərdɪˈveləp] *s* desarrollar incompletamente; (phot.) revelar incompletamente
underdeveloped countries [ˌʌndərdɪˈveləpt] *spl* países subdesarrollados
underdevelopment [ˌʌndərdɪˈveləpmənt] *s* desarrollo incompleto; (phot.) revelado incompleto
underdog [ˈʌndərˌdɔg] o [ˈʌndərˌdɑg] *s* perro perdedor; perdidoso, víctima; desvalido
underdone [ˈʌndərˌdʌn] o [ˌʌndərˈdʌn] *adj* soasado, a medio asar
underestimate [ˈʌndərˌestɪmɪt] *s* apreciación o estimación demasiado baja; presupuesto demasiado bajo; menosprecio; [ˌʌndərˈestɪmet] *va* avaluar o estimar en valor demasiado bajo; subestimar, menospreciar, tener (*a una persona o cosa*) en menos de lo que merece
underestimated [ˌʌndərˈestɪˌmetɪd] *adj* inestimado
underexpose [ˌʌndərekˈspoz] *va* (phot.) exponer insuficientemente
underexposure [ˌʌndərekˈspoʒər] *s* (phot.) subexposición
underfed [ˌʌndərˈfed] *pret & pp de* **underfeed**
underfeed [ˌʌndərˈfid] (*pret & pp:* **-fed**) *va* desnutrir
underfeeding [ˌʌndərˈfidɪŋ] *s* desnutrición
underfoot [ˌʌndərˈfʊt] *adj* debajo de los pies; en el suelo; (coll.) estorbando
undergarment [ˈʌndərˌgɑrmənt] *s* prenda de vestir interior
undergo [ˌʌndərˈgo] (*pret:* **-went;** *pp:* **-gone**) *va* experimentar, sufrir, padecer
undergraduate [ˌʌndərˈgrædʒʊɪt] *adj* no graduado; *s* alumno no graduado, estudiante del bachillerato
undergraduate course *s* asignatura o curso para el bachillerato
underground [ˈʌndərˈgraʊnd] *adj* subterráneo; clandestino; *adv* bajo tierra; clandestinamente; [ˈʌndərˌgraʊnd] *s* subterráneo; ferrocarril subterráneo; movimiento clandestino, fuerzas ocultas, resistencia
underground movement *s* movimiento oculto
underground railroad *s* ferrocarril subterráneo; (fig.) método clandestino de ayudar a los fugitivos
undergrowth [ˈʌndərˌgroθ] *s* maleza; pelaje corto
underhand [ˈʌndərˌhænd] *adj* taimado, socarrón, clandestino; (sport) hecho con las manos debajo de los hombros; *adv* taimadamente, socarronamente, clandestinamente; (sport) con las manos debajo de los hombros
underhanded [ˈʌndərˈhændɪd] *adj* taimado, socarrón, clandestino
underhung [ˈʌndərˌhʌŋ] *adj* suspendido; sobresaliente (*dícese de la quijada inferior*); con la quijada inferior sobresaliente
underlaid [ˌʌndərˈled] *pret & pp de* **underlay**
underlain [ˌʌndərˈlen] *pp de* **underlie**
underlap [ˌʌndərˈlæp] (*pret & pp:* **-lapped;** *ger:* **-lapping**) *va* extender por debajo de; *vn* extender por debajo
underlay [ˈʌndərˌle] *s* (print.) calzo, realce; [ˌʌndərˈle] (*pret & pp:* **-laid**) *va* (print.) calzar; poner por debajo; levantar, reforzar; *pret de* **underlie**
underlie [ˌʌndərˈlaɪ] (*pret:* **-lay;** *pp:* **-lain;** *ger:* **-lying**) *va* estar debajo de, extenderse debajo de; ser la razón fundamental de, ser la base de; sustentar, sostener
underline [ˌʌndərˈlaɪn] o [ˈʌndərˌlaɪn] *va* subrayar
underling [ˈʌndərlɪŋ] *s* inferior, subordinado; suboficial; paniaguado, secuaz servil
underlying [ˈʌndərˌlaɪɪŋ] *adj* subyacente; fundamental
undermine [ˌʌndərˈmaɪn] o [ˈʌndərˌmaɪn] *va* socavar, minar; (fig.) socavar, minar (*p.ej., la salud*)
undermost [ˈʌndərmost] *adj* (el) más bajo; *adv* a lo más bajo
underneath [ˌʌndərˈniθ] *s* parte baja, superficie inferior; *adj* inferior, más bajo; *adv* debajo; *prep* debajo de
undernourished [ˌʌndərˈnʌrɪʃt] *adj* desnutrido
undernourishment [ˌʌndərˈnʌrɪʃmənt] *s* desnutrición, subalimentación
underofficer [ˈʌndərˌɔfɪsər] o [ˈʌndərˌɑfɪsər] *s* subalterno, oficial subalterno; [ˌʌndərˈɔfɪsər] o [ˌʌndərˈɑfɪsər] *va* proveer de un número insuficiente de oficiales
underpants [ˈʌndərˌpænts] *spl* (coll.) calzoncillos
underpass [ˈʌndərˌpæs] o [ˈʌndərˌpɑs] *s* paso inferior; vía por bajo tierra
underpay [ˌʌndərˈpe] *s* pago insuficiente; (*pret & pp:* **-paid**) *va & vn* pagar insuficientemente
underpin [ˌʌndərˈpɪn] (*pret & pp:* **-pinned;** *ger:* **-pinning**) *va* apuntalar, socalzar
underpinning [ˈʌndərˌpɪnɪŋ] *s* apuntalamiento, socalzado; (coll.) las piernas de uno

underplot ['ʌndər,plɑt] *s* trama secundaria
underprivileged [,ʌndər'prɪvɪlɪdʒd] *adj* desamparado, desvalido
underproduction [,ʌndərprə'dʌkʃən] *s* baja producción
underrate [,ʌndər'ret] *va* menospreciar
underriver ['ʌndər,rɪvər] *adj* subfluvial
underscore ['ʌndər,skor] *s* línea de subrayar; [,ʌndər'skor] o ['ʌndər,skor] *va* subrayar
undersea ['ʌndər,si] *adj* submarino; [,ʌndər'si] *adv* bajo la superficie del mar
underseas [,ʌndər'siz] *adv* bajo la superficie del mar
undersecretary [,ʌndər'sɛkrɪ,tɛrɪ] *s* (*pl:* **-ies**) subsecretario
undersecretaryship [,ʌndər'sɛkrɪ,tɛrɪʃɪp] *s* subsecretaría
undersell [,ʌndər'sɛl] (*pret & pp:* **-sold**) *va* vender a menor precio que; malbaratar
underservant ['ʌndər,sʌrvənt] *s* criado inferior
undershirt ['ʌndər,ʃʌrt] *s* camiseta
undershot ['ʌndər,ʃɑt] *adj* que tiene saliente la mandíbula inferior; de corriente baja o inferior
undershot water wheel *s* rueda (hidráulica) de corriente baja o inferior
underside ['ʌndər,saɪd] *s* superficie inferior, superficie de fondo
undersign [,ʌndər'saɪn] o ['ʌndər,saɪn] *va* subscribir
undersigned ['ʌndər,saɪnd] *adj* infraescrito, abajo firmado
undersized ['ʌndər,saɪzd] *adj* de baja dimensión, de dimensión insuficiente, de infratamaño
underskirt ['ʌndər,skʌrt] *s* enaguas, refajo
undersleeve ['ʌndər,sliv] *s* manga interior
underslung ['ʌndər,slʌŋ] *adj* colgante, debajo del eje, debajo de los muelles
undersold [,ʌndər'sold] *pret & pp de* **undersell**
undersong ['ʌndər,sɔŋ] o ['ʌndər,sɑŋ] *s* canción acompañante; (fig.) sentido subyacente, sentido latente
understand [,ʌndər'stænd] (*pret & pp:* **-stood**) *va* comprender, entender; subentender, sobrentender (*una cosa que no está expresa*); (gram.) suplir; **be it understood** entiéndase; **to give to understand** dar a entender; **to understand each other** entenderse; *vn* comprender, entender
understandable [,ʌndər'stændəbəl] *adj* comprensible
understanding [,ʌndər'stændɪŋ] *adj* entendedor, inteligente; benévolo, tolerante; *s* entendimiento; comprensión; acuerdo; (philos.) entendimiento; **to come to an understanding** entenderse; **to come to an understanding with** llegar a un acuerdo con
understate [,ʌndər'stet] *va* exponer de un modo demasiado débil
understatement [,ʌndər'stetmənt] *s* exposición demasiado débil
understood [,ʌndər'stud] *pret & pp de* **understand**
understudy ['ʌndər,stʌdɪ] *s* (*pl:* **-ies**) (theat.) sobresaliente; (*pret & pp:* **-ied**) *va* aprender (*un papel*) para poder suplir a otro actor; aprender un papel para poder suplir (*a otro actor*); *vn* aprender un papel para poder suplir a otro actor
undertake [,ʌndər'tek] (*pret:* **-took;** *pp:* **-taken**) *va* emprender; comprometerse a; *vn* comprometerse; **to undertake to** + *inf* comprometerse a + *inf*
undertaker [,ʌndər'tekər] o ['ʌndər,tekər] *s* empresario; ['ʌndər,tekər] *s* empresario de pompas fúnebres, director de funeraria
undertaking [,ʌndər'tekɪŋ] *s* empresa; empeño; garantía; ['ʌndər,tekɪŋ] *s* funeraria, empresa funeraria
undertone ['ʌndər,ton] *s* voz baja; matiz suave, color apagado; fondo
undertook [,ʌndər'tuk] *pret de* **undertake**
undertow ['ʌndər,to] *s* resaca; contracorriente
undervaluation ['ʌndər,væljʊ'eʃən] *s* estimación baja
undervalue [,ʌndər'væljʊ] *va* estimar demasiado bajo
undervest ['ʌndər,vɛst] *s* camiseta
underwaist ['ʌndər,west] *s* jubón, corpiño
underwater ['ʌndər,wɔtər] o ['ʌndər,wɑtər] *adj* subacuático, submarino; inundado; entre aguas
underwear ['ʌndər,wɛr] *s* ropa interior
underweight ['ʌndər,wet] *s* peso escaso; *adj* de peso escaso
underwent [,ʌndər'wɛnt] *pret de* **undergo**
underwood ['ʌndər,wʊd] *s* maleza
underworld ['ʌndər,wʌrld] *s* mundo terrenal; mundo submarino; antípoda; averno, infierno; gente de mal vivir, mundo del vicio, bajos fondos sociales, inframundo
underwrite [,ʌndər'raɪt] o ['ʌndər,raɪt] (*pret:* **-wrote;** *pp:* **-written**) *va* subscribir; asegurar
underwriter ['ʌndər,raɪtər] *s* subscritor; asegurador; compañía aseguradora
underwritten [,ʌndər'rɪtən] o ['ʌndər,rɪtən] *pp de* **underwrite**
underwrote [,ʌndər'rot] o ['ʌndər,rot] *pret de* **underwrite**
undescribable [,ʌndɪ'skraɪbəbəl] *adj* indescriptible
undeserved [,ʌndɪ'zʌrvd] *adj* inmerecido
undesirable [,ʌndɪ'zaɪrəbəl] *adj & s* indeseable
undetachable [,ʌndɪ'tætʃəbəl] *adj* inamovible, inseparable
undeterminable [,ʌndɪ'tʌrmɪnəbəl] *adj* indeterminable
undevout [,ʌndɪ'vaʊt] *adj* indevoto
undigested [,ʌndɪ'dʒɛstɪd] *adj* indigesto
undid [ʌn'dɪd] *pret de* **undo**
undine [ʌn'din] o ['ʌndin] *s* (myth.) ondina
undiplomatic [,ʌndɪplə'mætɪk] *adj* poco diplomático
undiscernible [,ʌndɪ'zʌrnɪbəl] o [,ʌndɪ'sʌrnɪbəl] *adj* imperceptible, invisible
undisciplined [ʌn'dɪsɪplɪnd] *adj* indisciplinado
undiscriminating [,ʌndɪs'krɪmɪ,netɪŋ] *adj* sin sentido crítico, incapaz de distinguir bien
undisguised [,ʌndɪs'gaɪzd] *adj* sin disfraz; abierto, franco
undismayed [,ʌndɪs'med] *adj* impávido, intrépido; no desanimado
undisputed [,ʌndɪs'pjutɪd] *adj* incontestable, sin disputa
undistinguishable [,ʌndɪ'stɪŋgwɪʃəbəl] *adj* indistinguible
undistinguished [,ʌndɪ'stɪŋgwɪʃt] *adj* deslucido; no distinguido
undistorted [,ʌndɪs'tɔrtɪd] *adj* sin falsificación; (elec.) sin distorsión
undistorted output *s* (elec.) potencia de salida sin distorsión
undisturbed [,ʌndɪ'stʌrbd] *adj* sin tocar; imperturbado
undivided [,ʌndɪ'vaɪdɪd] *adj* indiviso
undo [ʌn'du] (*pret:* **-did;** *pp:* **-done**) *va* deshacer; anular; resolver, explicar
undoing [ʌn'duɪŋ] *s* desatadura; anulación; ruina, pérdida, destrucción
undone [ʌn'dʌn] *adj* sin hacer, por hacer; **to come undone** desatarse, deshacerse; **to leave nothing undone** no dejar nada por hacer; *pp de* **undo**
undoubted [ʌn'daʊtɪd] *adj* indudable
undoubtedly [ʌn'daʊtɪdlɪ] *adv* indudablemente
undramatic [,ʌndrə'mætɪk] *adj* no dramático, poco dramático
undraw [ʌn'drɔ] (*pret:* **-drew;** *pp:* **-drawn**) *va* abrir, tirar hacia fuera
undress ['ʌn,drɛs] o [ʌn'drɛs] *s* ropa de casa; (mil.) traje de cuartel; ['ʌn,drɛs] *adj* de trapillo, informal; [ʌn'drɛs] *va* desnudar; desadornar; desvendar (*una herida*); *vn* desnudarse
undrew [ʌn'dru] *pret de* **undraw**
undrinkable [ʌn'drɪŋkəbəl] *adj* impotable
undue [ʌn'dju] o [ʌn'du] *adj* indebido, impropio; excesivo
undulant ['ʌndjələnt] *adj* undulante, ondulante
undulant fever *s* (path.) fiebre ondulante

undulate ['ʌndjəlet] *adj* ondulado; *va* ondular (*el pelo*); hacer ondas en; *vn* ondular, undular
undulation [,ʌndjə'leʃən] *s* ondulación, undulación
undulatory ['ʌndjələ,torɪ] *adj* ondulatorio, undulatorio
unduly [ʌn'djulɪ] o [ʌn'dulɪ] *adv* indebidamente, impropiamente; excesivamente
undying [ʌn'daɪɪŋ] *adj* imperecedero
unearned [ʌn'ʌrnd] *adj* no ganado; inmerecido
unearned increment *s* mayor valía
unearth [ʌn'ʌrθ] *va* desenterrar; (fig.) descubrir
unearthly [ʌn'ʌrθlɪ] *adj* sobrenatural; espectral, fantástico
uneasy [ʌn'izɪ] *adj* inquieto; desgarbado; incómodo, no bien
uneatable [ʌn'itəbəl] *adj* no comestible, incomible
uneconomic [,ʌnikə'nɑmɪk] o [,ʌnɛkə'nɑmɪk] o **uneconomical** [,ʌnikə'nɑmɪkəl] o [,ʌnɛkə'nɑmɪkəl] *adj* antieconómico
uneducable [ʌn'ɛdʒəkəbəl] *adj* ineducable
uneducated [ʌn'ɛdʒə,ketɪd] *adj* ineducado
unemployable [,ʌnɛm'plɔɪəbəl] *adj* inutilizable; inútil para el trabajo
unemployed [,ʌnɛm'plɔɪd] *adj* cesante, desocupado; inutilizado; (com.) improductivo; *s* cesante, desocupado
unemployment [,ʌnɛm'plɔɪmənt] *s* cesantía, desocupación, desempleo
unemployment compensation *s* subsidios de paro
unemployment insurance *s* seguro de desocupación, seguro contra el paro obrero
unending [ʌn'ɛndɪŋ] *adj* inacabable, interminable
unenlightened [,ʌnɛn'laɪtənd] *adj* poco instruído, ignorante
unequal [ʌn'ikwəl] *adj* desigual; insuficiente; injusto, parcial; **unequal to** insuficiente para; no al nivel de; sin fuerzas para
unequaled o **unequalled** [ʌn'ikwəld] *adj* inigualado
unequally [ʌn'ikwəlɪ] *adv* desigualmente; injustamente, parcialmente
unequivocal [,ʌnɪ'kwɪvəkəl] *adj* inequívoco
unequivocally [,ʌnɪ'kwɪvəkəlɪ] *adv* inequívocamente
unerring [ʌn'ʌrɪŋ] o [ʌn'ɛrɪŋ] *adj* infalible, seguro
Unesco [ju'nɛsko] *s* Unesco
unessential [,ʌnɛ'sɛnʃəl] *adj* no esencial
unestimated [ʌn'ɛstɪ,metɪd] *adj* inestimado
unethical [ʌn'ɛθɪkəl] *adj* poco ético
uneven [ʌn'ivən] *adj* desigual, irregular; (math.) impar
unevenness [ʌn'ivənnɪs] *s* desigualdad, irregularidad; (math.) imparidad
uneventful [,ʌnɪ'vɛntfəl] *adj* sin acontecimientos notables, tranquilo
unexampled [,ʌnɛg'zæmpəld] o [,ʌnɛg'zɑmpəld] *adj* sin ejemplo, sin igual, sin par
unexceptionable [,ʌnɛk'sɛpʃənəbəl] *adj* irreprensible, irrecusable
unexceptional [,ʌnɛk'sɛpʃənəl] *adj* ordinario, usual; sin excepción
unexchangeable [,ʌnɛks'tʃendʒəbəl] *adj* incambiable
unexhausted [,ʌnɛg'zɔstɪd] *adj* inexhausto
unexpected [,ʌnɛk'spɛktɪd] *adj* inesperado
unexpectedly [,ʌnɛk'spɛktɪdlɪ] *adv* inesperadamente
unexpired [,ʌnɛk'spaɪrd] *adj* no expirado
unexplainable [,ʌnɛk'splenəbəl] *adj* inexplicable
unexplained [,ʌnɛk'splend] *adj* inexplicado
unexploited [,ʌnɛk'splɔɪtɪd] *adj* inexplotado
unexplored [,ʌnɛk'splord] *adj* inexplorado
unexposed [,ʌnɛk'spozd] *adj* (phot.) inexpuesto
unexpurgated [ʌn'ɛkspər,getɪd] *adj* no expurgado, sin expurgar
unextinguishable [,ʌnɛk'stɪŋgwɪʃəbəl] *adj* inapagable, inextinguible
unextinguished [,ʌnɛk'stɪŋgwɪʃt] *adj* inextinto
unfading [ʌn'fedɪŋ] *adj* sin descolorar; inmarcesible; (rad.) sin desvanecerse
unfailing [ʌn'felɪŋ] *adj* indefectible; inagotable
unfair [ʌn'fɛr] *adj* inicuo, injusto; falso, doble, desleal; desfavorable (*viento*); (sport) sucio
unfaithful [ʌn'feθfəl] *adj* infiel
unfaltering [ʌn'fɔltərɪŋ] *adj* resuelto, firme
unfamiliar [,ʌnfə'mɪljər] *adj* poco familiar; poco conocedor, no familiarizado
unfamiliarity [,ʌnfə,mɪlɪ'ærɪtɪ] *s* falta de familiaridad; desconocimiento
unfasten [ʌn'fæsən] o [ʌn'fɑsən] *va* desatar, desligar, desabrochar, soltar, desatacar
unfathomable [ʌn'fæðəməbəl] *adj* insondable
unfavorable [ʌn'fevərəbəl] *adj* desfavorable
unfeasible [ʌn'fizəbəl] *adj* impracticable
unfeathered [ʌn'fɛðərd] *adj* implume
unfeeling [ʌn'filɪŋ] *adj* insensible
unfeigned [ʌn'fend] *adj* sincero, verdadero
unfeignedly [ʌn'fenɪdlɪ] *adv* sinceramente, sin fingimiento
unfetter [ʌn'fɛtər] *va* desencadenar
unfilled [ʌn'fɪld] *adj* no lleno, vacante; por cumplir, pendiente
unfindable [ʌn'faɪndəbəl] *adj* inencontrable
unfinished [ʌn'fɪnɪʃt] *adj* sin acabar; mal acabado, imperfecto
unfit [ʌn'fɪt] *adj* incapaz, inhábil; impropio; (*pret & pp:* **-fitted;** *ger:* **-fitting**) *va* inhabilitar
unfitting [ʌn'fɪtɪŋ] *adj* impropio; indecoroso
unfix [ʌn'fɪks] *va* desatar, desprender, soltar
unflagging [ʌn'flægɪŋ] *adj* incansable, persistente
unfledged [ʌn'flɛdʒd] *adj* implume; inmaturo, inexperimentado
unflinching [ʌn'flɪntʃɪŋ] *adj* impávido, resuelto
unfold [ʌn'fold] *va* desplegar; *vn* desplegarse
unfordable [ʌn'fordəbəl] *adj* invadeable
unforeseeable [,ʌnfor'siəbəl] *adj* imprevisible
unforeseen [,ʌnfor'sin] *adj* imprevisto, inesperado
unforgettable [,ʌnfər'gɛtəbəl] *adj* inolvidable
unforgivable [,ʌnfər'gɪvəbəl] *adj* imperdonable
unformed [ʌn'fɔrmd] *adj* informe; crudo; rudimentario
unfortunate [ʌn'fɔrtʃənɪt] *adj & s* desgraciado
unfounded [ʌn'faʊndɪd] *adj* infundado
unfrequented [,ʌnfrɪ'kwɛntɪd] *adj* poco frecuentado
unfriended [ʌn'frɛndɪd] *adj* desamparado, sin amigos
unfriendly [ʌn'frɛndlɪ] *adj* inamistoso, poco amistoso; desfavorable
unfrock [ʌn'frɑk] *va* expulsar, degradar (*a un sacerdote*)
unfruitful [ʌn'frutfəl] *adj* infructuoso
unfulfilled [,ʌnfʊl'fɪld] *adj* incumplido
unfurl [ʌn'fʌrl] *va* desenrollar
unfurnished [ʌn'fʌrnɪʃt] *adj* desamueblado
ungainly [ʌn'genlɪ] *adj* desgarbado, torpe, feo
ungenerous [ʌn'dʒɛnərəs] *adj* poco generoso
ungentlemanly [ʌn'dʒɛntəlmənlɪ] *adj* poco caballeroso, malcriado, descortés
ungird [ʌn'gʌrd] *va* desceñir, descinchar
unglazed [ʌn'glezd] *adj* no vidriado; deslustrado; no satinado (*papel*); sin cristales (*ventana*)
ungodliness [ʌn'gɑdlɪnɪs] *s* impiedad, irreligión; maldad, perversidad; (coll.) atrocidad
ungodly [ʌn'gɑdlɪ] *adj* impío, irreligioso; malvado, perverso; (coll.) atroz
ungovernable [ʌn'gʌvərnəbəl] *adj* ingobernable; indisciplinado
ungraceful [ʌn'gresfəl] *adj* desgraciado, desgarbado
ungracious [ʌn'greʃəs] *adj* descortés; desgraciado, desagradable, sin gracia
ungrammatical [,ʌngrə'mætɪkəl] *adj* ingramatical
ungrateful [ʌn'gretfəl] *adj* ingrato, desagradecido
ungrounded [ʌn'graʊndɪd] *adj* infundado, inmotivado; poco instruído; (elec.) sin toma a tierra, sin retorno terrestre
ungrudgingly [ʌn'grʌdʒɪŋlɪ] *adv* de buena gana, sin quejarse

ungual ['ʌŋgwəl] *adj* unguinal, unguiculado
unguarded [ʌn'gɑrdɪd] *adj* indefenso; descuidado, imprudente
unguent ['ʌŋgwənt] *s* ungüento
unguiculate [ʌŋ'gwɪkjəlɪt] *adj* unguiculado
unguis ['ʌŋgwɪs] *s* (*pl:* **-gues** [gwiz]) (anat.) unguis
ungula ['ʌŋgjələ] *s* (*pl:* **-lae** [li]) uña; (bot.) uña; (zool. & geom.) úngula
ungular ['ʌŋgjələr] *adj* ungular
ungulate ['ʌŋgjəlet] o ['ʌŋgjəlɪt] *adj & s* (zool.) ungulado
unhallowed [ʌn'hælod] *adj* profano; malvado
unhand [ʌn'hænd] *va* quitar las manos a; soltar
unhandsome [ʌn'hænsəm] *adj* feo, desaliñado; descortés, indecoroso; poco generoso
unhandy [ʌn'hændɪ] *adj* desmañado; incómodo
unhappily [ʌn'hæpɪlɪ] *adv* infelizmente; desgraciadamente
unhappiness [ʌn'hæpɪnɪs] *s* infelicidad; desgracia
unhappy [ʌn'hæpɪ] *adj* infeliz; desgraciado
unharmed [ʌn'hɑrmd] *adj* incólume, ileso, indemne, sano y salvo
unharmonious [,ʌnhɑr'monɪəs] *adj* inarmónico
unharness [ʌn'hɑrnɪs] *va* desenjaezar, desguarnecer; desarmar; desenganchar
unhealthful [ʌn'hɛlθfəl] *adj* insalubre
unhealthy [ʌn'hɛlθɪ] *adj* malsano
unheard [ʌn'hʌrd] *adj* no oído; desconocido; sin ser oído
unheard-of [ʌn'hʌrd,ɑv] *adj* inaudito, nunca oído, nunca visto
unheeded [ʌn'hidɪd] *adj* desatendido
unheedful [ʌn'hidfəl] *adj* desatento
unhesitating [ʌn'hɛzɪ,tetɪŋ] *adj* resuelto, pronto, listo
unhinge [ʌn'hɪndʒ] *va* desgonzar; (fig.) desequilibrar, trastornar
unhitch [ʌn'hɪtʃ] *va* desenganchar
unholy [ʌn'holɪ] *adj* impío, malo
unhonored [ʌn'ɑnərd] *adj* sin honores, despreciado; protestado (*cheque*)
unhook [ʌn'hʊk] *va* desabrochar; desenganchar; descolgar; *vn* desabrocharse; desengancharse; descolgarse
unhoped-for [ʌn'hopt,fɔr] *adj* inesperado, no esperado
unhorse [ʌn'hɔrs] *va* desarzonar, desmontar
unhurriedly [ʌn'hʌrɪdlɪ] *adv* sin prisa
unhurt [ʌn'hʌrt] *adj* incólume, ileso
Uniat ['junɪæt] *adj & s* uniato
uniaxial [,junɪ'æksɪəl] *adj* uniáxico
unicameral [,junɪ'kæmərəl] *adj* unicameral
unicellular [,junɪ'sɛljələr] *adj* unicelular
unicorn ['junɪkɔrn] *adj* unicornio; *s* (myth. & Bib.) unicornio
unification [,junɪfɪ'keʃən] *s* unificación
uniflorous [,junɪ'florəs] *adj* (bot.) unifloro
unifoliate [,junɪ'folɪɪt] *adj* (bot.) unifoliado
uniform ['junɪfɔrm] *adj & s* uniforme; *va* uniformar
uniformity [,junɪ'fɔrmɪtɪ] *s* (*pl:* **-ties**) uniformidad
unify ['junɪfaɪ] (*pret & pp:* **-fied**) *va* unificar
unilateral [,junɪ'lætərəl] *adj* unilateral
unimpeachable [,ʌnɪm'pitʃəbəl] *adj* irrecusable, intachable
unimportance [,ʌnɪm'pɔrtəns] *s* poca importancia
unimportant [,ʌnɪm'pɔrtənt] *adj* poco importante
uninflammable [,ʌnɪn'flæməbəl] *adj* ininflamable
uninflected [,ʌnɪn'flɛktɪd] *adj* (gram.) sin inflexiones
uninhabitable [,ʌnɪn'hæbɪtəbəl] *adj* inhabitable
uninhabited [,ʌnɪn'hæbɪtɪd] *adj* inhabitado
uninspired [,ʌnɪn'spaɪrd] *adj* no inspirado, sin inspiración; aburrido, fastidioso
unintelligent [,ʌnɪn'tɛlɪdʒənt] *adj* ininteligente
unintelligible [,ʌnɪn'tɛlɪdʒɪbəl] *adj* ininteligible
uninterested [ʌn'ɪntərəstɪd] o [ʌn'ɪntrɪstɪd] *adj* desinteresado, poco interesado
uninteresting [ʌn'ɪntərɛstɪŋ] o [ʌn'ɪntrɪstɪŋ] *adj* poco interesante, falto de interés
uninterrupted [,ʌnɪntə'rʌptɪd] *adj* ininterrumpido, no interrumpido
union ['junjən] *s* unión; emblema de unión; sindicato, gremio obrero; (mach.) unión; *adj* gremial; (*cap.*) *s* Unión (*EE.UU.*)
union catalogue *s* catálogo colectivo (*de varias bibliotecas*)
unionism ['junjənɪzəm] *s* gremios obreros, sindicalismo, unionismo; (*cap.*) *s* Unionismo
unionist ['junjənɪst] *s* agremiado, sindicalista, unionista; (*cap.*) *s* Unionista
unionization [,junjənɪ'zeʃən] *s* agremiación
unionize ['junjənaɪz] *va* agremiar; *vn* agremiarse
Union Jack *s* pabellón nacional de la Gran Bretaña
Union of South Africa *s* Unión Sudafricana
Union of Soviet Socialist Republics *s* Unión de Repúblicas Socialistas Soviéticas
union shop *s* fábrica de obreros agremiados
union suit *s* traje interior de una sola pieza
uniparous [jʊ'nɪpərəs] *adj* (zool. & bot.) uníparo
uniped ['junɪpɛd] *adj* unípede
unipersonal [,junɪ'pʌrsənəl] *adj* unipersonal
unipolar [,junɪ'polər] *adj* (elec.) unipolar
unique [jʊ'nik] *adj* único (*en su género*)
uniqueness [jʊ'niknɪs] *s* unicidad
unisexual [,junɪ'sɛkʃʊəl] *adj* unisexual
unison ['junɪsən] o ['junɪzən] *s* concordancia, armonía; (mus.) unisonancia; **in unison** al unísono; **in unison with** al unísono de; *adj* (mus.) unísono
unit ['junɪt] *s* unidad; (mach. & elec.) grupo; *adj* unitario
Unitarian [,junɪ'tɛrɪən] *adj & s* unitario
Unitarianism [,junɪ'tɛrɪənɪzəm] *s* unitarismo
unitary ['junɪ,tɛrɪ] *adj* unitario
unitary theory *s* (chem.) teoría unitaria
unite [jʊ'naɪt] *va* unir; reunir, juntar; *vn* reunirse, juntarse
united [jʊ'naɪtɪd] *adj* unido
United Arab Republic *s* República Árabe Unida
United Kingdom *s* Reino Unido
United Nations *spl* Naciones Unidas
United States *adj* estadounidense; **the United States** *ssg* Estados Unidos *msg* o los Estados Unidos *mpl*
unitive ['junɪtɪv] *adj* unitivo
unity ['junɪtɪ] *s* (*pl:* **-ties**) unidad
univ. abr. de **universal** y **university**
Univ. abr. de **Universalist** y **University**
univalence [,junɪ'veləns] o [jʊ'nɪvələns] *s* (chem.) univalencia
univalent [,junɪ'velənt] o [jʊ'nɪvələnt] *adj* (chem.) univalente
univalve ['junɪ,vælv] *adj* (zool.) univalvo
universal [,junɪ'vʌrsəl] *adj* universal; *s* (log.) universal; (log.) proposición universal
Universal Bishop *s* obispo universal
universalism [,junɪ'vʌrsəlɪzəm] *s* universalismo; (*cap.*) *s* universalismo
universalist [,junɪ'vʌrsəlɪst] *s* universalista; (*cap.*) *s* universalista
universality [,junɪvʌr'sælɪtɪ] *s* (*pl:* **-ties**) universalidad
universalize [,junɪ'vʌrsəlaɪz] *va* universalizar
universal joint *s* (aut.) articulación universal, junta universal, cardán
universal language *s* lengua universal
universally [,junɪ'vʌrsəlɪ] *adv* universalmente
universe ['junɪvʌrs] *s* universo
university [,junɪ'vʌrsɪtɪ] *s* (*pl:* **-ties**) universidad; *adj* universitario
univocal [jʊ'nɪvəkəl] *adj* unívoco
unjoint [ʌn'dʒɔɪnt] *va* desunir; desencajar, desensamblar
unjust [ʌn'dʒʌst] *adj* injusto
unjustifiable [ʌn'dʒʌstɪ,faɪəbəl] *adj* injustificable
unjustified [ʌn'dʒʌstɪfaɪd] *adj* injustificado
unkempt [ʌn'kɛmpt] *adj* despeinado
unkind [ʌn'kaɪnd] *adj* poco amable; despiadado, brutal
unkindness [ʌn'kaɪndnɪs] *s* falta de amabilidad; tratamiento despiadado, acción brutal

unknit [ʌn'nɪt] (*pret & pp:* **-knitted** o **-knit; *ger:* -knitting**) *va* destejer; desfruncir
unknowable [ʌn'noəbəl] *adj* inconocible, incognoscible; insabible
unknowingly [ʌn'no·ɪŋlɪ] *adv* desconocidamente, sin saberlo
unknown [ʌn'non] *adj* desconocido, ignoto, incógnito; *s* desconocido; (math.) incógnita
unknown quantity *s* (math. & fig.) incógnita
unknown soldier *s* soldado desconocido
unlace [ʌn'les] *va* desenlazar; desatar (*p.ej., los cordones del zapato*)
unlade [ʌn'led] *va* descargar
unlatch [ʌn'lætʃ] *va* abrir levantando el picaporte
unlawful [ʌn'lɔfəl] *adj* ilegal; ilegítimo
unlawfully [ʌn'lɔfəlɪ] *adv* ilegalmente; ilegítimamente
unlearn [ʌn'lʌrn] *va* desaprender
unlearned [ʌn'lʌrnɪd] *adj* indocto; ignorante; [ʌn'lʌrnd] *adj* innato, no aprendido
unleash [ʌn'liʃ] *va* destraillar; soltar
unleavened [ʌn'lɛvənd] *adj* ázimo, sin levadura
unless [ʌn'lɛs] *prep* excepto; *conj* a menos que, a no ser que
unlettered [ʌn'lɛtərd] *adj* indocto, iletrado; analfabeto
unlike [ʌn'laɪk] *adj* desemejante; desemejante de; (dial.) improbable; (elec.) de nombres contrarios (*dícese, p.ej., de los polos de un imán*); (elec.) de signo contrario; *prep* a diferencia de
unlikelihood [ʌn'laɪklɪhud] *s* inverosimilitud, improbabilidad
unlikely [ʌn'laɪklɪ] *adj* inverosímil, improbable
unlikeness [ʌn'laɪknɪs] *s* disimilitud, desemejanza, diferencia
unlimber [ʌn'lɪmbər] *va* quitar el avantrén a (*un cañón*); preparar para la acción; *vn* prepararse para la acción
unlimited [ʌn'lɪmɪtɪd] *adj* ilimitado; indefinido
unlined [ʌn'laɪnd] *adj* sin forro; sin rayar (*papel*); sin arrugas (*rostro*)
unliquidated [ʌn'lɪkwɪ,detɪd] *adj* ilíquido
unload [ʌn'lod] *va* descargar (*una carga; un cañón*); exonerar, aliviar; (coll.) deshacerse de (*p.ej., mercancías*); *vn* descargar
unlock [ʌn'lɑk] *va* abrir; (print.) desapretar; (fig.) descubrir, revelar; *vn* abrirse
unlooked-for [ʌn'lukt,fɔr] *adj* inesperado, inopinado
unloose [ʌn'lus] *va* desatar, desencadenar, aflojar, soltar; *vn* desatarse, desencadenarse, aflojarse
unloosen [ʌn'lusən] *va* desatar, desencadenar, aflojar, soltar
unlosable [ʌn'luzəbəl] *adj* inamisible, imperdible
unloved [ʌn'lʌvd] *adj* desamado
unlovely [ʌn'lʌvlɪ] *adj* desgraciado, desgarbado
unloving [ʌn'lʌvɪŋ] *adj* desamorado
unlucky [ʌn'lʌkɪ] *adj* de mala suerte; desgraciado, desdichado; aciago, nefasto; **to be unlucky** tener mala suerte
unmake [ʌn'mek] (*pret & pp:* **-made**) *va* deshacer; arruinar, destruir
unman [ʌn'mæn] (*pret & pp:* **-manned; *ger:* -manning**) acobardar, desanimar; afeminar; privar de hombres; (mil.) desguarnecer (*una plaza, un castillo*)
unmanageable [ʌn'mænɪdʒəbəl] *adj* inmanejable
unmanly [ʌn'mænlɪ] *adj* afeminado, enervado; bajo, cobarde
unmannerly [ʌn'mænərlɪ] *adj* descortés, malcriado, mal educado; *adv* descortésmente
unmarketable [ʌn'mɑrkɪtəbəl] *adj* incomerciable
unmarriageable [ʌn'mærɪdʒəbəl] *adj* incasable
unmarried [ʌn'mærɪd] *adj* soltero
unmask [ʌn'mæsk] o [ʌn'mɑsk] *va* desenmascarar; *vn* desenmascararse
unmatchable [ʌn'mætʃəbəl] *adj* sin igual, incomparable
unmatched [ʌn'mætʃt] *adj* incomparable, único; desapareado
unmeaning [ʌn'minɪŋ] *adj* falto de significación; vacío, sin expresión, sin sentido
unmeasurable [ʌn'mɛʒərəbəl] *adj* inmensurable
unmeasured [ʌn'mɛʒərd] *adj* ilimitado; desenfrenado, inmoderado
unmeet [ʌn'mit] *adj* impropio, inconveniente
unmentionable [ʌn'mɛnʃənəbəl] *adj* que no se puede mencionar; infando; **unmentionables** *spl* cosas que no se deben mencionar; (hum.) prendas íntimas (*calzones, pantalones, etc.*)
unmerciful [ʌn'mʌrsɪfəl] *adj* inclemente, despiadado
unmerited [ʌn'mɛrɪtɪd] *adj* inmerecido
unmesh [ʌn'mɛʃ] *va* desengranar; *vn* desengranarse
unmindful [ʌn'maɪndfəl] *adj* desatento, descuidado; **to be unmindful of** no pensar en, olvidar (*p.ej., la hora*)
unmistakable [,ʌnmɪs'tekəbəl] *adj* inequívoco
unmitigated [ʌn'mɪtɪ,getɪd] *adj* no mitigado, duro; absoluto, redomado
unmixed o **unmixt** [ʌn'mɪkst] *adj* puro, sin mezcla
unmodulated [ʌn'mɑdjə,letɪd] *adj* sin modular
unmoor [ʌn'mur] *va* (naut.) desamarrar (*un buque*); (naut.) desaferrar (*las áncoras*)
unmoral [ʌn'mɑrəl] o [ʌn'mɔrəl] *adj* amoral
unmotivated [ʌn'motɪ,vetɪd] *adj* inmotivado
unmounted [ʌn'maʊntɪd] *adj* desmontado
unmovable [ʌn'muvəbəl] *adj* inmoble
unmoved [ʌn'muvd] *adj* inmoto; impasible, frío; inmoble, constante
unmuzzle [ʌn'mʌzəl] *va* desbozalar; (fig.) dejar hablar
unnatural [ʌn'nætʃərəl] *adj* innatural, contranatural, desnaturalizado; anormal; afectado
unnavigable [ʌn'nævɪgəbəl] *adj* innavegable
unnecessary [ʌn'nɛsə,sɛrɪ] *adj* innecesario
unnegotiable [,ʌnnɪ'goʃɪəbəl] *adj* innegociable; (coll.) incomerciable, intransitable
unnerve [ʌn'nʌrv] *va* acobardar, desconcertar, trastornar
unnoticeable [ʌn'notɪsəbəl] *adj* imperceptible
unnoticed [ʌn'notɪst] *adj* inadvertido
unnumbered [ʌn'nʌmbərd] *adj* innumerable; sin número
unobliging [,ʌnə'blaɪdʒɪŋ] *adj* poco amable, poco servicial
unobservant [,ʌnəb'zʌrvənt] *adj* inobservante
unobserved [,ʌnəb'zʌrvd] *adj* inadvertido
unobtainable [,ʌnəb'tenəbəl] *adj* inasequible
unobtrusive [,ʌnəb'trusɪv] *adj* discreto, reservado
unoccasioned [,ʌnə'keʒənd] *adj* inmotivado
unoccupied [ʌn'ɑkjəpaɪd] *adj* vacante, libre; desocupado, ocioso
unofficial [,ʌnə'fɪʃəl] *adj* oficioso, extraoficial
unopened [ʌn'opənd] *adj* no abierto, sin abrir; no cortado (*libro*)
unorganized [ʌn'ɔrgənaɪzd] *adj* inorganizado
unorthodox [ʌn'ɔrθədɑks] *adj* inortodoxo
unpack [ʌn'pæk] *va* desembalar, desempaquetar; vaciar
unpaid [ʌn'ped] *adj* sin pagar, por pagar
unpalatable [ʌn'pælətəbəl] *adj* desabrido, ingustable
unparalleled [ʌn'pærəlɛld] *adj* sin par, sin igual, incomparable
unpardonable [ʌn'pɑrdənəbəl] *adj* imperdonable
unparliamentary [,ʌnpɑrlə'mɛntərɪ] *adj* no parlamentario
unpatriotic [,ʌnpetrɪ'ɑtɪk] o [,ʌnpætrɪ'ɑtɪk] *adj* poco patriótico, antipatriótico
unpayable [ʌn'peəbəl] *adj* impagable
unpeople [ʌn'pipəl] *va* despoblar
unpeopled [ʌn'pipəld] *adj* despoblado
unperceived [,ʌnpər'sivd] *adj* inadvertido
unperturbable [,ʌnpər'tʌrbəbəl] *adj* imperturbable
unperturbed [,ʌnpər'tʌrbd] *adj* imperturbado
unpin [ʌn'pɪn] (*pret & pp:* **-pinned; *ger:* -pinning**) *va* desprender; desenclavijar
unplait [ʌn'plæt] o [ʌn'plet] *va* destrenzar

unplayable [ʌnˈpleəbəl] *adj* irrepresentable
unpleasant [ʌnˈplɛzənt] *adj* antipático, desagradable
unpleasantness [ʌnˈplɛzəntnɪs] *s* molestia; disgusto, desavenencia
unplumbed [ʌnˈplʌmd] *adj* no sondado; sin cañerías
unpolarized [ʌnˈpolərαɪzd] *adj* no polarizado
unpolluted [ˌʌnpəˈlutɪd] *adj* impoluto
unpopular [ʌnˈpɑpjələr] *adj* impopular
unpopularity [ʌnˌpɑpjəˈlærɪtɪ] *s* impopularidad
unpopulated [ʌnˈpɑpjəˌletɪd] *adj* despoblado
unpractical [ʌnˈpræktɪkəl] *adj* impráctico
unpracticed o **unpractised** [ʌnˈpræktɪst] *adj* inexperto; no practicado
unprecedented [ʌnˈprɛsɪˌdɛntɪd] *adj* inaudito, sin precedente
unpredictable [ˌʌnprɪˈdɪktəbəl] *adj* imposible de predecir; incierto, inconstante
unprejudiced [ʌnˈprɛdʒədɪst] *adj* imparcial; no perjudicado
unpremeditated [ˌʌnprɪˈmɛdɪˌtetɪd] *adj* impremeditado
unpremeditation [ˌʌnprɪˌmɛdɪˈteʃən] *s* impremeditación
unprepossessing [ˌʌnpripəˈzɛsɪŋ] *adj* poco atrayente
unpresentable [ˌʌnprɪˈzɛntəbəl] *adj* mal apersonado; impresentable
unpretending [ˌʌnprɪˈtɛndɪŋ] *adj* modesto
unpretentious [ˌʌnprɪˈtɛnʃəs] *adj* modesto, sencillo; poco ambicioso
unpreventable [ʌnprɪˈvɛntəbəl] *adj* inevitable
unprincipled [ʌnˈprɪnsɪpəld] *adj* malo, sin conciencia
unprintable [ʌnˈprɪntəbəl] *adj* que no puede imprimirse
unprinted [ʌnˈprɪntɪd] *adj* sin imprimir
unproductive [ˌʌnprəˈdʌktɪv] *adj* improductivo
unprofessional [ˌʌnprəˈfɛʃənəl] *adj* no profesional
unprofitable [ʌnˈprɑfɪtəbəl] *adj* inútil, infructuoso
unpronounceable [ˌʌnprəˈnaʊnsəbəl] *adj* impronunciable
unpropitious [ˌʌnprəˈpɪʃəs] *adj* impropicio
unprovoked [ˌʌnprəˈvokt] *adj* no provocado, sin provocación
unpublishable [ʌnˈpʌblɪʃəbəl] *adj* impublicable
unpublished [ʌnˈpʌblɪʃt] *adj* inédito
unpunished [ʌnˈpʌnɪʃt] *adj* impune
unpurchasable [ʌnˈpʌrtʃəsəbəl] *adj* incomprable
unqualifiable [ʌnˈkwɑlɪˌfaɪəbəl] *adj* incalificable
unqualified [ʌnˈkwɑlɪfaɪd] *adj* inepto, incompetente; absoluto, completo, ilimitado
unquenchable [ʌnˈkwɛntʃəbəl] *adj* inextinguible; insaciable
unquestionable [ʌnˈkwɛstʃənəbəl] *adj* incuestionable
unquestionably [ʌnˈkwɛstʃənəblɪ] *adv* incuestionablemente
unquestioned [ʌnˈkwɛstʃənd] *adj* no interrogado; no indagado; incontestable
unquiet [ʌnˈkwaɪət] *adj* agitado; inquieto
unquote [ʌnˈkwot] *va & vn* dejar de citar; **unquote** fin de la cita
unravel [ʌnˈrævəl] (*pret & pp:* **-eled** o **-elled;** *ger:* **-eling** o **-elling**) *va* desenredar, desenmarañar; *vn* desenredarse, desenmarañarse
unreachable [ʌnˈritʃəbəl] *adj* inalcanzable
unread [ʌnˈrɛd] *adj* no leído; indocto
unreadable [ʌnˈridəbəl] *adj* ilegible
unready [ʌnˈrɛdɪ] *adj* desprevenido; lento, lerdo
unreal [ʌnˈriəl] *adj* irreal
unreality [ˌʌnrɪˈælɪtɪ] *s* (*pl:* **-ties**) irrealidad
unrealizable [ʌnˈriəˌlaɪzəbəl] *adj* irrealizable
unreasonable [ʌnˈrizənəbəl] *adj* irrazonable, desrazonable
unreasonably [ʌnˈrizənəblɪ] *adv* irrazonablemente, desrazonablemente
unreasoning [ʌnˈrizənɪŋ] *adj* irracional
unrecognizable [ʌnˈrɛkəgˌnaɪzəbəl] *adj* irreconocible
unreconcilable [ʌnˈrɛkənˌsaɪləbəl] *adj* irreconciliable
unreconciled [ʌnˈrɛkənsaɪld] *adj* irreconciliado
unreconstructed [ʌnˌrikənˈstrʌktɪd] *adj* no reconstruído; (coll.) irreconciliado
unreel [ʌnˈril] *va* desenrollar; *vn* desenrollarse
unreeve [ʌnˈriv] *va* (naut.) despasar; *vn* (naut.) despasarse
unrefined [ˌʌnrɪˈfaɪnd] *adj* no refinado, impuro; tosco, grosero, rudo
unreflecting [ˌʌnrɪˈflɛktɪŋ] *adj* irreflexivo
unregarded [ˌʌnrɪˈgɑrdɪd] *adj* desatendido
unregenerate [ˌʌnrɪˈdʒɛnərɪt] *adj* irregenerado; impío, malvado
unrelenting [ˌʌnrɪˈlɛntɪŋ] *adj* inflexible, implacable, inexorable
unreliability [ˌʌnrɪˌlaɪəˈbɪlɪtɪ] *s* falta de confiabilidad, informalidad
unreliable [ˌʌnrɪˈlaɪəbəl] *adj* indigno de confianza, informal
unreligious [ˌʌnrɪˈlɪdʒəs] *adj* irreligioso
unremitting [ˌʌnrɪˈmɪtɪŋ] *adj* incesante; infatigable
unremunerated [ˌʌnrɪˈmjunəˌretɪd] *adj* irremunerado
unrenewable [ˌʌnrɪˈnjuəbəl] o [ˌʌnrɪˈnuəbəl] *adj* irrenovable; (com.) improrrogable
unrented [ʌnˈrɛntɪd] *adj* desalquilado
unrepaired [ˌʌnrɪˈpɛrd] *adj* descompuesto
unrepentant [ˌʌnrɪˈpɛntənt] *adj* impenitente
unreplaceable [ˌʌnrɪˈplesəbəl] *adj* irreemplazable
unrequited love [ˌʌnrɪˈkwaɪtɪd] *s* amor no correspondido
unreserved [ˌʌnrɪˈzʌrvd] *adj* libre, no reservado; franco, abierto
unreservedly [ˌʌnrɪˈzʌrvɪdlɪ] *adv* sin reserva; sin restricción
unresistant [ˌʌnrɪˈzɪstənt] *adj* no resistente
unresponsive [ˌʌnrɪˈspɑnsɪv] *adj* insensible, desinteresado; desobediente
unrest [ʌnˈrɛst] *s* intranquilidad, desorden
unrevoked [ˌʌnrɪˈvokt] *adj* irrevocado
unrhymed [ʌnˈraɪmd] *adj* no rimado
unriddle [ʌnˈrɪdəl] *va* descifrar, adivinar, explicar
unrig [ʌnˈrɪg] (*pret & pp:* **-rigged;** *ger:* **-rigging**) *va* (naut.) desaparejar
unrighteous [ʌnˈraɪtʃəs] *adj* malo, malvado, vicioso, injusto
unrighteousness [ʌnˈraɪtʃəsnɪs] *s* maldad, vicio, injusticia
unrightful [ʌnˈraɪtfəl] *adj* ilegítimo, injusto
unrimed [ʌnˈraɪmd] *adj* var. de **unrhymed**
unripe [ʌnˈraɪp] *adj* inmaturo; crudo
unrivaled o **unrivalled** [ʌnˈraɪvəld] *adj* sin rival, incomparable
unrobe [ʌnˈrob] *va* desarropar; *vn* desarroparse
unroll [ʌnˈrol] *va* desenrollar; desplegar; *vn* desenrollarse; desplegarse
unromantic [ˌʌnroˈmæntɪk] *adj* poco romántico
unroof [ʌnˈruf] o [ʌnˈrʊf] *va* destechar
unroot [ʌnˈrut] o [ʌnˈrʊt] *va* desarraigar; *vn* desarraigarse
unruffled [ʌnˈrʌfəld] *adj* sin fruncir, sin arrugar; tranquilo, sereno
unruled [ʌnˈruld] *adj* no gobernado; no rayado (*papel*)
unruly [ʌnˈrulɪ] *adj* ingobernable, revoltoso
unsaddle [ʌnˈsædəl] *va* desensillar (*un caballo*); desarzonar (*a una persona*)
unsafe [ʌnˈsef] *adj* inseguro
unsaid [ʌnˈsɛd] *adj* callado, no dicho; *pret & pp de* **unsay**
unsalable o **unsaleable** [ʌnˈseləbəl] *adj* invendible
unsanitary [ʌnˈsænɪˌtɛrɪ] *adj* insalubre, antihigiénico
unsatisfactory [ʌnˌsætɪsˈfæktərɪ] *adj* insatisfactorio, poco satisfactorio
unsatisfied [ʌnˈsætɪsfaɪd] *adj* insatisfecho
unsavory [ʌnˈsevərɪ] *adj* desabrido; (fig.) infame, deshonroso
unsay [ʌnˈse] (*pret & pp:* **-said**) *va* desdecirse de
unscathed [ʌnˈskeðd] *adj* ileso, incólume, sano y salvo

unscholarly [ʌn'skɑlərlɪ] *adj* falto de erudición; indigno de un erudito
unschooled [ʌn'skuld] *adj* indocto, ignorante
unscientific [ˌʌnsaɪən'tɪfɪk] *adj* no científico, poco científico, anticientífico
unscramble [ʌn'skræmbəl] *va* desenredar, desembrollar
unscrew [ʌn'skru] *va* destornillar; *vn* destornillarse
unscrupulous [ʌn'skrupjələs] *adj* inescrupuloso, poco escrupuloso
unseal [ʌn'sil] *va* desellar; (fig.) abrir
unsearchable [ʌn'sʌrtʃəbəl] *adj* inescrutable
unseasonable [ʌn'sizənəbəl] *adj* intempestivo
unseat [ʌn'sit] *va* quitar del asiento; desarzonar; destituir; echar abajo
unseaworthy [ʌn'siˌwʌrðɪ] *adj* innavegable
unseemly [ʌn'simlɪ] *adj* impropio, indecoroso; *adv* impropiamente, indecorosamente
unseen [ʌn'sin] *adj* no visto; invisible
unselfish [ʌn'sɛlfɪʃ] *adj* desinteresado, altruísta
unselfishness [ʌn'sɛlfɪʃnɪs] *s* desinterés, altruísmo
unsettle [ʌn'sɛtəl] *va* desarreglar, descomponer; inquietar, trastornar; *vn* desarreglarse, descomponerse; inquietarse, trastornarse
unsettled [ʌn'sɛtəld] *adj* desarreglado, descompuesto; inconstante; indeciso; inhabitado, despoblado; sin residencia fija; (com.) por pagar, no liquidado
unsex [ʌn'sɛks] *va* privar de la sexualidad
unshackle [ʌn'ʃækəl] *va* desherrar, desencadenar
unshakable o **unshakeable** [ʌn'ʃekəbəl] *adj* insacudible; firme; imperturbable
unshapely [ʌn'ʃeplɪ] *adj* contrahecho, deforme, desproporcionado
unshatterable [ʌn'ʃætərəbəl] *adj* inastillable
unshaven [ʌn'ʃevən] *adj* sin afeitar
unsheathe [ʌn'ʃið] *va* desenvainar
unshell [ʌn'ʃɛl] *va* descascarar
unship [ʌn'ʃɪp] (*pret & pp:* **-shipped;** *ger:* **-shipping**) *va* desembarcar; (coll.) deshacerse de; (naut.) desarmar (*un remo*); (naut.) desmontar (*el timón*)
unshod [ʌn'ʃɑd] *adj* descalzo; desherrado (*caballo*)
unshowy [ʌn'ʃo·ɪ] *adj* deslucido
unshrinkable [ʌn'ʃrɪŋkəbəl] *adj* inencogible
unshroud [ʌn'ʃraud] *va* desamortajar
unsightly [ʌn'saɪtlɪ] *adj* feo, repugnante
unsinkable [ʌn'sɪŋkəbəl] *adj* insumergible
unskilled [ʌn'skɪld] *adj* inexperto; desmañado
unskilled laborer *s* peón, bracero, operario no especializado
unskillful [ʌn'skɪlfəl] *adj* desmañado
unsling [ʌn'slɪŋ] (*pret & pp:* **-slung**) *va* descolgar; quitar del cabestrillo; (naut.) deslingar
unsnap [ʌn'snæp] (*pret & pp:* **-snapped;** *ger:* **-snapping**) *va* desabrochar
unsnarl [ʌn'snɑrl] *va* desenredar, desenmarañar
unsociability [ʌnˌsoʃə'bɪlɪtɪ] *s* insociabilidad
unsociable [ʌn'soʃəbəl] *adj* insociable
unsold [ʌn'sold] *adj* invendido
unsolder [ʌn'sɑdər] *va* desoldar; (fig.) dividir, separar
unsolvable [ʌn'sɑlvəbəl] *adj* insoluble, irresoluble
unsophisticated [ˌʌnsə'fɪstɪˌketɪd] *adj* cándido, natural, sencillo
unsound [ʌn'saund] *adj* poco firme; falso, erróneo; podrido; ligero (*sueño*)
unsparing [ʌn'spɛrɪŋ] *adj* liberal, generoso; cruel, despiadado
unspeakable [ʌn'spikəbəl] *adj* indecible; incalificable (*infame, atroz*)
unsportsmanlike [ʌn'sportsmənˌlaɪk] *adj* antideportivo
unspotted [ʌn'spɑtɪd] *adj* sin manchas, inmaculado
unstable [ʌn'stebəl] *adj* inestable
unsteady [ʌn'stɛdɪ] *adj* inseguro, inestable; inconstante, irresoluto; poco juicioso
unstep [ʌn'stɛp] (*pret & pp:* **-stepped;** *ger:* **-stepping**) *va* (naut.) desmontar (*p.ej., un mástil*)
unstinted [ʌn'stɪntɪd] *adj* ilimitado, liberal
unstinting [ʌn'stɪntɪŋ] *adj* porfiado, tenaz; generoso, liberal
unstitch [ʌn'stɪtʃ] *va* descoser
unstop [ʌn'stɑp] (*pret & pp:* **-stopped;** *ger:* **-stopping**) *va* destaponar (*una botella, las fosas nasales*)
unstrap [ʌn'stræp] (*pret & pp:* **-strapped;** *ger:* **-strapping**) *va* aflojar las correas de
unstressed [ʌn'strɛst] *adj* sin énfasis; (phonet.) inacentuado
unstring [ʌn'strɪŋ] (*pret & pp:* **-strung**) *va* desencordar, desencordelar; desensartar; debilitar, trastornar
unstrung [ʌn'strʌŋ] *adj* debilitado, trastornado, nervioso; *pret & pp de* **unstring**
unstudied [ʌn'stʌdɪd] *adj* natural, no afectado
unsubdued [ˌʌnsəb'djud] o [ˌʌnsəb'dud] *adj* indomado, insumiso
unsubmissive [ˌʌnsəb'mɪsɪv] *adj* insumiso
unsubstantial [ˌʌnsəb'stænʃəl] *adj* insubstancial
unsuccessful [ˌʌnsək'sɛsfəl] *adj* fracasado, sin éxito, impróspero, desairado
unsufferable [ʌn'sʌfərəbəl] *adj* inaguantable
unsuitability [ˌʌnsutə'bɪlɪtɪ] o [ˌʌnsjutə'bɪlɪtɪ] *s* inconveniencia; incompetencia
unsuitable [ʌn'sutəbəl] o [ʌn'sjutəbəl] *adj* inconveniente, inadecuado; incompetente
unsuited [ʌn'sutɪd] o [ʌn'sjutɪd] *adj* inadecuado; incompetente
unsullied [ʌn'sʌlɪd] *adj* inmaculado
unsung [ʌn'sʌŋ] *adj* no cantado
unsure [ʌn'ʃur] *adj* incierto; inseguro
unsurmised [ˌʌnsər'maɪzd] *adj* no conjeturado
unsurpassed [ˌʌnsər'pæst] o [ˌʌnsər'pɑst] *adj* insuperado, sin par
unsuspected [ˌʌnsə'spɛktɪd] *adj* insospechado
unsweetened [ʌn'switənd] *adj* no endulzado
unswept [ʌn'swɛpt] *adj* no barrido
unswerving [ʌn'swʌrvɪŋ] *adj* firme, inmutable, resoluto
unsymmetrical [ˌʌnsɪ'mɛtrɪkəl] *adj* asimétrico, disimétrico
unsympathetic [ˌʌnsɪmpə'θɛtɪk] *adj* incompasivo, indiferente
unsystematic [ˌʌnsɪstə'mætɪk] o **unsystematical** [ˌʌnsɪstə'mætɪkəl] *adj* sin sistema, no metódico
untactful [ʌn'tæktfəl] *adj* sin tacto, indiscreto
untainted [ʌn'tentɪd] *adj* incorrupto, sin mancha
untamable o **untameable** [ʌn'teməbəl] *adj* indomable
untamed [ʌn'temd] *adj* indomado
untangle [ʌn'tæŋgəl] *va* desenredar, desenmarañar
untaught [ʌn'tɔt] *adj* sin instrucción; natural, espontáneo
untaxed [ʌn'tækst] *adj* libre de impuesto
unteachable [ʌn'titʃəbəl] *adj* indócil
untempered [ʌn'tɛmpərd] *adj* sin templar
untenable [ʌn'tɛnəbəl] o [ʌn'tinəbəl] *adj* insostenible
untenanted [ʌn'tɛnəntɪd] *adj* sin arrendar, desocupado
unthankful [ʌn'θæŋkfəl] *adj* ingrato, desagradecido
unthatch [ʌn'θætʃ] *va* desbardar; (fig.) descubrir
unthinkable [ʌn'θɪŋkəbəl] *adj* impensable
unthinking [ʌn'θɪŋkɪŋ] *adj* irreflexivo; instintivo
unthoughtful [ʌn'θɔtfəl] *adj* irreflexivo; inconsiderado; aturdido
unthought-of [ʌn'θɔtˌɑv] *adj* no soñado, no imaginado; olvidado
unthread [ʌn'θrɛd] *va* desensartar; deshebrar, desenhebrar; desenredar; abrirse camino por
unthrifty [ʌn'θrɪftɪ] *adj* gastador, pródigo
untidy [ʌn'taɪdɪ] *adj* desaliñado, desaseado
untie [ʌn'taɪ] (*pret & pp:* **-tied;** *ger:* **-tying**) *va* desatar; soltar; *vn* desatarse
until [ʌn'tɪl] *prep* hasta; *conj* hasta que; **to wait until** + *ind* aguardar a que + *subj,* esperar a que + *subj*
untillable [ʌn'tɪləbəl] *adj* incultivable
untilled [ʌn'tɪld] *adj* inculto
untimely [ʌn'taɪmlɪ] *adj* intempestivo; pre-

maturo; *adv* intempestivamente; prematuramente
untiring [ʌn'taɪrɪŋ] *adj* incansable, infatigable
untitled [ʌn'taɪtəld] *adj* sin título
unto ['ʌntu] *prep* (archaic) a; (archaic) hasta
untold [ʌn'told] *adj* nunca dicho; inenarrable; incalculable
untouchable [ʌn'tʌtʃəbəl] *adj* intangible; *s* intocable (*individuo de una casta inferior en la India*)
untoward [ʌn'tord] *adj* desfavorable; terco, indócil; adverso, contrario, desdichado
untrained [ʌn'trend] *adj* indócil, indisciplinado; no adiestrado; no entrenado
untrammeled o **untrammelled** [ʌn'træməld] *adj* libre, sin trabas
untransferable [,ʌntræns'fʌrəbəl] *adj* intransferible
untranslatable [,ʌntræns'letəbəl] *adj* intraducible
untranslated [,ʌntræns'letɪd] *adj* sin traducir
untraveled o **untravelled** [ʌn'trævəld] *adj* que no ha viajado; aislado, inexplorado
untried [ʌn'traɪd] *adj* no probado
untrod [ʌn'trɑd] *adj* no pisado, no trillado
untrue [ʌn'tru] *adj* falso; inexacto; infiel; desalineado; desplomado
untruss [ʌn'trʌs] *va* desatar, desempaquetar; descargar; desarmar
untrustworthy [ʌn'trʌst,wʌrðɪ] *adj* indigno de confianza
untruth [ʌn'truθ] *s* falsedad, mentira
untruthful [ʌn'truθfəl] *adj* falso, mentiroso
untuck [ʌn'tʌk] *va* desenfaldar
untutored [ʌn'tjutərd] o [ʌn'tutərd] *adj* sin instrucción
untwine [ʌn'twaɪn] *va* desenroscar; desenmarañar; *vn* desenroscarse; desenmarañarse
untwist [ʌn'twɪst] *va* destorcer; desenmarañar; *vn* destorcerse; desenmarañarse
unused [ʌn'juzd] *adj* inutilizado, inusitado; deshabituado, no acostumbrado
unusual [ʌn'juʒuəl] *adj* inusual, extraordinario
unusually [ʌn'juʒuəlɪ] *adv* extraordinariamente
unutterable [ʌn'ʌtərəbəl] *adj* indecible, inexpresable
unutterably [ʌn'ʌtərəblɪ] *adv* indeciblemente, inexpresablemente
unvaccinated [ʌn'væksɪ,netɪd] *adj* sin vacunar
unvanquished [ʌn'væŋkwɪʃt] *adj* invicto
unvarnished [ʌn'vɑrnɪʃt] *adj* sin barnizar; (fig.) sencillo, sin adornos
unveil [ʌn'vel] *va* quitar el velo a; descubrir; inaugurar, develar, descubrir (*p.ej., una estatua*); *vn* quitarse el velo; descubrirse, revelarse
unveiling [ʌn'velɪŋ] *s* inauguración, develación (*de una estatua*)
unventilated [ʌn'ventɪ,letɪd] *adj* sin ventilación
unverified [ʌn'verɪfaɪd] *adj* sin verificar, sin comprobar
unvoice [ʌn'vɔɪs] *va* (phonet.) ensordecer, afonizar; *vn* (phonet.) ensordecerse, afonizarse
unvoiced [ʌn'vɔɪst] *adj* no expresado; (phonet.) insonoro, afonizado
unvoicing [ʌn'vɔɪsɪŋ] *s* (phonet.) afonización
unwanted [ʌn'wɑntɪd] *adj* indeseado
unwarrantable [ʌn'wɑrəntəbəl] o [ʌn'wɔrəntəbəl] *adj* injustificable
unwarranted [ʌn'wɑrəntɪd] o [ʌn'wɔrəntɪd] *adj* no justificado; desautorizado; no asegurado, sin garantía
unwary [ʌn'werɪ] *adj* incauto, imprudente
unwashed [ʌn'wɑʃt] o [ʌn'wɔʃt] *adj* sucio, sin lavar; **the great unwashed** la canalla, el populacho
unwavering [ʌn'wevərɪŋ] *adj* firme, resuelto, determinado
unweaned [ʌn'wind] *adj* sin destetar
unwearied [ʌn'wɪrɪd] *adj* no cansado; incansable
unweave [ʌn'wiv] (*pret:* **-wove;** *pp:* **-woven**) *va* destejer; desenmarañar; *vn* destejerse; desenmarañarse
unwed [ʌn'wed] o **unwedded** [ʌn'wedɪd] *adj* soltero, no casado
unwelcome [ʌn'welkəm] *adj* no bienvenido, mal acogido; importuno, molesto
unwell [ʌn'wel] *adj* enfermo, indispuesto; menstruante
unwept [ʌn'wept] *adj* no llorado; no vertido (*dícese de las lágrimas*)
unwholesome [ʌn'holsəm] *adj* insalubre
unwieldy [ʌn'wildɪ] *adj* pesado, abultado, inmanejable
unwilling [ʌn'wɪlɪŋ] *adj* desinclinado, maldispuesto; **willing or unwilling** que quiera o que no quiera
unwillingness [ʌn'wɪlɪŋnɪs] *s* desinclinación, mala gana
unwillingly [ʌn'wɪlɪŋlɪ] *adv* de mala gana
unwind [ʌn'waɪnd] (*pret & pp:* **-wound**) *va* desenvolver; (fig.) desenvolver (*p.ej., un cuento*); *vn* desenvolverse; distenderse (*el muelle del reloj*)
unwired [ʌn'waɪrd] *adj* sin alambres
unwise [ʌn'waɪz] *adj* mal aconsejado, indiscreto; tonto
unwitnessed [ʌn'wɪtnɪst] *adj* sin testigos
unwitting [ʌn'wɪtɪŋ] *adj* inconsciente, inadvertido
unwittingly [ʌn'wɪtɪŋlɪ] *adv* inconscientemente, inadvertidamente
unwomanly [ʌn'wumənlɪ] *adj* indigno de una mujer, poco propio de una mujer
unwonted [ʌn'wʌntɪd] *adj* desacostumbrado; inusitado
unworkable [ʌn'wʌrkəbəl] *adj* impracticable; irresoluble
unworkmanlike [ʌn'wʌrkmən,laɪk] *adj* chapucero; *adv* chapuceramente
unworldly [ʌn'wʌrldlɪ] *adj* no terrenal, no mundano, espiritual
unworthily [ʌn'wʌrðɪlɪ] *adv* indignamente
unworthiness [ʌn'wʌrðɪnɪs] *s* indignidad, desmerecimiento
unworthy [ʌn'wʌrðɪ] *adj* indigno, desmerecedor
unwound [ʌn'waund] *pret & pp de* **unwind**
unwounded [ʌn'wundɪd] *adj* ileso, sin heridas
unwrap [ʌn'ræp] (*pret & pp:* **-wrapped;** *ger:* **-wrapping**) *va* desenvolver; desempaquetar, desempapelar; *vn* desempaquetarse
unwrinkle [ʌn'rɪŋkəl] *va* desarrugar; *vn* desarrugarse
unwritten [ʌn'rɪtən] *adj* no escrito; en blanco; tradicional
unwritten law *s* ley no escrita; derecho de matar al seductor de la esposa o hija
unyielding [ʌn'jildɪŋ] *adj* terco; inflexible; insumiso
unyoke [ʌn'jok] *va* desuncir; *vn* desuncirse; desunirse
U.P. abr. de **United Press**
up [ʌp] *adv* arriba, en lo alto, en el aire; hacia arriba; para arriba; al norte; **to be all up with** no haber remedio para; **to be up** estar en lo alto, estar en el aire; estar levantado; vencer (*un plazo*); **to be up in arms** estar sobre las armas; protestar vehementemente; **to be up to a person** tocarle a uno; **to get up** levantarse; **to go up** subir; **to keep up** mantener; mantenerse firme; continuar; **to keep up with** correr parejas con; **up above** allá arriba; **up against it** (slang) en apuros; **up to** hasta; a la altura de; dispuesto para; al corriente de; armando, tramando; **what is up?** ¿qué pasa?; *prep* a lo alto de, en lo alto de; encima de; arriba de, hacia arriba de; sobre; subiendo; aguas arriba de (*cierto río*); **up the river** río arriba; **up the street** calle arriba; **up a tree** (slang) en apuros; *adj* ascendente; alto, elevado; en pie, derecho; de pie, levantado; levantado de la cama; acabado, terminado; cumplido; cercano; versado, al corriente; bajo consideración; **to be up and about** estar levantado (*dícese de uno que ha estado enfermo*); *s* altura; subida; prosperidad; **ups and downs** altibajos, vaivenes, vicisitudes; *va* levantar; (coll.) aumentar; *vn* levantarse; subir; animarse; **to up and** + *inf* (coll.) ponerse de repente a + *inf*
up-and-coming ['ʌpən'kʌmɪŋ] *adj* (coll.) emprendedor y prometedor
up-and-doing ['ʌpən'duɪŋ] *adj* (coll.) emprendedor

up-and-down [ˈʌpənˈdaʊn] *adj* vertical, perpendicular; (coll.) absoluto, categórico
up-and-up [ˈʌpənˈʌp] *s* subida progresiva; **on the up-and-up** (coll.) mejorándose; sin dolo, abiertamente
upas [ˈjupəs] *s* (bot.) upas (*árbol y resina*); (fig.) ponzoña
upborne [ʌpˈborn] *adj* sostenido; levantado en alto
upbraid [ʌpˈbred] *va* reconvenir; **to upbraid for** o **with** reconvenir con, de, por o sobre
upbraiding [ʌpˈbredɪŋ] *adj* recriminador; *s* recriminación, reconvención
upbringing [ˈʌpˌbrɪŋɪŋ) *s* educación
upbuild [ʌpˈbɪld] (*pret & pp:* **-built**) *va* construir, establecer, componer, armar
upcountry [ˈʌpˌkʌntrɪ] *s* (coll.) interior (del país); *adj* (coll.) del interior; *adv* en el interior, hacia el interior, tierra adentro
update [ʌpˈdet] *va* poner al día
upend [ʌpˈɛnd] *va* poner de punta, poner derecho; *vn* ponerse de punta, ponerse derecho
upgrade [ˈʌpˌgred] *s* pendiente en subida; **on the upgrade** ascendente; progresivo; *adj* ascendente; *adv* cuesta arriba; [ʌpˈgred] *va* mejorar la calidad de, adelantar a un nivel más alto, substituir un producto superior por (*uno inferior*)
upgrowth [ˈʌpˌgroθ] *s* crecimiento
upheaval [ʌpˈhivəl] *s* solevantamiento; (geol.) solevantamiento; (fig.) trastorno, cataclismo
upheave [ʌpˈhiv] *va* solevantar; *vn* solevantarse
upheld [ʌpˈhɛld] *pret & pp de* **uphold**
uphill [ˈʌpˌhɪl] *adj* ascendente; difícil, penoso; [ˌʌpˈhɪl] *adv* cuesta arriba
uphold [ʌpˈhold] (*pret & pp:* **-held**) *va* levantar en alto; sostener, apoyar; defender
upholster [ʌpˈholstər] *va* tapizar
upholsterer [ʌpˈholstərər] *s* tapicero
upholstery [ʌpˈholstərɪ] *s* (*pl:* **-ies**) tapicería
upkeep [ˈʌpˌkip] *s* conservación; gastos de conservación, gastos de entretenimiento
upland [ˈʌplənd] o [ˈʌpˌlænd] *s* terreno elevado, tierra alta; *adj* elevado, alto
upland cotton *s* algodón de altura, algodón de la Luisiana
upland plover *s* (orn.) batitú
uplift [ˈʌpˌlɪft] *s* levantamiento, elevación; mejora social; edificación; [ʌpˈlɪft] *va* levantar, elevar; edificar
upmost [ˈʌpmost] *adj* var. de **uppermost**
upon [əˈpɑn] *prep* en, sobre, encima de; hacia; contra; tras; **upon my honor!** ¡a fe mía!; **upon my word!** ¡por mi palabra!
upper [ˈʌpər] *adj* superior, alto; interior; exterior (*dícese de la ropa*); *s* pala (*del calzado*); **on one's uppers** con los zapatos sin suelas; (coll.) andrajoso, pobre
upper berth *s* litera alta
Upper Canada *s* el Alto Canadá (*hoy la provincia de Ontario*)
upper case *s* (print.) letra de caja alta
upper-case [ˈʌpərˌkes] *adj* (print.) de caja alta
upper-class [ˈʌpərˌklæs] o [ˈʌpərˌklɑs] *adj* de las altas clases, aristocrático; de tercer o cuarto año (*en las escuelas*)
upper classes *spl* altas clases
upperclassman [ˌʌpərˈklæsmən] o [ˌʌpərˈklɑsmən] *s* (*pl:* **-men**) estudiante de tercer o cuarto año
upper crust *s* (coll.) altas clases, alta sociedad
uppercut [ˈʌpərˌkʌt] *s* (box.) golpe de abajo arriba; (*pret & pp:* **-cut;** *ger:* **-cutting**) *va & vn* golpear de abajo arriba
upper hand *s* dominio, ventaja; **to have the upper hand** tener vara alta
Upper House *s* Cámara alta
upper lip *s* labio superior
upper middle class *s* alta burguesía
uppermost [ˈʌpərmost] *adj* (el) más alto, más elevado, supremo, último; predominante, principal; *adv* en lo más alto; en primer lugar
uppish [ˈʌpɪʃ] *adj* (coll.) arrogante, copetudo
upraise [ʌpˈrez] *va* levantar
uprear [ʌpˈrɪr] *va* levantar; *vn* levantarse
upright [ˈʌpˌraɪt] *adj* vertical, derecho; (fig.) recto, probo; *adv* verticalmente; *s* montante
uprightness [ˈʌpˌraɪtnɪs] *s* verticalidad; (fig.) rectitud, probidad
upright piano *s* piano vertical, piano recto
uprise [ˈʌpˌraɪz] *s* subida; [ʌpˈraɪz] (*pret:* **-rose;** *pp:* **-risen**) *vn* levantarse; subir; sublevarse
uprisen [ʌpˈrɪzən] *pp de* **uprise**
uprising [ʌpˈraɪzɪŋ] o [ˈʌpˌraɪzɪŋ] *s* levantamiento, alboroto popular, sublevación; pendiente en subida
uproar [ˈʌpˌror] *s* tumulto, alboroto, conmoción; rugido
uproarious [ʌpˈrorɪəs] *adj* tumultuoso
uproot [ʌpˈrut] o [ʌpˈrʊt] *va* desarraigar, descepar; (fig.) desarraigar
uprose [ʌpˈroz] *pret de* **uprise**
uprouse [ʌpˈraʊz] *va* despertar, excitar, mover
upset [ˈʌpˌsɛt] *s* vuelco; contratiempo, trastorno; enfermedad; disputa; [ʌpˈsɛt] o [ˈʌpˌsɛt] *adj* volcado; trastornado, perturbado; indispuesto; [ʌpˈsɛt] (*pret & pp:* **-set;** *ger:* **-setting**) *va* volcar; trastornar, perturbar; enfermar, indisponer; *vn* volcar
upset price *s* precio mínimo fijado en una subasta
upsetting [ʌpˈsɛtɪŋ] *adj* inquietante, desconcertante
upshot [ˈʌpˌʃɑt] *s* resultado; quid, esencia, toque
upside [ˈʌpˌsaɪd] *s* parte superior; **to turn upside down** volcar; trastornar; volcarse; trastornarse; **upside down** al revés, lo de arriba abajo; en confusión, revuelto
upstage [ˈʌpˌstedʒ] *adj* situado al fondo de la escena; (coll.) altanero, arrogante; [ˌʌpˈstedʒ] *adv* al fondo de la escena, hacia el fondo de la escena
upstairs [ˌʌpˈstɛrz] *adv* arriba; [ˈʌpˌstɛrz] *adj* de arriba; *s* piso de arriba; pisos superiores
upstanding [ʌpˈstændɪŋ] *adj* derecho, erguido; (fig.) recto, probo
upstart [ˈʌpˌstɑrt] *adj & s* advenedizo; presuntuoso
upstate [ˈʌpˌstet] *adj* (U.S.A.) interior, septentrional
upstream [ˈʌpˌstrim] *adv* aguas arriba, río arriba, contra la corriente
upstroke [ˈʌpˌstrok] *s* plumada ascendente; (mach.) carrera ascendente
upsurge [ˈʌpˌsʌrdʒ] *s* subida repentina (*p.ej., de precios*); [ʌpˈsʌrdʒ] *vn* subir repentinamente
upswing [ˈʌpˌswɪŋ] *s* movimiento hacia arriba; (fig.) mejora notable; **on the upswing** mejorando notablemente
uptake [ˈʌpˌtek] *s* levantamiento, subida; comprensión; canal de llamas ascendente; canal de ventilación; captación (*de un trazador radiactivo*)
upthrust [ˈʌpˌθrʌst] *s* solevantamiento; (geol.) solevantamiento
up-to-date [ˈʌptʊˌdet] *adj* que va hasta la fecha; moderno, reciente, de última moda, de última hora; al corriente
up-to-the-minute [ˈʌptʊðəˈmɪnɪt] *adj* moderno; al corriente
uptown [ˈʌpˌtaʊn] *adj* de arriba, de la parte alta de la ciudad; [ˈʌpˈtaʊn] *adv* arriba, hacia la parte alta de la ciudad
uptrend [ˈʌpˌtrɛnd] *s* tendencia al alza
upturn [ˈʌpˌtʌrn] *s* vuelta hacia arriba; mejora (*en los negocios, precios, etc.*); [ʌpˈtʌrn] *va* volver hacia arriba; *vn* volverse hacia arriba
upturned [ʌpˈtʌrnd] *adj* revuelto, invertido; arremangado; respingado
upward [ˈʌpwərd] *adj* ascendente; *adv* hacia arriba; **upward of** más de
upwardly [ˈʌpwərdlɪ] *adv* hacia arriba
upwards [ˈʌpwərdz] *adv* hacia arriba; **upwards of** más de
Ural [ˈjurəl] *adj* ural; **Urals** *spl* Urales, montes Urales
Ural-Altaic [ˈjurəlælˈteɪk] *adj & s* uraloaltaico
Uralian [juˈrelɪən] *adj* urálico
Ural Mountains *spl* montes Urales
Urania [juˈrenɪə] *s* (myth.) Urania
Uranian [juˈrenɪən] *adj* uranio
uranic [juˈrænɪk] *adj* (chem.) uránico
uraninite [juˈrænɪnaɪt] *s* (mineral.) uraninita
uranite [ˈjurənaɪt] *s* (mineral.) uranita
uranium [juˈrenɪəm] *s* (chem.) urano o uranio

uranographer [ˌjurəˈnɑgrəfər] *s* uranógrafo
uranography [ˌjurəˈnɑgrəfɪ] *s* uranografía
uranometry [ˌjurəˈnɑmɪtrɪ] *s* uranometría
uranous [ˈjurənəs] *adj* (chem.) uranoso
Uranus [ˈjurənəs] *s* (astr. & myth.) Urano
urao [uˈrɑo] *s* (mineral.) urao
urate [ˈjuret] *s* (chem.) urato
urban [ˈʌrbən] *adj* urbano (*perteneciente a la ciudad*); (*cap.*) *s* Urbano
urbane [ʌrˈben] *adj* urbano (*cortés, fino*)
urbanistic [ˌʌrbəˈnɪstɪk] *adj* urbanístico
urbanite [ˈʌrbənaɪt] *s* ciudadano
urbanity [ʌrˈbænɪtɪ] *s* urbanidad
urbanization [ˌʌrbənɪˈzeʃən] *s* urbanización
urbanize [ˈʌrbənaɪz] *va* urbanizar
urban renewal *s* renovación urbanística
urceolate [ˈʌrsɪəlet] *adj* urceolado
urchin [ˈʌrtʃɪn] *s* chiquillo, pilluelo, galopín; (ichth.) erizo; (mach.) erizo (*de la carda mecánica*)
Urdu [ˈurdu], [urˈdu] o [ʌrˈdu] *s* urdú
urea [juˈriə] o [ˈjurɪə] *s* (biochem.) urea
urease [ˈjurɪes] o [ˈjurɪez] *s* (biochem.) ureasa
uremia [juˈrimɪə] *s* (path.) uremia
uremic [juˈrimɪk] *adj* urémico
ureter [juˈritər] *s* (anat. & zool.) uréter
urethra [juˈriθrə] *s* (*pl:* **-thras** o **-thrae** [θri]) (anat.) uretra
urethral [juˈriθrəl] *adj* uretral
urethritis [ˌjurɪˈθraɪtɪs] *s* (path.) uretritis
urethroscope [juˈriθrəskop] *s* uretroscopio
urethroscopy [ˌjurɪˈθrɑskəpɪ] *s* uretroscopia
urge [ʌrdʒ] *s* impulso, instinto; *va* impeler, empujar; impulsar, incitar; apremiar, instar; pedir instantemente; **to urge to** + *inf* instar a que + *subj*; *vn* apresurarse; apremiar; presentar argumentos o pretensiones
urgency [ˈʌrdʒənsɪ] *s* (*pl:* **-cies**) urgencia; instancia, insistencia
urgent [ˈʌrdʒənt] *adj* urgente; insistente, apremiante
Uriah [juˈraɪə] *s* (Bib.) Urías
uric [ˈjurɪk] *adj* úrico
uric acid *s* (chem.) ácido úrico
urinal [ˈjurɪnəl] *s* orinal (*vaso*); urinal o urinario (*lugar*)
urinalysis [ˌjurɪˈnælɪsɪs] *s* (*pl:* **-ses** [siz]) urinálisis
urinary [ˈjurɪˌnerɪ] *adj* urinario; *s* (*pl:* **-ies**) urinal (*lugar*)
urinary calculus *s* (path.) cálculo urinario
urinary tract *s* (anat.) vías urinarias
urinate [ˈjurɪnet] *va* orinar (*p.ej., sangre*); *vn* orinar u orinarse
urination [ˌjurɪˈneʃən] *s* urinación, micción
urine [ˈjurɪn] *s* orina, orines
urn [ʌrn] *s* urna; cafetera o tetera con hornillo y grifo; (arch.) jarrón
urodelan [ˌjuroˈdilən] *adj & s* (zool.) urodelo
urogenital [ˌjuroˈdʒenɪtəl] *adj* urogenital
urolith [ˈjurolɪθ] *s* (path.) urolito
urolithiasis [ˌjurolɪˈθaɪəsɪs] *s* (path.) urolitiasis
urologic [ˌjuroˈlɑdʒɪk] o **urological** [ˌjuroˈlɑdʒɪkəl] *adj* urológico
urologist [jurˈɑlədʒɪst] *s* urólogo
urology [jurˈɑlədʒɪ] *s* urología
uropygial [ˌjuroˈpɪdʒɪəl] *adj* uropigal
uropygium [ˌjuroˈpɪdʒɪəm] *s* uropigio, rabadilla (*de las aves*)
uroscopy [jurˈɑskəpɪ] *s* uroscopia
urosis [jurˈosɪs] *s* (path.) urosis
Ursa Major [ˈʌrsəˈmedʒər] *s* (astr.) Osa Mayor
Ursa Minor [ˈʌrsəˈmaɪnər] *s* (astr.) Osa Menor
ursine [ˈʌrsaɪn] o [ˈʌrsɪn] *adj* ursino; velloso
ursine dasyure [ˈdæsɪjur] *s* (zool.) diablo de Tasmania
ursine howler *s* (zool.) aluato
Ursula [ˈʌrsjulə] *s* Úrsula
Ursuline [ˈʌrsjulɪn] o [ˈʌrsjulaɪn] *adj* ursulino; *s* ursulina
urticaceous [ˌʌrtɪˈkeʃəs] *adj* (bot.) urticáceo
urticant [ˈʌrtɪkənt] *adj* urticante
urticaria [ˌʌrtɪˈkerɪə] *s* (path.) urticaria
urtication [ˌʌrtɪˈkeʃən] *s* (med.) urticación
Uru. abr. de **Uruguay**
Uruguay [ˈjurəgwe] o [ˈjurəgwaɪ] *s* el Uruguay
Uruguayan [ˌjurəˈgweən] o [ˌjurəˈgwaɪən] *adj & s* uruguayo
urus [ˈjurəs] *s* (zool.) uro
U.S. abr. de **United States**
us [ʌs] *pron pers* nos; nosotros
U.S.A. abr. de **United States of America, United States Army** y **Union of South Africa**
usability [ˌjuzəˈbɪlɪtɪ] *s* disponibilidad
usable [ˈjuzəbəl] *adj* utilizable, aprovechable, usual
usage [ˈjusɪdʒ] o [ˈjuzɪdʒ] *s* uso
usance [ˈjuzəns] *s* (econ.) interés o renta (*beneficio sacado del dinero invertido o prestado*); (com.) plazo a que se debe pagar una letra de cambio; **at usance** al usado
U.S.C.G. abr. de **United States Coast Guard**
use [jus] *s* uso, empleo; **in use** en uso; **out of use** desusado; **to be of no use** no servir para nada; **to have no use for** no necesitar; no servirse de; (coll.) no tener buena opinión de, tener en poco; **to make use of** servirse de; **to put to use** servirse de, poner en uso; [juz] *va* usar, emplear; tratar; agotar, consumir; acostumbrar; **to use language** decir blasfemias; **to use up** agotar, consumir; (coll.) agotar, cansar, rendir; *vn* ir con frecuencia, concurrir con frecuencia; soler, p.ej., **I used to go out for a walk every morning** solía salir de paseo todas las mañanas o salía de paseo todas las mañanas
useable [ˈjuzəbəl] *adj* var. de **usable**
used [juzd] *adj* usado (*empleado; gastado por el uso; acostumbrado*); **used to** [ˈjustu] acostumbrado a
used car *s* coche usado, coche de segunda mano, coche de ocasión
useful [ˈjusfəl] *adj* útil
usefulness [ˈjusfəlnɪs] *s* utilidad
useless [ˈjuslɪs] *adj* inútil, inservible
uselessness [ˈjuslɪsnɪs] *s* inutilidad
user [ˈjuzər] *s* usuario; (law) usufructuario
U-shaped [ˈjuˌʃept] *adj* en forma de U
usher [ˈʌʃər] *s* acomodador (*p.ej., en el teatro*); ujier, portero; (Brit.) repetidor; *va* acomodar; anunciar, introducir; **to usher in** anunciar, introducir
usherette [ˌʌʃəˈret] *s* acomodadora
U.S.M. abr. de **United States Mail** y **United States Marine**
U.S.M.A. abr. de **United States Military Academy**
U.S.M.C. abr. de **United States Marine Corps**
U.S.N. abr. de **United States Navy**
U.S.N.A. abr. de **United States Naval Academy**
U.S.N.G. abr. de **United States National Guard**
U.S.S. abr. de **United States Senate** y **United States Ship, Steamer** o **Steamship**
U.S.S.R. o **USSR** abr. de **Union of Soviet Socialist Republics**
ustulation [ˌʌstʃəˈleʃən] *s* chamusquina, socarrina; (pharm.) ustulación
usu. abr. de **usual** y **usually**
usual [ˈjuʒuəl] *adj* usual; **as usual** como de costumbre
usually [ˈjuʒuəlɪ] *adv* usualmente
usucapion [ˌjuzjuˈkepɪɑn] *s* (law) usucapión
usucapt [ˈjuzjukæpt] *va* (law) usucapir
usufruct [ˈjuzjufrʌkt] *s* (law) usufructo; *va* usufructuar
usurer [ˈjuʒərər] *s* usurero
usurious [juˈʒurɪəs] *adj* usurario
usurp [juˈzʌrp] *va* usurpar
usurpation [ˌjuzʌrˈpeʃən] *s* usurpación
usurper [juˈzʌrpər] *s* usurpador
usury [ˈjuʒərɪ] *s* (*pl:* **-ries**) usura
Ut. abr. de **Utah**
utensil [juˈtensəl] *s* utensilio
uterine [ˈjutərɪn] o [ˈjutəraɪn] *adj* uterino
uterus [ˈjutərəs] *s* (*pl:* **-i** [aɪ]) (anat.) útero
utilitarian [ˌjutɪlɪˈterɪən] *adj* utilitario; utilitarista; *s* utilitarista
utilitarianism [ˌjutɪlɪˈterɪənɪzəm] *s* utilitarismo
utility [juˈtɪlɪtɪ] *s* (*pl:* **-ties**) utilidad; empresa de servicio público; *adj* para uso general

utility man *s* factótum, criado para todo; (baseball) suplente; (theat.) racionista
utilization [ˌjutɪlɪˈzeʃən] *s* utilización
utilize [ˈjutɪlaɪz] *va* utilizar
utmost [ˈʌtmost] *adj* sumo, supremo, extremo, último; más grande, mayor posible; más distante, más lejano; *s* más alto grado; **the utmost** lo sumo, lo mayor, lo más; **to do one's utmost** hacer todo lo posible; **to the utmost** a más no poder
utopia o **Utopia** [juˈtopɪə] *s* utopia o utopía
utopian o **Utopian** [juˈtopɪən] *adj* utópico; utopista; *s* utopista
utopianism [juˈtopɪənɪzəm] *s* utopismo
utricle [ˈjutrɪkəl] *s* (anat.) utrículo; (bot.) utrícula
utricular [juˈtrɪkjələr] *adj* utricular
utter [ˈʌtər] *adj* total, completo, absoluto, terminante; *va* proferir, pronunciar, lanzar; expresar, manifestar, dar a conocer; poner en circulación (*p.ej., moneda falsa*)
utterable [ˈʌtərəbəl] *adj* decible, articulable, pronunciable
utterance [ˈʌtərəns] *s* pronunciación; expresión, manifestación; declaración, palabras
utterly [ˈʌtərlɪ] *adv* totalmente, completamente, absolutamente, terminantemente
uttermost [ˈʌtərmost] *adj & s* var. de **utmost**
uvea [ˈjuvɪə] *s* (anat.) úvea
uvula [ˈjuvjələ] *s* (*pl:* **-las** o **-lae** [li]) (anat.) úvula
uvular [ˈjuvjələr] *adj* (anat. & phonet.) uvular
uvulitis [ˌjuvjəˈlaɪtɪs] *s* (path.) uvulitis
uxorial [ʌkˈsorɪəl] *adj* uxorio (*perteneciente a la esposa*)
uxoricide [ʌkˈsorɪsaɪd] *s* uxoricida (*marido*); uxoricidio (*acción*)
uxorious [ʌkˈsorɪəs] *adj* uxorio (*muy amante de su mujer y demasiado complaciente con ella*)
Uz [ʌz] *s* (Bib.) tierra de Hus
Uzbeg [ˈʌzbɛg] o **Uzbek** [ˈʌzbɛk] *s* uzbeco
Uzbekistan [ˌuzbɛkɪˈstɑn] *s* el Uzbekistán

V

V, v [vi] *s* (*pl:* **V's, v's** [viz]) vigésima segunda letra del alfabeto inglés.
v. abr. de **verb, verse, versus, vice-, vide** (Lat.) **see, voice, volt, voltage, volume** y **von**
v abr. de **volt**
V. abr. de **Venerable, Vice, Victoria, Viscount** y **Volunteer**
Va. abr. de **Virginia** (*EE.UU.*)
V.A. abr. de **Veterans' Administration, Vicar Apostolic** y **Vice-Admiral**
vacancy ['vekənsɪ] *s* (*pl:* **-cies**) vacío; vacancia, vacante (*empleo sin proveer*); apartamento o cuarto vacante; desocupación, ociosidad; vacuidad, vaciedad
vacant ['vekənt] *adj* vacío; vacante (*empleo, cuarto*); distraído, necio; vago (*dícese, p.ej., de la mirada*)
vacate ['veket] *va* dejar vacante, desocupar; anular, revocar; *vn* marcharse
vacation [ve'keʃən] *s* vacación; vacaciones; **to be on vacation** estar de vacaciones; **to go away on a vacation** o **to leave for a vacation** marcharse de vacaciones; *vn* tomar vacaciones
vacationist [ve'keʃənɪst] *s* vacacionista
vacations with pay *spl* vacaciones retribuídas, vacaciones en el trabajo
vaccinate ['væksɪnet] *va* vacunar
vaccination [,væksɪ'neʃən] *s* vacunación
vaccine ['væksin] o ['væksɪn] *s* vacuna
vaccine therapy *s* vacunoterapia
vacillate ['væsɪlet] *vn* vacilar
vacillating ['væsɪ,letɪŋ] *adj* vacilante
vacillation [,væsɪ'leʃən] *s* vacilación
vacuity [væ'kjuɪtɪ] *s* (*pl:* **-ties**) vacuidad
vacuo ['vækjuo]; **in vacuo** en el vacío
vacuole ['vækjuol] *s* (biol.) vacuola
vacuous ['vækjuəs] *adj* vacío; fatuo, necio
vacuum ['vækjuəm] *s* (*pl:* **-ums** o **-a** [ə]) vacío; *va* (coll.) limpiar con el aspirador, aspirar (*el polvo, las migajas*)
vacuum bottle *s* botella de vacío
vacuum brake *s* freno al vacío, freno de vacío
vacuum cleaner *s* aspirador de polvo
vacuum cup *s* ventosa
vacuum filter *s* filtro al vacío
vacuum pump *s* bomba al vacío
vacuum tank *s* (aut.) aspirador de gasolina, nodriza
vacuum tube *s* (elec.) tubo al vacío, tubo de vacío
vade mecum [,vedɪ'mikəm] *s* vademécum
vagabond ['vægəbɑnd] *adj & s* vagabundo
vagabondage ['vægəbɑndɪdʒ] *s* vagabundaje, vagabundeo
vagary [və'gerɪ] *s* (*pl:* **-ies**) capricho, extravagancia
vagina [və'dʒaɪnə] *s* (bot. & anat.) vagina
vaginal ['vædʒɪnəl] o [və'dʒaɪnəl] *adj* vaginal
vaginate ['vædʒɪnet] *adj* vaginado
vaginitis [,vædʒɪ'naɪtɪs] *s* (path.) vaginitis
vaginula [və'dʒɪnjələ] *s* (bot. & zool.) vagínula
vagitus [və'dʒaɪtəs] *s* (med.) vagido
vagrancy ['vegrənsɪ] *s* (*pl:* **-cies**) vagancia, vagabundaje
vagrant ['vegrənt] *adj* vagante, vagabundo; *s* vagabundo
vague [veg] *adj* vago
vagueness ['vegnɪs] *s* vaguedad
vagus ['vegəs] *s* (*pl:* **-gi** [dʒaɪ]) (anat.) vagus
vain [ven] *adj* vano; vanidoso; **in vain** en vano
vainglorious [,ven'glorɪəs] *adj* vanaglorioso
vainglory [,ven'glorɪ] *s* vanagloria
vainly ['venlɪ] *adv* vanamente; vanidosamente
vair [ver] *s* vero (*piel*); (her.) veros
valance ['væləns] *s* doselera (*cenefa del dosel*); guardamalleta (*sobre la cortina*)
vale [vel] *s* valle
valediction [,vælɪ'dɪkʃən] *s* despedida
valedictorian [,vælɪdɪk'torɪən] *s* alumno que pronuncia el discurso de despedida
valedictory [,vælɪ'dɪktərɪ] *s* (*pl:* **-ries**) discurso de despedida; *adj* de despedida
valence ['veləns] *s* (chem.) valencia
Valenciennes [,vælənsɪ'enz] *s* encaje de Valenciennes
valency ['velənsɪ] *s* (*pl:* **-cies**) var. de **valence**
valentine ['væləntaɪn] *s* tarjeta (*afectuosa o jocosa anónima*) del día de San Valentín; amado o amada (*escogida en ese día*); **St. Valentine** San Valentín
Valentine's Day *s* día de San Valentín; día de los enamorados, día de los corazones (*14 de febrero*)
vale of tears *s* valle de lágrimas
Vale of Tempe ['tempɪ] *s* (hist.) valle de Tempe
valerian [və'lɪrɪən] *s* (bot. & pharm.) valeriana
valet ['vælɪt] o ['væle] *s* paje, sirviente
valet de chambre [væ'ledə'ʃɑ̃brə] *s* paje de cámara, ayuda de cámara
valetudinarian [,vælɪ,tjudɪ'nerɪən] o [,vælɪtudɪ'nerɪən] *adj & s* valetudinario
Valhalla [væl'hælə] *s* (myth.) el Valhala
valiancy ['væljənsɪ] *s* (*pl:* **-cies**) valentía (*valor, ánimo; hazaña heroica*)
valiant ['væljənt] *adj* valiente
valid ['vælɪd] *adj* válido; vigente
validate ['vælɪdet] *va* validar
validation [,vælɪ'deʃən] *s* validación
validity [və'lɪdɪtɪ] *s* (*pl:* **-ties**) validez; vigencia
valise [və'lis] *s* maleta; velís (Am.)
Valkyrie [væl'kɪrɪ], ['vælkɪrɪ] o [væl'kaɪrɪ] *s* valquiria
vallation [væ'leʃən] *s* vallado
valley ['vælɪ] *s* valle; (arch.) lima hoya
valor ['vælər] *s* valor, coraje, ánimo
valorization [,vælərɪ'zeʃən] *s* valorización
valorize ['vælərаɪz] *va* valorizar
valorous ['vælərəs] *adj* valeroso
valour ['vælər] *s* (Brit.) var. de **valor**
valse [vɑls] *s* var. de **waltz**
valuable ['væljuəbəl] o ['væljəbəl] *adj* valioso (*que vale mucho*); valorable, estimable; **valuables** *spl* objetos de valor, joyas, alhajas
valuation [,vælju'eʃən] *s* valuación, valoración
value ['vælju] *s* valor; (mus.) valor; adquisición, inversión, p.ej., **a wonderful value** una adquisición extraordinaria, una inversión maravillosa; *va* valuar, valorar; estimar, tener en mucho
valued ['væljud] *adj* estimado, apreciado; valorado
valueless ['væljulɪs] *adj* sin valor
valuta [və'lutə] *s* (econ.) valuta
valvate ['vælvet] *adj* valvulado; valviforme
valve [vælv] *s* (anat., mach. & rad.) válvula; (biol.) valva; (bot.) ventalla (*de la vaina de una legumbre*); (mus.) llave; *va* gobernar por medio de válvulas
valve box *s* (mach.) caja de distribución
valve cap *s* tapita de válvula (*de neumático*)
valve chest *s* var. de **valve box**
valve gears *spl* distribución, mecanismo de distribución
valve-in-head ['vælvɪn'hed] *adj* con válvulas en la culata
valveless ['vælvlɪs] *adj* sin válvulas
valve lifter *s* levantaválvulas
valve seat *s* asiento de válvula
valve spring *s* muelle de válvula
valve stem *s* vástago de válvula
valvular ['vælvjələr] *adj* valvular
vamoose [væ'mus] *va* (slang) dejar rápidamente; *vn* (slang) marcharse rápidamente

vamp [væmp] *s* empella (*del calzado*); remiendo; (mus.) acompañamiento improvisado; (slang) vampiresa, mujer fatal; *va* poner empella a; remendar; enmendar, componer; (mus.) improvisar (*un acompañamiento*); (slang) coquetear con; **to vamp up** enmendar, componer; urdir para engañar; *vn* (mus.) improvisar; (slang) coquetear
vampire ['væmpaɪr] *s* vampiro; (zool.) vampiro; (fig.) vampiro (*concusionario*); mujer coqueta; vampiresa, mujer fatal (*mujer que sacrifica a su capricho a los hombres*)
van [væn] *s* carro de carga, camión, camión de mudanzas; (Brit.) furgón de equipajes; (mil.) vanguardia
vanadium [və'nedɪəm] *s* (chem.) vanadio
vanadium steel *s* acero al vanadio
Vandal ['vændəl] *adj* vándalo, vandálico; *s* vándalo; (*l.c.*) *adj* vandálico; *s* vándalo
vandalism ['vændəlɪzəm] *s* vandalismo
Vandyke beard [væn'daɪk] *s* barba puntiaguda
Vandyke collar *s* valona
vane [ven] *s* veleta (*para marcar la dirección del viento*); paleta (*de hélice*); barba (*de pluma*); aspa (*de molino*)
vang [væŋ] *s* (naut.) osta
vanguard ['væn,gɑrd] *s* (mil. & fig.) vanguardia; **in the vanguard** a vanguardia
vanilla [və'nɪlə] *s* (bot.) vainilla (*planta, fruto y extracto*)
vanillin ['vænɪlɪn] o [və'nɪlɪn] *s* (chem.) vainillina
vanish ['vænɪʃ] *vn* desvanecerse, desaparecer
vanishing cream *s* crema desvanecedora
vanishing point *s* punto de fuga, punto de desaparición; (perspective) punto de la vista
vanity ['vænɪtɪ] *s* (*pl:* **-ties**) vanidad; neceser de belleza, estuche de afeites; tocador
vanity case *s* neceser de belleza
vanity dresser o **table** *s* tocador
vanquish ['væŋkwɪʃ] *va* vencer, sujetar, dominar
vantage ['væntɪdʒ] o ['vɑntɪdʒ] *s* ventaja, superioridad
vantage ground *s* posición ventajosa
vanward ['vænwərd] *adj & adv* hacia el frente
vapid ['væpɪd] *adj* insípido
vapidity [væ'pɪdɪtɪ] *s* insipidez
vapor ['vepər] *s* vapor; niebla, bruma; vaho, exhalación; humo, quimera, sueño; *va* vaporizar; *vn* vaporear; jactarse
vaporable ['vepərəbəl] *adj* vaporable
vapor bath *s* baño de vapor
vapor heat *s* calefacción a vapor de muy baja presión
vaporish ['vepərɪʃ] *adj* vaporoso; melancólico
vaporization [,vepərɪ'zeʃən] *s* vaporización; (med.) vaporización
vaporize ['vepəraɪz] *va* vaporizar; *vn* vaporizarse
vaporizer ['vepə,raɪzər] *s* vaporizador
vaporous ['vepərəs] *adj* vaporoso; fugaz, inútil; vano, quimérico
vapor trail *s* (aer.) estela de vapor, rastro de condensación
vapory ['vepərɪ] *adj* vaporoso; melancólico, atrabilioso
var. abr. de **variant**
variability [,vɛrɪə'bɪlɪtɪ] *s* variabilidad
variable ['vɛrɪəbəl] *adj* variable; *s* (math.) variable
variable condenser *s* (elec.) condensador variable
variance ['vɛrɪəns] *s* variación, modificación, diferencia; desavenencia, desacuerdo; **at variance** en desacuerdo
variant ['vɛrɪənt] *adj & s* variante
variation [,vɛrɪ'eʃən] *s* variación
varicella [,værɪ'sɛlə] *s* (path.) varicela
varicocele ['værɪkə,sil] *s* (path.) varicocele
varicolored ['vɛrɪ,kʌlərd] *adj* abigarrado
varicose ['værɪkos] *adj* varicoso
varicose veins *spl* (path.) varices
varicosis [,værɪ'kosɪs] *s* (path.) varicosis
varicosity [,værɪ'kɑsɪtɪ] *s* (*pl:* **-ties**) varicosidad (*estado varicoso; varice*)
varied ['vɛrɪd] *adj* variado
variegate ['vɛrɪəget] o ['vɛrɪget] *va* jaspear, abigarrar
variegated ['vɛrɪə,getɪd] o ['vɛrɪ,getɪd] *adj* jaspeado, abigarrado
variegation [,vɛrɪə'geʃən] o [,vɛrɪ'geʃən] *s* jaspeado, abigarramiento
variety [və'raɪətɪ] *s* (*pl:* **-ties**) variedad; (theat.) variedades
variocoupler [,vɛrɪo'kʌplər] *s* (rad.) varioacoplador
variola [və'raɪələ] *s* (path.) viruela
varioloid ['vɛrɪələɪd] *s* (path.) varioloide
variolous [və'raɪələs] *adj* varioloso
variometer [,vɛrɪ'ɑmɪtər] *s* (elec., meteor. & rad.) variómetro
variorum [,vɛrɪ'orəm] *adj & s* variórum
various ['vɛrɪəs] *adj* vario; *adj pl* varios
varix ['vɛrɪks] *s* (*pl:* **varices** ['vɛrɪsiz]) (path.) varice o várice
varlet ['vɑrlɪt] *s* (archaic) lacayo, paje; (archaic) truhán, golfo
varmint ['vɑrmɪnt] *s* (coll. & dial.) bicho, sabandija; (coll. & dial.) golfo, bribón
varnish ['vɑrnɪʃ] *s* barniz; (fig.) capa, máscara, apariencia; *va* barnizar; (fig.) adornar, dar apariencia falsa a, encubrir
varnishing day *s* (f.a.) barnizado
varsity ['vɑrsɪtɪ] *s* (*pl:* **-ties**) (sport) universidad; (sport) equipo principal (*de la universidad*); *adj* (sport) universitario
varsovienne [,vær,so'vjɛn] *s* varsoviana (*baile y música*)
vary ['vɛrɪ] (*pret & pp:* **-ied**) *va & vn* variar
vas [væs] *s* (*pl:* **vasa** ['vesə]) (anat.) vaso
vascular ['væskjələr] *adj* (bot. & zool.) vascular
vasculous ['væskjələs] *adj* vasculoso
vase [ves] o [vez] *s* florero, jarrón; (arch.) copa, vaso
vasectomy [væ'sɛktəmɪ] *s* (*pl:* **-mies**) (surg.) vasectomía
vaseline ['væsəlin] *s* (trademark) vaselina
vasoligation [,væsolaɪ'geʃən] *s* (surg.) vasoligatura
vasomotor [,væso'motər] *adj* (physiol.) vasomotor
vassal ['væsəl] *adj & s* vasallo
vassalage ['væsəlɪdʒ] *s* vasallaje
vast [væst] o [vɑst] *adj* vasto
vastly ['væstlɪ] o ['vɑstlɪ] *adv* en sumo grado, sumamente
vastness ['væstnɪs] o ['vɑstnɪs] *s* vastedad
vat [væt] *s* tina, cuba
Vatican ['vætɪkən] *s* Vaticano
Vatican City *s* Ciudad del Vaticano, Ciudad Vaticana
vaticinate [və'tɪsɪnet] *va* vaticinar
vaudeville ['vodvɪl] o ['vɔdɪvɪl] *s* (theat.) variedades, teatro de variedades; (theat.) vaudeville, zarzuela
vault [vɔlt] *s* (arch. & anat.) bóveda; bóveda (*cripta*); bodega; cámara acorazada (*de un banco*); sepultura, tumba; bóveda celeste; salto; *va* abovedar; saltar; *vn* saltar
vaulted ['vɔltɪd] *adj* abovedado
vaulting ['vɔltɪŋ] *s* abovedado; salto
vaulting horse *s* potro de madera
vaunt [vɔnt] o [vɑnt] *s* jactancia; *va* jactarse de; *vn* jactarse
vb. abr. de **verb** y **verbal**
V.C. abr. de **Vice-Chancellor** y **Victoria Cross**
V.D. abr. de **venereal disease**
veal [vil] *s* carne de ternera
veal chop *s* chuleta de ternera
vector ['vɛktər] *adj* vectorial; *s* (biol. & math.) vector
Veda ['vedə] *s* Veda
Vedaic [ve'deɪk] *adj & s* védico
vedette [vɪ'dɛt] *s* centinela de avanzada; buque escucha
Vedic ['vedɪk] *adj & s* var. de **Vedaic**
Vedism ['vedɪzəm] *s* vedismo
veer [vɪr] *s* virada; *va* virar; soltar (*p.ej., un cabo*); *vn* virar; desviarse
veery ['vɪrɪ] *s* (*pl:* **-ies**) (orn.) tordo norteamericano (*Hylocichla fuscescens*)
Vega ['vigə] *s* (astr.) Vega
vegetable ['vɛdʒɪtəbəl] *adj* vegetal; *s* vegetal (*planta*); hortaliza, legumbre (*planta comestible*)

vegetable garden *s* huerto de hortalizas, huerto de legumbres, huerto de verduras
vegetable horsehair *s* crin vegetal
vegetable ivory *s* marfil vegetal
vegetable kingdom *s* reino vegetal
vegetable marrow *s* (bot.) calabaza (*variedad de Cucurbita Pepo*); (bot.) aguacate
vegetable mold *s* tierra vegetal, mantillo
vegetable oil *s* aceite vegetal
vegetable soup *s* sopa de hortelano, sopa de legumbres
vegetal ['vɛdʒɪtəl] *adj* vegetal
vegetarian [,vɛdʒɪ'tɛrɪən] *adj & s* vegetariano
vegetarianism [,vɛdʒɪ'tɛrɪənɪzəm] *s* vegetarianismo
vegetate ['vɛdʒɪtet] *vn* vegetar; (fig.) vegetar
vegetation [,vɛdʒɪ'teʃən] *s* vegetación
vegetative ['vɛdʒɪ,tetɪv] *adj* vegetativo
vehemence ['viɪməns] *s* vehemencia
vehement ['viɪmənt] *adj* vehemente
vehicle ['viɪkəl] *s* vehículo
vehicular [vɪ'hɪkjələr] *adj* vehicular
vehicular traffic *s* circulación rodada
Veii ['vijaɪ] *s* Veyos
veil [vel] *s* velo; (fig.) velo; **to take the veil** tomar el velo; *va* velar
veiling ['velɪŋ] *s* velo; material para velos
vein [ven] *s* vena; (fig.) rasgo; *va* jaspear, vetear
veined [vend] *adj* venoso, veteado
veining ['venɪŋ] *s* jaspeado; disposición a manera de venas
veinstone ['ven,ston] *s* (min.) ganga
velar ['vilər] *adj & s* (phonet.) velar
velarization [,vilərɪ'zeʃən] *s* (phonet.) velarización
velarize ['viləraɪz] *va* (phonet.) velarizar
velatura [,vɛlə'turə] *s* (paint.) veladura
vellum ['vɛləm] *s* vitela; papel avitelado; *adj* de vitela; avitelado
vellum paper *s* papel vitela, papel avitelado
velocipede [vɪ'lɑsɪpid] *s* velocípedo
velocity [vɪ'lɑsɪtɪ] *s* (*pl:* **-ties**) velocidad
velodrome ['vilədrom] *s* velódromo
velum ['viləm] *s* (*pl:* **-la** [lə]) (biol.) velo; (anat.) velo del paladar
velure [və'lur] *s* terciopelado; cepillo de pana; *va* cepillar con cepillo de pana
velvet ['vɛlvɪt] *s* terciopelo; vello, piel velluda; (slang) ganancia limpia; *adj* de terciopelo; aterciopelado
velvet glove *s* guante de terciopelo; **to handle with velvet gloves** tratar con cortesía superficial que encubre determinación inflexible
velvet grass *s* (bot.) heno blanco
velveteen [,vɛlvɪ'tin] *s* velludillo
velvet weaver *s* terciopelero
velvety ['vɛlvɪtɪ] *adj* aterciopelado
Ven. abr. de **Venerable** y **Venice**
venal ['vinəl] *adj* venal (*que se deja sobornar*)
venality [vi'nælɪtɪ] *s* venalidad
venation [vi'neʃən] *s* venación (*disposición de las venas*)
vend [vɛnd] *va* vender como buhonero; *vn* ser buhonero
Vendean [vɛn'diən] *adj & s* vandeano
vendee [vɛn'di] *s* comprador
vender ['vɛndər] *s* vendedor, buhonero
vendetta [vɛn'dɛtə] *s* vendetta, venganza entre una familia y otra
vending machine *s* distribuidor automático, tragaperras
vendor ['vɛndər] *s* vendedor, buhonero
vendue [vɛn'dju] o [vɛn'du] *s* almoneda, venduta
veneer [və'nɪr] *s* chapa, enchapado; (fig.) apariencia; *va* enchapar; (fig.) disfrazar
venerability [,vɛnərə'bɪlɪtɪ] *s* venerabilidad
venerable ['vɛnərəbəl] *adj* venerable
venerate ['vɛnəret] *va* venerar
veneration [,vɛnə'reʃən] *s* veneración
venereal [vɪ'nɪrɪəl] *adj* venéreo
venereal disease *s* enfermedad venérea
venery ['vɛnərɪ] *s* venus (*acto carnal*); (archaic) venación (*caza*)
Venetia [vɪ'niʃɪə] o [vɪ'niʃə] *s* Venecia (*provincia o distrito*)
Venetian [vɪ'niʃən] *adj & s* veneciano
Venetian blind *s* persiana de tiro, persiana interior americana
Venezuela [,vɛnɪ'zwilə] *s* Venezuela
Venezuelan [,vɛnɪ'zwilən] *adj & s* venezolano
Venezuelanism [,vɛnɪ'zwilənɪzəm] *s* venezolanismo
vengeance ['vɛndʒəns] *s* venganza; **with a vengeance** con violencia; con extremo, con creces
vengeful ['vɛndʒfəl] *adj* vengativo
venial ['vinɪəl] *adj* venial
veniality [,vinɪ'ælɪtɪ] *s* (*pl:* **-ties**) venialidad
venial sin *s* pecado venial
Venice ['vɛnɪs] *s* Venecia (*ciudad*)
venire [vɪ'naɪrɪ] *s* (law) auto de convocación del jurado
venireman [vɪ'naɪrɪmən] *s* (*pl:* **-men**) (law) persona convocada para jurado
venison ['vɛnɪzən] o ['vɛnzən] *s* carne de venado
venom ['vɛnəm] *s* veneno
venomous ['vɛnəməs] *adj* venenoso
venous ['vinəs] *adj* venal, venoso
vent [vɛnt] *s* orificio, agujero; ventosa, fogón (*oído del arma de fuego*); venteo; respiradero (*de un barril*); tapón; (found.) bravera; (mus.) orificio, agujero (*de un instrumento músico de viento*); (zool.) ano; abertura (*en una prenda de vestir*); chimenea (*del paracaídas*); **to give vent to** desahogar; *va* proveer de abertura; desahogar, expresar; **to vent one's spleen** descargar la bilis
ventage ['vɛntɪdʒ] *s* orificio, agujero
venthole ['vɛnt,hol] *s* venteo, respiradero (*en un barril*)
ventilate ['vɛntɪlet] *va* ventilar; (fig.) ventilar
ventilation [,vɛntɪ'leʃən] *s* ventilación
ventilator ['vɛntɪ,letər] *s* ventilador; extractor de aire
ventral ['vɛntrəl] *adj* ventral
ventrally ['vɛntrəlɪ] *adv* en posición ventral, en dirección ventral
ventricle ['vɛntrɪkəl] *s* (anat. & zool.) ventrículo
ventricular [vɛn'trɪkjələr] *adj* ventricular
ventriloquial [,vɛntrɪ'lokwɪəl] *adj* ventrílocuo
ventriloquism [vɛn'trɪləkwɪzəm] *s* ventriloquia
ventriloquist [vɛn'trɪləkwɪst] *s* ventrílocuo
ventriloquy [vɛn'trɪləkwɪ] *s* var. de **ventriloquism**
venture ['vɛntʃər] *s* empresa arriesgada, especulación; **at a venture** a la ventura; *va* aventurar; **to venture a guess** aventurar una suposición; *vn* aventurarse; **to venture on** arriesgarse en; **to venture out** arriesgarse fuera
venturesome ['vɛntʃərsəm] *adj* aventurero (*audaz, osado*); aventurado (*azaroso, peligroso*)
Venturi meter [vɛn'turɪ] *s* (trademark) venturímetro, medidor Venturi
Venturi tube *s* (hyd.) tubo Venturi
venturous ['vɛntʃərəs] *adj* aventurero; aventurado, peligroso
venue ['vɛnju] *s* (law) jurisdicción en que se ha cometido un crimen; (law) lugar donde se reúne el jurado
Venus ['vinəs] *s* (myth. & astr.) Venus; (fig.) Venus (*mujer de gran belleza*)
Venus's-flytrap ['vinəsɪz'flaɪ,træp] *s* (bot.) atrapamoscas, dionea
Venus's-looking-glass ['vinəsɪz'lʊkɪŋ,glæs] o ['vinəsɪz'lʊkɪŋ,glɑs] *s* (bot.) espejo de Venus
veracious [vɪ'reʃəs] *adj* veraz
veracity [vɪ'ræsɪtɪ] *s* (*pl:* **-ties**) veracidad
veranda o **verandah** [və'rændə] *s* terraza, galería
veratrine ['vɛrətrin] *s* (chem.) veratrina
verb [vʌrb] *s* (gram.) verbo; *adj* verbal
verbal ['vʌrbəl] *adj* verbal; (gram.) verbal; *s* (gram.) verbal
verbalism ['vʌrbəlɪzəm] *s* expresión verbal; verbalismo (*propensión a dar más importancia a las palabras que a los conceptos*); frase sin sentido o con poco sentido
verbalize ['vʌrbəlaɪz] *va* expresar por medio de palabras; (gram.) transformar en verbo; *vn* hablar con verbosidad, expresarse con verbosidad
verbatim [vər'betɪm] *adj* textual; *adv* al pie de la letra, palabra por palabra
verbena [vər'binə] *s* (bot.) verbena

verbenaceous [ˌvʌrbɪˈneʃəs] *adj* (bot.) verbenáceo
verbiage [ˈvʌrbɪɪdʒ] *s* verbosidad, palabrería
verbose [vərˈbos] *adj* verboso
verbosity [vərˈbɑsɪtɪ] *s* verbosidad
verdancy [ˈvʌrdənsɪ] *s* (*pl:* **-cies**) verdor; inocencia, sencillez
verdant [ˈvʌrdənt] *adj* verde; inocente, sencillo
verdict [ˈvʌrdɪkt] *s* veredicto
verdigris [ˈvʌrdɪgris] *s* cardenillo, verdete
verdure [ˈvʌrdʒər] *s* verdor
verdurous [ˈvʌrdʒərəs] *adj* verde y fresco, lozano, frondoso
verge [vʌrdʒ] *s* borde, margen; confín; báculo, vara; fuste (*de una columna*); **on the verge of** al borde de; **on the verge of** + *ger* a punto de + *inf; vn* acercarse; propender; **to verge on** o **upon** llegar casi hasta, rayar en; **to verge towards** propender a
verger [ˈvʌrdʒər] *s* sacristán; macero
Vergil [ˈvʌrdʒɪl] *s* var. de **Virgil**
Vergilian [vərˈdʒɪlɪən] *adj* var. de **Virgilian**
veriest [ˈvɛrɪɪst] *adj* extremo, sumo
verifiable [ˈvɛrɪˌfaɪəbəl] *adj* verificable
verification [ˌvɛrɪfɪˈkeʃən] *s* verificación
verify [ˈvɛrɪfaɪ] (*pret & pp:* **-fied**) *va* verificar, comprobar; (law) afirmar bajo juramento
verily [ˈvɛrɪlɪ] *adv* en verdad
verisimilar [ˌvɛrɪˈsɪmɪlər] *adj* verisímil
verisimilitude [ˌvɛrɪsɪˈmɪlɪtjud] o [ˌvɛrɪsɪˈmɪlɪtud] *s* verisimilitud
verism [ˈvɪrɪzəm] *s* verismo
veritable [ˈvɛrɪtəbəl] *adj* verdadero
veritably [ˈvɛrɪtəblɪ] *adv* verdaderamente
verity [ˈvɛrɪtɪ] *s* (*pl:* **-ties**) verdad
verjuice [ˈvʌrˌdʒus] *s* agrazada; acrimonia
verjuiced [ˈvʌrˌdʒust] *adj* agrio; de agrazada
vermeil [ˈvʌrmɪl] *s* plata, bronce o cobre sobredorados; (poet.) bermellón
vermicelli [ˌvʌrmɪˈsɛlɪ] *s* fideos
vermicidal [ˌvʌrmɪˈsaɪdəl] *adj* vermicida
vermicide [ˈvʌrmɪsaɪd] *s* vermicida
vermicular [vərˈmɪkjələr] *adj* vermicular
vermiform [ˈvʌrmɪfɔrm] *adj* vermiforme
vermiform appendix *s* (anat.) apéndice vermiforme
vermifuge [ˈvʌrmɪfjudʒ] *adj & s* (med.) vermífugo
vermilion [vərˈmɪljən] *s* bermellón; *adj* bermejo
vermilion flycatcher *s* (orn.) rubí
vermin [ˈvʌrmɪn] *spl* sabandijas (*animales o personas*); *ssg* sabandija (*persona*)
verminous [ˈvʌrmɪnəs] *adj* verminoso
vermis [ˈvʌrmɪs] *s* (anat.) vermis
vermouth [vərˈmuθ] o [ˈvʌrmuθ] *s* vermut
vernacular [vərˈnækjələr] *adj* vernáculo; *s* idioma vernáculo; idioma corriente; jerga (*lenguaje especial de un oficio o profesión*)
vernal [ˈvʌrnəl] *adj* vernal
vernal equinox *s* (astr.) equinoccio vernal o de primavera
vernal grass *s* (bot.) grama de olor o de los prados
vernally [ˈvʌrnəlɪ] *adv* primaveralmente
vernation [vərˈneʃən] *s* (bot.) vernación, prefoliación
vernier [ˈvʌrnɪər] o [ˈvʌrnɪr] *s* vernier
veronal [ˈvɛrənəl] *s* (trademark) veronal
Veronese [ˌvɛroˈniz] *adj* veronés; *s* (*pl:* **-nese**) veronés; el Veronés (*pintor*)
veronica [vəˈrɑnɪkə] *s* (bot.) verónica; lienzo de la Verónica; (taur.) verónica
Versailles [vɛrˈsaɪ] o [vərˈselz] *s* Versalles
versatile [ˈvʌrsətɪl] *adj* flexible, universal, hábil para muchas cosas; versátil (*inconstante*); (bot. & zool.) versátil
versatility [ˌvʌrsəˈtɪlɪtɪ] *s* (*pl:* **-ties**) flexibilidad, universalidad, variedad de habilidades; versatilidad (*inconstancia*)
verse [vʌrs] *s* verso; versículo (*en la Biblia*)
versed [vʌrst] *adj* versado; **versed in** versado en
versed sine *s* (trig.) seno verso
versemaker [ˈvʌrsˌmekər] *s* versificador
versicle [ˈvʌrsɪkəl] *s* (eccl.) versículo
versification [ˌvʌrsɪfɪˈkeʃən] *s* versificación
versifier [ˈvʌrsɪˌfaɪər] *s* versificador; poetastro
versify [ˈvʌrsɪfaɪ] (*pret & pp:* **-fied**) *va & vn* versificar
version [ˈvʌrʒən] o [ˈvʌrʃən] *s* versión; (obstet.) versión
verso [ˈvʌrso] *s* (*pl:* **-sos**) dorso, reverso; (print.) verso, vuelto
verst [vʌrst] *s* versta (*medida rusa igual a 3500 pies*)
versus [ˈvʌrsəs] *prep* contra
vertebra [ˈvʌrtɪbrə] *s* (*pl:* **-brae** [bri] o **-bras**) (anat. & zool.) vértebra
vertebral [ˈvʌrtɪbrəl] *adj* vertebral
vertebral column *s* (anat.) columna vertebral
vertebrate [ˈvʌrtɪbret] o [ˈvʌrtɪbrɪt] *adj & s* vertebrado
vertebrated [ˈvʌrtɪˌbretɪd] *adj* vertebrado
vertebration [ˌvʌrtɪˈbreʃən] *s* vertebración
vertex [ˈvʌrtɛks] *s* (*pl:* **-texes** o **-tices** [tɪsiz]) (math. & anat.) vértice; (astr.) cenit; ápice
vertical [ˈvʌrtɪkəl] *adj & s* vertical
vertical circle *s* (astr.) vertical
vertical hold *s* (telv.) bloqueo vertical
vertically [ˈvʌrtɪkəlɪ] *adv* verticalmente
vertical rudder *s* (aer.) timón de dirección
vertical stabilizer *s* (aer.) plano de dirección
verticil [ˈvʌrtɪsɪl] *s* (bot.) verticilo
verticilate [vərˈtɪsɪlet] *adj* (bot. & zool.) verticilado
vertiginous [vərˈtɪdʒɪnəs] *adj* vertiginoso
vertigo [ˈvʌrtɪgo] *s* (*pl:* **-gos** o **-goes**) vértigo; (vet.) modorra, vértigo
vervain [ˈvʌrven] *s* (bot.) verbena
verve [vʌrv] *s* energía, vigor, ánimo, viveza
very [ˈvɛrɪ] *adj* mismo, mismísimo; mero, puro; verdadero; *adv* muy; mucho, p.ej., **to be very hot** tener mucho calor
very high frequency *s* (rad. & telv.) frecuencia muy alta
vesical [ˈvɛsɪkəl] *adj* vesical
vesicant [ˈvɛsɪkənt] *adj & s* vesicante
vesicate [ˈvɛsɪket] *va* avejigar; *vn* avejigarse
vesicle [ˈvɛsɪkəl] *s* (anat., bot., path. & zool.) vesícula
vesicular [vɪˈsɪkjələr] *adj* vesicular
vesiculate [vɪˈsɪkjəlet] *adj* vesiculado
Vespasian [vɛsˈpeʒən] *s* Vespasiano
vesper [ˈvɛspər] *s* tarde, anochecer; oración de la tarde; campana que llama a vísperas; (*cap.*) *s* Véspero; **vespers** o **Vespers** *spl* (eccl.) vísperas; *adj* vespertino
vesper mouse *s* (zool.) rata de monte, rata silvestre
vespertine [ˈvɛspərtɪn] o [ˈvɛspərtaɪn] *adj* vespertino
vessel [ˈvɛsəl] *s* vasija, recipiente; bajel, buque, embarcación; (anat. & bot.) vaso
vest [vɛst] *s* chaleco; chaquetilla (*de mujer*); camiseta; *va* vestir; investir; conceder (*p.ej., poder*); **to vest with** investir de; *vn* vestirse; tener validez
Vesta [ˈvɛstə] *s* (myth.) Vesta
vestal [ˈvɛstəl] *adj* vestal; *s* vestal; virgen; monja
vestal virgin *s* vestal
vested [ˈvɛstɪd] *adj* revestido (*dícese, p.ej., de un prelado*); establecido por la ley
vested interests *spl* intereses creados
vestee [vɛsˈti] *s* pechera
vestibular [vɛsˈtɪbjələr] *adj* (anat.) vestibular
vestibule [ˈvɛstɪbjul] *s* vestíbulo; zaguán (*de una casa*); (anat.) vestíbulo (*del oído*)
vestibule car *s* (rail.) coche de vestíbulo
vestibule door *s* contrapuerta, portón
vestige [ˈvɛstɪdʒ] *s* vestigio; (biol.) vestigio
vestigial [vɛsˈtɪdʒɪəl] *adj* vestigial
vestment [ˈvɛstmənt] *s* vestidura
vest pocket *s* bolsillo de chaleco
vest-pocket [ˈvɛstˌpɑkɪt] *adj* diminuto, en miniatura
vestry [ˈvɛstrɪ] *s* (*pl:* **-tries**) sacristía; capilla; junta parroquial; reunión de la junta parroquial
vestryman [ˈvɛstrɪmən] *s* (*pl:* **-men**) miembro de la junta parroquial
vesture [ˈvɛstʃər] *s* vestidura; cubierta
Vesuvian [vɪˈsuvɪən] o [vɪˈsjuvɪən] *adj* vesubiano
Vesuvius [vɪˈsuvɪəs] o [vɪˈsjuvɪəs] *s* el Vesubio
vet. abr. de **veteran** y **veterinary**
vetch [vɛtʃ] *s* (bot.) vicia; (bot.) veza, arveja

veteran ['vɛtərən] *adj* veterano; *s* veterano; (mil.) veterano, ex combatiente
veterinarian [,vɛtərɪ'nɛrɪən] *s* veterinario
veterinary ['vɛtərɪ,nɛrɪ] *adj* veterinario; *s* (*pl:* **-ies**) veterinario
veterinary medicine *s* medicina veterinaria
vetiver ['vɛtɪvər] *s* (bot.) vetiver
veto ['vito] *s* (*pl:* **-toes**) veto; *adj* del veto; *va* vetar
vex [vɛks] *va* vejar
vexation [vɛks'eʃən] *s* vejación
vexatious [vɛks'eʃəs] *adj* vejante, vejatorio
vexedly ['vɛksɪdlɪ] *adv* irritadamente, con molestia
vexed question *s* cuestión batallona
V.F.W. abr. de **Veterans of Foreign Wars**
v.g. abr. de **verbi gratia** (Lat.) **for example**
VHF abr. de **very high frequency**
v.i. abr. de **intransitive verb**
V.I. abr. de **Virgin Islands**
via ['vaɪə] *prep* vía, p.ej., **via New York** vía Nueva York
viability [,vaɪə'bɪlɪtɪ] *s* viabilidad
viable ['vaɪəbəl] *adj* viable
viaduct ['vaɪədʌkt] *s* viaducto
vial ['vaɪəl] *s* frasco pequeño
viand ['vaɪənd] *s* vianda; **viands** *spl* manjares delicados, platos selectos
viaticum [vaɪ'ætɪkəm] *s* (*pl:* **-cums** o **-ca** [kə]) viático; (eccl.) viático
vibrant ['vaɪbrənt] *adj* vibrante; (phonet.) sonoro; (fig.) vibrante (*p.ej., estilo*); *s* (phonet.) sonora
vibrate ['vaɪbret] *va & vn* vibrar
vibratile ['vaɪbrətɪl] *adj* vibrátil
vibration [vaɪ'breʃən] *s* vibración
vibrative ['vaɪbrətɪv] *adj* vibratorio
vibrator ['vaɪbretər] *s* vibrador
vibratory ['vaɪbrə,torɪ] *adj* vibratorio
vibrio ['vɪbrɪo] *s* (*pl:* **-os**) (bact.) vibrio
vibrion ['vɪbrɪɑn] *s* (bact.) vibrión
viburnum [vaɪ'bʌrnəm] *s* (bot.) viburno, mundillo
vicar ['vɪkər] *s* vicario
vicarage ['vɪkərɪdʒ] *s* vicaría, vicariato; beneficio del vicario
vicar-general ['vɪkər'dʒɛnərəl] *s* (*pl:* **vicars-general**) vicario general
vicarial [vaɪ'kɛrɪəl] o [vɪ'kɛrɪəl] *adj* vicarial
vicarious [vaɪ'kɛrɪəs] o [vɪ'kɛrɪəs] *adj* vicario; sufrido por otro, experimentado por otro; (physiol.) vicario
vicarship ['vɪkərʃɪp] *s* vicaría, vicariato
vice [vaɪs] *s* vicio; (mach.) tornillo (*para sujetar el objeto que se ha de trabajar*)
vice-admiral [,vaɪs'ædmɪrəl] *s* vicealmirante
vice-admiralty [,vaɪs'ædmɪrəltɪ] *s* vicealmirantazgo
vice-chancellor [,vaɪs'tʃænsələr] o [,vaɪs'tʃɑnsələr] *s* vicecanciller
vice-Christ [,vaɪs'kraɪst] *s* vicecristo
vice-consul [,vaɪs'kɑnsəl] *s* vicecónsul
vice-consulate [,vaɪs'kɑnsəlɪt] *s* viceconsulado
vice-counsellor [,vaɪs'kaʊnsələr] *s* viceconsiliario
vicegerency [,vaɪs'dʒɪrənsɪ] *s* vicegerencia
vicegerent [,vaɪs'dʒɪrənt] *adj & s* vicegerente
vice-God [,vaɪs'gɑd] *s* vicediós
vice-governor [,vaɪs'gʌvərnər] *s* vicegobernador
vice-king [,vaɪs'kɪŋ] *s* virrey
vicennial [vaɪ'sɛnɪəl] *adj* vicenal
Vice Pres. abr. de **Vice-President**
vice-presidency [,vaɪs'prɛzɪdənsɪ] *s* vicepresidencia
vice-president [,vaɪs'prɛzɪdənt] *s* vicepresidente
vice-presidential [,vaɪsprɛzɪ'dɛnʃəl] *adj* vicepresidencial
vice-queen [,vaɪs'kwin] *s* virreina
vice-rector [,vaɪs'rɛktər] *s* vicerrector
viceregal [,vaɪs'rigəl] *adj* virreinal
viceregent [,vaɪs'ridʒənt] *s* vicerregente
viceroy ['vaɪsrɔɪ] *s* virrey
viceroyalty [,vaɪs'rɔɪəltɪ] *s* virreinato
vice-secretary [,vaɪs'sɛkrɪ,tɛrɪ] *s* vicesecretario
vice-secretaryship [,vaɪs'sɛkrɪ,tɛrɪʃɪp] *s* vicesecretaría
vice-treasurer [,vaɪs'trɛʒərər] *s* vicetesorero
vice versa ['vaɪsɪ'vʌrsə] *adv* viceversa
Vichy water ['vɪʃɪ] *s* agua de Vichy
vici ['vaɪsaɪ] *s* gamuza
vicinage ['vɪsɪnɪdʒ] *s* vecindad
vicinal ['vɪsɪnəl] *adj* vecinal
vicinity [vɪ'sɪnɪtɪ] *s* (*pl:* **-ties**) vecindad
vicious ['vɪʃəs] *adj* vicioso; ruin, arisco (*caballo*); bravo (*perro*)
vicious circle *s* círculo vicioso
vicissitude [vɪ'sɪsɪtjud] o [vɪ'sɪsɪtud] *s* vicisitud
victim ['vɪktɪm] *s* víctima
victimization [,vɪktɪmɪ'zeʃən] *s* inmolación; engaño, estafa
victimize ['vɪktɪmaɪz] *va* inmolar, hacer víctima; engañar, estafar
victor ['vɪktər] *s* vencedor
victoria [vɪk'torɪə] *s* victoria (*coche*); (bot.) victoria
Victorian [vɪk'torɪən] *adj & s* victoriano
Victorian age *s* época victoriana
victorious [vɪk'torɪəs] *adj* victorioso
victory ['vɪktərɪ] *s* (*pl:* **-ries**) victoria
victrola [vɪk'trolə] *s* (trademark) fonógrafo
victual ['vɪtəl] *s* (dial.) vitualla, alimento; **victuals** *spl* (coll. & dial.) vituallas, alimentos, víveres; (*pret & pp:* **-ualed** o **-ualled;** *ger:* **-ualing** o **-ualling**) *va* avituallar; *vn* avituallarse
victualer o **victualler** ['vɪtələr] *s* abastecedor; (mil.) comisario; hostelero
vicuña [vɪ'kunjə] o [vɪ'kjunə] *s* (zool.) vicuña (*animal, lana y tela*)
vid. abr. de **vide** (Lat.) **see**
videlicet [vɪ'dɛlɪsɛt] *adv* a saber, es decir
video ['vɪdɪo] *s* vídeo; *adj* de vídeo
videocast ['vɪdɪo,kæst] o ['vɪdɪo,kɑst] *s* teledifusión; (*pret & pp:* **-cast** o **-casted**) *va* teledifundir
video signal *s* videoseñal
video tape *s* cinta grabada de televisión
video-tape recording ['vɪdɪo,tep] *s* videograbación
video telephony *s* visiotelefonía
vidette [vɪ'dɛt] *s* var. de **vedette**
vie [vaɪ] (*pret & pp:* **vied;** *ger:* **vying**) *vn* competir, rivalizar
Vienna [vɪ'ɛnə] *s* Viena
Viennese [,viə'niz] *adj* vienés; *s* (*pl:* **-nese**) vienés
Viet-Namese [vi'ɛtnɑ'miz] o ['vitnə'miz] *adj* vietnamés o vietnamita; *s* (*pl:* **-ese**) vietnamés o vietnamita
view [vju] *s* vista; panorama, paisaje; opinión, parecer; inspección; intento, propósito; **in view of** en vista de; **on view** en exhibición; **to be on view** estar expuesto (*p.ej., un cadáver*); **to take a dim view of** mirar escépticamente, no entusiasmarse por; **with a view to** con el propósito de; en cuanto a; **with a view to** + *ger* con vistas a + *inf; va* ver, mirar; contemplar, considerar, pesar; examinar, inspeccionar
viewer ['vjuər] *s* espectador; inspector; televidente, telespectador; mirador para transparencias, proyector de transparencias
view finder *s* (phot.) visor
viewless ['vjulɪs] *adj* invisible; sin opinión
viewpoint ['vju,pɔɪnt] *s* punto de la vista (*sitio*); punto de vista (*opinión, ademán*)
vigesimal [vaɪ'dʒɛsɪməl] *adj* vigésimo; vigesimal
vigil ['vɪdʒɪl] *s* vigilia; **vigils** *spl* (eccl.) vigilia
vigilance ['vɪdʒɪləns] *f* vigilancia
vigilant ['vɪdʒɪlənt] *adj* vigilante
vigilante [,vɪdʒɪ'læntɪ] *s* vigilante
vignette [vɪn'jɛt] *s* viñeta
vigor ['vɪgər] *s* vigor
vigorous ['vɪgərəs] *adj* vigoroso
vigour ['vɪgər] *s* (Brit.) var. de **vigor**
viking o **Viking** ['vaɪkɪŋ] *s* vikingo, pirata escandinavo
vile [vaɪl] *adj* vil; repugnante
vilification [,vɪlɪfɪ'keʃən] *s* vilipendio, difamación
vilify ['vɪlɪfaɪ] (*pret & pp:* **-fied**) *va* vilipendiar, difamar
villa ['vɪlə] *s* villa, quinta
village ['vɪlɪdʒ] *s* aldea

villager [ˈvɪlɪdʒər] *s* aldeano
villain [ˈvɪlən] *s* malvado; malo, traidor (*de una novela o drama*); (hist.) villano
villainous [ˈvɪlənəs] *adj* malvado, villano
villainy [ˈvɪlənɪ] *s* (*pl:* **-ies**) villanía, maldad
villanelle [ˌvɪləˈnɛl] *s* villanela
villein [ˈvɪlən] *s* (hist.) villano
villeinage [ˈvɪlənɪdʒ] *s* (hist.) villanaje
villous [ˈvɪləs] *adj* velloso
villus [ˈvɪləs] *s* (*pl:* **-li** [laɪ]) (anat., bot. & zool.) vello
vim [vɪm] *s* fuerza, vigor, energía
vinaigrette [ˌvɪneˈgrɛt] *s* vinagrera
Vincennes [vɪnˈsɛnz] *s* Vincenas
Vincent [ˈvɪnsənt] *s* Vicente
vincible [ˈvɪnsɪbəl] *adj* vencible
vinculum [ˈvɪŋkjələm] *s* (*pl:* **-la** [lə]) vínculo
vindicate [ˈvɪndɪket] *va* vindicar; (law) vindicar, reivindicar
vindication [ˌvɪndɪˈkeʃən] *s* vindicación; (law) vindicación, reivindicación
vindicative [vɪnˈdɪkətɪv] o [ˈvɪndɪˌketɪv] *adj* vindicativo
vindicator [ˈvɪndɪˌketər] *s* vindicador
vindictive [vɪnˈdɪktɪv] *adj* vindicativo, vengativo
vine [vaɪn] *s* (bot.) enredadera; (bot.) vid, parra (*de uvas*)
vinedresser [ˈvaɪnˌdrɛsər] *s* viñador
vinegar [ˈvɪnɪgər] *s* vinagre
vinegar eel *s* (zool.) anguílula del vinagre
vinegarer [ˈvɪnɪgərər] *s* vinagrero
vinegar fly *s* (ent.) mosca del vinagre
vinegarish [ˈvɪnɪgərɪʃ] *adj* avinagrado
vinegary [ˈvɪnɪgərɪ] *adj* vinagroso (*gusto o genio*)
vinegrower [ˈvaɪnˌgroər] *s* vinícola, viñador
vineyard [ˈvɪnjərd] *s* viña, viñedo
vineyardist [ˈvɪnjərdɪst] *s* viñador
vinic [ˈvaɪnɪk] o [ˈvɪnɪk] *adj* vínico
vinification [ˌvɪnɪfɪˈkeʃən] *s* vinificación
vinous [ˈvaɪnəs] *adj* vinoso
vintage [ˈvɪntɪdʒ] *s* vendimia; cosecha de vino; (coll.) categoría, tipo, clase
vintager [ˈvɪntɪdʒər] *s* vendimiador
vintage wine *s* vino de buena cosecha
vintage year *s* año de buen vino
vintner [ˈvɪntnər] *s* vinatero
vinyl [ˈvaɪnɪl] o [ˈvɪnɪl] *s* (chem.) vinilo
vinyl acetate *s* (chem.) acetato de vinilo
vinyl alcohol *s* (chem.) alcohol vinílico
viol [ˈvaɪəl] *s* (mus.) viola; (naut.) virador
viola [vaɪˈolə] o [vɪˈolə] *s* (mus.) viola (*instrumento y persona*); [ˈvaɪolə] o [vaɪˈolə] *s* (bot.) viola
violable [ˈvaɪələbəl] *adj* violable
violaceous [ˌvaɪəˈleʃəs] *adj* violáceo
viola d'amore [viˈɔlɑ dɑˈmore] *s* (mus.) viola de amor
violate [ˈvaɪəlet] *va* violar
violation [ˌvaɪəˈleʃən] *s* violación
violator [ˈvaɪəˌletər] *s* violador
violence [ˈvaɪələns] *s* violencia
violent [ˈvaɪələnt] *adj* violento
violet [ˈvaɪəlɪt] *s* (bot.) violeta; violado (*color*); violeta (*color; colorante*); *adj* violado (*color*); violeta (*color y perfume*)
violet ray *s* rayo violeta
violet shift *s* (phys.) desviación hacia el violado del espectro
violin [ˌvaɪəˈlɪn] *s* violín (*instrumento y el que lo toca*)
violinist [ˌvaɪəˈlɪnɪst] *s* violinista
violist [ˈvaɪəlɪst] *s* viola (*persona*)
violle [vjɔl] *s* violle (*unidad fotométrica*)
violoncellist [ˌvaɪələnˈtʃɛlɪst] o [ˌviələnˈtʃɛlɪst] *s* violoncelista
violoncello [ˌvaɪələnˈtʃɛlo] o [ˌviələnˈtʃɛlo] *s* (*pl:* **-los**) (mus.) violoncelo
viosterol [vaɪˈɑstərɑl] *s* (pharm.) viosterol
viper [ˈvaɪpər] *s* (zool.) víbora; (fig.) víbora
viperine [ˈvaɪpərɪn] o [ˈvaɪpəraɪn] *adj* vipéreo o viperino
viperish [ˈvaɪpərɪʃ] o **viperous** [ˈvaɪpərəs] *adj* viperino; (fig.) viperino
viper's bugloss *s* (bot.) viborera
viper's-grass [ˈvaɪpərzˌgræs] o [ˈvaɪpərzˌgrɑs] *s* (bot.) escorzonera
virago [vɪˈrego] *s* (*pl:* **-goes** o **-gos**) mujer regañona
viral [ˈvaɪrəl] *adj* viral
virelay [ˈvɪrɪle] *s* virolai (*verso*)
vireo [ˈvɪrɪo] *s* (*pl:* **-os**) (orn.) vireo
virescence [vaɪˈrɛsəns] *s* (bot.) virescencia
virescent [vaɪˈrɛsənt] *adj* virescente
Virgil [ˈvʌrdʒɪl] *s* Virgilio
Virgilian [vərˈdʒɪlɪən] *adj* virgiliano
virgin [ˈvʌrdʒɪn] *s* virgen; (*cap.*) *s* (astr.) Virgen; **the Virgin** la Santísima Virgen; (*l.c.*) *adj* virgen
virginal [ˈvʌrdʒɪnəl] *adj* virginal; *s* (mus.) virginal, espineta
virgin birth *s* (theol.) parto virginal de María; (zool.) reproducción virginal o asexual (*partenogénesis*)
virgin cork *s* corcho bornizo, corcho virgen
Virginia [vərˈdʒɪnjə] *s* Virginia (*uno de los estados de los EE.UU.; nombre de mujer*)
Virginia creeper *s* (bot.) guau (*Parthenocissus quinquefolia*)
Virginian [vərˈdʒɪnjən] *adj & s* virginiano
Virginia snakeroot *s* (bot.) serpentaria virginiana, viperina de Virginia
Virginia stock *s* (bot.) mahonesa
Virgin Islands *spl* islas Vírgenes
virginity [vərˈdʒɪnɪtɪ] *s* virginidad
virginium [vərˈdʒɪnɪəm] *s* (chem.) virginio
Virgin Mary *s* Virgen María
Virgin Queen, the la reina virgen (*Isabel I de Inglaterra*)
virgin's-bower [ˈvʌrdʒɪnzˈbaʊər] *s* (bot.) clemátide
Virgo [ˈvʌrgo] *s* (astr.) Virgo
viridescence [ˌvɪrɪˈdɛsəns] *s* verdor
viridescent [ˌvɪrɪˈdɛsənt] *adj* verdoso
virile [ˈvɪrɪl] *adj* viril
virile member *s* (anat.) miembro viril
virility [vɪˈrɪlɪtɪ] *s* (*pl:* **-ties**) virilidad
virole [vɪˈrol] *s* (her.) virol
viroled [vɪˈrold] *adj* (her.) virolado
virological [ˌvaɪrəˈlɑdʒɪkəl] *adj* virológico
virologist [vaɪˈrɑlədʒɪst] *s* virólogo
virology [vaɪˈrɑlədʒɪ] *s* virología
virtual [ˈvʌrtʃʊəl] *adj* virtual
virtual image *s* (phys.) imagen virtual
virtuality [ˌvʌrtʃʊˈælɪtɪ] *s* virtualidad
virtually [ˈvʌrtʃʊəlɪ] *adv* virtualmente
virtue [ˈvʌrtʃʊ] *s* virtud; **by** o **in virtue of** en virtud de
virtuosity [ˌvʌrtʃʊˈɑsɪtɪ] *s* (*pl:* **-ties**) virtuosismo
virtuoso [ˌvʌrtʃʊˈoso] *s* (*pl:* **-sos** o **-si** [si]) virtuoso
virtuous [ˈvʌrtʃʊəs] *adj* virtuoso
virulence [ˈvɪrʊləns] o [ˈvɪrjələns] o **virulency** [ˈvɪrʊlənsɪ] o [ˈvɪrjələnsɪ] *s* virulencia
virulent [ˈvɪrʊlənt] o [ˈvɪrjələnt] *adj* virulento
virus [ˈvaɪrəs] *s* virus
Vis. o **Visc.** abr. de **Viscount**
visa [ˈvizə] *s* visa; *va* visar
visage [ˈvɪzɪdʒ] *s* semblante; apariencia
vis-à-vis [ˌvizəˈvi] *s* persona que está enfrente; coche con dos asientos enfrentados; sillón con dos asientos enfrentados; *adj* enfrentado; *adv* frente a frente; *prep* enfrente de; respecto de
Visayan [vɪˈsajən] *adj & s* bisayo o visayo
Visayan Islands *spl* islas Bisayas o Visayas
viscera [ˈvɪsərə] *spl* vísceras
visceral [ˈvɪsərəl] *adj* visceral
viscid [ˈvɪsɪd] *adj* viscoso
viscose [ˈvɪskos] *adj* viscoso; *s* viscosa
viscosity [vɪsˈkɑsɪtɪ] *s* viscosidad
viscount [ˈvaɪkaʊnt] *s* vizconde
viscountcy [ˈvaɪkaʊntsɪ] *s* (*pl:* **-cies**) vizcondado
viscountess [ˈvaɪkaʊntɪs] *s* vizcondesa
viscountship [ˈvaɪkaʊntʃɪp] *s* vizcongado
viscounty [ˈvaɪkaʊntɪ] *s* (*pl:* **-ties**) var. de **viscountship**
viscous [ˈvɪskəs] *adj* viscoso
vise [vaɪs] *s* (mach.) tornillo, torno
visé [ˈvize] o [vɪˈze] *s & va* var. de **visa**
Vishnu [ˈvɪʃnu] *s* Visnú
visibility [ˌvɪzɪˈbɪlɪtɪ] *s* visibilidad
visible [ˈvɪzɪbəl] *adj* visible
visibly [ˈvɪzɪblɪ] *adv* visiblemente
Visigoth [ˈvɪzɪgɑθ] *s* visigodo
Visigothic [ˌvɪzɪˈgɑθɪk] *adj* visigótico; *s* letra visigótica

vision [ˈvɪʒən] *s* visión; *va* ver en una visión, ver como en una visión; *vn* aparecer en una visión
visionary [ˈvɪʒən,ɛrɪ] *adj* visionario; *s* (*pl:* **-ies**) visionario
visit [ˈvɪzɪt] *s* visita; *va* visitar; mandar (*la peste, un castigo, etc.*); *vn* hacer visitas; visitarse
visitant [ˈvɪzɪtənt] *adj & s* visitante
visitation [,vɪzɪˈteʃən] *s* visitación; disposición divina, gracia o castigo del cielo; (*cap.*) *s* Visitación
visiting [ˈvɪzɪtɪŋ] *adj* visitador; de visita
visiting card *s* tarjeta de visita
visiting fireman *s* (coll.) personaje recibido con gran agasajo en país ajeno; (slang) forastero que se divierte en una gran ciudad
visiting hours *spl* horas de consulta
visiting nurse *s* enfermera ambulante
visiting professor *s* profesor visitante
visitor [ˈvɪzɪtər] *s* visitante; (sport) visitante
visor [ˈvaɪzər] o [ˈvɪzər] *s* visera (*del yelmo, de las gorras, del parabrisas del automóvil, etc.*); (fig.) máscara
vista [ˈvɪstə] *s* vista, panorama, perspectiva
Vistula [ˈvɪstjʊlə] *s* Vístula
visual [ˈvɪʒʊəl] *adj* visual; visible
visual acuity *s* acuidad
visualization [,vɪʒʊəlɪˈzeʃən] *s* representación en la mente, visualización
visualize [ˈvɪʒʊəlaɪz] *va* visualizar, representarse en la mente; *vn* representarse en la mente; (med.) hacerse visible
visual line *s* visual
visually [ˈvɪʒʊəlɪ] *adv* visualmente
visual purple *s* (biochem.) púrpura visual
vitaceous [vaɪˈteʃəs] *adj* (bot.) vitáceo
vital [ˈvaɪtəl] *adj* vital; mortal; **vitals** *spl* vísceras, partes vitales
vital force *s* fuerza vital
vitalism [ˈvaɪtəlɪzəm] *s* vitalismo
vitalist [ˈvaɪtəlɪst] *s* vitalista
vitalistic [,vaɪtəˈlɪstɪk] *adj* vitalista
vitality [vaɪˈtælɪtɪ] *s* vitalidad
vitalization [,vaɪtəlɪˈzeʃən] *s* vitalización
vitalize [ˈvaɪtəlaɪz] *va* vitalizar
vital statistics *ssg* estadística demográfica; *spl* estadísticas demográficas
vitamin o **vitamine** [ˈvaɪtəmɪn] *s* vitamina
vitamin deficiency *s* avitaminosis, carencia de vitaminas
vitaminic [,vaɪtəˈmɪnɪk] *adj* vitamínico
vitellin [vɪˈtɛlɪn] o [vaɪˈtɛlɪn] *s* (biochem.) vitelina
vitellus [vɪˈtɛləs] o [vaɪˈtɛləs] *s* vitelo, yema del huevo
vitiate [ˈvɪʃɪet] *va* viciar; (law) viciar
vitiation [,vɪʃɪˈeʃən] *s* viciación
viticultural [,vɪtɪˈkʌltʃərəl] o [,vaɪtɪˈkʌltʃərəl] *adj* vitícola
viticulture [ˈvɪtɪ,kʌltʃər] o [ˈvaɪtɪ,kʌltʃər] *s* viticultura
viticulturist [,vɪtɪˈkʌltʃərɪst] o [,vaɪtɪˈkʌltʃərɪst] *s* vitícola, viticultor
vitiligo [,vɪtɪˈlaɪgo] *s* (path.) vitíligo
vitreous [ˈvɪtrɪəs] *adj* vítreo
vitreous electricity *s* electricidad vítrea
vitreous humor *s* (anat.) humor vítreo
vitrifaction [,vɪtrɪˈfækʃən] *s* vitrificación
vitrifiable [,vɪtrɪˈfaɪəbəl] *adj* vitrificable
vitrification [,vɪtrɪfɪˈkeʃən] *s* var. de **vitrifaction**
vitrify [ˈvɪtrɪfaɪ] (*pret & pp:* **-fied**) *va* vitrificar; *vn* vitrificarse
vitriol [ˈvɪtrɪəl] *s* (chem.) vitriolo; (fig.) crítica cáustica
vitriolic [,vɪtrɪˈɑlɪk] *adj* (chem.) vitriólico; (fig.) cáustico, mordaz
vitriolize [ˈvɪtrɪəlaɪz] *va* vitriolizar (*impregnar de vitriolo*); vitriolar (*arrojar vitriolo a*)
vituperable [vaɪˈtjupərəbəl] o [vaɪˈtupərəbəl] *adj* vituperable
vituperate [vaɪˈtjupəret] o [vaɪˈtupəret] *va* vituperar
vituperation [vaɪ,tjupəˈreʃən] o [vaɪ,tupəˈreʃən] *s* vituperación, vituperio
vituperative [vaɪˈtjupə,retɪv] o [vaɪˈtupə,retɪv] *adj* vituperioso
vituperator [vaɪˈtjupə,retər] o [vaɪˈtupə,retər] *s* vituperador
viva [ˈvivɑ] *s* viva; *interj* ¡viva!
vivacious [vɪˈveʃəs] o [vaɪˈveʃəs] *adj* vivo, alegre, vivaracho, vivaz
vivacity [vɪˈvæsɪtɪ] o [vaɪˈvæsɪtɪ] *s* (*pl:* **-ties**) viveza, alegría
vivandière [vivɑ̃ˈdjɛr] *s* cantinera, vivandera
vivarium [vɪˈvɛrɪəm] *s* (*pl:* **-iums** o **-ia** [ɪə]) vivario
viva voce [ˈvaɪvəˈvosɪ] *adv* de viva voz
vive [viv] *interj* ¡viva!
Vivian [ˈvɪvɪən] *s* Viviana
vivid [ˈvɪvɪd] *adj* vivo
vivification [,vɪvɪfɪˈkeʃən] *s* vivificación
vivify [ˈvɪvɪfaɪ] (*pret & pp:* **-fied**) *va* vivificar
viviparous [vaɪˈvɪpərəs] *adj* vivíparo
vivisect [ˈvɪvɪsɛkt] o [,vɪvɪˈsɛkt] *va* disecar (*un animal vivo*); *vn* practicar la vivisección
vivisection [,vɪvɪˈsɛkʃən] *s* vivisección
vivisectionist [,vɪvɪˈsɛkʃənɪst] *s* viviseccionista
vivisector [ˈvɪvɪ,sɛktər] o [,vɪvɪˈsɛktər] *s* vivisector
vivisectorium [,vɪvɪsɛkˈtorɪəm] *s* vivisectorio
vixen [ˈvɪksən] *s* zorra (*hembra*); mujer regañona y colérica
vixenish [ˈvɪksənɪʃ] *adj* zorruno; regañona y colérica
viz. abr. de **videlicet** (Lat.) **to wit, namely**
vizard [ˈvɪzərd] *s* var. de **visor**
vizier [vɪˈzɪr] o [ˈvɪzjər] o **vizir** [vɪˈzɪr] *s* visir
vizor [ˈvaɪzər] o [ˈvɪzər] *s* var. de **visor**
vocab. abr. de **vocabulary**
vocable [ˈvokəbəl] *s* vocablo, voz
vocabulary [voˈkæbjə,lɛrɪ] *s* (*pl:* **-ies**) vocabulario
vocabulist [voˈkæbjəlɪst] *s* vocabulista, lexicógrafo
vocal [ˈvokəl] *adj* vocal; vocálico; expresivo
vocal cords *spl* (anat.) cuerdas vocales
vocalic [voˈkælɪk] *adj* vocálico
vocalism [ˈvokəlɪzəm] *s* (phonet.) vocalismo; canto, arte de cantar
vocalist [ˈvokəlɪst] *s* cantante, vocalista
vocalization [,vokəlɪˈzeʃən] *s* (mus. & phonet.) vocalización
vocalize [ˈvokəlaɪz] *va* (phonet.) vocalizar; emitir con la voz; cantar; *vn* (mus.) vocalizar; (phonet.) vocalizarse
vocally [ˈvokəlɪ] *adv* vocalmente; expresivamente
vocal music *s* música vocal
vocal organ *s* (anat.) órgano de la voz
vocation [voˈkeʃən] *s* vocación; (theol.) vocación
vocational [voˈkeʃənəl] *adj* práctico, vocacional
vocational guidance *s* guía vocacional
vocational school *s* escuela de artes y oficios
vocative [ˈvɑkətɪv] *adj & s* vocativo
vociferant [voˈsɪfərənt] *adj & s* vociferante
vociferate [voˈsɪfəret] *va & vn* vociferar
vociferation [vo,sɪfəˈreʃən] *s* vociferación, vocería
vociferous [voˈsɪfərəs] *adj* vociferador, vocinglero
vodka [ˈvɑdkə] *s* vodka
vogue [vog] *s* boga, moda; **in vogue** en boga, de moda
voice [vɔɪs] *s* voz; (gram. & mus.) voz; **in a loud voice** en voz alta; **in a low voice** en voz baja; **in voice** (mus.) en voz; **to raise one's voice** alzar la voz; **with one voice** a una voz; *va* expresar; divulgar; (mus.) regular el tono de (*un órgano*); (mus.) escribir la parte vocal de; (phonet.) sonorizar; *vn* (phonet.) sonorizarse
voice coil *s* (rad.) bobina móvil
voiceless [ˈvɔɪslɪs] *adj* mudo; (phonet.) mudo (*dícese de las consonantes oclusivas*)
voicing [ˈvɔɪsɪŋ] *s* (phonet.) sonorización
void [vɔɪd] *adj* vacío; nulo, inválido; vano; **void of** falto de, desprovisto de; *s* vacío, hueco; *va* vaciar; anular; evacuar
voidable [ˈvɔɪdəbəl] *adj* evacuable; anulable
voidance [ˈvɔɪdəns] *s* vaciamiento, evacuación; (eccl.) vacante
voile [vɔɪl] *s* espumilla
vol. abr. de **volume**
volant [ˈvolənt] *adj* volante; ligero; (her.) volante

volatile ['valətɪl] *adj* volátil
volatile oil *s* aceite volátil
volatility [,valə'tɪlɪtɪ] *s* volatilidad
volatilization [,valətɪlɪ'zeʃən] *s* volatilización
volatilize ['valətɪlaɪz] *va* volatilizar; *vn* volatilizarse
volcanic [val'kænɪk] *adj* volcánico
volcanic ashes *spl* (geol.) cenizas volcánicas
volcanic cone *s* (geol.) cono volcánico
volcanic mud *s* (geol.) lodo volcánico
volcanic neck *s* (geol.) cuello volcánico
volcanic rocks *spl* (geol.) rocas volcánicas
volcanism ['valkənɪzəm] *s* volcanismo
volcano [val'keno] *s* (*pl:* **-noes** o **-nos**) volcán; (fig.) volcán; **to be on the edge of a volcano** (fig.) estar sobre un volcán
volcanology [,valkən'alədʒɪ] *s* vulcanología
vole [vol] *s* (zool.) arvícola, rata de agua, campañol
volition [vo'lɪʃən] *s* volición
volitional [vo'lɪʃənəl] *adj* volitivo
volley ['valɪ] *s* descarga, lluvia (*de piedras, balas, etc.*); (mil.) descarga; (tennis) voleo; *va* (tennis) volear; *vn* lanzar una descarga
volleyball ['valɪ,bɔl] *s* volibol
volplane ['val,plen] *s* (aer.) planeo, vuelo planeado; *vn* (aer.) planear
vols. abr. de **volumes**
Volscian ['valʃən] *adj & s* volsco
volt [volt] *s* (elec.) voltio
voltage ['voltɪdʒ] *s* (elec.) voltaje
voltage amplification *s* (elec.) amplificación de tensión
voltage divider *s* (rad.) divisor de voltaje, partidor de tensión
voltage drop *s* (elec.) caída de tensión
voltage regulator *s* (elec.) regulador de tensión
voltage transformer *s* (elec.) transformador de tensión
voltaic [val'teɪk] *adj* voltaico
voltaic battery *s* (elec.) pila voltaica
voltaic cell *s* (elec.) célula voltaica
voltaic current *s* (elec.) corriente voltaica
voltaic electricity *s* electricidad voltaica
voltaic pile *s* (elec.) pila voltaica
Voltairian [val'tɛrɪən] *adj & s* volteriano
Voltairianism [val'tɛrɪənɪzəm] o **Voltairism** [val'tɛrɪzəm] *s* volterianismo
voltameter [val'tæmɪtər] *s* (phys.) voltámetro
voltammeter ['volt'æm,mitər] *s* (phys.) voltamperímetro
volt-ampere ['volt'æmpɪr] *s* (elec.) voltamperio
volte-face [,vɔlt'fas] *s* cambio de dirección; cambio de opinión; *vn* cambiar de dirección; cambiar de opinión
voltmeter ['volt,mitər] *s* (elec.) voltímetro
volubility [,valjə'bɪlɪtɪ] *s* facundia; volubilidad
voluble ['valjəbəl] *adj* facundo; voluble (*que fácilmente se puede mover alrededor*); (bot.) voluble
volume ['valjəm] *s* volumen (*libro; bulto; masa, p.ej., de agua*); tomo (*cada libro que forma parte de una obra*); volumen sonoro; (geom.) volumen; **to speak volumes** ser de suma significación
volume control *s* (rad.) regulación del volumen (sonoro); (rad.) regulador de volumen, control de volumen
volumeter [və'lumɪtər] *s* volúmetro
volumetric [,valjə'mɛtrɪk] *adj* volumétrico
voluminous [və'lumɪnəs] *adj* voluminoso
voluntarily ['valən,tɛrɪlɪ] *adv* voluntariamente
voluntarism ['valəntərɪzəm] *s* (philos.) voluntarismo
voluntary ['valən,tɛrɪ] *adj* voluntario; *s* (*pl:* **-ies**) acción voluntaria; (mus.) solo de órgano
voluntary manslaughter *s* (law) homicidio intencional sin premeditación
volunteer [,valən'tɪr] *adj* voluntario; de voluntarios; *va* ofrecer (*sus servicios*); *vn* servir como voluntario; ofrecerse
voluptuary [və'lʌptʃu,ɛrɪ] *s* (*pl:* **-ies**) voluptuoso; *adj* voluptuoso
voluptuous [və'lʌptʃuəs] *adj* voluptuoso
voluptuousness [və'lʌptʃuəsnɪs] *s* voluptuosidad
volute [və'lut] *s* (arch.) voluta; (fig.) voluta; (zool.) voluta (*cualquiera de los volútidos*); (zool.) vuelta (*de una concha en espiral*)
volva ['valvə] *s* (bot.) volva
volvulus ['valvjələs] *s* (path.) vólvulo
vomer ['vomər] *s* (anat.) vómer
vomicine ['vamɪsin] o ['vamɪsɪn] *s* (chem.) vomicina
vomit ['vamɪt] *s* vómito; vomitivo (*emético*); *va & vn* vomitar
vomitive ['vamɪtɪv] *adj & s* vomitivo
vomitory ['vamɪ,torɪ] *adj* vomitorio; *s* (*pl:* **-ries**) (arch.) vomitorio
vomiturition [,vamɪtʃu'rɪʃən] *s* (path.) vomiturición
voodoo ['vudu] *s* vodú; *adj* voduísta
voodooism ['vuduɪzəm] *s* voduísmo
voodooist ['vuduɪst] *s* voduísta
voodooistic [,vudu'ɪstɪk] *adj* voduísta
voracious [və'reʃəs] *adj* voraz
voracity [və'ræsɪtɪ] *s* voracidad
vortex ['vɔrtɛks] *s* (*pl:* **-texes** o **-tices** [tɪsiz]) vórtice
vorticella [,vɔrtɪ'sɛlə] *s* (*pl:* **-lae** [li]) (zool.) vorticela
Vosges [voʒ] *spl* Vosgos
votaress ['votərɪs] *s* partidaria, aficionada; monja, religiosa, mujer ligada por votos solemnes
votary ['votərɪ] *s* (*pl:* **-ries**) partidario, aficionado; monje, religioso, persona ligada por votos solemnes
vote [vot] *s* voto; *va* votar; **to vote down** derrotar por votación; **to vote in** elegir por votación; *vn* votar
vote-getter ['vot,gɛtər] *s* acaparador de votos; consigna que gana votos
vote of confidence *s* voto de confianza
voter ['votər] *s* votante
voting machine *s* máquina de votar, máquina electoral
voting paper *s* (Brit.) papeleta de votación
voting precinct *s* distrito electoral
votive ['votɪv] *adj* votivo
votive Mass *s* (eccl.) misa votiva
votive offering *s* voto, exvoto
vouch [vautʃ] *va* garantizar, atestiguar; *vn* salir fiador; **to vouch for** responder de (*una cosa*); responder por (*una persona*)
voucher ['vautʃər] *s* fiador, garante; comprobante (de pago); resguardo (*documento justificativo*)
vouchsafe [vautʃ'sef] *va* conceder, otorgar; servirse hacer o dar, dignarse hacer o dar; *vn* dignarse; **to vouchsafe to** + *inf* dignarse + *inf*
voussoir [vu'swar] *s* (arch.) dovela
vow [vau] *s* promesa solemne; voto (*a Dios, un santo, etc.*); *va* prometer solemnemente; votar; jurar; *vn* hacer voto; **to vow to** + *inf* hacer voto de + *inf*
vowel ['vauəl] *s* vocal; *adj* vocálico
vowel harmony *s* (philol.) armonía vocálica
vowelize ['vauəlaɪz] *va* vocalizar; puntar (*un texto hebreo o árabe*)
vowel point *s* punto vocálico (*de las lenguas hebrea, árabe, etc.*)
vowel system *s* sistema vocálico
voyage ['vɔɪɪdʒ] *s* viaje por mar, viaje por aire; *va* atravesar (*p.ej., el mar*); *vn* viajar por mar, viajar por aire
voyager ['vɔɪɪdʒər] *s* viajero por mar, viajero por aire
V.P. abr. de **Vice-President**
vs. abr. de **versus**
v.s. abr. de **vide supra** (Lat.) **see above**
V.S. abr. de **Veterinary Surgeon**
V-shaped ['vi,ʃept] *adj* en forma de V
v.t. abr. de **transitive verb**
Vt. abr. de **Vermont**
V-type engine ['vi,taɪp] *s* (aut.) motor tipo V
vug [vʌg] o [vug] *s* (min.) drusa, bolsa
Vul. abr. de **Vulgate**
Vulcan ['vʌlkən] *s* (myth.) Vulcano
Vulcanian [vʌl'kenɪən] *adj* vulcanio; (*l.c.*) *adj* vulcanio
vulcanism ['vʌlkənɪzəm] *s* vulcanismo
vulcanist ['vʌlkənɪst] *s* vulcanista
vulcanite ['vʌlkənaɪt] *s* vulcanita
vulcanization [,vʌlkənɪ'zeʃən] *s* vulcanización

vulcanize [ˈvʌlkənaɪz] *va* vulcanizar
vulcanized rubber *s* caucho vulcanizado
vulcanizer [ˈvʌlkən,aɪzər] *s* vulcanizador
vulcanology [,vʌlkənˈɑlədʒɪ] *s* var. de **volcanology**
vulg. abr. de **vulgar** y **vulgarly**
Vulg. abr. de **Vulgate**
vulgar [ˈvʌlgər] *adj* grosero; vulgar; *s* vulgo
vulgar fraction *s* (math.) fracción común
vulgarian [vʌlˈgɛrɪən] *s* persona grosera; advenedizo, nuevo rico
vulgarism [ˈvʌlgərɪzəm] *s* grosería; vulgarismo; vulgaridad
vulgarity [vʌlˈgærɪtɪ] *s* (*pl:* **-ties**) grosería; vulgaridad
vulgarization [,vʌlgərɪˈzeʃən] *s* vulgarización
vulgarize [ˈvʌlgəraɪz] *va* vulgarizar
vulgarizer [ˈvʌlgə,raɪzər] *s* vulgarizador
Vulgar Latin *s* latín vulgar, latín rústico
Vulgate [ˈvʌlget] *s* Vulgata
vulnerability [,vʌlnərəˈbɪlɪtɪ] *s* vulnerabilidad
vulnerable [ˈvʌlnərəbəl] *adj* vulnerable
vulnerary [ˈvʌlnə,rɛrɪ] *s* (*pl:* **-ies**) vulnerario; *adj* vulnerario
vulpine [ˈvʌlpaɪn] o [ˈvʌlpɪn] *adj* vulpino
vulpinite [ˈvʌlpɪnaɪt] *s* (mineral.) vulpinita
vulture [ˈvʌltʃər] *s* (orn.) buitre
vulturine [ˈvʌltʃəraɪn] o [ˈvʌltʃərɪn] *adj* buitrero
vulva [ˈvʌlvə] *s* (*pl:* **-vae** [vi] o **-vas**) (anat.) vulva
vulvar [ˈvʌlvər] *adj* vulvar
vulvitis [vʌlˈvaɪtɪs] *s* (path.) vulvitis
vying [ˈvaɪɪŋ] *adj* emulador; *ger de* **vie**
vyingly [ˈvaɪɪŋlɪ] *adv* rivalizando

W, w ['dʌbəlju] *s* (*pl:* **W's, w's** ['dʌbəljuz]) vigésima tercera letra del alfabeto inglés
w abr. de **watt**
w. abr. de **week, west, wide, width** y **wife**
W abr. de **watt** y **west**
W. abr. de **Wales, Wednesday, Welsh, west** y **western**
wabble ['wabəl] *s & vn* var. de **wobble**
wabbly ['wablɪ] *adj* var. de **wobbly**
wacky ['wækɪ] *adj* (*comp:* **-ier;** *super:* **-iest**) (slang) excéntrico, estrafalario
wad [wad] *s* bolita de algodón; fajo o lío (*de billetes, papeles, etc.*); taco (*que se pone en las escopetas*); (*pret & pp:* **wadded;** *ger:* **wadding**) *va* colocar algodón en; enliar; atapar; acolchonar, rellenar; atacar (*una escopeta*)
wadding ['wadɪŋ] *s* algodón (*bolitas de hebras de algodón*); taco; tapón; guata (*que se usa para acolchar*)
waddle ['wadəl] *s* anadeo; *vn* anadear
wade [wed] *s* vadeamiento; *va* vadear (*una corriente de agua*); *vn* caminar por terreno difícil, agua, nieve o barro; chapotear, andar descalzo por el agua; **to wade into** (coll.) meter el hombro a; (coll.) embestir con violencia; **to wade through** ir con dificultad por; leer con dificultad
wader ['wedər] *s* vadeador; bota alta impermeable; (orn.) zancuda, ave zancuda
wadi ['wadɪ] *s* (*pl:* **-dis**) uadi
wading bird *s* (orn.) ave zancuda
wady ['wadɪ] *s* (*pl:* **-dies**) var. de **wadi**
wafer ['wefər] *s* oblea (*para pegar sobres; píldora*); hostia (*oblea comestible*); (eccl.) hostia
wafery ['wefərɪ] *adj* delgado, ligero; fino y fácil de partir
waffle ['wafəl] *s* barquillo
waffle iron *s* barquillero (*molde*)
waft [wæft] o [waft] *s* ráfaga de aire, viento, olor, etc.; mecedura, fluctuación; movimiento (*de la mano*); *va* llevar por el aire; llevar a flote; *vn* moverse o flotar de un sitio a otro
wag [wæg] *s* meneo; bromista; (*pret & pp:* **wagged;** *ger:* **wagging**) *va* menear (*la cabeza; la cola*); *vn* menearse
wage [wedʒ] *s* salario, paga; **wages** *spl* salario, paga; galardón, premio; *va* emprender y continuar, perseguir; hacer (*guerra*), dar (*batalla*)
wage earner *s* asalariado
wager ['wedʒər] *s* apuesta; **to lay a wager** hacer una apuesta; *va & vn* apostar
wage scale *s* escala de salarios
wageworker ['wedʒ,wʌrkər] *s* asalariado
wageworking ['wedʒ,wʌrkɪŋ] *adj* asalariado
waggery ['wægərɪ] *s* (*pl:* **-ies**) broma, chanza; jocosidad
waggish ['wægɪʃ] *adj* bromista; divertido, gracioso
waggle ['wægəl] *s* meneo rápido; *va* menear rápidamente; *vn* menearse rápidamente
Wagnerian [vag'nɪrɪən] *adj & s* vagneriano
wagon ['wægən] *s* carro, furgón; (Brit.) vagón o coche (*de ferrocarril*); **on the wagon** (slang) sin tomar bebidas alcohólicas; **to hitch one's wagon to a star** poner el tiro muy alto
wagoner ['wægənər] *s* carretero
wagonette [,wægə'nɛt] *s* break, carricoche
wagonload ['wægən,lod] *s* carretada
wagon train *s* tren de furgones; (mil.) tren de equipajes
wagtail ['wæg,tel] *s* (orn.) aguanieves, aguzanieves, nevatilla
wahoo ['wahu] o [wa'hu] *s* (bot.) evónimo; (bot.) tilio; (bot.) olmo; (ichth.) peto
waif [wef] *s* expósito; granuja (*chiquillo vagabundo*); animal extraviado o abandonado; (law) cosa robada y soltada por el ladrón
wail [wel] *s* gemido, lamento; *vn* gemir, lamentarse, llorar quejándose de dolor
Wailing Wall *s* muro de los lamentos
wainscot ['wenskət] o ['wenskat] *s* arrimadillo, friso (*de madera*); (*pret & pp:* **-scoted** o **-scotted;** *ger:* **-scoting** o **-scotting**) *va* poner arrimadillo o friso a (*la parte inferior de una pared*)
wainscoting o **wainscotting** ['wenskətɪŋ] o ['wenskatɪŋ] *s* arrimadillo, friso; madera de entablado
wainwright ['wen,raɪt] *s* carretero
waist [west] *s* cintura, talle (*del cuerpo humano y del vestido*); blusa, corpiño
waistband ['west,bænd] *s* pretina
waistcloth ['west,klɔθ] o ['west,klaθ] *s* taparrabo
waistcoat ['west,kot] o ['wɛskət] *s* chaleco
waistline ['west,laɪn] *s* talle
wait [wet] *s* espera; **waits** *spl* murga de nochebuena; **to have a good wait** (coll.) esperar sentado; **to lie in wait** estar al acecho; **to lie in wait for** acechar, preparar una emboscada a; *va* esperar, aguardar; (coll.) aplazar, diferir; *vn* esperar, aguardar; **to wait for** esperar, aguardar; **to wait on** servir, despachar (*p.ej., a los parroquianos en una tienda*); visitar, ir a ver; acompañar, velar sobre; presentar respetos a; **to wait until** + *ind* esperar a que + *subj*
waiter ['wetər] *s* mozo de restaurante, camarero; azafate, bandeja; aguardador
waiting ['wetɪŋ] *s* espera; servicio; **in waiting** de honor (*dícese del caballero o la dama que sirve a un personaje real*); *adj* que espera; que sirve; de espera
waiting list *s* lista de espera
waiting maid *s* criada de servicio, doncella
waiting man *s* criado de servicio
waiting room *s* sala de espera; antesala (*p.ej., de un consultorio médico*)
waiting woman *s* criada de servicio, doncella
waitress ['wetrɪs] *s* moza de restaurante, camarera
waive [wev] *va* renunciar a (*p.ej., un derecho*); diferir, dilatar, poner a un lado
waiver ['wevər] *s* (law) renuncia
wake [wek] *s* vigilia; velatorio (*acción de velar a un difunto*); estela (*de un barco u otro objeto en movimiento*); **in the wake of** en la estela de; inmediatamente detrás de; (*pret:* **waked** o **woke;** *pp:* **waked**) *va & vn* despertar; resucitar; velar
wakeful ['wekfəl] *adj* desvelado
wakefulness ['wekfəlnɪs] *s* desvelo
wake knot *s* (her.) lago de amor
waken ['wekən] *va & vn* despertar
wake-robin ['wek,rabɪn] *s* (bot.) arisema; (bot.) aro; (bot.) trilio
Walachia [wa'lekɪə] *s* Valaquia
Walachian [wa'lekɪən] *adj & s* valaco
Waldenses [wal'dɛnsiz] *spl* valdenses
Waldensian [wal'dɛnsɪən] *adj & s* valdense
waldgrave ['wɔldgrev] *s* valdgrave
Waldo ['wɔldo] o ['waldo] *s* Ubaldo
wale [wel] *s* verdugón; (naut.) cinta; relieve (*que sobresale del tejido*); *va* levantar verdugones a
Wales [welz] *s* Gales, el país de Gales
walk [wɔk] *s* caminata (*distancia*); paseo (*acción*); andar, paso (*manera de andar o caminar*); andadura (*de una caballería*); alameda, paseo, vereda; cercado (*para animales*); carrera, condición; oficio, empleo; **at a walk** caminando; **to go for a walk** salir a pasear; **to take a walk** dar un paseo; *va* pasear (*a un niño, un caballo*); caminar (*recorrer caminando*); correr (*un espacio determinado*); ha-

cer andar (*y no correr*); llevar caminando; **to walk off** deshacerse de (*p.ej., un dolor de cabeza*) caminando; *vn* andar, caminar; pasear; ir despacio (*no corriendo*); conducirse, portarse; (baseball) pasar a primera base; **to walk away (from)** alejarse caminando (de); **to walk off with** cargar con, llevarse, robarse; **to walk out** salir repentinamente; declararse en huelga; **to walk out on** (coll.) abandonar, dejar airadamente, salir airadamente de

walkaway ['wɔkə,we] *s* (coll.) triunfo fácil

walker ['wɔkər] *s* caminante; paseante; peatón; andaderas

walkie-lookie ['wɔkɪ'lʊkɪ] *s* cámara televisora portátil

walkie-talkie ['wɔkɪ'tɔkɪ] *s* (rad.) transmisor-receptor portátil

walking beam *s* (mach.) balancín

walking delegate *s* delegado viajante de un gremio obrero

walking encyclopedia *s* (coll.) enciclopedia ambulante

walking papers *spl* (coll.) despedida (*de un empleo o cargo*)

walking stick *s* bastón; (ent.) espectro

walking typhoid fever *s* (path.) fiebre tifoidea ambulante o ambulatoria

walk-on ['wɔk,ɑn] *s* (theat.) parte de por medio

walkout ['wɔk,aʊt] *s* (coll.) huelga

walkover ['wɔk,ovər] *s* (coll.) triunfo fácil

wall [wɔl] *s* muro; pared (*entre dos habitaciones*); cerca (*muro que rodea, p.ej., un jardín*); muralla (*p.ej., de una fortificación*); pared (*de un tubo, vaso, caldera, etc.*); **to drive to the wall** poner entre la espada y la pared; **to go to the wall** entregarse, rendirse; fracasar; **to push to the wall** poner entre la espada y la pared; *va* emparedar, murar; amurallar; **to wall up** cerrar con muro

wallaby ['wɑləbɪ] *s* (*pl:* **-bies**) (zool.) ualabi (*especie de canguro*)

Wallachia [wɑ'lekɪə] *s* var. de **Walachia**

wallaroo [,wɑlə'ru] *s* (zool.) canguro de talla mayor (*del subgénero Osphranter*)

wallboard ['wɔl,bord] *s* cartón de yeso, cartón tabla

wallet ['wɑlɪt] *s* cartera de bolsillo; morral (*saco de provisiones*)

walleye ['wɔl,aɪ] *s* ojo de color muy pálido; ojo desviado hacia afuera; ojo saltón; estrabismo divergente; pez de ojos saltones

walleyed ['wɔl,aɪd] *adj* de ojos incoloros; de ojos desviados hacia afuera; de ojos saltones; de mirada vaga

walleyed herring *s* (ichth.) arenque de ojos grandes

wallflower ['wɔl,flaʊər] *s* (bot.) alhelí amarillo; (coll.) mujer que se queda sin bailar (*por no haber sido invitada a ello*); **to be a wallflower** (coll.) comer pavo

wall knot *s* (naut.) piña

Walloon [wɑ'lun] *adj* & *s* valón

wallop ['wɑləp] *s* (coll.) golpazo; (coll.) fuerza; (coll.) tunda, zurra; *va* (coll.) golpear fuertemente; (coll.) tundir, zurrar

wallow ['wɑlo] *s* revuelco (*acción*); revolcadero (*sitio*); *vn* revolcarse (*en el lodo; en los vicios*); nadar (*en riquezas*)

wallpaper ['wɔl,pepər] *s* papel de empapelar, papel pintado; *va* empapelar

wall plate *s* carrera, solera, viga de apoyo

wall rock *s* (geol. & min.) roca de respaldo

wall rocket *s* (bot.) jaramago

wall rue *s* (bot.) ruda de muros

wallwort ['wɔl,wʌrt] *s* (bot.) cañarroya

walnut ['wɔlnət] *s* (bot.) nogal (*árbol y madera*); nuez (*de nogal*)

Walpurgis night [vɑl'pʊrgɪs] *s* noche de Walpurgis

walpurgite [wɑl'pʌrdʒaɪt] o [wɑl'pʌrgaɪt] *s* (mineral.) valpurgita

walrus ['wɔlrəs] o ['wɑlrəs] *s* (zool.) morsa

Walter ['wɔltər] *s* Gualterio

waltz [wɔlts] *s* vals; *adj* de vals; *va* hacer valsar; *vn* valsar; girar, dar vueltas

wambly ['wɑmlɪ] o ['wæmlɪ] *adj* (dial.) trémulo, vacilante; (dial.) mareado, nauseado

wampum ['wɑmpəm] *s* cuentas de concha que usaban los pieles rojas como dinero; (slang) dinero

wan [wɑn] *adj* (*comp:* **wanner;** *super:* **wannest**) macilento; plomizo (*cielo*); obscuro, empañado

wand [wɑnd] *s* vara; varita de virtudes

wander ['wɑndər] *va* (poet.) atravesar o recorrer a la ventura; *vn* errar, vagar; extraviarse, perderse; **to wander about** o **around** errar o vagar de una parte a otra, andar acá y allá

wanderer ['wɑndərər] *s* vago, vagamundo; peregrino; prevaricador

wandering Jew *s* (bot.) matalí o sangría; (*caps.*) *s* Judío errante

wanderlust ['wɑndər,lʌst] *s* pasión de viajar, ansia de vagar

wane [wen] *s* mengua, disminución; decadencia, declinación; gema (*de un madero*); menguante (*de la luna*); **in** u **on the wane** menguando; decayendo, declinando; *vn* menguar, disminuir; decaer, declinar

wangle ['wæŋgəl] *va* sacudir; (coll.) mamar o mamarse (*p.ej., un buen destino*); (coll.) cazar (*adquirir con maña*); (coll.) adulterar (*p.ej., cuentas*); **to wangle into** + *ger* (coll.) persuadir con artimañas a + *inf; vn* (coll.) barajárselas; **to wangle through** (coll.) sacudirse bien (*salir con maña de un apuro*)

wanigan ['wɑnɪgən] *s* (U.S.A.) caja en que los gancheros guardan sus pertrechos; (U.S.A.) vivienda tosca de los gancheros, que flota en una balsa

wannish ['wɑnɪʃ] *adj* algo macilento

want [wɑnt] o [wɔnt] *s* deseo; necesidad; falta, carencia; **to be in want** estar necesitado; *va* desear; necesitar; carecer de; *vn* faltar; estar necesitado; **to want for** carecer de; necesitar; **to want to** + *inf* desear + *inf*

want ad *s* (coll.) anuncio clasificado

wanting ['wɑntɪŋ] o ['wɔntɪŋ] *adj* faltante (*que falta*); defectuoso, deficiente; **to be wanting** faltar; *prep* sin, menos, salvo

wanton ['wɑntən] *adj* insensible, perverso; caprichoso, irreflexivo; licencioso; lujoso; (poet.) lozano; (poet.) retozón; *s* libertino; *va* malgastar; *vn* retozar, juguetear

wantonness ['wɑntənnɪs] *s* insensibilidad, perversidad; capricho, irreflexión; libertinaje; lujo; (poet.) lozanía; (poet.) travesura

wapiti ['wɑpɪtɪ] *s* (*pl:* **-tis**) (zool.) uapití

war [wɔr] *s* guerra; **to be at war** estar en guerra; **to go to war** declarar la guerra, entrar en guerra; ir a la guerra (*como soldado*); (*pret & pp:* **warred;** *ger:* **warring**) *vn* guerrear; **to war on** guerrear con, hacer la guerra a

war baby *s* hijo de soldado, nacido durante una guerra; (coll.) industria o comercio fomentados por la guerra

War between the States *s* (U.S.A.) guerra entre Norte y Sur

warble ['wɔrbəl] *s* gorjeo, trino; *vn* gorjear, trinar

warbler ['wɔrblər] *s* gorjeador; (orn.) curruca; (orn.) candelita (*Setophaga ruticilla*)

war bond *s* bono de guerra

war bride *s* novia de guerra (*la recién casada con un soldado en tiempo de guerra*); (slang) industria o comercio fomentados por la guerra

war cloud *s* amenaza de guerra

war club *s* maza usada como arma

war crime *s* crimen de guerra

war criminal *s* criminal de guerra

war cry *s* grito de guerra

ward [wɔrd] *s* pupilo, menor o huérfano (*bajo tutela*); tutela, custodia; barrio, distrito (*de una ciudad*); crujía (*de un hospital*); guarda o rodaplancha (*de una llave*); guarda (*de la cerradura*); defensa, posición defensiva; *va* (archaic) guardar, vigilar; **to ward off** parar, detener, desviar

war dance *s* danza de guerra, danza guerrera

warden ['wɔrdən] *s* guardián; carcelero; alcalde; alcaide (*de una fortaleza*); capillero (*de una iglesia*); director (*de ciertas escuelas*)

warder ['wɔrdər] *s* guardián; (Brit.) carcelero

ward heeler *s* (coll.) muñidor (*de un cacique político*)

wardrobe ['wɔrd,rob] *s* guardarropa (*local; armario*); vestuario; (theat.) guardarropía

wardrobe trunk *s* baúl ropero, baúl perchero
wardroom [ˈwɔrd,rum] o [ˈwɔrd,rʊm] *s* (nav.) cuartel de oficiales; (Brit.) cuarto de guardia
wardship [ˈwɔrdʃɪp] *s* pupilaje, tutela
ware [wɛr] *s* loza de barro, artículos de alfarería; **wares** *spl* mercancías, efectos, géneros
war effort *s* esfuerzo bélico
warehouse [ˈwɛr,haʊs] *s* almacén; guardamuebles
warehouseman [ˈwɛr,haʊsmən] *s* (*pl:* **-men**) almacenero, guardalmacén; almacenista (*dueño*)
warfare [ˈwɔr,fɛr] *s* guerra
war game *s* supuesto táctico; juego de guerra
war god *s* dios de la guerra
war head *s* cabeza de combate, punta de combate (*de torpedo*)
war horse *s* caballo guerrero; (coll.) veterano, persona que ha tomado parte en muchas luchas y batallas
warily [ˈwɛrɪlɪ] *adv* cautelosamente
wariness [ˈwɛrɪnɪs] *s* cautela
warlike [ˈwɔr,laɪk] *adj* guerrero
war loan *s* empréstito de guerra
warlock [ˈwɔrlɑk] *s* (archaic) brujo, hechicero; (archaic) adivino, sortílego
war lord *s* jefe militar
warm [wɔrm) *adj* caliente (*que da calor*); templado (*ni frío ni caliente*); cálido, caluroso (*clima, país*); abrigador (*vestido, traje*); cálido (*color*); desagradable; (coll.) acomodado, bien de fortuna; (coll.) caliente (*cercano a lo que se busca*); (fig.) caluroso; **to be warm** hacer calor (*dícese del tiempo*); tener calor (*p.ej., una persona*); *va* calentar; hacer más amistoso, expresivo, etc.; acalorar; calentar (*una silla*); (coll.) zurrar; **to warm over** recalentar (*comida fría*); **to warm up** recalentar (*comida fría*); hacer más amistoso, expresivo, etc.; acalorar; *vn* calentarse; **to warm up** templar (*el tiempo*); hacerse más amistoso, expresivo, etc.; acalorarse; (sport) hacer ejercicios para entrar en calor
warm-blooded [ˈwɔrmˈblʌdɪd] *adj* apasionado, ardiente; (zool.) de sangre caliente
war memorial *s* monumento a los caídos
warm front *s* (meteor.) frente caliente
warm-hearted [ˈwɔrmˈhɑrtɪd] *adj* afectuoso, bondadoso, simpático
warming pan *s* mundillo, calentador de cama
warmish [ˈwɔrmɪʃ] *adj* algo caliente; algo caluroso
warmonger [ˈwɔr,mʌŋgər] *s* atizador de la guerra, fomentador de la guerra
warmth [wɔrmθ] *s* calor; ardor, entusiasmo; cordialidad, simpatía
warn [wɔrn] *va* avisar, advertir; aconsejar; amonestar
warning [ˈwɔrnɪŋ] *s* aviso, advertencia; *adj* amonestador
War Office *s* (Brit.) ministerio del Ejército
War of Independence *s* guerra de la Independencia
war of nerves *s* guerra de nervios
War of Secession *s* (U.S.A.) guerra de Secesión
War of the Roses *s* guerra de las dos Rosas
warp [wɔrp] *s* urdimbre (*de un tejido*); comba, alabeo (*de una tabla*); sesgo (*de la mente*); prejuicio; (naut.) espía; *va* combar, alabear, torcer; desviar; pervertir (*a una persona; el juicio de una persona; un texto*); (naut.) mover (*una embarcación*) con espía; *vn* combarse, alabearse, torcerse; desviarse; (naut.) espiarse
war paint *s* pintura que se ponen los pieles rojas para ir a la batalla; (coll.) ademán de amenaza; (coll.) colorete, atavíos, galas, trajes de lujo
warpath [ˈwɔr,pæθ] o [ˈwɔr,pɑθ] *s* senda que siguen los indios norteamericanos para atacar al enemigo; **to be on the warpath** estar preparado para la guerra; estar buscando pendencia
warplane [ˈwɔr,plen] *s* avión de guerra, avión militar
warrant [ˈwɑrənt] o [ˈwɔrənt] *s* autorización; decreto, orden; cédula, certificación; citación (*ante un juez*); justificación; garantía, promesa; *va* autorizar; justificar; garantizar, prometer; afirmar, asegurar
warrantable [ˈwɑrəntəbəl] o [ˈwɔrəntəbəl] *adj* garantizable; justificable
warrantee [,wɑrənˈti] o [,wɔrənˈti] *s* persona garantizada o afianzada
warranter [ˈwɑrəntər] o [ˈwɔrəntər] *s* garante
warrant officer *s* (mil.) suboficial de la clase de tropa; (nav.) contramaestre
warrantor [ˈwɑrəntɔr] o [ˈwɔrəntɔr] *s* (law) garante
warranty [ˈwɑrəntɪ] o [ˈwɔrəntɪ] *s* (*pl:* **-ties**) autorización; justificación; seguridad; (law) garantía
warren [ˈwɑrən] o [ˈwɔrən] *s* conejera; vivar (*donde se crían animales pequeños*); vedado; barrio o edificio densamente poblado
warrior [ˈwɑrɪər] o [ˈwɔrɪər] *s* guerrero
war risk insurance *s* seguros contra el riesgo de guerra
Warsaw [ˈwɔrsɔ] *s* Varsovia
Warsaw Pact *s* Tratado de Varsovia
war scare *s* psicosis de guerra
warship [ˈwɔr,ʃɪp] *s* buque de guerra
war strength *s* efectivos de guerra
wart [wɔrt] *s* verruga; (bot.) verruga
wart hog *s* (zool.) jabalí de verrugas
wartime [ˈwɔr,taɪm] *s* tiempo de guerra
war-torn [ˈwɔr,torn] *adj* devastado por la guerra
war to the death *s* guerra a muerte
warty [ˈwɔrtɪ] *adj* (*comp:* **-ier;** *super:* **-iest**) verrugoso
war whoop *s* grito de guerra (*especialmente de los pieles rojas*)
wary [ˈwɛrɪ] *adj* (*comp:* **-ier;** *super:* **-iest**) cauteloso (*dícese de una persona o de sus actos o dichos*); **wary of** cauteloso con
was [wɑz] o [wʌz] *primera y tercera personas del sg del pret de* **be**
Wash. abr. de **Washington**
wash [wɑʃ] o [wɔʃ] *s* lavado; jabonado (*ropa blanca que se ha de jabonar o se ha jabonado*); loción; alimento líquido; lavazas, despojos líquidos; batiente del agua; ruido del agua al batir; aluvión (*materia arrastrada y depositada por el agua*); charco, pantano; (aer.) disturbio aerodinámico, estela turbulenta; (paint.) lavado; (min.) grava aurífera; venta ficticia de acciones con el fin de manejar el mercado; *adj* lavable; *va* lavar; bañar, mojar; fregar (*la vajilla*); (mas., min., paint. & fig.) lavar; **to wash away** quitar lavando; derrubiar; llevarse (*el agua o las olas*); **to wash off** quitar lavando; *vn* lavarse; lavar la ropa; ser arrastrado y depositado por el agua; gastarse por la acción del agua: moverse, batir (*el agua*); (coll.) mantenerse firme
washable [ˈwɑʃəbəl] o [ˈwɔʃəbəl] *adj* lavable
wash-and-wear [ˈwɑʃəndˈwɛr] o [ˈwɔʃəndˈwɛr] *adj* de lava y pon
washbasin [ˈwɑʃ,besən] o [ˈwɔʃ,besən] *s* var. de **washbowl**
washbasket [ˈwɑʃ,bæskɪt] o [ˈwɔʃ,bæskɪt] *s* cesto de la colada
washboard [ˈwɑʃ,bord] o [ˈwɔʃ,bord] *s* lavadero, tabla de lavar; rodapié; (naut.) falca
wash bottle *s* (chem.) frasco lavador
washbowl [ˈwɑʃ,bol] o [ˈwɔʃ,bol] *s* jofaina, palangana
washcloth [ˈwɑʃ,klɔθ] o [ˈwɔʃ,klɔθ] *s* paño para lavarse
washday [ˈwɑʃ,de] o [ˈwɔʃ,de] *s* día de colada
washed-out [ˈwɑʃt,aʊt] o [ˈwɔʃt,aʊt] *adj* desteñido, descolorido; (coll.) debilitado, extenuado
washed-up [ˈwɑʃt,ʌp] o [ˈwɔʃt,ʌp] *adj* (slang) deslomado, derrengado; (slang) fracasado
washer [ˈwɑʃər] o [ˈwɔʃər] *s* lavador; lavadora o lavadora mecánica; arandela; disco de goma, zapatilla (*de una llave o grifo*); (phot.) lavador
washerwoman [ˈwɑʃər,wʊmən] o [ˈwɔʃər,wʊmən] *s* (*pl:* **-women**) lavandera
wash goods *spl* tejidos lavables, prendas lavables
washing [ˈwɑʃɪŋ] o [ˈwɔʃɪŋ] *s* lavado (*lavamiento; ropa lavada o por lavar*); (min.) lava;

washings *spl* lavadura (*agua sucia; rozadura de un cabo*)
washing machine *s* lavadora, lavadora mecánica, máquina de lavar
washing soda *s* sosa de lavar (*bicarbonato de sodio que se usa para blanquear la ropa*)
wash leather *s* gamuza (*piel*)
wash line *s* cordón de tender ropa
washout ['wɑʃ,aut] o ['wɔʃ,aut] *s* derrubio; (coll.) desilusión, fracaso
washrag ['wɑʃ,ræg] o ['wɔʃ,ræg] *s* paño para lavarse; paño de cocina
washroom ['wɑʃ,rum] o ['wɔʃ,rum] *s* gabinete de aseo, lavabo
wash sale *s* venta ficticia de acciones con el fin de manejar el mercado
washstand ['wɑʃ,stænd] o ['wɔʃ,stænd] *s* lavamanos (*palanganero; lavabo*)
washtub ['wɑʃ,tʌb] o ['wɔʃ,tʌb] *s* tina de lavar, cuba de colada; lavadero
wash water *s* agua de lavado; lavazas (*agua sucia*)
washwoman ['wɑʃ,wumən] o ['wɔʃ,wumən] *s* (*pl:* **-women**) lavandera
washy ['wɑʃɪ] o ['wɔʃɪ] *adj* (*comp:* **-ier;** *super:* **-iest**) aguado, diluído, débil; insulso, flojo
wasn't ['wɑzənt] o ['wʌzənt] contracción de **was not**
wasp [wɑsp] *s* (ent.) avispa
waspish ['wɑspɪʃ] *adj* colérico, rencoroso, irascible; como una avispa; ceñido, delgado
wasp-waisted ['wɑsp,westɪd] *adj* de talle de avispa
wassail ['wɑsəl] o ['wæsəl] *s* juerga de borrachera; cerveza o vino condimentados con especias (*que se toman en una juerga*); *interj* ¡salud!; *va* beber a la salud de; *vn* tomar parte en una juerga de borrachera
wassailer ['wɑsələr] o ['wæsələr] *s* juerguista, borrachón; brindador
wastage ['westɪdʒ] *s* pérdida, derroche, desgaste
waste [west] *s* derroche; pérdida (*p.ej., de tiempo*); decaimiento; basura, despojo, desecho, desperdicio; desgaste; despoblado, yermo; hilacha de algodón; (law) perjuicio causado por descuido del inquilino; **to go to waste** perderse, ser desperdiciado; **to lay waste** asolar, devastar, poner a fuego y sangre; *adj* desechado, inútil, sobrante; arruinado, desolado; yermo; (physiol.) excrementicio; *va* derrochar, malgastar, desperdiciar; desgastar; asolar, devastar; *vn* perderse; consumirse; mermar; **to waste away** decaer, consumirse
wastebasket ['west,bæskɪt] o ['west,bɑskɪt] *s* papelera (*cesto para papeles inútiles y desechos*)
wasteful ['westfəl] *adj* derrochador, manirroto, pródigo; devastador, ruinoso
waste paper *s* papel viejo, papeles usados
waste pipe *s* tubo de desagüe
waste product *s* producto de desecho; materia excretada
wastrel ['westrəl] *s* derrochador, malgastador; pródigo, perdido; cosa defectuosa o inútil, desecho
watch [wɑtʃ] *s* vigilancia; velación, vigilia; guardia; vigía; vigilante; reloj (*de bolsillo o de pulsera*); (mil.) centinela; (mil.) vigilia; (naut.) guardia; **to be on the watch for** estar a la mira de; tener cuidado con; **to keep watch** estar de guardia; **to keep watch over** velar (*p.ej., el sueño de una persona*); vigilar por o sobre; *adj* relojero; *va* mirar; velar, vigilar; guardar; tener cuidado con; *vn* mirar; velar (*no dormir*); **to watch for** acechar, esperar; **to watch out** tener cuidado; **to watch out for** estar a la mira de; guardarse de; tener cuidado con; **to watch over** velar (*p.ej., el sueño de una persona*); vigilar o velar por o sobre
watchcase ['wɑtʃ,kes] *s* caja de reloj
watch chain *s* cadena de reloj
watch charm *s* dije
watchdog ['wɑtʃ,dɔg] o ['wɑtʃ,dɑg] *s* perro de guarda, perro guardián; (fig.) fiel guardián
watch fire *s* hoguera encendida durante la noche (*p.ej., en un campamento*)
watchful ['wɑtʃfəl] *adj* desvelado, vigilante
watchfulness ['wɑtʃfəlnɪs] *s* desvelo, vigilancia
watchful waiting *s* espera vigilante
watch glass *s* cristal de reloj; (naut.) ampolleta de media hora
watchmaker ['wɑtʃ,mekər] *s* relojero
watchmaking ['wɑtʃ,mekɪŋ] *adj* relojero; *s* relojería
watchman ['wɑtʃmən] *s* (*pl:* **-men**) velador, vigilante, sereno
watchman's clock *s* reloj para vigilantes
watch meeting *s* oficio de noche vieja
watch night *s* noche vieja; oficio de noche vieja
watch pocket *s* relojera
watch spring *s* muelle de reloj
watch strap *s* pulsera
watchtower ['wɑtʃ,tauər] *s* garita, atalaya, vigía
watchword ['wɑtʃ,wʌrd] *s* santo y seña, contraseña; lema
watchwork ['wɑtʃ,wʌrk] *s* aparato de relojería
water ['wɔtər] o ['wɑtər] *s* agua; (com.) acciones emitidas sin el equivalente aumento de capital; **waters** *spl* aguas (*agua fluyente; agua batiente; agua mineral; agua de manantial; alta mar; visos de la seda, de las piedras preciosas*); **above water** (fig.) flotante; **by water** por agua, por barco; **like water** como agua (*pródigamente*); **of the first water** de lo mejor; **to back water** (naut. & fig.) ciar; **to carry water on both shoulders** nadar entre dos aguas, ser pancista; **to fish in troubled waters** pescar en río revuelto, pescar en agua turbia; **to go by water** ir por mar; **to hold water** retener el agua; (coll.) tener base firme, ser bien fundado; **to make water** hacer aguas (*orinar*); (naut.) hacer agua; **to pour** o **throw cold water on** echar un jarro de agua (fría) a, desanimar mostrando indiferencia; **to tread water** mantenerse a flote pataleando en el agua ‖ *adj* acuático; de agua; para agua ‖ *va* regar, rociar; aguar (*p.ej., el vino*); abrevar (*p.ej., el ganado*); proveer de agua; proveer de visos; (com.) emitir (*acciones*) sin el correspondiente aumento de capital ‖ *vn* llenarse de agua; abrevarse (*el ganado*); tomar agua (*p.ej., una locomotora*); llorar (*los ojos*); (naut.) hacer aguada
water back *s* caja de agua caliente
water ballast *s* (naut. & aer.) lastre de agua
water bath *s* baño de agua; baño maría
water beetle *s* (ent.) ditisco
water bird *s* ave acuática
water bottle *s* bolsa o botella para agua; cantimplora; vasija para recoger muestras de agua
water brain *s* (vet.) tornada
waterbuck ['wɔtər,bʌk] o ['wɑtər,bʌk] *s* (zool.) antílope acuático (*Kobus*)
water buffalo *s* (zool.) búfalo común; (zool.) carabao
water bug *s* (ent.) chinche de agua; (ent.) cucaracha
water carrier *s* aguador; barco para transporte de agua; cañería de agua; depósito de agua; nube de lluvia
water clock *s* reloj de agua
water closet *s* excusado, retrete, váter
water color *s* acuarela; color para acuarela
water-color ['wɔtər,kʌlər] o ['wɑtər,kʌlər] *adj* hecho a la acuarela
water-colorist ['wɔtər,kʌlərɪst] o ['wɑtər,kʌlərɪst] *s* acuarelista
water column *s* indicador de nivel del agua; (rail.) columna de agua
water-cooling ['wɔtər,kulɪŋ] o ['wɑtər,kulɪŋ] *s* refrigeración por agua
watercourse ['wɔtər,kors] o ['wɑtər,kors] *s* corriente de agua; lecho de corriente
watercraft ['wɔtər,kræft] o ['wɑtər,kræft] *s* embarcación, embarcaciones; destreza en la navegación; destreza en la natación o en los deportes acuáticos
water cress *s* (bot.) berro (*planta y hojas que se comen en ensalada*)
water cure *s* cura de aguas
water dog *s* perro de aguas; (coll.) buen nadador

water dropwort *s* (bot.) nabo del diablo
waterfall ['wɔtər,fɔl] o ['wɑtər,fɔl] *s* caída de agua, cascada
water fennel *s* (bot.) hinojo acuático, felandrio, enante
water flea *s* (ent.) pulga de agua
waterfowl ['wɔtər,faʊl] o ['wɑtər,faʊl] *s* ave acuática, aves acuáticas (*especialmente las palmípedas*)
water front *s* terreno ribereño (*especialmente de una ciudad*)
water gap *s* garganta u hondonada (*entre montañas por donde corre una corriente*)
water gas *s* gas de agua
water gate *s* abertura para el agua; compuerta
water germander *s* (bot.) escordio, ajote, camedrio acuático
water glass *s* vidrio soluble; vaso para beber agua
water hammer *s* choque de ariete, choque de agua; (phys.) martillo de agua (*tubo de vidrio*)
water heater *s* calentador de agua
water hemlock *s* (bot.) cicuta acuática; (bot.) felandrio, nabo del diablo
water hole *s* charco
water horehound *s* (bot.) marrubio acuático
water ice *s* sorbete, helado; hielo solidificado directamente del agua
wateriness ['wɔtərɪnɪs] o ['wɑtərɪnɪs] *s* acuosidad
watering can *s* regadera
watering place *s* aguadero, abrevadero; aguas minerales; baños, balneario
watering pot *s* regadera
watering trough *s* abrevadero, aguadero; (rail.) atarjea de alimentación
water jacket *s* camisa de agua
water level *s* nivel de agua; (naut.) línea de agua
water lily *s* (bot.) ninfea, nenúfar
water line *s* (naut.) línea de flotación, línea de agua; nivel de agua
water-logged ['wɔtər,lɔgd] o ['wɑtər,lɔgd] *adj* anegado, inundado; empapado
water main *s* cañería maestra
waterman ['wɔtərmən] o ['wɑtərmən] *s* (*pl:* **-men**) barquero; remero
watermark ['wɔtər,mɑrk] o ['wɑtər,mɑrk] *s* marca de agua, filigrana; marca de nivel de agua; *va* marcar (*papel*) al agua
watermelon ['wɔtər,mɛlən] o ['wɑtər,mɛlən] *s* (bot.) sandía (*planta y fruto*)
water meter *s* contador de agua
water mill *s* molino de agua
water moccasin *s* (zool.) mocasín de agua
water nymph *s* (myth.) ninfa de las aguas; (bot.) nenúfar
water of crystallization *s* (chem.) agua de cristalización
water ouzel *s* (orn.) tordo de agua, mirlo de agua
water parsnip *s* (bot.) berrera, arsáfraga
water pipe *s* cañería de agua
water plantain *s* (bot.) alisma
water polo *s* (sport) polo de agua, polo acuático
water power *s* fuerza de agua, fuerza hidráulica, hulla blanca
waterproof ['wɔtər,pruf] o ['wɑtər,pruf] *adj* impermeable; *s* material impermeable; impermeable (*sobretodo*); *va* impermeabilizar
waterproofing ['wɔtər,prufɪŋ] o ['wɑtər,prufɪŋ] *s* impermeabilización (*acción*); impermeabilizante (*material*)
water rat *s* (zool.) rata de agua, arvícola; (zool.) rata almizclada u ondatra
water seal *s* cierre hidráulico
watershed ['wɔtər,ʃɛd] o ['wɑtər,ʃɛd] *s* línea divisoria de las aguas; cuenca
water shrew *s* (zool.) musaraña de agua (*Neomys fodiens*)
waterside ['wɔtər,saɪd] o ['wɑtər,saɪd] *s* orilla, borde del agua
water ski *s* esquí acuático
water skiing *s* esquí acuático, esquiismo acuático
water skipper *s* var. de **water strider**
water snake *s* (zool.) culebra de agua
water-soak ['wɔtər,sok] o ['wɑtər,sok] *va* empapar de agua
water spaniel *s* perro de aguas
waterspout ['wɔtər,spaʊt] o ['wɑtər,spaʊt] *s* canalón (*para el agua del tejado*); manguera, boquilla de manguera; tromba marina; turbión, manga de agua
water sprite *s* espíritu de las aguas
water strider ['straɪdər] *s* (ent.) tejedor, zapatero
water supply *s* abastecimiento de agua
water-supply system ['wɔtərsə,plaɪ] o ['wɑtərsə,plaɪ] *s* fontanería
water table *s* (arch.) retallo de derrame; (eng.) capa freática
watertight *adj* ['wɔtər,taɪt] o ['wɑtər,taɪt] *adj* hermético, estanco; (fig.) seguro, que no deja lugar a malas interpretaciones
watertight compartment *s* (naut.) compartimiento estanco
water tower *s* arca de agua; torre de agua contra incendios
water-tube boiler ['wɔtər,tjub] o ['wɑtər,tjub] *s* caldera tubular de agua
water turkey *s* (orn.) anhinga
water vapor *s* vapor de agua
water wagon *s* (mil.) carro de agua; **to be on the water wagon** (slang) haber dejado de tomar bebidas alcohólicas
water wave *s* ondulación al agua (*en el peinado*)
waterway ['wɔtər,we] o ['wɑtər,we] *s* vía de agua, vía fluvial; canal (*para dejar pasar el agua*); (naut.) trancanil
water wheel *s* rueda hidráulica; turbina de agua; rueda de agua (*de la noria*); rueda de paletas (*del buque de ruedas*)
water wings *spl* nadaderas
waterworks ['wɔtər,wʌrks] o ['wɑtər,wʌrks] *ssg* o *spl* establecimiento para la distribución de las aguas; edificio con máquinas y bombas para la distribución de las aguas
waterworn ['wɔtər,worn] o ['wɑtər,worn] *adj* gastado o pulido por la acción del agua
watery ['wɔtərɪ] o ['wɑtərɪ] *adj* acuoso; aguado; mojado; lagrimoso, lloroso; evaporado, insípido; débil, pálido; que amenaza lluvia
watery grave *s* aguas en que tiene sepultura un cadáver
Watling Island ['wɑtlɪŋ] *s* Guanahaní o San Salvador (*isla de las Bahamas*)
watt [wɑt] *s* (elec.) vatio
wattage ['wɑtɪdʒ] *s* (elec.) vatiaje
watt-hour ['wɑt'aʊr] *s* (*pl:* **watt-hours**) (elec.) vatio-hora
watt-hour meter *s* (elec.) vatihorímetro
wattle ['wɑtəl] *s* zarzo, sebe; barba (*de ave*); barbilla (*de pez*); (bot.) acacia; *adj* construído con zarzo; *va* construir con zarzo; entretejer en forma de zarzo; amarrar con tiras de zarzo
wattmeter ['wɑt,mitər] *s* (elec.) vatímetro
wave [wev] *s* onda; onda u ondulación (*del cabello*); ola (*de calor o frío*); oleada (*p.ej., de huelgas*); señal hecha con la mano; (phys.) onda; (poet.) aguas, mar; *va* agitar, blandir (*p.ej., la espada*); ondear u ondular (*el cabello*); hacer señales con (*la mano o el pañuelo*); decir (*adiós*) con la mano; **to wave aside** apartar, rechazar; *vn* ondear, ondearse; hacer señales con la mano o el pañuelo
wave band *s* (rad.) banda de ondas
wave front *s* (phys.) frente de ondas
wave length *s* (phys.) longitud de onda
wavelet ['wevlɪt] *s* olita
wave motion *s* (phys.) ondulación, movimiento ondulatorio
waver ['wevər] *s* oscilación, vacilación; *vn* oscilar, vacilar
wave theory *s* (phys.) teoría ondulatoria (*de la luz*)
wave train *s* (phys.) tren de ondas
wave trap *s* (rad.) trampa de ondas
wavy ['wevɪ] *adj* (*comp:* **-ier;** *super:* **-iest**) ondeado; ondulado
wax [wæks] *s* cera; **to be wax in one's hands** ser como una cera; *va* encerar; cerotear (*el hilo*); *vn* hacerse, ponerse; crecer (*la luna*)
wax bean *s* habichuela, frijolillo
waxen ['wæksən] *adj* ceroso; plástico
wax myrtle *s* (bot.) árbol de la cera (*Myrica cerifera*)

wax palm *s* (bot.) palma de cera; (bot.) carnauba, palma negra (*Copernicia cerifera*)
wax paper *s* papel parafinado, papel encerado
wax plant *s* (bot.) monotropa; (bot.) flor de la cera (*Hoya carnosa*); (bot.) árbol de la cera (*Myrica cerifera*)
wax privet *s* (bot.) aligustre del Japón
wax taper *s* cerilla
wax tree *s* (bot.) trueno (*Ligustrum lucidum*); (bot.) fresno chino; (bot.) árbol de la cera (*Rhus verniciflus; Myrica cerifera*)
waxwing [ˈwæks,wɪŋ] *s* (orn.) ampélido
waxwork [ˈwæks,wʌrk] *s* figura o figuras de cera; **waxworks** *spl* museo de cera
waxy [ˈwæksɪ] *adj* (*comp:* **-ier;** *super:* **-iest**) ceroso
way [we] *s* vía, camino; pasaje; manera, modo; medio; costumbre, hábito; condición, estado; distancia; dirección, sentido; respecto; voluntad, p.ej., **he always wants his own way** quiere hacer siempre su voluntad; **ways** *spl* maneras, modales; anguilas (*para botar un barco al agua*); **across the way from** enfrente de, frente a; **a good way** un buen trecho; **a great way off** muy lejos; **all the way** por todo el camino; hasta el fin del camino; **all the way down to** o **up to** toda la distancia hasta; **any way** de cualquier modo, de todas maneras; **by the way** de paso; a propósito, dicho sea de paso; **by way of** por la vía de; por vía de, por modo de; a título de; a guisa de; **in a bad way** en mal estado; en malas condiciones; **in a big way** en gran escala; **in a small way** en pequeña escala; **in a way** de cierta manera, hasta cierto punto; **in every way** en todos respectos; **in my own way** a mi modo; **in no way** de ningún modo; **in the way of** en el ramo de, en la línea de; como; **in this way** de este modo; **once in a way** de vez en cuando; **on one's way** camino adelante; **on the way** en el camino; de paso; **on the way to** camino de, rumbo a; **on the way out** en dirección a la salida; saliendo; desapareciendo; **out of the way** hecho, despachado; fuera de lo común; fuera de orden; a un lado; escondido; inconveniente, impropio; **that way** por allí; de ese modo; **this way** por aquí; de este modo; **to be in the way** estorbar, incomodar; **to come one's way** seguir el mismo camino; caerle a uno en suerte, acontecerle a uno; **to feel one's way** tantear el camino; proceder con tiento; **to feel the same way** pasarle a uno lo mismo; ser de la misma opinión; **to find one's way** hallar el camino; **to force one's way** abrirse paso por fuerza; **to get into the way of** contraer la costumbre de; **to get out of the way** quitarse de en medio; quitarse de encima (*p.ej., un trabajo atrasado*); **to give way** ceder, retroceder; romperse (*p.ej., una cuerda*); fracasar; entregarse a las emociones propias; **to give way to** entregarse a (*p.ej., el dolor, el resentimiento*); **to go a long way towards** contribuir mucho a; **to go out of one's way** dar un rodeo; dar un rodeo innecesario; **to go out of one's way (for)** darse molestia (por), molestarse (por); **to go out of one's way to please** desvivirse por complacer; **to go the same way** llevar el mismo camino; **to have a way with** manejar bien, tener poder de persuasión con; **to have one's way** salirse con la suya; **to keep on one's way** seguir su camino; **to keep out of the way** estarse a un lado, no obstruir el paso; **to know one's way around** saber cómo entendérselas; **to lead the way** enseñar el camino, ir o entrar primero; **to lose one's way** perderse, andar perdido; **to make one's way** abrirse paso; avanzar; hacer carrera, acreditarse; **to make way** hacer lugar; ceder el paso; avanzar; **to make way for** dar paso a, hacer lugar para; **to mend one's ways** mejorar de conducta, mudar de vida; **to not know one's way around** estar en ayunas; **to not know which way to turn** no saber dónde meterse, no saber a qué atenerse; **to pave the way** preparar el terreno; **to put out of the way** poner (*una cosa*) donde no estorbe; quitar de en medio (*matar*); **to see one's way to** + *inf* ver el modo de, encontrar la manera de + *inf;* **to take one's way** irse, marcharse; **to wend one's way** seguir camino; **to wind one's way through** serpentear por; **to wing one's way** ir o avanzar volando; **to work one's way** abrirse camino, abrirse paso; **to work one's way through** pagar con su trabajo los gastos de (*p.ej., la universidad*); **under way** en marcha, en camino; pendiente; **which way?** ¿por dónde?
waybill [ˈwe,bɪl] *s* hoja de ruta
way down *s* bajada
wayfarer [ˈwe,fɛrər] *s* caminante
wayfaring [ˈwe,fɛrɪŋ] *adj* caminante
wayfaring tree *s* (bot.) barbadejo, morrionera
way in *s* entrada
waylaid [,weˈled] *pret & pp de* **waylay**
waylay [,weˈle] (*pret & pp:* **-laid**) *va* asechar; detener en el camino
way of life *s* manera de ser, modo de vivir
Way of St. James *s* Camino de Santiago (*Vía láctea*)
way out *s* salida
wayside [ˈwe,saɪd] *adj* del borde del camino, junto al camino; *s* borde del camino; **to fall by the wayside** desaparecer; fracasar
way station *s* (rail.) estación de paso, estación de tránsito, apeadero
way train *s* (rail.) tren ómnibus, tren carreta
way up *s* subida, subidero
wayward [ˈwewərd] *adj* descarriado; díscolo, voluntarioso; voltario, voluble
waywardness [ˈwewərdnɪs] *s* descarrío; voluntariedad; voltariedad
wayworn [ˈwe,worn] *adj* cansado de viajar, fatigado del viaje
w.c. abr. de **water closet** y **without charge**
W.C.T.U. abr. de **Women's Christian Temperance Union**
we [wi] *pron pers* nosotros
weak [wik] *adj* débil; (gram.) débil (*vocal; verbo*)
weaken [ˈwikən] *va* debilitar, enflaquecer; atenuar; *vn* debilitarse, enflaquecer; atenuarse
weaker sex *s* sexo débil
weakfish [ˈwik,fɪʃ] *s* (ichth.) pescadilla
weak-kneed [ˈwik,nid] *adj* flojo de rodillas; débil, cobarde
weakling [ˈwiklɪŋ] *adj & s* canijo, cobarde
weakly [ˈwiklɪ] *adj* (*comp:* **-lier;** *super:* **-liest**) débil, enfermizo, achacoso; *adv* débilmente
weak-minded [ˈwikˈmaɪndɪd] *adj* imbécil, mentecato; irresoluto, vacilante
weakness [ˈwiknɪs] *s* debilidad; lado débil; gusto, inclinación
weak side *s* lado débil
weal [wil] *s* verdugón; (archaic) bienestar
weald [wild] *s* (poet.) campo abierto
wealth [wɛlθ] *s* riqueza; abundancia
wealthy [ˈwɛlθɪ] *adj* (*comp:* **-ier;** *super:* **-iest**) rico
wean [win] *va* destetar; **to wean away from** apartar gradualmente de
weanling [ˈwinlɪŋ] *adj* recién destetado; *s* niño o animal recién destetado
weapon [ˈwɛpən] *s* arma
weaponeer [,wɛpənˈɪr] *s* perito en materia de armas nucleares
weaponry [ˈwɛpənrɪ] *s* (*pl:* **-ries**) armamento, sistema de armas
wear [wɛr] *s* uso (*de ropa*); ropa; desgaste, deterioro; durabilidad; estilo, moda; **for all kinds of wear** a todo llevar; **for everyday wear** para todo trote ‖ (*pret:* **wore;** *pp:* **worn**) *va* llevar o traer puesto, llevar, usar; calzar (*cierto tamaño de zapato o guante*); exhibir, mostrar; desgastar, deteriorar; agotar, cansar; hacer (*p.ej., un agujero*) por el roce o frotando; **to wear away** consumir, gastar; **to wear down** desgastar frotando; agotar, cansar (*p. ej., la paciencia de uno*); cansar hasta rendir (*a una persona*); **to wear out** consumir, gastar; agotar, cansar (*p.ej., la paciencia de uno*); acabar con; abusar de (*la hospitalidad de uno*) ‖ *vn* desgastarse, deteriorarse; durar; pasar, desaparecer; (naut.) virar; **to wear off** pasar, desaparecer; **to wear out** gastarse, usarse
wear and tear [tɛr] *s* desgaste o deterioro causado por el uso
weariness [ˈwɪrɪnɪs] *s* cansancio; aburrimiento

wearing apparel *s* ropaje, prendas de vestir
wearisome ['wɪrɪsəm] *adj* aburrido, fastidioso
weary ['wɪrɪ] *adj* (*comp:* **-rier;** *super:* **-riest**) cansado; aburrido; (*pret & pp:* **-ried**) *va* cansar; aburrir; *vn* cansarse; aburrirse
weasand ['wizənd] *s* tráquea; garganta
weasel ['wizəl] *s* (zool.) comadreja
weaseler ['wizələr] *s* pancista
weasel words *spl* palabras ambiguas (*dichas para quedar bien con todos*)
weather ['wɛðər] *s* tiempo; mal tiempo; **to be bad weather** hacer mal tiempo; **to be good weather** hacer buen tiempo; **to be under the weather** (coll.) estar indispuesto, sentirse mal; (coll.) estar borracho; *adj* meteorológico; atmosférico; (naut.) de barlovento; **to keep one's weather eye open** estar a la mira, espiar el peligro; *va* airear; solear; curar (*madera*) exponiéndola al aire, sol o lluvia; intemperizar; aguantar (*el temporal, la adversidad*); doblar (*un cabo*); dar inclinación a (*tablas, tejas, etc. para hacer caer el agua*); *vn* curtirse a la intemperie, desgastarse por la intemperie; resistir a la intemperie
weather beam *s* (naut.) costado de barlovento
weather-beaten ['wɛðər,bitən] *adj* curtido por la intemperie
weatherboard ['wɛðər,bord] *s* tabla de chilla, tabla solapada; *va* cubrir con tablas de chilla, cubrir con tablas solapadas
weather-bound ['wɛðər,baund] *adj* atrasado o detenido por el mal tiempo
Weather Bureau *s* departamento de señales meteorológicas
weathercock ['wɛðər,kɑk] *s* veleta; (fig.) veleta (*persona mudable*)
weathered oak *s* roble ahumado
weather gauge *s* (naut.) barlovento
weatherglass ['wɛðər,glæs] o ['wɛðər,glɑs] *s* barómetro, baroscopio u otro instrumento que indica la presión de la atmósfera, y por lo tanto, el estado del tiempo
weathering ['wɛðərɪŋ] *s* descomposición de la roca por los agentes atmosféricos; (constr.) declive de derrame
weatherman ['wɛðər,mæn] *s* (*pl:* **-men**) (coll.) pronosticador del tiempo, meteorologista; (coll.) oficina meteorológica
weather map *s* mapa meteorológico
weatherproof ['wɛðər,pruf] *adj* a prueba de la intemperie, a prueba del mal tiempo
weather strip *s* burlete, cierre hermético
weather-strip ['wɛðər,strɪp] (*pret & pp:* **-stripped;** *ger:* **-stripping**) *va* proveer de burletes
weather stripping *s* burlete, cierre hermético; burletes
weather vane *s* veleta
weather-wise ['wɛðər,waɪz] *adj* hábil en la pronosticación del tiempo
weave [wiv] *s* tejido; (*pret:* **wove** o **weaved;** *pp:* **woven** o **wove**) *va* tejer; (fig.) tejer (*un cuento, una intriga*); **to weave one's way** avanzar virando y cambiando de dirección; **to weave together** entrelazar; combinar; *vn* tejer; zigzaguear
weaver ['wivər] *s* tejedor; (orn.) tejedor
weaverbird ['wivər,bʌrd] *s* (orn.) tejedor
web [wɛb] *s* tela, tejido; tela (*p.ej., de araña*); membrana (*entre los dedos de ciertas aves*); barba (*de una pluma*); alma (*de los carriles, etc.*); paletón (*de la llave*); hoja (*de sierra, de espada*); (print.) rollo de papel continuo; (rad. & telv.) red; (fig.) tela, tejido, enredo, maraña
webbed [wɛbd] *adj* tejido; palmeado
webbing ['wɛbɪŋ] *s* tiras de tela (*que sirven para cinchas y para tapizar muebles*); borde tejido que se pone como refuerzo a las alfombras; membrana (*entre los dedos de ciertas aves*)
webfoot ['wɛb,fut] *s* (*pl:* **-feet**) pie palmeado; palmípedo
web-footed ['wɛb,futɪd] *adj* palmípedo, de pie palmeado
web frame *s* (naut.) cuaderna
web press *s* prensa que imprime en rollo de papel continuo
web-toed ['wɛb,tod] *adj* var. de **web-footed**
Wed. abr. de **Wednesday**
we'd [wid] contracción de **we had, we should** y **we would**
wed [wɛd] (*pret:* **wedded;** *pp:* **wedded** o **wed;** *ger:* **wedding**) *va* casar (*unir en matrimonio*); casarse con; *vn* casarse
wedding ['wɛdɪŋ] *s* bodas, matrimonio; *adj* de boda, nupcial
wedding cake *s* torta de boda
wedding day *s* día de bodas
wedding march *s* (mus.) marcha nupcial
wedding night *s* noche de bodas
wedding ring *s* anillo de boda
wedding trip *s* viaje de novios
wedge [wɛdʒ] *s* cuña; (mil.) cúneo; (fig.) cuña; *va* acuñar; apretar con cuña; apretar; encajar; *vn* avanzar con fuerza; estar encajado
wedlock ['wɛdlɑk] *s* matrimonio
Wednesday ['wɛnzdɪ] *s* miércoles
wee [wi] *adj* diminuto, menudo, pequeñito
weed [wid] *s* mala hierba; (coll.) cigarro, tabaco; (archaic) prenda de vestir; **weeds** *spl* ropa de luto; *va* desherbar, escardar; **to weed out** (fig.) escardar; (fig.) arrancar, extirpar
weeder ['widər] *s* desherbador, escardador (*persona*); escarda (*azada para escardar*)
weeding hoe *s* almocafre, escardillo
weed killer *s* matazarzas, matamalezas, herbicida
weedy ['widɪ] *adj* (*comp:* **-ier;** *super:* **-iest**) lleno de malas hierbas; débil, flaco; (coll.) torpe, lerdo, desgarbado
wee folk *spl* hadas
week [wik] *s* semana; **this day week** de hoy en ocho días; **week in, week out** semana tras semana
weekday ['wik,de] *s* día laborable, día de la semana que no sea el domingo; *adj* de o en un día laborable
weekend ['wik,ɛnd] *s* fin de semana; *adj* de o durante el fin de semana; *vn* pasar el fin de semana
weekly ['wiklɪ] *adj* semanal; *adv* semanalmente; *s* (*pl:* **-lies**) semanario
ween [win] *vn* (archaic) creer, imaginar, suponer
weep [wip] *s* (coll.) lloro; (orn.) ave fría; (*pret & pp:* **wept**) *va* llorar (*p.ej., la muerte de un amigo*); derramar (*lágrimas*); **to weep away** pasar (*la noche, la vida, etc.*) llorando; *vn* llorar; (plant path.) llorar
weeper ['wipər] *s* llorón; llorona, plañidera (*mujer alquilada para llorar en los entierros*)
weep hole *s* (eng.) cantimplora
weeping ['wipɪŋ] *adj* llorón, lloroso; (bot.) llorón; *s* lloro
weeping willow *s* (bot.) sauce llorón
weepy ['wipɪ] *adj* (*comp:* **-ier;** *super:* **-iest**) (coll.) lloroso
weevil ['wivəl] *s* (ent.) gorgojo (*de las familias Curculionidae y Lariidae*)
weevily o **weevilly** ['wivəlɪ] *adj* gorgojoso
weft [wɛft] *s* trama; tejido; humo
weigh [we] *va* pesar; agobiar, sobrecargar; (naut.) levantar (*el ancla*); (fig.) pesar; **to weigh down** agravar, hacer doblar bajo un peso; **to weigh one's words** pesar sus palabras; *vn* pesar; (naut.) levantar el ancla; (fig.) pesar (*tener influencia en el ánimo*); **to weigh in** (sport) pesarse (*un jockey*); **to weigh on** ser gravoso a
weighmaster ['we,mæstər] o ['we,mɑstər] *s* encargado de la báscula; balanzario (*en las casas de moneda*)
weight [wet] *s* peso; pesa (*de la balanza, el reloj, etc.; en la gimnasia*); (fig.) peso (*importancia; carga o gravamen*); **by weight** por peso; **to be worth its weight in gold** valer su peso en oro; **to lose weight** rebajar de peso; **to pull one's weight** hacer su parte; **to put on weight** ponerse gordo; **to throw one's weight around** (coll.) mandar arbitrariamente, hacer valer su poder; *va* cargar, gravar; sobrecargar; ponderar (*estadísticamente*)
weightless ['wetlɪs] *adj* ingrávido
weightlessness ['wetlɪsnɪs] ingravidez, gravedad nula
weighty ['wetɪ] *adj* (*comp:* **-ier;** *super:* **-iest**) pesado; gravoso; importante, influyente
weir [wɪr] *s* presa, vertedero; encañizada, pesquera

weird [wɪrd] *adj* misterioso, sobrenatural, horripilante; (coll.) extraño, raro
welch [wɛltʃ] *va* (slang) dejar de cumplir con; *vn* (slang) dejar de cumplir una apuesta u obligación; **to welch on** (slang) dejar de cumplir con
welcome [ˈwɛlkəm] *s* bienvenida, buena acogida; acogida; **to wear out one's welcome** abusar de la hospitalidad de una persona hasta serle molesto; *adj* bienvenido; grato, agradable; **you are welcome** sea Vd. bienvenido; no hay de qué; **you are welcome to it** está a la disposición de Vd., buen provecho le haga; *interj* ¡bienvenido!; *va* dar la bienvenida a; acoger, recibir con amabilidad y gusto
weld [wɛld] *s* autógena, soldadura autógena; (bot.) gualda; *va* soldar con autógena; (fig.) unificar, unir; *vn* soldarse; ser soldable
welder [ˈwɛldər] *s* soldador (*persona*); soldadora (*máquina*)
welding [ˈwɛldɪŋ] *s* autógena, soldadura autógena
welding torch *s* soplete soldador, antorcha soldadora
welfare [ˈwɛlˌfɛr] *s* bienestar; asistencia (*trabajo de auxilio social*)
welfare state *s* estado de beneficencia, estado socializante
welfare work *s* asistencia (*trabajo de auxilio social*)
welkin [ˈwɛlkɪn] *s* (archaic) bóveda celeste, firmamento
we'll [wil] contracción de **we shall** y **we will**
well [wɛl] *adj* bien; bien de salud; *adv* (*comp:* **better;** *super:* **best**) bien; muy; muy bien; mucho, p.ej., **he earned well over a hundred dollars** ganó mucho más de cien dólares; pues; pues bien; **as well** también; igualmente; **as well as** además de; así como, tanto como; *interj* ¡vaya!; *s* pozo; fuente, manantial; depósito (*de una pluma fuente*); *va* manar; *vn* manar, salir a borbotones
well-appointed [ˈwɛləˈpɔɪntɪd] *adj* bien amueblado, bien equipado
well-balanced [ˈwɛlˈbælənst] *adj* bien ajustado; (fig.) bien equilibrado, cuerdo, sensato
well-behaved [ˈwɛlbɪˈhevd] *adj* de buena conducta
well-being [ˈwɛlˈbiɪŋ] *s* bienestar
wellborn [ˈwɛlˈbɔrn] *adj* bien nacido
well-bred [ˈwɛlˈbrɛd] *adj* bien criado, cortés
well-content [ˈwɛlkənˈtɛnt] *adj* muy contento
well digger *s* pocero
well-disposed [ˈwɛldɪsˈpozd] *adj* bien dispuesto, bien intencionado
well-done [ˈwɛlˈdʌn] *adj* bien hecho; (cook.) bien asado
well-favored [ˈwɛlˈfevərd] *adj* bien parecido
well-featured [ˈwɛlˈfitʃərd] *adj* bien agestado, de buena cara
well-fed [ˈwɛlˈfɛd] *adj* bien comido, regordete
well-fixed [ˈwɛlˈfɪkst] *adj* (coll.) acomodado, próspero
well-found [ˈwɛlˈfaʊnd] *adj* bien provisto, bien equipado
well-founded [ˈwɛlˈfaʊndɪd] *adj* bien fundado
well-groomed [ˈwɛlˈgrumd] *adj* acicalado, de mucho aseo
wellhead [ˈwɛlˌhɛd] *s* venero, fuente, manantial
well-heeled [ˈwɛlˈhild] *adj* (slang) acomodado; **to be well-heeled** (slang) tener bien cubierto el riñón
well-informed [ˈwɛlɪnˈfɔrmd] *adj* bien enterado (*de un asunto*); culto
well-informed sources *spl* fuentes bien informadas
well-intentioned [ˈwɛlɪnˈtɛnʃənd] *adj* bien intencionado
well-kept [ˈwɛlˈkɛpt] *adj* bien cuidado, bien atendido
well-known [ˈwɛlˈnon] *adj* familiar; bien conocido
well-mannered [ˈwɛlˈmænərd] *adj* de buenos modales, cortés, urbano
well-meaning [ˈwɛlˈminɪŋ] *adj* bienintencionado
well-nigh [ˈwɛlˈnaɪ] *adv* casi
well-off [ˈwɛlˈɔf] o [ˈwɛlˈɑf] *adj* en buenas condiciones; acomodado, adinerado
well-ordered [ˈwɛlˈɔrdərd] *adj* bien ordenado, bien arreglado
well-preserved [ˈwɛlprɪˈzʌrvd] *adj* bien conservado
well-proportioned [ˈwɛlprəˈporʃənd] *adj* bien proporcionado
well-read [ˈwɛlˈrɛd] *adj* leído, muy leído
well-shaped [ˈwɛlˈʃept] *adj* bien formado; perfilado (*dícese de la nariz*)
well-spent [ˈwɛlˈspɛnt] *adj* bien empleado
well-spoken [ˈwɛlˈspokən] *adj* bienhablado; bien dicho
wellspring [ˈwɛlˌsprɪŋ] *s* fuente; fuente inagotable
well-stocked [ˈwɛlˈstɑkt] *adj* bien provisto
well-suited [ˈwɛlˈsjutɪd] o [ˈwɛlˈsutɪd] *adj* apropiado, conveniente
well sweep *s* cigoñal
well-tempered [ˈwɛlˈtɛmpərd] *adj* bien templado; (mus.) bien templado
well-thought-of [ˈwɛlˈθɔtˌɑv] *adj* bienquisto, bien mirado
well-thought-out [ˈwɛlˌθɔtˈaʊt] *adj* bien razonado
well-timed [ˈwɛlˈtaɪmd] *adj* oportuno
well-to-do [ˈwɛltəˈdu] *adj* acaudalado, acomodado
well-wisher [ˈwɛlˈwɪʃər] *s* amigo (*que desea suerte y fortuna a otra persona o empresa*)
well-worn [ˈwɛlˈworn] *adj* desgastado por el uso; trillado, vulgar
Welsh [wɛlʃ] *adj* galés; *spl* galeses; *ssg* galés (*idioma*); (*l.c.*) *va* (slang) defraudar, dejando de cumplir una apuesta u obligación; *vn* (slang) dejar de cumplir una apuesta u obligación; **to welsh on** (slang) defraudar, dejando de cumplir una apuesta u obligación
Welshman [ˈwɛlʃmən] *s* (*pl:* **-men**) galés
Welsh onion *s* (bot.) cebolleta, cebollino inglés
Welsh rabbit o **rarebit** *s* salsa de queso derretido con cerveza que se come sobre tostadas
welt [wɛlt] *s* vira (*del zapato*); ribete; (coll.) verdugón; (coll.) latigazo; *va* poner vira a; poner ribete a; (coll.) dar una paliza a
welter [ˈwɛltər] *s* confusión, conmoción; revuelco; *vn* revolcar; estar empapado
welterweight [ˈwɛltərˌwet] *s* (box.) peso mediano ligero, peso medio ligero; peso que se le pone a un caballo como ventaja para los otros que corren en la misma carrera
wen [wɛn] *s* lobanillo
wench [wɛntʃ] *s* muchacha; criada, moza; (archaic) ramera
wend [wɛnd] *va* seguir (*su camino*); *vn* seguir su camino; (*cap.*) *s* vendo
Wendish [ˈwɛndɪʃ] *adj* vendo; *s* vendo (*idioma*)
went [wɛnt] *pret de* **go**
wept [wɛpt] *pret & pp de* **weep**
we're [wɪr] contracción de **we are**
were [wʌr] *segunda persona del sg y primera, segunda y tercera personas del pl del pret de* **be; as it were** como si fuese, por decirlo así
weren't [wʌrnt] contracción de **were not**
werewolf [ˈwɪrˌwʊlf] o **werwolf** [ˈwʌrˌwʊlf] *s* (*pl:* **-wolves**) hombre convertido en lobo
Wesleyan [ˈwɛslɪən] *adj & s* wesleyano
west [wɛst] *s* oeste, occidente; *adj* occidental, del oeste; *adv* al oeste
West Berlin *s* el Berlín-Oeste
westerly [ˈwɛstərlɪ] *adj* occidental; que viene desde el oeste; que va hacia el oeste; *adv* desde el oeste; hacia el oeste; *s* (*pl:* **-lies**) viento del oeste
western [ˈwɛstərn] *adj* occidental; *s* cinta cinematográfica o historieta que se desarrolla en el oeste de los EE.UU.
Western Australia *s* la Australia Occidental
Western Church *s* Iglesia occidental
Western civilization *s* la civilización de occidente
Western Empire *s* Imperio de Occidente
westerner [ˈwɛstərnər] *s* habitante del oeste
Western Hemisphere *s* hemisferio occidental
westernization [ˌwɛstərnɪˈzeʃən] *s* occidentalización
westernize [ˈwɛstərnaɪz] *va* occidentalizar
westernmost [ˈwɛstərnmost] *adj* (el) más occidental
Western Roman Empire *s* var. de **Western Empire**

West Germany *s* la Alemania Occidental
West Indian *adj & s* antillano
West Indies *spl* Indias Occidentales
Westminster Abbey ['wɛst,mɪnstər] *s* la abadía de Wéstminster
west-northwest ['wɛst,nɔrθ'wɛst] *s* oesnoroeste, oesnorueste
Westphalia [wɛst'felɪə] *s* Vestfalia
Westphalian [wɛst'felɪən] *adj & s* vestfaliano
west-southwest ['wɛst,sauθ'wɛst] *s* oessudoeste, oessudueste
West Virginia *s* la Virginia Occidental, la Virginia del Oeste
westward ['wɛstwərd] *adj* que va hacia el oeste; *adv* hacia el oeste; *s* oeste
westwardly ['wɛstwərdlɪ] *adj* que va hacia el oeste; *adv* hacia el oeste
westwards ['wɛstwərdz] *adv* hacia el oeste
wet [wɛt] *adj* (*comp:* **wetter;** *super:* **wettest**) mojado; húmedo; fresco (*dícese de la pintura*); (coll.) antiprohibicionista; *s* líquido; humedad, lluvia; (coll.) antiprohibicionista; (*pret & pp:* **wet** *o* **wetted;** *ger:* **wetting**) *va* mojar; *vn* mojarse
wetback ['wɛt,bæk] *s* mojado (*bracero mejicano que ha pasado la frontera ilegalmente*)
wet battery *s* (elec.) batería líquida; (elec.) pila líquida
wet blanket *s* aguafiestas
wet cell *s* (elec.) pila húmeda
wet goods *spl* (com.) líquidos envasados; (coll.) licores, bebidas espiritosas
wether ['wɛðər] *s* carnero llano, carnero castrado
wetness ['wɛtnɪs] *s* humedad
wet nurse *s* ama de cría, nodriza
wet-nurse ['wɛt,nʌrs] *va* criar (*la nodriza al niño*)
wet season *s* estación de las lluvias
wettish ['wɛtɪʃ] *adj* algo mojado, húmedo
wet way *s* (chem.) vía húmeda
we've [wiv] contracción de **we have**
w.f. abr. de **wrong font**
w.g. abr. de **wire gauge**
whack [hwæk] *s* (coll.) golpe ruidoso; (coll.) prueba, tentativa; (coll.) parte; *va* (coll.) golpear ruidosamente
whacking ['hwækɪŋ] *adj* (coll.) desmesurado, enorme
whale [hwel] *s* (zool.) ballena; **a whale at tennis** (coll.) un as de tenis; **a whale for figures** (coll.) un genio para los números; **a whale of a difference** (coll.) una enorme diferencia; **a whale of a story** (coll.) una historia extraordinaria; **the Whale** (astr.) la Ballena; *va* (coll.) azotar; *vn* pescar ballenas
whaleback ['hwel,bæk] *s* (naut.) buque de carga con la cubierta superior redondeada en forma de lomo de ballena
whaleboat ['hwel,bot] *s* (naut.) ballenero (*embarcación menor de extremidades agudas*)
whalebone ['hwel,bon] *s* ballena (*lámina córnea; tira de tal lámina*)
whale louse *s* (zool.) piojo de mar
whale oil *s* aceite de ballena
whaler ['hwelər] *s* ballenero (*persona y embarcación*)
whaling ['hwelɪŋ] *adj* ballenero; *s* pesca de ballenas
whammy ['hwæmɪ] *s* (*pl:* **-mies**) (slang) mal de ojo; **to put a** *o* **the whammy on** (slang) hacer mal de ojo a
whang [hwæŋ] *s* (coll.) golpe resonante; *va & vn* (coll.) golpear de modo resonante
wharf [hwɔrf] *s* (*pl:* **wharves** *o* **wharfs**) muelle
wharfage ['hwɔrfɪdʒ] *s* empleo de un muelle; muellaje (*derecho o impuesto*); muelles
wharfinger ['hwɔrfɪndʒər] *s* dueño de muelle; encargado de un muelle
what [hwat] *pron interr* ¿qué?, p.ej., **what do you have in your hand?** ¿qué tiene Vd. en la mano?; ¿cuál?, p.ej., **what is the capital of Japan?** ¿cuál es la capital del Japón?; **what else?** ¿qué más?; *pron rel* lo que; *adj interr* ¿qué . . . ?; *adj rel* el (la, etc.) . . . que; *interj* ¡qué!; **and what not** y qué sé yo que más; **but what** que no, p.ej., **she is not so rich but what she needs help** no es tan rica que no necesite ayuda; **what a . . . !** ¡qué . . . !, p.ej., **what a man!** ¡qué hombre!; ¡qué . . . más o tan . . . !, p.ej., **what a beautiful day!** ¡qué día más hermoso!; **what about . . . ?** ¿qué le parece . . . ?; ¿qué hay en cuanto a . . . ?; **what for?** ¿para qué?, ¿por qué?; **what if?** ¿y si?; ¿qué será si?; **what of it?** ¿eso qué importa?; **what's what** (coll.) lo que hay, cuántas son cinco
whate'er [hwat'ɛr] *pron & adj* (poet.) var. de **whatever**
whatever [hwat'ɛvər] *pron* lo que, todo lo que, cualquier cosa que, sea lo que sea que; (coll.) ¿qué?, p.ej., **whatever do you mean?** ¿qué quiere Vd. decir?; *adj* cualquier . . . que
whatnot ['hwat,nat] *s* juguetero (*mueble*)
what's [hwats] contracción de **what is**
whatsoe'er [,hwatso'ɛr] *pron & adj* (poet.) var. de **whatsoever**
whatsoever [,hwatso'ɛvər] *pron & adj* var. de **whatever**
wheal [hwil] *s* roncha; *va* levantar roncha en
wheat [hwit] *s* (bot.) trigo (*planta y grano*)
wheatear ['hwit,ɪr] *s* (orn.) culiblanco
wheaten ['hwitən] *adj* triguero; hecho de trigo
wheat field *s* trigal
wheat smut *s* tizón del trigo
wheedle ['hwidəl] *va* engatusar; conseguir por medio de halagos
wheel [hwil] *s* rueda; (coll.) bicicleta; **wheels** *spl* maquinaria; **at the wheel** en el volante; (fig.) en el timón; *va* proveer de ruedas; mover por medio de ruedas; pasear (*a un niño en un cochecito*); hacer girar; dar forma por medio de una rueda de alfarero; *vn* girar, rodar; moverse suavemente; moverse por medio de ruedas; (coll.) ir o correr en bicicleta; **to wheel about** (mil.) conversar; **to wheel around** dar una vuelta; girar sobre los talones; cambiar de opinión
wheelbarrow ['hwil,bæro] *s* carretilla
wheel base *s* (aut.) batalla, distancia entre ejes
wheel chair *s* silla de ruedas, sillón de ruedas, cochecillo para inválidos
wheeler ['hwilər] *s* girador, rodador; caballo de varas; vapor de ruedas; (coll.) biciclista
wheel horse *s* caballo de varas; (fig.) persona que trabaja mucho y con eficiencia
wheelhouse ['hwil,haus] *s* (naut.) timonera, caseta del timón
wheel puller *s* (aut.) extractor de rueda, sacarruedas
wheelwright ['hwil,raɪt] *s* carretero, ruedero, carpintero de carretas
wheeze [hwiz] *s* resuello ruidoso; (slang) cuento viejo, chiste viejo; (slang) truco; *va* decir resollando con ruido; *vn* resollar con ruido, gañir
wheezy ['hwizɪ] *adj* (*comp:* **-ier;** *super:* **-iest**) que resuella con ruido
whelk [hwɛlk] *s* (zool.) buccino; pústula, barro
whelm [hwɛlm] *va* sobrepujar, subyugar; sumergir
whelp [hwɛlp] *s* cachorro (*de perro, león, oso, etc.*); calavera; diente (*de rueda de cadena*); **whelps** *spl* guardainfante (*del cabrestante*); *va & vn* parir
when [hwɛn] *adv* ¿cuándo?, p.ej., **when will he arrive?** ¿cuándo llegará? **I don't know when he will arrive** no sé cuándo llegará; *conj* cuando, p.ej., **I shall be here when he arrives** estaré aquí cuando llegue; en que, p.ej., **there are times when I like to be alone** hay ocasiones en que me gusta estar solo; que, p.ej., **the day when you were born** el dia que tú naciste
whence [hwɛns] *adv* ¿de dónde?; por eso, por tanto; de dónde; *conj* de donde
whencesoever [,hwɛnsso'ɛvər] *adv* de dondequiera; *conj* de dondequiera que
whene'er [hwɛn'ɛr] *conj* (poet.) var. de **whenever**
whenever [whɛn'ɛvər] *conj* cuando, cuando quiera que, siempre que
whensoever [,hwɛnso'ɛvər] *adv* cuando quiera; *conj* cuando quiera que
where [hwɛr] *adv* ¿dónde?, ¿adónde?, ¿en dónde?, p.ej., **where does he live?** ¿dónde vive?; **tell me where he lives** dígame dónde vive; *conj* donde, adonde, en donde, p.ej., **I can't find the house where he lives** no puedo hallar la casa donde vive

whereabout ['hwɛrə,baut] *adv & s* var. de **whereabouts**
whereabouts ['hwɛrə,bauts] *adv* en qué parte, dónde; *s* paradero
whereas [hwɛr'æz] *conj* mientras que; por cuanto, considerando que; *s* considerando
whereat [hwɛr'æt] *adv* con lo cual
whereby [hwɛr'baɪ] *adv* ¿cómo?; *conj* por donde, por medio del cual
where'er [hwɛr'ɛr] *conj* (poet.) dondequiera que
wherefore ['hwɛrfor] *adv* ¿por qué?; por eso, por tanto; *conj* por lo cual; *s* motivo, razón
wherefrom [hwɛr'frɑm] *adv* de dónde; ¿de dónde?
wherein [hwɛr'ɪn] *adv* ¿dónde?, ¿en qué?, ¿cómo?; *conj* donde, en el (la, etc.) que; en que, en lo cual
whereinto [hwɛr'ɪntu] o [,hwɛrɪn'tu] *conj* dentro de que, dentro de lo que
whereof [hwɛr'ɑv] *adv* ¿de qué?; *conj* de qué; de que
whereon [hwɛr'ɑn] *adv* ¿en qué?; *conj* en qué; en que
wheresoe'er [,hwɛrso'ɛr] *conj* (poet.) var. de **wheresoever**
wheresoever [,hwɛrso'ɛvər] *conj* dondequiera que
whereto [hwɛr'tu] *adv* ¿adónde?; ¿por qué?, ¿para qué?; *conj* adonde
whereunto [hwɛr'ʌntu] o [,hwɛrʌn'tu] *adv & conj* (archaic) var. de **whereto**
whereupon [,hwɛrə'pɑn] *adv* entonces, con lo cual, después de lo cual
wherever [hwɛr'ɛvər] *adv* (coll.) ¿dónde?; *conj* dondequiera que
wherewith [hwɛr'wɪð] o [hwɛr'wɪθ] *adv* ¿con qué?; *conj* con que, con el cual
wherewithal [,hwɛrwɪð'ɔl] *adv* (archaic) ¿con qué?; *conj* (archaic) con que, con el cual; ['hwɛrwɪðɔl] *s* cumquibus, dinero, medios
wherry ['hwɛrɪ] *s* (*pl:* **-ries**) esquife; (Brit.) chalana
whet [hwɛt] *s* afiladura, aguzadura; aperitivo; (*pret & pp:* **whetted;** *ger:* **whetting**) *va* afilar, aguzar; despertar, estimular; abrir (*el apetito*)
whether ['hwɛðər] *pron* (archaic) ¿cuál?; *conj* si, p.ej., **I don't know whether he will come** no sé si vendrá; **whether or no** en todo caso, de todas maneras; **whether or not** si . . . o no, ya sea que . . . o no
whetstone ['hwɛt,ston] *s* piedra de afilar
whew [hwju] *interj* ¡vaya!; ¡uf!
whey [hwe] *s* suero de la leche
which [hwɪtʃ] *pron interr* ¿cuál?; *pron rel* que, el (la, etc.) que; *adj interr* ¿qué . . . ?, ¿cuál de los (las) . . . ?; *adj rel* el (la, etc.) . . . que; **which is which** cuál es el uno y cuál el otro
whichever [hwɪtʃ'ɛvər] *pron rel* cualquiera; *adj rel* cualquier
whichsoever [,hwɪtʃso'ɛvər] *pron & adj rel* var. de **whichever**
whidah ['hwɪdə] o **whidah bird** *s* (orn.) viuda; (orn.) viuda de pecho rojo (*Steganura paradisea*)
whiff [hwɪf] *s* soplo, ráfaga; soplo fugaz, vaharada; bocanada, fumada; acceso, arranque; pizca, gustillo; descarga de metralla; (coll.) periquete, santiamén; **to get a whiff of** percibir un olor fugaz de; *va* soplar; fumar (*p.ej., una pipa*); fumar echando (*bocanadas de humo*); *vn* soplar; echar bocanadas
whiffet ['hwɪfɪt] *s* perrillo; soplillo; (coll.) mequetrefe
whiffle ['hwɪfəl] *va* soplar en ráfagas ligeras; *vn* soplar en ráfagas ligeras; cambiar de dirección; cambiar de opinión
whiffletree ['hwɪfəl,tri] *s* var. de **whippletree**
Whig [hwɪg] *s* whig (*miembro de un partido progresista*)
Whiggery ['hwɪgərɪ] *s* principios y prácticas políticas de los whigs
Whiggish ['hwɪgɪʃ] *adj* de los whigs, semejante a los whigs
while [hwaɪl] *conj* mientras que (*durante el tiempo que; a la vez que*); *s* rato; **a great while** o **a long while** largo rato; **a while ago** hace un rato; **between whiles** de vez en cuando; **the while** entretanto, mientras tanto; *va* pasar; **to while away** engañar o entretener (*el tiempo*); pasar (*p.ej. la mañana*) de un modo entretenido
whiles [hwaɪlz] *adv* (archaic & dial.) algunas veces; (archaic & dial.) mientras tanto; *conj* (archaic & dial.) mientras que
whilom ['hwaɪləm] *adj* antiguo, de antes; *adv* (archaic) antiguamente, en otro tiempo
whilst [hwaɪlst] *conj* mientras que
whim [hwɪm] *s* capricho, antojo; (min.) malacate
whimper ['hwɪmpər] *s* lloriqueo; *va* decir o expresar lloriqueando; *vn* lloriquear
whimsey ['hwɪmzɪ] *s* var. de **whimsy**
whimsical ['hwɪmzɪkəl] *adj* caprichoso, fantástico, extravagante
whimsicality [,hwɪmzɪ'kælɪtɪ] *s* (*pl:* **-ties**) capricho, fantasía, extravagancia
whimsy ['hwɪmzɪ] *s* (*pl:* **-sies**) capricho, antojo; amenidad arcaica, fantasía arcaica, humorismo anticuado
whin [hwɪn] *s* (bot.) tojo
whine [hwaɪn] *s* gimoteo, quejido lastimoso; *va* decir gimoteando, decir con quejidos lastimosos; *vn* gimotear, dar quejidos lastimosos
whinny ['hwɪnɪ] *s* (*pl:* **-nies**) relincho; (*pret & pp:* **-nied**) *vn* relinchar
whinstone ['hwɪn,ston] *s* roca basáltica
whiny ['hwaɪnɪ] *adj* quejicoso, quejumbroso
whip [hwɪp] *s* látigo; azote (*golpe*); batimiento; fusta (*de tronquista*); postre de nata y huevos batidos; mayoral (*pastor a cargo de los perros de caza*); carretero, cochero; miembro de un cuerpo legislativo que dirige y domina a sus copartidarios; cuerda y polea; (*pret & pp:* **whipped** o **whipt;** *ger:* **whipping**) *va* azotar, fustigar; mover, poner o sacar súbita y rápidamente; batir (*nata o huevos*); envolver (*un palo o cuerda*) con hilo o cuerda; pescar con caña en; sobrecoser; (coll.) derrotar, vencer; **to whip up** asir de repente; batir; hacer de prisa; avivar; **to whip out** sacar de repente; *vn* agitarse; arrojarse; moverse rápidamente; echar el anzuelo azotando el agua
whipcord ['hwɪp,kɔrd] *s* tralla; género basto y fuerte con costurones diagonales
whip hand *s* mano que maneja el látigo; dominio, mando, ventaja
whiplash ['hwɪp,læʃ] *s* tralla (*trencilla del extremo del látigo*)
whiplash injury *s* (path.) concusión de la espina cervical
whipped cream *s* crema o nata batida
whipper ['hwɪpər] *s* azotador; batidor
whipper-snapper ['hwɪpər,snæpər] *s* arrapiezo, títere, mequetrefe
whippet ['hwɪpɪt] *s* perro lebrel
whipping ['hwɪpɪŋ] *s* flagelación, paliza; (naut.) filástica, meollar
whipping boy *s* cabeza de turco, víctima inocente
whipping post *s* poste de flagelación
whippletree ['hwɪpəl,tri] *s* volea
whippoorwill [,hwɪpər'wɪl] *s* (orn.) chotacabras norteamericano, tapacamino, guabairo
whipsaw ['hwɪp,sɔ] *s* sierra cabrilla; *va* serrar con sierra cabrilla; (fig.) vencer sin remedio
whip snake *s* (zool.) chirrionera; (zool.) filodríada
whipstitch ['hwɪp,stɪtʃ] *s* sobrepuntada; *va* coser con sobrepuntada
whipstock ['hwɪp,stɑk] *s* puño del látigo
whir [hwʌr] *s* zumbido (*de algo que vuela o gira*); (*pret & pp:* **whirred;** *ger:* **whirring**) *va* hacer volar o girar zumbando; *vn* volver o girar zumbando
whirl [hwʌrl] *s* vuelta, giro; remolino, alboroto, ajetreo; vahido, vértigo; *va* hacer girar; llevar muy rápidamente; remolinear; *vn* dar vueltas, girar; remolinear; **my head whirls** siento vahido o vértigo
whirlibird ['hwʌrlɪ,bʌrd] *s* (slang) helicóptero
whirligig ['hwʌrlɪ,gɪg] *s* (ent.) escribano del agua, girino, tejedera; tiovivo; molinete, rehilandera
whirlpool ['hwʌrl,pul] *s* remolino; (fig.) remolino
whirlwind ['hwʌrl,wɪnd] *s* torbellino, manga de viento; (fig.) torbellino
whirr [hwʌr] *s, va & vn* var. de **whir**
whish [hwɪʃ] *s* zumbido suave; *vn* zumbar suavemente; moverse con zumbido suave

whisk [hwɪsk] *s* escobilla, cepillo; movimiento rápido; movimiento de la escobilla; batidor metálico; manojo de paja o heno; *va* cepillar; barrer; mover rápidamente; batir (*nata, huevos, etc.*); **to whisk out of sight** escamotear; *vn* moverse rápidamente
whisk broom *s* escobilla, cepillo de ropa
whisker [ˈhwɪskər] *s* pelo de la barba; (coll.) bigote o bigotes; **whiskers** *spl* barba o barbas (*pelo en la barba y en los carrillos*); patillas; bigotes (*p.ej., del gato*)
whiskered [ˈhwɪskərd] *adj* barbado; bigotudo
whiskey [ˈhwɪskɪ] *s* whisky; *adj* (coll.) aguardentoso (*dícese de la voz*)
whisky [ˈhwɪskɪ] *s* (*pl:* **-kies**) var. de **whiskey**
whisper [ˈhwɪspər] *s* cuchicheo, susurro; (fig.) susurro (*p.ej., del aura*); *va* decir al oído; decir al oído a; llevar susurrando; *vn* cuchichear, susurrar; (fig.) susurrar (*p.ej., el aura*)
whispering [ˈhwɪspərɪŋ] *s* cuchicheo; *adj* susurrador; susurrón (*que murmura en secreto*)
whist [hwɪst] *s* whist (*juego de naipes*); *adj* (archaic) callado; *interj* (archaic) ¡chitón!
whistle [ˈhwɪsəl] *s* silbido, silbo; silbato, pito; **to wet one's whistle** (coll.) remojar la palabra; *va* silbar (*una canción*); enviar, traer, llamar con un silbido; *vn* silbar (*una persona, una bala, el viento, etc.*); **to whistle for** (coll.) tener que arreglárselas sin; **to whistle for a taxi** silbarle a un taxi
whistler [ˈhwɪslər] *s* silbador; (zool.) marmota norteamericana (*Marmota caligata*)
whistle stop *s* (rail.) apeadero que el maquinista reconoce con una pitada; pueblecito
whit [hwɪt] *s* pizca; **not a whit** ni una pizca; **to not care a whit** no importarle a uno un bledo
white [hwaɪt] *adj* blanco (*como la nieve; aplícase también a las uvas, el vino, etc.*); reaccionario, realista; (coll.) honorable, justo; *s* blanco; vestido blanco; clara de huevo; blanco del ojo; reaccionario, realista; **whites** *spl* (path.) pérdidas blancas, flujo blanco; *va* blanquear; *vn* emblanquecerse
white ant *s* (ent.) comején, hormiga blanca
whitebait [ˈhwaɪtˌbet] *s* arenque de menor tamaño, arenque joven
whitebeam [ˈhwaɪtˌbim] *s* (bot.) mojera, mostellar
whitecap [ˈhwaɪtˌkæp] *s* cabrilla o paloma
white cedar *s* (bot.) cedro blanco de los pantanos; (bot.) tuya
white clover *s* (bot.) trébol blanco, trébol rampante
white coal *s* hulla blanca
white-collar [ˈhwaɪtˌkɑlər] *adj* de oficina; oficinesco (*empleo*)
white corpuscle *s* (physiol.) glóbulo blanco
whited sepulcher *s* sepulcro blanqueado (*hipócrita*)
white elephant *s* (fig.) elefante blanco
white feather *s* símbolo de cobardía; **to show the white feather** mostrarse cobarde
whitefish [ˈhwaɪtˌfɪʃ] *s* (ichth.) corégono
white flag *s* bandera blanca, bandera de paz
white flax *s* (bot.) camelina
white friar *s* fraile carmelita
white gold *s* oro blanco
white goods *spl* tejidos de hilo o algodón; ropa blanca; aparatos electrodomésticos
white goosefoot *s* (bot.) cenizo
white-haired [ˈhwaɪtˌherd] *adj* peliblanco; favorito, predilecto
white-headed [ˈhwaɪtˈhedɪd] *adj* de cabeza blanca; rubio (*de pelo*); (coll.) favorito
white-headed eagle *s* (orn.) águila de cabeza blanca
white heat *s* calor blanco; (fig.) fiebre, viva y ardorosa agitación; **to heat to a white heat** calentar al blanco
white horehound *s* (bot.) marrubio blanco
white horse *s* var. de **whitecap**
white-hot [ˈhwaɪtˈhɑt] *adj* calentado al blanco; (fig.) ardoroso, violento, excesivamente entusiasmado
White House *s* Casa Blanca
white lead [led] *s* albayalde, blanco de plomo
white lie *s* mentira inocente, mentira oficiosa
white-livered [ˈhwaɪtˈlɪvərd] *adj* macilento; cobarde, pusilánime
white magic *s* magia blanca
white mangrove *s* (bot.) mangle blanco
white matter *s* (anat.) materia blanca
white meat *s* pechuga, carne de la pechuga del ave; carne de ternera, carne de cerdo
whiten [ˈhwaɪtən] *va* blanquear, emblanquecer; *vn* blanquear, emblanquecerse; palidecer
whiteness [ˈhwaɪtnɪs] *s* blancura
white oak *s* (bot.) roble (*Quercus sessiliflora*); (bot.) roble blanco de América (*Quercus alba*)
white-of-egg [ˈhwaɪtəvˈɛg] *s* clara de huevo, blanco de huevo
white of the eye *s* blanco del ojo
white paper *s* papel blanco (*informe oficial*)
white pepper *s* pimienta blanca
white pine *s* (bot.) pino blanco (*Pinus strobus*)
white plague *s* peste blanca (*tisis*)
white poplar *s* (bot.) álamo blanco
White Russia *s* la Rusia Blanca
White Russian *s* ruso blanco
white sauce *s* salsa blanca
White Sea *s* mar Blanco
white slave *s* esclavo blanco; mujer vendida en la trata de blancas
white slavery *s* trata de blancas
white-tailed deer [ˈhwaɪtˌteld] *s* (zool.) ciervo de Virginia
white-tailed eagle *s* (orn.) águila marina
whitethorn [ˈhwaɪtˌθɔrn] *s* (bot.) espino, oxiacanto
whitethroat [ˈhwaɪtˌθrot] *s* (orn.) andahuertas, curruca (*Sylvia*); (orn.) gorrión de Pensilvania (*Zonotrichia albicollis*)
white-throated sparrow [ˈhwaɪtˌθrotɪd] *s* (orn.) gorrión de Pensilvania
white tie *s* corbatín blanco, traje de etiqueta
white vitriol *s* vitriolo blanco
whitewash [ˈhwaɪtˌwɑʃ] o [ˈhwaɪtˌwɔʃ] *s* jalbegue, encalado; encubrimiento de faltas; *va* enjalbegar, encalar, blanquear; encubrir (*faltas*); absolver sin justicia; (coll.) vencer (*a una persona*) sin que haya hecho tantos
white willow *s* (bot.) sauce blanco
white-winged dove [ˈhwaɪtˈwɪŋd] *s* (orn.) aliblanca, paloma de pitahaya
whitewood [ˈhwaɪtˌwʊd] *s* (bot.) liriodendro; (bot.) tilo
whither [ˈhwɪðər] *adv* ¿adónde?; adónde; *conj* adonde
whithersoever [ˌhwɪðərsoˈɛvər] *conj* adondequiera que
whiting [ˈhwaɪtɪŋ] *s* blanco de España; (ichth.) merluza; (ichth.) merlango; (ichth.) esciénido
whitish [ˈhwaɪtɪʃ] *adj* blanquecino, blancuzco
whitlow [ˈhwɪtlo] *s* (path.) panadizo
whitlow grass *s* (bot.) draba
whitlowwort [ˈhwɪtloˌwʌrt] *s* (bot.) nevadilla
Whitmonday [ˈhwɪtˈmʌndɪ] *s* lunes de Pentecostés
Whitsun [ˈhwɪtsən] *adj* de o del domingo de Pentecostés; de o de la semana de Pentecostés
Whitsunday [ˈhwɪtˈsʌndɪ] o [ˈhwɪtsənˌde] *s* domingo de Pentecostés
Whitsuntide [ˈhwɪtsənˌtaɪd] *s* semana de Pentecostés
whittle [ˈhwɪtəl] *s* (archaic) cuchillo; *va* sacar pedazos a (*un trozo de madera*) con un cuchillo o navaja; **to whittle away** o **down** rebajar o reducir poco a poco
whity [ˈhwaɪtɪ] *adj* var. de **whitish**
whiz o **whizz** [hwɪz] *s* sonido entre silbido y zumbido; (slang) fenómeno, perito; (*pret & pp:* **whizzed;** *ger:* **whizzing**) *va* mover produciendo un silbido; *vn* silbar; moverse produciendo un silbido, ir zumbando por el aire; **to whiz by** rehilar (*un arma arrojadiza*); pasar como una flecha
who [hu] *pron interr* ¿quién?; **who else?** ¿quién más?; *pron rel* que, quien; el que; **who's who** quién es el uno y quién el otro; quiénes son gente de importancia; **Who's Who** ¿Quién es quién? (*libro de biografías*)
whoa [hwo] o [wo] *interj* ¡so!
whodunit [huˈdʌnɪt] *s* (slang) novela policíaca corta
whoever [huˈɛvər] *pron interr* (coll.) ¿quién?; *pron rel* quienquiera que, cualquiera que; **whoever else** cualquier otro que
whole [hol] *adj* entero, todo; único, p.ej., **the**

whole interest for me was the money I made el único interés para mí era el dinero que gané; **made out of whole cloth** enteramente falso o imaginario; *s* conjunto, todo, total; **as a whole** en conjunto; **on the whole** en general; por la mayor parte
whole gale *s* (naut.) temporal
wholehearted [ˈhol,hartɪd] *adj* francote, cordial
whole hog; to go the whole hog (slang) entregarse sin reservas, llegar hasta el último límite, comprometerse a ultranza
wholeness [ˈholnɪs] *s* integridad, totalidad
whole note *s* (mus.) semibreve
whole number *s* número entero
whole rest *s* (mus.) pausa de semibreve
wholesale [ˈhol,sel] *s* venta al por mayor; *adj* al por mayor, mayorista; general; *va* vender al por mayor; *vn* vender al por mayor; venderse al por mayor
wholesaler [ˈhol,selər] *s* comerciante al por mayor, mayorista
wholesome [ˈholsəm] *adj* saludable; fresco, rollizo, lozano
whole step o **whole tone** *s* (mus.) tono completo
whole-wheat [ˈhol,hwit] *adj* hecho con harina de trigo entero
who'll [hul] contracción de **who shall** y de **who will**
wholly [ˈholɪ] *adv* enteramente, completamente
whom [hum] *pron interr* ¿a quién?; *pron rel* que, a quien; al que
whomsoever [,humsoˈɛvər] *pron rel* a quienquiera que
whoop [hup] o [hwup] *s* alarido, chillido; ululato; estertor, ruido jadeante (*peculiar de la tos ferina*); *va* decir a gritos; acosar gritando; **to whoop it up** (slang) armar una gritería, alborotar; *vn* gritar, chillar; ulular; toser con ruido jadeante
whoopee [ˈhwupi] o [ˈhwʊpi] *interj* (slang) ¡hurra!; *s* (slang) parranda; **to make whoopee** (slang) andar de parranda
whooping cough [ˈhupɪŋ] o [ˈhʊpɪŋ] *s* (path.) tos ferina, tos convulsiva
whooping crane *s* (orn.) toquilcoyote
whopper [ˈhwapər] *s* (coll.) enormidad; (coll.) mentirón
whopping [ˈhwapɪŋ] *adj* (coll.) enorme, grandísimo
whore [hor] *s* puta; *vn* putañear, putear
whorish [ˈhorɪʃ] *adj* putesco
whorl [hwʌrl] *s* espiral; espiral del caracol; (bot.) verticilo
whorled [hwʌrld] *adj* (bot.) verticilado
whortleberry [ˈhwʌrtəl,bɛrɪ] *s* (*pl:* **-ries**) (bot.) arándano, anavia
who's [huz] contracción de **who is**
whose [huz] *pron interr* ¿de quién?; *pron rel* de quien, cuyo
whosesoever [,huzsoˈɛvər] *pron rel* de quienquiera que
whoso [ˈhuso] *pron rel* (archaic) quienquiera que
whosoever [,husoˈɛvər] *pron rel* quienquiera que
why [hwaɪ] *adv* ¿por qué?; por qué; por lo que; por el que; **why not?** ¿cómo no?; *s* (*pl:* **whys**) porqué; *interj* ¡toma!; **why, certainly!** ¡desde luego!, ¡por supuesto!; **why, yes!** ¡claro!, ¡pues sí!
W.I. abr. de **West Indies** y **West Indian**
wick [wɪk] *s* pabilo, mecha
wicked [ˈwɪkɪd] *adj* malo, inicuo; travieso, revoltoso; (coll.) riguroso; (coll.) arisco; (coll.) molesto, desagradable
wickedness [ˈwɪkɪdnɪs] *s* maldad, iniquidad
wicker [ˈwɪkər] *s* mimbre; *adj* mimbroso; de mimbre
wickerwork [ˈwɪkər,wʌrk] *s* artículos de mimbre; cestería
wicket [ˈwɪkɪt] *s* portillo, postigo; ventanilla; (croquet) aro
wicking [ˈwɪkɪŋ] *s* torcida para pabilos y mechas
wide [waɪd] *adj* ancho; de ancho, p.ej., **two feet wide** dos pies de ancho; extenso; muy abierto; *adv* de par en par; **wide of** lejos de; **wide of the mark** errado (*tiro*); fuera de propósito; alejado de la verdad; *s* espacio ancho
wide-angle [ˈwaɪd,æŋgəl] *adj* (opt.) granangular, de ángulo ancho
wide-awake [ˈwaɪdə,wek] *adj* despabilado; (fig.) despabilado, listo, advertido
wide-eyed [ˈwaɪd,aɪd] *adj* con los ojos desmesuradamente abiertos
widely [ˈwaɪdlɪ] *adv* extensamente; completamente; muy; mucho
widen [ˈwaɪdən] *va* ensanchar; *vn* ensancharse
wide-open [ˈwaɪdˈopən] *adj* de par en par, abierto de par en par; **to be wide-open** tener (*una ciudad*) mano abierta para el juego
widespread [ˈwaɪd,sprɛd] *adj* extendido (*dícese de los brazos, alas, etc.*); difundido, dilatado, extenso; corriente
widgeon [ˈwɪdʒən] *s* (orn.) silbón, ánade silbador (*Anas penelope*); (orn.) lavanco (*Anas americana*)
widow [ˈwɪdo] *s* viuda; baceta o fondo (*en los naipes*); *va* dejar viuda
widow bird *s* var. de **whidah**
widower [ˈwɪdoər] *s* viudo
widowhood [ˈwɪdohʊd] *s* viudez
widow's mite *s* limosna dada gustosamente por una persona pobre
widow's weeds *spl* luto de viuda
width [wɪdθ] *s* anchura, ancho; extensión
wield [wild] *va* esgrimir (*la espada*); ejercer (*autoridad, el poder*)
wiener [ˈwinər] *s* embutido de carne de vaca y cerdo
wienerwurst [ˈwinər,wʌrst] *s* salchicha de carne de vaca y cerdo
wife [waɪf] *s* (*pl:* **wives**) esposa; (archaic) mujer; **to take a wife** tomar mujer; **to take to wife** casarse con
wifehood [ˈwaɪfhʊd] *s* estado de mujer casada
wifely [ˈwaɪflɪ] *adj* (*comp:* **-lier;** *super:* **-liest**) de esposa, de mujer casada
wig [wɪg] *s* peluca; (coll.) peluca (*persona que trae peluca; reprensión severa*)
wigged [wɪgd] *adj* de peluca, que trae peluca
wiggle [ˈwɪgəl] *s* meneo rápido; culebreo; *va* menear rápidamente; *vn* menearse rápidamente; culebrear
wiggler [ˈwɪglər] *s* persona que menea; persona o cosa que se menea; larva de mosquito
wiggly [ˈwɪglɪ] *adj* que se menea; ondulante
wigwag [ˈwɪg,wæg] *s* (nav.) comunicación por banderas; (*pret & pp:* **-wagged;** *ger:* **-wagging**) *va* mover de un lado para otro; (nav.) señalar moviendo banderas; *vn* moverse de un lado para otro; (nav.) hacer señales moviendo banderas
wigwam [ˈwɪgwam] *s* choza de forma cónica (*de los pieles rojas*)
wild [waɪld] *adj* salvaje; feroz, fiero; violento; frenético; descabellado; impetuoso; travieso; perdido (*tiro, bala, etc.*); (naut.) loco (*barco*); (coll.) loco; **wild about** (coll.) loco por; *adv* violentamente; disparatadamente; locamente; **to run wild** vivir desenfrenadamente; crecer salvaje o libre; *s* yermo, desierto, soledad; monte; **wilds** *spl* despoblado, monte
wild boar *s* (zool.) jabalí
wild card *s* comodín
wild carrot *s* (bot.) zanahoria silvestre
wildcat [ˈwaɪld,kæt] *s* (zool.) gato montés; (zool.) lince; luchador feroz; empresa arriesgada; locomotora sin tren; pozo de petróleo de exploración; *adj* quimérico; ilícito, ilegal; sin dominio; (*pret & pp:* **-catted;** *ger:* **-catting**) *va & vn* explorar por cuenta propia
wildcat strike *s* huelga no sancionada por el sindicato
wild duck *s* pato bravío
wildebeest [ˈwɪldə,bist] *s* (zool.) ñu, gnu
wilder [ˈwɪldər] *va* (archaic & poet.) confundir; (archaic & poet.) extraviar; *vn* (archaic & poet.) confundirse; (archaic & poet.) extraviarse
wilderness [ˈwɪldərnɪs] *s* yermo, desierto, soledad; gran cantidad, inmensidad
wild-eyed [ˈwaɪld,aɪd] *adj* con los ojos fijos locamente
wild fig *s* (bot.) higuera silvestre, cabrahigo; higo silvestre, cabrahigo (*fruto*)
wildfire [ˈwaɪld,faɪr] *s* fuego griego; fuego

fatuo; relámpago difuso (*sin trueno*); **to spread like wildfire** ser un reguero de pólvora, correr como pólvora en reguero
wild flower *s* flor del campo, flor silvestre
wild fowl *spl* aves de caza, ánades
wild goat *s* (zool.) cabra montés
wild goose *s* ganso bravo
wild-goose chase ['waɪld'gus] *s* caza de grillos, búsqueda o empresa hecha sin provecho
wild hazel *s* (bot.) nochizo
wild marjoram *s* (bot.) orégano
wildness ['waɪldnɪs] *s* selvatiquez; ferocidad, fiereza; violencia; travesura; locura, desvarío
wild oats *spl* avena loca, ballueca; (fig.) excesos juveniles, mocedad; **to sow one's wild oats** llevar (*los mozos*) una vida de excesos
wild olive *s* (bot.) acebuche, olivo silvestre; (bot.) ácana (*Sideroxylon mastichodendron*); acebuchina (*fruto*)
wild pansy *s* (bot.) trinitaria
wild rice *s* (bot.) arroz de los pieles rojas
wild sage *s* (bot.) gallocresta
wild thyme *s* (bot.) serpol
Wild West *s* oeste de los Estados Unidos durante la época de los pioneros
wildwood ['waɪld,wʊd] *s* bosque, floresta
wile [waɪl] *s* ardid, engaño; astucia; *va* engatusar; **to wile away** engañar o entretener (*el tiempo*)
wilful ['wɪlfəl] *adj* var. de **willful**
Wilhelmina [,wɪlhel'minə] o [,wɪlə'minə] *s* Guillermina
will [wɪl] *s* voluntad; (law) testamento; **at will** a voluntad; **to do the will of** cumplir la voluntad de; **with a will** con mucha voluntad; *va* querer; legar; *vn* querer; (*cond:* **would**) *v aux* se emplea para formar (1) el futuro de ind, p.ej., **he will arrive** llegará; (2) el futuro perfecto de ind, p.ej., **he will have arrived** habrá llegado; (3) el modo potencial, p.ej., **we cannot always do as we will** no siempre podemos hacer lo que queremos; y (4) el pres de ind, indicando costumbre, p.ej., **he will go for days without smoking** pasa días enteros sin fumar
willet ['wɪlɪt] *s* (orn.) sinfemia
willful ['wɪlfəl] *adj* voluntarioso; voluntario
willfully ['wɪlfəlɪ] *adv* voluntariosamente; voluntariamente
willfulness ['wɪlfəlnɪs] *s* voluntariedad
William ['wɪljəm] *s* Guillermo
William the Conqueror *s* Guillermo el Conquistador
willing ['wɪlɪŋ] *s* dispuesto; gustoso, pronto
willingly ['wɪlɪŋlɪ] *adv* de buena gana, gustosamente
willingness ['wɪlɪŋnɪs] *s* buena gana, buena voluntad, complacencia
will-o'-the-wisp ['wɪləðə'wɪsp] *s* fuego fatuo; ilusión, quimera
willow ['wɪlo] *s* (bot.) sauce
willow herb *s* (bot.) camenerio; (bot.) lisimaquia roja; (bot.) adelfilla pelosa
willowy ['wɪlo·ɪ] o ['wɪləwɪ] *adj* juncal, mimbreño; lleno de sauces; (fig.) juncal, esbelto, cimbreño
will power *s* fuerza de voluntad
will to power *s* (philos.) voluntad de poder
willy-nilly ['wɪlɪ'nɪlɪ] *adj* indeciso, vacilante; *adv* por malas o por buenas, quieras o no quieras
wilt [wɪlt] *va* marchitar; *vn* marchitarse; (fig.) marchitarse, languidecer; (coll.) acobardarse, perder el ánimo
wily ['waɪlɪ] *adj* (*comp:* **-ier**; *super:* **-iest**) artero, engañoso, astuto
wimble ['wɪmbəl] *s* barrena, taladro
wimple ['wɪmpəl] *s* griñón, impla; *va* cubrir con griñón o impla; rizar; (archaic) hacer caer en pliegues; *vn* rizarse (*p.ej., la superficie del agua*); (archaic) caer en pliegues
win [wɪn] *s* (coll.) triunfo, éxito; (*pret & pp:* **won**; *ger:* **winning**) *va* ganar; **to win over** conquistar (*ganar la voluntad de*); **to win something from someone** ganar algo a alguien; *vn* ganar, triunfar; **to win out** (coll.) ganar, triunfar; (coll.) tener éxito
wince [wɪns] *s* sobresalto; *vn* sobresaltarse (*de miedo, ante un peligro, etc.*)
winch [wɪntʃ] *s* torno, maquinilla; manubrio; *va* izar o cobrar con la maquinilla
wind [wɪnd] *s* viento (*corriente de aire; olor que deja la caza; ventosidad; vanidad y jactancia*); resuello, respiración; (mus.) instrumento de viento; **against the wind** contra el viento; **before the wind** (naut.) con el viento; **between wind and water** (naut.) cerca de la línea de flotación; (fig.) en sitio peligroso; **down the wind** con el viento; **in the eye** o **the teeth of the wind** (naut.) contra el viento; **into the wind** contra el viento; **off the wind** (naut.) de espalda al viento, con el viento; **on the wind** (naut.) de bolina; **to be in the wind** estar en el aire (*estar pendiente*); **to break wind** ventosear; **to get wind of** husmear, ventear; sospechar, descubrir; **to sail close to the wind** (naut.) ceñir el viento, navegar de bolina; rayar en lo inmoral o lo ilegal; ser formalista; **to take the wind out of one's sails** apagarle a uno los fuegos, dejar a uno súbitamente sin ventaja o sin apoyo ‖ *va* exponer al aire o al viento; husmear, ventear; dejar sin aliento; dejar recobrar el aliento ‖ [waɪnd] *s* vuelta, recodo; torcedura ‖ (*pret & pp:* **wound**) *va* enrollar, envolver; devanar; enroscar; torcer; ovillar (*el hilo*); dar cuerda a (*un reloj*); levantar con el cabrestante; rodear, ceñir (*p.ej., con los brazos*); entrelazar (*los brazos*); **to wind off** desenrollar, desenvolver; **to wind one's way through** serpentear por; **to wind up** enrollar, envolver; (coll.) poner punto final a ‖ *vn* enrollarse, envolverse; serpentear (*un camino*); dar vueltas; enroscarse; torcerse; alabearse, combarse; **to wind up** enrollarse; enroscarse; (baseball) tomar impulso; (coll.) acabar, terminar ‖ [waɪnd] o [wɪnd] (*pret & pp:* **winded** o **wound**) *va* sonar (*un instrumento de viento*)
windage ['wɪndɪdʒ] *s* (arti.) fuerza del viento para desviar el curso de un proyectil; (arti.) desvío de un proyectil por efecto del viento; (arti.) viento (*huelgo entre la bala y el ánima del cañón*); (mach.) fricción del aire
windbag ['wɪnd,bæg] *s* saco lleno de viento; (coll.) charlatán, palabrero
wind-blown ['wɪnd,blon] *adj* llevado por el viento; con el pelo cortado muy corto y peinado hacia la frente
windbreak ['wɪnd,brek] *s* guardavientos, abrigo o protección contra el viento
wind-broken ['wɪnd,brokən] *adj* (vet.) enfisematoso
wind cone *s* (aer.) cono de viento, indicador cónico de la dirección del viento
winded ['wɪndɪd] *adj* falto de respiración, sin resuello
windfall ['wɪnd,fɔl] *s* fruta caída del árbol (*por efecto del viento*); fortunón, golpe de suerte inesperado, cosa llovida del cielo
windflower ['wɪnd,flaʊər] *s* (bot.) anemone
windgall ['wɪnd,gɔl] *s* (vet.) aventadura
windiness ['wɪndɪnɪs] *s* ventosidad; vaciedad; vanidad, jactancia; verbosidad
winding ['waɪndɪŋ] *s* vuelta; torcedura; arrollamiento (*p.ej., de un alambre*); cuerda (*acción de dar cuerda al reloj*); (elec.) bobinado; *adj* sinuoso, tortuoso
winding machine *s* bobinadora
winding sheet *s* mortaja, sudario; chorro de cera que se ha corrido y endurecido en un lado de la vela o bujía
winding stairs *spl* escalera espiral, escalera de caracol
wind instrument *s* (mus.) instrumento de viento
windjammer ['wɪnd,dʒæmər] *s* (coll.) buque de vela; (coll.) tripulante de buque de vela
windlass ['wɪndləs] *s* torno, maquinilla; *va* izar o cobrar con el torno o la maquinilla
windless ['wɪndlɪs] *adj* sin viento; sin aliento
windmill ['wɪnd,mɪl] *s* molino de viento (*máquina; juguete de papel*); aeromotor, motor de viento; **windmills** *spl* (fig.) molinos de viento (*enemigos imaginarios*); **to tilt at windmills** luchar con los molinos de viento
window ['wɪndo] *s* ventana (*abertura en la pared; hoja u hojas de cristales con que se cierra*); ventanilla (*de coche; de los despachos de bille-*

tes; de un sobre); escaparate (*en la fachada de una tienda*); transparencia de celofán (*de una cartera*); *va* proveer de ventanas
window dresser *s* decorador de vitrinas o escaparates, escaparatista
window dressing *s* decoración de vitrinas o escaparates; (fig.) adorno de escaparate
window envelope *s* sobre de ventanilla
window frame *s* alfajía, marco de ventana
windowpane [ˈwɪndo,pen] *s* cristal, vidrio, hoja de vidrio
window regulator *s* (aut.) elevacristales
window sash *s* marco de vidriera
window screen *s* sobrevidriera; alambrera
window seat *s* asiento en la parte interior de un ventanal
window shade *s* visillo, transparente
window-shop [ˈwɪndo,ʃɑp] (*pret & pp:* **-shopped;** *ger:* **-shopping**) *vn* curiosear en las tiendas o mirando las vitrinas sin comprar
window-shopper [ˈwɪndo,ʃɑpər] *s* persona que curiosea en las tiendas o mirando las vitrinas sin comprar
window-shopping [ˈwɪndo,ʃɑpɪŋ] *s* curioseo en las tiendas o mirando las vitrinas sin comprar
window shutter *s* contraventana
window sill *s* repisa de ventana
window trimmer *s* decorador de vitrinas
windpipe [ˈwɪnd,paɪp] *s* (anat.) tráquea
windrow [ˈwɪndro] *s* hilera de heno puesto a secar; hilera de gavillas; hilera de hojas secas, hierba, árboles, etc., formada por el viento; *va* colocar o arreglar en hileras para secar
wind sail *s* (naut.) manguera
wind scale *s* escala de los vientos
wind shake *s* venteadura
windshield [ˈwɪnd,ʃild] *s* parabrisas o guardabrisa
windshield washer *s* lavaparabrisas, limpiacristales
windshield wiper *s* enjugaparabrisas, limpiaparabrisas, limpiavidrio
wind sock *s* (aer.) cono de viento
Windsor tie [ˈwɪnzər] *s* corbata ancha de seda atada en lazo
windstorm [ˈwɪnd,stɔrm] *s* ventarrón, viento impetuoso
wind tunnel *s* (aer.) túnel aéreo, túnel aerodinámico
wind-up [ˈwaɪnd,ʌp] *s* acabóse; conclusión; arreglo; (sport) final de partida; (baseball) movimiento circular del brazo del lanzador antes de lanzar la pelota
windward [ˈwɪndwərd] o [ˈwɪndərd] *adj* (naut.) de barlovento; *adv* (naut.) a barlovento; *s* (naut.) barlovento; **to turn to windward** (naut.) barloventear
Windward Islands [ˈwɪndwərd] *spl* islas de Barlovento
Windward Passage [ˈwɪndwərd] *s* paso de los Vientos
windy [ˈwɪndɪ] *adj* (*comp:* **-ier;** *super:* **-iest**) ventoso; vacío; palabrero; **it is windy** hace viento
wine [waɪn] *s* vino; *va* regalar u obsequiar con vino; *vn* beber vino
winebibber [ˈwaɪn,bɪbər] *s* bebedor de vino
wine cellar *s* bodega, candiotera
wine-colored [ˈwaɪn,kʌlərd] *adj* de color de vino, rojo obscuro
wine cooler *s* enfriadera, garapiñera
wine gallon *s* galón de 231 pulgadas cúbicas
wineglass [ˈwaɪn,glæs] o [ˈwaɪn,glɑs] *s* copa para vino
winegrower [ˈwaɪn,groər] *s* vinicultor
winegrowing [ˈwaɪn,gro·ɪŋ] *s* vinicultura; *adj* vinicultor
wine press *s* lagar; prensa de vino, prensa de lagar
winery [ˈwaɪnərɪ] *s* (*pl:* **-ies**) lagar (*edificio*)
winesap [ˈwaɪn,sæp] *s* manzana roja invernal
wineskin [ˈwaɪn,skɪn] *s* odre
wine steward *s* maestro de vinos
winetaster [ˈwaɪn,testər] *s* catavinos (*persona*); catavino (*tubo*)
wing [wɪŋ] *s* ala; facción, bando; vuelo; (theat.) bastidor, ala; (sport) ala (*jugador que está a un lado*); (hum.) brazo, pata delantera; **to be on the wing** estar volando; estar para irse; estar en pie y activo; **to be under the wing of** estar bajo el ala de; **to take wing** alzar el vuelo, irse volando; *va* dar alas a; herir en el ala o el brazo; volar a través de; acelerar; *vn* volar
wing case *s* (ent.) élitro
wing chair *s* sillón de orejas
wing collar *s* cuello doblado, cuello de pajarita
wing cover *s* var. de **wing case**
winged [wɪŋd] o [ˈwɪŋɪd] *adj* alado (*que tiene alas; rápido*); herido en el ala; (coll.) herido en el brazo; (poet.) elevado, sublime
wing load *s* (aer.) carga alar
wing nut *s* tuerca de aletas
wing-shaped [ˈwɪŋ,ʃept] *adj* alado
wingspread [ˈwɪŋ,sprɛd] *s* envergadura (*de ave o avión*)
Winifred [ˈwɪnɪfrɪd] *s* Genoveva
wink [wɪŋk] *s* guiño; parpadeo, pestañeo; parpadeo (*p.ej., de las estrellas*); **to not sleep a wink** no pegar los ojos; **to take forty winks** (coll.) descabezar el sueño; *va* guiñar (*el ojo*); expresar con un guiño; **to wink away** secar (*las lágrimas*) parpadeando; *vn* guiñar; parpadear, pestañear; señalar con un guiño; parpadear (*p.ej., las estrellas*); **to wink at** guiñar el ojo a; fingir no ver
winker [ˈwɪŋkər] *s* guiñador; anteojera (*de caballo*); (coll.) pestaña
winkle [ˈwɪŋkəl] *s* (zool.) litorina; (zool.) busicón
winner [ˈwɪnər] *s* ganador; premiado
Winnie [ˈwɪnɪ] *s* nombre abreviado de **Winifred**
winning [ˈwɪnɪŋ] *adj* ganancioso; triunfante, victorioso; atrayente, simpático, persuasivo; **winnings** *spl* ganancias
winning number *s* número premiado
winning post *s* (sport) poste de llegada
winning ways *spl* modales simpáticos, gracia, atractivo
winnow [ˈwɪno] *va* aventar; entresacar; batir (*las alas*); *vn* aventar; aletear
winnower [ˈwɪnoər] *s* aventador; máquina aventadora
winsome [ˈwɪnsəm] *adj* atrayente, simpático, gracioso
winter [ˈwɪntər] *s* invierno; *adj* invernal; *va* hacer invernar; *vn* invernar
winter cherry *s* (bot.) vejiga de perro, alquequenje, vejiguilla
wintergreen [ˈwɪntər,grin] *s* (bot.) pirola; (bot.) gaulteria, té del Canadá; aceite de gaulteria
winterkill [ˈwɪntər,kɪl] *va* matar por exposición a la intemperie durante el invierno; *vn* morir por exposición a la intemperie durante el invierno
winter rose *s* (bot.) eléboro negro
winter savory *s* (bot.) tomillo real, hisopillo
Winter's bark *s* canela de Magallanes, corteza de Winter
winter solstice *s* (astr.) solsticio hiemal
wintertide [ˈwɪntər,taɪd] *s* (poet.) invernada
wintertime [ˈwɪntər,taɪm] *s* invernada
winter wheat *s* trigo otoñal, trigo de invierno
wintery [ˈwɪntərɪ] *adj* invernal; frío, helado
wintriness [ˈwɪntrɪnɪs] *s* frío de invierno
wintry [ˈwɪntrɪ] *adj* (*comp:* **-trier;** *super:* **-triest**) invernal; frío, helado
winy [ˈwaɪnɪ] *adj* vinoso; vinolento
winze [wɪnz] *s* (min.) coladero
wipe [waɪp] *s* frotadura, limpiadura; *va* frotar para limpiar; enjugar (*p.ej., la cara, el sudor*); soldar frotando la juntura con un pedazo de cuero; **to wipe away** limpiar (*p.ej., las lágrimas*); **to wipe off** quitar frotando; **to wipe on** frotar (*una cosa*) sobre; **to wipe out** (coll.) borrar, cancelar; (coll.) aniquilar, destruir; (coll.) enjugar (*una deuda*)
wiper [ˈwaɪpər] *s* limpiador; paño, trapo; (elec.) contacto deslizante; (mach.) leva, álabe
wire [waɪr] *s* alambre; telégrafo; telegrama; **hold the wire** (coll.) no descuelgue; **to get under the wire** llegar o terminar con tiempo; **to pull wires** (coll.) tocar o mover resortes (*para lograr un fin*); (coll.) dirigir secretamente a otros; *adj* de alambre, hecho de alambre; *va* proveer de alambres; atar con alambre; atrapar por medio de alambres; alambrar (*ins-*

talar alambre conductor en); telegrafiar; *vn* telegrafiar
wire brush *s* cepillo de alambre
wire cutter *s* cortaalambres (*herramienta*)
wiredraw ['waɪr,drɔ] (*pret:* **-drew;** *pp:* **-drawn**) *va* trefilar; estrangular (*el agua o el vapor*); (fig.) prolongar con exceso; (fig.) torcer, falsear
wiredrawn ['waɪr,drɔn] *adj* trefilado; tratado con excesiva exactitud y precisión; *pp de* **wiredraw**
wiredrew ['waɪr,dru] *pret de* **wiredraw**
wired wireless *s* var. de **line radio**
wire fence *s* alambrada
wire gauge *s* calibre para alambres, calibrador de alambre
wire gauze *s* gasa de alambre
wire-haired ['waɪr,hɛrd] *adj* de pelo áspero (*perro*)
wireless ['waɪrlɪs] *adj* (elec.) inalámbrico, sin hilos; (Brit.) radiofónico; *s* (Brit.) receptor radiofónico; (Brit.) emisión radiofónica, comunicación radiofónica; *va* (Brit.) enviar o transmitir por radiofonía o radiotelegrafía
wireless telegraphy *s* telegrafía inalámbrica o sin hilos
wireless telephony *s* telefonía inalámbrica o sin hilos
wire mesh *s* malla de alambre
wire nail *s* alfiler de París, clavo de alambre
wire netting *s* tela metálica, red de alambre
wirephoto ['waɪr,foto] *s* (*pl:* **-tos**) (trademark) foto telegráfica
wire puller *s* (coll.) persona que mueve resortes (*para lograr un fin*)
wire pulling *s* (coll.) empleo de resortes (*para lograr un fin*)
wire recorder *s* magnetófono, aparato de grabación de alambre, aparato impresor del sonido en alambre, grabadora de alambre
wire recording *s* grabación de alambre
wire screen *s* tela de alambre
wire service *s* servicio telegráfico y telefónico; servicio telegráfico y telefónico de noticias turfistas
wire solder *s* alambre de soldadura
wire tapping *s* conexión telefónica o telegráfica secreta para interceptar mensajes
wire wheel *s* rueda de rayos de alambre
wirework ['waɪr,wʌrk] *s* alambrado, tela metálica; **wireworks** *spl* fábrica de objetos de alambre o de tela metálica; trefilería
wireworker ['waɪr,wʌrkər] *s* alambrero; trefilero
wireworm ['waɪr,wʌrm] *s* (zool.) larva de elatérido
wiring ['waɪrɪŋ] *s* (elec.) instalación de alambres eléctricos; (elec.) canalización, alambrado; (surg.) costura con alambre
wiry ['waɪrɪ] *adj* (*comp:* **-ier;** *super:* **-iest**) hecho de alambre; como alambre; cimbreante, delgado pero fuerte
Wis. o **Wisc.** abr. de **Wisconsin**
wis [wɪs] *va* (archaic) saber
wisdom ['wɪzdəm] *s* sabiduría, cordura
Wisdom of Solomon *s* (Bib.) Sabiduría de Salomón (*libro de la Apócrifa*)
wisdom tooth *s* muela del juicio, muela cordal; **to cut one's wisdom teeth** (coll.) salirle a uno las muelas del juicio (*ser prudente y mirado en sus acciones*)
wise [waɪz] *adj* sabio; listo; enterado, informado; juicioso, acertado (*p.ej., paso*); **to be wise to** (slang) estar al tanto de; (slang) conocer el juego de; **to get wise** (slang) caer en el chiste; **to put wise (to)** (slang) poner al tanto (de); (slang) poner al tanto del juego (de); *s* modo, manera, guisa; **in any wise** de cualquier modo; **in no wise** de ningún modo; **in this wise** así, en esta forma; *va* **to wise up** (slang) hacer caer en la cuenta; *vn* **to wise up** (slang) caer en la cuenta, caer en el chiste
wiseacre ['waɪz,ekər] *s* sabihondo
wisecrack ['waɪz,kræk] *s* (slang) cuchufleta, pulla; *vn* (slang) cuchufletear
wisecracker ['waɪz,krækər] *s* (slang) cuchufletero, pullista
wise guy *s* (slang) sábelotodo
Wise Men of the East *s* magos de Oriente
wish [wɪʃ] *s* deseo; **to make a wish** pensar en algo que se desea; *va* desear; dar (*p.ej., los buenos días*); **to wish something on someone** (coll.) lograr que una persona acepte una cosa que no desea; *vn* desear; **to wish for** desear, anhelar
wishbone ['wɪʃ,bon] *s* espoleta, hueso de la suerte
wishful ['wɪʃfəl] *adj* deseoso
wishful thinking *s* optimismo a ultranza; **to indulge in wishful thinking** forjarse ilusiones
wishing well *s* fuentecilla de los deseos
wishy-washy ['wɪʃɪ,wɑʃɪ] o ['wɪʃɪ,wɔʃɪ] *adj* aguado, diluído; débil, flojo, pobre
wisp [wɪsp] *s* manojito, puñado; jirón, mechón; rastro, vestigio; bandada; escobilla, cepillo
wispy ['wɪspɪ] *adj* (*comp:* **-ier;** *super:* **-iest**) sutil, ligero, delicado
wist [wɪst] *pret & pp de* **wit**
wistaria [wɪs'tɛrɪə] o **wisteria** [wɪs'tɪrɪə] *s* (bot.) vistaria
wistful ['wɪstfəl] *adj* ansioso, tristón, melancólico, pensativo
wistfulness ['wɪstfəlnɪs] *s* ansiedad, tristeza, melancolía
wit [wɪt] *s* ingenio; juicio, sentido; agudeza; chistoso; **to be at one's wits' end** estar para volverse loco, no saber qué hacer o decir; **to be out of one's wits** estar fuera de sí; **to have** o **to keep one's wits about one** conservar su presencia de ánimo; **to have the wit to** + *inf* tener el tino de + *inf;* **to live by one's wits** campar de golondro, vivir de gorra; **to lose one's wits** perder el juicio; **to use one's wits** valerse de su ingenio; (*primera y tercera personas del sg del pres de ind:* **wot;** *pl del pres de ind:* **wit;** *pret & pp:* **wist;** *ger:* **witting**) *va & vn* (archaic) saber; **to wit** a saber, es decir
witch [wɪtʃ] *s* bruja, hechicera; (fig.) hechicera (*mujer de encantos irresistibles*); (fig.) bruja (*mujer vieja y fea*); *adj* brujesco; *va* embrujar, hechizar
witchcraft ['wɪtʃ,kræft] o ['wɪtʃ,krɑft] *s* brujería
witch doctor *s* médico brujo (*en ciertas tribus africanas*)
witchery ['wɪtʃərɪ] *s* (*pl:* **-ies**) brujería; (fig.) hechicería
witches' Sabbath *s* aquelarre, junta nocturna de brujas, sábado
witch hazel *s* (bot.) hamamelis de Virginia, nogal de la brujería, planta del sortilegio; (bot.) carpe (*Carpinus betulus*); agua o loción de hamamelis, hamamelina
witch hunt *s* persecución de supuestos subversores, con fines políticos
witching ['wɪtʃɪŋ] *adj* hechicero, mágico, encantador
witenagemot ['wɪtənəgə,mot] *s* concejo de los antiguos anglosajones
with [wɪð] o [wɪθ] *prep* con; de, p.ej., **covered with snow** cubierto de nieve
withal [wɪð'ɔl] *adv* (archaic) además, también; *prep* (archaic) con
withdraw [wɪð'drɔ] o [wɪθ'drɔ] (*pret:* **-drew;** *pp:* **-drawn**) *va* retirar; *vn* retirarse; **to withdraw within oneself** recogerse en sí mismo
withdrawal [wɪð'drɔəl] o [wɪθ'drɔəl] *s* retiro; retirada
withdrawn [wɪð'drɔn] o [wɪθ'drɔn] *pp de* **withdraw**
withdrew [wɪð'dru] o [wɪθ'dru] *pret de* **withdraw**
withe [wɪθ], [wɪð] o [waɪð] *s* mimbre, junco
wither ['wɪðər] *va* marchitar; avergonzar, confundir; *vn* marchitarse; avergonzarse, confundirse; **withers** *spl* cruz (*del cuadrúpedo*)
withheld [wɪθ'hɛld] o [wɪð'hɛld] *pret & pp de* **withhold**
withhold [wɪθ'hold] o [wɪð'hold] (*pret & pp:* **-held**) *va* negar (*p.ej., un permiso*); suspender (*pago*); detener, retener, contener
withholding tax *s* descuento anticipado de los impuestos
within [wɪð'ɪn] *adv* dentro; *prep* dentro de; al alcance de; poco menos de; con un margen de,

con una diferencia de . . . más o menos, p.ej., **I can tell you when he will arrive within ten minutes** puedo decirle cuándo llegará con una diferencia de diez minutos más o menos
without [wɪ'ðaʊt] *adv* fuera; *prep* fuera de; más allá de; sin; **to do without** pasar sin; **without** + *ger* sin + *inf*, p.ej., **he left without saying good-bye** salió sin despedirse; sin que + *subj*, p.ej., **he came in without my seeing him** entró sin que yo le viese; *conj* (dial.) a menos que + *subj*
withstand [wɪθ'stænd] o [wɪð'stænd] (*pret & pp:* **-stood**) *va* aguantar, soportar, resistir
withstood [wɪθ'stʊd] o [wɪð'stʊd] *pret & pp de* **withstand**
withy ['wɪðɪ] o ['wɪθɪ] *s* (*pl:* **-ies**) mimbre, junco; banda o cabestro hechos de mimbre o junco; *adj* mimbreño
witless ['wɪtlɪs] *adj* insensato, estúpido, tonto
witness ['wɪtnɪs] *s* testigo (*persona*); testimonio (*evidencia*); **in witness whereof** en fe de lo cual; **to bear witness** dar testimonio; **to call to witness** nombrar testigo, tomar por testigo; *va* atestiguar o testimoniar; firmar como testigo; presenciar; mostrar; *vn* dar testimonio, servir de testigo
witness stand *s* puesto o mesa de los testigos
witticism ['wɪtɪsɪzəm] *s* agudeza, ocurrencia, dicho agudo
wittingly ['wɪtɪŋlɪ] *adv* adrede, a sabiendas
witty ['wɪtɪ] *adj* (*comp:* **-tier**; *super:* **-tiest**) agudo, ingenioso; chistoso, ocurrente
wive [waɪv] *va* casar, proveer de esposa; casarse con; *vn* casarse
wivern ['waɪvərn] *s* (her.) dragón
wizard ['wɪzərd] *s* brujo, hechicero, mago; (coll.) as, experto; *adj* mágico
wizardry ['wɪzərdrɪ] *s* magia
wizened ['wɪzənd] *adj* marchito; acartonado
wk. abr. de **week**
wks. abr. de **weeks** y **works**
w.l. abr. de **wave length**
w.long. abr. de **west longitude**
WNW, W.N.W. o **w.n.w.** abr. de **west-northwest**
wo [wo] *s & interj* var. de **woe**
woad [wod] *s* (bot.) glasto, hierba pastel
wobble ['wɑbəl] *s* bamboleo, tambaleo; *vn* bambolear, tambalear; bailar (*p.ej., una silla, una baldosa*); vacilar, cambiar, ser inconstante
wobbly ['wɑblɪ] *adj* tambaleante, inseguro
wobegone ['wobɪ,gɔn] o ['wobɪ,gɑn] *adj* var. de **woebegone**
woe [wo] *s* miseria, aflicción, pesar, infortunio; *interj* ¡ay!; **woe is me!** ¡ay de mí!
woebegone ['wobɪ,gɔn] o ['wobɪ,gɑn] *adj* cariacontecido, abatido
woeful o **woful** ['wofəl] *adj* miserable, triste, abatido; lastimoso
woke [wok] *pret de* **wake**
wold [wold] *s* rasa ondulada y sin bosques; (bot.) gualda
wolf [wʊlf] *s* (*pl:* **wolves**) (zool.) lobo; glotón cruel (*persona*); **to cry wolf** gritar ¡el lobo!, dar falsa alarma; **to keep the wolf from the door** defenderse de la pobreza, guardarse del hambre; *va* comer vorazmente; dar falsa alarma a; *vn* comer vorazmente; vivir como lobo; cazar lobos
wolf dog *s* perro lobero; perro de los esquimales; híbrido de perro y lobo
wolf fish *s* (ichth.) lobo de mar
wolfhound ['wʊlf,haʊnd] *s* galgo lobero
wolfish ['wʊlfɪʃ] *adj* lobuno; cruel, rapaz
wolf pack *s* grupo submarino a caza de presa
wolfram ['wʊlfrəm] *s* (chem.) volframio; (mineral.) volframita
wolframite ['wʊlfrəmaɪt] *s* (mineral.) volframita
wolf's-bane o **wolfsbane** ['wʊlfs,ben] *s* (bot.) matalobos
wolverine o **wolverene** [,wʊlvə'rin] o ['wʊlvərin] *s* (zool.) carcayú, glotón de América; (*cap.*) *s* natural o habitante del estado de Michigan, EE.UU.
woman ['wʊmən] *s* (*pl:* **women** ['wɪmɪn]) *s* mujer; criada; *adj* femenino; de mujer
woman hater *s* misógino, enemigo de las mujeres
womanhood ['wʊmənhʊd] *s* el sexo femenino, la mujer; las mujeres, la feminidad
womanish ['wʊmənɪʃ] *adj* mujeril, femenil, afeminado
womankind ['wʊmən,kaɪnd] *s* el sexo femenino, la mujer
womanlike ['wʊmən,laɪk] *adj* mujeril
womanly ['wʊmənlɪ] *adj* (*comp:* **-lier**; *super:* **-liest**) femenil, mujeril; *adv* femenilmente
woman of the world *s* mujer mundana
woman's rights *spl* derechos de la mujer
woman suffrage *s* sufragismo, sufragio femenino
woman-suffragist ['wʊmən'sʌfrədʒɪst] *s* sufragista
womb [wum] *s* (anat.) útero, matriz; (fig.) entrañas, seno
wombat ['wɑmbæt] *s* (zool.) tejón de Australia, fascólomo
women ['wɪmɪn] *pl de* **woman**
womenfolk ['wɪmɪn,fok] *spl* las mujeres
won [wʌn] *pret & pp de* **win**
wonder ['wʌndər] *s* maravilla; admiración; **for a wonder** por milagro; **no wonder** no es extraño; **to do wonders with** hacer maravillas con; **to work wonders** hacer milagros; *va* preguntarse, p.ej., **I wonder if it is true** me pregunto ¿será verdad?; *vn* maravillarse, admirarse; **to wonder at** maravillarse con o de, admirarse de
wonder drugs *spl* drogas prodigiosas, drogas milagrosas, drogas mágicas
wonderful ['wʌndərfəl] *adj* maravilloso
wonderland ['wʌndər,lænd] *s* tierra de las maravillas, reino de las hadas
wonderment ['wʌndərmənt] *s* asombro, sorpresa, admiración
wondrous ['wʌndrəs] *adj* maravilloso; *adv* maravillosamente
won't [wont] contracción de **will not**
wont [wʌnt] *adj* habituado, acostumbrado; **to be wont to** + *inf* soler + *inf*, acostumbrar + *inf*; *s* hábito, costumbre
wonted ['wʌntɪd] *adj* habitual, ordinario, acostumbrado
woo [wu] *va* cortejar (*a una mujer*); tratar de conquistar; tratar de persuadir
wood [wʊd] *s* madera; leña (*madera cortada para quemar*); objeto de madera; barril o pipa de madera; bosque; (mus.) instrumento de viento de madera; (print.) bloque de madera; **woods** *spl* bosque; (mus.) instrumentos de viento de madera; **out of the woods** libre de incertidumbre, libre de dificultades, libre de compromisos; fuera de peligro; **to take to the woods** andar a monte; *adj* de madera; *va* proveer de madera; obtener madera para
wood alcohol *s* alcohol de madera, alcohol metílico
wood anemone *s* (bot.) anemona silvestre
woodbine ['wʊd,baɪn] *s* (bot.) madreselva; (bot.) guau (*Parthenocissus quinquefolia*)
wood block *s* bloque de madera; adoquín de madera; (print.) grabado en madera
wood borer *s* (ent.) carcoma
wood carver *s* tallista
wood carving *s* labrado de madera
woodchuck ['wʊd,tʃʌk] *s* (zool.) marmota de América
woodcock ['wʊd,kɑk] *s* (orn.) chocha, becada
woodcraft ['wʊd,kræft] o ['wʊd,krɑft] *s* conocimiento de la vida del bosque; destreza en trabajos de madera
woodcut ['wʊd,kʌt] *s* (print.) grabado en madera
woodcutter ['wʊd,kʌtər] *s* leñador
wood duck *s* (orn.) juyuyo
wooded ['wʊdɪd] *adj* enselvado
wooden ['wʊdən] *adj* de madera, hecho de madera; vago (*dícese, p.ej., de la mirada*); torpe, estúpido; sin ánimo, sin color
wood engraving *s* (print.) grabado en madera
wooden-headed ['wʊdən,hɛdɪd] *adj* (coll.) torpe, estúpido
wooden horse *s* caballo de madera (*de que se sirvieron los griegos para invadir a Troya*); potro (*castigo*)
wooden shoe *s* zueco
woodenware ['wʊdən,wɛr] *s* utensilios de madera

wood germander *s* (bot.) camedrio de los bosques
wood grouse *s* (orn.) gallo de bosque
wood ibis *s* (orn.) bato, tántalo
woodland ['wudlənd] *s* bosque, arbolado; *adj* selvático
woodlander ['wudləndər] *s* habitante del bosque
wood lot *s* terreno de bosque
wood louse *s* (zool.) cochinilla de humedad; (ent.) reloj de la muerte
woodman ['wudmən] *s* (*pl:* **-men**) habitante del bosque; leñador; (Brit.) guardabosque
wood note *s* canto de pájaro silvestre
wood nymph *s* (myth.) napea, ninfa de los bosques; (ent.) mariposa (*del género Euthisanotia*); (orn.) colibrí sudamericano (*del género Thalurania*)
woodpecker ['wud,pɛkər] *s* (orn.) carpintero, picocarpintero
wood pigeon *s* (orn.) paloma torcaz (*Columba palumbus*); (orn.) paloma volcanera (*Columba fasciata*)
woodpile ['wud,paɪl] *s* montón de leña
wood pulp *s* pulpa de madera
woodruff ['wud,rʌf] *s* (bot.) asperilla, hepática estrellada, reina de los bosques
wood screw *s* tornillo para madera, tirafondo
woodshed ['wud,ʃɛd] *s* leñera
woodsman ['wudzmən] *s* (*pl:* **-men**) leñador; hombre acostumbrado a la vida del bosque
wood sorrel *s* (bot.) acederilla, acedera menor
woodsy ['wudzɪ] *adj* boscoso, selvático
wood tar *s* alquitrán vegetal
wood thrush *s* (orn.) tordo norteamericano (*Hylocichla mustelina*)
wood turning *s* torneo de madera
wood vinegar *s* vinagre de madera
woodwaxen ['wud,wæksən] *s* (bot.) retama de tintes o de tintoreros
wood wind *s* (mus.) instrumento de viento de madera; *spl* (mus.) instrumentos de viento de madera
wood-wind instrument ['wud,wɪnd] *s* (mus.) instrumento de viento de madera
woodwork ['wud,wʌrk] *s* ebanistería, obra de carpintería; maderaje
woodworker ['wud,wʌrkər] *s* ebanista, carpintero
woodworking ['wud,wʌrkɪŋ] *s* ebanistería, elaboración de maderas
woodworm ['wud,wʌrm] *s* (ent.) carcoma
woody ['wudɪ] *adj* (*comp:* **-ier;** *super:* **-iest**) arbolado, enselvado; leñoso
wooer ['wuər] *s* pretendiente, galán
woof [wuf] *s* trama; género, tejido; [wuf] *s* gruñido; *vn* gruñir (*p.ej., el perro*)
woofer ['wufər] *s* (rad.) altavoz para bajas audiofrecuencias, altavoz graves
wool [wul] *s* lana; **to pull the wool over one's eyes** (coll.) engañar a uno como un chino, hacerle chino a uno; *adj* de lana, hecho de lana
woold [wuld] *va* (naut.) encarcelar
woolen ['wulən] *adj* lanero; de lana, hecho de lana; *s* hilo de lana; tejido de lana; **woolens** *spl* géneros de lana, ropa de lana
woolgathering ['wul,gæðərɪŋ] *adj* absorto, distraído; *s* absorción, distracción
woolgrower ['wul,groər] *s* ganadero de ganado lanar
woollen ['wulən] *adj & s* var. de **woolen; woollens** *spl* var. de **woolens**
woolly ['wulɪ] *adj* (*comp:* **-lier;** *super:* **-liest**) lanoso, lanudo
woolman ['wulmən] *s* (*pl:* **-men**) lanero (*el que trata en lanas*)
woolpack ['wul,pæk] *s* fardo para llevar la lana; paquete de lana de 240 libras; cúmulo (*nubes amontonadas*)
woolsack ['wul,sæk] *s* saco de lana; (Brit.) cojín en el cual se sienta el Gran Canciller en la Cámara de los Lores; (Brit.) cargo o dignidad de Gran Canciller
wool stapler *s* lanero
wooly ['wulɪ] *adj* (*comp:* **-ier;** *super:* **-iest**) var. de **woolly**
woozy ['wuzɪ] o ['wuzɪ] *adj* (slang) confuso, vaguido; (slang) indispuesto
Worcestershire sauce ['wustərʃɪr] *s* salsa inglesa
word [wʌrd] *s* palabra; santo y seña, palabra de pase; orden *f*; (*cap.*) *s* (theol.) Verbo o Palabra (*segunda persona de la Santísima Trinidad*); **words** *spl* palabras mayores (*las injuriosas y ofensivas*); letra, palabra (*palabras de una canción*); **by word of mouth** de palabra, verbalmente; **in a word** en una palabra; **in other words** en otros términos; **mark my words!** ¡advierta lo que digo!; **my word!** ¡válgame Dios!; **the Word** la palabra de Dios (*la Escritura*); **to be as good as one's word** cumplir lo prometido; **to bring word** dar noticia; **to have a word with** hablar cuatro palabras con; **to have word from** recibir noticias de; **to have words** tener palabras, tener palabras mayores; **to keep one's word** cumplir su palabra; **to leave word** dejar dicho; **to put in a good word for** decir unas palabras en favor de; **to send word** mandar recado; **to send word that** mandar decir que; **to take a person at his word** tomarle la palabra a una persona; **to take the words out of one's mouth** quitarle a uno las palabras de la boca; **upon my word** palabra de honor; **upon my word!** ¡válgame Dios!; **word for word** palabra por palabra; *va* redactar, formular, expresar en palabras
wordage ['wʌrdɪdʒ] *s* palabras; fraseología; palabrería, verbosidad; número de palabras
word blindness *s* ceguera verbal, alexia
wordbook ['wʌrd,buk] *s* diccionario, vocabulario
word count *s* recuento de vocabulario
word deafness *s* sordera verbal, sordera psíquica, afasia sensorial
word element *s* (gram.) elemento de compuestos
word formation *s* (gram.) formación de palabras
word-for-word ['wʌrdfər'wʌrd] *adj* literal, ajustado palabra por palabra
wordiness ['wʌrdɪnɪs] *s* verbosidad
wording ['wʌrdɪŋ] *s* fraseología, manera de expresarse por medio de palabras
wordless ['wʌrdlɪs] *adj* falto de palabras; sin expresar
Word of God *s* palabra de Dios (*la Escritura*)
word of honor *s* palabra de honor
word order *s* (gram.) orden *m* de colocación
word picture *s* pintura por medio de la palabra
wordplay ['wʌrd,ple] *s* juego de palabras
word salad *s* esquizofasia (*lenguaje incoherente e incomprensible de la esquizofrenia*)
word sign *s* signo (*de la escritura jeroglífica; de la taquigrafía; del sistema Braille*)
word-slinger ['wʌrd,slɪŋər] *s* escritorcillo, escritor mercenario
word square *s* palabras cruzadas
wordstock ['wʌrd,stɑk] s léxico, vocabulario
wordy ['wʌrdɪ] *adj* (*comp:* **-ier;** *super:* **-iest**) verboso; verbal
wore [wor] *pret de* **wear**
work [wʌrk] *s* trabajo; obra (*resultado del trabajo; producción del espíritu; estructura en construcción; fortificación*); (sew.) labor; (phys.) trabajo; **works** *ssg* o *spl* fábrica, usina; *spl* mecanismo; movimiento (*p.ej., de un reloj*); (Bib.) obras; **at work** trabajando; en la oficina, en el taller, en la tienda, etc. (*es decir, no en casa*); **out of work** desempleado, sin trabajo; **to make short work of** concluir con prontitud; deshacerse de, sin rodeos; **to shoot the works** (slang) envidar el resto, jugar el todo por el todo; (slang) comprometerse a ultranza; **to throw out of work** privar de trabajo; quitar el empleo a ‖ *va* hacer trabajar; trabajar, obrar (*p.ej., la madera*); conseguir con esfuerzo; causar, producir; obrar (*p.ej., un milagro*); influir, persuadir; resolver; laborear, explotar (*una mina*); **to work in** meter, hacer entrar; **to work into** intercalar en (*p.ej., un discurso*); **to work it** (coll.) manejar las cosas, darse traza; **to work off** deshacerse de; **to work out** desarrollar, preparar; resolver; determinar (*su destino*); agotar (*una mina*); **to work up** preparar; estimular, excitar ‖ *vn* trabajar; funcionar, marchar; dar resultado;

obrar (*p.ej., un remedio*); **to work against** obrar en contra de; **to work free** o **loose** aflojarse (*con el movimiento o el uso*); **to work on** o **upon** tratar de influir o persuadir; **to work out** resultar; resolverse; (sport) entrenarse

workable [ˈwʌrkəbəl] *adj* practicable; manuable; explotable; laborable

workaday [ˈwʌrkəˌde] *adj* de cada día; práctico; ordinario, vulgar, prosaico

workbag [ˈwʌrkˌbæg] *s* saco de trabajo

workbench [ˈwʌrkˌbentʃ] *s* banco o mesa de trabajo, banco de taller

workbook [ˈwʌrkˌbuk] *s* libro de trabajo; libro de reglas; libro de ejercicios

workbox [ˈwʌrkˌbɑks] *s* caja de herramientas; caja de labor

workday [ˈwʌrkˌde] *s* día de trabajo, día laborable; jornada (*tiempo de duración del trabajo diario*); *adj* de cada día; práctico; ordinario, vulgar

worker [ˈwʌrkər] *s* trabajador, obrero; (ent.) obrera

work force *s* mano de obra, personal obrero

work horse *s* caballo de carga; yunque, trabajador esforzado

workhouse [ˈwʌrkˌhaus] *s* taller penitenciario; (Brit.) asilo de pobres donde los recogidos tienen que trabajar en el obrador

working [ˈwʌrkɪŋ] *s* funcionamiento; operación; explotación; **workings** *spl* (min.) labores; *adj* obrero; de trabajo; en funcionamiento

working agreement *s* ajuste, arreglo, modo de vivir

working capital *s* capital en giro

working class *s* clase obrera

working clothes *spl* traje de faena

working day *s* día de trabajo, día laborable; jornada (*tiempo de duración del trabajo diario*)

working-day [ˈwʌrkɪŋˌde] *adj* de cada día; práctico; ordinario, vulgar

working drawing *s* dibujo de trabajo, dibujo de guía

working face *s* (min.) fondo de laboreo

workinggirl [ˈwʌrkɪŋˌgʌrl] *s* trabajadora joven: obrera joven

working hours *spl* horas laborables, horas de trabajo, horas de jornada

working hypothesis *s* hipótesis de guía

working majority *s* mayoría suficiente

workingman [ˈwʌrkɪŋˌmæn] *s* (*pl:* **-men**) trabajador; obrero

working model *s* modelo de guía

working order *s* orden *m* de marcha

working speed *s* velocidad de régimen

working stroke *s* (mach.) carrera de trabajo

working voltage *s* (elec.) voltaje de régimen

workingwoman [ˈwʌrkɪŋˌwumən] *s* (*pl:* **-women**) trabajadora; obrera

workman [ˈwʌrkmən] *s* (*pl:* **-men**) trabajador; obrero; artífice

workmanlike [ˈwʌrkmənˌlaɪk] *adj* esmerado, primoroso, bien ejecutado; *adv* esmeradamente, primorosamente

workmanship [ˈwʌrkmənʃɪp] *s* destreza o habilidad en el trabajo; confección; hechura, obra

work of art *s* obra de arte

workout [ˈwʌrkˌaut] *s* ejercicio; prueba, ensayo

workpeople [ˈwʌrkˌpipəl] *spl* obreros

workroom [ˈwʌrkˌrum] o [ˈwʌrkˌrʊm] *s* obrador; sala de trabajo; gabinete de trabajo

workshop [ˈwʌrkˌʃɑp] *s* taller; (educ.) taller

work stoppage *s* paro

worktable [ˈwʌrkˌtebəl] *s* mesa de trabajo; mesa de labor

workwoman [ˈwʌrkˌwumən] *s* (*pl:* **-women**) trabajadora; obrera

world [wʌrld] *s* mundo; **a world of** la mar de; **for all the world** exactamente; **half the world** medio mundo (*mucha gente*); **in the world** en el mundo entero; alguna vez; **not for all the world** por nada del mundo; **since the world began** desde que el mundo es mundo; **the other world** el otro mundo (*la vida futura*); **the world over** por el mundo entero; **to bring into the world** echar al mundo; **to come into the world** venir al mundo; **to see the world** ver mundo; **to think the world of** tener un alto concepto de; **world without end** por los siglos de los siglos; *adj* mundial; mundano

world affairs *spl* asuntos internacionales

World Court *s* Tribunal Permanente de Justicia Internacional

world-famous [ˈwʌrldˈfeməs] *adj* mundialmente famoso

worldling [ˈwʌrldlɪŋ] *s* persona mundana

worldly [ˈwʌrldlɪ] *adj* (*comp:* **-lier;** *super:* **-liest**) mundano

worldly-minded [ˈwʌrldlɪˈmaɪndɪd] *adj* mundano, apegado a las cosas del mundo

worldly-wise [ˈwʌrldlɪˈwaɪz] *adj* que tiene mucho mundo

world map *s* mapamundi

world power *s* potencia mundial

World Series *s* (baseball) Serie Mundial

world view *s* concepto del mundo

World War *s* Guerra Mundial

world-weary [ˈwʌrldˌwɪrɪ] *adj* cansado de la vida

world-wide [ˈwʌrldˌwaɪd] *adj* mundial, global

worm [wʌrm] *s* gusano; serpentín; tornillo sin fin; (fig.) gusano (*persona despreciable*); (fig.) gusano (*de la conciencia*); **worms** *spl* (path.) lombrices; *va* limpiar de lombrices; conseguir o lograr por medio de artimañas; **to worm a secret out of a person** arrancar mañosamente un secreto a una persona; **to worm oneself into** insinuarse en; **to worm one's way through** atravesar serpenteando; *vn* arrastrarse, deslizarse, serpentear como un gusano

worm-eaten [ˈwʌrmˌitən] *adj* carcomido; apolillado; desgastado, inservible, viejo

worm gear *s* engranaje de tornillo sin fin

wormhole [ˈwʌrmˌhol] *s* agujero que deja la carcoma; apolilladura; agujero que hace el gusano

wormseed [ˈwʌrmˌsid] *s* (bot.) apasote, pazote

worm wheel *s* rueda de tornillo sin fin

wormwood [ˈwʌrmˌwud] *s* (bot.) ajenjo; (fig.) amargura

wormy [ˈwʌrmɪ] *adj* (*comp:* **-ier;** *super:* **-iest**) gusaniento, gusanoso; carcomido; apolillado; rastrero, servil

worn [worn] *adj* gastado, roto, raído; cansado, rendido; *pp de* **wear**

worn-out [ˈwornˌaut] *adj* muy gastado, inservible; consumido (*por el trabajo, las enfermedades, los vicios, etc.*)

worriment [ˈwʌrɪmənt] *s* (coll.) inquietud, preocupación; (coll.) molestia

worrisome [ˈwʌrɪsəm] *adj* inquietante; inquieto, aprensivo

worry [ˈwʌrɪ] *s* (*pl:* **-ries**) inquietud, preocupación; molestia; (*pret & pp:* **-ried**) *va* inquietar, preocupar; molestar; acosar; morder y sacudir; querer morder; **to be worried** estar inquieto; *vn* inquietarse, preocuparse; **don't worry** pierda Vd. cuidado; **to worry along** arreglárselas de algún modo

worse [wʌrs] *adj & adv comp* peor; **worse and worse** de mal en peor, cada vez peor; **worse than ever** peor que nunca; más que nunca; *s* peor

worsen [ˈwʌrsən] *va & vn* empeorar

worsening [ˈwʌrsənɪŋ] *s* empeoramiento

worship [ˈwʌrʃɪp] *s* adoración, culto; **your worship** vuestra merced; (*pret & pp:* **-shiped** o **-shipped;** *ger:* **-shiping** o **-shipping**) *va & vn* adorar, venerar

worshiper o **worshipper** [ˈwʌrʃɪpər] *s* adorador; devoto

worshipful [ˈwʌrʃɪpfəl] *adj* reverenciable; adorador

worst [wʌrst] *adj & adv super* peor; *s* (lo) peor; **at worst** a lo más; **if worst comes to worst** si pasa lo peor; **to get the worst of it** llevar la peor parte, salir perdiendo; **to give one the worst of it** darle a uno la peor parte, derrotar a uno; *va* derrotar, vencer

worsted [ˈwustɪd] *s* estambre; tela de estambre; *adj* de estambre

wort [wʌrt] *s* (bot.) planta, hierba; mosto de cerveza

worth [wʌrθ] *s* valor; valía; mérito; **a dollar's worth of** un dólar de; *adj* del valor de; digno de; **to be worth** valer; tener una fortuna de; **to be worth** + *ger* valer la pena de + *inf*, p.ej., **that city is not worth visiting** aquella ciudad no vale la pena de visitarse
worthiness [ˈwʌrðɪnɪs] *s* mérito
worthless [ˈwʌrθlɪs] *adj* sin valor, inútil, inservible; despreciable, indigno
worth while *adj*; **to be worth while** ser de mérito; valer la pena; **to be worth while to** + *inf* valer la pena + *inf*, p.ej., **it isn't worth while to go to the theater this evening** no vale la pena ir al teatro esta noche
worth-while [ˈwʌrθˈhwaɪl] *adj* de mérito, digno de atención, p.ej., **a worth-while book** un libro de mérito, un libro digno de atención
worthy [ˈwʌrðɪ] *adj* (*comp:* **-thier;** *super:* **-thiest**) digno; benemérito, meritorio; **worthy of** + *ger* digno de + *inf*; **worthy of note** digno de notarse; *s* (*pl:* **-thies**) benemérito, notable; (hum.) personaje
wot [wɑt] *primera y tercera personas del sg del pres de ind de* **wit**
would [wʊd] *v aux* se emplea para formar (1) el condicional presente, p.ej., **he said he would come** dijo que vendría; **he would come if he could** vendría si pudiese; (2) el condicional pasado, p.ej., **he would have come if he had been able** habría venido si hubiese podido; (3) el modo potencial, p.ej., **would that I knew it!** ¡ojalá que lo supiese!; (4) el imperf de ind, indicando costumbre, p.ej., **he would go for days without smoking** pasaba días enteros sin fumar
would-be [ˈwʊdˌbi] *adj* llamado; supuesto, p.ej., **a would-be pianist** un supuesto pianista; *s* presumido
wouldn't [ˈwʊdənt] contracción de **would not**
wound [wund] *s* herida; *va* herir; [waʊnd] *pret & pp de* **wind**
wounded [ˈwundɪd] *adj* herido; **the wounded** los heridos
wove [wov] *pret & pp de* **weave**
woven [ˈwovən] *pp de* **weave**
wow [waʊ] *interj* (coll.) ¡ax!; *s* ululación (*del disco fonográfico*); (slang) cosa muy graciosa; (slang) éxito rotundo; *va* (slang) arrebatar, entusiasmar
wrack [ræk] *s* naufragio; destrucción, ruina; (bot.) varec, quelpo, fuco, zostera de mar; algas que arroja el mar a la playa; **to go to wrack and ruin** arruinarse
wraith [reθ] *s* aparecido, espectro, fantasma
wrangle [ˈræŋgəl] *s* disputa, riña, pelotera; *va* disputar; pasar disputando; lograr disputando; rodear (*el ganado o las caballerías*); *vn* disputar, reñir, pelotear
wrangler [ˈræŋglər] *s* disputador, pendenciero; (Brit.) graduado con altos honores en matemáticas; (U.S.A.) ganadero, manadero
wrap [ræp] *s* abrigo; (*pret & pp:* **wrapped;** *ger:* **wrapping**) *va* envolver; **to be wrapped up in** estar prendado de, estar entregado a; estar envuelto en; **to wrap up** envolver; arropar; *vn* envolverse; **to wrap up** arroparse
wrap-around windshield [ˈræpəˌraund] *s* (aut.) parabrisas curvilíneo o panorámico
wrapper [ˈræpər] *s* envolvedor; envoltura; bata, peinador; faja (*de periódico o revista*); capa (*de tabaco*)
wrapping [ˈræpɪŋ] *s* envoltura; arropamiento
wrapping paper *s* papel de envolver o embalar, papel de estraza
wrasse [ræs] *s* (ichth.) labro; (ichth.) durdo (*Labrus bergylta*); (ichth.) tordo de mar (*Labrus mixtus*)
wrath [ræθ] o [rɑθ] *s* ira, cólera muy grande; venganza
wrathful [ˈræθfəl] o [ˈrɑθfəl] *adj* iracundo, colérico, furioso
wrathy [ˈræθɪ] o [ˈrɑθɪ] *adj* (*comp:* **-ier;** *super:* **-iest**) var. de **wrathful**
wreak [rik] *va* descargar (*la cólera*); infligir (*pena, castigo, venganza*)
wreath [riθ] *s* (*pl:* **wreaths** [riðz]) guirnalda; corona de laurel; corona (*funeral*); espiral (*p.ej., de humo*)
wreathe [rið] *va* enguirnaldar; tejer (*guirnaldas*); ceñir, envolver; *vn* enroscarse, moverse en anillos, elevarse en espirales (*p.ej., el humo*)
wreck [rɛk] *s* destrucción, ruina; naufragio; colisión o descarrilamiento (*p.ej., de un tren*); **to be a wreck** estar hecho un cascajo, estar hecho una ruina; *va* derribar; destruir, arruinar; hacer naufragar (*a un buque o una persona*); descarrilar (*un tren*); arrasar; *vn* arruinarse
wreckage [ˈrɛkɪdʒ] *s* destrucción, ruina; naufragio; despojos, restos; escombros (*de un edificio*); (fig.) naufragio (*p.ej., de las esperanzas de uno*)
wrecker [ˈrɛkər] *s* demoledor; descarrilador (*de trenes*); (aut.) camión de auxilio; (rail.) carro de auxilio, carro de grúa; (naut.) salvador de buques
wrecking ball *s* bola rompedora
wrecking car *s* (aut.) camión de auxilio; (rail.) carro de auxilio, carro de grúa
wrecking crane *s* grúa destructora; grúa de auxilio o de salvamento
wren [rɛn] *s* (orn.) buscareta, coletero, rey de zarza; (orn.) reyezuelo
wrench [rɛntʃ] *s* llave; torcedura violenta; dolor, pena, sufrimiento; *va* torcer violentamente; hacer daño a, torciendo; arrebatar torciendo; torcer (*el sentido de una frase*)
wrest [rɛst] *s* torsión violenta; llave para afinar pianos, arpas, etc.; *va* torcer violentamente, arrancar violentamente, arrebatar; torcer (*el sentido de una frase*); **to wrest something from someone** arrebatarle a uno una cosa
wrestle [ˈrɛsəl] *s* lucha; partido de lucha; *vn* (sport & fig.) luchar
wrestler [ˈrɛslər] *s* luchador
wrestling [ˈrɛslɪŋ] *s* lucha (*combate cuerpo a cuerpo*)
wrestling match *s* partido de lucha
wrest pin *s* clavija de piano
wrest plank *s* (mus.) clavijero (*del piano*)
wretch [rɛtʃ] *s* miserable (*persona desdichada; persona vil y despreciable*)
wretched [ˈrɛtʃɪd] *adj* miserable; pésimo, malísimo (*p.ej., trabajo*)
wretchedness [ˈrɛtʃɪdnɪs] *s* miseria; bajeza, ruindad, vileza
wrick [rɪk] *s* torcedura (*de un músculo o miembro*); *va* torcerse (*un músculo o miembro*)
wriggle [ˈrɪgəl] *s* meneo serpentino, culebreo; *va* menear rápidamente; introducir mañosamente; **to wriggle one's way into** colarse en; (fig.) colarse en; *vn* menearse rápidamente; culebrear, moverse serpenteando; **to wriggle away** escaparse culebreando; **to wriggle out of** escabullirse de, escaparse de
wriggler [ˈrɪglər] *s* persona que se menea; larva de mosquito
wriggly [ˈrɪglɪ] *adj* que se menea; sinuoso, tortuoso
wright [raɪt] *s* artífice
wring [rɪŋ] *s* torsión; expresión (*p.ej., del zumo*); (*pret & pp:* **wrung**) *va* torcer; retorcer (*las manos*); exprimir (*el zumo, la ropa, etc.*); arrancar (*dinero*); sacar por fuerza (*la verdad*); acongojar, afligir; **to wring out** exprimir (*la ropa*)
wringer [ˈrɪŋər] *s* exprimidor o secadora (*de la ropa acabada de lavar*)
wrinkle [ˈrɪŋkəl] *s* arruga; (coll.) truco, ardid; *va* arrugar; *vn* arrugarse
wrinkly [ˈrɪŋklɪ] *adj* (*comp:* **-klier;** *super:* **-kliest**) arrugado
wrist [rɪst] *s* (anat.) muñeca; codillo (*de los cuadrúpedos*)
wristband [ˈrɪstˌbænd] o [ˈrɪzbənd] *s* puño, bocamanga
wristlet [ˈrɪstlɪt] *s* brazalete; muñequera (*en la cual se lleva sujeto un reloj*); manguito para la muñeca
wrist pin *s* (mach.) eje o pasador de émbolo
wrist watch *s* reloj de pulsera
writ [rɪt] *s* escrito; (law) auto, mandato, orden *f* (*de la corte*)
write [raɪt] (*pret:* **wrote;** *pp:* **written**) *va* escribir; **to write down** poner por escrito; bajar el precio de; **to write off** cancelar (*una deuda*); **to write out** poner por escrito; escribir sin abreviar; **to write up** describir;

escribir en detalle; escribir una crónica de; poner al día (*un escrito*); subir el precio de; dar bombo a; *vn* escribir; **to write away** dejar correr la pluma, escribir a vuela pluma; **to write back** contestar por carta o por escrito; **to write on** seguir escribiendo; escribir acerca de
writer ['raɪtər] *s* escritor
writer's cramp *s* calambre de los escribientes
write-up ['raɪt,ʌp] *s* (coll.) relato; (coll.) crónica; (coll.) bombo; (coll.) valoración excesiva
writhe [raɪð] *vn* contorcerse; retorcerse (*a causa de un dolor*); sufrir angustia
writing ['raɪtɪŋ] *s* el escribir; escritura; profesión de escritor; escrito; **at this writing** al escribir ésta; **in one's own writing** de su puño y letra; **to put in writing** poner por escrito; *adj* de escribir
writing desk *s* escritorio
writing materials *spl* recado de escribir
writing pad *s* taco de escribir
writing paper *s* papel de escribir, papel de cartas
writing room *s* sala de escritura
writing table *s* mesa de escribir
writ of execution *s* (law) auto de ejecución
written ['rɪtən] *pp de* **write**
written accent *s* acento ortográfico
wrong [rɔŋ] o [rɑŋ] *adj* injusto; malo; equivocado; erróneo; impropio, poco conveniente; no . . . que se busca, p.ej., **this is the wrong house** ésta no es la casa que se busca; no . . . que se necesita, p.ej., **this is the wrong train** éste no es el tren que se necesita; no . . . que debe, p.ej., **he is going the wrong way** no sigue el camino que debe; **in the wrong place** descolocado, mal colocado; **to be wrong** no tener razón; tener la culpa; **to be wrong with** pasar algo a, p.ej., **something is wrong with the telephone** algo le pasa al teléfono; *adv* mal; por error; sin razón; al revés; **to go wrong** salir mal; ir por mal camino; darse a la mala vida; *s* mal, daño, perjuicio; agravio, injusticia; error; **to be in the wrong** no tener razón; tener la culpa; **to do wrong** obrar mal; *va* agraviar, ofender, hacer mal a, ser injusto con
wrongdoer ['rɔŋ,duər] o ['rɑŋ,duər] *s* malvado, malhechor
wrongdoing ['rɔŋ,duɪŋ] o ['rɑŋ,duɪŋ] *s* maldad, perversidad
wrongful ['rɔŋfəl] o ['rɑŋfəl] *adj* injusto, malo; equivocado; ilegal
wrong-headed ['rɔŋ,hɛdɪd] o ['rɑŋ,hɛdɪd] *adj* equivocado; terco, obstinado
wrongly ['rɔŋlɪ] o ['rɑŋlɪ] *adv* mal; por error; sin razón; al revés
wrongness ['rɔŋnɪs] o ['rɑŋnɪs] *s* injusticia; maldad; error; inexactitud
wrong number *s* (telp.) número errado, número equivocado
wrong side *s* revés, contrahaz; lado contrario (*del camino*); **to get out of bed on the wrong side** levantarse del izquierdo; **wrong side out** al revés
wrote [rot] *pret de* **write**
wroth [rɔθ] o [rɑθ] *adj* iracundo, colérico, furioso
wrought [rɔt] *adj* forjado; labrado; hecho al martillo
wrought iron *s* hierro dulce
wrought-up ['rɔt'ʌp] *adj* sobreexcitado, muy conmovido
wrung [rʌŋ] *pret & pp de* **wring**
wry [raɪ] *adj* (*comp:* **wrier;** *super:* **wriest**) torcido; tuerto; desviado, pervertido; terco; equivocado
wrybill ['raɪ,bɪl] *s* (orn.) anarrinco
wry face *s* mueca, mohín, gesto
wryneck ['raɪ,nɛk] *s* (orn.) torcecuello o tuercecuello; (path.) torticolis
WSW, W.S.W. o **w.s.w.** abr. de **west-southwest**
wt. abr. de **weight**
wulfenite ['wʊlfənaɪt] *s* (mineral.) wulfenita
W.Va. abr. de **West Virginia**
Wy. abr. de **Wyoming**
wych-elm ['wɪtʃ'ɛlm] *s* (bot.) olmo escocés
wych-hazel ['wɪtʃ'hezəl] *s* var. de **witch hazel**
Wycliffite o **Wyclifite** ['wɪklɪfaɪt] *adj & s* viclefita
wye level [waɪ] *s* (surv.) nivel de horquetas
Wyo. abr. de **Wyoming**
wyvern ['waɪvərn] *s* var. de **wivern**

X, x [ɛks] *s* (*pl:* **X's, x's** [ˈɛksɪz]) vigésima cuarta letra del alfabeto inglés
xanthaline [ˈzænθəlin] *s* (chem.) xantalina
xanthate [ˈzænθet] *s* (chem.) xantato
xanthein [ˈzænθiɪn] *s* (chem.) xanteína
xanthene [ˈzænθin] *s* (chem.) xanteno
xanthin [ˈzænθɪn] *s* (chem.) xantina
xanthine [ˈzænθin] o [ˈzænθɪn] *s* (biochem.) xantina
Xanthippe [zænˈtɪpɪ] *s* Jantipa o Jantipe; mujer pendenciera
xanthochroid [ˈzænθokrɔɪd] *adj* & *s* (anthrop.) xantocroide
xanthoderm [ˈzænθodʌrm] *s* (anthrop.) xantodermo
xanthogen [ˈzænθodʒɛn] *s* (chem.) xantógeno
xanthoma [zænˈθomə] *s* (*pl:* **-mata** [mətə] o **-mas**) (path.) xantoma
xanthophyll [ˈzænθofɪl] *s* (biochem.) xantofila
xanthopsia [zænˈθɑpsɪə] *s* (path.) xantopsia
xanthopsin [zænˈθɑpsɪn] *s* xantopsina
xanthosis [zænˈθosɪs] *s* (path.) xantosis
xanthous [ˈzænθəs] *adj* amarillo
xanthoxylin [zænˈθɑksɪlɪn] *s* (chem. & pharm.) xantoxilina
Xavier [ˈzævɪər] o [ˈzevɪər] *s* Javier
xebec [ˈzibɛk] *s* (naut.) jabeque
xenia [ˈzinɪə] *s* (bot.) xenia
xenogenesis [ˌzɛnəˈdʒɛnɪsɪs] *s* (biol.) xenogénesis
xenon [ˈzinɑn] o [ˈzɛnɑn] *s* (chem.) xeno o xenón
xenophobe [ˈzɛnofob] *s* xenófobo
xenophobia [ˌzɛnoˈfobɪə] *s* xenofobia
Xenophon [ˈzɛnəfən] *s* Jenofonte
xerophthalmia [ˌzɪrɑfˈθælmɪə] *s* (path.) xeroftalmía
xerophyte [ˈzɪrəfaɪt] *s* (bot.) xerófita
xerophytic [ˌzɪrəˈfɪtɪk] *adj* (bot.) xerófito
Xerxes [ˈzʌrksiz] *s* Jerjes
xiphisternum [ˌzɪfɪˈstʌrnəm] *s* (*pl:* **-na** [nə]) (anat.) xifisternón
xiphoid [ˈzɪfɔɪd] *adj* & *s* (anat.) xifoides
xiphosuran [ˌzɪfəˈsʊrən] *s* (zool.) jifosuro
Xmas [ˈkrɪsməs] *s* var. de **Christmas**
X ray *s* rayo X; radiografía; **X rays** *spl* rayos X
X-ray [ˈɛksˌre] *adj* radiográfico; [ˈɛksˈre] *va* radiografiar; tratar por medio de los rayos X
X-ray photograph *s* radiografía (*fotografía por los rayos X*)
xylan [ˈzaɪlæn] *s* (chem.) xilán
xylem [ˈzaɪlɛm] *s* (bot.) xilema
xylene [ˈzaɪlin] *s* (chem.) xileno
xylidine [ˈzaɪlɪdin] o [ˈzɪlɪdin] *s* (chem.) xilidina
xylobalsamum [ˌzaɪloˈbɔlsəməm] o [ˌzaɪloˈbælsəməm] *s* xilobálsamo
xylograph [ˈzaɪləgræf] o [ˈzaɪləgrɑf] *s* xilografía (*grabado*)
xylographer [zaɪˈlɑgrəfər] *s* xilógrafo
xylographic [ˌzaɪləˈgræfɪk] o **xylographical** [ˌzaɪləˈgræfɪkəl] *adj* xilográfico
xylography [zaɪˈlɑgrəfɪ] *s* xilografía (*arte*)
xylol [ˈzaɪlol] o [ˈzaɪlɑl] *s* (chem.) xilol
xylophagous [zaɪˈlɑfəgəs] *adj* xilófago
xylophone [ˈzaɪləfon] o [ˈzɪləfon] *s* (mus.) xilófono
xylose [ˈzaɪlos] *s* (chem.) xilosa
xyster [ˈzɪstər] *s* (surg.) xister

Y, y [waɪ] *s* (*pl:* **Y's, y's** [waɪz]) vigésima quinta letra del alfabeto inglés
-y *suffix adj* -ado, p.ej., **wavy** ondulado; -iento, p.ej., **hungry** hambriento; **dusty** polvoriento; -izo, p.ej., **coppery** cobrizo; **strawy** pajizo; -oso, p.ej., **juicy** jugoso; **rocky** rocoso; -udo, p.ej., **fleshy** carnudo; **hairy** peludo; *suffix s* -ía, p.ej., **glory** gloria; **victory** victoria; -ía, p.ej., **geology** geología; **philosophy** filosofía; *suffix dim* -ito, p.ej., **pussy** michito; **Johnny** Juanito
y. abr. de **yard** o **yards** y **year**
yacht [jɑt] *s* yate; *vn* pasear en yate; tomar parte en regatas en yate
yacht club *s* club náutico
yachting ['jɑtɪŋ] *adj* aficionado al deporte de los yates; *s* navegación en yate, paseo en yate
yacht race *s* regata de yates
yachtsman ['jɑtsmən] *s* (*pl:* **-men**) aficionado al deporte de los yates
yachtsmanship ['jɑtsmənʃɪp] *s* arte de navegar un yate
yackety-yack ['jækɪtɪ'jæk] *s* (slang) charla, palique
yah [jɑ] *interj* ¡bah!; ¡puf!
yahoo ['jɑhu] o ['jehu] *s* patán
Yahveh o **Yahweh** ['jɑwe] *s* (Bib.) Yahvé
yak [jæk] *s* (zool.) yac (*bóvido del Tibet*)
yam [jæm] *s* (bot.) ñame (*planta y raíz*); batata, camote, boniato
yank [jæŋk] *s* (coll.) tirón; (*cap.*) *adj & s* (slang) yanqui; (*l.c.*) *va* (coll.) sacar de un tirón; *vn* (coll.) dar un tirón, dar tirones
Yankee ['jæŋkɪ] *adj & s* yanqui
Yankeedom ['jæŋkɪdəm] *s* los yanquis; Yanquilandia
Yankeeism ['jæŋkɪɪzəm] *s* característica de los yanquis; yanquismo
yap [jæp] *s* (slang) ladrido corto; (slang) conversación necia y ruidosa; (*pret & pp:* **yapped;** *ger:* **yapping**) *vn* (slang) ladrar con ladrido corto; (slang) charlar necia y ruidosamente
yard [jɑrd] *s* yarda (*medida*); cercado, corral, patio; (naut.) verga; (rail.) patio; **to man the yards** (naut.) disponer la gente sobre las vergas; (naut.) disponerse sobre las vergas; **to square the yards** (naut.) poner las vergas en cruz; *va* acorralar
yardage ['jɑrdɪdʒ] *s* yardaje
yardarm ['jɑrd,ɑrm] *s* (naut.) penol, singlón
yardmaster ['jɑrd,mæstər] o ['jɑrd,mɑstər] *s* (rail.) superintendente del patio
yardstick ['jɑrd,stɪk] *s* yarda, vara de medir; (fig.) criterio, norma
yarn [jɑrn] *s* hilado, hilaza; (coll.) cuento, burlería; *vn* (coll.) inventar y contar historietas
yarn tester *s* cuentahilos
yarrow ['jæro] *s* (bot.) milenrama
yataghan ['jætəgæn] *s* yatagán
yaupon ['jɔpən] *s* (bot.) apalachina
yaw [jɔ] *s* (naut.) guiñada; (aer.) desvío; **yaws** *spl* (path.) frambesia; *vn* (naut.) guiñar; (aer.) desviarse; (fig.) desviarse del camino
yawl [jɔl] *s* (naut.) queche; (naut.) bote; (dial.) alarido, aullido; *vn* (dial.) dar alaridos, aullar
yawn [jɔn] *s* bostezo; abertura; *va* decir bostezando; *vn* bostezar; abrirse desmesuradamente
yawning ['jɔnɪŋ] *adj* bostezante; abierto desmesuradamente; *s* bostezos
yawp [jɔp] *s* (coll.) alarido; (coll.) plática ruidosa; *vn* (coll.) dar alaridos; (coll.) charlar ruidosamente; (coll.) bostezar ruidosamente
y-cleped o **y-clept** [ɪ'klɛpt] *adj* (archaic) llamado, nombrado
yd. abr. de **yard** o **yards**
yds. abr. de **yards**
ye [ji] *pron pers* (archaic) vosotros; [ðɪ] *art def* (archaic) el, la
yea [je] *s* sí (*voto afirmativo*); *adv* sí; sin duda; (archaic) además
yean [jin] *va & vn* parir (*la cabra, la oveja*)
yeanling ['jinlɪŋ] *s* cordero o cabrito mamantón
year [jɪr] *s* año; **years** *spl* años (*edad; época de la vida*); muchos años; **of late years** en estos últimos años; **year by year** año por año; **year in, year out** año tras año
yearbook ['jɪr,bʊk] *s* anuario
yearling ['jɪrlɪŋ] *adj & s* primal
yearlong ['jɪr,lɔŋ] o ['jɪr,lɑŋ] *adj* que dura un año; que dura años
yearly ['jɪrlɪ] *adj* anual; *adv* anualmente
yearn [jʌrn] *vn* suspirar; **to yearn for** suspirar por, anhelar por; sentir lástima por; **to yearn to** + *inf* anhelar + *inf*
yearning ['jʌrnɪŋ] *s* anhelo, deseo vivo
year of grace *s* año de gracia
yeast [jist] *s* levadura, fermento; espuma, jiste; pastilla de levadura
yeast cake *s* pastilla de levadura, levadura comprimida
yeasty ['jistɪ] *adj* de la levadura; espumoso; casquivano, frívolo
yegg [jɛg] *s* (slang) ladrón; (slang) ladrón de cajas fuertes
yelk [jɛlk] *s* var. de **yolk**
yell [jɛl] *s* grito, voz; *va* decir a gritos; *vn* gritar, dar voces
yellow ['jɛlo] *adj* amarillo; escandaloso, sensacional (*periodismo*); (coll.) blanco (*cobarde, miedoso*); *s* amarillo; yema de huevo; *vn* amarillecer
yellow-billed cuckoo ['jɛlo,bɪld] *s* (orn.) cuclillo de las lluvias
yellowbird ['jɛlo,bʌrd] *s* (orn.) jilguero de América; (orn.) dominguito; (orn.) oropéndola
yellow elder *s* (bot.) tronadora, trompetilla
yellow fever *s* (path.) fiebre amarilla
yellow flag *s* bandera amarilla; (bot.) lirio amarillo
yellowhammer ['jɛlo,hæmər] *s* (orn.) ave tonta; (orn.) picamaderos norteamericano
yellow goatsbeard *s* (bot.) salsifí de los prados
yellowish ['jɛlo·ɪʃ] *adj* amarillento
yellow jack *s* fiebre amarilla; bandera amarilla de cuarentena; (bot.) junquillo; (ichth.) jurel
yellow jacket *s* (ent.) avispa; (ent.) avispón
yellow jasmine *s* (bot.) jazmín; (bot.) jazmín silvestre (*Gelsemium sempervirens*)
yellow journalism *s* periodismo sensacional
yellowlegs ['jɛlo,lɛgz] *s* (*pl:* **-legs**) (orn.) sarapico (*Totanus flavipes*)
yellowness ['jɛlonɪs] *s* amarillez
yellow ocher *s* (mineral.) ocre amarillo
yellow oxide *s* óxido amarillo
yellow peril *s* peligro amarillo
yellow pine *s* (bot.) pino amarillo; (bot.) liriodendro
yellow poplar *s* (bot.) liriodendro
yellow poppy *s* (bot.) pamplina
Yellow River *s* río Amarillo
yellow sandalwood *s* (bot.) sándalo
Yellow Sea *s* mar Amarillo
yellow spot *s* (anat.) mancha amarilla
yellow streak *s* vena de cobarde, trazas de cobarde
yellowthroat ['jɛlo,θrot] *s* (orn.) pecho amarillo
yelp [jɛlp] *s* gañido (*del perro*); *va* decir con gritos; ahuyentar con gritos; *vn* gañir
yen [jɛn] *s* (coll.) deseo vivo; (*pret & pp:* **yenned;** *ger:* **yenning**) *vn* (coll.) anhelar

yeoman ['jomən] *s* (*pl:* **-men**) (Brit.) labrador acomodado, pequeño terrateniente; (archaic) guardia del rey, sirviente del rey; (naut.) oficinista de a bordo; (naut.) pañolero
yeomanly ['jomənlɪ] *adj* honrado, leal; firme, porfiado; *adv* valerosamente
yeoman of the guard *s* (Brit.) continuo
yeomanry ['jomənrɪ] *s* (Brit.) labradores acomodados, pequeños terratenientes; (archaic) guardias del rey; (naut.) pañoleros; (Brit.) caballería voluntaria
yeoman's service *s* buen servicio, ayuda leal
yes [jɛs] *adv* sí; además, aun; *s* (*pl:* **yeses**) sí; **to say yes** dar el sí (*convenir en el matrimonio*); (*pret & pp:* **yessed;** *ger:* **yessing**) *va* decir sí a; *vn* decir sí
yes man *s* (slang) hombre que asiente siempre y lo acepta todo
yesterday ['jɛstərdɪ] o ['jɛstərde] *adv & s* ayer; **the day before yesterday** anteayer
yestereve [,jɛstər'iv] o **yesterevening** [,jɛstər'ivnɪŋ] *adv* (archaic & poet.) ayer tarde; *s* (archaic & poet.) la tarde de ayer
yestermorn [,jɛstər'mɔrn] *adv* (archaic & poet.) ayer por la mañana; *s* (archaic & poet.) la mañana de ayer
yesternight [,jɛstər'naɪt] *adv* (archaic & poet.) anoche; *s* (archaic & poet.) la noche de ayer
yesteryear [,jɛstər'jɪr] *adv* (archaic & poet.) antaño; *s* (archaic & poet.) el año pasado
yestreen [,jɛs'trin] *adv* (Scottish & poet.) ayer tarde; *s* (Scottish & poet.) la tarde de ayer
yet [jɛt] *adv* todavía, aun; **as yet** hasta ahora; **not yet** todavía no; *conj* con todo, sin embargo
yew [ju] *s* (bot.) tejo
Yiddish ['jɪdɪʃ] *s* yídish
yield [jild] *s* producción; rédito; rendimiento; *va* producir; rendir, redituar; *vn* producir; rendir; rendirse, entregarse, someterse; acceder, ceder, consentir
yielding ['jildɪŋ] *adj* complaciente, dócil, sumiso; productivo; *s* sumisión, rendimiento
yipe [jaɪp] *interj* (coll.) grito de dolor, miedo, sorpresa, etc.
Y.M.C.A. abr. de **Young Men's Christian Association**
Y.M.H.A. abr. de **Young Men's Hebrew Association**
yod [jod] o [jɑd] *s* (philol.) yod
yodel ['jodəl] *s* canto que se hace cambiando frecuentemente de la voz natural a la voz de falsete y viceversa; (*pret & pp:* **-deled** o **-delled;** *ger:* **-deling** o **-delling**) *va & vn* cantar cambiando frecuentemente de la voz natural a la voz de falsete y viceversa
yodle ['jodəl] *s, va & vn* var. de **yodel**
yoga ['jogə] *s* yoga
yogi ['jogɪ] *s* yogui
yogurt ['jogurt] *s* yogurt
yo-heave-ho ['jo'hiv'ho] *interj* (naut.) ¡iza!
yoicks [jɔɪks] *interj* grito que se emplea para excitar los perros en la caza
yoke [jok] *s* yugo; yunta (*de bestias de trabajo*); percha para llevar cargas; hombrillo (*de la camisa*); parte superior de la falda en las caderas; (elec.) culata; (mach.) horquilla; **to throw off the yoke** sacudir el yugo; *va* uncir; acoplar, unir; oprimir, subyugar; *vn* estar unidos
yoke elm *s* (bot.) carpe, ojaranzo
yokefellow ['jok,fɛlo] *s* compañero de yugo; compañero de trabajo y sufrimiento; cónyuge (*marido o mujer*)
yokel ['jokəl] *s* patán
yokemate ['jok,met] var. de **yokefellow**
yolk [jok] *s* yema de huevo; churre en la lana de oveja
Yom Kippur [jɑm 'kɪpər] *s* día de propiciación que celebran los judíos al principio del año hebreo
yon [jɑn] o **yond** [jɑnd] *adj & adv* (archaic & dial.) var. de **yonder**
yonder ['jɑndər] *adj* aquel; de más allá; *adv* allí a la vista
yore [jor] *adv* (obs.) hace mucho tiempo, hace muchos años; *s* (obs.) otro tiempo; **of yore** antiguamente, en otro tiempo, antaño
Yorkshire pudding ['jɔrkʃɪr] *s* bizcocho de masa
you [ju] *pron pers sg & pl* tú, te; vosotros; usted, ustedes; le, la, les; **with you** contigo; consigo, p.ej., **you took it with you** lo llevó consigo; *pron indef* se, p.ej., **you cannot smoke here** no se puede fumar aquí
you'd [jud] contracción de **you had** y **you would**
you'll [jul] contracción de **you shall** y **you will**
young [jʌŋ] *adj* (*comp:* **younger** ['jʌŋgər]; *super:* **youngest** ['jʌŋgɪst]) joven; menor (de edad); reciente, temprano; tierno; inexperto; **the young** los jóvenes, la gente joven, la juventud; **with young** encinta, preñada; *spl* hijuelos
younger set *s* generación nueva, (los) jóvenes
young hopeful *s* muchacho que promete
youngish ['jʌŋɪʃ] *adj* bastante joven
youngling ['jʌŋlɪŋ] *adj & s* jovenzuelo; primal; novato
Young Men's Christian Association *s* Asociación de jóvenes cristianos, Asociación cristiana de jóvenes
young people *spl* jóvenes, gente joven, juventud
youngster ['jʌŋstər] *s* jovencito; niño, chiquito
younker ['jʌŋkər] *s* (archaic) niño, chiquito; (obs.) señorito
your [jur] *adj poss* tu, vuestro, su, el (o su) de Vd. o de Vds.
yours [jurz] *pron poss* tuyo, vuestro; suyo; de Vd., de Vds.; el tuyo, el vuestro; el suyo; el de Vd., el de Vds.; **of yours** tuyo, vuestro; suyo; de Vd., de Vds., p.ej., **a friend of yours** un amigo suyo, un amigo de Vd.; **yours truly** su seguro servidor, de Vd. atto. y S. S.; (coll.) este cura (*yo*)
yourself [jur'sɛlf] *pron* (*pl:* **-selves**) tú mismo; usted mismo; sí mismo; se; sí
youth [juθ] *s* (*pl:* **youths** [juθs] o [juðz]) juventud; jovenzuelo; *spl* jóvenes, gente joven, juventud
youthful ['juθfəl] *adj* juvenil
you've [juv] contracción de **you have**
yowl [jaul] *s* aullido, alarido; *vn* aullar, dar alaridos
yo-yo ['jo,jo] *s* (*pl:* **-yos**) diábolo
yr. abr. de **year** o **years**
yrs. abr. de **years**
ytterbium [ɪ'tʌrbɪəm] *s* (chem.) iterbio
yttrium ['ɪtrɪəm] *s* (chem.) itrio
Yucatan [,jukɑ'tɑn] o [,jukə'tæn] *s* el Yucatán
yucca ['jʌkə] *s* (bot.) yuca
Yugoslav ['jugo'slɑv] *adj & s* yugoeslavo
Yugoslavia ['jugo'slɑvɪə] *s* Yugoeslavia
Yugoslavic [,jugo'slɑvɪk] *adj* yugoeslavo
Yule [jul] *s* la Navidad; la pascua de Navidad
Yule log *s* nochebueno (*leño*)
Yuletide ['jul,taɪd] *s* la pascua de Navidad
Y.W.C.A. abr. de **Young Women's Christian Association**
Y.W.H.A. abr. de **Young Women's Hebrew Association**
ywis [ɪ'wɪs] *adv* (archaic) sin duda, ya lo creo

Z

Z, z [zi] *s* (*pl:* **Z's, z's** [ziz]) vigésima sexta letra del alfabeto inglés
Zaccheus [zæ'kiəs] *s* (Bib.) Zaqueo
Zachariah [,zækə'raɪə] *s* (Bib.) Zacarías
zaffer ['zæfər] *s* (mineral.) zafre
zany ['zenɪ] *s* (*pl:* **-nies**) tonto, necio; bufón, payaso
zeal [zil] *s* celo
Zealand ['zilənd] *s* la isla de Seeland (*Dinamarca*)
zealot ['zɛlət] *s* fanático
zealotry ['zɛlətrɪ] *s* fanatismo
zealous ['zɛləs] *adj* celoso (*que tiene gran entusiasmo*)
zebec ['zibɛk] *s* var. de **xebec**
Zebedee ['zɛbɪdi] *s* (Bib.) Zebedeo
zebra ['zibrə] *s* (zool.) cebra
zebra parakeet *s* (orn.) periquito de Australia
zebu ['zibju] *s* (zool.) cebú
Zech. abr. de **Zechariah**
Zechariah [,zɛkə'raɪə] *s* (Bib.) Zacarías
Zedekiah [,zɛdɪ'kaɪə] *s* (Bib.) Sedecías
zedoary ['zɛdo,ɛrɪ] *s* (pharm.) cedoaria
Zeeland ['zilənd] *s* la Zelanda o la Zelandia (*Holanda*)
Zeelander ['ziləndər] *s* celandés
zein ['ziɪn] *s* (biochem.) zeína
Zeitgeist ['tsaɪt,gaɪst] *s* espíritu de la época
zenith ['zinɪθ] *s* (astr. & fig.) cenit
Zeno ['zino] *s* Zenón
zeolite ['ziəlaɪt] *s* (mineral.) ceolita
Zeph. abr. de **Zephaniah**
Zephaniah [,zɛfə'naɪə] *s* (Bib.) Sofonías
zephyr ['zɛfər] *s* céfiro (*viento; tela*)
zeppelin o **Zeppelin** ['zɛpəlɪn] *s* zepelín
zero ['zɪro] *s* (*pl:* **-ros** o **-roes**) cero; *adj* nulo
zero gravity *s* gravedad nula
zero hour *s* (mil.) hora cero
zero weather *s* tiempo de cero grados, tiempo muy frío
zest [zɛst] *s* entusiasmo; gusto, sabor; cáscara de limón o naranja; *va* dar gusto o sabor a, sazonar
zeugma ['zjugmə] o ['zugmə] *s* (rhet.) zeugma; (rhet.) zeugma en que uno de los elementos de la construcción no es apropiado al sentido del verbo
Zeus [zus] o [zjus] *s* (myth.) Zeus
zigzag ['zɪg,zæg] *s* zigzag; *adj & adv* en zigzag; (*pret & pp:* **-zagged;** *ger:* **-zagging**) *va* mover en zigzag; *vn* zigzaguear
zinc [zɪŋk] *s* (chem.) cinc; (elec.) vara o cilindro de cinc (*de una pila húmeda*); (*pret & pp:* **zinced** [zɪŋkt] o **zincked;** *ger:* **zincing** ['zɪŋkɪŋ] o **zincking**) *va* cubrir con cinc; platear con cinc, cincar
zinc carbonate *s* (chem.) carbonato de cinc
zinc chloride *s* (chem.) cloruro de cinc
zinc etching *s* cincograbado; cincografía
zincograph ['zɪŋkəgræf] o ['zɪŋkəgrɑf] *s* cincograbado
zincography [zɪŋ'kɑgrəfɪ] *s* cincografía
zinc ointment *s* (pharm.) pomada o ungüento de cinc
zincous ['zɪŋkəs] *adj* cincoso
zinc oxide *s* (chem.) óxido de cinc
zinc sulfate *s* (chem.) sulfato de cinc
zinc sulfide *s* (chem.) sulfuro de cinc
zinc white *s* blanco de cinc
zingaro ['tsɪŋgɑro] *s* (*pl:* -ri [ri]) cíngaro
zingiberaceous [,zɪndʒɪbə'reʃəs] *adj* (bot.) cingiberáceo
zinnia ['zɪnɪə] *s* (bot.) rascamoño
Zion ['zaɪən] *s* Sión
Zionism ['zaɪənɪzəm] *s* sionismo
Zionist ['zaɪənɪst] *adj & s* sionista
zip [zɪp] *s* silbido, zumbido; (coll.) energía, vitalidad; (*pret & pp:* **zipped;** *ger:* **zipping**) *va* cerrar con cierre relámpago; *vn* silbar, zumbar; (coll.) actuar con energía, moverse con energía; **to zip by** (coll.) pasar rápidamente
zipper ['zɪpər] *s* cierre relámpago, cierre cremallera; (trademark) chanclo con cierre relámpago
zippy ['zɪpɪ] *adj* (*comp:* **-pier;** *super:* **-piest**) (coll.) animado, vivo, alegre
zircon ['zʌrkɑn] *s* (mineral.) circón
zirconate ['zʌrkənet] *s* (chem.) circonato
zirconia [zər'konɪə] *s* (chem.) circona
zirconium [zər'konɪəm] *s* (chem.) circonio
zither ['zɪθər] *s* (mus.) cítara (*instrumento músico con cuerdas tendidas horizontalmente*)
zithern ['zɪθərn] o **zittern** ['zɪtərn] *s* (mus.) cítara (*instrumento músico parecido a la guitarra; instrumento músico con cuerdas tendidas horizontalmente*)
zoanthropy [zo'ænθrəpɪ] *s* (path.) zoantropía
zodiac ['zodɪæk] *s* (astr.) zodíaco
zodiacal [zo'daɪəkəl] *adj* zodiacal
zoetrope ['zo·ɪtrop] *s* zootropo (*juguete*)
zona ['zonə] *s* (*pl:* **-nae** [ni]) zona (*lista; ceñidor*); (path.) zona
zonal ['zonəl] *adj* zonal
zone [zon] *s* zona; distrito postal; (poet.) zona (*ceñidor*); *va* dividir en zonas; marcar con zonas; ceñir
zoned [zond] *adj* zonado (*señalado con listas*); dividido en zonas; que lleva ceñidor
zone number *s* número del distrito postal
zoning ['zonɪŋ] *s* zonificación
zonule ['zonjʊl] *s* zonula
zoo [zu] *s* zoo (*parque zoológico*)
zoöcecidium [,zoəsɪ'sɪdɪəm] *s* (*pl:* **-a** [ə]) (zool.) zoocecidia
zoöchemical [,zoo'kɛmɪkəl] *adj* zooquímico
zoöchemistry [,zoo'kɛmɪstrɪ] *s* zooquímica
zoögeography [,zoodʒɪ'ɑgrəfɪ] *s* zoogeografía
zoögloea [,zoo'gliə] *s* (bact.) zooglea
zoögraphy [zo'ɑgrəfɪ] *s* zoografía
zoölogical [,zoə'lɑdʒɪkəl] *adj* zoológico
zoölogical garden *s* parque zoológico, jardín zoológico
zoölogist [zo'ɑlədʒɪst] *s* zoólogo
zoölogy [zo'ɑlədʒɪ] *s* zoología
zoom [zum] *s* zumbido; (aer.) empinadura; *va* (aer.) empinar; *vn* zumbar; (aer.) empinarse
zoömetric [,zoə'mɛtrɪk] *adj* zoométrico
zoömetry [zo'ɑmɪtrɪ] *s* zoometría
zoömorphism [,zoə'mɔrfɪzəm] *s* zoomorfismo
zoönosis [zo'ɑnəsɪs] *s* (path.) zoonosis
zoöparasite [,zoə'pærəsaɪt] *s* (zool.) zooparásito
zoöpathology [,zoəpə'θɑlədʒɪ] *s* zoopatología
zoöpery [zo'ɑpərɪ] *s* zooperia
zoöphilia [,zoə'fɪlɪə] *s* zoofilia
zoöphilous [zo'ɑfɪləs] *adj* zoófilo
zoöphyte ['zoəfaɪt] *s* (zool.) zoófito
zoöplankton [,zoə'plæŋktən] *s* (zool.) zooplancton
zoöplasty ['zoə,plæstɪ] *s* (surg.) zooplastia
zoöpsychology [,zoəsaɪ'kɑlədʒɪ] *s* zoopsicología
zoösporangium [,zoəspə'rændʒɪəm] *s* (*pl:* **-a** [ə]) (bot.) zoosporangio
zoöspore ['zoəspor] *s* (bot.) zoospora
zoötaxy ['zoə,tæksɪ] *s* zootaxia
zoötechny ['zoo,tɛknɪ] *s* zootecnia
zoötomy [zo'ɑtəmɪ] *s* zootomía
zoötoxin [,zoə'tɑksɪn] *s* zootoxina
zoot suit [zut] *s* (slang) traje con saco muy largo y pantalones holgados pero muy estrechos en los tobillos
Zoroaster [,zoro'æstər] *s* Zoroastro
Zoroastrian [,zoro'æstrɪən] *adj* zoroástrico, zoroastriano; *s* zoroastriano

Zoroastrianism [ˌzoroˈæstrɪənɪzəm] *s* zoroastrismo
zoster [ˈzɑstər] *s* (path.) zoster, zona
Zouave [zuˈɑv] *s* (mil.) zuavo
zounds [zaʊndz] *interj* (archaic) ¡ voto al diablo!
zucchetto [tsukˈkɛto] *s* (*pl:* **-tos**) (eccl.) solideo
Zulu [ˈzulu] *adj* zulú; *s* (*pl:* **-lus**) zulú
Zululand [ˈzuluˌlænd] *s* Zululandia
zwieback [ˈtswiˌbɑk] o [ˈswiˌbɑk] *s* bizcocho retostado
Zwinglian [ˈzwɪŋglɪən] o [ˈtsvɪŋlɪən] *adj & s* zuingliano
zygal [ˈzaɪgəl] *adj* cigal
zygodactyl [ˌzaɪgəˈdæktɪl] o [ˌzɪgəˈdæktɪl] *adj* (orn.) zigodáctilo; *s* (orn.) zigodáctila
zygoma [zaɪˈgomə] o [zɪˈgomə] *s* (*pl:* **-mata** [mətə]) (anat.) cigoma
zygomatic [ˌzaɪgoˈmætɪk] o [ˌzɪgoˈmætɪk] *adj* (anat.) cigomático
zygomatic arch *s* (anat.) arco cigomático
zygomatic bone *s* (anat.) hueso cigomático
zygomatic muscle *s* (anat.) músculo cigomático
zygomorphic [ˌzaɪgoˈmɔrfɪk] o [ˌzɪgoˈmɔrfɪk] o **zygomorphous** [ˌzaɪgoˈmɔrfəs] o [ˌzɪgoˈmɔrfəs] *adj* (biol.) zigomorfo
zygophyllaceous [ˌzaɪgofɪˈleʃəs] o [ˌzɪgofɪˈleʃəs] *adj* (bot.) cigofiláceo
zygosis [zaɪˈgosɪs] o [zɪˈgosɪs] *s* (bot. & zool.) cigosis
zygospore [ˈzaɪgəspor] o [ˈzɪgəspor] *s* (bot.) zigospora
zygote [ˈzaɪgot] o [ˈzɪgot] *s* (biol.) cigoto
zygotene [ˈzaɪgotin] o [ˈzɪgotin] *adj* (biol.) cigoteno
zymase [ˈzaɪmes] *s* (biochem.) zimasa
zyme [zaɪm] *s* (path.) cimo
zymogen [ˈzaɪmodʒən] o **zymogene** [ˈzaɪmodʒin] *s* (biochem.) cimógeno; (biol.) cimógeno, cimo excitador
zymogenesis [ˌzaɪmoˈdʒɛnɪsɪs] *s* (biochem.) cimogénesis
zymogenic [ˌzaɪmoˈdʒɛnɪk] *adj* cimógeno
zymogenic organism *s* (biol.) organismo cimógeno
zymology [zaɪˈmɑlədʒɪ] *s* cimología
zymolysis [zaɪˈmɑlɪsɪs] *s* (biochem.) cimólisis
zymometer [zaɪˈmɑmɪtər] *s* cimómetro
zymoplastic [ˌzaɪmoˈplæstɪk] *adj* (biochem.) cimoplástico
zymoscope [ˈzaɪmoskop] *s* cimoscopio
zymosimeter [ˌzaɪmoˈsɪmɪtər] *s* cimosímetro
zymosis [zaɪˈmosɪs] *s* (*pl:* **-ses** [siz]) cimosis
zymotic [zaɪˈmɑtɪk] *adj* cimótico
zymurgy [ˈzaɪmʌrdʒɪ] *s* cimurgia o cimotecnia
Zyrian [ˈzɪrɪən] *s* ziriano (*idioma finoúgrio*)

LABELS AND ABBREVIATIONS

abr. **abbreviation—abreviatura**
adj **adjective—adjetivo**
adv **adverb—adverbio**
(aer.) **aeronautics—aeronáutica**
(agr.) **agriculture—agricultura**
(alchem.) **alchemy—alquimia**
(alg.) **algebra—álgebra**
(Am.) **Spanish-American—hispanoamericano**
(anat.) **anatomy—anatomía**
(anthrop.) **anthropology—antropología**
(api.) **apiculture—apicultura**
(Arab.) **Arabic—arábigo**
(arch.) **architecture—arquitectura**
(archeol.) **archeology—arqueología**
(arith.) **arithmetic—aritmética**
(arm.) **armor—armadura**
art **article—artículo**
(arti.) **artillery—artillería**
(astr.) **astronomy—astronomía**
(astrol.) **astrology—astrología**
aug **augmentative—aumentativo**
(aut.) **automobiles—automóviles**
(bact.) **bacteriology—bacteriología**
(b.b.) **bookbinding—encuadernación**
(Bib.) **Biblical—bíblico**
(bibliog.) **bibliography—bibliografía**
(biochem.) **biochemistry—bioquímica**
(biog.) **biography—biografía**
(biol.) **biology—biología**
(bot.) **botany—botánica**
(box.) **boxing—boxeo**
(Brit.) **British—británico**
(*cap.*) **capital—mayúscula**
(carp.) **carpentry—carpintería**
(cf.) **compare—compárese**
(chem.) **chemistry—química**
(chron.) **chronology—cronología**
(coll.) **colloquial—familiar**
(com.) **commerce—comercio**
comp **comparative—comparativo**
conj **conjunction—conjunción**
(constr.) **construction—construcción**
(cook.) **cooking—cocina**
(cryst.) **crystallography—cristalografía**
def **definite—definido**
dem **demonstrative—demostrativo**
(dent.) **dentistry—dentistería**
(dial.) **dialectal—dialectal**
dim **diminutive—diminutivo**
(dipl.) **diplomacy—diplomacia**
(eccl.) **ecclesiastical—eclesiástico**
(econ.) **economics—economía**
(educ.) **education—educación**
(elec.) **electricity—electricidad**
(electron.) **electronics—electrónica**
(embryol.) **embryology—embriología**
(eng.) **engineering—ingeniería**
(ent.) **entomology—entomología**
(equit.) **horsemanship—equitación**
expl **expletive—partícula expletiva**
f **feminine noun—nombre femenino**
(f.a.) **fine arts—bellas artes**
(falc.) **falconry—cetrería**
fem **feminine—femenino**
(feud.) **feudalism—feudalismo**
(fig.) **figurative—figurado**
(fort.) **fortification—fortificación**
(found.) **foundry—fundición**
fpl **feminine noun plural—nombre femenino plural**
fsg **feminine noun singular—nombre femenino singular**
Fr. **French—francés**
fut **future—futuro**
(geog.) **geography—geografía**
(geol.) **geology—geología**
(geom.) **geometry—geometría**
ger **gerund—gerundio**
(gram.) **grammar—gramática**
(gun.) **gunnery—artillería**
(her.) **heraldry—heráldica**
(hist.) **history—historia**
(horol.) **horology—horología**
(hort.) **horticulture—horticultura**
(hum.) **humorous—jocoso**
(hunt.) **hunting—caza**
(hyd.) **hydraulics—hidráulica**
(ichth.) **ichthyology—ictiología**
(illit.) **illiterate—iliterato**
(immun.) **immunology—inmunología**
imperf **imperfect—imperfecto**
impers **impersonal—impersonal**
impv **imperative—imperativo**
ind **indicative—indicativo**
indecl **indeclinable—indeclinable**
indef **indefinite—indefinido**
inf **infinitive—infinitivo**
(ins.) **insurance—seguros**
(int. law) **international law—derecho internacional**
interj **interjection—interjección**
interr **interrogative—interrogativo**
invar **invariable—invariable**
(iron.) **ironical—irónico**
(jewel.) **jewelry—joyería**
(journ.) **journalism—periodismo**
(Lat.) **Latin—latín**
(*l.c.*) **lower case—letra de caja baja**